British National Bibliography

1982

The British National Bibliography has been published since 1950. The BNB Weekly Lists give new publications in classified subject order together with an author and title index. Indexes under authors and titles, and subjects for the month appear in the last issue of each month. Interim cumulations are published at four-monthly intervals, providing an up-to-date reference service to books published in Great Britain. Cumulations covering longer periods from 1950 are also available.

British National Bibliography

A Subject Catalogue of new British books received by the Copyright Receipt Office of the British Library, arranged according to the Dewey Decimal Classification and catalogued according to the Anglo-American Cataloguing Rules, with a full Author & Title Index, and a Subject Index

1982

Volume 1: Subject Catalogue

The British Library BIBLIOGRAPHIC SERVICES DIVISION

The British National Bibliography is compiled within
The British Library
BIBLIOGRAPHIC SERVICES DIVISION
2 Sheraton Street, London W1V 4BH
Telephone 01–636 1544
Telex 21462

ISBN 0-7123-10-12-6

ISSN 0007–1544

Computer-controlled phototypesetting by Computaprint Ltd London
Printed in Great Britain at the University Press, Oxford

Preface

The objects of the British National Bibliography are to list new works published in the British Isles to describe each work in detail and to give the subject matter of each work as precisely as possible. These operations are undertaken by a staff of qualified librarians. The material catalogued is based upon the items received, under the Copyright Act, 1911, by the Copyright Receipt Office of the British Library. Every endeavour is made to ensure the accuracy of the information given.

A few classes of publications are intentionally excluded, they are:

a) Periodicals (except the first issue of a new periodical and the first issue of a periodical under a new title)

b) Music (listed separately in the *British Catalogue of Music*)

c) Maps

d) Certain Government publications*

e) Publications without a British imprint, except those published in the Republic of Ireland.†

Hints for tracing information

This bibliography is in three sections: in the first, or Classified Subject Catalogue, the entries are arranged according to the Dewey Decimal system of subject classification; in the second the entries are arranged alphabetically by authors, titles, editors, series, etc.; the third section,. the Subject Index, is an alphabetical index of subjects appearing in the Classified Subject Catalogue. The fullest information about a book is given in the Classified Subject Catalogue, including the form of name used by the author in his books, the full title, edition, publisher, date of publication and the series as well as the number of pages, the kind of illustrations, the size, the International Standard Book Number and the price. A shorter entry is given in the Author & Title Index under the name of the author, including the short title, edition, publisher and price, the International Standard Book Number, Dewey Decimal Classification Number and BNB Number.

Authors, titles, editors, series, etc.

When the author of a book is known look under his name in the Author & Title Index. The information given there will be adequate for many purposes. If the fullest information about a book is required, refer to the entry in the Classified Subject Catalogue. This is easily found by means of the first reference number (the Dewey Decimal Classification Number) at the end of an entry in the Author & Title Index. The number is read as a decimal number. Thus, for example, the number 621 will be found after the number 598.2942 and before the number 621.384.

Books emanating from societies and other organisations are sometimes entered under the name of the society or organisation, while publications of governments are frequently entered under the name of the country or city for which they are responsible.

Books with diffuse or unknown authorship will be found entered under the first word of the title which is not an article.

Entries are made in the Author & Title Index under the titles of works, so that if the author is not known a work can be found by looking up its title in this Index.

If neither the author nor the title is known, it may still be possible to trace the work by means of the editor, illustrator, series, etc.

Subjects

One of the most important aspects of this bibliography is its exhaustive index to the subject matter of books. The Classified Subject Catalogue itself displays the works on a subject in such a way that the whole field of literature on that subject can be easily perused. The Subject Index lists all the subjects found in the Classified Subject Catalogue and shows by means of the class number (i.e. the Dewey Decimal Classification Number) where books on those subjects are listed in the Classified Subject Catalogue. For example, in the Subject Index under the word Africa is a full list of the places in the Classified Subject Catalogue where books in any way concerned with Africa may be found, thus:

Africa

Central Africa. Description & travel — *Illustrations*	916.7'04'0222
Common law countries. Commercial law — *Cases — Serials*	346.06'7'0264
East Africa. Birds	598.29676
Economic development — *Case studies*	330.96'0328
Freshwater gastropoda — *For medicine*	594'.3'096
North Africa — *Serials*	961'.048'05
Vertebrates. Cinematography — *Personal observations*	778.5'38596'0924

*Many titles published by Her Majesty's Stationery Office and included in its Selected Subscription Service to libraries are recorded in the British National Bibliography

The following categories of very specialised material are *not* included in B.N.B.:

Parliamentary Papers

House of Lords Papers and Bills, House of Lords Parliamentary Debates; House of Commons Papers relating solely to the business of the House, House of Commons Parliamentary Debates, House of Commons Bills; Local Acts, Private Acts, Church Assembly Measures.

Non-Parliamentary Papers

Such routine administrative publications as:

Amendments, Appeals, Awards; Circulars; Defence Guides, Lists and Specifications; Examination Papers; Forms, Licences; Memoranda; Notices; Orders; Regulations; Returns; Tax Cases; Warrants.

†Government publications of the Republic of Ireland are not included.

BLAISE filing rules

Entries in all sections of the British National Biliography are ordered according to the *BLAISE filing rules*, published by the British Library, Bibliographic Services Division, 2 Sheraton Street, London W1V 4BH.

Classification numbers

Entries in the British National Bibliography are classified by 19th edition of the Dewey Decimal Classification.

Bibliographic Descriptions

Entries in the Classified Subject Catalogue are prepared according to the requirements of the second edition of the Anglo-American Cataloguing Rules.

Publisher and place of publication

The place of publication is always given before the name of the publisher thus:

London : Harrap.

The address of a publisher is given in full in an entry if the address is not readily available elsewhere.
Where publisher and place of publication are not known, the abbreviations used are:

s.l.	sine loco—no place of publication.
s.n.	sine nomine—no publisher's name.

Collation

The collation is that part of the entry which describes the physical make-up of the book. The abbreviations used are:

v.	volumes.
p	pages. The preliminary pages, if they are separately numbered, are shown separately. For example, vii,222p. means seven preliminary pages are numbered with roman numerals and two hundred and twenty-two pages of text.
plates	pages not forming part of the main and preliminary sequences of pagination, generally containing illustrative matter, frequently numbered and sometimes on different paper.
ill	illustrations in the text or on plates.
col.ill	coloured illustrations.
facsims	facsimile reproductions.
geneal.table	genealogical table.
port	portrait.
cm	centimetres—used to give the height of a book.
pbk	paperback book.

International Standard Book Number

The International Standard Book Number (ISBN) relating to an individual book is given in the entry for that book in the Classified Subject Catalogue and in all related entries in the Author & Title Index. The International Standard Book Number consists of five parts; the initials ISBN; a country code; a publisher code; a title code and, finally, a 'check digit'. For example ISBN 0 406 55500 1 means:

ISBN	International Standard Book Number
0	UK/US group of publishers
406	Butterworth
55500	specific title; An introduction to English legal history, by J. H. Baker
1	the check digit (a device preventing incorrectly quoted numbers from being processed).

Prices

Prices given are those current at the time of appearance of an entry in the Weekly List.

Cataloguing in Publication (CIP)

When "CIP entry" appears in an annotation it indicates that the entry has been prepared from advance information supplied by the publisher and not from the book itself. CIP entries are revised when titles are published and deposited at the Copyright Receipt Office, and then bear the annotation "CIP rev."

An entry fully explained:

Derbyshire, Edward
Geomorphological processes / E. Derbyshire, K.J. Gregory, J.R. Hails. — London : Butterworths, 1981, c1979. — 312p :
ill,charts,maps ; 26cm. — (Studies in physical geography, ISSN 0142-6389)
Originally published: Folkestone : Dawson, 1979. — Bibliography: p290-305. — Includes index
ISBN 0-408-10735-9 (cased) : £12.50
ISBN 0-408-10739-1 (pbk) : £6.95
B81-11453

means

The main entry heading for this book is the first named author, Derbyshire, Edward. The title is: Geomorphological processes, and is written by E. Derbyshire, K.J. Gregory and J.R. Hails. It is published in London by Butterworths in 1981, and bears a copyright date of 1979. There are 312 pages, with illustrations, charts and maps, and the volume is approximately 26 cm. in height. This book is published as part of a series entitled Studies in physical geography which has the International Standard Serial Number (ISSN) 0142-6389. The title was originally published in Folkestone by Dawson in 1979 and includes a bibliography on pages 290–305 and an index. There are two International Standard Book Numbers (ISBN) for this book: the first one, 0-408-10735-9 is for the hardback (cased) edition, which was priced at £12.50 at the time of publication; the second, 0-408-10739-1 is for the paperback edition, which was priced at £6.95 at the time of publication. The catalogue record bears a BNB number of B81-11453

Outline of the Dewey Decimal Classification

000 Generalities

010 Bibliography
020 Library & Information Sciences
030 General Encyclopaedic Works
040
050 General Serial Publications
060 General Organizations & Museology
070 Journalism, Publishing, Newspapers
080 General Collections
090 Manuscripts & Book Rarities

100 Philosophy & Related Disciplines

110 Metaphysics
120 Epistemology, Causation, Humankind
130 Paranormal Phenomena & Arts
140 Specific Philosophical Viewpoints
150 Psychology
160 Logic
170 Ethics (Moral Philosophy)
180 Ancient, Medieval, Oriental
190 Modern Western Philosophy

200 Religion

210 Natural Religion
220 Bible
230 Christian Theology
240 Christian Moral & Devotional
250 Local Church & Religious Orders
260 Social & Ecclesiastical Theology
270 History & Geography of Church
280 Christian Denominations & Sects
290 Other & Comparative Religions

300 Social Sciences

310 Statistics
320 Political Science
330 Economics
340 Law
350 Public Administration
360 Social Problems & Services
370 Education
380 Commerce (Trade)
390 Customs, Etiquette, Folklore

400 Language

410 Linguistics
420 English & Anglo-Saxon Languages
430 Germanic Languages German
440 Romance Languages French
450 Italian, Romanian, Rhaeto-Romanic
460 Spanish & Portuguese Languages
470 Italic Languages Latin
480 Hellenic Languages Classical Greek
490 Other Languages

500 Pure Sciences

510 Mathematics
520 Astronomy & Allied Sciences
530 Physics
540 Chemistry & Allied Sciences
550 Science of Earth & Other Worlds
560 Palaeontology
570 Life Sciences
580 Botanical Sciences
590 Zoological Sciences

600 Technology (Applied Sciences)

610 Medical Sciences
620 Engineering & Allied Operations
630 Agriculture & Related Technologies
640 Home Economics & Family Living
650 Management & Auxiliary Services
660 Chemical & Related Technologies
670 Manufactures
680 Manufacture for Specific Uses
690 Buildings

700 The Arts

710 Civic & Landscape Art
720 Architecture
730 Plastic Arts Sculpture
740 Drawing, Decorative & Minor Arts
750 Painting & Paintings
760 Graphic Arts Prints
770 Photography & Photographs
780 Music
790 Recreational & Performing Arts

800 Literature (Belles-lettres)

810 American Literature in English
820 English & Anglo-Saxon Literatures
830 Literatures of Germanic Languages
840 Literatures of Romance Languages
850 Italian, Romanian, Rhaeto-Romanic
860 Spanish & Portuguese Literatures
870 Italic Literatures Latin
880 Hellenic Literatures Greek
890 Literatures of Other Languages

900 General Geography & History

910 General Geography Travel
920 General Biography & Genealogy
930 General History of Ancient World
940 General History of Europe
950 General History of Asia
960 General History of Africa
970 General History of North America
980 General History of South America
990 General History of Other Areas

Classified Subject Catalogue

001 — KNOWLEDGE

001 — General studies — *For technicians*

Denham, P.. General studies for technicians / P. Denham, H. Bamforth & J. Derbyshire. — London : Hutchinson, 1982. — 212p : ill,facsims,forms,maps ; 24cm. — (Hutchinson TEC texts)
Bibliography: p209-210. — Includes index
ISBN 0-09-145061-6 (pbk) : £5.95 : CIP rev.
B82-03742

001 — Great Britain. Colleges of further education & schools. Curriculum subjects: General studies — *For teaching*

Dixon, Katherine M.. General studies : a philosophical approach / by Katherine M. Dixon. — London (2 Chester House, Pages La., N10 1PR) : Christian Education Movement, [1982?]. — 6leaves ; 30cm. — (Occasional paper ; 3)
Unpriced (unbound) B82-34128

001 — Inquiry

Inquiry : a second level University course. — Milton Keynes : Open University Press
At head of title: The Open University
Units 10-11: Colour vision. — 1981. — 83p : ill(some col.) ; 30cm. — (U202 ; 10-11)
Ill on inside covers. — Includes bibliographies. — Contents: Unit 10: Colour vision 1 — Unit 11: Colour vision 2
ISBN 0-335-10070-8 (pbk) : Unpriced
B82-04959

Inquiry : a second level University course. — Milton Keynes : Open University Press
At head of title: The Open University
Unit 12-13: Scientific revolutions. — 1981. — 66p : ill(some col.),maps(some col,),ports ; 30cm. — (U202 ; 12-13)
Bibliography: p63. — Contents: Pt.1: The debate about scientific revolutions / by Stuart Brown — Pt.2: Plate tectonics : a case study on the development of new concepts concerning the nature and working of the earth's crust / by Chris Wilson — Pt.3: Plate tectonics : what kind of revolution? / by Stuart Wilson
ISBN 0-335-10071-6 (pbk) : Unpriced
B82-04960

Inquiry : a second level University course. — Milton Keynes : Open University Press
At head of title: The Open University
Unit 14: Objectivity in inquiry / Stuart Brown. — 1981. — 27p : ports ; 30cm. — (U202 ; 14)
Bibliography: p26-27
ISBN 0-335-10072-4 (pbk) : Unpriced
B82-04961

Inquiry. — Milton Keynes : Open University Press
At head of title: The Open University
Units 18-19: War and the media. — 1981. — 138p : ill,ports ; 30cm. — (U202 ; 18-19)
Includes bibliographies. — Contents: Unit 18: War and the media 1 — Unit 19: War and the media 2
ISBN 0-335-10074-0 (pbk) : Unpriced
B82-15024

Inquiry : a second level University course. — Milton Keynes : Open University Press
At head of title: The Open University
Unit 20: Inquiry in the social sciences. — 1981. — 33p : ill ; 30cm. — (U202 ; 20)
Bibliography: p32-33. — Contents: Introduction to social scientific inquiries — Unit 20: Inquiry in the social sciences — Some key questions on inquiry in the social sciences
ISBN 0-335-10075-9 (pbk) : Unpriced
B82-04953

Inquiry. — Milton Keynes : Open University Press
At head of title: The Open University
Units 21-23: Indentity : some social scientific inquiries. — 1981. — 124p : ill,maps,ports ; 30cm. — (U202 ; 21-23)
Includes bibliographies. — Contents: Unit 21: Inquiring about self — Unit 22: Inquiry in social anthropology — Unit 23: Welsh identity: problems of inquiry and society
ISBN 0-335-10076-7 (pbk) : Unpriced
B82-15023

001'.012 — Knowledge. Classification

Machlup, Fritz. The branches of learning / by Fritz Machlup. — Princeton ; Guildford : Princeton University Press, c1982. — xii,205p ; 25cm. — (Knowledge ; v.2)
Includes index
ISBN 0-691-04230-6 : £12.40 B82-37421

001.2 — SCHOLARSHIP AND LEARNING

001.2'092'4 — Scholarship. Collier, John Payne — *Biographies*

Ganzel, Dewey. Fortune and men's eyes : the career of John Payne Collier. — Oxford : Oxford University Press, July 1982. — [400]p
ISBN 0-19-212231-2 : £15.00 : CIP entry
B82-12534

001.2'092'4 — Scholarship. Erasmus, Desiderius — *Biographies*

Phillips, Margaret Mann. Erasmus and the northern Renaissance / Margaret Mann Phillips. — Rev. ed. — Woodbridge : Boydell Press, 1981. — vii,173p,[10]p of plates : ill,facsims,ports ; 23cm
Previous ed.: London : English Universities Press, 1949. — Bibliography: p165-166. — Includes index
ISBN 0-85115-151-5 : £12.00 : CIP rev.
B81-22590

001.3 — HUMANITIES

001.3'02462 — Humanities — *For engineering*

Engineering and humanities / edited by James H. Schaub and Sheila K. Dickison with M.D. Morris. — New York ; Chichester : Wiley, c1982. — xvi,503p : ill ; 26cm
Includes bibliographies
ISBN 0-471-08909-5 (pbk) : £23.25
B82-37990

001.3'028'54 — Humanities. Applications of digital computer systems

Computing in the humanities / edited by Peter C. Patton, Renee A. Holoien. — Aldershot : Gower, c1981. — xi,404p : ill ; 24cm. — (Lexington books series in computer science)
Includes bibliographies and index
ISBN 0-566-00490-9 : Unpriced : CIP rev.
B81-21560

001.3'028'54 — Humanities. Applications of digital computer systems — *Conference proceedings*

International Conference on Computing in the Humanities *(5th : 1981 : Ann Arbor)*. Computing in the humanities : papers from the Fifth International Conference on Computing in the Humanities, Ann Arbor, Michigan, May 1981 / edited by Richard W. Bailey. — Amsterdam ; Oxford : North-Holland, 1982. — viii,191p : ill ; 23cm
Includes bibliographies
ISBN 0-444-86423-7 : £21.10 B82-39840

001.3'05 — Humanities — *Serials*

British Academy. The proceedings of the British Academy. — Vol.66 [1980]. — Oxford : Oxford University Press, Mar.1982. — [520]p
ISBN 0-19-726013-6 : CIP entry B82-06023

001.3′07 — Educational institutions. Curriculum subjects: Humanities. Teaching
New movements in the social sciences and humanities. — London : Maurice Temple Smith, Apr.1982. — [288]p
ISBN 0-85117-193-1 : £12.95 : CIP entry
Primary classification 300′.7 B82-08422

001.3′07′1017671 — Islamic countries. Educational institutions. Curriculum subjects: Humanities. Teaching — *Islamic viewpoints*
Philosophy, literature and fine arts / edited by Seyyed Hossein Nasr. — Sevenoaks : Hodder & Stoughton, 1982. — viii,120p ; 24cm. — (Islamic education series)
ISBN 0-340-23612-4 : Unpriced : CIP rev. B82-07429

001.3′0973 — United States. Humanities
May, Ernest R.. Careers for humanists / Ernest R. May, Dorothy G. Blaney. — New York ; London : Academic Press, c1981. — xi,123p ; 24cm
Includes index
ISBN 0-12-480620-1 : £8.40 B82-30018

001.4 — RESEARCH

001.4 — Evaluation
Metaphors for evaluation : sources of new methods / Nick L. Smith, editor. — Beverly Hills ; London : Published in cooperation with the Northwest Regional Educational Laboratory [by] Sage, c1981. — 272p : ill,maps ; 23cm. — (New perspectives in evaluation ; v.1)
Includes bibliographies
ISBN 0-8039-1613-2 : Unpriced B82-09165

001.4 — Evaluation research
Borich, Gary D.. Programs and systems : an evaluation perspective / Gary D. Borich, Ron P. Jemellea. — New York ; London : Academic Press, c1982. — xiii,277p : ill ; 24cm. — (The Educational technology series)
Bibliography: p259-268. — Includes index
ISBN 0-12-118620-2 : £17.20 B82-29692

Methodological advances in evaluation research / edited by Ross F. Conner. — Beverly Hills ; London : Sage, published in co-operation with the Evaluation Research Society, c1981. — 159p : ill ; 23cm. — (Sage research progress series in evaluation ; v.10)
Includes bibliographies
ISBN 0-8039-1727-9 (cased) : Unpriced
ISBN 0-8039-1728-7 (pbk) : Unpriced B82-31890

Patton, Michael Quinn. Creative evaluation / Michael Quinn Patton ; foreword by Kay Adams. — Beverly Hills ; London : Sage, c1981. — 296p : ill ; 23cm
Bibliography: p289-295
ISBN 0-8039-1589-6 (cased) : Unpriced
ISBN 0-8039-1590-x (pbk) : £6.50 B82-11699

001.4 — Evaluation. Techniques
New techniques for evaluation / Nick L. Smith, editor. — Beverly Hills ; London : Published in cooperation with the Northwest Educational Laboratory [by] Sage, c1981. — 320p : ill ; 23cm. — (New perspectives in evaluation ; v.2)
Includes bibliographies
ISBN 0-8039-1612-4 : Unpriced B82-09167

001.4 — Research & development by European Community. Evaluation. Methodology — *Conference proceedings*
Evaluation of research and development : methods for evaluating the results of European Community R & D programmes : proceedings of the conference held in Brussels, Belgium, January 25-26, 1982 / edited by G. Boggio and R. Gallimore. — Dordrecht ; London : Reidel, c1982. — viii,133p : 1port ; 24cm
At head of title: Commission of the European Communities
ISBN 90-277-1425-8 : Unpriced B82-32400

001.4′024′24 — Research — *For construction industries — Manuals*
How to research. — Ascot : Chartered Institute of Building, Oct.1982. — 1v.
ISBN 0-906600-59-6 (pbk) : CIP entry B82-32319

001.4′025′4 — Europe. Research organisations — *Directories*
European Research Centres : a directory of organizations in science, technology, agriculture and medicine. — 5th ed. — London : Longman, Dec.1982. — 2v.. — (Longman reference on research series)
Previous ed.: 1977
ISBN 0-582-90012-3 : £155.00 : CIP entry B82-30336

001.4′025′41 — Great Britain. Research organisations — *Directories*
Research establishments. — Great Missenden : Data Research Group, [1981]. — 55leaves ; 30cm
Cover title
ISBN 0-86099-344-2 (pbk) : Unpriced B82-24683

001.4′03′21 — Research — *Encyclopaedias*
Calnan, James. One way to do research : the A-Z for those who must / James Calnan. — London : Heinemann, 1976. — viii,250p ; 19cm
Bibliography: p174-178
ISBN 0-433-05012-8 (pbk) : £2.95 B82-27288

001.4′0941 — Great Britain. Research by universities
Research in universities. — [London] : [Committee of Vice-Chancellors and Principals of the Universities of the United Kingdom], [1980]. — 55p ; 21cm
Cover title
ISBN 0-85143-069-4 (pbk) : Unpriced B82-16255

001.4′09421 — London. Universities: University of London. Research projects. Information sources: On-line referral services — *Feasibility studies*
Vickery, A.. Feasibility study for the University of London Online Referral Centre / prepared by A. Vickery. — [London] ([Senate House, Malet St, WC1E 7HU]) : [University of London], 1982. — 54p : ill,1form ; 30cm. — (BL R & D report ; 5713)
Unpriced (pbk) B82-26375

001.4′09425′42 — Research by University of Leicester — *Serials*
University of Leicester. Research report / University of Leicester. — 1980-81-. — [Leicester] : University of Leicester, 1981-. — v. ; 21cm
Annual. — Continues in part: University of Leicester. Annual report
ISSN 0263-757X = Research report - University of Leicester : Unpriced B82-32142

001.4′0973 — United States. Research by universities & colleges
Rosenzweig, Robert M.. The research universities and their patrons / Robert M. Rosenzweig with Barbara Turlington ; prepared under the auspices of the Association of American Universities. — Berkeley, [Calif.] ; London : University of California Press, c1982. — xiii,151p ; 22cm
Includes index
ISBN 0-520-04664-1 : Unpriced B82-36047

001.4′2 — Scholarship. Research. Methodology
Stibic, V.. Tools of the mind : techniques and methods for intellectual work / V. Stibic. — Amsterdam ; Oxford : North-Holland, 1982. — xiii,297p : ill ; 24cm
Bibliography: p269-286. — Includes index
ISBN 0-444-86444-x : Unpriced B82-39971

001.4′22 — Statistics
Ehrenberg, A. S. C.. Teachers′ guide to A primer in data reduction. — Chichester : Wiley, Oct.1982. — [100]p
ISBN 0-471-90086-9 (pbk) : £5.00 : CIP entry B82-29131

001.4′22 — Statistics. Misuse — *Questions & answers — For schools*
Phoney figures / [Schools Council Project on Statistical Education]. — Slough : Published for the Schools Council by Foulsham Educational, c1981. — 18p + teachers′ notes (18p ; 21cm) : ill ; 21cm. — (Statistics in your world)
ISBN 0-572-01080-x (pbk) : Unpriced
ISBN 0-572-01107-5 (teachers′ notes) : Unpriced B82-13024

001.4′225′028542 — Data: Tables. Analysis. Applications of digital computer systems. Programs: TAU program
Arm, Betty. An introduction to TAU / by Betty Arm and John Dixie. — [Fareham] : Methods Branch, Computer Division, OPCS, 1981. — 27p ; 30cm
Unpriced (pbk) B82-11190

The **Tau** system : an overview / Office of Population Censuses and Surveys. — [Fareham] : [OPCS], 1981. — 2p : 1ill ; 30cm
Unpriced (pbk) B82-11189

001.4′226 — Charts & graphs. Drawing — *Manuals*
Cardamone, Tom. Chart and graph preparation skills / Tom Cardamone ; illustrated by Tom Cardamone and Ann Kahaner. — New York ; London : Van Nostrand Reinhold, c1981. — 128p : ill(some col.) ; 25cm
Includes index
ISBN 0-442-26284-1 (cased) : £16.10
ISBN 0-442-26286-8 (pbk) : £8.45 B82-00851

001.4′226 — Graphs. Drawing. Applications of digital computer systems. Programming languages: Fortran language
Butland, J.. SIMPLEPLOT mark 2 : section 1 : plotting 2-dimensional data / J. Butland. — Bradford : Bradford University Research, c1982. — 92p : ill ; 21cm
Text on inside cover
ISBN 0-901945-45-5 (pbk) : Unpriced B82-24627

001.4′24 — Discrete systems. Simulations. Applications of digital computer systems
Bulgren, William G.. Discrete system simulation / William G. Bulgren. — Englewood Cliffs ; London : Prentice-Hall, c1982. — ix,230p : ill ; 25cm
Includes bibliographies and index
ISBN 0-13-215764-0 : £16.45 B82-29236

001.4′24 — Experiments. Design & analysis
Keppel, Geoffrey. Design and analysis : a researcher′s handbook / Geoffrey Keppel. — 2nd ed. — Englewood Cliffs ; London : Prentice-Hall, c1982. — xiii,669p : ill ; 24cm
Previous ed.: 1973. — Bibliography: p645-652. — Includes index
ISBN 0-13-200048-2 : Unpriced B82-28417

001.4′24 — Operations research
Taha, Hamdy A.. Operations research : an introduction / Hamdy A. Taha. — 3rd ed. — New York : Macmillan ; London : Collier Macmillan, c1982. — xiv,848p : ill ; 26cm
Previous ed.: 1976. — Includes index
ISBN 0-02-418860-3 (cased) : Unpriced
ISBN 0-02-977610-4 (Int. ed.) : £13.50 B82-36487

001.4′24 — Operations research — *Conference proceedings*
IFORS International Conference on Operational Research *(9th : 1981 : Hamburg)*. Operational research ′81 : proceedings of the ninth IFORS International Conference on Operational Research, Hamburg, Germany, July 20-24, 1981 = actes de la neuvième conférence internationale de recherche opérationnelle, Hambourg, Allemagne, juillet 20-24, 1981 / edited by J.P. Brans. — Amsterdam ; Oxford : North-Holland, c1981. — xx,984p : ill ; 23cm
Includes bibliographies and index
ISBN 0-444-86223-4 : £53.19 B82-13446

001.4′24 — Operations research. Optimisation. Mathematical models
Optimisation and control of dynamic operational research models / edited by Sypros G. Tzafesta. — Amsterdam ; Oxford : North-Holland, 1982. — xxii,437p : ill ; 23cm. — (North-Holland systems and control series ; v.4)
Includes bibliographies and index
ISBN 0-444-86380-x : £21.65 B82-39846

001.4′24 — Operations research. Problem solving — *Questions & answers*
Problem solving exercises in operational research. — Lancaster : Lancord
Vol.1 / edited by John Norman and Eric Ritchie. — c1981. — 174p : ill,2maps ; 21cm
ISBN 0-901699-84-5 (pbk) : Unpriced B82-09052

001.4'24 — Operations research. Problem solving — *Questions & answers* *continuation*

Solution guide to problem solving exercises in operational research / edited by Eric Ritchie. — Lancaster : Lancord
Vol.1. — c1982. — 125p : ill ; 21cm
ISBN 0-901699-87-x (pbk) : Unpriced
B82-31254

001.4'24 — Operations research. Stochastic processes

Kohlas, J.. Stochastic methods of operations research / J. Kohlas ; translated by A. Schmidt. — Cambridge : Cambridge University Press, 1982. — ix,224p ; 24cm
Translation of: Stochastische Methoden des Operations Research. — Includes index
ISBN 0-521-23899-4 (cased) : £17.50 : CIP rev.
ISBN 0-521-28292-6 (pbk) : £6.95 B82-15936

001.4'24 — Problem solving. Applications of digital computer systems

Scheid, Francis. Schaum's outline of theory and problems of computers and programming / by Francis Scheid. — New York ; London : McGraw-Hill, c1982. — 402p : ill ; 28cm. — (Schaum's outline series)
Includes index
ISBN 0-07-055196-0 (pbk) : Unpriced
B82-40613

001.4'24 — Problem solving. Applications of digital computer systems. Programming languages: Ada language

Mayoh, Brian. Problem solving with ADA / Brian Mayoh. — Chichester : Wiley, 1982. — viii,233p : ill,1port ; 24cm
Includes index
ISBN 0-471-10025-0 : £10.75 : CIP rev.
B81-15808

001.4'24 — Problem solving. Applications of digital computer systems. Programming languages: Basic language

Gustavson, Frances C.. Problem solving and BASIC : a modular approach / Frances G. Gustavson, Marian V. Sackson. — Chicago ; Henley-on-Thames : Science Research Associates, c1979. — x,251p : ill ; 24cm
Includes index
ISBN 0-574-21240-x (pbk) : Unpriced
B82-10991

001.4'24 — Simulations. Application of digital computer systems. Techniques

Law, Averill M.. Simulation modeling and analysis / Averill M. Law, W. David Kelton. — New York ; London : McGraw-Hill, c1982. — xiv,400p : ill ; 25cm. — (McGraw-Hill series in industrial engineering and management science)
Includes bibliographies and index
ISBN 0-07-036696-9 : £18.25 B82-02282

001.4'24 — Simulations. Applications of computer systems

Progress in modelling and simulation. — London : Academic Press, Apr.1982. — [450]p
ISBN 0-12-164780-3 : CIP entry B82-04139

001.4'24 — Simulations. Applications of digital computer systems

Spriet, Jan A.. Computer-aided modelling and simulation / by Jan A. Spriet and Ghislain C. Vansteenkiste. — London : Academic Press, 1982. — x,490p : ill ; 24cm. — (International lecture series in computer science)
Bibliography: p470-482. — Includes index
ISBN 0-12-659050-8 : £21.60 : CIP rev.
B81-31349

001.4'24 — Simulations. Applications of digital computer systems. Techniques

Payne, James A.. Introduction to simulation : programming techniques and methods of analysis / James A. Payne. — New York ; London : McGraw-Hill, c1982. — xii,324p : ill ; 25cm. — (McGraw-Hill computer science series)
Includes index
ISBN 0-07-048945-9 : £21.25 B82-33699

001.4'24'015115 — Operations research. Applications of graph theory

Boffey, T. B.. Graph theory in operations research / T.B. Boffey. — London : Macmillan, 1982. — x,301p : ill ; 25cm. — (Macmillan computer science series)
Bibliography: p288-297. — Includes index
ISBN 0-333-28213-2 (cased) : Unpriced
ISBN 0-333-28214-0 (pbk) : Unpriced
B82-19300

001.4'24'0724 — Operations research. Stochastic models

Heyman, Daniel P.. Stochastic models in operations research / Daniel P. Heyman, Matthew J. Sobel. — New York ; London : McGraw-Hill. — (McGraw-Hill series in quantitative methods for management)
Vol.1: Stochastic processes and operating characteristics. — c1982. — xii,548p : ill ; 25cm
Text on lining papers. — Includes bibliographies and index
ISBN 0-07-028631-0 : £22.50 B82-34508

001.4'24'076 — Operations research — *Questions & answers*

Bronson, Richard. Schaum's outline of theory and problems of operations research / Richard Bronson. — New York ; London : McGraw-Hill, c1982. — 328p : ill ; 28cm. — (Schaum's outline series)
Includes index
ISBN 0-07-007977-3 (pbk) : £5.95 B82-28049

001.4'24'091724 — Developing countries. Operations research. Applications

Selected readings in operational research for developing countries. — Birmingham : Operational Research Society, Oct.1982. — [240]p
ISBN 0-903440-03-2 (pbk) : £4.00 : CIP entry
B82-26714

001.4'33 — Surveys. Methodology

Marsh, Catherine. The survey method. — London : Allen & Unwin, Sept.1982. — [272]p. — (Contemporary social research series ; no.6)
ISBN 0-04-310014-7 (cased) : £14.95 : CIP entry
ISBN 0-04-310015-5 (pbk) : £6.95 B82-19076

001.4'34'028 — Experiments. Factorial design

Raktoe, B. L.. Factorial designs / B.L. Raktoe, A. Hedayat, W.T. Federer. — New York ; Chichester : Wiley, c1981. — xii,209p ; 24cm
Includes bibliographies and index
ISBN 0-471-09040-9 : £22.25 B82-09882

001.4'4 — Research. Awards: Rolex Awards for Enterprise. Projects

Spirit of enterprise : the 1981 Rolex awards / edited by Gregory B. Stone ; foreword by Lord Hunt ; preface by André J. Heiniger. — London : Harrap, 1981. — xx,460p : ill(some col.),1col.map,1port ; 25cm
Includes index
ISBN 0-245-53797-x : £7.95 B82-01812

001.5 — CYBERNETICS AND RELATED DISCIPLINES

001.5 — Great Britain. Information systems. Development. Role of industries — *Proposals*

PA International Group. A strategy for information technology / [by the PA International Group with a contribution from the Braxton Group]. — [London] ([Rochester House, 33 Greycoat St., SW1P 2QF]) : [PACTEL], c1981. — iii,44p : ill(some col.) ; 21cm
£3.50 (pbk) B82-21030

001.5 — Information processing — *Conference proceedings*

IFIP Congress 80 *(Tokyo and Melbourne)*. Information processing 80 : proceedings of IFIP Congress 80 : Tokyo, Japan October 6-9, 1980, Melbourne, Australia October 14-17, 1980 / edited by Simon Lavington. — Amsterdam ; Oxford : North-Holland, 1980. — xiii,1070p : ill ; 31cm. — (IFIP congress series ; v.8)
Includes index
ISBN 0-444-86034-7 : £40.85 B82-34693

001.5 — Information systems

Eaton, John. This is I.T. — Dedington : Philip Allan, Aug.1982. — [320]p
ISBN 0-86003-514-x (cased) : £14.00 : CIP entry
ISBN 0-86003-614-6 (pbk) : £6.95 B82-24338

Mader, Chris. Information systems : technology, economics, applications, management. — 2nd ed. — Chicago ; Henley-on-Thames : Science Research Associates, c1979. — x,398p : ill ; 25cm
Previou ed.: 1974. — Includes index
ISBN 0-574-21150-0 : £11.45 B82-02116

001.5 — Information systems — *Conference proceedings*

IFIP TC 8 Working Conference on Evolutionary Information Systems *(1981 : Budapest)*. Evolutionary information systems : proceedings of the IFIP TC 8 Working Conference on Evolutionary Information Systems, Budapest, Hungary, 1-3 September 1981 / [organised by Working Group 8.1 and 8.2, IFIP Technical Committee 8, Information Systems] ; edited by John Hawgood. — Amsterdam ; Oxford : North Holland, 1982. — x,272p : ill ; 23cm
ISBN 0-444-86359-1 : Unpriced B82-25703

001.5 — Information systems. Design

Lundeberg, Mats. Information systems development : a systematic approach / Mats Lundeberg, Göran Goldkuhl, Anders Nilsson. — Englewood Cliffs ; London : Prentice-Hall, c1981. — xii,337p : ill ; 25cm. — (Prentice-Hall advances in computing science and technology series)
Translation of: Systemering. — Bibliography: p331-332. — Includes index
ISBN 0-13-464677-0 : £18.70 B82-02231

001.5 — Information systems — *Encyclopaedias*

Meadows A. J.. Dictionary of new information technology / A.J. Meadows, M. Gordon, A. Singleton. — London : Kogan Page, 1982. — 206p : ill ; 23cm
ISBN 0-85038-531-8 : £11.95 : CIP rev.
B82-14919

001.5 — Information systems. Human factors — *Socials*

Behaviour & information technology. — Vol.1, no.1 (Jan.-Mar. 1982)-. — London : Taylor & Francis Ltd., 1982-. — v. : ill(some col.) ; 25cm
Quarterly
ISSN 0144-929X = Behaviour & information technology : £34.00 per year B82-22670

001.5 — Information systems — *Serials*

Information technology, research and development. — Vol.1, no.1 (Jan. 1982)-. — Sevenoaks : Butterworths, 1982-. — v. : ill ; 25cm
Quarterly
ISSN 0144-817X = Information technology, research and development : £40.00 per year to multiple reader institutions (£12.50 to individuals) B82-15169

001.5 — Microform based information systems & video based information systems — *Serials*

International journal of micrographics & video technology. — Vol.1, no.1 (1982)-. — Oxford : Pergamon, 1982-. — v. ; 25cm
Quarterly. — Merger of: Microdoc; and, Micropublishing of current periodicals
ISSN 0743-9636 = International journal of micrographics & video technology : £24.39 per year B82-38508

001.5 — United States. Information systems

Dizard, Wilson P.. The coming information age : an overview of technology, economics, and politics / Wilson P. Dizard. — New York ; London : Longman, c1982. — xv,213p : ill ; 24cm. — (Annenberg/Longman communication books)
Bibliography: p199-200. — Includes index
ISBN 0-582-28115-6 : £17.50 B82-33647

001.5′03′21 — Information systems — *Encyclopaedias*

Stokes, Adrian V.. Concise encyclopaedia of information technology. — Aldershot : Gower, Aug.1982. — [275]p
ISBN 0-566-03425-5 (cased) : £15.00 : CIP entry
ISBN 0-566-03456-5 (pbk) : £6.00 B82-15888

001.51 — Communication studies

McKeown, Neil. Case studies and projects in communication. — London : Methuen, Sept.1982. — [224]p. — (Studies in communication)
ISBN 0-416-30740-x (pbk) : £4.95 : CIP entry
B82-20173

001.51 — Comparative communication studies

Edelstein, Alex S.. Comparative communication research / Alex S. Edelstein. — Beverly Hills ; London : Sage, c1982. — 152p ; 23cm. — (Sage CommText series ; v.9)
Bibliography: p140-151
ISBN 0-8039-1750-3 (cased) : Unpriced
ISBN 0-8039-1751-1 (pbk) : £4.95 B82-24068

001.51 — Information systems. Human factors

Christie, Bruce. Face to file communication : a psychological approach to information systems / Bruce Christie. — Chichester : Wiley, c1981. — xii,306p : ill ; 24cm. — (Wiley series in information processing)
Bibliography: p281-293. — Includes index
ISBN 0-471-27939-0 : £14.50 : CIP rev.
B81-14986

001.51 — Man. Communication

Alder, Ronald B.. Understanding human communication / Ronald B. Adler, George Rodman. — New York ; London : Holt, Rinehart and Winston, c1982. — xiv,397p : ill ; 24cm
Includes index
ISBN 0-03-059468-5 (pbk) : £11.50
B82-25413

Contact : human communication : and its history / edited by Raymond Williams ; [contributions from] Ferruccio Rossi-Landi ... [et al.]. — London : Thames and Hudson, 1981. — 272p : ill(some col.),facsims,ports ; 28cm
Bibliography: p264-266. — Includes index
ISBN 0-500-01239-3 : £9.95 B82-03993

Firke, John. Introduction to communication studies. — London : Methuen, Mar.1982. — [150]p. — (Methuen studies in communication)
ISBN 0-416-74560-1 (cased) : £7.00 : CIP entry
ISBN 0-416-74570-9 (pbk) : £3.50 B82-01119

001.51 — Semiotics

Gillan, Garth. From sign to symbol / Garth Gillan. — Brighton : Harvester, 1982. — x,153p ; 23cm
ISBN 0-7108-0343-5 : £16.95 : CIP rev.
B81-31545

Hervey, Sándor. Semiotic perspectives. — London : Allen & Unwin, Nov.1982. — [304]p
ISBN 0-04-400026-x : £15.00 : CIP entry
B82-27818

Todorov, Tzvetan. Theories of the symbol. — Oxford : Blackwell, Feb.1982. — [340]p
Translation of: Théories du symbole
ISBN 0-631-10511-5 : £15.00 : CIP entry
B81-38327

001.51 — Semiotics — *Conference proceedings*

Semiotic Society of America. *Meeting (5th : 1980 : Lubbock)*. Semiotics 1980 / [proceedings of the fifth annual meeting of the Semiotic Society of America, held October 16-19, 1980, in Lubbock, Texas] ; compiled by Michael Herzfeld & Margot D. Lenhart. — New York ; London : Plenum Press, c1982. — xii,594p : ill ; 24cm
Includes bibliographies
ISBN 0-306-40827-9 : Unpriced B82-35331

001.51′01 — Communication — *Philosophical perspectives*

Libertson, Joseph. Proximity, Levinas, Blanchot, Bataille and communication / Joseph Libertson. — The Hague ; London : Nijhoff, 1982. — 355p ; 25cm. — (Phaenomenologica ; 87)
ISBN 90-247-2506-2 : Unpriced B82-34840

001.51′01 — Man. Communication — *Philosophical perspectives*

Kelly, John C.. A philosophy of communication : explorations for a systematic model / John C. Kelly. — London : Centre for the Study of Communications and Culture, 1981. — 192p ; 22cm. — (Communication and culture monographs)
Unpriced (pbk) B82-23414

001.51′014 — Man. Communication. Linguistic aspects

Saville-Troike, Muriel. The ethnography of communication : an introduction / Muriel Saville-Troike. — Oxford : Blackwell, 1982. — vii,290p ; 22cm. — (Language in society ; 3)
Bibliography: p253-281. — Includes index
ISBN 0-631-12781-x (cased) : Unpriced : CIP rev.
ISBN 0-631-12725-9 (pbk) : Unpriced
B81-34294

001.51′0246 — Communication — *For technicians*

Rowe, Brian. TEC communications for road transport / Brian Rowe and R.H. Jinks. — London : Hodder and Stoughton, c1982. — iv,140p : ill,1form,1map ; 22cm
ISBN 0-340-23045-2 (pbk) : £2.95 : CIP rev.
B82-07428

001.51′02461 — Communication — *Manuals* — *For medicine*

Smith, Voncile M.. [Communication for health professionals]. Communication for the health care team. — London : Harper & Row, Sept.1982. — [280]p
Originally published: Philadelphia : Lippincott, 1979
ISBN 0-06-318210-6 (pbk) : £6.50 : CIP entry
B82-20198

001.51′05 — Communication — *Serials*

Communication yearbook : an annual review published by the International Communication Association. — 1 (1977)-. — New Brunswick ; London : Translation Books, 1977-. — v. : ill ; 24cm
Description based on: 5 (1982)
Unpriced B82-32362

001.51′076 — Communication — *Questions & answers*

Cooper, Alan, *1941-*. Words in action : simple guidance and assignments in communication / Alan Cooper, Peter Leggott, Cyril Sprenger. — London : Edward Arnold, 1980. — iv,60p : ill,forms ; 25cm
ISBN 0-7131-0346-9 (pbk) : £2.25 : CIP rev.
B80-07191

001.53 — Cybernetics

Coiffet, Philippe. Modelling and control. — London : Kogan Page, Jan.1983. — [160]p. — (Robot technology ; 1)
Translation of: Modelisation et controle
ISBN 0-85038-533-4 : £22.50 : CIP entry
B82-35188

Rudall, B. H.. Computers and cybernetics / B.H. Rudall. — Tunbridge Wells : Abacus, 1981. — viii,188p : ill ; 25cm. — (Cybernetics and systems series ; 11)
Includes index
ISBN 0-85626-173-4 : Unpriced : CIP rev.
Primary classification 001.64 B81-13739

001.53′0331 — Cybernetics — *German & English dictionaries*

Junge, Hans-Dieter. Dictionary of technical cybernetics. — Oxford : Elsevier Scientific, Feb.1983. — [600]p
ISBN 0-444-99682-6 : £45.00 : CIP entry
B82-38305

001.53′2 — Bionics

Morecki, Adam. Cybernetic systems of limb movement in man, animals and robots. — Chichester : Ellis Horwood, Jan.1983. — [240]p
Translation of: Cybernetyczne systemy ruchu konczyn zwierzat i robotow
ISBN 0-85312-214-8 : £30.00 : CIP entry
B82-35191

001.53′4 — Pattern recognition — *Serials*

Progress in pattern recognition. — Vol.1-. — Amsterdam ; Oxford : North-Holland, c1981-. — v. : ill ; 23cm
£26.60 B82-14267

001.53′4 — Pattern recognition. Statistical methods

Devijver, Pierre A.. Pattern recognition : a statistical approach / Pierre A. Devijver and Josef Kittler. — Englewood Cliffs ; London : Prentice-Hall, c1982. — xiv,448p : ill ; 25cm
Includes bibliographies and index
ISBN 0-13-654236-0 : £24.95 : CIP rev.
B81-33846

001.53′4 — Pattern recognition. Syntactic methods

Fu, K. S.. Syntactic pattern recognition and applications / K.S. Fu. — Englewood Cliffs ; London : Prentice-Hall, c1982. — viii,596p : ill ; 24cm. — (Prentice-Hall advances in computing science and technology series)
Includes index
ISBN 0-13-880120-7 : £28.15 B82-16995

001.53′5 — Algebraic automata theory

Holcombe, W. M. L.. Algebraic automata theory / W.M.L. Holcombe. — Cambridge : Cambridge University Press, 1982. — xi,228p : ill ; 24cm. — (Cambridge studies in advanced mathematics ; 1)
Includes index
ISBN 0-521-23196-5 : £17.50 : CIP rev.
B82-23329

001.53′5 — Artificial intelligence

Andrew, A. M.. Artificial intelligence. — Tunbridge Wells : Abacus, Sept.1982. — [150]p
ISBN 0-85626-165-3 : £15.50 : CIP entry
B82-22816

001.53′5 — Artificial intelligence *related to* **human visual perception**

Howe, J. A. M.. AI2 vision notes / by Jim Howe. — Aberdeen : University of Aberdeen Department of Artificial Intelligence, [1979]. — 119leaves of various foliations : ill ; 30cm. — (D.A.I. occasional paper, ISSN 0144-4131 ; no.20)
Unpriced (spiral)
Also classified at 152.1′4 B82-13859

001.53′5′05 — Artificial intelligence — *Serials*

Machine intelligence. — 10. — Chichester : Ellis Horwood, Jan.1982. — [512]p
ISBN 0-85312-431-0 : £25.00 : CIP entry
ISSN 0076-2032 B82-02464

001.54′2 — Oral communication

Crable, Richard E.. Using communication : a new introduction for the 1980s / Richard E. Crable. — Boston [Mass.] ; London : Allyn and Bacon, c1982. — xx,358p : ill ; 25cm
Includes index
ISBN 0-205-07689-0 : Unpriced B82-26765

001.54′3 — Written communication

Smith, Frank, *1928-*. Writing and the writer / Frank Smith. — London : Heinemann Educational, 1982. — x,257p : ill ; 23cm
Bibliography: p239-248. — Includes index
ISBN 0-435-10815-8 (cased) : £9.50 : CIP rev.
ISBN 0-435-10816-6 (pbk) : Unpriced
B81-35033

001.54′3 — Written language

What writers know : the language, process, and structure of written discourse / edited by Martin Nystrand. — New York ; London : Academic Press, 1982. — xix,391p : ill ; 24cm
Includes bibliographies and index
ISBN 0-12-523480-5 : £21.20 B82-30130

001.54'36 — Cryptograms — *Collections*

Gleason, Norma. Cryptograms and spygrams / Norma Gleason. — New York : Dover ; London : Constable, 1981. — ix,112p ; 22cm
Bibliography: p101-102
ISBN 0-486-24036-3 (pbk) : £2.60 B82-13558

001.55'2 — Printed media. Information. Presentation

Wright, Patricia, *19---*. Designing information : some approaches, some problems and some suggestions / Patricia Wright. — London (Sheraton House, Great Chapel Street W1V 4BH) : British Library Research & Development Department, 1980. — 55p ; 30cm. — (Report ; no.5509)
Bibliography: p51-55
Unpriced (pbk) B82-35920

001.55'23 — Automated microform information retrieval systems

Horder, Alan. Automated retrieval of microforms : a guide and directory / Alan Horder. — Hertford : National Reprographic Centre for Documentation, 1980. — 65p ; 30cm. — (NRCd publication ; no.14) (British Library Research and Development Department report ; no.5590)
Also available on microfiche
ISBN 0-85267-182-2 (pbk) : Unpriced
ISBN 0-85267-183-0 (microfiche) : Unpriced B82-11053

001.55'23 — Remote access microform information retrieval systems

Horder, Alan. Remote access to microform stores : a guide and directory / Alan Horder. — Hertford : National Reprographic Centre for documentation, 1981. — 38p ; 30cm. — (NRCd publication ; no.16)
Bibliography: p37-38
ISBN 0-85267-197-0 (spiral) : Unpriced
ISBN 0-85267-198-9 (Microfiche) : Unpriced B82-05457

001.55'3'024092 — Audiovisual materials — *For librarianship*

Mitchell, Janet S.. Audio-visual workbook manuals : an outline of the media awareness study scheme at Leeds Polytechnic School of Librarianship / Janet S. Mitchell. — [Leeds] : Leeds Polytechnic School of Librarianship, 1981. — 87leaves : ill ; 30cm
ISBN 0-900738-26-x (pbk) : £15.00 B82-32343

001.55'3'05 — Audiovisual media — *Serials*

[**Stills** *(London)*]. Stills. — Vol.1, no.1 (Oct./Nov. 1980)-. — [London] ([BCM-Box 2117, WC1N 3XX]) : Stills Pub. Co. Ltd., 1980-. — v. : ill,ports ; 30cm
Quarterly
ISSN 0263-2608 = Stills (London) : £6.50 per year B82-22661

001.55'3'071142961 — Dyfed. Aberystwyth. Schools of librarianship: College of Librarianship, Wales. Curriculum subjects: Audiovisual materials

College of Librarianship, Wales. Non-book media at CLW : the approach to non-book materials at the College of Librarianship Wales. — Aberystwyth : College of Librarianship Wales, [1982?]. — [12]p : ill ; 21cm
Unpriced (unbound) B82-27865

001.56 — Europe. Gestures. Geographical aspects

Gestures : their origins and distribution / Desmond Morris ... [et al.]. — [St. Albans] : Triad, 1981, c1979. — xxi,296p : ill,maps ; 24cm
Originally published: London : Cape, 1979. — Bibliography: p274-291. — Includes index
ISBN 0-586-05361-1 (pbk) : £3.95 B82-11159

001.56 — Graphic communication

Smeets, René. Signs, symbols & ornaments / René Smeets. — New York ; London : Van Nostrand Reinhold, c1975 (1982 [printing]). — 176p : ill,facsims ; 24cm
Translation of: Ornament, symbol, & teken. — Includes index
ISBN 0-442-27800-4 (pbk) : £7.60 B82-30963

001.56 — Graphic communication. Research — *Conference proceedings*

Research in illustration / [proceedings of the conference held on 26/27 March in the Sallis Benney Hall, Faculty of Art & Design, Brighton Polytechnic] ; [chairman: John Vernon Lord] ; [conference organiser and proceedings editor Evelyn Goldsmith]. — Brighton (Grand Parade, Brighton BN2 2JY) : Brighton Polytechnic, c1982. — 2v. : ill ; 21cm
Unpriced (spiral) B82-35136

001.56 — Nonvocal communication

Kiernan, Chris. Signs and symbols. — London : Heinemann Educational, Dec.1982. — [288]p
ISBN 0-85473-129-6 (pbk) : £5.85 : CIP entry B82-37644

001.56 — Signs & symbols

Achen, Sven Tito. Symbols around us / Sven Tito Achen. — New York ; London : Van Nostrand Reinhold, 1978 (1981 [printing]). — 240p : ill,facsims,ports ; 21cm
Translation of: Symboler omkring os. — Includes index
ISBN 0-442-28261-3 (pbk) : £5.05 B82-13190

001.6 — DATA PROCESSING

001.6 — Data processing

Capper, Leonard. Computing. — London : Longman, May 1982. — [208]p. — (Questions & answers)
ISBN 0-582-41175-0 (pbk) : £2.95 : CIP entry B82-06927

Clare, C. P.. Data processing. — Tunbridge Wells : Abacus, Sept.1982. — [250]p
ISBN 0-85626-331-1 (pbk) : £9.95 : CIP entry B82-22817

Verzello, Robert J.. Data processing : systems and concepts / Robert J. Verzello, John Reutter III. — New York ; London : McGraw-Hill, c1982. — xv,539p : ill,forms ; 24cm
Includes index
ISBN 0-07-067325-x : £15.25 B82-34918

Zorkoczy, Peter. Information technology. — London : Pitman, Sept.1982. — [144]p
ISBN 0-273-01798-5 : £4.50 : CIP entry B82-25057

001.6 — Data processing systems

Stern, Robert A.. An introduction to computers and information processing / Robert A. Stern, Nancy Stern. — New York ; Chichester : Wiley, c1982. — xii,637p : ill(some col.),forms (some col.) ; 24cm
Previous ed.: published as Principles of data processing. 1979. — Bibliography: p529-537. — Includes index
ISBN 0-471-08723-8 : £13.40 B82-13289

Willmott, G.. Data processing and computer studies. — London : Arnold, Nov.1982. — [256]p
ISBN 0-7131-0746-4 (pbk) : £5.25 : CIP entry B82-27946

001.6 — Data processing systems. Design. Methodology — *For management*

Inman, William H.. Design review methodology for a data base environment / W.H. Inman, L.J. Friedman. — Englewood Cliffs ; London : Prentice-Hall, c1982. — xvi,284p : ill,forms ; 25cm. — (Prentice-Hall series in data processing management)
Bibliography: p239-240. — Includes index
ISBN 0-13-201392-4 : £18.70 B82-28159

001.6'024658 — Data processing — *For business studies*

Innes, Alexander E.. Data processing for business studies / A.E. Innes. — Plymouth, Macdonald and Evans, 1982. — xii,238p : ill,forms ; 22cm. — (The M & E BECbook series)
Bibliography: p229-231. — Includes index
ISBN 0-7121-0421-6 (pbk) : £4.95 B82-26613

Martin, Robert S. L.. An introduction to data processing / Robert S.L. Martin. — London : Holt, Rinehart and Winston, c1982. — ix,166p : ill ; 22cm. — (Holt business texts)
Includes index
ISBN 0-03-910299-8 (pbk) : £2.95 : CIP rev. B82-02657

001.6'024658 — Data processing — *For management*

Oliver, E. C.. Data processing : an instructional manual for business and accountancy students / E.C. Oliver, R.J. Chapman. — 4th ed. / revised and with additional material by J. Allen. — Winchester : D.P. Publications, 1979. — vii,303p : ill ; 22cm
Previous ed.: 1975. — Text on inside covers. — Includes index
ISBN 0-905435-08-7 (pbk) : Unpriced B82-05273

001.6'03'21 — Data processing — *Encyclopaedias*

Maynard, Jeff. Dictionary of data processing / Jeff Maynard. — 2nd ed. — London : Butterworths, 1981. — 275p : ill ; 23cm
Previous ed.: London : Newnes-Butterworths, 1975
ISBN 0-408-00591-2 : Unpriced : CIP rev. B81-34162

SRA data processing glossary / with concepts written by Robert C. Malstrom. — Chicago ; Henley-on-Thames : Science Research Associates, c1979. — vi,282p : ill ; 28cm
ISBN 0-574-21250-7 (pbk) : Unpriced B82-40119

001.6'068 — Data processing systems. Management — *Serials*

Advances in data processing management. — Vol.1-. — Philadelphia ; London : Heyden, 1980-. — v. : ill ; 24cm
Annual
£14.50 B82-18714

001.6'07 — Data processing services. Personnel. Training — *Directories — Serials*

Directory of training. — 1982. — Henley-on-Thames (Enterprise House, Badgemore Park, Henley-on-Thames, Oxon RG9 4NR) : Badgemore Park Enterprises, Jan.1982. — [500]p
ISBN 0-9507655-0-3 : £30.00 : CIP entry B81-35898

001.6'07'1141 — Great Britain. Data processing. Training courses — *Directories — Serials*

[Directory of training *(Henley-on-Thames)*].
Directory of training : the industry standard reference for DP education and training. — 1982-. — Henley-on-Thames (Enterprise House, Badgemore Park, Henley-on-Thames, Oxon. RG9 4NR) : Directory of Training, 1982-. — v. : ill,maps,ports ; 31cm
Annual. — Supplement: DOT plus
ISSN 0263-1237 = Directory of training (Henley-on-Thames) : £30.00 B82-18486

001.6'0722 — Data processing — *Case studies*

Aspinall, Brian. Case exercises in data processing. — London : McGraw-Hill, Sept.1982. — [160]p
ISBN 0-07-084653-7 (pbk) : £3.50 : CIP entry B82-19813

001.63 — Automated information processing systems

Information technology : the age of electronic information. — [London] : Department of Industry, c1981. — [16]p ; 21cm
Unpriced (pbk) B82-38366

001.63 — Automated information processing systems. Policies of governments — *Conference proceedings*

High Level Conference on Information, Computer and Communications Policies for the 80's *(1980 : Paris)*. Information, computer and communications policies for the 80's : an OECD report : proceedings of the High Level Conference on Information, Computer and Communications Policies for the 80's, Paris, 6th-8th October, 1980 / edited by Hans-Peter Gassmann. — Amsterdam ; Oxford : North-Holland, c1981. — xiii,276p : ill ; 23cm
ISBN 0-444-86327-3 : £20.21 B82-13441

001.63'092'4 — Automatic data processing. Hollerith, Herman — *Biographies*
Austrian, Geoffrey D.. Herman Hollerith : forgotten giant of information processing / Geoffrey D. Austrian. — New York ; Guildford : Columbia University Press, 1982. — xvi,418p : ill,ports ; 24cm
Bibliography: p403-406. — Includes index
ISBN 0-231-05146-8 : £14.40 B82-21497

001.64 — Computer sciences
Goldschlager, L.. Computer science : a modern introduction / by L. Goldschlager and A. Lister. — Englewood Cliffs ; London : Prentice-Hall, c1982. — xii,303p : ill ; 23cm. — (Prentice-Hall international series in computer science)
Includes bibliographies and index
ISBN 0-13-165704-6 (pbk) : £6.95 : CIP rev.
B82-01708

001.6'4 — Computer sciences — *Questions & answers*
McGettrick, Andrew D.. Graded problems in computer science. — London : Addison-Wesley, Sept.1982. — [256]p
ISBN 0-201-13787-9 (pbk) : £17.25 : CIP entry
B82-22418

001.64 — Computer systems
Berry, Adrian. The super-intelligent machine. — London : Cape, Feb.1983. — 1v.
ISBN 0-224-01967-8 : £7.50 : CIP entry
B82-37832

Computing and computers. — Milton Keynes : Open University Press. — (Mathematics : a second level course)
At head of title: The Open University
Data structures / prepared by D.C.S. Allison ... [et al.] and by the course team. — 1982. — 112p : ill. — (M252/PM252 ; DS)
ISBN 0-335-14071-8 (pbk) : Unpriced
B82-21190

Computing and computers. — Milton Keynes : Open University Press. — (Mathematics : a second level course)
At head of title: The Open University
Files and file processing / prepared by the course team in consultation with P.J.L. Wallis, M.J.R. Shave. — 1982. — 87p : ill ; 30cm. — (M252/PM252 ; F/FP)
ISBN 0-335-14070-x (pbk) : Unpriced
B82-21194

Computing and computers. — Milton Keynes : Open University Press. — (Mathematics : a second level course)
At head of title: The Open University
Introduction to database / prepared by the course team. — 1982. — 32p : ill ; 30cm. — (M252/PM252 ; DB)
ISBN 0-335-14082-3 (pbk) : Unpriced
B82-40140

Computing and computers. — Milton Keynes : Open University Press. — (Mathematics : a second level course)
At head of title: The Open University
Introduction to distributed computing / prepared by the course team. — 1982. — 39p : ill ; 30cm. — (M252/PM252 ; DC)
Includes bibliographies
ISBN 0-335-14083-1 (pbk) : Unpriced
B82-40141

Computing and computers. — Milton Keynes : Open University Press. — (Mathematics : a second level course)
At head of title: The Open University
Introduction to operating systems / prepared by the course team. — 1982. — 42p : ill ; 30cm. — (M252/PM252 ; OS)
ISBN 0-335-14075-0 (pbk) : Unpriced
B82-32035

Computing and computers. — Milton Keynes : Open University Press. — (Mathematics : a second level course)
At head of title: The Open University
Social implications of computing : from a supplement to the Times, 14 January 1982. — 1982. — 51p : 1ill ; 30cm. — (M252/PM252 ; SIC)
ISBN 0-335-14076-9 (pbk) : Unpriced
B82-40142

Computing and computers. — Milton Keynes : Open University Press. — (Mathematics : a second level course)
At head of title: The Open University
Systems analysis and design. — (M252/PM252 ; SAD)
Reference text / prepared by Patrick Raymont of the National Computing Centre Ltd and the Course Team. — 1982. — 38p : ill ; 30cm
ISBN 0-335-14074-2 (pbk) : Unpriced
B82-32036

Computing and computers. — Milton Keynes : Open University Press. — (Mathematics : a second level course)
At head of title: The Open University
Systems analysis and design
Study guide / prepared by the course team. — 1982. — 81p : ill ; 30cm. — (M252/PM252 ; SAD SG)
ISBN 0-335-14073-4 (pbk) : Unpriced
B82-32037

Condon, Ron. Introducing computers / Ron Condon. — [London] : [Macdonald], [1981?]. — 96p : ill(some col.),ports ; 20cm. — (Macdonald guidelines ; 42)
Bibliography: p89. — Includes index
ISBN 0-356-06442-5 (cased) : £3.95
ISBN 0-356-06042-x (pbk) : £2.50 B82-03544

Kindred, Alton R.. Introduction to computers / Alton R. Kindred. — 2nd ed. — Englewood Cliffs ; London : Prentice-Hall, c1982. — xviii,542p : ill,forms ; 24cm
Previous ed.: 1976. — Includes index
ISBN 0-13-480079-6 (pbk) : £14.20
B82-27563

Lawson, Harold W.. Understanding computer systems / Harold W. Lawson Jr. — 2nd ed. — Bromley (Old Orchard, Bickley Rd., Bromley, Kent BR1 2NE) : Chartwell-Bratt, c1979. — 150p : ill ; 30cm
Previous ed.: 197-?. — Text on inside cover
Unpriced (pbk) B82-35554

Selected essays in contemporary computing / edited by Alan Simpson. — Purley : Input Two-Nine, 1979. — 222p : ill ; 21cm
Includes bibliographies
ISBN 0-905897-28-5 (pbk) : Unpriced
B82-04096

001.64 — Computer systems — *Conference proceedings*
Eurocomp 78 *(Conference : Wembley Conference Centre)*. Eurocomp 78 : proceedings of the European Computing Congress 1978. — Uxbridge : Online Conferences, c1978. — xxxii,1088p : ill,maps,ports ; 29cm
ISBN 0-903796-23-6 : Unpriced B82-03523

Performance '81 *(Conference : Amsterdam)*. Performance '81 : proceeding of the 8th International Symposium on Computer Performance Modelling, Measurement and Evaluation, Amsterdam, 4-6 November, 1981 / [sponsored by IFIP Working Group 7.3 on Computer System Modelling and Netherlands Society of Informatics with the cooperation of ACM Sigmetrics, Royal Institute of Engineers, German Informatics Society] ; edited by F. J. Klystra. — Amsterdam ; Oxford : North-Holland, c1981. — xii,545p : ill ; 23cm
Includes bibliographies
ISBN 0-444-86330-3 : £31.98 B82-10560

001.64 — Computer systems. Design
LSI modular computer systems / Svetlana P. Kartashev, ed., Steven I. Kartashev, ed.. — Englewood Cliffs ; London : Prentice-Hall, c1982. — xxvii,643p : ill ; 24cm
Bibliography: p615-634. — Includes index
ISBN 0-13-201343-6 : £28.15 B82-32096

Siewiorek, Daniel P.. Computer structures : principles and examples / Daniel P. Siewiorek, C. Gordon Bell, Allen Newell. — New York ; London : McGraw-Hill, 1982. — xvi,926p : ill ; 25cm
Bibliography: p895-918. — Includes index
ISBN 0-07-057302-6 : £23.25 B82-03302

001.64 — Computer systems. Design faults. Tolerances
Anderson, T.. Fault tolerance. — London : Prentice-Hall, Sept.1981. — [288]p
ISBN 0-13-308254-7 : £13.95 : CIP entry
B81-25658

001.64 — Computer systems. Design. Human factors
User-friendly systems. — Maidenhead : Pergamon Infotech, c1981. — iv,439p : ill,ports ; 31cm. — (Infotech state of the art report. Series 9 ; no.4)
Editor: G. Murray. — Bibliography: p389-431. — Includes index
ISBN 0-08-028557-0 : Unpriced B82-00680

001.64 — Computer systems. Evaluation — *Conference proceedings*
Computer performance evaluation. — Uxbridge : Online Conferences, c1976. — 592p : ill ; 30cm
Conference papers. — Includes bibliographies
ISBN 0-903796-14-7 : Unpriced B82-03325

001.64 — Computer systems — *For children*
Frank, Mark. Discovering computers / by Mark Frank. — Harlow : Longman, 1982. — 96p : ill(some col.) ; 27cm
Includes index
ISBN 0-582-39061-3 : £6.95 : CIP rev.
B82-12990

001.64 — Computer systems — *For schools*
Bishop, Peter, *1949-*. Computing science / Peter Bishop. — Walton-on-Thames : Nelson, 1982. — xviii,362p : ill,1map ; 25cm
Includes index
ISBN 0-17-431267-9 (pbk) : Unpriced
B82-35349

Craddock, P.. An introduction to computer studies / P. Craddock and A.R. Haskins. — Exeter : Wheaton, 1982. — 159p : ill,facsims,1map,ports ; 22x24cm
Includes index
ISBN 0-08-025002-5 (pbk) : Unpriced
B82-35776

Shelley, John, *1940-*. Computer studies : a first course / John Shelley and Roger Hunt. — London : Pitman, c1980 (1982 [printing]). — x,225p : ill ; 25cm
Originally published: 1980. — Includes index
ISBN 0-273-01272-x (pbk) : Unpriced
B82-33657

001.64 — Computer systems. Instruction set processors. Design
Barbacci, Mario R.. The design and analysis of instruction set processors / Mario R. Barbacci, Daniel P. Siewiorek. — New York ; London : McGraw-Hill, c1982. — xvii,243p : ill ; 28cm. — (McGraw-Hill computer science series)
Bibliography: p237-238. — Includes index
ISBN 0-07-057303-4 (pbk) : Unpriced
B82-37582

001.64 — Computers — *For children*
Carter, Lionel. Using computers. — London : Knight, Dec.1982. — [160]p
ISBN 0-340-32062-1 (pbk) : £1.25 : CIP entry
B82-29651

001.64 — Data transmission
Bleazard, G. B.. Handbook of data communications. — Manchester : NCC Publications, Aug.1982. — [500]p
ISBN 0-85012-363-1 (pbk) : £12.50 : CIP entry
B82-17977

001.64 — Data transmission systems — *Conference proceedings*
International Conference on Performance of Data Communication Systems and their Applications *(1981 : Paris)*. Performance of data communication systems and their applications : proceedings of the International Conference on Performance of Data Communication Systems and their Applications, Paris, France 14-16 September, 1981 / edited by G. Pujolle ; [organized by École Nationale supérieure des Télécommunications (ENSY) and Institut National de Recherche en Informatique et en Automatique (INRIA) under the sponsorship of AFCET ... et al.]. — Amsterdam ; Oxford : North-Holland, c1981. — xi,431p : ill ; 23cm
ISBN 0-444-86283-8 : Unpriced B82-00836

001.64 — DEC digital computer systems — *Serials*

[Network *(Richmond)***]**. Network. — 1981-Aug. 1982. — Richmond, Surrey : Network, 1981-1982. — ?v. : ill ; 30cm
Quarterly. — Continued by: DEC user. — Description based on: Oct. 1981 issue
ISSN 0263-3280 = Network (Richmond) : Unpriced B82-36729

001.64 — Digital computer systems

Bradbeer, Robin. The computer book : an introduction to computers and computing / Robin Bradbeer, Peter De Bono, Peter Laurie ; additional material and editing by Susan Curran, David Allen. — London : British Broadcasting Corporation, 1982. — 208p : ill (some col.),ports ; 22cm
Published in conjunction with a BBC television series. — Includes index
ISBN 0-563-16484-0 (pbk) : £6.75 B82-13333

Computer science and technologies. — Tokyo : Ohm ; Amsterdam ; Oxford : North-Holland. — (Japan annual reviews in electronics, computers & telecommunications, ISSN 0167-5036)
1982 / editor T. Kitagawa. — c1982. — iv,365p : ill(some col.),ports ; 27cm
£65.96 B82-34284

Davis, William S.. The information age / William S. Davis, Allison McCormack. — Reading, Mass. ; London : Addison-Wesley, c1979. — xx,427p : ill ; 25cm
Includes index
ISBN 0-201-01101-8 : £13.60 B82-28660

Day, A. Colin. Illustrating computers (without much jargon) / Colin Day, Donald Alcock. — London : Pan in association with Heinemann Computers in Education, 1982. — 103p : ill ; 21cm
Includes index
ISBN 0-330-26599-7 (pbk) : £1.95 B82-15211

Fry, T. F.. Computer appreciation / T.F. Fry. — 3rd ed. — London : Butterworths, 1981. — 278p : ill ; 22cm
Previous ed.: 1975. — Includes index
ISBN 0-408-00492-4 (pbk) : Unpriced : CIP rev. B81-31722

Jaworski, Barbara. Computers : information and data / Barbara and John Jaworski. — Walton-on-Thames : Nelson, 1982. — ix,206p : ill ; 25cm
Includes index
ISBN 0-17-438126-3 (pbk) : Unpriced B82-29958

Lee, Graham. From hardware to software : an introduction to computers / Graham Lee. — London : Macmillan, 1982. — x,454p : ill ; 26cm. — (Macmillan computer science series)
Includes index
ISBN 0-333-33164-8 (cased) : Unpriced
ISBN 0-333-24363-3 (pbk) : Unpriced B82-35076

Peltu, Malcolm. Introducing computers. — Manchester : NCC Publications, Jan.1983. — [230]p
ISBN 0-85012-321-6 (pbk) : £5.50 : CIP entry B82-32857

Pfleeger, Charles P.. Machine organization : an introduction to the structure and programming of computing systems / Charles P. Pfleeger. — New York ; Chichester : Wiley, c1982. — xi,227p : ill ; 25cm
Includes index
ISBN 0-471-07970-7 : Unpriced B82-23945

Price, Wilson T.. Data processing : the fundamentals / Wilson T. Price. — New York ; London : Holt, Rinehart and Winston, c1982. — 185p : ill(some col.) ; 24cm
Includes index
ISBN 0-03-059744-7 (pbk) : £8.95 B82-25376

Rudall, B. H.. Computers and cybernetics / B.H. Rudall. — Tunbridge Wells : Abacus, 1981. — viii,188p : ill ; 25cm. — (Cybernetics and systems series ; 11)
Includes index
ISBN 0-85626-173-4 : Unpriced : CIP rev.
Also classified at 001.53 B81-13739

Willis, Neil. Introduction to computer architecture. — London : Pitman, Jan.1983. — [106]p
ISBN 0-273-01438-2 (pbk) : £5.95 : CIP entry B82-33718

Wright, G. G. L.. Mastering computers / G.G.L. Wright. — London : Macmillan, 1982. — xii,227p : ill ; 23cm. — (Macmillan master series)
Includes index
ISBN 0-333-31293-7 (cased) : £8.95
ISBN 0-333-30908-1 (pbk) : Unpriced B82-17105

001.64 — Digital computer systems. Applications

Weaver, Bryan. Computers and their uses / Bryan Weaver and Paul McGee. — London : Edward Arnold, 1982. — 66p : ill ; 25cm
ISBN 0-7131-0639-5 (pbk) : Unpriced : CIP rev. B82-10673

Weston, P. R.. Computers : applications and implications / P.R. Weston and M. Roberts. — London : Harrap, 1982. — vi,162p : ill,map,facsims ; 22cm
Includes index
ISBN 0-245-53634-5 (pbk) : £3.50 B82-16974

001.64 — Digital computer systems. Applications. Planning. Systems analysis

Millington, D.. Systems analysis and design for computer applications / D. Millington. — Chichester : Ellis Horwood, 1981. — 224p : ill ; 24cm. — (Computers and their applications ; 12)
Text on lining papers. — Includes index
ISBN 0-85312-249-0 (cased) : £16.50 : CIP rev.
ISBN 0-85312-415-9 (Student ed.) : £7.50 B81-12899

001.64 — Digital computer systems — *Conference proceedings*

International Conference on Fifth Generation Computer Systems *(1981 : Tokyo)*. Fifth generation computer systems : proceedings of the International Conference on Fifth Generation Computer Systems, Tokyo, Japan, October 19-22, 1981 / edited by T. Moto-Oka. — Amsterdam ; Oxford : North-Holland, c1982. — viii,287p : ill ; 27cm
Includes index
ISBN 0-444-86440-7 : £29.54 B82-38187

001.64 — Digital computer systems. Design

Iliffe, J. K.. Advanced computer design / J.K. Iliffe. — London : Prentice-Hall, c1982. — ix,469p : ill ; 24cm
Bibliography: p450-464. — Includes index
ISBN 0-13-011254-2 : £18.95 : CIP rev. B81-34419

Mehlmann, Marilyn. When people use computers : an approach to developing an interface / Marilyn Mehlmann. — Englewood Cliffs ; London : Prentice-Hall, c1981. — xvii,142p : ill ; 24cm. — (Prentice-Hall software series)
Bibliography: p135-136. — Includes index
ISBN 0-13-956219-2 : £11.25 B82-02234

Myers, Glenford J.. Advances in computer architecture / Glenford J. Myers. — 2nd ed. — New York ; Chichester : Wiley, c1982. — xix,545p : ill ; 24cm
Previous ed.: 1978. — Includes index
ISBN 0-471-07878-6 : £35.00 B82-28775

001.64 — Digital computer systems. Evaluation

Morris, Michael F.. Computer performance evaluation : tools and techniques for effective analysis / Michael F. Morris, Paul F. Roth. — New York ; London : Van Nostrand Reinhold, c1982. — xvii,260p : ill ; 24cm. — (Van Nostrand Reinhold data processing series)
Bibliography: p249-252. — Includes index
ISBN 0-442-80325-7 : £21.20 B82-09761

001.64 — Digital computer systems. Evaluation — *Conference proceedings*

Summer School on Computer Systems Performance Evaluation *(2nd : 1980 : Urbino)*. Experimental computer performance evaluation : lecture notes of the Second Summer School on Computer Systems Performance Evaluation, SOGESTA, Urbino, Italy, June 16-27, 1980 / sponsored by Istituto di analisi numerica del CNR, Pavia, Istituto di informatica e sistemistica, Università di Pavia, SOGESTA ; edited by Domenico Ferrari and Massimo Spadoni. — Amsterdam ; Oxford : North-Holland, 1981. — xvii,264p : ill ; 23cm
ISBN 0-444-86129-7 : £14.82 B82-40737

001.64 — Digital computer systems — *For business firms*

Beaman, I. R.. Small business computers for first-time users. — Manchester : NCC Publications, Nov.1982. — [230]p
ISBN 0-85012-374-7 (pbk) : £9.50 : CIP entry B82-29018

001.64 — Digital computer systems — *For children*

Fry, Tom. Computers. — London : Granada, Aug.1982. — [64]p. — (Granada guide series ; 23)
ISBN 0-246-11895-4 : £1.95 : CIP entry B82-15711

Gourlay, Carol. Computers and mathematics / Carol Gourlay. — London : Macdonald Educational, 1982. — 48p : col.ill ; 29cm. — (Visual science)
Includes index
ISBN 0-356-07112-x : Unpriced B82-16358

001.64 — Digital computer systems — *For schools*

Croft, G. M.. Computer studies. — London : Hodder and Stoughton, Dec.1982. — [320]p
ISBN 0-340-26899-9 (pbk) : £4.95 : CIP entry B82-29640

Seal, J. G.. Meet the computer. — Cheltenham : Thornes
Pupil's workbook. — Oct.1982. — [32]p
ISBN 0-85950-384-4 (pbk) : £1.15 : CIP entry B82-25758

Seal, J. G.. Meet the computer. — Cheltenham : Thornes. — Oct.1982
Teacher's guide. — [45]p
ISBN 0-85950-390-9 (pbk) : £2.00 : CIP entry B82-25759

001.64 — Digital computer systems: Hewlett-Packard HP1000 system — *Conference proceedings*

European HP1000 Users Conference *(1st : 1981 : Noordwijkerhout)*. HP1000 computer trends : proceedings of the First European HP1000 Users Conference, April 7-8, 1981, Noordwijkerhout, the Netherlands / edited by Matthijs Beekman, Albert Van Putten and Peter Zuidema. — Chertsey : Reedbooks, c1981. — xii,185p : ill ; 24cm
Includes index
ISBN 0-906544-09-2 (pbk) : Unpriced : CIP rev. B81-30905

001.64 — Digital computer systems. Parallel-processor systems

Hockney, R. W.. Parallel computers : architecture, programming and algorithms / R.W. Hockney, C.R. Jesshope. — Bristol : Hilger, c1981. — xiii,423p : ill ; 24cm
Bibliography: p401-412. — Includes index
ISBN 0-85274-422-6 : £22.50 : CIP rev. B81-27428

Parallel processing systems / edited by David J. Evans. — Cambridge : Cambridge University Press, 1982. — xi,399p : ill ; 24cm
Includes bibliographies and index
ISBN 0-521-24366-1 : £21.00 : CIP rev. B82-25488

001.64 — Digital computer systems. Pipelined systems. Design

Kogge, Peter M.. The architecture of pipelined computers / Peter M. Kogge. — Washington, [D.C.] ; London : Hemisphere, c1981. — xii,334p : ill ; 24cm. — (McGraw-Hill advanced computer science series)
Bibliography: p321-328. — Includes index
ISBN 0-07-035237-2 : £19.95 B82-22537

001.64 — Distributed automatic data processing systems

Bryan, G. C.. Distributed systems : for process monitoring and control / G.C. Bryan and I.G. Umbers ; prepared in collaboration with BP International. — Stevenage : Warren Spring Laboratory, [1982]. — 95p : ill ; 22x30cm
Text on lining papers
ISBN 0-85624-270-5 (pbk) : Unpriced
B82-28222

001.64 — Distributed automatic data processing systems. Management — *Serials*

Advances in distributed processing management. — Vol.1-. — Philadelphia ; London : Heyden, 1980-. — v. : ill ; 24cm
Annual
ISSN 0197-1433 = Advances in distributed processing management : £17.00 B82-11798

001.64 — Distributed digital computer systems

Lientz, Bennet P.. An introduction to distributed systems / Bennet P. Lientz. — Reading, Mass. ; London : Addison-Wesley, c1981. — 455p : ill ; 24cm
Includes index
ISBN 0-201-04297-5 (pbk) : £9.95 B82-33445

Needham, Roger M.. The Cambridge distributed computing system. — London : Addison-Wesley, Apr.1982. — [192]p. — (International computer science series)
ISBN 0-201-14092-6 (pbk) : £7.95 : CIP entry
B82-04293

001.64 — Distributed digital computer systems — *Conference proceedings*

Distributed processing. — [Uxbridge] : [Online Conferences], [c1977]. — 194leaves in various foliations : ill ; 29cm
Conference papers. — Includes bibliographies
Unpriced (pbk) B82-03320

001.64 — Great Britain. Computer systems. Users. Requirements

User requirements for data processing / report by the Project Committee on Future Requirements for Data Processing. — London (13 Mansfield St., W1M 0BP) : British Computer Society, 1978. — vi,26p ; 30cm
£15.00 (£10.00 to members of BCS) (pbk)
B82-40778

001.64 — Man. Interactions with computer systems — *Conference proceedings*

The **Psychology** of computer use. — London : Academic Press, Jan.1983. — [250]p. — (Computers and people)
Conference papers
ISBN 0-12-297420-4 : CIP entry B82-36125

001.64 — Natural language computer systems

Sager, Naomi. Natural language information processing : a computer grammar of English and its applications / Naomi Sager. — Reading, Mass. ; London : Addison-Wesley, 1981. — xv,399p : ill ; 25cm. — (Advanced book program)
Ill on lining papers. — Bibliography: p256-261. — Includes index
ISBN 0-201-06769-2 : £24.80 B82-35339

001.64 — Programmable electronic calculators. Use — *For business practices*

Hohenstein, C. Louis. Using programmable calculators for business / C. Louis Hohenstein. — New York ; Chichester : Wiley, c1982. — viii,296p : ill ; 26cm
Includes index
ISBN 0-471-08551-0 (pbk) : £6.50 B82-16016

001.64 — SERC PRIME digital computer systems — *Manuals*

PRIME manual, version 5. — Didcot (Chilton, Didcot, Oxon. OX11 0QY) : Science and Engineering Research Council, Rutherford Appleton Laboratory, Computing Division, 1981, c1982. — 494,13p : 1form ; 30cm
Includes index
Unpriced (spiral) B82-23768

001.64 — Text processing. Applications of digital computer systems

Teskey, F. N.. Principles of text processing / F.N. Teskey. — Chichester : Ellis Horwood, 1982. — 164p : ill ; 24cm. — (The Ellis Horwood series in computers and their applications ; 19)
Bibliography: p146-150. — Includes index
ISBN 0-85312-264-4 : £16.50 : CIP rev.
ISBN 0-85312-446-9 (student ed.) : Unpriced
B82-06051

001.64′24 — DEC PDP-11 minicomputer systems. Programming languages: Pascal language

MacEwen, Glenn H.. Introduction to computer systems : using the PDP-11 and Pascal / Glenn H. MacEwen. — New York ; London : McGraw-Hill, c1980. — xviii,462p : ill ; 25cm. — (McGraw-Hill computer science series)
Bibliography: p452-455. — Includes index
ISBN 0-07-044350-5 : £19.50 B82-14029

001.64′0207 — Computer systems — *Humour*

Kelly-Bootle, Stan. The Devil's DP dictionary / by Stan Kelly-Bootle. — New York ; London : McGraw-Hill, c1981. — xi,141p : ill ; 21cm
ISBN 0-07-034022-6 (pbk) : £3.95 B82-19787

001.64′0218 — Computer systems. Standards

Guides to computing standards : a series of reference documents on standards for computing and office automation. — Manchester : NCC Standardization Office
No.1: The making of standards / R.M. O'Connor. — 1981. — 28p : ill ; 30cm
Cover title. — Text on inside cover
ISBN 0-85012-305-4 (pbk) : Unpriced
B82-10929

Guides to computing standards : a series of reference documents on standards for computing and office automation. — Manchester : NCC Standardization Office
No.4: Flexible magnetic disk cartridges / C.R. Claber, J.B. Paterson. — 1981. — 24p : ill ; 30cm
Cover title. — Text on inside cover
ISBN 0-85012-306-2 (pbk) : Unpriced
B82-10930

Guides to computing standards : a series of reference documents on standards for computing and office automation. — Manchester : NCC Standardization Office
No.5: Magnetic disk packs and rigid disks / C.R. Claber. — 1981. — 20p : ill ; 30cm
Cover title. — Text on inside cover
ISBN 0-85012-307-0 (pbk) : Unpriced
B82-10931

Guides to computing standards : a series of reference documents on standards for computing and office automation. — Manchester : NCC Standardization Office
No.9: Character sets and coding / H.McG. Ross. — 1981. — 56p in various pagings : ill ; 30cm
Cover title. — Text on inside cover
ISBN 0-85012-308-9 (pbk) : Unpriced
B82-10932

Guides to computing standards : a series of reference documents on standards for computing and office automation. — Manchester : NCC Standardization Office
No.12: Safety / B. Roston. — 1981. — 14p : ill ; 30cm
Cover title. — Text on inside cover
ISBN 0-85012-309-7 (pbk) : Unpriced
B82-10933

Guides to computing standards : a series of reference documents on standards for computing and office automation. — Manchester : NCC Standardization Office
No.15: Programming languages / B. Meek. — 1981. — 32p ; 30cm
Cover title. — Text on inside cover
ISBN 0-85012-310-0 (pbk) : Unpriced
B82-10934

Guides to computing standards : a series of reference documents on standards for computing and office automation. — Manchester : NCC Standardization Office
No.16: Equipment interfaces / D.V. Blake. — 1981. — 48p : ill ; 30cm
Cover title. — Text on inside cover
ISBN 0-85012-311-9 (pbk) : Unpriced
B82-10935

Guides to computing standards : a series of reference documents on standards for computing and office automation. — Manchester : NCC Standardization Office
No.18: Stationery and printing of forms / V. Perriman. — 1981. — 14p : ill,forms ; 30cm
Cover title. — Text on inside cover
ISBN 0-85012-312-7 (pbk) : Unpriced
B82-10936

Guides to computing standards : a series of reference documents on standards for computing and office automation. — Manchester : NCC Standardization Office
No.21: Credit cards and automated transfer of funds / H.C. Way. — 1981. — 43p : ill ; 30cm
Cover title. — Text on inside cover
ISBN 0-85012-313-5 (pbk) : Unpriced
B82-10937

Guides to computing standards : a series of reference documents on standards for computing and office automation. — Manchester : NCC Standardization Office
No.22.1: Fundamental aspects / H.McG. Ross. — 1981. — 25p : ill ; 30cm
Cover title. — Text on inside cover
ISBN 0-85012-314-3 (pbk) : Unpriced
B82-10938

Guides to computing standards : a series of reference documents on standards for computing and office automation. — Manchester : NCC Standardization Office
No.22.2: Modem interfaces and connectors / G. Willis. — 1981. — 43p : ill ; 30cm
Cover title. — Text on inside cover
ISBN 0-85012-315-1 (pbk) : Unpriced
B82-10939

Guides to computing standards : a series of reference documents on standards for computing and office automation. — Manchester : NCC Standardization Office
No.22.3: Modems / G. Willis. — 1981. — 13p ; 30cm
Cover title. — Text on inside cover
ISBN 0-85012-316-x (pbk) : Unpriced
B82-10940

Guides to computing standards : a series of reference documents on standards for computing and office automation. — Manchester : NCC Standardization Office
No.22.6: Packet switched data networks / P. Dean. — 1981. — 19p ; 30cm
Cover title. — Text on inside cover
ISBN 0-85012-317-8 (pbk) : Unpriced
B82-10941

001.64′023 — Computer services — *Career guides* — *For graduates*

French, Jack. Up the EDP pyramid : the complete job hunting manual for computer professionals / Jack French. — New York ; Chichester : Wiley, c1981. — xii,185p : ill ; 24cm
Includes index
ISBN 0-471-08925-7 : £14.75 B82-07794

001.64′023′41 — Great Britain. Computer industries — *Career guides*

Carlyle, Dennis. Careers in computers. — London : Kogan Page, Feb.1983. — [100]p. — (Kogan Page careers series)
ISBN 0-85038-656-x (cased) : £6.95 : CIP entry
ISBN 0-85038-657-6 (pbk) : £2.50 B82-39284

Sharp, Angela. Working with computers / Angela Sharp. — London : Batsford, 1982. — 112p,[8]p of plates : ill ; 22cm. — (Careers series)
Includes index
ISBN 0-7134-0666-6 : £5.95 B82-17651

001.64'02341 — Great Britain. Computer industries — *Career guides*

Working with computers. — 3rd ed. — Manchester : NCC Publications, Apr.1982. — [50]p
Previous ed.: 1975
ISBN 0-85012-359-3 (pbk) : CIP entry
B82-07797

001.64'023'41 — Great Britain. Computer services — *Career guides — For graduates*

The **DOG** guide to computing / [editor Iris Rosier]. — [London] : [VNU Business Publications], [1981?]. — 48p : ill ; 25cm
Cover title
ISBN 0-86271-016-2 (pbk) : Unpriced
B82-05185

001.64'024362 — Digital computer systems — *For general practice — Serials*

Practice computing. — Vol.1, no.1 (Dec. 1981)-. — London (39 North Rd, N7 9DP) : Paradox Publications for ICI Pharmaceuticals Division, 1981-. — v. : ill,ports ; 28cm
Six issues yearly. — Description based on: Vol.1, no.2 (Feb. 1982)
ISSN 0262-0650 = Practice computing : Free to general practitioners B82-38507

001.64'02461 — Digital computer systems — *For medicine*

Covvey, H. Dominic. Computers in the practice of medicine / H. Dominic Covvey, Neil Harding McAlister. — Reading, Mass. ; London : Addison-Wesley. — (Addison-Wesley series, computers in the practice of medicine)
Vol.2: Issues in medical computing. — 1980. — xii,205p : ill ; 24cm
Includes bibliographies and index
ISBN 0-201-01249-9 : £12.95 B82-12655

001.64'02462 — Digital computer systems — *For engineering*

Adey, R. A.. Basic computational techniques for engineers. — London : Pentech Press, Sept.1982. — [236]p
ISBN 0-7273-0203-5 (cased) : £14.00 : CIP entry
ISBN 0-7273-0204-3 (pbk) : £7.50 B82-20395

001.64'024657 — Computer systems — *For accountancy*

Venables, Delia. Computers & word processors for accountants / by Delia Venables. — Uppingham (31 High St. East, Uppingham, Rutland, Leics. LE1 5 9PY) : European Study Conferences, [1981]. — 75p ; 30cm
Cover title
Unpriced (spiral) B82-23280

Venables, Delia. Computers & word processors for accountants : updating supplement / by Delia Venables. — Uppingham (31 High St. East, Uppingham, Rutland, Leics. LE15 9PY) : European Study Conferences, 1982. — 6leaves : ill ; 30cm
Unpriced (unbound) B82-23281

001.64'024657 — Digital computer systems — *For accountancy*

Perry, William E.. The accountants' guide to computer systems / William E. Perry. — New York ; Chichester : Wiley, c1982. — xi,286p : ill ; 24cm. — (Modern accounting perspectives and practice)
Includes index
ISBN 0-471-08992-3 : £23.00 B82-35303

001.64'024658 — Digital computer systems — *For small firms*

Cluff, Edward G.. Computerisation for the small business : a layman's guide for directors and senior line-management. — 2nd ed. / by Edward G. Cluff. — Purley : Input Two-Nine, [1979]. — 154p : ill ; 23cm
Previous ed.: 1977
ISBN 0-905897-33-1 (cased) : Unpriced
ISBN 0-905897-34-x (pbk) : Unpriced
B82-04095

001.64'025'41 — Great Britain. Computer services — *Directories*

NCC directory of computing services. — Manchester : NCC Information Services, Jan.1982. — [150]p
ISBN 0-85012-351-8 (pbk) : CIP entry
B82-02459

001.64'025'417 — Ireland *(Republic).* **Computer services** — *Directories — Serials*

Irish Computer Services Association. Company profile directory / the Irish Computer Services Association. — 1982-. — Dublin (Confederation House, Kildare St, Dublin 2) : The Association, 1982-. — v. ; 30cm
Two issues yearly
Unpriced B82-40043

001.64'03 — Computer systems — *Polyglot dictionaries*

The **Multilingual** computer dictionary / Alan Isaacs, editor. — London : Muller, c1981. — 332p ; 26cm
ISBN 0-584-95567-7 : £10.95 B82-00789

001.64'03'21 — Computer systems — *Encyclopaedias*

Anderson, R. G.. A dictionary of data processing and computer terms / R.G. Anderson. — Plymouth : Macdonald and Evans, 1982. — 106p ; 22cm
ISBN 0-7121-0429-1 (pbk) : £2.95 B82-19413

Dictionary of computing. — Chichester : Wiley, July 1982. — [325]p
ISBN 0-471-10468-x (cased) : £16.00 : CIP entry
ISBN 0-471-10469-8 (pbk) : £10.50
B82-14231

Sippl, Charles J.. The essential computer dictionary and speller : for secretaries, managers, and office personnel / Charles J. Sippl, JoAnne Coffman Mayer. — Englewood Cliffs ; London : Prentice-Hall, c1980. — v,258p : ill ; 23cm. — (A Spectrum book)
ISBN 0-13-284364-1 (cased) : £9.70
B82-37921

001.64'04 — ABC 80 microcomputer systems. Applications

Westh, Åke. Measurement and control with a small computer system : some applications of the ABC80 microcomputer. — Lund : Studentlitteratur ; Bromley : Chartwell-Bratt, 1981. — 125p : ill ; 23cm
Translation of: Stys och mät med ABC80. — Bibliography: p123. — Includes index
ISBN 0-86238-026-x (pbk) : Unpriced
B82-36844

001.64'04 — Apple II microcomputer systems

Dunn, Seamus. The Apple personal computer for beginners. — London : Prentice Hall, Sept.1982. — [288]p
ISBN 0-13-039149-2 (cased) : £8.95 : CIP entry
ISBN 0-13-039131-x (pbk) : £5.95 B82-19171

001.64'04 — Apple microcomputer systems — *Serials*

[Windfall *(Stockport)***]**. Windfall. — No.1 (July 1981)-. — Stockport (68 Chester Rd, Hazel Grove, Stockport SK7 5NY) : Europress, 1981-. — v. : ill ; 30cm
Monthly
ISSN 0262-4877 = Windfall (Stockport) : £12.00 per year B82-04922

001.64'04 — BBC microcomputer systems — *Manuals*

Dane, P. M.. Learning to use the BBC Microcomputer. — Aldershot : Gower, Sept.1982. — [120]p
ISBN 0-566-03452-2 (pbk) : £5.25 : CIP entry
B82-20211

001.64'04 — BBC microcomputer systems — *Serials*

BEEBUG : registered referral centre for the BBC project / independent national user group for the BBC Microcomputer. — Vol.1, no.1 (Apr. 1982)-. — St. Albans (P.O. Box 50, St. Albans, Herts. AL1 2AR) : BEEBUG, 1982-. — v. ; 21cm
Monthly. — Also entitled: BEEBUG newsletter
ISSN 0263-7561 = BEEBUG : £8.50 per year
B82-31732

Owl : the BBC microcomputer magazine. — Issue 1 (June 1982)-. — [Market Harborough] ([P.O. Box 50, Farndon Rd, Market Harborough, Leics.]) : [EMAP National Publications], 1982-. — v. : ill(some col.),ports ; 30cm
ISSN 0263-6883 = Owl : Unpriced
B82-29058

001.64'04 — Commodore PET microcomputer systems — *Manuals*

Marshall, Garry. Learning to live with the PET computer. — Aldershot : Gower, June 1982. — [120]p
ISBN 0-566-03427-1 (pbk) : £7.50 : CIP entry
B82-09431

001.64'04 — Commodore PET microcomputer systems — *Serials*

Printout : [the independent magazine for Pet users]. — Vol.1, no.1 (Dec. 1979)-. — [Newbury] ([P.O. Box 48, Newbury RG16 0BD, Berks.]) : Printout Publications, 1979-. — v. : ill ; 30cm
Monthly. — Subtitle varies
ISSN 0261-4499 = Printout : £11.40
B82-06792

001.64'04 — Commodore VIC microcomputer systems

Jones, A. J.. Mastering the VIC-20. — Chichester : Ellis Horwood, Jan.1983. — [208]p
ISBN 0-85312-506-6 : £12.50 : CIP entry
B82-37637

001.64'04 — Commodore VIC microcomputer systems — *Manuals*

Geere, Ron. Learning to use the VIC-20 computer. — Aldershot : Gower, Nov.1982. — [120]p
ISBN 0-566-03453-0 (pbk) : £5.25 : CIP entry
B82-26556

Hampshire, Nick. VIC revealed. — London : Duckworth, Nov.1982. — [272]p
ISBN 0-7156-1699-4 (pbk) : £9.95 : CIP entry
B82-33203

001.64'04 — Data General minicomputer systems. Design — *Personal observations*

Kidder, Tracy. The soul of a new machine / Tracy Kidder. — London : Allen Lane, 1982, c1981. — 254p ; 23cm
Originally published: Boston : Little, Brown, 1981
ISBN 0-7139-1482-3 : £7.50 B82-17719

001.64'04 — Data transmission. Applications of microcomputer systems

Derfler, Frank J.. Microcomputer data communication systems / Frank J. Derfler, Jr. — Englewood Cliffs ; London : Prentice-Hall, c1982. — ix,129p : ill ; 24cm. — (A Spectrum book)
Includes index
ISBN 0-13-580720-4 (cased) : Unpriced
ISBN 0-13-580712-3 (pbk) : £9.70 B82-24087

001.64'04 — Data transmission. Applications of minicomputer systems — *Conference proceedings*

The **Mini** in terminal-based systems. — [Uxbridge] : [Online Conferences], [c1977]. — 400p in various pagings : ill,maps ; 30cm
Conference papers
Unpriced (pbk) B82-03322

001.64'04 — IBM small digital computer systems — *Conference proceedings*

IBM : small systems. — Uxbridge : Online Conferences, c1979. — viii,122p : ill ; 29cm
Conference papers
ISBN 0-903796-47-3 (pbk) : Unpriced
B82-03326

001.64'04 — INTEL SDK-85 microcomputer systems

Rafiquzzaman, Mohamed. Microcomputer theory and applications with the INTEL SDK-85 / Mohamed Rafiquzzaman. — New York ; Chichester : Wiley, c1982. — xvii,600p ; 25cm
Bibliography: p563-564. — Includes index
ISBN 0-471-09631-8 : £16.60 B82-27759

001.64′04 — Laboratories. Minicomputer systems — *Study examples: DEC PDP-11 minicomputer systems*

Bourne, John R.. Laboratory minicomputing / John R. Bourne. — New York ; London : Academic Press, 1981. — x,297p : ill,forms ; 24cm. — (Notes and reports in computer science and applied mathematics ; 1)
Includes bibliographies and index
ISBN 0-12-119080-3 : £18.00 B82-10051

001.64′04 — Microcomputer systems

Danhof, Kenneth J.. Computing system fundamentals : an approach based on microcomputers / Kenneth J. Danhof, Carol L. Smith. — Reading, Mass. ; London : Addison-Wesley, c1981. — xi,331p : ill ; 25cm. — (Addison-Wesley series in computer science)
Bibliography: p321-323 . — Includes index
ISBN 0-201-01298-7 : £10.50 B82-38104

Deakin, Rose. Microcomputers : everything you ever wanted to know / Rose Deakin. — London : Sphere, 1982. — xv,172p ; 20cm
Cover title: Microcomputing. — Bibliography: p172
ISBN 0-7221-3010-4 (pbk) : £2.25 B82-21274

Flores, Ivan. Microcomputer systems / Ivan Flores, Christopher Terry. — New York ; London : Van Nostrand Reinhold, c1982. — xiv,290p : ill ; 24cm
Includes index
ISBN 0-442-26141-1 : £19.15 B82-35484

Introduction to microcomputers / editors Erik L. Dagless and David Aspinall. — London : Pitman, 1982. — xi,233p : ill ; 23cm. — (A Pitman international text)
Bibliography: p182-183. — Includes index
ISBN 0-273-01706-3 (pbk) : Unpriced : CIP rev. B81-28156

McGlynn, Daniel R.. Personal computing : home, professional and small business applications / Daniel R. McGlynn. — 2nd ed. — New York ; Chichester : Willey, 1982. — xii,335p : ill ; 26cm
Previous ed.: 1979. — Bibliography: p329-332. — Includes index
ISBN 0-471-86164-2 (pbk) : £11.65 B82-35994

Steinböck, Hans. Introduction to microcomputers / Hans Steinböck ; [translated from the German by H. Bibring]. — Berlin : Siemens ; London : Heyden, c1982. — 80p : ill ; 21cm. — (Pi ; 17)
Translation of: Einführung in die Mikrocomputertechnik
ISBN 0-85501-517-9 (pbk) : Unpriced : CIP rev. B82-02467

Ullmann, Julian R.. Microcomputer technology : an introduction / Julian R. Ullmann. — London : Pitman, 1982. — viii,260p : ill ; 23cm
Includes index
ISBN 0-273-01724-1 (pbk) : Unpriced : CIP rev. B82-07980

Wilson, F. A.. The pre-computer book. — London : Babani, Feb.1983. — [96]p. — (BP ; 115)
ISBN 0-85934-090-2 (pbk) : £1.95 : CIP entry B82-39596

Zaks, Rodnay. Your first computer : a guide to business and personal computing / Rodnay Zaks. — 2nd ed. — Berkeley, Calif. : Sybex ; Birmingham : the Computer Bookshop [distributor], 1980. — xv,258p : ill ; 22cm
Previous ed.: published as An introduction to personal and business computing. 1978. — Includes index
ISBN 0-89588-045-8 (pbk) : Unpriced B82-27398

001.64′04 — Microcomputer systems & microprocessor systems

Aumiaux, M.. Microprocessor systems / M. Aumiaux ; translation by Arleta Starza and David Brailsford. — Chichester : Wiley, c1982. — x,218p : ill ; 24cm. — (Wiley series in computing)
Translation of: Les systèmes à microprocesseur. — Includes index
ISBN 0-471-10129-x : £11.95 : CIP rev. B82-13248

Khambata, Adi J.. Microprocessors/microcomputers : architecture, software, and systems / Adi J. Khambata. — New York ; Chichester : Wiley, c1982. — xxiii,577p : ill ; 23cm
Includes index
ISBN 0-471-06490-4 : £15.95 B82-21536

Paker, Y.. Multi-microprocessor systems. — London : Academic Press, Feb.1983. — [250]p. — (APIC studies in data processing ; 18)
ISBN 0-12-543980-6 : CIP entry B82-36581

Rao, Guthikonda V.. Microprocessors and microcomputer systems / Guthikonda V. Rao. — 2nd ed. — New York ; London : Van Nostrand Reinhold, c1982. — xv,581p : ill ; 29cm
Previous ed.: 1978. — Includes index
ISBN 0-442-25626-4 : £36.50 B82-24926

Tocci, Ronald J.. Microprocessors and microcomputers : hardware and software / Ronald J. Tocci, Lester P. Laskowski. — 2nd ed. — Englewood Cliffs ; London : Prentice-Hall, c1982. — xii,404p : ill ; 24cm
Previous ed.: 1979. — Includes index
ISBN 0-13-581322-0 : £15.70 B82-16842

001.64′04 — Microcomputer systems — *Amateurs′ manuals*

McKirgan, David. The layman′s guide to home computing. — Cambridge (85 Castle St., Cambridge CA3 0AJ) : Great Ouse Press, Jan.1983. — [100]p
ISBN 0-907351-05-0 (pbk) : £2.00 : CIP entry B82-40927

001.64′04 — Microcomputer systems. Applications

Lane, J. E.. Microprocessors and information handling. — Manchester : NCC Publications, Sept.1981. — [60]p. — (Computing in the ′80s ; 4)
ISBN 0-85012-334-8 (pbk) : £4.00 : CIP entry B81-28150

Smith, F. J.. The computer : our silicon genie : an inaugural lecture delivered before the Queen′s University of Belfast on 16 December 1980 / F.J. Smith. — [Belfast] : Queen′s University of Belfast, c1980. — 35p : ill ; 21cm. — (New lecture series ; no.127)
ISBN 0-85389-202-4 (pbk) : £0.40 B82-12512

001.64′04 — Microcomputer systems. Design

Clements, Alan. Microcomputer design and construction : building your own system with the Motorola 6800 / Alan Clements. — Englewood Cliffs ; London : Prentice/Hall International, c1982. — xviii,520p : ill ; 24cm
Bibliography: p505-511. — Includes index
ISBN 0-13-580738-7 : £18.95 B82-38570

001.64′04 — Microcomputer systems — *For chldren*

Parker, David. Computing is easy. — London : Newnes Technical Books, June 1982. — [152]p
ISBN 0-408-01203-x (pbk) : £2.95 : CIP entry B82-10492

001.64′04 — Microcomputer systems — *Serials*

Don′t panic! : [the journal of Cambridge Microcomputer Club]. — Issue 1 (Nov. 1981)-. — [Cambridge] ([22a Castle St., Cambridge]) : Treacle Communications on behalf of the Club, 1981-. — v. : ill ; 30cm
Six issues yearly
ISSN 0262-9526 = Don′t panic! : £5.50 per year B82-12461

Which micro? & software review. — 1st issue (May-June 1982)-. — London (57(a) Hatton Garden, EC1B 1DT) : EMAP Business and Computer Publications, 1982-. — v. : ill(some col.),ports ; 30cm
Six issues yearly
ISSN 0262-673X = Which micro? & software review (corrected) : £0.85 B82-32176

001.64′04 — Microcomputer systems — *Study examples:* **Commodore PET microcomputer systems** — *Manuals*

Anderson, R. G.. Microcomputing / R.G. Anderson. — Plymouth : Macdonald and Evans, 1982. — xii,108p : ill ; 18cm. — (The M. & E. handbook series)
Bibliography: p104. — Includes index
ISBN 0-7121-1265-0 (pbk) : £1.95 B82-18031

001.64′04 — Micromputer systems. Interfaces with peripheral equipment

Zaks, Rodnay. Microprocessor interfacing techniques / Rodnay Zaks, Austin Lesea. — 3rd ed. — Berkeley, Calif. : Sybex ; Birmingham : the Computer Bookshop [distributor], c1979. — 456p : ill ; 22cm
Previous ed.: 1978. — Includes index
ISBN 0-89588-029-6 (pbk) : Unpriced B82-27396

001.64′04 — Microprocessor systems

Gilmore, Charles M.. Introduction to microprocessors / Charles M. Gilmore. — New York ; London : Gregg Division, McGraw-Hill, c1981. — x,310p : ill(some col.) ; 28cm. — (Basic skills in electricity and electronics)
Includes index
ISBN 0-07-023301-2 (pbk) : £11.50 B82-25222

Microprocessor-based systems Level IV. — London : Hutchinson Education, Dec.1982. — [512]p
ISBN 0-09-148911-3 (pbk) : £8.50 : CIP entry B82-32282

Sinclair, Ian R.. Practical microprocessor systems / Ian R. Sinclair. — Sevenoaks : Newnes Technical, 1981. — 139p : ill ; 22cm. — (Newnes microcomputer books)
Includes index
ISBN 0-408-00496-7 (pbk) : £4.95 : CIP rev. B81-31736

Wood, Alec, *1947-*. Microprocessors — your questions answered / Alec Wood. — London : Newnes Technical, 1982. — 155p : ill ; 22cm. — (Newnes microcomputer books)
Includes index
ISBN 0-408-00580-7 (pbk) : Unpriced : CIP rev. B81-25285

001.64′04 — Microprocessor systems — *Encyclopaedias — Polyglot texts*

International microcomputer dictionary. — Berkeley : Sybex ; Birmingham : The Computer Bookshop [distributor], c1981. — x,19p ; 17cm
ISBN 0-89588-067-9 (pbk) : Unpriced B82-27409

001.64′04 — Microprocessor systems — *For architecture*

Jarrett, Dennis. The handbook of computer systems for architects and designers. — London : New Technology Press, Oct.1982. — [228]p
ISBN 0-86330-210-6 (pbk) : £16.00 : CIP entry B82-31314

001.64′04 — Microprocessor systems — *For management*

Jones, W. S.William Stanley. Micro′s for managers / W.S. Jones and R.C. Peattie. — Stevenage : Peregrinus, c1981. — ix,158p : ill ; 23cm
Includes index
ISBN 0-906048-60-5 (pbk) : Unpriced : CIP rev. B81-27476

001.64'04 — Microprocessor systems. Interfaces with peripheral equipment

Bibbero, Robert J.. Microprocessor systems : interfacing and applications / Robert J. Bibbero, David M. Stern. — New York ; Chichester : Wiley, c1982. — xiv,195p : ill ; 24cm
Includes index
ISBN 0-471-05306-6 : £15.50 B82-34334

001.64'04 — Minicomputer systems

Minicomputers : a reference book for engineers, scientists and managers / [edited by] Y. Paker. — Tunbridge Wells : Abacus, 1981. — 505p : ill ; 24cm
Bibliography: p477-493. — Includes index
ISBN 0-85626-188-2 : Unpriced : CIP rev. B80-08075

001.64'04 — Minicomputer systems — *Conference proceedings*

Minicomputer forum : conference proceedings 1975. — Uxbridge : Online Conferences, [1975?]. — x,600p : ill ; 29cm
Unpriced B82-03524

Minicomputers and small business systems. — Uxbridge : Online Conferences, c1976. — 660p : ill ; 29cm
Conference proceedings
ISBN 0-903796-16-3 : Unpriced B82-03525

001.64'04 — Minicomputer systems. Evaluation & selection

Knight, P. A.. Installing a small business computer / P.A. Knight. — Manchester : NCC, 1981. — 111p : 1ill,forms ; 21cm
Bibliography: p109-111
ISBN 0-85012-343-7 (pbk) : Unpriced : CIP rev. B81-37593

001.64'04 — Motorola 6800 & 6802 microprocessor systems

Simpson, Robert J.. Introduction to 6800/6802 microprocessor systems : hardware, software and experimentation / Robert J. Simpson and Trevor J. Terrell. — London : Newnes Technical, 1982. — 238p : ill ; 22cm
Includes index
ISBN 0-408-01179-3 (pbk) : Unpriced : CIP rev. B81-36377

001.64'04 — Motorola 6800 microprocessor systems

Gault, James W.. Introduction to microcomputer-based digital systems / James W. Gault, Russell L. Pimmel. — New York ; London : McGraw-Hill, c1982. — xi,429p : ill ; 24cm. — (McGraw-Hill series in electrical engineering)
Text on lining papers. — Includes index
ISBN 0-07-023047-1 : £20.50 B82-25268

Newell, Sydney B.. Introduction to microcomputing / Sydney B. Newell. — New York ; London : Harper & Row, c1982. — xii,615p : ill ; 25cm
Includes index
ISBN 0-06-044802-4 : £12.50 B82-24028

001.64'04 — Motorola 6809 microprocessor systems

James, M.. The 6809 companion / by M. James. — London : Babani, 1982. — 88p ; 18cm
ISBN 0-85934-077-5 (pbk) : £1.95 : CIP rev. B82-04813

001.64'04 — Motorola 68000 microprocessor systems

MC 68000 16-bit microprocessor : user's manual / Motorola. — 3rd ed. — Englewood Cliffs, N.J. ; London : Prentice-Hall, c1982. — xv,231p : ill ; 25cm
Cover title: 16-bit microprocessor. — Previous ed.: 1980
ISBN 0-13-566703-8 (cased) : Unpriced
ISBN 0-13-566737-2 (limited ed.) : Unpriced
ISBN 0-13-566760-7 (special ed.) : Unpriced
ISBN 0-13-566695-3 (pbk) : Unpriced B82-28343

001.64'04 — Personal computer systems

Bradbeer, Robin. The personal computer book / Robin Bradbeer. — 2nd ed. — Aldershot : Gower, c1982. — 240p : ill ; 22cm
Previous ed.: 1980. — Bibliography: p197-220
ISBN 0-566-03445-x (cased) : Unpriced : CIP rev.
ISBN 0-566-03423-9 (pbk) : Unpriced B81-34724

Hickman, Ian. Get more from your personal computer. — London : Newnes Technical Books, Nov.1982. — [176]p
ISBN 0-408-01131-9 (pbk) : £4.95 : CIP entry B82-28249

Lafferty, Peter. Personal computing / Peter Lafferty. — London : Newnes Technical, 1981. — 91p : ill ; 17cm. — (Questions & answers)
Bibliography: p85-86. — Includes index
ISBN 0-408-00555-6 (pbk) : Unpriced : CIP rev. B81-20608

Nilles, Jock M.. Exploring the world of the personal computer / Jock M. Nilles. — Englewood Cliffs ; London : Prentice-Hall, c1982. — xviii,234p : ill ; 23cm. — (A Reward book)
Bibliography: p219-227. — Includes index
ISBN 0-13-297572-6 (pbk) : Unpriced B82-28419

Rodwell, Peter, *1951-*. Personal computers / Peter Rodwell. — London : W.H. Allen, 1982, c1981. — 117p ; 19cm
Includes index
ISBN 0-491-02777-x : £3.95 B82-13374

Zaks, Rodnay. Don't!, or, How to care for your computer / Rodnay Zaks. — Berkeley, Calif. : Sybex ; Birmingham : the Computer Bookshop [distributor], 1981. — xvi,218p : ill ; 22cm
Includes index
ISBN 0-89588-065-2 (pbk) : Unpriced B82-27399

001.64'04 — Personal computer systems — *Manuals*

Herbert, Frank. [Without me you're nothing]. The home computer handbook / Frank Herbert with Max Barnard. — London : Gollancz, 1981. — 297p : ill ; 23cm
Originally published: New York : Simon and Schuster, 1980
ISBN 0-575-03050-x : £7.95 B82-04333

Rodwell, Peter. Personal computers / Peter Rodwell. — [London] : Star, 1981. — 117p ; 18cm
Includes index
ISBN 0-352-31073-1 (pbk) : £1.50 B82-17842

001.64'04 — Personal computer systems — *Serials*

Personal computing today. — Vol.1, no.1 (Aug. 1982)-. — London : Argus Specialist Publications, 1982-. — v. : ill ; 30cm
Monthly
ISSN 0263-5542 = Personal computing today : £11.65 per year B82-36709

Your computer. — Vol.1 no.1 (June/July 1981)-. — Sutton (Quadrant House, The Quadrant, Sutton, Surrey SM2 5AS) : IPC Electrical-Electronic Press, 1981-. — v. : ill ; 30cm
Monthly. — Description based on: Vol.1 no.2 (Aug./Sept. 1981)
ISSN 0263-0885 = Your computer : £8.00 B82-18500

001.64'04 — Rockwell 6502 microprocessor systems. Applications. Projects — *Manuals*

Zaks, Rodnay. 6502 applications book / Rodnay Zaks. — Berkeley, Calif. : Sybex ; Birmingham : the Computer Bookshop [distributor], c1979. — 278p : ill,facsims ; 22cm. — (6502 series ; v.3)
Includes index
ISBN 0-89588-015-6 (pbk) : Unpriced B82-27391

001.64'04 — Sinclair ZX Spectrum microcomputer systems — *Manuals*

Bradbeer, Robin. Learning to use the ZX Spectrum. — Aldershot : Gower, Nov.1982. — [120]p. — (A Read-out publication)
ISBN 0-566-03481-6 : £5.25 : CIP entry B82-26558

Sinclair, Ian. The ZX Spectrum. — London : Granada, Oct.1982. — [128]p
ISBN 0-246-12018-5 (pbk) : £5.95 : CIP entry B82-28446

001.64'04 — Sinclair ZX80 & ZX81 microcomputer systems — *Practical information*

ZX 80.81 register : Youngs computer register : directory of dealers : classified list of programs, hardware sources, ZX publications, user clubs, features. — Halstead (2 Woodland Way, Gosfield, Halstead, Essex, CO9 1TH) : British Heritage Philatelics, [1982]. — 58p ; 21cm
Cover title. — Edited by M.W. Young, I.G. Young
Unpriced (pbk) B82-37957

001.64'04 — Sinclair ZX81 microcomputer systems — *Manuals*

Bradbeer, Robin. Learning to use the ZX81 computer. — Aldershot : Gower, Oct.1982. — [120]p
ISBN 0-566-03451-4 : £7.50 : CIP entry B82-23336

Hewson, Andrew D.. Hints & tips for the ZX81 / Andrew D. Hewson. — [Blewbury] : Hewson Consultants, c1981. — 76p ; 21cm
(pbk) B82-25015

Maunder, Bob. The ZX81 companion / by Bob Maunder. — Middlesbrough : LINSAC, 1981. — v,131p : ill ; 21cm
Includes index
ISBN 0-907211-01-1 (pbk) : £7.95 B82-24040

Terrell, Trevor J.. ZX81 user's handbook. — London : Newnes Technical, July 1982. — [160]p
ISBN 0-408-01223-4 (pbk) : £5.95 : CIP entry B82-12322

001.64'04 — Sinclair ZX81 microcomputer systems. Peripheral equipment

Wren-Hilton, Martin. The ZX81 add-on book. — Nantwich : Shiva, July 1982. — [100]p. — (Shiva's friendly micro series)
ISBN 0-906812-19-4 (pbk) : £6.50 : CIP entry B82-20873

001.64'04 — Small digital computer systems

Colloms, Martin. Computer controlled testing and instrumentation. — London : Pentech, Jan.1983. — [140]p
ISBN 0-7273-0310-4 : £12.50 : CIP entry B82-32630

001.64'04 — Small digital computer systems — *For business enterprise*

Smolin, C. Roger. How to buy the right small business computer system / C. Roger Smolin. — New York ; Chichester : Wiley, c1981. — ix,156p : ill ; 26cm
Includes index
ISBN 0-471-08494-8 (pbk) : £6.60 B82-05890

001.64'04 — Tandy TRS-80 microcomputer systems — *Manuals — For business firms*

Lewis, T. G.. The TRS-80 means business / by T.G. Lewis. — New York ; Chichester : Wiley, c1982. — ix,194p : ill ; 26cm
Includes index
ISBN 0-471-08239-2 (pbk) : £8.25 B82-18059

001.64'04 — Tandy TRS-80 microcomputer systems — *Serials*

Micro-80. — [Issue 1 (Dec. 1979)?]-. — Adelaide ; Tunbridge Wells (24 Woodhill Pk, Pembury, Tunbridge Wells, Kent TN2 4NW) : Micro-80, 1979-. — v. : ill ; 30cm
Monthly. — Description based on: Issue 11 (Oct. 1980)
£16.00 per year B82-19853

001.64'04 — Tandy TRS-80 Pocket Computer microcomputer systems — *Programmed instructions*

Inman, Don. Problem-solving on the TRS-80 pocket computer / Don Inman, Jim Conlan. — New York ; Chichester : Wiley, c1982. — 255p : ill ; 23cm
Includes index
ISBN 0-471-86808-6 (pbk) : Unpriced
ISBN 0-471-09270-3 (pbk) : £5.95 B82-21531

Spencer, Donald D.. Programming the TRS-80 pocket computer / Donald D. Spencer. — Englewood Cliffs ; London : Prentice-Hall, c1982. — x,142p : ill ; 23cm
Includes index
ISBN 0-13-730531-1 (pbk) : Unpriced
B82-39699

001.64'04 — Zilog Z8000 microprocessor systems

Fawcett, Bradly K.. The Z8000 microprocessor : a design handbook / Bradly K. Fawcett. — Englewood Cliffs ; London : Prentice-Hall, c1982. — x,310p : ill ; 24cm
Includes index
ISBN 0-13-983742-6 (cased) : Unpriced
ISBN 0-13-983734-5 (pbk) : £12.75
B82-37728

Z8000 CPU user's reference manual : Zilog. — Englewood Cliffs ; London : Prentice-Hall, c1982. — ix,290p : ill ; 24cm
ISBN 0-13-983908-9 (cased) : Unpriced
ISBN 0-13-983890-2 (pbk) : £10.45
B82-29485

001.64'04'02438 — Microcomputer systems — *For commerce*

Choosing and using a business microcomputer. — Aldershot : Gower, Mar.1982. — [200]p
ISBN 0-566-03405-0 (pbk) : £12.50 : CIP entry
B82-00195

001.64'04'024657 — Microcomputer systems — *For accountancy*

Forrest, A. T.. Microcomputers for the professional accountant. — Aldershot : Gower, Dec.1982. — [200]p
ISBN 0-566-03441-7 : £15.00 : CIP entry
B82-29445

001.64'04'02469 — Microcomputer systems — *For building industries — Serials*

[Microcomputer newsletter *(Bracknell)*]. Microcomputer newsletter / BSRIA. — No.1 (June 1982)-. — Bracknell (Old Bracknell Lane West, Bracknell, Berks. RG12 4AH) : Building Services Research and Information Association, 1982-. — v. : ill,ports ; 30cm
Quarterly
ISSN 0263-8908 = Microcomputer newsletter (Bracknell) : Unpriced B82-33871

001.64'04'0321 — Minicomputer & microcomputer systems — *Encyclopaedias*

Burton, Philip E.. A dictionary of minicomputing and microcomputing. — Chichester : Wiley, Aug.1982. — [368]p
ISBN 0-471-10499-x : £15.00 : CIP entry
B82-15820

001.64'05 — Computer sciences — *Serials*

GIGO. — 1979-. — Cambridge (c/o GIGO Editor, Computer Laboratory, Corn Exchange St., Cambridge, CB2 3QG) : Cambridge University Computer Society, 1979-. — v. : ill ; 21cm
Two issues yearly. — Description based on: Issue no.0100 (Easter Term 1982)
ISSN 0262-4052 = GIGO : £0.50 B82-31713

001.64'05 — Computer services — *Serials*

[On line *(Sunbury-on-Thames)*]. On line. — Vol.1, no.1 (1978)-. — [Sunbury-on-Thames] ([99 Staines Rd West, Sunbury-on-Thames, Middx]) : [BOC Computer Services], 1978-. — v. : ill,ports ; 30cm
Three issues yearly
ISSN 0263-2187 = On line (Sunbury-on-Thames) : Unpriced B82-19850

001.64'05 — Computer systems. Applications — *Serials*

[Computer applications *(Bradford)*]. Computer applications. — Vol.1, no.1 (1981)-. — Bradford : MCB Publications, 1981-. — v. : ill ; 25cm
Three issues yearly. — Each issue has a distinctive title
ISSN 0261-331x = Computer applications (Bradford) : Unpriced B82-06785

001.64'05 — Computer systems — *Serials*

What's new in computing. — Sept. 1981-. — London (Calderwood St., SE18 6QH) : Morgan-Grampian, 1981-. — v. : ill ; 30cm
Monthly. — Description based on: Oct. 1981
ISSN 0262-2734 = What's new in computing : £25.00 per year B82-05212

001.64'068 — Digital computer systems. Management — *Manuals*

Axelrod, C. Warren. Computer productivity : a planning guide for cost-effective management / C. Warren Axelrod. — New York ; Chichester : Wiley, c1982. — vii,254p : ill ; 24cm
Includes index
ISBN 0-471-07744-5 : £19.50 B82-28710

Bentley, Trevor J.. Management information systems and data processing / Trevor J. Bentley. — London : Holt, Rinehart and Winston, c1982. — x,249p : ill ; 25cm
Includes bibliographies and index
ISBN 0-03-910364-1 (pbk) : Unpriced : CIP rev. B82-10775

Longworth, Gordon. Management handbook of computer operations. — Manchester : NCC Publications, Aug.1982. — [460]p
ISBN 0-85012-360-7 (spiral) : CIP entry
B82-18479

001.64'068'5 — Digital computer systems. Project management

Collins, G. L.. Structured systems development techniques. — London : Pitman, Oct.1982. — [368]p
ISBN 0-273-01773-x : £16.00 : CIP entry
B82-20624

001.64'068'8 — Digital computer systems. Marketing — *Serials*

Computer confidential. — No.1-. — [Hove] ([27 Blatchington Rd, Hove, East Sussex BN3 3YL]) : [Peter Bartram Pub.], [1981]-. — v. ; 31cm
Monthly
ISSN 0263-1466 = Computer confidential : £95.00 per year B82-18494

001.64'07'073 — United States. Education. Curriculum subjects: Digital computer systems — *Conference proceedings*

Computer literacy : issues and directions for 1985 / edited by Robert J. Seidel, Ronald E. Anderson, Beverly Hunter. — New York ; London : Academic Press, 1982. — xvi,308p : ill ; 24cm
Based on the National computer literacy goals for 1985 conference, held at Reston, Virginia, Dec.18-20, 1980
ISBN 0-12-634960-6 : £15.20 B82-37236

001.64'0724 — Digital computer systems. Experiments

Hall, Douglas V.. Experiments in microprocessors and digital systems / Douglas V. Hall, Marybelle B. Hall. — New York ; London : McGraw-Hill, c1981. — ix,150p : ill ; 28cm
ISBN 0-07-025576-8 (pbk) : £5.75
Also classified at 621.3819'5835 B82-00533

001.64'076 — Digital computer systems — *Questions & answers*

Cross, T.. Computers study and revision / T. Cross, M. Quickfall. — [Glasgow] : Collins Educational, [1982?]. — [64]p : ill ; 30cm. — (Collins revision aids)
ISBN 0-00-197254-5 (pbk) : £1.50 B82-32056

001.64'07'8 — Educational institutions. Curriculum subjects: Computer systems. Teaching. Applications of educational technology — *Conference proceedings*

IFIP WG 3.4 Working Conference on Teaching Informatics Courses *(1981 : Vienna)*. Teaching informatics courses : guidelines for trainers and educationalists : proceedings of the IFIP WG 3.4 Working Conference on Teaching Informatics Courses held in Vienna, Austria, 21-24 July, 1981 / edited by H.L.W. Jackson ; [organised by Working Group 3.4 of IFIP Technical Committee 3, Education, International Federation for Information Processing]. — Amsterdam ; Oxford : North-Holland, 1982. — xii,265p : ill,forms ; 23cm
ISBN 0-444-86364-8 : £18.12 B82-24665

001.64'09172'4 — Developing countries. Digital computer systems — *Conference proceedings*

IFIP TC-9 International Seminar on Computers in Developing Nations *(1980 : Melbourne)*. Computers in developing nations : a one-day international seminar : proceedings of the IFIP TC-9 International Seminar on Computers in Developing Nations Melbourne, Australia, 13 October, 1980 / edited by John M. Bennett and Robert E. Kalman. — Amsterdam ; Oxford : North-Holland, c1981. — xv,272p : ill,1map ; 23cm
ISBN 0-444-86270-6 : £18.40 B82-01637

001.64'0947 — Soviet Union. Computer systems, *to 1981*

Ershov, A. P.. A.P. Ershov, the British lectures : four lectures presented by A.P. Ershov and delivered to British Computer Society audiences after his awards as Distinguished Fellow of the BCS. — London : Heyden, c1980. — xiii,57p : ill,ports ; 24cm
ISBN 0-85501-491-1 (pbk) : £12.00
B82-40779

001.64'0952 — Japan. Computer industries & services

Welke, H. J.. Data processing in Japan / H.J. Welke. — Amsterdam ; Oxford : North-Holland, 1982. — xi,198p : ill ; 23cm. — (Information research and resource reports ; v.1)
ISBN 0-444-86379-6 : Unpriced B82-34479

001.64'0956 — Middle East. Computer systems. Applications — *Serials*

Middle East computing. — [No.1]-. — Sutton (Quadrant House, the Quadrant, Sutton, Surrey SM2 5AS) : IPC Electrical-Electronic Press, 1981-. — v. : ill,ports ; 30cm
Quarterly
ISSN 0263-9203 = Middle East computing : £7.00 per year (free to computer users and selected suppliers in the Middle East)
B82-38505

001.64'2 — BBC microcomputer systems. Programming — *Manuals*

Williams, Peter. Programming the BBC microcomputer. — London : Newnes Technical, Oct.1982. — [160]p
ISBN 0-408-01302-8 (pbk) : £4.95 : CIP entry
B82-24025

001.64'2 — Commodore PET microcomputer systems. Programming — *Manuals*

West, Raeto. Programming the PET/CBM / Raeto West. — London : Level, 1982. — iv,503p : ill ; 26cm
Includes index
ISBN 0-9507650-0-7 (pbk) : Unpriced
B82-14633

001.64'2 — Digital computer systems. Functional programming

Functional programming and its applications : an advanced course / edited by J. Darlington, P. Henderson, D.A. Turner. — Cambridge : Cambridge University Press, 1982. — 306p : ill ; 24cm
Based on the CREST course on Functional Programming and its Applications held at the University of Newcastle upon Tyne in July 1980. — Includes bibliographies
ISBN 0-521-24503-6 : £12.50 : CIP rev.
B82-02451

001.64′2 — Digital computer systems. Parallel programs. Verification. Axiomatic techniques

Owicki, Susan Speer. Axiomatic proof techniques for parallel programs / Susan Speer Owicki. — New York ; London : Garland, 1980. — v,198p ; 24cm. — (Outstanding dissertations in the computer sciences)
Bibliography: p196-198
ISBN 0-8240-4413-4 : Unpriced B82-18913

001.64′2 — Digital computer systems. Programming

Chantler, Alan. Programming techniques and practice / Alan Chantler. — Manchester : NCC, 1981. — 177p : ill ; 21cm
Includes index
ISBN 0-85012-338-0 (pbk) : Unpriced : CIP rev. B81-28137

Fundamental structures of computer science / William A. Wulf ... [et al.]. — Reading, Mass. ; London : Addison-Wesley, c1981. — xviii,621p : ill ; 25cm
Includes index
ISBN 0-201-08725-1 : Unpriced B82-27984

Longworth, G.. Standards in programming : methods and procedures / G. Longworth. — Manchester : NCC Publications, 1981. — 1v.(loose-leaf) : ill ; 30cm
Bibliography: p195. — Includes index
ISBN 0-85012-341-0 : Unpriced : CIP rev. B81-21597

Meek, B. L.. Guide to good programming practice. — 2nd ed. — Chichester : Horwood, Sept.1982. — [194]p. — (Ellis Horwood series in computers and their applications)
Previous ed.: 1980
ISBN 0-85312-485-x : £12.50 : CIP entry B82-25764

Tools and notions for program construction. — Cambridge : Cambridge University Press, Aug.1982. — [398]p
ISBN 0-521-24801-9 : £15.00 : CIP entry B82-21726

001.64′2 — Digital computer systems. Programming — *Manuals*

Coats, R. B.. Software engineering for small computers. — London : Edward Arnold, Aug.1982. — [256]p
ISBN 0-7131-3472-0 (pbk) : £6.95 : CIP entry B82-15919

Reynolds, John C.. The craft of programming. — Hemel Hempstead : Prentice-Hall, May, 1981. — [416]p
ISBN 0-13-188862-5 : £14.95 : CIP entry B81-06602

001.64′2 — Digital computer systems. Programs. Design by users

Martin, James, *1933-*. Application development without programmers / James Martin. — Englewood Cliffs ; London : Prentice-Hall, c1982. — xvi,350p : ill(some col.) ; 25cm
Text and col.ill on lining papers. — Includes index
ISBN 0-13-038943-9 : £24.40 B82-21677

001.64′2 — Digital computer systems. Programs. Design — *Manuals*

Law, D. J.. Programmer workbenches. — Manchester : NCC Publications, May 1982. — [100]p
ISBN 0-85012-379-8 (spiral) : £6.50 : CIP entry B82-16508

001.64′2 — Digital computer systems. Programs. Development — *For teaching*

Design and development of programs as teaching material. — London : Council for Educational Technology, Nov.1982. — [96]p. — (Microelectronics Education Programme information guide, ISSN 0262-2181 ; 3)
ISBN 0-86184-076-3 (pbk) : £8.00 : CIP entry B82-35213

001.64′2 — Digital computer systems. Programs. Verification

Formal methods of program verification and specification / H.K. Berg ... [et al.]. — Englewood Cliffs ; London : Prentice-Hall, c1982. — xiv,207p : ill ; 24cm
Includes index
ISBN 0-13-328807-2 : £17.55 B82-40384

001.64′2 — Digital computer systems. Structured programming

Linger, Richard C.. Structured programming : theory and practice / Richard C. Linger, Harlan D. Mills, Bernard I. Witt. — Reading, Mass. ; London : Addison-Wesley, c1979. — xiv,402p : ill ; 25cm
Ill on lining papers. — Includes index
ISBN 0-201-14461-1 : £13.50 B82-10999

001.64′2 — Digital computer systems. Structured programming. Logical Construction of Programs

Gardner, Albert C.. Practical LCP : a direct approach to structured programming / Albert C. Gardner. — London : McGraw-Hill, c1981. — xii,218p : ill,forms ; 28cm
Bibliography: p216. — Includes index
ISBN 0-07-084561-1 (pbk) : £12.50 : CIP rev. B81-15867

001.64′2 — Microcomputer systems. Programming

Coan, David. How to design your computer programs. — Manchester : NCC Publications, Sept.1982. — [45]p
ISBN 0-85012-384-4 (pbk) : CIP entry B82-28583

001.64′2 — Microcomputer systems. Programs written in Basic language — *Collections*

Daines, Derrick. 26 BASIC programs for your micro / Derrick Daines. — London : Newnes Technical, 1982. — 124p : ill,2plans ; 24cm. — (Newnes microcomputer books)
ISBN 0-408-01204-8 (pbk) : Unpriced : CIP rev. B82-07266

001.64′2 — Microprogramming

Banerji, Dilip K.. Elements of microprogramming / Dilip K. Banerji, Jacques Raymond. — Englewood Cliffs ; London : Prentice-Hall, c1982. — xiii,434p : ill ; 24cm
Includes bibliographies and index
ISBN 0-13-267146-8 : £18.70 B82-16723

001.64′2 — Real time computer systems. Programming — *Conference proceedings*

Real-time programming 1981. — Oxford : Pergamon, June 1982. — [150]p. — (IFAC proceedings series)
Conference papers
ISBN 0-08-027613-x : £22.50 : CIP entry B82-12916

001.64′2 — Rockwell 6502 microcomputer systems. Programming — *Manuals*

Zaks, Rodnay. Programming the 6502 / Rodnay Zaks. — 3rd ed. — Berkeley, Calif. : Sybex ; Birmingham : the Computer Bookshop [distributor], 1980. — 386p : ill,forms ; 22cm. — (6502 series ; v.1)
Previous ed.: 1979?. — Includes index
ISBN 0-89588-046-6 (pbk) : Unpriced B82-27390

001.64′2 — Sinclair ZX Spectrum microcomputer systems. Programming — *Manuals*

Gee, S. H.. The Spectrum programmer. — London : Granada, Nov.1982. — [144]p
ISBN 0-246-12025-8 (pbk) : £5.95 : CIP entry B82-30579

Hartnell, Tim. The ZX Spectrum explored. — London : Sinclair Borwne, Oct.1982. — [224]p. — (A Sinclair computerguide)
ISBN 0-946195-00-5 (pbk) : £5.95 : CIP entry B82-29153

James, M.. The art of programming the ZX Spectrum. — London : Babani, Dec.1982. — [144]p. — (BP ; 119)
ISBN 0-85934-094-5 (pbk) : £2.95 : CIP entry B82-31311

James, M.. The Spectrum book of games. — London : Granada, Dec.1982. — [128]p
ISBN 0-246-12047-9 (pbk) : £7.95 : CIP entry B82-34090

001.64′2 — Sinclair ZX80 & ZX81 microcomputer systems & Acorn Atom microcomputer systems. Programming — *Serials*

[Interface *(London : 1981)*]. Interface. — Vol.1, issue 7 (Mar. 1981)-. — London (44-46 Earls Court Rd, W8 6EJ) : National ZX80 & ZX81 Users′ Club, 1981-. — v. : ill,ports ; 30cm
Weekly. — Continues: ZX80 interface, micro user
ISSN 0262-964X = Interface (London. 1981) : £9.50 per year B82-15773

001.64′2 — Sinclair ZX80 microcomputer systems. Programming — *Serials*

ZX80 interface, micro user. — Vol.1 (1980)-v.1, issue 6 (Feb. 1981). — London (44-46 Earls Court Rd, W8 6EJ) : National ZX80 Users′ Club, 1980-1981. — 6v. : ill,ports ; 30cm
Monthly. — Continued by: Interface (London : 1981). — Description based on: Vol.1, issue 5 (Jan. 1981)
Unpriced B82-15771

001.64′2 — Sinclair ZX81 microcomputer systems. Programming — *Manuals*

Bluston, H. S.. Mathematical and educational applications of the ZX81 microcomputer / H.S. Bluston. — Bedford (24 Elm Close, Bedford, MK41 8BZ) : Energy Consultancy, 1982. — 6leaves ; 30cm
£3.00 (pbk) B82-29220

Francis, Richard, *1957-*. The Cambridge collection : 30 programs for the ZX81 / Richard Francis. — Cambridge (22 Fox Hollow, Bar Hill, Cambridge CB3 8EP) : R. Francis, [1981]. — 64p ; 21cm
ISBN 0-9507658-1-3 (pbk) : £4.95 B82-04352

Hurley, Randle. The Sinclair ZX81 / Randle Hurley. — London : Macmillan, 1981. — vi,162p : ill ; 24cm
ISBN 0-333-32973-2 (pbk) : £6.95 B82-10834

James, M.. The art of programming the 1K ZX81 / by M. James & S.M. Gee. — London : Babani, 1982. — 86p ; 18cm
ISBN 0-85934-084-8 (pbk) : £1.95 : CIP rev. B82-13149

James, M.. The art of programming the 16K ZX81. — London : Babani, Nov.1982. — [144] p. — (BP114)
ISBN 0-85934-089-9 (pbk) : £2.50 : CIP entry B82-29421

Stewart, Ian, *1945-*. Peek poke byte & ram! Basic programming for the ZX81 / Ian Stewart, Robin Jones. — Nantwich : Shiva, c1982. — 109p : ill ; 24cm
Includes index
ISBN 0-906812-17-8 (pbk) : £4.95 B82-13693

001.64′2 — Zilog Z80 microprocessor systems. Programming — *Manuals*

Clark, K. L.. A micro-PROLOG primer / K.L. Clark, J.R. Ennals, F.G. McCabe. — 2nd ed. — London (36 Gorst Rd., SW11 6JE) : Logic Programming Associates, 1982. — 130p ; 21cm
Previous ed.: 1981. — Bibliography: p128-130
Unpriced (pbk) B82-35292

McCabe, F. G.. Micro-PROLOG 2.12 : programmer′s reference manual / F.G. McCabe. — Rev. 2nd ed., CP/M version. — [London] (36 Gorst Rd., SW11 6JE) : Logic Programming Associates, 1981. — 70p ; 30cm
Previous ed.: 1980
Unpriced (pbk) B82-35293

Zaks, Rodnay. Programming the Z80 / Rodnay Zaks. — 3rd ed. — Berkeley, Calif. : Sybex ; Birmingham : the Computer Bookshop [distributor], c1980. — 624p : ill ; 22cm
Previous ed.: 1980. — Includes index
ISBN 0-89588-069-5 (pbk) : Unpriced B82-27395

001.64′2 — Zilog Z8000 microprocessor systems. Programming — *Manuals*

Mateosian, Richard. Programming the Z8000 / Richard Mateosian. — Berkeley, Calif. : Sybex ; Birmingham : the Computer Bookshop [distributor], 1980. — xii,298p : ill ; 22cm
Includes index
ISBN 0-89588-032-6 (pbk) : Unpriced
B82-27394

001.64′2′015113 — Digital computer systems. Programming. Applications of mathematical logic

Logic programming / edited by K.L. Clark and S.-A. Tärnlund. — London : Academic Press, 1982. — xvii,366p : ill ; 24cm. — (APIC studies in data processing ; no.16)
Bibliography: p341-361. — Includes index
ISBN 0-12-175520-7 : £16.80 : CIP rev.
B82-08434

001.64′2′015113 — Digital computer systems. Programming. Applications of mathematical logic — *Conference proceedings*

Mathematical logic in computer science / edited by B. Dömölki and T. Gergely. — Amsterdam ; Oxford : North-Holland, c1981. — 758p : ill ; 25cm. — (Colloquia mathematica Societatis János Bolyai, ISSN 0139-3383 ; 26)
Conference papers
ISBN 0-444-85440-1 : £52.63 B82-11231

001.64′2′018 — Digital computer systems. Programming. Methodology

Theoretical foundations of programming methodology : lecture notes of an international summer school directed by F.L. Bauer, E.W. Dykstra and C.A.R. Hoare / edited by Manfred Broy and Gunther Schmidt. — Dordrecht ; London : Reidel published in cooperation with NATO Scientific Affairs Division, c1982. — xiii,658p : ill,music ; 25cm. — (Nato advanced study institutes series. Series C, Mathematical and physical sciences, ISSN 0377-2071 ; v.91)
ISBN 90-277-1460-6 (cased) : Unpriced
ISBN 90-277-1462-2 (pbk) : Unpriced
B82-40760

001.64′2′068 — Digital computer systems. Programming. Management — *Serials*

Advances in computer programming management. — Vol.1-. — Philadelphia ; London : Heyden, 1980-. — v. : ill ; 24cm
Annual
ISSN 0196-870x = Advances in computer programming management : £15.50
B82-11801

001.64′24 — Apple II microcomputer systems. Programming languages: Basic language — *Manuals*

Finkel, LeRoy. APPLE BASIC : data file programming / Leroy Finkel and Jerald R. Brown. — New York ; Chichester : Wiley, c1982. — ix,303p ; 26cm
Includes index
ISBN 0-471-09157-x (pbk) : £8.95 B82-13623

001.64′24 — Apple II microcomputer systems. Programming languages: Pascal language — *Manuals*

MacCallum, Iain. Pascal for the Apple. — London : Prentice-Hall, Jan.1983. — [512]p
ISBN 0-13-652891-0 (pbk) : £8.50 : CIP entry
B82-33471

001.64′24 — BBC microcomputer systems. Programming languages: Basic language — *Manuals*

Atherton, Roy. Structured programming with BBC Basic. — Chichester : Ellis Horwood, Jan.1983. — [205]p
ISBN 0-85312-547-3 : £14.50 : CIP entry
B82-36155

Cryer, Neil. BASIC programming on the BBC microcomputer / Neil Cryer and Pat Cryer. — Englewood Cliffs ; London : Prentice/Hall International, c1982. — xii,195p : ill ; 23cm
Includes index
ISBN 0-13-066407-3 (pbk) : £5.95 : CIP rev.
B81-39228

001.64′24 — Commodore PET microcomputer systems. Programming languages: Basic language — *Manuals*

Arotsky, J.. Introduction to microcomputing with the PET. — London : Edward Arnold, Oct.1982. — [288]p
ISBN 0-7131-3475-5 (pbk) : £5.95 : CIP entry
B82-26046

Haskell, Richard E.. PET/CBM BASIC / Richard Haskell. — Englewood Cliffs ; London : Prentice-Hall, c1982. — vi,154p : ill ; 29cm. — (A Spectrum book)
Includes index
ISBN 0-13-661769-7 (cased) : Unpriced
ISBN 0-13-661751-4 (pbk) : £9.70 B82-28196

001.64′24 — Commodore VIC microcomputer systems. Programming languages: Basic language — *Manuals*

Carter, L. R.. Learn computer programming with the Commodore VIC / L.R. Carter, E. Huzan. — London : Hodder and Stoughton, 1982. — xii,160p : ill ; 18cm. — (Teach yourself programming)
Bibliography: p154. — Includes index
ISBN 0-340-28070-0 (pbk) : £1.95 : CIP rev.
B81-35900

001.64′24 — DEC System 10 digital computer systems. Programming languages: Prolog — *Manuals*

Bowen, D. L.. DECsystem-10 Prolog user′s manual / D.L. Bowen. — [Edinburgh] : University of Edinburgh, Department of Artificial Intelligence, 1981. — 104p ; 30cm. — (D.A.I. occasional paper, ISSN 0144-4131 ; no.27)
'This manual corresponds to Prolog version 3.43'. — Supersedes occasional papers 15 & 19. — Bibliography: p98-99. — Includes index
Unpriced (spiral) B82-26845

001.64′24 — Digital computer systems. Coding

Mackenzie, Charles E.. Coded character sets, history and development / Charles E. Mackenzie. — Reading, Mass. ; London : Addison-Wesley, c1980. — xxi,513p : ill ; 25cm. — (The Systems programming series)
Ill on lining papers. — Includes index
ISBN 0-201-14460-3 : £15.95 B82-12654

001.64′24 — Digital computer systems. Portable programming languages

Wallis, P. J. L.. Portable programming / Peter J.L. Wallis. — London : Macmillan, 1982. — xiv,141p : ill ; 24cm. — (Macmillan computer science series)
Bibliography: p126-135. — Includes index
ISBN 0-333-31036-5 (pbk) : £5.95 B82-37416

001.64′24 — Digital computer systems. Programming language: Ada language

Ada-based system development methodology study report. — London ([123 Victoria St., SW1]) : Department of Industry, 1981. — 3v. : ill ; 30cm
Cover title
£35.00 (pbk) B82-10039

Barnes, J. G. P.. Programming in Ada / J.G.P. Barnes. — London : Addison-Wesley, c1982. — x,340p : ill ; 25cm. — (International computer science series)
Includes index
ISBN 0-201-13793-3 (cased) : £14.95 : CIP rev.
ISBN 0-201-13792-5 (pbk) : £8.50 B81-26783

Downes, Valerie A.. Programming embedded systems with Ada. — London : Prentice-Hall, Mar.1982. — [400]p
ISBN 0-13-730010-7 (pbk) : £8.50 : CIP entry
B82-02656

United Kingdom Ada study final technical report . — London ([123 Victoria St., SW1]) : Department of Industry, 1981. — 7v. : ill ; 30cm
Cover title
£75.00 (pbk) B82-10040

001.64′24 — Digital computer systems. Programming languages

Ghezzi, Carlo. Programming language concepts / Carlo Ghezzi, Mehdi Jazayeri. — New York ; Chichester : Wiley, c1982. — xvi,327p : ill ; 25cm
Bibliography: p295-320. — Includes index
ISBN 0-471-08755-6 : £18.45 B82-28181

001.64′24 — Digital computer systems. Programming languages: Ada language

Stratford-Collins, M. J.. ADA : a programmer′s conversion course / M.J. Stratford-Collins. — Chichester : Horwood, 1982. — 170p ; 24cm. — (The Ellis Horwood series in computers and their applications)
Includes index
ISBN 0-85312-250-4 : £16.50 : CIP rev.
ISBN 0-85312-444-2 (pbk) : Unpriced
B82-11094

Young, Stephen J.. An introduction to Ada. — Chichester : Ellis Horwood, Sept.1982. — [320] p. — (Ellis Horwood series in computers and their applications)
ISBN 0-85312-535-x : £25.00 : CIP entry
B82-28588

001.64′24 — Digital computer systems. Programming languages: Algol 60 language

ALGOL 60. — [London] ([13 Mansfield St., W1M 0PB]) : British Computer Society, [1982?]. — 50p ; 30cm
Articles from issues of the Computer journal. — Includes bibliographies and index
Unpriced (pbk) B82-40782

001.64′24 — Digital computer systems. Programming languages: ANS Cobol language — *Programmed instructions*

Ashley, Ruth. ANS COBOL / Ruth Ashley in consultation with Nancy B. Stern. — 2nd ed. — New York ; Chichester : Wiley, c1979. — ix,265p : ill ; 26cm
Previous ed.: 1974. — Includes index
ISBN 0-471-05136-5 (pbk) : £5.30 B82-01226

001.64′24 — Digital computer systems. Programming languages: APL language — *Conference proceedings*

International Conference on APL *(1980 : Leeuwenhorst Congress Centre)*. APL 80 : International Conference on APL, June 24-26, 1980 / [organised CRI (Leiden University Computer Centre) in cooperation with NGI (Netherlands Society for Informatics), ECI (European Cooperation in Informatics)] ; [responsible body SIC (Netherlands Foundation Informatics Congresses)] ; edited by Gijsbert van der Linden. — Amsterdam ; Oxford : North-Holland, 1980. — x,319p : ill ; 27cm
Includes index
ISBN 0-444-86015-0 : £20.87 B82-35059

001.64′24 — Digital computer systems. Programming languages: APL language — *Manuals*

Smith, Adrian. APL : a design handbook for commercial systems / Adrian Smith. — New York ; Chichester : Wiley, c1982. — ix,180p : ill,forms ; 24cm. — (Wiley series in information processing)
Bibliography: p176-177. — Includes index
ISBN 0-471-10092-7 : Unpriced : CIP rev.
B82-03606

001.64′24 — Digital computer systems. Programming languages: Applesoft language — *Manuals*

Presley, Bruce. A guide to programming in Apple soft / Bruce Presley. — [Lawrenceville, N.J.] : Lawrenceville Press ; New York ; London : distributed by Van Nostrand Reinhold, 1982. — 173p in various pagings : ill (some col.) ; 28cm
Includes index
ISBN 0-442-25890-9 (pbk) : £11.00
B82-30345

001.64′24 — Digital computer systems. Programming languages: Basic language

Gottfried, Byron S.. Schaum′s outline of theory and problems of programming with BASIC : including microcomputer BASIC / Byron S. Gottfried. — 2nd ed. — New York ; London : McGraw-Hill, c1982. — 282p : ill ; 28cm. — (Schaum′s outline series)
Previous ed.: 1975. — Includes index
ISBN 0-07-023855-3 (pbk) : £5.95 B82-37799

001.64'24 — Digital computer systems. Programming languages: Basic language *continuation*

Marateck, Samuel L.. BASIC / Samuel L. Marateck. — 2nd ed. — New York ; London : Academic Press, c1982. — xvi,475p : ill ; 27cm
Previous ed.: 1975. — Includes index
ISBN 0-12-470455-7 (pbk) : £11.20
B82-29966

001.64'24 — Digital computer systems. Programming languages: Basic language — *For Irish students*

Kelly, John, *1940-*. Computer studies : BASIC foundations / John Kelly ; cover design and cartoons Terry Myler ; diagrams Ann Murphy. — Dublin : Educational Company
2. — 1981. — 240p : ill ; 21cm
Text on inside cover. — Includes index
Unpriced (pbk) B82-02554

001.64'24 — Digital computer systems. Programming languages: Basic language — *For librarianship*

Hunter, Eric J.. The abc of BASIC : an introduction to programming for librarians. — London : Bingley, Sept.1982. — [128]p
ISBN 0-85157-355-x : £7.95 : CIP entry
B82-20527

001.64'24 — Digital computer systems. Programming languages: Basic language — *Manuals*

Bishop, Peter. Further computer programming in Basic / Peter Bishop. — Walton-on-Thames : Nelson, 1982. — 426p : ill ; 25cm
Includes index
ISBN 0-17-431266-0 (corrected : pbk) : £8.95
B82-34549

Cope, Tonia. Computing using basic : an interactive approach / Tonia Cope. — Chichester : Horwood, 1981. — 351p : ill ; 24cm. — (The Ellis Horwood series in computers and their applications)
Bibliography: p328-329. — Includes index
ISBN 0-85312-289-x (cased) : £15.00 : CIP rev.
ISBN 0-85312-385-3 (pbk) : Unpriced
B81-26694

Gosling, P. E.. Mastering computer programming / P.E. Gosling. — London : Macmillan, 1982. — vii,212p : ill,forms ; 23cm. — (Macmillan master series)
Bibliography: p209-210. — Includes index
ISBN 0-333-32018-2 : Unpriced
ISBN 0-333-32019-0 (pbk) : Unpriced
ISBN 0-333-32020-4 (export) B82-33850

Ledgard, Henry. Elementary BASIC. — London : Collins, Feb.1983. — [264]p
ISBN 0-00-217048-5 : £8.95 : CIP entry
B82-36458

Limbert, Ben. Ben Limbert's common-sense introduction to BASIC. — Wilmslow (75 Wilmslow Rd., Wilmslow, Cheshire SK9 3EN) : Designed Publications, Oct.1982. — [96]p
ISBN 0-946246-01-7 (pbk) : £2.95 : CIP entry
B82-33372

Marateck, Samuel L.. Instructor's manual for BASIC, second edition / by Samuel L. Marateck. — New York ; London : Academic Press, c1982. — 37p ; 23cm
ISBN 0-12-470456-5 (pbk) : Unpriced
B82-35119

Stephenson, A. P.. Beginner's guide to BASIC programming / A.P. Stephenson. — [London] : Newnes Technical, 1982. — 160p : ill ; 19cm
Includes index
ISBN 0-408-01184-x (pbk) : Unpriced : CIP rev. B82-19219

Wohl, Gerald. BASIC : a direct approach / Gerald Wohl, Mike Murach. — Chicago ; Henley-on-Thames : Science Research Associaties, c1977. — 69p : ill ; 28cm
Text on inside covers
ISBN 0-574-21125-x (pbk) : £3.25 B82-39343

001.64'24 — Digital computer systems. Programming languages: Basic language — *Manuals — For business practices*

Lott, Richard W.. BASIC with business applications / Richard W. Lott. — 2nd ed. — New York ; Chichester : Wiley, c1982. — xi,306p : ill ; 23cm
Previous ed.: 1977. — Bibliography: p302. — Includes index
ISBN 0-471-08560-x (pbk) : £11.45
B82-36953

001.64'24 — Digital computer systems. Programming languages: Basic language — *Manuals — For engineering & science*

Miller, Alan R.. Basic programs : for scientists and engineers / Alan R. Miller. — [Berkeley, Calif.] : Sybex ; Birmingham : Computer Bookshop [[distributor]], 1981. — xvii,318p : ill ; 23cm
Bibliography: p315-316. — Includes index
ISBN 0-89588-073-3 (pbk) : Unpriced
B82-27629

001.64'24 — Digital computer systems. Programming languages: Basic language — *Manuals — For hydraulic engineering*

Smith, P. D.. BASIC hydraulics. — London : Butterworths, June 1982. — [150]p
ISBN 0-408-01112-2 (pbk) : £6.50 : CIP entry
B82-10488

001.64'24 — Digital computer systems. Programming languages: Basic language — *Questions & answers*

Lamoitier, Jean-Pierre. Fifty Basic exercises / Jean-Pierre Lamoitier. — [Berkeley, Calif.] : Sybex ; Birmingham : Computer Bookshop [[distributor]], 1981. — xix,231p : ill ; 23cm
Translation of: Le Basic par la pratique. — Includes index
ISBN 0-89588-056-3 (pbk) : Unpriced
B82-27625

001.64'24 — Digital computer systems. Programming languages: Basic-Plus languages — *Manuals*

Price, Wilson T.. Elements of BASIC-plus programming / Wilson T. Price. — New York ; London : Holt, Rinehart and Winston, c1982. — xi,372p ; 23cm
Includes index
ISBN 0-03-060148-7 (pbk) : £11.50
B82-32838

001.64'24 — Digital computer systems. Programming languages: Cobol language

Brown, P. R.. COBOL control : possible United Kingdom measures for the improvement of COBOL portability. — Manchester : NCC Publications, Nov.1981. — [73]p
ISBN 0-85012-349-6 (pbk) : £6.50 : CIP entry
B81-38827

Davis, William S.. COBOL : an introduction to structured logic and modular program design / William S. Davis, Richard H. Fisher. — Reading, Mass. ; London : Addison-Wesley, c1979. — xix,552p : ill ; 24cm
Includes index
ISBN 0-201-01431-9 (pbk) : Unpriced
B82-20554

Fisher, Melinda. Computer programming in COBOL. — London : Hodder and Stoughton, Aug.1982. — [224]p. — (Teach yourself books)
ISBN 0-340-20383-8 (pbk) : £2.75 : CIP entry
B82-20625

Philippakis, Andreas S.. Advanced COBOL / A.S. Philippakis, Leonard J. Kazmier. — New York ; London : McGraw-Hill, c1982. — x,611p : ill ; 25cm
Includes index
ISBN 0-07-049806-7 : £18.95 B82-31562

Philippakis, Andreas S.. Structured COBOL / A.S. Philippakis, Leonard J. Kazmier. — 2nd ed. — New York ; London : McGraw-Hill, 1981. — xv,477p : ill ; 24cm
Previous ed.: 1977. — Includes index
ISBN 0-07-049801-6 (pbk) : £10.50
B82-14173

001.64'24 — Digital computer systems. Programming languages: Cobol language — *Manuals*

Parhin, Andrew, *1941-*. COBOL for students. — 2nd ed. — London : Edward Arnold, Sept.1982. — [216]p
Previous ed.: 1975
ISBN 0-7131-3477-1 (pbk) : £5.95 : CIP entry
B82-22809

001.64'24 — Digital computer systems. Programming languages: Comal language — *Manuals*

Christensen, Borge. Beginning COMAL / Borge Christensen. — Chichester : Ellis Horwood, 1982. — 332p : ill ; 24cm. — (The Ellis Horwood series in computers and their applications)
Includes index
ISBN 0-85312-435-3 (pbk) : Unpriced : CIP rev. B82-18586

001.64'24 — Digital computer systems. Programming languages — *Conference proceedings*

International Symposium on Algorithmic Languages *(1981 : Amsterdam)*. Algorithmic languages : proceedings of the International Symposium on Algorithmic Languages : a tribute to Prof. Dr. Ir. A. van Wijngaarden on the occasion of his retirement from the Mathematical Centre / edited by J.W. de Bakker and J.C. van Vliet ; [organized by the Mathematical Centre, Amsterdam, under the auspices of IFIP Technical Committee 2, Programming, International Federation for Information Processing]. — Amsterdam ; Oxford : North-Holland, 1981. — xxvi,431p : ill,1facsim,1port ; 23cm
ISBN 0-444-86285-4 : £23.45 B82-24667

001.64'24 — Digital computer systems. Programming languages: Forth language — *Manuals*

Brodie, Leo. Starting FORTH : an introduction to the FORTH language and operating systems for beginners and professionals / Leo Brodie ; with a foreword by Charles H. Moore. — Englewood Cliffs ; London : Prentice-Hall, c1981. — xvi,348p : ill,1port ; 24cm
ISBN 0-13-842930-8 (cased) : Unpriced
ISBN 0-13-842922-7 (pbk) : £11.95
B82-16707

001.64'24 — Digital computer systems. Programming languages: Fortran 77 language

Gibson, Glenn A.. Introduction to programming using FORTRAN 77 / Glenn A. Gibson and James R. Young. — Englewood Cliffs ; London : Prentice-Hall, c1982. — xv,461p : ill ; 24cm
Bibliography: p448-451. — Includes index
ISBN 0-13-493551-9 (pbk) : Unpriced
B82-36878

Monro, Donald M.. Fortran 77 / Donald M. Monro. — London : Edward Arnold, 1982. — vii,360p : ill,1map ; 28cm
Text on inside cover. — Includes index
ISBN 0-7131-2794-5 (pbk) : £9.50 : CIP rev.
B82-00167

001.64'24 — Digital computer systems. Programming languages: Fortran IV & Fortran 77 languages — *Manuals*

Calderbank, Valerie J.. A course on programming in FORTRAN. — 2nd ed. — London : Chapman and Hall, Sept.1982. — [120]p
Previous ed.: 1969
ISBN 0-412-24270-2 (cased) : £12.00 : CIP entry
ISBN 0-412-23790-3 (pbk) : £6.00 B82-19228

001.64'24 — Digital computer systems. Programming languages: Fortran language 77 — *Manuals*

Ellis, T. M. R.. A structural approach to Fortran 77 programming. — London : Addison-Wesley, June 1982. — [304]p. — (International computer science series ; 3)
ISBN 0-201-13790-9 (pbk) : £7.95 : CIP entry
B82-10461

001.64'24 — Digital computer systems. Programming languages: Fortran language — *Manuals*

Moore, Elmo. Introduction to FORTRAN and its applications / Elmo Moore. — Boston, [Mass.] ; London : Allyn and Bacon, c1982. — xiv,315p : ill ; 24cm. — (Allyn and Bacon computer science series)
Includes index
ISBN 0-205-07720-x (pbk) : Unpriced
B82-27106

001.64'24 — Digital computer systems. Programming languages: Fortran language. Optimization

Metcalf, Michael. FORTRAN optimization. — London : Academic Press, Nov.1982. — [230] p. — (APIC studies in data processing, ISSN 0067-2483 ; 17)
ISBN 0-12-492480-8 : CIP entry B82-29063

001.64'24 — Digital computer systems. Programming languages: Fortran language — *Questions & answers*

Moore, Elmo. Instructor's manual to accompany Introduction to FORTRAN and its applications / Elmo Moore. — Boston, Mass. ; London : Allyn and Bacon, c1982. — 63,[51]p : ill ; 28cm
Cover title. — Text, ill on inside covers
ISBN 0-205-07721-8 (pbk) : Unpriced
B82-29257

001.64'24 — Digital computer systems. Programming languages: Pascal language

Forsyth, Richard S.. Pascal at work and play. — London : Chapman and Hall, Sept.1982. — [320]p
ISBN 0-412-23370-3 (cased) : £15.00 : CIP entry
ISBN 0-412-23380-0 (pbk) : £6.95 B82-14088

Glinert, E. P.. Introduction to computer science using Pascal. — London : Prentice-Hall, Jan.1983. — [540]p
ISBN 0-13-479402-8 (pbk) : £8.95 : CIP entry
B82-33469

Kemp, R.. Pascal for students / R. Kemp. — London : Edward Arnold, 1982. — vi,225p : ill ; 25cm
Bibliography: p220-221. — Includes index
ISBN 0-7131-3447-x (pbk) : £5.95 : CIP rev.
B81-30611

Richards, James L.. PASCAL / James L. Richards. — New York ; London : Academic Press, c1982. — xi,482p : ill ; 27cm
Includes index
ISBN 0-12-587520-7 (pbk) : £11.20
B82-29967

Welsh, Jim. Introduction to Pascal / by Jim Welsh and John Elder. — 2nd ed. — Englewood Cliffs ; London : Prentice-Hall International, c1982. — xii,307p : ill ; 23cm. — (Prentice-Hall International series in computer science)
Previous ed.: 1979. — Includes index
ISBN 0-13-491530-5 (pbk) : Unpriced : CIP rev. B81-35789

Zaks, Rodnay. Introduction to Pascal : (includings UCSD Pascal) / Rodnay Zaks. — [Berkeley, Calif.] : Sybex ; Birmingham : Computer Bookshop [distributor], 1981. — xvii,422p : ill ; 23cm
Previous ed.: 197-?. — Includes index
ISBN 0-89588-066-0 (pbk) : Unpriced
B82-27630

001.64'24 — Digital computer systems. Programming languages: Pascal language. Compiler languages: Pascal-P language

Pemberton, Steven. Pascal implementation / Steven Pemberton and Martin Daniels. — Chichester : Ellis Horwood, 1982. — 2v. : ill ; 24cm. — (The Ellis Horwood series in computers and their applications ; 18)
Includes index
ISBN 0-85312-358-6 : £22.50
ISBN 0-85312-437-x (compiler : hbk)
ISBN 0-470-27325-9 (U.S.) B82-26292

Pemberton, Steven. Pascal implementation. — Student ed. — Chichester : Ellis Horwood, Jan.1983. — [254]p. — (The Ellis Horwood series in computers and their applications ; 18)
Previous ed.: 1982
ISBN 0-85312-589-9 (pbk) : £12.50 : CIP entry
ISBN 0-85312-588-0 (Book : pbk)
ISBN 0-85312-590-2 (Compiler : pbk)
B82-35190

001.64'24 — Digital computer systems. Programming languages: Pascal language — *Manuals*

Atkinson, Laurence V.. A student's guide to programming in Pascal. — Chichester : Wiley, Aug.1982. — [225]p
ISBN 0-471-10402-7 : £5.00 : CIP entry
B82-18473

Brown, P. J.. Pascal from BASIC. — London : Addison-Wesley, May 1982. — [192]p
ISBN 0-201-13789-5 (pbk) : £6.95 : CIP entry
B82-07526

Clark, Randy. The UCSD Pascal handbook : a reference and guidebook for programmers / Randy Clark, Stephen Koehler. — Englewood Cliffs ; London : Prentice-Hall, c1982. — xvi,356p : ill ; 24cm. — (Prentice-Hall software series)
Bibliography: p343-345. — Includes index
ISBN 0-13-935544-8 (cased) : Unpriced
ISBN 0-13-935536-7 (pbk) : £11.95
B82-16988

Jones, William B.. Programming concepts : a second course (with examples in Pascal) / William B. Jones. — Englewood Cliffs ; London : Prentice-Hall, c1982. — xiv,319p : ill ; 24cm
Bibliography: p308-310. — Includes index
ISBN 0-13-729970-2 : £14.95 B82-20069

Kennedy, Michael, *1939-*. PASCAL : program development with ten instruction PASCAL subset (TIPS) and standard PASCAL / Michael Kennedy, Martin B. Solomon. — Englewood Cliffs ; London : Prentice-Hall, c1982. — xxvi,532p : ill ; 24cm
1 folded sheet attached to inside back cover. — Includes index
ISBN 0-13-652735-3 (pbk) : £13.45
B82-16998

Ledgard, Henry. Elementary Pascal. — London : Collins, Feb.1983. — [264]p
ISBN 0-00-217049-3 : £8.95 : CIP entry
B82-37472

McGregor, James J.. Simple PASCAL / James J. McGregor and Alan H. Watt. — London : Pitman, 1981. — viii,182p ; 23cm
Includes index
ISBN 0-273-01704-7 (pbk) : Unpriced
B82-01777

Prather, Ronald E.. Problem-solving principles : programming with PASCAL / Ronald E. Prather. — Englewood Cliffs ; London : Prentice-Hall, c1982. — xiii,350p : ill ; 23cm. — (Prentice-Hall software series)
Bibliography: p336-337. — Includes index
ISBN 0-13-721316-6 (cased) : Unpriced
ISBN 0-13-721308-5 (pbk) : £11.95
B82-16997

Price, David, *1910-*. Pascal : a considerate approach / David Price. — Englewood Cliffs ; London : Prentice-Hall, c1982. — viii,194p : ill ; 25cm. — (A Spectrum book)
Includes index
ISBN 0-13-652818-x (cased) : Unpriced
ISBN 0-13-652800-7 (pbk) : £7.45 B82-28195

Schneider, G. Michael. Advanced programming and problem solving with Pascal / G. Michael Schneider, Steven C. Bruell. — New York ; Chichester : Wiley, c1981. — xiii,506p : ill ; 24cm
Includes index
ISBN 0-471-07876-x : £17.75 B82-06299

Tiberghien, Jacques. The Pascal handbook / Jacques Tiberghien. — [Berkeley, Calif.] : Sybex ; Birmingham : Computer Bookshop [[distributor]], 1981. — xix,473p : ill ; 23cm
Includes index
ISBN 0-89588-053-9 (pbk) : £13.95
B82-27627

001.64'24 — Digital computer systems. Programming languages: Pascal language — *Manuals — For science*

Miller, Alan R.. Pascal programs : for scientists and engineers / Alan R. Miller. — [Berkeley, Calif.] : Sybex ; Birmingham : Computer Bookshop [[distributor]], 1981. — xxi,374p : ill ; 23cm
Bibliography: p371-372. — Includes index
ISBN 0-89588-058-x (pbk) : Unpriced
B82-27626

001.64'24 — Digital computer systems. Programming languages: RPG language — *Manuals*

Mullish, Henry. RPG & RPG II primer : a modern approach / Henry Mullish, Richard Kestenbaum. — New York ; London : Holt, Rinehart and Winston, c1982. — x,189p : ill,forms ; 28cm
Includes index
ISBN 0-03-056918-4 (pbk) : £12.50
B82-15341

001.64'24 — Digital computer systems. Programming languages: S-algol

Cole, A. J. (Alfred John). An introduction to programming with S-algol. — Cambridge : Cambridge University Press, Sept.1982. — [184]p
ISBN 0-521-25001-3 : £7.95 : CIP entry
B82-29354

001.64'24 — Digital computer systems. Programming languages: Simula language

Simula begin / Graham M. Birtwistle ... [et al.]. — 2nd ed. — Lund : Studentlitteratur ; Bromley : Chartwell-Bratt, 1981. — 391p : ill ; 23cm
Previous ed.: 1973. — Includes index
ISBN 0-86238-009-x (pbk) : Unpriced
B82-35643

001.64'24 — Digital computer systems. Programs. Verification

McGettrick, Andrew D.. Program verification using Ada / Andrew D. McGettrick. — Cambridge : Cambridge University Press, 1982. — xii,345p : ill ; 24cm. — (Cambridge computer science texts ; 13)
Bibliography: p335-339. — Includes index
ISBN 0-521-24215-0 (cased) : £24.00 : CIP rev.
ISBN 0-521-28531-3 (pbk) : £8.95 B82-12692

001.64'24 — Digital computer systems. Structured programming. Programming languages: Cobol language — *Manuals*

Price, Wilson T.. Elements of structured COBOL programming. — 2nd ed. / Jack L. Olson, Wilson T. Price. — New York ; London : Holt, Rinehart and Winston, c1982. — xiii,380p : ill ; 28cm
Previous ed.: published as Elements of COBOL programming / Wilson T. Price, Jack L. Olson. Hinsdale : Dryden, 1977. — Includes index
ISBN 0-03-058052-8 (pbk) : £11.95
B82-15343

Topping, Anne L.. Business applications of structured COBOL programming / Anne L. Topping with Ian L. Gibbons. — Boston, [Mass.] ; London : Allyn and Bacon, c1982. — x,438p : ill ; 28cm
Includes index
ISBN 0-205-07750-1 (pbk) : £22.95
B82-35103

001.64'24 — Digital computer systems. Structured programming. Programming languages: Comal language

Atherton, Roy. Structured programming with COMAL / Roy Atherton. — Chichester : Ellis Horwood, 1982. — 266p : ill ; 24cm. — (The Ellis Horwood series in computers and their applications ; 17)
Bibliography: p212-213. — Includes index
ISBN 0-85312-416-7 (cased) : £18.50 : CIP rev.
ISBN 0-85312-423-x (pbk) : Unpriced
B82-06525

001.64'24 — Digital computer systems. Structured programming. Programming languages: Comal language — *Serials*

COMAL bulletin : structured methods in programming and education. — Vol.1, no.1 (Apr. 1982)-. — Chichester : Ellis Horwood, 1982-. — v. : ill ; 30cm
Six issues yearly
ISSN 0263-0478 = COMAL bulletin : Unpriced B82-40032

001.64'24 — Digital computer systems. Structured programming. Programming languages: Fortran 77 language

Seeds, Harice L.. Structuring FORTRAN 77 for business and general applications / Harice L. Seeds. — New York ; Chichester : Wiley, c1981. — x,512p : ill ; 23cm
Includes index
ISBN 0-471-07836-0 (pbk) : £10.85 B82-01807

001.64'24 — Digital computer systems. Structured programming. Programming languages: Pascal language

Koffman, Elliot B.. Problem solving and structured programming in PASCAL / Elliot B. Koffman. — Reading, Mass. ; London : Addison-Wesley, c1981. — xiv,430,[53]p : ill ; 24cm. — (Addison-Wesley series in computer science and information processing)
Includes index
ISBN 0-201-03893-5 (pbk) : £7.95 B82-14747

Tenenbaum, Aaron M.. Data structures using Pascal / Aaron M. Tenenbaum, Moshe J. Augenstein. — Englewood Cliffs ; London : Prentice-Hall, c1981. — xiv,545p : ill ; 25cm. — (Prentice-Hall software series)
Bibliography: p528-539. — Includes index
ISBN 0-13-196501-8 : £18.70 B82-02060

001.64'24 — Microcomputer systems. Programming languages

Marshall, G. J.. Programming languages for microcomputers. — London : Newnes Technical, Feb.1983. — [160]p
ISBN 0-408-01185-8 (pbk) : £5.50 : CIP entry B82-38298

001.64'24 — Microcomputer systems. Programming languages: Basic language — *Manuals*

Maynard, Jeff. BASIC for micros. — London : Newnes Technical, Feb.1983. — [144]p
ISBN 0-408-01224-2 (pbk) : £5.50 : CIP entry B82-38296

Prigmore, Clive. 30 hour basic / by Clive Prigmore. — Cambridge : National Extension College, c1981. — 248p : ill ; 22cm. — (National Extension College correspondence texts. Course ; no.M27)
Includes index
ISBN 0-86082-269-9 (spiral) : £5.50 B82-11455

Prigmore, Clive. 30 hour BASIC / by Clive Prigmore. — [Cambridge] : National Extension College, 1981 (1982 [printing]). — 254p : ill ; 21cm. — (National Extension College correspondence texts ; course no.MO27)
Includes index
ISBN 0-86082-269-9 (spiral) : £5.50 B82-39002

001.64'24 — Microcomputer systems. Programming languages: Pascal language. Translation from Basic language

Borgerson, Mark J.. A BASIC programmers guide to Pascal / by Mark J. Borgerson. — New York ; Chichester : Wiley, c1982. — viii,118p ; 26cm
Includes index
ISBN 0-471-09293-2 (pbk) : £6.75 B82-32732

001.64'24 — Microcomputer systems. Programming languages: Pascal — *Manuals*

Beer, M. D.. Programming microcomputers with PASCAL. — London : Granada, June 1982. — [256]p
ISBN 0-246-11619-6 (pbk) : £9.95 : CIP entry B82-10799

001.64'24 — Microcomputer systems. Programming languages: PROLOG

Ennals, J. R.. Beginning micro-PROLOG. — Chichester : Horwood, Nov.1982. — [192]p
ISBN 0-85312-517-1 : £12.50 : CIP entry B82-33205

001.64'24 — Motorola 6502 microcomputer systems. Programming languages: Assembly languages

Stephenson, A. P.. 6502 machine code for beginners. — London : Newnes Technical, Jan.1983. — [176]p
ISBN 0-408-01311-7 (pbk) : £5.50 : CIP entry B82-34440

001.64'24 — Real time digital computer systems. Programming languages

Young, Stephen J.. Real time languages : design and development / Stephen J. Young. — Chichester : Ellis Horwood, 1982. — 352p : ill ; 24cm. — (The Ellis Horwood series in computers and their applications ; 21)
Bibliography: p342-346. — Includes index
ISBN 0-85312-251-2 (cased) : £29.50 : CIP rev.
ISBN 0-85312-460-4 (pbk) : Unpriced B82-11784

001.64'24 — Sinclair ZX81 microcomputer systems. Programming languages: Basic language — *Manuals*

Norman, Robin. ZX81 BASIC book / Robin Norman. — London : Newnes Technical Books, 1982. — 165p : ill ; 22cm
Includes index
ISBN 0-408-01178-5 (pbk) : Unpriced : CIP rev. B81-34577

Prigmore, Clive. 30 hour BASIC : ZX81 edition / by Clive Prigmore ; adapted for ZX81 by Richard Freeman and Robert Horvath. — [Cambridge] : National Extension College, 1982. — 228p : ill ; 21cm. — (National Extension College correspondence texts ; course no.M27X)
Includes index
ISBN 0-86082-301-6 (spiral) : £5.50 B82-39003

001.64'24 — Tandy TRS-80 microcomputer systems. Programming languages: Basic language — *Manuals*

Andree, Richard V.. Explore computing with the TRS-80 (& common sense) : with programming in BASIC / Richard V. Andree & Josephine P. Andree. — Englewood Cliffs ; London : Prentice-Hall, c1982. — x,230p : ill ; 24cm
Text on lining papers. — Includes index
ISBN 0-13-296145-8 (cased) : Unpriced
ISBN 0-13-296137-7 (pbk) : £8.95 B82-20078

001.64'24 — Tandy TRS-80 microcomputer systems. Programming languages: Basic language — *Manuals* — *Programmed instructions*

Albrecht, Bob. TRS-80 color BASIC / Bob Albrecht. — New York ; Chichester : Wiley, c1982. — vi,378p : ill ; 26cm
Includes index
ISBN 0-471-09644-x (pbk) : £6.75 B82-37207

001.64'24'0287 — Digital computer systems. Programs. Testing

The **Correctness** problem in computer science / edited by R.S. Boyer and J. Strother Moore. — London : Academic Press, 1981. — xiii,279p : ill ; 24cm. — (International lecture series in computer science)
Includes bibliographies and index
ISBN 0-12-122920-3 : £14.20 : CIP rev. B81-23896

001.64'24'0287 — Digital computer systems. Programs. Testing — *Conference proceedings*

Summer School on Computer Program Testing *(1981 : Urbino)*. Computer program testing : proceedings of the Summer School on Computer Program Testing held at SOGESTA, Urbino, Italy June 29-July 3, 1981 / edited by B. Chandrasekaran and S. Radicchi. — Amsterdam ; Oxford : North-Holland, c1981. — viii,325p : ill,forms ; 23cm
Includes bibliographies
ISBN 0-444-86292-7 : £21.74 B82-07888

001.64'25 — Acorn Atom microcomputer systems & BBC microcomputer systems — *Programs*

Johnson-Davies, David. Practical programs : for the BBC computer and Acorn Atom / David Johnson-Davies. — Wilmslow : Sigma Technical, c1982. — 119p : ill ; 21cm
Bibliography: p119
ISBN 0-905104-14-5 (pbk) : £5.95 B82-24085

001.64'25 — Commodore PET 2/3/4/8000 microprocessor systems. Assembly programming — *Manuals*

Holmes, Peter, *1939-*. The Dr. Watson book of assembly language programming for Commodore PET 2-3-4-8000 / by Peter Holmes. — 2nd ed. — London : Dr. Watson Computer Press, 1981. — 201p in various pagings : ill ; 21cm
Previous ed.: 1981. — Includes index
ISBN 0-907792-02-2 (pbk) : Unpriced B82-32739

001.64'25 — Commodore PET 2/3000 microcomputer systems. Assembly programming — *Manuals*

Holmes, Peter, *1939-*. The Dr. Watson book of assembly-language programming for Commodore PET 2/3000 / by Peter Holmes. — London : Dr. Watson Computer Press, 1981. — 152p in various pagings : ill ; 30cm
Includes index
ISBN 0-907792-00-6 (pbk) : Unpriced B82-08735

001.64'25 — Commodore PET microcomputer systems. Assembly languages — *Manuals*

Holmes, Peter, *1939-*. The Dr Watson book of assembly-language programming for Commodore PET 2/3/4/8000 / by Peter Holmes. — [London] ([21 Colin Drive, NW9 6ES]) : [Dr Watson Computer Press], [c1981]. — 200p in various pagings : ill ; 30cm
Includes index
ISBN 0-907792-01-4 (pbk) : Unpriced B82-12381

001.64'25 — Commodore VIC 20 microcomputer systems. Assembly programming — *Manuals*

Holmes, Peter, *1939-*. The Dr. Watson book of assembly language programming for Commodore VIC 20 / by Peter Holmes. — London : Dr. Watson Computer Press, c1982. — 198p in various pagings : ill ; 30cm
Includes index
ISBN 0-907792-03-0 (pbk) : Unpriced B82-32740

001.64'25 — Computer systems. Software — *Conference proceedings*

Pragmatic programming & sensible software. — Uxbridge : Online Conferences, c1978. — xiii,572p : ill ; 29cm
Conference proceedings
ISBN 0-903796-20-1 : Unpriced B82-03522

001.64'25 — Computer systems. Software. Configuration management

Buckle, J. K.. Software configuration management / J.K. Buckle. — London : Macmillan, 1982. — xiii,152p : ill,forms ; 25cm. — (Macmillan computer science series)
Bibliography: p146-147. — Includes index
ISBN 0-333-30719-4 (cased) : £12.00
ISBN 0-333-33228-8 (pbk) : Unpriced B82-38783

001.64'25 — Computer systems. Software. Design. Engineering aspects — *Conference proceedings*

Software systems engineering. — Uxbridge : Online Conferences, c1976. — 544p : ill ; 29cm
Conference papers
ISBN 0-903796-15-5 (pbk) : Unpriced B82-03324

001.64'25 — DEC PDP-11 minicomputer systems. Software packages: SPSS — *Manuals*

Morrison, Nancy K.. SPSS-11 : the SPSS batch systems for the DEC PDP-11 / Nancy K. Morrison. — 2nd ed. — New York ; London : McGraw-Hill, c1982. — xvi,312p : ill ; 28cm
Previous ed.: 1980. — Bibliography: p306. — Includes index
ISBN 0-07-046546-0 (pbk) : £10.75 B82-31563

001.64′25 — Digital computer systems. Compilers. Writing — *Manuals*

A **Programming** methodology in compiler construction / J. Lewi ... [et al.]. — Amsterdam ; Oxford : North-Holland
Pt.2: Implementation. — 1982. — xxv,569p : ill,ports ; 23cm
Bibliography: p569
ISBN 0-444-86339-7 : £26.37 B82-27161

001.64′25 — Digital computer systems. Compilers. Writing. Recursive descent techniques

Davie, A. J. T.. Recursive descent compiling / A.J.T. Davie and R. Morrison. — Chichester : Ellis Horwood, 1981. — 195p : ill ; 24cm. — (The Ellis Horwood series in computers and their applications ; 14)
Text on lining papers. — Includes index
ISBN 0-85312-386-1 : £12.50 B82-03899

001.64′25 — Digital computer systems. CP/M operating systems — *Serials*

CPMUGUK : the journal of the UK CP/M Usergroup. — Vol.1, no.1-. — [Sudbury] ([c/o Andrew R.M. Clarke, Chilton Cottage, Chilton Corner, Sudbury, Suffolk]) : [CP/M User Group, U.K.], 1980-. — v. : ill ; 21-30cm
Irregular. — Subtitle varies. — Size varies
ISSN 0263-1555 = CPMUGUK : Unpriced B82-15168

001.64′25 — Digital computer systems: IBM system 360 & IBM system 370. Assembly languages: IBM 360-370 Operating System Assembler Language

Yarmish, Rina. Assembly language fundamentals : 360/370, OS/VS, DOS/VS / Rina Yarmish, Joshua Yarmish. — Reading, Mass. ; London : Addison-Wesley, c1979. — xvi,768p : ill ; 24cm
Includes index
ISBN 0-201-08798-7 : £16.00 B82-33444

001.64′25 — Digital computer systems: ICL 2976 system. Software packages — *Manuals*

Sharp, William, *19---*. First guide to the 2976 : an introductory description of the user facilities on the Glasgow University ICL 2976 Computer / William Sharp. — [Glasgow] ([The University, Glasgow G12 8QQ]) : University of Glasgow Computing Service, 1980. — viii,[103]p : 1map ; 21cm
Includes index
Unpriced (pbk) B82-02583

001.64′25 — Digital computer systems. Networks. Protocols

Computer network architectures and protocols / edited by Paul E. Green, Jr. — New York ; London : Plenum, 1982. — xvii,718p : ill ; 24cm. — (Applications of communications theory)
Includes index
ISBN 0-306-40788-4 : Unpriced B82-36621

001.64′25 — Digital computer systems. Operating systems

Calingaert, Peter. Operating system elements : a user perspective / Peter Calingaert. — Englewood Cliffs ; London : Prentice-Hall, c1982. — xv,240p : ill ; 24cm. — (Prentice-Hall software series)
Bibliography: p220-226. — Includes index
ISBN 0-13-637421-2 : £17.95 B82-16711

Lorin, Harold. Operating systems / Harold Lorin, Harvey M. Deitel. — Reading, Mass. ; London : Addison-Wesley, c1981. — xxi,378p : ill ; 25cm
Ill on lining papers. — Bibliography: p353-359. — Includes index
ISBN 0-201-14464-6 : Unpriced B82-27986

001.64′25 — Digital computer systems. Operating systems. Concurrent programming

Ben-Ari, M.. Principles of concurrent programming. — London : Prentice Hall, Sept.1982. — [350]p
ISBN 0-13-701078-8 (pbk) : £9.95 : CIP entry B82-19173

001.64′25 — Digital computer systems. Programming languages: APL language. Interpreters. Design

Zaks, Rodnay. A microprogrammed APL implementation / by Rodnay Zaks. — Berkeley : Sybex ; Birmingham : The Computer Bookshop [distributor], c1978. — viii,347p : ill ; 28cm
ISBN 0-89588-005-9 (pbk) : Unpriced B82-27408

001.64′25 — Digital computer systems. Programming languages. Compilers. Design & construction

Hunter, Robin. The design and construction of compilers / Robin Hunter. — Chichester : Wiley, c1981. — xii,272p : ill ; 24cm. — (Wiley series in computing)
Bibliography: p258-260. — Includes index
ISBN 0-471-28054-2 : £10.50 : CIP rev. B81-34411

001.64′25 — Digital computer systems. Programs. Decision tables

Welland, R.. Decision tables and computer programming. — London : Heyden, Sept.1981. — [250]p
ISBN 0-85501-708-2 : CIP entry B81-28274

001.64′25 — Digital computer systems. Query languages

Query languages : a unified approach / the British Computer Society, Query Language Group. — London : Heyden on behalf of the British Computer Society, c1981. — xi,105p : ill ; 24cm. — (Monographs in informatics)
Bibliography: p93-96. — Includes index
ISBN 0-85501-494-6 (pbk) : £12.00 : CIP rev. B81-14819

001.64′25 — Digital computer systems. Software

Fox, Joseph M.. Software and its development / Joseph M. Fox. — Englewood Cliffs ; London : Prentice-Hall, c1982. — xv,299p : ill ; 24cm
Inlcudes index
ISBN 0-13-822098-0 : £17.95 B82-31825

Sommerville, Ian. Software engineering. — London : Addison-Wesley, May 1982. — [300] p. — (International computer science series ; 5)
ISBN 0-201-13795-x (pbk) : £7.95 : CIP entry B82-09282

001.64′25 — Digital computer systems. Software. Development

Bjorner, D.. Formal specification and software development. — Hemel Hempstead : Prentice-Hall, Sept.1982. — [400]p
ISBN 0-13-329003-4 : £18.00 : CIP entry B82-19172

Gillett, Will D.. An introduction to engineered software / Will D. Gillett, Seymour V. Pollack. — New York ; London : Holt, Rinehart and Winston, c1982. — x,322p : ill ; 25cm. — (HRW series in computer science)
Includes index
ISBN 0-03-056902-8 : £20.95
ISBN 4-8337-0084-0 (International Edition) : £7.50 B82-29502

001.64′25 — Digital computer systems. Software. Development & maintenance. Management

Pressman, Roger S.. Software engineering : a practitioner's approach / Roger S. Pressman. — New York ; London : McGraw-Hill, c1982. — xvi,352p : ill ; 25cm. — (McGraw-Hill series in software engineering and technology)
Includes index
ISBN 0-07-050781-3 : £25.25 B82-29270

001.64′25 — Digital computer systems. Software. Development. Management

Bruce, Phillip. The software development project : planning and management / Phillip Bruce, Sam M. Pederson. — New York ; Chichester : Wiley, c1982. — xi,210p : ill,forms ; 29cm
Includes index
ISBN 0-471-06269-3 : £16.50 B82-24219

001.64′25 — Digital computer systems. Software packages: GOS

Description of the internal structure of GOS / Museum Documentation Association. — Duxford : The Association, 1980. — iv,29p ; 30cm
ISBN 0-905963-29-6 (spiral) : £7.50 (£5.00 to MDA members, £2.50 to GOS User Group members) B82-39101

001.64′25 — Digital computer systems. Software packages — *Lists*

NCC Information Services. NCC directory of computing software : catalogue (level 1) and summary tables (level 2) of NCC Information Services database of computing software / general editor Norman Candeland. — Manchester : NCC Information Services, 1980. — 206p in various pagings ; 30cm
Includes index
ISBN 0-85012-254-6 (pbk) : Unpriced : CIP rev. B80-17510

001.64′25 — Digital computer systems. Software packages: MINT

Machine-independent organic software tools. — 2nd ed. — London : Academic Press, Nov.1982. — [350]p
Previous ed.: 1980
ISBN 0-12-286982-6 : CIP entry B82-26860

001.64′25 — Digital computer systems. Software packages: SPSS

Norušis, Marija J.. SPSS introductory guide : basic statistics and operations / Marija J. Norusis ; series editors Norman H. Nie, C. Hadlai Hull. — New York ; London : McGraw-Hill, c1982. — xiv,173p : ill ; 29cm
Bibliography: p168-169. — Includes index
ISBN 0-07-047528-8 (pbk) : £7.75 B82-16012

001.64′25 — Digital computer systems. Software. Portability

Software portability : an advanced course / editor P.J. Brown ; invited contributors R.J. Allwood ... [et al.]. — Cambridge : Cambridge University Press, 1977 (1979 [printing]). — xiv,328p : ill ; 23cm
Includes bibliographies and index
ISBN 0-521-29725-7 (pbk) : £5.95 B82-08282

001.64′25 — Digital computer systems. Software. Quality control

Dunn, Robert, *1929-*. Quality assurance for computer software / Robert Dunn and Richard Ullman. — New York ; London : McGraw-Hill, c1982. — viii,351p : ill ; 24cm
Includes index
ISBN 0-07-018312-0 : £17.50 B82-02515

001.64′25 — Digital computer systems. Translators

Berry, Robert E.. Programming language translation / R.E. Berry. — Chichester : Ellis Horwood, 1982. — 175p : ill ; 24cm. — (The Ellis Horwood series in computers and their applications ; v.15)
Text on lining papers. — Includes index
ISBN 0-85312-379-9 (cased) : £15.00
ISBN 0-85312-430-2 (pbk) : Unpriced
ISBN 0-470-27305-4 (U.S.) B82-12299

001.64′25 — Digital computer systems. UNIX operating systems

Bourne, S. R.. The UNIX system. — London : Addison-Wesley, Oct.1982. — [320]p. — (International computer science series ; 6)
ISBN 0-201-13791-7 (pbk) : £9.95 : CIP entry B82-25923

001.64′25 — Great Britain. IBM computer systems. Software

IBM Computer Users' Association software survey. — [Ilford] ([55, Sunnymede Drive, Barkingside, Ilford, Essex]) : [The Association], 1980. — vii,185p ; 22x30cm
Unpriced (spiral) B82-09520

001.64′25 — ICL 2900 digital computer systems. Operating systems: EMAS. Programming languages: Prolog — *Manuals*

User's guide to EMAS Prolog / edited by Lawrence Byrd ; using material by D.L. Bowen ... [et al.]. — [Edinburgh] : Department of Artificial Intelligence, University of Edinburgh, 1981. — 36p ; 30cm. — (D.A.I. occasional paper, ISSN 0144-4131 ; no.26)
Unpriced (spiral) B82-17340

001.64′25 — Interactive computer systems. Software packages: SCSS — *Manuals*

SCSS : a user′s guide to the SCSS conversational system / Norman H. Nie ... [et al.]. — New York ; London : McGraw-Hill, c1980. — xxv,595p : ill ; 28cm
Bibliography: p581-583. — Includes index
ISBN 0-07-046538-x (cased) : £13.75
ISBN 0-07-046533-9 (pbk) : £8.95 B82-39121

001.64′25 — Macro processors

Cole, A. J. (Alfred John). Macro processors / A.J. Cole. — 2nd ed. — Cambridge : Cambridge University Press, 1981. — viii,254p ; 24cm. — (Cambridge computer science texts ; 4)
Previous ed.: 1976. — Includes index
ISBN 0-521-24259-2 (cased) : £12.00 : CIP rev.
ISBN 0-521-25860-7 (pbk) : £5.95 B81-32536

001.64′25 — Microcomputer systems & microprocessor systems. Software — *Serials*

Software & microsystems : a journal for practising engineers. — Vol.1, no.1 (Oct. 1981)-. — Stevenage : Institution of Electrical Engineers, 1981-. — v. : ill,ports ; 30cm
Six issues yearly
ISSN 0261-3182 = Software & microsystems : £27.00 per year B82-18507

001.64′25 — Microcomputer systems. Assembly languages

Stewart, Ian. Machine code and better Basic. — Nantwich : Shiva, July 1982. — [180]p. — (Shiva′s friendly micro series)
ISBN 0-906812-18-6 (pbk) : £7.50 : CIP entry
B82-22400

001.64′25 — Microcomputer systems. CP/M operating systems

Zaks, Rodnay. The CP/M handbook with MP/M / Rodnay Zaks. — Berkeley : Sybex ; Birmingham : The Computer Bookshop [distributor], c1980. — xiii,321p : ill ; 23cm
Includes index
ISBN 0-89588-048-2 (pbk) : Unpriced
B82-27410

001.64′25 — Minicomputer systems. Assembly programming

Cluley, J. C.. Programming for minicomputers / J.C. Cluley. — New York : Crane Russak ; London : Edward Arnold, 1979, c1978. — 275p : ill ; 23cm. — (Computer systems engineering series)
Bibliography: p263-270. — Includes index
ISBN 0-7131-2775-9 (pbk) : £9.75 B82-26915

001.64′25 — Sinclair ZX Spectrum microcomputer systems. Assembly languages — *Manuals*

Sinclair, Ian, *19---*. Introducing Spectrum machine code. — London : Granada, Jan.1983. — [208]p
ISBN 0-246-12082-7 (pbk) : £7.95 : CIP entry
B82-36129

001.64′25′0287 — Computer systems. Software. Testing

Deutsch, Michael S.. Software verification and validation : realistic project approaches / Michael S. Deutsch. — Englewood Cliffs ; London : Prentice-Hall, c1982. — xvi,327p : ill ; 25cm. — (Prentice-Hall series in software engineering)
Bibliography: p315-316. — Includes index
ISBN 0-13-822072-7 : £16-45 B82-28194

001.64′25′0288 — Data processing systems. Software. Maintenance. Management

Lientz, Bennet P.. Software maintenance management : a study of the maintenance of computer application software in 487 data processing organizations / Bennet P. Lientz, E. Burton Swanson. — Reading, Mass. ; London : Addison-Wesley, c1980. — 214p : ill ; 24cm
Bibliography: p178-184. — Includes index
ISBN 0-201-04205-3 (pbk) : £8.00 B82-12656

001.64′4 — Digital computer systems. Peripheral equipment

Eadie, Donald. A user′s guide to computer peripherals / Donald Eadie. — Englewood Cliffs ; London : Prentice-Hall, c1982. — x,244p : ill,2maps ; 24cm
Includes index
ISBN 0-13-939660-8 : £14.20 B82-33770

001.64′404 — Computer systems. Networks

Deasington, R. J.. A practical guide to computer communications and networking. — Chichester : Ellis Horwood, Sept.1982. — [120]p. — (Ellis Horwood series in computers and their applications)
ISBN 0-85312-405-1 : £16.00 : CIP entry
B82-22814

001.64′404 — Computer systems. Networks — *Conference proceedings*

IFIP Working Group 6·4 International Workshop on Local Networks *(1980 : Zürich)*. Local networks for computer communications : proceedings of the IFIP Working Group 6·4 International Workshop on Local Networks organized by IBM [Zürich Research Laboratory] Zürich, Switzerland, August 27-29, 1980 / edited by Anthony West and Philippe Janson. — Amsterdam ; Oxford : North-Holland, c1981. — xiii,470p : ill,2maps ; 23cm
Includes bibliographies
ISBN 0-444-86287-0 : £27.06 B82-01635

001.64′404 — Computer systems. Networks. Data transmission

Cole, Robert, *1952-*. Computer communications / Robert Cole. — London : Macmillan, 1982. — 200p : ill ; 25cm. — (Macmillan computer science series)
Bibliography: p192-194. — Includes index
ISBN 0-333-27892-5 (cased) : Unpriced
ISBN 0-333-27893-3 (pbk) : Unpriced
B82-10191

001.64′404 — Digital computer systems. Local networks

Franta, W. R.. Local networks : motivation, technology, and performance / W.R. Franta, Imrich Chlamtac. — Lexington, Mass. : Lexington Books ; [Aldershot] : Gower [distributor], 1982, c1981. — xx,481p : ill ; 24cm. — (Lexington Books series in computer science)
Includes index
ISBN 0-669-03779-6 : £29.50 B82-28318

Gee, K. C. E.. Local area networks — state of the art. — Manchester : NCC, July 1982. — [70]p
ISBN 0-85012-383-6 (pbk) : £7.00 : CIP entry
B82-21959

Local networks / Urwick Nexos. — Slough : Urwick Nexos Limited, [1981?]. — ii,47leaves : ill ; 30cm. — (Managing office automation) (Urwick Nexos report series ; 4)
Bibliography: p47
ISBN 0-907535-04-6 (pbk) : Unpriced
B82-09148

Local networks and distributed office systems. — Northwood Hills : Online Publications, Sept.1982
Vol.1: Network systems development. — [740]p
ISBN 0-903796-87-2 (pbk) : £50.00 : CIP entry
B82-29037

Local networks and distributed office systems. — Northwood Hills : Online Publications, Sept.1982
Vol.2: System selection and implementation. — [770]p
ISBN 0-903796-89-9 (pbk) : £45.00 : CIP entry
B82-29038

Tropper, Carl. Local computer network technologies / Carl Tropper. — New York ; London : Academic Press, 1981. — xi,144p : ill ; 24cm. — (Notes and reports in computer science and applied mathematics ; 2)
Includes index
ISBN 0-12-700850-0 (pbk) : £13.00
B82-18679

001.64′404 — Digital computer systems. Local networks — *Conference proceedings*

Office networks. — Aldershot : Gower, Feb.1983. — [100]p
Conference papers
ISBN 0-566-03031-4 (pbk) : £18.00 : CIP entry
B82-38723

001.64′404 — Digital computer systems. Networks

Gee, K. C. E.. Local area networks / K.C.E. Gee. — Manchester : NCC, 1982. — 253p : ill ; 22cm
Includes index
ISBN 0-85012-365-8 (pbk) : Unpriced : CIP rev. B82-23836

Gee, K. C. E.. Proprietary network architectures / K.C.E.Gee. — Manchester : NCC, 1981. — 258p : ill ; 31cm
Bibliography: p247-249. — Includes index
ISBN 0-85012-327-5 : £50.00 : CIP rev.
B81-18051

001.64′404 — Digital computer systems. Networks. Data transmission — *Conference proceedings*

COMNET ′81 *(Conference : Budapest)*. Networks from the user′s point of view : proceedings of the IFIP TC-6 Working Conference COMNET ′81, Budapest, Hungary, 11-15 May, 1981 / edited by Lászlo Csaba, Tibor Szentiványi, Katie Tarnay. — Amsterdam ; Oxford : North-Holland, c1981. — xvi,664p : ill ; 23cm
Includes index
ISBN 0-444-86291-9 : £36.80 B82-01634

001.64′404 — Digital computer systems. Networks. Data transmission. Design & analysis

Meijer, A.. Computer network architectures. — London : Pitman, Oct.1982. — [416]p
ISBN 0-273-01709-8 : £15.00 : CIP entry
B82-25190

001.64′404 — Digital computer systems. Networks. Data transmission. International political aspects

Freese, Jan. International data flow / Jan Freese ; with editorial assistance of G. Russell Pipe. — Lund, Sweden : Studentlitteratur ; Bromley : Chartwell-Bratt, c1979. — 71p : ill,1map ; 23cm
Bibliography: p71
ISBN 0-86238-010-3 (pbk) : Unpriced
B82-30915

001.64′404 — Distributed digital computer systems. Networks

Martin, James, *1933-*. Computer networks and distributed processing : software, techniques and architecture / James Martin. — Englewood Cliffs ; London : Prentice-Hall, c1981. — xiv,562p : ill(some col.) ; 25cm
Includes index
ISBN 0-13-165258-3 : £25.00 B82-07544

001.64′404 — On-line computer systems — *For small business firms*

Silver, Maurice A.. On-line computing for small businesses. — London : Pitman, Feb.1983. — [144]p
ISBN 0-273-01885-x (pbk) : £2.95 : CIP entry
B82-37821

001.64′404 — On-line information systems. Design — *Conference proceedings*

IFIP WG 8.1 Working Conference on Automated Tools for Information Systems Design and Development *(1982 : New Orleans)*. Automated tools for information systems design : proceedings of the IFIP WG 8.1 Working Conference on Automated Tools for Information Systems Design and Development, New Orleans, U.S.A., 26-28 January, 1982 / edited by Hans-Jochen Schneider and Anthony I. Wasserman. — Amsterdam ; Oxford : North-Holland, 1982. — ix,261p : ill ; 23cm
ISBN 0-444-86338-9 : £18.09 B82-13442

001.64′404′068 — Digital computer systems. Networks. Data transmission. Management — *Serials*

Advances in data communications management. — Vol.1-. — Philadelphia ; London : Heyden, 1980-. — v. : ill ; 24cm
Annual
ISSN 0197-1476 = Advances in data communications management : £15.50
B82-11799

001.64′42 — Associative machine-readable files. Management systems: CS4 system

Janning, Marianne. CS4 : an introduction to associative data bases and the CS4 system / Marianne Janning, Sam Nachmens, Stig Berild. — Lund : Studentlitteratur ; Bromley : Chartwell-Bratt, 1981. — 255p : ill ; 23cm
Includes index
ISBN 0-86238-012-x (pbk) : Unpriced B82-35642

001.64′42 — Data dictionary systems

Leong-Hong, Belkis W.. Data dictionary/directory systems : administration, implementation and usage / Belkis W. Leong-Hong, Bernard K. Plagman. — New York ; Chichester : Wiley, c1982. — xviii,328p : ill ; 24cm
Includes bibliographies and index
ISBN 0-471-05164-0 : Unpriced B82-38320

Van Duyn, J.. Developing a data dictionary system / J. Van Duyn. — Englewood Cliffs ; London : Prentice-Hall, c1982. — xiv,204p : ill,facsims ; 24cm
Bibliography: p191-193. — Includes index
ISBN 0-13-204289-4 : £18.75 B82-19948

001.64′42 — Data processing. Keyboarding — *Manuals*

Stananought, Joyce. Keyboarding for information : processing. — British ed. / adapted by Joyce Stananought ; from the book by Robert N. Hanson and D. Sue Rigby. — London : McGraw-Hill, c1982. — vi,90p : ill ; 23cm
ISBN 0-7084-6340-1 (spiral) : £1.95 B82-25966

001.64′42 — Data processing systems. Video discs

Sims, Robins J.. Optical data storage : thin film discs / by Robin J. Sims. — London : [City University Business School], c1981. — 55leaves : ill ; 30cm. — (Working paper / City University Business School, ISSN 0140-1041 ; no.31)
Unpriced (pbk) B82-09567

001.64′42 — Digital computer systems. Data. Input — *Manuals*

Lee, Iva Helen. Data entry : concepts and exercises / Iva Helen Lee. — New York ; Chichester : Wiley, c1982. — xi,355p : ill,forms ; 28cm
Includes index
ISBN 0-471-08605-3 (pbk) : £10.85 B82-18060

001.64′42 — Digital computer systems. Data. Structure

Beidler, John. An introduction to data structures / John Beidler. — Boston, [Mass.] ; London : Allyn and Bacon, 1982. — xv,213p : ill ; 25cm. — (Allyn and Bacon computer science series)
Bibliography: p205-210. — Includes index
ISBN 0-205-07711-0 : Unpriced B82-27060

Standish, Thomas A.. Data structure techniques / Thomas A. Standish. — Reading, Mass. ; London : Addison-Wesley, c1980. — xvi,447p : ill ; 24cm. — (Addison-Wesley series in computer science)
Bibliography: p409-434. — Includes index
ISBN 0-201-07256-4 : £9.95 B82-05155

001.64′42 — Digital computer systems. Storage devices

The **Applications** and benefits of Winchester disk technology : 16 February 1982, London : conference transcript. — London : Scientific and Technical Studies, c1982. — iii,80p : ill ; 30cm
ISBN 0-907822-01-0 (pbk) : £40.00 : CIP rev. B82-17237

001.64′42 — Distributed machine-readable files — *Conference proceedings*

International Seminar on Distributed Data Sharing Systems *(2nd : 1981 : Amsterdam)*. Distributed data sharing systems : proceedings of the second International Seminar on Distributed Data Sharing Systems held in Amsterdam, the Netherlands, 3-5 June, 1981 / [organized by Department of Mathematics and Informatics, Vrije Universiteit, Amsterdam and Institut national de récherche en informatique et en automatique (INRIA), Paris] ; [under the sponsorship of IGDD] ; edited by R.P. Van De Riet and W. Litwin. — Amsterdam ; Oxford : North-Holland, 1982. — xi,314p : ill ; 23cm
ISBN 0-444-86374-5 : £21.23 B82-28561

001.64′42 — Machine-readable files

Elbra, R. A.. Database for the small computer user. — Manchester : NCC Publications, Feb.1982. — [150]p
ISBN 0-85012-328-3 (pbk) : £8.50 : CIP entry B82-02458

Kroenke, David. Database : a professional′s primer / David Kroenke. — Chicago ; Henley-on-Thames : Science Research Associates, c1978. — xi,323p : ill ; 25cm
Ill on lining papers. — Bibliography: p317-319. — Includes index
ISBN 0-574-21210-8 : Unpriced B82-39705

Robinson, Hugh. Database analysis and design / Hugh Robinson. — England : Chartwell-Bratt, 1981. — viii,375p : ill ; 22cm. — (Hatfield Polytechnic computer science series)
Includes index
ISBN 0-86238-018-9 (pbk) : Unpriced B82-35648

001.64′42 — Machine-readable files — *Conference proceedings*

British National Conference on Databases *(1st : 1981 : Cambridge)*. Databases : proceedings of the 1st British National Conference on Databases held at Jesus College Cambridge, 13-14 July 1981 / edited by S.M. Deen, P. Hammersley. — London : Pentech, 1981. — 205p : ill ; 24cm
Includes index
ISBN 0-7273-0405-4 : Unpriced : CIP rev. B81-28813

001.64′42 — Machine-readable files. Data. Models

Tsichritzis, Dionysios C.. Data models / Dionysios C. Tsichritzis, Frederick H. Lochovsky. — Englewood Cliffs ; London : Prentice-Hall, c1982. — xiv,381p : ill ; 25cm. — (Prentice-Hall software series)
Bibliography: p343-365. — Includes index
ISBN 0-13-196428-3 : £18.70 B82-20544

001.64′42 — Machine-readable files. Design

Curtice, Robert M.. Logical data base design / Robert M. Curtice and Paul E. Jones, Jr. — New York ; London : Van Nostrand Reinhold, c1982. — xii,227p : ill,1form ; 26cm. — (Van Nostrand Reinhold data processing series)
Includes index
ISBN 0-442-24501-7 : £25.45 B82-30960

Hanson, Owen. Design of computer data files. — London : Pitman, Sept.1982. — [356]p
ISBN 0-273-01241-x : £16.00 : CIP entry B82-18871

Teorey, Toby J.. Design of database structures / Toby J. Teorey, James P. Fry. — Englewood Cliffs ; London : Prentice-Hall, 1982. — xv,492p : ill ; 24cm
Bibliography: p470-484. — Includes index
ISBN 0-13-200097-0 : Unpriced B82-38577

Warnier, Jean Dominique. Logical construction of systems / Jean Dominique Warnier. — New York ; London : Van Nostrand Reinhold, c1981. — ci,179p : ill ; 25cm
Translation of: Pratique de la construction d′un ensemble de données. — Bibliography: p177. — Includes index
ISBN 0-442-22556-3 : £19.50 B82-00747

001.64′42 — Machine-readable files. Management

Bradley, James. File and data base techniques / James Bradley. — New York ; London : Holt, Rinehart and Winston, c1982. — xiii,562p : ill ; 25cm. — (HRW series in computer science)
Includes bibliographies and index
ISBN 0-03-058673-9 : £18.95 B82-15347

Larson, James A.. Database management system anatomy / James A. Larson. — Lexington, Mass. : Lexington Books ; [Aldershot] : Gower [distributor], c1982. — xv,183p : ill ; 24cm. — (Lexington Books series in computer science)
Bibliography: p179-180. — Includes index
ISBN 0-669-04544-6 : £16.50 B82-28771

Mayne, Alan. Database management systems : a technical review / Alan Mayne. — Manchester : NCC, 1981. — 221p : ill ; 22cm
Bibliography: p207-208. — Includes index
ISBN 0-85012-323-2 (pbk) : Unpriced : CIP rev. B81-18064

001.64′42 — Machine-readable files. Management. Evaluation

King, Judy. Evaluating data base management systems / Judy King. — New York ; London : Van Nostrand Reinhold, c1981. — xviii,275p : ill ; 24cm. — (Van Nostrand Reinhold data processing series)
Bibliography: p261-263. — Includes index
ISBN 0-442-23994-7 : £18.65 B82-00850

001.64′42 — Machine-readable files. Management — *Serials*

Advances in data base management. — Vol.1-. — Philadelphia ; London : Heyden, 1980-. — v. : ill ; 24cm
Annual
£17.00 B82-18713

001.64′42 — Machine-readable files. Management systems — *Conference proceedings*

Database. — [Uxbridge] : [Online Conferences], [c1977]. — 287p in various pagings : ill ; 30cm
Conference papers
Unpriced (pbk) B82-03321

001.64′43 — Atari microcomputer systems. Sound effects & visual displays — *Manuals*

Moore, Herb. Atari sound and graphics / Herb Moore, Judy Lower, Bob Albrecht. — New York ; Chichester : Wiley, c1982. — vi,234p : ill ; 26cm. — (A self-teaching guide)
Includes index
ISBN 0-471-09593-1 (pbk) : Unpriced B82-36827

001.64′43 — Computer graphics — *Conference proceedings*

Computer graphics 82. — Northwood Hills : Online Publications, Oct.1982. — [320]p
Conference papers
ISBN 0-903796-92-9 (pbk) : £50.00 : CIP entry B82-29039

Eurographics ′81 *(Conference : Technische Hochschule Darmstadt)*. Eurographics ′81 : proceedings of the international conference and exhibition, Technische Hochschule Darmstadt, F.R. of Germany 9-11 September 1981 / edited by Jose L. Encarnacao. — Amsterdam ; Oxford : North-Holland, c1981. — xii,335p : ill,maps ; 23cm
Includes index
ISBN 0-444-86284-6 : Unpriced B82-19622

001.64′43 — Computer systems. Graphic displays

Angell, Ian O.. A practical introduction to computer graphics / Ian O. Angell. — London : Macmillan, 1981. — xiii,146p : ill ; 25cm. — (Macmillan computer science series)
Includes index
ISBN 0-333-31082-9 (cased) : £12.00 B82-06697

001.64′43 — Computer systems. Visual display terminals. Ergonomic aspects

Mackay, Colin, *1949-*. Human factors aspects of visual display unit operation / Colin Mackay ; [for the] Health and Safety Executive. — London : H.M.S.O., 1980. — iii,12p : ill ; 30cm. — (HSE research paper ; no.10)
ISBN 0-11-883408-8 (pbk) : £1.50 B82-20455

001.64'43 — Computer systems. Visual display terminals. Ergonomic aspects *continuation*

Vision and visual display units : course documentation / editor Veronica M. Reading. — [London] (Judd St, WC1H 9QS) : University of London, Institute of Ophthalmology, [c1981]. — 1v.(various pagings) : ill ; 30cm
Includes bibliographies
Unpriced (pbk) B82-07855

001.64'43 — Digital computer systems. Peripheral equipment: Printers

Condon, M. A.. Office printers : a practical evaluation guide. — Manchester : NCC Publications, Apr.1982. — [126]p. — (Office technology in the '80s ; 5)
ISBN 0-85012-371-2 (pbk) : £6.50 : CIP entry B82-17939

001.64'43 — Interactive computer systems with graphic displays

Scott, Joan E.. Introduction to interactive computer graphics / Joan E. Scott. — New York ; Chichester : Wiley, c1982. — xi,255p : ill,plans ; 24cm
Includes index
ISBN 0-471-05773-8 : £18.45
ISBN 0-471-86623-7 (pbk) : Unpriced B82-21800

001.64'43 — Microcomputer systems. Visual displays. Matrices

Anbarlian, Harry. An introduction to visicalc matrixing for APPLE & IBM / Harry Anbarlian. — New York ; London : McGraw-Hill, c1982. — xiii,252p ; 24cm
Includes index
ISBN 0-07-001605-4 (spiral) : £15.95 B82-39360

001.64'43 — Sinclair ZX Spectrum microcomputer systems. Graphic displays

Hampshire, Nick. Spectrum graphics. — London : Duckworth, Nov.1982. — [192]p
ISBN 0-7156-1700-1 (pbk) : £6.95 : CIP entry B82-33204

001.9 — CONTROVERSIAL KNOWLEDGE

001.9 — Controversial & spurious knowledge

The **Directory** of possibilities / edited by Colin Wilson and John Grant. — London : Corgi, 1982, c1981. — 303p,[32]p of plates : ill,ports ; 20cm
Originally published: Exeter : Webb & Bower, 1981. — Bibliography: p268-272. — Includes index
ISBN 0-552-11994-6 (pbk) : £2.50 B82-37811

001.9'3 — Curiosities

O'Donnell, J. M.. Curiosity won't kill you / J.M. O'Donnell. — Bognor Regis : New Horizon, c1982. — 91p : ill ; 21cm
ISBN 0-86116-036-3 : £3.50
Also classified at 133 B82-17488

The **Reader's** Digest book of strange stories, amazing facts : stories that are bizarre, unusual, odd, astonishing, incredible — but true. — London : Readers Digest Association, c1975 (1891 [printing]). — 607p : ill(some col.),ports ; 29cm
Includes index
Unpriced B82-05140

Steiger, Brad. Worlds before our own / Brad Steiger. — London : W.H. Allen, 1981, c1978. — 187p ; 18cm. — (A Star book)
Originally published: New York : Berkeley, 1978. — Bibliography: p186-187
ISBN 0-352-30815-x (pbk) : £1.50 B82-37017

Welfare, Simon. Arthur C. Clarke's mysterious world / Simon Welfare & John Fairley. — [London] : Fontana/Collins, 1982, c1980. — 320p : ill(some col.),maps(some col.),ports(some col.) ; 20cm
Based on the Yorkshire TV series. — Originally published: London : Collins, 1980. — Includes index
ISBN 0-00-636315-6 (pbk) : £4.50 B82-15247

001.9'3 — Curiosities. Theories

Däniken, Erich von. The stones of Kiribati : pathways to the gods? / by Erich von Däniken ; translated by Michael Heron. — London : Souvenir, 1982. — 267p,[16]p of plates : ill (some col.),ports(some col.) ; 23cm
Translation of: Reise nach Kiribati. — Bibliography: p259-262. — Includes index
ISBN 0-285-62523-3 : £7.95 B82-26981

Story, Ronald. Guardians of the universe? / Ronald Story. — London : New English Library, 1980 (1981 [printing]). — 207p,[48]p of plates : ill,maps,ports ; 18cm
Bibliography: p171-191. — Includes index
ISBN 0-450-04566-8 (pbk) : £1.75 B82-08667

001.9'4 — Mysteries — *For children*

Haining, Peter. The restless bones : and other true mysteries / Peter Haining ; illustrated by Ellis Nadler. — [London] : Armada, 1978 (1981 [printing]). — 125p : ill ; 19cm. — (An Armada original)
ISBN 0-00-691987-1 (pbk) : £0.85 B82-01917

Haining, Peter. The vampire terror : and other true mysteries / Peter Haining ; illustrated by Eric Kincaid. — London : Fontana, 1981. — 125p : ill ; 19cm. — (An Armada original)
ISBN 0-00-691954-5 (pbk) : £0.85 B82-01918

Hill, Gordon. Secrets of the unknown / Gordon Hill ; illustrated by Donald Harley. — 2nd impression. — [Sevenoaks] : Knight Books, 1979 (1980 [printing]). — 111p : ill ; 18cm
ISBN 0-340-24039-3 (pbk) : £0.70 : CIP rev. B79-22099

Mysteries / written by Christopher Fagg ... [et al.] ; illustrated by Michael Atkinson ... [et al.]. — London : Pan, 1981. — 128p : col.ill,col.maps,col.ports ; 22cm. — (A Piccolo explorer book)
Bibliography: p128. — Includes index. — Contents: Fabulous beasts — Sea mysteries — Lost cities — Missing treasure — Devils and demons — Ghosts
ISBN 0-330-26518-0 (pbk) : £1.95
Also classified at 398'.469 B82-01584

001.9'4'05 — Mysteries — *Serials*

Centre update. — No.1 (Apr. 1982)-. — Stockport (92 Hillcrest Rd, Offerton, Stockport, Cheshire SK2 5SE) : O.S.E.A.P., 1982-. — v. ; 30cm
Two issues yearly
ISSN 0262-7795 = Centre update : Unpriced B82-36694

001.9'4'09162 — Oceans. Mysteries, *1847-1969*

Harris, John, *1916-*. Without trace : the last voyages of eight ships / by John Harris. — London : Eyre Methuen, 1981. — 244p,[8]p of plates : ill,maps,1facsim,ports ; 24cm
Map on lining papers. — Bibliography: p237-238. — Includes index
ISBN 0-413-46170-x : £7.50 B82-17599

001.9'4'09162 — Oceans. Mysteries, *to 1981 — For children*

Abranson, Erik C.. Mysteries and legends of the sea. — London : Hodder & Stoughton Children's Books, Mar.1982. — [128]p
ISBN 0-340-27137-x : £4.95 : CIP entry B82-01713

001.9'4'094235 — Devon. Mysteries

Lauder, Rosemary Anne. Strange stories from Devon / Rosemary Anne Lauder & Michael Williams. — Bodmin : Bossiney Books, 1982. — 102p : ill,ports ; 20cm
ISBN 0-906456-61-4 (pbk) : £1.95 B82-28830

001.9'4'094237 — Cornwall. Mysteries

Williams, Michael, *1933-*. Strange happenings in Cornwall / Michael Williams. — Bodmin : Bossiney, 1981. — 104p : ill,ports ; 22cm
ISBN 0-906456-57-6 (pbk) : £1.75 B82-08210

001.9'4'094265 — Cambridgeshire. Mysteries — *Serials*

Cambridgeshire ancient mysteries : the magazine of earth mysteries, ancient enigmas, geomancy, terrestrial anomalies, paganism and local lore in Cambs. and nearby territories / [Cambridgeshire Ancient Mysteries Group]. — No.1 (Summer 1981)-no.2 (Autumn 1981). — Cambridge (142 Pheasant Rise, Bar Hill, Cambridge CB3 8SD) : Institute of Geomantic Research, 1981-1981. — 2v. : ill ; 30cm
Quarterly
£2.00 per year B82-07630

001.9'4'09429 — Wales. Mysteries

Barber, Chris, *1941-*. Mysterious Wales / Chris Barber. — Newton Abbot : David & Charles, c1982. — 243p : ill,1map ; 21cm
Bibliography: p233-234. — Includes index
ISBN 0-7153-8366-3 : £8.95 : CIP rev. B82-20380

001.9'4'094487 — France. Rennes-le-Château. Mysteries

Baigent, Michael. The holy blood and the Holy Grail / Michael Baigent, Richard Leigh and Henry Lincoln. — London : Cape, 1982. — xvi,445p,[24]p of plates : ill,maps,coats of arms,ports,geneal.tables ; 25cm
Bibliography: p395-405. — Includes index
ISBN 0-224-01735-7 : £8.95 : CIP rev. B81-34555

001.9'42 — Unidentified flying objects

Devereux, Paul. Earth lights : towards an understanding of the UFO enigma. — Wellingborough : Turnstone Press, Oct.1982. — [288]p
ISBN 0-85500-123-2 (cased) : £9.95 : CIP entry
ISBN 0-85500-124-0 (pbk) : £4.95 B82-24110

Hendry, Allan. The UFO handbook : a guide to investigating, evaluating and reporting UFO sightings / Allan Hendry ; foreword by J. Allen Hynek. — London : Sphere, 1980, c1979 (1981 [printing]). — xiii,297p : ill,facsims,1form,maps ; 26cm
Originally published: Garden City : Doubleday, 1979. — Bibliography: p295-297
ISBN 0-7221-4505-5 (pbk) : Unpriced B82-29491

The **House** of Lords UFO debate : illustrated full transcript / with preface by Lord Clancarty (Brinsley le Poer Trench) and notes by John Michell. — London : Open Head, 1979. — 115p : ill,ports ; 21cm
ISBN 0-9506772-0-5 (pbk) : £2.95 B82-11186

001.9'42 — Unidentified flying objects. Night observation — *Manuals*

Night observation exercise manual. — Crewe (30 Charlesworth St., Crewe, Cheshire, CW1 4DE) : Federation UFO Research assisted by A.R. Pace, [1982?]. — 17p : ill,forms ; 30cm
Unpriced (pbk) B82-16962

001.9'42'05 — Unidentified flying objects — *Serials*

NUFOIS news : a bulletin devoted to ufological notes and news, etc. — Vol.1, no. 1 (1981)-. — [Nottingham] ([443 Meadow La., Nottingham NG2 3GB]) : [Nottingham UFO Investigation Society], 1981-. — v. ; 30cm
Irregular. — Description based on: Vol.1, no.2 (1981)
ISSN 0262-9151 = NUFOIS news : £0.15 per issue B82-14268

001.9'42'072 — Unidentified flying objects. Investigation

UFO/IFO : a process of elimination : an investigative study / by SCUFORI & PROBE ; [edited by Ian Mrzyglod]. — [Swindon] ([29 Lethbridge Rd., Swindon, Wilts., SN1 4BY]) : SCUFORI/PROBE, [1982]. — 41p : ill,1map ; 21cm
Cover title. — Text and map on inside cover
ISBN 0-9507979-0-1 (pbk) : £0.80 B82-32050

001.9′42′072 — Unidentified flying objects. Investigation — *Serials*

OSEAP journal. — Vol.1, no.1 (Apr. 1982)-. — Crewe (170 Henry St., Crewe, Cheshire CW1 4BQ) : Organisation for Scientific Evaluation of Aerial Phenomena, 1982-. — v. : ill ; 30cm
Two issues yearly
ISSN 0262-5954 = OSEAP journal : £5.00 per year B82-31734

001.9′42′0942933 — Clwyd. Oakenholt. Unidentified flying objects. Claimed observations, *1976-1979*

Randles, Jenny. Alien contact : window on another world / Jenny Randles & Paul Whetnall. — Sudbury : Spearman, 1981. — viii,207p : ill ; 23cm
Bibliography: p201-202. — Includes index
ISBN 0-85435-444-1 : £5.25 B82-09155

Randles, Jenny. Alien contact. — London ; Coronet Books, Feb.1983. — [224]p
Originally published: Sudberry : Spearman, 1981
ISBN 0-340-32109-1 (pbk) : £1.25 : CIP entry B82-38065

001.9′42′0942962 — Dyfed. St. Bride′s Bay region. Unidentified flying objects. Claimed observations, *1977 - Reports, surveys*

Pugh, Randall. The Dyfed enigma. — Sevenoaks : Coronet Books, Aug.1981. — [192]p
Originally published: London : Faber, 1979
ISBN 0-340-26665-1 (pbk) : £1.50 : CIP entry B81-15819

001.9′42′0973 — United States. Unidentified flying objects. Claimed observations, *to 1979*

Gansberg, Judith M.. Direct encounters : UFO abductees tell their own story / Judith M. Gansberg and Alan L. Gansberg. — Sevenoaks : Coronet, 1981, c1980. — 191p ; 18cm
Originally published: New York : Walker, 1980. — Bibliography: p189-191
ISBN 0-340-26685-6 (pbk) : £1.25 : CIP rev. B81-22547

001.9′42′09742 — New Hampshire. Unidentified flying objects. Claimed observations, *1961*

Fuller, John G.. The interrupted journey : two lost hours aboard a flying saucer / John G. Fuller. — London : Corgi, 1981, c1966. — 386p ; 18cm
Originally published: New York : Dial Press, 1966 ; London : Souvenir, 1980
ISBN 0-552-11851-6 (pbk) : £1.50 B82-10210

001.9′44 — Bigfoot. Claimed observations, *to 1980*

Bord, Janet. Bigfoot casebook. — London : Granada, May 1982. — [240]p
ISBN 0-246-11397-9 : £8.95 : CIP entry B82-07404

001.9′44 — China. Wild men

Yuan, Zhenxin. Wild man : China′s yeti / Yuan Zhenxin & Huang Wanpo with Fan Jingquan, Zhou Xinyan ; [edited by Steve Moore]. — London (c/o 9/12 St Annes Court, W1) : Fortean times, c1981. — 23p : ill,1map ; 23cm. — (Fortean times occasional paper, ISSN 0260-5856 ; no.1)
Translation from the Chinese. — Cover title. — Text on inside cover. — Bibliography: p22
Unpriced (pbk) B82-05178

001.9′44 — Loch Ness monster

Dinsdale, Tim. Loch Ness monster / Tim Dinsdale. — 4th ed. — London : Routledge & Kegan Paul, 1982. — 218p,[16]p of plates : ill,maps,facsims,ports ; 22cm
Previous ed.: 1976
ISBN 0-7100-9022-6 (pbk) : £4.75 B82-24909

001.9′44 — Loch Ness monster. Claimed observations, *1933-1980*

Witchell, Nicholas. The Loch Ness story / Nicholas Witchell. — London : Corgi, 1982, c1974. — 207p : 1map,ports ; 18cm
Originally published: Lavenham : Dalton, 1974
ISBN 0-552-11933-4 (pbk) : £1.75 B82-25630

001.9′44 — Monsters — *For children*

Brett, Bernard. Monster or man? / [written by Bernard Brett and Dorothy D. Ward] ; [edited by Dorothy D. Ward] ; [illustrations by Michael Walls Studio]. — London : Marshall Cavendish, 1980. — 127p : ill(some col.) ; 22cm. — (Monsterbacks)
ISBN 0-85685-847-1 (pbk) : Unpriced B82-22937

001.9′44′0321 — Monsters — *Encyclopaedias*

Woodward, Ian. An A-Z of monsters / Ian Woodward ; illustrated by Johnny Pau. — London : Beaver, 1981. — 159p : ill ; 18cm. — (A Beaver original)
ISBN 0-600-20325-5 (pbk) : £0.95 B82-00975

001.9′5 — Hoaxes

Saunders, Richard. The world′s greatest hoaxes / Richard Saunders. — South Yarmouth, Mass. : Curley ; [Long Preston] : Distributed by Magna Print, c1980. — 316p ; 23cm
Published in large print
ISBN 0-89340-392-x : Unpriced B82-35134

002 — THE BOOK

002 — Books — *Critical studies*

The **Anti-booklist** / edited by Brian Redhead and Kenneth McLeish ; cartoons by Michael Heath. — London : Hodder and Stoughton, 1981. — 137p : ill ; 21cm
Includes index
ISBN 0-340-27084-5 (cased) : Unpriced : CIP rev.
ISBN 0-340-27447-6 (pbk) : £1.95 B81-25755

002′.075 — Books. Collecting

Chidley, John. Discovering book collecting / John Chidley. — Princes Risborough : Shire, 1982. — 80p : ill ; 18cm. — (The Discovering series ; 267)
Bibliography: p79. — Includes index
ISBN 0-85263-588-5 (pbk) : £1.25 B82-39399

Uden, Grant. Book collecting. — Woodbridge : Antique Collectors′ Club, Apr.1982. — [150]p
ISBN 0-907462-13-8 : £9.95 : CIP entry B82-05790

002′.075 — Rare books. Collecting — *Manuals*

Matthews, Jack. Collecting rare books : for pleasure and profit / by Jack Matthews. — Chicago ; London : Ohio University Press, 1981. — 307p,[16]p of plates : ill,facsims ; 24cm
Originally published: New York : Putnam, 1977. — Bibliography: p293-297. — Includes index
ISBN 0-8214-0610-8 (cased) : Unpriced
ISBN 0-8214-0611-6 (pbk) : £8.25 B82-30096

002′.09 — Books, *to 1980*

Books : their history, art, power, glory, infamy and suffering according to their creat ors, friends and enemies / [compiled by] Gerald Donaldson. — Oxford : Phaidon, 1981. — 128p : ill(some col.),facsims ; 25cm
Bibliography: p126-127. — Includes index
ISBN 0-7148-2236-1 : £8.95 B82-01922

002′.0938′5 — Ancient Greek books: Athenian books, *B.C.500-B.C.300*

Turner, E. G.. Athenian books in the fifth and fourth centuries B.C. : an inaugural lecture delivered at University College London 22 May 1951 / by E.G. Turner. — 2nd ed. — London : Published for the College by H.K. Lewis, 1977. — 23p,[1]leaf of plates : 1ill ; 26cm
Previous ed.: 1952
£0.80 (pbk) B82-17856

002′.75 — Book collectors - *Directories - Serials*

The **International** directory of book collectors. — 1981-83. — Beckenham (117 Kent House Rd, Beckenham, Kent BR3 1JJ) : Trigon Press, Apr.1981. — 1v.
ISBN 0-904929-20-5 : £16.00 : CIP entry B81-08932

003 — SYSTEMS

003 — Developing countries. Applications of general systems theory

Dependence and inequality. — Oxford : Pergamon, Aug.1982. — [342]p. — (Systems science and world order library)
ISBN 0-08-027952-x : £17.50 : CIP entry B82-20744

003 — Distributed parameter systems. Applications of optimal control theory

Ahmed, N. U.. Optimal control of distributed parameter systems / N.U. Ahmed, K.L. Teo. — New York ; Oxford : North-Holland, c1981. — xiii,430p ; 24cm
Bibliography: p409-425. — Includes index
ISBN 0-444-00559-5 : Unpriced B82-01656

003 — Dynamical systems. Instability — *For engineering*

Thompson, J. M. T.. Instabilities and catastrophes in science and engineering / J.M.T. Thompson. — Chichester : Wiley, c1982. — xvi,226p : ill ; 24cm
Includes index
ISBN 0-471-09973-2 (cased) : £14.50 : CIP rev.
ISBN 0-471-10071-4 (pbk) : Unpriced B81-34648

003 — Dynamical systems. Optimisation. Algorithms — *Conference proceedings*

Workshop on Numerical Techniques for Systems Engineering Problems *(1980 : Lexington, Ky.)*. Algorithms and theory in filtering and control : proceedings of the Workshop on Numerical Techniques for Systems Engineering Problems, part 1 / edited by D.C. Sorensen and R.J.-B. Wets ; [contributors] F.A. Badawi ... [et al.]. — Amsterdam ; Oxford : North-Holland, 1982. — x,159p : 1ill ; 24cm. — (Mathematical programming study ; 18)
ISBN 0-444-86399-0 (pbk) : £12.71 B82-38131

003 — General systems theory

Systems behaviour. — 3rd ed. / edited by Open Systems Group. — London : Harper and Row in association with the Open University Press, 1981. — 332p : ill ; 25cm. — (Open University set book)
Previous ed.: 1976. — Includes bibliographies and index
ISBN 0-06-318211-4 (cased) : Unpriced : CIP rev.
ISBN 0-06-318212-2 (pbk) : Unpriced B81-33971

Systems behaviour. — Milton Keynes : Open University Press. — (Technology : a second level course)
At head of title: The Open University
Module 1: Systems and how to describe them / prepared for the Systems Behaviour Course Team by Bill Mayon-White and Dick Morris. — 1982. — 64p : ill ; 30cm. — (T241 ; module 1)
′This module replaces the previous Module 1. Deep sea container ports′
ISBN 0-335-02613-3 (pbk) : Unpriced B82-21203

Systems behaviour / [Systems Behaviour Course Team]. — Milton Keynes : Open University Press. — (Technology : a second level course)
At head of title: The Open University
Module 2: Air traffic control : a man-machine system / Victor Bignell. — 1982. — 92p : ill,maps,1plan ; 30cm. — (T241 ; module 2)
ISBN 0-335-02614-1 (pbk) : Unpriced B82-32017

Systems behaviour / [Systems Behaviour Course Team]. — Milton Keynes : Open University Press. — (Technology : a second level course)
At head of title: The Open University
Module 3: Industrial social systems / prepared for the Systems Behaviour Course Team by Margaret Blunden. — 1982. — 98p : ill(some col.),1col.map ; 30cm. — (T241 ; module 3)
ISBN 0-335-02620-6 (pbk) : Unpriced B82-32016

003 — General systems theory *continuation*

Systems behaviour / [Systems Behaviour Course Team]. — Milton Keynes : Open University Press. — (Technology : a second level course)
At head of title: The Open University
Module 4: Government systems : planning and regulation of the British environment / prepared for the Systems Behaviour Course Team by Joyce Tait. — 1982. — 75p : ill(some col.),maps(some col.) ; 30cm. — (T241 ; module 4)
Bibliography: p74
ISBN 0-335-02621-4 (pbk) : Unpriced B82-32018

003 — Multidimensional systems theory

Bose, N. K. (Nirmal Kumar), *1940-*. Applied multidimensional systems theory / N.K. Bose. — New York ; London : Van Nostrand Reinhold, c1982. — xvi,411p : ill ; 24cm. — (Van Nostrand Reinhold electrical/computer science and engineering series)
Includes index
ISBN 0-442-27214-6 : £25.10 B82-21850

003 — Nonlinear systems. Systems analysis. Volterra theory & Wiener theory

Rugh, Wilson J.. Nonlinear system theory : the Volterra/Weiner approach / Wilson J. Rugh. — Baltimore ; London : Johns Hopkins University Press, c1981. — xiv,325p : ill ; 25cm. — (Johns Hopkins series in information sciences and systems)
Includes index
ISBN 0-8018-2549-0 : £22.75 B82-06991

003 — System development

Couger, J. Daniel. Advanced system development/feasibility techniques / J. Daniel Couger, Mel. A. Colter, Robert W. Knapp. — New York ; Chichester : Wiley, c1982. — xiii,506p : ill,forms ; 25cm
Includes bibliographies and index
ISBN 0-471-03141-0 : £20.00 B82-37206

003 — Systems analysis

Athey, Thomas H.. Systematic systems approach : an integrated method for solving systems problems / Thomas H. Athey. — Englewood Cliffs ; London : Prentice-Hall, c1982. — xiii,366p : ill ; 24cm
Bibliography: p355-360. — Includes index
ISBN 0-13-880914-3 : £18.70 B82-29231

Daniels, Alan. Basic systems analysis. — London : Pitman, Nov.1981. — [270]p
ISBN 0-273-01731-4 : £5.95 : CIP entry B81-30299

003 — Systems analysis — *Conference proceedings*

New approaches to systems analysis and design / organised in London 20 June 1979 by the British Computer Society ; edited by Peter Hammersley. — London : Heyden, c1982. — 33p : ill
Conference papers. — Reprinted from Computer journal. Vol.1, no.1 (Feb. 1980). — Includes bibliographies
ISBN 0-85501-492-x (unbound) : Unpriced B82-40783

Systems analysis and design : a foundation for the 1980's / [an invitational conference and workshop, Georgia State University, Atlanta, September 8-10, 1980] ; edited by William W. Cotterman ... [et al.] ; [organized by] Institute for Certification of Computer Professionals ; [sponsored by Computer Society of the Institute of Electrical ad Electronics Engineers, Association for Computing Machinery, Institute for Certification of Computer Professionals, Georgia State University]. — New York ; Oxford : North Holland, c1981. — 553p : ill ; 26cm
ISBN 0-444-00642-7 : £38.39 B82-00689

003 — Systems analysis. Mathematical models. Parameters. Estimation

Distributed parameter control systems. — Oxford : Pergamon, Oct.1982. — [525]p. — (International series on systems and control ; v.6)
ISBN 0-08-027624-5 : £30.00 : CIP entry B82-24705

003 — Systems. Failure. Diagnosis & detection — *Conference proceedings*

NATO Symposium on Human Detection and Diagnosis of System Failures *(1980 : Roskilde)*. Human detection and diagnosis of system failures / [proceedings of a NATO Symposium on Human Detection and Diagnosis of System Failures, held August 4-8, 1980, in Roskilde, Denmark] ; edited by Jens Rasmussen and William B. Rouse. — New York ; London : Published in cooperation with NATO Scientific Affairs Division [by] Plenum, c1981. — x,716p : ill ; 26cm. — (NATO conference series. III, Human factors ; v.15)
Includes index
ISBN 0-306-40744-2 : Unpriced B82-00671

003'.028'54 — Systems analysis. Optimisation. Applications of digital computer systems

Smith, David K.. Network optimisation practice : a computational guide. — Chichester : Ellis Horwood, May 1982. — [256]p
ISBN 0-85312-403-5 : £22.50 : CIP entry B82-11115

003'.0724 — Large scale systems. Mathematical models

Large scale systems / edited by Yacov Y. Haimes. — Amsterdam ; Oxford : North-Holland, 1982. — viii,183p : ill ; 23cm. — (Studies in management science and systems ; v.7)
Includes bibliographies
ISBN 0-444-86367-2 : £21.09 B82-38182

Mahmoud, Magdi S.. Large scale systems modelling / by Magdi S. Mahmoud and Madan G. Singh. — Oxford : Pergamon, 1981. — xi,326p : ill ; 24cm. — (International series on systems and control ; v.3)
Includes index
ISBN 0-08-027313-0 : £25.00 : CIP rev. B81-31355

003'.0724 — Systems. Simulation. Applications of digital computer systems — *Conference proceedings*

International Association for Mathematics and Computers in Simulation. *Congress (9th : 1979 : Sorrento)*. Simulation of Systems '79 : proceedings of the 9th IMACS Congress Sorrento, Italy September 24-28 1979 / [organized by Hybrid Computers Research Center of the National Research Council University of Naples, Italy] ; edited by L. Dekker, G. Savastano, G.C. Vansteenkiste. — New York ; Oxford : North Holland Publishing, 1980. — xvi,1169p : ill ; 27cm
Includes index
ISBN 0-444-86123-8 : £59.28 B82-11557

003.2'05 — Forecasting — *Serials*

Journal of forecasting. — Vol.1, issue 1 (Jan.-Mar. 1982)-. — Chichester : Wiley, 1982-. — v. : ill ; 26cm
Quarterly. — Description based on: Vol.1, no.2 (Apr.-June 1982)
ISSN 0277-6693 = Journal of forecasting : £28.50 per year B82-31723

010 — BIBLIOGRAPHY

010 — Bibliography

Stokes, Roy. The function of bibliography. — 2nd ed. — Aldershot : Gower, June 1982. — [275]p
Previous ed.: London : Deutsch, 1969
ISBN 0-566-03440-9 : £17.50 : CIP entry B82-09427

Vickers, Eric. Physical and descriptive bibliography : notes for guidance of students : revised and augmented / by Eric Vickers. — London : Polytechnic of North London, School of Librarianship and Information Studies, 1982. — 27p : ill ; 30cm
Text on inside cover. — Includes index
ISBN 0-900639-23-7 (pbk) : £0.65 B82-25622

011 — BIBLIOGRAPHIES

011'.02 — Libraries. Stock: Reference books — *Indexes*

Shearer, Benjamin F.. Finding the source : a thesaurus-index to the reference collection / compiled by Benjamin F. Shearer and Barbara Smith Shearer. — London : Aldwych, 1981. — xviii,545p ; 24cm. — (Studies in library science ; no.5)
ISBN 0-86172-024-5 : Unpriced B82-30526

011'.02 — Reference books — *Lists*

Chandler, George. How to find out : printed and on-line sources / G. Chandler. — 5th ed. — Oxford : Pergamon, 1982. — xviii,250p : ill ; 22cm
Previous ed.: 1974. — Includes index
ISBN 0-08-027433-1 : £7.50 : CIP rev. B81-17514

Cheney, Frances Neel. Fundamental reference sources / by Frances Neel Cheney and Wiley J. Williams. — 2nd ed. — Chicago : American Library Association ; London : Eurospan [distributor], c1980. — x,351p ; 25cm
Includes index
ISBN 0-8389-0308-8 : £9.50 B82-34660

Katz, Bill. Introduction to reference work / William A. Katz. — 4th ed. — New York ; London : McGraw-Hill. — (McGraw-Hill series in library education)
Previous ed.: 1978
Vol.1: Basic information sources. — c1982. — xii,398p ; 24cm
Includes bibliographies and index
ISBN 0-07-033333-5 : £15.25
Also classified at 025.5'2 B82-24908

Reference books for small and medium-sized libraries / compiled by the Ad Hoc Committee for the Third Edition of Reference Books for Small and Medium-sized Libraries, Reference and Adult Services Division, American Library Association ; Larry Earl Bone editor and chairperson. — Chicago : American Library Association ; London : Eurospan [distributor], 1979 (1980 printing). — xv,197p ; 23cm
Previous ed.: 1973. — Includes index
ISBN 0-8389-3227-4 (pbk) : £7.75 B82-34661

Walford's guide to reference material. — 4th ed. — London : Library Association
Previous ed.: 1975
Vol.2: Social & historical sciences, philosophy & religion. — June 1982. — [708]p
ISBN 0-85365-564-2 : £29.50 : CIP entry B82-10884

011'.02 — Reference books — *Lists* — *For small libraries*

Guide to reference sources for the small library / compiled by Karen Beales ... [et al.]. — Winchester : HATRICS, 1981. — 19p ; 21cm
ISBN 0-901903-10-8 (pbk) : £1.50 B82-05808

011'.03 — Free materials — *For children*

Free stuff for kids. — 2nd ed. — Watford : Exley, Sept.1982. — [128]p
Previous ed.: 1981
ISBN 0-905521-63-3 (cased) : £4.95 : CIP entry
ISBN 0-905521-69-2 (pbk) : £2.50 B82-21569

011'.3 — Books in Armenian, *1512-1850* — *Catalogues*

Nersessian, Vrej. Catalogue of early Armenian books : 1512-1850 / Vrej Nersessian. — London : British Library, 1980. — 172p,[8]p of plates : ill ; 29cm
Includes index
ISBN 0-904654-35-4 : £50.00 B82-28303

011'.31 — Manuscripts in Persian, *1580-1840* — *Lists*

India Office Library and Records. A descriptive catalogue of miscellaneous Persian Mughal documents from Akbar to Bahadur Shah II / M.Z.A. Shakeb. — London : India Office Library and Records, 1982. — 38p ; 30cm
ISBN 0-903359-37-5 (pbk) : Unpriced B82-31956

011′.31 — Manuscripts in Urdu — *Catalogues*

India Office Library and Records. Catalogue of the Urdu manuscripts in the India Office Library : supplementary to James Fuller Blumhardt's catalogue of 1926 / compiled by Salim al-Din Quraishi and Ursula Sims-Williams. — London : India Office Library and Records, 1978. — 101p ; 30cm
Includes index
ISBN 0-903359-15-4 (corrected) : £4.00
B82-39969

011′.31 — Scotland. Libraries. Stock: Manuscripts in Greek — *Catalogues*

Cunningham, I. C.. Greek manuscripts in Scotland : summary catalogue / Ian C. Cunningham. — Edinburgh : National Library of Scotland, 1982. — 27p ; 30cm
Text in English and Greek
ISBN 0-902220-48-9 (pbk) : Unpriced
B82-21469

011′.31 — Slavonic manuscripts — *Lists*

British Library. *Reference Division*. Slavonic manuscripts from the British Museum and Library. — London : [British Library Reference Division], 1978. — 60p,lviiip of plates : col.ill,col.facsims ; 23cm
Unpriced (pbk) B82-29542

011′.34 — Edinburgh. Libraries. Stock: Serials — *Catalogues*

Edinburgh University Library. A union list of current serials received in Edinburgh University Library and some other research libraries in Edinburgh / Edinburgh University Library. — [Edinburgh] ([George Sq., Edinburgh EH8 9LJ]) : [The Library], 1978. — viii,390p ; 30cm
Cover title
Unpriced B82-05352

011′.34 — Great Britain. Goethe institutes. Libraries. Stock: Serials in German — *Lists*

Books and information on Germany : newspapers and periodicals. — [London] ([50 Princes Gate, SW7 2PH]) : Goethe Institute Library, [1982]. — 19p ; 21x30cm
Resources of the 5 Goethe Institute Libraries in United Kingdom and Republic of Ireland
Unpriced (unbound) B82-23278

011′.34 — Great Britain. Libraries. Stock: Serials in South Asian languages — *Catalogues*

Shaw, Graham. The bibliography of South Asian periodicals. — Brighton : Harvester, Dec.1982. — [192]p
ISBN 0-7108-0470-9 : £30.00 : CIP entry
B82-30196

011′.34 — Suffolk. Libraries. Stock: Serials — *Catalogues*

S.U.L.I.S., Suffolk Union List of Serials / edited by R.T.M. Wilson. — [Ipswich] ([Rope Walk, Ipswich, 1P4 1LT]) : [Library of The Suffolk College of Higher and Further Education], 1981. — [31]p : ill ; 30cm
Unpriced (spiral) B82-07466

011′.35 — Newspapers with Durham *(County)* **imprints & newspapers with Northumberland imprints** — *Lists*

Durham and Northumberland. — London : British Library, Sept.1982. — [80]p. — (Bibliography of British newspapers)
ISBN 0-7123-0008-2 : £12.50 : CIP entry
B82-24355

011′.35 — Newspapers with Kent imprints — *Lists*

Kent. — London : British Library, Sept.1982. — [160]p. — (Bibliography of British newspapers)
ISBN 0-7123-0007-4 : £15.00 : CIP entry
B82-24354

011′.36 — Microforms — *Catalogues*

Bodleian Library. A guide to microform holdings in the Bodleian Library / compiled by Peter Snow. — Oxford : The Library, 1982. — 33p ; 21cm
ISBN 0-900177-86-1 (pbk) : Unpriced : CIP rev. B82-17891

011′.36′05 — Microforms in print — *Lists* — *Serials*

Guide to microforms in print. Author-title. — 1981. — London : Mansell, Sept.1981. — [840]p
ISBN 0-7201-1638-4 : £40.00 : CIP entry
ISSN 0164-0747 B81-26689

Guide to microforms in print. Subject. — 1981. — London : Mansell Publishing, Sept.1981. — [1200]p
ISBN 0-7201-1639-2 : £43.00 : CIP entry
B81-30272

011′.37 — Cinema films based on books & cinema films based on plays, *1975-1981* — *Lists*

Enser, A. G. S.. Filmed books and plays : a list of books and plays from which films have been made, 1975-81. — Aldershot : Gower, Nov.1982. — [96]p
ISBN 0-566-03475-1 : £6.00 : CIP entry
B82-26557

011′.37 — Cinema films — *Lists*

Movies on TV : 1982-1983 edition / edited by Stephen [i.e. Steven] H. Scheuer. — [9th ed.]. — Toronto ; London : Bantam, 1981. — 751p ; 18cm
Previous ed.: 1977?
ISBN 0-553-14806-0 (pbk) : £1.95 B82-27097

011′.37 — Great Britain. Cinema films. Repositories: National Film Archive. Stock — *Catalogues*

British Film Institute. National film archive catalogue / British Film Institute. — London : The Institute
Vol.1: Non-fiction films. — 1980. — xv,808p ; 31cm
Includes index
ISBN 0-85170-101-9 : £50.00 B82-25641

National Film Archive. Catalogue of stills, posters and designs / National Film Archive ; edited by Markku Salmi. — London : British Film Institute, c1982. — viii,574p ; 30cm
Includes index
ISBN 0-85170-129-9 (pbk) : Unpriced : CIP rev. B82-18581

011′.37 — London. Camden *(London Borough)*. **Educational film libraries: Film Library for Teacher Education. Stock** — *Catalogues* — *Serials*

Film Library for Teacher Education. Catalogue / Film Library for Teacher Education. — 197?-. — London (Paxton Place, Gipsy Rd, SE27 9SR) : National Audio-Visual Aids Library, [197-]-. — v. ; 21cm
Description based on: 1979-80 issue
ISSN 0262-9585 = Catalogue — Film Library for Teacher Education : Unpriced B82-14266

011′.37 — Scotland. Strathclyde Region. Glasgow. Educational film libraries: Higher Education Film & Video Library. Stock — *Catalogues*

Higher Education Film & Video Library. Catalogue supplement 1981 : more than 50 films and video recordings recently acquired for the Library / HEFVL, Higher Education Film & Video Library, a British Universities Film Council service. — London : British Universities Film Council, c1981. — iv,15p : ill ; 30cm
"The HEFVL supplement ... brings up to date the last HEFL Catalogue which was published in March 1980" — pii. — Index
ISBN 0-901299-29-4 (unbound) : £1.00 (£0.70 to members of BUFC) B82-01782

011′.38 — Northern Ireland. Public libraries: SELB Library Service. Stock: Videocassette tape recordings of educational television programmes — *Catalogues*

Television broadcasts for schools 1978-1981 : a library resource for teachers / SELB Library Service. — [Armagh] ([1 Markethill Rd., Armagh, N. Ireland B760 1NR]) : [The Service], [1980]. — xii,53p ; 30cm
Cover title
Unpriced (pbk) B82-17513

011′.44 — Books printed before 1801 — *Catalogues*

St. Deiniol's Library. A bibliography of books printed before 1800. — Hawarden : St Deiniol's Library
Vol.1: Biblical studies and patristics / compiled by Gordon C. Careless and Pamela Morris. — [1982?]. — 24leaves ; 30cm
ISBN 0-907450-00-8 (unbound) : Unpriced
B82-34707

011′.5 — Associations. Publications — *Lists* — *Serials*

Associations' publications in print. — 1981-. — New York ; London : Bowker, 1981-. — v. ; 28cm
Annual. — Published in two volumes every year
Unpriced B82-22653

011′.52 — European Community. Publications — *Lists* — *Serials*

European policies and legislative proposals : a monthly summary of European community and other documents for lawyers, executives and librarians. — Issue no.1 (Sept. 1981)-. — Ickwell (20 Caldecote Rd, Ickwell, Nr Biggleswade, Beds. SG18 9EH) : Euroinformation Ltd., 1981-. — v. ; 30cm
ISSN 0261-863x = European policies and legislative proposals : £24.00 per year
B82-06170

011′.625054 — Picture books for children: Picture books in English — *Bibliographies*

Cianciolo, Patricia Jean. Picture books for children / Patricia Jean Cianciolo. — 2nd ed. rev. and enl. — Chicago : American Library Association ; London : Eurospan [distributor], c1981. — xv,237p : ill ; 24cm
Previous ed.: 1973. — Includes index
ISBN 0-8389-0315-0 (pbk) : £9.50 B82-21313

011′.625054 — Picture books for children, *to 9 years:* **Picture books in English** — *Indexes*

Lima, Carolyn W.. A to zoo : subject access to children's picture books / Carolyn W. Lima. — New York ; London : Bowker, 1982. — xxi,464p ; 26cm
Bibliography: pxviii-xx. — Includes index
ISBN 0-8352-1400-1 : Unpriced B82-24499

011′.625054′05 — Children's books — *Bibliographies* — *Serials*

Children's books of the year. — 1981. — London : MacRea, July 1982. — [144]p
ISBN 0-86203-084-6 (pbk) : £4.25 : CIP entry
B82-16232

011′.6250544 — Books for primary school students — *Lists*

Harris, John, *19---*. Picture books and stories for nursery-first school children : an annotated bibliography / John Harris Winifred Whitehead. — [Sheffield] : Sheffield City Polytechnic Language Development Centre, 1980. — 169p ; 30cm
ISBN 0-903761-24-6 (pbk) : £1.00 B82-03064

011′.6250544 — Picture books for children, 9-13 years: Picture books in English — *Bibliographies*

Moss, Elaine. Picture books for young people 9-13 / Elaine Moss. — Stroud : Thimble, c1981. — 46p : ill,facsims ; 22cm. — (A Signal bookguide)
Includes index
ISBN 0-903355-07-8 (pbk) : £1.65 B82-13206

011′.7 — Books. Sequels — *Bibliographies*

Hicken, Marilyn E.. Sequels. — 7th ed. / compiled by Marilyn E. Hicken. — London : Association of Assistant Librarians
Vol.1: Adult books. — 1982. — 332p ; 24cm
Previous ed.: 1974. — Includes index
ISBN 0-900092-39-4 : £11.00 (£8.00 to members) B82-18393

015 — BIBLIOGRAPHIES OF WORKS FROM SPECIFIC PLACES

015.4'031 — Cambridgeshire. Cambridge. Museums: Fitzwilliam Museum. Stock: European illuminated manuscripts, *1200-1400 — Catalogues*
Fitzwilliam Museum. A descriptive catalogue of the additional illuminated manuscripts in the Fitzwilliam Museum acquired between 1895 and 1979 (excluding the McClean collection) / Francis Wormald and Phyllis M. Giles. — Cambridge : Cambridge University Press, 1982. — viii,xiii,808p,[64]p of plates : ill(some col.) ; 28cm
Includes index
ISBN 0-521-24581-8 : Unpriced
ISBN 0-521-24582-6 (v.2) : £70.00 B82-25790

015'.41 — Great Britain. Official publications: Documents not published by Great Britain. *Her Majesty's Stationery Office - Lists - Serials*
Catalogue of British official publications not published by HMSO. — 1980. — Cambridge : Chadwyck-Healey, May 1981. — [256]p
ISBN 0-85964-101-5 : £80.00 : CIP entry
ISSN 0260-5619 B81-12904

015.41'03 — Books with British imprints. National bibliographies: British National Bibliography. Books without international standard book numbers *— Study examples: British National Bibliography. Interim cumulation. January-April 1978*
Gagan, Christine. A sample survey and analysis of publications appearing in the British National Bibliography not carrying standard book numbers : final report / project undertaken for the BNB Research Fund by Christine Gagan. — [London] : [British Library Research & Development Department], 1980. — 65p ; 30cm. — (British National Bibliography Research Fund report ; no.8)
Unpriced (pbk) B82-09017

015.41'03'05 — Books with British imprints — *Lists — Serials*
British national bibliography. — 1981. — London : British Library, Bibliographic Services Division, Apr.1982. — 2v.
ISBN 0-900220-95-3 : £76.00 (£76.00 microfiche) : CIP entry
ISSN 0007-1544 B82-04705

015.41'034 — Serials with British imprints — *Lists*
Current British journals / edited by David P. Woodworth with the assistance of C.M. Goodair. — [3rd ed.]. — Wetherby : British Library Lending Division on behalf of the UK Serials Group, 1982. — vii,312p ; 30cm
Previous ed.: London : Library Association, 1972. — Includes index
ISBN 0-85350-182-3 (pbk) : Unpriced B82-24671

015.41'037 — Great Britain. Commercial television services: Granada Television. Television programmes *— Indexes*
Granada Television. Granada Television programme index : year twenty-one : 3 May 1956 to 2 May 1977. — London : Granada Television, 1977. — 132p ; 22cm
Unpriced (pbk) B82-24659

015.41'053 — British government publications: Inquiry reports. Chairmen & authors, *1800-1978 — Lists*
Richard, Stephen. British government publications : an index to chairmen of committees and commissions of inquiry / compiled by Stephen Richard for the Reference, Special and Information Section of the Library Association. — London : Library Association, 1982. — 3v. ; 31cm
Vol.2 originally published: 1974
ISBN 0-85365-743-2 : Unpriced : CIP rev.
ISBN 0-85365-427-1 (v.2) : £5.50
ISBN 0-85365-753-x (v.3) : Unpriced B81-30438

015.41'053 — Great Britain. Public bodies. Publications *— Bibliographies — For industries — Serials*
Business & government : a monthly survey of official publications for business and industry. — Issue 1 (Nov. 1981)-. — Cambridge : Chadwyck-Healey in association with H.M.S.O., 1981-. — v. ; 30cm
ISSN 0261-6807 = Business & government : £25.00 per year B82-18546

015.41'053'024658 — Great Britain. Public bodies. Publications *— Bibliographies — For personnel management — Serials*
Personnel & government : a monthly survey of official publications for personnel management. — Issue 1 (Nov. 1981)-. — Cambridge : Chadwyck-Healey in association with HMSO, 1981-. — v. ; 30cm
Also available on microfiche
ISSN 0261-6815 = Personnel & government : £25.00 per year B82-17252

015.41'062 — Young persons' books: Books for young persons in single-parent families: Books with British imprints *— Lists*
We don't all live with mum and dad : a guide to books for children living in one-parent families. — London (255 Kentish Town Rd., NW5 2LX) : One Parent Families, 1981. — 12p : ill ; 30cm
Cover title. — Ill. on inside cover
£0.50 (pbk) B82-06279

015.41'07 — Books for multiracial school students: Books with British imprints *— Bibliographies*
Whitehead, Winifred. Books in a multi-cultural society : an annotated bibliography of fiction, autobiography and poetry for schools / Winifred Whitehead. — [Sheffield] : [Sheffield City Polytechnic Language Development Centre], c1982. — 51p ; 30cm
ISBN 0-903761-56-4 : £0.55 B82-40464

015.41'07 — Theses accepted by British universities, *1716-1950 — Lists*
Retrospective index to theses of Great Britain and Ireland 1716-1950 / Roger R. Bilboul, editor ; Francis L. Kent associate editor. — Oxford : Clio
Vol.3: Life sciences. — c1977. — xi,327p : 1facsim ; 31cm
ISBN 0-903450-05-4 : £66.00
ISBN 0-903450-02-x (set) : Unpriced B82-23967

Retrospective index to theses of Great Britain and Ireland 1716-1950 / Roger R. Bilboul, editor ; Francis L. Kent, associate editor. — Santa Barbara : ABC-Clio ; Oxford : EBC -Clio
Cover title. — Text on inside cover
Addenda. — c1977. — iki,26p ; 30cm
ISBN 0-903450-12-7 (pbk) : Unpriced B82-23968

015.414'430625054 — Scotland. Strathclyde Region. Glasgow. Publishing industries: J. Lumsden & Son. Children's books *— Lists*
Roscoe, S.. James Lumsden & Son of Glasgow : their juvenile books and chapbooks / S. Roscoe & R.A. Brimmell. — Pinner : Private Libraries Association, c1981. — xxiv,134p : ill(some col.) ; 26cm
ISBN 0-900002-04-2 : £12.00 B82-16587

015.415'031 — Ireland *(Republic).* **Theological colleges. Libraries. Stock: Irish manuscripts** *— Catalogues — Irish texts*
Ó Fiannachta, Pádraig. Clár lamhscríbhinní Gaeilge : leabharlanna na cléire agus mionchnuasaigh / Pádraig Ó Fiannachta. — Baile Átha Claith [Dublin] : Institiúid Ard-Leinn Baile Átha Cliath
Fascúl 2. — 1980. — 239 ; 22cm
Unpriced (pbk) B82-23573

015.418'35 — Dublin. Organisations: Royal Dublin Society. Publications *— Lists*
Royal Dublin Society. A bibliography of the publications of the Royal Dublin Society from its foundation in the year 1731 together with a list of bibliographical material relative to the Society. — 3rd ed. — [Dublin] : [The Society], [1982]. — 53p ; 30cm
Previous ed.: 1953. — Includes index
ISBN 0-86027-011-4 (pbk) : Unpriced B82-36399

015.421'4203 — Books distributed by Library Association Publishing: Books with foreign imprints *— Lists — Serials*
Quality monitor / Library Science Book Distribution Service. — No.1 (July 1981)-. — London : Library Association Publishing, 1981-. — v. ; 30cm
Six issues yearly. — Description based on: No.2 (Oct. 1981)
ISSN 0261-2593 = Quality monitor : Unpriced B82-04906

015.44'3835 — Incunabula with Strasbourg imprints, *1480-1599 — Bibliographies*
Chrisman, Miriam Usher. Bibliography of Strasbourg imprints, 1480-1599. — London : Yale University Press, Nov.1982. — [432]p
ISBN 0-300-02891-1 : £27.50 : CIP entry B82-40331

015.47'053 — Eastern European government publications & Soviet government publications *— Lists*
Official publications of the Soviet Union and Eastern Europe 1945-1980 : a select annotated bibliography / edited by Gregory Walker. — London : Mansell, 1982. — xxviii,620p ; 25cm
Includes index
ISBN 0-7201-1641-4 : Unpriced : CIP rev. B82-09835

015.51'034 — Great Britain. National libraries: Science Reference Library. Stock: Serials with Chinese imprints *— Lists*
Science Reference Library. Periodicals from mainland China held by the Science Reference Library. — London : Science Reference Library, Aug.1982. — [60]p
ISBN 0-902914-68-5 (pbk) : £3.50 : CIP entry B82-20787

015.73'03 — Books with American imprints — *Lists*
Rinderknecht, Carol. A checklist of American imprints. — Metuchen, N.J. ; London : Scarecrow
1834 : items 22796-29893 / compiled by Carol Rinderknecht and Scott Bruntjen. — 1982. — 644p ; 23cm
ISBN 0-8108-1487-0 : £30.00 B82-38099

015.73'037 — Cinema films. American videorecordings *— Lists*
Consumer's handbook of video software / compiled by Videologs Inc. ; with an overview of home video by Charles Bensinger. — New York ; London : Van Nostrand Reinhold, 1981. — xiv,203p : ill,ports ; 21cm
ISBN 0-442-29007-1 (pbk) : £8.45 B82-13187

Pickard, Roy. Movies on video / Roy Pickard. — London : Muller, 1982. — 512p ; 20cm
Includes index
ISBN 0-584-11029-4 (pbk) : £3.95 : CIP rev. B82-14076

015.73'0625054 — Children's books in English: Books with American imprints, *1940-1970 — Bibliographies*
Notable children's books 1940-1970 / prepared by 1940-1970 Notable Children's Book Committee, Children's Services Division, American Library Association. — Chicago : The Association ; London : Eurospan [distributor], 1977. — x,84p ; 23cm
Includes index
£2.25 (pbk) B82-21310

015.73'0625054 — Children's books in English: Books with American imprints: Books in print — *Lists*
Let's read together : books for family enjoyment. — 4th ed. / Let's Read Together Revision Committee, Association for Library Service to Children, American Library Association. — Chicago : American Library Association ; London : distributed by Eurospan, 1981. — xii,111p ; 21cm
Previous ed.: / by the Special Committee of the National Congress of Parents and Teachers and the Children's Services Division, American Library Association. 1969. — Includes index
ISBN 0-8389-3253-3 (pbk) : £3.95 B82-21150

016 — BIBLIOGRAPHIES OF SPECIFIC SUBJECTS

016.001 — General studies — *Bibliographies — For teaching*
Schools Council. *General Studies Committee.* General studies. — London : National Book League, May 1982. — [36]p
ISBN 0-85353-370-9 (pbk) : £0.30 : CIP entry B82-17941

016.0012'092'4 — Scotland. Scholarship. Buchanan, George, *1506-1582 — Bibliographies*

Durkan, John. George Buchanan : (1506-1582) : Renaissance scholar and friend of Glasgow University : a quartercentenary exhibition : Glasgow University Library 17 May-7 August 1982 / catalogue by John Durkan, Stephen Rawles and Nigel Thorp. — [Glasgow] : Glasgow University Library, [1982]. — 13p ; 21cm
ISBN 0-85261-171-4 (pbk) : Unpriced B82-39051

016'.0013 — Humanities — *Bibliographies*

Ward, Philip. A lifetime's reading / Philip Ward. — Cambridge : Oleander, c1982. — xv,368p : ill ; 22cm
Includes index
ISBN 0-900891-73-4 (cased) : £13.50
ISBN 0-900891-74-2 (pbk) : £9.95 B82-24220

016.00155'3 — Scotland. Educational technology. Information services: Scottish Council For Educational Technology. *Information Service.* **Stock: Serial articles on films & transparencies** — *Catalogues*

Scottish Council for Educational Technology. *Information Service*. Journal articles on projected media : film, filmstrip. slide, OHP : articles appearing in the S.C.E.T. Information Service's holdings of journals dated March 1981-August 1981, received by the S.C.E.T. Information Service by August 1981 / compiled by Henry Brown. — [Glasgow] : [The Service], 1981. — 6p ; 31cm. — (SCET journals bibliography, ISSN 0260-972x ; no.3)
ISBN 0-86011-042-7 (unbound) : £0.25 B82-22373

016'.00164 — Computer systems — *Bibliographies — Serials*

Computer books review. — Vol.1, no.1 (1981)-. — London (322 St John St., EC1V 4QH) : A.P. Publications, 1981-. — v. ; 28cm
Quarterly
ISSN 0262-3552 = Computer books review (corrected) : £10.00 per year B82-03398

016.00164 — Digital computer systems — *Abstracts — Serials*

Computing news roundup / [NCC, the National Computing Centre, Information Services]. — 1980-. — [Manchester] ([Oxford Rd, Manchester M1 7ED]) : [NCC Information Services], 1980-. — v. ; 30cm
Monthly. — Description based on: Nov. 1980
ISSN 0262-9364 = Computing news roundup : £42.00 per year B82-15164

016'.00164'04 — Microcomputer systems — *Bibliographies*

What to read in microcomputing : a selective bibliography with annotations / edited by Carmen Saiady and Adrian V. Stokes. — Aldershot : Gower, c1982. — viii,103p ; 30cm
ISBN 0-566-03403-4 (pbk) : Unpriced B82-22963

016.00164'04 — Periodical articles on Commodore PET microcomputer systems — *Indexes*

Ryan, M. A. F.. The PET index. — Aldershot : Gower, June 1982. — [218]p
ISBN 0-566-03426-3 : £10.00 : CIP entry B82-09430

016.00164'2 — Microcomputer systems. Programs — *Bibliographies*

Pritchard, Alan. Small computer program index. — Bushey (21 Beechcroft Rd, Bushey, Herts. WD2 2JU) : Allm Books, Jan.1982. — [120]p
ISBN 0-9506784-1-4 : £15.00 : CIP entry B81-34969

016.00164'2 — Small digital computer systems. Programs — *Bibliographies — Serials*

Small computer program index. — Vol.1, no.1 (Jan. 1982)-. — Watford (21 Beechcroft Rd, Bushey, Watford, Herts. WD2 2JU) : ALLM Books, 1982-. — v. ; 30cm
Six issues yearly. — Annual index
ISSN 0261-7102 = Small computer program index : £15.00 per year B82-18508

016'.002 — Historical bibliography. Serials in English, *1933-1970 — Indexes*

Index to selected bibliographical journals. — Oxford : Oxford University Press, Mar.1982. — [256]p. — (Bibliographical Society publications for the years ... ; 1969 and 1970)
ISBN 0-19-721777-x : £25.00 : CIP entry B82-03354

016'.01 — Libraries. Published catalogues in English — *Lists*

Nelson, Bonnie R.. A guide to published library catalogs / Bonnie R. Nelson ; foreword by Lee Ash. — Metuchen ; London : Scarecrow, 1982. — xvi,342p ; 23cm
Includes index
ISBN 0-8108-1477-3 : £14.00 B82-29251

016.01546 — Books with Spanish imprints. Bibliographies — *Indexes*

Indice alfabetico de titulos-materias, correcciones, conexiones y adiciones del manual del librero Hispanoamericano de Antonio Palau Y Dulcet : primer hijo predilecto de la villa ducal de Montblanc / por Agustin Palau Claveras. — [Spain] : Palacete Palau Dulcet ; Oxford : Dolphin
T.1: A-Carvino. — 1981. — v,506p ; 28cm
ISBN 84-300-4752-2 (pbk) : Unpriced
Also classified at 016.0158 B82-15426

016.0158 — Books with Spanish American imprints. Bibliographies — *Indexes*

Indice alfabetico de titulos-materias, correcciones, conexiones y adiciones del manual del librero Hispanoamericano de Antonio Palau Y Dulcet : primer hijo predilecto de la villa ducal de Montblanc / por Agustin Palau Claveras. — [Spain] : Palacete Palau Dulcet ; Oxford : Dolphin
T.1: A-Carvino. — 1981. — v,506p ; 28cm
ISBN 84-300-4752-2 (pbk) : Unpriced
Primary classification 016.01546 B82-15426

016.016071 — United States. Libraries. Stock: Newspapers with American imprints. Indexes — *Catalogues*

Milner, Anita Cheek. Newspaper indexes : a location and subject guide for researchers / by Anita Cheek Milner. — Metuchen ; London : Scarecrow
Vol.3. — 1982. — 181p ; 23cm
ISBN 0-8108-1493-5 : £10.00 B82-17489

016'.0165 — Science. Abstracts journals & indexing journals — *Lists*

Science Reference Library. Abstracting and indexing periodicals in the Science Reference Library. — 2nd ed. / by B.A. Alexander. — London : Science Reference Library, c1982. — 54p ; 22x30cm
Previous ed.: 1975. — Includes index
ISBN 0-902914-69-3 (pbk) : £4.00 : CIP rev. B82-14925

016'.016789912 — Music. Sound recordings. Discographies — *Lists*

Christgau, Robert. Christgau's record guide. — London : Hutchinson, May 1982. — [480]p
ISBN 0-09-147891-x (pbk) : £5.95 : CIP entry B82-07965

016.02'072041 — Research reports on librarianship & information science: Reports on research financed by Great Britain. *Office for Scientific and Technical Information, 1968-1974* **& reports on research financed by British Library.** *Research and Development Department, 1974-1980 — Lists*

British Library. *Research and Development Department*. Complete list of OSTI and BL R & D reports : 1965-1980, report numbers 5001-5516 / British Library, Research & Development Department. — [London] : [The Department], [1980?]. — 60p ; 22cm
Cover title. — Includes index
ISBN 0-905984-55-2 (pbk) : Unpriced : CIP rev. B80-04635

British Library. *Research & Development Department*. Complete list of OSTI and BL R & D reports : 1965-1982, and report numbers 5001-5653. — London : [British Library Research & Development Department], 1982. — 117p ; 21cm
Cover title. — Includes index
ISBN 0-905984-82-x (pbk) : Unpriced : CIP rev. B82-04719

016.025'060014 — Research. Information. Communication & dissemination — *Bibliographies*

Mann, Margaret. Primary communications : a review of the literature since 1970 / by Margaret Mann. — Leicester : Primary Communications Research Centre, University of Leicester, 1981. — 63p ; 30cm. — (A Primary Communications Research publication, ISSN 0141-0261) (B.L. (R&D) report ; no.5678)
Includes index
ISBN 0-906083-20-6 (spiral) : Unpriced : CIP rev. B82-02483

016.0252'07'041 — Great Britain. Libraries. Stock. Information sources — *Bibliographies*

Downs, Robert B.. British and Irish library resources : a bibiographical guide / Robert B. Downs assisted by Elizabeth C. Downs. — Rev. and updated ed. — London : Mansell, 1981. — xiv,427p ; 29cm
Previous ed.: published as British library resources. 1973. — Includes index
ISBN 0-7201-1604-x : £38.50 B82-13981

016.0252'0973 — United States. Libraries. Stock. Acquisition — *Bibliographies*

Godden, Irene P.. Collection development and acquisitions, 1970-80 : an annotated, critical bibliography / compiled by Irene P. Godden, Karen W. Fachan, Patricia A. Smith with the assistance of Sandra Brug. — Metuchen ; London : Scarecrow, 1982. — vii,138p ; 23cm
Includes index
ISBN 0-8108-1499-4 : £8.80 B82-24793

016.0255'6 — Libraries. Users. Education — *Bibliographies*

Malley, Ian. Education in the use of libraries and information : a bibliography / by Ian Malley. — Loughborough : I. Malley
Pt.2: 1955-1969. — 1980. — 55p ; 30cm
ISBN 0-904641-15-5 (pbk) : £2.50 B82-40200

016.0276'63'0941 — Great Britain. Libraries. Services for handicapped persons — *Bibliographies*

Hay, Wendy. Library services for handicapped people : an annotated bibliography of British material 1970-1981 / Wendy Hay. — London : Library Association, 1982. — 33p ; 22cm
Includes index
ISBN 0-85365-824-2 (pbk) : Unpriced : CIP rev. B81-39241

016.0277 — Higher education institutions. Libraries — *Bibliographies*

Fanning, Jeff. Bibliography of further education libraries and their development / by Jeff Fanning. — [Southampton] (Warsash, Southampton, SO3 6ZL]) : [College of Nautical Studies], , [c1982]. — [15]p ; 30cm
Unpriced (pbk) B82-19941

016'.032 — Encyclopaedias in English — *Lists*

Walsh, James P.. Encyclopedia ratings, 1977-1978 / compiled by James P. Walsh. — Croydon (51 High St, Croydon, CR0 1QD) : Reference Books Research Publications, 1977. — 1folded sheet ; 21x36cm folded to 21x9cm
£0.25 B82-40427

Walsh, James P.. Encyclopedia ratings, 1978-1979 / compiled by James P. Walsh. — 2nd ed. — Croydon (51 High St, Croydon CR0 IQD) : Reference Books Research Publications, c1978. — 1folded sheet ; 21x24cm folded to 21x9cm
£0.50 B82-40428

016.0705'7 — London. Southwark *(London Borough).* **Polytechnics. Libraries: Polytechnic of the South Bank.** *Library.* **Stock: Documents on publishing academic documents** — *Catalogues*

Polytechnic of the South Bank. *Library*. Writing for publication : a bibliography / Polytechnic of the South Bank, Library, Southwark Site. — London : [The Library] ; London : Denny Publications [distributor], c1981. — ii,25p ; 30cm
Cover title. — Includes index
ISBN 0-905267-22-2 (pbk) : £1.50 B82-15205

016.133′092′4 — Occultism. Waite, A. E. Texts — *Bibliographies*
Gilbert, R. A.. A.E. Waite : a bibliography. — Wellingborough : Aquarian Press, Jan.1983. — [192]p
ISBN 0-85030-319-2 (pbk) : £9.95 : CIP entry
B82-32635

016.149′3 — Mysticism — *Bibliographies*
Pilgrimage of spiritual reading : a work in progress. — [Great Britain] : The Alexandria Foundation, c1982. — 142p ; 25cm
ISBN 0-900306-77-7 (pbk) : Unpriced
B82-37682

016.149′7′09171241 — Commonwealth countries. Free-thought — *Bibliographies*
Stein, Gordon. Freethought in the United Kingdom and the Commonwealth : a descriptive bibliography / Gordon Stein. — Westport ; London : Greenwood Press, 1981. — xxiii,193p ; 25cm
Includes bibliographies and index
ISBN 0-313-20869-7 : Unpriced B82-02245

016.15 — Psychology. Theses accepted by British universities, *1974-1979 — Lists*
Harris, Miriam. Psychology theses register / Miriam Harris. — London : Social Science Research Council, c1982. — 70p ; 30cm
'A register commissioned by the Psychology Committee'
ISBN 0-86226-028-0 (pbk) : Unpriced
B82-30488

016.15′01′5195 — Psychology. Applications of nonparametric statistical mathematics — *Bibliographies*
Singer, Bernard. Distribution-free methods for non-parametric problems : a classified and selected bibliography / Bernard Singer. — Leicester : British Psychological Society, c1979. — 66p ; 26cm
Originally published in the British Journal of Mathematical and Statistical Psychology, v.32 pt.1, 1979. — Includes index
ISBN 0-901715-10-7 : Unpriced B82-26850

016.181′45 — Yoga — *Bibliographies*
Jarrell, Howard R.. International yoga bibliography, 1950 to 1980 / by Howard R. Jarrell. — Metuchen ; London : Scarecrow, 1981. — ix,221p : ill ; 23cm
Includes index
ISBN 0-8108-1472-2 : £10.80 B82-17421

016.192 — English philosophy. Locke, John — *Bibliographies*
Hall, Ronald. Locke scholarship 1900-1980. — Edinburgh : Edinburgh University Press, June 1982. — [144]p
ISBN 0-85224-431-2 : £8.50 : CIP entry
B82-09870

016.2 — Religion — *Bibliographies — For teaching*
Resources for religious education in the primary & middle school / [Primary Department CEM]. — Updated. — [London] ([2 Chester House, Pages La., N10 1PR]) : [The Department], c1980. — 12p : 1ill ; 21cm
Previous ed.: 1978
Unpriced (unbound) B82-36994

016.2 — Religion. Teaching aids: Audiovisual materials — *Catalogues*
Jordanhill College of Education. *Audio-Visual Library.* Religion : a list of A-V materials for students and teachers / compiled by Linda Emery. — 2nd ed. — Glasgow (76 Southbrae Drive, Glasgow, G13 1PP) : Jordanhill College of Education Library, 1982. — iv,27p ; 21cm. — (Audio visual bibliographies ; no.9)
Previous ed.: 197-?
£0.25 (pbk) B82-35145

016.2′009171′7 — Communist countries. Religion — *Bibliographies*
Yule, Robert M.. Religion in Communist countries : a bibliography of books in English / compiled by Robert M. Yule. — Wellington [N.Z.] : New Zealand Society for the Study of Religion and Communism ; Keston (Heathfield Rd., Keston, Kent BR2 6BA) : Keston College, c1979. — 72p ; 21cm
Unpriced (pbk) B82-37456

016.209′2′4 — Christianity. Reckitt, Maurice B.. Works — *Bibliographies*
Howell-Thomas, Dorothy. Bibliography of the writings of Maurice B. Reckitt / compiled by Dorothy Howell-Thomas. — 2nd ed. — Durham (c/o Organising Secretary, Bede College, Durham DH1 1TA) : Christendom Trust, 1980. — 53leaves ; 30cm
Previous ed.: 1978?
Unpriced (pbk) B82-18034

016.2483′4 — Christian life. Meditation — *Bibliographies*
Vendy, Barry. Conversation piece : retreats & the life of prayer / by Barry Vendy. — [Great Britain] : Department of Ministry, [1982?]. — 6p ; 22cm
Unpriced (unbound) B82-27467

016.262′0242843 — Catholic Church. *Diocese of York. Archbishop (1398-1405 : Scrope).* **Episcopal registers —** *Abstracts*
Swanson, R. N.. A Calendar of the Register of Richard Scrope, Archbishop of York, 1398-1405 / R.N. Swanson. — York : Borthwick Institute of Historical Research
Pt.1. — 1981. — x,147p ; 25cm. — (Borthwick texts and calendars. Records of the northern province, ISSN 0305-8506 ; 8)
At head of title: University of York, Borthwick Institute of Historical Research. — Includes index
Unpriced (pbk) B82-05163

016.2629′83 — Devon. Exeter. Record repositories: Devon Record Office. Stock: Archives of Church of England. *Diocese of Exeter. Consistory Court — Lists*
Devon Record Office. The records of the Bishop of Exeter's Consistory Court to 1660 : a list with introduction / by J.A. Vage. — [Exeter] : Devon Record Office, c1981. — ii,17p ; 21cm. — (Handlist / Devon Record Office ; no.1)
ISBN 0-86114-354-x (pbk) : Unpriced
B82-20470

016.264 — Christian church. Public worship, *ca 600-1200 — Rites — Bibliographies*
Pfaff, Richard William. Medieval Latin liturgy : a select bibliography / Richard W. Pfaff. — Toronto ; London : University of Toronto Press, c1982. — xviii,129p ; 23cm. — (Toronto medieval bibliographies ; 9)
Includes index
ISBN 0-8020-5564-8 (cased) : Unpriced
ISBN 0-8020-6488-4 (pbk) : Unpriced
B82-39341

016.266′36 — Anglican missions: Church Missionary Society. *Africa (Group 3) Committee.* **Archives —** *Lists*
Church Missionary Society. Catalogue of the papers of the missions of the Africa (Group 3) Committee / catalogued by Rosemary A. Keen. — 2nd ed. — London : Church Missionary Society
Vol.1: West Africa (Sierra Leone) mission, 1803-1934. — 1981. — 95leaves ; 30cm
Previous ed.: 1979
£10.00 (pbk) B82-30188

Church Missionary Society. Catalogue of the papers of the missions of the Africa (Group 3) Committee / catalogued by Rosemary A. Keen. — London : Church Missionary Society
Vol.7: New Zealand mission 1809-1914. — 1981. — 92leaves ; 30cm
£6.00 (pbk) B82-14284

Church Missionary Society. *Africa (Group 3) Committee.* Catalogue of the papers of the missions of the Africa (Group 3) Committee. — London : Church Missionary Society
Vol.2: Nigeria missions 1844-1934. — 2nd ed. / catalogued by Rosemary A. Keen. — 1981. — 102leaves ; 30cm
Previous ed.: 1952?
Unpriced (pbk) B82-35142

016.283′092′4 — Church of England. Benson, Edward White. Correspondence — *Indexes*
Lambeth Palace Library. Index to the letters and papers of Edward White Benson : Archbishop of Canterbury 1883-1896 : in Lambeth Palace Library. — London : Mansell Publishing, 1980. — xii,240p : 1port ; 29cm. — (Calendars and indexes to the letters and papers of the Archbishops of Canterbury in Lambeth Palace Library ; v.3)
ISBN 0-7201-1615-5 : £20.00 : CIP rev.
B80-18967

016.283′092′4 — Church of England. Goodacre, Norman W. — *Bibliographies*
Goodacre, Selwyn H.. Norman W. Goodacre : an annotated hand-list of the printed writings / compiled by Selwyn H. Goodacre. — [Burton-on-Trent] ([69 Ashby Road, Woodville, Burton-on-Trent, Staffs.]) : [S.H. Goodcacre], 1982. — 43p ; 21cm
Limited ed. of 400 copies
Unpriced (pbk) B82-37069

016.283′42843 — Church of England. *Diocese of York.* **Historiology. Organisations: Borthwick Institute of Historical Research. Stock: Archives** *— Lists*
Borthwick Institute of Historical Research. A supplementary guide to the archive collections in the Borthwick Institute of Historical Research / [compiled by] David M. Smith. — [York] : The Institute, 1980. — i,77p ; 25cm. — (Borthwick texts and calendars. Records of the northern province, ISSN 0305-8506 ; 7)
Includes index
Unpriced (pbk) B82-16110

016.287 — Libraries. Stock: Books on Methodist churches — *Catalogues*
Methodist union catalog : pre-1976 imprints / edited by Kenneth E. Rowe. — Metuchen ; London : Scarecrow
Vol.5: G-Haz. — 1981. — xiii,357p ; 23cm
ISBN 0-8108-1454-4 : Unpriced B82-10848

016.2896′4281 — West Yorkshire *(Metropolitan County).* **Leeds. Universities. Libraries: Brotherton Library. Stock: Documents associated with Society of Friends in Yorkshire. Collections: Birkbeck Library —** *Catalogues*
Brotherton Library. Birkbeck Library : an alphabetical checklist of works in the Birkbeck Library of printed books dealing with Quakerism. — [Leeds] : [University of Leeds, Brotherton Library], 1981. — 103p ; 30cm
£4.00 (spiral) B82-19575

016.297′095491 — Pakistan. Muslim movements — *Bibliographies*
Hussain, Asaf. Islamic movements in Egypt, Pakistan and Iran. — London : Mansell, Feb.1983. — [180]p
ISBN 0-7201-1648-1 : £20.00 : CIP entry
Primary classification 016.297′0962
B82-39438

016.297′0955 — Iran. Muslim movements — *Bibliographies*
Hussain, Asaf. Islamic movements in Egypt, Pakistan and Iran. — London : Mansell, Feb.1983. — [180]p
ISBN 0-7201-1648-1 : £20.00 : CIP entry
Primary classification 016.297′0962
B82-39438

016.297′0962 — Egypt. Muslim movements — *Bibliographies*
Hussain, Asaf. Islamic movements in Egypt, Pakistan and Iran. — London : Mansell, Feb.1983. — [180]p
ISBN 0-7201-1648-1 : £20.00 : CIP entry
Also classified at 016.297′095491 ; 016.297′0955 B82-39438

016.297′38 — Islamic life. Hadj — *Bibliographies*
Khan, Zafarul-Islam. Hajj and Haramain. — London : Open Press, Sept.1982. — [100]p
ISBN 0-905081-12-9 (pbk) : £5.00 : CIP entry
B82-25730

016.3 — Social sciences — *Bibliographies — Serials*
A London bibliography of the social sciences. 15th supplement. — Vol.38 (1980). — London : Mansell, July 1981. — [912]p
ISBN 0-7201-1631-7 : £43.00 : CIP entry
ISSN 0076-051x B81-25698

016.301 — Sociology — *Bibliographies*

International bibliography of sociology. — Vol.30 (1980). — London : Tavistock, Feb.1982. — [500]p. — (International bibliography of the social sciences)
ISBN 0-422-80970-5 : £33.00 : CIP entry
ISSN 0085-2066 B82-00160

016.301'05 — Sociology. Serials — *Bibliographies*

Wepsiec, Jan. Sociology : an international bibliography of serial publications 1880-1980. — London : Mansell, Nov.1982. — [176]p
ISBN 0-7201-1652-x : £22.00 : CIP entry
B82-30580

016.3022 — Interpersonal relationships. Communication — *Bibliographies*

Tite, Catherine. A guide to media resources on interpersonal communication. — London : LLRS Publications, May 1982. — [30]p
ISBN 0-904264-64-5 (pbk) : £1.00 : CIP entry
B82-17940

016.3022'34 — Mass media. Audiovisual materials — *Lists*

Tite, Catherine. The mass media : a guide to audiovisual resources. — London (City of London Polytechnic, Calcutta House, Old Castle St., E1 7NT) : LLRS, July 1982. — [16]p
ISBN 0-904264-66-1 (pbk) : £1.00 : CIP entry
B82-25904

016.3046'6 — Great Britain. Birth control, *1922-1931* — *Bibliographies*

Doughan, David. Birth control : the equal knowledge campaign 1922-1931 : a select bibliography / compiled and annotated by David Doughan. — London : LLRS Publications, c1981. — 23p ; 30cm. — (Fawcett library papers ; no.3)
Includes index
ISBN 0-904264-58-0 (pbk) : £2.50 : CIP rev.
B81-31092

016.305 — Higher education institutions. Curriculum subjects: Social inequality. Teaching aids: Audiovisual materials — *Lists*

Van Haeften, Kate. Media resources on inequalities for lecturers / by Kate Van Haeften. — London : LLRS Publications, 1980. — 17p ; 30cm
Includes index
ISBN 0-904264-49-1 (pbk) : £1.00 : CIP rev.
B80-05175

016.3052'6 — Children's books in English: Books with American imprints. Special themes: Old age — *Bibliographies*

Horner, Catherine Townsend. The aging adult in children's books & nonprint media : an annotated bibliography / Catherine Townsend Horner. — Metuchen ; London : Scarecrow, 1982. — xxiii,242p ; 23cm
ISBN 0-8108-1475-7 : £12.00
Also classified at 016.3052'6 B82-17417

016.3052'6 — Children's audiovisual materials: Audiovisual materials with American imprints. Special themes: Old age — *Bibliographies*

Horner, Catherine Townsend. The aging adult in children's books & nonprint media : an annotated bibliography / Catherine Townsend Horner. — Metuchen ; London : Scarecrow, 1982. — xxiii,242p ; 23cm
ISBN 0-8108-1475-7 : £12.00
Primary classification 016.3052'6 B82-17417

016.3052'6'0973 — United States. Old age — *Bibliographies* — *For schools*

Learning about aging / the National Retired Teachers Association and the American Association of Retired Persons. — Chicago : American Library Association ; London : distributed by Eurospan, 1981. — vi,64p ; 23cm
Includes index
ISBN 0-8389-0324-x (pbk) : £3.25 B82-21145

016.3054 — Children's books in English: Books with American imprints. Special themes: Women — *Lists*

Newman, Joan E.. Girls are people too! : a bibliography of nontraditional female roles in children's books / by Joan E. Newman. — Metuchen ; London : Scarecrow, 1982. — viii,195p ; 23cm
Includes index
ISBN 0-8108-1500-1 : £10.00 B82-29249

016.3054 — Women — *Filmographies*

Women's movement : film catalogue / [edited and introduced by Sue Clayton]. — London (79 Wardour St., W1V 3TH) : Other Cinema, [1982]. — 43p : ill ; 30cm
Cover title. — Text on cover. — Bibliography: p1. — Includes index
£1.00 (pbk) B82-35674

016.3054'2 — Society. Role of women — *Bibliographies*

Een, JoAnn Delores. Women and society, citations 3601 to 6000 : an annotated bibliography / compiled and edited by JoAnn Delores Een, Marie B. Rosenberg-Dishman. — Beverley Hills ; London : Sage, c1978. — 277p ; 23cm
Includes index
ISBN 0-8039-0856-3 : Unpriced B82-14794

016.3054'2'094 — Western Europe. Society. Role of women, *to 1800* — *Bibliographies*

Frey, Linda. Women in Western European history : a select chronological, geographical, and topical bibliography from antiquity to the French Revolution / compiled and edited by Linda Frey, Marsha Frey and Joanne Schneider. — Brighton : Harvester, 1982. — lv,760p ; 25cm
Includes index
ISBN 0-7108-0447-4 : £50.00 : CIP rev.
B82-14056

016.3054'2'0973 — United States. Society. Role of women — *Bibliographies*

Haber, Barbara. Women in America : a guide to books, 1963-1975 : with an appendix on books published 1976-1979 / Barbara Haber. — Urbana ; London : University of Illinois Press, 1981. — xiii,262p ; 23cm
Originally published: Boston : G.K. Hall, 1978. — Bibliography: p246. — Includes index
ISBN 0-252-00826-x (pbk) : £7.00 B82-05729

016.3054'8896073 — United States. Negro women, *to 1979* — *Bibliographies*

Sims, Janet L.. The progress of Afro-American women : a selected bibliography and resource guide / compiled by Janet L. Sims ; foreword by Bettye Thomas. — Westport ; London : Greenwood Press, 1980. — xvi,378p ; 25cm
Includes index
ISBN 0-313-22083-2 : Unpriced B82-15056

016.3058'97'073 — United States. North American Indians. Relations with white persons — *Bibliographies*

Prucha, Francis Paul. Indian-white relations in the United States : a bibliography of works published, 1975-1980 / Francis Paul Prucha. — Lincoln [Neb.] ; London : University of Nebraska Press, c1982. — viii,179p ; 25cm
Includes index
ISBN 0-8032-3665-4 (cased) : Unpriced
ISBN 0-8032-8705-4 (pbk) : Unpriced
B82-38416

016.306 — Social anthropology — *Bibliographies* — *Serials*

International bibliography of social and cultural anthropology = Bibliographie internationale d'anthropologie sociale et culturelle. — Vol.24 (1978). — London : Tavistock, Nov.1981. — [560]p. — (International bibliography of the social sciences)
ISBN 0-422-80930-6 : £33.00 : CIP entry
ISSN 0085-2074 B81-30160

International bibliography of social and cultural anthropology. — Vol.25 (1979). — London : Tavistock, Oct.1982. — [450]p. — (International bibliography of the social sciences)
ISBN 0-422-80940-3 : £35.00 : CIP entry
ISSN 0085-2074 B82-24012

016.306'092'4 — Kent. Canterbury. Universities. Libraries: Kent University Library. Exhibits: Items associated with Powell-Cotton, P. H. G. — *Catalogues*

Nicklin, Keith. Powell-Cotton : man & museum : an exhibition, Kent University Library, April 21-May 16, 1981 / [written by Keith Nicklin]. — Canterbury : University of Kent at Canterbury, 1981. — [16]p : ill,1map,1plan,ports ; 21cm
Catalgue to accompany the exhibition
Unpriced (unbound) B82-08493

016.306'48 — Leisure, recreation & tourism. Theses accepted by British universities, *to 1980* — *Lists*

Gilbert, G. A.. A register of theses on recreation, leisure and tourism presented for higher degrees in the United Kingdom / compiled by G.A. Gilbert. — 2nd ed. / rev. and enl. by A. Howarth. — Walsall : West Midlands College of Higher Education Library, 1981. — [38]p ; 21cm
Previous ed.: 1979. — Includes index
ISBN 0-906693-01-2 (spiral) : Unpriced
B82-07739

016.3067 — Great Britain. Sexual liberation movements. Bibliographies, *1977-1978* — *Indexes*

Thomas, Mavis. Sexual politics in Britain during 1977 and 1978. — Brighton : Harvester Press Microform Publications, Dec.1981. — [30]p
ISBN 0-86257-007-7 (pbk) : £4.00 : CIP entry
B81-35903

016.307'14 — Community development — *Bibliographies*

Davies, Anne. CETU's list of information on community arts, community development and non-formal education / compiled by Anne Davies. — Nottingham : University of Nottingham Department of Adult Education, c1981. — ii,128p ; 21cm
ISBN 0-902031-55-4 (pbk) : Unpriced
Also classified at 016.7 B82-03024

016.307'2'0942 — England. Urban regions. Population. Mobility *related to* **housing market** — *Bibliographies*

Cockett, Ian. Housing and migration / compiled by Ian Cockett. — London : Greater London Council, 1978, c1977. — 18,5p ; 30cm. — (Research bibliography / Greater London Council ; no.89)
Includes index
ISBN 0-7168-0975-3 (pbk) : £1.75
Also classified at 016.3635'0942 B82-25305

016.3077'6 — Great Britain. Urban regions. Inner areas. Social aspects — *Bibliographies*

Lambert, Claire M.. Inner cities : a select list of material / compiled by Claire M. Lambert. — [London] : Departments of the Environment and Transport. — (Bibliography ; no.194, supplement no.3)
Supplement no.3: A select list of supplementary references. — 1979. — 52p ; 30cm
Cover title
Unpriced (pbk) B82-35919

016.312'09428'27 — South Yorkshire *(Metropolitan County)*. **Doncaster region. Population. Censuses**, *1851* — *Indexes*

Index to 1851 census. — Doncaster : Doncaster Society for Family History
Vol.1: Kirk Bramwith, Fenwick & Moss. — 1981. — 24p : 1map ; 21cm
Cover title. — Text on inside covers
ISBN 0-9506934-1-3 (pbk) : Unpriced
B82-00996

Index to 1851 census. — Doncaster : Doncaster Society for Family History in conjunction with Doncaster M.B.C.
Cover title. — Text on inside covers
Vol.2: Norton & Campsall. — 1982. — 28p : 1map ; 21cm
ISBN 0-9506934-2-1 (pbk) : Unpriced
B82-28713

016.314 — Europe. Statistics — *Bibliographies*

Harvey, Joan M.. Statistics Europe : sources for social, economic and market research / Joan M. Harvey. — Ed. 4, rev. and enl. — Beckenham : CBD Research, 1981. — xiv,508p ; 31cm
Previous ed.: 1976. — Includes index
ISBN 0-900246-36-7 : £42.50 B82-07084

016.314 — European Community statistical publications — *Indexes*

Ramsay, Anne. Eurostat index : a detailed keyword subject index to the statistical series published by the Statistical Office of the European Communities : with notes on the series / compiled by Anne Ramsay. — Edinburgh : Capital Planning Information, c1981. — 152p ; 30cm
ISBN 0-906011-15-9 (pbk) : Unpriced : CIP rev. B81-30628

016.317 — America. Social conditions. Statistics — *For marketing* — *Bibliographies*

Harvey, Joan M.. Statistics America : sources for social, economic and market research : (North, Central & South America) / Joan M. Harvey. — Ed.2, rev. and enl. — Beckenham : CBD Research, 1980. — xiii,385p ; 31cm. — (A CBD research publication)
Previous ed.: 1973. — Includes index
ISBN 0-900246-33-2 : £43.50 B82-32198

016.32 — Politics - *Bibliographies*

International bibliography of political science = Bibliographie internationale de science politique. — Vol.28, (1979). — London : Tavistock, June 1981. — [600]p. — (International bibliography of the social sciences = Bibliographie internationale des sciences sociales)
ISBN 0-422-80920-9 : £32.50 : CIP entry B81-12339

016.32 — Politics — *Bibliographies*

International bibliography of political science. — Vol.29 (1980). — London : Tavistock, Feb.1982. — [600]p. — (International bibliography of the social sciences)
ISBN 0-422-80990-x : £32.50 : CIP entry
ISSN 0085-2058 B82-00159

016.320941 — Great Britain. Right-wing political movements, *1978* — *Bibliographies*

Harris, Brenda. The radical right and patriotic movements in Britin during 1978 : a bibliographical guide. — Brighton : Harvester, Nov.1982. — [50]p
ISBN 0-86257-014-x (pbk) : £4.50 : CIP entry B82-32865

016.3234 — Human rights — *Bibliographies*

Falconer, Alan, *1945-*. What to read on human rights / by Alan Falconer. — London (2 Eaton Gate, SW1W 9BL) : British Churches' Advisory Forum on Human Rights, British Council of Churches, c1980. — 6p ; 21cm
£0.40 (unbound) B82-13781

016.3271'16 — Persian Gulf countries. International security — *Bibliographies*

Newman, David, *1956-*. The security of Gulf oil : an introductory bibliography / by David Newman, Ewan Anderson, Gerald Blake. — Durham : University of Durham, Centre for Middle Eastern and Islamic Studies, 1982. — 55p ; 21cm. — (Occasional papers series / University of Durham Centre for Middle Eastern and Islamic Studies, ISSN 0307-0654 ; no.13)
Unpriced (pbk) B82-25116

016.328'41'073 — Great Britain. Parliaments. Members, *1660-1761.* **Lists** — *Lists*

A Register of Parliamentary lists, 1660-1761. — Leicester (University Rd., Leicester LE1 7RH) : University of Leicester, History Department. — (Occasional publications / University of Leicester. History Department, ISSN 0144-3739 ; no.3)
Supplement. — Dec.1982. — [28]p
ISBN 0-906696-02-x (pbk) : £1.00 : CIP entry B82-35232

016.33 — Economics — *Bibliographies* — *Serials*

International bibliography of economics. — Vol.29 (1980). — London : Tavistock, Sept.1982. — [600]p. — (International bibliography of the social sciences)
ISBN 0-422-81000-2 : £35.00 : CIP entry
ISSN 0085-204x B82-22423

016.33 — London. Camden *(London Borough).* **Universities. Libraries: University of London.** *Library.* **Stock: Documents on economics. Collections: Goldsmiths' Library of Economic Literature** — *Catalogues*

University of London. *Library.* Catalogue of the Goldsmiths' Library of Economic Literature. — London : Athlone Press
Vol.3. — Apr.1982. — [336]p
ISBN 0-485-15012-3 : £60.00 : CIP entry
ISBN 0-485-15016-6 (set) : £200.00 B82-01117

016.33 — London. Camden *(London Borough).* **Universities. Libraries: University of London** *Library.* **Stock: Documents on economics. Collections: Goldsmiths' Library of Economic Literature** — *Catalogues*

University of London. *Library.* Catalogue of the Goldsmiths' Library of Economic Literature. — London : Athlone Press
Vol.4. — Sept.1982. — [560]p
ISBN 0-485-15013-1 : £75.00 : CIP entry
ISBN 0-485-15016-6 (set) : £200.00 B82-19535

016.33'005 — Economics. Serials: Economica, *1959-1981* — *Indexes*

Economica index to volumes 26-48 1959-1981. — Clevedon : Tieto, Nov.1982. — [340]p
ISBN 0-905028-06-6 (pbk) : £15.00 : CIP entry
ISSN 0013-0427 B82-37487

016.33112'5'0941 — Great Britain. Employment. Labour, *to 1978.* **Theses accepted by British & American universities** — *Lists*

Gilbert, Victor F.. Labour and social history theses : American, British and Irish university theses and dissertations in the field of British and Irish labour history, presented between 1900 and 1978 / compiled by Victor F. Gilbert. — London : Mansell, 1982. — x,194p ; 26cm
Includes index
ISBN 0-7201-1647-3 : Unpriced : CIP rev. B82-04885

016.3314'0941 — Great Britain. Women. Employment, *1914-1918.* **Interviews. Sound tape recordings** — *Catalogues*

Imperial War Museum. *Department of Sound Records.* War work 1914-18 : medicine and welfare, industry and agriculture. — [London] : Imperial War Museum, Dept. of Sound Records, [1982?]. — 35p ; 21cm. — (Oral history recordings)
Unpriced (pbk) B82-26784

016.3315'9 — Handicapped persons. Employment — *Bibliographies*

Simpson, Struan. Employment for handicapped people : bibliography / compiled by Struan Simpson. — London : Disabled Living Foundation, c1981. — viii,72p ; 30cm
Includes index
ISBN 0-906544-08-4 (pbk) : Unpriced : CIP rev. B81-32537

016.3317'02'0941 — Great Britain. Careers. Choice. Books — *Indexes* — *For teaching*

March, Gerald. Starting points : a guide to planning & resourcing careers education / by Gerald March. — [Revised ed.]. — Exeter : March, 1982, c1981. — 132p : forms ; 21cm
Previous ed.: 1981. — Bibliography: p131
ISBN 0-9508038-0-4 (sprial) : Unpriced B82-32063

016.3321'028'54 — Banking. Applications of digital computer systems — *Bibliographies*

Banking and finance : an annotated bibliography / co-ordinator P.J. Down ; compilers G.G. Ramirez, D.P. Best. — London : Heyden on behalf of the British Computer Society, c1982. — vi,27p ; 21cm. — (Use of computers for national development)
ISBN 0-85501-695-7 (pbk) : £7.00 : CIP rev. B81-40228

016.33376'13'094111 — Scotland. Highlands & Islands. Rural regions. Land use, *to 1980* — *Bibliographies*

Mather, A. S.. An annotated bibliography of rural land use in the Highlands and Islands of Scotland / by A.S. Mather and R.J. Ardern. — Old Aberdeen : Department of Geography University of Aberdeen, 1981. — 193p ; 30cm. — (O'Dell memorial monograph, ISSN 0141-1454 ; no.9)
Unpriced (1mappbk) B82-07537

016.33379'09172'4 — Developing countries. Rural regions. Energy resources — *Bibliographies*

Barnett, Andrew. Rural energy and the Third World. — Oxford : Pergamon, July 1982. — [302]p
ISBN 0-08-028953-3 (cased) : £18.00 : CIP entry
ISBN 0-08-028954-1 (pbk) : £9.00 B82-12405

016.33379'0941 — Great Britain. *Departments of the Environment and Transport Library.* **Stock: Documents on environmental aspects of energy resources** — *Catalogues*

Great Britain. *Departments of the Environment and Transport Library.* Energy and the environment : a select list of materials based on the DOE/DTp library / compiled by Claire M. Lambert. — London (2 Marsham St., SW1P 3EB) : Departments of the Environment and Transport, c1980. — ii,48p ; 30cm. — (Bibliography series / Headquarters library Department of the Environment, Department of Transport ; 190a)
£1.15 (pbk) B82-13861

016.33379'12 — Energy. Supply & demand. Forecasts — *Bibliographies*

Great Britain. *Department of Energy. Library.* Energy forecasts : selected references 1974 to 1978 / [compiled by Charlotte Atkinson]. — London (Thames House South, Millbank, SW1P 4QJ) : Department of Energy Library, c1979. — 20p ; 21cm. — (Energy bibliographies ; 1979/1)
Includes index
Unpriced (pbk) B82-35796

016.33379'16'0941 — Great Britain. Energy resources. Conservation — *Bibliographies*

Great Britain. *Department of Energy. Library.* Energy conservation in the United Kingdom : selected references 1974 to mid 1979 / [compiled by Graham Hurford]. — London (Thames House South, Millbank, SW1P 4QJ) : Department of Energy Library, c1979. — 68p ; 21cm. — (Energy bibliographies ; 1979/2)
Includes index
Unpriced (pbk) B82-35798

016.33391'0028'54 — Natural resources: Water. Management. Applications of digital computer systems — *Bibliographies*

McEvoy, J. E.. Water resource management : an annotated bibliography / editor R.A. Newell ; compilers J.E. McEvoy, J.R. Bessant, K.E. Dickson. — London : Heyden on behalf of the British Computer Society, c1982. — vi,71p ; 21cm. — (Use of computers for national development)
ISBN 0-85501-693-0 : £7.00 : CIP rev. B81-40231

016.33391'63 — Northumberland. Kielder region. Natural resources: Water. Reservoirs: Kielder Water — *Bibliographies*

Kielder water scheme : a bibliography. — 4th ed. — [Gosforth] ([Northumbria House, Regent Centre, Gosforth, Newcastle-upon-Tyne, NE3 3PX]) : Library & Information Service, 1982. — 12p ; 30cm
Previous ed.: 1980?
Unpriced (unbound) B82-32920

016.334'683'094 — Western Europe. Agricultural cooperatives, *1975-1980* — *Bibliographies*

Agricultural co-operatives in Western Europe. — Slough (Farnham House, Farnham Royal, Slough SL2 3BN) : Commonwealth Agricultural Bureaux, c1980. — [36]p ; 21x30cm. — (Commonwealth Agricultural Bureaux annotated bibliographies. General series, ISSN 0141-593x)
Includes index
Unpriced (pbk) B82-27995

016.3356'0943 — Germany. National socialism, *1919-1945* **—** *Bibliographies*

Kehr, Helen. The Nazi era, 1919-1945. — London : Mansell, May 1982. — [400]p
ISBN 0-7201-1618-x : £20.00 : CIP entry
B82-07597

016.3356'0943 — West Midlands *(Metropolitan County).* **Birmingham. Public libraries: Birmingham Public Libraries.** *Reference Library.* **Stock: Documents on national socialism in Germany —** *Catalogues*

Birmingham Public Libraries. *Reference Library.* National Socialist literature : in Birmingham Reference Library : a bibliography / with an introduction by Lord Dacre of Glanton (formerly Hugh Trevor-Roper). — [Birmingham] : Social Sciences Department, Brimingham Public Libraries, 1980. — x,74p ; 30cm
Includes index
ISBN 0-7093-0021-2 : £3.50 : CIP rev.
B80-13178

016.3371'4 — Western European countries. Integration, *1957-1980.* **Theses —** *Lists*

Siemers, J. P.. European integration : select international bibliography of theses and dissertations = Europäische Integration : internationales Auswahlverzeichnis von Dissertationen und Diplomarbeiten = Intégration Européenne : bibliographie internationale sélective de theses et mémoires : 1957-1980 / J.P. Siemers, E.H. Siemers-Hidma ; preface Ralph Dahrendorf. — 2nd rev. and enl. ed. — The Hague ; London : Nijhoff, 1981. — xxx,412p ; 24cm
English, French and German text. — Previous ed.: 1956?. — Includes index
ISBN 90-247-2542-9 : Unpriced B82-00482

016.3381'094 — Europe. Agricultural industries, *1975-1980.* **Geographical factors —** *Bibliographies*

Problems and policies of agriculture in the less-favoured area of Europe (1975-1980). — Slough (Farnham House, Farnham Royal, Slough SL2 3BN) : Commonwealth Agricultural Bureaux, c1981. — iii,111p : ill ; 21x30cm. — (Commonwealth Agricultural Bureaux annotated bibliographies. General series, ISSN 0141-593x ; annotated bibliography no.R45)
Unpriced (spiral) B82-27996

016.3381'61 — Agricultural industries. Applications of digital computer systems — *Bibliographies*

Ramirez, G. G.. Agriculture : an annotated bibliography / editors G.P. Tottle ; compilers G.G. Ramirez, D.P. Best, J.R. Bessant. — London : Heyden on behalf of the British Computer Society, c1982. — viii,42p ; 21cm. — (Use of computers for national development)
ISBN 0-85501-694-9 (pbk) : £7.00 : CIP rev.
B81-40229

016.3381'9'1724 — Developing countries. Food supply. Shortages — *Bibliographies*

Ball, Nicole. World hunger : a guide to the economic and political dimensions / Nicole Ball. — Santa Barbara ; Oxford : ABC-Clio, c1981. — xxiii,386p : 1ill ; 24cm. — (The War/peace bibliography series ; 15)
Includes index
ISBN 0-87436-308-x : £27.95 B82-27406

016.3382'724'0941 — Great Britain. Coal industries — *Bibliographies*

Benson, John, *1945 July 23-*. Bibliography of the British coal industry : secondary literature, parliamentary and departmental papers, mineral maps and plans and a guide to sources / compiled and occasionally annotated by John Benson, Robert G. Neville and Charles H. Thompson. — Oxford : Published for the National Coal Board by Oxford University Press, 1981. — vii,760p ; 23cm
Includes index
ISBN 0-19-920120-x : £45.00 : CIP rev.
B81-31194

016.3384'7677'0095492 — Great Britain. National libraries: India Office Library and Records. Stock: Manuscripts in Bengali: Manuscripts on textile industries & trades in Bangladesh, *1774-1814* **—** *Lists*

India Office Library and Records. Factory correspondence and other Bengali documents in the India Office Library and Records : supplementary to J.F. Blumhardt's Catalogue of the Bengali and Assamese MMS in the library of the India Office (1924) / [compiled by] Anisuzzaman ; published under the auspices of the British Academy Oriental Documents Committee. — [London] : India Office Library and Records, 1981. — iii,300p : 1map,facsims ; 30cm. — (Oriental documents ; 4)
ISBN 0-903359-31-6 (pbk) : Unpriced : CIP rev. B81-07461

016.3384'7677653'094252 — Nottinghamshire. Lace industries, *to 1920* **—** *Bibliographies*

Robinson, Susan, *1955-*. An introductory bibliography of the hosiery and lace industries in Nottingham and district to 1920 : with Nottingham locations / by Susan Robinson and Michael Brook. — Nottingham : University of Nottingham Library, 1982. — iv,14p ; 30cm
£1.30 (pbk)
Primary classification 016.3384'76873'094252
B82-21834

016.3384'7686'0942 — England. Provincial towns. Book industries & trades, *to 1850* **—** *Bibliographies*

Feather, John. The English provincial book trade before 1850 : a checklist of secondary sources / by John Feather. — Oxford : Oxford Bibliographical Society, 1981. — vi,37p ; 26cm. — (Occasional publications / Oxford Bibliographical Society ; no.16)
Includes index
ISBN 0-901420-37-9 (pbk) : Unpriced
B82-05691

016.3384'76873'094252 — Nottinghamshire. Hosiery & knitwear industries, *to 1920* **—** *Bibliographies*

Robinson, Susan, *1955-*. An introductory bibliography of the hosiery and lace industries in Nottingham and district to 1920 : with Nottingham locations / by Susan Robinson and Michael Brook. — Nottingham : University of Nottingham Library, 1982. — iv,14p ; 30cm
£1.30 (pbk)
Also classified at 016.3384'7677653'094252
B82-21834

016.3386'42 — Small firms — *Bibliographies* **—** *Serials*

The **London** Business School small business bibliography. — 1980-. — London (Sussex Place, Regent's Park, NW1 4SA) : London Graduate School of Business Studies, 1980-. — v. ; 30cm
Updated by supplements between cumulated editions
ISSN 0263-5259 = London Business School small business bibliography : Unpriced
B82-23582

016.33891'4'041 — European Community. Membership of Great Britain. Documents, *1981* **—** *Lists*

Ayles, Sarah. Britain and Europe during 1981 : a bibliographical guide : an author, title and chronological index to British primary source material on European integration / compiled by Sarah Ayles. — Brighton : Harvester Microfrom, 1982. — 139p ; 21cm. — (Harvester / Primary social sources)
Includes index
ISBN 0-86257-011-5 (pbk) : Unpriced
B82-25280

016.34 — Law — *Bibliographies*

Law books 1876-1981 : books and serials on law and its related subjects. — New York ; London : Bowker, c1981. — 4v.(xviii,5039p) ; 29cm
Includes index
ISBN 0-8352-1397-8 : Unpriced
ISBN 0-8352-1469-9 (v.1)
ISBN 0-8352-1470-2 (v.2)
ISBN 0-8352-1471-0 (v.3)
ISBN 0-8352-1472-9 (v.4) B82-17422

016.341'0266'41 — Great Britain. Treaties. Ratifications, accessions & withdrawals — *Lists*

Great Britain. Third supplementary list of ratifications, accessions, withdrawal, etc. for 1981. — London : H.M.S.O., [1982]. — 32p ; 25cm. — (Treaty series ; no.34 (1981)) (Cmnd. ; 8461)
ISBN 0-10-184610-x (unbound) : £2.65
B82-18674

Great Britain. Third supplementary list of ratifications, accessions, withdrawals, etc. for 1980. — London : H.M.S.O., [1980]. — 23p ; 25cm. — (Treaty series ; no.91 (1980)) (Cmnd. ; 8090)
ISBN 0-10-180900-x (unbound) : £2.10
B82-15131

016.341'094 — European Economic Community. Law — *Indexes*

Guide to EEC-legislation / editors Alfred E. Kellermann ... [et al.] ; secretary to the editors Jan S. de Jongh. — Amsterdam ; Oxford : North-Holland
At head of title: T.M.C. Asser Institute — The Hague
Suppl.3: (1.7.1978-1.7.1981). — 1981. — xvi,1172p ; 30cm
Includes index
Unpriced (pbk) B82-09496

016.3416'9 — War criminals. Trials, *to 1976* **—** *Bibliographies*

Lewis, John R. (John Rodney). Uncertain judgment : a bibliography of war crimes trials / compiled by John R. Lewis. — Santa Barbara ; Oxford : ABC-Clio, 1979. — xxxii,251p ; 24cm. — (The War/peace bibliography series ; 8)
Includes index
ISBN 0-87436-288-1 : £15.95 B82-02741

016.3423'97 — Aviation. Law — *Bibliographies*

Heere, Wybo P.. International bibliography of air law / Wybo P. Heere. — The Hague ; London : Nijhoff
Supplement 1977-1980. — 1981. — xxxviii,356p ; 25cm
Includes index
Unpriced B82-04272

016.34363 — Liability. Law — *Bibliographies*

Veljanovski, Čento G.. Legal liability and negligence / by Cento G. Veljanovski. — Oxford : Centre for Socio-Legal Studies, 1979. — [32]p ; 21cm. — (Bibliography in law and economics ; no.2)
ISBN 0-86226-009-4 (pbk) : Unpriced
B82-30882

016.344103'7869 — Great Britain. Buildings. Construction. Law — *Abstracts*

Harlow, P. A.. Contracts and building law / compiled by P.A. Harlow. — Ascot : Chartered Institute of Building
Includes index
Vol.2: A review of the literature 1977-1980. — [1981]. — 99p ; 30cm
ISBN 0-906600-43-x (pbk) : Unpriced : CIP rev. B81-18063

016.3442 — England. Law. Texts, *1700-1800* **—** *Bibliographies*

Adams, J. N. (John Norman). A bibliography of eighteenth century legal literature : a subject and author catalogue of law treatises and all law related literature held in the main legal collections in England / by J.N. Adams and G. Averley ; with historical and technical assistance from F.J.G. Robinson ; for the BELL Project at the University of Kent in Canterbury. — Newcastle upon Tyne : Avero, 1982. — xvi,900p ; 31cm + prospectus(6p : 30cm ; pbk)
Six microfiche in pocket
ISBN 0-907977-01-4 : Unpriced : CIP rev.
B82-14529

016.344203'14 — Great Britain. ***Public Record Office.*** **Stock: Records of cases on prizes from naval operations by Great Britain.** ***Royal Navy*** **in Great Britain.** ***High Court of Admiralty — Indexes***

Great Britain. *High Court of Admiralty.* Prize papers (HCA 32/260-493) index 1776-1786 / High Court of Admiralty. — London : Swift, 1982. — 165p ; 33cm. — (Publications / List & Index Society ; v.183)
At head of title: List & Index Society
£7.60 (Subscribers only) B82-23832

Great Britain. *High Court of Admiralty.* Prize papers (HCA 32/494-930) index 1793-1803 / High Court of Admiralty. — London : Swift, 1982. — 212p ; 33cm. — (Publications / List & Index Society ; v.184)
At head of title: List & Index Society
£9.00 (Subscribers only) B82-23835

016.3442064'38 — Great Britain. ***Public Record Office.*** **Stock: Letters patent in archives of England and Wales.** ***Augmentation Office, 1216-1625 — Indexes***

England and Wales. *Augmentation Office.* Letters patent (original) E 313/1-14) index of persons and subjects Henry III-Charles I / Exchequer, Augmentation Office. — London : Swift, 1982. — 121p ; 33cm. — (Publications / List & Index Society ; v.185)
At head of title: List & Index Society
£6.50 (Subscribers only) B82-21436

016.344207'2 — England. Quarter sessions. Records *— Catalogues*

Gibson, J. S. W.. Quarter sessions records for family historians : a select list / compiled by J.S.W. Gibson. — Plymouth : Federation of Family History Societies, 1982. — 32p ; 21cm
Text on inside cover
ISBN 0-907099-15-7 (pbk) : £1.00 B82-31015

016.344207'26 — Great Britain. ***Public Record Office.*** **Stock: Chancery patent rolls** *— Lists — Latin texts — Manuscripts — Facsimiles*

Great Britain. *Court of Chancery.* Chancery patent rolls (Contemporary) (C66) 14 Jas. I. — London : Swift, 1982. — 179p ; 33cm. — (Publications / List & Index Society ; v.187)
At head of title: List & Index Society
£8.50 (Subscribers only) B82-21437

016.3520423'1 — Wiltshire. Parish records *— Lists*

Carter, Barbara J.. Location of documents for Wiltshire parishes / [compiled] by Barbara J. Carter. — Swindon : B.J. Carter
Pt.4: Hindon to Marlborough. — 1981. — [76]p ; 21cm
ISBN 0-9507586-3-9 (pbk) : £2.00 B82-11005

016.3544103'12 — Great Britain. ***Public Record Office.*** **Stock: Archives of Great Britain.** ***Lord Steward's Department — Lists***

Lord Stewards Department (LS 1-4, 6-13) list 1598-1870. — London : Swift, 1982. — 56p ; 33cm. — (Publications / List & Index Society ; v.186)
At head of title: List & Index Society
£5.00 (Subscribers only) B82-21438

016.355'009438 — Poland. ***Wojsko — History — Bibliographies — Polish texts — Serials***

Materiały do historii Wojska Polskiego. — No.1-. — Londyn [London] (c/o Polish Institute, 20 Princes Gate, SW7 1QA) : Dr T. Kryska-Karski, 1982-. — v. ; 24cm
ISSN 0263-1539 = Materiały do historii Wojska Polskiego : £1.50 per issue B82-20893

016.3551'342 — British military forces. Decorations: Victoria Cross *— Bibliographies*

Reid, D. I.. The Victoria Cross 1856-1981 : a select bibliography / D.I. Reid. — London (St Mary's Rd, Ealing, W5 5RF) : School of Library and Information Studies, Ealing College of Higher Education, c1981. — 11leaves ; 30cm. — (Ealing miscellany ; no.24)
Unpriced (unbound) B82-35093

016.3554'0941 — Military operations by British military forces. Archives. Collections: Liddell Hart Centre for Military Archives. Stock *— Catalogues*

Liddell Hart Centre for Military Archives. King's College London Liddell Hart Centre for Military Archives : consolidated list of accessions. — [London] : [Kings College London], [1981?]. — 38leaves ; 30cm
ISBN 0-901324-23-x (spiral) : Unpriced B82-22588

016.358'18'0941 — Army operations by Great Britain. ***Army, 1919-1939.*** **Armoured combat vehicles. Interviews. Sound tape recordings** *— Catalogues*

Imperial War Museum. *Department of Sound Records.* Mechanisation of the British Army 1919-39. — [London] : Imperial War Museum, Dept. of Sound Records, [1982?]. — [34]p ; 21cm. — (Oral history recordings)
Unpriced (pbk) B82-26780

016.3584'00947 — Union of Soviet Socialist Republics. ***Voenno-vozdushnye sily, 1939-1980 — Bibliographies***

Smith, Myron J.. The Soviet air and strategic rocket forces 1939-1980 : a guide to sources in English / Myron J. Smith ; with foreword by Kenneth R. Whiting. — Santa Barbara ; Oxford : ABC-Clio, c1981. — xliv,321p ; 24cm. — (The War/peace bibliography series ; 10)
Includes index
ISBN 0-87436-306-3 : £26.95 B82-02963

016.3591'0941 — Great Britain. ***Royal Navy.*** **Sailors. Naval life,** ***1910-1922.*** **Interviews. Sound tape recordings** *— Catalogues*

Imperial War Museum. *Department of Sound Records.* Lower deck 1910-22. — [London] : Imperial War Museum, Dept. of Sound Records, [1982?]. — 34p ; 21cm. — (Oral history recordings)
Unpriced (pbk) B82-26778

016.361 — London. Southwark ***(London Borough).*** **Polytechnics. Libraries: Polytechnic of the South Bank.** ***Library.*** **Stock: Documents on welfare services** *— Catalogues*

Polytechnic of the South Bank. *Library.* Guide to literature searching in nursing, community health and social services / Polytechnic of the South Bank, Library, Southwark Site. — 2nd rev. ed. — London : [The Library] ; London : Denny Publications [distributor], c1981. — 41p : ill,1plan ; 21cm
Cover title. — Previous ed.: published as Guide to literature searching in nursing and community health. 197-?
ISBN 0-905267-24-9 (pbk) : £1.00 B82-15206

016.361 — Welfare work. Reference books *— Lists*

Conrad, James H.. Reference source in social work : an annotated bibliography / by James H. Conrad. — Metuchen ; London : Scarecrow, 1982. — vi,201p ; 22cm
Includes index
ISBN 0-8108-1503-6 : £12.00 B82-31799

016.361'06 — Community information. Information sources: Ephemera with British imprints: Ephemera in Asian languages *— Lists*

Community information (Asian languages) directory. — London : Commission for Racial Equality in association with National Association of Citizens' Advice Bureaux, 1980. — vi,89p ; 21cm
ISBN 0-902355-92-9 (pbk) : £1.00 B82-16022

016.361'06 — Community information. Information sources: Ephemera with British imprints *— Lists*

Watson, Joyce. Bibliography of ephemeral community information materials / Joyce Watson. — Leeds : Public Libraries Management Research Unit, School of Librarianship, Leeds Polytechnic
Pt.2: An assessment of BNB coverage of Housing and education titles from January 1977 to April 1979. — 1979. — 183p ; 30cm
Unpriced (pbk) B82-21715

016.3617 — Voluntary work *— Abstracts — Serials*

Voluntary forum abstracts. — Vol.1, issue no.1 (Mar. 1982)-. — London : National Council for Voluntary Organisations, 1982-. — v. ; 30cm
Six issues yearly
ISSN 0262-8570 = Voluntary forum abstracts : £9.00 per year B82-27645

016.3617'0941 — Great Britain. Voluntary organisations. Fund raising *— Bibliographies*

Bates, Susan. Fundraising and grant aid for voluntary organisations : a guide to the literature / compiled by Susan Bates. — London : Information Department NCVO, 1981. — 45p ; 30cm
Cover title. — Includes index
ISBN 0-7199-1078-1 (pbk) : £1.00 B82-09482

016.3621'0941 — Great Britain. National health services *— Bibliographies*

Best, K. W.. A select bibliography on the National Health Service / by K.W. Best. — London : Department of Health and Social Security Library, 1980. — 73p ; 30cm. — (Bibliography series / Department of Health and Social Security Library ; no.130)
Includes index
ISBN 0-902650-12-2 (pbk) : £2.00 B82-16405

016.3621'09427 — North-west England. Health services. Archives *— Lists*

Coyne, Liz. A guide to the records of health services in the Manchester region (Kendal to Crewe) / by Liz Coyne, Dennis Doyle and John Pickstone. — [Manchester] : [Department of History of Science and Technology, UMIST], c1981. — 2v. : maps ; 30cm. — (Occasional publication / Department of History of Science and Technology UMIST, ISSN 0260-1052 ; nos.3 and 4)
Includes index
ISBN 0-907362-02-8 (pbk) : Unpriced
ISBN 0-907362-03-6 (pt.2) : £2.50 B82-19619

016.3621'9892 — Hospitals. Patients: Children. Care. Psychosocial aspects *— Abstracts*

Akins, Dianna L.. The hospitalized child : psychosocial issues : an abstracted bibliography / Dianna Lyell Akins, Gillian S. Mace, and Faren R. Akins. — New York ; London : IFI/Plenum, c1981. — vii,294p ; 26cm. — (IFI data base library)
Includes index
ISBN 0-306-65199-8 : Unpriced B82-02767

016.3622'0896873 — United States. Spanish Americans. Mental health *— Bibliographies*

Newton, Frank. Hispanic mental health research : a reference guide / Frank Newton, Esteban L. Olmedo, Amado M. Padilla. — Berkeley, [Calif.] ; London : University of California Press, c1982. — 685p ; 26cm
Bibliography: p5. — Includes index
ISBN 0-520-04166-6 : Unpriced B82-36050

016.3622'08997 — North American Indians. Mental health *— Bibliographies*

Kelso, Dianne R.. Bibliography of North American Indian mental health / compiled by Dianne R. Kelso and Carolyn L. Attneave ; prepared under the auspices of the White Cloud Center. — Westport ; London : Greenwood Press, 1981. — xxviii,411p ; 25cm
Includes index
ISBN 0-313-22930-9 : Unpriced B82-18023

016.3624 — Scotland. Strathclyde Region. Hamilton. Colleges. Libraries: Bell College of Technology. ***Library.*** **Stock: Documents on physical handicaps** *— Catalogues*

Bell College of Technology. *Library.* Bibliography of publications on disability : held in Bell College of Technology Library : compiled to complement Signpost 81 : a festival to mark the international year of disabled people, organised by Strathclyde Regional Council Social Work Department Lanark Division in collaboration with Bell College of Technology on 24th, 25th and 26th November 1981 at Regional Council Buildings and Bell College of Technology Hamilton. — Hamilton : Bell College of Technology Library, 1981. — 19p ; 30cm
ISBN 0-906249-05-8 (unbound) : £1.00
B82-10903

016.3624'088054 — Handicapped children. Children's books — *Lists*

Smyth, Margaret, *1952-*. Count me in : books for and about disabled children / compiled by Margaret Smyth. — Towcester : Library Association Youth Libraries Group, 1981. — 28p : ill ; 21cm. — (Pamphlet / Library Association Youth Libraries Group ; no.23)
Includes index
ISBN 0-85365-924-9 (pbk) : £1.20 B82-00673

016.3624'1'0941 — Great Britain. Partially sighted persons. Social conditions — *Bibliographies*

Cameron, Agnes T.. Partial sight : bibliography on the living problems of partially sighted people / compiled by Agnes T. Cameron. — 2nd ed. — London : Disabled Living Foundation, c1981. — viii,116p ; 30cm
Previous ed.: 1977. — Includes index
ISBN 0-906544-07-6 (pbk) : Unpriced : CIP rev. B81-39240

016.3631'1 — Industrial health & industrial safety — *Bibliographies*

Health and safety at work : a select bibliography. — Birmingham (Science and Technology Department, Central Library, Chamberlain Sq., Birmingham B3 3HQ) : Birmingham Public Libraries, 1979. — (Technical bibliographies, ISSN 0308-4191 ; 11c)
3rd supplement / compiled by John F. Skidmore. — 79p ; 30cm
£6.00 (pbk) B82-17710

016.3631'79 — Chemical laboratories. Safety measures — *Abstracts* — *Serials*

Laboratory hazards bulletin / Royal Society of Chemistry. — Apr. 1981 ; 1981, no.1-. — Nottingham : The Society, 1981-. — v. : ill ; 30cm
Monthly. — Introductory no. issued Apr. 1981
ISSN 0261-2917 = Laboratory hazards bulletin : £50.00 per year B82-06175

016.3635'0942 — England. Urban regions. Housing market *related to* **mobility of population** — *Bibliographies*

Cockett, Ien. Housing and migration / compiled by Ien Cockett. — London : Greater London Council, 1978, c1977. — 18,5p ; 30cm. — (Research bibliography / Greater London Council ; no.89)
Includes index
ISBN 0-7168-0975-3 (pbk) : £1.75
Primary classification 016.307'2'0942
B82-25305

016.3636'9'0973 — United States. Buildings of historical importance. Preservation, *1941-1975* — *Bibliographies*

Tubesing, Richard. Architectural preservation in the United States, 1941-1975 : a bibliography of federal, state, and local government publications / Richard Tubesing. — New York ; London : Garland, 1978. — xvii,452p ; 23cm. — (Garland reference library of the humanities ; v.61)
Includes index
ISBN 0-8240-9937-0 : Unpriced B82-28353

016.3681'1'00942591 — London *(City)*. **Public libraries: Guildhall Library. Stock: Fire insurance policies for Milton Keynes region,** *1710-1731* — *Indexes*

Index to the fire insurance policies held at the Guildhall Library, London covering the Milton Keynes area for the period 1710 to 1731 and the year 1793 / compiled by Brian L. Giggins. — [Milton Keynes] (Wavendon Tower, Wavendon, Milton Keynes MK17 8LX) : Milton Keynes Development Corporation, 1981. — 36p : forms ; 30cm
Unpriced (spiral) B82-11029

016.36946'3'0941 — Great Britain. Girls' organisations: Girl Guides Association, *to 1930* — *Bibliographies*

Pickles, Diane J.. A select bibliography of the founding and history of the Girl Guide Movement in the United Kingdom, 1907-1930 / Diane J. Pickles. — London (St Mary's Rd, Ealing, W5 5RF) : School of Library and Information Studies, Ealing College of Higher Education, c1981. — 14p ; 30cm. — (Ealing miscellany ; no.22)
Includes index
Unpriced (unbound) B82-35094

016.37 — Education — *Bibliographies*

Education literature 1907-1932 / edited by Malcolm Hamilton. — New York ; London : Garland
Facsims of: Bibliography of education 1907-1911/12 and Record of current educational publications, United States Office of Education, Jan.1912-Jan./Mar.1932 published by the U.S. Govt. Printing Office, Washington, D.C.
Vols.4-6: Indexing done from 1910 through Jan.1914. — 1979. — ca330p ; 24cm
ISBN 0-8240-3701-4 : Unpriced B82-14352

Education literature 1907-1932 / edited by Malcolm Hamilton. — New York ; London : Garland
Facsims of: Bibliography of education 1907-1911/12 and Record of current educational publications, United States Office of Education, Jan.1912-Jan./Mar.1932 published by the U.S. Govt. Printing Office, Washington, D.C.
Vols.7-8: Indexing done from Feb.1914 through Jan.1916. — 1979. — ca400p ; 24cm
ISBN 0-8240-3702-2 : Unpriced B82-14351

Education literature 1907-1932 / edited by Malcolm Hamilton. — New York ; London : Garland
Facsims of: Bibliography of education 1907-1911/12 and Record of current educational publications, United States Office of Education, Jan.1912-Jan./Mar.1932 published by the U.S. Govt. Printing Office, Washington, D.C.
Vols.11-12: Indexing done from Feb.1918 through Jan.1920. — 1979. — ca340p ; 24cm
ISBN 0-8240-3704-9 : Unpriced B82-14350

Education literature 1907-1932 / edited by Malcolm Hamilton. — New York ; London : Garland
Facsims of: Bibliography of education 1907-1911/12 and Record of current educational publications, United States Office of Education, Jan.1912-Jan./Mar.1932 published by the U.S. Govt. Printing Office, Washington, D.C.
Vols.17-18: Indexing done from 1927 through 1928. — 1979. — ca360p ; 24cm
ISBN 0-8240-3708-1 : Unpriced B82-14347

Education literature 1907-1932 / edited by Malcolm Hamilton. — New York ; London : Garland
Facsims of: Bibliography of education 1907-1911/12 and Record of current educational publications, United States Office of Education, Jan.1912-Jan./Mar.1932 published by the U.S. Govt. Printing Office, Washington, D.C.
Vols.19-20: Indexing done from 1929 through 1930. — 1979. — ca300p ; 24cm
ISBN 0-8240-3709-x : Unpriced B82-14348

Education literature 1907-1932 / edited by Malcolm Hamilton. — New York ; London : Garland
Facsims of: Bibliography of education 1907-1911/12 and Record of current educational publications, United States Office of Education, Jan.1912-Jan./Mar.1932 published by the U.S. Govt. Printing Office, Washington, D.C.
Vols.21-25: Indexing done from 1931 through March 1932. — 1979. — ca530p ; 24cm
ISBN 0-8240-3710-3 : Unpriced B82-14349

016.37 — Education. Serial articles — *Indexes* — *Serials*

British education index. — Vol.17 (Jan.-Dec.1981). — London : The British Library, Bibliographic Services Division, Apr.1982. — [304]p
ISBN 0-900220-96-1 : £22.00 : CIP entry
ISSN 0007-0637 B82-05771

016.37 — Education. Theses accepted by British higher education institutions — *Lists*

Register of advanced studies in further and higher education : originating in the colleges of education (technical). — 2nd ed. / (edited by Jean Lovell). — London : Garnett College, 1980. — [93]leaves ; 30cm
Previous ed.: Bolton : Bolton College of Education (Technical), 1976. — Includes index
ISBN 0-906498-01-5 (pbk) : £2.50 B82-03935

016.37 — Hampshire. Southampton. Universities. Libraries: University of Southampton. *Library.* **Stock: Reference books on education**

Bibliographical aids and reference tools for the literature of education : a guide to works in the Education Library with some reference to works in other parts of the University Library. — 5th ed. / edited by Joan V. Marder. — Southampton : University of Southampton. Library, 1981. — iv,49p ; 30cm. — (User's guides / University of Southampton, Library)
Previous ed.: Southampton : Southampton University Press, 1978. — Includes index
ISBN 0-85432-221-3 (pbk) : £2.50 B82-10093

016.37019 — Education. Sociological perspectives — *Bibliographies*

Bibliography / research conducted by past and present members of the Centre and by others associated with it ; University of Edinburgh, Centre for Educational Sociology. — [Edinburgh] (7 Buccleuch Place, Edinburgh EH8 9LN) : Centre for Educational Sociology, [1982]. — 56p ; 30cm
Unpriced (pbk) B82-29209

016.370'28'54 — Education. Applications of information retrieval systems using digital computer systems — *Bibliographies*

Maddison, John, *19---*. Information technology and education. — Milton Keynes : Open University Press, Oct.1982. — [256]p
ISBN 0-335-10183-6 : £14.95 : CIP entry
B82-25514

016.37'07'30942166 — London. Wandsworth *(London Borough)*. **Colleges of education: Whitelands College. Archives** — *Catalogues*

Whitelands College. Whitelands College archive catalogue / compiled by Helen Henstridge. — London (West Hill, SW15 3SN) : The college, 1979. — 131p ; 21cm
At head of title: Roehampton Institute of Higher Education
Unpriced (pbk) B82-09259

016.37'07'78 — Great Britain. Education. Applications of microelectronics — *Bibliographies*

Maddison, John, *19---*. National education and the microelectronics revolution : an annotated bibliography and a media resources list : with a survey essay on educational and training aspects of the new technology / by John Maddison. — Clevedon : Clevedon Printing Co., 1980. — 67p ; 32cm
Includes index
ISBN 0-9505919-1-2 (pbk) : Unpriced
B82-11552

016.37'0917'4927 — Arab countries. Education, *1956-1978* — *Bibliographies*

Pantelidis, Veronica S.. Arab Education 1956-1978 : a bibliography / Veronica S. Pantelidis. — London : Mansell, 1982. — xvii,552p ; 24cm
Includes index
ISBN 0-7201-1588-4 : £45.00 : CIP rev.
B82-07596

016.3713 — Scotland. Educational technology. Information services: Scottish Council for Educational Technology. *Information Service.* **Stock: Serial articles on distance study** — *Catalogues*

Scottish Council for Educational Technology. *Information Service.* Journal articles on educational broadcasting and open learning systems : articles appearing in the S.C.E.T. Information Service's holdings of journals dated April 1981-September 1981, received by the S.C.E.T. Information Service by September 1981 / compiled by Andrew Foley. — Glasgow : The Service, 1981. — 10p ; 30cm. — (SCET journals bibliography, ISSN 0260-972x ; no.4)
ISBN 0-86011-043-5 (unbound) : £0.25
B82-22374

016.3713'07'8 — Educational technology — *Bibliographies*

Green, Douglas A.. An index to collected essays on eductional media and technology / Douglas A. Green. — Metuchen ; London : Scarecrow, 1982. — vii,188p ; 23cm
Bibliography: p181-188. — Includes index
ISBN 0-8108-1490-0 : £10.00 B82-22977

016.3713'3'0973 — United States. Schools. Teaching aids: Audiovisual materials — *Lists*
The **Complete** media monitor : guides to learning resources / [compiled] by Mary Robinson Sive. — Methuchen ; London : Scarecrow Press, 1981. — 196p : ill ; 29cm
Includes a reprint of all Media monitor issues (1977-1980)
ISBN 0-8108-1466-8 : £10.80 B82-11466

016.3724 — Children, to 7 years. Reading skills. Development — *Bibliographies*
Friedlander, Janet. Early reading development : a bibliography / compiled by Janet Friedlander ; classification and introductions to the literature by Elizabeth Hunter-Grundin and Hans U. Grundin. — London : Harper & Row, 1981. — xxiv,446p ; 26cm
Includes index
ISBN 0-06-318161-4 : Unpriced : CIP rev. B81-20551

016.3727'3 — Primary schools. Curriculum subjects: Mathematics. Concepts — *Bibliographies — For teaching*
Turnbull, Joanna. Maths links : a classroom guide to school mathematics and published resources / Joanna Turnbull. — Stafford : NARE, 1981. — 174p,[5]leaves of folded plates : ill,forms ; 30cm
Bibliography: p171. — Includes index
ISBN 0-906730-03-1 (pbk) : Unpriced B82-19940

016.3732'36 — United States. Children, 10-14 years. Education — *Bibliographies*
Blyth, Dale A.. Philosophy, policies, and programs for early adolescent education : an annotated bibliography / compiled by Dale A. Blyth and Elizabeth Lueder Karnes. — Westport ; London : Greenwood, 1981. — xix,689p ; 25cm
Includes index
ISBN 0-313-22687-3 : Unpriced B82-17881

016.374'012 — Adult numeracy education — *Bibliographies*
Numeracy resource guide. — London (252 Western Ave., W3) : Adult Literacy Support Services Fund, [1979]. — 9p ; 30cm
£0.20 (unbound) B82-40585

016.378'11 — Great Britain. Higher education institutions. Staff development — *Bibliographies*
Cryer, Pat. Academic staff development in higher education : a catalogue of resource materials / Pat Cryer. — London : Council for Educational Technology with the Institute for Educational Technology, University of Surrey, 1982. — vii,55p ; 22cm
ISBN 0-86184-069-0 (pbk) : £4.00 : CIP rev. B82-08117

016.378'1552 — Great Britain. Higher education institutions. Sandwich courses — *Bibliographies*
Samuelson, J.. Sandwich courses : an annotated bibliography / compiled by J. Samuelson and H. Saxby ; incorporating Supplement 1972-1975 compiled by D.J. Worboys. — [Guildford] : University of Surrey Library, [1980]. — 50leaves ; 30cm. — (Library bibliography)
Cover title. — Includes index
ISBN 0-902471-03-1 (pbk) : Unpriced
ISBN 0-902471-04-x B82-15260

016.378'173 — Higher education. Teaching aids: Audiovisual materials — *Lists — For teaching in higher education institutions*
Audio-visual materials for higher education, 1981-82 / editor: James Ballantyne. — Update ed. — London : British Universities Film Council, c1981
'... updates the four-part edition published in October 1979 ...' — Foreword
Supplement. — xx,110p ; 30cm
ISBN 0-901299-28-6 (pbk) : £8.00 (£7.00 to BUFC members) : CIP rev. B81-24628

016.37873 — United States. Higher education — *Bibliographies*
Quay, Richard H.. Index to anthologies on postsecondary education 1960-1978 / compiled by Richard H. Quay. — Westport ; London : Greenwood Press, 1980. — li,342p ; 25cm
Includes index
ISBN 0-313-21272-4 : Unpriced B82-14981

016.3801'025 — Great Britain. National libraries: Science Reference Library. Stock: Serials containing directories of industries & trades — *Catalogues*
Rahman, H.. Trade directories in journals. — 3rd ed. — London (25 Southampton Buildings, Chancery Lane, WC2A 1AW) : The Library, Jan.1983. — [20]p
Previous ed.: 1981
ISBN 0-7123-0701-x (pbk) : £2.00 : CIP entry B82-39297

Science Reference Library. Trade directories in journals : a list of those appearing within numbered parts of serials / the British Library Science Reference Library ; [compiled by] D.M. King and A. Larkin. — London : The Library, [1980]. — 13p ; 30cm
Includes index
ISBN 0-902914-55-3 (unbound) : £1.00 : CIP rev. B80-12195

016.3805 — Great Britain. Transport. Research organisations: Transport and Road Research Laboratory. Publications — *Lists*
Transport and Road Research Laboratory. Transport and Road Research Laboratory index of publications for 1975-1979. — [Crowthorne] ([Old Wokingham Rd., Crowthorne, Berks. RG7 6AU]) : [The Laboratory], [1980?]. — v,187p ; 21cm
Unpriced (pbk) B82-13863

016.3805 — Transport. Documents on transport — *Lists*
Publications and working papers in transport from British universities and polytechnics. — London (University College London, [Gower Street, WC1E 6BT]) : Universities Transport Study Group. — (UTSG occasional publication, ISSN 0140-5594 ; no.10)
3rd issue: 1979-1980 / edited by Saskia Fry. — 1981. — 143p ; 30cm
Unpriced (pbk) B82-19755

016.381'1 — Shopping centres — *Bibliographies*
Managed shopping centres bibliography. — Reading (26 Queen Victoria St., Reading, Berks. RG1 2TG) : Unit for Retail Planning Information, 1979. — 64p ; 30cm. — (URPI ; B4)
Cover title
Unpriced (pbk) B82-19924

016.3871'64 — Freight transport. Shipping. Ships. Bulk cargoes. Terminals. Cargo handling — *Bibliographies*
Law, Peter R.. Bulk cargoes — terminals and handling equipment / compiler Peter R. Law. — London : ICHCA, c1982. — 8leaves ; 30cm. — (Information Service Library bibliography ; no.19) (An ICHCA information access publication)
ISBN 0-906297-25-7 (pbk) : Unpriced B82-27579

016.3872'45 — Bulk cargoes. Freight transport. Shipping — *Bibliographies*
Law, Peter R.. Bulk cargoes — handling & transport of bulk commodities / compiler Peter R. Law. — London : ICHCA, c1982. — 6leaves ; 30cm. — (Information Service Library bibliography ; no.20) (An ICHCA information access publication)
ISBN 0-906297-26-5 (pbk) : Unpriced B82-27580

016.3872'45 — Freight transport. Shipping. Bulk carrying ships — *Bibliographies*
Law, Peter R.. Bulk cargoes — bulk carrying vessels / compiler Peter R. Law. — London : ICHCA, c1982. — [4]leaves ; 30cm. — (Information Service Library bibliography ; no.18) (An ICHCA information access publication)
ISBN 0-906297-24-9 (pbk) : Unpriced B82-27581

016.3877'44 — Air freight transport — *Bibliographies*
Law, Peter R.. Air Cargo / prepared by Peter R. Law. — 2nd ed. — London : International Cargo Handling Co-ordination Association, 1980, c1979. — 19leaves ; 30cm. — (Information service library bibliography ; no.2) (An ICHCA information access publication)
Previous ed.: 1979
ISBN 0-906297-18-4 (pbk) : Unpriced B82-38344

016.3884'1 — Urban regions. Road traffic. Environmental aspects — *Bibliographies*
Chu, Chen. Environmental effects of urban road traffic : an annotated bibliography / Chen Chu. — 2nd ed. — London : Centre for Environmental Studies, 1974. — 97p ; 30cm. — (Information paper / Centre for Environmental Studies ; 26)
Previous ed.: 1972. — Includes index
£1.00 (pbk) B82-08892

016.407 — Languages. Teaching — *Abstracts — Serials*
Language teaching : the international abstracting journal for language teachers and applied linguists. — Vol.15, no.1 (Jan. 1982)-. — Cambridge : Cambridge University Press, 1982-. — v. ; 21cm
Quarterly. — Continues: Language teaching & linguistics. Abstracts
ISSN 0261-4448 = Language teaching : £20.00 per year B82-36723

016.4281 — English language. Words. Lists — *Bibliographies — For psycholinguistics*
Lesser, Ruth. An annotated bibliography of verbal materials : for use in psycholinguistic and neurolinguistic experimentation. — Newcastle upon Tyne : Grevatt & Grevatt, July 1982. — [24]p
ISBN 0-9507918-2-2 (pbk) : £1.50 : CIP entry B82-18596

016.428'6 — English language. Reading books. Special subjects: General knowledge — *Bibliographies*
Heeks, Peggy. Ways of knowing : information books for 7 to 9 year olds. — Stroud (Lockwood Station Rd., South Woodchester, Stroud, Glos.) : Thimble Press, Nov.1982. — [40]p. — (Signal bookguides)
ISBN 0-903355-11-6 (pbk) : £1.90 : CIP entry B82-33361

016.44 — French language — *Bibliographies*
Osburn, Charles B.. Research and reference guide to French studies / Charles B. Osburn. — 2nd ed. — Metuchen ; London : Scarecrow, 1981. — xxxvii,532p ; 23cm
Previous ed.: 1968. — Includes index
ISBN 0-8108-1440-4 : £26.00
Also classified at 016.84 B82-17413

016.475 — Latin language. Grammar. Manuscripts in English, *1400-1500* — *Bibliographies*
Thomson, David, *1952-*. A descriptive catalogue of Middle English grammatical texts / David Thomson. — New York ; London : Garland, 1979. — xvii,369p ; 23cm. — (Garland reference library of the humanities ; v.171)
Bibliography: p352-369. — Includes index
ISBN 0-8240-9765-3 : Unpriced B82-10721

016.492'7 — Arabic language — *Bibliographies*
Bakalla, M. H.. Arabic linguistics : an introduction and bibliography. — 2nd rev. ed. — London : Mansell, Nov.1982. — [750]p
Previous ed. published as: Bibliography of Arabic linguistics. 1975
ISBN 0-7201-1583-3 : £33.50 : CIP entry B82-26405

016.496 — African languages. Dictionaries — *Lists*
Hendrix, Melvin K.. An international bibliography of African lexicons / Melvin K. Hendrix. — Metuchen ; London : Scarecrow, 1982. — xxi,348p : 2maps ; 23cm
Includes index
ISBN 0-8108-1478-1 : £18.00 B82-35106

016.497 — Californian Indian languages — *Bibliographies*
Bright, William. Bibliography of the languages of native California : including closely related languages of adjacent areas / William Bright. — Metuchen ; London : Scarecrow Press, 1982. — x,220p ; 23cm. — (Native American bibliography series ; no.3)
Includes index
ISBN 0-8108-1547-8 : £13.20 B82-38911

016.5 — Great Britain. Science. Organisations: Royal Society. Publications: Serials. Articles. Authors — *Indexes*

Royal Society. Decennial index 1971-1980 : index of authors in proceedings, philosophical transactions and biographical memoirs / Royal Society. — London : Royal Society, 1981. — 260p ; 26cm
ISBN 0-85403-181-2 : Unpriced B82-16388

016.5 — Science — *Bibliographies*

Grogan, Denis. Science and technology : an introduction to the literature / Denis Grogan. — 4th ed. — London : Bingley, 1982. — 400p ; 22cm
Previous ed.: 1976. — Includes bibliographies and index
ISBN 0-85157-315-0 (cased) : Unpriced : CIP rev.
ISBN 0-85157-340-1 (pbk) : Unpriced
Also classified at 016.6 B82-01165

016.5'05 — Science. Serials with Japanese imprints — *Lists*

Gibson, Robert W.. Japanese scientific and technical literature : a subject guide / Robert W. Gibson, Jr. and Barbara K. Kunkel. — Aldershot : Gower, 1981. — xv,560p : ill ; 29cm
Bibliography: pxv. — Includes index
ISBN 0-566-00505-0 : Unpriced : CIP rev.
Also classified at 016.6'05 B81-34286

016.509 — Science. Historiology. Reference books — *Lists*

Jayawardene, S. A.. Reference books for the historian of science : a handlist / compiled by S.A. Jayawardene. — London : Science Museum, 1982. — xiv,229p ; 21cm. — (Occasional publications / Science Museum Library, ISSN 0262-4818 ; 2)
Includes index
ISBN 0-901805-14-9 (pbk) : Unpriced : CIP rev. B82-03386

Lorch, R. P.. Aids to research in the history of science / compiled by R.P. Lorch. — [Rev. list]. — Manchester ([P.O. Box 88, Manchester M60 1QD]) : [University of Manchester Institute of Science and Technology], 1980. — 14p ; 21cm
Cover title. — Previous ed.: 1977
£1.20 (pbk) B82-12127

016.509 — Science — *History* — *Bibliographies*

ISIS cumulative bibliography : a bibliography of the history of science formed from ISIS critical bibliographies 1-90, 1913-65. — London : Mansell Publishing in conjunction with the History of Science Society
Vol.4: Civilizations and periods : prehistory to Middle Ages / edited by Magda Whitrow. — 1982. — xviii,457p ; 29cm
ISBN 0-7201-1642-2 : Unpriced
ISBN 0-7201-0549-8 (set) : £100.00 B82-39959

ISIS cumulative bibliography : a bibliography of the history of science formed from ISIS critical bibliographies 1-90, 1913-65. — London : Mansell Publishing in conjunction with the History of Science Society
Vol.5: Civilizations and periods : 15th to 19th centuries / edited by Magda Whitrow. — 1982. — xi,573p ; 29cm
Includes index
ISBN 0-7201-1643-0 : Unpriced
ISBN 0-7201-0549-8 (set) : £100.00 B82-39960

ISIS Cumulative bibliography 1966-1975 : a bibliography of the history of science formed from ISIS critical bibliographies 91-100 : indexing literature published from 1965 through 1974 / edited by John Neu. — London : Mansell Publishing in conjunction with the History of Science Society
Vol.1: Personalities and institutions. — 1980. — xxix,483p ; 29cm
ISBN 0-7201-1515-9 : £44.00 : CIP rev.
ISBN 0-7201-0550-1 (set) : Unpriced B79-35640

016.522'19413'4 — Edinburgh. Astronomical observatories: Royal Observatory, Edinburgh. Archives, *1764-1937* — *Catalogues*

Royal Observatory, Edinburgh. Catalogue of the archives of the Royal Observatory, Edinburgh 1764-1937. — Edinburgh (Blackford Hill, Edinburgh) : The Observatory, Dec.1981. — [55]p
ISBN 0-902553-24-0 : CIP entry B82-00178

016.5304 — Matter. Thermal properties — *Bibliographies*

Thermophysical properties research literature retrieval guide : 1900-1980 / editors J.F. Chaney ... [et al.]. — [New ed.]. — New York ; London : IFI/Plenum
V.5: Oxide mixtures and minerals. — c1982. — [321]p in various pagings ; 29cm
Previous ed.: 1967. — Text on lining papers. — Includes index
ISBN 0-306-67225-1 : Unpriced B82-31340

Thermophysical properties research literature retrieval guide : 1900-1980 / editors J.F. Chaney ... [et al.]. — [New ed.]. — New York ; London : IFI/Plenum
V.6: Mixtures and solutions. — c1982. — [496]p ; 29cm
Previous ed.: 1967. — Text on lining papers. — Includes index
ISBN 0-306-67226-x : Unpriced B82-31341

Thermophysical properties research literature retrieval guide : 1900-1980 / editors J.F. Chaney ... [et al.]. — New York ; London : IFI/Plenum
V.7: Coatings, systems, composite, foods, animal and vegetable products. — 1982. — [639]p in various pagings ; 29cm
Previous ed.: 1967. — Text on lining papers. — Includes index
ISBN 0-306-67227-8 : Unpriced B82-31342

016.5397'3 — Particle accelerators. Targets — *Bibliographies*

Jaklovsky, Jozef. Preparation of nuclear targets : a comprehensive bibliography / Jozef Jaklovsky. — New York ; London : IFI/Plenum, c1981. — 324p ; 26cm. — (IFI data base library)
Includes index
ISBN 0-306-65200-5 : Unpriced B82-01473

016.54'05 — Great Britain. National libraries: Science Reference Library. Stock: Serials on chemistry — *Catalogues*

Science Reference Library. Periodicals on chemistry held by the Science Reference Library. — 2nd ed. — London : Science Reference Library, Aug.1982. — [73]p
Previous ed. 1980
ISBN 0-7123-0700-1 (pbk) : £5.00 : CIP entry B82-22410

016.5412'8 — Chemistry. Quantum theory — *Bibliographies*

Ohno, K.. Quantum chemistry literature data base : bibliography of ab initio calculations for 1978-1980 / K. Ohno, K. Morokuma. — Amsterdam ; Oxford : Elsevier Scientific, 1982. — ix,459p : ill ; 25cm. — (Physical sciences data ; 12)
ISBN 0-444-42074-6 : £47.87 : CIP rev.
ISBN 0-444-41689-7 B82-11264

016.5412'8 — Molecules. Wave functions — *Bibliographies*

Richards, W. G.. A bibliography of ab initio molecular wave functions / W.G. Richards, T.E.H. Walker, R.K. Hinkley. — Oxford : Clarendon
Supplement for 1978-80 / by N.G. Richards ... [et al.]. — 1981. — xxxix,463p ; 24cm. — (Oxford science research papers)
Includes index
ISBN 0-19-855367-6 (pbk) : £35.00 : CIP rev. B81-21633

016.5413'416 — Solutions. Excess thermodynamic properties & mixing thermodynamic properties — *Bibliographies*

Wisniak, Jaime. Mixing and excess thermodynamic properties : a literature source book. — Oxford : Elsevier Scientific. — (Physical sciences data ; 11)
Supplement 1. — Apr.1982. — [752]p
ISBN 0-444-42072-x : CIP entry B82-10671

016.5413'6 — Fluid mixtures. Low temperature properties — *Bibliographies*

Hiza, M. J.. Equilibrium properties of fluid mixtures 2 : a bibliography of experimental data on selected fluids / M.J. Hiza, A.J. Kidnay and R.C. Miller. — New York ; London : IFI/Plenum, c1982. — vii,246p ; 29cm. — (NSRDS bibliographic series)
Updates Equilibrium properties of fluid mixtures. 1975
ISBN 0-306-66002-4 : Unpriced B82-33177

016.543'0894 — Combined liquid chromatography & mass spectrometry — *Abstracts* — *Serials*

Liquid chromatography mass spectrometry abstracts. — Vol.1, no.1 (Nov. 1981)-. — London (261a Finchley Rd., NW3 6LU) : PRM Science & Technology Agency, 1981-. — v. ; 21cm
Two issues yearly (1981-1982), quarterly (1983-)
ISSN 0262-4168 = Liquid chromatography mass spectrometry abstracts : Unpriced B82-14770

016.547 — Organic compounds. Documents on organic compounds - *Indexes*

Lewis, D. A.. Index of reviews in organic chemistry. — London : Royal Society of Chemistry, Apr.1981
1980 supplement to the second cumulative volume. — 1v.
ISBN 0-85186-549-6 (pbk) : CIP entry B81-05142

016.548'5 — Crystals. Growth — *Bibliographies*

Keesee, A. M.. Crystal growth bibliography : supplement / compiled by A.M. Keesee, T.F. Connolly, and G.C. Battle, Jr. ; with a foreword by Lynn A. Boatner. — New York ; London : IFI/Plenum, c1981. — 262p ; 28cm. — (Solid state physics literature guides ; v.11)
ISBN 0-306-68331-8 : Unpriced B82-17722

016.551 — London. Camden *(London Borough)*. **Universities. Colleges. Libraries: University College, London.** *Library.* **Stock: Manuscripts of Greenaugh, George Bellas** — *Lists*

University College, London. *Library.* A list of the papers and correspondence of George Bellas Greenough (1778-1855) : held in the Manuscripts Room, University College London Library / compiled by Jacqueline Golden. — [London] : University College London, 1981. — 46p ; 21cm
Bibliography: p10. — Includes index
ISBN 0-902137-27-1 (pbk) : Unpriced B82-17633

016.551'09 — Geology, *to 1978* — *Bibliographies*

Sarjeant, William A. S.. Geologists and the history of geology : an international bibliography from the origins to 1978 / by William A.S. Sargeant. — London : Macmillan, 1980. — 5v.(4526p) ; 27cm. — (Macmillan reference books)
Includes index
ISBN 0-333-29393-2 : Unpriced B82-17272

016.5517'9 — Quaternary tephra — *Bibliographies*

World bibliography and index of quaternary tephra : supplement 1 / edited by Dorothy B. Vitaliano. — Norwich : Geo Books, c1982. — 194p ; 21cm. — (Geo Abstracts bibliography ; no.9)
Includes index
ISBN 0-86094-072-1 (pbk) : £7.10 B82-26928

016.5532'8 — Scotland. Grampian Region. Aberdeen. Public libraries: Aberdeen City Libraries. *Commercial and Technical Department.* **Stock: Documents on natural gas & petroleum** — *Catalogues*

Bibliography of material on oil and gas. — 3rd ed. / compiled by the staff of Aberdeen City Libraries. — [Aberdeen] ([Rosemount Viaduct, Aberdeen AB9 1GU]) : [City of Aberdeen, Libraries Department], 1981. — 101p ; 30cm
At head of title: Aberdeen City Libraries, Commercial and Technical Department. — Previous ed.: 1979
Unpriced (spiral) B82-01497

016.55716′22 — Nova Scotia. Halifax County. Geological features — *Bibliographies*

Leidemer, Nelle L.. Geology of Halifax County : a selected bibliography / compiled by Nelle L. Leidemer. — 2nd rev. ed. / revised by Fred Kennedy. — London : Vine, 1981. — 59p ; 28cm. — (Occasional paper / Dalhousie University School of Library Service, ISSN 0318-7403 ; 5)
ISBN 0-7703-0142-8 (pbk) : Unpriced B82-39321

016.5573 — United States. Geological features — *Bibliographies*

Corbin, John B.. An index of state geological survey publications issued in series / compiled by John B. Corbin. — Metuchen ; London : Scarecrow Press
Supplement 1963-1980. — 1982. — xi,449p ; 23cm
Includes index
ISBN 0-8108-1501-x : Unpriced B82-29213

016.565′7 — Quaternary strata. Fossil insects — *Bibliographies*

Buckland, P. C.. A bibliography of quaternary entomology / P.C. Buckland. — Birmingham : Department of Geography, University of Birmingham, 1980. — 25p : ill ; 30cm. — (Working paper series / University of Birmingham. Department of Geography ; no.11)
Cover title
ISBN 0-7044-0566-0 (pbk) : £0.60 B82-23559

016.574′028 — Biology. Use of ultrasonic waves — *Bibliographies*

Ultrasound in biomedicine : cumulative bibliography of the world literature in ultrasound in medicine and biology to 1978 / editors Denis White ... [et al.]. — Oxford : Pergamon, 1982. — 722p ; 25cm
ISBN 0-08-027374-2 : £50.00 : CIP rev.
Primary classification 016.61′028 B81-32602

016.574′.092′4 — Nottinghamshire. Nottingham. Universities. Libraries: University of Nottinghamshire. *Manuscripts Department.* **Stock: Correspondence of Pentland, Joseph: University of Nottingham.** *Manuscripts Department* — *Catalogues*

University of Nottingham. *Manuscripts Department.* The letters of Joseph Pentland to Rev. William Buckland, 1820-1822 / University of Nottingham, Manuscripts Department, University Library. — [Nottingham] : [University of Nottingham], [1981?]. — 4p ; 30cm
£1.00 (pbk) B82-06306

016.5742′9′028 — Immunology. Laboratory techniques. Automation — *Bibliographies*

Palmer, Wendy J.. Rapid & automated methods in microbiology & immunology : a bibliography : 1976-1980 / compiled & edited by Wendy J. Palmer ; advisor E.S. Krudy. — London : Information Retrieval, c1981. — 265p ; 23cm
Includes index
ISBN 0-904147-19-3 (pbk) : Unpriced
Primary classification 016.576′028 B82-41106

016.57487′3282 — Organisms. Recombinant DNA — *Abstracts* — *Serials*

Recombinant DNA. — Vol.1, no.1 (Jan. 1982)-. — Sheffield (Sheffield S10 2TN) : University of Sheffield Biomedical Information Service, 1982-. — v. ; 30cm
Monthly. — Description based on: Vol.1, no.5 (May 1982)
ISSN 0261-4979 = Recombinant DNA : £35.00 per year B82-38510

016.576′028 — Microbiology. Laboratory techniques. Automation — *Bibliographies*

Palmer, Wendy J.. Rapid & automated methods in microbiology & immunology : a bibliography : 1976-1980 / compiled & edited by Wendy J. Palmer ; advisor E.S. Krudy. — London : Information Retrieval, c1981. — 265p ; 23cm
Includes index
ISBN 0-904147-19-3 (pbk) : Unpriced
Also classified at 016.5742′9′028 B82-41106

016.58′05 — London. Richmond-upon-Thames *(London Borough).* **Botanical gardens. Libraries: Royal Botanic Gardens** *(Kew). Library.* **Stock: Serials** — *Catalogues* — *Serials*

Royal Botanic Gardens *(Kew). Library.* Current awareness list / Royal Botanic Gardens, Kew. Library. — No.1 (Jan. 1982)-. — [Kew] ([Kew, Surrey TW9 3AE]) : [The Library], 1982-. — v. ; 30cm
Monthly
ISSN 0263-4740 = Current awareness list - Royal Botanic Gardens Kew. Library : Unpriced B82-26148

016.59159 — Animals. Sounds. Sound recordings — *Discographies* — *For cinematography*

Kettle, Ron. Sources of natural sound for wildlife film-makers / by Ron Kettle, Dominic Couzens, Jeffery Boswall. — 2nd corrected impression. — [London] ([29 Exhibition Rd., SW7 2AS]) : British Library of Wildlife Sounds The British Institute of Recorded Sound, 1981. — 28p : 1map ; 30cm
Originally published: 1981. — Bibliography: p28
Unpriced (pbk) B82-11560

016.59901′9256 — Mammals. Proteinases — *Bibliographies*

McDonald, J. K.. Mammalian proteases : a glossary and bibliography. — London : Academic Press, July 1982
Vol.2. — [300]p
ISBN 0-12-079502-7 : CIP entry
Primary classification 599.01′9256 B82-12437

016.6 — Technology — *Bibliographies*

Grogan, Denis. Science and technology : an introduction to the literature / Denis Grogan. — 4th ed. — London : Bingley, 1982. — 400p ; 22cm
Previous ed.: 1976. — Includes bibliographies and index
ISBN 0-85157-315-0 (cased) : Unpriced : CIP rev.
ISBN 0-85157-340-1 (pbk) : Unpriced
Primary classification 016.5 B82-01165

Thomson, Alan W.. Books for BEC and TEC : a list of current and forthcoming titles / compiled by Alan W. Thomson. — Oxford : Seabrook, 1982. — [50]p ; 30cm
Includes index
ISBN 0-946104-00-x (pbk) : £2.50
Primary classification 016.658 B82-41109

016.6′014 — Technology. Terminology — *Bibliographies* — *Serials*

Catchword and trade name index (CATNI). — Vol.1, no.1 (Mar. 1981)-. — London : Library Association Publishing, 1981-. — v. ; 30cm
Quarterly, cumulated in Dec. issue. — Supplement to: CTI
ISSN 0261-0191 = Catchword and trade name index (CATNI) : £45.00 (to full subscribers to CTI)
Also classified at 016.6′0275 B82-15765

016.602′18 — Technology. Standards — *Lists*

Surrey and Sussex Libraries in Co-operation. Location key to British & foreign standards / compiled by Hilary Ingram, David Picken. — Worthing : Surrey & Sussex Libraries in Co-operation, 1980. — 24p ; 30cm
£3.50 (£2.50 to members of Saslic) (pbk) B82-36493

016.6′0275 — Technology. Trade names — *Bibliographies* — *Serials*

Catchword and trade name index (CATNI). — Vol.1, no.1 (Mar. 1981)-. — London : Library Association Publishing, 1981-. — v. ; 30cm
Quarterly, cumulated in Dec. issue. — Supplement to: CTI
ISSN 0261-0191 = Catchword and trade name index (CATNI) : £45.00 (to full subscribers to CTI)
Primary classification 016.6′014 B82-15765

016.6′05 — Technology. Serials with Japanese imprints — *Lists*

Gibson, Robert W.. Japanese scientific and technical literature : a subject guide / Robert W. Gibson, Jr. and Barbara K. Kunkel. — Aldershot : Gower, 1981. — xv,560p : ill ; 29cm
Bibliography: pxv. — Includes index
ISBN 0-566-00505-0 : Unpriced : CIP rev.
Primary classification 016.5′05 B81-34286

016.608 — Great Britain. National libraries: Science Reference Library. Stock: Serials on industrial property — *Catalogues*

Science Reference Library. Industrial property literature in the Science Reference Library : holdings from the UK, the European Patent Office and WIPO (PCT). — Revised [ed.]. — London : The Library, 1982. — 17p ; 30cm. — (Aids to readers, ISSN 0306-4301 ; no.26)
Previous ed.: 1980
Unpriced (pbk) B82-26623

016.60874 — European patents — *Abstracts, 1956-1981* — *Collections*

Fysh, Michael. Industrial property citator. — London : European Law Centre, Sept.1982. — [270]p
ISBN 0-907451-04-7 : £40.00 : CIP entry B82-21580

016.61 — Edinburgh. Libraries. Stock: Books on medicine: Books with European imprints: Books printed between 1500 & 1600 — *Catalogues*

Bird, D. T.. A catalogue of sixteenth-century medical books in Edinburgh libraries / compiled by D.T. Bird. — Edinburgh : Royal College of Physicians of Edinburgh, 1982. — xxxii,298p : ill,facsims ; 30cm
Includes index
ISBN 0-85405-039-6 : £45.00 B82-25033

016.61 — Essex. Chelmsford. Libraries: Graves Medical Audiovisual Library. Stock: Audiovisual aids on medicine — *Catalogues* — *Serials*

Graves Medical Audiovisual Library. Catalogue : audio-cassettes and slides / Graves Medical Audiovisual Library. — 1977-. — Chelmsford (PO Box 99, Chelmsford, Essex CM2 9BJ) : The Library, 1977-. — v. ; 30cm
Annual. — Continues: Royal College of General Practitioners. Medical Recording Service Foundation. Catalogue. — Description based on: Jan. 1979 issue
ISSN 0144-7610 = Catalogue - Graves Medical Audiovisual Library : Unpriced B82-25477

016.61 — Man. Medical aspects — *Bibliographies*

Sunday times self-help directory. — 2nd ed. — London : Granada, Apr.1982. — [320]p
Previous ed.: London : Times Newspapers, 1975
ISBN 0-246-11304-9 (pbk) : £3.95 : CIP entry
Primary classification 361′.0025′41 B82-04317

016.61 — Medicine — *Bibliographies*

Mathers, Nancy M.. The medical profession : a bibliography / Nancy M. Mathers. — [Leeds] : University of Leeds, Library of the Nuffield Centre for Health Services Studies, 1979. — 8p ; 30cm
Unpriced (pbk) B82-12954

Morton, Leslie T.. A medical bibliography (Garrison and Morton). — 4th ed. — Aldershot : Gower, July 1982. — [950]p. — (A Grafton book)
Previous ed.: London : Deutsch, 1970
ISBN 0-566-03438-7 : £37.50 : CIP entry B82-12977

016.61 — Medicine — *Bibliographies* — *Serials* — *For health visiting*

HVA current awareness bulletin. — No.1 (Oct 1981)-. — London (36 Ecclestone Sq., SW1V 1PF) : [Health Visitors′ Association], 1981-. — v.1 ; 30cm
Quarterly
ISSN 0262-172x = Current awareness bulletin - HVA : Unpriced B82-08453

016.610′28 — Great Britain. National Libraries: Science Reference Library. Stock : Documents on medical equipment — *Catalogues*

Oates, Judith. Medical equipment. — London : British Library, Science Reference Library, Nov.1981. — [12]p. — (Guidelines / Science Reference Library)
ISBN 0-902914-64-2 (pbk) : CIP entry B81-30884

016.610′28 — Medical equipment. Documents on medical equipment — *Catalogues*
Oates, Judith. Medical equipment. — 2nd ed. — London : British Library, Science Reference Library, Nov.1982. — [11]p. — (Guidelines (Science Reference Library), ISSN 0306-4298)
Previous ed.: 1981
ISBN 0-7123-0704-4 (pbk) : CIP entry B82-29435

016.61′028 — Medicine. Use of ultrasonic waves — *Bibliographies*
Ultrasound in biomedicine : cumulative bibliography of the world literature in ultrasound in medicine and biology to 1978 / editors Denis White ... [et al.]. — Oxford : Pergamon, 1982. — 722p ; 25cm
ISBN 0-08-027374-2 : £50.00 : CIP rev.
Also classified at 016.574′028 B81-32602

016.612′01522 — Man. Body fluids. Gas-liquid chromatography — *Bibliographies*
Signeur, Austin V.. Literature guide to the GLC of body fluids / Austin V. Signeur. — New York ; London : Plenum, c1982. — ix,385p ; 28cm. — (IFI data base library)
Includes index
ISBN 0-306-65203-x : Unpriced B82-31339

016.612′6′00880565 — Old persons. Sexuality — *Bibliographies*
Wharton, George F.. Sexuality and aging : an annotated bibliography / by George F. Wharton, III. — Metuchen, N.J. ; London : Scarecrow, 1981. — viii,251p : ill ; 23cm
Includes index
ISBN 0-8108-1427-7 : £12.00 B82-05356

016.612′78 — Man. Language skills. Physiological aspects — *Bibliographies*
Dingwall, William Orr. Language and the brain : a bibliography and guide / William Orr Dingwall. — New York ; London : Garland
Vol.2. — 1981. — viii,p595-1017 ; 23cm
Includes index
ISBN 0-8240-9495-6 : Unpriced B82-37174

016.6132 — Man. Diet — *Bibliographies*
Freedman, Robert L.. Human food uses : a cross-cultural comprehensive annotated bibliography / compiled by Robert L. Freedman. — Westport ; London : Greenwood Press, 1981. — xxxvii,552p ; 29cm
Includes index
ISBN 0-313-22901-5 : Unpriced B82-02822

016.6132′8 — Man. Diet. Role of fibre. Medical aspects — *Bibliographies*
Freuchen, Anne. The importance of fibre in the diet with special reference to the colon : a select annotated bibliography / Anne Freuchen. — London (St Mary′s Rd, Ealing, W5 5RF) : School of Library and Information Studies, Ealing College of Higher Education, c1981. — 23leaves ; 30cm. — (Ealing miscellany ; no.27)
Unpriced (unbound) B82-35095

016.6137 — Physical education. Theses accepted by British uiversities — *Lists*
Keighley, J. S.. PERDAS : 1950-1980 : a list of theses, dissertations and projects on physical education, recreation, dance, athletics and sport, presented at United Kingdom universities / compiled by J.S. Keighley. — Lancaster : LISE, 1981. — 184leaves ; 17x22cm
Cover title. — Previous ed.: published as Bibliography of studies in physical education / compiled by L.B. Hendry. London : Physical Education Association of Great Britain and Northern Ireland, 1973. — Text on inside cover. — Includes index
ISBN 0-901922-11-0 (pbk) : £4.50 B82-12108

016.6137′09 — Physical education, *to 1980*. Theses accepted by British universities — *Lists*
Cox, R. W.. Theses and dissertations of the history of sport, physical education, recreation and dance, approved for higher degrees and advanced diplomas in British Universities 1900-1981 / compiled by R.W. Cox. — [Liverpool] : [University of Liverpool], 1982. — 13,[16]p ; 30cm. — (Occasional publication ; no.1)
Includes index
Unpriced (spiral)
Also classified at 016.79′009 ; 016.796′09 B82-30890

Cox, R. W.. Theses for higher degrees in progress on the history of sport, physical education and recreation in British universities / R.W. Cox. — [Liverpool] : [University of Liverpool], 1982. — [4]leaves ; 30cm. — (Occasional publication ; no.2)
Unpriced (spiral)
Also classified at 016.79′009 ; 016.796′09 B82-30891

016.6137′0941 — Great Britain. Physical education, *to 1980*. Theses accepted by American universities — *Lists*
Cox, R. W.. American theses on the history of British sport and physical education / R.W. Cox. — [Liverpool] : [University of Liverpool], 1982. — 4leaves ; 30cm. — (Occasional publication ; no.3)
Unpriced (spiral)
Also classified at 016.796′0941 B82-30889

016.6138′5 — Tobacco smoking. Health aspects — *Bibliographies*
Berton, Alberta D.. Smoking and health : a comprehensive bibliography / compiled by Alberta D. Berton, assisted by K. Bernice Odom. — New York ; London : IFI/Plenum, c1980. — 530p ; 28cm. — (Biomedical information guides ; v.3)
ISBN 0-306-65184-x : Unpriced B82-35684

016.6139′432 — Oral contraceptives — *Abstracts*
Kolbe, Helen K.. Oral contraceptives abstracts : a guide to the literature, 1977-1979 / compiled from the PoPLINE data base by Helen K. Kolbe. — New York ; London : IFI/Plenum, c1980. — 563p ; 28cm. — (Population information library ; v.2)
Includes index
ISBN 0-306-65192-0 : Unpriced B82-40741

016.6139′435 — Intrauterine devices — *Abstracts*
Kolbe, Helen K.. Intrauterine devices abstracts : a guide to the literature, 1976-1979 / compiled from the PoPLINE data base by Helen K. Kolbe. — New York ; London : IFI/Plenum, c1980. — 571p ; 28cm. — (Population information library ; v.1)
Includes index
ISBN 0-306-65191-2 : Unpriced B82-40740

016.6139′5′07 — Sex education — *Bibliographies*
Speight, A. Edwin. Sex education : a guide to resources / A. Edwin Speight. — Sheffield : Sheffield City Libraries, 1982. — 135p ; 21cm
Includes index
ISBN 0-900660-82-1 (pbk) : £4.95 B82-21780

016.6144′4 — Hospitals. Patients. Nosocomial infections — *Abstracts* — *Serials*
Hospital acquired infection : a selection of abstracts from the literature on hospital-acquired infection and its control. — Vol.1, no.1 (1981)-. — London ([2 Queen Anne St., W.1.]) : Royal Society of Medicine, 1981-. — v. ; 25cm
Two issues yearly
ISSN 0262-2173 = Hospital acquired infection : Unpriced B82-12465

016.615′1 — Drugs — *Bibliographies*
Londos, Eutychia G.. Compendium of current source materials for drugs / by Eutychia G. Londos. — Metuchen ; London : Scarecrow, 1982. — ii,140p ; 28cm
Includes index
ISBN 0-8108-1507-9 (pbk) : £10.00 B82-24794

016.615′31 — Drugs. Constituents. Polymers — *Bibliographies*
Pharmaceutical applications of polymers : a selected bibliography / edited by Richard Juniper. — Shrewsbury : Rubber and Plastics Research Association, c1981. — x,245p ; 21cm
Includes index
ISBN 0-902348-23-x (pbk) : Unpriced B82-17637

016.6155′8 — Medicine. Drug therapy. Documents on drug therapy — *Indexes*
Fukushima, Hiroyuki. Index guide to rational drug therapy / Hiroyuki Fukushima, Toshiro Okazaki, Michiko Noguchi. — Amsterdam ; Oxford : Excerpta Medica, 1982. — xvi,387p ; 25cm
Includes index
ISBN 90-219-3074-9 : Unpriced
ISBN 0-444-90273-2 (Elsevier Science) B82-32387

016.61607′575 — Nuclear medicine — *Bibliographies*
Berton, Alberta D.. Nuclear medicine : a comprehensive bibliography / compiled by Alberta D. Berton assisted by K. Bernice Odom. — New York ; London : IFI/Plenum, c1980. — 351p ; 28cm. — (Biomedical information guides ; v.2)
ISBN 0-306-65178-5 : Unpriced B82-35685

016.6161 — Man. Cardiovascular system. Diseases — *Bibliographies* — *Serials*
Current medical literature. Cardiovascular medicine / the Royal Society of Medicine. — Vol.1, no.1 (Oct. 1981)-. — London ([2 Queen Anne St., W1M 0BR]) : The Society, 1981-. — v. ; 25cm
Six issues yearly
ISSN 0261-3352 = Current medical literature. Cardiovascular medicine : £15.00 per year B82-15158

016.6163′005 — Man. Digestive system. Diseases — *Abstracts* — *Serials*
Current medical literature. Gastroenterology / the Royal Society of Medicine. — Vol.1, no.1 (June 1982)-. — London ([2 Queen Anne St, W.1]) : The Society, 1982-. — v. ; 25cm
Six issues yearly
ISSN 0263-2659 = Current medical literature. Gastroenterology : £15.00 per year B82-40069

016.6163′65 — Man. Gall bladder. Cholesterol gallstones. Therapy. Use of chenodeoxycholic acid — *Bibliographies*
Hofmann, Alan F.. Bile, bile acids, gallstones and gallstone dissolution. — Lancaster : MTP Press, Dec.1982. — [330]p
ISBN 0-85200-497-4 : £19.50 : CIP entry B82-35230

016.6164′62 — Man. Diabetes. Conference proceedings — *Abstracts*
Belfiore, Francesco. Reviewed contents of major diabetes congresses / Francesco Belfiore. — Basel ; London : Karger, 1981. — vii,162p ; 25cm. — (Frontiers in diabetes ; v.1)
Bibliography: p118-151. — Includes index
ISBN 3-8055-3414-0 : £28.30 B82-11589

016.6166′3 — Man. Incontinence — *Bibliographies*
Mandelstam, Dorothy. Incontinence : bibliography / compiled by Dorothy Mandelstam, Philippa Lane. — London : Disabled Living Foundation, c1981. — 104p ; 30cm
Includes index
ISBN 0-906544-06-8 (pbk) : Unpriced : CIP rev. B81-30278

016.61689′07′078 — Great Britain. Higher education institutions. Curriculum subjects: Medicine. Psychopathology. Teaching aids: Audiovisual materials — *Lists*
Tite, Catherine. A guide to media resources in psychopathology / by Catherine Tite. — London : LLRS Publications, 1982. — i,26p ; 30cm
Includes index
ISBN 0-904264-63-7 (pbk) : Unpriced : CIP rev. B82-14397

016.61689′156 — Medicine. Family therapy — *Bibliographies*
Family therapy and research : an annotated bibliography of articles, books, videotapes, and films published 1950-1979 / Ira D. Glick ... [et al.]. — 2nd ed. — New York ; London : Grune & Stratton, c1982. — xi,308p ; 27cm
Previous ed.: 1971. — Includes index
ISBN 0-8089-1431-6 : £26.20 B82-27133

016.62'000425'02854 — Engineering. Design. Applications of computer systems — *Bibliographies*

Computer aided design : an introductory bibliography / edited by J. Acland and D. Lane. — London : The Library, The Institution of Electrical Engineers, 1981. — 1v (various pagings) ; 21cm
Includes index
ISBN 0-85296-255-x (pbk) : £10.00
B82-22835

016.62'0009417 — Ireland *(Republic).* **Engineering,** *1760-1980 — Bibliographies*

Hughes, Noel J.. Irish engineering 1760-1960 / Noel J. Hughes. — [Dublin] : Institution of Engineers of Ireland, 1982. — viii,159p : ill,facsims,maps,plans ; 21cm
Includes index
ISBN 0-9502359-1-1 (pbk) : £6.00 B82-33660

016.6201'06 — Fluid engineering — *Bibliographies — Serials*

Current fluid engineering titles. — Vol.1, issue 1 (1981)-. — Cranfield : BHRA Fluid Engineering, 1981-. — v. ; 21cm
Monthly
ISSN 0261-2437 = Current fluid engineering titles : £110.00 per year B82-06787

016.6201'1296 — Materials. Thermal properties — *Bibliographies*

Thermophysical properties research literature retrieval guide : 1900-1980 / editors J.F. Chaney ... [et al.]. — New York ; London : IFI/Plenum
Text on inside covers
Vol.1: Elements. — c1982. — 801p in various pagings ; 29cm
ISBN 0-306-67221-9 : Unpriced B82-29962

Thermophysical properties research literature retrieval guide : 1900-1980 / editors J.F. Chaney ... [et al.]. — New York ; London : IFI/Plenum
Text on inside covers
Vol.2: Inorganic compounds. — c1982. — 1092p in various pagings ; 29cm
ISBN 0-306-67222-7 : Unpriced B82-29963

Thermophysical properties research literature retrieval guide : 1900-1980 / editors J.F. Chaney ... [et al.]. — New York ; London : IFI/Plenum
Text on inside covers
Vol.3: Organic compounds and polymeric materials. — c1982. — 628p in various pagings ; 29cm
ISBN 0-306-67223-5 : Unpriced B82-29964

Thermophysical properties research literature retrieval guide : 1900-1980 / editors J.F. Chaney ... [et al.]. — New York ; London : IFI/Plenum
Text on inside covers
Vol.4: Alloys, intermetallic compounds, and cermets. — c1982. — 734p in various pagings ; 29cm
ISBN 0-306-67224-3 : Unpriced B82-29965

016.6202'3 — Noise — *Bibliographies*

Great Britain. *Departments of the Environment and Transport Library.* Noise : a select list of supplementary material based on D.O.E./D.Tp. Library / edited by Claire M. Lambert. — London (2 Marsham St., SW1P 3EB) : Departments of the Environment and Transport, c1980. — 18p : ill ; 30cm. — (Bibliography series / Headquarters Library. Department of the Environment, Department of Transport ; no.148e, suppl.1)
Unpriced (pbk) B82-36203

016.62'04162 — Offshore engineering — *Bibliographies*

Myers, Arnold. Current bibliography of offshore technology and offshore literature classification / Arnold Myers. — Berkhamsted : ASR Marketing, 1981. — v,93p ; 30cm
Includes index
ISBN 0-906528-01-1 (pbk) : Unpriced
B82-04268

016.6213'05 — Great Britain. Electrical engineering. Research organisations. Information centres: ERA Technology Ltd.. *Information Centre.* **Stock: Serials —** *Catalogues*

ERA Technology Ltd.. *Information Centre.* Periodicals holdings / Information Centre. — Leatherhead (Cleeve Rd., Leatherhead, Surrey KT22 7SA) : ERA Technology, 1982. — 16,viip ; 30cm
Unpriced (spiral) B82-27382

016.62131'2134 — Electricity supply. Generation by wave power — *Bibliographies*

Hughes, Fay E.. Wave power : a select bibliography. — [Birmingham] ([Chamberlain Sq, Birmingham B3 3HQ]) : [Science and Technology Dept, Central Library], [198-]. — 22p ; 30cm. — (Technical bibliographies / Birmingham Public Libraries, ISSN 0308-4191 ; 13)
Compiled by Fay E. Hughes
£3.66 (unbound) B82-26627

016.621319'3 — Electric equipment. Conductors. Patents — *Abstracts*

Cables, conductors, insulators : materials. — London (128 Theobalds Rd, WC1X 8RP) : Derwent, c1982. — 561p : ill ; 30cm. — (Electrical patents abridgments. Series 1 ; 1975-79)
Unpriced (pbk) B82-39894

016.62137 — Electric measuring instruments. Patents — *Abstracts*

Measuring electric variables : general. — London : Derwent, c1982. — 1v(various pagings) : ill ; 30cm. — (Electrical patents abridgements. Series 1)
Unpriced (pbk) B82-30523

016.6213815 — Digital electronic equipment. Design. Applications of digital computer systems — *Bibliographies*

vanCleemput, W. M.. Computer aided design of digital systems : a bibliography / [compiled by] W.M. vanCleemput. — London : Pitman. — (Digital system design series)
Includes index
Vol.4: 1977-79. — 1979, c1980. — viii,196p : ill ; 28cm
ISBN 0-273-08451-8 (pbk) : Unpriced
B82-01878

016.6213815'2 — Semiconductor devices. Implementation of ions — *Bibliographies*

Agajanian, A. H.. Ion implantation in microelectronics : a comprehensive bibliography / A.H. Agajanian. — New York ; London : IFI/Plenum, c1981. — x,255p ; 26cm. — (Computer science information guides ; v.1)
Includes index
ISBN 0-306-65198-x : Unpriced B82-02765

016.621381'71 — Microelectronic devices — *Bibliographies*

Bibliography on microelectronics applications / MAP. — [London] ([MAP Information Centre, Room 524, Dean Bradley House, 52 Horseferry Rd., S.W.1]) : MAP, 1981. — 30p ; 30cm
Cover title
Unpriced (pbk) B82-38329

Information technology : a bibliography. — [London] ([123 Victoria St., SW1E 6RB]) : Department of Industry Ashdown House Library, c1982. — 61p ; 30cm. — (Industry bibliographies ; 1982/1)
Unpriced (pbk) B82-38331

016.6213819'5833 — Digital computers. Magnetic discs. Patents — *Abstracts*

Dynamic information storage : disc drives : general. — London (128 Theobalds Rd, WC1X 8RP) : Derwent, c1982. — 537p : ill ; 30cm. — (Electrical patents abridgments. Series 1 ; 1975-79)
Unpriced (pbk) B82-39893

016.6213819'5833 — Digital computers. Static storage devices. Patents — *Abstracts*

Static information storage. — London (128 Theobalds Rd, WC1X 8RP) : Derwent, c1982. — 2v. : ill ; 30cm. — (Electrical patents abridgments. Series 1 ; 1975-79)
Unpriced (pbk) B82-39892

016.6213841'51 — Amateur radio equipment. Serial articles — *Indexes*

Weston, Colin. Amateur radio equipment index / Colin Weston. — Aberdeen (14 Abbotshall Place, Cults, Aberdeen AB1 9JB) : Amber Documentation Centre, c1982. — 18p ; 30cm
£2.00 (pbk) B82-25013

016.621385'09'04 — London. Libraries. Stock: Books on telephony, *1878-1940 — Catalogues*

Cave, J. F.. Telephony 1878-1940 : a bibliographic guide to six major holdings of books in London / compiled by J.F. Cave. — Barnet (Trent Park, Cock Fosters Rd, Barnet, Herts.) : Middlesex Polytechic, 1980. — 22leaves ; 31cm
Unpriced (pbk) B82-11045

016.621389'32 — Scotland. Educational technology. Information services: Scottish Council for Educational Technology. *Information Service.* **Stock: Serial articles on sound recording —** *Catalogues*

Scottish Council for Educational Technology. *Information Service.* Journal articles on audio : articles appearing in the S.C.E.T. Information Service's holdings of journals dated October 1980-May 1981, received by the S.C.E.T. Information Service by May 1981 / compiled by Jo Crozier. — Glasgow : The Service, 1981. — 15p ; 26cm. — (SCET journals bibliography, ISSN 0260-972x ; no.1)
ISBN 0-86011-039-7 (unbound) : £0.25
B82-22377

Scottish Council for Educational Technology. *Information Service.* Journal articles on audio (2) : articles appearing in the S.C.E.T. Information Service's holdings of journals dated June 1981-November 1981, received by the S.C.E.T. Information Service by November 1981 / compiled by Andrew Foley. — [Glasgow] : [The Service], 1981. — 6p ; 30cm. — (SCET journals bibliography, ISSN 0260-972x ; no.5)
ISBN 0-86011-046-x (unbound) : £0.25
B82-22372

016.6214 — Great Britain. Alternative energy sources — *Bibliographies*

Alternative energy sources for the United Kingdom : a selection of recent publications. — London (Thames House South, Millbank, SW1P 4QT) : Department of Energy Library, c1978. — 8p ; 21cm. — (Energy bibliographies ; 1978/1)
Includes index
Unpriced (pbk) B82-35797

016.6214 — Stirling engines — *Bibliographies*

Jankowska, Elizabeth. The Stirling Engine : a select bibliography / [compiled by Elizabeth Jankowska and others]. — [Birmingham] ([Paradise Circus, Birmingham B3 3HQ]) : [Science and Technology Department, Central Library], [1981?]. — 12p ; 30cm. — (Technical bibliographies / Birmingham Public Libraries, ISSN 0308-4191 ; 12)
Cover title. — Text on inside covers
Unpriced (pbk) B82-08843

016.62147'0973 — United States. Solar energy. Government publications — *Lists*

McAninch, Sandra. Sun power : a bibliography of United States Government documents on solar energy / compiled by Sandra McAninch. — Westport, Conn. ; London : Greenwood Press, 1981. — xx,944p ; 25cm
Includes index
ISBN 0-313-20992-8 : Unpriced B82-02229

016.62148 — Nuclear power — *Bibliographies*

Chester, Kerry. Nuclear energy and the nuclear industry. — London : British Library, Science Reference Library, Oct.1982. — [35]p. — (Guidelines, ISSN 0306-4298)
ISBN 0-7123-0703-6 (pbk) : CIP entry
B82-28569

016.62148'38 — Radioactive waste materials. Disposal — *Abstracts*

Heckman, Richard A.. Nuclear waste management abstracts / Richard A. Heckman and Camille Minichino. — New York ; London : IFI/Plenum, c1982. — 104p : ill ; 28cm. — (IFI data base library)
Includes index
ISBN 0-306-65202-1 : Unpriced B82-28814

016.6219'3 — Jet cutting — *Abstracts*

Jet cutting technology / a review & bibliography ; editor Robin Brown ; reviewers R.D. Lee ... [et al.]. — Cranfield : BHRA Fluid Engineering, [1982?]. — 188p : ill ; 30cm. — (BHRA fluid engineering series ; v.9)
Includes index
ISBN 0-906085-64-0 (pbk) : Unpriced : CIP rev. B82-05779

016.6238 — London. Greenwich *(London Borough).* **Museums: National Maritime Museum. Stock: Manuscripts** — *Catalogues*

National Maritime Museum. Guide to the manuscripts in the National Maritime Museum. — London : Mansell
Vol.2: Public records, business records and artificial collections / edited by R.J.B. Knight. — 1980. — xxxiii,216p : 1facsim ; 25cm
Includes index
ISBN 0-7201-1591-4 : £17.50 B82-02834

016.624 — Great Britain. Civil engineering. Organisations: Institution of Civil Engineers. Publications — *Indexes*

Holmstrom, J. Edwin. Analytical index to the publications of the Institution of Civil Engineers, January 1975-December 1979 / compiled by J. Edwin Holmstrom. — London : Institution of Civil Engineers, c1979. — 164p ; 22cm
ISBN 0-7277-0116-9 : £10.00 B82-18030

016.6241'042 — Quantity surveying — *Abstracts*

Harlow, P. A.. A decade of quantity surveying : review of the literature 1970-1979 / compiled by P.A. Harlow. — Ascot : Institute of Building, 1980. — 82p ; 30cm
Includes index
ISBN 0-906600-28-6 (pbk) : £3.50 (£2.80 to members of the Institute) B82-39538

016.6241'5136 — London. Westminster *(London Borough).* **Universities. Libraries: Imperial College of Science and Technology Department of Civil Engineering.** *Library.* **Stock: Documents on soil mechanics** — *Catalogues*

Imperial College of Science and Technology. A bibliographical catalogue of the collection of works on soil mechanics 1764-1950 / A.W. Skempton. — London : Imperial College, 1981. — 73p : ill,facsims ; 24cm
Limited ed. of 200 copies. — Includes index
Unpriced B82-06395

016.6252'61'0941 — Great Britain. Steam locomotives. Sound recordings — *Discographies*

Palm, Jim. Railways on record / Tim Palm. — Weston-Super-Mare : Avon Anglia, c1980. — 128p ; 21cm
ISBN 0-905466-36-5 (pbk) : £7.50 B82-11038

Palm, Jim. Railways on record / compiled by Jim Palm. — Weston-Super-Mare : Avon Anglia
Appendix 2: [Additions March 1980 to December 1981]. — c1982. — 14p ; 21cm
ISBN 0-905466-50-0 (unbound) : Unpriced B82-40241

016.627 — Solids. Hydraulic transport — *Bibliographies*

International Cargo Handling Co-ordination Association. Bulk cargoes : handling and transport of solids by slurry systems and pipeline / compiler Peter R. Law. — London : International Cargo Handling Co-ordination Association, 1981. — 4p ; 30cm. — (Information service library bibliography ; no.21) (An ICHCA information access publication)
ISBN 0-906297-21-4 (pbk) : £4.00 (£2.00 to members) B82-20700

016.6298'92 — Industrial robots — *Bibliographies*

Industrial robotics : a bibliography / edited by D. Lane and J. Acland. — London : Library, Institution of Electrical Engineers, 1981. — [146]p ; 30cm
ISBN 0-85296-249-5 (spiral) : £10.50 B82-09924

016.63'05 — Great Britain. National libraries: Science Reference Library. Stock: Serials on agriculture — *Catalogues*
Science Reference Library. Periodicals on agriculture held by the Science Reference Library. — London : Science Reference Library
Pt.1: Agricultural research and industry / G. Jackson. — [1981?]. — v,[78p]p ; 21x30cm
Cover title. — Includes index
ISBN 0-902914-66-9 (pbk) : Unpriced : CIP rev. B81-32005

016.63'0941 — Great Britain. Agriculture, *1793-1839* — *Bibliographies*
Fussell, G. E.. The old English farming books. — London (35 Palace Court, W2 4LS) : Pindar Press
Vol.3: 1793-1839. — Oct.1981. — [304]p
ISBN 0-907132-03-0 : £27.00 : CIP entry B81-27994

016.632'58 — Agricultural industries. Smallholdings. Crops. Weeds. Control measures — *Bibliographies*
Compton, J. A. F.. Small farm weed control : an annotated bibliography / compiled and edited by J.A.F. Compton. — London : Intermediate Technology Development Group, 1982. — iv,170p ; 28cm
£4.95 (pbk) B82-29323

016.6331'197 — Developing countries. Pre-harvest wheat. Pests: Insects. Control — *Bibliographies*
Southam, E.. Insect pests of pre-harvest wheat and their control in the developing world : 1975-1980 / compiled by E. Southam and P. Schofield. — London : Centre for Overseas Pest Research, 1981. — 62p ; 30cm. — (COPR information service annotated bibliographies series ; no.1)
ISBN 0-85135-124-7 (pbk) : £13.00 B82-33069

016.6333'043 — Crops: Legumes. Pollination by insects — *Bibliographies*
Woyke, H. W.. Insect pollination of papilionaceae vegetable crops. — London : International Bee Research Association, Dec.1981. — 1v.. — (IBRA bibliography ; no.28)
ISBN 0-86098-096-0 : £4.00 : CIP entry B81-30907

016.6349 — Forestry — *Bibliographies*
Helliwell, Dennis Rodney. Options in forestry. — Funtington : Packard, Apr.1982. — 1v.
ISBN 0-906527-08-2 (cased) : £4.95 : CIP entry
ISBN 0-906527-09-0 (pbk) : £2.50 B82-14198

016.635'61 — Pepos. Pollination by insects — *Bibliographies*
Woyke, H. W.. Insect pollination of Cucurbitaceae vegetable crops. — London : International Bee Research Association, Sept.1981. — 1v.. — (IBRA bibliography ; no.27)
ISBN 0-86098-095-2 : £6.00 : CIP entry B81-25663

016.6361 — Connecticut. New Haven. Art galleries: Yale Center for British Art. Stock: Books on horses as livestock. Collections: Paul Mellon Collection — *Catalogues*
Podeschi, John B.. Books on the horse and horsemanship : riding, hunting, breeding & racing 1400-1941 / a catalogue compiled by John B. Podeschi. — London : Tate Gallery for the Yale Center for British Art, 1981. — xvii,427p,[18]leaves of plates : ill(some col.),2maps,music,facsims,1plan,ports (some col.),1geneal.table ; 30cm. — (The Paul Mellon collection) (Sport in art and books)
Bibliography: pxvii. — Includes index
ISBN 0-905005-53-8 : Unpriced B82-22082

016.6361 — Great Britain. National libraries: Science Reference Library. Stock: Documents on horses as livestock — *Catalogues*
Science Reference Library. Bloodstock, equine breeds and types : sources of information and the literature of husbandry and management. — London : [Science Reference Library], [1979]. — 23p ; 30cm. — (Guideline / Science Reference Library)
Stock held by the Science Reference Library
ISBN 0-902914-50-2 (unbound) : Unpriced : CIP rev.
Also classified at 016.6361'6 B79-28367

016'.636'1 — Livestock: Horses, *1851-1967* — *Bibliographies*
Grimshaw, Anne. Hippobibliography 1851-1967. — London : Library Association, Dec.1981. — [372]p
ISBN 0-85365-533-2 : £35.00 : CIP entry B81-31725

016.6361 — Livestock: Horses — *Bibliographies*
Smith, Myson J.. Equestrian studies : the Salem College guide to sources in English, 1950-1980 / Myron J. Smith, Jr. — Metuchen, N.J. ; London : Scarecrow, 1981. — x,361p : 1port ; 23cm
Includes index
ISBN 0-8108-1423-4 : £14.00 B82-05355

016.6361'6 — Great Britain. National libraries: Science Reference Library. Stock: Documents on ponies as livestock — *Catalogues*
Science Reference Library. Bloodstock, equine breeds and types : sources of information and the literature of husbandry and management. — London : [Science Reference Library], [1979]. — 23p ; 30cm. — (Guideline / Science Reference Library)
Stock held by the Science Reference Library
ISBN 0-902914-50-2 (unbound) : Unpriced : CIP rev.
Primary classification 016.6361 B79-28367

016.638'1 — Books on bee-keeping — *Lists*
International Bee Research Association. Apicultural reference books for developing countries. — Gerrards Cross : International Bee Research Association, Apr.1982. — [8]p. — (Source materials for apiculture ; no.8)
ISBN 0-86098-118-5 (pbk) : £1.00 : CIP entry B82-16504

016.638'1'05 — Bee-keeping. Serials — *Lists*
International Bee Research Association. List of serial publications : that have provided material relevant to bees and beekeeping : with their standard abbreviations currently used by the International Bee Research Association. — Gerrards Cross : The Association, 1978. — 91p ; 30cm
ISBN 0-86098-056-1 (pbk) : £8.50 B82-37311

016.638'142 — Bee-keeping equipment. Standards — *Bibliographies*
World-wide standards for hive products except honey and for equipment used in beekeeping and in processing hive products. — London : International Bee Research Association, 1979. — 12p ; 31cm. — (IBRA bibliography ; no.24)
ISBN 0-86098-021-9 (pbk) : £3.00 : CIP rev.
Primary classification 016.638'16 B79-36622

016.638'16 — Hive products. Standards — *Bibliographies*
World-wide standards for hive products except honey and for equipment used in beekeeping and in processing hive products. — London : International Bee Research Association, 1979. — 12p ; 31cm. — (IBRA bibliography ; no.24)
ISBN 0-86098-021-9 (pbk) : £3.00 : CIP rev.
Also classified at 016.638'142 B79-36622

016.6399'0941 — Great Britain. Urban regions. Nature conservation — *Bibliographies*
New life for old space : a guide to handbooks and leaflets covering the principles and methods of converting small urban sites into nature areas in Britain. — Rev. — London (c/o The Linnean Society, Burlington House, Piccadilly, W.1) : Produced by the Ecological Parks Trust in association with the Nature Conservancy Council, 1982. — [8]p : ill ; 30cm
Unpriced (unbound) B82-29311

016.64 — Home economics. Books in English: Books published 1700-1800 — *Lists*
Maclean, Virginia. A short-title catalogue of household and cookery books published in the English tongue 1701-1800 / Virginia Maclean. — London : Prospect, 1981. — xxiv,197p : facsims ; 28cm
Includes index
ISBN 0-907325-06-8 : £20.00 B82-08611

016.6413'009 — Food, *to 1981* — *Bibliographies*
Sutton, David C.. The history of food : a preliminary bibliography of printed sources / compiled by David C. Sutton. — Coventry : Chapelfields, 1982. — 24p ; 22cm
ISBN 0-86279-019-0 (pbk) : £1.00 B82-13379

016.658 — Business studies — *Bibliographies*
Thomson, Alan W.. Books for BEC and TEC : a list of current and forthcoming titles / compiled by Alan W. Thomson. — Oxford : Seabrook, 1982. — [50]p ; 30cm
Includes index
ISBN 0-946104-00-x (pbk) : £2.50
Also classified at 016.6 B82-41109

016.658 — Management — *Bibliographies — For librarianship*
Baldwin, Clive. Management : a selected annotated bibliography / compiled by Clive Baldwin and Marsaili Cameron. — Bradford : MCB, c1979. — 89p ; 25cm
ISBN 0-905440-89-7 (pbk) : Unpriced
B82-22044

016.658 — Management. Theses accepted by British universities — *Lists — Serials*
Selected list of U.K. theses and dissertations in management studies. — 1975-. — [Henley-on-Thames] ([Greenlands, Henley-on-Thames, Oxon RG9 3AU]) : [Administrative Staff College Library], 1976-. — v. ; 21cm
Annual. — Sponsored by: British Business Schools Libraries Group. — Description based on: 1980 issue
ISSN 0140-7414 = Selected list of U.K. theses and dissertations in management studies : Unpriced B82-19858

016.658'00722 — Management. Case studies — *Bibliographies*
Cases in management : a select bibliography. — Cranfield : Case Clearing House of Great Britain and Ireland
Vol.2. — c1981. — xxviii,259p ; 30cm
ISBN 0-907815-00-6 (pbk) : Unpriced : CIP rev. B82-01352

016.658'022'0941 — Great Britain. Small firms. Organisation — *Bibliographies*
Shipp, Jennifer. Starting your own business : a bibliographical guide / [compiled by] Jennifer Shipp. — Biggleswade (8 Ashby Drive, Caldecote, Biggleswade, Beds. SG18 9DJ) : Clover, c1982. — 109p ; 21cm
£4.60 (spiral) B82-40178

016.6583'124 — Organisations. Personnel. Training — *Abstracts — Serials*
APTT : abstracts on productivity, technology and training. — No.1 (July 1982)-. — Camberley (Chynoweth, Crawley Ridge, Camberley, Surrey GU15 2AJ) : John Russell Associates, 1982-. — v. ; 30cm
Six issues yearly
ISSN 0263-2349 = APTT. Abstracts on productivity, technology and training : Unpriced B82-38540

016.6584'071244 — Great Britain. Managers. Industrial training. Curriculum subjects: Industrial relations. Teaching aids: Audiovisual materials — *Lists*
Employment Relations Ltd.. Industrial relations training : catalogue of audio visual materials. — Cambridge (62, Hills Rd, Cambridge, CB2 1LA) : Employment Relations, 1981. — 176p ; 21cm
Includes index
Unpriced (pbk) B82-25961

016.6588'3 — Great Britain. National libraries: Science Reference Library. Stock: Market research surveys — *Catalogues*
Science Reference Library. Market research and industry surveys : a classified list of books and periodicals held by the Science Reference Library / E. Barta. — London : The Library, [1982]. — 66p ; 30cm
ISBN 0-902914-63-4 (pbk) : £4.00 : CIP rev.
B81-34960

016.6602 — Chemical vapour deposition — *Bibliographies*
Hawkins, Donald T.. Chemical vapor deposition, 1960-1980 : a bibliography / edited by Donald T. Hawkins ; with a foreword by McDonald Robinson. — New York ; London : IFI/Plenum, c1981. — xi,737p : 1ill ; 28cm. — (IFI data base library)
Includes index
ISBN 0-306-65201-3 : Unpriced B82-14548

016.6602'8425 — Vapour-liquid equilibria. Technical data — *Bibliographies*
Wichterle, Ivan. Vapor-liquid equilibrium data bibliography: supplement III. — Oxford : Elsevier Scientific, July 1982. — [322]p
ISBN 0-444-42097-5 : CIP entry B82-21371

016.662'6 — Energy sources: Biomass — *Abstracts — Serials*
Biomass abstracts / IEA Biomass Conversion Technical Information Service. — Vol.5, no.4 (Oct. 1981)-. — [Dublin] ([Institute for Industrial Research and Standards, Ballymun Road, Dublin 9]) : The Service, 1981-. — v. ; 29cm
Prepared by: the Information Technology Group of the Institute for Industrial Research and Standards in conjunction with the National Board for Science and Technology. — Continues: Current awareness bulletin (IEA Biomass Conversion Technical Information Service)
Unpriced B82-27647

016.6626'24 — Coal. Transport — *Bibliographies*
International Cargo Handling Co-ordination Association. Transport and handling of coal / compiler Peter R. Law. — London : International Cargo Handling Co-ordination Association, 1981. — 7p ; 30cm. — (Information service library bibliography ; no.3) (An ICHCA information access publication)
ISBN 0-906297-23-0 (pbk) : £4.00 (£2.00 to members) B82-20699

016.662'65 — Fuels: Wood & wood waste — *Abstracts*
Retrospective search on wood stoves / prepared by the Information Technology Group of the Institute for Industrial Research and Standards, Ireland, in conjunction with the National Board for Science and Technology. — [Dublin] : IEA Biomass Conversion Technical Information Service, 1980. — 134p ; 30cm
Unpriced (pbk) B82-35951

016.664'028 — Great Britain. Food. Commercial preservation. Research organisations: Campden Food Preservation Research Association. Publications, *1950-1980* — *Lists*
Campden Food Preservation Research Association. List of publications 1950-1980. — Chipping Campden (Chipping Campden, Gloucestershire, GL55 6LD) : Campden Food Preservation Research Association, [1980]. — [69]p : ill,facsims ; 30cm
Cover title. — Includes index
Unpriced (pbk) B82-14887

016.6684'226 — Epoxy powder coatings — *Bibliographies*
Chandler, R. H.. New epoxy powder coatings 1973-1979 / by R.H. Chandler. — Braintree (P.O. Box 55, Braintree, Essex) : R.H. Chandler, c1979. — ii,92p : ill ; 30cm. — (Bibliographies in paint technology, ISSN 0067-7094 ; no.33)
Bibliography: p44-86. — Includes index
Unpriced (pbk) B82-02541

016.669'141 — Great Britain. Iron. Production. Use of coke — *Bibliographies*
Dobson, Philippa. The 250th anniversary of the first successful use of coke in ironmaking : a select bibliography / Philippa Dobson. — London (St Mary's Rd, Ealing, W5 5RF) : School of Library and Information Studies, Ealing College of Higher Education, c1981. — 12leaves ; 30cm. — (Ealing miscellany ; no.25)
Includes index
Unpriced (unbound) B82-35092

016.674'134 — Wood. Chemical properties — *Abstracts*
Retrospective search on wood and wood residues as a source of chemcials [i.e chemicals] / prepared by the Information Technology Group of the Institute for Industrial Research and Standards, Ireland in conjunction with the National Board for Science and Technology. — Dublin : IEA Biomass Conversion, Technical Information Service, 1980. — 219p ; 30cm
Unpriced (pbk) B82-35057

016.683'82 — Cutlery — *Bibliographies*
Cutlery : a bibliography. — 2nd ed. / compiled by Sylvia Pybus, Marie Bairstow, Elizabeth Wright and others. — Sheffield : Sheffield City Libraries, 1982. — 69p ; 31cm
Previous ed.: 1961
ISBN 0-900660-84-8 (pbk) : £2.50 B82-36783

016.6841 — Furniture. Manufacture — *Bibliographies*
Furniture Industry Research Association. *Library*. Furniture literature 1979-1981 / compiled by Patricia Bristow. — Stevenage (Maxwell Rd., Stevenage, Herts. SG1 2EW) : Furniture Industry Research Association, [1982?]. — 244p ; 30cm
Stock of the Furniture Industry Research Association Library
£15.00 (£7.50 to members) (spiral) B82-41138

016.69'0068'1 — Buildings. Design. Life cycle costing
Building Services Research and Information Association. Life cycle & failure data. — Bracknell : Building Services Research and Information Association, 1982. — 4p ; 30cm. — (BSRIA bibliography)
ISBN 0-86022-165-2 (unbound) : Unpriced
B82-34246

016.696 — Swimming pools. Engineering services. Design & construction — *Bibliographies*
Loyd, Stephen. Building services for swimming pools : an annotated bibliography / Stephen Loyd. — [Bracknell] : [Building Services Research & Information Association], 1981. — 23p ; 30cm. — (Bibliography)
ISBN 0-86022-145-8 (pbk) : Unpriced
B82-13819

016.7 — Community arts — *Bibliographies*
Davies, Anne. CETU's list of information on community arts, community development and non-formal education / compiled by Anne Davies. — Nottingham : University of Nottingham Department of Adult Education, c1981. — ii,128p ; 21cm
ISBN 0-902031-55-4 (pbk) : Unpriced
Primary classification 016.307'14 B82-03024

016.7 — Visual arts — *Bibliographies*
Art books 1876-1949 : including an international index of current serial publications / [prepared by R.R. Bowker Company]. — New York ; London : Bowker, c1981. — xviii,780p ; 29cm
Includes index
ISBN 0-8352-1370-6 : Unpriced B82-04006

Art books 1950-1979 : including an international directory of museum collection catalogs. — New York : Bowker, c1979. — li,1500p ; 29cm
ISBN 0-8352-1189-4 : £49.50 B82-25367

016.704'0396073 — American negro visual arts, *to 1980* — *Bibliographies*
Igoe, Lynn Moody. 250 years of Afro-American art : an annotated bibliography / Lynn Moody Igoe with James Igoe. — New York ; London : Bowker, 1981. — xxv,1266p ; 25cm
ISBN 0-8352-1376-5 : £87.75 B82-13575

016.709'011 — Primitive visual arts — *Bibliographies*
Tribal and ethnic art. — Oxford : Clio Press, Dec.1981. — [99]p. — (Modern art bibliographical series ; 1)
ISBN 0-903450-60-7 : £15.00 : CIP entry
B82-01347

016.709'2'2 — Visual artists. Biographies — *Indexes*
Havlice, Patricia Pate. Index to artistic biography / by Patricia Pate Havlice. — Metuchen ; London : Scarecrow
1st supplement. — 1981. — viii,953p ; 23cm
Bibliography: pv-viii
ISBN 0-8108-1446-3 : £36.00 B82-17415

016.709'41 — British visual arts, *500-1500* — *Bibliographies*
Swanton, Michael. Medieval art in Britain : a select bibliography / compiled by M.J. Swanton. — London : Portico, 1981. — 64p ; 24cm
ISBN 0-907810-00-4 (pbk) : Unpriced
B82-12749

016.711'7'02854 — Transport. Planning. Applications of digital computer systems — *Bibliographies*

Transportation : an annotated bibliography / co-ordinator R. Buckingham ; compilers A. Costain ... [et al.]. — London : Heyden on behalf of the British Computer Society, c1982. — x,28p ; 21cm. — (Use of computers for national development)
ISBN 0-85501-696-5 (pbk) : £7.00 : CIP rev.
B81-40230

016.72'06'041 — Great Britain. Architectural design. Organisations: Royal Institute of British Architects. Archives — *Lists*

Bassett, Philippa. Lists of historical records retained by the Royal Institute of British Architects / compiled by Philippa Bassett as part of a research project funded by the Social Science Research Council. — [Birmingham] : Centre for Urban and Regional Studies, University of Birmingham, 1980. — xiii,29leaves ; 30cm
Unpriced (pbk) B82-15238

016.725'71 — Restaurants. Architectural design — *Bibliographies*

Restaurant design : a reading list. — Croydon : Property Services Agency Library Service, 1979. — 23p ; 29cm
Includes index
ISBN 0-86177-040-4 (pbk) : £2.15 B82-17317

016.74164 — Illustrations: Illustrations for books & serials, ***1900-1980*****. Special subjects: Latin America,** ***to 1980*** **—** *Lists*

Wilgus, A. Curtis. Latin America : a guide to illustrations / A. Curtis Wilgus. — Metuchen ; London : Scarecrow, 1981. — xxviii,250p ; 23cm
Includes index
ISBN 0-8108-1459-5 : Unpriced B82-10850

016.7455'088054 — Handicrafts for children — *Bibliographies*

Gallivan, Marion F.. Fun for kids : an index to children's craft books / by Marion F. Gallivan. — Metuchen, N.J. ; London : Scarecrow, 1981. — vii,340p ; 23cm
Bibliography: p3-20
ISBN 0-8108-1439-0 : £12.00 B82-05357

016.7485 — Stained glass — *Bibliographies*

Evans, David. A bibliography of stained glass. — Woodbridge : Boydell & Brewer, July 1982. — [224]p
ISBN 0-85991-087-3 : £40.00 : CIP entry
B82-17910

016.7485'028'8 — Painted glass. Conservation — *Bibliographies*

Newton, R. G.. The deterioration and conservation of painted glass : a critical bibliography. — 2nd ed. — Oxford : Oxford University Press for the British Academy, Nov.1982. — [103]p. — (Corpus vitrearum medii aevi, Great Britain. Occasional paper ; 2)
Previous ed.: 1974
ISBN 0-19-726017-9 (pbk) : £4.00 : CIP entry
B82-27030

016.75913 — American paintings. Regionalism — *Bibliographies*

Guedon, Mary Scholz. Regionalist art : Thomas Hart Benton, John Steuart Curry, and Grant Wood : a guide to the literature / by Mary Scholz Guedon. — Metuchen, N.J. ; London : Scarecrow, 1982. — xvii,191p : ill ; 23cm
Includes index
ISBN 0-8108-1543-5 : £10.80 B82-38097

016.77 — Books on photography: Books with British imprints, ***1839-1875*** **—** *Bibliographies*

Gernsheim, Helmut. Incunabula of British photography. — London : Scolar Press, Oct.1982. — [160]p
ISBN 0-85967-657-9 : £30.00 : CIP entry
B82-24124

016.77 — Photography — *Bibliographies*

Photography. — Oxford : Clio, Aug.1982. — [390]p. — (Modern art bibliographical series ; 2)
ISBN 0-903450-59-3 : £35.00 : CIP entry
B82-24337

016.77859'92 — Scotland. Educational technology. Information services: Scottish Council for Educational Technology. ***Information Service.*** **Stock: Serial articles on videorecording —** *Catalogues*

Scottish Council for Educational Technology. *Information Service*. Journal articles on video : articles appearing in the S.C.E.T. Information Service's holdings of journals dated January 1981-June 1981, received by the S.C.E.T. Information Service by June 1981 / compiled by Jim Mackechnie. — Glasgow : The Service, 1981. — 14p ; 30cm. — (SCET journals bibliography, ISSN 0260-972x ; no.2)
ISBN 0-86011-041-9 (unbound) : £0.25
B82-22375

Scottish Council for Educational Technology. *Information Service*. Journal articles on video (2) : articles appearing in the S.C.E.T. Information Service's holdings of journals dated July 1981-December 1981, received by the S.C.E.T. Information Service by December 1981 / compiled by Margaret Duff. — Glasgow : The Service, 1981. — 10p ; 30cm. — (SCET journals bibliography, ISSN 0260-972x ; no.6)
ISBN 0-86011-049-4 (unbound) : £0.25
B82-22376

016.78 — Merseyside ***(Metropolitan County)*****. Liverpool. Public music libraries: Liverpool City Libraries.** ***Music Library*** **—** *Catalogues*

Liverpool City Libraries. Catalogue of the music library / Liverpool City Libraries. — Liverpool (William Brown St., Liverpool L3 8EW) : Brown, Picton and Hornby Libraries
Vol.2. — 1981. — 865p ; 24cm
Unpriced (pbk) B82-22960

016.78 — Music & musical scores — *Bibliographies — Serials*

British catalogue of music. — 1981. — London : British Library, Bibliographic Services Division, June 1982. — [130]p
ISBN 0-900220-97-x : £21.00 : CIP entry
ISSN 0068-1407 B82-10260

016.78 — Music — *Bibliographies — German texts*

Bibliographie des Musikschrifttums / herausgegeben vom Staatlichen Institut für Musikforschung Preußicher Kulturbesitz ; [Bearbeitung und Redaktion Elisabeth Wilker unter Mitarbeit von Gitta Borchert, Irmelind Roth und Claudia Wegner]. — Mainz ; London : Schott, c1981. — xvii,484p ; 25cm
Includes index
ISBN 3-7957-1475-3 : £27.00 B82-37970

016.78 — Musical scores — *Lists*

British Library. The catalogue of printed music in the British Library in 1980. — London : Saur
7: Bochn-Brahe / [editor Laureen Baillie]. — 1982. — 382p ; 31cm
ISBN 0-86291-304-7 : Unpriced
ISBN 0-86291-300-4 (set) : Unpriced
B82-38571

British Library. The catalogue of printed music in the British Library to 1980. — London : Saur
3: Bach, J.S.-Barre / [editor Laureen Baillie]. — 1981. — 384p ; 31cm
ISBN 0-85157-903-5 : Unpriced
ISBN 0-85157-900-0 (set) B82-02876

British Library. The catalogue of printed music in the British Library to 1980. — London : Saur
4: Barri-Bels / [editor Laureen Baillie]. — 1981. — 408p ; 31cm
ISBN 0-86291-301-2 : Unpriced
ISBN 0-85157-900-0 (set) B82-02875

British Library. The catalogue of printed music in the British Library to 1980. — London : Saur
5: Belta-Bienb / [editor Laureen Baillie]. — 1981. — 376p ; 31cm
ISBN 0-86291-302-0 : Unpriced
ISBN 0-86291-300-4 (set) B82-17017

British Library. The catalogue of printed music in the British Library to 1980 / [editor Laureen Baillie]. — London : Saur
6: Biere - Bochm. — 1982. — 368p ; 31cm
ISBN 0-86291-303-9 : Unpriced
ISBN 0-86291-300-4 (set) : Unpriced
B82-31103

British Library. The catalogue of printed music in the British Library to 1980. — London : Saur
8: Brahm-Brow / [editor Laureen Baillie]. — 1982. — 376p ; 31cm
ISBN 0-86291-305-5 : Unpriced
ISBN 0-86291-300-4 (set) : Unpriced
B82-38572

016.78 — Oxfordshire. Oxford. Universities. Colleges: Christ Church ***(University of Oxford). Library.*** **Stock: Music —** *Catalogues*

Bray, Roger. The music collection of Christ Church, Oxford. — Brighton : Harvester Press Microform Publications, Dec.1981. — [75]p
ISBN 0-86257-006-9 (pbk) : £4.50 : CIP entry
B81-35897

Carter, Tim. The music collection of Christ Church, Oxford : a listing and guide to part three. — Brighton : Harvester Press Microform Publications, May 1982. — [40]p
ISBN 0-86257-013-1 (pbk) : £4.50 : CIP entry
B82-16506

016.78'09'02 — European music, ***900-1700*****. Manuscripts —** *Catalogues*

Cambridge music manuscripts, 900-1700 / edited by Iain Fenlon. — Cambridge : Cambridge University Press, 1982. — xiii,174p : ill,facsims (some col.),music ; 26cm
Published to accompany an exhibition at the Fitzwilliam Museum, Cambridge, 1982
ISBN 0-521-24452-8 : £30.00 : CIP rev.
B82-15939

016.78'092'4 — Australian music. Williamson, Malcolm — *Lists*

Malcolm Williamson : (born 1931) : a catalogue to celebrate the composer's 50th birthday. — London : Weinberger, c1981. — 35p : 1music,1port ; 25cm
List of sound discs: p27-29. — Includes index
Unpriced (pbk) B82-04195

016.78'092'4 — English music. Purcell, Henry — *Discographies*

Greenhalgh, Michael. The music of Henry Purcell : a guide for librarians, listeners & students / by Michael Greenhalgh. — Eastcote : M.J. Greenhalgh, 1982. — 40p ; 22cm. — (English music guides, ISSN 0262-6403 ; 1)
Includes index
ISBN 0-907949-00-2 (pbk) : Unpriced : CIP rev. B82-07837

016.780'92'4 — English music. Vaughan Williams, Ralph — *Bibliographies*

Kennedy, Michael, *1926-*. A catalogue of the works of Ralph Vaughan Williams. — Rev. ed. — Oxford : Oxford Univesity Press, June 1982. — [336]p
Previous ed.: 1964
ISBN 0-19-315452-8 : £15.00 : CIP entry
B82-10440

016.78'092'4 — French music. Berlioz, Hector — *Bibliographies*

Berlioz Society. Library of books, scores, periodicals, gramophone records, etc. / the Berlioz Society. — [Esher] ([c/o I.W.C. Martin, 10 Manor Court, Station Approach, Hinchley Wood, Esher, Surrey KT10 0SP]) : The Society, 1981. — 8p ; 21cm
Unpriced (unbound) B82-31337

Hopkinson, Cecil. A bibliography of the musical and literary works of Hector Berlioz : 1803-1869 : with histories of the French music publishers concerned / by Cecil Hopkinson. — 2nd ed. / incorporating the author's additions and corrections edited by Richard MacNutt ; with a new foreword by Alec Hyatt King. — Tunbridge Wells : MacNutt, 1980. — xix,230,[20]p of plates : facsims,1port ; 29cm
Previous ed.: Edinburgh : Edinburgh Bibliographical Society, 1951. — Includes index
ISBN 0-907180-00-0 : £38.00 : CIP rev.
B80-11714

016.78'092'4 — Russian music. Rachmaninoff, Sergei — *Lists*

Threlfall, Robert. A catalogue of the compositions of S. Rachmaninoff / by Robert Threlfall and Geoffrey Norris. — London : Scolar, 1982. — 218p : facsims,2ports ; 26cm
Includes index
ISBN 0-85967-617-x : £30.00 B82-18052

016.7817'296 — Negro music — *Bibliographies*

Bibliography of black music. — Westport ; London : Greenwood. — (The Greenwood encyclopedia of black music, ISSN 0272-0264)
Vol.1: Reference materials / Dominique-René de Lerma ; foreword by Jessie Carney Smith. — 1981. — xv,124p ; 29cm
ISBN 0-313-21340-2 : Unpriced B82-02823

016.7817'296073 — American negro music, *to 1979* — *Bibliographies*

Skowronski, JoAnn. Black music in America : a bibliography / JoAnn Skowronski. — Metuchen ; London : Scarecrow Press, 1981. — ix,723p ; 23cm
Includes index
ISBN 0-8108-1443-9 : £30.00 B82-11462

016.781742 — English music, *1700-1800* — *Catalogues*

University of St Andrews. *Library*. Catalogue of the Finzi collection in St Andrews University Library / compiled by Cedric Thorpe Davie. — St Andrews : St Andrews University Library, 1982. — v,71p ; 30cm
Includes index
ISBN 0-900897-04-x (pbk) : Unpriced
B82-39046

016.783 — American negro religious choral music — *Bibliographies*

White, Evelyn Davidson. Choral music by Afro-American composers : a selected annotated bibliography / compiled by Evelyn Davidson White. — Metuchen, N.J. ; London : Scarecrow, 1981. — v,167p : music ; 29cm
Bibliography: p143-146. — List of sound discs: p146-163. — Includes index
ISBN 0-8108-1451-x : £14.00 B82-05362

016.7834'52 — Religious cantatas — *Lists*

Evans, Margaret R.. Sacred cantatas : an annotated bibliography, 1960-1979 / by Margaret R. Evans. — Jefferson ; London : McFarland, 1982. — xviii,188p ; 24cm
Includes index
ISBN 0-89950-044-7 : Unpriced B82-37985

016.784 — Avon. Public libraries: Avon County Library. Stock: Choral music. Choral sets — *Catalogues*

Avon County Library. Orchestral and choral sets / Avon County Library. — Bristol : County Public Relations and Publicity Department
Supplement. — 1981. — 15p ; 21cm
ISBN 0-86063-123-0 (unbound) : Unpriced
Primary classification 016.785 B82-12220

016.784 — Somerset. Wellington. Public music libraries: Somerset County Music Library. Stock: Vocal music. Vocal music sets — *Catalogues*

Somerset. *Library Service*. Catalogue of sets of vocal music 1981. — [Bridgwater] : Somerset County Council, Library Service, 1981. — 235p ; 30cm
Includes index
ISBN 0-86183-017-2 (pbk) : £1.80 B82-11954

016.7844'944 — Folk songs in French — *Bibliographies*

Scales, R. P.. La musique et les chants traditionnels de la France : a short bibliography of French folk music / R.P. Scales. — London (St Mary's Rd, Ealing, W5 5RF) : School of Library and Information Studies, Ealing College of Higher Education, c1981. — 24leaves ; 30cm. — (Ealing miscellany ; no.26)
English and French text. — Includes index
Unpriced (unbound) B82-35091

016.7845'4'009 — Rock music, *to 1978* — *Bibliographies*

Kendrick, Terry A.. Rock music / compiled by Terry A. Kendrick. — Penzance : Library Association, Public Libraries Group, 1981. — 27p ; 19cm. — (Readers' guide / Library Association. Public Libraries Group ; no.37)
Includes index
ISBN 0-85365-724-6 (pbk) : £1.10 B82-40557

016.785 — Avon. Public libraries: Avon County Library. Stock: Orchestral music. Orchestral sets — *Catalogues*

Avon County Library. Orchestral and choral sets / Avon County Library. — Bristol : County Public Relations and Publicity Department
Supplement. — 1981. — 15p ; 21cm
ISBN 0-86063-123-0 (unbound) : Unpriced
Also classified at 016.784 B82-12220

016.785 — Great Britain. Libraries. Stock: Orchestral music. Orchestral sets — *Catalogues*

Compton, Sheila. British union catalogue of orchestral sets. — Bristol (c/o 24 Beckington Rd, Bristol BS3 5EB) : IAML (UK)/Polytechnic of North London, Oct.1982. — [360]p
ISBN 0-900639-14-8 (pbk) : £38.00 : CIP entry
B82-29036

016.785'09 — Orchestral music, *1723-1970* — *Lists*

Daniels, David. Orchestral music : a handbook / David Daniels. — 2nd ed. — Metuchen ; London : Scarecrow, 1982. — xii,413p ; 23cm
Previous ed.: 1972
ISBN 0-8108-1484-6 : £16.00 B82-22975

016.786'092'2 — Keyboard music. Women composers — *Bibliographies*

Meggett, Joan M.. Keyboard music by women composers : a catalog and bibliography / compiled by Joan M. Meggett ; foreword by Nancy Fierro. — Westport, Conn. ; London : Greenwood Press, 1981. — xx,210p ; 25cm
ISBN 0-313-22833-7 : £22.95 B82-18181

016.7899'12 — Music, *ca 800-1775.* **Sound recordings** — *Discographies* — *Serials*

Early music discography. Volume 1, Record index / compiled by Trevor Croucher. — 1981 ed.-. — London : The Library Association, 1981-. — v. ; 21cm
Annual
ISSN 0262-5776 = Early music discography. Volume 1. Record index : Unpriced
B82-07639

Early music discography. Volume 2, Composer, plainsong, anonymous work and performer indexes / compiled by Trevor Croucher. — 1981 ed.-. — London : The Library Association, 1981-. — v. ; 21cm
Annual
ISSN 0262-5784 = Early music discography. Volume 2. Composer, plainsong, anonymous work and performer indexes : Unpriced
B82-07640

016.7899'12 — Music. Melodiya long-playing sound discs — *Discographies*

Bennett, John R. (John Reginald). Melodiya : a Soviet Russian L.P. discography / compiled by John R. Bennett ; foreword by Boris Semeonoff and Anatali Zheleznу. — Westport ; London : Greenwood Press, c1981. — xxii,832p ; 24cm. — (Discographies ; no.6)
Includes index
ISBN 0-313-22596-6 : Unpriced B82-17882

016.7899'12 — Music. Sound recordings — *Discographies*

Cohn, Arthur. Recorded classical music : a critical guide to compositions and performances / Arthur Cohn. — New York : Schirmer ; London : Collier Macmillan, c1981. — xi,2164p ; 25cm
Includes index
ISBN 0-02-870640-4 : £50-00 B82-19764

016.7899'12 — Music, *to ca 1750.* **Sound recordings. Discographies**

Croucher, Trevor. Early music discography. — London : Library Association, May 1981. — 2v.
ISBN 0-85365-613-4 (pbk) : £15.00 : CIP entry
B81-04261

016.7899'12 — Pop music, *1949-1980* **Sound discs: Singles** — *Discographies*

Pelletier, Paul Maurice. British London (American) complete singles catalogue 1949-1980. — Chessington (P.O. Box 18F, Chessington, Surrey KT9 1UZ) : Record Information Services, May 1982. — [128]p. — (Record Information Services British popular series, ISSN 0262-320x ; 2)
ISBN 0-907872-01-8 (pbk) : £3.50 : CIP entry
B82-07697

016.7899'12 — Pop music. Long-playing sound discs, *to 1979* — *Discographies*

The **Rolling** Stone record guide : reviews and ratings of almost 10,000 currently available rock, pop, soul, country, blues, jazz, and gospel albums / edited by Dave Marsh with John Swenson. — London : Virgin, 1980, c1979. — xxi,631p : ill,ports ; 24cm
Originally published: New York : Random House, 1979. — Bibliography: p625-631
ISBN 0-907080-00-6 (pbk) : £5.25 B82-21775

016.7899'12 — Popular music. British Capitol 45 r.p.m. sound discs — Discographies

Pelletier, Paul Maurice. British Capitol 45 r.p.m. singles catalogue. — Chessington (P.O. Box 18F, Chessington, Surrey KT9 1UZ) : Record Information Services, Feb.1982. — [64]p. — (Record information services British popular series, ISSN 0262-320x ; 1)
ISBN 0-907872-00-x (pbk) : £2.50 : CIP entry
B82-02486

016.7899'1245 — Pop music. Sound discs: British number one singles, *1952-1981* — *Discographies*

The **Guinness** book of 500 number one hits. — Enfield : Guinness Superlatives, Oct.1982. — [264]p
ISBN 0-85112-250-7 (pbk) : £5.95 : CIP entry
B82-24744

016.7899'1245'00922 — English pop music. Shadows. Sound recordings — *Discographies*

Geddes, George T.. The Shadows : a history and discography / by George Geddes. — Glasgow (102 Dorchester Ave., Glasgow, G12 0EB) : G. and M. Geddes, 1981. — 178p ; 30cm
Bibliography: p173-175
£5.00 (spiral)
Primary classification 784.5'0092'2 B82-03930

016.7899'125'0666 — Popular music. Big bands. Sound discs — *Discograpies*

Big bands / edited by Peter Gammond and Raymond Horricks. — Cambridge : Stephens, 1981. — 183p : 1facsim,ports ; 24cm. — (Music on record ; 2)
Bibliography: p178-183
ISBN 0-85059-495-2 : £8.95 : CIP rev.
B81-30333

016.79'009 — Recreation, *to 1980.* **Theses accepted by British universities** — *Lists*

Cox, R. W.. Theses and dissertations of the history of sport, physical education, recreation and dance, approved for higher degrees and advanced diplomas in British Universities 1900-1981 / compiled by R.W. Cox. — [Liverpool] : [University of Liverpool], 1982. — 13,[16]p ; 30cm. — (Occasional publication ; no.1)
Includes index
Unpriced (spiral)
Primary classification 016.6137'09 B82-30890

Cox, R. W.. Theses for higher degrees in progress on the history of sport, physical education and recreation in British universities / R.W. Cox. — [Liverpool] : [University of Liverpool], 1982. — [4]leaves ; 30cm. — (Occasional publication ; no.2)
Unpriced (spiral)
Primary classification 016.6137'09 B82-30891

016.7902'05 — Lancashire. Lancaster. Universities. Libraries: University of Lancaster. *Library.* **Stock: Serials on performing arts** — *Catalogues*

University of Lancaster. *Library*. Performing arts serials / University of Lancaster library. — Lancaster : The Library, 1976. — viii,27p ; 21cm
Includes index
ISBN 0-901699-40-3 (pbk) : £0.25 (£0.40 by post) B82-25851

016.79143 — United States. 8mm cinema films & 16mm cinema films: Feature films — *Lists*

Limbacher, James L.. Feature films on 8mm, 16mm, and videotape : a directory of feature films available for rental, sale, and lease in the United States and Canada : with a serials section, an index of directors, and an index of foreign-language films / compiled and edited by James L. Limbacher. — 7th ed. — New York ; London : Bowker, 1982. — ix,481p ; 29cm
Previous ed.: 1979. — Bibliography: p471. — Includes index
ISBN 0-8352-1486-9 : Unpriced B82-39054

016.79143′0233′0922 — American cinema films, *1929-1979.* **Directors** — *Filmographies*

Langman, Larry. A guide to American film directors : the sound era, 1929-1979 / Larry Langman. — Metuchen ; London : Scarecrow, 1981. — 2v ; 23cm
Includes index
£23.60 B82-19793

016.79143′026′0979494 — California. Los Angeles. Hollywood. Cinema films. Costumes — *Bibliographies*

Prichard, Susan Perez. Film costume : an annotated bibliography / Susan Perez Prichard. — Metuchen ; London : Scarecrow, 1981. — xiii,563p ; 23cm
Includes index
ISBN 0-8108-1437-4 : £26.00 B82-17482

016.79143′09′0915 — Cinema films: Science fiction films, *1889-1981*

Willis, Donald C.. Horror and science fiction films II / by Donald C. Willis. — Metuchen ; London : Scarecrow, 1982. — xiv,474p ; 22cm
ISBN 0-8108-1517-6 : £22.80
Primary classification 016.79143′09′0916
B82-31807

016.79143′09′0916 — Cinema films: Horror films, *1889-1981* — *Lists*

Willis, Donald C.. Horror and science fiction films II / by Donald C. Willis. — Metuchen ; London : Scarecrow, 1982. — xiv,474p ; 22cm
ISBN 0-8108-1517-6 : £22.80
Also classified at 016.79143′09′0915
B82-31807

016.79143′09′09382 — Cinema films. Special subjects: Bible — *Filmographies*

Campbell, Richard H.. The Bible on film : a checklist, 1897-1980 / Richard H. Campbell and Michael R. Pitts. — Metuchen ; London : Scarecrow, 1981. — ix,214p : ill ; 23cm
Includes index
ISBN 0-8108-1473-0 : £10.00 B82-17481

016.79143′0994 — Australian cinema films, *to 1977* — *Filmographies*

Pike, Andrew. Australian film 1900-1977 : a guide to feature film production / by Andrew Pike and Ross Cooper. — Melbourne ; Oxford : Oxford University Press in association with The Australian Film Institute, 1980. — xi,448p,[8]p of plates : ill(some col.),facsims,ports ; 22x28cm
Bibliography: p413. — Includes index
ISBN 0-19-554213-4 (cased) : £50.00
ISBN 0-19-554332-7 (pbk) : Unpriced
B82-37219

016.7915′3 — New Mexico. Sante Fe. Universities. Libraries: University of New Mexico. *Fine Arts Library.* **Stock: Documents on puppetry. Collections: Batchelder-McPharlin Collection** — *Catalogues*

Miller, George B.. Puppetry library : an annotated bibliography based on the Batchelder-McPharlin Collection at the University of New Mexico / compiled and edited by George B. Miller, Jr., Janet S. Harris and William E. Hannaford, Jr. ; foreword by Marjorie Batchelder McPharlin. — Westport, Conn. ; London : Greenwood, 1981. — xxiv,172p ; 24cm
Includes index
ISBN 0-313-21359-3 : Unpriced B82-02874

016.792 — Theatre — *Bibliographies*

Watts, Susan. Stagecraft and theatre / compiled by Susan Watts. — Penzance : Library Association, Public Libraries Group, 1981. — 24p ; 19cm. — (Readers′ guide / Library Association. Public Libraries Group ; no.35)
Includes index
ISBN 0-85365-704-1 (pbk) : £1.10 B82-40556

016.796′09 — Sports, *to 1980.* **Theses accepted by British universities** — *Lists*

Cox, R. W.. Theses and dissertations of the history of sport, physical education, recreation and dance, approved for higher degrees and advanced diplomas in British Universities 1900-1981 / compiled by R.W. Cox. — [Liverpool] : [University of Liverpool], 1982. — 13,[16]p ; 30cm. — (Occasional publication ; no.1)
Includes index
Unpriced (spiral)
Primary classification 016.6137′09 B82-30890

Cox, R. W.. Theses for higher degrees in progress on the history of sport, physical education and recreation in British universities / R.W. Cox. — [Liverpool] : [University of Liverpool], 1982. — [4]leaves ; 30cm. — (Occasional publication ; no.2)
Unpriced (spiral)
Primary classification 016.6137′09 B82-30891

016.796′0941 — Great Britain. Sports, *to 1980.* **Theses accepted by American universities** — *Lists*

Cox, R. W.. American theses on the history of British sport and physical education / R.W. Cox. — [Liverpool] : [University of Liverpool], 1982. — 4leaves ; 30cm. — (Occasional publication ; no.3)
Unpriced (spiral)
Primary classification 016.6137′0941
B82-30889

016.8 — Literature. Reference books — *Lists*

Kehler, Dorothea. Problems in literary research : a guide to selected reference works / Dorothea Kehler. — 2nd ed., rev. and enl. — Metuchen ; London : Scarecrow, 1981. — ix,186p ; 23cm + instructor′s index(66p ; 22cm)
Previous ed.: 1975. — Includes index
ISBN 0-8108-1452-8 : Unpriced
ISBN 0-8108-1453-6 (instructor′s index) : Unpriced B82-10845

016.801′92 — Literature, *to 1980.* **Psychological aspects** — *Bibliographies*

Psychoanalysis, psychology, and literature : a bibliography / edited by Norman Kiell. — 2nd ed. — Metuchen ; London : Scarecrow, 1982. — 2v.(xiv,1269p) ; 23cm
Previous ed.: published in 1 vol. Madison : University of Wisconsin Press, 1963. — Includes index
ISBN 0-8108-1421-8 : £52.00 B82-22979

016.80881 — Great Britain. Arts. Patronage. Organisations. Libraries: Arts Council of Great Britain. *Poetry Library.* **Stock** — *Catalogues*

Arts Council of Great Britain. *Poetry Library.* The Poetry Library of the Arts Council of Great Britain : short-title catalogue / compiled with a postscript by Jonathan Barker ; introduction by Philip Larkin. — 6th ed. rev. and enl. — London : Arts Council of Great Britain, 1981. — 149p : ports ; 22cm
Previous ed.: published as Short-title catalogue, the Poetry Library of the Arts Council of Great Britain. 1973
ISBN 0-85635-394-9 (cased) : £5.95 : CIP rev.
ISBN 0-85635-395-7 (pbk) : £2.95 B81-28132

016.80882 — Avon. Public libraries: Avon County Library. Stock: Drama in European languages. Play sets. Collections: County Drama Collection — *Catalogues*

Avon County Library. Playsets : first supplement (to July 1980) / Avon County Library. — Bristol : The Library, [1980]. — 30p ; 19cm
ISBN 0-86063-102-8 (pbk) : Unpriced
B82-25112

016.80882 — Drama. Texts — *Bibliographies*

The **Guide** to selecting plays for performance. — 84th ed. — London : French, [1981?]. — ca 520p ; 23x11cm
Spine title: The complete guide to selecting plays. — Compiled by Samuel French Ltd. — Previous ed.: 1978. — Includes index
Unpriced (pbk) B82-11616

016.80882 — Northern England. Public libraries: Northern Regional Library System. Stock: Drama. Play sets — *Lists*

Play sets in the Northern Region. Supplement — September 1979. — [Newcastle upon Tyne] ([Central Library, Newcastle upon Tyne, NE99 1MC]) : [Northern Regional Library System], [1979]. — 14p ; 30cm
£0.15 (unbound) B82-40578

016.80885 — Speeches, *to 1980.* **Anthologies in English** — *Indexes*

Speech index : an index to collections of world famous orations and speeches for various occasions. — 4th ed. — Metuchen ; London : Scarecrow
Supplement, 1966-1980 / by Charity Mitchell. — 1982. — xviii,466p ; 23cm
″Cumulates the 1966-1970 and 1971-1975 supplements to the fourth edition of Roberta Sutton′s Speech index″ — Pref
ISBN 0-8108-1518-4 : £23.60 B82-35107

016.8092′9358 — Drama in European languages, *1816-1976:* **Dramatisations of fiction in English by Scott,** *Sir* **Walter. Texts** — *Bibliographies*

Ford, Richard, *1948 Sept.10-*. Dramatisations of Scott′s novels : a catalogue / Richard Ford. — Oxford : Oxford Bibliographical Society, 1979. — xvi,52p ; 26cm. — (Occasional publication / Oxford Bibliographical Society ; no.12)
Includes index
ISBN 0-901420-33-6 (pbk) : £5.00 B82-24194

016.810′8′0358 — English literature. American writers, *1945-.* **Special subjects: Vietnamese wars. Texts** — *Bibliographies*

Newman, John, *1942-*. Vietnam War literature : an annotated bibliography of imaginative works about Americans fighting in Vietnam / by John Newman. — Metuchen ; London : Scarecrow, 1982. — xii,117p ; 22cm
Includes index
ISBN 0-8108-1514-1 : £8.00 B82-31801

016.8108′0897 — English literature. North American Indian writers — *Bibliographies*

Littlefield, Daniel F.. A biobibliography of native American writers, 1772-1924 / by Daniel F. Littlefield, Jr. and James W. Parins. — Metuchen ; London : Scarecrow, 1981. — xvii,343p ; 23cm. — (Native American bibliography series ; no.2)
Includes index
ISBN 0-8108-1463-3 : £15.60
Also classified at 810.9′897 B82-08577

016.8109 — English literature. American writers, *to 1976.* **Criticism. Serials,** *1950-1977* — *Indexes*

Corse, Larry B.. Articles on American and British literature : an index to selected periodicals, 1950-1977 / compiled by Larry B. Corse and Sandra Corse. — Chicago ; London : Swallow Press, c1981. — xii,413p ; 29cm
ISBN 0-8040-0408-0 : £22.50
Also classified at 016.8209 B82-30092

016.811′52 — Poetry in English. American writers. Pound, Ezra — *Bibliographies*

Gallup, Donald. A bibliography of Ezra Pound. — 3rd ed. — Godalming (Foxbury Meadow, Godalming, Surrey GU8 4AE) : St. Pauls′ Bibliography, Dec.1982. — [500]p. — (St. Pauls′ bibliographies ; no.7)
Originally published: London : Hart-Davis, 1963
ISBN 0-906795-07-9 : £18.00 : CIP entry
B82-30746

016.813′3 — Fiction in English. American writers. Hawthorne, Nathaniel. Criticism — *Bibliographies*

Boswell, Jeanetta. Nathaniel Hawthorne and the critics : a checklist of criticism 1900-1978 / by Jeanetta Boswell. — Metuchen ; London : Scarecrow, 1982. — x,273p ; 23cm. — (The Scarecrow author bibliographies ; no.57)
Includes index
ISBN 0-8108-1471-4 : £14.00 B82-22974

016.813'4 — Fiction in English. American writers. James, Henry, *1843-1916*. Criticism — *Bibliographies*

Edel, Leon. A bibliography of Henry James. — 3rd ed. — Oxford : Clarendon, Oct.1981. — [448]p. — (Soho bibliographies)
Previous ed.: 1961
ISBN 0-19-818186-8 : £20.00 : CIP entry
B81-25845

016.813'52 — Fiction in English. American writers. Cozzens, James Gould. Texts — *Bibliographies*

Bruccoli, Matthew J. (Matthew Joseph), *1931-*. James Gould Cozzens : a descriptive bibliography / Matthew J. Bruccoli. — Pittsburgh : University of Pittsburgh Press ; London : Feffer and Simons, 1981. — xiii,193p : ill,facsims ; 25cm. — (Pittsburgh series in bibliography)
Bibliography: p185. — Includes index
ISBN 0-8229-3435-3 : Unpriced B82-23744

016.813'54'0809282 — Children's stories in English. American writers, *1945-* — *Lists*

Popular reading for children : a collection of the Booklist columns / [selected by] Barbara Elleman. — Chicago : American Library Association ; London : Distributed by Eurospan, 1981. — 60p ; 23cm
Includes index
ISBN 0-8389-0322-3 (pbk) : £2.95 B82-21147

016.82 — English literature. Bibliography & textual criticism, *1890-1969*. Bibliograpies — *Indexes*

Howard-Hill, T. H.. British literary bibliography and textual criticism 1890-1969 : an index / T.H. Howard-Hill. — Oxford : Clarendon, 1980. — xix,409p ; 24cm. — (Index to British literary bibliography ; v.6)
ISBN 0-19-818180-9 : £40.00 : CIP rev.
B80-03001

016.8208 — English literature. Manuscripts — *Indexes*

Index of English literary manuscripts. — London : Mansell
Vol.1: 1450-1625 / compiled by Peter Beal. — 1980. — 2v. : facsims ; 29cm
ISBN 0-7201-0807-1 : £130.00 : CIP rev.
ISBN 0-7201-0808-x (pt.1)
ISBN 0-7201-0809-8 (pt.2) B79-12224

Index of English literary manuscripts. — London : Mansell
Vol.4: 1800-1900 / compiled by Barbara Rosenbaum and Pamela White
Pt.1: Arnold-Gissing. — 1982. — xxxii,831p,23p of plates : facsims ; 29cm
ISBN 0-7201-1587-6 : £80.00 : CIP rev.
ISBN 0-7201-0898-5 (set) B81-31081

016.8208'09282 — Children's literature in English, *to 1977* — *Bibliographies*

Smith, Elva S.. Elva S. Smith's The history of children's literature : a syllabus with selected bibliographies. — Rev. and enl. ed. / by Margaret Hodges and Susan Steinfirst. — Chicago : American Library Association ; London : distributed by Eurospan, 1980. — xiii,290p : ill ; 27cm
Previous ed.: published as The history of children's literature. 1937. — Includes index
ISBN 0-8389-0286-3 : £31.50 B82-21151

016.8208'09282 — English literature. Compositions by children, *to 1981* — *Bibliographies*

Wilson, Jane B.. Children's writings : a bibliography of works in English / compiled by Jane B. Wilson. — Jefferson ; London : McFarland, 1982. — xviii,169p ; 24cm
Includes index
ISBN 0-89950-043-9 : Unpriced B82-39481

016.8208'0941693 — English literature. Donegal *(County)* writers, *to 1980* — *Bibliographies*

O'Hanrahan, Brenda. Donegal authors : a bibliography / Brenda O'Hanrahan. — Blackrock : Irish Academic Press, c1982. — 275p ; 22cm
Bibliography: p269-272. — Includes index
ISBN 0-7165-0095-7 : £25.00 B82-29756

016.8209 — English literature. Criticism. Summers, Montague — *Bibliographies*

Smith, Timothy d'Arch. A bibliography of the work of Montague Summers. — 2nd rev. ed. — Wellingborough : Aquarian Press, Jan.1983. — [176]p
Previous ed.: London : Vane, 1964
ISBN 0-85030-317-6 : £9.95 : CIP entry
B82-32634

016.820'9 — English literature. Modernism — *Bibliographies*

Davies, Alistair. An annotated bibliography of modernism. — Brighton : Harvester Press, June 1982. — [192]p
ISBN 0-7108-0031-2 : £28.00 : CIP entry
B82-10865

016.8209 — English literature, *to 1976*. Criticism. Serials, *1950-1977* — *Indexes*

Corse, Larry B.. Articles on American and British literature : an index to selected periodicals, 1950-1977 / compiled by Larry B. Corse and Sandra Corse. — Chicago ; London : Swallow Press, c1981. — xii,413p ; 29cm
ISBN 0-8040-0408-0 : £22.50
Primary classification 016.8109 B82-30092

016.82'09006 — English literature. Book reviews: Serial articles with British imprints, *1747-1800* — *Indexes*

Ward, William S.. Literary reviews in British periodicals 1789-1797 : a bibliography : with a supplementary list of general (non-review) articles on literary subjects / compiled by William S. Ward. — New York ; London : Garland, 1979. — xvii,342p ; 23cm. — (Garland reference library of the humanities ; v.172)
ISBN 0-8240-9763-7 : Unpriced B82-26813

016.8209'35206642 — English literature. Special themes: Male homosexuality — *Bibliographies*

Young, Ian, *1945-*. The male homosexual in literature : a bibliography / by Ian Young with essays by Ian Young, Graham Jackson and Rictor Norton. — 2nd ed. — Metuchen, N.J. ; London : Scarecrow, 1982. — x,350p ; 23cm
Previous ed.: 1975. — Includes index
ISBN 0-8108-1529-x : £16.00 B82-38098

016.821'4 — New Zealand. Wellington. Public reference libraries: Alexander Turnbull Library. Stock: Documents associated with Milton, John, *1608-1674* — *Catalogues*

Alexander Turnbull Library. A descriptive catalogue of the Milton collection in the Alexander Turnbull Library, Wellington, New Zealand : describing works printed before 1801 held in the Library at December 1975 / compiled by K.A. Coleridge. — Oxford : Published for the Alexander Turnbull Library, National Library of New Zealand by Oxford University Press, 1980. — xxv,536,[54]p of plates : facsims ; 23cm
Bibliography: p509-516. — Includes index
ISBN 0-19-920110-2 : £35.00 : CIP rev.
B80-01011

016.821'4 — Poetry in English. King, Henry, *1592-1669*. Texts — *Bibliographies*

Keynes, *Sir* Geoffrey. A bibliography of Henry King D.D., Bishop of Chichester / by Geoffrey Keynes. — London : Cleverdon ; Godalming : St Paul's Bibliographies [distributor], 1977. — xxiv,117p : facsims ; 24
Includes index
ISBN 0-906795-18-4 : Unpriced B82-39796

016.821'5'08 — Poetry in English, *1702-1800* — *Indexes*

Forster, Harold. Supplements to Dodsley's collection of poems / by Harold Forster. — Oxford : Oxford Bibliographical Society, 1980. — ix,106p : ill,facsims ; 25cm. — (Occasional publication / Oxford Bibliographical Society ; no.15)
ISBN 0-901420-36-0 (pbk) : Unpriced
B82-12731

016.821'6 — Nottinghamshire. Nottingham. Universities. Libraries: University of Nottingham. *Manuscripts Department*. Stock: Documents of White, Henry Kirke — *Catalogues*

University of Nottingham. *Manuscripts Department*. The papers of Henry Kirke White 1785-1806 / University of Nottingham, Manuscripts Department. — [Nottingham] : [University of Nottingham], [1981?]. — 31p ; 30cm
£1.50 (pbk) B82-06124

016.821'8 — Poetry in English. Mangan, James Clarence — *Bibliographies*

Chutto, Jacques. The James Clarence Mangan bibliography. — Dublin : Wolfhound Press, Oct.1981. — [200]p. — (Irish literary bibliographies ; 2)
ISBN 0-905473-48-5 : £20.00 : CIP entry
B81-30201

016.821'8 — Poetry in English. Swinburne, Algernon Charles. Criticism — *Bibliographies*

Beetz, Kirk H.. Algernon Charles Swinburne : a bibliography of secondary works, 1861-1980 / by Kirk H. Beetz. — Metuchen, N.J. ; London : Scarecrow, 1982. — viii,227p ; 23cm. — (The Scarecrow author bibliographies ; 61)
Includes index
ISBN 0-8108-1541-9 : £13.20 B82-38102

016.821'912 — Poetry in English. Housman, A. E. — *Bibliographies*

Sparrow, John. A.E. Housman. — New rev. ed. — Godalming (Foxbury Meadow, Godalming, Surrey) : St. Paul's Bibliographies, Sept.1981. — [72]p
Previous ed.: / by John Carter and John Sparrow. London : Hart-Davis, 1952
ISBN 0-906795-05-2 : £10.00 : CIP entry
B81-25896

016.821'914 — Poetry in English. Hughes, Ted — *Bibliographies*

Sagar, Keith. Ted Hughes : a bibliography 1946-1980. — London : Mansell, Oct.1982. — [256]p
ISBN 0-7201-1654-6 : £15.00 : CIP entry
B82-23025

016.822 — Great Britain. National libraries: British Library. *Reference Division*. Stock: Drama in English, *ca 1600-ca 1800*. Collections: Garrick Collection — *Catalogues*

Kahrl, George M.. The Garrick Collection of old English plays. — London : British Library Reference Division, Sept.1982. — [320]p
ISBN 0-7123-0004-x : CIP entry B82-21095

016.822'008 — Greater Manchester *(Metropolitan County)*. Stockport. Public libraries: Stockport Central Library. Stock: Drama in English. Play sets — *Lists*

Stockport Central Library. Sets of plays in the stock of Stockport Central Library. — Stockport : Metropolitan Borough of Stockport, Recreation and Culture Division, Central Lending Library, 1980. — 18,[24]p ; 21cm
ISBN 0-905164-25-3 (unbound) : Unpriced
B82-19328

016.822'912 — Drama in English. Shaw, Bernard — *Bibliographies*

Laurence, Dan H.. A bibliography of Bernard Shaw. — Oxford : Clarendon Press, Nov.1982. — 2v. ([900]p). — (The Soho bibliographies ; 22)
ISBN 0-19-818179-5 : £50.00 : CIP entry
B82-26878

016.823'008'09282 — Children's stories in English — *Bibliographies*

Dixon, Bob. Now read on. — London : Pluto, Aug.1982. — [160]p
ISBN 0-86104-383-9 (pbk) : £3.95 : CIP entry
B82-22406

Frend, Patricia M.. Junior fiction index / Patricia M. Frend. — 4th ed. — London : Association of Assistant Librarians, 1981. — 50p ; 25cm
Previous ed.: 1977
ISBN 0-900092-38-6 (pbk) : Unpriced
B82-18335

016.823'0876'08 — Science fiction short stories in English, *1945-.* Anthologies — *Indexes*

Fletcher, Marilyn P.. Science fiction story index 1950-1979. — 2nd ed. / Marilyn P. Fletcher. — Chicago : American Library Association ; London [distributor], 1981. — xi,610p ; 28cm
Previous ed.: / Frederick Siemon. 1971. — Includes index
ISBN 0-8389-0320-7 (pbk) : £15.25 B82-21314

016.823'5 — Fiction in English, *1702-1800* — *Catalogues*

Hardy, J. C.. A catalogue of English prose fiction : mainly of the eighteenth century from a private library / by J.C. Hardy. — Foss (Fernich, Foss, [Pitlochry, Perthshire PH16 5NG]) : K.D. Duval, c1982. — 171p ; 22cm
Unpriced (pbk) B82-37763

016.823'7 — Fiction in English. Austen, Jane — *Bibliographies*

Gilson, David. A bibliography of Jane Austen / by David Gilson. — Oxford : Clarendon, 1982. — 877p,8leaves of plates : ill,facsims ; 23cm. — (The Soho biliographies ; 21)
Includes index
ISBN 0-19-818173-6 : £50.00 : CIP rev. B82-18548

016.823'8 — Fiction in English. Brontë, Charlotte. Manuscripts — *Lists*

Alexander, Christine. A bibliography of the manuscripts of Charlotte Brontë. — Haworth (Bronte Parsonage, Haworth, Keighley, West Yorkshire BD22 8DR) : Brontë Society, Oct.1982. — [204]p
ISBN 0-9505829-1-3 : £10.00 : CIP entry B82-32890

016.823'8 — West Midlands *(Metropolitan County).* Coventry. Universities. Libraries: University of Warwick. *Library.* Exhibits: Documents associated with Eliot, George — *Catalogues*

George Eliot : the making of a novelist : a centenary exhibition / devised and arranged by John Preston and Audrey Cooper. — [Coventry] ([Coventry CV4 7AL]) : [University of Warwick Library], 1980. — 14p : 1ill,1facsim ; 21cm
Catalogue of publications presented at the exhibition
Unpriced (pbk) B82-21711

016.823'912 — Fiction in English. Doyle, *Sir* Arthur Conan — *Bibliographies*

Green, Richard Lancelyn. A bibliography of A. Conan Doyle. — Oxford : Clarendon Press, Nov.1982. — [420]p. — (The Soho bibliographies ; 23)
ISBN 0-19-818190-6 : £40.00 : CIP entry B82-26879

016.823'912 — Fiction in English. Firbank, Ronald — *Bibliographies*

Benkovitz, Miriam J.. A bibliography of Ronald Firbank / by Miriam J. Benkovitz. — 2nd ed. — Oxford : Clarendon Press, 1982. — xv,106p ; 23cm. — (The Soho bibliographies ; 16)
Previous ed.: London : Hart-Davis, 1963. — Includes index
ISBN 0-19-818188-4 : £17.50 : CIP rev. B82-07513

016.823'912 — Fiction in English. Lawrence, D. H. — *Bibliographies*

Roberts, Warren. A bibliography of D.H. Lawrence. — 2nd ed. — Cambridge : Cambridge University Press, Sept.1982. — [644]p
Previous ed.: London : Hart-Davis, 1963
ISBN 0-521-22295-8 : £45.00 : CIP entry B82-26225

016.823'912 — Fiction in English. Webb, Mary, *1881-1927* — *Bibliographies*

Dickins, Gordon. Mary Webb : a narrative bibliography of her life and works / by Gordon Dickins. — Shrewsbury : Shropshire Libraries, 1981. — 33p : ill ; 21cm
ISBN 0-903802-17-1 (pbk) : £0.95 B82-07564

016.823'912 — Fiction in English. Woolf, Virginia — *Bibliographies*

Kirkpatrick, B. J.. A bibliography of Virginia Woolf / by B.J. Kirkpatrick. — 3rd ed. — Oxford : Clarendon Press, 1980. — xiii,268p,[3] leaves of plates : ill,facsims ; 23cm. — (The Soho biliographies ; 9)
Previous ed.: London : Hart-Davis, 1967. — Includes index
ISBN 0-19-818185-x : £23.50 : CIP rev. B80-34403

016.823'914 — Fiction in English. Lessing, Doris. Criticism — *Bibligraphies*

Seligman, Dee. Doris Lessing : an annotated bibliography of criticism / compiled by Dee Seligman. — Westport, Conn. ; London : Greenwood Press, 1981. — xv,139p ; 24cm
Includes index
ISBN 0-313-21270-8 : Unpriced B82-02189

016.823'914 — Fiction in English. Quin, Ann — *Bibliographies*

Willmott, R. D.. A bibliography of works by and about Ann Quin / R.D. Willmott. — London (St Mary's Rd, Ealing, W5 5RF) : School of Library and Information Studies, Ealing College of Higher Education, c1981. — 13leaves ; 30cm. — (Ealing miscellany ; no.23)
Includes index
Unpriced (unbound) B82-36480

016.828 — English literature. Australian writers. Wright, Judith — *Bibliographies*

Walker, Shirley. Judith Wright / Shirley Walker. — Melbourne ; Oxford : Oxford University Press, 1981. — ix,213p ; 22cm. — (Australian bibliographies)
Includes index
ISBN 0-19-554234-7 (pbk) : £11.00 B82-41067

016.828'808 — Prose in English. Stevenson, Robert Louis. Texts — *Bibliographies*

Swearingen, Roger G.. The prose writings of Robert Louis Stevenson : a guide / by Roger G. Swearingen. — London : Macmillan, 1980. — xxiii,217p : ill ; 24cm
Includes index
ISBN 0-333-27652-3 : £15.00 : CIP rev. B80-03451

016.83 — German literature, *to 1980.* Translations into English language — *Lists*

O'Neill, Patrick, *1945-*. German literature in English translation : a select bibliography / Patrick O'Neill. — Toronto ; London : University of Toronto Press, c1981. — xii,242p ; 24cm
Includes index
ISBN 0-8020-2409-2 : £17.50 B82-13933

016.831'912 — Poetry in German. Arp, Hans — *Bibliographies — Polyglot texts*

Bleikasten, Aimée. Arp : bibliographie / by Aimée Bleikasten. — London : Grant & Cutler
Text in French, German and English
Vol.1: Écrits/dichtung. — 1981. — 173p ; 23cm. — (Research bibliographies & checklists ; 31.1)
Includes index
ISBN 0-7293-0091-9 (pbk) : Unpriced
Also classified at 016.841'912 B82-35236

016.839'5 — Fiction in Scandinavian languages, *1900-.* Criticism — *Bibliographies*

Budd, John. Eight Scandinavian novelists : criticism and reviews in English / compiled by John Budd. — Westport, Conn. ; London : Greenwood, 1981. — viii,180p ; 24cm
Includes index
ISBN 0-313-22869-8 : Unpriced B82-02615

016.84 — French literature — *Bibliographies*

Osburn, Charles B.. Research and reference guide to French studies / Charles B. Osburn. — 2nd ed. — Metuchen ; London : Scarecrow, 1981. — xxxvii,532p ; 23cm
Previous ed.: 1968. — Includes index
ISBN 0-8108-1440-4 : £26.00
Primary classification 016.44 B82-17413

016.841'912 — Poetry in French. Arp, Hans — *Bibliographies — Polyglot texts*

Bleikasten, Aimée. Arp : bibliographie / by Aimée Bleikasten. — London : Grant & Cutler
Text in French, German and English
Vol.1: Écrits/dichtung. — 1981. — 173p ; 23cm. — (Research bibliographies & checklists ; 31.1)
Includes index
ISBN 0-7293-0091-9 (pbk) : Unpriced
Primary classification 016.831'912 B82-35236

016.842'7 — Drama in French. Hugo, Victor — *Bibliographies*

Doyle, Ruth Lestha. Victor Hugo's drama : an annotated bibliography 1900-1980 / compiled by Ruth Lestha Doyle. — Westport ; London : Greenwood Press, 1981. — x,217p ; 25cm
Includes index
ISBN 0-313-22884-1 : Unpriced B82-18021

016.843'8 — Fiction in French. Maupassant, Guy de. Criticism — *Bibliographies*

Artinian, Robert Willard. Maupassant criticism : a centennial bibliography 1880-1979 / compiled by Robert Willard Artinian with Artine Artinian. — Jefferson ; London : McFarland, 1982. — xxii,178p ; 22cm
Includes index
ISBN 0-89950-046-3 : £20.95 B82-38736

016.848'91209 — French literature. Genêt, Jean. Criticism — *Bibliographies*

Webb, Richard C.. Jean Genet and his critics : an annotated bibliography, 1943-1980 / by Richard C. Webb with the assistance of Suzanne A. Webb. — Metuchen ; London : Scarecrow, 1982. — xii,600p ; 23cm. — (Scarecrow author bibliographies ; no.58)
Includes index
ISBN 0-8108-1512-5 : £28.00 B82-39025

016.8609'972 — Spanish literature. Mexican writers, *to 1980.* Criticism — *Bibliographies*

Foster, David William. Mexican literature : a bibliography of secondary sources / by David William Foster. — Metuchen ; London : Scarecrow, 1981. — xxv,386p ; 23cm
Includes index
ISBN 0-8108-1449-8 : Unpriced B82-10846

016.862 — Drama in Spanish. Comedias sueltas, *to 1833* — *Catalogues*

Bergman, Hannah E.. A catalogue of Comedias sueltas in the New York Public Library / by Hannah E. Bergman and Szilvia E. Szmuk. — London : Grant & Cutler
Text in English and Spanish
Vol.2. — 1981. — p161-310 ; 23cm. — (Research bibliographies & checklists ; 32.2)
Includes index
ISBN 0-7293-0113-3 (pbk) : Unpriced B82-35237

016.8692'2 — Drama in Portuguese. Vicente, Gil — *Bibliographies*

Stathatos, Constantine C.. A Gil Vicente bibliography : (1940-1975) / by Constantine C. Stathatos ; with a preface by Thomas R. Hart. — London : Grant & Cutler, 1980. — 132p ; 22cm. — (Research bibliographies & checklists ; 30)
Includes index
ISBN 0-7293-0089-7 (pbk) : £6.80 B82-17583

016.88009 — Classical literatures. Criticism — *Bibliographies*

Gwinup, Thomas. Greek and Roman authors : a checklist of criticism / by Thomas Gwinup and Fidelia Dickinson. — 2nd ed. — Metuchen ; London : Scarecrow, 1982. — xii,280p ; 23cm
Previous ed.: 1973
ISBN 0-8108-1528-1 : £14.00 B82-37699

016.891'55'62 — Letters in Persian, *1777-1810* — *Lists*

India Office Library and Records. A descriptive catalogue of Persian letters from Arcot and Baroda / M.Z.A. Shakeb. — London : India Office Library and Records, 1982. — iv,13p ; 30cm
ISBN 0-903359-36-7 (pbk) : Unpriced B82-31955

016.8916'612 — Poetry in Welsh. Jones, T. Gwynn (Thomas Gwynn), *1871-1949 — Bibliographies — Welsh texts*

Roberts, D. Hywel E.Llyfryddiaeth Thomas Gwynn Jones = The bibliography of Thomas Gwynn Jones / golygwyd gan D. Hywel E. Roberts. — Caerdydd : Cyhoeddwyd ar ran Bwrdd Gwybodau Celtaidd Prifysgol Cymru [gan] Gwasg Prifysgol Cymru, 1981. — xvi,350p ; 23cm
Includes a brief introduction in English. — Includes index
ISBN 0-7083-0757-4 : Unpriced : CIP rev. B81-23840

016.905 — Historical events. Serials — *Lists*

Historical periodicals directory / Eric H. Boehm, Barbara H. Pope and Marie S. Ensign. — Santa Barbara ; Oxford : ABC-Clio, c1981. — (Clio periodicals directories)
Includes index
Vol.1: USA and Canada / Marie S. Ensign, editor. — xii,180p ; 29cm
ISBN 0-87436-018-8 : £55.00 B82-27400

016.909'097671 — Theses on Islamic civilization: Theses accepted by British and Irish universities, *1880-1978 — Lists*

Sluglett, Peter. Theses on Islam, the Middle East and North-West Africa 1880-1978. — London : Mansell, Nov.1982. — [154]p
ISBN 0-7201-1651-1 : £16.00 : CIP entry B82-29429

016.912'4129 — Scotland. Fife Region. Dunfermline. Public libraries: Dunfermline Central Library. Stock: Local maps of Fife Region — *Catalogues*

Dunfermline Central Library. A guide to local maps & plans held in Dunfermline Central Library's Local History Collection. — [Dunfermline] ([Central Library, Abbot St., Dunfermline]) : Dunfermline District Libraries, 1978. — 9p ; 30cm
Cover title
Unpriced (pbk) B82-08887

016.91421 — London. Geographical features — *Bibliographies*

Dolphin, Philippa. The London region. — London : Mansell, Oct.1981. — [368]p
ISBN 0-7201-1598-1 : £25.00 : CIP entry B81-27406

016.916'005 — Africa — *Bibliographies — Serials*

International African bibliography 1973-1978. — London : Maxwell, Oct.1982. — [368]p
ISBN 0-7201-1565-5 : £60.00 : CIP entry
ISSN 0262-7973 B82-23024

016.918'042 — Oxfordshire. Oxford. Universities. Libraries: Bodleian Library. Exhibits: Items associated with travel in Latin America by Europeans, *ca 1800-1900 — Catalogues*

McNeil, R. A.. Europeans in Latin America : Humboldt to Hudson : catalogue of an exhibition held in the Bodleian Library, December 1980-April 1981 / prepared by R.A. McNeil & M.D. Deas. — Oxford : Bodleian Library, 1980. — ix,63p : ill ; 22cm
ISBN 0-900177-78-0 (pbk) : Unpriced B82-17061

016.9198 — Polar regions. Geographical features — *Bibliographies — Serials*

Recent polar and glaciological literature. — 1 (1981)-. — Cambridge (Lensfield Rd, Cambridge CB2 1ER) : Scott Polar Research Institute, 1981-. — v. ; 21cm
Three issues yearly. — Continues: Recent polar literature
ISSN 0263-547x = Recent polar and glaciological literature : £10.50 per year B82-27654

016.929'2 — Cornwall. Truro. Record repositories: Cornwall County and Diocesan Record Office. Stock: Family trees — *Catalogues*

Cornwall County and Diocesan Record Office. Handlist of pedigrees and heraldic documents. — [Truro] ([County Hall, Truro, Cornwall TR1 3AY]) : Cornwall County and Diocesan Record Office], c1981. — 18p,A-Jp of plates : ill,coat of arms,facsims ; 30cm. — (Handlist ; no.3)
Bibliography: p15. — Includes index
Unpriced (pbk) B82-06302

016.929'2'0941 — Great Britain. Families. Genealogical aspects — *Bibliographies*

Current publications by member societies / Federation of Family History Societies. — Plymouth : Federation of Family History Societies, 1982. — 23p ; 21cm
ISBN 0-907099-13-0 (pbk) : Unpriced B82-21838

016.929'341 — Great Britain. Genealogy. Organisations: Society of Genealogists. Stock: Directories & poll-books of Great Britain — *Catalogues*

Society of Genealogists. Catalogue of directories and poll books in the possession of the Society of Genealogists. — 3rd ed. / edited by L.W.L. Edwards. — London : Society of Genealogists, 1979. — 56p ; 21cm
Previous ed.: 1974
ISBN 0-901878-41-3 (pbk) : £1.00 B82-08177

016.929'342 — England. Repositories. Stock: Bishops' transcripts of parish registers — *Catalogues*

Gibson, J. S. W.. Bishops transcripts and marriage licences : bonds and allegations : a guide to their location and indexes / compiled by J.S.W. Gibson. — 2nd ed. — Banbury : Gulliver, and the Federation of Family History Societies, 1982. — 32p ; 21cm
Previous ed.: 1981. — Text on inside cover
ISBN 0-907099-12-2 (pbk) : £1.00
ISBN 0-906428-11-4 (Gulliver)
Also classified at 016.929'342 B82-31017

016.929'342 — England. Repositories. Stock: Records of marriage licences — *Catalogues*

Gibson, J. S. W.. Bishops transcripts and marriage licences : bonds and allegations : a guide to their location and indexes / compiled by J.S.W. Gibson. — 2nd ed. — Banbury : Gulliver, and the Federation of Family History Societies, 1982. — 32p ; 21cm
Previous ed.: 1981. — Text on inside cover
ISBN 0-907099-12-2 (pbk) : £1.00
ISBN 0-906428-11-4 (Gulliver)
Primary classification 016.929'342 B82-31017

016.929'342 — Great Britain. Genealogy. Organisations. Libraries: Society of Genealogists. *Library.* **Stock: English marriage licences** — *Catalogues*

Marriage licences : abstracts and indexes in the library of the Society of Genealogists / compiled by Lydia Collins. — London : Society of Genealogists, 1981. — 19p ; 21cm
ISBN 0-901878-48-0 (pbk) : £0.90 B82-17454

016.929'3421 — Inner London. Parish registers, *1538-1837 — Lists*

Graham, Norman H.. The genealogist's consolidated guide to parish registers copies and indexes in the Inner London area 1538 to 1837 / compiled and arranged by Norman H. Graham. — Rev. & updated ed. — Birchington : N.H. Graham, 1981. — a-b,129p : 1map ; 16x22cm
Previous ed.: 1976. — Includes index
ISBN 0-9505003-4-8 (pbk) : £3.00 B82-01306

016.929'34241 — Gloucestershire. Genealogical sources — *Lists*

Gloucestershire Record Office. Handlist of genealogical sources / compiled by M.E. Richards (with the assistance of H.C. Martin). — [Gloucester] : Gloucestershire Record Office, 1982. — iv,139p ; 30cm
Bibliography: pi
ISBN 0-904950-46-8 (pbk) : £2.50 B82-28841

016.929'342574 — Church of England. *Archdeaconry of Oxford. Archdeaconry Court &* **Church of England.** *Diocese of Oxford. Bishop's Court.* **Probate records,** *1516-1732 — Indexes*

Cheyne, Ernest. Probate records of the courts of the Bishop and Archdeacon of Oxford 1516-1732 / based on an index compiled by Ernest Cheyne ; revised by D.M. Barratt. — Cambridge : British Record Society
Vol.1: A-K. — 1981. — xv,337p : 1map ; 25cm. — (The Index library)
ISBN 0-901505-09-9 (pbk) : Unpriced B82-03851

016.929'34271 — Church of England. *Diocese of Chester. Probate Registry.* **Probate records,** *1834-1837 — Indexes*

Church of England. *Diocese of Chester. Probate Registry.* Index to wills and administrations formerly preserved in the Probate Registry, Chester 1834-1837 / edited by Florence Dickinson. — [Chester] : Record Society of Lancashire and Cheshire, 1980. — viii,219p ; 24cm. — (Publications / Record Society of Lancashire and Cheshire ; v.120)
ISBN 0-902593-09-9 : Unpriced B82-22742

016.932'007'2 — Egyptology — *Bibliographies — Serials*

Annual Egyptological bibliography. — 1978. — Warminster : Aris & Phillips, Apr.1982. — [280]p
ISBN 0-85668-204-7 : £20.00 : CIP entry B82-07841

016.932'.007'2 — Egyptology - *Bibliographies - Serials*

Annual Egyptological bibliography = Bibliographie Egyptologique annuelle. — 1977. — Warminster : Aris & Phillips, Apr.1981. — [256]p
ISBN 0-85668-186-5 : £15.00 : CIP entry B81-06067

016.9361'31804 — Scotland. Central Region. Falkirk *(District).* **Ancient Roman antiquities** — *Bibliographies*

A Select bibliography and source guide to the Romans in Falkirk District. — Falkirk : Falkirk District Council, Department of Libraries and Museums, 1982. — [104]p ; 30cm
ISBN 0-906586-20-8 (pbk) : Unpriced B82-26506

016.9403'162'0941 — Great Britain. Conscientious objection, *1914-1918.* **Interviews. Sound tape recordings** — *Catalogues*

Imperial War Museum. *Department of Sound Records.* The anti-war movement 1914-1918. — [London] : Imperial War Museum, Dept. of Sound Records, [1982?]. — 19p ; 21cm. — (Oral history recordings)
Unpriced (pbk) B82-26783

016.9404'144 — World War 1. Western Front. Army operations by Great Britain. *Army.* **Interviews. Sound tape recordings** — *Catalogues*

Imperial War Museum. *Department of Sound Records.* Western Front 1914-18. — [London] : Imperial War Museum, Dept. of Sound Records, [1982?]. — 37p ; 21cm. — (Oral history recordings)
Unpriced (pbk) B82-26782

016.9404'4941 — World War 1. Air operations by British air forces. Interviews. Sound tape recordings — *Catalogues*

Imperial War Museum. *Department of Sound Records.* Military and naval aviation 1914-18. — [London] : Imperial War Museum, Dept. of Sound Records, [1982?]. — 26p ; 21cm. — (Oral history recordings)
Unpriced (pbk) B82-26785

016.94054'8 — World War 2. Interviews. Sound recordings — *Lists*

Imperial War Museum. *Department of Sound Records.* 'The World at War' 1939-1945 : Thames Television recorded interviews. — [2nd ed.]. — [London] ([Lambeth Rd, SE1 6HZ]) : Imperial War Museum, Department of Sound Records, [1980]. — 29p ; 21cm
Previous ed.: 1977. — Includes index
Unpriced (pbk) B82-28939

016.941 — Great Britain — *History — Bibliographies — Serials*

Annual bibliography of British and Irish history. — Publications of 1980. — Brighton : Harvester Press, Sept.1981. — 1v.
ISBN 0-7108-0361-3 : CIP entry B81-23879

Annual bibliography of British and Irish history. — Publications of 1981. — Brighton : Harvester Press, Sept.1982. — [224]p
ISBN 0-7108-0452-0 : £22.50 : CIP entry B82-21389

016.94107′3′0924 — Great Britain. Politics. Burke, Edmund, *1729-1797* **—** *Bibliographies*

Todd, William B.. A bibliography of Edmund Burke. — Godalming (Foxbury Meadow, Godalming, Surrey) : St. Paul′s Bibliographies, Feb.1982. — [336]p. — (St. Paul′s bibliographies ; 5)
Originally published: London : Hart-Davis, 1964
ISBN 0-906795-03-6 : £16.00 : CIP entry
B81-25895

016.941081 — Higher education institutions. Curriculum subjects: Great Britain, *1800-1950.* **Teaching aids: Audiovisual materials —** *Lists*

Van Haeften, Kate. Media resources in British 19th and 20th century history for lecturers / by Kate Van Haeften. — London : LLRS Publications, 1980. — 23p ; 30cm
Includes index
ISBN 0-904264-50-5 (pbk) : £1.00 : CIP rev.
B80-09556

016.941081′092′2 — Great Britain. Victoria, *Queen of Great Britain.* **Family —** *Bibliographies*

Van der Kiste, John. Queen Victoria′s family : a select bibliography / John van der Kiste. — Biggleswade (8 Ashby Drive, Caldecote, Biggleswade, Beds.) : Clover, c1982. — vi,68p ; 21cm
Includes index
£4.90 (spiral) B82-20609

016.9411 — Scotland — *Bibliographies*

Grant, Eric G.. Scotland. — Oxford : Clio Press, Feb.1982. — [224]p. — (World bibliographical series ; v.34)
ISBN 0-903450-64-x : £23.00 : CIP entry
B82-02478

016.9414′23 — Scotland. Strathclyde Region. Islay. Documents on Islay in stock of Museum of Islay Life — *Catalogues*

Museum of Islay Life. Library list. — Rev. [ed.]. — Port Charlotte (Isle of Islay, Argyll) : Islay Museums Trust, 1981. — 13leaves ; 30cm
Previous ed.: 19---
Unpriced (unbound) B82-25048

016.9415 — Ireland, *ca 1600-1980* **—** *Bibliographies*

Shannon, Michael Owen. Modern Ireland : a bibliography on politics, planning, research and development / compiled and edited by Michael Owen Shannon. — London : Library Association, 1981. — xxvi,733p ; 24cm
Includes index
ISBN 0-85365-914-1 : Unpriced : CIP rev.
B82-01417

016.9415081 — British government publications, *1800-1900.* **Special subjects: Ireland —** *Abstracts*

Maltby, Arthur. Ireland in the nineteenth century : a breviate of official publications / by Arthur Maltby, Jean Maltby. — Oxford : Pergamon, 1979. — xxix,269p : facsims ; 26cm. — (Guides to official publications ; v.4)
Includes index
ISBN 0-08-023688-x : £20.00 : CIP rev.
B79-33872

016.9416 — Northern Ireland — *Bibliographies — Serials*

N. Ireland — local studies list. — No.1 (1981)-. — [Ballymena] ([c/o J.P.E. Francis, Ballymena, Co. Antrim]) : North Eastern Education & Library Board], 1981-. — v. ; 30cm
Two issues yearly. — Continues: Northern Ireland local history
ISSN 0262-8643 = N. Ireland, local studies list : Unpriced B82-11144

016.9416′54 — Down *(District).* **Strangford Lough,** *to 1980* **—** *Bibliographies*

Strangford Lough : a select source list. — [Ballynahinch] ([Windmill Hill, Ballynahinch, Co. Down BT2 48OH]) : [South Eastern Education & Library Service], 1981. — [44]p : 1ill ; 30cm
Unpriced (unbound) B82-08059

016.942 — Leicestershire. Leicester. Universities: University of Leicester. *Department of English Local History.* **Academic personnel. Publications —** *Lists*

Everitt, Alan. English local history at Leicester 1948-1978 : a bibliography of writings by members of the Department of English Local History, University of Leicester / compiled by Alan Everitt & Margery Tranter. — Leicester : Department of English Local History, University of Leicester, c1981. — 87p ; 21cm
Bibliography: p87. — Includes index
ISBN 0-907647-00-6 (pbk) : Unpriced
B82-03437

016.94203′8 — England. Peasants′ Revolt — *Bibliographies*

Newfield, Gabriel. The rising of 1381 : an annotated bibliography with special reference to St Albans / Gabriel Newfield. — Hatfield : School of Social Sciences, Hatfield Polytechnic, 1981. — 19p ; 21cm. — (Social sciences occasional papers ; no.3)
Cover title
ISBN 0-900458-13-5 (pbk) : £0.50 B82-11037

016.94206′6′0924 — Cambridgeshire. Cambridge. Libraries: Pepys Library — *Catalogues*

Pepys Library. Catalogue of the Pepys Library at Magdalene College, Cambridge. — Woodbridge : Brewer
Vol.5: Manuscirpts. — 1981
Includes index
Part 2: Modern. — xxxvi,275p ; 31cm
ISBN 0-85991-078-4 : £75.00 : CIP rev.
B81-19204

016.942081 — Nottinghamshire. Nottingham. Universities. Libraries: University of Nottingham. *Manuscripts Department.* **Stock: Documents of Denison,** *Sir* **William —** *Catalogues*

University of Nottingham. *Manuscripts Department.* Papers of Sir William Denison 1819-1915 / University of Nottingham, Manuscripts Department. — [Nottingham] : [The Department], [1981?]. — 15p ; 30cm
£1.00 (pbk) B82-00940

016.942081′092′4 — Berkshire. Windsor. Castles. Libraries: Windsor Castle. *Royal Library.* **Stock: Manuscripts collected by Jackson, J. E. (John Edward). Collections: Jackson Collections —** *Catalogues*

Windsor Castle. *Royal Library.* Catalogue of the Jackson Collection of manuscript fragments in the Royal Library Windsor Castle : with a memoir of Canon J.E. Jackson and a list of his works / by Jenny Stratford. — London : Academic Press, 1981. — xiii,106p,11p of plates : facsims,1port ; 24cm
Includes index
ISBN 0-12-672980-8 : £9.50 B82-18352

016.9421 — Illustrated books on London, *1604-1851* **—** *Catalogues*

Adams, Bernard. London illustrated 1604-1851. — London : Library Association, Nov.1982. — [492]p
ISBN 0-85365-734-3 (cased) : £68.00 : CIP entry
ISBN 0-85365-566-9 (limited ed) : £160.00
B82-29423

016.9422 — South-east England, *to 1980* **—** *Bibliographies*

Branson, C. E.. South east England / compiled by C.E. Branson. — Penzance : Library Association Public Libraries Group, 1981. — 26p ; 19cm. — (Readers′ guide / Library Association. Public Libraries Group ; no.29)
ISBN 0-85365-644-4 (pbk) : £1.10 B82-40555

016.9422′3 — Kent. Public libraries. Stock: Books on Kent — *Catalogues*

Bennett, George, *1912-*. The Kent bibliography : a finding list of Kent material in the public libraries of the county and of the adjoining London boroughs / compiled by the late George Bennett ; hon. editors Wyn Bergess and Carleton Earl. — London : Library Association, London and Home Counties Branch
Supplement / compiled and edited by Wyn Bergess. — 1981. — vii,368p ; 30cm
At head of title: Library Association, London and Home Counties Branch, Kent Sub-Branch. — Includes index
ISBN 0-902119-30-3 (pbk) : £9.50 B82-13282

016.9422′5 — East & West Sussex, *500-1500* **—** *Bibliographies*

Farrant, Sue. Medieval Sussex : a bibliography / by Sue Farrant. — Brighton : Centre for Continuing Education, University of Sussex, 1980. — 40p ; 21cm. — (Occasional paper / University of Sussex Centre for Continuing Education, ISSN 0306-1108 ; no.10)
Includes index
ISBN 0-904242-11-0 (pbk) : £0.60 B82-13904

016.9422′62 — West Sussex. Petworth. Country houses: Petworth House. Archives — *Catalogues*

The **Petworth** House archives : a catalogue / edited by Alison McCann ; with a foreword by the Lord Egremont. — Chichester : West Sussex County Council
Vol.2. — 1979. — xi,111p,jp of plates : ill,facsims ; 25cm
Includes index
ISBN 0-900801-42-5 : Unpriced B82-25020

016.9425′4 — Leicestershire. Churches — *Bibliographies*

A **Bibliography** of Leicestershire churches / [general editor David Parsons]. — Leicester : Department of Adult Education, University of Leicester
Pt.2: Newspaper sources / compiled by Geoffrey K. Brandwood. — c1980. — 94p ; 21cm
ISBN 0-901507-17-2 (pbk) : Unpriced
B82-19329

016.9425′42081′05 — Leicestershire. Leicester. Serials, *1850-1874* **—** *Indexes*

The **Leicester** newspapers 1850-74 : a guide for historians / edited by R.L. Greenall. — [Leicester] ([University Rd, Leicester LE1 7RH]) : University of Leicester, Department of Adult Education, 1980. — viii,61p : ill,ports ; 21cm
£1.50 (pbk) B82-16111

016.9426 — East Anglia. Theses — *Lists*

Henney, Janice. East Anglian studies : theses completed / compiled and edited by Janice Henney in collaboration with Victor Morgan. — Norwich : Centre for East Anglian Studies, 1982. — x,99p ; 21cm
Bibliography: px. — Includes index
ISBN 0-906219-10-8 (pbk) : Unpriced
B82-21225

016.9427′1 — Cheshire. Chester. Record repositories: Cheshire Record Office. Stock — *Lists*

Cheshire Record Office. Cheshire Record Office and Chester Diocesan Record Office / [Cheshire County Council]. — [Rev.]. — Chester (The Castle, Chester CH1 2DN) : [Cheshire Record Office], [1982?]. — 42leaves in various foliations : 1map ; 30cm
Previous ed.: 1977
£1.00 (pbk) B82-20958

016.945′634 — Vatican, *to 1982* **—** *Bibliographies*

Walsh, Michael J.. Vatican City State. — Oxford : Clio Press, Feb.1983. — [120]p. — (World bibliographical series ; v.41)
ISBN 0-903450-72-0 : £12.00 : CIP entry
B82-39834

016.946081 — Spanish Civil War. Military operations by International Brigades. British units. Interviews. Sound tape recordings — *Catalogues*

Imperial War Museum. *Department of Sound Records.* British involvement in the Spanish Civil War 1936-1939. — [London] : Imperial War Museum, Dept. of Sound Records, [1982?]. — 27p ; 21cm. — (Oral history recordings)
Unpriced (pbk) B82-26786

016.946′89 — Gibraltar — *Bibliographies*

Green, Muriel M.. A Gibraltar bibliography : a supplement / by Muriel M. Green. — [London] : University of London, Institute of Commonwealth Studies, 1981. — p109-136 ; 30cm
Includes index
ISBN 0-902499-28-9 (pbk) : Unpriced
B82-06389

016.947 — Soviet Union, *to 1980* **—** *Bibliographies*
Davies, Richard, *1949-*. Russian and Russian-related material from the Brotherton Library's collections : catalogue of an exhibition held to mark the establishment of the Leeds Russian archive : 25 May 1982 / compiled by Richard Davies and Michael Holman. — [Leeds] : [The Library], [1982]. — 16p ; 21cm
Cover title
Unpriced (unbound) B82-40225

016.94897 — Finland — *Bibliographies*
Screen, J. E. O.. Finland / J.E.O. Screen. — Oxford : Clio Press, 1981. — 212p : 1map ; 22cm. — (World bibliographical series ; v.31)
Includes index
ISBN 0-903450-55-0 : £21.75 : CIP rev. B81-09471

016.9493'5 — Luxembourg, *to 1980* **—** *Bibliographies*
Hury, Carlo. Luxembourg / Carlo Hury, Jules Christophory, compilers. — Oxford : Clio Press, c1981. — xx,184p : 1map ; 23cm. — (World bibliographical series ; v.23)
Includes index
ISBN 0-903450-37-2 : Unpriced B82-03905

016.9495 — Byzantine civilization — *Bibliographies*
Literature in various Byzantine disciplines 1892-1977. — London : Published for the Dumbarton Oaks Center for Byzantine Studies [by] Mansell. — (Dumbarton Oaks bibliographies ; Series 2)
Vol.1: Epigraphy / edited by Jelisaveta Stanojevich Allen and Ihor Ševčenko. — 1981. — xx,386p ; 29cm
Includes index
ISBN 0-7201-1586-8 : £47.00 : CIP rev.
ISBN 0-7201-0216-2 (set) : Unpriced B81-21538

016.9495'074 — Greece. Political events, *1944-1952* **—** *Bibliographies*
Fleischer, Hagen. Greece in the 1940s : a bibliographic companion / bibliographies by Hagen Fleischer, Steven Bowman ; John O. Iatrides, editor. — Hanover, N.H. ; London : University Press of New England, 1981. — viii,94p ; 23cm. — (Modern Greek Studies Association series ; 5)
Companion to: Greece in the 1940s : a nation in crisis
ISBN 0-87451-199-2 (pbk) : £10.50 B82-13931

016.951 — China — *Bibliographies*
Tanis, Norman E.. China in books : a basic bibliography in western language / compiled by Norman E. Tanis, David L. Perkins, Justine Pinto. — Greenwich, Conn. : Jai Press ; London (3 Henrietta St., WC2E 8LU) : Distributed by Jaicon Press, c1979. — xvi,328p ; 24cm. — (Foundations in library and information science ; v.4)
Includes index
ISBN 0-89232-071-0 : £27.30 B82-02076

016'.952 — Great Britain. Libraries. Stock: Documents on local history of Japan: Documents in Japanese — *Catalogues*
Bunn, J. M.. A union list of Japanese local histories in British libraries / compiled by J.M. Bunn and A.D.S. Roberts ; with an introduction by J.M. Bunn. — Oxford : Bodleian Library, 1981. — xvii,406p ; 20cm
Japanese text, English preface, notes and introduction. — Includes index
ISBN 0-900177-83-7 (pbk) : Unpriced : CIP rev. B81-30618

016.953'53 — Oman — *Bibliographies*
Clements, Frank A.. Oman / Frank A. Clements, compiler. — Oxford : Clio Press, c1981. — xv,216p : 1map ; 22cm. — (World bibliographical series ; v.29)
Includes index
ISBN 0-903450-43-7 : £23.00 B82-11574

016.953'63 — Qatar — *Bibliographies*
Unwin, P. T. H.. Qatar. — Oxford : Clio Press, July 1982. — [200]p. — (World bibliographical series ; 36)
ISBN 0-903450-66-6 : £20.00 : CIP entry B82-17907

016.953'67 — Kuwait. Political agencies: British Political Agency *(Kuwait).* **Stock: Documents on Kuwait: Documents in Arabic -** *Lists*
British Political Agency *(Kuwait).* Arabic documents in the archives of the British Political Agency, Kuwait, 1904-1919. — London : India Office Library and Records, July 1981. — 1v.. — (British Academy oriental documents ; 5)
ISBN 0-903359-32-4 (pbk) : CIP entry B81-15839

016.954 — South Asia, *to 1980* **—** *Bibliographies*
Patterson, Maureen L. P.. South Asian civilizations : a bibliographic synthesis / Maureen L.P. Patterson in colla beration with William J. Alspaugh. — Chicago ; London : University of Chicago Press, 1981. — xxxvii,853p : 2maps ; 29cm
Includes index
ISBN 0-226-64910-5 : £12.00 B82-22272

016.95403'5 — India. Army operations by Great Britain. *Army, 1919-1939.* **Interviews. Sound tape recordings —** *Catalogues*
Imperial War Museum. *Department of Sound Records.* The British Army in India 1919-39. — [London] : Imperial War Museum, Dept. of Sound Records, [1982?]. — 43p ; 21cm. — (Oral history recordings)
Unpriced (pbk) B82-26781

016.95403'5 — India. Britons. Social life, *ca 1900-1947.* **Interviews —** *Catalogues*
Plain tales from the Raj : a catalogue of the BBC recordings. — London : India Office Library and Records, Jan.1982. — 1v.
ISBN 0-903359-34-0 (pbk) : CIP entry B81-33841

016.955 — Iran — *Bibliographies*
Bibliographical guide to Persia. — Brighton : Harvester, Dec.1982. — [300]p
ISBN 0-7108-0412-1 : £35.00 : CIP entry B82-30085

016.956 — Great Britain. *Foreign and Commonwealth Office.* **Libraries: India Office Library and Records. Stock: Documents on Middle East —** *Lists*
India Office Library and Records. A brief guide to sources for Middle East studies in the India Office Records. — London : India Office Library and Records, Jan.1982. — [20]p
ISBN 0-903359-35-9 (pbk) : CIP entry B82-06059

016.956'03 — Middle East. Army operations by Great Britain. *Army, 1919-1939.* **Interviews. Sound tape recordings —** *Catalogues*
Imperial War Museum. *Department of Sound Records.* Middle East : British military personnel 1919-39. — [London] : Imperial War Museum, Dept. of Sound Records, [1982?]. — 44p ; 21cm. — (Oral history recordings)
Unpriced (pbk) B82-26779

016.9561 — Turkey — *Bibliographies*
Güçlü, Meral. Turkey / Meral Güçlü compiler. — Oxford : Clio, c1981. — xli,331p : 1map ; 23cm. — (World bibliographical series ; v.27)
Includes index
ISBN 0-903450-39-9 : £35.00 : CIP rev. B81-28122

016.95645 — Cyprus — *Bibliographies*
Kitromilides, Paschalis. Cyprus / Paschalis M. Kitromilides, Marios L. Evriviades, compilers. — Oxford : Clio, c1982. — xx,193p : maps ; 21cm. — (World bibliographical series ; v.28)
Includes index
ISBN 0-903450-40-2 : £22.00 : CIP rev. B81-36039

016.96'02'0922 — Africa. Influence of Scotsmen, *1600-1980* **—** *Bibliographies*
Scotland & Africa. — Edinburgh : National Library of Scotland, 1982. — 63p : ill,1facsim,ports ; 25cm
Published to accompany an exhibition at the National Library of Scotland. — Includes index
ISBN 0-902220-50-0 (pbk) : Unpriced B82-31182

016.961'1 — Tunisia — *Bibliographies*
Findlay, Allan M.. Tunisia / Allan M. Findlay, Anne M. Findlay, Richard I. Lawless compilers. — Oxford : Clio, c1982. — xxviii,251p : 1map ; 22cm. — (World bibliographical series ; v.33)
Includes index
ISBN 0-903450-63-1 : £28.00 : CIP rev. B82-02477

016.9624 — Sudan — *Bibliographies*
Daly, Martin. Sudan. — Oxford : Clio Press, Dec.1982. — [180]p. — (World bibliographical series ; 40)
ISBN 0-903450-70-4 : £18.00 : CIP entry B82-32317

016.963 — Ethiopia, *to 1980* **—** *Bibliographies*
Rosenfeld, Chris Prouty. Historical dictionary of Ethiopia / by Chris Prouty and Eugene Rosenfeld. — Metuchen ; London : Scarecrow, 1981. — xv,436p : 1map ; 23cm. — (African historical dictionaries ; no.32)
Bibliography: p192-407. — Includes index
ISBN 0-8108-1448-x : £20.00
Primary classification 963'.003'21 B82-17418

016.965 — Algeria, *to 1980* **—** *Bibliographies*
Lawless, Richard I.. Algeria / Richard I. Lawless, compiler. — Oxford : Clio Press, c1980. — xxxii,215p : 1map ; 23cm. — (World bibliographical series ; v.19)
Includes index
ISBN 0-903450-32-1 : Unpriced B82-02689

016.9676'2 — Kenya — *Bibliographies*
Collison, Robert. Kenya / Robert L. Collison compiler. — Oxford : Clio, c1982. — xxix,157p : 1map ; 22cm. — (World bibliographical series ; v.25)
Includes index
ISBN 0-903450-34-8 : £18.00 : CIP rev. B82-03131

016.968'3 — Swaziland — *Bibliographies*
Nyeko, Balam. Swaziland. — Oxford : Clio Press, Dec.1982. — [180]p. — (World bibliographical series ; 24)
ISBN 0-903450-35-6 : £18.00 : CIP entry B82-32316

016.972 — Chicanos — *Abstracts*
Robinson, Barbara J.. The Mexican American : a critical guide to research aids / by Barbara J. Robinson, J. Cordell Robinson ; foreword by Carlos E. Cortes. — Greenwich, Conn. : Jai Press ; London : distributed by Jaicon Press, c1980. — xv,287p ; 24cm. — (Foundations in library and information science ; v.1)
Includes index
ISBN 0-89232-006-0 : £27.85 B82-03911

016.97281 — Guatemala — *Bibliographies*
Franklin, Woodman B.. Guatemala / Woodman B. Franklin compiler. — Oxford : Clio, c1981. — xiv,109p : 1map ; 23cm. — (World bibliographical series ; v.9)
Includes index
ISBN 0-903450-24-0 : £15.00 : CIP rev. B81-31542

016.97287 — Panama — *Bibliographies*
Langstaff, Eleanor DeSelms. Panama. — Oxford : Clio Press, Aug.1982. — [200]p. — (World bibliographical series ; 14)
ISBN 0-903450-26-7 : £20.00 : CIP entry B82-20790

016.97294 — Haiti — *Bibliographies*
Chambers, Frances. Haiti. — Oxford : Clio, Feb.1983. — [190]p. — (World bibliographical series ; 39)
ISBN 0-903450-69-0 : £19.00 : CIP entry B82-40314

016.973 — American culture, *ca 1850-1977* **—** *Bibliographies*
Handbook of American popular culture / edited by M. Thomas Inge. — Westport ; London : Greenwood Press
Includes bibliographies and index
Vol.2. — 1980. — x,423p ; 25cm
ISBN 0-313-21363-1 : Unpriced B82-14968

016.973 — Cornwall. Truro. Record repositories: Cornwall County and Diocesan Record Office. Stock: Documents on United States, ***1843-1903*** **—** ***Catalogues***

Cornwall County and Diocesan Record Office. The United States of America : maps, letters, diaries. — [Truro] ([County Hall, Truro, Cornwall, TR1 3AY]) : [Cornwall County and Diocesan Record Office], c1981. — 36p,[4]p of plates : ill,facsims ; 30cm. — (Handlist ; no.1)
Unpriced (pbk) B82-06301

016.973 — Great Britain. Repositories. Stock: Manuscripts on United States — ***Lists***

A Guide to the manuscripts relating to America in Great Britain and Ireland. — Rev. ed., edited by John W. Raimo / (under the general supervision of Dennis Welland). — London : Published for the British Association for American Studies by Meckler Books / Mansell Publishing, c1979. — xxv,467p ; 29cm
Previous ed.: London : Oxford University Press, 1961. — Includes index
ISBN 0-7201-0818-7 : £27.50 : CIP rev.
B79-18846

016.973 — United States — ***Bibliographies***

Heard, J. Norman. Bookman's guide to Americana / J. Norman Heard. — 8th ed. — Metuchen, N.J. ; London : Scarecrow, 1981. — ix,284p ; 23cm
Previous ed.: 1977
ISBN 0-8108-1457-9 : £14.00 B82-03953

Herstein, Sheila R.. United States of America / Sheila R. Herstein, Naomi C. Robbins, compilers. — Oxford : Clio, 1982. — xii,307p : 1map ; 23cm. — (World bibliographical series ; v.16)
Includes index
ISBN 0-903450-29-1 : £32.00 : CIP rev.
B81-34780

016.9736'2 — Mexican War — ***Bibliographies***

Tutorow, Norman E.. The Mexican-American war : an annotated bibliography / compiled and edited by Norman E. Tutorow. — Westport ; London : Greenwood, 1981. — xxix,427p ; 29cm
Includes index
ISBN 0-313-22181-2 : Unpriced B82-02821

016.98 — Latin America — ***Bibliographies***

Delorme, Robert L.. Latin America : social science information sources, 1967-1979 / Robert L. Delorme. — Santa Barbara ; Oxford : ABC-Clio, c1981. — ix,262p ; 29cm
Includes index
ISBN 0-87436-292-x : £21.75 B82-02740

016.98 — Latin America. Reference books — ***Lists***

Woods, Richard D.. Reference materials on Latin America in English : the humanities / by Richard D. Woods. — Metuchen ; London : Scarecrow, 1980 ; [Folkestone] : [Bailey and Swinfen] [[distributor]]. — xii,639p ; 23cm
Includes index
ISBN 0-8108-1294-0 : £22.75 B82-16109

017 — SUBJECT CATALOGUES

017'.534 — Essex. Public libraries: Essex County Library. Stock: Directories — ***Subject catalogues***

Essex County Library. *Technical Library Service.* Subject index to directories and some reference books : a short-title check list / Essex County Library Technical Library Service. — [Chelmsford] : [Essex Libraries], 1981. — 71p ; 30cm
ISBN 0-903630-12-5 (spiral) : £2.00
B82-08912

018 — AUTHOR CATALOGUES

018'.1 — Great Britain. National libraries: British Library. ***Department of Printed Books.*** **Stock —** ***Author catalogues***

British Library. The British Library general catalogue of printed books to 1975. — London : Bingley
67: Colum to Congr / [managing editor Jim Emmett]. — 1980. — 522p ; 31cm
ISBN 0-85157-587-0 : £38.00 : CIP rev.
ISBN 0-85157-520-x (set) : £11,800
B80-13677

British Library. The British Library general catalogue of printed books to 1975 / [managing editor Jim Emmett]. — London : Saur
93: Einem-Ellis / [editor Judi Vernau]. — 1981. — 538p ; 31cm
ISBN 0-86291-004-8 : Unpriced : CIP rev.
ISBN 0-86291-000-5 (set) : Unpriced
B81-30989

British Library. The British Library general catalogue of printed books to 1975 / [managing editor Jim Emmett]. — London : Saur
94: Ellis-Engla / [editor Judi Vernau]. — 1981. — 538p ; 31cm
ISBN 0-86291-005-6 : Unpriced : CIP rev.
ISBN 0-86291-000-5 (set) : Unpriced
B81-30988

British Library. The British Library general catalogue of printed books to 1975 / [managing editor Jim Emmett]. — London : Saur
95: England, 1-492 / [editor Judi Vernau]. — 1981. — 492p ; 31cm
ISBN 0-86291-008-0 : Unpriced : CIP rev.
ISBN 0-86291-006-4 (England sequence)
ISBN 0-85157-520-x (set) : Unpriced
B81-30994

British Library. The British Library general catalogue of printed books to 1975 / [managing editor Jim Emmett]. — London : Saur
96: England, 493-985 / [editor Judi Vernau]. — 1981. — p493-985 ; 31cm
ISBN 0-86291-007-2 : Unpriced : CIP rev.
ISBN 0-86291-006-4 (England sequence)
ISBN 0-85157-520-x (set) : Unpriced
B81-30987

British Library. The British Library general catalogue of printed books to 1975 / [managing editor Jim Emmett]. — London : Saur
97: England, 986-1478 / [editor Judi Vernau]. — 1981. — p986-1478 ; 31cm
ISBN 0-86291-009-9 : Unpriced
ISBN 0-86291-006-4 (England sequence)
ISBN 0-86291-000-5 (set) : Unpriced
B82-09509

British Library. The British Library general catalogue of printed books to 1975 / [managing editor Jim Emmett]. — London : Saur
98: England, 1479-1971 / [editor Judi Vernau]. — 1981. — p1479-1971 ; 31cm
ISBN 0-86291-010-2 : Unpriced
ISBN 0-86291-006-4 (England sequence)
ISBN 0-86291-000-5 (set) : Unpriced
B82-09510

British Library. The British Library general catalogue of printed books to 1975 / [managing editor Jim Emmett]. — London : Saur
99: England, 1972-2464 / [editor Judi Vernau]. — 1981. — p1972-2464 ; 31cm
ISBN 0-86291-011-0 : Unpriced
ISBN 0-86291-006-4 (England sequence)
ISBN 0-86291-000-5 (set) : Unpriced
B82-09511

British Library. The British Library general catalogue of printed books to 1975 / [managing editor Jim Emmett]. — London : Saur
100: England, 2465-2957 / [editor Judi Vernau]. — 1981. — p2465-2957 ; 31cm
ISBN 0-86291-012-9 : Unpriced
ISBN 0-86291-006-4 (England sequence)
ISBN 0-86291-000-5 (set) : Unpriced
B82-09512

British Library. The British Library general catalogue of printed books to 1975 / [managing editor Jim Emmett]. — London : Saur
101: Engla-Equiv / [editor Judi Vernau]. — 1981. — 522p ; 31cm
ISBN 0-86291-013-7 : Unpriced : CIP rev.
ISBN 0-86291-000-5 (set) : Unpriced
B81-34720

British Library. The British Library general catalogue of printed books to 1975 / [managing editor Jim Emmett]. — London : Saur
102: Equiv-Esser / [editor Judi Vernau]. — 1981. — 522p ; 31cm
ISBN 0-86291-014-5 : Unpriced : CIP rev.
ISBN 0-86291-000-5 (set) : Unpriced
B81-34721

British Library. The British Library general catalogue of printed books to 1975. — London : Saur
103: Esser-Evans / [editor Judi Vernau]. — 1981. — 522p ; 31cm
ISBN 0-86291-015-3 : Unpriced : CIP rev.
ISBN 0-85157-520-x (set) : Unpriced
B81-34722

British Library. The British Library general catalogue of printed books to 1975. — London : Saur
104: Evans-Fabre / [editor Judi Vernau]. — 1981. — 522p ; 31cm
ISBN 0-86291-016-1 : Unpriced : CIP rev.
ISBN 0-85157-520-x (set) : Unpriced
B81-38849

British Library. The British Library general catalogue of printed books to 1975. — London : Saur
105: Fabre-Farnu / [editor Judi Vernau]. — 1981. — 522p ; 31cm
ISBN 0-86291-017-x : Unpriced : CIP rev.
ISBN 0-85157-520-x (set) : Unpriced
B81-38294

British Library. The British Library general catalogue of printed books to 1975. — London : Saur
106: Farnu-Felka / [editor Judi Vernau]. — 1981. — 522p ; 31cm
ISBN 0-86291-018-8 : Unpriced : CIP rev.
ISBN 0-85157-520-x (set) : Unpriced
B82-01343

British Library. The British Library general catalogue of printed books to 1975. — London : Saur
107: Felka-Fesca / [editor Judi Vernau]. — 1981. — 522p ; 31cm
ISBN 0-86291-019-6 : Unpriced : CIP rev.
ISBN 0-85157-520-x (set) : Unpriced
B82-01344

British Library. The British Library general catalogue of printed books to 1975. — London : Saur
108: Fesca-Finla / [editor Judi Vernau]. — 1981. — 522p ; 31cm
ISBN 0-86291-020-x : Unpriced : CIP rev.
ISBN 0-85157-520-x (set) : Unpriced
B82-01345

British Library. The British Library general catalogue of printed books to 1975. — London : Saur
109: Finla-Flamm / [editor Judi Vernau]. — 1981. — 490p ; 31cm
ISBN 0-86291-021-8 : Unpriced
ISBN 0-85157-520-x (set) : Unpriced
B82-14158

British Library. The British Library general catalogue of printed books to 1975. — London : Saur
110: Flamm-Fogg / [editor Judi Vernau]. — 1981. — 490p ; 31cm
ISBN 0-86291-022-6 : Unpriced
ISBN 0-85157-520-x (set) : Unpriced
B82-14159

British Library. The British Library general catalogue of printed books to 1975. — London : Saur
111: Fogg-Forst / [editor Judi Vernau]. — 1981. — 490p ; 31cm
ISBN 0-86291-023-4 : Unpriced
ISBN 0-85157-520-x (set) : Unpriced
B82-31228

British Library. The British Library general catalogue of printed books to 1975. — London : Saur
112: Forst-Franc / [editor Judi Vernau]. — 1981. — 490p ; 31cm
ISBN 0-86291-024-2 : Unpriced
ISBN 0-85157-520-x (set) : Unpriced
B82-35539

British Library. The British Library general catalogue of printed books to 1975. — London : Saur
113: France / [editor Judi Vernau]. — 1981. — 474p ; 31cm
ISBN 0-86291-025-0 : Unpriced (set) : Unpriced B82-31230

018′.1 — Great Britain. National libraries: British Library. *Department of Printed Books.* **Stock —** *Author catalogues* *continuation*

British Library. The British Library general catalogue of printed books to 1975. — London : Saur
114: France-Frank / [editor Judi Vernau]. — 1982. — 244p ; 31cm
ISBN 0-86291-026-9 : Unpriced : CIP rev.
ISBN 0-85157-520-x (set) : Unpriced
B82-08407

British Library. The British Library general catalogue of printed books to 1975. — London : Saur
115: Frank-Freem / [editor Judi Vernau]. — 1982. — 474p ; 31cm
ISBN 0-86291-027-7 : Unpriced : CIP rev.
ISBN 0-85157-520-x (set) : Unpriced
B82-08408

British Library. The British Library general catalogue of printed books to 1975. — London : Saur
116: Freem-Frimo / [editor Judi Vernau]. — 1982. — 474p ; 31cm
ISBN 0-86291-028-5 : Unpriced : CIP rev.
ISBN 0-85157-520-x (set) : Unpriced
B82-10656

British Library. The British Library general catalogue of printed books to 1975. — London : Saur
117: Frimo-Furet / [editor Judi Vernau]. — 1982. — 474p ; 31cm
ISBN 0-86291-029-3 : Unpriced : CIP rev.
ISBN 0-85157-520-x (set) : Unpriced
B82-10655

British Library. The British Library general catalogue of printed books to 1975. — London : Saur
118: Furet-Galfr / [editor Judi Vernau]. — 1982. — 474p ; 31cm
ISBN 0-86291-030-7 : Unpriced : CIP rev.
ISBN 0-85156-720-x (set) : Unpriced
B82-10661

British Library. The British Library general catalogue of printed books to 1975. — London : Saur
119: Galfr-Garde / [editor Judi Vernau]. — 1982. — 474p ; 31cm
ISBN 0-86291-031-5 : Unpriced : CIP rev.
ISBN 0-85157-520-x (set) : Unpriced
B82-10662

British Library. The British Library general catalogue of printed books to 1975. — London : Saur
120: Garde-Gaudi / [editor Judi Vernau]. — 1982. — 474p ; 31cm
ISBN 0-86291-032-3 : Unpriced : CIP rev.
ISBN 0-85157-520-x (set) : Unpriced
B82-10676

British Library. The British Library general catalogue of printed books to 1975. — London : Saur
121: Gaudi-Gener / [editor Judi Vernau]. — 1982. — 474p ; 31cm
ISBN 0-86291-033-1 (corrected) : Unpriced : CIP rev.
ISBN 0-85157-520-x (set) : Unpriced
B82-10677

British Library. The British Library general catalogue of printed books to 1975. — London : Saur
122: Gener-Germa / [editor Judi Vernau]. — 1982. — 474p ; 31cm
ISBN 0-86291-034-x : Unpriced : CIP rev.
ISBN 0-85157-520-x (set) : Unpriced
B82-13482

British Library. The British Library general catalogue of printed books to 1975. — London : Saur
123: Germa-Gessn / [editor Judi Vernau]. — 1982. — 474p ; 31cm
ISBN 0-86291-035-8 : Unpriced : CIP rev.
ISBN 0-85157-520-x (set) : Unpriced
B82-14932

British Library. The British Library general catalogue of printed books to 1975. — London : Saur
124: Gessn-Gilca / [editor Judi Vernau]. — 1982. — 474p ; 31cm
ISBN 0-86291-036-6 : Unpriced : CIP rev.
ISBN 0-85157-520-x (set) : Unpriced
B82-13481

British Library. The British Library general catalogue of printed books to 1975. — London : Saur
125: Gilca-Gjedd / [editor Judi Vernau]. — 1982. — 474p ; 31cm
ISBN 0-86291-037-4 : Unpriced : CIP rev.
ISBN 0-85157-520-x (set) : Unpriced
B82-13480

British Library. The British Library general catalogue of printed books to 1975. — London : Saur
126: Gjedd-Godle / [editor Judi Vernau]. — 1982. — 474p ; 31cm
ISBN 0-86291-038-2 : Unpriced
ISBN 0-85157-520-x (set) : Unpriced
B82-36689

British Library. The British Library general catalogue of printed books to 1975. — London : Saur
127: Godle-Golds / [editor Judi Vernau]. — 1982. — 474p ; 31cm
ISBN 0-86291-039-0 : Unpriced : CIP rev.
ISBN 0-85157-520-x (set) : Unpriced
B82-14933

British Library. The British Library general catalogue of printed books to 1975. — London : Saur
128: Golds-Gordo / [editor Judi Vernau]. — 1982. — 474p ; 31cm
ISBN 0-86291-040-4 : Unpriced : CIP rev.
ISBN 0-85157-520-x (set) : Unpriced
B82-22395

British Library. The British Library general catalogue of printed books to 1975. — London : Saur
129: Gordo-Gover / [editor Judi Vernau]. — 1982. — 474p ; 31cm
ISBN 0-86291-041-2 : Unpriced : CIP rev.
ISBN 0-85157-520-x (set) : Unpriced
B82-17902

British Library. The British Library general catalogue of printed books to 1975. — London : Saur
130: Gover-Grass / [editor Judi Vernau]. — 1982. — 474p ; 31cm
ISBN 0-86291-042-0 : Unpriced : CIP rev.
ISBN 0-85157-520-x (set) : Unpriced
B82-17903

British Library. The British Library general catalogue of printed books to 1975. — London : Saur
131: Grass-Green / [editor Judi Vernau]. — 1982. — 474p ; 31cm
ISBN 0-86291-043-9 : Unpriced
ISBN 0-85157-520-x (set) : Unpriced
B82-31231

British Library. The British Library general catalogue of printed books to 1975. — London : Saur
132: Green-Griff / [editor Judi Vernau]. — 1982. — 474p ; 31cm
ISBN 0-86291-044-7 : Unpriced : CIP rev.
ISBN 0-85157-520-x (set) : Unpriced
B82-17909

British Library. The British Library general catalogue of printed books to 1975. — London : Saur
133: Griff-Grove. — June 1982. — [480]p
ISBN 0-86291-045-5 : CIP entry
ISBN 0-85157-520-x (set) : Unpriced
B82-22397

British Library. The British Library general catalogue of printed books to 1975. — London : Saur
134: Grove-Guibe. — June 1982. — [480]p
ISBN 0-86291-046-3 : CIP entry
ISBN 0-85157-520-x (set) : Unpriced
B82-17949

British Library. The British Library general catalogue of printed books to 1975. — London : Saur
135: Guibert-Guthrie. — July 1982. — [480]p
ISBN 0-86291-047-1 : CIP entry
ISBN 0-85157-520-x (set) : Unpriced
B82-17957

British Library. The British Library general catalogue of printed books to 1975. — London : Saur
136: Guthr-Haeke. — July 1982. — [480]p
ISBN 0-86291-048-x : CIP entry
ISBN 0-85157-520-x (set) : Unpriced
B82-17956

British Library. The British Library general catalogue of printed books to 1975. — London : Saur
137: Hacke-Hall. — July 1982. — [474]p
ISBN 0-86291-049-8 : CIP entry
ISBN 0-85157-520-x (set) : Unpriced
B82-21118

British Library. The British Library general catalogue of printed books to 1975. — London : Saur
138: Hall-Hamme. — July 1982. — [474]p
ISBN 0-86291-050-1 : CIP entry
ISBN 0-85157-520-x (set) : Unpriced
B82-23837

British Library. The British Library general catalogue of printed books to 1975. — London : Saur
139: Hamme-Hards / [editor Judi Vernau]. — 1982. — 474p ; 31cm
ISBN 0-86291-051-x : Unpriced : CIP rev.
ISBN 0-85157-520-x (set) : Unpriced
B82-21119

British Library. The British Library general catalogue of printed books to 1975. — London : Saur
140: Hards-Harri / [editor Judi Vernau]. — 1982. — 474p ; 31cm
ISBN 0-86291-052-8 : Unpriced : CIP rev.
ISBN 0-85157-520-x (set) : Unpriced
B82-21120

British Library. The British Library general catalogue of printed books to 1975. — London : Saur
141: Harri-Hatsc / [editor Judi Vernau]. — 1982. — 474p ; 31cm
ISBN 0-86291-053-6 : Unpriced : CIP rev.
ISBN 0-85157-520-x (set) : Unpriced
B82-26700

British Library. The British Library general catalogue of printed books to 1975. — London : Saur
142: Hatsc-Hayne / [editor Judi Vernau]. — 1982. — 474p ; 31cm
ISBN 0-86291-054-4 : Unpriced : CIP rev.
ISBN 0-85157-520-x (set) : Unpriced
B82-23849

British Library. The British Library general catalogue of printed books to 1975. — London : Saur
143: Hayne-Heide / [editor Judi Vernau]. — 1982. — 474p ; 31cm
ISBN 0-86291-055-2 : Unpriced : CIP rev.
ISBN 0-85157-520-x (set) : Unpriced
B82-23847

British Library. The British Library general catalogue of printed books to 1975. — London : Saur
144: Heide-Hende / [editor Judi Vernau]. — 1982. — 474p ; 31cm
ISBN 0-86291-056-0 : Unpriced : CIP rev.
ISBN 0-85157-520-x (set) : Unpriced
B82-23848

British Library. The British Library general catalogue of printed books to 1975. — London : Saur
145: Hende-Herbi. — Sept.1982. — [474]p
ISBN 0-86291-057-9 : CIP entry
ISBN 0-85157-520-x (set) : Unpriced
B82-23857

018′.1 — Great Britain. National libraries: British Library. *Department of Printed Books.* **Stock —** *Author catalogues* *continuation*

British Library. The British Library general catalogue of printed books to 1975. — London : Saur
146: Herbi-Herzo. — Sept.1982. — [474]p
ISBN 0-86291-058-7 : CIP entry
ISBN 0-85157-520-x (set) : Unpriced
B82-23858

British Library. The British Library general catalogue of printed books to 1975. — London : Saur
147: Herzo-Highm. — Sept.1982. — [474]p
ISBN 0-86291-059-5 : CIP entry
ISBN 0-85157-520-x (set) : Unpriced
B82-28602

British Library. The British Library general catalogue of printed books to 1975. — London : Saur
148: Highm-Hirsc. — Sept.1982. — [474]p
ISBN 0-86291-060-9 : CIP entry
ISBN 0-85157-520-x (set) : Unpriced
B82-26081

British Library. The British Library general catalogue of printed books to 1975. — London : Saur
149: Hirsc-Hoeld. — Sept.1982. — [474]p
ISBN 0-86291-061-7 : CIP entry
ISBN 0-85157-520-x (set) : Unpriced
B82-26082

British Library. The British Library general catalogue of printed books to 1975. — London : Saur
150: Hoeld-Holla. — Sept.1982. — [474]p
ISBN 0-86291-062-5 : CIP entry
ISBN 0-85157-520-x (set) : Unpriced
B82-25729

British Library. The British Library general catalogue of printed books to 1975. — London : Saur, Sept.1982
151: Holla-Honde. — [474]p
ISBN 0-86291-063-3 : CIP entry
ISBN 0-85157-520-x (set) : Unpriced
B82-25728

British Library. The British Library general catalogue of printed books to 1975. — London : Saur
152: Honde-Hornb. — Sept.1982. — [474]p
ISBN 0-86291-064-1 : CIP entry
ISBN 0-85157-520-x (set) : Unpriced
B82-27194

British Library. The British Library general catalogue of printed books to 1975. — London : Saur
153: Horub-Howcr. — Sept.1982. — [474]p
ISBN 0-86291-067-6 : CIP entry
ISBN 0-85157-520-x (set) : Unpriced
B82-28603

British Library. The British Library general catalogue of printed books to 1975. — London : Saur
154: Howcr-Hughe. — Sept.1982. — [474]p
ISBN 0-86291-068-4 : CIP entry
ISBN 0-85157-520-x (set) : Unpriced
B82-28604

British Library. The British Library general catalogue of printed books to 1975. — London : Saur
Vol.155: Hughe-Hunt. — Sept.1982. — [474]p
ISBN 0-86291-069-2 : CIP entry B82-32880

British Library. The British Library general catalogue of printed books to 1975. — London : Saur
Vol.156: Hunt-Hymna. — Oct.1982. — [510]p
ISBN 0-86291-070-6 : CIP entry B82-32881

British Library. The British Library general catalogue of printed books to 1975. — London : Saur
Vol.157: Hymna-Illus. — Oct.1982. — [474]p
ISBN 0-86291-071-4 : CIP entry B82-32882

British Library. The British Library general catalogue of printed books to 1975. — London : Saur
Vol.158: Illus-Innes. — Oct.1982. — [474]p
ISBN 0-86291-072-2 : CIP entry B82-32883

British Library. The British Library general catalogue of printed books to 1975. — London : Saur
Vol.159: Innes-Inter. — Oct.1982. — [474]p
ISBN 0-86291-073-0 : CIP entry B82-32884

British Library. The British Library general catalogue of printed books to 1975. — London : Saur
Vol.160: Inter-Irwin. — Oct.1982. — [474]p
ISBN 0-86291-074-9 : CIP entry B82-36294

British Library. The British Library general catalogue of printed books to 1975. — London : Saur
Vol.161: Irwin-J., F.W.. — Nov.1982. — [474]p
ISBN 0-86291-075-7 : CIP entry B82-36295

British Library. The British Library general catalogue of printed books to 1975. — London : Saur
Vol.162: J.G.-Jahrb. — Nov.1982. — [474]p
ISBN 0-86291-076-5 B82-37641

British Library. The British Library general catalogue of printed books to 1975. — London : Saur
Vol.163: Jahrb-Jaque. — Nov.1982. — [474]p
ISBN 0-86291-077-3 : CIP entry B82-40919

British Library. The British Library general catalogue of printed books to 1975. — London : Saur
Vol.164: Jacque-Jerem. — Nov.1982. — [474]p
ISBN 0-86291-078-1 B82-37640

British Library. The British Library general catalogue of printed books to 1975. — London : Saur
Vol.165: Jerem-Jezie. — Dec.1982. — [474]p
ISBN 0-86291-079-x : CIP entry B82-40345

British Library. The British Library general catalogue of printed books to 1975. — London : Saur
Vol.166: Jezie-Johns. — Dec.1982. — 1v.
ISBN 0-86291-080-3 : CIP entry B82-40343

British Library. The British Library general catalogue of printed books to 1975. — London : Saur
Vol.167: Johns-Jones. — Jan.1983. — 1v.
ISBN 0-86291-081-1 : CIP entry B82-40920

British Library. The British Library general catalogue of printed books to 1975. — London : Saur
England — subheadings index. — Sept.1982. — [200]p
ISBN 0-86291-065-x : CIP entry B82-32879

British Library. The British Library general catalogue of printed books to 1975. — London : Saur
England — titles index. — Sept.1982. — [656]p
ISBN 0-86291-066-8 : CIP entry B82-32315

018′.1221 — England. Legal deposit libraries. Stock: Books in English: Books published between 1701 & 1800. Author catalogues: Author Union Catalogue — *Indexes*

Robinson, F. J. G.. Eighteenth-century British books : an index to the foreign and provincial imprints in the author union catalogue / compiled by F.J.G. & J.M. Robinson and C. Wadham ; cartography by D. Hume. — Newcastle upon Tyne : Avero, 1982. — x,320p : facsims,maps ; 31cm + prospectus 1sheet : 30cm ; 1map
Nine folded sheets (maps) in pocket
ISBN 0-907977-00-6 : £250.00 : CIP rev.
B82-14205

018′.1291439 — Great Britain. National libraries: India Office Library and Records. Stock: Books in Urdu, *1800-1920* **—** *Catalogues*

India Office Library. Catalogue of Urdu books in the India Office Library, 1800-1920 : (supplementary to James Fuller Blumhardt's catalogue of 1900) / compiled by Salim Al-din Quraishi. — London : India Office Library and Records, 1982. — xii,280p ; 30cm
Includes index
Unpriced (pbk) B82-25796

018′.131 — Bible societies: British and Foreign Bible Society. *Library.* **Stock: Manuscripts —** *Catalogues*

Falivene, M. Rosaria. Historical catalogue of the manuscripts of Bible House Library. — London : British & Foreign Bible Society, Aug.1982. — 1v.
ISBN 0-564-07162-5 (pbk) : CIP entry
B82-16484

018′.131 — Great Britain. National libraries: British Library. *Department of Manuscripts.* **Stock: Acquisitions,** *1961-* **—** *Catalogues*

British Library. *Department of Manuscripts.* 'Rough register' of acquisitions of the Department of Manuscripts British Library 1976-1980. — London : Swift, 1982. — 256p ; 33cm. — (Special series / List & Index Society ; v.15)
At head of title: List & Index Society
£11.80(£9.50 to members) B82-21432

018′.131 — Great Britain. National libraries: British Library. *Department of Manuscripts.* **Stock: Acquisitions —** *Catalogues*

British Library. Catalogue of additions to the manuscripts, 1951-1955 / The British Library. — London : The Library, c1982. — 2v.(xi,701p) ; 24cm
Limited ed. of 500 copies. — Includes index
ISBN 0-904654-69-9 : £90.00 : CIP rev.
B81-34661

018′.131 — Great Britain. National libraries: India Office Library and Records. Stock: Manuscripts in Sinhalese — *Catalogues*

India Office Library and Records. Catalogue of the Sinhalese manuscripts in the India Office Library / compiled by D.J. Wijayaratne in collaboration with A.S. Kulasuriya ; edited by C.H.B. Reynolds. — London : India Office Library and Records, 1981. — viii,73p ; 30cm
Includes index
ISBN 0-903359-33-2 (pbk) : Unpriced : CIP rev. B81-20654

018′.131 — Spain. Libraries. Stock: Manuscripts in Arabic — *Lists*

Imamuddin, S. M.. Hispano-Arab libraries. — London (68a Delancey St., NW1 2RY) : Ta Ha Publishers, Sept.1982. — [42]p
Originally published: Karachi : Pakistan Historical Society, 1961
ISBN 0-907461-29-8 (pbk) : £1.50 : CIP entry
Primary classification 027.6′7 B82-31324

018′.134 — Great Britain. National libraries: British Library. *Lending Division.* **Stock: Periodicals: Translations into English language —** *Lists*

Journals in translation. — 3rd ed. — Boston Spa : British Library Lending Division, Aug.1982. — [175]p
Previous ed.: 1978
ISBN 0-7123-2000-8 : £25.00 : CIP entry
B82-18477

018′.134 — Hereford and Worcester. Special libraries. Stock: Serials — *Title catalogues — Serials*

Hereford and Worcester Association of Technical Libraries. Union list of periodicals / Hereford and Worcester Association of Technical Libraries. — 6th ed. (Summer 1978)-. — Redditch (The Library, Redditch College, Redditch, Worcs. B98 8DW) : The Association, 1978-. — v. ; 30cm
Irregular. — Continues: County of Hereford and Worcester Association of Technical Libraries. Union list of periodicals. — Description based on: 7th ed. (Autumn 1981)
ISSN 0262-4702 = Union list of periodicals - Hereford and Worcester Association of Technical Libraries : £5.00 B82-04076

018′.134 — Scotland. National libraries: National Library of Scotland. Stock: Serials — *Catalogues*

National Library of Scotland. Current periodicals / [National Library of Scotland]. — Edinburgh : The Library, 1982, c1981. — 250p : 1form ; 30cm
ISBN 0-902220-47-0 (pbk) : £6.00 B82-19109

018′.142 — Oxfordshire. Oxford. Universities: University of Oxford. Libraries. Stock: Incunabula — *Author catalogues*

Rhodes, Dennis E.. A catalogue of incunabula in all the libraries of Oxford University outside the Bodleian / Dennis E. Rhodes. — Oxford : Clarendon, 1982. — xli,444p,viiip of plates : facsims ; 22cm
Bibliography: pxl-xli. — Includes index
ISBN 0-19-818175-2 : £40.00 : CIP rev. B81-22549

018′.144 — England. Legal deposit libraries. Stock: Books with British imprints: Books published between 1701 & 1800 — *Author catalogues*

Eighteenth-century British book : an author union catalogue : extracted from the British Museum Catalogue of Printed Books, the Catalogues of the Bodleian Library and of the University Library, Cambridge / by F.J.G. Robinson ... [et al.]. — Folkestone : Dawson [for] Project for Historical Biobibliography
Vol.4: M-R. — 1981. — xvi,715p ; 30cm
ISBN 0-7129-1023-9 : Unpriced B82-03028

Eighteenth-century British books : an author union catalogue extracted from the British Museum General Catalogue of Printed Books, the catalogues of the Bodleian Library and of the University Library, Cambridge / by F.J.G. Robinson ... [et al.]. — Folkestone : Dawson [for] Project for Historical Biobibliography
Vol.5: S-Z. — 1981. — xvi,707p ; 31cm
ISBN 0-7129-1023-9 : Unpriced B82-11682

018′.23 — Ancient Rome. Historiography. Gibbon, Edward. Personal property: Books — *Author catalogues*

The **Library** of Edward Gibbon : a catalogue / edited and introduced by Geoffrey Keynes Kt. — 2nd ed. — [Godalming] : St Paul′s Bibliographies, 1980. — 293p,[11]p of plates : ill,facsims,1port ; 24cm
Previous ed.: London : Cape, 1940
ISBN 0-906795-02-8 : £12.00 : CIP rev. B80-05178

018′.244 — Clwyd. Hawarden. Private libraries: St. Deiniol′s Library. Stock: Rare books. Collections: Glynne Library — *Author catalogues*

St. Deiniol′s Library. A bibliography of the Glynne Library : a collection of rare books dating from the 16th to the 19th century at St. Deiniol′s Library / compiled by Diana C. MacIntyre. — [Hawarden] : [St. Deiniol′s Library], [1981]. — 40leaves ; 29cm
Cover title
£1.80 (pbk) B82-19747

018′.244 — Scotland. Grampian Region. Elgin. Abbeys. Libraries: Pluscarden Library. Stock: Books printed before 1801 — *Author catalogues*

Pluscarden Abbey. Benedictine Abbey of Our Lady and St John the Baptist and St Andrew, Pluscarden : catalogue of books printed before 1801 / compiled and with introduction by D.W. Doughty ; and foreword by the Abbot of Pluscarden. — St Andrews : University Library, 1980. — xviii,48p : ill ; 21cm
Bibliography: pxiv-xviii. — Includes index
ISBN 0-900897-03-1 (pbk) : £1.50 B82-10823

019 — DICTIONARY CATALOGUES

019.091 — Great Britain. National libraries: British Library. *Department of Printed Books*. Stock: Acquisitions, *1961-1970* — *Subject catalogues*

British Library. *Department of Printed Books*. Subject index of modern books acquired 1961-1970. — London : British Library Reference Division Publications, Dec.1982. — 12v.
ISBN 0-904654-55-9 : CIP entry B82-30741

020 — LIBRARY AND INFORMATION SCIENCES

020 — Comparative librarianship

Simsova, Sylva. A primer of comparative librarianship / Sylva Simsova. — London : Bingley, 1982. — 95p : ill ; 23cm
Bibliography: p80-82. — Includes index
ISBN 0-85157-341-x : Unpriced : CIP rev. B81-31527

020 — Librarianship

Contemporary developments in librarianship : an international handbook / edited by Miles M. Jackson. — London : Library Association, 1981. — xxxii,619p ; 29cm
Includes bibliographies and index
ISBN 0-85365-834-x : Unpriced : CIP rev. B82-04798

Modern library practice. — 2nd ed. — Buckden (45 Park Rd., Buckden, Cambs. PE18 9SL) : Elm Publications, Oct.1982. — [352]p
Previous ed. published as: Library practice. 1977
ISBN 0-9505828-5-9 (pbk) : £8.90 : CIP entry B82-30297

020 — Librarianship & information science

Pratt, Allan D.. The information of the image / Allan D. Pratt. — Norwood, N.J. : Ablex ; London (3 Henrietta St., WC2E 8LU) : Eurospan [distributor], c1982. — v,117p : ill ; 24cm. — (Libraries and librarianship)
Includes bibliographies and index
ISBN 0-89391-055-4 : £12.00 B82-27699

020 — Librarianship — *Conference proceedings*

Library Association. *Reference, Special and Information Section. Study Group (27th : 1979 : Winchester)*. Proceedings of the 27th Annual Study Group, Winchester 30th March to 2nd April 1979 / the Library Association, Reference, Special and Information Section ; edited by Ann Penniall. — London : The Section, [1979?]. — 40p ; 21cm
Cover title
ISBN 0-85365-573-1 (pbk) : Unpriced : CIP rev. B80-07645

020 — Librarianship — *Manuals* — *For non-professional personnel*

Chirgwin, F. John. The library assistant′s manual. — 2nd, rev. ed. — London : Bingley, Sept.1982. — [135]p. — (Outlines of modern librarianship)
Previous ed.: 1978
ISBN 0-85157-350-9 : £6.50 : CIP entry B82-20529

020′.148 — Librarianship & information science — *Abbreviations*

Montgomery, A. C.. Acronyms and abbreviations in library and information work. — London : Library Association, Mar.1982. — [132]p
ISBN 0-85365-904-4 (pbk) : £7.00 : CIP entry B82-01416

020′.23′41 — Great Britain. Librarianship — *Career guides*

Kinross, John, *1933-*. Careers in librarianship / John Kinross. — Northampton : Hamilton House, 1982. — 44p ; 21cm. — (Careerscope ; 7)
Bibliography: p43-44
ISBN 0-906888-26-3 (pbk) : Unpriced B82-17430

020′.28′542 — Librarianship. Applications of digital computer systems. Programming

Davis, Charles H.. Illustrative computer programming for libraries : selected examples for information specialists / Charles H. Davis. — 2nd ed. / Charles H. Davis and Gerald W. Lundeen. — London : Aldwych, 1981. — xii,129p : ill ; 22cm
Previous ed.: Westport, Conn. : Greenwood, 1974. — Bibliography: p123-124. — Includes index
ISBN 0-86172-027-x : £11.50 B82-30925

020′.5 — Information service & libraries — *Serials* — *For research libraries*

Outlook on research libraries : the monthly review of national and international developments influencing research library management. — Vol.1, no.1 (Oct. 1978)-. — Lausanne ; Oxford : Elsevier Sequoia, 1978-. — v. ; 30cm
Description based on: Vol.3, no.5 (May 1981)
ISSN 0165-2818 = Outlook on research libraries : Unpriced B82-10111

020′.622′41 — Great Britain. Librarianship. Organisations: Library Association — *Serials*

Library Association. The Library Association year book. — 1982. — London : The Association, Mar.1982. — [400]p
ISBN 0-85365-525-1 : £13.75 : CIP entry
ISSN 0075-9066 B82-02640

020′.7 — Comparative librarianship. Information sources — *Lists*

Mackee, Monique. A handbook of comparative librarianship. — 3rd ed. — London : Bingley, Feb.1983. — [550]p
Previous ed.: 1975
ISBN 0-85157-348-7 : £30.00 : CIP entry B82-39594

020′.7 — Developing countries. Librarians. Professional education — *Conference proceedings*

Unesco-IFLA Conference Seminar on Library Education Programmes in Developing Countries *(1980 : University of the Philippines)*. Library education programmes in developing countries with special reference to Asia. — London : Library Association, July 1982. — [170]p
ISBN 0-85365-655-x (pbk) : £7.50 : CIP entry B82-13141

020′.7′041 — Great Britain. Librarians. Professional education, *to 1980*

Bramley, Gerald. Apprentice to graduate : a history of library education in the United Kingdom / Gerald Bramley. — London : Bingley, 1981. — 218p ; 23cm
Includes index
ISBN 0-85157-343-6 : Unpriced : CIP rev. B81-24670

020′.7′1 — Librarians. Professional education. Courses — *Directories*

World guide to library schools and training courses in documentation = Guide mondial des écoles de bibliothécaires et documentalistes. — 2nd ed. — London : Bingley, 1981. — 549p ; 23cm
Text in English and French. — Previous ed.: / Unesco, 1972. — Includes index
ISBN 0-85157-309-6 : £25.00 : CIP rev. B81-20190

020′.7′1141 — Great Britain. Schools of librarianship — *Directories*

Ward, N. J.. Which library school? / compiled by N.J. Ward on behalf of the A.A.L. Students′ Committee. — 2nd ed. — London : Association of Assistant Librarians with assistance from Harold Hill & Son, 1982. — 40p ; 21cm
Previous ed.: 1980
ISBN 0-900092-40-8 (pbk) : £1.50 (£1.20 to members) B82-19044

020′.7′1142547 — Leicestershire. Loughborough. Schools of librarianship: Loughborough University of Technology. *Department of Library and Information Studies*

Loughborough University of Technology. *Department of Library and Information Studies*. Department of Library and Information Studies : departmental profile : the first decade. — [Loughborough] : Loughborough University, 1981. — 231p,[5]leaves of plates : ill,1plan,1port ; 30cm
Unpriced (pbk) B82-36896

020′.7′1143 — West Germany. Medical professional education information scientists

Kostrewski, Barbara. Education in medical information in West Germany : final report : report to the British Library R & D Department on project numbers S1/V/047 / Barbara Kostrewski. — [London] ([Northampton Square, London EC1V 0HB]) : Centre for Information Science, City University, 1980. — 63p : ill,(1 facsim) ; 30cm. — (BL R & D report ; 5582)
Unpriced (pbk) B82-36191

020′.7′1173 — United States. Schools of librarianship. Teaching methods

Havard-Williams, P.. Teaching methods in North American library schools : report to British Library Research and Development Department of study visit overseas / by P. Havard-Williams and J.M. Brittain. — Loughborough : Department of Library and Information Studies, Loughborough University, 1982. — 67p ; 30cm. — (BL R & D report ; 5712)
Cover title. — Bibliography: p63
Unpriced (pbk) B82-24642

020′.7′15 — Great Britain. Libraries. Personnel. Training. Curriculum subjects: Machine-readable files. Searching

Keenan, S.. Training requirements for online intermediaries / S. Keenan and A. Vickery. — [Loughborough] : [Loughborough University, Department of Library and Information Studies], 1982. — 164p : ill,1form ; 30cm. — (Report ; no.5724)
Unpriced (unbound) B82-40945

020′.76 — Librarianship — *Questions & answers*

Ritchie, Sheila. Modern library practice. — Buckden (45 Park Rd., Buckden, Cambs. PE18 9SL) : Elm Publications, Oct.1982
Tutor′s pack: Advanced (B). — [60]p
ISBN 0-9505828-7-5 (unbound) : £15.95 : CIP entry B82-30298

Ritchie, Sheila. Modern library practice. — Buckden (45 Park Rd., Buckden, Cambs. PE18 9SL) : Elm Publications, Nov.1982
Tutor′s pack: Basic (A). — [40]p
ISBN 0-9505828-6-7 (unbound) : £11.95 : CIP entry B82-30299

020′.7′8 — Great Britain. Schools of librarianship. Teaching. Implications of digital computer systems

Smith, Joan M.. Workshop on New Technology and Library-Information Science Education, Newcastle upon Tyne Polytechnic, April 13th-16th, 1981 : summary of proceedings : report to the British Library Research and Development Department on Project SI/G/508 / Joan M. Smith, Ian S. Simpson, D. Alasdair Kemp. — [Newcastle upon Tyne] ([Ellison Bldg., Ellison Place, Newcastle upon Tyne NE1 8ST]) : School of Librarianship and Information Studies, Newcastle upon Tyne Polytechnic, 1981. — 24p ; 30cm. — (Report ; 5668)
Unpriced (pbk) B82-10918

020′.7′8 — United States. Librarians. Professional education. Teaching aids: Simulations

Guy, Leonard C.. Simulation in library education : a report on a workshop and subsequent visits to library schools on the eastern seaboard of the U.S.A. / Leonard C. Guy. — [London] : Ealing College of Higher Education, 1982. — 5p : ill ; 30cm. — (BL R & D report ; 5701)
Cover title
Unpriced (pbk) B82-20477

020′.9172′4 — Developing countries. Librarianship & information science. Development. Role of Great Britain — *Conference proceedings*

The **British** commitment overseas : a transcript of seminar discussions held at the Library Association Study School and National Conference, Brighton. — London : International and Comparative Librarianship Group, 1979. — ii,71leaves ; 30cm
ISBN 0-906904-00-5 (pbk) : £1.25 : CIP rev. B79-31459

020′.941 — Great Britain. Librarianship

A **Librarian′s** handbook / compiled by L.J. Taylor. — London : Library Association
Vol.2: Supplementary papers and documents containing new policy statements, standards of service and memoranda of evidence and a fully revised directory section. — 1980. — xxi,1181p ; 24cm
Includes index
ISBN 0-85365-651-7 (pbk) : £25.00 (£20.00 to members of L.A.) : CIP rev. B80-06259

020′.941 — Great Britain. Librarianship & information science

British librarianship and information work, 1976-1980. — London : Library Association
Vol.1: General libraries and the profession. — July 1982. — [300]p
ISBN 0-85365-763-7 : £29.50 : CIP entry B82-14934

British librarianship and information work, 1976-1980. — London : Library Association
Vol.2: Special libraries, materials and processes. — Nov.1982. — [300]p
ISBN 0-85365-825-0 : £29.50 : CIP entry B82-26321

020′.941 — Great Britain. Libraries & information services — *Serials*

Great Britain. *Office of Arts and Libraries*. Report by the Minister for the Arts on library and information matters during ... — London : H.M.S.O., 1981-. — v. ; 25cm. — (Cmnd. ; 8454)
Annual
ISSN 0262-740x = Report by the Minister of the Arts on library and information matters during .. : £2.30 B82-12453

020′.9411 — Scotland. Librarianship — *Conference proceedings*

Peebles ′82. — Glasgow : Scottish Library Association, Sept.1982. — [83]p
Conference papers
ISBN 0-900649-52-6 (pbk) : £3.60 : CIP entry B82-35224

020′.9426′59 — Cambridgeshire. Cambridge. Libraries & information services — *For librarianship* — *Serials*

BUNC : Bibliographical Unit news (Cambridgeshire). — Issue no.1 (Jan. 1980)-. — Cambridge (Central Library, 7 Lion Yard, Cambridge CB2 3QD) : The Unit, 1980-. — v. ; 30cm
Monthly. — Description based on: Issue no.24 (Mar. 1982)
Unpriced B82-26138

020′.973 — United States. Librarianship & information science — *Conference proceedings*

An **Information** agenda for the 1980′s : proceedings of a colloquium June 17-18, 1980 / Carlton C. Rochell, editor. — Chicago : American Library Association ; London : distributed by Eurospan, 1981. — xiii,119p : ill,ports ; 23cm
ISBN 0-8389-0336-3 (pbk) : £6.50 B82-39801

021 — LIBRARY RELATIONSHIPS

021 — Librarians. Communication with readers

Powell, Judith W.. Peoplework : communications dynamics for librarians / Judith W. Powell and Robert B. LeLieuvre. — Chicago : American Library Association ; London : Eurospan [distributor], 1979. — ix,189p ; 23cm
Includes bibliographies and index
ISBN 0-8389-0290-1 (pbk) : £5.50 B82-34658

021 — Repositories. Planning — *Comparative studies*

National repository plans and programmes : a comparative study of existing plans and possible models / Capital Planning Information. — Wetherby : IFLA International Office for UAP, c1982. — ii,133p ; 30cm
Bibliography: p113-133
ISBN 0-7123-2001-6 (pbk) : Unpriced B82-30846

021.6 — LIBRARY COOPERATION AND NETWORKS

021.6′4 — Librarianship. Cooperation

Sewell, P. H.. Resource sharing : co-operation and co-ordination in library and information services / Philip H. Sewell. — London : Deutsch, 1981. — 159p ; 23cm. — (A Grafton book)
Bibliography: p147-152. — Includes index
ISBN 0-233-97342-7 : £12.50 : CIP rev. B81-28801

021.6′4 — Librarianship. International cooperation

Chandler, George. International and national library and information services : a review of some recent developments 1970-1980 / by George Chandler. — Oxford : Pergamon, 1982. — xii,275p : facsims ; 22cm. — (Recent advances in library and information services ; v.2)
Includes index
ISBN 0-08-025793-3 : £9.75 : CIP rev.
Primary classification 027.5 B81-34467

021.6′4′02854 — South-east England. Libraries. Cooperation. Organisations: London and South Eastern Library Region. Services. Applications of digital computer systems

Plaister, Jean M.. Regional library cooperation : computing in LASER. — London : Library Association, July 1982. — [50]p. — (Case studies in library automation)
ISBN 0-85365-954-0 (pbk) : £5.75 : CIP entry B82-19288

021.6′4′0941 — Great Britain. Libraries. Cooperation

Garside, Kenneth. Library co-operation at a time of financial constraints / by Kenneth Garside. — London : [University of London. Library Resources Co-ordinating Committee], 1981. — 17p ; 21cm. — (Occasional publication ; 1)
Cover title
Unpriced (pbk) B82-30888

021.6′5′0973 — United States. Libraries. Networks, *to 1980*

Martin, Susan K.. Library networks, 1981-82 / by Susan K. Martin. — White Plains : Knowledge Industry Publications ; London : Eurospan [distributor], c1981. — 160p ; 29cm. — (The Professional librarian series)
Bibliography: p154-156. — Includes index
ISBN 0-914236-55-5 (cased) : Unpriced
ISBN 0-914236-66-0 (pbk) : Unpriced B82-12205

021.7 — LIBRARY PROMOTION

021.7 — Libraries & information services. Services. Marketing

The **Marketing** of library and information services / edited by Blaise Cronin. — London : Aslib, 1981. — 360p : ill ; 26cm. — (Aslib reader series ; v.4)
Includes bibliographies and index
ISBN 0-85142-153-9 (cased) : £17.00(£14.50 to members)
ISBN 0-85142-154-7 (pbk) : £10.00(£8.50 to members) B82-29510

021.7 — Libraries. Public relations

Harrison, K. C.. Public relations for librarians. — 2nd rev. ed. — Aldershot : Gower, Dec.1982. — [120]p
Previous ed.: London : Deutsch, 1973
ISBN 0-566-03454-9 : £4.50 : CIP entry B82-30060

021.7′0973 — United States. Public libraries. Public relations — *Manuals*

Edsall, Marian S.. Library promotion handbook / Marian S. Edsall. — Phoenix : Oryx ; London : Mansell Publishing, c1980. — 244p : ill,forms ; 29cm. — (A Neal-Schuman professional book)
Bibliography: p195-201. — Includes index
ISBN 0-7201-0832-2 : £11.50 : CIP rev. B79-37135

022.9 — LIBRARIES. EQUIPMENT, FURNITURE, FURNISHINGS

022′.9 — Great Britain. Libraries. Applications of Prestel — *Conference proceedings*
Prestel and its use in libraries : proceedings of a seminar held at Washington Town Centre Library on Friday 14th September 1979 / edited by A.C. McDonald and P.J. Atkinson ; organised by Library Association University, College and Research Section, Northern Group, Library Association Reference, Special and Information Section, Northern Group, NETWORK. — Newcastle upon Tyne (c/o P.J. Atkinson, The Library, Newcastle upon Tyne Polytechnic, Ellison Building, Ellison Place, Newcastle upon Tyne NE1 8ST) : Library Association University, College and Research Section, c1979. — 52p : 2ill ; 30cm
Bibliography: p47-52
ISBN 0-85365-682-7 (pbk) : £3.50 : CIP rev.
B79-33879

022′.9 — United States. Libraries. Automation
The **Professional** librarian′s reader in library automation and technology / introduction by Susan K. Martin. — White Plains, N.Y. : Knowledge Industry ; London : Eurospan [distributor], c1980. — vii,201p : ill,forms ; 29cm. — (Professional librarian series)
Bibliography: p197-201
ISBN 0-914236-59-8 (cased) : Unpriced
B82-08809

023.9 — LIBRARY STAFF. PERSONNEL MANAGEMENT

023′.9 — Libraries. Personnel management
Cowley, John. Personnel management. — London : Bingley, Aug.1982. — [112]p. — (Outlines of modern librarianship)
ISBN 0-85157-324-x : £6.25 : CIP entry
B82-15875

Jones, Noragh. Staff management in library and information work. — Aldershot : Gower, June 1982. — [350]p
ISBN 0-566-03430-1 : £15.00 : CIP entry
B82-09426

025 — LIBRARY OPERATIONS

025′.0028′54 — Great Briain. Libraries. Applications of computer systems — *Conference proceedings*
Minis, micros and terminals for libraries and information services : proceedings of the conference organized jointly by the Institute of Information Scientists and the Information Retrieval Specialist Group of the British Computer Society, held at the National Computing Centre, Manchester, 6-7 November 1980 / edited by Alan Gilchrist. — London : Heyden on behalf of The British Computer Society, c1981. — viii,121p : ill ; 24cm. — (The British Computer Society workshop series)
Includes index
ISBN 0-85501-712-0 (pbk) : Unpriced
B82-10088

025′.0028′54 — Great Britain. Librarians. Professional education. Curriculum subjects: Applications of digital computer systems in libraries. Teaching — *Case studies*
The **Teaching** of computer appreciation and library automation / A.J. Oulton ... [et al.]. — [London] : British Library ; Boston Spa : Distributed by British Library Lending Division, 1981. — viii,118p : forms ; 30cm. — (British Library research and development reports, ISSN 0308-2385 ; no.5647)
Bibliography: p79-83
ISBN 0-905984-75-7 (pbk) : Unpriced
B82-05463

025′.0028′54 — Great Britain. Libraries. Automation. Teaching aids: Digital computer systems. Software packages: LATP
Eyre, John, *1930-*. LATP (Library Automation Teaching Package) : final report : being a review of the project, the use made of the package and the lessons to be learned / John Eyre. — [London] : Polytechnic of North London, School of Librarianship, 1982. — 2v. : ill,forms ; 30cm. — (BL R & D report ; 5709)
"Report to the British Library Research & Development Department"
Unpriced (spiral) B82-24637

025′.0028′54 — Hertfordshire. Hatfield. Polytechnics. Libraries: Hatfield Polytechnic. *Library*. Automation, *to 1981*
Bagley, D. E.. Automation in a polytechnic library. — London : Library Association, Nov.1982. — [58]p. — (Case studies in library automation)
ISBN 0-85365-964-8 : £6.75 : CIP entry
B82-32312

025′.0028′54 — Libraries. Applications of digital computer systems: Free text systems
Ashford, John H.. Studies in the application of free text package systems. — London : Library Association, Mar.1982. — [48]p. — (Case studies in library automation)
ISBN 0-85365-535-9 (pbk) : £7.75 : CIP entry
B82-06527

025′.0028′54 — Libraries. Automation. Management
Cohen, Elaine. Automation, space management, and productivity : a guide for libraries / Elaine Cohen, Aaron Cohen. — New York ; London : Bowker, 1981, c1982. — viii,221p,[4]p of plates : ill(some col.),plans ; 27cm
Bibliography: p209-213. — Includes index
ISBN 0-8352-1398-6 : Unpriced B82-24500

025′.0028′54 — North Yorkshire. Public libraries: North Yorkshire County Library. On-line computer systems
Hughes, Angela M.. North Yorkshire Library on line system / Angela M. Hughes. — Northallerton : Computer Services, 1980. — 19 [i.e. 53] leaves : ill,1maps,forms ; 30cm
ISBN 0-902021-10-9 (pbk) : Unpriced
B82-11044

025′.0028′5404 — Great Britain. Libraries. Microcomputer systems — *Directories*
Microcomputer applications in libraries and information retrieval : a dirctory of users / compiled by Paul. F. Burton. — Edinburgh (24 Milton Road East, Edinburgh, EH15 2PP) : Library, Leith Nautical College, 1981. — viii,38p : ill ; 30cm
Bibliography: p32-36
Unpriced (spiral) B82-00741

025′.0028′5404 — Libraries. Applications of microcomputer systems — *Serials*
Library micromation news. — No.1 (May 1982)-. — London (c/o Phillips Petroleum Co. U.K., Southside, 105 Victoria St, SW1E 6QR) : A. Dawson, 1982-. — v. ; 30cm
Irregular
ISSN 0262-7841 = Library micromation news : Unpriced B82-38503

025′.0028′5404 — Small libraries. Small digital computer systems
Minis and micros : smaller computers : for smaller libraries? / edited by A. Rennie McElroy. — London : Library Associaton, Colleges of Further and Higher Education Group, 1980. — 44p : ill ; 21cm. — (CoFHE occasional publications ; 6)
Bibliography: p34-44
ISBN 0-85365-903-6 (pbk) : Unpriced
B82-00687

025.04 — LIBRARIES. INFORMATION STORAGE AND RETRIEVAL SYSTEMS

025′.04 — Bedfordshire. Public libraries: Bedfordshire County Library. On-line bibliographic information retrieval services. Use
Ebrahim, Heidi. Experimental use of on-line terminals in public libraries : the establishment and operation of an online information retrieval service in Bedfordshire, January 1980-September 1981 : report of the British Library Research and Development Department on project SI/9/354 / Heidi Ebrahim. — [Bedford] : Bedfordshire County Library, 1982. — 12leaves ; 30cm. — (BL R & D report ; 5716)
Unpriced (unbound) B82-26629

025′.04 — European Community countries. On-line information retrieval services: EURONET DIANE
LUCIS guide to EURONET-DIANE databases / compiled and edited by Angela Batten and Gerald Fitzmaurice. — [London] : University of London, 1980. — 1v.(loose-leaf) ; 32cm
Includes index
ISBN 0-7187-0562-9 : Unpriced B82-06348

025′.04 — Great Britain. Information services & special libraries. On-line information processing systems: ADLIB — *Manuals*
Ross, M. R. (Madeleine Rachel). ADLIB design : an ADaptive LIBrary management system / M.R. Ross ; and K.C. Butchers [editor]. — Maidenhead : Lipman Management Resources, c1982. — 112p ; 30cm
Includes index
ISBN 0-906168-03-1 (spiral) : £25.00
B82-31579

025′.04 — Great Britain. Linguistic data banks. Organisation. Feasibility studies
Sager, J. C.. Feasibility study of the establishment of a terminological data bank in U.K. / J.C. Sager and J. McNaught. — [Manchester] : Centre for Computational Linguistics, University of Manchester Institute of Science and Technology, 1981. — iii,114p in various pagings ; 30cm. — (British Library R. & D. report ; no.5642)
Bibliography: p39-57
Unpriced (spiral) B82-02029

025′.04 — Great Britain. National libraries: British Library. On-line information processing systems: BLAISE — *Manuals*
British Library. *Bibliographic Services Division*. BLAISE LINE user manual / The British Library Bibliographic Services Division. — London : British Library Automated Services Department, 1982. — 1v.(loose-leaf) ; 30cm
Issued in parts
ISBN 0-7123-1000-2 : Unpriced : CIP rev.
B82-14487

025′.04 — Great Britain. National libraries: British Library. On-line information processing systems: BLAISE — *Manuals* — *Serials*
BLAISE. BLAISE mini manual. — [Ist ed. (1980)]-. — [London] ([2 Sheraton St., W1V 4BH]) : BLAISE, [1980]-. — v. ; 30cm
Annual
ISSN 0262-835x = BLAISE mini manual : £5.00 B82-09683

BLAISE-LINK mini manual. — 1982. — London (2 Sheraton St., W1V 4BH) : British Library Automated Services Dept., May 1982. — [179]p
ISBN 0-7123-1003-7 (spiral) : £10.00 (1 copy free to subscribers) : CIP entry
ISSN 0262-8562 B82-16480

025′.04 — Great Britain. National libraries: British Library. On-line information retrieval services: BLAISE — *Manuals* — *Serials*
BLAISE-LINE mini manual. — 1982. — London (2 Sheraton St., W1V 4BH) : British Library Automated Services Dept., May 1982. — [66]p
ISBN 0-7123-1002-9 (spiral) : £10.00 (1 copy free to subscribers) : CIP entry
ISSN 0262-8554 B82-16481

025′.04 — Great Britain. Public libraries. On-line information retrieval services
The **On-line** public library. — London : British Library, July 1982. — [113]p. — (Library and information research reports, ISSN 0263-1709 ; v.1)
ISBN 0-7123-3002-x (pbk) : £8.00 : CIP entry
B82-25723

025′.04 — Information retrieval. Applications of video discs
Horder, Alan. Video discs : their application to information storage and retrieval / Alan Horder. — 2nd ed. — Hertford : National Reprograhic Centre for documentation, 1981. — 50p ; 30cm. — (British Library research and development reports, ISSN 0308-2385 ; no.5671) (NRCd publication ; no.17)
Previous ed.: 1979. — Bibliography: p47-50
ISBN 0-85267-199-7 (spiral) : £7.00 (£6.00 to members of NRCd)
ISBN 0-85267-200-4 (microfiche) : £3.50
B82-09169

025'.04 — On-line information retrieval systems. Design. Human factors — ***Conference proceedings***

Informatics 6 *(Conference : 1981 : Oxford).* The design of information systems for human beings : Informatics 6 : proceedings of a conference held by the Aslib Informatics Group, Oxford, 24 September 1981 / edited by Kevin P. Jones and Heather Taylor. — London : Aslib, c1981. — 96p : ill ; 30cm
ISBN 0-85142-156-3 (pbk) : Unpriced B82-29564

025'.04 — Scotland. Grampian Region. Aberdeen. Public libraries: Aberdeen City Libraries. On-line bibliographic information retrieval services. Use

Dickson, Muriel. Experimental use of on-line terminals in public libraries: phase two, Scotland : the on-line information retrieval service at Aberdeen City Libraries : report for the period October 1979-September 1981 : report to the British Library Research and Development Department on project SI/G/338 / Muriel Dickson. — Aberdeen ([Rosemount Viaduct, Aberdeen]) : Aberdeen City Libraries, 1981. — 28,[20]leaves : ill ; 30cm. — (Report ; no.SI/G/338) (Report ; no.5688)
Unpriced (spiral) B82-14480

025'.04 — Scotland. Public libraries. On-line bibliographic information retrieval services. Use

Armstrong, Norma. Experimental use of online terminals in public libraries: phase 2: Scotland : report to the British Library Research and Development Department on project SI/G/G339 : for the period April 1980-September 1981 / Norma Armstrong and Ronald Davies. — Edinburgh : Edinburgh City Libraries, 1981. — v,26leaves : facsims,forms ; 30cm. — (BL R & D report ; 5683)
Unpriced (pbk) B82-15466

025'.04 — Scotland. Strathclyde Region. Glasgow. Public libraries: Glasgow District Libraries. On-line bibliographic information retrieval services. Use

Gillespie, Roy. The experimental use of on-line terminals in public libraries : phase two (Scotland) / Roy Gillespie, Doreen Kean. — Glasgow ([The Mitchell Library, North St, Glasgow 3]) : Glasgow District Libraries, 1982. — [27]leaves : ill,forms ; 30cm. — (BL R & D report ; 5676)
Unpriced (pbk) B82-26376

025'.04 — West Yorkshire ***(Metropolitan County).*** **Bradford** ***(District).*** **Public libraries: Metropolitan Bradford Libraries. On-line information retrieval services. Establishment**

Hoyle, Harry B.. The on-line information retrieval service at Metropolitan Bradford libraries : its establishment and operation, December 1979-September 1981 / Harry B. Hoyle. — [Great Britain] : [S.n.], 1982. — 15,[7]leaves ; 30cm. — ([BL R & D report] ; [5657])
"Final report to the British Library Research and Development Department of Project S1/G/353". — Cover title
Unpriced (spiral) B82-24640

025'.04 — West Yorkshire ***(Metropolitan County).*** **Leeds. Public libraries: Leeds City Libraries. On-line bibliographic information retrieval services. Use**

McKenna, Graham. On-line information retrieval at Leeds City Libraries : a report on the research project funded by the British Library from March 1980-September 1981 / Graham McKenna. — [Leeds] : [Leeds City Libraries], 1981. — 14leaves ; 30cm. — (B.L. R & D report ; no.5703)
Unpriced (pbk) B82-26630

025'.06070595 — Government publications. Documentation

Government publications : key papers / edited by Bernard M. Fry and Peter Hernon. — Oxford : Pergamon, 1981. — xii,814p : ill,facsims,forms ; 26cm. — (Guides to official publications ; v.8)
Bibliography: p753-810. — Includes index. — Papers from the first seven vols. (1973-1980) of 'Government publications review' and published as Supplement No.1 1981 of that journal
ISBN 0-08-025216-8 : £42.00 : CIP rev. B81-10428

025'.063 — Information services on social sciences

The **Social** sciences. — London (500 Chesham House, 150 Regent St., W1R 5FA) : Rossendale, July 1982. — [140]p
ISBN 0-946138-00-1 (pbk) : £10.00 : CIP entry B82-22403

025'.063 — Social sciences. On-line bibliographic information retrieval services. Machine-readable files

Foster, Allan. Which database? : an evaluative guide to online bibliographic databases in business and the social sciences / Allan Foster. — Hartlepool : Headland, 1981. — 102p ; 30cm
Bibliography: p98-99
ISBN 0-906889-03-0 (spiral) : £14.95 B82-01891

025'.063628286 — Family planning services. Documentation

Forget, Jacqueline P.. Practical documentation : a training package for librarians / Jacqueline P. Forget. — London (18 Lower Regent St., SW1Y 4PW) : International Planned Parenthood Federation
Module 2: Documents, documentation, documentalists. — 1978. — 1portfolio ; 31cm
£2.00 B82-19035

Forget, Jacqueline P.. Practical documentation : a training package for librarians / Jacqueline P. Forget. — London (18 Lower Regent St., SW1Y 4PW) : International Planned Parenthood Federation
Module 3: Cataloguing, classification and indexing, key to information retrieval. — 1978. — 1portfolio ; 31cm
£3.00 B82-19033

Forget, Jacqueline P.. Practical documentation : a training package for librarians / Jacqueline P. Forget. — London (18 Lower Regent St., SW1Y 4PW) : International Planned Parenthood Federation
Module 4: Acquisition and entry of documents policy and process. — 1978. — 1portfolio : forms ; 31cm
£2.00 B82-19038

Forget, Jacqueline P.. Practical documentation : a training package for librarians / Jacqueline P. Forget. — London (18 Lower Regent St., SW1Y 4PW) : International Planned Parenthood Federation
Module 5: Installation, equipment, layout and conservation of collections. — 1978. — 1portfolio : 1ill,2forms ; 31cm
£3.00 B82-19037

Forget, Jacqueline P.. Practical documentation : a training package for librarians / Jacqueline P. Forget. — London (18 Lower Regent St., SW1Y 4PW) : International Planned Parenthood Federation
Module 6: Reference work methods and sources. — 1978. — 1portfolio ; 31cm
£2.00 B82-19032

Forget, Jacqueline P.. Practical documentation : a training package for librarians / Jacqueline P. Forget. — London (18 Lower Regent St., SW1Y 4PW) : International Planned Parenthood Federation
Module 7: Consultation, loan, dissemination, copyright. — 1978. — 1portfolio : forms ; 31cm
£2.00 B82-19036

Forget, Jacqueline P.. Practical documentation : a training package for librarians / Jacqueline P. Forget. — London (18 Lower Regent St., SW1Y 4PW) : International Planned Parenthood Federation
Module 8: Documentation products, preparation of bibliographies, abstracts, low cost fact sheets and leaflets. — 1979. — 1portfolio : ill,facsims ; 31cm
£3.00 B82-19034

Forget, Jacqueline P.. Practical documentation : a training package for librarians / Jacqueline P. Forget. — London (18 Lower Regent St., SW1Y 4PW) : International Planned Parenthood Federation
Module 9: Audio visual materials storage and information processing. — 1979. — 1portfolio : ill ; 31cm
£2.00 B82-19039

Forget, Jacqueline P.. Practical documentation : a training package for librarians / Jacqueline P. Forget. — London (18 Lower Regent St., SW1Y 4PW) : International Planned Parenthood Federation
Module 10: Management issues in documentation centres. — 1978. — 1portfolio ; 31cm
£2.00 B82-22192

025'.064 — Great Britain. Linguistic data banks — ***Feasibility studies***

Sager, J. C.. Specifications of a linguistic data bank for the U.K. / J.C. Sager and J. McNaught. — [Manchester] : Centre for Computational Linguistics, University of Manchester Institute of Science and Technology, [1981?]. — ii,50leaves : ill ; 30cm. — (CCL/UMIST ; no.81/10) (British Library R. & D. report ; no.5644)
Bibliography: leaves 40-50
£5.50 (spiral) B82-03992

025'.064 — Western Europe. Linguistic data banks

Sager, J. C.. Selective survey of existing linguistic data banks in Europe / J.C. Sager and J. McNaught. — [Manchester] : Centre for Computational Linguistics, University of Manchester Institute of Science and Technology, [1981?]. — iii,72leaves ; 30cm. — (CCL/UMIST ; no.81/9) (British Library R. & D. report ; no.5643)
Bibliography: leaves 61-72
£7.50 (spiral) B82-03991

025'.0652 — Astronomy. Data retrieval services using digital computer systems

International Astronomical Union. *Colloquium (64th : 1981 : Strasbourg).* Automated data retrieval in astronomy : proceedings of the 64th Colloquium of the International Astronomical Union held in Strasbourg, France, July 7-10, 1981 / edited by C. Jaschek and W. Heintz. — Dordrecht ; London : Reidel, c1982. — xx,324p : ill ; 25cm. — (Astrophysics and space science library ; v.97)
Includes 3 chapters in French. — Includes index
ISBN 90-277-1435-5 : Unpriced B82-34838

025'.06608 — Great Britain. Patents. Information retrieval services: UK Patents Information Network — ***Serials***

PIN bulletin / UK Patents Information Network, the British Library. — No.1 (Dec. 1981)-. — London (25 Southampton Buildings, WC2A 1AW) : Science Reference Library, Reference Division, British Library, 1981-. — v. : ill,ports ; 30cm
Quarterly
ISSN 0261-7234 = PIN bulletin : Unpriced B82-13413

025'.06608 — Western Europe. Patents. Information retrieval services — ***Directories***

Patent information and documentation in Western Europe : an inventory of services available to the public / edited by H. Bank, M. Fenat-Haessig and M. Roland. — 2nd rev. and enl. ed. — München ; London : Saur, 1981. — 268p : facsims ; 25cm
At head of title: Commission of the European Communities. — Previous ed.: 1976
ISBN 3-598-10158-9 : Unpriced B82-25289

025'.0660874 — European Community countries. Patents. Information retrieval

Finding information from patents : instructors manual. — Newcastle upon Tyne : Newcastle upon Tyne Polytechnic Products, c1981. — 1v.(looseleaf) : ill,2maps ; 30cm + Students handbook(93p : ill,2maps ; 30cm)
Cover title: Patents Europe : instructors manual : finding information from patents
ISBN 0-906471-18-4 : Unpriced
ISBN 0-906471-17-6 (Students handbook) : Unpriced B82-35552

025′.06608741 — Great Britain. Information on patents. Use by industries

Stephenson, J.. The use of patent information in industry. — London : British Library Research & Development Department, Sept.1982. — [81] p. — (Library and information research reports, ISSN 0263-1709 ; 4)
ISBN 0-7123-3005-4 (pbk) : CIP entry
B82-29106

025′.0661 — Medicine. Documents on medicine. Information retrieval services using digital computer systems: Medlars. International MEDLARS Workshop *(1981 : Cologne)*

Johnston, S. M.. Report on international MEDLARS workshop Cologne, Federal Republic of Germany / S.M. Johnston. — [London] ([Whitehall Place, SW1]) : ADAS, [1982]. — 5p ; 30cm
Unpriced (unbound) B82-16553

025′.06627 — Hydraulic engineering. On-line information retrieval services: Fluidex

Guide to the FLUIDEX database / edited by C. Walker. — Bedford : BHRA Fluid Engineeering, c1981. — 63p : ill ; 30cm
Includes index
ISBN 0-906085-62-4 (pbk) : Unpriced : CIP rev. B81-30980

025′.06627 — Hydraulic engineering. On-line information retrieval services: Fluidex. Primary journals — *Lists*

List of periodicals scanned and abstracted for inclusion in the FLUIDEX database / [edited by C. Walker, J. White, L. Williams]. — Bedford : BHRA Fluid Engineeering, c1981. — 16p ; 30cm
Cover title
Unpriced (pbk) B82-04786

025′.0663 — Agriculture. Information retrieval services using digital computer systems. Machine-readable files — *Comparative studies*

White, J. D.. Bibliometric evaluation of the CAB, CAIN and BIOSIS data bases / J.D. White, J. Davison and D. Harris. — [Loughborough] : Loughborough University, 1982. — v,59p ; 30cm + 3microfiche(ill ; 11x15cm). — (British Library R & D report ; no.5660)
Unpriced (pbk) B82-27576

025.1 — LIBRARY ADMINISTRATION

025.1 — Libraries. Management

Library management without bias / edited by Ching-Chih Chen. — Greenwich, Conn. : Jai Press ; London (3 Henrietta St., WC2E 8LU) : Distributed by Jaicon Press, c1980. — xxviii,225p : ill,forms,ports ; 24cm. — (Foundations in library and information science ; v.13)
Conference proceedings. — Includes bibliographies and index
ISBN 0-89232-163-6 : £22.85 B82-02082

Studies in library management. — London : Bingley
Vol.7 / edited by Anthony Vaughan. — 1982. — 237p : ill,2forms ; 23cm
ISBN 0-85157-322-3 : Unpriced : CIP rev.
B82-07021

025.1 — Libraries. Management — *Conference proceedings*

Marketing the library. — Newcastle upon Tyne (c/o P.M. Judd, Newcastle upon Tyne Polytechnic Library, Ellison Building, Ellison Place, Newcastle upon Tyne NE1 8ST) : Association of Assistant Librarians, Northern Division, July 1981. — [130]p
Conference papers
ISBN 0-9506682-1-4 (pbk) : £4.00 : CIP entry
B81-23736

025.1′05 — Libraries. Management — *Serials*

Information and library manager. — Vol.1, no.1 (June 1981)-. — Buckden (45 Park Rd, Buckden, Cambridgeshire) : ELM Publications, 1981-. — v. ; 30cm
Quarterly
ISSN 0260-6879 = Information and library manager : £16.00 per year B82-22666

025.1′07′1141 — Great Britain. Librarians. Professional education. Curriculum subjects: Library management. Simulation games: Bishopsbury Simulation

Guy, Leonard C.. The Bishopsbury simulation : Decisions: a teaching package / by Leonard C. Guy, Stuart E. Mills, Janet Shuter. — [London] : Ealing College of Higher Education, 1982. — 166p in various pagings : ill,forms ; 30cm. — (BL R & D report ; 5699)
Unpriced (pbk) B82-22370

Guy, Leonard C.. Decisions teaching package dissemination phase : preparation of the Bishopsbury simulation for publication. Final report for the period February-June 1981 / by Leonard C. Guy. — [London] : [Ealing College of Higher Education], [1982]. — 6p ; 30cm. — (BL R & D report ; 5700)
Unpriced (pbk) B82-23652

025.1′07′1141 — Great Britain. Librarians. Professional education. Curriculum subjects: Library management. Simulation games: Bishopsbury Simulation. Evaluation by students

Jones, K. H.. The Leeds evaluation of the Bishopsbury case study / by Ken Jones and Noragh Jones. — Leeds : School of Librarianship, Leeds Polytechnic, 1981. — 88p ; 30cm
ISBN 0-900738-25-1 (pbk) : £15.00
B82-16347

025.1′072042547 — Great Britain. Libraries. Management. Research organisations: Loughborough University of Technology. *Centre for Library and Information Management.* **Research projects,** *1978-1980*

Report to the British Library Research and Development Department covering the period January 1978-February 1980 / Library Management Research Unit and Centre for Library and Information Management, Department of Library and Information Studies, Loughborough University of Technology. — Loughborough : CLAIM, c1980. — v,23p ; 30cm. — (Report ; no.4) (British Library research & development reports ; no.5572)
ISBN 0-904924-28-9 (pbk) : £3.00 B82-16182

025.1′072042547 — Great Britain. Libraries. Management. Research organisations: Loughborough University of Technology. *Centre for Library and Information Management.* **Research projects,** *1980-1981*

Loughborough University of Technology. *Centre for Library and Information Management.* The work of the Centre for Library and Information Management, 1 March 1980-28 February 1981. — Loughborough : The Centre, [1981]. — v,24p ; 30cm. — (Report / CLAIM, ISSN 0261-0302 ; no.9)
Unpriced (pbk) B82-05833

025.1′0941 — Great Britain. Libraries. Management. Effects of financial constraints — *Conference proceedings*

Library management in times of economic constraints : papers read at a one day seminar organized by the School of Librarianship and Information Studies in May 1981. — [Liverpool] : Liverpool Polytechnic, School of Librarianship and Information Studies, [1981]. — i,15p ; 30cm. — (Occasional paper ; 13)
Cover title. — Contents: The public library / by Patrick D. Gee — The university library / by A. Graham Mackenzie — The polytechnic library / by D.H. Revill
ISBN 0-901537-17-9 (pbk) : £2.50 B82-05182

025.1′0973 — United States. Libraries. Management — *Serials*

Advances in library administration and organization. — Vol.1 (1982)-. — Greenwich, Conn. ; London : JAI, 1982-. — v. : ill ; 24cm
Unpriced B82-33852

025.1′1 — London *(City).* **Polytechnics. Libraries: City of London Polytechnic.** *Library and Learning Resources Service.* **Budgeting. Planning, programming, budgeting systems**

Library work plan 1982/83. — London (City of London Polytechnic, Calcutta House, Old Castle St., E1 7NT) : LLRS Publications, Dec.1982. — [25]p
ISBN 0-904264-67-x (pbk) : £1.00 : CIP entry
B82-36162

Pankhurst, Rita. Library work plan 1981/82. — London (City of London Polytechnic, Calcutta House, Old Castle St., E1 7NT) : LLRS Publications, Jan.1982. — [15]p
ISBN 0-904264-61-0 (pbk) : £1.00 : CIP entry
B82-02480

025.1′1 — United States. Academic libraries. Financial management

Martin, Murray S.. Budgetary control in academic libraries / by Murray S. Martin. — Greenwich, Conn. : Jai Press ; London (3 Henrietta St., WC2E 8LU) : Distributed by Jaicon Press, c1978. — x,219p : ill ; 24cm. — (Foundations in library and information science ; v.5)
Bibliography: p209-212. — Includes index
ISBN 0-89232-010-9 : £24.50 B82-02111

025.17 — Great Britain. Public libraries. Stock: Fiction — *Conference proceedings*

The **Librarian** and the novel / compiled and with an introduction by John Dixon. — London ([Sales Officer, 38 Parkstone Ave., Hornchurch, Essex RM11 3LW]) : Association of Assistant Librarians, South East Division, 1981. — 47p ; 21cm. — (Fiction papers ; 1)
'Based on papers given at an AALSED day school on 1st October 1980 at Holborn Library'
Unpriced (pbk) B82-15121

025.17 — Great Britain. Public records. Selection. Modern public records — *Critical studies*

Modern public records : the Government response to the report of the Wilson Committee. — London : H.M.S.O., [1982]. — ii,29p ; 25cm. — (Cmnd. ; 8531)
At head of title: Lord Chancellor's Department
ISBN 0-10-185310-6 (unbound) : £2.65
Also classified at 323.44′5 B82-31676

025.17 — United States. Libraries. Stock: Documents for subcultures

Alternative materials in libraries / edited by James P. Danky and Elliott Shore. — Metuchen ; London : Scarecrow, 1982. — ix,245p ; 23cm
Bibliography: p183-206. — Includes index
ISBN 0-8108-1508-7 : £12.80 B82-29253

025.17′16 — Libraries. Stock: Rare books. Organisation — *Manuals*

Cave, Roderick. Rare book librarianship / Roderick Cave. — 2nd, rev. ed. — London : Bingley, 1982. — 162p,xvip of plates : ill,facsims ; 23cm
Previous ed.: 1976. — Bibliography: p148-153. — Includes index
ISBN 0-85157-328-2 : Unpriced : CIP rev.
B82-09868

025.17′32 — Libraries. Stock: Serials. Management. Effects of cooperation — *Conference proceedings*

U.K. Serials Group. *Conference (1981 : University of Manchester).* Resource sharing : its impact on serials. — Newcastle upon Tyne (c/o M. E. Graham, Newcastle upon Tyne Polytechnic Library, Newcastle upon Tyne NE1 8ST) : U.K. Serials Group, Feb.1982. — [120]p. — (Serials monograph, ISSN 0141-1810)
ISBN 0-906148-03-0 (pbk) : £4.50 : CIP entry
B82-07133

025.17′32′0941 — Great Britain. Libraries. Stock: Serials. Management. Automation — *Conference proceedings*

UK Serials Group. *Conference (1980 : South Glamorgan Institute of Higher Education).* Automation and serials : proceedings of the UK Serials Group Conference held at South Glamorgan Institute of Higher Education, Cardiff 31 March-3 April 1980 / edited by Margaret E. Graham. — [Newcastle upon Tyne?] : UK Serials Group, c1981. — 120p : ill ; 21cm. — (Serials monograph, ISSN 0141-1810 ; no.3)
ISBN 0-906148-02-2 (pbk) : Unpriced
B82-14320

025.17'34'0942732 — Greater Manchester *(Metropolitan County)*. Salford. Universities. Libraries: University of Salford. *Library*. Stock: Documents published by Great Britain. *Her Majesty's Stationery Office*

University of Salford. *Library*. A guide to HMSO publications / University of Salford Library. — [Salford] : [The Library], [1980]. — 13p : plans ; 21cm
Cover title. — Includes index
Unpriced (pbk) B82-26586

025.17'6 — Libraries. Stock: Maps. Collections. Administration

Nichols, Harold. Map librarianship / Harold Nichols. — 2nd ed. — London : Bingley, 1982. — 272p ; 23cm
Previous ed.: 1976. — Bibliography: p258-266. — Includes index
ISBN 0-85157-327-4 : Unpriced : CIP rev. B82-04788

025.17'73 — Great Britain. Film libraries — *Directories — For youth work in Northern Ireland*

Film libraries / The Standing Conference of Youth Organisations in Northern Ireland. — Belfast : SCOYO, 1979. — 10p ; 30cm
Cover title
ISBN 0-906797-04-7 (pbk) : £0.25 B82-00096

025.17'73 — Great Britain. Higher education institutions. Libraries. Stock: Transparencies. Collections. Organisation

Bradfield, V. J.. Slide collections : a user requirement survey : final report for the period April to August 1976 : report to the British Library on project SI/G/183 / V.J. Bradfield ; project director S.R. Gadsden. — Leicester : Library, Leicester Polytechnic, 1976. — 205p : ill,1form ; 30cm. — (BL report ; no.5309)
Unpriced (pbk) B82-35124

025.17'94 — Libraries. Stock: Microforms

Folcarelli, Ralph J.. The microform connection : a basic guide for libraries / Ralph J. Folcarelli, Arthur C. Tannenbaum and Ralph C. Ferragamo. — New York ; London : Bowker, 1982. — x,210p : ill ; 26cm
Bibliography: p181-193. — Includes index
ISBN 0-8352-1475-3 : Unpriced B82-21264

Gabriel, Michael R.. The microform revolution in libraries / by Michael R. Gabriel, Dorothy P. Ladd. — Greenwich, Conn. : JAI, c1980 ; London : Distributed by JAICON. — ix,176p : ill ; 24cm. — (Foundations in library and information science ; v.3)
Bibliography: p162-164. — Includes index
ISBN 0-89232-008-7 : £22.85 B82-05606

025.17'94'0973 — United States. Libraries. Stock: Microforms. Management

Boss, Richard W.. Developing microform reading facilities / by Richard W. Boss with Deborah Raikes. — Westport, Conn. ; London : Microform Review, [1981]. — 198p : ill ; 29cm. — (Microform Review series in library micrographics management)
Bibliography: p179-188. — Includes index
ISBN 0-913672-09-2 : £29.50 B82-16954

025.1'974 — Public libraries. Administration

Stoakley, R. J.. Presenting the library service / Roger Stoakley. — London : Bingley, 1982. — 109p ; 23cm. — (Outlines of modern librarianship)
Includes bibliographies and index
ISBN 0-85157-320-7 : Unpriced : CIP rev. B81-34572

025.1'97473 — United States. Public libraries. Management

Jenkins, Harold R.. Management of a public library / by Harold R. Jenkins. — Greenwich, Conn. : Jai Press ; London (3 Henrietta St., WC2E 8LU) : Distributed by Jaicon Press, c1980. — x,258p : forms ; 24cm. — (Foundations in library and information science ; v.8)
Includes index
ISBN 0-89232-038-9 : £22.85 B82-02078

Local public library administration. — 2nd ed. / completely revised by Ellen Altman, editor in cooperation with the International City Management Association. — Chicago : American Library Association ; London : Eurospan [distributor], 1980. — ix,251p : il ; 27cm
Previous ed.: United States : International City Management Association, 1964. — Includes bibliographies and index
ISBN 0-8389-0307-x : Unpriced B82-38975

025.1'977 — Academic libraries. Management. Decision-making. Information systems

McClure, Charles R.. Information for academic library decision making : the case for organizational information management / Charles R. McClure. — London : Aldwych, 1980. — xvi,227p : ill ; 22cm
Bibliography: p211-219. — Includes index
ISBN 0-86172-011-3 : £19.50 B82-31080

025.1'978 — Schools. Libraries. Administration

Herring, James E.. School librarianship / James E. Herring. — London : Bingley, 1982. — 116p ; 22cm. — (Outlines of modern librarianship)
Bibliography: p97-101. — Includes index
ISBN 0-85157-347-9 : Unpriced : CIP rev. B82-13133

025.1'978'0941 — Great Britain. Schools. Libraries. Organisation — *For children*

Carr, Louie. Libraries without tears / by Louie Carr. — Elland (22 Castlegate House, Elland, Yorks. HX5 ORN) : L. Carr, c1982. — 33p : ill ; 21cm
ISBN 0-9507950-0-3 (pbk) : £1.00 B82-14626

025.2 — LIBRARY ACQUISITIONS

025.2 — Great Britain. Public libraries. Stock: Books in Punjabi. Acquisition — *Inquiry reports*

Rait, S. K.. Acquisition, cataloguing and transliteration of Punjabi literature in the public libraries of the United Kingdom : final report for the period March 1980-October 1981 : report to the British Library Research and Development Department on Project SI/G/378 / S.K. Rait. — [Leeds] ([28 Park Place, Leeds, LS1 2SY]) : School of Librarianship, Leeds Polytechnic, 1981. — ii,42leaves ; 30cm. — (Report ; no.5681)
Unpriced (unbound)
Also classified at 025.3 B82-14186

025.2'1 — Libraries. Stock. Acquisition. Selection. National cooperation — *Comparative studies*

Collins, Judith. National acquisition policies and systems : a comparative study of existing systems and possible models / Judith Collins and Ruth Finer. — Wetherby : IFLA International Office for UAP, 1982. — vi,219p ; 21
Bibliography: p160-221
ISBN 0-85350-185-8 (pbk) : Unpriced B82-24669

025.2'1'0941 — Great Britain. Libraries. Stock: Books. Selection — *Manuals*

Whittaker, Kenneth. Systematic evaluation : methods and sources for assessing books / Kenneth Whittaker. — London : Bingley, 1982. — 154p : facsims ; 22cm. — (Outlines of modern librarianship)
Bibliography: p148-150. — Includes index
ISBN 0-85157-344-4 : Unpriced : CIP rev. B82-10880

025.2'1'0973 — United States. Libraries. Stock. Acquisition. Selection

Collection development in libraries : a treatise / edited by Robert D. Stueart, George B. Miller, Jr.. — Greenwich, Conn. : Jai ; London : distributed by Jaicon, c1980. — 2v.(602p) : ill ; 24cm. — (Foundations in library and information science ; v.10)
Includes bibliographies and index
ISBN 0-89232-106-7 : £52.45
ISBN 0-89232-162-8 (pt.B) B82-05919

025.2'16 — North-east England. Academic libraries. Stock. Relegation — *Conference proceedings*

Stock relegation practice in major academic libraries in North-east England. — Sunderland (c/o Mrs M. Watson, Secretary, Sunderland Polytechnic Library, Chester Rd, Sunderland SR1 3SD) : Library Association, University College & Research Section, Northern Group, Oct.1982. — [63]p
Conference papers
ISBN 0-85365-546-4 (pbk) : £5.00 : CIP entry B82-30317

025.2'33 — United States. Publishers. Stock: Books. Supply to libraries — *Practical information*

Kim, Ung Chon. Policies of publishers : a handbook for order librarians / by Ung Chon Kim. — 1982 ed. — Metuchen ; London : Scarecrow, 1982. — xi,161p ; 27cm
Previous ed.: 1978
ISBN 0-8108-1527-3 (pbk) : £12.00 B82-31800

025.2'6'0973 — United States. Libraries. Stock. Gifts & exchanges. Organisation

Lane, Alfred H.. Gifts and exchange manual / Alfred H. Lane. — London : Aldwych, 1980. — xi,121p : ill,facsims,forms ; 24cm
Includes bibliographies and index
ISBN 0-86172-007-5 : £12.50 B82-30924

025.3 — LIBRARIES. BIBLIOGRAPHIC ANALYSIS AND CONTROL

025.3 — Bibliographic control

Anderson, Dorothy, *1923-*. UBC : a survey of Universal Bibliographic Control. — London (c/o British Library Reference Division, Great Russell St., WC1B 3DG) : IFLA International Office for UBC, June 1982. — [50]p. — (Occasional papers / The IFLA International Office for UBC, ISSN 0309-9202 ; 10)
ISBN 0-903043-38-6 (pbk) : £8.00 : CIP entry B82-14212

025.3 — Bibliographic data. Standardisation

IFLA International Office for UBC. Standard practices in the preparation of bibliographic records. — London (c/o British Library, Reference Division, Great Russell Street, WC1B 3DG) : IFLA International Office for UBC, Apr.1982. — [47]p. — (Occasional paper / IFLA International Office for UBC, ISSN 0309-9202 ; no.9)
ISBN 0-903043-37-8 (pbk) : £10.00 : CIP entry B82-16199

025.3 — Documents. Cataloguing

Hunter, Eric J.. Cataloguing. — 2nd rev. and expanded ed. — London : Bingley, Dec.1982. — [230]p
Previous ed.: 1979
ISBN 0-85157-358-4 : £9.25 : CIP entry
ISBN 0-85157-354-1 (pbk) : £6.95 B82-30735

025.3 — Documents. Cataloguing — *Conference proceedings*

The **Nature** and future of the catalog : proceedings of the ALA's Information Science and Automation Division's 1975 and 1977 Institutes on the Catalog / edited by Maurice J. Freedman and S. Michael Malinconico. — Phoenix : Oryx ; London : Mansell Publishing, 1979. — xvi,317p : ill,forms ; 26cm. — (A Neal-Schuman professional book)
Includes index
ISBN 0-7201-0908-6 : £10.00 : CIP rev. B80-05181

025.3 — Documents. Cataloguing in publication — *Conference proceedings*

Cataloguing in publication : what is happening? : proceedings of a one-day seminar held at the Library Association on 21st October 1981. — London : Library Association Cataloguing & Indexing Group, 1982. — 16p ; 30cm
ISBN 0-85365-645-2 (unbound) : £3.50 B82-22039

025.3 — Great Britain. Extra-MARC materials. Cataloguing

Plaister, Jean. EMMA : report of a research project undertaken by LASER into the qualitative and quantitive cataloguing input from selected libraries not processed by the British Library and related MARC services / by Jean Plaister, Peter Smith, Robin Yeates. — London (33/34 Alfred Place, WC1E 7DP) : LASER, [1982?]. — [90]p,[96]leaves ; 30cm. — (BLR & DD report ; 5720)
Bibliography: Appendix IV
Unpriced (pbk) B82-31362

025.3 — Great Britain. Public libraries. Stock: Books in Punjabi. Cataloguing — *Inquiry reports*

Rait, S. K.. Acquisition, cataloguing and transliteration of Punjabi literature in the public libraries of the United Kingdom : final report for the period March 1980-October 1981 : report to the British Library Research and Development Department on Project SI/G/378 / S.K. Rait. — [Leeds] ([28 Park Place, Leeds, LS1 2SY]) : School of Librarianship, Leeds Polytechnic, 1981. — ii,42leaves ; 30cm. — (Report ; no.5681)
Unpriced (unbound)
Primary classification 025.2 B82-14186

025.3 — Libraries. Catalogues. Closing — *Conference proceedings*

Closing the Catalog : proceedings of the 1978 and 1979 Library and Information Technology Association Institutes / edited by D. Kaye Gapen and Bonnie Juergens. — Phoenix : Oryx ; London : Mansell Publishing, 1980. — xiv,194p ; 24cm
Includes bibliographies and index
ISBN 0-7201-1622-8 : £10.00 : CIP rev.
B80-18972

025.3′028′54 — Great Britain. National libraries: British Library. MARC services. Use by British libraries

Ralls, Marion. The use of MARC records : results of a survey / by Marion Ralls with the assistance of Frances Hendrix and John Foulkes. — [Huntingdon] ([c/o Grasshopper Press, 12 Church St., Fenstanton, Huntingdon, Cambs PE18 9JL]) : Marc Users' Group, 1982. — 46p : ill,forms ; 30cm
ISBN 0-905463-03-x (unbound) : £8.00
B82-38845

025.3′028′5442 — Great Britain. National libraries: British Library. Cataloguing services: LOCAS — *Manuals*

BLAISE. LOCAS user manual / BLAISE, British Library Automated Information Service. — London : British Library, Bibliographic Services Division, c1981. — 1v.(loose-leaf) ; 32cm
ISBN 0-900220-94-5 : Unpriced : CIP rev.
B81-34213

025.3′068 — United States. Libraries. Cataloguing departments. Management

Foster, Donald L.. Managing the catalog department / by Donald L. Foster. — 2nd ed. — Metuchen ; London : Scarecrow, 1982. — viii,236p ; 23cm
Previous ed.: 197-?. — Bibliography: p228-232. — Includes index
ISBN 0-8108-1486-2 : £12.00 B82-29252

025.3′1 — Libraries. Catalogues. Data

Seal, Alan. Full and short entry catalogues. — Aldershot : Gower, Dec.1982. — [160]p
ISBN 0-566-03484-0 : £15.00 : CIP entry
B82-30061

Seal, Alan. Full and short entry catalogues : library needs and uses. — Bath (The Library, University of Bath, Claverton Down, Bath, BA2 7AY) : Centre for Catalogue Research, Jan.1982. — [130]p. — (BLRD report ; 5669)
ISBN 0-86197-032-2 : £10.00 : CIP entry
B82-01342

025.3′13 — Great Britain. Libraries. COM catalogues. Readability

Reynolds, L.. Visual presentation of information in COM library catalogues / L. Reynolds. — London : British Library, c1979. — 2v. : ill ; 30cm. — (British Library research & development reports, ISSN 0308-2385 ; no.5472)
Also available on microfiche
ISBN 0-905984-34-x (spiral) : £8.00 : CIP rev.
B79-12229

025.3′13 — Libraries. Card catalogues. Unit cards. Use — *Programmed instructions*

Elrod, J. McRee. Construction and adaptation of the unit card / by J. McRee Elrod. — 3rd ed. — Metuchen ; London : Scarecrow, 1980 ; [Folkestone] : [Bailey & Swinfen] [[distributor]]. — viii,72p : facsims,forms ; 22cm. — (Modern library practices series ; no.1)
'Updated for use with AACR2'. — Previous ed.: 1978
ISBN 0-8108-1336-x (pbk) : £3.85 B82-15066

025.3′17 — Libraries. Card catalogues. Filing — *Programmed instructions*

Carothers, Diane Foxhill. Self-instruction manual for filing catalog cards / Diane Foxhill Carothers. — Chicago : American Library Association ; London : Eurospan [distributor], c1981. — v,120p ; 28cm
ISBN 0-8389-0326-6 (pbk) : £5.75 B82-21316

Elrod, J. McRee. Filing in the public catalog and shelf list / by J. McRee Elrod. — 3rd ed. — Metuchen ; London : Scarecrow, 1980 ; [Folkestone] : [Bailey & Swinfen] [[distributor]]. — vii,81p : forms ; 22cm. — (Modern library practices series ; no.2)
Previous ed.: 1978
ISBN 0-8108-1337-8 (pbk) : £8.40 B82-15067

025.3′2 — Documents. Author & descriptive cataloguing. Rules: Anglo-American cataloguing rules. 2nd ed — *Manuals*

Hoffmann, Christa F. B.. Getting ready for AACR2 : the cataloguer's guide / by Christa F.B. Hoffmann ; serials examples by Sally C. Tseng. — White Plains, N.Y. : Knowledge Industry ; London : Eurospan [distributor], c1980. — iii,225p : ill,forms ; 28cm. — (Professional librarian series)
Includes index
ISBN 0-914236-64-4 (pbk) : Unpriced
B82-08806

Maxwell, Margaret F.. Handbook for AACR2 : explaining and illustrating Anglo-American cataloguing rules second edition / by Margaret F. Maxwell. — Chicago : American Library Association, c1980 (1981 printing) ; London : distributed by Eurospan. — xi,463p : facsims ; 25cm
Includes index
ISBN 0-8389-0301-0 (pbk) : £14.95
B82-21149

025.3′2′0285442 — Documents. Descriptive cataloguing. Machine-readable files: UK MARC records — *Samplers* — *Serials*

British Library. *Bibliographic Services Division.* Cataloguing practice notes for UKMARC records. — No.1-. — [London] : [The British Library, Bibliographic Services Division], 1981-. — v. ; 30cm
Irregular
ISSN 0262-0278 = Cataloguing practice notes for UKMARC records : Unpriced B82-14767

025.3′22 — Catholic Church. Latin rites, *1563-*. Descriptive cataloguing. Uniform titles — *Lists*

International Federation of Library Associations and Institutions. *Working Group on Uniform Headings for Liturgical Works.* List of uniform titles for liturgical works of the Latin rites of the Catholic Church / recommended by the Working Group on Uniform Headings for Liturgical Works, International Federation of Library Associations and Institutions. — 2nd ed. — London : IFLA International Office for UBC, 1981. — x,17p ; 30cm
Previous ed.: 1975. — Bibliography: p3
ISBN 0-903043-35-1 (pbk) : Unpriced : CIP rev. B81-24625

025.3′22 — Documents. Author cataloguing. Corporate author headings

Carpenter, Michael. Corporate authorship : its role in library cataloging / Michael Carpenter. — Westport, Conn. ; London : Greenwood, 1981. — x,200p ; 24cm. — (Contributions in librarianship and information science ; no.34)
Includes index
ISBN 0-313-22065-4 : Unpriced B82-02619

025.3′22 — Documents. Author cataloguing. Personal author headings — *Standards*

Supplement to Names of persons: national usages for entry in catalogues. Third edition / compiled by the IFLA International Office for UBC. — London : The Office, 1980. — xii,49p ; 30cm
Includes index
ISBN 0-903043-30-0 (pbk) : £7.50 : CIP rev.
B80-30630

025.3′22′077 — Documents. Author cataloguing. Headings — *Programmed instructions*

Elrod, J. McRee. Choice of main and added entries / by J. McRee Elrod. — 3rd ed. — Metuchen ; London : Scarecrow, 1980 ; [Folkestone] : [Bailey & Swinfen] [[distributor]]. — viii,82p : forms ; 22cm. — (Modern library practices series ; no.4)
'Updated for use with AACR2'. — Previous ed.: 1978
ISBN 0-8108-1339-4 (pbk) : £3.85 B82-15069

025.3′24 — Monographs. Descriptive cataloguing. Rules: International Federation of Library Associations and Institutions. ISBD(M) - International standard bibliographic description for monographic publications — *Questions & answers*

Ravilious, C. P.. Manual of annotated ISBD(M) examples / compiled by C.P. Ravilious. — London : IFLA International Office for UBC, 1981. — viii,106p : facsims ; 30cm
Includes index
ISBN 0-903043-36-x (pbk) : £10.00 : CIP rev.
B81-40232

025.3′4 — Audiovisual materials. Author & descriptive cataloguing rules. Rules: Anglo-American cataloguing rules. 2nd ed — *Critical studies*

Croghan, Antony. On cataloguing : non-book media and Anglo American cataloguing rules / by Antony Croghan. — London : Coburgh, 1982, c1981. — v,124p ; 21cm
Bibliography: p118. — Includes index
Unpriced (pbk) B82-37544

025.3′432 — Serials. Descriptive cataloguing

Smith, Lynn S.. A practical approach to serials cataloging / by Lynn S. Smith. — Greenwich, Conn. : Jai Press ; London : distributed by Jaicon Press, c1978. — xx,424p : ill ; 24cm. — (Foundations in library and information science ; v.2)
Bibliography: p397-413. — Includes index
ISBN 0-89232-007-9 : £26.20 B82-02010

025.3′434 — Official publications. Bibliographic control

The **Bibliographic** control of official publications. — Oxford : Pergamon, Oct.1982. — [172]p. — (Guides to official publications ; v.11)
ISBN 0-08-027419-6 : £12.50 : CIP entry
B82-25507

025.3′434 — United Nations. Official publications. Bibliographic control

Clews, John. Documentation of the UN system. — London : IFLA International Office for UBC, Sept.1981. — [26]p. — (The IFLA International Office for UBC occasional papers, ISSN 0309-9202 ; no.8)
ISBN 0-903043-34-3 (pbk) : £5.00 : CIP entry
B81-28108

025.3′46 — Cartographic materials. Descriptive cataloguing — *Rules*

Cartographic materials : a manual of interpretation for AACR2. — London : Library Association, Nov.1982. — [416]p
ISBN 0-85365-855-2 : £35.00 : CIP entry
B82-23843

025.3′47 — Audiovisual materials with British imprints. Cataloguing. Projects: Learning Materials Recording Study

Ferris, D. J.. Learning materials recording study : report of a study funded by the British Library Research and Development Department / D.J. Ferris. — London : Council for Educational Technnology, 1981. — x,94p : facsims ; 31cm. — (British Library R & D report ; no.5661)
ISBN 0-86184-052-6 (pbk) : £8.00 B82-02924

025.3′47′076 — Audiovisual materials. Cataloguing — *Questions & answers*

Fleischer, Eugene. Cataloguing audiovisual materials : a manual based on the Anglo-American cataloguing rules II / by Eugene Fleischer and Helen Goodman ; conceived and illustrated by Eugene Fleischer. — New York : Neal-Schuman ; London : Mansell, c1980. — xi,388p : ill ; 28cm
Includes index
ISBN 0-7201-1625-2 (pbk) : £11.00 : CIP rev. B80-32818

025.3′49 — Digital computer systems. Software. Bibliographic control — *Conference proceedings*

Libraries and computer materials : a seminar held at the White Horse Hotel, Dorking, 13-14 March 1981 / edited by Paul Baxter. — [London] : [British Library], 1982. — 42p : ill ; 30cm. — (BL R & D report ; no.5690)
Unpriced (pbk) B82-16789

025.4 — LIBRARIES. SUBJECT ANALYSIS AND CONTROL

025.4 — Documents. Automatic subject indexing & classification. Effectiveness

Harding, P.. Automatic indexing and classification for mechanised information retrieval / P. Harding. — London : Inspec, 1982. — 109p : ill ; 30cm. — ([BL R & D report ; 5723])
'Final report to the British Library R & D Department on Project number SI/G/235'
Unpriced (pbk) B82-40943

025.4′028 — Documents. Abstracting

Rowley, J. E.. Abstracting and indexing / Jennifer E. Rowley. — London : Bingley, 1982. — 155p : ill ; 23cm. — (Outlines of modern librarianship)
Bibliography: p147-151. — Includes index
ISBN 0-85157-336-3 : Unpriced : CIP rev.
Also classified at 025.4′8 B81-30413

025.4′2 — Documents. Classification

Foskett, A. C.. The subject approach to information / by A.C. Foskett. — 4th ed. — London : Bingley, 1982. — xvii,574p : ill ; 23cm
Previous ed.: 1977. — Includes bibliographies and index
ISBN 0-85157-313-4 (cased) : Unpriced : CIP rev.
ISBN 0-85157-339-8 (pbk) : Unpriced
Also classified at 025.4′8 B81-31076

025.4′2′077 — Documents. Classification — *Programmed instructions*

Elrod, J. McRee. Classification / by J. McRee Elrod. — 3rd ed. — Metuchen ; London : Scarecrow, 1980 ; [Folkestone] : [Bailey & Swinfen] [[distributor]]. — viii,79p : forms ; 22cm. — (Modern library practices series ; no.3)
'For use with LC or Dewey'. — Previous ed.: 1978
ISBN 0-8108-1338-6 (pbk) : £3.85 B82-15068

025.4′31′077 — Documents. Subject classification schemes: Dewey Decimal Classification. 19th edition — *Programmed instructions*

Batty, C. D.. An introduction to the nineteenth edition of the Dewey decimal classification / C.D. Batty. — London : Bingley, 1981. — [121]p ; 23cm
Includes index
ISBN 0-85157-303-7 : £5.50 : CIP rev. B81-18037

025.4′66381 — Bee-keeping. Documents on bee-keeping. Subject classification schemes: Universal Decimal Classification — *Indexes*

English alphabetical subject index to Universal Decimal Classification numbers used by the International Bee Research Association in apiculture abstracts and in subject indexes. — 3rd enlarged ed. — London : The Association, 1979. — vi,114p ; 30cm
Previous ed.: 1971
ISBN 0-86098-057-x (pbk) : £12.50 : CIP rev. B79-17199

025.4′7 — Documents. Subject indexing. Library of Congress & Sears subject headings — *Programmed instructions*

Elrod, J. McRee. Choice of subject headings / by J. McRee Elrod. — 3rd ed. — Metuchen ; London : Scarecrow, 1980 ; [Folkestone] : [Bailey & Swinfen] [[distributor]]. — viii,49p : forms ; 22cm. — (Modern library practice series ; no.5)
Previous ed.: 1978
ISBN 0-8108-1340-8 (corrected : pbk) : £3.85 B82-17009

025.4′8 — Documents. Printed subject indexes

Wheatley, Alan. Manual on printed subject indexes / Alan Wheatley. — Aberystwyth : Department of Information Systems Studies, College of Librarianship Wales, 1978. — xiv,426p : ill ; 30cm. — (Report / College of Librarianship Wales. Department of Information Systems Studies ; no.5680)
Unpriced (spiral) B82-12096

025.4′8 — Documents. Subject indexing

Foskett, A. C.. The subject approach to information / by A.C. Foskett. — 4th ed. — London : Bingley, 1982. — xvii,574p : ill ; 23cm
Previous ed.: 1977. — Includes bibliographies and index
ISBN 0-85157-313-4 (cased) : Unpriced : CIP rev.
ISBN 0-85157-339-8 (pbk) : Unpriced
Primary classification 025.4′2 B81-31076

Rowley, J. E.. Abstracting and indexing / Jennifer E. Rowley. — London : Bingley, 1982. — 155p : ill ; 23cm. — (Outlines of modern librarianship)
Bibliography: p147-151. — Includes index
ISBN 0-85157-336-3 : Unpriced : CIP rev.
Primary classification 025.4′028 B81-30413

025.4′8 — Drug therapy. Serial articles. Abstracts journals: National drug information abstracts. Indexing. Applications of digital computer systems

Bishop, J. M. (Jacqueline Margaret). The application of computer indexing to the operation of an N.H.S. pharmacy-based regional drug information centre : short report of a project supported by the King's Fund / J.M. Bishop. — [London] ([St. Thomas St., SE1 9RT]) : S.E. Thames Regional Drug Information Centre, Pharmacy Dept., Guy's Hospital, 1981. — [60]leaves : forms ; 30cm
Unpriced (pbk) B82-09555

025.4′8′077 — Documents. Subject indexing — *Programmed instructions*

Brown, A. G. (Alan George). An introduction to subject indexing / A.G. Brown in collaboration with D.W. Langridge and J. Mills. — 2nd ed. — London : Bingley, 1982. — [250]p ; 22cm
Previous ed.: 1976. — Includes index
ISBN 0-85157-331-2 : Unpriced : CIP rev. B81-38856

025.4′82 — Librarians. Professional education. Curriculum subjects: Documents. Automated subject indexing. Schemes: KWAC & NEPHIS. Teaching aids: Microcomputer systems. Software packages — *Manuals*

Armstrong, C. J.. Microcomputer printed subject indexes teaching package / C.J. Armstrong and E.M. Keen. — [London] : British Library, c1982. — (British Library research and development reports, ISSN 0308-2385 ; no.5710)
Part 1: Workbook for NEPHIS and KWAC. — 57p : 1form ; 30cm
ISBN 0-7123-3000-3 (pbk) : Unpriced : CIP rev. B82-11491

Armstrong, C. J.. Microcomputer printed subject indexes teaching package / C.J. Armstrong and E.M. Keen. — [London] : British Library, c1982. — (British Library research and development reports, ISSN 0308-2385 ; no.5711)
Part 2: Manual for teaching NEPHIS and KWAC. — 59p : forms ; 30cm
ISBN 0-7123-3001-1 (pbk) : Unpriced : CIP rev. B82-11490

025.4′9362293 — Drug abuse — *Thesauri*

ISDD thesaurus : keywords relating to the non-medical use of drugs and drug dependence / edited and revised by Philip Defriez. — 1st definitive ed. — London (3 Blackburn Rd., N.W.6) : Institute for the Study of Drug Dependence, 1980. — 224p in various pagings : ill ; 21x31cm
Cover title. — Includes index
Unpriced (spiral) B82-38655

025.4′93627 — Social services for young persons — *Thesauri*

Aitchison, Jean. Thesaurus on youth : an integrated classification and thesaurus for youth affairs and related topics / compiled by Jean Aitchison in association with Inese A. Smith and Susan Thompson. — Leicester : NYB, 1981. — xx,530p ; 30cm
Includes index
ISBN 0-86155-044-7 (pbk) : Unpriced B82-10924

025.4′938134 — Consumer protection — *Thesauri*

Askew, Colin. Thesaurus of consumer terms / compiled by Colin Askew. — London : Consumers' Association
Part 2: Alphabetically structured display. — 1982. — xxix,289p : ill ; 29cm
ISBN 0-85202-228-x (pbk) : £30.00 B82-39631

025.4′953 — Physics — *Thesauri*

Physics thesaurus. — [London] : British Library Bibliographic Services Division, Bibliographic Systems & Standards Office, 1981. — iv,46leaves ; 30cm
Cover title. — Alternate pages blank
£5.00 (spiral) B82-25282

025.4′96 — Technology — *Thesauri*

British Standards Institution. BSI ROOT thesaurus. — Hemel Hempstead : British Standards Institution, 1981. — 2v. ; 31cm
Spine title: ROOT thesaurus. — Includes index
ISBN 0-905877-57-8 : Unpriced B82-04350

025.4′9627 — Hydraulic engineering — *Thesauri*

The **Thesaurus** : for fluid engineering / edited by N.G. Guy. — Bedford : BHRA Fluid Engineering, c1981. — xiii,128p ; 30cm
ISBN 0-906085-57-8 (pbk) : Unpriced : CIP rev. B81-25117

025.4′96381 — Bee-keeping. Subject headings — *Lists*

List of subject categories used for the IBRA collection of historical and contemporary beekeeping material. — Gerrards Cross : International Bee Research Association, 1978. — 6leaves ; 31cm. — (L14)
ISBN 0-86098-018-9 (pbk) : £0.50 B82-36243

025.4′965 — Business practices — *Thesauri*

Newman, Steve. SCIMP/SCANP thesaurus. — 4th ed. / prepared by Steve Newman. — [Manchester] ([Booth St. West, Manchester MI5 6PB]) : European Business School Librarians Group, 1981. — 200p ; 30cm
Previous ed.: 1980?
Unpriced (spiral) B82-31106

025.4′96626 — Energy sources: Biomass — *Thesauri* — *Serials*

Biomass thesaurus. — Sept. 1979-. — Dublin (Institute for Industrial Research and Standards, Ballymun Rd, Dublin 9) : IEA Biomass Conversion Technical Information Service, 1979-. — v. ; 30cm
Prepared by: the Information Technology Group of the Institute for Industrial Research and Standards in conjunction with the National Board for Science and Technology
Unpriced B82-32352

025.4'9663'3 — Brewing. Subject headings — *Lists*

EBC thesaurus. — 2nd ed. — Oxford : IRL Press, July 1982. — 2v. ([380 ; 380]p.)
Previous ed.: s.l. : European Brewery Convention, 1976
ISBN 0-904147-39-8 (pbk) : £50.00 : CIP entry B82-17987

025.5 — LIBRARY SERVICES TO USERS

025.5'2 — Great Britain. Non-computer-based information services — *Lists*

Dewe, A.. British information services not available online : a select list / compiled by Ainslie Dewe with Mary Ann Colyer. — London : Aslib, c1980. — 105p ; 21cm
Includes index
ISBN 0-85142-137-7 (pbk) : £5.75 B82-35369

025.5'2 — Information services. Organisation — *For personnel of citizens' advice bureaux*

Turner, Christopher. The management of information / by Christopher Turner and Les Collins. — Birmingham : National Association of Citizens Advice Bureaux, West Midlands Area, 1981. — 74leaves : 1ill ; 30cm. — (Organiser training. Unit 3)
Unpriced (spiral) B82-01877

025.5'2 — Libraries. Reference services

Katz, Bill. Introduction to reference work / William A. Katz. — 4th ed. — New York ; London : McGraw-Hill. — (McGraw-Hill series in library education)
Previous ed.: 1978
Vol.2: Reference services and reference processes. — c1982. — x,309p ; 24cm
Includes bibliographies and index
ISBN 0-07-033334-3 : £16.25 B82-40612

Thomas, Diana M.. The effective reference librarian / Diana M. Thomas, Ann T. Hinckley, Elizabeth R. Eisenbach. — New York ; London : Academic Press, c1981. — ix,214p : ill,facsims ; 24cm. — (Library and information science)
Includes bibliographies and index
ISBN 0-12-688720-9 : £11.60 B82-02204

025.5'2 — Reference libraries. Information services — *Manuals*

Katz, Bill. Introduction to reference work / William A. Katz. — 4th ed. — New York ; London : McGraw-Hill. — (McGraw-Hill series in library education)
Previous ed.: 1978
Vol.1: Basic information sources. — c1982. — xii,398p ; 24cm
Includes bibliographies and index
ISBN 0-07-033333-5 : £15.25
Primary classification 011'.02 B82-24908

025.5'2 — United States. Information broking services. Organisation & management — *Manuals*

Warnken, Kelly. The information brokers : how to start and operate your own fee-based service / by Kelly Warnken. — New York ; London : Bowker, 1981. — ix,154p ; 24cm. — (Information management series ; 2)
Bibliography: p133-146. — Includes index
ISBN 0-8352-1347-1 : Unpriced B82-04003

025.5'2'024338 — Great Britain. Information services — *For industries* — *Directories*

Technical services for industry : technical information and other services available from government departments and associated organisations / Department of Industry. — London ([Ashdown House, Victoria St., SW1E 6RB]) : The Department, 1981. — 360p ; 21cm
Includes index
Unpriced (pbk) B82-38484

025.5'2'02542496 — West Midlands *(Metropolitan County).* **Birmingham. Information services: West Midlands Library and Information Network** — *Directories*

West Midlands Library and Information Network . Weslink members' directory and union list of resources. — 2nd ed. / compiled by K.A. Small. — Redditch : West Midlands Library and Information Network, 1981. — 51p ; 30cm
Previous ed.: published as Members' directory and union list of standards, reports and patents, 1976
ISBN 0-905894-01-4 (pbk) : £4.00 B82-02681

025.5'2'028 — England. Public libraries. Reference services. Videotex services: Prestel. Use

Sullivan, Catherine, *19---.* Impact of Prestel on public library branch services / Catherine Sullivan. — London : Aslib Research & Consultancy Division, 1981. — iv,58p ; 30cm. — (British Library research and development report ; no.5694)
ISBN 0-85142-159-8 (spiral) : £8.00 B82-27577

Yeates, R.. Prestel in the public library. — Boston Spa : British Library Lending Division, July 1982. — [134]p. — (Library and information research reports, ISSN 0263-1709 ; 2)
ISBN 0-7123-3003-8 (pbk) : £8.50 : CIP entry B82-20771

025.5'2'028 — England. Public libraries. Reference services. Viewdata services: Prestel. Use

Sullivan, Catherine, *19---.* The impact of Prestel on public library reference activities / Catherine Sullivan, David Oliver. — London : Aslib Research & Consultancy Division, 1981. — 2,iv,99p : forms ; 30cm. — (British Library research and development report ; no.5654)
Bibliography: p98-99
ISBN 0-85142-151-2 (spiral) : Unpriced B82-14471

025.5'2'068 — Information services. Management

Tricker, Robert Ian. Effective information management. — Oxford (25 Beaumont St., Oxford OX1 2NP) : Beaumont Executive Press, June 1982. — [204]p
ISBN 0-946065-00-4 (pbk) : £5.95 : CIP entry B82-18595

025.52'0941 — Great Britain. Libraries. Reference services — *Conference proceedings*

Library Association. *Reference, Special and Information Section. Annual Study Group (29th : 1981 : Newcastle-upon-Tyne).* Proceedings of the 29th Annual Study Group, Newcastle-upon-Tyne, 10th-13th April 1981. — London (16 Springfield, Ovington, Northumberland NE42 6EH) : The Section, Oct.1981. — 1v.
ISBN 0-85365-864-1 (pbk) : £4.00 (£3.20 to members) : CIP entry B81-32088

025.5'2'0973 — United States. Libraries. Information services

Reference and information services : a new reader / compiled by Bill Katz and Anne Clifford. — Metuchen ; London : Scarecrow, 1982. — ix,421p : ill,1form ; 23cm
Previous ed.: 1978
ISBN 0-8108-1483-8 : £14.00 B82-17419

025.5'23 — Great Britain. International cooperative information services

East, Harry, *1936-.* UK cooperation in international information systems : a study conducted for the British Library Research and Development Department / Harry East. — London : School of Library, Archive and Information Studies, University College, London, 1978. — iii,100p ; 30cm. — ([BL R & D report] ; [5698])
Bibliography: p96-100
Unpriced (spiral) B82-24641

025.5'24 — Great Britain. National libraries: British Library. On-line bibliographic information retrieval services: BLAISE — *Manuals*

British Library. *Bibliographic Services Division.* BLAISE LINK user manual. — London : British Library, Bibliographic Services Division, Apr.1982. — 1v.(loose-leaf)
ISBN 0-7123-1001-0 : £25.00 (1 copy free to BLAISE subscribers) : CIP entry B82-14486

025.5'24 — Information retrieval systems. Design & organisation

Booth, Pat F.. Information filing and finding. — Buckden (45 Park Rd., Buckden, Cambs. PE18 9SL) [Elm Publications], Sept.1982. — [288]p
ISBN 0-946139-00-8 (pbk) : £7.90 : CIP entry B82-30296

025.5'24 — On-line bibliographic information retrieval services. Machine-readable files: UK MARC records. Searching. Use of keywords & international standard book numbers — *Study examples: BLAISE*

Curwen, Anthony G.. The use of ISBNs compared with keywords as means of retrieving bibliographic records on-line : project undertaken for the BNB Research Fund January-November 1979 / report by Anthony G. Curwen. — Aberystwyth : College of Librarianship Wales, 1980. — 16p : 1ill ; 30cm. — (British National Bibliography Research Fund report ; no.7)
Unpriced (pbk) B82-03855

025.5'24 — On-line information retrieval systems — *For librarianship*

The Library and information manager's guide to online services / Ryan E. Hoover with Alice H. Bahr ... [et al.]. — White Plains, N.Y. : Knowledge Industry ; London : Eurospan [distributor], c1980. — v,270p : ill,forms ; 29cm. — (Professional librarian series)
Bibliography: p263-265. — Includes index
ISBN 0-914236-60-1 (cased) : Unpriced
ISBN 0-914236-52-0 (pbk) : Unpriced B82-08807

025.5'24 — On-line information retrieval. Teaching. Use of viewdata systems. Evaluation

Maslin, J. M.. Evaluation of the use of viewdata for on-line training / J.M. Maslin, M. Thompson and M.Y. Gates. — [Leatherhead] ([Randalls Rd., Leatherhead, Surrey KT22 7RU]) : Pira, 1981. — 65p : forms ; 31cm. — (British Library R & D report ; no.5658) (Pira viewdata report ; no.3)
Bibliography: p6
Unpriced (spiral) B82-05183

025.5'24 — Scotland. Central Region. Falkirk. Public libraries: Falkirk Library. *Reference and Information Department.* **On-line information retrieval services. Projects,** *1980-1981*

Falkirk District Libraries : on-line information retrieval project, March 1980-Sept. 1981 : final report to the British Library Research and Development Department on Project SI/G/342. — Falkirk (c/o Margaret Sharp, Hope St., Falkirk) : Falkirk District Libraries, 1981. — 16leaves ; 30cm. — (Report ; no.5682)
Unpriced (unbound) B82-14318

025.5'24 — West Sussex. Public libraries: West Sussex County Council Library Service. On-line bibliographic information retrieval services. Use, *1980-1981*

Wood, A. F.. Experimental use of on-line terminals in public libraries : final report for the period January 1980- December 1981 : report to the British Library Research and Development Department on Project S1/G 352 / A.F. Wood. — [Chichester] : West Sussex County Council Library Service, 1982. — 18p ; 30cm. — (Report ; no.5708)
Unpriced (pbk) B82-22365

025.5'24'02854 — Libraries. On-line bibliographic information retrieval. Techniques. Teaching

Scott, Aldyth D.. Teaching and training for on-line work in libraries : final report for the period June 1978-June 1980 : report to the British Library Research and Development Department on Project S1/G/270 / Aldyth D. Scott. — [Brighton] : School of Librarianship, Department of Communication and European Studies, Brighton Polytechnic, 1980. — 67p : ill ; 30cm. — (BL R & D report ; 5604)
Unpriced (pbk) B82-02425

025.5'24'071173 — United States. Schools of librarianship. Curriculum subjects: On-line information retrieval. Teaching — *Case studies*

Large, J. A.. Teaching online searching in American library schools : report to the British Library Research and Development Department / by J.A. Large. — [London] : [British Library Research and Development Department], 1982. — 24p ; 29cm. — (BL R & D report ; 5692)
Bibliography: p23
Unpriced (pbk) B82-17702

025.5′24′072 — Information retrieval. Research. Use of on-line bibliographic information retrieval services

Cleverdon, Cyril. An investigation into the use of operational data-bases for research into information retrieval / by Cyril Cleverdon. — [London] : [British Library Research and Development Department], 1977. — 44p ; 24cm. — (BL R & D report ; 5696)
Unpriced (pbk) B82-17701

025.5′24′0724 — Information retrieval. Stochastic models

Van Rijsbergen, C. J.. New models in probabilistic information retrieval / C.J. van Rijsbergen, S.E. Robertson and M.F. Porter. — Cambridge (Corn Exchange St., Cambridge CB2 3QG) : Computer Laboratory, University of Cambridge, c1980. — 123p ; 30cm. — (British Library R & D report ; no.5587)
Unpriced (pbk) B82-11054

025.5′25 — Great Britain. Education. SDI services — *Feasibility studies*

Hounsell, Dai. Bibliographic and information services in education : final report to the British Library Research and Development Department on project SI/CT/011 / by Dai Hounsell, Philip Payne and Irene Willett. — [Bailrigg] ([Cartmel College, Bailrigg, Lancaster LA1 4YL]) : University of Lancaster Centre for Educational Research and Development, 1980. — 110,[52]p : ill,forms ; 30cm. — (Report ; no.5610)
Bibliography: p109-110
Unpriced (pbk) B82-11396

025.5′25 — Libraries. Non-computer-based SDI services

Whitehall, T.. Personal current awareness service : a handbook of techniques for manual SDI / T. Whitehall. — London : British Library, c1979. — v,119p : ill ; 30cm. — (British Library research and development reports, ISSN 0308-2385 ; no.5502)
Bibliography: p94-96. — Includes index
ISBN 0-905984-43-9 (spiral) : Unpriced
B82-26374

025.5′25′025417 — Ireland *(Republic)*. **Special libraries. Current awareness services** — *Directories*

Hughes, N.. Current awareness services in Irish university and special libraries / N. Hughes and D. O′Connell. — Dublin : Library Association of Ireland, University and Special Libraries Section, 1981. — i,32p ; 22cm
ISBN 0-946037-00-0 (pbk) : £3.00 (Irish)
B82-23390

025.5′6 — Europe. Libraries. Stock. Classification. Guiding signs, *to 1850:* **Visual arts**

Masson, André. The pictorial catalogue : mural decoration in libraries : the Lyell Lectures, Oxford 1972-1973 / André Masson ; translated by David Gerard. — Oxford : Clarendon, 1981. — xiii,81p,[17]p of plates : ill,ports ; 23cm
Translated from the French. — Includes index
ISBN 0-19-818159-0 : £10.50 : CIP rev.
B81-30311

025.5′6 — Great Britain. Libraries. Graphics. Resource centres — *Proposals*

Cronin, Blaise. A national graphics resource centre for libraries in the United Kingdom / by Blaise Cronin. — London : Aslib, c1981. — 43,[38]p : ill,1form ; 30cm. — (Aslib occasional publication ; no.26) (British Library research and development report ; no.5646)
ISBN 0-85142-149-0 (pbk) : Unpriced
B82-14472

025.5′6 — Libraries. Information retrieval. Teaching. Programmes. Design

Bantly, Harold A.. Information searching : a handbook for designing & creating instructional programs. — Rev. ed. / compiled by Janet L. Freedman and Harold A. Bantly. — Metuchen ; London : Scarecrow, 1982. — ix,198p : ill ; 29cm
Previous ed.: Boston : Massachusetts Board of Library Commissioners, 1979. — Bibliography: p185-196. — Includes index
ISBN 0-8108-1509-5 : £12.80 B82-37695

025.5′6 — Libraries. Use — *Forecasts*

Thompson, James, *1932-*. The end of libraries. — London : Bingley, Sept.1982. — [128]p
ISBN 0-85157-349-5 : £9.75 : CIP entry
B82-20528

025.5′6 — Libraries. Use — *Questions & answers*

Kirby, John. Basic library skills : a checklist / John Kirby. — Sheffield : PAVIC Publications, c1982. — 12leaves ; 30cm. — (Gems ; 12)
Cover title
ISBN 0-903761-85-8 (spiral) : Unpriced
B82-39030

025.5′6 — Libraries. Users. Education

Rice, James, *1946-*. Teaching library use : a guide for library instruction / James Rice, Jr. — Westport, Conn. ; London : Greenwood Press, 1981. — vi,169p ; 22cm. — (Contributions in librarianship and information science ; no.37)
Bibliography: p157-166. — Includes index
ISBN 0-313-21485-9 : £18.95 B82-18372

025.5′6 — Libraries. Users. Education — *Conference proceedings*

Second international conference on library user education : Keble College Oxford 7-10 July 1981 : proceedings / edited by Peter Fox. — Loughborough : INFUSE, 1981. — 148p : ill ; 21cm
ISBN 0-904641-17-1 (pbk) : Unpriced
B82-22473

025.5′677′028 — Great Britain. Higher education institutions. Libraries. Users. Education. Use of audiovisual materials

Malley, Ian. Survey of audiovisual programmes produced for user education in UK academic libraries / Ian Malley and Sue Moys. — Loughborough : INFUSE, 1982. — 24p ; 30cm
ISBN 0-904641-18-x (pbk) : £3.00 B82-28408

025.5′677′0941 — Great Britain. Higher education institutions. Libraries. Guidance for users. Role of travelling seminars. Projects: Travelling Workshops Experiment

Clark, Daphne. Students and libraries : based on the Travelling Workshops Experiment′s work teaching information-handling skills / Daphne Clark. — Newcastle upon Tyne : Newcastle upon Tyne Polytechnic Products, c1981. — 32p : ill,facsims,forms ; 15x21cm
Bibliography: p30-32
ISBN 0-906471-13-3 (pbk) : Unpriced
B82-11599

025.5′87441 — Great Britain. Public libraries. Use

Houghton, A.. Access to public libraries / A. Houghton, C. Norrie. — Reading (201 King′s Rd., Reading RG1 4LH) : Local Government Operational Research Unit, [1981]. — 55p : ill ; 30cm
£10.00 (spiral) B82-02881

025.5′8′77 — Higher education institutions. Libraries. Catalogues. Use by readers. Analysis

Reader failure at the shelf. — Loughborough (University of Technology, Loughborough, Leics. LE11 3TU) : Centre for Library and Information Management, Jan.1982. — [38]p. — (Aids to library administration, ISSN 0261-0222 ; no.2) (British Library research and development reports, ISSN 0308-2385 ; no.5666)
ISBN 0-904924-33-5 (pbk) : £5.00 : CIP entry
B82-03134

025.5′8774212 — Great Britain. Polytechnics. Libraries. Use by part-time students — *Study examples: City of London Polytechnic. Library*

Payne, Philip, *1952-*. The use of books and libraries by part-time business studies students at a polytechnic : a follow-up study / by Philip Payne. — London : LLRS, 1981. — iii,42p : ill,forms ; 30cm
Bibliography: p42
ISBN 0-904264-59-9 (pbk) : £15.00 : CIP rev.
B82-01348

025.6 — LIBRARY CIRCULATION SERVICES

025.6 — Scotland. Public libraries. Stock: Videorecordings. Lending — *Conference proceedings*

The **Lending** of video by Public libraries : papers presented at a one day school arranged by the Scottish Library Association, West of Scotland Branch, 24th June 1981. — Motherwell : The Association, c1981. — 56p ; 21cm
ISBN 0-900649-31-3 (pbk) : Unpriced : CIP rev. B82-03129

025.6 — United States. Libraries. Automated charging systems

Bahr, Alice Harrison. Automated library circulation systems, 1979-1980. — 2nd ed. / by Alice Harrison Bahr. — White Plains, N.Y. : Knowledge Industry Publications ; London : Distributed by Eurospan, c1979. — 105p : ill ; 27cm
Previous ed.: published as Automated library circulation systems, 1977-78 / Paula Dranov. 1977. — Bibliography: p101-102. — Includes index
ISBN 0-914236-34-2 (pbk) : Unpriced
B82-11945

025.6′2 — England. Libraries. Stock. Inter-library loans. Road transport

Inter-regional transport scheme : users list. — [Boston Spa] : British Library Lending Division, 1982. — 114,60p ; 30cm
Cover title. — Includes index
Unpriced (pbk) B82-31813

Library transport schemes : inter-regional transfer : user′s guide. — [Boston Spa] : [British Library Lending Division], 1982. — 10p : maps ; 30cm
Unpriced (unbound) B82-31812

025.6′2 — Libraries. Stock. International inter-library loans

Kefford, Brian. International interlibrary lending : a review of the literature / Brian Kefford. — Boston Spa : IFLA Office for International Lending, 1982. — v,41p ; 21cm
ISBN 0-85350-184-x (pbk) : Unpriced
B82-30870

025.8 — LIBRARIES. MAINTENANCE AND PRESERVATION OF COLLECTIONS

025.8 — Great Britain. Archives. Storage. Machine-readable files

Machine readable data archiving : abridged version of June 1980 report to Central Computer and Telecommunications Agency/Public Record Office Management / [prepared by R.G. Fiddes ... et al.]. — London : Civil Service Department, c1981. — 43p : ill ; 30cm
£1.00 (pbk) B82-37601

025.8 — Higher education institutions. Libraries. Stock. Regulation & storage

The **Relegation** and storage of material in academic libraries : a literature review / L. Gilder ... [et al.]. — Loughborough : Centre for Library and Information Management, Dept. of Library and Information Studies, Loughborough University, [c1980]. — 77p : 1ill ; 30cm. — (Report / CLAIM ; no.3)
Bibliography: p 63-75. — Includes index
ISBN 0-904924-24-6 (pbk) : Unpriced
B82-36202

025.8 — Libraries. Stock. Conservation, physical arrangement & stock control

Hubbard, William J.. Stack management : a practical guide to shelving and maintaining library collections / William J. Hubbard. — [Revision]. — Chicago : American Library Association ; London : Distributed by Eurospan, 1981. — viii,102p : plans ; 23cm
Previous ed.: published as Shelf work in libraries / by W.H. Jesse. 1952. — Includes index
ISBN 0-8389-0319-3 (pbk) : £5.75 B82-21146

025.8'1 — England. Public libraries. Stock. Arrangement

Alternative arrangement : new approaches to public library stock / [edited] by Patricia Ainley and Barry Totterdell. — London : Association of Assistant Librarians published with assistance from Holmes McDougall, 1982. — 135p : ill ; 22cm
ISBN 0-900092-41-6 (pbk) : £5.50 (£4.50 to members) B82-31244

025.8'2'0973 — United States. Libraries. Stock. Theft. Security measures

Bahr, Alice Harrison. Book theft and library security systems, 1981-82 / by Alice Harrison Bahr. — New York : Knowledge Industry ; London : Eurospan [[distributor]], c1981. — iii,157p : ill ; 28cm. — (Professional librarian series)
Bibliography: p143-151. — Includes index
ISBN 0-914236-71-7 (pbk) : Unpriced B82-17479

025.8'4 — Documents. Conservation — *Manuals*

Baynes-Cope, A. D.. Caring for books and documents / A.D. Baynes-Cope ; with line illustrations by Sture Åkerström. — London : Published for the Trustees of the British Museum by British Museum Publications, c1980. — 32p : ill ; 26cm
Bibliography: p31-32
ISBN 0-7141-2006-5 : £2.50 B82-21234

025.8'4 — Great Britain. Cinema films. Repositories: National Film Archive. Stock: Cinema films. Cinematographic materials: Nitrate films. Conservation — *Inquiry reports*

Great Britain. *Parliament. House of Commons. Education, Science and Arts Committee.* Fourth report from the Education, Science and Arts Committee : session 1981-82 : public and private funding of the arts : interim report on the nitrate problem at the National Film Archive : together with a memorandum. — London : H.M.S.O., 1982. — v,6p ; 25cm. — ([H.C.] ; 240)
ISBN 0-10-224082-5 (unbound) : £1.50 B82-25644

025.8'4 — Libraries. Stock. Conservation

Harrison, Alice W.. The conservation of library materials / by Alice W. Harrison. — London : Vine, 1981. — 210p ; 29cm. — (Occasional paper / Dalhousie University Libraries and Dalhousie University School of Library Service, ISSN 0138-7403 ; 28)
Includes bibliographies
ISBN 0-7703-0164-9 (spiral) : Unpriced B82-20733

026 — SPECIAL LIBRARIES

026'.000941 — Great Britain. Special libraries. Technological innovation

Singleton, Alan. Information technology in industrial information services. — Leicester (University of Leicester LE1 7RH) : Primary Communications Research Centre, June 1982. — [56]p. — (A Primary Communications Research Publication, ISSN 0141-0261)
ISBN 0-906083-22-2 (spiral) : £6.00 : CIP entry B82-14964

026'.0013 — United States. Public libraries. Stock: Humanities — *Conference proceedings*

The **Role** of the humanities in the public library / edited by Robert N. Broadus with the assistance of Brian Nielsen. — Chicago : American Library Association ; London : Eurospan [distributor], 1979. — vi,213p ; 24cm
ISBN 0-8389-0297-9 : £15.25 B82-34659

026'.297 — Great Britain. Libraries. Stock: Documents on Islam

Collections in British libraries on middle Eastern and Islamic studies / edited by Paul Auchterlonie. — Durham (Elvet Hill, Durham DH1 3TR) : Centre for Middle Eastern Studies, University of Durham, c1981. — 98p ; 21cm. — (Occasional papers series, ISSN 0307-0654 ; no.12 (1982))
Includes bibliographies
Unpriced (pbk)
Also classified at 026'.956 B82-18670

026'.3 — West Midlands *(Metropolitan County).* **Coventry. Record repositories: University of Warwick.** *Modern Records Centre.* **Stock**

University of Warwick. *Modern Records Centre.* Supplement to the Guide to the Modern Records Centre, University of Warwick Library / compiled by Richard Storey & Susan Edwards. — Coventry : The Library, 1981. — 116p : 1ill ; 21cm. — (Occasional publications / University of Warwick Library ; no.9)
Bibliography: p94. — Includes index
ISBN 0-903220-10-5 (pbk) : £3.00 B82-06268

026'.3'00254 — Europe. Social sciences. Information services — *Directories*

Gabrovska, Svobodozarya. European guide to social science information and documentation services / compiled by Svobodozarya Gabrovska for the European Cooperation in Social Science Information and Documentation ; editors Svobodozarya Gabrovska, Manfred Biskup, Anna Bossilkova. — Oxford : Pergamon, 1982. — v,234p : 1form ; 26cm
Includes index
ISBN 0-08-028927-4 : £17.50 : CIP rev. B82-03087

026'.33188'0941 — Great Britain. Trade unions. Information services. Provision

Backhouse, Roger. Information services for trades unionists / Roger Backhouse. — Buckden : Elm, 1982. — 35p ; 30cm. — (Information and library manager occasional papers, ISSN 0262-9755 ; no.1) (British Library research and development report ; no.5695)
ISBN 0-9505828-4-0 (pbk) : £4.95 : CIP rev. B82-14401

026'.3337'0941 — Great Britain. Environmental studies. Information services — *Lists*

Moody, Mary. Environmental information services in the United Kingdom / a report prepared for DOE-DTp Library in December 1980 by Mary Moody. — [London] : Departments of the Environment and Transport, c1981. — 11,[32]p ; 30cm. — (Occasional paper ; no.8)
Bibliography: 15p
ISBN 0-7184-0192-1 (pbk) : £2.20 B82-06129

026'.361 — Social services. Information services. Organisation — *Manuals*

Mathews, R. Mark. Matching clients and services : information and referral / R. Mark Mathews, Stephen B. Fawcett ; published in cooperation with the Continuing Education Program in the Human Services of the University of Michigan School of Social Work. — Beverly Hills ; London : Sage, c1981. — 160p : ill,forms ; 22cm. — (A Sage human services guide ; 21)
Bibliography: p159
ISBN 0-8039-1619-1 (pbk) : Unpriced B82-08573

026'.375001 — United States. Higher education institutions. Libraries. Stock: Documents on curriculum development in schools. Collections. Management

Clark, Alice S.. Managing curriculum materials in the academic library / Alice S. Clark. — Metuchen ; London : Scarecrow, 1982. — vi,221p : forms ; 23cm
Includes index
ISBN 0-8108-1482-x : £11.20 B82-22978

026'.5 — Oxfordshire. Oxford. Universities: University of Oxford. Scientific libraries

Shaw, Dennis F.. Oxford University Press science libraries : a guide / by Dennis F. Shaw. — Oxford : Bodleian Library, 1981. — 83p : 1ill ; 22cm
ISBN 0-900177-82-9 (cased) : Unpriced
ISBN 0-900177-84-5 (pbk) : Unpriced B82-01493

026'.61 — Great Britain. Hospitals. Information services & libraries. Role — *Study examples: Guy's Hospital*

Childs, Susan. The experiences of a clinical librarian in medicine : report to the British Library Research and Development Department on Project S1/G/262 : final report for the peroid July 1978 to June 1980 / Susan Childs. — London : Guy's Hospital Medical School, 1980. — iv,58p ; 30cm. — (Report ; no.5687)
Unpriced (pbk) B82-15467

026'.61 — Great Britain. Medicine. Information services

Ford, G. (Geoffrey). The provision and use of medical literature : summary report and conclusions / G. Ford. — London : British Library Research and Development Department, c1979. — iv,17p ; 30cm. — (The British Library research and development reports, ISSN 0308-2385 ; no.5510)
Bibliography: p17
ISBN 0-905984-47-1 (pbk) : Unpriced B82-35926

026'.61'02541 — Great Britain. Medical libraries — *Directories*

Linton, W. D.. Directory of medical and health care libraries in the United Kingdom and Republic of Ireland. — 5th ed. — London : Library Association, Oct.1982. — [236]p
Previous ed.: published as Directory of medical libraries in the British Isles. 1976
ISBN 0-85365-536-7 (pbk) : £12.00(£5.75 to members) : CIP entry B82-31308

026'.61'0973 — United States. Information services on medicine

Developing consumer health information services / edited by Alan M. Rees. — New York ; London : Bowker, 1982. — x,296p : ill,1plan,1form ; 24cm. — (Consumer information series)
Includes index
ISBN 0-8352-1473-7 : Unpriced B82-24498

026'.615822'0971 — Canada. Information services on physiotherapy — *Proposals*

Lloyd, Hazel A.. The information needs of physiotherapists with a guide to physiotherapy collections for community general hospitals. — 2nd ed., rev. and expanded / M. Doreen E. Fraser, Hazel A. Lloyd. — [London] : [Vine Press], 1981. — 72p ; 28cm. — (Occasional paper / Dalhousie University Libraries/Dalhousie University School of Library Service, ISSN 0318-7403 ; no.13)
Previous ed.: published as The Information needs of physiotherapists in the Atlantic provinces, with suggested physiotherapy working collections for small hospitals. 1977. — Bibliography: p31-72
Unpriced (pbk) B82-14654

026'.617 — Great Britain. Medicine. Surgery. Role of hospital information services & libraries — *Study examples: Guy's Hospital*

Moore, Alison. The clinical librarian in the department of surgery : a report of two years' experience : report to the British Library Research and Development Department on Project S1/G/262 : final report for the period July 1978-June 1980 / Alison Moore. — London : Wills Library, Guy's Hospital Medical School, 1980. — v,75p ; 30cm. — (Report ; no.5686)
Bibliography: p70
Unpriced (pbk) B82-15464

026'.63 — Malawi. Agriculture. Information services. Role of mass media

Perraton, Hilary. Mass media for agricultural extension in Malawi / Hilary Perraton, Dean Jamison and François Orivel. — Cambridge : International Extension College, 1982. — viii,51p : 2ill ; 30cm
Bibliography: p50-51
ISBN 0-903632-21-7 (pbk) : Unpriced B82-36036

026'.65 — Great Britain. Information services for business firms. Organisation

Campbell, Malcolm J.. Business information services : some aspects of structure organisation and problems / Malcolm J. Campbell. — 2nd ed. — London : Bingley, 1981. — 179p ; 23cm
Previous ed.: 1974. — Includes index
ISBN 0-85157-321-5 : Unpriced : CIP rev. B81-18084

026'.65 — Great Britain. Information services for small business firms

Information and the small manufacturing firm. — Edinburgh : Capital Planning Information, Aug.1982. — [160]p
ISBN 0-906011-17-5 (pbk) : £9.75 : CIP entry B82-21971

026'.658 — Great Britain. National libraries: British Library. Information services on business

British Library. *Working Group on Business Information*. Business information : the role of the British Library : report of the British Library Working Group on Business Information 1980. — Rev. ed. with progress report. — [London] : British Library, 1982. — 11p ; 21cm
Previous ed.: 1980
Unpriced (unbound) B82-24790

026'.669'00941 — Great Britain. Metals industries. Information services

Metals Society. *Metals Information Review Committee*. Scientific and technical information in the metals industry : report of the Metals Information Review Committee / L. Jones and J. Vaughan. — [London] : British Library ; Boston Spa : distributed by Publications, The British Library Lending Division, 1982. — vii,110p : forms ; 30cm. — (British Library research and development reports, ISSN 0308-2385 ; no.5717)
Bibliography: p48-56
ISBN 0-7123-3008-9 (pbk) : Unpriced : CIP rev. B82-21746

026'.7 — Art libraries. Organisations: International Federation of Library Associations and Institutions. ***Section of Art Libraries — Serials***

International Federation of Library Associations and Institutions. *Section of Art Libraries*. Newsletter / International Federation of Library Associations and Institutions, Special Libraries Division, Section of Art Libraries. — No.2 (July 1981)-. — [London] ([c/o Vera Kaden, National Art Library, Victoria and Albert Museum, South Kensington, SW7 2RL]) : The Section, 1981-. — v. ; 30cm
Two issues yearly. — Continues: Round Table of Art Librarians. Newssheet
ISSN 0261-152x = Newsletter - IFLA. Special Libraries Division. Section of Art Libraries : Unpriced B82-04901

026'.781773 — American music, ***1776-1945.*** **Information services** ***— Directories***

Resources of American music history : a directory of source materials from colonial times to World War II / D.W. Krummel ... [et al.]. — Urbana ; London : University of Illinois Press, c1981. — 463p ; 29cm. — (Music in American life)
Includes index
ISBN 0-252-00828-6 : £49.00 B82-09775

026'.9291 — Great Britain. ***Public Record Office.*** **Stock: Genealogical sources**

Cox, Jane, *1942-*. Tracing your ancestors in the Public Record Office / by Jane Cox and Timothy Padfield. — London : H.M.S.O., 1981. — viii,92p : ill,3facsims ; 25cm. — (Public Record Office handbooks ; no.19)
Includes bibliographies
ISBN 0-11-440114-4 (pbk) : £3.95 B82-08677

Great Britain. *Public Record Office*. Genealogy : a selection of leaflets / Public Record Office. — [London] : P.R.O., [1981]. — [75]p : 1map ; 30cm
Includes bibliographies
Unpriced (spiral) B82-14432

026'.9291 — London ***(City).*** **Public libraries: Guildhall Library. Stock: Genealogical sources**

Guildhall Library. A guide to genealogical sources in Guildhall Library. — 2nd ed., rev.. — [London] ([Guildhall, EC2P 2EJ]) : Corporation of London, [1981]. — 44p ; 21cm
Previous ed.: 1979. — Includes index
Unpriced (pbk) B82-03030

026'.929341 — Great Britain. Record repositories. Stock: Probate records ***— Directories***

Gibson, J. S. W.. A simplified guide to probate jurisdictions : where to look for wills / compiled by J.S.W. Gibson. — 2nd ed. — Banbury : Gulliver and the Federation of Family History Societies, 1982. — x,62p : ill,maps ; 21cm
Previous ed.: 1980
ISBN 0-906428-10-6 (pbk) : £2.00
ISBN 0-907099-11-4 (Federation of Family History Societies) B82-14667

026'.929342234 — Great Britain. ***Public Record Office.*** **Stock: Probate records of Church of England.** ***Province of Canterbury. Prerogative Court***

Great Britain. *Public Record Office*. The records of the Prerogative Court of Canterbury and the death duty registers / Jane Cox. — [London] : Public Record Office, 1980. — 40p ; 30cm
A provisional guide, pending preparation of a more complete guide to be published as a PRO handbook. — Cover title: The Prerogative Court of Canterbury. — Includes bibliographies
£1.50 (spiral) B82-14429

026'.94 — Great Britain. Libraries. European Documentation Centres ***— Serials***

[EDC newsletter *(Association of EDC Librarians)*]. EDC newsletter. — No.11 (Nov. 1980)-. — [Newcastle upon Tyne] ([c/o Mrs. A. Ramsay, Newcastle upon Tyne Polytechnic EDC, Ellison Place, Newcastle upon Tyne NE1 8ST]) : [Association of EDC Librarians], 1980-. — v. ; 30cm
Irregular. — Continues: Northern EDC newsletter. — Description based on: No.13 (May 1981)
ISSN 0262-9216 = EDC newsletter (Association of EDC Librarians) : £5.00 per year B82-11816

Northern EDC newsletter. — No.1 (Oct. 1978)-no.10 (Aug. 1980). — [Newcastle upon Tyne] ([c/o Mrs. A. Ramsay, Newcastle upon Tyne Polytechnic EDC, Ellison Place, Newcastle upon Tyne NE1 8ST]) : [s.n.], 1978-1980. — 10v. ; 30cm
Irregular. — Continued by.: EDC newsletter (Association of EDC Librarians). — Description based on: No.5 (July 1979)
Unpriced B82-11817

026'.941 — Great Britain. Public libraries. Local history collections. Organisations: Library Association. ***Local Studies Group — Serials***

[Newsletter *(Library Association. Local Studies Group)*]. Newsletter / the Library Association, Local Studies Group. — No.1 (Nov. 1977)-. — Birmingham (c/o B.M. Hall, Department of Librarianship, Birmingham Polytechnic, Perry Bar, Birmingham B42 2SU) : The Group, 1977-. — v. ; 30cm
Two issues yearly
ISSN 0261-9970 = Newsletter - Library Association. Local Studies Group : Unpriced B82-08466

026'.941 — Great Britain. ***Public Record Office.*** **Stock: Local history. Historical sources**

Great Britain. *Public Record Office*. Local history : a selection of leaflets / Public Record Office. — [London] : P.R.O., [1980]. — [36]p ; 30cm
Includes bibliographies
Unpriced (spiral) B82-14434

026'.94765 — London. Barnet ***(London Borough).*** **Private libraries: Francis Skaryna Byelorussian Library and Museum,** ***1971-1981***

Francis Skaryna Byelorussian Library and Museum. The Francis Skaryna Byelorussian Library and Museum 1971-1981. — London ([37 Holden Rd., N12 8HS]) : The Library, 1981. — 24p : facsims ; 25cm
Author: Alexander Nadson. — Bibliography: p19
Unpriced (pbk) B82-31409

026'.956 — Great Britain. Libraries holding documents on Middle East ***— Directories***

Netton, Ian Richard. Middle East materials in United Kingdom and Irish libraries. — London : Library Association, Jan.1983. — [128]p
ISBN 0-85365-526-x (pbk) : £15.00 : CIP entry B82-36304

026'.956 — Great Britain. Libraries. Stock: Documents on Middle East

Collections in British libraries on middle Eastern and Islamic studies / edited by Paul Auchterlonie. — Durham (Elvet Hill, Durham DH1 3TR) : Centre for Middle Eastern Studies, University of Durham, c1981. — 98p ; 21cm. — (Occasional papers series, ISSN 0307-0654 ; no.12 (1982))
Includes bibliographies
Unpriced (pbk)
Primary classification 026'.297 B82-18670

026'.9591 — Great Britain. National libraries: India Office Library and Records. Stock: Documents on Burma, ***to 1948***

India Office Library and Records. A brief guide to the sources for the study of Burma in the India Office records / [compiled by] Andrew Griffin. — London : India Office Library & Records, 1979. — iv,25p : 1map,ports ; 30cm
ISBN 0-903359-19-7 (pbk) : Unpriced : CIP rev. B79-32199

026'.973 — Great Britain. Libraries holding documents on United States ***— Directories***

Snow, Peter, *1947-*. The United States : a guide to library holdings in the UK / compiled by Peter Snow. — Wetherby : British Library Lending Division in association with SCONUL, c1982. — xxiii,717p ; 24cm
Includes index
ISBN 0-85350-183-1 : Unpriced B82-24670

026'.973 — London. Universities: University of London. Libraries. Stock: Documents on American studies

American studies collections in the University of London : a guide to libraries. — London : University of London, Institute of United States Studies, 1981. — 30p ; 22cm
Includes index
£1.00 (pbk) B82-09820

027 — LIBRARIES

027 — Libraries ***— For children***

Peacock, Frank. Let's go to the library / Frank Peacock ; general editor Henry Pluckrose ; photography by G.W. Hales. — London : Watts, c1975 (1982 [printing]). — 31p : col.ill ; 22cm. — (Let's go series)
ISBN 0-85166-587-x : £2.99 B82-26836

027 — Libraries. Implications of technological innovations

Library Association. The impact of new technology on libraries and information centres. — London : Library Association, Aug.1982. — [48]p. — (Library Association pamphlet ; 38)
ISBN 0-85365-925-7 (pbk) : £4.75 : CIP entry B82-25725

027'.0025'41 — Great Britain. Libraries. Directories

Libraries in the United Kingdom and the Republic of Ireland. — 9th ed. — London : Library Association, July 1981. — [174]p
Previous ed.: 1979
ISBN 0-85365-803-x (pbk) : £9.50 : CIP entry B81-14457

027'.0025'41 — Great Britain. Libraries — ***Directories — Serials***

Guide to government department and other libraries. — 1982. — London : Science Reference Library, Mar.1982. — [95]p
ISBN 0-902914-67-7 (pbk) : £9.00 : CIP entry B82-08411

027'.0025'41 — Great Britain. Libraries - ***Directories - Serials***

Libraries, museums and art galleries year book. — 1978-1979. — Cambridge : James Clarke, May 1981. — [272]p
ISBN 0-227-67835-4 : £23.00 : CIP entry
ISSN 0075-899x
Also classified at 069'.025'41 ; 708'.0025'41 B81-14963

027'.0025'4121 — Scotland. Grampian Region. Libraries ***— Directories***

A Directory of library resources in the North-East of Scotland. — 3rd ed., compiled by Susan Semple. — Aberdeen : Aberdeen and North of Scotland Library and Information Co-operative Service, 1982. — 53p ; 21cm
Previous ed.: 1979. — Includes index
Unpriced (pbk) B82-36858

027'.0025'4259 — Buckinghamshire. Libraries — ***Directories***

Directory of resources in public, special and academic libraries in Buckinghamshire. — [Aylesbury] : Buckinghamshire County Council, County Library, 1982. — 1v.(looseleaf) ; 22cm
Cover title. — Includes index
ISBN 0-86059-236-7 : £5.00 B82-40255

027'.0025'6 — Africa. Libraries — *Directories*
The **African** book world and press : a directory / edited by Hans M. Zell = Répertoire du livre et de la presse en Afrique / editée par Hans M. Zell. — 2nd ed. = 2e éd. — London : Zell, 1980. — xxiv,244p : ill ; 31cm
English and French text. — Previous ed.: 1977
ISBN 0-905450-06-x : £35.00 : CIP rev.
Also classified at 338.7'686'0256 B80-21286

027'.0072041 — Great Britain. Libraries. Research projects. Management
Moore, Nick. How to do library research. — London : Library Association, Feb.1983. — [156]p
ISBN 0-85365-905-2 : £9.50 : CIP entry
B82-37483

027'.00723 — Libraries. Surveys. Methodology
Line, Maurice B.. Library surveys : an introduction to the use, planning, procedure and presentation of surveys / Maurice B. Line. — 2nd ed. / revised by Sue Stone. — London : Bingley, 1982. — 162p : ill ; 23cm
Previous ed.: 1967. — Bibliography: p154-156. — Includes index
ISBN 0-85157-346-0 : Unpriced : CIP rev.
B82-04789

027.041 — Great Britain. Libraries. Services — *Conference proceedings*
Library Association. *Conference (1981 : Cliftonville)*. Papers : learning through life : Cliftonville 1981. — London : Library Association, c1981. — 206p : ill ; 23cm
At head of title: The Library Association Conference. — Includes bibliographies and index
ISBN 0-85365-994-x (pbk) : Unpriced : CIP rev. B82-12829

Scottish Library Association. *Conference (67th : 1981 : Peebles)*. Peebles '81 : proceedings of the 67th Annual Conference of the Scottish Library Association 25-28 May 1981 : 'themes for the times, a consideration of some of the major issues confronting libraries in the 1980s' / editor Alan G.D. White with Alan F. Taylor. — Glasgow : The Association, 1981. — 91p : ill,ports ; 21cm
ISBN 0-900649-27-5 (pbk) : Unpriced
B82-02989

027.047 — Soviet Union. Archives & manuscripts. Repositories
Grimsted, Patricia Kennedy. Archives and manuscript repositories in the USSR / Patricia Kennedy Grimsted. — Princeton ; Guildford : Princeton University Press
[2]: Estonia, Latvia, Lithuania, and Belorussia. — c1981. — xliii,929p ; 25cm + 1pamphlet (16p : 1map ; 23cm). — (Studies of the Russian Institute, Columbia University) (Harvard Ukrainian series)
Includes index
ISBN 0-691-05279-4 : £42.20 B82-12478

027.066'3 — Senegal. Libraries, *to 1976*
Maack, Mary Niles. Libraries in Senegal : continuity and change in an emerging nation / Mary Niles Maack. — Chicago : American Library Association ; London : distributed by Eurospan, 1981. — xiii,280p : maps,1plan ; 23cm
Bibliography: p263-271. — Includes index
ISBN 0-8389-0321-5 (pbk) : £15.25
B82-21144

027.073 — United States. Libraries. Activities — *Manuals*
Robotham, John S.. Library programs : how to select, plan and produce them / by John S. Robotham and Lydia LaFleur. — 2nd ed. — Metuchen, N.J. ; London : Scarecrow, 1981. — xii,352p : ill,facsims,forms ; 23cm
Previous ed.: 1976. — Bibliography: p332-341. — Includes index
ISBN 0-8108-1422-6 : £14.00 B82-05359

027.094 — Australia. Libraries
Biskup, Peter. Australian libraries. — 3rd ed. / Peter Biskup and Doreen M. Goodman. — London : Bingley, 1982. — vii,221p ; 23cm
Previous ed.: / by John Balnaves & Peter Biskup. 1975. — Includes bibliographies and index
ISBN 0-85157-326-6 : Unpriced : CIP rev.
B82-13104

027.1 — PRIVATE AND FAMILY LIBRARIES

027'.1'42876 — Tyne and Wear *(Metropolitan County)*. **Newcastle upon Tyne. Public libraries: Newcastle Central Library. Stock: Documents owned by Thomlinson, Robert. Collections: Dr Thomlinson's Library**
Newcastle Central Library. The Thomlinson Library : an introduction / by Susan Jeffery. — Newcastle upon Tyne : Newcastle upon Tyne City Libraries, 1981. — 15p : ill,1map,1facsim ; 22cm
£1.50 (pbk) B82-22189

027.4 — PUBLIC LIBRARIES

027.4 — Public libraries — *For children*
Kent, Graeme. The public library / Graeme Kent. — Hove : Wayland, 1982. — 64p : ill,facsims,ports ; 22cm. — (In the High Street)
Bibliography: p62. — Includes index
ISBN 0-85340-974-9 : £4.25 B82-39795

027.4'025'42 — England. Dual use libraries — *Directories*
Directory of dual use libraries / [compiled by] Society of County Children's & Education Librarians. — Chelmsford : Essex Libraries, c1981. — [25]leaves ; 30cm
Cover title. — Bibliography: leaf 25
ISBN 0-903630-14-1 (spiral) : £2.50
B82-19577

027.4'025'421 — London. Public libraries — *Directories*
Directory of London public libraries. — 7th ed. / edited by Lawrence H. Cudby. — London : Association of London Chief Librarians, 1982. — 167p ; 28cm
Previous ed.: 1978
ISBN 0-902814-05-2 (pbk) : Unpriced
B82-15991

027.4'072041 — Great Britain. Public libraries. Research
Seminar for research officers in public libraries : held at the Institute of Local Government Studies, 21-23 February 1979 / [report by] Steve Rogers. — [Birmingham] ([P.O. Box 363, Birmingham B15 2TT]) : Birmingham University, [1981?]. — 59p in various pagings ; 30cm. — (Report ; no.5672)
Unpriced (pbk) B82-11395

027.4'092'4 — Public libraries. Greenwood, Thomas, *1851-1908* — *Biographies*
Prichard, R. J.. Thomas Greenwood : public library enthusiast / by R.J. Prichard. — Biggleswade (8 Ashby Drive, Caldecote, Biggleswade, Beds. SG18 9DJ) : Clover, 1981. — vi,61p,[1]leaf of plates : ill,facsims, 1port ; 21cm. — (Library history series ; 5)
Includes index
£4.80 (spiral) B82-03314

027.441 — Great Britain. Public libraries — *Comparative studies*
Inter library comparisons : pilot comparison with public libraries / Centre for Interfirm Comparison. — [London] : British Library, c1981. — 20,ii,[57]p ; 30cm. — (British Library research & development reports ; no.5638)
ISBN 0-905984-74-9 (spiral) : Unpriced : CIP rev. B81-23891

027.441 — Great Britain. Public libraries. Services. Expenditure by local authorities. Reduction. Effects, *1980-1982*
Driver, E. H. C.. Coping with the cuts : the effect on public libraries of the reduction in public expenditure 1980/82 / E.H.C. Driver for British Library Research & Development Department. — [London] : [Library Association], [1982?]. — 18leaves ; 30cm. — (BL R & D report ; 5684)
Unpriced (unbound) B82-26628

027.4422'36 — Kent. Sevenoaks. Public libraries. Services, *to 1980*
Swan, Peter, *1944-*. A short history of library services in Sevenoaks 1905-1980 / Peter Swan. — [Sevenoaks] ([H.Q. Library, The Drive, Sevenoaks, Kent TN13 3AB]) : Kent County Library, [1980]. — 16p : ill,ports ; 30cm
Published to mark the 75th anniversary of the opening, in 1905, of the Carnegie Free Public Library in the Drive
£0.50 (pbk) B82-08813

027.4425'9 — Buckinghamshire. Public libraries: Buckinghamshire County Library. Services — *Practical information*
Buckinghamshire County Library. Your library service in Buckinghamshire. — [Aylesbury] : Buckinghamshire County Council County Library, [1981]. — 11p : ill ; 21cm
Cover title
ISBN 0-86059-128-x (pbk) : Unpriced
B82-02892

027.4426 — East Anglia. Public libraries. Stock: Non-fiction for adults. Provision & use — *Comparative studies*
Smith, Judy. Book use in East Anglia / Judy Smith. — [London] : British Library, 1980. — ii,111p : ill,maps ; 30cm. — (British Library research & development reports, ISSN 0308-2385 ; no.5514)
Bibliography: p109-110
ISBN 0-905984-50-1 (spiral) : £7.50 : CIP rev.
B79-35142

027.5 — GOVERNMENT LIBRARIES

027.5 — National libraries
Chandler, George. International and national library and information services : a review of some recent developments 1970-1980 / by George Chandler. — Oxford : Pergamon, 1982. — xii,275p : facsims ; 22cm. — (Recent advances in library and information services ; v.2)
Includes index
ISBN 0-08-025793-3 : £9.75 : CIP rev.
Also classified at 021.6'4 B81-34467

027.5 — National libraries & information services — *Conference proceedings*
Library Association. *International Workshop (1st : 1981 : London)*. The development of national library and information services : papers given at the first Library Association International Workshop, London, 1981. — London : The Association, Dec.1982. — [128]p
ISBN 0-85365-784-x : £12.50 : CIP entry
B82-37501

027.5'025'41 — Great Britain. Record repositories — *Directories*
Record repositories in Great Britain : a geographical directory. — 7th ed. — London : H.M.S.O., 1982. — 31p ; 25cm
At head of title: Royal Commission on Historical Manuscripts. — Includes index
ISBN 0-11-440160-8 (pbk) : £2.50 B82-35972

027.5'025'42 — England. Record repositories — *Directories*
Gibson, J. S. W.. Record offices : how to find them / Jeremy Gibson and Pamela Peskett. — 2nd ed. — Plymouth : Federation of Family History Societies, 1982. — 44p : maps ; 21cm
Previous ed.: 1981. — Text and maps on inside covers
ISBN 0-907099-16-5 (pbk) : £1.00 B82-34551

027.541'05 — Great Britain. National libraries: British Library — *Serials*
[Newsletter *(British Library. American Trust for the British Library)*]. Newsletter / the American Trust for the British Library. — No.1 (Fall 1980)-. — London : The British Library, Reference Division Publications, 1980-. — v. : ill,ports ; 28cm
Two issues yearly
ISSN 0260-3667 = Newsletter - American Trust for the British Library : Unpriced
B82-10132

027.542 — England. Record repositories. Stock — *For postgraduate research*

Emmison, F. G.. Material for theses in local record offices and libraries / compiled by F.G. Emmison and W.J. Smith. — London (59a Kennington Park Rd., SE11 4JH) : The Historical Association for the Emmison Retirement Gift Committee, [1982]. — iv,48p ; 21cm. — (Helps for students of history ; 87)
Includes index
£1.40 (pbk) B82-37374

027.5429 — Wales. National libraries: National Library of Wales, *to 1973*

National Library of Wales. Trysorfa cenedi : hanes Llyfrgell Genedlaethol Cymru = A nation's treasury : the story of the National Library of Wales. — Aberystwyth : National Library of Wales, 1982. — [56]p : ill(some col.),1col.coat of arms,facsims,1map,1col.plan,ports(some col.) ; 21cm
English and Welsh text
ISBN 0-907158-04-8 (pbk) : Unpriced B82-31923

027.6 — LIBRARIES FOR SPECIAL GROUPS AND SPECIFIC ORGANISATIONS

027.62'5'0941 — Great Britain. Libraries. Services for children

Library work with young people : the research perspective / proceedings of a conference of the Library and Information Research Group, held at the National Children's Bureau, London, 28 October 1981 ; edited by Lesley Gilder. — London : Rossendale, [1982?]. — 80p ; 25cm
Includes bibliographies
ISBN 0-946138-01-x (pbk) : Unpriced : CIP rev. B82-21121

027.62'6 — Libraries. Services for adolescents

Directions for library service to young adults / Young Adult Services Division, American Library Association Services Statement Development Committee, Penny Jeffrey, chairperson. — Chicago : American Library Association ; London : Eurospan [distributor], c1977 (1979 printing). — vi,24p ; 23cm
Bibliography: p21-24
ISBN 0-8389-3198-7 (pbk) : £2.25 B82-21311

027.6'3 — Great Britain. Public libraries. Services for disadvantaged persons

Coleman, Patricia M.. Whose problem? : the public library and the disadvantaged / by Patricia M. Coleman. — London : Association of Assistant Librarians (Group of the Library Association, with assistance from Harold Hill), 1981. — 80p ; 21cm
Bibliography: p72-75
ISBN 0-900092-37-8 (pbk) : £3.50 (£3.00 to members) B82-00828

027.6'3 — Great Britain. Public libraries. Services for negro communities

Alexander, Ziggi. Library service and Afro-Caribbean communities / by Ziggi Alexander. — London : Association of Assistant Librarians, 1982. — 56p ; 22cm
Bibliography: p55-56
ISBN 0-900092-43-2 (pbk) : £3.00 (£2.50 to members of the Association of Assistant Librarians) B82-35631

027.6'3 — Great Britain. Public libraries. Services for teenagers

Marshall, Margaret R.. The state of public library services to teenagers in Britain 1981. — London : British Library Research & Development Dept., Oct.1982. — [74]p. — (Library and information research reports, ISSN 0263-1709 ; 5)
ISBN 0-7123-3006-2 (pbk) : CIP entry B82-33208

027.6'3 — London. Public libraries. Services. Requirements of students of West Indian self-help schools

Wellum, Jessica. Black children in the library : a brief survey of the library needs of pupils attending the West Indian supplementary education schemes in London / by Jessica Wellum. — [London] : School of Librarianship, Polytechnic of North London, 1981. — 46p : ill ; 30cm. — (Research report / Polytechnic of North London School of Librarianship, ISSN 0143-8549 ; no.8)
Bibliography: p37
ISBN 0-900639-21-0 (pbk) : £1.40 B82-18703

027.6'3 — Netherlands. Public libraries. Services for disadvantaged persons

Brown, Roy. Outreach in the Netherlands : an experiment in Public Library Service to disadvantaged groups with particular reference to the role of the Nederlands Bibliotheek en Lektuur Centrum (NBLC) : report to the British Library Research & Development Division / by Roy Brown. — [Brighton] ([c/o Central Library, Church St., Brighton, E. Sussex]) : Public Libraries Research Group, 1981. — 23,ixp ; 30cm. — (BL R & D report ; 5689)
Unpriced (spiral) B82-15465

027.6'62'0941 — Great Britain. Hospitals. Libraries

Hospital libraries and work with the disabled in the community / compiled and edited by Mona E. Going. — 3rd ed. / in collaboration with Jean M. Clarke. — London : Library Association, 1981, c1982. — xii,311p : ill ; 23cm
Previous ed.: 1973. — Bibliography: p301-304. — Includes index
ISBN 0-85365-723-8 (pbk) : Unpriced : CIP rev. B81-27997

027.6'63 — Great Britain. Public libraries. Services for mentally handicapped persons

Pearlman, Della. No choice : library services for the mentally handicapped / Della Pearlman. — London : Library Association, 1982. — 61p ; 22cm
Bibliography: p51-59. — Includes index
ISBN 0-85365-543-x (pbk) : Unpriced : CIP rev. B81-31508

027.6'65 — Dorset. Isle of Portland. Borstals. Libraries: Portland Borstal. *Library*

Portland Borstal : a review of the library provision. — [Dorchester] : Dorset County Library, 1981. — 6p : 2plans ; 30cm
Cover title
ISBN 0-85216-304-5 (pbk) : £0.75 B82-27302

027.6'65'0973 — United States. Prisons. Libraries. Organisation

Bayley, Linda. Jail library service : a guide for librarians and jail administrators / Linda Bayley, Leni Greenfield, Flynn Nogueira ; prepared for the Association of Specialized and Cooperative Library Agencies, a division of the American Library Association. — Chicago : American Library Association ; London : Eurospan [distributor], 1981. — ix,114p ; 28cm
Bibliography: p113-114
ISBN 0-8389-3258-4 (pbk) : £12.25 B82-21317

027.6'65'0973 — United States. Prisons. Libraries. Services. Discussion groups. Organisation

Schexnaydre, Linda. Workshops for jail library service : a planning manual / Linda Schexnaydre, Kaylyn Robbins ; prepared for the Association of Specialized and Co-operative Library Agencies, a division of the American Libraries Association. — Chicago : American Library Association ; London : Eurospan [distributor], 1981. — xii,115p : ill ; 28cm
Bibliography: p115
£12.25 (pbk) B82-24910

027.6'7 — Spain. Islamic libraries, *to 1981*

Imamuddin, S. M.. Hispano-Arab libraries. — London (68a Delancey St., NW1 2RY) : Ta Ha Publishers, Sept.1982. — [42]p
Originally published: Karachi : Pakistan Historical Society, 1961
ISBN 0-907461-29-8 (pbk) : £1.50 : CIP entry
Also classified at 018'.131 B82-31324

027.6'7'0942165 — London. Lambeth *(London Borough).* **Episcopal palaces. Libraries: Lambeth Palace Library. Stock**

Bill, E. G. W.. Unexpected collections at Lambeth Palace Library / by E.G.W. Bill. — London : [University of London. Library Resources Co-ordinating Committee], 1982. — 10p ; 21cm. — (Occasional publications ; 2)
Cover title
Unpriced (pbk) B82-30883

027.7 — COLLEGE AND UNIVERSITY LIBRARIES

027.7'0941 — Great Britain. Academic libraries — *Conference proceedings*

Gemeinsame Probleme von Staats- und Hochschulbibliotheken in Großbritannien und der Bundesrepublik Deutschland : Tagung englischer und deutscher Bibliothekare in Konstanz, Mai 1981 = Common themes in academic librarianship in the Federal Republic of Germany and in the United Kingdom : meeting of British and German librarians in Konstanz, May 1981. — Berlin : Deutsches Bibliotheksinstitut ; London : Standing Conference of National and University Libraries, 1981. — 285p ; 21cm. — (Dbi-materialien ; 10)
German and English text. — At head of title: Deutsche Forschungsgemeinschaft, Standing Conference of National and University Libraries
ISBN 0-900210-06-0 (pbk) : £5.00
Primary classification 027.7'0943 B82-12958

027.7'0941 — Great Britain. Colleges. Libraries — *Standards*

College libraries : guidelines for professional service and resource provision. — 3rd ed. — London : Library Association, 1982. — 64p ; 21cm
Previous ed.: 1971. — Includes index
ISBN 0-85365-635-5 (pbk) : Unpriced : CIP rev. B82-07820

027.7'0942 — England. Colleges. Libraries — *National Association of Teachers in Further and Higher Education viewpoints*

National Association of Teachers in Further and Higher Education. College libraries : policy statement / NATFHE. — London (Hamilton House, Mabledon Place, WC1H 9BH) : National Association of Teachers in Further and Higher Education, 1982. — 20p ; 21cm
Bibliography: p20
£0.55 (£0.45 to members) (pbk) B82-24379

027.7'0943 — West Germany. Academic libraries *— Conference proceedings — German texts*

Gemeinsame Probleme von Staats- und Hochschulbibliotheken in Großbritannien und der Bundesrepublik Deutschland : Tagung englischer und deutscher Bibliothekare in Konstanz, Mai 1981 = Common themes in academic librarianship in the Federal Republic of Germany and in the United Kingdom : meeting of British and German librarians in Konstanz, May 1981. — Berlin : Deutsches Bibliotheksinstitut ; London : Standing Conference of National and University Libraries, 1981. — 285p ; 21cm. — (Dbi-materialien ; 10)
German and English text. — At head of title: Deutsche Forschungsgemeinschaft, Standing Conference of National and University Libraries
ISBN 0-900210-06-0 (pbk) : £5.00
Also classified at 027.7'0941 B82-12958

027.7'0973 — United States. Higher education institutions. Librarianship, *to ca 1940*

Shiflett, Orvin Lee. Origins of American academic librarianship / by Orvin Lee Shiflett. — Norwood, N.J. : Ablex ; London (3 Henrietta St., WC2E 8LU) : Eurospan [distributor], c1981. — xxii,308p ; 24cm. — (Libraries and librarianship)
Bibliography: p279-300. — Includes index
ISBN 0-89391-082-1 : £16.95 B82-27698

027.7′0973 — United States. Higher education institutions. Libraries — *Conference proceedings*

Association of College and Research Libraries. *National Conference (1st : 1978 : Boston, Mass.).* New horizons for academic libraries : papers presented at the First National Conference of the Association of College and Research Libraries, Boston, Massachusetts, November 8-11, 1978 / edited by Robert D. Stueart and Richard D. Johnson. — New York ; London : Saur, 1979. — viii,583p : ill,maps,1plan,forms ; 26cm
Includes bibliographies
ISBN 0-89664-093-0 : £29.50 : CIP rev. B79-13270

027.7413′4′09 — Edinburgh. Universities. Libraries: Edinburgh University Library, *1580-1980*

Edinburgh University Library. Edinburgh University Library 1580-1980 : a collection of historical essays / edited by Jean R. Guild and Alexander Law. — Edinburgh : The Library, 1982. — x,237p,16p of plates : ill,facsims ; 26cm
Bibliography: p205-217. — Includes index
ISBN 0-907182-01-1 : Unpriced B82-29312

027.7414′43 — Scotland. Strathclyde Region. Glasgow. Universities. Libraries: Andersonian Library — *Visitors′ guides*

Frame, Edith. The Andersonian library get-about book / by Edith Frame. — 2nd rev. ed. — Glasgow : Andersonian Library, University of Strathclyde, 1981. — 20p : ill ; 21cm
Previous ed.: 1980
ISBN 0-907380-01-8 (pbk) : Unpriced B82-16593

027.7426′723 — Essex. Colchester. Universities. Libraries: University of Essex. *Library — Visitors′ guides*

University of Essex. *Library.* What′s in it for you?. — [Colchester] ([The University, Wivenhoe Park, Colchester CO4 3SQ]) : Essex University Library, 1981. — 16p : ill,plans ; 22cm
Unpriced (pbk) B82-13120

027.7427′32 — Greater Manchester *(Metropolitan County).* **Salford. Universities. Libraries: University of Salford.** *Library — Visitors′ guides*

University of Salford. *Library.* Guide to the library / the University of Salford Library. — [Salford] : [The Library], 1981. — 14p : plans ; 21cm
Cover title
Unpriced (pbk) B82-26590

027.8 — SCHOOL LIBRARIES

027.8′028′5404 — Great Britain. Schools. Libraries. Applications of microcomputer systems

The **Microelectronics** revolution and its implications for the school library / the Library Association School Libraries Group. — Mansfield (c/o Education Library Service, Central Library, Westgate, Mansfield, Notts.) : The Group, c1982. — 11p : 1ill ; 22cm
Bibliography: p7
£1.00 (unbound) B82-14661

027.8′0941 — Great Britain. Schools. Libraries

Ray, Sheila G.. Library service to schools. — 3rd ed. — London : Library Association, Sept.1982. — [72]p. — (Library Association pamphlet ; 39)
Previous ed.: 1972
ISBN 0-85365-953-2 : £6.75 : CIP entry B82-28589

027′8′223 — Nova Scotia. Secondary schools. Librarians. Role. Perception by teachers

Rainforth, John. Perceptions of the high school librarian / by John Rainforth. — London : Vine Press, 1981. — xi,121p ; 28cm. — (Occasional paper / Dalhousie University Libraries and Dalhousie School of Library Service, ISSN 0318-7403 ; 27)
Bibliography: p102-106
ISBN 0-7703-0168-1 (pbk) : Unpriced B82-14655

028.1 — BOOK REVIEWS

028.1 — Books in English — *Reviews*

James, Clive. From the land of shadows / Clive James. — London : Cape, 1982, c1981. — 294p ; 23cm
Includes index
ISBN 0-224-02021-8 : £7.95 : CIP rev. B82-07104

028.1′05 — Books in English — *Reviews — Serials*

Views & reviews. — Vol.1, no.1-. — Ashford (24 Falcon Way, Ashford, Kent TN23 2UP) : C. Ingham, 1981-. — v. ; 30cm
Six issues yearly
ISSN 0263-1792 = Views & reviews : £3.00 per year B82-18504

028.1′2 — Reference books with American imprints — *Reviews*

Reference and subscription books reviews 1979-1980 : a compilation of evaluations appearing in Reference and subscription books reviews, September 1, 1979-July 15, 1980, within vol.76 of Booklist / prepared by the American Library Association, Reference and Subscription Books Review Committee ; edited by Helen K. Wright. — Chicago : American Library Association ; London : Europspan [distributor], 1981, c1980. — xiv,134p ; 28cm
ISBN 0-8389-3256-8 (pbk) : £15.00 B82-21315

028.5 — READING AND USE OF OTHER INFORMATION MEDIA BY CHILDREN AND YOUNG ADULTS

028.5 — Children′s books. Racism & sexism

Racism and sexism in children′s books. — London : Writers and Readers, 1979. — 147p : ill ; 21cm
Edited by Judith Stinton
ISBN 0-906495-19-9 : £4.95 B82-01371

028.5 — Children′s books. Racism & sexism — *Educational Institute of Scotland viewpoints*

Racism and sexism in children′s books. — Edinburgh : Educational Institute of Scotland, [1979]. — 8p ; 21cm
Bibliography: p8
Unpriced (unbound) B82-03332

028.5 — Great Britain. Children′s books. Information sources — *Lists*

Children′s books : an information guide. — London : National Book League, Apr.1982. — [36]p
ISBN 0-85353-369-5 (pbk) : £1.70 : CIP entry B82-11785

028.5 — Picture books for gifted children: Picture books in English: Books for children, 4-7 years — *For teaching*

Polette, Nancy. Picture books for gifted programs / by Nancy Polette. — Metuchen ; London : Scarecrow Press, 1981. — viii,220p ; 23cm
Bibliography: p193-208. — Includes index
ISBN 0-8108-1461-7 : £10.00 B82-11464

028.5′3′055 — Children, 13-15 years. Reading habits — *Study regions: South Yorkshire (Metropolitan County). Sheffield*

Heather, Pauline. Young people′s reading : a study of the leisure reading of 13-15 year olds / Pauline Heather. — Sheffield : Centre for Research on User Studies, University of Sheffield, 1981. — vi,139p : ill ; 30cm. — (CRUS occasional paper, ISSN 0140-3834 ; 6) (BLR & DD report ; no.5650)
Bibliography: p16-17
ISBN 0-906088-05-4 (pbk) : Unpriced B82-19346

028.5′34 — Children′s books — *Collectors′ guides*

Quayle, Eric. A collector′s guide to early children′s books. — Newton Abbot : David & Charles, Jan.1983. — [256]p
ISBN 0-7153-8307-8 : £14.95 : CIP entry B82-32610

028.5′34′0942 — England. Children′s books, *to 1910*

Darton, F. J. Harvey. Children′s books in England : five centuries of social life / F.J. Harvey Darton. — 3rd ed. / revised by Brian Alderson. — Cambridge : Cambridge University Press, 1982. — xviii,398p : ill,facsims ; 26cm
Previous ed.: 1958. — Bibliography: p362-371. — Includes index
ISBN 0-521-24020-4 (cased) : £12.95 : CIP rev. B81-37003

028.5′344 — Children′s books: Books for children, 5-11 years — *For teaching*

Bennett, Jill. A choice of stories / Jill Bennett. — Oxford : School Library Association, 1982. — 32p ; 21cm. — (Books in the primary school)
Includes bibliographies
ISBN 0-900641-40-1 (pbk) : £1.80 (£1.30 to SLA members) B82-15371

028.5′35 — London. Westminster *(London Borough).* **Public libraries: Westminster City Libraries. Stock: Books. Reading by adolescents. Promotion. Projects: Bookmaster scheme**

Bird, J.. Young teenage reading habits. — London : British Library Research & Development Dept., Aug.1982. — [119]p. — (British National Bibliography Research Fund report ; 9)
ISBN 0-7123-3007-0 (pbk) : £9.00 : CIP entry B82-25906

028.7 — USE OF BOOKS AND OTHER MEDIA AS SOURCES OF INFORMATION

028.7 — Information sources — *Manuals*

Lancaster, Fred. Find out for yourself / [written by Fred Lancaster] ; [illustrated by Gillian Hurry] ; [photographs by Lisa Mackson]. — Cambridge : Basic Skills Unit, c1981. — 42p + Tutor′s notes([4]p : 1ill ; 30cm) : ill,facsims,1map ; 30cm
Includes index
ISBN 0-86082-203-6 (pbk) : £1.90 B82-38352

028.7 — Reference books. Use — *For African students*

Allan, Alastair. Look it up : reference skills for situational writing. — London : Heinemann, 1980. — 88p : forms ; 22cm
Includes index
ISBN 0-435-92010-3 (pbk) : £1.75 : CIP rev. B80-26045

028.7 — Reference books. Use — *For schools*

Weston, Paul. Look up, find out. — London : Bell & Hyman, Sept.1981. — [64]p
ISBN 0-7135-1266-0 (pbk) : £1.75 : CIP entry B81-23751

028.9 — READING INTERESTS AND HABITS

028′.9′0899510421 — London. Chinese immigrants. Reading habits — *For librarianship*

Chin, Wey Tze. Information sheets on Chinese readers / by Wey Tze Chin and Sylva Simsova. — London : School of Librarianship, Polytechnic of North London, 1981. — 211p : ill,maps,forms ; 30cm. — (Research report / Polytechnic of North London. School of Librarianship, ISSN 0143-8549 ; no.7) (British Library R & D report ; no.5670)
English and Chinese text
ISBN 0-900639-20-2 (pbk) : £4.20 B82-13526

Simsova, Sylva. Library needs of Chinese in London / by Sylva Simsova and Wey Tze Chin. — London : Polytechnic of North London, School of Librarianship and Information Studies, 1982. — 194p : maps ; 30cm. — (British Library R & D report ; no.5718) (Research report / Polytechnic of North London. School of Librarianship and Information Studies ; no.9)
Bibliography: p187-194
ISBN 0-900639-22-9 (pbk) : £5.00 B82-

030 — ENCYCLOPAEDIAS

030′.94 — Encyclopaedias in European languages, *1674-1760 — Critical studies*

Notable encyclopedias of the seventeenth and eighteenth centuries : nine predecessors of the encyclopédie / edited by Frank A. Kafker. — Oxford : The Voltaire Foundation, 1981. — 252p ; 24cm. — (Studies on Voltaire and the eighteenth century, ISSN 0435-2866 ; 194)
Includes bibliographies and index
ISBN 0-7294-0256-8 : Unpriced B82-17344

031 — AMERICAN ENCYCLOPAEDIAS

031′.02 — Miscellaneous facts — *American collections*

Asimov, Isaac. The book of facts. — London : Hodder & Stoughton. — (Coronet books)
Originally published: 1980
Vol.2. — Dec.1981. — [336]p
ISBN 0-340-27268-6 : £1.50 : CIP entry B81-31467

Asimov, Isaac. Isaac Asimov′s book of facts. — London : Hodder and Stoughton, Apr.1981
Originally published: New York : Red Dembner Enterprises Corp., 1979 ; London : Hodder and Stoughton, 1980
Vol.1. — [560]p
ISBN 0-340-26218-4 (pbk) : £1.25 : CIP entry B81-02650

Wallechinsky, David. The People′s almanac [no.] 3 / by David Wallechinsky and Irving Wallace. — Toronto ; London : Bantam, 1981. — 722p,[8]p of plates : ill,col.maps,ports ; 24cm
Includes index
ISBN 0-553-01352-1 (pbk) : £3.95 B82-21595

032 — ENGLISH ENCYCLOPAEDIAS

032 — Children′s encyclopaedias in English — *Texts*

Piccolo explorer encyclopedia / edited by Bill Bruce ; contributors: Michael Chinery ... [et al.]. — London : Pan, 1981 (1982 [printing]). — 223p : ill(some col.),charts,maps(some col.),col.ports ; 22cm. — (A Piccolo explorer book)
Includes index
ISBN 0-330-26362-5 : £2.95 B82-25832

Turner, Dorothy. The A-Z colour encyclopedia / Dorothy Turner. — London : Macmillan, 1982. — [97]p : col.ill,col.maps,music,col.ports ; 30cm
Map on lining papers
ISBN 0-333-30871-9 : £3.95 B82-20901

032 — Children′s encyclopaedias in English — *Welsh texts*

Concise children′s encyclopaedia. — London : Ward Lock, Sept.1982. — [420]p
ISBN 0-7063-6215-2 : £7.95 : CIP entry B82-20018

032 — Encyclopaedias in English — *Texts*

Everyman′s fact finder. — London : Dent, Oct.1982. — [448]p
ISBN 0-460-04569-5 : £8.95 : CIP entry B82-23993

032′.02 — Miscellaneous facts — *Collections*

Bailey, Andrew. A day in the life of the world. — London : Hutchinson, Oct.1982. — [122]p
ISBN 0-09-147701-8 (pbk) : £0.99 : CIP entry B82-25081

Brandreth, Gyles. The amazing almanac / Gyles Brandreth. — London : Pelham, 1981. — 191p : ill ; 20cm
ISBN 0-7207-1384-6 (pbk) : £1.95 B82-05364

Frost, David, *1939 Apr.7-.* I could have kicked myself / compiled and written by David Frost and Michael Deakin ; illustrated by William Rushton. — London : Deutsch, 1982. — 142p : ill ; 24cm
ISBN 0-233-97419-9 : £4.95 B82-27307

The **Guinness** book of answers : a handbook of general knowledge. — 4th ed. / general editor Norris McWhirter ; assistant editor Moira F. Stowe ; art editor David Roberts. — London : Guinness Superlatives, c1982. — 368p : ill (some col.),maps(some col.),coats of arms,ports ; 31cm
Previous ed.: 1980. — Map and text on lining paper. — Includes index
ISBN 0-85112-236-1 : £6.95 : CIP rev. B82-04993

Hawkins, Colin. It′s a fact : and it′s very funny / Colin Hawkins. — London : ITV Books in association with Michael Joseph, 1982. — [40]p : col.ill ; 23cm
ISBN 0-900727-97-7 : £2.95 B82-39940

Pile, Stephen. The book of heroic failures : the official handbook of the Not Terribly Good Club of Great Britain : by Stephen Pile / with Cartoons by Bill Tidy. — London : Futura, 1980, c1979 (1981 [printing]). — 216p : ill ; 18cm
Originally published: London : Routledge and Kegan Paul, 1979
ISBN 0-7088-1908-7 (pbk) : £1.25 B82-00837

Speddy, Robert. The Guinness pocket book of facts / Robert Speddy. — Enfield : Guinness Superlatives, c1982. — 160p : ill ; 22cm
Includes index
ISBN 0-85112-223-x : £3.95 : CIP rev. B82-12827

Strong, Roy. The English year. — Exeter : Webb & Bower, Sept.1982. — [224]p
ISBN 0-906671-29-9 : £9.95 : CIP entry B82-21999

What′s what in the 1980′s : a dictionary of contemporary history, literature, arts, technology, medicine, music, cinema, theatre, controversies, fads, movements and events / edited by Christopher Pick. — London : Europa, 1982. — 399p ; 22cm
ISBN 0-905118-69-3 : £18.00 : CIP rev. B82-02481

032′.02 — Miscellaneous facts — *Collections — For children*

James, Paul. The fact-a-minute book / Paul James. — [London] : Sparrow, 1982. — 153p ; 18cm
ISBN 0-09-927360-8 (pbk) : £0.95 B82-16534

Piddock, Helen. The Tiswas book of fizzling facts / compiled by Helen Piddock ; compiled by Helen Piddock ; illustrated by Mike Miller. — London : Carousel, 1982. — 138p : ill ; 20cm
ISBN 0-552-54201-6 (pbk) : £0.85 B82-21596

032′.02 — Miscellaneous facts — *Collections — For schools*

Purton, Rowland W.. Spring and summer days. — Oxford : Blackwell, Jan.1983. — [272]p
ISBN 0-631-13203-1 : £5.95 : CIP entry B82-32520

032′.02 — Records of achievement — *Collections — For children*

Brandreth, Gyles. The crazy book of world records / Gyles Brandreth ; illustrated by Mike Miller. — [London] : Carousel, [1982]. — 138p : ill ; 20cm
ISBN 0-552-54196-6 (pbk) : £0.85 B82-18699

032′.02 — Records of achievement — *Collections — Serials*

Guinness book of records. — 28th ed. (1982). — Enfield : Guinness Superlatives, Oct.1981. — [352]p
ISBN 0-85112-232-9 : £4.99 : CIP entry B81-24647

Guinness book of records. — 29th ed. (1983). — Enfield : Guinness Superlatives, Oct.1982. — [352]p
ISBN 0-85112-251-5 : £5.75 : CIP entry B82-24258

051 — AMERICAN SERIALS

051 — General serials in English: Serials with American imprints: Century magazine, *to 1909*

John, Arthur. The best years of the Century : Richard Watson Gilder, Scribner′s monthly, and the Century magazine 1870-1909 / Arthur John. — Urbana ; London : University of Illinois Press, c1981. — xii,296p,[12]p of plates : ill,facsims,ports ; 24cm
Includes index
ISBN 0-252-00857-x : £14.00 B82-14328

051 — Serials for negroes: Serials in English: Serials with American imprints, *1838-1909*

Bullock, Penelope L.. The Afro-American periodical press 1838-1909 / Penelope L. Bullock. — Baton Rouge ; London : Louisiana State University Press, c1981. — xiv,330p : ill,facsims,ports ; 24cm
Bibliography: p311-313. — Includes index
ISBN 0-8071-0663-1 : £17.50 B82-15450

052 — ENGLISH SERIALS

052 — Adolescent girls′ serials in English — *Texts*

Girl & dreamer. — No.67 (22nd May 1982)-. — London : IPC Magazines, 1982-. — v. : ill (some col.),ports(some col.) ; 30cm
Weekly. — Merger of: Girl (London : 1981); and, Dreamer (London)
£0.22 B82-33867

Heartbeat. — No.1 (1981)-. — London : IPC Magazines, 1981-. — v. : ill(some col.),ports (some col.) ; 30cm
Weekly. — Description based on: No.3 (17th Oct. 1981)
ISSN 0262-348x = Heartbeat : £0.22 per issue B82-14771

My guy & heartbeat. — No.205 (17th Apr. 1982)-. — London : IPC Magazines, 1982-. — v. : ill(some col.),ports(some col.) ; 30cm
Weekly. — Merger of: My guy; and, Heartbeat
£0.24 B82-33865

Oh boy! and Mates. — No.239 (5th Sept. 1981)-. — London : IPC Magazines, 1981-. — v. : ill (some col.),ports ; 30cm
Weekly. — Merger of: Oh boy! and Fab ; and, Mates and Pink
ISSN 0262-3730 = Oh boy! and Mates : £0.22 per issue B82-03392

Photo-love annual. — 1981-. — London : IPC Magazines, 1980-. — v. : ill(some col.) ; 28cm
Continues: Photo-love weekly annual. — Supplement to: Photo-love weekly
ISSN 0263-2403 = Photo-love annual : £2.00 B82-18723

Photo-love with photo secret love. — No.146 (6th Feb. 1982)-. — London : IPC Magazines, 1982-. — v. : ill(some col.),ports(some col.) ; 30cm
Weekly. — Merger of: Photo-love weekly; and, Photo secret love
£0.26 B82-33866

Tammy and Jinty. — 28th Nov. 1981-. — London : IPC Magazines, 1981-. — v. : chiefly ill ; 28cm
Weekly. — Merger of: Tammy (1981); and, Jinty (1981)
ISSN 0262-7450 = Tammy and Jinty : £0.14 per issue B82-14247

052 — Boys′ serials in English — *Texts*

Attack picture library. — [1982]-. — London : IPC Magazines, 1982-. — v. : chiefly ill ; 17cm
Annual
£0.50 per issue B82-32167

052 — Children′s serials in English — *Texts*

Worzel Gummidge. — Vol.1, no.1 (Oct. 1981)-. — London (205 Kentish Town Rd., NW5) : Marvel Comics, 1981-. — v. : chiefly ill ; 28cm
Monthly
ISSN 0262-9097 = Worzel Gummidge : £4.80 per year B82-11826

052 — General serials in English — *Texts*

Nine to five. — Issue 1 (8 Feb. 1982)-. — London (2 Swallow Place, W1R 7AA) : Nine to Five Magazine, 1982-. — v. : ill,ports ; 29cm
Weekly
ISSN 0263-5380 = Nine to five : Unpriced B82-25484

[Revue *(London : 1979)***]**. Revue. — No.1 (Sept. 28, 1979)-. — London (234 Old St., EC1V 9DD) : Revue Publications, 1979-. — v. : ill,ports ; 41cm
Weekly. — Description based on: No.53 (Nov. 1, 1980)
ISSN 0263-5208 = Revue (London. 1979) : £0.20 per issue B82-26156

052 — Men's serials in English — *Texts*

[Executive *(London)***]**. Executive. — No.1 (May 1982)-. — London (Lonsdale Chambers, 27 Chancery La., WC2A 1NT) : Fragilion Ltd., 1982-. — v. : ill(some col.),ports ; 30cm
Monthly. — Also entitled: Executive international
ISSN 0263-8258 = Executive (London) : £14.25 per year B82-30487

052 — Serials for Mauritian immigrants in Great Britain — *Texts*

APWM newsletter. — No.1 (1979)-. — London (135 Mitcham Rd., SW17 9PE) : Association for the Promotion of the Welfare of Mauritians in the U.K., 1979-. — v. ; 30cm
Quarterly. — Description based on: No.8 (Nov. 1981)
ISSN 0262-8511 = APWM newsletter : Unpriced B82-32171

052 — Women's serials in English — *Texts*

Busy mums. — Oct. 1981-. — Norwich (130 Ber St., Norwich NR1 3AQ) : Printel, 1981-. — v. : ill ; 30cm
Monthly
ISSN 0263-5755 = Busy mums : £0.35 per issue B82-26141

[IT *(Dublin)***]**. IT. — No.1 (1979)-. — [Dublin] (Marino Grove, Marino Ave. West, Killiney, [Dublin]) : IT magazine, [1979]-. — v. : col.ill,ports ; 28cm
Monthly. — Cover title: IT magazine. — Continues: Irish tatler and sketch. — Description based on: No.26, (Jan. 1982)
£0.60 per issue B82-13410

[Options *(London)***]**. Options. — Apr. 1982-. — London : IPC Magazines, 1982-. — v. : ill (some col.),ports ; 30cm
Monthly
ISSN 0263-2624 = Options (London) : £0.60 per issue B82-22669

052'.024658 — Serials with British imprints — *Directories — For public relations*

PR planner : United Kingdom : a service of Media Information Limited. — London (Hale House, 290-296 Green Lanes N13 5TP) : Media Information Group, [1982?]. — 1v.(loose-leaf) : maps ; 32cm
Unpriced B82-25279

052'.09 — Serials with British imprints, *1830-1900 — Critical studies*

The **Victorian** periodical press : samplings and soundings / edited by Joanne Shattock and Michael Wolff. — [Leicester] : Leicester University Press, 1982. — xix,400p,[12]p of plates : ill,facsims, ports ; 24cm
Includes index
ISBN 0-7185-1190-5 : £28.00 : CIP rev. B81-35852

060 — GENERAL ORGANISATIONS

060 — Conferences & exhibitions — *Serials*

Meetings international. — No.1 (Mar.-Apr. 1982)-. — Croydon (PO Box 109, Maclaren House, Croydon CR9 1QH) : Maclaren, 1982-. — v. : ill(some col.),ports ; 30cm
Text in English and French
ISSN 0263-4724 = Meetings international : £16.00 per year B82-26146

060 — Great Britain. Exhibitions, *1900-1979*

Fletcher, F. A.. British and foreign exhibitions and their postcards / by F.A. Fletcher & A.D. Brooks. — [London] (3-9 Dane St, WC1) : Fleetway Press
Pt 2: 1915-1979. — [1980]. — 68p : ill(some col.),facsims,maps,plans ; 30cm
£3.25 (pbk)
Primary classification 769'.49941 B82-40964

060 — Learned institutions — *Directories — Serials*

The **World** of learning. — 32nd ed. (1981-82). — London : Europa, Jan.1982. — 2v.([11042]p)
ISBN 0-905118-70-7 : CIP entry
ISSN 0084-2117 B81-34566

060'.25 — Learned institutions — *Directories — Serials*

The **World** of learning. — 1982-83. — London : Europa, Jan.1983. — [2136]p
ISBN 0-905118-82-0 : £54.00 : CIP entry
ISSN 0084-2117 B82-33242

062 — Great Britain. Organisations

Anderson, Pamela. Simple steps to public life / Pamela Anderson, Mary Stott & Fay Weldon ; research by Betty Jerman ; illustrations by Tony Bethall. — London : Virago, 1980. — 44p : ill ; 22cm. — (Virago handbook ; 6)
ISBN 0-86068-122-x (pbk) : £1.50 B82-40616

062'.025 — Great Britain. Voluntary organisations — *Directories — Serials*

Voluntary organisations : an NCVO directory. — 1980/81-. — London : Bedford Square Press, 1980-. — v. ; 15x21cm
Annual. — Continues: Voluntary social services
ISSN 0263-3922 = Voluntary organisations : £3.95 B82-19863

062'.28 — Isle of Wight. Organisations — *Directories*

Join the club : a list of clubs, societies and organisations in the Isle of Wight. — Newport, Isle of Wight : Isle of Wight County Library, 1981. — [32]p ; 30cm
ISBN 0-906328-17-9 (unbound) : Unpriced B82-14601

062'.9134 — Scotland. Learned societies: Royal Society of Edinburgh. Fellows, *to 1882 — Lists*

Gaffney, Clare. Index of Fellows of the Royal Society of Edinburgh elected from 1783 to 1882 : containing their dates of birth, death and election to that Society, primary occupation or institutional affiliation / compiled by Clare Gaffney, assisted by Patrick Murray and Dawn Gilmour ; edited and introduced by Eric G. Forbes. — [Edinburgh] ([University of Edinburgh, Old College, Edinburgh]) : [E.G. Forbes], [1980?]. — [153]p : 1map ; 30cm
At head of title: Manpower Services Commission (STEP) Project for the preservation of Scotland's cultural heritage
Unpriced (unbound) B82-27471

062'.91617 — Carrickfergus *(District)***. Whitehead. Organisations** — *Directories*

Whitehead : local information. — Ballymena ([182, Galgorm Rd., Ballymena BT42 1HN]) : North Eastern Education and Library Board, 1981. — 21p ; 25cm
Cover title
Unpriced (pbk) B82-09521

068'.94 — Australia. Voluntary organisations. Political aspects

Scott, David. The social and political uses of voluntary organisations in Australia. — London : Allen & Unwin, Jan.1982. — [170]p
ISBN 0-08-686251-0 (cased) : £10.95 : CIP entry
ISBN 0-08-686259-6 (pbk) : £4.95 B81-33755

069 — MUSEUMS

069'.025'41 — Great Britain. Museums — *Directories*

Johnstone, Clive. The Which? heritage guide / Clive Johnstone and Winifred Weston. — London : Consumers' Association and Hodder & Stoughton, c1981. — 458p : ill,maps ; 21cm
Includes index
ISBN 0-340-26585-x (pbk) : £4.95
Primary classification 914.1 B82-02587

069'.025'41 — Great Britain. Museums - *Directories - Serials*

Libraries, museums and art galleries year book. — 1978-1979. — Cambridge : James Clarke, May 1981. — [272]p
ISBN 0-227-67835-4 : £23.00 : CIP entry
ISSN 0075-899x
Primary classification 027'.0025'41 B81-14963

069'.025'411 — Scotland. Museums — *Directories*

Museums and galleries in Scotland : a guide to over 300 museums and galleries throughout Scotland. — [Edinburgh] : Council for Museums and Galleries in Scotland, [1981]. — 96p : ill,1map,ports ; 21cm
Cover title. — Includes index
ISBN 0-85419-196-8 (pbk) : £1.50 B82-09748

069'.025'4137 — Scotland. Borders Region. Museums — *Directories*

Museums. — Newtown St. Boswells (Newtown St. Boswells, Roxburghshire) : Borders Regional Council, 1982. — 1folded sheet([6]p) : map ; 21cm. — (The Scottish Borders)
Unpriced B82-32912

069'.025'4233 — Dorset. Museums — *Directories*

Dorset. *Education Committee*. Directory of museums in Dorset. — [Dorchester, Dorset] : [Dorset County Education Committee], 1982. — 14p ; 21cm
Cover title
ISBN 0-85216-302-9 (pbk) : £0.20 B82-38241

069'.0941 — Great Britain. Museums — *Visitors' guides*

The **Good** museums guide / [edited by] Kenneth Hudson. — London : Macmillan, 1980. — 277p : ill,maps,1form ; 23cm
Includes index
ISBN 0-333-28549-2 (cased) : £12.00
ISBN 0-333-28550-6 (pbk) : Unpriced B82-22485

069'.09411 — Scotland. National museums — *Inquiry reports*

A **Heritage** for Scotland : Scotland's national museums and galleries : the next 25 years : report of a committee appointed by the Secretary of State for Scotland under the chairmanship of Dr. Alwyn Williams. — Edinburgh : H.M.S.O., 1981. — xi,105p : maps ; 25cm
ISBN 0-11-491746-9 (pbk) : £5.20 B82-00700

069'.09419'45 — Limerick *(County)***. Limerick. Museums: Hunt Museum** — *Visitors' guides*

Doran, Patrick F.. The Hunt Museum / by Patrick F. Doran. — Limerick : The Craggaunowen Project, 1981. — 16p,xip of plates : ill ; 25cm
Unpriced (pbk) B82-08220

069'.09421'42 — London. Camden *(London Borough)***. Museums: British Museum,** *to 1980*

Caygill, Marjorie L.. The story of the British Museum. — London : British Museum Publications, May 1981. — [64]p
ISBN 0-7141-8039-4 (pbk) : £3.50 : CIP entry B81-04206

069'.09421'42 — London. Camden *(London Borough)***. Museums: British Museum** - *Visitors' guides*

British Museum. British Museum guide and map. — London : British Museum Publications, July 1981. — 1v.
ISBN 0-7141-2011-1 (pbk) : £1.00 : CIP entry B81-14444

069'.09422'82 — Isle of Wight. East Cowes. Country houses: Osborne House. Stock — *Catalogues*

Great Britain. *Department of the Environment*. Catalogue of the principal items on view at Osborne House / Department of the Environment. — 2nd ed. — London : H.M.S.O., 1980. — 15p : 2plans,ports ; 21cm
Previous ed.: 1965
ISBN 0-11-670833-6 (pbk) : £0.40 B82-16414

069'.09423'96 — Avon. Weston-super-Mare. Museums: Woodspring Museum — *Visitors' guides*

Woodspring Museum. Woodspring Museum, Weston-super-Mare. — Weston-super-Mare (Burlington St., Weston-super-Mare, Avon BS23 1PR) : The Museum, [1980]. — [12]p : ill,2ports ; 20x21cm
Cover title
£0.65 (pbk) B82-16532

069'09425'74 — Oxfordshire. Oxford. Museums: Ashmolean Museum — *Serials*

Ashmolean Museum. Annual report of the Visitors of the Ashmolean Museum / University of Oxford. — 1977-1978-. — Oxford : O.U.P., 1979-. — v. : ill ; 22cm
Annual. — Cover title: Annual report of the Ashmolean Museum Oxford. — Supplement to: Oxford University gazette. — Continues: Ashmolean Museum. Report of the visitors. — Description based on: 1979-1980 issue
ISSN 0262-7493 = Annual report of the visitors of the Ashmolean Museum : £2.25
B82-14262

069'.09427'63 — Lancashire. Rawtenstall. Museums: Rossendale Museum — *Visitors' guides*

Rossendale Museum. Rossendale Museum, Lancashire : a brief history and guide with a catalogue of the Rossendale Collection. — 4th ed. — Rossendale : Rossendale Museum, 1981. — 41p : ill ; 16x22cm
Previous ed.: 197-. — Ill on inside covers
£0.20 (pbk) B82-05103

069'.09428'69 — Durham *(County)*. Beamish. Museums: North of England Open Air Museum — *Serials*

North of England Open Air Museum. *Friends of the North of England Open Air Museum.* Friends' magazine / Friends of the North of England Open Air Museum. — No.1 (Winter 1981/2)-. — Stanley (Beamish, Stanley, Co. Durham DH9 ORG) : The Friends, 1981-. — v. : ill ; 21cm
Annual. — Continues in part: North of England Open Air Museum. Friends of the North of England Open Air Museum. Newsletter
ISSN 0263-1326 = Friends' magazine - Friends of the North of England Open Air Museum : Unpriced B82-17244

069'.09429 — Wales. Museums — *Inquiry reports*

Morris, Brian, *1930-*. Report on museums in Wales / by Brian Morris ; [for the] Standing Commission on Museums and Galleries. — London : H.M.S.O., [1981]. — 50p : 1map ; 25cm
ISBN 0-11-290368-1 (pbk) : £3.25 B82-13832

069'.0947'453 — Russia *(RSFSR)*. Lenigrad. Museums: Gosudarstvennyĭ russkiĭ muzeĭ — *Visitors' guides*

Gubarev, A.. The Russian Museum : a guide / A. Gubarev. — Moscow : Progress Publishers ; [London] : distributed by Central Books, c1981. — 174p : ill(some col.),col.plans,ports (some col.) ; 17cm
Translation of: Russkiĭ Muzeĭ. — Plans and text on lining papers. — Includes index
ISBN 0-7147-1754-1 : £3.50 B82-38235

069.1 — Great Britain. Museums. Gift shops — *Serials*

[Newsletter *(Group for Museum Publishing and Shop Management)*]. Newsletter / Group for Museum Publishing and Shop Management. — Issue no.1 (1979)-. — Birmingham (T. Jones, treasurer, c/o the Publications Unit, Birmingham City Museum and Art Gallery, Birmingham B3 3DH) : The Group, 1979-. — v. : ill ; 30cm
Two issues yearly. — Description based on: Issue no.5 (Spring 1981)
ISSN 0262-1401 = Newsletter - Group for Museum Publishing and Shop Management : £2.00 per year B82-17255

069'.33 — England. Countryside. Outdoor recreation sites. Information signs — *Manuals*

Allwood, John. Information signs for the countryside : a guide to their production / compiled by John Allwood. — Cheltenham : Countryside Commission, c1981. — v,84p : ill ; 30cm. — (CCP ; 132)
Bibliography: p84
ISBN 0-86170-017-1 (spiral) : £6.10
B82-03990

069.5'2 — Great Britain. Museums. Stock. Documentation. Organisations: Museum Documentation Association

Museum Documentation Association. Introduction to the Museum Documentation Association / Museum Documentation Association. — Duxford : The Association, 1980. — iii,27p ; 30cm
ISBN 0-905963-31-8 (spiral) : £2.25 (£1.50 to members of MDA) B82-39099

069.5'2 — Museums. Stock. Documentation. Application of digital computer systems. Software packages: GOS — *Manuals*

Porter, M. F.. How to use GOS / by M.F. Porter. — Duxford : Museum Documentation Association, 1980. — vi,79p ; 30cm
ISBN 0-905963-30-x (spiral) : £7.50 (£5.00 to MDA members, £2.50 to GOS User Group members) B82-39105

069.5'2 — Museums. Stock. Documentation. Applications of digital computer systems. Software packages: GOS

Guide to GOS / Museum Documentation Association. — Duxford : The Association, 1980. — iv,26p ; 30cm
ISBN 0-905963-24-5 (spiral) : £2.25 (£1.50 to members of the MDA) B82-39098

069.5'2 — Museums. Stock. Documentation. Applications of digital computer systems. Software packages: GOS — *Manuals*

GOS : a first primer. — Duxford : Museum Documentation Association, 1981. — iv,60p ; 30cm
Bibliography: p58. — Includes index
ISBN 0-905963-46-6 (spiral) : Unpriced
B82-21502

069.5'2 — Museums. Stock. Documentation systems: MDA system

Data definition language and data standard / Museum Documentation Association. — Duxford : The Association, 1980. — vi,140p : ill,forms ; 30cm. — (Museum documentation system)
ISBN 0-905963-26-1 (spiral) : £20.00 (£14.00 to members of MDA) B82-39104

Guide to the Museum documentation system / Museum Documentation Association. — Duxford : The Association, 1980. — iv,50p : ill,forms ; 30cm. — (Museum documentation system)
ISBN 0-905963-22-9 (spiral) : £5.00 (£3.50 to members of MDA) B82-39103

Neufeld, Steven D.. The MDA systems and services : a user's view / Steven D. Neufeld. — Duxford : Museum Documentation Association, 1981. — v,115p : 2forms ; 30cm. — (MDA occasional paper, ISSN 0140-7198 ; 6)
Bibliography: p115
ISBN 0-905963-42-3 (spiral) : Unpriced
B82-00816

069.5'2 — Museums. Stock. Documentation systems: MDA system — *Manuals*

Entry form instructions. — Duxford : Museum Documentation Association, 1981. — iv,32p : forms ; 30cm. — (Museum documentation system)
Bibliography: p28
ISBN 0-905963-37-7 (spiral) : Unpriced
B82-21505

Exit form instructions. — Duxford : Museum Documentation Association, 1981. — iv,19p : forms ; 30cm. — (Museum documentation system)
Bibliography: p17
ISBN 0-905963-38-5 (spiral) : Unpriced
B82-21506

Guide to the Museum Documentation System. — Duxford : Museum Documentation Association, 1981. — iv,42,[64]p : samples ; 30cm. — (Museum documentation system)
Previous ed.: 1980
ISBN 0-905963-45-8 (spiral) : Unpriced
B82-21503

Practical museum documentation. — Duxford : Museum Documentation Association, 1981. — viii,188p : forms ; 30cm. — (Museum documentation system)
Previous ed.: 1980. — Bibliography: p169-177. — Includes index
ISBN 0-905963-41-5 (spiral) : Unpriced
B82-21504

Transfer of title form instructions. — Duxford : Museum Documentation Association, 1981. — iv,18p : forms ; 30cm. — (Museum documentation system)
Bibliography: p17
ISBN 0-905963-39-3 (spiral) : Unpriced
B82-21507

069.5'2 — Museums. Stock: Mass produced goods. Documentation systems: MDA system

Technology card instructions / Museum Documentation Association. — Duxford : The Association, 1979. — iii,46p : forms ; 30cm. — (Museum documentation system)
Sample cards on 5 sheets in envelope attached to back cover. — Bibliography: p46
ISBN 0-905963-08-3 (spiral) : £2.25 (£1.50 to members of MDA) B82-39102

069.5'3 — Great Britain. Museums. Stock: Artefacts. Storage — *Conference proceedings*

Archaeological storage / Society of Museum Archaeologists and Yorkshire & Humberside Federation of Museums & Art Galleries. — [Lincoln] ([c/o A.J. White, Lincolnshire City and County Museum, Broadgate, Lincoln]) : [The Society], 1981. — 37p : ill ; 30cm
Conference papers. — Cover title
Unpriced (pbk) B82-18894

069.5'3 — Great Britain. Museums. Stock. Conservation — *Inquiry reports*

Great Britain. *Working Party on Conservation.* Report by a Working Party on Conservation 1980 / Standing Commission on Museums and Galleries. — London : H.M.S.O., 1980. — 45p ; 25cm
ISBN 0-11-290357-6 (unbound) : £3.00
B82-13678

069.5'3 — Iron antiquities. Conservation — *Conference proceedings*

Conservation of iron / edited by R.W. Clarke and S.M. Blackshaw. — [Greenwich?] : Trustees of the National Maritime Museum, [1982]. — ix,73p : ill ; 30cm. — (Maritime monographs and reports, ISSN 0307-8590 ; no.53-1982)
Conference proceedings. — Includes bibliographies
ISBN 0-905555-59-7 (pbk) : Unpriced
B82-32824

069'.63 — Great Britain. Art objects. Curators & conservators. Training

Cannon-Brookes, Peter. After Gulbenkian : a study paper towards the training of conservators and curators of works of art / foreword by Sir Norman Reid ; Peter Cannon-Brookes. — Birmingham (c/o Publications Unit, City Museums & Art Gallery, Birmingham, B3 3DH) : Peter Cannon-Brookes, c1976. — 28p ; 21cm
£0.50 (pbk) B82-37019

070 — JOURNALISM, PUBLISHING, NEWSPAPERS

070'.023'41 — Great Britain. Journalism — *Career guides*

Attwood, Tony. Careers in journalism / Tony Attwood. — Totnes : Hamilton House, 1981. — 24p ; 21cm. — (Careerscope ; 2)
ISBN 0-906888-19-0 (pbk) : Unpriced
B82-03069

070'.023'41 — Great Britain. Journalism — *Career guides* *continuation*
Conner, Edwina. Working on a newspaper / Edwina Conner ; photography by Tim Humphrey. — Hove : Wayland, 1982. — 94p : ill,ports ; 25cm. — (People at work)
Includes index
ISBN 0-85340-978-1 : £4.95 B82-39793

070'.025'41 — Great Britain. Newspapers — *Directories — Serials*
PIMS media directory. — Jan. 1981-. — London (4 St John's Place, EC1M 4AH) : Press Information & Mailing Services, 1981-. — v. ; 26x31cm
Monthly. — Continues: PRADS media lists
ISSN 0261-5169 = PIMS media directory (corrected) : Unpriced
Also classified at 384.54'025'41 B82-11810

070'.068'4 — United States. Newspaper publishing industries. Companies. Organisational change
Smith, Anthony, *1938-*. Goodbye Gutenberg : the newspaper revolution of the 1980's / Anthony Smith. — Oxford : Oxford University Press, 1980 (1981 [printing]). — xiii,367p : ill ; 21cm
Includes index
ISBN 0-19-285118-7 (pbk) : £3.95 B82-13948

070.1 — NEWS MEDIA

070.1'72 — Community newspapers. Production
Designing a community paper : publishing your own newspaper. — Aberdeen (163 King St, Aberdeen People's Press), [1982?]. — [4]p : ill,facsims ; 30cm
Unpriced (unbound) B82-18394

070.1'9 — Great Britain. Television programmes: News programmes
More bad news / Glasgow University Media Group ; [the authors are Peter Beharrell et al.]. — London : Routledge and Kegan Paul, 1980. — xviii,483p : ill,ports ; 23cm. — (Bad news ; v.2)
Includes index
ISBN 0-7100-0414-1 (pbk) : £17.50 : CIP rev. B79-34382

070.1'9'0924 — Great Britain. Television services: News reporting services: Independent Television News. Journalism — *Personal observations*
Cullen, Sarah. In praise of panic / Sarah Cullen ; with illustrations by Mac. — London : Joseph, 1982. — 206p : ill ; 23cm
ISBN 0-7181-2073-6 : £7.95 B82-13710

070.1'9'0973 — United States. Radio & television programmes: News programmes. Journalism
Broussard, E. Joseph. Writing and reporting broadcast news / E. Joseph Broussard, Jack F. Holgate. — New York : Macmillan ; London : Collier Macmillan, c1982. — x,191p : forms ; 28cm
Includes index
ISBN 0-02-315270-2 (pbk) : Unpriced B82-33409

070.4 — JOURNALISM. TECHNIQUES AND TYPES

070.4'12 — Newspapers. Editorial policies
Walker, Martin. Powers of the press. — London : Quartet Books, June 1982. — [416]p
ISBN 0-7043-2271-4 (pbk) : £15.00 : CIP entry B82-13507

070.4'15 — Newspapers. Copy-editing — *Manuals*
Baskette, Floyd K.. The art of editing. — 3rd ed. / Floyd K. Baskette, Jack Z. Sissors, Brian S. Brooks. — New York : Macmillan ; London : Collier Macmillan, c1982. — vii,504p : ill,facsims,ports ; 27cm
Previous ed.: 1977. — Includes index
ISBN 0-02-306280-0 : £15.50 B82-36485

Garst, Robert E.. Headlines and deadlines : a manual for copy editors / by Robert E. Garst and Theodore M. Bernstein. — 4th ed. — New York ; Guildford : Columbia University Press, 1982. — xiii,227p : ill ; 21cm
Previous ed.: London : Oxford University Press, 1961. — Includes index
ISBN 0-231-04816-5 (cased) : Unpriced
ISBN 0-231-04817-3 (pbk) : Unpriced B82-37312

070.4'3 — Journalism. Reporting
MacDougall, Curtis D.. Interpretative reporting / Curtis D. MacDougall. — 8th ed. — London : Macmillan, c1982. — xviii,588p ; 24cm
Previous ed.: 1977. — Includes index
ISBN 0-02-373120-6 (pbk) : £8.95 B82-26283

070.4'3'0926 — Great Britain. Newspapers. Reporters — *Case studies — For children*
Cuckson, Pippa. A day with a reporter / Pippa Cuckson and Tim Humphrey. — Hove : Wayland, 1982. — 55p : ill,ports ; 24cm. — (A day in the life)
Bibliography: p55
ISBN 0-85340-902-1 : £3.25 B82-28022

070.4'3'0973 — United States. News. Reporting
Izard, Ralph S.. Reporting the citizens' news : public affairs reporting in modern society / Ralph S. Izard. — New York ; London : Holt, Rinehart and Winston, c1982. — xvii,390p : forms,ports ; 25cm
Includes index
ISBN 0-03-057366-1 : Unpriced B82-27633

070.4'33 — Foreign news. Reporting. Political aspects
Crisis in international news : policies and prospects / Jim Richstad and Michael H. Anderson, editors. — New York ; Guildford : Columbia University Press, 1981. — xxiv,473p ; 24cm
Bibliography: p451-455. — Includes index
ISBN 0-231-05254-5 (cased) : £20.50
ISBN 0-231-05255-3 (pbk) : £9.00 B82-05616

070.4'33'092'4 — Foreign correspondents, *1950-1978 — Personal observations*
Behr, Edward. Anyone here been raped and speaks English. — London : New English Library, Feb.1982. — [256]p
Originally published: New York : Viking Press, 1978 ; London : H. Hamilton, 1981
ISBN 0-450-05360-1 (pbk) : £1.75 : CIP entry B81-36205

070.4'4930362'09416 — Northern Ireland. Violence. Reporting by news media
Hawthorne, James. Reporting violence — lessons from Northern Ireland? : a speech / given by James Hawthorne ... to the Edinburgh International Radio Festival at the Royal College of Physicians, Edinburgh, 21 August 1981. — London : British Broadcasting Corporation, [1981]. — 14p ; 21cm
Unpriced (pbk) B82-08223

070.4'4930542 — Newspapers with British imprints. Male chauvinism — *Collections*
Naked ape : an anthology of male chauvinism from the Guardian / edited by Andrew Veitch. — London : Duckworth, 1981. — 64p : ill,facsims ; 22cm
ISBN 0-7156-1614-5 (pbk) : £1.95 B82-00566

Naked ape 2. — London : Duckworth, Sept.1982. — [64]p
ISBN 0-7156-1685-4 (pbk) : £1.95 : CIP entry B82-25912

070.4'493058'00941 — Great Britain. Race relations. Reporting by mass media
Cohen, Phil. It ain't half racist, Mum : fighting racism in the media. — London : Comedia, Dec.1982. — [128]p
ISBN 0-906890-31-4 (cased) : £7.50 : CIP entry
ISBN 0-906890-30-6 (pbk) : £2.50 B82-40925

070.4'49320941 — Great Britain. Politics. Reporting by British Broadcasting Corporation
Howard, George, *1920-*. Broadcasting and politics : a speech / given by George Howard. — London (35 Marylebone High St. W1N 4AA) : British Broadcasting Corporation, 1982. — 14p ; 21cm
Unpriced (pbk) B82-40564

070.4'4933 — Economic conditions. Newspapers: Financial times. Journalists: Subject specialists — *Directories*
Financial Times Ltd. Journalists available for broadcasting & public speaking / [issued by Sheelagh Wilson]. — [London] : [Financial Times], [1982]. — 21p ; 30cm
Cover title
Unpriced (pbk) B82-24384

070.4'4935839 — Nuclear weapons. Reporting by mass media
Nukespeak : the media and the bomb / edited by Crispin Aubrey. — London : Comedia, 1982. — 135p : ill,facsims ; 22cm. — (Comedia/Minority Press Group series ; no.9)
ISBN 0-906890-27-6 (cased) : Unpriced
ISBN 0-906890-27-6 (pbk) : £2.50 B82-40854

070.4'496 — Technological innovation. Reporting by Engineer, *The , 1856-1980*
The **Innovative** engineer : 125 years of The Engineer / [editor John Pullin]. — London (Morgan-Grampian House, Calderwood Steet, SE18 6QH) : Morgan-Grampian, c1981. — 232p,[7]leaves of plates (some folded) : ill(some col.),facsims,plans ; 31cm
£8.50 (pbk) B82-11634

070.4'49796352'0924 — Golf. Reporting. Ward-Thomas, Pat — *Biographies*
Ward-Thomas, Pat. Not only golf : an autobiography / Pat Ward-Thomas. — London : Hodder and Stoughton, 1981. — 206p,[8]p of plates : ill,ports ; 24cm
Includes index
ISBN 0-340-26756-9 : £7.95 : CIP rev. B81-30128

070.4'499420858 — England. Riots. Reporting by television, *1981 (July)*
Tumber, Howard. Television and the riots : a report for the Broadcasting Research Unit of the British Film Institute / Howard Tumber. — London : BFI, 1982. — viii,54p ; 21cm
Bibliography: p54
ISBN 0-85170-120-5 (pbk) : Unpriced : CIP rev. B82-12816

070.5 — PUBLISHING

070.5 — Anti-Jewish forgeries: Protocols of the learned elders of Zion. Publication, *1945-1980*
The **Post** war career of the Protocols of Zion / [Institute of Jewish Affair]. — London (11 Hertford St., W1Y 7DX) : Institute of Jewish Affairs, 1981. — 12p ; 24cm. — (Research report / Institute of Jewish Affairs ; no.15)
Unpriced (unbound) B82-13824

070.5 — Drama in English. Shakespeare, William. First Folio. Publication
Connell, Charles. They gave us Shakespeare : John Heminge & Henry Condell / by Charles Connell. — Stocksfield : Oriel, 1982. — 110p,15leaves of plates : ill,1facsim,ports ; 23cm
Bibliography: p110
ISBN 0-85362-193-4 : £6.95 B82-27042

070.5 — Great Britain. Christianity. Books. Publishing — *Personal observations*
England, Edward, *1930-*. An unfading vision : the adventure of books / Edward England. — London : Hodder and Stoughton, 1982. — 159p ; 18cm. — (Hodder Christian paperbacks)
ISBN 0-340-27603-7 (pbk) : £1.75 : CIP rev. B81-36221

070.5 — Ireland, Isle of Man & Scotland. Law. Documents on law. Publishing
Law publishing and legal information : small jurisdictions of the British Isles / edited by William Twining and Jennifer Uglow. — London : Sweet & Maxwell, 1981. — 181p ; 22cm
Bibliography: p150-178. — Includes index
ISBN 0-421-28930-9 (pbk) : £10.00 : CIP rev. B81-30511

070.5 — London. Camden *(London Borough)*. **Museums. Libraries: British Museum.** *Department of Printed Books.* **Stock. Catalogues: Catalogue of the printed books in the library of the British Museum. Publication,** *1881-1900*
McCrimmon, Barbara. Power, politics, and print : the publication of the British Museum Catalogue 1881-1900 / Barbara McCrimmon. — Hamden, Conn. : Linnet ; London : Bingley, 1981. — 186p ; 23cm
Includes index
ISBN 0-85157-342-8 : £12.50 B82-01799

070.5 — Printing & publishing — *Amateurs' manuals*
Cohen, Colin. Print it! / Colin Cohen. — Tadworth : Kaye & Ward, 1981. — 128p : ill ; 21cm
ISBN 0-7182-1256-8 (pbk) : £3.95 : CIP rev. B81-19200

070.5'03 — Printing & publishing — *Polyglot dictionaries*
The **Multilingual** dictionary of printing and publishing / Alan Isaacs, editor. — London : Muller, c1981. — 289p ; 26cm
ISBN 0-584-95569-3 : £10.95 B82-00791

070.5'05 — Publishing — *Amateurs' manuals — Serials*
Wordsmith : a monthly report on the art of writing, publishing & being published. — Vol.1, no.1 (Oct. 1981)-. — [Oxford] ([P.O. Box 125, Oxford]) : [Research Associates], 1981-. — v. ; 30cm
Description based on: Vol.1, no.4 (Jan. 1982)
ISSN 0262-6748 = Wordsmith : Unpriced
Primary classification 808'.02'05 B82-22696

070.5'068'8 — Churches. Bookstalls. Management
Thorn, Eric A.. Project the right image : a practical handbook for Christian bookstall organisers / by Eric A. Thorn. — Maidstone : Third Day Enterprises, 1981. — 11p : ill ; 21cm
ISBN 0-9505912-6-2 (pbk) : £0.60 B82-09646

070.5'068'8 — Great Britain. Bookselling, *to 1980*
Mumby, Frank Arthur. Mumby's publishing & bookselling in the 20th century. — 6th ed. — London : Bell & Hyman, Dec.1982. — [256]p
Previous ed. published as: Publishing and bookselling ... London : Cape, 1974
ISBN 0-7135-1341-1 : £12.95 : CIP entry
Primary classification 070.5'0941 B82-30210

070.5'092'2 — Great Britain. Publishing. Unwin, *Sir* **Stanley,** *1884-1968.* **Interpersonal relationships with Unwin, David,** *1918-* — *Personal observations*
Unwin, David, *1918-*. Fifty years with Father : a relationship / David Unwin. — London : Allen & Unwin, 1982. — 150p : 1port ; 22cm
ISBN 0-04-920065-8 : Unpriced : CIP rev. B82-03715

070.5'092'4 — Great Britain. Publishing. Athill, Diana — *Biographies*
Athill, Diana. Instead of a letter / Diana Athill. — London : Robin Clark, 1981, c1976. — 223p ; 20cm
Originally published: London : Chatto and Windus, 1963
ISBN 0-86072-053-5 (pbk) : £3.50 B82-08201

070.5'092'4 — Great Britain. Publishing. Woolf, Leonard — *Biographies*
Woolf, Leonard. An autobiography / Leonard Woolf. — Oxford : Oxford University Press
Vol.2: 1911-1969. — 1980. — 527p,[32]p of plates : ill,ports ; 20cm
Includes index. — Contents: Beginning again. Originally published: London : Hogarth, 1964 — Downhill all the way. Originally published: London : Hogarth, 1967 — The journey not the arrival matters. Originally published: London : Hogarth, 1969
ISBN 0-19-281290-4 (pbk) : £5.95 : CIP rev. B80-12206

070.5'0941 — Great Britain. Community publishing
The **Republic** of letters : working class writing and local publishing / Paddy Maguire ... [et al.] ; edited by Dave Morley and Ken Worpole. — London : Comedia, 1982. — ix,155p : facsims ; 23cm. — (Comedia/Minority Press Group series ; no.6)
Bibliography: p153
ISBN 0-906890-13-6 (cased) : £8.50
ISBN 0-906890-12-8 (pbk) : £2.95 B82-30687

070.5'0941 — Great Britain. Publishing
Legal and financial aspects of publishing : proceedings of the IBIS/PCRC conference / editor, J. Collins. — Leicester : Primary Communications Research Centre, University of Leicester, 1980. — viii,28p ; 30cm. — (BL (R & D) report ; no.5564)
Bibliography: p25-28
ISBN 0-906083-11-7 (pbk) : Unpriced B82-38639

070.5'0941 — Great Britain. Publishing, *to 1980*
Mumby, Frank Arthur. Mumby's publishing & bookselling in the 20th century. — 6th ed. — London : Bell & Hyman, Dec.1982. — [256]p
Previous ed. published as: Publishing and bookselling ... London : Cape, 1974
ISBN 0-7135-1341-1 : £12.95 : CIP entry
Also classified at 070.5'068'8 B82-30210

070.5'0973 — United States. Books. Publishing
Dessauer, John P.. Book publishing : what it is, what it does / John P. Dessauer. — 2nd ed. — New York ; London : Bowker, 1981. — xiii,230p ; 24cm
Previous ed.: New York : Bowker, 1974. — Bibliography: p217-218. — Includes index
ISBN 0-8352-1325-0 (cased) : Unpriced
ISBN 0-8352-1326-9 (pbk) : Unpriced B82-03999

070.5'0973 — United States. Publishing — *Encyclopaedias*
Brownstone, David M.. The dictionary of publishing / David M. Brownstone, Irene M. Franck. — New York ; London : Van Nostrand Reinhold, c1982. — vii,302p : ill ; 24cm
ISBN 0-442-25874-7 : £16.10 B82-23711

070.5'7 — Science. Documents on science: Documents with European imprints. Publishing, *to 1980*
Development of science publishing in Europe / edited by A.J. Meadows. — Amsterdam ; Oxford : Elsevier Science, 1980. — ix,269p ; 25cm
Includes bibliographies
ISBN 0-444-41915-2 : £25.00 : CIP rev. B80-18152

070.5'72 — United States. Magazines for women. Publishing. Nast, Condé — *Biographies*
Seebohm, Caroline. The man who was Vogue : the life and times of Condé Nast / Caroline Seebohm. — London : Weidenfeld and Nicolson, 1982. — viii,390p : ill,ports ; 24cm
Originally published: New York : Viking Press, 1982. — Includes index
ISBN 0-297-78048-4 : £12.50 B82-39315

070.5'794 — Great Britain. Christian songs. Publishing — *Practical information*
Acott, Dennis. The Christian songwriters' handbook / general editor Eric A. Thorn ; prepared by Dennis Acott and Mal Grosch. — Maidstone : Third Day Enterprises, c1977 (1979 [printing]). — 11p ; 21cm
ISBN 0-9505912-2-x (pbk) : Unpriced : CIP rev. B79-29158

070.5'795 — American government publications: Microforms
Hernon, Peter. Microforms and government information / by Peter Hernon. — Westport, Conn. ; London : Microform Review, c1981. — viii,287p : ill,forms ; 24cm. — (Microform Review series in library micrographics management)
Bibliography: p269-277. — Includes index
ISBN 0-913672-12-2 : £22.50 B82-16953

070.5'93 — Great Britain. Books. Publishing by authors
Knowles, C. M.. Self-publishers and their books : report of project carried out by the Primary Communications Research Centre, Leicester, England : this project was funded by the British Library Research & Development Department / C.M. Knowles. — [Leicester] ([University of Leicester LE1 7RH]) : [Primary Communications Research Centre], 1981. — iv,102,[17]leaves : ill ; 30cm. — (British Library research and development reports, ISSN 0308-2385 ; no.5674)
Cover title. — Bibliography: leaves 99-102
Unpriced (spiral) B82-14184

070.5'95 — Great Britain. Public bodies. Publications
Richard, Stephen. Directory of British official publications : a guide to sources / compiled by Stephen Richard. — London : Mansell, 1981. — xxxii,360p ; 25cm
Includes index
ISBN 0-7201-1596-5 : Unpriced : CIP rev. B81-27392

070.5'95'0941 — Great Britain. Official publications
Butcher, David. Official publications in Britain. — London : Bingley, Jan.1983. — [160]p. — (Outlines of modern librarianship)
ISBN 0-85157-351-7 : £7.95: CIP entry B82-33107

070.9 — NEWSPAPERS AND JOURNALISM. HISTORICAL TREATMENT

070'.92'4 — Australia. Journalism. Murdoch, *Sir* **Keith,** *1885-1952* — *Biographies*
Zwar, Desmond. In search of Keith Murdoch / Desmond Zwar. — South Melbourne ; London : Macmillan, 1980. — 130p,[4]p of plates : ill (some col.),1facsim,ports(1col.) ; 27cm
Includes index
ISBN 0-333-29973-6 : Unpriced B82-36782

070'.92'4 — Great Britain. Journalism. Hopkinson, *Sir* **Tom** — *Biographies*
Hopkinson, *Sir* **Tom**. Of this our time. — London : Hutchinson, Apr.1982. — [288]p
ISBN 0-09-147860-x : £8.95 : CIP entry B82-04126

070'.92'4 — Great Britain. Journalism. Johnson, Frank — *Biographies*
Johnson, Frank. Out of order. — London : Robson, Oct.1982. — [208]p
ISBN 0-86051-190-1 : £6.50 : CIP entry B82-24140

070'.92'4 — Great Britain. Journalism. Lambert, Derek — *Biographies*
Lambert, Derek. Unquote / Derek Lambert. — London : Arlington, 1981. — 186p ; 23cm
ISBN 0-85140-543-6 : £6.50 : CIP rev. B81-30315

070'.92'4 — Great Britain. Journalism. Russell, William Howard — *Biographies*
Hankinson, Alan. Man of wars. — London : Heinemann Educational, Oct.1982. — [320]p
ISBN 0-435-32395-4 : £12.50 : CIP entry B82-23995

070'.92'4 — Great Britain. Journalism. Wooldridge, Ian — *Biographies*
Wooldridge, Ian. Right hand window smoking. — London : Collins, Sept.1982. — [96]p
ISBN 0-00-216660-7 : £5.95 : CIP entry B82-19068

070'.92'4 — Journalism. Bruce Lockhart, *Sir* **Robert** — *Correspondence, diaries, etc*
Bruce Lockhart, *Sir* **Robert**. The diaries of Sir Robert Bruce Lockhart / edited by Kenneth Young. — London : Macmillan
Vol.2: 1939-1965. — 1980. — 800p,[1]leaf of plates : 1port ; 24cm
Includes index
ISBN 0-333-18480-7 : £30.00 B82-06895

070'.92'4 — Journalism. Muggeridge, Malcolm — *Biographies*
Hunter, Ian, *1945-*. Malcolm Muggeridge : a life / by Ian Hunter. — [Glasgow] : Fontana/Collins, 1981. — 270p : ports ; 20cm
Originally published: London : Collins, 1980. — Bibliography: p257-258. — Includes index
ISBN 0-00-626510-3 (pbk) : £2.50 B82-18956

070'.92'4 — Scotland. Journalism. Webster, Jack — *Biographies*
Webster, Jack. A grain of truth : a Scottish journalist remembers / Jack Webster. — Edinburgh : Harris, 1981. — viii,200p,[12]p of plates : ill,ports ; 22cm
ISBN 0-86228-028-1 : £6.95 B82-28834

070'.92'4 — United States. Journalism. Reed, John, *1887-1920* — *Biographies*
Rosenstone, Robert A.. Romantic revolutionary : a biography of John Reed / Robert A. Rosenstone. — Harmondsworth : Penguin, 1982, c1975. — xiv,443p ; 20cm
Originally published: New York : Knopf, 1975. — Bibliography: p411-430. — Includes index
ISBN 0-14-006374-9 (pbk) : £2.95 B82-22492

070′.92′4 — Wales. Journalism. Rhys, E. Prosser — *Biographies* — *Welsh texts*

Hincks, Rhisiart. E. Prosser Rhys : 1901-1945 / Rhisiart Hincks. — Llandysul : Gwasg Gomer, 1980. — 201p,[12]p of plates : ill,ports ; 23cm
Bibliography: p187-190. — Includes index
ISBN 0-85088-903-0 : £4.95 B82-28306

071/079 — NEWSPAPERS AND JOURNALISM. GEOGRAPHICAL TREATMENT

072 — Evening newspapers with British imprints, *to 1980*

Clark, Peter A., *1930-*. Sixteen million readers : evening newspapers in the UK / Peter A. Clark. — London : Holt, Rinehart and Winston with the Advertising Association, c1981. — 97p ; 22cm
Four appendices on folded leaves in pocket. — Bibliography: p92-94. — Includes index
ISBN 0-03-910296-3 : £15.00 : CIP rev.
B81-20528

072 — Newspapers with English imprints: Guardian. Editing, *1956-1975* — *Personal observations*

Hetherington, Alastair. Guardian years / Alastair Hetherington. — London : Chatto & Windus, 1981. — x,382p,[8]p of plates : ill,ports ; 23cm
Includes index
ISBN 0-7011-2552-7 : £15.00 : CIP rev.
B81-23843

072′.1 — Evening newspapers with London imprints — *Forecasts*

Lind, Harold. The future of evening newspapers in London and the regions : a forecast to 1985 / by Harold Lind. — London (44 Earlham St., WC2H 9LA) : Admap, c1981. — 25p : 1port ; 30cm
£10.00 (pbk) B82-09553

072′.1 — Newspapers with London imprints: Newspapers in Bengali — *Texts*

Bajrakanṭha : a Bengali newsweekly. — 1 ma barsha, 1 ma saṅkhyā (9 i akṭabora 1981 iṃ)-. — London (63 Hanbury St., E1) : Joy Bangla Publications, 1981-. — v. : ill,ports ; 45cm
Description based on: 1 ma barsha 4 rtha saṅkhyā (30 śe akṭabora 1981 iṃ)
ISSN 0263-0370 = Bajrakanṭha : £0.20 per issue B82-14777

072′.1 — Newspapers with London imprints — *Texts*

Irish observer : serving the Irish in Britain. — Vol.1, no.1 (15th May 1982)-. — London (16a Craven Park Rd., N.W.10) : Noturn Publishing, 1982-. — v. : ill,ports ; 43cm
Weekly
ISSN 0263-886X = Irish observer : £0.20
B82-32359

The **Mail** on Sunday. — May 2 1982-. — London : Associated Newspapers, 1982-. — v. : ill,maps,ports ; 40cm
Weekly
ISSN 0263-8878 = Mail on Sunday : £0.28
B82-32358

072′.91443 — Newspapers with Scottish imprints: Newspapers with Strathclyde Region imprints: Newspapers with Glasgow imprints: Glasgow Herald, *to 1983*

Philipps, Alastair. Glasgow's Herald 1783-1983. — Glasgow : Drew, Oct.1982. — [192]p
ISBN 0-86267-008-x : £9.95 : CIP entry
B82-24603

072′.91486 — Scotland. Dumfries and Galloway Region. Newspapers: Dumfries and Galloway Standard and Advertiser, *to 1979* — *Indexes*

A **Local** index of the Dumfries and Galloway standard and advertiser and its predecessors over 200 years. — Dumfries (Sangspiel, 35 Rosemount St., Dumfries) : James Urquhart
Vol.3: The Dumfries courier, 1832 & 1833 as addendum to volume 1, the Dumfries & Galloway standard & advertiser, 1861-1880 / [general editor James Urquhart]. — 1981. — xxii,565p,[1]folded leaf of plates : 2ill,1facsim,2maps ; 30cm
Ill on inside cover
ISBN 0-9507033-3-8 (pbk) : £20.00
B82-29569

072′.9149 — Newspapers with Scottish imprints: Galloway Advertiser & Wigtownshire Free Press, *1843-1914* — *Indexes*

Wigtown free press index. — Dumfries (Catherine St., Dumfries DG1 4DY) : Dumfries and Galloway Regional Library Service
Vol.1: Personal names 1843-1880. — Dec.1982. — [416]p
ISBN 0-946280-00-2 : £20.00 : CIP entry
B82-37668

079′.495 — Greece. Press, *1967-1974*

McDonald, Robert. Pillar & tinderbox : the Greek press and the dictatorship. — London : Boyars, Oct.1982. — [288]p
ISBN 0-7145-2781-5 : £12.95 : CIP entry
B82-24736

080 — GENERAL COLLECTIONS

080 — Cars. Graffiti

Graffiti on wheels : the highway code of car stickers / compiled by Max Hodes ; illustrated by John Jenson. — London : W.H. Allen, 1981. — [144]p ; 18cm. — (A star book)
ISBN 0-352-30999-7 (pbk) : £1.25 B82-07897

080 — Graffiti — *Illustrations*

The **Golden** graffiti awards / collected and introduced by Roger Kilroy ; illustrated by McLachlan. — London : Corgi, 1981. — 96p : chiefly ill ; 20cm
ISBN 0-552-11812-5 (pbk) : £1.25 B82-04345

080 — Quotations, *1800-1940* — *Anthologies*

Madan, Geoffrey. Geoffrey Madan's notebooks : a selection / edited by J.A. Gere and John Sparrow ; with a foreword by Harold Macmillan. — Oxford : Oxford University Press, 1981. — xx,136p : 1port ; 22cm
ISBN 0-19-215870-8 : £7.95 : CIP rev.
B81-22469

080 — Quotations, *1945-1980* — *Anthologies* — *English texts*

A **Dictionary** of contemporary quotations / compiled by Jonathon Green. — London : Pan, 1982. — 454p ; 20cm
Includes index
ISBN 0-330-26534-2 (pbk) : £2.50 B82-37689

080 — Quotations, *1945-1981* — *Anthologies* — *English texts*

A **Dictionary** of contemporary quotations / compiled by Jonathon Green. — Newton Abbot : David & Charles, c1982. — 454p ; 24cm
Includes index
ISBN 0-7153-8417-1 : £9.95 : CIP rev.
B82-18478

080 — Quotations — *Anthologies* — *For public speaking*

Quotations for speakers / [compiled by] Norman Weed. — Newton Abbot : David & Charles, c1981. — [62]p ; 22cm
ISBN 0-7153-8111-3 : £3.50 : CIP rev.
B81-22505

080 — Quotations. Negro writers, *to 1980* — *Anthologies* — *English texts*

Quotations in black / compiled and edited by Anita King. — Westport ; London : Greenwood, 1981. — xviii,344p ; 24cm
ISBN 0-313-22128-6 : Unpriced B82-17879

080 — Quotations. Special subjects: Politics — *Anthologies*

Rogers, Michael. Political quotes. — Newton Abbot : David and Charles, Oct.1982. — [64]p
ISBN 0-7153-8378-7 : £3.50 : CIP entry
B82-23015

080 — Quotations, *to 1979* — *Anthologies* — *English texts*

The **Concise** Oxford dictionary of quotations. — 2nd ed. — Oxford : Oxford University Press, 1981. — 464p ; 21cm
Previous ed.: 1964. — Includes index
ISBN 0-19-211588-x (cased) : £7.50 : CIP rev.
ISBN 0-19-281324-2 (pbk) : £2.95 B81-22478

Nigel Rees presents The quote-unquote book of love, death and the universe / with illustrations by Michael Ffolkes. — London : Allen & Unwin, 1980. — 128p : ill ; 26cm
Includes index
ISBN 0-04-827022-9 : £4.95 : CIP rev.
B80-10732

080 — Quotations, *to 1980* — *Anthologies* — *English texts*

As cedar trees beside the waters / [compiled by] Edwin Hemingway Pleasants. — Bognor Regis : New Horizon, c1982. — 44p,[9]leaves of plates : ill ; 21cm
ISBN 0-86116-514-4 : £3.95 B82-19403

Don't quote me / compiled by Don Atyeo & Jonathon Green ; cartoons by Edward Barker. — London : Hamlyn, 1981. — viii,216p : ill ; 18cm
ISBN 0-600-20387-5 (pbk) : £1.00 B82-00082

More of who said that? : quotations and biographies of famous people / selected and compiled by Renie Gee. — Newton Abbot : David & Charles, c1981. — 64p ; 22cm
Bibliography: p61. — Includes index
ISBN 0-7153-8275-6 : £2.95 : CIP rev.
Also classified at 920′.02 B81-28073

[The 'Quote-Unquote' book of love, death and the universe]. Quote-Unquote 2 : a galaxy of quotations and quizzes on love, death and the universe / Nigel Rees ; illustrated by Michael ffolkes. — London : Unwin, 1982. — 160p : ill ; 18cm
Originally published: London : Allen & Unwin, 1980. — Includes index
ISBN 0-04-827031-8 (pbk) : £1.50 : CIP rev.
B81-33899

081 — General essays in English. American writers — *Texts*

All too true. — London : Quartet Books, May 1982. — [128]p
ISBN 0-7043-2327-3 : £1.95 : CIP entry
B82-13495

Asimov, Isaac. Opus : a selection from the first 200 books / by Isaac Asimov. — London : Granada, 1982, c1979. — 672p ; 18cm. — (A Panther book)
Originally published: London : Deutsch, 1980
ISBN 0-586-05128-7 (pbk) : £2.50 B82-30993

Tolson, M. B.. Caviar and cabbage : selected columns by Melvin B. Tolson from the Washington tribune, 1937-1944 / edited with an introduction, by Robert M. Farnsworth. — Columbia ; London : University of Missouri Press, 1982. — x,278p : ill,1port ; 22cm
Includes index
ISBN 0-8262-0348-5 : £15.00 B82-40261

082 — Anthologies in English — *Texts*

The **second** bedside book : an anthology / edited by Julian Shuckburgh. — London : Windward, 1981. — 255p : ill ; 25cm
Bibliography: p254-255
ISBN 0-7112-0207-9 : £7.95 B82-00723

The **Woman's** Hour book / edited by Wyn Knowles and Kay Edwards ; introduced by Sue MacGregor ; illustrations by Phillida Gili. — London : Sidgwick & Jackson, 1981. — 256p : ill ; 23cm
Bibliography: p254-256
ISBN 0-283-98821-5 : £6.50
ISBN 0-563-20013-8 (BBC) B82-03561

082 — Children's annuals in English — *Texts*

Carter, Margaret. The mother book of play pages : fun and games, things to make / [written by Margaret Carter] ; [designed by Ivan Radley] ; [drawings by Malcolm Bird]. — London : IPC Magazines, c1981. — 47p : chiefly ill(some col.) ; 31cm. — (A Fleetway annual)
Cover title
ISBN 0-85037-525-8 : Unpriced B82-30187

Judge Dredd annual. — 1981-. — London : IPC Magazines, 1980-. — v. : chiefly ill ; 28cm
ISSN 0263-2411 = Judge Dredd annual : £1.80 B82-18527

082 — Children's annuals in English — *Texts continuation*

Speed annual. — 1981-. — London : IPC Magazines, 1980-. — v. : chiefly ill ; 28cm
Supplement to: Speed
ISSN 0263-3906 = Speed annual : £1.80 B82-19870

[The Topper book *(1981)*]. The Topper book. — 1982-. — London : D.C. Thomson, 1981-. — v. : chiefly ill ; 28cm
Annual. — Continues: The Topper and Sparky fun book. — Supplement to: The Topper
ISSN 0262-4656 = Topper book (1981) : £1.55 B82-03422

082 — General essays in English — *Anthologies*

Amazing Times. — London : Allen and Unwin, Oct.1982. — [256]p
ISBN 0-04-808033-0 : £7.50 : CIP entry B82-23098

The **Best** of the Saturday book / edited by John Hadfield. — London : Hutchinson, 1981. — 306p : ill(some col.),ports(some col.) ; 24cm
Ill on lining papers
ISBN 0-09-145990-7 : £12.95 B82-02030

Sunday best / edited by Donald Trelford ; introduction by Clive James. — London : Observer, 1981. — 224p : ill ; 23cm
Includes index
ISBN 0-575-03071-2 : £6.95 B82-05717

082 — General essays in English. Saudi Arabian writers — *Texts*

Algosaibi, Ghazi A.. Arabian essays / Ghazi A. Algosaibi. — London : Kegan Paul International, 1982. — 117p ; 23cm
ISBN 0-7103-0019-0 : £9.50 B82-39943

082 — General essays in English — *Texts*

Amis, Kingsley. What became of Jane Austen? : and other questions / Kingsley Amis. — Harmondsworth : Penguin, 1981, c1970. — 216p ; 19cm
Originally published: London : Cape, 1970
ISBN 0-14-005509-6 (pbk) : £1.95 B82-08527

Cameron, James. The best of Cameron / James Cameron. — London : New English Library, c1981. — xiv,349p,[17]p of plates : ill,ports ; 24cm
Includes index
ISBN 0-450-04881-0 : £9.95 : CIP rev. B81-32009

Carter, Angela, *1940-*. Nothing sacred. — London : Virago, Oct.1982. — [192]p
ISBN 0-86068-269-2 (pbk) : £3.50 : CIP entry B82-24147

Coleridge, Nicholas. Tunnel vision : ephemeral writings / Nicholas Coleridge. — London : Quartet, 1981. — 214p : ill ; 24cm
ISBN 0-7043-2295-1 : £7.95 : CIP rev. B81-28146

Junor, John. The best of JJ / John Junor ; illustrations by Bill Martin. — London : Sidgwick & Jackson, 1981. — vii,175p : ill,facsims ; 23cm
ISBN 0-283-98820-7 : £6.50 B82-03560

Koestler, Arthur. Kaleidoscope. — Danube ed. — London : Hutchinson, Oct.1981. — 1v.
ISBN 0-09-145950-8 : £9.95 : CIP entry B81-26768

Levin, Bernard. Speaking up. — London : Cape, Mar.1982. — [352]p
ISBN 0-224-01729-2 : £8.50 : CIP entry B82-01127

Mallinson, Arnold. The leaning tower, or, Out of the perpendicular. — Oxford (Corpus Christi College, Oxford OX1 4JF) : Robert Dugdale, Apr.1982. — [224]p
ISBN 0-9503880-9-2 : £5.95 : CIP entry B82-08106

More, *Sir* **Thomas,** *Saint*. The complete works of St. Thomas More. — New Haven ; London : Yale University Press
Bibliography: p593-600. — Includes index
Vol.6: [A dialogue concerning heresies] / edited by Thomas M.C. Lawler, Germain Marc'hadour and Richard C. Marius. — c1981. — 2v.(xiv,888p,[14]leaves of plates) : ill,facsims ; 25cm
ISBN 0-300-02211-5 (cased) : Unpriced B82-08944

Muggeridge, Malcolm. Some answers / Malcolm Muggeridge ; compiled and edited by Michael Bowen. — London : Methuen, 1982. — 125p ; 23cm
Selected answers from Any questions?
ISBN 0-413-49940-5 : £5.50 : CIP rev. B82-15786

Philip, *Prince, consort of Elizabeth II, Queen of Great Britain*. A question of balance / H.R.H. the Duke of Edinburgh. — Salisbury : Michael Russell, 1982. — 142p ; 23cm
ISBN 0-85955-087-7 : £5.95 B82-31959

Whitehorn, Katharine. View from a column / Katharine Whitehorn. — London : Eyre Methuen, 1981. — 180p ; 23cm
ISBN 0-413-48620-6 : £5.95 B82-33777

082 — General knowledge

Reader's Digest library of modern knowledge / [edited by Reader's Digest Association]. — 3rd ed. — London : Reader's Digest Association, 1981. — 3v.(1408) : ill(some col.),charts(some col.),col.maps,music,facsims,ports ; 31cm
Previous ed.: 1979. — Text on lining papers. — Includes index
£29.95 B82-00041

082 — General knowledge — *For children*

Boys' pocket book. — Bristol : Purnell, 1982. — 128p : ill,1map,ports ; 19cm
ISBN 0-361-05386-x (pbk) : £1.50 B82-35132

Cassell discovery books. — London : Cassell
Set 4: Sporting events / R.E. Wigglesworth. — 1981. — 4v. : ill,ports ; 19cm
Text on inside covers. — Includes indexes. — Contents: Wimbledon — The Olympic Games — The TT — The World Cup
ISBN 0-304-30274-0 (pbk) : Unpriced B82-14874

Cassell discovery books. — London : Cassell
Set 5: Pets / Kevin Philbin. — 1981. — 4v. : ill ; 19cm
Text on inside covers. — Includes index. — Contents: Dogs — Ponies — Cats — Small pets
ISBN 0-304-30634-7 (pbk) : Unpriced B82-14875

Cassell discovery books. — London : Cassell
Set 6: People / Sam McBratney. — 1981. — 4v. : ill,ports ; 19cm
Text on inside covers. — Includes index. — Contents: Prince Charles — Elvis Presley — Mary Peters — Muhammad Ali
ISBN 0-304-30636-3 (pbk) : Unpriced B82-14876

Girls' pocket book. — Bristol : Purnell, 1982. — 128p : ill,1map,ports ; 19cm
ISBN 0-361-05385-1 (pbk) : £1.50 B82-35131

How to hold a crocodile / the Diagram Group. — London : Sidgwick & Jackson, 1981. — 191p : ill ; 28cm
Includes index
ISBN 0-283-98831-2 (cased) : £7.95
ISBN 0-283-98832-0 (pbk) : £4.95 B82-03653

082 — General knowledge — *Questions & answers — For schools*

Phillips, H. M. (Harry Mervyn). Timebreak too / H.M. Phillips. — Welwyn : Nisbet, 1982. — 32p ; 19cm
ISBN 0-7202-0820-3 (pbk) : £0.75 B82-36240

082 — General knowledge — *Topics for discussion groups*

Another look at our world : a book of current knowledge & interests for group study. — Birmingham (Norfolk House, Smallbrook Queensway, Birmingham, B5 4LJ) : NASO, 1982. — 202p ; 19cm
Includes bibliographies
Unpriced (pbk) B82-09763

Another look at our world : a book of current knowledge & interests for group study. — Birmingham (Norfolk House, Smallbrook, Queensway, Birmingham B5 4LJ) : NASO, 1982. — 207p ; 19cm
Unpriced (pbk) B82-20474

Our life and time : a book of current knowledge & interests for group study. — London (Drayton House, Gordon St., WC1H 0BE) : NASO, 1980. — 206p ; 19cm
Includes bibliographies
Unpriced (pbk) B82-40689

082 — Girls' annuals in English — *Texts*

[Blue jeans *(Annual)*]. Blue jeans. — 1982-. — London : D.C. Thomson, 1981-. — v. : ill (some col.) ; 28cm
Annual. — Continues: Blue jeans annual. — Supplement to: Blue jeans (Weekly)
ISSN 0262-4214 = Blue jeans (Annual) : £1.70 B82-03423

Girl annual. — 1982-. — London : IPC Magazines, 1981-. — v. : ill(some col.),ports ; 28cm
Annual. — Supplement to: Girl (London : 1981)
ISSN 0262-9208 = Girl annual : £2.25 B82-11156

[Patches *(Annual)*]. Patches. — 1982-. — London : D.C. Thomson, 1981-. — v. : ill,ports ; 28cm
Annual
ISSN 0262-3560 = Patches (Annual) : £1.70 B82-04899

Photo secret love annual. — 1982-. — London : IPC Magazines, c1981-. — v. : ill(some col.),col.ports ; 28cm
Supplement to: Photo secret love
ISSN 0262-9119 = Photo Secret Love annual : £2.25 B82-12462

082 — Graffiti in English — *Anthologies*

Graffiti 4. — London : Allen and Unwin, Sept.1982. — [144]p
ISBN 0-04-827066-0 (pbk) : £1.50 : CIP entry B82-19085

The **Graffiti** file / [compiled by] Nigel Rees. — London : Allen & Unwin, 1981. — 352p : ill ; 21cm
ISBN 0-04-827049-0 : Unpriced : CIP rev. B81-25870

More Irish graffiti / by Sean Kilroy. — Dublin : Mercier, c1982. — 48p ; 18cm
ISBN 0-85342-673-2 (pbk) : £1.15 (Irish) B82-39170

Rees, NigelGraffiti 2 / [compiled by] Nigel Rees. — London : Unwin Paperbacks, 1980. — 144p : ill ; 18cm
ISBN 0-04-827023-7 (pbk) : £1.25 : CIP rev. B80-18142

The **Writing** on the wall : a collection of good old British graffiti — / [compiled] by Mark Barker ; with cartoons by Larry. — London : Clare, c1979. — 93p : ill ; 15x23cm
ISBN 0-906549-01-9 : Unpriced B82-00933

082 — Grafitti in English — *Anthologies — For children*

Rogers, Janet. Crazy graffiti / Janet Rogers ; illustrated by David Mostyn. — London : Hamlyn, 1982. — 95p : ill ; 18cm
ISBN 0-600-20542-8 (pbk) : £0.85 B82-24875

082 — Quotations in English, *ca 1400-1981.* **Special subjects: Travel** — *Anthologies*

The **Travellers'** dictionary of quotations. — London : Routledge, Oct.1982. — [200]p
ISBN 0-7100-0992-5 : £12.50 : CIP entry
B82-23204

082 — Quotations. Women writers, *to 1979* — *Anthologies — English texts*

Violets and vinegar : an anthology of women's writings and sayings / chosen by Jilly Cooper and Tom Hartman. — [London] : Corgi, 1982, c1980. — 302p ; 18cm
Originally published: London : Allen & Unwin, 1980. — Includes index
ISBN 0-552-11869-9 (pbk) : £1.65 B82-14449

082'.05 — General essays in English — *Anthologies — Serials*

The **Bedside** Guardian. — 30. — London : Collins, Nov.1981. — [250]p
ISBN 0-00-216356-x : £6.95 : CIP entry
B81-28762

The **Bedside** Guardian. — 31. — London : Collins, Nov.1982. — [252]p
ISBN 0-00-216497-3 : £6.95 : CIP entry
B82-29853

The **Pick** of the Herald. — 1. — Glasgow : Drew, Oct.1982. — [224]p
ISBN 0-86267-011-x (pbk) : £2.25 : CIP entry
B82-24604

082'.05 — General knowledge — *For children — Serials*

World of knowledge annual. — 1981-. — London : IPC Magazines, 1980-. — v. : ill(some col.) ; 28cm
Supplement to: World of knowledge
ISSN 0263-1547 = World of Knowledge annual : £2.40 B82-18722

083'.1 — General essays in German — *English texts*

Marx, Karl. [Selections]. The essential Marx : the non-economic writings — a selection / edited, with new translations, by Saul K. Padover. — New York : New American Library ; London : New English Library, 1979, c1978. — x,438p ; 18cm. — (A Mentor book)
Bibliography: p403-405. — Includes index
ISBN 0-451-61709-6 (pbk) : Unpriced
B82-12858

084'.1 — General essays in French — *English texts*

Serres, Michel. Hermes : literature, science, philosophy / by Michel Serres ; edited by Josué V. Harari & David F. Bell. — Baltimore ; London : Johns Hopkins University Press, c1982. — xl,168p ; 24cm
Translations from the French. — Includes index
ISBN 0-8018-2454-0 : Unpriced B82-36868

087'.85 — General essays in Polish — *Texts*

Laks, Szymon. Taryfa ulgowa kosztuje drożej / Szymon Laks. — Londyn : Oficyna Poetów i Malarzy, 1982. — 118p ; 22cm
Includes index
Unpriced (pbk) B82-31543

Świdzińska, Halina. Absurdyści i iluzjoniści : eseje refleksje rozważania / Halina Swidzińska. — Londyn : OPiM, 1981. — 168p,[4]p of plates : ill,ports ; 22cm
Unpriced (pbk) B82-25113

087'.86 — General essays in Czech — *English texts*

Janáček, Leoš. Janáček : leaves from his life / edited and translated by Vilem and Margaret Tausky. — London : Kahn & Averill, 1982. — 159p : ill,music,ports ; 21cm
Translated from the Czech
ISBN 0-900707-68-2 : £4.95 : CIP rev.
B81-37587

089'.71 — Gwent. Usk. Graffiti in Latin

Boon, George C.. The coins / George C. Boon. Inscriptions and graffiti / Mark Hassall with other contributions by R.P. Wright and George C. Boon. — Cardiff : Published on behalf of the Board of Celtic Studies of the University of Wales [by] University of Wales Press, 1982. — 72p,[2]p of plates : ill ; 30cm. — (Report on the excavations at Usk 1965-1976)
ISBN 0-7083-0789-2 : Unpriced
ISBN 0-7083-0741-8 (set)
Primary classification 737.4937 B82-36889

089'.71 — Quotations in Latin — *Anthologies — Latin-English parallel texts*

Cree, Anthony. Cree's Shorter dictionary of useful and familiar Latin quotations / compiled by Anthony Cree. — Oxford : Hannon, c1974 (1979 printing). — [25]p : ill ; 21cm
Unpriced (pbk) B82-28228

089'.9162 — General essays in Irish — *Texts*

Ó Néill, Séamus. Lamh dhearg abu! : aistí agus dréachtaí / le Séamus Ó Néill. — Baile Átha Cliath [Dublin] (29 Sráid Uí Chonaill Íoch, Baile Átha Cliath 1) : Foilseacháin Náisiúnta Teoronta, 1982. — 221p ; 19cm
£5.00 B82-21686

089'.9166 — General essays in Welsh — *Texts*

Owen, William, *1935-*. Llacio'r gengal : sgyrsiau ac ysgrifau / gan William Owen. — Llandysul : Gwasg Gomer, 1982. — 93p ; 19cm
ISBN 0-85088-636-8 (pbk) : £1.60 B82-27246

Roberts, Selyf. Hel meddyliau : ysgrifau a cherddi / Selyf Roberts. — [Denbigh] : Gwasg Gee, c1982. — 84p ; 22cm
£2.00 (pbk) B82-37870

090 — RARE BOOKS

090 — Antiquarian books with European imprints & European manuscripts, *1306-1892* — *Festschriften*

Fine books and book collecting : books and manuscripts acquired from Alan G. Thomas and described by his customers on the occasion of his seventieth birthday / edited by Christopher de Hamel and Richard A. Linenthal. — Leamington Spa : Hall, 1981. — x,72p : ill,facsims ; 31cm
ISBN 0-907471-03-x : £15.00 : CIP rev.
B81-24615

091 — MANUSCRIPTS

091 — Byzantine illuminated manuscripts: Psalters & lectionaries — *Critical studies*

Weitzmann, Kurt. Byzantine liturgical psalters and gospels / Kurt Weitzmann. — London : Variorum, 1980. — 322p in various pagings : ill,1port ; 31cm. — (Collected studies series ; CS 119)
Includes four chapters in German. — Facsim reprints. — Includes index
ISBN 0-86078-064-3 : £65.00 : CIP rev.
B80-17526

091 — Hertfordshire. St Albans. Abbeys: St Albans Abbey, *1066-1235.* **Stock: Manuscripts**

Thomson, Rodney M.. Manuscripts from St Albans Abbey 1066-1235. — Woodbridge : Boydell and Brewer, July 1982. — [256]p
ISBN 0-85991-085-7 : £45.00 : CIP entry
B82-13154

091'.0941 — British illuminated manuscripts, *1190-1285*

Morgan, N. J.. Early Gothic manuscripts / by Nigel Morgan. — London : Harvey Miller. — (A Survey of manuscripts illuminated in the British Isles ; 5)
1: 1190-1250. — c1982. — 276p : ill(some col.) ; 34cm
Bibliography: p42-45. — Includes index
ISBN 0-19-921026-8 : Unpriced B82-34864

094 — BOOKS NOTABLE FOR PRINTING

094 — Books printed by Kelmscott Press: Works of Geoffrey Chaucer now newly imprinted - *Critical studies*

Robinson, Duncan. William Morris, Edward Burne-Jones and the Kelmscott Chaucer. — London : Gordon Fraser, July 1981. — [160]p
ISBN 0-86092-038-0 : £30.00 : CIP entry
B81-14439

095 — BOOKS NOTABLE FOR BINDINGS

095'.074'02142 — Great Britain. National libraries: British Library. *Department of Printed Books.* **Stock: Books. Bindings,** *ca 1200-1900.* **Collections: Henry Davis Gift**

Foot, Mirjam. A collection of bookbindings. — London : British Library
Vol.2: A catalogue of North-European bindings. — Dec.1982. — [445]p
ISBN 0-904654-73-7 : CIP entry B82-30742

098 — BOOKS NOTABLE FOR CONTENT

098'.3'0922 — English literature. Forgeries by Wise, Thomas James & Forman, H. Buxton

Barker, Nicolas. A sequel to an enquiry : the forgeries of H. Buxton Forman and T.J. Wise re-examined. — London : Scolar, July 1982. — [422]p
ISBN 0-85967-638-2 : £27.50 : CIP entry
B82-13153

098'.3'0924 — English literature. Forgeries. Wise, Thomas James

Carter, John, *1905-1976.* An enquiry into the nature of certain nineteenth century pamphlets. — 2nd ed. — London : Scolar Press, July 1982. — [422]p
Previous ed.: London : Constable, 1934
ISBN 0-85967-637-4 : £27.50 : CIP entry
B82-13152

099 — BOOKS NOTABLE FOR FORMAT

099 — Miniature books — *Buyers' guides — Serials*

Gleniffer news : newsletter of the private press of Helen & Ian MacDonald. — No.1 (1977)-no.4 (1980). — Paisley (11 Low Rd., Catlehead, Paisley PA2 6AQ) : Gleniffer Press, 1977-1980. — 4v. ; 30cm
Annual. — Description based on: No.4 (1980)
ISSN 0143-8743 = Gleniffer news : Unpriced
B82-09686

099 — Miniature books, *to 1980*

Brady, Louis W.. Miniature books : their history from the beginnings to the present day / by Louis W. Brady. — London : Sheppard, 1981. — 221p : ill(some col.),1port ; 22cm
Bibliography: p203-207. — Includes index
ISBN 0-900661-23-2 : £9.00 B82-02603

100 — PHILOSOPHY AND RELATED DISCIPLINES

100 — Dialectics — *Philosophical perspectives*

Kharin, ÎÛ. A.. Fundamentals of dialectics / Yu. A. Kharin. — Moscow : Progress Publishers ; [London] : Distributed by Central Books, 1981. — 255p : ill ; 21cm
Translation of: Nachala dialektiki
ISBN 0-7147-1669-3 : £2.95 B82-06706

100 — Philosophy — *Critical studies*

Basic concepts in philosophy / edited by Zak Van Straaten. — Cape Town ; Oxford : Oxford University Press, 1981. — xii,264p : ill ; 22cm
Includes bibliographies
ISBN 0-19-570288-3 : £11.95 B82-08288

Cornman, James W.. Philosophical problems and arguments : an introduction. — 3rd ed. / James W. Cornman, Keith Lehrer, George S. Pappas. — London : Macmillan, c1982. — xviii,366p ; 25cm
Previous ed.: 1974. — Bibliography: p327-354. — Includes index
ISBN 0-02-325120-4 : £12.95 B82-26282

100 — Philosophy — *Critical studies continuation*

Marxism and alternatives : towards the conceptual interaction among Soviet philosophy, neo-Thomism, pragmatism, and phenomenology / Tom Rockmore ... [et al.]. — Dordrecht ; London : Reidel, c1981. — xiv,311p : ill ; 23cm. — (Sovietica ; v.45)
Includes index
ISBN 90-277-1285-9 : Unpriced B82-06116

Philosophical problems. — Milton Keynes : Open University Press. — (Arts : a third level course)
At head of cover title: The Open University
Units 10-11: Philosophical logic / prepared for the Course Team by Simon Blackburn. — 1980. — 65p : ill ; 30cm. — (A313 ; 10-11)
Bibliography: p63-65
ISBN 0-335-11020-7 (pbk) : Unpriced B82-04651

La **Philosophie** contemporaine : chroniques nouvelles = contemporary philosophy : a new survey / edited by Guttorm Fløistad. — The Hague ; London : Nijhoff, 1981
'Published under the auspices of the International Council of Philosophy and Humanistic Studies and of the International Federation of Philosophical Studies, with the support of UNESCO' — T.p. verso. — Half title: International Institute of Philosophy. Institut International de Philosophie. — Includes bibliographies and index
Vol.1: Philosophy of language, editor G. Fløistad. Philosophical logic, co-editor G. H. von Wright. — lx,404p : ill,25cm
ISBN 90-247-2451-1 : Unpriced B82-00479

Philosophy of science / prepared for the course team by Janet Radcliffe Richards. — Milton Keynes : Open University Press. — (Arts : a third level course)
At head of title: The Open University
Units 23-24: Philosophical problems. — 1981. — 66p : ill ; 30cm. — (A313 ; 23-24)
Bibliography: p66
ISBN 0-335-11026-6 (pbk) : Unpriced B82-15050

100 — Philosophy — *Texts* — *Interviews*

Magee, Bryan. Men of ideas. — Oxford : Oxford University Press, Sept.1982. — [288]p
Originally published: London : British Broadcasting Corporation, 1978
ISBN 0-19-283034-1 (pbk) : £3.50 : CIP entry B82-18989

101 — Philosophy — *Philosophical perspectives*

Pettit, Philip. Philosophy and the human sciences / by Philip Pettit. — [Bradford] : University of Bradford, [1979?]. — 27p ; 21cm
An inaugural lecture delivered at the University of Bradford on 23 January 1979
Unpriced (pbk) B82-14573

101'.4 — Philosophy. Language

Chatterjee, Margaret. The language of philosophy / by Margaret Chatterjee. — The Hague ; London : Nijhoff, 1981. — viii,140p ; 25cm. — (Martinus Nijhoff philosophy library ; v.4)
Includes index
ISBN 90-247-2372-8 : Unpriced B82-03858

105 — Philosophy — *Serials*

Philosophical investigations. — Vol.1, no.1 (Winter 1978)-. — Oxford : Blackwell, 1978-. — v. ; 22cm
Quarterly. — Published: Decatur, Ill. : Philosophical Investigations, 1978-1980. — Description based on: Vol.5, no.1 (Jan. 1982)
ISSN 0190-0536 = Philosophical investigations : £19.50 per year B82-24770

109 — Philosophy, *to 1960* — *Comparative studies*

Wedberg, Anders. A history of philosophy. — Oxford : Clarendon Press
Translation of: Filosofins historia
Vol.2: The modern age to Romanticism. — Oct.1982. — [270]p
ISBN 0-19-824640-4 (cased) : £12.50 : CIP entry
ISBN 0-19-824692-7 (pbk) : £4.50 B82-23690

109'.04 — Philosophy, *1945-1980* — *Critical studies*

Handbook of world philosophy : contemporary developments since 1945 / edited by John R. Burr. — London : Aldwych, 1981, c1980. — xxiii,641p ; 24cm
Originally published: Westport, Conn. : Greenwood, 1980. — Includes bibliographies and index
ISBN 0-86172-014-8 : £34.50 B82-30926

110 — METAPHYSICS

110 — Archetypes. Psychosocial aspects

Stevens, Anthony. Archetype : a natural history of the self / Anthony Stevens. — London : Rougledge & Kegan Paul, 1982. — 324p : ill ; 25cm
Bibliography: p302-309. — Includes index
ISBN 0-7100-0980-1 : £12.50 : CIP rev. B82-04473

110 — Metaphysics

Schlesinger, George N.. Metaphysics. — Oxford : Blackwell, Sept.1982. — [256]p
ISBN 0-631-13124-8 (cased) : £17.50 : CIP entry
ISBN 0-631-13125-6 (pbk) : £6.95 B82-23853

110 — Metaphysics. Aristotle. 'Physics' — *Critical studies*

Waterlow, Sarah. Nature, change, and agency in Aristotle's Physics : a philosophical study / Sarah Waterlow. — Oxford : Clarendon, 1982. — 269p ; 23cm
Bibliography: p263-266. — Includes index
ISBN 0-19-824653-6 : £17.50 : CIP rev. B82-07516

110'.92'4 — Metaphysics. Theories of Moore, G. E.

O'Connor, David. The metaphysics of G.E. Moore / David O'Connor. — Dordrecht ; London : Reidel, c1982. — x,180p ; 23cm. — (Philosophical studies series in philosophy ; v.25)
Bibliography: p169-173. — Includes index
ISBN 90-277-1352-9 : Unpriced B82-25210

111 — ONTOLOGY

111 — Identity — *Philosophical perspectives*

Hirsch, Eli. The concept of identity / Eli Hirsch. — New York ; Oxford : Oxford University Press, 1982. — x,318p : ill ; 23cm
Part One originally published: as The persistence of objects. Philadelphia : University Science Center, 1976. — Includes index
ISBN 0-19-502995-x : £14.50 B82-34511

111'.092'4 — Ontology. Theories of Tillich, Paul

Thompson, Ian E.. Being and meaning : Paul Tillich's theory of meaning, truth and logic / by Ian E. Thompson. — Edinburgh, Edinburgh University Press, c1981. — x,244p ; 22cm
Bibliography: p223-231. — Includes index
ISBN 0-85224-388-x : Unpriced B82-02321

111'.092'4 — Ontology. Theories of Udayaṇācārya

Tachikawa, Musashi. The structure of the world in Udayana's realism : a study of the Lakṣaṇāvalī and the Kiraṇāvali / by Musashi Tachikawa. — Dordrecht ; London : Reidel, c1981. — xiv,180p : ill ; 24cm. — (Studies of classical India ; v.4)
Bibliography: p163-168. — Includes index
ISBN 90-277-1291-3 : Unpriced B82-17271

111'.1 — Existence. Aristotle. De generatione et corruptione — *Texts with commentaries*

Aristotle. [De generatione et corruptione. English]. Aristotle's De generatione et corruptione. — Oxford : Clarendon Press, July 1982. — [250]p. — (Clarendon Aristotle series)
ISBN 0-19-872062-9 (cased) : £12.50 : CIP entry
ISBN 0-19-872063-7 (pbk) : £6.25 B82-12553

111'.1 — Existence — *Philosophical perspectives*

Williams, C. J. F.. What is existence? / C.J.F. Williams. — Oxford : Clarendon, 1981. — xviii,359p ; 23cm. — (Clarendon library of logic and philosophy)
Bibliography: p345-350. — Includes index
ISBN 0-19-824429-0 : £17.50 : CIP rev. B81-13802

111'.6'09 — Continuity & infinity. Theories, *to 1300*

Infinity and continuity in ancient and medieval thought / edited by Norman Kretzmann. — Ithaca ; London : Cornell University Press, 1982. — 367p ; 24cm
Bibliography: p341-350. — Includes index
ISBN 0-8014-1444-x : £20.75 B82-35760

111'.83'0924 — Truth. Theories of Ghandhi, M. K.

Richards, Glyn. The philosophy of Gandhi. — London : Curzon Press, Feb.1982. — [176]p
ISBN 0-7007-0150-8 : £5.50 : CIP entry B82-02453

111'.85 — Aesthetics

Pole, David. Aesthetics, form and emotion. — London : Duckworth, Apr.1982. — [256]p
ISBN 0-7156-1608-0 : £24.00 : CIP entry B82-04877

Scruton, Roger. Art and imagination : a study in the philosophy of mind / Roger Scruton. — London : Rougledge & Kegan Paul, 1982, c1974. — viii,259p : music ; 22cm
Originally published: London : Methuen, 1974. — Bibliography: p250-253. — Includes index
ISBN 0-7100-9014-5 (pbk) : £7.95 B82-16882

Sharpe, R. A.. What art is : an introduction to contemporary aesthetics. — Brighton : Harvester Press, June 1982. — [192]p
ISBN 0-7108-0456-3 : CIP entry B82-12154

Tatarkiewicz, Władysław. A history of six ideas : an essay in aesthetics / by Władysław Tatarkiewicz. — The Hague ; London : Nijhoff, 1980. — xiii,383p : ill ; 25cm. — (Melbourne international philosophy series ; v.5)
Translation of: Dzieje sześciu pojeć. — Bibliography: p349-374. — Includes index
ISBN 90-247-2233-0 : Unpriced B82-40812

111'.85'0924 — Aesthetics. Theories of Kant, Immanuel

Essays in Kant's aesthetics / edited and introduced by Ted Cohen & Paul Guyer. — Chicago ; London : University of Chicago Press, 1982. — x,323p ; 24cm
Bibliography: p307-323
ISBN 0-226-11226-8 : Unpriced B82-35315

113 — METAPHYSICS. COSMOLOGY

113 — Cosmology

Hoyle, Fred. Facts and dogmas in cosmology and elsewhere / Fred Hoyle. — Cambridge : Cambridge University Press, 1982. — 16p ; 19cm. — (The Rede lecture ; 1982)
Cover title
ISBN 0-521-27268-8 (pbk) : £1.75 B82-38757

Munitz, Milton K.. Space, time and creation : philosophical aspects of scientific cosmology / Milton K. Munitz. — 2nd ed. — New York : Dover ; London : Constable, 1981. — viii,184p ; 22cm
Previous ed.: Glencoe, Ill. : Free Press, 1957. — Includes index
ISBN 0-486-24220-x (pbk) : £3.00 B82-29993

113 — Nature, *ca 1500-ca 1700* — *Philosophical perspectives*

Merchant, Carolyn. The death of nature. — London : Wildwood House, Sept.1981. — [368]p
ISBN 0-7045-3049-x : £6.95 : CIP entry B81-23793

113 — Nature — *Philosophical perspectives*

Krishnamurti, J.. Krishnamurti's journal / J. Krishnamurti ; foreword by Mary Lutyens. — London : Gollancz ; Bombay : B.I. Publications, 1982. — 100p ; 21cm
ISBN 0-575-03040-2 : £4.95 B82-14582

115 — METAPHYSICS. TIME

115 — Time — *Philosophical perspectives*

Chapman, T.. Time : a philosophical analysis / T. Chapman. — Dordrecht ; London : Reidel, c1982. — xv,162p : ill ; 23cm. — (Synthese library ; v.159)
Bibliography: p156-160. — Includes index
ISBN 90-277-1465-7 : Unpriced B82-40152

Jaques, Elliott. The form of time. — London : Heinemann Educational, Apr.1982. — [288]p
ISBN 0-435-82480-5 : £12.50 : CIP entry
B82-09197

Mellor, D. H.. Real time / D.H. Mellor. — Cambridge : Cambridge University Press, 1981. — xi,203p ; 24cm
Bibliography: p188-200. — Includes index
ISBN 0-521-24133-2 : £17.50 : CIP rev.
B81-31280

116 — METAPHYSICS. EVOLUTION

116 — Evolution — *Philosophical perspectives*

The **Philosophy** of evolution / [edited by] U.J. Jensen and R. Harré. — Brighton : Harvester Press, 1981. — vii,299p ; 22cm. — (Harvester studies in philosophy ; 26)
Conference papers. — Includes index
ISBN 0-7108-0072-x : £20.00 : CIP rev.
B81-22602

121 — EPISTEMOLOGY

121 — Epistemology

Adorno, Theodor W.. Against epistemology. — Oxford : Blackwell, Oct.1982. — [256]p
Translation of: Zur Metakritik der Erkenntnistheorie
ISBN 0-631-12843-3 : £17.50 : CIP entry
B82-23166

O'Connor, D. J. (Daniel John). Introduction to the theory of knowledge / D.J. O'Connor and Brian Carr. — Brighton : Harvester, 1982. — ix,211p ; 23cm
Bibliography: p204-208. — Includes index
ISBN 0-85527-487-5 (cased) : £18.95 : CIP rev.
ISBN 0-7108-0445-8 (pbk) : Unpriced
B82-03381

121 — Epistemology — *Conference proceedings*

Common denominators in art and science. — Aberdeen : Aberdeen University Press, Feb.1983. — [220]p
Conference papers
ISBN 0-08-028457-4 : £14.00 : CIP entry
B82-36474

121 — Epistemology. Evolutionary aspects

Learning, development, and culture : essays in evolutionary epistemology. — Chichester : Wiley, Dec.1982. — [500]p
ISBN 0-471-10219-9 : £25.00 : CIP entry
B82-30818

121 — Epistemology. Kant, Immanuel. Kritik der reinen Vernunft — *Critical studies*

Atkinson, R. F.. Kant's first Critique / R.F. Atkinson ; an original lecture delivered in the University of Exeter on 23 January 1981. — [Exeter] : University of Exeter, 1981. — 11p ; 22cm
ISBN 0-85989-118-6 (pbk) : £0.60 B82-06272

Kant on pure reason / edited by Ralph C.S. Walker. — Oxford : Oxford University Press, 1982. — 201p : ill ; 21cm ; 1982. — (Oxford readings in philosophy)
Bibliography: p196-201. — Includes index
ISBN 0-19-875056-0 : £3.95 : CIP rev.
B82-12554

Pippin, Robert B.. Kant's theory of form : an essay on the Critique of pure reason / Robert B. Pippin. — New Haven ; London : Yale University Press, c1982. — xii,247p ; 25cm
Bibliography: p233-242. — Includes index
ISBN 0-300-02659-5 : £16.50 : CIP rev.
B82-21083

121 — Epistemology *related to* **ethics**

White, Morton. What is and what ought to be done : an essay on ethics and epistemology / Morton White. — New York ; Oxford : Oxford University Press, 1981. — x,131p ; 23cm
Includes index
ISBN 0-19-502916-x : £8.95
Primary classification 170 B82-02987

121 — Experience — *Philosophical perspectives*

Stevenson, Leslie. The metaphysics of experience. — Oxford : Clarendon Press, July 1982. — [120]p
ISBN 0-19-824655-2 : £7.95 : CIP entry
B82-12548

121 — Intentionality — *Philosophical perspectives*

Thought and object : essays on intentionality / edited by Andrew Woodfield. — Oxford : Clarendon, 1981. — xi,316p ; 23cm
Bibliography: p299-309. — Includes index
ISBN 0-19-824606-4 : £16.00 : CIP rev.
B81-34387

121 — Knowledge — *Anthroposophical viewpoints*

Steiner, Rudolf. A theory of knowledge implicit in Goethe's world conception / by Rudolf Steiner. — 3rd ed. — Spring Valley, N.Y. : Anthroposophic Press ; London (38 Museum St., WC1) : Rudolf Steiner Press [[distributor]], 1978, c1968. — xx,131p ; 21cm
Translation of: Grundlinien einer Erkenntnistheorie der Goetheschen Weltanschauung. — Previous ed.: 1968
Unpriced (pbk) B82-05076

121 — Knowledge — *Philosophical perspectives*

Chisholm, Roderick M.. The foundations of knowing / Roderick M. Chisholm. — Brighton : Harvester, 1982. — viii,216p ; 24cm
Includes index
ISBN 0-7108-0373-7 (corrected) : £22.50 : CIP rev. B82-02661

Fichte, Johann Gottlieb. Science of knowledge. — Cambridge : Cambridge University Press, Aug.1982. — [320]p. — (Texts in German philosophy)
Translation of: Wissenschaftslehre
ISBN 0-521-25018-8 (cased) : £20.00 : CIP entry
ISBN 0-521-27050-2 (pbk) : £6.95 B82-26250

Trusted, Jennifer. An introduction to the philosophy of knowledge / Jennifer Trusted. — London : Macmillan, 1981. — xii,271p : ill ; 23cm
Bibliography: p266-267. — Includes index
ISBN 0-333-32296-7 (cased) : Unpriced
ISBN 0-333-32297-5 (pbk) : Unpriced
B82-20927

121 — Knowledge. Philosophical perspectives. Locke, John, *1632-1704*. Essay concerning human understanding — *Critical studies*

Jenkins, John. Understanding Locke. — Edinburgh : Edinburgh University Press, Nov.1982. — [264]p
ISBN 0-85224-442-8 (cased) : £12.00 : CIP entry
ISBN 0-85224-449-5 (pbk) : £6.50 B82-26312

121'.09 — Knowledge. Theories, *to 1981*

Degenhardt, M. A. B.. Education and the value of knowledge. — London : Allen & Unwin, Aug.1982. — [128]p. — (Introductory studies in philosophy of education)
ISBN 0-04-370115-9 (cased) : £7.95 : CIP entry
ISBN 0-04-370116-7 (pbk) : £3.50 B82-15637

121'.092'4 — Knowledge. Theories of Petar II Petrović Njegoš, *Prince-Bishop of Montenegro* — *Serbo-Croatian texts*

Prvulović, Žika Rad.. Njegoševa teorija saznanja i sistem / Žika Rad. Prvulović. — Birmingham : Lazarica, 1981. — 127p ; 18cm
Serbo-Croatian title transliterated. — Bibliography: p121-123. — Includes index
£2.50 (pbk) B82-17011

121'.2 — Other minds. Theories of Wittgenstein, Ludwig

Wittgenstein and the problem of other minds / edited by Harold Morick. — [Atlantic Highlands] : Humanities Press ; [Brighton] : Harvester Press, 1981, c1967. — xxiii,231p ; 22cm
Originally published: New York ; London : McGraw-Hill, 1967. — Bibliography: p227-231
ISBN 0-7108-0346-x (pbk) : £4.95 B82-16144

121'.3 — Man. Perception — *Philosophical perspectives*

Wittgenstein, Ludwig. Remarks on the philosophy of psychology / Ludwig Wittgenstein. — Oxford : Blackwell
Vol.1 / edited by G.E.M. Anscombe and G.H. von Wright ; translated by G.E.M. Anscombe. — 1980. — vi,218p : ill ; 23cm
Parallel German and English text. — Includes index
ISBN 0-631-12541-8 : £16.50 : CIP rev.
Primary classification 153.4 B80-20140

Wittgenstein, Ludwig. Remarks on the philosophy of psychology / Ludwig Wittgenstein. — Oxford : Blackwell
Vol.2 / edited by G.H. Von Wright and Heikki Nyman ; translated by G.G. Luckhardt and M.A.E. Ave. — 1980. — 143[i.e.249]p ; 23cm
Parallel German and English text. — Includes index
ISBN 0-631-12551-5 : £13.50 : CIP rev.
Primary classification 153.4 B80-20141

121'.3 — Reality. Perception by man — *Phenomenological perspectives*

Merleau-Ponty, Maurice. Phenomenology of perception / by M. Merleau-Ponty ; translated from the French by Colin Smith. — London : Routledge & Kegan Paul, 1962 (1981 [printing]). — xxi,466p ; 22cm
Translation of: Phénoménologie de la perception. — Bibliography: p457-462. — Includes index
ISBN 0-7100-0994-1 (pbk) : £7.95 B82-23261

121'.5 — Knowledge. Scepticism — *Philosophical perspectives*

Klein, Peter D. (Peter David). Certainty : a refutation of scepticism / Peter D. Klein. — Brighton : Harvester, 1981. — xiv,242p : ill ; 24cm
Includes index
ISBN 0-7108-0369-9 : £22.50 : CIP rev.
B81-32056

121'.6 — Belief. Rationality & relativism — *Philosophical perspectives*

Rationality and relativism. — Oxford : Blackwell, Sept.1982. — [288]p
ISBN 0-631-12773-9 (cased) : £12.00 : CIP entry
ISBN 0-631-13126-4 (pbk) : £4.95 B82-20280

121'.6 — Belief. Relations with science. Theories, *ca 1800-ca 1930*

Science and belief : from Darwin to Einstein. — Milton Keynes : Open University Press. — (Arts : a third level course)
At head of title: The Open University
Block 4: Modern physics and problems of knowledge / prepared for the Course Team by Paul M. Clark ... [et al.]. — 1981. — 153p : ill,ports ; 30cm. — (A381 ; block 4 (6-9))
Bibliography: p153. — Contents: Unit 6: Einstein : philosophical belief and physical theory — Unit 7: Introduction to quantum theory — Unit 8: Quantum theory ; the Bohr-Einstein debate — Unit 9: Physics and society
ISBN 0-335-11003-7 (pbk) : Unpriced
Also classified at 501 B82-04649

Science and belief : from Darwin to Einstein. — Milton Keynes : Open University Press. — (Arts : a third level course)
At head of title: The Open University
Block 5: The mystery of life / prepared for the Course Team by David Goodman and Robert Olby. — 1981. — 53p : ill,ports ; 30cm. — (A381 ; block 5 (10,11))
Bibliography: p52-53. — Contents: Unit 10: The origins of life : discussions in the later nineteenth century — Unit 11: The nature of life : discovery in the twentieth century
ISBN 0-335-11004-5 (pbk) : Unpriced
Also classified at 501 B82-04650

121′.6 — Inquiry — *Philosophical perspectives*

Rescher, Nicholas. Empirical inquiry / Nicholas Rescher. — London : Athlone Press, 1982. — xii,291p : ill ; 22cm
Originally published: Totowa : Rowman and Littlefield, 1981. — Includes index
ISBN 0-485-30009-5 : £15.00 : CIP rev. B81-36219

121′.68 — Hermeneutics

Ricoeur, Paul. Paul Ricoeur hermeneutics and the human sciences : essays on language, action and interpretation / edited, translated and introduced by John B. Thompson. — Cambridge : Cambridge University Press, 1981. — viii,314p ; 24cm
Translation from the French. — Bibliography: p306-308. — Includes index
ISBN 0-521-23497-2 (cased) : £20.00 : CIP rev.
ISBN 0-521-28002-8 (pbk) : £6.95 B81-35921

Schutz, Alfred. Life forms and meaning structure / Alfred Schutz ; translated, introduced, and annotated by Helmut R. Wagner. — London : Routledge & Kegan Paul, 1982. — vi,217p ; 23cm. — (The International library of phenomenology and moral sciences)
Translation of: Lebensformen und Sinnstruktur. — Includes index
ISBN 0-7100-9201-6 : £11.95 B82-30180

121′.8 — Values — *Philosophical perspectives*

Plato. Hippias Major. — Oxford : Basil Blackwell, June 1982. — [224]p
ISBN 0-631-13091-8 : £10.00 : CIP entry B82-09450

121′.8′05 — Values — *Serials*

The **Tanner** lectures on human values. — 1 (1980)-. — Salt Lake City, Utah : University of Utah Press ; Cambridge : Cambridge University Press, 1980-. — v. ; 25cm
Annual
£12.50 B82-11808

122 — CAUSATION

122 — Karma

Baker, Douglas, *1922-*. Karmic laws : the esoteric philosophy of disease and rebirth. — 2nd ed. — Wellingborough : Aquarian, June 1982. — [96]p
Previous ed.: 1977
ISBN 0-85030-299-4 (pbk) : £2.95 : CIP entry B82-09839

123 — DETERMINISM AND INDETERMINISM

123 — Determinism & free will — *Philosophical perspectives*

Denyer, Nicholas. Time, action & necessity : a proof of free will / Nicholas Denyer. — London : Duckworth, 1981. — 103p ; 22cm
ISBN 0-7156-1530-0 : £8.95 B82-00565

Free will. — Oxford : Oxford University Press, Sept.1982. — [180]p. — (Oxford readings in philosophy)
ISBN 0-19-875054-4 (pbk) : £3.50 : CIP entry B82-18981

126 — THE SELF

126 — Self — *Philosophical perspectives*

Armour, Leslie. The conceptualization of the inner life : a philosophical exploration / by Leslie Armour and Edward T. Bartlett, III. — Atlantic Highlands : Humanities ; Gloucester : distributed by Sutton, c1980. — vii,314p ; 23cm
ISBN 0-391-01759-4 : Unpriced B82-38122

Lewis, Hywel D.. The elusive self : based on the Gifford lectures delivered in the University of Edinburgh / Hywel D. Lewis. — London : Macmillan, 1982. — viii,202p ; 23cm
Includes index
ISBN 0-333-29106-9 : £12.00 B82-28391

The **Mind's** I : fantasies and reflections on self and soul / composed and arranged by Douglas R. Hofstadter and Daniel C. Dennett. — Brighton : Harvester Press, 1981. — vii,501p : ill ; 24cm
Bibliography: p465-482. — Includes index
ISBN 0-7108-0352-4 : £9.95
Also classified at 128′.1 B82-03645

Versfeld, Martin. Our selves / Marthinus Vensfeld. — Cape Town : David Philip ; London : Global [distributor], 1979. — 175p ; 18cm
Bibliography: p174-175
ISBN 0-949968-80-3 (pbk) : £6.80 B82-00090

128 — HUMANKIND

128 — Man

Dürckheim, Karlfried, *Graf von*. Our twofold origin. — London : Allen & Unwin, Nov.1982. — [192]p
Translation of: Vom doppelten Ursprung des Menschen
ISBN 0-04-291017-x : £9.95 : CIP entry B82-27183

Tagger, Joseph. OYDJ & I / by Joseph Tagger. — [Cambridge] ([c/o Diana Gonzaner, 19 Priory Rd., Cambridge]) : [J. Tagger], c1981. — 82p ; 20cm
Unpriced (pbk) B82-08045

128 — Man — *Anthroposophical viewpoints*

Lauer, Hans E.. Aggression and repression in the individual and society / Hans E. Lauer ; translated by K. Castelliz and B. Saunders Davies. — London : Rudolf Steiner Press, c1981. — 111p ; 19cm. — (Pharos books)
Translation of: Aggression und Repression im individuellen und sozialen Bereich. — Bibliography: p110-111
ISBN 0-85440-359-0 (pbk) : £2.95 B82-22949

128 — Man. Philosophical perspectives. Heidegger, Martin. Sein und Zeit — *Critical studies*

Blitz, Mark. Heidegger's Being and time and the possibility of political philosophy / Mark Blitz. — Ithaca ; London : Cornell University Press, 1981. — 260p ; 23cm
Includes index
ISBN 0-8014-1320-6 : £13.75 B82-24374

128′.092′4 — Man. Theories of Weininger, Otto

Mayne, Ellen. Otto Weininger on the character of man : twenty-first Foundation lecture, 1981 / Ellen Mayne. — Ditchling (1 Dymocks Manor, East End La., Ditchling, Sussex) : New Atlantis Foundation, 1982. — 21p ; 22cm
Cover title
Unpriced (pbk) B82-17427

128′.1 — Man. Soul — *Philosophical perspectives*

The **Mind's** I : fantasies and reflections on self and soul / composed and arranged by Douglas R. Hofstadter and Daniel C. Dennett. — Brighton : Harvester Press, 1981. — vii,501p : ill ; 24cm
Bibliography: p465-482. — Includes index
ISBN 0-7108-0352-4 : £9.95
Primary classification 126 B82-03645

128′.2 — Man. Mind *related to* **brain**

Kuhlenbeck, Hartwig. The human brain and its universe / Hartwig Kuhlenbeck ; edited by Joachim Gerlach. — 2nd rev. and enl. ed. — Basel ; London : Karger
Vol.1: The world of natural sciences and its phenomenology. — c1982. — xiii,281p : ill ; 24cm
Previous ed.: published in 1 vol. as Brain and consciousness. 1957. — Bibliography: p265-276. — Includes index
ISBN 3-8055-1817-x : £48.00
Also classified at 612′.82 B82-28702

Kuhlenbeck, Hartwig. The human brain and its universe / Hartwig Kuhlenbeck ; edited by Joachim Gerlach. — 2nd rev. and enl. ed. — Basel ; London : Karger
Vol.2: The brain and its mind. — c1982. — xiii,374p : ill ; 24cm
Previous ed.: published in 1 vol. as Brain and consciousness. 1957. — Bibliography: p347-368. — Includes index
ISBN 3-8055-2403-x : £67.25
Also classified at 612′.82 B82-28703

128′.2 — Mind

Hampden-Turner, Charles. Maps of the mind / [Charles Hampden-Turner]. — London : Mitchell Beazley, c1981. — 224p : ill(some col.) ; 25cm
Bibliography: p213-219. — Includes index
ISBN 0-85533-293-x : £6.95 B82-33572

128′.2 — Mind — *Philosophical perspectives*

Introduction to the philosophy of mind : readings from Descartes to Strawson / edited by Harold Morick. — [Atlantic Highlands] : Humanities Press ; [Brighton] : Harvester Press, 1981, c1970. — xvii,315p : 1ill ; 22cm
Originally published: Glenview, Ill. : Scott, Foresman, 1970. — Bibliography: p309-311. — Includes index
ISBN 0-7108-0341-9 (pbk) : £5.95 B82-16143

McGinn, Colin. The character of mind. — Oxford : Oxford University Press, Oct.1982. — [176]p. — (OPUS)
ISBN 0-19-219171-3 (cased) : £9.95 : CIP entry
ISBN 0-19-289159-6 (pbk) : £3.95 B82-23662

Mind, brain and function : essays in the philosophy of mind. — Brighton : Harvester Press, June 1982. — [208]p. — (Harvester studies in philosophy)
ISBN 0-7108-0435-0 : £18.95 : CIP entry B82-09601

The **Philosophy** of mind / edited by V.C. Chappell. — New York : Dover ; London : Constable, 1981. — ix,178p ; 22cm
Bibliography: p173-178
ISBN 0-486-24212-9 (pbk) : £2.50 B82-29998

Readings in philosophy of psychology. — London : Methuen
Vol.1 / edited by Ned Block. — c1980. — vi,312p ; 26cm
Includes bibliographies and index
ISBN 0-416-74200-9 : £10.95 B82-39129

128′.2′0924 — Man. Mind. Theories of Kant, Immanuel

Ameriks, Karl. Kant's theory of mind : an analysis of the paralogisms of pure reason / Karl Ameriks. — Oxford : Clarendon Press, 1982. — ix,314p ; 23cm
Bibliography: p302-309. — Includes index
ISBN 0-19-824661-7 : £15.00 : CIP rev. B82-01084

128′.4 — Man. Actions — *Philosophical perspectives*

Hampshire, Stuart. Thought and action / by Stuart Hampshire. — New ed. — London : Chatto & Windus, 1982. — 298p ; 23cm
Previous ed.: 1959. — Includes index
ISBN 0-7011-2604-3 : £10.00 : CIP rev. B82-20297

128′.4 — Man. Actions — *Philosophical perspectives — Conference proceedings*

The **Analysis** of action. — Cambridge : Cambridge University Press, July 1982. — [420]p. — (European studies in social psychology)
Conference papers
ISBN 0-521-24229-0 (cased) : £29.50 : CIP entry
ISBN 0-521-28644-1 (pbk) : £9.95 B82-19255

128′.5 — Life — *Theosophical viewpoints*

Adams, D. H. O.. The meaning and purpose of life / D.H.O. Adams. — London (77 Twyford Abbey Rd., NW10 7ET) : [D.H.O. Adams], c1981. — 64p : music ; 21cm
Cover title
Unpriced (pbk) B82-05937

Adams, D. H. O.. The way of harmony : a sensible philosophy for the twentieth century / D.H.O. Adams. — [London] ([77 Twyford Abbey Rd., NW10 7ET]) : [D.H.O. Adams], [c1976]. — 44p ; 22cm
Cover title
Unpriced (pbk) B82-05936

128'.5 — Life — *Theosophical viewpoints continuation*

Steiner, Rudolf. Rosicrucian esotericism / by Rudolf Steiner ; [translated from the German by D.S. Osmond]. — New York : Anthroposophic Press ; London : Rudolf Steiner Press, 1978. — iv,122p ; 21cm
Lectures given at the Fifth Congress of the Federation of European Sections of the Theosophical Society, May 30th and June 12, 1909
ISBN 0-910142-78-5 : £3.50 B82-40811

129 — ORIGIN AND DESTINY OF INDIVIDUAL SOULS

129 — Future life — *Philosophical perspectives*

Badham, Paul. Immortality or extinction? / Paul and Linda Badham. — London : Macmillan, 1982. — ix,146p ; 23cm. — (Library of philosophy and religion)
Bibliography: p142-143. — Includes index
ISBN 0-333-25933-5 : Unpriced B82-28687

129 — Immortality — *Philosophical perspectives*

Chapman, James. Qed, quiz & credo / by James Chapman. — Gravesend (30 Brenchley Ave., Gravesend, Kent) : Qedist Publications, c1981. — 57p ; 15cm
Unpriced (pbk) B82-37432

131 — PARAPSYCHOLOGICAL AND OCCULT TECHNIQUES FOR ACHIEVEMENT OF WELL-BEING, HAPPINESS, SUCCESS

131 — Personal success. Parapsychological aspects

McNeil, Sandra. Psi-kinetic power / by Sandra McNeil. — Wellingborough : Excalibur, 1981, c1980. — 251p : ill ; 22cm
Originally published: West Nyack, N.Y. : Parker, 1980
ISBN 0-85454-081-4 (pbk) : £3.50 : CIP rev. B81-30425

133 — PARAPSYCHOLOGY AND OCCULTISM

133 — Candles. Burning. Occult aspects

Vinci, Leo. The book of practical candle magic / by Leo Vinci ; illustrations by Roger L. Fitzpatrick. — Wellingborough : Aquarian, 1981. — 127p : ill ; 22cm
Includes index
ISBN 0-85030-271-4 (pbk) : £2.95 : CIP rev. B81-20532

133 — Colour. Occult aspects

Kent, Win. The aura and you / Win Kent. — London (33 St. Leonards Court, St. Leonards Rd., East Sheen, SW14 7NG) : International Association of Colour Healers, [1981?]. — 16p : ill ; 26cm
Cover title
Unpriced (pbk) B82-05142

Kent, Win. The living power of colour / Win Kent. — London (33 St. Leonards Court, St. Leonards Rd., East Sheen, SW14 7NG) : International Association of Colour Healers, [1981?]. — 14p ; 26cm
Cover title
Unpriced (pbk) B82-05144

Kent, Win. The mystic wisdom of colour / Win Kent. — London (33 St. Leonards Court, St. Leonards Rd., East Sheen, SW14 7NG) : International Association of Colour Healers, [1981?]. — 14p ; 26cm
Cover title
Unpriced (pbk) B82-05143

133 — Eckankar

Twitchell, Paul. The flute of God / Paul Twitchell. — London (79 Gloucester Rd., SW7 4SS) : Eckankar, U.K. Satsang Society, [1982]. — 184p ; 18cm
Originally published: Menlo Park, Calif. : Illuminated Way Press, 1970. — Includes index
Unpriced (pbk) B82-37956

133 — Gemstones. Occult aspects

Uyldert, Mellie. The magic of precious stones / by Mellie Uyldert ; translated from the Dutch by Transcript. — Wellingborough : Turnstone, 1981. — 160p : ill ; 22cm
Translation of: Verborgen krachten der edelstenen. — Includes index
ISBN 0-85500-138-0 (pbk) : £3.95 : CIP rev. B81-27427

133 — Life. Occult aspects

Alder, Vera Stanley. The finding of the 'Third Eye'. — London : Rider, Sept.1982. — [192]p
Originally published: 1938
ISBN 0-09-149961-5 (pbk) : £2.95 : CIP entry B82-25054

133 — Man. Invisibility. Occult aspects

Richards, Steve. Invisibility : mastering the art of vanishing / by Steve Richards. — Wellingborough : Aquarian, 1982. — 160p : ill ; 22cm
Includes index
ISBN 0-85030-305-2 (cased) : Unpriced : CIP rev.
ISBN 0-85030-281-1 (pbk) : £3.50 B82-06252

133 — Man. Occult aspects

Jayarajah, Aloy. God, man and the universe / Aloy Jayarajah. — Ilfracombe : Stockwell, 1981. — 71p ; 18cm
ISBN 0-7223-1521-x (pbk) : £2.10 B82-06351

133 — Occult practices. Exercises

Knight, Gareth. Occult exercises and practices : gateways to the four 'worlds' of occultism / by Gareth Knight. — Rev., enl., and reset. — Wellingborough : Aquarian, 1982. — 96p : ill ; 18cm
Previous ed.: 1976. — Includes index
ISBN 0-85030-296-x (pbk) : £0.95 : CIP rev. B82-00296

133 — Occult practices. Initiation

Bailey, Alice A.. Initiation, human and solar / by Alice A. Bailey. — New York ; London : Lucis, c1951 (1980 printing). — xv,240p : 1ill ; 20cm
Originally published: New York : Lucifer, 1922. — Includes index
Unpriced (pbk) B82-00941

133 — Occultism

Butler, W. E.. Apprenticed to magic. — Wellingborough : Aquarian Press, Aug.1981. — [112]p
Originally published: 1962
ISBN 0-85030-284-6 (pbk) : £2.95 : CIP entry B81-22608

Regardie, Israel. Foundations of practical magic. — Wellingborough : Aquarian Press, Sept.1982. — [160]p
Originally published: 1979
ISBN 0-85030-315-x : £2.95 : CIP entry B82-21396

Scott, Cyril. The greater awareness : a sequel to An outline of modern occultism / by Cyril Scott. — London : Routledge & Kegan Paul, 1936 (1981 [printing]). — xii,243p ; 19cm
ISBN 0-7100-0953-4 (pbk) : £3.50 B82-07914

Student, A.. The occult and paranormal world : an area where physics and paraphysics, science and religion, meet and merge / A. Student. — Bognor Regis : New Horizon, c1982. — 49p : 1ill ; 21cm
Bibliography: p48
ISBN 0-86116-801-1 : £4.95 B82-22448

Wilson, Robert Anton. The illuminati papers / Robert Anton Wilson. — London : Sphere, 1982, c1980. — ix,149p : ill ; 24cm
Originally published: San Francisco : And/Or Press, 1980
ISBN 0-7221-9225-8 (pbk) : £3.50 B82-24201

133 — Occultism. Meditation

Cooke, Grace. Meditation / Grace Cooke. — 2nd ed. — Liss : White Eagle Publishing Trust, 1965 (1980 [printing]). — 167p ; 18cm
Previous ed.: 1955
ISBN 0-85487-011-3 : £2.75 B82-02835

133 — Occultism. Self-development — *Manuals*

Stuart, Vincent. Changing mind / Vincent G. Stuart. — Boulder ; London : Shambhala, 1981 ; London : Distributed by Routledge & Kegan Paul. — 74p ; 21cm
ISBN 0-87773-206-x : £4.95 B82-03274

133 — Paranormal phenomena

Eysenck, H. J.. Explaining the unexplained : mysteries of the paranormal / Hans J. Eysenck and Carl Sargent. — London : Weidenfeld and Nicolson, c1982. — 192p : ill,ports ; 25cm
Bibliography: p188-189. — Includes index
ISBN 0-297-78068-9 : £9.95 B82-26752

Lethbridge, T. C.. The essential T.C. Lethbridge / edited by Tom Graves and Janet Hoult ; foreword by Colin Wilson. — London : Granada, 1982, c1980. — 267p : ill ; 18cm. — (A Panther book)
Originally published: London : Routledge and Kegan Paul, 1980. — Includes index
ISBN 0-586-05077-9 (pbk) : £1.95 B82-16155

O'Donnell, J. M.. Curiosity won't kill you / J.M. O'Donnell. — Bognor Regis : New Horizon, c1982. — 91p : ill ; 21cm
ISBN 0-86116-036-3 : £3.50
Primary classification 001.9'3 B82-17488

Randall, John L.. Psychokinesis : a study of paranormal forces through the ages / John L. Randall. — London : Souvenir, 1982. — 256p,[8]p of plates : ill,ports ; 23cm
Bibliography: p239-250. — Includes index
ISBN 0-285-62540-3 : £8.95 B82-39072

133 — Paranormal phenomena. Attitudes of society

Evans, Hilary. Intrusions : society and the paranormal / Hilary Evans. — London : Routledge & Kegan Paul, 1982. — x,206p : ill,facsims,ports ; 23cm
Port on inside cover. — Bibliography: p196-201. — Includes index
ISBN 0-7100-0927-5 (pbk) : £5.95 B82-17452

133 — Parapsychology

Alcock, James E.. Parapsychology, science or magic? : a psychological perspective / by James E. Alcock. — Oxford : Pergamon, 1981. — xi,224p ; 26cm. — (Pergamon international library)
Bibliography: p197-211. — Includes index
ISBN 0-08-025773-9 (cased) : Unpriced : CIP rev.
ISBN 0-08-025772-0 (pbk) : £7.25 B81-02083

Dubrov, A. P.. Parapsychology and contemporary science / A.P. Dubrov and V.N. Pushkin. — New York ; London : Consultants Bureau, 1982. — vi,221p : ill ; 26cm
Translation of: Parapsikhologi͡a i sovremennoe estestvoznanie. — Bibliography: p198-214. — Includes index
ISBN 0-306-10973-5 : Unpriced B82-31519

133 — Parapsychology — *Christian viewpoints*

Fryer, C. E. J.. A hand in dialogue. — Cambridge : James Clarke, Dec.1982. — [128]p
ISBN 0-227-67841-9 : £7.50 : CIP entry B82-40346

133 — Supernatural

The **Encyclopedia** of horror / edited by Richard Davis. — London : Octopus, 1981. — 192p : ill(some col.),facsims,ports ; 31cm
Text, ill on lining papers. — List of films: p185-188. — Includes index
ISBN 0-7064-1507-8 : £6.95 B82-03922

133 — Time. Occult aspects

Forman, Joan. The mask of time : the mystery factor in timeslips, precognition and hindsight / Joan Forman. — London : Corgi, 1981, c1978. — 302p ; 18cm
Originally published: London : Macdonald and Jane's, 1978. — Bibliography: p289-292. — Includes index
ISBN 0-552-11823-0 (pbk) : £1.50 B82-04180

133 — Unity. Occult aspects

Seven essays on unity / by Heshmatullah Dowlatshahi (Heshmatussultan) and six members of the New Universal Union. — London : [New Universal Union], 198-?. — 64p : ill ; 19cm
Unpriced (pbk) B82-23114

133′.05 — Occultism — *Serials*

British journal of Ma′at. — Vol.1, no.1 (1982)-. — London (BM Box 8640, WC1N 3XX) : Cosmic Pub. Co., 1982-. — v. : ill ; 22cm
Official organ of: Ordo Occultus Dea
ISSN 0263-385x = British journal of Ma′at : £3.00 per issue B82-25476

Nine worlds : earthly mysteries and cosmic truths. — Issue no.8-. — London (BM/Nine Worlds, WC1N 3XX) : [s.n.], 1982-. — v. ; 33cm
Quarterly. — Continues: Occult world
ISSN 0263-208X = Nine worlds (corrected) : £1.80 per year B82-19861

Prytania. — [Vol.1, no.1] (May 1982)-. — Lowestoft (126 Bevan St., Lowestoft, Suffolk NR32 2AQ) : Biophysical Research, 1982-. — v. : ill ; 30cm
Quarterly
ISSN 0263-5097 = Prytania : £3.00 per year B82-31704

133′.05 — Paranormal phenomena — *Serials*

Common ground : studies at the fringe of human experience. — No.1 (May 1981)-. — Leicester (14 Northfold Rd, Knighton, Leicester) : K. & S. McClure, 1981-. — v. : ill ; 21cm
Quarterly
ISSN 0261-6572 = Common ground : £4.00 per year B82-04914

The **Supernaturalist**. — Issue 1-. — Wickford (c/o A. Collins, 19 St Davids Way, Wickford, Essex SS11 8EX) : Parasearch Organisation, 1981-. — v. : ill ; 21cm
Irregular
ISSN 0262-849x = Supernaturalist : £1.50 B82-13403

133′.07 — Occultism. Organisations. Members. Training

Fortune, Dion. The esoteric orders and their work. — Wellingborough : Aquarian Press, June 1982. — [144]p
ISBN 0-85030-310-9 (pbk) : £3.50 : CIP entry B82-10877

133′.072 — Science. Research — *Sociological perspectives — Study examples: Research into paranormal phenomena*

Collins, H. M.. Frames of meaning : the social construction of extraordinary science / H.M. Collins and T.J. Pinch. — London : Routledge & Kegan Paul, 1982. — x,210p : ill,1plan ; 23cm
Bibliography: p195-204. — Includes index
ISBN 0-7100-9011-0 : £12.50 B82-14738

133′.09′03 — Occultism, *ca 1400-1980*

King, Francis, *1904-*. The rebirth of magic / Francis King and Isabel Sutherland. — [London] : Corgi, 1982. — 217p ; 18cm
ISBN 0-552-11880-x (pbk) : £1.50 B82-14456

133′.09′04 — Occultism, *1900-1982*

Webb, James. The occult establishment. — Glasgow (20 Park Circus, Glasgow G3 6BE) : Richard Drew, Nov.1981. — [544]p
Originally published: La Salle, Ill. : Open Court Publishing Co., 1976
ISBN 0-904002-82-9 : £9.50 : CIP entry B81-30891

133′.092′4 — Occultism. Leadbeater, C. W. — *Biographies*

Tillett, Gregory. The elder brother : a biography of Charles Webster Leadbeater / Gregory Tillett. — London : Routledge & Kegan Paul, 1982. — xii,337p,16p of plates : ill,1facsim,ports ; 25cm
Bibliography: p316-330. — Includes index
ISBN 0-7100-0926-7 : £12.50 B82-30996

133′.092′4 — Occultism — *Personal observations*

Marriott, Sara. From the centre / Sara Marriott. — Findhorn : Findhorn Publications, 1981. — 204p : ill ; 22cm
ISBN 0-905249-47-x (pbk) : £2.75 B82-09519

133′.0951′25 — Hong Kong. Paranormal phenomena — *Case studies*

Emmons, Charles F.. Chinese ghosts and ESP : a study of paranormal beliefs and experiences / by Charles F. Emmons. — Metuchen ; London : Scarecrow, 1982. — ix,297p : ill,1plan,1port ; 23cm
Bibliography: p277-285. — Includes index
ISBN 0-8108-1492-7 : £14.00 B82-22973

133.1 — GHOSTS

133.1 — Ghosts — *For children*

Brett, Bernard. Ghosts, ghouls and spirits / [written by Bernard Brett and Dorothy D. Ward] ; [edited by Dorothy D. Ward] ; [illustrations by Michael Wells Studio]. — London : Marshall Cavendish, 1980. — 126p : ill(some col.),1plan ; 23cm. — (Monsterbacks)
ISBN 0-85685-849-8 (pbk) : £1.95 B82-22935

Brett, Bernard. A young person′s guide to ghosts / Bernard Brett ; with illustrations by the author. — London : Granada, 1981. — 96p : ill ; 18cm. — (A Dragon book)
ISBN 0-583-30466-4 (pbk) : £0.85 B82-09537

133.1′03′21 — Ghosts — *Encyclopaedias*

Haining, Peter. A dictionary of ghosts / by Peter Haining. — London : Hale, 1982. — 270p : ill,facsims,ports ; 23cm
ISBN 0-7091-9622-9 : £9.50 B82-23605

133.1′0941 — Great Britain. Ghosts, *1750-1980* — *For children*

The **Tiswas** book of ghastly ghosts / compiled by Helen Piddock ; illustrated by Daniel Woods. — London : Carousel, 1981. — 95p : ill ; 20cm
ISBN 0-552-54186-9 (pbk) : £0.85 B82-04339

133.1′0941 — Great Britain. Ghosts — *Case studies*

MacKenzie, Andrew. Hauntings and apparitions / Andrew MacKenzie. — London : Heinemann published on behalf of the Society for Psychical Research, 1982. — xv,240p,[16]p of plates : ill,ports ; 23cm
Bibliography: p228-236. — Includes index
ISBN 0-434-44051-5 : £8.50 B82-30650

133.1′09422′7 — Hampshire. Ghosts

Brode, Anthony. Haunted Hampshire / Anthony Brode ; with illustrations by Don Osmond. — Newbury : Countryside Books, 1981. — 93p : ill ; 22cm
Includes index
ISBN 0-905392-11-6 (pbk) : £2.50 B82-06668

133.1′09423′5 — Devon. Ghosts

Underwood, Peter, *1923-*. Ghosts of Devon / Peter Underwood. — Bodmin : Bossiney, 1982. — 112p : ill,ports ; 22cm
Bibliography: p109
ISBN 0-906456-62-2 (pbk) : £1.95 B82-36003

133.1′09424′8 — Warwickshire. Ghosts

Atkins, Meg Elizabeth. Haunted Warwickshire : a gazetteer of ghosts and legends / by Meg Elizabeth Atkins ; photography by Percy G. Moss. — London : Hale, 1981. — 189,[12]p of plates : ill,1map ; 23cm
Bibliography: p181-182. — Includes index
ISBN 0-7091-9131-6 : £8.95 B82-03284

133.1′09428′43 — North Yorkshire. York. Ghosts

Mitchell, John V.. Ghosts of an ancient city / John V. Mitchell ; illustrated by John Brown. — [York] ([c/o Herald Rusholmes, P.O. Box 21, 15 Convey St., York Y01 1YT]) : [Cerialis], [1981]. — 72p : ill,1port ; 20x21cm
Previous ed.: 1974
£2.25 (pbk) B82-09026

133.1′22 — Great Britain. Haunted castles

Ronson, Mark. Haunted castles / Mark Ronson. — [London] : Beaver, 1982. — 159p,[8]p of plates : maps ; 18cm
ISBN 0-600-20481-2 (pbk) : £1.00 B82-25888

133.1′22 — Great Britain. Haunted stately homes — *Visitors′ guides*

Alexander, Marc. Haunted houses you may visit / Marc Alexander. — London : Sphere, 1982. — 184p : 1map ; 18cm
Includes index
ISBN 0-7221-1118-5 (pbk) : £1.50 B82-29175

133.1′22 — United States. Haunted houses

Winer, Richard. More haunted houses / by Richard Winer and Nancy Osborn Ishmael. — Toronto ; London : Bantam, 1981. — 193p,[8]p of plates : ill,ports ; 18cm
Includes index
ISBN 0-553-14243-7 (pbk) : £1.25 B82-04177

133.1′294215 — London. Tower Hamlets *(London Borough)*. **Castles: Tower of London. Ghosts**

Abbott, G.. Ghosts of the Tower of London / G. Abbott. — London : Heinemann, 1980 (1981 [printing]). — 85p : ill,1plan,ports ; 20cm
Bibliography: p85
ISBN 0-434-00595-9 (pbk) : £1.95 B82-27323

133.1′4 — Poltergeists

Wilson, Colin, *1931-*. Poltergeist! : a study in destructive haunting / Colin Wilson. — London : New English Library, 1981. — 382p : 1ill ; 23cm
Bibliography: p365-369. — Includes index
ISBN 0-450-04880-2 : £7.95 : CIP rev. B81-32010

Wilson, Colin, *1931-*. Poltergeist. — London : New English Library, Dec.1982. — [384]p
Originally published: 1981
ISBN 0-450-05452-7 (pbk) : £2.50 : CIP entry B82-30086

133.3 — DIVINATORY ARTS

133.3 — Prophecies, *1555-1566* — *Texts with commentaries*

Houghton-Brown, Geoffrey. The Popes, Rome and the church : according to the oracles of Nostradamus 1555-2055 / by Geoffrey Houghton-Brown. — [London] ([29 Thurloe Sq., S.W.7]) : [G. Houghton-Brown], 1981. — 64p ; 22cm
£2.00 (pbk) B82-10616

133.3 — Prophecies, *ca 1512-1561* — *Texts*

Shipton, *Mother*. [Mother Shipton]. Mother Shipton′s prophecies : the earliest editions / with an introduction. — Maidstone : Mann, 1978 (1979 [printing]). — xxvii,78p : ill ; 17cm
ISBN 0-7041-0076-2 (pbk) : £1.95 B82-01674

133.3 — Psychic phenomena: Divination. Use of crystal balls, magic mirrors & pendulums — *Manuals*

The **Pendulum**, crystal ball and magic mirror : their use in magical practice / taken by Noud van den Eerenbeemt from the instructions of an esoteric Lodge ; introduction by W.N. Schors ; translated from the Dutch by Transcript. — Wellingborough : Aquarian, 1982. — 64p : ill ; 22cm
Translation of: Pendel-, kristal- en speigelmagie
ISBN 0-85030-270-6 (pbk) : Unpriced : CIP rev. B81-35840

133.3 — World events. Prophecies

Lemesurier, Peter. The Armageddon script : prophecy in action / Peter Lemesurier. — Salisbury : Element Books, 1981. — 255p ; 24cm
Bibliography: p254-255. — Includes index
ISBN 0-906540-19-4 : £7.95 B82-39858

133.3′23 — Dowsing

Whitlock, Ralph. Water divining : and other dowsing : a practical guide / Ralph Whitlock. — Newton Abbot : David & Charles, c1982. — 144p : ill ; 23cm
Bibliography: p137-139. — Includes index
ISBN 0-7153-8220-9 : £5.95 : CIP rev. B82-04869

133.3′23 — Radiaesthesia. Use of pendulums

Kent, Win. Pendulum power — is it for you? / Win Kent. — London (33 St. Leonards Court, St. Leonards Rd., East Sheen, SW14 7NG) : International Association of Colour Healers, [1981?]. — 12p ; 26cm
Cover title
Unpriced (pbk) B82-05145

133.3'23'09415 — Ireland. Dowsing
McIvor, John A.. Divining in Ireland / John A. McIvor. — Stillorgon : Gilbert Dalton, 1980. — 63p : ill,1map,1port ; 18cm
ISBN 0-86233-017-3 (pbk) : £1.80 B82-23138

133.3'24 — Fortune-telling
Darlinda. Darlinda : telling the future / foreword by Diana Dors. — Glasgow : Molendinar, 1981. — 196p : ill ; 20cm
ISBN 0-904002-66-7 (pbk) : £2.95 B82-31683

Hill, Douglas. Fortune telling / Douglas Hill ; illustrated by John Beswick. — London : Hamlyn, 1972 (1982 [printing]). — 159p : col.ill,col.ports ; 19cm
Bibliography: p156. — Includes index
ISBN 0-600-33791-x (cased) : £2.99
ISBN 0-600-32835-x (pbk) : £1.75 B82-37049

133.3'2424 — Tarot cards
Waite, Arthur Edward. The key to the tarot : being fragments of a secret tradition under the veil of divination / Arthur Edward Waite. — [New] ed. — London : Rider, 1982. — xxii,170p ; 18cm
Previous ed.: 1972. — Bibliography: p151-170
ISBN 0-09-149571-7 (pbk) : £1.95 B82-31358

133.3'2424 — Tarot cards. Major arcana. Meaning
Wirth, Oswald. Introduction to the study of the Tarot / by Oswald Wirth ; translated from the French by Transcript. — Wellingborough : Aquarian, 1981. — 62p : ill ; 22cm
Translaton of: L'etude du Tarot
ISBN 0-85030-263-3 (pbk) : £2.25 : CIP rev. B81-14901

133.3'2429 — Fortune-telling. Use of playing cards — *Manuals*
Dee, Nerys. Fortune-telling by playing cards : a new guide to the ancient art of cartomancy / by Nerys Dee. — Wellingborough : Aquarian, 1982. — 159p : ill ; 22cm
Includes index
ISBN 0-85030-266-8 (pbk : corrected) : £3.50 : CIP rev. B82-04974

133.3'3 — Fortune-telling. Use of mah-jongg — *Manuals*
Walters, Derek. Your future revealed by the Mah Jongg / Derek Walters. — Wellingborough : Aquarian, 1982. — 192p : ill ; 22cm
Bibliography: p189-190. — Includes index
ISBN 0-85030-290-0 (pbk) : £4.50 : CIP rev. B82-13083

133.3'3'0321 — Symbolism — *Encyclopaedias*
Chetwynd, Tom. Dictionary of symbols / Tom Chetwynd. — London : Granada, 1982. — xv,459p : ill ; 20cm. — (A Paladin book)
Includes index
ISBN 0-586-08351-0 (pbk) : £2.95 B82-36665

133.3'33 — Feng-shui
Skinner, Stephen. The living earth manual of feng-shui : Chinese geomancy / Stephen Skinner. — London : Routledge & Kegan Paul, 1982. — xii,129p : ill ; 22cm
Includes Chinese words (transliterated) and glossary. — Bibliography: p122-123. — Includes index
ISBN 0-7100-9077-3 (pbk) : £4.95 B82-37013

133.4 — MAGIC, WITCHCRAFT, DEMONOLOGY

133.4'23 — Werewolves — *For children*
Brett, Bernard. Werewolves : and other weird creatures / [written by Bernard Brett and Dorothy D. Ward] ; [edited by Dorothy D. Ward] ; [illustrations by Michael Wells Studio]. — London : Marshall Cavendish, 1980. — 127p : ill(some col.) ; 22cm. — (Monsterbacks)
ISBN 0-85685-846-3 (pbk) : Unpriced B82-22934

133.4'26'0924 — British Columbia. Victoria. Demonic possession — *Childhood reminiscences*
Smith, Michelle. Michelle remembers / Michelle Smith and Lawrence Pazder. — London : Sphere, 1981, c1980 (1982 [printing]). — xix,298p,[8]p of plates : ill,ports ; 18cm
Originally published: New York : Congdon & Lattes, 1980
ISBN 0-7221-7958-8 (pbk) : £1.75 B82-16577

133.4'3 — Magic & witchcraft — *For children*
Brett, Bernard. A young person's guide to witchcraft / Bernard Brett ; with illustrations by the author. — London : Granada, 1981. — 124p : ill ; 18cm. — (A Dragon book)
ISBN 0-583-30465-6 (pbk) : £0.85 B82-00793

133.4'3 — Magic — *Manuals*
Green, Marian. Magic for the Aquarian age. — Wellingborough : Aquarian Press, Feb.1983. — [160]p
ISBN 0-85030-318-4 (pbk) : £3.95 : CIP entry B82-39466

133.4'3 — Magic. Rituals
Ashcroft-Nowicki, Dolores. First steps in ritual. — Wellingborough : Aquarian Press, Aug.1982. — [96]p
ISBN 0-85030-314-1 (pbk) : £2.95 : CIP entry B82-15851

133.4'3 — Magic, *to ca 1912*
Lévi, Éliphas. The history of magic. — London : Rider, Sept.1982. — [384]p
Translation of: Histoire de la magie. — Originally published: 1913
ISBN 0-09-150041-9 (pbk) : £2.95 : CIP entry B82-19816

133.4'3 — Witchcraft
Haining, Peter. Witchcraft and black magic / Peter Haining ; illustrated by Jan Parker. — London : Hamlyn, 1971 (1982 [printing]), 1982. — 159p : col.ill,col.ports ; 19cm
Bibliography: p156. — Includes index
ISBN 0-600-33789-8 (cased) : £2.99
ISBN 0-600-39221-x (pbk) : £1.75 B82-36013

Jong, Erica. Witches. — London : Granada, Apr.1982. — [168]p
ISBN 0-246-11805-9 : £12.50 : CIP entry B82-04319

Witchcraft and sorcery : selected readings / edited by Max Marwick. — 2nd ed. — Harmondsworth : Penguin, 1982. — 496p ; 20cm
Previous ed.: 1970. — Bibliography: p477-479. — Includes index
ISBN 0-14-080457-9 (pbk) : £4.95 B82-23221

133.4'3'0932 — Ancient Egyptian magic
Farr, Florence. Egyptian magic / by Florence Farr ; introduction by Timothy d'Arch Smith. — Wellingborough : Aquarian Press, 1982. — 85p : ill ; 22cm. — (Studies in hermetic tradition)
Originally published in Westcott's Collectanea Hermetica series 1896. — Bibliography: pxvi-xvii
ISBN 0-85030-277-3 (pbk) : Unpriced : CIP rev. B81-36971

133.4'3'09415 — Ireland. Witchcraft
Seymour, St. John D.. Irish witchcraft and demonology. — Kilkenny : Roberts Books, Dec.1981. — [288]p
Originally published: Dublin : Hodges, Figgis & Co., 1913
ISBN 0-907561-04-7 (pbk) : CIP entry B81-34219

133.4'3'095951 — Peninsular Malaysian magic
Endicott, Kirk Michael. An analysis of Malay magic / Kirk Michael Endicott. — Kuala Lumpur ; Oxford : Oxford University Press, 1970 (1981 [printing]). — viii,188p,[1]leaf of plates : 1ill ; 22cm. — (Oxford in Asia paperbacks)
Bibliography: p180-183. — Includes index
ISBN 0-19-582513-6 (pbk) : £6.75 B82-31502

133.5 — ASTROLOGY

133.5 — Astrology
Anrias, David. Through the eyes of the masters : meditations and portraits / by David Anrias ; with an introduction by the author of "The initiate", etc.. — 3rd ed. — London : Routledge & Kegan Paul, 1947 (1980 [printing]). — xvi,76p,[9]leaves of plates : 1ill,ports ; 21cm
Previous ed.: 1936
ISBN 0-7100-1016-8 (cased) : £3.75
ISBN 0-7100-0701-9 (pbk) : £2.50 B82-13744

Eysenck, H. J.. Astrology : science or superstition. — London : Maurice Temple Smith, Jan.1982. — [288]p
ISBN 0-85117-214-8 : £9.00 : CIP entry B81-33833

Ledbury, John. Introduction to astrology / John Ledbury. — [London] ([BCM-SCL Quest, WC1N 3XX]) : [Marian Green], [c1981]. — 36p : ill ; 26cm
Unpriced (pbk) B82-12221

Lind, Ingrid. Astrologically speaking / by Ingrid Lind. — Romford : L.N. Fowler, c1981. — 267p : ill ; 23cm
ISBN 0-85243-366-2 (pbk) : £6.95 B82-20095

MacLeod, Charlotte. Trusting : astrology for sceptics / Charlotte MacLeod ; illustrated by the author. — Wellingborough : Turnstone, 1973, c1972 (1980 [printing]). — viii,308p : ill ; 22cm
Originally published: New York : Macmillan, 1972 ; Wellingborough : Turnstone, 1973. — Bibliography: p296-297. — Includes index
ISBN 0-85500-106-2 (pbk) : Unpriced B82-07706

Rathgeb, Marlene Masini. Success signs : a practical astrological guide to career fulfilment / Marlene Masini Rathgeb. — London : New English Library, 1982, c1981. — x,245p ; 22cm
Originally published: New York : St. Martin's Press, 1981
ISBN 0-450-05353-9 (pbk) : £2.25 : CIP rev. B81-37582

Sepharial. [The manual of astrology in four books]. The manual of astrology / by Sepharial. — London : Foulsham, c1979. — viii,228p : ill ; 23cm
Originally published: 1962
ISBN 0-572-01029-x : £5.50 B82-25200

Seymour-Smith, Martin. The new astrologer / Martin Seymour-Smith. — London : Sidgwick & Jackson, 1981. — 320p : ill,ports ; 26cm
Includes index
ISBN 0-283-98758-8 : £10.00 B82-08062

133.5 — Astrology — *Manuals*
Sakoian, Frances. The astrologer's handbook / Frances Sakoian and Louis S. Acker. — Harmondsworth : Penguin, 1981, c1973. — xiv,461p : ill ; 20cm
Originally published: New York : Harper and Row, 1973 ; London : P. Davies, 1974. — Includes index
ISBN 0-14-005336-0 (pbk) : £2.50 B82-07293

Thornton, Penny. Synastry : a comprehensive guide to the astrology of relationships / by Penny Thornton. — Wellingborough : Aquarian, 1982. — 157p : ill ; 22cm. — (An Aquarian astrology handbook)
Bibliography: p159. — Includes index
ISBN 0-85030-276-5 (pbk) : £3.95 : CIP rev. B82-13082

133.5'09 — Astrology, *to 1981*
Arthur, Hugh. Astrology / Hugh Arthur. — Feltham : Hamlyn, 1982. — ill(some col.),charts ; 18cm. — (Hamlyn all-colour paperbacks)
Includes index
ISBN 0-600-30274-1 (pbk) : £1.75 B82-24315

133.5'09 — Astrology, *to 1981 — For schools*
Gilchrist, Cherry. Astrology / Cherry Gilchrist. — London : Batsford Academic and Educational, 1982. — 71p : ill,facsims,ports ; 26cm. — (History in focus)
Bibliography: p70. — Includes index
ISBN 0-7134-3543-7 : £5.95 B82-22246

133.5'0951 — Chinese astrology
Lau, Theodora. The handbook of Chinese horoscopes / by Theodora Lau ; calligraphy by Kenneth Lau. — London : Arrow, 1981, c1979. — xi,314p : ill ; 18cm
Originally published: London : Souvenir, 1979
ISBN 0-09-924690-2 (pbk) : £1.95 B82-08313

133.5′0951 — Chinese astrology *continuation*

Poulson, Derek. The way to Chinese astrology. — London : Unwin Paperbacks, Dec.1982. — [176]p
ISBN 0-04-133010-2 : £5.50 : CIP entry B82-29860

Wilhelm, Hans. Hans Wilhelm′s Chinese horoscopes. — London : Pan, 1980 (1981 printing). — 205p : ill ; 20cm
ISBN 0-330-26209-2 (pbk) : £1.50 B82-10741

133.5′2 — Signs of the zodiac

Wilhelm, Hans. Hans Wilhelm′s fun signs : the most accurate zodiac guide ever drawn. — London : Pan, 1981. — 203p : ill ; 20cm
ISBN 0-330-26557-1 (pbk) : £1.50 B82-08257

133.5′2 — Signs of the zodiac — *Poems*

Steiner, Rudolf. Twelve cosmic moods / Rudolf Steiner ; [English version H. Falck-Ytter] ; [design, layout and calligraphy Rae Wilmot]. — [Bristol?] ([6 Hillside, Cotham, Bristol 6]) : [R. Wilmot], c1982. — [30]p ; 21cm
Translation of: Zwölf Stimmungen. — Parallel German text and English translation. — Limited ed. of 500 copies
Unpriced (pbk) B82-40501

133.5′4 — Astrological predictions — *Horoscopes*

Acora, *Gypsy*. Your wheel of fortune / Gypsy Acora. — Bodmin : Bossiney, c1981. — 46p : ill,ports ; 21cm
Cover title
ISBN 0-906456-58-4 (pbk) : £0.60 B82-20337

Freeman, Martin. Forecasting by astrology. — Wellingborough : Aquarian, Nov.1982. — [128]p
ISBN 0-85030-297-8 (pbk) : £3.95 : CIP entry B82-26415

Paterson, Sarah. Superstars : star signs for the 80s / Sarah Paterson ; drawings by Julie Smith. — London : Elm Tree, 1982. — 195p : ill ; 23cm
ISBN 0-241-10797-0 : £6.95 : CIP rev. B82-14363

Penn, June. Astrology mirror : your stars in 1982 : a month-by-month, sign-by-sign guide to the year ahead / by June Penn. — London : Mirror Books, 1981. — 26p : ill(some col.),ports ; 36cm. — (A Daily Mirror astrology special)
ISBN 0-85939-273-2 (unbound) : £0.50 B82-09023

Petrie, Ann. Everything you ever wanted to know about astrology but thought you shouldn′t ask. — London : Eyre Methuen, July 1981. — [192]p
ISBN 0-413-48360-6 : £6.50 : CIP entry B81-13870

Petrie, Ann. Everything you ever wanted to know about astrology but thought you shouldn′t ask / Ann Petrie. — London : Methuen, 1982, c1981. — 181p : ill ; 20cm
Originally published: London : Eyre Methuen, 1981
ISBN 0-413-50500-6 (pbk) : £1.50 B82-33994

Tracey, Kim. Predictions 1983 / Kim Tracey. — London : Sphere, 1982. — ix,116p ; 18cm
ISBN 0-7221-8563-4 (pbk) : £1.25 B82-39058

133.5′4 — Astrological predictions. Horoscopes. Interpretation — *Manuals*

Freeman, Martin. How to interpret a birth chart : a guide to the analysis and synthesis of astrological charts / by Martin Freeman. — Wellingborough : Aquarian, 1981. — 128p : ill ; 22cm. — (An Aquarian astrology handbook)
Includes index
ISBN 0-85030-249-8 (pbk) : £2.95 : CIP rev. B81-19181

133.5′5 — Astrology. Ephemerides — *Texts*

The **Concise** planetary ephemeris for 1900 to 1950 A.D. at midnight : given at midnight ephemeris time in the true longitude and true declination coordinates of date. — Medford, Mass. : Hieratic Publishing ; Romford : Distributed by Fowler, c1979. — [318]p ; 24cm
English text, introduction in English, French, Spanish, Italian and German
ISBN 0-915820-05-6 (cased) : Unpriced
ISBN 0-915820-06-4 (pbk) : Unpriced B82-21606

133.5′81554 — Young persons. Development — *Horoscopes* — *For parents*

King, Teri. Your child and the zodiac / Teri King. — London : Sphere, 1982, c1980. — x,272p ; 18cm
Originally published: London : Angus and Robertson, 1980
ISBN 0-7221-5234-5 (pbk) : £1.50 B82-36549

133.5′83054 — Women. Interpersonal relationships — *Horoscopes*

Bennett, Judith. Sex signs : every woman′s astrological and psychological guide to love, men, sex, anger and personal power / Judith Bennett. — London : Pan in association with Macmillan, 1981, c1980. — 481p : ill ; 18cm. — (Pan original)
Originally published: New York : St. Martin′s Press, 1980
ISBN 0-330-26500-8 (pbk) : £1.95 B82-01598

133.5′830681 — Marriage & divorce — *Horoscopes*

King, Teri. Marriage divorce & astrology / by Teri King. — London : Allison & Busby, 1982. — viii,152p : ill ; 23cm
ISBN 0-85031-465-8 : £6.95 : CIP rev. B82-11088

133.5′8574 — Astrology. Biochemical aspects

Sawtell, Vanda. Astrology and biochemistry. — Rev., enl., and reset ed. — Wellingborough : Thorsons, Oct.1982. — [96]p
Previous ed.: London : Health Science Press, 1947
ISBN 0-7225-0778-x (pbk) : £0.95 : CIP entry B82-24243

133.6 — PALMISTRY

133.6 — Sex relations. Prediction. Use of palmistry

Shap, Mark. Am I a good lover? : the answer is in the palm of your hand / by Mark Shap & Alan Kahn ; photographs by Marili Forastieri. — London : W.H. Allen, 1981. — [62]p : ill ; 19x26cm. — (A Star book)
Originally published: New York : St Martin′s Press, 1981
ISBN 0-352-31059-6 (pbk) : £2.95 B82-03043

133.8 — PSYCHIC PHENOMENA

133.8 — Man. Psychic powers. Development — *Manuals*

McNeil, Sandra. Your super, natural mind / by Sandra McNeil. — London : Angus & Robertson, 1981. — 186p : ill ; 24cm. — (A Nicholson Press book)
Originally published: Toronto : Methuen, 1981. — Includes index
ISBN 0-207-95983-8 (cased) : Unpriced
ISBN 0-207-95984-6 (pbk) : Unpriced B82-18340

133.8 — Man. Psychic powers. Induction. Applications of hypnotism

Edmunds, Simeon. The psychic power of hypnosis : paranormal abilities and the hypnotic state / by Simeon Edmunds. — 2nd ed. — Wellingborough : Aquarian, 1982. — 96p ; 18cm
Previous ed.: 1968. — Includes index
ISBN 0-85030-291-9 (pbk) : £0.95 B82-00388

133.8′072 — Psychic phenomena. Research, *1880-1982*

Psychical research. — Wellingborough : Aquarian, Sept.1982. — [320]p
ISBN 0-85030-316-8 (pbk) : £5.95 : CIP entry B82-20485

133.8′072041 — Great Britain. Psychic phenomena. Research organisations: Society for Psychical Research, *to 1982*

Haynes, Renée. The Society for Psychical Research 1882-1982 : a history / Renée Haynes. — London : Macdonald, 1982. — xv,240p ; 23cm
Includes index
ISBN 0-356-07875-2 : £7.95 B82-37223

133.8′8′0724 — United States. Psychokinesis. Research organisations: SORRAT. Experiments, *1961-1981*

Richards, John Thomas. SORRAT : a history of the Neihardt psychokinesis experiments, 1961-1981 / by John Thomas Richards. — Metuchen ; London : Scarecrow, 1982. — xiv,338p,[2]leaves of plates : ill,ports ; 23cm
Bibliography: p312-323. — Includes index
ISBN 0-8108-1491-9 : £14.00 B82-29264

133.9 — SPIRITUALISM

133.9 — Astral projection

Blackmore, Susan J.. Beyond the body : an investigation of out-of-the-body experiences / Susan J. Blackmore. — London : Heinemann published on behalf of the Society for Psychical Research, 1982. — xv,271p,[16]p of plates : ill ; 23cm
Bibliography: p253-264. — Includes index
ISBN 0-434-07470-5 : £8.50 B82-30651

Mitchell, Janet Lee. Out-of-body experiences : a handbook / by Janet Lee Mitchell. — Jefferson, N.C. ; London : McFarland, 1981. — xi,128p ; 24cm
Bibliography: p115-124 . — Includes index
ISBN 0-89950-031-5 : £9.75 B82-11627

133.9 — Astral projection — *Personal observations*

Sculthorp, Frederick C.. Excursions to the spirit world : a report of personal experiences during conscious astral projections / by Frederick C. Sculthorp ; with an introduction and a short survey of the subject by Karl E. Müller. — 2nd ed. — London : Greater World Association Trust, 1969 (1981 [printing]). — 158p ; 19cm
Previous ed.: London : Almorris, 1961
ISBN 0-900413-29-8 (pbk) : £2.25 B82-38365

133.9 — Spiritualism

Doyle, *Sir* **Arthur Conan**. The new revelation ; and, The vital message / by Arthur Conan Doyle. — London : Psychic Press, 1981. — 163p,[2]p of plates : ill,1facsim,ports ; 20cm
ISBN 0-85384-056-3 : £4.50 B82-19425

133.9 — Spiritualism — *Christian viewpoints*

Findlay, Robert. One tree of the wood : a justification for good mediumship within the Christian Churches / by Robert Findlay ... of the Churches′ Fellowship for Psychical and Spiritual Studies (Scotland). — [Alexandria] ([Boturich, Alexandria, Dunbartonshire, G83 8LX]) : [R. Findlay], [1981]. — 8p ; 21cm
£0.20 (pbk) B82-24381

Findlay, Robert. The parable of the rope and the river : a talk given to the Bournemouth branch of the Churches′ Fellowship for Psychical and Spiritual Studies on Sat. 2 May 1981 / by Robert Findlay ... of the CFPSS (Scotland). — Alexandria (Boturich, Alexandria, Dunbartonshire, G83 8LX) : R. Findlay, [1981]. — 32p ; 21cm
Bibliography: p25-26
£0.20 (pbk) B82-24380

133.9′01′3 — Psychic phenomena: Group reincarnation

Guirdham, Arthur. We are one another : a record of group reincarnation / by Arthur Guirdham. — Wellingborough : Turnstone, 1982, c1974. — 227p,[2]p of plates : ill ; 22cm
Originally published: Jersey : Neville Spearman, 1974
ISBN 0-85500-166-6 (pbk) : £3.95 : CIP rev. B82-13143

133.9'01'3 — Psychic phenomena: Reincarnation

Brennan, J. H.. Reincarnation : five keys to past lives / by J.H. Brennan. — 2nd ed., rev., enl. and reset. — Wellingborough : Aquarian Press, c1981. — 94p ; 18cm
Previous ed.: published as Five keys to past lives, 1971. — Includes index
ISBN 0-85030-275-7 (pbk) : £0.95 : CIP rev. B81-15924

133.9'01'3 — Psychic phenomena: Reincarnation — *Case studies*

Guirdham, Arthur. The Cathars and reincarnation : the record of a past life in thirteenth-century France / by Arthur Guirdham. — Wellingborough : Turnstone, 1982, c1970. — 207p : ill ; 22cm
Originally published: London : Spearman, 1970. — Bibliography: p199-204. — Includes index
ISBN 0-85500-165-8 (pbk) : £3.95 : CIP rev. B82-13142

133.9'092'4 — Spiritualism — *Personal observations*

Iba, Zaid. A kalox marvellous yawn / Zaid Iba. — Bognor Regis : New Horizon, c1981. — 281p ; 21cm
Bibliography: p1-4
ISBN 0-86116-144-0 : £5.50 B82-05456

133.9'1'0924 — Spiritualism. Mediums. Home, Daniel Dunglas — *Biographies*

Jenkins, Elizabeth. The shadow and the light : a defence of Daniel Dunglas Home, the medium. — London : Hamilton, Nov.1982. — [352]p
ISBN 0-241-10892-6 : £12.95 : CIP entry B82-27375

133.9'1'0924 — Spiritualism. Mediums: Stokes, Doris — *Biographies*

Stokes, Doris. More voices in my ear / Doris Stokes with Linda Dearsley. — London : Macdonald Futura, 1981. — 223p,[8]p of plates : ill,ports ; 18cm. — (A Futura book)
ISBN 0-7088-2100-6 (pbk) : £1.50 B82-00521

Stokes, Doris. More voices in my ear : the autobiography of a medium / Doris Stokes and Linda Dearsley. — Henley on Thames : Aidan Ellis, 1981. — 223p,[8]p of plates : ill,ports ; 23cm
ISBN 0-85628-105-0 : £6.95 : CIP rev. B81-14913

133.9'3 — Scotland. Grampian Region. Findhorn. Occult communities: Findhorn Foundation. Communication with extraterrestrial life — *Personal observations*

Maclean, Dorothy. To hear the angels sing : an odyssey of co-creation with the devic kingdom / Dorothy Maclean. — Forres : Findhorn, 1980. — xiii,217p : ill,ports ; 22cm
ISBN 0-905249-42-9 (pbk) : £2.50 B82-01678

133.9'3 — Spiritualism. Automatic communication — *Texts*

A **World** within a world : X-7 reporting : transmissions from Russia on the theory and practice of solar light radiations by the group known as X-7. — St. Helier : Spearman, 1981, c1979. — 121p ; 23cm
Originally published: Forres : Findhorn, 1979
ISBN 0-85978-096-1 (cased) : £4.95
ISBN 0-85978-055-4 (pbk) : Unpriced B82-25003

133.9'3 — Spiritualism. Communication — *Personal observations*

Stevenson, Victoria. [The triumph of love]. Love after death : her unique story of communication beyond the grave / Victoria Stevenson. — [London] : Corgi, 1981, c1980. — 124p ; 18cm
Originally published: London : Arlington, 1980
ISBN 0-552-11860-5 (pbk) : £1.25 B82-14448

Wheatley, J. B.. Spiritual realms : the after life experiences of a lawyer / by J.B. Wheatley ; foreword by P.D. Rommaynne. — London : Greater World Association Trust, c1981. — 124p ; 19cm
ISBN 0-900413-31-x (pbk) : £2.95 B82-14171

133.9'3 — Spiritualism. Communication — *Texts*

Cleeve, Brian. The seven mansions / Brian Cleeve. — London : Watkins, c1980. — 195p ; 21cm
Unpriced (pbk) B82-20977

Lascelles, *Dr. (Spirit)*. The magic invisible : based on the teachings of Dr Lascelles received through his medium the late C.A. Simpson / edited and collated by Stanley King. — Maidstone (Addington Park, Maidstone, Kent ME19 5BL) : Seekers Trust, c1982. — 159p ; 19cm
Unpriced (pbk) B82-39404

Osiris *(Spirit)*. The book of truth, or, The voice of Osiris. — 5th ed. / inspirationally dictated through El Eros (H.C. Randall-Stevens). — London (La Maison de Leoville, St. Ouen, Jersey, Channel Islands) : Knights Templars of Aquarius, 1976. — 1v.(various pagings) : ill,1map ; 25cm
Previous ed.: 196-?. — Includes index. — With: The teachings of Osiris / with commentary inspirationally dictated by the Master Adolemaiu through El Eros (H.C. Randall-Stevens). 2nd. augm. ed. Previous ed.: 1958
Unpriced B82-31275

Randall-Stevens, H. C.. Six inspirational stories / by H.C. and Margaret Randall-Stevens (El Eros - El Erua). — Jersey (La Maison de Leoville, St. Ouen, Jersey, Channel Islands) : Knights Templars of Aquarius, 1982. — 58p ; 22cm
Unpriced (pbk) B82-31276

White Eagle *(Spirit)*. The path of the soul : the great initiations of every man / White Eagle. — Liss : White Eagle Publishing Trust, 1959 (1975 [printing]). — 79p ; 20cm
ISBN 0-85487-020-2 : £0.85 B82-02838

White Eagle *(Spirit)*. The way of the Sun. — Liss : White Eagle Publishing Trust, Nov.1982. — [128]p
ISBN 0-85487-055-5 : £3.50 : CIP entry B82-29143

135 — DREAMS AND THE MYSTIC TRADITIONS

135'.4 — Cabala

Fortune, Dion. The mystical qabalah / by Dion Fortune. — London : E. Benn, 1958, c1957 (1980 [printing]). — viii,327p : ill ; 23cm
Originally published: London : Williams and Norgate, 1935. — Includes index
ISBN 0-510-41001-4 : £6.50 : CIP rev. B79-18045

Lévi, Éliphas. The book of splendours. — Wellingborough : Aquarian Press, Sept.1981. — [192]p
Translation of: Le livre des splendeurs. — Originally published: 1973
ISBN 0-85030-245-5 (pbk) : £3.50 : CIP entry B81-20472

Lévi, Éliphas. The great secret. — Wellingborough : Aquarian Press, Sept.1981. — [192]p
Translation of: Le grand arcane. — Originally published: Wellingborough : Thorsons, 1975
ISBN 0-85030-243-9 (pbk) : £3.50 : CIP entry B81-20471

Richardson, Alan, *1951-*. An introduction to the mystical qabalah / by Alan Richardson. — 2nd ed., rev., enl. and reset. — Wellingborough : Aquarian Press, c1981. — 94p : ill ; 18cm
Previous ed.: 1974
ISBN 0-85030-264-1 (pbk) : £0.95 : CIP rev. B81-24677

Stirling, William. The canon : an exposition of the pagan mystery perpetuated in the Cabala as the rule of all the arts / William Stirling ; preface by R.B. Cunninghame Graham. — 3rd ed. / foreword by John Michell. — London : Research into Lost Knowledge Organisation, 1981. — xxii,409p : ill ; 22cm
Previous ed.: London : Garnstone, 1974. — Includes index
ISBN 0-902103-07-5 (pbk) : Unpriced B82-03518

135'.4 — Occult practices. Initiation. Cabalistic interpretations

Perkins, Keith. Egyptian life and the tree of life / by Keith Perkins and Karen Johnson. — London (25 Circle Gardens, Merton Park, SW1 3JX) : International Order of Kabbalists, [1982?]. — [9]p ; 30cm
Unpriced (pbk) B82-22201

135'.43 — Rosicrucianism

Bernard, Raymond. The invisible empire / by Raymond Bernard. — 3rd ed. — London (181A Lavender Hill, SW11 5TE) : Francis Bacon Lodge, 1982. — ii,74p : ill,1map ; 22cm
Translated from the French. — Previous ed.: 1981
Unpriced (pbk) B82-34054

Bernard, Raymond. The secret houses of the Rose-Croix / by Raymond Bernard. — London (181A Lavender Hill, SW11 5TE) : Francis Bacon Lodge, 1982. — ii,78p ; 22cm
Translated from the French. — Previous ed.: 1982
Unpriced (pbk) B82-34051

Bernard, Raymond. A secret meeting in Rome / by Raymond Bernard. — 4th ed. — London (181A Lavender Hill, SW11 5TE) : Francis Bacon Lodge, 1982. — 11p ; 22cm
Translated from the French. — Previous ed.: 1981
Unpriced (pbk) B82-34052

Bernard, Raymond. Strange encounters / by Raymond Bernard. — London (181A Lavender Hill, SW11 5TE) : Francis Bacon Lodge, 1982. — ii,38p ; 22cm
Translated from the French. — Previous ed.: 1981
Unpriced (pbk) B82-34053

Lewis, H. Spencer. The divinity of man / by H. Spencer Lewis. — 2nd ed. — London (181A Lavender Hill, SW11 5TE) : Francis Bacon Lodge, 1982. — iv,38p ; 21cm
Previous ed.: 1965
Unpriced (pbk) B82-34050

135'.43 — Rosicrucianism. Andreae, Johann Valentin. Chymical wedding of Christian Rosenkreutz — *Critical studies*

Stok, Hans van der. Contemplations on the chymical wedding of Christian Rosenkreutz / Hans van der Stok. — Whitby : Camphill Press on behalf of the Association of Camphill Communities (in Britain), 1981. — 55p : ill ; 19cm
ISBN 0-904145-31-x (pbk) : Unpriced B82-26669

137 — ANALYTIC AND DIVINATORY GRAPHOLOGY

137 — Graphology — *Manuals*

West, Peter, *1939-*. Graphology : understanding what handwriting reveals / by Peter West. — Wellingborough : Aquarian Press, 1981. — 95p : ill,facsim ; 18cm
Includes index
ISBN 0-85030-260-9 (pbk) : £0.95 : CIP rev. B81-18093

140 — PHILOSOPHICAL VIEWPOINTS

141 — Philosophy. Idealism

Foster, John, *1941 May 5-*. The case for idealism / John Foster. — London : Routledge & Kegan Paul, 1982. — ix,309p : ill ; 23cm. — (International library of philosophy)
Includes index
ISBN 0-7100-9019-6 : £12.50 B82-30181

141 — Philosophy. Idealism *continuation*

Idealism past and present / edited by Godfrey Vesey. — Cambridge : Cambridge University Press, c1982. — 290p ; 24cm. — (Royal Institute of Philosphy lecture series ; 13)
'Supplement to Philosophy'. — Includes index
ISBN 0-521-28905-x (pbk) : Unpriced B82-32020

141'.3'0974 — New England. Transcendentalism, *1830-1850*

Rose, Anne C.. Transcendentalism as a social movement, 1830-1850 / Anne C. Rose. — New Haven ; London : Yale University Press, c1981. — xii,269p ; 25cm
Bibliography: p245-258. — Includes index
ISBN 0-300-02587-4 : Unpriced : CIP rev. B81-35028

142'.7 — Phenomenology

Husserl, Edmund. Edmund Husserl : phenomenology and the foundations of the sciences. — The Hague ; London : Nijhoff. — (Edmund Husserl collected works ; v.1)
3rd bk.: Ideas pertaining to a pure phenomenology and to a phenomenological philosophy / translated by Ted E. Klein and William E. Pohl. — 1980. — xviii,130p ; 25cm
Translation of: Edmund Husserl, Ideen zu einer reinen Phänomenologie und phänomenologischen Philosophie. — Includes index
ISBN 90-247-2093-1 : Unpriced B82-13339

Spiegelberg, Herbert. The context of the phenomenological movement / Herbert Spiegelberg. — The Hague ; London : Nijhoff, 1981. — xvi,239p : ill ; 25cm. — (Phaenomenologica ; 80)
Includes index. — Includes the text of 1 letter in German
ISBN 90-247-2392-2 : Unpriced B82-02727

142'.7 — Phenomenology — *Festschriften*

Pfänder-Studien / Herausgegeben von Herbert Spiegelberg und Eberhard Avé-Lallemant. — The Hague ; London : Nijhoff, 1982. — xiv,384p : 1port ; 25cm. — (Phaenomenologica ; 84)
Bibliography: p359-379. — Includes index
ISBN 90-247-2490-2 : Unpriced
ISBN 90-247-2490-2 (series) B82-40765

142'.7'09 — Phenomenology. Theories, *to 1980*

Spiegelberg, Herbert. The Phenomenological Movement : a historical introduction / Herbert Spiegelberg. — 3rd rev. and enl. ed. / with the collaboration of Karl Schuhmann. — The Hague ; London : Nijhoff, 1982. — xlviii,768p,[19]leaves of plates : facsims,ports ; 25cm. — (Phaenomenologica ; 5-6)
Previous ed.: The Hague : Nijhoff, 1965. — Includes bibliographies and index
ISBN 90-247-2577-1 (cased) : Unpriced
ISBN 90-247-2535-6 (pbk) : Unpriced B82-14563

142'.78 — Existentialism

The **Existentialist** tradition : selected writings / edited by Nino Langiulli. — [Atlantic Highlands], [N.J.] : Humanities ; [Brighton] : Harvester, 1981, c1971. — xii,459p ; 21cm
Includes bibliographies
ISBN 0-7108-0326-5 (pbk) : £7.95 B82-12101

144 — Humanism

Bailey, Charles. What it means to be a humanist. — Ely : EARO, c1977. — 16p : ports ; 15x21cm. — (What it means to be)
Cover title. — Author: Charles Bailey
ISBN 0-904463-60-5 (pbk) : £0.70 B82-30533

Ehrenfeld, David W.. The arrogance of humanism / David Ehrenfeld. — Oxford : Oxford University Press, 1981, c1978. — xiv,286p ; 21cm. — (A Galaxy book)
Originally published: New York : Oxford University Press, 1978. — Bibliography: p271-279. — Includes index
ISBN 0-19-502890-2 (pbk) : £3.95 B82-00506

144'.09469 — Portugal. Humanism, *1500-1600*

Hooykaas, R.. Humanism and the voyages of discovery in 16th century Portuguese science and letters / R. Hooykaas. — Amsterdam ; Oxford : North-Holland, 1979. — 67p ; 24cm. — (Mededelingen der Koninklijke Nederlandse akademie van Wetenschappen, Afd Letterkunde. Nieuwe reeks ; d.42, no.4)
Pages also numbered 99-159
ISBN 0-7204-8487-1 (pbk) : Unpriced
Also classified at 910'.9469 B82-05450

145 — Ideology — *Psychological perspectives*

Billig, Michael. Ideology and social psychology. — Oxford : Basil Blackwell, Sept.1982. — [256]p
ISBN 0-631-13063-2 : £12.50 : CIP entry B82-20291

145 — Ideology. Theories of Lenin, V.I. ; Mannheim, Karl & Marx, Karl

Carlsnaes, Walter. The concept of ideology and political analysis : a critical examination of its usage by Marx, Lenin and Mannheim / Walter Carlsnaes. — Westport, Conn. ; London : Greenwood, 1981. — xii,274p ; 22cm. — (Contributions in philosophy, ISSN 0084-926x ; no.17)
Bibliography: p249-261. — Includes index
ISBN 0-313-22267-3 : Unpriced B82-02614

145 — Ideology. Theories of Marxists

Seliger, Martin. The Marxist conception of ideology : a critical essay / Martin Seliger. — Cambridge : Cambridge University Press, 1977 (1979 [printing]). — xiii,229p ; 22cm. — (International studies)
Bibliography: p211-218. — Includes index
ISBN 0-521-29625-0 (pbk) : £6.50 B82-17642

146'.3 — Materialism

Bunge, Mario. Scientific materialism / Mario Bunge. — Dordrecht ; London : Reidel, 1981. — xiv,219p : ill ; 23cm. — (Episteme ; v.9)
Bibliography: p209-213. — Includes index
ISBN 90-277-1304-9 (cased) : Unpriced
ISBN 90-277-1305-7 (pbk) : Unpriced B82-00484

Robinson, Howard. Matter and sense : a critique of contemporary materialism. — Cambridge : Cambridge University Press, Aug.1982. — [140]p. — (Cambridge studies in philosophy)
ISBN 0-521-24471-4 : £13.50 : CIP entry B82-25497

148 — Great Britain. Liberals. Influence of socialism, *ca 1860-ca 1960*

Clarke, Peter, *1942-*. Liberals and social democrats / Peter Clarke. — Cambridge : Cambridge University Press, 1978 (1981 [printing]). — xiii,344p ; 23cm
Bibliography: p291-334. — Includes index
ISBN 0-521-28651-4 (pbk) : £7.95 : CIP rev. B81-31606

149'.2 — Philosophy. Realism

Rosenberg, Jay F.. One world and our knowledge of it : the problematic of realism in post-Kantian perspective / Jay F. Rosenberg. — Dordrecht ; London : Reidel, 1980. — xv,209p : ill ; 23cm. — (Philosophical studies series in philosophy ; v.23)
Bibliography: p201-202. — Includes index
ISBN 90-277-1136-4 : Unpriced B82-16888

149'.3 — Grail Movement

Abd-ru-shin. In the light of truth : the Grail message / Abd-ru-shin. — Vomperberg : Bernhardt ; London : Grail Foundation, 1979, c1971. — 1061p ; 22cm
ISBN 3-87860-093-3 : Unpriced B82-26667

149'.3 — Mysticism

A.E.. The descent of the gods, comprising the mystical writings of G.W. Russell, AE. — Gerrards Cross : Smythe, Nov.1982. — [800]p
ISBN 0-901072-44-3 : £30.00 : CIP entry B82-26718

Understanding mysticism / edited by Richard Woods. — London : Athlone, 1981, c1980. — xi,586p ; 22cm
Originally published: Garden City, N.Y. : Image Books, 1980. — Bibliography: p564-575. — Includes index
ISBN 0-485-11219-1 (cased) : Unpriced
ISBN 0-485-12037-2 (pbk) : Unpriced B82-28184

Wainwright, William J.. Mysticism : a study of its nature, cognitive value and moral implications / William J. Wainwright. — Brighton : Wayland, 1981. — xv,245p ; 22cm
Bibliography: p234-242. — Includes index
ISBN 0-7108-0062-2 : £22.50 : CIP rev. B81-27953

149'.8 — Nihilism

Rosen, Stanley. Nihilism. — London : Yale University Press, Feb.1982. — [268]p
Originally published: 1969
ISBN 0-300-02847-4 (pbk) : £4.95 : CIP entry B82-07091

149'.94 — Philosophical logic. Wittgenstein, Ludwig. Philosophical investigations — *Commentaries*

Baker, G. P.. An analytical commentary on Wittgenstein's Philosophical investigations. — Oxford : Blackwell, June 1982. — [352]p
Originally published as part of Vol.1 of An analytical commentary on the Philosophical investigations. 1980
ISBN 0-631-13069-1 (pbk) : £5.95 : CIP entry B82-09455

149'.94 — Philosophical logic. Wittgenstein, Ludwig. Philosophical investigations — *Critical studies*

Baker, G. P.. Wittgenstein : understanding and meaning. — Oxford : Blackwell, June 1982. — [400]p
Originally published as part of v.1 of An analytical commentary on the Philosophical investigations. 1980
ISBN 0-631-13071-3 (pbk) : £5.95 : CIP entry B82-09457

149'.943 — Philosophical logic

Grayling, A. C.. An introduction to philosophical logic / A.C. Grayling. — Brighton : Harvester, 1982. — 300p ; 23cm
Includes index
ISBN 0-85527-514-6 (cased) : £20.00 : CIP rev.
ISBN 0-7108-0421-1 (pbk) : £6.95 B82-13145

149'.946 — Natural language. Reference — *Philosophical perspectives*

Evans, Gareth. The varieties of reference. — Oxford : Clarendon Press, Nov.1982. — [432]p
ISBN 0-19-824685-4 (cased) : £15.00 : CIP entry
ISBN 0-19-824686-2 (pbk) : £5.95 B82-26876

Salmon, Nathan U.. Reference and essence / Nathan U. Salmon. — Oxford : Basil Blackwell, 1982. — xvi,293p ; 23cm
Bibliography: p265-278. — Includes index
ISBN 0-631-13004-7 (cased) : Unpriced : CIP rev.
ISBN 0-631-13005-5 (pbk) : Unpriced B82-01158

149'.96 — Structuralism

The **Logic** of culture : advances in structural theory and methods / Ino Rossi: and contributors. — London : Tavistock, 1982. — viii,296p : ill ; 24cm
Includes bibliographies and index
ISBN 0-422-77760-9 : Unpriced B82-39370

Seung, T. K.. Structuralism and hermeneutics / T.K. Seung. — New York ; Guildford : Columbia University Press, 1982. — xiii,310p ; 22cm
Includes index
ISBN 0-231-05278-2 : £16.20 B82-19501

150 — PSYCHOLOGY

150 — Man. Behaviour

Coleman, James C.. Contemporary psychology and effective behaviour / James C. Coleman. — 4th ed. — Glenview ; London : Scott, Foresman, c1979. — 493p : ill(some col.) ; 26cm
Previous ed.: 1974. — Ill on lining papers. — Bibliography: p465-473. — Includes index
ISBN 0-673-15202-2 : £16.75 B82-40999

Drake, Roger A.. The effects of a motive for cognitive simplicity on social perceptual errors / Roger A. Drake. — [Sheffield] : Sheffield City Polytechnic, Faculty of Business and Management Studies, Department of Hotel & Catering Studies and Home Economics, c1982. — 73leaves ; 30cm
Bibliography: leaves 66-72
ISBN 0-903761-55-6 (spiral) : Unpriced B82-29919

Ferster, Charles B.. Behavior principles. — 3rd ed. / Charles B. Ferster, Stuart A. Culbertson. — Englewood Cliffs ; London : Prentice-Hall, c1982. — xii,386p : ill ; 24cm
Previous ed.: 1975. — Includes index
ISBN 0-13-072520-x : £15.70 B82-28155

Friedman, Myles I.. Human nature and predictability / Myles I. Friedman, Martha R. Willis. — Lexington, Mass. : Lexington Books, c1981 ; [Aldershot] : Gower [distributor], 1982. — xvi,346p : ill ; 24cm
Bibliography: p307-334. — Includes index
ISBN 0-669-04684-1 : £18.50 B82-21167

The **Fundamental** connection between nature and nurture : a review of the evidence / edited by Walter R. Gove, G. Russell Carpenter. — Lexington, Mass. : Lexington ; [Aldershot] : Gower [distributor], c1982. — vi,312p : ill ; 24cm
Includes bibliographies and index
ISBN 0-669-04483-0 : £21.00 B82-31791

Toda, Masanao. Man, robot, and society : models and speculations / Masanao Toda ; with an introduction by Hans F.M. Crombag. — Boston, [Mass.] ; London : Nijhoff, c1982. — xviii,235p : ill ; 24cm
Includes bibliographies
ISBN 0-89838-060-x : Unpriced B82-05345

150 — Man. Behaviour *expounded by* attitudes to problems

Burnand, Gordon. Via focal problems : a problems approach to psychology and social science / Gordon Burnand. — High Wycombe : Leadership, c1982. — 275p ; 22cm
Inlcudes index
ISBN 0-907774-00-8 (pbk) : £7.25 B82-20535

150 — Man. Instinctive behaviour. Relationships with language. Theories of Wittgenstein, Ludwig

Malcolm, Norman. Wittgenstein : the relation of language to instinctive behaviour : J.R. Jones memorial lecture delivered at the college on May 12, 1981 / by Norman Malcolm. — Swansea : University College of Swansea, 1981. — 26p ; 21cm
ISBN 0-86076-024-3 (pbk) : Unpriced B82-00581

150 — Man. Play. Psychological aspects

Micklem, Niel. Playing consequences / by Niel Micklem. — [London] ([c/o Hon. Sec., 37 Hogarth Hill, N.W.11]) : [Guild of Pastoral Psychology], [1982?]. — 15p ; 18cm. — (Guild lecture / Guild of Pastoral Psychology, ISSN 0434-9253 ; no.207)
Text on inside cover
£0.75 (pbk) B82-28965

150 — Mind. Psychological aspects

Marková, Ivana. Paradigms, thought and language. — Chichester : Wiley, Aug.1982. — [270]p
ISBN 0-471-10196-6 : £15.95 : CIP entry B82-23317

150 — Psychology

Barnes-Gutteridge, William. Psychology / William Barnes-Gutteridge ; illustrated by Whitecroft Designs. — [London] : Hamlyn Paperbacks, 1982, c1974. — 159p : col.ill,col.ports ; 18cm
Originally published: 1974. — Bibliography: p156. — Includes index
£1.75 (pbk) B82-36016

Bourne, Lyle E.. Psychology / Lyle E. Bourne, Jr., Bruce R. Ekstrand. — 4th ed. — New York ; London : Holt, Rinehart and Winston, 1982. — xxvi,581p,[8]p of plates : ill(some col.) ; 26cm
Previous ed.: 1979. — Bibliography: p551-559. — Includes index
ISBN 0-03-059688-2 : £15.50 B82-25418

Bruner, Jerome S.. On knowing : essays for the left hand / Jerome S. Bruner. — Expanded ed. — Cambridge, Mass. ; London : Belknap Press, 1979 (1980 printing). — xii,189p : ill ; 21cm
Previous ed.: 1962
ISBN 0-674-63525-6 (cased) : Unpriced
ISBN 0-674-63525-6 (pbk) : Unpriced B82-08212

Essentials of psychology / John P. Houston ... [et al.]. — New York ; London : Academic Press, c1981. — xv,529,[60]p,[4]p of plates : ill(some col.),ports ; 27cm
Previous ed.: published as Invitation to psychology. 1979. — Bibliography: pR1-R16. — Includes index
ISBN 0-12-356858-7 (pbk) : £9.00 B82-04247

Goodale, Robert A.. Experiencing psychology / Robert A. Goodale, Elaine Ruth Goldberg ; Benjamin Kleinmuntz ... [et al.]. — Chicago ; Henley-on-Thames : Science Research Associates, c1978. — viii,767p : ill(some col.) ; 25cm
Includes bibliographies and index
ISBN 0-574-42025-8 : £9.30 B82-02113

Introduction to psychology. — Milton Keynes : Open University Press. — (Social sciences : a second level course)
At head of title: The Open University
Block 2: Psychology of the person. — 1981. — 90p : ill ; 30cm. — (DS262 ; 8,9)
Includes bibliographies and index. — Contents: Unit 8: Social contexts — Unit 9: Humanistic perspectives
ISBN 0-335-12042-3 (pbk) : Unpriced B82-04548

Introduction to psychology. — Milton Keynes : Open University Press. — (Social sciences : a second level course)
At head of title: The Open University
Block 4: Perspectives and problems. — 1981. — 108p : ill,plans ; 30cm. — (DS262 ; 11,12-13,14,15)
Includes bibliographies and index. — Contents: Unit 11: Similarities and differences — Units 12-13: Projects — Unit 14: Cognitive psychology — Unit 15: Understanding people
ISBN 0-335-12045-8 (pbk) : Unpriced B82-04547

Lefton, Lester A.. Psychology / Lester A. Lefton. — 2nd ed. — Boston ; London : Allyn & Bacon, c1982. — xviii,733p : ill(some col.) ; 26cm + Test booklet(various pagings ; 28cm)
Previous ed.: 1979. — Ill on lining papers. — Bibliography: p705-733. — Includes index
ISBN 0-205-07590-8 : Unpriced B82-27858

Morris, Charles G.. Psychology : an introduction / Charles G. Morris ; with the editorial staff of Prentice-Hall. — 4th ed. — Englewood Cliffs ; London : Prentice-Hall, c1982. — xv,603p : ill (some col.),ports ; 27cm
Previous ed.: 1979. — Bibliography: p561-582. — Includes index
ISBN 0-13-734293-4 : £14.95 B82-21694

Principles of psychology / Richard H. Price ... [et al.]. — New York ; London : Holt, Rinehart and Winston, c1982. — xvii,650p : ill ; 27cm
Bibliography: p589-621. — Includes index
ISBN 0-03-048411-1 : £9.95 B82-27789

Romanyshyn, Robert D.. Psychological life : from science to metaphor / by Robert D. Romanyshyn. — Milton Keynes : Open University Press, 1982. — xvii,209p : ill ; 24cm
Bibliography: p197-203. — Includes index
ISBN 0-335-10108-9 : £11.95 : CIP rev. B82-22405

Silverman, Robert E.. Psychology / Robert E. Silverman. — 4th ed. — Englewood Cliffs ; London : Prentice-Hall, c1982. — xxi,573p : ill (some col.),ports ; 28cm
Previous ed.: 1978. — Ill on lining papers. — Bibliography: p533-549. — Includes index
ISBN 0-13-733550-4 : Unpriced B82-28424

Smith, Ronald E.. Psychology : the frontiers of behavior / Ronald E. Smith, Irwin G. Sarason, Barbara R. Sarason. — 2nd ed. — New York ; London : Harper & Row, c1982. — xvi,[4]p of plates : ill(some col.),maps,col.plans,ports ; 29cm
Previous ed.: 1978. — Bibliography: p679-704. — Includes index
ISBN 0-06-045729-5 : £9.50 B82-21902

Taylor, Ann, *1937-*. Introducing psychology. — 2nd ed. / Ann Taylor, Wladyslaw Sluckin ... [et al.]. — Harmondsworth : Penguin, 1982. — 755p : ill ; 20cm. — (Penguin education)
Previous ed.: / by D.S. Wright, Ann Taylor, et al. 1970. — Bibliography: p659-730. — Includes index
ISBN 0-14-080456-0 (pbk) : £5.95 B82-40767

150 — Psychology — *For schools*

Beer, Jonathan. Experiments in psychology : a workbook for students / Jonathan Beer. — London : Weidenfeld and Nicolson, c1982. — viii,328p : ill ; 22cm
Includes bibliographies and index
ISBN 0-297-78080-8 (pbk) : £5.95 B82-28980

150'.1 — Man. Behaviour. Theories

Maze, J. R.. The meaning of behaviour. — London : Allen and Unwin, Feb.1983. — [216]p
ISBN 0-04-150081-4 : £16.50 : CIP entry B82-36440

150'.1 — Psychology — *Philosophical perspectives*

James, William, *1842-1910*. The principles of psychology / William James. — Cambridge, Mass. ; London : Harvard University Press, 1981. — 3v.(lxviii,1740p) : ill,1port ; 24cm. — (The works of William James)
Includes index
ISBN 0-674-70559-9 : Unpriced
ISBN 0-674-70555-6 (v.3) : £17.50 B82-13666

Kendler, Howard H.. Psychology : a science in conflict / Howard H. Kendler. — New York ; Oxford : Oxford University Press, 1981. — vii,390p ; 22cm
Bibliography: p372-384. — Includes index
ISBN 0-19-502900-3 (cased) : £15.00
ISBN 0-19-502901-1 (pbk) : Unpriced B82-05900

Valentine, Elizabeth R.. Conceptual issues in psychology. — London : Allen & Unwin, Nov.1982. — [224]p
ISBN 0-04-150079-2 (cased) : £12.00 : CIP entry
ISBN 0-04-150080-6 (pbk) : £5.95 B82-27801

150'.1 — Psychology. Soviet theories. Concepts: Activity

The **Concept** of activity in Soviet psychology / translated and edited by James V. Wertsch. — Armonk, N.Y. : Sharpe ; London : distributed by Eurospan, c1981. — xi,441p : ill ; 22cm
Translation from the Russian. — Includes bibliographies
ISBN 0-87332-158-8 : £22.50 B82-17305

150'.1 — Psychology. Theories

Cosgrove, Mark P.. Psychology gone awry : four psychological world views / Mark P. Cosgrove. — Leicester : Inter-Varsity, 1982. — 144p ; 18cm
Previous ed.: Grand Rapids, Mich.: Zondervan, 1979. — Includes index
ISBN 0-85110-432-0 (pbk) : Unpriced : CIP rev. B81-40265

150′.1 — Psychology. Theories *continuation*

Eiser, J. Richard. Attitudes in psychology : an inaugural lecture delivered in the University of Exeter on 7 November 1980 / J. Richard Eiser. — Exeter : University of Exeter, 1981. — 15p : ill ; 21cm
Bibliography: p15
ISBN 0-85989-128-3 (pbk) : £0.60 B82-09643

150′.1 — Psychology. Theories, *1800-1900*

Robinson, Daniel N.. Toward a science of human nature : essays on the psychologies of Mill, Hegel, Wundt and James / Daniel N. Robinson. — Chicago ; London : University of Chicago Press, 1982. — xiii,258p ; 22cm
Includes index
ISBN 0-231-05174-3 : £19.80 B82-21493

150.19′32 — Psychodynamics

Bridger, Harold. Consultative work with communities and organisations towards a psychodynamic image of man. — Aberdeen : Aberdeen University Press, June 1981. — [42] p. — (The Malcolm Miller lecture, ISSN 0144-1663 ; 1980)
ISBN 0-08-025751-8 (pbk) : £1.25 : CIP entry B81-14783

150.19′5 — Psychoanalysis

Langs, Robert. Technique in transition / Robert Langs. — New York ; London : Aronson ; London : Distributed by Eurospan, c1978. — xvi,725p ; 24cm. — (Classical psychoanalysis and its applications)
Includes bibliographies and index
ISBN 0-87668-349-9 : Unpriced B82-23969

Loewenstein, Rudolph M.. Practice and precept in psychoanalytic technique. — London : Yale University Press, Sept.1982. — [240]p
ISBN 0-300-02531-9 : £17.50 : CIP entry B82-29117

Malcolm, Janet. Psychoanalysis : the impossible profession / Janet Malcolm. — London : Picador, 1982, c1981. — 174p ; 20cm
Originally published: New York : Knopf, 1981. — Bibliography: p169-174
ISBN 0-330-26737-x (pbk) : £1.95 B82-15111

Schafer, Roy. A new language for psychoanalysis. — London : Yale University Press, Oct.1981. — [416]p
ISBN 0-300-02761-3 : £6.95 : CIP entry B81-31942

150.19′5 — Psychoanalysis. Theories of Lacan, Jaques *related to* feminism

Gallop, Jane. Feminism and psychoanalysis : the daughter's seduction / Jane Gallop. — London : Macmillan, 1982. — xv,164p : 1ill ; 23cm. — (Language, discourse, society)
Bibliography: p158-160. — Includes index
ISBN 0-333-29471-8 (cased) : £15.00
ISBN 0-333-29472-6 (pbk) : £4.15
Also classified at 305.4′2 B82-37756

150.19′5′0944 — France. Psychoanalysis. Political aspects, *ca 1950-1978 — Sociological perspectives*

Turkle, Sherry. Psychoanalytic politics : Freud's French revolution / Sherry Turkle. — London : Burnett in association with Deutsch, 1979, c1978. — x,278p ; 21cm
Originally published: New York : Basic Books, 1978. — Includes index
ISBN 0-233-97183-1 (pbk) : £5.50 B82-39319

150.19′52 — Psychoanalysis. Freud, Sigmund — *Biographies*

Clark, Ronald W.. Freud : the man and the cause / Ronald W. Clark. — London : Granada, 1982, c1980. — 652p,[16]p of plates : ill,1geneal.table,ports ; 20cm
Originally published: London : Cape, 1980. — Bibliography: p533-547. — Includes index
ISBN 0-586-08395-2 (pbk) : £3.95 B82-29736

150.19′52 — Psychoanalysis. Freud, Sigmund — *Critical studies*

Fromm, Erich. Greatness and limitations of Freud's thought / Erich Fromm. — London : Abacus, 1982, c1980. — ix,147p ; 20cm
Originally published: London : Cape, 1980. — Bibliography: p139-141. — Includes index
ISBN 0-349-11341-6 (pbk) : £1.95 B82-36964

Rieff, Philip. Freud : the mind of the moralist / Philip Rieff. — 3rd ed. — Chicago ; London : University of Chicago Press, 1979. — xxv,440p ; 21cm
Previous ed.: Garden City, N.Y. : Doubleday, 1961. — Includes index
ISBN 0-226-71640-6 (cased) : Unpriced
ISBN 0-226-71639-2 (pbk) : £4.90 B82-21490

Steele, Robert S.. Freud and Jung : conflicts of interpretation / Robert S. Steele ; with consulting editor Susan V. Swinney. — London : Routledge & Kegan Paul, 1982. — x,390p ; 23cm
Bibliography: p376-384. — Includes index
ISBN 0-7100-9067-6 : £14.95
Also classified at 150.19′54 B82-28430

150.19′52 — Psychoanalysis. Freud, Sigmund — *Critical studies — Welsh texts*

Pritchard Jones, Harri. Freud / Harri Pritchard Jones. — [Denbigh] : Gwasg Gee, 1982. — 83p ; 19cm. — (Y Meddwl modern)
Bibliography: p82-83
£1.90 (pbk) B82-39998

150.19′52 — Psychoanalysis. Freudian system. Testing, *to 1980*

Kline, Paul. Fact and fantasy in Freudian theory / Paul Kline. — 2nd ed. — London : Methuen, 1981. — xi,510p ; 25cm
Previous ed.: 1972. — Bibliography: p448-493. — Includes index
ISBN 0-416-72640-2 : £22.00 : CIP rev. B81-31747

150.19′52 — Psychoanalysis. Theories of Freud, Sigmund

Draenos, Stan. Freud's odyssey. — London : Yale University Press, Sept.1982. — [178]p
ISBN 0-300-02791-5 : £14.50 : CIP entry B82-29124

Nagera, Humberto. Basic psychoanalytic concepts on metapsychology, conflicts, anxiety : and other subjects / by Humberto Nagera and A. Colonna ... [et al.] ; [edited by Humberto Nagera]. — London : Maresfield, 1981. — 233p ; 21cm. — (The Hampstead Clinic psychoanalytic library ; v.4)
Originally published: London : Allen & Unwin, 1970. — Includes index
ISBN 0-9507146-6-6 (pbk) : Unpriced B82-11681

Van Herik, Judith. Freud : on femininity and faith / Judith Van Herik. — Berkeley ; London : University of California Press, c1982. — xiii,216p : 1ill ; 24cm
Bibliography: p201-207. — Includes index
ISBN 0-520-04368-5 : £17.50 B82-34359

150.19′52′0207 — Psychoanalysis. Theories of Freud, Sigmund — *Cartoons*

Appignanesi, Richard. Freud : for beginners / text by Richard Appignanesi ; illustrations by Oscar Zarate. — London : Writers and Readers, 1979. — 174p : ill,1port ; 22cm
Bibliography: p174
ISBN 0-906386-04-7 (cased) : £3.95
ISBN 0-906389-09-8 (pbk) : Unpriced B82-01372

150.19′52′0924 — Psychology. Reich, Wilhelm — *Biographies*

Wilson, Colin, *1931-*. The quest for Wilhelm Reich / Colin Wilson. — London : Granada, 1981 (1982 [printing]). — xiv,306p ; 18cm. — (A Panther book)
Bibliography: p295-297. — Includes index
ISBN 0-586-04852-9 (pbk) : £1.95 B82-33877

150.19′52′0924 — Psychology. Reich, Wilhelm — *Correspondence, diaries, etc.*

Reich, Wilhelm. Record of a friendship : the correspondence between Wilhelm Reich and A.S. Neill : 1936-1957 / edited, and with an introduction, by Beverley R. Placzek. — London : Gollancz, 1982, c1981. — xviii,429p : 1port ; 24cm
Originally published: New York : Farrar, Straus, Giroux, 1981. — Includes index
ISBN 0-575-03054-2 : £12.50
Also classified at 371.2′012′0924 B82-10195

150.19′52′0924 — Psychology. Reich, Wilhelm — *Critical studies*

Cohen, Ira H.. Ideology and unconsciousness : Reich, Freud, and Marx / Ira H. Cohen. — New York ; London : New York University Press, 1982. — ix,235p : 1ill ; 24cm
Bibliography: p227-231. — Includes index
ISBN 0-8147-1383-1 : £24.15 B82-36369

150.19′54 — Psychoanalysis. Jung, C. G. — *Critical studies*

Steele, Robert S.. Freud and Jung : conflicts of interpretation / Robert S. Steele ; with consulting editor Susan V. Swinney. — London : Routledge & Kegan Paul, 1982. — x,390p ; 23cm
Bibliography: p376-384. — Includes index
ISBN 0-7100-9067-6 : £14.95
Primary classification 150.19′52 B82-28430

150.19′54 — Psychoanalysis. Jungian system

Mattoon, Mary Ann. Jungian psychology in perspective / Mary Ann Mattoon. — New York : Free Press ; London : Collier Macmillan, c1981. — xvi,334p : ill ; 24cm
Bibliography: p285-320. — Includes index
ISBN 0-02-920440-2 : £11.95 B82-18900

150.19′54 — Psychology. Projection. Theories of Jung, C. G.

Franz, Marie-Louise von. Projection and re-collection in Jungian psychology : reflections of the soul / Marie-Louise von Franz ; translated by William H. Kennedy. — La Salle ; London : Open Court, c1980. — 253p : ill ; 22cm. — (The Reality of the psyche series)
Translation of: Spiegelungen der Seele. — Bibliography: p233-240. — Includes index
ISBN 0-87548-357-7 : Unpriced B82-10992

150′.2461 — Man. Behaviour — *For medical personnel*

Understanding human behavior in health and illness / edited by Richard C. Simons, Herbert Pardes. — 2nd ed. — Baltimore ; London : Williams & Wilkins, c1981. — xx,733p : ill ; 21cm
Previous ed.: 1977. — Includes bibliographies and index
ISBN 0-683-07740-6 : Unpriced B82-03748

150′.2461 — Psychology — *For medicine*

Psychology and medicine / [edited by] David Griffiths. — London : Macmillan, 1981. — xii,491p : ill ; 26cm. — (Psychology for professional groups)
Includes bibliographies and index
ISBN 0-333-31862-5 (cased) : £12.50
ISBN 0-333-31877-3 (pbk) : Unpriced B82-06963

150′.2461 — Psychology — *For physiotherapy*

Psychology for physiotherapists / [edited by] E.N. Dunkin. — London : Macmillan, 1981. — x,401p : ill ; 26cm. — (Psychology for professional groups)
Includes bibliographies and index
ISBN 0-333-31857-9 (cased) : £12.50
ISBN 0-333-31884-6 (pbk) : Unpriced B82-06959

150′.24618 — Psychology — *For speech disorder therapy*

Purser, Harry. Psychology for speech therapists / Harry Purser. — London : Macmillan, 1982. — viii,375p : ill ; 26cm. — (Psychology for professional groups)
Bibliography: p363-370. — Includes index
ISBN 0-333-31855-2 (cased) : £12.50
ISBN 0-333-31885-4 (pbk) : Unpriced B82-33838

150′.28′7 — Man. Psychological testing — *Questions & answers*

Thornton, George C.. Exercises in psychological testing / George C. Thornton III and Eugene R. Oetting. — 2nd ed. — New York ; London : Harper & Row, c1982. — viii,341p : ill,forms ; 28cm
Previous ed.: 19---. — Includes bibliographies
ISBN 0-06-044909-8 (pbk) : £7.95 B82-26273

150′.28′7 — Psychological tests

Aiken, Lewis R.. Psychological testing and assessment / Lewis R. Aiken. — 4th ed. — Boston ; London : Allyn and Bacon, c1982. — ix,454p : ill,forms ; 25cm + Instructor′s manual(vi,96p ; 22cm) + Study guide(v,191p ; 24cm)
Previous ed.: 1979. — Bibliography: p429-442. — Includes index
ISBN 0-205-07610-6 : Unpriced
ISBN 0-205-07611-4 (instructor′s manual)
ISBN 0-205-07612-2 (study guide) B82-27109

Anastasi, Anne. Psychological testing / Anne Anastasi. — 5th ed. — New York : Macmillan ; London : Collier Macmillan, c1982. — xiii,784p : ill ; 25cm
Previous ed.: 1976. — Bibliography: p683-751. — Includes index
ISBN 0-02-302960-9 (cased) : £13.95
ISBN 0-02-977510-8 (pbk) : £8.50 B82-18898

Jensen, Arthur R.. Straight talk about mental tests / Arthur R. Jensen. — London : Methuen, 1981. — xiv,269p : ill ; 25cm
Bibliography: p260-262. — Includes index
ISBN 0-416-32300-6 : £8.95 : CIP rev.
B81-14866

150′.3′21 — Man. Behaviour — *Encyclopaedias*

Statt, David A.. A dictionary of human behaviour / David Statt. — London : Harper & Row, 1981. — 132p : ill ; 22cm
ISBN 0-06-318191-6 : Unpriced : CIP rev.
B81-22569

150′.3′21 — Psychology — *Encyclopaedias*

ABC of psychology / general editor Leonard Kristal ; associate editor Leonard Kristal ; associate editors Michael Argyle ... [et al.]. — Harmondsworth : Penguin, 1982. — 253p : ill,ports ; 21cm. — (Pelican books)
Originally published: London : Joseph, 1981
ISBN 0-14-022366-5 (pbk) : £4.95 B82-30515

150′.5 — Descriptive psychology — *Serials*

Advances in descriptive psychology : official annual publication of the Society for Descriptive Psychology. — Vol.1 (1981)-. — Greenwich, Conn. : JAI Press ; London (3 Henrietta St., WC 2E 8LU) : Distributed by JAICON Press, 1981-. — v. ; 24cm
£26.50 B82-03429

150′.7 — Education. Curriculum subjects: Psychology. Teaching

Silberberg, Alan. Instructor′s manual for Gleitman′s Psychology / Alan Silberberg, Henry Gleitman ; with a guide to audiovisual materials [by] James B. Maas. — New York ; London : Norton, c1981. — vi,184p : ill ; 23cm
ISBN 0-393-95105-7 (pbk) : £3.75 B82-32727

150′.7′1173 — United States. Higher education institutions. Curriculum subjects: Historiology of psychology. Teaching

Benjamin, Ludy T.. Teaching history of psychology : a handbook / Ludy T. Benjamin, Jr. — New York ; London : Academic Press, c1981. — viii,109p ; 24cm
Includes bibliographies and index
ISBN 0-12-633065-4 (pbk) : £3.60 B82-32791

150′.72 — Psychology. Research. Methodology

Mook, Douglas G.. Psychological research : strategy and tactics / Douglas G. Mook. — New York ; London : Harper & Row, c1982. — xx,475p : ill,ports ; 25cm
Bibliography: p455-464. — Includes index
ISBN 0-397-47414-8 : £9.50 B82-21904

150′.72 — Psychology. Research. Methodology — *Questions & answers — For teaching*

McCormick, Nancy Keeler. Instructor′s manual to accompany Lewin: Understanding psychological research / prepared by Nancy Keeler McCormick and Ann Polinger. — New York ; Chichester : Wiley, c1979. — 103p ; 24cm
ISBN 0-471-05037-7 (pbk) : £4.10 B82-13989

150′.72 — Psychology. Research. Statistical methods

Reference handbook of research and statistical methods in psychology : for students and professionals / R.M. Yaremko ... [et al.]. — New York ; London : Harper & Row, c1982. — xxx,335p : ill ; 24cm
ISBN 0-06-047332-0 (pbk) : £7.95 B82-11961

150′.72042659 — Research by Great Britain. ***MRC Applied Psychology Unit — Serials***

Great Britain. ***MRC Applied Psychology Unit.*** Progress report for the period ... / MRC Applied Psychology Unit. — 1974-1978-. — Cambridge (15 Chaucer Rd., Cambridge CB2 2EF) : The Unit, [1978]-. — v. ; 21cm
Irregular. — Description based on: 1978-1981 issue
ISSN 0263-0397 = Progress report - MRC Applied Psychology Unit : Unpriced
B82-14769

150′.724 — Experimental psychology. Methodology

Jung, John. The experimenter′s challenge : methods and issues in psychological research / John Jung. — New York : Macmillan ; London : Collier Macmillan, c1982. — x,429p : ill ; 24cm
Includes bibliographies and index
ISBN 0-02-361510-9 : Unpriced B82-33415

150′.724 — Psychology. Experiments. Ethical aspects — *Conference proceedings*

The **Ethics** of psychological research. — Oxford : Pergamon, Jan.1982. — [84]p
ISBN 0-08-028116-8 : £8.15 : CIP entry
B82-05378

150′.724 — Psychology. Stochastic models

Wickens, Thomas D.. Models for behavior : stochastic processes in psychology / Thomas D. Wickens. — Oxford : Freeman, c1982. — xiv,353p : ill ; 24cm. — (A Series of books in psychology)
Bibliography: p343-346. — Includes index
ISBN 0-7167-1352-7 (cased) : £20.95
ISBN 0-7167-1353-5 (pbk) : Unpriced
B82-34387

150′.76 — Psychology — *Questions & answers*

Valvatne, Laura. Keeping pace : an active reading study guide to accompany Lefton′s Psychology, 2nd ed. / by Laura Valvatne. — Boston ; London : Allyn & Bacon, c1982. — x,351p : ill ; 28cm
ISBN 0-205-07594-0 (pbk) : Unpriced
B82-27859

150′.9 — Psychology, *to 1980*

Brennan, James F.. History and systems of psychology / James F. Brennan. — Englewood Cliffs ; London : Prentice-Hall, c1982. — x,374p : ill,maps,ports ; 24cm
Includes bibliographies and index
ISBN 0-13-392209-x : £15.70 B82-23415

O′Neil, W. M.. The beginnings of modern psychology / W.M. O′Neil. — 2nd rev. ed. — Brighton : Harvester, 1982. — x,145p ; 23cm
Previous ed.: Harmondsworth : Penguin, 1968. — Bibliography: p130-142. — Includes index
ISBN 0-7108-0334-6 (cased) : £15.95 : CIP rev.
ISBN 0-7108-0329-x (pbk) : Unpriced
B81-33847

150′.951 — China. Psychology

Brown, L. B.. Psychology in contemporary China / L.B. Brown. — Oxford : Pergamon, 1981. — xi,291p ; 26cm
Bibliography: p269-280. — Includes index
ISBN 0-08-026063-2 : Unpriced B82-08046

152 — PHYSIOLOGICAL PSYCHOLOGY

152 — Man. Orifices. Psychological aspects

Malik, S. M. A.. The oral concept of the world : a study in the origins of human thought / by S.M.A. Malik. — Worcester Park : Roseneath Scientific, c1982. — 32p ; 22cm
Includes index
ISBN 0-903306-16-6 (pbk) : £4.80 B82-26984

152 — Neuropsychology

Hebb, Donald. The conceptual nervous system. — Oxford : Pergamon, Nov.1982. — [308]p. — (Foundations and philosophy of science and technology)
ISBN 0-08-027418-8 : £15.00 : CIP entry
B82-28721

152′.076 — Man. Behaviour. Physiological aspects — *Questions & answers*

Standish, Leanna J.. A workbook for Carlson′s Physiology of behavior. 2nd ed. / Leanna J. Standish. — Boston [Mass.] ; London : Allyn and Bacon, c1981. — 340p : ill ; 28cm
ISBN 0-205-07264-x (pbk) : £4.95 B82-08545

152.1 — PSYCHOLOGY. SENSORY PERCEPTION

152.1 — Man. Sensory perception

Schiffman, Harvey Richard. Sensation and perception : an integrated approach / Harvey Richard Schiffman. — 2nd ed. — New York ; Chichester : Wiley, c1982. — xii,540p : ill ; 25cm
Previous ed.: 1976. — Bibliography: p462-518. — Includes index
ISBN 0-471-08208-2 : £19.60 B82-27763

152.1′4 — Man. Face. Recognition. Role of visual perception

Perceiving and remembering faces / edited by Graham Davies, Hadyn Ellis and John Shepherd. — London : Academic, 1981. — xv,329p : ill ; 24cm. — (Academic Press series in cognition and perception)
Bibliography: p287-323. — Includes index
ISBN 0-12-206220-5 : £19.20 : CIP rev.
B81-26771

152.1′4 — Man. Visual perception *related to* **artificial intelligence**

Howe, J. A. M.. AI2 vision notes / by Jim Howe. — Aberdeen : University of Aberdeen Department of Artificial Intelligence, [1979]. — 119leaves of various foliations : ill ; 30cm. — (D.A.I. occasional paper, ISSN 0144-4131 ; no.20)
Unpriced (spiral)
Primary classification 001.53′5 B82-13859

152.1′4 — Man. Visual perception. Role of cognition

Heijden, A. H. C. van der. Short-term visual information forgetting / A.H.C. van der Heijden. — London : Routledge & Kegan Paul, 1981. — xv,240p : ill ; 23cm. — (International library of psychology)
Bibliography: p219-231. — Includes index
ISBN 0-7100-0851-1 : £13.50 B82-05454

152.1′4 — Visual perception

Weale, R. A.. Focus on vision. — London : Hodder & Stoughton, Mar.1982. — [224]p
ISBN 0-340-24839-4 (pbk) : £5.65 : CIP entry
B82-01834

152.1′42 — Man. Visual perception. Orientation

Howard, Ian P.. Human visual orientation / Ian P. Howard. — Chichester : Wiley, c1982. — xi,697p : ill ; 24cm
Bibliography: p588-669. — Includes index
ISBN 0-471-27946-3 : £25.00 B82-18067

152.1′48 — Optical illusions. Analysis. Applications of statistical mathematics — *Questions & answers — For schools*

Seeing is believing / [Schools Council Project on Statistical Education]. — Slough : Published for the Schools Council by Foulsham Educational, c1981. — 20p + teachers′ notes (24p ; 21cm) : ill ; 21cm. — (Statistics in your world)
ISBN 0-572-01075-3 (pbk) : Unpriced
ISBN 0-572-01102-4 (teachers′ notes) : Unpriced B82-13026

152.1′5 — Man. Auditory perception

Moore, Brian C. J.. An introduction to the psychology of hearing / Brian C.J. Moore. — 2nd ed. — London : Academic Press, 1982. — 293p : ill ; 24cm
Previous ed.: London : Macmillan, 1977. — Bibliography: p268-285. — Includes index
ISBN 0-12-505620-6 (cased) : £14.50 : CIP rev.
ISBN 0-12-505622-2 (pbk) : Unpriced
B82-00327

152.1'5 — Man. Auditory perception *continuation*

Rosemary, Martin E.. Sound and hearing. — London : Edward Arnold, Sept.1982. — [64]p. — (The Institute of Biology's studies in biology, ISSN 0537-9024 ; no.145)
ISBN 0-7131-2850-x : £2.25 : CIP entry B82-20034

152.1'66 — Odours. Perception by man

Engen, Trygg. The perception of odors / Trygg Engen. — New York ; London : Academic, 1982. — xi,202p : ill ; 24cm. — (Academic Press series in cognition and perception)
Bibliography: p173-195. — Includes index
ISBN 0-12-239350-3 : £16.00 B82-38077

152.1'82 — Man. Tactile perception

Montagu, Ashley. Touching : the human significance of the skin / Ashley Montagu. — 2nd ed. — New York ; London : Harper & Row, c1978. — x,384p : ill ; 21cm
Previous ed.: New York ; London : Columbia University Press, 1971. — Includes index
ISBN 0-06-090630-8 (pbk) : £3.95 B82-08248

Tactual perception : a sourcebook / edited by William Schiff and Emerson Foulke. — Cambridge : Cambridge University Press, 1982. — xiii,465p : ill ; 24cm
Includes bibliographies and index
ISBN 0-521-24095-6 : £25.00 B82-29930

152.3 — PSYCHOLOGY. MOVEMENTS AND MOTOR FUNCTIONS

152.3 — Man. Motor skills. Development — *For physical education*

Singer, Robert N.. The learning of motor skills / Robert N. Singer. — New York : Macmillan ; London : Collier Macmillan, c1982. — xii,244p : ill ; 27cm
Includes bibliographies and index
ISBN 0-02-410790-5 : £12.95 B82-26197

Stallings, Loretta M.. Motor learning : from theory to practice / Loretta M. Stallings. — St. Louis, Mo. ; London : Mosby, 1982. — xi,259p : ill,forms ; 24cm
Includes bibliographies and index
ISBN 0-8016-4768-1 (pbk) : £10.00 B82-31859

152.3'24 — Man. Instincts. Theories of Freud, Sigmund

Nagera, Humberto. Basic psychoanalytic concepts on the theory of instincts / by Humberto Nagera and S. Baker ... [et al.] ; [edited by Humberto Nagera]. — London : Maresfield, 1981. — 136p ; 21cm. — (The Hampstead Clinic psychoanalytic library ; v.3)
Originally published: London : Allen & Unwin, 1970. — Includes index
ISBN 0-9507146-5-8 (pbk) : Unpriced B82-11679

152.3'34 — Psychomotor skills. Learning by man — *Information processing perspectives*

Kerr, Robert, *19---*. Psychomotor learning / Robert Kerr. — Philadelphia ; London : Saunders College, c1982. — xv,350p : ill ; 24cm
Bibliography: p317-337. — Includes index
£18.95 B82-23130

152.3'85 — Man. Motor activities. Coordination

Motor coordination / edited by Arnold L. Towe and Erich S. Luschei. — New York ; London : Plenum, c1981. — xvi,640p : ill ; 26cm. — (Handbook of behavioral neurobiology ; v.5)
Includes bibliographies and index
ISBN 0-306-40613-6 : Unpriced B82-14700

152.4 — PSYCHOLOGY. EMOTIONS AND FEELINGS

152.4 — Guilt

Coleman, Vernon. Guilt / Vernon Coleman. — London : Sheldon, 1982. — 87p ; 20cm. — (Overcoming common problems)
Includes index
ISBN 0-85969-363-5 (pbk) : £1.95 B82-28403

152.4 — Jealousy

Hauck, Paul. Jealousy / Paul Hauck. — London : Sheldon, 1982, c1981. — 140p ; 21cm. — (Overcoming common problems)
Originally published: Philadelphia : Westminster Press, 1981
ISBN 0-85969-350-3 (cased) : £5.95
ISBN 0-85969-349-x (pbk) : £2.50 B82-20144

152.4 — Love. Psychological aspects

Malik, S. M. A.. Philism : a study in human love and its complications / by S.M.A. Malik. — Worcester Park : Roseneath Scientific, c1982. — 39p ; 21cm
Includes index
ISBN 0-903306-15-8 (pbk) : £5.85 B82-26964

152.4 — Man. Anger. Control

Hauck, Paul. Calm down / Paul Hauck. — London : Sheldon, 1980. — 128p ; 20cm. — (Overcoming common problems)
Includes index
ISBN 0-85969-319-8 (pbk) : £2.50 B82-26499

152.4 — Man. Emotions & feelings

Dobson, James, *1936-*. Emotions : can you trust them? / James Dobson. — London : Hodder and Stoughton, 1982, c1980. — 143p ; 18cm
Originally published: Ventura, Calif. : GL Regal, 1980. — Includes bibliographies
ISBN 0-340-28196-0 (pbk) : £1.50 : CIP rev. B82-09421

152.4 — Man. Fear

Hauck, Paul. Why be afraid? : how to overcome your fears / Paul Hauck. — London : Sheldon, 1981, c1975. — viii,86p ; 20cm. — (Overcoming common problems)
Originally published: Philadelphia : Westminster, 1975
ISBN 0-85969-337-6 (pbk) : £1.95 B82-40624

152.4 — Shame — *Psychoanalytical perspectives*

Wurmser, Léon. The mask of shame / Léon Wurmser. — Baltimore ; London : Johns Hopkins University Press, c1981. — xiii,345p ; 24cm
Bibliography: p326. — Includes index
ISBN 0-8018-2527-x : £17.50 B82-12184

152.8 — PSYCHOPHYSICS

152.8 — Man. Behaviour. Assessment — *Manuals*

Macdonald, Ian, *19---*. Manual for the Chart of initiative and independence (C.I.I.) : including manual of activities / Ian Macdonald and Terry Couchman. — Windsor : NFER Publishing, 1980. — 71p : ill,facsims ; 30cm
ISBN 0-7005-0253-x (pbk) : Unpriced B82-36981

153 — PSYCHOLOGY. INTELLIGENCE, INTELLECTUAL AND CONSCIOUS MENTAL PROCESSES

153 — Man. Consciousness

Aspects of consciousness. — London : Academic Press
Vol.3: Awareness and self-awareness. — Sept.1982. — [345]p
ISBN 0-12-708803-2 : CIP entry B82-18736

Harth, Erich. Windows on the mind. — Brighton : Harvester Press, Sept.1982. — [286]p
ISBN 0-7108-0477-6 : £12.00 : CIP entry B82-20648

Miller, Robert. Meaning and purpose in the intact brain : a philosophical, psychological, and biological account of conscious processes / Robert Miller. — Oxford : Clarendon Press, 1981. — ix,239p : ill ; 24cm. — (Oxford science publications)
Bibliography: p205-224. — Includes index
ISBN 0-19-857579-3 : £20.00 : CIP rev. B81-26751

153 — Man. Mental processes

Hunt, Morton. The universe within. — Brighton : Harvester Press, Sept.1982. — [416]p
ISBN 0-7108-0437-7 : £12.95 : CIP entry B82-23850

153.1 — PSYCHOLOGY. MEMORY AND LEARNING

153.1 — Man. Learning & memory

Hall, John F. (John Fry). An invitation to learning and memory / John F. Hall. — Boston, [Mass.] : Allyn and Bacon, c1982. — vi,312p : ill ; 24cm
Bibliography: p267-298. — Includes index
ISBN 0-205-07608-4 : £18.95 B82-20613

153.1'2 — Man. Memory

Loftus, Elizabeth F.. Memory : surprising new insights into how we remember and why we forget / Elizabeth Loftus. — Reading, Mass. ; London : Addison-Wesley, c1980. — xv,207p : ill ; 25cm
Includes index
ISBN 0-201-04473-0 (cased) : £6.60
ISBN 0-201-04474-9 (pbk) : Unpriced B82-33447

153.1'2 — Man. Memory. Effects of age differences

Foulds, Alison M.. Age differences in aspects of memory performance / by Alison M. Foulds. — Nottingham : Department of Adult Education, University of Nottingham, c1981. — ii,28p ; 21cm. — (Adults ; 5)
Includes bibliographies
ISBN 0-902031-50-3 (pbk) : Unpriced B82-17451

153.1'5 — Learning by adults

Smith, Robert M.. Learning how to learn. — Milton Keynes : Open University Press, Jan.1983. — [192]p
ISBN 0-335-10115-1 : £12.95 : CIP entry B82-33726

153.1'5 — Learning by man

Borger, Robert. The psychology of learning / Robert Borger and A.E.M. Seaborne. — 2nd ed. — Harmondsworth : Penguin, 1982. — 281p : ill ; 20cm. — (Penguin education)
Previous ed.: 1966. — Bibliography: p265-272. — Includes index
ISBN 0-14-080443-9 (pbk) : £2.95 B82-41154

153.1'5 — Learning by man. Psychological aspects

Navarick, Douglas J.. Principles of learning : from laboratory to field / Douglas J. Navarick. — Reading, Mass. ; London : Addison-Wesley, c1979. — xi,436p : ill ; 24cm
Bibliography: p408-422. — Includes index
ISBN 0-201-05204-0 : £14.40 B82-28659

Petrie, Hugh G.. The dilemma of enquiry and learning / Hugh G. Petrie. — Chicago ; London : University of Chicago Press, c1981. — viii,238p : ill ; 23cm. — (Chicago originals)
Bibliography: p225-233. — Includes index
ISBN 0-226-66349-3 (pbk) : £12.00 B82-20090

153.1'5 — Learning by man. Theories

Hergenhahn, B. R.. An introduction to theories of learning / B.R. Hergenhahn. — 2nd ed. — Englewood Cliffs ; London : Prentice-Hall, c1982. — x,454p : ill,ports ; 24cm
Previous ed.: 1976. — Bibliography: p434-445. — Includes index
ISBN 0-13-498725-x : £15.70 B82-16989

153.1'5 — Learning — *For children*

Learning. — [London] : Save the Children Fund, 1981. — 31p : col.ill,1col.map ; 27cm. — (Round the world)
ISBN 0-333-30678-3 : £1.95 B82-07006

153.1'5 — Learning. Role of visual perception

Sless, David. Learning and visual communication / David Sless. — London : Croom Helm, c1981. — 208p : ill ; 23cm. — (New patterns of learning series) (A Halsted Press book)
Bibliography: p189-199. — Includes index
ISBN 0-7099-2319-8 : £11.95 : CIP rev. B81-22596

153.1'5 — Learning. Theories

Talyzina, Nina. The psychology of learning : theories of learning and programmed instruction / Nina Talyzina. — Moscow : Progress ; [London] : distributed by Central Books, c1981. — 341p ; 21cm
Translation of: Psikhologii͡a obuchenii͡a
ISBN 0-7147-1670-7 : £3.95 B82-19974

153.1'5 — Man. Information processing

Anderson, Norman H.. Foundations of information integration theory / Norman H. Anderson. — New York ; London : Academic Press, 1981. — xvi,423p : ill ; 24cm. — (Information integration theory)
Bibliography: p389-410. — Includes index
ISBN 0-12-058101-9 : £23.80 B82-18353

153.1'5'024372 — Learning by man. Theories — *For teaching*

Bigge, Morris L.. Learning theories for teachers / Morris L. Bigge. — 4th ed. — New York ; London : Harper & Row, c1982. — xi,356p : ill ; 24cm
Previous ed.: 1976. — Includes bibliographies and index
ISBN 0-06-040673-9 (pbk) : £7.95 B82-11966

153.1'5'05 — Learning by man — *Serials*

Human learning : journal of practical research and applications. — Vol.1, no.1 (Jan.-Mar. 1982)-. — Chichester : Wiley, 1982-. — v. ; 25cm
Quarterly
ISSN 0277-6707 = Human learning : £35.00 per year B82-22702

153.2 — PSYCHOLOGY. IDEATION

153.2'3 — Concepts. Psychological aspects

Smith, Edward E.. Categories and concepts / Edward E. Smith and Douglas L. Medin. — Cambrige, Mass. ; London : Harvard University Press, 1981. — viii,203p : ill ; 24cm. — (Cognitive science series ; 4)
Bibliography: p191-199. — Includes index
ISBN 0-674-10275-4 : £10.50 B82-03866

153.3 — PSYCHOLOGY. IMAGINATION AND IMAGERY

153.3'2 — Mental images

Imagery / edited by Ned Block. — Cambridge, Mass. ; London : MIT Press, c1981. — 261p : ill ; 24cm. — (A Bradford book)
Bibliography: p247-258. — Includes index
ISBN 0-262-02168-4 (cased) : £10.50
ISBN 0-262-52072-9 (pbk) : Unpriced
B82-21008

153.3'5 — Creative thought

Perkins, D. N.. The mind's best work / D.N. Perkins. — Cambridge, Mass. ; London : Harvard University Press, 1981. — ix,314p : ill ; 24cm
Bibliography: p301-309. — Includes index
ISBN 0-674-57627-6 : £11.80 B82-11915

153.3'5 — Man. Creativity

Hayward, T. Curtis. Bees of the invisible : creative play and divine possession / T. Curtis Hayward. — [London] ([c/o Hon. Sec., 37 Hogarth Hill, N.W.11]) : [Guild of Pastoral Psychology], [1982?]. — 23p ; 18cm. — (Guild lecture / Guild of Pastoral Psychology, ISSN 0434-9253 ; no.206)
Text on inside cover
£0.75 (pbk) B82-28964

153.3'5'01 — Creativity — *Philosophical perspectives*

The **Concept** of creativity in science and art / edited by Denis Dutton and Michael Krausz. — The Hague ; London : Nijhoff, c1981. — 212p ; 25cm. — (Martinus Nijhoff philosophy library ; . v.6)
Includes index
ISBN 90-247-2418-x : Unpriced
ISBN 90-247-2344-2 (set) : Unpriced
B82-05347

153.4 — PSYCHOLOGY. COGNITION

153.4 — Man. Cognition

Cohen, Gillian. The psychology of cognition. — 2nd ed. — London : Academic Press, Feb.1983. — [280]p
Previous ed.: 1977
ISBN 0-12-178760-5 (cased) : CIP entry
ISBN 0-12-178762-1 (pbk) : Unpriced
B82-36583

Gilhooly, K. J.. Thinking. — London : Academic Press, Oct.1982. — [220]p
ISBN 0-12-283480-1 (cased) : CIP entry
ISBN 0-12-283482-8 (pbk) : Unpriced
B82-24938

Glass, Arnold Lewis. Cognition / Arnold Lewis Glass, Keith James Holyoak, John Lester Santa. — Reading, Mass. ; London : Addison-Wesley, c1979. — xix,521p : ill ; 24cm
Bibliography: p449-491. — Includes index
ISBN 0-201-02449-7 (pbk) : £8.40 B82-05699

Wessels, Michael G.. Cognitive psychology / Michael G. Wessells. — New York ; London : Harper & Row, c1982. — x,403p : ill ; 24cm
Bibliography: p363-395. — Includes index
ISBN 0-06-047009-7 : £10.50 B82-14551

153.4 — Man. Cognition. Biological aspects

Maturana, Humberto R.. Autopoiesis and cognition : the realization of the living / Humberto R. Maturana and Francisco J. Varela ; with a preface to Autopoiesis by Sir Stafford Beer. — Dordrecht ; London : Reidel, c1980. — xxx,141p : 1ill ; 25cm. — (Boston studies in the philosophy of science ; v.42)
Bibliography: p139-140. — Includes index
ISBN 90-277-1015-5 (cased) : Unpriced
ISBN 90-277-1016-3 (pbk) : Unpriced
Also classified at 612'.001 B82-37353

153.4 — Man. Cognition — *Conference proceedings*

Knowledge and representation / edited by Beatrice de Gelder. — London : Routledge & Kegan Paul, 1982. — xii,218p : ill ; 23cm. — (International library of psychology)
Conference papers. — Includes bibliographies and index
ISBN 0-7100-0922-4 : £12.50 B82-38564

153.4 — Man. Cognition. Neuropsychological aspects

The **Neuropsychology** of cognitive function : proceedings of a Royal Society discussion meeting, held on 18 and 19 November 1981 / organized and edited by D.E. Broadbent and L. Weiskrantz. — London : Royal Society, 1982. — 226p : ill ; 31cm
Originally published: in Philosophical transactions of the Royal Society of London, series B, vol.298 (no.1089), p1-226. — Includes bibliographies
ISBN 0-85403-190-1 : £27.80 B82-39925

Normality and pathology in cognitive functions / edited by Andrew W. Ellis. — London : Academic Press, 1981. — xi,327p : ill ; 24cm
Includes bibliographies and index
ISBN 0-12-237480-0 : £19.20 : CIP rev.
B82-07265

153.4 — Man. Cognition — *Philosophical perspectives*

Wittgenstein, Ludwig. Remarks on the philosophy of psychology / Ludwig Wittgenstein. — Oxford : Blackwell
Vol.1 / edited by G.E.M. Anscombe and G.H. von Wright ; translated by G.E.M. Anscombe. — 1980. — vi,218p : ill ; 23cm
Parallel German and English text. — Includes index
ISBN 0-631-12541-8 : £16.50 : CIP rev.
Also classified at 121'.3 B80-20140

Wittgenstein, Ludwig. Remarks on the philosophy of psychology / Ludwig Wittgenstein. — Oxford : Blackwell
Vol.2 / edited by G.H. Von Wright and Heikki Nyman ; translated by G.G. Luckhardt and M.A.E. Ave. — 1980. — 143[i.e.249]p ; 23cm
Parallel German and English text. — Includes index
ISBN 0-631-12551-5 : £13.50 : CIP rev.
Also classified at 121'.3 B80-20141

153.4 — Man. Cognition. Psychosocial aspects

Social cognition : perspectives on everyday understanding / [edited by] Joseph P. Forgas. — London : published in cooperation with European Association of Experimental Social Psychology by Academic Press, 1981. — xiii,281p : ill ; 24cm. — (European monographs in social psychology ; 26)
Includes bibliographies and index
ISBN 0-12-263560-4 (cased) : Unpriced : CIP rev.
ISBN 0-12-263562-0 (pbk) : Unpriced
B81-27352

153.4 — Man. Cognition *related to* **social behaviour** — *Conference proceedings*

Cognitive Analysis of Socio-Psychological Processes *(Conference : 1981 : Aix-en-Provence).* Cognitive analysis of social behavior : proceedings of the NATO advanced study institute on "The cognitive analysis of socio-psychological processes", Aix-en-Provence, France, July 12-31, 1981 / edited by Jean-Paul Codol and Jacques-Philippe Leyens. — The Hague ; London : Nijhoff, 1982. — xv,304p : ill ; 25cm. — (NATO advanced study institutes series. Series D, Behavioural and social sciences ; no.13)
Includes 3 chapters in French. — Includes bibliographies and index
ISBN 90-247-2701-4 : Unpriced
Also classified at 302 B82-34841

153.4 — Man. Cognition. Role of language

Luriĭa, A. R.. Language and cognition / Alexander R. Luria ; edited by James V. Wertsch. — Washington, D.C. : Winston ; New York ; Chichester : Wiley, c1982. — vii,264p : ill ; 24cm
Translated from the Russian. — Bibliography: p247-257. — Includes index
ISBN 0-471-09302-5 : £17.50 B82-15406

153.4 — Man. Cognition. Role of memory

Tulving, Endel. Elements of episodic memory. — Oxford : Clarendon Press, Oct.1982. — [400]p. — (Oxford psychology series ; 2)
ISBN 0-19-852102-2 : £23.00 : CIP entry
B82-23695

153.4 — Man. Cognitive development — *Marxist viewpoints*

Leont'ev, A. N.. Problems of the development of the mind / A.N. Leontyev. — Moscow : Progress Publishers ; [London] : Distributed by Central Books, 1981. — 454p : ill ; 21cm
Translation of: Problemy razvitiĭa psikhiki. — Includes index
ISBN 0-7147-1673-1 : £4.95 B82-06705

153.4 — Pakistan. Qalandar. Cognitive development. Cultural factors

Berland, Joseph C.. No five fingers are alike : cognitive amplifiers in social context / Joseph C. Berland. — Cambridge, Mass. ; London : Harvard University Press, 1982. — xii,246p : ill,1map ; 25cm
Bibliography: p217-237. — Includes index
ISBN 0-674-62540-4 : Unpriced B82-35318

153.4'028'7 — Man. Cognition. Assessment

Cognitive assessment / edited by Thomas V. Merluzzi, Carol R. Glass and Myles Genest. — New York ; London : Guilford, c1981. — xvi,532p : ill ; 24cm. — (The Guilford clinical psychology and psychotherapy series)
Includes bibliographies and index
ISBN 0-89862-001-5 : £22.00 B82-05619

153.4'0724 — Man. Cognition. Experiments

Workshops in cognitive processes / A. Bennett ... [et al.]. — [2nd ed.]. — London : Routledge & Kegan Paul, 1981. — xiii,176p ; 22cm
Previous ed.: Kensington, N.S.W. : New South Wales University Press, 1978 ; London : Routledge and Kegan Paul, 1980. — Includes bibliographies
ISBN 0-7100-0932-1 (pbk) : £4.95 B82-02757

153.4'2 — Thought processes

Blanshard, Brand. The nature of thought / by Brand Blanshard. — London : Allen & Unwin, 1939 (1978 [printing]). — 2v. ; 23cm. — (The Muirhead library of philosophy)
Includes index
ISBN 0-85527-545-6 : £25.00 B82-23791

153.4′3 — Rationality — *Philosophical perspectives*
Putnam, Hilary. Reason, truth and history / Hilary Putnam. — Cambridge : Cambridge University Press, 1981. — xii,222p ; 22cm
Includes index
ISBN 0-521-23035-7 (cased) : £15.00 : CIP rev.
ISBN 0-521-29776-1 (pbk) : £4.95 B81-32534

153.4′33 — Man. Deductive reasoning. Psychological aspects
Evans, Jonathan St. B. T.. The psychology of deductive reasoning / Jonathan St. B.T. Evans. — London : Routledge & Kegan Paul, 1982. — 277p : ill ; 23cm. — (International library of psychology)
Bibliography: p258-272. — Includes index
ISBN 0-7100-0923-2 : £12.95 B82-17447

153.4′4 — Man. Intuition
Bastick, Tony. Intuition : how we think and act / Tony Bastick. — Chichester : Wiley, c1982. — xxiv,494p : ill ; 24cm
Bibliography: p392-419. — Includes index
ISBN 0-471-27992-7 : £21.00 : CIP rev.
B81-34478

153.4′6 — Judgment
Judgement under uncertainty : heuristics and biases / edited by Daniel Kahneman, Paul Slovic, Amas Tversky. — Cambridge : Cambridge University Press, 1982. — xiii,555p : ill ; 24cm
Bibliography: p521-551. — Includes index
ISBN 0-521-24064-6 (cased) : £25.00
ISBN 0-521-28414-7 (pbk) : £9.95 B82-29932

153.6 — PSYCHOLOGY. COMMUNICATION

153.6 — Communication skills — *Questions & answers — For schools*
The **Life** and work box : assignments in communication skills for general education. — London : E. Arnold, May 1982. — [96]p
ISBN 0-7131-0717-0 : £35.00 : CIP entry
B82-11105

153.6 — Written communication. Psychological aspects
The **Psychology** of written communication : selected readings / edited by James Hartley. — London : Kogan Page, 1980. — 301p : ill,forms ; 23cm
Includes bibliographies and index
ISBN 0-85038-282-3 : £12.00 B82-24373

153.6′072 — Nonverbal communication. Psychological aspects. Research. Methodology
Handbook of methods in nonverbal behavior research / edited by Klaus R. Scherer and Paul Ekman. — Cambridge : Cambridge University Press, 1982. — xii,593p : ill ; 25cm. — (Studies in emotion and social interaction)
Includes bibliographies and index
ISBN 0-521-23614-2 (cased) : £30.00
ISBN 0-521-28072-9 (pbk) : £12.50
B82-32496

153.7 — PSYCHOLOGY. PERCEPTUAL PROCESSES

153.7′0724 — Man. Perception. Experiments
Power, R. P.. Workshops in perception / R.P. Power, S. Hausfeld, A. Gorta. — London : Routledge & Kegan Paul, 1981. — x,182p : ill ; 22cm
Includes bibliographies
ISBN 0-7100-0931-3 (pbk) : £4.95 B82-02759

153.7′33 — Man. Vigilance. Psychological aspects
Davies, D. R.. The psychology of vigilance / D.R. Davies, R. Parasuraman. — London : Academic Press, 1982. — 288p : ill ; 24cm. — (Organizational and occupational psychology)
Bibliography: p228-270. — Includes index
ISBN 0-12-206180-2 : £15.80 : CIP rev.
B81-35916

153.7′36 — Man. Subliminal perception
Dixon, Norman F.. Preconscious processing / Norman F. Dixon. — Chichester : Wiley, c1981. — vi,313p : ill ; 24cm
Bibliography: p268-298. — Includes index
ISBN 0-471-27982-x : £14.95 : CIP rev.
B81-28015

153.8 — PSYCHOLOGY. VOLITION

153.8 — Man. Achievement motivation
Raynor, Joel O.. Motivation, career striving and aging / Joel O. Raynor, Elliot E. Entin with contributions by Eileen T. Brown ... [et al.]. — Washington [D.C.] ; London : Hemispher ; London : McGraw-Hill [[distributor]], c1982. — x,406p : ill ; 24cm
Bibliography: p379-392. — Includes index
ISBN 0-07-051274-4 : Unpriced B82-40614

153.8 — Man. Motivation
Apter, Michael J.. The experience of motivation : the theory of psychological reversals / Michael J. Apter. — London : Academic Press, 1982. — ix,378p : ill ; 24cm
Bibliography: p334-357. — Includes index
ISBN 0-12-058920-6 : £16.80 : CIP rev.
B81-36036

153.8 — Man. Reactive behaviour
Brehm, Sharon S.. Psychological reactance : a theory of freedom and control / Sharon S. Brehm, Jack W. Brehm. — New York ; London : Academic Press, 1981. — xiii,432p : ill ; 24cm
Bibliography: p398-419. — Includes index
ISBN 0-12-129840-x : £24.20 B82-12969

153.8′3 — Decision making — *For students*
Decision making. — Manchester : Manchester University Press, Sept.1982. — [384]p
ISBN 0-7190-0890-5 (cased) : £11.00 : CIP entry
ISBN 0-7190-0891-3 (pbk) : £3.50 B82-20382

153.8′3 — Decision making. Psychological aspects
Kozielecki, Józef. Psychological decision theory / Józef Kozielecki [translated by Bogusław A. Jankowski]. — Dordrecht ; London : Reidel, c1981. — xvi,403p : ill ; 23cm. — (Theory and decision library ; v.24)
'Revised edition based on the original Polish, Psychologiczna teoria decyzji'. — Bibliography: p377-395. — Includes index
ISBN 90-277-1051-1 : Unpriced B82-27300

153.8′5 — Man. Behaviour modification
Progress in behavior modification / edited by Michel Hersen, Richard M. Eisler, Peter M. Miller. — New York ; London : Academic Press
Vol.10. — 1980. — xiv,243p : ill ; 24cm
Includes bibliographies and index
ISBN 0-12-535610-2 : Unpriced B82-07736

Sulzer-Azaroff, Beth. Applying behavioral analysis : a program for developing professional competence / Beth Sulzer-Azaroff, Ellen P. Reese. — New York ; London : Holt, Rinehart and Winston, c1982. — xx,419p : ill,forms ; 26cm
Bibliography: p407-411
ISBN 0-03-049291-2 (pbk) : £8.95 B82-25401

153.8′5 — Man. Behaviour modification — *For welfare work*
Sheldon, Brian. Behaviour modification. — London : Tavistock, Sept.1982. — [240]p. — (Tavistock library of social work practice)
ISBN 0-422-77060-4 (cased) : £9.95 : CIP entry
ISBN 0-422-77070-1 (pbk) : £4.95 B82-19669

153.9 — PSYCHOLOGY. INTELLIGENCE AND APTITUDES

153.9 — Man. Intelligence
Clifton, F.. Humans and intelligence : a chain of essays / by F. Clifton, between 1961 and 1979. — [Westcliffe-on-Sea] ([47 Gainsborough Drive, Westcliffe-on-Sea, Essex]) : [F. Clifton], 1980. — 158p : 2ill ; 22cm
Unpriced (unbound) B82-40547

153.9 — Man. Intelligence. Theories
Davis, Don D.. The unique animal : the origin, nature & consequences of human intelligence / by Don D. Davis. — London : Prytaneum, 1981. — 336p : ill ; 22cm
Bibliography: p321-329. — Includes index
ISBN 0-907152-02-3 (cased) : £12.95 : CIP rev.
ISBN 0-907152-01-5 (pbk) : £6.95 B81-28564

153.9 — Man. Skills *related to* **knowledge** — *Philosophical perspectives*
Krejci, Jaroslav. Specialised or general knowledge? : strategy for harmonisation : inaugural lecture delivered on the 24th January 1979 / Jaroslav Krejci. — [Lancaster] : University of Lancaster, [1979?]. — 12p ; 22cm
Unpriced (unbound) B82-25460

154.6 — PSYCHOLOGY. SLEEP PHENOMENA

154.6′3 — Dreams. Control
Saint-Denys, Hervey de. Dreams and how to guide them / Hervey de Saint-Denys ; translated by Nicholas Fry ; edited with an introduction by Morton Schatzman. — London : Duckworth, 1982. — 168p ; 23cm
Translation of: Les rêves et les moyens de les diriger. — Includes index
ISBN 0-7156-1584-x : Unpriced : CIP rev.
B81-28165

154.6′3′088054 — Children. Dreams — *Comparative studies*
Foulkes, David, *1935-*. Children's dreams : longitudinal studies / David Foulkes. — New York ; Chichester : Wiley, 1982. — xi,477p ; 24cm
Bibliography: p305-313 . — Includes index
ISBN 0-471-08181-7 : £24.00 B82-18202

154.6′3′0924 — Dreams. Theories of Freud, Sigmund
Nagera, Humberto. Basic psychoanalytic concepts on the theory of dreams / by Humberto Nagera and S. Baker ... [et al.] ; [edited by Humberto Nagera]. — London : Maresfield, 1981. — 121p ; 21cm. — (The Hampstead Clinic psychoanalytic library ; v.2)
Originally published: London : Allen & Unwin, 1969. — Includes index
ISBN 0-9507146-4-x (pbk) : Unpriced
B82-11680

154.6′32 — Erotic dreams. Interpretation. Psychological aspects — *Case studies*
Sterling, Richard. [1,001 erotic dreams interpreted]. 1,001 erotic dreams / Richard Sterling. — London : Sphere, 1982, c1976. — 292p ; 18cm
Originally published: / by Graham Masterton. Chicago : Regnery, 1976
ISBN 0-7221-6011-9 (pbk) : £1.75 B82-16569

154.6′34 — Dreams — *Psychoanalytical perspectives*
Rycroft, Charles. The innocence of dreams / Charles Rycroft. — Oxford : Oxford University Press, 1981, c1979. — v,184p ; 20cm. — (Oxford paperbacks)
Originally published: London : Hogarth, 1979. — Includes index
ISBN 0-19-281315-3 (pbk) : £2.25 : CIP rev.
B81-25792

154.7 — HYPNOTISM

154.7 — Auto-suggestion
Romen, A. S.. Self-suggestion : and its influence on the human organism / A.S. Romen ; translated and edited by A.J. Lewis and Valentina Forsky. — Armonk, N.Y. : Sharpe ; London : distributed by Eurospan, c1981. — xii,223p : ill ; 24cm
Translation of: Samovnushenie i ego vliianie na organizm cheloveka
ISBN 0-87332-195-2 : £16.95 B82-17300

154.7 — Hypnotism
Haward, L. R. C.. Hypnosis in the service of research / L.R.C. Haward. — [Guildford] ([Guildford, Surrey GU2 5XH]) : [University of Surrey], [1979?]. — 16p ; 21cm. — (University of Surrey inaugural lecture)
Cover title
Unpriced (pbk) B82-26650

Wagstaff, Graham F.. Hypnosis, compliance and belief / Graham F. Wagstaff. — Brighton : Wayland, 1981. — x,262p ; 22cm
Bibliography: p221-252. — Includes index
ISBN 0-7108-0017-7 : £22.50 B82-06549

154.7 — Hypnotism. Methodology
Chester, Roland John. Hypnotism in East and West : twenty hypnotic methods / by Roland John Chester. — London : Octagon, c1982. — 23p ; 21cm
ISBN 0-900860-98-7 (pbk) : £3.50 B82-25030

154.7'6 — Self-hypnotism — *Manuals*
Shone, R. (Ronald). Autohypnosis : a step-by-step guide to self-hypnosis / by Ronald Shone. — Wellingborough : Thorsons, 1982. — 159p : ill ; 22cm
Includes index
ISBN 0-7225-0738-0 (pbk) : £3.50 : CIP rev. B82-00384

155 — DIFFERENTIAL AND GENETIC PSYCHOLOGY

155 — Developmental psychology
Handbook of developmental psychology / Benjamin B. Wolman editor ; George Stricker associate editor ; Steven J. Ellman, Patricia Keith-Spiegel, David S. Palermo consulting editors. — Englewood Cliffs ; London : Prentice-Hall, c1982. — xv,960p : ill ; 29cm
Includes bibliographies and index
ISBN 0-13-372599-5 : £59.95 B82-29831

Review of human development / edited by Tiffany M. Field ... [et al.]. — New York ; Chichester : Wiley, c1982. — xix,664p : ill ; 26cm
Includes bibliographies and index
ISBN 0-471-08116-7 : Unpriced B82-38982

155 — Man. Development
Ambron, Sueann Robinson. Lifespan human development / Sueann Robinson Ambron, David Brodzinsky. — 2nd ed. — New York ; London : Holt, Rinehart and Winston, c1982. — xiv,650p : ill ; 25cm
Previous ed.: 1979. — Bibliography: p631-650. — Includes index
ISBN 0-03-059812-5 : £17.50 B82-25375

Kaluger, George. Human development : the span of life / George Kaluger, Meriem Fair Kaluger. — 2nd ed. — St. Louis ; London : Mosby, 1979. — xii,530p : ill ; 26cm
Previous ed.: 1974. — Includes index
ISBN 0-8016-2610-2 : £14.00 B82-24772

Perroux, François. A new concept of development. — London : Croom Helm, Jan.1983. — [160]p
ISBN 0-7099-2040-7 : £9.95 : CIP entry B82-32549

155 — Man. Development. Psychosocial aspects
The **Life** cycle : readings in human development / [edited by] Laurence D. Steinberg with the assistance of Lynn J. Mandelbaum. — New York ; Guildford : Columbia University Press, 1981. — xiv,379p ; 24cm
Includes bibliographies
ISBN 0-231-05110-7 (cased) : £17.50
ISBN 0-231-05111-5 (pbk) : £8.70 B82-10942

155 — Persons, 15-60 years. Development
Present and past in middle life / edited by Dorothy H. Eichorn ... [et al.]. — New York ; London : Academic Press, 1981. — xviii,500p : ill ; 24cm
Bibliography: p473-491. — Includes index
ISBN 0-12-233680-1 : £22.80 B82-28067

155'.024362 — Man. Development — *For welfare work*
Specht, Riva. Human development : a social work perspective / Riva Specht, Grace J. Craig. — Englewood Cliffs ; London : Prentice-Hall, c1982. — xii,372p : ill ; 24cm
Bibliography: p326-351. — Includes index
ISBN 0-13-444778-6 : £14.95 B82-16713

155'.0724 — Man. Psychological development. Models
Models of man / edited by Antony J. Chapman and Dylan M. Jones. — Leicester : British Psychological Society, c1980. — xv,414p ; 21cm
Bibliography: p373-396. — Includes index
ISBN 0-901715-12-3 (cased) : £12.50
ISBN 0-901715-11-5 (pbk) : Unpriced B82-38727

155.2 — INDIVIDUAL PSYCHOLOGY, PERSONALITY

155.2 — Man. Behaviour. Personal construct theory. Repertory grid technique. Data. Analysis. Applications of digital computer systems. Programs
Higginbotham, Peter. The GAB computer program for the analysis of repertory grid data / by Peter Higginbotham and D. Bannister. — [London] : [Medical Research Council, Publications Group], [1982]. — [40]p ; 21cm + Notes(2leaves ; 30cm)
Cover title
Unpriced (pbk) B82-31242

155.2 — Man. Identity
Pegasus : on identity / [editor Gregory Vitiello]. — [London] ([54 Victoria St, SW1E 6QB]) : Mobil Services Co., [1981?]. — 72p : ill(some col.),ports ; 25cm
Poster on folded sheet as insert
Unpriced (pbk) B82-06140

155.2 — Man. Individuation — *Psycho-analytical perspectives*
Lambert, Kenneth, *1910-*. Analysis, repair and individuation / Kenneth Lambert. — London : Published for the Society of Analytical Psychology, London by Academic Press, 1981. — xiv,234p ; 24cm. — (The Library of analytical psychology ; vol.5)
Bibliography: p218-224. — Includes index
ISBN 0-12-434640-5 : £12.50 : CIP rev. B81-11934

155.2 — Personality
Hampson, Sarah E.. The construction of personality : an introduction / Sarah E. Hampson. — London : Routledge & Kegan Paul, 1982. — 319p : ill ; 23cm. — (Introduction to modern psychology)
Bibliography: p287-310. — Includes index
ISBN 0-7100-0872-4 (cased) : £11.95
ISBN 0-7100-0873-2 (pbk) : £5.95 B82-13276

155.2 — Personality. Theories
Hettema, P. J.. Personality and adaption / P.J. Hettema. — Amsterdam ; Oxford : North-Holland Publishing, 1979. — x,228p : ill ; 23cm. — (Advances in psychology ; 2)
Bibliography: p195-209. — Includes index
ISBN 0-444-85380-4 : Unpriced B82-17885

Mangan, G. L.. The biology of human conduct : East-West models of temperament and personality / by G.L. Mangan. — Oxford : Pergamon, 1982. — xi,571p : ill ; 24cm. — (International series in experimental psychology ; v.25)
Bibliography: p465-542. — Includes index
ISBN 0-08-026781-5 : £35.00 : CIP rev. B81-31719

Smith, Barry D.. Theoretical approaches to personality / Barry D. Smith, Harold J. Vetter. — Englewood Cliffs ; London : Prentice-Hall, c1982. — xi,404p : ill ; 24cm
Includes bibliographies and index
ISBN 0-13-913491-3 : £14.95 B82-16981

Stolorow, Robert D.. Faces in a cloud : subjectivity in personality theory / Robert D. Stolorow and George E. Atwood. — New York ; London : Aronson ; London : Distributed by Eurospan, c1979. — 217p ; 24cm
Includes bibliographies and index
ISBN 0-87668-305-7 : £8.75 B82-23970

155.2 — Psychology. Attribution theory
Attributions and psychological change : applications of attributional theories to clinical and education practice / edited by Charles Antaki and Chris Brewin. — London : Academic Press, 1982. — xv,250p : ill ; 24cm
Includes bibliographies and index
ISBN 0-12-058780-7 : £14.20 : CIP rev. B82-12436

155.2 — Self — *Psychological perspectives*
Claxton, Guy. Wholly human : Western and Eastern visions of the self and its perfection / Guy Claxton (Swami Anand Ageha). — London : Routledge & Kegan Paul, 1981. — 211p : ill ; 22cm
Bibliography: p207-208. — Includes index
ISBN 0-7100-9004-8 (pbk) : £4.95 B82-02756

155.2'32 — Man. Aggression
Aggression and violence / edited by Peter Marsh and Anne Campbell. — Oxford : Basil Blackwell, 1982. — vi,242p : ill ; 24cm
Includes bibliographies and index
ISBN 0-631-12742-9 : £12.00 : CIP rev.
Primary classification 303.6'2 B81-22627

Multidisciplinary approaches to aggression research / edited by Paul F. Brain and David Benton. — Amsterdam ; Oxford : Elsevier/North-Holland Biomedical, 1981. — xvi,549p : ill ; 25cm
Includes bibliographies and index
ISBN 0-444-80317-3 : Unpriced
Also classified at 156'.24 B82-01652

155.2'32 — Man. Locus of control
Research with the locus of control construct / edited by Herbert M. Lefcourt. — New York ; London : Academic Press
Vol.1: Assessment methods. — 1981. — xiv,391p : ill ; 24cm
Includes bibliographies and index
ISBN 0-12-443201-8 : £21.20 B82-02209

155.2'5 — Man. Self-discipline. Development
Hauck, Paul. How to do what you want to do / Paul Hauck. — London : Sheldon, 1982, c1976. — 96p ; 20cm. — (Overcoming common problems)
Originally published: Philadelphia : Westminster, 1976
ISBN 0-85969-361-9 (pbk) : £1.95 B82-29729

155.2'5 — Personality. Development
Kegan, Robert. The evolving self : problem and process in human development / Robert Kegan. — Cambridge, Mass. ; London : Harvard University Press, 1982. — xi,318p : ill ; 25cm
Bibliography: p299-307. — Includes index
ISBN 0-674-27230-7 : £17.50 B82-33393

155.2'8 — Personality. Assessment
Lanyon, Richard I.. Personality assessment / Richard I. Lanyon, Leonard D. Goodstein. — 2nd ed. — New York ; Chichester : Wiley, c1982. — xiii,311p : ill ; 24cm
Previous ed.: 1971. — Bibliography: p257-292. — Includes index
ISBN 0-471-04087-8 : £18.50 B82-34341

155.3 — SEX PSYCHOLOGY

155.3 — Great Britain. Man. Sexual behaviour, *1700-1800*
Sexuality in eighteenth-century Britain. — Manchester : Manchester University Press, May 1982. — [288]p
ISBN 0-7190-0865-4 : £18.50 : CIP entry B82-07587

155.3 — Man. Sexual behaviour. Prediction. Applications of graphology
Marne, Patricia. Crime and sex in handwriting / Patricia Marne. — London : Constable, 1981. — 150p : ill,facsims ; 23cm
Bibliography: p150
ISBN 0-09-464320-2 : £6.95
Primary classification 364.3 B82-06383

155.3 — Man. Sexual behaviour — *Psychoanalytical perspectives*
Kahn, Sandra S.. The Kahn report on sexual preference / Sandra S. Kahn with Jean Davis. — London : W.H. Allen, 1981. — 278p ; 22cm
Includes index
ISBN 0-491-02605-6 : £6.95 B82-30561

155.3 — Women. Sexual behaviour
Women's sexual experience : explorations of the Dark continent / edited by Martha Kirkpatrick. — New York ; London : Plenum, c1982. — xv,328p ; 24cm. — (Women in context)
Includes bibliographies and index
ISBN 0-306-40793-0 : Unpriced B82-31407

155.3′0723 — Man. Sexual behaviour. Research. Interviewing. Recording. Techniques — *Case studies*

Pomeroy, Wardell B.. Taking a sex history : interviewing and recording / Wardell B. Pomeroy, Carol C. Flax, Connie Christine Wheeler. — New York : Free Press ; London : Collier Macmillan, c1982. — 329p : forms ; 27cm
Includes index
ISBN 0-02-925370-5 : Unpriced B82-33417

155.3′1′0924 — Libido. Theories of Freud, Sigmund

Nagera, Humberto. Basic psychoanalytic concepts on the libido theory / by Humberto Nagera and S. Baker ... [et al.] ; [edited by Humberto Nagera]. — London : Maresfield, 1981. — 194p ; 21cm. — (The Hampstead Clinic psychoanalytic library ; v.1)
Originally published: London : Allen & Unwin, 1969. — Includes index
ISBN 0-9507146-3-1 (pbk) : Unpriced B82-11678

155.3′32 — Men. Psychobiological aspects

Brothers, Joyce. What every woman should know about men. — London : Granada, July 1982. — [268]p
Originally published: New York : Simon and Schuster, 1981
ISBN 0-246-11880-6 : £8.95 : CIP entry B82-12235

155.4 — CHILD PSYCHOLOGY

155.4 — Children. Behaviour. Development

Richman, N.. Pre-school to school : a behavioural study. — London : Academic Press, Sept.1982. — [260]p. — (Behavioural development)
ISBN 0-12-587940-7 : CIP entry B82-19165

155.4 — Children. Development

Fahlberg, Vera. Child development / Vera Fahlberg. — [Michigan?] : Michigan Dept. of Social Services ; London : British Association for Adoption & Fostering, 1982. — 99p : ill,forms ; 22cm. — (Practice series / British Agencies for Adoption and Fostering, ISSN 0260-0803 ; 7)
Bibliography: p99
ISBN 0-903534-40-1 (pbk) : £3.00 B82-39630

Leslie, Shirley. Children growing up / by Shirley Leslie ; illustrated by Vic Mitchell. — London : Scripture Union, c1982. — 126p : ill ; 22cm
ISBN 0-85421-955-2 (pbk) : £2.50 B82-31414

155.4 — Children. Development. Assessment: Observation methods

Earle, Patty T.. Child development : an observation manual / Patty T. Earle, Cosby S. Rogers, Jean G. Wall. — Englewood Cliffs ; London : Prentice-Hall, c1982. — xiv,230p : ill,forms ; 28cm
ISBN 0-13-130427-5 (pbk) : £9.70 B82-29466

155.4 — Children. Development. Cultural factors

Cultural perspectives on child development / edited by Daniel A. Wagner, Harold W. Stevenson. — Oxford : Freeman, c1982. — xiv,315p : ill ; 25cm. — (A Series of books in psychology)
Bibliography: p280-303. — Includes index
ISBN 0-7167-1289-x (cased) : £14.80
ISBN 0-7167-1290-3 (pbk) : £7.60 B82-23936

155.4 — Children. Development — *For schools*

Askew, Susan. Growing and changing : roles, relationships and responsibilities / Susan Askew and Eileen Carnell. — London : Edward Arnold, 1982. — vii,86p : ill ; 25cm
Includes index
ISBN 0-7131-0567-4 (pbk) : £2.75 : CIP rev. B81-22488

Sylva, Kathy. Child development : a first course. — London : Grant McIntyre, Mar.1982. — [200]p
ISBN 0-86216-053-7 (cased) : £9.95 : CIP entry
ISBN 0-86216-054-5 (pbk) : £3.95 B82-00376

155.4 — Children. Development. Role of interpersonal relationships with fathers

The **Role** of the father in child development / edited by Michael E. Lamb. — 2nd ed., completely rev. and updated. — New York ; Chichester : Wiley, c1981. — xiv,582p : ill ; 24cm
Previous ed.: 1976. — Includes bibliographies and index
ISBN 0-471-07739-9 : £21.00 B82-08621

155.4 — Children. Emotional problems — *Encyclopaedias — For parents*

Crabtree, Tom. An A-Z of children's emotional problems. — London : Allen and Unwin, Feb.1983. — [288]p
Originally published: London : Elm Tree, 1981
ISBN 0-04-649018-3 (pbk) : £2.95 : CIP entry B82-36448

155.4 — Children. Psychological development — *Psychoanalytical perspectives*

Freud, Anna. Psychoanalytic psychology of normal development : 1970-1980 / Anna Freud. — London : Hogarth, 1982. — ix,389p ; 23cm. — (The International psycho-analytical library ; no.112)
Bibliography: p363-372. — Includes index
ISBN 0-7012-0543-1 : £15.00 : CIP rev. B82-00226

155.4′0240431 — Children. Development — *For parents*

Pickard, P. M.. Has our child talent? / by Phyllis M. Pickard ; illustrated by Peter Ripper. — Knebworth : Pullen, c1981. — [24]p : ill(some col.) ; 20x21cm
Text, ill on inside covers
ISBN 0-907616-04-6 (pbk) : £2.00 B82-12863

155.4′072 — Children. Development. Research. Methodology

Strategies and techniques of child study / edited by Ross Vasta ; foreword by Paul H. Mussen. — New York ; London : Academic Press, c1982. — xvi,358p : ill ; 24cm
Includes bibliographies and index
ISBN 0-12-715080-3 (cased) : £21.60
ISBN 0-12-715082-x (pbk) : £9.95 B82-29694

155.4′092′4 — Children. Psychology. Theories of Winnicott, D. W.

Davis, Madeleine. Boundary and space : an introducton to the work of D.W. Winnicott / by Madeleine Davis and David Wallbridge. — London : Karnac, c1981. — xiv,196p ; 24cm
Includes index
ISBN 0-9507146-7-4 : £9.00 B82-11528

155.4′09931 — New Zealand. Children, to 12 years. Development

Smith, Anne B.. Understanding children's development. — London : Allen & Unwin, Sept.1982. — [230]p
ISBN 0-86861-228-6 : £7.95 : CIP entry B82-22819

155.4′12 — Children. Emotions. Measurement — *Conference proceedings*

Measuring emotions in infants and children : based on seminars sponsored by the Committee on Social and Affective Development During Childhood of the Social Science Research Council / edited by Carroll E. Izard. — Cambridge : Cambridge University Press, 1982. — x,347p : ill ; 24cm. — (Cambridge studies in social and emotional development)
Includes bibliographies and index
ISBN 0-521-24171-5 : £20.00 B82-26368

155.4′12 — Children. Psychomotor skills. Teaching

Werner, Peter H.. Learning through movement : teaching cognitive content through physical activities / Peter H. Werner, Elsie C. Burton. — St. Louis ; London : Mosby, 1979. — ix,319p : ill,maps ; 26cm
Includes bibliographies and index
ISBN 0-8016-5415-7 (pbk) : £9.50 B82-19323

155.4′12 — Children, to 12 years. Motor skills. Development

The **Development** of movement control and co-ordination / edited by J.A. Scott Kelso and Jane E. Clark. — Chichester : Wiley, c1982. — xii,370p : ill ; 24cm. — (Wiley series in developmental psychology)
Includes bibliographies and index
ISBN 0-471-10048-x : £22.00 : CIP rev. B82-01103

155.4′13 — Children. Cognition. Social aspects

Social cognition : studies of the development of understanding / edited by George Butterworth and Paul Light. — Brighton : Harvester, 1982. — xiv,265p : ill ; 23cm. — ([The developing boby and mind] ; [no.2])
Conference proceedings. — Includes bibliographies and index
ISBN 0-7108-0095-9 : £22.50 : CIP rev. B81-30602

155.4′13 — Children. Cognitive development

U-shaped behavioral growth / edited by Sidney Strauss with Ruth Stavy. — New York ; London : Academic Press, 1982. — xiv,301p : ill ; 24cm. — (Developmental psychology series)
Includes bibliographies and index
ISBN 0-12-673020-2 : £19.20 B82-30013

Wachs, Theodore D.. Early experience and human development / Theodore D. Wachs and Gerald E. Gruen. — New York ; London : Plenum, c1982. — xi,297p ; 24cm
Bibliography: p251-284. — Includes index
ISBN 0-306-40685-3 : Unpriced B82-37760

155.4′13 — Children. Cognitive development *related to* **acquisition of language skills**

Children thinking through language / edited by Michael Beveridge. — London : Edward Arnold, 1982. — x,272p : ill ; 22cm
Includes bibliographies and index
ISBN 0-7131-6352-6 (pbk) : £7.95 : CIP rev.
Primary classification 401′.9 B81-37563

155.4′13 — Children. Cognitive development. Theories of Piaget, Jean

Infancy and epistemology : an evluation of Piaget's theory / edited by George Butterworth. — Brighton : Harvester, 1981. — x,267p : ill ; 23cm. — ([The developing body and mind] ; [no.1])
Includes bibliographies and index
ISBN 0-85527-497-2 : £22.50 : CIP rev. B81-23847

Jean Piaget : consensus and controversy / edited by Sohan Modgil and Celia Modgil ; finale incorporating Jean Piaget's contemporary thinking by Bärbel Inhelder. — London : Holt, Rinehart and Winston, c1982. — 446p : ill ; 25cm
Includes bibliographies and index
ISBN 0-03-910352-8 : £17.95 : CIP rev. B81-33925

155.4′13 — Children. Development. Role of acquisition of communication skills

Communication in development / edited by W.P. Robinson. — London : Published in cooperation with European Association of Experimental Social Psychology by Academic Press, 1981. — xiv,292p : ill ; 24cm. — (European monographs in social psychology ; 24)
Includes bibliographies and index
ISBN 0-12-590140-2 : £19.40 : CIP rev. B81-13424

155.4′13 — Children. Intelligence. Measurement

Sattler, Jerome M.. Student's manual to accompany Assessment of children's intelligence and special abilities. 2nd ed. / Jerome M. Sattler. — Boston ; London : Allyn and Bacon, c1982. — 241p ; 24cm
ISBN 0-205-07728-5 (pbk) : £1.00 B82-08546

155.4′13 — Children. Intelligence. Measurement — *For teaching*

Sattler, Jerome M.. Instructor's manual to accompany Sattler's Assessment of children's intelligence and special abilities. 2nd ed. / Jerome M. Sattler, Marjorie L. Lewis. — Boston ; London : Allyn and Bacon, c1982. — 149p ; 24cm
ISBN 0-205-07379-4 (pbk) : £1.00 B82-08548

155.4'13 — Children. Intelligence tests — *Collections*

Arkwright, R. M.. Helping your child with home tests : for grammar and comprehensive school entrance / R.M. Arkwright. — 4th ed. — London : Harrap, 1981. — 94p : ill ; 19cm
Previous ed. published as: Home tests for grammar and comprehensive school entrance, 1970
ISBN 0-245-53786-4 (pbk) : £1.75
Also classified at 428 ; 510'.76 B82-01489

Kitto-Jones, A.. Test your intelligence / A. Kitto-Jones. — Glasgow : Gibson, c1982. — 96p : ill ; 21cm
ISBN 0-7169-5516-4 (pbk) : Unpriced B82-40640

155.4'13 — Children. Mental development

Piaget, Jean. The essential Piaget / edited by Howard E. Gruber and J. Jacques Vonèche. — London : Routledge & Kegan Paul, 1977 (1982 [printing]). — xlii,881p : ill,1port ; 24cm
Bibliography: p861-866. — Includes index
ISBN 0-7100-9213-x (pbk) : £8.95 B82-20431

155.4'13 — Children. Oral communication — *Conference proceedings*

Children's oral communication skills / edited by W. Patrick Dickson. — New York ; London : Academic Press, 1981. — xv,394p : ill ; 24cm. — (Developmental psychology series)
Conference papers. — Includes bibliographies and index
ISBN 0-12-215450-9 : £19.60 B82-10146

155.4'13 — Children. Reasoning skills — *Questions & answers — For children*

Test your child's reasoning ability. — Sevenoaks : Produced exclusively for W.H. Smith by Hodder and Stoughton, 1982. — [32]p : ill ; 25cm
ISBN 0-340-28054-9 (pbk) : £0.60 B82-27678

155.4'13 — Learning by children — *For schools*

Bennett, Olivia. Learning in life / Olivia Bennett. — London : Macmillan Education in association with the Save the Children Fund and the Commonwealth Institute, 1982. — 48p : col.ill ; 26cm. — (Patterns of living)
Text on lining papers. — Includes index
ISBN 0-333-31195-7 : Unpriced B82-33383

155.4'13 — Learning by children. Influence of personality

Personality and learning. — Milton Keynes : Open University Press. — (Educational studies : a second level course)
At head of title: The Open University
Block 2: Personality theories and dimensions / prepared for the course team by Peter Barnes. — 2nd ed., completely rev. — 1982. — 57p : ill ; 30cm. — (E201 ; block 2)
Previous ed.: 1976. — Bibliography: p55-57
ISBN 0-335-06517-1 (pbk) : Unpriced B82-21191

Personality and learning. — Milton Keynes : Open University Press. — (Educational studies : a second level course)
At head of title: The Open University
Block 9: Problems of adjustment and learning / prepared by Bill Gillham for the course team. — 1982. — 63p : ill ; 30cm. — (E201 ; block 9)
Previous ed.: 1976. — Bibliography: p60-63
ISBN 0-335-06518-x (pbk) : Unpriced B82-40656

155.4'13 — Learning by children. Role of play — *For parents*

Isenberg, Joan P.. Playthings as learning tools : a parents' guide / Joan P. Isenberg and Judith E. Jacobs. — New York ; Chichester : Wiley, c1982. — 176p : ill ; 23cm. — (Wiley parent education series)
ISBN 0-471-09042-5 (pbk) : Unpriced B82-28182

155.4'13 — Man. Musical ability. Psychological aspects

Shuter-Dyson, Rosamund. The psychology of musical ability. — 2nd ed. — London : Methuen, Nov.1981. — [384]p
Previous ed.: 1968
ISBN 0-416-71300-9 : £15.00 : CIP entry B81-30459

155.4'13 — Time. Perception by children

The **Developmental** psychology of time / edited by William J. Friedman. — New York ; London : Academic, 1982. — xii,286p : ill ; 24cm. — (Developmental psychology series)
Includes bibliographies and index
ISBN 0-12-268320-x : £19.20 B82-38078

155.4'18 — Children. Communication skills. Development. Role of playgroups

McMahon, Linnet. Talking with children : resource materials for tutors and group leaders / by Linnet McMahon and Yvonne Cranstoun. — Reading : Southern Region Pre-School Playgroups Association, [1981?]. — 194p in various pagings : ill ; 30cm
Cover title
ISBN 0-901755-27-3 (pbk) : Unpriced B82-05137

155.4'18 — Children. Development. Role of narcissism & Oedipus complex

Hamilton, Victoria. Narcissus and Oedipus : the children of psychoanalysis / Victoria Hamilton. — London : Routledge & Kegan Paul, 1982. — xi,313p ; 23cm
Bibliography: p295-303. — Includes index
ISBN 0-7100-0869-4 : £12.50 B82-23811

155.4'18 — Children. Interpersonal relationships with mothers. Psychological aspects

Bowlby, John. Attachment and loss / by John Bowlby. — London : Hogarth
Vol.1: Attachment. — 2nd ed. — 1982. — xx,425p ; 23cm. — (The International psycho-analytical library ; 79)
Bibliography: p379-399. — Includes index
ISBN 0-7012-0544-x : £15.00 : CIP rev. B82-11305

155.4'18 — Children. Interpersonal relationships with parents. Psychobiological aspects

The **Development** of attachment and affiliative systems / edited by Robert N. Emde and Robert J. Harmon. — New York ; London : Plenum, c1982. — xx,311p : ill ; 24cm. — (Topics in developmental psychobiology)
Conference papers. — Includes bibliographies and index
ISBN 0-306-40849-x : Unpriced B82-38663

155.4'18 — Children. Moral development

Siegal, Michael. Fairness in children : a social-cognitive approach to the study of moral development / Michael Siegal. — London : Academic Press, 1982. — 207p : ill ; 24cm
Bibliography: p181-203. — Includes index
ISBN 0-12-641380-0 : £16.80 : CIP rev. B82-07490

155.4'18 — Children. Sexual development — *For parents*

Jackson, Stevi. Childhood and sexuality / Stevi Jackson. — Oxford : Blackwell, 1982. — 184p ; 19cm. — (Understanding everyday experience)
Bibliography: p183-184
ISBN 0-631-12871-9 (cased) : Unpriced : CIP rev.
ISBN 0-631-12949-9 (pbk) : Unpriced B82-04590

155.4'18 — Children. Temperament — *Conference proceedings*

Temperamental differences in infants and young children. — London : Pitman, June 1982. — [320]p. — (Ciba Foundation symposium series ; 89)
Conference papers
ISBN 0-272-79653-0 : £22.50 : CIP entry B82-09993

155.4'18 — United States. Children. Communication skills. Appraisal. Tests. Evaluation

Evaluation of appraisal techniques in speech and language pathology / editor Frederic L. Darley ; associate editors Warren H. Fay ... [et al.]. — Reading, Mass. ; London : Addison-Wesley, c1979. — xiii,274p : ill ; 25cm. — (Addison-Wesley series in speech pathology and audiology)
Includes bibliographies
ISBN 0-201-01276-6 : Unpriced B82-13352

155.4'18'0287 — Young persons, 5-18 years. Personality. Development. Projective tests: Columbus test — *Manuals*

Langeveld, M. J.. The Columbus : picture analysis of growth towards maturity / M.J. Langeveld ; translated by G. Uildriks. — 3rd unchanged ed. — Basel ; London : Karger, c1981. — 72p ; 24cm + 24 cards(ill;23cm)
Translation of: Columbus. — Previous ed.: 1976. — Cards in pocket. — Bibliography: p68-72
ISBN 3-8055-2529-x (pbk) : £23.25 B82-04217

155.4'22 — Babies, 9-13 months. Cognitive development — *Case studies*

Bates, Elizabeth. The emergence of symbols : cognition and communication in infancy / Elizabeth Bates with the collaboration of Laura Benigni ... [et al.]. — New York ; London : Academic Press, 1979. — xvi,387p : ill ; 24cm. — (Language, thought, and culture)
Bibliography: p371-381. — Includes index
ISBN 0-12-081540-0 : £22.60 B82-11647

155.4'22 — Babies. Development

Bower, T. G. R.. Development in infancy / T.G.R. Bower. — 2nd ed. — Oxford : Freeman, c1982. — x,304p : ill ; 24cm. — (A Series of books in psychology)
Previous ed.: 1974. — Bibliography: p280-296. — Includes index
ISBN 0-7167-1301-2 (cased) : £14.80
ISBN 0-7167-1302-0 (pbk) : Unpriced B82-34385

Stirrat, Gordon M.. You and your baby. — London : Norman & Hobhouse, May 1982. — [192]p
ISBN 0-906908-81-7 (pbk) : £3.95 : CIP entry B82-17235

155.4'22 — Babies, *to 2 years.* **Development. Role of interpersonal relationships with parents**

Kaye, Kenneth. The mental and social life of babies. — Brighton : Harvester Press, Sept.1982. — [304]p. — (The Developing body and mind ; 3)
ISBN 0-7108-0416-4 : CIP entry B82-19842

155.4'22 — Babies, to 6 months. Development. Teaching aids: Exercises — *For parents*

Koch, Jaroslav. [Total baby development]. Superbaby / Jaroslav Koch. — London : Orbis, 1982, c1976. — ix,351p : ill ; 22cm
Translation of: Vychova kojence v rodině. — Originally published: New York : Wyden, 1976. — Includes index
ISBN 0-85613-411-2 (pbk) : £5.95 B82-24026

155.4'22 — Babies. Visual perception

Bronson, Gordon W.. The scanning patterns of human infants : implications for visual learning / Gordon W. Bronson ; with a commentary by Richard N. Aslin. — Norwood, N.J. : Ablex, c1982 ; London : Distributed by Eurospan. — xiv,136p : ill ; 24cm. — (Monographs in infancy)
Includes bibliographies and index
ISBN 0-89391-114-3 : Unpriced B82-39724

155.4'22 — Children, 1-3 years. Self perception

Kagan, Jerome. The second year : the emergence of self-awareness / Jerome Kagan with Robin Mount ... [et al.]. — Cambridge, Mass. ; London : Harvard University Press, 1981. — viii,163p : ill ; 25cm
Bibliography: p153-160. — Includes index
ISBN 0-674-79662-4 : £9.00 B82-11871

155.4'22 — Children, to 5 years. Cognitive development

Action and thought : from sensorimotor schemes to symbolic operations / edited by George E. Forman. — New York ; London : Academic Press, 1982. — xvii,352p : ill ; 24cm. — (Developmental psychology series)
Includes bibliographies and index
ISBN 0-12-262220-0 : £23.20 B82-30109

155.4'22 — Children, to 5 years. Development

In the beginning : readings on infancy / edited by Jay Belsky. — New York ; Guildford : Columbia University Press, 1982. — xi,310p : ill ; 24cm
Bibliography: p287-310
ISBN 0-231-05114-x (cased) : £21.10
ISBN 0-231-05115-8 (pbk) : £8.80 B82-10646

155.4'22 — Children, to 5 years. Development. Assessment

Sheridan, Mary D.. [Children's developmental progress from birth to five years]. From birth to five years : children's developmental progress / Mary D. Sheridan. — 3rd and expanded ed. — Windsor : NFER-Nelson, 1975 (1981 [printing]). — 74p : ill ; 25cm
Previous ed.: 1973
ISBN 0-85633-074-4 (pbk) : £2.95 B82-07924

155.4'22 — Children, to 5 years. Development — *For child care*

Hicks, Patricia. Introduction to child development / Patricia Hicks. — Harlow : Longman, 1981. — 160p : ill ; 22cm. — (Longman early childhood education)
Bibliography: p154-155. — Includes index
ISBN 0-582-36149-4 (pbk) : £3.95 : CIP rev. B81-25692

155.4'22 — Children, to 5 years. Development. Teaching aids: Activities

Bailey, Rebecca Anne. The dynamic self : activities to enhance infant development / Rebecca Anne Bailey, Elsie Carter Burton. — St. Louis ; London : Mosby, 1982. — viii,195p : ill ; 24cm
Bibliography: p188-189. — Includes index
ISBN 0-8016-0438-9 (pbk) : £8.50 B82-08260

155.4'22 — Children, to 5 years. Psychological development

Gillham, Bill. Child psychology : the child to five years / Bill Gillham and Kim Plunkett. — Sevenoaks : Hodder and Stoughton, 1982. — 135p : ill ; 18cm
Bibliography: p120-127. — Includes index
ISBN 0-340-25112-3 (pbk) : £1.95 : CIP rev. B81-33984

155.4'22 — Newborn babies. Interpersonal relationships with parents. Psychological aspects

Klaus, Marshall H.. Parent-infant bonding / Marshall H. Klaus, John H. Kennell. — 2nd ed. — St. Louis, Mo. ; London : Mosby, 1982. — xix,214p : ill,1plan,1port ; 25cm
Previous ed.: published as Maternal-infant bonding. 1976. — Bibliography: p293-308. — Includes index
ISBN 0-8016-2686-2 (cased) : £13.50
ISBN 0-8016-2685-4 (pbk) : £9.75 B82-22839

155.4'22 — Newborn babies. Psychobiological aspects

Psychobiology of the human newborn. — Chichester : Wiley, Sept.1982. — [416]p. — (Developmental psychology series)
ISBN 0-471-10093-5 : £16.00 : CIP entry B82-19518

155.4'23 — Children, 3-5 years. Communication. Development

Lloyd, Peter, *1942-*. Information and meaning in child communication / Peter Lloyd, Michael Beveridge. — London : Academic Press, 1981. — xii,196p : ill ; 24cm. — (Applied language studies)
Bibliography: p185-194. — Includes index
ISBN 0-12-453520-8 : £13.60 : CIP rev. B81-31342

155.4'24 — Children, 8-14 years. Social development. Assessment. Methodology

Schofield, W. N.. A review of the literature on methods of assessing the personal and social development of young people / by W.N. Schofield. — [London] ([Department of Education and Science, Elizabeth House, York Rd., S.E.1]) : Assessment of Performance Unit, 1981. — iii,92p ; 30cm
Cover title: Personal and social development literature review 1980. — Bibliography: p64-71
Unpriced (pbk) B82-17341

155.4'33 — Girls. Psychological development

Early female development : current psychoanalytic views / edited by Dale Mendell. — Lancaster : M.T.P. Press, c1982. — 256p : ill ; 24cm
Includes bibliographies and index
ISBN 0-85200-586-5 : £20.25 B82-39876

155.4'43 — Children. Interpersonal relationships with siblings

Dunn, Judy. Siblings. — London : Grant McIntyre, Feb.1982. — [240]p
ISBN 0-86216-045-6 (cased) : £12.95 : CIP entry
ISBN 0-86216-078-2 (pbk) : £5.95 B81-36042

155.4'44 — Identical twins. Behavior. Influence of heredity & environmental factors — *Case studies*

Watson, Peter, *1943-*. Twins : an investigation into the strange coincidences in the lives of separated twins / Peter Watson. — London : Hutchinson, 1981. — 207p : ill,ports ; 23cm
ISBN 0-09-145330-5 : £7.50 : CIP rev. B81-12320

155'.4'51 — Handicapped children, to 5 years. Development

Chazan, Maurice. The early years / Maurice Chazan and Alice F. Laing. — Milton Keynes : Open University Press, 1982. — viii,120p ; 24cm. — (Children with special needs)
Includes bibliographies and index
ISBN 0-335-10050-3 (cased) : £11.95 : CIP rev.
ISBN 0-335-10052-x (pbk) : £4.95 B81-36982

155.4'528 — Mentally handicapped children. Development — *For teaching*

Perkins, E. A.. Developmental checklist / authors E.A. Perkins, P.D. Taylor, A.C.M. Capie. — 2nd ed. — Kidderminster : British Institute of Mental Handicap, 1980. — 15p ; 21cm
This checklist is taken from: Helping the retarded — a systematic approach / E.A. Perkins, P.D. Taylor, A.C.M. Capie, 2nd ed. — Previous ed.: 1976
ISBN 0-906054-25-7 (unbound) : Unpriced B82-35269

155.4'55 — Gifted children

Lowenstein, L. F.. The psychological problems of gifted children / L.F. Lowenstein. — Knebworth : Pullen, c1981. — ii,68p ; 21cm
Bibliography: p57-66
ISBN 0-907616-03-8 (pbk) : £3.75 B82-12864

155.4'55092'6 — Gifted children. Development — *Case studies*

Deakin, Michael. The children on the hill. — London : Quartet Books, Feb.1982. — [120]p
Originally published: London : Deutsch, 1972
ISBN 0-7043-3086-5 (pbk) : £1.95 : CIP entry B81-40248

155.4'567 — France. Aveyron. Feral children: Victor, *of Aveyron*

Shattuck, Roger. The forbidden experiment. — London : Quartet Books, Oct.1981. — [240]p
Originally published: London : Secker and Warburg, 1980
ISBN 0-7043-3383-x (pbk) : £3.50 : CIP entry B81-28117

155.4'567 — Spain. Feral children: Pantoja, Marcos Rodríquez — *Biographies*

Janer Manila, Gabriel. Marcos, wild child of the Sierra Morena / Gabriel Janer Manila ; translated by Deborah Bonner. — London : Souvenir, 1982. — 167p,[8]p of plates : ill,ports ; 23cm
Translated from the Spanish
ISBN 0-285-64924-8 : £8.95 B82-23964

155.4'567'0996941 — Socially disadvantaged children. Psychology — *Study regions: Hawaii. Kauai*

Werner, Emmy E.. Vulnerable but invincible : a longitudinal study of resilient children and youth / Emmy E. Werner, Ruth S. Smith ; foreword by Norman Garmezy. — New York ; London : McGraw-Hill, c1982. — xxii,228p ; 24cm
Bibliography: p209-217. — Includes index
ISBN 0-07-069445-1 : £14.50 B82-15984

155.5 — PSYCHOLOGY OF ADOLESCENTS

155.5 — Adolescents. Psychology

Fadely, Jack L.. Confrontation in adolescence / Jack L. Fadely, Virginia N. Hosler. — St. Louis ; London : C.V. Mosby, 1979. — xiii,147p : ill ; 25cm
Includes bibliographies and index
ISBN 0-8016-1553-4 (pbk) : £9.50 B82-33561

155.6 — PSYCHOLOGY OF ADULTS

155.6 — Adulthood. Crises. Psychological aspects

Golan, Naomi. Passing through transitions : a guide for practitioners / Naomi Golan. — New York : Free Press ; London : Collier Macmillan, c1981. — xxii,330p ; 25cm
Bibliography: p301-323. — Includes index
ISBN 0-02-912070-5 : £13.95 B82-20402

155.6 — Adulthood. Psychological aspects

Rogers, Dorothy, *1914-*. The adult years : an introduction to aging / Dorothy Rogers. — 2nd ed. — Englewood Cliffs ; London : Prentice-Hall, c1982. — xvi,445p : ill ; 25cm
Previous ed.: 1979. — Bibliography: p420-440. — Includes index
ISBN 0-13-008961-3 : £15.70 B82-23645

155.6 — Adults. Ageing. Psychological aspects

Freese, Arthur S.. The end of senility / Arthur S. Freese. — South Yarmouth : John Curley ; [Skipton] : Magna Print [distributor], 1979, c1978. — xx,287p ; 22cm
Originally published: New York : Arbor House, 1978. — Published in large print. — Bibliography: p282-287
ISBN 0-89340-189-7 : £4.75 B82-15100

Kausler, Donald H.. Experimental psychology and human aging / Donald H. Kausler. — New York ; Chichester : Wiley, c1982. — x,720p : ill ; 25cm
Bibliography: p637-687. — Includes index
ISBN 0-471-08163-9 : £18.20 B82-34520

155.6 — Adults. Psychological development

Readings in adult psychology : contemporary perspectives / edited by Lawrence R. Allman, Dennis T. Jaffe. — 2nd ed. — New York ; London : Harper & Row, c1982. — xii,407p : ill ; 28cm. — (Harper & Row's contemporary perspectives reader series)
Previous ed.: 197-?. — Includes bibliographies
ISBN 0-06-040234-2 (pbk) : £5.95 B82-28708

155.6'33 — Middle age. Personal adjustment of women, 30-50 years — *Interviews*

Bailey, Caroline. Beginning in the middle. — London : Quartet, Nov.1982. — [320]p
ISBN 0-7043-2348-6 : £10.95 : CIP entry B82-29082

155.6'33 — Women. Dependency — *Feminist viewpoints*

Dowling, Colette. The Cinderella complex : women's hidden fear of independence / Colette Dowling. — [London] : Fontana, 1982. — 254p ; 18cm
Originally published: New York : Summit Books, 1981. — Bibliography: p243-254
ISBN 0-00-636481-0 (pbk) : £1.75 B82-26610

Dowling, Colette. The Cinderella complex : women's hidden fear of independence / Colette Dowling. — London : Joseph, 1982, c1981. — 254p ; 23cm
Originally published: New York : Summit, 1981. — Bibliography: p243-254
ISBN 0-7181-2119-8 : £8.95 B82-25330

155.6'33 — Women. Psychological development

Gilligan, Carol. In a different voice : psychological theory and women's development / Carol Gilligan. — Cambridge, Mass. ; London : Harvard University Press, 1982. — vi,184p ; 24cm
Bibliography: p177-180. — Includes index
ISBN 0-674-44543-0 : £10.50 B82-36043

155.6'33 — Women. Psychology

Harding, Esther. The way of all women. — London : Rider Books, Feb.1983. — [286]p
ISBN 0-09-150021-4 (pbk) : £2.95 : CIP entry B82-36437

155.6'33 — Women. Psychology — *Feminist viewpoints*

Eichenbaum, Luise. Outside in-inside out : women's psychology : a feminist psychoanalytic approach / Luise Eichenbaum and Susie Orbach. — Harmondsworth : Penguin, 1982. — 133p ; 20cm. — (Pelican books)
Bibliography: p125-128. — Includes index
ISBN 0-14-022296-0 (pbk) : £1.95 B82-30357

155.6′71 — Dementia patients. Premorbid intelligence. Assessment. Tests: National Adult Reading Test

Nelson, Hazel E.. National adult reading test (NART) : for the assessment of premorbid intelligence in patients with dementia / Hazel E. Nelson. — Windsor : NFER-Nelson, c1982. — 3v. : 1form ; 30cm
ISBN 0-7005-0475-3 : Unpriced
ISBN 0-7005-0474-5 (answer/record sheet) : (Sold in packs of 25) £2.05
ISBN 0-7005-0484-2 (pronunciation guide) : £0.95 B82-25462

155.8 — ETHNOPSYCHOLOGY AND NATIONAL PSYCHOLOGY

155.8 — Man. Behaviour. Cultural factors — *Anthropological perspectives*

Clark, Grahame. The identity of man. — London : Methuen, Sept.1982. — [224]p
ISBN 0-416-33560-8 (cased) : £15.00 : CIP entry
ISBN 0-416-33550-0 (pbk) : £5.95 B82-18753

155.8′2 — Ethnic groups. Identity. Personal construct theory. Repertory grid technique. Applications of digital computer systems. Programs

Weinreich, Peter. Manual for identity exploration using personal constructs / Peter Weinreich. — Birmingham (St Peter′s College, College Rd., Saltley, Birmingham B8 3TE) : Social Science Research Council, Research Unit on Ethnic Relations, c1980. — 49,[45]p : forms ; 30cm. — (Working papers on ethnic relations, ISSN 0309-6394)
Bibliography: p[43]-[45]
£2.50 (pbk) B82-20232

155.8′496073 — United States. Negroes. Intelligence. Theories

Garrett, Henry E.. IQ and racial differences / by Henry E. Garrett. — Torrance, Calif. : Noontide Press ; Brighton : Historical Review Press, c1980. — 57p : ill ; 19cm
Bibliography: p55-57
ISBN 0-906879-35-3 (pbk) : Unpriced B82-03644

155.9 — ENVIRONMENTAL PSYCHOLOGY

155.9 — Man. Behaviour. Environmental factors

Jochim, Michael A.. Strategies for survival : cultural behaviour in an ecological context / Michael A. Jochim. — New York ; London : Academic Press, c1981. — x,233p : ill,maps ; 24cm
Bibliography: p214-230. — Includes index
ISBN 0-12-385460-1 : £12.40 B82-02071

155.9 — Man. Intelligence & ability — *Psychological perspectives*

Genius and eminence. — Oxford : Pergamon, Jan.1983. — [300]p. — (International series in experimental social psychology ; v.5)
ISBN 0-08-028105-2 : £17.50 : CIP entry B82-33608

155.9′05 — Man. Behaviour. Environmental factors — *Serials*

Human behavior and environment : advances in theory and research. — Vol.1-. — New York ; London : Plenum, 1976-. — v. ; 23cm
Description based on: Vol.5
ISSN 0148-8686 = Human behavior and environment : Unpriced B82-18517

155.9092′472 — Environmental psychology - *For architects*

Brebner, John. Environmental psychology for architects. — London : Applied Science, May 1981. — [224]p. — (Architectural science series)
ISBN 0-85334-969-x : £18.00 : CIP entry B81-08851

155.9′37 — Bereaved persons. Self-help — *Manuals*

Kirsch, Charlotte. A survivor′s manual. — London : Jill Norman and Hobhouse, June 1982. — [192]p
ISBN 0-906908-61-2 (pbk) : £3.95 : CIP entry B82-10897

155.9′37 — Bereavement. Psychosocial aspects

Bowling, Ann. Life after a death. — London : Tavistock, Nov.1982. — [256]p
ISBN 0-422-78230-0 : £12.00 : CIP entry B82-27510

155.9′37 — Death. Attitudes. Psychological aspects

Rowe, Dorothy. The construction of life and death / Dorothy Rowe. — Chichester ; New York : Wiley, c1982. — xiii,218p : ill ; 24cm
Bibliography: p210-214. — Includes index
ISBN 0-471-10064-1 : £12.50 : CIP rev. B82-03604

155.9′37 — Death. Psychological aspects — *Conference proceedins*

Death and dying : a quality of life / edited by Patricia F. Pegg and Erno Metze. — London : Pitman, 1981. — x,190p : ill ; 24cm
Includes bibliographies and index
ISBN 0-272-79606-9 : Unpriced : CIP rev. B81-23887

155.9′37 — United States. Grief. Personal adjustment of women

Silverman, Phyllis R.. Helping women cope with grief / Phyllis R. Silverman. — Beverly Hills ; London : Published in coooperation with the Continuing Education Program in the Human Services of the University of Michigan School of Social Work [by] Sage, c1981. — 111p ; 22cm. — (A Sage human services guide ; 24)
Includes bibliographies
ISBN 0-8039-1735-x (pbk) : Unpriced B82-21866

155′.9′62 — Imprisonment. Psychological aspects

Coping with imprisonment / edited by Nicolette Parisi. — Beverly Hills ; London : Sage, c1982. — 160p : ill ; 22cm. — (Perspectives in criminal justice ; 3)
Published in cooperation with the Academy of Criminal Justice Sciences. — Includes bibliographies
ISBN 0-8039-1785-6 (cased) : Unpriced
ISBN 0-8039-1786-4 (pbk) : Unpriced B82-25692

156 — COMPARATIVE PSYCHOLOGY

156 — Man. Behaviour *compared with* **behaviour of primates**

Passingham, R. E.. The human primate / R.E. Passingham. — Oxford : Freeman, c1982. — xii,390p : ill,maps ; 24cm
Bibliography: p334-380. — Includes index
ISBN 0-7167-1356-x (cased) : £14.95
ISBN 0-7167-1357-8 (pbk) : £7.50 B82-35532

156.2 — ANIMAL PSYCHOLOGY. PHYSIOLOGICAL PSYCHOLOGY

156′.24 — Laboratory animals: Vertebrates. Aggression

Multidisciplinary approaches to aggression research / edited by Paul F. Brain and David Benton. — Amsterdam ; Oxford : Elsevier/North-Holland Biomedical, 1981. — xvi,549p : ill ; 25cm
Includes bibliographies and index
ISBN 0-444-80317-3 : Unpriced
Primary classification 155.2′32 B82-01652

156′.242 — Animals. Emotions. Expression — *Early works*

Darwin, Charles. The expression of emotions in man and animals / Charles Darwin ; introduced by S.J. Rachman. — London : Friedman, 1979. — xiii,vi,374p,[12]p of plates : ill ; 22cm
Facsim of ed. published: London : Murray, 1872. — Bibliography: pxiii. — Includes index
ISBN 0-904014-39-8 : Unpriced B82-30449

156.3 — ANIMAL PSYCHOLOGY. INTELLIGENCE AND INTELLECTUAL PROCESSES

156′.315 — Deaf persons. Sign languages: American Sign Language. Learning by gorillas — *Personal observations*

Patterson, Francine. The education of Koko / Francine Patterson & Eugene Linden ; photographs by Ronald H. Cohn. — London : Deutsch, 1982, c1981. — xiv,224p,[8]p of plates : ill(some col.),ports ; 24cm
Bibliography: p215-216 . — Includes index
ISBN 0-233-97431-8 : £7.95 B82-23383

157 — ABNORMAL PSYCHOLOGY

157′.7 — Homosexuality — *Psychoanalytical perspectives*

Socarides, Charles W.. Homosexuality / Charles W. Socarides. — New York ; London : Aronson ; London : Distributed by Eurospan, c1978. — cvii,642p ; 24cm
Bibliography: p603-626. — Includes index
ISBN 0-87668-355-3 : Unpriced B82-23966

157.9 — CLINICAL PSYCHOLOGY

157′.9 — Clinical psychology

Kendall, Philip C.. Clinical psychology : scientific and professional dimensions / Philip C. Kendall, Julian D. Norton-Ford. — New York ; Chichester : Wiley, c1982. — 699p : ill ; 25cm
Bibliography: p595-675. — Includes index
ISBN 0-471-04350-8 : £16.25 B82-27762

157′.9′05 — Clinical psychology — *Serials*

Clinical psychology review. — Vol.1, no.1 (1981)-. — New York ; Oxford : Pergamon, 1981-. — v. : ill ; 26cm
Quarterly
Unpriced B82-07632

157′.9′072 — Clinical psychology. Research. Methodology

Handbook of research methods in clinical psychology / edited by Philip C. Kendall, James N. Butcher. — New York ; Chichester : Wiley, c1982. — xvi,728p : ill ; 26cm. — (Wiley series on personality processes, ISSN 0195-4008)
Includes bibliographies and index
ISBN 0-471-07980-4 : £38.75 B82-37993

158 — APPLIED PSYCHOLOGY

158 — Applied psychology

Beck, Robert C.. Applying psychology : understanding people / Robert C. Beck. — Englewood Cliffs ; London : Prentice-Hall, c1982. — x,484p : ill ; 25cm
Bibliography: p463-474. — Includes index
ISBN 0-13-043463-9 : £15.70 B82-31909

Psychology in practice. — Chichester : Wiley, Dec.1982. — [300]p
ISBN 0-471-10411-6 : £16.00 : CIP entry B82-30826

158 — Negotiation — *Manuals*

Kennedy, Gavin. Everything is negotiable!. — London : Business Books, Nov.1982. — [272]p
ISBN 0-09-149770-1 : £12.95 : CIP entry B82-30576

158′.1 — Man. Personal problems. Solutions

Morris, Sarah. Coping with crisis / Sarah Morris. — South Yarmouth, Mass. : John Curley, c1978 ; [Long Preston] : Distributed by Magna. — 227p ; 23cm
Published in large print. — Bibliography: p222-227
ISBN 0-89340-193-5 : £5.25 B82-05855

158′.1 — Personal success. Use of self-hypnotism — *Manuals*

Hariman, Jusuf. How to use the power of self-hypnosis / by Jusuf Hariman. — Wellingborough : Thorsons, 1981. — 128p ; 22cm
Bibliography: p127-128
ISBN 0-7225-0728-3 (pbk) : £2.95 : CIP rev. B81-31536

158′.1 — Personal success. Use of subordination — *Manuals*

Ellis, Derek. Subordinate sex. — London : Arlington Books, June 1982. — [208]p
ISBN 0-85140-550-9 : £9.95 : CIP entry B82-13103

158′.1 — Self-assertion — *Manuals*

Dickson, Anne. A woman in your own right. — London : Quartet Books, Sept.1982. — [176]p
ISBN 0-7043-3420-8 (pbk) : £4.95 : CIP entry B82-29008

158′.1 — Self-assertion — *Manuals* *continuation*

Hauck, Paul. How to stand up for yourself / Paul Hauck. — London : Sheldon, 1981, c1979. — x,85p ; 20cm. — (Overcoming common problems)
Originally published: Philadelphia: Westminster, 1979
ISBN 0-85969-335-x (pbk) : £1.95 B82-40623

158′.1 — Self-assertion — *Manuals — For women*

Butler, Pamela. Self-assertion for women / Pamela Butler. — New ed. — Cambridge [Mass.] ; London : Harper & Row, c1981. — 335p : ill ; 23cm
Previous ed.: San Francisco : Canfield, c1976. — Bibliography: p322-328. — Includes index
ISBN 0-06-250121-6 (pbk) : £4.95 B82-10037

158′.1 — Self-development — *Manuals*

Dyer, Wayne W.. The sky′s the limit / Wayne W. Dyer. — London : Granada, 1981, c1980 (1982 [printing]). — 446p ; 18cm. — (A Mayflower book)
Originally published: New York : Simon & Schuster, 1980
ISBN 0-583-13477-7 (pbk) : £1.95 B82-38554

Woodcock, Mike. Fifty activities for self-development. — Aldershot : Gower, Mar.1982. — [250]p
ISBN 0-566-02372-5 : £27.50 : CIP entry
B82-00194

158′.1 — Self-discovery

Krystal, Phyllis. Cutting the ties that bind : how to achieve liberation from false security and negative conditioning / by Phyllis Krystal. — Wellingborough : Turnstone, 1982. — 192p : ill ; 22cm
ISBN 0-85500-162-3 (pbk) : £4.50 : CIP rev.
B82-07031

Wilson, Colin. Access to inner worlds. — London : Hutchinson, Feb.1983. — 1v.
ISBN 0-09-150080-x (cased) : £6.95 : CIP entry
ISBN 0-09-150081-8 (pbk) : £3.95 B82-36457

158′.1 — Self-realisation

Ferrucci, Piero. What we may be : the visions and techniques of psychosynthesis / by Piero Ferrucci ; foreword by Laura Huxley. — Wellingborough : Turnstone, 1982. — 250p : ill ; 22cm
Bibliography: p243-244. — Includes index
ISBN 0-85500-153-4 (pbk) : £4.95 : CIP rev.
B82-04803

Individuals as producers of their development : a life-span perspective / edited by Richard M. Lerner, Nancy A. Busch-Rossnagel ; with a foreword by Orville G. Brim, Jr. — New York ; London : Academic, 1981. — xxi,503p : ill ; 24cm
Includes bibliographies and index
ISBN 0-12-444550-0 : £27.50 B82-02033

Wilber, Ken. No boundary : eastern and western approaches to personal growth / Ken Wilber. — Boulder [Colo.] ; London : Shambhala ; London : Routledge & Kegan Paul [Distributor], 1981, c1979. — 160p ; 23cm
Originally published: Los Angeles : Center Publications, 1979. — Includes bibliographies and index
ISBN 0-394-74881-6 (pbk) : £4.95 B82-13305

158′.1 — Self-realisation — *For Irish students*

Gill, Albert. Plan your future, 2 : a programme for middle school students / Albert Gill and Michael McCoy. — Dublin : Educational Company of Ireland, 1982. — 92p : ill,forms ; 21cm
Unpriced (pbk) B82-25667

158′.1 — Self-realisation — *Manuals*

Brennan, J. H.. Getting what you want. — Wellingborough : Excalibur, Nov.1982. — [160]p
ISBN 0-85454-083-0 (pbk) : £3.50 : CIP entry
B82-26322

Jensen, E. A.. On your head : expand your potential — private and business — in 84 days / E.A. Jensen. — Enl. and rev. ed. — Brighton : E.A. Jensen, 1981. — 121p ; 22cm
Previous ed.: 1972
ISBN 0-9507437-0-4 (pbk) : £3.50 B82-28334

Rainwater, Janette. You′re in charge! : a guide to becoming your own therapist / by Janette Rainwater. — Wellingborough : Turnstone, 1981, c1979. — 221p ; 22cm
Originally published: Los Angeles : Guild of Tutors Press, 1979. — Bibliography: p212-216. — Includes index
ISBN 0-85500-156-9 (pbk) : £3.75 : CIP rev.
B81-18162

Taylor, F. J. (Frederick John), *1912-*. The right way to a good job / by F.J. Taylor. — London : Business Books, 1979. — x,174p ; 22cm
Includes index
ISBN 0-220-66364-5 (pbk) : £5.05 B82-30652

158′.1 — Self-realisation — *Manuals — For persons, 50 years-*

Torrie, Margaret. Completing the circle : new ways of life after fifty / by Margaret Torrie. — Wellingborough : Turnstone, 1982. — 96p ; 22cm
Bibliography: p93-96
ISBN 0-85500-167-4 (pbk) : £2.95 : CIP rev.
B82-04800

158′.1 — Self-realisation — *Serials*

Human potential resources. — Dec. 1977-. — Lincoln (P.O. Box 10, Lincoln LN5 8XE) : LSG, 1977-. — v. : ill,ports ; 29cm
Quarterly
ISSN 0263-5100 = Human potential resources : Unpriced B82-40060

Share it : a magazine to celebrate & promote awareness of our true identity. — 1-. — Ipswich (c/o Anne Seward, Roots, Church La., Playford, Ipswich IP6 9DS) : [s.n.], [1981?]-. — v. : ill ; 21cm
Two issues yearly. — Continues: The Nacton newsletter
ISSN 0262-9356 = Share it : £1.00 per issue
B82-11833

158′.1 — Self-realisation — *Stories, anecdotes*

Mandino, Og. The greatest gift in the world / Augustus Mandino. — London : Sheldon, 1981, c1968. — 104p ; 21cm
Originally published: New York : Fell, 1968
ISBN 0-85969-351-1 : £3.95 B82-08476

158′.12 — Meditation

Eastcott, Michael J.. The silent path. — London : Rider, Feb.1983. — [176]p
ISBN 0-09-149971-2 (pbk) : £2.95 : CIP entry
B82-36435

LeShan, Lawrence. How to meditate. — Wellingborough : Turnstone, Feb.1983. — [144]p
Originally published: Boston : Hall, 1974
ISBN 0-85500-175-5 (pbk) : £3.50 : CIP entry
B82-39609

Long, Barry. Meditation : a foundation course / Barry Long. — [London] : Barry Long Centre, 1969 (1982 [printing]). — 25p ; 21cm
Cover title
ISBN 0-9508050-0-9 (pbk) : Unpriced
B82-28847

Steinbrecher, Edwin C.. The inner guide meditation. — Wellingborough : Aquarian Press, Nov.1982. — [224]p
ISBN 0-85030-300-1 (pbk) : £4.50 : CIP entry
B82-28754

158′.12 — Meditation. Techniques

Laurie, Sanders G.. Centering : the power of meditation. — Wellingborough : Excalibur Books, June 1982. — [192]p
ISBN 0-85454-082-2 (pbk) : £3.50 : CIP entry
B82-10216

158′.12 — Self-development. Role of meditation

Alder, Vera Stanley. The fifth dimension. — London : Rider, Feb.1983. — [240]p
ISBN 0-09-149951-8 (pbk) : £2.95 : CIP entry
B82-36434

158′.12 — Transcendental meditation

Allan, John, *1950-*. TM : a Cosmic confidence trick : transcendental meditation analysed / John Allan. — Leicester : Inter-Varsity, 1980. — 61p ; 18cm
Bibliography: p61
ISBN 0-85110-243-3 (pbk) : £0.75 : CIP rev.
B80-19003

Fenn, Mair. An introduction to T.M. / by Mair Fenn. — Dublin : Mercier, c1978 (1979 [printing]). — 96p ; 18cm. — (Self-improvement series)
Bibliography: p95
ISBN 0-85342-539-6 (pbk) : Unpriced
B82-23920

Hollings, Robert. Transcendental meditation : an introduction to the practice and aims of TM / by Robert Hollings. — Wellingborough : Aquarian, 1982. — 96p ; 18cm
Includes index
ISBN 0-85030-240-4 (pbk) : £0.95 : CIP rev.
B82-00387

158′.12′09 — Meditation, *to 1981*

Johnson, Willard. Riding the ox home : a history of meditation from Shamanism to science / Willard Johnson. — London : Rider, 1982. — 261p : ill ; 22cm
Bibliography: p242-246. — Includes index
ISBN 0-09-146291-6 (pbk) : £5.50 : CIP rev.
B81-30343

158′.2 — Interpersonal relationships. Communication — *Manuals*

Phillips, Keri. The management of interpersonal skills training. — Aldershot : Gower, Jan.1983. — [284]p
ISBN 0-566-02286-9 : £15.00 : CIP entry
B82-32442

158′.2 — Interpersonal relationships. Communication. Psychological aspects — *Conference proceedings*

Guy′s Hospital Symposium on the Individual Frame of Reference *(1st : 1980)*. Personal meanings. — Chichester : Wiley, Dec.1982. — [170]p
ISBN 0-471-10220-2 : £14.95 : CIP entry
B82-30819

158′.2 — Interpersonal relationships — *Manuals*

Crabtree, Tom. The search for love : a guide to your relationships / by Tom Crabtree. — London : Ebury, 1982. — 159p : ill ; 23cm. — (A Cosmopolitan book)
ISBN 0-85223-225-x : £6.95 B82-32570

Garner, Alan, *1950-*. Conversationally speaking / by Alan Garner. — New York ; London : McGraw-Hill, 1981, c1980. — xiii,186p : ill ; 21cm
Bibliography: p175-180. — Includes index
ISBN 0-07-022885-x (pbk) : £3.95 B82-03530

158′.2 — Interpersonal relationships. Psychological aspects

Duck, Steve. Friends for life. — Brighton : Harvester Press, Feb.1983. — [208]p
ISBN 0-7108-0481-4 : £12.95 : CIP entry
B82-38901

The Place of attachment in human behavior / edited by Colin Murray Parkes and Joan Stevenson-Hinde. — London : Tavistock, 1982. — xvi,331p : ill ; 25cm
Conference papers. — Includes bibliographies and index
ISBN 0-422-77600-9 : Unpriced : CIP rev.
B82-04059

Semin, G. R.. The accountability of conduct. — London : Academic Press, Jan.1983. — [192]p. — (European monographs in social psychology ; 33)
ISBN 0-12-636650-0 : CIP entry B82-36322

158'.2 — Man. Helping behaviour. Psychological aspects

Cooperation and helping behaviour : theories and research / edited by Valerian J. Derlega, Janusz Grzelak. — New York ; London : Academic Press, c1982. — xvii,452p : ill ; 24cm
Includes bibliographies and index
ISBN 0-12-210820-5 : £25.60 B82-29689

158'.2 — Man. Shyness. Alleviation — *Manuals*

Powell, Barbara. Overcoming shyness : practical scripts for everyday encounters / Barbara Powell. — Toronto ; London : McGraw-Hill, c1979. — 203p ; 21cm
Includes index
ISBN 0-07-050570-5 : £6.95 B82-14168

158.3 — Counselling psychology

Nelson-Jones, Richard. The theory and practice of counselling psychology / Richard Nelson-Jones. — London : Holt, Rinehart and Winston, 1982. — x,533p : ill ; 25cm
Includes index
ISBN 0-03-910350-1 (pbk) : £7.50 : CIP rev. B81-34486

158'.3 — Interviewing — *Manuals*

Molyneaux, Dorothy. Effective interviewing : techniques and analysis / Dorothy Molyneaux, Vera W. Lane. — Boston [Mass.] ; London : Allyn and Bacon, c1982. — viii,244p : forms ; 24cm
Includes bibliographies and index
ISBN 0-205-07564-9 : £18.95 B82-14669

158.5 — Negotiation — *Manuals*

Fisher, Roger, *1922-*. Getting to yes : negotiating agreement without giving in / Roger Fisher and William Ury with Bruce Patton, editor. — London : Hutchinson, 1982, c1981. — xiii,165p ; 23cm
Originally published: Boston, Mass. : Houghton Mifflin, 1981
ISBN 0-09-149370-6 : £6.95 : CIP rev. B82-09279

Sparks, Donald B.. The dynamics of effective negotiation / Donald B. Sparks. — Houston ; London : Gulf, c1982. — xi,162p : forms ; 22cm
Bibliography: p158. — Includes index
ISBN 0-87201-582-3 : Unpriced B82-39862

158.7 — Industrial psychology

Psychology at work / edited by Peter Warr. — 2nd ed. — Harmondsworth : Penguin, 1978 (1981 [printing]). — 448p : ill ; 20cm. — (Penguin education) (The Open University set book)
Bibliography: p376-428. — Includes index
ISBN 0-14-080284-3 (pbk) : £2.95 B82-11611

Rambo, William W.. Work and organizational behavior / William W. Rambo. — New York ; London : Holt, Rinehart and Winston, 1982. — xvi,542p : ill,forms ; 25cm
Bibliography: p486-521. — Includes index
ISBN 0-03-056133-7 : £17.95 B82-25826

Schultz, Duane P.. Psychology and industry today : an introduction to industrial and organizational psychology / Duane P. Schultz. — 3rd ed. — New York : Macmillan ; London : Collier Macmillan, c1982. — xiii,509p : ill ; 24cm
Previous ed.: 1978. — Includes bibliographies and index
ISBN 0-02-408020-9 : £14.95 B82-19510

The **Theory** and practice of organizational psychology : a collection of original essays / edited by Nigel Nicholson and Toby D. Wall. — London : Academic, 1982. — ix,261p : ill ; 24cm. — (Organizational and occupational psychology)
Includes bibliographies and index
ISBN 0-12-518040-3 : £16.40 : CIP rev. B81-36060

158.7 — Industries. Machine operators. Stress. Effects of machine-pacing — *Conference proceedings*

Machine pacing and occupational stress : proceedings of the international conference, Purdue University, March 1981 / edited by Gavriel Salvendy and M.J. Smith. — London : Taylor & Francis, 1981. — x,374p : ill ; 24cm
Includes bibliographies and index
ISBN 0-85066-225-7 : £19.75 : CIP rev. B81-30886

158.7 — Industries. Personnel. Stress

Stress, work design, and productivity / edited by E.N. Corlett and J. Richardson. — Chichester : Wiley, c1981. — xvi,271p : ill ; 24cm. — (Wiley series on studies in occupational stress)
Includes bibliographies and index
ISBN 0-471-28044-5 : £15.00 : CIP rev. B81-33799

158.7 — Man. Organisational behaviour

Organizational behavior and management : a contingency approach / edited by Henry L. Tosi, W. Clay Hamner. — 3rd ed. — New York ; Chichester : Wiley, c1982. — x,581p : ill ; 24cm. — (St. Clair series in management and organizational behavior)
Previous ed.: Chicago : St. Clair, 1977
ISBN 0-471-08504-9 (pbk) : £12.15 B82-27760

158.7 — Personnel. Stress

McLean, Alan A.. Work stress / Alan A. McLean. — Reading, Mass. ; London : Addison-Wesley, c1979. — xiv,142p : ill ; 21cm. — (Addison-Wesley series on occupational stress)
Includes bibliographies and index
ISBN 0-201-04592-3 (pbk) : £5.20 B82-37943

158.7 — Personnel. Stress — *Case studies*

Coping with stress at work : case studies from industry / edited by Judi Marshall and Cary L. Cooper. — Aldershot : Gower, c1981. — xvi,236p : ill ; 23cm
Includes bibliographies and index
ISBN 0-566-02338-5 : Unpriced : CIP rev. B81-30967

158.7 — Personnel. Stress. Psychophysiological aspects

French, John R. P.. The mechanisms of job stress and strain. — Chichester : Wiley, Sept.1982. — [200]p. — (Wiley series on studies in occupational stress)
ISBN 0-471-10177-x : £15.00 : CIP entry B82-19525

158.7'05 — Man. Organisational behaviour — *Serials*

Research in organizational behavior : an annual series of analytical essays and critical reviews. — Vol.1 (1979)-. — Greenwich, Conn. : JAI Press ; London (3 Henrietta St., WC2E 8LU) : Distributed by JAICON Press, 1979-. — v. ; 24cm
ISSN 0191-3085 = Research in organizational behavior : Unpriced B82-02362

158.7'0973 — United States. Man. Organisational behaviour — *Questions & answers*

Experiences in management and organizational behavior / Douglas T. Hall ... [et al.]. — 2nd ed. — New York ; Chichester : Wiley, c1982. — xiii,444p : ill,facsims,forms ; 24cm. — (St. Clair series in management and organizational behavior)
Previous ed.: Chicago : St. Clair Press, 1975. — Includes bibliographies
ISBN 0-471-08210-4 (pbk) : £7.65 B82-13619

160 — LOGIC

160 — Dialectics. Theories of Hegel, Georg Wilhelm Friedrich

Rosen, Michael. Hegel's dialectic and its criticism. — Cambridge : Cambridge University Press, Oct.1982. — [199]p
ISBN 0-521-24484-6 : £17.50 : CIP entry B82-29374

160 — Lateral thought — *For management*

De Bono, Edward. Lateral thinking for management : a handbook / Edward de Bono. — Harmondsworth : Penguin, 1982, c1971. — 225p : ill ; 20cm. — (Pelican books)
Originally published: London : McGraw-Hill, 1971
ISBN 0-14-022373-8 (pbk) : £2.50 B82-36664

160 — Logic

Copi, Irving M.. Introduction to logic / Irving M. Copi. — 6th ed. — New York : Macmillan ; London : Collier Macmillan, c1982. — xiv,604p : ill ; 24cm
Previous ed.: 1978. — Text on inside cover. — Includes index
ISBN 0-02-324920-x (cased) : £13.95
ISBN 0-02-977520-5 (pbk) : Unpriced B82-19512

Gibson, Roland. Logic as history of science and experience of art / Roland Gibson. — London : Heinemann Educational, 1982. — 140p : ill ; 24cm
Includes index
ISBN 0-435-83340-5 (pbk) : £12.00 : CIP rev. B82-04068

Miller, Richard W.. Study guide for Irving M. Copi's Introduction to logic, sixth edition / by Richard W. Miller. — New York ; Macmillan ; London : Collier Macmillan, c1982. — iii,247p : ill ; 26cm
ISBN 0-02-381180-3 (pbk) : Unpriced B82-33692

Sommers, Fred. The logic of natural language / Fred Sommers. — Oxford : Clarendon, 1982. — xvii,469p : ill ; 22cm. — (Clarendon library of logic and philosophy)
Bibliography: p457-463. — Includes index
ISBN 0-19-824425-8 : £19.50 : CIP rev. B82-01538

160 — Logic. Definitions — *Philosophical perspectives*

Gorskiĭ, D. P.. Definition : (logico-methodological problems) / D.P. Gorsky. — Moscow : Progress ; [London] : distributed by Central, c1981. — 272p ; 21cm
Translation of: Opredelenie. — Includes index
ISBN 0-7147-1751-7 : £4.95 B82-37038

160 — Logic — *Early works*

Paulus, *Venetus*. [Logica magna]. Pauli Veneti Logica magna. — Oxford : Published for the British Academy by the Oxford University Press. — (Classical and medieval logic texts ; 4)
Prima pars: Tractatus de scire et dubitare / edited with an English translation and notes by Patricia Clarke. — 1981. — xxii,216p ; 26cm
Parallel Latin text and English translation, English introduction and notes. — Includes index
ISBN 0-19-726003-9 : £40.00 B82-13949

160 — Logic — *Philosophical perspectives* — *Conference proceedings*

Logic and philosophy : International Institute of Philosophy symposium in Düsseldorf 27 August-1 September 1978 / edited by G.H. von Wright. — The Hague ; London : Nijhoff, 1980. — viii,84p ; 25cm
Includes bibliographies and index
ISBN 90-247-2271-3 B82-11042

160 — Logical thought

Shaw, Patrick. Logic and its limits / Patrick Shaw. — London : Pan in association with Heinemann Educational, 1981. — 255p : ill ; 20cm. — (Pan philosophy) (A Pan original)
Bibliography: p246-249. — Includes index
ISBN 0-330-26519-9 (pbk) : £2.50 B82-01581

160 — Man. Actions. Role of reasoning — *Philosophical perspectives*

Castañeda, Hector-Neri. Thinking and doing : the philosophical foundations of institutions / Hector-Neri Castañeda. — Dordrecht ; London : Reidel, 1975 (1982 [printing]). — xviii,366p ; 23cm. — (Pallas paperbacks)
Includes index
ISBN 90-277-1375-8 (pbk) : Unpriced B82-11237

160 — Modal logic

Ruzsa, Imre. Modal logic with descriptions / by Imre Ruzsa. — The Hague ; London : Nijhoff, 1981. — 135p ; 25cm. — (Nijhoff international philosophy series ; v.10)
Translation from the Hungarian. — Bibliography: p129. — Includes index
ISBN 90-247-2473-2 : Unpriced B82-02729

160′.92′4 — Modal logic. Theories of Aristotle

Waterlow, Sarah. Passage and possibility : a study of Aristotle's modal concepts / by Sarah Waterlow. — Oxford : Clarendon, 1982. — 165p ; 22cm
Includes index
ISBN 0-19-824656-0 : £10.50 : CIP rev. B82-12549

161 — Logic. Induction

Prys Williams, A. G.. Applicable inductive logic / A.G. Prys Williams. — London : Edsall, 1982. — x,179p : ill ; 24cm
Bibliography: p170-172
ISBN 0-902623-33-8 (corrected) : Unpriced B82-37415

Studies in inductive logic and probability / Rudolf Carnap and Richard C. Jeffrey editors. — Berkeley ; London : University of California Press
Vol.2 / Richard C. Jeffrey, editor. — c1980. — 305p : ill ; 24cm
Includes index
ISBN 0-520-03826-6 : £12.00
Primary classification 519.2 B82-40424

165 — Logic. Paradoxes — *Philosophical perspectives — Early works*

Buridan, John. John Buridan on self-reference. — Cambridge : Cambridge University Press, Sept.1982. — [248]p
ISBN 0-521-28864-9 (pbk) : £20.00 : CIP entry B82-33343

168 — Argument

Inglis, John. Clear thinking : an introduction / written jointly by John Inglis and Roger Lewis. — Cambridge : National Extension College, c1980. — 78p : ill ; 21cm. — (National Extension College course ; no.ED14)
Unpriced (pbk) B82-40274

169 — Analogy

Ross, J. F.. Portraying analogy / J.F. Ross. — Cambridge : Cambridge University Press, 1981. — xi,244p : ill,music ; 23cm. — (Cambridge studies in philosophy)
Bibliography: p223-234. — Includes index
ISBN 0-521-23805-6 : £20.00 : CIP rev. B82-15935

170 — ETHICS

170 — Ethics

Aristotle. [Ethics (Eudemian). English]. Aristotle's Eudemian Ethics : books I, II, and VIII / translated with a commentary by Michael Woods. — Oxford : Clarendon Press, 1982. — xii,234p ; 21cm. — (Clarendon Aristotle series)
Bibliography: p223-226. — Includes index
ISBN 0-19-872060-2 (cased) : £11.50 : CIP rev.
ISBN 0-19-872061-0 (pbk) : Unpriced B81-31457

Ethics in hard times / edited by Arthur L. Caplan and Daniel Callahan. — New York ; London : Plenum, c1981. — xv,296p ; 22cm. — (The Hastings Center series in ethics)
Includes index
ISBN 0-306-40790-6 : Unpriced B82-14759

Ferguson, Adam. Principles of moral and political science / Adam Ferguson. — New York ; London : Garland, 1978. — 2v ; 24cm. — (British philosophers and theologians of the 17th & 18th centuries)
Facsim of: edition published Edinburgh : Printed for A. Strahan, T. Cadell and W. Creech, 1792
ISBN 0-8240-1772-2 : Unpriced B82-23392

Hare, R. M.. Moral thinking : its levels, method, and point / by R.M. Hare. — Oxford : Clarendon, 1981. — viii,242p ; 21cm
Bibliography: p229-236. — Includes index
ISBN 0-19-824659-5 (cased) : £11.00 : CIP rev.
ISBN 0-19-824660-9 (pbk) : Unpriced B81-31452

Kupperman, Joel J.. The foundations of morality. — London : Allen & Unwin, Nov.1982. — [176]p. — (Unwin education books)
ISBN 0-04-370124-8 (cased) : £10.00 : CIP entry
ISBN 0-04-370125-6 (pbk) : £4.50 B82-27184

Midgley, Mary. Heart and mind : the varieties of moral experience / Mary Midgley. — Brighton : Harvester, 1981. — x,176p ; 22cm
Includes index
ISBN 0-7108-0048-7 : £16.95 : CIP rev. B81-23884

Midgley, Mary. Heart and mind. — London : Methuen, Jan.1983. — [176]p
Originally published: Brighton : Harvester, 1981
ISBN 0-416-34430-5 (pbk) : £3.95 : CIP entry B82-34452

Philosophical ethics : an introduction to moral philosophy / [compiled by] Tom L. Beauchamp. — New York ; London : McGraw-Hill, c1982. — xv,396p ; 25cm
Includes bibliographies and index
ISBN 0-07-004203-9 : £14.25 B82-14172

The **Roots** of ethics : science, religion and values / edited by Daniel Callahan and H. Tristram Engelhardt Jr.. — New York ; London : Plenum, c1981. — xiii,450p ; 24cm. — (The Hastings Center series in ethics)
Includes index
ISBN 0-306-40796-5 : Unpriced B82-14758

Scheffler, Samuel. The rejection of consequentialism : a philosophical investigation of the considerations underlying rival moral conceptions / by Samuel Scheffler. — Oxford : Clarendon, 1982. — viii,133p ; 23cm
Includes index
ISBN 0-19-824657-9 : £9.00 : CIP rev. B82-10451

Williams, Bernard. Moral luck : philosophical papers 1973-1980 / Bernard Williams. — Cambridge : Cambridge University Press, 1981. — xiii,173p ; 24cm
ISBN 0-521-24372-6 (cased) : £16.50 : CIP rev.
ISBN 0-521-28691-3 (pbk) : £5.95 B81-34006

170 — Ethics. Plato. Protagoras — *Commentaries*

Hubbard, B. A. F.. Plato's Protagoras. — London : Duckworth, July 1982. — [132]p
ISBN 0-7156-1640-4 : £18.00 : CIP entry B82-12935

170 — Ethics *related to* **epistemology**

White, Morton. What is and what ought to be done : an essay on ethics and epistemology / Morton White. — New York ; Oxford : Oxford University Press, 1981. — x,131p ; 23cm
Includes index
ISBN 0-19-502916-x : £8.95
Also classified at 121 B82-02987

170 — Moral judgement — *Philosophical perspectives*

Sperry, Roger. Science & moral priority. — Oxford : Blackwell, Oct.1982. — [160]p
ISBN 0-631-13199-x : £10.50 : CIP entry B82-23171

170 — Moral philosophy

Mullen, Peter. Working with morality. — London : Arnold, Dec.1982. — [96]p
ISBN 0-7131-0844-4 (pbk) : £2.50 : CIP entry B82-29444

170 — Morals

Morality in the making. — Chichester : Wiley, Feb.1983. — [288]p. — (Wiley series in developmental psychology)
ISBN 0-471-10423-x : £17.75 : CIP entry B82-38708

170 — Obligation. Ethical aspects

Fishkin, James S.. The limits of obligation / James S. Fishkin. — New Haven ; London : Yale University Press, c1982. — viii,184p : ill ; 22cm
Includes index
ISBN 0-300-02747-8 : £12.95 : CIP rev. B82-07097

170 — Promises. Ethical aspects

Atiyah, P. S.. Promises, morals, and law. — Oxford : Oxford University Press, Jan.1983. — [226]p
Originally published: Oxford : Clarendon, 1981
ISBN 0-19-825479-2 (pbk) : £5.95 : CIP entry B82-33482

170 — Social ethics

Barrow, Robin. Injustice, inequality and ethics : a philosophical introduction to moral problems / Robin Barrow. — Brighton : Wheatsheaf, 1982. — xii,204p ; 23cm
Bibliography: p199-202. — Includes index
ISBN 0-7108-0165-3 (cased) : £18.95 : CIP rev.
ISBN 0-7108-0170-x (pbk) : Unpriced B82-12151

170′.14 — Ethics. Linguistic aspects

Forrester, Mary Gore. Moral language / Mary Gore Forrester. — Madison ; London : University of Wisconsin Press, 1982. — xii,222p ; 22cm
Bibliography: p199-204. — Includes index
ISBN 0-299-08630-5 : Unpriced B82-38420

170′.2′0242 — Japan. Samurai. Personal conduct. Ethics — *Early works*

Yamamoto, Tsunetomo. Hagakure : the book of the samurai / Yamamoto Tsunetomo ; translated by William Scott Wilson. — Tokyo : Kodansha International ; Oxford : distributed by Phaidon, 1979 (1980 printing). — 180p ; 20cm
Translation of the Japanese. — Bibliography: p179-180
ISBN 0-87011-378-x : Unpriced B82-12879

170′.42′0933 — Ancient Israeli moral philosophy *compared with* **Ancient Greek moral philosophy**

Kimpel, Ben. Philosophies of life of the ancient Greeks and Israelites : an analysis of their parallels / Ben Kimpel. — New York : Philosophical Library ; London : Prior [distributor], c1981. — xviii,331p ; 23cm
ISBN 0-8022-2371-0 : Unpriced
Also classified at 170′.42′0938 B82-22020

170′.42′0938 — Ancient Greek moral philosophy *compared with* **Ancient Israeli moral philosophy**

Kimpel, Ben. Philosophies of life of the ancient Greeks and Israelites : an analysis of their parallels / Ben Kimpel. — New York : Philosophical Library ; London : Prior [distributor], c1981. — xviii,331p ; 23cm
ISBN 0-8022-2371-0 : Unpriced
Primary classification 170′.42′0933 B82-22020

170′.724 — Ethics. Mathematical models

Lefebvre, Vladimir A.. Algebra of conscience : a comparative analysis of Western and Soviet ethical systems / Vladimir A. Lefebvre ; with a foreword by Anatol Rapoport. — Dordrecht ; London : Reidel, c1982. — xxvii,194p : ill ; 23cm. — (Theory and decision library ; v.26)
Bibliography: p186-187. — Includes index
ISBN 90-277-1301-4 : Unpriced B82-30375

170′.92′4 — Ethics. Theories of Locke, John, *1632-1704*

Colman, John. John Locke's moral philosophy. — Edinburgh : Edinburgh University Press, Oct.1982. — [300]p
ISBN 0-85224-445-2 : £15.00 : CIP entry B82-25945

170′.973 — United States. Social ethics

Tipton, Steven M.. Getting saved from the sixties : moral meaning in conversion and cultural change / Steven M. Tipton ; foreword by Robert N. Bellah. — Berkeley, [Calif.] ; London : University of California Press, c1982. — xviii,364p ; 24cm
Bibliography: p349-356. — Includes index
ISBN 0-520-03868-1 : Unpriced B82-28298

171 — ETHICS. SYSTEMS AND DOCTRINES

171 — Ethics. Scepticism. Theories of Hume, David

Wright, John P.. The sceptical realism of David Hume. — Manchester : Manchester University Press, Sept.1982. — [224]p. — (Studies in intellectual history)
ISBN 0-7190-0882-4 : £15.00 : CIP entry
B82-20381

171'.2 — Ethics. Theories of empiricists, *to 1978* **—** *Philosophical perspectives*

Maris, C. W.. Critique of the empiricist explanation of morality : is there a natural equivalent of categorical morality? / C.W. Maris ; [translated by Jane Fenoulhet]. — Deventer ; London : Kluwer, 1981. — xx,475p ; 25cm
Translation of: Een natuurlijk equivalent van de plicht?. — Bibliography: p463-470. — Includes index
ISBN 90-654-4011-9 (pbk) : Unpriced
B82-10262

171'.4 — Pleasure. Philosophical perspectives. Theories of Ancient Greek writers

Gosling, J. C. B.. The Greeks on pleasure. — Oxford : Clarendon Press, July 1982. — [448]p
ISBN 0-19-824666-8 : £22.50 : CIP entry
B82-13230

171'.5 — Utilitarianism

Utilitarianism and beyond / edited by Amartya Sen and Bernard Williams. — Cambridge : Cambridge University Press, 1982. — vii,290p ; 24cm
Bibliography: p279-290
ISBN 0-521-24296-7 (cased) : £20.00 : CIP rev.
ISBN 0-521-28771-5 (pbk) : £7.50 B82-12691

172 — POLITICAL ETHICS

172 — Politics. Irreversible decision making. Ethical aspects

Pearce, D. W.. Ethics, irreversibility, future generations and the social rate of discount / by David Pearce. — [Aberdeen] : [University of Aberdeen, Department of Political Economy], [1982]. — 37leaves : ill ; 30cm. — (Discussion paper / University of Aberdeen. Department of Political Economy, ISSN 0143-4543 ; 82-01)
Unpriced (pbk) B82-19620

172'.0973 — United States. Politics. Ethical aspects

Public duties : the moral obligations of government officials / edited by Joel L. Fleishman, Lance Liebman, Mark H. Moore. — Cambridge, Mass. ; London : Harvard University Press, 1981. — x,316p ; 25cm
Includes index
ISBN 0-674-72231-0 : £15.75 B82-13730

172'.2 — United States. Administrators. Professional conduct. Ethics

Cooper, Terry L.. The responsible administrator : an approach to ethics for the administrative role / Terry L. Cooper. — Port Washington ; London : National University Publications : Kennikat, 1982. — viii,175p ; 22cm. — (Series in political science)
Bibliography: p171-175
ISBN 0-8046-9292-0 : £14.85 B82-24796

172'.4 — Foreign relations. Ethical aspects

Hare, J. E.. Ethics and international affairs / J.E. Hare and Carey B. Joynt. — London : Macmillan, 1982. — vii,208p ; 23cm
Includes index
ISBN 0-333-27853-4 : £17.50 B82-32227

172'.4 — International relations. Ethical aspects

Howard, Michael, *1922-*. Ethics and power in international politics / Michael Howard. — London ([86 Leadenhall St., E.C.3]) : Council on Christian Approaches to Defence and Disarmament (British Group), [1978]. — 19p ; 21cm
£1.00 (unbound) B82-36770

172'.4 — International relations. Ethical aspects — *Festschriften*

Explorations in ethics and international relations : essays in honour of Sydney D. Bailey / edited by Nicholas A. Sims. — London : Croom Helm, c1981. — xi,210p : 1port ; 23cm
Bibliography: p202-204. — Includes index
ISBN 0-7099-2300-7 : £10.95 : CIP rev.
B81-21505

172'.42 — Nuclear warfare. Deterrence. Ethical aspects

Ethics and nuclear deterrence / edited by Geoffrey Goodwin. — London : Croom Helm, c1982. — 199p : ill ; 23cm
Includes index
ISBN 0-7099-1129-7 : £11.95 : CIP rev.
B82-04467

Phipps, John-Francis. Time and the bomb / John-Francis Phipps. — [Oxford] : [Pica], c1982. — 45p ; 21cm
ISBN 0-907213-03-0 (pbk) : £1.50 B82-36859

172'.42 — Nuclear warfare. Ethical aspects — *For schools*

The **Nuclear** age / researched & written by the Humanities Peace Education Scheme ; designed & illustrated by Paul Knight ; edited by Brenda Lealman. — London : Christian Education Movement, 1982. — 82p : ill ; 28cm
Bibliography: p80-81
ISBN 0-905022-78-5 (pbk) : Unpriced
B82-34004

174 — PROFESSIONAL AND OCCUPATIONAL ETHICS

174'.2 — Great Britain. National health services. Patients. Behaviour modification. Ethical aspects — *Proposals*

Behaviour modification : report of a joint working party to formulate ethical guidelines for the conduct of programmes of behaviour modification in the National Health Service : a consultative document with suggested guidelines / Royal College of Psychiatrists, Royal College of Nursing, British Psychological Society. — London : H.M.S.O., 1980. — 51p ; 25cm
ISBN 0-11-320732-8 (pbk) : £3.30 B82-16410

174'.2 — Medicine. Behaviour therapy. Ethical aspects

Macklin, Ruth. Man, mind, and morality : the ethics of behavior control / Ruth Macklin. — Englewood Cliffs ; London : Prentice-Hall, c1982. — x,130p ; 23cm. — (Prentice-Hall series in the philosophy of medicine)
Includes bibliographies and index
ISBN 0-13-551127-5 (pbk) : £5.65 B82-16996

174'.2 — Medicine. Ethics

Campbell, Alastair. In that case. — London : Darton Longman & Todd, Oct.1982. — [144]p
ISBN 0-232-51557-3 (pbk) : £4.95 : CIP entry
B82-24710

Jonsen, Albert R.. Clinical ethics : a practical approach to ethical decisions in clinical medicine / Albert R. Jonsen, Mark Siegler, William J. Winslade. — New York : Macmillan ; London : Baillière Tindall, c1982. — xvii,187p ; 19cm
Includes bibliographies and index
ISBN 0-02-361360-2 : Unpriced B82-34729

McLean, Sheila. Medicine, morals and the law. — Aldershot : Gower, Jan.1983. — [224]p
ISBN 0-566-00533-6 : £15.00 : CIP entry
B82-32434

174'.2 — Medicine. Ethics — *Conference proceedings*

New knowledge in the biomedical sciences : some moral applications of its acquisition, possession, and use / edited by William B. Bondeson ... [et al.]. — Dordrecht ; London : Reidel, 1982. — xviii,224p ; 23cm. — (Philosophy and medicine ; v.10)
Conference proceedings. — Includes bibliographies and index
ISBN 90-277-1319-7 : Unpriced B82-17270

174'.2 — Medicine. Nursing. Ethics

Benjamin, Martin. Ethics in nursing / Martin Benjamin, Joy Curtis. — New York ; Oxford : Oxford University Press, c1981. — xii,180p ; 24cm
Bibliography: p170-174. — Includes index
ISBN 0-19-502836-8 (cased) : Unpriced
B82-05632

174'.2 — Medicine. Triage. Ethical aspects

Winslow, Gerald R.. Triage and justice / Gerald R. Winslow. — Berkeley ; London : University of California Press, 1982. — xi,228p ; 23cm
Bibliography: p207-221, — Includes index
ISBN 0-520-04328-6 : £15.00 B82-31096

174'.2 — Mentally handicapped persons. Behaviour modification. Ethical aspects — *Conference proceedings*

Ethical implications of behaviour modification : with special reference to mental handicap : proceedings of the conference held at Lea Castle Hospital, Wolverley, Kidderminster on Friday, 23rd January, 1976 / chairman: Chris Williams ; discussion leader: Evan Jones. — 2nd ed. — Kidderminster : British Institute of Mental Handicap, 1981. — iii,51p ; 21cm
Previous ed.: 1977. — Includes bibliographies
ISBN 0-906054-07-9 (pbk) : £2.70 B82-40092

174'.24 — Terminally ill patients. Care. Ethical aspects

Dilemmas of dying : a study in the ethics of terminal care / edited by Ian Thompson. — Edinburgh : Edinburgh University Press, c1979. — xx,227p ; 23cm
Bibliography: p203-216. — Includes index
ISBN 0-85224-367-7 (cased) : £10.00
ISBN 0-85224-378-2 (pbk) : Unpriced
B82-16136

Sherrill, John. Mother's song. — London : Hodder & Stoughton, Jan.1983. — [144]p
ISBN 0-340-32642-5 (pbk) : £1.50 : CIP entry
B82-36314

174'.4 — Business enterprise. Ethics

Bowie, Norman E.. Business ethics / Norman Bowie. — Englewood Cliffs ; London : Prentice-Hall, c1982. — xiii,159p ; 23cm. — (Prentice-Hall series in occupational ethics)
Includes index
ISBN 0-13-095901-4 (pbk) : £6.70 B82-20056

174'.9301 — Social sciences. Research. Ethical aspects

Ethical issues in social science research / edited by Tom L. Beauchamp ... [et al.]. — Baltimore ; London : Johns Hopkins University Press, c1982. — xii,436p ; 24cm
Bibliography: p417-422. — Includes index
ISBN 0-8018-2655-1 (cased) : Unpriced
ISBN 0-8018-2656-x (pbk) : Unpriced
B82-36042

Reynolds, Paul Davidson. Ethics and social science research / Paul Davidson Reynolds. — Englewood Cliffs ; London : Prentice-Hall, c1982. — xiv,191p : 1ill ; 23cm. — (Prentice-Hall methods and theories in the social sciences series)
Bibliography: p170-181. — Includes index
ISBN 0-13-290965-0 (pbk) : £7.45 B82-24090

174'.9301 — Social sciences. Research methods: Covert participant observation. Ethical aspects

Social research ethics : an examination of the merits of covert participant observation / edited by Martin Bulmer. — London : Macmillan, 1982. — xiv,284p ; 23cm
Bibliography: p252-258
ISBN 0-333-29198-0 (cased) : Unpriced
ISBN 0-333-29199-9 (pbk) : Unpriced
B82-22538

174'.9362'0973 — United States. Welfare work. Ethical aspects

Reamer, Frederic G.. Ethical dilemmas in social service / Frederic G. Reamer. — New York ; Guildford : Columbia University Press, 1982. — xiii,280p ; 24cm
Includes index
ISBN 0-231-05188-3 : £13.00 B82-39009

174′.95 — Science. Ethical aspects

Morley, David, *1947-*. The sensitive scientist : report of a British Association study group / David Morley. — London : SCM, 1978. — viii,131p ; 22cm
Bibliography: p130-131
ISBN 0-334-01386-0 (pbk) : £2.95 B82-32813

174′.962 — Engineering. Ethical aspects

Unger, Stephen H.. Controlling technology : ethics and the responsible engineer / Stephen H. Unger. — New York ; London : Holt, Rinehart and Winston, c1982. — x,192p ; 24cm
Bibliography: p180-186. — Includes index
ISBN 0-03-060282-3 (pbk) : Unpriced B82-35783

174′.991 — Geographers. Professional conduct

Mitchell, Bruce. Relevance and ethics in geography. — London : Longman, Jan.1983. — [240]p
ISBN 0-582-30035-5 : £12.95 : CIP entry B82-32464

176 — ETHICS OF SEX AND REPRODUCTION

176 — Sex — *Philosophical aspects*

Evola, Julius. The metaphysics of sex. — London : East-West Publications, Jan.1983. — [336]p
Translation of: Metafisica del sesso
ISBN 0-85692-053-3 (pbk) : £5.95 : CIP entry B82-36305

177 — ETHICS OF SOCIAL RELATIONS

177 — Man. Social behaviour. Ethical aspects

Sabini, John, *1947-*. Moralities of everyday life / John Sabini, Maury Silver. — Oxford ; Oxford : Oxford University Press, 1982. — xi,238p ; 22cm
Bibliography: p231-238
ISBN 0-19-503016-8 (cased) : £14.50
ISBN 0-19-503017-6 (pbk) : Unpriced B82-37005

177′.6 — Friendship. Role of altruism — *Philosophical perspectives*

Blum, Lawrence A.. Friendship, altruism and morality / Lawrence A. Blum. — London : Routledge & Kegan Paul, 1980. — x,234p ; 22cm. — (International library of philosophy)
Bibliography: p229-232. — Includes index
ISBN 0-7100-0582-2 : £10.00 : CIP rev. B80-26454

179 — MISCELLANEOUS ETHICAL NORMS

179 — Justice — *Philosophical perspectives*

Buchanan, Allen E.. Marx and justice : the radical critique of liberalism. — London : Methuen, June 1982. — [224]p
ISBN 0-416-33450-4 : £9.95 : CIP entry B82-10504

Sandal, Michael J.. Liberalism and the limits of justice. — Cambridge : Cambridge University Press, Sept.1982. — [190]p
ISBN 0-521-24501-x (cased) : £17.50 : CIP entry
ISBN 0-521-27077-4 (pbk) : £5.95 B82-29359

179 — Justice. Theories of Hume, David

Harrison, Jonathan. Hume's theory of justice / Jonathan Harrison. — Oxford : Clarendon Press, 1981. — xxiii,304p ; 23cm
Includes index
ISBN 0-19-824619-6 : £16.00 B82-21356

179.3 — ETHICS. TREATMENT OF ANIMALS

179′.3 — Animals. Treatment by man. Ethics

Bharij, A. S.. Man and the cow / A.S. Bharij. — Bognor Regis : New Horizon, c1982. — 62p ; 21cm
ISBN 0-86116-311-7 : £3.25 B82-09558

179.7 — ETHICS. RESPECT AND DISRESPECT FOR HUMAN LIFE

179′.7 — Suicide — *Philosophical perspectives*

Battin, M. Pabst. Ethical issues in suicide / Margaret Pabst Battin. — Englewood Cliffs ; London : Prentice-Hall, c1982. — viii,200p ; 23cm. — (Prentice-Hall series in the philosophy of medicine)
Includes index
ISBN 0-13-290155-2 (pbk) : £8.20 B82-31823

179.9 — ETHICS. VIRTUES

179′.9 — Supererogation. Ethics

Heyd, David. Supererogation : its status in ethical theory / David Heyd. — Cambridge : Cambridge University Press, 1982. — vii,191p ; 23cm. — (Cambridge studies in philosophy)
Bibliography: p174-188. — Includes index
ISBN 0-521-23935-4 : £14.00 : CIP rev. B82-11518

180 — ANCIENT, MEDIEVAL, ORIENTAL PHILOSOPHY

180 — Ancient Roman philosophy. Boethius — *Critical studies*

Boethius : his life, thought and influence / edited by Margaret Gibson. — Oxford : Blackwell, 1981. — xxv,451p,[1]leaf of plates : ill,facsims,music,ports ; 24cm
Includes index
ISBN 0-631-11141-7 : £25.00 : CIP rev. B81-21475

Chadwick, Henry. Boethius : the consolations of music, logic, theolgy and philosophy / Henry Chadwick. — Oxford : Clarendon, 1981. — xv,313p ; 22cm
Bibliography: p261-284. — Includes index
ISBN 0-19-826447-x : £18.00 : CIP rev. B81-30543

180′.938 — Ancient Greek philosophy — *Critical studies* — *Festschriften*

Language and logos : studies in ancient Greek philosophy presented to G.E.L. Owen / edited by Malcolm Schofield and Martha Craven Nussbaum. — Cambridge : Cambridge University Press, 1982. — xiii,359p : 1port ; 24cm
Includes bibliography: p339-341. — Includes index
ISBN 0-521-23640-1 : £27.50 : CIP rev. B82-12681

180′.938 — Ancient Greek thought, *to B.C.500*

Vernant, Jean-Pierre. The origins of Greek thought / Jean-Pierre Vernant ; translated from the French. — London : Methuen, 1982. — 144p ; 22cm
Translation of: Les origines de la pensée grecque. — Bibliography: p133-135. — Includes index
ISBN 0-416-34310-4 : Unpriced B82-38394

180′.938 — Classical philosophy — *Critical studies*

Armstrong, A. H.. An introduction to ancient philosophy. — 3rd ed. — London : Methuen, Oct.1981. — [260]p
Originally published: 1965
ISBN 0-416-69310-5 (pbk) : £4.25 : CIP entry B81-28834

181 — ORIENTAL PHILOSOPHY

181 — Oriental philosophy. Theories

New research on current philosophical systems. — [London] : [Octagon], [c1982]. — 36p ; 21cm
Cover title. — Bibliography: p32
ISBN 0-86304-016-0 (pbk) : £2.50 B82-25031

181′.06 — Jewish philosophy — *Texts*

Philo, *of Alexandria*. The contemplative life ; The giants and selections / Philo of Alexandria ; translation and introduction by David Winston ; preface by John Dillon. — London : SPCK, 1981. — xxi,425p ; 23cm. — (The Classics of Western spirituality)
Translation from the Greek. — Originally published: New York : Paulist Press, c1981. — Bibliography: p393-395. — Includes index
ISBN 0-281-03806-6 (pbk) : £8.50 B82-08478

181′.07 — Islamic philosophy, *to 1981*

Fakhry, Majid. A history of Islamic philosophy. — 2nd ed. — London : Longman, Sept.1982. — [416]p
Previous ed.: New York ; London : Columbia University Press, 1970
ISBN 0-582-78324-0 : £14.95 : CIP entry B82-19810

181′.09512 — East Asia. Neo-Confucianism, *to ca 1700*

De Bary, William Theodore. Neo-Confucian orthodoxy and the learning of the mind-and-heart / Wm. Theodore de Bary. — New York ; Guildford : Columbia University Press, 1981. — xviii,267p ; 24cm
Bibliography: p269-272. — Includes index
ISBN 0-231-05228-6 : £20.00 B82-10945

181′.09512 — Neo-Confucianism, *1100-1200*

Tillman, Hoyt Cleveland. Utilitarian Confucianism : Ch'en Liang's challenge to Chu Hsi / Hoyt Cleveland Tillman. — [Cambridge, Mass.] : Council on East Asian Studies, Harvard University ; Cambridge, Mass. ; London : Distributed by Harvard University Press, 1982. — xvi,304p ; 24cm. — (Harvard East Asian monographs ; 101)
Includes Chinese glossary. — Bibliography: p271-287. — Includes index
ISBN 0-674-93176-9 : £24.50 B82-33395

181′.11 — Chinese philosophy — *Texts with commentaries*

Zhuang zi. The seven Inner Chapters and other writings from the book Chuang-tzŭ / Chuang-tzŭ ; translated by A.C. Graham. — London : Allen & Unwin, 1981. — viii,293p ; 22cm
Translated from the Chinese. — Includes index
ISBN 0-04-299010-6 : Unpriced : CIP rev. B81-28778

181′.11 — Chinese philosophy. Zhuang zi — *Commentaries*

Graham, A. C.. Chuang-tzŭ : textual notes to a partial translation / A.C. Graham. — London : School of Oriental and African Studies, University of London, 1982. — xiii,65p ; 25cm
Companion volume to Chang-tzŭ: the seven inner chapters
ISBN 0-7286-0089-7 (pbk) : £3.00 : CIP rev. B81-30590

181′.4 — Indian philosophy — *Critical studies*

Koller, John M.. The Indian way / John M. Koller. — London : Macmillan, c1982. — x,406p : ill,1map ; 24cm. — (Asian perspectives)
Map on inside cover. — Bibliography: p391. — Includes index
ISBN 0-02-365800-2 (pbk) : £6.95 B82-26287

181′.4 — Indian philosophy. Krishnamurti, Jiddu — *Biographies*

Lutyens, Mary. Krishnamurti : the years of fulfilment. — London : Murray, Oct.1982. — [352]p
ISBN 0-7195-3979-x : £12.50 : CIP entry B82-23022

181′.4 — Indian philosophy — *Texts*

Krishnamurti, J.. Freedom from the known. — London : Gollancz, Jan.1983. — [128]p
Originally published: 1969
ISBN 0-575-03264-2 (pbk) : £4.95 : CIP entry B82-32463

181′.4′0321 — Indian philosophy — *Encyclopaedias*

Encyclopedia of Indian philosophies / edited by Karl H. Potter. — Princeton ; Guildford : Princeton University Press
Advaita Vedanta up to Śaṃkara and his pupils. — c1981. — x,635p ; 25cm
Includes index
ISBN 0-691-07182-9 : £31.80 B82-05653

181′.45 — Hatha-yoga — *Manuals*

Bernard, Theos. Hatha yoga. — London : Hutchinson, Sept.1982. — [112]p
Originally published: 1950
ISBN 0-09-150051-6 (pbk) : £2.95 : CIP entry B82-20618

181′.45 — Hatha-yoga — *Manuals*
continuation

Iyengar, B. K. S.. The concise light on yoga : yoga dipika / B.K.A. Iyengar ; foreword by Yehudi Menuhin. — Abridged ed. — London : Unwin paperbacks, 1980. — xii,240p : ill ; 18cm
Previous ed.: i.e. 2nd ed. published as Light on yoga. London : Allen & Unwin, 1968. — Includes index
ISBN 0-04-149056-8 (pbk) : £2.50 : CIP rev. B80-20156

181′.45 — Layayoga

Goswami, Shyam Sundar. Layayoga : an advanced method of concentration / Shyam Sundar Goswami ; foreword by Acharyya Karunamoya Saraswati. — London : Routledge & Kegan Paul, 1980. — xix,342p,28p of plates : col.ill ; 25cm
Bibliography: p335-337. — Includes index
ISBN 0-7100-0078-2 : £17.50 : CIP rev. B79-26880

181′.45 — Raja-yoga

Yesudian, Selvarajan. Raja yoga / Selvarajan Yesudian and Elisabeth Haich. — London : Unwin paperbacks, 1980. — 160p ; 20cm. — (Mandala books)
Translation of: Yoga in den zwei Welten. — Originally published: as Yoga uniting East and West. London : Allen and Unwin, 1956 ; and as Raja Yoga. London : Allen and Unwin, 1970
ISBN 0-04-149055-x (pbk) : £2.25 : CIP rev. B79-33900

181′.45 — Yoga

Brunton, Paul. The hidden teaching beyond yoga. — London : Rider, Sept.1982. — [368]p
Originally published: New York : Dutton ; London : Rider, 1941
ISBN 0-09-149991-7 (pbk) : £2.95 : CIP entry B82-20617

Gent, John. Yoga seeker / by John Gent. — Mansfield (136 Oak Tree La., Mansfield, Notts. NG18 3HR) : J. Gent
Action plan 5: Healing therapy. — 1982. — [8]p ; 21cm
Cover title. — Text on covers
£0.50 (pbk) B82-20962

Gent, John. Yoga seeker / John Gent. — Mansfield (136 Oak Tree La., Mansfield, Notts. NG18 3HR) : J. Gent
Action plan 6: Personal ecology. — 1982. — [8]p ; 21cm
Cover title. — Text on covers
£0.50 (pbk) B82-38247

Iyengar, B. K. S.. Light on yoga : yoga dipika / B.K.S. Iyengar ; foreword by Yehudi Menuhin. — 2nd ed. — London : Unwin Paperbacks, 1968, c1976 ([printing]). — 544p : ill ; 19cm
Previous ed.: London : Allen & Unwin, 1966. — Includes index
ISBN 0-04-149035-5 (pbk) : £4.95 B82-40512

Wood, Ernest, *1883-1965*. Yoga / Ernest Wood. — Repr. with revisions. — Harmondsworth : Penguin, 1962 (1982 [printing]). — 271p ; 20cm
Bibliography: p259-261. — Includes index
ISBN 0-14-020448-2 (pbk) : £2.25 B82-40774

Yesudian, Selvarajan. Self-reliance through yoga : aspects of yoga wisdom / collected and commented on by the author Selvarajan Yesudian. — Rev. and expanded ed. — London : Unwin Paperbacks, 1979. — x,222p ; 20cm. — (Mandala books)
Translation of: Selbsterziehung durch Yoga. — Previous ed.: published as A yoga miscellany. London : Allen & Unwin, 1963 ; and as Self-reliance through yoga. London : Allen and Unwin, 1975
ISBN 0-04-149054-1 (pbk) : £2.75 : CIP rev. B79-20616

181′.45 — Yoga. Shri Dada Sanghita

Shastri, Hari Prasad. The heart of the Eastern mystical teaching : Shri Dada Sanghita / by Hari Prasad Shastri. — 3rd ed. — London : Shanti Sadan, 1979. — 330p : 1port ; 22cm
Previous ed.: 1954. — Includes index
ISBN 0-85424-030-6 (pbk) : Unpriced B82-09968

181′.452 — Yoga. Patanjali — *Texts*

Patanjali. [Yoga sūtras. English]. Effortless being : the Yoga sutras of Patanjali / a new translation by Alistair Shearer ; photographs by Richard Lannoy. — London : Wildwood House in association with Arnold Heinemann, 1982. — 128p : ill ; 25cm
Translated from the Hindi
ISBN 0-7045-0398-0 (pbk) : £5.95 : CIP rev. B82-09199

181′.452 — Yoga. Patanjali. Yoga sutras — *Texts with commentaries*

Patanjali. The Yoga-Sútra of Patañjali : new translation and commentary / Georg Feuerstein. — Folkestone : Dawson, 1979. — xiii,179p ; 23cm
Translated from the Sanskrit. — Bibliography: p173-174. — Includes index
ISBN 0-7129-0915-x : £10.00 : CIP rev. B79-20617

181′.482 — Shankara vedanta

Śaṅkarácárya. The crest jewel of wisdom. — Dulverton : Watkins, Oct.1981. — [116]p
ISBN 0-7224-0191-4 (pbk) : £3.50 : CIP entry B81-27431

181′.5 — Iranian philosophy. Sadr al-Dīn Shīrāzī, Muhammad ibn Ibrāhīm — *Critical studies*

Morris, James Winston. The wisdom of the throne : an introduction to the philosophy of Mulla Sadra / James Winston Morris. — Princeton ; Guildford : Princeton University Press, c1981. — xiii,275p ; 25cm. — (UNESCO collection of representative works. Arabic series) (Princeton library of Asian translations)
Bibliography: p259-262. — Includes index. — Includes a translation of al-Hikmah al-ʻarshīyah
ISBN 0-691-06493-8 : £17.60 B82-11657

181′.9 — Islamic philosophy. Ikhwán al-Safá′ — *Critical studies*

Netton, Ian Richard. Muslim neoplatonists. — London : Allen & Unwin, Oct.1982. — [176]p
ISBN 0-04-297043-1 : £12.50 : CIP entry B82-23087

182 — PRE-SOCRATIC PHILOSOPHY

182′.1 — Ionian philosophy — *Texts*

Anaximander, *of Miletus*. The Anaximander fragment. — [Carnwarth] : Wild Hawthorn Press, [1982?]. — [24]p : ill ; 12cm
Translations from the classical Greek
Unpriced (pbk) B82-17839

182′.5 — Ancient Greek philosophy. Empedocles — *Texts*

Empedocles. Empedocles : the extant fragments / edited, with an introduction, commentary, and concordance, by M.R. Wright. — New Haven ; London : Yale, 1981. — vii,364p ; 24cm
Greek text, English introduction, translation and commentary. — Bibliography: p299-309. — Includes index
ISBN 0-300-02475-4 : Unpriced : CIP rev. B81-30246

184 — PLATONIC PHILOSOPHY

184 — Ancient Greek philosophy. Plato — *Critical studies*

Hare, R. M.. Plato. — Oxford : Oxford University Press, Oct.1982. — [178]p. — (Past masters)
ISBN 0-19-287586-8 (cased) : £5.95 : CIP entry
ISBN 0-19-287585-x (pbk) : £1.50 B82-23676

Teloh, Henry. The development of Plato′s metaphysics / Henry Teloh. — University Park ; London : Pennsylvania State University Press, c1981. — xiii,256p ; 24cm
Bibliography: p219-226. — Includes index
ISBN 0-271-00268-9 : Unpriced B82-02049

184 — Ancient Greek philosophy. Plato. Phaedrus — *Critical studies*

Ficino, Marsilio. Marsilio Ficino and the Phaedran charioteer / introduction, texts, translations by Michael J.B. Allen. — Berkeley ; London : University of California Press, c1981. — viii,274p : 1facsim ; 24cm. — (Publications of the Centre for Medieval and Renaissance Studies, UCLA ; 14)
Parallel Latin text and English translation, English introduction and notes. — Bibliography: p257-263. — Includes index
ISBN 0-520-04222-0 : £18.50 B82-06976

185 — ARISTOTELIAN PHILOSOPHY

185 — Ancient Greek philosophy. Aristotle — *Critical studies*

Barnes, Jonathan. Aristotle. — Oxford : Oxford University Press, Oct.1982. — [96]p. — (Past masters)
ISBN 0-19-287582-5 (cased) : £5.95 : CIP entry
ISBN 0-19-287581-7 (pbk) : £1.50 B82-23675

Edel, Abraham. Aristotle and his philosophy / Abraham Edel. — London : Croom Helm, c1982. — xii,479p ; 24cm
Bibliography: p461-469. — Includes index
ISBN 0-7099-0906-3 : £14.95 B82-31741

186 — SCEPTIC AND NEOPLATONIC PHILOSOPHY

186′.4 — Ancient Greek philosophy. Neoplatonism — *Greek texts*

Plotinus. Plotini opera. — Oxford : Clarendon Press. — (Oxford classical texts)
Tomus 3: Enneas 6. — Mar.1982. — [350]p
ISBN 0-19-814591-8 : £12.50 : CIP entry B82-01089

186′.4 — Ancient Greek philosophy. Plotinus. Ennead V.1 — *Commentaries*

Atkinson, Michael. Plotinus : Ennead V.1 on the three principal hypostases. — Oxford : Oxford University Press, Nov.1982. — [320]p. — (Oxford classical and philosophical monographs)
Includes original Greek text and English translation
ISBN 0-19-814719-8 : £17.50 : CIP entry B82-29000

186′.4 — Neoplatonism — *Conference proceedings*

Soul and the structure of being in late neoplatonism : Syrianus, Proclus and Simplicius : papers and discussions of a colloquium held at Liverpool, 15-16 April 1982 / edited by H.J. Blumenthal and A.C. Lloyd. — Liverpool : Liverpool University Press, 1982. — vii,95p ; 22cm
Includes contributions in French
ISBN 0-85323-404-3 (pbk) : £6.50 B82-40389

189 — MEDIAEVAL WESTERN PHILOSOPHY

189 — Christian philosophy, *150-1475* — *Critical studies*

Gilson, Etienne. History of Christian philosophy in the Middle Ages / Etienne Gilson. — London : Sheed and Ward, 1955 (1980 [printing]). — xvii,829p ; 22cm
Bibliography: p549. — Includes index
ISBN 0-7220-4114-4 (pbk) : £15.00 B82-14983

189 — English philosophy. Grosseteste, Robert — *Critical studies*

McEvoy, James. The philosophy of Robert Grosseteste / James McEvoy. — Oxford : Clarendon, 1982. — xviii,560p : 1ill ; 23cm
Bibliography: p521-547. — Includes index
ISBN 0-19-824645-5 : £35.00 : CIP rev. B82-10450

189 — European thought, *ca 1100-1384*

Smalley, Beryl. Studies in medieval thought and learning from Abelard to Wyclif. — London (35 Gloucester Ave., NW1 7AX) : Hambledon Press, Dec.1981. — [455]p. — (History series ; 6)
ISBN 0-9506882-6-6 : £25.00 : CIP entry B81-31521

189 — Western philosophy, *1100-1600* **—** *Critical studies*

The **Cambridge** history of later medieval philosophy : from the rediscovery of Aristotle to the disintegration of scholasticism 1100-1600 / editors Norman Kretzmann, Anthony Kenny, Jan Pinborg ; associate editor Eleonore Stump. — Cambridge : Cambridge University Press, 1982. — xiv,1035p ; 23cm
Bibliography: p893-977. — Includes index
ISBN 0-521-22605-8 : £40.00 : CIP rev.
B82-12139

190 — MODERN WESTERN PHILOSOPHY

190 — Analytic philosophy — *Critical studies*

The **Need** for interpretation : contemporary conceptions of the philosopher's task. — London : Athlone Press, July 1982. — [192]p
ISBN 0-485-11224-8 : £14.00 : CIP entry
B82-13512

190 — Western philosophy — *Critical studies*

Derrida, Jacques. Margins of philosophy. — Brighton : Harvester, Oct.1982. — [256]p
Translation of: Marges de la philosophie
ISBN 0-7108-0454-7 : £18.95 : CIP entry
B82-28481

Lacey, A. R.. Modern philosophy : an introduction / A.R. Lacey. — Boston, Mass. ; London : Routledge & Kegan Paul, 1982. — 246p ; 22cm
Bibliography: p221-234. — Includes index
ISBN 0-7100-0935-6 (cased) : £7.95
ISBN 0-7100-0974-7 (pbk) : £3.95 B82-13768

190'.9 — European philosophy, *1600-1975* **—** *Critical studies*

Quinton, Anthony. Thoughts and thinkers / Anthony Quinton. — London : Duckworth, 1982. — x,365p ; 26cm
Includes index
ISBN 0-7156-1150-x : £28.00 : CIP rev.
B78-24831

190'.9 — Western philosophy, *to 1981* **—** *Critical studies*

Wedberg, Anders. A history of philosophy. — Oxford : Clarendon Press, Aug.1982
Vol.1: Antiquity and the Middle Ages. — [200]p
Translation of: Filosofinshistoria. Antiken och medeltiden
ISBN 0-19-824639-0 : £10.50 : CIP entry
B82-15682

190'.9'032 — European philosophy, *ca 1630-1740* **—** *Critical studies*

Loeb, Louis E.. From Descartes to Hume : continental mataphysics and the development of modern philosophy / Louis E. Loeb. — Ithaca ; London : Cornell University Press, c1981. — 382p ; 24cm
Bibliography: p365-373. — Includes index
ISBN 0-8014-1289-7 : £17.25 B82-02061

190'.9'04 — European thought, *1870-1976*

Biddiss, Michael D.. The age of the masses : ideas and society in Europe since 1870 / Michael D. Biddiss. — Hassocks : Harvester, 1977. — 379p ; 23cm
Originally published: Harmondsworth : Penguin, 1977. — Bibliography: p357-362. — Includes index
ISBN 0-85527-790-4 : Unpriced : CIP rev.
B77-12283

191 — American philosophy. Kyburg, Henry E & Levi, Isaac — *Critical studies*

Henry E. Kyburg, Jr & Isaac Levi / edited by Radu J. Bogdan. — Dordrecht ; London : Reidel, c1982. — xi,322p : ill,2 ports ; 24cm. — (Profiles (Reidel) ; v.3)
Includes bibliographies and index
ISBN 90-277-1308-1 (cased) : Unpriced
ISBN 90-277-1309-x (pbk) : Unpriced
B82-17269

191 — American philosophy. Marcuse, Herbert — *Biographies*

Kätz, Barry. Herbert Marcuse and the art of liberation : an intellectual biography / Barry Kätz. — London : NLB, 1982. — 234p : ill,facsims ; 22cm
Bibliography: p222-230. — Includes index
ISBN 0-86091-050-4 (cased) : £15.00 : CIP rev.
(pbk) : Unpriced B82-30332

191 — American philosophy. Peirce, Charles S. — *Critical studies*

Almeder, Robert F.. The philosophy of Charles S. Peirce : a critical introduction / Robert Almeder. — Oxford : Blackwell, 1980. — ix,205p ; 23cm. — (APQ library of philosophy)
Bibliography: p186-191. — Includes index
ISBN 0-631-12492-6 : £15.00 : CIP rev.
B80-08592

191 — American philosophy — *Texts*

Nozick, Robert. Philosophical explanations. — Oxford : Clarendon Press, Oct.1981. — [720]p
ISBN 0-19-824672-2 : £15.00 : CIP entry
B81-26718

Quine, W. V.. Theories and things / W.V. Quine. — Cambridge, Mass. ; London : Harvard University Press, 1981. — 219p ; 22cm
Bibliography: p209-213. — Includes index
ISBN 0-674-87925-2 : £8.75 B82-11872

191 — Canadian philosophy, *1850-1950* **—** *Critical studies*

Armour, Leslie. The faces of reason : an essay on philosophy and culture in English Canada 1850-1950 / Leslie Armour and Elizabeth Trott. — Waterloo, Ont. : Wilfrid Laurier University Press ; Gerrards Cross : Distributed by Colin Smythe, c1981. — xxvi,548p : ports ; 24cm
Includes index
ISBN 0-88920-107-2 : Unpriced B82-19628

192 — British philosophy. Influence of Malebranche, Nicolas, *ca 1700-1799*

McCracken, Charles J.. Malebranche and British philosophy. — Oxford : Oxford University Press, Sept.1982. — [520]p
ISBN 0-19-824664-1 : £30.00 : CIP entry
B82-22417

192 — English philosophy. Bacon, Francis, *Viscount St. Albans - Biographies*

Fuller, Jean Overton. Francis Bacon. — London : East-West, Apr.1981. — [400]p
ISBN 0-85692-069-x : £10.00 : CIP entry
B81-06885

192 — English philosophy. Bacon, Francis, *Viscount St. Albans — Critical studies — Serials*

The **Francis** Bacon Research Trust journal. — Ser.1, vol.1-. — Northampton (The Dairy Office, Castle Ashby, Northampton NN7 1LJ) : The Trust, 1981-. — v. : ill ; 26cm
Irregular
ISSN 0262-8228 = Francis Bacon Research Trust journal : Unpriced B82-09067

192 — English philosophy. Bentham, Jeremy & Coleridge, Samuel Taylor — *Critical studies*

Mill, John Stuart. Mill on Bentham and Coleridge / with an introduction by F.R. Leavis. — Cambridge : Cambridge University Press, 1980. — 168p ; 22cm
Originally published: London : Chatto & Windus, 1950
ISBN 0-521-23330-5 (cased) : £9.50 : CIP rev.
ISBN 0-521-29917-9 (pbk) : £3.50 B80-18580

192 — English philosophy. Bentham, Jeremy — *Correspondence, diaries, etc.*

Bentham, Jeremy. The correspondence of Jeremy Bentham. — London : Athlone Press. — (The Collected works of Jeremy Bentham)
Vol.4: October 1788 to December 1793 / edited by Alexander Taylor Milne. — 1981. — xlii,506p,[1]leaf of plates : 1port ; 24cm
Includes index
ISBN 0-485-13204-4 : £45.00 : CIP rev.
B81-08809

Bentham, Jeremy. The correspondence of Jeremy Bentham. — London : Athlone Press. — (The Collected works of Jeremy Bentham)
Vol.5: January 1794 to December 1797 / edited by Alexander Taylor Milne. — 1981. — xviii,403p : 1plan ; 24cm
Includes index
ISBN 0-485-13205-2 : £40.00 : CIP rev.
B81-08810

192 — English philosophy. Bentham, Jeremy — *Critical studies*

Hart, H. L. A.. Essays on Bentham. — Oxford : Clarendon Press, Sept.1982. — [250]p
ISBN 0-19-825348-6 (cased) : £15.00 : CIP entry
ISBN 0-19-825468-7 (pbk) : £6.95 B82-18973

192 — English philosophy. Bradley, F. H. Principles of logic — *Critical studies*

Manser, Anthony. Bradley's logic. — Oxford : Blackwell, Dec.1982. — [280]p
ISBN 0-631-13139-6 : £17.50 : CIP entry
B82-30049

192 — English philosophy. Koestler, Arthur — *Biographies*

Hamilton, Iain. Koestler : a biography / Iain Hamilton. — London : Secker & Warburg, 1982. — xviii,397p ; 24cm
Bibliography: p365-366. — Includes index
ISBN 0-436-19101-6 : £12.00 B82-25102

192 — English philosophy. Locke, John, *1632-1704* **—** *Correspondence, diaries, etc.*

Locke, John, *1632-1704*. The correspondence of John Locke / edited by E.S. de Beer. — Oxford : Clarendon. — (The Clarendon edition of the works of John Locke. The correspondence)
Vol.7: Letters nos.2665-3286. — 1982. — vii,789p ; 23cm
Includes letters in Latin and French. — Includes index
ISBN 0-19-824564-5 : £45.00 : CIP rev.
B81-30529

192 — English philosophy. Mill, John Stuart — *Biographies*

Mill, John Stuart. Autobiography and literary essays / by John Stuart Mill ; edited by John M. Robson and Jack Stillinger. — Toronto : University of Toronto Press ; London : Routledge & Kegan Paul, c1981. — liv,766p : facsims ; 25cm. — (Collected works of John Stuart Mill ; v.1)
Includes index
ISBN 0-7100-0718-3 : £32.50
Also classified at 820.9'007 B82-17794

192 — English philosophy. Popper, Karl R. — *Biographies*

Popper, Karl R.. Unended quest : an intellectual autobiography / Karl Popper. — Rev. ed. — [London] : Fontana, 1976 (1982 [printing]). — 270p ; 20cm
Previous ed.: published as Autobiography of Karl Popper in The philosophy of Karl Popper. La Salle, Ill. : Open Court, 1974. — List of works: p241-251. — Includes index
ISBN 0-00-636592-2 (pbk) : £2.50 B82-34487

192 — English philosophy. Popper, Karl R. — *Critical studies*

Burke, T. E.. The philosophy of Popper. — Manchester : Manchester University Press, Feb.1983. — [200]p
ISBN 0-7190-0904-9 (cased) : £17.50 : CIP entry
ISBN 0-7190-0911-1 (pbk) : £6.50 B82-39459

O'Hear, Anthony. Karl Popper / Anthony O'Hear. — London : Routledge & Kegan Paul, 1980 (1982 [printing]). — xii,219p ; 24cm. — (The Arguments of the philosophers)
Bibliography: p208-212. — Includes index
ISBN 0-7100-9334-9 (pbk) : £4.95 B82-37015

192 — English philosophy — *Texts*

Bealer, George. Quality and concept / George Bealer. — Oxford : Clarendon Press, 1982. — viii,311p ; 23cm. — (Clarendon library of logic and philosophy)
Bibliography: p285-291. — Includes index
ISBN 0-19-824428-2 : £20.00 : CIP rev.
B81-31451

192 — English philosophy — *Texts continuation*

Conway, Anne, *1631-1679*. The principles of the most ancient and modern philosophy / by Anne Conway ; edited and with an introduction by Peter Loptson. — The Hague ; London : Nijhoff, 1982. — 252p : ill ; 25cm. — (Archives internationales d'histoire des idées = International archives of the history of ideas ; 101)
Latin and English translations, English introduction. — Includes index
ISBN 90-247-2671-9 : Unpriced
ISBN 90-247-2433-3 B82-39339

Dummett, Michael. Truth and other enigmas / Michael Dummett. — London : Duckworth, 1978. — lviii,470p ; 24cm
Includes index
ISBN 0-7156-1650-1 (pbk) : £9.95 B82-37800

Warnock, G. J.. Morality and language. — Oxford : Basil Blackwell, Aug.1982. — [240]p
ISBN 0-631-13098-5 : £17.50 : CIP entry B82-15898

Wittgenstein, Ludwig. Last writings. — Oxford : Blackwell
Vol.1. — Sept.1982. — [300]p
ISBN 0-631-12895-6 : £15.00 : CIP entry B82-20282

192 — English philosophy. Whitehead, Alfred North *related to* **theories of poetry of Wordsworth, William,** *1770-1850*

Cappon, Alexander P.. About Wordsworth and Whitehead : a prelude to philosophy / by Alexander P. Cappon. — New York : Philosophical Library ; London : George Prior [distributor], c1982. — xi,190p ; 22cm
Includes index
ISBN 0-8022-2386-9 : £9.50
Also classified at 808.1'092'4 B82-24278

192 — English philosophy. Wittgenstein, Ludwig — *Critical studies*

Wittgenstein and his times. — Oxford : Blackwell, June 1981. — [144]p
ISBN 0-631-11161-1 : £7.95 : CIP entry B81-10483

192 — English philosophy. Wittgenstein, Ludwig — *Critical studies — Conference proceedings*

Perspectives on the philosophy of Wittgenstein. — Oxford : Blackwell, Sept.1981. — [256]p
Conference papers
ISBN 0-631-19550-5 : £9.50 : CIP entry B81-22617

192 — English philosophy. Wittgenstein, Ludwig — *Personal observations*

Wright, G. H. von. Wittgenstein. — Oxford : Blackwell, June 1982. — [224]p
ISBN 0-631-13099-3 : £9.50 : CIP entry B82-09458

192 — English thought, *1700-1800*

Stephen, *Sir* **Leslie**. Selected writings in British intellectual history / Leslie Stephen ; edited and with an introduction by Noël Annan. — Chicago ; London : University of Chicago Press, 1979. — xx,297p ; 23cm. — (Classics of British historical literature)
Bibliography: pxxix-xxx
ISBN 0-226-77255-1 : £11.95 B82-23315

192 — Irish philosophy. Berkeley, George — *Critical studies*

Urmson, J. O.. Berkeley / J.O. Urmson. — Oxford : Oxford University Press, 1982. — 90p ; 19cm. — (Past masters)
Bibliography: p88. — Includes index
ISBN 0-19-287547-7 (cased) : Unpriced : CIP rev.
ISBN 0-19-287546-9 (pbk) : £1.25 B82-00882

Warnock, G. J.. Berkeley. — 3rd ed. — Oxford : Basil Blackwell, Aug.1982. — [240]p
Previous ed.: Harmondsworth : Penguin, 1969
ISBN 0-631-13097-7 (cased) : £15.00 : CIP entry
ISBN 0-631-13119-1 (pbk) : £4.95 B82-15899

192 — Scottish philosophy. Hume, David, *1711-1776 — Critical studies*

Norton, David Fate. David Hume : common-sense moralist, sceptical metaphysician / David Fate Norton. — Princeton ; Guildford : Princeton University Press, c1982. — xii,329p ; 23cm
Bibliography: p311-322. — Includes index
ISBN 0-691-07265-5 : £17.70 B82-34456

192 — Scottish philosophy. Hume, David — *Critical studies*

Jones, Peter. Hume's sentiments : their Ciceronian and French context. — Edinburgh : Edinburgh University Press, Nov.1982. — [280]p
ISBN 0-85224-443-6 : £15.00 : CIP entry B82-26313

192 — Scottish philosophy — *Texts*

Smith, Adam, *1723-1790*. Essays on philosophical subjects / Adam Smith ; edited by W.P.D. Wightman and J.C. Bryce. — Oxford : Clarendon, 1980. — ix,358p ; 24cm. — (The Glasgow edition of the works and correspondence of Adam Smith)
Originally published: London : T. Caddell, Jnr & W. Davies, 1795. — Bibliography: pviii-ix. — Includes index. — Includes Dugald Stewart's Account of Adam Smith / edited by I.S. Ross
ISBN 0-19-828187-0 : £14.00 : CIP rev. B79-29176

192 — Welsh philosophy. Price, Richard, *b. 1723 — Correspondence, diaries, etc.*

Price, Richard, *b. 1723*. The correspondence of Richard Price. — Cardiff : University of Wales Press
Vol.1. — Jan.1983. — [310]p
ISBN 0-7083-0819-8 : £20.00 : CIP entry B82-32525

193 — Austrian philosophy. Steiner, Rudolf — *Biographies*

Carlgren, Frans. Rudolf Steiner : and anthroposophy / [text Frans Carlgren] ; [arrangement Anne Klingborg] ; [translation Joan and Siegfried Rudel]. — 4th ed. — London : Rudolf Steiner, 1979. — 51p,32p of plates : ill,ports ; 17cm
Translation from the German. — Previous ed.: 197-?
£2.00 (pbk) B82-05078

193 — German philosophy, *1789-1939*. **Sociopolitical aspects**

Lukács, Georg. The destruction of reason / Georg Lukács ; translated by Peter Palmer. — London : Merlin, c1980. — 865p : ill ; 23cm. — ([International library of social and political thought])
Translation from the German. — Includes index
ISBN 0-85036-247-4 : £12.50 B82-05674

193 — German philosophy, *1945-1980 — Critical studies*

Bubner, Rüdiger. Modern German philosophy / Rüdiger Bubner ; translated by Eric Matthews. — Cambridge : Cambridge University Press, 1981. — xi,223p ; 22cm
Translation from the German. — Includes index
ISBN 0-521-22908-1 (cased) : £18.50 : CIP rev.
ISBN 0-521-29711-7 (pbk) : £5.95 B81-31281

193 — German philosophy. Bloch, Ernst — *Critical studies*

Hudson, Wayne. The Marxist philosophy of Ernst Bloch / Wayne Hudson. — London : Macmillan, 1982. — 289p ; 23cm
Bibliography: p254-278. — Includes index
ISBN 0-333-25664-6 : Unpriced B82-25244

193 — German philosophy. Feuerbach, Ludwig — *Critical studies*

Wartofsky, Marx W.. Feuerbach. — Cambridge : Cambridge University Press, Sept.1982. — [460]p
Originally published: 1977
ISBN 0-521-28929-7 (pbk) : £9.95 : CIP entry B82-19541

193 — German philosophy. Frege, Gottlob — *Critical studies*

Currie, Gregory. Frege : an introduction to his philosophy / Gregory Currie. — Brighton : Harvester, 1982. — xi,212p : ill ; 23cm
Bibliography: p198-208. — Includes index
ISBN 0-85527-826-9 : £20.00 : CIP rev. B82-12168

Dummett, Michael. The interpretation of Frege's philosophy / Michael Dummett. — London : Duckworth, 1981. — xviii,621p ; 25cm
Bibliography: p604-612. — Includes index
ISBN 0-7156-1450-9 : £35.00 : CIP rev. B80-29039

193 — German philosophy. Habermas, Jürgen — *Critical studies*

Habermas : critical debates / edited by John B. Thompson and David Held. — London : Macmillan, 1982. — vii,324p ; 25cm. — (Contemporary social theory)
Bibliography: p318-322
ISBN 0-333-27549-7 (cased) : Unpriced
ISBN 0-333-27557-9 (pbk) : Unpriced B82-33851

Kortian, Garbis. Metacritique : the philosophical argument of Jürgen Habermas / Garbis Kortian ; translated by John Raffan ; with an introductory essay by Charles Taylor and Alan Montefiore. — Cambridge : Cambridge University Press, 1980. — 134p ; 23cm
Translation of: Métacritique. — Includes index
ISBN 0-521-22374-1 (cased) : £11.00 : CIP rev.
ISBN 0-521-29618-8 (pbk) : £3.75 B80-19586

193 — German philosophy. Hegel, Georg Wilhelm Friedrich, *1801-1806 — Critical studies*

Harris, H. S.. Hegel's development : night thoughts (Jena 1801-1806). — Oxford : Clarendon, Sept.1982. — [600]p
ISBN 0-19-824654-4 : £40.00 : CIP entry B82-18998

193 — German philosophy. Hegel, Georg Wilhelm Friedrich — *Critical studies*

Gadamer, Hans-Georg. Hegel's dialectic. — London : Yale University Press, Feb.1982. — [130]p
Translated from the German. — Originally published: 1976
ISBN 0-300-02842-3 (pbk) : £3.45 : CIP entry B82-07096

Rosen, Stanley. G.F.W. Hegel. — London : Yale University Press, Feb.1982. — [320]p
Originally published: 1974
ISBN 0-300-02848-2 (pbk) : £5.50 : CIP entry B82-07090

193 — German philosophy. Hegel, Georg Wilhelm Friedrich — *Critical studies — Serials*

The **Bulletin** of the Hegel Society of Great Britain. — No.1 (Spring/Summer 1980)-. — [Oxford] ([c/o Dr Z.A. Pelczynski, Pembroke College, Oxford OX1 1DW]) : The Society, 1980-. — v. ; 21cm
Two issues yearly
ISSN 0263-5232 = Bulletin of the Hegel Society of Great Britain : £3.00 per year B82-26135

193 — German philosophy. Heidegger, Martin — *Critical studies*

Halliburton, David. Poetic thinking : an approach to Heidegger / David Halliburton. — Chicago ; London : University of Chicago Press, 1981. — xii,235p : ill ; 24cm
Includes index
ISBN 0-226-31372-7 : Unpriced B82-35072

Zimmerman, Michael E.. Eclipse of the self : the development of Heidegger's concept of authenticity / Michael E. Zimmerman. — Athens [Ohio] ; London : Ohio University Press, c1981. — xxx,331p ; 24cm
Bibliography: p299-311. — Includes index
ISBN 0-8214-0570-5 (cased) : Unpriced
ISBN 0-8214-0601-9 (pbk) : £7.45 B82-30095

193 — German philosophy. Husserl, Edmund — *Critical studies*

International Phenomenology Conference *(6th : 1976 : University of Arezzo/Siena).* The teleologies in Husserlian phenomenology : the irreducible element in man, part III : telos as the pivotal factor of contextual phenomenology : papers read at the VIth International Phenomenology Conference, University of Arezzo/Siena, July 1-July 6, 1976 / organized by the International Husserl and Phenomenological Research Society ... [et al.] ; edited by Anna-Teresa Tymieniecka. — Dordrecht ; London : Reidel, c1979. — xvi,495p : 1facsim ; 23cm. — (Analecta Husserliana ; v.9)
Includes 2 chapters in French. — Bibliography: p469-484. — Includes index
ISBN 90-277-0981-5 : Unpriced B82-37358

193 — German philosophy. Husserl, Edmund. Influence of Hume, David, *1711-1776*

Murphy, Richard T. (Richard Timothy). Hume and Husserl : towards radical subjectivism / Richard T. Murphy. — The Hague ; London : Nijhoff, 1980. — 148p ; 25cm. — (Phaenomenologica ; 79)
Bibliography: p141-144. — Includes index
ISBN 90-247-2172-5 : Unpriced B82-41031

193 — German philosophy. Jaspers, Karl — *Critical studies*

Young-Bruehl, Elisabeth. Freedon and Karl Jaspers's philosophy / Elisabeth Young-Bruehl. — New Haven ; London : Yale University Press, c1981. — xiv,233p ; 22cm
Bibliography: p219-227. — Includes index
ISBN 0-300-02629-3 : Unpriced B82-08934

193 — German philosophy. Kant, Immanuel — *Biographies*

Cassirer, Ernst. Kant's life and thought / Ernst Cassirer ; translated by James Haden ; introduction by Stephan Körner. — New Haven, Conn. ; London : Yale University Press, c1981. — xxiii,429p ; 25cm
Translation of: Kants Leben und Lehre. — Includes index
ISBN 0-300-02358-8 : £17.50 : CIP rev. B82-01315

193 — German philosophy. Kant, Immanuel — *Critical studies*

Scruton, Roger. Kant / Roger Scruton. — Oxford : Oxford University Press, 1982. — 99p ; 19cm. — (Past masters)
Bibliography: p95-96. — Includes index
ISBN 0-19-287578-7 (cased) : Unpriced : CIP rev.
ISBN 0-19-287577-9 (pbk) : £1.25 B82-00885

Walker, Ralph C. S.. Kant / Ralph C.S. Walker. — London : Routledge & Kegan Paul, 1978 (1982 [printing]). — xii,200p ; 24cm. — (The Arguments of the philosophers)
Bibliography: p193-198. — Includes index
ISBN 0-7100-0009-x (pbk) : £4.95 B82-38563

193 — German philosophy. Leibniz, Gottfried Wilhelm — *Critical studies*

Leibniz : metaphysics and philosophy of science / edited by R.S. Woolhouse. — Oxford : Oxford University Press, 1981. — viii,182p ; 21cm
Bibliography: p176-179. — Includes index
ISBN 0-19-875050-1 (pbk) : £3.50 : CIP rev. B81-31458

193 — German philosophy. Nietzsche, Friedrich — *Critical studies*

Deleuze, Gilles. Nietzsche and philosophy. — London : Athlone Press, Aug.1982. — [240]p
Translation of: Nietzsche et la philosophie
ISBN 0-485-11233-7 : £14.50 : CIP entry B82-15821

Stern, J. P.. A study of Nietzsche / J.P. Stern. — Cambridge : Cambridge University Press, 1979 (1981 [printing]). — xi,220p ; 21cm. — (Major European authors)
Bibliography: p212-214. — Includes index
ISBN 0-521-28380-9 (pbk) : £6.95 : CIP rev. B81-32595

193 — German philosophy. Nietzsche, Friedrich. Influence of Wagner, Richard

Hollinrake, Roger. Nietzsche, Wagner : and the philosophy of pessimism / by Roger Hollinrake. — London : Allen & Unwin, 1982. — x,308p : facsims ; 23cm
Bibliography: p284-308
ISBN 0-04-921029-7 : Unpriced B82-32981

193 — German philosophy. Schopenhauer, Arthur — *Critical studies*

Magee, Bryan. The philosophy of Schopenhauer. — Oxford : Clarendon Press, Jan.1983. — [450]p
ISBN 0-19-824673-0 : £20.00 : CIP entry B82-32845

193 — German philosophy — *Texts*

Buber, Martin. The way of man. — Dulverton : Robinbson & Watkins, Aug.1982. — [44]p
ISBN 0-7224-0199-x (pbk) : £3.00 : CIP entry B82-25934

Eckhart, *Meister*. German sermons & treatises / Meister Eckhart ; translated with introduction and notes by M.O'C. Walshe. — London : Watkins
Translation of: Deutsche Predigten und Traktate
Vol.2. — 1981. — viii,350p ; 22cm
ISBN 0-7224-0190-6 (pbk) : Unpriced : CIP rev. B81-26699

Gadamer, Hans-Georg. Reason in the age of science / Hans-Georg Gadamer ; translated by Frederick G. Lawrence. — Cambridge, Mass. ; London : MIT, c1981. — xxxiii,179p ; 21cm. — (Studies in contemporary German social thought ; 2)
Translations from the German. — Includes index
ISBN 0-262-07085-5 : £12.25 B82-35672

Hahn, Hans. Empiricism, logic, and mathematics : philosophical papers / Hans Hahn ; edited by Brian McGuinness ; with an introduction by Karl Menger. — Dordrecht ; London : Reidel, c1980. — xix,139p : 1port ; 23cm. — (Vienna Circle collection ; v.13)
Bibliography: p132-135. — Includes index
ISBN 90-277-1065-1 (cased) : Unpriced
ISBN 90-277-1066-x (pbk) : Unpriced B82-40722

Husserl, Edmund. Husserl : shorter works / edited by Peter McCormick and Frederick A. Elliston. — Notre Dame, Ind. : University of Notre Dame Press ; Brighton : Harvester Press, 1981. — xix,440p ; 26cm
Bibliography: p381-430. — Includes index
ISBN 0-7108-0351-6 : £22.50 B82-18338

Leibniz, Gottfried Wilhelm. New essays on human understanding. — Abridged ed. — Cambridge : Cambridge University Press, Oct.1982. — [292]p
Translation and abridgement of: Nouveaux essais sur l'entendement humain
ISBN 0-521-28539-9 (pbk) : £6.50 : CIP entry B82-26252

Nietzsche, Friedrich. Daybreak : thoughts on the prejudices of morality / Friedrich Nietzsche ; translated by R.J. Hollingdale ; with an introduction by Michael Tanner. — Cambridge : Cambridge University Press, 1982. — xvii,233p ; 23cm. — (Texts in German philosophy)
Translation of: Morgenröthe. — Includes index
ISBN 0-521-24396-3 (cased) : £12.00 : CIP rev.
ISBN 0-521-28662-x (pbk) : £3.95 B82-15938

Nietzsche, Friedrich. Philosophy and truth : selections from Nietzsche's notebooks of the early 1870's / translated and edited with an introduction and notes by Daniel Breazeale ; with a foreword by Walter Kaufmann. — Atlantic Highlands, N.J. : Humanities Press ; Hassocks : Harvester Press, 1979. — lxix,165p ; 24cm
Bibliography: plxvii-lxix
ISBN 0-85527-327-5 : Unpriced B82-08623

193 — Ideology. Theories of Marx, Karl

Parekh, Bhikhu. Marx's theory of ideology / Bhikhu Parekh. — London : Croom Helm, c1982. — 247p ; 23cm
Bibliography: p243-245. — Includes index
ISBN 0-7099-0045-7 : £14.95 : CIP rev. B81-16372

193 — Phenomenology. Theories of Husserl, Edmund

Apriori and world : European contributions to Husserlian phenomenology / edited and translated by William McKenna, Robert M. Harlan and Laurence E. Winters ; with an introduction by J.N. Mohanty. — The Hague ; London : Nijhoff, 1981. — x,244p ; 25cm. — (Martinus Nijhoff philosophy texts ; v.2)
ISBN 90-247-2375-2 : Unpriced B82-07452

193 — Phenomenology. Theories of Husserl, Edmund — *French texts*

Valdinoci, Serge. Les fondements de la phénomenologie Husserlienne / Serge Valdinoci. — The Hague ; London : Nijhoff, 1982. — ix,302p ; 25cm. — (Phaenomenologica ; 85)
Bibliography: p293-302. — Includes index
ISBN 90-247-2504-6 : Unpriced B82-40858

193 — Phenomenology. Theories of Husserl, Edmund — *German texts*

Yamaguchi, Ichiro. Passive Synthesis und Intersubjektivität bei Edmund Husserl / Ichiro Yamaguchi. — The Hague ; London : Nijhoff, 1982. — xiii,164p ; 25cm. — (Phaenomenologica ; 86)
Bibliography: p145-148. — Includes index
ISBN 90-247-2505-4 : Unpriced B82-40857

194 — French philosophy. Derrida, Jacques — *Interviews*

Derrida, Jacques. Positions / Jacques Derrida ; translated and annotated by Alan Bass. — London : Athlone, 1981. — vii,114p ; 21cm
Translated from the French
ISBN 0-485-30000-1 : £10.95 B82-27715

194 — French philosophy. Diderot, Denis — *Critical studies*

Mason, John Hope. The irresistible Diderot. — London : Quartet Books, June 1982. — [288]p
ISBN 0-7043-2277-3 : £15.00 : CIP entry B82-13505

194 — French philosophy. Merleau-Ponty, Maurice — *Critical studies*

Merleau - Ponty : perception, structure, language : a collection of essays / edited by John Sallis. — Atlantic Highlands : Humanities ; Gloucester : distributed by Sutton, c1981. — 173p ; 24cm
Originally published in Research in phenomenology, vol.10, 1980. — Includes bibliographies
ISBN 0-391-02382-9 : Unpriced B82-38121

194 — French philosophy. Pascal, Blaise — *Critical studies*

Nelson, Robert J.. Pascal : adversary and advocate / by Robert J. Nelson. — Cambridge, Mass. ; London : Harvard University Press, 1981. — vi,286p : ill ; 25cm
Bibliography: p278-279. — Includes index
ISBN 0-674-65615-6 : £15.75 B82-27039

194 — French philosophy. Postel, Guillaume — *Critical studies*

Kuntz, Marion Leathers Daniels. Guillaume Postel : prophet of the restitution of all things, his life and thought / by Marion L. Kuntz. — The Hague ; London : Nijhoff, 1981. — xv,270p : ill,facsims ; 25cm. — (Archives internationales d'histoire des idees = International archives of the history of ideas ; 98)
Bibliography: p178-233. — Includes index
ISBN 90-247-2523-2 : Unpriced B82-03460

194 — French philosophy. Rousseau, Jean-Jacques — *Correspondence, diaries, etc.* — *French texts*

Rousseau, Jean-Jacques. Correspondance complete de Jean Jacques Rousseau. — ed. critique, établie et annotée par R.A. Leigh. — Oxford (Taylor Institution [St. Giles, Oxford OX1 3NA]) : Voltaire Foundation
T.38: Avril 1770-décembre 1771. — 1981. — xxiv,389p ; 25cm
French text. — Includes index
ISBN 0-7294-0263-0 : £32.00 B82-14859

194 — French philosophy. Rousseau, Jean-Jacques — *Critical studies* — *Conference proceedings*

Rousseau after two hundred years : proceedings of the Cambridge Bicentennial Colloquium / edited by R.A. Leigh. — Cambridge : Cambridge University Press, 1982. — xv,299p ; 24cm
Includes four chapters in English. — Includes index
ISBN 0-521-23753-x : £30.00 : CIP rev.
B82-04856

194 — French philosophy. Sorel, Georges — *Critical studies*

Stanley, John, *1937-*. The sociology of virtue : the political & social theories of George Sorel / John Stanley. — Berkeley ; London : University of California Press, c1981. — 387p ; 24cm
Bibliography: p343-376
ISBN 0-520-03790-1 : £21.00 B82-28102

194 — French philosophy — *Texts*

Derrida, Jacques. Dissemination / Jacques Derrida ; translated, with an introduction and additional notes, by Barbara Johnson. — London : Athlone, 1981. — xxxiii,366p : ill ; 24cm
Translation of: La Dissémination
ISBN 0-485-30005-2 : £25.00 : CIP rev.
B81-28162

194 — French philosophy — *Texts* — *Correspondence, diaries, etc.*

Descartes, René. Philosophical letters / Descartes ; translated and edited by Anthony Kenny. — Oxford : Blackwell, 1981, c1970. — xv,270p ; 22cm
Translation from the French. — Originally published: Oxford : Clarendon Press, 1970. — Bibliography: pviii. — Includes index
ISBN 0-631-12818-2 (pbk) : £4.95 : CIP rev.
B81-16930

194 — Materialism. Theories of Proudhon, P.-J.

Condit, Stephen. Proudhonist materialism & revolutionary doctrine / [Stephen Condit]. — Sanday : Cienfuegos, 1982. — 43p ; 22cm
ISBN 0-904564-49-5 (pbk) : £1.00 : CIP rev.
B82-05774

194 — Philosophy. Personalism. Theories of Mounier, Emmanuel, *1930-1950*

Hellman, John. Emmanuel Mounier and the new Catholic Left 1930-1950 / John Hellman. — Toronto ; London : University of Toronto Press, c1981. — viii,357p ; 24cm
Bibliography: p333-336. — Includes index
ISBN 0-8020-2399-1 : £24.50 B82-06993

195 — Italian philosophy. Bruno, Giordano — *Critical studies*

Yates, Frances A.. Lull & Bruno / Frances A. Yates. — London : Routledge & Kegan Paul
Vol.1. — 1982. — xii,279p,[32]p of plates : ill,facsims,ports ; 24cm. — (Collected essays : Frances A. Yates ; v.1)
Includes index
ISBN 0-7100-0952-6 : £12.50
Also classified at 196'.1 B82-26599

195 — Italian philosophy. Ficino, Marsilio — *Correspondence, diaries, etc.*

Ficino, Marsilio. [Epistolae. English]. The letters of Marsilio Ficino / translated from the Latin by members of the Language Department of the School of Economic Science, London. — London : Shepheard-Walwyn
'Being a translation of Liber IV'. — Facsims on lining papers. — Bibliography: p154-156. — Includes index
Vol.3. — 1981. — xiv,162p : facsims ; 24cm
ISBN 0-85683-045-3 : £8.00 : CIP rev.
B81-14449

195 — Italian philosophy — *Texts*

Vico, Giambattista. Vico : selected writings / edited and translated by Leon Pompa. — Cambridge : Cambridge University Press, 1982. — xvii,279 : ill ; 24cm
Translated from the Italian and the Latin. — Bibliography: p271-272. — Includes index
ISBN 0-521-23514-6 : £20.00 : CIP rev.
ISBN 0-521-28014-1 (pbk) : Unpriced
B82-11501

195 — Italian philosophy. Vico, Giambattista — *Critical studies*

Vicos : past and present / edited by Giorgio Tagliacozzo. — Atlantic Highlands : Humanities ; Gloucester : distributed by Sutton, c1981. — xvi,266p : 1ill ; 23cm
Includes bibliographies and index
ISBN 0-391-02228-8 : Unpriced B82-38118

196'.1 — Spanish philosophy. Ferrater Mora, J. — *Critical studies*

Transparencies : philosophical essays in honor of J. Ferrater Mora / edited by Priscilla Cohn. — Atlantic Highlands : Humanities ; Gloucester : distributed by Sutton, c1981. — xxiii,235p ; 24cm
Bibliography: p202-232
ISBN 0-391-02361-6 : Unpriced B82-38124

196'.1 — Spanish philosophy. Lull, Ramón — *Critical studies*

Yates, Frances A.. Lull & Bruno / Frances A. Yates. — London : Routledge & Kegan Paul
Vol.1. — 1982. — xii,279p,[32]p of plates : ill,facsims,ports ; 24cm. — (Collected essays : Frances A. Yates ; v.1)
Includes index
ISBN 0-7100-0952-6 : £12.50
Primary classification 195 B82-26599

196'.1 — Spanish philosophy — *Texts*

Trías, Eugenio. The artist and the city / Eugenio Trías ; translated by Kenneth Krabbenhoft. — New York ; Guildford : Columbia University Press, 1982. — xx,154p ; 22cm. — (European perspectives)
Translation of: El artista y la ciudad. — Includes index
ISBN 0-231-05286-3 : £13.00 B82-36925

197'.2 — Russian philosophy. Gurdjieff, G. I., *1943-1945* — *Personal observations*

Zuber, René. Who are you Monsieur Gurdjieff? / René Zuber ; translated by Jenny Koralek ; with a foreword by P.L. Travers. — London : Routledge & Kegan Paul, 1980. — viii,82p ; 18cm
Translation of: Qui êtes-vous Monsieur Gurdjieff?
ISBN 0-7100-0674-8 (pbk) : £2.95 : CIP rev.
B80-20160

197'.2 — Russian philosophy. Gurdjieff, G. I. — *Critical studies*

Thomasson, Henri. The pursuit of the present : journal of twenty years in the Gurdjieff work / Henri Thomasson ; translated by Rina Hands. — [Amersham] : Avebury, 1980. — 205p ; 23cm
Translation of: Batailles pour le présent
ISBN 0-86127-001-0 : £7.00 : CIP rev.
B80-02303

197'.2 — Russian philosophy. Gurdjieff, George. All and everything — *Indexes*

Guide and index to G.I. Gurdjieff's All and everything, Beelzebub's tales to his grandson. — London : Routledge & Kegan Paul, 1979, c1973. — 680p ; 17cm
Originally published: Toronto : Society for Traditional Studies, 1971
ISBN 0-919608-01-9 : £12.95 B82-39701

197'.2 — Russian philosophy. Ouspensky, P. D.. In search of the miraculous — *Indexes*

An Index to In search of the miraculous. — Ellingstring : Coombe Springs, c1982. — viii,48p : ill ; 21cm
ISBN 0-900306-67-x (pbk) : Unpriced
B82-37685

197'.2 — Russian philosophy — *Texts*

Ouspensky, P. D.. Tertium Organum : the third canon of thought a key to enigmas of the world / P.D. Ouspensky ; revised translation by E. Kadloubovsky and the author ; first translated from the Russian by Nicholas Bessaraboff and Claude Bragdon. — London : Routledge & Kegan Paul, 1981 (1982 [printing]). — xvi,298p : ill ; 24cm
Translation of: Tertium Organum. — Includes index
ISBN 0-7100-0843-0 (pbk) : £5.25 B82-39707

197'.2 — Soviet philosophy — *Texts* — *Collections*

Philosophy in the USSR : problems of historical materialism / [translated from the Russian by Sergei Syrovatkin]. — Moscow : Progress ; [London] : Distributed by Central, c1981. — 317p ; 21cm
Translation of: Filosofiīa v SSSR. — Bibliography: p295-308. — Includes index
ISBN 0-7147-1699-5 : £3.25 B82-29280

198'.1 — Norwegian philosophy. Naess, Arne — *Critical studies* — *Festschriften*

In sceptical wonder : inquiries into the philosophy of Arne Naess on the occasion of his 70th birthday / edited by Ingemund Gullvåg and Jon Wetlesen. — Oslo : Universitetsforlaget ; London : Global [distributor], c1982. — 328p : 1port ; 23cm
Bibliography: p315-319
ISBN 82-00-05867-0 : £25.00 B82-37360

199'.439 — Hungarian philosophy. Lukács, György — *Critical studies*

Lukács revalued. — Oxford : Blackwell, Jan.1983. — [220]p
ISBN 0-631-13159-0 : £15.00 : CIP entry
B82-32516

200 — RELIGION, CHRISTIANITY

200 — Christianity

Bühlmann, Walbert. The chosen peoples / Walbert Bühlmann ; translated from the German by Robert R. Barr. — Slough : St. Paul, 1982. — xiv,285p : ill ; 23cm
Includes index
ISBN 0-85439-200-9 : £10.00 B82-23244

Heiner, Wolfgang. Jesus is different. — Exeter : Paternoster, Nov.1982. — [112]p
Translation of: Warum unbedingt Jesus?
ISBN 0-85364-344-x (pbk) : £2.00 : CIP entry
B82-27220

Priestland, Gerald. Priestland's progress : one man's search for Christianity now / Gerald Priestland. — London : British Broadcasting Corporation, 1981. — 224p ; 20cm
Bibliography: p222-224
ISBN 0-563-17968-6 (pbk) : £3.50 B82-08350

World Christian encyclopedia : a comparative study of churches and religions in the modern world AD 1900-2000 / edited by David B. Barrett. — Nairobi ; Oxford : Oxford University Press, 1982. — xii,1010p : ill(some col.),maps(some col.),ports ; 32cm
Includes bibliographies and index
ISBN 0-19-572435-6 : £55.00 B82-34301

200 — Christianity *compared with* **Buddhism** — *Philosophical perspectives*

Smart, Ninian. Beyond ideology : religion and the future of western civilization : Gifford lectures delivered in the University of Edinburgh, 1979-1980 / Ninian Smart. — London : Collins, 1981. — 350p ; 21cm
Bibliography: p314-331. — Includes index
ISBN 0-00-215846-9 : £9.95 : CIP rev.
Also classified at 294.3 B81-20622

200 — Christianity - *For African students - For schools*

Developing in Christ. — London : Chapman, Oct.1981
Course 2: Teacher's handbook. — [198]p
ISBN 0-225-66299-x (pbk) : £5.50 : CIP entry
B81-08867

200 — Christianity — *For schools*

Hughes, Richard M.. Christianity : then and now / Richard Hughes. — Oxford : Oxford University Press, c1981. — 80p : ill(some col.),maps(some col.),1port ; 28cm. — (A Secondary religious education course ; Book 1)
Bibliography: p80
ISBN 0-19-918134-9 (pbk) : Unpriced
B82-15413

Thompson, Jan. Christian belief and practice / Jan Thompson. — London : Edward Arnold, 1982. — 74p : ill,1map ; 21cm
Includes index
ISBN 0-7131-0713-8 (pbk) : Unpriced : CIP rev.
B82-20032

200 — Christianity *related to* **Marxism**

Christianity & Marxism. — Exeter : Paternoster Press, Apr.1982. — [144]p
ISBN 0-85364-289-3 (pbk) : £3.20 : CIP entry
Also classified at 335.4 B82-05745

200 — Christianity — *Ukrainian texts*

Zhyzhka, Mariîa. ÎAkim idesh shlîakhom? : rozdumy / Mariîa Zhyzhka. — Kembridzh : Nakladom Zenoviîa Zhyzhky, 1980. — 176p : ill,1port ; 19cm
Includes index
Unpriced B82-03940

200 — Religion

Faculty of Theology, University College, Cardiff : Jubilee 1931-1981 : commemorative lecture by Professor Glanmor Williams, University College, Swansea and other lectures delivered to celebrate the jubilee of the faculty. — [Cardiff] ([University College, Cardiff, Law Building, P.O. Box 78, Cardiff CF1 1XL]) : [The Faculty], 1981. — 57p ; 21cm
Bibliography: p56-57
£0.80 (pbk) B82-06881

The **Nature** of religious man : tradition and experience : a symposium / organized by the Institute for Cultural Research ; edited by D.B. Fry. — London : Octagon, c1982. — xxii,219p ; 23cm
Bibliography: p216-217
ISBN 0-900860-67-7 : £8.00 B82-29272

Sharpe, Eric J.. Understanding religion. — London : Duckworth, Jan.1983. — [208]p
ISBN 0-7156-1657-9 : £18.00 : CIP entry
B82-32616

200 — Religion — *For schools*

Bruce, Ray. Beginning religion / Ray Bruce, Jane Wallbank. — London : Edward Arnold, 1982. — 96p : ill ; 25cm
Includes index
ISBN 0-7131-0571-2 (pbk) : £2.25 : CIP rev.
B81-22487

Collinson, Celia. Believers : worship in a multi-faith community / Celia Collinson and Campbell Miller ; photographs by Nick Hedges and David Richardson. — London : Edward Arnold, 1981. — 95p : ill,facsims ; 25cm
Includes index
ISBN 0-7131-0525-9 (pbk) : £2.50 : CIP rev.
B81-14835

Pitcher, Roy. Religion meets the new age / Roy Pitcher. — Harlow : Longman, 1981. — 112p : ill(some col.),ports(some col.) ; 24cm. — (The Developing world. Religion ; v.5)
Includes index
ISBN 0-582-21495-5 (pbk) : £2.95 B82-10042

200 — Religions

Brown, David, *1922-1982*. All their splendour : world faiths : a way to community / David Brown ; with a preface by Robert Runcie. — Glasgow : Collins, c1982. — 223p ; 18cm
Bibliography: p223
ISBN 0-00-626484-0 (pbk) : £1.95 B82-32764

The **Religious** world : communities of faith / Richard C. Bush ... [et al.] ; Robert F. Weir, general editor. — New York : Macmillan ; London : Collier Macmillan, 1982. — xvi,396p : ill,maps(some col.) ; 25cm
Maps on lining papers. — Includes bibliographies and index
ISBN 0-02-317480-3 : Unpriced B82-40792

The **World's** religions / consulting editors [R. Pierce Beaver ... et al.]. — Tring : Lion, 1982. — 448p : ill(some col.),maps(some col.). — (A Lion handbook)
Ill on lining papers. — Includes index
ISBN 0-85648-187-4 : £9.95 B82-23784

200 — Religions — *For schools*

Cole, W. Owen. Five religions in the twentieth century / W. Owen Cole. — Amersham : Hulton, 1981 (1982 [printing]). — 254p : ill,maps,plans,ports ; 25cm
Bibliography: p231-234. — Includes index
ISBN 0-7175-1100-6 : £5.45 B82-31040

Comparative religions : a modern textbook / Douglas Charing ... [et al.] ; [edited by W. Owen Cole]. — Poole : Blandford, 1982. — 256p : ill ; 23cm
Bibliography: p248-249. — Includes index
ISBN 0-7137-1077-2 (cased) : £6.95 : CIP rev.
ISBN 0-7137-1266-x (pbk) : £3.95 B82-06246

200′.1 — Philosophy of religion

Kolakowski, Leszek. Religion / Leszek Kolakowski. — New York ; Oxford : Oxford University Press, 1982. — 235p ; 22cm
Includes index
ISBN 0-19-520372-0 : £9.50 B82-27765

200′.1 — Religion. Faith — *Philosophical perspectives*

Swinburne, Richard. Faith and reason. — Oxford : Oxford University Press, Dec.1981. — [264]p
ISBN 0-19-824663-3 : £16.00 : CIP entry
B81-31453

200′.1 — Religion — *Philosophical perspectives*

Contemporary philosophy of religion / edited by Steven M. Cahn, David Shatz. — New York ; Oxford : Oxford University Press, 1982. — x,310p ; 23cm
Bibliography: p301-310
ISBN 0-19-503009-5 (pbk) : Unpriced
B82-27083

Davies, Brian, *19---*. An introduction to the philosophy of religion / Brian Davies. — Oxford : Oxford University Press, 1982. — x,144p ; 23cm. — (OPUS)
Bibliography: p140-142. — Includes index
ISBN 0-19-219158-6 (cased) : £9.95 : CIP rev.
ISBN 0-19-289145-6 (pbk) : Unpriced
B82-00889

Fries, Jakob Friedrich. Dialogues on morality and religion. — Oxford : Basil Blackwell, June 1982. — [272]p
Selected translations from: Julius und Evagoras
ISBN 0-631-10071-7 : £15.00 : CIP entry
B82-09452

James, William, *1842-1910*. Essays in religion and morality / William James. — Cambridge, Mass. ; London : Harvard University Press, 1982. — xxviii,345p : 1port ; 24cm. — (The Works of William James)
Includes index
ISBN 0-674-26735-4 : £17.50 B82-33392

Kolakowski, Leszek. Religion : if there is no God — : on God, the Devil, sin and other worries of the so-called philosophy of religion / Leszek Kolakowski. — [Glasgow] : Fontana, 1982. — 235p ; 18cm. — (Fontana masterguides)
Includes index
ISBN 0-00-635967-1 (pbk) : £2.50 B82-18953

Radhakrishnan, S.. An idealist view of life / Radhakrishnan. — 2nd ed. — London : Unwin paperbacks, 1980. — 279p ; 20cm. — (Mandala books)
Previous ed.: London : Allen and Unwin, 1932. — Includes index
ISBN 0-04-141009-2 (pbk) : £2.95 : CIP rev.
B80-20161

Santayana, George. Reason in religion : volume three of 'The life of reason' / George Santayana. — New York : Dover ; London : Constable, 1982. — vii,279p ; 21cm
Originally published: New York : Scribner's 1905
ISBN 0-486-24253-6 (pbk) : £3.40 B82-40189

200′.1 — Religion — *Philosophical perspectives — German texts*

Stavenhagen, Kurt. Absolute Stellungnahmen : eine ontologische Untersuchung über das Wesen der Religion / Kurt Stavenhagen. — New York ; London : Garland, 1979. — x,224p ; 23cm. — (Phenomenology)
Text in German. — Facsim of ed. published: Erlangen : Philosophischen Akademie, 1925
ISBN 0-8240-9557-x : Unpriced B82-18889

200′.1′4 — Religious language. Secularisation

Fenn, Richard K.. Liturgies and trials. — Oxford : Blackwell, Sept.1981. — [208]p
ISBN 0-631-12786-0 : £9.50 : CIP entry
B81-22628

200′.1′9 — Religion. Theories of Freud, Sigmund

Küng, Hans. Freud and the problem of God / Hans Küng ; translated by Edward Quinn. — New Haven ; London : Yale University Press, 1979. — ix,126p ; 21cm. — (The Terry lectures)
Translated from the German. — Includes index
ISBN 0-300-02350-2 (cased) : Unpriced : CIP rev.
ISBN 0-300-02597-1 (pbk) : £2.50

200′.1′9 — Religion. Theories of Jung, C. G.

Holt, David. Jung and the third person / by David Holt. — [London] : [Guild of Pastoral Psychology], [1981?]. — 23p ; 19cm
Unpriced (unbound) B82-15025

200′.3′21 — Religion — *Encyclopaedias*

Man, myth and magic. — London : Marshall Cavendish, Feb.1983. — 12v.
ISBN 0-86307-041-8 : CIP entry
Primary classification 291.1′3′0321 B82-39822

200′.5 — Religion — *Serials*

Doubting Thomas' viewsletter. — Vol.1, no.1 (1982)-. — Berkhamsted (c/o J. Sprague, 3 Greenway, Berkhamsted, Herts. HP4 3JD) : [s.n.], 1982-. — v. ; 21cm
ISSN 0263-2330 = Doubting Thomas' viewsletter : Unpriced B82-20886

200′.7 — Great Britain. Religious education teachers. Interviewing — *Case studies*

Shepherd, Robin. R.E. post interview : simulation exercise / Robin Shepherd. — [London] ([2 Chester House, Pages La., N10 1PR]) : Christian Education Movement, Secondary R.E. Department, [1982?]. — [12]p ; 30cm
Unpriced (unbound) B82-37002

200′.71 — Schools. Curriculum subjects: Religion. Research

Webster, Derek H.. Playing hide and seek with God : some themes in contemporary research in religious education / Derek H. Webster. — [London] ([2 Chester House, Pages La., N10 1PR]) : [Christian Education Movement], c1981. — 18p ; 21cm
Paper presented at Exeter University to the C.E.M. Easter Vacation Course, April 1981. — Cover title. — Text on inside front cover. — Bibliography: p18
Unpriced (pbk) B82-37000

200′.7′1041 — Great Britain. Schools. Curriculum subjects: Religion. Teaching

Religious education 5-18 years : approaches for non-specialist teachers / CEM. — London : Christian Education Movement, c1980. — 42p ; 30cm
ISBN 0-905022-67-x (pbk) : Unpriced
B82-36398

Sutcliffe, John, *1933-*. Teacher awareness in religious education / John M. Sutcliffe. — [London] ([2 Chester House, Pages La., N10 1PR]) : [Christian Education Movement], 1981. — 10p ; 21cm
Paper presented at Exeter University to the C.E.M. Easter Vacation Course, April 1981. — Cover title. — Text on inside front covers
Unpriced (pbk) B82-37001

200'.7'1041 — Great Britain. Schools. Curriculum subjects: Religions — *For teaching*
Approaching world religions / edited by Robert Jackson. — London : Murray, 1982. — xii,196p : ill ; 22cm. — (World religions in education)
Includes index
ISBN 0-7195-3913-7 (pbk) : £3.75 : CIP rev.
B82-07592

200'.7'1041 — Great Britain. Schools. Curriculum subjects: Religions — *Serials* — *For teaching*
Shap mailing. — 1978-. — Solihull (7 Alderbrook Rd, Solihull, W. Midlands B91 1NH) : Commission for Racial Equality for Shap Working Party, 1978-. — v. ; 30cm
Annual
ISSN 0263-3876 = Shap mailing : £1.00
B82-26154

200'.7'1041 — Great Britain. Schools. Religious education — *Christian Education Movement viewpoints*
The **Nature** of R.E. : paper / prepared by the Secondary Religious Education Department of the Christian Education Movement. — London (2 Chester House, Pages La., N10 1PR) : Christian Education Movement, c1980. — 3p ; 30cm
Unpriced (unbound) B82-35654

200'.7'1041 — Great Britain. Secondary schools. Religious education. Attitudes of students
Parker, Stephen, *1951-*. "— In case you meet some religious people" : an account of an RE survey conducted with four sets of third year mixed ability pupils / by Stephen Parker. — London (2 Chester House, Pages La., N10 1PR) : Christian Education Movement, [1982?]. — 7leaves ; 30cm. — (Occasional paper ; 4)
Unpriced (unbound) B82-34127

200'.7'10411 — Scotland. Schools. Religious education. Curriculum. Development
Curriculum guidelines for religious education. — Glasgow (c/o The Secretary, Scottish Curriculum Development Service, Glasgow Centre, Jordanhill College of Education, 76 Southbrae Drive, Glasgow G13 1PP) : Consultative Committee on the Curriculum, Scottish Central Committee on Religious Education, c1981. — ix,18p ; 21cm. — (Bulletin ; 2)
Unpriced (pbk) B82-33071

200'.7'10411 — Scotland. Schools. Religious education. Curriculum. Development — *Conference proceedings*
Curriculum, examinations & inspection in religious education : the Scottish context : a report of a religious education forum held in Dundee College of Education, 30-31 October 1981. — Dundee : Department of Learning Resources, Dundee College of Education, c1982. — 42p : ill ; 21cm
Cover title. — Text on inside cover
ISBN 0-903765-07-1 (pbk) : Unpriced
B82-23400

200'.7'1042 — England. Schools. Curriculum subjects: Religion. Syllabuses: Agreed Syllabus
Implementing the agreed syllabus. — London : Christian Education Movement, c1981. — 74p ; 30cm. — (Professional papers / Christian Education Movement ; 2)
ISBN 0-905022-72-6 (pbk) : Unpriced
B82-12049

200'.76 — England. Secondary schools. Students, 16 years-. Religious education. Examinations
Current issues in examinations. — London : Christian Education Movement, c1981. — 52p : forms ; 30cm. — (Professional papers / Christian Education Movement ; 3)
ISBN 0-905022-77-7 (pbk) : Unpriced
B82-05607

200'.92'4 — Religion. Theories of Hamann, Johann Georg
German, Terence J.. Hamann on language and religion / Terence J. German. — Oxford : Oxford University Press, 1981. — viii,187p ; 23cm. — (Oxford theological monographs)
Bibliography: p176-184. — Includes index
ISBN 0-19-826717-7 : £12.50 : CIP rev.
Primary classification 409'.2'4 B81-26752

200'.947 — Eastern Europe & Soviet Union. Religion
Eastern Europe : its people and our church / the Bishops' Conference of England and Wales Committee for Europe. — London : Catholic Truth Society, 1981. — 22p : 1map ; 19cm
Text, map on inside covers. — Bibliography: p21-22
ISBN 0-85183-444-2 (pbk) : £0.40 B82-02688

200'.97292 — Jamaica. Religions, *to 1981*
Morris, Ivor. Obeah, Christ and Rastaman : Jamaica and its religion. — Cambridge : Clarke, July 1982. — [128]p
ISBN 0-227-67831-1 : £7.50 : CIP entry
B82-18461

200'.973 — United States. Religion, *to 1980.* **Cultural aspects**
Moseley, James G.. A cultural history of religion in America / James G. Moseley. — Westport, Conn. ; London : Greenwood Press, 1981. — xviii,183p ; 22cm. — (Contributions to the study of religion, ISSN 0196-7053 ; no.2)
Bibliography: p167-178. — Includes index
ISBN 0-313-22479-x : £18.95 B82-18184

201 — CHRISTIANITY. PHILOSOPHY AND THEORY

201 — Christianity. Belief
Clark, Robert E. D.. God beyond nature / Robert E.D. Clark. — Exeter : Paternoster, c1982. — 112p : ill ; 18cm
Includes index
ISBN 0-85364-320-2 (pbk) : £1.95 : CIP rev.
B82-01414

Kennedy, D. James. Why I believe / D. James Kennedy. — London : Lakeland, 1980. — 164p ; 18cm
ISBN 0-551-00888-1 (pbk) : £1.50 B82-34794

201 — Christianity — *Philosophical perspectives*
Butler, B. C.. An appraoch to Christianity / Christopher Butler. — London : Fount, 1981. — 300p ; 20cm
ISBN 0-00-626388-7 (pbk) : £2.95 B82-04017

201'.9 — Christianity. Psychological aspects
Hanaghan, Jonathan. The beast factor : (forging passion into power) / Jonathan Hanaghan. — Enniskerry (the Egotist Press, Glaskenny, Enniskerry, Co. Wicklow) : Tansy Books, 1979. — 97p,[3]p of plates : ill,ports ; 22cm
Compiled from recorded talks given by the author
Unpriced B82-37061

Hanaghan, Jonathan. [The beast factor]. Forging passion into power / by Jonathan Hanaghan ; with a preface by Kenneth S. Woodroofe. — Dublin : Runa, c1981. — 97p,[3]p of plates : ill,ports ; 21cm
Compiled from recorded talks by the author. — Originally published without preface: Enniskerry : Tansy Books, 1979
Unpriced (pbk) B82-37062

205 — CHRISTIANITY. SERIALS

205 — Christianity — *Gujarati texts* — *Serials*
Prabhu sāthe che. — 1-. — [Smethwick] ([c/o The Editor, 163 Dibble Rd, Smethwick, Warley, W. Midlands B67 7PT]) : [s.n.], [1979]-. — v. ; 30cm
ISSN 0262-3250 = Prabhu sāthe che : Unpriced B82-02383

206 — CHRISTIANITY. ORGANISATIONS

206 — Christianity. Organisations — *Directories* — *Serials*
UK Christian handbook. — 1983. — London : Evangelical Alliance. — [416]p
ISBN 0-9505952-3-3 (pbk) : £10.00 : CIP entry
B82-28618

207 — CHRISTIANITY. STUDY AND TEACHING

207 — Christian religious education
O'Leary, D. J.. Love and meaning in religious education : an incarnational approach to teaching Christianity / D.J. O'Leary and T. Sallnow. — Oxford : Oxford University Press, 1982. — 147p ; 21cm
ISBN 0-19-918141-1 (pbk) : Unpriced
B82-15414

Rummary, Gerard. Growing into faith. — London : Darton Longman & Todd, Aug.1982. — [128]p
ISBN 0-232-51482-8 (pbk) : £3.95 : CIP entry
B82-19251

207'.1 — Schools. Christian religious education. Teaching — *Manuals*
Discovering the church. — 2nd ed. — London : CEM, c1978. — 20p : illl ; 30cm. — (Dimension ; 1)
Previous ed.: 197-?. — Text on inside cover
ISBN 0-905022-39-4 (pbk) : Unpriced
B82-40967

207'.38 — Schools. Christian religious education. Use of visual arts — *For teaching*
Grist, Ken. Batik, collage and all that graffiti : ideas for art in religious education / Ken Grist. — Leigh-on-Sea : Mayhew, 1978. — 80p : ill ; 21cm
ISBN 0-905725-45-x (pbk) : £2.50 B82-01822

207'.41 — Great Britain. Schools. Christian religious education — *For teaching*
New directions in religious education / edited and introduced by John Hull. — Lewes : Falmer, 1982. — xvi,215p : ill ; 24cm
Includes index
ISBN 0-905273-31-1 (cased) : £10.95
ISBN 0-905273-30-3 (pbk) : £5.95 B82-32418

207'.41 — Great Britain. Schools. Curriculum subjects: Christian religious education. Political aspects. Teaching — *Proposals*
Kibble, David G.. Politics in the context of religious education / by David G. Kibble. — Bramcote : Grove, 1982. — 25p ; 21cm. — (Grove booklet on ethics, ISSN 0305-4241 ; 45)
Text on inside cover
ISBN 0-907536-15-8 (pbk) : £0.70 B82-17700

207'.41 — Great Britain. Schools. Curriculum subjects: Christianity — *Conference proceedings*
Christianity in the classroom. — London : Christian Education Movement, 1978. — 42p ; 21cm
Conference papers
ISBN 0-905022-26-2 (pbk) : Unpriced
B82-36995

207'.41 — Great Britain. Secondary schools. Christian religious education — *For teaching*
Religious education in secondary schools / edited by Norman Richards. — London ([130 City Rd, EC1V 2NJ]) : Association of Christian Teachers. — (RE booklet series ; no.2)
1. — 1978. — 32p ; 21cm
Bibliography: On inside cover
£0.65 (pbk) B82-12487

207'.4185 — Ireland *(Republic).* **Maynooth. Theological colleges: St. Patrick's College** *(Maynooth).* **Students,** *1795-1895* — *Lists*
Hamell, Patrick J.. Maynooth : students and ordinations index 1795-1895 / by Patrick J. Hamell. — Birr ([St. Brendan's] Birr, Co. Offaly, Ireland) : P.J. Hamell, [1982]. — 199p ; 24cm
Unpriced B82-36766

207'.42496 — West Midlands *(Metropolitan County).* **Birmingham. Theological colleges: Woodbrooke College,** *1953-1978*
Woodbrooke College. Woodbrooke 1953-1978 : a documentary account of Woodbrooke's third 25 years / by F. Ralph Barlow ; edited by David B. Gray. — York : Sessions in association with Woodbrooke College, 1982. — xii,182p : ill,1plan,ports ; 21cm
Includes index
ISBN 0-900657-65-0 (pbk) : £3.00 B82-17837

207'.45632 — Italy. Rome. Catholic seminaries: Venerable English College, Rome, *to 1979*
Williams, Michael E.. The Venerable English College, Rome : a history : 1579-1979 / Michael E. Williams. — London : Associated Catholic on behalf of the College, 1979. — xii,256p,[28]p of plates : ill,1port ; 24cm
Bibliography: p243-247. — Includes index
ISBN 0-904359-24-7 : £5.95 B82-36649

209 — CHRISTIANITY. HISTORICAL AND GEOGRAPHICAL TREATMENT

209 — Christianity, *to 1881 — Poems*
Garrett, Arthur. The folk of Christendom / by Arthur Garrett. — New York : Philosophical Library ; London : Prior [distributor], c1981. — 520p : ill,ports ; 29cm
ISBN 0-8022-2363-x : Unpriced B82-12034

209'.2'2 — Christians, *to ca 65 — Stories for children*
The **First** Christians / editorial committee René Berthier, Jeanne-Marie Faure, Marie-Hélène Sigaut ; illustrated by Lizzie Napoli ; translated by Jane Collins. — London : Hodder and Stoughton, 1980. — 48p : col.ill,1col.map ; 29cm. — (Hodder & Stoughton Bible albums ; no.7)
Translation of: Les premiers Chrétiens. — Map on inside cover
ISBN 0-340-25332-0 (pbk) : £1.30 : CIP rev. B80-05777

209'.2'2 — Theology. Barth, Karl & Bultmann, Rudolf correspondence, diaries, etc.
Barth, Karl. Karl Barth-Rudolf Bultmann letters 1922-1966 / edited by Bernd Jaspert ; translated and edited by Geoffrey W. Bromiley. — Edinburgh : T. & T. Clark, 1982, c1971. — xiii,192p ; 23cm
Translation of: 'Karl Barth-Rudolf Bultmann : Briefwechsel, 1922-1966, V, Vol.1, of t'Karl Barth Gesamtausgabe'. — Bibliography: p186-192. — Includes index
ISBN 0-567-09334-4 : £6.95 B82-40630

209'.2'4 — Christianity. Theories of Lewis, C. S.
Purtill, Richard L.. C.S. Lewis's case for the Christian faith / Richard L. Purtill. — San Francisco ; London : Harper & Row, c1981. — xi,146p ; 22cm
Bibliography: p141-144. — Includes index
ISBN 0-06-066711-7 : Unpriced B82-37979

209'.2'4 — Theology. Lampe, G. W. H. — *Biographies*
G.W.H. Lampe : Christian, scholar, churchman : a memoir by friends / edited by C.F.D. Moule. — London : Mowbray, 1982. — ix,144p ; 22cm
ISBN 0-264-66864-2 (pbk) : £5.95 : CIP rev. B82-12718

209'.429 — Wales. Christianity. Effects of revival of Welsh culture, *1890-1914 — Welsh texts*
Jones, R. Tudur. Ffydd ac argyfwng cenedl : Cristionogaeth a diwylliant yng Nghymru 1890-1914 / R. Tudur Jones. — Abertawe [Swansea] : Tŷ John Penry
Cyfrol 1: Prysurdeb a phryder. — 1981. — 249p ; 22cm
ISBN 0-903701-24-3 : £8.00 B82-16389

Jones, R. Tudur. Ffydd ac argyfwng cenedl : Cristionogaeth a diwylliant yng Nghymru 1890-1914 / R. Tudur Jones. — Abertawe [Swansea] : Tŷ John Penry
Cyfrol 2: Dryswch a diwygiad. — 1982. — 305p ; 23cm
Includes index
ISBN 0-903701-48-0 : £7.00 B82-33179

209'.47 — Russia. Christianity, *ca 900-1300*
Poppe, Andrzej. The rise of Christian Russia. — London : Variorum, Sept.1982. — [346]p. — (Collected studies series ; CS157)
ISBN 0-86078-105-4 : £26.00 : CIP entry B82-21399

209'.669 — Nigeria. Christianity, *to 1964*
Varieties of Christian experience in Nigeria / edited by Elizabeth Isichei. — London : Macmillan, 1982. — x,211p,[4]p of plates : ill,1map,3ports ; 23cm
Includes index
ISBN 0-333-31027-6 : £17.60 B82-32333

210 — NATURAL THEOLOGY

211'.092'4 — God. Theories of Vallone, Yves de
O'Higgins, James. Yves de Vallone : the making of an esprit-fort / by James O'Higgins. — The Hague ; London : Nijhoff, 1982. — 248p ; 25cm. — (Archives internationales d'histoire des idées = International archives of the history of ideas ; 97)
Bibliography: p233-238. — Includes index
ISBN 90-247-2520-8 : Unpriced B82-25209

211'.5'0924 — Deism. Theories of Toland, John, *1670-1722*
Sullivan, Robert E.. John Toland and the deist controversy : a study in adaptations / Robert E. Sullivan. — Cambridge, Mass. ; London : Harvard University Press, 1982. — viii,355p : ill ; 24cm. — (Harvard historical studies ; v.101)
Bibliography: p336-344. — Includes index
ISBN 0-674-48050-3 : £19.25 B82-32837

212'.1 — God. Existence
Dumitriu, Petru. To the unknown God / Petru Dumitriu ; translated from the French by James Kirkup. — London : Collins, 1982. — 247p ; 21cm
Translation of: Au Dieu inconnu
ISBN 0-00-216358-6 (pbk) : £5.95 : CIP rev. B82-19061

Küng, Hans. Does God exist? : an answer for today / Hans Küng ; translated by Edward Quinn. — London : Collins, 1980. — xxiv,839p ; 24cm
Translation of: Existiert Gott?. — Includes index
ISBN 0-00-215147-2 : £12.00 B82-12306

212'.1 — God. Existence — *Catholic viewpoints*
Davies, Brian, *1951-.* Does God exist? / Brian Davies. — London : Catholic Truth Society, 1982. — 7p ; 19cm
ISBN 0-85183-453-1 (pbk) : £0.30 B82-15997

212'.1 — God. Existence — *Early works*
Herbert of Cherbury, Edward Herbert, *Baron.* A dialogue between a tutor and his pupil / Edward Herbert. — New York ; London : Garland, 1979. — 272p ; 23cm. — (British philosophers and theologians of the 17th & 18th centuries)
Facsim. of: 1768 ed., London : W. Bathoe, 1768
ISBN 0-8240-1779-x : Unpriced B82-08717

212'.1 — God. Existence — *Philosophical perspectives*
Mackie, J. L.. The miracle of Theism. — Oxford : Clarendon Press, Sept.1982. — [320]p
ISBN 0-19-824665-x (cased) : £10.50 : CIP entry
ISBN 0-19-824682-x (pbk) : £3.95 B82-18974

212'.1'01 — God. Existence — *Philosophical perspectives*
Meynell, Hugo A.. The intelligible universe : a cosmological argument / Hugo A. Meynell. — London : Macmillan, 1982. — 153p ; 23cm. — (New studies in the philosophy of religion)
Includes index
ISBN 0-333-28102-0 : Unpriced B82-28394

Ward, Keith, *1938-.* Rational theology and the creativity of God / Keith Ward. — Oxford : Blackwell, 1982. — 240p ; 23cm
Bibliography: p235-237. — Includes index
ISBN 0-631-12597-3 : Unpriced : CIP rev. B81-14877

213 — Christian doctrine *related to* **Cosmology —** *Early works*
Boehme, Jacob. The signature of all things and other writings. — Cambridge : James Clarke, Feb.1982. — [304]p
Translated from the Latin. — Originally published: 1969
ISBN 0-227-67853-2 (pbk) : £5.50 : CIP entry B82-08405

213 — Organisms. Evolution. Theories — *Christian viewpoints*
Cameron, N. M. de S.. Evolution and the authority of the Bible. — Exeter : Paternoster Press, Oct.1982. — [112]p
ISBN 0-85364-326-1 (pbk) : £3.00 : CIP entry B82-24106

215 — Christian doctrine *related to* **science**
Nebelsick, Harold P.. Theology and science in mutual modification / Harold P. Nebelsick. — Belfast : Christian Journals, 1981. — 192p ; 23cm. — (Theology and scientific culture ; v.2)
Includes index
ISBN 0-904302-76-8 : Unpriced : CIP rev. B81-36989

The **Sciences** and theology in the twentieth century / edited by A.R. Peacocke. — Stocksfield : Oriel, 1981. — xviii,309p ; 23cm. — (Oxford international symposia)
Includes index
ISBN 0-85362-188-8 : Unpriced B82-23252

215 — Religion *related to* **science**
Burhoe, Ralph Wendell. Toward [sic] a scientific theology / Ralph Wendell Burhoe. — Belfast : Christian Journals, 1981. — 240p ; 23cm
Includes index
ISBN 0-904302-70-9 : Unpriced : CIP rev. B81-07452

220 — BIBLE

220 — Bible — *For Nigerian students*
Horton, R. H.. Handbook of Bible knowledge studies for class 1 in secondary schools in Nigeria. — London : Edward Arnold, Aug.1982. — [128]p
ISBN 0-7131-8089-7 (pbk) : £1.50 : CIP entry B82-17210

220'.07 — Bible. Teaching — *Manuals*
Morrison, Jean C.. Growing fellowship : six "do-it-yourself" Bible studies for Women's Guild meetings / designed by Jean C. Morrison. — [Edinburgh] : Church of Scotland Women's Guild, [1982]. — 42p : ill ; 22cm
ISBN 0-86153-042-x (pbk) : £1.00 B82-29850

220'.076 — Bible — *Questions & answers*
Coates, Mick. 'Hill top' quiz book / presented by 'Mick' Coates. — Ilkeston : Moorley's Bible & Bookshop
No.2. — [1981?]. — 32p ; 21cm
ISBN 0-86071-121-8 (pbk) : £0.40 B82-05567

Mills, Daphne. The road to Emmaus / by Daphne Mills. — Rev. ed. — Poole : Celebration, c1979. — 127p : ill ; 21cm
Previous ed.: in 3v. S.l. : s.n., 1968. — Bibliography: p122-123
ISBN 0-906309-11-5 (pbk) : £1.95 : CIP rev. B80-09573

220'.092'4 — Bible study. Bruce, F.F. — *Biographies*
Bruce, F. F.. In retrospect : remembrance of things past / F.F. Bruce. — London : Pickering & Inglis, 1980. — viii,319p,[8]p of plates : ill,ports ; 21cm
ISBN 0-7208-0471-x : £7.50 B82-40809

220.1'3 — Bible. Authority
Packer, J. I.. [Freedom and authority]. Freedom, authority & Scripture / J.I. Packer ; foreword by Charles W. Colson. — Leicester : Inter-Varsity Press, 1982, c1981. — 61p ; 18cm
Originally published: U.S.A. : s.n., 1981?
ISBN 0-85110-445-2 (pbk) : £0.95 : CIP rev. B82-04990

Stott, John R. W.. The Bible. — Leicester : Inter-Varsity Press, Oct.1982. — [80]p
ISBN 0-85110-439-8 (pbk) : £0.95 : CIP entry B82-24235

Welch, Charles H.. True, from the beginning : or evidence that all scripture is given by inspiration of God / by Charles H. Welch. — Rev. ed. — London : Berean Publishing, 1977. — 58p : ill ; 21cm
Previous ed.: i.e. 2nd ed. 1958
ISBN 0-85156-056-3 (pbk) : Unpriced B82-35176

220.1′3 — Bible. Authority. Theories of Lewis, C. S.

Christensen, Michael J.. C.S. Lewis on scripture : his thoughts on the nature of biblical inspiration, the role of revelation and the question of inerrancy / Michael J. Christensen ; foreword by Owen Barfield ; introduction by Clyde S. Kilby. — London : Hodder and Stoughton, 1980, c1979. — 120p ; 18cm. — (Hodder Christian paperbacks)
Originally published: Waco : Word Books, c1979. — Bibliography: p117-120
ISBN 0-340-25336-3 (pbk) : £1.25 : CIP rev. B80-09967

220.1′5 — Bible. Prophecy

Southwell, Peter. Prophecy. — London : Hodder and Stoughton, Sept.1982. — [128]p
ISBN 0-340-27238-4 (pbk) : £4.50 : CIP entry B82-18807

220.3′21 — Bible — *Encyclopaedias*

The **International** standard Bible encyclopedia. — Exeter : Paternoster Press
Vol.2 (E-J). — Apr.1982. — [1023]p
ISBN 0-85364-304-0 : £22.00 : CIP entry B82-04736

The **New** Bible dictionary. — 2nd ed. (completely rev. and reset). — Leicester : Inter-Varsity Press, Mar.1982. — [1324]p
Previous ed.: 1962
ISBN 0-85110-630-7 : £17.50 : CIP entry B82-01562

220.4′4 — Bible. *Hebrew.* Interpretation — *Festschriften*

Interpreting the Hebrew Bible : essays in honour of E.I.J. Rosenthal / edited by J.A. Emerton and Stefan C. Reif. — Cambridge : Cambridge University Press, c1982. — xv,318p : ill,1port ; 23cm. — (University of Cambridge oriental publications ; no.32)
Includes index
ISBN 0-521-24424-2 : £22.50 : CIP rev. B82-21723

220.4′4 — Bible. *Hebrew.* Textual criticism

Weingreen, J.. Introduction to the critical study of the text of the Hebrew Bible / J. Weingreen. — Oxford : Clarendon Press, 1982. — 103p ; 22cm
Bibliography: p98. — Includes index
ISBN 0-19-815453-4 : £5.50 : CIP rev. B80-22868

220.4′8′014 — Bible. *Greek.* Words — *Greek & English dictionaries*

Vine, W. E.. Expository dictionary of Bible words / by W.E. Vine. — London : Marshall Morgan & Scott, 1981. — 351,127p ; 23cm
Contents: An expository dictionary of New Testament words. Originally published: London : Oliphants, 1940 — Expository dictionary of Old Testament words. Originally published: London : Marshall Morgan & Scott, 1979
ISBN 0-551-00913-6 : £11.95 : CIP rev. B81-28339

220.5′2 — Bible. *English. New International. Selections — Texts*

[Bible. *English. New International. Selections. 1982*]. Daily light. — London : Hodder & Stoughton, Nov.1982. — [368]p
ISBN 0-340-32393-0 (pbk) : £1.95 : CIP entry B82-29004

220.5′2 — Bible. *English. New International — Texts*

[Bible. *English. New International. 1981*]. The Holy Bible : New International Version. — London : Hodder & Stoughton, Nov.1981. — [1182]p
ISBN 0-340-27818-8 (pbk) : £3.75 : CIP entry B81-31159

[Bible. *English. New International. 1982*]. The Holy Bible : New International Version. — Pocket ed. — London : Hodder and Stoughton, Mar.1982. — [1240]p
ISBN 0-340-27617-7 : £3.95 : CIP entry B82-00246

[Bible. *English. New International. 1982*]The **Holy** Bible : New International version. — Illustrated ed. — London : Hodder & Stoughton, July 1982. — [1200]p
ISBN 0-340-27852-8 : £5.50 : CIP entry B82-12244

220.5′2 — Bible. *English. Today′s English. Selections — Texts*

[Bible. *English. Today′s English. Selections. 1981*] **Words** of hope. — Large print ed. — Tring : Lion, 1981, c1976. — 44p : col.ill ; 19cm
Originally published: as A word of hope. 1976
ISBN 0-85648-412-1 (pbk) : £0.95 B82-06387

220.5′2 — Bible. *English. Today′s English — Texts*

[Bible. *English. Today′s English. 1979*]. Good news Bible : with Deuterocanonical Books/Apocrypha : today′s English version. — Glasgow : Collins, 1979. — x,931,231,377p : ill,maps ; 22cm
Maps on lining papers. — Includes index
ISBN 0-00-512682-7 : Unpriced B82-19433

220.5′2 — Bible — *Texts — Quotations*

[Bible. *English. Selections. 1982*]. The lion concise book of Bible quotations / compiled by Martin H. Manser. — Tring : Lion, 1982. — 240p ; 22cm
ISBN 0-85648-365-6 (cased) : Unpriced
ISBN 0-85648-167-x (pbk) : £4.95 B82-21035

220.5′2 — Bible. Translations into English language

Hammond, Gerald. The making of the English Bible. — Manchester : Carcanet, Sept.1982. — [224]p
ISBN 0-85635-433-3 : £9.95 : CIP entry B82-21991

220.5′2′00924 — Bible. Translation. Coverdale, Miles — *Biographies*

Lupton, Lewis. Endurance / by Lewis Lupton. — London (2 Milnthorpe Rd., W4 3DX) : Olive Tree, 1979. — 192p : ill,maps,music,facsims ; 23cm. — (A History of the Geneva Bible ; v.11)
′ ... the first of two volumes devoted to a biography of Miles Coverdale′. — Ill on lining papers
£10.40 (£7.62 to subscribers) B82-11646

220.5′2036 — Bible. *English. Authorized — Quotations*

[Bible. *English. Authorized. Selections. 1980*] **Book** of Biblical quotations / edited by Anthony J. Castagno with Faye C. Allen, Joseph M. Castagno under the direction of Lawrence Urdang. — London : Pickering & Inglis, 1981, c1980. — 271p ; 21cm
Originally published as: A Treasury of Biblical quotations. Nashville : Nelson, c1980
ISBN 0-7208-0485-x (pbk) : £3.95 B82-00141

A **Treasury** of biblical quotations / edited by Jennifer Speake. — London : Hamlyn, 1982. — xv,203p ; 22cm
Includes index
ISBN 0-600-33247-0 : £5.95 B82-40748

220.5′2036 — Bible. *English. Authorized. Selections — Texts*

[Bible. *English. Authorized. Selections. 1981*]. Book of Bible lists / [compiled by] J.L. Meredith. — London : Pickering & Inglis, 1981, c1980. — 286p : ill ; 21cm
Originally published: as Meredith′s book of Bible lists. Minneapolis, Minn. : Bethany Fellowship, c1980. — Bibliography: p285-286
ISBN 0-7208-0498-1 (pbk) : £3.95 B82-05045

[Bible. *English. Authorized. Selections. 1981*] **Words** of peace. — Authorized Version ed. — Tring : Lion, 1981. — 44p : col.ill ; 19cm
Previous ed.: published as A word of peace. 1978
ISBN 0-85648-420-2 (cased) : Unpriced
ISBN 0-85648-426-1 (pbk) : £0.95 B82-06386

220.5′2038 — Bible. *English. Authorized.* Translation

Opfell, Olga S.. The King James Bible translators / Olga S. Opfell. — Jefferson ; London : McFarland, 1982. — v,173p : 1ill ; 24cm
Bibliography: p163-165. — Includes index
ISBN 0-89950-041-2 : £13.25 B82-37700

220.5′204 — Bible. *English. Revised standard — Texts*

[Bible. *English. Revised. 1981*]. The Holy Bible : the revised version containing the Old and New Testaments. — London : Octopus, 1981. — 894p in various pagings,[14]p of plates : col.ill,3col.maps ; 29cm
ISBN 0-7064-1704-6 : Unpriced B82-04229

220.5′209 — Bible. *English. Taylor — Texts*

[Bible. *English. Taylor. 1971*]. The living Bible. — Eastbourne : Kingsway, 1979, c1971. — xii,1216p : ill ; 20cm
Originally published: New York: Tyndale House ; London : Hodder and Stoughton, 1971. — Full leather
ISBN 0-86065-014-6 (cased) : £12.50
ISBN 0-86065-067-7 (pbk) : £3.25
ISBN 0-86065-013-8 (Imitation leather) : £8.95
ISBN 0-86065-011-1 (Hbk : grey) : £4.25
ISBN 0-86065-012-x (Hbk : white) : £4.25
ISBN 0-902088-53-x (U.S. : Hbk)
ISBN 0-902088-75-0 (U.S. : pbk) B82-23423

220.5′9162 — Bible. *Irish. Maynooth — Texts*

[Bible. *Irish. Maynooth. 1981*]. An Bíobla naofa : arna aistriú ón mbuntéacs faoi threoir ó Easpaig na hEireann maille le Réamhrá agus Brollaigh. — Maigh Nuad [Maynooth] ([c/o St Patrick′s College, Maynooth, Co. Kildare]) : An Sagart, 1981. — 263p,[6]leaves of plates : col.ill,4maps,col.facsims ; 28cm
Maps on lining papers
Unpriced B82-03025

220.6 — Bible — *Critical studies*

Ferguson, Sinclair B.. Handle with care! : a guide to using the Bible / Sinclair B. Ferguson. — London : Hodder and Stoughton, 1982. — 121p ; 20cm
ISBN 0-340-28197-9 (pbk) : £3.95 : CIP rev. B82-12237

Penny, Michael. The Bible — myth or message? / Michael Penny. — London : Triangle, 1982. — lx,132p : ill,maps ; 18cm
ISBN 0-281-03813-9 (pbk) : £1.95 B82-20149

Williams, James G.. Those who ponder proverbs : aphoristic thinking and biblical literature / James G. Williams. — Sheffield : Almond, 1981. — 128p : ill ; 23cm. — (Bible and literature series, ISSN 0260-4493 ; 2)
Bibliography: p113-120. — Includes index
ISBN 0-907459-02-1 (cased) : £14.95 : CIP rev.
ISBN 0-907459-03-x (pbk) : £5.95 B81-11953

220.6 — Bible — *Critical studies — Conference proceedings*

International Congress on Biblical Studies *(6th : 1978 : Oxford)*. Studia biblica 1978 : Sixth International Congress on Biblical Studies, Oxford 3-7 April 1978. — Sheffield : JSOT Press. — (Journal for the study of the New Testament supplement series ; 3)
3: Papers on Paul and other New Testament authors / edited by E.A. Livingstone. — 1980. — 468p ; 22cm
Includes 1 paper in German, and 1 paper in French
ISBN 0-905774-27-2 : Unpriced B82-01658

220.6 — Bible — *Critical studies — Welsh texts*

Bara′r bywyd : darlleniadau Beiblaidd dyddiol. — Pen-y-bont ar Ogwr [Bridgend] : Gwasg Efengylaidd Cymru
Rhif 12: 1 Samuel / Gwilym Ll. Humphreys. — 1982. — 62p ; 19cm
ISBN 0-900898-67-4 (pbk) : £0.85 B82-35402

220.6 — Bible. Criticism

Anderson, Bernhard W.. The living word of the Bible / Bernhard W. Anderson. — London : SCM, 1979. — 118p ; 22cm
Bibliography: p111-118
ISBN 0-334-00920-0 (pbk) : £2.95 B82-00078

220.6 — Bible — *Expositions*

Barr, James. Holy scripture. — Oxford : Clarendon Press, Jan.1983. — [186]p
ISBN 0-19-826323-6 (cased) : £9.50 : CIP entry
ISBN 0-19-826324-4 (pbk) : £2.95 B82-36324

220.6 — Bible — *Expositions continuation*

Mathews, Oliver, *1900-*. The Bible : unclaimed legacy / Oliver Mathews. — Edinburgh : Floris Books, 1981. — 125p ; 22cm
ISBN 0-903540-47-9 (pbk) : £5.75 : CIP rev. B81-20563

Moore, E.. The address on the envelope / by E. Moore. — 3rd ed. — London (52a Wilson St., EC2A 2ER) : Berean Publishing, 1980 (1976 [printing]). — 16p ; 21cm
Previous ed.: 1968
Unpriced (pbk) B82-34762

Welch, Charles H.. The key of knowledge, or, The dispensational truth / by Charles H. Welch. — London (52a Wilson St., E.C.2) : Berean Publishing, [1980?]. — 20p ; 21cm
Cover title
Unpriced (pbk) B82-35965

Welch, Charles H.. Steps through scripture / by Charles H. Welch. — London (52a Wilson St., E.C.2) : Berean Publishing, [1980?]. — 20p ; 21cm
Cover title
Unpriced (pbk) B82-35964

Welch, Charles H.. "Things most surely believed" / by Charles H. Welch. — London (52a Wilson St., EC2A 2ER) : Berean Publishing, [1980?]. — 69p ; 18cm
Unpriced (pbk) B82-35966

Welch, Charles H.. United, yet divided / by Charles H. Welch. — Rev. ed. — London : Berean Publishing, 1976. — 40p ; 21cm
Previous ed.: 1957
ISBN 0-85156-057-1 (pbk) : Unpriced B82-35180

220.6 — Bible. Interpretation

Brown, Raymond E.. The critical meaning of the Bible / Raymond E. Brown. — [London] : Chapman, 1982, c1981. — x,150p ; 21cm
Originally published: New York : Paulist Press, 1981. — Includes index
ISBN 0-225-66325-2 (pbk) : £4.95 B82-26268

Wilder, Amos N.. Jesus' parables and the war of myths : essays on imagination in the Scripture / Amos N. Wilder ; edited, with a preface by James Breech. — London : SPCK, 1982. — 168p ; 24cm
ISBN 0-281-04008-7 : £10.00 B82-37372

220.7 — Bible — *Commentaries — Welsh texts*

Bara'r bywyd : darlleniadau Beiblaidd dyddiol. — Pen-y-bont ar Ogwr [Bridgend] : Gwasg Efengylaidd Cymru
Rhif 9: Llyfr yr Actau / Gwyn Davies. — 1981. — 63p ; 19cm
ISBN 0-900898-63-1 (pbk) : £0.85 B82-02287

Bara'r bywyd : darlleniadau Beiblaidd dyddiol. — Pen-y-bont ar Ogwr [Bridgend] : Gwasg Efengylaidd Cymru
Rhif 10: Barnwyr-Ruth / Gwyn Davies. — 1981. — 64p ; 19cm
ISBN 0-900898-64-x (pbk) : £0.85 B82-15222

Bara'r bywyd : darlleniadau Beiblaidd dyddiol. — [Bridgend] : Gwasg Efengylaidd Cymru
Rhif 11: Philipiaid-2 Thesaloniaid / Gwyn Davies. — 1982. — 63p ; 19cm
ISBN 0-900898-65-8 (pbk) : £0.85 B82-25612

220.8'3054 — Bible. Special subjects: Women

Williams, James G.. Women recounted. — Sheffield (24 Tapton Crescent Rd., Sheffield S10 5DA) : Almond Press, Dec.1982. — [128] p. — (Bible and literature series, ISSN 0260-4493 ; 6)
ISBN 0-907459-18-8 (cased) : £14.95 : CIP entry
ISBN 0-907459-19-6 (pbk) : £5.95 B82-30721

220.8'30542 — Bible. Special subjects: Society. Role of women

LaHaye, Beverly. I am a woman by God's design / Beverly LaHaye. — Eastbourne : Kingsway, 1981, c1980. — 128p ; 18cm
Originally published: Old Tappan, N.J. : Revell, 1980
ISBN 0-86065-157-6 (pbk) : £1.25 B82-00715

220.8'30689 — Bible. Special subjects: Divorce

Williams, John, *1928-*. For every cause? : the question of divorce / John Williams. — Exeter : Paternoster, c1981. — 96p ; 18cm
Bibliography: p90-92. — Includes index
ISBN 0-85364-330-x (pbk) : £1.60 : CIP rev. B82-01415

220.8'574 — Bible. Special subjects: Organisms

Feliks, Yehuda. Nature and man in the Bible : chapters in biblical ecology / Yehuda Feliks. — London : Soncino Press, c1981. — xiv,294p : ill ; 26cm
Bibliography: p281-285. — Includes index
ISBN 0-900689-19-6 : Unpriced B82-39474

220.8'58213 — Bible. Special subjects: Flowering plants

Chancellor, John. The flowers and fruits of the Bible / John Chancellor ; illustrated by W.H. McCheane. — Exeter : Webb & Bower, 1982. — 64p : col.ill ; 29cm
Bibliography: p64
ISBN 0-906671-53-1 : £5.95 : CIP rev. B82-01407

220.8'613 — Bible. Special subjects: Man. Health

Gregson, A. H.. A doctor looks at the Bible / A.H. Gregson. — Bognor Regis : New Horizon, c1982. — 169p ; 22cm
ISBN 0-86116-432-6 : £5.25 B82-09559

220.9 — BIBLICAL GEOGRAPHY AND HISTORY

220.9'3 — Bible. Historicity. Archaeological sources

Thompson, J. A.. The Bible and archaeology. — Revised ed. — Exeter : Paternoster Press, Feb.1982. — [512]p
Previous ed.: 1963
ISBN 0-85364-347-4 : £9.00 : CIP entry B82-02466

220.9'5 — Ancient Middle East, *to ca 70.* **Historical sources: Bible**

Allen, John Catling. Pictorial Bible atlas / J. Catling Allen ; with maps drawn by Malcolm Porter. — [Amersham] : Hulton, [c1980]. — 64p : ill(some col.),col.maps,2facsims ; 27cm
ISBN 0-7175-0991-5 (cased) : £3.50
ISBN 0-7175-0857-9 (pbk) : £2.25 B82-09524

220.9'505 — Bible — *Stories for children*

Bruce, F. F.. A first Bible history atlas. — Exeter : Paternoster, Nov.1981. — [96]p
ISBN 0-85364-312-1 : £4.95 : CIP entry B81-30424

Christie-Murray, David. The all-colour children's Bible / David Christie-Murray ; illustrated by Ken Petts ... [et al.]. — London : Hamlyn, 1982. — 414p : col.ill ; 27cm
Text ... first published in 1974 in ... Hamlyn Bible for children
ISBN 0-600-36650-2 : £4.50 B82-37314

Hunt, P. J. (Patricia Joan). Bible stories / written by Patricia Hunt ; illustrated by Angus McBride. — London : Ward Lock, 1981. — 248p : col.ill,maps(some col.) ; 28cm
Ill on lining papers
ISBN 0-7063-5805-8 : £4.95 : CIP rev. B81-25872

Knowles, Andrew. Fount children's Bible / Andrew Knowles ; illustrated by Bert Bouman. — London : Fount Paperbacks, 1981. — 445p : col.ill ; 19cm
ISBN 0-00-625894-8 (pbk) : £3.95 B82-01919

Marshall, Catherine. Catherine Marshall's story Bible / illustrated by children. — London : Hodder and Stoughton, c1982. — 196p : col.ill ; 33cm
Illustrations originally published with French text
ISBN 0-340-28525-7 : £8.95 : CIP rev. B82-21087

Patston, A. G.. A visual background to the Bible / A.G. Patston ; illustrated by the author. — Exeter : Relgious Education Press, 1981. — 63p : ill,1map ; 25cm
ISBN 0-08-025626-0 (pbk) : £1.25 B82-05464

Penny, Sylvia. The great plan of God / by Sylvia and Michael Penny. — London (52a Wilson St, EC2A 2ER) : Berean Publishing, c1981. — 65p ; 21cm
ISBN 0-85156-084-9 (pbk) : Unpriced B82-34759

Snashall, Hazel. The Bible story / Hazel Snashall ; artwork by Anne Farncombe. — Redhill : National Christian Education Council
Bk.5. — 1980. — 32p : col.ill,1col.map ; 23cm
ISBN 0-7197-0264-x (pbk) : Unpriced B82-17618

Snashall, Hazel. The Bible story / Hazel Snashall ; artwork by Anne Farncombe. — Redhill : National Christian Education Council
Bk.6. — 1980. — 32p : col.ill,2col.maps ; 23cm
ISBN 0-7197-0265-8 (pbk) : Unpriced B82-17619

Wangerin, Walter. [The Bible]. Purnell's illustrated Bible / by Walter Wangerin, Jr. — Bristol : Purnell, 1982. — 432p : col.ill,col.maps ; 26cm
Originally published: Chicago : Rand McNally, 1981. — Includes index
ISBN 0-361-05297-9 : Unpriced B82-23619

221 — OLD TESTAMENT

221 — Bible. O.T.. Quotations in Bible. N.T.

Hanson, Anthony Tyrrell. The New Testament interpretation of scripture / Anthony Tyrrell Hanson. — London : SPCK, 1980. — xi,237p ; 23cm
Bibliography: p212-223. — Includes index
ISBN 0-281-03702-7 : £12.50
Primary classification 225 B82-08375

221.4'4 — Bible. O.T. *Hebrew.* **Narrative** — *Critical studies*

Alter, Robert. The art of Biblical narratives. — London : Allen & Unwin, Feb.1982. — [200]p
ISBN 0-04-801022-7 : £10.00 : CIP entry B82-02438

221.5'2 — Bible. O.T.. *English. Selections — Texts*

[Bible. O.T.. *English. Selections. 1979*]. The Old Testament : in the dialect of the Black Country. — Tipton : Black Country Society
Pt.2: The books of Joshua, Judges, Ruth, Job, Jonah, the first and second books of Samuel / by Kate Fletcher ; [edited and produced by Harold Parsons]. — 1979. — 88p ; 19cm
ISBN 0-904015-17-3 (pbk) : £0.80 B82-09091

221.6 — Bible. O.T. — *Critical studies*

Art and meaning : rhetoric in Biblical literature. — Sheffield : JSOT Press, June 1982. — [280] p. — (Journal for the study of the Old Testament. Supplement series, ISSN 0309-0787 ; 19)
ISBN 0-905774-38-8 (cased) : £12.50 : CIP entry
ISBN 0-905774-39-6 (pbk) : £8.95 B82-14963

Beginning Old Testament study. — London : SPCK, Jan.1983. — [144]p
ISBN 0-281-03840-6 (pbk) : £3.95 : CIP entry B82-33722

Fontaine, Carole R.. Traditional sayings in the Old Testament : a contextual study / Carole R. Fontaine. — Sheffield : Almond, 1982. — viii,279p : ill ; 23cm. — (Bible and literature series, ISSN 0260-4493 ; 5)
Bibliography: p253-268. — Includes index
ISBN 0-907459-08-0 (cased) : £17.95 : CIP rev.
ISBN 0-907459-09-9 (pbk) : £8.95 B82-05789

Gunneweg, A. H. J.. Understanding the Old Testament / A.H.J. Gunneweg ; [translated by John Bowden]. — London : SCM, 1978. — vi,265p ; 23cm. — (Old Testament library)
Translation of: Vom Verstehen des Alten Testaments. — Bibliography: p240-254. — Includes index
ISBN 0-334-01727-0 : £7.00 B82-41085

221.6 — Bible. O.T. — *Critical studies continuation*

Images of man and God : Old Testament short stories in literary focus / editor Burke O. Long. — Sheffield : Almond, 1981. — 127p : 1ill ; 23cm. — (Bible and literature series, ISSN 0260-4493 ; 1)
Includes index
ISBN 0-907459-00-5 (cased) : £14.95
ISBN 0-907459-01-3 (pbk) : £5.95 B82-39534

Lohfink, Norbert. Great themes from the Old Testament / by Norbert Lohfink ; translated by Ronald Walls. — Chicago : Franciscan Herald ; Edinburgh : T & T Clark, 1982. — x,267p ; 21cm
Translation of: Unsere grossen Wörter Das Alte Testament zu Themen dieser Jahre
£7.95 B82-39773

221.6 — Bible. O.T. — *Expositions*

Bradley, A. G.. A.L.I.C.E. : through the dark glass : Another Look Into Christian Education / A.G. Bradley. — Bognor Regis : New Horizon, c1982. — 126p ; 21cm
ISBN 0-86116-206-4 : £4.25 B82-06353

Brook, Peggy M.. The Bible as our life / Peggy M. Brook. — London : Foundational, [1982]. — 163p ; 22cm
Unpriced (pbk) B82-26792

Bush, F. W.. Old Testament survey. — Leicester : Inter-Varsity Press, Oct.1982. — [600]p
ISBN 0-85110-631-5 : £15.00 : CIP entry B82-24237

Goldsworthy, Graeme. Gospel and Kingdom : a Christian interpretation of the Old Testament / Graeme Goldsworthy. — Exeter : Paternoster Press, c1981. — 124p ; 22cm
Includes index
ISBN 0-85364-218-4 (pbk) : £2.50 : CIP rev. B80-17542

221.6 — Bible. O.T. Theology

Goldingay, John. Approaches to Old Testament interpretation. — Leicester : Inter-Varsity Press, Oct.1981. — [176]p. — (Issues in contemporary theology)
ISBN 0-85111-404-0 (pbk) : £3.50 : CIP entry B81-24674

221.6 — Bible. O.T. Theology *related to* **N.T. theology**

Bruce, F. F.. This is that : the New Testament development of some Old Testament themes. — Exeter : Paternoster Press, Jan.1982. — [128]p
Originally published: 1968
ISBN 0-85364-168-4 (pbk) : £2.40 : CIP entry
Primary classification 225.6 B82-02465

221.6'09'034 — Bible. O.T.. Interpretation, *1870-1975*

Day, John, *1948-*. Recent Old Testament scholarship / by John Day. — London (2 Chester House, Pages La., N10 1PR) : Christian Education Movement, [1982?]. — 12leaves ; 30cm. — (Occasional paper ; 2)
Bibliography: p12
Unpriced (unbound) B82-34129

221.6'6 — Bible. O.T.. Irony

Good, Edwin M.. Irony in the Old Testament / Edwin M. Good. — 2nd ed. — Sheffield : Almond, 1981, c1965. — 256p ; 22cm. — (Bible and literature series, ISSN 0260-4493 ; 3)
Previous ed.: Philadelphia : Westminster, 1965. — Includes index
ISBN 0-907459-05-6 (pbk) : £5.95 : CIP rev. B81-12376

221.7 — Bible. O.T. — *Commentaries*

Bridgland, Cyril. Pocket guide to the Old Testament / Cyril Bridgland. — Leicester : Inter-Varsity Press, 1982. — 240p : ill,maps ; 18cm
Includes bibliographies
ISBN 0-85110-436-3 (pbk) : £2.75 : CIP rev. B82-04989

221.7 — Bible. O.T. — *Commentaries — For West African students*

Okafor, S. N. O.. Bible knowledge for School Certificate : Old Testament / S.N.O. Okafor ; advisor, Reverend Dr. Etok. — London : Macmillan Education, 1981. — vi,90p : 3maps ; 22cm
Includes index
ISBN 0-333-31976-1 (pbk) : Unpriced B82-28536

Tarrant, C. J. C.. From the united monarchy to the fall of Samaria / C.J.C. Tarrant. — Harlow : Longman, 1981. — vi,138p : ill,maps ; 22cm. — (Certificate Bible knowledge)
ISBN 0-582-65082-8 (pbk) : £1.20 B82-23065

221.8'1 — Bible. O.T. Special subjects: Wisdom — *Critical studies*

Morgan, Donn F.. Wisdom in the Old Testament traditions. — Oxford : Blackwell, Oct.1981. — [180]p
ISBN 0-631-12948-0 : £12.00 : CIP entry B81-26703

221.8'29163 — Bible. O.T. Prophets

Duncan, George B.. A preacher among the prophets / George B. Duncan. — London : Hodder and Stoughton, 1981. — 176p ; 18cm
ISBN 0-340-26356-3 (pbk) : £1.95 : CIP rev. B81-23954

221.8'29163 — Bible. O.T.. Prophets — *Festschriften*

Israel's prophetic tradition : essays in honour of Peter R. Ackroyd / edited by Richard Coggins, Anthony Phillips and Michael Knibb. — Cambridge : Cambridge University Press, 1982. — xxi,272p : 1port ; 23cm
Includes bibliographies and index
ISBN 0-521-24223-1 : £21.00 : CIP rev. B82-14530

221.8'29163 — Bible. O.T.. Prophets — *Stories for children*

Kent, David. The time of the prophets / David Kent ; illustrated by Harry Bishop, John Keay and Rob McCaig. — London : Kingfisher, 1981. — 22p : col.ill ; 23cm. — (Kingfisher explorer books. Bible stories ; bk.4)
Includes index
ISBN 0-86272-020-6 : £1.95 : CIP rev. B81-27974

221.8'5356 — Bible. O.T. Special subjects: Colour terms

Brenner, Athalya. Colour terms in the Old Testament. — Sheffield : Journal for the Study of the Old Testament, Dec.1982. — [300]p. — (Journal for the Study of the Old Testament supplement series, ISSN 0309-0787 ; 21)
ISBN 0-905774-42-6 (cased) : CIP entry
ISBN 0-905774-43-4 (pbk) B82-30324

221.8'933 — Bible. O.T.. Special subjects: Ancient Israel. Kings — *Stories for children*

Kent, David. Kings of Israel / by David Kent ; illustrated by Harry Bishop, John Keay and Rob McCaig. — London : Pan, 1981. — 22p : col.ill ; 22cm. — (Piccolo explorer books. Bible stories ; bk.3)
Includes index
ISBN 0-330-26496-6 (pbk) : £0.85 B82-01764

Kent, David. Kings of Israel / David Kent ; illustrated by Harry Bishop, John Keay and Rob McCaig. — London : Kingfisher, 1981. — 22p : col.ill ; 23cm. — (Kingfisher explorer books. Bible stories ; bk.3)
Includes index
ISBN 0-86272-019-2 : £1.95 : CIP rev. B81-28079

221.8'935 — Bible. O.T. Special subjects: Syro-Ephraimite War

Thompson, Michael E. W.. Situation and theology : Old Testament interpretations of Syro-Ephraimite War. — Sheffield (24 Tapton Crescent Rd., Sheffield S10 5DA) : Almond Press, Dec.1982. — [168]p. — (Prophets and historians, ISSN 0263-6492 ; 1)
ISBN 0-907459-14-5 (cased) : £15.95 : CIP entry
ISBN 0-907459-15-3 (pbk) : £6.95 B82-30722

221.9'22 — Bible. O.T. — *Biographies*

Comay, Joan. Who's who in the Old Testament together with the Apocrypha. — London : Hodder & Stoughton, Feb.1982. — [432]p. — (Teach yourself books)
Originally published: London : Weidenfeld & Nicolson, 1971
ISBN 0-340-27176-0 (pbk) : £2.95 : CIP entry B81-36355

221.9'22'0222 — Bible. O.T.. Characters — *Illustrations*

Stern, Jossi. People of the book : an artistic exploration of the Bible / by Jossi Stern ; edited and designed by Dave Foster ; with contribution by Teddy Kollek. — London : Collins, 1979. — 125p : ill(some col.),ports (some col.) ; 26cm
Includes index
ISBN 0-00-513001-8 : £5.95 B82-18642

221.9'24 — Bible. O.T.. David, *King of Israel*

Palau, Luis. Heart after God / Luis Palau. — London : Lakeland, 1980, c1978. — 127p ; 18cm
Originally published: Portland : Multnomah, 1978
ISBN 0-551-00825-3 (pbk) : £1.25 B82-25285

221.9'24 — Bible. O.T. David, *King of Israel — Stories for children*

Butcher, Geoffrey. David. — London : Hodder & Stoughton Children's Books, Jan.1983. — [24] p. — (First Bible stories)
ISBN 0-340-28341-6 (pbk) : £0.60 : CIP entry B82-33734

221.9'24 — Bible. O.T.. David, *King of Israel — Stories for children*

Robertson, Jenny. David the shepherd king / text by Jenny Robertson ; illustrations by Alan Parry. — London : Scripture Union, 1981. — [28]p : col.ill ; 27cm. — (A Ladybird Bible book)
ISBN 0-85421-937-4 : Unpriced
ISBN 0-7214-0580-0 (Ladybird) B82-01503

Williams-Ellis, Virginia. Stories about David / stories retold by Virginia Williams-Ellis ; illustrated by Harry Bishop. — London : Dean, c1981. — 28p : ill(some col.) ; 20cm. — (Day by day)
ISBN 0-603-00273-0 : Unpriced B82-26805

221.9'5 — Ancient Middle East. Jews, *to B.C. 586.* **Historical sources: Bible. O.T.**

Jacobson, Dan. The story of the stories : the chosen people and its God. — London : Secker & Warburg, June 1982. — [211]p
ISBN 0-436-22048-2 : £7.95 : CIP entry B82-09723

221.9'505 — Bible. O.T. — *Stories for children*

Bailey, John, *1940 Nov.4-*. Stories from the Old Testament / retold by John Bailey. — London : Beaver, 1982. — 191p : col.ill,2maps(some col.) ; 18cm
ISBN 0-600-20507-x (pbk) : £1.95 B82-24279

Kent, David. The time of the prophets / by David Kent ; illustrated by Harry Bishop, John Keay and Rob McCaig. — London : Pan, 1981. — 22p : col.ill ; 22cm. — (Piccolo explorer books. Bible stories ; bk.4)
Includes index
ISBN 0-330-26497-4 (pbk) : £0.85 B82-00970

222'.077 — Bible. O.T. Historical books — *Texts with commentaries*

[**Bible. O.T.. Historical Books**. *English. Today's English. 1982*]. Old Testament history : Joshua, Judges, Ruth, 1 Samuel, 2 Samuel, 1 Kings, 2 Kings, 1 Chronicles, 2 Chronicles, Ezra, Nehemiah, Esther. — London : Bible Society, [1982]. — p241-528 : ill(some col.),1geneal.table,col.maps ; 23cm. — (Special edition Good News Bible ; 2)
ISBN 0-564-06891-8 (pbk) : Unpriced B82-25677

222'.0924 — Bible. O.T. Historical books. Solomon, *King of Israel* — *Stories for children*

Robertson, Jenny. King Solomon / text by Jenny Robertson ; illustrations by Alan Parry. — London : Scripture Union, 1982. — [28]p : col.ill ; 27x13cm. — (A Ladybird Bible book ; 10)
Text, ill on lining papers
ISBN 0-85421-950-1 : Unpriced
ISBN 0-7214-0581-9 (Ladybird) : Unpriced
B82-25891

222'.1077 — Bible. O.T. Pentateuch — *Texts with commentaries*

[Bible. O.T.. Pentateuch. *English. Today's English. 1982*]. Creation and the Law : Genesis, Exodus, Leviticus, Numbers, Deuteronomy. — London : Bible Society, [1982]. — 240p : ill(some col.),3geneal.tables,col.maps ; 23cm. — (Special edition Good News Bible ; 1)
ISBN 0-564-06881-0 (pbk) : Unpriced
B82-25676

222'.1106 — Bible. O.T. Genesis — *Expositions*

McKeating, Henry. Why bother with Adam and Eve? / Henry McKeating. — Guildford : Lutterworth, 1982. — 57p ; 19cm. — (Anselm books)
ISBN 0-7188-2533-0 (pbk) : £0.95 B82-13122

Maher, Michael. When God made a promise : a Christian appreciation of Genesis / Michael Maher. — Manchester : Koinonia, c1976. — 120p ; 16cm
Bibliography: p9
ISBN 0-86088-002-8 (pbk) : Unpriced
B82-04394

222'.11068 — Bible. O.T. Genesis. Creation. Symbolism

Greenlaw, Jean-Pierre. Discovery of the form of forms and creative symbolism / by Jean-Pierre Greenlaw. — [Henley-on-Thames] ([White Cottage, 37, Manor Rd., Henley-on-Thames, RG9 1LU]) : [J.-P. Greenlaw], [198-?]. — 21p : ill ; 21cm
Unpriced (unbound) B82-06583

Greenlaw, Jean-Pierre. The form of forms : forma pleromae Christi. — [Henley-on-Thames] ([White Cottage, 37, Manor Rd., Henley-on-Thames, RG9 1LU]) : [J.-P. Greenlaw], [1980]. — 4p : ill(some col.) ; 21cm
Written by Jean-Pierre Greenlaw. — Ill on inside covers
Unpriced B82-06584

Greenlaw, Jean-Pierre. The heavens and the firmament : the second day of creation / by Jean-Paul Greenlaw. — [Henley-on-Thames] (White Cottage, 37, Manor Rd., Henley-on-Thames RG9 1LU]) : [J.-P. Greenlaw], [1981?]. — 25p,[13]p of plates : ill,facsims ; 34cm. — (A creative symbolism book) (The eight days of creation ; v.2)
Unpriced (pbk) B82-06582

Greenlaw, Jean-Pierre. The 'mandala' : the first day of creation : darkness and light : an explanation of the first symbols of creation / written and illustrated by Jean-Pierre Greenlaw. — Henley-on-Thames ([c/o White Cottage, 37, Manor Rd., Henley-on-Thames, RG9 1LU]) : Vermont Press, [1980]. — 41p : ill ; 19x21cm. — (A creative symbolism book)
Unpriced (pbk) B82-06581

222'.1107 — Bible. O.T. Genesis XX1V-XXXV1 — *Commentaries*

Wallace, Ronald S.. Isaac and Jacob : Genesis 24-36 / Ronald S. Wallace. — London : Triangle, 1982. — xiv,144p ; 18cm. — (The Bible for every day)
Bibliography: p143-144
ISBN 0-281-03844-9 (pbk) : £1.85 B82-21685

222'.11077 — Bible. O.T. Genesis I-XI — *Text with commentaries*

Asimov, Isaac. In the beginning / Isaac Asimov. — South Yarmouth : John Curley ; [Ripley] : Distributed by Magna Print, c1981. — 496p ; 22cm
Published in large print. — Includes index
ISBN 0-89340-367-9 : Unpriced B82-17284

Asimov, Isaac. In the beginning. — London : New English Library, Dec.1982. — [240]p
Originally published: South Yarmouth : John Curly, 1981
ISBN 0-450-05507-8 (pbk) : £1.75 : CIP entry
B82-30087

Harrington, Wilfrid J.. In the beginning God : Genesis 1-11 / Wilfrid Harrington. — Manchester (19 Langdale Drive, Bury, Greater Manchester) : Koinonia, c1976. — 143p ; 21cm
Bibliography: p142-143
Unpriced (pbk) B82-04396

222'.11077 — Bible. O.T. Genesis — *Texts with commentaries*

Gibson, John C. L.. Genesis / John C.L. Gibson. — Edinburgh : Saint Andrew. — (The Daily Study Bible)
Bibliography: p321-322. — Includes index
Vol.2. — c1982. — vi,322p ; 19cm
ISBN 0-7152-0539-0 (pbk) : £2.95 B82-30545

222'.110922 — Bible. O.T. Genesis. Adam & Eve — *Stories for children*

Caseley, Judith. The garden of Eden / Judith Caseley. — [London] : Abelard, 1982. — [26]p : col.ill ; 25cm
ISBN 0-200-72746-x : £4.95 : CIP rev.
B82-04291

222'.110924 — Bible. O.T. Genesis. Abraham — *Stories for children*

Robertson, Jenny. Abraham's family / text by Jenny Robertson ; illustrations by Alan Parry. — London : Scripture Union/Ladybird, 1980. — [28]p : col.ill ; 27cm. — (A Ladbybird Bible book)
Text and ill on lining papers
ISBN 0-85421-894-7 : £0.75
ISBN 0-7214-0574-6 (Ladybird) B82-13747

Williams-Ellis, Virginia. Day by day stories about Abraham / stories retold by Virginia Williams-Ellis ; illustrated by Harry Bishop. — London : Dean, 1982. — 28p : ill(some col.) ; 21cm
ISBN 0-603-00319-2 : £0.95 B82-34962

222'.110924 — Bible. O.T. Genesis. Adam — *Stories for children*

Butcher, Geoffrey. Adam : the story of the Creation / written and illustrated by Geoffrey Butcher. — London : Hodder and Stoughton, 1982. — [28]p : col.ill ; 18cm. — (First Bible stories)
ISBN 0-340-28185-5 (pbk) : £0.60 : CIP rev.
B82-06504

222'.110924 — Bible. O.T. Genesis. Jacob — *Stories for children*

Williams-Ellis, Virginia. Day by day stories about Jacob / stories retold by Virginia Williams-Ellis ; illustrated by Harry Bishop. — London : Dean, 1982. — 28p : ill(some col.) ; 21cm
ISBN 0-603-00320-6 : £0.95 B82-36418

222'.110924 — Bible. O.T. Genesis. Joseph *(Biblical patriarch)* — *Stories for children*

Butcher, Geoffrey. Joseph : the coat of many colours / written and illustrated by Geoffrey Butcher. — London : Hodder and Stoughton, 1982. — [28]p : col.ill ; 18cm. — (First Bible stories)
ISBN 0-340-28183-9 (pbk) : £0.60 : CIP rev.
B82-06502

Williams-Ellis, Virginia. Stories about Joseph / stories retold by Virginia Williams-Ellis ; illustrated by Gwen Green. — London : Dean, c1981. — 28p : ill(some col.) ; 20cm. — (Day by day)
ISBN 0-603-00274-9 : Unpriced B82-26664

222'.110924 — Bible. O.T. Genesis. Noah — *Stories for children*

Butcher, Geoffrey. Noah : the story of the Ark / written and illustrated by Geoffrey Butcher. — London : Hodder and Stoughton, 1982. — [28]p : col.ill ; 18cm. — (First Bible stories)
ISBN 0-340-28184-7 (pbk) : £0.60 : CIP rev.
B82-06503

222'.1109505 — Bible. O.T. Genesis. Creation — *Stories for children*

Van der Meer, Ron. Oh Lord! / by Ron and Atie van der Meer. — London : Macmillan Children's, 1979 (1981 [printing]). — [30]p : chiefly col.ill ; 25cm
ISBN 0-333-32180-4 (pbk) : £1.50 B82-05973

Vries, C. M. de. When God made our world / [illustrations by Anna-Hermine Müller] ; [Dutch text by C.M. de Vries] ; [English text adapted by Felicity Clayton Smith]. — 1st English ed. — Tring : Lion, 1982. — [16]p : col.ill ; 20cm. — (A Bible Story picture-book)
Translation of: Wat God ons gegeven heeft. — Text, ill on lining papers
ISBN 0-85648-134-3 : £0.95 B82-36904

222'.1109505 — Bible. O.T. Genesis. Noah's Ark — *Stories for children*

Vries, C. M. de. The boat that Noah made / [illustrations by Anna-Hermine Müller] ; [Dutch text by C.M. de Vries] ; [English text adapted by Felicity Clayton Smith]. — Tring : Lion, 1982. — [18]p : col.ill ; 20cm. — (A Bible Story picture-book)
Translation of: Noach vertrouwt op God. — Text, ill on lining papers
ISBN 0-85648-135-1 : £0.95 B82-36908

Williams-Ellis, Virginia. Noah's ark / [story retold by Virginia Williams-Ellis] ; [illustrated by Anna Dzierzek]. — London : Dean, c1981. — [10]p : col.ill ; 21cm. — (A Dean board book)
ISBN 0-603-00243-9 : Unpriced B82-26663

Williams-Ellis, Virginia. Noah's ark / story retold by Virginia Williams-Ellis ; illustrated by J.B. Long. — London : Dean, 1981. — [26]p : col.ill ; 32cm. — (An Everyday picture book)
New ed. — Previous ed. / by Aileen E. Passmore. 1968
ISBN 0-603-00287-0 : Unpriced B82-27478

222'.1109505 — Bible. O.T. Genesis — *Stories for children*

Kent, David. The desert people / David Kent ; illustrated by Harry Bishop. — London : Kingfisher, 1981. — 22p : col.ill ; 23cm. — (Kingfisher explorer books. Bible stories ; bk.1)
Includes index
ISBN 0-86272-017-6 : £1.95 : CIP rev.
B81-28039

222'.1206 — Bible. O.T. Exodus — *Expositions*

Maher, Michael. When God formed a people : a Christian appreciation of Exodus / Michael Maher. — Manchester : Koinonia, [1978]. — 152p ; 18cm
Bibliography: p6
ISBN 0-86088-013-3 (pbk) : £1.95 B82-04392

222'.1207 — Bible. O.T. Exodus XXXII-XXXIV — *Commentaries*

Moberly, Walter. At the mountain of God. — Sheffield : JSOT Press, Dec.1982. — [252]p. — (Journal for the Study of the Old Testament supplement series, ISSN 0309-0787 ; 22)
ISBN 0-905774-44-2 : CIP entry B82-39267

222'.12077 — Bible. O.T. Exodus — *Texts with commentaries*

Ellison, H. L.. Exodus / H.L. Ellison. — Edinburgh : Saint Andrew, c1982. — xi,203p ; 19cm. — (The Daily study Bible)
ISBN 0-7152-0493-9 (pbk) : £2.95 B82-29469

222'.120924 — Bible. O.T. Exodus. Moses *(Prophet)*. Childhood — *Stories for children*

Wever, Hinke Baukje. The baby in the basket / [illustrations by Anna-Hermine Müller] ; [Dutch text by Hinke Baukje Wever and Job Heeger] ; [English text adapted by Felicity Clayton Smith]. — Tring : Lion, 1982. — [18]p : col.ill ; 20cm. — (A Bible Story picture-book)
Translation of: Het kind in het mandje. — Text, ill on lining papers
ISBN 0-85648-136-x : £0.95 B82-36906

Williams-Ellis, Virginia. Moses in the bulrushes / [story retold by Virginia Williams-Ellis] ; [illustrated by Anna Dzierzek]. — London : Dean, c1981. — [10]p : col.ill ; 21cm. — (A Dean board book)
ISBN 0-603-00242-0 : Unpriced B82-26803

222′.120924 — Bible. O.T. Exodus. Moses *(Prophet) — Stories for children*

Butcher, Geoffrey. Moses : the escape from Egypt / written and illustrated by Geoffrey Butcher. — London : Hodder and Stoughton, 1982. — [28]p : col.ill ; 18cm. — (First Bible stories)
ISBN 0-340-28182-0 (pbk) : £0.60 : CIP rev. B82-06501

Williams-Ellis, Virginia. Day by day stories about Moses / stories retold by Virginia Williams-Ellis ; illustrated by Gwen Green. — London : Dean, c1981. — 28p : ill(some col.) ; 20cm
ISBN 0-603-00271-4 : Unpriced B82-26109

222′.1209505 — Bible. O.T. Exodus — *Stories for children*

Kent, David. Escape from Egypt / David Kent ; illustrated by Harry Bishop and Roger Payne. — London : Kingfisher, 1981. — 21p : col.ill ; 23cm. — (Kingfisher explorer books. Bible stories ; bk.2)
Includes index
ISBN 0-86272-018-4 : £1.95 : CIP rev. B81-27976

222′.1606 — Ten Commandments — *Expositions*

Abd-ru-shin. The Ten Commandments of God ; The Lord's Prayer / explained to mankind by Abd-ru-shin. — Vomperberg : Bernhardt ; Sidcup : Grail Foundation, c1979. — 67p ; 20cm
Translation from the German
ISBN 3-87860-094-1 : Unpriced B82-28377

Schaeffer, Edith. Lifelines : the ten commandments for today. — London : Hodder and Stoughton, Sept.1982. — [224]p
ISBN 0-340-27897-8 (pbk) : £4.50 : CIP entry B82-18745

222′.320922 — Bible. O.T. Judges. Gideon & Samson — *Stories for children*

Robertson, Jenny. Gideon and Samson / text by Jenny Robertson ; illustrations by Alan Parry. — London : Scripture Union, 1981. — [28]p : col.ill ; 27cm. — (A Ladybird Bible book)
ISBN 0-85421-935-8 : Unpriced
ISBN 0-7214-0578-9 (Ladybird) B82-01502

222′.320924 — Bible. O.T. Judges. Samson — *Stories for children*

Williams-Ellis, Virginia. Day by day stories about Samson / stories retold by Virginia Williams-Ellis ; illustrated by Harry Bishop. — London : Dean, 1982. — 28p : ill(some col.) ; 21cm
ISBN 0-603-00321-4 : £0.95 B82-36417

222′.3506 — Bible. O.T. Ruth — *Expositions*

Atkinson, David. The wings of refuge : the message of the book of Ruth. — Leicester : Inter-Varsity Press, Jan.1983. — [256]p. — (The Bible speaks today)
ISBN 0-85110-708-7 (pbk) : £4.75 : CIP entry B82-32638

222′.406 — Bible. O.T. Samuel — *Expositions — For West African students*

Williams, David, *19---*. From the institution of the Monarchy to the fall of the Northern Kingdom / David and Bridget Williams. — [London] : Collins, 1981. — 224p : ill,2maps ; 21cm. — (Bible knowledge for the West African school certificate)
ISBN 0-00-326134-4 (pbk) : £2.35
Also classified at 222′.506 B82-10028

222′.406 — Bible. O.T. Samuel. Special subjects: Succession — *Critical studies*

Rost, Leonhard. The succession to the throne of David. — Sheffield : Almond Press, Aug.1982. — [160]p. — (Historic texts and interpreters in Biblical scholarship, ISSN 0263-1199 ; 1)
Translation of: Die Überlieferung von der Thronnachfolge Davids
ISBN 0-907459-12-9 (cased) : £15.95 : CIP entry
ISBN 0-907459-13-7 (pbk) : £6.95 B82-18482

222′.40922 — Bible. O.T. Samuel. Characters: Samuel & Saul, *King of Israel — Stories for children*

Williams-Ellis, Virginia. Day by day stories about Samuel / stories retold by Virginia Williams-Ellis ; illustrated by Harry Bishop. — London : Dean, 1982. — 28p : ill(some col.) ; 21cm
ISBN 0-603-00322-2 : £0.95 B82-34963

222′.40922 — Bible. O.T. Samuel. Samuel & Saul — *Stories for children*

Robertson, Jenny. Samuel and Saul / text by Jenny Robertson ; illustrations by Alan Parry. — London : Scripture Union, 1981. — [28]p : col.ill ; 27cm. — (A Ladybird Bible book)
ISBN 0-85421-936-6 : Unpriced
ISBN 0-7214-0579-7 (Ladybird) B82-01504

222′.430922 — Bible. O.T. Samuel, 1st. David, *King of Israel* **& Goliath** — *Stories for children*

Purves, John. King David / by John Purves ; illustrated by Martin Reiner. — Loughborough : Ladybird, c1981. — 51p : col.ill ; 18cm. — (Ladybird Bible stories. Series 813)
Col. ill on lining papers
ISBN 0-7214-0668-8 : £0.50 B82-15109

Watkins, Peter, *1934-*. David and the giant / retold by Peter Watkins ; illustrated by Jan Martin. — London : MacRae, 1981. — 46p : ill ; 21cm. — (Blackbird books)
ISBN 0-86203-054-4 : £2.75 : CIP rev.
ISBN 0-531-04356-8 (U.S.) B81-20173

222′.430924 — Bible. O.T. Samuel, 1st. David, *King of Israel.* **Childhood** — *Stories for children*

Williams-Ellis, Virginia. David the shepherd boy / [story retold by Virginia Williams-Ellis] ; [illustrated by Anna Dzierzek]. — London : Dean, c1981. — [10]p : col.ill ; 21cm. — (A Dean board book)
ISBN 0-603-00241-2 : Unpriced B82-26804

222′.506 — Bible. O.T. Kings — *Expositions — For West African students*

Williams, David, *19---*. From the institution of the Monarchy to the fall of the Northern Kingdom / David and Bridget Williams. — [London] : Collins, 1981. — 224p : ill,2maps ; 21cm. — (Bible knowledge for the West African school certificate)
ISBN 0-00-326134-4 (pbk) : £2.35
Primary classification 222′.406 B82-10028

222′.50924 — Bible. O.T.. Characters: Elisha — *Devotional works*

Stewart, Alexander, *1870-1937*. A prophet of grace : an expository & devotional study of the life of Elisha / by Alexander Stewart. — Edinburgh (15 North Bank St., Edinburgh, EH1 2LS) : Knox, [1982?]. — 268p ; 22cm
Originally published: Edinburgh : Henderson, 1925
Unpriced B82-24657

222′.50924 — Bible. O.T.. Elijah — *Stories for children*

Robertson, Jenny. Elijah and Elisha / text by Jenny Robertson ; illustrations by Alan Parry. — London : Scripture Union, 1982. — [28]p : col.ill ; 27x13cm. — (A Ladybird Bible book)
Text, ill on lining papers
ISBN 0-85421-951-x : Unpriced
ISBN 0-7214-0582-7 (Ladybird) : Unpriced
Also classified at 222′.540924 B82-25890

222′.540924 — Bible. O.T. Kings, 2nd. Elisha — *Stories for children*

Robertson, Jenny. Elijah and Elisha / text by Jenny Robertson ; illustrations by Alan Parry. — London : Scripture Union, 1982. — [28]p : col.ill ; 27x13cm. — (A Ladybird Bible book)
Text, ill on lining papers
ISBN 0-85421-951-x : Unpriced
ISBN 0-7214-0582-7 (Ladybird) : Unpriced
Primary classification 222′.50924 B82-25890

223′.077 — Bible. O.T.. Poetical books — *Texts with commentaries*

[Bible. O.T. *English. Today's English. Selections. 1982*]. Poems, proverbs and wisdom : Job, Psalms, Proverbs, Ecclesiastes, Song of Songs. — London : Bible Society, [1982]. — p529-672 : ill(some col.) ; 23cm. — (Special edition Good News Bible ; 3)
ISBN 0-564-06901-9 (pbk) : Unpriced B82-25675

223′.2 — Bible. O.T. Psalms XXIII. *English. Authorized — Texts*

[Bible. O.T. Psalms of XXIII. *English. Authorized. 1982*]. The Lord is my shepherd : the twenty-third psalm / illustrated by Tasha Tudor. — Guildford : Lutterworth, 1982, c1980. — [26]p : col.ill ; 21cm
Originally published: New York : Philomel, 1980. — Ill on lining papers
ISBN 0-7188-2541-1 : £2.95 B82-31063

223′.2052 — Bible. O.T. Psalms. *English. Today's English. Selections — Texts*

[Bible. O.T. Psalms. *English. Today's English. Selections. 1981*]**Songs** from green pastures : selections from the Psalms / edited by Jørgen Vium Olesen. — Tring : Lion, 1981. — 77p : chiefly col.ill ; 26cm
ISBN 0-85648-322-2 : £4.95 B82-02600

223′.205203 — Bible. O.T. Psalms. *English Authorized — Texts*

[Bible. O.T. Psalms. *English. Authorized. 1982*]. The Book of Psalms. — London : Muller, Sept.1982. — [352]p
ISBN 0-584-11023-5 : £9.95 : CIP entry B82-20279

223′.206 — Bible. O.T. Psalms — *Expositions*

Barclay, William, *1907-1978*. The Lord is my shepherd : expositions of selected psalms / by William Barclay ; with an introduction by Allan Galloway. — [London] : Fount, 1982. — 153p ; 18cm
Originally published: Glasgow : Collins, 1980
ISBN 0-00-626477-8 (pbk) : £1.50 B82-26614

Bonhoeffer, Dietrich. The psalms : prayer book of the Bible / Dietrich Bonhoeffer ; [translation by Sister Isabel Mary]. — Oxford : SLG, c1982. — 25p ; 21cm
Translation of: Das Gebetbuch der Bibel
ISBN 0-7283-0092-3 (pbk) : £0.60 B82-20732

Maher, Michael. Lord, open my lips : the Psalms of morning and evening prayer / Michael Maher. — Manchester : Koinonia, c1977. — 218p ; 19cm
Bibliography: p217. — Includes index
ISBN 0-86088-006-0 (pbk) : £1.50 B82-04393

Westermann, Claus. Praise and lament in the psalms / Claus Westermann ; translated by Keith R. Crim and Richard N. Soulen. — Edinburgh : T. & T. Clark, c1981, c1965. — vii,301p ; 21cm
Translation of: Das Loben Gottes in den Psalmen. — Originally published as: The praise of God in the psalms. Atlanta : John Knox Press, 1965 ; London : Epworth, 1966. — Bibliography: p281-286. — Includes index
ISBN 0-567-29110-3 (pbk) : £4.95 B82-36489

223′.206 — Bible. O.T. Psalms XLII-XLIX — *Critical studies*

Goulder, M. D.. The psalms of the Sons of Korah. — Sheffield : Journal for the Study of the Old Testament, Dec.1982. — [300]p. — (Journal for the Study of the Old Testament supplement series, ISSN 0309-0787 ; 20)
ISBN 0-905774-40-x (cased) : £13.50 (£9.50 to subscribers) : CIP entry
ISBN 0-905774-41-8 (pbk) : £8.95 (£5.95 to subscribers) B82-30323

223′.206 — Bible. O.T. Psalms XXIII — *Expositions*

Keller, W. Phillip. A shepherd looks at Psalm 23 / by Phillip Keller. — London : Pickering & Inglis, 1976, c1970 (1981 [printing]). — [144]p : ill ; 21cm
Originally published: Grand Rapids : Zondervan, 1970
ISBN 0-7208-0378-0 (pbk) : £1.95 B82-19643

223′.207 — Bible. O.T. Psalms - *Commentaries*

Anderson, A. A.. Psalms. — London : Marshall, Morgan & Scott, July 1981. — (The New Century Bible commentary)
Vol.1: (Psalms 1-72). — [527]p
ISBN 0-551-00846-6 (pbk) : £6.95 : CIP entry B81-18167

223′.207 — Bible. O.T. Psalms - *Commentaries continuation*

Anderson, A. A.. Psalms. — London : Marshall, Morgan & Scott, July 1981. — (The New Century Bible commentary)
Vol.2: (Psalms 73-150). — [446]p
ISBN 0-551-00847-4 (pbk) : £5.95 : CIP entry
B81-18168

223′.9044 — Bible. O.T. Song of Solomon. *English & Hebrew — Texts*

[Bible. O.T. Song of Solomon. *English & Hebrew . Falk. 1982*]. Love lyrics from the Bible : a translation and literary study of the Song of Songs / Marcia Falk. — Sheffield : Almond, 1982. — 142p ; 23cm. — (Bible and literature series, ISSN 0260-4493 ; 4)
Parallel Hebrew text and English translation, English commentary and notes. — Bibliography: p136-142
ISBN 0-907459-06-4 (cased) : £14.95 : CIP rev.
ISBN 0-907459-07-2 (pbk) : £5.95 B82-05788

224 — Bible. O.T. Former prophets — *Textual criticisms*

Nelson, Richard D.. The double redaction of the Deuteronomistic history / Richard D. Nelson. — Sheffield : JSOT, 1981. — 185p ; 23cm. — (Journal for the study of the Old Testament supplement series, ISSN 0309-0787 ; 18)
Bibliography: p151-166. — Includes index
ISBN 0-905774-33-7 (cased) : Unpriced : CIP rev.
ISBN 0-905774-34-3 (pbk) : Unpriced
B81-35893

224′.007′1 — Schools. Curriculum subjects: Bible. O.T. Prophets. Teaching — *Manuals*

Undy, Harry. Discovering the later prophets / text by Harry Undy ; illustrations by Sue Howells. — London : CEM, c1978. — 20p : ill,1map ; 30cm. — (Dimension ; 4)
Text on inside cover
ISBN 0-905022-38-6 (pbk) : Unpriced
B82-40968

224′.077 — Bible. O.T. Prophets — *Texts with commentaries*

[Bible. O.T.. Prophets. *English. Today′s English. 1982*]. The Prophets : Isaiah, Jeremiah, Lamentations, Ezekiel, Daniel, Hosea, Joel, Amos, Obadiah, Jonah, Micah, Nahum, Habbakuk, Zephaniah, Haggai, Zechariah, Malachi. — London : Bible Society, [1982]. — p673-912 : ill,col.maps ; 23cm. — (Special edition Good News Bible ; 4)
ISBN 0-564-06911-6 (pbk) : Unpriced
B82-25678

224′.1 — Bible. O.T. Isaiah. Servant songs — *Commentaries*

Ellison, H. L.. The servant of Jehovah. — Exeter : Paternoster, Nov.1982. — [32]p
ISBN 0-85364-254-0 (pbk) : £0.90 : CIP entry
B82-32311

224′.106 — Bible. O.T. Isaiah. Special subjects: Ethics — *Expositions*

Davies, Eryl W.. Prophecy and ethics : Isaiah and the ethical tradition of Israel / Eryl W. Davies. — Sheffield : JSOT Press, 1981. — 184p ; 23cm. — (Journal for the study of the Old Testament supplement series, ISSN 0309-0787 ; 16)
Bibliography: p150-172. — Includes index
ISBN 0-905774-26-4 : Unpriced : CIP rev.
B81-14400

224′.106 — Bible. O.T. Isaiah XXI — *Expositions*

Macintosh, A. A.. Isaiah XXI : a palimpsest / A.A. Macintosh. — Cambridge : Cambridge University Press, 1980. — xi,156p ; 22cm
Bibliography: p144-150. — Includes index
ISBN 0-521-22943-x : £12.50 : CIP rev.
B80-25118

224′.305209 — Bible. O.T. Lamentations. *English. Jackson — Texts*

[Bible. O.T.. Lamentations. *English. Jackson. 1980*]. Five griefsongs over a fallen city : being versions of the Lamentations of Jeremiah by Gordon Jackson / with illustrations by Paul Jackson. — Lincoln (1 Stonefield Ave., Lincoln) : Asgill, 1980. — [19]p : ill ; 25cm
Limited ed. of 400 numbered copies
£1.00 (pbk) B82-18178

224′.4068 — Bible. O.T. Ezekiel. Cabalistic interpretations

Lévi, Éliphas. The mysteries of the Qabalah : or the occult agreement of the two Testaments / by Eliphas Lévi. — Wellingborough : Aquarian, 1974 (1981 [printing]). — 285p : ill,plans ; 22cm. — (Studies in hermetic tradition)
Translation of: Les mystères de la Kabbale
ISBN 0-85030-274-9 (pbk) : £4.95 : CIP rev.
Also classified at 228′.068 B81-32054

224′.509505 — Bible. O.T. Daniel — *Stories for children*

Butcher, Geoffrey. Daniel. — London : Hodder & Stoughton Children′s Books, Jan.1983. — [24]p. — (First Bible stories)
ISBN 0-340-28340-8 (pbk) : £0.60 : CIP entry
B82-33733

224′.5′09505 — Bible. O.T. Daniel — *Stories for children*

Williams-Ellis, Virginia. Day by day stories about Daniel / stories retold by Virginia Williams-Ellis ; illustrated by Harry Bishop. — London : Dean, c1981. — 28p : ill(some col.) ; 20cm
ISBN 0-603-00272-2 : Unpriced B82-27477

224′.6077 — Bible. O.T. Hosea — *Texts with commentaries*

Kidner, Derek. Love to the loveless : the story and message of Hosea / Derek Kidner. — Leicester : Inter-Varsity, 1981. — 142p : 2maps ; 20cm. — (The Bible speaks today)
Bibliography: p9-10
ISBN 0-85110-703-6 (pbk) : £3.25 : CIP rev.
B81-24676

224′.95052034 — Bible. O.T. Habakkuk III, 10-11. *English. Authorised — Illustrations*

[Bible. O.T.. Habakkuk. III, 10-11. *English. Authorised. 1979*]. Habakkuk : 3 : 10, 11. — Crosby ([51 York Ave., Great Crosby, Liverpool L23 5RN]) : Cracked Bell Press, 1979. — [8]p : chiefly col.ill ; 17cm
Unpriced (unbound) B82-27270

225 — NEW TESTAMENT

225 — Bible. N.T.. Quotations. Sources: Bible. O.T.

Hanson, Anthony Tyrrell. The New Testament interpretation of scripture / Anthony Tyrrell Hanson. — London : SPCK, 1980. — xi,237p ; 23cm
Bibliography: p212-223. — Includes index
ISBN 0-281-03702-7 : £12.50
Also classified at 221 B82-08375

225 — Bible. N.T. Theology — *Encyclopaedias*

The **New** international dictionary of New Testament theology. — 2nd ed. — Exeter : Paternoster Press, Aug.1981
Translation of: Theologisches Begriffslexikon zum Neuen Testament
Vol.2. — [1058]p
Previous ed.: 1976
ISBN 0-85364-331-8 : £26.00 : CIP entry
B81-23902

The **New** international dictionary of New Testament theology. — 2nd ed. — Exeter : Paternoster Press, Aug.1981
Translation of: Theologisches Begriffslexikon zum Neuen Testament
Vol.3. — [1514]p
Previous ed.: 1978
ISBN 0-85364-332-6 : £32.00 : CIP entry
B81-23903

225.15 — Bible. N.T. Prophecy

Boring, M. Eugene. Sayings of the risen Jesus. — Cambridge : Cambridge University Press, Sept.1982. — [332]p. — (Society for New Testament Studies. Monograph series ; 46)
ISBN 0-521-24117-0 : £21.00 : CIP entry
B82-20201

225.4′8 — Bible. N.T.. *Greek.* **Textual criticism** — *Festschriften*

New Testament textual criticism : its significance for exegesis : essays in honour of Bruce M. Metzger / edited by Eldon Jay Epp and Gordon D. Fee. — Oxford : Clarendon, 1981. — xxviii,410p,[1]leaf of plates : 1port ; 23cm
Includes 4 contributions in German and 1 in French. — Bibliography: pxix-xxviii. — Includes index
ISBN 0-19-826175-6 : £40.00 : CIP rev.
B80-18160

225.5′2 — Bible. N.T. *English. Today′s English. Selections — Texts*

[Bible. N.T.. *English. Today′s English. Selections. 1977*]. New life in Christ. — London : Bible Society, c1977. — 1folded sheet : ill ; 21x30cm folded to 21x10cm
ISBN 0-564-07681-3 : Unpriced B82-37998

225.6 — Bible. N.T. — *Critical studies*

Gundry, Robert H.. A survey of the New Testament / Robert H. Gundry. — Exeter : Paternoster, 1979, c1970. — xvi,400p : ill,maps ; 23cm
Originally published: Grand Rapids : Zondervan, 1970. — Includes index
ISBN 0-85364-111-0 (pbk) : £6.80 B82-15000

Moule, C. F. D.. The birth of the New Testament / C.F.D. Moule. — 3rd ed., rev. and rewritten. — London : Adam & Charles Black, 1981. — xii,382p ; 22cm. — (Black′s New Testament commentaries)
Previous ed.: 1966. — Bibliography: p343-382. — Includes index
ISBN 0-7136-2133-8 (pbk) : £9.95 : CIP rev.
B81-02119

Spivey, Robert A.. Anatomy of the New Testament : a guide to its structure and meaning / Robert A. Spivey, D. Moody Smith. — 3rd ed. — New York : Macmillan ; London : Collier Macmillan, c1982. — xviii,539p : ill,maps(some col.),1facsim,plans,ports ; 25cm
Previous ed.: 1974. — Maps on lining papers. — Bibliography: p510-515. — Includes index
ISBN 0-02-415300-1 : £13.95 B82-26203

225.6 — Bible. N.T. — *Expositions*

Balchin, John. Pocket readers guide to the Bible : Matthew - Corinthians / John Balchin. — [London] : Scripture Union, 1981. — [208]p : col.ill ; 17cm
ISBN 0-85421-939-0 : £2.95 B82-05524

Marshall, I. Howard. God′s word in man′s words. — London : Hodder & Stoughton, Nov.1982. — [160]p
ISBN 0-340-32337-x (pbk) : £3.95 : CIP entry
B82-27333

Welch, Charles H.. Fundamentals and the mystery : a refutation of the charge, that they who hold to the ″prison epistles″ do not teach the fundamentals of the faith / by Charles H. Welch. — London (52a Wilson St., E.C.2) : Berean Publishing, [1980?]. — 14p ; 20cm
Cover title
Unpriced (pbk) B82-35962

Welch, Charles H.. Right division / by Charles H. Welch. — London (52a Wilson St., EC2A 2ER) : Berean Publishing, [1980?]. — 12p ; 19cm
Unpriced (unbound) B82-35963

225.6 — Bible. N.T.. Interpretation

Moule, C. F. D.. Essays in New Testament interpretation / C.F.D. Moule. — Cambridge : Cambridge University Press, 1982. — xiii,327p ; 23cm
Includes index
ISBN 0-521-23783-1 : £18.00 : CIP rev.
B82-13130

225.6 — Bible. N.T. Theology *related to* **O.T. theology**

Bruce, F. F.. This is that : the New Testament development of some Old Testament themes. — Exeter : Paternoster Press, Jan.1982. — [128]p
Originally published: 1968
ISBN 0-85364-168-4 (pbk) : £2.40 : CIP entry
Also classified at 221.6 B82-02465

225.6 — Church of England. Sermons. Special subjects: Bible. N.T. — *Sermon outlines*
Cleverley Ford, D. W.. More preaching from the New Testament / D. W. Cleverley Ford. — London : Mowbray, 1982. — ix,116p ; 22cm
ISBN 0-264-66832-4 (pbk) : £3.50 B82-31274

225.9′22 — Bible. N.T. — *Biographies*
Brownrigg, Ronald. Who′s who in the New Testament. — London : Hodder & Stoughton, Feb.1982. — [320]p. — (Teach yourself books)
Originally published: London : Weidenfeld & Nicolson, 1971
ISBN 0-340-27177-9 (pbk) : £2.95 : CIP entry B81-36356

225.9′24 — Bible. N.T.: John, *the Apostle, Saint* — *For teaching*
I was there! : 10 studies from the Bible on the life of John the Apostle / prepared by WEC Youth. — Gerrards Cross (Bulstrode, Gerrards Cross, Bucks. SL9 8SZ) : [WEC Youth], [1981?]. — 76p : ill,1map ; 21cm. — (Combined Bible studies for 8-10′s and 11-14′s)
Unpriced (pbk) B82-06594

I was there! : ten studies on the life of the Apostle John / prepared by WEC Youth. — Gerrards Cross (Bulstrode, Gerrards Cross, Bucks. SL9 8SZ) : [WEC Youth], [1981?]. — 52p ; 21cm. — (Bible character study for youth)
Unpriced (pbk) B82-06595

225.9′24 — Bible. N.T.. Paul, *the Apostle, Saint*
Barrett, C. K.. Essays on Paul / C.K. Barrett. — London : SPCK, 1982. — x,170p ; 23cm
Includes index
ISBN 0-281-03833-3 : £10.50 B82-16247

King, Nicholas. Paul the Apostle / Nicholas King. — London : Catholic Truth Society, 1982. — [17]p ; 19cm. — (B543)
ISBN 0-85183-449-3 (unbound) : £0.45 B82-22328

Welch, Charles H.. Who then is Paul? / by Charles H. Welch. — London (52a Wilson St., E.C.2) : Berean Publishing, [1980?]. — 24p ; 21cm
Cover title
Unpriced (pbk) B82-35969

225.9′24 — Bible. N.T.. Paul, *the Apostle, Saint* — *Biographies*
Copestake, Reginald H.. Learning about St Paul / by Reginald H. Copestake. — London : Mowbray, 1982. — 32p ; 15cm. — (Enquirer′s library)
Bibliography: p32
ISBN 0-264-66866-9 (pbk) : £0.60 B82-41124

Jeffery, Colin. Saint Paul / by Colin Jeffery and Paul Dunn. — London : Catholic Truth Society, 1981. — 13p ; 18cm
ISBN 0-85183-423-x (pbk) : £0.35 B82-17798

225.9′24 — Bible. N.T.. Paul, *the Apostle, Saint* — *Festschriften*
Paul and Paulinism : essays in honour of C.K. Barrett / edited by M.D. Hooker and S.G. Wilson. — London : SPCK, 1982. — xxvii,404p,[1]leaf of plates : 1port ; 23cm
Bibliography: p373-381. — Includes index
ISBN 0-281-03835-x : £21.00 (£25.00 after 1.10.82) B82-31267

225.9′24 — Bible. N.T. Paul, *the Apostle, Saint.* **Local associations: Mediterranean region**
Bruce, F. F.. Places they knew : Jesus and Paul / F.F. Bruce. — London : Ark, 1981. — 128p : ill(some col.),maps(some col.),plans ; 28cm
Spine title. — Includes index
ISBN 0-86201-110-8 : £5.95
Primary classification 232.9′01 B82-05602

225.9′24 — Bible. N.T.. Paul, *the Apostle, Saint* — *Stories for children*
Robertson, Jenny. Paul the prisoner / text by Jenny Robertson ; illustrations by Alan Parry. — London : Scripture Union/Ladybird, 1980. — [28]p : col.ill ; 27cm. — (A Ladybird Bible book)
Text and ill on lining papers
ISBN 0-85421-893-9 : £0.75
ISBN 0-7214-0573-8 (Ladybird) B82-13746

225.9′24 — Bible. N.T.. Peter, *the Apostle, Saint*
O′Collins, Gerald. What Peter does for the Church / Gerald O′Collins. — London : Catholic Truth Society, 1982. — 16p ; 19cm
ISBN 0-85183-484-1 (pbk) : £0.35 B82-35626

225.9′505 — Bible. N.T. — *Stories for children*
Bailey, John, *1940 Nov.4-*. Stories from the New Testament / retold by John Bailey. — London : Beaver, 1982. — 127p : col.ill,2maps(some col.) ; 18cm
ISBN 0-600-20508-8 (pbk) : £1.75 B82-24280

Kent, David. The last journey / David Kent ; illustrated by Gwen Green, Francis Phillips and Martin Reiner. — London : Kingfisher, 1981. — 22p : col.ill ; 23cm. — (Kingfisher explorer books. Bible stories ; bk.6)
Includes index
ISBN 0-86272-022-2 : £1.95 : CIP rev. B81-27975

226′.059166 — Bible. N.T. Gospels. *Welsh. Selections* — *Texts*
[Bible. N.T.. Gospels. *Welsh. Selections. 1981*]. Iesu a ddywedodd. — Abertawe [Swansea] : Tŷ John Penry, 1981. — 60p : col.ill ; 20cm
Originally published: as Great words of Jesus, with English captions to the illustrations. Tring : Lion Publishing, 1979
ISBN 0-903701-42-1 (pbk) : £0.95 B82-16387

[Bible. N.T.. Gospels. *Welsh. Selections. 1981*]. Bywyd Iesu. — Abertawe [Swansea] : Tŷ John Penry, 1981. — 60p : col.ill ; 20cm
Originally published: as The life of Jesus, with English captions to the illustrations. Tring : Lion Publishing, 1979
ISBN 0-903701-43-x (pbk) : £0.95 B82-16386

226′.06 — Bible. N. T. Synoptic Gospels. Marcan hypothesis
Stoldt, Hans-Herbert. History and criticism of the Marcan hypothesis / Hans-Herbert Stoldt ; translated and edited by Donald L. Niewyk ; introduction by William R. Farmer. — Macon, Ga. : Mercer University Press ; Edinburgh : T. & T. Clark, 1980. — xviii,302p ; 22cm. — ([Studies of the New Testament and its world])
Translation of: Geschichte und Kritik der Markushypothese. — Bibliography: p281-283. — Includes index
ISBN 0-567-09310-7 : £7.95 B82-08792

226′.06 — Bible. N.T. Gospels - *Psychological perspectives*
Nicoll, Maurice. The mark. — London : Watkins, Apr.1981. — 1v.
ISBN 0-7224-0195-7 (pbk) : CIP entry B81-05140

226′.06 — Bible. N.T. Synoptic Gospels — *Comparative studies*
Orchard, Bernard. Matthew, Luke & Mark / Bernard Orchard. — 2nd ed. — Manchester : Koinonia, 1977. — viii,151p ; 21cm. — (The Griesbach solution to the synoptic question ; v.1)
Previous ed.: 1976. — Bibliography: p142-146. — Includes index
ISBN 0-86088-009-5 (pbk) : Unpriced B82-04390

226′.06 — Bible. N.T. Synoptic Gospels — *Expositions*
Crane, Thomas E.. The Synoptics : Mark, Matthew and Luke interpret the Gospel. — London : Sheed & Ward, Mar.1982. — [224]p
ISBN 0-7220-8711-x (pbk) : £7.50 : CIP entry B82-10659

226′.06 — Catholic Church. Sermons. Special subjects: Bible. N.T. Gospels — *Sermon outlines — For church year*
McGinlay, Hugh. Celebrating God′s word : introducing the Gospel readings for Sundays and feasts, Year C / Hugh McGinlay. — Great Wakering : Mayhew-McCrimmon, 1979. — 72p ; 21cm
ISBN 0-85597-283-1 (pbk) : £1.30 B82-19962

226′.07 — Bible. N.T. Gospels — *Commentaries*
Explaining the gospels : an illustrated introduction. — London : Scripture Union, c1981. — 350p : ill(some col.),maps(some col.),col.ports,1col.geneal.table ; 27cm
Includes index
ISBN 0-85421-954-4 : Unpriced B82-24430

226′.077 — Bible. N.T. Gospels — *Texts with commentaries*
[Bible. N.T.. Gospels. *English. Today′s English. 1982*]. New Testament history : the Gospels and Acts : Matthew, Mark, Luke, John, Acts. — London : Bible Society, [1982]. — p913-1104 : ill(some col.),col.maps ; 23cm. — (Special edition Good News Bible ; 5)
ISBN 0-564-06921-3 (pbk) : Unpriced B82-25680

226′.206 — Bible. N.T. Matthew — *Expositions*
Balchin, John. Matthew : the promise of salvation / [author John Balchin] ; [photography Alan Hayward, Robert Gainer Hunt, Paul Marsh]. — [London] : Scripture Union, 1981. — [24]p : col.ill ; 17cm. — (Discovering Bible books)
Text on inside covers
ISBN 0-85421-926-9 (pbk) : £0.40 B82-05534

Scroggie, W. Graham. Dr. W. Graham Scroggie on Matthew & Mark. — London : Ark Publishing, 1981. — 131p ; 21cm
ISBN 0-86201-091-8 (pbk) : Unpriced
Also classified at 226′.306 B82-05522

226′.207 — Bible. N.T. Matthew — *Commentaries — For West African students*
Tarrant, C. J. C.. Matthew and the Acts of the Apostles 1-15 / C.J.C. Tarrant. — Harlow : Longman, 1982. — v,153p : ill,maps ; 22cm. — (Certificate Bible knowledge)
ISBN 0-582-65096-8 (pbk) : £1.30
Also classified at 226′.607 B82-23064

Williams, David, *19---*. The gospel of Matthew / David and Bridget Williams. — [Glasgow] : Collins, 1982. — 192p : 2maps ; 21cm. — (Bible knowledge for the West African School Certificate)
ISBN 0-00-326135-2 (pbk) : £1.75 B82-31751

226′.2077 — Bible. N.T. Matthew. *English - Texts with commentaries*
Beare, Francis Wright. The Gospel according to Matthew. — Oxford : Blackwell, June 1981. — [576]p
ISBN 0-631-12528-0 : £25.00 : CIP entry B81-14416

226′.306 — Bible. N.T. Mark — *Expositions*
Balchin, John. Mark : the message of salvation / [author John Balchin] ; [photography Alan Hayward, Robert Gainer Hunt, Paul Marsh]. — [London] : Scripture Union, 1981. — [24]p : col.ill ; 17cm. — (Discovering Bible books)
Text on inside covers
ISBN 0-85421-927-7 (pbk) : £0.40 B82-05533

Martin, Ralph P.. Mark : evangelist and theologian / by Ralph P. Martin. — Exeter : Paternoster, c1972 (1979 [printing]). — 240p ; 22cm
Bibliography: p227-235. — Includes index
ISBN 0-85364-253-2 (pbk) : £4.20 : CIP rev. B79-14383

Scroggie, W. Graham. Dr. W. Graham Scroggie on Matthew & Mark. — London : Ark Publishing, 1981. — 131p ; 21cm
ISBN 0-86201-091-8 (pbk) : Unpriced
Primary classification 226′.206 B82-05522

226′.3077 — Bible. N.T. Mark — *Texts with commentaries*
Harrington, Wilfrid J.. Mark / Wilfrid Harrington. — Dublin (7 Lower Abbey St., Dublin) : Veritas, c1979. — xvi,253p ; 21cm. — (New Testament message ; v.4)
Bibliography: p251-253
Unpriced (pbk) B82-26366

226'.4'0076 — Bible. N.T. Luke — *Questions & answers*

Mills, Daphne. Come walk with Jesus : introductory bible study to the Road to Emmaus / by Daphne Mills. — Poole : Celebration, 1980. — 32p : ill ; 21cm
ISBN 0-906309-12-3 (pbk) : £0.75 : CIP rev. B80-09585

226'.4'05203 — Bible. N.T. Luke II. *English. Authorized — Texts — For children*

Watts, Bernadette. The Christmas story. — London : Abelard-Schuman, Sept.1982. — [32]p
ISBN 0-200-72791-5 : £4.95 : CIP entry B82-18968

226'.406 — Bible. N.T. Luke — *Expositions*

Balchin, John. Luke : the scope of salvation / [author John Balchin] ; [photography Alan Hayward, Robert Gainer Hunt, Paul Marsh]. — [London] : Scripture Union, 1981. — [24]p : col.ill ; 17cm. — (Discovering Bible books)
Text on inside covers
ISBN 0-85421-928-5 (pbk) : £0.40 B82-05532

Marshall, I. Howard. Luke : historian and theologian / by I. Howard Marshall. — 2nd ed. — Exeter : Paternoster, c1970 (1979 [printing]). — 238p ; 22cm
Includes index
ISBN 0-85364-252-4 (pbk) : £4.20 : CIP rev. B79-14384

Scroggie, W. Graham. Dr. W. Graham Scroggie on Luke & John. — London : Ark Publishing, 1981. — 155p ; 21cm
ISBN 0-86201-092-6 (pbk) : Unpriced
Also classified at 226'.506 B82-05521

226'.406 — Bible. N.T. Luke — *Topics for discussion groups*

Nilsen, Mary Ylvisaker. Real living : a small-group life experience with the Gospel of Luke / by Mary Ylvisaker Nilsen. — English ed. / adapted by Wendy S. Robins. — London : Bible Society, 1981. — 204p : ill ; 21cm
Previous ed.: Minneapolis : Winston Press, 1977
ISBN 0-564-04442-3 (pbk) : £2.95 B82-14019

Nilsen, Mary Ylvisaker. Real living : a small-group life experience with the Gospel of Luke / by Mary Ylvisaker Nilsen. — London : Bible Society
Leader's guide. — English ed. / adapted by Wendy S. Robins. — c1981. — 36p : ill ; 21cm
Previous ed.: Minneapolis : Winston Press, 1977
ISBN 0-564-07122-6 (pbk) : £0.50 B82-14020

226'.4'07 — Bible. N.T. Luke — *Commentaries*

Barrell, E. V.. An introduction to St Luke. — London : Murray, Feb.1982. — [224]p
ISBN 0-7195-3903-x (pbk) : £2.25 : CIP entry B81-35851

226'.407 — Bible. N.T. Luke — *Commentaries*

Ellis, E. Earle. The Gospel of Luke. — London : Marshall, Morgan & Scott, July 1981. — [324] p. — (The New Century Bible commentary)
ISBN 0-551-00849-0 (pbk) : £4.95 : CIP entry B81-20643

226'.4'07 — Bible. N.T. Luke — *Commentaries — For schools*

Dickson, Kwesi. The Gospel according to Luke. — London : Darton, Longman & Todd, Apr.1982. — [208]p
ISBN 0-232-51556-5 : £1.75 : CIP entry B82-04304

226'.5052 — Bible. N.T. John. *English. New International — Texts*

[Bible. N.T. John. *English. New International. 1982*]The **Offer** of life. — London : Hodder & Stoughton, Oct.1982. — [64]p
ISBN 0-340-32242-x : £0.95 : CIP entry B82-33207

226'.506 — Bible. N.T. John — *Expositions*

Balchin, John. John : the truth of salvation / [author John Balchin] ; [photography Alan Hayward, Robert Gainer Hunt, Paul Marsh]. — [London] : Scripture Union, 1981. — [24]p : col.ill ; 17cm. — (Discovering Bible books)
Text on inside covers
ISBN 0-85421-929-3 (pbk) : £0.40 B82-05529

Barrett, C. K.. Essays on John / C.K. Barrett. — London : SPCK, 1982. — viii,167p ; 23cm
ISBN 0-281-03834-1 : £10.50 B82-28993

Scroggie, W. Graham. Dr. W. Graham Scroggie on Luke & John. — London : Ark Publishing, 1981. — 155p ; 21cm
ISBN 0-86201-092-6 (pbk) : Unpriced
Primary classification 226'.406 B82-05521

Welch, Charles H.. John and the mystery / by C.H. Welch. — London (52a Wilson St., EC2A 2ER) : Berean Publishing, [198-?]. — 19p ; 21cm
Cover title
Unpriced (unbound) B82-34760

226'.507 — Bible. N.T. John — *Commentaries*

Lindars, Barnabas. The Gospel of John. — London : Marshall, Morgan & Scott, July 1981. — [648]p. — (The New Century Bible commentary)
ISBN 0-551-00848-2 (pbk) : £7.95 : CIP entry B81-20647

226'.606 — Bible. N.T. Acts — *Expositions*

Balchin, John. Acts : the power of salvation / [author John Balchin] ; [photography Alan Hayward, Robert Gainer Hunt, Paul Marsh]. — [London] : Scripture Union, 1981. — [24]p : col.ill ; 17cm. — (Discovering Bible books)
Text on inside covers
ISBN 0-85421-930-7 (pbk) : £0.40 B82-05530

Maddox, Robert. The purpose of Luke — Acts / by Robert Maddox ; edited by John Riches. — Edinburgh : T. & T. Clark, 1982. — 218p ; 22cm. — (Studies of the New Testament and its world)
"Originally published in Forschungen zur Religion und Literatur des Alten und Neuen Testaments" — t.p. verso. — Bibliography: p190-201. — Includes index
ISBN 0-567-09312-3 : £9.95 B82-32506

Welch, Charles H.. 'Acts 13 or 28?' / by Charles H. Welch. — London : Berean Publishing, 1957 (1981 [printing]). — 20p ; 21cm
ISBN 0-85156-075-x (corrected : pbk) : Unpriced B82-35177

226'.607 — Bible. N.T. Acts — *Commentaries — Welsh texts*

Griffiths, Eifion Wyn. Ffordd y ffydd : detholiad o Lyfr yr Actau / Eifion Wyn Griffiths. — [Caernarfon] ([c/o Calvinistic Methodist Book Agency, Heol Ddewi, Caernarfon, Gwynedd LL55 1ER]) : Gwasg Pantycelyn, c1981. — 172p ; 18cm
Bibliography: p171-172
Unpriced (pbk) B82-02286

226'.607 — Bible N.T. Acts I-XV — *Commentaries — For West African students*

Tarrant, C. J. C.. Matthew and the Acts of the Apostles 1-15 / C.J.C. Tarrant. — Harlow : Longman, 1982. — v,153p : ill,maps ; 22cm. — (Certificate Bible knowledge)
ISBN 0-582-65096-8 (pbk) : £1.30
Primary classification 226'.207 B82-23064

226'.6077 — Bible. N.T. Acts — *Texts with commentaries*

[Bible. N.T. Acts of the Apostles. *English. Revised Standard. 1982*]. [Bible. N.T. Acts of the Apostles. English. Revised Standard. 1982]. The Acts of the Apostles / R.H. Horton, E.O.N. Aghaegbuna. — London : Arnold, 1982. — xii,198p : ill(some col.),maps ; 23cm. — (Bible knowledge)
Bibliography: pxii
ISBN 0-7131-8084-6 (pbk) : £2.40 B82-36010

226'.60924 — Bible. N.T. Acts. Paul, *the Apostle, Saint — Stories for children*

Paul, the churchbuilder / editorial committee René Berthier, Jean-Marie Faure, Marie-Hélène Sigaut ; illustrated by Lizzie Napoli ; translated by Jane Collins. — London : Hodder and Stoughton, 1980. — 48p : col.ill,1col.map ; 29cm. — (Hodder & Stoughton Bible albums ; no.9)
Translation of: Paul, le bâtisseur d'églises. — Map on inside cover
ISBN 0-340-25333-9 (pbk) : £1.30 : CIP rev. B80-05778

Paul, the convert / editorial committee René Berthier, Jeanne-Marie Faure, Marie-Hélène Sigaut ; illustrated by Régine and Bruno Le Sourd ; translated by Jane Collins. — London : Hodder and Stoughton, 1980. — 46p : col.ill,1col.map ; 29cm. — (Hodder & Stoughton Bible albums ; no.8)
Translation of: Paul, le converti. — Map on inside cover
ISBN 0-340-25334-7 (pbk) : £1.30 : CIP rev. B80-05779

Paul, witness to the Gospel / editorial committee René Berthier, Jeanne-Marie Faure, Marie-Hélène Sigaut ; illustrated by Lizzie Napoli ; translated by Jane Collins. — London : Hodder and Stoughton, 1980. — 48p : col.ill,1map ; 29cm. — (Hodder & Stoughton Bible albums ; no.10)
Translation of: Paul, le temoin de l'Evangile. — Map on inside cover
ISBN 0-340-25335-5 (pbk) : £1.30 : CIP rev. B80-05780

226'.6'09505 — Bible. N.T. Acts - *Stories for children*

Jones, Roger. Saints alive!. — Redhill : National Christian Education Council, May 1981. — [64]p
ISBN 0-7197-0292-5 (pbk) : £3.00 : CIP entry B81-06047

226'.7'00222 — Jesus Christ. Miracles — *Illustrations — For schools*

Mullen, Peter. Jesus : miracles, signs and wonders in pictures : written by Peter Mullen / drawn by Martin Pitts. — London : Edward Arnold, 1982. — ill,1map ; 25cm
ISBN 0-7131-0711-1 (pbk) : Unpriced : CIP rev. B82-06915

226'.706 — Bible. N.T. John. Miracles — *Expositions*

Holloway, Richard. Signs of glory. — London : Darton Longman & Todd, Oct.1982. — [128]p
ISBN 0-232-51542-5 (pbk) : £2.95 : CIP entry B82-24709

226'.706 — Jesus Christ. Miracles: Cursing of the fig-tree — *Critical studies*

Telford, William R.. The barren temple and the withered tree : a redaction-critical analysis of the cursing of the fig-tree pericope in Mark's Gospel and its relation to the cleansing of the temple tradition / William R. Telford. — Sheffield : JSOT Press, 1980. — xvi,319p ; 22cm. — (Journal for the study of the New Testament supplement series, ISSN 0143-2108 ; 1)
Bibliography: p270-286. — Includes index
ISBN 0-905774-20-5 : £9.95 (£6.95 to subscribers) : CIP rev. B80-04657

226'.709505 — Bible. N.T. Luke. Miracles — *Stories for children*

[Bible. N.T. Gospels. Luke XI, 1-11. *English. 1982*]. Jesus and the fisherman / illustrated by Gordon Stowell. — London : Scripture Union, 1982. — [23]p : col.ill ; 10cm. — (Little fish books about Jesus)
Text on inside cover
ISBN 0-85421-967-6 (pbk) : Unpriced B82-37184

226'.709505 — Bible. N.T.. Miracles — *Stories for children*

[Bible. N.T. Gospels. Matthew IX, 18-26. *English . 1982*]. Jesus heals / illustrated by Gordon Stowell. — London : Scripture Union, 1982. — [23]p : col.ill ; 10cm. — (Little fish books about Jesus)
Text on inside cover
ISBN 0-85421-964-1 (pbk) : Unpriced B82-37180

226'.709505 — Jesus Christ. Miracles: Feeding of the five thousand — *Stories for children*

[Bible. N.T. Gospels. Mark VI, 30-44. *English. 1982*]. Jesus feeds the people / illustrated by Gordon Stowell. — London : Scripture Union, 1982. — [23]p : col.ill ; 10cm. — (Little fish books about Jesus)
Text on inside cover
ISBN 0-85421-968-4 (pbk) : Unpriced B82-37187

226'.709505 — Jesus Christ. Miracles: Raising of Jairus' daughter — *Stories for children*

Wever, Hinke Baukje. The little girl who was ill / [illustrations by Anna-Hermine Müller] ; [Dutch text by Hinke Baukje Wever and Job Heeger] ; [English text adapted by Felicity Clayton Smith]. — 1st English ed. — Tring : Lion, 1982. — [18]p : col.ill ; 20cm. — (A Bible story picture-book)
Translation of: Meisje sta op. — Ill on inside back cover
ISBN 0-85648-393-1 : £0.95 B82-40183

226'.806 — Bible. N.T.. Parables — *Expositions*

Stamp, Clifford. "Without a parable spake he not unto them" / Clifford Stamp and Rosalie Maas. — Poole (5 Canford Court, Cliffe Drive, Canford Cliffs, Poole, Dorset, BH13 7JD) : C. Stamp and R. Mass
No.4. — c1981. — 50p ; 21cm
Unpriced (pbk) B82-11195

Stamp, Clifford. "Without a parable spake he not unto them" / Clifford Stamp and Rosalie Maas. — Poole (5 Canford Court, Cliff Drive, Canford Cliffs, Poole, Dorset, BH13 7JD) : C. Stamp and R. Maas
No.5. — 1981. — 52p ; 21cm
Unpriced (pbk) B82-39756

Stamp, Clifford. "Without a parable spake he not unto them" / Clifford Stamp and Rosalie Maas. — Poole (5 Canford Court, Cliff Drive, Canford Cliffs, Poole, Dorset BH13 7Th) : C. Stamp and R. Maas
No.6. — 1982. — 52p ; 21cm
Unpriced (pbk) B82-39757

Stamp, Clifford. "Without a parable spake he not unto them" / Clifford Stamp and Rosalie Maas. — Poole (5 Canford Court, Cliff Drive, Canford Cliffs, Poole, Dorset BH13 7JD) : C. Stamp and R. Maas
No.7. — 1982. — 56p ; 21cm
Unpriced (pbk) B82-39758

226'.806 — Bible. N.T.. Parables: Prodigal Son — *Expositions*

De Witt, John Richard. Amazing love : the parable of the prodigal son / John R. De Witt. — Edinburgh : Banner of Truth Trust, 1981. — 160p : ill ; 19cm
ISBN 0-85151-328-x (pbk) : £1.95 B82-12884

226'.8'06 — Bible. N.T. Parables - *Psychological perspectives*

Nicoll, Maurice. The new man. — London : Watkins, Apr.1981. — 1v.
ISBN 0-7224-0194-9 (pbk) : CIP entry B81-05139

226'.809505 — Bible. N.T. Luke. Parables — *Stories for children*

[Bible. N.T. Gospels. Luke XV, 3-32. *English. 1982*]. Jesus tells some stories / illustrated by Gordon Stowell. — London : Scripture Union, 1982. — [23]p : col.ill ; 10cm. — (Little fish books about Jesus)
Text on inside cover
ISBN 0-85421-969-2 (pbk) : Unpriced B82-37182

226'.809505 — Bible. N.T.. Parables: Good Samaritan — *Stories for children*

[Bible. N.T. Gospels. Luke X, 25-37. *English. 1982*]. Jesus teaches / illustrated by Gordon Stowell. — London : Scripture Union, 1982. — [23]p : col.ill ; 10cm. — (Little fish books about Jesus)
Text on inside cover
ISBN 0-85421-965-x (pbk) : Unpriced B82-37183

226'.809505 — Bible. N.T.. Parables: Lost sheep — *Stories for children*

Vries, C. M. de. The Shepherd and the lost sheep / [illustrations by Anna-Hermine Müller] ; [Dutch text by C.M. de Vries] ; [English text adapted by Felicity Clayton Smith]. — Tring : Lion, 1982. — [18]p : col.ill ; 20cm. — (A Bible Story picture-book)
Translation of: Het Schaapje dat gevonden werd. — Text, ill on lining papers
ISBN 0-85648-397-4 : £0.95 B82-36907

226'.9'06 — Sermon on the Mount — *Expositions*

Thielicke, Helmut. Life can begin again. — Cambridge : James Clarke, Feb.1982. — [224]p
Translation of: Das Leben kann noch einmal beginnen. — Originally published: 1966
ISBN 0-227-67854-0 (pbk) : £4.95 : CIP entry B82-08404

226'.9606 — Lord's Prayer — *Expositions*

Brain, Derrick. Wrestling with prayer / (outline of the Lord's Prayer) : companion to Wrestling with spirituals / by Derrick Brain. — Bognor Regis : New Horizon, c1982. — 84p ; 21cm
ISBN 0-86116-626-4 : £4.50 B82-32816

227'.077 — Bible. N.T. Epistles — *Texts with commentaries*

[Bible. N.T.. Epistles. *English. Today's English. 1982*]. The Letters : Romans, 1 Corinthians, 2 Corinthians, Galatians, Ephesians, Philippians, Collossians, 1 Thessalonians, 2 Thessalonians, 1 Timothy, 2 Timothy, Titus, Philemon, Hebrews, James, 1 Peter, 2 Peter, 1 John, 2 John, 3 John, Jude. — London : Bible Society, [1982]. — p1105-1248 : ill(some col.),1col.map ; 23cm. — (Special edition Good News Bible ; 6)
Includes the Revelation to John
ISBN 0-564-06931-0 (pbk) : Unpriced B82-25679

227'.08'30336 — Bible. N.T. Epistles. Special subjects: Authority

Munro, Winsome. Authority in Paul and Peter. — Cambridge : Cambridge University Press, Nov.1982. — [248]p. — (Society for New Testament Studies. Monograph series ; 45)
ISBN 0-521-23694-0 : £15.00 : CIP entry B82-26232

227'.106 — Bible. N.T. Romans — *Expositions*

Balchin, John. Romans : the way of salvation / [author John Balchin] ; [photography Alan Hayward, Robert Gainer Hunt, Paul Marsh]. — [London] : Scripture Union, 1981. — [24]p : col.ill ; 17cm. — (Discovering Bible books)
Text on inside covers
ISBN 0-85421-931-5 (pbk) : £0.40 B82-05531

227'.1077 — Bible. N.T. Romans — *Texts with commentaries*

Hendriksen, William. Romans / William Hendriksen. — Edinburgh : Banner of Truth Trust
Vol.2: Ch.9-16. — 1981. — vii,p305-535 ; 23cm. — (New Testament commentary)
Bibliography: p531-535
ISBN 0-85151-336-0 : £5.95 B82-10820

227'.206 — Bible. N.T. Corinthians, 1st — *Expositions*

Balchin, John. 1 Corinthians : the reality of salvation / [author John Balchin] ; [photography Alan Hayward, Robert Gainer Hunt, Paul Marsh]. — [London] : Scripture Union, 1981. — [24]p : col.ill ; 17cm. — (Discovering Bible books)
Text on inside covers
ISBN 0-85421-932-3 (pbk) : £0.40 B82-05527

227'.206 — Bible. N.T. Corinthians — *Expositions*

Green, Michael, *1930-*. To Corinth with love : the vital relevance today of Paul's advice to the Corinthian church / by Michael Green. — London : Hodder and Stoughton, 1982. — 175p ; 18cm. — (Hodder Christian paperbacks)
ISBN 0-340-28226-6 (pbk) : £1.50 : CIP rev. B82-10797

227'.306 — Bible. N.T. Corinthians, 2nd — *Expositions*

Balchin, John. 2 Corinthians : the experience of salvation / [author John Balchin] ; [photography Alan Hayward, Robert Gainer Hunt, Paul Marsh]. — [London] : Scripture Union, 1981. — [24]p : col.ill ; 17cm. — (Discovering Bible books)
Text on inside covers
ISBN 0-85421-933-1 (pbk) : £0.40 B82-05528

227'.406 — Bible. N.T. Galatians I — *Expositions*

Cragg, Kenneth. Paul and Peter : meeting in Jerusalem / Kenneth Cragg. — [London] : BRF, 1980. — 96p ; 20cm. — (BRF book club ; no.7)
ISBN 0-900164-52-2 (pbk) : £1.75 B82-15084

227'.407 — Bible. N.T. Galatians. Greek — *Commentaries*

Bruce, F. F.. The Epistle of Paul to the Galatians : a commentary on the Greek text. — Exeter : Paternoster Press, Aug.1982. — [336]p. — (The New international Greek Testament commentary ; 2)
ISBN 0-85364-299-0 (cased) : £12.00 : CIP entry
ISBN 0-85364-300-8 (pbk) : £8.00 B82-16663

227'.506 — Bible. N.T. Ephesians — *Expositions*

Detzler, Wayne. Living words in Ephesians / Wayne Detzler. — Welwyn : Evangelical, 1981. — 140p ; 22cm
ISBN 0-85234-157-1 (pbk) : Unpriced B82-13541

227'.7077 — Bible. N.T. Colossians — *Texts with commentaries*

Schweizer, Eduard. The letter to the Colossians : a commentary / Eduard Schweizer ; translated by Andrew Chester. — London : SPCK, 1982. — 319p ; 22cm
Translated from the German. — Bibliography: p303-312. — Includes index
ISBN 0-281-03856-2 : £12.50 B82-33541

227'.8107 — Bible. N.T. Thessalonians — *Texts with commentaries*

Wilson, Geoffrey B.. 1 & 2 Thessalonians : a digest of reformed comment / Geoffrey B. Wilson. — Edinburgh : Banner of Truth Trust, 1982. — 128p ; 18cm
Bibliography: p126-128
ISBN 0-85151-339-5 (pbk) : £1.75 B82-31399

227'.83077 — Bible. N.T. Pastoral Epistles — *Texts with commentaries*

Wilson, Geoffrey B.. The Pastoral Epistles : a digest of reformed comment / Geoffrey B. Wilson. — Edinburgh : Banner of Truth Trust, 1982. — 173p ; 18cm
Bibliography: p171-173
ISBN 0-85151-335-2 (pbk) : £1.95 B82-31400

227'.8706 — Bible. N.T. Hebrews — *Expositions*

Brown, Raymond, *1928-*. Christ above all : the message of Hebrews / Raymond Brown. — Leicester : Inter-Varsity, 1982. — 272p ; 20cm. — (The Bible speaks today)
Bibliography: p11-12
ISBN 0-85110-702-8 (pbk) : Unpriced : CIP rev. B82-01449

227'.8706 — Bible. N.T. Hebrews. Special subjects: Perfection — *Critical studies*

Peterson, David. Hebrews and perfection. — Cambridge : Cambridge University Press, Nov.1982. — [328]p. — (Society for New Testament Studies monograph series ; 47)
ISBN 0-521-24408-0 : £21.00 : CIP entry B82-29393

227'.8707 — Bible. N.T. Hebrews — *Commentaries*

Guthrie, Donald. The letter to the Hebrews. — Leicester : Inter-Varsity Press, Apr.1982. — [256]p. — (The Tyndale New Testament commentaries)
ISBN 0-85111-636-1 (cased) : £5.00 : CIP entry
ISBN 0-85111-837-2 (pbk) B82-06522

227′.91077 — Bible. N.T. Epistle of James — *Texts with commentaries*
Davids, Peter. The Epistle of James. — Exeter : Paternoster Press, June 1982. — [250]p. — (The New international Greek testament commentary)
ISBN 0-85364-334-2 (cased) : £8.00 : CIP entry
ISBN 0-85364-335-0 (pbk) : £5.00 B82-10215

227′.92077 — Bible. N.T. Peter — *Texts with commentaries*
Nisbet, Alexander. An exposition of 1 & 2 Peter / Alexander Nisbet. — Edinburgh : Banner of Truth Trust, 1982. — 300p : ill ; 23cm. — (A Geneva series commentary)
Originally published: S.l. : s.n., 1658. — Ill on lining papers
ISBN 0-85151-338-7 : £5.95 B82-37980

228′.06 — Bible. N.T. Revelation — *Expositions*
Lawrence, D. H.. Apocalypse / D.H. Lawrence ; edited by Mara Kalnins ; introduction by Melvyn Bragg. — London : Granada, 1981, c1980. — xii,178p ; 19cm. — (The Cambridge edition of the works of D.H. Lawrence)
Originally published: Cambridge : Cambridge University Press, 1980
ISBN 0-246-11683-8 (cased) : £6.95
ISBN 0-586-05273-9 (pbk) : Unpriced B82-09245

Lawrence, D. H.. Apocalypse and the writings on Revelation / D.H. Lawrence ; edited by Mara Kalnins. — Cambridge : Cambridge University Press, c1980. — xiii,249p ; 23cm. — (The works of D.H. Lawrence)
ISBN 0-521-22407-1 : £12.50 : CIP rev. B80-25123

228′.068 — Bible. N.T. Revelation. Cabalistic interpretations
Lévi, Éliphas. The mysteries of the Qabalah : or the occult agreement of the two Testaments / by Eliphas Lévi. — Wellingborough : Aquarian, 1974 (1981 [printing]). — 285p : ill,plans ; 22cm. — (Studies in hermetic tradition)
Translation of: Les mystères de la Kabbale
ISBN 0-85030-274-9 (pbk) : £4.95 : CIP rev.
Primary classification 224′.4068 B81-32054

230 — CHRISTIAN THEOLOGY, CHRISTIAN DOCTRINE

230 — Christian doctrine
Allen, Stuart. What is a Christian? / by Stuart Allen. — London : Berean Publishing, [198-?]. — 7p ; 17cm
Unpriced (unbound) B82-35172

Broadie, Elsie. I believe / by Elsie Broadie. — Redhill : NCEC, 1981. — 96p ; 20cm
ISBN 0-7197-0312-3 (pbk) : £2.00 B82-08554

Chapman, Colin, *1938-*. The case for Christianity / Colin Chapman. — Tring : Lion, 1981. — 313p : ill(some col.),ports(some col.) ; 23cm. — (A Lion handbook)
Includes index
ISBN 0-85648-371-0 : £7.95 B82-06385

Findlay, Robert. Turn again / by Robert Findlay. — Alexandria, Dunbartonshire (Boturich, Alexandria, Dunbartonshire G83 8LX) : R. Findlay, 1979. — viii,48p ; 21cm
£0.50 (pbk) B82-21786

Lewis, Edward, *1913-*. The sacrament of the Word / by Edward Lewis. — [Denbigh] ([Chapel St., Denbigh, Clwyd]) : Gwasg Gee, [1981]. — 135p ; 19cm
£1.50 (pbk) B82-12203

Packer, J. I.. God's words : studies of key Bible themes / J.I. Packer. — Leicester : Inter-Varsity, 1981. — 223p ; 18cm
Includes index
ISBN 0-85110-434-7 (pbk) : Unpriced : CIP rev. B81-30614

Penny, Michael. What on earth is a / [Michael Penny]. — London : Berean Publishing, [198-?]. — [4]p ; 21cm
Unpriced (unbound) B82-35173

Rubie, Graham J.. God's inheritance in the saints / Graham J. Rubie. — [Sevenoaks] ([20 Knole Way, Sevenoaks, Kent TN13 3RS]) : [G.J. Rubie], [1981?]. — 47p ; 21cm
Unpriced (pbk) B82-07538

Urquhart, Colin. In Christ Jesus / Colin Urquhart. — London : Hodder and Stoughton, 1981. — 302p : ill ; 18cm. — (Hodder Christian paperbacks)
ISBN 0-340-27601-0 (pbk) : £1.75 : CIP rev. B81-30127

Ward, Keith. Holding fast to God. — London : SPCK, Oct.1982. — [176]p
ISBN 0-281-04022-2 (pbk) : £4.95 : CIP entry B82-23475

Welch, Charles H.. Usefulness at the expense of faithfulness / [Charles H. Welch]. — London : Berean Publishing, [198-?]. — [4]p ; 21cm
Unpriced (unbound) B82-35175

Welch, Charles H.. Wise — or otherwise? / [Charles H. Welch]. — London : Berean Publishing, [198-?]. — [4]p ; 21cm
Unpriced (unbound) B82-35174

230 — Christian doctrine — *Conference proceedings*
Purity and power : Keswick ministry from Dick Lucas, Alan Flavelle, Philip Hacking, David Jackman & others / edited by David Porter. — Bromley : STL Books, c1981. — 189p ; 18cm
Conference papers
ISBN 0-903843-59-5 (pbk) : £1.75 B82-08367

Tracts for our times, 1833-1983. — London (St Mary's Presbytery, 30 Bourne St., SW1W 8JJ) : St Mary's, Bourne St., Jan.1983. — [112]p
Conference papers
ISBN 0-9508516-0-4 (pbk) : £2.00 : CIP entry B82-40297

Witness to the spirit : essays on revelation, spirit, redemption / edited by Wilfrid Harrington. — Dublin : Irish Biblical Association, c1979. — 166p ; 21cm. — (Proceedings of the Irish Biblical Association ; no.3)
Conference papers
ISBN 0-86088-017-6 (pbk) : £2.50 B82-04395

230 — Christian doctrine — *For schools*
Erricker, Clive. Christian experience / Clive Erricker. — Guildford : Lutterworth Educational, [c1982]. — 32p : ill ; 30cm. — (The Chichester project ; 3)
Text on inside covers. — Bibliography: p32
ISBN 0-7188-2497-0 (pbk) : Unpriced B82-20341

230 — Christian theology
Chadwick, Henry. Frontiers of theology : an inaugural lecture delivered before the University of Cambridge on 5 May 1981 / Henry Chadwick. — Cambridge : Cambridge University Press, 1981. — 15p ; 22cm
Cover title
ISBN 0-521-28630-1 (pbk) : £1.50 B82-15277

Milne, Bruce. Know the truth : a handbook of Christian belief / Bruce Milne ; foreword by J.I. Packer. — Leicester : Inter-Varsity Press, 1982. — 288p ; 20cm
Bibliography: p13. — Includes index
ISBN 0-85110-707-9 (pbk) : £3.95 : CIP rev. B82-04991

Whitehouse, W. A.. The authority of grace : essays in response to Karl Barth / by W.A. Whitehouse ; edited by Ann Loades. — Edinburgh : T. & T. Clark, 1981. — xxiv,247p ; 23cm
List of works: pxxi-xxiv. — Includes index
ISBN 0-567-09308-5 (pbk) : £4.95 B82-00426

230 — Christian theology — *Conference proceedings*
Latin America/UK Theological Consultation *(1980 : Birmingham)*. Putting theology to work : papers of the Latin America/UK Theological Consultation at Fircroft, May 1980 / edited by Derek Winter. — London : Conference for World Mission, 1980. — v,93p ; 21cm
ISBN 0-85169-079-3 (pbk) : Unpriced B82-16890

230 — Dogmatic theology. Applications of axiomatic set theory
Carnes, John R.. Axiomatics and dogmatics. — Belfast : Christian Journals, May1982. — 1v.. — (Theology and scientific culture ; v.4)
ISBN 0-904302-79-2 : £9.50 : CIP entry B82-16212

230′.01 — Christian theology — *Philosophical perspectives — Festschriften*
The **Philosophical** frontiers of Christian theology : essays presented to D.M. Mackinnon / edited by Brian Hebblethwaite and Stewart Sutherland. — Cambridge : Cambridge University Press, 1982. — ix,252p : ill ; 23cm
Bibliography: p239-248. — Includes index
ISBN 0-521-24012-3 : £17.50 : CIP rev. B81-39210

230′.014 — Christian doctrine. Hermeneutics. Linguistic aspects
The **Autonomy** of religious belief : a critical inquiry / edited with an introduction by Frederick J. Crosson. — Notre Dame, Ind. ; London : University of Notre Dame Press, c1981. — 162p ; 22cm. — (University of Notre Dame studies in the philosophy of religion ; no.2)
ISBN 0-268-00596-6 : £10.45 B82-15445

230′.03′21 — Bible. N.T.. Theology — *Encyclopaedias*
Brown, Colin, *1932-*. New international dictionary of New Testament theology. — Exeter : Paternoster
Addenda. — July 1982. — [20]p
ISBN 0-85364-360-1 (pbk) : £0.50 : CIP entry B82-21112

230′.03′21 — Bible. Theology — *Encyclopaedias*
Bauer encyclopedia of biblical theology / edited by Johannes B. Bauer. — London : Sheed and Ward, 1982, c1970. — 2v.(xxxiii,1141p) ; 22cm
Translation of: Bibeltheologisches Wörterbuch. — Originally published in 1 vol.: 1970. — Includes index
ISBN 0-7220-3420-2 (pbk) : £22.50 B82-24153

230′.03′21 — Theology — *Encyclopaedias*
Turner, Nicholas. Handbook for Biblical studies / Nicholas Turner. — Oxford : Basil Blackwell, 1982. — xi,145p : ill,2maps ; 23cm
ISBN 0-631-12939-1 (cased) : Unpriced : CIP rev.
ISBN 0-631-13025-x (pbk) : Unpriced B82-06942

230′.044′0941 — Great Britain. Protestant churches. Christian doctrine. Influence of thories of evolution of Darwin, Charles, *1870-1900*
Moore, James R.. The post Darwinian controversies : a study of the Protestant struggle to come to terms with Darwin in Great Britain and America 1870-1900 / James R. Moore. — Cambridge : Cambridge University Press, 1979 (1981 [printing]). — xi,514p ; 23cm
Bibliography: p401-469. — Includes index
ISBN 0-521-28517-8 (pbk) : £9.95
Also classified at 230′.044′0973 B82-04567

230′.044′0973 — United States. Protestant churches. Christian doctrine. Influence of theories of evolution of Darwin, Charles, *1870-1900*
Moore, James R.. The post Darwinian controversies : a study of the Protestant struggle to come to terms with Darwin in Great Britain and America 1870-1900 / James R. Moore. — Cambridge : Cambridge University Press, 1979 (1981 [printing]). — xi,514p ; 23cm
Bibliography: p401-469. — Includes index
ISBN 0-521-28517-8 (pbk) : £9.95
Primary classification 230′.044′0941 B82-04567

230'.05 — Christian doctrine — *Serials*

The **Gospel** truth. — No.1 (May 1980)-. — [London] ([c/o M. Grimshaw, 109 Upper Tollington Park, N4 4ND]) : [Tollington Park Baptist Church], 1980-. — v. : ill ; 21cm
Quarterly
ISSN 0263-5216 = Gospel truth : Unpriced
B82-36716

230'.09 — Christian doctrine, *to ca 1935*

Richardson, Alan, *1905-1975.* Creeds in the making : a short introduction to the history of Christian doctrine / Alan Richardson. — London : SCM, 1935 (1979 [printing]). — 128p ; 20cm
ISBN 0-334-00264-8 (pbk) : £2.25 B82-03782

230'.09 — Christian theology. Influence of scientific theories, *to 1981*

Torrance, Thomas F.. Transformation and convergence in the frame of knowledge. — Belfast : Christian Journals, Oct.1982. — [240]p
ISBN 0-904302-78-4 : £12.50 : CIP entry
B82-24621

230'.09'015 — Christian doctrine, *ca 250*

[Didascalia apostolorum. *English. Selections*]. The liturgical portions of the Didascalia / translation and textual introduction by Sebastian Brock ; selection and general introduction by Michael Vasey. — Bramcote : Grove, 1982. — 33p ; 22cm. — (Grove liturgical study, ISSN 0306-0608 ; no.29)
Text on inside cover
£1.40 (pbk) B82-25339

230'.09'015 — Christian doctrine, *to ca 200*

Houlden, J. L.. What did the first Christians believe? / Leslie Houlden. — Guildford : Lutterworth, 1982. — 60p ; 19cm. — (Anselm books)
ISBN 0-7188-2515-2 (pbk) : £0.95 B82-13123

230'.1'3 — Turkey. Antioch. Christian Church. Christian theology, *ca 100-700*

Wallace-Hadrill, D. S.. Christian Antioch : a study of early Christian thought in the East. — Cambridge : Cambridge University Press, Oct.1982. — [232]p
ISBN 0-521-23425-5 : £17.50 : CIP entry
B82-29385

230'.14 — Church Fathers, *325-636.* Christian doctrine — *Anthologies*

Later Christian Fathers. — Oxford : Oxford University Press, Jan.1982. — [304]p. — (Oxford paperbacks)
Originally published: 1970
ISBN 0-19-283012-0 (pbk) : £2.95 : CIP entry
B82-03353

230'.19 — Orthodox Eastern Church. Christian doctrine

Ware, Kallistos. The orthodox way / by Kallistos Ware. — London : Mowbray, 1979 (1981 [printing]). — 204p ; 18cm. — (Mowbrays popular Christian paperbacks)
Includes index
ISBN 0-264-66578-3 (pbk) : £1.75 B82-12782

230'.2 — Catholic Church. Christian doctrine

John Paul II, *Pope.* Beloved young people : Pope John Paul II speaks to the world's youth / the words of Pope John Paul II ; photographs by Vittoriano Rastelli. — London : Hodder and Stoughton, 1982. — 96p : col.ill,col.ports ; 29cm
Translated from the Italian. — Ill on lining papers
ISBN 0-340-27966-4 : £4.95 : CIP rev.
B82-03833

Leonard, Ellen. George Tyrrell and the Catholic tradition. — London : Darton Longman & Todd, May 1982. — [208]p
ISBN 0-232-51558-1 (pbk) : £7.50 : CIP entry
B82-07658

O'Mahoney, Gerald. Abba! Father! : a personal catechism of the Catholic faith / by Gerald O'Mahony. — Slough : St. Paul, 1981. — xii,146p ; 21cm
ISBN 0-85439-194-0 (pbk) : £3.25 B82-00130

Promise : something beautiful in an ugly world, something happy in a sad society. — [Thornton Heath] (14 Sovereign Rd., Thornton Heath, Surrey CR4 6DU) : Evangelical Times, [1982]. — 8p : ill(some col.),ports(some col.) ; 30cm
Unpriced (unbound) B82-25011

Rahner, Karl. Theological investigations / by Karl Rahner. — London : Darton, Longman & Todd
Vol.20: Concern for the Church / translated by Edward Quinn. — 1981. — 191p ; 23cm
'A translation of selected articles from Schriften zur Theologie XIV'. — Includes index
ISBN 0-232-51538-7 : £14.50 : CIP rev.
B81-34407

Redford, John. What Catholics believe — : — in twenty lessons / John Redford. — London : CTS, 1981. — 42p ; 19cm
ISBN 0-85183-428-0 (pbk) : £0.40 B82-09409

Richards, Michael. The Church 2001 / by Michael Richards ; writings from The clergy review and other sources, edited with additional material by Peter Jennings. — Slough : St. Paul, 1982. — xxi,329p ; 23cm
ISBN 0-85439-202-5 : £10.00 B82-23243

Romero, Oscar Arnulfo. Romero martyr for liberation. — London (22 Coleman Fields, N1 7AF) : Catholic Institute for International Relations, Feb.1982. — [84]p
Translated extracts from La voz de los sin voz
ISBN 0-904393-71-2 (pbk) : £1.50 : CIP entry
B82-03133

Sheed, F. J.. Theology and sanity / F.J. Sheed. — Rev. and enl. ed. — London : Sheed and Ward, 1978 (1981 [printing]). — xv,333p ; 22cm. — (Stagbooks)
Includes index
ISBN 0-7220-9017-x (pbk) : £6.50 B82-04688

230'.2 — Catholic Church. Christian doctrine — *Correspondence, diaries, etc.*

Giordani, Igino. Diary of fire / by Igino Giordani. — London : New City, 1981. — viii,118p ; 19cm
Translation of: Diario di fuoco
ISBN 0-904287-17-3 (pbk) : Unpriced
B82-26525

230'.2 — Catholic Church. Christian doctrine — *Early works*

Eckhart, *Meister.* Meister Eckhart : the essential sermons, commentaries, treatises, and defense / translation and introduction by Edmund Colledge and Bernard McGinn ; preface by Huston Smith. — London : SPCK, 1981. — xviii,366p ; 23cm. — (The Classics of Western spirituality)
Translation of Latin and German works. — Bibliography: p349-353. — Includes index
ISBN 0-281-03848-1 (pbk) : £8.50 B82-20146

230'.2 — Catholic Church. Christian doctrine — *Polish texts*

John Paul II, *Pope.* Jan Paweł II : człowiek modlitwy / przygotował Zdzisław J. Peszkowski. — London : Veritas Foundation Publication Centre, 1981. — 184p,[6]leaves of plates : ports ; 19cm. — (Biblioteka polska. Seria niebieska ; tom 30)
Unpriced B82-25331

Thomas, *Aquinas, Saint.* [Summa theologiae. Polish]. Summa teologiczna / św. Tomasz z Akwinu. — London : Veritas Foundation. — (Biblioteka polska. Seria tomistyczna ; t.26)
Tom 8: Rządy Boże ... / przełożył [z łaciny] i o objaśnieniami zaopatrzył o. Pius Bełch ... — 1981. — 271p,[1]leaf of plates : 1port ; 19cm
Translation of: Summa theologiae. Vol.1 : 103-119
Unpriced B82-35583

Thomas, *Aquinas, Saint.* [Summa theologiae. Polish]. Suma teologiczna / św. Tomasz z Akwinu. — London : Veritas Foundation. — (Biblioteka polska. Seria tomistyczna ; t.27)
Tom 32: Małżeństwo ... / przełożył [z łaciny] i objaśnieniami zaopatrzył o. Feliks W. Bednarski ... — 1982. — 409p,[2]leaves of plates : 2ports ; 19cm
Translation of: Summa theologiae. Suppl. : 41-68
Unpriced B82-35582

230'.2'0924 — Catholic Church. Christian doctrine. Theories of Küng, Hans

Scheffezyk, Leo. On being a Christian : the Hans Küng debate / Leo Scheffezyk ; [translation by Peadar Mac Seumais]. — Blackrock, Co. Dublin : Four Courts Press, 1982, c1980. — 98p ; 23cm
Translation of: Kursänderung des Glaubens?
ISBN 0-906127-57-2 (cased) : Unpriced
ISBN 0-906127-58-0 (pbk) : £2.50 B82-20599

230'.2'0924 — Catholic Church. Christian doctrine. Theories of Teilhard de Chardin, Pierre

Faricy, Robert. Christian faith and my everyday life : the spiritual doctrine of Teilhard de Chardin / Robert Faricy. — Slough : St. Paul, 1981. — 102p ; 21cm
Bibliography: p102
ISBN 0-85439-197-5 (pbk) : £1.95 B82-05681

230'.2415 — Ireland. Catholic Church. Christian doctrine, *to 1900*

Irish spirituality / edited by Michael Maher. — Dublin : Veritas, 1981. — 152p ; 22cm
Includes bibliographies
ISBN 0-86217-039-7 (pbk) : £3.50 B82-20324

230'.3 — Anglican churches. Christian doctrine

Wolf, William J.. The spirit of Anglicanism : Hooker, Maurice, Temple / William J. Wolf, editor, John E. Booty, Owen C. Thomas. — Edinburgh : T. & T. Clark, 1982. — ix,212p : ports ; 21cm
Originally published: Wilton, Conn. : Morehouse-Barlow, 1979. — Bibliography: p205-212
ISBN 0-567-29111-1 (pbk) : £4.95 B82-28229

230'.3 — Church of England. Christian doctrine

Believing in the church : the corporate nature of faith / a report by the Doctrine Commission of the Church of England. — London : SPCK, 1981. — ix,310p ; 22cm
Includes index
ISBN 0-281-03839-2 (pbk) : £8.50 B82-08183

Church of England. *Archbishops' Commission on Christian Doctrine.* Doctrine in the Church of England (1938) : the report of the Commission on Christian Doctrine appointed by the Archbishops of Canterbury and York. — Repr. with a new introduction / by G.W.H. Lampe. — London : SPCK, 1982. — lx,242p ; 22cm
Originally published: 1938
ISBN 0-281-03847-3 (pbk) : £8.50 B82-20148

Hill, Rowland E.. I believe and trust : an exposition of the Christian faith based on the Affirmations made in the Baptism and Confirmation services in the alternative service book 1980 / by Rowland E. Hill ; foreword by Cuthbert Bardsley. — London : Mowbray, 1982. — 47p ; 21cm
ISBN 0-264-66859-6 (pbk) : £1.25 B82-22933

230'.3 — Church of England. Christian doctrine — *Facsimiles*

Sibbes, Richard. [The complete works of Richard Sibbes]. Works of Richard Sibbes. — Edinburgh : Banner of Truth Trust
Facsim of: ed. published Edinburgh: J. Nichol, 1862-64
Vol.7: Miscellaneous sermons & indices / edited by Alexander B. Grosart. — 1982. — xi,604p ; 23cm
Includes index
ISBN 0-85151-341-7 : £7.50 B82-31921

230'.3'0924 — Church of England. Christian doctrine. Theories of Taylor, Jeremy, ***1613-1667***

Porter, Harry Boone. Jeremy Taylor : liturgist (1613-1667) / by Harry Boone Porter. — [London] : Alcuin Club, 1979. — vii,185,[18]p : ill ; 22cm. — (Alcuin Club collections ; no.61)
Includes index
ISBN 0-281-03736-1 (pbk) : £6.95 B82-14335

230'.42'0924 — Reformed Churches. Christian doctrine. Theories of Calvin, Jean

Helm, Paul. Calvin and the Calvinists / Paul Helm. — Edinburgh : Banner of Truth Trust, 1982. — 84p ; 22cm
Includes index
ISBN 0-85151-344-1 (pbk) : £2.25 B82-37739

230'.58 — Congregational churches. Christian doctrine

Hodgkins, Harold. The Congregational way : apostolic legacy, ministry, unity, freedom / Harold Hodgkins. — Nottingham ([12 Canal St., Nottingham NG1 7EH]) : Congregational Federation, 1982. — 180p ; 22cm
Bibliography: p168-175. — Includes index
£5.00 B82-34569

230'.59 — Puritanism. Christian doctrine

Bunyan, John. Some Gospel-truths opened ; A vindication of Some Gospel-truths opened ; A few sighs from Hell / John Bunyan ; edited by T.L. Underwood with the assistance of Roger Sharrock. — Oxford : Clarendon, 1980. — lvi,402p : 3facsims ; 23cm. — (The Miscellaneous works of John Bunyan)
Facsim reprint of: Some Gospel-truths opened. London : Printed for J. Wright the Younger, 1656 — Facsim reprint of: A vindication of Some Gospel-truths opened. London : Printed for Matthias Cowley, 1657 — Facsim reprint of: A few sighs from Hell. London : Printed for Ralph Wood by M. Wright, 1658. — Bibliography: pxiii
ISBN 0-19-812730-8 : £25.00 : CIP rev.
B78-32425

230'.6 — Baptist churches. Christian doctrine

Clarke, Robert, *1903-*. The heart of the evangelical faith / Robert Clarke. — Ilfracombe : Stockwell, 1981. — 155p ; 19cm
ISBN 0-7223-1501-5 : £5.50 B82-12283

230'.673 — Seventh-Day Adventists. Christian doctrine

Ball, Bryan W.. The English connection. — Cambridge : James Clarke, June 1981. — 1v.
ISBN 0-227-67844-3 : £7.50 : CIP entry
B81-15860

230'.7 — Methodist churches. Christian doctrine

Wesley, John. The works of John Wesley. — Oxford : Clarendon Press, Jan.1983. — (The Oxford edition of the works of John Wesley)
Vol.7: A collection of hymns for the use of the people called Methodists. — [600]p
ISBN 0-19-812529-1 : £40.00 : CIP entry
B82-33485

Wesley, John. The works of John Wesley / [General editor Frank Baker]. — Oxford : Clarendon. — (Oxford edition of the works of John Wesley)
Vol.25
Letters 1: 1721-1739 / edited by Frank Baker. — 1980. — xxii,763p,[5]p of plates : facsims ; 23cm
Bibliography: pxvi-xix. — Includes index
ISBN 0-19-812545-3 : £35.00 : CIP rev.
B79-12739

Wesley, John. The works of John Wesley / edited by Frank Baker. — Oxford : Clarendon. — (The Oxford edition of the works of John Wesley)
Vol.26: Letters 2 : 1740-1755. — 1982. — xx,684p,[8]leaves : facsims ; 22cm
Bibliography: pxv-xx. — Includes index
ISBN 0-19-812546-1 : £35.00 : CIP rev.
B80-06764

230'.94'0924 — New Church. Christian doctrine. Theories of Swedenborg, Emanuel

Kingslake, Brian. Swedenborg explores the spiritual dimension : an introduction to the New Church / by Brian Kingslake. — London : Seminar, 1981. — 176p ; 20cm
ISBN 0-907295-09-6 (pbk) : Unpriced
B82-03651

230'.96 — Society of Friends. Christian doctrine

Priestland, Gerald. Reasonable uncertainty : a Quaker approach to doctrine / by Gerald Priestland. — London : Quaker Home Service, 1982. — 67p ; 19cm. — (Swarthmore lecture)
Text on inside covers
ISBN 0-85245-161-x (pbk) : £2.00 B82-40228

230'.99 — Brethren. Christian doctrine

Burr, E. C.. Enlargement : meetings in Villa Grove December 1979 / E.C. Burr. — London (50 Red Post Hill, SE24 9JQ) : E.C. Burr, 1979. — 162p ; 17cm
£1.40 (pbk) B82-09808

Renton, J.. The assembly's appreciation of Christ : meetings in Macduff, September 1978 / J. Renton. — London (20 Red Post Hill, SE24 9JQ) : E.C. Burr, [1978]. — 156p ; 17cm
£1.40 (pbk) B82-02394

Symington, J. H.. Confirmation in the way : Woodlands / J.H. Symington ; editor, Wilbert J. Seed. — Kingston [-upon-Thames] ([2, Upper Teddington Rd.,] Kingston, Surrey KT1 4DX) : Bible & Gospel Trust, c1982. — 227p ; 15cm. — (JHS ; v.100)
Unpriced (pbk) B82-23133

Symington, J. H.. Conspicuous as full grown : Bristol October 1981 / J.H. Symington ; editor, Wilbert J. Seed. — Kingston [-upon-Thames] ([2, Upper Teddington Rd.,] Kingston, Surrey KT1 4DX) : Bible & Gospel Trust, c1981. — 243p ; 15cm. — (JHS ; v.97)
Unpriced (pbk) B82-23135

Symington, J. H.. How we save ourselves and the brethren : Toronto, January 1982 / J.H. Symington ; editor, Wilbert J. Seed. — Kingston ([2 Upper Teddington Rd., Kingston-upon-Thames], KT1 4DX) : Bible & Gospel Trust, 1982. — 279p ; 16cm. — (JHS ; v.101)
Unpriced (pbk) B82-31808

Symington, J. H.. Ministry of J.H. Symington : August 1981 / editor, Wilbert J. Seed. — Kingston [-upon-Thames] ([2, Upper Teddington Rd.,] Kingston, Surrey KT1 4DX) : Bible & Gospel Trust, c1981. — 185p ; 15cm. — (JHS ; v.95)
Unpriced (pbk) B82-23131

Symington, J. H.. Ministry of J.H. Symington : 1976-77. — Kingston [-upon-Thames] ([2, Upper Teddington Rd.,] Kingston, Surrey KT1 4DX) : Bible & Gospel Trust, c1981. — 342p ; 15cm. — (JHS ; v.94)
Unpriced (pbk) B82-23132

Symington, J. H.. Ministry of J.H. Symington : 1977-78 / editor, Wilbert J. Seed. — Kingston [-upon-Thames] ([2, Upper Teddington Rd.,] Kingston, Surrey KT1 4DX) : Bible & Gospel Trust, c1981. — 366p ; 15cm. — (JHS ; v.98)
Unpriced (pbk) B82-23137

Symington, J. H.. Standing by the cross of Jesus : Omaha November 1981 / J.H. Symington ; editor, Wilbert J. Seed. — Kingston [-upon-Thames] ([2, Upper Teddington Rd.,] Kingston, Surrey KT1 4DX) : Bible & Gospel Trust, c1981. — 264p ; 15cm. — (JHS ; v.99)
Unpriced (pbk) B82-23134

Symington, J. H.. When your obedience shall have been fulfilled : Chicago, February 1982 / J.H. Symington ; editor, Wilbert J. Seed. — Kingston ([2 Upper Teddington Rd., Kingston-upon-Thames], KT1 4DX) : Bible & Gospel Trust, 1982. — 231p ; 16cm. — (JHS ; v.102)
Unpriced (pbk) B82-31809

Symington, J. H.. Ye ought, O men, to have hearkened to me : Toronto September 1981 / J.H. Symington. — Kingston [-upon-Thames] ([2, Upper Teddington Rd.,] Kingston, Surrey KT1 4DX) : Bible & Gospel Trust, c1981. — 199p ; 15cm. — (JHS ; v.96)
Unpriced (pbk) B82-23136

Taylor, J. (James), *19---*. Ministry of J. Taylor Jr. — Kingston ([2 Upper Teddington Rd., Kingston-upon-Thames,] KT1 4DX) : Bible & Gospel Trust
Vol.139: Sydney, January 1970 / editor: Wilbert J. Seed. — 1982. — 220p ; 16cm
Unpriced (pbk) B82-33397

Taylor, J. (James), *19---*. Ministry of J. Taylor Jr. — Kingston ([2 Teddington Rd., Kingston-upon-Thames,] KT1 4DX) : Bible & Gospel Trust
Vol. 140: Adelaide & Brisbane, January 1970 / editor: Wilbert J. Seed. — 1982. — 171p ; 16cm
Unpriced (pbk) B82-33398

Taylor, R.. Perseverance : meetings in London April 1981 / R. Taylor [et al.]. — London (50 Red Post Hill, SE24 9JQ) : Burr, 1981. — 177p ; 17cm
£1.40 (pbk) B82-10983

The **Unfolding** of the truth : meeting in Melbourne, January 1981 / A.J.E. Welch. — London (50 Red Post Hill SE24 9JO) : E.C. Burr, [1981]. — 141p ; 17cm
Unpriced (pbk) B82-25234

230'.99 — Brethren. Christian doctrine — ***Serials***

Christian Brethren review : the journal of the Christian Brethren Research Fellowship. — No.31/32 (Feb. 1982)-. — Berkhamsted (c/o Dr J. Boyes, 13 The Meads, Northchurch, Berkhamsted, Herts. HP4 3QX) : The Fellowship ; Exeter : Paternoster Press [distributor], 1982-. — v. ; 21cm
Irregular. — Spine title: Christian Brethren review journal. — Continues: CBRF
ISSN 0263-466x = Christian Brethren review (corrected) : £3.50 B82-25480

230'.99 — Church of Jesus Christ on Earth by the Prophet Simon Kimbangu. Christian doctrine

Out of Africa : Kimbanguism / with introductory chapters by Peter Manicom. — London : Christian Education Movement, 1979. — 66p : 1port ; 21cm. — (CEM student theology series)
Mainly a statement of the theology of the Church of Jesus Christ on Earth by the Prophet Simon Kimbangu, written by Joseph Diangienda and translated from the French
ISBN 0-905022-55-6 (pbk) : Unpriced
B82-35652

230'.99 — Salvation Army. Christian doctrine

The **Doctrine** we adorn. — London : The Salvation Army, 1982. — 142p ; 19cm
ISBN 0-85412-387-3 (pbk) : Unpriced
B82-39772

231 — CHRISTIAN DOCTRINE. GOD

231 — Bible. O.T. Special subjects: Christian doctrine. God. Hiddenness

Balentine, Samuel E.. The hidden God. — Oxford : Oxford University Press, Dec.1982. — [192]p. — (Oxford theological monographs)
ISBN 0-19-826719-3 : £13.50 : CIP entry
B82-29624

231 — Bible. O.T.. Special subjects: God — ***Expositions***

Schmidt, Werner H.. The faith of the Old Testament. — Oxford : Blackwell, Jan.1983. — [320]p
Translation of: Alttestamentlicher Glaube in seiner Geschichte
ISBN 0-631-13177-9 : £15.00 : CIP entry
B82-32517

231 — Christian doctrine. God

Beasley-Murray, George. The coming of God. — Exeter : Paternoster, Oct.1982. — [64]p
ISBN 0-85364-350-4 (pbk) : £1.20 : CIP entry
B82-25088

231 — Christian doctrine. God *continuation*

Boulding, Maria. The coming of God. — London : SPCK, Oct.1982. — [192]p
ISBN 0-281-04009-5 (pbk) : £4.95 : CIP entry B82-23472

Hartshorne, Charles. The divine relativity. — London : Yale University Press, July 1982. — [164]p
Originally published: 1948
ISBN 0-300-02880-6 (pbk) : £3.95 : CIP entry B82-22781

Moreland, David. God. — London : Darton Longman & Todd, July 1982. — [64]p
ISBN 0-232-51465-8 (pbk) : £1.95 : CIP entry B82-18563

Sidebottom, E. M.. Good news of God. — London : Darton Longman & Todd, June 1982. — [176]p
ISBN 0-232-51564-6 (pbk) : £6.50 : CIP entry B82-18564

Welch, Charles H.. Is God a person : the Bible's answer / by Charles H. Welch. — Rev. ed. — London (52a Wilson St., EC2A 2ER) : Berean Publishing, 1978. — 60p ; 21cm
Previous ed.: 1964
Unpriced (pbk) B82-34761

231'.044 — Christian doctrine. Trinity

Adam, Peter. Living the Trinity / by Peter Adam. — Bramcote : Grove, 1982. — 20p ; 22cm. — (Grove spirituality series, ISSN 0262-799x ; no.1)
Bibliography: p20
ISBN 0-907536-17-4 (pbk) : £0.70 B82-24287

231'.3 — Bible. N.T.. Special subjects: Christian doctrine. Holy Spirit — *Expositions*

Wiley, John, *1947-*. The spirit of the risen Lord / John Wiley. — London : Catholic Truth Society, 1981. — 10p ; 19cm. — (CTS ; Do 532)
ISBN 0-85183-438-8 (pbk) : £0.25 B82-08483

231'.3 — Bible. Special subjects: Christian doctrine. Holy Spirit — *Expositions*

Allen, Stuart. Pentecost / by Stuart Allen. — Rev. ed. — London : Berean Publishing, 1977. — 27p ; 21cm
Previous ed.: Sulhamstead : H. Joy, 1939
ISBN 0-85156-068-7 (pbk) : Unpriced B82-35171

231'.3 — Christian doctrine. Holy Spirit

Poonen, Zac. Radiating His glory : the spirit-filled life / Zac Poonen. — Eastbourne : Kingsway, 1982. — 87p : ill ; 18cm
ISBN 0-86065-165-7 (pbk) : £1.25 B82-19356

231'.3 — Christian doctrine. Holy Spirit — *Devotional works*

Marshall, Catherine. The helper / Catherine Marshall. — London : Hodder and Stoughton, 1978 (1980 [printing]). — 192p ; 18cm. — (Hodder Christian paperbacks)
Originally published: Lincoln, Va. : Chosen Books ; London : Hodder and Stoughton, 1978
ISBN 0-340-25693-1 (pbk) : £1.25 : CIP rev. B80-10937

231'.4 — Bible. Special subjects: Christian doctrine. Refuge — *Expositions*

Welch, Charles H.. The eternal God is thy refuge : studies designed to encourage the believer in times of stress / by Charles H. Welch. — [London] ([52a Wilson St., EC2A 2ER]) : [Berean Publishing], [1980?]. — 16p ; 21cm
Cover title
Unpriced (pbk) B82-35960

231'.6 — Christian doctrine. God. Love

Bernard, *of Clairvaux, Saint*. On the love of God = De diligendo Deo / Saint Bernard. — London : Mowbray, 1950, c1961 (1982 [printing]). — 94p ; 14cm
ISBN 0-264-66837-5 (pbk) : £1.50 B82-28940

231.7 — Christian doctrine. God. Relationship with man — *Latvian texts*

Cirsis, Pēteris. Viss mans — tavs / Peteris Cirsis. — Londonā ([Southwell House, 39 Fitzjohn's Ave. N.W.3]) : Autora uzdevoms
Otra 2 : Cilvēkam tuvais Dievs. — 1981. — 306p ; 22cm
Unpriced B82-20969

231.7'2 — Bible. Special subjects: Christian doctrine. Kingdom of God

Gray, John, *1913-*. The biblical doctrine of the reign of God / by John Gray. — Edinburgh : T. & T. Clark, 1979. — xiii,401p ; 23cm
Includes index
ISBN 0-567-09300-x : Unpriced B82-24186

231.7'2 — Bible. Special subjects: Christian doctrine. Kingdom of God — *Expositions*

Welch, Charles H.. Strangers and sojourners with me / C.H. Welch. — London : Berean Publishing, 1965 (1979 [printing]). — 18p ; 21cm
Cover title
ISBN 0-85156-052-0 (pbk) : Unpriced B82-35178

231.7'3 — Mexico. Guadalupe Hidalgo. Mary, *Mother of Jesus Christ*. Manifestations: Our Lady of Guadalupe

Johnston, Francis. The wonder of Guadalupe : the origin and cult of the miraculous image of the Blessed Virgin in Mexico / by Francis Johnston. — Chulmleigh : Augustine Publishing, 1981. — 143p : ill,1port ; 21cm
Text on inside covers. — Bibliography: p141. — Includes index
ISBN 0-85172-729-8 (pbk) : Unpriced B82-22013

231.7'3'01 — Christians. Miracles. Theories, *1000-1215*

Ward, Benedicta. Miracles and the medieval mind. — London : Scolar Press, June 1982. — [336]p
ISBN 0-85967-609-9 : £15.00 : CIP entry B82-11123

231.7'4 — Bible. Special subjects: Christian doctrine. Revelation

Englezakis, Benedict. New and old in God's revelation. — Cambridge : Clarke, July 1982. — [128]p
ISBN 0-227-67755-2 : £9.95 : CIP entry B82-21765

231.7'4 — Christian doctrine. Revelation

Abraham, William J.. Divine revelation and the limits of historical criticism / William J. Abraham. — Oxford : Oxford University Press, 1982. — 222p ; 23cm
Includes index
ISBN 0-19-826665-0 : £13.50 : CIP rev. B82-07517

231.7'45 — Christian doctrine. Prophecy

The **Burden** of prophecy / edited by Neil McIlwraith. — Birmingham : SCM, 1982. — 81p : 1ill ; 21cm. — (Studies in prophecy ; no.1)
ISBN 0-906359-14-7 (pbk) : £0.75 B82-15993

Gill, Robin. Prophecy and praxis. — London : Marshall Morgan & Scott, Nov.1981. — [144] p. — (Contemporary Christian studies)
ISBN 0-551-00918-7 (pbk) : £5.95 : CIP entry B81-34215

231.7'65 — Christian doctrine. Creation *related to* theories of evolution of organisms

Newell, Norman D.. Creation and evolution : myth or reality? / Norman D. Newell. — New York ; Guildford : Columbia University Press, 1982. — xxxii,201p : ill,maps ; 24cm. — (Convergence)
Bibliography: p201
ISBN 0-231-05348-7 : £14.40 B82-32688

231'.8 — Bible. N.T. Special subjects: Suffering

Suffering and martyrdom in the New Testament : studies presented to G.M. Styler by the Cambridge New Testament Seminar / edited by William Horbury and Brian McNeil. — Cambridge : Cambridge University Press, 1981. — xxi,217p ; 23cm
Includes index
ISBN 0-521-23482-4 : £17.50 : CIP rev.
Also classified at 272'.1 B81-19191

231'.8 — Catholic Church. Christian doctrine. God. Mercy

John Paul II, *Pope*. Dives in misericordia : encyclical letter of the supreme Pontiff John Paul II on the mercy of God. — Abbots Langley (74 Gallows Hill La., Abbots Langley, Herts. WD5 0BZ) : Infoform, [1980]. — 87p ; 22cm
Translation of: Dives in misericordia. — Originally published: London : Catholic Truth Society, 1980
Unpriced (unbound) B82-21931

John Paul II, *Pope*. Dives in misericordia : encyclical letter of the supreme Pontiff John Paul II on the mercy of God / [translation Vatican Polyglot Press]. — London : Catholic Truth Society, 1980. — 83p ; 19cm
Translated from the Latin. — Cover title
ISBN 0-85183-399-3 (pbk) : £0.75 B82-17395

231'.8 — Christian doctrine. Theodicy — *Philosophical perspectives*

Encountering evil : live options in theodicy / Stephen T. Davis, editor ; [contributions by] John B. Cobb, Jr ... [et al.]. — Edinburgh : T. & T. Clark, c1981. — 182p ; 23cm
ISBN 0-567-29107-3 (pbk) : £3.95 B82-15366

231'.8 — Suffering — *Christian viewpoints*

Endersbee, Mary. Suffering : a Christian response / by Mary Endersbee. — London : Mowbray, 1981. — 30p ; 15cm. — (Enquirer's library)
Bibliography: p30
ISBN 0-264-66745-x (pbk) : £0.60 B82-02106

Graham, Billy. Till Armageddon. — London : Hodder & Stoughton, Jan.1983. — [224]p
Originally published: 1981
ISBN 0-340-32644-1 (pbk) : £1.75 : CIP entry B82-36313

231'.8 — Suffering — *Christian viewpoints — Early works — Facsimiles*

Tritheim, Johann von. A three-fold mirrour of mans vanitie and miserie 1633 / Johann von Tritheim. — Ilkley : Scolar, 1978. — 364p ; 20cm. — (English recusant literature, 1558-1640 ; 386)
Facsim. of: ed. published Doway : Lawrence Kellam, 1633
ISBN 0-85967-505-x : Unpriced B82-35410

232 — JESUS CHRIST

232 — Bible. N.T. Gospels. Special subjects: Jesus Christ

Vermes, Geza. The Gospel of Jesus the Jew / by Geza Vermes. — Newcastle-upon-Tyne : University of Newcastle-upon-Tyne, 1981. — viii,64p ; 21cm. — (The Riddell memorial lectures ; 48th series)
Lectures delivered at the University of Newcastle upon Tyne on 17, 18 and 19 March 1981. — Bibliography: p60-64
ISBN 0-7017-0029-7 (pbk) : Unpriced B82-22036

232 — Bible. N.T. Gospels. Special subjects: Jesus Christ. Names: Son of Man — *Expositions*

Lindars, Barnabas. Jesus Son of Man. — London : SPCK, Feb.1983. — [256]p
ISBN 0-281-04016-8 : £12.50 : CIP entry B82-37863

232 — Bible. N.T.. Special subjects: Christian doctrine. Jesus Christ — *Expositions*

Beer, John S.. Who is Jesus? / John S. Beer. — Guildford : Lutterworth, 1982. — 56p ; 19cm. — (Anselm books)
ISBN 0-7188-2516-0 (pbk) : £0.95 B82-13125

232 — Christology

Stanton, Graham N.. Who is Jesus? / by Graham N. Stanton. — London (2 Chester House, Pages La., N10 1PR) : Christian Education Movement, [1982?]. — 4leaves ; 30cm. — (Occasional paper ; 1)
Originally published: King's Theological Review, 111, 1, Spring 1980
Unpriced (unbound) B82-34130

232 — Christology — *Festschriften*

Christ the Lord. — Leicester : Inter-Varsity Press, Sept.1982. — [320]p
ISBN 0-85111-744-9 : £8.50 : CIP entry B82-20494

232 — Jesus Christ

Day, David, *1936-*. This Jesus — / David Day. — 2nd ed. — Leicester : Inter-Varsity, 1981. — 113p ; 18cm
Previous ed: 1980
ISBN 0-85110-429-0 (pbk) : £1.25 B82-32242

Marsh, John. Who does he think he is?. — Leicester : Inter-Varsity Press, Sept.1982. — [64]p
ISBN 0-85110-441-x (pbk) : £0.95 : CIP entry B82-20493

Sanders, J. Oswald. The incomparable Christ : the person and work of Jesus / J. Oswald Sanders. — London : Triangle, 1982. — 256p : ill ; 1982
Originally published: London : Marshall, Morgan and Scott, 1971
ISBN 0-281-03845-7 : £1.95 B82-24372

Wiley, John, *1947-*. Who was Jesus Christ? / John Wiley. — London : Catholic Truth Society, 1981. — 11p ; 19cm
Cover title
ISBN 0-85183-437-x (pbk) : £0.30 B82-08299

Winter, David. The search for the real Jesus / David Winter. — London : Hodder and Stoughton, c1982. — 156p ; 20cm. — (Ecclesia books)
Bibliography: p150
ISBN 0-340-26932-4 (pbk) : £4.50 : CIP rev. B82-10011

232 — Jesus Christ — *Devotional works*

John Paul II, *Pope*. Sign of contradiction / Karol Wojtyla, Pope John Paul II. — London : Hodder and Stoughton, 1980, c1979. — xii,206p ; 18cm
Translation of: Segno di contraddizione. — Originally published: Slough : St Paul Publications, 1979
ISBN 0-340-24700-2 (pbk) : £1.40 : CIP rev. B80-01029

232 — Jesus Christ — *For children*

Tell us about Jesus / [illustrations T. Dessaut] ; [translation Helen M. Wynne]. — Slough : St. Paul, 1981. — 141p : col.ill,maps ; 22cm
Translation of: Parlez-nous de Jesus
ISBN 0-85439-193-2 (pbk) : Unpriced B82-08899

232 — Jesus Christ — *For schools*

Shannon, Trevor. Jesus / Trevor Shannon. — Guildford : Lutterworth Educational, [c1982]. — 32p : ill,1map,1plan,ports ; 30cm. — (The Chichester project ; 4)
Text on inside covers. — Bibliography on inside back cover
ISBN 0-7188-2498-9 (pbk) : Unpriced B82-20338

232'.092'2 — Christian doctrine. Jesus Christ. Theories of Origen *compared with* **theories of Teilhard de Chardin, Pierre**

Lyons, J. A.. The cosmic Christ in Origen and Teilhard de Chardin : a comparative study / by J.A. Lyons. — Oxford : Oxford University Press, 1982. — x,236p ; 23cm
Bibliography: p222-231. — Includes index
ISBN 0-19-826721-5 : Unpriced : CIP rev. B81-34381

232'.1 — Armenian Apostolic Orthodox Church. Christian doctrine. Jesus Christ. Incarnation. Book of letters — *Critical studies*

Frivold, Leif. The Incarnation : a study of the doctrine of the Incarnation in the Armenian Church in the 5th and 6th centuries according to the Book of Letters / Leif Frivold. — Oslo : Universitetsforlaget ; London : Global Book [distributor], c1981. — 236p : facsims ; 22cm
Includes Armenian text with English translation. — Bibliography: p227-232. — Includes index
ISBN 82-00-05684-8 (pbk) : £10.85 B82-01025

232'.1 — Jesus Christ. Incarnation

Dunn, James D. G.. Christology in the making : a New Testament inquiry into the origins of the doctrine of the incarnation / James D.G. Dunn. — London : SCM Press, 1980. — xvii,443p ; 23cm
Bibliography: p354-403. — Includes index
ISBN 0-334-00237-0 (pbk) : £10.50 B82-05865

God incarnate : story and belief / edited by A.E. Harvey. — London : SPCK, 1981. — viii,104p ; 22cm
Includes index
ISBN 0-281-03832-5 (pbk) : £3.95 B82-08184

Haughton, Rosemary. The passionate God / Rosemary Haughton. — [New] ed. — London : Darton, Longman and Todd, 1982, c1981. — 344p ; 22cm
Previous ed.: 1981. — Bibliography: p336-337. — Includes index
ISBN 0-232-51567-0 (pbk) : £8.95 : CIP rev.
Primary classification 232'.5 B82-05384

232'.3 — Christian doctrine. Atonement

Wallace, Ronald. The atoning death of Christ. — London : Marshall, Morgan & Scott, July 1981. — [160]p. — (Foundations for faith)
ISBN 0-551-00855-5 (pbk) : £4.95 : CIP entry B81-20597

232'.4 — Bible. Special subjects: Jesus Christ. Sacrifice — *Questions & answers*

Parker, R. G.. The importance of Christ's sufferings / R.G. Parker. — Birmingham (47, Woodbridge Rd, Moseley, Birmingham B13 9DZ) : R.G. Parker, [1982]. — 7leaves ; 30cm
Unpriced (unbound) B82-31777

232'.5 — Jesus Christ. Resurrection

Derrett, J. Duncan M.. The Anastasis : the Resurrection of Jesus as an historical event / by J. Duncan M. Derrett. — Shipston-on-Stour : P. Drinkwater, 1982. — xiv,166p ; 23cm
Bibliography: p143-153. — Includes index
ISBN 0-9505751-9-4 (pbk) : £5.00 B82-35831

Green, Michael,. The day death died / Michael Green. — Leicester : Inter-Varsity, 1982. — 96p ; 18cm
ISBN 0-85110-438-x (pbk) : Unpriced : CIP rev. B82-01728

Haughton, Rosemary. The passionate God / Rosemary Haughton. — [New] ed. — London : Darton, Longman and Todd, 1982, c1981. — 344p ; 22cm
Previous ed.: 1981. — Bibliography: p336-337. — Includes index
ISBN 0-232-51567-0 (pbk) : £8.95 : CIP rev.
Also classified at 232'.1 B82-05384

Williams, Rowan. Resurrection : interpreting the Easter gospel / Rowan Williams. — London : Darton, Longman & Todd, 1982. — ix,129p ; 22cm
Includes index
ISBN 0-232-51546-8 : £4.75 : CIP rev. B82-06494

232'.6 — Jesus Christ. Second coming

Preparation for the latter rain : quotations from the Spirit of Prophecy / compiled by B.E. Wagner. — [Great Britain?] : [B.E. Wagner?], 1981?]. — 32p ; 22cm
Cover title
Unpriced (pbk) B82-12100

Sanders, J. Oswald. Certainties of Christ's Second Coming / J. Oswald Sanders. — Eastbourne : Kingsway, 1982, c1977. — 128p ; 18cm
Originally published: Philippines : OMF, c1977
ISBN 0-86065-180-0 (pbk) : £1.35 B82-29474

Travis, Stephen. I believe in the second coming of Jesus. — London : Hodder & Stoughton, Feb.1982. — [256]p
ISBN 0-340-27164-7 (pbk) : £4.95 : CIP entry B81-36354

232'.6 — Jesus Christ. Second coming — *Occult viewpoints* — *Serials*

[Wayfarer *(Lodge of the Star)*]. The Wayfarer : Lodge of the Star newsletter. — Issue no.1-. — Brentwood (57, Warescot Rd., Brentwood, Essex CM15 9HH) : The Lodge, 1982-. — v. ; 30cm
Quarterly
ISSN 0263-127X = Wayfarer (Lodge of the Star) : Unpriced B82-32178

232'.8 — Bible. Special subjects: Jesus Christ. Humanity — *Expositions*

Pollard, T. E.. Fullness of humanity : Christ's humanness and ours / T.E. Pollard. — Sheffield : Almond, 1982. — 126p ; 23cm. — (The Croall lectures ; 1980)
Includes index
ISBN 0-907459-10-2 (cased) : £9.95 : CIP rev.
ISBN 0-907459-11-0 (pbk) : £5.95 B82-10900

232'.8 — Bible. Special subjects: Jesus Christ. Lordship — *Expositions*

Chrisope, T. Alan. Jesus is Lord : a study in the unity of confessing Jesus as Lord and Saviour in the New Testament / T. Alan Chrisope. — Welwyn : Evangelical Press, 1982. — 112p ; 20cm
Bibliography: p96-101
ISBN 0-85234-160-1 (pbk) : £1.95 B82-37448

232'.8 — Jesus Christ. Divinity

Drain, John. The deity of the Lord Jesus Christ / [by John Drain]. — Bromley (6, Georgian Close, Bromley, Kent) : Hayes Press, [1982?]. — 12p ; 15cm
Unpriced (pbk) B82-21475

Welch, Charles H.. The deity of Christ / by Charles H. Welch. — Rev. ed. — London : Berean Publishing, 1977. — 53p ; 21cm
Previous ed.: 1949
ISBN 0-85156-031-8 (pbk) : Unpriced B82-34758

232.9'01 — Jesus Christ — *Biographies*

Stewart, Desmond. The foreigner : a search for the first-century Jesus / Desmond Stewart. — London : Hamilton, 1981. — x,181p : 3maps ; 24cm
Bibliography: p168-169. — Includes index
ISBN 0-241-10686-9 : £9.95 : CIP rev. B81-26779

Turrall-Clarke, Robert. A life of Jesus Christ / Robert Turrall-Clarke. — [Cambridge] : Cambridge Academic, 1981. — vi,151p ; 21cm
Cover title
ISBN 0-907971-00-8 (pbk) : Unpriced B82-18038

232.9'01 — Jesus Christ — *Biographies* — *For children*

Dickens, Charles, *1812-1870*. The life of our Lord / written expressly for his children by Charles Dickens. — Philadelphia : Westminster ; London : Associated Newspapers, 1981. — 127p : ill,2facsims ; 25cm
Facsim. of: ed. published 1934
ISBN 0-85969-352-x : Unpriced B82-08180

The story of Jesus : retold for young children / illustrations by Gwen Green. — Maidenhead : Purnell, 1981. — 45p : col.ill ; 27cm
ISBN 0-361-05069-0 : £2.99 B82-00719

232.9′01 — Jesus Christ — *Biographies — Stories for children*

Ashley, Elizabeth. A child′s stories of Jesus / written by Elizabeth Ashley ; illustrated by Anna Dzierzek. — London : Dean, 1978 (1981 [printing]). — [27]p : col.ill ; 32cm. — (An Everyday picture book)
ISBN 0-603-08501-6 : Unpriced B82-29680

Kent, David. The last journey / by David Kent ; illustrated by Gwen Green, Francis Phillips and Martin Reiner. — London : Pan, 1981. — 22p : col.ill ; 22cm. — (Bible stories) (A Piccolo explorer book)
Includes index
ISBN 0-330-26560-1 (pbk) : £0.85 B82-08130

Kent, David. Miracles and parables / David Kent ; illustrated by Gwen Green ... [et al.]. — London : Pan, 1981. — 21p : col.ill ; 22cm. — (Bible stories) (A Piccolo explorer book)
Includes index
ISBN 0-330-26561-x (pbk) : £0.85 B82-08129

Kent, David. Miracles and parables / David Kent ; illustrated by Gwen Green ... [et al.]. — London : Kingfisher, 1981. — 21p : col.ill ; 23cm. — (Kingfisher explorer books. Bible stories ; bk.5)
Includes index
ISBN 0-86272-021-4 : £1.95 : CIP rev.
B81-27977

Tallach, Isobel. The life of Jesus : for the very young / by Isobel Tallach ; illustrated by Lawrence Littleton Evans. — Edinburgh : Banner of Truth Trust, 1982. — [32]p : col.ill ; 21cm
ISBN 0-85151-345-x (pbk) : £0.85 B82-22585

232.9′01 — Jesus Christ. Local associations: Mediterranean region

Bruce, F. F.. Places they knew : Jesus and Paul / F.F. Bruce. — London : Ark, 1981. — 128p : ill(some col.),maps(some col.),plans ; 28cm
Spine title. — Includes index
ISBN 0-86201-110-8 : £5.95
Also classified at 225.9′24 B82-05602

232.9′04 — Jesus Christ. Discipleship

Hengel, Martin. The charismatic leader and his followers / by Martin Hengel ; translated by James C.G. Greig ; edited by John Riches. — Edinburgh : T. & T. Clark, 1981. — xiii,111p ; 22cm. — (Studies of the New Testament and its world)
Translation of: Nachfolge und Charisma. — Bibliography: p93-94. — Includes index
ISBN 0-567-03001-6 : £7.95 B82-08791

232.9′08 — Jesus Christ. Historicity

Harvey, A. E.. Jesus and the constraints of history / A.E. Harvey. — London : Duckworth, 1982. — 184p ; 24cm. — (The Bampton lectures ; 1980)
Includes index
ISBN 0-7156-1597-1 : £7.50 : CIP rev.
B81-36394

232.9′08 — Jesus Christ. Historicity — *For schools*

Chappell, K. R.. Investigating Jesus / K.R. Chappell. — London : Edward Arnold, 1982. — vi,74p : ill,facsims,1map ; 25cm
Bibliography: p74
ISBN 0-7131-0638-7 (pbk) : Unpriced : CIP rev. B82-01186

232.91 — Catholic Church. Christian doctrine. Mary, *Mother of Jesus Christ*

McNamara, Kevin. Mary, the Mother of God / Kevin McNamara. — London : Catholic Truth Society, 1982. — 21p ; 19cm. — (The Teaching of Pope John Paul II)
ISBN 0-85183-478-7 (pbk) : £0.45 B82-26911

232.91 — Christian doctrine. Mary, *Mother of Jesus Christ*

Mary′s place in Christian dialogue : occasional papers of the Ecumenical Society of the Blessed Virgin Mary 1970-1980 / edited by Alberic Stacpoole. — Slough : St. Paul, 1982. — xvi,281p ; 23cm
ISBN 0-85439-201-7 : £1.00 B82-26802

232.91 — Mary, *Mother of Jesus Christ — Biographies — Stories for children*

Butcher, Geoffrey. Mary — the mother of Jesus. — London : Hodder & Stoughton, Feb.1983. — 1v.. — (First Bible stories)
ISBN 0-340-28702-0 (pbk) : £0.60 : CIP entry
B82-38039

232.91 — Mary, *Mother of Jesus Christ — Devotional works*

Nassan, Maurice. More meditations on Mary / Maurice Nassan. — London : Catholic Truth Society, 1982. — 32p ; 17cm
ISBN 0-85183-482-5 (pbk) : £0.40 B82-33842

Robinson, Gweneth E.. The joy of Mary : a vision / Gweneth E. Robinson. — Holsworthy : Unity Teaching and Healing Trust, c1981. — 31p : ill ; 22cm
ISBN 0-907707-00-9 (pbk) : Unpriced
B82-01529

232.9′21 — Jesus Christ. Nativity — *Dramatisations — For schools*

Murcott, Peter. Closer than you think / by Peter Murcott ; freely adapted from an old Russian Christmas story. — Ilkeston : Moorley′s, [1981]. — 20p : music ; 21cm
ISBN 0-86071-124-2 (pbk) : Unpriced
B82-00598

232.9′21 — Jesus Christ. Nativity — *Stories for children*

[Bible. N.T. Gospels. *English. Selections. 1982*]. Jesus is born / illustrated by Gordon Stowell. — London : Scripture Union, 1982. — [23]p : col.ill ; 10cm. — (Little fish books about Jesus)
Text on inside cover
ISBN 0-85421-963-3 (pbk) : Unpriced
B82-37185

The **Christmas** pageant / illustrated by Tomie de Paola ; text [retold] from the stories of Matthew and Luke. — London : Fontana, 1981, c1978. — [32]p : col.ill ; 16x21cm. — (Picture lions)
Originally published: Minneapolis : Winston, 1978 ; London : Methuen, 1979
ISBN 0-00-661878-2 (pbk) : £0.90 B82-03192

Passmore, Aileen E.. My baby Jesus pop-up book / [written by Aileen E. Passmore] ; [illustrations by Janet & Anne Grahame Johnstone]. — London : Dean, c1982, c1970. — [8]p : col.ill ; 24cm
Cover title. — Text and ill on lining papers
ISBN 0-603-02027-5 : Unpriced B82-25975

Vries, C. M. de. When Jesus was born / [illustrations by Anna-Hermine Müller] ; [Dutch text by C.M. de Vries] ; [English text adapted by Felicity Clayton Smith]. — 1st English ed. — Tring : Lion, 1982. — [18]p : col.ill ; 20cm. — (A Bible Story picture-book)
Translation of: Zij vonden het kind. — Text, ill on lining papers
ISBN 0-85648-137-8 : £0.95 B82-36905

Williams-Ellis, Virginia. The baby Jesus / [story retold by Virginia Williams-Ellis] ; [illustrated by Anna Dzierzek]. — London : Dean, c1981. — [10]p : col.ill ; 21cm. — (A Dean board book)
ISBN 0-603-00240-4 : Unpriced B82-26662

232.9′23 — Bible. N.T.. Magi — *Stories, anecdotes*

Traynor-Moravska, Stella. The story of the Three Kings / Stella Traynor-Moravska. — Bognor Regis : New Horizon, c1981. — 54p,[10]leaves of plates : ill ; 21cm
ISBN 0-86116-516-0 : £3.25 B82-09557

232.9′23 — Star of Bethlehem. Theories

Hughes, David, *1941-*. The star of Bethlehem mystery / David Hughes. — [London] : Corgi, 1981, c1979. — 253p : ill,2maps ; 18cm
Originally published: London : Dent, 1979. — Bibliography: p235-241. — Includes index
ISBN 0-552-11842-7 (pbk) : £1.75 B82-08042

232.9′4 — Bible. N.T.. John, *the Baptist, Saint — Stories for children*

Butcher, Geoffrey. John — the story of the Baptist. — London : Hodder & Stoughton, Feb.1983. — 1v.. — (First Bible stories)
ISBN 0-340-28701-2 (pbk) : £0.60 : CIP entry
B82-38038

232.9′54 — Jesus Christ. Teachings — *Expositions*

Neil, William. More difficult sayings of Jesus / William Neil and Stephen H. Travis. — London : Mowbray, 1981. — vi,128p ; 30cm. — (Mowbray′s Christian studies)
ISBN 0-264-66552-x (pbk) : £2.25 B82-18194

232.9′54 — Jesus Christ. Teachings — *Stories for children*

[Bible. N.T. Gospels. *English. Selections. 1982*]. Jesus loves / illustrated by Gordon Stowell. — London : Scripture Union, 1982. — [23]p : col.ill ; 10cm. — (Little fish books about Jesus)
Text on inside cover
ISBN 0-85421-966-8 (pbk) : Unpriced
B82-37181

232.9′6 — Catholics. Christian life. Prayer. Stations of the Cross — *Devotional works*

Freeman-Grenville, G. S. P.. The Stations of the Cross. — London : East-West Publications, Apr.1982. — [32]p
ISBN 0-85692-083-5 (pbk) : £1.50 : CIP entry
B82-06054

232.9′6 — Jesus Christ. Passion *compared with* **tragedy in literature**

Anderson, David, *1919-*. The passion of man in gospel and literature / David Anderson. — [London] : BRF, 1980. — 104p ; 20cm. — (BRF book club ; no.8)
Includes index
ISBN 0-900164-53-0 (pbk) : £1.75
Also classified at 809′.916 B82-15085

232.9′62 — Jesus Christ. Trial

Gray, Alastair H.. The trial of Jesus / Alastair H. Gray. — [Methil] ([The Manse, 14 Methilbrae, Methil, Fife]) : [A.H. Gray], [1981]. — 7p : ill ; 20cm
Unpriced (unbound) B82-29206

232.9′63 — Jesus Christ. Crucifixion — *Meditations*

Murray, Andrew. The secret of the cross. — London : Marshall, Morgan & Scott, Feb.1982. — [32]p. — (The Secret series)
ISBN 0-551-00934-9 (pbk) : £6.00 : CIP entry
B82-07800

232.9′7 — Jesus Christ. Post-resurrection appearances

Moore, T. V.. The last days of Jesus : the appearances of our Lord during the forty days between the Resurrection and Ascension / T.V. Moore. — Edinburgh : Banner of Truth Trust, 1981. — 212p ; 19cm
Originally published: 1858
ISBN 0-85151-321-2 (pbk) : £1.95 B82-12885

232.9′7 — Jesus Christ. Resurrection — *Stories for children*

[Bible. N.T. Gospels. John XX, 1-18. *English. 1982*]. Jesus lives! / illustrated by Gordon Stowell. — London : Scripture Union, 1982. — [23]p : col.ill ; 10cm. — (Little fish books about Jesus)
Text on inside cover
ISBN 0-85421-970-6 (pbk) : Unpriced
B82-37186

233 — CHRISTIAN DOCTRINE. HUMANKIND

233 — Christian doctrine. Man

Balthasar, Hans Urs von. Man in history : a theological study / Hans Urs von Balthasar. — London : Sheed and Ward, 1968 (1982 [printing]). — 341p ; 22cm. — (Stagbooks)
Translation of: Das Ganze im Fragment. — Includes index
ISBN 0-7220-5218-9 (pbk) : £9.50 B82-32766

Gosden, Vernon J.. All the power you need / Vernon J. Gosden. — London : Japan Evangelistic Band, c1977. — 48p ; 19cm
ISBN 0-902846-08-6 (pbk) : £0.50 B82-17186

233′.1 — Christian doctrine. Creation

Torrance, Thomas F.. Divine and contingent order. — Oxford : Oxford University Press, Sept.1981. — [144]p
ISBN 0-19-826658-8 : £9.50 : CIP entry
B81-21609

233′.11′05 — Christian doctrine. Creation — *Serials*

[Rainbow *(Glasgow)***]**. Rainbow : an easily read and understood contribution to the creation and evolution debate. — No.1 (Oct. 1981)-. — Glasgow (51 Cloan Cres., Bishopbriggs, Glasgow G64 2HN) : Biblical Creation Society, 1981-. — v. ; 21cm
ISSN 0262-5466 = Rainbow (Glasgow) : Unpriced B82-06176

233′.5′0924 — Christian doctrine. Humanity. Theories of Barth, Karl

McLean, Stuart D.. Humanity in the thought of Karl Barth / by Stuart D. McLean. — Edinburgh : T & T Clark, c1981. — viii,202p ; 23cm
Includes index
ISBN 0-567-09304-2 : £5.95 B82-19726

233′.7 — Christian doctrine. Freedom

Bennett, John G.. The way to be free / J.G. Bennett. — New York : Weiser ; Ripon : Coombe Springs Press [distributor], 1980. — 196p ; 21cm
ISBN 0-87728-491-1 (pbk) : £3.95 B82-36187

234 — CHRISTIAN DOCTRINE. SALVATION AND GRACE

234 — Christian doctrine. Assurance

Griffiths, Michael, *1928-*. How can I be sure? / Michael C. Griffiths. — 2nd ed. — Leicester : Inter-Varsity Press, c1980. — 47p ; 18cm
Previous ed.: published as Christian assurance. London : Inter-Varsity Fellowship, 1962
ISBN 0-85110-244-1 (pbk) : £0.65 : CIP rev.
B80-21361

234 — Christian doctrine. Holiness

Aumann, Jordan. Spiritual theology / Jordan Aumann. — London : Sheed and Ward, c1980 (1982 [printing]). — 441p ; 22cm. — (Stagbooks)
ISBN 0-7220-8518-4 (pbk) : £9.50 B82-32763

Häring, Bernard. Called to holiness / Bernard Häring. — Slough : St Paul, 1982. — 73p ; 21cm
ISBN 0-85439-199-1 (pbk) : £1.95 B82-15082

Marshall, Walter. Gospel mystery of sanctification / Walter Marshall. — [Welwyn] : [Evangelical], [1981]. — 257p ; 22cm
Originally published: London : s.n., 1692
ISBN 0-85234-158-x (pbk) : Unpriced
B82-24170

234 — Christian doctrine. Salvation

Welch, Charles H.. Things that accompany salvation : Hebrews 6:9 / [Charles H. Welch]. — London (52a Wilson St., EC2A 2ER) : Berean Publishing, [1980?]. — [4]p ; 20cm
Unpriced (unbound) B82-35968

234′.12 — Christian church. Gifts of the Holy Spirit

Gray, Tony R.. You will have power / Tony R. Gray. — [Basingstoke] : [Olive Tree], [1978] ([1979 printing]). — 58p ; 19cm
Cover title
ISBN 0-906645-00-x (pbk) : Unpriced
B82-09089

234′.12 — Christian doctrine. Gifts of the Holy Spirit

Horabin, Peter R.. God's spiritual gifts / by Peter R. Horabin. — Brighton (65 Eastbrook Rd., Portslade, Brighton, Sussex) : Outreach for Jesus, 1981. — 91p ; 18cm
£1.50 (pbk) B82-14286

234′.16 — Christian doctrine. Sacraments

Lavery, Hugh. Sacraments. — London : Darton Longman & Todd, July 1982. — [96]p
ISBN 0-232-51504-2 (pbk) : £2.95 : CIP entry
B82-18562

234′.161 — Bible. Special subjects: Christian doctrine. Baptism

Allen, Stuart. Baptism / by Stuart Allen. — London (52a Wilson St., EC2A 2ER) : Berean Publishing, [198-?]. — 13p ; 21cm
Cover title
Unpriced (pbk) B82-34757

234′.5 — Bible. Special subjects: Christian doctrine. Reconciliation — *Expositions*

Welch, Charles H.. The reconciliation of all things / by Charles H. Welch. — London (52a Wilson St., EC2A 2ER) : Berean Publishing, [1980?]. — 48p ; 20cm
£0.15 (pbk) B82-35961

235 — CHRISTIAN DOCTRINE. SPIRITUAL BEINGS

235′.2 — Christian church. Saints. Veneration, *to 600*

Brown, Peter, *1935 July 26-*. The cult of the saints : its rise and function in Latin Christianity / Peter Brown. — London : SCM, 1981. — xv,187p ; 23cm
Includes index
ISBN 0-334-00285-0 : £6.95 B82-21325

235′.3 — Christian doctrine. Angels & principalities. Theories of Paul, *the Apostle, Saint*

Carr, Wesley. Angels and principalities : the background, meaning and development of the Pauline phrase hai archai kai hai exousiai / Wesley Carr. — Cambridge : Cambridge University Press, 1981. — xii,242p ; 23cm. — (Monograph series / Society for New Testament Studies)
Bibliography: p212-228. — Includes index
ISBN 0-521-23429-8 : £13.50 : CIP rev.
B81-32013

235′.47 — Christian doctrine. Satan

Russell, Jeffrey Burton. Satan : the early Christian tradition / Jeffrey Burton Russell. — Ithaca ; London : Cornell University Press, c1981. — 258p : ill,facsims ; 24cm
Bibliography: p242-252. — Includes index
ISBN 0-8014-1267-6 : £14.00 B82-11911

Welch, Charles H.. Satan : his snares, devices and goal : a brief examination of an exhaustive theme, intended as a warning as the day of Apostacy approaches / [C.H. Welch]. — London : Berean Publishing, 1968 (1980 [printing]). — 18p ; 21cm
ISBN 0-85156-079-2 (pbk) : Unpriced
B82-35179

236 — CHRISTIAN DOCTRINE. ESCHATOLOGY

236 — Apocalyptic literature, *to 200*

Rowland, Christopher. The open heaven : a study of apocalyptic in Judaism and early Christianity / Christopher Rowland. — London : SPCK, 1982. — xiii,562p ; 24cm
Bibliography: p520-545. — Includes index
ISBN 0-281-03784-1 : £22.50 B82-28851

236′.2 — Christian doctrine. Future life

MacGregor, Geddes. Reincarnation as a Christian hope / Geddes MacGregor. — London : Macmillan, 1982. — xi,161p ; 23cm. — (Library of philosophy and religion)
Includes index
ISBN 0-333-31986-9 : Unpriced B82-28426

236′.2 — Future life — *Christian viewpoints*

Rawlings, Maurice. Before death comes / Maurice S. Rawlings. — London : Sheldon, 1980. — 178p ; 22cm
ISBN 0-85969-324-4 (pbk) : £2.50
Also classified at 248.4 B82-13741

236′.3 — Christian doctrine. End of the world

Goetz, William. Apocalypse next / William Goetz. — Eastbourne : Kingsway, 1982, c1980. — 319p ; 18cm
Originally published: Beaverlodge, Alta. : Horizon House, 1980. — Bibliography: p315-318
ISBN 0-86065-179-7 (pbk) : £1.95 B82-28978

238 — CHRISTIAN DOCTRINE. CREEDS, CONFESSIONS OF FAITH, COVENANTS, CATECHISMS

238′.1 — Christian church. Creeds, *to ca 810*

Kelly, J. N. D.. Early Christian creeds / J.N.D. Kelly. — 3rd ed. — Harlow : Longman, 1972 (1981 [printing]). — xi,446p ; 22cm
Includes some Greek-English, Latin-English parallel text. — Previous ed.: 1960. — Bibliography: px. — Includes index
ISBN 0-582-49219-x (pbk) : £7.50 : CIP rev.
B81-30889

238′.11 — Apostles' Creed — *Expositions*

Day, Colin, *1948-*. I believe / Colin Day. — Eastbourne : Falcon, 1982. — 94p : ill ; 18cm
ISBN 0-86239-004-4 (pbk) : £1.25 B82-37089

McEwen, James S.. I believe — / James S. McEwen. — Edinburgh : The Saint Andrew Press, 1982. — 64p ; 20cm
ISBN 0-7152-0498-x (pbk) : £1.50 B82-19426

238′.42 — Germany. Reformed churches. Christian doctrine. Catechisms: Heidelberger Katechismus — *Critical studies*

Barth, Karl. [The Heidelberg Catechism for today]. Learning Jesus Christ through the Heidelberg catechism / Karl Barth ; translated by Shirley C. Guthrie, Jr. — Grand Rapids : Eerdmans ; Edinburgh : distributed by Clark, [1982], c1964. — 141p ; 21cm
Translation of: Die ehristliche Lehre nach dem Heidelberger Katechismus ; and, Einführung in den Heidelberger Katechismus. — Originally published: Richmond, Va. : John Knox ; London : Epworth, 1964
ISBN 0-8028-1893-5 (pbk) : £3.75 B82-41068

238′.52 — Presbyterian churches. Confessions of faith: Westminster Assembly, *(1643).* **Westminster Confession. Use,** *to 1980*

The **Westminster** Confession in the Church today : papers prepared for the Church of Scotland Panel on Doctrine / edited by Alasdair I.C. Heron. — Edinburgh : Saint Andrew Press, 1982. — vii,154p,1folded leaf : 1ill ; 22cm
Bibliography: p150-152
ISBN 0-7152-0497-1 : £4.00 B82-17180

239 — CHRISTIAN DOCTRINE. APOLOGETICS AND POLEMICS

239′.3 — Christian doctrine. Apologetics against pagans — *Early works*

Tatian. Oratio ad Graecos and fragments / Tatian ; edited and translated by Molly Whittaker. — Oxford : Clarendon Press, 1982. — xxv,92p ; 23cm. — (Oxford early Christian texts)
Parallel Greek text and English translation. — Bibliography : pxxiii-xxv. — Includes index
ISBN 0-19-826809-2 : £11.50 : CIP rev.
B82-15683

241 — CHRISTIANITY. MORAL THEOLOGY

241 — Bible. Special subjects: Ethics

Gerhardsson, Birger. The ethos of the Bible. — London : Darton Longman & Todd, Nov.1982. — [160]p
Translation of: Med hela ditt hjärta
ISBN 0-232-51579-4 (pbk) : £5.95 : CIP entry
B82-30340

241 — Christian ethics

Brown, David. Choices. — Oxford : Blackwell, Jan.1983. — [160]p. — (Faith and the future)
ISBN 0-631-13182-5 (cased) : £9.50 : CIP entry
ISBN 0-631-13222-8 (pbk) : £3.50 B82-32518

Field, David, *1921-*. Real questions / David Field & Peter Toon. — Tring : Lion, 1982. — 96p : ill(some col.) ; 25cm
ISBN 0-85648-347-8 : £4.95 B82-21323

Gustafson, James M.. Christ and the moral life / James M. Gustafson. — Chicago ; London : University of Chicago Press, 1979, c1968. — xi,275p ; 21cm. — (A Phoenix book)
Originally published: New York : Harper & Row, 1968. — Includes index
ISBN 0-226-31109-0 (pbk) : £3.90 B82-22547

241 — Christian ethics *continuation*
Gustafson, James M.. Theology and ethics / James M. Gustafson. — Oxford : Basil Blackwell, c1981. — xii,345p ; 24cm
Includes index
ISBN 0-631-12945-6 : £15.00 : CIP rev. B81-28022

Hebblethwaite, Brian. The adequacy of Christian ethics. — London : Marshall Morgan & Scott, Nov.1981. — [144]p. — (Contemporary Christian studies)
ISBN 0-551-00919-5 (pbk) : £5.95 : CIP entry B81-34214

Peschke, C. Henry. Christian ethics : a presentation of general moral theology in the light of Vatican II / by C. Henry Peschke. — Alcester ([Arden Forest industrial estate, Alcester, Warwickshire]) : Goodliffe Neal, 1975 (1981 printing). — 2v ; 22cm
Bibliography: pxvii,xii. — Includes index
Unpriced (pbk) B82-33685

241 — Christian ethics — *For schools*
Chignell, M. A.. Perspectives : a handbook of Christian responsibility / M.A. Chignell. — London : Edward Arnold, 1981. — viii,199p ; 22cm
ISBN 0-7131-0614-x (pbk) : £3.25 : CIP rev. B81-31552

241 — Christian social ethics
Hauerwas, Stanley. A community of character : toward a constructive Christian social ethic / Stanley Hauerwas. — Notre Dame ; London : University of Notre Dame Press, c1981. — x,298p ; 23cm
Includes index
ISBN 0-268-00733-0 (pbk) : £5.55 B82-01300

241 — Christian social ethics — *Evangelical viewpoints — Conference proceedings*
Essays in evangelical social ethics / edited by David F. Wright. — Exeter : Paternoster, [1980?]. — 192p ; 23cm
Conference proceedings. — Includes bibliographies and index
ISBN 0-85364-288-5 (cased) : £7.50
ISBN 0-85364-290-7 (pbk) : Unpriced B82-05134

241 — Protestant ethics *compared with* **Catholic ethics**
Gustafson, James M.. Protestant and Roman Catholic ethics / James M. Gustafson. — London : SCM, 1979, c1978. — xii,192p ; 23cm
Originally published: Chicago ; London : University of Chicago Press, 1978. — Includes index
ISBN 0-334-01332-1 : £6.50 B82-03779

241'.042 — Catholic Church. Casuistry — *Early works*
Elizabethan casuistry / [edited] by P.J. Holmes. — [London] : Catholic Record Society, 1981. — 130p ; 23cm. — (Catholic Record Society publications. (records series) ; v.67)
Includes index
Unpriced B82-08139

241'.09 — Christian ethics, *to 1980*
White, R. E. O.. The insights of history / R.E.O. White. — Exeter : Paternoster, c1981. — 442p ; 25cm. — (The Changing continuity of Christian ethics ; v.2)
Bibliography: p379-384. — Includes index
ISBN 0-85364-282-6 (cased) : £12.50
ISBN 0-85364-283-4 (pbk) : Unpriced B82-05135

241'.2 — Christian doctrine. Divine law
Monk, C. A.. The law of the Lord is perfect / by C.A. Monk. — Essex (c/o 1 Donald Way, Chelmsford, Essex CM2 9JB) : Bible Spreading Union, [198-?]. — 8p ; 22cm
Unpriced (unbound) B82-28327

241'.3 — Christian doctrine. Sin
Welch, Charles H.. Sin and its relation to God / by Charles H. Welch. — London (52a Wilson St., E.C.2) : Berean Publishing, [198-?]. — 14p ; 21cm
Cover title
Unpriced (pbk) B82-35967

241'.4 — Christian life. Compassion
McNeil, Donald P.. Compassion : a reflection on the Christian life. — London : Darton Longman & Todd, Sept.1982. — [160]p
ISBN 0-232-51578-6 (pbk) : £2.95 : CIP entry B82-25178

241'.642 — Medicine. Ethics — *Christian viewpoints*
Scorer, C. Gordon. A Christian framework for medical ethics / C. Gordon Scorer. — London : Christian Medical Fellowship, 1980. — 19p ; 21cm
Bibliography: p17
ISBN 0-85111-972-7 (pbk) : £0.50 B82-13182

241'.6424 — Euthanasia — *Christian viewpoints*
Purcell, William. Euthanasia / by William Purcell. — London : Mowbray, 1981. — 31p ; 15cm. — (Enquirer's library)
Bibliography: p31
ISBN 0-264-66725-5 (pbk) : £0.60 B82-14741

241'.66 — Sex relations. Ethics — *Catholic viewpoints*
John Paul II, *Pope*. Love and responsibility / Karol Wojtyla (Pope John Paul II) ; translated by H.T. Willetts. — Rev. ed. — London : Collins : Fount, 1982, c1981. — 319p ; 18cm
Translation of: Milosc i odpowiedzialnosc. — Originally published: London : Collins, 1981. — Includes index
ISBN 0-00-626112-4 (pbk) : £1.95 B82-21905

241'.693 — Animals. Treatment by man. Ethics — *Christian viewpoints*
Griffiths, Richard, *1943-*. The human use of animals / by Richard Griffiths. — Bramcote : Grove, 1982. — 24p ; 22cm. — (Grove booklet on ethics, ISSN 0305-4241 ; 46)
ISBN 0-907536-20-4 (pbk) : £0.70 B82-25340

241'.697 — Life. Ethical aspects — *Christian viewpoints*
Braine, David. Medical ethics and human life / David Braine. — Aberdeen : Palladio, 1982. — 49p ; 21cm
Bibliography: p36-42
ISBN 0-905292-01-4 (pbk) : £1.25 : CIP rev. B81-39233

242 — CHRISTIANITY. DEVOTIONAL LITERATURE

242 — Carmelites. Christian life — *Devotional works*
Laurent, *Frère*. The practice of the presence of God : the conversations, letters, ways and spiritual principles of Brother Lawrence, from his own literary remains and the writings of Joseph De Beaufort / translated by E.M. Blaiklock. — London : Hodder and Stoughton, 1982. — 93p ; 18cm. — (Hodder Christian paperbacks)
Translation of: La pratique de la présence de Dieu
ISBN 0-340-26937-5 (pbk) : £1.25 : CIP rev. B81-33985

242 — Catholics. Christian life — *Devotional works*
Canals, Salvatore. Jesus as friend / Salvatore Canals ; [translation Michael Adams]. — Dublin : Four Courts, c1979. — 117p ; 22cm
Translation of: Ascetica meditata
ISBN 0-906127-10-6 (cased) : £6.00
ISBN 0-906127-11-4 (pbk) : Unpriced B82-01002

Escrivá de Balaguer, Josemaría. The way / Josemaría Escrivá de Balaguer. — Dublin : Four Courts, c1981. — 178p ; 15cm
Translation of: Camino. — Includes index
Unpriced (pbk) B82-00993

John Paul II, *Pope*. Things of the spirit / Pope John Paul II ; compiled by Kathryn Spink. — London : SPCK, 1982. — 55p ; 17cm
ISBN 0-281-03869-4 (pbk) : £1.25 B82-28852

Smith, John-Venard. The interior castle / St. Teresa of Avila ; a simplified version prepared by John-Venard Smith. — 3rd ed. — Manchester ([19 Langdale Drive, Bury, Greater Manchester]) : Koinonia, [1978]. — 150p ; 18cm
Previous ed.: 1974
£1.25 (pbk) B82-04391

242 — Catholics. Christian life — *Devotional works — Irish texts*
Escrivá de Balaguer, Josemaría. Bealach / Josemaría Escrivá de Balaguer ; Tóniás Tóibín a d'aistrigh ón Spáinnis. — Dublin : Four Courts, c1980. — 218p ; 19cm
Translation of: Camino. — Includes index
Unpriced B82-00994

242 — Catholics. Christian life. Teresa, *of Avila, Saint.* **Castillo interior** — *Critical studies*
O'Donoghue, Noel Dermot. With inward glory crowned : a guide to St. Teresa of Avila's Interior Castle / Noel Dermot O'Donoghue ; edited by Thomas Curran. — Dublin : Carmelite Centre of Spirituality, c1981. — 57p ; 20cm. — (Living flame series ; v.16)
ISBN 0-86088-027-3 (pbk) : Unpriced B82-04413

242 — Christian life — *Allegories*
Sister of Malling Abbey. The play of wisdom / by a Sister of Malling Abbey ; foreword by Martin Israel. — London : Mowbray, 1981. — 122p ; 18cm
Originally published: [S.l.] : St Mary's Abbey, 1980
ISBN 0-264-66826-x (pbk) : £1.50 B82-00555

Way, Robert. The garden of the Beloved / Robert Way ; illustrations by Laszlo Kubinyi. — London : Sheldon, 1975, c1974 (1981 [printing]). — 71p : ill ; 22cm
ISBN 0-85969-359-7 (cased) : Unpriced
ISBN 0-85969-348-1 (pbk) : £2.25 B82-08181

242 — Christian life — *Devotional works*
Andrew, *Father, SDC*. [Meditations for every day. Selections]. Harold A.T. Bennett's selection from Father Andrew's Meditations for every day. — London : Mowbray, c1981. — ix,182p ; 20cm
Includes index
ISBN 0-264-66792-1 (pbk) : £2.95 B82-14040

Appleton, George. Glimpses of faith : one hundred meditations for today / by George Appleton. — London : Mowbray, 1982, c1981. — viii,100p ; 18cm
ISBN 0-264-66788-3 (pbk) : £1.50 B82-11569

The **Bridge** is love : an anthology of hope / collected by Elizabeth Bassett ; foreword by Sir John Betjeman. — London : Darton, Longman and Todd, 1981. — 180p ; 23cm
Bibliography: p171-180. — Includes index
ISBN 0-232-51541-7 : £5.95 : CIP rev. B81-33635

Clark, Kelly James. Quiet times for Christian growth / Kelly James Clark. — British ed. — Leicester : Inter-Varsity, 1981, c1979. — 61p ; 13cm
Previous ed.: 1979. — Includes bibliographies
ISBN 0-85110-245-x (pbk) : £0.50 : CIP rev. B81-10498

Gibbard, Mark. Jesus, liberation and love : meditative reflections on our believing and praying, maturity and service / by Mark Gibbard. — London : Mowbray, 1982. — 128p ; 19cm. — (Mowbray's popular Christian paperbacks)
ISBN 0-264-66550-3 (pbk) : £1.75 B82-19118

Julian, *of Norwich*. [Revelations of divine love. Selections]. Revelations of divine love / Julian of Norwich ; readings selected and modernised by James Walsh. — London : Catholic Truth Society, 1981. — 58p ; 13cm
Bibliography: p58
ISBN 0-85183-429-9 (pbk) : Unpriced B82-00023

242 — Christian life — *Devotional works continuation*

Murray, Andrew, *1828-1917*. Working for God / Andrew Murray. — London : Lakeland, c1979. — 128p ; 18cm
ISBN 0-551-00810-5 (pbk) : £1.25 B82-14431

Neville, Derek. The garden of silence ; and Put off thy shoes / by Derek Neville ; foreword by Henry Thomas Hamblin. — 1st rev. ed. — Evesham : James, 1979. — 79p ; 19cm
Previous ed. i.e. 2nd ed. of Garden of silence. Croydon : Derek Neville, 1942. — Previous ed. of : Put off thy shoes. Croydon : Derek Neville, 1942
ISBN 0-85305-209-3 (pbk) : £1.25 : CIP rev. B79-33914

Pearce, Yvonne. Thoughts from a hospital chapel / by Yvonne Pearce. — Ilkeston : Moorley's, [1981?]. — 44p : ill ; 21cm
ISBN 0-86071-133-1 (pbk) : £0.65 B82-05465

Schlink, Basilea. Hidden in His hands / Basilea Schlink. — 1st British ed. — London : Marshall, Morgan & Scott, 1979. — 96p ; 16cm
Translation of: Wir bergen uns in Deine Hand. — Translation of: 'Wir bergen uns in Deine Hand'. Darmstadt-Eberstadt : Verlag Evangelische Marienschwesternschaft, 1969
ISBN 0-551-05590-1 (pbk) : £0.85 : CIP rev. B78-40030

Teresa, *Mother*. A gift for God / Mother Teresa of Calcutta ; compiled and introduced by Malcolm Muggeridge. — London : Collins : Fount Paperbacks, 1981. — 96p : ill,ports ; 19cm
Originally published: London : Collins, 1975
ISBN 0-00-626446-8 (pbk) : £1.00 B82-01921

Turner, Joan. Close encounters / by Joan Turner. — Belfast : Long Bridge under the auspices of the Christian Renewal Centre, Belfast Cathedral
Pt.1. — 1980. — 12p ; 21cm
ISBN 0-9506727-1-8 (pbk) : £1.00 B82-02545

Turner, Joan. Close encounters / by Joan Turner. — Belfast : Long Bridge under the auspices of the Christian Renewal Centre, Belfast Cathedral
Pt.2: Lent. — c1980. — [24]p ; 21cm
ISBN 0-9506727-2-6 (pbk) : Unpriced B82-02546

Tyler, Jill. Breakthrough : poems and prayers for living and loving / Jill Tyler. — Manchester : Koinonia, c1977. — 109p ; 18cm
ISBN 0-86088-005-2 (pbk) : £0.95 B82-03553

Walton, Michael. Peace river / by Michael Walton. — [Beer] : [M. Walton], [c1981]. — [251]p : ill,music ; 23cm
ISBN 0-9507000-0-2 : Unpriced : CIP rev. B80-19592

Wharton, Michael, *19---*. Time to stop and think / Michael Wharton. — Ilfracombe : Stockwell
Vol.1: Christian devotional poetry. — 1980. — 64p ; 15cm
ISBN 0-7223-1422-1 : £2.84 B82-17565

White Eagle *(Spirit)*. The still voice : a White Eagle of meditation. — Liss : White Eagle Publishing Trust, 1981. — xiii,113p ; 18cm
ISBN 0-85487-049-0 : £2.50 : CIP rev. B81-21591

242 — Christian life. Mysticism — *Devotional works*

Crawford, Charles. The cell of self-knowledge : early English mystical teatises / [translated and adapted by Charles Crawford & John Griffiths] ; [edited with an introduction by John Griffiths]. — Dublin : Gill and Macmillan, 1981. — 128p : ill ; 20cm. — (Gill's spiritual classics)
ISBN 0-7171-1157-1 (pbk) : £3.50 B82-08673

Crawford, Charles. A mirror for simple souls / by a French mystic of the thirteenth century ; [edited, translated and adapted by Charles Crawford]. — Dublin : Gill and Macmillan, 1981. — 159p : ill ; 20cm. — (Gill's spiritual classics)
ISBN 0-7171-1158-x (pbk) : £4.50 B82-08674

Griffiths, John, *19---*. A letter from Jesus Christ : to the soul that really loves him / by John of Landsberg ; [edited, translated and adapted by John Griffiths]. — Dublin : Gill and Macmillan, 1981. — 144p : ill ; 20cm. — (Gill's spiritual classics)
Adaptation of: The epistle of Jesus Christ to the faithful soul
ISBN 0-7171-1159-8 (pbk) : £3.50 B82-08672

Griffiths, John, *19---*. A letter of private direction and other treatises / by a fourteenth-century English mystic ; [edited, translated and adapted by John Griffiths]. — Dublin : Gill and Macmillan, 1981. — 127p : ill ; 20cm. — (Gill's spiritual classics)
ISBN 0-7171-1160-1 (pbk) : £3.50 B82-08671

Julian, *of Norwich*. [Revelations of divine love. Selections. English]. Revelations of divine love / Julian of Norwich ; compiled by Roger L. Roberts. — London : Mowbray, 1981. — 61p ; 14cm. — (Treasures from the spiritual classics ; 3)
Extracts reprinted from Julian of Norwich's Revelations of divine love edited by Grace Warrack from the MS in the British Museum, and published (tenth edition) in 1934 by Methuen
ISBN 0-264-66785-9 (cased) : £3.50
ISBN 0-264-66763-8 (pbk) : Unpriced B82-09414

Thomas, *à Kempis*. [De imitatio Christi. Selections. English]. The imitation of Christ / Thomas A Kempis ; compiled by Roger L. Roberts. — London : Mowbray, 1981. — 64p ; 14cm. — (Treasures from the spiritual classics ; 2)
Translation of: De imitatio Christi. — Extracts reprinted from an edition of Thomas à Kempis' The imitation of Christ published by Cambridge University Press sometime before 1916, itself based on the English version of 1620 by F.B.
ISBN 0-264-66784-0 (cased) : £3.50
ISBN 0-264-66760-3 (pbk) : Unpriced B82-09413

242 — England. Puritans. Christian life — *Devotional works — Collections*

Apples of gold. — Ossett : Zoar
Vol.2. — 1980. — 279p : ill(some col.),facsims,ports ; 19cm
ISBN 0-904435-43-1 : Unpriced B82-08963

242 — Moral Re-Armament. Christian life — *Devotional works*

Almond, Harry. Foundations for faith / compiled by Harry Almond. — London : Grosvenor, 1980. — 61p ; 19cm
Originally published: New York : Moral Re-Armament, 1975. — Bibliography: p7
ISBN 0-901269-52-2 (pbk) : £1.25 B82-25258

242'.2 — Adolescents. Christian life — *Daily readings*

Barclay, William, *1907-1978*. Marching orders : daily readings for younger people. — Evesham : Arthur James, May 1982. — [192]p
Originally published: London : Hodder & Stoughton, 1973
ISBN 0-85305-251-4 (pbk) : £1.50 : CIP entry B82-16207

242'.2 — Bible — *Daily readings*

Lane, G. Eric. Daily Bible readings / devised, compiled and arranged by G. Eric Lane. — London : Rushworth Literature Enterprise, 1977 (1978 [printing]). — 64p ; 21cm
ISBN 0-900329-17-3 (pbk) : Unpriced B82-08521

242'.2 — Bible — *Daily readings — For adolescents*

Discovering the Bible. — Redhill : International Bible Reading
Pt.2. — c1980. — 192p ; 18cm
ISBN 0-7197-0260-7 (pbk) : Unpriced : CIP rev. B80-18586

242'.2 — Bible. N.T. Luke — *Daily readings — For Lent*

Wood, Maurice A. P.. Into the way of peace : readings in St Luke's Gospel / Maurice Wood. — London : Triangle, 1982. — 126p ; 18cm
ISBN 0-281-03846-5 (pbk) : £1.25 B82-16071

242'.2 — Christian life — *Daily readings*

Barclay, William, *1907-1978*. Through the year with William Barclay. — Evesham : Arthur James, Nov.1982. — [382]p
Originally published: London : Hodder and Stoughton, 1971
ISBN 0-85305-252-2 (pbk) : £1.95 : CIP entry B82-29032

Carmichael, Amy. Whispers of his power : selections for daily reading. — London (Holy Trinity Church, Marylebone Rd, NW1 4DU) : Triangle, Sept.1982. — [256]p. — (A Dohnavur book)
ISBN 0-281-03864-3 (pbk) : £1.95 : CIP entry B82-18880

Discovery : wider horizons in today's world / [editor Stephan Welch]. — London (2 Elizabeth St., SW1W 9RQ) : Bible Reading Fellowship
New series 3: Growing
Pt.1. — 1981. — 80p : ill ; 19cm
Cover title
Unpriced (pbk) B82-23577

Duncan, Denis. A day at a time : a thought and a prayer for each day of the year / by Denis Duncan. — Evesham : James. — (Amulree paperback ; no.3)
Pt.2: January-June. — 1980. — 110p ; 20cm
ISBN 0-85305-227-1 (pbk) : £3.25 : CIP rev. B80-19593

Hughes, Bill. The door is open : readings and prayers / Bill Hughes. — Ilkeston : Moorley's Bible & Bookshop, [1982?]. — 30p ; 21cm
ISBN 0-86071-143-9 (pbk) : £0.55 B82-18395

Hughes, Selwyn. Every day reflections / Selwyn Hughes. — Eastbourne : Kingsway, 1981. — [373]p ; 18cm
ISBN 0-86065-154-1 (pbk) : £2.50 B82-05850

Mitchell, Fred. At break of day / Fred Mitchell. — Eastbourne : Kingsway, 1981, c1959. — 372p ; 18cm
Originally published: London : Marshall, Morgan & Scott, 1959
ISBN 0-86065-156-8 (pbk) : £2.50 B82-00714

Praise in all our days : common prayer at Taizé : liturgies for the entire year in modern English / [translated by Emily Chisholm]. — London : Mowbray, 1981. — 341p ; 19cm
Translation of: La louange des jours
ISBN 0-264-66794-8 (pbk) : £4.95 B82-08020

Temple, William. Daily readings from William Temple / compiled by Hugh C. Warner. — London : Mowbray, 1981, 1948. — 279p ; 20cm
Originally published: London : Hodder & Stoughton, 1948. — Includes index
ISBN 0-264-66804-9 (pbk) : £3.50 B82-01231

Ten Boom, Corrie. This day is the Lord's / Corrie ten Boon. — Sevenoaks : Hodder and Stoughton ; [Alresford] : Christian Literature Crusade, 1980, c1979 (1981 [printing]). — 192p ; 18cm
Originally published: Old Tappan : Revell, 1979
ISBN 0-340-27158-2 (pbk) : £1.50 : CIP rev. B81-22454

Watson, David, *1933-*. Through the year with David Watson. — London : Hodder & Stoughton, Nov.1982. — [392]p
ISBN 0-340-32636-0 (cased) : £7.95 : CIP entry
ISBN 0-340-28714-4 (pbk) : £5.95 B82-28731

242′.2 — Christian life — *Daily readings continuation*

Wyszynski, Stefan. A piece of bread : 365 guide-lines for each day of the year / Stefan Wyszynski. — Slough : St. Paul Publications, 1982. — 140p ; 21cm
Translation of: Druga kromka chleba
ISBN 0-85439-215-7 (pbk) : £2.95 B82-35785

242′.2 — Christian life. Family worship — *Daily readings*

Time for the family. — London : Scripture Union
[Vol.1]: [Red]. — [c1982]. — [64]p : ill,maps,music,ports ; 30cm
ISBN 0-85421-961-7 (pbk) : £1.50 B82-40558

Time for the family. — London : Scripture Union
[Vol.2]: [Green]. — c1982. — [66]p : ill,maps,ports ; 30cm
ISBN 0-85421-986-2 (pbk) : £1.50 B82-40559

242′.33 — Christian life — *Devotional works — For Christmas*

What is Christmas?. — London (Ealing Abbey, W5 2DY) : Living Parish Pamphlets
Book 1. — [1982?]. — 16p : ill(some col.) ; 25cm
Cover title
£0.40 (pbk) B82-13727

What is Christmas?. — London (Ealing Abbey, W5 2DY) : Living Parish Pamphlets
Book 2. — [1982]. — 31p : ill ; 25cm
Cover title
£0.80 (pbk) B82-13728

242′.34 — Christian life — *Devotional works — For Lent*

What is Easter?. — London (Ealing Abbey, W5 2DY) : Living Parish Pamphlets
Book 1. — c1982. — 16p : ill(some col.) ; 25cm
Cover title
£0.40 (pbk) B82-13725

What is Easter?. — London (Ealing Abbey, W5 2DY) : Living Parish Pamphlets
Book 2. — c1982. — 32p : ill ; 25cm
Cover title
£0.80 (pbk) B82-13726

242′.5 — Bible — *Devotional works*

Briscoe, Margaret. Take my yoke / Margaret Briscoe. — Bude : M. Briscoe, 1982. — 32p ; 18cm
ISBN 0-7223-1570-8 (pbk) : Unpriced B82-36186

Koyama, Kosuke. Three mile an hour God / Kosuke Koyama. — London : SCM, 1979. — viii,146p ; 22cm
ISBN 0-334-01648-7 (pbk) : £2.95 B82-04228

242′.5 — Bible. N.T. Matthew — *Devotional works*

Lambeth, J. R.. Meditating with Matthew / J.R. Lambeth. — Bognor Regis : New Horizon, c1982. — 58p ; 21cm
ISBN 0-86116-554-3 : £3.25 B82-05677

242′.5 — Bible. O.T. Psalms — *Devotional works*

Snowden, Rita F.. Discoveries that delight : a fresh love of the psalms / Rita F. Snowden. — London : Fount, 1982. — 159p ; 18cm
ISBN 0-00-626180-9 (pbk) : £1.50 B82-26611

242′.5 — Lord's Prayer — *Devotional works*

Wyszynski, Stefan. 'Our Father — ' : meditations / Stefan Wyszynski ; [translated from the German by Dame Mary Groves]. — Slough : St. Paul, 1982. — 109p ; 21cm
Translation of: Vater unser
ISBN 0-85439-216-5 (pbk) : £3.95 B82-39861

242′.72 — Catholics. Christian life. Devotions to Jesus Christ — *Early works — Facsimiles*

Hymns to Christ : and a concert of miniatures / [edited by Costante Berselli] ; [icongraphic research by M. Luisa Badenchini] ; [translated from the Italian by Sr Mary of Jesus]. — Slough : St Paul Publications, 1982. — 125p : col.ill ; 25cm
Translation of: Inni a Cristo e un concerto di miniature. — Includes index
ISBN 0-85439-210-6 : £10.00 B82-39566

242′.723 — Christian life. Prayers: God be in my head — *Devotional works*

Simms, George, *1910-*. In my understanding / George Simms. — Dublin : Gill and Macmillan, 1982. — 150p ; 21cm
ISBN 0-7171-1103-2 (pbk) : £4.95 B82-22255

242′.74 — Catholics. Christian life. Prayer. Rosary — *Devotional works*

Escrivá de Balaguer, Josemaría. Holy Rosary / by Josemaria Escriva de Balaguer ; with wood-engravings by David Jones. — Dublin : Four Courts, c1979. — 49p : ill ; 17cm
ISBN 0-906127-15-7 (cased) : Unpriced
ISBN 0-906127-14-9 (pbk) : Unpriced B82-00989

McGarry, Columba. Meditations on the rosary / Columba McGarry ; drawings by Laurent Maka-Novapari. — Great Wakering : Mayhew-McCrimmon, 1982. — 48p : ill ; 15cm
ISBN 0-85597-332-3 (pbk) : £0.60 B82-28958

Prazan, Ceslaus. Grasping the rosary / Ceslaus Prazan ; edited from the Hausa publication Theresa McNeal ; drawings Cornelia Bock. — Great Wakering : Mayhew-McCrimmon, 1982. — 63p : ill ; 15cm
ISBN 0-85597-333-1 (pbk) : £0.75 B82-28957

242′.74 — Catholics. Christian life. Prayer. Rosary — *Devotional works — Irish texts*

Escrivá de Balaguer, Josemaría. An Choroin Mhuire Naofa / Josemaría Escrivá de Balaguer. — Dublin : Four Courts, c1979. — 46p : ill ; 17cm
ISBN 0-906127-18-1 : Unpriced B82-00990

242′.74 — Catholics. Christian life. Prayer. Rosary — *Manuals*

Hollings, Michael. The Chaplet of Mary / by Michael Hollings. — Great Wakering : Mayhew-McCrimmon, 1982. — 32p ; 15cm
ISBN 0-85597-331-5 (pbk) : £0.60 B82-25394

242′.8 — Christian life. Prayer — *Prayer-books*

A Book of prayers. — London : MacRae, Oct.1982. — [160]p
ISBN 0-86203-108-7 : £7.95 : CIP entry B82-25931

242′.8 — Christian life — *Prayers & readings*

Godwin, John, *1922-*. Lessons from life and legend : epilogues suitable for youth groups, Christian discussion groups, etc. / by John Godwin. — Ilkeston : Moorley's, [1982?]. — 77p ; 21cm
ISBN 0-86071-120-x (pbk) : £1.20 B82-17751

242′.8 — Christian life — *Prayers & readings — Welsh texts*

Davies, T. J.. Cip : cyfrol o sgyrsiau a gweddïau myfyrdodol / gan T.J. Davies. — Llandybie : C. Davies, c1982. — 108p ; 18cm
£1.50 (pbk) B82-24644

242′.8 — Christian life. Prayers — *Collections*

And now a prayer / edited by F.G. Doubleday ; [written by] William Barclay ... [et al.]. — Ilkeston : Moorley's Bible & Bookshop, c1982. — 100p ; 21cm
ISBN 0-86071-149-8 (pbk) : £1.45 B82-34023

Bittleston, Adam. Meditative prayers for today / Adam Bittleston. — 6th ed. — Edinburgh : Floris, 1982. — 56p ; 13cm
Previous ed.: London : Christian Community Press, 1975
ISBN 0-903540-54-1 : £1.95 B82-35574

Hutchison, Harry. Have a word with God : original prayers for personal use / by Harry Hutchison. — Andover : Eyre & Spottiswoode, 1981, c1980. — ii,91p ; 17cm
ISBN 0-413-80200-0 (pbk) : £1.95 B82-17570

Laing, Allan M.. Prayers and graces : a little book of extraordinary piety / collected by Allan M. Laing ; with illustrations by Mervyn Peake. — London : Pan, 1981. — 127p : ill ; 18cm
Contents: Prayers and graces. Originally published: London : Gollancz, 1944 — More prayers and graces. Originally published: London : Gollancz, 1957
ISBN 0-330-26533-4 (pbk) : £1.25 B82-04250

Lee, Helen. This is my home, Lord : a woman's prayers / by Helen Lee ; foreword by Brenda Blanch. — London : Mowbray, 1982. — 120p ; 18cm. — (Mowbray's popular Christian paperworks)
Includes index
ISBN 0-264-66856-1 (pbk) : £1.50 B82-23636

McKeating, Henry. More everyday prayers. — Nutfield : National Christian Education Council, Mar.1982. — [96]p
ISBN 0-7197-0325-5 (pbk) : £1.50 : CIP entry B82-11085

Mayne, Michael. Prayers for pastoral occasions / compiled by Michael Mayne. — London : Mowbray, 1982. — 47p ; 15cm
Includes index
ISBN 0-264-66568-6 (pbk) : £1.00 B82-28054

Micklem, Nathaniel. Prayers and praises / originaly compiled by Nathaniel Micklem. — Rev. ed. — Edinburgh : Saint Andrew, 1982. — 124p ; 17cm
Previous ed.: i.e. 2nd rev. ed. London : Independent Press, 1954
ISBN 0-7152-0541-2 (pbk) : £2.00 B82-29476

Praying together : in word and song / Taizé. — Oxford : Mowbrays, c1981. — 32p : music ; 21cm
Translation from the French. — Cover title
ISBN 0-264-66852-9 (pbk) : £1.50
Also classified at 264′.2 B82-26960

Short prayers for the long day / compiled by Giles and Melville Harcourt. — London : Collins, 1978 (1982 [printing]). — 142p ; 18cm
ISBN 0-00-599592-2 (corrected : pbk) : £1.75 B82-17008

242′.802 — Catholics. Christian life. Prayers — *Collections*

John Paul II, *Pope*. Prayers of Pope John Paul II / edited by John F. McDonald ; foreword by Bishop Agnellus Andrew. — Slough : St. Paul, 1982. — 104p ; 21cm
Translated from the Italian
ISBN 0-85439-214-9 (pbk) : £2.95 B82-21621

242′.803 — Anglicans. Christian life. Prayers — *Collections*

Front line praying. — London : Bible Reading Fellowship, Sept.1981. — [208]p
ISBN 0-900164-56-5 (pbk) : £2.25 : CIP entry B81-30302

242′.806 — Baptists. Christian life. Prayers — *Collections — For church year*

Wallace, Jamie. There's a time and a place : prayers for the Christian year / Jamie Wallace. — London : Collins, 1982. — 159p : ill ; 19cm
Includes index
ISBN 0-00-599697-x (pbk) : £2.50 B82-32653

242′.82 — Children. Christian life. Prayers — *Collections*

Campbell, Elspeth. Sometimes I get lonely : psalm 42 for children / by Elspeth Campbell ; illustrated by Jane E. Nelson. — London : Pickering & Inglis, 1981. — [24]p : ill(some col.) ; 18x22cm. — (David and I talk to God)
ISBN 0-7208-2298-x (pbk) : £0.75 B82-02295

Campbell, Elspeth. Sometimes I get scared : psalm 23 for children / by Elspeth Campbell ; illustrated by Jane E. Nelson. — London : Pickering & Inglis, 1981. — [24]p : ill(some col.) ; 18x22cm. — (David and I talk to God)
ISBN 0-7208-2295-5 (pbk) : £0.75 B82-02294

242′.82 — Children. Christian life. Prayers — *Collections* *continuation*

Campbell, Elspeth. What can I say to you, God? : verses from the psalms on prayer / by Elspeth Campbell ; illustrated by Jane E. Nelson. — London : Pickering & Inglis, 1981. — [24]p : ill(some col.) ; 18x22cm. — (David and I talk to God)
ISBN 0-7208-2296-3 (pbk) : £0.75 B82-02293

Campbell, Elspeth. Where are you, God? : psalm 139 for children / by Elspeth Campbell ; illustrated by Jane E. Nelson. — London : Pickering & Inglis, 1981. — [24]p : ill(some col.) ; 18x22cm. — (David and I talk to God)
ISBN 0-7208-2297-1 (pbk) : £0.75 B82-02296

Little one′s prayers / [illustrations by Janet and Anne Grahame Johnstone]. — London : Dean, c1982, c1968. — [8]p : col.ill ; 24cm
Cover title. — Text and ill on lining papers
ISBN 0-603-02001-1 : Unpriced B82-25972

Pearson, Muriel. A time for prayer / Muriel Pearson. — London : Edward Arnold, 1981. — 48p : ill ; 22cm
ISBN 0-7131-0604-2 (pbk) : £1.50 : CIP rev.
B81-31551

Prayers / edited by Jane Carruth. — Bristol : Purnell, 1976 (1982 [printing]). — [28]p : col.ill ; 25cm. — (My first colour library)
ISBN 0-361-03491-1 : Unpriced B82-25842

Thomas, Joan Gale. Our Father : the Lord′s prayer arranged in picture and rhyme for people who are still very young / Joan Gale Thomas. — London : Mowbrays, 1940 (1979 [printing]). — [24]p : ill(some col.) ; 21cm
ISBN 0-264-66703-4 (pbk) : £0.95 B82-23426

242′.82 — Children. Christian life. Prayers — *Collections — Welsh texts*

Smeltzer, Patricia. [Thank you for a drink of water. Welsh]. Diolch yn fawr am lymaid o ddŵr / Patricia a Victor Smeltzer ; addasiad Cymraeg gan Aneurin Jenkins-Jones. — Caernarfon (Ffordd Ddewi, Caernarfon LL556 1ER, Gwynedd) : Gwasg Pontycelyn, 1982, c1980. — [24]p : col.ill ; 24cm
Translation of: Thank you for a drink of water
£0.75 (pbk) B82-40461

Smeltzer, Patricia. [Thank you for a pair of jeans. Welsh]. Diolch yn fawr am bâro jîns / Patricia a Victor Smeltzer ; addasiad Cymraeg gan Aneurin Jenkins-Jones. — Caernarfon (Ffordd Ddewi, Caernarfon LL55 1ER, Gwynedd) : Gwasg Pantycelyn, 1982, c1980. — [24]p : col.ill ; 24cm
Translation of: Thank you for a pair of jeans
£0.75 (pbk) B82-40462

246 — ART IN CHRISTIANITY

246′.55 — Christian church. Symbols

Hare Duke, Michael. Stories, signs and sacraments in the emerging church / Michael Hare Duke. — London : Mowbray, c1982. — ix,114p ; 20cm. — (Mowbray′s emerging church series)
ISBN 0-264-66797-2 (pbk) : £2.25 B82-19119

247 — CHURCH FURNISHINGS AND RELATED ARTICLES

247′.792 — Bible O.T. Exodus. Aaron. Ceremonial clothing

Tiller, Lawrence V.. Garments for glory and for beauty / by Lawrence V. Tiller. — Cheltenham (PO Box 38, Cheltenham, Glos.) : [Grenehurst Press], c1981. — 80p : ill,1port ; 20cm
Unpriced (pbk) B82-08684

247′.792 — Christian church. Clerical clothing. Abolition

Brown, Roger Lee. How to rid your church of vestments : some practical advice. — [Cardiff] ([The Vicarage, Merthyr Rd, Tongwynlais, Cardiff CF4 7LF) : R.L. Brown, 1982. — 7p ; 21cm
Author: Roger Lee Brown
Unpriced (unbound) B82-35599

248 — CHRISTIAN EXPERIENCE, PRACTICE, LIFE

248 — Man. Identity — *Christian viewpoints*

Identity. — [London] ([2 Chester House, Pages Lane, N10]) : [Christian Education Movement], c1982. — [4] : 1ill ; 21cm. — (1999 this future is mine)
Unpriced (unbound) B82-18695

248 — Man. Stress — *Christian viewpoints*

McPheat, W. Scott. Coping with life. — London : Hodder & Stoughton, Jan.1982. — [144]p
ISBN 0-340-27471-9 (pbk) : £1.50 : CIP entry
B81-34122

248.2 — Christian life. Doubt

Simpson, James A.. Doubts are not enough / James A. Simpson. — Edinburgh : Saint Andrew, 1982. — vii,136p ; 20cm
ISBN 0-7152-0501-3 (pbk) : £3.65 B82-29470

248.2 — Christian life. Religious experiences, *1399-1618 — Study examples: Saints. Apparitions — Study regions: Spain*

Christian, William A. (William Armistead), *1944-*. Apparitions in late medieval and renaissance Spain / by William A. Christian Jr. — Princeton ; Guildford : Princeton University Press, c1981. — vi,349p,[8]p of plates : ill,3maps ; 23cm
English text, Spanish documentary appendix. — Includes index
ISBN 0-691-05326-x : £14.50 B82-00069

248.2′2 — Christian life. Mysticism — *Early works*

The **Cloud** of unknowing / edited with an introduction by James Walsh ; preface by Simon Tugwell. — London : SPCK, 1981. — xxvi,293p ; 23cm. — (The Classics of Western spirituality)
Bibliography: p267-276. — Includes index
ISBN 0-281-03729-9 (pbk) : £7.50 B82-16250

248.2′2′01 — Christian life. Mysticism. Theories, *to ca 260*

Louth, Andrew. The origins of the Christian mystical tradition from Plato to Denys. — Oxford : Clarendon Press, Apr.1981. — [192]p
ISBN 0-19-826655-3 : £12.50 : CIP entry
B81-00735

248.2′2′0924 — Christian life. Mysticism. Francis, *of Assisi, Saint*

Moorman, John R. H.. Richest of poor men : the spirituality of St Francis of Assisi / John R.H. Moorman. — London : Darton Longman & Todd, 1977 (1982 [printing]). — 110p ; 22cm
Bibliography: p110
ISBN 0-232-51562-x (pbk) : £2.95 B82-19963

248.2′2′0924 — Christian life. Mysticism — *Personal observations*

Rolle, Richard. [Incendium amoris]. The fire of love / Richard Rolle ; translated into modern English with an introduction by Clifton Wolters. — Harmondsworth : Penguin, 1972 (1981 [printing]). — 192p ; 19cm
ISBN 0-14-044256-1 (pbk) : £1.50 B82-09952

248.2′2′0942 — England. Christian life. Mysticism, *1300-1416*

Ryder, Andrew. Visions of light : the English spiritual writers of the fourteenth century / Andrew Ryder ; edited by Thomas Curran. — Dublin : Carmelite Centre of Spirituality, c1981. — 56p ; 20cm. — (Living flame series ; v.12)
Originally published: in Mount Carmel
ISBN 0-86088-023-0 (pbk) : Unpriced
B82-04411

248.2′46 — Christianity. Conversion of criminals — *Personal observations*

Greenaway, Brian. Hell′s Angel / Brian Greenaway with Brian Kellock. — Tring : Lion, 1982. — 144p ; 18cm
ISBN 0-85648-389-3 (pbk) : £1.50 B82-24166

248.2′46 — Christianity. Conversion of Muslims — *Conference proceedings*

Chambésy Dialogue Consultation *(Conference : 1976)*. Christian mission and Islamic da′wah : proceedings of the Chambésy Dialogue Consultation. — Leicester : Islamic Foundation, c1982. — 103p ; 22cm
ISBN 0-86037-110-7 (pbk) : Unpriced : CIP rev.
Also classified at 297′.42 B82-03126

248.2′46 — Christianity. Conversion of Muslims — *Personal observations*

Hirji-Walji, Hass. Escape from Islam / Hass Hirji-Walji & Jaryl Strong. — Eastbourne : Kingsway, 1981. — 128p ; 18cm
ISBN 0-86065-166-5 (pbk) : £1.25 B82-05852

248.2′46 — Christianity. Conversion of Muslims — *Personal observations — Collections*

Jesus : more than a prophet / edited by R.W.F. Wootton. — Leicester : Inter-Varsity Press, 1982. — 80p ; 18cm
ISBN 0-85110-422-3 (pbk) : £1.25 : CIP rev.
B81-30613

248.2′46 — Christianity. Conversion of non-Christians

Winter, David. Converted to Christianity / by David Winter. — London : Mowbray, 1981. — 30p ; 15cm. — (Enquirer′s library)
Bibliography: p30
ISBN 0-264-66750-6 (pbk) : £0.60 B82-02109

248.2′46 — Europe. Christianity. Conversion of Jews. Wurmbrand, Judy — *Biographies*

Wurmbrand, Judy. Escape from the grip / by Judy Wurmbrand. — London : Hodder and Stoughton, 1979. — 126p ; 18cm. — (Hodder Christian paperbacks)
ISBN 0-340-27150-7 (pbk) : £1.25 : CIP rev.
B81-34651

248.2′5 — Moral Re-Armament. Christian life — *Case studies*

Piguet, Charles. The world at the turning : experiments with Moral Re-Armament / by Charles Piguet and Michel Sentis ; foreword by Cardinal König ; translated by Ailsa Hamilton. — London : Grosvenor, 1982. — xii,116p : ill ; 19cm
Translation of: Ce Monde que Dieu nous confie. Also available in Italian as Questo mondo nelle nostre mani. — Bibliography: p116
ISBN 0-901269-67-0 (cased) : Unpriced
ISBN 0-901269-68-9 (pbk) : £1.95 B82-23921

248.2′9 — Christian life. Baptism in the Holy Spirit

Harper, Michael, *1931-*. Power for the body of Christ / Michael Harper. — Rev. ed. — Eastbourne : Kingsway, 1981. — 86p ; 18cm
Previous ed.: London : Fountain Trust, 1964
ISBN 0-86065-151-7 (pbk) : £1.25 B82-05848

248.3 — Christian life. Devotions

Murray, Andrew. The secret of adoration. — London : Marshall, Morgan & Scott, Feb.1982. — [32]p. — (The Secret series)
ISBN 0-551-00933-0 (pbk) : £6.00 : CIP entry
B82-07972

248.3′2 — Bible. Special subjects: Prayer — *Expositions*

Appleton, George. Praying with the Bible. — London : Bible Reading Fellowship, Oct.1981. — [72]p
ISBN 0-900164-57-3 : £1.25 : CIP entry
B81-30977

248.3′2 — Catholics. Christian life. Prayer

Murphy, Columcille. Prayer and community / Columcille Murphy ; edited by Thomas Curran. — Dublin : Carmelite Centre of Spirituality, c1979. — 48p ; 20cm. — (Living flame series ; v.9)
ISBN 0-86088-020-6 (pbk) : Unpriced
B82-04410

248.3'2 — Catholics. Christian life. Prayer — *Manuals*

Hughes, John Jay. Praying in silence : an introduction to centering prayer — an ancient form of Christian meditation rediscovered / John Jay Hughes. — London : Catholic Truth Society, 1982. — 8p ; 19cm
Cover title. — Bibliography: p8
ISBN 0-85183-462-0 (pbk) : £0.30 B82-17632

248.3'2 — Catholics. Christian life. Prayer — *Personal observations*

Henaghan, John. Pathways to God / John Henaghan ; edited by Thomas Curran. — Dublin : Carmelite Centre of Spirituality, c1981. — 59p ; 20cm. — (Living flame series ; v.13)
Originally published: St Columban, Neb. : St Columban's Foreign Mission Society, 1939
ISBN 0-86088-024-9 (pbk) : Unpriced
B82-04405

248.3'2 — Christian life. Prayer

Baelz, Peter. Does God answer prayer? / Peter Baelz. — London : Darton, Longman & Todd, 1982. — 55p ; 20cm
ISBN 0-232-51554-9 (pbk) : £1.95 : CIP rev.
B82-07530

Baughen, Michael. The prayer principle / by Michael Baughen. — London : Mowbray, 1981. — 133p ; 18cm. — (Mowbray's popular Christian paperbacks)
ISBN 0-264-66701-8 (pbk) : £1.50 B82-12373

Fife, Eric. Prayer : common sense and the Bible / by Eric Fife. — Bromley : Send the Light Trust, 1977, c1976. — 91p ; 18cm
Originally published: Grand Rapids : Zondervan, 1976
Unpriced (pbk) B82-05302

Llewelyn, Robert. With pity not with blame. — London : Darton Longman & Todd, Oct.1982. — [144]p
ISBN 0-232-51577-8 (pbk) : £3.95 : CIP entry
B82-30339

Murray, Andrew. The secret of united prayer. — London : Marshall, Morgan & Scott, Feb.1982. — [32]p. — (The Secret series)
ISBN 0-551-00936-5 (pbk) : £6.00 : CIP entry
B82-07802

Rahner, Karl. Happiness through prayer / Karl Rahner. — London : Burns & Oates, 1958 (1978 [printing]). — 107p ; 22cm
Translated from the German
ISBN 0-86012-062-7 (pbk) : Unpriced
B82-41030

Ramsey, Michael. Be still and know : a study in the life of prayer / Michael Ramsey ; with a foreword by the Archbishop of Canterbury. — London : Collins in associaiton with Faith Press, 1982. — 127p ; 18cm
Bibliography: p125-127
ISBN 0-00-626350-x (pbk) : £1.25 B82-15113

248.3'2 — Christian life. Prayer — *Manuals*

Martin, Linette. Practical praying. — London (Holy Trinity Church, Marylebone Rd, NW1 4DU) : Triangle, Sept.1982. — [112]p
ISBN 0-281-03863-5 (pbk) : £1.75 : CIP entry
B82-18879

248.3'2 — Franciscans. Christian life. Prayer — *Early works*

Osuna, Francisco de. Francisco de Osuna : the Third spiritual alphabet / translation and introduction by Mary E. Giles ; preface by Kieran Kavanaugh. — London : SPCK, 1981. — xvi,624p ; 23cm. — (The Classics of Western spirituality)
Translated from the Spanish. — Bibliography: p610. — Includes index
ISBN 0-281-03850-3 (pbk) : £12.50
B82-20145

248.3'2 — Orthodox Eastern churches. Christian life. Prayer — *Early works*

The **Philokalia** : the complete text / compiled by St Nikodimos of the Holy Mountain and St Makarios of Corinth ; translated from the Greek and edited by G.E.H. Palmer, Philip Sherrard, Kallistos Ware with the assistance of the Holy Transfiguration Monastery ... [et al.]. — London : Faber
Vol.2. — 1981. — 414p ; 23cm
Includes index
ISBN 0-571-11725-2 : £12.95 : CIP rev.
B81-25326

248.3'2'088054 — Children. Christian life. Prayer — *For children*

Doney, Meryl. The Piccolo book of prayers / Meryl Doney ; illustrated by Chris Molan. — London : Piccolo, 1981. — 143p : ill ; 18cm
ISBN 0-330-26517-2 (pbk) : £1.25 B82-04234

248.3'2'088054 — Children. Christian life. Prayer — *For teaching*

Cardwell, Ruth. Helping children to pray / Ruth Cardwell. — Pinner : Grail, 1981. — 83p : ill ; 21cm
Bibliography: p82-83
ISBN 0-901829-59-5 (pbk) : £1.90 B82-06356

248.3'2'0924 — Catholics. Christian life. Prayer. Theories of Teresa, *of Avila, Saint*

ALverez, Thomas. Living with God : St Teresa's concept of prayer / Thomas Alverez ; translated by Christopher O'Mahony & Dominica Horia ; edited by Thomas Curran. — Dublin : Carmelite Centre of Spirituality, c1980. — 47p ; 20cm. — (Living flame series ; v.11)
Translated from the Spanish
ISBN 0-86088-022-2 (pbk) : Unpriced
B82-04409

Lantry, Jerome. Saint Teresa on prayer / Jerome Lantry ; edited by Thomas Curran. — Dublin : Carmelite Centre of Spirituality, [c1981]. — 57p ; 20cm. — (Living flame series ; v.14)
Cover title
ISBN 0-86088-025-7 (pbk) : Unpriced
B82-04408

248.3'4 — Christian life. Contemplation

Coulson, Robert. Into God : an exercise in contemplation / R.G. Coulson. — Great Missenden (c/o The Lee Vicarage, Great Missenden, Bucks. HP16 9LZ) : R.G. Coulson, c1981. — 175p ; 22cm
Originally published: London : J. Murray, 1956. — Includes index
ISBN 0-9503505-1-6 (pbk) : Unpriced
B82-03783

248.3'4 — Christian life. Meditation groups. Organisation — *Manuals*

Trudinger, Ron. Cells for life : home groups : God's strategy for church growth / Ron Trudinger. — Basingstoke : Olive Tree, 1979. — 123p ; 18cm
ISBN 0-906645-01-8 (pbk) : Unpriced
B82-13121

248.3'4 — Christian life. Meditation — *Manuals*

Spink, Peter. The path of the mystic. — London : Darton Longman & Todd, Jan.1983. — [96]p
ISBN 0-232-51563-8 : £2.50 : CIP entry
B82-36303

248.3'4 — Christian life. Meditation. Role of hatha-yoga

Amaldas, Brahmachari. Yoga and contemplation / Brahmachari Amaldas ; foreword by Bede Griffiths. — London : Darton, Longman and Todd, 1981. — xiii,146p : ill ; 20cm
ISBN 0-232-51530-1 (pbk) : £2.95 : CIP rev.
B81-11923

248.4 — Bereaved persons. Grief — *Christian viewpoints*

Ainsworth-Smith, Ian. Letting go : caring for the dying and the bereaved / Ian Ainsworth-Smith and Peter Speck. — London : SPCK, 1982. — xii,153p : ill,1form ; 22cm. — (New library of pastoral care)
Bibliography: p150-151. — Includes index
ISBN 0-281-03861-9 (pbk) : £3.95 B82-34732

248.4 — Bible. N.T. Special themes: Christian life. Joy

Morrice, William G.. Joy in the New Testament. — Exeter : Paternoster Press, Nov.1982. — [160]p
ISBN 0-85364-340-7 (pbk) : £4.00 : CIP entry
B82-26319

248.4 — Bible. Special subjects: Christian life. Guidance

Brooks, Peter, *1918-*. What the Bible says about — / by 'Peter' Brooks. — London : Mowbray, 1982. — 112p ; 18cm
ISBN 0-264-66823-5 : £1.50 B82-18027

248.4 — Christian life

Carter, Phyllis. Stewardship and sharing / by Phyllis Carter. — London : Mowbray, 1981. — 31p ; 15cm. — (Enquirer's library)
Bibliography: p31
ISBN 0-264-66748-4 (pbk) : £0.60 B82-02107

Dalrymple, John. The Cross a pasture. — London : Darton Longman & Todd, Feb.1983. — [144]p
ISBN 0-232-51545-x : £2.95 : CIP entry
B82-37658

Erasmus, Desiderius. Enchiridion militis Christiani : an English version / Erasmus ; edited by Anne M. O'Donnell. — Oxford : Published for the Early English Text Society by the Oxford University Press, 1981. — liii,322p : 1ill ; 23cm
Bibliography: pxi-xiii. — Includes index
ISBN 0-19-722284-6 : £23.00 : CIP rev.
B81-15938

Foster, Richard J.. Freedom of simplicity / Richard J. Foster. — London : Triangle, 1981. — viii,200p ; 18cm
Originally published: San Francisco : Harper & Row, 1981. — Includes index
ISBN 0-281-03818-x (pbk) : £1.75 B82-08471

Getting nowhere fast. — Swindon : Bible Societies, 1982. — 1sheet : col.ill ; 21x30cm folded to 21x10cm
ISBN 0-564-04642-6 : Unpriced B82-28911

Go in peace. — Swindon : Bible Societies, 1982. — 1sheet : col.ill ; 21x30cm folded to 21x10cm
ISBN 0-564-04582-9 : Unpriced B82-28914

Guild of Pastoral Psychology. *Spring Conference (1979)*. The search for meaning / Guild Spring Conference, 1979 ; by Wendy Robinson and Christopher Bryant. — [London] (9 Phoenix House, 5 Waverley Rd, N8 9QU) : The Guild of Pastoral Psychology, [1979]. — 39p ; 19cm. — (Guild lecture ; no.196)
Conference papers
Unpriced (unbound) B82-40436

Harmony. — Swindon : Bible Societies, 1982. — 1sheet : col.ill ; 21x30cm folded to 21x10cm
ISBN 0-564-04652-3 : Unpriced B82-28915

Harper, Michael, *1931-*. Walk in the spirit / Michael Harper. — Rev. ed. — Eastbourne : Kingsway, 1981. — 91p ; 18cm
Previous ed.: London : Hodder & Stoughton, 1968
ISBN 0-86065-150-9 (pbk) : £1.25 B82-00712

Hirst, C. W.. Jacob's ladder / C.W. & M. Hirst. — Ilfracombe : Stockwell, 1982. — 147p ; 19cm
ISBN 0-7223-1568-6 (pbk) : £2.50 B82-36185

Horne, Brian. A world to gain. — London : Darton Longman & Todd, Feb.1983. — [96]p
ISBN 0-232-51543-3 : £2.50 : CIP entry
B82-37657

Hurnard, Hannah. Hinds' feet on high places / Hannah Hurnard. — Eastbourne : Kingsway, 1982. — 158p ; 18cm
Originally published: London : Christian Literature Crusade, 1955
ISBN 0-86065-192-4 (pbk) : £1.60 B82-37088

248.4 — Christian life *continuation*

Hutchinson, Harry. A faith that conquers / by Harry Hutchinson. — Edinburgh : Saint Andrew, 1982. — ix,134p ; 18cm
ISBN 0-7152-0462-9 (pbk) : £3.65 B82-29477

Is the world falling apart?. — Swindon : Bible Societies, 1982. — 1sheet : col.ill ; 21x30cm folded to 21x10cm
ISBN 0-564-04622-1 : Unpriced B82-28909

Jugan, Jeanne. Sayings of Jeanne Jugan : foundress of the Little Sisters of the Poor. — London : Catholic Truth Society, 1982. — vii,60p : ill,1facsim,1port ; 17cm
ISBN 0-85183-472-8 (pbk) : £0.85 B82-33173

Keller, W. Phillip. Walking with God / W. Phillip Keller. — Eastbourne : Kingsway, 1982, c1980. — 160p ; 18cm
Originally published: Old Tappan, N.J. : F.H. Revell Co., c1980
ISBN 0-86065-169-x (pbk) : £1.35 B82-19359

Lealman, Brenda. Knowing and unknowing / Brenda Lealman and Edward Robinson. — [London] : Christian Education Movement, c1981. — 63p : ill(some col.) ; 21cm + Teacher's handbook(19p ; 21cm). — (Exploration into experience)
ISBN 0-905022-75-0 (pbk) : Unpriced
ISBN 0-905022-76-9 (Teacher's handbook) B82-05272

Maddocks, Morris. The Christian adventure. — London : SPCK, Jan.1983. — [144]p
ISBN 0-281-04032-x (pbk) : £1.50 : CIP entry B82-33723

Mathews, R. Arthur. Born for battle / R. Arthur Mathews. — Robesonia, Pa. ; Sevenoaks : OMF Books ; Bromley : STL Books, 1981, c1978. — 182p ; 18cm
Originally published: Robesonia, Pa. ; Sevenoaks : OMF, 1978
ISBN 0-903843-57-9 (pbk) : £1.35
ISBN 0-85363-143-3 (OMF Books) : Unpriced B82-19318

Murray, Andrew. The secret of fellowship. — London : Marshall, Morgan & Scott, Feb.1982. — [32]p. — (The Secret series)
ISBN 0-551-00935-7 (pbk) : £6.00 : CIP entry B82-07801

Northey, James. My father's house / by James Northey. — London : Salvationist, 1981. — 125p ; 22cm
Includes index
ISBN 0-85412-381-4 (pbk) : Unpriced B82-13284

Perry, John. Christian leadership. — London : Hodder & Stoughton, Feb.1983. — [96]p
ISBN 0-340-27803-x (pbk) : £1.75 : CIP entry B82-38042

Phillips, Keith. The making of a disciple / Keith Phillips. — Eastbourne : Kingsway, 1982, c1981. — 157p : ill ; 18cm
Originally published: Old Tappan : Revell, 1981
ISBN 0-86065-193-2 (pbk) : £1.60 B82-37086

Picking up the pieces. — Swindon : Bible Societies, 1982. — 1sheet : col.ill ; 21x30cm folded to 21x10cm
ISBN 0-564-04602-7 : Unpriced B82-28913

Reaching out of the darkness. — Swindon : Bible Societies, 1982. — 1sheet : col.ill ; 21x30cm folded to 21x10cm
ISBN 0-564-04632-9 : Unpriced B82-28910

Robinson, Arthur W.. The personal life of the Christian / Arthur W. Robinson. — [Rev. ed.]. — Oxford : Oxford University Press, 1980. — xi,80p ; 20cm
Previous ed.: published as The personal life of the clergy. London : Longmans, 1902
ISBN 0-19-213427-2 (pbk) : £1.95 B82-38469

Sergiev, Ivan Il'ich. The spiritual counsels of Father John of Kronstadt. — Cambridge : James Clarke, Feb.1982. — [256]p
Translated from the Russian. — Originally published: 1967
ISBN 0-227-67856-7 (pbk) : £4.95 : CIP entry B82-07101

Sugden, Chris. Radical discipleship. — London : Marshall Morgan & Scott, May 1981. — [160] p. — (Marshalls paperbacks)
ISBN 0-551-00901-2 (pbk) : £1.50 : CIP entry B81-12885

Trudinger, Ron. Built to last / Ron Trudinger. — Rev. ed. — Eastbourne : Kingsway, 1982. — 192p ; 18cm
Previous ed. published as Master plan. Basingstoke : Olive Tree, 1980
ISBN 0-86065-185-1 (pbk) : £1.75 B82-36935

True wealth?. — Swindon : Bible Societies, 1982. — 1sheet : col.ill ; 21x30cm folded to 21x10cm
ISBN 0-564-04612-4 : Unpriced B82-28912

Urch, Elizabeth. Ladders up to heaven / by Elizabeth Urch. — Evesham : James
Part 4: Worship. — 1982. — 69p : music ; 20cm
Includes index
ISBN 0-85305-235-2 (pbk) : £1.95 : CIP rev. B82-07120

What it means to be a Christian. — Ely : EARO, Resource and Technology Centre, c1977. — 16p : ill,1port ; 15x21cm
ISBN 0-904463-43-5 (pbk) : £0.70 B82-13778

Whiter than snow. — Swindon : Bible Societies, 1982. — 1sheet : col.ill ; 21x30cm folded to 21x10cm
ISBN 0-564-04592-6 : Unpriced B82-28908

Wilkerson, David. Have you felt like giving up lately? / David Wilkerson. — Eastbourne : Kingsway, 1981, c1980. — 157p ; 18cm
Originally published: Old Tappan, N.J. : Revell, 1980
ISBN 0-86065-163-0 (pbk) : £1.50 B82-00711

248.4 — Christian life. Creativity

Rookmaaker, H. R.. The creative gift : the arts and the Christian life / H.R. Rookmaaker. — Leicester : Inter-Varsity Press, 1982, c1981. — 158p ; 22cm
Originally published: Westchester, Ill. : Cornerstone Books, 1981
ISBN 0-85110-706-0 (pbk) : Unpriced : CIP rev. B82-10879

248.4 — Christian life. Dependence

Vanstone, W. H.. The stature of waiting. — London : Darton Longman & Todd, Oct.1982. — [144]p
ISBN 0-232-51573-5 (pbk) : £4.50 : CIP entry B82-26221

248.4 — Christian life. Faith

Holloway, Richard. Beyond belief : the Christian encounter with God / Richard Holloway. — London : Mowbray, 1982, c1981. — ix,164p ; 20cm. — (Mowbray's Christian studies)
Originally published: Grand Rapids, Mich. : Eerdmans, 1981
ISBN 0-264-66721-2 (pbk) : £2.50 B82-23635

Urquhart, Colin. Faith for the future. — London : Hodder & Stoughton, Oct.1982. — [192]p
ISBN 0-340-32262-4 (pbk) : £1.75 : CIP entry B82-24846

248.4 — Christian life. Faith — *Personal observations*

Grabham, Olive. Marks of faith / Olive Grabham. — Braunton : Merlin Books, 1982. — 20p ; 21cm
ISBN 0-86303-023-8 (pbk) : £0.60 B82-41115

248.4 — Christian life. Faith — *Topics for discussion groups*

Talking together : study material for house groups. — Redhill : National Christian Education Council, c1982
1: Raw materials of faith / by Donald Hilton. — 20p ; 21cm
ISBN 0-7197-0336-0 (pbk) : Unpriced B82-41114

248.4 — Christian life — *For East African students* — *For schools*

Christian living today : Christian religious education for secondary schools : a study of life themes. — London : Chapman
Prepared at the Pastoral Institute of Eastern Africa
Teacher's handbook. — 1981. — xv,326p : ill ; 24cm
ISBN 0-225-66307-4 (pbk) : Unpriced : CIP rev. B81-26705

248.4 — Christian life — *For schools*

Hughes, Richard M.. The kingdom of Heaven / Richard Hughes. — Oxford : Oxford University Press, c1982. — 80p : ill(some col.),facsims,col.maps,ports(some col.) ; 28cm. — (A Secondary religious education course ; bk.2)
Bibliography: p80
ISBN 0-19-918135-7 (pbk) : Unpriced B82-39061

248.4 — Christian life. Guidance

Ferguson, Sinclair B.. Discovering God's will / Sinclair B. Ferguson. — Edinburgh : The Banner of Truth Trust, 1981. — 126p ; 18cm
Bibliography: p126
ISBN 0-85151-334-4 (pbk) : £1.60 B82-16964

248.4 — Christian life. Love

Harper, Michael, *1931-*. The love affair / Michael Harper. — London : Hodder and Stoughton, 1982. — 237p ; 20cm
ISBN 0-340-28202-9 (pbk) : £4.95 : CIP rev. B82-07950

248.4 — Christian life — *Manuals*

Dammers, A. H.. Life style : a parable of sharing / by A.H. Dammers. — Wellingborough : Turnstone, 1982. — 224p ; 22cm
ISBN 0-85500-159-3 (cased) : Unpriced : CIP rev.
ISBN 0-85500-160-7 (pbk) : £4.95 B82-01419

Finney, John. Saints alive! : the Christian life in the power of the Spirit / John Finney, Felicity Lawson. — Ilkeston : published on behalf of Anglican Renewal Ministries by Moorley's, [1981]. — 41p : ill ; 21cm + link-work booklet (24p ; 21cm)
ISBN 0-86071-136-6 (spiral) : £1.40
ISBN 0-86071-137-4 (link-work booklet) : £0.40 B82-13119

248.4 — Christian life — *Personal observations*

Andrew, *Brother*. Building in a broken world / Brother Andrew. — Eastbourne : Kingsway, 1982, c1981. — 141p ; 18cm
ISBN 0-86065-170-3 (pbk) : £1.35 B82-19358

Arnott, Anne. The Brethren : an autobiography of a Plymouth Brethren childhood / by Anne Arnott. — London : Mowbray, 1969 (1982 [printing]). — xi,196p ; 20cm. — (Mowbray religious reprint)
ISBN 0-264-66873-1 (pbk) : £2.95 B82-34798

Barfield, Janice. You can fly / Janice Barfield. — London : Pickering & Inglis, 1981. — 128p ; 19cm
ISBN 0-7208-0507-4 (pbk) : £1.60 B82-02843

Beasley, Mary. Back from the brink / by Mary Beasley ; foreword by Don Wilkerson. — London : Mowbray, 1982. — viii,150p ; 18cm. — (Mowbray's popular Christian paperbacks)
ISBN 0-264-66858-8 (pbk) : £1.75 : CIP rev. B82-19823

248.4 — Christian life — *Personal observations continuation*

Copley, Derek. My chains fell off : openness to God, ourselves and others / by Derek Copley & Mary Austin ; illustrated by Bob Bond. — Exeter : Paternoster, c1982. — ix,150p : ill ; 18cm
ISBN 0-85364-314-8 (pbk) : £2.20 : CIP rev. B82-01564

Dehqani-Tafti, H. B.. Design of my world / by H.B. Dehqani-Tafti. — Guildford : Lutterworth, 1982. — 80p ; 19cm
Originally published: London : United Society for Christian Literature, 1959
ISBN 0-7188-2525-x (pbk) : Unpriced B82-19789

Elliot, Elisabeth. All that was ever ours : personal perceptions on her turbulent life / Elisabeth Elliot. — London : Pickering & Inglis, 1982. — x,173p ; 21cm
ISBN 0-7208-0483-3 (pbk) : £2.50 B82-23776

Evans, Colleen Townsend. The vine life / Colleen Townsend Evans. — London : Hodder and Stoughton, 1982, c1980. — 135p ; 18cm. — (Hodder Christian paperbacks)
Originally published: Lincoln, Va. : Chosen Books, c1980
ISBN 0-340-27736-x (pbk) : £1.50 : CIP rev. B82-03815

Fewtrell, Sheila. Pathfinder and the liberating spirit / Sheila Fewtrell. — Bognor Regis : New Horizon, c1982. — 106p : ill ; 22cm
ISBN 0-86116-727-9 : £3.95 B82-27155

Haile, Peter. The difference God makes / Peter Haile. — Eastbourne : Kingsway, 1982, c1981. — 96p ; 18cm
Originally published: Downers Grove, Ill. : Inter-Varsity Press, 1981
ISBN 0-86065-184-3 (pbk) : £1.25 B82-34913

Kerr, Cecil. Just a moment / by Cecil Kerr. — Belfast : Christian Journals, 1982. — 96p ; 22cm
ISBN 0-904302-77-6 (pbk) : Unpriced B82-31635

Larsson, Flora. From my treasure chest / by Flora Larsson. — London : Salvationist Publishing and Supplies, 1981. — 117p ; 22cm
ISBN 0-85412-378-4 (pbk) : £1.95 B82-10706

Lemon, Fred. Breakthrough. — London : Marshall Morgan & Scott, Oct.1981. — [160]p. — (Marshalls paperbacks)
ISBN 0-551-00920-9 (pbk) : £1.50 : CIP entry B81-30640

L'Engle, Madeleine. Walking on water / Madeleine L'Engle. — Tring : Lion Publishing, 1982, c1980. — 191p ; 18cm
Originally published: Wheaton, Ill. : Harold Shaw, 1980
ISBN 0-85648-395-8 (pbk) : £1.75 B82-29532

Lubich, Chiara. The word of life / by Chiara Lubich. — London : New City, 1981. — 57p ; 19cm
Translation of: Parola di vita
ISBN 0-904287-21-1 (pbk) : Unpriced B82-26524

Marshall, Catherine. Meeting God at every turn : a personal family story / Catherine Marshall. — London : Hodder and Stoughton, 1981. — 354p : ports ; 23cm
ISBN 0-340-27155-8 : £5.25 : CIP rev. B81-22495

Osman, May. Through laughter and tears / by May Osman. — Cheltenham : Elim Publications, 1982. — 94p ; 19cm
£1.50 (pbk) B82-37429

Peale, Norman Vincent. The positive power of Jesus Christ / by Norman Vincent Peale. — London : Hodder and Stoughton, 1980 (1981 [printing]). — 266p ; 18cm. — (Hodder Christian paperbacks)
ISBN 0-340-27156-6 (pbk) : £1.75 : CIP rev. B81-31264

Suarez, Federico. The narrow gate / Federico Suarez. — Blackrock : Four Courts, c1982. — 128p ; 22cm
Translation of: La puerta angosta
ISBN 0-906127-60-2 (pbk) : Unpriced B82-29849

Tchividjian, Gigi. A woman's search for serenity / Gigi Tchividjian. — Eastbourne : Kingsway, 1982, c1981. — 158p ; 18cm
Originally published: Old Tappan : Revell, 1981
ISBN 0-86065-183-5 (pbk) : £1.50 B82-35183

248.4 — Christian life. Self-realisation — *For schools*

Donnelly, Noel. The evolving self / Noel Donnelly. — London (Ealing Abbey, W5 2DY) : A-V Publications, 1976. — 50p : ill(some col.) ; 25cm
Unpriced (pbk) B82-13610

248.4 — Christian life. Spirituality

Botting, Michael. A beginner's guide to spirituality / by Michael Botting. — Bramcote : Grove Books, 1982. — 24p ; 22cm. — (Grove spirituality series, ISSN 0262-799x ; no.2)
Bibliography: p24
ISBN 0-907536-25-5 (pbk) : £0.70 B82-39627

MacQuarrie, John. Paths in spirituality / John MacQuarrie. — London : SCM, 1972 (1979 [printing]). — 134p ; 22cm
Includes index
ISBN 0-334-01243-0 (pbk) : £2.95 B82-04227

248.4 — Christian life. Spirituality, *1100-1300*

Bynum, Caroline Walker. Jesus as mother : studies in the spirituality of the high Middle Ages / Caroline Walker Bynum. — Berkeley ; London : University of California Press, c1982. — xiv,279p : ill ; 25cm
Includes index
ISBN 0-520-04194-1 : £21.50 B82-40215

248.4 — Christian life — *Stories for children*

Kingslake, Brian. Angel stories / by Brian Kingslake ; cover and illustrations by G. Roland Smith. — Evesham : James, 1982. — 94p : ill ; 20cm. — (The World of Brian Kingslake)
ISBN 0-85305-250-6 (pbk) : £1.50 : CIP rev. B82-18444

248.4 — Christian life — *Topics for discussion groups*

Anstey, Jill. Caring & sharing : study guides for individuals and groups / Jill Anstey, Barbara Grimes, Margaret Maidment. — Sutherland, N.S.W. : Albatross ; Tring : Lion, c1982. — 112p ; 18cm
ISBN 0-85648-384-2 (pbk) : £1.50 B82-24169

248.4 — Death — *Christian viewpoints*

Rawlings, Maurice. Before death comes / Maurice S. Rawlings. — London : Sheldon, 1980. — 178p ; 22cm
ISBN 0-85969-324-4 (pbk) : £2.50
Primary classification 236'.2 B82-13741

248.4 — Death — *Christian viewpoints* — *Personal observations*

Malz, Betty. My glimpse of eternity / Betty Malz. — London : Hodder and Stoughton, 1982, c1977. — 125p ; 18cm. — (Hodder Christian paperbacks)
Originally published: Waco, Tex. : Chosen Books, 1977
ISBN 0-340-22816-4 (pbk) : £1.25 : CIP rev. B81-35688

248.4 — Grief — *Christian viewpoints*

Read, Dennis R.. Growing through grief / Dennis R. Read. — London (136 Rosendale Rd., SE21 8LG) : Fellowship of Independent Evangelical Churches, [1982?]. — 16p ; 22cm
Unpriced (pbk) B82-24210

248.4 — Loneliness — *Christian viewpoints*

Moore, Sebastian. The inner loneliness. — London : Darton Longman & Todd, Oct.1982. — [128]p
ISBN 0-232-51575-1 : £4.95 : CIP entry B82-24711

248.4 — Love — *Christian viewpoints*

Dominian, Jack. The growth of love and sex / Jack Dominian. — London : Darton, Longman & Todd in association with the National Children's Home, 1982. — 91p ; 20cm
ISBN 0-232-51566-2 (pbk) : £2.95 : CIP rev.
Also classified at 261.8'357'088054 B82-11268

248.4 — Man. Emotional problems — *Christian viewpoints*

Lutzer, Erwin. Managing your emotions / Erwin Lutzer. — Eastbourne : Kingsway, 1982, c1981. — 159p ; 18cm
Originally published: Chappaqua, N.Y. : Christian Herald, c1981
ISBN 0-86065-168-1 (pbk) : £1.50 B82-19357

248.4'024054 — Christian life — *For young persons*

Quinn, Antonia. Living true from cradle to grave / Antonia Quinn. — Ilfracombe : Stockwell, 1981. — 82p ; 18cm
ISBN 0-7223-1493-0 (pbk) : £1.75 B82-12280

248.4'05 — Christian life — *For children* — *Serials*

[Orbit *(London : 1982)***]**. Orbit : the USPG/CMS magazine for children. — Vol.1, no.1-. — London (15 Tufton St., SW1P 3QQ) : USPG, 1982-. — v. : ill ; 30cm
ISSN 0263-8894 = Orbit (London. 1982) : £0.15 B82-33869

248.4'05 — Christian life — *Serials*

[New life *(Sheffield)***]**. The new life : news of what God is doing in South Yorkshire. — No.1 (New Year 1982)-. — Sheffield (6 Viola Bank, Stocksbridge, Sheffield S30 5FZ) : C. Gardner, 1982-. — v. : ill,ports ; 30cm
ISSN 0263-2470 = New life (Sheffield) : £0.15 per issue B82-20877

248.4'07 — Christian life. Experiential learning

Williams, Michael, *1942-*. Learning through experience / by Michael Williams. — Bramcote : Grove Books, 1981. — 25p : ill ; 21cm. — (Grove pastoral series, ISSN 0144-171x ; no.8)
ISBN 0-907536-11-5 (pbk) : £0.70 B82-11383

248.4'0947 — Soviet Union. Christian life

Bordeaux, Michael. Risen indeed. — London : Darton Longman & Todd, Jan.1983. — [112]p
ISBN 0-232-51506-9 : £3.95 : CIP entry B82-36302

248.4'63'0933 — Palestine. Christian pilgrimages to Jerusalem, *312-460*

Hunt, E. D.. Holy Land pilgrimage in the later Roman Empire AD 312-460 / E.D. Hunt. — Oxford : Clarendon Press, 1982. — x,269p ; 23cm
Bibliography: p249-361. — Includes index
ISBN 0-19-826438-0 : £16.50 : CIP rev. B81-34386

248.4'63'094253 — Lincolnshire. Christian pilgrimages, *ca 1150-1540*

Ambrose, Timothy. Pilgrims in medieval Lincolnshire / [compiled and written by Timothy Ambrose]. — [Lincoln] ([City and County Museum, Broadgate, Lincoln]) : Lincolnshire Museums, c1979. — 6p : ill ; 30cm. — (Information sheet / Lincolnshire Museums. Archaeology series ; no.6)
Bibliography: p6
Unpriced (unbound) B82-23422

248.4'7 — Christian life. Donation

Maiden, Peter. Take my silver. — Exeter : Paternoster, Oct.1982. — [48]p
ISBN 0-85364-352-0 (pbk) : £0.90 : CIP entry B82-26713

248.4'7 — Christian life. Self-denial

Chantry, Walter J.. The shadow of the cross : studies in self-denial / Walter J. Chantry. — Edinburgh : The Banner of Truth Trust, 1981. — 79p ; 19cm
ISBN 0-85151-331-x (pbk) : £1.25 B82-16966

248.4′7 — Christian life. Simplicity

Lifestyle in the eighties : an evangelical commitment to simple lifestyle / edited by Ronald J. Sider. — Exeter : Paternoster, c1982. — 256p : 1ill ; 22cm. — (Contemporary issues in social ethics ; v.1)
Includes index
ISBN 0-85364-327-x (pbk) : £5.80 : CIP rev. B81-31079

248.4′82 — Africa. Catholics. Christian life

Gregoire, Nicole. Africa : our way to be other Christs / Nicole Gregoire, Michael McGrath. — London : Chapman, 1981. — 196p ; 20cm
Includes index
ISBN 0-225-66289-2 (pbk) : Unpriced B82-07469

248.4′82 — Catholics. Christian life — *Early works*

Teresa, *of Avila, Saint*. The complete works of Saint Teresa of Jesus / translated and edited by E. Alison Peers ; from the critical edition of P. Silverio de Santa Teresa. — London : Sheed and Ward, 1946 (1982 [printing]). — 3v. ; 22cm
Translation from the Spanish. — Bibliography: v.3, p379-387. — Includes index
ISBN 0-7220-2541-6 (pbk) : £21.00
ISBN 0-7220-2542-4 (v.2) : £7.50
ISBN 0-7220-2543-2 (v.3) : £7.50 B82-34705

248.4′82 — Catholics. Christian life — *For schools*

Clemson, Josephine. Living and growing / Josephine Clemson. — Catholic ed. — Walton-on-Thames : Nelson, 1982. — 68p : ill,ports ; 25cm. — (Living plus ; bk.3)
ISBN 0-17-437023-7 (pbk) : Unpriced B82-27069

248.4′82 — Catholics. Christian life. Gratitude

Fenn, Francis. Thank you! / by Francis Fenn. — London : Catholic Truth Society, 1981. — 12p ; 19cm
ISBN 0-85183-435-3 (pbk) : £0.35 B82-05017

248.4′82 — Catholics. Christian life — *Personal observations*

Orione, Luigi. The restless apostle / from the writings of Don Orione ; foreword by Christopher Butler. — London : Darton, Longman & Todd, 1981. — 146p : ill,facsims ; 22cm
Includes index
ISBN 0-232-51547-6 (pbk) : £4.00 : CIP rev. B81-30509

Why I am still a Catholic / Bernard Bergonzi ... [et al.] ; edited by Robert Nowell. — London : Collins, 1982. — 157p ; 21cm
Bibliography: p155
ISBN 0-00-215247-9 (pbk) : £4.95 : CIP rev. B82-07654

248.4′82 — Catholics. Christian life — *Quotations — Collections*

The **Wisdom** of the Popes / compiled and edited by Tony Castle. — London : Catholic Truth Society, 1981. — 16p ; 14cm
Text on inside cover
ISBN 0-85183-440-x (pbk) : £0.30 B82-09494

248.4′82 — Catholics. Christian life — *Topics for discussion groups*

Work and witness : ′the Easter People′ in daily life. — Slough : St. Paul, 1981. — 24p ; 22cm. — (The Easter People discussion outlines ; 5)
ISBN 0-85439-208-4 (pbk) : £0.65 B82-08765

248.4′82 — South Africa. Catholics. Christian life

Zwane, Mandlenkhosi. Black Christians and the church in South Africa : a talk given by Mandlenkhosi Zwane. — London : CIIR, [1982]. — 1folded sheet(([6]p)) : ill ; 30cm. — (Church in the world ; 4)
ISBN 0-904393-43-7 : £0.10 B82-30629

248.4′83 — Anglicans. Christian life

Robson, Peter, *19---*. Kite-string : creative tension for Anglicans / by Peter Robson. — Consett (The Vicarage, Blanchland, Consett, Durham, DH8 9ST) : P. Robson, [1981?]. — [46]p ; 21cm
Bibliography: p46
Unpriced (pbk) B82-05861

248.4′83 — Anglicans. Christian life — *Correspondence, diaries, etc.*

Andrew, *Father, SDC*. [The life and letters of Father Andrew. Selections]. The life and letters of Father Andrew / compiled by Roger L. Roberts. — London : Mowbray, 1981. — 64p ; 14cm. — (Treasures from the spiritual classics ; 5)
ISBN 0-264-66793-x (cased) : £3.50
ISBN 0-264-66389-6 (pbk) : Unpriced B82-09416

248.4′83 — Anglicans. Christian life — *Early works*

Law, William. [A serious call to a devout and holy life. Selections]. A serious call to a devout and holy life / William Law ; compiled by Roger L. Roberts. — London : Mowbray, 1981. — 60p ; 14cm. — (Treasures from the spiritual classics ; 1)
Extracts reprinted from William Law′s A serious call to a devout and holy life edited by Robert F. Horton. London : Dent, 1898
ISBN 0-264-66783-2 (cased) : £3.50
ISBN 0-264-66762-x (pbk) : Unpriced B82-09412

Taylor, Jeremy, *1613-1667*. [The rule and exercises of holy living. Selections]. The rule and exercises of holy living Vol. two ; and, The rule and exercises of holy dying / Jeremy Taylor ; compiled by Roger L. Roberts. — London : Mowbray, 1981. — 63p ; 15cm. — (Treasures from the spiritual classics ; 4)
Extracts from editions published: London : Dent, 1900-1901
ISBN 0-264-66786-7 (cased) : £3.50
ISBN 0-264-66761-1 (pbk) : Unpriced B82-09415

248.4′83 — Anglicans. Christian life — *Personal observations*

Israel, Martin. Precarious living : the path to life / by Martin Israel. — London : Mowbray, 1982, c1976. — 190p ; 22cm
Originally published: London : Hodder and Stoughton, 1976
ISBN 0-264-66884-7 (pbk) : £3.50 B82-39790

248.4′83 — Anglicans. Christian life. Spirituality, *to 1982*

Moorman, John R. H.. The Anglican spiritual tradition. — London : Darton Longman & Todd, Jan.1983. — [192]p
ISBN 0-232-51455-0 (pbk) : £6.95 : CIP entry B82-33499

248.4′83 — Church of England. Sermons. Special subjects: Christian life — *Texts — For women′s groups*

Booth, Marjorie R.. ′Hidden music′ : talks to women / Marjorie R. Booth. — Ilkeston : Moorley′s Bible & Bookshop, [1981?]. — 59p ; 21cm
ISBN 0-86071-110-2 (pbk) : Unpriced B82-07480

248.4′83043 — Church of England. Clergy. Wives. Christan life

Jackson, Ruth, *1932-*. Battered clergy wives / Ruth Jackson. — Bognor Regis : New Horizon, c1982. — 72p ; 21cm
ISBN 0-86116-595-0 : £3.25
Primary classification 361.1′0941 B82-09560

248.4′841 — Lutherans. Christian life — *Early works*

Arndt, Johann. True Christianity / Johann Arndt ; translation and introduction by Peter Erb ; preface by Heiko A. Oberman. — London : SPCK, 1979. — xvii,301p ; 23cm. — (The Classics of Western spirituality)
Translation of: Book 1 and part of books 2-6 of Wahres Christenthum
ISBN 0-281-03696-9 (pbk) : £6.50 B82-11926

248′.5 — Bible. N.T.. Special subjects: Discipleship

Samuel, Vinay Kumar. The meaning and cost of discipleship / by Vinay Kumar Samuel. — Bombay : Bombay Urban Industrial League for Development ; Exeter : Paternoster Press [distributor], 1981. — 56p ; 22cm. — (Bishop Joshi memorial lectures ; 1980) (A BUILD publication)
ISBN 0-85364-342-3 (pbk) : £0.70 B82-04343

248′.5 — Christian church. Personal evangelism — *Manuals*

Pointer, Roy. Tell what God has done / by Roy Pointer. — Swindon : [British & Foreign Bible Society], c1982. — 35p : ill ; 15cm
Cover title
ISBN 0-564-04662-0 (pbk) : Unpriced B82-24624

248′.5 — Christian life. Discipleship

Watson, David, *1933-*. Discipleship / by David Watson. — London : Hodder and Stoughton, 1981. — 287p : ill ; 20cm
Bibliography: p285-287
ISBN 0-340-26572-8 (pbk) : £3.95 : CIP rev. B81-30134

248.8′2 — Children. Christian life — *For parents*

Stroud, Marion. The gift of a child / written and compiled by Marion Stroud. — Tring : Lion, 1982. — [62]p : col.ill ; 25cm
ISBN 0-85648-406-7 : £4.95 B82-32939

248.8′2′0222 — Children. Christian life — *For children — Illustrations*

Grey, Donald. Dick and his dad / drawn by Donald Grey. — Gerrards Cross (Bulstrode, Gerrards Cross, Bucks, SL9 8SZ) : WEC Youth, [1980]. — 32p : chiefly ill ; 12x18cm
Cover title
£0.15 (pbk) B82-22233

Grey, Donald. Raj and Rani / drawn by Donald Grey. — Gerrards Cross (Bulstrode, Gerrards Cross, Bucks. SL9 8SZ) : WEC Youth, [1980]. — 32p : chiefly ill ; 12x18cm
Cover title
£0.15 (pbk) B82-22232

248.8′42 — Middle-aged men. Christian life

Conway, Jim. Men in mid-life crisis. — Exeter : Paternoster Press, May 1982. — [224]p
Originally published: Elgin, Ill. : D.C. Cook, 1978
ISBN 0-85364-318-0 (pbk) : £4.20 : CIP entry B82-07678

248.8′43 — Women. Christian life

Sanford, Ruth. With God my helper. — London : Marshall, Morgan & Scott, Feb.1982. — [160] p. — (Marshalls paperbacks)
ISBN 0-551-00965-9 (pbk) : £1.60 : CIP entry B82-07806

248.8′6 — Bereavement. Personal adjustment — *Christian viewpoints*

Richardson, Jean, *1925-*. A death in the family / Jean Richardson. — Tring : Lion, 1979 (1982 [printing]). — 108p : ill ; 18cm. — (A Lion guide)
ISBN 0-85648-390-7 (pbk) : £1.50 B82-37753

248.8′6 — Man. Kidneys. Chronic renal failure. Personal adjustment — *Christian viewpoints*

Moffat, George. Yet will I rejoice : a rare poignant glimpse into the loving ways of God / George Moffat with Janice Moffat. — London : Pickering & Inglis, 1982. — 96p ; 19cm
ISBN 0-7208-0511-2 (pbk) : Unpriced B82-23775

248.8′6 — Man. Loss. Personal adjustment — *Christian viewpoints*

Price, Eugenia. Getting through the night. — London (Holy Trinity Church, Marylebone Rd., NW1 4DU) : Triangle, Sept.1982. — [96]p
ISBN 0-281-04011-7 (pbk) : £1.50 : CIP entry B82-18822

248.8′6 — Man. Sickness — *Christian viewpoints*

Heimbucher, Kurt. In times of illness / [based on the original German text by Kurt Heimbucher]. — Tring : Lion, c1982. — 44p : col.ill ; 20cm
ISBN 0-85648-434-2 : £2.50 B82-30967

248.8′6 — Man. Stress — *Christian viewpoints*

Thompson, Peter, *1926-*. Triumphing under stress / Peter Thompson. — Eastbourne : Kingsway, 1981. — 58p ; 18cm
ISBN 0-86065-159-2 (pbk) : £0.95 B82-05853

248.8'6 — Man. Terminal cancer. Personal adjustment — *Christian viewpoints*

Kopp, Ruth Lewshenia. Encounter with terminal illness / Ruth Lewshenia Kopp with Stephen Sorenson. — Tring : Lion, 1981. — 223p ; 18cm
ISBN 0-85648-369-9 (pbk) : £2.95 B82-09807

248.8'6 — Paralysed persons. Christian life — *Personal observationas*

Sinclair, Max. Halfway to Heaven / Max Sinclair with Carolyn Armitage. — London : Hodder and Stoughton, 1982. — 188p ; 18cm. — (Hodder Christian paperbacks)
ISBN 0-340-26336-9 (pbk) : £1.50 : CIP rev. B81-25749

248.8'6 — Physically handicapped married couples. Christian life — *Personal observations*

Creed, Richard. Together for God / Richard and Sandra Creed with Anne Townsend. — London : Triangle, c1981. — 96p ; 18cm
ISBN 0-281-03817-1 (pbk) : £1.50 B82-08178

248'.892 — Church of England. Clergy. Clerical life, ***1930-1980*** — *Personal observations*

Nichols, M. W. H.. Dry breasts / M.W.H. Nichols. — Ilfracombe : Stockwell, 1982. — 156p ; 22cm
ISBN 0-7223-1555-4 (pbk) : £2.95 B82-37940

248.8'94 — Catholic religious communities. Christian life. Sources of evidence: Bible

Moloney, Francis J.. Disciples and prophets : a biblical model for the religious life / Francis J. Moloney. — London : Darton, Longman and Todd, 1980 (1982 [printing]). — xiii,225p ; 22cm
Bibliography: p203-209. — Includes index
ISBN 0-232-51572-7 (pbk) : £4.95 : CIP rev. B82-10770

248.8'942 — Trappists. Christian life — *Personal observations*

Schellenberger, Bernardin. Nomad of the spirit : reflections of a young monastic / Bernardin Schellenberger. — London : Sheed and Ward, 1981. — 105p ; 20cm
Translation of: Ein anderes Leben
ISBN 0-7220-6212-5 (pbk) : £4.50 B82-19431

248.8'9438 — Anchoresses. Christian life. Manuals: Ancren Riwle — *Critical studies*

Georgianna, Linda. The solitary self : individuality in the Ancrene Wisse / Linda Georgianna. — Cambridge, Mass. ; London : Harvard University Press, 1981. — xii,169p ; 24cm
Includes index
ISBN 0-674-81751-6 : £11.50 B82-03921

249 — CHRISTIAN OBSERVANCES IN FAMILY LIFE

249 — Baptist families. Christian life

LaHaye, Tim F.. Spirit-controlled family / Tim & Bev LaHaye. — Eastbourne : Kingsway, 1980, c1978. — 188p ; 18cm
Originally published: Wheaton : Tyndale House, 1966 ; London : Coverdale House, 1973
ISBN 0-86065-094-4 (pbk) : £1.50 B82-32395

249 — Catholics. Families. Christian life — *Topics for discussion groups*

Called to be holy : prayer, worship and action among 'the Easter People'. — Slough : St. Paul, 1981. — 24p ; 22cm. — (The Easter People discussion outlines ; 6)
ISBN 0-85439-209-2 (pbk) : £0.65 B82-08766

Faith and family : marriage and family life within 'the Easter People'. — Slough : St. Paul, 1981. — 24p ; 22cm. — (The Easter People discussion outlines ; 4)
ISBN 0-85439-207-6 (pbk) : £0.65 B82-08764

The **New** priority : adult formation for 'the Easter People'. — Slough : St. Paul, 1981. — 24p ; 22cm. — (The Easter People discussion outlines ; 3)
ISBN 0-85439-206-8 (pbk) : £0.65 B82-08763

249 — Christian life. Family worship

Richardson, Mary K.. The family liturgy book / compiled by Mary K. Richardson. — Leigh-on-Sea : Mayhew, 1977. — 111p ; 21cm
ISBN 0-905725-36-0 (pbk) : £2.50 B82-01758

249 — Families. Christian life. Prayers for the sick — *Manuals*

MacNutt, Francis. The prayer that heals : praying for healing in the family / Francis MacNutt. — London : Hodder and Stoughton, 1982, c1981. — 116p ; 18cm. — (Hodder Christian paperbacks)
Originally published: Notre Dame, Ind. : Ave Maria Press, 1981
ISBN 0-340-28079-4 (pbk) : £1.25
ISBN 0-340-26411-x B82-30448

251 — CHRISTIAN CHURCH. PREACHING

251 — Christian church. Preaching

Stott, John R. W.. I believe in preaching / John Stott. — London : Hodder and Stoughton, 1982. — 351p ; 22cm
Bibliography: p341-351
ISBN 0-340-27564-2 (pbk) : £5.95 : CIP rev. B81-36364

251 — Christian church. Preaching — *Manuals*

Ireson, Gordon W.. A handbook of parish preaching / by Gordon W. Ireson. — London : Mowbray, 1982. — xi,145p ; 19cm
Includes index
ISBN 0-264-66857-x (pbk) : £3.75 B82-40404

The **Living** word. — Alton : Redemptorist
Cycle 'B'. — c1982
Part 2 / contributors John Trenchard (general editor) ... [et al.]. — [64]p ; 21cm
ISBN 0-85231-053-6 (pbk) : Unpriced B82-17377

Spurgeon, C. H.. Lectures to my students : the art of preaching. — London : Marshall, Morgan & Scott, Feb.1982. — [448]p. — (Marshalls study library)
ISBN 0-551-05299-6 (pbk) : £5.95 : CIP entry B82-07807

251 — Christian church. Preaching. Use of Bible

Fuller, Reginald H.. The use of the Bible in preaching / Reginald H. Fuller. — London : Bible Reading Fellowship, 1981. — 79p ; 22cm. — (BRF book club ; no.9)
Bibliography: p75-79
ISBN 0-900164-54-9 (pbk) : £1.75 B82-15083

251 — Christian church. Preaching. Use of Bible. O.T.

Gowan, Donald E.. Reclaiming the Old Testament for the Christian pulpit / Donald E. Gowan. — Edinburgh : T. & T. Clark, 1981, c1980. — vi,163p ; 23cm
Originally published: Atlanta : John Knox Press, 1980. — Includes index
ISBN 0-567-29106-5 (pbk) : £4.50 B82-15367

251 — Church of England. Eucharist. Preaching

Bunting, Ian. Preaching at communion / by Ian Bunting. — Bramcote : Grove Books
(1). — 1981. — 25p ; 22cm. — (Grove worship series, ISSN 0144-1728 ; no.78)
Text on inside cover
ISBN 0-907536-10-7 (pbk) : £0.60 B82-06339

Bunting, Ian. Preaching at Communion / by Ian Bunting. — Bramcote : Grove. — (Grove worship series, ISSN 0144-1728 ; no.79)
(2). — 1982. — 24p ; 21cm
ISBN 0-907536-14-x (pbk) : £0.70 B82-17699

251'.02 — Church of England. Sermons — *Sermon outlines — For church year*

Cleverley Ford, D. W.. Preaching on special occasions / D.W. Cleverley Ford. — London : Mowbray
Vol.2. — 1982. — viii,134p ; 22cm
ISBN 0-264-66777-8 (pbk) : £3.50 B82-14039

Runcorn, D. B.. Preaching at the parish communion : ASB gospels — Sundays: year one / D.B. Runcorn. — London : Mowbray, 1982. — vii,135p ; 22cm. — (Mowbray's sermon outline series)
ISBN 0-264-66801-4 (pbk) : £3.75 B82-34797

252 — CHRISTIAN CHURCH. SERMONS

252'.02 — Catholic Church. Sermons — *Anglo-Norman texts*

Bozon, Nicholas. Nine verse sermons by Nicholas Bozon : the art of an Anglo-Norman poet and preacher / Brian J. Levy. — Oxford : Society for the Study of Mediaeval Languages and Literature, 1981. — 98p ; 22cm. — (Medium Aevum monographs. New series ; 11)
ISBN 0-907570-01-1 (pbk) : Unpriced : CIP rev. B81-32587

252'.02 — Catholic Church. Sermons — *Texts*

Escrivá de Balaguer, Josemaría. Friends of God : homilies / Josemaría Escrivá de Balaguer. — Dublin : Four Courts, 1981. — xxii,296p,[18] leaves of plates : col.ill ; 22cm
Translation of: Amigos de Dios. — Includes index
ISBN 0-906127-41-6 (cased) : Unpriced
ISBN 0-906127-40-8 (pbk) : Unpriced
ISBN 0-906127-42-4 (De Luxe ed.) : Unpriced B82-00991

Escrivá de Balaguer, Josemaría. Friends of God : homilies / Josemaría Escrivá de Balaguer. — London : Scepter, 1981. — xii,296p : ill ; 21cm
Translation of: Amigos de Dios. — Includes index
ISBN 0-906138-03-5 (cased) : Unpriced
ISBN 0-906138-02-7 (pbk) : Unpriced
ISBN 0-906138-04-3 (De Luxe) : Unpriced B82-08931

John Paul II, *Pope*. The Pope in Britain : collected homilies and speeches. — Slough : St Paul, 1982. — vi,106p ; 21cm
Author: Pope John Paul II
ISBN 0-85439-217-3 (pbk) : £2.95 B82-33544

252'.02 — Catholic Church. Sermons — *Texts — For church year*

The **Living** word. — Alton : Redemptorist
Cycle 'C'
Pt.1 / contributors John Trenchard (general editor) ... [et al.]. — c1979. — [64]p ; 21cm. — (A Redemptorist publication)
ISBN 0-85231-058-7 (pbk) : Unpriced B82-24425

The **Living** word. — Alton : Redemptorist
Cycle 'C'
Pt.2 / contributors John Trenchard (general editor) ... [et al.]. — c1980. — [64]p ; 21cm. — (A Redemptorist publication)
ISBN 0-85231-060-9 (pbk) : Unpriced B82-24426

The **Living** word. — Alton : Redemptorist
Cycle 'C'
Pt.3 / contributors John Trenchard (general editor) ... [et al.]. — c1980. — [64]p ; 21cm. — (A Redemptorist publication)
ISBN 0-85231-061-7 (pbk) : Unpriced B82-24427

The **Living** word. — Alton : Redemptorist
Cycle 'C'
Pt.4 / contributors John Trenchard (general editor) ... [et al.]. — c1980. — [64]p ; 21cm. — (A Redemptorist publication)
ISBN 0-85231-063-3 (pbk) : Unpriced B82-24428

The **Living** word. — Alton : Redemptorist
Cycle 'A'
Pt.1 / contributors John Trenchard (general editor) ... [et al.]. — c1980. — [64]p ; 21cm. — (A Redemptorist publication)
ISBN 0-85231-064-1 (pbk) : Unpriced B82-24423

252′.02 — Catholic Church. Sermons — *Texts — For church year* *continuation*

The **Living** word. — Alton : Redemptorist. — (A Redemptorist publication)
Cycle 'B'
Part 3 / contributors John Trenchard (general editor) ... [et al.]. — c1982. — [64]p ; 21cm
ISBN 0-85231-054-4 (pbk) : Unpriced B82-29508

The **Living** word. — Alton : Redemptorist
Cycle 'B'
Pt.4 / contributors John Trenchard (general editor) ... [et al.]. — c1979. — [64]p ; 21cm. — (A Redemptorist publication)
ISBN 0-85231-041-2 (pbk) : Unpriced B82-24424

252′.03 — Church of England. Sermons — *Texts*

Johnson, Samuel. Sermons / Samuel Johnson ; edited by Jean Hagstrum and James Gray. — New Haven ; London : Yale University Press, 1978. — lix,354p : facsims ; 23cm. — (The Yale edition of the works of Samuel Johnson ; v.14)
Includes index
ISBN 0-300-02104-6 : £16.20 B82-41049

252′.04 — Continental Protestant churches. Sermons — *Texts*

Gollwitzer, Helmut. The way to life : sermons in a time of world crisis / by Helmut Gollwitzer ; translated by David Cairns. — Edinburgh : Clark, 1981. — xiii,153p ; 23cm
Translation of: Wendung zum Leben
ISBN 0-567-09322-0 : £8.95 B82-28186

252′.04 — Lollards. Sermons — *Anthologies*

Wycliffite sermons. — Oxford : Oxford University Press, Aug.1982. — (Oxford English texts)
Vol.1. — [672]p
ISBN 0-19-812704-9 : £25.00 : CIP entry B82-15681

252′.058 — Union of Welsh Independents. Sermons — *Welsh texts*

Jenkins, Emlyn G.. Cyfoeth ei ras : cyfrol o bregethau / Emlyn G. Jenkins. — Abertawe [Swansea] : Tŷ John Penry, 1982. — 87p ; 22cm
ISBN 0-903701-49-9 (pbk) : £2.00 B82-33178

253 — CHRISTIAN CHURCH. CLERGY AND PASTORAL WORK

253 — Christian church. Pastoral work

Wright, Frank, *1922-*. The pastoral nature of the ministry / Frank Wright. — London : SCM, 1980 (1981 [printing]). — 89p ; 22cm
ISBN 0-334-01212-0 (pbk) : £2.95 B82-41086

253 — Christian church. Pastoral work. Role of laity

Comerford, Monica. Many ministries / Monica Comerford, Christine Dodd. — London : Catholic Truth Society, 1982. — 16p ; 18cm
Text on inside cover
ISBN 0-85183-455-8 (pbk) : £0.45 B82-24996

253 — Soviet Union. Catholic Church. Pastoral work — *Correspondence, diaries, etc*

Bukowinski, Władysław. A priest in Russia / Wladyslaw Bukowinski ; [selected and translated by Alexander Tomsky]. — London : Incorporated Catholic Truth Society, 1982. — 16p ; 19cm
Text on inside covers. — Cover title
ISBN 0-85183-456-6 (pbk) : £0.40 B82-19579

253′.2 — Church of England. Rectors. Clerical life — *Early works*

Herbert, George. The country parson ; The temple / George Herbert ; edited, with an introduction by John N. Wall, Jr. ; preface by A.M. Allchin. — London : SPCK, 1981. — xxii,354p ; 23cm. — (The Classics of Western spirituality)
Originally published: New York : Paulist Press, c1981. — Bibliography: p335-339. — Includes index
ISBN 0-281-03821-x (pbk) : £8.50
Also classified at 821′.3 B82-08474

253′.2′0922 — Great Britain. Rural regions. Christian church. Clergy, *1616-1880 — Correspondence, diaries, etc.*

Brander, Michael. The country divine / Michael Brander. — Edinburgh : St Andrew, 1981. — xiii,213p : ill,1map ; 20cm
Bibliography: p212-213
ISBN 0-7152-0492-0 : £3.90 B82-13538

253.5 — Christian church. Pastoral work. Counselling

Lake, Frank. Tight corners in pastoral counselling / Frank Lake. — London : Darton, Longman and Todd, 1981. — xvii,187p ; 22cm
Includes index
ISBN 0-232-51309-0 (pbk) : £4.95 : CIP rev. B81-11957

253.5 — Christian church. Pastoral work. Counselling — *Manuals*

Hughes, Selwyn. The Christian counsellor's pocket guide / Selwyn Hughes. — Eastbourne : Kingsway, 1982. — 96p ; 18cm
ISBN 0-86065-153-3 (pbk) : £1.50 B82-19354

Jacobs, Michael, *1941-*. Still small voice : a practical introduction to counselling for pastors and other helpers / Michael Jacobs. — London : SPCK, 1982. — x,182p ; 22cm. — (New library of pastoral care)
Bibliography: p179-180. — Includes index
ISBN 0-281-03852-x (pbk) : £3.95 B82-34733

253.5 — Christian counselling

Peterson, Evelyn H.. Who cares? : a handbook of Christian counselling / by Evelyn H. Peterson. — Exeter : Paternoster Press, c1980. — 181p ; 22cm
Bibliography: p177-178. — Includes index
ISBN 0-85364-272-9 (pbk) : £3.20 : CIP rev. B80-19027

253.5 — Counselling — *Manuals — For Christians*

Chave-Jones, Myra. The gift of helping. — Leicester : Inter-Varsity Press, Nov.1982. — [112]p
ISBN 0-85110-444-4 (pbk) : CIP entry B82-27033

253.7′0880623 — England. Urban regions. Working classes. Evangelism by Christian church

Joslin, Roy. Urban harvest / Roy Joslin. — Welwyn : Evangelical Press, 1982. — 327p ; 22cm
ISBN 0-85234-159-8 (pbk) : £4.95 B82-37447

254 — CHRISTIAN CHURCH. PARISH WORK. ORGANISATION

254′.5 — Church of Scotland. Membership

Levack, John G.. The potential church : lectures on the meaning of church membership under the terms of the Chalmers Lectureship Trust / by John G. Levack. — Edinburgh : Saint Andrew Press, 1982. — xiii,133p ; 20cm
ISBN 0-7152-0542-0 (pbk) : £4.50 B82-21227

254.8 — Church of England. Parishes. Financial management. Covenants

Parish Covenant Funding programme (C. of E. Parishes) : step-by-step guidebook, introduction & parts I, II & III : Thwaite Parish Funding. — Cockermouth (Wentwood, Greysouthern, Cockermouth, Cumbria, CA13 0UQ) : Thwaite Funding Consultants, c1981. — 1v. : ill ; 30cm
Cover title
Unpriced (spiral) B82-09022

254.8 — Church of England. Parishes. Fund raising. Covenants — *Manuals*

The **Recurring-income** parish covenant programme, administration, printing and secretarial guide. — Cockermouth (Westwood, Greysouthern, Cockermouth, Cumbria CA13 0UQ) : Thwaite Funding Consultants, c1981. — 19leaves : ill,forms ; 30cm
Specimen documents in plastic pockets as inserts
Unpriced (spiral) B82-26357

254.8 — England. Tithes

Kendall, R. T.. Tithing. — London : Hodder & Stoughton, Aug.1982. — [96]p
ISBN 0-340-28201-0 (pbk) : £1.25 : CIP entry B82-15743

254.8 — Europe. Tithes, *ca 1400-1800.* **Research**

Le Roy Ladurie, Emmanuel. Tithe and agrarian history from the fourteenth to the nineteenth century : an essay in comparative history / Emmanuel Le Roy Ladurie, Joseph Goy ; translated by Susan Burke. — Cambridge : Cambridge University Press, 1982. — ix,206p : ill ; 23cm
Translation of the French. — Bibliography: p205-206
ISBN 0-521-23974-5 : £17.50 : CIP rev. B81-39256

254.8 — Suffolk. Boxford. Church of England, *1529-1561 — Accounts*

Boxford churchwardens' accounts 1530-1561 / edited by Peter Northeast. — Woodbridge, Suffolk : Published by the Boydell Press for the Suffolk Records Society, 1982. — xv,108p : ill,1map ; 24cm. — (Vol.23)
Bibliography: pix-x. — Includes index
ISBN 0-85115-160-4 : £12.00 : CIP rev. B81-33648

254.8 — United States. Churches. Taxation

Weber, Paul J.. Private churches and public money : church-government fiscal relations / Paul J. Weber and Dennis A. Gilbert. — Westport ; London : Greenwood, 1981. — xx,260p ; 22cm. — (Contributions to the study of religion, ISSN 0196-7053 ; no.1)
Bibliography: p239-253. — Includes index
ISBN 0-313-22484-6 : Unpriced B82-02034

255 — CHRISTIANITY. RELIGIOUS CONGREGATIONS AND ORDERS

255 — Catholics. Community life

Murphy, Columcille. Community in Christ / Columcille Murphy ; edited by Thomas Curran. — Dublin : Carmelite Centre of Spirituality, c1979. — 46p ; 20cm. — (Living flame series ; v.8)
Unpriced (pbk) B82-04415

255′.1′00922 — England. Benedictines. Monasticism — *Personal observations — Collections*

A **Touch** of God : eight monastic journeys / edited by Maria Boulding ; introduction by Philip Jebb. — London : SPCK, 1982. — viii,180p ; 22cm
ISBN 0-281-03853-8 (pbk) : £4.95 B82-26853

255′.106 — Benedictines. Community life. Benedict, *Saint.* **Regula** — *Expositions*

Parry, David. Rule of Saint Benedict. — London : Darton, Longman & Todd, Dec.1982. — [144]p
ISBN 0-232-51585-9 (cased) : £3.50 : CIP entry
ISBN 0-232-51584-0 (pbk) : £1.95 B82-32288

255′.8 — Anglican churches. Franciscans

Williams, Barrie. The Franciscan revival in the Anglican communion. — London : Darton Longman & Todd, Sept.1982. — [208]p
ISBN 0-232-51549-2 (pbk) : £6.50 : CIP entry B82-25058

255′.98 — Community of St Mary the Virgin — *Personal observations*

Kirsty, *Sister*. The choice / by Sister Kirsty. — London : Hodder and Stoughton, 1982. — 256p ; 18cm. — (Hodder Christian paperbacks)
ISBN 0-340-26345-8 (pbk) : £1.95 : CIP rev. B82-07434

259 — CHRISTIAN CHURCH. PAROCHIAL ACTIVITIES

259′.2′0941 — Great Britain. Church of England. Pastoral work with young persons — *Proposals*

Towards a policy for work with young people : a discussion paper produced for the General Synod Board of Education by a working party consisting largely of young people. — [London] : CIO, 1982. — 31p : ill ; 22cm
Bibliography: p30-31
Unpriced (unbound) B82-18951

259′.22 — United Reformed Church. Children. Activities

Junior work book. — Rev. ed. — [London] : United Reformed Church, Church Life Department, 1981. — 39p : ill ; 21cm
Previous ed.: London : Churches of Christ Christian Education Department, 197-?
ISBN 0-902256-50-5 (pbk) : £0.60 B82-20343

259′.4 — Christian church. Pastoral work with physically handicapped persons

Van Dongen-Garrad, Jessie. Invisible barriers : caring for physically disabled people. — London : SPCK, Oct.1982. — [192]p. — (New library of pastoral care)
ISBN 0-281-04014-1 (pbk) : £3.95 : CIP entry B82-23474

259′.8 — Christian church. Parish life. Group activities: Drama. Use of Bible — *Manuals*

Stickley, Steve. Using the Bible in drama / Steve and Janet Stickley and Jim Belben. — London : Bible Society, c1980 (1981 [printing]). — 96p : ill ; 20cm. — (Using the Bible series ; 3)
Bibliography: p96
ISBN 0-564-00990-3 (pbk) : Unpriced B82-20993

260 — CHRISTIANITY. SOCIAL AND ECCLESIASTICAL THEOLOGY

260 — Bible. N.T.. Special subjects: Christian church — *Expositions*

Drane, John W.. The life of the early church / John W. Drane. — Tring : Lion, 1982. — 144p : ill,maps,facsims,1port ; 24cm
Bibliography: p142-143. — Includes index
ISBN 0-85648-348-6 (pbk) : £3.95 B82-23750

260 — Christian church

Allen, Stuart. The Church / by Stuart Allen. — London (52a Wilson St., EC2A 2ER) : Berean Publishing, [198-?]. — 7p ; 21cm
Unpriced (Unpriced) B82-34763

Moltmann, Jürgen. The Church in the power of the Spirit : a contribution to Messianic ecclesiology / Jürgen Moltmann ; [translated by Margaret Kohl]. — London : SCM, 1977 (1981 [printing]). — xvii,407p ; 22cm
Translation of : Kirche in der Kraft des Geistes. — Includes index
ISBN 0-334-01942-7 (pbk) : £6.50 B82-41084

Watson, David, *1933-*. I believe in the Church / by David Watson. — London : Hodder and Stoughton, 1982, c1978. — 386p : ill ; 18cm + study guide(73p : ill ; 18cm). — (Hodder Christian paperbacks)
Originally published: 1978
ISBN 0-340-27565-0 (pbk) : £2.25 : CIP rev.
ISBN 0-340-28206-1 (Study guide) : £0.95 B82-11756

Watson, David, *1933-*. Study guide to I believe in the Church. — London : Hodder and Stoughton, June 1982. — [96]p
ISBN 0-340-28206-1 (pbk) : £0.95 : CIP entry B82-12137

261 — CHRISTIANITY. SOCIAL THEOLOGY

261 — Authority — *Christian viewpoints*

Dominian, Jack. Authority : a Christian interpretation of the psychological evolution of authority / Jack Dominian. — London : Darton, Longman and Todd, 1981, c1976. — iii,107p ; 22cm
Originally published: London : Burns & Oates, 1976
ISBN 0-232-51552-2 (pbk) : £3.95 : CIP rev. B81-31178

261 — Christian church. Worldliness

White, John, *1924 Mar.5-*. Flirting with the world. — London : Hodder & Stoughton, Feb.1983. — [160]p
ISBN 0-340-32474-0 (pbk) : £1.50 : CIP entry B82-36315

261 — Civilization, *to 1980* — *Christian viewpoints*

Newbigin, Edith. The development of the human race / by Edith Newbigin. — Liverpool (47 Reeds Rd, Huyton, Liverpool L36 7SL) : [E. Newbigin], [1981?]. — 119p ; 21cm
Bibliography: p119
Unpriced (pbk) B82-11918

261 — Education — *Christian viewpoints*

Catherwood, *Sir* Fred. Education — a better way? : the 1977 Annual Lecture of the Association of Christian Teachers given at the Polytechnic of Central London on 15th January 1977 / Sir Fred Catherwood. — London (47 Marylebone Lane, W1M 6AX) : Association of Christian Teachers, 1977. — 15p ; 21cm
£0.10 (pbk) B82-35149

May, Philip R.. Which way to teach? / Philip R. May. — Leicester : Inter-Varsity, 1981. — 176p ; 18cm
Bibliography: p176
ISBN 0-85110-428-2 (pbk) : Unpriced : CIP rev. B81-22554

Newbigin, Edith. I am who I am / by Edith Newbigin. — Liverpool (47 Reeds Rd, Huyton, Liverpool L36 7SL) : [E. Newbigin], [1981?]. — 115p : ill ; 21cm
Bibliography: p114-115
Unpriced (pbk) B82-11924

261 — Middle East — *Christian viewpoints*

Tatford, Frederick A.. The Middle East / by Fredk. A. Tatford. — Bath (1 Widcombe Crescent, Bath, BA2 6AQ) : Echoes, [1982]. — 16p : ill,1map ; 19cm
£0.10 (unbound) B82-31664

261 — Society — *Christian viewpoints*

Christians and the future of social democracy / edited by Michael H. Taylor. — Ormskirk : Hesketh, 1982. — 168p ; 22cm
ISBN 0-905777-32-8 : £18.50 B82-39634

Eliot, T. S.. The idea of a Christian society and other writings. — 2nd ed. — London : Faber, Sept.1982. — [192]p
Previous ed.: 1939
ISBN 0-571-18069-8 (cased) : £9.95 : CIP entry
ISBN 0-571-11891-7 (pbk) : £3.50 B82-28467

Newbigin, Edith. Life is for living / Edith Newbigin. — [Liverpool] (47 Reeds Rd, Huyton, Liverpool L36 7SL) : [E. Newbigin], [1981?]. — 111p ; 21cm
Bibliography: p111
Unpriced (pbk) B82-11921

Robinson, John A. T.. The roots of a radical / John A.T. Robinson. — London : SCM, 1980. — viii,168p ; 22cm
Bibliography: p164-166. — Includes index
ISBN 0-334-02321-1 (pbk) : £3.50 B82-29269

Storkey, Alan. A Christian social perspective / Alan Storkey. — Leicester : Inter-Varsity, 1979. — 416p ; 22cm
Includes index
ISBN 0-85110-593-9 (pbk) : £8.95 B82-22926

261.1 — Environment — *Christian viewpoints*

Attfield, Robin. The ethics of environmental concern. — Oxford : Blackwell, Sept.1982. — [224]p
ISBN 0-631-13137-x : £15.00 : CIP entry B82-20288

261.1 — Society. Role of Christian church

Hill, Clifford. The day comes : a prophetic view of the contemporary world / Clifford Hill. — London : Collins : Fount, 1982. — 350p : ill,maps ; 18cm
Bibliography: p345-350
ISBN 0-00-626521-9 (pbk) : £2.50 B82-26724

261.1 — Society. Role of Christian church — *Catholic viewpoints*

Schillebeeckx, Edward. World and church / Edward Schillebeeckx. — London : Sheed and Ward, 1982, c1971. — vii,308p ; 22cm
Translation of: Wereld en Kerk. — Originally published: 1971
ISBN 0-7220-9812-x (pbk) : £8.50 B82-19436

261.1′09 — Society. Role of Christianity, *400-ca 1500*

Brown, Peter, *1935-*. Society and the holy in late antiquity / Peter Brown. — London : Faber, 1982. — vii,347p ; 24cm
Includes index
ISBN 0-571-11686-8 : £10.50 : CIP rev. B82-03111

261.1′094 — Europe. Society. Role of Christians

Hume, George Basil. 'The truth concerning man —' : some reflections on the Christian contribution to the future of Europe / Basil Hume. — London : Catholic Truth Society, 1982. — 16p ; 19cm
ISBN 0-85183-464-7 (pbk) : £0.40 B82-33005

261.1′0941 — Great Britain. Society. Role of Christian church

Caribbean Christian challenge : the report of the ecumenical team from the Caribbean who visited Britain in the autumn of 1981, under the auspices of the Conference for World Mission, the British Council of Churches. — London (2 Eaton Gate SW1W 9BL) : Conference for World Mission, British Council of Churches, 1981. — 71p ; 30cm
£0.60 (pbk) B82-17402

261.1′09415 — Ireland. Society. Role of Catholic Church, *1780-1845*

Connolly, S. J.. Priests and people in pre-famine Ireland 1780-1845 / S.J. Connolly. — Dublin : Gill and Macmillan, 1982. — 338p : 1map ; 23cm
Bibliography: p314-329 . — Includes index
ISBN 0-7171-0955-0 : £17.00 B82-15370

261.1′095 — Asia. Society. Role of Catholic Church

Kim, Stephen. Development and underdevelopment in Asia / [Stephen Kim]. — London : CIIR, c1980. — 1folded sheet([6]p) : ill ; 30cm. — (Church in the world ; 7)
Translated from French
ISBN 0-904393-60-7 : £0.10 B82-30630

261.2 — Non-Christian religions. Attitudes of Christianity

Christianity and other faiths. — Exeter : Paternoster Press, Oct.1982. — [64]p
ISBN 0-85364-363-6 (pbk) : £0.90 : CIP entry B82-30316

261.2 — Non-Christian sects. Attitudes of Christianity

Who are they? : new religious groups : how should we respond? / [produced by the Mission and Other Faiths Committee, the World Church and Mission Department, The United Reformed Church]. — London : United Reformed Church, [1982?]. — 8p ; 21cm
Cover title. — Text on inside cover
ISBN 0-902256-52-1 (pbk) : £0.35 B82-30675

261.2′1 — Europe. German speaking countries. Christianity. Relations with Marxism, *1870-1970*

Bentley, James. Between Marx and Christ : the dialogue in German-speaking Europe 1870-1970 / James Bentley. — London : Verso, 1982. — xi,191p ; 21cm
Bibliography: p166-185. — Includes index
ISBN 0-86091-048-2 (cased) : £12.00 : CIP rev.
ISBN 0-89091-748-7 (pbk) : Unpriced
Also classified at 335.4′0943 B82-01576

261.2′6 — Christian church. Relations with Judaism, *70-1978*

Stevens, George H.. Strife between brothers / George H. Stevens. — London : Olive Press, 1979. — 64p ; 18cm
ISBN 0-904054-13-6 (pbk) : £1.00
Also classified at 296.3′872 B82-05428

261.5′1 — Knowledge. Acquisition. Attitudes of Catholic Church — *Study examples: Rais, Gilles de, baron*

Crowley, Aleister. The banned lecture : Gilles de Rais : to have been delivered before the Oxford University Poetry Society on the evening of Monday February 3rd, 1930 / by Aleister Crowley. — [Carnforth] ([White Scar, Ingleton, via Carnforth, Lancs.]) : [Society for the Propagation of Religious Truth], [c1982]. — [24]p ; 19cm
Unpriced (pbk) B82-20932

261.5′15 — Children, to 5 years. Development — *Christian viewpoints — Topics for discussion groups*
Durran, Maggie. Beginnings / Maggie Durran. — [Poole] : Post Green Press, 1982. — 96p : ill,1form ; 21x31cm. — (A Take time to grow course)
ISBN 0-906309-22-0 (spiral) : £1.95
B82-41018

261.5′15 — Man. Failures — *Christian viewpoints*
Blair, Charles. The other side of failure. — London : Hodder and Stoughton, Aug.1982. — [240]p
ISBN 0-340-28199-5 (pbk) : £1.75 : CIP entry
B82-15742

261.5′5 — Science — *Christian viewpoints*
Wright, V.. The relevance of Christianity in a scientific age / V. Wright. — London : Christian Medical Fellowship, 1981. — 18p ; 18cm
ISBN 0-906747-06-6 (pbk) : £0.45 B82-04191

261.5′6 — Great Britain. Society. Effectgs of technological development — *Christian viewpoints*
Bleakley, David. In place of work — the sufficient society : a study of technology from the point of view of people / David Bleakley. — London : SCM Press, 1981. — 119p ; 22cm
Includes index
ISBN 0-334-00691-0 (pbk) : £3.95 B82-22477

261.5′6 — Medicine — *Christian viewpoints*
Light in the darkness : disabled lives? : papers on some contemporary medical problems / collected by the Medical Committee, Order of Christian Unity. — [London] : Unity, c1981. — viii,109p ; 22cm
Bibliography: p101. — Includes index
ISBN 0-7289-0010-6 (pbk) : £2.25 B82-14038

261.5′6 — Psychotherapy — *Christian viewpoints*
Dunstan, G. R.. Therapy and care. — Aberdeen : Aberdeen University Press, Mar.1982. — [26]p. — (The Malcolm Millar lecture, ISSN 0144-1663 ; 1981)
ISBN 0-08-028467-1 (pbk) : £1.00 : CIP entry
B82-10665

261.5′7 — Arts — *Christian viewpoints*
Wilson, John, *1926-*. One of the richest gifts : an introductory study of the arts from a Christian world-view / John Wilson. — Edinburgh : Handsel, 1981. — viii,124p ; 22cm
Bibliography: p125
ISBN 0-905312-17-1 (pbk) : £5.00 B82-09265

261.7 — Great Britain. Political parties: Conservative Party. Policies — *Christian viewpoints*
Thatcherism : the Jubilee Lent lectures, 1980 / edited by Kenneth Leech. — London (St Mary's House, Eastway, E9) : Jubilee Publications, [1982?]. — 40p ; 21cm
£0.50 (unbound) B82-17757

261.7 — Latin America. Human rights. Protection. Role of Catholic Church
Lernoux, Penny. Cry of the people : the struggle for human rights in Latin America — the Catholic Church in conflict with U.S. policy / Penny Lernoux. — Harmondsworth : Penguin, 1982. — xxiv,535p ; 20cm
Originally published: New York : Doubleday, 1980. — Includes index
ISBN 0-14-006047-2 (pbk) : £2.95 B82-22488

261.7 — Latin America. Politics — *Christian viewpoints*
Gonzalez, Peter Asael. Prophets of revolution. — London : Hodder & Stoughton, Nov.1982. — [192]p
ISBN 0-340-32372-8 (pbk) : £1.75 : CIP entry
B82-29443

261.7 — Marxism — *Christian viewpoints*
Lash, Nicholas. A matter of hope : a theologian's reflections on the thought of Karl Marx / Nicholas Lash. — London : Darton, Longman and Todd, 1981. — 312p ; 23cm
Bibliography: p293-298. — Includes index
ISBN 0-232-51494-1 : £14.95 : CIP rev.
B81-26790

Turner, Denys. Marxism and Christianity. — Oxford : Blackwell, Sept.1982. — [224]p
ISBN 0-631-13118-3 : £12.50 : CIP entry
B82-20285

261.7 — Philippines. Politics. Violence — *Catholic viewpoints*
Catholic Church. *Catholic Bishops' Conference of the Philippines*. The Philippines : exhortation against violence : a joint pastoral letter of the Philippine hierarchy / [for the Catholic Bishops' Conference of the Philippines]. — London : CIIR, [1982?]. — [4]p : ill ; 30cm. — (Church in the world ; 6)
ISBN 0-904393-50-x (unbound) : £0.10
B82-30626

261.7 — Political theology
Cobb, John B.. Process theology as political theology. — Manchester : Manchester University Press, Mar.1982. — [160]p
ISBN 0-7190-0869-7 (pbk) : £7.50 : CIP entry
B82-06047

261.7 — Politics. Role of Christian church
Davis, Charles. Theology and political society : the Halsean lectures in the University of Cambridge 1978 / Charles Davis. — Cambridge : Cambridge University Press, 1980. — ix,196p ; 23cm
Bibliography: p187-194. — Includes index
ISBN 0-521-22538-8 : £9.50 : CIP rev.
B80-29073

Griffiths, Brian, *1941-*. Morality and the market place. — London : Hodder & Stoughton, Sept.1982. — [160]p
ISBN 0-340-26354-7 (pbk) : £5.50 : CIP entry
B82-18744

Hinchliff, Peter. Holiness and politics / Peter Hinchliff. — London : Darton, Longman and Todd, 1982. — ix,213p ; 22cm
Includes index
ISBN 0-232-51502-6 (pbk) : £8.95 : CIP rev.
B82-10573

261.7 — Politics. Violence — *Catholic viewpoints*
McDonagh, Enda. Violence and political change / Enda McDonagh. — [London] ([22 Coleman Fields, N1 7AF]) : Catholic Institute for International Relations, c1978. — 19p ; 21cm
Text on inside cover
£0.25 (pbk) B82-11563

261.7 — South Africa. Apartheid — *Catholic Institute for International Relations viewpoints*
South Africa in the 1980s. — London : Catholic Institute for International Relations, [1980]. — 43p ; 22cm
ISBN 0-904393-54-2 (pbk) : £0.75 B82-15065

261.7 — South Africa. Apartheid. Policies of government, *1978-1980 — South African Council of Churches viewpoints*
Tutu, Desmond. Bishop Desmond Tutu — the voice of one crying in the wilderness : a collection of his recent statements in the struggle for justice in South Africa / introduced and edited by John Webster ; foreword by Trevor Huddleston. — London : Mowbray, 1982. — 125p,[8]p of plates : ill,ports ; 20cm. — (Mowbray's emerging church series)
Bibliography: p125
ISBN 0-264-66827-8 (pbk) : £2.50 : CIP rev.
B81-40257

261.7 — South Africa. Politics. Role of Christian church
Catholic Institute for International Relations. War and conscience in South Africa. — London : Catholic Institute for International Relations, Oct.1982. — [80]p
ISBN 0-904393-73-9 (pbk) : £2.00 : CIP entry
B82-40921

261.7 — Southern Africa. Politics. Violence, *ca 1965-1980 — Christian viewpoints*
Kaunda, Kenneth David. Kaunda on violence / Kenneth David Kaunda ; edited by Colin M. Morris. — London : Sphere, 1982, c1980. — 184p ; 18cm
Originally published: London : Collins, 1980
ISBN 0-7221-5174-8 (pbk) : £1.50 B82-11198

261.7′05 — Politics. Role of Christian church — *Serials*
[The Link *(Walsall)*]. The Link : (formerly Wake up! magazine). — Vol.1, no.1 (1981)-. — Walsall (47a Sutton Rd., Walsall, W. Midlands WS1 2PQ) : Christian Israel Foundation, 1981-. — v. : ill,maps ; 22cm
Continues: Wake up!. — Description based on: Vol.1, no.5 (Dec. 1981)
ISSN 0263-0389 = Link (Walsall) : Unpriced
B82-14768

261.7′094 — Europe. Politics. Religious aspects
Religion in West European politics / edited by Suzanne Berger. — London : Cass, 1982. — 191p : ill ; 23cm
ISBN 0-7146-3218-x : £15.00 : CIP rev.
B82-14383

261.8 — Bolivia. Social conditions — *Evangelical Methodist Church in Bolivia viewpoints*
Manifesto to the nation. — London (PO Box no.1, London SW1W 9BW) : Christian Aid, c1976. — [8]p ; 21cm. — (Viewpoint)
Prepared by the Evangelical Methodist Church in Bolivia
£0.05 (unbound) B82-11243

261.8 — Great Britain. Liberation theology
Drummond, Terry. Liberation theology and the British situation / Terry Drummond. — [London] ([St Mary's House, Eastway, E9]) : Jubilee Group, [1982?]. — 7leaves ; 30cm
£0.35 (unbound) B82-17762

261.8 — Social development. Role of Christian church — *Evangelical viewpoints*
Evangelicals and development : toward a theology of social change / edited by Ronald J. Sider. — Exeter : Paternoster Press, c1981. — 123p ; 22cm. — (Contemporary issues in social ethics ; v.2)
Conference papers. — Includes index
ISBN 0-85364-329-6 (pbk) : £3.40 : CIP rev.
B81-30286

261.8′3 — England. Police — *Christian viewpoints*
Forster, Greg. 'To live good' : the police and the community / by Greg Forster. — Bramcote : Grove Books, c1982. — 25p ; 22cm. — (Grove booklets on ethics, ISSN 0305-4241 ; no.47)
ISBN 0-907536-28-x (pbk) : £0.70 B82-40939

261.8′3 — Great Britain. Cities — *Christian viewpoints*
Cities. — London : CEM, c1981. — [4]p : ill ; 21cm. — (1999 this future is mine)
Unpriced (unbound) B82-05104

261.8′3′0941 — Great Britain. Social problems — *Christian viewpoints*
Sheppard, David. Bias to the poor. — London : Hodder & Stoughton, Jan.1983. — [320]p
ISBN 0-340-32484-8 (cased) : £9.95 : CIP entry
ISBN 0-340-32370-1 (pbk) : £6.95 B82-34083

261.8′321 — Man. Sickness — *Christian viewpoints*
Autton, Norman. Making use of illness / by Norman Autton. — London : Mowbray, 1981. — 32p ; 15cm. — (Enquirer's library)
Bibliography: p32
ISBN 0-264-66833-2 (pbk) : £0.60 B82-14740

261.8′324 — Handicapped persons — *Christian viewpoints*
Handicap. — [London] ([2 Chester House, Pages Lane, N10]) : [Christian Education Movement], c1982. — [4]p : 1ill ; 21cm. — (1999 this future is mine)
Unpriced (unbound) B82-18693

261.8′3258 — Poverty. Alleviation. Role of Christian church
Winter, Colin. The breaking process / Colin Winter. — London : SCM, 1981. — 117p ; 20cm
ISBN 0-334-00139-0 (pbk) : £2.50 B82-18388

261.8′34235 — Adolescence — *Christian viewpoints*
Dobson, James C.. Preparing for adolescence / James Dobson. — Eastbourne : Kingsway, 1982, c1978. — 155p ; 18cm
Originally published: Santa Ana : Vision House, c1978
ISBN 0-86065-167-3 (pbk) : £1.60 B82-29475

261.8′3426 — Old age. Personal adjustment — *Christian viewpoints*

Blaiklock, E. M.. Between the sunset and the stars / E.M. Blaiklock. — London : Hodder and Stoughton, 1982. — 95p ; 18cm. — (Hodder Christian paperbacks)
ISBN 0-340-27602-9 (pbk) : £1.25 : CIP rev. B82-12261

Sanders, J. Oswald. Enjoying growing old / J. Oswald Sanders. — Eastbourne : Kingsway, 1981. — 157p ; 18cm
Includes index
ISBN 0-86065-158-4 (pbk) : £1.50 B82-00713

261.8′3426 — Retirement. Personal adjustment of personnel — *Christian viewpoints*

Purcell, William. The Christian in retirement / by William Purcell. — London : Mowbray, 1982. — 119p ; 18cm
ISBN 0-264-66557-0 (pbk) : £1.75 B82-41081

261.8′343 — Masculinity — *Christian viewpoints*

Elliot, Elisabeth. The mark of a man / Elisabeth Elliot. — London : Hodder and Stoughton, 1981. — 176p ; 18cm. — (Hodder Christian paperbacks)
Originally published: Old Tappan, N.J. : Revell, 1981
ISBN 0-340-27566-9 (pbk) : £1.75 : CIP rev. B81-25753

261.8′3442 — Society. Role of women. Attitudes of Christian church — *Feminist viewpoints*

Dowell, Susan. Dispossessed daughters of Eve : faith and feminism / Susan Dowell and Linda Hurcombe. — London : SCM, 1981. — xi,148p ; 22cm
Includes index
ISBN 0-334-00321-0 (pbk) : £4.50 B82-32811

261.8′3456 — Great Britain. Poverty. Attitudes of Christian church

Paget-Wilkes, Michael. Poverty, revolution and the Church / by Michael Paget-Wilkes ; with a preface by Trevor Huddleston. — Exeter : Paternoster Press, c1981. — 142p ; 22cm
ISBN 0-85364-285-0 (pbk) : £3.80 : CIP rev. B80-21371

261.8′357 — Courtship — *Christian viewpoints*

Huggett, Joyce. Growing into love. — Leicester : Inter-Varsity Press, Oct.1982. — [128]p
ISBN 0-85110-446-0 (pbk) : £1.50 : CIP entry B82-24236

261.8′357 — Sex relations — *Christian viewpoints*

McDowell, Josh. Givers, takers and other kinds of lovers / Josh McDowell and Paul Lewis. — 1st British ed. — Eastbourne : Kingsway, 1981. — 94p ; 18cm
Previous ed.: Wheaton, Ill. : Tyndale, c1980
ISBN 0-86065-108-8 (pbk) : £1.25 B82-12372

Patey, Edward H.. Christians and sex / by Edward H. Patey. — London : Mowbray, 1981. — 31p ; 15cm. — (Enquirer′s library)
Bibliography: p31
ISBN 0-264-66746-8 (pbk) : £0.60 B82-08011

261.8′357′088054 — Young persons. Sexuality — *Christian viewpoints*

Dominian, Jack. The growth of love and sex / Jack Dominian. — London : Darton, Longman & Todd in association with the National Children′s Home, 1982. — 91p ; 20cm
ISBN 0-232-51566-2 (pbk) : £2.95 : CIP rev.
Primary classification 248.4 B82-11268

261.8′35732 — Man. Virginity — *Christian viewpoints — Early works*

Hali meiðhad / edited by Bella Millett. — London : Published for the Early English Text Society by the Oxford University Press, 1982. — 84p : 1facsim ; 23cm
Middle English text, English introduction and notes. — Bibliography: pviii-xi
ISBN 0-19-722286-2 : £6.00 : CIP rev. B82-18456

261.8′35766 — Homosexuality — *Christian viewpoints*

Pastoral Approaches to Homosexuality *(Conference : 1980 : Pitlochry)*. The Pitlochry papers : the papers read to the 'Pastoral Approaches to Homosexuality' Conference held at Bonskeid House near Pitlochry 18-20 April 1980 / edited in consultation with the authors by James Anthony and Ian C. Dunn ; with an introduction by Ian C. Dunn. — Edinburgh (60 Broughton St., Edinburgh EH1 3SA) : Scottish Homosexual Rights Group, 1981. — 64p : 1facsim ; 21cm
Unpriced (pbk) B82-38581

261.8′35766 — Homosexuality — *Society of Friends viewpoints*

Furlong, Monica. Shrinking and clinging / Monica Furlong. Transition to openness / Erica F. Vere. Postcript to Homosexuality from the inside / David Blamires. — [Faringdon] ([10 The Row, Hinton Waldrist, Faringdon, Oxon SN7 8RS]) : Friends Homosexual Fellowship, 1981. — [8]p ; 21cm
Unpriced (unbound) B82-21421

Meeting gay friends : essays / by members of the Friends Homosexual Fellowship ; edited by John Banks and Martina Weitsch ; with an afterword by Mary D.E. Guillemard. — Manchester : The Fellowship, c1982. — 92p ; 21cm
Bibliography: p91-92
ISBN 0-9508031-0-3 (pbk) : £2.40 : CIP rev. B82-13525

261.8′35766′0942 — England. Homosexuality. Attitudes of Christian church

Anglican, Catholic and Methodist statements on homosexuality : a response from the Friends Homosexual Fellowship. — Faringdon (10 The Row, Hinton Waldrist, Faringdon, Oxford SN7 8RS) : Friends Homosexual Fellowship, 1980. — [8]p ; 21cm
Unpriced (unbound) B82-21422

261.8′358 — Childbirth — *Christian viewpoints*

Cooke, Jenny. Childbirth : a Christian perspective / by Jenny Cooke. — Bramcote : Grove Books, 1981. — 25p ; 22cm. — (Grove booklet on ethics, ISSN 0305-4241 ; no.43)
ISBN 0-907536-08-5 (pbk) : £0.60 B82-02576

261.8′358 — Marriage — *Christian viewpoints*

Dominian, Jack. Marriage, faith and love / Jack Dominian. — London : Darton, Longman and Todd, 1981. — 279p ; 23cm
Includes index
ISBN 0-232-51548-4 : £7.50 : CIP rev. B81-28207

Huggett, Joyce. Two into one? : relating in Christian marriage / Joyce Huggett. — Leicester : Inter-Varsity, 1981. — 128p ; 18cm
ISBN 0-85110-424-x (pbk) : Unpriced : CIP rev. B81-20135

261.8′3581 — Marriage — *Catholic viewpoints*

Baggot, Tony. Enjoy a happy marriage / Tony Baggot. — Dublin : Mercier Press, c1979 (1981 [printing]). — 64p : ill ; 18cm
ISBN 0-85342-614-7 (pbk) : £1.30 B82-32892

Churchill, Anthony, *1947-*. Marriage and the family / Anthony Churchill. — London : Catholic Truth Society, 1982. — 14p ; 19cm. — (The Teaching of Pope John Paul II)
ISBN 0-85183-492-2 (pbk) : £0.35
Also classified at 261.8′3585 B82-28840

261.8′3581 — Marriage — *Christian viewpoints*

Batchelor, Mary. Getting married in church / Mary Batchelor. — Tring : Lion, 1979 (1982 [printing]). — 96p : ill ; 18cm. — (A Lion guide)
ISBN 0-85648-399-0 (pbk) : £1.50 B82-37754

Foley, Michael, *1936-*. Marriage : a relationship : preparation and fulfilment / Michael Foley. — London : Darton, Longman and Todd, 1981. — 88p ; 20cm
Bibliography: p85. — Includes index
ISBN 0-232-51544-1 (pbk) : £1.95 : CIP rev. B81-26792

Lee, Helen. Why get married? / by Helen Lee. — London : Mowbray, 1981. — 29p ; 15cm. — (Enquirer′s library)
Bibliography: p29
ISBN 0-264-66749-2 (pbk) : £0.60 B82-02108

Thatcher, Floyd. Long term marriage : a search for the ingredients of a lifetime partnership / Floyd & Harriett Thatcher. — London : Hodder and Stoughton, 1982, c1980. — 238p ; 18cm. — (Hodder Christian paperbacks)
Bibliography: p229-232
ISBN 0-340-27597-9 (pbk) : £1.95 : CIP rev. B81-33923

261.8′3581 — Marriage — *Church of England viewpoints*

Patey, Edward H.. 'I give you this ring' : a study course about marriage with points for discussion (addressed to those looking forward to their wedding in church) / by Edward H. Patey. — London : Mowbray, 1982. — 64p ; 21cm
Bibliography: p64
ISBN 0-264-66847-2 (pbk) : £1.50 B82-33172

261.8′3584′0941 — Great Britain. Remarriage — *Christian viewpoints*

Kelly, Kevin T.. Divorce and second marriage : facing the challenge / Kevin T. Kelly. — London : Collins, 1982. — 111p ; 18cm
ISBN 0-00-599722-4 (pbk) : £2.00 B82-40411

261.8′3585 — Family life — *Catholic viewpoints*

Churchill, Anthony, *1947-*. Marriage and the family / Anthony Churchill. — London : Catholic Truth Society, 1982. — 14p ; 19cm. — (The Teaching of Pope John Paul II)
ISBN 0-85183-492-2 (pbk) : £0.35
Primary classification 261.8′3581 B82-28840

John Paul II, *Pope*. Apostolic exhortation of His Holiness Pope John Paul II to the episcopate, to the clergy and to faithful of the whole Catholic Church regarding the role of the Christian family in the modern world. — London : Catholic Truth Society, 1981. — 174p ; 19cm
Translation of: Familiaris Consortio. — Cover title
ISBN 0-85183-469-8 (pbk) : £1.50 B82-14154

261.8′3585 — Family life — *Catholic viewpoints — Polish texts*

Catholic Church. *Pope (1978- : John Paul II)*. Pouczenie apostolskie O zadaniach rodziny chrześcijańskiej w świecie współczesnym / Jan Paweł II ; [tłumaczenie z łaciny]. — London : Veritas Foundation, 1982. — 102p ; 22cm
Cover title: Pouczenie apostolskie o zadananiach rodziny chrześcijańskiej w świecie współczesnym
Unpriced (pbk) B82-38578

261.8′3585 — Family life — *Christian viewpoints*

Christenson, Larry. The Christian family / Larry Christenson. — Eastbourne : Kingsway, 1981, c1970. — 216p ; 18cm
Originally published: Minneapolis : Bethany Fellowship, 1970 ; London : Fountain Trust, 1971
ISBN 0-86065-152-5 (pbk) : £1.50 B82-00709

Newbigin, Edith. The human family / by Edith Newbigin. — Liverpool (47 Reeds Rd, Huyton, Liverpool L36 7SL) : [E. Newbigin], [1981?]. — 115p ; 21cm
Bibliography: p115
Unpriced (pbk) B82-14014

261.8′35872 — Married couples. Interpersonal relationships — *Christian viewpoints*

Dobson, James, *1936-*. [What wives wish their husbands knew about women]. Man to man about women : — what wives wish their husbands knew about women / James Dobson. — Eastbourne : Kingsway, 1981, c1975. — 175p : ill ; 18cm
Originally published: Wheaton : Tyndale House, 1975 ; London : Coverdale House, 1976
ISBN 0-902088-87-4 (pbk) : £1.35 B82-16809

261.8′358743 — Women. Childbirth. Pregnancy & childbirth — *Christian viewpoints*
Williamson, Anne. Having a baby / Anne Williamson. — Tring : Lion, c1982. — 92p : ill ; 18cm. — (A Lion guide)
ISBN 0-85648-411-3 (pbk) : £1.50 B82-37752

261.8′3588 — Living alone — *Christian viewpoints*
Israel, Martin. Living alone : the inward journey to fellowship / Martin Israel. — London : SPCK, 1982. — ix,132p ; 22cm. — (New library of pastoral care)
ISBN 0-281-03854-6 (pbk) : £3.95 : CIP rev. B82-18877

261.8′3589 — Divorce — *Christian viewpoints*
Green, Wendy. The Christian and divorce / Wendy Green. — London : Mowbray, 1981. — 132p ; 18cm
Bibliography: p131-132
ISBN 0-264-66796-4 (pbk) : £1.75 B82-11256

Green, Wendy. Divorce / by Wendy Green. — London : Mowbray, c1981. — 30p ; 15cm. — (Enquirer′s library)
Bibliography: p30
ISBN 0-264-66831-6 (pbk) : £0.60 B82-14739

261.8′3589 — Divorce. Personal adjustment of women — *Christian viewpoints — Personal observations*
Furlong, Monica. Divorce : one woman′s view / Monica Furlong. — London : Mothers′ Union, c1981. — 28p : 1port ; 21cm
Cover title
ISBN 0-85943-037-5 (pbk) : £0.80 B82-08039

261.8′36 — Environment. Conservation — *Christian viewpoints*
Moss, Rowland. The earth in our hands / Rowland Moss. — Leicester : Inter-Varsity Press, 1982. — 125p ; 18cm
Bibliography: p125
ISBN 0-85110-427-4 (pbk) : £1.65 : CIP rev. B81-25655

261.8′362 — Natural resources: Water — *Christian viewpoints*
Water. — London : Christian Education Movement, c1981. — 4p ; 21cm. — (1999 this future is mine)
Unpriced (unbound) B82-05109

261.8′36632 — Childlessness — *Christian viewpoints*
Choices in childlessness : the report of a working party set up in July 1979 under the auspices of the Free Church Federal Council and the British Council of Churches. — London : Free Church Federal Council, 1982. — vii,55p ; 21cm
£0.80 (pbk) B82-25950

261.8′5 — Capitalism *related to* **Protestant ethics. Theories of Weber, Max**
Marshall, Gordon. In search of the spirit of capitalism. — London : Hutchinson Education, Nov.1981. — [240]p
ISBN 0-09-145650-9 (pbk) : £12.00 : CIP entry
ISBN 0-09-145651-7 (pbk) : £4.95 B81-28842

261.8′5 — Developing countries. Rural regions. Economic development. Role of Christian church
Batchelor, Peter. People in rural development / Peter Batchelor. — Exeter : Paternoster Press, c1981. — xii,157p : ill ; 22cm
Bibliography: p156-157
ISBN 0-85364-310-5 (pbk) : £3.40 : CIP rev. B81-28184

261.8′5 — Economic conditions — *Christian viewpoints*
Webley, Simon. What shall it profit — ? / Simon Webley. — Eastbourne : Kingsway, 1981. — 92p ; 18cm
ISBN 0-86065-164-9 (pbk) : £1.25 B82-05851

261.8′5 — Economic development. Inequalities. Alleviation. Independent Commission on International Development Issues. North-South, a programme for survival — *Catholic viewpoints*
O′Mahony, Patrick J.. Brandt : the Christian connection / [Patrick O′Mahony]. — London : Catholic Truth Society, 1982. — 15p ; 19cm
ISBN 0-85183-493-0 (pbk) : £0.35 B82-41070

261.8′5 — Economics — *Christian viewpoints*
Richards, Paul, *1945-*. False gods and wrong economics / by Paul Richards. — London (PO Box no.1, London SW9 8BH) : Christian Aid, c1977. — [12]p ; 21cm. — (Viewpoint)
£0.10 (unbound) B82-11242

261.8′5 — Employment — *Catholic viewpoints*
Catholic Church. *Pope (1978- : John Paul II)*. Encyclical Laborem exercens : addressed by the supreme pontif John Paul II to his venerable brothers in the episcopate, to the priests, to the religious families, to the sons and daughters of the church and to all men and women of good will on human work on the ninetieth anniversary of rerum navarum. — London : Incorporated Catholic Truth Society, 1981. — 99p ; 18cm
Translation of: Laborem exercens
ISBN 0-85183-447-7 (pbk) : £1.00 B82-00631

Crawley, Eduardo. This is human work : simplification of the encyclical Laborem exercens of Pope John Paul II / text simplified by Eduardo Crawley. — Pinner : The Grail, 1982. — 63p ; 19cm
ISBN 0-901829-67-6 (pbk) : £0.85
ISBN 0-85183-471-x (Catholic Truth Society) : £0.85 B82-25886

261.8′5 — Employment — *Catholic viewpoints — Polish texts*
Catholic Church. *Pope (1978- : John Paul II)*. [Laborem exercens. Polish]. Encyklika laborem exercens = O pracy ludzkiej / Jan Paweł II ; [tłumaczenie z łaciny]. — London : Veritas Foundation Publication Centre, 1981. — 102p ; 19cm
Unpriced (pbk) B82-11337

261.8′5 — Energy resources. Conservation — *Christian viewpoints*
Hodgson, Peter. World energy needs and resources / by Peter Hodgson. — Bramcote : Grove Books, 1981. — 25p ; 22cm. — (Grove booklet on ethics, ISSN 0305-4241 ; 44)
Bibliography: p25
ISBN 0-907536-12-3 (pbk) : £0.70 B82-11382

261.8′5 — Great Britain. Nuclear power — *Christian viewpoints*
Habgood, John. The proliferation of nuclear technology / John S. Habgood. — London (c/o Publications Department, British Council of Churches, 10 Eaton Gate, S.W.1) : Council on Christian Approaches to Defence and Disarmament, 1977. — 15p ; 26cm
£0.15 (unbound) B82-36769

261.8′5 — Industrialised countries. Socioeconomic aspects — *Christian viewpoints*
Bigman, Sidney. The creative / by Sidney Bigman. — Ramsey : A.M.F., 1981. — 303p ; 23cm
ISBN 0-907385-00-1 : £9.95 B82-09889

261.8′5 — Socialism — *Christian viewpoints*
Hay, Donald A.. A Christian critique of socialism / by Donald A. Hay. — Bramcote : Grove, 1982. — 48p ; 22cm. — (Grove booklet on ethics, ISSN 0305-4241 ; no.5b)
ISBN 0-907536-22-0 (pbk) : £1.40 B82-33257

261.8′5 — South America. Poverty — *Catholic viewpoints*
Conferencia General Del Episcopado Latinoamericano *(3rd : 1979 : Puebla)*. The poor : the Church′s first priority : an extract from the conclusions of the Puebla conference. — London : CIIR, 1979 (1981 [printing]). — 1folded sheet([6]p) : ill ; 30cm. — (Church in the world ; 3)
Translated from the Spanish. — Conclusion from the 3rd Conferencia General Del Episcopado Latinoamericano, Puebla, 1979
ISBN 0-904393-35-6 : £0.10 B82-30631

261.8′5 — Work — *Christian viewpoints*
Attwood, David. The spade and the thistle : the place of work today / by David Attwood. — Bramcote : Grove Books, 1980. — 23p ; 22cm. — (Grove booklet on ethics, ISSN 0305-4241 : no.38)
ISBN 0-905422-91-0 (pbk) : £0.50 B82-16527

Ballard, Paul H.. Towards a contemporary theology of work / Paul H. Ballard ; foreword, Noel Davies. — Cardiff ([University College, Cardiff, Law Building, P.O. Box 78, CF1 1XL]) : Collegiate Centre of Theology, Faculty of Theology, University College, Cardiff in association with the Industrial Committee, Council of Churches for Wales, 1982. — 72p ; 30cm. — (Holi ; 3)
Bibliography: p69-71
£1.80 (pbk) B82-31781

McCormack, Arthur. Human work / Arthur McCormack. — London : Catholic Truth Society, 1982. — 18p ; 19cm. — (The Teaching of Pope John Paul II)
ISBN 0-85183-497-3 (pbk) : £0.40 B82-33056

The **Person** in work : a programme of enquiries into the place of work in society based on the encyclical letter of Pope John Paul II, Laborem exercens. — London (106 Clapham Rd., SW9 0JX) : World of Work (a service of FSA), 1982. — 39p : ill ; 19cm
£0.75 (pbk) B82-38364

Right to work?. — London (93 Gloucester Place, W1H 4AA) : Current Affairs Committee, Baptist Mens Movement, 1981. — 49p in various pagings : forms ; 21cm. — (Current affairs study pack ; no.2)
Cover title. — Bibliography: 1p
£0.50 (pbk) B82-14795

Work. — London : CEM, c1981. — [4]p : ill ; 22cm. — (1999 this future is mine)
Unpriced (unbound) B82-05113

261.8′73 — Guerilla warfare — *Christian viewpoints*
Harries, Richard. Should a Christian support guerillas? / Richard Harries. — Guildford : Lutterworth, 1982. — 60p ; 19cm. — (Anselm books)
ISBN 0-7188-2517-9 (pbk) : £0.95 B82-13124

261.8′73 — Just war. Theories, *1740-1980*
Johnson, James Turner. Just war tradition and the restraint of war : a moral and historical inquiry / James Turner Johnson. — Princeton ; Guildford : Princeton University Press, c1981. — xxxv,380p ; 23cm
Bibliography: p367-376. — Includes index
ISBN 0-691-07263-9 : £20.20 B82-03196

261.8′73 — Nuclear weapons. Proliferation — *Christian viewpoints*
The **Church** and the bomb. — London : Hodder & Stoughton, Oct.1982. — [160]p
ISBN 0-340-32371-x (pbk) : £4.50 : CIP entry B82-25189

261.8′73 — Pacifism — *Anglican viewpoints*
Dransfield, P.. Christians and war : ″why I am not a pacifist″, the pacifist reply / by P. Dransfield. — Huddersfield (19a Longlands Rd., Slaithwaite, Huddersfield, West Yorkshire) : P. Dransfield, 1981. — [12]p : ill ; 21cm
Cover title. — Text on inside covers
Unpriced (pbk) B82-13695

261.8′73 — Peace — *Catholic viewpoints*
Beresford, Robert. Peace / Robert Beresford. — London : Catholic Truth Society, 1982. — 18p ; 19cm. — (The Teaching of Pope John Paul II)
ISBN 0-85183-499-x (pbk) : £0.40 B82-35401

261.8′73 — Peace — *Christian viewpoints*
Peace. — [London] ([2 Chester House, Pages Lane, N10]) : [Christian Education Movement], c1982. — [4]p : 1ill ; 21cm. — (1999 this future is mine)
Unpriced (unbound) B82-18694

261.8′73 — War — *Christian viewpoints*
Council on Christian Approaches to Defence and Disarmament. *British Group*. Council on Christian Approaches to Defence and Disarmament British Group. — [London] ([St. Katherine Cree, 86 Leadenhall St., EC3A 3DH]) : The Council, 1980. — 1folded sheet ; 21cm
Unpriced (unbound) B82-36771

261.8′73 — War — *Christian viewpoints* *continuation*

Hehir, J. Bryan. The Church and the arms race : reflections on theology, politics and Christian witness / J. Bryan Hehir. — Abbots Langley : Catholic Information Services, c1982. — 23p ; 22cm
'A study prepared for the Commission for International Justice and Peace of England and Wales as a contribution to discussion'
ISBN 0-905241-10-x (pbk) : £0.40 B82-40016

262 — CHRISTIAN CHURCH. GOVERNMENT AND ORGANISATION

262′.0011 — Ecumenism

Anglican-Roman Catholic International Commission. Elucidations : eucharistic doctrine, ministry and ordination / Anglican-Roman Catholic International Commission. — London : SPCK, 1979. — 19p ; 19cm
ISBN 0-281-03735-3 (unbound) : £0.45
ISBN 0-85183-200-8 (Catholic Truth Society) B82-29914

262′.0017 — Christian church. Renewal

Cotterell, Peter. Church alive! : a fresh look at church growth / Peter Cotterell. — Leicester : Inter-Varsity, 1981. — 127p : ill ; 18cm
Bibliography: p123-127
ISBN 0-85110-431-2 (pbk) : Unpriced : CIP rev. B81-20134

Walker, Tom. Renew us by your spirit / Tom Walker. — London : Hodder and Stoughton, 1982. — 143p ; 18cm. — (Hodder Christian paperbacks)
ISBN 0-340-26601-5 : £1.50 : CIP rev. B81-36350

262′.0017 — Christian church. Renewal. Charismatic aspects

Suenens, Léon Joseph. Charismatic renewal and social action : a dialogue / Léon-Joseph Suenens, Helder Camara. — London : Darton, Longman and Todd, 1980, c1979. — 98p ; 22cm. — (Malines document ; 3)
ISBN 0-232-51468-2 (pbk) : £1.95 B82-40688

262′.0017 — Christian church. Renewal — *Serials*

[Grass-roots *(Poole)*]. Grass-roots : God's people : a force for renewal in society today. — Vol.8, no.1 (Jan./Feb. 1982)-. — Poole (57 Dorchester Rd, Lytchett Minster, Poole, Dorset BH16 6JE) : Celebration Pub., 1982-. — v. : ill,ports ; 29cm
Six issues yearly. — Journal of: Post Green Community. — Continues: TR
ISSN 0262-4753 = Grass-roots (Poole) : £3.95 per year B82-18495

262′.0092′4 — English ecclesiology. Hooker, Richard, *1553 or 4-1600*

Faulkner, Robert K.. Richard Hooker and the politics of a Christian England / Robert K. Faulkner. — Berkeley ; London : University of California Press, c1981. — vi,190p : 1port ; 25cm
Includes index
ISBN 0-520-03993-9 : £15.75 B82-13760

262′.02 — Catholic Church. Renewal — *Serials*

Agapé. — Vol.1, no.1 (Jan. 1982)-. — Southport (11 York Rd, Birkdale, Southport, Merseyside PR8 2AD) : Emmaus Family of Prayer, 1982-. — ill,music ; 26cm
Monthly. — Continues: Maranatha
ISSN 0261-5630 = Agapé : £7.75 per year B82-22663

262′.02411 — Scotland. Christian church. Organisation structure, *1100-1198* — *Readings from contemporary sources*

Somerville, Robert, *1940-*. Scotia pontificia : papal letters to Scotland before the Pontificate of Innocent III / Robert Somerville. — Oxford : Clarendon, 1982. — xiii,177p : 1facsim ; 25cm
Includes Latin text. — Bibliography: px-xiii. — Includes index
ISBN 0-19-822433-8 : £25.00 : CIP rev. B81-28851

262′.0242534 — Catholic Church. *Diocese of Lincoln. Bishop (1405-1419 : Repingdon).* **Episcopal registers** — *Latin texts*

Catholic Church. *Diocese of Lincoln. Bishop (1405-1419 : Repingdon).* The register of Bishop Philip Repingdon 1405-1419 / edited by Margaret Archer. — [Lincoln?] : Lincoln Record Society. — (The Publications of the Lincoln Record Society ; v.74)
Vol.3 Memoranda 1414-1419. — 1982. — 327p ; 26cm
Latin texts, English introduction and notes. — Includes index
Unpriced B82-19348

262′.0342 — Church of England. Renewal — *Catholic viewpoints*

Hollings, Michael. Hearts not garments : Christ is our peace / Michael Hollings. — London : Darton, Longman and Todd, 1982. — viii,83p ; 22cm
ISBN 0-232-51539-5 (pbk) : £2.50 : CIP rev. B81-37527

262′.0342534 — Church of England. *Diocese of Lincoln.* **Administration,** *1521-1547*

Bowker, Margaret. The Henrician reformation : the diocese of Lincoln under John Longland 1521-1547 / Margaret Bowker. — Cambridge : Cambridge University Press, 1981. — xx,229p : ill,maps ; 24cm
Bibliography: p188-193. — Includes index
ISBN 0-521-23639-8 : £21.00 B82-01006

262′.05232 — United Reformed Church. Administration — *Inquiry reports*

United Reformed Church. The United Reformed Church : this section of reports to Assembly 1982 contains material relating to the Covenant proposals, with resolutions, to be brought to the Assembly by the World Church and Mission Department. — [London] ([86, Tavistock Place, WC1H 9RT]) : [United Reformed Church], [1982]. — 8p ; 21cm
Unpriced (unbound) B82-21770

262′.12 — Christian church. Bishops

Bishops, but what kind? : reflections on episcopacy / collected and edited by Peter Moore. — London : SPCK, 1982. — xi,176p ; 22cm
ISBN 0-281-03860-0 (pbk) : £4.95 B82-34734

262′.13 — Christian church. Role of papacy

Metcalfe, John, *1932-*. A question for Pope John Paul II from John Metcalfe. — Penn : John Metcalfe Publishing Trust, 1980. — 100p ; 21cm
ISBN 0-9506366-4-9 (pbk) : £1.25 B82-16020

262′.13 — Papacy. Power

Hudson, Henry T.. Papal power : its origns and development / Henry T. Hudson. — Welwyn : Evangelical, 1981. — 133p ; 22cm
ISBN 0-85234-151-2 (pbk) : Unpriced B82-24167

262′.13 — Papacy. Relations with England, *1100-1300*

Cheney, C. R.. The papacy and England 12th-14th centuries : historical and legal studies / C.R. Cheney. — London : Variorum Reprints, 1982. — 346p in various pagings : ill,1facsim ; 24cm. — (Collected studies series ; CS154)
Includes Latin texts. — Facsimile reprints. — Includes index
ISBN 0-86078-099-6 : Unpriced : CIP rev.
Primary classification 942.03 B82-01571

262′.13 — Popes. Authority

Stewart, Richard L.. The Pope and the Church / Richard L. Stewart. — London : Catholic Truth Society, 1982. — [16]p ; 18cm
ISBN 0-85183-474-4 (pbk) : £0.35 B82-25885

262′.13′09 — Papacy, *312-1981*

Martin, Malachi. The decline and fall of the Roman Church / Malachi Martin. — London : Secker & Warburg, 1982, c1981. — 309p ; 24cm
ISBN 0-436-27336-5 : £6.95 B82-06381

262′.13′09 — Papacy, *to 1963*

Milton, Joyce. The feathered serpent and the Cross : the pre-Columbian god-kings : the Papal States / Joyce Milton, Robert A. Orsi, Norman Harrison ; preface by Jeffrey R. Parsons. — London : Cassell, 1980. — 168p : col.ill,col.maps,col.ports ; 31cm. — (The Rise and fall of empires)
Includes index
ISBN 0-304-30724-6 : £7.95
Also classified at 980′.01 B82-24800

262′.13′09 — Papacy, *to 1981*

Cheetham, Nicolas. Keepers of the keys : the Pope in history / Nicolas Cheetham. — London : Macdonald & Co., 1982. — viii,340p : ill,ports ; 23cm
Bibliography: p313-315. — Includes index
ISBN 0-356-08584-8 : £14.95 B82-25556

262′.13′0904 — Papacy, *1914-1978*

Holmes, J. Derek. The Papacy in the modern world, 1914-1978 / J. Derek Holmes. — London : Burns & Oates, 1981. — 275p : ill,ports ; 22cm
Bibliography: p263-268. — Includes index
ISBN 0-86012-076-7 : Unpriced B82-33695

262′.131 — Papacy. Infallibility

Crowley, Patrick. Infallibility in the Church / Patrick Crowley. — London : Catholic Truth Society, 1982. — 24p ; 19cm
Cover title. — Text on inside covers
ISBN 0-85183-481-7 (pbk) : £0.45 B82-32894

262′.14 — Christian church. Ministry

Green, Michael, *1930-*. A servant ministry?. — London : Hodder & Stoughton, Sept.1982. — [128]p
ISBN 0-340-28195-2 (pbk) : £1.25 : CIP entry B82-18790

262′.14 — Christian church. Women's ministry

Draper, G. I. A. D.. The ordination of women / G.I.A.D. Draper. — London (24, Tufton St) : Mothers' Union, [1982]. — 16p ; 22cm. — (The Mary Sumner lecture ; 1981)
Cover title
Unpriced (pbk) B82-27443

262′.142 — Catholic Church. Ministry — *Topics for discussion groups*

For others : the ministry and mission of 'the Easter People'. — Slough : St. Paul, 1981. — 24p ; 22cm. — (The Easter People discussion outlines ; 2)
ISBN 0-85439-205-x (pbk) : £0.65 B82-08762

262′.143 — Church of England. Ministry

Kirkman, Harold. Five years longer : reflections on the ministry now / by Harold Kirkman ; with a foreword by Simon M. Bannister. — Todmorden (3 Black Dyke, Mankinholes Bank, Todmorden, Lancashire OL14 6JA) : H. Kirkman, 1981. — xi,83p ; 23cm
£2.40 (pbk) B82-02879

262′.14342 — England. Rural regions. Church of England. Clergy, *to 1981*

Goodenough, Simon. The country parson. — Newton Abbot : David & Charles, Jan.1983. — [192]p
ISBN 0-7153-8238-1 : £7.95 : CIP entry B82-32608

262′.14342845 — North Yorkshire. Selby. Church of England. St James' Church, *Selby.* **Deaconesses. Parish work** — *Personal observations*

Cundiff, Margaret. Called to be me. — London : SPCK, Oct.1982. — [128]p
ISBN 0-281-04013-3 (pbk) : £1.75 : CIP entry B82-23473

262′.15 — Christian church. Role of women

Davies, Margaret, *1911-*. Circles of community : a study guide : towards a renewed community of women and men in church and society, based on a World Council of Churches consultation, Sheffield, 1981 / by Margaret and Rupert Davies. — London : British Council of Churches, c1982. — 15p : ill,ports ; 30cm
Bibliography: p15
ISBN 0-85169-091-2 (unbound) : £0.50 B82-23282

262'.15 — Church of Scotland. Elders. Duties

Macdonald, William Caldwell. The elder : his character and duties / William Caldwell Macdonald. — Rev. ed. — Edinburgh : Saint Andrew Press, 1982. — iv,28p ; 18cm
Previous ed.: Stirling : Stirling Tract Enterprise, 1958
£0.75 (pbk) B82-26448

The **Office** of Elder in the Church of Scotland : a brief statement / prepared by the Panel on Doctrine. — Rev. ed. — Edinburgh : Saint Andrew on behalf of the Panel on Doctrine of the General Assembly of the Church of Scotland, 1975 (1979 [printing]). — 6p ; 19cm
Cover title. — Previous ed.: 1964
ISBN 0-7152-0330-4 (pbk) : £0.20 B82-30913

262'.72 — Christian church. Unity

Allchin, A. M.. The dynamic of tradition / A.M. Allchin. — London : Darton, Longman & Todd, 1981. — viii,151p ; 22cm
Includes index
ISBN 0-232-51516-6 (pbk) : £4.50 : CIP rev. B81-13490

Hale, Robert. Canterbury and Rome : sister churches : a Roman Catholic monk reflects upon reunion in diversity / Robert Hale ; foreword by Alan C. Clark ; afterword by A.M. Allchin. — London : Darton, Longman and Todd, 1982. — x,188p ; 22cm
Bibliography: p182-183. — Includes index
ISBN 0-232-51555-7 (pbk) : £5.95 : CIP rev. B82-10758

262'.72 — Christian church. Unity. Inquiry reports — *Critical studies*

Observations : on the final report of the Anglican-Roman Catholic International Commission / Sacred Congregation for the Doctrine of the Faith. — London : Catholic Truth Society, 1982. — [12]p ; 18cm
Text on inside cover
ISBN 0-85183-498-1 (pbk) : £0.35 B82-30175

262.9'094 — Europe. Christian church. Canon law, *900-1500*

Kuttner, Stephan. Medieval councils, decretals and collections of canon law : selected essays / Stephan Kuttner. — London : Variorum, 1980. — 380p ; 24cm. — (Collected studies series ; CS 126)
Includes chapters in French and German. — Facsim reprints. — Includes index
ISBN 0-86078-071-6 : £22.00 : CIP rev. B80-13204

262.9'0942 — England. Catholic Church. Canon law, *1140-1200*

Duggan, Charles. Canon law in medieval England : the Becket dispute and decretal collections / Charles Duggan. — London : Variorum, Mar.1982. — 340p in various pagings : facsims,1port ; 24cm. — (Collected studies series ; CS151)
Includes texts in Latin. — Facsimile reprints. — Includes index
ISBN 0-86078-103-8 : Unpriced : CIP rev. B82-01575

262.9'0942 — England. Ecclesiastical law, *1100-1400*

Cheney, Christopher R.. The English church and its laws, 12th-14th centuries. — London : Variorum, Sept.1982. — [348]p. — (Collected studies series ; CS160)
ISBN 0-86078-108-9 : £26.00 : CIP entry B82-21402

262.9'83 — Church of England. *Province of Canterbury.* **Ecclesiastical courts,** *1200-1301 — Cases*

Select cases from the ecclesiastical courts of the Province of Canterbury c.1200-1301 / edited for the Selden Society by Norma Adams and Charles Donahue Jr. — London : Selden Society, 1981. — xxx,756p,[1]leaf of plates : 1facsim ; 26cm. — (Publications of the Selden Society ; v.95)
English and Latin text. — Bibliography: pxxiv-xxx. — Includes index
Unpriced B82-02894

263 — CHRISTIANITY. DAYS, TIMES, PLACES OF RELIGIOUS OBSERVANCE

263'.042411 — Scotland. Shrines: Wells — *Gazetteers*

Morris, Ruth. Scottish healing wells : healing, holy, wishing and fairy wells of the mainland of Scotland / Ruth and Frank Morris. — Sandy : Alethea Press, 1982. — 211p : ill ; 22cm
Bibliography: p191-202. — Includes index
ISBN 0-907859-00-3 : £7.50 B82-26510

263'.9 — Catholic Church. Church year

Fenn, Francis. The Church's year / Francis Fenn. — London : Catholic Truth Society, 1982. — [12]p ; 19cm
ISBN 0-85183-450-7 (pbk) : £0.35 B82-33841

263'.9 — Christian festivals — *Anthroposophical viewpoints*

Steiner, Rudolf. Christmas, Easter, Ascension and Pentecost, Michaelmas : the festivals and their meaning / Rudolf Steiner. — London : Rudolf Steiner Press, 1981. — 399p ; 22cm
Lectures given between 1904 and 1924. — Translated from the German. — Cover title: The festivals and their meaning
ISBN 0-85440-370-1 (cased) : Unpriced
ISBN 0-85440-380-9 (pbk) : £6.50 B82-22950

263'.9'0941 — Great Britian. Christian festivals

Christian celebrations. — London : Christian Education Movement, [1982?]. — 15p : ill ; 22cm
Cover title. — Text on inside covers
ISBN 0-905022-15-7 (pbk) : Unpriced B82-36996

Watkins, Peter, *1934-*. Here's the year / Peter Watkins & Erica Hughes ; illustrated by Gill Tomblin. — London : Julia MacRae Books, 1981. — 128p : ill ; 24cm
Includes index
ISBN 0-86203-046-3 : £5.75 : CIP rev. B81-30341

263'.91 — Christian church. Christmas. Celebration — *For teaching*

Celebrating Christmas / [compiled by Susan Tompkins ... et al.] ; [editor Susan Tompkins]. — London : Christian Education Movement, c1978. — 54p : ill,music ; 26cm
Cover title. — Bibliography: p53-54
ISBN 0-905022-31-9 (pbk) : Unpriced B82-36999

264 — CHRISTIAN CHURCH. PUBLIC WORSHIP

264 — Christian church. Public worship

Wray, Daniel E.. The importance of the local church / Daniel E. Wray. — Edinburgh : Banner of Truth Trust, 1981. — 15p ; 19cm
ISBN 0-85151-330-1 (pbk) : £0.40 B82-14735

264 — Christian church. Public worship. Activities: Drama

Burbridge, Paul. Time to act : sketches and guidelines for biblical drama / by Paul Burbridge & Murray Watts. — London : Hodder and Stoughton, 1979. — 127p ; 18cm. — (Hodder Christian paperbacks)
ISBN 0-340-24699-5 (pbk) : £1.00 B82-24190

264 — Christian church. Public worship. Activities: Folk arts

Barker, Martha Keys. Building worship together : Fisherfolk resources for worship and teaching / Martha Keys Barker and The Fisherfolk. — [Poole] : Celebration, 1981. — 126p ; 18cm
List of sound recordings: p125-126
ISBN 0-906309-21-2 (pbk) : £1.35 : CIP rev. B81-28131

264 — Christian church. Public worship. Influence of Luther, Martin. Liturgical aspects

Spinks, Bryan D.. Luther's liturgical criteria and his reform of the canon of the Mass / Bryan Spinks. — Bramcote : Grove Books, 1982. — 40p : music ; 22cm. — (Grove liturgical study, ISSN 0306-0608 ; no.30)
Text on inside cover
ISBN 0-907536-24-7 (pbk) : £1.40 B82-39626

264 — Christian church. Public worship. Liturgical aspects

Getting the liturgy right : essays / by the Joint Liturgical Group on Practical Liturgical Principles for Today ; edited by R.C.D. Jasper. — London : SPCK, 1982. — vii,103p ; 22cm
ISBN 0-281-03841-4 (pbk) : £4.50 B82-28853

Liturgy reshaped. — London : SPCK, Sept.1982. — [192]p
ISBN 0-281-03865-1 : £8.50 : CIP entry B82-18820

264 — Christian church. Sailors. Public worship — *Rites*

Seafarers prayer book. — Great Wakering : Mayhew-McCrimmon, 1977. — 143p : ill ; 15cm
ISBN 0-85597-208-4 (pbk) : Unpriced B82-29934

264 — Christian church. Worship — *For schools*

Rankin, John. Christian worship / John Rankin. — Guildford : Lutterworth Educational, [c1982]. — 32p : ill ; 30cm. — (The Chichester project ; 1)
Text on inside covers. — Bibliography on inside back cover
ISBN 0-7188-2499-7 (pbk) : Unpriced B82-20339

264 — Great Britain. Christian church. Homosexual couples. Services of blessing

Exploring lifestyles : an introduction to services of blessing for gay couples / [Jim Cotter, editor]. — London (BM Box 6914, WC1V 6XX) : Gay Christian Movement, 1980. — 30p ; 21cm
Text on inside cover
£0.40 (pbk) B82-21483

264'.019 — Orthodox Eastern Church. Public worship. Troparia & kontakia — *Collections*

The **Menaion** : Troparia and Kontakia. — [Fakenham] : [Monastery of Saint Seraphim of Sarov]
December. — c1980. — 21p ; 21cm
Cover title
ISBN 0-907410-04-9 (pbk) : Unpriced
ISBN 0-907410-00-6 (set) : Unpriced B82-40552

The **Menaion** : Troparia and Kontakia. — Fakenham : Monastery of Saint Seraphim of Sarov
January. — c1980. — 30p ; 21cm
Cover title
ISBN 0-907410-05-7 (pbk) : Unpriced
ISBN 0-907410-00-6 (set) : Unpriced B82-23576

The **Menaion** : Troparia and Kontakia. — [Fakenham] : [Monastery of Saint Seraphim of Sarov]
November. — [1980?]. — 28p ; 21cm
Cover title
ISBN 0-907410-03-0 (pbk) : Unpriced
ISBN 0-907410-00-6 (set) : Unpriced B82-40551

The **Menaion** : Troparia and Kontakia. — [Fakenham] : [Monastery of Saint Seraphim of Sarov]
October. — [1980?]. — 28p ; 21cm
Cover title
ISBN 0-907410-02-2 (pbk) : Unpriced
ISBN 0-907410-00-6 (set) : Unpriced B82-40550

The **Menaion** : Troparia and Kontakia. — [Fakenham] : [Monastery of Saint Seraphim of Sarov]
September. — [1980?]. — 25p ; 21cm
Cover title
ISBN 0-907410-01-4 (pbk) : Unpriced
ISBN 0-907410-00-6 (set) : Unpriced B82-40549

264'.01903 — Orthodox Eastern Church. Matins — *Rites*

Orthodox Eastern Church. [Matins]. Daily matins of the Orthodox Church. — Fakenham : Monastery of Saint Seraphim of Sarov, 1982. — 40p ; 21cm
ISBN 0-907410-22-7 (pbk) : £1.00 B82-22932

264'.0193 — Ekklēsia tēs Hellados. Matins. Canons — *Rites*

Canons of Sunday matins / translated from the Greek [by] Mother Katherine. — Whitby : Greek Orthodox Monastery of the Assumption. — (Library of Orthodox thinking. Pamphlet ; no.6)
(Tones 5-8). — New ed. — 1982. — 44p ; 22cm
Previous ed.: 19--
ISBN 0-903455-28-5 (pbk) : £1.45
ISBN 0-903455-26-9 (set) B82-21781

264'.02 — Catholic Church. Public worship

Crichton, J. D.. Christian celebration : the Mass, the sacraments, the prayer of the church / J.D. Crichton. — London : Geoffrey Chapman, 1981. — xii,134p ; 22cm
Includes index
ISBN 0-225-66314-7 (pbk) : Unpriced B82-14792

264'.02 — Catholic Church. Public worship. Lectionaries — *Commentaries*

McLaughlin, Vincent. Reading in church : a guide to cycle C / Vincent McLaughlin. — Great Wakering : Mayhew-McCrimmon, 1979. — 135p ; 21cm
ISBN 0-85597-284-x (pbk) : £2.50 B82-21442

264'.02013 — Catholic Church. Public worship. Prayers — *Collections*

Catholic prayer book / edited by Anthony Bullen. — 3rd rev. ed. — London : Darton, Longman & Todd, 1982. — 207p ; 17cm
Previous ed.: 1977. — Includes index
ISBN 0-232-51570-0 (cased) : £5.95 : CIP rev.
ISBN 0-232-51569-7 (Limp) : £2.50 B82-08443

Challoner, Richard. [The garden of the Soul. Selections]. The garden of the soul / by Richard Challoner. — [Lancaster?] : Printed for the Challoner Society by Darlington Carmel, 1981. — 26p ; 14cm
Originally published: S.l. : s.n., 1740
Unpriced (pbk) B82-41146

264'.0202 — Catholic Church. Eucharist. Music

Music in the parish mass / the Bishops' Conference of England and Wales. — London : Catholic Truth Society, 1981. — vi,73p ; 19cm + supplement(7p ; 19cm)
Includes index
ISBN 0-85183-445-0 (pbk) : £2.50 B82-11188

264'.02034 — Catholic Church. Public worship. Bible readings by lectors — *Manuals*

Wijngaards, John N. M.. Reading God's words to others / John N.M. Wijngaards. — Great Wakering : Mayhew-McCrimmon, 1981. — 104p : ill ; 21cm
Includes index
ISBN 0-85597-315-3 (pbk) : £2.00 B82-09120

264'.02036 — Catholic Church. Eucharist

Coyle, Tom. This is our Mass / Tom Coyle. — London : Collins Liturgical, 1982. — 141p : ill ; 18cm
ISBN 0-00-599700-3 (pbk) : £2.25 B82-35429

Flood, Edmund. The Mass in practice / Edmund Flood. — London (7a Henry Rd., N4 2LH) : St. Thomas Centre for Pastoral Liturgy, [1981?]. — 40p : ill ; 19cm
Cover title. — Text on inside covers
Unpriced (pbk) B82-13771

Morland, David. The Eucharist and justice : do this in memory of me : a document prepared for the Commission for International Justice and Peace of England and Wales as a contribution to discussion / David Morland. — London : Published by Infoform for the Commission, c1980. — 25p ; 21cm
£0.50 (pbk) B82-00140

264'.02036 — Catholic Church. Eucharist — *Devotional works*
The **Worship** of the Eucharist including the new rite of benediction and night prayers for Sundays / [compiled by Stephen Dean]. — Rev. ed. — London : Catholic Truth Society, c1981. — 77p ; 14cm
Previous ed.: published as The mystery of the Eucharist. 1979
ISBN 0-85183-446-9 (pbk) : Unpriced B82-15335

264'.02036 — Wales. Catholic Church. Feasts. Eucharist. Eucharistic prayers — *Collections*
Catholic Church. Proper for Wales : masses for the feasts of Welsh saints to be used in the Archdiocese of Cardiff and the Diocese of Menevia / [compilation by S.G.A. Luff and Byron Harries]. — Cardiff ([c/o S.G.A. Luff , Our Lady's Church, College View, Llandovery, Dyfed]) : [Roman Catholic Province of Wales], 1981. — 27p ; 24cm
Parallel English and Latin texts. — Added t.p. in Latin
Unpriced (pbk) B82-06126

264'.023 — Africa. Catholic Church. Eucharist — *Rites*
Catholic Church. [Mass]. Worship! : a mass book for Africa : the Order of Mass with prayers and hymns for use at Mass / edited by Anthony Gittins. — London : Collins, 1981. — 63p : col.ill ; 17cm
Includes index
ISBN 0-00-599686-4 (pbk) : Unpriced B82-02537

264'.023 — Catholic Church. Eucharist — *Rites*
Catholic Church. [Missal]. The new Sunday missal : texts approved for use in England & Wales, Ireland, Scotland & Africa / foreword by Cardinal Hume ; commentary by Ernest Sands ; illustrations by Guillem Ramos-Poquí. — London : Chapman, 1982. — xvi,1040p : ill ; 17cm
ISBN 0-225-66329-5 : Unpriced
ISBN 0-225-66327-9 (blue standard ed.)
ISBN 0-225-66330-9 (white de-luxe ed.) B82-30976

The **Sunday** missal : Sunday masses for the entire three-year cycle complete in one volume : texts approved for use in England & Wales, Scotland, Ireland, Africa / edited by Harold Winstone ; illustrations by Meinrad Craighead. — Rev. ed. — London : Collins, 1977 (1982 [printing]). — 832p : ill,music ; 16cm
ISBN 0-00-599698-8 (pbk) : Unpriced B82-15333

The **Sunday** Missal : Sunday masses for the entire three-year cycle complete in one volume : texts approved for use in England & Wales, Scotland, Ireland, Africa / edited by Harold Winstone ; illustrations by Meinrad Craighead. — Rev. ed. — London : Collins, 1977 (1982 [printing]). — 832p : ill ; 17cm
Previous ed.: 1975
ISBN 0-00-599724-0 (pbk) : Unpriced B82-35126

264'.023 — Wales. Catholic Church. Feasts — *Rites*
Catholic Church. Proper for Wales : divine office for the feasts of Welsh saints to be used in the Archdiocese of Cardiff and the Diocese of Menevia / [compilation by S.G.A. Luff and Byron Harries]. — Cardiff ([c/o S.G.A. Luff, Our Lady's Church, College View, Llandovery, Dyfed]) : [Roman Catholic Province of Wales]. — 104p ; 17cm
Parallel English and Latin texts. — Added t.p. in Latin
Unpriced (pbk) B82-06121

264'.029 — Catholic Church. Public worship — *Lectionaries*
Catholic Church. [Missal]. Lectionary. — Rev. ed. / revised by decree of the Second Vatican council and published by authority of Pope Paul VI. — London : Collins, 1981. — 3v. ; 26cm
ISBN 0-00-599694-5 : Unpriced
ISBN 0-00-599653-8 (v.1)
ISBN 0-00-599654-6 (v.2)
ISBN 0-00-599655-4 (v.3)
ISBN 0-225-66322-8 (Cassell : set)
ISBN 0-225-66258-2 (Cassell : v.1)
ISBN 0-225-66259-0 (Cassell : v.2)
ISBN 0-225-66297-5 (Cassell : v.3) B82-28175

264'.03 — Church of England. Holy Week services
Austerberry, David. Celebrating Holy Week : a guide for priest and people / by David Austerberry ; foreword by the Bishop of Lichfield. — London : Mowbray, 1982. — 64p : ill ; 21cm
Bibliography: p17
ISBN 0-264-66844-8 (pbk) : £1.75 B82-17170

264'.03 — Church of England. Public worship
Harrison, D. E. W.. Worship in the Church of England / D.E.W. Harrison and Michael C. Sansom. — New and rev. ed. — London : SPCK, 1982. — viii,181p ; 20cm
Previous ed.: published as Common Prayer in the Church of England. 1969. — Includes index
ISBN 0-281-03843-0 (pbk) : £3.95 B82-20147

264'.03 — Church of England. Public worship — *For children*
Kenneth, *Brother, CGA*. Bells are ringing! / words by Brother Kenneth ; pictures by Berit Karlsson. — [London] : CIO, c1981. — [48]p : col.ill ; 13x19cm
Translation of: Fest i Guds hus!
ISBN 0-7151-0403-9 (pbk) : £1.50 B82-05914

264'.03 — Church of England. Public worship. Prayer — *Prayer books*
Church of England. [The Book of Common Prayer. Selections]. The beauty of the Book of Common Prayer / selections, scribed & decorated by G.E. Pallant-Sidaway. — Burgh-by-Sands ([Fort House, Burgh-by-Sands, Carlisle, Cumbria, CA5 6AW]) : Fort House Publications, [1981]. — 32p : ill ; 21cm
Text on inside cover
ISBN 0-9505901-1-8 (pbk) : Unpriced B82-07740

New parish prayers. — London : Hodder and Stoughton, Oct.1982. — [224]p
ISBN 0-340-27237-6 : £6.95 : CIP entry B82-24819

264'.03 — Church of England. Public worship — *Rites*
Church of England. [Alternative Service Book]. Alternative Service Book. — London : Hodder & Stoughton, Nov.1981. — [1296]p
ISBN 0-340-27562-6 : £11.95 : CIP entry
ISBN 0-340-27563-4 (Bonded leather ed.) : £13.95 B81-30135

Church of England. [Alternative Service Book]. Alternative Service Book. — London : Hodder & Stoughton, May 1982. — [1296]p
ISBN 0-340-28220-7 (cased) : £13.95 : CIP entry
ISBN 0-340-28221-5 (Rexine ed.) : £11.95 B82-10684

Church of England. Morning and evening prayer. — London : Hodder & Stoughton, Mar.1982. — [72]p
ISBN 0-340-28219-3 (pbk) : £0.60 : CIP entry B82-03104

Further alternative rules to order the service together with an additional alternative lectionary : authorized for optional use in conjunction with the calendar and services of the Book of Common Prayer and with any other services authorized for use in the Church of England, when no specific provision is made. — London : CIO, 1981. — 44p ; 21cm
ISBN 0-7151-3694-1 (unbound) : £1.20 B82-03054

264'.03 — Church of England. Public worship. Rituals: Church of England. Alternative service book — *Critical studies*
No alternative : the Prayer Book controversy / edited by David Martin & Peter Mullen. — Oxford : Basil Blackwell, 1981. — xvii,238p ; 22cm
Includes index
ISBN 0-631-12974-x (cased) : £9.50 : CIP rev.
ISBN 0-631-12975-8 (pbk) : £3.95 B81-31228

264'.03 — Church of England. Public worship. Services — *Rites*
Jackson, Lawrence. Services for special occasions / Lawrence Jackson. — London : Mowbray, 1982. — x,166p ; 22cm
ISBN 0-264-66771-9 (pbk) : £3.95 B82-18196

264'.03 — Church of England. Ritualism. Lowder, Charles — *Biographies*

Ellsworth, L. E.. Charles Lowder and the Ritualist Movement. — London : Darton, Longman & Todd, Nov.1981. — [208]p
ISBN 0-232-51535-2 : £9.95 : CIP entry B81-28815

264'.03 — East Sussex. Brighton. Church of England. Ritualism. Revival by Purchas, John

Butler, Michael J.. Scarlet cassocks, tippets and the mysterious black powder (the Purchas Judgement 1871) / by Michael J. Butler. — Hove (9 Brunswick Sq., Hove, E. Sussex BN3 1EN) : Chichester Diocesan Fund and Board of Finance, 1981. — 15p ; 22cm
Unpriced (unbound) B82-05249

264'.0301 — Church of England. Public worship. Prayer. Prayer books — *Expositions*

Liturgy and worship : a companion to the prayer books of the Anglican Communion / edited by W.K. Lowther Clarke with the assistance of Charles Harris. — London : SPCK, 1932 (1981 [printing]). — vii,868p ; 23cm
Includes index
ISBN 0-281-00726-8 : £15.00 B82-08475

264'.03036 — Church of England. Eucharist. Liturgical aspects

Perham, Michael. The eucharist / Michael Perham. — 2nd ed., rev. and reset. — London : SPCK for the Alcuin Club, 1981. — ix,65p : ill ; 22cm. — (Alcuin Club manuals ; no.1)
Previous ed.: 1978
ISBN 0-281-03836-8 (pbk) : £1.95 B82-08321

264'.035 — Church of England. Eucharist. Activities for children

Francis, Leslie Roose. His spirit is with us : a project approach to Christian nurture based on the Rite A. Communion service / Leslie Francis. — London : Collins, 1981. — 238p : ill ; 21cm
ISBN 0-00-599684-8 (pbk) : £5.00 B82-05562

264'.035 — Church of England. Eucharist — *Lectionaries*

Introduction to the readings at Holy Communion : based on the Sunday themes of the Alternative Lectionary / compiled by William C. Collins. — London : Mowbray, c1980
Year 1. — 80p ; 21cm
ISBN 0-264-66767-0 (pbk) : £1.75 B82-23574

Introductions to the readings at Holy Communion : based on the Sunday themes of the Alternative Lectionary / compiled by William C. Collins. — London : Mowbray
Year 2. — 1981. — 80p ; 21cm
ISBN 0-264-66803-0 (pbk) : £1.75 B82-08022

264'.035 — Church of England. Eucharist — *Rites* — *For children*

Children's communion book : rite B adapted from The alternative service book 1980. — Oxford : Mowbray, 1982. — 24p : col.ill ; 22cm
Cover title. — Text and ill on inside covers
ISBN 0-264-66871-5 (pbk) : £1.00 B82-22952

264'.035 — Church of England. Marriage — *Rites*

Church of England. [The marriage service]. The marriage service. — London : Hodder & Stoughton, Mar.1982. — [24]p
ISBN 0-340-28169-3 (pbk) : £0.35 : CIP entry B82-04698

264'.035 — Church of England. Public worship. Rituals: Church of England. Alternative service book. Eucharist. Prayers of intercession — *Collections*

Intercessions for use with The Order for Holy Communion Rite A in The alternative service book 1980 / with an introduction and suggested prayers by Colin Semper. — Rev. ed. — London : Mowbray, 1982. — 32p ; 17cm
Previous ed. published as: Intercessions at Holy Communion services for use with Series 1 and 2 or Series 3. 1978
ISBN 0-264-66799-9 (pbk) : £0.75 B82-22938

264'.035 — Church of England. Public worship. Rituals: Church of England. Alternative service book. Marriage — *Commentaries*

Mullett, John. To love and to cherish — : a guide to the marriage service in "The alternative service book 1980" / John Mullett ; foreword by the Archbishop of York. — Luton : Cortney, 1982. — iv,28p ; 21cm
ISBN 0-904378-16-0 (pbk) : £0.90 B82-28784

264'.052034 — Church of Scotland. Public worship — *Lectionaries*

Room to grow / [Woman's Guild]. — Edinburgh (121 George St., Edinburgh, EH2 4YN) : The Guild, [1982]. — 12p ; 22cm. — (Theme booklet ; 16)
£0.30 (pbk) B82-14659

264'.0523202 — United Reformed Church. Public worship. Hymns. Words — *Anthologies*

Hymns from Twickenham Green / edited by Brian Louis Pearce. — [Twickenham Green] : United Reformed Church, 1982. — [32]p ; 20cm
ISBN 0-9501639-8-8 (pbk) : £0.75 B82-31338

264'.2 — Christian church. Public worship. Hymns — *Anthologies*

Praying together : in word and song / Taizé. — Oxford : Mowbrays, c1981. — 32p : music ; 21cm
Translation from the French. — Cover title
ISBN 0-264-66852-9 (pbk) : £1.50
Primary classification 242'.8 B82-26960

To him be praise : hymns to Christ in the first millennium of the Church / edited by Costante Berselli ; [translated from the Italian by Sr. Mary of Jesus]. — Slough : St Paul Publications, 1982. — 141p ; 21cm
Translation of: Inni a Cristo nel primo millennio della Chiesa. — Includes index
ISBN 0-85439-211-4 (pbk) : £3.95 B82-29346

264'.2 — Christian church. Public worship. Hymns — *Collections* — *For schools*

Harvest time : an anthology / arranged by Kenneth Pont. — London : Oxford University Press Music Department, c1982. — 17p : music ; 28cm
Text and music on inside covers
ISBN 0-19-330617-4 (pbk) : Unpriced B82-39414

264'.2 — Christian church. Public worship. Hymns — *Critical studies*

Wright, David R.. Praises with understanding. — Exeter : Paternoster, Oct.1982. — [32]p
ISBN 0-85364-355-5 (pbk) : £1.50 : CIP entry B82-25089

264'.2 — Christian church. Public worship. Hymns, *to 1000.* **Special subjects: Mary,** *Mother of Jesus Christ.* **Words** — *Anthologies*

Sing the joys of Mary : hymns from the first millen[n]ium of the eastern and western Churches / edited by Costante Berselli and Georges Gharib ; [translated from the Italian by Phil Jenkins]. — Slough : St Paul Publications, 1982. — 136p ; 21cm
Translation of: Lodi alla Madonna. — Includes index
ISBN 0-85439-188-6 (pbk) : £3.95 B82-29347

264'.2 — Christian church. Public worship. Hymns. Words — *Anthologies*

Alexander's hymns. — Large print ed. — London : Marshall Morgan & Scott
3. — Sept.1981. — [160]p
ISBN 0-551-00911-x (pbk) : £1.60 : CIP entry B81-28334

The **Greater** World Christian Spiritualist hymn book. — [London] : [Greater World Christian Spiritualist Association], [1981?]. — 41p ; 19cm
Includes index
ISBN 0-900413-26-3 (pbk) : Unpriced B82-00768

Hymns for today's church. — Words ed. — London : Hodder & Stoughton, Nov.1982. — [736]p
ISBN 0-340-27046-2 : £2.95 : CIP entry B82-28729

Jesus praise : words : a songbook for all occasions / [compiled by Norman Warren, David Peacock] ; [words arranged by Michael Perry] ; [edited by Simon Jenkins]. — London : Scripture Union, 1982. — [106]p ; 14cm
Includes index
ISBN 0-85421-962-5 (pbk) : £0.95 B82-28199

264'.2 — Christian church. Public worship. Hymns. Words. Modernisation

Idle, Christopher. Hymns in today's language? / by Christopher Idle. — Bramcote : Grove Books, 1982. — 24p ; 22cm. — (Grove worship series, ISSN 0144-1728 ; no.81)
ISBN 0-907536-27-1 (pbk) : £0.70 B82-40941

264'.2 — Christian church. Public worship. Hymns. Words — *Texts*

Bayly, Albert F.. Rejoice together : hymns and verse / by Albert F. Bayly. — Chelmsford (3 Church La., Springfield, Chelmsford, Essex CM1 5SF) : A.F. Bayly, 1982. — [78]p ; 19cm
Unpriced (pbk) B82-34204

Green, Fred Pratt. The hymns and ballads of Fred Pratt Green / with commentary by Bernard Braley. — Carol Stream, Ill. : Hope ; London : Stainer & Bell, 1982. — xvii,268p,[8]p of plates : ill,music,facsims,ports ; 21cm
Bibliography: p240-242. — Includes index
ISBN 0-85249-612-5 (pbk) : £5.00 : CIP rev. B82-09872

John and Charles Wesley : selected prayers, hymns, journal notes, sermons, letters and treaties / edited, with an introduction by Frank Whaling ; preface by Albert C. Outler. — London : SPCK, 1981. — xvii,412p ; 23cm. — (The Classics of Western spirituality)
Bibliography: p389-393. — Includes index
ISBN 0-281-03838-4 (pbk) : £8.95
Primary classification 287'.092'4 B82-16246

Thorn, Eric A.. The chosen few / Eric A. Thorn. — Maidstone : Third Day Enterprises, 1977 (1979 [printing]). — [16]p ; 21cm
Text on inside cover
ISBN 0-9505912-3-8 (pbk) : Unpriced : CIP rev. B79-28424

264'.2'05 — Christian church. Public worship. Hymns — *Serials*

News of hymnody. — Issue no.1 (Jan. 1982)-. — Bramcote : Grove Books, 1982-. — v. ; 22x56cm. folded to 22x14cm
Quarterly. — Sponsored by: S.P.C.K.
ISSN 0263-2306 = News of hymnody : £1.00 per year B82-19847

264'.2'0922 — Christian church. Public worship. Hymns. Words. British writers, *ca 1800-1900* — *Critical studies*

Watson, J. R. (John Richard), *1934-*. The Victorian hymn : an inaugural lecture / by J.R. Watson. — Durham : University of Durham, 1981. — 23p ; 22cm
£0.60 (pbk) B82-02509

264'.3 — Christian church. Eucharist. Lectionaries — *Commentaries*

This is the word of the Lord. — London : Bible Reading Fellowship
Year C: The year of Luke / edited by Robin Duckworth. — 1982. — 167p : 2maps ; 20cm
ISBN 0-19-826666-9 (pbk) : £3.25 : CIP rev. B82-23691

This is the word of the Lord / edited by Robin Duckworth. — London : Bible Reading Fellowship
Year A: The year of Mark. — 1980. — 174p : 2maps ; 20cm
ISBN 0-19-213248-2 (pbk) : £2.50 : CIP rev. B80-12721

This is the word of the Lord. — London : Bible Reading Fellowship ; Oxford : Oxford University Press
Year B: The year of Mark / edited by Robin Duckworth. — 1981. — 164p : 2maps ; 20cm
ISBN 0-19-826662-6 (pbk) : £2.95 : CIP rev. B81-26742

264'.36 — Christian church. Eucharist. Attitudes of Voltaire

Trapnell, William H.. Voltaire and the Eucharist / William H. Trapnell. — Oxford : Voltaire Foundation at the Taylor Institution, 1981. — 219p ; 24cm. — (Studies on Voltaire and the eighteenth century, ISSN 0435-2866 ; 198)
Bibliography: p205-208. — Includes index
ISBN 0-7294-0264-9 : Unpriced B82-19506

264'.36 — Christian church. Eucharist. Eucharistic prayers

Cuming, G. J.. He gave thanks : an introduction to the Eucharistic prayer / by Geoffrey Cuming. — Bramcote : Grove Books, 1981. — 33p ; 22cm. — (Grove liturgical study, ISSN 0306-0608 ; no.28)
ISBN 0-907536-13-1 (pbk) : £1.25 B82-13805

264'.36 — Christian church. Eucharist. Participation of children, to 10 years, *to 1980*

Holeton, David. Infant communion — then and now / by David Holeton. — Bramcote : Grove Books, 1981. — 31p ; 22cm. — (Grove liturgical study, ISSN 0306-0608 ; no.27)
ISBN 0-907536-09-3 (pbk) : £1.25 B82-02570

265 — CHRISTIAN RITES, CEREMONIES, ORDINANCES

265'.1 — Catholic Church. Baptism — *Topics for discussion groups*

Easter in us : introduction : baptism and its implications for the faith and life of 'the Easter People'. — Slough : St. Paul, 1981. — 24p ; 22cm. — (The Easter People discussion outlines ; 1)
ISBN 0-85439-204-1 (pbk) : £0.65 B82-08761

265'.1 — Christian church. Baptism

Cryer, Neville B.. Learning about baptism / by Neville B. Cryer. — London : Mowbray, 1982. — 32p ; 15cm. — (Enquirer's library)
Bibliography: p32
ISBN 0-264-66853-7 (pbk) : £0.60 B82-41126

265'.12 — Christian church. Infant baptism

Marcel, Pierre Ch.. The Biblical doctrine of infant baptism. — Cambridge : James Clarke, Feb.1982. — [256]p
Translated from the French. — Originally published: 1953
ISBN 0-227-67855-9 (pbk) : £4.95 : CIP entry B82-07100

265'.2 — Catholic Church. Confirmation candidates. Teaching

Araujo, Christina. I am sending you : a guideline course for preparing candidates for the Sacrament of Confirmation / Christina Araujo. — Great Wakering : Mayhew McCrimmon, 1982. — 72p ; 21cm
ISBN 0-85597-317-x (pbk) : Unpriced B82-37073

265'.5 — Christian doctrine. Sacraments: Marriage. Liturgical aspects, *to 1981*

Stevenson, Kenneth W.. Nuptial blessing. — London : SPCK, Oct.1982. — [272]p. — (Alcuin Club collections ; 64)
ISBN 0-281-04027-3 (pbk) : £10.50 : CIP entry B82-23477

265'.82 — Bible. Special subjects: Ministry of healing

Martin, Trevor. Kingdom healing. — London : Marshall Morgan & Scott, May 1981. — [160] p. — (Marshalls paperbacks)
ISBN 0-551-00902-0 (pbk) : £1.50 : CIP entry B81-12886

265'.82 — Christian church. Ministry of healing

Hutchison, Harry. Healing through worship / by Harry Hutchison. — Andover : Eyre & Spottiswoode, 1981, c1980. — ii,136p ; 17cm
ISBN 0-413-80190-x (pbk) : £2.50 B82-17569

265'.9 — Christian church. Public worship. Kissing

Buchanan, Colin, *1934-*. The kiss of peace / by Colin Buchanan. — Bramcote : Grove, 1982. — 25p ; 22cm. — (Grove worship series ; no.80)
ISBN 0-907536-21-2 (pbk) : Unpriced B82-32347

266 — CHRISTIAN MISSIONS

266 — Bible. Special subjects: Christian missions

Simon and Sarah look at mission in the Bible. — London (93 Gloucester Pl., W1H 4AA) : Young People's Department, Baptist Missionary Society, [1981?]. — [4]p : ill ; 30cm
Unpriced (unbound) B82-02503

266 — Christian church. Mission

Beeby, Dan. Mission and missions / by Dan Beeby. — London : Christian Education Movement, 1979. — 91p : 2maps ; 21cm. — (CEM student theology series)
ISBN 0-905022-54-8 (pbk) : Unpriced B82-36997

266 — Christian church. Mission — *Conference proceedings*

Conway, Martin. Through the eyes of the poor / Martin Conway. — London : Conference for World Mission, 1980. — 29p ; 21cm
Text on inside cover
ISBN 0-900540-18-4 (pbk) : £0.60 B82-13183

266 — Christian missions

Coggan, Donald. Mission to the world : the Chavasse memorial lectures 1981 / Donald Coggan. — London : Hodder and Stoughton, 1982. — 93p ; 20cm
ISBN 0-340-28268-1 (pbk) : £4.95 : CIP rev. B82-06029

Cotterell, Peter. The eleventh commandment : Church and mission today / Peter Cotterell. — Leicester : Inter-Varsity, 1981. — 174p : ill ; 22cm
Bibliography: p166-171. — Includes index
ISBN 0-85110-705-2 (pbk) : £4.75 : CIP rev. B81-30569

266 — Christian missions — *Evangelical viewpoints*

Davies, John D.. The faith abroad. — Oxford : Blackwell, Jan.1983. — [160]p
ISBN 0-631-13183-3 (cased) : £9.50 : CIP entry
ISBN 0-631-13221-x (pbk) : £3.50 B82-32519

Walls, Andrew F.. Evangelical views on mission and development / by Andrew F. Walls and Jim Punton. — London (PO Box No.1, SW1W 9BW) : Christian Aid, c1975. — 11p ; 21cm. — (Viewpoint)
£0.05 (unbound) B82-03776

266'.009172'4 — Developing countries. Christian missions

Edgington, David W.. Christians and the Third World. — Exeter : Paternoster Press, May 1982. — [144]p
ISBN 0-85364-286-9 (pbk) : £3.80 : CIP entry B82-14961

266'.009172'4 — Developing countries. Christian missions — *Serials*

[Horizons *(London : 1981)*]. Horizons : magazine of the Regions Beyond Missionary Union. — Summer 1981-. — London (186 Kennington Park Rd, SE11 4BT) : RBMU, 1981-. — v. : ill,facsims,ports ; 30cm
Quarterly. — Continues: Regions beyond
ISSN 0262-3358 = Horizons (London. 1981) : £2.00 per year B82-02391

266'.009172'4 — Developing countries. Christian missions: Summer Institute of Linguistics

Stoll, David. The modern evangelists. — London : Zed Press, Oct.1982. — [352]p
ISBN 0-86232-111-5 (cased) : £18.95 : CIP entry
ISBN 0-86232-112-3 (pbk) : £6.95 B82-24585

266'.0092'2 — China. Christian missions: China Inland Mission. Women missionaries, *to 1950* — *Biographies*

Thompson, Phyllis, *1906-*. Each to her post : six women of the China Inland Mission : Amelia Hudson Broomhall, Jennie Hudson Taylor, Margaret King, Jessie Gregg, Jessie McDonald, Lilian Hamer / Phyllis Thompson. — London : Hodder and Stoughton, 1982. — 158p ; 18cm. — (Hodder Christian paperbacks)
ISBN 0-340-26933-2 (pbk) : £1.75 : CIP rev. B81-36353

266'.0092'2 — China. Christian missions. Missionaries, *1930-1939* — *Biographies*

Kuhn, Isobel. Second-mile people / Isobel Kuhn. — Sevenoaks : OMF, 1982. — 154p : ill ; 18cm
ISBN 0-85363-145-x (pbk) : £1.50 B82-36773

266'.0092'4 — Burma. Christian missions. Judson, Ann Hasseltine — *Biographies*

Beasley, Ina. Pagodas and prisons : the life of Ann Hasseltine Judson (1789-1826) / by Ina Beasley. — London : LLRS, 1982. — 21p ; 21cm. — (Fawcett library papers ; no.5)
ISBN 0-904264-62-9 (pbk) : Unpriced : CIP rev. B82-03387

266'.0092'4 — China. Christian missions. Taylor, Hudson — *Biographies*

Broomhall, A. J.. Hudson Taylor & China's open century. — London : Hodder & Stoughton, Jan.1983
Bk.3: If I had a thousand lives. — [288]p
ISBN 0-340-32392-2 (pbk) : £4.50 : CIP entry B82-34414

Broomhall, H. J.. Hudson Taylor and China's open century. — London : Hodder & Stoughton
Bk.2. — Nov.1981. — [432]p
ISBN 0-340-27561-8 (pbk) : £3.25 : CIP entry B81-31157

266'.0092'4 — Nigeria. Christian missions: Qua Iboe Mission. Dickson, Herbert W. — *Biographies*

Dickson, Herbert W.. All the days of my life : recollections of Herbert W. Dickson / as told to Jean S. Corbett. — Belfast : Qua Iboe Mission, 1981. — 190p : 2maps ; 19cm. — (A Qua Iboe Mission publication)
ISBN 0-9507657-0-8 (pbk) : £1.50 B82-10987

266'.0092'4 — Pakistan. Christian missions: International Christian Fellowship — *Personal observations*

Fitzsimons, Lionel. Panorama Pakistan / Lionel Fitzsimons. — [Hounslow] ([20 Vicarage Farm Rd., Hounslow, Middx TW3 4NW]) : ICF, [1982?]. — 31p : ill,ports ; 17cm
£0.50 (pbk) B82-21681

266'.0095 — Far East. Christian missions: Overseas Missionary Fellowship

Lane, Denis. Keeping body and soul together / Denis Lane. — Sevenoaks : OMF, [1982?]. — 94p ; 19cm
ISBN 0-85363-144-1 (pbk) : £1.20 B82-25686

266'.00952 — Japan. Protestant missions, *to 1981*

Gosden, Eric W.. The other ninety-nine : the persisting challenge of present-day Japan / Eric W. Gosden. — London : Marshalls : Japan Evangelistic Band, 1982. — 125p ; 18cm
ISBN 0-551-01001-0 (pbk) : £1.40 B82-38397

266'.009549'2 — Bangladesh. Christian missions

Khan, Abdul Karim. Christian mission in Bangladesh : a survey / by Abdul Karim Khan. — Leicester : Islamic Foundation, [1982?]. — 30p ; 30cm. — (Study paper / Islamic Foundation ; no.3)
ISBN 0-86037-100-x (pbk) : Unpriced B82-23565

266'.009866'41 — Ecuador. Napo-Pastaza. Christian missions to Aucas, *1956-1980*

Hefley, James. Unstilled voices / James and Marti Hefley. — London : Hodder and Stoughton, 1982, c1981. — 236p,[16]p of plates : ill,ports ; 18cm. — (Hodder Christian paperbacks)
ISBN 0-340-27284-8 : £1.95 : CIP rev. B81-34650

266'.022 — Kent. Ramsgate. Sailors. Church of England missions: Sailors Church *(Ramsgate), to 1982*

Beer, Edward A. R.. The Sailors Home and Harbour Mission, Ramsgate : a brief history / by Edward A.R. Beer. — [Ramsgate] ([27 Southwood Rd., Ramsgate]) : [E.A.R. Beer], c1982. — 12p : ill ; 22cm
Unpriced (unbound) B82-22460

266′.022′09421 — London. Christian missions: London City Mission

Seymour, Stanley. London — day by day / by Stanley Seymour. — London (175 Tower Bridge Rd., SE1 2AH) : London City Mission, [1981]. — 119p,[5]p of plates : ill ; 19cm
£1.25 (pbk) B82-01874

266′.2′0924 — Africa. Catholic missions. Libermann, Francis — *Biographies*

O'Carroll, Michael. Francis Libermann : Apostle of Africa / Michael O'Carroll. — London : Catholic Truth Society, 1982. — 19p ; 19cm
Cover title. — Text on inside covers
ISBN 0-85183-473-6 (pbk) : £0.35 B82-28312

266′.2′0924 — India. Catholic missions. Nobili, Roberto de — *Biographies*

Gallagher, John, *1911-*. Apostle of India : the story of Roberto de Nobili / by John Gallagher. — London : CTS, 1982. — 12p ; 19cm
ISBN 0-85183-463-9 (pbk) : £0.45 B82-18915

266′.2′0924 — India *(Republic)*. **Catholic missions. Teresa,** *Mother — Biographies — For children*

Sebba, Anne. Mother Teresa / Anne Sebba ; illustrated by Paul Crompton. — London : MacRae, 1982. — 42p : ill,1map,ports ; 21cm. — (Blackbird books)
ISBN 0-86203-064-1 : £2.75 : CIP rev.
B81-36045

266′.251 — China. American Catholic missions, *1915-1956*

Breslin, Thomas A.. China, American Catholicism, and the missionary / Thomas A. Breslin. — University Park ; London : The Pennsylvania State University Press, c1980. — 144p : maps ; 24cm
Bibliography : p134-138. — Includes index
ISBN 0-271-00259-x : £12.00 B82-35656

266′.342 — England. Church of England missions: Additional Curates Society — *Serials*

[Good news *(Birmingham)*]. Good news / Additional Curates Society for England & Wales. — Vol.48, no.1 (Michaelmas 1981)-. — Birmingham (246a Washwood Heath Rd., Birmingham B8 2XS) : The Society, 1981-. — v. : ill,ports ; 21cm
Three issues yearly. — Continues: Home mission news
ISSN 0262-2874 = Good news (Birmingham) : £0.10 per issue B82-01075

266′.99 — Argentina. Brethren missions, *1882-1982*

Tatford, Frederick A.. A new day in Argentina : centenary 1882-1982 / by Dr Fredk. A. Tatford. — [Bath] ([1 Widcombe Cres., Bath]) : Echoes of Service, [1982?]. — 16p : ill,1maps ; 19cm
Cover title. — Map on inside cover
Unpriced (pbk) B82-40011

266′.99 — Christian missions — *Study examples: Literature Crusades*

Khan, Abdul Karim. Christian literature crusade : case study of a missionary organisation / by Abdul Karim Khan. — Leicester : The Islamic Foundation, c1981. — 19p ; 30cm. — (Situation report ; no.5)
Unpriced (pbk) B82-12866

267 — CHRISTIAN ASSOCIATIONS FOR RELIGIOUS WORK

267 — Christian communities — *For schools*

Brown, Alan, *1944-*. Christian communities / Alan Brown. — Guildford : Lutterworth Educational, [c1982]. — 32p : ill,1map ; 30cm. — (The Chichester project ; 2)
Text on inside covers. — Bibliography on inside back cover
ISBN 0-7188-2455-5 (pbk) : Unpriced
B82-20340

267′.13′0924 — Dorset. Post Green. Religious communities: Post Green Community. Community life — *Personal observations*

Lees, Tom. Another man / Tom Lees with Jeanne Hinton. — London : Hodder and Stoughton, 1980. — 156p ; 18cm. — (Hodder Christian paperbacks)
ISBN 0-340-25684-2 (pbk) : £1.50 : CIP rev.
B80-13700

267′.15′0924 — Salvation Army. Booth, Catherine, *1829-1890 — Stories, anecdotes*

Barnes, Cyril. Words of Catherine Booth / by Cyril Barnes. — London : Salvationist Publishing and Supplies, c1981. — 85p : ill,ports ; 19cm
ISBN 0-85412-379-2 (pbk) : Unpriced
B82-10922

267′.15′0924 — Salvation Army. Calliss, Gladys — *Biographies*

Coutts, Frederick. More than one homeland : a biography of Commissioner Gladys Callis / by Frederick Coutts. — London : Salvationist Pub., 1981. — 107p ; 22cm
ISBN 0-85412-390-3 (pbk) : Unpriced
B82-23116

267′.15′0924 — Salvation Army. Higgins, Edward, *1864-1947 — Biographies*

Harris, William. Storm pilot : the story of the life and leadership of General Edward J. Higgins / by William Harris ; author's manuscript prepared for publication by Cyril J. Barnes. — London : Salvationist, 1981. — 109p,[1]leaf of plates : 2ports ; 22cm
ISBN 0-85412-386-5 (pbk) : Unpriced
B82-13283

267′.15′0954 — India. Salvation Army, *to 1980*

Smith, Solveig. By love compelled : the Salvation Army's one hundred years in India and adjacent lands / Solveig Smith. — London : Salvationist Pub., 1981. — 202p,[4]p of plates : ill,1map,ports ; 22cm
Bibliography: p192-193
ISBN 0-85412-385-7 (pbk) : Unpriced
B82-23115

267′.182 — Catholic organisations: Catholic Institute for International Relations, *to 1980*

Walsh, Michael J.. From sword to ploughshare : Sword of the spirit to Catholic Institute for International Relations 1940-1980 / by Michael Walsh. — London : Catholic Institute for International Relations, 1980. — 39p : ill,facsims,ports ; 26cm
ISBN 0-904393-53-4 (pbk) : £1.00 B82-15237

267′.182 — Catholic organisations: Opus Dei

Illanes, José Luis. On the theology of work. — Blackrock : Four Courts Press, Nov.1982. — [108]p
Translation of: La sanctificación del trabajo
ISBN 0-906127-55-6 (cased) : CIP entry
ISBN 0-906127-56-4 (pbk) : £3.50 B82-35227

267′.182′05 — Catholic organisations: Focolare Movement — *Serials*

Focolare news. — Vol.1, no.1 (Aug. 1982)-. — London (57 Twyford Ave., W3 9PZ) : Mariapolis Ltd., 1982-. — v. : ill,maps ; 29cm
Monthly
ISSN 0263-6018 = Focolare news : £4.00 per year B82-40057

267′.182′0924 — Catholic organisations: Opus Dei. Escrivá de Balaguer, Josemaría — *Biographies*

Bernal, Salvador. Msgr. Josemaría Escrivá de Balaguer : a profile of the founder of Opus Dei / Salvador Bernal. — London : Scepter, 1977. — 343p ; 22cm
Translation of: Mons. Josemaría Escrivá de Balaguer
ISBN 0-906138-01-9 (cased) : Unpriced
ISBN 0-906138-00-0 (pbk) : Unpriced
B82-08930

267′.182′0924 — Catholic organisations: Opus Dei. Escrivá de Balaguer, Josemaría — *Interviews*

Escrivá de Balaguer, Josemaría. Conversations with Mgr Escrivá de Balaguer. — Dublin : Four Courts, c1980. — 147p ; 22cm
Includes index
Unpriced B82-03226

267′.182′0924 — Legion of Mary. Duff, Frank — *Biographies*

Ripley, Francis J.. Frank Duff : a memoir / by Francis J. Ripley. — London : Catholic Truth Society, 1981. — 16p : ill ; 18cm
Cover title
ISBN 0-85183-442-6 (pbk) : £0.40 B82-07562

267′.183′05 — Church Army — *Serials*

Church Army. Centenary news. Church Army. — Issue no.1 (June 1981)-. — [London] ([Independents Rd, Blackheath, SE3 9LG]) : Church Army, 1981-. — v. : ill,ports ; 42cm
Description based on: Issue no.3 (Sept. 1981)
Unpriced B82-11145

267′.18342352 — Devon. Lynton. Church of England religious communities: Lee Abbey, *to 1980*

More, Richard. Growing in faith : the Lee Abbey story / Richard More. — London : Hodder and Stoughton, 1982. — 184p,[8]p of plates : ill,1map,ports ; 18cm. — (Hodder Christian paperbacks)
ISBN 0-340-26353-9 (pbk) : £1.95 : CIP rev.
B82-12254

267′.3942842 — North Yorkshire. Harrogate. Men's Christian organisations: Harrogate YMCA

Grass roots? : a discussion document for the movement, based on the Harrogate experience / YMCA. — [Leeds] ([35 Albion Place, Leeds 1]) : [Yorkshire and Humberside Region of YMCA], [1982?]. — 24p : ill ; 21cm
Cover title. — Text on inside cover
£1-00 (pbk) B82-31413

267′.44242 — England. Women's Catholic organisations: Catholic Women's League, *to 1981*

Catholic Women's League. Yesterday recalled : a jubilee history of the Catholic Women's League 1906-1981 / compiled by Marjorie Ryan. — London (National Headquarters, 48 Great Peter St, SW1P 2HA) : The League, [1981]. — 34p : 1port ; 21cm
Text on inside covers
Unpriced (pbk) B82-05678

267′.4452411 — Women's Church of Scotland organisations: Church of Scotland. *Women's Guild.* **Meetings. Organisation** — *Manuals*

Vision unlimited / [Church of Scotland Woman's Guild]. — Edinburgh (121 George St., Edinburgh EH2 4YN) : The Guild, [1982]. — 17p ; 21cm. — (Theme booklet ; 15)
Text on inside covers
£0.25 (pbk) B82-29568

267′.4452411 — Women's Church of Scotland organisations: Church of Scotland. *Women's Guild, to 1980*

Church of Scotland. *Woman's Guild*. A history of the Woman's Guild. — [Edinburgh] ([121 George St., Edinburgh EH2 4YN]) : [Church of Scotland], [1981?]. — 8p ; 21cm
Cover title
ISBN 0-86153-040-3 (pbk) : £0.50 B82-08900

267′.6′0941 — Great Britain. Christian youth work

Milson, Fred. Youth in the local church / Fred Milson. — [Leicester] : [National Youth Bureau], [1981]. — 11p ; 30cm
Cover title. — Text on inside cover
ISBN 0-86155-050-1 (pbk) : £0.80 B82-10925

267′.7′094167 — Belfast. Boys' Christian organisations: Boys' Brigade. *Belfast Battalion, to 1978*

Boys' Brigade. *Belfast Battalion*. Firm and deep : an historic account of the formation The 1st Belfast (1st Irish) Company, The Boy's Brigade and the subsequent formation and development of The Belfast Battalion / by William R. Kelly. — Belfast : The Boy's Brigade Belfast Battalion, [1982?]. — 205p : ill,ports ; 25cm
Bibliography: p195. — Includes index
ISBN 0-9506410-0-6 : Unpriced B82-25613

268 — CHRISTIANITY. RELIGIOUS TRAINING AND INSTRUCTION

268′.3 — Africa. Catholic Church. Catechists. Duties — *Manuals*

McGrath, Michael. Africa : our way to be God's messengers : a handbook for Catechists / Michael McGrath and Nicole Gregoire. — [London] : Chapman, c1979. — vi,183p : ill ; 18cm
ISBN 0-225-66246-9 (pbk) : £1.25 : CIP rev.
B79-12257

268'.432 — Christian religious education — *For Church of Scotland Sunday school teaching*

Children of the way : a programme for Sunday school. — Edinburgh : St Andrew
Bk.1: For children of ages 5-7 / editor: David P. Munro. — c1981. — 3v. : ill,music ; 30cm
ISBN 0-7152-0470-8 (pbk) : Unpriced
ISBN 0-7152-0471-6 (Term 2)
ISBN 0-7152-0472-4 (Term 3) B82-39641

Children of the way : a programme for Sunday School. — Edinburgh : Saint Andrew
Bk.2: For children of ages 5-7 : (primary school grades 1-3) / editor David G. Hamilton ; contributors Alistair Bennett ... [et al.]. — [1982]. — 3v. : ill,music ; 30cm
ISBN 0-7152-0502-1 (pbk) : £2.80
ISBN 0-7152-0503-x (Term 2)
ISBN 0-7152-0504-8 (Term 3) B82-27166

Children of the way : a programme for Sunday School. — Edinburgh : Saint Andrew
Bk.5: For children of ages 8 and 9 : (primary school grades 4 and 5) / editor David G. Hamilton ; contributors Anne Carruthers ... [et al.]. — [1982]. — 3v. : ill,music ; 30cm
ISBN 0-7152-0507-2 (pbk) : £2.80
ISBN 0-7152-0508-0 (Term 2)
ISBN 0-7152-0509-9 (Term 3) B82-27167

Children of the way : a programme for Sunday School. — Edinburgh : Saint Andrew
Bk.7: For children of ages 10 and 11 : (primary school grades 6 and 7) / editor David G. Hamilton ; contributors Marina Brown ... [et al.]. — [1982]. — 3v. : ill ; 30cm
ISBN 0-7152-0512-9 (pbk) : £2.80
ISBN 0-7152-0513-7 (Term 2)
ISBN 0-7152-0514-5 (Term 3) B82-27168

268'.6 — Christian church. Single-parent families. Discussion groups — *Manuals*

One big family : practical guidelines for parishes on meeting the pastoral needs of one-parent families. — London (106 Clapham Rd., SW9 0JX) : Family and Social Action, 1981 (1982 [printing]). — 36p : ill ; 21cm
£0.50 (pbk) B82-38360

268'.6 — United States. Lutheran churches. Christian doctrine. Catechetics. Influence of Luther, Martin. Kleine Katechismus, *1638-1850*

Repp, Arthur C.. Luther's Catechism comes to America : theological effects on the issues of the Small Catechism prepared in or for America prior to 1850 / by Arthur C. Repp. — Metuchen ; London : Scarecrow and the American Theological Library Association, 1982. — xiv,297p,[16]p of plates : facsims ; 23cm. — (ATLA monograph series ; no.18)
Bibliography: p239-248. — Includes index
ISBN 0-8108-1546-x : £18.00 B82-39022

269 — CHRISTIANITY. SPIRITUAL RENEWAL

269 — Christian life. Spiritual renewal

Bridge, Donald. More than tongues can tell. — London : Hodder and Stoughton, Sept.1982. — [128]p
ISBN 0-340-32018-4 (pbk) : £1.50 : CIP entry B82-18781

Watson, David, *1933-*. Be filled with the Spirit / David Watson. — Eastbourne : Falcon, 1982. — 16p ; 18cm
Bibliography: p16
ISBN 0-86239-002-8 (unbound) : £0.25 B82-19353

269'.2 — Catholic Church. Sermons. Special subjects: Evangelism — *Sermon outlines*

Now is the hour of mission : for use on Sunday 11th October 1981 and on World Mission Sunday 18th October 1981. — [London] : [Association for the Propagation of the Faith], [1981?]. — 8p : 1map,1col.port ; 21cm
Unpriced (unbound) B82-02685

269'.2 — Christian church. Evangelism

Bassett, Paul. God's way / Paul Bassett. — Welwyn : Evangelical, 1981. — 143p ; 22cm
ISBN 0-85234-147-4 (pbk) : Unpriced B82-09809

Light upon the word : an anthology of Evangelical spiritual writings / selected and introduced by Herbert F. Stevenson. — London : Mowbrays, 1979. — 182p ; 23cm
Includes index
ISBN 0-264-66565-1 (cased) : £6.75
ISBN 0-264-66468-x (pbk) B82-32833

Wallis, Jim. The call to conversion / Jim Wallis. — Tring : Lion, 1982, c1981. — xviii,190p ; 18cm
Originally published: New York : Harper & Row, 1981. — Bibliography: p180-186. — Includes index
ISBN 0-85648-391-5 (corrected : pbk) : £1.50 B82-18321

Wooderson, Michael. Good news down the street / by Michael Wooderson. — Bramcote : Grove, 1982. — 25p ; 22cm. — (Grove pastoral series, ISSN 0144-171x)
Text on inside cover
ISBN 0-907536-18-2 (pbk) : £0.70 B82-24286

Wright, Eric. Tell the world : apostolic patterns for evangelism and missions / Eric Wright. — Welwyn : Evangelical, 1981. — 144p ; 18cm
ISBN 0-85234-156-3 (pbk) : Unpriced B82-13542

269'.2 — Christian church. Evangelism — *Evangelical Methodist Church in Bolivia viewpoints*

Second manifesto to the nation. — London (PO Box no.1, London SW1W 9BW) : Christian Aid, [1974?]. — [8]p ; 21cm. — (Viewpoint)
Prepared by the Evangelical Methodist Church in Bolivia
£0.05 (unbound) B82-11241

269'.2 — Christian church. Evangelism. Role of social responsibility

Evangelism and social responsibility. — Exeter : Paternoster Press, Oct.1982. — [64]p
ISBN 0-85364-364-4 (pbk) : £1.00 : CIP entry B82-29138

269'.2'0924 — Christian church. Evangelism. Luff, Ernest — *Biographies*

Bridge, Donald W.. God has resources. — Exeter : Paternoster Press, July 1982. — [80]p
ISBN 0-85364-311-3 (pbk) : £1.10 : CIP entry B82-19278

269'.2'0924 — Christian church. Evangelism — *Personal observations*

Tozer, A. W.. Echoes from Eden : the voices of God calling man / by A.W. Tozer. — Bromley : STL, 1981. — 121p ; 18cm
ISBN 0-903843-45-5 (pbk) : £1.20 B82-06390

Verwer, George. Hunger for reality / George Verwer. — 2nd British ed. — Bromley : STL, 1977, c1972 (1979 [printing]). — 96p ; 18cm
Previous ed.: published as Come! Live! Die!. Wheaton, Ill.: Tyndale House Publishers, 1972; London : Hodder and Stoughton, 1973
ISBN 0-903843-19-6 (pbk) : £0.75 B82-01265

269'.2'0924 — Christian church. Evangelism. Pink, Arthur W. — *Biographies*

Murray, Iain H.. Arthur W. Pink : his life and thought / Iain H. Murray. — Edinburgh : The Banner of Truth Trust, 1981. — 272p,[8]p of plates ; 18cm
Includes index
ISBN 0-85151-332-8 (pbk) : £2.45 B82-16967

269'.2'0924 — Christian church. Evangelism. Ten Boom, Corrie — *Biographies*

Watson, Jean, *1936-*. Corrie : watchmaker's daughter / Jean Watson. — Eastbourne : Kingsway, 1982. — 159p : ill ; 18cm
ISBN 0-86065-171-1 (pbk) : £1.60 B82-19355

269'.2'0924 — Christian church. Evangelism. Ten Boom, Corrie — *Biographies* — *For schools*

Wallington, David. The secret room : the story of Corrie Ten Boom / David Wallington. — Exeter : Religious Education Press, 1981. — 30p : ill,ports ; 21cm. — (Faith in action series)
Bibliography: p29
ISBN 0-08-026416-6 (pbk) : £0.65
ISBN 0-08-026415-8 (pbk) : Unpriced (non net) B82-12065

269'.2'0924 — Cuba. Christian church. Evangelism — *Personal observations*

White, Tom, *1947-*. God's missiles over Cuba / Tom White. — London : Triangle, 1982. — xx,221p : ill,ports ; 18cm
ISBN 0-281-03858-9 (pbk) : £1.75 B82-36939

269'.2'0924 — Japan. Christian church. Evangelism, *1923-1970* — *Personal observations*

Kogo, Shotaro. Earthquake evangelist : a spiritual odyssey / by Shotaro Kogo. — London : Japan Evangelistic Band, c1977. — 79p,[4]p of plates : ill,ports ; 19cm
ISBN 0-902846-09-4 (pbk) : £0.70 B82-22223

269'.2'0941 — Great Britain. Christian church. Evangelism. Jackopson, Vic — *Biographies*

Jackopson, Vic. From prison to pulpit. — London : Marshall Morgan & Scott, Sept.1981. — [128]p. — (Marshalls paperbacks)
ISBN 0-551-00916-0 (pbk) : £1.25 : CIP entry B81-27904

269'.2'0941 — Great Britain. Urban regions. Christian church. Evangelism — *Serials*

ECUM bulletin. — [198?]-. — London (130 City Rd, EC1V 2NJ) : Evangelical Coalition for Urban Mission, [198-]-. — v. ; 30cm
Description based on: No.2 (Winter '81)
ISSN 0263-662X = ECUM bulletin : Unpriced B82-28867

269'.2'0941 — Great Britain. Urban regions. Inner areas. Evangelism by United Reformed Church

Johansen-Berg, John. Good news to the poor : new enterprise in mission for the United Reformed Church / [John Johansen-Berg, Henry Gordon, Philip Woods]. — London : The Church, [1982]. — 17p ; 21cm
ISBN 0-902256-53-x (unbound) : £0.15 B82-27067

269'.24 — East Sussex. Eastbourne. Pentecostal churches. Revivals, *ca 1920-1930.* **Role of Jeffreys, George**

Homan, Roger. Principal George Jeffreys and the pentecostal revival / by Roger Homan. — Hove (Diocesan Church House, 9 Brunswick Sq., Hove, E. Sussex BN3 1EN) : [Diocese of Chichester], [1981]. — 8p : 1port ; 21cm
Bibliography: p8
£0.10 (unbound) B82-04369

269'.24'09 — Christian church. Revivals, *to 1845* — *Early works* — *Facsimiles*

Gillies, John. Historical collections of accounts of revival / John Gillies. — Revised and enlarged. — [Edinburgh] : Banner of Truth Trust, 1981. — xvi,582p ; 27cm
Facsim of: Rev. ed. published Kelso : John Rutherford, 1845. — Includes index
ISBN 0-85151-325-5 : £11.95 B82-10826

269'.24'0924 — East Africa. Christian church. Revivals, *1927-1965* — *Personal observations* — *Correspondence, diaries, etc.*

Church, J. E.. Quest for the highest : an autobiographical account of the East African Revival / by J.E. Church. — Exeter : Paternoster Press, c1981. — 284p : ill,map,facsims,ports ; 22cm
Includes index
ISBN 0-85364-328-8 (pbk) : Unpriced : CIP rev. B81-22691

269'.24'0942256 — East Sussex. Brighton. Christian church. Revivals, *ca 1850-1900*

Hales, E. E. Y.. The religious revival in Victorian Brighton / by E.E.Y. Hales. — Hove (Diocesan Church House, 9 Brunswick Sq., Hove, E. Sussex BN3 1EN) : [Diocese of Chichester], [1981]. — 8p : ill ; 21cm
£0.10 (unbound) B82-04368

269'.24'09429 — Wales. Christian church. Revivals, *1800-1900* — *Festschriften* — *Welsh texts*

Gwanwyn Duw : diwygwyr a diwygiadau : cyfrol deyrnged i Gomer Morgan Roberts / golygwyd gan J.E. Wynne Davies. — Caernarfon ([Llyfrfa'r Methodistiaid Calfinaidd, Heol Ddewi, Caernarfon, Gwynedd LL55 1ER]) : Gwasg Pantycelyn, c1982. — 205p,[9]p of plates : ill,ports ; 22cm
Bibliography: p186-205
£4.95 B82-28809

269'.24'097479 — West New York *(State).* **Christian church. Revivals,** *1800-1850*

Cross, Whitney R.. The burned-over district : the social and intellectual history of enthusiastic religion in western New York, 1800-1850 / Whitney R. Cross. — Ithaca ; London : Cornell University Press, 1950 (1982 printing). — xiii,383p : maps ; 22cm
Includes index
ISBN 0-8014-9232-7 (pbk) : £6.75 B82-35754

269'.6 — Retreat houses. Christian life. Spiritual renewal

Baldwin, Joanna. Learning about retreats / by Joanna Baldwin. — London : Mowbray, 1982. — 30p ; 15cm. — (Enquirer's library)
Bibliography: p30
ISBN 0-264-66885-5 (pbk) : £0.60 B82-41123

269'.6'02541 — Great Britain. Retreat houses — *Directories*

Gerard, Geoffrey. Away from it all : a guide to retreat houses / Geoffrey Gerard. — 3rd ed. — Guildford : Lutterworth, 1982. — 96p : ill,maps ; 22cm
Previous ed.: 1979. — Includes index
ISBN 0-7188-2536-5 (pbk) : £2.25 B82-12210

269'.6'0941464 — Scotland. Strathclyde Region. Girvan. Retreat houses: Trochrague Guest House, *to 1981*

McGhee, Susan. The history of Trochrague Guest House / by Susan McGhee. — Girvan (Trochrague Guest House, Girvan KA26 9QB) : Sisters of St. Joseph of Cluny, [1981?]. — 23p : ill,2geneal.tables,1map ; 22cm
Unpriced (pbk) B82-26356

270 — CHRISTIAN CHURCH. HISTORICAL AND GEOGRAPHICAL TREATMENT

270 — Christian church, *ca 500-1500 — French texts*

Gaudemet, Jean. La Société ecclésiastique dans l' Occident médiéval / Jean Gaudemet. — London : Variorum, 1980. — 338p in various pagings : 1port ; 24cm. — (Collected studies series ; CS 116)
Facsim reprint. — Includes index
ISBN 0-86078-061-9 : £22.00 : CIP rev.
B80-01501

270 — Christian church, *ca 600-1500*

Birkin, John L.. The Thyatira Church age : a study in the restoration of the church / [John L. Birkin]. — [Caerphilly] ([40 Alexander Court, Lansbury Park, Caerphilly, M. Glamorgan, CF8 1RJ]) : [J.L. Birkin], [c1979]. — 61p ; 22cm. — (Studies / John L. Birkin ; no.6)
Cover title
£0.50 (pbk) B82-23439

270 — Christian church, *ca 600-ca 1500 — French texts*

Congar, Yves. Droit ancien et structures ecclésiales. — London : Variorum, Sept.1982. — [312]p. — (Collected studies series ; C5159)
ISBN 0-86078-107-0 : £26.00 : CIP entry
B82-21401

270 — Christian church. Growth

Gibbs, Eddie. I believe in church growth / by Eddie Gibbs. — London : Hodder and Stoughton, 1981. — 460p : ill,maps ; 22cm. — ('I believe' series)
Bibliography: p454-460
ISBN 0-340-26352-0 (pbk) : £5.95 : CIP rev.
B81-22492

270 — Christian church — *History*

History of the Church / edited by Hubert Jedin and John Dolan. — London : Burns & Oates
Translation of: Handbuch der Kirchengeschichte
Vol.5: Reformation and counter reformation / by Erwin Iserloh, Joseph Glazik, Hubert Jedin ; translated by Anselm Biggs and Peter W. Becker. — 1980. — xx,795p ; 24cm
Bibliography: p649-755. — Includes index
ISBN 0-86012-087-2 : Unpriced B82-16112

270 — Christian church, *to 1978*

Turner, Joan. New wine, fresh skins! : a short and simple account of the Church ... / [by Joan Turner]. — [Belfast] : J. Turner, 1979. — 76p ; 21cm
Limited ed
ISBN 0-9506727-0-x (pbk) : Unpriced
B82-02539

270 — Saints — *Biographies*

Chaundler, Christine. A year book of saints / by Christine Chaundler. — Rev. ed. / revised by Brother Kenneth ; with illustrations by Nicholas Rous. — London : Mowbray, 1981. — 181p : ill ; 20cm
Previous ed.: 1978. — Includes index
ISBN 0-264-66838-3 (pbk) : £2.95 B82-09135

Delaney, John J.. Dictionary of saints / by John J. Delaney. — Tadworth : Kaye & Ward, 1982. — 647p ; 25cm
ISBN 0-7182-2170-2 : £12.50 B82-32249

Farmer, David Hugh. The Oxford dictionary of saints. — Oxford : Oxford University Press, Sept.1982. — [464]p
Originally published: Oxford : Clarendon Press, 1978
ISBN 0-19-283036-8 (pbk) : £2.95 : CIP entry
B82-18990

270 — Saints — *Biographies — For schools*

Green, Victor J.. Saints for all seasons / Victor J. Green. — Poole : Blandford, 1982. — 137p ; 20cm. — (A Blandford assembly book)
Includes index
ISBN 0-7137-1193-0 : £3.95 : CIP rev.
B82-15830

270 — Saints — *Calendars*

Kenneth, *Brother, CGA*. A pocket calendar of saints and people to remember / by Brother Kenneth CGA. — London : Mowbray, 1981. — 80p ; 16cm
Bibliography: p3. — Includes index
ISBN 0-264-66835-9 (cased) : £2.95
ISBN 0-264-66716-6 (pbk) : Unpriced
B82-14005

270 — Saints — *Polish texts*

Mirewicz, Jerzy. Wychowawcy Europy / Jerzy Mirewicz. — Londyn : Księża Jezuici, 1981. — 132p ; 22cm
Unpriced (pbk) B82-12733

270.1 — Christian church, *to 500*

Chadwick, Henry. History and thought of the early church. — London : Variorum, Sept.1982. — [344]p. — (Collected studies series ; CS164)
ISBN 0-86078-112-7 : £26.00 : CIP entry
B82-21406

270.1 — Christian church, *to ca 60 — Stories for children*

The **Birth** of the church / editorial committee René Berthier, Jeanne-Marie Faure, Marie-Hélène Sigaut ; illustrated by Regine and Bruno Le Sourd ; translated by Jane Collins. — London : Hodder and Stoughton, 1980. — 48p : col.ill,1col.map ; 29cm
Translation of: La naissance de l'église. — Map on inside cover
ISBN 0-340-25331-2 (pbk) : £1.30 : CIP rev.
B80-05787

270.1 — Christian church, *to ca 600*

Bruce, F. F.. The spreading flame : the rise and progress of Christianity from its first beginnings to the conversion of the English. — Exeter : Paternoster Press, Oct.1982. — [432]p
Originally published: 1958
ISBN 0-85364-348-2 (pbk) : £7.00 : CIP entry
B82-24107

270.1 — Patristics — *Conference proceedings*

Studia patristica. — Oxford : Pergamon
Conference papers
Vol.XVII. — Sept.1982. — [1520]p
ISBN 0-08-025779-8 : £85.00 : CIP entry
B82-32842

270.2 — Ancient Rome. Christian church, *300-500*

Barnes, Timothy D.. Constantine and Eusebius / Timothy D. Barnes. — Cambridge, Mass. ; London : Harvard University Press, 1981. — vi,458p : 1map ; 24cm
Bibliography: p406-442. — Includes index
ISBN 0-674-16530-6 : £24.50 B82-13738

270.2 — Christian church, *ca 475-920 — Polish texts*

Koczy, Leon. Kościół w okresie wczesnego średniowiecza / Leon Koczy. — Glasgow (42 Cecil St., Glasgow W2) : Instytut Polski i Muzeum Gen. Sikorskiego, Biblioteka w Szkocji, 1981. — 31p ; 21cm
Unpriced (pbk) B82-11338

270.2'092'4 — Christian church. Augustine, *Saint, Bishop of Hippo — Biographies*

McDonagh, Gabriel. St Augustine of Hippo / Gabriel McDonagh. — London : Catholic Truth Society, 1982. — 19p ; 19cm
ISBN 0-85183-488-4 (pbk) : £0.45 B82-30676

270.2'092'4 — Christian church. Columba, *Saint, of Iona — Stories, anecdotes*

Thompson, Rosemary C.. The dove of the church : or Colomcille / by Rosemary C. Thompson ; illustrated by a member of a religious community. — Iona : Iona Community, c1980. — 40p : col.ill ; 26cm
Unpriced (pbk) B82-26297

270.2'092'4 — Christian church. Columban, *Saint*

Griffiths, Liam. Saint Columban / by Liam Griffiths ; illustrated by Janet Wilcox. — London : Catholic Truth Society, 1981. — 24p : col.ill ; 19cm
Text on inside cover
ISBN 0-85183-426-4 (pbk) : £0.60 B82-09408

270.2'092'4 — Christian church. John, *the Almsgiver, Saint — Biographies — Early works*

The **Life** of Saint John the Almsgiver / edited by Kenneth Urwin. — London : Anglo-Norman Text Society, 1980. — 2v. : 1facsim ; 23cm. — (Anglo-Norman texts ; nos.38-39)
Anglo-Norman text, English introduction and notes. — Includes index
Unpriced B82-40355

270.2'092'4 — Christian church. Patrick, *Saint.* **Local associations: Ireland**

De Breffny, Brian. In the steps of St. Patrick / Brian de Breffny ; photographs by George Mott ; with 40 illustrations, line drawings and maps. — London : Thames and Hudson, c1982. — 176p : ill,2maps ; 25cm
Bibliography: p170-173. — Includes index
ISBN 0-500-24110-4 : £6.50 B82-20414

270.2'092'4 — Christian church. Wilfrid, *Saint — Biographies*

Orbach, Ann. Wilfrid and the Church of England / by Ann Orbach. — Hove (Diocesan Church House, 9 Brunswick Sq., Hove, E. Sussex BN3 1EN) : [Diocese of Chichester], [1981]. — 23p : ill ; 21cm
Cover title
Unpriced (pbk) B82-04374

270.2'092'4 — Christian church. Wilfrid, *Saint — Chronologies*

Gudgeon, Michael. Wilfrid / Michael Gudgeon. — Hove (Diocesan Church House, 9 Brunswick Sq., Hove, E. Sussex BN3 1EN) : [Diocese of Chichester], [1981]. — 6p ; 21cm
Cover title
£0.07 (pbk) B82-04375

270.2'092'4 — Libya. Ptolemaïs. Christian church. Synesius, *of Cyrene, Bishop of Ptolemaïs — Biographies*

Bregman, Jay. Synesius of Cyrene : philosopher-bishop / Jay Bregman. — Berkeley ; London : University of California Press, c1982. — xi,206p ; 25cm. — (The Transformation of the classical heritage ; 2)
Bibliography: p185-193. — Includes index
ISBN 0-520-04192-5 : £18.75 B82-41100

270.5 — Catholic Church. Great Schism

MacCarron, Daniel. The Great Schism : antipopes who split the Church / Daniel MacCarron. — Dublin : DMC Universal, 1982. — v,265p,[8]p of plates : ill,ports ; 23cm
ISBN 0-9507808-0-4 : £5.95 B82-32897

270.6 — Christian church. Counter-Reformation
Wright, A. D. (Anthony David), *1947-*. The Counter-Reformation : Catholic Europe and the non-Christian world / A.D. Wright. — London : Weidenfeld and Nicolson, c1982. — 344p ; 24cm
Bibliography: p295-327. — Includes index
ISBN 0-297-78011-5 : £18.50 B82-21672

270.6 — Christian church. Reformation
Atkinson, James. Martin Luther and the birth of Protestantism. — Revised ed. — London : Marshall, Morgan & Scott, Feb.1982. — [368]p
Previous ed.: Harmondsworth : Penguin, 1968
ISBN 0-551-00923-3 (pbk) : £5.95 : CIP entry B82-07971

270.6 — England & Germany. Christian church. Reformation, *1536-1604*
Dickens, A. G.. Reformation studies. — London (35 Gloucester Ave., NW1 7AX) : Hambledon Press, June 1982. — [618]p. — (History series ; v.9)
ISBN 0-907628-04-4 : £24.00 : CIP entry B82-11117

270.6'092'4 — Christian church. Luther, Martin — *Biographies*
Todd, John M.. Luther. — London : H. Hamilton, Feb.1982. — [288]p
ISBN 0-241-10703-2 : £15.00 : CIP entry B81-35793

270.6'092'4 — Christian church. Tyndale, William — *Biographies*
Edwards, Brian H.. God's outlaw / Brian H. Edwards. — 2nd ed. — Welwyn : Evangelical, 1982. — 174p : ill,facsims,ports ; 22cm
Previous ed.: 1976. — Bibliography: p171-174
ISBN 0-85234-161-x (pbk) : Unpriced B82-19319

270.8'2 — Christian church. Ecumenical movement. Activities — *For Christian religious education*
United in Christ : an approach to ecumenical education in secondary schools / general editor Josephine Clemson ; contributors and advisers P. Ryan ... [et al.]. — Slough : St. Paul, 1981. — 122p ; 22cm
Includes index
ISBN 0-85439-196-7 (pbk) : £2.95 B82-05676

270.8'26 — Christian church. Ecumenical movement, *1963-1981 — Catholic viewpoints*
Yarnold, Edward. They are in earnest : Christian unity in the statements of Paul VI, John Paul I, John Paul II / Edward Yarnold ; foreword by the Archbishop of Canterbury. — Slough : St. Paul, 1982. — x,257p ; 23cm
Includes index
ISBN 0-85439-212-2 : £10.00 B82-26801

270.8'28 — Christian church. Charismatic movement
Grossmann, Siegfried. Stewards of God's grace / Siegfried Grossmann ; translated by Michael Freeman. — Exeter : Paternoster Press, c1981. — 192p ; 22cm
Translation of: Haushalter der Gnade Gottes. — Bibliography: p184-192
ISBN 0-85364-287-7 (pbk) : £4.20 B82-04341

271 — CHRISTIAN CHURCH HISTORY. RELIGIOUS CONGREGATIONS AND ORDERS

271'.009415 — Ireland. Christianity. Monasticism. Reform, *750-900*
O'Dwyer, Peter. Céli dé : spiritual reform in Ireland 750-900 / Peter O'Dwyer. — 2nd ed. rev. — Dublin : Editions Tailliura, 1981. — xv,213p : ill,facsims ; 23cm
Appendix of Latin hymns and prayers. — Previous ed.: Dublin : Carmelite Publications, 1977. — Ill, facsims on lining papers. — Includes index
ISBN 0-906553-01-6 : £13.00 B82-14175

271'.00942 — England. Religious orders, *547-1982*
Desmond, Helena. Religious life in England & Wales : historical background / Helena Desmond. — Abbots Langley (74 Gallows Hill La., Abbots Langley, Herts. WD5 0BZ) : Catholic Information Services, [1982]. — 12p ; 21cm. — (A Signum publication)
Unpriced (unbound) B82-37926

271'.009428'1 — Yorkshire. Monasteries, *to 1980*
Spence, Joan. The medieval monasteries of Yorkshire / by Joan and Bill Spence ; foreword by Basil Hume ; drawings by Judith Gilbert ; calligraphy by Duncan Spence. — Helmsley : Ambo, c1981. — 116p : ill,plans ; 22cm
ISBN 0-906641-01-2 (cased) : Unpriced
ISBN 0-906641-00-4 (pbk) : Unpriced B82-06892

271'.00944 — France. Monasteries, *1100-1200 — French texts*
Dubois, Jacques. Histoire monastique en France au XIIe siècle. — London : Variorum, Sept.1982. — [342]p. — (Collected studies series ; CS161)
ISBN 0-86078-109-7 : £26.00 : CIP entry B82-21403

271'.1'024 — Benedictines. Benedict, *Saint — Biographies — Early works*
Gregory I, *Pope*. Saint Benedict : a translation of Gregory the Great's Life of Benedict / by Justin McCann ; introduced by Pearse Cusack ; edited by Thomas Curran. — Dublin : Carmelite Centre of Spirituality, c1980. — 59p : 2ill ; 20cm. — (Living flame series ; v.10)
Translation of: Dialogues bk.2
ISBN 0-86088-021-4 (pbk) : Unpriced B82-04406

271'.1'042644 — Suffolk. Bury St Edmunds. Abbeys: Bury St Edmunds Abbey. Community life, *1173-1202 — For schools*
Scarfe, Norman. A monk named Jocelin : life in an abbey in medieval England / Norman Scarfe. — Edinburgh : Chambers, c1976. — 48p : ill,maps,facsims,plans ; 25cm. — (The Way it was. Norman invasions)
Text on inside covers. — Bibliography: p48. — Includes index
ISBN 0-550-75521-7 (pbk) : Unpriced B82-25840

271'.1'04453 — France. Vendôme. Abbeys: Abbaye de la Trinité *(Vendôme), 1032-1187*
Johnson, Penelope D.. Prayer, patronage, and power : the Abbey of La Trinité, Vendôme 1032-1187 / by Penelope D. Johnson. — New York : New York University Press, 1981. — xii,213p : ill,geneal.tables,maps ; 24cm
Bibliography: p194-207. — Includes index
ISBN 0-8147-4162-2 : £13.00 B82-38744

271'.12'024 — Cistercians. Aelred, *Saint — Critical studies*
Squire, Aelred. Aelred of Rievaulx : a study / Aelred Squire. — London : S.P.C.K., 1969 (1981 [printing]). — xiii,177p : 1facsim ; 23cm
Bibliography: p153. — Includes index
ISBN 0-281-03851-1 : £7.50 B82-16074

271'.125'024 — Trappists. Merton, Thomas — *Biographies*
Furlong, Monica. Merton : a biography / Monica Furlong. — London : Fount, 1982, c1980. — xx,342p,8p of plates : ill,ports ; 20cm
Originally published: London : Collins, 1980. — Includes index
ISBN 0-00-626478-6 (pbk) : £2.50 B82-31646

271'.2'024 — Religious orders: Dominicans. Dominic, *Saint*
Tugwell, Simon. Saint Dominic and the Order of Preachers / Simon Tugwell. — London : Incorporated Catholic Truth Society, 1981. — 16p ; 19cm
Cover title
ISBN 0-85183-436-1 (pbk) : £0.35
ISBN 0-907271-08-1 (Dominican Publications) B82-08746

271'.3'024 — Franciscans. Francis, *of Assisi, Saint*
Carretto, Carlo. I, Francis : the spirit of St Francis of Assisi / Carlo Carretto. — London : Collins, 1982. — 164p ; 21cm
Translation of: Io, Francesco
ISBN 0-00-215352-1 (pbk) : £3.95 : CIP rev. B82-19060

271'.3'024 — Franciscans. Francis, *of Assisi, Saint — Biographies*
Allen, Elizabeth, *1928-*. The patron saint of animals / by Elizabeth Allen. — 2nd ed. — Glasgow : Brown, Son & Ferguson, 1981. — 78p : 1ill ; 19cm
Previous ed.: 1962
ISBN 0-85174-396-x (pbk) : £4.00 B82-12291

Halley, Shelagh. Francis of Assisi / Shelagh Halley. — London : Catholic Truth Society, 1982. — 13p ; 19cm
ISBN 0-85183-468-x (pbk) : £0.30 B82-24992

Schnieper, Xavier. Saint Francis of Assisi / text by Xavier Schnieper ; photographs by Dennis Stock. — London : Muller, 1981. — 127p : ill (some col.) ; 22x27cm
ISBN 0-584-97080-3 : £6.95 B82-00808

271'.3'024 — Franciscans. Francis, *of Assisi, Saint — Critical studies*
Murphy, Elizabeth. Saint Francis and his message / Elizabeth Murphy ; edited by Thomas M. Curran. — Dublin : Carmelite Centre of Spirituality, c1979. — 47p ; 20cm. — (Living flame series ; v.7)
Bibliography: p45
ISBN 0-86088-018-4 (pbk) : Unpriced B82-04407

271'.3'024 — Franciscans. Francis, *of Assisi, Saint — Stories for children*
Rose, Elizabeth. How St Francis tamed the wolf. — London : Bodley Head, Oct.1982. — [32]p
Originally published: London : Faber, 1958
ISBN 0-370-30506-x : £4.50 : CIP entry B82-24452

271'.3'042 — England. Franciscans, *to 1982*
Moorman, John R. H.. The Franciscans in England / by John R.H. Moorman. — London : Mowbray, 1974 (1982 [printing]). — vi,122p ; 20cm. — (Mowbray's Christian studies)
ISBN 0-264-66849-9 (pbk) : £2.25 B82-23637

271'.36'024 — Capuchins. Joseph, *Père — Biographies*
Huxley, Aldous. Grey eminence : a study in religion and politics / Aldous Huxley. — [St Albans] : Triad Granada, 1982. — 303p ; 18cm
Originally published: London : Chatto & Windus, 1941. — Includes index
ISBN 0-586-05477-4 (pbk) : £1.95 B82-40714

271'.4'024 — Augustinians. Solminihac, Alain de — *Biographies*
Egger, Carlo. Blessed Alain de Solminihac : Canon Regular of St. Augustine and Bishop of Cahors / by Carlo Egger. — London : Catholic Truth Society, 1981. — [12]p ; 17cm
ISBN 0-85183-439-6 (pbk) : £0.45 B82-08736

271'.53'024 — Jesuits. Bellarmino, Roberto, *Saint — Biographies*
Gallagher, John, *1911-*. Saint Robert Bellarmine / by John Gallagher. — London : Catholic Truth Society, 1980. — 15p ; 19cm
ISBN 0-85183-378-0 (pbk) : £0.25 B82-16108

271'.71'042 — England. Carthusians, *to 1980*
Carthusians : an historical and spiritual study / devised and compiled from Carthusian sources by J.D. Lee ; with foreword by Michael G. Bowen. — London (23 The Slade, SE18 2NB) : Henry VI Society, 1981. — 53p : ill,1plan,1port ; 26cm
Bibliography: On inside cover
£1.50 (pbk) B82-03462

271'.78'024 — Christian Brothers. *Irish Christian Brothers.* Rice, Edmund Ignatius — *Biographies*
Rushe, Desmond. Edmund Rice : the man and his times / Desmond Rushe. — Dublin : Gill and Macmillan, 1981. — xi,156p,[8]p of plates : ill,2maps ; 23cm
Includes Index
ISBN 0-7171-1116-4 (cased) : £9.00
ISBN 0-7171-1161-x (pbk) : Unpriced B82-08590

271'.79 — Brothers of St. Patrick. Howlin, Aloysius — *Biographies*
Walker, Linus H.. Once a soldier — / Linus H. Walker. — Galway : Patrician Brothers, 1977. — 44p ; 19cm
Unpriced (pbk) B82-14574

271'.79 — Brothers of St. Patrick. Tierney, Gerard — *Biographies*
Walker, Linus H.. Fruit that will last / Linus H. Walker. — [Galway] ([Nuris Island, Galway, Republic of Ireland]) : [L.H. Walker?], [1979?]. — 25p ; 19cm
Unpriced (unbound) B82-11244

271′.79 — Knights of Malta, *to 1630*
Luttrell, Anthony. Latin Greece, the Hospitallers and the Crusades, 1291-1440. — London : Variorum, Sept.1982. — [322]p. — (Collected studies series ; CS158)
ISBN 0-86078-106-2 : £26.00 : CIP entry
B82-21400

271′.79 — Templars *(Order of chivalry), to 1314*
Howarth, Stephen. The Knights Templar / Stephen Howarth. — London : Collins, 1982. — 321p,[12]p of plates : ill,1map ; 24cm
Bibliography: p313-316p. — Includes index
ISBN 0-00-216452-3 : £9.95 : CIP rev.
B81-33974

Partner, Peter. The murdered magicians : the Templars and their myth / Peter Partner. — Oxford : Oxford University Press, 1982, c1981. — xxi,209p,[10]p of plates : ill,1 map ; 23cm
Bibliography: p195-203. — Includes index
ISBN 0-19-215847-3 : £12.95 : CIP rev.
B82-04157

271′.91′024 — Sisters of Charity *(Ireland).* **Walker, Mary Charles** — *Biographies*
Cooke, Colman. Mary Charles Walker : the nun of Calabar / Colman Cooke. — Dublin (3 Serpentine Ave., Dublin 4) : Four Courts Press, c1980. — 207p ; 22cm
Unpriced B82-01768

271′.97 — Congregation of the Religious of Jesus and Mary. Thévenet, Claudine — *Biographies*
Chiasson, Laurentine. Unless a wheat grain dies — : Claudine Thévenet, 1774-1837 (Mother Mary St. Ignatius), foundress of the Congregation of the Religious of Jesus and Mary / Laurentine Chiasson ; translated by Evangeline Flynne. — London : Religious of Jesus and Mary, c1981. — 144p : ill,1map,facsims,ports ; 20cm
Translation of: Si le grain ne meurt —. — Bibliography: p143-144
ISBN 0-9507750-0-2 (pbk) : Unpriced
B82-02434

271′.97 — Egypt. Cairo. Catholic Church. Nuns: Emmanuelle, *Sister* — *Biographies*
Emmanuelle, *Sister*. Sister with the ragpickers. — London : SPCK, Nov.1982. — [192]p
Translation of: Chiffonnière avec les chiffonniers
ISBN 0-281-04018-4 (pbk) : £1.75 : CIP entry
B82-27377

271′.97 — Society of Marie Auxiliatrice. Soubiran, Marie Thérèse de — *Biographies*
McCarthy, F. J.. Unless the grain of wheat : a life of Marie Thérèse de Soubiran, foundress of the congregation of Marie Auxiliatrice / F.J. McCarthy. — London : Catholic Truth Society, 1982. — 10p ; 19cm
ISBN 0-85183-479-5 (pbk) : £0.35 B82-35835

271′.971′024 — Carmelites. Teresa, *of Avila, Saint — Biographies*
Clissold, Stephen. St Teresa of Avila / Stephen Clissold. — London : Sheldon, 1979 (1982 [printing]). — xv,272p : 1map ; 22cm
Includes index
ISBN 0-85969-347-3 (pbk) : Unpriced
B82-35101

271′.971′024 — Carmelites. Teresa, *of Avila, Saint — Conference proceedings*
Teresa de Jesús and her world : papers of a conference held at Trinity and All Saints′ College on October 24th and 25th 1981 in preparation for commemoration of the quartercentenary of the death of Saint Teresa of Avila (1515-1582) / edited by Margaret A. Rees. — Leeds : Trinity and All Saints′ College, 1981. — 103p ; 21cm
ISBN 0-9507984-0-1 (pbk) : Unpriced : CIP rev. B82-07135

271′.971′024 — Carmelites. Teresa, *of Avila, Saint — Critical studies*
McCaffrey, Eugene. Introduction to the writings of St Teresa of Avila / Eugene McCaffrey ; edited by Thomas Curran. — Dublin : Carmelite Centre of Spirituality, c1981. — 58p ; 20cm. — (Living flame series ; v.15)
ISBN 0-86088-026-5 (pbk) : Unpriced
B82-04412

271′.971′024 — Carmelites. Thérèse, *de Lisieux, Saint — Biographies*
Boyce, Philip. Spiritual exodus of John Henry Newman & Thérèse of Lisieux / Philip Boyce ; edited by Thomas Curran. — Dublin : Carmelite Centre of Spirituality, c1979. — 48p ; 20cm. — (Living flame series ; v.6)
ISBN 0-86088-016-8 (pbk) : £0.60
Also classified at 282′.092′4 B82-04414

272 — CHRISTIAN CHURCH HISTORY. PERSECUTIONS

272′.1 — Bible. N.T. Special subjects: Martyrdom
Suffering and martyrdom in the New Testament : studies presented to G.M. Styler by the Cambridge New Testament Seminar / edited by William Horbury and Brian McNeil. — Cambridge : Cambridge University Press, 1981. — xxi,217p ; 23cm
Includes index
ISBN 0-521-23482-4 : £17.50 : CIP rev.
Primary classification 231′.8 B81-19191

272′.8 — Massachusetts. Salem. Witches. Persecution, *1692*
The **Witches** of Salem : a documentary narrative / edited by Roger Thompson ; lino-cuts by Clare Melinsky. — London ([202 Great Suffolk Street, SE1]) : Folio Society, 1982. — 194p : ill ; 23cm
In slip case
£9.25 B82-16305

272′.8 — Scotland. Fife Region. Dunfermline *(District).* **Witches. Persecution,** *1620-1710.* **Historical scources**
The **17th** century witch craze in West Fife : a guide to the printed sources. — [Dunfermline] ([Central Library, Abbot St., Dunfermline, Fife]) : Dunfermline District Libraries, 1980. — 30leaves ; 30cm
Bibliography: p28-30
Unpriced (pbk) B82-08534

272′.8 — Scotland. Witches. Persecution, *1590-1700*
Larner, Christina. Enemies of God : the witch-hunt in Scotland / Christina Larner ; with a foreword by Norman Cohn. — Baltimore : Johns Hopkins University Press ; London : Chatto & Windus, 1981. — x,244p : maps ; 23cm
Bibliography: p229-235. — Includes index
ISBN 0-8018-2699-3 : £12.25 B82-11912

272′.9 — Soviet Union. Baptist churches. Persecution — *Personal observations*
Hartfield, Hermann. Irina / Hermann Hartfield. — London : Hodder & Stoughton, 1982, c1980. — 316p ; 18cm
ISBN 0-340-27898-6 (pbk) : £1.95 : CIP rev.
B82-07443

272′.9′09498 — Romania. Christian church. Persecution
Romanian report. — [Great Britain] : Society for the Study of Religion and Communism, [1982?]. — 48p ; 28cm
Cover title
Unpriced (spiral) B82-37454

273 — CHRISTIAN CHURCH HISTORY. DOCTRINAL CONTROVERSIES AND HERESIES

273 — Christian dualism, *to ca 1300*
Runciman, Steven. The Medieval manichee : a study of the Christian dualist heresy / by Steven Runciman. — Cambridge : Cambridge University Press, 1947 (1982 [printing]). — x,214p ; 23cm
Bibliography: p189-201. — Includes index
ISBN 0-521-06166-0 (cased) : £19.50 : CIP rev.
ISBN 0-521-28926-2 (pbk) : £6.95 B82-12678

273′.1 — Anti-gnostic doctrine
Vallée, Gérard. A study in anti-Gnostic polemics : Irenaeus, Hippolytus, and Epiphanius : Gérard Vallée. — Waterloo, Ont. : Published for the Canadian Corporation for Studies in Religion/Corporation canadienne des sciences religieuses by Wilfrid Laurier University Press ; Gerrards Cross : Smythe [distributor], c1981. — xi,114p ; 23cm. — (Studies in Christianity and Judaism = Études sur le christianisme et le judaïsme, ISSN 0711-5903 ; 1)
Bibliography: p105-114
ISBN 0-919812-14-7 (pbk) : Unpriced
B82-19144

273′.6 — France. Christian church. Heresies, *1200-1300 — French texts*
Dossat, Yves. Eglise et hérésie en France au XIIIe siècle / Yves Dossat. — London : Variorum Reprints, 1982. — 364p in various pagings : 1port ; 24cm. — (Collected studies series ; CS147)
Facsimile reprints. — Includes index
ISBN 0-86078-094-5 : Unpriced : CIP rev.
B82-01566

274 — CHRISTIAN CHURCH. EUROPE

274′.05 — Europe. Christian church, *1250-1550*
Ozment, Steven E.. The age of reform. — London : Yale University Press, Nov.1981. — [472]p
ISBN 0-300-02760-5 (pbk) : £6.25 : CIP entry
B81-34957

274′.08 — Western Europe. Christian church, *1789-1970*
McLeod, Hugh. Religion and the people of Western Europe 1789-1970 / Hugh McLeod. — Oxford : Oxford University Press, 1981. — vii,169p : 2maps ; 20cm. — (OPUS)
Bibliography: p154-158. — Includes index
ISBN 0-19-289101-4 (cased) : £8.95 : CIP rev.
ISBN 0-19-215832-5 (pbk) : £3.95 B81-22609

274.1′0828 — Great Britain. Christian church
Churches in Britain / [editor Harry Undy]. — London : Christian Education Movement, [1979?]. — 1portfolio : ill ; 28cm. — (Topic folder ; no.4)
ISBN 0-905022-23-8 : Unpriced B82-35405

Cuthbert, Nick. Rise up and build / Nick Cuthbert. — Eastbourne : Kingsway, 1982. — 119p ; 18cm
ISBN 0-86065-189-4 (pbk) : £1.35 B82-37087

274.11′06 — Scotland. Christian church. Reformation, *1500-1600*
Cowan, Ian B.. The Scottish Reformation : Church and society in sixteenth century Scotland / Ian E. Cowan. — London : Weidenfeld and Nicolson, c1982. — x,244p : 1map ; 23cm
Bibliography: p224-230. — Includes index
ISBN 0-297-78029-8 : £11.95 B82-37909

274.13′406 — Edinburgh. Christian church. Reformation, *1540-1590*
Lynch, Michael, *1946-*. Edinburgh and the Reformation / Michael Lynch. — Edinburgh : Donald, c1981. — xv,416p : maps ; 25cm
Bibliography: p398-407. — Includes index
ISBN 0-85976-069-3 : £18.00 B82-06002

274.15′0092′2 — Ireland. Saints, *to 1980*
Montague, H. Patrick. The saints and martyrs of Ireland / H. Patrick Montague. — Gerrards Cross : Smythe, 1981. — 138p ; 23cm
Bibliography: p137-138
ISBN 0-86140-106-9 (cased) : £5.95 : CIP rev.
ISBN 0-86140-107-7 (pbk) : £2.25 B81-21592

274.2 — England. Christian church, *871-1204 — Readings from contemporary sources*
Councils & synods with other documents relating to the English church. — Oxford : Clarendon Press
1: 871-1204. — Oct.1981. — [1230]p
ISBN 0-19-822394-3 : £48.00 : CIP entry
B81-25745

274.205 — Catholic Church. *Diocese of York.* **Lollards & Protestants**

Dickens, A. G.. Lollards and Protestants in the Diocese of York. — 2nd ed. — London (35 Gloucester Ave., NW1 7AX) : Hambledon Press, July 1982. — [280]p. — (History series ; no.10)
Previous ed.: London : University of Hull, 1959
ISBN 0-907628-05-2 (cased) : £15.00 : CIP entry
ISBN 0-907628-06-5 (pbk) : £5.95 B82-13275

274.22′5 — East & West Sussex. Christian church, *to 1962*

Studies in Sussex church history / edited by M.J. Kitch. — London : Leopard's Head Press in association with the Centre for Continuing Education, University of Sussex, 1981. — xv,264p,6p of plates,[1]folded leaf of plates : ill,maps,ports ; 26cm
Includes bibliographies and index
ISBN 0-904920-03-8 : £14.50 B82-02018

274.22′5′00922 — East Sussex. Saints, *600-1000*

Saxon saints. — Hove (9 Brunswick Sq., Hove, E. Sussex BN3 1EN) : Chichester Diocesan Fund and Board of Finance, 1981. — 4p : 1ill ; 21cm
Unpriced (unbound) B82-05932

274.28′13 — West Yorkshire *(Metropolitan County).* **Dewsbury. Christian church,** *to 1350*

Scargill, Christopher M.. The origins of the church in Dewsbury and its role in the conversion of Northumbria / by Christopher M. Scargill. — [Dewsbury] ([19 Staincliffe Rd., Dewsbury, W. Yorkshire WF13 4ET]) : [C.M. Scargill], [1982]. — 8p : ill ; 30cm
Unpriced (unbound) B82-35815

274.3′06 — Germany. Christian church. Reformation. Role of popular printed propaganda, *1520-1570*

Scribner, R. W.. For the sake of simple folk : popular propaganda for the German Reformation / R.W. Scribner. — Cambridge : Cambridge University Press, 1981. — xi,299p : ill,facsims ; 24cm. — (Cambridge studies in oral and literate culture ; 2)
Bibliography: p281-293. — Includes index
ISBN 0-521-24192-8 : £25.00 : CIP rev. B81-31259

275 — CHRISTIAN CHURCH. ASIA

275.1′082′0922 — China. Christian church. Nee, Watchman; Wang, Mingdao & Yang, David — *Biographies*

Lyall, Leslie T.. Three of China's mighty men / by Leslie Lyall. — [Sevenoaks] : Hodder and Stoughton, 1980, c1973. — 144p ; 18cm. — (Hodder Christian paperbacks)
Originally published: London : Overseas Missionary Fellowship Books, 1973. — Bibliography: p144
ISBN 0-340-25561-7 (pbk) : £1.40 : CIP rev. B80-10943

275.1′082′0924 — China. Christian church. Wang, Mingdao — *Biographies*

Wang, Mingdao. A stone made smooth / Wong Ming-dao. — Southampton : Mayflower Christian Books, c1981. — 245p : ill,1map,ports ; 21cm
Translated from the Chinese
ISBN 0-907821-00-6 (pbk) : Unpriced B82-40088

277 — CHRISTIAN CHURCH. NORTH AMERICA

277.28′0828 — Central America. Christian church

Jerez, Cesar. The church in Central America : faith, hope and love in a suffering church / Cesar Jerez. — London : Catholic Institute for International Relations, c1980. — 30p : 1map ; 21cm
Cover title
ISBN 0-904393-61-5 (pbk) : £0.40 B82-15064

280 — CHRISTIAN CHURCH. DENOMINATIONS AND SECTS

280′.092′4 — Christian church. Hurding, Roger — *Biographies*

Hurding, Roger. As trees walking. — Exeter : Paternoster, Nov.1982. — [224]p
ISBN 0-85364-354-7 (pbk) : £4.00 : CIP entry B82-26320

280′.4 — East & West Sussex. Nonconformist churches, *to 1900*

Caplan, Neil, *19---*. Sussex dissent / by Neil Caplan. — Hove (9 Brunswick Sq., Hove, E. Sussex BN3 1EN) : Chichester Diocesan Fund and Board of Finance, 1981. — 8p : 1ill ; 22cm
£0.10 (unbound) B82-05246

280′.4 — Gloucestershire. Dursley. Nonconformists, *ca 1661-ca 1981*

Evans, David E.. As mad as a hatter. — Gloucester : Alan Sutton, Nov.1982. — [240]p
ISBN 0-904387-90-9 : £7.50 : CIP entry B82-28762

280′.4 — Romania. Nonconformist churches

Michael-Titus, C.. Romania under pressure : report III / C. Michael-Titus. — London : Panopticum, 1982. — 47p : ill,facsims ; 21cm
Includes facsimiles of Romanian letters etc.
ISBN 0-907256-05-8 (pbk) : Unpriced B82-14625

280′.4 — Wales. Nonconformist churches, *1800-1920*

Davies, E. T. (Ebenezer Thomas). Religion and society in the nineteenth century / E.T. Davies. — Llandybïe : Christopher Davies, 1981. — 100p,[8]p of plates : ill,ports ; 21cm. — (A New history of Wales)
Bibliography: p98-100. — Includes index
ISBN 0-7154-0602-7 (pbk) : £3.95 B82-14542

280′.4′0942 — England. Protestantism, *1559-1625*

Collinson, Patrick. The religion of Protestants : the church in English society 1559-1625. — Oxford : Clarendon Press, June 1982. — [270]p
ISBN 0-19-822685-3 : £17.50 : CIP entry B82-10449

281 — CHRISTIAN CHURCH. PRIMITIVE AND ORIENTAL CHURCHES

281.9′092′4 — Russkaia pravoslavnaia tserkov. Skobtsova, Maria — *Biographies*

Hackel, Sergei. Pearl of great price : the life of Mother Maria Skobtsova 1891-1945 / Sergei Hackel ; foreword by Metropolitan Anthony of Sourozh. — Rev ed. — London : Darton, Longman and Todd, 1982. — xv,160p : ill,ports ; 22cm
Previous ed.: published as One, of great price. 1965. — Bibliography: p150-153. — Includes index
ISBN 0-232-51540-9 (pbk) : £4.95 : CIP rev. B81-30268

281.9′5483 — India *(Republic).* **Malabar. St. Thomas Christians,** *to 1980*

Brown, Leslie. The Indian Christians of St. Thomas : an account of the ancient Syrian church of Malabar / by Leslie Brown. — Reissued with additional chapter. — Cambridge : University Press, 1982. — xii,327p,[7]p of plates : ill,1map,1port ; 23cm
Originally published: 1956. — Bibliography: p318-324. — Includes index
ISBN 0-521-21258-8 : £18.00 : CIP rev. B82-12683

282 — CATHOLIC CHURCH

282 — Catholic Church

Catholic Church. *Pope (1978- : John Paul II).* Encyclical redemptor hominis addressed by the supreme pontiff John Paul II to his venerable brothers in the episcopate, the priests, the religious families, the sons and daughters of the Church and to all men and women of goodwill at the beginning of his papal ministry. — London : Catholic Truth Society, [198-]. — 103p ; 19cm
£0.70 (pbk) B82-22526

Coomaraswamy, Rama P.. The destruction of the Christian tradition. — London : Perennial Books ; Wellingborough : Thorsons [distributor], May 1981. — [228]p
ISBN 0-900588-20-9 (pbk) : £6.95 : CIP entry B81-12310

Nichols, Peter, *1928-*. The Pope's divisions : the Roman Catholic church today / Peter Nichols. — Harmondsworth : Penguin, 1982, c1981. — 382p ; 20cm
Originally published: Faber, 1981. — Includes index
ISBN 0-14-006368-4 (pbk) : £2.95 B82-27840

Pironio, Eduardo F.. We wish to see Jesus / Eduardo F. Pironio. — Slough : St. Paul Publications, c1982. — x,214p ; 22cm
Translation of: Queremos ver a Jesús
ISBN 0-85439-198-3 (pbk) : £4.50 B82-20718

282 — Catholic Church. Relations with Anglican churches

Anglican-Roman Catholic International Commission. The final report : Windsor, September 1981. — London : CTS/SPCK, 1982. — iii,122p ; 19cm
At head of title: Anglican-Roman Catholic International Commission
ISBN 0-85183-451-5 (pbk) : £1.95
ISBN 0-281-03859-7 (SPCK)
Also classified at 283 B82-25026

282 — Catholic Church. Relations with Church of England, *1530-1981*

Pawley, Bernard. Rome and Canterbury through four centuries : a study of the relations between the Church of Rome and the Anglican Churches 1530-1981 / by Bernard and Margaret Pawley. — Updated and rev. ed. — London : Mowbray, 1981. — xi,387p ; 22cm
Previous ed.: 1974. — Bibliography: p355-370. — Includes index
ISBN 0-264-66415-9 (pbk) : £4.95 : CIP rev.
Also classified at 283′.42 B81-30186

282 — Catholic Church — *Stories, anecdotes*

Gallagher, John, *1911-*. Scenes from a priestly life / John Gallagher ; with illustrations by John Ryan. — London : Catholic Truth Society, 1982. — 32p : ill ; 18cm
ISBN 0-85183-452-3 (pbk) : £0.45 B82-15334

282′.09 — Catholic Church, *to 1980* — *For African students*

McGrath, Michael. Africa : our way as God's people / M. McGrath, Nicole Gregoire. — London : Mission Book Service, c1981. — viii,227p ; 22cm
Bibliography: p225
ISBN 0-9507888-0-5 (pbk) : £2.00 B82-13713

282′.092′4 — Catholic Church. Challoner, Richard — *Biographies*

Challoner and his Church : a Catholic bishop in Georgian England / edited by Eamon Duffy ; foreword by Cardinal Hume. — London : Darton, Longman & Todd, 1981. — x,203p : ill,1facsim,1port ; 23cm
Includes index
ISBN 0-232-51527-1 : £9.95 : CIP rev. B81-26791

Holmes, Eleanor. Bishop Richard Challoner 1691-1781 / by Eleanor Holmes. — Hove (Diocesan Church House, 9 Brunswick Sq., Hove, E. Sussex BN3 1EN) : [Diocese of Chichester], [1981]. — 7p : 1port ; 21cm
Unpriced (unbound) B82-04367

282′.092′4 — Catholic Church. Costa, Alexandrina da — *Biographies*

Johnston, Francis. Alexandrina : the agony and the glory / Francis Johnston ; translation assistance by Anne Croshaw. — Dublin : Veritas, 1979. — viii,87p ; 19cm
Includes passages translated from the Italian
ISBN 0-905092-68-6 (pbk) : Unpriced B82-17755

282'.092'4 — Catholic Church. Howard, Philip, *Saint — Biographies*

Philip Howard : (carefree courtier to saint). — Hove (Diocesan Church House, 9 Brunswick Sq., Hove, E. Sussex BN3 1EN) : [Diocese of Chichester], [1981]. — 8p : ill,1coat of arms ; 21cm
Unpriced (unbound) B82-04373

282'.092'4 — Catholic Church. John Paul II, *Pope, 1979-1981*

St John-Stevas, Norman. Pope John Paul II : his travels and mission / Norman St John-Stevas. — London : Faber, 1982. — 159p : col.ill,col.ports ; 25cm
Includes index
ISBN 0-571-11908-5 (pbk) : £4.95 : CIP rev. B82-06233

282'.092'4 — Catholic Church. John Paul II, *Pope — Biographies*

Bergin, Jane. Pope John Paul II : a welcome visitor : an appreciation in words and pictures in celebration of his visit to Britain May 28-June 2 1982 / [text Jane Bergin] ; [design Peter Butler] ; [editor Psyche Pirie] ; [production editor Primrose Minney]. — London : IPC Magazines, [1982?]. — 126p : ill (some col.),1col.coat of arms,ports(some col.) ; 28cm
ISBN 0-85037-539-8 (pbk) : £1.95 B82-24879

Dean, Stephen. Pope John Paul II / Stephen Dean. — London : Catholic Truth Society, 1982. — 40p ; 19cm
Text on inside covers
ISBN 0-85183-483-3 (pbk) : £0.65 B82-28319

Felici. Pope John Paul II : his life and work : a pictorial record / [photographers Felici, Mari] ; [author George Bull]. — Bristol : Published in association with the official Vatican publishers by Purnell, 1982. — 31p : chiefly ill(some col.),ports(some col.) ; 30cm
Cover title. — Text on inside covers
ISBN 0-361-05432-7 (pbk) : £1.95 B82-23620

Hebblethwaite, Peter. Introducing John Paul II : the populist Pope / Peter Hebblethwaite. — London : Collins : Fount, 1982. — 192p ; 18cm
Includes index
ISBN 0-00-626346-1 (pbk) : £1.50 B82-22555

Johnson, Paul. Pope John Paul II and the Catholic restoration / Paul Johnson. — London : Weidenfeld and Nicolson, c1982. — vii,216p ; 23cm
Includes index
ISBN 0-297-78059-x : £8.95 B82-16431

Johnson, Paul. Pope John Paul II and the Catholic restoration / Paul Johnson. — Large print ed. — Bath : Chivers, 1982. — 341p ; 23cm. — (A Lythway book)
Originally published: London : Weidenfeld & Nicolson, 1982
ISBN 0-85119-877-5 : Unpriced : CIP rev. B82-12844

Lake, Frank. With respect : a doctor's response to a healing Pope / Frank Lake. — London : Darton, Longman and Todd, 1982. — xxiii,327p ; 22cm
Bibliography: p310-312. — Includes index
ISBN 0-232-51565-4 (pbk) : £6.95 : CIP rev. B82-06027

Longford, Frank Pakenham, *Earl of*. Pope John Paul II : an authorized biography / Lord Longford. — London : Joseph, 1982. — 224p : ill(some col.),ports(some col.) ; 26cm
Includes index
ISBN 0-7181-2127-9 : £8.95 B82-21142

Lyte, Charles. His Holiness Pope John Paul II : a man for all people / [written by Charles Lyte]. — London : Mirror Books, 1982. — 30p : ill (some col.),ports(some col.) ; 36cm + 1col.port (18cm)
ISBN 0-85939-311-9 (unbound) : £0.60 B82-33671

282'.092'4 — Catholic Church. John Paul II, *Pope — Biographies — For children*

Collins, Joan, *1917-*. His Holiness Pope John Paul II / written by Joan Collins. — Loughborough : Ladybird, c1982. — 51p : col.ill,1col.map,1col.coat of arms,col.ports ; 18cm
Ports on lining papers
ISBN 0-7214-0733-1 : £0.50 B82-25884

Craig, Mary, *1928-*. Pope John Paul II / Mary Craig ; illustrated by Karen Heywood. — Harmondsworth : Puffin, 1982. — 80p : ill,ports ; 18cm
Includes index
ISBN 0-14-031543-8 (pbk) : £0.90 B82-28678

Craig, Mary, *1928-*. Pope John Paul II / Mary Craig ; illustrated by Karen Heywood. — London : Hamilton, 1982. — 64p : ill,ports ; 22cm. — (Profiles (Hamilton))
ISBN 0-241-10711-3 : £3.25 B82-20814

Lewis, Brenda Ralph. Pope John Paul II : his story for children / Brenda Ralph Lewis. — Bristol : Purnell, 1982. — [46]p : ill(some col.),ports(some col.) ; 27cm
ISBN 0-361-05436-x : £2.95 B82-31192

282'.092'4 — Catholic church. John Paul II, *Pope — Biographies — Polish texts*

Nowakowski, Tadeusz. W bagażniku jego świątobliwości / Tadeusz Nowakowski. — Londyn ([9 Charleville Road, W.14]) : Polska Fundacja Kulturalna, 1981. — 132p,[16]p of plates : ill,ports ; 22cm
Test in Polish
Unpriced (pbk) B82-14668

282'.092'4 — Catholic church. John Paul II, *Pope — Illustrations*

Rastelli, Vittoriano. John Paul II : Welcome to Britain. — London : Hodder & Stoughton, Mar.1982. — [64]p. — (Coronet books)
ISBN 0-340-28355-6 (pbk) : £2.50 : CIP entry B82-02650

282'.092'4 — Catholic Church. John Paul II, *Pope — Illustrations — For children*

Wynn, Wilton. Pope John Paul II gift book. — London : Hodder & Stoughton Children's Books, Oct.1982. — [64]p
ISBN 0-340-28194-4 : £9.95 : CIP entry B82-27350

282'.092'4 — Catholic Church. Maycock, Hugh — *Biographies*

Allchin, A. M.. Francis Hugh Maycock : a tribute / A.M. Allchin and others. — Oxford : SLG Press, c1981. — 21p : ports ; 21cm
ISBN 0-7283-0091-5 (pbk) : £0.40 B82-03849

282'.092'4 — Catholic Church. Merry del Val, Rafael — *Biographies*

Buehrle, Marie C.. Rafael, Cardinal Merry del Val / Marie C. Buehrle. — Houston : Lumen Christi ; Dublin : Four Courts, c1981. — 308p ; 22cm
Unpriced (corrected) B82-02407

282'.092'4 — Catholic Church. Molyneux, Terence *— Correspondence, diaries, etc.*

Molyneux, Terence. Dear friends, shalom! : the collected letters of Terence Molyneux / edited by T.A. Collins. — Middleton : Hopwood, 1982. — 71p : 1port ; 20cm
ISBN 0-9507669-1-7 (cased) : Unpriced
ISBN 0-9507669-0-9 (pbk) : Unpriced B82-14763

282'.092'4 — Colombia. Catholic Church. Torres, Camilo — *Biographies*

Watson, John, *19---*. Camilo Torres / John Watson. — Bognor Regis : New Horizon, c1981. — 69p ; 21cm
ISBN 0-86116-570-5 : £3.25 B82-04436

282'.092'4 — El Salvador. Catholic Church. Romero, Oscar Arnulfo — *Biographies*

Erdozáin, Plácido. Archbishop Romero : martyr of Salvador / Plácido Erdozaín ; translated by John McFadden and Ruth Warner ; foreword by Jorge Lara-Brand. — Guildford : Lutterworth, 1981, c1980. — xxiii,98p,[5]p of plates : ill,ports ; 22cm
Translation of: Monseñor Romero: mártir de la Iglesia Popular
ISBN 0-7188-2528-4 (pbk) : £2.95 B82-03186

282'.092'4 — England. Catholic Church. Clitherow, Margaret, *Saint — Biographies*

Halley, Shelagh. St. Margaret Clitherow / by Shelagh Halley. — [London] : Catholic Truth Society, [1981?]. — [16]p ; 18cm
Cover title
ISBN 0-85183-434-5 (pbk) : £0.35 B82-07565

282'.092'4 — England. Catholic Church. Newman, John Henry — *Biographies*

Boyce, Philip. Spiritual exodus of John Henry Newman & Thérèse of Lisieux / Philip Boyce ; edited by Thomas Curran. — Dublin : Carmelite Centre of Spirituality, c1979. — 48p ; 20cm. — (Living flame series ; v.6)
ISBN 0-86088-016-8 (pbk) : £0.60
Primary classification 271'.971'024 B82-04414

Martin, Brian. John Henry Newman : his life and work / Brian Martin. — London : Chatto & Windus, 1982. — 160p : ill,facsims,ports ; 25cm
Includes index
ISBN 0-7011-2588-8 : £8.95 : CIP rev. B82-07671

282'.092'4 — England. Catholic Church. Newman, John Henry — *Correspondence, diaries, etc.*

Newman, John Henry. A packet of letters : a selection from the correspondence of John Henry Newman. — Oxford : Clarendon, Feb.1983. — [194]p
ISBN 0-19-826442-9 : £6.50 : CIP entry B82-36596

282'.092'4 — England. Catholic Church. Southwell, Robert, *Saint — Biographies*

Nassan, Maurice. Saint Robert Southwell : poet and martyr / Maurice Nassan. — London : Catholic Truth Society, [1982]. — 8p ; 19cm
ISBN 0-85183-476-0 (pbk) : £0.40 B82-35834

282'.092'4 — Great Britain. Visits by John Paul II, *Pope, 1982*

Jennings, Peter. The Pope in Britain. — London : Bodley Head, July 1982. — [128]p
ISBN 0-370-30925-1 : £7.95 : CIP entry B82-17923

282'.092'4 — Great Britain. Visits by John Paul II, *Pope — Illustrations*

The **Man** from Rome / photographers John Shelley ... [et al.]. — [Great Britain] : Quiller with Argus Sales & Distribution, c1982. — [48]p : chiefly col.ill,col.ports ; 30cm
ISBN 0-907621-14-7 (pbk) : £2.25 B82-35421

282'.092'4 — Poland. Catholic Church. Kolbe, Maksymilian — *Biographies*

Dewar, Diana. Saint of Auschwitz. — London : Darton Longman & Todd, Oct.1982. — [160]p
ISBN 0-232-51574-3 (pbk) : £4.95 : CIP entry B82-27025

282'.41 — Great Britain. Catholic Church. Archives. Organisations: Catholic Archives Society — *Serials*

[CAS newsletter *(Catholic Archives Society)***]**.
CAS newsletter : bulletin of the Catholic Archives Society. — [Vol.1?], no.1 (Spring 1980)-. — [Oxford] ([c/o M.A. Kuhn-Régnier, 4A Polstead Rd., Oxford]) : [The Society], 1980-. — v. ; 30cm
Description based on: Vol.1, no.3 (Summer 1981)
ISSN 0262-6896 = CAS newsletter (Catholic Archives Society) : Unpriced B82-10124

282'.411 — Scotland. Catholic Church, *to 1982*

Cooney, John. Scotland and the Papacy / John Cooney. — Edinburgh : Harris, 1982. — 126p ; 23cm
Bibliography: p119-126
ISBN 0-86228-052-4 (cased) : £8.95
ISBN 0-86228-053-2 (pbk) : £4.95 B82-28835

282'.415 — Ireland. Catholic Church, *1600-1800.* **Sociopolitical aspects**
Corish, Patrick J.. The Catholic community in the seventeenth and eighteenth centuries / Patrick J. Corish. — Dublin (Ballymount Rd., Walkinstown, Dublin 12) : Helicon, 1981. — vii,156p ; 21cm. — (Helicon history of Ireland)
Includes index
Unpriced (pbk) B82-08203

282'.42 — England. Catholic Church
Flood, Edmund. Tomorrow's Church? : a plain man's guide to A time for building / Edmund Flood. — [Southend-on-Sea] : [Mayhew-McCrimmon], [1981?]. — 24p : ill ; 21cm
Cover title
ISBN 0-85597-196-7 (pbk) : Unpriced B82-13770

282'.42 — England. Catholic Church, *1563-1688*
Lingard, John[History of England. *Selections*]. The English Catholics : extracts from The history of England / John Lingard ; edited with an introduction by J.A. Hilton. — Wigan ([23 Swinley La., Wigan, Lancs.]) : North West Catholic History Society, 1981. — i,19p ; 19cm
Bibliography: p19
Unpriced (pbk) B82-05658

282'.42 — England. Catholic Church. Attitudes of society, *1860-1870*
Arnstein, Walter L.. Protestant versus Catholic in mid-Victorian England : Mr. Newdegate and the nuns / Walter L. Arnstein. — Columbia ; London : University of Missouri Press, 1982. — viii,271p : ill,ports ; 22cm
Bibliography: p253-262. — Includes index
ISBN 0-8262-0354-x : £15.00 B82-40260

282'.42 — England. Catholic Church. Recusants, *1534-1830*
Brooks, Leslie. Faith never lost / by Leslie Brooks. — Farnborough, [Hants.] : L. Brooks, c1982. — 16p : ill ; 21cm
ISBN 0-9508118-0-7 (pbk) : £1.00 B82-33065

282'.42496 — West Midlands *(Metropolitan County).* **Birmingham. Great Barr. Catholic Church. Holy Name Church** *(Great Barr), to 1981*
Holy Name Church *(Great Barr).* A short history / by Elisabeth Chattell. — Birmingham (The Presbytery, 9 Cross Lane, Great Barr, Birmingham B43 6LN) : Holy Name Church, Great Barr, 1982. — 39p : ill ; 22cm
Cover title: Parish history
£0.50 (pbk) B82-39755

282'.438 — Poland. Catholic Church
Tomsky, Alexander. Catholic Poland / Alexander Tomsky. — Keston (Heathfield Rd., Keston, Kent BR2 6BA) : Keston College in association with Aid to the Church in Need, 1982. — 20p : ill,1port ; 19cm. — (Keston College book ; no.18)
Cover title. — Text on inside cover
£0.60 (pbk) B82-32769

282'.438 — Poland. Catholic Church, *1945-1980.* **Sociopolitical aspects**
Pomian-Srzednicki, Maciej. Religious change in contemporary Poland : secularization and politics / Maciej Pomian-Srzednicki. — London : Routledge & Kegan Paul, 1982. — xii,227p ; 23cm. — (International library of sociology)
Bibliography: p223-226. — Includes index
ISBN 0-7100-9245-8 : £12.50 B82-31000

282'.68 — South Africa. Catholic Church
Catholic Church. *Southern African Catholic Bishops' Conference. Plenary Session (1977).* Southern African Catholic bishops' statements / [Southern African Catholic Bishops' Conference Plenary Session, 1977]. — London : CIIR, [1982?]. — 1folded sheet([6]p) : ill ; 30cm. — (Church in the world ; 1)
ISBN 0-904393-19-4 : £0.10 B82-30627

282'.68 — South Africa. Catholic Church. Political aspects
Walshe, Peter. Church versus state in South Africa. — London : Hurst, Jan.1983. — [234]p
ISBN 0-905838-81-5 : £12.50 : CIP entry B82-39303

282'.83 — Chile. Catholic Church. Political aspects
Smith, Brian H.. The Church and politics in Chile : challenges to modern Catholicism / Brian H. Smith. — Princeton ; Guildford : Princeton University Press, c1982. — xiii,383p ; 25cm
Bibliography: p357-375. — Includes index
ISBN 0-691-07629-4 (cased) : £21.20
ISBN 0-691-10119-1 (pbk) : £6.90 B82-29212

283 — ANGLICAN CHURCHES

283 — Anglican churches. Charismatic movement
Gunstone, John. Pentecostal Anglicans. — London : Hodder & Stoughton, Nov.1982. — [320]p
ISBN 0-340-26936-7 (pbk) : £5.50 : CIP entry B82-27340

283 — Anglican churches — *Conference proceedings*
Anglican Consultative Council. *Meeting (5th : 1981 : Newcastle upon Tyne).* ACC-5 / Anglican Consultative Council Fifth Meeting, Newcastle upon Tyne, England 8-18 September 1981. — London : ACC, 1981. — 84p ; 21cm
Includes index
ISBN 0-9507305-2-1 (pbk) : £1.25 B82-11731

283 — Anglican churches. Relations with Catholic Church
Anglican-Roman Catholic International Commission. The final report : Windsor, September 1981. — London : CTS/SPCK, 1982. — iii,122p ; 19cm
At head of title: Anglican-Roman Catholic International Commission
ISBN 0-85183-451-5 (pbk) : £1.95
ISBN 0-281-03859-7 (SPCK)
Primary classification 282 B82-25026

283'.092'2 — East Sussex. Brighton. Church of England. Role of Wagner *(Family), 1824-1902*
Homan, Roger. The Wagners in Brighton / by Roger Homan. — Hove (Diocesan Church House, 9 Brunswick Sq., Hove, E. Sussex BN3 1EN) : [Diocese of Chichester], [1981]. — 8p : 1ill ; 21cm
Bibliography: p8
Unpriced (unbound) B82-04370

283'.092'2 — London. Richmond upon Thames *(London Borough).* **Barnes. Church of England. St Mary's Church** *(Barnes).* **Rectors,** *1635-1944*
Whale, John, *1931-*. One church, one lord / John Whale. — London : SCM, 1979. — xii,180p : ill,port ; 22cm
Includes index
ISBN 0-334-01184-1 (pbk) : £3.50 B82-01682

283'.092'4 — Avon. Bristol region. Church of England. Parish life, *ca 1844 — Personal observations*
Leech, Joseph. Rural rides of the Bristol churchgoer. — Gloucester : A. Sutton, May 1982. — [320]p
ISBN 0-904387-50-x (cased) : £8.95 : CIP entry
ISBN 0-904387-68-2 (pbk) : £4.95 B82-11983

283'.092'4 — Church of England. Bell, George, *1883-1958 — Biographies*
Mason, Lancelot. George Bell, Bishop of Chichester 1920-1958 / by Lancelot Mason. — Hove (9 Brunswick Sq., Hove, E. Sussex BN3 1EN) : Chichester Diocesan Fund and Board of Finance, [1981?]. — 18p : 1port ; 22cm
Unpriced (unbound) B82-05243

283'.092'4 — Church of England. Bulley, Cyril — *Biographies*
Bulley, Cyril. The glass of time : the autobiography of Cyril Bulley, 63rd Bishop of Carlisle. — Bognor Regis : New Horizon, c1982. — iii,261p,[8]p of plates : ill,ports ; 22cm
Includes index
ISBN 0-86116-545-4 : £6.75 B82-26922

283'.092'4 — Church of England. Coggan, Donald — *Biographies*
Daniels, Robin. Conversations with Coggan. — London : Hodder & Stoughton, Feb.1983. — [160]p
ISBN 0-340-32638-7 : £7.95 : CIP entry B82-38036

283'.092'4 — Church of England. Hanbury, William — *Biographies*
Prophet, John, *1910-*. Church Langton and William Hanbury / John Prophet ; drawings by the author. — Wymondham : Sycamore, 1982. — 151p : ill,1coat of arms,maps,ports ; 32cm
Limited ed. of 250 numbered copies. — Bibliography: p146. — Includes index
ISBN 0-905837-08-8 : £36.00 B82-34381

283'.092'4 — Church of England. Hannington, James — *Biographies*
Butler, Michael J.. James Hannington of Hurstpierpoint and East Africa / by Michael J. Butler. — Hove (9 Brunswick Sq., Hove, E. Sussex BN3 1EN) : Chichester Diocesan Fund and Board of Finance, [1981?]. — 11p : 1ill ; 22cm
Unpriced (unbound) B82-05248

283'.092'4 — Church of England. Neale, John Mason — *Biographies*
Gabriel, *SSM.* John Mason Neale 1818-1866 / [Gabriel SSM]. — Hove (9 Brunswick Sq., Hove, E. Sussex BN3 1EN) : Chichester Diocesan Fund and Board of Finance, [1981]. — 6p : 1port ; 21cm
Unpriced (unbound) B82-05933

283'.092'4 — Church of England. Pusey, E. B. — *Biographies*
Lough, A. G.. Dr. Pusey - restorer of the Church / by A.G. Lough. — Newton Abbot : A.G. Lough, c1981. — 166p : 1port ; 21cm
Bibliography: p166
ISBN 0-9504675-1-0 (pbk) : £4.50 B82-13583

Prestige, G. L.. Pusey / by Leonard Prestige ; with introduction by Cheslyn Jones. — London : Mowbray, 1982. — xv,176p ; 20cm. — (Mowbray religious reprint)
Originally published: London : Philip Allan, 1933. — Includes index
ISBN 0-264-66869-3 (pbk) : £3.50 B82-34795

283'.092'4 — Church of England. Stockwood, Mervyn — *Biographies*
Stockwood, Mervyn. Chanctonbury ring. — London : Hodder & Stoughton, Sept.1982. — [224]p
ISBN 0-340-27568-5 : £9.95 : CIP entry B82-18792

283'.092'4 — Church of England. Woodward, George — *Correspondence, diaries, etc.*
Woodward, George. A parson in the Vale of White Horse. — Gloucester : Alan Sutton, Nov.1982. — [160]p
ISBN 0-86299-025-4 (pbk) : £3.95 : CIP entry B82-29035

283'.092'4 — Church of England. Wright, Philip, *1908- — Biographies*
Wright, Philip, *1908-*. Country padre / by Philip Wright. — Rev. ed. — Baldock : Egon, 1981. — 102p : ill,ports ; 22cm
Previous ed.: 1980
ISBN 0-905858-13-1 : £4.95 B82-38146

283'.092'4 — East Sussex. Brighton. Church of England. Robertson, Friedrick — *Biographies*
Allen, George, *19---*. Frederick Robertson of Brighton / by George Allen. — Hove (Diocesan Church House, 9 Brunswick Sq., Hove, E. Sussex BN3 1EN) : [Diocese of Chichester], [1981]. — 11p : 1ill ; 21cm
Unpriced (unbound) B82-04371

283'.092'4 — Hampshire. Abbotts Ann. Church of England. Best, Samuel — *Biographies*
Geddes, Alastair. Samuel Best & the Hampshire labourer / Alastair Geddes. — Andover : Andover Local History Society, [1981?]. — 64p : 1ill,1port ; 21cm
ISBN 0-903755-11-4 (pbk) : Unpriced B82-09953

283'.092'4 — Kent. Kingston. Church of England. Parish life, *1918-1939 — Personal observations — Correspondence, diaries, etc.*

Potts, Robert. Kingston between the wars : writings of Canon Robert Potts. — [Canterbury] ([3 Whitelocks Close, Kingston, Canterbury, Kent CT4 6JG]) : [Kingston Village Society], 1981. — 20p,[4]p of plates : ill,1port ; 21cm. — (A Kingston Village Society publication)
Cover title
Unpriced (pbk) B82-11884

283'.092'4 — London. Redbridge *(London Borough).* **Wanstead. Church of England. Parish life,** *ca 1952-1967 — Personal observations*

Eastment, Winifred. Down at the vicarage / by Winifred Eastment (S.O. Green) ; illustrated by John Clarke. — Letchworth : Egon, 1979, c1967. — 261p : ill ; 23cm
Originally published: Letchworth : Letchworth Printers, 1967
ISBN 0-905858-08-5 : £4.95 B82-04689

283'.3 — Free Church of England, *to 1978*

Vital facts. — Rev. and repr. — Fleetwood (c/o The Rector, St. Paul's Rectory, Lowther Rd., Fleetwood, Lancs. FY7 7AS) : Free Church of England, 1979. — 26p ; 15cm. — (FCE publications)
Previous ed.: i.e. rev. ed., 1949
£0.10 (unbound) B82-02863

283'.411'05 — Episcopal Church in Scotland — *Serials*

Newscan : the news magazine of the Scottish Episcopal Church. — Issue no.1 (Jan. 1982)-. — Newburgh (c/o Ivybank, High St., Newburgh, Fife) : Executive Committee of the Representative Church Council of the Episcopal Church ; Paisley (18 Gordon St., Paisley PA1 1XB, Renfrewshire) : James Paton Ltd. [distributor], [1981]-. — v. : ill,ports ; 40cm
Monthly. — Continues in part: Outlook (Paisley)
ISSN 0263-2497 = Newscan (corrected) : £2.30 per year B82-22659

283'.41182 — Scotland. Highland Region. Kyle of Lochalsh. Episcopal Church in Scotland. St. Donnan's Episcopal Church *(Lochalsh), to 1981*

Earle, J. B. F.. The making of St. Donnan's Episcopal Church, Lochalsh. — [Kyle] ([Carnmore, Kyle, Ross-shire IV40 8BB]) : [J.B.F. Earle], [1981]. — 8p ; 21cm
Author: J.B.F. Earle. — Bibliography: p8
Unpriced (pbk) B82-27273

283'.42 — Church of England. Charismatic movement

The **Charismatic** movement in the Church of England. — London : CIO, 1981. — 65p ; 21cm
Bibliography: p52
ISBN 0-7151-4751-x (pbk) : £1.95 B82-00834

283'.42 — Church of England. Establishment by England and Wales. *Parliament, 1559*

Jones, Norman L.. Faith by statute : Parliament and the Settlement of Religion 1559. — London : Swift, Oct.1982. — [246]p
ISBN 0-901050-84-9 : £17.50 : CIP entry B82-27203

283'.42 — Church of England. Evangelicalism, *to 1977 — Conference proceedings*

The **Evangelical** succession in the Church of England / edited by D.N. Samuel. — Cambridge : James Clarke, c1979. — 123p ; 18cm
Conference papers
ISBN 0-227-67834-6 (pbk) : £2.75 : CIP rev. B79-16346

283'.42 — Church of England — *For children*

Baker, Kenneth, *1930-.* Your church / [illustrations by Derek Lucas] ; [text by by Kenneth Baker]. — Oxford : Mowbray, 1982. — [16]p : col.ill ; 21cm
Text on inside covers
ISBN 0-264-66834-0 (pbk) : £1.00 B82-41083

283'.42 — Church of England — *For confirmation candidates*

Wilkinson, Raymond. My confirmation search-book / Raymond Wilkinson. — 8th ed rev. / foreword by Gerald A. Ellison. — London : Mowbray [1980]. — 64p : ill ; 22cm
Previous ed.: London : Faith, 1978
64p, 22cm (pbk) B82-38961

283'.42 — Church of England. Relations with Catholic Church, *1530-1981*

Pawley, Bernard. Rome and Canterbury through four centuries : a study of the relations between the Church of Rome and the Anglican Churches 1530-1981 / by Bernard and Margaret Pawley. — Updated and rev. ed. — London : Mowbray, 1981. — xi,387p ; 22cm
Previous ed.: 1974. — Bibliography: p355-370. — Includes index
ISBN 0-264-66415-9 (pbk) : £4.95 : CIP rev.
Primary classification 282 B81-30186

283'.42 — Church of England, *to 1979*

Smith, Michael, *19---.* Learning about the Church of England / by Michael Smith. — London : Mowbray, 1982. — 31p ; 15cm. — (Enquirer's library)
ISBN 0-264-66892-8 (pbk) : £0.60 B82-41125

283'.42 — Church of England. Union with Catholic Church — *Church of England viewpoints*

Authority and community. — London : SPCK, Oct.1982. — [160]p
ISBN 0-281-04025-7 (pbk) : £3.95 : CIP entry B82-23476

283'.42165 — London. Lambeth *(London Borough).* **North Lambeth. Church of England. Parish life** *— For children*

Fairclough, Chris. A day with a vicar / Chris Fairclough. — Hove : Wayland, 1981. — 55p : ill ; 24cm. — (A Day in the life)
Bibliography: p55
ISBN 0-85340-836-x : £3.25 B82-06542

283'.42185 — London. Brent *(London Borough).* **Wembley. Church of England. St John the Evangelist** *(Church : Wembley), to 1940*

Brock, Richard E.. St John the Evangelist Wembley : the church & parish / by Richard E. Brock. — [Wembley] ([25, Forty Ave., Wembley, Middx HA9 8JL]) : Wembley History Society, 1981. — [20]p : ill,1plan,ports ; 16x20cm
Ill on inside cover
Unpriced (pbk) B82-29559

283'.42393 — Avon. Bristol. Bedminster. Church of England. St. Paul's Church *(Bedminster), to 1914*

Cleeve, Ronald E.. St. Paul's Bedminster : the formative years. — Bristol (108, Sylvia Avenue, Bristol BS3 5BZ) : Ronald E. Cleeve, 1981. — 68p ; 30cm
Cover title. — Author: Ronald E. Cleeve
£1.50 (pbk) B82-05368

283'.42463 — Staffordshire. Stoke-on-Trent. Tunstall. Church of England. Christ Church *(Tunstall), to 1982*

Llewellyn, John G.. The story of Christ Church, Tunstall : Stoke-on-Trent, 1832-1982 / by John G. Llewellyn. — 90p : ill,1plan,ports ; 21cm
Unpriced (pbk) B82-35819

283'.42674 — Hertfordshire. Waltham Cross. Church of England. Christ Church *(Waltham Cross), to 1975*

Edwards, Jack. Christ Church Waltham Cross Hertfordshire : a short history / by Jack Edwards. — Rev. ed. — Cheshunt (48 Albury Ride, Cheshunt) : [J. Edwards], 1978. — 8p : 1ill ; 21cm
Cover title. — Previous ed.: s.l. : s.n., 19--?
Unpriced (pbk) B82-09475

283'.4287'0924 — Tyne and Wear *(Metropolitan County).* **Church of England. Parish life —** *Personal observations*

Arnott, Anne. The unexpected call / by Anne Arnott. — London : Hodder and Stoughton, 1981. — 159p : ill ; 18cm
ISBN 0-340-26360-1 (pbk) : £1.75 : CIP rev. B81-24620

283'.46915 — Portugal. Oporto. Church of England. Church of St James *(Oporto), to 1981*

Delaforce, John. Anglicans abroad : the history of the Chaplaincy and Church of St James at Oporto / John Delaforce. — London : SPCK, 1982. — ix,140p : ill,1facsim,3ports ; 22cm
Bibliography: p141
ISBN 0-281-03842-2 (pbk) : £3.00 B82-18385

284 — PROTESTANT DENOMINATIONS OF CONTINENTAL ORIGIN

284.1'092'4 — Lutheran churches. Bonhoeffer, Dietrich — *Biographies*

Major, David. Dietrich Bonhoeffer / by David Major. — London : Christian Education Movement, 1979. — 55p : 1port ; 21cm. — (CEM student theology series)
Bibliography: p55
ISBN 0-905022-46-7 (pbk) : Unpriced B82-36998

284.1'092'4 — Lutheran churches. Bonhoeffer, Dietrich — *Biographies — Welsh texts*

Williams, Harri. Bonhoeffer / Harri Williams. — [Denbigh] ([Chapel St., Denbigh, Clwyd]) : Gwasg Gee, 1981. — 109p ; 19cm. — (Y Meddwl modern)
Bibliography: p109
£1.50 (pbk) B82-12199

284.2'0924 — Reformed churches. Calvin, Jean — *Biographies*

Potter, G. R.. John Calvin. — London : Edward Arnold, Jan.1983. — [192]p. — (Documents of modern history)
ISBN 0-7131-6381-x : £5.50 : CIP entry B82-40910

285.1 — PRESBYTERIAN CHURCHES OF UNITED STATES ORIGIN

285'.1'0924 — United States. Presbyterian churches. Buechner, Frederick — *Biographies*

Buechner, Frederick. The sacred journey. — London : Chatto & Windus, Sept.1982. — [128]p
ISBN 0-7011-2645-0 : £4.95 : CIP entry B82-20303

285.2 — PRESBYTERIAN CHURCHES OF BRITISH COMMONWEALTH ORIGIN

285'.2'0924 — Church of Scotland. Campbell, Duncan, *1898-1972 — Biographies*

Woolsey, Andrew A.. Channel of revival : a biography of Duncan Campbell / by Andrew A. Woolsey. — Edinburgh : Faith Mission, 1974 (1982 [printing]). — 191p,1leaf of plate : 1port ; 18cm
ISBN 0-9508058-0-7 (pbk) : Unpriced B82-27431

285'.2'0924 — Countess of Huntingdon's Connexion. Huntingdon, Selina Hastings, *Countess of — Biographies*

Stanley, Gladys. Selina, Countess of Huntingdon / by Gladys Stanley and Gillian Allen. — Hove (9 Brunswick Sq., Hove, E. Sussex BN3 1EN) : Chichester Diocesan Fund and Board of Finance, [1981?]. — 10p : 1port ; 21cm
£0.10 (unbound) B82-05245

285'.2'0924 — England. Presbyterian churches. Henry, Philip — *Biographies*

Lewis, Peter, *1945-.* Philip Henry : (1631-1696) : from palace to pulpit / by Peter Lewis. — London ([78A Chiltern St., W1N 2HB]) : [Evangelical Library], 1981. — 23p : 1port ; 22cm. — (Annual lecture of the Evangelical Library)
Unpriced (pbk) B82-12110

285'.2'0924 — Free Church of Scotland. Macdonald, John, *1779-1849 — Biographies*

Kennedy, John, *1819-1884.* The apostle of the north : the life and labours of the Rev. John Macdonald, D.D., of Ferintosh / by John Kennedy. — [2nd] ed. / with illustrations and appendices by Rev. Principal Macleod. — Glasgow (133 Woodlands Rd., Glasgow G3 6LE) : Free Presbyterian, 1978. — 292p : 2ports ; 19cm
Previous ed.: London : s.n., 1866
£3.00 (pbk) B82-28989

285′.2′0924 — Northern Ireland. Presbyterian Church in Ireland. Cooke, Henry, *1788-1868 — Biographies*
Holmes, Finlay. Henry Cooke / by Finlay Holmes. — Belfast : Christian Journals, 1981. — vii,214p ; 23cm
Bibliography: p214. — Includes index
ISBN 0-904302-75-x : Unpriced : CIP rev. B81-34223

285′.232′09 — United Reformed Church, *to 1981*
Taylor, John H.. Tell me about the URC : the United Reformed Church at a glance / by John H. Taylor. — Rev. — London : Church Life Department, United Reformed Church, 1981. — [8]p : ill,1map ; 21cm
Cover title. — Previous ed.: 1978. — Text on inside covers
ISBN 0-902256-44-0 (pbk) : £0.35 B82-01469

285′.2411 — Scotland. Covenanters, *to 1688*
Purves, Jock. Fair sunshine : character studies of the Scottish Covenanters / Jock Purves. — Edinburgh : Banner of Truth Trust, 1968 (1982 [printing]). — 206p ; 18cm
Bibliography: p205-206
ISBN 0-85151-136-8 (pbk) : £2.45 B82-37736

285′.241225 — Scotland. Grampian Region. Fraserburgh. Church of Scotland: Fraserburgh South Church, *to 1980*
Fraserburgh South Church. Centenary magazine : 1880-1980 / Fraserburgh South Church. — [Fraserburgh] ([The South Manse, 15 Victoria St, Fraserburgh, Aberdeenshire AB4 5PJ]) : [The Church], [1980?]. — 25p : ill,ports ; 22cm
Cover title
Unpriced (pbk) B82-26602

285′.24127 — Scotland. Tayside Region. Dundee. Church of Scotland. St David's North Parish Church *(Dundee), to 1980*
Fraser, Margaret. St. David's North Parish Church : Strathmore Avenue, Dundee / text by Margaret Fraser ; photographs by Ron Gazzard. — [Dundee] ([Strathmore Ave., Dundee]) : [St. David's North Parish Church], [1981?]. — [12]p : ill,ports ; 15cm
£1.00 (unbound) B82-00461

285′.241295 — Scotland. Fife Region. Denbeath. United Free Church of Scotland: Denbeath Parish Church, *to 1980*
Denbeath Parish Church. A history of Denbeath Church / by Graham D.S. Deans. — Methil ([9 Chemiss Rd, Methilhill, Fife, KY8 2BS]) : Congregational Board of Denbeath Parish Church, 1980. — 28p,[4]p of plates : ports ; 22cm
Cover title
£0.50 (pbk) B82-35113

285′.241318 — Scotland. Central Region. Muiravonside. Church of Scotland. Muiravonside Parish Church, *to 1981*
Muiravonside Parish Church. Muiravonside Parish Church 1806-1981. — [Muiravonside] ([c/o Minister at Muiravonside, Muiravonside, E. Stirlingshire]) : [The Parish Church], [1982?]. — 24p : ill,ports ; 20cm
Unpriced (pbk) B82-29558

285′.242134 — London. Kensington and Chelsea *(London Borough).* **United Reformed Church: St. John's United Reformed Church,** *1962-1975*
Macklin, George C.. The last years 1962-1975 / by George C. Macklin. — London ([Allen St., W.8]) : St. John's Presbyterian Church (United Reformed), Kensington, [1981]. — 15p ; 23cm
Unpriced (pbk) B82-14298

285′.242195 — London. Richmond upon Thames *(London Borough).* **Twickenham. United Reformed Church: Twickenham United Reformed Church,** *to 1981*
Twickenham United Reformed Church. Chapel next the green : the story of Twickenham Congregational Church (Twickenham United Reformed Church 1972-) / A.C. Bryer. — Twickenham (72 Heathfield South, Twickenham, TW2 7SS) : B.L. Pearce for Twickenham United Reformed Church, 1982. — 64p : ill,facsims,1plan,ports ; 22cm
Text and facsim on inside covers
ISBN 0-9501639-9-6 (pbk) : £2.00 B82-31892

285′.2427612 — Lancashire. Tunley. United Reformed Church. Tunley United Reformed Church, *to 1980*
Mackay, W. G.. A history of the Tunley congregation : founded in 1662 and church built in 1691 / W.G. Mackay. — [Preston] ([1 Cumberland Ave., Leyland, Preston PR5 1BE]) : [W.G. Mackay], [1981?]. — 54p : ill,2plans,ports ; 21cm
Bibliography: p53
Unpriced (pbk) B82-04198

285′.242925 — Gwynedd. Rhosgadfan. Presbyterian Church of Wales. Capel Cesarea *(Rhosgadfan), to 1981 — Welsh texts*
Capel Cesarea *(Rhosgadfan).* 1881-1981 canmlwyddiant Capel Cesarea : (agor y trydydd capel). — [Llandwrog Uchaf] ([Tŷ'r Ysgol, Bronyfoel, Llandwrog Uchaf, Caernarfon, Gwynedd]) : [Capel Cesarea], 1981. — 8p ; 24cm
Cover title
£0.50 (pbk) B82-08536

285′.256944 — Jerusalem. Church of Scotland. St. Andrew's Church and Hospice *(Jerusalem), to 1980*
Jubilee : the Scots memorial, Jerusalem St. Andrew's Church and Hospice. — [Edinburgh] : [Society of Friends of St Andrew's, Jerusalem], [1982]. — 8p ; 21cm
Cover title
Unpriced (unbound) B82-25959

285.9 — PURITANISM

285′.9′0722 — England. Puritanism, *1560-1600 — Case studies*
Lake, Peter. Moderate puritans and the Elizabethan church / Peter Lake. — Cambridge : Cambridge University Press, 1982. — viii,357p ; 23cm
Bibliography: p343-347. — Includes index
ISBN 0-521-24010-7 : £27.50 : CIP rev. B82-11517

285′.9′0924 — England. Puritanism. Martin, Christopher, *d.1621 — Biographies*
Carpenter, R. J.. Christopher Martin, Great Burstead and the Mayflower / by R.J. Carpenter. — Chelmsford (28 Ravensbourne Drive, Chelmsford, Essex) : Barstable Books, 1982. — 14p,[4]p of plates : ill,facsims, ; 22cm
Unpriced (pbk) B82-38238

285′.9′0942 — England. Puritanism, *1558-1603*
Collinson, Patrick. The Elizabethan Puritan movement / Patrick Collinson. — London : Methuen, 1982. — 527p ; 23cm
Originally published: London : Cape, 1967. — Bibliography: p468-470. — Includes index
ISBN 0-416-34000-8 : Unpriced : CIP rev. B82-07970

285′.9′0974 — New England. Puritanism, *ca 1606-1700*
Adair, John. Founding fathers : the Puritans in England and America. — London : Dent, Oct.1982. — [288]p
ISBN 0-460-04421-4 : £12.95 : CIP entry B82-23990

286 — BAPTIST CHURCHES

286′.141425 — Scotland. Strathclyde Region. Helensburgh. Baptist churches. Helensburgh Baptist Church, *to 1981*
Helensburgh Baptist Church. The first hundred years : 1881-1981 / Helensburgh Baptist Church. — [Helensburgh] : [Helensburgh Baptist Church], [1982?]. — [8]p ; 21cm
Cover title
Unpriced (pbk) B82-33644

286′.142188 — London. Haringey *(London Borough).* **Wood Green. Baptist churches. Westbury Avenue Baptist Church** *(Wood Green), to 1981*
Smith, David R.. Living stones : the story of the believers who comprise the Baptist Church on Westbury Avenue, in Wood Green, in the Borough of Haringay, North London N22 65A / by David Rushworth Smith. — London : [Rushworth Literature Enterprise], 1981. — 36p : ill,maps,ports ; 21cm
Text on inside covers
ISBN 0-900329-20-3 (pbk) : Unpriced B82-05305

286′.142192 — London. Sutton *(London Borough).* **Carshalton. Baptist churches. Carshalton Beeches Baptist Free Church,** *to 1981*
Carshalton Beeches Baptist Free Church 1931-1981. — [Carshalton Beeches] ([67 Warnham Court Rd., Carshalton Beeches, Surrey]) : [L.E. Wigley], [1981]. — 20p : ill,ports ; 21cm
Unpriced (pbk) B82-09099

286′.142285 — Isle of Wight. Sandown. Baptist churches: Sandown Baptist Church, *to 1980*
Fancutt, Walter. His excellent greatness : the story of Sandown Baptist Church and its ministers, 1882-1982 / by Walter Fancutt. — [Ventnor] ([4b St Boniface Gardens, Ventnor, I.O.W. PO38 1NN]) : [W. Fancutt], [1982]. — 20p ; 22cm
£0.75 (pbk) B82-36636

286.6 — CHURCHES OF CHRIST

286.6′092′4 — Churches of Christ in Great Britain and Ireland. Robinson, William, *1888-1963 — Biographies*
WR — the man and his work : a brief account of the life and work of William Robinson, M.A., B.Sc., D.D. 1888-1963 / edited by James Gray. — Birmingham (1856A Persbore Rd., Birmingham B30 3AS) : Churches of Christ, Publication Department (Berean Press), 1978. — 135p : ports ; 22cm
Bibliography: p134-135
£2.00 (pbk) B82-17062

287 — METHODIST CHURCHES

287′.092′4 — Methodist churches. Wesley, John *— Biographies — For children*
John Wesley : missionary to the English. — London : Marshall, Morgan & Scott, Feb.1982. — [96]p. — (Heroes of the cross)
ISBN 0-551-00945-4 (pbk) : £0.95 : CIP entry B82-08121

287′.092′4 — Methodist churches. Wesley, John *— Correspondence, diaries, etc*
John and Charles Wesley : selected prayers, hymns, journal notes, sermons, letters and treaties / edited, with an introduction by Frank Whaling ; preface by Albert C. Outler. — London : SPCK, 1981. — xvii,412p ; 23cm. — (The Classics of Western spirituality)
Bibliography: p389-393. — Includes index
ISBN 0-281-03838-4 (pbk) : £8.95
Also classified at 264′.2 B82-16246

287′.1′0924 — Methodist Church. Chadwick, Samuel *— Biographies*
Bowden, Kenneth F.. Samuel Chadwick and Stacksteads / compiled by K.F. Bowden. — Bacup ('Cadeby', 34, Fernhill Cres., Bacup, Lancs.) : Privately published on behalf of Stacksteads Methodist Church, [1982]. — 24p,[4]p of plates : 2ill,1facsim,3ports ; 22cm
Facsim on inside cover
£1.00 (pbk) B82-27066

287′.1′0924 — Methodist Church. Whitefield, George *— Biographies*
Pollock, John, *1923-*. George Whitefield : and the great awakening / by John Pollock. — Tring : Lion, 1982, c1972. — x,272p ; 18cm. — (A Lion paperback)
Originally published : New York : Doubleday, 1972 ; London : Hodder & Stoughton, 1973
ISBN 0-85648-273-0 (pbk) : £2.50 B82-31703

287′.142511 — Derbyshire. Hayfield. Methodist Church. St. John's Methodist Church *(Hayfield), to 1982*
St. John's Methodist Church Hayfield 1782-1982 : a bicentenary history incorporating the 1932 third jubilee publication / foreword by Robert Barker. — [Hayfield] ([c/o Rev. R. Barker, 120 Church Rd., New Mills, Stockport SK12 4PF]) : [St. John's Methodist Church], [1982]. — 28p : ill,ports ; 19cm
Unpriced (pbk) B82-30169

287′.1429 — Wales. Methodist Church, *1700-1800 — Welsh texts*
Morgan, Derec Llwyd. Y diwygiad mawr / gan Derec Llwyd Morgan. — Llandysul : Gwasg Gomer, 1981. — xi,320p ; 22cm
Includes index
ISBN 0-85088-755-0 : £6.75 B82-12784

287′.5′0924 — Methodist Church. Soper of Kingsway, Donald, *Baron* **—** *Biographies*

Purrell, William. Odd man out. — Oxford : Mowbray, Jan.1983. — [200]p
Originally published: as Portrait of Soper. 1972
ISBN 0-264-66906-1 (pbk) : £3.50 : CIP entry
B82-32847

287′.5411 — Scotland. Methodist Church, *1800-1857 — Correspondence, diaries, etc.*

Scottish Methodism in the early Victorian period : the Scottish correspondence of the Rev. Jabez Bunting 1800-57 / edited by A.J. Hayes and D.A. Gowland. — Edinburgh : Edinburgh University Press, c1981. — viii,144p,[16]p of plates : ill,facsims,ports ; 24cm
Includes index
ISBN 0-85224-412-6 : £8.00 B82-05299

287′.542142 — London. Camden *(London Borough)*. **Methodist Church: Gospel Oak Methodist Church,** *to 1981*

Gospel Oak Methodist Church : centenary. — [London] : [The Church], 1982. — [12]p : ill,1port
Unpriced (pbk) B82-31370

287′.542194 — London. Kingston upon Thames *(London Borough)*. **Surbiton. Methodist Church: Surbiton Hill Methodist Church,** *to 1982*

Surbiton Hill Methodist Church. The chapel on the hill : a history of Surbiton Hill Methodist Church : 1882-1982 / by Pendry Morris. — [Surbiton] ([118 Elgar Ave., Surbiton, Surrey KT5 9JR]) : [The author for the Church Council, Surbiton Hill Methodist Church], [1981]. — xi,91p : ill,maps,ports ; 21cm
Includes index
Unpriced B82-11184

287′.542256 — East Sussex. Brighton. Methodist churches. Dorset Gardens Methodist Church, *to 1980*

Wright, J. L.. Dorset Gardens and the Dome / by J.L. Wright. — Hove (9 Brunswick Sq., Hove, E. Sussex BN3 1EN) : Chichester Diocesan Fund and Board of Finance, [1981]. — 15p : 1ill ; 21cm
Unpriced (unbound) B82-05931

287′.542313 — Wiltshire. Swindon. Methodist Church. Bath Road Methodist Church *(Swindon), 1880-1980*

Carter, E. R.. History of Bath Road Methodist Church Swindon 1880-1980 / by E.R. Carter. — Swindon : [E.R. Carter], 1981. — 81p,[4]p of plates : ill ; 22cm
ISBN 0-9507586-7-1 (pbk) : £1.50 B82-11925

287′.542385 — Somerset. West Somerset *(District)*. **Methodist churches. Circuits: Methodist Church.** *West Somerset Circuit*

Pointon, A. G.. Methodists in West Somerset : their place and influence in the life of the community : the story of the West Somerset Circuit, 1790-1980 / by A.G. Pointon. — Minehead (1 Millbridge Rd., Minehead, Somerset, TA24 8AG) : A.G. Pointon, 1982. — v,106p : 1ill ; 22cm
Bibliography: p103. — Includes index
£2.75 (pbk) B82-33758

287′.542531 — Lincolnshire. Nettleton. Methodist churches, *to 1900*

Mumby, Eileen H.. Methodism in Nettleton / Eileen H. Mumby ; foreword by John Minor. — [Nettleton] ([2 Orb Cottage, Cooks La., Nettleton, Lincoln LN7 6NL]) : [E.M. Mumby], [1982]. — 12leaves : 1ill ; 30cm
Unpriced (pbk) B82-31332

287′.542821 — South Yorkshire *(Metropolitan County)*. **Bents Green. Methodist Church. Bents Green Methodist Church,** *to 1982*

Manning, Anthony J.. Bents Green Methodist Church : 1932-1982 : a commemorative booklet to mark the golden jubilee / by Anthony J. Manning. — Sheffield (174 Millhouses Lane, Sheffield 7) : G.H. Tattershall, c1981. — 64p : ill,1map,1plan,ports ; 21cm
Text and ill. on inside covers
£1.25 (pbk) B82-05680

288 — UNITARIAN CHURCHES

288′.092′4 — Great Britain. Unitarian churches. Downing, A. B. — *Festschriften*

The **Downing** flavour : Arthur Benjamin Downing (1915-1980) / a memorial volume compiled and edited by H. John McLachlan. — [England?] : [s.n.] ; Sheffield (112, Brincliffe Edge Rd., Sheffield S11 9BX) : distributor: J. McLachlan (Liverpool : Codeprint Ltd.), c1982. — 48p,[1]p of plates : 1port ; 21cm
Includes one passage in German, with English translation
Unpriced B82-36898

288′.092′4 — New England. Unitarian churches. Judd, Sylvester — *Biographies*

Hathaway, Richard D.. Sylvester Judd's New England / Richard D. Hathaway. — University Park ; London : Pennsylvania State University Press, c1981. — 362p : ill,1port ; 22cm
Bibliography: p351-355. — Includes index
ISBN 0-271-00307-3 : Unpriced B82-38140

289 — NEW CHURCH, SOCIETY OF FRIENDS, BRETHREN, PENTECOSTAL CHURCHES, ETC

289 — New England. Christian sects, *1770-1820*

Marini, Stephen A.. Radical sects of revolutionary New England / Stephen A. Marini. — Cambridge, Mass. ; London : Harvard University Press, 1982. — 213p ; 25cm
Bibliography: p194-206. — Includes index
ISBN 0-674-74625-2 : £11.55 B82-34324

289 — Russia. Christian sects, *1860-1917*

Klibanov, A. I.. History of religious sectarianism in Russia (1860s-1917) / by A.I. Klibanov ; translated by Ethel Dunn ; edited by Stephen P. Dunn. — Oxford : Pergamon, 1982. — xv,450p : maps ; 24cm
Translation of: Istoriia religioznogo sektantstva v Rossii, 60-e gody XIXv.-1917g.. —
Bibliography: p429-439. — Includes index
ISBN 0-08-026794-7 : £25.00 : CIP rev.
B82-00286

289.3 — CHURCH OF JESUS CHRIST OF LATTER-DAY SAINTS

289.3′092′4 — Church of Jesus Christ of Latter-day Saints. Kimball, Heber C — *Biographies*

Kimball, Stanley B.. Heber C. Kimball : Mormon patriarch and pioneer / Stanley B. Kimball. — Urbana ; London : University of Illinois Press, c1981. — xv,343p,[22]p of plates : ill,facsims,1plan,ports ; 24cm
Maps on lining papers. — Includes index
ISBN 0-252-00854-5 : £12.60 B82-05725

289.3′792 — Utah. Church of Jesus Christ of Latter-day Saints, *1830-1937*

Stegner, Wallace. Mormon country / by Wallace Stegner. — Lincoln [Neb.] ; London : University of Nebraska Press, 1981. — x,362p ; 21cm
Originally published: New York : Duell, Sloan & Pearce, 1942. — Includes index
ISBN 0-8032-4129-1 : £16.05 B82-35899

289.4 — NEW CHURCH

289.4′092′4 — New Church. Swedenborg, Emanuel — *Biographies — Illustrations*

Hasler, Christopher. Emanuel Swedenborg / by Christopher Hasler and John Kaczmarcyck. — [London] ([20 Bloomsbury Way WC1A 2TH]) : [The Swedenborg Society], [1982?]. — 31p : ill ; 30cm
ISBN 0-901381-52-7 (unbound) : Unpriced
B82-39771

289.6 — SOCIETY OF FRIENDS

289.6 — Society of Friends

Firth, David. Familiar friend : commentaries from The Friend / David Firth. — London : Quaker Home Service, 1982. — 97p ; 19cm
ISBN 0-85245-159-8 (pbk) : £2.00 B82-39766

289.6′09 — Society of Friends, *to 1937*

Brayshaw, A. Neave. The Quakers : their story and message / by A. Neave Brayshaw. — 3rd ed. rev.. — York : William Sessions Book Trust, 1938 (1982 [printing]). — 354p : 1port ; 19cm
Previous ed.: London : Swarthmore, 1927. — Includes index
ISBN 0-900657-64-2 (pbk) : Unpriced
B82-39751

289.6′41 — Great Britain. Society of Friends

Allen, Richard, *1908-*. Growing points in the Quaker tradition / Richard Allen. — Rev. ed. — Sutton (12 Boston Court, Christchurch Park, Sutton, Surrey SM2 5TJ) : R. Allen, 1982. — 35p ; 21cm
ISBN 0-9508171-0-4 (pbk) : £0.45 B82-41021

289.6′4225 — East & West Sussex. Quakers, *to ca 1700*

Stanley, Gladys. The suffering of the Quakers in Sussex / by Gladys Stanley. — Hove (Diocesan Church House, 9 Brunswick Sq., Hove, E. Sussex BN3 1EN) : [Diocese of Chichester], [1981]. — 8p : 1ill ; 21cm
Unpriced (unbound) B82-04372

289.6′42516 — Derbyshire. Fritchley. Quakers, *to 1980*

Lowndes, Walter. The Quakers of Fritchley, 1863-1980 / Walter Lowndes. — Fritchley ([c/o The Meeting Librarian, 30 Horsley Rd., Kilburn, Derby]) : Friends Meeting House, 1980, c1981. — vii,272p : ill,facims,1plan,ports,1geneal.table ; 22cm
Limited ed. of 200 copies
£5.50 (pbk) B82-09957

289.6′42644 — Suffolk. Bury St Edmunds. Society of Friends, *to 1982*

Curtayne, Betty. 300 years of Quakerism in Bury St. Edmunds, Suffolk / text by Betty Curtayne. — [Bury St Edmunds] ([c/o Suffolk Record Office, Bury St Edmunds' Branch, School Hall St., Bury St Edmunds, IP33 1RX]) : Bury St Edmunds Meeting of the Religious Society of Friends, 1982. — 30p : 2facsims ; 22cm
£1.20 (pbk) B82-14663

289.6′42819 — Society of Friends. *Leeds Meeting, 1692-1712 — Minutes*

Leeds Friends' minute book : 1692-1712 / edited by Jean and Russell Mortimer. — [Leeds] ([Claremont, Clarendon Rd, Leeds LS2 9NZ]) : Yorkshire Archaeological Society, 1980. — li,269p ; 23cm. — (Record series ; v.139 for the years 1977 and 1978)
Bibliography: pxlvi-xlix. — Includes index
£14.90 B82-13115

289.9 — ASSEMBLIES OF GOD, BRETHREN, PENTECOSTAL CHURCHES, ETC

289.9 — England. Christadelphians. Thomas, John, *1805-1871 — Biographies*

Blore, Charles B.. Dr John Thomas : his family and the background of his times / by Charles B. Blore ; art work by Daniel and Sylvia Harrison. — Northampton (Hatikvah, 163 Billing Rd., Northampton NN1 5RS) : C.B. Blore, c1982. — 32p : ill,1geneal.table,1map ; 21cm
Unpriced (pbk) B82-31788

289.9 — People's Temple, *to 1978*

Naipaul, Shiva. Black and white / Shiva Naipaul. — London : Abacus, 1981, c1980. — 279p ; 20cm
Originally published: London : H. Hamilton, 1980
ISBN 0-349-12491-4 (pbk) : £2.50 B82-07080

Violence and religious commitment : implications of Jim Jones's People's Temple Movement / edited by Ken Levi. — University Park ; London : Pennsylvania State University Press, c1982. — xv,207p ; 24cm
Bibliography: p192-204. — Includes index
ISBN 0-271-00296-4 : Unpriced B82-38143

289.9 — Unification Church
Elkins, Chris. Heavenly deception / Chris Elkins. — Eastbourne : Kingsway, 1982, c1980. — 128p ; 18cm
Originally published: Wheaton, Ill. : Tyndale House, 1980
ISBN 0-86065-172-x (pbk) : £1.35 B82-34914

289.9 — Unification Church — *Personal observations*
Swatland, Susan. My life with the Moonies. — London : New English Library, Mar.1982. — [160]p
ISBN 0-450-05403-9 (pbk) : £1.25 : CIP entry B82-01987

289.9 — West Sussex. Society of Dependents, *to 1980*
Homan, Roger. The Sussex Cokelers / by Roger Homan. — Hove (9 Brunswick Sq., Hove, E. Sussex BN3 1EN) : Chichester Diocesan Fund and Board of Finance, 1981. — 8p : 1port ; 22cm
Unpriced (unbound) B82-05241

289.9 — West Yorkshire *(Metropolitan County).* **Stapleton. Brotherhood Church** *(Stapleton), to 1981*
Brotherhood Church *(Stapleton).* A history of the Brotherhood Church / A.G. Higgins. — Stapleton (Stapleton, nr. Pontefract, Yorks.) : Brotherhood Church, c1982. — 148p,[11]p of plates : ill,ports ; 26cm
Includes index
Unpriced B82-27389

289.9'2 — Jehovah's Witnesses — *Catholic viewpoints*
Ripley, Francis J.. Jehovah's Witnesses / Francis J. Ripley. — Rev. and updated. — London : Catholic Truth Society, 1982. — 17p ; 18cm
ISBN 0-85183-465-5 (pbk) : £0.35 B82-30173

290 — NON-CHRISTIAN RELIGIONS

290 — Muggletonians, *ca 1600-1699*
Hill, Christopher. The world of the Muggletonians. — London : Temple Smith, Sept.1982. — [256]p
ISBN 0-85117-226-1 : £12.50 : CIP entry B82-20186

291 — COMPARATIVE RELIGION

291 — Religions — *Comparative studies*
Peters, F. E.. Children of Abraham : Judaism — Christianity — Islam / F.E. Peters. — Princeton ; Guildford : Princeton University Press, c1982. — xi,225p ; 23cm
Includes index
ISBN 0-691-07267-1 : £10.30 B82-31198

Religious organization and religious experience / edited by J. Davis. — London : Academic Press, 1982. — ix,215p ; 24cm. — (A.S.A. monograph ; 21)
Includes bibliographies and index
ISBN 0-12-206580-8 : £12.00 : CIP rev. B82-00325

291'.03'21 — Non-Christian religions — *Encyclopaedias*
Parrinder, Geoffrey. Dictionary of non-Christian religions / Geoffrey Parrinder. — 2nd ed. — Amersham : Hulton, 1981. — 320p : ill ; 24cm
Previous ed.: 1971. — Bibliography: p318-320
ISBN 0-7175-0972-9 : £6.50 B82-09523

291'.03'21 — Religions — *Encyclopaedias*
Jones, Arthur A.. Illustrated dictionary of world religions / Arthur A. Jones. — Exeter : Religious Education Press, 1982. — 286p : ill,ports ; 25cm
ISBN 0-08-024176-x (cased) : Unpriced
ISBN 0-08-026441-7 (pbk) : £6.50 B82-32263

291'.092'4 — Religion. Historiography. Eliade, Mircea — *Biographies*
Eliade, Mircea. Autobiography / Mircea Eliade ; translated from the Romanian by Mac Linscott Ricketts. — San Francisco ; London : Harper & Row
Vol.1: 1907-1937, journey east, journey west. — c1981. — ix,335p : 1port ; 25cm
Includes index
ISBN 0-06-062142-7 : £12.50 B82-11962

291'.0941 — Britons. Religious beliefs, *to 1540 — For schools*
Pearce, R. T.. Stones, bones and gods : discovering the beliefs of primitive man in Britain / R.T. Pearce. — London : Ward Lock Educational, 1982. — 96p : ill,2plans ; 21cm
Includes bibliographies and index
ISBN 0-7062-4041-3 (pbk) : £1.95 B82-33059

291.1'3 — Myths — *Anthologies*
Mercer, John, *1934-*. The stories of vanishing peoples : a book for children / prepared by John Mercer ; illustrated by Tony Evora. — London : Allison & Busby, 1982. — 128p : ill,maps ; 23cm
ISBN 0-85031-421-6 (cased) : £5.95 : CIP rev.
ISBN 0-85031-422-4 (pbk) : Unpriced B81-28832

291.1'3 — South-eastern European myths. Historical sources: Artefacts, *B.C.6500-B.C.3500*
Gimbutas, Marija. The goddesses and gods of Old Europe : 6500-3500 BC : myths and cult images / Marija Gimbutas. — New and updated ed. / with 252 illustrations, 171 text figures and 8 maps. — London : Thames and Hudson, c1982. — 304p : ill,maps ; 25cm
Previous ed.: published as Gods and goddesses of Old Europe, 7000 to 3500 BC. 1974. — Bibliography: p256-269. — Includes index
ISBN 0-500-27238-7 (pbk) : £5.95 B82-19968

291.1'3'0321 — Mythology — *Encyclopaedias*
Larousse world mythology / edited by Pierre Grimal ; [translated by Patricia Beardsworth]. — London : Hamlyn, 1965 (1981 [printing]). — 560p,[40]p of plates : ill(some col.) ; 29cm
Translations from: Mythologies de la Méditerranée au Gange and Mythologies des steppes, des iles et des forêts. — Bibliography: p546-547. — Includes index
ISBN 0-600-33225-x (pbk) : £7.95 B82-08038

Man, myth and magic. — London : Marshall Cavendish, Feb.1983. — 12v.
ISBN 0-86307-041-8 : CIP entry
Also classified at 200'.3'21 B82-39822

291.1'3'0321 — Mythology — *Encyclopaedias — Facsimiles*
Bell, John, *1745-1831*. Bell's new pantheon / John Bell ; introduction by Robert D. Richardson, Jr. — New York ; London : Garland, 1979. — 2v.(vi,407,329p,[39]p of plates) : ill ; 29cm. — (Myth & romanticism)
Facsim. of: ed. published London : printed by and for J. Bell, 1790
ISBN 0-8240-3553-4 : Unpriced B82-14679

291.2 — Religions. Doctrines — *For children*
Dent, Jenny. The giant jigsaw. — Liss : White Eagle Publishing Trust, Nov.1982. — [32]p. — ('Spiritual teaching for children' series ; bk.3)
ISBN 0-85487-053-9 (pbk) : £1.25 : CIP entry B82-29141

Dent, Jenny. God loves us all. — Liss : White Eagle Publishing Trust, Nov.1982. — [32]p. — ('Spiritual teaching for children' series ; bk.1)
ISBN 0-85487-051-2 (pbk) : £1.25 : CIP entry B82-29139

Dent, Jenny. Where is heaven?. — Liss : White Eagle Publishing Trust, Nov.1982. — [32]p. — ('Spiritual teaching for children' series ; bk.2)
ISBN 0-85487-052-0 (pbk) : £1.25 : CIP entry B82-29140

291.2'11'0321 — Gods — *Encyclopaedias*
Carlyon, Richard. A guide to the gods / compiled by Richard Carlyon. — London : Heinemann, 1981. — 401p ; 25cm
Includes index
ISBN 0-434-98005-6 (cased) : £10.00
ISBN 0-434-98023-4 (pbk) : £5.95 B82-17047

291.2'12 — Great Britain. Non-Christian religions. Sun cults
Toulson, Shirley. The winter solstice. — London : Jill Norman & Hobhouse, Nov.1981. — [160]p
ISBN 0-906908-25-6 : £7.50 : CIP entry B81-30620

291.2'12 — Tibet. Mount Kailas. Religious aspects
Snelling, John. The sacred mountain. — London : Wildwood, June 1982. — [256]p
ISBN 0-7045-3055-4 : £7.95 : CIP entry B82-10863

291.2'13 — Myths. Special subjects: Women. Psychological aspects
Harding, M. Esther. Woman's mysteries, ancient and modern. — London : Rider, Sept.1982. — [256]p
Originally published: London : Longmans, 1935
ISBN 0-09-150061-3 (pbk) : £2.95 : CIP entry B82-20619

291.2'15 — Angels — *Theosophical viewpoints*
Devas and men : a compilation of the theosophical studies on the angelic kingdom / by the Southern Centre of Theosophy, Robe, South Australia. — Adyar ; London : Theosophical, 1977. — xi,369p,[2]p of plate : ill (some col.) ; 25cm
Unpriced B82-09369

291.2'3 — Future life
Russell, Edward Wriothesley. Prospects of eternity / Edward Wriothesley Russell. — Sudbury : Spearman, 1982. — vii,152p : 1form ; 23cm
ISBN 0-85435-394-1 : £5.50 B82-25005

291.2'3 — Myths. Special subjects: Paradise. Origins
Ford, Julian. The story of Paradise / by Julian Ford. — Richmond : H & B Publications, 1981. — vi,165p : ill ; 22cm
ISBN 0-9506371-2-2 (pbk) : £2.00 B82-03575

291.2'37 — Reincarnation
Rawlings, Maurice. Life wish : reincarnation : reality or hoax? / Maurice Rawlings. — London : Triangle, 1982. — 148p ; 18cm
Originally published: Nashville : T. Nelson, 1981
ISBN 0-281-03857-0 (pbk) : £1.75 : CIP rev. B82-18878

291.3'6 — Pagan festivals — *Calendars — Serials*
Pennick's Endsville pagan almanack. — 1980 C.E.-. — Cambridge ([c/o Mr. N. Pennick, 142 Pheasant Rise, Bar Hill, Cambridge CB3 8SD]) : [Fenris-Wolf/Institute of Geomantic Research/Cambridge Ancient Mysteries Group Complex], 1980-. — v. : ill ; 30cm
Annual. — Continues: Pennick's Endsville almanack
ISSN 0262-7736 = Pennick's Endsville pagan almanack : Unpriced B82-07626

291.4'2 — India. Religious life. Mysticism
Bharati, Agehananda. The light at the centre : context and pretext of modern mysticism. — London : East-West Publications, Apr.1982. — [256]p
ISBN 0-85692-084-3 (pbk) : £4.95 : CIP entry B82-06257

291.4'2 — India. Religious life. Mysticism — *Personal observations*
Belfrage, Sally. Flowers of emptiness / Sally Belfrage. — London : Women's Press 1981. — 240p : 1port ; 20cm
ISBN 0-7043-3875-0 (pbk) : £3.95 : CIP rev. B81-30352

291.4'2 — Religious experiences
Hay, David, *1935-*. Exploring inner space : scientists and religious experience / David Hay. — Harmondsworth : Penguin, 1982. — 256p ; 20cm
Bibliography: p236-246. — Includes index
ISBN 0-14-022340-1 (pbk) : £2.95 B82-18147

291.4'2 — Religious life. Mysticism
Suzuki, Daisetz Teitaro. Mysticism : Christian and Buddhist / Daisetsu Teitaro Suzuki. — London : Unwin Paperbacks, 1979. — 152p ; 20cm. — (Mandala books)
Originally published: New York: Harper ; London : Allen & Unwin, 1957
ISBN 0-04-149053-3 (pbk) : Unpriced : CIP rev. B79-30511

291.4'2 — Religious life. Mysticism, *ca 1100-ca 1400*

Bancroft, Anne. The luminous vision : six medieval mystics and their teachings. — London : Allen & Unwin, Nov.1982. — [208]p
ISBN 0-04-189001-9 : £12.50 : CIP entry
B82-27806

291.4'3 — Prayers for mealtimes — *Prayers & readings — Collections*

A **Book** of graces / compiled by Carolyn Martin ; illustrations by Bert Wharton. — [Sevenoaks] : Hodder and Stoughton, 1980. — 221p : ill ; 18cm
Includes index
ISBN 0-340-25761-x (pbk) : £1.75 : CIP rev.
B80-13693

291.4'3 — Religious life. Meditation

Pearce, Joseph Chilton. The bond of power. — London : Routledge & Kegan Paul, June 1982. — [192]p
Originally published: New York : Dutton, 1981
ISBN 0-7100-9278-4 (pbk) : £5.95 : CIP entry
B82-09598

291.4'4 — Religious life

Cupitt, Don. Taking leave of God / Don Cupitt. — London : SCM Press, 1980 (1981 [printing]). — xiii,174p ; 22cm
Includes index
ISBN 0-334-01596-0 (pbk) : £4.95 B82-05901

Griffiths, Bede. The marriage of East and West / Bede Griffiths. — London : Collins, 1982. — 224p ; 22cm
Includes index
ISBN 0-00-215529-x (pbk) : £5.95 B82-23125

291.4'4'0924 — India *(Republic)*. **Religious life** — *Personal observations*

Pullar, Philippa. The shortest journey / by Philippa Pullar. — London : Hamilton, 1981. — x,262p : 1map ; 23cm
ISBN 0-241-10685-0 : £9.95 : CIP rev.
B81-24614

291.4'4'09519 — Korea. Religious life — *Illustrations*

Michaud, Jean-Claude. Korea / Jean-Claude and Roland Michaud ; [translated from the French by Alexis Gregory]. — London : Thomas and Hudson, 1981. — 23p, [80]p of plates : chiefly ill(some col.),maps ; 27x31cm
ISBN 0-500-24113-9 : £20.00 B82-01308

291.6 — Religious leaders — *For children*

Dent, Jenny. Great teachers. — Liss : White Eagle Publishing Trust, Nov.1982. — [32]p. — ('Spiritual teaching for children' series ; bk.4)
ISBN 0-85487-054-7 (pbk) : £1.25 : CIP entry
B82-29142

291.6'092'4 — India *(Republic)*. **Poona. Religious leaders: Rajneesh,** *Bhagwan Shree*. **Religious life** — *Personal observations*

Satya Bharti, *Ma*. Death comes dancing : celebrating life with Bhagwan Shree Rajneesh / Ma Satya Bharti. — London : Routledge and Kegan Paul, 1981. — viii,183p ; 22cm
ISBN 0-7100-0705-1 (pbk) : £4.95 B82-18036

291.6'2 — Primitive socities. Shamanism

Heusch, Luc de. Why marry her? : society and symbolic structures / Luc de Heusch ; translated by Janet Lloyd. — Cambridge : Cambridge University Press, c1981. — vi,218p : ill ; 24cm. — (Cambridge studies in social anthropology ; 33)
Translated from the French. — Bibliography: p208-214. — Includes index
ISBN 0-521-22460-8 : £19.50 : CIP rev.
Primary classification 305 B81-30495

291.6'2 — Shamanism

Drury, Nevill. The shaman and the magician : journeys between the worlds / Nevill Drury. — London : Routledge & Kegan Paul, 1982. — xii,129p : ill ; 22cm
Bibliography: p119-126. — Includes index
ISBN 0-7100-0910-0 (pbk) : £3.95 B82-28425

Halifax, Joan. Shaman : the wounded healer / Joan Halifax. — London : Thames and Hudson, c1982. — 96p : ill(some col.) ; 28cm
Bibliography: p96
ISBN 0-500-81029-x (pbk) : £3.95 B82-29492

291.6'3 — Prophets

Scrutton, Robert J.. The message of the Masters / Robert Scrutton ; edited by Kenneth Johnson. — St. Helier : Spearman, 1982. — xiv,261p : ill,maps ; 23cm
ISBN 0-85978-091-0 : £6.50 B82-25004

291.6'3 — Religions. Founders — *For children*

Gray, Iain A. S.. The founders' file / Iain A.S. Gray, Donald M. McFarlan. — London : Blackie, 1982. — 19pamphlets : ill ; 21cm
In plastic bag
ISBN 0-216-91163-x (unbound) : Unpriced
B82-21818

291.8'2 — Sacred works

Davies, Robin. Holy books / Robin Davies. — London : Longman, 1981. — 64p : ill,2maps,facsims,2ports ; 24cm. — (The Religious dimension)
Includes index
ISBN 0-582-23008-x (pbk) : £1.30 B82-16889

291.8'2 — Sacred works — *Stories for children*

Bull, Norman J.. Stories from world religions. — Edinburgh : Oliver & Boyd. — (Wide range)
1 / Norman J. Bull, Reginald J. Ferris. — c1982. — 128p : ill(some col.) ; 20cm
ISBN 0-05-003370-0 (pbk) : Unpriced
B82-26466

291.9 — United States. Negro messianic movements, *to 1981*

Moses, Wilson Jeremiah. Black messiahs and Uncle Toms : social and literary manipulations of a religious myth / Wilson Jeremiah Moses. — University Park ; London : Pennsylvania State University Press, c1982. — xii,278p ; 24cm
Bibliography: p261-270. — Includes index
ISBN 0-271-00294-8 : Unpriced B82-38136

292 — CLASSICAL RELIGIONS

292'.13 — Ancient Greek myths — *Anthologies — For children — Welsh texts*

Phillips, Juli. Chwedlau gwlad Groeg / Juli Phillips ; lluniau gan Alison Jenkins. — Caerdydd : Gwasg y Dref Wen, c1981. — 63p : ill ; 19cm. — (Cyfres y wiwer)
£1.70 (pbk) B82-10639

292'.13 — Ancient Greek myths. Special subjects: Fabulous beasts — *Critical studies*

Lloyd-Jones, Hugh. Mythical beasts / Hugh Lloyd-Jones ; sculptures by Marcelle Quinton. — London : Duckworth, 1980. — 70p : ill ; 26cm
ISBN 0-7156-1439-8 (cased) : £15.00 : CIP rev.
ISBN 0-7156-1503-3 (pbk) : £5.95 B80-10567

292'.13 — Ancient Greek myths — *Structuralist perspectives*

Myth, religion and society : structuralist essays / by M. Detienne ... [et al.] ; edited by R.L. Gordon ; with an introduction by R.G.A. Buxton. — Cambridge : Cambridge University Press, 1981. — xvii,306p : ill ; 24cm
Bibliography: p272-290. — Includes index
ISBN 0-521-22780-1 (cased) : £20.00 : CIP rev.
ISBN 0-521-29640-4 (pbk) : £6.95 B81-40270

Vernant, Jean-Pierre. Myth and society in ancient Greece / Jean-Pierre Vernant ; translated from the French by Janet Lloyd. — London : Methuen, 1982, c1980. — x,242p ; 22cm
Translation of: Mythe et société en Grèce ancienne. — Originally published: Brighton : Harvester, 1979
ISBN 0-416-33830-5 (pbk) : Unpriced : CIP rev. B82-06748

292'.13 — Classical myths: Rape of Lucretia

Donaldson, Ian. The rapes of Lucretia. — Oxford : Clarendon Press, Sept.1982. — [184]p
ISBN 0-19-812638-7 : £15.00 : CIP entry
B82-18979

292'.13'0321 — Classical mythology — *Encyclopaedias*

Stapleton, Michael. The Hamlyn concise dictionary of Greek and Roman mythology / Michael Stapleton ; introduction by Stewart Perowne. — Concise ed. — London : Hamlyn, 1982. — xi,306p ; 15cm
Previous ed.: published as A dictionary of Greek and Roman mythology. 1978. — Bibliography: p289. — Includes index
ISBN 0-600-33237-3 (pbk) : £1.50 B82-35259

292'.13'076 — Classical myths — *Questions & answers*

Partington-Greive, J.. Classics by questions / by J. Partington-Greive ; drawings by Peter McGlashon. — Thirsk : Crakehill
Vol.1: The Greek legends. — c1982. — 52p : ill ; 21cm
Text and map on inside covers
ISBN 0-907105-08-4 (pbk) : Unpriced
B82-28313

Partington-Greive, J.. Classics by questions / by J. Partington-Greive ; drawings by Peter McGlashon. — Thirsk : Crakehill
Vol.2: The Trojan legends. — c1982. — 48p : ill ; 21cm
Text and map on inside covers
ISBN 0-907105-09-2 (pbk) : Unpriced
B82-28314

Partington-Greive, J.. Classics by questions / J. Partington-Greive ; drawings by Peter McGlashon. — Thirsk : Crakehill
Vol.3: The Roman legends. — c1982. — 44p : ill ; 21cm
Text and map on inside covers
ISBN 0-907105-10-6 (pbk) : Unpriced
B82-28315

292'.211 — Ancient Greek religion. Dionysos

Danielou, Alain. Shiva and Dionysus. — London : East-West Publications, Apr.1982. — [288]p
Translation of: Shiva et Dionysos
ISBN 0-85692-054-1 (pbk) : £4.95 : CIP entry
Primary classification 294.5'513 B82-06256

292'.211 — Classical religions. Gods & goddesses

Laing, Jennifer. The Greek and Roman gods : a pocket guide / Jennifer Laing. — Newton Abbot : David & Charles, c1982. — 63p : 1map ; 22cm
Includes index
ISBN 0-7153-8292-6 : £3.50 : CIP rev.
B82-15840

292'.3 — Ancient Rome. Religious cults, *1-500*

Godwin, Joscelyn. Mystery religions : in the ancient world / Joscelyn Godwin. — London : Thames and Hudson, c1981. — 176p : ill,ports ; 24cm
Bibliography: p172. — Includes index
ISBN 0-500-27271-9 (pbk) : £4.50 B82-29493

293 — GERMANIC NON-CHRISTIAN RELIGIONS

293 — Norse religion

Pennick, Nigel. The 18th rune / by Nigel Pennick. — Cambridge (142 Pheasant Rise, Bar Hill, Cambridge CB3 8SD) : Fenris-Wolf, 1982. — 11p ; 22cm. — (Fenris-Wolf pagan paper ; no.1)
Unpriced (unbound) B82-30635

293'.13 — Norse myths — *Anthologies*

Crossley-Holland, Kevin. The Norse myths / introduced and retold by Kevin Crossley-Holland. — Harmondsworth : Penguin, 1982, c1980. — xli,276p : ill ; 23cm
Originally published: London: Deutsch, 1980. — Bibliography: p254-261. — Includes index
ISBN 0-14-006056-1 (pbk) : £4.95 B82-30517

293'.9 — England. Odinism, *681-1980*

Yeowell, John. Hidden gods / John Yeowell. — London : Raven Banner, c1982. — 19p ; 21cm
Bibliography: p19
Unpriced (pbk) B82-24691

294 — RELIGIONS OF INDIC ORIGIN

294 — Asian religions

Iqbal, Muhammad, *1938-*. East meets West : a background to some Asian faiths. — 3rd ed. rev. / Muhammad Iqbal in collaboration with Dharam Kumar Vohra and Sardar Arjan Kirpal Singh ; foreword by David Lane. — London : Commission for Racial Equality, 1981. — 130p ; 21cm
Previous ed.: 1973. — Includes bibliographies and index
ISBN 0-902355-94-5 (pbk) : £1.50 B82-05048

294 — Tantrism

Walker, Benjamin. Tantrism. — Wellingborough : Aquarian Press, Oct.1982. — [192]p
ISBN 0-85030-272-2 (cased) : £8.95 : CIP entry
ISBN 0-85030-273-0 (pbk) : £4.50 B82-24270

294.3 — BUDDHISM

294.3 — Buddhism *compared with* **Christianity** — *Philosophical perspectives*

Smart, Ninian. Beyond ideology : religion and the future of western civilization : Gifford lectures delivered in the University of Edinburgh, 1979-1980 / Ninian Smart. — London : Collins, 1981. — 350p ; 21cm
Bibliography: p314-331. — Includes index
ISBN 0-00-215846-9 : £9.95 : CIP rev.
Primary classification 200 B81-20622

294.3 — Buddhism — *For children*

Patrick, Martha. Buddhists and Buddhism / Martha Patrick. — Hove : Wayland, 1982. — 63p : ill ; 22cm. — (Beliefs and believers)
Bibliography: p61. — Includes index
ISBN 0-85340-906-4 : £3.95 B82-16516

294.3 — Buddhism — *For schools*

Buddhism / [editor Harry Undy]. — London : Christian Education Movement, [1979?]. — 1portfolio : ill,maps ; 26cm. — (Topic folder ; no.5)
Includes bibliographies
ISBN 0-905022-50-5 : Unpriced B82-24187

294.3 — Buddhism — *Welsh texts*

Harris, J. G.. Arweiniad at Bwdhaeth / J. Glyndwr Harris. — Abertawe [Swansea] : C. Davies, c1980. — 139p : ill,col.maps ; 22cm. — (Cyfres crefyddau'r byd)
Bibliography: p129-132. — Includes index
ISBN 0-7154-0579-9 (pbk) : £3.50 B82-17004

294.3'09 — Buddhism, *to 1978*

Conze, Edward. A short history of Buddhism. — London : Unwin Paperbacks, Nov.1982. — [160]p
Originally published: 1980
ISBN 0-04-294123-7 (pbk) : £2.95 : CIP entry B82-27830

294.3'09'014 — Buddhism, *ca B.C.500-A.D.1500*

Ikeda, Daisaku. Buddhism, the first millennium / Daisaku Ikeda ; translated by Burton Watson. — Tokyo : Kodansha International ; Oxford : Phaidon [distributor], c1977. — 172p ; 24cm
Translation of: Watakushi no bukkyō kan. — Bibliography: p155-158. — Includes index
ISBN 0-87011-321-6 : £5.95 B82-02056

294.3'4 — Buddhist life. Mysticism

Govinda, Anagarika Brahmacari. Foundations of Tibetan mysticism. — London : Rider Books, Feb.1983. — [320]p
ISBN 0-09-150031-1 (pbk) : £2.95 : CIP entry B82-36438

294.3'422 — Mahayana Buddhism. Bodhisattva docrine

The **Bodhisattva** doctrine in Buddhism / edited and introduced by Leslie S. Kawamura. — Waterloo, Ont. : Published for the Canadian Corporation for Studies in Religion/Corporation canadienne des sciences religieuses by Wilfrid Laurier University Press ; Gerrards Cross : Smythe [distributor], c1981. — xxi,272p ; 23cm. — (SR supplements ; 10)
Conference papers. — Includes index
ISBN 0-919812-12-0 (pbk) : Unpriced B82-19145

294.3'443 — Buddhist life. Meditation — *Manuals — Pali texts*

The **Yogāvacara's** manual of Indian mysticism as practised by Buddhists / edited by T.W. Rhys Davids. — London : The Pali Text Society, 1981. — xxxi,105p ; 23cm
Pali text with English introduction. — Includes index
Unpriced B82-17607

294.3'443 — Theravada Buddhist life. Meditation

Goldstein, Joseph, *1944-*. The experience of insight : a natural unfolding / by Joseph Goldstein ; introduction by Ram Dass ; preface by Robert Hall. — London : Wildwood, 1981, c1976. — xi,171p ; 20cm
Originally published: Santa Cruz : Unity Press, 1976. — Bibliography: p171
ISBN 0-7045-0370-0 (pbk) : £3.95 B82-02846

294.3'443 — Vipaśyanā

Dhiravamsa. Dynamic meditation : the release and cure of pain and suffering. — Wellingborough : Turnstone Press, May 1982. — [256]p
ISBN 0-85500-163-1 (pbk) : £4.95 : CIP entry B82-07032

294.3'444 — Buddhist life. Pātimokkha — *Commentaries — Pali texts*

Buddhaghosa. Kaṅkhāvitaraṇi nāma Mātikaṭṭhakathā : Buddhaghosa's commentary on The Pātimokkha / edited by Dorothy Maskell (née stede). — London : The Pali Text Society, 1981. — xiii,216p ; 23cm
Pali text with English introduction. — Includes index
Unpriced B82-17608

294.3'444 — Mahayana Buddhist life. Skilful means

Pye, Michael, *1939-*. Skilful means : a concept in Mahayana Buddhism / Michael Pye. — London : Duckworth, 1978. — viii,211p ; 26cm
Bibliography: p198-202. — Includes index
ISBN 0-7156-1266-2 (cased) : £32.00
ISBN 0-7156-1624-2 (pbk) : £7.95 B82-08758

294.3'4447 — Japan. Hermits. Buddhist life, *1207-1212 — Personal observations*

Kamo, Chōmei. Notebook of a ten square rush-mat sized world : a fugitive essay ... / by the Buddhist recluse Kamo No Chomei ; adapted from the Japanese by Thomas Rowe and Anthony Kerrigan ; with illustrations adapted from old Japanese woodcuts. — Dublin : Dolmen, 1979. — 40p : ill ; 23cm. — (Dolmen texts ; 3)
Translation of: Hōjōki
ISBN 0-85105-343-2 : £4.50 B82-02200

294.3'5 — Buddhist ethics

Aśoka, *King of Magadha*. The edicts of Asoka / edited and translated by N.A. Nikam and Richard McKeon. — Chicago ; London : University of Chicago Press, 1959 (1978 [printing]). — xxv,68p : 1map ; 23cm. — (Midway reprint)
ISBN 0-226-58611-1 (pbk) : £3.50 B82-21491

294.3'5699 — Tibetan Buddhist life. Compassion

Tsoṅ-kha-pa Blo-bzaṅ-grags-pa. Compassion in Tibetan Buddhism / Tsong-ka-pa ; edited and translated by Jeffrey Hopkins ; co-editor Lati Rinbochay ; assistant editors Anne Klein and Elizabeth Napper. — London : Rider, 1980. — 254p ; 22cm
Translated from the Tibetan. — Bibliography: p237-247. — Includes Meditations of a Tantric abbot / by Kensur Lekden, edited and translated by Jeffrey Hopkins, associate Barbara Frye
ISBN 0-09-143261-8 (corrected : pbk) : £4.95 B82-16947

294.3'61'09515 — Tibet. Lamas — *Childhood reminiscences*

Lobsang Rampa, T.. Tibetan sage / T. Lobsang Rampa. — [London] : Corgi, 1980. — 158p ; 18cm
ISBN 0-552-11563-0 (pbk) : £1.00 B82-17138

294.3'62'0924 — Tibetan Buddhism. Mi-la-ras-pa — *Biographies*

Ras-chun-rdo-rje-grags-pa.
[Rje-brtsun-mi-la-ras-pa'i-rnam-thar. English]. The life of Milarepa / a new translation from the Tibetan by Lobsang P. Lhalungpa in collaboration with Far West Translations. — London : Granada, 1979, c1977. — xxxii,220p,[8]p of plates : ill(some col.) ; 20cm. — (A Paladin U.K. original)
Author: Ras-chun-rdo-rje-grags-pa. — Originally published: New York : Dutton, 1977
ISBN 0-586-08325-1 (pbk) : £1.95 B82-07872

294.3'82 — Buddhism. Scriptures — *Khotanese texts*

Khotanese Buddhist texts / [edited by] H.W. Bailey. — Rev. ed. — Cambridge : Cambridge University Press, 1981. — x,157p ; 26cm. — (University of Cambridge oriental publications ; no.31)
Khotanese text, English preface. — Previous ed.: London : Taylor's Foreign Press, 1951
ISBN 0-521-23717-3 : £27.50 : CIP rev. B81-30496

294.3'82 — Theravada Buddhism. Scriptures — *Indexes*

Index to the Kathāvatthu / compiled by Tetsuya Tabata ... [et al.]. — London : Pali Text Society, c1982. — 246p ; 23cm. — (Text series ; no.174)
Text in Pali, foreword and preface in English
Unpriced B82-40437

294.3'82 — Theravada Buddhism. Scriptures — *Texts*

[Tipiṭaka. Abhidhammapiṭaka. *English*]. Conditional relations (Paṭṭhāna). — London : The Pali Text Society
Vol.2 : being vol.II of the Chaṭṭhasaṅgāyana text of the seventh book of the Abhidhamma Piṭaka / a translation by U Nārada Mūla Paṭṭhāna Sayadaw assisted by Thein Nyun. — 1981. — cii,599p ; 23cm. — (Translation series ; no.42)
ISBN 0-7100-0968-2 : Unpriced B82-17606

294.3'91 — Theravada Buddhism

Collins, Steven. Selfless persons : imagery and thought in Theraváda Buddhism / Steven Collins. — Cambridge : Cambridge University Press, 1982. — ix,323p ; 24cm
Bibliography: p310-317. — Includes index
ISBN 0-521-24081-6 : £22.50 : CIP rev. B82-14505

294.3'92 — Mahayana Buddhism

Wisdom energy 2. — Ulverston : Wisdom Culture, 1979. — 94p : ill,ports ; 25cm
ISBN 0-86171-001-0 (pbk) : £2.30 B82-12180

294.3'923 — Tibetan Buddhism

MacDonald-Bayne, M.. Life everlasting / M. MacDonald-Bayne. — Romford : Fowler, c1981. — 165p ; 19cm
ISBN 0-85243-365-4 : £3.95 B82-00930

Rinpochey, Khetsun Sangpo. Tantric practice in Nying-ma. — London : Hutchinson, Nov.1982. — [1v.]
ISBN 0-09-146130-8 : £7.95 : CIP entry B82-30341

294.3'923'0924 — Tibetan Buddhism. Evans-Wentz, W. Y. — *Biographies*

Winkler, Ken. Pilgrim of the clear light / Ken Winkler. — Berkeley : Dawnfire Books ; Gerrards Cross : Colin Smythe, c1982. — xvi,114p : ill,ports ; 22cm
Includes index
ISBN 0-86140-126-3 (pbk) : Unpriced : CIP rev. B82-07130

294.3'927 — Zen Buddhism

Stryk, Lucien. Encounter with Zen : writings on poetry and Zen / Lucien Stryk. — Chicago ; London : Ohio University Press, c1981. — ix,259p ; 23cm
ISBN 0-8040-0405-6 (cased) : Unpriced
ISBN 0-8040-0406-4 (pbk) : £6.75 B82-33010

Suzuki, Daisetz Teitaro. An introduction to Zen Buddhism. — London : Rider, Feb.1983. — [144]p
ISBN 0-09-151121-6 (pbk) : £2.95 : CIP entry B82-36608

294.3′927 — Zen Buddhism *continuation*

Suzuki, Daisetz Teitaro. Living by Zen. — London : Rider, Sept.1982. — [192]p
Originally published: 1950
ISBN 0-09-149981-x (pbk) : £2.95 : CIP entry B82-20616

The **Three** pillars of Zen : teaching, practice and enlightenment / compiled and edited with translations, introductions and notes by Philip Kapleau ; foreword by Houston Smith. — Rev. and expanded ed. — London : Rider, 1980. — xxii,400p : ill ; 22cm
Previous ed.: New York : Harper and Row, 1966. — Includes index
ISBN 0-09-142031-8 (pbk) : £4.95 : CIP rev. B80-08606

Zen : poems, prayers, sermons, anecdotes, interviews / selected and translated by Lucien Stryk and Takashi Ikemoto. — 2nd ed. — Chicago ; London : Swallow Press, c1981. — xlv,160p,8p of plates : ill,1facsim ; 23cm
Translation from the Japanese. — Previous ed.: Garden City, N.Y. : Anchor Books, 1965
ISBN 0-8040-0377-7 (cased) : Unpriced
ISBN 0-8040-0378-5 (pbk) : Unpriced B82-29186

294.3′928 — Nichiren Shōshū Buddhism

The **Buddhism** of the Sun. — Richmond (1 The Green, Richmond, Surrey TW9 1PL) : Nichiren Shoshu of the United Kingdom, Nov.1982. — [128]p
ISBN 0-9508274-0-1 (pbk) : £2.50 : CIP entry B82-28620

294.5 — HINDUISM

294.5 — Hinduism

Bahree, Patricia. The Hindu world / Patricia Bahree. — London : Macdonald, 1982. — 45p : col.ill,1col.map ; 29cm. — (Religions of the world)
Bibliography: p44. — Includes index
ISBN 0-356-07521-4 : £3.95 B82-37622

Brockington, J. L.. The sacred thread : Hinduism in its continuity and diversity / J.L. Brockington. — Edinburgh : Edinburgh University Press, c1981. — ix,222p : ill,1facsim ; 18cm
Bibliography: p210-216. — Includes index
ISBN 0-85224-393-6 (pbk) : £4.00 B82-03059

Kinsley, David R.. Hinduism : a cultural perspective / David R. Kinsley. — Englewood Cliffs ; London : Prentice-Hall, c1982. — xi,164p : ill,1map,plans,2ports ; 23cm. — (Prentice-Hall series in world religions)
Bibliography: p158-160. — Includes index
ISBN 0-13-388975-0 (pbk) : £5.95 B82-20055

294.5 — Hinduism. Deva, Amrito, *Swami* — *Biographies*

Deva, Amrito, *Swami*. Coming home. — London : Wildwood House, Oct.1981. — [208]p
ISBN 0-7045-3053-8 : £7.95 : CIP entry B81-28063

294.5 — Hinduism — *For children*

Mitter, Partha. Hindus and Hinduism / Partha and Swasti Mitter. — Hove : Wayland, 1982. — 64p : ill ; 22cm. — (Beliefs and believers)
Bibliography: p61. — Includes index
ISBN 0-85340-908-0 : £3.95 B82-16515

294.5 — Hinduism — *Welsh texts*

Harris, J. G.. Arweiniad at Hindwaeth / J. Glyndwr Harris. — Abertawe [Swansea] : C. Davies, c1980. — 128p : ill,2col.maps,facsims ; 22cm. — (Cyfres crefyddau′r byd)
Bibliography: p122-123. — Includes index
ISBN 0-7154-0578-0 (pbk) : £3.50 B82-17003

294.5′01 — Hinduism — *Philosophical perspectives*

Rammohun Roy, *Raja*. The only true God. — Newcastle upon Tyne (9 Rectory Drive, Newcastle upon Tyne NE3 1XT) : Grevatt and Grevatt, Nov.1982. — [56]p
Translation from the Bengali and Sanskrit
ISBN 0-9507918-1-4 (pbk) : £2.20 : CIP entry B82-29417

294.5′07′1041 — Great Britain. Schools. Curriculum subjects: Hinduism — *For teaching*

A **Handbook** of Hinduism / Hinduism Working Party: Jackie Joicey ... [et al.] ; editor Dermot Killingley ; illustrations Siew-yue Killingley. — [Newcastle upon Tyne] ([Pendower Hall Teachers′ Centre, West Rd., Newcastle upon Tyne, NE15 6PP]) : Newcastle upon Tyne Education Committee, c1980. — iv,110p ; 30cm
Bibliography: p101-109
Unpriced (pbk) B82-09093

294.5′0954 — India *(Republic)*. Hinduism

Radhakrishnan, S.. The Hindu view of life / Radhakrishnan. — London : Unwin Paperbacks, 1980. — 92p ; 20cm. — (Mandala books)
Originally published: London : Allen & Unwin, 1927
ISBN 0-04-294115-6 (pbk) : £1.95 : CIP rev. B80-20197

294.5′211 — Great Britain. National libraries: British Library. *Department of Oriental Manuscripts and Printed Books*. Stock: Eastern Indian manuscripts. Special subjects: Hindu myths. Krishna — *Critical studies*

Losty, Jeremiah P.. Krishna : a Hindu vision of God : scenes from the life of Krishna illustrated in Orissan and other eastern Indian manuscripts in the British Library / Jeremiah P. Losty. — London : British Library, c1980. — 53p : ill(some col.) ; 24cm. — (British Library booklets)
Text, ill on inside covers. — Bibliography: p53
ISBN 0-904654-51-6 (pbk) : £1.50 : CIP rev. B80-32923

294.5′211′0924 — Hindu doctrine. God. Theories of Śaṅkaracārya

Alston, A. J.. Śaṃkara on the absolute / by A.J. Alston. — London (29 Chepstow Villas [W11 3DR]) : Shanti Sadan, 1980 (1981 [printing]). — ix,259p ; 21cm. — (A Śaṃkara source-book ; v.1)
Bibliography: p241-253
Unpriced (pbk) B82-09640

294.5′212 — Hindu myths. Special themes: Animals & sex relations. Symbolic aspects

O′Flaherty, Wendy Doniger. Women, androgynes, and other mythical beasts / Wendy Doniger O′Flaherty. — Chicago ; London : University of Chicago Press, c1980. — xviii,382p,[8]p of plates : ill ; 25cm
Bibliography: p345-362. — Includes index
ISBN 0-226-61849-8 : £16.20 B82-00401

294.5′22 — Hindu doctrine. Man. Soul. Theories of Śaṅkaracārya

Alston, A. J.. Śaṃkara on the soul / by A.J. Alston. — London (29 Chepstow Villas [W11 3DR]) : Shanti Sadan, c1981. — ix,195p ; 21cm. — (A Śaṃkara source-book ; v.3)
Bibliography: p185-190
Unpriced (pbk) B82-09638

294.5′24′0924 — Hindu doctrine. Creation. Theories of Śaṅkaracārya

Alston, A. J.. Śaṃkara on the creation / by A.J. Alston. — London (29 Chepstow Villas [W11 3DR]) : Shanti Sadan, c1980. — vii,249p ; 21cm. — (A Śaṃkara source-book ; v.2)
Bibliography: p237-243
Unpriced (pbk) B82-09639

294.5′42 — Hindu life. Self-realisation

Mata, Daya. [Qualities of a devotee]. Only love / by Daya Mata. — London : Fudge, 1980, c1976. — xvi,277p,[23]p of plates : ill,ports ; 20cm
Originally published: Los Angeles : Self-Realization Fellowship, 1976
ISBN 0-87612-215-2 : £4.50 B82-40568

294.5′43 — Hatha-yoga. Kundalini

Mookerjee, Ajit. Kundalini : the arousal of the inner energy / Ajit Mookerjee. — London : Thames and Hudson, c1982. — 112p : ill(some col.),facsims(some col.) ; 26cm
Bibliography: p101-102. — Includes index
ISBN 0-500-27240-9 (pbk) : £4.95 B82-14864

Sivananda Radha, *Swami*. Kundalini : yoga for the west / Swami Sivananda Radha ; with a foreword by Herbert V. Guenther ; and an introduction by Stanley Krippner. — Boulder [Colo.] ; London : Shambhala ; London : Routledge & Kegan Paul [Distributor], 1981, c1978. — xxii,357p : ill,2ports ; 23cm
Originally published: Spokane, W.A. : Timeless Books, 1978. — Bibliography: p341-345. — Includes index
ISBN 0-394-74884-0 (pbk) : £6.95 B82-13307

294.5′44 — India *(Republic)*. Varanasi. Hindu life

Eck, Diana L.. Banaras. — London : Routledge & K. Paul, Dec.1982. — [413]p
ISBN 0-7100-9430-2 : £15.00 : CIP entry B82-30589

294.5′513 — Sivaism

Danielou, Alain. Shiva and Dionysus. — London : East-West Publications, Apr.1982. — [288]p
Translation of: Shiva et Dionysos
ISBN 0-85692-054-1 (pbk) : £4.95 : CIP entry
Also classified at 292′.211 B82-06256

294.5′61 — Hinduism. Prabhavananda, *Swami*. Interpersonal relationships with Isherwood, Christopher

Isherwood, Christopher. My guru and his disciple / Christopher Isherwood. — [London] : Magnum, 1981, c1980. — 338p ; 17cm
Originally published: London : Eyre Methuen, 1980
ISBN 0-417-05590-0 (pbk) : £1.95
Primary classification 823′.912 B82-17571

294.5′61 — Hinduism. Shraddhānanda, *Swami* — *Biographies*

Jordens, J. T. F.. Swāmī Shraddhānanda : his life and causes / J.T.F. Jordens. — Delhi ; Oxford : Oxford University Press, 1981. — xv,210p,[9]p of plates : ill,ports ; 22cm
Bibliography: p197-203. — Includes index
ISBN 0-19-561252-3 : £8.95 B82-05424

294.5′65 — Illinois. Chicago. International Society for Krishna Consciousness — *Personal observations*

Yanoff, Morris. Where is Joey? : lost among the Hare Krishnas / Morris Yanoff. — Chicago ; London : Swallow Press, c1981 (1982 [printing]). — x,260p ; 24cm
ISBN 0-8040-0414-5 : £12.00 B82-40493

294.5′9218 — Hinduism. Upanishads. Kenapanishad — *Expositions*

Rajneesh, *Bhagwan Shree*. The supreme doctrine : discourses on the kenopanishad / Bhagwan Shree Rajneesh ; compilation by Ma Yoga Vivek ; editors Swami Prem Chinmaya, Ma Ananda Prem. — London : Routledge & Kegan Paul, 1980. — xiv,468p : ports ; 22cm
Includes text in Hindi. — Originally published: Poona : Rajneesh Foundation, 1977
ISBN 0-7100-0572-5 (pbk) : £5.95 : CIP rev. B80-10946

294.6 — SIKHISM

294.6 — Sikhism — *For children*

Kapoor, Sukhbir S.. Sikhs and Sikhism / Sukhbir S. Kapoor. — Hove : Wayland, 1982. — 64p : ill ; 22cm. — (Beliefs and believers)
Bibliography: p81. — Includes index
ISBN 0-85340-907-2 : £3.95 B82-16514

294.6′0954 — India. Sikhism, *1467-1708*

Cole, W. Owen. Sikhism and its Indian context 1467-1708. — London : Darton, Longman & Todd, July 1982. — [352]p
ISBN 0-232-51508-5 : £12.50 : CIP entry B82-12565

294.6′61 — Sikhism. Gurus, *to 1980*

Cole, W. Owen. The guru in Sikhism / W. Owen Cole. — London : Darton, Longman & Todd, 1982. — xi,115p ; 22cm
Bibliography: p108-110. — Includes index
ISBN 0-232-51509-3 (pbk) : £3.95 : CIP rev. B82-02653

294.6'82 — Sikhism. Adi-Granth. Nānak, *Guru*. Hymns. Words — *Punjabi & English dictionaries*

Shackle, C.. A Gurū Nānak glossary / compiled by C. Shackle. — London : School of Oriental and African Studies, University of London, 1981. — xxxi,276p ; 22cm
Entries in the Gurmukhi script, with romanized transcription and English definitions
ISBN 0-7286-0074-9 (pbk) : £10.00 : CIP rev. B80-21394

294.6'82 — Sikhism. Scriptures — *Texts*

Shackle, C.. An introduction to the sacred language of the Sikhs. — London : School of Oriental and African Studies, Jan.1983. — [224]p
ISBN 0-7286-0107-9 (pbk) : £7.00 : CIP entry B82-40303

296 — JUDAISM

296 — Judaism

Marmur, Dow. Beyond survival : reflections on the future of Judaism / Dow Marmur. — London : Darton Longman & Todd, 1982. — xviii,218p ; 22cm
Includes index
ISBN 0-232-51456-9 (pbk) : £7.95 : CIP rev. B82-01314

The **Witness** of the Jews to God / David H.S. Lyon ... [et al.] ; edited by David W. Torrance. — Edinburgh : Handsel, 1982. — viii,180p ; 22cm
ISBN 0-905312-18-x (pbk) : £4.25 B82-13334

296'.09'01 — Judaism, *to 100*

Stone, Michael E.. Scriptures, sects and visions. — Oxford : Blackwell, Jan.1982. — [160]p
Originally published: Petersham, N.S.W. : Maitland Publications, 1980
ISBN 0-631-13008-x : £7.95 : CIP entry B81-34784

296'.09'01 — Judaism, *to ca B.C.100*

Fohrer, Georg. History of Israelite religion / Georg Fohrer ; translated by David E. Green. — London : SPCK, 1973, c1972 (1981 [printing]). — 416p ; 22cm. — (SPCK large paperbacks ; 36)
Translation of: Geschichte der Israelitischen Religion. — Originally published: Nashville : Abingdon, 1972. — Includes index
ISBN 0-281-03825-2 (pbk) : £7.50 B82-08185

296'.0941 — Great Britain. Judaism

Hear, O Israel : (information for Christians). — London (189 Whitechapel Rd., E1 1DN) : Messianic Testimony, [1982?]. — 1folded sheet : ill,1map ; 21cm
Unpriced B82-35413

296.1'206 — Judaism. Talmud — *Expositions*

Davidmann, M.. Freedom now, freedom for ever / M. Davidmann. — [Stanmore] : Social Organisation, [1982, c1978]. — 4v. : ill,1geneal.table ; 30cm
Originally published: 1978
ISBN 0-85192-022-5 (pbk) : £17.95
ISBN 0-85192-023-3 (v.2) : £4.90
ISBN 0-85192-024-1 (v.3) : £4.90
ISBN 0-85192-025-x (v.4) : £4.90 B82-35769

296.1'2306 — Judaism. Mishnah — *Critical studies*

Neusner, Jacob. Judaism : the evidence of the Mishnah / Jacob Neusner. — Chicago ; London : University of Chicago Press, 1981. — xix,419p ; 24cm
Includes index
ISBN 0-226-57617-5 : £15.00 B82-09575

296.1'2407 — Judaism. Talmud Yerushalmi — *Texts with commentaries*

[Talmud Yerushalmi. *English*]. The Talmud of the land of Israel : a preliminary translation and explanation / translated by Jacob Neusner. — Chicago ; London : University of Chicago Press. — (Chicago studies in the history of Judaism)
Vol.34: Horayot and Niddah. — c1982. — xiii,243p ; 24cm
Includes index
ISBN 0-226-57694-9 : £17.50 B82-38449

296.1'6 — Judaism. Cabala

Halevi, Z'ev ben Shimon. Tree of life. — London : Rider, Feb.1983. — [208]p
ISBN 0-09-150011-7 (pbk) : £2.95 : CIP entry B82-36436

Hoffman, Edward. The way of splendor : Jewish mysticism and modern psychology / Edward Hoffman. — Boulder [Colo.] ; London : Shambhala ; London : Routledge & Kegan Paul [Distributor], 1981. — viii,247p : ill ; 22cm
Bibliography: p235-243. — Includes index
ISBN 0-394-52152-8 (cased) : Unpriced
ISBN 0-394-74885-9 (pbk) : £5.95
ISBN 0-87773-209-4 (U.S.)
ISBN 0-87773-210-8 (pbk : U.S.) B82-13306

296.1'72 — Jewish law. Codes: Maimonides. Code of Maimonides — *Expositions*

Twersky, Isadore. Introduction to the Code of Maimonides (Mishneh Torah). — London : Yale University Press, Mar.1982. — [656]p. — (Yale Judaica series ; 22)
ISBN 0-300-02846-6 (pbk) : £7.95 : CIP entry B82-12886

296.1'8 — Bible. O.T.. Special subjects. Jewish law — *Critical studies*

Boecker, Hans Jochen. Law and the administration of justice in the Old Testament and ancient East / Hans Jochen Boecker ; translated by Jeremy Moiser. — London : SPCK, 1980. — 224p ; 22cm
Translated from the German. — Bibliography: p209-218. — Includes index
ISBN 0-281-03792-2 (pbk) : £8.50 B82-39797

296.1'8 — Jewish law — *Codes*

Maimonides. The book of knowledge : from the Mishnah Torah of Maimonides / translated from the Hebrew by H.M. Russell and J. Weinberg. — Edinburgh : Royal College of Physicians of Edinburgh, 1981. — xi,135p ; 22cm. — (Publication / Royal College of Physicians of Edinburgh ; no.55)
Translated from the Hebrew
ISBN 0-85405-038-8 (pbk) : Unpriced B82-13530

296.3'87 — Jewish doctrine. Israel

Davies, W. D. *(1911-)*. The territorial dimension of Judaism / W.D. Davies. — Berkeley ; London : University of California Press, c1982. — xviii,169p ; 22cm. — ([A Quantum book])
Bibliography: p149-156. — Includes index
ISBN 0-520-04331-6 : £11.25 B82-31090

296.3'872 — Judaism. Relations with Christian church, *70-1978*

Stevens, George H.. Strife between brothers / George H. Stevens. — London : Olive Press, 1979. — 64p ; 18cm
ISBN 0-904054-13-6 (pbk) : £1.00
Primary classification 261.2'6 B82-05428

296.6'1'0924 — Judaism. Rabbis: Jung, Leo — *Biographies*

Jung, Leo. The path of a pioneer : the autobiography of Leo Jung. — London : Soncino, c1980. — xix,408p,[8]p of plates : 1ill,facsims,ports ; 24cm. — (The Jewish library ; 8)
Unpriced B82-41047

296.7'1'0924 — Jewish life. Mysticism. Scholem, Gershom. Interpersonal relationships with Benjamin, Walter — *Personal observations*

Scholem, Gershom. Walter Benjamin : the story of a friendship. — London : Faber, Aug.1982. — [242]p
Translation of: Walter Benjamin : die Geschichte einer Freundschaft
ISBN 0-571-11970-0 : £10.00 : CIP entry
Primary classification 801'.95'0924 B82-18577

296.7'4 — Jewish life — *Personal observations*

Bermant, Chaim. On the other hand / Chaim Bermant. — London : Robson, 1982. — 160p ; 23cm
ISBN 0-86051-185-5 : £6.95 : CIP rev. B82-20869

297 — ISLAM

297 — Islam

Gilsenan, Michael. Recognizing Islam. — London : Croom Helm, July 1982. — [288]p
ISBN 0-7099-1119-x : £12.95 : CIP entry B82-17208

Martin, Richard C.. Islam : a cultural perspective / Richard C. Martin. — Englewood Cliffs ; London : Prentice-Hall, c1982. — xiii,178p : ill,2maps ; 23cm. — (Prentice-Hall series in world religions)
Bibliography: p172-174. — Includes index
ISBN 0-13-506345-0 (pbk) : £5.95 B82-20077

Sarwar, Ghulam. Islam : beliefs and teachings. — 2nd ed. — London (130 Stroud Green Rd, N4 3RZ) : Muslim Educational Trust, Mar.1982. — [192]p
ISBN 0-907261-03-5 (pbk) : £1.50 : CIP entry B82-06064

Tames, Richard. The Muslim world / Richard Tames. — London : Macdonald, 1982. — 45p : col.ill,col.maps ; 29cm. — (Religions of the world)
Bibliography: p43. — Includes index
ISBN 0-356-07520-6 : £3.95 B82-37623

Waddy, Charis. The Muslim mind. — 2nd ed. — London : Longman, Sept.1982. — [216]p
Previous ed.: 1976
ISBN 0-582-78346-1 (cased) : £10.95 : CIP entry
ISBN 0-582-78345-3 (pbk) : £3.95 B82-20275

297 — Islam — *Christian viewpoints*

Ali, Michael Nazir. Islam : a Christian perspective. — Exeter : Paternoster Press, June 1982. — [192]p
Originally published: London : Marshall Morgan & Scott, 1980
ISBN 0-85364-333-4 (pbk) : £4.40 : CIP entry B82-12017

Goldsmith, Martin. Islam and Christian witness. — London : Hodder & Stoughton, Nov.1982. — [160]p
ISBN 0-340-26968-5 (pbk) : £1.75 : CIP entry B82-27338

Miller, William M.. A Christian's response to Islam / William M. Miller. — Bromley : STL, 1981, c1976. — 178p ; 18cm
Originally published: Nutley, N.J. : Presbyterian and Reformed Publishing, 1976. — Bibliography: p177-178
ISBN 0-903843-56-0 (pbk) B82-06394

297 — Islam — *For children*

Murad, Khurram. Love your God. — Leicester : Islamic Foundation, Dec.1982. — [36]p. — (Muslim children's history ; 11)
ISBN 0-86037-108-5 (pbk) : £0.95 : CIP entry B82-39265

297 — Islam — *For schools*

Thompson, Jan. Islamic belief and practice / Jan Thompson. — London : Edward Arnold, 1981. — 66p : ill,maps,facsims ; 21cm
Includes index
ISBN 0-7131-0586-0 (pbk) : £1.60 : CIP rev. B81-28032

297 — Islam — *Welsh texts*

Harris, J. G.. Arweiniad at Islam / J. Glyndwr Harris. — Caernarfon (Lôn Ddewi, Caernarfon LL55 1ER) : Gwasg Pantycelyn, 1981. — 138p : ill,maps(some col.),1port ; 22cm. — (Cyfres crefyddau'r byd)
Bibliography: p130-131. — Includes index
£4.00 (pbk) B82-41003

297 — Muslims: Martyrs

Muṭahharī, Murtaẓā. The martyr / Murtaza Mutahhary. — Karachi : Islamic Seminary Pakistan ; London (284 Kilburn High Rd., NW6 2DP) : Islamic Seminary [distributor], 1979 (1980 printing). — 61p ; 18cm
Translated from the Persian
Unpriced (pbk) B82-13617

297'.05 — Islam — *Serials*

an-Nūr / diterbitkan dan diedarkan percuma oleh jabatan penuntut malaysia London. — [Bilangan 1, tahun 1 (4 Jumada al-Ukhra 1400) [11 July 1980]]-. — London (44 Bryanston Sq., W1H 8AJ) : Malaysian Students Department, 1981-. — v. ; 30cm
Monthly. — Text in Malay and English, some Arabic translations. — Also entitled: an-Nuur. — Description based on: Bilangan 6, Tahun 2 (25 Zulhijjah 1401) [23 October 1981]
ISSN 0262-0693 = an-Nūr : Unpriced B82-17249

297'.07'1041 — Great Britain. Schools. Curriculum subjects: Islam — *For teaching*

A **Handbook** on Islam / Islam Working Party: C. Brannen ... [et al.] ; editor Zoë Jenkins. — [Newcastle upon Tyne] ([Pendower Hall Teachers' Centre, West Rd., Newcastle upon Tyne, NE15 6PP]) : Newcastle upon Tyne Education Committee, 1980. — vi,46p ; 30cm
Bibliography: p43-46
Unpriced (pbk) B82-09092

Tames, Richard. Approaches to Islam / Richard Tames. — London : Murray, 1982. — 264p : ill ; 22cm. — (World religions in education)
Includes bibliographies and index
ISBN 0-7195-3914-5 (pbk) : £3.95 : CIP rev. B82-14945

297'.09 — Islam, *to 1981*

Voll, John Obert. Islam : continuity and change in the modern world. — London : Longman, Nov.1982. — [400]p
ISBN 0-582-78343-7 : £18.95 : CIP entry B82-26543

297'.095 — Asia. Islam

The **Crescent** in the East : Islam in Asia Minor / edited by Raphael Israeli. — London : Curzon, 1982. — 245p : 1map ; 22cm
ISBN 0-7007-0143-5 : £6.75 : CIP rev. B82-08415

297'.0966 — West Africa. Islam, *to 1980*

Clarke, Peter B. (Peter Bernard). West Africa and Islam : a study of religious development from the 8th to the 20th century / by Peter B. Clarke. — London : Edward Arnold, 1982. — viii,275p : ill,maps ; 23cm
Bibliography: p268-270. — Includes index
ISBN 0-7131-8029-3 (pbk) : £5.50 : CIP rev. B81-37564

297'.0966 — West Africa. Islam, *to 1981*

Hiskett, Mervyn. The development of Islam in West Africa. — London : Longman, Dec.1982. — [360]p
ISBN 0-582-64692-8 (cased) : £15.00 : CIP entry
ISBN 0-582-64694-4 (pbk) : £5.95 B82-30068

297'.1224 — Islam. Koran. *English & Arabic — Texts*

Doi, A. Rahman I.. Introduction to the Qur'an / A. Rahman I. Doi. — Sevenoaks : Arewa, 1981. — v,90p ; 22cm
Bibliography: p90. — Includes selections from the text of the Qur'an in Arabic, with transliteration and English translation
ISBN 0-340-26705-4 (pbk) : £1.50 : CIP rev.
Primary classification 297'.1226 B81-13581

[**Koran**. *English & Arabic. 1981*]. The Quran : the eternal revelation vouchsafed to Muhammad the Seal of the Prophets / Arabic text with a new translation by Muhammad Zafrulla Khan. — 3rd ed., rev. — London : Curzon, 1981. — lx,673p ; 22cm
Parallel Arabic text and English translation, preface and introduction in English. — Previous ed.: 1975. — Includes index
ISBN 0-7007-0148-6 : £6.50 : CIP rev. B81-39227

297'.1225'21 — Islam. Koran — *English texts*

[**Koran**. *English. 1982*]. The Koran interpreted. — Oxford : Oxford University Press, Nov.1982. — [688]p. — (The World's classics)
Originally published: London : Allen & Unwin, 1955
ISBN 0-19-281628-4 (pbk) : £1.50 : CIP entry B82-26898

[**Koran**. *English. Selections*]. Gleanings from the glorious Quran / [compiled by] Aziz Ahmed. — Karachi ; Oxford : Oxford University Press, 1980. — xxi,104p ; 22cm
Selections from the Koran, translated by Marmaduke Pickthall, and originally published in The meaning of the glorious Koran
ISBN 0-19-577280-6 (pbk) : £3.50 B82-00504

297'.1225'21 — Islam. Koran. *English — Texts*

[**Koran**. *English. Selections. 1980*]. Selections from the Koran / by Sirdar Ikbal Ali Shah. — London : Octagon, 1980. — xiii,94p ; 20cm
Translated from the Arabic
ISBN 0-900860-85-5 : Unpriced B82-21524

297'.1226 — Islam. Koran — *Critical studies — For West African students*

Doi, A. Rahman I.. Introduction to the Qur'an / A. Rahman I. Doi. — Sevenoaks : Arewa, 1981. — v,90p ; 22cm
Bibliography: p90. — Includes selections from the text of the Qur'an in Arabic, with transliteration and English translation
ISBN 0-340-26705-4 (pbk) : £1.50 : CIP rev.
Also classified at 297'.1224 B81-13581

Lemu, B. Aisha. The Qur'an. — London : Hodder & Stoughton, Feb.1983. — [64]p. — (Junior Islamic studies ; bk.2A)
ISBN 0-340-32791-x (pbk) : £1.50 : CIP entry B82-36316

297'.1226 — Islam. Koran — *Expositions*

Khalifa, Mohammad. The sublime Qur'an and orientalism. — London : Longman, Sept.1982. — [288]p
ISBN 0-582-78036-5 : £9.95 : CIP entry B82-20273

Muṭahharī, Murtaẓā. Master and mastership. — Karachi : Islamic Seminary Pakistan ; London (284 Kilburn High Rd., NW6 2DP) : Islamic Seminary [distributor], 1980. — 74p ; 18cm
Translated from the Persian. — Written by Murtaza Mutahhary
Unpriced (pbk) B82-13615

297'.1228 — Islam. Koran. Special subjects: Christianity

Denffer, Ahmad von. Christians in the Qur'an and the Sunna : an assessment from the sources to help define our relationship / Ahmad von Denffer. — Leicester : Islamic Foundation, 1979. — 46p ; 30cm. — (Seminar papers ; 2)
Bibliography: p45-46
ISBN 0-86037-056-9 (pbk) : Unpriced B82-32805

297'.1228 — Islam. Koran. Special subjects: Elementary particles

at-Tarjumana, 'A'isha 'Abd ar-Rahman. The subatomic world in the Qur'an / Aisha 'Abd ar-Rahman at-Tarjumana. — Norwich : Diwan, 1981, c1980. — 31p ; 18cm. — (The Darqawi Institute papers)
ISBN 0-906512-08-5 (pbk) : Unpriced B82-17140

297'.1229 — Islam. Koran. Sūrat al-Hujurāt — *Critical studies*

Ahsan, Muhammad Manazir. The Islamic attitude to social relations in the light of Sūra al-Hujurat, verses 10-12 / Muhammad Manazir Ahsan. — Leicester : Islamic Foundation, c1979. — 13p ; 30cm. — (Seminar papers ; 3)
ISBN 0-86037-052-6 (pbk) : Unpriced B82-32806

297'.12404 — Islam. Hadith — *Critical studies — For West African students*

Doi, A. Rahman I.. Introduction to the Hadith : traditions of prophet Muhammad / A. Rahman I. Doi. — Sevenoaks : Arewa, 1981. — 130p ; 22cm
Bibliography: p130. — Includes selections from the text of the Hadith in Arabic, with transliteration and English translation
ISBN 0-340-26706-2 (pbk) : £1.75 : CIP rev.
Also classified at 297'.1240521 B81-21650

297'.1240521 — Islam. Hadith. *English & Arabic — Texts*

Doi, A. Rahman I.. Introduction to the Hadith : traditions of prophet Muhammad / A. Rahman I. Doi. — Sevenoaks : Arewa, 1981. — 130p ; 22cm
Bibliography: p130. — Includes selections from the text of the Hadith in Arabic, with transliteration and English translation
ISBN 0-340-26706-2 (pbk) : £1.75 : CIP rev.
Primary classification 297'.12404 B81-21650

297'.1240531 — Islam. Hadith — *German texts*

Denffer, Ahmad von. Ein Tag mit dem Propheten. — Leicester : Islamic Foundation, Jan.1982. — [128]p
Translation of: A day with the Prophet
ISBN 0-86037-106-9 (pbk) : £1.95 : CIP entry B82-00179

297'.19785 — Macroeconomics — *Islamic viewpoints*

Metwally, Mokhtar M.. Macroeconomic models of Islamic doctrines / M.M. Metwally. — London : J.K. Publishers, c1981. — x,78p : ill ; 22cm
Bibliography: p75-76. — Includes index
ISBN 0-906216-89-3 (pbk) : £4.00 B82-12378

297'.2 — Islamic doctrine

aṣ-Ṣadr, Muḥammad Bāqir. HE : his messenger and his message / [Muhammad Baqir Al Sadr]. — Karachi : Islamic Seminary Pakistan ; London (284 Kilburn High Rd., NW6 2DB) : Islamic Seminary [distributor], 1980. — 109p ; 21cm
Translation from the Arabic
Unpriced (pbk) B82-14439

Rationality of Islam. — Rev. and enl. — Karachi : Islamic Seminary Pakistan ; London (284 Kilburn High Rd., NW6 2DP) : Islamic Seminary [distributor], 1980. — 168p ; 21cm
Translated from the Arabic. — Previous ed.: 1978
Unpriced (pbk) B82-13614

Universal Islamic declaration. — London (16 Grosvenor Crescent, SW1) : Islamic Council of Europe, 1980. — 20p ; 15x21cm
£0.50 (pbk) B82-28384

297'.2 — Islamic doctrine — *For children*

Children's guide to Islam. — Karachi : Islamic Seminary Pakistan ; London (284 Kilburn High Rd., NW6 2DB) : Islamic Seminary [distributor], 1980. — 109p : ill ; 22cm
Unpriced (pbk) B82-14440

297'.2 — Sufi doctrine

Key concepts in Sufi understanding / edited by Hafiz Jamal. — London (BM/Sufi Studies, WC1V 6XX) : Society for Sufi Studies, c1980. — 47p ; 21cm
£2.50 (pbk) B82-17131

Visits to Sufi centres : some recent research papers on Sufis and Sufism. — London : BM/Sufi Studies, WC1V 6XX : Society for Sufi Studies, c1980. — 35p ; 21cm
£2.50 (pbk) B82-17132

297'.20413 — Malikite Islamic doctrine — *For West African students*

Doi, A. Rahman I.. The cardinal principles of Islam : according to the Maliki system / A. Rahman I. Doi. — Sevenoaks : Arewa, 1981. — ix,144p ; 22cm
Bibliography: p143-144
ISBN 0-340-26704-6 (pbk) : £2.00 : CIP rev. B81-07475

297'.211 — Islamic doctrine. Polytheism

Surty, M. I. H. Ismail. The Qur'amic concept of al-Shirk. — London (68A Delancey St., NW1 7RY) : Ta-Ha, Mar.1982. — [70]p
ISBN 0-907461-25-5 (pbk) : £0.70 : CIP entry B82-11970

297'.23 — Islamic doctrine. Mahdi

aṣ-Ṣadr, Muḥammad Bāqir. The awaited saviour / [Baqir Al-Sadr]. — Karachi : Islamic Seminary Pakistan ; London (284 Kilburn High Rd., NW6 2DB) : Islamic Seminary [distributor], c1979. — 109p ; 18cm
Translated from the Arabic
Unpriced (pbk) B82-15384

297'.4 — Sufism

ad-Darqāwī, Muhammad al-'Arabī ibn Ahmad. The Darqawi way : letters from the shaykh to the fugara / Mawlay al-Arabi ad-Darqawi. — Norwich, Diwan, 1981, c1979. — 325p ; 18cm
ISBN 0-906512-06-9 (pbk) : Unpriced B82-17139

Gairdner, W. H. T.. Theories, practices and training systems of a Sufi school / by W.H.T. Gairdner. — London : BM/Sufi Studies, WC1V 6XX : Society for Sufi Studies, c1980. — 33p ; 21cm
£3.00 (pbk) B82-17130

Hossain, Seyyed F.. The Sufis of today / by Seyyed F. Hossain. — London : [Octagon], 1981. — 27p ; 22cm
£2.50 (pbk) B82-17128

Idries Shah. Evenings with Idries Shah : Sufi discussions collected by R. Easterling and Kamil Hanafy. — [London] ([14 Baker St., W1M 1DA]) : [Octagon], c1981. — 40p ; 22cm
£3.00 (pbk) B82-13205

Idries Shah. Letters and lectures : of Idries Shah / compiled and edited by Adam Musa. — [London] ([14 Baker St., W1M 1DA]) : [Octagon], c1981. — 40p ; 21cm
£2.50 (pbk) B82-13204

Idries Shah. Thinkers of the east : studies in experientialism / Idries Shah. — London : Octagon, 1977, c1982 (1982 [printing]). — 198p ; 23cm
Originally published: London : Cape, 1971
ISBN 0-900860-46-4 : Unpriced B82-21660

In a Sufi monastery : and other papers / by N. Siddiqi ... [et al.]. — London (13 Marylebone Rd., NW1 5JB) : Designist Communications, c1982. — 35p ; 21cm
£2.50 (pbk) B82-31700

Mir Valiuddin. Contemplative disciplines in Sufism / Mir Valiuddin ; edited by Gulshan Khakee. — London : East-West Publications, c1980. — xxvii,173p ; 22cm
Bibliography: p167-173
ISBN 0-85692-007-x : £5.95 : CIP rev. B80-06289

Ritual, initiation and secrets in Sufi circles. — London : BM/Sufi Studies, WC1V 6XX : Society for Sufi Studies, c1980. — 48p ; 21cm
£2.50 (pbk) B82-17129

Stoddart, William. Sufism. — Wellingborough : Aquarian, May 1982. — [96]p
Originally published: Wellingborough : Thorsons, 1976
ISBN 0-85030-303-6 (pbk) : £2.95 : CIP entry B82-07843

Sufi principles, action, learning methods, imitators, meeting-places - and the Western seeker / papers by: Humayun Abbas ... [et al.]. — London (BM/Sufi Studies, WC1V 6XX) : Society for Sufi Studies, c1980. — 64p ; 30cm
Cover title
£2.50 (pbk) B82-17101

297'.4 — Sufism — *Early works*

Ibn 'Atā'Allāh al-Iskandarī, Ahmad ibn Muhammad. The book of wisdom : Ibn 'Ata'Illah. Intimate conversations / Kwaja Abdullah Ansari : introduction, translation and notes of The book of wisdom by Victor Danner and of Intimate conversations by Wheeler M. Thackston / preface by Annemarie Schimmel. — London : SPCK, 1979, c1978. — ix,233p ; 23cm. — (The Classics of Western spirituality)
Translation of: Ibn 'Atā'Allāh's al-Hikam al-Atā'iyah, from the Arabic and of al-Ansārī's Munājāt, from the Persian. — Originally published: New York : Paulist Press, 1978. — Includes index
ISBN 0-281-03689-6 (pbk) : £6.50 B82-12292

Waliullah, *Shah.* The sacred knowledge of the higher functions of the mind : : Altaf al-Quds / by Shah Waliullah of Delhi ; translated by G. N. Jalbani ; revised and edited by David Pendlebury. — London : Octagon, c1982. — vii,103p ; 23cm
Translation of: Altaf-al-quds fi ma'arifat lataifin-nafs
ISBN 0-900860-93-6 : £7.00 B82-40716

297'.4'0922 — Nimatullahi Sufism — *Biographies*

Nurbakhsh, Javad. Masters of the path : a history of the masters of the Nimatullahi Sufi Order / Javad Nurbakhsh. — New York ; London : Khaniqahi-Nimatullahi, c1980. — 130p : ill,ports ; 21cm
Includes index
ISBN 0-933546-03-3 (pbk) : Unpriced B82-17392

297'.4'0924 — Egypt. Sufism. Al-Sha'rānī, 'Abd al-Wahhāb ibn Ahmad — *Critical studies*

Winter, Michael, *1934-.* Society and religion in early Ottoman Egypt : studies in the writings of 'Abd al-Wahhāb al-Sha'rānī / Michael Winter. — New Brunswick ; London : Transaction Books, c1982. — ix,345p ; 24cm. — (Studies in Islamic culture and history)
Bibliography: p318-326. — Includes index
ISBN 0-87855-351-7 : £29.00 B82-12033

297'.4'0924 — Sufism — *Personal observations*

Dervish, H. B. M.. Journeys with a Sufi master / by H.B.M. Dervish ; [translated by A.W.T. Tiragi] ; [edited by A.L. Griffiths] ; [revised by Adib Jamalian]. — London : Octagon, c1982. — xvi,243p ; 23cm
Translated from the Arabic
ISBN 0-900860-95-2 : £8.00 B82-40721

297'.42 — Islam. Conversion of Christians — *Conference proceedings*

Chambésy Dialogue Consultation *(Conference : 1976).* Christian mission and Islamic da'wah : proceedings of the Chambésy Dialogue Consultation. — Leicester : Islamic Foundation, c1982. — 103p ; 22cm
ISBN 0-86037-110-7 (pbk) : Unpriced : CIP rev.
Primary classification 248.2'46 B82-03126

297'.42 — Sufism. Dervishes — *Conference proceedings*

Documents on contemporary Dervish communities : a symposium / collected, edited and arranged by Roy Weaver Davidson. — London : Octagon, [c1982]. — 28p ; 21cm
Bibliography: p28
ISBN 0-86304-015-2 (pbk) : £2.50 B82-25032

297'.42'0924 — Islamic life. Mysticism. Ghani, Ghassem — *Correspondence, diaries, etc.*

Ghani, Ghassem. The memoirs of Dr Ghassem Ghani. — London : Cyrus Ghani ; London : Ithaca [distributor]
Urdu text
Vol.5: The letters of Kamal al-Molk and Mohammad Qazvini to Ghassem Ghani. — 1981. — 328p,[12]p of plates : ill,facsims,ports ; 23cm
Unpriced B82-01454

Ghani, Ghassem. The memoirs of Dr Ghassem Ghani. — London : Cyrus Ghani ; London : Ithaca [distributor]
Parallel Urdu text and English translation. — Opposite pages bear duplicate numbering
Vol.6: A comparison of the translation into English of a selection of the poems of Hafiz by Gertrude Bell with the original text. — 1981. — 3,101,101p ; 23cm
Unpriced B82-01455

297'.43 — Islamic life. Prayer

al-'Alawī al-Mustaghanimī, Ahmad ibn Mu s tafa. The two invocations : the unique name : the prayer on the prophet / by Shaykh al-'Alawi. — Norwich : Diwan, c1980. — 43p ; 18cm
ISBN 0-906512-05-0 (pbk) : £1.00 B82-17141

297'.43 — Islamic life. Prayer — *For children*

al-Asifi, Mehdi. Al salat / [Allama Mehdi Asifi]. — Karachi : Islamic Seminary Pakistan ; London (284 Kilburn High Rd., NW6 2DB) : Islamic Seminary Publications, 1980. — 98p : ill ; 22cm
Translation from the Arabic
Unpriced (pbk) B82-14890

297'.43 — Sufi life — *Allegories*

al-Muqaddasī, Muḥammad ibn Aḥmad. Revelation of the secrets of the birds and flowers / by Sheikh Izzidin son of Abdusalam son of Alimad son of Ghanim, Al-Muqaddisi ; [translated from the Arabic by Irene Hoare and Darya Galy] ; [translation edited by Denise Winn]. — London : Octagon, 1980. — 73,118p ; 22cm
Arabic text, English translation
ISBN 0-900860-75-8 : Unpriced B82-21709

297'.44 — Islamic life

Islam : a code of social life / [translation M. Fazal Haq]. — Karachi : Islamic Seminary Pakistan ; London (284 Kilburn High Rd., NW6 2DP) : Islamic Seminary [distributor], 1980. — 190,76p ; 22cm
Text in English and Arabic
Unpriced (pbk) B82-13613

Roberts, D. S.. Islam : a Westerner's guide / D.S. Roberts. — Feltham : Hamlyn, 1982, c1981. — 181p : maps ; 18cm
Originally published: London : Kogan Page, 1981
ISBN 0-600-20346-8 (pbk) : £1.50 B82-14467

What it means to be a Muslim. — Ely : EARO, Resource and Technology Centre, c1977. — 16p : ill ; 15x21cm
ISBN 0-904463-44-3 (pbk) : £0.70 B82-13782

297'.44 — Islamic life. Love — *For children*

Murad, Khurram. Love your brother, love your neighbour. — Leicester : Islamic Foundation, Oct.1982. — [36]p. — (Muslim children's library ; 9)
ISBN 0-86037-115-8 (pbk) : £0.95 : CIP entry B82-29033

297'.44 — Sufi life

Idries Shah. Seeker after truth : a handbook : from tales, discussions and teachings, letters and lectures / by Idries Shah. — London : Octagon, c1982. — viii,214p ; 23cm
ISBN 0-900860-91-x : £8.00 B82-24991

Thurlnas, Chawan. Current Sufi activity : work, literature, groups and techniques / by Chawan Thurlnas. — [London] : [Octagon], c1980. — 40p : 1ill ; 21cm
Bibliography: p39-40
£2.50 (pbk) B82-17134

297'.446 — Islamic life. Fasting

Hamidullah, Muhammad. Why fast? : spiritual & temporal study of fast in Islam / Muhammad Hamidullah. — 2nd ed. repr. — Luton : Apex, [1982?]. — 19p ; 22cm. — (Centre culturel islamique Paris series ; 10)
Previous ed.: 197-?
ISBN 0-904812-41-3 (unbound) : Unpriced B82-38167

297'.55 — Muslim pilgrimages to Mecca

Guellouz, Ezzedine. Pilgrimage to Mecca / [introduction Touhami Nagra] ; [text Ezzedine Guellouz] ; [photographer Abdelaziz Frikha]. — London : East-West Publications, 1980. — 208p : ill(some col.),col.maps ; 34cm
Ill on lining papers
ISBN 0-85692-059-2 : £25.00 B82-25202

297'.63 — Islam. Muhammad *(Prophet)* — *Biographies*

Lings, Martin. Muhammad. — London : Allen & Unwin, Jan.1983. — [384]p
ISBN 0-04-297042-3 : £12.50 : CIP entry B82-33596

297'.63 — Islam. Muhammad *(Prophet)* — *Biographies* *continuation*

Rahman, Afzalur. Muhammad. — London (78 Gillespie Rd, N5 1LN) : Muslim Schools Trust, Dec.1981. — [300]p
ISBN 0-907052-11-8 (cased) : £5.00 : CIP entry
ISBN 0-907052-10-x (pbk) : £3.00 B81-31520

297'.63 — Islam. Muhammad *(Prophet)* — *Stories for children*

Tarantino, Mardijah Aldrich. Marvellous stories from the life of Muhammad / Mardijah Aldrich Tarantino. — Leicester : Islamic Foundation, c1982. — 120p : ill(some col.) ; 21cm. — (Muslim children's library)
ISBN 0-86037-103-4 (pbk) : Unpriced : CIP rev. B81-39250

297'.89 — Bahaism

Nakhjavání, Bahíyyih. Response / by Bahíyyih Nakhjavání. — Oxford : Ronald, c1981. — x,134p ; 22cm
Bibliography: p125-126
ISBN 0-85398-106-x (cased) : £3.85
ISBN 0-85398-107-8 (pbk) : Unpriced B82-12104

297'.89 — Iran. Bahais. Persecution, *1979-1981*

Nash, Geoffrey. Iran's secret pogrom : the conspiracy to wipe out the Baha'is / Geoffrey Nash. — Sudbury : Spearman, 1982. — 156p : ill,facsims,ports ; 23cm
Bibliography: p155-156
ISBN 0-85435-005-5 (cased) : £4.95
ISBN 0-85435-015-2 (pbk) : Unpriced B82-25006

297'.89 — Iran. Bahais. Persecution, *1980-1981*

Sears, William. A cry from the heart : the Bahá'is in Iran / by William Sears. — Oxford : Ronald, 1982. — 219p : ill,facsims,ports ; 21cm
ISBN 0-85398-133-7 (cased) : £3.75
ISBN 0-85398-134-5 (pbk) : £1.15 B82-25325

297'.89 — Iran. Bahais. Persecution, *to 1979*

Cooper, Roger. The Baha'is of Iran / by Roger Cooper. — London (36 Craven St., WC2N 5NG) : Minority Rights Group, 1982. — 16p : 1ill ; 30cm. — (Report / Minority Rights Group, ISSN 0305-6252 ; no.51)
£1.20 (pbk) B82-26619

297'.89 — Iran. Hurmuzak. Bahais. Persecution, *1955*

Labíb, Muhammad. The seven martyrs of Hurmuzak / by Muhammad Labíb ; translated from the Persian and with a foreword by Moojan Momen. — Oxford : Ronald, c1981. — xiii,63p : ill,1geneal.table,maps,ports ; 21cm
Translated from the Persian
ISBN 0-85398-105-1 (cased) : Unpriced
ISBN 0-85398-104-3 (pbk) : £1.70 B82-31680

297'.89'0924 — Bahaism. Kelsey, Curtis — *Biographies*

Rutstein, Nathan. He loved and served : the story of Curtis Kelsey / by Nathan Rutstein. — Oxford : Ronald, 1982. — 185p,[12]p of plates : ill,ports ; 22cm
ISBN 0-85398-120-5 (cased) : £5.25
ISBN 0-85398-121-3 (pbk) : Unpriced B82-35763

297'.89'0924 — Bahaism. K h ánum — *Biographies*

Gail, Marzieh. Khánum / as remembered by Marzieh Gail. — Oxford : George Ronald, c1981. — 40p,[1]leaf of plates : 1col.port ; 21cm
ISBN 0-85398-112-4 : Unpriced B82-26612

297'.89'0956 — Middle East. Bahaism, *to 1979*

Braun, Eunice. A crown of beauty : the Bahá'í faith and the Holy Land / written by Eunice Braun ; concept and design by Hugh E. Chance. — Oxford : George Ronald, c1982. — 103p : ill(some col.),maps,1col.port ; 28cm
Map on lining papers. — Bibliography: p103
ISBN 0-85398-139-6 (cased) : £7.50
ISBN 0-85398-140-x (pbk) : Unpriced B82-37910

297'.892 — Bahai doctrine

Shoghi, *effendi*. The dispensation of Bahá'u'lláh / by Shoghi Effendi. — London : Bahá'í Publishing Trust, 1981, c1947. — 69p ; 19cm
ISBN 0-900125-46-2 (pbk) : £0.95 B82-19708

297'.8944 — Bahai life

Excellence in all things / compiled by the Research Department of the Universal House of Justice. — Oakham : Bahá'í Publishing Trust, 1981. — iii leaves,18p ; 21cm
£0.70 (unbound) B82-19709

297'.8982 — Bahaism. Scriptures — *Texts with commentaries*

Bahá Ulláh. These perspicuous verses : a passage from the writings of Bahá'u'lláh / with notes by Robert W. McLaughlin. — Oxford : George Ronald, c1982. — 94p ; 22cm
ISBN 0-85398-118-3 (cased) : £3.50
ISBN 0-85398-119-1 (pbk) : Unpriced B82-26616

299.1/4 — NON-CHRISTIAN RELIGIONS. INDO-EUROPEAN, SEMITIC, HAMITIC, URAL-ALTAIC

299'.31 — Ancient Egyptian myths — *For children*

Pinch, Geraldine. Gods and pharaohs from Egyptian mythology. — London : Peter Lowe, Sept.1982. — [136]p
ISBN 0-85654-043-9 : £4.95 : CIP entry B82-22436

299'.31 — Ancient Egyptian religion

David, Rosalie. The ancient Egyptians : religious beliefs and practices / A. Rosalie David. — London : Routledge & Kegan Paul, 1982. — xvi,260p,[16]p of plates : ill,maps,plans,ports ; 23cm. — (Library of religious beliefs and practices)
Includes bibliographies and index
ISBN 0-7100-0877-5 (cased) : £9.95
ISBN 0-7100-0878-3 (pbk) : £5.95 B82-24905

Lamy, Lucie. Egyptian mysteries : new light on ancient knowledge / Lucie Lamy. — London : Thames and Hudson, c1981. — 96p : ill(some col.),1map ; 28cm. — (Art and imagination)
Bibliography: p96
ISBN 0-500-81024-9 (pbk) : £3.95 B82-01789

299'.31 — Ancient Egyptian religion. Gods & goddesses

Shorter, Alan W.. The Egyptian gods : a handbook / by Alan W. Shorter. — London : Routledge & Kegan Paul, 1937 (1981 [printing]). — xii,143p,[4]p of plates : ill,1facsim ; 19cm
ISBN 0-7100-0982-8 (pbk) : £2.60 B82-00569

299.5 — NON-CHRISTIAN RELIGIONS OF EAST AND SOUTHEAST ASIAN ORIGIN

299'.51'0901 — Chinese religions, *B.C.202-A.D.220*

Loewe, Michael. Chinese ideas of life and death : faith, myth and reason in the Han period (202 BC-AD 220) / by Michael Loewe. — London : Allen & Unwin, 1982. — x,226p ; 23cm
Bibliography: p191-202. — Includes index
ISBN 0-04-180001-x : £12.50 : CIP rev. B82-15623

299'.514 — Taoism

Allen, G. F.. Taoist words of wisdom. — Dulverton : Watkins, Sept.1982. — [200]p
ISBN 0-7224-0198-1 : £3.00 : CIP entry B82-25939

Cooper, J. C. (Jean Campbell). Yin and yang : the Taoist harmony of opposites / by J.C. Cooper. — Wellingborough : Aquarian, 1981. — 128p : ill ; 22cm
Includes index
ISBN 0-85030-265-x (pbk) : £3.50 : CIP rev. B81-27971

Durrell, Lawrence. A smile in the mind's eye / Lawrence Durrell. — London : Granada, 1982, c1980. — 93p ; 20cm. — (A Paladin book)
Originally published: London : Wildwood House, 1980
ISBN 0-586-08378-2 (pbk) : £1.95 B82-19894

Jefferson, R. B.. The doctrine of the elixir / [R.B. Jefferson]. — Ellingstring : Coombe Springs, 1982. — 24p : 2ill,1port ; 21cm
Originally published: s.l. : Institute for the Comparative Study of History, Philosophy and the Sciences, 1981
ISBN 0-900306-15-7 (pbk) : Unpriced B82-38587

299'.51482 — Taoism. Scriptures — *Texts*

Lao Tzu. Tao tê Ching. — New ed. — London : Unwin Paperbacks, Oct.1982. — [128]p
Translation from the Chinese. — Previous ed.: 1976
ISBN 0-04-299011-4 (pbk) : £2.95 : CIP entry B82-25082

299'.56 — Japan. Shamanism

Blacker, Carmen. The Catalpa bow : a study of shamanistic practices in Japan. — London : Allen & Unwin, Feb.1982. — [376]p
ISBN 0-04-398006-6 : £4.95 : CIP entry B82-01312

299.6 — NON-CHRISTIAN RELIGIONS OF BLACK AFRICAN AND NEGRO ORIGIN

299'.683 — Nigeria. Inbo. Religious beliefs

Metuh, Emefie Ikenga. God and man in African religion : a case study of the Igbo of Nigeria / Emefie Ikenga Metuh. — London : Geoffrey Chapman, 1981. — xiv,181p : ill,maps ; 22cm
Bibliography: p176-181
ISBN 0-225-66279-5 (pbk) : Unpriced : CIP rev. B81-14468

299.7 — NON-CHRISTIAN RELIGIONS OF NORTH AMERICAN INDIAN ORIGIN

299'.72 — Navaho myths — *Texts*

Haile, Berard. The upward moving and emergence way : the Gishin Biye' version / Berard Haile ; Karl W. Luckert, editor ; Navajo orthography by Irvy W. Goossen. — Lincoln, [Neb.] ; London : University of Nebraska Press, c1981. — xv,238p : ill ; 24cm. — (American tribal religions ; v.7)
ISBN 0-8032-2320-x (cased) : Unpriced
ISBN 0-8032-7212-x (pbk) : £8.40 B82-19491

299'.72 — North American Indian myths — *Anthologies*

Wood, Marion. Spirits, heroes & hunters from North American Indian mythology / text by Marion Wood ; illustrations by John Sibbick. — [London] : Peter Lowe, c1981. — 132p : ill (some col.),chart,1col.map ; 28cm
Includes index
ISBN 0-85654-040-4 : £4.95 : CIP rev. B81-20620

299'.75 — Guatemala. Maya religion. Divination

Colby, Benjamin N.. The daykeeper : the life and discourse of an Ixil diviner / Benjamin N. Colby and Lore M. Colby. — Cambridge, Mass. ; London : Harvard University Press, 1981. — xii,333p : ill ; 24cm
Bibliography: p315-324. — Includes index
ISBN 0-674-19409-8 : £17.50 B82-03867

299'.75 — Mexico. Yacqui. Shamanism — *Personal observations*

Castaneda, Carlos. The eagle's gift / Carlos Castaneda. — Harmondsworth : Penguin, 1982, c1981. — 281p ; 18cm
Originally published: London : Hodder & Stoughton, 1981
ISBN 0-14-005999-7 (pbk) : £1.95 B82-40805

299'.75 — Navaho religious life. Prayer

Gill, Sam D.. Sacred words : a study of Navajo religion and prayer / Sam D. Gill. — Westport, Conn. ; London : Greenwood Press, 1981. — xxvi,257p : ill ; 22cm. — (Contributions in intercultural and comparative studies, ISSN 0147-1031 ; no.4)
Bibliography: p237-243. — Includes index
ISBN 0-313-22165-0 : Unpriced B82-02532

299.9 — NON-CHRISTIAN RELIGIONS OF AUSTRONESIAN, OCEANIC, MISCELLANEOUS ORIGIN

299′.93 — Astronomy — *New Universal Union viewpoints*

Dowlatshahi, Heshmatullah. Ten questions to prominent scientists (astronomy) / by Heshmatullah Dowlatshahi (Heshmatussultan). — Teheran ; London : N.U.U., 1980. — 16p : ill ; 19cm
Unpriced (pbk) B82-21331

299′.93 — New Universal Union doctrine

Dowlatshahi, Heshmatullah. New thoughts from the new philosophy 1 / by Heshmatullah Dowlatshahi (Heshmatussultan). — Teheran ; London : N.U.U., 1980. — 30p : 1port ; 19cm
£0.75 (pbk) B82-21328

Dowlatshahi, Heshmatullah. New thoughts from the new philosophy II / by Heshmatullah Dowlatshahi (Heshmatussultan). — Teheran ; London : N.U.U., 1980. — 28p : 1port ; 19cm
£0.75 (pbk) B82-21329

Dowlatshahi, Heshmatullah. New thoughts from the new philosophy III / by Heshmatullah Dowlatshahi (Heshmatussultan) and N.U.U. members, J. Dana-Haeri ... [et al.]. — London : [N.U.U.], 1981. — 24p : ill ; 19cm
£1.00 (pbk) B82-21330

Dowlatshahi, Heshmatullah. Spring thoughts / by Heshmatullah Dowlatshahi (Heshmatussultan) the founder and rahnamoon and six members of the New Universal Union. — Teheran ; London : N.U.U., c1981. — 61p : ports ; 19cm
£1.00 (pbk) B82-21327

Fluid growth. — London (347 Long Lane, N2) : New Universal Union, 1982. — 69p : ill ; 19cm
Text on inside cover
£1.00 (pbk) B82-39066

299′.932 — Gnosticism

Pagels, Elaine. The gnostic gospels / Elaine Pagels. — Harmondsworth : Penguin, 1982, c1979. — 184p ; 20cm. — (Pelican books)
Originally published: New York : Random House, 1979 ; London : Weidenfeld and Nicolson, 1980. — Includes index
ISBN 0-14-022358-4 (pbk) : £2.25 B82-37612

299′.933 — Subud

Bissing, Hubert von. Songs of submission. — Cambridge : James Clarke, Feb.1982. — [192]p
Originally published: 1962
ISBN 0-227-67852-4 (pbk) : £3.95 : CIP entry B82-08403

Sumohadiwidjojo, Muhammad-Subuh. Four talks by Bapak / Muhammad-Subuh Sumohadiwidjojo. — Tunbridge Wells (55 The Pantiles, Tunbridge Wells, Kent TN2 5TE) : Subud Publications International, 1981. — 48p ; 22cm. — (New directions ; 2)
Unpriced (pbk) B82-12094

Sumohadiwidjojo, Muhammad-Subuh. New directions : four talks given at the Sixth Subud World Congress, Toronto, August 13-19,1979; and three talks in London ... / Muhammad-Subuh Sumohadiwidjojo. — Tunbridge Wells (55, The Pantiles, Tunbridge Wells, Kent TN2 5TE) : Subud, 1980. — 128p : ill,ports ; 22cm
Unpriced (pbk) B82-00769

299′.933′05 — Subud — *Serials*

Subud world : the official organ of the International Subud Committee for the Subud Brotherhood International Foundation, incorporating Pewarta Kejiwaan Subud, Subud world news, Zone one news, Aneka Subud and the newsletters of S. Widjojo, Amanco, the Kalimaktan [i.e. Kalimantan] Project, SES and SBIF (S & H). — Vol.1 no.1 (Sept. 1981)-. — Tunbridge Wells (55 The Pantiles, Tunbridge Wells, Kent) : Subud Publications International, 1981-. — v. : ill(some col.),maps,ports ; 30cm
Six issues yearly. — Continues: Subud world news. — Description based on: Vol.1, no.2 (Oct./Nov. 1981)
ISSN 0263-4155 = Subud world : Unpriced B82-23597

299′.934 — Theosophy

Blavatsky, H. P.. [The Secret doctrine. 3. Occultism]. The esoteric writings of Helena Petrovna Blavatsky : a synthesis of science, philosophy and religion. — Wheaton ; London : Theosophical Publishing House, c1980. — 500p,[5]leaves of plates(some folded) : ill(some col.) ; 23cm. — (Quest books)
Originally published: 1897. — Includes index
ISBN 0-8356-0535-3 (pbk) : Unpriced B82-34847

White, John, *1939-*. A practical guide to death and dying / John White. — Wheaton ; London : Theosophical Publishing House, c1980. — xiii,171p ; 21cm. — (A Quest book)
ISBN 0-8356-0539-6 (pbk) : Unpriced B82-34846

299′.935 — Anthroposophy

Harwood, A. C.. The way of a child / A.C. Harwood. — London : Rudolf Steiner, 1979. — 142p ; 19cm. — (Pharos)
ISBN 0-85440-352-3 (pbk) : £2.25 B82-05081

Lievegoed, Bernard. Phases : crisis and development in the individual / Bernard Lievegoed ; translated by H.S. Lake. — London : Rudolf Steiner, 1979. — 250p ; 19cm. — (Pharos)
Translation of: De Levensloop van de mens. — Bibliography: p247-250
ISBN 0-85440-353-1 (pbk) : £2.95 B82-05083

Steiner, Rudolf. The evolution of consciousness / Rudolf Steiner ; translated by V.E. Watkin and C. Davy. — London : Rudolf Steiner, 1979. — 198p ; 19cm. — (Pharos)
Translation of: Initiations - Erkenntnis
ISBN 0-85440-351-5 (pbk) : Unpriced B82-05082

Steiner, Rudolf. The philosophy of freedom : a basis for a modern world conception / Rudolf Steiner ; translated by Michael Wilson. — London : Rudolf Steiner, 1979. — xxx,233p ; 19cm. — (Pharos)
Translation of: Die Philosophie der Freiheit. — Includes index
ISBN 0-85440-350-7 (pbk) : Unpriced B82-05080

300 — SOCIAL SCIENCES

300 — Social sciences

Social sciences : a foundation course. — Milton Keynes : Open University Press
At head of title: The Open University
Block 1: Studying society. — 1981. — 81p : ill,ports ; 30cm. — (D102 ; block 1 (units 3 and 4))
Contents: Unit 2: Making sense of society — Unit 4: The social sciences
ISBN 0-335-12081-4 (pbk) : Unpriced B82-21179

Social sciences : a foundation course. — Milton Keynes : Open University Press
At head of title: The Open University
[Block 1]: [Studying society]. — 1981
Studying at university / prepared for the course team by Andy Northedge. — 34p : ill ; 30cm. — (D102 ; block 1 (SAU))
ISBN 0-335-12096-2 (pbk) : Unpriced B82-21180

Social sciences : a foundation course. — Milton Keynes : Open University Press
At head of title: The Open University
Block 2: The economy : a social process. — 1981. — 76p : ill,facsims,1map,ports ; 30cm. — (D102 ; block 2 (units 8 and 9))
Includes bibliographies. — Contents: Unit 8: Modern Britain : economic crises — Unit 9: Review A
ISBN 0-335-12097-0 (pbk) : Unpriced B82-31936

Social sciences : a foundation course. — Milton Keynes : Open University Press
At head of title: The Open University
Block 2: The economy : a social process. — 1982. — 53p : ill,facsims,ports ; 30cm. — (D102 ; block 2 (unit 5))
Bibliography: p53. — Contents: Introduction to Block 2 — Unit 5: Modern Britain: the economic base
ISBN 0-335-12082-2 (pbk) : Unpriced B82-21181

Social sciences : a foundation course. — Milton Keynes : Open University Press
At head of title: The Open University
Block 2: The economy : a social process. — 1982. — 100p : ill,facsims ; 30cm. — (D102 ; block 2, units 6 and 7)
Includes bibliographies. — Contents: Unit 6: How is production organized? — Unit 7: How do we know what to produce?
ISBN 0-335-12083-0 (pbk) : Unpriced B82-21182

Social sciences : a foundation course. — Milton Keynes : Open University Press
At head of title: The Open University
Block 3: The production of social divisions. — 1982. — 88p : ill,1facsim,1map ; 30cm. — (D102 ; block 3, units 10 and 11)
Includes bibliographies. — Contents: Introduction — Unit 10: Class divisions in modern Britain — Unit 11: Race and class
ISBN 0-335-12084-9 (pbk) : Unpriced B82-31934

Social sciences : a foundation course. — Milton Keynes : Open University Press
At head of title: The Open University
Block 3: The production of social divisions. — 1982. — 72p : ill ; 30cm. — (D102 ; block 3, units 12-13)
Includes bibliographies. — Contents: Introduction — Unit 12: Gender and class — Unit 13: Review B
ISBN 0-335-12085-7 (pbk) : Unpriced B82-31927

Social sciences : a foundation course. — Milton Keynes : Open University Press
At head of title: The Open University
[Block 4]: [Politics, legitimacy and the state]
Unit 18: Why do social scientists disagree? / [prepared for the course team by Tony Walton]. — 1982. — 32p : ill,ports ; 30cm. — (D102 ; block 4, unit 18)
Cover title. — Bibliography: p32
ISBN 0-335-12088-1 (pbk) : Unpriced B82-31933

Social sciences : a foundation course. — Milton Keynes : Open University Press
At head of title: The Open University
Block 4: Politics, legitimacy and the state. — 1982. — 89p : ill,facsims,1map,ports ; 30cm. — (D102 ; block 4 (units 14 and 15))
Includes bibliographies. — Contents: Introduction — Unit 14: Why do people accept the authority of the state — Unit 15: Democracy and popular participation
ISBN 0-335-12086-5 (pbk) : Unpriced B82-31929

Social sciences : a foundation course. — Milton Keynes : Open University Press
At head of title: The Open University
Block 4: Politics, legitimacy and the state. — 1982. — 61p : ill,facsims ; 30cm. — (D102 ; block 4 (units 16 and 17))
Includes bibliographies. — Contents: Unit 16: The making of public policy — Unit 17: Competing theories of the state
ISBN 0-335-12087-3 (pbk) : Unpriced B82-31928

300 — Social sciences *continuation*

Social sciences : a foundation course. — Milton Keynes : Open University Press
At head of title: The Open University
Block 5: Conformity, consensus and conflict. — 1982. — 100p : ill ; 30cm. — (D102 ; Block 5, units 19-20)
Bibliography: p100. — Contents: Introduction — Unit 19: Is conformity necessary for social cohesion? — Unit 20: How is social integration achieved?
ISBN 0-335-12089-x (pbk) : Unpriced
B82-34149

Social sciences : a foundation course. — Milton Keynes : Open University Press
At head of title: The Open University
[Block 5]: Conformity, consensus and conflict. — 1982. — 78p : ill ; 30cm. — (D102 ; Block 5, units 21-22)
Contents: Unit 21: Managing conflict, producing consent — Unit 22: Review C
ISBN 0-335-12090-3 (pbk) : Unpriced
B82-34151

Social sciences : a foundation course. — Milton Keynes : Open University Press
At head of title: The Open University
Block 6: Social change, geography and policy. — 1982. — 48p : ill,1col.map ; 30cm. — (D102 ; block 6 (unit 25))
Contents: Unit 25: social problems, policies and plans
ISBN 0-335-12092-x (pbk) : Unpriced
B82-40653

Social sciences : a foundation course. — Milton Keynes : Open University Press. — (D102 ; b block 6 (unit 26))
At head of title: The Open University
Block 6: Social change, geography and policy. — 1982. — 41p : ill,col.maps,ports ; 30cm
Bibliography: p40-41. — Contents: Unit 26: Local action and social change, racism and the inner city
ISBN 0-335-12099-7 (pbk) : Unpriced
B82-40651

Social sciences : a foundation course. — Milton Keynes : Open University Press
At head of title: The Open University
Block 7: The individual and society. — 1982. — 82p : ill ; 30cm. — (D102 ; block 7 (units 27-28))
Includes bibliographies. — Contents: Introduction — Unit 27: The person, determined or autonomous? — Unit 28: Individual aggression and social conflict
ISBN 0-335-12093-8 (pbk) : Unpriced
B82-40650

300 — Social sciences. Applications of general systems theory

Laszlo, Ervin. Systems science and world order. — Oxford : Pergamon, Jan.1983. — [273]p. — (Systems science and world order library)
ISBN 0-08-028924-x : £17.50 : CIP entry
B82-37474

300 — Social sciences. Occult aspects

Douglas, Graham. Physics astrology and semiotics / by Graham Douglas. — [London] : [G.J. Douglas], [c1981]. — i,71p : ill ; 21cm
Cover title
ISBN 0-9507947-0-8 (pbk) : £3.00 B82-11618

300 — Social sciences. Systems analysis

Systems methodology in social science research : recent developments / edited by Roger Cavallo. — Boston, [Mass.] ; London : Kluwer Nijhoff, c1982. — x,194p : ill ; 24cm. — (Frontiers in systems research. Implications for the social sciences ; v.2)
Includes bibliographies and index
ISBN 0-89838-044-8 : Unpriced B82-34780

300 — Society. Role of social sciences

MacRae, Duncan. The social function of social science. — London : Yale University Press, Apr.1981. — [367]p
Originally published: 1976
ISBN 0-300-02670-6 (pbk) : £5.00 : CIP entry
B81-10005

300′.1 — Social sciences. Applications of dialectics

Mitroff, Ian I.. Creating a dialectical social science : concepts, methods and models / Ian I. Mitroff and Richard O. Mason. — Dordrecht ; London : Reidel, c1981. — ix,189p : ill ; 23cm. — (Theory and decision library ; v.25)
Bibliography: p176-186. — Includes index
ISBN 90-277-1268-9 : Unpriced B82-09385

300′.1 — Social sciences - *Philosophical perspectives*

Van Parijs, Philippe. Evolutionary exploration in the social sciences. — London : Tavistock, July 1981. — [288]p
ISBN 0-422-77860-5 : £14.50 : CIP entry
B81-13469

300′.1 — Social sciences. Reasoning

Meehan, Eugene J.. Reasoned argument in social science : linking research to policy / Eugene J. Meehan. — Westport, Conn. ; London : Greenwood Press, 1981. — xvi,218p : ill ; 22cm. — (Contributions in political science, ISSN 0147-1066 ; no.53)
Bibliography: p205-212. — Includes index
ISBN 0-313-22481-1 : Unpriced B82-01950

300′.1′51955 — Social sciences. Time series. Analysis. Applications of digital computer systems. Software packages: Gottman-Williams programs — *Manuals*

Williams, Esther A.. A users′ guide to the Gottman-Williams time-series analysis computer programs for social scientists / Esther A. Williams, John M. Gottman. — Cambridge : Cambridge University Press, 1982. — 98p ; 23cm
ISBN 0-521-28059-1 (pbk) : £6.50 B82-26775

300′.2461 — Behavioural sciences — *For medicine* — *For Nigerian students*

Erinosho, Olayiwola A.. Behavioural science for nursing and medical students in Nigeria / by Olayiwola A. Erinosho with D.S. Usman and Felicia Mkpume. — London : Allen & Unwin, 1981. — 86p ; 22cm
Bibliography: p81-83. — Includes index
ISBN 0-04-362047-7 (pbk) : Unpriced : CIP rev. B81-24599

300′.28 — Social sciences. Statistical methods

Blalock, Hubert M.. Conceptualization and measurement in the social sciences / Hubert M. Blalock, Jr. — Beverly Hills ; London : Sage, c1982. — 285p : ill ; 23cm
Bibliography: p273-279. — Includes index
ISBN 0-8039-1804-6 : £15.00 B82-38163

Cohen, Louis. Statistics for social scientists. — London : Harper & Row, June 1982. — [320]p : ill
ISBN 0-06-318219-x (cased) : £11.95 : CIP entry
ISBN 0-06-318220-3 (pbk) : £5.95 B82-12128

Social measurement : current issues / George W. Bohrnstedt, Edgar F. Borgatta, editors. — Beverly Hills ; London : Sage, c1981. — 254p : ill ; 23cm
Includes bibliographies
ISBN 0-8039-1595-0 (cased) : Unpriced
ISBN 0-8039-1596-9 (pbk) : 6.50 B82-07903

300′.28′5425 — Social sciences. Software packages: SPSS — *Manuals*

Sours, Keith J.. SCSS short guide : an introduction to the SCSS conversational system / Keith J. Sours. — New York ; London : McGraw-Hill, c1982. — ix,134p ; 29cm
Includes index
ISBN 0-07-046539-8 (pbk) : £5.75 B82-02504

300′.28′7 — Social sciences. Measurement. Magnitude scaling

Lodge, Milton. Magnitude scaling : quantitative measurement of opinions / Milton Lodge. — Beverly Hills ; London : Sage, c1981. — 87p : ill ; 22cm. — (Quantitative applications in the social sciences ; no.07-025) (Sage university papers)
Bibliography: p83-85
ISBN 0-8039-1747-3 (pbk) : £2.50 B82-17083

300′.5 — Social sciences — *Serials*

The **Year** book of social policy in Britain. — 1980-1981. — London : Routledge & Kegan Paul, Apr.1982. — [260]p
ISBN 0-7100-9083-8 : £12.50 : CIP entry
B82-12148

300′.7 — Educational institutions. Curriculum subjects: Social sciences. Teaching

New movements in the social sciences and humanities. — London : Maurice Temple Smith, Apr.1982. — [288]p
ISBN 0-85117-193-1 : £12.95 : CIP entry
Also classified at 001.3′07 B82-08422

300′.72 — Behavioural sciences. Research. Methodology

Agnew, Neil McK.. The science game : an introduction to research in the behavioral sciences / Neil McK. Agnew, Sandra W. Pyke. — 3rd ed. — Englewood Cliffs ; London : Prentice-Hall, c1982. — xiv,285p : ill,1map ; 23cm
Previous ed.: 1978. — Bibliography: p269-276. — Includes index
ISBN 0-13-795260-0 (pbk) : £8.95 B82-31822

300′.72 — Social sciences. Fieldwork — *Manuals*

Field study : a sourcebook for experiential learning / Lenore Borzak editor. — Beverly Hills ; London : Sage, c1981. — 320p : ill ; 23cm
Includes bibliographies
ISBN 0-8039-1614-0 (cased) : Unpriced
ISBN 0-8039-0050-3 (pbk) : £6.50 B82-11695

300′.72 — Social sciences. Research

Blalock, Ann Bonar. Introduction to social research. — 2nd ed. / Ann Bonar Blalock, Hubert M. Blalock, Jr.. — Englewood Cliffs ; London : Prentice-Hall, c1982. — xiii,153p : ill ; 24cm. — (Prentice-Hall foundations of modern sociology series)
Previous ed.: 1970. — Bibliography: p149-150. — Includes index
ISBN 0-13-496810-7 (cased) : Unpriced
ISBN 0-13-496802-6 (pbk) B82-28418

300′.72 — Social sciences. Research. Methodology

Bailey, Kenneth D.. Methods of social research / Kenneth D. Bailey. — 2nd ed. — New York : Free Press ; London : Collier Macmillan, c1982. — xxii,553p : ill,1form ; 25cm
Previous ed.: 1978. — Bibliography: p523-539. — Includes index
ISBN 0-02-901280-5 : £15.95 B82-30023

Nachmias, Chava. Research methods in the social sciences / Chava Nachmias, David Nachmias. — Alternate 2nd ed., without statistics. — London : Edward Arnold, 1982, c1981. — xvi,358p : ill ; 24cm
Previous ed.: 1976. — Includes bibliographies and index
ISBN 0-7131-6283-x (pbk) : £7.95 : CIP rev.
B82-04486

300′.72 — Social sciences. Research. Methodology — *For African students*

Peil, Margaret. Social science research methods : an African handbook / Margaret Peil with contributions by Peter K. Mitchell and Douglas Rimmer. — London : Hodder and Stoughton, 1982. — vi,234p : ill,maps ; 24cm
Bibliography: p226-231. — Includes index
ISBN 0-340-26205-2 (pbk) : £6.95 : CIP rev.
B82-01837

300′.72 — Social sciences. Research projects. Design

Spector, Paul E.. Research designs / Paul E. Spector. — Beverly Hills ; London : Sage, c1981. — 80p : ill ; 22cm. — (Quantitative applications in the social sciences ; no.07-023) (Sage university papers)
Bibliography: p78-80
ISBN 0-8039-1709-0 (pbk) : £2.50 B82-17082

300′.72 — Social sciences. Research. Quantitative methods

Glass, Gene V.. Meta-analysis in social research / Gene V. Glass, Barry McGraw and Mary Lee Smith. — Beverly Hills ; London : Sage, c1981. — 279p : ill ; 23cm
Bibliography: p257-270. — Includes index
ISBN 0-8039-9700-0 (corrected) : £17.00
B82-10513

300'.72041 — Great Britain. *Social Science Research Council — Inquiry reports*

Rothschild, Nathaniel Mayer Victor, *Baron.* An enquiry into the Social Science Research Council / by Lord Rothschild. — London : H.M.S.O., 1982. — vi,114p ; 25cm. — (Cmnd. ; 8554)
ISBN 0-10-185540-0 (pbk) : £6.50 B82-32029

300'.72041 — Great Britain. *Social Science Research Council — Serials*

Great Britain. *Social Science Research Council.* Social Science Research Council annual report. — 1980/81-. — London : The Council, 1981-. — v. : ill,ports ; 30cm
Continues: Great Britain. Social Science Research Council. Report of the Social Science Research Council, April ... -March ...
ISSN 0262-5482 = Social Science Research annual report (London) : £3.00 B82-06783

300'.72041 — Social sciences. Research. Commissioning by British government departments

Blume, Stuart S.. The commissioning of social research by central government : a report commissioned by the Research Careers Executive Panel / Stuart S. Blume. — London : Social Science Research Council ; Merstham : School Government Publishing Co. [distributor], c1982. — 59p ; 30cm
ISBN 0-86226-038-8 (pbk) : Unpriced B82-30847

Kogan, Maurice. Government's commissioning of research : a case study / Maurice Kogan, Nancy Korman, Mary Henkel. — [Uxbridge] ([Uxbridge, Middx, UB8 3PH]) : Department of Government, Brunel University, c1980. — 57p : 2ill ; 22cm
Bibliography: p54-57
£1.00 (pbk) B82-37922

300'.7'2041 — Social sciences. Research in British Institutions — *Directories*

Research in British universities, polytechnics and colleges : Vol.2, Biological sciences. — 2nd ed. (1981). — Boston Spa (RBUPC Office, British Library Lending Division, Boston Spa, Wetherby, W.Yorks., LS23 7B9) : British Library, June 1981. — [655]p
ISBN 0-900220-88-0 (pbk) : £20.00 : CIP entry
ISSN 0143-0734
Primary classification 507'.2041 B81-13546

300'.72041 — Social sciences. Research in British institutions — *Directories — Serials*

Research in British universities, polytechnics and colleges. Vol.3, Social sciences. — 2nd ed. (1981). — Wetherby : British Library Lending Division, RBUPC Office, Aug.1981. — [450]p
ISBN 0-900220-89-9 (pbk) : £20.00 : CIP entry
ISSN 0143-0742 B81-25109

Research in British universities, polytechnics and colleges. Vol.3, Social sciences. — 1982. — Wetherby : British Library Lending Division, RBUPC Office, July 1982. — [500]p
ISBN 0-7123-2005-9 (pbk) : £23.00 : CIP entry
ISBN 0-7123-2002-4 (set) : Unpriced
ISSN 0143-0742 B82-14524

300'.72041 — Social sciences. Research projects supported by Great Britain. *Social Science Research Council*

The **Contribution** to published literature of postgraduate research in the social sciences. — London : Social Science Research Council, 1980. — 36p ; 30cm
Includes bibliographies
ISBN 0-86226-045-0 (pbk) : Unpriced B82-20233

300'.720415 — Social sciences. Research in Irish institutions — *Lists*

O'Sullivan, Florence, *1941-.* Register of current social science research in Ireland 1981 / compiled by Florence O'Sullivan. — Dublin : The Economic and Social Research Institute, 1982. — xiii,72p ; 24cm
Includes index
ISBN 0-7070-0050-5 (pbk) : £3.00 B82-40451

300'.72073 — United States. Social sciences. Research. Methodology

Saxe, Leonard. Social experiments : methods for design and evaluation / Leonard Saxe, Michelle Fine ; introduction by Donald T. Campbell. — Beverly Hills ; London : Sage, c1981. — 267p : ill ; 22cm. — (Sage library of social research ; v.131)
Bibliography: p243-256. — Includes index
ISBN 0-8039-1710-4 (cased) : Unpriced
ISBN 0-8039-1711-2 (pbk) : Unpriced B82-21916

300'.722 — Social sciences. Longitudinal studies

Longitudinal research : methods and uses in behavioral science / edited by Fini Schulsinger, Sarnoff A. Mednick, Joachim Knop. — Boston ; London : Nijhoff, c1981. — x,326p : ill ; 24cm. — (Longitudinal research in the behavioral, social, and medical sciences ; 1)
Bibliography: p297-319. — Includes index
ISBN 0-89838-056-1 : Unpriced B82-08508

300.722 — Social sciences. Research. Historical sources

Historical sources and the social scientist. — Milton Keynes : Open University Press. — (Social sciences : a third level course)
At head of title: The Open University
Units 6-8: Introduction to historical psephology. — 1982. — 126p : ill,facsims ; 30cm. — (D301. Second series ; 6-8)
Bibliography: p119-125
ISBN 0-335-04819-6 (pbk) : Unpriced B82-32214

Historical sources and the social scientist. — Milton Keynes : Open University Press. — (Social sciences : a third level course)
At head of title: The Open University
Units 9-10: Patterns and processes of internal migration. — 1982. — 104p : ill(some col.),maps(some col.) ; 30cm. — (D301. Second series ; units 9-10)
Bibliography: p99-102
ISBN 0-335-04821-8 (pbk) : Unpriced B82-32212

Historical sources and the social scientist. — Milton Keynes : Open University Press. — (Social sciences : a third level course)
At head of title: The Open University
A guide to nineteenth-century census enumerators' books. — 1982. — 46p : ill,facsims ; 30cm. — (D301. Second series ; GCEB)
Bibliography: p45-46
ISBN 0-335-04823-4 (pbk) : Unpriced B82-32213

300'.723 — Great Britain. Social sciences. Research. Information sources: Social surveys

Hakim, C.. Secondary analysis in social research : a guide to data sources and with examples / Catherine Hakim methods ; forewords by Michael Posner. — London : Allen & Unwin, 1982. — xiv,202p ; 23cm. — (Contemporary social research series ; 5)
Bibliography: p185-195. — Includes index
ISBN 0-04-312015-6 (cased) : Unpriced : CIP rev.
ISBN 0-04-312016-4 (pbk) : Unpriced B82-15625

300'.723 — Social sciences. Field studies. Methodology

Field research : a sourcebook and field manual / edited by Robert G. Burgess. — London : Allen & Unwin, 1982. — xii,286p ; 26cm. — (Contemporary social research series ; 4)
Bibliography: p264-279. — Includes index
ISBN 0-04-312013-x (cased) : Unpriced : CIP rev.
ISBN 0-04-312014-8 (pbk) : Unpriced B82-10575

300'.724 — Social sciences. Linear models

Linear models in social research / edited by Peter V. Marsden. — Beverly Hills ; London : Sage, c1981. — 336p : ill ; 22cm
Bibliography: p319-332
ISBN 0-8039-1721-x (cased) : Unpriced
ISBN 0-8039-1722-8 (pbk) : £7.95 B82-21511

300'.724 — Social sciences. Simulation games

Greenblat, Cathy S.. Principles and practices of gaming-simulation / Cathy Stein Greenblat, Richard D. Duke. — Beverly Hills ; London : Sage, c1981. — 283p : ill,1form ; 22cm
'Many of the chapters have been revised from' Gaming-Simulation. Beverly Hills : Sage ; New York ; London : Wiley, [distributor], 1975. — Bibliography: p255-280
ISBN 0-8039-1675-2 (cased) : Unpriced
ISBN 0-8039-1676-0 (pbk) : £6.50 B82-21510

300'.724 — Social sciences. Stochastic models

Bartholomew, David J.. Stochastic models for social processes / D. J. Bartholomew. — 3rd ed. — Chichester : Wiley, c1982. — xii,365p : ill ; 24cm. — (Wiley series in probability and mathematical statistics)
Previous ed.: 1973. — Text on lining papers. — Bibliography: p324-352. — Includes index
ISBN 0-471-28040-2 : £18.50 : CIP rev.
ISBN 0-471-09978-3 (pbk) : £8.95 B81-33798

300'.92'4 — Social sciences. Theories of Schutz, Alfred

Thomason, Burke C.. Making sense of reification : Alfred Schutz and constructionist theory / Burke C. Thomason ; foreword by Tom Bottomore. — London : Macmillan, 1982. — xvi,203p ; 22cm
Bibliography: p188-196. — Includes index
ISBN 0-333-31497-2 : Unpriced B82-32931

301 — SOCIOLOGY

301 — Anthropology

Bloch, Maurice. Marxism and anthropology. — Oxford : Clarendon Press, Feb.1983. — [192]p. — (Marxist introductions)
ISBN 0-19-876091-4 : £8.95 : CIP entry B82-36325

Haviland, William A.. Anthropology / William A. Haviland. — 3rd ed. — New York ; London : Holt, Rinehart and Winston, c1982. — xix,698p,[16]p of plates : ill(some col.),maps (some col.),ports ; 24cm
Previous ed.: 1978. — Bibliography: p670-679. — Includes index
ISBN 0-03-059279-8 (pbk) : £13.50 B82-15361

Lewis, John, *19---.* Anthropology made simple. — London : Heinemann, Nov.1982. — [294]p. — (Made simple books)
Originally published: London : W.H. Allen, 1969
ISBN 0-434-98567-8 (pbk) : £2.95 : CIP entry B82-31295

301 — Anthropology. Psychological aspects

Jahoda, G.. Psychology and anthropology. — London : Academic Press, Nov.1982. — [300]p
ISBN 0-12-379820-5 : CIP entry B82-26861

301 — Ethnomethodology

Handel, Warren. Ethnomethodology : how people make sense / Warren Handel. — Englewood Cliffs ; London : Prentice-Hall, c1982. — xii,170p ; 23cm
Bibliography: p160-165. — Includes index
ISBN 0-13-291708-4 (pbk) : £7.45 B82-20058

301 — Man. Needs — *Sociological perspectives*

Springborg, Patricia. The problem of human needs and the critique of civilisation / Patricia Springborg. — London : Allen & Unwin, 1981. — 293p ; 24cm
Bibliography: p275-286. — Includes index
ISBN 0-04-301133-0 : Unpriced : CIP rev. B81-20148

301 — Marxist sociology

Weiner, Richard R.. Cultural Marxism and political sociology / Richard R. Weiner ; preface by Ira Katznelson. — Beverly Hills ; London : Sage, c1981. — 271p : ill ; 22cm. — (Sage library of social research ; v.125)
Bibliography: p247-258. — Includes index
ISBN 0-8039-1644-2 (cased) : Unpriced B82-07376

301 — Social processes

Curtis, Richard K.. Evolution or extinction : the choice before us : a systems approach to the study of the future / by Richard K. Curtis. — Oxford : Pergamon, 1982. — xviii,447p ; 24cm. — (Systems science and world order library)
Bibliography: p404-422. — Includes index
ISBN 0-08-027933-3 (cased) : Unpriced : CIP rev.
ISBN 0-08-027932-5 (pbk) : £12.50
B82-11997

301 — Social systems

Luhmann, Niklas. The differentiation of society / Niklas Luhmann ; translated by Stephen Holmes and Charles Larmore. — New York ; Guildford : Columbia University Press, c1982. — xxxvii,482p ; 24cm. — (European perspectives)
Bibliography: p415-456. — Includes index
ISBN 0-231-04996-x : £24.60 B82-19580

Ramos, Alberto Guerreiro. The new science of organizations : a reconceptualization of the Wealth of nations / Alberto Guerreiro Ramos. — Toronto ; London : University of Toronto Press, c1981. — xiv,210p ; 24cm
Includes bibliographies and index
ISBN 0-8020-5527-3 : £17.50 B82-06984

301 — Social systems. Cybernetics aspects

Aulin, Arvid. The cybernetic laws of social progress : towards a critical social philosophy and a criticism of Marxism / by Arvid Aulin. — Oxford : Pergamon, 1982. — vii,218p : ill,1map ; 24cm. — (Systems science and world order library) (Pergamon international library)
Bibliography: p210-211. — Includes index
ISBN 0-08-025782-8 : £22.50 : CIP rev.
B81-31804

301 — Social systems. Sociopolitical aspects

Bieńkowski, W.. Theory and reality : the development of social systems / W. Bienkowski ; translated from Polish by Jane Cave. — London : Allison & Busby, 1981. — 303p ; 23cm
Translated from the Polish. — Includes index
ISBN 0-85031-401-1 (cased) : £10.95 : CIP rev.
ISBN 0-85031-402-x (pbk) : Unpriced
B81-13516

301 — Society

The **Schumacher** Lectures / edited with an introduction by Satish Kumar. — London : Abacus, 1982, c1980. — xvii,198p : ill ; 20cm
Originally published: London : Blond & Briggs, 1980. — Includes bibliography
ISBN 0-349-12118-4 (pbk) : £2.50 B82-16570

301 — Society — *Anthropological perspectives* — *For schools*

Barber, C. Renate. Life journeys : an anthropological primer / C.R. Barber. — Exeter : Wheaton, 1981. — 100p : ill ; 22cm
Includes bibliographies and index
ISBN 0-08-027396-3 (cased) : Unpriced
ISBN 0-08-026420-4 (pbk) : Unpriced
B82-05705

301 — Society — *For schools*

Hawthorn, Ruth. Asking about society / Ruth Hawthorn. — Cambridge : Cambridge University Press, 1981. — v,130p : ill ; 25cm
Includes index
ISBN 0-521-28069-9 (pbk) : £3.45 B82-32326

Nobbs, Jack. Modern society : social studies for CSE / Jack Nobbs. — 2nd ed. — London : Allen & Unwin, 1981. — 200p : ill,maps,facsims ; 25cm
Previous ed.: 1976. — Includes index
ISBN 0-04-301134-9 (pbk) : Unpriced : CIP rev. B81-20094

301 — Society. Role of information

McGarry, K. J.. The changing context of information : an introductory analysis / K.J. McGarry. — London : Bingley, 1981. — 189p ; 23cm
Bibliography: p152-186. — Includes index
ISBN 0-85157-325-8 : Unpriced : CIP rev.
B81-27403

301 — Society — *Sociological perspectives*

Hirschman, Albert O.. Shifting involvements : private interest and public action. — Oxford : Martin Robertson, Apr.1982. — [160]p
Originally published: Princeton, N.J. : Princeton University Press, 1981
ISBN 0-85520-487-7 (cased) : £10.00 : CIP entry
ISBN 0-85520-490-7 (pbk) : £5.95 B82-04804

301 — Society. Theories

Campbell, Tom. Seven theories of human society / Tom Campbell. — London : Clarendon Press, c1981. — 244p ; 21cm
Includes index
ISBN 0-19-876104-x (cased) : Unpriced : CIP rev.
ISBN 0-19-876105-8 (pbk) : £3.95 B81-18166

301 — Society. Theories *related to* **politics**

Social theory and political practice. — Oxford : Clarendon, Feb.1983. — [190]p
ISBN 0-19-827447-5 (cased) : £15.00 : CIP entry
ISBN 0-19-827448-3 (pbk) : £5.95 B82-36603

301 — Sociology

Advances in social theory and methodology : toward an integration of micro- and macro-sociologies / edited by K. Knorr-Cetina and A.V. Cicourel. — Boston, [Mass.] ; London : Routledge & Kegan Paul, 1981. — xii,325p ; 22cm
Includes index
ISBN 0-7100-0946-1 (cased) : £12.50
ISBN 0-7100-0947-x (pbk) : Unpriced
B82-13574

Alexander, Jeffrey C.. Theoretical logic in sociology / Jeffrey C. Alexander. — London : Routledge & Kegan Paul. — (International library of sociology)
Vol.1: Positivism, presuppositions and current controversies. — 1982. — xvi,234p ; 24cm
Includes index
ISBN 0-7100-9049-8 : £16.95 : CIP rev.
B82-01210

Alexander, Jeffrey C.. Theoretical logic in sociology. — London : Routledge and Kegan Paul. — (International library of sociology)
Vol.2: The antinomies of classical thought : Marx and Durkheim. — Sept.1982. — [250]p
ISBN 0-7100-9289-x : £15.00 : CIP entry
B82-21094

Berger, Peter L.. Sociology reinterpreted : an essay on method and vocation / Peter L. Berger, Hansfried Kellner. — Harmondsworth : Penguin, 1982, c1981. — 176p : ill ; 18cm. — (Pelican books)
Originally published: New York : Anchor Press, 1981. — Bibliography: p167-170. — Includes index
ISBN 0-14-022430-0 (pbk) : £1.75 B82-30358

Culture, ideology and social process : a reader / edited by Tony Bennett ... [et al.] at the Open University. — London : Batsford Academic and Educational in association with Open University Press, 1981. — 312p,[8]p of plates : ill,facsims ; 22cm. — (Open University Press set book)
Includes bibliographies and index
ISBN 0-7134-4314-6 (pbk) : £6.95 : CIP rev.
B81-30386

Giddens, Anthony. Sociology : a brief but critical introduction / Anthony Giddens. — London : Macmillan, 1982. — viii,182p ; 23cm
Includes index
ISBN 0-333-30928-6 (cased) : Unpriced
ISBN 0-333-30929-4 (pbk) : Unpriced
B82-39996

Haralambos, Michael. Sociology : themes and perspectives / Michael Haralambos with Robin Heald. — Slough : University Tutorial Press, 1980 (1981 [printing]). — xiv,594p ; 23cm
Bibliography: p560-584. — Includes index
ISBN 0-7231-0812-9 (cased) : £8.00
ISBN 0-7231-0793-9 (pbk) : Unpriced
B82-34910

Henderson, Penny. Sociology A Level : a course leading to the Sociology GCE A Level exam. of the Associated Examining and Joint Matriculation Boards / by Penny Henderson. — Cambridge : National Extension College, c1981. — 3v. : ill ; 30cm. — (National Extension College correspondence texts ; course no.HS23)
Includes bibliographies
ISBN 0-86082-238-9 (pbk) : Unpriced
ISBN 0-86082-235-4 (v.1)
ISBN 0-86082-236-2 (v.2)
ISBN 0-86082-237-0 (v.3) B82-38348

Hess, Beth B.. Sociology / Beth B. Hess, Elizabeth W. Markson, Peter J. Stein. — London : Macmillan, c1982. — xvi,653p : ill (some col.) ; 26cm
Bibliography: p-607-625. — Includes index
ISBN 0-02-354120-2 : £9.95 B82-26285

Hobbs, Donald A.. Sociology and the human experience / Donald A. Hobbs, Stuart J. Blank. — 3rd ed. — New York ; Chichester : Wiley, c1982. — xvii,536p : ill ; 24cm
Previous ed.: 1978. — Includes bibliographies and index
ISBN 0-471-08281-3 (pbk) : £10.20
B82-18225

An **Introduction** to sociology. — Milton Keynes : Open University Press. — (Social sciences : a second level course)
At head of title: The Open University
Block 3: Comparison and change
Study section 19: Feudalism and capitalism / prepared for the course team by Paul Keleman. — 1980. — 35p : ill ; 30cm. — (D207 ; block 3, study section 19)
Bibliography: p34-35
ISBN 0-335-12018-0 (pbk) : Unpriced
B82-04549

An **Introduction** to sociology. — Milton Keynes : Open University Press. — (Social sciences : a second level course)
At head of title: The Open University
Block 3: Comparison and change
Study section 20: Community / prepared for the course team by Howard Newby. — 1980. — 42p : ill ; 30cm. — (D207 ; block 3, study section 20)
Bibliography: p40-42
ISBN 0-335-12019-9 (pbk) : Unpriced
B82-04551

An **Introduction** to sociology. — Milton Keynes : Open University Press. — (Social sciences : a second level course)
At head of title: The Open University
Block 3: Comparison and change
Study section 21: Organizations / prepared for the course team by Graeme Salaman. — 1980. — 47p : ill ; 30cm. — (D207 ; block 3, study section 21)
Bibliography: p45-47
ISBN 0-335-12020-2 (pbk) : Unpriced
B82-04550

An **Introduction** to sociology. — Milton Keynes : Open University Press. — (Social sciences : a second level course)
At head of title: The Open University
Block 3: Comparison and change
Study section 22: Power and ideology in work organizations : Britain and Japan / prepared for the course team by Craig R. Littler. — 1981. — 52p : ill ; 30cm. — (D207 ; block 3, study section 22)
Bibliography: p47-50
ISBN 0-335-12021-0 (pbk) : Unpriced
B82-17528

Lenski, Gerhard. Human societies : an introduction to macrosociology / Gerhard Lenski, Jean Lenski. — 4th ed. — New York ; London : McGraw-Hill, c1982. — xiv,514p : ill,ports ; 25cm
Previous ed.: 1978. — Includes index
ISBN 0-07-037176-8 : £16.50 B82-16011

Moore, Stephen. Sociology. — London : Hodder and Stoughton, Aug.1982. — [288]p. — (Teach yourself books)
ISBN 0-340-26945-6 (pbk) : £2.75 : CIP entry
B82-18566

301 — Sociology *continuation*

Readings for introducing sociology / [edited by] Richard F. Larson, Ronald J. Knapp. — New York ; Oxford : Oxford University Press, 1982. — x,293p : ill ; 24cm
Includes bibliographies
ISBN 0-19-503007-9 (pbk) : £7.75 B82-33305

Ritzer, George. Sociology : experiencing a changing society / George Ritzer, Kenneth C.W. Kammeyer, Norman R. Yetman. — 2nd ed. — Boston ; London : Allyn & Bacon, c1982. — 551p : ill(some col.) ; 24cm + 2test banks
Previous ed.: 1979. — Ill on lining papers. — Bibliography: p515-536. — Includes index
ISBN 0-205-07363-8 : Unpriced B82-27857

Sherman, Howard J.. Sociology : traditional and radical perspectives. — London : Harper and Row, July 1982. — [448]p
Originally published: New York : Harper & Row, 1979
ISBN 0-06-318190-8 (pbk) : £5.95 : CIP entry B82-16485

Society and the social sciences : an introduction / edited by David Potter with James Anderson ... [et al.] for the Social Sciences Foundation Course Team at the Open University. — London : Routledge & Kegan Paul in association with Open University Press, 1981. — ix,449p : ill ; 21cm. — (An Open University set book)
Includes index
ISBN 0-7100-0943-7 (pbk) : £2.40 : CIP rev. B81-30601

Sociological theory : a book of readings / edited by Lewis A. Coser, Bernard Rosenberg. — 5th ed. — London : Macmillan, c1982. — xviii,603p ; 24cm
Previous ed.: 1976. — Includes index
ISBN 0-02-325220-0 : £8.95 B82-26286

Sociology : the state of the art / edited by Tom Bottomore, Stefan Nowak, Magdalena Sokolowska ; sponsored by the International Sociological Association/ISA. — London : Sage, c1982. — 378p ; 23cm
Includes bibliographies
ISBN 0-8039-9790-6 (cased) : Unpriced : CIP rev.
ISBN 0-8039-9791-4 (pbk) : £4.95 B82-00304

Thompson, Jane L.. Sociology made simple / Jane L. Thompson. — London : Heinemann, c1982. — xiii,288p : ill ; 23cm. — (Made simple books)
Includes bibliographies and index
ISBN 0-434-98507-4 (cased) : £5.95
ISBN 0-434-98508-2 (pbk) : £2.95 B82-17166

Yorburg, Betty. Introduction to sociology / Betty Yorburg. — New York ; London : Harper & Row, c1982. — xx,486p : ill ; 25cm
Includes index
ISBN 0-06-047333-9 : Unpriced B82-34911

301 — Sociology — *For schools*

Burgen, Andrew D.. Comprehension exercises in sociology. — Cheltenham : Thornes, Apr.1982. — [196]p
ISBN 0-85950-327-5 (pbk) : £2.45 : CIP entry B82-04815

Randall, F.. Basic sociology. — 4th ed. / F. Randall. — Plymouth : Macdonald and Evans, 1981. — viii,200p ; 19cm. — (The M & E handbook series)
Previous ed.: /by F.J. Wright, 1975. — Bibliography: p181-186.. — Includes index
ISBN 0-7121-0291-4 (pbk) : £2.75 B82-01910

301 — Sociology *related to* **economics**

Economics and sociology : towards an integration / edited by T. Huppes. — Boston [Mass.] ; London : Kluwer, c1976 (1982 [printing]). — vii,178p ; 24cm
ISBN 0-89838-093-6 : Unpriced
Primary classification 330 B82-24573

301 — Sociology *related to* **historiology**

Tilly, Charles. As sociology meets history / Charles Tilly. — New York ; London : Academic Press, c1981. — xiii,237p : ill ; 24cm. — (Studies in social discontinuity)
Bibliography: p217-232. — Includes index
ISBN 0-12-691280-7 : £16.60
Also classified at 907′.2 B82-30132

301 — United States. Personal life styles — *Sociological perspectives*

Sobel, Michael E.. Lifestyle and social structure : concepts, definitions, analyses / Michael E. Sobel. — New York ; London : Academic Press, c1981. — xi,226p : ill ; 24cm. — (Quantitative studies in social relations)
Bibliography: p213-220. — Includes index
ISBN 0-12-654280-5 : £17.60 B82-21257

301′.01 — Sociology. Classical theories

The **Future** of the sociological classics / edited by Buford Rhea. — London : Allen & Unwin, 1981. — xi,212p ; 23cm
Bibliography: p195-208. — Includes index
ISBN 0-04-301136-5 (cased) : Unpriced : CIP rev.
ISBN 0-04-301137-3 (pbk) : Unpriced B81-28777

301′.01 — Sociology. Critical theory

Geuss, Raymond. The idea of a critical theory : Habermas and the Frankfurt School / Raymond Geuss. — Cambridge : Cambridge University Press, 1981. — xii,100p ; 23cm. — (Modern European philosophy)
Bibliography: p96-97. — Includes index
ISBN 0-521-24072-7 (cased) : £10.00 : CIP rev.
ISBN 0-521-28422-8 (pbk) : £3.75 B81-32524

301′.01 — Sociology. Functionalism

Turner, Jonathan H.. Functionalism / Jonathan H. Turner, Alexandra Maryanski. — Menlo Park ; London : Benjamin/Cummings, c1979. — 147p ; 23cm. — (The Benjamin/Cummings series in contemporary sociology)
Includes index
ISBN 0-8053-9338-2 (pbk) : Unpriced B82-28200

301′.01 — Sociology — *Philosophical perspectives*

Halfpenny, Peter. Positivism and sociology. — London : Allen & Unwin, Oct.1982. — [144]p. — (Controversies in sociology ; 13)
ISBN 0-04-300084-3 (cased) : £10.95 : CIP entry
ISBN 0-04-300085-1 (pbk) : £4.50 B82-23088

301′.01 — Sociology. Theories

Hall, John A.. Diagnoses of our time : six views on our social condition / John A. Hall. — London : Heinemann Educational, 1981. — vi,283p ; 23cm
Bibliography: p266-275. — Includes index
ISBN 0-435-82402-3 : £16.50 : CIP rev. B81-12344

Luckmann, Thomas. Life-world and social realities. — London : Heinemann Educational, Nov.1981. — [224]p
Translation of: Lebenswelt und Gesellschaft
ISBN 0-435-82550-x : £13.50 : CIP entry B81-30307

Menzies, Ken. Sociological theory in use / Ken Menzies. — London : Routledge & Kegan Paul, 1982. — x,250p : ill ; 23cm
Bibliography: p214-237. — Includes index
ISBN 0-7100-0892-9 (cased) : £9.95
ISBN 0-7100-0893-7 (pbk) : £4.95 B82-14736

301′.01 — Sociology. Theories, *1950-1980*

Collins, Randall. Sociology since midcentury : essays in theory cumulation / Randall Collins. — New York ; London : Academic Press, c1981. — x,365p : maps ; 24cm
Bibliography: p341-351. — Includes index
ISBN 0-12-181340-1 : £18.20 B82-12965

301′.01 — Sociology. Theories — *Serials*

Current perspectives in social theory : a research annual. — Vol.1 (1980)-. — Greenwich, Conn. : JAI Press ; London (3 Henrietta St., WC2E 8LU) : Distributed by JAICON Press, 1980-. — v. : ill ; 24cm
Unpriced B82-03403

301′.018 — Comparative sociology. Methodology

International comparative research. — Oxford : Pergamon, Oct.1982. — [184]p
ISBN 0-08-027960-0 : £17.50 : CIP entry B82-28435

301′.01′8 — Sociology. Methodology. Implications of philosophy of science

Tudor, Andrew. Beyond empiricism : philosophy of science in sociology / Andrew Tudor. — London : Routledge & Kegan Paul, 1982. — xi,213p : ill ; 22cm. — (Monographs in social theory)
Includes index
ISBN 0-7100-0925-9 (pbk) : £4.95 B82-25673

301′.024372 — Sociology — *For teaching*

Handbook for sociology teachers. — London : Heinemann Educational, Oct.1982. — [320]p
ISBN 0-435-82597-6 (pbk) : £10.50 : CIP entry B82-23999

301′.024613 — Sociology — *For nursing*

Chapman, Christine M.. Sociology for nurses / Christine M. Chapman. — 2nd ed. — London : Baillière Tindall, 1982. — viii,210p : ill ; 19cm. — (Nurses′ aids series)
Previous ed.: 1977. — Includes bibliographies and index
ISBN 0-7020-0940-7 (pbk) : £3.50 : CIP rev. B82-20008

301′.05 — Sociology. Comparative studies — *Serials*

Comparative social research : an annual publication. — Vol.2 (1979)-. — Greenwich, Conn. : JAI Press ; London (3 Henrietta St., WC2E 8LU) : Distributed by JAICON Press, 1979-. — v. : ill ; 24cm
An official publication of: the Comparative Interdisciplinary Studies Society (CISS), from v.3 (1980). — Continues: Comparative studies in sociology. — Indexes: Author index to preceding volumes in every issue. Subject index to preceding volumes in every issue from v.3
ISSN 0195-6310 = Comparative social research : Unpriced B82-04915

301′.072 — Sociology. Research. Factor analysis & measurement

Factor analysis and measurement in sociological research : a multi-dimensional perspective / editors David J. Jackson and Edgar F. Borgatta. — London : Sage, c1981. — 313p : ill ; 23cm. — (Sage studies in international sociology ; 21)
Includes bibliographies
ISBN 0-8039-9814-7 (cased) : Unpriced
ISBN 0-8039-9815-5 (pbk) : Unpriced B82-00143

301′.072 — Sociology. Research. Methodology

Rose, Gerry. Deciphering sociological research / Gerry Rose. — London : Macmillan, 1982. — ix,325p : ill ; 23cm. — (Contemporary social theory)
Bibliography: p314-319. — Includes index
ISBN 0-333-28557-3 (cased) : £12.95
ISBN 0-333-28558-1 (pbk) : Unpriced B82-32221

301′.07207 — North America. Anthropology. Research. Methodology

Anthropologists at home in North America : methods and issues in the study of one′s own society / Donald A. Messerschmidt, editor. — Cambridge : Cambridge University Press, 1981. — x,310p : ill ; 24cm
Bibliography: p281-299. — Includes index
ISBN 0-521-24067-0 (cased) : £20.00
ISBN 0-521-28419-8 (pbk) : Unpriced B82-15255

301′.076 — Sociology — *Questions & answers*

Jeffries, Patricia Ann. Experiencing sociology : a study guide to accompany Ritzer, Kammeyer, and Yetman′s Sociology : 2nd edition / Patricia Ann Jeffries and Vincent Jeffries. — Boston ; London : Allyn & Bacon, c1982. — ix,164p : ill ; 24cm
ISBN 0-205-07378-6 (pbk) : Unpriced B82-27860

301'.09'034 — Sociology. Theories, *1880-1980*

Inglis, Fred. Radical earnestness : English social theory 1880-1980. — Oxford : Martin Robertson, Aug.1982. — [252]p
ISBN 0-85520-328-5 (cased) : £12.50 : CIP entry
ISBN 0-85520-401-x (pbk) : £5.50 B82-16664

301'.09'04 — Sociology, *1945-1980*

The **State** of sociology : problems and prospects / James F. Short, Jr. editor. — Beverly Hills ; London : Sage, c1981. — 303p ; 23cm
Includes bibliographies
ISBN 0-8039-1657-4 (cased) : Unpriced
ISBN 0-8039-1658-2 (pbk) : £6.50 B82-17081

301'.0917'671 — Islamic countries — *Sociological perspectives*

Issues in the Islamic movement 1981-82. — London : Open Press, Jan.1983. — [400]p
ISBN 0-905081-13-7 (cased) : £13.95 : CIP entry
ISBN 0-905081-14-5 (pbk) : £6.95 B82-37462

301'.092'4 — Anthropology. Cesara, Manda — *Biographies*

Cesara, Manda. Reflections of a woman anthropologist : no hiding place / Manda Cesara. — London : Academic Press, 1982. — x,234p : ill ; 24cm. — (Studies in anthropology)
Bibliography: p229-232. — Includes index
ISBN 0-12-164880-x : £10.80 : CIP rev.
B82-12438

301'.092'4 — Anthropology. Leenhardt, Maurice — *Biographies*

Clifford, James, *1945-*. Person and myth : Maurice Leenhardt in the Melanesian world / James Clifford. — Berkeley ; London : University of California Press, c1982. — xi,270p : ill,1map,ports ; 24cm
Bibliography: p257-264. — Includes index
ISBN 0-520-04247-6 : £21.50 B82-37064

301'.092'4 — Society. Theories of Ellul, Jacques

Jacques Ellul : interpretive essays / edited by Clifford G. Christians and Jay M. Van Hook. — Urbana ; London : University of Illinois Press, c1981. — xiii,336p ; 23cm
Bibliography: p325-328. — List of works: p310-324. — Includes index
ISBN 0-252-00812-x (cased) : Unpriced
ISBN 0-252-00890-1 (pbk) : £6.30 B82-13568

301'.092'4 — Society. Theories of Marx, Karl

Carver, Terrell. Marx's social theory. — Oxford : Oxford University Press, Oct.1982. — [128]p. — (OPUS)
ISBN 0-19-219170-5 (cased) : £7.95 : CIP entry
ISBN 0-19-289158-8 (pbk) : £2.95 B82-23661

301'.092'4 — Sociology. Durkheim, Emile — *Critical studies*

Thompson, Kenneth. Emile Durkheim. — Chichester : Ellis Horwood, Jan.1982. — [128]p
ISBN 0-85312-394-2 (cased) : £6.50 : CIP entry
ISBN 0-85312-419-1 (pbk) : £2.95 B82-00185

301'.092'4 — Sociology. Theories of Freud, Sigmund

Bocock, Robert. Sigmund Freud. — Chichester : Ellis Horwood, Jan.1983. — [128]p. — (Key sociologists)
ISBN 0-85312-511-2 : £7.25 : CIP entry
B82-37636

301'.092'4 — Sociology. Theories of Parsons, Talcott

Bourricaud, François. The sociology of Talcott Parsons / François Bourricaud ; translated by Arthur Goldhammer ; foreword by Harry M. Johnson. — Chicago ; London : University of Chicago Press, 1981, c1977. — xv,326p ; 23cm. — (Chicago originals)
Translation of: L'individualisme institutionnel. — Bibliography: p313-314. — Includes index
ISBN 0-226-06755-6 (pbk) : £16.10
B82-03781

Savage, Stephen P.. The theories of Talcott Parsons : the social relations of action / Stephen P. Savage. — London : Macmillan, 1981. — xiii,279p ; 23cm
Bibliography: p251-274. — Includes index
ISBN 0-333-24565-2 : £20.00 B82-06659

301'.092'4 — Sociology. Theories of Weber, Max

Schluchter, Wolfgang. The rise of Western rationalism : Max Weber's developmental history / Wolfgang Schluchter ; translated, with an introduction, by Guenther Roth. — Berkeley London : University of California Press, c1981. — xxvii,178p ; 24cm
Translation of: Die Entwicklung des okzidentalen Rationalismus. — Includes index
ISBN 0-520-04060-0 : Unpriced B82-16923

301'.092'4 — Sociology. Weber, Max — *Critical studies*

Parkin, Frank. Max Weber. — Chichester : Ellis Horwood, Jan.1982. — [108]p
ISBN 0-85312-393-4 (cased) : £6.50 : CIP entry
ISBN 0-85312-409-4 (pbk) : £2.95 B82-00184

301'.092'4 — Sociology. Weber, Max — *Critical studies — Welsh texts*

Roberts, Ellis. Weber. — [Denbigh] : Gwasg Gee, 1982. — 84p : 2ill ; 19cm. — (Y Meddwl modern)
Bibliography: p84
£1.90 (pbk) B82-39999

301'.0941 — Great Britain — *Sociological perspectives*

Noble, Trevor. Structure and change in modern Britain / Trevor Noble. — London : Batsford Academic and Educational, 1981. — 416p ; 22cm
Includes index
ISBN 0-7134-3691-3 (pbk) : £7.95 : CIP rev.
B81-27936

301'.0941 — Great Britain. Sociology, *1950-1980*

Practice and progress : British sociology 1950-1980. — London : Allen & Unwin, Sept.1981. — [240]p
ISBN 0-04-301131-4 (cased) : £12.50 : CIP entry
ISBN 0-04-301132-2 (pbk) : £4.95 B81-20149

301'.0973 — United States. Sociology. Theories, *1870-1970*

Bierstedt, Robert. American sociological theory : a critical history / Robert Bierstedt. — New York ; London : Academic Press, 1981. — xiv,525p ; 24cm
Includes index
ISBN 0-12-097480-0 : £25.80
ISBN 0-12-097482-7 (pbk) : Unpriced
B82-10054

302 — SOCIAL INTERACTION

302 — Cognitive social psychology

Cognitive social psychology / edited by Albert H. Hastorf, Alice M. Isen. — New York ; Oxford : Elsevier/North-Holland, c1982. — x,362p : ill ; 24cm
Includes bibliographies and index
ISBN 0-444-00617-6 : Unpriced B82-19317

Mower White, C. J.. Consistency in cognitive social behaviour : an introduction to social psychology / C.J. Mower White. — London : Routledge & Kegan Paul, 1982. — vi,201p ; 23cm. — (Introductions to modern psychology)
Bibliography: p171-194. — Includes index
ISBN 0-7100-9028-5 (cased) : £10.95
ISBN 0-7100-9029-3 (pbk) : £5.95 B82-33963

302 — Developmental social psychology

Blank, Thomas O.. A social psychology of developing adults / Thomas O. Blank. — New York ; Chichester : Wiley, c1982. — xvi,325p ; 24cm. — (Wiley series on personality processes, ISSN 0195-4008)
Text on lining papers. — Bibliography: p291-310. — Includes index
ISBN 0-471-08787-4 : £22.25 B82-32051

Developmental social psychology : theory and research / edited by Sharon S. Brehm, Saul M. Kassin, Frederick X. Gibbons. — New York ; Oxford : Oxford University Press, 1981. — xii,376p : ill ; 24cm
Bibliography: p315-356. — Includes index
ISBN 0-19-502840-6 (cased) : £15.00
ISBN 0-19-502841-6 (pbk) : £9.00 B82-01001

302 — Empathy — *Sociological perspectives*

Empathy, fantasy and helping / Ezra Stotland ... [et al.]. — Beverly Hills ; London : Sage, c1978. — 162p ; 23cm. — (Sage library of social research ; v.65)
Bibliography: p117-122. — Includes index
ISBN 0-8039-0984-5 (cased) : £15.50
ISBN 0-8039-0983-7 (pbk) : Unpriced
B82-02414

302 — Folly. Sociocultural aspects

Zijderveld, Anton C.. Reality in a looking-glass : rationality through an analysis of traditional folly / Anton C. Zijderveld. — London : Routledge & Kegan Paul, 1982. — ix,199p : ill ; 23cm. — (International library of sociology)
Includes index
ISBN 0-7100-0949-6 : £12.50 B82-23814

302 — Friendship

Bell, Robert R.. Worlds of friendship / Robert R. Bell. — Beverly Hills ; London : Sage, c1981. — 216p ; 22cm. — (Sociological observations ; 12)
Bibliography: p203-209. — Includes index
ISBN 0-8039-1723-6 (cased) : Unpriced
.ISBN 0-8039-1724-4 (pbk) : £6.50 B82-21514

302 — Great Britain. Social skills — *For school leavers*

Joyce, Stephen. New horizons / Stephen Joyce. — Glasgow : Collins
3: Relationships. — 1981. — 32p : ill ; 23cm
ISBN 0-00-327882-4 (pbk) : £0.65 B82-05565

302 — Great Britain. Social skills — *For young persons*

Maxfield, Brenda. Social and life skills assignment worksheets. — London : Edward Arnold, Nov.1982. — [64]p
ISBN 0-7131-0812-6 : £30.00 : CIP entry
B82-27957

Parsons, C. J.. Assignments in communication : social and life skills / C.J. Parsons. — London : Edward Arnold, 1982. — iv,92p : ill,1map,facsims,plans,forms ; 28cm
ISBN 0-7131-0518-6 (pbk) : £3.50 : CIP rev.
B82-01185

302 — Interpersonal relationships

Hamachek, Don E.. Encounters with others : interpersonal relationships and you / Don E. Hamachek. — New York ; London : Holt, Rinehart and Winston, c1982. — viii,254p : ill ; 24cm
Includes index
ISBN 0-03-088411-x (pbk) : Unpriced
B82-20709

Personal relationships / editors Steve Duck and Robin Gilmour. — London : Academic Press
3: Personal relationships in disorder. — 1981. — xvi,278p ; 24cm
Bibliography: p235-265. — Includes index
ISBN 0-12-222803-0 : £12.20 : CIP rev.
B81-22558

Personal relationships / editors Steve Duck and Robin Gilmour. — London : Academic Press
4: Dissolving personal relationships / edited by Steve Duck. — 1982. — xiii,307p : ill ; 24cm
Bibliography: p263-289. — Includes index
ISBN 0-12-222804-9 : £16.00 : CIP rev.
B82-12439

302 — Interpersonal relationships. Political aspects

Colman, Marshall. Continuous excursions : politics and personal life / Marshall Colman. — London : Pluto, 1982. — 134p ; 19cm
Includes index
ISBN 0-86104-357-x (pbk) : £3.95 B82-20685

302 — Man. Actions. Social psychology

Cranach, M. von. Goal-directed action. — London : Academic Press, Aug.1982. — [400] p. — (European monographs in social psychology ; no.30)
Translation of: Zielgerichtetes Handeln
ISBN 0-12-724760-2 : CIP entry B82-15671

302 — Man. Collective behaviour

Rose, Jerry D.. Outbreaks : the sociology of collective behaviour / Jerry D. Rose. — New York : Free ; London : Collier Macmillan, c1982. — viii,278p ; 24cm
Bibliography: p255-259. — Includes index
ISBN 0-02-926790-0 (pbk) : £6.95 B82-29742

302 — Man. Collective behaviour. Momentum

Adler, Peter. Momentum : a theory of social action / Peter Adler ; foreword by Marvin B. Scott. — Beverly Hills ; London : Sage, c1981. — 190p ; 23cm. — (Sociological observations ; 11)
Bibliography: p185-190
ISBN 0-8039-1307-9 (cased) : Unpriced
ISBN 0-8039-1581-0 (pbk) : £6.50 B82-07904

302 — Man. Psychosocial development. Teaching aids: Games — *Collections*

Newstrom, John W.. Games trainers play : experiential learning exercises / John W. Newstrom and Edward E. Scannell. — New York ; London : McGraw Hill, c1980. — xvi,303p : ill,forms ; 28cm
Alternate pages blank
ISBN 0-07-046408-1 (pbk) : £9.95 B82-33705

302 — Man. Social behaviour

Barash, David P.. Sociobiology and behavior / David P. Barash ; foreword by Edward O. Wilson. — 2nd ed. — London : Hodder and Stoughton, c1982. — xiv,426p : ill,ports ; 27cm. — (Biological science texts)
Previous ed.: Oxford : Elsevier, 1977. — Bibliography: p395-419. — Includes index
ISBN 0-340-28460-9 : £8.95 : CIP rev. B82-10475

Baron, Robert A.. Exploring social psychology / Robert A. Baron, Donn Byrne. — 2nd ed. — Boston ; London : Allyn and Bacon, c1982. — xi,350p : ill ; 24cm
Previous ed.: 1979. — Bibliography: p306-339. — Includes index
ISBN 0-205-07606-8 (pbk) : £11.50 B82-17784

The **Psychology** of social situations : selected readings / edited by Adrian Furnham and Michael Argyle. — Oxford : Pergamon, 1981. — lvi,492p : ill ; 24cm. — (Pergamon international library)
Includes bibliographies and index
ISBN 0-08-024319-3 (cased) : Unpriced
ISBN 0-08-023719-3 (pbk) : £9.95 B82-05703

302 — Man. Social behaviour. Evolution

Reynolds, Peter C.. On the evolution of human behavior : the argument from animals to man / Peter C. Reynolds. — Berkeley ; London : University of California Press, c1981. — xi,272p : ill ; 24cm
Includes bibliographies and index
ISBN 0-520-04294-8 (cased) : £20.00
ISBN 0-520-04416-9 (pbk) : £6.25 B82-11914

302 — Man. Social behaviour *related to* **cognition** — *Conference proceedings*

Cognitive Analysis of Socio-Psychological Processes *(Conference : 1981 : Aix-en-Provence).* Cognitive analysis of social behavior : proceedings of the NATO advanced study institute on "The cognitive analysis of socio-psychological processes", Aix-en-Provence, France, July 12-31, 1981 / edited by Jean-Paul Codol and Jacques-Philippe Leyens. — The Hague ; London : Nijhoff, 1982. — xv,304p : ill ; 25cm. — (NATO advanced study institutes series. Series D, Behavioural and social sciences ; no.13)
Includes 3 chapters in French. — Includes bibliographies and index
ISBN 90-247-2701-4 : Unpriced
Primary classification 153.4 B82-34841

302 — Man. Social behaviour — *Soviet viewpoints*

Bueva, L. P.. Man : his behaviour and social relations / L.P. Bueva. — Moscow : Progress ; [London] : distributed by Central Books, c1981. — 253p ; 17cm
Translation of: Chelovek
ISBN 0-7147-1710-x (pbk) : £1.95 B82-19609

302 — Man. Social behaviour. Unintended effects

Boudon, Raymond. The unintended consequences of social action / Raymond Boudon. — London : Macmillan, 1982. — vii,232p : ill ; 23cm
Includes index
ISBN 0-333-25845-2 : Unpriced B82-33843

302 — Man. Social development. Theories

Armstrong, Albert. Mind and muscle : 9000 B.C.-2000 A.D. : a new analysis of man's social, psychological and economic history / by Albert Armstrong. — Hatfield (13 White Lion House, Town Centre Hatfield, Herts.) : Armstrong Publications, [1981?]. — 54p : ill ; 21cm
ISBN 0-9507007-0-3 (pbk) : £1.30 B82-07704

302 — Man. Social relations

Hirst, Paul. Social relations and human attributes. — London : Tavistock, Dec.1981. — [300]p. — (Social science paperbacks ; 229)
ISBN 0-422-77220-8 (pbk) : £10.50 : CIP entry
ISBN 0-422-77230-5 (pbk) : £4.95 B81-31704

302 — Mediation

Lachs, John. Responsibility and the individual in modern society / John Lachs. — Brighton : Harvester, 1981. — 145p ; 23cm
ISBN 0-7108-0308-7 : £13.95 : CIP rev. B81-20520

302 — Personnel. Social skills

Social skills and work / edited by Michael Argyle. — London : Methuen, 1981. — xix,227p : ill ; 21cm
Bibliography: p218-220. — Includes index
ISBN 0-416-73000-0 (cased) : Unpriced : CIP rev.
ISBN 0-416-73010-8 (pbk) : £3.95 B81-30567

302 — Social life. Style

Crisp, Quentin. Doing it with style / Quentin Crisp and Donald Carroll ; with drawings by Jonathan Hills. — London : Eyre Methuen, 1981. — 157p : ill ; 21cm
Includes index
ISBN 0-413-47490-9 : £5.95 B82-17558

302 — Social psychology

Confronting social issues : applications of social psychology / edited by Peter Stringer. — London : Published in cooperation with European Association of Experimental Social Psychology by Academic. — (European monographs in social psychology ; 28)
Vol.1. — 1982. — xiv,238p : ill ; 24cm
Includes bibliographies and index
ISBN 0-12-673801-7 : Unpriced : CIP rev. B81-35912

Confronting social issues. — London : Academic Press. — (European monographs in social psychology ; no.29)
Vol.2. — Aug.1982. — [240]p
ISBN 0-12-673802-5 : CIP entry B82-15670

Feld, Sheila. Social psychology for social work and the mental health professions / Sheila Feld & Norma Radin. — New York ; Guildford : Columbia University Press, 1982. — x,581p ; 24cm
Bibliography: p499-559. — Includes index
ISBN 0-231-04190-x : £13.00 B82-36923

McCall, George J.. Social psychology : a sociological approach / George J. McCall, J.L. Simmons ; with glossary prepared by Nola Simmons. — New York : Free Press ; London : Collier Macmillan, c1982. — xxi,502p : ill ; 25cm
Bibliography: p457-481. — Includes index
ISBN 0-02-920640-5 : £15.50 B82-30029

Readings in social psychology : contemporary perspectives / Dennis Krebs editor. — 2nd ed. — New York ; London : Harper & Row, c1982. — 361p : ill,ports ; 28cm. — (Harper & Row's contemporary perspectives reader series)
Previous ed.: 1976. — Includes bibliographies
ISBN 0-06-043769-3 (pbk) : Unpriced B82-08630

Shaw, Marvin E.. Theories of social psychology / Marvin E. Shaw, Philip R. Costanzo. — 2nd ed. — New York ; London : McGraw-Hill, c1982. — xiii,482p : ill ; 25cm. — (McGraw-Hill series in psychology)
Previous ed.: 1970. — Bibliography: p421-457. — Includes index
ISBN 0-07-056512-0 : £20.75 B82-24907

Smithson, Michael. Dimensions of helping behaviour. — Oxford : Pergamon, Jan.1983. — [165]p. — (The International series in experimental social psychology ; v.6)
ISBN 0-08-027412-9 : £9.95 : CIP entry B82-33606

Social identity and intergroup relations. — Cambridge : Cambridge University Press, Oct.1982. — [544]p. — (European studies in social psychology)
ISBN 0-521-24616-4 : £35.00 : CIP entry B82-29373

Social psychology : a gateway course for the Open University / authors: Graham Richards ... [et al.] ; [editors: Raymond Jobling and Anthony Heath]. — Cambridge : National Extension College, 1970 (1978-1981 [printing]). — 2v.(189p) : ill ; 30cm. — (National Extension College correspondence texts ; course no.HS1)
ISBN 0-86082-082-3 (pbk) : Unpriced
ISBN 0-86082-080-7 (v.1) : Unpriced B82-38359

Social psychology and behavioral medicine / edited by J. Richard Eiser. — Chichester : Wiley, c1982. — xiv,588p : ill ; 24cm
Includes bibliographies and index
ISBN 0-471-27994-3 : £19.95 : CIP rev. B81-23739

302 — Social skills — *Manuals*

Handbook of social skills. — London : Methuen
Vol.1: Social skills and health. — Nov.1981. — [745]p
ISBN 0-416-72980-0 (cased) : £8.50 : CIP entry
ISBN 0-416-72990-8 (pbk) : £3.95 B81-30568

302 — Sociology. Exchange theory

Networks, exchange and coercion : the elementary theory and its applications / edited by David Willer, Bo Anderson. — New York ; Oxford : Elsevier, c1981. — xii,240p : ill ; 24cm
Includes bibliographies and index
ISBN 0-444-99078-x : Unpriced B82-02007

302 — Symbolic interactionism — *Serials*

Studies in symbolic interation : a research annual. — Vol.1 (1978)-. — Greenwich, Conn. : JAI Press ; London (3 Henrietta St., WC2E 8LU) : Distributed by JAICON Press, 1978-. — v. ; 24cm
Description based on: Vol.20 (1979)
ISSN 0163-2396 = Studies in symbolic interaction : Unpriced B82-05216

302 — Tourists. Social behaviour. Psychological aspects

Pearce, Philip L.. The social psychology of tourist behaviour. — Oxford : Pergamon, July 1982. — [142]p. — (International series in experimental social psychology ; 3)
ISBN 0-08-025794-1 : £9.50 : CIP entry B82-12410

302'.024372 — Man. Social behaviour — *For teaching*

Smith, Gene F.. Instructor's manual to accompany Exploring social psychology, second edition / prepared by Gene F. Smith, Bem P. Allen. — Boston ; London : Allyn and Bacon, c1982. — vi,190,28p : ill ; 24cm
Includes bibliographies
ISBN 0-205-07607-6 (pbk) : £1.00 B82-17782

302'.024613 — Interpersonal relationships — *For practical nursing*

Becker, Betty Glore. Vocational and personal adjustment in practical nursing / Betty Glore Becker, Dolores T. Fendler. — 4th ed. / with a chapter on ethical and legal aspects by Laura Reilly and James Abrams. — St. Louis ; London : Mosby, 1982. — ix,180p : ill ; 23cm
Previous ed.: 1978. — Includes bibliographies and index
ISBN 0-8016-0566-0 (pbk) : £7.50
Primary classification 610.73 B82-31870

302'.024613 — Social skills — *For nursing*

French, Peter. Social skills for nursing practice. — London : Croom Helm, Oct.1982. — [256]p
ISBN 0-7099-1009-6 (pbk) : £6.95 : CIP entry B82-23191

302'.05 — Applied social psychology — *Serials*

Applied social psychology annual / sponsored by the Society for the Psychological Study of Social Issues (SPSSI). — Vol.1-. — Beverly Hills, Calif. ; London : Sage Publications, 1980-. — v. : ill ; 22cm
Description based on: 2
ISSN 0196-4151 = Applied social psychology annual : Unpriced B82-15162

302'.05 — Social psychology — *Serials*

Progress in applied social psychology. — Vol.1-. — Chichester : Wiley, 1981-. — v. ; 24cm
£17.50 B82-06797

302'.07 — Social skills. Teaching

Developments in social skills training. — London : Academic Press, Feb.1983. — [328]p
ISBN 0-12-656620-8 : CIP entry B82-36574

302'.07 — Social skills. Teaching — *Manuals*

Wilkinson, Jill. Social skills training manual : assessment, programme design, and management of training / Jill Wilkinson and Sandra Canter. — Chichester : Wiley, c1982. — xii,148p : forms ; 24cm
Bibliography: p145-148
ISBN 0-471-10056-0 (cased) : £14.95 : CIP rev.
ISBN 0-471-10067-6 (pbk) : Unpriced B82-01135

302'.07 — Social skills. Teaching methods

Improving interpersonal relations : some approaches to social skill training / edited by Cary L. Cooper. — Aldershot : Gower, c1981. — x,129p : ill ; 23cm
Includes bibliographies
ISBN 0-566-02277-x : Unpriced : CIP rev. B81-07913

302'.07'12417 — Ireland *(Republic)*. **Secondary schools. Curriculum subjects: Social skills** — *For teaching*

Gill, Albert. Teacher's guide to Plan your future 1,2,3 / Albert Gill and Michael McCoy. — Dublin (Ballymount Rd., Walkinstown, Dublin 12) : The Educational Company, 1982. — 7p ; 22cm
Unpriced (unbound) B82-27123

302'.072 — Man. Social behaviour. Research methods: Observation

Fassnacht, G.. Theory and practice of observing behaviour. — London : Academic Press, Oct.1982. — [230]p. — (Behavioural development)
Translation of: Systematische Verhaltensbeobachtung
ISBN 0-12-249780-5 : CIP entry B82-24936

302'.092'4 — Social adjustment. Theories of Adler, Alfred

Crandall, James E.. Theory and measurement of social interest : empirical tests of Alfred Adler's concept / James E. Crandall. — New York ; Guildford : Columbia University Press, 1981. — xi,181p : ill ; 22cm
Bibliography: p163-173. — Includes index
ISBN 0-231-05256-1 : £15.80 B82-10651

302'.09417 — Ireland *(Republic)*. **Social skills** — *For school leavers*

Gill, Albert. Plan your future, 3 : a programme for senior students and school leavers / Albert Gill and Michael McCoy. — Dublin : Educational Company, 1982. — 140p : ill,forms ; 21cm
Bibliography: p137
Unpriced (pbk) B82-34489

302.1'2 — Man. Perception — *Sociological perspectives*

Essays in the sociology of perception / edited by Mary Douglas. — London : Routledge & Kegan Paul published in co-operation with the Russell Sage Foundation, 1982. — viii,340p : ill ; 24cm
Includes bibliographies and index
ISBN 0-7100-0881-3 (pbk) : £7.95 B82-23739

302.1'2 — Social identity

Hardison, O. B.. Entering the maze : identity and change in modern culture / O.B. Hardison, Jr. — New York ; Oxford : Oxford University Press, 1981. — xiv,304p ; 22cm
ISBN 0-19-502953-4 : £13.00 B82-37007

302.1'2 — Western Europe. Society. Perception by middle classes, *1775-1915*

Lowe, Donald M.. History of bourgeois perception / Donald M. Lowe. — Brighton : Harvester, 1982. — ix,206p : ill ; 24cm
Includes index
ISBN 0-7108-0383-4 : £18.95 B82-33840

302.1'3 — Social choice

Margolis, Howard. Selfishness, altruism and rationality : a theory of social choice / Howard Margolis. — Cambridge : Cambridge University Press, 1982. — xii,194p : ill ; 24cm
Bibliography: p189-191. — Includes index
ISBN 0-521-24068-9 : £18.00 B82-29927

Rational man and irrational society? : an introduction and sourcebook / edited by Brian Barry and Russell Hardin. — Beverly Hills ; London : Sage, c1982. — 413p : ill ; 22cm
Bibliography: p391-400. — Includes index
ISBN 0-8039-1850-x (cased) : Unpriced
ISBN 0-8039-1851-8 (pbk) : £9.95 B82-38451

302.1'3'0724 — Social choice. Mathematical models

Lehrer, Keith. Rational consensus in science and society : a philosophical and mathematical study / by Keith Lehrer and Carl Wagner. — Dordrecht ; London : Reidel, c1981. — ix,165p ; 23cm. — (Philosophical studies series in philosophy ; v.24)
Bibliography: p154-157. — Includes index
ISBN 90-277-1306-5 (cased) : Unpriced
ISBN 90-277-1307-3 (pbk) : Unpriced B82-05342

302.2 — Cross-cultural communication

Cultures in contact : studies in cross-cultural interaction / edited by Stephen Bochner. — Oxford : Pergamon, 1982. — xiv,232p : ill ; 24cm. — (International series in experimental social psychology ; v.1)
Includes bibliographies and index
ISBN 0-08-025805-0 (cased) : Unpriced : CIP rev.
ISBN 0-08-028919-3 (pbk) : £7.95 B82-12896

302.2 — Interpersonal relationships. Communication

Berger, Charles R.. Language and social knowledge. — London : Arnold, Dec.1982. — [224]p. — (The Social psychology of language)
ISBN 0-7131-6196-5 (pbk) : £7.50 : CIP entry B82-30207

Schramm, Wilbur. Men, women, messages, and media : understanding human communication / Wilbur Schramm, William E. Porter. — 2nd ed. — New York ; London : Harper & Row, c1982. — ix,278p : ill ; 24cm
Previous ed.: published as Men, messages, and media. 1973. — Includes bibliographies and index
ISBN 0-06-045798-8 (pbk) : £7.95 B82-26276

302.2 — Man. Communication. Social aspects

Ong, Walter J.. Orality and literacy. — London : Methuen, Oct.1982. — [224]p. — (New accents)
ISBN 0-416-71370-x (cased) : £7.50 : CIP entry
ISBN 0-416-71380-7 (pbk) : £3.95 B82-23981

302.2 — Symbolism

Cooper, J. C.. Symbolism. — Wellingborough : Aquarian, Nov.1982. — [128]p
ISBN 0-85030-279-x (pbk) : £3.95 : CIP entry B82-26414

302.2'024658 — Man. Communication — *For business studies*

Lord, Gordon A.. It's my business to know : studies in communication / Gordon A. Lord. — London : McGraw-Hill, c1982. — xi,170p : ill,1map,1plan ; 25cm
Includes bibliographies and index
ISBN 0-07-084654-5 (pbk) : £4.95 : CIP rev. B82-07239

Shackleton, Jenny. Beyond words / Jenny Shackleton, Colin Blundell, Roger Bailey. — St. Albans : Hart-Davis Educational, c1982. — 192p : ill ; 30cm
Bibliography: p188. — Includes index
ISBN 0-247-13006-0 (pbk) : Unpriced B82-24517

Wolff, Margaret, *1947-*. Communicating at work / Margaret Wolff, Graham Collins. — Walton-on-Thames : Nelson, 1982. — 153p : ill,facsims,1form,1map ; 25cm. — (Nelson BEC books. National level : people and communication)
Includes index
ISBN 0-17-741129-5 (pbk) : £4.25 B82-29463

302.2'05 — Communication. Social aspects — *Serials*

Studies in communications : a research annual. — Vol.1 (1980)-. — Greenwich, Conn. : JAI Press ; London (3 Henrietta St., WC2E 8LU) : Distributed by JAICON Press, 1980-. — v. ; 24cm
ISSN 0275-7982 = Studies in communications : Unpriced B82-05213

302.2'09182'1 — Western world. Social development. Role of literacy, *1066-1980*

Literacy and social development in the West : a reader / edited by Harvey J. Graff. — Cambridge : Cambridge University Press, 1981. — ix,340p : ill ; 24cm. — (Cambridge studies in oral and literate culture)
ISBN 0-521-23954-0 (cased) : £19.50
ISBN 0-521-28372-8 (pbk) : £6.50 B82-18921

302.2'09595'1 — Malaysia. Pahang. Rural regions. Communication systems. Social aspects

Wilder, William D.. Communication, social structure and development in rural Malaysia. — London : Athlone Press, Nov.1982. — [224]p. — (London School of Economics monographs on social anthropology, ISSN 0077-1024 ; 56)
ISBN 0-485-19556-9 : £18.00 : CIP entry B82-27502

302.2'09666'2 — Literacy. Psychological aspects — *Sample populations: Vai — Study regions: Liberia*

Scribner, Sylvia. The psychology of literacy / Sylvia Scribner, Michael Cole. — Cambridge, Mass. ; London : Harvard University Press, 1981. — xii,335p,8p of plates : ill,1map,1plan ; 25cm
Bibliography: p321-329. — Includes index
ISBN 0-674-72115-2 : £15.00 B82-11876

302.2'2 — Reading. Ethnomethodological analysis

McHoul, A. W.. Telling how texts talk : essays on reading and ethnomethodology / A.W. McHoul. — London : Routledge & Kegan Paul, 1982. — xi,163p : ill ; 23cm. — (The International library of phenomenology and moral sciences)
Bibliography: p148-154. — Includes index
ISBN 0-7100-9047-1 : £9.95 B82-23255

302.2'234 — Great Britain. Magazines for women, *1949-1980 — Sociological perspectives*
Ferguson, Marjorie. Forever feminine. — London : Heinemann Educational, Jan.1983. — [256]p
ISBN 0-435-82301-9 (cased) : £14.50 : CIP entry
ISBN 0-435-82302-7 (pbk) : £6.50 B82-35218

302.2'24 — Alaska. Athapaskan speaking communities. Verbal communication with English speaking communities. Cultural aspects
Scollon, Ron. Narrative, literacy and face in interethnic communication / by Ron Scollon and Suzanne B.K. Scollon. — Norwood, N.J. : Ablex ; London (3 Henrietta St., WC2E 8LU) : Eurospan [distributor], c1981. — xiv,209p : ill ; 24cm. — (Advances in discourse processes, ISSN 0164-0224 ; v.7)
Bibliography: p203-209
ISBN 0-89391-076-7 (unbound) : £13.95
ISBN 0-89391-086-4 (pbk) : Unpriced
B82-27696

302.2'24 — Professional personnel. Interpersonal relationships. Communication. Linguistic aspects
Delaware Symposium on Language Studies *(2nd)*. Linguistics and the professions : proceedings of the Second Annual Delaware Symposium on Language Studies / Robert J. Di Pietro editor. — Norwood, N.J. : Ablex, c1982 ; London : Distributed by Eurospan. — xv,272p : ill ; 24cm. — (Advances in discourse processes ; v.8)
Includes bibliographies and index
ISBN 0-89391-092-9 (cased) : Unpriced
ISBN 0-89391-120-8 (pbk) : Unpriced
B82-39726

302.2'3 — American cinema films. Sociopolitical aspects
Cinema, politics and society in America / edited by Philip Davies and Brian Neve. — Manchester : Manchester University Press, 1981. — 266p ; 23cm
Includes index
ISBN 0-7190-0832-8 : £14.50 : CIP rev.
B81-27989

302.2'3 — Society. Role of mass media
Culture, society and the media. — London : Methuen, Mar.1982. — [300]p
ISBN 0-416-73500-2 (cased) : £11.00 : CIP entry
ISBN 0-416-73510-x (pbk) : £6.50 B82-01118

302.2'32 — England. Books. Readership, *1700-1800*
Books and their readers in eighteenth-century England / edited by Isabel Rivers. — [Leicester] : Leicester University Press, 1982. — xi,267p ; 24cm
Includes index
ISBN 0-7185-1189-1 : £15.00 : CIP rev.
B82-16510

302.2'32 — English popular literature, *1578-1700.* **Readership**
Spufford, Margaret. Small books and pleasant histories : popular fiction and its readership in seventeenth-century England / Margaret Spufford. — London : Methuen, 1981. — xxi,275p,[4]p of plates : ill,maps,facsims ; 22cm
Includes index
ISBN 0-416-74150-9 : £14.95 : CIP rev.
B81-03145

302.2'32 — Newspapers & magazines. Readership. Surveys *— Conference proceedings*
Readership research : theory and practice : proceedings of the first international symposium, New Orleans, 1981 / edited by Harry Henry. — London : Sigmatext, c1982. — 527p : ill ; 25cm
ISBN 0-907338-02-x : Unpriced : CIP rev.
B81-38850

302.2'32 — Printed media. Effects of technological innovation
The **Future** of the printed word : the impact and the implications of the new communications technology / edited by Philip Hills. — Milton Keynes : Open University Press, 1981, c1980. — 172p : ill ; 22cm
Originally published: London : Pinter, 1980. — Includes bibliographies
ISBN 0-335-10048-1 (pbk) : £4.95 : CIP rev.
B81-23952

302.2'32 — Printed media, *to 1981*
Small, Christopher. The printed word. — Aberdeen : Aberdeen University Press, Sept.1982. — [144]p
ISBN 0-08-025766-6 (cased) : £11.50 : CIP entry
ISBN 0-08-025767-4 (pbk) : £6.50 B82-19098

302.2'32 — Western world. Book industries & trades *— Sociological perspectives*
Gedin, Per. Literature in the marketplace. — London : Faber, Sept.1982. — [256]p
Translation of: Litteraturen i verkligheten. — Originally published: 1977
ISBN 0-571-11948-4 (pbk) : £3.95 : CIP entry
B82-28465

302.2'324 — Great Britain. Serials in English. Readership. Surveys. Organisations: JICNARS. National Readership Survey. Methodology
NRS development : a report on the Cumberland Lodge Research Programme / prepared by the Development Working Party for the Technical Sub-Committee of JICNARS. — [London] ([44 Belgrave Square, SW1X 8QS]) : [JICNARS], 1980. — 32,xxiii,5p : ill ; 30cm
Unpriced (pbk) B82-37307

302.2'34 — Communication. Effects of mass media
Language, image, media. — Oxford : Blackwell, Jan.1983. — [250]p
ISBN 0-631-12704-6 (cased) : £16.00 : CIP entry
ISBN 0-631-12726-7 (pbk) : £5.95 B82-32513

302.2'34 — Great Britain. Local media *— Lists — Serials*
PIMS townslist : a town by town guide to regional media coverage. — 1981-2-. — London (Faber Court, St. John's Place, EC1M 4AH) : Press Information and Mailing Services, 1981-. — v. ; 26x32cm
Annual. — Continues: PRADS towns list
ISSN 0262-7345 = PIMS townslist : Unpriced
B82-14271

302.2'34 — Mass communication
Hiebert, Ray Eldon. Mass media III : an introduction to modern communication / Ray Eldon Hiebert, Donald F. Ungurait, Thomas W. Bohn. — New York ; London : Longman, c1982. — x,643p : ill,facsims,ports ; 24cm
Bibliography: p608-631. — Includes index
ISBN 0-582-28223-3 (pbk) : Unpriced
B82-34307

302.2'34 — Mass media
Perspectives on mass communications / [editors] Warren K. Agee, Phillip H. Ault, Edwin Emery. — New York ; London : Harper & Row, c1982. — xv,476p : ill,ports ; 24cm
Includes index
ISBN 0-06-040174-5 (pbk) : £9.50 B82-28714

302.2'34 — Mass media. Content analysis. Methodology
Berger, Arthur Asa. Media analysis techniques / Arthur Asa Berger. — Beverly Hills ; London : Sage, c1982. — 159p ; 23cm. — (The Sage Commtext series ; v.10)
Bibliography: p158. — Includes index
ISBN 0-8039-0613-7 (cased) : Unpriced
ISBN 0-8039-0614-5 (pbk) : £5.50 B82-38111

302.2'34 — Mass media. Social aspects
Davison, W. Phillips. Mass media : systems and effects / W. Phillips Davison, James Boylan, Frederick T.C. Yu. — 2nd ed. — New York ; London : Holt, Rinehart and Winston, c1982. — x,264p ; 24cm
Previous ed.: New York : Praeger, 1976. — Bibliography: p-230-252. — Includes index
ISBN 0-03-052481-4 (pbk) : £11.95
B82-25372

De Fleur, Melvin L.. Theories of mass communication. — 4th ed. / Melvin L. De Fleur, Sandra J. Ball-Rokeach. — New York ; London : Longman, c1982. — xiii,263p : ill ; 24cm
Previous ed.: 1977. — Includes index
ISBN 0-582-28278-0 (cased) : Unpriced
ISBN 0-582-28277-2 (pbk) : £1.95 B82-34306

Howitt, Dennis. The mass media and social problems / by Dennis Howitt. — Oxford : Pergamon, 1982. — viii,204p ; 34cm. — (International series in experimental social psychology ; v.2)
Bibliography: p180-195. — Includes index
ISBN 0-08-026759-9 (cased) : Unpriced : CIP rev.
ISBN 0-08-028918-5 (pbk) : £5.50 B82-03734

302.2'34 — News media
Hartley, John, *1933-*. Understanding news / John Hartley. — London : Methuen, 1982. — xiii,203p : ill,facsims,ports ; 20cm. — (Studies in communication)
Bibliography: p193-197. — Includes index
ISBN 0-416-74540-7 (cased) : Unpriced : CIP rev.
ISBN 0-416-74550-4 (pbk) : Unpriced
B82-11525

World press encyclopedia / edited by George Thomas Kurian ; indexed by Marjorie B. Bank and James Johnson. — London : Mansell, 1982. — 2v.(xix,1202p) : ill ; 29cm
Includes bibliographies and index
ISBN 0-7201-1646-5 : Unpriced : CIP rev.
ISBN 0-7201-1644-9 (v.1) : Unpriced
ISBN 0-7201-1645-7 (v.2) : Unpriced
B82-02643

302.2'34'0710411 — Scotland. Educational institutions. Curriculum subjects: Mass media *— Conference proceedings*
Media Education Conference *(1980 : Glasgow)*. Media education : a report on the Media Education Conference jointly held by the Scottish Film Council, Jordanhill College of Education and the Scottish Council for Educational Technology at Dowanhill, Glasgow on November 29th 1980 / edited by Kevin Cowle. — Glasgow : Scottish Film Council, 1981. — 101p in various pagings : facsims,ports ; 30cm
ISBN 0-86011-040-0 (spiral) : Unpriced
B82-00771

302.2'34'0724 — Mass communication. Mathematical models
McQuail, Denis. Communication models : for the study of mass communications / Denis McQuail and Sven Windahl. — London : Longman, 1981. — 110p : ill ; 21cm
Includes bibliographies and index
ISBN 0-582-29572-6 (pbk) : £2.95 : CIP rev.
B81-28084

302.2'34'09174927 — Arab countries. Society. Role of news media. Political aspects
Rugh, William A.. as-Sihāfah al-'arabiyyah = The Arab press : news media and political process in the Arab world / William A. Rugh. — London : Croom Helm, 1979. — xviii,205p ; 24cm
Includes index
ISBN 0-7099-0181-x : £11.50 B82-08513

302.2'34'0941 — Great Britain. Mass media. Relations with business firms *— Manuals — For businessmen*
The **Headline** business : a businessman's guide to working with the media / [compiled by Squire Barraclough for the CBI Information Directorate]. — [London] : Confederation of British Industry in association with Abbey Life Assurance Co. Ltd., c1981. — 112p : ill ; 21cm
Cover title
£2.50 (pbk)
Primary classification 658.4'5 B82-06373

302.2'34'0941 — Great Britain. Society. Effects of mass media
Fox, Julian. The power of the media / Julian Fox. — Hove : Wayland, 1981. — 72p : ill,facsims,ports ; 24cm. — (People, politics and powers)
Bibliography: p70. — Includes index
ISBN 0-85340-897-1 : £4.50 B82-03883

302.2'34'0951 — China. Mass communication
Howkins, John, *1945-*. Mass communication in China / John Howkins. — New York ; London : Longman, c1982. — xvii,160p : ill,1map ; 24cm. — (Annenberg/Longman communication books)
Bibliography: p148-152. — Includes index
ISBN 0-582-28264-0 : Unpriced B82-33645

302.2′34′0973 — United States. Mass media

Agee, Warren K.. Introduction to mass communications / Warren K. Agee, Phillip H. Ault, Edwin Emery. — 7th ed. — New York ; Cambridge : Harper & Row, c1982. — xiii,498p : ill,1map,2facsims,ports ; 24cm
Previous ed.: 1979. — Bibliography: p438-476. — Includes index
ISBN 0-06-040175-3 (pbk) : £10.95 B82-22927

Sandman, Peter M.. Media : an introductory analysis of American mass communications / Peter M. Sandman, David M. Rubin, David B. Sachsman. — 3rd ed. — Englewood Cliffs ; London : Prentice-Hall, c1982. — vii,525p ; 24cm
Previous ed.: 1976. — Includes bibliographies and index
ISBN 0-13-572545-3 (pbk) : £11.20 B82-24093

302.2′34′0994 — Australia. Mass media. Public opinion, *1940-1980*

Mayer, Henry. The media. — London : Allen & Unwin, Nov.1982. — [224]p
ISBN 0-86861-348-7 : £20.00 : CIP entry B82-26089

302.2′343′09 — Cinema films, *to 1980.* **Social aspects**

Reader, Keith. Cultures on celluloid / Keith Reader. — London : Quartet, 1981. — 216p,[8]p of plates : ill ; 25cm
Bibliography: p200-202. — List of films: p203-209. — Includes index
ISBN 0-7043-2272-2 : £11.50 : CIP rev. B81-25707

302.2′344′0941 — Great Britain. Society. Role of broadcasting services, *1918-1939*

Pegg, Mark. Broadcasting and society 1918-1939. — London : Croom Helm, Dec.1982. — [240]p
ISBN 0-7099-2039-3 : £11.95 : CIP entry B82-30590

302.2′345 — Capitalist countries. Society. Role of television

Birîukov, N. S.. Television in the West and its doctrines / N.S. Biryukov ; [translated from the Russian by Yuri Sviridov]. — Moscow : Progress ; [London] : distributed by Central, c1981. — 206p ; 21cm
Translation of: Televidenie zapada i ego doktriny
ISBN 0-7147-1696-0 : £2.95 B82-29295

302.2′345′0973 — United States. Television services. Social aspects

Esslin, Martin. The age of television / Martin Esslin. — Oxford : Freeman, c1982. — 138p : ill,ports ; 25cm
Bibliography: p127-129. — Includes index
ISBN 0-7167-1337-3 (cased) : £11.90
ISBN 0-7167-1338-1 (pbk) : £5.50 B82-29338

302.3 — Bargaining

Bacharach, Samuel B.. Bargaining : power, tactics, and outcomes / Samuel B. Bacharach, Edward J. Lawler. — San Francisco ; London : Jossey-Bass, 1981. — xviii,234p : ill ; 24cm. — (The Jossey-Bass social and behavioral science series)
Bibliography: p215-224. — Includes index
ISBN 0-87589-498-4 : £13.75 B82-11702

302.3 — Group dynamics

Johnson, David W.. Joining together : group theory and group skills / David W. Johnson, Frank P. Johnson. — 2nd ed. — Englewood Cliffs ; London : Prentice Hall, 1982. — xv,510p : ill ; 24cm
Previous ed.: 1975. — Includes bibliographies and index
ISBN 0-13-510396-7 (pbk) : Unpriced B82-34703

Randall, Rosemary. Co-operative and community group dynamics : — or your meetings needn′t be so appalling / text Rosemary Randall and John Southgate ; illustrations Frances Tomlinson. — London : Barefoot, c1980. — 53p : ill ; 30cm
Cover title. — Bibliography: p53
ISBN 0-9506273-1-3 (pbk) : £1.50 : CIP rev. B80-17555

302.3 — Groups. Decision making — *Conference proceedings*

Group decision making / edited by Hermann Brandstätter, James H. Davis, Gisela Stocker-Kreichgauer. — London : Published in cooperation with European Association of Experimental Social Psychology by Academic Press, 1982. — xvi,557p : ill ; 24cm. — (European monographs in social psychology ; 25)
Conference proceedings. — Includes bibliographies and index
ISBN 0-12-125820-3 : £21.80 : CIP rev. B82-00322

302.3 — Negotiation. Psychosocial aspects

Pruitt, Dean G.. Negotiation behavior / Dean G. Pruitt. — New York ; London : Academic Press, 1981. — xii,263p : ill ; 24cm. — (Organizational and occupational psychology)
Bibliography: p237-249. — Includes index
ISBN 0-12-566250-5 : £14.00 B82-22237

302.3 — Social groups. Interpersonal relationships. Social psychology

Intergroup behaviour. — Oxford : Basil Blackwell, July 1981. — [256]p
ISBN 0-631-11711-3 (cased) : £12.50 : CIP entry
ISBN 0-631-12718-6 (pbk) : £5.50 B81-14970

302.3′3 — France. Crowds. Psychology. Theories, *1878-1900*

Barrows, Susanna. Distorting mirrors : visions of the crowd in late nineteenth-century France / Susanna Barrows. — New Haven ; London : Yale University Press, c1981. — ix,221p ; 22cm
Bibliography: p199-213. — Includes index
ISBN 0-300-02588-2 : Unpriced : CIP rev.
Also classified at 306′.2 B81-34718

302.3′3 — Man. Crowds. Behaviour. Psychosocial aspects

Canetti, Elias. Crowds and power / Elias Canetti ; translated from the German by Carol Stewart. — Harmondsworth : Penguin, 1973 (1981 printing). — 575p ; 20cm
Originally published: London : Gollancz, 1962. — Bibliography: p563-575
ISBN 0-14-003616-4 (pbk) : £2.95 B82-08522

302.3′46′024658 — Interpersonal relationships. Face to face communication — *For management*

Honey, Peter. Face to face : business communication for results / Peter Honey. — American ed. — Englewood Cliffs ; London : Prentice Hall, c1978. — xvi,207p ; 21cm. — (A Spectrum book)
Originally published: London : Institute of Personnel Management, 1976
ISBN 0-13-298620-5 (cased) : Unpriced
ISBN 0-13-298612-4 (pbk)
ISBN 0-85292-287-6 (IPM) B82-39859

302.3′5 — Organisational behaviour

Hutton, Geoffrey, *1928-*. Thinking about systems, ideas and action / by Geoffrey Hutton. — Bath : University of Bath. — (Working paper / Centre for the Study of Organizational Change and Development ; 80/05)
6: On responsibility in research. — c1980. — 18p : 1ill ; 21cm
Bibliography: p18
ISBN 0-86197-028-4 (pbk) : Unpriced B82-35803

Mohr, Lawrence B.. Explaining organizational behavior / Lawrence B. Mohr. — San Francisco ; London : Jossey-Bass, 1982. — xv,260p ; 24cm. — (The Jossey-Bass social and behavioral science series)
Bibliography: p228-245. — Includes index
ISBN 0-87589-514-x : Unpriced B82-32918

302.3′5 — Organisations. Commitment of personnel

Mowday, Richard T.. Employee-organization linkages : the psychology of commitment, absenteeism and turnover / Richard T. Mowday, Lyman W. Porter, Richard M. Steers. — New York ; London : Academic Press, 1982. — x,253p : ill ; 24cm. — (Organizational and occupational psychology)
Bibliography: p231-244. — Includes index
ISBN 0-12-509370-5 : £16.60 B82-30111

302.3′5 — Organisations. Design

Designing organisations for satisfaction and efficiency / edited by Karen Legge and Enid Mumford. — Farnborough, Hants. : Gower, c1978. — ix,144p : ill ; 23cm. — (A Personnel review monograph)
Includes bibliographies
ISBN 0-566-02102-1 : Unpriced : CIP rev. B78-22480

302.3′5 — Organisations. Middle range theories — *Conference proceedings*

Middle range theory and the study of organizations / edited by Craig C. Pinder, Larry F. Moore. — Boston, [Mass.] ; London : Nijhoff, c1980. — xiv,413p : ill ; 24cm
Papers presented at a conference held Aug.1-3, 1978 at the University of British Columbia, Vancouver. — Includes bibliographies
ISBN 0-89838-021-9 : Unpriced B82-12871

302.3′5 — Organisations. Personnel. Behaviour — *For management*

Mitchell, Terence R.. People in organisations : an introduction to organizational behavior / Terence R. Mitchell. — 2nd ed. — New York ; London : McGraw-Hill, 1982. — xvi,590p : ill ; 24cm. — (McGraw-Hill series in management)
Previous ed.: 1978. — Includes bibliographies and index
ISBN 0-07-042532-9 : £16.75 B82-25879

302.3′5 — Organisations — *Sociological perspectives*

Hall, Richard H.. Organizations : structure and process / Richard H. Hall. — 3rd ed. — Englewood Cliffs ; London : Prentice-Hall, c1982. — xii,356p : ill ; 24cm. — (Prentice-Hall series in sociology)
Previous ed.: 1977. — Bibliography: p327-349. — Includes index
ISBN 0-13-641993-3 : £15.70 B82-23238

302.3′5 — Organisations — *Sociological perspectives — For Nigerian students*

Ogunniyi, ′Dayo. Social organizations and institutions / ′Dayo Ogunniyi. — 2nd ed. — London : Evans, 1981. — 76p : ill,maps,ports ; 25cm. — (Social studies for schools and colleges ; bk.1)
Previous ed.: 1977
ISBN 0-237-50656-4 (pbk) : Unpriced B82-03569

Ogunniyi, ′Dayo. Social organizations and institutions / ′Dayo Ogunniyi. — Rev. ed. — London : Evans. — (Social studies for schools and colleges ; bk.1)
Previous ed.: 1978
Teacher′s book. — 1982. — 72p ; 22cm
ISBN 0-237-50657-2 (pbk) : Unpriced B82-18288

302.3′5 — Organisations. Theories

Perspectives on organization design and behavior / edited by Andrew H. Van de Ven and William F. Joyce. — New York ; Chichester : Wiley, c1981. — xxiii,486p : ill ; 24cm. — (Wiley series on organizational assessment and change, ISSN 0194-0120)
Includes bibliographies and index
ISBN 0-471-09358-0 : £22.00 B82-11633

302.3′5 — Organisations. Theories — *For management*

Jackson, John H.. Organization theory : a macro perspective for management / John H. Jackson, Cyril P. Morgan. — 2nd ed. — Englewood Cliffs ; London : Prentice-Hall, 1982. — xv,413p : ill ; 24cm
Previous ed.: 1978. — Bibliography: p386-398. — Includes index
ISBN 0-13-641415-x : £17.20 B82-35160

302.3′5 — United States. Industries. Large companies. Social aspects — *Case studies*

Sethi, S. Prakash. Up against the corporate wall : modern corporations and social issues of the eighties / S. Prakash Sethi. — 4th ed. — Englewood Cliffs ; London : Prentice-Hall, c1982. — xvi,480p : ill,facsims ; 25cm
Previous ed.: 1977. — Includes bibliographies
ISBN 0-13-938316-6 (cased) : Unpriced
ISBN 0-13-938308-5 (pbk) : £10.45 B82-20542

302.3'5 — United States. Organisations. Deviance — *Sociological perspectives*

Corporate and governmental deviance : problems of organizational behavior in contemporary society / [edited by] M. David Ermann, Richard J. Lundman. — 2nd ed. — New York ; Oxford : Oxford University Press, 1982. — x,294p ; 21cm
Previous ed.: 1978
ISBN 0-19-503036-2 (pbk) : £5.95 B82-41062

302.3'5'024658 — Organisations — *For business studies*

Edwards, G. J.. The organization in its environment / G.J. Edwards, A.C. Kellar. — London : McGraw-Hill. — (McGraw-Hill business education courses)
Bk.2: The complex society. — c1980. — xviii,226p : ill
Includes index
ISBN 0-07-084630-8 (pbk) : £3.75 : CIP rev. B80-10949

Gallant, Cyril. The world of work / Cyril Gallant. — New York ; London : McGraw-Hill, c1981. — ix,240p : ill,1map,plans,forms ; 25cm. — (McGraw-Hill business education courses)
Includes index
ISBN 0-07-084246-9 (pbk) : £4.50 : CIP rev. B81-11967

Livesey, Frank. The organisation in its environment / F. Livesey, G.K. Pople, P.J. Davies. — London : Longman. — (Longman business education series)
Vol.1: Lecturers' manual. — 1980. — 69p ; 30cm
ISBN 0-582-41582-9 (spiral) : £2.50 : CIP rev. B79-35677

302.3'5'05 — Organisations — *Sociological perspectives — Serials*

The **International** yearbook of organization studies. — 1981. — London : Routledge & Kegan Paul, Dec.1981. — [306]p
ISBN 0-7100-0996-8 : £18.00 : CIP entry B81-36993

302.3'5'0722 — Organisational behaviour — *Case studies*

White, Donald D.. Action in organizations / Donald D. White, H. William Vroman. — 2nd ed. — Boston, Mass. ; London : Allyn and Bacon, c1982. — xii,425p : ill,facsims ; 24cm
Previous ed.: [1977?]. — Includes index
ISBN 0-205-07353-0 (pbk) : Unpriced B82-02804

302.5'42 — Camp behaviour, *to 1981*

Booth, Mark. Camp. — London : Quartet, Oct.1982. — [192]p
ISBN 0-7043-2353-2 : £12.50 : CIP entry B82-29011

302.5'42 — Deviance

Higgins, Paul C.. Understanding deviance / Paul C. Higgins, Richard R. Butler ; [editors were Eric M. Munson and Barry Benjamin]. — New York ; London : McGraw-Hill, c1982. — xi,292p ; 24cm
Bibliography: p263-280. — Includes index
ISBN 0-07-028776-7 (pbk) : £8.95 B82-22229

302.5'42 — Deviance. Social control

Gibbs, Jack P.. Norms, deviance, and social control : conceptual matters / Jack P. Gibbs. — New York ; Oxford : Elsevier, c1981. — xii,190p ; 24cm
Bibliography: p169-181. — Includes index
ISBN 0-444-01551-5 : Unpriced B82-02145

302.5'42 — Deviance — *Sociological perspectives*

Best, Joel. Organizing deviance / Joel Best, David F. Luckenbill. — Englewood Cliffs ; London : Prentice-Hall, c1982. — xii,288p ; 23cm
Bibliography: p262-275. — Includes index
ISBN 0-13-641605-5 (pbk) : £9.70 B82-20064

Downes, David. Understanding deviance : a guide to the sociology of crime and rule-breaking. — Oxford : Clarendon, July 1982. — [320]p
ISBN 0-19-876086-8 (cased) : £12.50 : CIP entry
ISBN 0-19-876087-6 (pbk) : £7.95 B82-12555

Images of deviance / edited by Stanley Cohen. — Harmondsworth : Penguin, 1971 (1982 [printing]). — 255p : ill ; 20cm. — (Penguin education)
Bibliography: p25
ISBN 0-14-080450-1 (pbk) : £1.95 B82-33149

302.5'44 — Alienation

Alienation : problems of meaning, theory and method / edited y R. Felix Geyer and David Schweitzer. — London : Routledge & Kegan Paul, 1981. — xv,283p : ill ; 23cm
Conference papers. — Includes bibliographies
ISBN 0-7100-0835-x : £12.50 B82-05453

Baxter, Brian. Alienation and authenticity. — London : Tavistock, Dec.1982. — [240]p
ISBN 0-422-78280-7 : £14.00 : CIP entry B82-29796

302.5'44'01 — Alienation — *Philosophical perspectives*

Keyan, Rostam. Being and alienation / Rostam Keyan. — New York : Philosophical Library ; London : George Prior [distributor], c1981. — 430p ; 22cm
Includes index
ISBN 0-8022-2235-8 : £6.50 B82-13954

Shoham, S. Giora. The violence of silence. — Northwood : Science Reviews, Dec.1982. — [300]p
ISBN 0-905927-06-0 (pbk) : £15.00 : CIP entry B82-30614

302.5'44'0924 — Alienation. Theories of Marx, Karl

Wallimann, Isidor. Estrangement : Marx's conception of human nature and the division of labor / Isidor Wallimann ; foreword by Gunter W. Remmling. — Westport ; London : Greenwood, 1981. — xxiv,195p ; 22cm. — (Contributions in philosophy, ISSN 0084-926x ; no.16)
Bibliography: p177-189. — Includes index
ISBN 0-313-22096-4 : Unpriced B82-02002

302.5'45 — Loneliness

Kurtz, Irma. Loneliness. — Oxford : Blackwell, Nov.1982. — [128]p. — (Understanding everyday experience)
ISBN 0-631-12578-7 (cased) : £9.95 : CIP entry
ISBN 0-631-13084-5 (pbk) : £2.95 B82-32860

Loneliness : a sourcebook of current theory, research and therapy / edited by Letitia Anne Peplau, Daniel Perlman. — New York ; Chichester : Wiley, c1982. — xvii,430p ; 25cm. — (Wiley series on personality processes)
Bibliography: p407-417. — Includes index
ISBN 0-471-08028-4 : £29.50 B82-36683

303 — SOCIAL PROCESSES

303.3 — Power — *Sociological perspectives*

Beecham, Yvonne. Power and conflict / Yvonne Beecham, Julia Fiehn, Jo Gates ; cartoons by Chris Madden ... [et al.]. — London : Harrap, 1982. — 63p : ill ; 28cm. — (Themes in sociology)
ISBN 0-245-53254-4 (pbk) : £2.25
Also classified at 303.6 B82-40465

303.3'2 — Children. Socialisation

Blunden, Ruth. Social development / Ruth Blunden. — Lancaster : MTP Press, c1982. — 160p : ill ; 23cm. — (Studies in developmental paediatrics ; v.4)
Bibliography: p143-153. — Includes index
ISBN 0-85200-304-8 : Unpriced : CIP rev. B81-35857

303.3'2 — Villages. Children. Socialisation. Cultural factors — *Comparative studies*

Whiting, Beatrice B.. Children of six cultures : a psycho-cultural analysis / Beatrice B. Whiting and John W.M. Whiting in collaboration with Richard Longabaugh ; based on data collected by John and Ann Fischer ... [et al.]. — Cambridge, Mass. ; London : Harvard University Press, c1975 (1979 [printing]). — xiv,237p : ill,maps,plans ; 20cm
Bibliography: p221-227. — Includes index
ISBN 0-674-11645-3 (cased) : Unpriced
ISBN 0-674-11648-8 (pbk) : £4.20 B82-02731

303.3'27 — United States. Ethnic minorities. Children. Socialisation. Role of television services

Television and the socialization of the minority child / edited by Gordon L. Berry, Claudia Mitchell-Kernan. — New York ; London : Academic, 1982. — xvii,289p ; 24cm
Conference papers. — Includes bibliographies and index
ISBN 0-12-093220-2 : £16.20 B82-38081

303.3'3'0942 — England. Social control. Implications of special education

Ford, Julienne. Special education and social control : invisible disasters / Julienne Ford, Denis Mongon and Maurice Whelan. — London : Routledge & Kegan Paul, 1982. — ix,179p : ill ; 23cm
Bibliography: p172-177. — Includes index
ISBN 0-7100-0951-8 : £7.95 B82-32502

303.3'4 — Leadership — *Manuals*

Adair, John, *1934-*. Effective leadership. — Aldershot : Gower, Jan.1983. — [200]p
ISBN 0-566-02411-x : £12.50 : CIP entry B82-36147

Gordon, Thomas. Leader effectiveness training : L.E.T. : the no-lose way to release the productive potential of people / Thomas Gordon. — London : Futura, 1979, c1977. — vi,278p : ill ; 18cm
Originally published: New York : Wyden Books, 1977. — Includes index
ISBN 0-7088-1449-2 (pbk) : £1.10 B82-08797

303.3'4 — Leadership. Role of universities

Adair, John, *1934-*. Developing tomorrow's leaders : a university contribution / John Adair. — [Guildford] ([Guildford, Surrey GU2 5XH]) : [University of Surrey], [1981?]. — 22p : ill ; 21cm. — (University of Surrey inaugural lecture)
Cover title
Unpriced (pbk) B82-26654

303.3'4'01 — Leadership. Theories, *to ca 1980*

Hodgkinson, Christopher. The philosophy of leadership. — Oxford : Blackwell, Feb.1983. — [224]p
ISBN 0-631-13082-9 : £12.00 : CIP entry B82-38863

Stogdill, Ralph M.. Stogdill's handbook of leadership : a survey of theory and research. — Rev. and expanded ed. / by Bernard M. Bass. — New York : Free Press ; London : Collier Macmillan, c1981. — xviii,356p ; 26cm
Previous ed.: 1974. — Bibliography: p618-808. — Includes index
ISBN 0-02-901820-x : £27.95 B82-18007

303.3'6 — Authority — *Philosophical perspectives*

Watt, E. D.. Authority / E.D. Watt. — London : Croom Helm, c1982. — 124p ; 23cm. — (Croom Helm international series in social and political thought)
Bibliography: p109-121. — Includes index
ISBN 0-7099-2741-x (cased) : £9.95 : CIP rev.
ISBN 0-7099-2742-8 (pbk) : Unpriced B82-06518

303.3'72 — India *(Republic)* **& Nepal. Social values** — *Anthropological perspectives*

Culture and morality : essays in honour of Christoph von Fürer-Haimendorf / edited by Adrian C. Mayer. — Delhi ; Oxford : Oxford University Press, 1981. — xv,270p,[1]leaf of plates : 1port ; 23cm
Includes bibliographies and index
ISBN 0-19-561257-4 : Unpriced B82-31222

303.3'75 — Germany. Propaganda. Role of cinema films, *1933-1945*

Welch, David. Propaganda and the German cinema 1933-1945. — Oxford : Clarendon, Feb.1983. — [420]p
ISBN 0-19-822598-9 (pbk) : £19.50 : CIP entry B82-36602

303.3'75'091713 — Western anti-Soviet propaganda — *Soviet viewpoints*

Artemov, V.. Information abused : critical essays / Vladimir Artemov ; [translated from the Russian by Dmitry Belyavsky]. — Moscow : Progress Publishers ; [London] : distributed by Central Books, c1981. — 214p ; 17cm
Translation of: Zloupotreblenie informatsieĭ
ISBN 0-7147-1763-0 (pbk) : £1.50 B82-38233

303.3'8 — Public. Attitudes. Measurement. Methodology — *Case studies*

Some issues in the methodology of attitude research / contributions by E.E. Davis ... [et al.] ; with an appendix by B.J. Whelan. — Dublin : Economic and Social Research Institute, 1980. — xiii,153p ; 21cm. — (Policy research series ; no.3)
Includes bibliographies
ISBN 0-7070-0035-1 (pbk) : Unpriced
B82-35802

303.3'8'0941 — Great Britain. Public opinion, *1981*

Webb, Norman L.. The Gallup report : your opinions in 1981 / Norman Webb and Robert Wybrow. — London : Sphere, 1982. — 192p ; 20cm
ISBN 0-7221-9023-9 (pbk) : £2.25 B82-24540

303.3'85 — Prejudice. Psychosocial aspects

Levin, Jack, *1941-*. The functions of discrimination and prejudice / Jack Levin, William C. Levin. — 2nd ed. — New York ; London : Harper & Row, c1982. — xiv,258p : ill ; 21cm
Previous ed.: published as Functions of prejudice, 1975. — Bibliography: p249. — Includes index
ISBN 0-06-043964-5 (pbk) : £7.95
Also classified at 305 B82-16588

303.3'879192 — Lithuanians. National identity — *Lithuanian texts*

Štromas, Aleksandras. Politinė samonė Lietuvoje ir joje astispindinčios krašto ateities vižijos / su Ţomo Venclovos komentarias ; Aleksandras Štromas. — Londonas : Nida, 1980. — 101p : ports ; 19cm
Unpriced (pbk) B82-20908

303.4 — Industrialised societies. Social change — *Conference proceedings*

The **Poverty** of progress. — Oxford : Pergamon, Feb.1982. — [275]p
Conference papers
ISBN 0-08-028906-1 : £17.00 : CIP entry
B81-35946

303.4 — Industrialised societies. Social change. Geographical aspects

Geographical agenda for a changing world : a report commissioned by the SSRC Human Geography Committee / edited by B.T. Robson and J. Rees. — London : SSRC, c1982. — ii,162p : ill ; 30cm
Includes bibliographies
ISBN 0-86226-039-6 (pbk) : £5.00 B82-30857

303.4 — Organisational change

Koolhaas, Jan. Organization dissonance and change / Jan Koolhaas. — Chichester : Wiley, c1982. — xvii,208p : ill ; 24cm
Bibliography: p200-203. — Includes index
ISBN 0-471-10140-0 : £12.75 : CIP rev.
B82-13252

303.4 — Social change

Lauer, Robert H.. Perspectives on social change / Robert H. Lauer. — 3rd ed. — Boston [Mass.] ; London : Allyn and Bacon, c1982. — vi,378p : ill ; 24cm
Previous ed.: 1977. — Includes index
ISBN 0-205-07561-4 : Unpriced B82-08538

303.4 — World — *Forecasts*

O'Neill, Gerard K.. 2081 : a hopeful view of the human future / Gerard K. O'Neill. — London : Cape, 1981. — 248p : ill ; 25cm
Bibliography: p269-274. — Includes index
ISBN 0-224-01677-6 : £6.95 : CIP rev.
B81-27445

303.4'05 — Social change — *Serials*

Research in social movements, conflicts and change : an annual compilation of research. — Vol.1 (1978)-. — Greenwich, Conn. : JAI Press ; London (3 Henrietta St., WC2E 8LU) : Distributed by JAICON Press, 1978-. — v. ; 24cm
ISSN 0163-786x = Research in social movements, conflicts and change : £24.50
B82-02359

303.4'0724 — Social change. Mathematical models

Kessler, Ronald C.. Linear panel analysis : models of quantitative change / Ronald C. Kessler, David F. Greenberg. — New York ; London ; Academic Press, c1981. — x,203p : ill ; 24cm. — (Quantitative studies in social relations)
Bibliography: p189-197. — Includes index
ISBN 0-12-405750-0 : £14.20 B82-04242

303.4'09182'1 — Western world. Social change

Williams, Trevor A.. Learning to manage our futures : the participative redesign of societies in turbulent transition / Trevor A. Williams ; with an afterword by Fred E. Emery. — New York ; Chichester : Wiley, c1982. — xi,211p : ill ; 24cm
Bibliography: p203-206. — Includes index
ISBN 0-471-08135-3 : £17.75 B82-26264

303.4'0947 — Eastern Europe. Social conditions — *Forecasts*

Eastern Europe in the 1980s / edited by Stephen Fischer-Galati. — Boulder : Westview Press ; London : Croom Helm, 1981. — xvii,291p ; 24cm
Includes index
ISBN 0-7099-1005-3 : £15.95 B82-00018

303.4'4 — Progress

Progress and its discontents / edited by Gabriel A. Almond, Marvin Chodorow & Roy Harvey Pearce ; sponsored by the Western Center of the American Academy of Arts and Sciences. — Berkeley ; London : University of California Press, c1982. — xiv,565p : ill ; 24cm
Conference papers. — Includes index
ISBN 0-520-04478-9 : £20.75 B82-39732

303.4'4 — Social systems. Development

Teune, Henry. The developmental logic of social systems / Henry Teune, Zdravko Mlinar. — Beverly Hills ; London : Sage, c1978. — 175p : ill ; 23cm. — (Sage library of social research ; v.60)
ISBN 0-8039-0900-4 (cased) : £15.50
ISBN 0-8039-0901-2 (pbk) : Unpriced
B82-09090

303.4'4'01 — Progress. Theories, *to 1979*

Olson, Theodore. Millennialism, utopianism and progress / Theodore Olson. — Toronto ; London : University of Toronto Press, c1982. — x,320p ; 24cm
Bibliography: p299-309. — Includes index
ISBN 0-8020-5506-0 : Unpriced B82-35662

303.4'82 — International relations

Bandyopadhyaya, Jayantanuja. North over South : a non-western perspective of international relations / Jayantanuja Bandyopadhyaya. — Brighton : Harvester Press, 1982. — ix,290p : ill ; 22cm
Bibliography: p270-281. — Includes index
ISBN 0-7108-0344-3 : £18.95 : CIP rev.
B81-33888

Krippendorff, Ekkehart. International relations as a social science / by E. Krippendorff. — Brighton : Harvester, 1982. — ix,192p ; 23cm
Translation of: Internationale Beziehungen als Wissenschaft. — Bibliography: p183-192
ISBN 0-7108-0480-6 : £16.95 : CIP rev.
B82-09602

303.4'82 — International relations. Role of ethnic groups

Ethnic identities in a transnational world / edited by John F. Stack, Jr.. — Westport, Conn. ; London : Greenwood Press, 1981. — xiii,223p ; 22cm. — (Contributions in political science, ISSN 0147-1466 ; no.52)
Bibliography: p207-215. — Includes index
ISBN 0-313-21088-8 : £20.95 B82-18366

303.4'82'09411 — Scotland. Relations with United States, *1700-1800.* **Historical sources**

Brock, William R.. Scotus Americanus : a survey of the sources for links between Scotland and America in the eighteenth century. — Edinburgh : Edinburgh University Press, Jan.1982. — [320]p
ISBN 0-85224-420-7 : £15.00 : CIP entry
Also classified at 303.4'82'0973 B81-37529

303.4'82'0973 — United States. Relations with Scotland, *1700-1800.* **Historical sources**

Brock, William R.. Scotus Americanus : a survey of the sources for links between Scotland and America in the eighteenth century. — Edinburgh : Edinburgh University Press, Jan.1982. — [320]p
ISBN 0-85224-420-7 : £15.00 : CIP entry
Primary classification 303.4'82'09411
B81-37529

303.4'821724 — Developing countries. International relations

Mushkat, M.. The Third World and peace. — Aldershot : Gower, Aug.1982. — [450]p
ISBN 0-566-00559-x : £12.50 : CIP entry
B82-15882

303.4'824'0415 — Western Europe. Relations with Ireland, *400-1200* — *Festschriften*

Ireland in early mediaeval Europe : studies in memory of Kathleen Hughes / edited by Dorothy Whitelock, Rosamond McKitterick, David Dumville. — Cambridge : Cambridge University Press, 1982. — x,406p,[16]p of plates : ill,1port ; 24cm
Includes index
ISBN 0-521-23547-2 : £39.00 : CIP rev.
Primary classification 303.4'82415'04
B81-14958

303.4'824'047 — Western Europe. Cooperation with Eastern Europe — *Socialist viewpoints*

Benn, Tony. European unity : a new perspective / Tony Benn. — Nottingham (Bertrand Russell House, Gamble Street, Nottingham, NG7 4ET) : Spokesman for the Bertrand Russell Peace Foundation, [1981]. — 15p ; 21cm. — (Spokesman pamphlet ; no.75)
Text of a lecture delivered under the auspices of the British Broadcasting Corporation and the Gulbenkian Foundation, 19 March 1981
£0.50 (unbound)
Also classified at 303.4'8247'04 B82-17674

303.4'82415'04 — Ireland. Relations with Western Europe, *400-1200* — *Festschriften*

Ireland in early mediaeval Europe : studies in memory of Kathleen Hughes / edited by Dorothy Whitelock, Rosamond McKitterick, David Dumville. — Cambridge : Cambridge University Press, 1982. — x,406p,[16]p of plates : ill,1port ; 24cm
Includes index
ISBN 0-521-23547-2 : £39.00 : CIP rev.
Also classified at 303.4'824'0415 B81-14958

303.4'82415'042 — Ireland. Relations with England, *1200-1500*

England and Ireland in the later middle ages : essays in honour of Jocelyn Otway-Ruthven / edited by James Lydon. — Blackrock, Co. Dublin : Irish Academic Press, 1981. — xii,273p : 3maps,1port ; 22cm
List of works by A.J. Otway-Ruthven: p255-263. — Includes index
ISBN 0-7165-0070-1 : Unpriced
Primary classification 303.4'8242'0415
B82-14670

303.4'8242'0415 — England. Relations with Ireland, *1200-1500*

England and Ireland in the later middle ages : essays in honour of Jocelyn Otway-Ruthven / edited by James Lydon. — Blackrock, Co. Dublin : Irish Academic Press, 1981. — xii,273p : 3maps,1port ; 22cm
List of works by A.J. Otway-Ruthven: p255-263. — Includes index
ISBN 0-7165-0070-1 : Unpriced
Also classified at 303.4'82415'042 B82-14670

303.4'8247'04 — Eastern Europe. Cooperation with Western Europe — *Socialist viewpoints*

Benn, Tony. European unity : a new perspective / Tony Benn. — Nottingham (Bertrand Russell House, Gamble Street, Nottingham, NG7 4ET) : Spokesman for the Bertrand Russell Peace Foundation, [1981]. — 15p ; 21cm. — (Spokesman pamphlet ; no.75)
Text of a lecture delivered under the auspices of the British Broadcasting Corporation and the Gulbenkian Foundation, 19 March 1981
£0.50 (unbound)
Primary classification 303.4'824'047
B82-17674

303.4'8247'0495 — Eastern Europe. Relations with Byzantine Empire, *ca 700-ca 1400*

Obolensky, Dimitri. The Byzantine inheritance of Eastern Europe / Dimitri Obolensky. — London : Variorum Reprints, 1982. — 300p in various pagings : ill,1port ; 24cm. — (Collected studies series ; CS156)
Includes 1 paper in French. — Facsimile reprints. — Includes index
ISBN 0-86078-102-x : Unpriced : CIP rev.
Also classified at 303.4'82495'047 B82-01574

303.4'82495'047 — Byzantine Empire. Relations with Eastern Europe, *ca 700-ca 1450*

Obolensky, Dimitri. The Byzantine inheritance of Eastern Europe / Dimitri Obolensky. — London : Variorum Reprints, 1982. — 300p in various pagings : ill,1port ; 24cm. — (Collected studies series ; CS156)
Includes 1 paper in French. — Facsimile reprints. — Includes index
ISBN 0-86078-102-x : Unpriced : CIP rev.
Primary classification 303.4'8247'0495
B82-01574

303.4'824972 — Yugoslavia. Dubrovnik. International relations, *1200-1600*

Krekić, Bariša. Dubrovnik, Italy and the Balkans in the late Middle Ages / Bariša Krekić. — London : Variorum Reprints, c1980. — 332p in various pagings : 1port ; 24cm
Text in English, chapters in French and Italian. — Includes index
ISBN 0-86078-070-8 : £22.00 : CIP rev.
B80-17558

303.4'8268'073 — South Africa. Relations with United States. Attitudes of American public

The **American** people and South Africa : publics, elites, and policymaking processes / edited by Alfred O. Hero, Jr., John Barratt. — Lexington, Mass. : Lexington Books, c1981 ; [Aldershot] : Gower [distributor], 1982. — ix,229p ; 24cm
Conference papers. — Includes index
ISBN 0-669-04320-6 : £15.50
Primary classification 303.4'8273'068
B82-21164

303.4'826894 — Zambia. Western Province. Lozi civilization. Influence of European colonialists, *1876-1896*

Prins, Gwyn. The hidden hippopotamus : reappraisal in African history : the early colonial experience in western Zambia / Gwyn Prins. — Cambridge : Cambridge University Press, 1980. — xvi,319p : ill,maps,ports ; 24cm. — (African studies series, ISSN 0065-406x ; 28)
Bibliography: p306-309. — Includes index
ISBN 0-521-22915-4 : £20.00 : CIP rev.
B80-25170

303.4'8273 — United States. Cultural relations, *to 1976*

For better or worse : the American influence in the world / edited by Allen F. Davis. — Westport, Conn. ; London : Greenwood, 1981. — xiv,195p : ill,facsims ; 24cm. — (Contributions in American studies ; no.51)
Includes index
ISBN 0-313-22342-4 : Unpriced B82-02618

303.4'8273'068 — United States. Relations with South Africa. Attitudes of American public

The **American** people and South Africa : publics, elites, and policymaking processes / edited by Alfred O. Hero, Jr., John Barratt. — Lexington, Mass. : Lexington Books, c1981 ; [Aldershot] : Gower [distributor], 1982. — ix,229p ; 24cm
Conference papers. — Includes index
ISBN 0-669-04320-6 : £15.50
Also classified at 303.4'8268'073 B82-21164

303.4'83 — Computer systems. Social aspects — *Forecasts*

Evans, Christopher. The mighty micro : the impact of the computer revolution. — New ed. — London : Gollancz, Jan.1982. — [272]p
Previous ed.: 1979
ISBN 0-575-03122-0 : £6.95 : CIP entry
B81-40245

303.4'83 — Developing countries. Society. Effects of technological development

Duller, H. J.. Development technology / H.J. Duller. — London : Routledge & Kegan Paul, 1982. — 192p ; 22cm. — (International library of anthropology)
Bibliography: p173-190. — Includes index
ISBN 0-7100-0990-9 (pbk) : £5.95 B82-30999

303.4'83 — Developing countries. Technological innovation. Socioeconomic aspects

The **Economics** of new technology in developing countries. — London : Pinter, Apr.1982. — [256]p
ISBN 0-86187-216-9 : £14.25 : CIP entry
B82-09193

303.4'83 — Great Britain. Society. Effects of microelectronic devices

The **Impact** of microelectronics technology / edited by Mervyn A. Jack. — Edinburgh : Edinburgh University Press, c1982. — x,120p : ill ; 24cm
Bibliography: p118. — Includes index
ISBN 0-85224-426-6 (pbk) : £5.50 : CIP rev.
B82-07024

303.4'83 — Great Britain. Society. Effects of technological development in information systems

Butler, David, *19---*. Britain and the information society / David Butler. — London : Published by Heyden on behalf of the British Computer Society, c1981. — 34p ; 21cm. — (The British Computer Society lecture series ; . 3)
Bibliography: p31-34
ISBN 0-85501-699-x (pbk) : £6.00 : CIP rev.
B81-20468

Information technology revolution / [compiled by] Robert Irvine Smith, Bob Campbell. — York : Longman, 1981. — 248p : ill,3ports ; 30cm
Bibliography: p238-247
ISBN 0-582-39635-2 (pbk) : £8.95 B82-15196

303.4'83 — Industrial development — *Sociological perspectives*

Cooke, P. N.. Inter-regional class relations and the redevelopment process / by Philip Cooke ; a paper from the Wales Regionalism Group. — Cardiff (King Edward VII Ave., Cardiff CF1 3NU) : Dept. of Town Planning, University of Wales Institute of Science and Technology, 1981. — iii,50p ; 30cm. — (Papers in planning research ; 36)
Bibliography: p46-48
Unpriced (pbk) B82-26826

303.4'83 — Scientists. Social responsibility

The **Social** responsibilities of scientists : proceedings of a joint meeting on 5 June 1980 of the Royal Society and the American Philosophical Society, held in the rooms of the Royal Society. — London : Royal Society, 1980. — 50p ; 21cm
ISBN 0-85403-157-x (pbk) : Unpriced
B82-37920

303.4'83 — Social values. Effects of scientific innovation

Graham, Loren R.. Between science and values / Loren R. Graham. — New York ; Guildford : Columbia University Press, 1981. — x,449p : ill ; 24cm
Bibliography: p415-439. — Includes index
ISBN 0-231-05192-1 : £14.00 B82-10648

303.4'83 — Society. Effects of microelectronic devices

Microchips with everything. — London : Comedia, Jan.1983. — [128]p
ISBN 0-906890-33-0 (cased) : £9.50 : CIP entry
ISBN 0-906890-32-2 (pbk) : £3.50 B82-40299

Microelectronics and society : for better or for worse : a report to the Club of Rome / edited by Günter Friedrichs and Adam Schaff. — Oxford : Pergamon, 1982. — xii,353p,4p of plates : ill ; 22cm. — (Pergamon international library)
ISBN 0-08-028956-8 (cased) : Unpriced : CIP rev.
ISBN 0-08-028955-x (pbk) : £7.50 B82-03345

303.4'83 — Society. Role of science

Agassi, Joseph. Science and society : studies in the sociology of science / Joseph Agassi. — Dordrecht ; London : Reidel, c1981. — xxi,531p ; 23cm. — (Boston studies in the philosophy of science ; v.65)
Bibliography: p502-511. — Includes index
ISBN 90-277-1244-1 (cased) : Unpriced
ISBN 90-277-1245-x (pbk) : Unpriced
B82-04389

303.4'83 — Society. Role of science & technology — *Soviet viewpoints*

Bobrov, L. V.. Grounds for optimism / L.V. Bobrov ; translated from the Russian by H. Campbell Creighton. — 2nd ed. — Moscow : Mir ; [London] : distributed by Central Books, 1981. — 246p : ill ; 17cm
Translation of: Fundament optimizma. — Previous ed.: 1973
ISBN 0-7147-1685-5 (pbk) : £1.95 B82-19617

303.4'83 — Technological change — *French texts*

Salomon, J. J.. Prométhée empêtré : la résistance au changement technique. — Oxford : Pergamon, Dec.1981. — [160]p. — (Collection futuribles)
ISBN 0-08-027064-6 (pbk) : £3.45 : CIP entry
B81-36984

303.4'83'09 — Society. Role of technology, *to 1974*

Technology and culture : an anthology / edited by Melvin Kranzberg and William H. Davenport. — New York : New American Library ; London : New English Library, 1975, c1972. — vii,364p ; 21cm. — (A Meridian book)
Originally published: New York : Schocken Books, 1972
Unpriced (pbk) B82-12856

303.4'83'0941 — Great Britain. Industrialisation, *1750-1851.* **Social aspects** — *For schools*

Jamieson, Alan. The Industrial Revolution. — London : E. Arnold, Sept.1982. — [64]p
ISBN 0-7131-0653-0 (pbk) : £1.95 : CIP entry
B82-20030

303.4'83'0942 — England. Industrialisation, *1850-1980.* **Social aspects**

Weiner, Martin J.. English culture and the decline of the industrial spirit 1850-1980 / Martin J. Weiner. — Cambridge : Cambridge University Press, 1981 (1982 [printing]). — xi,217p ; 23cm
Includes index
ISBN 0-521-27034-0 (pbk) : £4.95 B82-36428

303.4'83'0942 — England. Rural regions. Social change. Effects of technological development, *1580-1800*

Butlin, R. A.. The transformation of rural England c. 1580-1800 : a study in historical geography / R.A. Butlin. — Oxford : Oxford University Press, 1982. — 64p ; 21cm. — (Theory and practice in geography)
Bibliography: p58-64
ISBN 0-19-874046-8 (pbk) : £2.50 : CIP rev.
B81-33903

303.4'83'09427 — Northern England. Industrialisation. Social aspects, *ca 1850-ca 1900*

Joyce, Patrick, *1945-*. Work, society and politics : the culture of the factory in later Victorian England / Patrick Joyce. — London : Methuen, 1982, c1980. — xxv,356p : ill ; 22cm
Originally published: Brighton : Harvester, 1980. — Includes index
ISBN 0-416-32800-8 (pbk) : Unpriced : CIP rev. B82-12333

303.4′83′0954 — India. Industrialisation, *1874-1975.* **Social aspects**

Sen, Anupam. The state, industrialization and class formations in India : a neo-Marxist perspective on colonialism, underdevelopment and development / Anupam Sen. — London : Routledge & Kegan Paul, 1982. — xii,289p ; 23cm
Bibliography: p269-280. — Includes index
ISBN 0-7100-0888-0 : £14.95 B82-33282

303.4′832 — United States. Cars. Driving. Social aspects

Dunn, Halbert B.. The automobilic syndrome : or symptoms of syndromic driving : which is a disease of American society and suggestions on what we may be able to do about it ... / by Halbert B. Dunn. — [London] ([32 The Cedars, St. Stephen′s Rd, W13 8JF]) : H.B. Dunn, c1981. — viii,164p ; 21cm
Bibliography: p163-164
Unpriced (pbk) B82-29826

303.4′833 — Europe. Society. Effects of letterpress printing

Eisenstein, Elizabeth L.. The printing press as an agent of change : communications and cultural transformations in early-modern Europe / Elizabeth L. Eisenstein. — Cambridge : Cambridge University Press, 1979 (1980 [printing]). — xxi,794p ; 23cm
Bibliography: p709-767. — Includes index
ISBN 0-521-29955-1 (pbk) B82-18179

303.4′833 — Society. Effects of information processing systems — *Conference proceedings*

Information society : for richer, for poorer : selected papers from a conference held at the Selsdon Park Hotel, London, 25-29 January, 1982 / edited by Niels Bjørn-Andersen ... [et al.]. — Amsterdam ; Oxford : North-Holland, 1982. — xv,320p : ill ; 23cm. — (Information research and resource reports ; v.2)
Includes one chapter in French
ISBN 0-444-86426-1 : £24.02 B82-34292

303.4′833 — Society. Role of telecommunication systems — *Forecasts*

Martin, James, *1933-*. [The wired society]. Telematic society : a challenge for tomorrow / James Martin. — Englewood Cliffs ; London : Prentice-Hall, c1981. — ix,244p : 1ill ; 24cm
Originally published: 1978. — Includes index
ISBN 0-13-902460-3 : £9.70 B82-07541

Telecommunications and Productivity *(Conference : 1980 : New York).* Telecommunications and productivity : based on the International Conference sponsored by the Center for Science and Technology, Graduate School of Public Administration, New York University, January 29-30, 1980 / edited by Mitchell L. Moss. — Reading, Mass. ; London : Addison Wesley, 1981. — xx,376p : ill ; 25cm. — (Advanced book program)
Includes index
ISBN 0-201-04649-0 : £24.80 B82-40221

303.4′834 — Society. Effects of automated information processing systems — *Conference proceedings*

The **Humane** use of human ideas. — Oxford : Pergamon, Oct.1982. — [240]p
Conference papers
ISBN 0-08-027941-4 (cased) : £20.00 : CIP entry
ISBN 0-08-027942-2 (pbk) : £10.00 B82-24955

303.4′834 — Society. Effects of microprocessors

Curnow, Ray. The silicon factor : living with the microprocessor : a National Extension College discussion pack linked to the BBC tv series The silicon factor / Ray Curnow and Susan Curran. — 1st ed., Repr. with amendments. — Cambridge : National Extension College, 1980, c1979. — 72p : ill ; 30cm
Includes bibliographies
ISBN 0-86082-156-0 (pbk) : Unpriced B82-35364

303.4′84 — China. Social reform, *1900-1980 compared with* **social reform in Soviet Union,** *1900-1980*
Rosenberg, William G.. Transforming Russia and China : revolutionary struggle in the twentieth century / William G. Rosenberg and Marilyn B. Young. — New York ; Oxford : Oxford University Press, 1982. — xix,397p ; 21cm
Bibliography: p363-372. — Includes index
ISBN 0-19-502965-8 (cased) : Unpriced
ISBN 0-19-502966-6 (pbk) : £4.95
Primary classification 303.4′84 B82-21226

303.4′84 — Great Britain. Social reform, *1870-1950*
Thane, Pat. Foundations of the welfare state / Pat Thane. — London : Longman, 1982. — x,383p ; 20cm. — (Social policy in modern Britain)
Bibliography: p364-365. — Includes index
ISBN 0-582-29515-7 (pbk) : £5.75 : CIP rev. B82-06923

303.4′84 — Great Britain. Social reform. Role of Fitzpatrick, *Sir* **Jeremiah,** *1763-1802*
MacDonagh, Oliver. The inspector general : Sir Jeremiah Fitzpatrick and the politics of social reform, 1783-1802 / Oliver MacDonagh. — London : Croom Helm, c1981. — 344p : maps,2facsims,1form ; 23cm
Bibliography: p332-339. — Includes index
ISBN 0-85664-421-8 : £19.95 : CIP rev. B81-10010

303.4′84 — Social movements
Gorz, André. Farewell to the working class. — London : Pluto Press, Nov.1982. — [160]p
Translation of: Adieux au prolétariat
ISBN 0-86104-364-2 (pbk) : £3.50 : CIP entry B82-30331

Roberts, Ron E.. Social movements : between the balcony and the barricade / Ron E. Roberts, Robert Marsh Kloss. — 2nd ed. — St. Louis, Mo. ; London : Mosby, 1979. — xiii,245p : ill,facsims ; 26cm
Previous ed.: 1974. — Bibliography: p227-239. — Includes index
ISBN 0-8016-4135-7 (pbk) : Unpriced B82-21892

303.4′84 — Soviet Union. Social reform, *1900-1980 compared with* **social reform in China,** *1900-1980*
Rosenberg, William G.. Transforming Russia and China : revolutionary struggle in the twentieth century / William G. Rosenberg and Marilyn B. Young. — New York ; Oxford : Oxford University Press, 1982. — xix,397p ; 21cm
Bibliography: p363-372. — Includes index
ISBN 0-19-502965-8 (cased) : Unpriced
ISBN 0-19-502966-6 (pbk) : £4.95
Also classified at 303.4′84 B82-21226

303.4′9 — Civilization — *Forecasts*
Higgins, Ronald. The seventh enemy : the human factor in the global crisis / Ronald Higgins. — Updated ed. — London : Hodder and Stoughton, 1982, c1978. — 303p ; 23cm
Includes index
ISBN 0-340-27575-8 (pbk) : £5.95 : CIP rev. B81-22582

Sakharov, Andreĭ D.. Progress, coexistence and intellectual freedom / Andrei D. Sakharov ; translated from the Russian by the New York Times ; with introduction, afterword and notes by Harrison E. Salisbury. — Harmondsworth : Penguin, 1969, c1968 (1982 [printing]). — 136p ; 18cm
Originally published: London : Deutsch, 1968
ISBN 0-14-021118-7 (pbk) : £1.50 B82-29672

303.4′9 — Social conditions — *Forecasts* — *For children*
Ardley, Neil. School, work and play / Neil Ardley. — London : Watts, [1981]. — 37p : col.ill ; 30cm. — (World of tommorow)
Includes index
ISBN 0-85166-932-8 (pbk) : £3.99 B82-05552

303.4′9 — Society. Development — *Philosophical perspectives* — *Forecasts* — *Conference proceedings*
Visions of desirable societies. — Oxford : Pergamon, Feb.1983. — [288]p. — (Systems science and world order library)
Conference papers
ISBN 0-08-026089-6 : £20.00 : CIP entry B82-36469

303.4′9 — World. Destruction — *Forecasts*
Berlitz, Charles. Doomsday 1999 A.D. / Charles Berlitz ; with collaboration, maps and drawings by J. Manson Valentine. — London : Souvenir, 1981. — 226p : ill,maps ; 23cm
Originally published: New York : Doubleday, 1981. — Bibliography: p214-216. — Includes index
ISBN 0-285-62508-x : £6.95 B82-01623

303.4′9 — World — *Forecasts*
Peccei, Aurelio. One hundred pages for the future : reflections of the President of the Club of Rome / Aurelio Peccei. — New York ; Oxford : Pergamon, c1981. — 191p : ill ; 21cm
Text and ill on lining papers
ISBN 0-08-028110-9 : £6.50 B82-09083

Peccei, Aurelio. One hundred pages for the future : reflections of the President of the Club of Rome / Aurelio Peccei. — London : Macdonald, 1982. — 191p : ill ; 18cm. — (A Futura book)
Originally published: New York ; London : Pergamon, 1981
ISBN 0-7088-2165-0 (pbk) : £1.75 B82-16945

Tilms, Richard A.. Judgement of Jupiter / Richard A. Tilms. — London : New English Library, 1980, (1981 [printing]). — 136p : ill ; 18cm
ISBN 0-450-05153-6 (pbk) : £1.25 B82-04767

Wallechinsky, David. The People′s almanac presents the book of predictions / [compiled by] David Wallechinsky, Amy Wallace, Irving Wallace. — London : Corgi, 1982, c1981. — xviii,513p : ill,1map,ports ; 18cm
Originally published: London : Elm Tree Books, 1981. — Includes index
ISBN 0-552-11885-0 (pbk) : £1.95 B82-18419

303.4′9 — World wars — *Forecasts*
Hackett, *Sir* **John**. The Third World War : the untold story / Sir John Hackett. — London : Sidgwick & Jackson, 1982. — xvii,446p : ill,maps ; 24cm
Includes index
ISBN 0-283-98863-0 : £9.95 B82-33391

303.4′9 — World wars — *Forecasts* — *Polish texts*
Barański, Jan. Na drodze do trzeciej wojny światowej / Jan Barański. — London : Veritas Foundation Publication Centre, 1981. — 119p ; 19cm
Unpriced (pbk) B82-14018

303.4′9′0321 — Futurology — *Encyclopaedias*
Insight. — London : Marshall Cavendish, Feb.1983. — 20v.
ISBN 0-86307-069-8 (pbk) : CIP entry B82-39823

303.4′941 — Great Britain. Social conditions — *Forecasts*
Bellini, James. Rule Britannia : a progress report for Domesday 1986 / James Bellini. — [London] : ABACUS, 1982, c1981. — xv,280p : ill,2geneal.tables ; 20cm
Originally published: London : Cape, 1981. — Bibliography: p273-274. — Includes index
ISBN 0-349-10299-6 (pbk) : £2.75 B82-33813

Martin, William H.. Leisure & work : the choices for 1991 and 2001 / by W.H. Martin & S. Mason. — Sudbury : Leisure Consultants, 1982. — 283p : ill ; 30cm
Bibliography: p275-283
ISBN 0-9504627-2-1 (spiral) : Unpriced B82-21228

303.4′95695 — Jordan. Social development — *Forecasts*
Jordan : the five year plan for economic and social development 1981-1985 : a summary of development prospects and priorities and of opportunities in Jordan for British firms. — London (33 Bury St, SW1Y 6AX) : Committee for Middle East Trade, 1982. — vi,50p : 1map ; 30cm. — (A Comet report)
£5.00 (spiral) B82-29539

303.4'973 — United States. Social change — *Forecasts*

Ferguson, Marilyn. The aquarian conspiracy : personal and social transformation in the 1980s / Marilyn Ferguson ; foreword by Max Lerner. — London : Granada, 1982, c1980. — 495p ; 20cm
Originally published: New York : St. Martin, 1980 ; London : Routledge & Kegan Paul, 1981. — Includes index
ISBN 0-586-08390-1 (pbk) : £2.95 B82-29737

Hawken, Paul. Seven tomorrows : toward a voluntary history / Paul Hawken, James Ogilvy, Peter Schwartz. — Toronto ; London : Bantam, 1982. — vi,235p : ill ; 21cm
Bibliography: p229-235
ISBN 0-553-01367-x (pbk) : £3.95 B82-29845

303.6 — Social conflict

Beecham, Yvonne. Power and conflict / Yvonne Beecham, Julia Fiehn, Jo Gates ; cartoons by Chris Madden ... [et al.]. — London : Harrap, 1982. — 63p : ill ; 28cm. — (Themes in sociology)
ISBN 0-245-53254-4 (pbk) : £2.25
Primary classification 303.3 B82-40465

Kriesberg, Louis. Social conflicts / Louis Kriesberg. — 2nd ed. — Englewood Cliffs ; London : Prentice-Hall, c1982. — xiii,349p : ill ; 23cm. — (Prentice-Hall series in sociology)
Previous ed.: published as The sociology of social conflicts. 1973. — Includes bibliographies and index
ISBN 0-13-815589-5 (pbk) : £11.95
B82-16710

303.6'01 — Social conflict. Theories

Schellenberg, James A.. The science of conflict / James A. Schellenberg. — New York ; Oxford : Oxford University Press, 1982. — vii,291p ; 22cm
Bibliography: p275-283. — Includes index
ISBN 0-19-502973-9 : £12.00
ISBN 0-19-502974-7 (pbk) : Unpriced
B82-33542

303.6'0938 — Ancient Greece. Social conflict. Political aspects, ***B.C.750-B.C.330***

Lintott, Andrew. Violence, civil strife and revolution in the classical city 750-330 BC / Andrew Lintott. — London : Croom Helm, c1982. — 289p ; 23cm
Bibliography: p274-282. — Includes index
ISBN 0-7099-1605-1 : £13.95 : CIP rev.
B81-31428

303.6'094 — Europe. Social protest

Holt, Stephen C.. Democracy and direct action in contemporary Europe : based on an address given by Stephen Holt ... at a seminar held at St Edmund Hall, Oxford in August 1981 ... — Exeter (7 Cathedral Close, Exeter, Devon EX1 1EZ) : European-Atlantic Movement, [1982?]. — 12p : 1ill ; 22cm
Cover title. — Bibliography: p12
Unpriced (pbk) B82-35505

303.6'0941 — Great Britain. Social protest. Role of women, ***1800-1850***

Thomis, Malcolm I.. Women in protest 1800-1850 / Malcolm I. Thomis and Jennifer Grimmett. — London : Croom Helm, c1982. — 166p ; 23cm
Includes index
ISBN 0-7099-2407-0 : £11.95 : CIP rev.
B81-37559

303.6'1 — Tribal societies. Non-aggression — *Anthropological perspectives*

Learning non-aggression : the experience of non-literate societies / edited by Ashley Montagu. — Oxford : Oxford University Press, 1978. — 235p : ill ; 21cm. — (A Galaxy book)
Includes bibliographies
ISBN 0-19-502342-0 (cased) : Unpriced
ISBN 0-19-502343-9 (pbk) : £3.50 B82-09492

303.6'2 — Southern Africa. Tswana. Disputes — *Anthropological perspective*

Comaroff, John L.. Rules and processes : the cultural logic of dispute in an African context / John L. Comaroff, Simon Roberts. — Chicago ; London : University of Chicago, 1981. — ix,293p : ill,geneal.tables ; 23cm
Bibliography: p277-288. — Includes index
ISBN 0-226-11424-4 : £19.25 B82-03915

303.6'2 — Violence

Aggression and violence / edited by Peter Marsh and Anne Campbell. — Oxford : Basil Blackwell, 1982. — vi,242p : ill ; 24cm
Includes bibliographies and index
ISBN 0-631-12742-9 : £12.00 : CIP rev.
Also classified at 155.2'32 B81-22627

303.6'2'072073 — United States. Violence. Research

Violence and the politics of research / edited by Willard Gaylin, Ruth Macklin and Tabitha M. Powledge. — New York ; London : Plenum, c1981. — xvi,256p ; 22cm. — (The Hastings Center series in ethics)
Includes index
ISBN 0-306-40789-2 : Unpriced B82-20898

303.6'2'0973 — United States. Violence

Violence in America : historical & comparative perspectives / Hugh Davis Graham, Ted Robert Gurr, editors. — Rev. ed.. — Beverly Hills ; London : Sage, c1979. — 528p : ill ; 24cm
Previous ed.: New York, London : Bantam, 1969. — Includes index
ISBN 0-8039-0963-2 (corrected : cased) : £17.00
ISBN 0-8039-0964-0 (pbk) : Unpriced
B82-08754

303.6'4'01 — Revolution. Theories, ***1848-1940***

Löwy, Michael. The politics of combined and uneven development : the theory of permanent revolution / Michael Löwy. — London : NLB, 1981. — 242p ; 23cm
Includes index
ISBN 0-86091-023-7 (cased) : £12.00 : CIP rev.
ISBN 0-86091-740-1 (pbk) : Unpriced
B81-33637

303.6'6 — War. Social aspects — *For schools*

War and society. — London (6 Endsleigh St., W.C.1) : Peace Education Project [[1982?]]. — 1case : ill ; 30cm. — (Peace Education Project study pack ; 1)
Unpriced B82-39359

304 — HUMAN ECOLOGY, GENETIC FACTORS, POPULATION, ETC

304.2 — Environment. Effects of man

Eckholm, Erik P.. Down to earth : environment and human needs / Erik P. Eckholm. — London : Pluto Press, 1982. — xv,238p ; 20cm
Includes index
ISBN 0-86104-381-2 (pbk) : £3.95 B82-31891

304.2 — Environment. Effects of man — *For schools*

Fawcett, Richard. Environment. — London : Edward Arnold, Apr.1981. — [64]p. — (Systematic secondary series)
ISBN 0-7131-0485-6 (pbk) : £2.00 : CIP entry
B81-03168

304.2 — Environment. Perception by man

Pocock, D. C. D.. The view from the bridge : experience and recall of landscape / D.C.D. Pocock. — [Durham] : Department of Geography, University of Durham, 1982. — 34p : ill ; 25cm. — (Occasional publications. (New series), ISSN 0307-0913 ; no.17)
Unpriced (pbk) B82-37375

Valued environments / edited by John R. Gold & Jacquelin Burgess. — London : Allen & Unwin, 1982. — xi,206p : ill,maps ; 24cm
Conference papers. — Includes index
ISBN 0-04-710001-x : Unpriced : CIP rev.
B82-03708

Walter, J. A.. The human home : the myth of the sacred environment / J.A. Walter. — Tring : Lion, 1982. — 224p ; 18cm. — (A Lion paperback)
Includes index
ISBN 0-85648-394-x (pbk) : £1.95 B82-31702

304.2 — Environment. Sociopolitical aspects

Cotgrove, Stephen. Catastrophe or cornucopia : the environment, politics and the future / Stephen Cotgrove. — Chichester : Wiley, c1982. — xi,154p ; 24cm
Bibliography: p140-149. — Includes index
ISBN 0-471-10079-x (cased) : £16.00 : CIP rev.
ISBN 0-471-10166-4 (pbk) : Unpriced
B82-03605

304.2 — Environmental studies

Education and environment. — Northwood : Science Reviews, Sept.1981. — [300]p
ISBN 0-905927-75-3 (pbk) : £9.50 : CIP entry
B81-25136

304.2 — Human geography

Applied geography : selected perspectives / John W. Frazier editor. — Englewood Cliffs ; London : Prentice-Hall, c1982. — xv,333p : ill,maps ; 25cm
Includes index
ISBN 0-13-040451-9 : £16.45 B82-16854

Conflict, politics and the urban scene. — London : Longman, July 1982. — [288]p
ISBN 0-582-30062-2 (cased) : £13.00 : CIP entry
ISBN 0-582-30064-9 (pbk) : £6.95 B82-12988

De Blij, Harm J.. Human geography : culture, society and space / Harm J. de Blij. — 2/e. — New York ; Chichester : Wiley, c1982. — xii,656p : ill(some col.),col.maps ; 25cm
Previous ed.: 1977. — Includes bibliographies and index
ISBN 0-471-08557-x : £19.95 B82-18224

Drew, David. Man-environment processes. — London : Allen & Unwin, Nov.1982. — [152]p
ISBN 0-04-551063-6 (pbk) : £4.95 : CIP entry
B82-27819

Ellen, Roy. Environment, subsistence and system : the ecology of small-scale social formations. — Cambridge : Cambridge University Press, Oct.1982. — [328]p. — (Themes in the social sciences)
ISBN 0-521-24458-7 (cased) : £21.00 : CIP entry
ISBN 0-521-28703-0 (pbk) : £7.50 B82-26242

Fundamentals of human geography. — Milton Keynes : Open University Press. — (Social sciences : a second level course)
At head of title: The Open University
Section 1: Man & environment. — 1977 (1981 [printing]). — 145p : ill(some col.),maps(some col.) ; 30cm. — (D204 ; Section 1, units 4-6)
Includes bibliographies. — Contents: Units 4-6, parts 1 and 2
ISBN 0-335-07201-1 (pbk) : Unpriced
B82-21211

Hopkins, Ian. An introduction to human geography / Ian Hopkins. — London : Weidenfeld and Nicolson, c1982. — x,217p,[8]p of plates : ill,maps ; 22cm
Includes index
ISBN 0-297-78085-9 (cased) : £8.95
ISBN 0-297-78120-0 (pbk) : £4.50 B82-26750

Jordan, Terry G.. The human mosaic : a thematic introduction to cultural geography / Terry G. Jordan, Lester Rowntree. — New York ; London : Harper & Row, c1982. — xv,444p : ill,col.maps ; 29cm
Previous ed.: 1979. — Maps on lining papers. — Includes bibliographies and index
ISBN 0-06-043461-9 : £14.95 B82-22889

304.2 — Human geography. Behavioural aspects

Behavioral problems in geography revisited / edited by Kevin R. Cox and Reginald G. Golledge. — New York ; London : Methuen, 1981. — xxix,290p : ill ; 23cm
Includes index
ISBN 0-416-72430-2 (cased) : Unpriced : CIP rev.
ISBN 0-416-72440-x (pbk) : £5.95 B81-31537

304.2 — Human geography — *Conference proceedings*

Institutions and geographical patterns. — London : Croom Helm, July 1982. — [352]p. — (Croom Helm series in geography and environment)
Conference papers
ISBN 0-7099-1011-8 : £13.95 : CIP entry
B82-17207

304.2 — Human geography — *For schools*

Briggs, Ken. Human geography. — London : Hodder & Stoughton, July 1982. — [192]p
ISBN 0-340-16116-7 (pbk) : £3.95 : CIP entry
B82-12246

Renwick, Malcolm. Going places / Malcolm Renwick and Bill Pick. — Walton-on-Thames : Nelson
Text, ill on inside cover
3. — 1980 (1982 [printing]). — 64p : ill(some col.),maps,plans ; 28cm
ISBN 0-17-425424-5 (pbk) : Unpriced
B82-36097

304.2 — Human geography — *For West African students*

Lewis, G. E. D.. Human geography for West Africa. — London : Hodder and Stoughton, July 1982. — [160]p
ISBN 0-340-27596-0 (pbk) : £3.25 : CIP entry
B82-12260

304.2 — Human geography — *Humanistic perspectives*

Relph, Edward. Rational landscapes and humanistic geography / Edward Relph. — London : Croom Helm, c1981. — 231p ; 23cm. — (Croom Helm series in geography and environment)
Bibliography: p215-223. — Includes index
ISBN 0-7099-0016-3 : £14.95 : CIP rev.
B81-16373

304.2 — Human geography. Spatial aspects

Kirby, Andrew. The politics of location. — London : Methuen, Dec.1982. — [224]p
ISBN 0-416-33900-x (cased) : £10.50 : CIP entry
ISBN 0-416-33910-7 (pbk) : £5.50 B82-29760

304.2 — Man. Ecology

Catton, William R.. Overshoot / William R. Catton, Jr. — Urbana ; London : University of Illinois Press, c1980. — xvii,298p ; 24cm
Bibliography: p269. — Includes index
ISBN 0-252-00818-9 : £11.50 B82-39348

Novik, I.. Society and nature : socio-ecological problems / Ilya Novik ; translated from the Russian by H. Campbell Creighton. — Moscow : Progress ; [London] : Distributed by Central, c1981. — 300p ; 19cm
Translation of: Obshchestvo i priroda
ISBN 0-7147-1702-9 : £2.25 B82-29275

Social problems of man's environment : where we live and work / under the general editorship of P. Fedoseyev and T. Timofeyev. — Moscow : Progress, 1981 ; [London] : Distributed by Central Books. — 333p ; 21cm
Translation of: O sot͡sial'nykh problemakh sredy obitanii͡a i truda cheloveka
ISBN 0-7147-1760-6 : £3.95 B82-39313

304.2 — Man. Relationships with animals

Hall, Rebecca. Animals are equal : an exploration of animal consciousness / Rebecca Hall. — London : Wildwood House, 1980 (1981 [printing]). — viii,256p : 1ill ; 22cm
Includes index
ISBN 0-7045-0438-3 (pbk) : Unpriced
Primary classification 591.6 B82-37452

304.2 — Man. Territoriality

Ericksen, E. Gordon. The territorial experience : human ecology as symbolic interaction / by E. Gordon Ericksen ; foreword by Herbert Blumer. — Austin ; London : University of Texas Press, c1980. — xx,204p ; 24cm
Bibliography: p175-197. — Includes index
ISBN 0-292-78038-9 : £14.00 B82-13563

304.2 — United States. Environment. Risks. Perception by man. Sociopolitical aspects

Douglas, Mary. Risk and culture : an essay on the selection of technical and environmental dangers / Mary Douglas and Aaron Wildavsky. — Berkeley ; London : University of California Press, c1982. — ix,221p ; 22cm
Includes index
ISBN 0-520-04491-6 : £11.25 B82-40210

304.2'01 — Human geography — *Philosophical perspectives*

Johnston, Ronald A. J.. Philosophy and human geography. — London : Edward Arnold, Jan.1983. — [160]p
ISBN 0-7131-6385-2 (pbk) : £5.95 : CIP entry
B82-32593

304.2'03'21 — Human geography — *Encyclopaedias*

The **Dictionary** of human geography / edited by R.J. Johnston. — Oxford : Blackwell Reference, 1981. — xxiii,411p ; 26cm
Includes bibliographies and index
ISBN 0-631-10721-5 : £19.50 : CIP rev.
B81-21493

304.2'0941 — Great Britain. Human geographical features — *For schools*

Kemp, Richard. The British Isles / Richard Kemp. — London : Edward Arnold, 1981. — 128p : ill,maps,plans ; 24cm. — (Patterns of development)
ISBN 0-7131-0339-6 (pbk) : £3.95 B82-00584

304.2'0967 — Africa. Tropical regions. Human geographical features — *For African students*

Udo, Reuben K.. The human geography of tropical Africa / Reuben K. Udo. — Idadan : Heinemann Educational (Nigeria) ; London : Heinemann Educational, 1982. — xii,244p : ill,maps,ports ; 25cm
Bibliography: p234-237. — Includes index
ISBN 0-435-95919-0 (pbk) : £6.95 : CIP rev.
B81-34565

304.2'09794'85 — California. Tulare Lake region. Social change, *to 1980.* **Environmental aspects**

Preston, William L.. Vanishing landscapes : land and life in the Tulare Lake Basin / William L. Preston. — Berkeley ; London : University of California Press, c1981. — x,278p,[16]p of plates : ill,maps ; 26cm
Bibliography: p251-270. — Includes index
ISBN 0-520-04053-8 : Unpriced B82-16913

304.2'0985'24 — Peru. Satipo. Social conditions, *1930-1975 — Anthropological perspectives*

Shoemaker, Robin. The peasants of El Dorado : conflict and contradiction in a Peruvian frontier settlement / Robin Shoemaker. — Ithaca, N.Y. ; London : Cornell University Press, c1981. — 265p : ill,1map ; 23cm
Bibliography: p253-260. — Includes index
ISBN 0-8014-1390-7 : £13.75 B82-11841

304.2'0994 — Australia. Environment. Effects of man, *1788-1980*

Bolton, G. C., *1931-*. Spoils and spoilers : Australians make their environment 1788-1980 / Geoffrey Bolton. — Sydney ; London : Allen & Unwin, 1981. — 197p : ill,maps,1plan ; 22cm. — (The Australian experience)
Bibliography: p185-186. — Includes index
ISBN 0-86861-218-9 (cased) : Unpriced
ISBN 0-86861-226-x (pbk) : Unpriced
B82-01223

304.2'5 — Desertification. Ecology — *Sociological perspectives*

Desertification and development. — London : Academic Press, Sept.1982. — [430]p
ISBN 0-12-658050-2 : CIP entry B82-19166

304.5 — Human sociobiology — *Philosophical perspectives*

Trigg, Roger. The shaping of man : philosophical aspects of sociobiology. — Oxford : Basil Blackwell, May 1982. — [172]p
ISBN 0-631-13023-3 (cased) : £12.00 : CIP entry
ISBN 0-631-13028-4 (pbk) : £4.50 B82-06940

304.5 — Man. Genetics. Social aspects

Nagle, James J.. Heredity and human affairs / James J. Nagle. — 2nd ed. — St. Louis ; London : Mosby, 1979. — xvi,379p : ill,1map,1port ; 26cm + Instructor's supplement(31p : ill ; 26cm)
Previous ed.: 1974. — Includes bibliographies and index
ISBN 0-8016-3621-3 (pbk) : £12.75
B82-24782

304.5 — Sociobiology

Current problems in sociobiology / edited by King's College Sociobiology Group, Cambridge. — Cambridge : Cambridge University Press, 1982. — xi,394p : ill ; 24cm
Conference papers. — Includes bibliographies and index
ISBN 0-521-24203-7 (cased) : £27.50 : CIP rev.
ISBN 0-521-28520-8 (pbk) : £9.95 B82-25489

304.6 — Demography. Techniques — *For African students*

Kpedekpo, G. M. K.. Essentials of demographic analysis for Africa / G.M.K. Kpedekpo. — London : Heinemann, 1982. — xii,210p : ill,1form ; 26cm. — (Studies in the economics of Africa)
Includes bibliographies and index
ISBN 0-435-97390-8 (cased) : £15.00 : CIP rev.
ISBN 0-435-97391-6 (pbk) : Unpriced
B79-36663

304.6 — England. Population. Censuses, *1981 — Serials*

1981 census user guide. — 1-. — [London] ([10 Kingsway WC2B 6JP]) : [Office of Population Censuses and Surveys], [1981]-. — v. ; 30cm
At head of title: Census geography. —
Description based on: 2
Unpriced B82-10116

304.6 — England. Population. Official statistics. Mapping. Techniques

The **OPCS** LP zone mapping package Charmap. — [London] : [Office of Population Censuses and Surveys], [1980]. — [30]leaves : maps(some col.) ; 30cm
Cover title. — Includes index
Unpriced (spiral) B82-37302

304.6 — Great Britain. Population. Censuses, *1981.* **Functional regions**

Appropriate areas for census analysis : an outline of functional regions / by M.G. Coombes ... [et al.]. — [Newcastle upon Tyne] : University of Newcastle upon Tyne. Centre for Urban and Regional Development Studies, 1982. — 31,13p : ill,maps ; 30cm. — (Discussion paper, ISSN 0140-6515 ; no.41)
Unpriced (unbound) B82-27742

304.6 — Population — *Early works*

Malthus, T. R.. An essay on the principle of population / T.R. Malthus. — [7th. ed.] / introduction by T.H. Hollingsworth. — London : Dent, 1973 (1982 [printing]). — xxxiv,284p ; 18cm. — (Everyman's library)
Facsim. of ed. published: London : Reeves and Turner, 1872. — Bibliography: pxxxiii-xxxiv. — Includes index
ISBN 0-460-01692-x (pbk) : £3.95 B82-37241

304.6 — Population — *For schools*

Greasley, Brian. Population and urbanization : Brian Greasley, Michael Younger. — London : Harrap, 1982. — 63p : ill,facsims,maps(some col.),plans ; 28cm. — (Harrap's world topic geography)
ISBN 0-245-53698-1 (pbk) : £2.25 B82-28241

304.6 — Population. Geographical aspects

Hornby, William F.. An introduction to population geography / William F. Hornby, Melvyn Jones. — Cambridge : Cambridge University Press, 1980 (1982 [printing]). — 168p : ill,map,1plan ; 25cm. — (Studies in human geography ; 1)
Bibliography: p162-164. — Includes index
ISBN 0-521-21395-9 (pbk) : £4.95 B82-38839

Woods, Robert. Theoretical population geography / Robert Woods. — London : Longman, 1982. — xiv,220p : ill,maps ; 22cm
Bibliography: p185-215. — Includes index
ISBN 0-582-30029-0 (pbk) : £5.95 : CIP rev.
B82-00241

304.6′01′5195 — Population. Analysis. Applications of statistical mathematics — *Questions & answers — For schools*

Multiplying people / [Schools Council Project on Statistical Education]. — Slough : Published for the Schools Council by Foulsham Educational, c1981. — 20p + teachers′ notes (20p ; 21cm) : ill ; 21cm. — (Statistics in your world)
ISBN 0-572-01083-4 (pbk) : Unpriced
ISBN 0-572-01102-4 (teachers′ notes) : Unpriced B82-13025

304.6′09172′4 — Developing countries. Population — *For schools*

Price, Gillian. Population and food resources in the developing world. — London : Edward Arnold, Sept.1982. — [64]p. — (Patterns of development ; 5)
ISBN 0-7131-0454-6 (pbk) : £2.25 : CIP entry
Also classified at 338.1′09172′4 B82-20028

304.6′0917′4927 — Arab countries. Population

Omran, Abdel-Rahim. Population in the Arab world : problems & prospects / Abdel-Rahim Omran. — New York : United Nations Fund for Population Activities ; London : Croom Helm, 1980. — xxii,215p : ill,maps ; 24cm
Bibliography: p199-204. — Includes index
ISBN 0-7099-1904-2 : £13.95 B82-38306

304.6′0941 — Great Britain. Ethnic minorities. Demographic aspects

Demography of immigrants and minority groups in the United Kingdom. — London : Academic Press, Dec.1982. — [290]p
Conference papers
ISBN 0-12-179780-5 : CIP entry B82-29876

304.6′0941 — Great Britain. Population, *1850-1980.* **Demographic & socioeconomic aspects**

Population and society in Britain 1850-1980 / edited by Theo Barker and Michael Drake. — London : Batsford Academic and Educational, 1982. — 221p : maps ; 22cm
Includes bibliographies and index
ISBN 0-7134-3676-x (pbk) : £6.95 : CIP rev. B82-06954

304.6′0941 — Great Britain. Population, *1971.* **Demographic aspects** — *For schools*

People and work / compiled by Roger Robinson ... [et al.]. — York : Longman, 1981. — 198p : ill,maps ; 30cm
ISBN 0-582-39634-4 (pbk) : £7.25 B82-07574

304.6′09411 — Scotland. Population — *Forecasts*

Knight, Peter. Population projections, Scotland, 1977 based / Peter Knight. — Edinburgh (Trinity Park House, South Trinity Rd, Edinburgh EH5 3SQ) : Information Services Division, Scottish Health Service Common Services Agency, [1982?]. — [4]p ; 30cm. — (Occasional papers ; 4)
Unpriced (unbound) B82-40984

304′.6′09415 — Ireland. Population, *1300-1700.* **Historical sources**

Mac Niocaill, Gearóid. Irish population before Petty : problems and possibilities : O′Donnell lecture delivered at University College Galway, May 1981 / by Gearóid Mac Niocaill. — [Dublin] : National University of Ireland, [1981]. — 11p ; 22cm. — (O′Donnell lecture)
£0.50 (pbk) B82-18032

304.6′0942 — England. Population, *1541-1871*

Wrigley, E. A.. The population history of England, 1541-1871 : a reconstruction / E.A. Wrigley and R.S. Schofield with contributions by Ronald Lee and Jim Oeppen. — London : Edward Arnold for the Cambridge Group for the History of Population and Social Structure, 1981. — xv,779p,[1]folded leaf of plates : ill,maps ; 25cm. — (Studies in social and demographic history)
Bibliography: p741-757. — Includes index
ISBN 0-7131-6264-3 : £45.00 : CIP rev. B80-32949

304.6′0942 — England. Population — *Forecasts*

Davis, P. R. (Peter Reginald). Man, health and technology, the next 100 years? / P.R. Davis. — [Guildford] ([Guildford, Surrey GU2 5XH]) : [University of Surrey], [1977?]. — 11p : ill ; 21cm. — (University of Surrey university lecture)
Cover title
Unpriced (pbk) B82-26657

304.6′09422′75 — Hampshire. Boldre & Brockenhurst. Population, *1817* — *Early works*

Comyn, Henry. Comyn′s New Forest : 1817 directory of life in the parishes of Boldre & Brockenhurst / edited by Jude James. — Ringwood : Newsome in conjunction with Lymington Historical Record Society, 1982. — 189p : ill,facsims,maps,ports ; 31cm
Maps on lining papers. — Bibliography: p189. — Includes index
ISBN 0-906742-01-3 : £17.50 B82-33068

304.6′09425′81 — Hertfordshire. North Hertfordshire *(District).* **Population** — *Forecasts — For environment planning*

Population topic study / [North Hertfordshire District Council]. — [Letchworth] ([Council Offices, Gernon Rd., Letchworth, Herts. SG6 3JF]) : [The Council], 1978. — iii,37p : ill,1map ; 30cm. — (North Hertfordshire district plan. Topic studies)
£0.60 (pbk) B82-11583

304.6′09429′85 — West Glamorgan. Glyncorrwg, *to ca 1850.* **Demographic aspects**

Brown, Roger Lee. The population of the hamlet of Glyncorrwg, a demographic survey ; and, the Jenkin family of Corrwg Fechan a revised statement : two papers on the history of Glynworrwg / by Roger Lee Brown. — Tongwynlais (The Vicarage, Merthyr Rd, Tongwynlais, Cardiff CF4 7LF) : R.L. Brown, 1982. — 37p : geneal.tables,2maps ; 21cm
Limited ed. of 200 copies
£1.00 (pbk) B82-35596

304.6′0951 — China. Population, *1949-1979*

Population theory in China / edited with an introduction by H. Yuan Tien. — New York ; Sharpe ; London : Croom Helm, 1980. — x,129p ; 24cm
Includes bibliographies
ISBN 0-7099-0444-4 : £8.95 B82-37451

304.6′096 — Africa. Population. Distribution

Redistribution of population in Africa / edited by John I. Clarke and Leszek A. Kosiński. — London : Heinemann, 1982. — x,212p : ill,maps ; 29cm
Includes bibliographies and index
ISBN 0-435-95030-4 : £19.50 : CIP rev.
ISBN 0-435-95031-2 (pbk) : £7.50 B81-21630

304.6′0981 — Brazil. Population. Policies of government. Political aspects

McDonough, Peter. The politics of population in Brazil : elite ambivalence and public demand / by Peter McDonough and Amaury DeSouza. — Austin ; London : University of Texas Press, c1981. — xii,178p : ill ; 24cm. — (The Texas Pan American series)
Bibliography: p161-173. — Includes index
ISBN 0-292-76466-9 : £14.00 B82-12770

304.6′0985 — Peru. Population, *1520-1620*

Cook, Noble David. Demographic collapse : Indian Peru, 1520-1620 / Noble David Cook. — Cambridge : Cambridge University Press, 1981. — x,310p : ill,maps ; 22cm. — (Cambridge Latin American studies ; 41)
Bibliography: p281-297. — Includes index
ISBN 0-521-23995-8 : £22.50 B82-16195

304.6′2 — Population. Economic aspects — *Serials*

Research in population economics : a research annual. — Vol.1 (1978)-. — Greenwich, Conn. : JAI Press ; London (3 Henrietta St., WC2E 8LU) : Distributed by JAICON Press, 1978-. — v. ; 24cm
Description based on: Vol.2 (1980)
ISSN 0163-7878 = Research in population economics : £26.20 B82-03433

304.6′2 — Population. Growth

Salk, Jonas. World population and human values : a new reality / Jonas Salk and Jonathan Salk. — Cambridge [Mass.] ; London : Harper & Row, c1981. — xviii,170p : ill ; 29cm
Bibliography: p169-170
ISBN 0-06-013778-9 (cased) : £7.95
ISBN 0-06-090907-2 (pbk) : Unpriced B82-10038

304.6′2 — Population. Growth. Economic aspects

Simon, Julian L.. The ultimate resource / by Julian L. Simon. — Oxford : Martin Robertson, 1981. — x,415p : ill ; 24cm
Bibliography: p387-403. — Includes index
ISBN 0-85520-440-0 : £9.50 : CIP rev. B81-30339

304.6′2 — Population. Growth. Forecasting. Techniques

Population estimates : methods for small area analysis / edited by Everett S. Lee, Harold F. Goldsmith. — Beverly Hills ; London : Sage, c1982. — 248p : ill ; 23cm
Conference papers. — Includes bibliographies
ISBN 0-8039-1812-7 : £15.50 B82-38165

304.6′2 — Population. Growth. Geographical aspects

Sivamurthy, M.. Growth and structure of human population in the presence of migration. — London : Academic Press, Apr.1982. — [250]p. — (Studies in population)
ISBN 0-12-647250-5 : CIP entry B82-11506

304.6′2 — Population. Growth. Socioeconomic aspects — *Conference proceedings*

Population and the world economy in the 21st century. — Oxford : Blackwell, Sept.1982. — [200]p
Conference papers
ISBN 0-631-12964-2 : £12.50 : CIP entry B82-22429

304.6′2′091821 — Western world. Population. Growth, *1955-1970.* **Socioeconomic aspects**

Steinberg, Ira S.. The new lost generation : the population boom and public policy / Ira S. Steinberg. — Oxford : Martin Robertson, 1982. — x,160p ; 22cm
Bibliography: p155-157. — Includes index
ISBN 0-85520-293-9 (cased) : £15.00 : CIP rev.
ISBN 0-85520-402-8 (pbk) : £5.95 B81-08805

304.6′2′0941 — Great Britain. Population. Change, *1971-1979*

Mounsey, Helen. Comparison of population changes within Great Britain 1971-75 and 1975-79 / Helen Mounsey and John I. Clarke. — [Durham] : University of Durham, Department of Geography, Census Research Unit, 1981. — 17p : col.ill,col.maps ; 30cm
Unpriced (pbk) B82-23834

304.6′2′0941 — Great Britain. Population. Decline. Socioeconomic aspects

Population change and social planning : social and economic implications of the recent decline in fertility in the United Kingdom and the Federal Republic of Germany / edited by David Eversley and Wolfgang Köllmann ; with contributions by Adelheid Gräfin zu Castell Rüdenhausen ... [et al.]. — London : Edward Arnold, 1982. — ix,485p : ill,1map ; 24cm
Bibliography: p441-446. — Includes index
ISBN 0-7131-6345-3 : £45.00 : CIP rev.
Also classified at 304.6′2′0943 B81-37562

304.6′2′0942 — England. Population. Growth — *Forecasts*

Population projections area : population projections by sex and age for standard regions, counties, London boroughs and metropolitan districts of England from mid-1977 / Office of Population Censuses and Surveys. — London : H.M.S.O., 1980. — 75p ; 30cm. — (Series PP3 ; no.3)
ISBN 0-11-690737-1 (pbk) : £6.00 B82-18627

304.6′2′0942276 — Hampshire. Southampton. Population. Growth, *1960-1981.* Socioeconomic aspects

Dimensions of change in a growth area : Southampton since 1960 / edited by C.M. Mason and M.E. Witherick. — Aldershot : Gower, c1981. — xi,271p : ill ; 23cm
Includes bibliographies
ISBN 0-566-00426-7 : Unpriced : CIP rev. B81-34279

304.6′2′0943 — West Germany. Population. Decline. Socioeconomic aspects

Population change and social planning : social and economic implications of the recent decline in fertility in the United Kingdom and the Federal Republic of Germany / edited by David Eversley and Wolfgang Köllmann ; with contributions by Adelheid Gräfin zu Castell Rüdenhausen ... [et al.]. — London : Edward Arnold, 1982. — ix,485p : ill,1map ; 24cm
Bibliography: p441-446. — Includes index
ISBN 0-7131-6345-3 : £45.00 : CIP rev.
Primary classification 304.6′2′0941 B81-37562

304.6′2′096 — Africa. Population. Growth — *Conference proceedings*

Population growth and economic development in Africa / edited by S.H. Ominde and C.N. Ejiogu. — London : Heinemann in association with the Population Council, New York, 1972 (1981 [printing]). — xxii,421p : ill,maps ; 28cm
Conference papers. — Includes bibliographies and index
ISBN 0-435-97470-x (pbk) : £12.50 B82-01875

304.6′3 — Childbirth. Ethnographic aspects — *Conference proceedings*

Ethnography of fertility and birth / edited by Carol P. MacCormack. — London : Academic Press, 1982. — x,293p : ill ; 24cm
Conference papers. — Includes bibliographies and index
ISBN 0-12-463550-4 : £14.00 : CIP rev.
Primary classification 304.6′32 B82-04143

304.6′3 — Population. Fertility *- Sociological perspectives - Conference proceedings*

Changing patterns of conception and fertility. — London : Academic Press, June 1981. — [200]p
Conference papers
ISBN 0-12-171350-4 : CIP entry B81-08913

304.6′3′091722 — Developed countries. Population. Fertility

Andorka, Rudolf. Determinants of fertility in advanced societies. — London : Methuen, Feb.1982. — [444]p
Originally published: 1978
ISBN 0-416-67350-3 (pbk) : £5.95 : CIP entry B81-35714

304.6′32 — Man. Fertility. Ethnographic aspects — *Conference proceedings*

Ethnography of fertility and birth / edited by Carol P. MacCormack. — London : Academic Press, 1982. — x,293p : ill ; 24cm
Conference papers. — Includes bibliographies and index
ISBN 0-12-463550-4 : £14.00 : CIP rev.
Also classified at 304.6′3 B82-04143

304.6′32′09744 — Massachusetts. Population. Fertility, *1765-1860.* Socioeconomic factors

Vinovskis, Maris A.. Fertility in Massachusetts from the Revolution to the Civil War / Maris A. Vinovskis. — New York ; London : Academic Press, c1981. — xii,253p : ill,1map ; 24cm
Bibliography: p233-245. — Includes index
ISBN 0-12-722040-2 : £18.20 B82-18683

304.6′34′091724 — Developing countries. Families. Size. Socioeconomic aspects

Caldwell, John C. (John Charles). Theory of fertility decline / John C. Caldwell. — London : Academic Press, c1982. — xi,386p ; 24cm. — (Population and social structure)
Bibliography: p369-386
ISBN 0-12-155080-x : £11.80 : CIP rev. B82-00324

304.6′4 — England. Deaths due to respiratory diseases, *1951-1975*

Trends in respiratory mortality 1951-1975 / Office of Population Censuses and Surveys. — London : H.M.S.O., 1981. — viii,55p : ill ; 30cm. — (Series DH1 ; no.7)
ISBN 0-11-690786-x (pbk) : £6.20 B82-11666

304.6′4 — England. Man. Perinatal mortality rate & neonatal mortality rate. Great Britain. *Parliament. House of Commons. Social Services Committee.* **Second report ... session 1979-80** — *Critical studies*

Great Britain. *Department of Health and Social Security.* Reply to the second report from the Social Services Committee on perinatal and neonatal mortality / Department of Health and Social Security. — London : H.M.S.O., [1980]. — v,80p ; 25cm. — (Cmnd. ; 8084)
ISBN 0-10-180840-2 (pbk) : £4.60 B82-15137

304.6′4 — England. Man. Perinatal mortality rate & neonatal mortality rate — *Inquiry reports*

Great Britain. *Parliament. House of Commons. Social Services Committee.* Second report from the Social Services Committee, session 1979-80 : perinatal and neonatal mortality : together with the proceedings of the committee, the minutes of evidence (including evidence taken by the Social Services and Employment Sub-Committee of the Expenditure Committee in session 1978-79) and appendices. — London : H.M.S.O., [1980]
Vol.3: Evidence : (21 February-28 March 1979). — xivp,p337-674 : ill,1map ; 25cm. — ([HC] ; 663-II)
ISBN 0-10-009189-x (pbk) : £10.90 B82-10966

Great Britain. *Parliament. House of Commons. Social Services Committee.* Second report from the Social Services Committee, session 1979-80 : perinatal and neonatal mortality : together with the proceedings of the committee, the minutes of evidence (including evidence taken by the Social Services and Employment Sub-Committee of the Expenditure Committee in session 1978-79) and appendices. — London : H.M.S.O., [1980]
Vol.4: Evidence : (16 January-4 March 1980). — xiv,566p : ill,maps ; 25cm. — ([HC] ; 663-IV)
ISBN 0-10-009199-7 (pbk : corrected) : £12.40 B82-10965

304.6′4′0942 — England. Mortality rate, *1971-1975*

Fox, A. J. (Anthony John). Longitudinal study : socio-demographic mortality differentials : a first report on mortality in 1971-1975 according to 1971 census characteristics, based on data collected in OPCS Longitudinal study / A.J. Fox, P.O. Goldblatt. — London : H.M.S.O., 1982. — xxii,227p : ill,forms ; 30cm. — (Series LS ; no.1)
At head of title: Office of Population Censuses and Surveys. — Includes index
ISBN 0-11-690906-4 (pbk) : £11.70 B82-40197

304.6′6 — Population. Control. Economic aspects

And the poor get children : radical perspectives on population dynamics / edited by Karen L. Michaelson. — New York ; London : Monthly Review, c1981. — 269p : ill,2maps ; 21cm
Bibliography: p247-262. — Includes index
£8.65 (corrected : cased)
ISBN 0-85345-553-8 (pbk) : Unpriced B82-17073

304.6′6 — United Nations Fund for Population Activities, *to 1979 — Spanish texts*

Salas, Rafael M.. Ayuda internacional en población. — Oxford : Pergamon, Aug.1981. — [537]p
ISBN 0-08-026099-3 (cased) : £9.50 : CIP entry
ISBN 0-08-026098-5 (pbk) : £8.75 B81-19213

304.6′66 — Family planning

Planned parenthood and women′s development. — London : International Planned Parenthood Federation, Apr.1982. — [68]p
ISBN 0-86089-048-1 (pbk) : £5.50 : CIP entry B82-12813

304.6′66′09411 — Scotland. Family planning — *Serials*

Themes in family planning / Social Demographic Research Group, Department of Sociology, Edinburgh University [and] Scottish Health Education Group. — Report no.1-. — Edinburgh (Health Education Centre, Woodburn House, Canaan La., Edinburgh EH10 4SG) : Scottish Health Education Group, 1979-. — v. : maps ; 30cm
Quarterly. — Description based on: Report no.4
ISSN 0262-1193 = Themes in family planning : Unpriced B82-02375

304.8 — Glacial epoch. Land bridges. Migration. Anthropological aspects — *Conference proceedings*

Quaternary land bridges. — London : Academic Press, July 1982. — [540]p
Conference papers
ISBN 0-12-260450-4 : CIP entry B82-12441

304.8′09 — Migration. Geographical aspects

Lewis, G. J.. Human migration : a geographical perspective / G.J. Lewis. — London : Croom Helm, c1982. — 220p : ill,maps ; 23cm. — (Croom Helm series in geography and environment)
Bibliography: p192-216. — Includes index
ISBN 0-7099-0007-4 : £13.95 : CIP rev. B81-34304

304.8′0947 — Russia. Urban regions. Migration from rural regions, *1890-1900.* Spatial aspects

Rowland, Richard H.. Spatial patterns of urban in-migration in late nineteenth century Russia : a factor analytic approach / by R.H. Rowland. — Norwich : Geo Abstracts for the Historical Geography Study Group of the Institute of British Geographers, c1982. — 43p : maps ; 21cm. — (Historical geography research series, ISSN 0143-683x ; no.10)
ISBN 0-86094-112-4 (pbk) : Unpriced B82-40442

304.8′0964 — Morocco. Emigration, *1960-1980*

Findlay, Anne M.. Migration studies in Tunisia and Morocco / Anne Findlay and Allan Findlay. — [Glasgow] : [University of Glasgow, Department of Geography], [1980]. — 22p : 1ill,maps ; 30cm. — (Occasional papers / Geography Department Glasgow University ; no.3)
Bibliography: p21-22
Unpriced (spiral)
Primary classification 304.8′2′09611 B82-27871

304.8′2′0941 — Great Britain. Population. Internal migration to rural regions. Policies of local authorities. Economic aspects

Rural settlement policy and economics / Nigel Curry (ed). — Gloucester : Department of Town and Country Planning, Gloucestershire College of Arts and Technology, 1981. — 52p : ill,3maps ; 30cm. — (Gloucestershire papers in local planning, ISSN 0144-4875 ; Issue no.12)
Cover title. — Bibliography: p49-51
Unpriced B82-16000

304.8′2′09611 — Tunisia. Internal migration, *1966-1975*

Findlay, Anne M.. Migration studies in Tunisia and Morocco / Anne Findlay and Allan Findlay. — [Glasgow] : [University of Glasgow, Department of Geography], [1980]. — 22p : 1ill,maps ; 30cm. — (Occasional papers / Geography Department Glasgow University ; no.3)
Bibliography: p21-22
Unpriced (spiral)
Also classified at 304.8′0964 B82-27871

304.8′2′0975 — United States. Southern states. Migration, *1900-1950*

Fligstein, Neil. Going North : migration of blacks and whites from the South, 1900-1950 / Neil Fligstein. — New York ; London : Academic Press, 1981. — xiv,230p : ill,maps ; 24cm. — (Quantitative studies in social relations)
Bibliography: p215-223. — Includes index
ISBN 0-12-260720-1 : £16.20 B82-30112

304.8′36′034 — India & Sri Lanka. Dravidians. Migration to Europe, *ca B.C.3000*

Tambimuttu, Paulinus. Europe and the Dravidians / by Paulinus Tambimuttu. — London : P. Tambimuttu, 1979 (1980 [printing]). — iii,68p ; 22cm
ISBN 0-9506823-1-4 (cased) : Unpriced
ISBN 0-9506823-2-2 (pbk) : £2.00 B82-16618

304.8′41 — Great Britain. Immigration, *to 1980 — For schools*

Bodey, Hugh. Immigrants and emigrants / Hugh Bodey. — London : Batsford Academic and Educational, 1982. — 72p : ill ; 26cm. — (History in focus)
Bibliography: p70. — Includes index
ISBN 0-7134-3564-x : £5.95 B82-36938

304.8′411′071 — Scotland. Highlands. Emigration to Canada, *ca 1770-ca 1815*

Bumstead, J. M.. The people′s clearance : Highland emigration to British North America, 1770-1815. — Edinburgh : Edinburgh University Press, May 1982. — [200]p
ISBN 0-85224-419-3 : £10.00 : CIP entry
B82-07023

304.8′73′05195 — South Korea. Emigration to United States

Illsoo, Kim. New urban immigrants : the Korean community in New York / Illsoo Kim. — Princeton ; Guildford : Princeton University Press, c1981. — xvi,329p ; 25cm
Bibliography: p321-323. — Includes index
ISBN 0-691-09355-5 : £18.80
Primary classification 305.8′957′07471
B82-02601

305 — SOCIAL STRATIFICATION

305 — Discrimination. Psychosocial aspects

Levin, Jack, *1941-*. The functions of discrimination and prejudice / Jack Levin, William C. Levin. — 2nd ed. — New York ; London : Harper & Row, c1982. — xiv,258p : ill ; 21cm
Previous ed.: published as Functions of prejudice, 1975. — Bibliography: p249. — Includes index
ISBN 0-06-043964-5 (pbk) : £7.95
Primary classification 303.3′85 B82-16588

305 — Equality

Dahrendorf, Ralf. Life chances : approaches to social and political theory / Ralf Dahrendorf. — London : Weidenfeld and Nicolson, c1979. — ix,181p ; 23cm
Includes index
ISBN 0-297-77682-7 : £10.00
Also classified at 323.44 B82-33506

Rae, Douglas W.. Equalities / Douglas Rae, and Douglas Yates ... [et al.]. — Cambridge, Mass. ; London : Harvard University Press, 1981. — viii,210p : ill ; 24cm
Bibliography: p193-204. — Includes index
ISBN 0-674-25980-7 : £13.65 B82-13732

305 — Persons: Freaks. Social aspects

Fiedler, Leslie A.. Freaks : myths and images of the secret self / Leslie Fiedler. — Harmondsworth : Penguin, 1981, c1978. — 367p : ill,facsims,ports ; 24cm
Originally published: New York : Simon and Schuster, 1978. — Bibliography: p349-353. — Includes index
ISBN 0-14-005426-x (pbk) : £4.95 B82-07295

305 — Primitive societies. Social structure — *Anthropological perspectives*

Heusch, Luc de. Why marry her? : society and symbolic structures / Luc de Heusch ; translated by Janet Lloyd. — Cambridge : Cambridge University Press, c1981. — vi,218p : ill ; 24cm. — (Cambridge studies in social anthropology ; 33)
Translated from the French. — Bibliography: p208-214. — Includes index
ISBN 0-521-22460-8 : £19.50 : CIP rev.
Also classified at 291.6′2 B81-30495

305 — Social discrimination. Intervention by governments

Little, Alan, *1934-*. 'Loading the law' : a study of transmitted deprivation, ethnic minorities and affirmative action / Alan Little, Diana Robbins. — London : Commission for Racial Equality, 1982. — 67p ; 21cm
Text on inside covers. — Bibliography: p63-67
ISBN 0-902355-98-8 (pbk) : £1.50 B82-38579

Little, Alan, *1934-*. 'Loading the law' : the study of transmitted deprivation, ethnic and affirmative action : summary / Alan Little, Diana Robbins. — London : Commission for Racial Equality, 1982. — 14p ; 21cm
ISBN 0-907920-14-4 (unbound) : Unpriced
B82-38580

305 — Social inequality

Hurst, Charles E.. The anatomy of social inequality / Charles E. Hurst. — St. Louis ; London : Mosby, 1979. — xiv,356p : ill ; 25cm
Bibliography: p322-344. — Includes index
ISBN 0-8016-2314-6 : £15.00 B82-28889

Rethinking social inequality. — Aldershot : Gower, Aug.1982. — [272]p
ISBN 0-566-00557-3 : £12.50 : CIP entry
B82-15881

305 — Social structure

Wilhelmsen, Jens-J.. Man and structures / Jens-J. Wilhelmsen. — Rev. ed. — London : Grosvenor, 1982. — vii,87p ; 18cm
Previous ed.: 1977
ISBN 0-901269-64-6 (pbk) : £1.50 B82-17604

305 — United States. Cultural pluralism

Morgan, Gordon Daniel. America without ethnicity / Gordon Daniel Morgan. — Port Washington : Kennikat ; London : National University Publications, 1981. — 137p ; 22cm
Bibliography: p125-133. — Includes index
ISBN 0-8046-9293-9 : Unpriced B82-17484

305′.00995′3 — Papua New Guinea. Highlands. Tribes. Social inequality — *Anthropological perspectives*

Strathern, Andrew. Inequality in New Guinea Highlands societies. — Cambridge : Cambridge University Press, Oct.1982. — [200]p. — (Cambridge papers in social anthropology ; 11)
ISBN 0-521-24489-7 : £19.50 : CIP entry
B82-29375

305′.01 — Equality — *Philosophical perspectives*

Flew, Antony. The politics of Procrustes : contradictions of enforced equality / Antony Flew. — London : Temple Smith, 1981. — 216p ; 23cm
Bibliography: p195-209. — Includes index
ISBN 0-85117-204-0 : £9.95 B82-24030

305′.01 — Social structure — *Philosophical perspectives*

Santayana, George. Reason in society : volume two of "The life of reason" / George Santayana. — New York : Dover ; London : Constable & Co., 1980. — viii,205p ; 21cm
Originally published: New York : Scribner′s sons, 1905
ISBN 0-486-24003-7 (pbk) : £1.95 B82-17137

305′.05 — Social minorities — *Serials*

Immigrants & minorities. — Vol.1, no.1 (Mar. 1982)-. — London : Frank Cass, 1982-. — v. ; 22cm
Three issues yearly
ISSN 0261-9288 = Immigrants & minorities : £30.00 per year B82-22694

305′.05 — Social mobility & stratification — *Serials*

Research in social stratification and mobility : a research annual. — Vol.1 (1981)-. — Greenwich, Conn. : JAI Press ; London (3 Henrietta St., WC2E 8LU) : Distributed by JAICON Press, 1981-. — v. ; 24cm
£24.50 B82-02369

305′.0938 — Ancient Greece. Social structure

Finley, M. I.. Economy and society in Ancient Greece / by M.I. Finley ; edited with an introduction by Brent D. Shaw and Richard P. Saller. — London : Chatto & Windus, 1981. — xxvi,326p ; 23cm
Bibliography: p298-318. — Includes index
ISBN 0-7011-2549-7 : £15.00 : CIP rev.
B81-07617

305′.094 — Europe. Social minorities. Sociopolitical aspects

Mugny, Gabriel. The power of minorities. — London : Academic Press, Oct.1982. — [200]p. — (European monographs in social psychology ; 31)
ISBN 0-12-509720-4 : CIP entry B82-24939

305′.094 — Europe. Social structure, *to ca 1000*

Ranking, resource and exchange : aspects of the archaeology of early European society. — Cambridge : Cambridge University Press, July 1982. — [176]p. — (New directions in archaeology)
ISBN 0-521-24282-7 : £18.50 : CIP entry
B82-26240

305′.0941 — Great Britain. Social equality. Effects of distribution of expenditure on public welfare services

Le Grand, Julian. The strategy of equality : redistribution and the social services / Julian Le Grand. — London : Allen & Unwin, 1982. — viii,192p : ill ; 23cm
Bibliography: p176-186. — Includes index
ISBN 0-04-336074-2 (cased) : Unpriced : CIP rev.
ISBN 0-04-336075-0 (pbk) : Unpriced
B81-33918

305′.0941 — Great Britain. Social inequality

Brown, Muriel. Despite the welfare state : a report on the SSRC/DHSS programme of research into transmitted deprivation / Muriel Brown and Nicola Madge. — London : Heinemann Educational, 1982. — xi,388p ; 23cm. — (Studies in deprivation and disadvantage)
Bibliography: p361-378. — Includes index
ISBN 0-435-82095-8 (cased) : £14.50 : CIP rev.
ISBN 0-435-82096-6 (pbk) : Unpriced
B82-11763

305′.0942 — England. Social structure, *ca 1940 — Socialist viewpoints*

Orwell, George. The lion and the unicorn : socialism and the English genius / George Orwell ; with an introduction by Bernard Cick. — Harmondsworth : Penguin, 1982, c1941. — 123p ; 18cm
Originally published: London : Secker & Warburg, 1941
ISBN 0-14-006327-7 (pbk) : £1.25 B82-30251

305′.09429 — Wales. Social structure

Cooke, P. N.. Local class structure in Wales / by P.N. Cooke ; a paper from the Wales Regionalism Group. — Cardiff (King Edward VII Ave., Cardiff CF1 3NU) : Dept. of Town Planning, University of Wales Institute of Science and Technology, 1981. — 35p ; 30cm. — (Papers in planning research ; 31)
Bibliography: p32-33
Unpriced (pbk) B82-26830

305′.09429′87 — Urban regions. Social structure. Research. Applications of multivariate analysis — *Study regions: Cardiff Region*

Davies, Wayne K. D.. Urban social structure : a multivariate-structural analysis of Cardiff and its region. — Cardiff : University of Wales Press, Nov.1982. — [174]p. — (Social science monographs, ISSN 0307-0042 ; 8)
ISBN 0-7083-0833-3 (pbk) : £5.00 : CIP entry
B82-29436

305′.0947 — Eastern Europe. Social structure, *1945-1980*

Tarniewski, Marek. The new regime. — London : Allison & Busby, Dec.1981. — [192]p
ISBN 0-85031-417-8 (cased) : £9.95 : CIP entry
ISBN 0-85031-418-6 (pbk) : £4.95 B81-31628

305′.0947 — Soviet Union. Social inequality
Lane, David. The end of social inequality?. — London : Allen & Unwin, Sept.1982. — [208]p
ISBN 0-04-323024-5 (cased) : £12.95 : CIP entry
ISBN 0-04-323025-3 (pbk) : £4.95 B82-19077

305′.097 — North America. Urban regions. Social structure, *ca 1800-ca 1900*
Katz, Michael B.. The social organisation of early industrial capitalism / Michael B. Katz, Michael J. Doucet, Mark J. Stern. — Cambridge, Mass. ; London : Harvard University Press, 1982. — xiii,444p ; 24cm
Includes index
ISBN 0-674-81445-2 : £26.25 B82-33389

305′.0973 — United States. Social equality, *to 1980*
Redenius, Charles. The American ideal of equality : from Jefferson's Declaration to the Burger Court / Charles Redenius. — Port Washington ; London : National University Publications : Kennikat, 1981. — 166p ; 22cm. — (Series in political science)
Bibliography: p158-161. — Includes index
ISBN 0-8046-9282-3 : £14.85 B82-02829

305′.0973 — United States. Social minorities
The **Minority** report : an introduction to racial, ethnic, and gender relations / [edited by] Anthony Gary Dworkin and Rosalind J. Dworkin. — 2nd ed. — New York ; London : Holt, Rinehart and Winston, c1982. — xi,407p : ill ; 24cm
Previous ed.: New York : Praeger, 1976. — Includes bibliographies and index
ISBN 0-03-055186-2 (pbk) : £8.95 B82-25373

305′.0982′54 — Argentina. Córdoba. Social mobility & stratification, *1870-1914*
Szuchman, Mark D.. Mobility and integration in urban Argentina : Córdoba in the liberal era / by Mark D. Szuchman. — Austin ; London : University of Texas Press, c1980. — xi,236p : 2maps ; 24cm. — (Latin American monographs ; no.52)
Bibliography: p207-231. — Includes index
ISBN 0-292-75057-9 : £14.00 B82-12769

305.2 — Man. Transitions — *Conference proceedings*
Major transitions in the human life cycle / edited by Alvin C. Eurich. — Lexington, Mass. : Lexington Books ; [Aldershot] : Gower [distributor], 1982, c1981. — xi,528p : ill ; 24cm
Papers from 4 conferences sponsored by the Academy for Educational Development. — Bibliography: p509-511. — Includes index
ISBN 0-669-04559-4 : Unpriced B82-14755

305.2′3 — Childhood — *Sociological perspectives*
The **Sociology** of childhood : essential readings / edited by Chris Jenks. — London : Batsford Academic and Educational, 1982. — 299p ; 22cm
Bibliography: p289-290. — Includes index
ISBN 0-7134-3695-6 (cased) : Unpriced : CIP rev.
ISBN 0-7134-3696-4 (pbk) : £6.95 B81-33838

305.2′3 — Children. Development — *Sociological perspectives*
Papalia, Diane E.. A child's world : infancy through adolescence / Diane E. Papalia, Sally Wendkos Olds. — 3rd ed. — New York ; London : McGraw-Hill, c1982. — ix,692p : ill (some col.),ports ; 25cm
Previous ed.: 1979. — Bibliography: p637-671. — Includes index
ISBN 0-07-048464-3 : £14.95 B82-37579

305.2′3 — Children. Interpersonal relationships with babysitters — *For children*
Althea. My babysitter / by Althea ; illustrated by Helen Herbert. — Cambridge : Dinosaur, c1981. — [24]p : col.ill ; 16x19cm. — (Dinosaur's Althea books)
ISBN 0-85122-303-6 (cased) : £2.25
ISBN 0-85122-160-2 (pbk) : Unpriced B82-08276

305.2′3 — Children. Sex roles. Development
Pitcher, E.. Boys and girls at play. — Brighton : Harvester Press, Feb.1983. — [192]p
ISBN 0-7108-0493-8 : £15.95 : CIP entry B82-38902

305.2′3 — Great Britain. Children. Emigration to Commonwealth countries, *to 1952*
Wagner, Gillian. Children of the Empire / Gillian Wagner. — London : Weidenfeld and Nicolson, c1982. — xix,248p,[12]p of plates : ill,facsims,ports ; 23cm
Bibliography: p267-273. — Includes index
ISBN 0-297-78047-6 : £10.95 B82-14631

305.2′3 — Great Britain. Middle class girls. Social conditions, *1837-1901*
Gorham, Deborah. The Victorian girl and the feminine ideal. — London : Croom Helm, June 1982. — [224]p
ISBN 0-85664-913-9 : £13.95 : CIP entry B82-10221

305.2′3 — London. Young persons, 16-25 years. Attitudes — *Sociological perspectives*
Francis, Leslie J.. Youth in transit. — Aldershot : Gower, June 1982. — [196]p
ISBN 0-566-00530-1 : £12.50 : CIP entry B82-09428

305.2′3 — Northern India *(Republic).* **Rural regions. Girls. Sex discrimination,** *1789-1980.* **Cultural factors**
Miller, Barbara D.. The endangered sex : neglect of female children in rural North India / Barbara D. Miller. — Ithaca ; London : Cornell University Press, c1981. — 201p : ill,maps ; 24cm
Bibliography: p175-196. — Includes index
ISBN 0-8014-1371-0 : £12.25 B82-02055

305.2′3 — Working class children, *1800-1981.* **Social conditions**
Seabrook, Jeremy. Working-class childhood. — London : Gollancz, Sept.1982. — [224]p
ISBN 0-575-03147-6 (cased) : £9.95 : CIP entry
ISBN 0-575-03198-0 (pbk) B82-20187

305.2′3 — Young persons. Interpersonal relationships — *For young persons*
Stewart, Bill, *1923-*. You — and all the others : a guide to personal relationships / Bill Stewart. — Harmondsworth : Kestrel, 1982. — 112p : ill ; 21cm
ISBN 0-7226-5689-0 : £4.95 B82-39942

305.2′3 — Young persons. Social development — *Structuralist perspectives*
Social development in youth : structure and content / volume editors J.A. Meacham and N.R. Santilli. — Basel ; London : Karger, 1981. — xi,186p ; 23cm. — (Contributions to human development ; v.5)
Includes bibliographies and index
ISBN 3-8055-2868-x (pbk) : £21.90 B82-03753

305.2′3 — Young persons. Social skills. Teaching — *Manuals*
McGuire, James. Life after school : a social skills curriculum / by James McGuire and Philip Priestley. — Oxford : Pergamon, 1981. — xi,230p : ill,1facsim ; 21cm. — (Pergamon international library)
Bibliography: p214-221. — Includes index
ISBN 0-08-025192-7 (cased) : Unpriced : CIP rev.
ISBN 0-08-025193-5 (pbk) : £5.00 B81-21554

305.2′3′0882971 — Great Britain. Young Muslims. Social aspects
Anwar, Muhammad. Young Muslims in a multi-cultural society : their educational needs and policy implications : the British case / Muhammad Anwar. — Leicester : Islamic Foundation, c1982. — 24p ; 21cm
ISBN 0-86037-105-0 (pbk) : Unpriced B82-21948

305.2′3′09 — Society. Role of children, *to 1980*
Sommerville, C. John. The rise and fall of childhood / C. John Sommerville. — Beverly Hills ; London : Sage, c1982. — 255p ; 23cm. — (Sage library of social research ; v.140)
Bibliography: p243-250. — Includes index
ISBN 0-8039-1823-2 (cased) : Unpriced
ISBN 0-8039-1824-0 (pbk) : £6.50 B82-38159

305.2′3′0924 — Great Britain. Socially disadvantaged young persons: Gaskin, Graham — *Biographies*
MacVeigh, James. Gaskin. — London : Cape, Sept.1982. — [272]p
ISBN 0-224-01997-x : £7.50 : CIP entry B82-25520

305.2′3′094 — Europe. Young persons. Cultural processes, *1770-1973*
Gillis, John R.. Youth and history : tradition and change in European age relations, 1770 - present / John R. Gillis. — Expanded student ed. — New York ; London : Academic Press, c1981. — xiv,250p : ill ; 23cm. — (Studies in social discontinuity)
Previous ed.: 1974. — Bibliography: p231-244. — Includes index
ISBN 0-12-785264-6 (pbk) : £6.40 B82-02072

305.2′3′094 — Western Europe. Children, to 8 years — *Conference proceedings*
From birth to eight : young children in European society in the 1980's / a council for cultural co-operation conference, organized by the School Education Division of the Council of Europe. — Windsor : NFER-Nelson, c1979. — 168p ; 25cm
Bibliography: p160-168
ISBN 0-85633-225-9 (pbk) : £9.95 B82-07920

305.2′3′09416 — Northern Ireland. Children. Social conditions
Harbison, Jeremy. A society under stress : children and young people in Northern Ireland / Jeremy and Joan Harbison. — Shepton Mallet : Open Books, 1980. — xii,200p : ill,maps ; 23cm
Bibliography: p177-189. — Includes index
ISBN 0-7291-0128-2 : £9.95 B82-03262

305.2′3′09417 — Ireland *(Republic).* **Society. Role of young persons**
Challenge for young Ireland / edited [by] David Medcalf. — Dublin (6 Waterloo Rd., Dublin 6) : National Youth Council of Ireland, c1980. — 56p : ports ; 21cm
£1.50 (pbk) B82-13184

305.2′3′0942 — England. Children. Social conditions, *1800-1914*
Walvin, James. A child's world : a social history of English childhood, 1800-1914 / James Walvin. — Harmondsworth : Penguin, 1982. — 236p ; 20cm
Bibliography: p204-208. — Includes index
ISBN 0-14-022389-4 (pbk) : £2.95 B82-22090

305.2′3′09427 — North-west England. Urban regions. Children. Social conditions, *1780-1900*
Cruickshank, Marjorie. Children and industry : child health and welfare in north-east textile towns during the nineteenth century / Marjorie Cruickshank. — Manchester : Manchester University Press, c1981. — viii,189p : ill,1map ; 23cm
Bibliography: p178-184. — Includes index
ISBN 0-7190-0809-3 : £14.50 : CIP rev. B81-28053

305.2′3′0973 — United States. Children. Equality of opportunity. Social aspects
De Lone, Richard H.. Small futures : children, inequality, and the limits of liberal reform / by Richard H. de Lone for the Carnegie Council on Children. — New York ; London : Harcourt Brace Jovanovich, c1979. — xiv,258p ; 25cm
Includes index
ISBN 0-15-183128-9 : £8.40 B82-13549

305.2′34 — Great Britain. Working class girls. Expectations — *Sociological perspectives*
Steedman, Carolyn. The tidy house. — London : Virago, Feb.1983. — [224]p
ISBN 0-86068-321-4 (cased) : £9.95 : CIP entry
ISBN 0-86068-326-5 (pbk) : £5.95 B82-39828

305.2′35 — Adolescence
Conger, John Janeway. Adolescence : generation under pressure / John Conger. — London : Harper & Row, c1979. — 128p : ill(some col.) ; 24cm. — (The Life cycle series)
Includes index
ISBN 0-06-318100-2 (cased) : £4.95
ISBN 0-06-318099-5 (pbk) : Unpriced B82-03769

305.2'35 — Adolescents. Behaviour. Psychosocial aspects
Rutter, Michael. Changing youth in a changing society : patterns of adolescent development and disorder / Michael Rutter. — London : Nuffield Provincial Hospitals Trust, 1979. — xii,323p : ill ; 23cm
At head of title: The Rock Carling Fellowship 1979. — Bibliography: p295-323
ISBN 0-900574-31-3 : Unpriced B82-03519

305.2'35 — Qatar. Young men. Social identity. Effects of social change — *Study examples: University of Qatar. Students*
Melikian, Levon H.. Jassim : a study in the psychosocial development of a young man in Qatar / Levon H. Melikian. — London : Longman, 1981. — 112p ; 23cm
Bibliography: p109-112
ISBN 0-582-78035-7 : £11.95 B82-19430

305.2'35'0207 — Adolescent boys. Interpersonal relationships with adolescent girls — *Humour*
Ephron, Delia. Teenage romance, or, How to die of embarrassment. — London : Gollancz, Sept.1982. — [128]p
Originally published: New York : Viking Press, 1981
ISBN 0-575-03146-8 (pbk) : £2.95 : CIP entry B82-19557

305.2'35'0973 — United States. Adolescents. Social development
Seltzer, Vivian Center. Adolescent social development : dynamic functional interaction / Vivian Center Seltzer. — [Lexington, Mass.] : Lexington Books ; [Aldershot] : Gower [distributor], 1982. — xii,286p ; 24cm
Bibliography: p255-271. — Includes index
ISBN 0-669-04511-x : £21.00 B82-27879

305.2'4'0973 — United States. Adulthood
Turner, Jeffrey S.. Contemporary adulthood / Jeffrey S. Turner, Donald B. Helms. — 2nd ed. — New York ; London : Holt, Rinehart and Winston, c1982. — xiv,400p : ill ; 25cm
Previous ed.: Philadelphia : Saunders, 1979. — Bibliography: p369-387. — Includes index
ISBN 0-03-060143-6 : £11.50 B82-25368

305.2'42 — London. Persons, 26-39 years. Attitudes — *Sociological perspectives*
Francis, Leslie J.. Experiences of adulthood. — Aldershot : Gower, Nov.1982. — [232]p
ISBN 0-566-00562-x : £12.50 : CIP entry B82-26547

305.2'44 — Middle age
Fiske, Marjorie. Middle age : the prime of life? / Marjorie Fiske. — London : Harper & Row, c1979. — 128p : ill(some col.) ; 24cm. — (The Life cycle series)
Includes index
ISBN 0-06-318103-7 (cased) : £4.95
ISBN 0-06-318104-5 (pbk) : Unpriced B82-03768

305.2'44 — Middle age. Personal adjustment
Hepworth, Mike. Surviving middle age / Mike Hepworth and Mike Featherstone. — Oxford : Blackwell, 1982. — 204p ; 19cm. — (Understanding everyday experience)
Bibliography: p178-190. — Includes index
ISBN 0-631-12751-8 (cased) : Unpriced : CIP rev.
ISBN 0-631-12955-3 (pbk) : Unpriced B82-04583

305.2'44'088041 — United States. Middle age. Personal adjustment of men — *Case studies*
Farrell, Michael P.. Men at midlife / Michael P. Farrell, Stanley D. Rosenberg. — Boston, Mass. : Auburn House ; London : distributed by Eurospan, c1981. — xiv,242p : ill ; 25cm
Bibliography: p227-235. — Includes index
ISBN 0-86569-073-1 (cased) : £16.25
ISBN 0-86569-062-6 (pbk) : Unpriced B82-14306

305.2'6 — Adults. Ageing. Social aspects
Ageing and life course transitions. — London : Tavistock, Oct.1982. — [280]p
ISBN 0-422-78360-9 : £16.00 : CIP entry B82-24011

Carlson, Avis D.. In the fullness of time / Avis D. Carlson. — South Yarmouth : Curley ; [Skipton] : Magna Print [distributor], 1979, c1977. — xxiii,388p ; 22cm
Originally published: Chicago : Regnery, 1977. — Published in large print
ISBN 0-89340-172-2 : £4.75 B82-14861

305.2'6 — Australia. Old age — *Sociological perspectives*
Russell, Cherry. The aging experience. — London : Allen & Unwin, Jan.1982. — [350]p
ISBN 0-86861-267-7 : £15.00 : CIP entry B81-34071

305.2'6 — Old age
Aiken, Lewis R.. Later life / Lewis R. Aiken. — 2nd ed. — New York ; London : Holt, Rinehart and Winston, c1982. — ix,308p : ill ; 25cm
Previous ed.: Philadelphia ; London : Saunders, 1978. — Bibliography: p284-296. — Includes index
ISBN 0-03-059751-x : £15.95 B82-25404

Skeet, Muriel. The third age : a guide for elderly people, their families and friends / Muriel Skeet ; foreword by David Hobman. — London : Darton, Longman and Todd in association with Age Concern England and the Disabled Living Foundation, 1982. — xvi,220p : 1ill ; 22cm
Bibliography: p210-213. — Includes index
ISBN 0-232-51484-4 (pbk) : 6.95 : CIP rev. B81-16390

305.2'6 — Old persons — *For schools*
Van Zwanenberg, Fiona. Getting together : a work card pack for juniors / [written by Fiona van Zwanenberg] ; [illustrations by Susan Hellard] ; [designed by Carlos Sapochnik]. — London : Help the Aged Education Dept., c1981. — 1portfolio(12 cards) : ill ; 30cm
ISBN 0-905852-13-3 (unbound) : Unpriced B82-41130

305.2'6'091821 — Western world. Old persons. Social conditions. Geographical aspects
Geographical perspectives on the elderly / edited by A.M. Warnes. — Chichester : Wiley, c1982. — xviii,478p : ill,maps,plans ; 24cm
Bibliography: p449-465. — Includes index
ISBN 0-471-09976-7 : Unpriced : CIP rev. B81-35731

305.2'6'0922 — Old age — *Personal observations — Collections*
Bid the world good-night : a symposium / edited and produced by Ralph Ricketts. — London : Search, 1981. — 210p ; 22cm
ISBN 0-85532-446-5 (pbk) : £3.95
Also classified at 306.9'0922 B82-03033

305.2'6'0924 — Old age — *Personal observations*
The **Turn** of the years / with an introduction by Paul Theroux. — Salisbury : Michael Russell, 1982. — 48p : ill ; 19cm
Contents: The seasons' course / selected engravings by Reynolds Stone — As old as the century / V.S. Pritchett
ISBN 0-85955-085-0 : £3.95
Also classified at 769.92'4 B82-31960

305.2'6'0941 — Great Britain. Old persons — *For schools*
People not 'pensioners'. — Rev. 3rd ed. — London : Help the Aged, Education Department, c1981. — 29p : ill,ports ; 30cm
Cover title. — Previous ed.: 1978. — Text and ill. on inside covers
ISBN 0-905852-14-1 (pbk) : Unpriced B82-40560

305.2'6'0941 — Great Britain. Old persons. Social aspects — *Conference proceedings*
British Society of Gerontology. *Conference (1980 : Aberdeen)*. Current trends in British gerontology : proceedings of the 1980 conference of the British Society of Gerontology / edited by Rex Taylor and Anne Gilmore. — Aldershot : Gower, c1982. — x,230p : ill ; 23cm
Includes bibliographies
ISBN 0-566-00495-x : Unpriced : CIP rev. B81-31608

305.2'6'0942 — England. Old age — *Sociological perspectives*
Pincus, Lily. The challenge of a long life / Lily Pincus with a contribution by Aleda Erskine. — London : Faber, 1981. — 152p ; 23cm
Bibliography: p151-152
ISBN 0-571-11775-9 : £5.95 : CIP rev. B81-25305

305.2'6'0954 — India *(Republic)*. **Old persons** — *For schools*
Hubley, John, *19---*. Growing old : an Indian experience / by John & Penny Hubley for Help the Aged Education Department. — Senior ed. — [London] : [Help the Aged Education Department], c1980. — [24]p : ill ; 21cm
ISBN 0-905852-09-5 (unbound) : Unpriced B82-40563

305.2'6'0973 — United States. Old persons
Neuhaus, Ruby Hart. Successful aging / Ruby Hart Neuhaus, Robert Henry Neuhaus. — New York ; Chichester : Wiley, c1982. — xviii,285p ; 24cm
Bibliography: p250-274. — Includes index
ISBN 0-471-08448-4 : £12.50
Primary classification 612'.67 B82-26472

305.2'6'0973 — United States. Old persons. Socioeconomic aspects
Aging / editors Aliza Kolker, Paul I. Ahmed. — New York ; Oxford : Elsevier Biomedical, c1982. — xx,290p ; 24cm. — (Coping with medical issues)
Includes bibliographies and index
ISBN 0-444-00664-8 : Unpriced B82-33795

305.3 — Man. Sexes. Cultural aspects
Sexual meanings : the cultural construction of gender and sexuality / edited by Sherry B. Ortner and Harriet Whitehead. — Cambridge : Cambridge University Press, 1981. — x,435p ; 25cm
Includes bibliographies and index
ISBN 0-521-23965-6 (cased) : £25.00
ISBN 0-521-28375-2 (pbk) : £7.95 B82-13982

305.3 — Men. Interpersonal relationships with women — *Feminist viewpoints*
Lazarre, Jane. On loving men / by Jane Lazarre. — London : Virago, 1981, c1980. — 181p ; 20cm
Originally published: New York : Dial, 1980. — Bibliography: p179-181
ISBN 0-86068-206-4 (pbk) : £3.50 : CIP rev. B81-30401

305.3 — Sex differences. Social aspects — *Anthropological perspectives*
Archer, John, *1944-*. Sex and gender / John Archer and Barbara Lloyd. — Harmondsworth : Penguin, 1982. — 265p : ill ; 20cm. — (Pelican books)
Bibliography: p227-245. — Includes index
ISBN 0-14-022194-8 (pbk) : £2.95 B82-37813

305.3 — Sex roles — *Conference proceedings*
Sex role attitudes and cultural change / edited by Ira Gross, John Downing and Adma D'Heurle. — Dordrecht ; London : Reidel, c1982. — vii,213p : ill ; 25cm. — (Priority issues in mental health ; v.3)
Conference papers. — Includes bibliographies and index
ISBN 90-277-1340-5 : Unpriced B82-21455

305.3'05 — Sex roles. Social aspects — *Serials*
Research in the interweave of social roles : women and men : a research annual. — Vol.1 (1980)-. — Greenwich, Conn. : JAI Press ; London (3 Henrietta St., WC2E 8LU) : Distributed by JAICON Press, 1980-. — v. ; 24cm
ISSN 0272-2801 = Research in the interweave of social roles, women and men : £24.50 B82-02351

305.3'0880633 — Primitive societies. Sex roles — *Comparative studies*
Sanday, Peggy Reeves. Female power and male dominance : on the origins of sexual inequality / Peggy Reeves Sanday. — Cambridge : Cambridge University Press, 1981. — xvii,295p : ill ; 24cm
Bibliography: p275-283. — Includes index
ISBN 0-521-23618-5 (cased) : £20.00
ISBN 0-521-28075-3 (pbk) : £6.95 B82-21361

305.3′09 — Sexism, *to 1981*
Janssen-Jurreit, Marielouise. Sexism : the male monopoly on history and thought / Marielouise Janssen-Jurreit ; translated from the German by Verne Moberg. — London : Pluto, 1982. — 376p ; 20cm
Translation (shortened and reworked) of: Sexismus : Über die Abteilung der Frauenfrage
ISBN 0-86104-315-4 (pbk) : £4.95 B82-23771

305.3′0941 — Great Britain. Sex roles
Reid, Ivan. Sex differences in Britain. — London : Grant McIntyre, July 1982. — [280]p
ISBN 0-86216-064-2 (cased) : £14.95 : CIP entry
ISBN 0-86216-065-0 (pbk) : £5.95 B82-17958

305.3′0944 — France. Peasant communities. Marriage. Sex roles, *ca 1800-1982*
Segalen, Martine. Love and power in the peasant family. — Oxford : Blackwell, Jan.1983. — [256]p
Translation of: Mari et femme dans la société paysanne
ISBN 0-631-12626-0 : £12.50 : CIP entry B82-32512

305.3′1 — Masculinity
Pleck, Joseph H.. The myth of masculinity / Joseph H. Pleck. — Cambridge, Mass. ; London : MIT Press, c1981. — ix,229p ; 24cm
Bibliography: p189-216. — Includes index
ISBN 0-262-16081-1 : £12.25 B82-03918

305.3′1′0973 — United States. Adulthood. Personal adjustment of young men
Hogan, Dennis P.. Transitions and social change : the early lives of American men / Dennis P. Hogan. — New York ; London : Academic Press, 1981. — xiv,232p : ill ; 24cm. — (Studies in population)
Bibliography: p221-225. — Includes index
ISBN 0-12-352080-0 : £17.60 B82-10057

305.3′2′0952 — Japan. Men. Self-development, *to ca 1970.* **Social aspects**
Kinmonth, Earl H.. The self-made man in Meiji Japanese thought : from Samurai to salary man / Earl H. Kinmonth. — Berkeley ; London : University of California Press, c1981. — xi,385p : ill,forms ; 24cm
Bibliography: p357-371. — Includes index
ISBN 0-520-04159-3 : Unpriced B82-16912

305.3′3 — Husbands. Careers. Role of wives
Finch, Janet. Married to the job. — London : Allen & Unwin, Feb.1983. — [224]p
ISBN 0-04-301149-7 : £10.00 : CIP entry B82-36442

305.3′8896073 — United States. Negro men. Social conditions
Black men / edited by Lawrence E. Gary. — Beverly Hills ; London : Sage, c1981. — 295p ; 21cm. — (Sage focus edition ; 31)
Includes bibliographies
ISBN 0-8039-1654-x (cased) : Unpriced
ISBN 0-8039-1655-8 (pbk) : £6.50 B82-17074

305′.4 — Science — *Sociological perspectives*
Science in context. — Milton Keynes : Open University Press, Mar.1982. — [250]p
ISBN 0-335-10054-6 (pbk) : £5.95 : CIP entry B82-01870

305.4 — Women — *Anthropological perspectives*
Fisher, Helen E.. The sex contract : the evolution of human behaviour. — London : Granada, June 1982. — [224]p
ISBN 0-246-11768-0 : £7.95 : CIP entry B82-09989

305.4 — Women. Sex roles. Implications of behaviour of female primates
Hrdy, Sarah Blaffer. The woman that never evolved / Sarah Blaffer Hrdy. — Cambridge, Mass. ; London : Harvard University Press, 1981. — ix,256p : ill ; 25cm
Includes index
ISBN 0-674-95540-4 : £12.25 B82-11868

305.4 — Women's studies
Women in futures research. — Oxford : Pergamon, Aug.1981. — [124]p
ISBN 0-08-028100-1 : £6.25 : CIP entry B81-23791

305.4′06041 — Great Britain. Women's organisations: National Federation of Women's Institutes. Annual general meetings
National Federation of Women's Institutes. All about the AGM : with guidance for WI delegates. — London : WI Books, c1982. — 1folded sheet(8p) ; 18cm
ISBN 0-900556-72-2 (unbound) : Unpriced B82-31156

305.4′09411 — Scotland. Women, *1080-1980*
Marshall, Rosalind K.. Virgins and viragos : a history of women in Scotland from 1080 to 1980. — London : Collins, Aug.1982. — [368]p
ISBN 0-00-216039-0 : £12.50 : CIP entry B82-15616

305.4′096 — Africa. Women — *Illustrations*
Murray, Maggie. Our own freedom / photographs by Maggie Murray ; introduction and comments by Buchi Emecheta. — London : Sheba, 1981. — 112p : ill ; 22cm
ISBN 0-907179-09-6 (pbk) : £3.75 B82-18410

305.4′2 — Feminism
Feminist theory. — Brighton : Harvester, Oct.1982. — [312]p
ISBN 0-7108-0444-x (pbk) : £6.95 : CIP entry B82-28480

Richards, Janet Radcliffe. The sceptical feminist : a philosophical enquiry / Janet Radcliffe Richards. — Harmondsworth : Penguin, 1982, c1980. — 369p ; 19cm
Originally published: London : Routledge & Kegan Paul, 1980. — Includes index
ISBN 0-14-022341-x (pbk) : £2.50 B82-18153

305.4′2 — Feminism — *Philosophical perspectives*
McMillan, Carol. Women, reason and nature. — Oxford : Basil Blackwell, June 1982. — [160]p. — (Values and philosophical inquiry)
ISBN 0-631-12496-9 : £9.50 : CIP entry B82-09451

305.4′2 — Feminism *related to* **Marxism** — *Socialist viewpoints*
Women and revolution : a discussion of the unhappy marriage of marxism and feminism / edited by Lydia Sargent. — London : Pluto, 1981. — xxxi,373p ; 21cm
ISBN 0-86104-340-5 (pbk) : £3.95
Primary classification 335.4 B82-20689

305.4′2 — Feminism *related to* **theories of psychoanalysis of Lacan, Jacques**
Gallop, Jane. Feminism and psychoanalysis : the daughter's seduction / Jane Gallop. — London : Macmillan, 1982. — xv,164p : 1ill ; 23cm. — (Language, discourse, society)
Bibliography: p158-160. — Includes index
ISBN 0-333-29471-8 (cased) : £15.00
ISBN 0-333-29472-6 (pbk) : £4.15
Primary classification 150.19′5 B82-37756

305.4′2 — Feminism. Theories, *to ca 1930*
Feminist theorists. — London : Women's Press, July 1982. — [240]p
ISBN 0-7043-3889-0 (pbk) : £4.95 : CIP entry B82-13005

305.4′2 — Feminists. Interpersonal relationships with men — *Conference proceedings*
On the problem of men. — London : Women's Press, May 1982. — [288]p
Conference papers
ISBN 0-7043-3887-4 (pbk) : £4.95 : CIP entry B82-07672

305.4′2 — Great Britain. Women's liberation movements, *1968-1981* — *Feminist viewpoints*
Coote, Anna. Sweet freedom : the struggle for women's liberation. — Oxford : Blackwell, Apr.1982. — [192]p
ISBN 0-631-12555-8 (cased) : £7.50 : CIP entry B82-04587

305.4′2 — Society. Role of women
Munson, Beryl. The long walk : a report on the United Nations Mid-Decade Conference for Women, July 1980 at the Bella Centre, Copenhagen and the associated forum at the Amagher University, Copenhagen / Beryl Munson. — [Gravesend] : Victoria Press, 1981. — 81p ; 21cm
ISBN 0-907165-03-6 (pbk) : Unpriced B82-28333

Oakley, Ann. Subject women / Ann Oakley. — [London] : Fontana, 1982, c1981. — x,406p : ill ; 18cm
Originally published: Oxford : Martin Robertson, 1981. — Bibliography: p342-392. — Includes index
ISBN 0-00-635730-x (pbk) : £2.75 B82-31650

305.4′2 — Society. Role of women. Biological factors — *Feminist viewpoints*
Sayers, Janet. Biological politics. — London : Tavistock, Feb.1982. — [200]p
ISBN 0-422-77870-2 (cased) : £10.50 : CIP entry
ISBN 0-422-77880-x (pbk) : £4.95 B81-35727

305.4′2 — Society. Role of women — *Early works*
Wollstonecraft, Mary. Vindication of the rights of woman / Mary Wollstonecraft ; edited with an introduction by Miriam Brody Kramnick. — Harmondsworth : Penguin, 1982. — 319p : 1facsim ; 18cm. — (Penguin English library)
Originally published: London : J. Johnson, 1792. — Bibliography: p73-74
ISBN 0-14-043199-3 (pbk) : £1.75 B82-30255

305.4′2 — Society. Role of women — *Feminist viewpoints*
Friedan, Betty. The feminine mystique / Betty Friedan. — Harmondsworth : Penguin, 1965, c1963 (1982 [printing]). — 366p ; 20cm. — (Pelican books)
Originally published: London : Gollancz, 1963. — Includes index
ISBN 0-14-022408-4 (pbk) : £2.95 B82-30519

Friedan, Betty. The second stage / Betty Friedan ; introduction by Carolyn Faulder and Sandra Brown. — London : Joseph, 1982, c1981. — 348p ; 23cm
Originally published: New York : Summit, 1981
ISBN 0-7181-2139-2 : £8.95 B82-31743

Spare rib reader / edited by Marsha Rowe. — Harmondsworth : Penguin, 1982. — 620p : ill,facsims ; 20cm
Includes index
ISBN 0-14-005250-x (pbk) : £4.95 B82-37812

Women, power and political systems / edited by Margherita Rendel with the assistance of Georgina Ashworth. — London : Croom Helm, 1981. — 262p : ill ; 23cm
Includes bibliographies and index
ISBN 0-7099-2204-3 : £12.95 : CIP rev. B81-14904

305.4′2 — Society. Role of women. Influence of social change — *Conference proceedings*
Women and world change : equity issues in development / edited by Naomi Black and Ann Baker Cottrell. — Beverly Hills ; London : Sage, c1981. — 288p ; 23cm. — (Sage focus editions ; 38)
Conference papers. — Includes bibliographies
ISBN 0-8039-1700-7 (cased) : Unpriced
ISBN 0-8039-1701-5 (pbk) : £6.50 B82-11694

305.4′2 — Society. Role of women — *Marxist feminist viewpoints*
Delphy, Christine. The main enemy : a materialist analysis of women's oppression / by Christine Delphy. — London : Women's Research and Resources Centre, 1977 (1980 [printing]). — v,66p ; 22cm. — (Explorations in feminism ; no.3)
Translated from the French
ISBN 0-905969-02-2 (pbk) : £1.00 B82-18406

305.4'2 — Society. Role of women. Political aspects. Theories, *to 1980*

Elshtain, Jean Bethke. Public man, private woman : women in social and political thought / Jean Bethke Elshtain. — Oxford : Robertson, c1981. — xviii,378p ; 23cm
Bibliography: p355-372. — Includes index
ISBN 0-85520-470-2 (cased) : £17.50 : CIP rev.
ISBN 0-85520-471-0 (pbk) : £5.95 B81-26697

305.4'2 — Society. Role of women — *Socialist viewpoints*

Of marriage and the market. — London : C.S.E. Books, Oct.1981. — [224]p
ISBN 0-906336-24-4 (cased) : £12.00 : CIP entry
ISBN 0-906336-25-2 (pbk) : £4.95 B81-28116

305.4'2 — Society. Role of women, *to 1977 — Feminist viewpoints*

Fisher, Elizabeth. Women's creation : sexual evolution and the shaping of society / Elizabeth Fisher. — London : Wildwood House, 1980, c1979. — xvii,484p,[8]p of plates : ill ; 21cm
Originally published: Garden City, N.Y. : Anchor, 1979. — Bibliography: p431-449. — Includes index
ISBN 0-7045-0399-9 (pbk) : £2.95 B82-30665

305.4'2 — Women. Attitudes of society — *Feminist viewpoints*

Dworkin, Andrea. Our blood. — London : Women's Press, Apr.1982. — [128]p
ISBN 0-7043-3886-6 (pbk) : £3.50 : CIP entry B82-06238

305.4'2 — Women. Oppression by men. Economic aspects

Marshall, Kate. Real freedom. — London (38 Electric Ave., SW9 8JR) : Junius Publications, Nov.1982. — [112]p
ISBN 0-9508404-0-8 (pbk) : £1.95 : CIP entry B82-35211

305.4'2 — Women's liberation groups. Organisation

Freeman, Jo. The tyranny of structurelessness / by Jo Freeman. — London (c/o 5 Caledonian Rd., N1 9DX) : Dark Star, [1982?]. — 8p ; 22cm
Cover title. — Originally published: U.S.A. : Women's Liberation Movement, 1970
£0.35 (pbk) B82-38843

305.4'2'0207 — Feminism — *Humour*

Tweedie, Jill. Letters from a fainthearted feminist / introduced [i.e. written] by Jill Tweedie ; illustrated by Merrily Harpur. — London : Robson, 1982. — 144p : ill ; 22cm
ISBN 0-86051-171-5 : £5.95 : CIP rev. B82-05752

305.4'2'05 — Women. Equality of opportunity — *Serials*

Equal opportunities international. — Vol.1, no.1 (1981)-. — Hull (Enholmes Hall, Patrington, Hull, N. Humberside HU12 0PR) : Barmarick, 1981-. — v. : ill ; 31cm
Quarterly. — Description based on: Vol.1, no.2 (1981)
ISSN 0261-0159 = Equal opportunities international : Unpriced B82-29044

305.4'2'06041 — Great Britain. Women's organisations: National Federation of Women's Institutes

National Federation of Women's Institutes. The WI handbook. — Rev. ed. — London : WI, 1982. — 143p ; 21cm
Previous ed.: 1972. — Includes index
ISBN 0-900556-73-0 (pbk) : Unpriced : CIP rev. B82-12808

305.4'2'08996073 — United States. Society. Role of negro women, *to 1980 — Feminist viewpoints*

Hooks, Bell. Ain't I a woman : black women and feminism / by bell hooks. — London : Pluto, 1982, c1981. — 205p ; 21cm
Bibliography: p197-202. — Includes index
ISBN 0-86104-379-0 (pbk) : £3.95 B82-38149

305.4'2'09 — Feminism, *to 1980*

Banks, Olive. Faces of feminism : a study of feminism as a social movement / Olive Banks. — Oxford : Martin Robertson, 1981. — 285p ; 23cm
Bibliography: p264-279. — Includes index
ISBN 0-85520-261-0 (cased) : Unpriced : CIP rev.
ISBN 0-85520-260-2 (pbk) : £5.50 B81-13752

Charvet, John. Feminism / John Charvet. — London : Dent, 1982. — 159p ; 23cm. — (Modern Ideologies)
Bibliography: p155-156. — Includes index
ISBN 0-460-10255-9 (cased) : £7.95 : CIP rev.
ISBN 0-460-11255-4 (pbk) : Unpriced B81-36232

305.4'2'09 — Feminism, *to ca 1930 — Comparative studies*

Evans, Richard J.. The feminists : women's emancipation movements in Europe, America and Australasia, 1840-1920 / Richard J. Evans. — Rev. ed. — London : Croom Helm, 1979, c1977. — 266p ; 22cm
Previous ed.: 1977. — Includes index
ISBN 0-85664-212-6 (cased) : Unpriced
ISBN 0-85664-977-5 (pbk) : £4.95 B82-11612

305.4'2'091724 — Developing countries. Social development. Role of women

May, Nicky. Of conjuring and caring : women in development / compiled by Nicky May ; edited by Georgina Ashworth. — London : Change, [1982]. — [28]p ; 21x30cm. — (Change international reports. Women and society)
Text on inside covers. — Bibliography: p27-28
ISBN 0-907236-06-5 (pbk) : £2.00 B82-29498

305.4'2'091724 — Developing countries. Society. Role of women. Effects of population change

Women's roles and population trends in the Third World : a study prepared for the International Labour Office within the framework of the World Employment Programme with the financial support of the United Nations Fund for Population Activities / edited by Richard Anker, Mayra Buvinic and Nadia H. Youssef. — London : Croom Helm, c1982. — 287p ; 23cm
Includes bibliographies and index
ISBN 0-7099-0508-4 : £15.95 : CIP rev. B81-25711

305.4'2'091724 — Developing countries. Women — *Sociological perspectives*

Third world. — London : Zed Press, Oct.1982. — [272]p
ISBN 0-86232-017-8 (cased) : £14.95 : CIP entry
ISBN 0-86232-029-1 (pbk) : £6.50 B82-33360

305.4'2'09174927 — Arab countries. Society. Role of women

Minces, Juliette. The house of obedience : women in Arab society / Juliette Minces ; translated by Michael Pallis. — London : Zed, 1982. — 114p ; 23cm. — ([Women in the Third World series])
Translation of: La femme dans le monde arabe. — Bibliography: p113-114
ISBN 0-86232-012-7 (cased) : Unpriced : CIP rev.
ISBN 0-86232-063-1 (pbk) : £4.95 B82-02471

305.4'2'0924 — Feminism. Wilson, Elizabeth — *Biographies*

Wilson, Elizabeth. Mirror writing. — London : Virago, Jan.1982. — [176]p
ISBN 0-86068-241-2 (pbk) : £3.50 : CIP entry B81-33763

305.4'2'0924 — Great Britain. Working class women. Social conditions, *1894-1914 — Personal observations*

Nield Chew, Doris. The life and writings of Ada Nield Chew / remembered and collected by Doris Nield Chew ; with a foreword by Anna Davin. — London : Virago, 1982. — xxiv,255p,8p of plates : ports ; 20cm
ISBN 0-86068-294-3 (pbk) : £4.50 : CIP rev. B82-10239

305.4'2'0937 — Ancient Rome. Society. Role of women

Women's life in Greece and Rome / [edited by] Mary R. Lefkowitz and Maureen B. Fant. — London : Duckworth, 1982. — xvi,294p ; 24cm
Includes index
ISBN 0-7156-1434-7 : £24.00 : CIP rev.
Also classified at 305.4'2'0938 B81-28805

305.4'2'0938 — Ancient Greece. Society. Role of women

Lefkowitz, Mary R.. Heroines and hysterics / Mary R. Lefkowitz. — London : Duckworth, 1981. — ix,96p ; 23cm
Includes index
ISBN 0-7156-1518-1 : £8.95
Also classified at 880.9'352042 B82-08759

Women's life in Greece and Rome / [edited by] Mary R. Lefkowitz and Maureen B. Fant. — London : Duckworth, 1982. — xvi,294p ; 24cm
Includes index
ISBN 0-7156-1434-7 : £24.00 : CIP rev.
Primary classification 305.4'2'0937 B81-28805

305.4'2'094 — Europe. Society. Role of women, *1789-1945 — Readings from contemporary sources*

European women : a documentary history, 1789-1945. — Brighton : Harvester, Nov.1982. — [256]p
ISBN 0-7108-0479-2 (pbk) : £5.95 : CIP entry B82-28750

305.4'2'094 — Western Europe. Society. Role of women, *ca 500-ca 1500*

Lucas, Angela M.. Women in the Middle Ages : religion, marriage and letters. — Brighton : Harvester Press, Aug.1982. — 1v.
ISBN 0-7108-0348-6 : CIP entry B82-16651

305.4'2'0941 — Great Britain. Feminism, *1918-1968*

Doughan, David. Lobbying for liberation : British feminism 1918-1968 : based on the first Vera Douie memorial lecture, given before the Friends of the Fawcett Library at the City of London Polytechnic on October 17th, 1979 / by David Doughan. — London (Calcutta House, Old Castle St. E1 7NT) : LLRS Publications, c1980. — 14p : 1port ; 30cm. — (The Vera Douie memorial lecture ; 1979)
ISBN 0-904264-45-9 (pbk) : Unpriced : CIP rev. B80-03048

305.4'2'0941 — Great Britain. Society. Role of women

The **Changing** experience of women. — Oxford : Robertson, Sept.1982. — [416]p
ISBN 0-85520-517-2 (cased) : £15.00 : CIP entry
ISBN 0-85520-518-0 (pbk) : £5.95 B82-20840

Women in the eighties / a survey conducted by Tesco. — [Waltham Cross] ([Tesco House, PO Box 18, Delamare Rd, Cheshunt, Waltham Cross, Herts. EN8 9SL]) : Tesco, [1982?]. — 22leaves : ill ; 30cm
Cover title
Unpriced (spiral) B82-32907

305.4'2'0941 — Great Britain. Society. Role of women, *1911-1917*

West, Rebecca. The young Rebecca : writings of Rebecca West 1911-17 / selected and introduced by Jane Marcus. — London : Macmillan in association with Virago, 1982. — x,402p,[8]p of plates : ports ; 24cm
Includes index
ISBN 0-333-25589-5 : £9.95 B82-35080

305.4'2'0941 — Great Britain. Society. Role of women, *1960-1980 — Feminist viewpoints*

Coote, Anna. Sweet freedom : the struggle for women's liberation / Anna Coote and Beatrix Campbell ; illustrations by Christine Roche. — London : Pan, 1982. — 257p : ill ; 20cm. — (Picador original)
Includes index
ISBN 0-330-26511-3 (pbk) : £1.95 B82-20428

305.4'2'0941 — Great Britain. Society. Role of women — *For schools*
McConnell, Eileen. Women / Elieen McConnell. — London : Batsford Academic and Educational, 1982. — 72p : ill,ports ; 26cm. — (Living today)
Bibliography: p69-70. — Includes index
ISBN 0-7134-3970-x : £5.95 B82-30750

305.4'2'0941 — Great Britain. Women. Emancipation, *to 1906*. **Social aspects**
Black, Eugene C.. Feminists, liberalism, and morality : the unresolvable triangle / by Eugene C. Black. — London : LLRS, 1981. — 41p ; 30cm
ISBN 0-904264-57-2 (pbk) : Unpriced B82-08341

305.4'2'0941 — Great Britain. Women. Equality of opportunity — *Feminist viewpoints — For adolescent girls*
Feminism for girls : an adventure story / edited by Angela McRobbie and Trisha McCabe. — London : Routledge & Kegan Paul, 1981. — 212p : ill ; 24cm
ISBN 0-7100-0961-5 (pbk) : £5.95 B82-08165

305.4'2'0941 — Great Britain. Women. Equality of opportunity. Projects. Financial assistance by Great Britain. *Equal Opportunities Commission, 1976-1981*
'Grants for equality' : research and educational activities funded by the Equal Opportunities Commission 1976-1981. — Manchester : Equal Opportunities Commission, 1981. — 64p : ill,1col.map ; 21cm
Col. map inside back cover
ISBN 0-905829-40-9 (pbk) : Unpriced B82-30843

305.4'2'0941 — Great Britain. Women. Social conditions
Women rule OK. — Cambridge : National Extension College, 1980. — 32p : ill ; 15x20cm
Includes bibliographies
ISBN 0-86082-207-9 (pbk) : Unpriced B82-26917

Women's welfare — women's rights. — London : Croom Helm, Dec.1982. — [224]p
ISBN 0-7099-1610-8 : £11.95 : CIP entry B82-36149

305.4'2'0941 — Great Britain. Women. Social conditions, *1960-1980*
Ingham, Mary. Now we are thirty : women of the breakthrough generation / Mary Ingham. — London : Eyre Methuen, 1981. — 244p ; 23cm
ISBN 0-413-47750-9 (cased) : £8.50 : CIP rev.
ISBN 0-413-49300-8 (pbk) : Unpriced B81-25311

305.4'2'0941 — Great Britain. Women. Social control — *Conference proceedings*
Controlling women : the normal and the deviant / edited by Bridget Hutter and Gillian Williams. — London : Croom Helm in association with the Oxford University Women's Studies Committee, c1981. — 207p ; 23cm. — (The Oxford women's series)
Conference papers. — Includes bibliographies and index
ISBN 0-7099-0469-x (cased) : £10.95 : CIP rev.
ISBN 0-7099-1218-8 (pbk) : £6.95 B81-14893

305.4'2'0941 — Great Britain. Women's liberation movements, *1970-1980 — Socialist Workers' Party viewpoints*
Paczuska, Anna. Sisters and workers / Anna Paczusca [i.e. Paczuska]. — London : Produced for the SWP by Socialist Unlimited, 1980. — 54p : ill,facsims,2ports ; 21cm
ISBN 0-905998-16-2 (pbk) : £0.60 B82-17148

305.4'2'0942 — England. Society. Role of women, *ca 1780-ca 1850 — Feminist viewpoints*
Davidoff, Leonore. Life is duty, praise and prayer : some contributions of the new women's history / Leonore Davidoff. — London (City of London Polytechnic, Calcutta House, Old Castle St., E1 7NT) : LLRS, 1981. — 22p : 1ill,1map,1geneal.table ; 30cm. — (Fawcett library papers ; no.4)
Bibliography: p21-22
ISBN 0-904264-60-2 (pbk) : £2.00 : CIP rev. B82-01349

305.4'2'0944 — France. Feminism, *to 1980*
New French feminisms : an anthology / edited and with introductions by Elaine Marks & Isabelle de Courtivron. — Brighton : Harvester, 1981, c1980. — xiii,279p ; 21cm
Originally published: Amherst : University of Massachusetts Press, 1980. — Bibliography: p265-270. — Includes index
ISBN 0-7108-0354-0 (pbk) : £5.95 B82-02415

305.4'2'09485 — Sweden. Women. Equality of opportunity
Scott, Hilda. Sweden's "right to be human" : sex-role equality : the goal and the reality / Hilda Scott. — London : Allison & Busby, 1982. — 191p ; 23cm
Includes index
ISBN 0-85031-452-6 (cased) : £8.95 : CIP rev.
ISBN 0-85031-453-4 (pbk) : Unpriced B81-35839

305.4'2'095 — Asia. Rural regions. Women. Social conditons — *Case studies*
The **Endless** day : some case material on Asian rural women / edited by T. Scarlett Epstein and Rosemary A. Watts. — Oxford : Pergamon, 1981. — xii,179p,[8]p of plates : ill ; 22cm. — (Pergamon international library) (Women in development series ; v.3)
Bibliography: p173-179
ISBN 0-08-028106-0 : Unpriced : CIP rev. B81-31356

305.4'2'0951 — China. Society. Role of women, *1900-1949*
Siu, Bobby. Women of China : imperialism and women's resistance 1900-1949 / Bobby Siu. — London : Zed, 1982, c1981. — xiv,208p ; 23cm. — ([Women in the Third World series])
Bibliography: p193-208
ISBN 0-905762-58-4 (cased) : Unpriced : CIP rev.
ISBN 0-905762-63-0 (pbk) : £5.95 B81-20524

305.4'2'095353 — Oman. Society. Role of women
Wikan, Unni. Behind the veil in Arabia : women in Oman / Unni Wikan. — Baltimore ; London : Johns Hopkins University Press, c1982. — xiii,314p : ill,1map ; 24cm
Bibliography: p305-307. — Includes index
ISBN 0-8018-2729-9 : £15.00 B82-34983

305.4'2'095492 — Bangladesh. Rural regions. Women. Social conditions
Abdullah, Tahrunnessa A.. Village women of Bangladesh : prospects for change : a study / prepared for the International Labour Office within the framework of the World Employment Programme by Tahrunnessa A. Abdullah and Sondra A. Zeidenstein. — Oxford : Pergamon, 1982. — xx,246p,[8]p of plates : ill ; 22cm. — (Women in development ; v.4) (Pergamon international library)
Bibliography: p234-246
ISBN 0-08-026795-5 : £10.00 : CIP rev. B81-34725

305.4'2'0956 — Middle East. Islamic countries. Society. Role of women, *ca 600-1980*
Minai, Naila. Women in Islam : tradition and transition in the Middle East / Naila Minai. — London : Murray, c1981. — xvi,283p ; 22cm
Bibliography: p273-278. — Includes index
ISBN 0-7195-3882-3 : £8.95 B82-00669

305.4'2'096 — Africa. Economic development. Role of women. Social aspects
African women in the development process / edited by Nici Nelson. — London : Cass, 1981. — viii,136p ; 23cm
Originally published: in Journal of development studies, v.17 no.3. — Includes bibliographies
ISBN 0-7146-3175-2 (cased) : £13.50 : CIP rev.
ISBN 0-7146-4032-8 (pbk) : £8.50 B81-14460

305.4'2'09624 — Sudan. Society. Role of women
Hall, Marjorie J.. Sisters under the sun : the story of Sudanese women / Marjorie Hall and Bakhita Amin Ismail. — London : Longman, 1981. — viii,264p,[16]p of plates : ill(some col.),ports ; 23cm
Includes index
ISBN 0-582-78017-9 : £12.00 : CIP rev. B81-23842

305.4'2'0973 — United States. Feminism,
Rosenberg, Rosalind. Beyond separate spheres : intellectual roots of modern feminism. — London : Yale University Press, July 1982. — [352]p
ISBN 0-300-02695-1 : £15.50 : CIP entry B82-22784

305.4'2'0973 — United States. Society. Role of women, *1941-1945*
Anderson, Karen. Wartime women : sex roles, family relations, and the status of women during World War II / Karen Anderson. — Westport, Conn. ; London : Greenwood Press, 1981. — 198p ; 22cm. — (Contributions in women's studies, ISSN 0147-104x ; no.20)
Bibliography: p183-192. — Includes index
ISBN 0-313-20884-0 : Unpriced B82-01952

305'.4'2'0973 — United States. Society. Role of women — *Conference proceedings*
Toward the second decade : the impact of the women's movement on American institutions / edited by Betty Justice and Renate Pore. — Westport ; London : Greenwood Press, 1981. — xii,242p ; 22cm. — (Contributions in women's studies, ISSN 0147-104x ; no.25)
Bibliography: p225-232. — Includes index
ISBN 0-313-22110-3 : Unpriced B82-18017

305.4'2'0973 — United States. Women, *to 1981 — Sociological perspectives*
Women's America : refocusing the past / [edited by] Linda K. Kerber, Jane De Hart Mathews. — New York ; Oxford : Oxford University Press, 1982. — xi,478p ; 25cm
Bibliography: p455-461. — Includes index
ISBN 0-19-502982-8 (cased) : £16.00
ISBN 0-19-502983-6 (pbk) : Unpriced B82-41061

305.4'2'0994 — Australia. Society. Role of women — *Feminist viewpoints*
Australian women : feminist perspectives / edited by Norma Grieve and Patricia Grimshaw. — Melbourne ; London : Oxford University Press, 1981. — xv,333p ; 20cm
Includes index
ISBN 0-19-554293-2 (pbk) : £7.95 B82-08290

305.4'3 — United States. Women. Family life. Effects of careers
Tittle, Carol Kehr. Careers and family : sex roles and adolescent life plans / Carol Kehr Tittle. — Beverly Hills ; London : Sage, c1981. — 319p : ill ; 23cm. — (Sage library of social research ; v.121)
Bibliography: p253-264. — Includes index
ISBN 0-8039-1352-4 (cased) : Unpriced
ISBN 0-8039-1353-2 (pbk) : £6.50 B82-07908

305.4'3'00806942 — India *(Republic)*. **Kerala. Poor working women** — *Case studies*
Gulati, Leela. Profiles in female poverty : a study of five poor working women in Kerala / by Leela Gulati ; with a foreword by Marvin Harris. — Oxford : Pergamon, 1982. — ix,179p ; 22cm. — (Women in development ; v.5) (Pergamon international library)
Originally published: Delhi : Hindustan Publishing Corporation, 1981. — Bibliography: p174-175. — Includes index
ISBN 0-08-027922-8 : £10.00 : CIP rev. B82-12417

305.4'3'00947 — Soviet Union. Women. Employment. Social aspects
Women, work and family : in the Soviet Union / edited with an introduction by Gail Warshofsky Lapidus ; [translated by Vladimir Talmy]. — New York ; London : Sharpe ; London : Distributed by Eurospan, c1982. — xlvi,311p : ill ; 24cm
Translated from the Russian. — Bibliography: pxliii-xlvi
ISBN 0-87332-181-2 : £15.95 B82-23790

305.4'3'0941 — Great Britain. Working mothers — *Practical information*
Garner, Lesley. How to survive as a working mother / Lesley Garner. — Harmondsworth : Penguin, 1982, c1980. — 192p ; 18cm
Originally published: London : Jill Garner, 1980. — Bibliography: p181-185. — Includes index
ISBN 0-14-046525-1 (pbk) : £1.25 B82-26440

305.4'3351 — Politics. Women leaders, *to 1981*

Millan, Betty. Monstrous regiment. — Windsor Forest (Shooters Lodge, Windsor Forest, Berks. SL4 4SY) : Kensal Press, Oct.1982. — [288]p
ISBN 0-946041-01-6 : £12.50 : CIP entry B82-24618

305.4'3613'0973 — United States. Women nurses. Socialisation

Socialization, sexism, and stereotyping : women's issues in nursing / edited by Janet Muff. — St. Louis, Mo. ; London : Mosby, 1982. — xxi,434p : ill ; 24cm
Includes index
ISBN 0-8016-3581-0 (pbk) : £10.75 B82-31860

305.4'3649 — Capitalist societies. Women. Housework. Political aspects — *Feminist viewpoints*

The **Politics** of housework / edited by Ellen Malos. — Rev. ed. — London : Allison & Busby, 1982. — 250p ; 20cm
Previous ed.: 1980. — Bibliography: p239-245. — Includes index
ISBN 0-85031-462-3 (pbk) : £3.95 B82-28016

305.4'3649'06041 — Great Britain. Housewives. Organisations: National Housewives Register, *to 1980*

Jerman, Betty. The lively-minded women : the first twenty years of the National Housewives Register / Betty Jerman. — London : Heinemann, 1981. — 236p,[8]p of plates : ill,ports ; 22cm
Bibliography: p229. — Includes index
ISBN 0-434-37400-8 : £9.50 B82-14149

305.4'3677 — India *(Republic).* **Andhra Pradesh. Home-based lace industries. Women personnel. Social conditions**

Mies, Maria. The lace makers of Narsapur : Indian housewives in the world market. — London : Zed, July 1982. — [144]p
ISBN 0-86232-032-1 (pbk) : £4.50 : CIP entry B82-15922

305.4'8 — Middle-aged women

Women in the middle years : current knowledge and directions for research and policy / sponsored by the Social Science Research Council ; edited by Janet Zollinger Giele. — New York ; Chichester : Wiley, c1982. — xiii,283p : ill ; 24cm. — (Wiley series on personality processes, ISSN 0195-4008)
Includes index
ISBN 0-471-09611-3 : £23.50 B82-32709

305.4'8 — Northern France. Middle class women. Social conditions, *1800-1900*

Smith, Bonnie G.. Ladies of the leisure class : the bourgeoises of northen France in the nineteenth century / Bonnie G. Smith. — Princeton ; Guildford : Princeton University Press, c1981. — x,303p,[8]p of plates : ill,ports ; 23cm
Bibliography: p269-296. — Includes index
ISBN 0-691-05330-8 (cased) : £15.00
ISBN 0-691-10121-3 (pbk) : £7.10 B82-05883

305.4'889275694'05692 — Lebanon. Palestinian Arab refugees. Women. Social conditions

Bendt, Ingela. We shall return. — London : Zed Press, July 1982. — [144]p
Translation of: Vi ska tilbaka till var jord
ISBN 0-86232-042-9 (cased) : £12.95 : CIP entry
ISBN 0-86232-087-9 (pbk) : £5.50 B82-20786

305.4'88948 — Sri Lanka. Thoppukadu. Tamils. Women — *Sociological perspectives*

Skjonsberg, Else. A special caste? : Tamil women of Sri Lanka. — London : Zed Press, Aug.1982. — [160]p
ISBN 0-86232-071-2 : £13.95 : CIP entry B82-21117

305.4'8896073 — United States. Negro women. Social conditions — *Marxist viewpoints*

Davis, Angela. Women, race and class. — London : Women's Press, Sept.1982. — [276]p
ISBN 0-7043-3892-0 (pbk) : £4.95 : CIP entry B82-25063

305.4'8896073 — United States. Negro women — *Sociological perspectives*

The **Afro-American** woman : struggles and images / edited by Sharon Harley and Rosalyn Terborg-Penn. — Port Washington ; London : National University Publications, 1978 (1981 [printing]). — xiii,137p ; 21cm. — (Series in American studies)
Includes index
ISBN 0-8046-9294-7 (pbk) : £8.45 B82-29216

305.4'89 — Great Britain. Middle class women, *1830-1880*

Branca, Patricia. Silent sisterhood : middle-class women in the Victorian home / Patricia Branca. — London : Croom Helm, 1975 (1977 [printing]). — 170p : ill ; 22cm
Bibliography: p158-166. — Includes index
ISBN 0-85664-698-9 (pbk) : Unpriced B82-34657

305.4'89'00880622 — Europe. Women intellectuals, *1100-1820*

Beyond their sex : learned women of the European past / edited by Patricia H. Labalme. — New York ; London : New York University Press, c1980. — xx,188p : ill,facsims,ports ; 24cm
Includes index
ISBN 0-8147-4998-4 : £13.80 B82-35942

305.5 — Inequality. Theories

Green, Philip. The pursuit of inequality / Philip Green. — Oxford : Robertson, 1981. — x,320p ; 22cm
Includes index
ISBN 0-85520-446-x : £12.50 : CIP rev. B81-10014

305.5 — Social class

Classes, power, and conflict : classical and contemporary debates / edited by Anthony Giddens and David Held. — Basingstoke : Macmillan, 1982. — x,646p ; 24cm. — (Contemporary social theory)
Includes bibliographies
ISBN 0-333-32289-4 (cased) : Unpriced
ISBN 0-333-32290-8 (pbk) : Unpriced B82-39989

305.5 — Social class — *Festschriften*

Social class and the division of labour. — Cambridge : Cambridge University Press, Nov.1982. — [353]p
ISBN 0-521-24597-4 (cased) : £20.00 : CIP entry
ISBN 0-521-28809-6 (pbk) : £6.95 B82-26243

305.5'01 — Social class. Theories, *to 1981*

Calvert, Peter. The concept of class : an historical introduction / Peter Calvert. — London : Hutchinson, 1982. — 254p ; 23cm. — (Hutchinson university library)
Bibliography: p217-229. — Includes index
ISBN 0-09-146670-9 (cased) : £12.00 : CIP rev.
ISBN 0-09-146671-7 (pbk) : £5.50 B82-03745

305.5'072042 — England. Social class, *ca 1700-1900.* **Historiography**

History and class. — Oxford : Blackwell, Jan.1983. — [256]p
ISBN 0-631-13016-0 (cased) : £15.00 : CIP entry
ISBN 0-631-13135-3 (pbk) : &5.95 B82-32514

305.5'0938 — Ancient Greece. Social classes. Conflict

De Ste. Croix, G. E. M.. The class struggle in the ancient Greek world : from the Archaic Age to the Arab Conquests / G.E.M. de Ste. Croix. — London : Duckworth, 1981. — xi,732p,[1]leaf of plate : 1col.ill ; 26cm
Bibliography: p665-699. — Includes index
ISBN 0-7156-0738-3 : £38.00 : CIP rev. B81-17500

305.5'0941 — England. Poor persons. Social conditions, *1849-1852* — *Early works*

Labour and the poor in England and Wales, 1849-1852. — London : Cass, Sept.1981
Vol.1: Lancashire, Cheshire, Yorkshire. — [288]p
ISBN 0-7146-2907-3 : £12.50 : CIP entry B81-21486

305.5'09424'96 — West Midlands *(Metropolitan County).* **Birmingham. Social classes** *compared with* **social classes in Sheffield,** *1830-1914*

Smith, Dennis. Conflict and compromise : class formation in English society 1830-1914 : a comparative study of Birmingham and Sheffield / Dennis Smith. — London : Routledge & Kegan Paul, 1982. — xiii,338p : ill ; 24cm
Bibliography: p297-325. — Includes index
ISBN 0-7100-0969-0 : £17.95
Also classified at 305.5'09428'21 B82-26257

305.5'09428'21 — South Yorkshire *(Metropolitan County).* **Sheffield. Social classes** *compared with* **social classes in Birmingham,** *1830-1914*

Smith, Dennis. Conflict and compromise : class formation in English society 1830-1914 : a comparative study of Birmingham and Sheffield / Dennis Smith. — London : Routledge & Kegan Paul, 1982. — xiii,338p : ill ; 24cm
Bibliography: p297-325. — Includes index
ISBN 0-7100-0969-0 : £17.95
Primary classification 305.5'09424'96 B82-26257

305.5'0951 — China. Social classes. Conflict, *1949-1980*

Kraus, Richard Curt. Class conflict in Chinese socialism / Richard Curt Kraus. — New York ; Guildford : Columbia University Press, 1981. — x,243p : ill ; 24cm. — (Studies of the East Asian Institute)
Includes index
ISBN 0-231-05182-4 : £15.80 B82-10652

305.5'0954'82 — India *(Republic).* **Tamil Nadu** *(State).* **Thanjavur. Villages. Social classes,** *1770-1953* — *Comparative studies*

Gough, Kathleen. Rural society in southeast India / Kathleen Gough. — Cambridge : Cambridge University Press, 1981. — xiv,458p : ill,maps ; 24cm. — (Cambridge studies in social anthropology ; 38)
Bibliography: p441-446. — Includes index
ISBN 0-521-23889-7 : £29.50 B82-24222

305.5'098 — Developing countries. Social classes. Conflict, *1945-1980* — *Study regions: Latin America*

Petras, James. Class, state, and power in the Third World : with case studies on class conflict in Latin America / James F. Petras with Morris H. Morley, Peter DeWitt and A. Eugene Havens. — Montclair : Allanheld, Osmun ; London : Zed Press, 1981. — xv,285p : ill ; 25cm. — (Imperialism series)
Includes index
ISBN 0-86232-096-8 : £16.95 B82-01003

305.5'0994 — Australia. Social class

Chamberlain, Chris. Class consciousness in Australia. — London : Allen and Unwin, Jan.1983. — [184]p. — (Studies in society)
ISBN 0-86861-021-6 : £6.95 : CIP entry B82-33237

305.5'122'0954 — India *(Republic).* **Caste system** — *Sociological perspectives*

Béteille, André. The backward classes and the new social order : The Ambedkar Memorial Lectures delivered under the auspices of the University of Bombay / André Béteille. — Delhi ; London : Oxford University Press, 1981. — 51p ; 22cm
ISBN 0-19-561386-4 (pbk) : £1.25 B82-39768

305.5'122'0954 — South Asia. Castes

Caste ideology and interaction / edited by Dennis B. McGilvray. — Cambridge : Cambridge University Press, 1982. — x,255p : ill ; 23cm. — (Cambridge papers in social anthropology ; no.9)
Bibliography: p236-247. — Includes index
ISBN 0-521-24145-6 : £19.50 : CIP rev. B82-21728

305.5'2 — Europe. Knights, *800-1450* — *For children*

Gibson, Michael, *1936-*. All about knights / [author Michael Gibson] ; [editor Trisha Pike]. — London : Marshall Cavendish, 1981. — 29p : col.ill,col.coats of arms ; 30cm. — (Enigma) (An All colour fact book)
Text, ill on lining papers
ISBN 0-85685-967-2 : Unpriced B82-06079

305.5'2 — Europe. Knights, *to ca 1600 — Illustrations*

Heller, Julek. Knights. — London : Hutchinson, Oct.1982. — [192]p
ISBN 0-09-150210-1 (pbk) : £9.95 : CIP entry
B82-24973

305.5'2 — France. Nobility, *1789-1799*

Higonnet, Patrice. Class, ideology, and the rights of nobles during the French revolution / by Patrice Higonnet. — Oxford : Clarendon Press, 1981. — xvii,358p,leaf of plate : 1facsim ; 23cm
Includes index
ISBN 0-19-822583-0 : £22.50 : CIP rev.
B81-28186

305.5'2 — Germany. Elites. Moral standards, *1871-1945 — Sociological perspectives*

Baum, Rainer C.. The holocaust and the German elite : genocide and national suicide in Germany, 1871-1945 / Rainer C. Baum. — Totowa : Rowman and Littlefield ; London : Croom Helm, 1981. — ix,374p : forms ; 25cm
Bibliography: p353-364. — Includes index
ISBN 0-7099-0656-0 : £19.95
ISBN 0-8476-6970-x (U.S.) B82-07147

305.5'2 — Great Britain. Hereditary peers

Winchester, Simon. Their noble lordships : the hereditary peerage today / Simon Winchester. — London : Faber, 1981. — 317p,[8]p of plates : maps,ports ; 23cm
Bibliography: p307-308. — Includes index
ISBN 0-571-11069-x : £7.95 : CIP rev.
B81-20558

305.5'2 — Great Britain. Upper classes. Families. Members. Anti-social behaviour, *ca 1600-ca 1910*

Sykes, Christopher Simon. Black sheep. — London : Chatto & Windus, May 1982. — [256]p
ISBN 0-7011-2548-9 : £8.95 : CIP entry
B82-14208

305.5'2 — Japan. Samurai, *to 1868*

Storry, Richard. The way of the samurai / Richard Storry ; photographs by Werner Forman. — London : Orbis, 1978 (1982 [printing]). — 128p : col.ill,1col.map ; 30cm. — (Echoes of the ancient world)
Bibliography: p124-125. — Includes index
ISBN 0-85613-404-x (pbk) : £5.95 B82-11968

Turnbull, S.. The book of the Samurai. — London : Arms & Armour Press, Dec.1982. — [192]p
ISBN 0-85368-538-x : £10.95 : CIP entry
B82-30715

305.5'2'01 — Elites. Theories

Bottomore, Tom. Elites and society / T.B. Bottomore. — Harmondsworth : Penguin, 1966, c1964 (1982 [printing]). — 160p ; 20cm
Originally published: London : Watts, 1964. — Bibliography: p151-158. — Includes index
ISBN 0-14-020782-1 (pbk) : £1.95 B82-23220

305.5'2'0941 — Great Britain. Power elites — *Interviews*

Griffin, Brian. Power : British management in focus. — London : Travelling Light, Oct.1981. — [128]p
ISBN 0-906333-13-x : £8.95 : CIP entry
B81-26700

305.5'2'0941 — Great Britain. Upper classes. Social values

Mackwood, Neil. In & out : a lighthearted guide to contemporary society / by Neil Mackwood ; preface by Lord Burghersh ; drawings by Lucy. — London : Pan, 1980. — xvi,158p : ill ; 18cm. — (Debrett's 1980-1981)
ISBN 0-330-26330-7 (pbk) : £1.25 B82-13742

305.5'2'0944 — France. Elites, *1850-1980 — Sociological perspectives*

Elites in France : origins, reproduction and power. — London : Frances Pinter, Nov.1981. — [272]p
ISBN 0-903804-90-5 : £13.75 : CIP entry
B82-00176

305.5'2'095493 — Sri Lanka. Karāva caste groups, *1500-1931*

Roberts, Michael, *19---*. Caste conflict and elite formation : the rise of a Karāva elite in Sri Lanka 1500-1931 / Michael Roberts. — Cambridge : Cambridge University Press, 1982. — xxviii,382p : ill,maps ; 23cm. — (Cambridge South Asian studies ; 24)
Bibliography: p341-363. — Includes index
ISBN 0-521-23210-4 : £30.00 : CIP rev.
B81-34655

305.5'2'096216 — Egypt. Cairo. Elites, *1400-1500*

Petry, Carl F.. The civilian elite of Cairo in the later Middle Ages / Carl F. Petry. — Princeton, N.J. ; Guildford : Princeton University Press, c1981. — xxiv,475p : ill,geneal.tables,maps ; 25cm. — (Princeton studies on the Near East)
Bibliography: p436-447. — Includes index
ISBN 0-691-05329-4 : £24.40 B82-28233

305.5'223'094 — Western Europe. Nobility, *ca 1000-ca 1400 — French texts*

Genicot, Léopold. La noblesse dans l'Occident médiéval. — London : Variorum, Sept.1982. — [356]p. — (Collected studies series ; CS163)
ISBN 0-86078-111-9 : £26.00 : CIP entry
B82-21405

305.5'234 — England. Gentlemen, *to 1981*

Mason, Philip. The English gentleman. — London : Deutsch, Sept.1982. — [240]p
ISBN 0-233-97489-x : £9.95 : CIP entry
B82-18844

305.5'5'0942 — England. Middle classes, *to 1980*

Bradley, Ian, *1950-*. The English middle classes are alive and kicking / Ian Bradley. — London : Collins, 1982. — 240p ; 22cm
Includes index
ISBN 0-00-216276-8 (pbk) : £6.95 : CIP rev.
B81-33975

305.5'52'091717 — Communist countries. Visits by Western intellectuals, *1928-1978*

Hollander, Paul. Political pilgrims : travels of Western intellectuals to the Soviet Union, China and Cuba 1928-1978 / Paul Hollander. — New York ; Oxford : Oxford University Press, 1981. — xvi,524p ; 24cm
Bibliography: p505-516. — Includes index
ISBN 0-19-502937-2 : £15.00 B82-08287

305.5'52'0924 — Intellectuals, *1900-1980 — Personal observations*

Berlin, Isaiah. Personal impressions. — Oxford : Oxford University Press, Oct.1982. — [256]p. — (Selected writings / Isaiah Berlin) (Oxford paperbacks)
Originally published: London : Hogarth Press, 1980
ISBN 0-19-283029-5 (pbk) : £2.95 : CIP entry
Also classified at 909.82'092'2 B82-23673

305.5'52'0951 — China. Society. Role of intellectuals, *ca 1840-1949*

Grieder, Jerome B.. Intellectuals and the state in modern China : a narrative history / Jerome B. Grieder. — New York : Free Press ; London : Collier Macmillan, c1981. — xix,395p ; 25cm. — (The Transformation of modern China series)
Bibliography: p378-383. — Includes index
ISBN 0-02-912810-2 : £15.95 B82-18005

305.5'54 — Western world. Small firms. Owners — *Sociological perspectives*

Scase, Richard. The entrepreneurial middle class / Richard Scase and Robert Goffee. — London : Croom Helm, c1982. — 212p : ill ; 23cm. — (Social analysis)
Bibliography: p203-210. — Includes index
ISBN 0-7099-0450-9 : £14.95 : CIP rev.
B81-34308

305.5'6 — Great Britain. Poverty, *1945-1980*

Berthoud, Richard. Poverty and the development of anti-poverty policy in the United Kingdom / Richard Berthoud and Joan C. Brown with Steven Cooper ; a report to the Commission of the European Communities. — London : Heinemann Educational, 1981. — xvi,288p : ill,maps ; 23cm
At head of title: Policy Studies Institute. — Includes index
ISBN 0-435-83102-x : £13.50 : CIP rev.
B81-30260

305.5'6 — Great Britain. Poverty. Political aspects

MacGregor, Susanne. The politics of poverty / Susanne MacGregor. — London : Longman, 1981. — vii,193p ; 20cm. — (Politics today)
Bibliography: p181-186. — Includes index
ISBN 0-582-29524-6 (pbk) : £2.95 : CIP rev.
B81-30184

305.5'6 — Great Britain. Working classes, *1838-1900*

Holbrook-Jones, Mike. Supremacy and subordination of labour. — London : Heinemann Educational, Apr.1982. — [224]p
ISBN 0-435-82417-1 : £13.50 : CIP entry
B82-04066

305.5'6 — Ireland (Republic). Poverty

Joyce, L.. Irish national report on poverty and policies to combat poverty. — Dublin (59 Lansdowne Road, Dublin 4) : Institute of Public Administration, Sept.1981. — 2v.[300]p
ISBN 0-906980-04-6 (pbk) : £14.00 : CIP entry
B81-30276

305.5'62 — Europe. Migrant personnel. Social integration. Research projects — *Lists*

Social integration of migrant workers and other ethnic minorities : a documentation of current research / edited by Matthias Herfurth and Huberta Hogeweg-de Haart ; with an introduction by Michel Oriol. — Oxford : Pergamon, 1982. — xxi,265p : 1form ; 26cm
Includes index
ISBN 0-08-028957-6 : £20.00 : CIP rev.
B82-03346

305.5'62 — Migrant personnel. Social conditions

Living in two cultures : the socio-cultural situation of migrant workers and their families. — Aldershot : Gower, 1982. — xv,325p ; 22cm
Includes index
ISBN 0-566-00459-3 (pbk) : Unpriced : CIP rev. B81-15907

305.5'62 — Oxfordshire. Oxford. Fishing communities & inland waterway freight transport communities. Social conditions, *1500-1900*

Prior, Mary. Fisher Row : fishermen, bargemen, and canal boatmen in Oxford, 1500-1900 / by Mary Prior. — Oxford : Clarendon, 1982. — xxiv,406p,[4]p of plates : ill,maps,facsims,plans,ports,geneal.tables ; 23cm
Bibliography: p375-386. — Includes index
ISBN 0-19-822649-7 : £22.50 : CIP rev.
B81-32045

305.5'62 — Scotland. Migrant personnel. Social integration — *Conference proceedings*

Way of life : integration and immigration / edited by Anthony Jackson. — London : Social Science Research Council, [1982?]. — 84p ; 21cm. — (North Sea Oil Panel occasional paper ; no.12)
Conference papers. — Includes bibliographies
ISBN 0-86226-076-0 (pbk) : £1.80 B82-38927

305.5'62'0941 — Great Britain. Working classes, *1840-1980*

Social conflict and the political order in modern Britain / edited by James E. Cronin and Johathan Schneer. — London : Croom Helm, c1982. — 221p ; 22cm. — (Croom Helm studies in society and history)
Includes index
ISBN 0-7099-0708-7 : £13.95 : CIP rev.
B81-34314

305.5'62'0941 — Great Britain. Working classes. Attitudes, *1800-1900 — Sources of data: Working classes. Autobiographies*

Vincent, David. Bread, knowledge and freedom. — London : Methuen, Dec.1982. — [221]p
Originally published: London : Europa, 1981
ISBN 0-416-34510-7 (pbk) : £4.95 : CIP entry
B82-29762

305.5'62'0941 — Great Britain. Working classes. Class consciousness

Porter, Marilyn. Home, work and class consciousness. — Manchester : Manchester University Press, Jan.1983. — [200]p
ISBN 0-7190-0899-9 : £20.00 : CIP entry
B82-32620

305.5'62'09411 — Scotland. Working classes, *to 1981*
Capital and class in Scotland / edited by Tony Dickson. — Edinburgh : Donald, c1982. — vi,286p ; 25cm
Bibliography: p278-281. — Includes index
ISBN 0-85976-065-0 : £16.00 B82-31552

305.5'62'0943 — Germany. Working classes. Social conditions, *1888-1933*
The German working class 1888-1933 : the politics of everyday life / edited by Richard J. Evans. — London : Croom Helm, c1982. — 259p ; 23cm
Includes index
ISBN 0-7099-0431-2 : £14.95 : CIP rev. B81-31442

305.5'62'0947 — Soviet Union. Personnel. Social conditions
The Soviet worker : illusions and realities / edited by Leonard Schapiro and Joseph Godson. — London : Macmillan, 1981 (1982 [printing]). — xii,291p ; 22cm
Includes index
ISBN 0-333-28847-5 (pbk) : £4.95 B82-32223

305.5'63 — England. Agricultural industries. Personnel: Harvesters. Social conditions, *1840-1900*
Morgan, David Hoseason. Harvesters and harvesting 1840-1900 : a study of the rural proletariat / David Hoseason Morgan. — London : Croom Helm, c1982. — 224p : ill ; 23cm
Bibliography: p206-220. — Includes index
ISBN 0-7099-1735-x : £12.95 : CIP rev. B81-31429

305.5'63 — Latin America. Peasants — *Sociological perspectives*
Singelmann, Peter. Structures of domination and peasant movements in Latin America / Peter Singelmann. — Columbia ; London : University of Missouri Press, 1981. — 248p : ill ; 23cm
Bibliography: p224-241. — Includes index
ISBN 0-8262-0307-8 : £14.00 B82-26973

305.5'63'0942 — England. Agricultural industries. Farms. Servants. Social conditions, *ca 1550-1850*
Kussmaul, Ann. Servants in husbandry in early modern England / Ann Kussmaul. — Cambridge : Cambridge University Press, 1981. — xii,233p : ill,maps ; 24cm. — (Interdisciplinary perspectives on modern history)
Bibliography: p205-229. — Includes index
ISBN 0-521-23566-9 : £19.50 B82-04563

305.5'63'094256 — Bedfordshire. Agricultural industries. Personnel. Social conditions, *1800-1900*
Agar, Nigel E.. The Bedfordshire farm worker in the nineteenth century / by Nigel E. Agar. — [Bedford] : Bedfordshire Historical Record Society, 1981. — ix,213p,[8]p of plates : ill,ports ; 21cm. — (The Publications of the Bedfordshire Historical Record Society ; v.60)
Includes index
ISBN 0-85155-042-8 (pbk) : Unpriced B82-05460

305.5'67'0924 — Slavery. Equiano, Oiaudah — *Biographies — For schools*
Milsome, John. Olaudah Equiano : the slave who helped to end the slave trade / John R. Milsome. — London : Longman, 1969 (1976 [printing]). — 59p : ill,maps ; 20cm. — (Makers of African history)
ISBN 0-582-60901-1 (pbk) : £0.65 B82-00424

305.5'67'09757 — South Carolina. Rice plantations. Personnel: Slaves. Ethnicity. Attitudes of owners
Littlefield, Daniel C.. Rice and slaves : ethnicity and the slave trade in colonial South Carolina / Daniel C. Littlefield. — Baton Rouge ; London : Louisianan State University Press, c1981. — xii,199p : ill,maps,1facsim ; 24cm
Bibliography: p179-193. — Includes index
ISBN 0-8071-0794-8 : £12.20 B82-09918

305.5'68 — England. Tramps: Stacey, Joseph — *Biographies*
Vose, John D.. Diary of a tramp / John D. Vose. — St. Ives : United Writers, c1981. — 199p ; 22cm
ISBN 0-901976-70-9 : £6.95 B82-20154

305.5'68 — India *(Republic).* **Dusadhs. Caste status**
Chaman, Devendradatta Saneheesingh. Dusadhs, are they the Gehlote Rajputs? / by Devendradatta Saneheesingh Chaman. — [London] ([7 Crown Close, Lymington Rd., N.W.6.]) : Author & editor (DSC), 1981. — 32p : 1port ; 21cm
Unpriced (pbk) B82-14301

305.5'68 — India *(Republic).* **Punjab. Untouchables. Social conditions,** *1920-1980*
Juergensmeyer, Mark. Religion as social vision : the movement against Untouchability in 20th-century Punjab / Mark Juergensmeyer. — Berkeley ; London : University of California Press, c1982. — x,357p[12]p of plates : ill,1map,ports ; 23cm
Bibliography: p321-346. — Includes index
ISBN 0-520-04301-4 : £21.00 B82-28106

305.5'68 — United States. Slums. Residents: Vagrants — *Sociological perspectives — Case studies*
Miller, Ronald J.. The demolition of skid row / Ronald J. Miller. — Lexington, Mass. : Lexington ; [Aldershot] : Gower [distributor], c1982. — xi,147p : 1map ; 24cm
Bibliography: p133-139. — Includes index
ISBN 0-669-04563-2 : £13.50 B82-31795

305.5'68 — United States. Tramps. Social conditions — *Personal observations*
Harper, Douglas A.. Good company / Douglas A. Harper. — Chicago ; London : University of Chicago Press, 1982. — ix,172p,[52]p of plates : ill ; 25cm
Ill on lining papers. — Bibliography: p163-164
ISBN 0-226-31686-6 : Unpriced B82-35311

305.5'69'091724 — Developing countries. Urban regions. Poverty
Lloyd, P. C.. A Third World proletariat? / Peter Lloyd. — London : Allen & Unwin, 1982. — 139p ; 22cm. — (Controversies in sociology ; 11)
Bibliography: p126-134. — Includes index
ISBN 0-04-301140-3 (cased) : Unpriced : CIP rev.
ISBN 0-04-301141-1 (pbk) : Unpriced B81-35941

305.5'69'0924 — London. Poor persons. Social conditions, *1850.* **Research. Mayhew, Henry** — *Biographies*
Humpherys, Anne. Travels into the poor man's country : the work of Henry Mayhew / Anne Humpherys. — Firle : Caliban, [1982]. — xiv,240p : ill,1facsim,2ports ; 23cm
Originally published: Athens, Ga. : University of Georgia Press, 1977. — Bibliography: p227-232. — Includes index
ISBN 0-904573-29-x : £10.00 B82-38852

305.5'69'0941 — England. Poor persons. Social conditions, *1849-1852 — Early works*
Labour and the poor in England and Wales 1849-1852. — London : Cass
Vol.2: Northumberland and Durham, Staffordshire, the Midlands. — Sept.1982. — [224]p
ISBN 0-7146-2960-x : £18.00 : CIP entry B82-19805

Labour and the poor in England and Wales 1849-1852. — London : Cass
Vol.3: The mining and manufacturing districts of South Wales and North Wales. — Oct.1982. — [256]p
ISBN 0-7146-2961-8 : £18.00 : CIP entry B82-30571

305.5'69'09417 — Ireland *(Republic).* **Poverty**
One million poor? : the challenge of Irish inequality / edited by Stanislaus Kennedy. — Dublin : Turoe Press, c1981. — vi,272p ; 22cm
ISBN 0-905223-30-6 (pbk) : Unpriced B82-24533

305.5'69'09421 — London. Poor persons. Social conditions, *1849-1850 — Early works*
Mayhew, Henry. The Morning chronicle survey of labour and the poor : the metropolitan districts / Henry Mayhew. — Horsham : Caliban
Vol.2. — 1981. — 335p ; 23cm
Includes index
ISBN 0-904573-21-4 : £15.00 B82-06081

Mayhew, Henry. The Morning chronicle survey of labour and the poor : the metropolitan districts / Henry Mayhew. — Horsham : Caliban
Vol.3. — 1981. — 277p ; 23cm
Includes index
ISBN 0-904573-22-2 : £15.00 B82-06082

Mayhew, Henry. The Morning Chronicle survey of labour and the poor : the metropolitan districts / Henry Mayhew. — Horsham : Caliban
Vol.4. — 1981. — 245p ; 23cm
Includes index
ISBN 0-904573-23-0 : £20.00 B82-24306

Mayhew, Henry. The Morning chronicle survey of labour and the poor : the metropolitan districts / Henry Mayhew. — Horsham : Caliban
Vol.5. — 1982. — 248p ; 23cm
Includes index
ISBN 0-904573-24-9 : £20.00 B82-26725

Mayhew, Henry. The Morning Chronicle survey of labour and the poor : the metropolitan districts / Henry Mayhew. — Horsham : Caliban
Vol.6. — 1982. — 265p ; 23cm
Includes index
ISBN 0-904573-25-7 : £20.00 B82-32064

305.5'69'0942645 — Suffolk. Hoxne. Poverty, *1780-1880*
People, poverty and protest in Hoxne hundred 1780-1880 / Nora E. Coleman ... [et al.]. — [Sreffing] ([Mill Green, Sreffing, Suffolk]) : [N. Evans?], c1982. — 83p : ill,1facsim,maps ; 21x30cm
Text on inside covers. — Bibliography: p83
Unpriced (spiral) B82-32928

305.5'69'095492 — Bangladesh. Rural regions. Poor persons. Effects of technological innovation in rice processing
Greeley, Martin. Rural technology, rural institutions and the rural poorest / by Martin Greeley. — Brighton : Institute of Development Studies, 1980. — 20p ; 21cm. — (Discussion paper, ISSN 0308-5864 ; 154)
Bibliography: p19-20
£0.60 (pbk) B82-32253

305.5'69'096 — Africa. Urban regions. Poverty. Political aspects
Sandbrook, Richard. The politics of basic needs : urban aspects of assaulting poverty in Africa / Richard Sandbrook. — London : Heinemann, 1982. — vi,250p ; 22cm
Includes index
ISBN 0-435-96537-9 (pbk) : £5.95 : CIP rev B81-30164

305.6'00947 — Soviet Union. Religious minorities
Bourdeaux, Michael. Religious minorities in the Soviet Union / a report prepared for the Minority Rights Group by Michael Bourdeaux and two associates, Kathleen Matchett and Cornelia Gerstenmaier. — 3rd ed. — London (36 Craven St., WC2N 5NG) : Minority Rights Group, 1977. — 28p ; 30cm. — (Report (Minority Rights Group), ISSN 0305-6252 ; no.1)
Previous ed.: 1973?. — Bibliography: p28-29
£1.20 (pbk) B82-36910

305.6'2'04286 — Durham *(County).* **Durham. Catholic communities,** *1624-1861*
Tweedy, J. M.. Popish Elvet / J.M. Tweedy. — [Old Elvet] ([St. Cuthbert's, Old Elvet, Durham DH1 3HL]) : [J.M. Tweedy]
Part 1: The history of St. Cuthbert's, Durham. — [1981]. — ii,167p,[1]leaf of plates : ill,2maps,1plan,1port ; 21cm
£2.30 (pbk) B82-17406

305.7'96392'09676 — East Africa. Swahili speaking persons. Cultural processes, *ca 1900*
Mtoro bin Mwinyi Bakari. The customs of the Swahili people : the Desturi za Waswahili of Mtoro bin Mwinyi Bakari and other Swahili persons / edited and translated into English by J.W.T. Allen ; compiled in memoriam with notes and studies by various Makerere colleagues, African, American, Asian, British and European. — Berkeley ; London : University of California Press, 1981. — xv,342p ; 24cm
Translation of: Desturi za Waswahili. — Map on lining papers. — Bibliography: p313-327. — Includes index
ISBN 0-520-04122-4 : £17.50 B82-31094

305.8 — Coloured racial groups. Expansion — *Early works*
Stoddard, Lothrop. The rising tide of colour : against white world-supremacy / by Lothrop Stoddard ; with an introduction by Madison Grant. — Brighton : Historical Review Press, 1981. — xxxii,320p ; 21cm
Originally published: New York : Scribner, 1920. — Includes index
ISBN 0-906879-70-1 (pbk) : Unpriced B82-04400

305.8 — Ethnic groups
Ethnocultural processes and national problems in the modern world / edited by I.R. Grigulevich and S. Ya. Kozlov ; translated from the Russian by H. Campbell Creighton. — Moscow : Progress Publishers ; [London] : Distributed by Central Books, 1981. — 383p ; 21cm
Translation of: Étnokul'turnye prot͡sessy i nat͡sional'nye problemy v sovremennom mire. — Includes index
ISBN 0-7147-1674-x : £2.95 B82-06707

Murdock, George Peter. Atlas of world cultures / George Peter Murdock. — Pittsburgh : University of Pittsburgh Press ; London : Feffer and Simons, c1981. — 151p ; 24cm
Includes bibliographies and index
ISBN 0-8229-3432-9 : Unpriced B82-23749

305.8 — Race — *Racial Preservation Society viewpoints*
Isherwood, H. B.. Racial kinship : the dominant factor in nationhood / by H.B. Isherwood. — Southam (Chapel Ascote Farm, Ladbroke, Southam, Warwickshire) : Racial Preservation Society, 1974. — 35p ; 22cm
Bibliography: p34-35
£0.30 (pbk) B82-04351

305.8 — Race relations
Blalock, Hubert M.. Race and ethnic relations / Hubert M. Blalock Jr. — Englewood Cliffs ; London : Prentice-Hall, c1982. — x,133p : ill ; 24cm. — (Prentice-Hall foundations of modern sociology series)
Includes index
ISBN 0-13-750182-x (cased) : Unpriced
ISBN 0-13-750174-9 (pbk) : £5.95 B82-16698

305.8 — Racial equality
Isherwood, H. B.. Race and politics : the myth of racial equality / by H.B. Isherwood. — Southam (Chapel Ascote, Ladbroke, Southam, Warwickshire) : Racial Preservation Society, 1978. — 30p ; 22cm
Bibliography: p29-30
Unpriced (pbk) B82-04404

305.8 — Racism
Fyfe, Christopher. Race, empire and post-empire / Christopher Fyfe. — [Edinburgh] ([Adam Ferguson Building, 40 George Square, Edinburgh, EH8 9LL]) : [Centre of African Studies, University of Edinburgh], [1980]. — 10p ; 21cm
The Africanus Horton memorial lecture, 1979: sponsored by the Centre of African Studies, University of Edinburgh, and Fourah Bay College, University of Sierra Leone. — Cover title
Unpriced (pbk) B82-20661

Roots of racism. — London : Institute of Race Relations
Bk.1 / [maps by Sandra Oakins]. — c1982. — iv,28p : ill,1facsim,maps,ports ; 22x30cm
Includes bibliographies
ISBN 0-85001-023-3 (pbk) : £1.00 B82-38390

305.8'005 — Race relations — *Serials*
Research in race and ethnic relations : a research annual. — Vol.1 (1979)-. — Greenwich, Conn. : JAI Press ; London (3 Henrietta St., WC2E 8LU) : Distributed by JAICON Press, 1979-. — v. ; 24cm
ISSN 0195-7449 = Research in race and ethnic relations : £22.85 B82-02370

305.8'005 — Racial discrimination — *Serials*
[Bulletin *(International Organisation for the Elimination of All Forms of Racial Discrimination)*]. Bulletin / the International Organisation for the Elimination of All Forms of Racial Discrimination. — [Vol.1 (1981)?]-. — London (35 Ludgate Hill, EC4M 7JN) : The Organisation, [1981?]-. — v. ; 21cm
Description based on: Vol.2, no.2,3,4 (Dec. 1981)
Unpriced B82-40068

305.8'006'0424 — England. Midlands. Ethnic minorities. Organisations — *Directories*
Directory of ethnic minority organisations : Midlands and Wales. — London : Commission for Racial Equality, 1980 (1982 [printing]). — 84p : 1map ; 30cm
Text on inside cover
ISBN 0-907920-05-5 (pbk) : £1.00
Also classified at 305.8'006'0429 B82-35522

305.8'006'0429 — Wales. Ethnic minorities. Organisations — *Directories*
Directory of ethnic minority organisations : Midlands and Wales. — London : Commission for Racial Equality, 1980 (1982 [printing]). — 84p : 1map ; 30cm
Text on inside cover
ISBN 0-907920-05-5 (pbk) : £1.00
Primary classification 305.8'006'0424 B82-35522

305.8'0088796 — British coloured sportsmen. Social aspects
Cashmore, Ernest. Black sportsmen / Ernest Cashmore. — London : Routledge & Kegan Paul, 1982. — xiv,226p : ports ; 22cm
Bibliography: p213-220. — Includes index
ISBN 0-7100-9054-4 (pbk) : £5.95 B82-39420

305.8'009 — Racism, *to 1981* **—** *For schools*
Patterns of racism : book two. — London : Institute of Race Relations, c1982. — 44p : ill,1coat of arms,maps,ports ; 21x30cm
Text on inside cover. — Includes bibliographies
ISBN 0-85001-024-1 (pbk) : £1.50 B82-39049

305.8'0094 — Europe. Racial groups, *to 1920*
Stoddard, Lothrop. Racial realities in Europe / by Lothrop Stoddard. — Brighton : Historical Review Press, 1981. — xv,252p : 1map ; 21cm
Originally published: New York : Scribner, 1924. — Includes index
ISBN 0-906879-60-4 (pbk) : Unpriced B82-04401

305.8'00941 — Great Britain. Ethnic minorities. Effects of environment planning — *Conference proceedings*
Planning for a multi-racial Britain : the proceedings of the Bolton conference 1981 / edited by M. Madden. — Liverpool : Department of Civic Design, University of Liverpool, [1981]. — ii,65leaves ; 30cm. — (Working paper / Department of Civic Design, University of Liverpool, ISSN 0309-8753 ; WP17)
ISBN 0-906109-09-4 (pbk) : Unpriced B82-05825

305.8'00941 — Great Britain. Race relations
The Empire strikes back. — London : Hutchinson Education, Oct.1982. — [320]p
ISBN 0-09-149380-3 (cased) : £12.00 : CIP entry
ISBN 0-09-149381-1 (pbk) : £5.95 B82-24963

Ethnic minorities and community relations. — Milton Keynes : Open University Press
At head of title: The Open University
Block 1. — 1982
Unit 4: Ethnic disadvantage in Britain / prepared by Sheila Allen for the course team. — 40p : ill ; 30cm
Bibliography: p36-40
ISBN 0-335-13142-5 (pbk) : Unpriced B82-21184

Ethnic minorities and community relations. — Milton Keynes : Open University Press. — (Educational studies : a third level course)
At head of title: The Open University
Block 1. — 1982. — 88p : ill,1map ; 30cm. — (E354 : block 1, units 2-3)
Includes bibliographies. — Contents: Unit 2: Migration and settlement in Britain — Unit 3: Migrant labour in Europe
ISBN 0-335-13141-7 (pbk) : Unpriced B82-21183

Ethnic minorities and community relations. — Milton Keynes : Open University Press. — (Educational studies : a third level course)
At head of title: The Open University
Block 2
Unit 5-6: Race, identity and British society. — 1982. — 80p : ill ; 30cm. — (E354 ; block 2, units 5-6)
Includes bibliographies
ISBN 0-335-13143-3 (pbk) : Unpriced B82-32000

Ethnic minorities and community relations. — Milton Keynes : Open University Press. — (Educational studies : a third level course)
At head of title: The Open University
Block 2
Unit 7: Race relations and the law. — 1982. — 70p : ill ; 30cm. — (E354 ; block 2, unit 7)
Includes bibliographies
ISBN 0-335-13149-2 (unbound) : Unpriced B82-31999

Ethnic minorities and community relations. — Milton Keynes : Open University Press. — (Educational studies : a third level course)
At head of title: The Open University
Block 3. — 1982
Units 8-9: Minority experience. — 127p : ill ; 30cm. — (E354 ; block 3, units 8-9)
Includes bibliographies
ISBN 0-335-13144-1 (pbk) : Unpriced B82-31997

Ethnic minorities and community relations. — Milton Keynes : Open University Press. — (Educational studies : a third level course)
At head of title: The Open University
Block 3
Unit 10: The experience of black minorities in Britain / prepared by Bhikhu Parekh for the Course Team. — 1982. — 24p : ill ; 30cm. — (E354 ; block 3, unit 10)
Bibliography: p24
ISBN 0-335-13145-x (pbk) : Unpriced B82-31996

Ethnic minorities and community relations. — Milton Keynes : Open University Press. — (Educational studies : a third level course)
At head of title: The Open University
Block 4: Ethnic minorities and education. — 1982. — 92p : ill ; 30cm. — (E354 ; Block 4, units 13-14)
Bibliography: p91-92. — Contents: Unit 13: Ethnic minorities and educational policy 1960-80 — Unit 14: Multicultural education : curriculum issues for schools
ISBN 0-335-13147-6 (pbk) : Unpriced B82-34150

Ethnic minorities and community relations. — Milton Keynes : Open University Press. — (Educational studies : a third level course)
At head of title: The Open University
Using the literature and resources / prepared by Magnus John for the Course Team. — 1982. — 18p ; 30cm. — (E354 ; UL)
Includes index
ISBN 0-335-13150-6 (pbk) : Unpriced B82-31998

'Race' in Britain : continuity and change / edited by Charles Husband. — London : Hutchinson, 1982. — 329p : ill ; 24cm. — (Hutchinson university library)
Includes index
ISBN 0-09-146911-2 (pbk) : £6.95 : CIP rev. B81-35904

305.8'00941 — Great Britain. Race relations, *1953-1980*
Kapo, Remi. A savage culture. — London : Quartet, Sept.1981. — 1v.
ISBN 0-7043-2302-8 (pbk) : £2.95 : CIP entry B81-28464

305.8'00941 — Great Britain. Race relations. Attitudes of public

Race relations in 1981 : an attitude survey. — London (Elliot House, 10-12 Allington St., SW1E 5EH) : Commission for Racial Equality, 1981. — 17p ; 30cm
Unpriced (unbound) B82-11168

305.8'00941 — Great Britain. Race relations. Influence of mass media

Jones, Clement, *1915-*. Race and the media : thirty years' misunderstanding / Clement Jones. — London : Commission for Racial Equality, 1982. — 20p ; 21cm. — (Occasional paper series ; no.1)
Bibliography: p20
ISBN 0-907920-02-0 (pbk) : Unpriced
B82-36207

Troyna, Barry. Public awareness and the media : a study of reporting on race / Barry Troyna. — London : Commission for Racial Equality, 1981. — 95p ; 21cm
Text on inside covers. — Bibliography: p91-92
ISBN 0-902355-96-1 (pbk) : Unpriced
B82-04952

305.8'00941 — Great Britain. Race relations. Role of community work

Community work and racism / edited by Ashok Ohri, Basil Manning, Paul Curno. — London : Routledge & Kegan Paul, 1982. — xiv,188p ; 23cm. — (Community work series ; 7)
Includes index
ISBN 0-7100-9032-3 (pbk) : £5.95 B82-24998

305.8'00941 — Great Britain. Race relations. Role of local authorities

Local government and racial equality. — London : Commission for Racial Equality, 1982. — 54p ; 21cm
ISBN 0-902355-99-6 (unbound) : Unpriced
B82-31241

305.8'00941 — Great Britain. Race relations — *Serials*

Race and immigration : the Runnymede Trust bulletin. — No.142 (Apr. 1982)-. — London (37A Gray's Inn Rd, WC1 8PS) : The Trust, 1982-. — v. ; 21cm
Monthly. — Continues: Bulletin (Runnymede Trust)
ISSN 0262-9925 = Race and immigration : £8.00 per year B82-27660

305.8'00941 — Great Britain. Racial discrimination. Great Britain. *Parliament. House of Commons. Home Affairs Committee.* Fifth report ... session 1980-81 — *Critical studies*

Great Britain. The government reply to the fifth report from the Home Affairs Committee session 1980-81 HC424 : racial disadvantage. — London : H.M.S.O., [1982]. — 27p ; 25cm. — (Cmnd. ; 8476)
ISBN 0-10-184760-2 (unbound) : £2.65
B82-20564

305'.8'00941 — Great Britain. Racial discrimination. Policies of government. Implementation by local authorities

Young, Ken, *1943-*. Policy and practice in the multi-racial city / Ken Young, Naomi Connelly. — London : Policy Studies Institute, c1981. — vi,175p ; 21cm. — ([Report] ; no.598)
Includes bibliographies
ISBN 0-85374-194-8 (pbk) : £6.50 B82-10089

305.8'00941 — Great Britain. Racism

Race & racism : a handbook for Lambeth NALGO members / [prepared by the Race Equality Sub-Group of Lambeth NALGO]. — [London] ([c/o June Dawes, Lambeth Town Hall, Brixton Hill, Brixton, SW2 1RW]) : [The Sub-Group], [1981]. — 28p ; 21cm
Cover title. — Bibliography: p28
Unpriced (pbk) B82-13280

305.8'00941 — Great Britain. Urban regions. Ethnic groups. Segregation. Geographical aspects — *Conference proceedings*

Social interaction and ethnic segregation / edited by Peter Jackson, Susan J. Smith. — London : Academic Press, 1981. — x,235p : ill,maps ; 26cm. — (Institute of British Geographers special publication ; no.12)
Conference papers. — Includes bibliographies and index
ISBN 0-12-379080-8 : £16.00 : CIP rev.
B81-31340

305.8'00941 — Great Britain. Urban regions. Ethnic minorities. Segregation *compared with* segregration of ethnic minorities in urban regions in United States — *Conference proceedings*

Ethnic segregation in cities / edited by Ceri Peach, Vaughan Robinson and Susan Smith. — London : Croom Helm, c1981. — 258p : ill,maps ; 23cm
Conference papers. — Includes bibliographies and index
ISBN 0-7099-2012-1 : £12.95 : CIP rev.
Also classified at 305.8'00973 B81-25715

305.8'00941 — Great Britain. Young coloured persons. Social conditions

Black youth in crisis. — London : Allen & Unwin, Nov.1982. — [192]p
ISBN 0-04-362052-3 (cased) : £10.95 : CIP entry
ISBN 0-04-362053-1 (pbk) : £4.95 B82-27812

305.8'009421 — London. Ethnic minorities. Harassment

Great Britain. *Commission for Racial Equality.* CRE's evidence to GLC Police Committee inquiry into racial harassment. — London (Elliot House, 10-12 Allington St., SW1E 5EH) : Commission for Racial Equality, 1981. — 17p ; 30cm
Unpriced (unbound) B82-11169

305.8'009421'84 — London. Ealing *(London Borough).* Southall. Race relations, *1950-1981* — *Campaign Against Racism and Fascism viewpoints*

Southall : the birth of a black community / Campaign Against Racism and Fascism/Southall Rights. — London : Institute of Race Relations, c1981. — 70p,[4]p of plates : ill,1map ; 21cm
Ill on inside covers. — Bibliography: p65-66
ISBN 0-85001-022-5 (pbk) : £1.30 B82-00037

305.8'009421'85 — London. Brent *(London Borough).* Coloured persons. Social conditions — *Serials*

Black insight : a monthly newspaper for the black community by the black community of Brent. — No.1 (Sept. 1981)-. — London (c/o 13 Nicoll Rd, Harlesden, NW10) : [s.n.], 1981-. — v. : ill,ports ; 40cm
ISSN 0262-6381 = Black insight : £0.20 per issue B82-06782

305.8'009424'98 — West Midlands *(Metropolitan County).* Coventry. Racial conflict — *Coventry Workers Against Racism viewpoints*

Ghost town / Coventry Workers Against Racism. — [London] ([BCM JPLTD, WC1N 3XX]) : Junius, 1981. — 13p : ill ; 22cm. — (Revolutionary Communist pamphlets, ISSN 0141-8874 ; no.11)
Cover title. — Text on inside cover
£0.20 (pbk) B82-05870

305.8'00947 — Soviet Union. Ethnic minorities

Sheehy, Ann. The Crimean Tatars, Volga Germans and Meskhetians : Soviet treatment of some national minorities. — 3rd ed. / by Ann Sheehy and Bohdan Nahaylo. — London (36 Craven St., WC2N 5NG) : Minority Rights Group, 1980. — 28p : 1map ; 30cm. — (Report (Minority Rights Group), ISSN 0305-6252 ; no.6)
Previous ed.: 1973. — Bibliography: p28
£0.75 (pbk) B82-36912

305.8'009492 — Ethnic minorities. Formation. Effects of immigration — *Study regions: Netherlands, 1945-1975*

Amersfoort, Hans van. Immigration and the formation of minority groups : the Dutch experience 1945-1975 / Hans Van Amersfoort ; translated from Dutch by Robert Lyng. — Cambridge : Cambridge University Press, 1982. — vii,234p : ill ; 23cm
Translation of: Immigratie en minderheidsvorming. — Bibliography: p217-227. — Includes index
ISBN 0-521-23293-7 : £19.50 : CIP rev.
B82-26000

305.8'00953'53 — Oman. Tribes. Cultural processes

Carter, J. R. L.. Tribes in Oman / J.R.L. Carter. — London : Peninsular Publishing, 1982. — 176p : ill(some col.),geneal.tables,1map,col.ports ; 31cm
Bibliography: p174. — Includes index
ISBN 0-907151-02-7 : £25.95 B82-37221

305.8'00954 — India *(Republic).* Ethnic groups. Preferential treatment

Weiner, Myron. India's preferential policies : migrants, the middle classes, and ethnic equality / Myron Weiner and Mary Fainsod Katzenstein with K.V. Narayana Rao. — Chicago ; London : University of Chicago Press, 1981. — vii,184p : 3maps ; 23cm. — (Chicago originals)
Includes index
ISBN 0-226-88577-1 (pbk) : £11.10
B82-22273

305.8'009597 — Vietnam. Central Higlands. Ethnic groups, *1954-1976*

Hickey, Gerald Cannon. Free in the forest : ethnohistory of the Vietnamese Central Highlands 1954-1976 / Gerald Cannon Hickey. — New Haven ; London : Yale University Press, c1982. — xxi,350p : ill,geneal.tables,maps ; 24cm
Includes index
ISBN 0-300-02437-1 : £21.00 : CIP rev.
B82-21369

305.8'00973 — United States. Race relations

Farley, John E.. Majority — minority relations / John E. Farley. — Englewood Cliffs ; London : Pentice-Hall, c1982. — xii,451p : ill ; 25cm
Bibliography: p405-431
ISBN 0-13-545574-x : £14.95 B82-35169

Report of a BYC study tour on race relations in the USA. — London (57 Chalton St., NW1 1HU) : British Youth Council, [1980]. — 25p ; 30cm
Cover title
Unpriced (pbk) B82-38466

305.8'00973 — United States. Race relations. Role of verbal communication

Kochman, Thomas. Black and white styles in conflict / Thomas Kochman. — Chicago ; London : University of Chicago Press, 1981. — vi,177p ; 23cm
Bibliography: p167-172. — Includes index
ISBN 0-226-44954-8 : £9.10 B82-13672

305.8'00973 — United States. Racial discrimination, *1830-1980*

Toplin, Robert Brent. Freedom and prejudice : the legacy of slavery in the United States and Brazil / Robert Brent Toplin. — Westport, Conn. ; London : Greenwood Press, 1981. — xxvi,134p ; 22cm. — (Contributions in Afro-American and African studies, ISSN 0069-9624 ; no.56)
Bibliography: p121-127. — Includes index
ISBN 0-313-22008-5 : Unpriced
Also classified at 305.8'00981 B82-01947

305.8'00973 — United States. Racism, *1776-1900.* Socioeconomic aspects

Takaki, Ronald T.. Iron cages : race and culture in nineteenth-century America / Ronald T. Takaki. — Seattle ; London : University of Washington Press, 1982. — xviii,361p : ill ; 24cm
Originally published: New York : Knopf, 1979 ; London : Athlone, 1980. — Bibliography: p333-349. — Includes index
ISBN 0-295-95904-5 (pbk) : Unpriced
B82-37621

305.8′00973 — United States. Racism, *to 1850*

Horsman, Reginald. Race and manifest destiny : the origins of American racial Anglo-Saxonism / Reginald Horsman. — Cambridge, Mass. ; London : Harvard University Press, 1981. — 367p ; 24cm
Includes index
ISBN 0-674-74572-8 : £13.50 B82-11875

305.8′00973 — United States. Urban regions. Ethnic minorities. Segregation *compared with* **segregation of ethnic minorities in urban regions in Great Britain** — *Conference proceedings*

Ethnic segregation in cities / edited by Ceri Peach, Vaughan Robinson and Susan Smith. — London : Croom Helm, c1981. — 258p : ill,maps ; 23cm
Conference papers. — Includes bibliographies and index
ISBN 0-7099-2012-1 : £12.95 : CIP rev.
Primary classification 305.8′00941 B81-25715

305.8′009747′1 — Urban regions. Ethnic groups. Identity. Spatial aspects — *Study regions: New York (City). Manhattan*

Jackson, Peter, *1955-*. Ethnic groups and boundaries : 'ordered segmentation' in urban neighbourhoods / Peter Jackson. — Oxford : Oxford Publishing, 1980. — 29p : maps ; 22cm. — (Research paper / University of Oxford School of Geography, ISSN 0305-8190 ; no.26)
Bibliography: p25-29
Unpriced (pbk) B82-15077

305.8′00981 — Brazil. Racial discrimination, *1830-1980*

Toplin, Robert Brent. Freedom and prejudice : the legacy of slavery in the United States and Brazil / Robert Brent Toplin. — Westport, Conn. ; London : Greenwood Press, 1981. — xxvi,134p ; 22cm. — (Contributions in Afro-American and African studies, ISSN 0069-9624 ; no.56)
Bibliography: p121-127. — Includes index
ISBN 0-313-22008-5 : Unpriced
Primary classification 305.8′00973 B82-01947

305.8′00994 — Australia. Ethnic minorities

Martin, Jean. The ethnic dimension. — London : Allen and Unwin, Jan.1982. — [185]p. — (Studies in society ; 9)
ISBN 0-86861-235-9 : £12.00 : CIP entry B81-33896

305.8′13 — United States. White persons. Effects of racism — *Conference proceedings*

Impacts of racism on white Americans / edited by Benjamin P. Bowser, Raymond G. Hunt. — Beverly Hills ; London : Published in cooperation with the Institute for the Study of Contemporary Social Problems [by] Sage, c1981. — 288p ; 22cm. — (Sage focus editions ; 36)
Conference papers. — Bibliography: p261-276. — Includes index
ISBN 0-8039-1593-4 (cased) : Unpriced
ISBN 0-8039-1594-2 (pbk) : £6.50 B82-17079

305.8′51′074797 — New York *(State).* **Buffalo. Italian immigrant families. Social conditions,** *1880-1930*

Yans-McLaughlin, Virginia. Family and community : Italian immigrants in Buffalo, 1880-1930 / Virginia Yans-McLaughlin. — Urbana, Ill. ; London : University of Illinois Press, 1982, c1977. — 286p : 1map ; 21cm
Originally published: Ithaca : Cornell University Press, 1977. — Bibliography: p267-279. — Includes index
ISBN 0-252-00916-9 (pbk) : Unpriced B82-38139

305.8′687295′073 — United States. Puerto Ricans. Social aspects

The Puerto Rican community and its children on the mainland : a source book for teachers, social workers and other professionals / [edited] by Francesco Cordasco and Eugene Bucchioni. — 3rd rev. ed. — Metuchen ; London : Scarecrow, 1982. — xi,457p ; 22cm
Previous ed.: 1972. — Bibliography: p441-450. — Includes index
ISBN 0-8108-1506-0 : £18.00 B82-31802

305.8′895 — Cyprus. Greek Cypriot refugees: Argaki refugees, *1974-1975* — *Anthropological perspectives*

Loizos, Peter. The heart grown bitter : a chronicle of Cypriot war refugees / Peter Loizos. — Cambridge : Cambridge University Press, 1981. — xii,219p : ill,maps,ports ; 24cm
Bibliography: p214-216. — Includes index
ISBN 0-521-24230-4 (cased) : £17.50
ISBN 0-521-28546-1 (pbk) : £5.95 B82-04564

305.8′9159 — Iran. Bakhtiari. Social conditions — *French texts*

Digard, Jean-Pierre. Techniques des nomades baxtyâri d'Iran / Jean-Pierre Digard. — Cambridge : Cambridge University Press, c1981. — x,273p : ill,2maps,plans,geneal.tables ; 24cm. — (Production pastorale et société)
Bibliography: p253-260. — Includes index
ISBN 0-521-24375-0 : £22.50 : CIP rev.
ISBN 2-901725-41-4 (cased) : France
ISBN 2-901725-30-9 (pbk) : France B82-03108

305.8′9159 — Pakistan. Swat. Pathans — *Anthropological perspectives*

Lindholm, Charles. Generosity and jealousy : the Swat Pukhtun of Northern Pakistan / Charles Lindholm. — New York ; Guildford : Columbia University Press, 1982. — xxxii,321p : ill,maps ; 24cm
Bibliography: p301-309. — Includes index
ISBN 0-231-05398-3 (cased) : £20.80
ISBN 0-231-05399-1 (pbk) : £10.40 B82-39004

305.8′9162 — Ireland. Anglo-Irish communities, *to 1921*

Beckett, J. C.. The Anglo-Irish tradition. — Belfast : Blackstaff, Oct.1982. — [160]p
Originally published: London : Faber, 1976
ISBN 0-85640-280-x (pbk) : £3.95 : CIP entry B82-28591

305.8′9162′041 — Great Britain. Irish, *1950-1976.* **Social aspects**

Irish people in British society. — London (c/o Carlton Community Centre, Granville Rd., Kilburn NW6 7RA) : Brent Irish Advisory Service, c1979. — 7p ; 30cm
Cover title
Unpriced (pbk) B82-19337

305.8′9162′073 — United States. Irish immigrants, *1760-1820*

Doyle, David Noel. Ireland, Irishmen and revolutionary America, 1760-1820 / David Noel Doyle. — Dublin : Published for the Cultural Relations Committee of Ireland by Mercier, 1981. — xix,257p : ill,2facsims,ports ; 20cm
Bibliography: p231-257
ISBN 0-85342-590-6 (pbk) : £4.95 B82-33757

305.8′91811′041 — Great Britain. Bulgarian communities — *Serials*

Vesti : bi͡uletin na Bŭlgarskata kulturno-prosvetna obshtina vŭv Velikobritani͡a : bulletin of the Bulgarian Community in Great Britain for Culture, Education & Church Affairs. — [R.1, broĭ 1 (i͡uni 1980)?]-. — London (c/o Dr M. Kusseff, 81 Ridge Rd, Hornsey [N8]) : The Community, 1980-. — v. ; 29cm
Irregular. — Text in English and Bulgarian. — Description based on: Broĭ [4]
ISSN 0263-256X = Vesti : Unpriced B82-22676

305.8′924′042 — England. Philosemitism, *1603-1655*

Katz, David S.. Philo-semitism and the readmission of the Jews to England 1603-1655 / David S. Katz. — Oxford : Clarendon, 1982. — viii,286p ; 23cm. — (Oxford historical monographs)
Bibliography: p245-271. — Includes index
ISBN 0-19-821885-0 : £17.50 : CIP rev. B81-34388

305.8′924′0494 — Jews. Racial discrimination by society. Measurement — *Study regions: Switzerland*

May, Michael. Can prejudice be measured? : two case studies on antisemitism in Switzerland / [Michael May]. — London (11 Hertford St., W1Y 7DX) : IJA, 1981. — 15p ; 24cm. — (Research report / Institute of Jewish Affairs ; no.18)
Unpriced (unbound) B82-27690

305.8′924′05694 — Israel. American Jewish immigrants. Social conditions

Avruch, Kevin. American immigrants in Israel : social identities and change / Kevin Avruch. — Chicago ; London : University of Chicago Press, c1981. — x,243p ; 23cm
Bibliography: p219-231. — Includes index
ISBN 0-226-03241-8 : £15.40 B82-03754

305.8′948 — India *(Republic).* **Andhra Pradesh. Gonds. Cultural processes**

Fürer-Haimendorf, Christoph von. The Gonds of Andhra Pradesh : tradition and change in an Indian tribe / Christoph von Fürer-Haimendorf in collaboration with Elizabeth von Fürer-Haimendorf. — London : Allen & Unwin, 1979. — ix,569p,[12]p of plates : ill,maps ; 24cm. — (School of Oriental and African Studies studies on modern Asia and Africa ; no.12)
Maps on lining papers. — Bibliography: p563-565. — Includes index
ISBN 0-04-301090-3 : £18.00 : CIP rev. B78-24899

305.8′948 — India *(Republic).* **Ghat Mountains. Hill Pandaram. Social structure**

Morris, Brian, *1936-*. Forest traders : a socio-economic study of the Hill Pandaram / by Brian Morris. — London : Athlone Press, 1982. — xiii,219p ; 23cm. — (London School of Economics monographs on social anthropology, ISSN 0077-1074 ; no.55)
Bibliography: p211-217. — Includes index
ISBN 0-485-19555-0 : £18.00 : CIP rev. B82-07668

305.8′948 — Sri Lanka. Tamils. Social conditions, *to 1979*

Schwarz, Walter. The Tamils of Sri Lanka / by Walter Schwarz. — Rev ed. — London (36 Craven St, WC2N 5NG) : Minority Rights Group, 1979. — 16p : 1map ; 30cm. — (Report, ISSN 0305-6252 ; no.25)
Previous ed.: 1975. — Bibliography: p16
£1.20 (pbk) B82-17711

305.8′948′05413 — India *(Republic).* **Orissa** *(State).* **Kond Hills. Konds. Cultural processes** — *Anthropological perspectives*

Boal, Barbara. The Konds : human sacrifice and religious change. — Warminster : Aris & Phillips, Mar.1982. — [304]p
ISBN 0-85668-154-7 (pbk) : £15.00 : CIP entry B82-05748

305.8′951′059 — South-east Asia. Chinese, *to 1980.* **Sociopolitical aspects**

Wang, Gungwu. Community and nation. — London : Allen & Unwin, Jan.1982. — [290]p. — (Southeast Asia publications series / Asian Studies Association of Australia ; no.6)
ISBN 0-86861-347-9 : £15.00 : CIP entry B81-35873

305.8′951′05954 — Malaysia. Sarawak. Society. Role of Chinese immigrants, *to 1979*

Chin, John M.. The Sarawak Chinese / John M. Chin. — Kuala Lumpur ; Oxford : Oxford University Press, 1981. — xv,158p,8p of plates : ill,maps,ports ; 22cm. — (Oxford in Asia paperbacks)
Maps on inside covers. — Bibliography: p143-147. — Includes index
ISBN 0-19-580470-8 (pbk) : £7.75 B82-05423

305.8′951′07471 — New York *(City).* **Chinese. Social conditions**

Wong, Bernard P.. Chinatown : economic adaptation and ethnic identity of the Chinese / by Bernard P. Wong. — New York ; London : Holt, Rinehart and Winston, c1982. — xiv,110p : ill,maps ; 24cm. — (Case studies in cultural anthropology)
Bibliography: p109-110
ISBN 0-03-058906-1 (pbk) : £4.50 B82-25820

305.8′957′052 — Japan. Koreans. Social conditions

Lee, Changsoo. Koreans in Japan : ethnic conflict and accommodation / Changsoo Lee and George De Vos with contributions by Dae-Gyun Chung ... [et al.] ; foreword by Robert A. Scalapino. — Berkeley ; London : University of California Press, c1981. — xiv ; 24cm
Bibliography: p417-424. — Includes index
ISBN 0-520-04258-1 : £22.75 B82-28104

305.8′957′07471 — New York *(City)*. South Korean immigrant communities

Illsoo, Kim. New urban immigrants : the Korean community in New York / Illsoo Kim. — Princeton ; Guildford : Princeton University Press, c1981. — xvi,329p ; 25cm
Bibliography: p321-323. — Includes index
ISBN 0-691-09355-5 : £18.80
Also classified at 304.8′73′05195 B82-02601

305.8′96 — Negroes. Racial discrimination by society

Sivanandan, A.. A different hunger : writings on black resistance / A. Sivanandan. — London : Pluto, c1982. — xi,171p ; 20cm
ISBN 0-86104-371-5 (pbk) : £3.95 B82-28405

305.8′96′024 — Great Britain. Racism — *Negro viewpoints — Personal observations*

Kapo, Remi. A savage culture : racism — a black British view / Remi Kapo. — London : Quartet, 1981. — xiv,146p ; 20cm
ISBN 0-7043-3392-9 (pbk) : £2.50 B82-00139

305.8′96′073 — United States. Negro ghettos

The **Ghetto** : readings with interpretations / edited by Joe T. Darden. — Port Washington : Kennikat ; London : National University Publications, 1981. — xi,243p ; 22cm
Bibliography: p227-240. — Includes index
ISBN 0-8046-9277-7 : Unpriced
ISBN 0-8046-9279-3 (pbk) : Unpriced
B82-17483

305.8′96073 — United States. Negroes. Interpersonal relationships with Africans — *Case studies*

Moikobu, Josephine Moraa. Blood and flesh : Black American and African indentifications / Josephine Moraa Moikobu. — Westport, Conn. ; London : Greenwood Press, 1981. — xiii,226p ; 22cm. — (Contributions in Afro-American and African studies ; no.59)
Bibliography: p205-217. — Includes index
ISBN 0-313-22549-4 : £18.95 B82-18187

305.8′96073 — United States. Negroes. Social conditions

Swan, L. Alex. Survival and progress : the Afro-American experience / L. Alex Swan. — Westport ; London : Greenwood Press, 1981. — xxiii,251p : ill ; 25cm. — (Contributions in Afro-American and African studies, ISSN 0069-9624 ; no.58)
Bibliography: p239-243. — Includes index
ISBN 0-313-22480-3 : Unpriced B82-02244

305.8′96073 — United States. Single negroes. Social aspects

Staples, Robert. The world of black singles : changing patterns of male/female relations / Robert Staples. — Westport ; London : Greenwood Press, 1981. — xxi,259p ; 22cm. — (Contributions in Afro-American and African studies, ISSN 0069-9624 ; no.57)
Bibliography: p247-252. — Includes index
ISBN 0-313-22478-1 : Unpriced B82-02246

305.8′96073 — United States. Urban regions. Free negroes. Social conditions, *1800-1850*

Curry, Leonard P.. The free black in urban America 1800-1850 : the shadow of the dream / Leonard P. Curry. — Chicago ; London : University of Chicago Press, 1981. — xix,346p : ill ; 24cm
Bibliography: p275-279. — Includes index
ISBN 0-226-13124-6 : £17.50 B82-03913

305.8′963′06751 — Zaire. Kongo. Social conditions, *1700-1800 — French texts*

Gonçalves, António C.. La symbolisation politique : Le prophétisme Kongo au XVIIIème siècle / António C. Gonçalves. — München ; London : Weltforum, c1980. — vi,137p ; 22cm. — (Materialien zu Entwicklung und Politik ; 19)
Bibliography: p127-137
Unpriced B82-28017

305.8′969729′0421 — London. West Indians. Social conditions

Cottle, Thomas J.. Black testimony : the voices of Britain′s West Indians / Thomas J. Cottle. — London : Wildwood House, 1978. — 184p ; 23cm
ISBN 0-7045-3011-2 : £6.95 B82-39753

305.8′97 — Hunter-gatherer peoples — *Anthropological perspectives — Study examples: North American Indians*

Hunter-gatherer foraging strategies : ethnographic and archeological analyses / edited by Bruce Winterhalder and Eric Alden Smith. — Chicago ; London : University of Chicago Press, 1981. — x,268p : ill,maps ; 25cm
Bibliography: p233-261. — Includes index
ISBN 0-226-90216-1 (cased) : £15.00
ISBN 0-226-90218-8 (pbk) : Unpriced
B82-21689

305.8′97 — Mexico. Aztecs — *Anthropological perspectives*

Berdan, Frances F.. The Aztecs of central Mexico : an imperial society / Frances F. Berdan. — New York ; London : Holt, Rinehart and Winston, c1982. — xi,195p : ill,maps,plan ; 24cm. — (Case studies in cultural anthropology)
Bibliography: p189-195
ISBN 0-03-055736-4 (pbk) : £5.95 B82-18934

305.8′97 — Mexico. Santiago Yaitepec. Chatino Indians — *Anthropological perspectives*

Greenberg, James B.. Santiago′s sword : Chatino peasant religion and economics / James B. Greenberg. — Berkeley ; London : University of California Press, c1981. — xii,227p : ill,maps ; 23cm
Bibliography: p209-220. — Includes index
ISBN 0-520-04135-6 : £13.00 B82-12191

305.8′97 — New Mexico. Zuñi Indians — *Anthropological perspectives*

Cushing, Frank Hamilton. Zuñi : selected writings of Frank Hamilton Cushing / edited, with an introduction, by Jesse Green ; foreword by Fred Eggan. — Lincoln, [Neb.] ; London : University of Nebraska Press, 1981, c1979. — xiv,447p : ill,2maps,3ports ; 21cm. — (A Bison book ; 779)
Originally published: 1979. — Bibliography: p431-438. — Includes index
ISBN 0-8032-7007-0 (pbk) : £5.95 B82-19496

305.8′97 — North America. Kwakiutl. Cultural processes

Walens, Stanley. Feasting with cannibals : an essay on Kwakiutl cosmology / Stanley Walens. — Princeton ; Guildford : Princeton University Press, c 1981. — xi,191p,[8]p of plates : ill ; 25cm
Bibliography: p173-187. — Includes index
ISBN 0-691-09392-x : £10.20 B82-20795

305.8′97 — Plains Indians. Cultural processes, *to ca 1910*

Bancroft-Hunt, Norman. The Indians : of the Great Plains / text by Norman Bancroft-Hunt ; photographs by Werner Forman. — London : Orbis, 1982, c1981. — 128p : col.ill,col.maps ; 31cm. — (Echoes of the ancient world)
Ill on lining papers. — Bibliography: p127. — Includes index
ISBN 0-85613-338-8 : £10.00 B82-23924

305.8′9922 — Indonesia. West Sumatra *(Province)*. Minangkabaus. Social conditions, *1850-1970*

Kato, Tsuyoshi. Matriliny and migration : evolving Minangkabau traditions in Indonesia / Tsuyoshi Kato. — Ithaca ; London : Cornell University Press, 1982. — 267p : ill,maps ; 23cm
Bibliography: p253-262. — Includes index
ISBN 0-8014-1411-3 : £15.75 B82-22616

305.8′994 — Polynesians. Cultural processes

Burt, Ben. Polynesians / Ben Burt. — London : British Museum Publications, c1981. — 16p : ill,1map,1port ; 24cm. — (Discovering other cultures)
Cover title. — At head of series title: Museum of Mankind. — Ill on inside covers. — Bibliography: p16
ISBN 0-7141-1566-5 (pbk) : Unpriced
B82-39889

305.8′995 — Solomon Islands. Malaita. Kwara′ae. Cultural processes

Burt, Ben. Solomon Islanders : the Kwara′ae / Ben Burt. — London : British Museum Publications, c1981. — 16p : ill,2maps,ports ; 24cm. — (Discovering other cultures)
Cover title. — At head of series title: Museum of Mankind. — Ill on inside covers. — Bibliography: p16
ISBN 0-7141-1565-7 (pbk) : Unpriced
B82-39890

305.9′0652 — United States. Society. Role of single persons

Cargan, Leonard. Singles : myths and realities / Leonard Cargan, Matthew Melko ; published in cooperation with National Council on Family Relations. — Beverly Hills ; London : Sage, c1982. — 287p : ill ; 23cm. — (New perspectives on family)
Bibliography: p283-286
ISBN 0-8039-1806-2 (cased) : Unpriced
ISBN 0-8039-1807-0 (pbk) : £6.50 B82-38161

305.9′08162 — Man. Deafness — *Sociological perspectives*

Nash, Jeffrey E.. Deafness in society / Jeffrey E. Nash, Anedith Nash. — Lexington : Lexington Books, c1981 ; [Aldershot] : Gower [distributor], 1982. — xi,125p ; 24cm
Bibliography: p111-120. — Includes index
ISBN 0-669-04590-x : £13.50 B82-18261

305.9′0824 — Man. Mental illness — *Sociological perspectives*

Horwitz, Allan V.. The social control of mental illness / Allan V. Horwitz. — New York ; London : Academic Press, 1982. — xi,212p ; 24cm. — (Studies on law and social control)
Bibliography: p187-204. — Includes index
ISBN 0-12-356180-9 : £13.00 B82-29601

305′.9′0824 — Man. Mental illness — *Sociological perspectives*

Mangen, Stephen P.. Sociology and mental health. — Edinburgh : Churchill Livingstone, Sept.1982. — [160]p
ISBN 0-443-02378-6 (pbk) : £3.95 : CIP entry
B82-24348

305.9′362 — England. Higher education institutions. Curriculum subjects: Community work & youth work. Ex-students. Careers, *1970-1978*

Holmes, John, *1946-*. Professionalisation : a misleading myth? : a study of the careers of ex-students of youth and community work courses in England and Wales from 1970 to 1978 / by John Holmes. — Leicester : National Youth Bureau, 1981. — 294p : ill,maps,forms ; 30cm
Bibliography: p293-294
ISBN 0-86155-045-5 (pbk) : £4.95 B82-14035

305.9′613 — Medicine. Nursing — *Sociological perspectives*

Murray, Ruth Beckmann. Nursing concepts for health promotion / Ruth Beckmann Murray, Judith Proctor Zentner. — Englewood Cliffs ; London : Prentice-Hall, c1979. — xviii,525p ; 24cm
Previous ed.: 1975. — Includes bibliographies and index
ISBN 0-13-627638-5 (cased) : £13.45
ISBN 0-13-627620-2 (pbk) : Unpriced
B82-07153

Schurr, Margaret C.. Nursing — image or reality?. — London : Hodder and Stoughton, Oct.1982. — [160]p
ISBN 0-340-28186-3 (pbk) : £5.25 : CIP entry
B82-24824

Smith, James P.. Sociology and nursing / James P. Smith. — 2nd ed. — Edinburgh : Churchill Livingstone, 1981. — ix,234p : ill ; 22cm. — (Churchill Livingstone nursing text)
Previous ed.: 1976. — Includes bibliographies and index
ISBN 0-443-02274-7 (pbk) : Unpriced
B82-05205

305.9′613 — United States. Student nurses. Socialisation
Cohen, Helen A.. The nurse′s quest for a professional indentity / Helen A. Cohen. — Menlo Park, Calif. ; London : Addison-Wesley, c1981. — ix,214p : ill ; 24cm
Bibliography: p188-211. — Includes index
ISBN 0-201-00956-0 (cased) : Unpriced
ISBN 0-201-01157-3 (pbk) : £8.00 B82-33443

305.9′63 — Philippines. Palawan. San José. Agricultural industries. Migrant personnel. Social inequality
Eder, James F.. Who shall succeed? : agricultural development and social inequality on a Philippine frontier / James F. Eder. — Cambridge : Cambridge University Press, 1982. — xv,264p : ill,maps ; 24cm
Bibliography: p253-258. — Includes index
ISBN 0-521-24218-5 : £20.00 B82-31126

305.9′635 — United States. Iceberg lettuce industries. Organisation structure — *Sociological perspectives*
Friedland, William H.. Manufacturing green gold : capital, labor and technology in the lettuce industry / William H. Friedland, Amy E. Barton, Robert J. Thomas. — Cambridge : Cambridge University Press, 1981. — x,159p : ill ; 24cm. — (The Arnold and Caroline Rose monograph series of the American Sociological Association)
Bibliography: p149-156. — Includes index
ISBN 0-521-24284-3 (cased) : £15.00
ISBN 0-521-28584-4 (pbk) : Unpriced
B82-08356

305.9′658 — West Midlands *(Metropolitan County)*. Coventry. Executives. Careers — *Sociological perspectives*
Lee, Gloria L.. Who gets to the top? : a sociological study of business executives / Gloria L. Lee. — Aldershot : Gower, 1981. — xiv,160p : ill ; 23cm
Bibliography: p149-153. — Includes index
ISBN 0-566-00497-6 : Unpriced : CIP rev.
B81-30283

305.9′68′094923 — Netherlands. Delft. Craftsmen. Socioeconomic status, *1560-1714*
Montias, John Michael. Artists and artisans in Delft : a socio-economic study of the seventeenth century / John Michael Montias. — Princeton ; Guildford : Princeton University Press, c1982. — xvi,424p : ill,ports ; 24cm
Bibliography: p395-402. — Includes index
ISBN 0-691-03986-0 (cased) : £25.80
ISBN 0-691-10129-9 (pbk) : Unpriced
Also classified at 305.9′7′094923 B82-25817

305.9′7′094923 — Netherlands. Delft. Artists. Socioeconomic status, *1560-1714*
Montias, John Michael. Artists and artisans in Delft : a socio-economic study of the seventeenth century / John Michael Montias. — Princeton ; Guildford : Princeton University Press, c1982. — xvi,424p : ill,ports ; 24cm
Bibliography: p395-402. — Inlcudes index
ISBN 0-691-03986-0 (cased) : £25.80
ISBN 0-691-10129-9 (pbk) : Unpriced
Primary classification 305.9′68′094923
B82-25817

306 — CULTURE AND INSTITUTIONS

306 — Civilization. Socioeconomic aspects — *For schools*
Ghaye, Tony. Man. — London : Macmillan Education, Feb.1983. — [88]p. — (Discovering geography)
ISBN 0-333-28403-8 (pbk) : £2.35 : CIP entry
B82-37859

306 — Cultural processes. Economic aspects — *Anthropological perspectives*
Douglas, Mary. In the active voice / Mary Douglas. — London : Routlege & Kegan Paul, 1982. — xi,306p : ill,maps ; 23cm
Includes bibliographies and index
ISBN 0-7100-9065-x : £9.95 B82-26597

306 — Culture
Scruton, Roger. The politics of culture and other essays / Roger Scruton. — Manchester : Carcanet, 1981. — 245p : music ; 23cm
Includes index
ISBN 0-85635-362-0 : £8.95 : CIP rev.
B81-16898

306 — Culture — *Sociological perspectives*
Apple, Michael W.. Education and power / Michael W. Apple. — Boston [Mass.] ; London : Routledge & Kegan Paul, 1982. — vii,218p ; 24cm
Bibliography: p203-211. — Includes index
ISBN 0-7100-0977-1 : £10.95 B82-33964

Mannheim, Karl. Structures of thinking / Karl Mannheim ; text and translation edited and introduced by David Kettler, Volker Meja and Nico Stehr ; translated by Jeremy J. Shapiro and Shierry Weber Nicholsen. — London : Routledge & Kegan Paul, 1982. — 292p ; 23cm. — (International library of sociology)
Translation of: Strukturen des Denkens. — Includes index
ISBN 0-7100-0936-4 : £14.00 B82-16881

306 — Death. Attitudes of society, *to 1980*
Mirrors of mortality : studies in the social history of death / edited by Joachim Whaley. — London : Europa, c1981. — viii,252p,[12]p of plates : ill ; 24cm. — (Europa social history of human experience)
Includes index
ISBN 0-905118-67-7 : £19.50 : CIP rev.
B81-28036

306 — France. Death. Attitudes of society, *1700-1800*
McManners, John. Death and the Enlightenment : changing attitudes to death among Christians and unbelievers in eighteenth-century France / John McManners. — Oxford : Clarendon, 1981. — vii,619p ; 23cm
Bibliography: p569-604. — Includes index
ISBN 0-19-826440-2 : £17.50 : CIP rev.
B81-34416

306 — Gathering communities & hunting communities — *Anthropological perspectives*
Politics and history in band societies. — Cambridge : Cambridge University Press, Oct.1982. — [498]p
ISBN 0-521-24063-8 (cased) : £29.50 : CIP entry
ISBN 0-521-28412-0 (pbk) : £9.95 B82-26237

306 — International relations
Change and the study of international relations. — London : Pinter, May 1981. — [225]p
ISBN 0-903804-83-2 : £13.50 : CIP entry
B81-10431

306 — Social anthropology
Augé, Marc. The anthropological circle : symbol, function, history / Marc Augé ; translated by Martin Thom. — Cambridge : Cambridge University Press, 1982. — vii,131p ; 24cm. — (Cambridge studies in social anthropology)
Translation of: Symbole, fonction, histoire. — Includes index
ISBN 0-521-23236-8 (cased) : £12.50 : CIP rev.
ISBN 0-521-28548-8 (pbk) : £4.95 B81-33801

Leach, Edmund. Social anthropology / Edmund Leach. — [Glasgow] : Fontana, 1982. — 254p ; 18cm. — (Fontana masterguides)
Bibliography: p245-248. — Includes index
ISBN 0-00-635533-1 (pbk) : £2.50 B82-18955

Leach, Edmund. Social anthropology / Edmund Leach. — New York ; Oxford : Oxford University Press, 1982. — 320p : ill ; 22cm
Bibliography: p245-248. — Includes index
ISBN 0-19-520371-2 : £9.50 B82-27095

Lewis, I. M.. Social anthropology in perspective : the relevance of social anthropology / I.M. Lewis. — Harmondsworth : Penguin, 1976 (1981 [printing]). — 386p : ill ; 20cm. — (Penguin education)
Bibliography: p360-370. — Includes index
ISBN 0-14-080453-6 (pbk) : £3.95 B82-07291

Needham, Rodney. Circumstantial deliveries / Rodney Needham. — Berkeley ; London : University of California Press, c1981. — xiii,119p ; 21cm. — (A Quantum book)
Bibliography: p111-114. — Includes index
ISBN 0-520-04389-8 : £9.00 B82-28097

306 — Social anthropology — *Marxist viewpoints*
The **Anthropology** of pre-capitalist societies / edited by Joel S. Kahn and Josep R. Llobera. — London : Macmillan, 1981. — xii,329p : ill ; 23cm. — (Critical social studies)
Includes bibliographies
ISBN 0-333-23417-0 (cased) : Unpriced : CIP rev.
ISBN 0-333-23418-9 (pbk) : Unpriced
B80-35671

306 — Time. Allocation — *Anthropological perspectives*
Carlstein, Tommy. Time resources, society and ecology. — London : Allen and Unwin, Mar.1982
Vol.1: Preindustrial societies. — [200]p
ISBN 0-04-300082-7 (cased) : £12.00 : CIP entry
ISBN 0-04-300083-5 (pbk) : £6.95 B82-00274

306 — Time — *Sociological perspectives*
Zerubavel, Eviatar. Hidden rhythms : schedules and calendars in social life / Eviatar Zerubavel. — Chicago ; London : University of Chicago Press, 1981. — xix,201p ; 23cm
Includes index
ISBN 0-226-98162-2 : £15.75 B82-13667

306′.02493 — Social anthropology — *For archaeology*
Hodder, Ian. The present past : an introduction to anthropology for archaeologists. — London : Batsford, Aug.1982. — [240]p
ISBN 0-7134-2527-x : £12.50 : CIP entry
B82-15920

306′.03′21 — Culture — *Encyclopaedias*
Pocket heritage dictionary. — Harlow : Longman, 1982. — 280p ; 12cm. — (Longman top pocket series)
ISBN 0-582-55548-5 (pbk) : £0.75 B82-29198

306′.092′4 — Social anthropology. Evans-Pritchard, *Sir* Edward — *Critical studies — Welsh texts*
Jenkins, Dafydd. Evans-Pritchard / Dafydd Jenkins. — [Denbigh] : Gwasg Gee, 1982. — 112p ; 19cm. — (Y Meddwl modern)
Bibliography: p112
£1.90 (pbk) B82-40001

306′.09866 — Ecuador. Society — *Anthropological perspectives*
Cultural transformations and ethnicity in modern Ecuador / edited by Norman E. Whitten, Jr. — Urbana ; London : University of Illinois Press, c1981. — xvii,811p : ill,maps ; 24cm
Includes bibliographies and index
ISBN 0-252-00832-4 : £23.80 B82-19645

306′.1 — British popular culture
Popular culture. — Milton Keynes : Open University Press. — (A second level course)
At head of title: The Open University
Block 5: Politics, ideology and popular culture (2). — 1982. — 92p : ill,facsims ; 30cm. — (U203 ; block 5, units 21, 22 and 23)
Includes bibliographies. — Contents: Unit 21: James Bond as popular hero — Unit 22: Television police series and law and order — Unit 23: Class, sex and the family in situation comedy
ISBN 0-335-10129-1 (pbk) : Unpriced
B82-35787

Popular culture. — Milton Keynes : Open University Press
At head of title: The Open University
Form and meaning (1). — 1981. — 98p : ill,facsims ; 30cm. — (U203 ; block 4, units 13, 14 and 15)
Includes bibliographies. — Contents: Introduction to block 4 — Unit 13: Readers, viewers and texts — Unit 14: Meaning, image and ideology — Unit 15: Reading and realism
ISBN 0-335-10126-7 (pbk) : Unpriced
B82-31986

Popular culture. — Milton Keynes : Open University Press
At head of title: The Open University
Form and meaning (2). — 1981. — 75p : ill,music ; 30cm. — (U203 ; block 4, units 16 and 17)
Includes bibliographies. — Contents: Unit 16: 'Reading' popular music — Unit 17: Pleasure
ISBN 0-335-10127-5 (pbk) : Unpriced
B82-31984

306'.1 — British popular culture *continuation*

Popular culture. — Milton Keynes : Open University Press
At head of title: The Open University
Politics, ideology and popular culture (1). — 1981. — 92p : ill ; 30cm. — (U203 ; block 5, units 18 and 19/20)
Includes bibliographies. — Contents: Introduction to block 5 — Unit 18: Popular culture and hegemony in post-war Britain — Unit 19: Pop culture, pop music and post-war youth : subcultures — Unit 20: Pop culture, pop music and post-war youth : countercultures
ISBN 0-335-10128-3 (pbk) : Unpriced
B82-31987

Popular culture. — Milton Keynes : Open University Press
At head of title: The Open University
Popular culture : themes and issues (1). — 1981. — 86p : ill,facsims,ports ; 30cm. — (U203 ; block 1, units 1/2)
Includes bibliographies. — Contents: Units 1/2: Christmas, a case study
ISBN 0-335-10120-8 (pbk) : Unpriced
B82-21185

Popular culture. — Milton Keynes : Open University Press
At head of title: The Open University
Popular culture : themes and issues (2). — 1981. — 34p ; 30cm. — (U203 ; block 1, unit 3)
Bibliography: p34. — Contents: Unit 3: Popular culture, history and theory
ISBN 0-335-10121-6 (pbk) : Unpriced
B82-21188

Popular culture. — Milton Keynes : Open University Press
At head of title: The Open University
Popular culture and everyday life (1). — 1981. — 66p : ill,1facsim ; 30cm. — (U203 ; block 3, units 9 and 10)
Includes bibliographies. — Contents: Introduction to block 3 — Unit 9: Approaches to the study of everyday life — Unit 10: Leisure activities : home and neighbourhood
ISBN 0-335-10124-0 (pbk) : Unpriced
B82-31985

Popular culture. — Milton Keynes : Open University Press
At head of title: The Open University
Popular culture and everyday life (2). — 1981. — 68p : ill,facsims ; 30cm. — (U203 ; block 3, units 11 and 12)
Includes bibliographies. — Contents: Unit 11: Holidays — Unit 12: Interpreting television
ISBN 0-335-10125-9 (pbk) : Unpriced
B82-31983

Popular culture. — Milton Keynes : Open University Press
At head of title: The Open University
The Historical development of popular culture in Britain (2). — 1981. — 85p : ill,facsims ; 30cm. — (U203 ; block 2, units 7 and 8)
Includes bibliographies. — Contents: Unit 7: British cinema in the 1930s — Unit 8: Radio in World War II
ISBN 0-335-10123-2 (pbk) : Unpriced
B82-21186

306'.1 — British popular culture, ***ca 1800-ca 1980***

Popular culture : past and present : a reader / edited by Bernard Waites, Tony Bennett and Graham Martin. — London : Croom Helm in association with The Open University Press, c1982. — 326p ; 22cm
Includes bibliographies and index
ISBN 0-7099-1909-3 (pbk) : £5.25 : CIP rev.
B81-25714

306'.1 — English popular culture, ***1800-1900***

Popular culture and custom in nineteenth-century England / edited by Robert D. Storch. — London : Croom Helm, c1982. — 213p ; 23cm
Includes index
ISBN 0-7099-0453-3 : £13.95 : CIP rev.
B82-04625

306'.1'05 — Alternative society — ***Serials***

Northern lights : a new journal for a new age. — Vol.1, no.1 (Apr.-May 82)-. — [Leeds] ([99 Meadow La., Leeds, LS11 5DW]) : [Northern Lights], 1982-. — v. : ill,plans,ports ; 30cm
Six issues yearly
ISSN 0263-5496 = Northern lights : £0.60
B82-28854

306'.1'0941 — Great Britain. Alternative society — ***Illustrations***

Eco-socialism in a nutshell. — [London] : SERA, c1980. — 23p : ill ; 21cm
ISBN 0-906495-65-2 (pbk) : £0.50 B82-22022

306'.1'09417 — Ireland ***(Republic).*** **Alternative society —** ***Serials***

North-west newsletter. — [No.1]-. — Boyle (c/o Ms. M. Sachs, Aughnafinigan, Knockvicar, Boyle, Co. Roscommon, [Ireland]) : [s.n.], [197-]-. — v. : ill ; 30cm
Six issues yearly. — Description based on: No.24 (Sept./Oct. 1981)
Unpriced B82-23601

306'.2 — African countries. Politics. Leadership, ***1945-1981***

Cartwright, J.. Political leadership in Africa. — London : Croom Helm, Jan.1983. — [320]p
ISBN 0-7099-0751-6 : £15.95 : CIP entry
B82-40913

306'.2 — Children. Political socialisation

Stevens, Olive. Children talking politics. — Oxford : Martin Robertson, July 1982. — [192] p. — (Issues and ideas in education)
ISBN 0-85520-489-3 (cased) : £12.50 : CIP entry
ISBN 0-85520-492-3 (pbk) : £4.95 B82-13144

306'.2 — France. Crowds, ***1878-1900.*** **Political behaviour**

Barrows, Susanna. Distorting mirrors : visions of the crowd in late nineteenth-century France / Susanna Barrows. — New Haven ; London : Yale University Press, c1981. — ix,221p ; 22cm
Bibliography: p199-213. — Includes index
ISBN 0-300-02588-2 : Unpriced : CIP rev.
Primary classification 302.3'3 B81-34718

306'.2 — France. Working classes. Political behaviour

DeAngelis, Richard A.. Blue-collar workers and politics : a French paradox / Richard A. DeAngelis. — London : Croom Helm published in association with Flinders University of South Australia, c1982. — 286p ; 23cm
'Published in association with Flinders University of South Australia' — Title page. — Bibliography: p268-279. — Includes index
ISBN 0-7099-0815-6 : £12.95 : CIP rev.
B82-07673

306'.2 — Great Britain & United States. Electoral systems — ***Sociological perspectives***

McLean, Iain. Dealing in votes. — Oxford : Martin Robertson, Apr.1982. — [256]p
ISBN 0-85520-472-9 (cased) : £12.50 : CIP entry
ISBN 0-85520-473-7 (pbk) : £4.95 B82-04799

306'.2 — Great Britain. ***Parliament. House of Commons.*** **Women members,** ***to 1978 — Sociological perspectives***

Vallance, Elizabeth. Women in the House. — London : Athlone Press, Jan.1982. — [224]p
Originally published: 1979
ISBN 0-485-11229-9 (pbk) : £4.95 : CIP entry
B82-00163

306'.2 — Great Britain. Politics. Leadership, ***1916-1978.*** **Psychology**

Margach, James. The anatomy of power : an enquiry into the personality of leadership / by James Margach. — London : W.H. Allen, 1981, c1979. — 164p ; 20cm. — (A Star book)
Originally published: 1979. — Includes index
ISBN 0-352-30699-8 (pbk) : £1.95 B82-33968

306'.2 — Great Britain. Politics. Participation of senior civil servants

Rose, Richard, *1933-*. The political status of higher civil servants in Britain / by Richard Rose. — Glasgow (University of Strathclyde, Glasgow, G1 1XQ) : Centre for the Study of Public Policy, 1981. — 43p ; 30cm. — (Studies in public policy, ISSN 0140-8240 ; no.92)
Unpriced (pbk) B82-12868

306'.2 — Great Britain. Secondary schools. Students. Political socialisation. Influence of political behaviour of teachers

Ewens, D. C.. The case of the institutionalized deviant : from political socialization to political control / D.C. Ewens. — London : Polytechnic of Central London, School of Social Sciences and Business Studies, 1981. — 54,xxiiip : ill ; 30cm. — (Research working paper / Polytechnic of Central London. School of Social Sciences and Business Studies ; no.15)
Bibliography: pxvii-xxxiii
Unpriced (spiral) B82-11600

306'.2 — Political behaviour — ***Sociological perspectives***

Sociobiology and human politics / edited by Elliott White. — Lexington, Mass. : Lexington Books, c1981 ; [Aldershot] : Gower, 1982. — xiii,290p ; 24cm
Includes bibliographies and index
ISBN 0-669-03602-1 : £16.50 B82-08646

306'.2 — Political identity. Psychological aspects — ***Study regions: South Africa***

Du Preez, Peter. [The politics of identity]. Social psychology of politics. — Oxford : Blackwell, June 1982. — [188]p
Originally published as: The politics of identity. 1980
ISBN 0-631-13035-7 (pbk) : £5.50 : CIP entry
B82-12834

306'.2 — Political stability

Political equilibrium / edited by Peter C. Ordeshook, Kenneth A. Shepsle. — Boston, Mass. ; London : Kluwer Nijhoff, c1982. — xiii,210p : ill ; 24cm. — (Studies in public choice)
Bibliography: p197-207
ISBN 0-89838-073-1 : Unpriced B82-31277

306'.2 — Politics. Participation of public — ***Comparative studies***

Verba, Sidney. Participation and political equality / Sidney Verba, Norman H. Nie, Jae-On Kim. — Cambridge : Cambridge University Press, 1978 (1980 [printing]). — xxi,393p : ill ; 23cm
Bibliography: p376-386. — Includes index
ISBN 0-521-29721-4 (pbk) : £7.95 B82-08279

306'.2 — Politics. Patronage — ***Sociological perspectives***

Political clientelism, patronage, and development / edited by S.N. Eisenstadt and René Lemarchand. — Beverly Hills ; London : Sage, c1981. — 332p ; 22cm. — (Contemporary political sociology ; v.3)
Bibliography: p298-330
ISBN 0-8039-9794-9 (cased) : Unpriced : CIP rev.
ISBN 0-8039-9795-7 (pbk) : Unpriced
B81-19169

306'.2 — Politics. Role of ethnic groups — ***Sociological perspectives***

The Politics of territorial identity : studies of developments in the European peripheries. — London : Sage, May 1982. — [500]p
ISBN 0-8039-9788-4 : £17.00 : CIP entry
B82-07828

306'.2 — Politics — ***Sociological perspectives***

Wasburn, Philo C.. Political sociology : approaches, concepts, hypotheses / Philo C. Wasburn. — Englewood Cliffs, N.J. ; London : Prentice-Hall, c1982. — viii,374p ; 24cm
Includes index
ISBN 0-13-684860-5 : Unpriced B82-28341

306'.2 — State. Power. Theories — ***Marxist viewpoints***

Dragstedt, A. J.. State, power & bureaucracy : a Marxist critique of sociological theories / by A.J. Dragstedt ; with two essays by C. Slaughter. — London : New Park, c1981. — 135p ; 21cm
ISBN 0-902030-83-3 (pbk) : £3.00 B82-36965

306′.2 — Western world. Political socialisation

Sewell, John. Public affairs and the successor generation : a project report / compiled by John Sewell. — Exeter (7 Cathedral Close, Exeter, Devon [EX1 1EZ]) : European-Atlantic Movement, [1982?]. — 22p ; 21cm
Cover title
Unpriced (pbk) B82-35508

306′.2′05 — Politics — *Sociological perspectives — Serials*

Political power and social theory : a research annual. — Vol.1 (1980)-. — Greenwich, Conn. : JAI Press ; London (3 Henrietta St., WC2E 8LU) : Distributed by JAICON Press, 1980-. — v. : ill ; 24cm
ISSN 0198-8719 = Political power and social theory : £24.50 B82-02363

306′.2′088042 — United States. Politics. Participation of women

Gelb, Joyce. Women and public policies / Joyce Gelb and Marian Lief Palley. — Princeton ; Guildford : Princeton University Press, c1982. — xiv,198p ; 23cm
Includes index
ISBN 0-691-07639-1 (cased) : £13.10
ISBN 0-691-02209-7 (pbk) : £4.90 B82-39749

306′.2′08997 — Wyoming. Arapaho. Government, *1851-1978 — Anthropological perspectives*

Fowler, Loretta. Arapahoe politics, 1851-1978 : symbols in crises of authority / Loretta Fowler ; foreword by Fred Eggan. — Lincoln [Neb.] ; London : University of Nebraska Press, c1982. — xx,373p,16p of plates : ill,maps,ports ; 24cm
Bibliography: p348-356. — Includes index
ISBN 0-8032-1956-3 : Unpriced B82-37238

306′.2′0943 — Germany. Political events, *1933-1945 — Sociological perspectives*

Weinstein, Fred. The dynamics of Nazism : leadership, ideology and the holocaust / Fred Weinstein. — New York ; London : Academic Press, c1980. — xviii,168p ; 24cm. — (Studies in social discontinuity)
Includes index
ISBN 0-12-742480-6 : £9.00 B82-10045

306′.2′0943 — Germany. Politics, *1888-1918.* **Social aspects**

Society and politics in Wilhelmine Germany / edited by Richard J. Evans. — London : Croom Helm, 1980, c1978. — 305p ; 22cm
Originally published: 1978. — Includes index
ISBN 0-7099-0429-0 (pbk) : Unpriced B82-38557

306′.2′0951 — China. Political institutions — *Anthropological perspectives*

Ahern, Emily Martin. Chinese ritual and politics / Emily Martin Ahern. — Cambridge : Cambridge University Press, 1981. — ix,144p : ill ; 24cm. — (Cambridge studies in social anthropology)
Bibliography: p120-128. — Includes index
ISBN 0-521-23690-8 : £14.50 : CIP rev. B81-34587

306′.2′097274 — Mexico. Oaxaca *(State).* **Zapotecs. Political development,** *to ca 500.* **Archaeological sources**

Spencer, Charles S.. The Cuicatlán Cañada and Monte Albán : a study of primary state formation / Charles S. Spencer. — New York ; London : Academic Press, 1982. — xx,326p : ill,maps,plans ; 25cm. — (Studies in archaeology)
Bibliography: p309-318. — Includes index
ISBN 0-12-656680-1 : £25.80 B82-39503

306′.2′09728 — Central America. Political development, *to ca 1530 — Anthropological perspectives — Conference proceedings*

The **Transition** to statehood in the new world / edited by Grant D. Jones, Robert R. Kautz. — Cambridge : Cambridge University Press, 1981. — ix,254p : ill,1map ; 24cm. — (New directions in archaeology)
Conference papers. — Bibliography: p228-248. — Includes index
ISBN 0-521-24075-1 : £17.50 B82-13955

306′.23 — Western Europe. Society. Role of parliaments, *1460-1943 — Conference proceedings*

Irish Conference of Historians *(1981 : Dublin).* Parliament and community. — Belfast : Appletree Press, Feb.1983. — [248]p. — (Historical studies, ISSN 0075-0743 ; 14)
ISBN 0-904651-93-2 : £13.00 : CIP entry B82-39838

306′.24 — Eastern Europe. Public administration. Bureaucracy — *Sociological perspectives*

Hirszowicz, Maria. The bureaucratic Leviathan. — Oxford : Robertson, June 1982. — [220]p
Originally published: 1980
ISBN 0-85520-515-6 (pbk) : £5.95 : CIP entry B82-12850

306′.24 — England. Local government. Policies. Formulation — *Sociological perspectives*

Approaches in public policy / edited by Steve Leach and John Stewart. — London : For the Institute of Local Government Studies, University of Birmingham [by] Allen & Unwin, 1982. — 263p : ill,1map ; 24cm
Bibliography: p243-258. — Includes index
ISBN 0-04-658236-3 (cased) : Unpriced : CIP rev.
ISBN 0-04-658237-1 (pbk) : Unpriced B82-15645

306′.26 — Political groups — *Sociological perspectives*

Private patronage and public power : political clientelism in the modern state. — London : Frances Pinter, Apr.1982. — [256]p
ISBN 0-86187-223-1 : £14.75 : CIP entry B82-04835

306′.27 — Africa. Military governments. Social aspects

Odetola, Olatunde. Military regimes and development. — London : Allen & Unwin, Nov.1982. — [240]p
ISBN 0-04-301154-3 (pbk) : £4.50 : CIP entry B82-27803

306′.27 — Military operations. Strategy. Social aspects

Atkinson, Alexander. Social order and the general theory of strategy / Alexander Atkinson. — London : Routledge & Kegan Paul, 1981. — xi,305p ; 22cm
Bibliography: p293-305
ISBN 0-7100-0907-0 (pbk) : £8.50 B82-08166

306′.27 — Society. Role of military forces — *Soviet viewpoints*

Dolgopolov, Evgeniĭ. The army and the revolutionary transformation of society / Yevgeny Dolgopolov ; [translated from the Russian by Lilia Nakhapetyan]. — Moscow : Progress Publishers ; [London] : distributed by Central Books, c1981. — 111p ; 20cm
Translation of: Armii͡a i revoli͡ut͡sionnye preobrazovanii͡a obshchestva
ISBN 0-7147-1769-x (pbk) : £1.50 B82-38230

306′.27′0904 — Society. Role of military forces, *1945-1980 — Conference proceedings*

Civil-military relations : regional perspectives / edited by Morris Janowitz. — Beverly Hills ; London : Published in cooperation with the Inter-University Seminar on Armed Forces and Society [by] Sage, c1981. — 288p ; 23cm
Conference papers
ISBN 0-8039-1666-3 : £15.50 B82-13977

306′.27′0941 — Great Britain. Society. Role of British military forces

Troops for tomorrow / Peace Force Scotland. — Kirkcaldy (The Lantern House, Olympia Arcade, Kirkcaldy, KY1 1QF) : Peace Force Scotland, [1982]. — [4]p : ill ; 21cm. — (Fact sheet ; 10)
Bibliography: p4
Unpriced (unbound) B82-27597

306′.3 — Ancient Rome. Personal patronage, *B.C.30-A.D.235*

Saller, Richard P.. Personal patronage under the early empire / Richard P. Saller. — Cambridge : Cambridge University Press, 1982. — ix,222p : geneal.tables,1map ; 24cm
Bibliography: p209-216. — Includes index
ISBN 0-521-23300-3 : £18.50 : CIP rev. B82-12140

306′.3 — Australia. Industrial relations. Strikes, *to 1980 — Sociological perspectives*

Waters, Malcolm. Strikes in Australia : a sociological account of industrial conflict. — London : Allen & Unwin, Apr.1982. — [320]p. — (Studies in society)
ISBN 0-86861-204-9 : £15.00 : CIP entry B82-06265

306′.3 — Australia. Work — *Sociological perspectives*

The **Future** of work. — London : Allen & Unwin, Jan.1982. — [200]p
ISBN 0-86861-283-9 : £12.00 : CIP entry B81-34076

306′.3 — Economic conditions — *Sociological perspectives*

Hopkins, Terence K.. World systems analysis : theory and methodology / Terence K. Hopkins, Immanuel Wallerstein. — Beverly Hills ; London : Sage, c1982. — 200p ; 22cm. — (Explorations in the world economy ; 1)
Three associate authors are named on the title page. — Bibliography: p193-199
ISBN 0-8039-1810-0 (cased) : Unpriced
ISBN 0-8039-1811-9 (pbk) : £6.50 B82-38164

306′.3 — Economic development — *Anthropological perspectives — Serials*

Research in economic anthropology : an annual compilation of research. — Vol.1 (1978)-. — Greenwich, Conn. : JAI Press ; London (3 Henrietta St., WC2E 8LU) : Distributed by JAICON Press, 1978-. — v. : ill ; 24cm
Supplement: Research in economic anthropology. Supplement
ISSN 0190-1281 = Research in economic anthropology : £26.20 B82-02348

Research in economic anthropology : a research annual. Supplement. — Vol.1 (1980)-. — Greenwich, Conn. : JAI Press ; London (3 Henrietta St., WC2E 8LU) : Distributed by JAICON Press, 1980-. — v. ; 24cm
Supplement to: Research in economic anthropology
£26.20 B82-02349

306′.3 — Economic development — *Sociological perspectives*

Peattie, Lisa. Thinking about development / Lisa Peattie. — New York ; London : Plenum, c1981. — x,198p ; 22cm. — (Environment, development, and public policy. Cities and development)
Includes index
ISBN 0-306-40761-2 : Unpriced B82-22468

306′.3 — Food — *Anthropological perspectives*

Goody, Jack. Cooking, cuisine and class : a study in comparative sociology / Jack Goody. — Cambridge : Cambridge University Press, 1982. — viii,253p ; 24cm. — (Themes in the social sciences)
Bibliography: p234-245. — Includes index
ISBN 0-521-24455-2 : £19.50 : CIP rev. B82-12722

306′.3 — Great Britain. Society. Role of business firms

Donnelly, Graham. The firm in society / Graham Donnelly. — London : Longman, 1981. — 370p : ill ; 22cm
Includes bibliographies and index
ISBN 0-582-41592-6 (pbk) : £5.95 : CIP rev. B81-03158

306′.3 — Great Britain. Unemployment. Social aspects

Seabrook, Jeremy. Unemployment. — London : Quartet Books, Mar.1982. — [256]p
ISBN 0-7043-2325-7 : £9.95 : CIP entry B82-01162

306′.3 — Great Britain. Work — *Personal observations*

Leighton, Martin. Men at work. — London : Jill Norman, Sept.1981. — [192]p
ISBN 0-906908-38-8 : £6.95 : CIP entry B81-21579

306'.3 — Job redesign — *Sociological perspectives*
Autonomy and control at the workplace : contexts for job redesign / edited by John E. Kelly and Chris W. Clegg. — London : Croom Helm, c1982. — 213p : ill ; 23cm. — (Social analysis)
Bibliography: p181-204. — Includes index
ISBN 0-7099-0410-x : £13.95 : CIP rev.
B81-31441

306'.3 — Money — *Anthropological perspectives*
Crump, Thomas. The phenomenon of money / Thomas Crump. — London : Routledge & Kegan Paul, 1981. — xiii,366p ; 23cm
Bibliography: p341-356. — Includes index
ISBN 0-7100-0856-2 : £17.50 : CIP rev.
B81-28080

306'.3 — Papua New Guinea. Highlands. Food. Production — *Anthropological perspectives*
Sillitoe, Paul. Roots of the earth : crops in the highlands of Papua New Guinea. — Manchester : Manchester University Press, Jan.1983. — [320]p
ISBN 0-7190-0874-3 : £30.00 : CIP entry
B82-32619

306'.3 — United States. Old persons. Economic conditions — *Forecasts*
Olson, Lawrence, *1945-*. The elderly and the future economy / Lawrence Olson, Christopher Caton, Martin Duffy ; with contributions by Michael Shannon, Robert Tannenwald. — Lexington : Lexington Books, c1981 ; [Aldershot] : Gower [distributor], 1982. — xviii,195p : ill ; 24cm
Bibliography: p185-187. — Includes index
ISBN 0-669-04651-5 : £14.50 B82-18260

306'.3 — Women. Economic conditions
Leghorn, Lisa. Woman's worth : sexual economics and the world of woman / Lisa Leghorn and Katherine Parker. — Boston, Mass. ; London : Routledge & Kegan Paul, 1981. — xiii,356p ; 22cm
Includes index
ISBN 0-7100-0836-8 : £12.00 : CIP rev.
ISBN 0-7100-0855-4 (pbk) : £5.95 B81-21498

306'.3 — Work. Attitudes of personnel. Evaluation. Techniques
The **Experience** of work : a compendium and review of 249 measures and their use / John D. Cook ... [et al.]. — London : Academic, 1981. — vii,335p ; 24cm. — (Organizational and occupational psychology)
Bibliography: p265-312. — Includes index
ISBN 0-12-187050-2 : £16.80 : CIP rev.
B81-28791

306'.3 — Work. Change
Clutterbuck, David. The re-making of work : changing work patterns and how to capitalize on them / David Clutterbuck and Roy Hill. — London : Grant-McIntyre, 1981. — 216p ; 23cm
Bibliography: p209-211. — Includes index
ISBN 0-86216-044-8 : £8.95 : CIP rev.
B81-31077

306'.3'088042 — East Africa. Women. Economic conditions — *Case studies*
Obbo, Christine. African women : their struggle for economic independence / Christine Obbo. — London : Hutchinson University Library for Africa in association with Zed Press, 1982, c1980. — x,166p : ill,1map ; 22cm
Originally published: London : Zed, 1980. — Bibliography: p165-166
ISBN 0-905762-48-7 (pbk) : Unpriced
B82-39556

306'.32 — Property — *Sociological perspectives*
Property and social relations / edited by Peter G. Hollowell. — London : Heinemann, 1982. — 209p ; 21cm
Includes index
ISBN 0-435-82435-x (pbk) : £8.50 : CIP rev.
B81-35694

306'.36 — Business enterprise — *Sociological perspectives*
Honour, T. F.. The sociology of business. — London : Croom Helm, Aug.1982. — [240]p
ISBN 0-7099-0333-2 (cased) : £13.95 : CIP entry
ISBN 0-7099-1245-5 (pbk) : £6.95 B82-15903

306'.36 — Capitalist countries. Industries. Industrial relations, *1870-1981* — *Sociological perspectives*
Littler, Craig R.. The development of the labour process in capitalist societies. — London : Heinemann Educational, Nov.1982. — [256]p
ISBN 0-435-82540-2 (cased) : £14.50 : CIP entry
ISBN 0-435-82541-0 (pbk) : £5.95 B82-27506

306'.36 — Great Britain. Employment. Social aspects
Diversity and decomposition in the labour market . — Aldershot : Gower, Sept.1982. — [220]p
ISBN 0-566-00556-5 : £12.50 : CIP entry
B82-19544

Whitehead, A. K.. People and employment / A.K. Whitehead, L. Baruch ; with contributions from E.M. Wilson, O.D. Jones, D. Golding. — London : Butterworths, 1981. — xiii,278p : ill ; 24cm
Includes bibliographies and index
ISBN 0-408-10691-3 (cased) : £10.00 : CIP rev.
ISBN 0-408-10692-1 (pbk) : £5.95 B81-23950

306'.36 — Great Britain. First employment. Personal adjustment of school leavers
West, Michael. The transition from school to work. — London : Croom Helm, July 1982. — [240]p
ISBN 0-7099-2758-4 : £11.95 : CIP entry
B82-22430

306'.36 — Great Britain. Manufacturing industries. Supervisors — *Sociological perspectives*
Child, John. Lost managers : supervisors in industry and society / by John Child and Bruce Partridge. — Cambridge : Cambridge University Press, 1982. — xiv,241p ; 23cm. — (Management and industrial relations series ; 1)
Bibliography: p227-234. — Includes index
ISBN 0-521-23356-9 (cased) : £16.50 : CIP rev.
ISBN 0-521-29931-4 (pbk) : £5.95 B82-12719

306'.36 — Great Britain. Society. Role of business firms
Business in the Community. Handbook for action / Business in the Community. — London (91 Waterloo Rd., SE1) : Business in the Community working group, [1982?]. — [16]p : ill,ports ; 30cm
Unpriced (pbk) B82-24156

306'.36 — Great Britain. Work patterns. Economic aspects
Bosworth, Derek L.. Work patterns : an economic analysis / Derek L. Bosworth, Peter J. Dawkins. — Aldershot : Gower, c1981. — viii,265p : ill ; 23cm
Bibliography: p249-257. — Includes index
ISBN 0-566-00310-4 : Unpriced : CIP rev.
B81-06603

306'.36 — Industrial sociology
Hirszowicz, Maria. Industrial sociology : an introduction / Maria Hirszowicz ; with a guide to the literature by Peter Cook. — Oxford : Robertson, 1981. — ix,303p : ill ; 23cm
Bibliography: p270-291. — Includes index
ISBN 0-85520-425-7 (cased) : £17.50 : CIP rev.
ISBN 0-85520-426-5 (pbk) : £5.95 B81-16861

306'.36 — Industrialised societies. Work — *Sociological perspectives*
Kahn, Robert L.. Work and health / Robert L. Kahn. — New York ; Chichester : Wiley, c1981. — xvi,198p : ill ; 22cm. — (Wiley series on organizational assessment and change)
Bibliography: p185-194. — Includes index
ISBN 0-471-05749-5 : £14.75 B82-01054

306'.36 — Industries. Organisation structure — *Sociological perspectives*
Power, efficiency and institutions. — London : Heinemann Educational, Sept.1982. — [256]p
ISBN 0-435-82315-9 : £13.00 : CIP entry
B82-24350

306'.36 — Organisations. New personnel. Career expectations
Williams, Allan P. O.. Factors related to career aspirations of new entrants into a stratified occupational system / by Allan P.O. Williams and Sally Woodward. — London (Basinghall St, EC2V 5AH) : Gresham College, c1981. — 27leaves : ill ; 30cm. — (Working paper / City University Business School, ISSN 0140-1041 ; no.34)
Unpriced (pbk) B82-16002

306'.36 — Organisations. Personnel. Careers — *Sociological perspectives*
Brown, Alan J.. The structure of career opportunities in organisations / Alan J. Brown. — Coventry : Centre for Industrial, Economic and Business Research, University of Warwick, 1981. — 47p ; 31cm. — (Discussion paper. General series / Centre for Industrial, Economic and Business Research, University of Warwick ; no.95)
Bibliography: p43-47
Unpriced (pbk) B82-21611

306'.36 — Overseas residence. Personal adjustment of personnel
Torbiörn, Ingemar. Living abroad : personal adjustment and personnel policy in the overseas setting / Ingemar Torbiörn. — Chichester : Wiley, c1982. — xi,187p : ill ; 24cm. — (Wiley series on studies in occupational stress)
Bibliography: p177-181. — Includes index
ISBN 0-471-10094-3 : £12.95 : CIP rev.
B82-13243

306'.36 — Scotland. Cotton manufacturing industries, *ca 1830*. **Social aspects** — *For schools*
Scottish Central Committee on Social Subjects. *History Working Party S1 and S2*. Living & working in a cotton town about 150 years ago / Scottish Central Committee on Social Subjects, History Working Party SI and SII. — [Glasgow] : [The Party]
Set C. — [1980?]. — 41p : ill ; 30cm
Cover title. — Bibliography: p7
Unpriced (pbk) B82-22850

Scottish Central Committee on Social Subjects. *History Working Party S1 and S2*. Living & working in a cotton town about 150 years ago / Scottish Central Committee on Social Subjects, History Working Party SI and SII. — [Glasgow] : [The Party]
Set D. — [1980?]. — 56p : ill,2maps ; 30cm
Cover title. — Bibliography: p10
Unpriced (pbk) B82-22849

Scottish Central Committee on Social Subjects. *History Working Party S1 and S2*. Living & working in a cotton town about 150 years ago / Scottish Central Committee on Social Subjects, History Working Party SI and SII. — [Glasgow] : [The Party]
Set A. — [1980?]. — 48p : ill,1map ; 30cm
Cover title. — Bibliography: p9
Unpriced (spiral) B82-22851

306'.36 — Unemployment. Personal adjustment of white-collar personnel
Fineman, Stephen. White collar unemployment. — Chichester : Wiley, Jan.1983. — [180]p. — (Wiley series on organisational change and development)
ISBN 0-471-10490-6 : £12.00 : CIP entry
B82-34620

306'.36 — United States. Labour market — *Sociological perspectives*
Sociological perspectives on labor markets / edited by Ivar Berg. — New York ; London : Academic Press, c1981. — xvii,374p : ill ; 24cm. — (Quantitative studies in social relations)
Includes bibliographies and index
ISBN 0-12-089650-8 : £20.60 B82-02067

306'.36 — United States. Society. Role of business firms
Partridge, Scott H.. Cases in business and society / Scott H. Partridge. — Englewood Cliffs ; London : Prentice-Hall, c1982. — xx,361p : ill,1map ; 24cm
ISBN 0-13-117606-4 (pbk) : £11.20
B82-16855

306'.36 — Work — *For children*
Working. — [London] : Save the Children Fund, 1981. — 31p : col.ill,1col.map ; 27cm. — (Round the world)
ISBN 0-333-30677-5 : £1.95 B82-07007

306'.36 — Work. Psychosocial aspects
The **Degradation** of work? : skill, deskilling and the labour process / edited by Stephen Wood. — London : Hutchinson, 1982. — 238p : ill ; 23cm
Bibliography: p213-229. — Includes index
ISBN 0-09-145400-x : £15.00 : CIP rev. B81-28841

306'.36 — Work. Social aspects
Work, workers and work organizations : a view from social work / edited by Sheila H. Akabas, Paul A. Kurzman. — Englewood Cliffs ; London : Prentice-Hall, c1982. — xiv,242p ; 24cm. — (Prentice-Hall series in social work practice)
Includes index
ISBN 0-13-965335-x : £14.20 B82-24088

306'.36 — Work — *Sociological perspectives*
Johns, Ruth I.. Work. — 2nd ed. — London (Henrietta House, 9 Henrietta Place, W1M 9AG) : Action Resource Centre, May 1982. — [13]p
Previous ed.: 1980
ISBN 0-946100-01-2 (unbound) : £2.50 : CIP entry B82-17899

306'.36 — Working life — *For schools*
Bennett, Olivia. Working life / Olivia Bennett. — London : Macmillan Education in association with the Save the Children Fund and the Commonwealth Institute, 1982. — 48p : col.ill ; 26cm. — (Patterns of living)
Text on lining papers. — Includes index
ISBN 0-333-31196-5 : Unpriced B82-33382

306'.36'05 — Work — *Sociological perspectives — Serials*
Research in the sociology of work : a research annual. — Vol.1 (1981)-. — Greenwich, Conn. : JAI Press ; London (3 Henrietta St., WC2E 8LU) : Distributed by JAICON Press, 1981-. — v. ; 24cm
£30.00 B82-02355

306'.36'0924 — Great Britain. Work — *Personal observations — For young people*
Merry, Robert. I started work / Robert Merry. — Cambridge : Basic Skills Unit, c1981. — 24p : ill,1port ; 21cm
Unpriced (pbk) B82-39001

306'.36'0941 — Work & leisure — *For schools*
O'Mara, Vincent. Work and leisure / Vincent O'Mara. — London : Batsford Academic and Educational, 1982. — 72p : ill ; 26cm. — (Living today)
Bibliography: p70. — Includes index
ISBN 0-7134-3576-3 : £5.95 B82-30753

306'.36'0973 — United States. Work. Social aspects
Varieties of work / Phyllis L. Stewart, Muriel G. Cantor, editors. — Beverly Hills ; London : Sage, c1982. — 308p ; 22cm
Bibliography: p279-300 . — Includes index
ISBN 0-8039-1813-5 (cased) : Unpriced
ISBN 0-8039-1814-3 (pbk) : £7.95 B82-38112

306'.362 — Slavery — *Anti-abolitionist viewpoints — Readings from contemporary sources*
The **Ideology** of slavery : proslavery thought in the Antebellum South, 1830-1860 / edited, with an introduction, by Drew Gilpin Faust. — Baton Rouge ; London : Louisiana State University Press, c1981. — x,306p ; 24cm. — (Library of Southern civilization)
Bibliography: p301-306
ISBN 0-8071-0855-3 (cased) : Unpriced
ISBN 0-8071-0892-8 (pbk) : £6.30 B82-15446

306'.362'094 — Europe. Slavery, *to 1500*
Dockés, Pierre. Medieval slavery and liberation / Pierre Dockés ; translated by Arthur Goldhammer. — London : Methuen, 1982. — vii,291p ; 24cm
Translation of: La liberation medievale. — Includes index
ISBN 0-416-33970-0 : Unpriced : CIP rev. B82-04052

306'.362'09469 — Portugal. Negro slavery, *1441-1555*
Saunders, A. C. de C. M.. A social history of black slaves and freedmen in Portugal 1441-1555 / A.C. De C.M. Saunders. — Cambridge : Cambridge University Press, 1982. — xviii,283p,[4]p of plates : ill,maps ; 24cm. — (Cambridge Iberian and Latin American studies)
Bibliography: p224-265. — Includes index
ISBN 0-521-23150-7 : £27.50 : CIP rev. B82-00236

306'.362'096 — Africa. Slavery, *to 1920*
The **Ideology** of slavery in Africa / Paul E. Lovejoy editor. — Beverly Hills ; London : Sage, c1981. — 311p : maps ; 22cm. — (Sage series on African modernization and development ; v.6)
Conference papers. — Includes bibliographies
ISBN 0-8039-1664-7 (cased) : Unpriced
ISBN 0-8039-1665-5 (pbk) : £7.50 B82-17084

306'.362'0966 — West Africa. Slavery — *For Caribbean students*
Halcrow, Elizabeth M.. Canes and chains : a study of sugar and slavery / Elizabeth M. Halcrow. — Kingston, [Jamaica] ; London : Heinemann, 1982. — viii,88p : ill,1map ; 22cm. — (Heinemann CXC history)
Bibliography: p87-88
ISBN 0-435-98223-0 (pbk) : £1.00 : CIP rev. B82-01954

306'.38 — England. Retirement. Planning
Coleman, Allin. Preparation for retirement in England and Wales. — Leicester : National Institute of Adult Education, Aug.1982. — [120]p
ISBN 0-900559-45-4 : £5.25 : CIP entry B82-26090

306'.38'0924 — United States. Retirement — *Personal observations*
Gresham, Perry E.. With wings as eagles / Perry E. Gresham. — South Yarmouth : Curley ; [Skipton] : Magna Print, [1981], c1980. — 275p ; 22cm
Originally published: Winter Park : Anna, 1980. — Published in large print
ISBN 0-89340-352-0 : Unpriced B82-05835

306'.38'0941 — Great Britain. Retirement
Curry, Jennifer. Enjoying retirement : getting the most from the rest of your life / Jennifer Curry. — Feltham : Hamlyn paperbacks, 1982. — 219p : ill ; 18cm
Bibliography: p217-218
ISBN 0-600-20550-9 (pbk) : £1.50 B82-36515

Parker, Stanley. Work and retirement / Stanley Parker. — London : Allen & Unwin, 1982. — 203p ; 23cm
Bibliography: p180-194. — Includes index
ISBN 0-04-658238-x (cased) : Unpriced : CIP rev.
ISBN 0-04-658239-8 (pbk) : £4.95 B82-15646

Towards a happier retirement. — London : New Opportunity Press, Jan.1983. — [180]p
ISBN 0-86263-044-4 (cased) : £9.95 : CIP entry
ISBN 0-86263-043-6 (pbk) : £4.25 B82-37645

306'.38'0941 — Great Britain. Retirement. Policies of government — *Forecasts — Conference proceedings*
Retirement policy : the next fifty years / edited by Michael Fogarty. — London : Heinemann, 1982. — viii,216p : ill ; 23cm. — (Joint studies in public policy ; 5)
Conference proceedings. — Includes index
ISBN 0-435-83320-0 (cased) : £14.00 : CIP rev.
ISBN 0-435-83321-9 (pbk) : £6.50 B82-12343

306'.38'0973 — United States. Retirement
Aging and retirement : prospects, planning, and policy / edited by Neil G. McCluskey, Edgar F. Borgatta. — Beverly Hills ; London : Sage, c1981. — 233p : ill ; 23cm. — (Sage focus editions ; 43)
Includes bibliographies and index
ISBN 0-8039-1756-2 (cased) : Unpriced
ISBN 0-8039-1757-0 (pbk) : £6.50 B82-24070

Economics of aging : the future of retirement / edited by Malcolm H. Morrison. — New York ; London : Van Nostrand Reinhold, c1982. — xxi,294p : ill ; 24cm
Includes index
ISBN 0-442-25553-5 : £20.40 B82-14303

306'.38'0973 — United States. Retirement — *Comparative studies*
Work and retirement : a longitudinal study of men / edited by Herbert S. Parnes with contributions by Gilbert Nestel ... [et al.]. — Cambridge, Mass. ; London : MIT Press, c1981. — xxi,293p : ill ; 24cm
Includes bibliographies and index
ISBN 0-262-16079-x : £21.00 B82-03917

306'.4 — Alcoholic drinks. Consumption. Social aspects
Economics and alcohol. — London : Croom Helm, Nov.1982. — [304]p
ISBN 0-7099-1132-7 : £14.95 : CIP entry B82-27935

306'.4 — Great Britain. Leisure. Social aspects
Roberts, Kenneth, *1940-*. Leisure / Kenneth Roberts. — 2nd ed. — London : Longman, 1981. — 140p ; 20cm. — (Aspects of modern sociology. The social structure of modern Britain)
Previous ed.: 1970. — Includes index
ISBN 0-582-29556-4 (pbk) : £3.95 : CIP rev. B81-31371

306'.4 — Leisure — *Sociological perspectives*
Jenkins, Clive. The leisure shock. — London : Eyre Methuen, Sept.1981. — [182]p
ISBN 0-413-48200-6 (cased) : £8.95 : CIP entry
ISBN 0-413-48210-3 (pbk) : £4.25 B81-23911

306'.4 — Magic — *Sociological perspectives*
O'Keefe, Daniel. Stolen lightning : the social theory of magic. — Oxford : Martin Robertson, Apr.1982. — [540]p
ISBN 0-85520-486-9 : £15.00 : CIP entry B82-09307

306'.4 — Nuclear power. Social aspects
Addinall, Eric. Nuclear power in perspective. — London : Kogan Page, Jan.1982. — [240]p
ISBN 0-85038-510-5 : £9.95 : CIP entry B81-40253

306'.4 — Nuclear power. Social aspects — *Conference proceedings — French texts*
Energie nucléaire et société. — Oxford : Pergamon, Oct.1981. — [310]p
Conference papers
ISBN 0-08-027077-8 (pbk) : £12.90 : CIP entry B81-31945

306'.4 — Science. Research. Social aspects
Brannigan, Augustine. The social basis of scientific discoveries / Augustine Brannigan. — Cambridge : Cambridge University Press, 1981. — xi,212p ; 24cm
Bibliography: p201-209. — Includes index
ISBN 0-521-23695-9 (cased) : £12.50 : CIP rev.
ISBN 0-521-28163-6 (pbk) : £4.95 B81-25817

306'.4 — Science. Social aspects
Ziman, John. Puzzles, problems and enigmas : occasional pieces on the human aspects of science / John Ziman. — Cambridge : Cambridge University Press, 1981. — ix,373p : ill ; 24cm
Includes index
ISBN 0-521-23659-2 : £12.50 : CIP rev. B81-31278

306'.4 — Science, *to 1979*. **Social aspects** — *Philosophical perspectives*
Lamb, D.. The philosophy of scientific development. — Amersham : Avebury, Dec.1981. — [240]p
ISBN 0-86127-104-1 (cased) : £12.00 : CIP entry
ISBN 0-86127-115-7 (pbk) : £6.95 B81-33882

306'.4 — United States. Society. Role of household objects. Psychological aspects

Csikszentmihalyi, Mihaly. The meaning of things : domestic symbols and the self / Mihaly Csikszentmihalyi and Eugene Rochberg-Halton. — Cambridge : Cambridge University Press, 1981. — xiv,304p ; 24cm
Bibliography: p290-297. — Includes index
ISBN 0-521-23919-2 (cased) : £20.00
ISBN 0-521-28774-x (pbk) : Unpriced
B82-07389

306'.42 — Knowledge — *Sociological perspectives*

The **Knowledge** cycle / edited by Robert F. Rich. — Beverly Hills ; London : Sage, c1981. — 222p ; 23cm. — (Sage focus editions ; 35)
Includes bibliographies and index
ISBN 0-8039-1686-8 (cased) : Unpriced
ISBN 0-8039-1687-6 (pbk) : Unpriced
B82-07906

306'.42 — Sociology. Structuralism

Structural sociology / edited by Ino Rossi. — New York ; Guildford : Columbia University Press, 1982. — xv,363p : ill ; 24cm
Includes bibligraphies and index
ISBN 0-231-04846-7 : £25.30 B82-28060

306'.45 — Alternative science — *Sociological perspectives*

Capra, Fritjof. The turning point : science, society, and the rising culture / Fritjof Capra. — London : Wildwood House, 1982. — 516p ; 23cm
Bibliography: p482-494. — Includes index
ISBN 0-7045-3054-6 : £9.50 : CIP rev.
B82-08421

306'.45 — Australia. Botany, *to ca 1980.* **Social aspects**

People and plants in Australia / edited by D.J. and S.G. M. Carr. — Sydney ; London : Academic Press, 1981. — xxi,416p : ill,maps,3facsims,ports ; 24cm
Includes index
ISBN 0-12-160720-8 (cased) : Unpriced
ISBN 0-12-160722-4 (pbk) : £12.60
B82-07551

Plants and man in Australia / edited by D.J. and S.G.M. Carr. — Sydney ; London : Academic Press, 1981. — xiv,313p : ill,2maps,2ports ; 24cm
Includes bibliographies and index
ISBN 0-12-160723-2 (cased) : Unpriced
ISBN 0-12-160724-0 (pbk) : £12.60
B82-07550

306'.45 — Biology. Social aspects, *1840-1940*

Biology, medicine and society 1840-1940 / edited by Charles Webster. — Cambridge : Cambridge University Press, 1981. — ix,344p : 1ill ; 23cm. — (Past and present publications)
Includes index
ISBN 0-521-23770-x : £22.50 : CIP rev.
Also classified at 610'.09'034 B81-30183

306'.45 — Great Britain. Statistical mathematics. Social aspects, *1865-1930*

MacKenzie, Donald A.. Statistics in Britain 1865-1930 : the social construction of scientific knowledge / Donald A. MacKenzie. — Edinburgh : Edinburgh University Press, 1981. — viii,306p : ill ; 23cm
Bibliography: p272-301. — Includes index
ISBN 0-85224-369-3 : £12.50 B82-26615

306'.45 — Medicine — *Sociological perspectives*

The **Problem** of medical knowledge. — Edinburgh : Edinburgh University Press, June 1982. — [200]p
ISBN 0-85224-417-7 : £12.00 : CIP entry
B82-14392

306'.45 — Molecular biology. Research. Social aspects

Holliday, Robin. The science of human progress / by Robin Holliday. — Oxford : Oxford University Press, 1980. — ix,121p ; 23cm
Includes index
ISBN 0-19-854711-0 : £6.95 B82-10203

306'.45 — Peninsular Malaysia. Selangor. Carey Island. Ma' Betisék. Beliefs. Special subjects: Organisms

Karim, Wazir-Jahan Begum. Ma' Betisék concepts of living things / by Wazir-Jahan Begum Karim. — London : Athlone Press, c1981. — xv,270p : ill,maps ; 23cm. — (London School of Economics monographs on social anthropology ; 54)
Bibliography: p265-268. — Includes index
ISBN 0-485-19554-2 : £16.00 : CIP rev.
B81-30560

306'.45 — Science & technology. Social aspects

A **Guide** to the culture of science, technology and medicine / general editor Paul T. Durbin. — New York : Free Press ; London : Collier Macmillan, c1980. — xl,723p ; 27cm
Includes bibliographies and index
ISBN 0-02-907820-2 : Unpriced B82-37369

306'.45 — Science. Research organisations — *Sociological perspectives*

Scientific establishments and hierarchies / edited by Norbert Elias, Herminio Martins and Richard Whitley. — Dordrecht ; London : Reidel, c1982. — 368p ; 23cm. — (Sociology of the sciences ; v.6)
Includes index
ISBN 90-277-1322-7 (cased) : Unpriced
ISBN 90-277-1323-5 (pbk) : Unpriced
B82-25207

306'.45 — Science. Research. Social aspects

. Scientific research and social goals. — Oxford : Pergamon, Apr.1982. — [250]p
ISBN 0-08-028118-4 : £17.50 : CIP entry
B82-11981

306'.45'0924 — Science. Sociological perspectives. Theories of Kuhn, Thomas S. — *Critical studies*

Barnes, Barry. T.S. Kuhn and social science / Barry Barnes. — London : Macmillan, 1982. — xiv,135p : ill ; 23cm. — (Theoretical traditions in the social sciences)
Bibliography: p127-131. — Includes index
ISBN 0-333-28936-6 (cased) : Unpriced
ISBN 0-333-28937-4 (pbk) B82-23369

306'.45'0941 — Great Britain. Science. Cultural aspects, *1780-1850*

Metropolis and province. — London : Hutchinson Education, Feb.1983. — [328]p
ISBN 0-09-145180-9 : £15.00 : CIP entry
B82-36454

306'.46 — Computer systems & telecommunication systems. Social aspects

Williams, Frederick, *1933-*. The communications revolution / Frederick Williams. — Beverly Hills ; London : Sage, c1982. — 291p : ill ; 23cm
Bibliography: p281-285. — Includes index
ISBN 0-8039-1782-1 (cased) : Unpriced
ISBN 0-8039-1783-x (pbk) : £7.95 B82-24072

306'.46 — Computer systems. Software. Social aspects

Baber, Robert Laurence. Software reflected : the socially responsible programming of our computers / Robert Laurence Baber. — Amsterdam ; Oxford : North-Holland, 1982. — ix,192p : ill,1map ; 23cm
Bibliography: p191-192
ISBN 0-444-86372-9 : £16.99 B82-28643

306'.46 — Medicine — *Sociological perspectives*

Eyles, John. The social geography of medicine and health. — London : Croom Helm, Jan.1983. — [256]p
ISBN 0-7099-0257-3 : £7.95 : CIP entry
B82-32546

Sociology as applied to medicine / the Sociology Teachers Group from London Medical Schools ; edited by Donald L. Patrick and Graham Scambler ; with a Foreword by Margot Jeffreys. — London : Baillière Tindall, 1982. — xiv,255p : ill ; 22cm. — (Concise medical textbooks)
Bibliography: p251. — Includes index
ISBN 0-7020-0899-0 (pbk) : £6.50 : CIP rev.
B81-35817

306'.46 — Microprocessor systems. Social aspects

Webster, Robin. Microprocessors today / Robin Webster. — Kingswood : Kaye & Ward, 1981, c1982. — 78p : ill,1facsim,ports ; 22cm. — (Today series)
Bibliography: p76. — Includes index
ISBN 0-7182-0463-8 : £4.95 B82-24440

306'.46 — Technological change. Social aspects

Norman, Colin, *1946-*. The god that limps : science and technology in the eighties / Colin Norman. — New York ; London : Norton, c1981. — 224p ; 22cm. — (A Worldwatch Institute book)
Includes index
ISBN 0-393-01504-1 : £10.50 B82-32729

306'.46 — Technological development. Social aspects

Aspects of the economic and social impact of new technology. — London : Polytechnic of Central London, School of Social Sciences and Business Studies, 1982. — 24p ; 30cm. — (Research working paper ; no.17)
Cover title. — Bibliography: p15. — Contents: Satellite business / Gareth Locksley — Can the unions survive the new technology? / Gareth Locksley & J.R. Shackleton
Unpriced (spiral) B82-29570

306'.46 — Technological innovation. Social aspects

Gosling, William. The kingdom of sand : essays to salute a world in process of being born / William Gosling. — London : Council for Educational Technology, 1981. — 98p : ill,1port ; 22cm. — (Occasional paper ; 9)
ISBN 0-86184-053-4 (pbk) : £4.50 : CIP rev.
B81-33633

306'.46 — Technology. Social aspects — *Forecasts*

Stephens, K. G.. Microelectronics and energy in the 1980s and beyond / K.G. Stephens. — [Guildford] ([Guildford, Surrey GU2 5XH]) : [University of Surrey], [1979?]. — 35p : ill ; 21cm. — (University of Surrey inaugural lecture)
Cover title. — Bibliography: p35
Unpriced (pbk) B82-26643

306'.46 — Technology. Social control

Collingridge, David. The social control of technology / David Collingridge. — London : Pinter, 1980 (1982 [printing]). — 200p : ill ; 23cm
Includes bibliographies and index
ISBN 0-903804-72-7 : £13.50 B82-39778

306'.46 — Telecommunication. Social aspects — *Forecasts — Conference proceedings*

Communications in the twenty-first century / edited by Robert W. Haigh, George Gerbner, Richard B. Byrne. — New York ; Chichester : Wiley, c1981. — xviii,240p : ill ; 24cm
Conference papers. — Bibliography: p223-225. — Includes index
ISBN 0-471-09910-4 : £14.00 B82-14151

306'.47 — Arts — *Sociological perspectives*

Hauser, Arnold. The sociology of art / Arnold Hauser ; translated by Kenneth J. Northcott. — London : Routledge & Kegan Paul, 1982. — xxi,776p ; 24cm
Translation of: Soziologie der Kunst
ISBN 0-7100-9231-8 : £19.95 B82-38432

306'.47'05 — Arts — *Sociological perspectives — Serials*

Research in sociology of knowledge, sciences and art : a research annual. — Vol.1 (1978)-. — Greenwich, Conn. : JAI Press ; London (3 Henrietta St., WC2E 8LU) : Distributed by JAICON Press, 1978-. — v. : ill ; 24cm
Description based on : Vol.2 (1979)
ISSN 0163-0180 = Research in sociology of knowledge, sciences and art : £22.85
B82-02342

306'.48 — England. Working classes. Leisure activities, *1590-1914*

Popular culture and class conflict 1590-1914 : explorations in the history of labour and leisure / edited by Eileen Yeo and Stephen Yeo. — Brighton : Harvester, 1981. — xii,315p ; 24cm
Includes index
ISBN 0-85527-123-x : £25.00 B82-00030

306'.48 — Scotland. Canals: Edinburgh and Glasgow Union Canal. Recreational use. Projects, *1979-1981*

Union Canal : report of a two year project 1979-81 / sponsors: Countryside Commission for Scotland and Lothian Regional Council, Central Regional Council. — [Perth] : [Countryside Commission for Scotland], [1981?]. — 24p : ill,facsims,maps ; 30cm
Facsims on inside covers. — Bibliography: p22
ISBN 0-902226-55-x (pbk) : Unpriced
B82-31333

306'.48 — Vacations — *Serials*

Holidays & holiday homes : the informative holiday magazine. — Vol.1, no.1 (1979)-. — London (100 Fleet St., E.C.4) : Holidays and Holiday Homes Pub. Co., 1979-. — v. : ill (some col.),maps,ports ; 30cm
Six issues yearly. — Description based on: Vol.3, no.3 (Apr./May 1982)
ISSN 0263-6638 = Holidays & holiday homes : £8.50 per year B82-28879

306'.48'05 — Leisure, recreation & tourism — *Serials*

Leisure studies : the journal of the Leisure Studies Association. — Vol.1, no.1 (Jan. 1982)-. — London : E. & F.N. Spon, 1982-. v. ; 24cm
Three issues yearly
ISSN 0261-4367 = Leisure studies : £25.00 per year B82-30476

306'.48'0723 — Leisure activities. Surveys — *Manuals*

Recreation site survey manual. — London : Chapman and Hall, Dec.1982. — [150]p
ISBN 0-419-12680-5 (pbk) : £15.00 : CIP entry
B82-29774

306'.48'088054 — London. Hammersmith and Fulham *(London Borough).* **Aconmore & Coningham. Young persons, to 19 years. Leisure activities**

Noble, Paul. Recreational needs : a survey of children and young people. — [London] ([Town Hall, King St., Hammersmith, W6 9JU]) : Hammersmith & Fulham, 1981. — [72]p : maps ; 30cm. — (Research report ; 50)
Written by Paul Noble and Sue Williams
Unpriced (pbk) B82-06132

306'.48'0880544 — California. Oakland. Children, 11-12 years. Leisure activities — *Sociological perspectives*

The **Serious** business of growing up : a study of children's lives outside school / Elliot A. Medrich ... [et al.]. — Berkeley ; London : University of California Press, c1982. — xvii,402p : forms ; 24cm
Includes index
ISBN 0-520-04296-4 : £17.50 B82-31177

306'.48'088055 — Great Britain. Adolescents. Leisure activities

Hendry, L. B.. Growing up and going out. — Aberdeen : Aberdeen University Press, Jan.1983. — [192]p
ISBN 0-08-025768-2 (cased) : £9.00 : CIP entry
ISBN 0-08-025769-0 (pbk) : £5.00 B82-33628

306'.48'0941 — Great Britain. Leisure activities

Purves, Libby. Britain at play. — London : Robson, Oct.1982. — [208]p
ISBN 0-86051-192-8 : £6.50 : CIP entry
B82-24142

306'.48'094288 — Northumberland. National parks: Northumberland National Park. Visitors, *1980* — *Statistics*

The **1980** visitor surveys. — Hexham : Northumberland National Park & Countryside Committee, 1981. — 62p,[10]p of plates : ill,maps ; 30cm. — (Occasional paper ; no.4)
ISBN 0-907632-04-1 (spiral) : Unpriced
B82-14037

306'.48'0973 — Leisure. Social aspects — *Study regions: United States*

Stebbins, Robert A.. Amateurs : on the margin between work and leisure / Robert A. Stebbins ; foreword by Max Kaplan. — Beverly Hills ; London : Sage, c1979. — 280p ; 23cm. — (Sociological observations ; 6)
Bibliography: p273-277
ISBN 0-8039-1200-5 (cased) : £15.50
ISBN 0-8039-1201-3 (pbk) : Unpriced
B82-38158

306'.48'0973 — United States. Leisure & recreation

Kelly, John R.. Leisure / John R. Kelly. — Englewood Cliffs ; London : Prentice-Hall, c1982. — vi,426p : ill ; 25cm
Includes bibliographies and index
ISBN 0-13-530055-x : £14.20 B82-16712

306'.482 — United States. Poker. Social aspects

Hayano, David M.. Poker faces : the life and work of professional card players / David M. Hayano. — Berkeley ; London : University of California Press, c1982. — xii,205p : 1plan ; 24cm
Bibliography: p189-200. — Includes index
ISBN 0-520-04492-4 : £13.50 B82-34356

306'.483'088042 — Sportswomen. Social aspects — *Conference proceedings*

International Congress on Women and Sport *(1980 : Rome).* The female athlete : a socio-psychological and kinanthropometric approach : selected papers of the International Congress on Women and Sport, Rome, Italy, July 4-8, 1980 / volume editors J. Borms, M. Hebbelinck and A. Venerando. — Basel ; London : Karger, c1981. — xiii,218p : ill ; 25cm. — (Medicine and sport ; v.15)
Includes bibliographies and index
ISBN 3-8055-2739-x : £36.00
Primary classification 573'.6 B82-21666

306'.483'0968 — South Africa. Sports. Racial aspects

Archer, Robert. The South African game : sport and racism in South Africa. — London : Zed Press, June 1982. — [368]p
ISBN 0-86232-066-6 (cased) : £18.95 : CIP entry
ISBN 0-86232-082-8 (pbk) : £5.95 B82-14929

306'.483'0973 — United States. Sports — *Sociological perspectives*

Coakley, Jay J.. Sport in society : issues and controversies / Jay J. Coakley. — 2nd ed. — St. Louis ; London : Mosby, 1982. — ix,335p : ill ; 24cm
Previous ed.: 1978. — Bibliography: p292-317. — Includes index
ISBN 0-8016-1119-9 (pbk) : £10.00
B82-31877

306'.484 — Oxfordshire. Adderbury region. Folk songs in English. Singing, *1800-1900.* **Social aspects**

Pickering, Michael. Village song & culture : a study based on the Blunt collection of song from Adderbury North Oxfordshire / Michael Pickering. — London : Croom Helm, c1982. — 187p ; 22cm
Bibliography: p182-184. — Includes index
ISBN 0-7099-0059-7 : £12.50 B82-16117

306'.488 — Reading. Learning by man. Sociocultural factors

Finn, Patrick J.. Failure in learning to read : the impact of social and cultural factors on learning to read : a talk / by Patrick J. Finn. — Edinburgh : W.E.A. South East Scotland, [1980]. — 18p : ill ; 21cm. — (A WEASES publication)
Text on inside cover. — Bibliography: p18
ISBN 0-902303-01-5 (pbk) : £0.50 B82-09747

306'.6 — Ancient Israel. Prophets. Role — *Sociological perspectives*

Petersen, David L.. The roles of Israel's prophets / David L. Petersen. — Sheffield : JSOT, c1981. — 131p ; 23cm. — (Journal for the study of the Old Testament supplement series, ISSN 0309-0787 ; 17)
Bibliography: p120-124. — Includes index
ISBN 0-905774-32-9 (cased) : Unpriced : CIP rev.
ISBN 0-905774-34-5 (pbk) : Unpriced
B81-21594

306'.6 — East Sussex. Eastbourne. Christian life. Social aspects, *1735-1920*

Neville, Graham. Religion and society in Eastbourne 1735-1920 / Graham Neville. — Eastbourne (c/o Harold Spears, 30 East Dean Rd, Eastbourne, BN20 8EE) : Eastbourne Local History Society, 1982. — 32p : ill,ports ; 21cm
Bibliography: p30
Unpriced (pbk) B82-22325

306'.6 — Islam. Social aspects — *Early works*

Ibn Taymiya, al-Shaykh al-Iman Abdul Abbas Ahmad. [al-Risāla fi 'l-hisba. English]. Public duties in Islam. — Leicester (223 London Rd, Leicester LE2 1ZE) : Islamic Foundation, Mar.1982. — [112]p. — (Islamic economic series ; no.3)
Translation of: al-Risāla fi 'l-hisba
ISBN 0-86037-114-x (cased) : £4.95 : CIP entry
ISBN 0-86037-113-1 (pbk) : £2.25 B82-06055

306'.6 — Madagascar. Mayotte. Inhabitants. Trances. Cultural aspects

Lambek, Michael. Human spirits : a cultural account of trance in Mayotte / Michael Lambek. — Cambridge : Cambridge University Press, 1981. — xix,219p : ill,1map ; 24cm. — (Cambridge studies in cultural systems ; 6)
Bibliography: p208-212. — Includes index
ISBN 0-521-23844-7 (cased) : £17.50
ISBN 0-521-28255-1 (pbk) : Unpriced
B82-13751

306'.6 — Morocco. Islam. Social aspects — *Study regions: Boujad*

Eickelman, Dale F.. Moroccan Islam : tradition and society in a pilgrimage centre / by Dale F. Eickelman. — Austin ; London : University of Texas Press, 1976 (1981 printing). — xvi,303p : ill,1map,1geneal.table ; 23cm. — (Modern Middle East series ; no.1)
Bibliography: p287-296. — Includes index
ISBN 0-292-75062-5 : £6.65 B82-05728

306'.6 — North Yorkshire. Staithes. Religious life. Social aspects, *1975-1976*

Clark, David, *1953-*. Between pulpit and pew : folk religion in a North Yorkshire fishing village / David Clark. — Cambridge : Cambridge University Press, 1982. — xii,186p : ill,maps ; 24cm
Bibliography: p175-183. — Includes index
ISBN 0-521-24071-9 : £13.50 : CIP rev.
B82-12695

306'.6 — Primitive religions — *Anthropological perspectives*

Ferguson, John, *1921-*. Gods many and lords many : a study in primal religions / by John Ferguson. — Guildford : Lutterworth Educational, 1982. — vii,118p : ill ; 21cm
Bibliography: p115-118. — Includes index
ISBN 0-7188-2496-2 (pbk) : £4.95 B82-19785

Gill, Sam D.. Beyond "the primitive" : the religions of nonliterate peoples / Sam D. Gill. — Englewood Cliffs ; London : Prentice-Hall, c1982. — xvii,120p ; 23cm. — (Prentice-Hall series in world religions)
Bibliography: p113-116. — Includes index
ISBN 0-13-076034-x (pbk) : £5.95 B82-16703

306'.6 — Religion — *Sociological perspectives*

Wilson, Bryan R.. Religion in sociological perspective / Bryan Wilson. — Oxford : Oxford University Press, 1982. — vii,187p ; 22cm
Includes index
ISBN 0-19-826663-4 (cased) : £8.50 : CIP rev.
ISBN 0-19-826664-2 (pbk) : Unpriced
B81-34380

306'.6 — Secularisation — *Sociological perspectives*

Berger, Peter L.. Modernisation and religion / P.L. Berger. — Dublin : Economic and Social Research Institute, c1981. — 20p ; 21cm. — (Fourteenth Geary Lecture, 1981)
ISBN 0-7070-0046-7 (pbk) : £2.00 B82-19476

306′.6 — United States. Catholic Church. Religious orders for women — *Sociological perspectives*

Ebaugh, Helen Rose Fuchs. Out of the cloister : a study of organizational dilemmas / Helen Rose Fuchs Ebaugh. — Austin ; London : University of Texas Press, c1977. — xxii,155p : 2ill,forms ; 24cm
Bibliography: p149-155
ISBN 0-292-76007-8 : £9.35 B82-35392

306′.6 — Western culture. Secularisation — *Islamic viewpoints*

Nasr, Seyyed Hossein. Knowledge and the sacred : the Gifford lectures 1981 / Seyyed Hossein Nasr. — Edinburgh : Edinburgh University Press, c1981. — ix,341p ; 24cm
Includes index
ISBN 0-85224-433-9 : £11.00 B82-18341

306′.6′088042 — Religion. Role of women

Women′s religious experience. — Beckenham : Croom Helm, Jan.1983. — [224]p
ISBN 0-7099-1232-3 (cased) : £13.95 : CIP entry
ISBN 0-7099-1239-0 (pbk) : £9.95 B82-36148

306′.6′0937 — Ancient Rome. Society. Role of religion, *to ca 395*

Wardman, Alan. Religion and statecraft among the Romans. — London : Granada, Sept.1982. — [340]p
ISBN 0-246-11743-5 : £12.50 : CIP entry B82-18859

306.7 — Celebrities. Sex relations

Elson, Howard. The superstuds / Howard Elson. — London : Sphere, 1982, c1980. — 120p : ports ; 17cm
Originally published: London : Proteus, 1980
ISBN 0-7221-3289-1 : £1.75 B82-24633

306.7 — Cohabiting persons. Interpersonal relationships — *Manuals*

Sager, Clifford J.. Intimate partners : hidden patterns in love relationships / Clifford J. Sager and Bernice Hunt. — New York ; London : McGraw-Hill, c1979 (1981 [printing]). — vii,194p ; 21cm. — (McGraw-Hill paperbacks)
ISBN 0-07-054428-x (pbk) : £3.50 B82-02331

306.7 — Great Britain. Young persons. Courtship — *Study regions: West Glamorgan. Swansea — Sociological perspectives*

Leonard, Diana. Sex and generation : a study of courtship and weddings. — London : Tavistock, Apr.1982. — [320]p. — (Social science paperbacks)
Originally published: 1980
ISBN 0-422-78220-3 (pbk) : £5.50 : CIP entry B82-04061
Also classified at 392′.5′0942982

306.7 — Sex relations

Beers, Laura. Physical love / [Laura Beers] ; [editor Brenda Marshall]. — London : Marshall Cavendish, c1979. — 80p : ill(some col.) ; 28cm. — (Your body)
Includes index
ISBN 0-85685-353-4 (pbk) : £0.99 B82-37310

Francoeur, Robert T.. Becoming a sexual person / Robert T. Francoeur. — New York ; Chichester : Wiley, c1982. — xx,752,[62]p : ill (some col.),1col.map,facsims,ports ; 24cm
Bibliography: p[1]-[20]. — Includes index
ISBN 0-471-07848-4 : £15.50 B82-27702

Gerber, Albert B.. The book of sex lists / compiled by Albert B. Gerber. — London : W.H. Allen, 1982, c1981. — 256p ; 16cm. — (A star book)
Originally published: Secaucus, N.J. : L. Stuart, 1981
ISBN 0-352-31152-5 (pbk) : £1.95 B82-39017

Meeks, Linda Brower. Human sexuality : making responsible decisions / Linda Meeks, Philip Heit ; illustrated by James C. Bower. — Philadelphia : Saunders College, c1982. — xx,503p : ill(some col.),ports ; 25cm
Includes bibliographies and index
ISBN 0-03-058366-7 : £13.50 B82-16905

Phillips, Debora. Sexual confidence / Debora Phillips with Robert Judd. — London : Futura, 1982, c1980. — x,227p ; 18cm
Originally published: Boston : Houghton Mifflin, 1980. — Includes index
ISBN 0-7088-2185-5 (pbk) : £1.75 B82-24096

Tiefer, Leonore. Human sexuality : feelings and functions / Leonore Tiefer. — London : Harper & Row, c1979. — 128p : ill(some col.) ; 24cm. — (The Life cycle series)
Includes index
ISBN 0-06-318111-8 (cased) : Unpriced
ISBN 0-06-318112-6 (pbk) : £2.50 B82-22206

306.7 — Sex relations — *For children*

Pickering, Lucienne. Boys talk / Lucienne Pickering. — London : Chapman, 1981. — 93p : ill ; 21cm
ISBN 0-225-66309-0 (pbk) : Unpriced : CIP rev. B81-20123

Pickering, Lucienne. Girls talk / Lucienne Pickering. — London : Chapman, 1981. — 92p : ill ; 21cm
ISBN 0-225-66310-4 (pbk) : Unpriced : CIP rev. B81-20122

306.7 — Sex relations. Implications of body types

Harris, Anthony, *1937-*. Love bodies / Anthony Harris. — London : Arrow, 1982. — 175p ; 18cm
ISBN 0-09-927880-4 (pbk) : £1.50 B82-21782

306.7 — United States. Adolescent girls. Sexual intercourse & pregnancy. Social aspects

Zelnik, Melvin. Sex and pregnancy in adolescence / Melvin Zelnik, John F. Kantner, Kathleen Ford. — Beverly Hills ; London : Sage, c1981. — 272p : ill ; 22cm. — (Sage library of social research ; v.133)
Bibliography: p265-269
ISBN 0-8039-1733-3 (cased) : Unpriced
ISBN 0-8039-1734-1 (pbk) : £6.50 B82-17085

306.7 — Western world. Sex. Attitudes of children, 5 to 15 years — *Comparative studies*

Goldman, Ronald. Children′s sexual thinking : a comparative study of children aged 5 to 15 years in Australia, North America, Britain and Sweden / Ronald and Juliette Goldman. — London : Routledge & Kegan Paul, 1982. — xviii,485p : ill ; 23cm
Bibliography: p451-470. — Includes index
ISBN 0-7100-0883-x : £11.95 B82-23257

306.7′0207 — Sex relations — *Humour*

Once a week is ample : being quotations compiled by Gerard Macdonald from the most respected sources of advice to the male and female, written with delicacy and refinement. — London : Hutchinson, 1981. — 61p : ill ; 20cm
Bibliography: p7-8
ISBN 0-09-146500-1 : £2.50 : CIP rev. B81-26797

Parker, Cliff. How to avoid sex. — London : New English Library, Nov.1982. — [144]p
ISBN 0-450-05519-1 (pbk) : £1.50 : CIP entry B82-27528

Vernon, Edward. Aphrodisiacs. — London : Severn House, Oct.1982. — [96]p
ISBN 0-7278-3004-x : £4.95 : CIP entry B82-24248

306.7′024042 — Sex relations — *For women*

Penney, Alexandra. How to make love to a man / by Alexandra Penney ; special consultant Norman F. Stevens Jr. — London : Macmillan, 1982, c1981. — 143p ; 20cm
Originally published: New York : C.N. Potter, 1981
ISBN 0-333-33519-8 (pbk) : £1.95 B82-32378

306.7′05 — Sex relations — *Serials*

Escort. — Vol.1, no.1-. — London (2 Archer St., W1V 7HE) : Paul Raymond Publications, [1981?]-. — v. : ill(chiefly col.) ; 30cm
Monthly. — Description based on: Vol.1, no.7
£0.65 per issue B82-01067

Silk swingers. — Vol.2, no.5 (Nov./Dec.)-. — [London] ([P.O. Box 128, SE1 8QL]) : [Kentfern Ltd.], [1981]-. — v. : ill ; 21cm
Six issues yearly. — Merger of: Silk ; and, Experience swingers
£12.00 per year B82-09063

306.7′088042 — United States. Women. Sex relations

Hite, Shere. The Hite report : a nationwide study of female sexuality / Shere Hite. — London : Corgi, 1981, c1976. — 633p ; 18cm
Originally published: New York : Macmillan, 1976 ; London : Collier Macmillan, 1977
ISBN 0-552-11829-x (pbk) : £1.95 B82-04179

Wolfe, Linda. The Cosmo report / Linda Wolfe. — London : Corgi, 1982, c1981. — 432p ; 18cm
Originally published: New York : Arbor House, 1981. — Includes index
ISBN 0-552-12015-4 (pbk) : £1.95 B82-40193

306.7′088042 — Women. Sex relations — *Feminist viewpoints*

Meulenbelt, Anja. For ourselves : from women′s point of view : our bodies and sexuality / text Anja Meulenbelt, Johanna′s daughter ; interviews Ariane Amsberg ; drawings Jolet Leenhouts ; photographs Sjan Bijman ... [et al.] ; ... English translation Ann Oosthuizen with help from Marij van Helmond ; English edition edited by Jill Nicholls with help from Tina Reid. — London : Sheba Feminist, 1981. — 255p : ill ; 22cm
Translation of: Voor onszelf. — Includes bibliographies
ISBN 0-907179-01-0 (pbk) : £4.50 B82-06083

306.7′088042 — Women. Sex relations — *Humour*

Tickle my fancy and colour me pink. — London : Virago, Nov.1982. — [48]p
ISBN 0-86068-334-6 (pbk) : £1.95 : CIP entry B82-26349

306.7′088042 — Women. Sexuality. Effects of masochism — *Feminist viewpoints*

Marcus, Maria. A taste for pain : on masochism and female sexuality / by Maria Marcus ; translated from the Danish by Joan Tate. — London : Souvenir Press, 1981. — 267p ; 22cm. — (A Condor book)
Translation of: Den frygtelige sandhed, en brugsbog om kvinder og masokisme
ISBN 0-285-62497-0 (cased) : £8.95
ISBN 0-285-64956-6 (pbk) : £5.95 B82-01938

306.7′088055 — Adolescents. Sex relations

Stoppard, Miriam. Talking sex. — London : Gollancz, Sept.1982. — [128]p
ISBN 0-575-03150-6 : £4.95 : CIP entry B82-18759

306.7′0880565 — Old persons. Sex relations — *For medicine*

Croft, Lesley Hoyt. Sexuality in later life : a counseling guide for physicians / Lesley Hoyt Croft. — Boston, Mass. ; Bristol : Wright, 1982. — vi,197p : ill ; 23cm
Includes bibliographies and index
ISBN 0-7236-7002-1 (pbk) : Unpriced : CIP rev. B81-34778

306.7′0880816 — Physically handicapped persons. Sex relations

Sexuality and physical disability : personal perspectives / edited by David G. Bullard, Susan E. Knight. — St. Louis ; London : Mosby, 1981. — xv,318p : ill ; 24cm
Bibliography: p310-312. — Includes index
ISBN 0-8016-0861-9 (pbk) : £13.00 B82-08259

306.7′09181′2 — Western world. Sex relations. Attitudes of society

Haddon, Celia. The limits of sex / Celia Haddon. — London : Joseph, 1982. — 202p ; 23cm
Bibliography: p189-200. — Includes index
ISBN 0-7181-2079-5 : £7.95 B82-13711

306.7′09181′2 — Western world. Sex relations, ***to 1980***
Gathorne-Hardy, Jonathan. Love, sex, marriage and divorce / Jonathan Gathorne-Hardy. — London : Cape, 1981. — 384p ; 23cm
Includes index
ISBN 0-224-01602-4 : £8.50 : CIP rev. B81-27340

306.7′092′4 — Sex relations. Research. Kinsey, A. C.
Pomeroy, Wardell B.. Dr Kinsey and the Institute for Sex Research. — 2nd ed. — London : Yale University Press, Oct.1982. — [480]p
Previous ed.: New York : Harper & Row, 1972 ; London : Nelson, 1972
ISBN 0-300-02916-0 (cased) : £23.00 : CIP entry
ISBN 0-300-02801-6 (pbk) : £7.95 B82-36130

306.7′0941 — Great Britain. Sex relations. Attitudes of society, ***1837-1979***
Weeks, Jeffrey. Sex, politics and society : the regulation of sexuality since 1800 / Jeffrey Weeks. — London : Longman, 1981. — xiii,306p ; 23cm. — (Themes in British social history)
Includes index
ISBN 0-582-48333-6 (cased) : £11.00
ISBN 0-582-48334-4 (pbk) : Unpriced B82-03219

306.7′0954 — India. Sex relations
Kokkoka. The Koka Shastra. — London : Allen & Unwin, Nov.1982. — [176]p
Translated from the Sanskrit
ISBN 0-04-891050-3 (pbk) : £1.95 : CIP entry B82-27826

306.7′0954 — India. Sex relations — ***Early works***
Vatsyayana. The Kama Sutra of Vatsyayana / translated by Sir Richard Burton and F. F. Arbuthnot ; edited with a preface by W.G. Archer ; introduction by K.M. Panikkar. — London : Unwin Paperbacks, 1981. — 295p ; 20cm
Translated from the Sanskrit. — Originally published: Benares : Kama Shastra Society of London and Benares, 1883. — Bibliography: p79
ISBN 0-04-891049-x (cased) : Unpriced : CIP rev.
ISBN 0-04-891048-1 (pbk) : £1.95 B81-09492

306.7′37′01 — Illegitimacy — ***Philosophical perspectives***
Teichman, Jenny. Illegitimacy : a philosophical examination / Jenny Teichman. — Oxford : Blackwell, 1982. — 200p ; 23cm
Includes index
ISBN 0-631-12807-7 : £12.00 : CIP rev. B81-34295

306.7′42′02542132 — London. Covent Garden. Prostitutes, ***1793 — Directories — Facsimiles***
Harris′s list of Covent Garden ladies, or, Men of pleasure′s kalender for the year 1793. — Edinburgh : Harris, 1982. — viii,106p ; 18cm
Facsim of: ed. published London : Ranger, 1793
ISBN 0-86228-040-0 : Unpriced : CIP rev. B81-39214

306.7′6 — Great Britain. Paedophilia
Paedophilia and public morals. — London (BM 1151, WC1V 6XX) : Campaign Against Public Morals, [1980?]. — 58p : ill,facsims,ports ; 21cm
£0.95 (pbk) B82-24654

306.7′6 — Society. Role of homosexuals — ***Marxist viewpoints***
Fernbach, David. The spiral path : a gay contribution to human survival / David Fernbach. — Boston : Alyson ; London : Gay Men′s Press, 1981. — 236p ; 20cm
ISBN 0-907040-07-1 (pbk) : £3.75 : CIP rev. B81-09465

306.7′6′0942 — England. Homosexuality, ***1550-1600***
Bray, Alan. Homosexuality in Renaissance England. — London (Priory Ave., N8 7RN) : Gay Men′s Press, Apr.1982. — [152]p
ISBN 0-907040-13-6 (pbk) : £2.95 : CIP entry B82-05787

306.7′66′024362 — Homosexuality — ***For counselling***
Moses, A. Elfin. Counseling lesbian women and gay men : a life-issues approach / A. Elfin Moses, Robert O. Hawkins, Jr. — St. Louis ; London : Mosby, 1982. — xv,263p : 2ports ; 24cm
Bibliography: p231-252. — Includes index
ISBN 0-8016-3563-2 (pbk) : £9.75 B82-16565

306.7′66′09421 — London. Homosexuals
Building the London gay community / London Gay Workshops Collective. — London (5 Caledonian Rd., N.1) : The Collective, 1982. — 32p : ill ; 21cm
Text on inside cover
£0.50 (pbk) B82-31410

306.7′66′0973 — United States. Homosexuals
White, Edmund. States of desire : travels in gay America / Edmund White. — London : Deutsch, 1980. — xi,336p ; 22cm
ISBN 0-233-97301-x : £5.95 B82-31265

306.7′662′01 — Male homosexuality. Theories, ***ca 1860-1980***
Dannecker, Martin. Theories of homosexuality / Martin Dannecker. — London : Gay Men′s Press, 1981. — 123p ; 19cm
Translation of: Der Homosexuelle und die Homosexualität
ISBN 0-907040-05-5 (pbk) : £1.95 : CIP rev. B81-26701

306.7′662′05 — Male homosexuality — ***Serials***
Capital gay / a weekly newspaper published by gay men. — June 26 1981-. — [London] ([38 Mount Pleasant, WC1X 0AP]) : [Capital Gay], 1981-. — v. : ill,ports ; 37cm
£0.20 per issue B82-40048

306.7′662′088055 — Homosexual male adolescents. Sexual intercourse. Age of consent — ***Homosexual viewpoints***
The Age taboo : gay male sexuality, power and consent / Daniel Tsang, editor. — Boston : Alyson ; London : Gay Men′s Press, 1981. — 178p ; 22cm
Bibliography: p167-173. — Includes index
ISBN 0-907040-11-x (pbk) : £3.25 B82-15081

306.7′662′0973 — United States. Male homosexual movements — ***Interviews***
Praunheim, Rosa von. Army of lovers / Rosa von Praunheim. — London : Gay Men′s Press, 1980. — 207p : ill ; 20cm
Translation of: Armee der Liebenden
ISBN 0-907040-00-4 (pbk) : £3.95 : CIP rev. B80-06297

306.7′663 — Lesbian mothers
Hanscombe, Gillian E.. Rocking the cradle : lesbian mothers : a challenge in family living / Gillian E. Hanscombe and Jackie Forster. — London : Sheba, 1982. — 172p ; 21cm
Originally published: London : Owen, 1981. — Bibliography: p170-172. — Includes index
ISBN 0-907179-13-4 (pbk) : Unpriced B82-31697

306.7′663′0880692 — United States. Detention institutions. Lesbianism — ***Case studies***
Propper, Alice M.. Prison homosexuality : myth and reality / Alice M. Propper. — Lexington, Mass. : Lexington Books, c1981 ; [Aldershot] : Gower [distributor], 1982. — xi,237p : ill ; 24cm
Bibliography: p207-227. — Includes index
ISBN 0-669-03628-5 : £17.50 B82-21169

306.7′7′0924 — Great Britain. Transvestism. Pepper, John — ***Biographies***
Pepper, John. A man′s tale. — London : Quartet Books, May 1982. — [192]p
ISBN 0-7043-2326-5 : £6.95 : CIP entry B82-13494

306.7′75 — Flagellomania — ***Serials***
[Janus ***(London)*****]**. Janus. — [No.9?]-. — London (40 Old Compton St., W1) : Gatisle, 1982-. — v. : ill(some col.) ; 29cm
Continues: New Janus. — Description based on: No.9
£3.00 B82-15776

New Janus. — [No.1?]-. — Liverpool (53 Queen Victoria St., Liverpool) : Misline Ltd. ; [London] ([40 Old Compton St., W1]) : [Gatisle Ltd.] [distributor], [1981]-[1982?]. — 8v. : ill(some col.) ; 29cm
Monthly. — Continued by: Janus (London). — Description based on: No.5
£3.00 per issue B82-08459

306.7′77 — Father-daughter incest
Herman, Judith Lewis. Father-daughter incest / Judith Lewis Herman with Lisa Hirschman. — Cambridge, Mass. ; London : Harvard University Press, 1981. — xi,282p ; 25cm
Includes index
ISBN 0-674-29505-6 : £11.20 B82-03920

306.7′77 — Incest
Goodwin, Jean. Sexual abuse : incest victims and their families / Jean Goodwin with contributions. — Boston [Mass.] ; Bristol : John Wright, 1982. — xii,209p ; 24cm
Includes index
ISBN 0-7236-7012-9 : Unpriced : CIP rev. B82-00362

Renvoize, Jean. Incest : a family pattern / Jean Renvoize. — London : Routledge & Kegan Paul, 1982. — viii,224p ; 23cm
Bibliography : p217-220. — Includes index
ISBN 0-7100-9073-0 : £7.95 : CIP rev. B82-01726

306.8 — Families — ***For children***
Families. — [London] : Save the Children Fund, 1981. — 31p : col.ill,1col.map ; 27cm. — (Round the world)
ISBN 0-333-30675-9 : £1.95 B82-07005

306.8 — Families - ***Sociological perspectives***
Rediscovery of the family and other lectures. — Aberdeen : Aberdeen University Press, Aug.1981. — [112]p. — (Sister Marie Hilda memorial lectures 1954-1973)
ISBN 0-08-025754-2 (pbk) : £5.00 : CIP entry B81-15807

306.8 — Marriage
Mackay, Dougal. Marriage does matter. — Loughton : Piatkus, Jan.1982. — [256]p
ISBN 0-86188-123-0 : £6.95 : CIP entry B81-33759

306.8 — Marriage. Attitudes of homosexuals
Maddox, Brenda. The marrying kind : homosexuality and marriage. — London : Granada, Apr.1982. — [256]p
ISBN 0-246-11189-5 : £7.95 : CIP entry B82-04316

306.8′0941 — Great Britain. Families, ***1900-1939 — Sociological perspectives***
Gittins, Diana. Social change and the family structure. — London : Hutchinson Education, Feb.1982. — [256]p
ISBN 0-09-145490-5 (cased) : £12.00 : CIP entry
ISBN 0-09-145491-3 (pbk) : £5.95 B81-35948

306.8′0941 — Great Britain. Marriage, ***1100-1980.*** **Social aspects**
Marriage and society : studies in the social history of marriage / edited by R.B. Outhwaite. — London : Europa, c1981. — viii,284p : ill ; 24cm. — (Europa social history of human experience)
Includes index
ISBN 0-905118-62-6 : £19.50 : CIP rev. B81-27389

306.8′1 — Marriage
Bernard, Jessie. The future of marriage. — 2nd ed. — London : Yale University Press, Nov.1982. — [384]p
Previous ed.: New York : World, 1972
ISBN 0-300-02912-8 (cased) : £19.50 : CIP entry
ISBN 0-300-02853-9 (pbk) : £6.95 B82-40330

Eysenck, H. J.. I do : your guide to a happy marriage. — London : Century Publishing, Oct.1982. — [192]p
ISBN 0-7126-0008-6 : £6.95 : CIP entry B82-23885

306.8′1 — Marriage *continuation*

Hauck, Paul. Making marriage work / Paul Hauck. — London : Sheldon, 1981, c1977. — viii,88p ; 20cm. — (Overcoming common problems)
Originally published: Philadelphia : Westminster, 1977
ISBN 0-85969-336-8 (pbk) : £1.95 B82-40625

306.8′1 — Marriage & divorce

Alvarez, A.. Life after marriage : scenes from divorce / A. Alvarez. — London : Macmillan, 1982. — 268p ; 23cm
ISBN 0-333-24161-4 : £8.95 B82-38794

306.8′1′0941 — Great Britain. Marriage — *Manuals*

Getting married / [authors: Elizabeth Penrose ... [et al.]. — [London] : British Medical Association, [c1982]. — 110p : ill(some col.) ; 20cm. — (A Family doctor special)
Unpriced (unbound) B82-20444

306.8′1′0941 — Great Britain. Marriage. Social aspects

The **Future** of marriage : a report by a research sub-committee of the Society of Conservative Lawyers. — London : Conservative Political Centre, 1981. — [31]p ; 21cm
Bibliography: p31
ISBN 0-85070-664-5 (pbk) : £1.00 B82-28415

306.8′1′0952 — Japan. Marriage

Hendry, Joy. Marriage in changing Japan : community and society / Joy Hendry. — London : Croom Helm, c1981. — 274p : ill,maps ; 23cm
Bibliography: p254-268. — Includes index
ISBN 0-7099-0166-6 : £14.95 : CIP rev.
B80-17561

306.8′1′0973 — United States. Marriage & divorce, *1945-1980*

Cherlin, Andrew J.. Marriage, divorce, remarriage / Andrew J. Cherlin. — Cambridge, Mass. ; London : Harvard University Press, 1981. — xiv,142p : ill ; 25cm. — (Social trends in the United States)
Includes index
ISBN 0-674-55080-3 : £19.80 B82-14160

306.8′1′0994295 — Australia. Northern Territory. Port Keats. Australian aborigines. Marriage — *Anthropological perspectives*

Falkenberg, Aslaug. The affinal relationship system : a new approach to kinship and marriage among the Australian Aborigines at Port Keats / Aslaug and Johannes Falkenberg. — Oslo : Universitetsforlaget ; London : Global Book Resources [[distributor]], c1981. — 206p : ill,2maps ; 23cm. — (Oslo studies in social anthropology ; no.1)
Bibliography: p201-202. — Includes index
ISBN 82-00-05563-9 : £12.85
Also classified at 306.8′3′0994295 B82-01788

306.8′3′072041 — Kinship. Research in Great Britain, *1898-1931*

Langham, Ian. The building of British social anthropology : W.H.R. Rivers and his Cambridge disciples in the development of kinship studies, 1898-1931 / Ian Langham. — Dordrecht ; London : Reidel, c1981. — xxxii,392p,[8]p of plates : ill,ports ; 23cm. — (Studies in the history of modern science ; v.8)
Includes index
ISBN 90-277-1264-6 (cased) : Unpriced
ISBN 90-277-1265-4 (pbk) : Unpriced
B82-06115

306.8′3′0954 — South Asia. Dravidians. Kinship

Trautmann, Thomas R.. Dravidian kinship / Thomas R. Trautmann. — Cambridge : Cambridge University Press, 1981. — xvii,472p : ill,maps ; 24cm. — (Cambridge studies in social anthropology ; 36)
Bibliography: p447-462. — Includes index
ISBN 0-521-23703-3 : £35.00 B82-18238

306.8′3′0994295 — Australia. Northern Territory. Port Keats. Australian aborigines. Kinship — *Anthropological perspectives*

Falkenberg, Aslaug. The affinal relationship system : a new approach to kinship and marriage among the Australian Aborigines at Port Keats / Aslaug and Johannes Falkenberg. — Oslo : Universitetsforlaget ; London : Global Book Resources [[distributor]], c1981. — 206p : ill,2maps ; 23cm. — (Oslo studies in social anthropology ; no.1)
Bibliography: p201-202. — Includes index
ISBN 82-00-05563-9 : £12.85
Primary classification 306.8′1′0994295
B82-01788

306.8′46′0942165 — London. Lambeth *(London Borough).* **Brixton. Interracial marriage**

Benson, Susan. Ambiguous ethnicity : interracial families in London / Susan Benson. — Cambridge : Cambridge University Press, 1981. — ix,172p : ill,maps ; 23cm. — (Changing cultures)
Bibliography: p158-168. — Includes index
ISBN 0-521-23017-9 (cased) : £16.50 : CIP rev.
ISBN 0-521-29769-9 (pbk) : £5.50 B82-03106

306.8′5 — Families

The **Family** in the eighties. — London (106 Clapham Rd., SW9 0JX) : Family & Social Action, [1982]. — 24p : ill ; 25cm
£0.75 (unbound) B82-35531

Goode, William J.. The family / William J. Goode. — 2nd ed. — Englewood Cliffs ; London : Prentice-Hall, c1982. — xviii,200p : 1ill ; 24cm. — (Prentice-Hall foundations of modern sociology series)
Previous ed.: 1964. — Includes index
ISBN 0-13-301762-1 (cased) : Unpriced
ISBN 0-13-301754-0 (pbk) : £6.70 B82-28160

Leslie, Gerald R.. The family in social context / Gerald R. Leslie. — 5th ed. — New York ; Oxford : Oxford University Press, 1982. — viii,663p : ill ; 25cm
Previous ed.: 1979. — Includes bibliographies and index
ISBN 0-19-502975-5 : £13.50 B82-27301

Philosophy, children and the family / edited by Albert C. Cafagna, Richard T. Peterson and Craig A. Staudenbaur. — New York ; London : Plenum, c1982. — xiv,377p ; 26cm. — (Child nurturance ; v.1)
Includes bibliographies and index
ISBN 0-306-41003-6 : Unpriced B82-31527

306.8′5 — Families. Economic aspects

Becker, Gary S.. A treatise on the family / Gary S. Becker. — Cambridge, Mass. ; London : Harvard University Press, 1981. — xii,288p : ill ; 25cm
Bibliography: p259-277. — Includes index
ISBN 0-674-90696-9 : £12.00 B82-13978

306.8′5 — Families. Political aspects. Theories

The **Family** in political thought / edited by Jean Bethke Elshtain. — Brighton : Harvester, 1982. — viii,354p ; 24cm
Includes index
ISBN 0-7108-0426-1 : £22.50 : CIP rev.
B82-06240

306.8′5 — Families — *Sociological perspectives*

Barrett, Michéle. The anti-social family. — London : Verso, Sept.1982. — [192]p
ISBN 0-86091-052-0 (cased) : £12.50 : CIP entry
ISBN 0-86091-751-7 (pbk) : £3.50 B82-21116

306.8′5′01 — Families. Theories

Contemporary theories about the family : research-based theories / edited by Wesley R. Burr ... [et al.]. — New York : Free Press ; London : Collier Macmillan
Vol.1. — c1979. — xii,668p : ill ; 25cm
Includes bibliographies and index
ISBN 0-02-904940-7 : £18.95 B82-14138

306.8′5′0883527 — West Africa. Family life — *Study examples: Akan civil servants — Study regions: Ghana*

Oppong, Christine. [Marriage among a matrilineal elite]. Middle class African marriage : a family study of Ghanaian senior civil servants / Christine Oppong. — London : Allen & Unwin, 1981. — xx,190p : 2ill,1map ; 22cm
Originally published: Cambridge : Cambridge University Press, 1974. — Bibliography: p166-177. — Includes index
ISBN 0-04-301138-1 (pbk) : Unpriced : CIP rev. B81-28147

306.8′5′088616 — Doctors. Family life. Effects of careers

Gerber, Lane A.. Married to their careers : career and family dilemmas in doctors′ lives. — London : Tavistock, Feb.1983. — [250]p
ISBN 0-422-78240-8 (cased) : £9.50 : CIP entry
ISBN 0-422-78250-5 (pbk) : £4.95 B82-38302

306.8′5′08996073 — United States. Negro families

Black families / edited by Harriette Pipes McAdoo. — Beverly Hills ; London : Sage, c1981. — 303p : ill ; 23cm. — (Sage focus editions ; 41)
Includes bibliographies
ISBN 0-8039-1741-4 (cased) : Unpriced
ISBN 0-8039-1742-2 (pbk) : £6.50 B82-24073

306.8′5′08996073 — United States. Negro families. Psychosocial aspects

The **Afro-American** family : assessment, treatment, and research issues / edited by Barbara Ann Bass, Gail Elizabeth Wyatt, Gloria Johnson Powell. — New York ; London : Grune & Stratton, c1982. — xix,364p ; 24cm. — (Seminars in psychiatry)
Conference papers. — Includes index
ISBN 0-8089-1377-8 : £13.00 B82-32792

306.8′5′09 — Families. Social aspects, *to 1980*

Mount, Ferdinand. The subversive family : an alternative history of love and marriage / Ferdinand Mount. — London : Cape, 1982. — 282p ; 23cm
Bibliography: p272-276. — Includes index
ISBN 0-224-01999-6 : £9.50 : CIP rev.
B82-14227

306.8′5′094 — Europe. Families, *ca 1350-1982*

Mitterauer, Michael. The European family : patriarchy to partnership from the Middle Ages to the present / Michael Mitterauer and Reinhard Sieder ; translated by Karla Oosterveen and Manfred Hörzinger. — Oxford : Blackwell, 1982. — xv,235p ; 24cm
Translation of: Vom Patriarchat zur Partnerschaft. — Bibliography: p178-226. — Includes index
ISBN 0-631-12913-8 (cased) : Unpriced : CIP rev.
ISBN 0-631-12923-5 (pbk) : Unpriced
B81-30168

306.8′5′0941 — Great Britain. Families — *Sociological perspectives*

Symposium on Priority for the Family *(1981 : London).* Family matters. — Oxford : Pergamon, Nov.1982. — [160]p
ISBN 0-08-028928-2 : £9.95 : CIP entry
B82-26212

306.8′5′0941 — Great Britain. Families — *Statistics*

Rimmer, Lesley. Families in focus / Lesley Rimmer. — London : Study Commission on the Family, c1981. — 79p : ill ; 21cm. — (Occasional paper / Study Commission on the Family ; no.6)
Bibliography: p74-79
ISBN 0-907051-08-1 (pbk) : £3.00 B82-04348

306.8′5′0941 — Great Britain. Family life. Attitudes of women

Rossiter, Chris. Women, work and the family : a report of a survey of Townswoman readers / Chris Rossiter. — London : Study Commission on the Family, c1980. — 25p : 1form ; 30cm
ISBN 0-907051-07-3 (spiral) : Unpriced
B82-29514

306.8′5′094415 — France. Rennes. Family life — *For children*

Regan, Mary. French family. — London : A. & C. Black, Sept.1982. — [32]p. — (Beans)
ISBN 0-7136-2216-4 : £2.95 : CIP entry B82-20355

306.8′5′0973 — United States. Families. Influence of social change, *1960-1980*

Masnick, George. The nation′s families : 1960-1990 / George Masnick and Mary Jo Bane with Neal Baer ... [et al.]. — Boston, Mass. : Auburn House ; London : distributed by Eurospan, c1980. — xv,175p : ill ; 25cm. — (A Joint Center outlook report)
Bibliography: p117-120
ISBN 0-86569-050-2 : £14.50 B82-14165

306.8′5′0973 — United States. Families — *Sociological perspectives*

Levitan, Sar A.. What′s happening to the American family? / Sar A. Levitan and Richard S. Belous. — Baltimore ; London : Johns Hopkins University Press, c1981. — ix,206p : ill ; 24cm
Includes index
ISBN 0-8018-2690-x (cased) : Unpriced
ISBN 0-8018-2691-8 (pbk) : Unpriced B82-16986

306.8′5′0973 — United States. Families. Sociological perspectives, *1865-1940*

Howard, Ronald L.. A social history of American family sociology, 1865-1940 / Ronald L. Howard with an additional chapter on Early family sociology in Europe by Louis Th. van Leeuwen ; edited by John Mogey. — Westport, Conn. ; London : Greenwood Press, 1981. — xiii,150p ; 22cm. — (Contributions in family studies, ISSN 0147-1023 ; no.4)
Includes index
ISBN 0-313-22767-5 : Unpriced B82-01948

306.8′5′0973 — United States. Family life — *Feminist viewpoints*

Rethinking the family : some feminist questions / edited by Barrie Thorne with Marilyn Yalom ; prepared under the auspices of the Centre for Research on Women, Stanford University. — New York ; London : Longman, c1982. — x,246p ; 23cm
Includes index
ISBN 0-582-28265-9 (pbk) : £5.95 B82-20970

306.8′7 — Families. Interpersonal relationships

Reiss, David. The family′s construction of reality / David Reiss. — Cambridge, Mass. ; London : Harvard University Press, 1981. — xiii,426p : ill ; 24cm
Bibliography: p401-402. — Includes index
ISBN 0-674-29415-7 : £17.50 B82-13733

306.8′7 — Families. Interpersonal relationships — *Conference proceedings*

Family strengths 3 : roots of well-being / edited by Nick Stinnett ... [et al.]. — Lincoln ; London : University of Nebraska Press, c1981. — x,395p ; 23cm
Conference papers. — Includes bibliographies
ISBN 0-8032-4128-3 (cased) : Unpriced
ISBN 0-8032-9124-8 (pbk) : Unpriced B82-02187

306.8′7 — Families. Interpersonal relationships. Exchange theory

Family relationships : rewards and costs / edited by F. Ivan Nye. — Beverly Hills ; London : Sage, c1982. — 264p : ill ; 23cm. — (Sage focus editions ; 46)
Includes bibliographies
ISBN 0-8039-1770-8 (cased) : Unpriced
ISBN 0-8039-1771-6 (pbk) : Unpriced B82-25197

306.8′7 — Grandmothers. Interpersonal relationships with grandchildren — *Childhood reminiscences — Collections*

To grandma with love / compiled and edited by Jack Hallam ; designed by Victor Shreeve and Peter Snowball. — London : Souvenir, 1981. — 176p : ill,1facsim,port ; 28cm
ISBN 0-285-62454-7 : £8.95 B82-04933

306.8′7 — Great Britain. Families. Violence

Violence in the family : theory and practice in social work / Social Work Services Group, Scottish Education Department. — Edinburgh : H.M.S.O., 1982. — vii,70p ; 21cm
Includes bibliographies
ISBN 0-11-491991-7 (pbk) : £3.75 B82-23763

306.8′7 — United States. Old persons. Family life — *Sociological perspectives*

Aging : stability and change in the family / edited by Robert W. Fogel ... [et al.]. — New York ; London : Academic Press, c1981. — xx,341p ; 24cm
Includes bibliographies and index
ISBN 0-12-040003-0 (cased) : £19.60
ISBN 0-12-040023-5 (pbk) : £9.60 B82-30138

306.8′72 — Marriage. Interpersonal relationships. Assessment — *Behaviourist perspectives*

Assessing marriage : new behavioral approaches / edited by Erik E. Filsinger and Robert A. Lewis. — Beverly Hills ; London : Published in cooperation with the National Council on Family Relations [by] Sage, c1981. — 300p : ill ; 22cm. — (Sage focus editions ; 34)
Includes bibliographies
ISBN 0-8039-1570-5 (cased) : Unpriced
ISBN 0-8039-1571-3 (pbk) : £6.50 B82-17080

306.8′72 — Married couples. Interpersonal relationships. Love. Communication — *Manuals*

Swihart, Judson J.. How do you say ′I love you′? / Judson Swihart. — Eastbourne : Kingsway, 1978, c1977 (1982 [printing]). — 94p ; 18cm
Originally published: Downers Grove, Ill. : Intervarsity Press, c1977
ISBN 0-86065-017-0 (pbk) : £1.35 B82-32485

306.8′74 — Children, 1-3 years. Interpersonal relationships with parents — *For parents*

Crowe, Brenda. Living with a toddler / Brenda Crowe ; foreword by Willem van der Eyken. — London : Unwin Paperbacks, 1982. — vii,246p ; 20cm
Originally published: London : Allen and Unwin, 1980
ISBN 0-04-649015-9 (pbk) : £2.50 : CIP rev. B82-00276

306.8′74 — Children. Interpersonal relationships with adults — *Children′s viewpoints*

Dear adults — / selected and edited by Alan Davies ... [et al.]. — London : Published for the General Synod Board of Education by CIO Publishing, 1981. — 72p ; 21cm
ISBN 0-7151-0402-0 (pbk) : £2.20 B82-15080

306.8′74 — Parenthood

Backett, Kathryn C.. Mothers and fathers : a study of the development and negotiation of parental behaviour / Kathryn C. Backett. — London : Macmillan, 1982. — x,251p ; 23cm. — (Edinburgh studies in sociology)
Bibliography: p246-248. — Includes index
ISBN 0-333-28112-8 : Unpriced B82-39990

Ourselves and our children : a book by and for parents / the Boston Women′s Health Book Collective. — British ed. — Harmondsworth : Penguin, 1981. — 464p : ill,ports ; 21cm
Previous ed.: New York : Random House, 1978. — Bibliography: p435-449. — Includes index
ISBN 0-14-005439-1 (pbk) : £4.50 B82-07292

306.8′74 — Parenthood. Personal adjustment of married couples

Clulow, Christopher F.. To have and to hold : marriage, the first baby and preparing couples for parenthood. — Aberdeen : Aberdeen University Press, Sept.1982. — [152]p
ISBN 0-08-028470-1 (cased) : £9.50 : CIP entry
ISBN 0-08-028471-x (pbk) : £5.50 B82-18732

306.8′74′07041 — Great Britain. Parent education

Pugh, GillianA Job for life / education and support for parents. — London (8 Wakley Street, EC4 7QE) : National Children′s Bureau, c1982. — 12p ; 21cm
Cover title. — Written by Gillian Pugh, Joan Kidd and Kate Torkington. Published jointly by National Children′s Bureau, National Children′s Home and National Marriage Guidance Council
Unpriced (pbk) B82-20534

306.8′742 — Daughters. Interpersonal relationships with fathers

Woolfolk, William. Daddy′s little girl : the unspoken bargain between fathers and their daughters / William Woolfolk with Donna Woolfolk Cross. — Englewood Cliffs ; London : Prentice-Hall, c1982. — 220p ; 23cm
Includes index
ISBN 0-13-196345-7 : £9.70 B82-28826

306.8′742′0941 — Great Britain. Families. Role of fathers

The Father figure / edited by Lorna McKee & Margaret O′Brien. — London : Tavistock, 1982. — xii,239p ; 23cm
Bibliography: p208-277. — Includes index
ISBN 0-422-77720-x (cased) : Unpriced : CIP rev.
ISBN 0-422-77730-7 (pbk) : Unpriced B82-09736

306.8′743 — Motherhood

Dally, Ann. Inventing motherhood : the consequences of an ideal / by Ann Dally. — London : Burnett, 1982. — 360p ; 25cm
Bibliography: p346-356. — Includes index
ISBN 0-09-147240-7 (cased) : £12.95 : CIP rev.
ISBN 0-09-147241-5 (pbk) : £5.95 B82-10606

306.8′743′0924 — Motherhood — *Personal observations*

Nicholson, Joyce. The heartache of motherhood. — London : Sheldon, Sept.1982. — [112]p. — (Overcoming common problems)
ISBN 0-85969-369-4 (pbk) : £2.95 : CIP entry B82-20848

306.8′743′0944 — France. Motherhood. Attitudes of women, *1680-1980*

Badinter, Elisabeth. The myth of motherhood : an historical view of the maternal instinct / Elisabeth Badinter ; foreword by Francine du Plessix Gray. — xxiii,359p ; 21cm
Translation of: L′Amour en plus. — Includes index
ISBN 0-285-64941-8 (cased) : £8.95 B82-10209

306.8′743′09775 — United States. Babies. Home care by mothers — *Sociological perspectives — Study regions: Wisconsin*

Slesinger, Doris Peyser. Mothercraft and infant health : a sociodemographic and sociocultural approach / Doris Peyser Slesinger. — Lexington, Mass. : Lexington Books, c1981 ; [Aldershot] : Gower [distributor], 1982. — xxi,202p : ill ; 24cm
Bibliography: p189-196. — Includes index
ISBN 0-669-04562-4 : £14.50 B82-13993

306.8′8 — Bereaved persons. Counselling

Bereavement counseling : a multidisciplinary handbook / edited by B. Mark Schoenberg. — Westport ; London : Greenwood Press, 1980. — xii,266p ; 25cm
Includes bibliographies and index
ISBN 0-313-21434-4 : Unpriced B82-15054

306.8′8 — Bereavement. Personal adjustment — *For Christian welfare work*

Archer, Mary. They shall be comforted / by Mary Archer. — Redhill (Robert Denholm House, Nutfield, Redhill, Surrey RH1 4HW) : NCEC, [1981?]. — [8]p ; 21cm
£0.10 (unbound) B82-08557

306.8′8 — Bereavement. Personal adjustment of fathers — *Personal observations*

Leach, Christopher, *1925-*. Letter to a younger son / Christopher Leach. — London : Arrow, 1982, c1981. — 155p ; 18cm
Originally published: London : Dent, 1981
ISBN 0-09-927280-6 (pbk) : £1.25 B82-13371

306.8′8 — Bereavement. Personal adjustment of mothers — *Personal observations*

D′Arcy, Paula. Song for Sarah / Paula D′Arcy. — Tring : Lion, 1981, c1979. — 124p ; 23cm
Originally published: Wheaton : H. Shaw, 1979
ISBN 0-85648-424-5 : £2.95 B82-06388

306.8′8 — Bereavement. Personal adjustment — *Personal observations — Collections*

Losses : talking about bereavement / compiled and edited by Rosamond Richardson. — Shepton Mallet : Open Books, 1980. — xxiii,204p ; 23cm
Bibliography: p202-204
ISBN 0-7291-0188-6 : £5.95 B82-17099

306.8′8 — Divorce or widowhood. Personal adjustment of women — *Manuals*

Bunyan, Katharine. Second time single / Katharine Bunyan & Rosemary de Herez Smyth. — Bognor Regis : New Horizon, c1982. — 115p ; 22cm
ISBN 0-86116-607-8 : £4.50 B82-10272

306.8′8 — Perinatal death. Personal adjustment of families

Borg, Suban. When pregnancy fails. — London : Routledge & Kegan Paul, Oct.1982. — [217]p
ISBN 0-7100-9309-8 (pbk) : £4.50 : CIP entry B82-24734

306.8′9 — Children. Effects of divorce

Inglis, Ruth. Must divorce hurt the children? / Ruth Inglis. — London : Temple Smith, 1982. — 176p ; 23cm
Bibliography: p169-173. — Includes index
ISBN 0-85117-220-2 : £7.95 : CIP rev. B81-33832

306.8′9 — Divorce. Personal adjustment — *Manuals*

Ambrose, Peter. Surviving divorce. — Brighton : Harvester Press, Oct.1982. — [192]p
ISBN 0-7108-0378-8 (cased) : £15.95 : CIP entry
ISBN 0-7108-0417-2 (pbk) : £5.95 B82-23180

306.8′9 — Divorce — *Practical information*

Obërg, Bente. I′m leaving. — London : Jill Norman and Hobhouse, May 1982. — [192]p
Translation of: Nu gar jag
ISBN 0-906908-17-5 (pbk) : £3.95 : CIP entry B82-07702

306.8′9 — Great Britain. Wives. Sale, *1550-1928*

Menefee, Samuel Pyeatt. Wives for sale : an ethnographic study of British popular divorce / Samuel Pyeatt Menefee. — Oxford : Blackwell, 1981. — ix,336p : 1ill,maps,facsims ; 24cm
Ill on lining papers. — Bibliography: p320-332. — Includes index
ISBN 0-631-11871-3 : £15.00 : CIP rev. B81-10489

306.8′9 — Married persons. Separation. Personal adjustment — *Manuals*

Dineen, Jacqueline. Going solo : starting out again after separation. — London : Unwin Paperbacks, 1982. — 130p ; 19cm
Bibliography: p126-127. — Includes index
ISBN 0-04-347005-x (pbk) : £2.25 : CIP rev. B82-07229

306.8′9′0924 — Great Britain. Women. Divorce — *Personal observations*

Fordham, Kate. No pit too deep : the diary of a divorce / Kate Fordham. — Tring : Lion, 1982. — 159p ; 18cm
ISBN 0-85648-392-3 (pbk) : £1.50 B82-17133

306.8′9′09417 — Ireland *(Republic)*. **Divorce —** *Irish Council for Civil Liberties viewpoints*

Duncan, William, *1944-*. The case for divorce in the Irish Republic / a report commissioned by the Irish Council for Civil Liberties ; William Duncan. — Rev. ed. with postscript. — Dublin ([Liberty Hall, Dublin 1]) : The Council, 1982. — 107p ; 21cm. — (ICCL report ; no.5)
Previous ed.: 1979
Unpriced (pbk) B82-34725

306.8′9′0942 — England. Married persons. Separation & divorce — *Manuals*

Black, Jill M.. Divorce : the things you thought you′d never need to know / by Jill M. Black. — Kingswood : Elliot Right Way, c1982. — 192p ; 18cm. — (Paperfronts)
Includes index
ISBN 0-7160-0674-x (pbk) : £0.75 B82-23917

306.8′9′09931 — New Zealand. Divorce, *1867-1980*

Phillips, Roderick. Divorce in New Zealand : a social history / Roderick Phillips. — Auckland ; Oxford : Oxford University Press, c1981. — 154p : ill ; 22cm
Bibliography: p149-152. — Includes index
ISBN 0-19-558077-x (pbk) : £7.75 B82-33307

306.9 — Death

Parkes, Colin Murray. Facing death / by Colin Murray Parkes. — Cambridge : National Extension College in association with London Weekend Television, 1981. — 24p ; 21cm
Bibliography: p24
ISBN 0-86082-216-8 (pbk) : Unpriced B82-40271

Sabom, Michael B.. Recollections of death : a medical investigation / Michael B. Sabom. — New York ; London : Harper & Row, c1982. — xii,224p : ill ; 25cm
Includes index
ISBN 0-06-014895-0 : £6.95 B82-16592

306′.9 — Death — *Anthropological perspectives*

Death and the regeneration of life. — Cambridge : Cambridge University Press, Jan.1983. — [248]p
ISBN 0-521-24875-2 (cased) : £18.50 : CIP entry
ISBN 0-521-27037-5 (pbk) : £5.95 B82-32430

306.9 — Western world. Death. Attitudes of society, *1200-1977*

Ariès, Philippe. The hour of our death / by Philippe Ariès ; translated from the French by Helen Weaver. — London : Allen Lane, 1981. — xvii,651p,[24]p of plates : ill ; 25cm
Translation of: L′homme devant la mort. — Includes index
ISBN 0-7139-1207-3 : £14.95 B82-21774

306.9′07′073 — United States. Death. Information sources

Death education : annotated resource guide / Hannelore Wass ... [et al.]. — Washington, [D.C] ; London : Hemisphere, c1980. — xi,303p ; 24cm
Includes index
ISBN 0-89116-170-8 : £21.50 B82-24550

306.9′0922 — Death — *Personal observations — Collections*

Bid the world good-night : a symposium / edited and produced by Ralph Ricketts. — London : Search, 1981. — 210p ; 22cm
ISBN 0-85532-446-5 (pbk) : £3.95
Primary classification 305.2′6′0922 B82-03033

306.9′093 — Ancient world. Death. Attitudes of society — *Polyglot texts*

La **Mort**, les morts dans les sociétés anciennes / sous la direction de Gherardo Gnoli et Jean-Pierre Vernant. — Cambridge : Cambridge University Press, 1982. — xvi,505p : ill ; 24cm
French and Italian text
ISBN 0-521-22322-9 : £25.00 B82-18237

306.9′0973 — United States. Man. Dying. Social aspects

Backer, Barbara A.. Death and dying : individuals and institutions / Barbara A. Backer, Natalie Hannon, A. Russell. — New York ; Chichester : Wiley, c1982. — x,332p : ill ; 24cm
Includes bibliographies and index
ISBN 0-471-08715-7 : £12.50 B82-18247

307 — COMMUNITIES

307 — Communities

Community as a social ideal. — London : Arnold, Dec.1982. — [192]p. — (Ideas and ideologies)
ISBN 0-7131-6180-9 (pbk) : £6.00 : CIP entry B82-30206

307 — Communities — *For children*

Sproule, Anna. Living together / Anna Sproule. — London : Macdonald Educational, 1982. — 30p : ill(some col.) ; 29cm. — (My first encyclopedia ; 2)
Includes index
ISBN 0-356-07818-3 : £2.95 B82-35812

307 — Community studies — *Study regions: Australia, Great Britain & United States*

Wild, R. A.. Australian community studies and beyond. — London : Allen & Unwin, Dec.1981. — [241]p. — (Studies in society ; 7)
ISBN 0-86861-219-7 : £18.00 : CIP entry B81-31540

307 — Human settlements

Wallis, Elizabeth B.. Settlement. — London : Edward Arnold, Apr.1981. — [64]p. — (Systematic secondary series)
ISBN 0-7131-0499-6 (pbk) : £2.00 : CIP entry B81-00023

307 — Human settlements — *Conference proceedings*

Policies for human settlement and their implementation. — London : Commonwealth Human Ecology Council, c1980. — 118p ; 21cm
Conference proceedings. — Cover title
ISBN 0-904713-05-9 (pbk) : £2.95 B82-23942

307 — Human settlements — *For schools*

Calcutt, Julia. Settlement. — London : Edward Arnold, Nov.1982. — [64]p. — (Foundation geography)
ISBN 0-7131-0665-4 (pbk) : £2.00 : CIP entry B82-27955

Ghaye, Tony. Settlements. — London : Macmillan Education, Feb.1983. — [72]p. — (Discovering geography)
ISBN 0-333-28401-1 (pbk) : £2.25 : CIP entry B82-37858

Hayes, John, *1946-*. Villages, towns and cities / John Hayes. — London : Hutchinson, 1980. — 32p : ill,maps,1port ; 22x30cm. — (Down to earth)
ISBN 0-09-138631-4 (unbound) : £0.50 : CIP rev. B79-14416

307′.06′041 — Great Britain. Community relations councils

The **Nature** and funding of local race relations work : community relations councils. — London : 10 Allington St., SW1E 5EH : Commission for Racial Equality, 1980. — 18p ; 21cm
Unpriced (pbk) B82-16893

307′.09425′11 — England. South Pennines. Human settlements, *to ca 1980*

Breakell, Bill. Man and the Pennine landscape / [written and designed by Bill Breakell]. — Hebden Bridge : Pennine Heritage Network, c1982. — 1folded sheet : ill(some col.) ; 59x21cm folded to 21x15cm
ISBN 0-907613-09-8 : Unpriced B82-37742

307′.12 — Cities. Social planning — *Comparative studies*

City, economy and society : a comparative reader / edited by Allan Cochrane, Chris Hamnett and Linda McDowell. — London : Harper & Row in association with the Open University Press, 1981. — xviii,236p : ill,maps,plans ; 25cm. — (Open University set book)
Includes bibliographies and index
ISBN 0-06-318205-x (cased) : Unpriced : CIP rev.
ISBN 0-06-318206-8 (pbk) : Unpriced B81-33969

307′.12′0722 — Asia. Developing countries. Urban regions. Planning — *Case studies*

Urban planning practice in developing countries / editors, John L. Taylor and David G. Williams. — Oxford : Pergamon, 1982. — x,357p : ill,maps ; 24cm. — ([Urban and regional planning series] ; [v.25]) (Pergamon international library)
Includes bibliographies
ISBN 0-08-022225-0 : £19.50 : CIP rev. B81-31805

307'.12'091724 — Developing countries. Urban regions. Social planning — *Conference proceedings*
Problem cities in search of solutions : Delhi, Nairobi, Lusaka : papers and proceedings of the annual Habitat Forum conferences 1980/81 / edited by Thomas L. Blair. — [London] : Polytechnic of Central London, School of Environment, c1981. — xiv,159p : ill ; 30cm. — (Papers and proceedings ; 6th v.)
Unpriced (pbk) B82-03652

307'.12'0941 — Great Britain. Cities. Inner areas. Social planning. Policies of government
Booth, Simon A. S.. Government and area approaches : the growth of mangos / Simon A.S. Booth & Douglas Pitt. — Glasgow (McCance Building, 16 Richmond St., Glasgow, G1 1XQ) : Centre for the Study of Public Policy, University of Strathclyde, 1982. — 32p ; 21cm. — (Studies in public policy ; no.101)
Bibliography: p26-29
£1.75 (pbk) B82-40787

307'.12'0941 — Great Britain. Rural regions. Social planning. Policies of local authorities, *1945-1980*
Review of rural settlement policies 1945-1980 / prepared for Directorate of Rural Affairs ... [et al.], prepared by Martin and Voorhees Associates. — London (112 Strand, WC2R 0AA) : Martin and Voorhees Associates, 1980. — v,224,[28]p : ill,maps ; 30cm
Unpriced (pbk) B82-17859

307'.12'0941 — Great Britain. Urban regions. Social planning. Projects: Urban Programme
The **Urban** programme : the partnership at work. — [London] ([2 Marsham St., SW1P 3EB]) : Department of the Environment, 1981. — 48p : ill,3plans ; 30cm
Cover title
Unpriced (pbk) B82-35523

307'.12'0954 — India *(Republic).* **Urban regions. Social planning**
Hall, Derek. A spatial analysis of urban community development policy in India / Derek Hall. — Letchworth : Research Studies Press, c1980. — ix,180p : ill,maps ; 29cm. — (Geography and public policy research studies ; 1)
Bibliography: p161-177. — Includes index
ISBN 0-471-27862-9 (pbk) : £15.00 : CIP rev. B80-34546

307'.12'0977132 — United States. Urban regions. Social planning. Simulations — *Study regions: Ohio. Cleveland*
Bradbury, Katharine L.. Futures for a declining city : simulations for the Cleveland area / Katharine L. Bradbury, Anthony Downs, Kenneth A. Small. — New York ; London : Academic Press, c1981. — xiii,247p : ill ; 24cm. — (Studies in urban economics)
Includes index
ISBN 0-12-123580-7 : £18.00 B82-21256

307'.12'098 — Latin America. Urban regions. Social planning
Urbanization in contemporary Latin America : critical approaches to the analysis of urban issues. — Chichester : Wiley, Sept.1982. — [350]p
ISBN 0-471-10183-4 : £20.00 : CIP entry B82-19526

307'.14'091724 — Developing countries. Urban regions. Social development. Projects. Monitoring & evaluation
Rakodi, Carole. The role of monitoring and evaluation in the planning process, with special reference to squatter area upgrading programmes in developing countries / by Carole Rakodi. — Cardiff (King Edward VII Av, Cardiff, CF1 3NU, Wales) : Dept. of Town Planning, University of Wales, Institute of Science and Technology, 1981. — iileaves,60p ; 30cm. — (Papers in planning research ; 29)
Bibliography: p54-58
Unpriced (pbk) B82-25637

307'.14'091734 — Rural regions. Community development — *Serials*
Progress in rural extension and community development. — Vol.1-. — Chichester : Wiley, 1982-. — v. ; 24cm
Unpriced B82-24767

307'.14'094 — Europe. Urban regions. Growth
Urban Europe. — Oxford : Pergamon
Vol.1: A study of growth and decline / by Leo van den Berg ... [et al.] for the European Coordination Centre for Research and Documentation in Social Sciences. — 1982. — xxii,162p : ill,maps ; 24cm
ISBN 0-08-023156-x : £18.00 : CIP rev. B81-31806

307'.14'0941 — Great Britain. Community development. Role of cooperatives — *Case studies*
Stettner, Leonora. Community co-operatives their potential for rural and urban development / by Leonora Stettner. — [Oxford] : Plunkett Foundation for Co-operative Studies, 1981. — v,62p ; 21cm. — (Plunkett development series, ISSN 0143-8484 ; 3)
Bibliography: p61-62
ISBN 0-85042-045-8 (pbk) : Unpriced B82-08594

307'.14'09417 — Ireland *(Republic).* **Community development**
Overseas Institute for Community Development. *Summer School (5th : 1979 : Dundrum and Killala).* Report : Fifth Summer School 1979 held at Gort Muire, Dundrum, Co. Dublin and Sea Angling Centre, Killala, Co. Mayo 10th-14th September, 1979 : theme: Community development. Ensuring social progress through popular participation — an evaluation. — Dublin (c/o Poverty Combat, 8 Charlemont St., Dublin 2) : Overseas Institute for Community Development, [1979?]. — 4,57leaves ; 21cm
Unpriced (spiral) B82-31046

307'.14'0942975 — Mid Glamorgan. Merthyr Tydfil. Urban development. Spatial models, *1851*
Carter, Harold. Merthyr Tydfil in 1851. — Cardiff : University of Wales Press, Nov.1982. — [140]p. — (Social science monographs / University of Wales. Board of Celtic Studies ; no.7)
ISBN 0-7083-0825-2 (pbk) : £5.00 : CIP entry B82-29437

307'.14'0973 — United States. Urban regions. Neighbourhoods. Development
Neighborhoods in urban America / edited by Ronald H. Bayor. — Port Washington, N.Y. ; London : National University Publications : Kennikat, 1982. — ix,252p ; 22cm. — (Interdisciplinary urban series)
Bibliography: p247-252
ISBN 0-8046-9284-x : Unpriced B82-31901

Yin, Robert K.. Conserving America's neighborhoods / Robert K. Yin. — New York ; London : Plenum, c1982. — xvii,195p : ill,1map ; 24cm. — (Environment, development and public policy. Cities and development)
Includes bibliographies and index
ISBN 0-306-40795-7 : Unpriced B82-20988

307'.14'0974827 — United States. Urban development. Entrepreneurship — *Study regions: Pennsylvania. Lehigh Valley, 1800-1920*
Folsom, Burton W.. Urban capitalists : entrepreneurs and city growth in Pennsylvania's Lackawanna and Lehigh regions, 1800-1920 / Burton W. Folsom, Jr. — Baltimore ; London : Johns Hopkins University Press, c1981. — xiv,191p : ill,maps,ports,1geneal.table ; 24cm. — (Studies in industry and society ; 1)
Includes index
ISBN 0-8018-2520-2 : £11.50
Primary classification 307'.14'0974836 B82-02236

307'.14'0974836 — United States. Urban development. Entrepreneurship — *Study regions: Pennsylvania. Lackawanna Valley, 1800-1920*
Folsom, Burton W.. Urban capitalists : entrepreneurs and city growth in Pennsylvania's Lackawanna and Lehigh regions, 1800-1920 / Burton W. Folsom, Jr. — Baltimore ; London : Johns Hopkins University Press, c1981. — xiv,191p : ill,maps,ports,1geneal.table ; 24cm. — (Studies in industry and society ; 1)
Includes index
ISBN 0-8018-2520-2 : £11.50
Also classified at 307'.14'0974827 B82-02236

307'.2 — Massachusetts. Internal migration, *1700-1800.* **Social aspects** — *Study regions: Beverly & Wenham*
Jones, Douglas Lamar. Village and seaport : migration and society in eighteenth-century Massachusetts / Douglas Lamar Jones. — Hanover, N.H. : Published for Tufts University by University Press of New England, 1981. — xx,167p : ill,1map,facsims ; 23cm
Bibliography: p129-133. — Includes index
ISBN 0-87451-200-x : £10.50 B82-13929

307'.2'0724 — United States. Urban regions. Population. Mobility *related to* **housing market. Mathematical models**
Pollakowski, Henry O.. Urban housing markets and residential location / Henry O. Pollakowski. — Lexington, Mass. : Lexington ; [Aldershot] : Gower [distributor], c1982. — xvii,141p : ill ; 24cm
Bibliography: p129-137. — Includes index
ISBN 0-669-02773-1 : £15.00
Also classified at 363.5'0724 B82-31792

307'.2'0724 — Urban regions. Population. Mobility. Dynamic models
Pickles, A. R.. Intra-urban migration dynamics for a heterogeneous population / by A.R. Pickles, R. Crouchley and R.B. Davies. — Cardiff (King Edward VII Ave., Cardiff CF1 3NU) : Dept. of Town Planning, University of Wales Institute of Science and Technology, 1981. — 1,17p : ill ; 30cm. — (Papers in planning research ; 34)
Bibliography: p15
Unpriced (pbk) B82-26827

307'.2'0724 — Urban regions. Population. Mobility. Stochastic models
Pickles, A. R.. Movers and stayers / by A.R. Pickles, R. Crouchley, and R.B. Davies. — Cardiff (King Edward VII Ave., Cardiff CF1 3NU) : Dept. of Town Planning, University of Wales Institute of Science and Technology, 1981. — i,13p : ill ; 30cm. — (Papers in planning research ; 33)
Unpriced (pbk) B82-26828

307'.2'091724 — Developing countries. Urban regions. Population. Distribution. Planning
Richardson, Harry W.. National urban development strategies : Norma Wilkinson memorial lecture 1980 / H.W. Richardson. — Reading : Department of Geography, University of Reading, 1981. — i,33p ; 21cm. — (Geographical papers / University of Reading. Department of Geography, ISSN 0305-5914 ; no.76)
ISBN 0-7049-0664-3 (corrected : pbk) : Unpriced B82-15070

307'.2'0941 — Great Britain. Urban regions, *1951-1971.* **Demographic aspects**
British cities : an analysis of urban change / Nigel Spence ... [et al.]. — Oxford : Pergamon, 1982. — xx,310p : ill,maps ; 26cm. — (Urban and regional planning series ; v.26)
ISBN 0-08-028931-2 : £20.00 : CIP rev. B82-03737

307'.2'0942184 — London. Ealing *(London Borough).* **Population. Change,** *1971-1981*
A **Note** on population changes in the London Borough of Ealing at ward level, 1971-1981 : an examination of preliminary figures from the 1981 Census of Population / prepared by the Borough Plan Section. — [London] : [London Borough of Ealing], 1981. — [5] leaves : 1maps ; 30cm
At head of title: London Borough of Ealing, Technical Services Group, Town Planning Division
ISBN 0-86192-009-0 (pbk) : Unpriced B82-15093

307'.2'0942496 — Urban regions. Population. Mobility *related to* **housing market** — *Study regions: West Midlands (Metropolitan County). Birmingham*
Ford, Robert G.. Intra-urban migration and British housing submarkets / by Robert G. Ford and Geoffrey C. Smith. — [Birmingham] : [Department of Geography, University of Birmingham], 1979. — 82p : ill,1map ; 30cm. — (Occasional publication / Department of Geography ; no.9)
Cover title. — Bibliography: p79-82
£1.00 (corrected : pbk)
Also classified at 363.5'0942496 B82-02399

307′.2′095525 — Iran. Teheran. Urban regions. Migrants from rural regions. Social conditions, *1950-1976*

Kazemi, Farhad. Poverty and revolution in Iran : the migrant poor, urban marginality and politics / Farhad Kazemi. — New York ; London : New York University Press, c1980. — 180p : ill ; 24cm
Bibliography: p157-176. — Includes index
ISBN 0-8147-4576-8 : £13.00 B82-38742

307′.2′0973 — United States. Local communities. Population. Change. Social aspects

Baldassare, Mark. The growth dilemma : residents′ views and local population change in the United States / Mark Baldassare. — Berkeley ; London : University of California Press, c1981. — ix,175p : 1map ; 23cm
Bibliography: p157-167. — Includes index
ISBN 0-520-04302-2 : Unpriced B82-16919

307′.336 — Great Britain. Housing, *1945-1982 — Sociological perspectives*

Murie, Alan. Housing inequality and deprivation. — London : Heinemann Educational, Jan.1983. — [320]p. — (SSRC/DHSS studies in deprivation and disadvantage ; 7)
ISBN 0-435-82626-3 : £13.50 : CIP entry B82-34586

307.7′2 — Rural regions. Human settlements

Bunce, Michael. Rural settlement in an urban world / Michael Bunce. — London : Croom Helm, c1982. — 219p : ill,maps ; 23cm
Includes index
ISBN 0-7099-0651-x : £12.95 : CIP rev. B81-31080

307.7′2′07204 — Europe. Rural communities. Research

Rural community studies in Europe. — Oxford : Pergamon
Vol.2. — Oct.1982. — [282]p
ISBN 0-08-026094-2 : £19.50 : CIP entry B82-28438

307.7′2′094244 — Hereford and Worcester. Worcestershire. Rural regions. Human settlements, *to 1855.* **Geographical aspects**

Field and forest : an historical geography of Warwickshire and Worcestershire / edited by T.R. Slater and P.J. Jarvis. — Norwich, Geo Books, 1982. — ix,396p : ill,facsims,maps,1port ; 24cm
Includes index
ISBN 0-86094-099-3 : £13.50
Primary classification 307.7′2′094248 B82-23495

307.7′2′094248 — Warwickshire. Rural regions. Human settlements, *to 1855.* **Geographical aspects**

Field and forest : an historical geography of Warwickshire and Worcestershire / edited by T.R. Slater and P.J. Jarvis. — Norwich, Geo Books, 1982. — ix,396p : ill,facsims,maps,1port ; 24cm
Includes index
ISBN 0-86094-099-3 : £13.50
Also classified at 307.7′2′094244 B82-23495

307.7′2′094952 — Greece. Helos Plain. Rural regions. Human settlements, *to ca 1970*

Wagstaff, J. Malcolm. The development of rural settlements : a study of the Helos Plain in southern Greece / J.M. Wagstaff. — [Amersham] : Avebury, 1982. — 166p : ill,maps,plans ; 22cm
Bibliography: p149-162. — Includes index
ISBN 0-86127-302-8 (pbk) : Unpriced : CIP rev. B81-21522

307.7′2′095694 — Israel. Arab villages. Social change, *1950-1980.* **Geographical aspects**

Bar-Gal, Y.. Geographical changes in the traditional Arab villages in Northern Israel / by Y. Bar-Gal and A. Soffer. — Durham : University of Durham, Centre for Middle Eastern and Islamic Studies, 1981. — vii,88p : ill,maps ; 21cm. — (Occasional papers series, ISSN 0307-0654 ; no.9)
Bibliography: p85-88
Unpriced (pbk) B82-11402

307.7′4 — Scotland. Peri-urban regions — *Conference proceedings*

Where town meets country. — Aberdeen : Aberdeen University Press, Jan.1982. — [150]p
Conference papers
ISBN 0-08-028442-6 (cased) : £9.50 : CIP entry
ISBN 0-08-028443-4 (pbk) : £6.50 B81-34635

307.7′4′0941 — Great Britain. Suburbs, *1920-1939*

Oliver, Paul. Dunroamin : the suburban semi and its enemies / Paul Oliver, Ian Davis, Ian Bentley. — London : Barrie & Jenkins, 1981. — 223p : ill,facsims,plans ; 25cm
Bibliography: p217. — Includes index
ISBN 0-09-145930-3 : £16.00 : CIP rev. B81-26782

307.7′4′0942 — England. Suburbs, *to 1939*

The **Rise** of suburbia / edited by F.M.L. Thompson. — Leicester : Leicester University Press, 1982. — xii,274p : ill,maps,plans ; 24cm. — (Themes in urban history)
Includes index
ISBN 0-7185-1177-8 : £22.00 : CIP rev. B82-04878

307.76 — Urban development — *Conference proceedings*

World Congress of Engineers and Architects in Israel *(5th : 1979 : Israel).* Urban development and urban renewal. — London : George Godwin, Sept.1981. — [296]p. — (International forum series)
ISBN 0-7114-5728-x : £16.00 : CIP entry B81-23853

307.7′6 — Urban regions

Urban change and conflict : an interdisciplinary reader / edited by Andrew Blowers ... [et al.] at the Open University. — London : Harper & Row in association with the Open University Press, 1982, c1981. — xii,220p : ill,maps ; 25cm. — (Open University set book)
Includes bibliographies and index
ISBN 0-06-318203-3 (cased) : Unpriced : CIP rev.
ISBN 0-06-318204-1 (pbk) : Unpriced B81-34487

Urban change and conflict. — Milton Keynes : Open University Press. — (Social sciences : a second level course)
At head of title: The Open University
Block 2 : Market processes 1 : forces in urban and regional development / block coordinator Christopher Brook. — 1982. — 87p : ill(some col.),maps(some col.) ; 30cm. — (D202 ; block 2, units 5 and 6)
Includes bibliographies. — Contents: Unit 5: City development in a hinterland — Unit 6: Migration and urban change
ISBN 0-335-12057-1 (pbk) : Unpriced B82-21216

Urban change and conflict. — Milton Keynes : Open University Press. — (Social sciences : a second level course)
At head of title: The Open University
Block 2 : Market processes 1 : forces in urban and regional development / block coordinator Christopher Brook. — 1982. — 100p : ill(some col.),maps(some col.) ; 30cm. — (D202 ; block 2, units 7 and 8)
Includes bibliographies. — Contents: Unit 7: The emergence of a system of cities — Unit 8: The evolving metropolitan area
ISBN 0-335-12058-x (pbk) : Unpriced B82-21215

Urban change and conflict. — Milton Keynes : Open University Press. — (Social sciences : a second level course)
At head of title: The Open University
Block 3: Market processes 2 : the internal structure of the city / block coordinator Chris Hamnett. — 1982. — 103p : ill(some col.),maps(some col.) ; 30cm. — (D202 ; block 3, units 9 and 10)
Includes bibliographies. — Contents: Unit 9: Urban land use and the property development industry — Unit 10: Industry and employment in urban areas
ISBN 0-335-12059-8 (pbk) : Unpriced B82-21218

Urban change and conflict. — Milton Keynes : Open University Press. — (Social sciences : a second level course)
At head of title: The Open University
Block 3: Market processes 2 : the internal structure of the city / block coordinator Chris Hamnett. — 1982. — 95p : ill(some col.),maps (some col.) ; 30cm. — (D202 ; block 3, units 11 and 12)
Includes bibliographies. — Contents: Unit 11: City centres, condemned or reprieved? — Unit 12: Urban housing markets
ISBN 0-335-12060-1 (pbk) : Unpriced B82-21217

Urban change and conflict. — Milton Keynes : Open University Press. — (Social sciences : a second level course)
At head of title: The Open University
Block 4: Conflict and stability in urban society / block co-ordinators Allan Cochrane and Linda McDowell. — 1982. — 111p : ill,maps ; 30cm. — (D202 ; block 4, unit 13, 14 and 15)
Includes bibliographies. — Contents: Unit 12: Class, status, location and life-style — Unit 14: Community and the city — Unit 15: Race, ethnicity and urban change
ISBN 0-335-12061-x (pbk) : Unpriced B82-32216

Urban change and conflict. — Milton Keynes : Open University Press. — (Social science : a second level course)
At head of title: The Open University
Block 4: Conflict and stability in urban society / block coordinators Allan Cochrane and Linda McDowell. — 1982. — 143p : ill(some col.),col.maps ; 30cm. — (D202 ; block 4, units 16, 17 and 18)
Includes bibliographies. — Contents: Unit 16: Is there an urban crisis? — Unit 17: Urban government and public services — Unit 18: Political issues and urban policy-making
ISBN 0-335-12062-8 (pbk) : Unpriced B82-32217

Urban change and conflict. — Milton Keynes : Open University Press. — (Social sciences : a second level course)
At head of title: The Open University
Block 5: State intervention 1 : planning and market processes / block coordinator: Andrew Blowers. — 1982. — 140p : ill(some col.),maps (some col.) ; 30cm. — (D202 ; block 5, units 19, 20 and 21)
Includes bibliographies. — Contents: Unit 19: The British planning system — Unit 20: Finance and planning in land and property development — Unit 21: Regional planning
ISBN 0-335-12063-6 (pbk) : Unpriced B82-34533

Urban change and conflict. — Milton Keynes : Open University Press. — (Social sciences : a second level course)
At head of title: The Open University
Block 5: State intervention 1 : planning and market processes / block coordinator: Andrew Blowers. — 1982. — 87p : ill,1col.facsim,col.plans ; 30cm. — (D202 ; block, 5, units 22 and 23)
Includes bibliographies. — Contents: Unit 22: Local planning — Unit 23: The effects of town and country planning in Britain
ISBN 0-335-12064-4 (pbk) : Unpriced B82-34534

Urban change and conflict. — Milton Keynes : Open University Press. — (Social sciences : a second level course)
At head of title: The Open University
Block 6: State intervention 2 : urban public services and state investment / block coordinator Stephen Potter. — 1982. — 148p : ill(some col.) ; 30cm. — (D202 ; block 6, units 26-28b)
Contents: Unit 26: Public housing — Unit 27: The transport policy crisis — Unit 28a: The new town experience — Unit 28b: The inner-city crisis
ISBN 0-335-12066-0 (pbk) : Unpriced B82-40661

307.7′6 — Urban regions — *For schools*

Punnett, Neil. Towns and cities / Neil Punnett, Peter Webber. — Basingstoke : Macmillan Education, 1982. — 74p : ill,maps ; 25cm. — (Geography in focus)
Includes index
ISBN 0-333-29530-7 (pbk) : £2.25 : CIP rev. B82-01852

307.7'6 — Urban regions. Social development — *Conference proceedings*

New perspectives in urban change and conflict / edited by Michael Harloe. — London : Heinemann Educational, 1981. — 265p ; 23cm
Conference proceedings. — Bibliography: p250-261. — Includes index
ISBN 0-435-82404-x : £15.00 : CIP rev. B81-23767

307.7'6 — Urban regions — *Sociological perspectives*

City, class and capital : new developments in the political economy of cities and regions / edited by Michael Harloe and Elizabeth Lebas. — London : Edward Arnold, 1981. — xxxiii,188p ; 22cm
Includes bibliographies and index
ISBN 0-7131-6346-1 (pbk) : £6.95 : CIP rev. B81-25733

307.7'6 — Urban sociology

Forrest, Ray. Urban political economy and social theory : critical essays in urban studies / Ray Forrest, Jeff Henderson and Peter Williams. — Aldershot : Gower, c1982. — x,220p ; 23cm
Bibliography: p203-220
ISBN 0-566-00493-3 : Unpriced : CIP rev. B82-09730

Gold, Harry, *19---*. The sociology of urban life / Harry Gold. — Englewood Cliffs ; London : Prentice-Hall, c1982. — x,421p : ill ; 24cm
Includes bibliographies and index
ISBN 0-13-821371-2 : £15.70 B82-21696

307.7'6'05 — Urban sociology — *Serials*

Papers in urban and regional studies. — No.1 (Feb. 1977)-. — Birmingham (P.O. Box 363, Birmingham B15 2TT) : Centre for Urban and Regional Studies, University of Birmingham, 1977-. — v. ; 21cm
Irregular. — Description based on: No.4 (1980)
ISSN 0263-9017 = Papers in urban and regional studies : £1.50 B82-36724

307.7'6'0724 — Urban regions. Mathematical models

Foot, David, *1939-*. Operational urban models : an introduction / David Foot. — London : Methuen, 1981. — xviii,231p : ill,maps ; 22cm
Bibliography: p214-220. — Includes index
ISBN 0-416-73320-4 (cased) : Unpriced : CIP rev.
ISBN 0-416-73330-1 (pbk) : £5.95 B81-30396

307.7'6'091724 — Developing countries. Cities — *For schools*

Massingham, Bryan. Cities and industry in the developing world / Bryan Massingham. — London : Edward Arnold, 1981. — 64p : ill,maps ; 24cm. — (Patterns of development)
ISBN 0-7131-0455-4 (pbk) : £2.25 : CIP rev.
Also classified at 338.09172'4 B81-23832

307.7'6'091724 — Developing countries. Urban development

Gilbert, Alan. Cities, poverty, and development. — Oxford : Oxford University Press, July 1982. — [288]p
ISBN 0-19-874083-2 (cased) : £12.50 : CIP entry
ISBN 0-19-874084-0 (pbk) : £5.95 B82-13229

307.7'6'091724 — Developing countries. Urban regions. Social planning — *Case studies*

Problems and planning in Third World cities / edited by Michael Pacione. — London : Croom Helm, 1981. — 290p : ill,maps ; 23cm
Includes bibliographies and index
ISBN 0-7099-0192-5 : £12.95 : CIP rev. B81-21502

307.7'6'091812 — Western world. Urban regions. Human geographical features

Knox, Paul L. Urban social geography : an introduction / Paul Knox. — London : Longman, 1982. — viii,243p : ill,maps,1facsim ; 25cm
Bibliography: p213-235. — Includes index
ISBN 0-582-30044-4 (pbk) : £7.95 : CIP rev. B81-22551

307.7'6'0941 — Great Britain. Cities. Inner areas. Social planning

Lawless, Paul. Britain's inner cities. — London : Harper and Row, May 1981. — [224]p
ISBN 0-06-318184-3 (cased) : £8.95 : CIP entry
ISBN 0-06-318185-1 (pbk) : £4.95 B81-06605

307.7'6'0941 — Great Britain. Urban regions. Structure, *1800-1900*

The Structure of nineteenth century cities / edited by James H. Johnson and Colin G. Pooley. — London : Croom Helm, c1982. — 312p : ill ; 23cm
Includes bibliographies and index
ISBN 0-7099-1412-1 : £13.95 : CIP rev. B82-02629

307.7'6'09411 — Scotland. Urban regions, *to 1950*

Scottish urban history. — Aberdeen : Aberdeen University Press, Oct.1982. — [240]p
ISBN 0-08-025762-3 : £11.00 : CIP entry B82-24948

307.7'6'09417 — Ireland *(Republic)*. **Urban regions. Development**

Stokes, Dermot. Urban Ireland. — Dublin : O'Brien Press, Aug.1982. — [96]p
ISBN 0-86278-017-9 : £9.00 : CIP entry B82-17221

307.7'6'0944 — France. Urbanisation, *1800-1900*

French cities in the nineteenth century / edited by John M. Merriman. — London : Hutchinson, 1982. — 304p : ill,2maps ; 23cm. — (Hutchinson university library)
Bibliography: p287-293. — Includes index
ISBN 0-09-145200-7 : £17.50 : CIP rev. B81-34507

307.7'6'094672 — Spain. Barcelona. Urbanisation, *to 1980*

Lowder, Stella. The evolution and identity of urban social areas : the case of Barcelona / Stella Lowder. — [Glasgow] : [University of Glasgow, Department of Geography], [1980]. — 37p : ill,maps ; 30cm. — (Occasional papers / Geography Department Glasgow University ; no.4)
Unpriced (spiral) B82-27872

307.7'6'0952 — Japan. Urban regions, *to 1981*

Kornhauser, David. Japan : geographical background to urban-industrial development. — 2nd ed. — London : Longman, Sept.1982. — [192]p. — (The World's landscapes)
Previous ed. published as: Urban Japan. 1976
ISBN 0-582-30081-9 : £5.95 : CIP entry B82-20262

307.7'6'0973 — United States. Urban regions

Johnston, R. J. The American urban system : a geographical perspective / R.J. Johnston. — London : Longman, 1982. — xii,348p : ill,maps ; 23cm
Includes bibliographies and index
ISBN 0-582-30101-7 (pbk) : £6.95 : CIP rev. B82-00211

307.7'6'09943 — Queensland. Open Cut. Working class communities. Social conditions

Williams, Claire. Open Cut. — London : Allen & Unwin, Jan.1982. — [218]p. — (Studies in society ; 8)
ISBN 0-86861-299-5 : £12.00 : CIP entry B81-33932

307.7'62'094585 — Malta. Casals — *Case studies*

Gibb, A.. Siggiewi : a Maltese casal / A. Gibb, J.W. Shearer, D. Kennedy. — [Glasgow] : [University of Glasgow, Department of Geography], [1980]. — 5p,[1]folded leaf of plates : 1ill,1col.map ; 30cm. — (Occasional papers / Geography Department Glasgow University ; no.2)
Bibliography: p5
Unpriced (spiral) B82-27868

307.7'62'09515 — Tibet. Villages. Social conditions

Dargvay, Eva K.. Tibetan village communities. — Warminster : Aris and Phillips, Nov.1982. — [120]p. — (Central Asian studies)
ISBN 0-85668-151-2 (pbk) : CIP entry B82-28759

307.7'64'09034 — Cities, *1800-1980* — *Conference proceedings*

Modern industrial cities : history, policy, and survival / edited by Bruce M. Stave. — Beverly Hills ; London : Sage, c1981. — 307p : ill,maps ; 23cm. — (Sage focus editions ; 44)
Conference papers. — Includes index
ISBN 0-8039-1760-0 (corrected: cased) : Unpriced
ISBN 0-08-391760-0
ISBN 0-8039-1761-9 (pbk) : £6.50 B82-24069

307.7'64'091724 — Developing countries. Cities — *For schools*

Jones, Melvyn. Developing cities / Melvyn Jones. — Walton-on-Thames : Nelson for the Schools Council, 1982. — 48p : ill(some col.),maps (some col.),plans ; 28cm. — (Geography and change)
ISBN 0-17-434182-2 (pbk) : Unpriced B82-29552

307.7'64'0942 — England. Cities. Social aspects, *1860-1914*

Briggs, Asa. Cities and countrysides : British and American experience : (1860-1914) / by Asa Briggs. — Leicester : Victorian Studies Centre, University of Leicester, 1982. — 20p ; 22cm. — (The H.J. Dyos memorial lecture)
ISBN 0-9500518-9-6 (pbk) : Unpriced
Also classified at 307.7'64'0973 B82-34651

Dyos, H. J.. Exploring the urban past : essays in urban history / by H.J. Dyos ; edited by David Cannadine and David Reeder. — Cambridge : Cambridge University Press, 1982. — xix,258p ; 24cm
ISBN 0-521-24624-5 (cased) : Unpriced : CIP rev.
ISBN 0-521-28848-7 (pbk) : Unpriced B82-20760

307.7'64'0954 — South Asia. Cities, *1700-1979* — *Conference proceedings*

The City in South Asia : pre-modern and modern / edited by Kenneth Ballhatchet and John Harrison. — London : Curzon, 1980. — xiii,342p : ill,maps ; 23cm. — (Collected papers on South Asia, ISSN 0141-0156 ; no.3)
ISBN 0-7007-0133-8 : £6.00 : CIP rev. B80-18602

307.7'64'0973 — United States. Cities

Internal structure of the city : readings on urban form, growth, and policy / edited by Larry S. Bourne. — 2nd ed. — New York ; Oxford : Oxford University Press, 1982. — xi,629p : ill,maps ; 24cm
Previous ed.: 1971. — Bibliography: p619-629
ISBN 0-19-503032-x (pbk) : £7.50 B82-34507

307.7'64'0973 — United States. Cities. Social aspects, *1860-1914*

Briggs, Asa. Cities and countrysides : British and American experience : (1860-1914) / by Asa Briggs. — Leicester : Victorian Studies Centre, University of Leicester, 1982. — 20p ; 22cm. — (The H.J. Dyos memorial lecture)
ISBN 0-9500518-9-6 (pbk) : Unpriced
Primary classification 307.7'64'0942 B82-34651

307.7'64'0973 — United States. Cities, *to 1978*

American urban history : an interpretive reader with commentaries / edited by Alexander B. Callow, Jr. — 3rd ed. — New York ; Oxford : Oxford University Press, 1982. — x,566p : ill ; 23cm
Previous ed.: 1973
ISBN 0-19-502981-x (pbk) : £8.95 B82-31569

307.7'66'096894 — Zambia. Copperbelt. Urbanisation. Social aspects

Epstein, A. L.. Urbanization and kinship : the domestic domain on the Copperbelt of Zambia 1950-1956 / A.L. Epstein. — London : Academic Press, 1981. — xii,364p : ill,1geneal.table ; 24cm. — (Studies in anthropology)
Bibliography: p355-359. — Includes index
ISBN 0-12-240520-x : £16.80 : CIP rev. B81-31337

307.7′72 — Middle East. Nomadic tribes. Effects of social change, *559 B.C.-323 B.C. — French texts*

Briant, Pierre. Etat et pasteurs au Moyen-orient ancien / Pierre Briant. — Cambridge : Cambridge University Press, 1982. — 267p : ill,maps ; 24cm
Bibliography: p241-253. — Includes index
ISBN 0-521-24376-9 : £25.00 B82-26776

307.7′72 — North America. Arctic. Nomadic hunter-gatherer communities — *Anthropological perspectives*

Riches, David. Northern nomadic hunter-gatherers : a humanistic approach / David Riches. — London : Academic Press, 1982. — xii,240p ; 24cm. — (Studies in anthropology)
Bibliography: p226-234. — Includes index
ISBN 0-12-587620-3 : £11.80 : CIP rev.
B82-07488

307.7′74′09794 — California. Rural regions. Communes — *Sociological perspectives — Case studies*

Berger, Bennett M.. The survival of a counterculture : ideological work and everyday life among rural communards / by Bennett M. Berger. — Berkeley ; London : University of California Press, c1981. — xiv,264p ; 22cm
Bibliography: p243-249. — Includes index
ISBN 0-520-02388-9 : £11.25 B82-02222

307.7′76′095694 — Israel. Kibbutzim. Social change, *to 1975 — Case studies*

Rayman, Paula M.. The kibbutz community and nation building / Paula Rayman. — Princeton ; Guildford : Princeton University Press, c1981. — xiv,308p ; 23cm
Bibliography: p281-294. — Includes index
ISBN 0-691-09391-1 (cased) : £17.60
ISBN 0-691-10124-8 (pbk) : Unpriced
B82-14169

310 — STATISTICS

310 — Social sciences. Statistics — *For African students*

Lerche, C. O.. Social and economic statistics : a foundation course for African students. — London : Longman, Jan.1983. — [192]p
ISBN 0-582-64332-5 (pbk) : £3.95 : CIP entry
B82-32470

312 — POPULATION STATISTICS

312′.09411′35 — Scotland. Shetland. Inhabitants, *1872 — Lists*

Sandison, Alexander. Some inhabitants in Shetland in 1872 / compiled by A. Sandison. — London : A. Sandison, 1980. — 34p ; 30cm
Limited ed. of 50 copies. — Includes index
ISBN 0-9506191-1-6 (pbk) : £10.00
B82-12307

312′.09414′23 — Scotland. Strathclyde Region. Islay. Inhabitants, *1655-1871 — Lists*

Booth, C. G.. A list of Islay people / compiled for the Museum of Islay Life by C.G. Booth. — [Port Charlotte] ([Isle of Islay, Argyll]) : [Islay Museums Trust], 1982. — 30leaves ; 30cm
Unpriced (unbound) B82-25049

312′.099312′2 — New Zealand. Auckland. Population, *1976 — Census tables*

Taylor, M. A.. Population patterns : Auckland at the 1976 census / by M.A. Taylor, M.S. Putterill, J.R. Dart assisted by J.B. Oliver & E.F. Schwarz. — [Auckland] : Auckland University Press ; [Oxford] : Oxford University Press, 1980. — 110p in various pagings : ill,maps ; 30cm
Accompanied by tracings of selected Auckland census area units and local authority areas
ISBN 0-19-647990-8 (pbk) : £6.95 B82-31269

312′.2′0723 — Survival data. Statistical analysis

Miller, Rupert G.. Survival analysis / Rupert G. Miller, Jr ; notes by Gail Gong ; problem solutions by Alvaro Muñoz. — New York ; Chichester : Wiley, c1981. — xi,238p : ill ; 23cm. — (Wiley series in probability and mathematical statistics)
Bibliography: p213-229. — Includes index
ISBN 0-471-09434-x (pbk) : £12.25
B82-10186

312′.27 — England. Drownings, *1976 — Statistics*

Drowning statistics, England and Wales, 1976. — London : Home Office Scientific Advisory Branch, 1980. — 46p : ill ; 21cm. — (Accident studies)
ISBN 0-86252-000-2 (pbk) : £3.00 B82-06593

312′.3′0942 — England. Morbidity, *1968-1978 — Sources of data: Hospitals. In-patients — Statistics*

Trends in morbidity 1968-1978 applying surveillance techniques to the hospital in-patient enquiry : England and Wales / Department of Health and Social Security, Office of Population Censuses and Surveys, Welsh Office. — [London] : [Office of Population Censuses and Surveys], [1981]. — xii,141p ; 21x31cm
ISBN 0-906197-25-2 (spiral) : Unpriced
B82-00666

312′.3994′009411 — Scotland. Man. Cancer — *Statistics*

Cancer registration and survival statistics Scotland 1963-1977 : Scottish cancer registration scheme. — Edinburgh (Trinity Park House, South Trinity Rd, Edinburgh EH5 3SQ) : Information Services Division, Scottish Health Services Common Services Agency, 1981. — 72p : ill,1map ; 21x30cm
Cover title
Unpriced (spiral) B82-34362

312′.3994′00942 — England. Man. Cancer — *Statistics*

Cancer statistics : incidence, survival and mortality in England and Wales / [J.R. Toms ... et al.]. — London : H.M.S.O., 1981. — xxviii,114p : ill,maps ; 30cm. — (Studies on medical and population subjects ; no.46)
At head of title: Office of Population Censuses and Surveys, Cancer Research Campaign
ISBN 0-11-690787-8 (pbk) : £14.50
B82-11689

312′.9 — England. Households. Social conditions, *1978-1979 — Statistics*

National dwelling and housing survey : phases II and III / Department of the Environm,ent. — London : H.M.S.O., 1980. — 318p : form ; 30cm
ISBN 0-11-751487-x (pbk) : £25.00
B82-18621

314 — GENERAL STATISTICS OF EUROPE

314.1′07 — Great Britain. Social conditions. Statistics. Information sources

Statistical sources / [the Statistical Sources Course Team]. — Milton Keynes : Open University Press. — (Social sciences : a second level course)
At head of title: The Open University
Audiovision handbook 2: Audio. — 1982. — 31p : ill ; 30cm. — (D291 ; AVH2)
ISBN 0-335-04645-2 (unbound) : Unpriced
B82-40655

Statistical sources / [the Statistical Sources Course Team]. — Milton Keynes : Open University Press. — (Social sciences : a second level course)
At head of title: The Open University
Do statistics influence policy? / prepared for the course team by Ray Thomas. — 1980 (1981 [printing]). — 26p ; 30cm. — (D291)
Bibliography: p25-26
ISBN 0-335-04629-0 (unbound) : Unpriced
B82-04552

Statistical sources / [the Statistical Sources Course Team]. — Milton Keynes : Open University Press. — (Social sciences : a second level course) (D291)
At head of title: The Open University
Labour and income. — 1982. — 110p : ill ; 30cm
Includes bibliographies. — Contents: Part 1: The labour force — Part 2: Income
ISBN 0-335-04646-0 (pbk) : Unpriced
B82-34539

Statistical sources / [the Statistical Sources Course Team]. — Milton Keynes : Open University Press. — (Social sciences : a second level course)
At head of title: The Open University
Transport statistics : sources with car taxation case study / prepared for the Course Team by S. Potter and S. Cousins. — 1981. — 27p : ill ; 30cm. — (D291)
Bibliography: p26
ISBN 0-335-04633-9 (unbound) : Unpriced
B82-04553

314.1′07 — Great Britain. Statistics. Information sources

Rendall, F. J.. Statistical sources and techniques. — Maidenhead : McGraw-Hill, Feb.1983. — [256]p
ISBN 0-07-084658-8 (pbk) : £6.50 : CIP entry
B82-36476

314.2′05 — England. Counties. Social conditions, *1981 — Statistics — Serials*

OPCS county monitor : census 1981. — CEN 81 CM 1-. — London (10 Kingsway, WC2B 6JP) : Information Branch (Dept. M), Office of Population Censuses and Surveys, 1981-. — v. ; 30cm
Irregular. — Title on binder: County monitors, England and Wales. — Issues not published in numerical sequence. — Description based on: CEN 81 CM 23 (13 Oct. 1981)
ISSN 0261-2216 = OPCS county monitor : £0.30 B82-10121

314.2′05 — England. Social conditions — *Statistics — Serials*

OPCS monitor. [Social survey] / Office of Population Censuses & Surveys. — SS 81/1 (27 Oct. 1981)-. — London (10 Kingsway, WC2B 6JP) : Information Branch (Dept. M), Office of Population Censuses & Surveys, 1981-. — v. : ill ; 30cm
Irregular
ISSN 0262-8392 = OPCS monitor. SS : Unpriced B82-10120

314.29′05 — Wales. Counties. Social conditions, *1981 — Statistics — Welsh texts — Serials*

[Blaengyfrif sirol *(Great Britain. Office of Population Censuses and Surveys)*]. Blaengyfrif sirol : cyfrifiad 1981 / Swyddfa Cyfrif ac Adolygu′r Boblogaeth. — CEN 81 CM 47-. — Llundain [London] (10 Kingsway WC2B 6JP) : Cang n Hysbysrswydd (Adr M), Swyddfa Cyfrif ac Adolygu′r Boblogaeth, 1981-. — v. ; 30cm
Irregular. — Welsh edition of: OPCS county monitor. — Issues not published in numerical sequence. — Description based on: CEN 81 CM 52 (Tach. 1981)
ISSN 0262-7167 = Blaengyfrif sirol - Swyddfa Cyfrif ac Adolygu′r Boblogaeth (corrected) : £0.30 B82-10122

315 — GENERAL STATISTICS OF ASIA

315.1′249 — Taiwan — *Statistics — For marketing*

Taiwan market data. — Farnborough : Gower, Oct.1981. — [150]p
ISBN 0-566-02307-5 (pbk) : £25.00 : CIP entry
B81-27950

315.1′25 — Hong Kong — *Statistics — For marketing*

Hong Kong and Macau market data. — Farnborough, Hants. : Gower, Nov.1981. — [150]p
ISBN 0-566-02310-5 (pbk) : £25.00 : CIP entry
B81-31257

315.19′5 — South Korea — *Statistics — For marketing*

South Korea market data. — Farnborough : Gower, Nov.1981. — [150]p
ISBN 0-566-02309-1 (pbk) : £25.00 : CIP entry
B81-31256

315.99 — Philippines — *Statistics — For marketing*

Philippines market data. — Farnborough : Gower, Oct.1981. — [150]p
ISBN 0-566-02308-3 (pbk) : £25.00 : CIP entry
B81-28047

318 — GENERAL STATISTICS OF SOUTH AMERICA

318.3 — Chile. Social conditions, *to 1980 — Statistics*
Mamalakis, Markos J.. Historical statistics of Chile / compiled by Markos J. Mamalakis. — Westport, Conn. ; London : Greenwood Press
Bibliography: pxxxix-li
Vol.2: Demography and labor force. — 1980. — li,420p ; 29cm
ISBN 0-313-20854-9 : Unpriced B82-19345

319 — GENERAL STATISTICS OF OCEANIA, ATLANTIC OCEAN ISLANDS, ETC

319.31 — New Zealand — *Statistics — For marketing*
New Zealand and Pacific islands. — Aldershot : Gower, Aug.1982. — [150]p. — (The Markets of Asia/Pacific)
ISBN 0-566-02313-x (pbk) : £25.00 : CIP entry B82-29132

320 — POLITICAL SCIENCE

320 — Politics
al-Qadhdhāfi, Mu'ammar. The green book / Muammar al-Qadhafi. — London : Martin Brian & O'Keeffe
Pt.1: The solution of the problem of democracy : 'the authority of the people'. — 1976. — 32,48p : ill ; 19cm
Added t.p. in Arabic. — English and Arabic text
ISBN 0-85616-410-0 (pbk) : Unpriced
Also classified at 330 B82-21787

Blondel, Jean. The discipline of politics / Jean Blondel. — London : Butterworths, 1981. — viii,222p ; 23cm
Includes bibliographies and index
ISBN 0-408-10681-6 (cased) : Unpriced : CIP rev.
ISBN 0-408-10785-5 (pbk) : Unpriced B81-16928

Crick, Bernard. In defence of politics / Bernard Crick. — 2nd Pelican ed. — Harmondsworth : Penguin, 1982. — 240p ; 20cm. — (Pelican books)
Previous ed.: i.e. rev. ed. 1964
ISBN 0-14-020655-8 (pbk) : £2.95 B82-40948

Deutsch, Karl W.. Politics and government : how people decide their fate / Karl W. Deutsch. — 3rd ed. — Boston ; London : Houghton Mifflin, c1980. — xxxii,656,xxviip : ill,maps ; 25cm
Previous ed.: 1974. — Includes bibliographies and index
ISBN 0-395-28486-4 : £16.50 B82-24275

Levine, Herbert M.. Political issues debated : an introduction to politics / Herbert M. Levine. — Englewood Cliffs, N.J. ; London : Prentice-Hall, c1982. — xiii,319p ; 24cm
Includes bibliographies and index
ISBN 0-13-685032-4 : Unpriced B82-28349

Mackintosh, John P.. John P. Mackintosh on parliament and social democracy / edited and introduced by David Marquand. — London : Longman, 1982. — vii,279p ; 22cm
Bibliography: p259-271. — Includes index
ISBN 0-582-29587-4 (pbk) : £7.95 : CIP rev. B82-06926

Ponton, Geoffrey. Introduction to politics / Geoffrey Ponton and Peter Gill (in collaboration with John Vogler). — Oxford : Robertson, 1982. — xii,268p ; 24cm
Includes bibliographies and index
ISBN 0-85520-466-4 (cased) : Unpriced : CIP rev.
ISBN 0-85520-467-2 (pbk) : Unpriced B81-35703

Ranney, Austin. Governing : an introduction to political science / Austin Ranney. — 3rd ed. — New York ; London : Holt, Rinehart and Winston, 1982. — xi,544p : ill,facsims,ports ; 25cm
Previous ed.: New York : Dryden, 1975. — Includes bibliographies and index
ISBN 0-03-045106-x : £14.95 B82-19437

World politics / [the D233 World Politics Course Team]. — Milton Keynes : Open University Press. — (Social sciences : a second level course)
At head of title: The Open University
[Block 5]: A third perspective : dominance and dependence / prepared by the course team. — 1981. — 169p : ill,maps,ports ; 30cm. — (D233 ; V (12-15))
Includes bibliographies. — Contents: Paper 12: The Lomé Convention, a case study — Paper 13: The structuralist approach, key concepts — Paper 14: Imperialism, modes of dominance and dependence — Paper 15: Capitalism, its instruments and effects
ISBN 0-335-12029-6 (pbk) : Unpriced B82-17527

320 — Politics — *Early works*
Madison, James. The mind of the founder : sources of the political thought of James Madison / edited with introduction and commentary by Marvin Meyers. — Rev. ed. — Hanover [N.H.] ; London : Published for Brandeis University Press by University Press of New England, 1981. — lvi,449p ; 22cm
Previous ed.: Indianapolis : Bobbs-Merrill, 1973. — Bibliography: pliii-lvi. — Includes index
ISBN 0-87451-201-8 (pbk) : £7.00 B82-13762

320'.01 — Politics — *Philosophical perspectives*
Contemporary political philosophy : radical studies / edited by Keith Graham. — Cambridge : Cambridge University Press, 1982. — 159p ; 23cm
Includes bibliographies
ISBN 0-521-24551-6 (cased) : £12.50 : CIP rev.
ISBN 0-521-28783-9 (pbk) : £4.50 B82-11526

Grimond, Jo. Is political philosophy based on a mistake? / Jo Grimond. — London (9 Poland St., W1V 3DG) : Poland Street Publications, [1981?]. — 15p ; 22cm. — (The Romanes lecture 1980)
Unpriced (pbk) B82-26666

320'.01 — Politics. Philosophical perspectives
Iyer, Raghavan. Parapolitics : toward the City of Man / Raghavan Iyer. — New York ; Oxford : Oxford University Press, 1979. — viii,381p : ill ; 22cm
Includes index
ISBN 0-19-502596-2 : £9.75 B82-14603

320'.01 — Politics — *Philosophical perspectives*
Shapiro, Michael J.. Language and political understanding : the politics of discursive practices / Michael J. Shapiro. — New Haven ; London : Yale University Press, c1981. — x,253p : ill ; 25cm
Includes index
ISBN 0-300-02590-4 : Unpriced : CIP rev. B81-34719

320'.01 — Politics — *Philosophical perspectives — Early works*
al-Fārābī, Abū Naṣr. [Ārā' ahl al-madīnah al-fāḍilah. English]. Al-Farabi on the perfect state. — Oxford : Clarendon Press, Apr.1982. — [57]p
Translation of: Ārā' ahl al-madīnah al-fāḍilah
ISBN 0-19-824505-x : £15.00 : CIP entry B82-14955

320'.01 — Politics. Theories
Contemporary political theory / edited by J.S. Bains, R.B. Jain. — Atlantic Highlands : Humanities ; Gloucester : distributed by Sutton, c1980. — xv,185p ; 23cm
Includes index
ISBN 0-391-01901-5 : Unpriced B82-38119

Goodin, Robert E.. Political theory and public policy. — Oxford : Blackwell, July 1982. — [256]p
ISBN 0-631-12965-0 (cased) : £15.00 : CIP entry
ISBN 0-631-13104-3 (pbk) : £4.95 B82-14241

Krishna, Daya. Political development : a critical perspective / Daya Krishna. — Delhi ; Oxford : Oxford University Press, 1979. — x,211p ; 23cm
Includes index
ISBN 0-19-561117-9 : £5.75 B82-14607

Perspectives in political theory / edited by J.S. Bains, R.B. Jain. — Atlantic Highlands : Humanities ; Gloucester : distributed by Sutton, 1980. — xi,207p ; 23cm
Includes index
ISBN 0-391-01900-7 : Unpriced B82-38116

320'.01 — Politics. Theories — *Early works*
Hobbes, Thomas. Leviathan / Thomas Hobbes ; edited with an introduction by C.B. Macpherson. — Harmondsworth : Penguin, 1968 (1981 [printing]). — 728p ; 18cm
Originally published: London : Andrew Crooke, 1651
ISBN 0-14-043195-0 (pbk) : £2.25 B82-08031

320'.01 — Politics. Theories — *Feminist viewpoints*
O'Brien, Mary. The politics of reproduction / Mary O'Brien. — Boston, Mass. ; London : Routledge & Kegan Paul, 1981. — x,240p ; 22cm
Bibliography: p227-233. — Includes index
ISBN 0-7100-0810-4 : £11.95 : CIP rev. B81-13724

320'.01 — Politics. Theories — *Festschriften*
The Nature of political theory. — Oxford : Clarendon Press, Jan.1983. — [240]p
ISBN 0-19-827441-6 : £17.50 : CIP entry B82-33486

320'.01 — Politics. Theories — *Latin texts*
Hobbes, Thomas. De cive : the Latin version. — Oxford : Clarendon Press, Oct.1982. — [292]p. — (The Clarendon edition of the philosophical works of Thomas Hobbes ; v.2)
ISBN 0-19-824385-5 : £25.00 : CIP entry B82-26695

320'.01 — Politics. Theories of Locke, John
Dunn, John. The political thought of John Locke. — Cambridge : Cambridge University Press, Sept.1982. — [290]p
Originally published: 1969
ISBN 0-521-27139-8 (pbk) : £7.50 : CIP entry B82-21730

320'.05 — Politics — *Serials*
Focal point : issued to the Focus Policy Group. — [198?]-. — London (Suite 411, 76 Shoe La., E.C.4) : [Focalpoint], [198-]-. — v. : ill,facsims,ports ; 30cm
Description based on: Apr. 14th 1981
ISSN 0263-6662 = Focal point : £0.20 B82-29050

[Politics *(Manchester)*]. Politics / the Political Studies Association of the United Kingdom. — Vol.1, no.1 (Apr. 1981)-. — Manchester : The Association, 1981-. — v. ; 30cm
Two issues yearly. — Description based on: Vol.2, no.1 (Apr. 1982)
ISSN 0263-3957 = Politics (Manchester) : Unpriced B82-27651

320'.07'1 — Western world. Schools. Students. Political education
Political education in flux / edited by Derek Heater and Judith A. Gillespie. — London : Sage, c1981. — 302p : ill ; 23cm. — (Sage annual reviews of social and educational change ; v.3)
Includes bibliographies
ISBN 0-8039-9822-8 : Unpriced : CIP rev. B81-20612

320'.07'1041 — Great Britain. Educational institutions. Curriculum subjects: Politics
Brennan, Tom. Political education and democracy / Tom Brennan. — Cambridge : Cambridge University Press, 1981. — 149p ; 22cm
Bibliography: p122-133
ISBN 0-521-28267-5 (pbk) : £3.95 : CIP rev. B81-28845

320'.07'1141 — Great Britain. Polytechnics & universities. Curriculum subjects: Politics — *Comparative studies*
Bristow, Steve. Politics in polytechnics / by Steve Bristow & Vicky Randall. — [London] ([School of Social Sciences and Business, Polytechnic of Central London, 70 Great Portland St., W1]) : Political Studies Association of the United Kingdom, 1981. — iv,42p ; 30cm. — (Studies in public policy, ISSN 0140-8240 ; no.95)
Unpriced (pbk) B82-12867

320'.072 — Political science. Research. Methodology

Strategies of political inquiry / edited by Elinor Ostrom. — Beverly Hills ; London : Sage, c1982. — 224p : ill ; 24cm. — (A Sage Focus edition)
Includes bibliographies
ISBN 0-8039-1817-8 (cased) : Unpriced
ISBN 0-8039-1818-6 (pbk) : £7.25 B82-38110

320'.072 — Political science. Research. Quantitative methods

Schware, Robert. Quantification in the history of political thought : toward a qualitative approach / Robert Schware. — Westport ; London : Greenwood, 1981. — 168p ; 22cm. — (Contributions in political science, ISSN 0147-1066 ; no.55)
Bibliography: p155-162. — Includes index
ISBN 0-313-22228-2 : Unpriced B82-02006

320'.09'04 — Politics — *Philosophical perspectives, 1900-1980*

Parekh, B. C.. Contemporary political thinkers. — Oxford : Martin Robertson, Feb.1982. — [224]p
ISBN 0-85520-337-4 (cased) : £10.00 : CIP entry
ISBN 0-85520-336-6 (pbk) : £3.95 B81-35705

320'.096 — Africa. Political science

Political science in Africa. — London : Zed Press, Sept.1982. — [272]p
ISBN 0-86232-033-x (cased) : £14.95 : CIP entry
ISBN 0-86232-034-8 (pbk) : £6.50 B82-20183

320.1 — POLITICS. THE STATE

320.1 — State — *Socialist viewpoints*

Bukharin, N.. Selected writings on the state and the transition to socialism. — Nottingham : Spokesman, Oct.1982. — [351]p
Translation from the Russian
ISBN 0-85124-275-8 : £15.00 : CIP entry B82-32302

320.1'01 — State. Theories — *Early works*

Machiavelli, Niccolò. The prince / by Niccolo Machiavelli ; translated by Daniel Donno ; edited with an introduction by the translator. — Toronto ; London : Bantam, 1966 (1981 [printing]). — 146p ; 17cm : 1map. — (A Bantam classic)
Bibliography: p146
ISBN 0-553-21029-7 (pbk) : £0.85 B82-25133

320.1'01 — State. Theories. Nozick, Robert. Anarchy, state and utopia — *Critical studies*

Reading Nozick : essays on Anarchy, state and utopia / edited with an introduction by Jeffrey Paul. — Oxford : Basil Blackwell, 1982, c1981. — xi,418p ; 22cm
Originally published: Totowa : Rowman & Littlefield, 1981. — Bibliography: p412-416
ISBN 0-631-12977-4 (cased) : Unpriced : CIP rev.
ISBN 0-631-12978-2 (pbk) : Unpriced B81-34296

320.1'024092 — States. Names — *Lists* — *For cataloguing*

IFLA International Office for UBC. Names of states : an authority list of language forms for catalogue entries / compiled by the IFLA International Office of UBC. — London : The Office, 1981. — viii,49p ; 30cm
At head of title: International Federation of Library Associations and Institutions
ISBN 0-903043-32-7 (pbk) : Unpriced B82-08593

320.1'09182'1 — Western world. State, *1200-1981*

Elias, Norbert. The civilizing process / Norbert Elias ; translated by Edmund Jephcott. — Oxford : Blackwell, 1982
[Vol.2]: State formation and civilization. — viii,376p ; 23cm.
Translation of: Über den Prozess der Zivilisation. Bd.2. — Includes index
ISBN 0-631-19680-3 : £19.50 : CIP rev.
Primary classification 395'.09182'1 B81-10486

320.1'094 — State. Theories of Western European writers

Dyson, Kenneth H. F.. The state tradition in Western Europe. — Oxford : Robertson, June 1982. — [320]p
Originally published: 1980
ISBN 0-85520-510-5 (pbk) : £6.50 : CIP entry B82-12163

320.1'0994 — Australia. State. Role, *1840-ca 1950*

Sydney Labour History Group. What rough beast?. — London : Allen & Unwin, Jan.1983. — [276]p
ISBN 0-86861-332-0 : £15.00 : CIP entry B82-33235

320.1'2 — Geopolitics. Mackinder, *Sir* Halford — *Biographies*

Parker, W. H. (William Henry). Mackinder : geography as an aid to statecraft / W.H. Parker. — Oxford : Clarendon Press, 1982. — vi,295p : maps,1port ; 23cm
Bibliography: p262-282. — Includes index
ISBN 0-19-823235-7 : £15.00 : CIP rev. B82-13127

320.1'2 — Politics. Geographical aspects

Short, John R.. An introduction to political geography / John R. Short. — London : Routledge & Kegan Paul, 1982. — xiii,193p : ill,1facsim,maps ; 23cm
Bibliography: p179-185. — Includes index
ISBN 0-7100-0964-x (cased) : £10.00
ISBN 0-7100-0965-8 (pbk) : £5.95 B82-32503

320.1'2'05 — Politics. Geographical aspects — *Serials*

Political geography quarterly. — Vol.1, no.1 (Jan. 1982)-. — Sevenoaks : Butterworths, 1982-. — v. ; 25cm
ISSN 0260-9827 = Political geography quarterly : £30.00 (£12.50 for individuals) B82-17240

320.1'2'091824 — Red Sea countries. Politics. Geographical factors

Lapidoth-Eschelbacher, Ruth. The Red Sea and the Gulf of Aden / Ruth Lapidoth-Eschelbacher. — The Hague ; London : Nijhoff, 1982. — xiv,265p : maps ; 25cm. — (International straits of the world ; 5)
Includes index
ISBN 90-247-2501-1 : Unpriced B82-34543

320.1'2'09981 — Norway. Spitzbergen, *1907-1935.* **International political aspects**

Singh, Elen C.. The Spitsbergen (Svalbard) question : United States foreign policy 1907-1935 / Elen C. Singh. — Oslo : Universitetsforlaget, c1980 ; Henley on Thames : [Distributed by] Global. — 244p : 1ill,2maps ; 22cm
Bibliography: p179-184
ISBN 82-00-01971-3 (pbk) : £12.35 B82-20956

320.1'57 — National independence. Role of United Nations

Pomerance, Michla. Self-determination in law and practice : the new doctrine in the United Nations / by Michla Pomerance. — Hague ; London : Nijhoff, 1982. — xi,154p ; 25cm
Bibliography: p130-138. — Includes index
ISBN 90-247-2594-1 : Unpriced B82-30373

320.3 — COMPARATIVE POLITICS

320.3 — Comparative politics

Calvert, Peter. Politics, power and revolution. — Brighton : Harvester Press, Oct.1982. — [208]p
ISBN 0-7108-0167-x (cased) : £16.95 : CIP entry
ISBN 0-7108-0196-3 (pbk) : £4.95 B82-23178

320.3 — Politics — *Comparative studies*

Bertsch, Gary K.. Comparing political systems : power and policy in three worlds / Gary K. Bertsch, Robert P. Clark, David M. Wood. — 2nd ed. — New York ; Chichester : Wiley, c1982. — viii,548p : ill,maps,ports ; 25cm
Previous ed.: 1978. — Includes bibliographies and index
ISBN 0-471-08446-8 : £17.20 B82-34738

Roskin, Michael G.. Countries and concepts : an introduction to comparative politics / Michael G. Roskin. — Englewood Cliffs ; London : Prentice-Hall, c1982. — xxv,401p : ill,maps,ports ; 25cm
Includes bibliographies and index
ISBN 0-13-184325-7 : £14.95 B82-33776

320.3'09171'7 — Communist countries. Politics — *Comparative studies*

Bertsch, Gary K.. Power and policy in communist systems / Gary K. Bertsch. — 2nd ed. — New York ; Chichester : Wiley, c1982. — x,192p : ill,maps,ports ; 24cm
Previous ed.: 1978. — Includes bibliographies and index
ISBN 0-471-09005-0 (pbk) : £8.85 B82-28035

320.3'09172'4 — Developing countries. Politics — *Comparative studies*

Clark, Robert P.. Power and policy in the Third World / Robert P. Clark. — 2nd ed. — New York ; Chichester : Wiley, c1982. — viii,168p : ill,1map ; 24cm
Previous ed.: 1978. — Includes bibliographies and index
ISBN 0-471-09008-5 (pbk) : £7.00 B82-28036

Gamer, Robert E.. The developing nations : a comparative perspective / Robert E. Gamer. — 2nd ed. — Boston, Mass. ; London : Allyn and Bacon, c1982. — xiii,422p : ill,1map ; 25cm
Previous ed.: 1976. — Map on lining papers. — Includes index
ISBN 0-205-07647-5 : £16.95 B82-27673

320.3'094 — Western Europe. Politics — *Comparative studies*

Wood, David M.. Power and policy in Western European democracies / David M. Wood. — 2nd ed. — New York ; Chichester : Wiley, c1982. — x,177p : ill,maps,ports ; 24cm
Previous ed.: 1978. — Includes bibliographies and index
ISBN 0-471-09006-9 (pbk) : £8.85 B82-27758

320.3'0967 — Africa. Tropical regions. Political systems, *1945-1975* — *Comparative studies*

Collier, Ruth Berins. Regimes in tropical Africa : changing forms of supremacy, 1945-1975 / Ruth Berins Collier. — Berkeley ; London : University of California Press, c1982. — xi,221p : ill,1maps ; 23cm
Bibliography: p181-207. — Includes index
ISBN 0-520-04313-8 : £19.50 B82-31179

320.4 — GOVERNMENT. STRUCTURE, FUNCTIONS, ACTIVITIES

320.441 — Great Britain. Civics

Harvey, J.. The British constitution and politics. — 5th ed. — London : Macmillan Education, May 1982. — [650]p
Previous ed.: 1977
ISBN 0-333-32697-0 (pbk) : £3.95 : CIP entry B82-07425

Randall, F.. British government and politics / F. Randall. — 2nd ed. — Plymouth : Macdonald and Evans, 1981. — ix,276p ; 18cm. — (The M & E handbook series)
Previous ed.: 1979. — Bibliography: p252-256. — Includes index
ISBN 0-7121-0292-2 (pbk) : £3.50 B82-05077

320.441 — Great Britain. Civics — *For schools*

Harvey, J.. How Britain is governed. — 3rd ed. — London : Macmillan, Feb.1983. — [276]p
Previous ed.: 1975
ISBN 0-333-33608-9 (pbk) : £4.95 : CIP entry B82-37862

320.473 — United States. Civics

Getz, Robert S.. The politics and process of American government / Robert S. Getz, Frank B. Feigert. — Boston, Mass. ; London : Allyn and Bacon, c1982. — xvii,590p : ill,maps,plan,ports ; 25cm
Includes bibliographies and index
ISBN 0-205-06862-6 : £20.95 B82-19600

320.473 — United States. Civics *continuation*

Miller, Arthur Selwyn. Democratic dictatorship : the emergent constitution of control / Arthur Selwyn Miller. — Westport, Conn. ; London : Greenwood Press, 1981. — xvi,268p ; 25cm. — (Contributions in American studies, ISSN 0084-9227 ; no.54)
Bibliography: p257-263. — Includes index
ISBN 0-313-22836-1 : Unpriced B82-02143

Saye, Albert B.. Principles of American government / Albert B. Saye, John F. Allums, Merritt B. Pound. — 9th ed. — Englewood Cliffs ; London : Prentice-Hall, c1982. — ix,372p : ill,maps,ports ; 23cm
Previous ed.: 1978. — Includes bibliographies and index
ISBN 0-13-701110-5 (pbk) : £10.45 B82-20068

Sherrill, Kenneth S.. Power, policy and participation : an introduction to American government / Kenneth S. Sherrill, David J. Vogler. — Cambridge, [Mass.] ; London : Harper & Row, c1982. — xviii,621p : ill,ports ; 24cm
Previous ed.: 1977. — Includes bibliographies and index
ISBN 0-06-046120-9 (pbk) : Unpriced B82-34018

320.5 — POLITICAL THEORIES AND IDEOLOGIES

320.5 — Political ideologies

Goodwin, Barbara. Using political ideas / Barbara Goodwin. — Chichester : Wiley, c1982. — v,294p ; 24cm
Includes bibliographies and index
ISBN 0-471-10115-x (cased) : £14.95 : CIP rev.
ISBN 0-471-10116-8 (pbk) : Unpriced B82-09703

320.5 — Politics. Concepts: Left & right

Laponce, J. A.. Left and right : the topography of political perceptions / J.A. Laponce. — Toronto ; London : University of Toronto Press, c1981. — xi,292p : ill ; 23cm
ISBN 0-8020-5533-8 : £24.50 B82-13932

320.5′09182′1 — Western world. Politics. Theories, *to 1981*

Nelson, Brian R.. Western political thought : from Socrates to the age of ideology / Brian R. Nelson. — Englewood Cliffs ; London : Prentice-Hall, c1982. — xv,367p ; 25cm
Bibliography: p343-349. — Includes index
ISBN 0-13-951640-9 : £14.95 B82-31827

320.5′092′2 — Politics. Theories of Hobbes, Thomas & Locke, John

Leyden, W. von. Hobbes and Locke : the politics of freedom and obligation / W. von Leyden. — London : Macmillan, 1981, c1982. — x,253p ; 23cm
Includes index
ISBN 0-333-27688-4 : £20.00 B82-20952

320.5′092′4 — Politics. Theories of Arendt, Hannah

Parekh, Bhikhu. Hannah Arendt and the search for a new political philosophy / Bhikhu Parekh. — London : Macmillan, 1981. — xiii,198p ; 23cm
Bibliography: p194-195. — Includes index
ISBN 0-333-30474-8 : £20.00 B82-06655

320.5′092′4 — Politics. Theories of Hegel, Georg Wilhelm Friedrich

Ritter, Joachim. Hegel and the French Revolution : essays on the philosophy of right / Joachim Ritter ; translated with an introduction by Richard Dien Winfield. — Cambridge, Mass. ; London : MIT, c1982. — xii,191p ; 21cm. — (Studies in contemporary German social thought)
Translated from the German
ISBN 0-262-18105-3 : £15.75 B82-37521

320.5′092′4 — Politics. Theories of Hume, David

Miller, David. Philosophy and ideology in Hume's political thought / by David Miller. — Oxford : Clarendon, 1981. — ix,218p ; 22cm
Bibliography: p206-213. — Includes index
ISBN 0-19-824658-7 : £15.00 : CIP rev. B81-36967

320.5′092′4 — Politics. Theories of Kant, Immanuel

Williams, Howard. Kant's political philosophy. — Oxford : Blackwell, Jan.1983. — [320]p
ISBN 0-631-13123-x : £20.00 : CIP entry B82-32515

320.5′092′4 — Politics. Theories of Plato

Hall, Robert W.. Plato / Robert W. Hall. — London : Allen & Unwin, 1981. — 168p ; 23cm. — (Political thinkers ; 9)
Bibliography: p160-165. — Includes index
ISBN 0-04-320145-8 (cased) : Unpriced : CIP rev.
ISBN 0-04-320146-6 (pbk) : Unpriced B81-28776

320.5′092′4 — Politics. Theories of Spence, Thomas

Spence, Thomas. The political works of Thomas Spence. — Newcastle upon Tyne (20 Great North Rd, Newcastle upon Tyne NE2 4PS) : Avero (Eighteenth-century) Publications, Aug.1982. — [166]p
ISBN 0-907977-02-2 : £4.75 : CIP entry B82-24702

320.5′092′4 — Politics. Theories of Yeats, W. B.

Freyer, Grattan. W.B. Yeats and the anti-democratic tradition / Grattan Freyer. — Dublin : Gill and Macmillan, 1981. — x,143p ; 22cm
Includes index
ISBN 0-7171-0893-7 : £12.00 B82-13470

320.5′09714 — Quebec *(Province)*. **Political ideologies,** *1760-1980*

Monière, Denis. Ideologies in Quebec : the historical development / Denis Monière ; translated by Richard Howard. — Toronto ; London : University of Toronto Press, c1981. — x,328p ; 24cm
Translation of: Le développement des idéologies au Québec
ISBN 0-8020-5452-8 (cased) : £21.00
ISBN 0-8020-6358-6 (pbk) : Unpriced B82-06979

320.5′1 — Political ideologies: Liberalism

Saunders, James H.. Modern Liberalism : a pathway into tomorrow's world / James H. Saunders. — Hythe (21 Fisher Close, Hythe, Kent, CT21 6AB) : New Creation Enterprises, [1982]. — 12p ; 21cm. — (The Orpington initiative ; pamphlet no.10)
£1.00 (pbk) B82-30663

Spragens, Thomas A.. The irony of liberal reason / Thomas A. Spragens Jr. — Chicago ; London : University of Chicago Press, 1981. — xii,443p ; 24cm
Includes index
ISBN 0-226-76975-5 : Unpriced B82-35319

320.5′1 — Politics. Liberalist theories

Gaus, Gerald F.. The modern liberal theory of man. — London : Croom Helm, Jan.1983. — [335]p
ISBN 0-7099-1127-0 : £15.95 : CIP entry B82-35208

320.5′1′0924 — Politics. Arendt, Hannah — *Biographies*

Young-Bruehl, Elizabeth. Hannah Arendt, for love of the world. — London : Yale University Press, May 1982. — [616]p
ISBN 0-300-02660-9 : £12.95 : CIP entry B82-17897

320.5′1′0941 — Great Britain. Political ideologies: Liberalism, *ca 1640-ca 1870*

Eisenach, Eldon J.. Two worlds of liberalism : religion and politics in Hobbes, Locke, and Mill / Eldon J. Eisenach. — Chicago ; London : University of Chicago, 1981. — x,262p ; 23cm
Includes index
ISBN 0-226-19533-3 (pbk) : £13.50 B82-03914

320.5′1′0941 — Great Britain. Political ideologies: Liberalism, *to 1981*

Saunders, James H.. Liberalism revitalised / James H. Saunders. — Hythe (21 Fisher Close, Hythe, Kent, CT21 6AB) : New Creation Enterprises, [1982]. — 20p ; 21cm. — (The Orpington initiative ; pamphlet no.1)
£1.00 (pbk) B82-30655

320.5′1′0943 — Germany. Political ideologies: Liberalism, *1770-1914*

Sheehan, James J.. German liberalism in the nineteenth century / James J. Sheehan. — London : Methuen, 1982, c1978. — 411p : ill ; 24cm
Originally published: Chicago : University of Chicago Press, 1978. — Bibliography: p367-398. — Includes index
ISBN 0-416-32910-1 (pbk) : Unpriced : CIP rev. B82-12335

320.5′12 — United States. Political ideologies: Individualism — *Early works*

Hoover, Herbert. American individualism / Herbert Hoover. — New York ; London : Garland, 1979. — 72p ; 19cm. — (The History of the United States, 1876-1976)
Facsim of: 1st ed. Garden City, New York : Doubleday, Page & Co, 1922
ISBN 0-8240-9704-1 : Unpriced B82-18911

320.5′12 — United States. Political ideologies: Individualism, *to 1979*

Pole, J. R.. American individualism and the promise of progress : an inaugural lecture delivered before the University of Oxford on 14 February 1980 / by J.R. Pole. — Oxford : Clarendon, 1980. — 33p ; 22cm
ISBN 0-19-951526-3 (pbk) : £1.95 B82-13117

320.5′2′0903 — Political ideologies: Conservatism, *1750-1980*

The **Portable** conservative reader / edited, with an introduction and notes by Russell Kirk. — Harmondsworth : Penguin, 1982. — xl,723p ; 19cm. — (The Viking portable library)
Bibliography: p711-712. — Includes index
ISBN 0-14-015095-1 (pbk) : £3.50 B82-37607

320.5′3′0941 — Great Britain. Left-wing radical movements, *1914-1918*

Carsten, F. L.. War against war : British and German radical movements in the First World War / F.L. Carsten. — London : Batsford Academic and Educational, 1982. — 285p ; 23cm
Bibliography: p266-276. — Includes index
ISBN 0-7134-3697-2 : £12.50 : CIP rev.
Also classified at 320.5′3′0943 B81-37574

320.5′3′0941 — Great Britain. Left-wing radical movements, *1931-1941*

Jupp, James. The radical left in Britain : 1931-1941 / James Jupp. — London : Cass, 1982. — viii,261p ; 22cm
Bibliography: p233-248. — Includes index
ISBN 0-7146-3123-x : £16.00 B82-29710

320.5′3′0941 — Great Britain. Political ideologies: Collectivism, *ca 1880-1980*

Beer, Samuel H.. Modern British politics. — 3rd ed. — London : Faber, June 1982. — [450]p
Previous ed.: 1969
ISBN 0-571-18064-7 (pbk) : £3.95 : CIP entry B82-14240

320.5′3′0943 — Germany. Left-wing radical movements, *1914-1918*

Carsten, F. L.. War against war : British and German radical movements in the First World War / F.L. Carsten. — London : Batsford Academic and Educational, 1982. — 285p ; 23cm
Bibliography: p266-276. — Includes index
ISBN 0-7134-3697-2 : £12.50 : CIP rev.
Primary classification 320.5′3′0941 B81-37574

320.5′315′0924 — Politics. Theories of Benn, Tony

Freeman, Alan. The Benn heresy. — London : Pluto, Aug.1982. — [192]p
ISBN 0-86104-363-4 (pbk) : £3.50 : CIP entry B82-22408

320.5′315′0924 — Politics. Theories of Gramsci, Antonio

Approaches to Gramsci / edited by Anne Showstack Sassoon. — London : Writers and Readers, 1982. — 254p : ill,1facsim,ports ; 22cm
Bibliography: p251-254
ISBN 0-906495-55-5 (cased) : £7.95
ISBN 0-906495-56-3 (pbk) : Unpriced B82-39784

320.5'315'0924 — Politics. Theories of Gramsci, Antonio *continuation*
Femia, Joseph V.. Gramsci's political thought : hegemony, consciousness, and the revolutionary process by Joseph V. Femia. — Oxford : Clarendon, 1981. — ix,303p ; 23cm
Bibliography: p286-298. — Includes index
ISBN 0-19-827251-0 : £17.50 : CIP rev.
B81-30336

320.5'32'0722 — Communism, *1945-1980.* Political aspects — *Case studies*
The **Withering** away of the state? : party and state under Communism / edited by Leslie Holmes. — London : Sage, c1981. — 294p ; 23cm. — (Sage modern politics series ; v.6)
Includes index
ISBN 0-8039-9796-5 (cased) : Unpriced : CIP rev.
ISBN 0-8039-9797-3 (pbk) : £6.95 B81-13569

320.5'32'0924 — Politics. Theories of Trotskiĭ, L.
Molyneux, John, *1948-*. Leon Trotsky's theory of revolution / John Molyneux. — Brighton : Harvester Press, 1981. — xii,252p ; 22cm
Includes index
ISBN 0-85527-948-6 : £20.00 : CIP rev.
B82-00338

320.5'32'0924 — Politics. Theories of Trotskiĭ, L. — *Cartoons*
Tariq Ali. Trotsky : for beginners / Tariq Ali & Phil Evans. — London : Writers and Readers, 1980. — 174p : ill,facsims,ports ; 22cm
Bibliography: p166-167
ISBN 0-906495-27-x (cased) : £4.95
ISBN 0-906495-28-8 (pbk) : Unpriced
B82-01376

320.5'4 — Nationalism
Breuilly, John. Nationalism and the state / John Breuilly. — Manchester : Manchester University Press, c1982. — x,421p ; 24cm
Bibliography: p402-412. — Includes index
ISBN 0-7190-0692-9 : £25.00 : CIP rev.
B82-01426

320.5'4 — Nationalism — *Festschriften*
Nationalism : essays in honor of Louis L. Snyder / edited by Michael Palumbo and William O. Shanahan ; foreword by Arthur Schlesinger, Jr. — Westport, Conn. ; London : Greenwood Press, 1981. — x,219p ; 22cm. — (Contributions in political science, ISSN 0147-1066 ; no.65. Global perspectives in history and politics)
Bibliography: p208-211. — Includes index
ISBN 0-313-23176-1 : £20.95 B82-18185

320.5'4'09 — Nationalism, *to 1977*
Seton-Watson, Hugh. Nations and states. — London : Methuen, Apr.1982. — [580]p
Originally published: 1977
ISBN 0-416-33820-8 (pbk) : £5.95 : CIP entry
B82-04051

320.5'4'094 — Europe. Nationalism
Brugmans, Hendrik. The crisis in the traditional nation state : is the nation state obsolete? : based on an address given by Hendrik Brugmans ... at a seminar at St Edmund Hall, Oxford in August 1981 ... — Exeter (7 Cathedral Close, Exeter, Devon EX1 1EZ) : European-Atlantic Movement, [1982?]. — 12p ; 21cm
Cover title. — Bibliography: p11-12
Unpriced (pbk) B82-35504

320.5'4'094 — Europe. Nationalism *related to* **socialism,** *1848-1940*
Talmon, J. L.. The myth of the nation and the vision of revolution : the origins of ideological polarisation in the twentieth century / J.L. Talmon. — London : Secker & Warburg, 1981, c1980. — xviii,632p ; 24cm
Includes index
ISBN 0-436-51399-4 : £15.00
Also classified at 335'.0094 B82-02607

320.5'4'094 — Pan-Europeanism — *Serials*
The **Paneuropean**. — No.1 (Michaelmas 1981)-. — London (54 Eaton Sq., SW1) : The Pan-Europe Club, 1981-. — v. ; 30cm
Quarterly
ISSN 0261-4197 = Paneuropean : Unpriced
B82-04905

320.5'4'0941 — Great Britain. Nationalism, *1640-1975* — *Marxist viewpoints*
Nairn, Tom. The break-up of Britain. — London : NLB, Sept.1981. — [380]p
Originally published: 1977
ISBN 0-86091-706-1 (pbk) : £4.50 : CIP entry
B81-30224

320.5'4'09411 — Scotland. Nationalism. Role of Scottish Gaelic language
Hendry, Joy. Literature and language : the way forward / by Joy Hendry. — Edinburgh (6 North Charlotte St., Edinburgh EH21 4JH) : Heritage Committee of Scottish National Party, [1981]. — 20p ; 21cm. — (Heritage of Scotland)
Cover title. — Text on inside covers. — Bibliography: p20
£1.00 (pbk) B82-31258

320.5'4'09415 — Ireland. Nationalism, *1800-ca 1965*
Garvin, Tom. The evolution of Irish nationalist politics / Tom Garvin. — Dublin : Gill and Macmillan, 1981. — xii,244p : ill,1map ; 23cm
Includes index
ISBN 0-7171-1105-9 : £15.00 B82-10282

320.5'4'09415 — Ireland. Nationalism, *to 1981*
Boyce, D. George. Nationalism in Ireland / D. George Boyce. — London : Croom Helm, c1982. — 441p : maps ; 23cm
Bibliography: p396-429. — Includes index
ISBN 0-85664-705-5 : £14.95 : CIP rev.
ISBN 0-7171-1219-5 (Gill and Macmillan)
B81-31652

320.5'4'09415 — Ireland. Partition. Attitudes of De Valera, Eamon, *1917-1973*
Bowman, John. De Valera and the Ulster Question, 1917-1973. — Oxford : Clarendon, Nov.1982. — [384]p
ISBN 0-19-822681-0 : £17.50 : CIP entry
B82-26872

320.5'4'09561 — Pan-Turkism, *1900-1980*
Landau, Jacob M.. Pan-Turkism in Turkey : a study of irredentism / by Jacob M. Landau. — London : C. Hurst, 1981. — 219p : 1ill,1facsim ; 23cm
Bibliography: p190-206. — Includes index
ISBN 0-905838-57-2 : £11.50 : CIP rev.
B81-30624

320.5'4'0973 — United States. Nationalism
Oliver, Revilo P.. America's decline : the education of a conservative / by Revilo P. Oliver. — London : Londinium, c1981. — xi,375p : ill ; 22cm
ISBN 0-906832-01-2 (pbk) : Unpriced
B82-04402

320.5'5 — Politics. Theories of Calvin, Jean
Höpfl, Harro. The Christian polity of John Calvin / Harro Höpfl. — Cambridge : Cambridge University Press, 1982. — x,303p ; 23cm. — (Cambridge studies in the history and theory of politics)
Bibliography: p290-297. — Includes index
ISBN 0-521-24417-x : £27.50 : CIP rev.
B82-19257

320.8 — LOCAL GOVERNMENT. FORMS AND THEORETICAL ASPECTS

320.8'09421 — London boroughs. Local government. Politics — *Case studies*
Glassberg, Andrew D.. Representation and urban community / Andrew D. Glassberg. — London : Macmillan, 1981. — ix,232p ; 23cm
Bibliography: p221-227. — Includes index
ISBN 0-333-28878-5 : £20.00 B82-07278

320.9 — POLITICS. HISTORICAL AND GEOGRAPHICAL TREATMENT

320.9 — Political systems. Analysis
Easton, David. A framework for political analysis / David Easton. — Chicago ; London : University of Chicago Press, 1979. — xviii,142p : ill ; 23cm
Originally published: Englewood Cliffs : Prentice-Hall, 1965
ISBN 0-226-18015-8 (pbk) : £2.45 B82-21492

320.9'04 — Politics, *1945-1981*
Calvocoressi, Peter. World politics since 1945 / Peter Calvocoressi. — 4th ed. — London : Longman, 1982. — xi,516p ; 22cm
Previous ed.: 1977. — Includes index
ISBN 0-582-29586-6 (pbk) : Unpriced : CIP rev. B81-37554

320.9172'4 — Developing countries. Political development
Somjee, A. H.. Political capacity in developing societies / A.H. Somjee. — London : Macmillan, 1982. — xi,124p ; 23cm
Includes index
ISBN 0-333-28719-3 : £15.00 B82-28523

Tames, Richard. Case studies of emergent nations / Richard Tames. — Glasgow : Blackie, 1982. — 76p : ill,maps,ports,21cm. — (Crossroads)
Bibliography: p74-76. — Includes index
ISBN 0-216-91067-6 (pbk) : £1.95 B82-40017

320.9172'4 — Developing countries. Political development. Theories
Higgott, Richard A.. Political development theory. — London : Croom Helm, Jan.1983. — [208]p. — (Croom Helm international series in social and political thought)
ISBN 0-7099-1252-8 (cased) : £11.95 : CIP entry
ISBN 0-7099-1257-9 (pbk) : £5.50 B82-32553

320.9172'4 — Developing countries. Politics. Effects of American imperialism & British imperialism, *1815-1980*
Smith, Tony, *1942-*. The pattern of imperialism : the United States, Great Britain, and the late-industrializing world since 1815 / Tony Smith. — Cambridge : Cambridge University Press, 1981. — xi,308p : maps ; 24cm
Bibliography: p284-304. — Includes index
ISBN 0-521-23619-3 (cased) : Unpriced
ISBN 0-521-28076-1 (pbk) : Unpriced
B82-23055

320.917'671 — Islamic countries. Politics
Mortimer, Edward. Faith and power. — London : Faber, Sept.1982. — [587]p
ISBN 0-571-11944-1 (cased) : £10.50 : CIP entry
ISBN 0-571-11978-6 (pbk) : £5.95 B82-25172

320.9'4 — Western Europe. Frontier regions. Politics
Frontier regions in Western Europe. — London : Cass, Oct.1982. — [144]p
First appeared in a special issue on 'Frontier regions in Western Europe' of West European politics, Vol.5, no.4
ISBN 0-7146-3217-1 : £15.00 : CIP entry
B82-32874

320.94 — Western Europe. Politics
Policy styles in Western Europe. — London : Allen & Unwin, Nov.1982. — [224]p
ISBN 0-04-350062-5 : £15.00 : CIP entry
B82-27811

320.941 — Great Britain. Anti-fascist movements — *Serials*
[Searchlight *(London)*]. Searchlight : the anti-fascist monthly, incorporating CARF. — No.26 (Aug. 1977)-. — London (37B New Cavendish St., W1M 8JR) : Searchlight Publishing, 1977-. — v. : ill,ports ; 30cm
Subtitle varies. — Continues: Searchlight on the struggle against racism and fascism. — Absorbed: CARF, 1979. — Description based on: No.76 (Oct. 1981)
ISSN 0262-4591 = Searchlight (London) : £8.00 per year B82-05234

320.941 — Great Britain. Left-wing political movements, *1904-1981*
Kaur, Prunella. Go fourth & multiply : the political anatomy of the British left groups / by Prunella Kaur. — Bristol (Box 99, Full Marks Bookshop, 110 Cheltenham Rd, Bristol 6) : Dialogue of the Deaf, [1982?]. — 21p : 1ill ; 30cm
£0.30 (unbound) B82-23045

320.941 — Great Britain. Politics
Beer, Samuel H.. Britain against itself. — London : Faber, June 1982. — [224]p
ISBN 0-571-11918-2 : £8.50 : CIP entry
B82-12918

320.941 — Great Britain. Politics *continuation*

Mackintosh, John P.. The government and politics of Britain / John P. Mackintosh. — 5th ed. / revised and updated by Peter Richards. — London : Hutchinson, 1982. — 244p ; 22cm. — (Hutchinson university library)
Previous ed.: 1977. — Bibliography: p231-232.. — Includes index
ISBN 0-09-145531-6 (pbk) : £4.95 : CIP rev. B81-20181

Stacey, Roger. Public administration : the political environment / Roger Stacey and John Oliver. — Plymouth : Macdonald and Evans, 1980. — viii,296p : ill,maps ; 22cm. — (The M & E BECbook series)
Includes index
ISBN 0-7121-1681-8 (pbk) : £4.50 B82-27086

320.941 — Great Britain. Politics, *1754-1757*

Clark, J. C. D.. The dynamics of change : the crisis of the 1750s and the English Party systems / J.C.D. Clark. — Cambridge : Cambridge University Press, 1982. — xiii,615p : ill ; 24cm. — (Cambridge studies in the history and theory of politics)
Bibliography: p563-606. — Includes index
ISBN 0-521-23830-7 : £37.50 : CIP rev. B82-11500

320.941 — Great Britain. Politics, *1760-1770*

Brewer, John, *1947-*. Party ideology and popular politics at the accession of George III / John Brewer. — Cambridge : Cambridge University Press, 1976 (1981 [printing]). — xi,382p : ill ; 23cm
Bibliography: p325-368. — Includes index
ISBN 0-521-28701-4 (pbk) : £9.95 : CIP rev. B81-31607

320.941 — Great Britain. Politics, *1867-1939*

Pugh, Martin. The making of modern British politics 1867-1939 / Martin Pugh. — Oxford : Basil Blackwell, 1982. — xi,377p : ill ; 24cm
Bibliography: p309-327. — Includes index
ISBN 0-631-12919-7 (cased) : Unpriced : CIP rev.
ISBN 0-631-12985-5 (pbk) : Unpriced B82-06941

320.941 — Great Britain. Politics, *1945-1980 — For schools*

Macfarlane, L. J.. Issues in British politics since 1945 / L.J. Macfarlane. — 2nd ed. — Harlow : Longman, 1981. — x,181p ; 20cm. — (Political realities)
Previous ed.: 1975. — Includes bibliographies and index
ISBN 0-582-35328-9 (pbk) : £2.95 B82-18358

320.941 — Great Britain. Politics, *1951-1955*

Seldon, Anthony. Churchill's Indian summer : the Conservative government, 1951-55 / Anthony Seldon. — London : Hodder and Stoughton, 1981. — xvii,667p,[8]p of plates : ports ; 25cm
Bibliography: p627-645. — Includes index
ISBN 0-340-25456-4 : £14.95 : CIP rev. B81-26736

320.941 — Great Britain. Politics, *ca 1830-1980*

Greenleaf, W. H.. The British political tradition. — London : Methuen
Vol.1: The rise of collectivism. — Nov.1982. — [380]p
ISBN 0-416-15570-7 : £15.00 : CIP entry B82-28286

320.941 — Great Britain. Politics — *Proposals*

Rodgers, William, *1928-*. The politics of change / William Rodgers. — London : Secker & Warburg, 1982. — v,199p ; 24cm
Includes index
ISBN 0-436-42080-5 (cased) : £7.95
ISBN 0-436-42081-3 (pbk) : Unpriced B82-23216

320.941 — Great Britain. Politics, *to 1981*

Greenleaf, W. H.. The British political tradition. — London : Methuen
Vol.2: The ideological heritage. — Nov.1982. — [480]p
ISBN 0-416-34660-x : £15.00 : CIP entry B82-28293

320.941 — Great Britain. Radical movements, *1776-1848*

Royle, Edward. Radicalism and reform 1776-1848. — Brighton : Harvester Press, June 1982. — [208]p
ISBN 0-7108-0382-6 : £18.95 : CIP entry B82-09600

320.941 — Great Britain. Right-wing radical movements, *1900-1914*

Nationalist and racialist movements in Britain and Germany before 1914 / edited by Paul Kennedy and Anthony Nicholls. — London : Macmillan in association with St Antony's College, Oxford, 1981. — xi,210p ; 23cm. — (St. Antony's/Macmillan series)
Conference papers. — Includes index
ISBN 0-333-27378-8 : £20.00
Also classified at 320.943 B82-10811

320.941 — Scotland. Union with England, *1707*. Political aspects — *Early works*

Fletcher, Andrew. State of the controversy betwixt united and separate parliaments / Andrew Fletcher ; with an introduction by P.H. Scott. — Edinburgh : Printed for the Saltire Society by William Blackwood, 1982. — 34p ; 19cm. — (Saltire pamphlets. New series ; no.3)
Cover title: United and separate parliaments. — Originally published: 1706
ISBN 0-85411-025-9 (pbk) : £1.00 B82-40944

320.941'092'2 — Great Britain. Radicalism, *1600-1700 — Biographies*

Biographical dictionary of British radicals in the seventeenth century / edited by Richard L. Greaves and Robert Zaller. — Brighton : Harvester Press
Vol.1: A-F. — 1982. — xxxiii,308p ; 24cm
ISBN 0-85527-133-7 : £40.00 : CIP rev. B81-30368

320.941'092'4 — Great Britain. Radicalism, *1603-1691 — Biographies*

The **Biographical** dictionary of British radicals in the seventeenth century. — Brighton : Harvester Press
Vol.2. — Nov.1982. — [224]p
ISBN 0-7108-0430-x : £40.00 : CIP entry B82-27929

320.9411 — Scotland. Politics, *1560-1800*

New perspective on the politics and culture of early modern Scotland / edited by John Dwyer, Roger A. Mason and Alexander Murdoch. — Edinburgh : Donald, [1982]. — vii,329p : 2maps ; 24cm
Includes index
ISBN 0-85976-066-9 : £15.00 B82-37745

320.9411 — Scotland. Politics, *1963-1977*

Mackintosh, John P.. John P. Mackintosh on Scotland / edited and introduced by H.M. Drucker. — London : Longman, 1982. — viii,232p ; 22cm
Includes index
ISBN 0-582-29574-2 (pbk) : Unpriced : CIP rev. B82-06925

320.9412'25 — Scotland. Grampian Region. Peterhead. Politics

Bealey, Frank. The politics of independence. — Aberdeen : Aberdeen University Press, Apr.1981. — [272]p
ISBN 0-08-025736-4 : £15.00 : CIP entry B81-00762

320.9415 — Ireland. Unification — *Fine Gael viewpoints*

Fine Gael. Ireland : our future together / Fine Gael. — [Dublin] ([151 Upper Mount St, Dublin 2]) : [Fine Gael], [1979]. — 46p : 2ports ; 22cm
Unpriced (pbk) B82-26985

320.9416 — Northern Ireland. Politics, *1690-1990*

Bleakley, David. Ireland and Britain 1690-1990 : a search for peace / David Bleakley. — [New Malden] ([9 Coombe Rd, New Malden, Surrey KT3 5AU]) : Fellowship of Reconciliation, [1982]. — 20p ; 21cm. — (Alex Wood memorial lecture)
Cover title
£0.60 (pbk) B82-33066

320.9416 — Northern Ireland. Unionism, *1920-1980 — 'Workers' Weekly' viewpoints*

Unionism or devolution? : a word to some Unionists who have forgotten the Unionism of Carson & Craig. — Belfast (10 Athol St., Belfast, 12) : Workers' Weekly, 1981. — 14p ; 26cm
Cover title
Unpriced (pbk) B82-04225

320.9417 — Ireland *(Republic)*. Politics, *1926-1981*

Chubb, Basil. The government and politics of Ireland. — 2nd ed. — London : Longman, Sept.1982. — [416]p
Previous ed.: London : Oxford University Press, 1974
ISBN 0-582-29635-8 (pbk) : £7.95 : CIP entry B82-19809

320.942 — England. Politics, *1485-1714*

Elton, G. R.. Studies in Tudor and Stuart politics and government. — Cambridge : Cambridge University Press
Vol.3. — Oct.1982. — [512]p
ISBN 0-521-24893-0 : £27.50 : CIP entry B82-40319

320.9421 — London. Politics, *1837-1981*

Young, Ken, *1943-*. Metropolitan London : politics and urban change 1837-1981 / Ken Young and Patricia L. Garside. — London : Edward Arnold, 1982. — xiv,401p : ill,maps ; 24cm. — (Studies in urban history ; 6)
Bibliography: p359-390. — Includes index
ISBN 0-7131-6331-3 : £25.00 : CIP rev. B82-04487

320.9421 — London. Radical movements, *1796-1821*

Hone, J. Ann. For the cause of truth : radicalism in London 1796-1821 / J. Ann Hone. — Oxford : Clarendon, 1982. — 412p ; 23cm. — (Oxford historical monographs)
Bibliography: p365-392. — Includes index
ISBN 0-19-821887-7 : £19.50 : CIP rev. B81-35763

320.943 — Germany. Right-wing radical movements, *1900-1914*

Nationalist and racialist movements in Britain and Germany before 1914 / edited by Paul Kennedy and Anthony Nicholls. — London : Macmillan in association with St Antony's College, Oxford, 1981. — xi,210p ; 23cm. — (St. Antony's/Macmillan series)
Conference papers. — Includes index
ISBN 0-333-27378-8 : £20.00
Primary classification 320.941 B82-10811

320.943 — West Germany. Politics

Beyme, Klaus von. The political system of the Federal Republic of Germany. — London : Gower, Jan.1983. — [200]p
ISBN 0-566-00537-9 : £15.00 : CIP entry B82-32435

Conradt, David P.. The German polity / David P. Conradt. — 2nd ed. — New York ; London : Longman, [c1982]. — xvi,272p : 1ill ; 23cm
Previous ed.: 1977. — Bibliography: p242-248. — Includes index
ISBN 0-582-28191-1 (pbk) : £6.95 B82-39551

Smith, Gordon, *1927-*. Democracy in Western Germany. — 2nd ed. — London : Heinemann Educational, Dec.1981. — [240]p
Previous ed.: 1979
ISBN 0-435-83792-3 (cased) : £9.50 : CIP entry
ISBN 0-435-83793-1 (pbk) : £5.50 B81-31702

The **West** German model : perspectives on a stable state / edited by William E. Paterson and Gordon Smith. — London : Cass, 1981. — v,176p : 1ill ; 23cm
ISBN 0-7146-3180-9 (cased) : £13.50 : CIP rev.
ISBN 0-7146-4034-4 (pbk) : £8.50 B81-18034

320.943 — West Germany. Politics, *1945-1981*

Party government and political culture in Western Germany / edited by Herbert Döring and Gordon Smith. — London : Macmillan, 1982. — ix,227p ; 23cm
Includes index
ISBN 0-333-29082-8 : £20.00 B82-20951

320.9438 — Poland. Politics. Cultural factors

Podgórecki, Adam. The Polish burial of Marxist ideology / Adam Podgórecki. — London : Poets' and Painters' Press, 1981. — 29p ; 22cm
Unpriced (pbk) B82-00732

320.9439 — Hungary. Politics, *1825-1945*

Janos, Andrew C.. The politics of backwardness in Hungary : 1825-1945 / Andrew C. Janos. — Princeton, N.J. ; Guildford : Princeton University Press, 1982. — xxxvi,370p : 3maps ; 25cm
Bibliography: p325-343. — Includes index
ISBN 0-691-07633-2 (cased) : £19.30
ISBN 0-691-10123-x (pbk) : £8.90 B82-24506

320.944 — France. Left-wing political movements

Nugent, Neill. The Left in France / Neill Nugent and David Lowe. — London : Macmillan, 1982. — ix,275p : ill ; 23cm
Bibliography: p270-271. — Includes index
ISBN 0-333-24135-5 : £15.00 B82-28522

320.944 — France. Politics, *1785-1795 — Readings from contemporary sources*

The **French** Revolution : the fall of the ancien régime to the Thermidorian reaction, 1785-1795 / [compiled by] John Hardman. — London : Edward Arnold, 1981. — xiv,240p ; 20cm. — (Documents of modern history)
Bibliography: p203. — Includes index
ISBN 0-7131-6327-5 (pbk) : £4.95 : CIP rev. B81-30346

320.944 — France. Radicalism, *1866-1885*

Auspitz, Katherine. The radical bourgeoisie : the Ligue de l'enseignement and the origins of the Third Republic 1866-1885 / Katherine Auspitz. — Cambridge : Cambridge University Press, 1982. — x,237p ; 24cm
Bibliography: p222-234. — Includes index
ISBN 0-521-23861-7 : Unpriced B82-30684

320.945 — Italy. Politics

Marengo, Franco Damaso. Rules of the Italian political game / Franco Damaso Marengo. — Aldershot : Gower, c1981. — x,134p ; 23cm
ISBN 0-566-00301-5 : Unpriced : CIP rev. B81-30194

320.946 — Iberian Peninsula. Politics

Kohler, Beate. Political forces in Spain, Greece and Portugal. — London : Butterworths, Aug.1982. — [288]p. — (Butterworths European studies)
Translation of: Politischer Umbruch in Südeuropa
ISBN 0-408-10796-0 : £18.00 : CIP entry
Also classified at 320.9495 B82-17198

320.946 — Spain. Politics, *1975-1981*

Maravall, José. The transition to democracy in Spain / José Maravall. — London : Croom Helm, c1982. — 213p : ill ; 23cm
Includes index
ISBN 0-7099-1714-7 : £14.95 : CIP rev. B82-09590

320.947 — Soviet Union. Politics

Barry, Donald D.. Contemporary Soviet politics : an introduction / Donald D. Barry, Carol Barner-Barry. — 2nd ed. — Englewood Cliffs ; London : Prentice-Hall, c1982. — xi,420p : 1map ; 23cm
Previous ed.: 1978. — Bibliography: p357-358. — Includes index
ISBN 0-13-170191-6 (pbk) : £9.70 B82-20054

Soviet politics / [The D334 'Soviet politics' Course Team]. — Milton Keynes : Open University Press. — (Social sciences : a third level course)
At head of title: The Open University
[Block] 2: The machinery of rule / prepared for the Course Team by Paul G. Lewis, Robert A. Clifton and Peter Frank. — 1982. — 67p : ill ; 30cm. — (D334 ; 11(6-8))
Includes bibliographies. — Contents: Questions 6-8
ISBN 0-335-12101-2 (pbk) : Unpriced B82-21213

Soviet politics / [The D334 'Soviet Politics' Course Team]. — Milton Keynes : Open University Press. — (Social sciences : a third level course)
At head of title: The Open University
[Block] 3: Policy and leadership in the Soviet Union / prepared for the Course Team by Franklyn Griffiths ... [et al.]. — 1982. — 111p : ill,maps,ports ; 30cm. — (D334 ; iii (9-13))
Includes bibliographies. — Contents: Questions 9-13
ISBN 0-335-12102-0 (pbk) : Unpriced B82-32209

Soviet politics / [the D334 'Soviet Politics' Course Team]. — Milton Keynes : Open University Press. — (Social sciences : a third level course)
At head of title: The Open University
[Block 4]: Conceptual approaches to Soviet politics / prepared for the course team by Paul G. Lewis and Robert A. Clifton. — 1982. — 69p : ill ; 30cm. — (D334 ; 4 (14-16))
Includes bibliographies. — Contents: Questions 14-16
ISBN 0-335-12103-9 (pbk) : Unpriced B82-40137

Soviet politics / [The D334 'Soviet politics' Course Team]. — Milton Keynes : Open University Press. — (Social sciences : a third level course)
At head of title: The Open University
Readings in Soviet politics / edited for the course team by P.G. Lewis, R.A. Clifton and F.G. Castles. — 1982. — 243p ; 30cm. — (D334)
Includes index
ISBN 0-335-12104-7 (pbk) : Unpriced B82-21212

320.947 — Soviet Union. Politics, *1917-1924*

Sirianni, Carmen. Workers' control and socialist democracy. — London : Verso/NLB, Nov.1982. — [352]p
ISBN 0-86091-054-7 (cased) : £17.50 : CIP entry
ISBN 0-86091-754-1 (pbk) : £6.95 B82-29031

320.947 — Soviet Union. Politics, *1946-1953*

Hahn, Werner G.. Postwar Soviet politics : the fall of Zhdanov and the defeat of moderation, 1946-53 / Werner G. Hahn. — Ithaca ; London : Cornell University Press, 1982. — 243p ; 23cm
Bibliography: p225-231. — Includes index
ISBN 0-8014-1410-5 : £17.00 B82-35755

320.947 — Soviet Union. Politics, *1953-1980*

Bialer, Seweryn. Stalin's successors : leadership, stability and change in the Soviet Union / Seweryn Bialer. — Cambridge : Cambridge University Press, 1980 (1981 [printing]). — vii,312p ; 23cm
Includes index
ISBN 0-521-28906-8 (pbk) : £6.50 B82-36885

Breslauer, George W.. Khrushchev and Brezhnev as leaders. — London : Allen & Unwin, Dec.1982. — [336]p
ISBN 0-04-329040-x (cased) : £14.95 : CIP entry
ISBN 0-04-329041-8 (pbk) : £6.95 B82-29861

320'.948 — Scandinavia. Politics

Elder, Neil. The consensual democracies? : the government and politics of the Scandinavian states. — Oxford : Martin Robertson, June 1982. — [224]p
ISBN 0-85520-423-0 : £12.50 : CIP entry B82-11787

320.9494 — Switzerland. Politics *— Socialist viewpoints*

Ziegler, Jean. Switzerland exposed / Jean Ziegler ; translated from the French by Rosemary Sheed Middleton. — London : Allison & Busby, 1978. — 173p ; 21cm
Translation of: Une Suisse au-dessus de tout soupçon. — Includes index
ISBN 0-85031-351-1 (cased) : Unpriced
ISBN 0-85031-247-7
Also classified at 332.1'09494 B82-15001

320.9495 — Greece. Politics

Kohler, Beate. Political forces in Spain, Greece and Portugal. — London : Butterworths, Aug.1982. — [288]p. — (Butterworths European studies)
Translation of: Politischer Umbruch in Südeuropa
ISBN 0-408-10796-0 : £18.00 : CIP entry
Primary classification 320.946 B82-17198

320.9497 — Yugoslavia. Politics

Krishna Moorthy, K.. After Tito what? / by K. Krishna Moorthy. — Atlantic Highlands : Humanities ; Gloucester : distributed by Sutton, 1980. — xv,207p : ill ; 23cm
Bibliography: p201-202. — Includes index
ISBN 0-391-02063-3 : Unpriced B82-38123

320.9497 — Yugoslavia. Politics. Reform — *Serbo-Croatian texts*

Demokratske reforme / Uredili Vane Ivanović i Aleksa Djilas. — London : Demokratske Reforme, 1982. — 163p ; 22cm
Serbo-Croation text, English introduction and summaries
Unpriced (pbk) B82-25290

320.951 — China. Politics, *1949-1977*

Ahn, Byung-joon. Chinese politics and the Cultural Revolution : dynamics of policy processes / Byung-joon Ahn. — Seattle ; London : University of Washington Press, c1976. — xi,392p ; 24cm. — (Publications on Asia of the Institute for Comparative and Foreign Area Studies ; no.30)
Bibliography: p359-381. — Includes index
ISBN 0-295-95515-5 : £13.05 B82-30760

320.951 — China. Politics, *1949-1980*

Waller, Derek J.. The government and politics of the People's Republic of China / Derek J. Waller. — 3rd ed. — London : Hutchinson, 1981. — 228p : ill,1map ; 23cm
Previous ed.: 1973. — Bibliography: p202-219. — Includes index
ISBN 0-09-144300-8 (cased) : £12.00 : CIP rev.
ISBN 0-09-144301-6 (pbk) : £4.95 B81-16394

320.951 — China. Politics, *ca 1920-1980*

Saich, Tony. China : politics and government / Tony Saich. — London : Macmillan, 1981. — xiii,265p : ill,2maps ; 23cm. — (China in focus series)
Bibliography: p254-261. — Includes index
ISBN 0-333-28742-8 (cased) : Unpriced
ISBN 0-333-28743-6 (pbk) : Unpriced B82-06663

320.9'52 — Japan. Politics, *1941-1945*

Shillony, Ben-Ami. Politics and culture in wartime Japan. — Oxford : Clarendon, Oct.1981. — [272]p
ISBN 0-19-821573-8 : £17.50 : CIP entry B81-25846

320.952 — Japan. Politics, *1945-1981*

Stockwin, J. A. A.. Japan : divided politics in a growth economy / J.A.A. Stockwin. — 2nd ed. — London : Weidenfeld and Nicolson, 1982. — xii,333p : 2maps ; 22cm. — (Modern governments)
Previous ed.: 1975. — Bibliography: p311-316. — Includes index
ISBN 0-297-77933-8 (cased) : £15.50
ISBN 0-297-77934-6 (pbk) : £8.50 B82-17275

320.9536 — Arabia. Gulf States. Politics. Role of Gulf Co-operation Council

Al-Nafisi, Abdallah Fahd. Gulf Co-operation Council : political and strategic frame-work. — London (68a Delancey St., NW1 7RY) : Ta-Ha, July 1982. — [80]p
Translation of: Majlis al-tāāwan al-khaliji-al-Itār al-Siyasi wa-al-Istratiji
ISBN 0-907461-27-1 (pbk) : £3.00 : CIP entry B82-22401

320.953'6 — Arabia. Gulf States. Politics. Role of Gulf Co-operation Council *— Arabic texts*

Al-Nafisi, Abdallah Fahd. Majlis al-tāāwan al-khaliji-al-Itār al-Siyasi wa-al-Istratiji. — London (68a Delancey St., NW1 7RY) : Ta-Ha, July 1982. — [80]p
ISBN 0-907461-28-x (pbk) : £3.00 : CIP entry B82-22402

320.954 — India *(Republic).* **Gandhi, Indira. Political speeches,** *1966-1982 — Collections*

Gandhi, Indira. Peoples and problems. — London : Hodder & Stoughton, Sept.1982. — [256]p
ISBN 0-340-28659-8 : £8.95 : CIP entry B82-21732

320.954 — South Asia. Politics

The **States** of South Asia : problems of national integration. — London : Hurst, Sept.1982. — [340]p
ISBN 0-905838-69-6 : £13.50 : CIP entry B82-21739

320.954′7 — Western India. Princely states. Politics, *1857-1930*

Copland, Ian. The British Raj and the Indian princes : paramountcy in Western India, 1857-1930 / Ian Copland. — London : Sangam, 1982. — xiii,345p : ill,1map ; 22cm
Bibliography: p319-337. — Includes index
ISBN 0-86131-245-7 : £6.95 B82-26748

320.9549′1 — Pakistan. Political development, *to 1981*

Pakistan's roots of dictatorship. — London : Zed Press, Nov.1982. — [448]p
ISBN 0-86232-046-1 : £22.50 : CIP entry B82-26066

320.955 — Iran. Politics, *900-1500*

Lambton, Ann K. S.. Theory and practice in medieval Persian government / A.K.S. Lambton. — London : Variorum, 1980. — 332p in various pagings ; 24cm. — (Collected studies series ; CS122)
Facsim reprints. — Includes index
ISBN 0-86078-067-8 : £22.00 : CIP rev. B80-17569

320.95694 — Israel. Politics

Galnoor, Itzhak. Steering the polity : communication and politics in Israel / Itzhak Galnoor. — Beverly Hills ; London : Sage, c1982. — xii,410p ; 23cm
Bibliography: p379-399. — Includes index
ISBN 0-8039-1340-0 : £18.95 B82-38113

320.958′1 — Afghanistan. Politics, *1965-1980*

Male, Beverley. Revolutionary Afghanistan : a reappraisal / Beverley Male. — London : Croom Helm, c1982. — 229p ; 22cm
Bibliography: p216-220. — Includes index
ISBN 0-7099-1716-3 : £13.95 : CIP rev. B81-33894

320.9597 — Vietnam. Political movements, *1920-1945*

Marr, David G.. Vietnamese tradition on trial, 1920-1945 / David G. Marr. — Berkeley ; London : University of California Press, c1981. — xi,468p : ill,facsims,1port ; 24cm
Bibliography: p429-452. — Includes index
ISBN 0-520-04180-1 : £17.50 B82-13758

320.96 — Africa. Political systems, *1960-1981.* **Socioeconomic aspects**

Young, Crawford. Ideology and development in Africa / Crawford Young. — New Haven ; London : Yale University, c1982. — xviii,376p : ill,1map ; 21cm. — (A Council on Foreign Relations book)
Includes index
ISBN 0-300-02744-3 : Unpriced : CIP rev. B82-13478

320.96 — Africa. Politics

Jackson, Robert H.. Personal rule in black Africa : prince, autocrat, prophet, tyrant / Robert H. Jackson and Carl G. Rosberg. — Berkeley ; London : University of California Press, c1982. — xi,316p : 1map ; 24cm
Includes index
ISBN 0-520-04185-2 : £17.50 B82-28101

320.96 — Africa. Politics, *ca 1945-1980*

Palmberg, Mai. The struggle for Africa. — London : Zed Press, Jan.1983. — [256]p
Translation of: Befrielse kampen i Afrika
ISBN 0-86232-100-x (cased) : £14.95 : CIP entry
ISBN 0-86232-101-8 (pbk) : £5.95 B82-34095

320.96′0922 — Africa. Politics. Women leaders, *to ca 1921 — Biographies*

Sweetman, David. Women leaders in African history. — London : Heinemann Educational, Sept.1982. — 1v.
ISBN 0-435-94480-0 (pbk) : £2.95 : CIP entry B82-20632

320.962′05 — Egypt. Politics *— Serials*

The **Egyptian** runner. — No.1 (Aug. 1981)-. — London ([P.O.Box no.455, NW5 1DF]) : Committee for Peace, Democracy and Development in Egypt, 1981-. — v. ; 30cm
Irregular
ISSN 0263-4775 = Egyptian runner : £1.20 for 6 issues B82-27638

320.9627 — Sudan. Dār Fūr. Politics, *ca 1720-1916 — Readings from contemporary sources*

Land in Dār Fūr : charters and related documents from the Dār Fūr sultanate. — Cambridge : Cambridge University Press, Jan.1983. — [168]p. — (Fontes historiae Africanae. Series Arabica ; 3)
ISBN 0-521-24643-1 : £17.50 : CIP entry B82-40898

320.9667 — Ghana. Politics, *1957-1966*

Amonoo, Ben. Ghana 1957-1966 : the politics of institutional dualism / Ben Amonoo. — London : Allen & Unwin, 1981. — x,242p ; 23cm
Bibliography: p232-239. — Includes index
ISBN 0-04-320147-4 (cased) : Unpriced : CIP rev.
ISBN 0-04-320148-2 (pbk) : Unpriced B81-33921

320.9′67 — Africa south of the Sahara. Politics, *1945-1980 — Sub-Saharan viewpoints*

The **African** liberation reader. — London : Zed Press, June 1982
Vol.1: The anatomy of colonialism. — [224]p
ISBN 0-86232-067-4 : £16.95 : CIP entry B82-10253

The **African** liberation reader. — London : Zed Press, June 1982
Vol.2: The national liberation movements. — [224]p
ISBN 0-86232-068-2 : £16.95 : CIP entry B82-10254

320.967 — Africa south of the Sahara. Politics, *1945-1980 — Sub-Saharan viewpoints*

The **African** liberation reader. — London : Zed Press
Vol.3: The strategy of liberation. — Sept.1982. — [224]p
ISBN 0-86232-069-0 : £16.95 : CIP entry B82-21557

320.9′67 — Africa South of the Sahara. Politics, *1945-1980 — Sub-Saharan viewpoints*

Who is the enemy?. — London : Zed Press, June 1982. — [640]p
ISBN 0-86232-028-3 (pbk) : £16.95 : CIP entry B82-12851

320.968 — South Africa. Politics

Thompson, Leonard. South African politics. — London : Yale University Press, June 1982. — [288]p
ISBN 0-300-02779-6 : £4.50 : CIP entry B82-21084

320.968 — South Africa. Politics, *to 1981*

Thompson, Leonard. South African politics / Leonard Thompson and Andrew Prior. — New York ; London : Yale University Press, c1982. — xiii,255p : 2maps ; 22cm
Includes index
ISBN 0-300-02767-2 (cased) : Unpriced : CIP rev.
ISBN 0-300-02779-6 (pbk) : Unpriced B82-18443

320.973 — United States. Politics

Holsworth, Robert D.. American politics and everyday life / Robert D. Holsworth, J. Harry Wray. — New York ; Chichester : Wiley, c1982. — xv,204p : ill ; 23cm
Bibliography: p194-200. — Includes index
ISBN 0-471-08645-2 (pbk) : £7.00 B82-39914

Lees, John D.. American politics today / J.D. Lees, R.A. Maidment and M. Tappin. — Manchester : Manchester University Press, 1982. — viii,189p ; 21cm
Includes bibliographies
ISBN 0-7190-0895-6 (cased) : £9.50 : CIP rev.
ISBN 0-7190-0867-0 (pbk) : Unpriced B82-07588

Public values & private power in American politics / edited by J. David Greenstone. — Chicago ; London : University of Chicago Press, c1982. — xiv,286p,[12]p of plates : ill,ports ; 24cm
Includes index
ISBN 0-226-30716-6 : Unpriced B82-35317

320.973 — United States. Politics, *1970-1982*

Grant, Alan R.. The American political process. — 2nd ed. — London : Heinemann Educational, Sept.1982. — [320]p
Previous ed.: 1979
ISBN 0-435-83357-x (pbk) : £5.50 : CIP entry B82-25055

320.973 — United States. Politics. Attitudes of public

Sniderman, Paul M.. A question of loyalty / Paul M. Sniderman. — Berkeley ; London : University of California Press, c1981. — x,186p : ill ; 22cm
Includes index
ISBN 0-520-04196-8 (cased) : £13.25
ISBN 0-520-04413-4 (pbk) : Unpriced B82-06998

320.973 — United States. Politics. Role of political ideologies, *to 1980*

Huntington, Samuel P.. American politics : the promise of disharmony / Samuel P. Huntington. — Cambridge, Mass. ; London : Harvard University Press, 1981. — viii,303p : ill ; 25cm
Includes index
ISBN 0-674-03020-6 : £10.50 B82-11869

320.973′03′21 — United States. Politics *— Encyclopaedias*

Plano, Jack C.. The American political dictionary / Jack C. Plano, Milton Greenberg. — 6th ed. — New York ; London : Holt, Rinehart and Winston, c1982. — viii,472p ; 25cm
Previous ed.: 1979. — Includes index
ISBN 0-03-061514-3 (cased) : Unpriced
ISBN 0-03-060127-4 (pbk) : £7.95 B82-25410

320.9747 — New York *(State).* **Politics**

Zimmerman, Joseph F.. The government and politics of New York State / Joseph F. Zimmerman. — New York ; London : New York University Press, 1981. — xiii,398p ; 24cm
Bibliography: p353-378. — Includes index
ISBN 0-8147-9657-5 : £26.00 B82-38743

320.9747 — New York *(State).* **Politics,** *1760-1790*

Countryman, Edward. A people in revolution : the American Revolution and political society in New York, 1760-1790 / Edward Countryman. — Baltimore ; London : Johns Hopkins University Press, c1981. — xviii,388p : 2maps ; 24cm. — (The Johns Hopkins University studies in historical and political science. 99th series ; v.2)
Includes index
ISBN 0-8018-2625-x : £17.25 B82-12190

320.9757 — South Carolina. Politics, *1815-1845*

Peterson, Merrill D.. Olive branch and sword — the compromise of 1833 / Merrill D. Peterson. — Baton Rouge ; London : Louisiana State University Press, c1982. — 132p ; 23cm. — (The Walter Lynwood Fleming lectures in southern history)
Includes index
ISBN 0-8071-0894-4 : £11.25 B82-40268

320.9761 — Alabama. Politics, *1800-1860*

Thornton, J. Mills. Politics and power in a slave society / Alabama, 1800-1860 ; J. Mills Thornton III. — Baton Rouge ; London : Louisiana State University Press, 1981, c1978. — xxiv,492p : ill,maps ; 23cm
Originally published: Ann Arbor : Xerox University Microfilms, 1976. — Bibliography: p475-480. — Includes index
ISBN 0-8071-0891-x (pbk) : £6.95 B82-15448

320.981 — Brazil. Political power
McDonough, Peter. Power and ideology in Brazil / Peter McDonough. — Princeton ; Guildford : Princeton University Press, c1981. — xxxiv,326p : ill ; 25cm
Bibliography: p295-322. — Includes index
ISBN 0-691-07628-6 (cased) : £17.60
ISBN 0-691-02203-8 (pbk) : £5.65 B82-09526

320.994 — Australia. Politics, *1970-1979*
A **Fractured** Federation?. — London : Allen and Unwin, Jan.1983. — [128]p
ISBN 0-86861-109-3 : £15.00 : CIP entry B82-33239

321 — POLITICS. FORMS OF STATES

321 — Political integration
Political co-operation in divided societies : a series of papers relevant to the conflict in Northern Ireland / edited by Desmond Rea. — Dublin : Gill and Macmillan, 1982. — 353p : 1ill ; 23cm
Includes bibliographies
ISBN 0-7171-1162-8 : £25.00 B82-31559

321 — Regional self-government — *Proposals*
Rougemont, Denis de. The future is our concern. — Oxford : Pergamon, Dec.1982. — [254]p. — (System science and world order library) (Pergamon international library)
ISBN 0-08-027395-5 (cased) : £22.50 : CIP entry
ISBN 0-08-027394-7 (pbk) : £10.00 B82-29868

321.02 — Federalism
Forsyth, Murray. Unions of states : the theory and practice of confederation / Murray Forsyth. — [Leicester] : Leicester University Press, 1981. — xii,236p ; 22cm
Includes index
ISBN 0-7185-1188-3 (cased) : £13.00 : CIP rev.
ISBN 0-7185-1221-9 (pbk) : Unpriced B81-20638

King, Preston. Federalism and federation / Preston King. — London : Croom Helm, c1982. — 159p ; 23cm. — (Croom Helm international series in social and political thought)
Bibliography: p149-155. — Includes index
ISBN 0-7099-1515-2 (cased) : £9.95 : CIP rev.
ISBN 0-7099-1520-9 (pbk) : Unpriced B82-09589

321'.04 — European Community countries. Political cooperation
Allen, David, *1949-*. European political cooperation : towards a foreign policy for Western Europe / David Allen, Reinhardt Rummel and Wolfgang Wessels. — London : Butterworth Scientific, 1982. — viii,184p ; 24cm. — (Butterworths European studies)
Translated from the German. — Includes index
ISBN 0-408-10663-8 : Unpriced : CIP rev. B82-10493

Great Britain. *Foreign and Commonwealth Office*. Report on European political co-operation : (approved by the Foreign Ministers of the ten member states of the European Communities at their meeting in London on 13 October 1981) / presented to Parliament by the Secretary of State for Foreign and Commonwealth Affairs ... — London : H.M.S.O., [1981]. — 7p ; 25cm. — (Miscellaneous ; no.25 (1981)) (Cmnd. ; 8424)
ISBN 0-10-184240-6 (unbound) : £1.15 B82-09573

321'.04 — South-east Asian countries. Political cooperation
Jorgensen-Dahl, Arnfinn. Regional organization and order in South-East Asia / Arnfinn Jorgensen-Dahl. — London : Macmillan, 1982. — xvii,278p ; 23cm
Includes index
ISBN 0-333-30663-5 : £20.00 B82-38782

321'.05 — Nation states
The **Nation** state. — Oxford : Robertson, June 1982. — [224]p
Originally published: 1981
ISBN 0-85520-516-4 (pbk) : £5.95 : CIP entry B82-12167

321.06'09 — City states, *to 1800*
The **City-state** in five cultures / edited and with an introduction by Robert Griffeth and Carol G. Thomas. — Santa Barbara ; Oxford : ABC-Clio, c1981. — xx,237p : ill,maps,plans ; 24cm
Text on lining papers. — Bibliography: p209-220. — Includes index
ISBN 0-87436-316-0 : £15.00 B82-27405

321.06'0945 — Italy. Signorial states, *1250-1500*
Law, John E.. The Lords of Renaissance Italy : the signori, 1250-1500 / John E. Law. — London : Historical Association, c1981. — 36p : 1map ; 22cm. — (General series ; 102)
Bibliography: p34-35
ISBN 0-85278-247-0 (pbk) : Unpriced B82-03504

321'.07 — Utopianism, *1516-1630 — Critical studies*
Eliav-Feldon, Miriam. Realistic utopias. — Oxford : Clarendon Press, June 1982. — [230] p. — (Oxford historical monographs)
ISBN 0-19-821889-3 : £17.50 : CIP entry B82-10446

321'.07 — Utopianism. Theories of Bakunin, Mikhail Aleksandrovich
Kelly, Aileen. Mikhail Bakunin. — Oxford : Clarendon Press, Sept.1982. — [320]p
ISBN 0-19-827244-8 : £15.00 : CIP entry B82-18972

321'.07 — Utopianism. Theories of European writers, *1800-1850*
Taylor, Keith. The political ideas of the utopian socialists / Keith Taylor. — London : Cass, 1982. — ix,238p ; 23cm
Bibliography: p218-225. — Includes index
ISBN 0-7146-3089-6 : £14.50 : CIP rev. B81-31286

321'.07 — Utopias. Plato. Republic — *Critical studies*
Cross, R. C. (Robert Craigie). Plato's Republic : a philosophical commentary / R.C. Cross and A.D. Woozley. — London : Macmillan, 1964 (1980 [printing]). — xv,295p ; 22cm
Bibliography: p289-291. — Includes index
ISBN 0-333-19302-4 (pbk) : £4.95 : CIP rev. B78-30427

321'.07 — Utopias, *to 1980*
Goodwin, Barbara. The politics of Utopia. — London : Hutchinson Education, Sept.1982. — [276]p
ISBN 0-09-149000-6 (cased) : £10.00 : CIP entry
ISBN 0-09-149001-4 (pbk £5.95) B82-19150

321.1 — Prehistoric government
Haas, Jonathan. The evolution of the prehistoric state / Jonathan Haas. — New York ; Guildford : Columbia University Press, 1982. — x,251p ; 24cm
Bibliography: p219-241. — Includes index
ISBN 0-231-05338-x : £18.55 B82-38907

321.6'0947 — Russia. Absolutism, *1613-1801*
Dukes, Paul, *1934-*. The making of Russian absolutism 1613-1801 / Paul Dukes. — London : Longman, 1982. — 197p : maps ; 24cm. — (Longman history of Russia)
Bibliography: p187-188. — Includes index
ISBN 0-582-48684-x (cased) : Unpriced
ISBN 0-582-48685-8 (pbk) : £5.95 B82-14616

321.8 — Democracies. Politics. Pluralism
Dahl, Robert A.. Dilemmas of pluralist democracy. — London : Yale University Press, July 1982. — [232]p. — (Yale studies in political science ; 31)
ISBN 0-300-02543-2 : £14.50 : CIP entry B82-22786

321.8 — Politics. Pluralism, *to 1978*
Ehrlich, Stanislaw. Pluralism on and off course. — Oxford : Pergamon, Aug.1982. — [300]p
ISBN 0-08-028114-1 (cased) : £20.00 : CIP entry
ISBN 0-08-027936-8 (pbk) : £9.75 B82-19248

321.8 — Representative institutions — *History — Serials*
Parliaments, estates & representation = Parlements, états & représentation. — Vol.1, pt.1 (June 1981)-. — Clevedon (c/o Tieto Ltd., 4 Bellevue Mansions, Bellevue Rd, Clevedon, Avon BS21 7NU) : Published for the International Commission for the History of Representative and Parliamentary Institutions by Pageant Pub., 1981-. — v. ; 25cm
Two issues yearly. — Text in English and French
ISSN 0260-6755 = Parliaments, estates & representation : £16.00 per year B82-06178

321.8'01 — Democracy. Liberalist theories
Levine, Andrew. Liberal democracy : a critique of its theory / Andrew Levine. — New York ; Guildford : Columbia University Press, 1981. — 216p : ill ; 22cm
Includes index
ISBN 0-231-05250-2 : £17.50 B82-10943

321.8'042'09669 — Nigeria. Presidential government
Nwabueze, B. O.. The presidential constitution of Nigeria. — London : C. Hurst, Mar.1982. — [558]p
ISBN 0-905838-60-2 : £16.50 : CIP entry B82-00298

321.8'043 — Europe. Coalition governments, *1945-1980*
Government coalitions in Western democracies / edited by Eric C. Browne, John Dreijmanis. — New York ; London : Longman, c1982. — x,384p : ill ; 23cm
Bibliography: p358-375. — Includes index
ISBN 0-582-28218-7 (cased) : Unpriced
ISBN 0-582-28219-5 (pbk) : £9.95 B82-33648

321.8'09181'2 — Western world. Democracy
Nordlinger, Eric A.. On the autonomy of the democratic state / Eric A. Nordlinger. — Cambridge, Mass. ; London : Harvard University Press, 1981. — viii,239p : ill ; 24cm
Includes index
ISBN 0-674-63407-1 : £14.00 B82-03919

321.8'0941 — Great Britain. Democracy, *1867-1980*
Miliband, Ralph. Capitalist democracy in Britain. — Oxford : Oxford University Press, Oct.1982. — [192]p
ISBN 0-19-827445-9 : £8.95 : CIP entry B82-24708

321.8'0941 — Great Britain. Democracy — *Socialist viewpoints*
Benn, Tony. Arguments for democracy / Tony Benn ; edited by Chris Mullin. — Harmondsworth : Penguin, 1982, c1981. — xiv,257p ; 18cm
Originally published: London : Cape, 1981. — Includes index
ISBN 0-14-006157-6 (pbk) : £1.75 B82-40946

321.8'0951 — China. Democracy, *1905-1914*
Fincher, John H.. Chinese democracy : the self-government movement in local, provincial and national politics, 1905-1914 / John H. Fincher. — London : Croom Helm, c1981. — 276p ; 23cm
ISBN 0-7099-0463-0 : £17.95 : CIP rev.
ISBN 0-7081-1267-6 (Australia) B80-12263

321.9 — Corporatism
Patterns of corporatist policy-making. — London : Sage, July 1982. — [298]p. — (Sage modern politics series ; v.7)
ISBN 0-8039-9832-5 (cased) : £15.50 : CIP entry
ISBN 0-8039-9833-3 (pbk) : £7.50 B82-13081

321.9'09'04 — Authoritarianism, *ca 1900-1980*
Perlmutter, Amos. Modern authoritarianism : a comparative institutional analysis / Amos Perlmutter. — New Haven ; London : Yale University Press, c1981. — xiv,194p : ill ; 22cm
Includes index
ISBN 0-300-02640-4 : Unpriced : CIP rev. B81-35025

321.9'2 — Communist governments. Establishment, *1917-1981*

Szajkowski, Bogdan. The establishment of Marxist regimes. — London : Butterworths, Aug.1982. — [224]p
ISBN 0-408-10834-7 (cased) : £12.00 : CIP entry
ISBN 0-408-10833-9 (pbk) : £6.95 B82-15782

321.92'0947 — Soviet Union. Democratic centralism, *1905-1980*

Waller, Michael. Democratic centralism : an historical commentary / Michael Waller. — Manchester : Manchester University Press, c1981. — 155p ; 25cm
Includes index
ISBN 0-7190-0802-6 : £14.50 : CIP rev.
B81-17502

322 — POLITICS. RELATION OF STATE TO ORGANISED GROUPS

322'.1 — Western world. Politics. Role of Catholics, *1790-1971*

Whyte, John H.. Catholics in western democracies : a study in political behaviour / John H. Whyte. — Dublin : Gill and Macmillan, 1981. — 193p ; 23cm
Bibliography: p158-183. — Includes index
ISBN 0-7171-1129-6 : £13.00 B82-09134

322'.1'0941 — Great Britain. Politics. Role of Nonconformists, *1870-1914*

Bebbington, D. W.. The Nonconformist conscience : chapel and politics, 1870-1914 / D.W. Bebbington. — London : Allen & Unwin, 1982. — x,193p ; 23cm
Includes index
ISBN 0-04-942173-5 : Unpriced : CIP rev.
B81-33897

322'.1'09411 — Church of Scotland. Relations with state, *1600-1700 — Readings from contemporary sources*

The **Party-coloured** mind : prose relating to the conflict of church and state in seventeenth century Scotland / edited by David Reid. — Edinburgh : Scottish Academic Press, 1982. — x,221p ; 23cm. — (The Association for Scottish Literary Studies ; no.11)
Includes index
ISBN 0-7073-0304-4 : Unpriced B82-39482

322'.2'09 — Working class movements, *to ca 1900 — Marxist viewpoints*

The **International** working-class movement : problems of history and theory / introduction by B.N. Ponomarev. — Moscow : Progress Publishers ; [London] : Distributed by Central Books
Translation of: Mezhdunarodnoe rabochee dvizhenie
Vol.1: The origins of the proletariat and its evolution as a revolutionary class / [translated from the Russian by Yuri Shirokov and Campbell Creighton]. — c1980. — 674p ; 23cm
Includes index
ISBN 0-7147-1640-5 : £4.50 B82-02703

322'.2'0922 — Great Britain. Working class movements. Lovell, Bob & Lovell, Sarah — *Biographies*

Frow, Edmund. Bob and Sarah Lovell : crusaders for a better society / by Edmund and Ruth Frow. — Manchester (111, Kings Rd., Old Trafford, Manchester M16 9NU) : Working Class Movement Library, [1982?]. — 25p : ill,ports ; 30cm
Unpriced (pbk) B82-17845

322'.2'0924 — Great Britain. Working class movements. Benson, Ernie — *Biographies*

Benson, Ernie. To struggle is to live : a working class autobiography / [Ernie Benson]. — Newcastle upon Tyne : People's Publications
Vol.2: Starve or rebel. — 1980. — 280p : facsims,1port ; 22cm
ISBN 0-906917-04-2 (cased) : Unpriced
ISBN 0-906917-05-0 (pbk) : £1.90 B82-27119

322'.2'0924 — Kent. Tomists. Courtenary, *Sir* **William —** *Biographies*

Robinson, Beverley. The Red Lion : a re-assessment of the leader of the Tomists of Kent, 'Sir William Courtenay'/John Nichols Tom, killed in Bossenden Wood, 1838 / by Beverley Robinson. — Newcastle upon Tyne : People's Publications, 1980. — xix,65p : ill,facsims,ports ; 21cm
ISBN 0-906917-03-4 (pbk) : Unpriced
B82-30091

322'.2'0941 — Great Britain. Politics. Role of trade unions, *to 1981*

Trade unions in British politics. — London : Longman, Nov.1982. — [320]p
ISBN 0-582-49184-3 (pbk) : £6.50 : CIP entry
B82-26539

322'.2'0942 — England. Working class movements, *1700-1951*

Brown, Kenneth D.. The English labour movement 1700-1951. — Dublin : Gill and Macmillan, 1982. — 322p ; 23cm
Includes index
ISBN 0-7171-0870-8 : £20.00 B82-24308

322'.2'0945 — Italy. Working class movements. Autonomy, *1964-1979 — Marxist-Leninist viewpoints*

Working class autonomy and the crisis : Italian Marxist texts of the theory and practice of a class movement : 1964-79. — London (2a St. Paul's Rd., N1) : Red Notes, 1979. — x,202p : ill,1facsim ; 30cm
ISBN 0-906305-05-5 (pbk) : £3.95 B82-01479

322'.2'09669 — Nigeria. Politics. Role of trade unions, *1945-1978*

Cohen, Robin. Labour and politics in Nigeria / Robin Cohen. — London : Heinemann, 1974 (1981 [printing]). — xv,304p : ill ; 22cm
Bibliography: p274-291. — Includes index
ISBN 0-435-96150-0 (pbk) : £5.50 B82-05074

322.4'2 — Middle East. Politics. Violence, *1882-1976*

Hirst, David. The gun and the olive branch : the roots of violence in the Middle East / David Hirst. — London : Futura, 1978, c1977. — 367p ; 18cm
Originally published: London : Faber, 1977. — Includes index
ISBN 0-7088-1401-8 (pbk) : £1.25 B82-35487

322.4'2 — Revolutions. Political aspects
Revolutionary theory and political reality. — Brighton : Harvester Books, Feb.1983. — [240]p
ISBN 0-7108-0194-7 : CIP entry B82-38899

322.4'2 — Separatist movements
National separatism / edited by Colin H. Williams. — Cardiff : University of Wales Press, 1982. — ix,317p : ill,maps ; 23cm
Includes index
ISBN 0-7083-0798-1 : Unpriced : CIP rev.
B81-34301

322.4'2 — Socialist revolution. Role of working classes
Timofeev, T. T.. Workers in society : polemical essays / Timur Timofeyev. — Moscow : Progress ; [London] : distributed by Central, 1981. — 319p ; 21cm
Translation of: Rabochie v obshchestve. — Includes index
ISBN 0-7147-1775-4 : £3.95 B82-37037

322.4'2 — Socialist revolution. Theories
Dunayevskaya, Raya. Philosophy and revolution. — Brighton : Harvester Press, Apr.1982. — [392]p
Originally published: New York : Delacorte Press, 1973
ISBN 0-7108-0303-6 (pbk) : £6.50 : CIP entry
B82-04476

322.4'2 — Terrorism
Dobson, Christopher. Terror! : the West fights back / Christopher Dobson and Ronald Payne. — London : Macmillan, 1982. — 218p ; 23cm
Bibliography: p207-209. — Includes index
ISBN 0-333-29417-3 (cased) : Unpriced
ISBN 0-333-29418-1 (Papermac) : Unpriced
B82-38771

322.4'2 — Terrorism — *Conference proceedings*
Contemporary terror : studies in sub-state violence / edited by David Carlton and Carlo Schaerf. — London : Macmillan, 1981. — xvi,231p ; 23cm
Includes index
ISBN 0-333-27207-2 : £20.00 B82-06897

322.4'2 — Terrorism. Influence of reporting of terrorism by news media
Schmid, Alex P.. Violence as communication : insurgent terrorism and the Western news media. — London : Sage Publications, Feb.1982. — [284]p
ISBN 0-8039-9789-2 : £17.00 : CIP entry
B81-37586

322.4'2'088042 — Nicaragua. Revolutionary movements. Role of women, *1930-1979 — Interviews*
Randall, Margaret, *1936-*. Sandino's daughters : testimonies of Nicaraguan women in struggle / Margaret Randall ; Lynda Yanz, editor. — London : Zed, 1981. — ix,220p : ill,ports ; 21cm
ISBN 0-919888-34-8 (cased) : Unpriced
ISBN 0-919888-33-x (pbk) : £4.95 B82-32092

322.4'2'09047 — International terrorism, *1968-1979 — Chronologies*
Mickolus, Edward F.. Transnational terrorism : a chronology of events, 1968-1979 / Edward F. Mickolus. — London : Aldwych, 1980. — xxxviii,967p ; 24cm
Bibliography: pxxxi-xxxvi. — Includes index
ISBN 0-86172-013-x : £55.00 B82-31085

322.4'2'0924 — Clare *(County)*. **Revolutionary movements: Irish Volunteers.** *Western Division, 1st, 1913-1921 — Personal observations*
Brennan, Michael, *1896-*. The war in Clare 1911-1921 : personal memoirs of the Irish war of independence / Michael Brennan. — Dublin : Four Courts, 1980. — 112p : maps ; 23cm
Maps on lining papers. — Includes index
ISBN 0-906127-26-2 : £5.00 B82-00995

322.4'2'0924 — Ghana. Nationalist movements. Role of Nkrumah, Kwame, *1947-1957*
James, C. L. R.. Nkrumah and the Ghana revolution / C.L.R. James. — London : Allison & Busby, 1977 (1982 [printing]). — 224p ; 20cm
Includes index
ISBN 0-85031-461-5 (pbk) : £3.95 : CIP rev.
B82-05415

322.4'2'0924 — Ireland. Marxist movements. Role of Connolly, James
Mac an Bheatha, Proinsias. James Connolly and the workers' republic / Proinsias Mac an Bheatha. — Baile Átha Cliath (29 Sráid Uí Chonaill, Íocht., Baile Átha Cliath 1) : Foilseacháin Naísúnta Teoranta, c1978. — 90p : ill,1port ; 18cm
£1.25 (pbk) B82-14332

322.4'2'0924 — Ireland. Revolutionary movements: Irish Republican Army. Barry, Tom — *Biographies*
Ryan, Meda. The Tom Barry story / Meda Ryan. — Dublin : Mercier, c1982. — 207p : 1map ; 19cm
Bibliography: p202-203. — Includes index
ISBN 0-85342-672-4 (pbk) : £4.20 B82-35765

322.4'2'0924 — Ireland. Revolutionary movements: Irish Republican Army. Flood, Matt — *Biographies*
Hammond, Bill. Soldier of the rearguard : the story of Matt Flood and the Active Service Column / by Bill Hammond. — Fermoy : Éigse Mainistreach, 1977. — 69p : ports ; 18cm
£1.50 (pbk) B82-16135

322.4'2'0924 — Ireland. Revolutionary movements: Provisional IRA. Sands, Bobby
Bobby Sands : portrait of a hunger striker / [produced by the Troops Out Movement (Central London Branch)]. — London (1 North End Road, London W14 8ST) : Information on Ireland, [1981]. — 1sheet : ill (some col.),1port ; 61x43cm folded to 31x22cm + writings from the blocks / by Bobby Sands (1sheet ; 43x30cm)
£0.25 B82-13457

322.4'2'0924 — Ireland. Revolutionary movements. Role of Davitt, Michael, *1865-1882*

Moody, T. W.. Davitt and Irish revolution, 1846-82 / by T.W. Moody. — Oxford : Clarendon, 1981. — xxiv,674p,[12]p of plates : ill,maps,facsims,ports ; 24cm
Bibliography: p579-633. — Includes index
ISBN 0-19-822382-x : £22.50 : CIP rev. B81-15840

322.4'2'0924 — Namibia. Nationalist movements: SWAPO. Ya-Otto, John — *Biographies*

Ya-Otto, John. Battlefront Namibia : an autobiography / John Ya-Otto with Ole Gjerstad and Michael Mercer. — London : Heinemann, 1982. — 151p ; 19cm
ISBN 0-435-90244-x (pbk) : £1.95 B82-09154

322.4'2'0924 — Russia. Revolutionary movements, *1914-1917 — Personal observations*

Shlîapnikov, A.. On the eve of 1917 / Alexander Shlyapnikov ; translated from the Russian by Richard Chappell. — London : Allison & Busby, 1982. — xii,237p ; 23cm
Translation of: Kanun semnadtsatogo goda. — Includes index
ISBN 0-85031-376-7 (cased) : £10.95 : CIP rev.
ISBN 0-85031-377-5 (pbk) B80-21499

322.4'2'0924 — United States. Revolutionary movements: Symbionese Liberation Army. Hearst, Patricia Campbell, *1974-1979 — Biographies*

Hearst, Patricia Campbell. Every secret thing. — London : Methuen, Feb.1982. — [480]p
ISBN 0-413-50460-3 : £7.95 : CIP entry B82-02448

322.4'2'094 — European Community countries. Terrorism

Terrorism : a challenge to the state. — Oxford : Robertson, June 1982. — [260]p
Originally published: 1981
ISBN 0-85520-511-3 (pbk) : £5.95 : CIP entry B82-12164

Terrorism in Europe. — London : Croom Helm, July 1982. — [224]p
ISBN 0-7099-0728-1 : £12.95 : CIP entry B82-18466

322.4'2'0942 — England. Irish revolutionary movements: Fenian Brotherhood, *1865-1872*

Quinlivan, Patrick. The Fenians in England 1865-1872 : a sense of insecurity / Patrick Quinlivan and Paul Rose. — London : Calder, 1982. — 196p,[18]p of plates : ill,ports ; 23cm. — (Historical perspectives)
Bibliography: p175-185. — Includes index
ISBN 0-7145-3775-6 : £10.95 : CIP rev. B80-17570

322.4'2'0943 — West Germany. Guerilla movements, *to 1978*

The **German** guerrilla : terror, reaction, and resistance. — Sanday : Cienfuegos, [1981]. — 106p : ill,ports ; 22cm
Translation from the German
ISBN 0-904564-36-3 (pbk) : £2.00 : CIP rev. B80-04089

322.4'2'09438 — Poland. Nationalist movements, *1830-1863*

Walicki, Andrzej. Philosophy and romantic nationalism : the case of Poland / by Andrzej Walicki. — Oxford : Clarendon, 1982. — 415p ; 23cm
Includes index
ISBN 0-19-827250-2 : £20.00 : CIP rev. B82-10453

322.4'2'094436 — France. Paris. Republican revolutionary movements: Sans-culottes, *1789-1792*

Rose, R. B.. The making of the Sans-culottes. — Manchester : Manchester University Press, Nov.1982. — [224]p
ISBN 0-7190-0879-4 : £19.50 : CIP entry B82-29016

322.4'2'094461 — France. Vendée. Peasant counter-revolutionary movements, *1770-1796*

Sutherland, Donald. The Chouans : the social origins of popular counter-revolution in Upper Brittany, 1770-1796. — Oxford : Clarendon Press, July 1982. — [400]p
ISBN 0-19-822579-2 : £25.00 : CIP entry B82-12547

322.4'2'0954 — India *(Republic).* **Revolutionary movements: Naxalite Movement. Uprising,** *1967*

Banerjee, Sumanta. India's simmering revolution. — London : Zed Press, Aug.1982. — [464]p
ISBN 0-86232-038-0 (pbk) : £7.95 : CIP entry B82-19289

322.4'2'0955 — Iran. Islamic revolutionary movements

Algar, Hamid. The Islamic Revolution in Iran : transcript of a four-lecture course given by Hamid Algar at the Muslim Institute London / editor Kalim Siddiqui. — London : Open Press in association with the Muslim Institute, 1980. — x,70,9p : ill,ports ; 30cm
Bibliography: p70
ISBN 0-905081-04-8 (pbk) : £4.00 : CIP rev. B80-25015

322.4'2'095694 — Palestinian Arab resistance movements: Palestine Liberation Organisation. International recognition

The **International** status of the PLO / [Institute of Jewish Affairs]. — London (11 Hertford St., W1Y 7DX) : Institute of Jewish Affairs, 1981. — 8p ; 24cm. — (Research report / Institute of Jewish Affairs ; no.16)
Unpriced (unbound) B82-13823

322.4'2'095694 — Palestinian Arab resistance movements: Palestine Liberation Organisation. Manifestos: Palestinian National Covenant, *to 1977 — Commentaries*

Harkabi, Y.. The Palestinian Covenant and its meaning / Y. Harkabi. — London : Valentine, Mitchell, 1979. — 159p ; 23cm
Bibliography: p102-103
ISBN 0-85303-200-9 (cased) : Unpriced : CIP rev.
ISBN 0-85303-201-7 (pbk) : Unpriced B79-12288

322.4'2'097284 — El Salvador. Revolutionary movementss, *to 1979*

Revolutionary strategy in El Salvador. — London (29 Islington Park St., N.1) : Tricontinental Society, [1981?]. — 44p : ill,1port ; 30cm
£1.00 (pbk) B82-29490

322.4'2'09788 — Colorado. Racial discrimination. Organisations: Ku Klux Klan, *1920-1930*

Goldberg, Robert Alan. Hooded empire : the Ku Klux Klan in Colorado / Robert Alan Goldberg. — Urbana ; London : University of Illinois Press, c1981. — xv,255p : 1ill,2maps ; 24cm
Bibliography: p219-243. — Includes index
ISBN 0-252-00848-0 : £9.95 B82-06391

322.4'2'0982 — Argentina. Urban guerrilla movements: Montoneros, *1968-1981*

Gillespie, Richard. Soldiers of Perón. — Oxford : Clarendon Press, Dec.1982. — [350]p
ISBN 0-19-821131-7 : £19.50 : CIP entry B82-29898

322.4'3 — Great Britain. Pro-Arab pressure groups *— Jewish viewpoints*

The **Pro-Arab** lobby in Britain. — London (11 Hertford St., W1Y 7DX) : IJA, 1981. — 18p ; 24cm. — (Research report / Institute of Jewish Affairs ; nos.22 & 23)
Unpriced (unbound) B82-27692

322.4'3 — Pressure groups

Willetts, Peter. Pressure groups in the global system. — London : Pinter, Apr.1982. — [256]p
ISBN 0-903804-86-7 (cased) : £14.50 : CIP entry
ISBN 0-86187-224-x (pbk) : £5.95 B82-11977

322.4'3 — Pressure groups. Organisation — *Manuals*

Jelfs, Martin. Manual for action / Martin Jelfs ; revised by Sandy Merritt. — London : Action Resources Group, 1982. — 81p ; 30cm
Bibliography: p79-80. — Includes index
ISBN 0-9508181-0-0 (pbk) : £2.50 B82-40562

322.4'3'094 — European Community countries. Interest groups. Relations with Commission of the European Communities. *Economic and Social Committee*

European interest groups and their relationship with the Economic and Social Committee / Economic and Social Committee of the European Communities, General Secretariat, Directorate General Studies and Documentation Division. — Farnborough, Hants. : Saxon House, c1980. — ix,453p : ill ; 23cm
Includes bibliographies
ISBN 0-566-00365-1 (corrected) : £25.00 : CIP rev. B80-07243

322.4'3'094 — European Community. Interest groups

Kirchner, Emil Joseph. The role of interest groups in the European Community / Emil Kirchner, Konrad Schwaiger. — Aldershot : Gower, c1981. — xi,178p : ill ; 23cm
Bibliography: p167-170. — Includes index
ISBN 0-566-00257-4 : Unpriced : CIP rev. B81-16365

322.4'3'0951242 — China. Chekiang. Political elites, *1912-1927*

Schoppa, R. Keith. Chinese elites and political change : Zhejiang Province in the early twentieth century / R. Keith Schoppa. — Cambridge, Mass. ; London : Harvard University Press, 1982. — viii,280p : 3maps ; 24cm. — (Harvard East Asian series ; 96)
Includes Chinese glossary. — Bibliography: p251-265. — Includes index
ISBN 0-674-12325-5 : £21.00 B82-33388

322.4'3'0973 — United States. Politics. Role of interest groups

Hrebenar, Ronald J.. Interest group politics in America / Ronald J. Hrebenar, Ruth K. Scott. — Englewood Cliffs ; London : Prentice-Hall, c1982. — xi,275p : ill,facsims ; 23cm
Includes index
ISBN 0-13-469254-3 (pbk) : £8.95 B82-23648

322.4'3'0973 — United States. Pressure groups — *Encyclopaedias*

Schapsmeier, Edward L.. Political parties and civic action groups / Edward L. Schapsmeier and Frederick H. Schapsmeier. — Westport, Conn. ; London : Greenwood Press, 1981. — xxxiii,554p ; 25cm. — (The Greenwood encyclopedia of American institutions)
Includes index
ISBN 0-313-21442-5 : £37.00 B82-18365

322.4'4'0924 — Chartism. O'Connor, Feargus, *1832-1842*

Epstein, James. The lion of freedom : Feargus O'Connor and the Chartist movement, 1832-1842 / James Epstein. — London : Croom Helm, c1982. — 327p ; 23cm. — (Croom Helm social history series)
Includes index
ISBN 0-85664-922-8 : £14.95 : CIP rev. B81-33774

322.4'4'0941 — Chartism, *1837-1848 — Readings from contemporary sources*

Chartism and society : an anthology of documents / edited by F.C. Mather. — London : Bell & Hyman, 1980. — 319p ; 23cm
Bibliography: p303-310. — Includes index
ISBN 0-7135-1114-1 : £15.00 : CIP rev. B80-05802

322.4'4'0941 — North America. Slavery. British abolitionist movements, *ca 1790-1863*

Antislavery reconsidered : new perspectives on the abolitionists / edited by Lewis Perry and Michael Fellman. — Baton Rouge ; London : Louisiana State University Press, 1981, c1979. — xvi,348p ; 23cm
Originally published: 1979. — Includes index
ISBN 0-8071-0889-8 (pbk) : £6.30
Primary classification 322.4'4'0973 B82-09919

322.4'4'0941 — Slavery. British abolitionist movements, *to 1833*
Slavery and British society 1776-1846 / edited by James Walvin. — London : Macmillan, 1982. — 272p : ill ; 22cm. — (Problems in focus series)
Includes index
ISBN 0-333-28073-3 (cased) : Unpriced
ISBN 0-333-28074-1 (pbk) : Unpriced
B82-32930

322.4'4'09411 — Slavery. Scottish abolitionist movements, *1833-1861*
Rice, C. Duncan. The Scots abolitionists 1833-1861 / C. Duncan Rice. — Baton Rouge ; London : Louisiana State University Press, c1981. — xii,221p ; 24cm
Includes index
ISBN 0-8071-0861-8 (cased) : Unpriced
ISBN 0-8071-0898-7 (pbk) : Unpriced
B82-34771

322.44'0942 — England. Rural regions. Protest movements, *1548-1900*
An **Atlas** of rural protest in Britain 1548-1900. — London : Croom Helm, Oct.1982. — [208]p. — (Croom Helm historical geography series)
ISBN 0-7099-0703-6 : £14.95 : CIP entry
B82-25733

322.4'4'09421 — London. Chartism, *1838-1848*
Goodway, David. London Chartism 1838-1848 / David Goodway. — Cambridge : Cambridge University Press, 1982. — xvii,333p : ill,1map,1facsim,ports ; 24cm
Bibliography: p301-323. — Includes index
ISBN 0-521-23867-6 : £22.50 : CIP rev.
B82-03615

322.4'4'094299 — Gwent. Chartism, *to 1840*
Davies, James. The Chartist movement in Monmouthshire / James Davies. — Newport : Starling, 1981. — vi,51p,[24]p of plates : ill,1map,facsims,ports ; 23cm
Facsim of: 1st ed. Newport : Newport Chartist Centenary Committee, 1939. — Text on inside covers
ISBN 0-903434-45-8 : Unpriced B82-17287

322.4'4'09433 — Germany. Bavaria. Politics. Dissent, *1933-1945*
Kershaw, Ian. Popular opinion and political dissent in the Third Reich. — Oxford : Clarendon, Feb.1983. — [450]p
ISBN 0-19-821922-9 : £22.50 : CIP entry
B82-36601

322.4'4'0947312 — Soviet Union. Moscow. Dissidents. Social life
Rubenstein, Joshua. Soviet dissidents. — London : Wildwood House, Aug.1981. — [320]p
ISBN 0-7045-3062-7 : £8.50 : CIP entry
B81-23804

322.4'4'0973 — North America. Slavery. American abolitionist movements, *1793-1867*
Antislavery reconsidered : new perspectives on the abolitionists / edited by Lewis Perry and Michael Fellman. — Baton Rouge ; London : Louisiana State University Press, 1981, c1979. — xvi,348p ; 23cm
Originally published: 1979. — Includes index
ISBN 0-8071-0889-8 (pbk) : £6.30
Also classified at 322.4'4'0941 B82-09919

322.4'4'0973 — Slavery. American abolitionist movements, *1830-1865*
Friedman, Lawrence J.. Gregarious saints : self and community in American abolitionism, 1830-1870 / Lawrence J. Friedman. — Cambridge : Cambridge University Press, 1982. — xi,344p ; 24cm
Bibliography: p333-336. — Includes index
ISBN 0-521-24429-3 (cased) : £20.00
ISBN 0-521-27015-4 (pbk) : Unpriced
B82-34878

322.4'4'098153 — Brazil. Urban regions. Populism, *1925-1945 — Study regions: Rio de Janeiro*
Conniff, Michael L.. Urban politics in Brazil : the rise of populism, 1925-1945 / Michael L. Conniff. — Pittsburgh : University of Pittsburgh Press ; London : Feffer and Simons, c1981. — xix,227p : ill,ports ; 24cm. — (Pitt Latin American series)
Bibliography: p209-219. — Includes index
ISBN 0-8229-3438-8 : Unpriced B82-23748

322.4'4'0985 — Peru. Populism, *1930-1931*
Stein, Steve. Populism in Peru : the emergence of the masses and the politics of social control / Steve Stein. — Madison ; London : University of Wisconsin Press, 1980. — xvi,296p : ill,ports ; 24cm
Bibliography: p276-292. — Includes index
£16.05 B82-40491

322'.5 — Politics. Role of military forces
Soldiers, peasants, and bureaucrats : civil-military relations in communist and modernizing societies / edited by Roman Kolkowicz and Andrzej Korbonski. — London : Allen & Unwin, 1982. — 340p : ill,maps ; 24cm
Published under the auspices of the Center for International and Strategic Affairs, University of California, Los Angeles. — Includes index
ISBN 0-04-322007-x : Unpriced : CIP rev.
B81-35924

322'.5'09669 — Nigeria. Politics. Role of military forces, *1966-1979*
Adekson, J. 'Bayo. Nigeria in search of a stable civil-military system / J. 'Bayo Adekson. — Aldershot : Gower, 1981. — xi,164p : 1map ; 23cm
Includes index
ISBN 0-566-00431-3 : Unpriced : CIP rev.
B81-14972

323 — POLITICS. RELATION OF STATE TO INDIVIDUALS AND SOCIAL CLASSES

323.1'06'01 — Social minorities. Civil rights. Organisations: Minority Rights Group
The **Minority** Rights Group : aims, work, reports. — London : The Group, 1981. — 4p ; 30cm
Unpriced (unbound) B82-05426

323.1'1 — Ethnic groups. National independence
Smith, Anthony D.. The ethnic revival / Anthony D. Smith. — Cambridge : Cambridge University Press, 1981. — xiv,240p ; 24cm. — (Themes in the social sciences)
Bibliography: p218-235. — Includes index
ISBN 0-521-23267-8 (cased) : £15.00 : CIP rev.
ISBN 0-521-29885-7 (pbk) : £4.95 B81-27943

323.1'1 — Ethnic groups. National independence — *Case studies*
Ronen, Dov. The quest for self-determination. — London : Yale University Press, Feb.1982. — [192]p
Originally published: 1979
ISBN 0-300-02840-7 (pbk) : £3.95 : CIP entry
B82-07093

323.1'1924'01821 — Western world. Anti-Jewish movements. Political aspects, *1945-1981*
Rubinstein, W. D.. The Left, the Right and the Jews. — London : Croom Helm, Sept.1982. — [240]p
ISBN 0-7099-0204-2 : £11.96 : CIP entry
B82-25061

323.1'1924'04 — Europe. Anti-Jewish movements. Role of friars, *1215-1350*
Cohen, Jeremy. The friars and the Jews : the evolution of medieval anti-Judaism / Jeremy Cohen. — Ithaca ; London : Cornell University Press, 1982. — 301p ; 24cm
Bibliography: p267-294. — Includes index
ISBN 0-8014-1406-7 : £17.00 B82-35756

323.1'197'077 — United States. North American Indians. Policies of government. Influence of trade between W.G. & G.W. Ewing & North American Indians in Mid-West region, *1827-1854*
Trennert, Robert A.. Indian traders on the middle border : the House of Ewing 1827-54 / Robert A. Trennert, Jr. — Lincoln [Neb.] ; London : University of Nebraska Press, c1981. — xiii,271p : 2maps,2ports ; 23cm
Bibliography: p247-257. — Includes index
ISBN 0-8032-4407-x : £12.60 B82-09773

323.1'4 — Europe. Ethnic groups. Nationalism
Krejčí, Jaroslav. Ethnic and political nations in Europe / Jaroslav Krejčí and Vítězslav Velímský. — London : Croom Helm, c1981. — 279p : ill,3maps ; 23cm
Bibliography: p273-274. — Includes index
ISBN 0-85664-988-0 : £14.95 : CIP rev.
B80-33021

323.1'68 — South Africa. Apartheid
Saul, John S.. The crisis in South Africa : class defense, class revolution / John S. Saul and Stephen Gelb. — New York ; London : Monthly Review, c1981. — 156p ; 23cm
ISBN 0-85345-594-5 (cased) : £6.50
ISBN 0-85345-593-7 (pbk) : Unpriced
B82-16976

323.1'68 — South Africa. Apartheid. Geographical aspects
Living under apartheid. — London : Allen & Unwin, Oct.1982. — [304]p
ISBN 0-04-309110-5 : £18.00 : CIP entry
B82-25083

323.1'68 — South Africa. Apartheid. Protest movements by coloured women
'Apartheid - you shall be crushed' : women's fight against apartheid. — Lusaka ; London (P.O. Box 28, 28 Penton Rd, N1 9PR) : African National Congress (SA), [1981?]. — 32p : ill,1map,ports ; 21cm
Unpriced (pbk) B82-05655

323.1'68'05 — Southern Africa. Race relations. Political aspects — *International Defence and Aid Fund viewpoints — Serials*
Briefing paper on Southern Africa / International Defence & Aid Fund. — No.1 (Mar. 1981)-. — London (104 Newgate St., EC1 7AP) : The Fund, 1981-. — v. ; 30cm
Three issues yearly
ISSN 0262-3781 = Briefing paper on Southern Africa : Unpriced B82-03426

323.1'687 — South Africa. Cape Town. Apartheid, *1950-1981*
Western, John. Outcast Cape Town. — London : Allen & Unwin, Feb.1982. — [361]p
ISBN 0-04-301139-x : £13.95 : CIP entry
B81-35940

323.1'73 — United States. Politics. Representation of disadvantaged persons
Dluhy, Milan J.. Changing the system : political advocacy for disadvantaged groups / Milan J. Dluhy. — Beverly Hills ; London : Published in cooperation with the Continuing Education Program in the Human Services of the University of Michigan School of Social Work [by] Sage, c1981. — 117p ; 22cm. — (A Sage human services guide ; 24)
Includes index
ISBN 0-8039-1726-0 (pbk) : Unpriced
B82-21865

323.3 — England. Working classes. Radicalism, *1790-1830*
Calhoun, Craig Jackson. Before the working class. — Oxford : Blackwell, Sept.1981. — [272]p
ISBN 0-631-12905-7 : £12.50 : CIP entry
B81-22645

323.3'2 — Eastern Europe. Politics. Role of working classes — *Conference proceedings*
Blue collar workers in Eastern Europe / edited by Jan F. Triska, Charles Gati. — London : Allen & Unwin, 1981. — xvi,302p ; 24cm
Includes bibliographies and index
ISBN 0-04-321027-9 (cased) : Unpriced : CIP rev. B81-28786

323.3'4 — Politics. Role of women
Williams, Shirley, *1930-*. Women in politics / Shirley Williams. — [London] : Bedford College, University of London, [c1980]. — 7p ; 25cm. — (The Fawcett lecture ; 1979-80)
Cover title
ISBN 0-900145-57-9 (pbk) : £0.85 B82-40823

323.3'4'0941 — Great Britain. Women. Civil rights — *Practical information*
Coote, Anna. Women's rights : a practical guide / Anna Coote and Tess Gill ; drawings by Posy Simmonds. — 3rd ed. — Harmondsworth : Penguin, 1981. — 555p : ill ; 20cm
Previous ed.: 1977. — Includes index
ISBN 0-14-046532-4 (pbk) : £3.95 B82-08024

323.3'4'0968 — South Africa. Politics. Role of women

Walker, Cherryl. Women and resistance in South Africa. — London : Onyx Press, Nov.1982. — [288]p
ISBN 0-906383-14-5 (cased) : £12.95 : CIP entry
ISBN 0-906383-15-3 (pbk) : £4.95 B82-33365

323.3'4'0968 — Southern Africa. Women. Political movements

You have struck a rock : women and political repression in Southern Africa. — London : International Defence & Aid Fund, 1980. — 24p : ill,1maps,ports ; 15x21cm
ISBN 0-904759-38-5 (pbk) : £0.20 B82-13185

323.4 — CIVIL RIGHTS

323.4 — Amnesty International

Power, Jonathan. Amnesty International, the human rights story. — Oxford : Pergamon, Aug.1981. — [200]p
ISBN 0-08-028902-9 : £10.00 : CIP entry B81-22578

323.4 — Children. Rights — *Philosophical perspectives*

Wringe, C. A.. Children's rights : a philosophical study / C.A. Wringe. — London : Routledge & Kegan Paul, 1981. — xi,180p ; 23cm. — (International library of the philosophy of education)
Bibliography: p173-176. — Includes index
ISBN 0-7100-0852-x : £12.50 : CIP rev. B81-30598

323.4 — Human rights

Human rights / edited by J. Roland Pennock and John W. Chapman. — New York ; London : New York University Press, 1981. — xvi,303p ; 22cm. — (Nomos ; 23)
Includes index
ISBN 0-8147-6578-5 : £18.60 B82-38251

323.4 — Human rights. Economic aspects

Madeley, John. Human rights begin with breakfast / by John Madeley. — Oxford : Pergamon on behalf of the United Nations Association of Great Britain and Northern Ireland, 1982. — 47p ; 22cm
ISBN 0-08-028926-6 (pbk) : £2.95 : CIP rev. B82-12404

323.4 — Human rights — *Islamic viewpoints*

Universal Islamic declaration of human rights. — London (16 Grosvenor Crescent, SW1) : Islamic Council, 1981. — 19p ; 15x21cm
£1.00 (pbk) B82-28385

323.4 — Social justice

Ackerman, Bruce A.. Social justice in the liberal state. — London : Yale University Press, Nov.1981. — [408]p
ISBN 0-300-02757-5 (pbk) : £6.25 : CIP entry B81-34716

323.4 — Social justice — *Conference proceedings*

Social justice / edited by Randolph L. Braham. — Boston, Mass. ; London : Nijhoff, c1981. — xvi,170p : ill ; 24cm
Conference papers
ISBN 0-89838-063-4 : Unpriced B82-04419

323.4'01 — Human rights — *Philosophical perspectives*

The **Philosophy** of human rights : international perspectives / edited by Alan S. Rosenbaum. — London : Aldwych, 1981, c1980. — xv,269p ; 24cm. — (Studies in human rights ; no.1)
Originally published: Westport, Conn. : Greenwood, 1980. — Bibliography: p253-256. — Includes index
ISBN 0-86172-016-4 : £19.95 B82-31081

323.4'05 — Civil rights — *Serials*

[Bulletin *(International Campaign Against Repression)*]. Bulletin / International Campaign Against Repression. — [No.1] (Apr. 1980)-. — London (Flat 1, 1 Maberley Cres., SE19) : ICAR, 1980-. — v. ; 30cm
ISSN 0263-9823 = Bulletin - International Campaign Against Repression : £0.20 per issue B82-40071

Freedom in the world : political rights and civil liberties. — 1978-. — [Oxford] : [Clio Press], 1978-. — v. : maps ; 25cm
Annual. — Description based on: 1981 issue
£21.00 B82-11811

323.4'06'073 — United States. Civil rights. Organisations: Fund for the Republic, *to 1980*

Kelly, Frank K.. Court of reason : Robert Hutchins and the Fund for the Republic / Frank K. Kelly. — New York : Free Press ; London : Collier Macmillan, c1981. — xii,722p ; 25cm
Includes index
ISBN 0-02-918030-9 : £13.95 B82-18904

323.4'088054 — Great Britain. Young persons. Rights — *For young persons*

Rae, Maggie. First rights : a guide to legal rights for young people / Maggie Rae, Patricia Hewitt and Barry Hugill ; illustrations by Corinne Pearlman. — 2nd ed., with revisions and corrections. — London : National Council for Civil Liberties, 1981. — 112p : ill ; 21cm. — (NCCL know your rights handbooks)
Previous ed.: 1979
ISBN 0-901108-95-2 (pbk) : £1.25 B82-39946

323.4'088055 — Scotland. Adolescents. Rights — *Practical information*

Basic rights information for young people : on benefits, police, sex, employment, housing, drugs, homosexuality, etc. — Edinburgh (132, Lauriston Place) : Edinburgh Citizens Rights Office, [1982?]. — [20]p : ill ; 22cm
Cover title. — Produced by: Bob Stead. — Text on inside covers
Unpriced (pbk) B82-36899

323.4'09'04 — Human rights, *1948-1978*

Oestreicher, Paul. Thirty years of human rights / by Paul Oestreicher. — London (2 Eaton Gate, SW1W 9BL) : British Churches' Advisory Forum on Human Rights and the Christian Institute Fund Trustees, c1980. — 8p ; 21cm
Cover title
£0.30 (pbk) B82-13780

323.4'092'4 — United States. Negroes. Civil rights movements. King, Martin Luther

Kondrashov, Stanislav. The life and death of Martin Luther King / Stanislav Kondrashov. — Moscow : Progress ; [London] : distributed by Central, c1981. — 260p ; 17cm
Translation of: Zhizn' i smert' Martina Līūtera Kinga
ISBN 0-7147-1697-9 (pbk) : £1.95 B82-29719

323.4'0941 — Great Britain. Civil rights

Hewitt, Patricia. The abuse of power : civil liberties in the United Kingdom / Patricia Hewitt. — Oxford : Robertson, 1982. — xiv,295p ; 24cm. — (Law in society series)
Bibliography: p267-279. — Includes index
ISBN 0-85520-379-x (cased) : £15.00 : CIP rev.
ISBN 0-85520-380-3 (pbk) : £4.95 B81-33645

323.4'0943 — West Germany. Human rights

Russell Tribunal 3 on the State of Human Rights in the Federal Republic of Germany. Censorship, legal defence and the domestic intelligence service in West Germany : conclusions of the Final Session of the Third Russell Tribunal. — Nottingham (Bertrand Russell House, Gamble Street, Nottingham, NG7 4ET) : Bertrand Russell Peace Foundation, [1979]. — 24p ; 21cm. — (Spokesman pamphlet ; no.69)
£0.40 (unbound) B82-17671

323.44 — Freedom

Dahrendorf, Ralf. Life chances : approaches to social and political theory / Ralf Dahrendorf. — London : Weidenfeld and Nicolson, c1979. — ix,181p ; 23cm
Includes index
ISBN 0-297-77682-7 : £10.00
Primary classification 305 B82-33506

Ruffin, R. W. B.. Are we free enough to care? : the challenge that a world in need poses to Americans / R.W.B. Ruffin. — London : MRA Books, [1982?]. — 15p ; 21cm
Unpriced (corrected : pbk) B82-40511

323.44 — Liberty

Mill, John Stuart. On liberty / John Stuart Mill ; edited with an introduction by Gertrude Himmelfarb. — Harmondsworth : Penguin, 1982. — 186p : 1facsim ; 19cm. — (Penguin English library)
Originally published: London : Parker, 1859
ISBN 0-14-043207-8 (pbk) : £1.50 B82-30254

323.44 — Liberty. Implications of theories of justice

Hayek, F. A.. Law, legislation and liberty : a new statement of the liberal principles of justice and political economy / F.A. Hayek. — London : Routledge & Kegan Paul, 1982. — xxi,180,191,244p ; 22cm
Originally published in 3 vols.. — Includes index
ISBN 0-7100-9211-3 (pbk) : £5.95 : CIP rev. B82-04474

323.44'0947 — Soviet Union. Personal freedom — *Soviet viewpoints*

Medvedev, F. E.. Human rights and freedoms in the USSR / F. Medvedev, G. Kulikov ; [translated from the Russian by Lyudmila Lezhneva]. — Moscow : Progress Publishers ; [London] : distributed by Central Books, c1981. — 255p ; 19cm
Translation of: Svobody i prava cheloveka v SSSR
ISBN 0-7147-1750-9 : £2.50 B82-38232

323.44'3'0922 — United States. Trade unions: Industrial Workers of the World. Freedom of speech, *1909-1916 — Personal observations — Collections*

Fellow workers and friends : I.W.W. free-speech fights as told by participants / edited by Philip S. Foner. — Westport ; London : Greenwood Press, 1981. — viii,242p ; 22cm. — (Contributions in American history ; no.92)
Includes index
ISBN 0-313-20660-0 : Unpriced B82-18025

323.44'3'0941 — Great Britain. Mass media. Freedom of speech

Francis, Richard, *1934-*. What price free speech? : a paper given by Richard Francis ... to the Law Society Conference in Coventry, Saturday 27 February 1982. — London : British Broadcasting Corporation, [1982]. — 16p ; 21cm
Unpriced (pbk) B82-38945

323.44'5 — Freedom of information

Freedom of information trends in the information age. — London : Cass, Nov.1982. — [180]p. — (Journal of media law and practice ; 3, no.1)
ISBN 0-7146-3221-x : £12.50 : CIP entry B82-32295

323.44'5 — Great Britain. Consumers. Effects of official secrets

Consuming secrets : how official secrecy affects everyday life in Britain / edited by Rosemary Delbridge and Martin Smith ; foreword by Harold Evans. — London : Burnett, 1982. — x,249p ; 22cm
At head of title: The National Consumer Council. — Bibliography: p239-241. — Includes index
ISBN 0-09-147590-2 (cased) : Unpriced : CIP rev.
ISBN 0-09-147591-0 (pbk) : £4.95 B82-07103

323.44'5 — Great Britain. Public records. Access. Rights of public. Modern public records — *Critical studies*

Modern public records : the Government response to the report of the Wilson Committee. — London : H.M.S.O., [1982]. — ii,29p ; 25cm. — (Cmnd. ; 8531)
At head of title: Lord Chancellor's Department
ISBN 0-10-185310-6 (unbound) : £2.65
Primary classification 025.17 B82-31676

323.44'8 — Great Britain. Privacy. Encroachment by computer systems. Control

The **External** auditor as privacy inspector. — Manchester : NCC Publications, July 1982. — [51]p
ISBN 0-85012-381-x (pbk) : £6.50 : CIP entry B82-29019

323.44′8′0941 — Great Britain. Privacy. Encroachment — *Labour Party (Great Britain) viewpoints*

Personal information and privacy : a Labour Party discussion document. — [London] : The Party, [1981]. — 15p ; 21cm. — (Socialism in the 80s)
Cover title
ISBN 0-86117-071-7 (pbk) : £0.40
Also classified at 323.44′83′0941 B82-05515

323.44′8′0941 — Great Britain. Privacy. Encroachment — *National Council of Civil Liberties viewpoints*

Hewitt, Patricia. Privacy : the information gatherers / Patricia Hewitt. — London : National Council for Civil Liberties, c1977 (1980 [printing]). — 98p ; 21cm
ISBN 0-901108-68-5 (pbk) : £1.75
Also classified at 323.44′83′0941 B82-14426

323.44′83 — Privacy. Encroachment by data processing systems

Simons, G. L.. Privacy in the computer age. — Manchester : NCC Publications, Nov.1982. — [120]p
ISBN 0-85012-348-8 (pbk) : £9.50 : CIP entry
B82-26410

323.44′83′0941 — Great Britain. Confidential information. Misuse — *Labour Party (Great Britain) viewpoints*

Personal information and privacy : a Labour Party discussion document. — [London] : The Party, [1981]. — 15p ; 21cm. — (Socialism in the 80s)
Cover title
ISBN 0-86117-071-7 (pbk) : £0.40
Primary classification 323.44′8′0941
B82-05515

323.44′83′0941 — Great Britain. Confidential information. Misuse — *National Council of Civil Liberties viewpoints*

Hewitt, Patricia. Privacy : the information gatherers / Patricia Hewitt. — London : National Council for Civil Liberties, c1977 (1980 [printing]). — 98p ; 21cm
ISBN 0-901108-68-5 (pbk) : £1.75
Primary classification 323.44′8′0941
B82-14426

323.4′9 — United Nations. Petitions: Petitions concerning deprivation of human rights

Zuijdwijk, Ton J. M.. Petitioning the United Nations : a study in human rights / Ton J.M. Zuijdwijk. — Aldershot : Gower, 1982. — xv,397p ; 23cm
Bibliography: p383-389. — Includes index
ISBN 0-566-00463-1 : Unpriced : CIP rev.
B81-34281

323.4′9′09437 — Czechoslovakia. Human rights. Deprivation, *1968-1980*

On freedom and power. — London : Allison & Busby, Dec.1981. — 1v.
ISBN 0-85031-415-1 (cased) : £9.95 : CIP entry
ISBN 0-85031-416-x (pbk) : £4.95 B81-31627

323.4′9′095491 — Pakistan. Human rights. Deprivation, *1977-1981*

Pakistan : human rights violations and the decline of the rule of law. — London : Amnesty International Publications, 1982. — 54p : ill,ports ; 30cm. — (An Amnesty International report)
ISBN 0-86210-041-0 (pbk) : Unpriced
B82-23121

323.6 — CITIZENSHIP

323.6′29 — American citizenship, *1900-1917.* **Acquisition by Puerto Ricans,** *1900-1917*

Cabranes, José A.. Citizenship and the American empire : notes on the legislative history of the United States citizenship of Puerto Ricans / José A. Cabranes. — New Haven, [Conn.] ; London : Yale University Press, 1979. — viii,101p ; 24cm
Originally published: in University of Pennsylvania law review 127 U.Pa.L.Rev.391 (1978)
ISBN 0-300-02325-1 : £7.00 B82-02430

324 — THE POLITICAL PROCESS. POLITICAL PARTIES, ELECTIONS

324.2 — Communist parties, *1919-1980*

Narkiewicz, Olga A.. Marxism and the reality of power 1919-1980 / Olga A. Narkiewicz. — London : Croom Helm, c1981. — 337p : ill ; 23cm
Bibliography: p324-330. — Includes index
ISBN 0-85664-806-x : £14.95 : CIP rev.
B81-27965

324.2′3 — United States. Political parties. General election manifestos, *1980* — *Collections*

Johnson, Donald Bruce. National party platforms of 1980 : supplement to National party platforms, 1840-1976 / compiled by Donald Bruce Johnson. — Urbana ; London : University of Illinois Press, c1982. — 233p ; 26cm
Includes index
ISBN 0-252-00923-1 (pbk) : £11.25
B82-35666

324.24 — Western Europe. Political parties

Western European party systems. — London : Sage, Feb.1983. — [480]p
ISBN 0-8039-9769-8 : £16.00 : CIP entry
B82-32633

324.24′05 — Western Europe. Centre Right political parties

Moderates and Conservatives in Western Europe. — London : Heinemann Educational, May 1982. — [256]p
ISBN 0-435-83615-3 : £14.50 : CIP entry
B82-10682

324.241′009 — Great Britain. Political parties, *1760-1832*

O′Gorman, Frank. The emergence of the British two-party system 1760-1832 / Frank O′Gorman. — London : Edward Arnold, 1982. — xi,132p ; 22cm. — (Foundations of modern history)
Bibliography: p123-126. — Includes index
ISBN 0-7131-6293-7 (pbk) : £4.50 : CIP rev.
B82-07575

324.241′009 — Great Britain. Political parties, *1867-1980*

Ball, Alan R.. British political parties : the emergence of a modern party system / Alan R. Ball. — London : Macmillan, 1981. — xiv,292p ; 23cm
Bibliography: p277-286. — Includes index
ISBN 0-333-30497-7 (cased) : Unpriced
ISBN 0-333-30498-5 (pbk) : unpriced
B82-06644

324.241′02 — Great Britain. Political parties: Tory Party, *1714-1760*

Colley, Linda. In defiance of oligarchy : the Tory Party 1714-60 / Linda Colley. — Cambridge : Cambridge University Press, 1982. — viii,375p : ill ; 24cm
Includes index
ISBN 0-521-23982-6 : £25.00 : CIP rev.
B82-00231

324.24104 — Great Britain. Political parties: Conservative Party

Norton, Philip. Conservatives and conservatism / Philip Norton and Arthur Aughey. — London : Temple Smith, 1981. — 334p : ill ; 23cm
Bibliography: p320-322. — Includes index
ISBN 0-85117-211-3 : £12.50
ISBN 0-85117-212-1 (pbk) : Unpriced
B82-38398

324.24104 — Great Britain. Political parties: Conservative Party. Policies, *1945-1981* — *Proposals*

Conservative & Labour Party conference decisions 1945-1981. — Chichester (18 Lincoln Green, Chichester, West Sussex) : Parliamentary Research Services, Sept.1982. — 1v.
ISBN 0-900178-08-6 (pbk) : £10.00 : CIP entry
Also classified at 324.24107 B82-29150

324.24106′09 — Great Britain. Political parties: Liberal Party, *1910-1931*

Adelman, Paul. The decline of the Liberal Party 1910-1931 / Paul Adelman. — Harlow : Longman, 1981. — x,94p ; 20cm. — (Seminar studies in history)
Bibliography: p85-91. — Includes index
ISBN 0-582-35327-0 (pbk) : £1.75 : CIP rev.
B81-30294

324.24107 — Great Britain. Political parties: Labour Party *(Great Britain)*

The Politics of the Labour Party / edited by Dennis Kavanagh. — London : Allen & Unwin, 1982. — 220p : ill ; 22cm
Includes index
ISBN 0-04-329037-x (cased) : Unpriced : CIP rev.
ISBN 0-04-329038-8 (pbk) : Unpriced
B82-07225

324.24107 — Great Britain. Political parties: Labour Party *(Great Britain).* **Leaders. Accountability**

Democracy and accountability in the Labour Party / edited by John B. Burnell. — [Nottingham] : Spokesman for the Institute for Workers′ Control, 1980. — 87p ; 19cm
ISBN 0-85124-299-5 (cased) : £6.00
ISBN 0-85124-300-2 (pbk) : Unpriced
B82-14581

324.24107 — Great Britain. Political parties: Labour Party *(Great Britain).* **Organisation structure,** *1973-1981*

Kogan, David. The battle for the Labcur Party / David Kogan & Maurice Kogan. — [London] : Fontana, 1982. — 160p,[4]p of plates : ill,ports ; 18cm
Includes index
ISBN 0-00-636512-4 (pbk) : £1.75 B82-15116

324.24107 — Great Britain. Political parties: Labour Party *(Great Britain).* **Policies,** *1945-1981* — *Proposals*

Conservative & Labour Party conference decisions 1945-1981. — Chichester (18 Lincoln Green, Chichester, West Sussex) : Parliamentary Research Services, Sept.1982. — 1v.
ISBN 0-900178-08-6 (pbk) : £10.00 : CIP entry
Primary classification 324.24104 B82-29150

324.24107 — Great Britain. Political parties: Labour Party *(Great Britain).* **Reform** — *Proposals*

Kogan, David. The battle for the Labour Party. — London : Kogan Page, Feb.1982. — [160]p
ISBN 0-85038-540-7 : £6.00 : CIP entry
B82-00146

Kogan, David. The battle for the Labour Party. — 2nd ed. — London : Kogan Page, Feb.1983. — [200]p
Previous ed.: 1982
ISBN 0-85038-654-3 (cased) : £7.95 : CIP entry
ISBN 0-85038-655-1 (pbk) : £3.95 B82-39283

324.24107 — Great Britain. Political parties: Labour Party *(Great Britain).* **Trotskyism**

Webster, David, *1945-*. The Labour Party and the new left / David Webster. — London : Fabian Society, 1981. — 32p ; 22cm. — (Fabian tract, ISSN 0307-7535 ; 477)
Cover title. — Text on inside cover
ISBN 0-7163-0477-5 (pbk) : Unpriced
B82-02712

324.24107 — Great Britain. Political patries: Labour Party *(Great Britain). Young Socialists, 1981-1982*

Reports : for the 21st National Conference of the Labour Party Young Socialists : Spa Royal Hall, South Marine Drive, Bridlington, Saturday, Sunday and Monday 10, 11 and 12 April 1982. — [London] ([144 Walworth Rd, SE17]) : [Labour Party Young Socialists National Committee], [1982]. — 9p ; 30cm
£0.10 (unbound) B82-25252

324.24107'05 — Great Britain. Political parties: Labour Party *(Great Britain)* — *Serials*

New socialist. — No.1 (Sept./Oct. '81)-. — London : Labour Party, 1981-. — v. : ill,ports ; 30cm
Six issues yearly
ISSN 0261-6912 = New socialist : £3.75 yearly (£7.50 to multi-reader institutions) B82-06179

324.24107'09 — Great Britain. Political parties: Labour Party *(Great Britain), 1931-1979*

Howell, David. British social democracy : a study in development and decay / David Howell. — [2nd ed.]. — London : Croom Helm, 1980. — 342p ; 22cm
Previous ed.: 1976. — Bibliography: p325-333. — Includes index
ISBN 0-7099-0428-2 (pbk) : £5.95 B82-37090

324.24107'09 — Great Britain. Political parties: Labour Party *(Great Britain), 1945-1980*

Warde, Alan. Consensus and beyond : the development of Labour Party strategy since the Second World War / Alan Warde. — Manchester : Manchester University Press, c1982. — 243p ; 24cm
Bibliography: p222-238. — Includes index
ISBN 0-7190-0849-2 : £19.50 : CIP rev. B81-33829

324.24107'09 — Great Britain. Political parties: Labour Party *(Great Britain), 1960-1980*

Hodgson, Geoff. Labour at the crossroads : the political and economic challenge to the Labour Party in the 1980s / Geoff Hodgson. — Oxford : Robertson, 1981. — x,257p : ill ; 23cm
Includes index
ISBN 0-85520-462-1 (cased) : Unpriced : CIP rev.
ISBN 0-85520-463-x (pbk) : £4.95 B81-20567

324.24107'092'2 — London. Wandsworth *(London Borough).* **Putney. Political parties: Labour Party** *(Great Britain). Putney Labour Party — Personal observations — Collections*

Jenkins, Hugh, *1908-.* Rank and file / Hugh Jenkins. — London : Croom Helm, c1980. — 181p ; 22cm
Includes index
ISBN 0-7099-0331-6 (cased) : £9.95 : CIP rev.
ISBN 0-7099-1400-8 (pbk) : £3.95 B80-21478

324.24107'09426'41 — Suffolk. Lowestoft. Political parties: Lowestoft Constituency Labour Party, *to 1945*

Mathew, Don. From two boys and a dog to political power : the Labour Party in the Lowestoft constituency 1918-1945 / Don Mathew. — Lowestoft : Lowestoft Constituency Labour Party, 1979. — 53p : ill ; 21cm
ISBN 0-9506497-0-8 (pbk) : £1.00 B82-27457

324.241'0938 — Great Britain. Political parties: National Front, *to 1980*

Taylor, Stan. The National Front in English politics / Stan Taylor. — London : Macmillan, 1982. — xvii,212p ; 23cm
Bibliography: p199-205. — Includes index
ISBN 0-333-27741-4 : £20.00 B82-20911

324.241'0972 — Great Britain. Political parties: Social Democratic Party — *Labour Party (Great Britain) viewpoints*

The Soft centre : the true story of the SDP / cartoons by Fluck and Austin ; with a foreword by Michael Foot. — London : Labour Party, [1982]. — 35p : ill,ports ; 30cm. — (Labour weekly special booklet)
£0.60 (unbound) B82-25028

324.241'0972'09 — Great Britain. Political parties: Social Democratic Party, *to 1981*

Bradley, Ian, *1950-.* Breaking the mould? : the birth and prospects of the Social Democratic Party / Ian Bradley. — Oxford : Robertson, 1981. — xiv,172p : ill ; 22cm
Bibliography: p165-166. — Includes index
ISBN 0-85520-468-0 (cased) : Unpriced : CIP rev.
ISBN 0-85520-469-9 (pbk) : £2.95 B81-21549

324.241'0972'09411 — Scotland. Political parties: Social Democratic Party — *Serials*

Scottish democrat : newsletter for social democrats in Scotland. — No.1 (July 1981)-. — Glasgow (c/o SDP, 70 Hillington Rd South, Glasgow G52) : SDP Interim Scottish Liaison Committee, 1981-. — v. : ill,ports ; 30cm
Quarterly
ISSN 0261-3379 = Scottish democrat : Unpriced B82-11824

324.2415'074 — Ireland. Political parties: Labour Party *(Ireland).* **Influence of Stalin, I.**

Stalin and the Irish working class. — Belfast : British and Irish Communist Organisation, 1979. — 18p ; 21cm
Reprinted from "Irish Communist" December 1979, no.169
Unpriced (unbound) B82-04197

324.2417'074 — Ireland (Republic). Political parties: Irish Labour Party, *1957-1981*

Gallagher, Michael. The Irish Labour Party in transition 1957-81. — Manchester : Manchester University Press, May 1982. — [240]p
ISBN 0-7190-0866-2 : £16.50 : CIP entry B82-07675

324.2429'03 — Wales. Political parties: Plaid Cymru, *to 1980 — Personal observations*

Williams, Phil, *1939-.* Voice from the valleys / Phil Williams. — Aberystwyth : Plaid Cymru, 1981. — 112p ; 18cm
ISBN 0-905077-18-0 (pbk) : Unpriced B82-06878

324.243'038 — Germany. Political parties: Nationalsozialistische Deutsche Arbeiter-Partei. Political ideologies, *1939-1945*

Herzstein, Robert Edwin. When Nazi dreams come true : the Third Reich's internal struggle over the future of Europe after a German victory : a look at the Nazi mentality 1939-45 / Robert Edwin Herzstein. — [London] : Abacus, 1982. — xi,301p,[8]p of plates : ill,maps,ports ; 20cm
Bibliography: p283-291. — Includes index
ISBN 0-349-11680-6 (pbk) : £2.95 B82-11196

324.243'038'0922 — Germany. Political parties: Nationalsozialistische Deutsche Arbeiter-Partei. Members, *1933-1945 — Biographies*

Wistrich, Robert S.. Who's who in Nazi Germany / Robert Wistrich. — London : Weidenfeld and Nicolson, c1982. — 359p ; 25cm
Bibliography: p353-359
ISBN 0-297-78109-x : £10.95 B82-32754

324.243'072'09 — Germany. Political parties: Sozialdemokratische Partei Deutschlands, *to 1914*

Steenson, Gary P.. 'Not one man! Not one penny!' : German social democracy, 1863-1914 / Gary P. Steenson. — Pittsburgh : University of Pittsburgh Press ; London : Feffer and Simons, c1981. — xvi,288p ; 24cm
Bibliography: p265-273. — Includes index
ISBN 0-8229-3440-x (cased) : Unpriced
ISBN 0-8229-5329-3 (pbk) : Unpriced B82-23746

324.243'072'094355 — West Germany. Düsseldorf. Political parties: Sozialdemokratische Partei Deutschlands, *1890-1920*

Nolan, Mary. Social democracy and society : working-class radicalism in Düsseldorf, 1890-1920 / Mary Nolan. — Cambridge : Cambridge University Press, 1981. — xi,376p ; 24cm
Bibliography: p354-370. — Includes index
ISBN 0-521-23473-5 : £27.50 B82-08317

324.244 — France. Political parties

Contemporary French political parties / edited by David S. Bell. — London : Croom Helm, c1982. — 199p ; 23cm
Includes index
ISBN 0-7099-0633-1 : £13.95 : CIP rev. B81-37555

324.244'02 — France. Political parties: Ligue des patriotes, *1882-1900*

Rutkoff, Peter M.. Revanche & revision : the Ligue des Patriotes and the origins of the radical Right in France, 1882-1900 / by Peter M. Rutkoff. — Athens [Ohio] ; London : Ohio University Press, c1981. — 182p ; 24cm
Bibliography: p169-178. — Includes index
ISBN 0-8214-0589-6 : £12.35 B82-30093

324.244'07'09 — France. Left-wing political parties, *to 1982*

The **Left** in France. — Nottingham : Spokesman, Dec.1982. — [200]p
ISBN 0-85124-349-5 (cased) : £14.50 : CIP entry
ISBN 0-85124-350-9 (pbk) : £3.50 B82-32304

324.244'075 — France. Political parties: Parti communiste français. Relations with Confédération générale du travail, *to 1981*

Ross, George. Workers and communists in France : from Popular Front to Eurocommunism / George Ross. — Berkeley ; London : University of California Press, c1982. — xvi,357p ; 25cm
Bibliography: p337-347. — Includes index
ISBN 0-520-04075-9 : £22.50
Also classified at 331.88'06'044 B82-31178

324.245'075'09 — Italy. Political parties: Partito comunista italiano, *to 1979*

The **Italian** Communist Party : yesterday, today, and tomorrow / edited by Simon Serfaty and Lawrence Gray. — London : Aldwych, 1981, c1980. — xii,256p ; 24cm. — (European studies ; no.5)
Originally published: Westport, Conn. : Greenwood, 1980. — Includes index
ISBN 0-86172-015-6 : £23.95 B82-31082

324.245'08 — Italy. Political parties: Democrazia cristiana, *to 1981*

Furlong, Paul. The Italian Christian Democrats : from Catholic movement to conservative party / by Paul Furlong. — [Hull] ([Hull, HU6 7RX]) : University of Hull, Department of Politics, 1982. — 45,iiip : 2ills,2maps ; 30cm. — (Hull papers in politics, ISSN 0142-7377 ; no.25)
Bibliography: pi-iii
Unpriced (pbk) B82-23444

324.247'075 — Soviet Union. Political parties. Conferences: Kommunisticheskaîa partiîa Sovetskogo Soîuza. *S'ezd (26th : 1981 : Moscow) — Conference proceedings*

Kommunisticheskaîa partiîa Sovetskogo Soîuza. *S"ezd (26th : 1981 : Moscow).* Documents and resolutions : the 26th Congress of the Communist Party of the Soviet Union, Moscow, February 23-March 3, 1981. — Moscow : Novosti ; [London] : distributed by Central, 1981. — 245p ; 20cm
Translation of: Dokumenty i rezolîutsii
ISBN 0-7147-1711-8 (pbk) : Unpriced B82-29721

324.247'075 — Soviet Union. Political parties: Kommunisticheskaîa partiîa Sovetskogo soîuza. S"ezd (20th : 1956: Moscow) — *Correspondence, diaries, etc.*

Vidali, Vittorio. Diary of the 20th congress of the Soviet Communist Party. — London : Journeyman Press, Nov.1982. — [208]p
Translation of: Diario del XX congresso
ISBN 0-904526-44-5 (pbk) : £3.75 : CIP entry B82-30586

324.247'075 — Soviet Union. Political parties: Kommunisticheskaîa partiîa Sovetskogo Soîuza, *to 1981*

The **CPSU** : stages of history. — 3rd enl ed. — Moscow : Novosti, 1980 ; [London] : Distributed by Central Books. — 110p : ill,facsims,ports ; 21cm
Previous ed.: 1977
ISBN 0-7147-1644-8 (pbk) : £0.95 B82-02534

324.2495'075 — Greece. Political parties: Kommounistikon Komma tēs Hellados, *1940-1944*

Loulis, John C.. The Greek Communist Party, 1940-1944 / John C. Loulis. — London : Croom Helm, c1982. — 224p : ill ; 23cm
Bibliography: p207-220. — Includes index
ISBN 0-7099-1612-4 : £12.50 : CIP rev. B81-34781

324.251'075 — China. Political parties: Zhong guo gong chan dang, *to 1981*

Resolution on CPC history : 1949-81. — Oxford : Pergamon, 1981. — 126p ; 19cm
Translation of: Guan yu Zhong guo gong chan dang li shi de jue yi
ISBN 0-08-028958-4 (pbk) : £2.00 : CIP rev. B81-32091

324.2736 — United States. Presidents. Democratic Party primary elections, *1972-1976*

Lengle, James I.. Representation and presidential primaries : the Democratic Party in the post-reform era / James I. Lengle. — Westport, Conn. ; London : Greenwood Press, 1981. — xi,131p : ill ; 25cm. — (Contributions in political science, ISSN 0147-1066 ; no.57)
Bibliography: p123-126. — Includes index
ISBN 0-313-22482-x : £20.95 B82-18183

324.294 — Australia. Political parties, *1966-1981*

Jupp, James. Party politics : Australia 1966-81. — London : Allen & Unwin, Jan.1982. — [309]p
ISBN 0-86861-315-0 : £18.00 : CIP entry B81-36041

324.294 — Australia. Political parties, *to 1981*

Jaensch, Dean. The Australian party system. — London : Allen and Unwin, Jan.1983. — [224]p
ISBN 0-86861-077-1 : £8.95 : CIP entry B82-33238

324.294'03 — Australia. Right-wing political parties. Policies

Australia and the new right. — London : Allen & Unwin, Apr.1982. — [200]p
ISBN 0-86861-188-3 : £15.00 : CIP entry B82-06264

324'.3 — France. Jacobin clubs, *1791*

Kennedy, Michael L.. The Jacobin Clubs in the French Revolution : the first years / Michael L. Kennedy. — Princeton ; Guildford : Princeton University Press, c1982. — xii,381p : ill,1map ; 23cm
Includes index
ISBN 0-691-05337-5 : £19.00 B82-20608

324'.4'0973 — United States. Politics. Role of interest groups

Wilson, Graham K.. Interest groups in the United States / Graham K. Wilson. — Oxford : Clarendon Press, 1981. — ix,161p ; 22cm
Bibliography: p154-158. — Includes index
ISBN 0-19-827425-4 (cased) : £12.95 : CIP rev.
ISBN 0-19-876095-7 (pbk) : Unpriced B81-26743

324.6 — Democracies. Electorates. Voting behaviour. Theories

Riker, William H.. Liberalism against populism : a confrontation between the theory of democracy and the theory of social choice / William H. Riker. — Oxford : Freeman, c1982. — xix,311p : ill ; 24cm
Bibliography: p299-305. — Includes index
ISBN 0-7167-1245-8 (cased) : £19.95
ISBN 0-7167-1246-6 (pbk) : Unpriced B82-34388

324.6'05 — Elections — *Serials*

Electoral studies : an international journal. — Vol.1, no.1 (Apr. 1982)-. — Guildford : Butterworth Scientific, 1982-. — v. : ill ; 25cm
Three issues yearly
ISSN 0261-3794 = Electoral studies : £30.00 per year B82-27653

324.6'2'094 — European Community countries. Electorate. Voting rights

Berghe, Guido van den. European rights for European citizens. — Aldershot : Gower, July 1982. — [248]p
ISBN 0-566-00524-7 : £15.00 : CIP entry B82-09429

324.6'3 — European Parliament. British members. Direct election

Marquand, David. The European Parliament and European integration : have direct elections made a difference / by David Marquand. — Manchester (CIS Building, Miller St., Manchester M60 0AL) : Manchester Statistical Society, [1980?]. — 16p ; 20cm
£2.50 (pbk) B82-29239

324.6'3 — Great Britain. Proportional representation

Fear, G. H. L.. Proportional representation as an electoral system for Great Britain (with notes on the present system) : a critical analysis / by G.H.L. Fear. — Liverpool (26 Warwick Ave., Crosby, Liverpool 23) : G.H.L. Fear, [1981?]. — 24p ; 21cm
£1.50 (pbk) B82-08300

Lakeman, Enid. Power to elect : the case for proportional representation / Enid Lakeman. — London : Heinemann, c1982. — xiv,178p : ill,1map,1port ; 22cm
Ill and text on inside front cover. — Bibliography: p172-173. — Includes index
ISBN 0-434-40220-6 (pbk) : £6.95 B82-37624

324.6'3 — United States. Proportional representation

Balinski, M. L.. Fair representation : meeting the ideal of one man, one vote / Michel L. Balinski and H. Peyton Young. — New Haven ; London : Yale University Press, c1982. — xi,191p : ill ; 25cm
Includes index
ISBN 0-300-02724-9 : £20.00 : CIP rev. B82-14202

324.6'4'0941 — Great Britain. Electoral registration. Proposed extension. Attitudes of public

Manners, A. J.. Extending the electoral register — 2 : two surveys of public acceptability / A.J. Manners, I. Rauta. — London : Office of Population Censuses and Surveys, 1981. — vi,62p : forms ; 30cm. — (Occasional paper ; 21)
ISBN 0-906197-21-x (pbk) : £1.00 B82-11950

324.6'5 — Great Britain. Elections. Use of single transferable vote — *Proposals*

The **Case** for the single transferable vote : giving voting power to every elector, The Electoral Reform Society. — London (6, Chancel St., Blackfriars, SE1 OUX) : The Society, [1981]. — 21p : ill ; 21cm
Cover title. — Bibliography: p21
£1.00 (pbk) B82-05868

324.7'3'0973 — United States. Presidents. Elections. Influence of mass media

Rubin, Richard L.. Press, party and presidency / Richard L. Rubin. — New York ; London : Norton, c1981. — x,246p : ill ; 22cm
Includes index
ISBN 0-393-01497-5 (cased) : £13.50
ISBN 0-393-95206-1 (pbk) : £4.95 B82-34638

324.94 — Western Europe. Electorate. Voting behaviour, *1968-1981*

Sallnow, John. An electoral atlas of Europe 1968-1981 : a political geographic compendium including 76 maps / John Sallnow and Anna John ; cartography by Sarah K. Webber. — London : Butterworth Scientific, 1982. — 149p : maps ; 26cm. — (Butterworths European studies)
Includes index
ISBN 0-408-10800-2 : £20.00 : CIP rev. B82-04041

324.94'0557 — European Parliament. Members. Elections, *1979*

Lodge, Juliet. Direct elections to the European Parliament : a Community perspective / Juliet Lodge and Valentine Herman. — London : Macmillan, 1982. — xiv,322p ; 23cm
Bibliography: p302-309. — Includes index
ISBN 0-333-25955-6 : £20.00 B82-20947

324.94'0557 — European Parliament. Members. Elections, *1979- — Statistics*

Craig, F. W. S.. European votes / compiled and edited by F.W.S. Craig and T.T. Mackie. — Chichester : Parliamentary Research Services
1: European parliamentary election results 1979. — 1980. — viii,152p ; 25cm
Includes index
ISBN 0-900178-19-1 (pbk) : £6.50 : CIP rev. B80-10481

324.941'081 — Great Britain. Electorate. Voting behaviour, *1832-1969 — For schools — Welsh texts*

Price, Emyr. Ennill y bleidlais. — Cardiff : University of Wales, Apr.1982. — [28]p. — (Project Defnyddiau Ac Adonddau y Swyddfa Gymreig. Hanes ; v.2)
ISBN 0-7083-0822-8 (unbound) : £1.50 : CIP entry B82-16511

324.941'082 — Great Britain. *Parliament. House of Commons.* **Members. Elections,** *1918-1949 — Statistics*

Craig, F. W. S.. British Parliamentary election results, 1918-1949. — 3rd ed. — Chichester : Parliamentary Research Services, Jan.1983. — [804]p
Previous ed.: London : Macmillan, 1977
ISBN 0-900178-06-x : £25.00 : CIP entry B82-33245

324.941'0856'0724 — Great Britain. Electorate. Voting behaviour, *1959-1974.* **Models**

How voters decide : a longitudinal study of political attitudes and voting extending over fifteen years / Hilde T. Himmelweit ... [et al.]. — London : Academic Press in cooperation with European Association of Experimental Social Pschology, 1981. — xvi,276p : ill ; 24cm. — (European monographs in social psychology ; 27)
Bibliography: p256-262. — Includes index
ISBN 0-12-348950-4 (cased) : Unpriced : CIP rev.
ISBN 0-12-348952-0 (pbk) : Unpriced B81-31336

324.941'0857 — Great Britain. *Parliament. House of Commons.* **Members. Elections,** *1950-1973 — Statistics*

Craig, F. W. S.. British parliamentary election results 1950-1973. — 2nd ed. — Chichester : Parliamentary Research Services, Jan.1983. — [800]p
Previous ed.: London : Political Reference Services, 1974
ISBN 0-900178-07-8 : £25.00 : CIP entry B82-35234

324.941'0857 — Great Britain. *Parliament. House of Commons.* **Members. Elections,** *1974-1979 — Statistics*

Craig, F. W. S.. Britain votes / compiled and edited by F.W.S. Craig. — Chichester : Parliamentary Research Services
2: British parliamentary election results 1974-1979. — 1980. — xii,292p ; 25cm
Includes index
ISBN 0-900178-18-3 (pbk) : £8.50 : CIP rev. B80-08627

324.941'0857 — Great Britain. *Parliament. House of Commons.* **Members. General elections,** *1979*

Political communications : the General Election campaign of 1979 / edited by Robert M. Worcester, Martin Harrop. — London : Allen & Unwin, 1982. — ix,181p : facsims ; 23cm
Conference papers. — Includes index
ISBN 0-04-324007-0 : Unpriced : CIP rev. B82-09266

324.9421'0858 — Greater London Council. Members. Elections, *1981 — Statistics*

Greater London Council. *Intelligence Unit.* Greater London Council election : 7 May 1981 / compiled in the Director-General's Department of the Greater London Council by the Intelligence Unit from information supplied by the Returning Officers. — [London] : [The Council], [1981]. — 17p : 1map ; 30cm
Cover title
ISBN 0-7168-1202-9 (pbk) : £3.00 B82-13278

324.9421'860857 — Harrow. *Borough Council.* **Members. Elections,** *1978 — Statistics*

Gray, Colin J.. Harrow votes : the London Borough of Harrow, from 1978 : a companion to Harrow's 1982 Borough Election / compiled and edited by Colin J. Gray. — Harrow (11 Lulworth Gardens, Harrow, Middx HA2 9NW) : C.J. Gray, [1981]. — 53p : 1map ; 30cm
Includes index
£1.80 (unbound) B82-12092

324.943'085 — Germany. Elections, *1918-1933*

Hamilton, Richard F.. Who voted for Hitler? / Richard F. Hamilton. — Princeton ; Guildford : Princeton University Press, c1982. — xv,664p : maps ; 25cm
Includes index
ISBN 0-691-09395-4 (cased) : £35.30
ISBN 0-691-10132-9 (ltd. pbk) : Unpriced B82-34870

324.947'0853 — Union of Soviet Socialist Republic. *Verkhovnyĭ sovet.* **Members. Elections,** *1979 — Personal observations*

Medvedev, Roĭ A.. How I ran for election and how I lost / by Roy A. Medvedev ; [translated from the Russian by Erica J. Brown]. — Nottingham (Bertrand Russell House, Gamble Street, Nottingham, NG7 4ET) : Bertrand Russell Peace Foundation, [1979]. — 5p ; 21cm. — (Spokesman pamphlet ; no.68)
£0.20 (unbound) B82-17672

324.9595'1053 — Peninsular Malaysia. Elections, *1978*

Malaysian politics and the 1978 election / edited by Harold Crouch, Lee Kam Hing and Michael Ong. — Kuala Lumpur ; Oxford : Oxford University Press, 1980. — xiv,330p : ill ; 23cm
Includes index
ISBN 0-19-580464-3 (cased) : £15.50
ISBN 0-19-580481-3 (pbk) : Unpriced B82-00502

324.9669'05 — Nigeria. *Parliament.* **Members. General elections,** *1979*

The **Nigerian** 1979 elections / edited by Oyeleye Oyediran. — Lagos : Macmillan Nigeria ; London : Macmillan, 1981. — xi,182p : maps ; 23cm. — (Contemporary African issues series)
ISBN 0-333-31785-8 (cased) : Unpriced
ISBN 0-333-31786-6 (pbk) : Unpriced B82-06702

324.96891'04 — Rhodesia. *Parliament.* **Members. General elections,** *1979*

Palley, Claire. The Rhodesian election campaign : on whether elections were fair and free and whether principles required for Rhodesian independence have been satisfied / C. Palley. — London (1, Cambridge Terrace, Regent's Park, N.W.1) : Catholic Institute for International Relations, c1979. — 36p ; 30cm
Unpriced (spiral) B82-11898

324.97284'052 — El Salvador. *Asamblea Constituyente.* **Members. General elections,** *1982 — Inquiry reports*

Galsworthy, *Sir* **John,** *1919-*. Report on the election in El Salvador on 28 March 1982 / by Sir John Galsworthy and Derek W. Bowett, 7 April 1982 ; presented to Parliament by the Secretary of State for Foreign and Commonwealth Affairs ... — London : H.M.S.O., [1982]. — 23p : 1ill,1 map ; 25cm. — (Cmnd. ; 8553)
ISBN 0-10-185530-3 (unbound) : £2.55 B82-29925

324.973 — United States. Electorate. Voting behaviour, *to 1980.* **Analysis**

Analyzing electoral history : a guide to the study of American voter behavior / edited by Jerome M. Clubb, William H. Flanigan, Nancy H. Zingale. — Beverly Hills ; London : Sage, c1981. — 310p : ill ; 22cm. — (Sage focus editions ; 33)
Includes index
ISBN 0-8039-1673-6 (cased) : Unpriced
ISBN 0-8039-1674-4 (pbk) : £6.50 B82-17078

324.973 — United States. Presidents. Election. Procedure, *1783-1844*

McCormick, Richard P.. The presidential game : the origins of American presidential politics / Richard P. McCormick. — New York ; Oxford : Oxford University Press, 1982. — 279p ; 22cm
Includes index
ISBN 0-19-503015-x : £14.00 B82-33306

324.973 — United States. Presidents. Elections, *1787-1850.* **Campaigns**

Heale, M. J.. The presidential quest : candidates and images in American political culture, 1787-1852 / M.J. Heale. — Harlow : Longman, 1982. — xi,268p ; 22cm
Includes index
ISBN 0-582-29542-4 (pbk) : £5.95 : CIP rev. B82-06924

324.973'00212 — United States. Governors. Elections, *1775-1978 — Statistics*

Glashan, Roy R.. American governors and gubernatorial elections 1775-1978 / compiled by Roy R. Glashan. — [Westport, Conn.] : Meckler ; London : Mansell Publishing, c1979. — 370p ; 24cm
Bibliography: p348-363
ISBN 0-7201-1511-6 : £30.00 : CIP rev. B79-29917

324.973'0926 — United States. *Congress.* **Members. Elections,** *1978*

Congressional elections / edited by Louis Sandy Maisel and Joseph Cooper. — Beverley Hills ; London : Sage, c1981. — 280p : ill ; 23cm. — (Sage electoral studies yearbook ; v.6)
Includes bibliographies
ISBN 0-8039-1568-3 (cased) : Unpriced
ISBN 0-8039-1569-1 (pbk) : £7.50 B82-00945

324.973'0926 — United States. Presidents. Elections, *1980.* **Campaigns**

Drew, Elizabeth. Portrait of an election : the 1980 presidential campaign / Elizabeth Drew. — London : Routledge & Kegan Paul, 1981. — 459p ; 25cm
Originally published: New York : Simon & Schuster, 1981. — Includes index
ISBN 0-7100-9021-8 : £10.95 B82-07913

324.973'0927 — United States. *Congress.* **Members. Elections. Voting behaviour of electorate. Influence of economic conditions**

Jacobson, Gary C.. Strategy and choice in congressional elections / Gary C. Jacobson and Samuel Kernell. — New Haven ; London : Yale University Press, c1981. — xiii,111p ; 22cm
Includes index
ISBN 0-300-02690-0 : £10.50 : CIP rev. B82-01324

325.2 — POLITICS. EMIGRATION

325'.21'0924 — Thailand. Laotian refugees — *Personal observations*

Nickerson, Ruth. Promise of dawn : pages from a Thailand diary / Ruth Nickerson. — Tring : Lion, 1982. — [56]p : ill(some col.) ; 20cm. — (A Lion book)
ISBN 0-85648-480-6 : £2.50 B82-21033

325'.21'094 — European Jewish refugees. Policies of United States government, *1945-1950*

Dinnerstein, Leonard. America and the survivors of the holocaust / Leonard Dinnerstein. — New York ; Guildford : Columbia University Press, 1982. — xiv,409p : ill,maps,ports ; 24cm. — (Contemporary American history series)
Bibliography: p373-396. — Includes index
ISBN 0-231-04176-4 : £14.40 B82-28059

325'.21'097294 — United States. Haitian refugees, *to 1981*

Stepick, Alex. Haitian refugees in the U.S. / by Alex Stepick with the assistance of Dale Frederick Swartz. — London (36 Craven St, WC2N 5NG) : Minority Rights Group, 1982. — 20p : ill,2maps ; 30cm. — (Report / Minority Rights Group, ISSN 0305-6252 ; no.52)
Bibliography: p17-18
£1.20 (pbk) B82-26378

325.3 — COLONIAL ADMINISTRATION

325'.3'0922 — British colonies. Governors — *Biographies*

Kirk-Greene, A. H. M.. A biographical dictionary of the British colonial governors / Anthony H.M. Kirk-Greene. — Brighton, Harvester
Vol.1: Africa. — 1980. — 320p ; 22cm
ISBN 0-85527-383-6 : £30.00 : CIP rev. B80-09998

325'.31'41 — British colonies. Colonial administration. Financial management, *1895-1902*

Kesner, Richard M.. Economic control and colonial development : crown colony financial management in the age of Joseph Chamberlain / Richard M. Kesner. — Oxford : Clio, 1981. — xvii,305p ; 24cm
Bibliography: p277-299. — Includes index
ISBN 0-903450-51-8 : £21.75 B82-27403

325'.31'41 — British colonies. Colonial administration. Role of women — *Interviews*

Voices and echoes : tales from colonial women. — London : Quartet, Feb.1983. — 1v.
ISBN 0-7043-2366-4 : CIP entry B82-40312

325'.31'41096 — Africa. British colonies. Colonial administration, *1938-1948*

Pearce, Robert D.. The turning point in Africa : British colonial policy 1938-48 / R.D. Pearce. — London : Cass, 1982. — 223p ; 23cm
Bibliography: p211-217. — Includes index
ISBN 0-7146-3160-4 : £15.00 : CIP rev. B81-24672

325'.32 — Imperialism

Reynolds, Charles. Modes of imperialism / Charles Reynolds. — Oxford : Martin Robertson, 1981. — viii,263p ; 24cm
Bibliography: p249-257. — Includes index
ISBN 0-85520-339-0 : Unpriced : CIP rev. B81-05137

325'.32'094 — European imperialism, *1815-1960*

Kiernan, V. G.. European empires from conquest to collapse, 1815-1960 / V.G. Kiernan. — [London] : Fontana, 1982. — 285p ; 20cm. — (Fontana history of European war and society)
Bibliography: p255-269. — Includes index
ISBN 0-00-634826-2 (pbk) : £2.95 B82-22560

Kiernan, V. G.. European empires from conquest to collapse 1815-1960 / V.G. Kiernan. — [Leicester] : Leicester University Press in association with Fontana, 1982. — 285p ; 23cm. — (Fontana history of European war and society)
Bibliography: p255-269. — Includes index
ISBN 0-7185-1228-6 : £12.00 : CIP rev. B82-08120

325'.32'0941 — British imperialism, *to 1976*

Johnston, W. Ross. Great Britain great Empire : an evaluation of the British imperial experience / W. Ross Johnston. — St. Lucia ; London : University of Queensland Press, c1981. — xvii,207p ; 22cm. — (University of Queensland Press scholar's library)
Includes index
ISBN 0-7022-1576-7 : £16.70 B82-16714

325'.32'0941 — Imperialism. Theories — *Study examples: British imperialism, 1880-1914*

Baumgart, Winfried. Imperialism : the idea and reality of British and French colonial expansion, 1880-1914 / by Winfried Baumgart ; translated by the author with the assistance of Ben V. Mast ; with a preface by Henri Brunschwig. — Rev. ed. — Oxford : Oxford University Press, 1982. — xi,239p : ill,1map ; 23cm
Translation of: Der Imperialismus. — Bibliography: p213-231. — Includes index
ISBN 0-19-873040-3 (cased) : £15.00 : CIP rev.
ISBN 0-19-873040-3 (pbk) : £5.95
Also classified at 325'.32'0944 B82-07521

325'.32'0944 — Imperialism. Theories — *Study examples: French imperialism, 1880-1914*

Baumgart, Winfried. Imperialism : the idea and reality of British and French colonial expansion, 1880-1914 / by Winfried Baumgart ; translated by the author with the assistance of Ben V. Mast ; with a preface by Henri Brunschwig. — Rev. ed. — Oxford : Oxford University Press, 1982. — xi,239p : ill,1map ; 23cm
Translation of: Der Imperialismus. — Bibliography: p213-231. — Includes index
ISBN 0-19-873040-3 (cased) : £15.00 : CIP rev.
ISBN 0-19-873040-3 (pbk) : £5.95
Primary classification 325'.32'0941 B82-07521

325'.32'0947 — Russian imperialism. Soviet historiography

Enteen, George M.. Soviet historians and the study of Russian imperialism / by George M. Enteen, Tatiana Gorn and Cheryl Kern. — University Park ; London : Pennsylvania State University Press, c1979. — ix,60p ; 23cm. — (Pennsylvania State University studies ; no.45)
Bibliography: p60
ISBN 0-271-00211-5 (pbk) : Unpriced B82-37324

325'.341'0954 — India. Colonial administration by Great Britain, *1914-1947* — *Personal observations*

Jardine, Lionel. They called me an 'impeccable imperialist' / Lionel Jardine. — India : R.M. Lala ; London : Grosvenor Books [[distributor]], 1979. — xi,78p,[8]p of plates : ill,ports ; 19cm
Map on lining papers
ISBN 0-901269-41-7 : £2.95 B82-09823

325'.341'0954 — India. Colonial administration by Great Britain, *1930-1947* — *Personal observations* — *Collections*

The **District** Officer in India 1930-1947 / [edited by] Roland Hunt and John Harrison. — London : Scolar, 1980. — xxxii,255p,[1]folded leaf of plates : map(some col.) ; 24cm
Bibliography: pxxxi-xxxii. — Includes index
ISBN 0-85967-560-2 : £17.50 : CIP rev. B80-03058

The **District** officer in India 1930-1947 / [compiled by] Ronald Hunt and John Harrison. — London : Scolar Press, 1980 (1982 [printing]). — xxxii,255p : maps ; 23cm
Includes bibliographies and index
ISBN 0-85967-660-9 (pbk) : £6.95 : CIP rev. B82-00171

325'.341'0954 — India. Colonial administration by Great Britain, *1942-1947.* **State papers** — *Collections*

The **Transfer** of power 1942-47 / editor-in-chief Nicholas Mansergh. — London : H.M.S.O.. — (Constitutional relations between Britain and India)
Vol.10: The Mountbatten Viceroyalty formulation of a plan 22 March-30 May 1947 / editor Penderel Moon asssisted by David M. Blake and Lionel Carter. — 1981. — cxxvi,1077p,[5]p of plates : ill,1facsim,ports ; 28cm
Includes index
ISBN 0-11-580085-9 : £60.00 B82-25291

325'.341'0954 — India. Princely states. Colonial administration by Great Britain, *1905-1939*

Ashton, S. R.. British policy towards the Indian States 1905-1939 / S.R. Ashton. — London : Curzon, 1982. — xiii,231p : 1map ; 23cm. — (London studies on South Asia, ISSN 0142-601x ; no.2)
Bibliography: p216-224. — Includes index
ISBN 0-7007-0146-x : Unpriced : CIP rev. B82-01336

325'.341'09669 — Nigeria. Colonial administration by Great Britain, *1900-1948*

White, Jeremy. Central administration in Nigeria, 1914-1948 : the problem of polarity / Jeremy White ; foreword by Adebayo Adedeji. — Dublin : Irish Academic Press, 1981. — 369p : 2 maps ; 23cm
Bibliography: p354-362. — Includes index
ISBN 0-7165-0057-4 : £17.50 B82-01902

325'.341'0974 — New England. British colonies. Colonial administration, *1675-1715*

Johnson, Richard R.. Adjustment to empire : the New England colonies 1675-1715 / Richard R. Johnson. — [Leicester] : Leicester University Press, 1981. — xx,470p : 1maps ; 24cm
Bibliography: p423-452. — Includes index
ISBN 0-7185-1208-1 : £22.00 B82-07364

325'.3469'096 — Africa. Portuguese colonies. Colonial administration, *to 1974*

Newitt, Malyn. Portugal in Africa : the last hundred years / by Malyn Newitt. — London : Hurst, c1981. — viii,278p : maps ; 23cm
Also published: Harlow : Longman, 1981. — Bibliography: p250-263. — Includes index
ISBN 0-905838-37-8 (cased) : £11.50 : CIP rev.
ISBN 0-905838-49-1 (pbk) : Unpriced B81-09470

325.4/9 — POLITICS. MIGRATION. GEOGRAPHICAL TREATMENT

325.6 — Africa. Colonial administration, *1870-1960*

Colonialism in Africa 1870-1960 / edited by L.H. Gann and Peter Duignan. — Cambridge : Cambridge University Press, 1969 (1981 [printing]). — 2v. : ill,maps ; 23cm
Includes index
ISBN 0-521-07373-1 (pbk) : Unpriced : CIP rev.
ISBN 0-521-07732-x
ISBN 0-521-28648-4 (v.1) : £12.50
ISBN 0-521-28649-2 (v.2) : £12.50 B81-36238

327 — FOREIGN RELATIONS

327 — Foreign relations

Cohen, Raymond. International politics : the rules of the game / Raymond Cohen. — London : Longman, 1981. — vi,186p ; 22cm
Includes index
ISBN 0-582-29558-0 (pbk) : £3.50 : CIP rev. B81-25875

The **Community** of states. — London : Allen & Unwin, Nov.1982. — [208]p
ISBN 0-04-320151-2 : £15.00 : CIP entry B82-27804

Couloumbis, Theodore A.. Introduction to international relations : power and justice / Theodore A. Couloumbis, James H. Wolfe. — 2nd ed. — Englewood Cliffs ; London : Prentice-Hall, c1982. — xvi,411p ; 24cm
Previous ed.: 1978. — Includes bibliographies and index
ISBN 0-13-485292-3 : £14.95 B82-16993

Holsti, K. J.. Why nations realign : foreign policy restructuring in the postwar world / K.J. Holsti with Miguel Monterichard ... [et al.]. — London : Allen & Unwin, 1982. — xi,225p : ill ; 24cm
Includes index
ISBN 0-04-351062-0 : Unpriced : CIP rev. B82-07227

Jensen, Lloyd. Explaining foreign policy / Lloyd Jensen. — Englewood Cliffs ; London : Prentice-Hall, c1982. — x,278p ; 23cm
Includes index
ISBN 0-13-295600-4 (pbk) : £8.20 B82-20053

Russett, Bruce M.. World politics : the menu for choice / Bruce Russett, Harvey Starr. — Oxford : W.H. Freeman, c1981. — xii,596p : ill,maps,2ports ; 24cm
Maps on lining papers. — Includes index
ISBN 0-7167-1283-0 : Unpriced B82-08398

Stegenga, James A.. The global community : a brief introduction to international relations. — 2nd ed. / James A. Stegenga, W. Andrew Axline. — New York ; London : Harper & Row, c1982. — x,190p : ill ; 21cm
Previous ed.: / by W. Andrew Axline and James A. Stegenga. New York : Dodd, Mead, 1972. — Includes bibliographies and index
ISBN 0-06-040404-3 (pbk) : £6.95 B82-11967

327 — Foreign relations. Change

Gilpin, Robert. War and change in world politics / Robert Gilpin. — Cambridge : Cambridge University Press, 1981. — xiv,272p ; 24cm
Bibliography: p245-259. — Includes index
ISBN 0-521-24018-2 : £15.00 B82-07157

327 — Foreign relations. Influence of nationalism

Boundaries : national autonomy and its limits / edited by Peter G. Brown and Henry Shue. — Totowa, N.J. : Rowman and Littlefield ; London : Distributed by Prior, 1981. — xvii,216p ; 25cm. — (Maryland studies in public philosophy)
Includes index
ISBN 0-8476-7011-2 (cased) : Unpriced
ISBN 0-8476-7048-1 (pbk) : Unpriced B82-12099

327'.05 — Foreign relations — *Serials*

The **Ditchley** newsletter. — No.1 (Spring 1981)-. — Enstone (Ditchley Park, Enstone, OX7 4ER) : Ditchley Foundation, 1981-. — v. ; 30cm
Three issues yearly. — Continues: The Ditchley journal
ISSN 0262-8015 = Ditchley newsletter : Free to Foundation supporters B82-09078

327'.059 — South-east Asia. Foreign relations with China

Tajima, Takashi. China and South-East Asia : strategic interests and policy prospects / by Takashi Tajima. — London : International Institute for Strategic Studies, 1981. — 38p : ill ; 25cm. — (Adelphi papers, ISSN 0567-932x ; no.172)
Cover title
ISBN 0-86079-054-1 (pbk) : Unpriced
Primary classification 327.51059 B82-20706

327'.09'04 — Foreign relations, *1945-1980*

Griffith, William E.. The superpowers and regional tensions : the USSR, the United States, and Europe / William E. Griffith. — Lexington, Mass. : Lexington Books ; [Aldershot] : Gower [distributor], c1982. — vii,135p ; 24cm
Includes index
ISBN 0-669-04702-3 : £13.50 B82-28773

327'.09'04 — Great powers. Foreign relations, *1945-1980* — *For schools*

Sayer, John, *1942-*. Super power rivalry / John Sayer. — London : Edward Aronld, 1981. — 48p : ill,maps,ports ; 24cm. — (Links : twentieth century world history books)
Bibliography: p46. — Includes index
ISBN 0-7131-0538-0 (pbk) : £1.80 : CIP rev. B81-13736

327'.09'042 — Foreign relations, *1919-1939*

Carr, Edward Hallett. The twenty years' crisis, 1919-1939 : an introduction to the study of international relations : by E.H. Carr. — 2nd ed. — London : Macmillan, 1946 (1981 [printing]). — xiv,243p ; 23cm
Previous ed.: 1939. — Includes index
ISBN 0-333-06913-7 (cased) : £15.00
ISBN 0-333-31228-7 (pbk) : Unpriced B82-38575

327'.09171'241 — Commonwealth Heads of Government Meeting *(1981: Melbourne).* **Decisions**

Commonwealth heads of government meeting, Melbourne, 30 September-7 October 1981 : communiqué. — London : H.M.S.O., [1981]. — 23p ; 25cm. — (Cmnd. ; 8412)
ISBN 0-10-184120-5 (unbound) : £2.30 B82-11539

327'.09171'3 — Western bloc countries. Foreign relations with communist countries

Halliday, Fred. The origins of the second cold war. — London : Verso, May 1982. — [160]p
ISBN 0-86091-053-9 (cased) : £10.00 : CIP entry
ISBN 0-86091-752-5 (pbk) : £2.95
Also classified at 327'.09171'7 B82-12910

327'.09171'3 — Western bloc countries. Foreign relations with Eastern Europe

East West relations and the future of Eastern Europe : politics and economics / edited by Morris Bornstein, Zvi Gitelman and William Zimmerman. — London : Allen & Unwin, 1981. — x,301p : ill ; 24cm
Includes index
ISBN 0-04-330317-x : Unpriced : CIP rev.
Primary classification 327'.0947 B81-15887

327'.09171'3 — Western bloc countries. Foreign relations with Middle East, *1950-1980*

The **Middle** East and the Western alliance / edited by Steven L. Spiegel. — London : Allen & Unwin published under the auspices of the Center for International and Strategic Affairs, University of California, 1982. — 252p ; 25cm
Includes index
ISBN 0-04-327067-0 : £15.00 : CIP rev.
Primary classification 327'.0956 B82-16225

327'.09171'3 — Western bloc countries. Foreign relations with South Africa

Barber, James, *1931-*. The West and South Africa / James Barber, Jesmond Blumenfeld and Christopher R. Hill. — London : Royal Institute of International Affairs : Routledge and Kegan Paul, 1982. — 106p ; 22cm. — (Chatham House papers, ISSN 0143-5795 ; 14)
ISBN 0-7100-9232-6 (pbk) : £3.95 : CIP rev.
Also classified at 327.680171'3 B82-11260

327'.09171'3 — Western bloc countries. Foreign relations with Soviet Union

Roberts, *Sir* **Frank**, *1907-*. East-West tensions world wide : based on an address given by Sir Frank Roberts ... at a seminar held at St Edmund Hall, Oxford in August 1981 ... — Exeter (7 Cathedral Close, Exeter, Devon EX1 1EZ) : European-Atlantic Movement, [1982?]. — 12p ; 22cm
Cover title. — Bibliography: p11
Unpriced (pbk)
Primary classification 327.470171'3 B82-35507

327'.09171'7 — Communist countries. Foreign relations with Western bloc countries

Halliday, Fred. The origins of the second cold war. — London : Verso, May 1982. — [160]p
ISBN 0-86091-053-9 (cased) : £10.00 : CIP entry
ISBN 0-86091-752-5 (pbk) : £2.95
Primary classification 327'.09171'3 B82-12910

327'.09172'4 — Developing countries. Foreign relations with developing countries, *1917-1979*

The **Soviet** Union and the Third World / edited by E.J. Feuchtwanger and Peter Nailor. — London : Macmillan, 1981. — vi,229p : ill ; 23cm
Includes index
ISBN 0-333-28736-3 : £20.00
Primary classification 327.470172'4 B82-06656

327'.09172'4 — Developing countries. Foreign relations with European Community countries

The **EEC** and the Third World / edited by K.B. Lall, H.S. Chopra. — Atlantic Highlands : Humanities ; Gloucester : distributed by Sutton, c1981. — xx,452p : ill ; 23cm
Includes index
ISBN 0-391-02004-8 : Unpriced
Primary classification 327'.094 B82-38141

327'.0917'4927 — Arab countries. Foreign relations with Africa

Beshir, Mohamed Omer. Terramedia : themes in Afro-Arab relations / Mohamed Omer Beshir. — London : Ithaca, 1982. — 205p ; 22cm
Bibliography: p173-205
Unpriced (pbk)
Primary classification 327'.096 B82-33285

327'.0917'4927 — Arab countries. Foreign relations with Israel

Rodinson, Maxime. Israel and the Arabs / Maxime Rodinson ; translated by Michael Perl and Brian Pearce. — 2nd ed. — [Harmondsworth] : Penguin, 1982. — 364p ; 20cm. — (Pelican books)
Translated from the French. — Previous ed.: 1968. — Includes index
ISBN 0-14-022445-9 (pbk) : £3.50
Primary classification 327.5694017'4927 B82-37608

327'.0917'4927 — Arab countries. Foreign relations with Israel, *1964-1971 — Personal observations*

Riad, Mahmoud. The struggle for peace in the Middle East / Mahmoud Riad. — London : Quartet, 1981. — 365p,[9]p of plates : 1map,ports ; 24cm
Includes index
ISBN 0-7043-2297-8 : £11.95 : CIP rev.
Also classified at 327.5694017'4927 B81-25709

327'.0917'7 — North Atlantic Treaty Organization countries. Foreign relations with Soviet Union

Critchley, Julian. The North Atlantic Alliance and the Soviet Union in the 1980s / Julian Critchley. — London : Macmillan, 1982. — 210p ; 23cm
Includes index
ISBN 0-333-29469-6 : £15.00
Also classified at 327.47017'7 B82-20946

327'.09182'1 — Caribbean countries. Foreign relations with United States, *to 1980*

Perkins, Whitney T.. Constraint of empire : the United States and Caribbean interventions / Whitney T. Perkins. — Oxford : Clio, 1981. — xv,282p ; 24cm
Bibliography: p268-274. — Includes index
ISBN 0-903450-52-6 : £21.75
Primary classification 327.730182'1 B82-27401

327'.09182'1 — Caribbean countries. Foreign relations with United States, *to 1981 — For Caribbean students*

Stewart, Rosemarie. The United States and the Caribbean. — London : Heinemann Educational, Aug.1982. — [64]p. — (Heinemann CXC history)
ISBN 0-435-98230-3 (pbk) : £1.00 : CIP entry
Primary classification 327.730182'1 B82-19660

327'.09182'3 — South China Sea. Islands. International political aspects, *to 1980*

Samuels, Marwyn S.. Contest for the South China Sea / Marwyn S. Samuels. — New York ; London : Methuen, 1982. — xiii,203p : ill,maps ; 24cm
Bibliography: p173-177. — Includes index
ISBN 0-416-33140-8 : Unpriced : CIP rev. B82-10505

327'.094 — Europe. Foreign relations with United States. Diplomacy, *1919-1941*

U.S. diplomats in Europe, 1919-1941 / edited by Kenneth Paul Jones ; foreword by Alexander DeConde. — Santa Barbara ; Oxford : ABC-Clio, c1981. — xxiii,240p : 2maps,ports ; 24cm
Bibliography: p225-229. — Includes index
ISBN 0-87436-311-x : £22.95
Primary classification 327.7304 B82-02742

327'.094 — Europe. Foreign relations with United States. Policies of United States government, *1937-1939*

Graebner, Norman A.. Roosevelt and the search for a European policy 1937-1939 : an inaugural lecture delivered before the University of Oxford on 21 May 1979 / by Norman A. Graebner. — Oxford : Clarendon, 1980. — 47p ; 22cm
ISBN 0-19-951524-7 (pbk) : £1.95 : CIP rev.
Primary classification 327.7304 B80-13243

327'.094 — European Community countries. Foreign relations with developing countries

The **EEC** and the Third World / edited by K.B. Lall, H.S. Chopra. — Atlantic Highlands : Humanities ; Gloucester : distributed by Sutton, c1981. — xx,452p : ill ; 23cm
Includes index
ISBN 0-391-02004-8 : Unpriced
Also classified at 327'.09172'4 B82-38141

327'.094 — European Community. Foreign relations

Bailey, Richard. The European connection. — Oxford : Pergamon, Feb.1983. — [250]p
ISBN 0-08-026775-0 : £10.50 : CIP entry
ISBN 0-08-026774-2 (pbk) : £6.95 B82-36470

327'.094 — European Community. Foreign relations with United States — *Conference proceedings*

The **United** States and the European Community : new administrations and continuing problems : papers presented at a conference held at Cumberland Lodge, Windsor Great Park, on 5th and 6th of May 1981 and organised by the University Association for Contemporary European Studies in conjunction with the United States Mission to the European Community / edited by Michael Smith. — London : University Association for Contemporary European Studies, c1981. — iv,65p : ill ; 22cm
ISBN 0-906384-05-2 (pbk) : £1.80
Also classified at 327.7304 B82-20097

327'.094 — Western Europe. Foreign relations with United States, *1945-1977*

Grosser, Alfred. The Western alliance : European-American relations since 1945 / Alfred Grosser ; translated by Michael Shaw ; with a foreword by Stanley Hoffmann. — London : Macmillan, 1980. — xxiv,375p ; 23cm
Translation of: Les Occidentaux. — Includes index
ISBN 0-333-29271-5 (cased) : £12.50 : CIP rev.
ISBN 0-333-29259-6 (pbk) : £3.95
Also classified at 327.7304 B80-18182

327'.0947 — Eastern Europe. Foreign relations with Western bloc countries

East West relations and the future of Eastern Europe : politics and economics / edited by Morris Bornstein, Zvi Gitelman and William Zimmerman. — London : Allen & Unwin, 1981. — x,301p : ill ; 24cm
Includes index
ISBN 0-04-330317-x : Unpriced : CIP rev.
Also classified at 327'.09171'3 B81-15887

327'.095 — Asia. Foreign relations with Great Britain, *1795-1800*

Ingram, Edward, *1940-*. Commitment to empire : prophecies of the great game in Asia 1797-1800 / by Edward Ingram. — Oxford : Clarendon, 1981. — xvi,431p : maps ; 22cm
Bibliography: p402-423. — Includes index
ISBN 0-19-822662-4 : £22.50 : CIP rev.
Primary classification 327.4105 B81-15801

327'.0953'6 — Persian Gulf countries. Foreign relations

Security in the Persian Gulf. — Aldershot : Published for the International Institute for Strategic Studies by Gower
3: Modernization, political development and stability / Avi Plascov. — c1982. — viii,183p ; 22cm
Includes index
ISBN 0-566-00450-x (pbk) : Unpriced : CIP rev. B82-01721

Security in the Persian Gulf. — Aldershot : Published for the International Institute for Strategic Studies by Gower
4: The role of outside powers / Shahram Chubin. — c1982. — v,180p ; 22cm
Includes index
ISBN 0-566-00449-6 (pbk) : Unpriced : CIP rev. B82-01134

327'.0956 — Middle East. Foreign relations with China, *1955-1975 — Case studies*

Behbehani, Hashim S. H.. China's foreign policy in the Arab world, 1955-75 : three case studies / Hashim S.H. Behbehani. — London : Kegan Paul International, 1981. — xiv,426p : 1map ; 22cm
Bibliography: p394-422. — Includes index
ISBN 0-7103-0008-5 : £25.00 : CIP rev.
Primary classification 327.51056 B81-21479

327'.0956 — Middle East. Foreign relations with Western bloc countries, *1950-1980*

The **Middle** East and the Western alliance / edited by Steven L. Spiegel. — London : Allen & Unwin published under the auspices of the Center for International and Strategic Affairs, University of California, 1982. — 252p ; 25cm
Includes index
ISBN 0-04-327067-0 : £15.00 : CIP rev.
Also classified at 327'.09171'3 B82-16225

327'.096 — Africa. Foreign relations with Arab countries

Beshir, Mohamed Omer. Terramedia : themes in Afro-Arab relations / Mohamed Omer Beshir. — London : Ithaca, 1982. — 205p ; 22cm
Bibliography: p173-205
Unpriced (pbk)
Also classified at 327'.0917'4927 B82-33285

327'.096 — Africa. Foreign relations with Soviet Union, *1917-1977*

USSR and countries of Africa : (friendship, cooperation, support for the anti-imperialist struggle) / general editor E.A. Tarabrin ; [translated from the Russian by David Fidlon and Stanislav Ponomarenko]. — Moscow : Progress ; [London] : distributed by Central Books, c1980. — 319p ; 21cm
Translation of: SSSR i strany Afriki. — Includes index
ISBN 0-7147-1684-7 : £3.25
Primary classification 327.4706 B82-19611

327'.098 — Latin America. Foreign relations with United States. Policies of United States government. Influence of human rights movement, *1960-1980*

Schoultz, Lars. Human rights and United States policy toward Latin America / Lars Schoultz. — Princeton ; Guildford : Princeton University Press, c1981. — xvii,421p ; 25cm
Bibliography: p381-405. — Includes index
ISBN 0-691-07630-8 (cased) : £22.80
ISBN 0-691-02204-6 (pbk) : Unpriced
Primary classification 327.7308 B82-13308

327.1 — War & peace. Theories, *1795-1870*

Gallie, W. B.. Philosophers of peace and war : Kant, Clausewitz, Marx, Engels and Tolstoy / W.B. Gallie. — Cambridge : Cambridge University Press, 1978 (1980 [printing]). — x,147p ; 23cm. — (The Wiles lectures given at the Queen's University Belfast)
Bibliography: p142-143
ISBN 0-521-29651-x (pbk) : Unpriced B82-01765

327.1'01 — Foreign relations. Theories

Dougherty, James E.. Contending theories of international relations : a comprehensive survey / James E. Dougherty, Robert L. Pfaltzgraff. — 2nd ed. — New York ; London : Harper & Row, c1981. — xv,592p ; 24cm
Previous ed.: 1971. — Includes index
ISBN 0-06-045215-3 (pbk) : £8.95 B82-01881

Linklater, Andrew. Men and citizens in the theory of international relations / Andrew Linklater. — London : Macmillan, 1982. — xii,232p ; 23cm
Bibliography: p222-227. — Includes index
ISBN 0-333-32001-8 : £15.00 B82-20954

327.1'01'9 — Foreign relations. Adaptive behaviour

Smith, Steven M.. Foreign policy adaptation / Steven M. Smith. — Aldershot : Gower, 1981. — vii,152p : ill ; 23cm
Includes index
ISBN 0-566-00370-8 : Unpriced : CIP rev. B81-21562

327.1'12'0904 — Balance of power, *1943-*

Thompson, Kenneth W.. Cold war theories / Kenneth W. Thompson. — Baton Rouge ; London : Louisiana State University Press
Vol.1: World polarization, 1943-1953. — 1981. — 216p ; 24cm
Includes index
ISBN 0-8071-0876-6 : £13.30 B82-22619

327.1'12'0904 — Balance of power, *1945-1980*

Cameron, Neil, *1920-*. The global balance of power / by Neil Cameron. — Leeds : University of Leeds, [1982]. — p83-98 ; 21cm. — (The thirty-sixth Montague Burton lecture on international relations)
Lecture given at Leeds, 9 March 1981. — 'Published as an offprint of The University of Leeds Review 1981'. — Cover title. — Text on inside cover
Unpriced (pbk) B82-28900

Millar, T. B.. The East-West strategic balance / T.B. Millar. — London : Allen & Unwin, 1981. — xxx,199p : ill,maps ; 23cm
Includes index
ISBN 0-04-355015-0 (cased) : Unpriced : CIP rev.
ISBN 0-04-355017-7 (pbk) : Unpriced B81-25104

327.1'12'0947 — Eastern Europe. Balance of power, *1940-1955*

Witnesses to the origins of the cold war / edited by Thomas T. Hammond. — Seattle ; London : University of Washington Press, c1982. — 318p ; 24cm. — (Publications on Russia and Eastern Europe of the School of International Studies ; v.10)
Includes index
ISBN 0-295-95892-8 : Unpriced B82-37677

327.1'16 — Europe. International security

European security, nuclear weapons and public confidence / edited by William Gutteridge assisted by Marian Dobrosielski and Jorma Miettinen. — London : Macmillan, 1982. — xiii,236p : ill,maps ; 22cm
Includes index
ISBN 0-333-30959-6 : £20.00 B82-28651

327.1'16 — Indian Ocean. International security aspects

Ahsan, Syed Akhtar. Strategic concepts of the Indian Ocean / Syed Akhtar Ahsan. — Maidstone : Mann in association with Wajidalis, 1981, c1979. — 184p ; 25cm
ISBN 0-7041-0204-8 : £15.00 B82-01675

327.1'16 — Persian Gulf countries. International security

Chubin, Shahram. Security in the Gulf. — Aldershot : Gower, Sept.1982. — [620]p. — (The Adelphi library ; 7)
ISBN 0-566-00452-6 : £20.00 : CIP entry B82-19543

Litwak, Robert. Sources of inter-state conflict / Robert Litwak. — Aldershot : Published for the International Institute for Strategic Studies by Gower, 1981. — xii,105p : ill,3maps ; 22cm. — (Security in the Persian Gulf ; 2)
Includes index
ISBN 0-566-00451-8 (pbk) : Unpriced : CIP rev. B81-14975

Oil and security in the Arab Gulf : the proceedings of an international symposium / James Akins ... [et al.]. — London : Arab Research Centre, c1980. — 48p ; 25cm. — (Arab papers. Symposia and seminar report series : the first symposium ; no.5)
Available in Arabic
ISBN 0-907233-05-8 (pbk) : £1.25 B82-39730

327.1'16 — Western Europe. International security

Burrows, Bernard. The defence of Western Europe / Bernard Burrows and Geoffrey Edwards. — London : Butterworth Scientific, 1982. — 155p ; 25cm. — (Butterworths European studies)
Includes index
ISBN 0-408-10702-2 : £16.00 : CIP rev. B82-10494

The **Crisis** in western security / edited by Lawrence S. Hagen. — London : Croom Helm, c1982. — 247p : ill,maps ; 23cm
Includes index
ISBN 0-7099-1214-5 : £13.95 : CIP rev. B81-37557

327.1'2 — Espionage — *Amateurs' manuals — For children*

Brandreth, Gyles. 1000 secrets : the greatest book of spycraft ever known / Gyles Brandreth ; illustrated by Peter Stevenson. — [London] : Carousel, 1982. — 196p : ill ; 20cm
ISBN 0-552-54207-5 (pbk) : £0.95 B82-29732

327.1'2'09 — Espionage, *to 1980 — For children*

The **Beaver** book of spy stories / [compiled by] George Kay ; illustrated by Peter Dennis. — London : Beaver, 1982. — 159p : ill ; 18cm
ISBN 0-600-20544-4 (pbk) : £1.00 B82-36479

327.1'2'09 — Espionage, *to 1987*

Davis, Richard, *1935-*. Spies : the true story / Richard Davis. — London : Hutchinson, 1982. — 144p ; 21cm
ISBN 0-09-149420-6 : £5.50 : CIP rev. B82-20193

327.1'2'091724 — Developing countries. Subversive activities. Role of United States. *Central Intelligence Agency, 1945-1977*

Kumar, Satish. CIA and the Third World : a study in Crypto-Diplomacy / Satish Kumar. — London : Zed Press, 1981. — vi,200p ; 23cm
Includes index
ISBN 0-86232-055-0 : £12.95 B82-01004

327.1'2'0924 — Australian intelligence services, *ca 1940-1980 — Personal observations*

Mathams, R. J.. Sub Rosa : memoirs of an Australian intelligence analyst. — London : Allen & Unwin, Jan.1983. — 1v.
ISBN 0-86861-380-0 : £15.00 : CIP entry B82-33233

327.1'2'0924 — Espionage — *Personal observations*

Deacon, Richard. With my little eye. — London : Muller, Oct.1982. — [256]p
ISBN 0-584-11032-4 : £8.95 : CIP entry B82-23364

327.1'2'0941 — British secret services. Infiltration by Soviet secret services, *ca 1940-1980*

Pincher, Chapman. Their trade is treachery / Chapman Pincher. — [New ed]. — London : Sidgwick & Jackson, 1982. — xi,317p ; 19cm
Previous ed.: 1981. — Includes index
ISBN 0-283-98847-9 (pbk) : £1.75 B82-16941

327.1'2'0947 — Nuclear weapons. Soviet espionage, *1943-1953*

Hyde, H. Montgomery. The atom bomb spies / H. Montgomery Hyde. — London : Sphere, 1982, c1980. — 341p,[8]p of plates : ill,ports ; 18cm
Originally published: London : Hamilton, 1980. — Bibliography: p333-335. — Includes index
ISBN 0-7221-4863-1 (pbk) : £2.25 B82-21272

327.1'2'0947 — Union of Soviet Socialist Republics. *Komitet gosudarstvennoĭ bezopasnosti, to 1980*

Rositzke, Harry A.. The KGB : the eyes of Russia / Harry Rositzke. — London : Sidgwick & Jackson, 1982, c1981. — xiii,295p ; 25cm
Originally published: Garden City, N.Y. : Doubleday, 1981. — Includes index
ISBN 0-283-98823-1 : £8.95 B82-12066

327.1'2'0952 — Japanese secret services, *to 1980*

Deacon, Richard. A history of the Japanese secret service / Richard Deacon. — London : Frederick Muller, 1982. — 306p,[8]p of plates : ill,1map,ports ; 23cm
Bibliography: p291-294. — Includes index
ISBN 0-584-10383-2 : £12.95 : CIP rev. B81-39248

327.1'2'0956 — Middle East. Intelligence operations by Western intelligence services, *1898-1926*

Winstone, H. V. F.. The illicit adventure : the story of political and military intelligence in the Middle East from 1898 to 1926. — London : Cape, Sept.1982. — [416]p
ISBN 0-224-01582-6 : £8.95 : CIP entry B82-19004

327.1'2'0973 — United States. National security. Role of intelligence services

Intelligence policy and national security / edited by Robert L. Pfaltzgraff, Jr., Uri Ra'anan and Warren Milberg. — London : Macmillan, 1981. — x,318p : ill ; 25cm
Includes index
ISBN 0-333-30728-3 : £25.00 B82-11648

327.1'6'091724 — Developing countries. Conflict. International security aspects

Third-world conflict and international security / edited by Christoph Bertram. — London : Macmillan, 1982. — 121p ; 26cm. — (An IISS book)
Conference papers. — At head of title: International Institute for Strategic Studies
ISBN 0-333-32955-4 : £15.00 B82-20945

327.1′7′0948 — Scandinavian countries. International cooperation
Turner, Barry. The other European community : integration and co-operation in Nordic Europe / Barry Turner with Gunilla Nordquist. — London : Weidenfeld and Nicolson, c1982. — vii,307p : 1map ; 22cm
Bibliography: p298-300. — Includes index
ISBN 0-297-77792-0 (cased) : £12.95
ISBN 0-297-78137-5 (pbk) : £7.95 B82-24209

327.1′72 — Arab countries. Conflict with Israel. Peacemaking. Role of European Community — *Israeli viewpoints*
Argov, Shlomo. Europe and Arab-Israeli peacemaking : a critique / by Shlomo Argov. — Leeds : University of Leeds, [1982]. — 12p ; 21cm. — (The Twenty-second Selig Brodetsky memorial lecture)
Lecture given at Leeds, 18 May 1981. — 'Published as an offprint of The University of Leeds Review 1981'. — Cover title. — Text on inside cover
Unpriced (pbk) B82-28896

327.1′72 — Peace. Maintenance — *World Parliament of the People for Peace viewpoints*
World Parliament of the Peoples for Peace. Safeguarding peace is the common task of all peoples : materials of the World Parliament of the Peoples for Peace. — Moscow : Novosti, c1977 ; [London] : distributed by Central Books. — 39p ; 17cm
Translation from the Russian
ISBN 0-7147-1645-6 (pbk) : £0.25 B82-02962

327.1′72 — Peace movements: Bertrand Russell Peace Foundation, *to 1980*
Bertrand Russell Peace Foundation. The Bertrand Russell Peace Foundation : its aims and work. — Nottingham (Bertrand Russell House, Gamble Street, Nottingham, NG7 4ET) : Bertrand Russell Peace Foundation, [1981]. — 15p : ill,3ports ; 21cm. — (Spokesman pamphlet ; no.73)
£0.30 (unbound) B82-17668

327.1′72 — Peace studies
Contemporary peace research / edited by Ghanshyam Pardesi ; advisory editors Anatol Rapoport, Ekkehart Krippendorff. — Brighton : Harvester, 1982. — xi,374p ; 23cm
Includes bibliographies and index
ISBN 0-7108-0485-7 : £22.50 : CIP rev. B82-12155

327.1′72 — Ukraine. Artek. Youth peace movements: Global Children′s Festival for Peace, Friendship and Cooperation *(1st : 1977 : Artek)*
Morton, Miriam. Young teens blaze paths to peace : the story of the first global children′s festival for peace, friendship, cooperation / Miriam Morton ; foreword by Benjamin Spock. — Moscow : Progress ; [London] : Distributed by Central Books, c1981. — 109p,[24]p of plates : ill,1facsim ; 20cm
ISBN 0-7147-1747-9 (pbk) : Unpriced B82-38835

327.1′72 — Women′s peace movements — *Serials*
Women′s peace review. — 1-. — London : Women′s Press, Nov.1982. — v.
ISBN 0-7043-3901-3 : CIP entry
ISSN 0263-5135 B82-27962

327.1′72′06042 — England. Pacifism. Organisations: Friends of Peace, *to 1815*
Cookson, J. E.. The friends of peace : anti-war liberalism in England, 1793-1815 / J.E. Cookson. — Cambridge : Cambridge University Press, 1982. — vi,330p ; 23cm
Bibliography: p293-315. — Includes index
ISBN 0-521-23928-1 : £24.00 : CIP rev. B81-37551

327.1′72′071041 — Great Britain. Educational institutions. Curriculum subjects: Peace studies. Teaching
Hicks, David, *1942-*. Education for peace : what does it mean? : some thoughts for the 1980s : this paper is a revision of a lecture given to the International Association for Christian Education seminar on 12th May 1981 at Bad Marienberg in West Germany / David Hicks. — Lancaster : S. Martin′s College, [1981]. — 18p ; 30cm. — (Occasional paper / Centre for Peace Studies ; no.1)
Unpriced (spiral) B82-38841

327.1′72′0924 — Pacifism. Partridge, Frances — *Biographies*
Partridge, Frances. Memories. — London : Robin Clark, June 1982. — [244]p
Originally published: London : Gollancz, 1981
ISBN 0-86072-056-x (pbk) : £2.95 : CIP entry B82-10241

327.1′72′094 — Europe. Peace movements, *to 1980*
Disarming Europe. — London : Merlin, May 1982. — [220]p
ISBN 0-85036-277-6 (cased) : £10.00 : CIP entry
ISBN 0-85036-278-4 (pbk) : £3.60 B82-12824

327.1′74 — Arms control
The **Arms** race and arms control / SIPRI. — London : Taylor & Francis, 1982. — xiii,242p : ill,maps ; 19cm
Includes index
ISBN 0-85066-232-x (pbk) : £3.95 : CIP rev.
Primary classification 355.8′2 B82-21752

Davis, Michael J.. Address to the United Nations Second Special Session on Disarmament : New York, June 1982. — [Windsor] : Council for Arms Control, [1982]. — 9p ; 30cm
Cover title. — 'Written and presented at United Nations by Michael J. Davis′ — inside cover
Unpriced (pbk) B82-37098

327.1′74 — Arms control. International cooperation
Goldblat, Jozef. Agreements for arms control : a critical survey / Jozef Goldblat. — London : Taylor & Francis, 1982. — xvi,387p : ill,maps ; 24cm
Bibliography: p378-382. — Includes index
ISBN 0-85066-229-x : £18.50 : CIP rev. B82-11987

327.1′74 — Disarmament
Debate on disarmament / edited by Michael Clarke and Marjorie Mowlam ; contributors E.P. Thompson ... [et al.]. — London : Routledge & Kegan Paul, 1982. — 143p ; 22cm
Bibliography: p133-138. — Includes index
ISBN 0-7100-9269-5 (pbk) : £3.95 B82-28431

Faramazı͡an, R. A.. Disarmament and the economy / R. Faramazyan ; [translated from the Russian by Joseph Shapiro]. — Moscow : Progress ; [London] : distributed by Central, c1981. — 172p ; 21cm
Translation of: Razoruzhenie i ėkonomika
ISBN 0-7147-1726-6 : £2.95 B82-29289

FitzGerald, Brigid. Towards disarmament : the second UN Special Session — and beyond / [researched and written by Brigid FitzGerald]. — London : United World Trust, c1981. — 39p : ill ; 30cm
Bibliography: p30
ISBN 0-9507900-0-1 (pbk) : £1.50 B82-16611

Militarization and arms production. — London : Croom Helm, Aug.1982. — [288]p
ISBN 0-7099-2422-4 : £12.95 : CIP entry B82-18476

Sanger, Clyde. Safe & sound. — London : Zed Press, Sept.1982. — [128]p
ISBN 0-86232-121-2 (cased) : £10.95 : CIP entry
ISBN 0-86232-122-0 (pbk) : £4.95 B82-21745

Thompson, E. P.. Zero option. — London : Merlin Press, May 1982. — [240]p
ISBN 0-85036-287-3 (cased) : £10.00 : CIP entry
ISBN 0-85036-288-1 (pbk) : £3.60 B82-14946

327.1′74 — Disarmament — *Communist viewpoints — Conference proceedings*
Vstrecha kommunisticheskikh i rabochikh partiĭ Evropy za mir i razoruzhenie *(1980 : Paris)*. Meeting of European Communist and Workers′ Parties for Peace and Disarmament : Paris, 28-29 April 1980. — Moscow : Progress Publishers ; [London] : Distributed by Central Books, 1980. — 204p ; 18cm
Translation of: Vstrecha kommunisticheskikh i rabochikh partiĭ Evropy za mir i razoruzhenie
ISBN 0-7147-1681-2 : £1.95 B82-06711

327.1′74 — Disarmament. Human factors — *Conference proceedings*
Disarmament : the human factor : proceedings of a colloquium on the societal context for disarmament / sponsored by UNITAR and the Planetary Citizens and held at the United Nations, New York ; edited by Ervin Laszlo and Donald Keys. — Oxford : Pergamon, 1981. — x,164p ; 24cm
Includes index
ISBN 0-08-024703-2 (cased) : £10.50
ISBN 0-08-028129-x (pbk) : Unpriced B82-00138

327.1′74 — Nuclear disarmament
Apocalypse now? / Earl Mountbatten, Lord Noel-Baker, Lord Zuckerman. — Nottingham : Spokesman for the Atlantic Peace Foundation in support of the World Disarmament Campaign, 1980 (1981 [printing]). — 64p ; 22cm
Contents: The final abyss? / Earl Mountbatten of Burma — Defeat is indivisible / Lord Zuckerman — The prospect of disarmament / Lord Noel-Baker
ISBN 0-85124-297-9 (pbk) : £1.50 B82-39519

Give peace a chance!. — London (21 Little Russell St., WC1A 2HN) : World Disarmament Campaign, 1981. — 1folded sheet : ill ; 42x60cm folded to 21x20cm
Unpriced (unbound) B82-40869

Jack, Homer A.. Lessening the nuclear threat : a defence of unilateralism / Homer A. Jack. — London : Lindsey, 1982. — 26p ; 21cm. — (The 1982 Essex Hall lecture)
Unpriced (pbk) B82-27455

A **Matter** of choice / [produced by the Malvern Oxfam group and sponsored by the Malvern Society of Friends and by the World Disarmament Campaign]. — [London] ([21 Little Russell St., WC1A 2HN]) : [World Disarmament Campaign], 1979. — 1folded sheet : ill ; 36x51cm folded to 18x19cm
Unpriced (unbound) B82-40867

Towards a world at peace / [sponsored by Hereford Peace Council]. — [London] ([21 Little Russell St., WC1A 2HN]) : [World Disarmament Campaign], 1982. — 1folded sheet : ill ; 59x21cm folded to 10x21cm
£0.03 (unbound) B82-40868

327.1′74 — Nuclear disarmament — *Campaign for Nuclear Disarmament viewpoints*
Thompson, E. P.. Protest and survive / E.P. Thompson. — 2nd (rev.) ed. — [Nottingham] : [Campaign for Nuclear Disarmament] : [Bertrand Russell Peace Foundation], [1980]. — 33p : 1ill,1map ; 21cm. — (Spokesman pamphlet ; no.71)
Previous ed. (i.e. 2nd ed.): 1980
£0.45 (unbound) B82-17676

327.1′74 — Nuclear disarmament — *Correspondence, diaries, etc*
Thompson, E. P.. Human rights and disarmament : an exchange of letters between E.P. Thompson & Vaclav Racek. — Nottingham (Bertrand Russell House, Gamble Street, Nottingham, NG7 4ET) : Spokesman for END and The Bertrand Russell Peace Foundation, [1981]. — 24p ; 21cm. — (Spokesman pamphlet ; no.77)
£0.60 (unbound) B82-17673

327.1′74 — Nuclear disarmament. Political aspects
Ryle, Martin H.. The politics of nuclear disarmament / Martin H. Ryle. — London : Pluto, 1981. — 108p ; 20cm. — (Militarism, state and society)
ISBN 0-86104-353-7 (pbk) : £2.50 B82-20697

327.1′74 — Nuclear disarmament. Role of scientists — *Conference proceedings*
Scientists, the arms race and disarmament : a Unesco/Pugwash symposium / general editor Joseph Rotblat. — London : Taylor & Francis, 1982. — viii,323p ; 24cm
Includes index
ISBN 0-85066-234-6 : Unpriced B82-38746

327.1'74 — Nuclear weapons. Proliferation. Control
Dunn, Lewis A.. Controlling the bomb : nuclear proliferation in the 1980s / Lewis A. Dunn. — New Haven ; London : Yale University Press, c1982. — xii,209p : 1map ; 22cm. — (A Twentieth Century Fund report)
Includes index
ISBN 0-300-02820-2 (cased) : £14.95 : CIP rev.
ISBN 0-300-02821-0 (pbk) B82-13486

327.1'74 — Nuclear weapons. Testing. Prohibition. Treaties. Negotiations. Participation of United States, *1958-1963*
Seaborg, Glenn T.. Kennedy, Khrushchev and the test ban / Glenn T. Seaborg with the assistance of Benjamin S. Loeb ; foreword by W. Averell Harriman. — Berkeley ; London : University of California Press, c1981. — xvi,320p,[16]p of plates : 1ill,ports ; 25cm
Includes index
ISBN 0-520-04332-4 : £12.00 B82-22618

327.1'74'05 — Arms control & disarmament — *Serials*
[Bulletin *(Council for Arms Control)*]. Bulletin / the Council for Arms Control. — No.1 (Feb. 1982)-. — Windsor (5 High St., Windsor, Berks. SL4 1LD) : The Council, 1982-. — v. ; 30cm
ISSN 0263-8010 = Bulletin - Council for Arms Control : Unpriced B82-32157

. World armaments and disarmament. — 1982. — Basingstoke : Taylor & Francis, May 1982. — [500]p
ISBN 0-85066-230-3 : £21.00 : CIP entry
ISSN 0347-2205 B82-11986

327.1'74'076 — Nuclear disarmament — *Questions & answers*
A **Quiz** for peace / quiz produced by the Malvern Oxfam Group, sponsored by the Malvern Society of Friends. — [London] ([21 Little Russell St., WC1A 2HN]) : [World Disarmament Campaign], 1980. — 1folded sheet : ill ; 60x21cm folded to 10x21cm
Unpriced (pbk) B82-40866

327.1'74'0904 — Disarmament, *ca 1945-1981*
Ferguson, John, *1921-*. Disarmament : the unanswerable case / John Ferguson. — London : Heinemann, c1982. — 106p ; 22cm
Bibliography: p99-100. — Includes index
ISBN 0-434-25706-0 (pbk) : £3.50 B82-17168

327.1'74'094 — Europe. Nuclear disarmament — *Bertrand Russell Peace Foundation viewpoints*
Coates, Ken. European nuclear disarmament / Ken Coates. — Nottingham (Bertrand Russell House, Gamble Street, Nottingham, NG7 4ET) : Bertrand Russell Peace Foundation, [1981]. — 24p ; 21cm. — (Spokesman pamphlet ; no.72)
£0.50 (unbound) B82-17666

327.1'74'094 — Europe. Nuclear disarmament — *Proposals*
Myrdal, Alva. Steps towards European nuclear disarmament : two papers for the Rome Consultation on European nuclear disarmament, sponsored by signatories to the "Russell" appeal and the Bertrand Russell Peace Foundation / Kalevi Sorsa and Alva Myrdal ; introduced by Ken Coates. — Nottingham : Spokesman, 1981. — 79p : 2maps ; 22cm
ISBN 0-85124-304-5 (pbk) : £1.95 B82-08302

327.1'74'094 — Europe. Nuclear disarmament — *Serials*
END newsletter / European Nuclear Disarmament. — No.1 (1981)-. — London ([227 Seven Sisters Rd, N4]) : END, 1981-. — v. ; 30cm
Six issues yearly. — Description based on: No.3 (Dec. 1981)
ISSN 0263-2195 = END newsletter : Unpriced B82-19851

327.1'74'0941 — Disarmament. Policies of British government
Peace and disarmament : a short guide to British government policy / [prepared by the Central Office of Information]. — London (Downing St. (East), SW1A 2AH) : Arms Control and Disarmament Research Unit, Foreign and Commonwealth Office, 1982. — 15p ; 21cm
Unpriced (pbk) B82-32957

327.1'74'0941 — Great Britain. Nuclear disarmament. Campaigns — *Manuals*
Scott, Gavin, *1950-*. How to get rid of the bomb : a peace action handbook / Gavin Scott. — [London] : Fontana, 1982. — 189p : ill,forms,2maps ; 20cm
ISBN 0-00-636542-6 (pbk) : £1.95 B82-31649

327.1'74'0941 — Great Britain. Nuclear disarmament — *Labour Party (Great Britain) viewpoints*
No Cruise, no Trident, no nuclear weapons / the Labour Party. — [London] : The Party, [1981]. — 23p : ill ; 30cm
Bibliography: p22-23
ISBN 0-86117-083-0 (unbound) : £0.60 B82-05516

327.1'74'0941 — Great Britain. Nuclear disarmament — *Labour Party (Great Britain). Young Socialists viewpoints*
Socialists & nuclear disarmament. — [London] ([144 Walworth Rd, SE17]) : [Labour Party Young Socialists National Committee], [1982]. — 14p : 1ill ; 30cm. — (LPYS conference document ; 1982)
£0.20 (unbound) B82-25253

327.1'74'0941 — Great Britain. Nuclear disarmament movements — *Communist viewpoints*
Nuclear politics : articles on the political history of the Campaign for Nuclear Disarmament reprinted from The Communist, August-October, 1980. — Belfast (10 Athol St, Belfast BT12 4GX) : British and Irish Communist Organistation, 1981. — 41p ; 23cm (pbk) B82-04193

327.1'74'0941 — Great Britain. Nuclear disarmament movements. Group activities
Flint, Ray. 'The people's scenario' : averting a nuclear holocaust in a northern seaport / by Ray Flint. — [Hull] : [Ray Flint], 1982. — vi,25p ; 21cm
ISBN 0-9507960-0-x (pbk) : £0.90 B82-19970

327.1'74'0942812 — West Yorkshire *(Metropolitan County)*. Halifax. Nuclear disarmament movements — *Serials*
Halifax Nuclear Disarmament Group. Bulletin / Halifax Nuclear Disarmament Group. — No.1 (1980)-. — [Halifax] ([c/o J. Harber, 1 Bankhouse La., Salterhebble, Halifax]) : The Group, 1980-. — v. ; 32cm
Description based on: No.7 (July 1981)
ISSN 0262-3587 = Bulletin - Halifax Nuclear Disarmament Group : Unpriced B82-10128

327.1'74'0942812 — West Yorkshire *(Metropolitan County)*. Hebden Bridge. Nuclear disarmament movements — *Serials*
Hebden Bridge European Nuclear Disarmament. Bulletin / Hebden Bridge European Nuclear Disarmament. — No.1-. — [Hebden Bridge] ([c/o The Secretary, Hebden Bridge E.N.D., 5 Eaves Mount, Hebden Bridge, West Yorkshire]) : HBEND, [1980?]-. — v. ; 30cm
Description based on: No.8
ISSN 0262-3595 = Bulletin - Hebden Bridge European Nuclear Disarmament : Unpriced B82-10127

327.1'74'0973 — United States. Arms control
Arms control and defense postures in the 1980s / edited by Richard Burt ; foreword by Robert E. Osgood. — Boulder, Colo. : Westview ; London : Croom Helm, 1982. — x,230p ; 24cm
Includes index
ISBN 0-7099-0624-2 : £15.95 B82-37777

327.2 — Capitalist countries. Foreign relations. Diplomacy
Borisov, I. B.. Modern diplomacy of capitalist powers. — Oxford : Pergamon, Dec.1982. — [396]p
Translation of: Sovremennaîa diplomatiîa burzhuaznykh gosudarstv
ISBN 0-08-028173-7 : £35.00 : CIP entry B82-40885

327.2 — Foreign relations. Diplomacy
Watson, Adam, *1914-*. Diplomacy. — London : Eyre Methuen, Mar.1982. — [256]p
ISBN 0-413-48190-5 : £8.95 : CIP entry B82-01995

327.2 — Foreign relations. Negotiations
Zartman, I. William. The practical negotiator / I. William Zartman and Maureen R. Berman. — New Haven ; London : Yale University Press, c1982. — xiii,250p ; 22cm
Bibliography: p237-243. — Includes index
ISBN 0-300-02523-8 : £14.00 : CIP rev. B82-02444

327.2'09171'241 — Commonwealth countries. Foreign relations. Diplomacy, *1966-1979*
Papadopoulos, Andrestinos N.. Multilateral diplomacy within the Commonwealth : a decade of expansion / Andrestinos N. Papadopoulos. — The Hague ; London : Nijhoff, 1982. — ix,172p ; 25cm
Bibliography: p161-163. — Includes index
ISBN 90-247-2568-2 : Unpriced B82-27294

327.2'092'4 — Belgian diplomatic service. Eeman, Harold, *1942-1958 — Biographies*
Eeman, Harold. Clouds over the sun : memories of a diplomat 1942-1958 / by Harold Eeman ; illustrated by the author. — London : Hale, 1981. — 239p : ill ; 23cm
Ill on lining papers. — Sheet containing additional text inserted on p.89
ISBN 0-7091-8981-8 : £8.75 B82-22224

327.2'092'4 — Great Britain. Foreign relations. Diplomacy. Temple, *Sir* William — *Biographies*
Faber, Richard. The brave courtier : Sir William Temple. — London : Faber, Feb.1983. — [256]p
ISBN 0-571-11982-4 : CIP entry B82-38695

327.2'092'4 — United States. Foreign relations. Kissinger, Henry A., *1973-1974 — Biographies*
Kissinger, Henry A.. Years of upheaval / Henry Kissinger. — London : Weidenfeld and Nicolson, 1982. — xxi,1283p,[40]p of plates : ill,maps,ports ; 25cm
Includes index
ISBN 0-7181-2115-5 : £15.95 B82-21342

327.3/9 — FOREIGN RELATIONS OF SPECIFIC COUNTRIES

327.41 — Great Britain. Foreign relations, *1919-1939 — Correspondence, diaries, etc*
Great Britain. *Foreign Office*. Documents on British foreign policy 1919-1939. First series. — London : H.M.S.O.
Papers from the Foreign Office archives
Vol.22: [Central Europe and the Balkans 1921 Albania 1921-2] / edited by W.N. Medlicott and Douglas Dakin assisted by Gillian Bennett. — 1980. — cxii,885p ; 25cm
ISBN 0-11-591555-9 : £45.00 B82-05642

327.41 — Great Britain. Foreign relations, *1945-1981*
Verrier, Anthony. Through the looking glass : British foreign policy in an age of illusions. — London : Cape, Feb.1983. — [400]p
ISBN 0-224-01979-1 : £12.50 : CIP entry B82-37833

327.41 — Great Britain. Foreign relations. Policies of government. Implications of Soviet invasion of Afghanistan. Great Britain. *Parliament. House of Commons. Foreign Affairs Committee.* Fifth report ... session 1979-80 — *Critical studies*
Great Britain. *Foreign and Commonwealth Office*. Fifth report from the Foreign Affairs Committee, sesion 1979/80 : Afghanistan : the Soviet invasion and its consequences for British policy : observations by the Secretary of State for Foreign and Commonwealth Affairs. — London : H.M.S.O., [1980]. — 5p ; 25cm. — (Miscellaneous ; no.23 (1980)) (Cmnd. ; 8068)
ISBN 0-10-180680-9 (unbound) : £1.10 B82-14718

327.41 — Great Britain. *Security Commission.* Reports — *Critical studies*
Statement on the recommendations of the Security Commission. — London : H.M.S.O., [1982]. — 14p ; 25cm. — (Cmnd. ; 8540)
ISBN 0-10-185400-5 (unbound) : £1.90 B82-31675

327.410417 — Great Britain. Foreign relations with Ireland *(Republic) — Inquiry reports*

Anglo-Irish joint studies : joint report and studies. — London : H.M.S.O., [1981]. — 39p ; 25cm. — (Cmnd. ; 8414)
ISBN 0-10-184140-x (unbound) : £3.05
Also classified at 327.417041 B82-11541

327.41043 — Great Britain. Foreign relations with Germany, *1858-1900.* **Role of Victoria,** *Empress, consort of Frederick III, Emperor of Germany*

Sinclair, Andrew. The other Victoria : the Princess Royal and the great game of Europe / Andrew Sinclair. — London : Weidenfeld and Nicolson, 1981. — 282p,[24]p of plates : ill,ports,2geneal.tables ; 25cm
Bibliography: p265-267. — Includes index
ISBN 0-297-77987-7 : £10.00
Also classified at 327.43041 B82-08505

327.41043 — Great Britain. Foreign relations with Germany, *1860-1914*

Kennedy, Paul M.. The rise of the Anglo-German antagonism 1860-1914 / Paul M. Kennedy. — London : Allen & Unwin, 1982. — xiv,604p ; 24cm
Originally published: 1980. — Bibliography: p550-586. — Includes index
ISBN 0-04-940064-9 (pbk) : Unpriced : CIP rev.
Also classified at 327.43041 B82-00280

327.41044 — Great Britain. Foreign relations with France, *1200-1500*

Chaplais, Pierre. Essays in medieval diplomacy and administration. — London (35 Gloucester Ave., NW1 7AX) : Hambledon Press, May 1981. — [428]p
ISBN 0-9506882-2-3 : £30.00 : CIP entry
Also classified at 327.44041 B81-07466

327.41047 — Great Britain. Foreign relations with Soviet Union, *1941-1947*

Rothwell, V. H.. Britain and the Cold War 1941-1947 / Victor Rothwell. — London : Cape, 1982. — 551p ; 22cm
Includes index
ISBN 0-224-01478-1 : £16.00 : CIP rev.
Also classified at 327.47041 B81-33977

327.41047 — Great Britain. Foreign relations with Soviet Union, *to 1981*

Northedge, F. S.. Britain and Soviet Communism : the impact of a revolution / F.S. Northedge and Audrey Wells. — London : Macmillan, 1982. — viii,280p ; 23cm
Bibliography: p249-254. — Includes index
ISBN 0-333-27192-0 (cased) : Unpriced
ISBN 0-333-27193-9 (pbk) : Unpriced
Also classified at 327.47041 B82-34915

327.4105 — Great Britain. Foreign relations with Asia, *1795-1800*

Ingram, Edward, *1940-*. Commitment to empire : prophecies of the great game in Asia 1797-1800 / by Edward Ingram. — Oxford : Clarendon, 1981. — xvi,431p : maps ; 22cm
Bibliography: p402-423. — Includes index
ISBN 0-19-822662-4 : £22.50 : CIP rev.
Also classified at 327'.095 B81-15801

327.41051 — Great Britain. Foreign relations with China, *1839-1860 — Correspondence, diaries, etc.*

Anglo-Chinese relations 1839-1860. — Oxford : Oxford University Press for the British Academy, Nov.1982. — [398]p. — (Oriental documents ; 7)
ISBN 0-19-726014-4 : CIP entry
Also classified at 327.51041 B82-33328

327.41052 — Great Britain. Foreign relations with Japan, *1919-1952 — Conference proceedings*

Anglo-Japanese Conference on the History of the Second World War *(1979 : London).*
Anglo-Japanese alienation 1919-1952 : papers of the Anglo-Japanese Conference on the History of the Second World War / edited by Ian Nish. — Cambridge : Cambridge University Press, 1982. — x,305p ; 23cm. — (International studies)
Includes index
ISBN 0-521-24061-1 : £20.00 : CIP rev.
Also classified at 327.52041 B82-14497

327.41052 — Great Britain. Foreign relations with Japan, *1945-1952*

Buckley, Roger. Occupation diplomacy : Britain, the United States and Japan, 1945-1952. — Cambridge : Cambridge University Press, Nov.1982. — [296]p. — (International studies)
ISBN 0-521-23567-7 : £22.50 : CIP entry
Also classified at 327.52041 B82-29395

327.41056 — Great Britain. Foreign relations with Ottoman Empire. Policies of government, *1908-1914*

Heller, Joseph. British policy towards the Ottoman Empire 1908-1914. — London : Cass, June 1982. — [240]p
ISBN 0-7146-3127-2 : £15.00 : CIP entry
Also classified at 327.56041 B82-09613

327.41'0561 — Great Britain. Foreign relations with Turkey, *1919-1938*

Evans, Stephen F.. The slow rapprochement. — Beverley : Eothen Press, Dec.1982. — [123]p
ISBN 0-906719-04-6 (pbk) : £4.50 : CIP entry
Also classified at 327.561'041 B82-40922

327.41071 — Great Britain. Foreign relations with Canada. Role of King, W. L. Mackenzie, *1921-1948*

Britain and Canada in the age of Mackenzie King. — [London] ([Canada House, Trafalgar Square, SW1Y 5BJ]) : [Canadian High Commission]. — (Canada House lecture series ; no.4)
Part 1: The outstanding imperialist : Mackenzie King and the British / by Norman Hillmer. — [1982]. — 13p ; 21cm
Lecture presented at Canada House, 14 November 1978. — Cover title
Unpriced (pbk)
Primary classification 327.71041 B82-26847

327.41073 — Great Britain. Foreign relations with United States, *1937-1941*

Reynolds, David. The creation of the Anglo-American Alliance, 1937-41 : a study in competitive co-operation / David Reynolds. — London : Europa, 1981. — xiii,397p ; 24cm
Bibliography: p373-390. — Includes index
ISBN 0-905118-68-5 : £20.00 : CIP rev.
Also classified at 327.73041 B81-27466

327.41073 — Great Britain. Foreign relations with United States, *1944-1947*

Hathaway, Robert M.. Ambiguous partnership : Britain and America, 1944-1947 / Robert M. Hathaway. — New York ; Guildford : Columbia University Press, 1981. — x,410p ; 24cm. — (Contemporary American history series)
Bibliography: p383-400. — Includes index
ISBN 0-231-04452-6 : £17.50
Also classified at 327.73041 B82-10654

327.417041 — Ireland *(Republic).* **Foreign relations with Great Britain** *— Inquiry reports*

Anglo-Irish joint studies : joint report and studies. — London : H.M.S.O., [1981]. — 39p ; 25cm. — (Cmnd. ; 8414)
ISBN 0-10-184140-x (unbound) : £3.05
Primary classification 327.410417 B82-11541

327.43 — Germany. Foreign relations with China & Japan, *1931-1938*

Fox, John P. (John Patrick). Germany and the Far Eastern crisis 1931-1938 : a study in diplomacy and ideology / John P. Fox. — Oxford : Clarendon, 1982. — ix,445p : 3maps ; 22cm
Bibliography: p401-419. — Includes index
ISBN 0-19-822573-3 : £20.00 : CIP rev.
Also classified at 327.51 ; 327.52 B81-34389

327.43 — West Germany. Foreign relations, *1955-1980*

The Foreign policy of West Germany : formation and contents / editors Ekkehart Krippendorf, Volker Rittberger. — London : Sage, c1980. — 372p : ill ; 22cm. — (German political studies, ISSN 0307-7233 ; v.4)
Bibliography: p271-372
ISBN 0-8039-9818-x (cased) : £12.50 : CIP rev.
ISBN 0-8039-9819-8 (pbk) : £6.00 B80-06304

327.43041 — Germany. Foreign relations with Great Britain, *1858-1900.* **Role of Victoria,** *Empress, consort of Frederick III, Emperor of Germany*

Sinclair, Andrew. The other Victoria : the Princess Royal and the great game of Europe / Andrew Sinclair. — London : Weidenfeld and Nicolson, 1981. — 282p,[24]p of plates : ill,ports,2geneal.tables ; 25cm
Bibliography: p265-267. — Includes index
ISBN 0-297-77987-7 : £10.00
Primary classification 327.41043 B82-08505

327.43041 — Germany. Foreign relations with Great Britain, *1860-1914*

Kennedy, Paul M.. The rise of the Anglo-German antagonism 1860-1914 / Paul M. Kennedy. — London : Allen & Unwin, 1982. — xiv,604p ; 24cm
Originally published: 1980. — Bibliography: p550-586. — Includes index
ISBN 0-04-940064-9 (pbk) : Unpriced : CIP rev.
Primary classification 327.41043 B82-00280

327.43047 — West Germany. Foreign relations with Soviet Union, *1955-1980*

Stent, Angela. From embargo to ostpolitik : the political economy of West German-Soviet relations, 1955-1980 / Angela Stent. — Cambridge : Cambridge University Press, 1981. — xvi,328p ; 23cm. — (Soviet and East European studies)
Bibliography: p304-315. — Includes index
ISBN 0-521-23667-3 : £22.50
Also classified at 327.47043 B82-17873

327.44 — France. Foreign policies, *1914-1919*

Stevenson, D.. French war aims against Germany 1914-1919. — Oxford : Clarendon Press, Mar.1982. — [320]p
ISBN 0-19-822574-1 : £19.50 : CIP entry
B82-01082

327.44041 — France. Foreign relations with Great Britain, *1200-1500*

Chaplais, Pierre. Essays in medieval diplomacy and administration. — London (35 Gloucester Ave., NW1 7AX) : Hambledon Press, May 1981. — [428]p
ISBN 0-9506882-2-3 : £30.00 : CIP entry
Primary classification 327.41044 B81-07466

327.44073 — France. Foreign relations with United States. Role of Napoléon I, *Emperor of the French*

Murat, Inès. Napoleon and the American dream / Inès Murat ; translated by Frances Frenaye. — Baton Rouge ; London : Louisiana State University Press, c1981. — 243p ; 24cm
Translation of: Napoléon et le rêve américain. — Bibliography: p231-237. — Includes index
ISBN 0-8071-0770-0 : £12.20
Also classified at 327.73044 B82-09774

327.45 — Italy. Foreign relations. Influence of Catholic Church, *1929-1935*

Kent, Peter C.. The Pope and the Duce : the international impact of the Lateran Agreements / Peter C. Kent. — London : Macmillan, 1981. — ix,248p,[8]p of plates : ports ; 23cm
Bibliography: p227-236. — Includes index
ISBN 0-333-27774-0 : £20.00 B82-06645

327.46 — Spain. Foreign relations, *1898-1978*

Spain in the twentieth-century world : essays on Spanish diplomacy, 1898-1978 / edited by James W. Cortada. — London : Aldwych, 1980. — xiii,294p ; 23cm
Includes index
ISBN 0-86172-005-9 : £19.50 B82-30928

327.47 — Soviet Union. Foreign relations, *1917-1980*

Lebedev, N. I.. Great October and today's world. — Oxford : Pergamon, Feb.1982. — [350]p
Translation of: Velikiĭ oktiabr'i perestroĭka mezhdunarodnykh otnosheniĭ
ISBN 0-08-023607-3 : £20.00 : CIP entry
B81-40259

327.47 — Soviet Union. Foreign relations — *Forecasts*

Walker, *Sir* Walter. The next domino? / Sir Walter Walker. — London : Corgi, 1982, c1980. — xix,364p : ill,maps ; 20cm
Originally published: London : Covenant, 1980. — Includes index
ISBN 0-552-99020-5 (pbk) : £3.95 B82-40194

327.47 — Soviet Union. Foreign relations. Policies of government

Bykov, O.. The priorities of Soviet foreign policy today / O. Bykov, V. Razmerov, D. Tomashevsky ; [translated from the Russian by Stanislav Ponomarenko]. — Moscow : Progress Publishers ; [London] : distributed by Central Books, c1981. — 213p ; 19cm
Translation of: Aktual'nye problemy vneshneĭ politiki SSSR
ISBN 0-7147-1767-3 : £2.25 B82-38237

Halliday, Fred. Threat from the East? : Soviet policy from Afghanistan and Iran to the Horn of Africa / Fred Halliday. — Rev. ed. — Harmondsworth : Penguin, 1982. — 149p ; 19cm. — (Pelican books)
Previous ed.: Washington, D.C. : Institute for Policy Studies, 1981
ISBN 0-14-022448-3 (pbk) : £1.75 B82-37613

Sen Gupta, Bhabani. The Afghan syndrome : how to live with Soviet power / Bhabani Sen Gupta. — London : Croom Helm, 1982. — x,296p ; 23cm
Includes index
ISBN 0-7099-0477-0 : £12.95 B82-37776

What about Russia? / Peace Force Scotland. — Kirkcaldy (The Lantern House, Olympia Arcade, Kirkcaldy, KY1 1QF) : Peace Force Scotland, [1982]. — [4]p : ill ; 21cm. — (Fact sheet ; 8)
Bibliography: p4
Unpriced (unbound) B82-27595

327.47 — Soviet Union. Foreign relations. Policies of government, *1917-1980*

Adomeit, Hannes. Soviet risk-taking and crisis behavior : a theoretical and empirical analysis / Hannes Adomeit. — London : Allen & Unwin, 1982. — viii,375p : ill ; 24cm. — (Studies of the Russian Institute, Columbia University)
Bibliography: p348-362. — Includes index
ISBN 0-04-335043-7 : £27.50 : CIP rev.
B82-00894

327.470171'3 — Soviet Union. Foreign relations with Western bloc countries

Roberts, *Sir* Frank, *1907-*. East-West tensions world wide : based on an address given by Sir Frank Roberts ... at a seminar held at St Edmund Hall, Oxford in August 1981 ... — Exeter (7 Cathedral Close, Exeter, Devon EX1 1EZ) : European-Atlantic Movement, [1982?]. — 12p ; 22cm
Cover title. — Bibliography: p11
Unpriced (pbk)
Also classified at 327'.09171'3 B82-35507

327.470172'4 — Soviet Union. Foreign relations with developing countries, *1917-1979*

The **Soviet** Union and the Third World / edited by E.J. Feuchtwanger and Peter Nailor. — London : Macmillan, 1981. — vi,229p : ill ; 23cm
Includes index
ISBN 0-333-28736-3 : £20.00
Also classified at 327'.09172'4 B82-06656

327.47017'7 — Soviet Union. Foreign relations with North Atlantic Treaty Organization countries

Critchley, Julian. The North Atlantic Alliance and the Soviet Union in the 1980s / Julian Critchley. — London : Macmillan, 1982. — 210p ; 23cm
Includes index
ISBN 0-333-29469-6 : £15.00
Primary classification 327'.0917'7 B82-20946

327.47041 — Soviet anti-British espionage, *1930-1965*

Boyle, Andrew. The climate of treason / Andrew Boyle. — 2nd ed. — London : Hutchinson, 1982, c1980. — 574p,[8]p of plates : ports ; 23cm
Originally published: London : Coronet, 1980. — Includes index
ISBN 0-09-143060-7 : £12.95 B82-15407

327.47041 — Soviet anti-British espionage, *1930-1965 — Personal observations*

Straight, Michael. After long silence. — London : Collins, Feb.1983. — [448]p
ISBN 0-00-217001-9 : £12.95 : CIP entry
B82-36462

327.47041 — Soviet Union. Foreign relations with Great Britain, *1941-1947*

Rothwell, V. H.. Britain and the Cold War 1941-1947 / Victor Rothwell. — London : Cape, 1982. — 551p ; 22cm
Includes index
ISBN 0-224-01478-1 : £16.00 : CIP rev.
Primary classification 327.41047 B81-33977

327.47041 — Soviet Union. Foreign relations with Great Britain, *to 1981*

Northedge, F. S.. Britain and Soviet Communism : the impact of a revolution / F.S. Northedge and Audrey Wells. — London : Macmillan, 1982. — viii,280p ; 23cm
Bibliography: p249-254. — Includes index
ISBN 0-333-27192-0 (cased) : Unpriced
ISBN 0-333-27193-9 (pbk) : Unpriced
Primary classification 327.41047 B82-34915

327.47043 — Soviet Union. Foreign relations with West Germany, *1955-1980*

Stent, Angela. From embargo to ostpolitik : the political economy of West German-Soviet relations, 1955-1980 / Angela Stent. — Cambridge : Cambridge University Press, 1981. — xvi,328p ; 23cm. — (Soviet and East European studies)
Bibliography: p304-315. — Includes index
ISBN 0-521-23667-3 : £22.50
Primary classification 327.43047 B82-17873

327.47051 — Soviet Union. Foreign relations with China

The **China** factor : Peking and the superpowers / edited by Gerald Segal. — London : Croom Helm, c1982. — 210p ; 23cm
Bibliography: p193-204. — Includes index
ISBN 0-7099-2308-2 : £12.95 : CIP rev.
Primary classification 327.51047 B81-30538

327.47051 — Soviet Union. Foreign relations with China, *1970-1979 — Conference proceedings*

The **Sino-Soviet** conflict : a global perspective / edited by Herbert J. Ellison. — Seattle ; London : University of Washington Press, c1982. — xxii,408p : 3maps ; 24cm
Includes index
ISBN 0-295-95854-5 (cased) : Unpriced
ISBN 0-295-95873-1 (pbk) : Unpriced
Also classified at 327.51047 B82-35900

327.470536 — Soviet Union. Foreign relations with Persian Gulf countries

Yodfat, Aryeh Y.. The Soviet Union and the Arabian peninsula. — London : Croom Helm, Dec.1982. — [192]p
ISBN 0-7099-2904-8 : £10.95 : CIP entry
Also classified at 327.53'6'047 B82-30810

327.47058'1 — Soviet Union. Foreign relations with Afghanistan, *1917-1980*

Maprayil, Cyriac. The Soviets and Afghanistan / by Cyriac Maprayil. — London (53 Carlingford Rd., N15) : Cosmic, 1982. — xii,165p ; 21cm
Includes index
Unpriced (pbk)
Primary classification 327.58'1'047 B82-25650

327.4706 — Soviet Union. Foreign relations with Africa, *1917-1977*

USSR and countries of Africa : (friendship, cooperation, support for the anti-imperialist struggle) / general editor E.A. Tarabrin ; [translated from the Russian by David Fidlon and Stanislav Ponomarenko]. — Moscow : Progress ; [London] : distributed by Central Books, c1980. — 319p ; 21cm
Translation of: SSSR i strany Afriki. — Includes index
ISBN 0-7147-1684-7 : £3.25
Also classified at 327'.096 B82-19611

327.47073 — Soviet Union. Foreign relations with United States

Liska, George. Russia and the road to appeasement : cycles of East-West conflict in war and peace / George Liska. — Baltimore ; London : Johns Hopkins University Press, c1982. — xv,261p ; 24cm
Bibliography: p253-254. — Includes index
ISBN 0-8018-2763-9 : Unpriced
Also classified at 327.73047 B82-36870

327.485 — Sweden. Foreign relations. Neutrality

Neutralism in action / Peace Force Scotland. — Kirkcaldy (The Lantern House, Olympia Arcade, Kirkcaldy, KY1 1QF) : Peace Force Scotland, [1982]. — [4]p : ill,1map ; 21cm. — (Fact sheet ; 9)
Bibliography: p4
Unpriced (unbound)
Also classified at 327.494 B82-27596

327.4897 — Finland. Foreign relations

Kekkonen, Urho. A president's view / Urho Kekkonen ; translated by Gregory Coogan. — London : Heinemann, 1982. — 195p : ill ; 19cm
Translation from the Finnish. — Ill on lining papers
ISBN 0-434-38631-6 : £6.95 B82-17048

327.4897 — Finland. Foreign relations, *1808-1914*

Paasivirta, Juhani. Finland and Europe : international crises in the period of autonomy 1808-1914 / by Juhani Paasivirta ; translated from the Finnish by Anthony F. Upton and Sirkka R. Upton ; edited and abridged by D.G. Kirby. — London : Hurst, 1981. — xii,270p : 1map ; 23cm
Translation of: Suomi ja Eurooppa. — Bibliography: p253-266. — Includes index
ISBN 0-905838-55-6 : £13.50 : CIP rev.
B81-30973

327.494 — Switzerland. Foreign relations. Neutrality

Neutralism in action / Peace Force Scotland. — Kirkcaldy (The Lantern House, Olympia Arcade, Kirkcaldy, KY1 1QF) : Peace Force Scotland, [1982]. — [4]p : ill,1map ; 21cm. — (Fact sheet ; 9)
Bibliography: p4
Unpriced (unbound)
Primary classification 327.485 B82-27596

327.495073 — Greece. Foreign relations with United States, *1943-1949*

Wittner, Lawrence S.. American intervention in Greece, 1943-1949 / Lawrence S. Wittner. — New York ; Guildford : Columbia University Press, 1982. — xii,445p ; 24cm. — (Contemporary American history series)
Bibliography: p409-430. — Includes index
ISBN 0-231-04196-9 : £14.40
Primary classification 327.730495 B82-28062

327.51 — China. Foreign relations, *1960-1970*

Segal, Gerald. The great power triangle / Gerald Segal. — London : Macmillan, 1982. — viii,195p : ill ; 23cm
Includes index
ISBN 0-333-31842-0 : £15.00 B82-20939

327.51 — China. Foreign relations with Germany & Japan, *1931-1938*

Fox, John P. (John Patrick). Germany and the Far Eastern crisis 1931-1938 : a study in diplomacy and ideology / John P. Fox. — Oxford : Clarendon, 1982. — ix,445p : 3maps ; 22cm
Bibliography: p401-419. — Includes index
ISBN 0-19-822573-3 : £20.00 : CIP rev.
Primary classification 327.43 B81-34389

327.51041 — China. Foreign relations with Great Britain, *1839-1860 — Correspondence, diaries, etc.*

Anglo-Chinese relations 1839-1860. — Oxford : Oxford University Press for the British Academy, Nov.1982. — [398]p. — (Oriental documents ; 7)
ISBN 0-19-726014-4 : CIP entry
Primary classification 327.41051 B82-33328

327.51047 — China. Foreign relations with Soviet Union

The **China** factor : Peking and the superpowers / edited by Gerald Segal. — London : Croom Helm, c1982. — 210p ; 23cm
Bibliography: p193-204. — Includes index
ISBN 0-7099-2308-2 : £12.95 : CIP rev.
Also classified at 327.51073 ; 327.47051 ; 327.73051 B81-30538

327.51047 — China. Foreign relations with Soviet Union, *1970-1979 — Conference proceedings*

The **Sino-Soviet** conflict : a global perspective / edited by Herbert J. Ellison. — Seattle ; London : University of Washington Press, c1982. — xxii,408p : 3maps ; 24cm
Includes index
ISBN 0-295-95854-5 (cased) : Unpriced
ISBN 0-295-95873-1 (pbk) : Unpriced
Primary classification 327.47051 B82-35900

327.51051′35 — China. Foreign relations with Nan Chao, *618-897*

Backus, Charles. The Nan-chao kingdom and Tang China's southwestern frontier / Charles Backus. — Cambridge : Cambridge University Press, 1981. — xii,224p : ill,maps ; 24cm. — (Cambridge studies in Chinese history, literature and institutions)
Bibliography: p204-218. — Includes index
ISBN 0-521-22733-x : £17.50 : CIP rev.
Also classified at 327.51′35′051 B82-01359

327.51052 — China. Foreign relations with Japan, *1949-1980*

Jain, R. K. (Rajendra Kumar). China and Japan 1949-1980 / R.K. Jain. — Thoroughly rev. and expanded 2nd ed. — Oxford : Robertson, 1981. — xxii,339p ; 23cm
Previous ed.: published as China and Japan 1949-1976. 1977. — Bibliography: p324-330. — Includes index
ISBN 0-85520-415-x : £20.00 : CIP rev.
Also classified at 327.52051 B81-20577

327.51054 — China. Foreign relations with South Asia. Policies of Chinese government, *1947-1980*

China-South Asian relations 1947-1980. — Brighton : Harvester Press, Sept.1981. — 2v.[(640;728p)]
ISBN 0-7108-0356-7 : £60.00 : CIP entry
Also classified at 327.54051 B81-21471

327.51056 — China. Foreign relations with Middle East, *1955-1975 — Case studies*

Behbehani, Hashim S. H.. China's foreign policy in the Arab world, 1955-75 : three case studies / Hashim S.H. Behbehani. — London : Kegan Paul International, 1981. — xiv,426p : 1map ; 22cm
Bibliography: p394-422. — Includes index
ISBN 0-7103-0008-5 : £25.00 : CIP rev.
Also classified at 327′.0956 B81-21479

327.51059 — China. Foreign relations with South-east Asia

Tajima, Takashi. China and South-East Asia : strategic interests and policy prospects / by Takashi Tajima. — London : International Institute for Strategic Studies, 1981. — 38p : ill ; 25cm. — (Adelphi papers, ISSN 0567-932x ; no.172)
Cover title
ISBN 0-86079-054-1 (pbk) : Unpriced
Also classified at 327′.059 B82-20706

327.51073 — China. Foreign relations with United States

The **China** factor : Peking and the superpowers / edited by Gerald Segal. — London : Croom Helm, c1982. — 210p ; 23cm
Bibliography: p193-204. — Includes index
ISBN 0-7099-2308-2 : £12.95 : CIP rev.
Primary classification 327.51047 B81-30538

The **Future** of US-China relations / edited by John Bryan Starr. — New York ; London : New York University Press, 1981. — xiii,270p ; 22cm. — (UNA-USA policy studies book series)
Includes index
ISBN 0-8147-7818-6 : £18.60
Primary classification 327.73051 B82-36368

327.51′35′051 — China. Nan Chao. Foreign relations with China, *618-897*

Backus, Charles. The Nan-chao kingdom and Tang China's southwestern frontier / Charles Backus. — Cambridge : Cambridge University Press, 1981. — xii,224p : ill,maps ; 24cm. — (Cambridge studies in Chinese history, literature and institutions)
Bibliography: p204-218. — Includes index
ISBN 0-521-22733-x : £17.50 : CIP rev.
Primary classification 327.51051′35 B82-01359

327.52 — Japan. Foreign relations with Germany & China, *1931-1938*

Fox, John P. (John Patrick). Germany and the Far Eastern crisis 1931-1938 : a study in diplomacy and ideology / John P. Fox. — Oxford : Clarendon, 1982. — ix,445p : 3maps ; 22cm
Bibliography: p401-419. — Includes index
ISBN 0-19-822573-3 : £20.00 : CIP rev.
Primary classification 327.43 B81-34389

327.52041 — Japan. Foreign relations with Great Britain, *1919-1952 — Conference proceedings*

Anglo-Japanese Conference on the History of the Second World War *(1979 : London).*
Anglo-Japanese alienation 1919-1952 : papers of the Anglo-Japanese Conference on the History of the Second World War / edited by Ian Nish. — Cambridge : Cambridge University Press, 1982. — x,305p ; 23cm. — (International studies)
Includes index
ISBN 0-521-24061-1 : £20.00 : CIP rev.
Primary classification 327.41052 B82-14497

327.52041 — Japan. Foreign relations with Great Britain, *1945-1952*

Buckley, Roger. Occupation diplomacy : Britain, the United States and Japan, 1945-1952. — Cambridge : Cambridge University Press, Nov.1982. — [296]p. — (International studies)
ISBN 0-521-23567-7 : £22.50 : CIP entry
Primary classification 327.41052 B82-29395

327.52051 — Japan. Foreign relations with China, *1949-1980*

Jain, R. K. (Rajendra Kumar). China and Japan 1949-1980 / R.K. Jain. — Thoroughly rev. and expanded 2nd ed. — Oxford : Robertson, 1981. — xxii,339p ; 23cm
Previous ed.: published as China and Japan 1949-1976. 1977. — Bibliography: p324-330. — Includes index
ISBN 0-85520-415-x : £20.00 : CIP rev.
Primary classification 327.51052 B81-20577

327.53′6′047 — Persian Gulf countries. Foreign relations with Soviet Union

Yodfat, Aryeh Y.. The Soviet Union and the Arabian peninsula. — London : Croom Helm, Dec.1982. — [192]p
ISBN 0-7099-2904-8 : £10.95 : CIP entry
Primary classification 327.470536 B82-30810

327.54 — India *(Republic).* **Foreign relations,** *1947-1974*

Appadorai, A.. The domestic roots of India's foreign policy 1947-1972 / A. Appadorai. — Delhi ; Oxford : Oxford University Press, 1981. — viii,244p ; 23cm
Includes index
ISBN 0-19-561144-6 : £7.75 B82-31501

327.54051 — South Asia. Foreign relations with China. Policies of Chinese government, *1947-1980*

China-South Asian relations 1947-1980. — Brighton : Harvester Press, Sept.1981. — 2v.[(640;728p)]
ISBN 0-7108-0356-7 : £60.00 : CIP entry
Primary classification 327.51054 B81-21471

327.55073 — Iran. Foreign relations with United States, *1941-1980*

Rubin, Barry. Paved with good intentions : the American experience in Iran / Barry Rubin. — Harmondsworth : Penguin, 1981, c1980. — xii,426p,[8]p of plates : ill,ports ; 20cm
Originally published: Oxford : Oxford University Press, 1980. — Bibliography: p402-416. — Includes index
ISBN 0-14-005964-4 (pbk) : £1.95
Also classified at 327.73055 B82-18146

327.56041 — Ottoman Empire. Foreign relations with Great Britain. Policies of government, *1908-1914*

Heller, Joseph. British policy towards the Ottoman Empire 1908-1914. — London : Cass, June 1982. — [240]p
ISBN 0-7146-3127-2 : £15.00 : CIP entry
Primary classification 327.41056 B82-09613

327.561′041 — Turkey. Foreign relations with Great Britain, *1919-1938*

Evans, Stephen F.. The slow rapprochement. — Beverley : Eothen Press, Dec.1982. — [123]p
ISBN 0-906719-04-6 (pbk) : £4.50 : CIP entry
Primary classification 327.41′0561 B82-40922

327.5694017′4927 — Israel. Foreign relations with Arab countries

Rodinson, Maxime. Israel and the Arabs / Maxime Rodinson ; translated by Michael Perl and Brian Pearce. — 2nd ed. — [Harmondsworth] : Penguin, 1982. — 364p ; 20cm. — (Pelican books)
Translated from the French. — Previous ed.: 1968. — Includes index
ISBN 0-14-022445-9 (pbk) : £3.50
Also classified at 327′.0917′4927 B82-37608

327.5694017′4927 — Israel. Foreign relations with Arab countries, *1964-1971 — Personal observations*

Riad, Mahmoud. The struggle for peace in the Middle East / Mahmoud Riad. — London : Quartet, 1981. — 365p,[9]p of plates : 1map,ports ; 24cm
Includes index
ISBN 0-7043-2297-8 : £11.95 : CIP rev.
Primary classification 327′.0917′4927 B81-25709

327.5694073 — Israel. Foreign relations with United States, *to 1981*

Glick, Edward Bernard. The triangular connection : America, Israel and American Jews / Edward Bernard Glick. — London : Allen & Unwin, 1982. — 174p ; 23cm
Bibliography: p166-170. — Includes index
ISBN 0-04-353008-7 : £12.50 : CIP rev.
Primary classification 327.7305694 B82-15633

327.58′1′047 — Afghanistan. Foreign relations with Soviet Union, *1917-1980*

Maprayil, Cyriac. The Soviets and Afghanistan / by Cyriac Maprayil. — London (53 Carlingford Rd., N15) : Cosmic, 1982. — xii,165p ; 21cm
Includes index
Unpriced (pbk)
Also classified at 327.47058′1 B82-25650

327.65 — Algeria. Foreign relations, *1962-1978 — German texts*

Lauff, Rudolf J.. Die Außenpolitik Algeriens 1962-1978 : Phasen und Bezugsfelder / von Rudolf J. Lauff. — München ; London : Weltforum Verlag, c1981. — iv,227p ; 21cm. — (Afrika-Studien ; nr.107)
German text. — At head of title: IFO-Institut für Wirtschaftsforschung Abteilung Entwicklungsländer. — Bibliography: p221-227
ISBN 3-8039-0198-7 : Unpriced B82-12222

327.680171′3 — South Africa. Foreign relations with Western bloc countries

Barber, James, *1931-.* The West and South Africa / James Barber, Jesmond Blumenfeld and Christopher R. Hill. — London : Royal Institute of International Affairs : Routledge and Kegan Paul, 1982. — 106p ; 22cm. — (Chatham House papers, ISSN 0143-5795 ; 14)
ISBN 0-7100-9232-6 (pbk) : £3.95 : CIP rev.
Primary classification 327′.09171′3 B82-11260

327.68073 — South Africa. Foreign relations with United States

Study Commission on U.S. Policy Toward Southern Africa. South Africa : time running out / the report of the Study Commission on U.S. Policy Toward Southern Africa. — Berkeley ; London : University of California Press, c1981. — xxvii,517p,[24]p of plates : ill,col.maps,ports ; 24cm
Bibliography: p479-490. — Includes index
ISBN 0-520-04594-7 (corrected : cased) : Unpriced
ISBN 0-520-04547-5 (pbk) : Unpriced
Primary classification 968.06′3 B82-17876

327.71 — Canada. Foreign relations — *History*
Stacey, C. P.. Canada and the age of conflict : a history of Canadian external policies / C.P. Stacey. — Toronto ; London : University of Toronto Press
Vol.2: 1921-1948, the Mackenzie King era. — c1981. — x,491p : ill,ports ; 24cm
Includes index
ISBN 0-8020-2397-5 (cased) : £21.00
ISBN 0-8020-6420-5 (pbk) : Unpriced
B82-06992

327.71041 — Canada. Foreign relations with Great Britain. Role of King, W. L. Mackenzie, *1921-1948*
Britain and Canada in the age of Mackenzie King. — [London] ([Canada House, Trafalgar Square, SW1Y 5BJ]) : [Canadian High Commission]. — (Canada House lecture series ; no.4)
Part 1: The outstanding imperialist : Mackenzie King and the British / by Norman Hillmer. — [1982]. — 13p ; 21cm
Lecture presented at Canada House, 14 November 1978. — Cover title
Unpriced (pbk)
Also classified at 327.41071 B82-26847

327.73 — United States. Foreign relations, *1945-1981*
Gaddis, John Lewis. Strategies of containment : a critical appraisal of postwar American national security policy / John Lewis Gaddis. — New York ; Oxford : Oxford University Press, 1982. — xi,432p ; 24cm
Bibliography: p411-422. — Includes index
ISBN 0-19-502944-5 : £16.50 B82-26516

327.73 — United States. Foreign relations. Influence of international law, *1945-1980*
Perkins, John A.. The prudent peace : law as foreign policy / John A. Perkins. — Chicago ; London : University of Chicago Press, 1981. — xvi,246p ; 24cm
Bibliography: p229-239. — Includes index
ISBN 0-226-65873-2 : £16.80 B82-09671

327.73 — United States. Foreign relations. Policies of government, *1970-1980*
Chomsky, Noam. Towards a new Cold War : essays on the current crisis and how we got there / Noam Chomsky. — London : Sinclair Browne, 1982. — 498p ; 25cm
Includes index
ISBN 0-86300-019-3 (cased) : £12.95 : CIP rev.
ISBN 0-86300-020-7 (pbk) : £5.95 B82-10258

327.73 — United States. Foreign relations. Policies of government, *1981*
Van Slyck, Philip. Strategies for the 1980s : lessons of Cuba, Vietnam, and Afghanistan / Philip van Slyck ; foreword Daniel P. Moynihan. — Oxford : Clio Press, 1981. — xvi,108p ; 22cm. — (A Freedom House Book)
Bibliography: p101-102. — Includes index
ISBN 0-903450-57-7 : £10.95 B82-02738

327.73 — United States. Foreign relations. Policies of government. Decision making
Spanier, John. Foreign policy and the democratic dilemmas / John Spanier, Eric M. Uslaner. — 3rd ed. — New York ; London : Holt, Rinehart and Winston, c1982. — xi,264p ; 24cm
Previous ed.: published as How American foreign policy is made. 1978. — Bibliography: p253-255. — Includes index
ISBN 0-03-060141-x (pbk) : £9.95 B82-15339

327.73 — United States. Foreign relations. Policies of government. Formulation
Bloomfield, Lincoln P.. The foreign policy process : a modern primer / Lincoln P. Bloomfield. — Englewood Cliffs ; London : Prentice-Hall, c1982. — xv,237p : ill ; 23cm
Bibliography: p223-228. — Includes index
ISBN 0-13-326504-8 (pbk) : £7.45 B82-20052

327.73 — United States. National security. Policies of government
International Institute for Strategic Studies. *Conference (23rd : 1981 : Williamsburg).* America's security in the 1980s / IISS annual conference papers. — London : International Institute for Strategic Studies, 1982. — 2pts. : 1ill ; 25cm. — (Adelphi papers, ISSN 0567-932x ; nos.173-174)
ISBN 0-86079-058-4 (pbk) : Unpriced
ISBN 0-86079-059-2 (pt.2) : £2.50 B82-40441

Jordan, Amos A.. American national security : policy and process / Amos A. Jordan, William J. Taylor, Jr. and associates. — Baltimore ; London : Johns Hopkins University Press, c1981. — xiv,604p : ill,maps ; 24cm
Includes bibliographies and index
ISBN 0-8018-2640-3 (cased) : £21.00
ISBN 0-8018-2641-1 (pbk) : Unpriced
B82-06983

327.73'0092'4 — United States. Foreign relations. Role of Roosevelt, Theodore, *1901-1909*
Marks, Frederick W.. Velvet on iron : the diplomacy of Theodore Roosevelt / Frederick W. Marks III. — Lincoln, Neb. ; London : University of Nebraska Press, c1979 (1982 [printing]). — xiv,247p ; 21cm
Bibliography: p213-240. — Includes index
ISBN 0-8032-8115-3 (pbk) : Unpriced
B82-38137

327.730182'1 — United States. Foreign relations with Caribbean countries, *to 1980*
Perkins, Whitney T.. Constraint of empire : the United States and Caribbean interventions / Whitney T. Perkins. — Oxford : Clio, 1981. — xv,282p ; 24cm
Bibliography: p268-274. — Includes index
ISBN 0-903450-52-6 : £21.75
Also classified at 327'.09182'1 B82-27401

327.730182'1 — United States. Foreign relations with Caribbean countries, *to 1981 — For Caribbean students*
Stewart, Rosemarie. The United States and the Caribbean. — London : Heinemann Educational, Aug.1982. — [64]p. — (Heinemann CXC history)
ISBN 0-435-98230-3 (pbk) : £1.00 : CIP entry
Also classified at 327'.09182'1 B82-19660

327.7304 — United States. Foreign relations with Europe. Diplomacy, *1919-1941*
U.S. diplomats in Europe, 1919-1941 / edited by Kenneth Paul Jones ; foreword by Alexander DeConde. — Santa Barbara ; Oxford : ABC-Clio, c1981. — xxiii,240p : 2maps,ports ; 24cm
Bibliography: p225-229. — Includes index
ISBN 0-87436-311-x : £22.95
Also classified at 327'.094 B82-02742

327.7304 — United States. Foreign relations with Europe. Policies of government, *1937-1939*
Graebner, Norman A.. Roosevelt and the search for a European policy 1937-1939 : an inaugural lecture delivered before the University of Oxford on 21 May 1979 / by Norman A. Graebner. — Oxford : Clarendon, 1980. — 47p ; 22cm
ISBN 0-19-951524-7 (pbk) : £1.95 : CIP rev.
Also classified at 327'.094 B80-13243

327.7304 — United States. Foreign relations with European Community — *Conference proceedings*
The **United** States and the European Community : new administrations and continuing problems : papers presented at a conference held at Cumberland Lodge, Windsor Great Park, on 5th and 6th of May 1981 and organised by the University Association for Contemporary European Studies in conjunction with the United States Mission to the European Community / edited by Michael Smith. — London : University Association for Contemporary European Studies, c1981. — iv,65p : ill ; 22cm
ISBN 0-906384-05-2 (pbk) : £1.80
Primary classification 327'.094 B82-20097

327.7304 — United States. Foreign relations with Western Europe, *1945-1977*
Grosser, Alfred. The Western alliance : European-American relations since 1945 / Alfred Grosser ; translated by Michael Shaw ; with a foreword by Stanley Hoffmann. — London : Macmillan, 1980. — xxiv,375p ; 23cm
Translation of: Les Occidentaux. — Includes index
ISBN 0-333-29271-5 (cased) : £12.50 : CIP rev.
ISBN 0-333-29259-6 (pbk) : £3.95
Primary classification 327'.094 B80-18182

327.73041 — United States. Foreign relations with Great Britain, *1937-1941*
Reynolds, David. The creation of the Anglo-American Alliance, 1937-41 : a study in competitive co-operation / David Reynolds. — London : Europa, 1981. — xiii,397p ; 24cm
Bibliography: p373-390. — Includes index
ISBN 0-905118-68-5 : £20.00 : CIP rev.
Primary classification 327.41073 B81-27466

327.73041 — United States. Foreign relations with Great Britain, *1944-1947*
Hathaway, Robert M.. Ambiguous partnership : Britain and America, 1944-1947 / Robert M. Hathaway. — New York ; Guildford : Columbia University Press, 1981. — x,410p ; 24cm. — (Contemporary American history series)
Bibliography: p383-400. — Includes index
ISBN 0-231-04452-6 : £17.50
Primary classification 327.41073 B82-10654

327.73044 — United States. Foreign relations with France. Role of Napoléon I, *Emperor of the French*
Murat, Inès. Napoleon and the American dream / Inès Murat ; translated by Frances Frenaye. — Baton Rouge ; London : Louisiana State University Press, c1981. — 243p ; 24cm
Translation of: Napoléon et le rêve américain. — Bibliography: p231-237. — Includes index
ISBN 0-8071-0770-0 : £12.20
Primary classification 327.44073 B82-09774

327.73047 — United States. Foreign relations with Soviet Union
Liska, George. Russia and the road to appeasement : cycles of East-West conflict in war and peace / George Liska. — Baltimore ; London : Johns Hopkins University Press, c1982. — xv,261p ; 24cm
Bibliography: p253-254. — Includes index
ISBN 0-8018-2763-9 : Unpriced
Primary classification 327.47073 B82-36870

327.730495 — United States. Foreign relations with Greece, *1943-1949*
Wittner, Lawrence S.. American intervention in Greece, 1943-1949 / Lawrence S. Wittner. — New York ; Guildford : Columbia University Press, 1982. — xii,445p ; 24cm. — (Contemporary American history series)
Bibliography: p409-430. — Includes index
ISBN 0-231-04196-9 : £14.40
Also classified at 327.495073 B82-28062

327.73051 — United States. Foreign relations with China
The **China** factor : Peking and the superpowers / edited by Gerald Segal. — London : Croom Helm, c1982. — 210p ; 23cm
Bibliography: p193-204. — Includes index
ISBN 0-7099-2308-2 : £12.95 : CIP rev.
Primary classification 327.51047 B81-30538

The **Future** of US-China relations / edited by John Bryan Starr. — New York ; London : New York University Press, 1981. — xiii,270p ; 22cm. — (UNA-USA policy studies book series)
Includes index
ISBN 0-8147-7818-6 : £18.60
Also classified at 327.51073 B82-36368

327.73055 — United States. Foreign relations with Iran, *1941-1980*
Rubin, Barry. Paved with good intentions : the American experience in Iran / Barry Rubin. — Harmondsworth : Penguin, 1981, c1980. — xii,426p,[8]p of plates : ill,ports ; 20cm
Originally published: Oxford : Oxford University Press, 1980. — Bibliography: p402-416. — Includes index
ISBN 0-14-005964-4 (pbk) : £1.95
Primary classification 327.55073 B82-18146

327.7305694 — United States. Foreign relations with Israel, *to 1981*
Glick, Edward Bernard. The triangular connection : America, Israel and American Jews / Edward Bernard Glick. — London : Allen & Unwin, 1982. — 174p ; 23cm
Bibliography: p166-170. — Includes index
ISBN 0-04-353008-7 : £12.50 : CIP rev.
Also classified at 327.5694073 B82-15633

327.73068 — United States. Foreign relations with South Africa
Study Commission on U.S. Policy Toward Southern Africa. South Africa : time running out / the report of the Study Commission on U.S. Policy Toward Southern Africa. — Berkeley ; London : University of California Press, c1981. — xxvii,517p,[24]p of plates : ill,col.maps,ports ; 24cm
Bibliography: p479-490. — Includes index
ISBN 0-520-04594-7 (corrected : cased) : Unpriced
ISBN 0-520-04547-5 (pbk) : Unpriced
Primary classification 968.06'3 B82-17876

327.7308 — United States. Foreign relations with Latin America. Policies of United States government. Influence of human rights movements, *1960-1980*
Schoultz, Lars. Human rights and United States policy toward Latin America / Lars Schoultz. — Princeton ; Guildford : Princeton University Press, c1981. — xvii,421p ; 25cm
Bibliography: p381-405. — Includes index
ISBN 0-691-07630-8 (cased) : £22.80
ISBN 0-691-02204-6 (pbk) : Unpriced
Also classified at 327'.098 B82-13308

327.94 — Australia. Foreign relations
Phillips, Dennis. Cold war 2 and Australia. — London : Allen and Unwin, Feb.1983. — [144]p
ISBN 0-86861-133-6 : £12.50 : CIP entry
B82-36310

328 — LEGISLATURES, PARLIAMENTS

328'.2 — Scotland. Elected assemblies. Devolution of powers of British government. Referendums
The **Referendum** experience, Scotland 1979. — Aberdeen : Aberdeen University Press, Oct.1981. — [224]p
ISBN 0-08-025734-8 : £11.00 : CIP entry
B81-24601

328'.2 — Wales. Elected assemblies. Devolution of powers of British government. Referendums, *1979*
Cledwyn of Penrhos, Cledwyn Hughes, *Baron*. The referendum : the end of an era : a lecture delivered to the Guild of Graduates of the University of Wales at the Lliw Valley National Eisteddfod, 1980 / by the Lord Cledwyn. — Cardiff : University of Wales Press, 1981. — 14,14p ; 21cm
Includes the text in Welsh, printed tête-bêche, under the title Y refferendwm
ISBN 0-7083-0808-2 (pbk) : Unpriced : CIP rev. B81-34302

The **Welsh** veto. — Cardiff : University of Wales Press, Dec.1982. — [268]p
ISBN 0-7083-0831-7 : £8.95 : CIP entry
B82-30830

328'.3'091717 — Communist countries. Legislatures — *Comparative studies*
Communist legislatures in comparative perspective / edited by Daniel Nelson and Stephen White. — London : Macmillan, 1982. — 201p ; 22cm
Includes bibliographies and index
ISBN 0-333-31938-9 : Unpriced B82-28653

328'.3'094 — Europe. Legislatures. Names — *Lists* — *For cataloguing*
List of uniform headings for higher legislative and ministerial bodies in European countries / compiled by the USSR Cataloguing Committee. — 2nd ed. rev. — London : IFLA International Office for UBC, 1979. — x,53p ; 30cm
English introduction, text in various languages. — Previous ed.: London : IFLA Committee on Cataloguing, 1975. — Includes index
ISBN 0-903043-23-8 (pbk) : £8.00 : CIP rev.
Primary classification 351.004'094 B79-34030

328'.3'096 — Africa. Legislatures. Names — *Lists* — *For cataloguing*
African legislative and ministerial bodies : list of Uniform headings for higher legislative and ministerial bodies in African countries / compiled by the IFLA International Office for UBC in association with the African Standing Conference on Bibliographic Control. — London : The Office, 1980. — viii,37p ; 30cm
English and French text with one chapter in parallel French and Kirundi. — Includes index
ISBN 0-903043-25-4 (pbk) : £6.00 : CIP rev.
Primary classification 351.004'096 B80-12296

328.41 — Great Britain. *Parliament*
The **British** Parliament / [prepared by Reference Division, Central Office of Information]. — 11th ed. — London : H.M.S.O., 1980. — 61p : 2plans ; 21cm
Previous ed.: 1975. — Bibliography: p60-61
ISBN 0-11-701006-5 (pbk) : £3.60 B82-16060

328.41 — Great Britain. *Parliament.* **Public information services. Provision,** *to 1979*
Bond, Maurice. The development of public information services at Westminster / by M.F. Bond. — London : Information Office, House of Lords, 1979. — 20p ; 21cm. — (House of Lords factsheets ; no.5)
Originally published: in The Table, v.47(1979)
Unpriced (pbk) B82-21925

328.41'04 — Great Britain. Government. Policies. Queen's Speech — *Texts*
Great Britain. *Sovereign (1952- : Elizabeth II).* Her Majesty's most gracious speech to both Houses of Parliament : delivered on Wednesday, 4th November 1981. — London : H.M.S.O., [1981]. — 3p ; 25cm
ISBN 0-10-499982-9 (unbound) : £0.70
B82-06334

328.41'05 — Great Britain. *Parliament.* **Debates. Procedure** — *For schools*
Debates : how parliament discusses things. — [London] : [Public Information Office, House of Commons], [1980]. — 11p : ill,plans ; 30cm. — (Education sheets ; 2)
Unpriced (unbound) B82-00066

328.41'05 — Great Britain. *Parliament. House of Commons.* **Procedure**
Marshall, Edmund. Parliament and the public / Edmund Marshall. — London : Macmillan, 1982. — xi,142p : 2facsims,1plan ; 23cm
Bibliography: p139. — Includes index
ISBN 0-333-31480-8 : £15.00 B82-28396

328.41'05 — Great Britain. *Parliament.* **State opening**
The **State** opening of Parliament / [compiled by Maurice Bond on behalf of the House of Lords Information Office]. — London : House of Lords Information Office, 1980. — 11p : 1plan ; 30cm. — (House of Lords factsheets ; no.6)
Unpriced (pbk) B82-21355

328.41'071 — Great Britain. *Parliament. House of Lords*
Baldwin, Nicholas. The House of Lords : its constitution and functions / Nicholas Baldwin. — [Exeter] : [Exeter Research Group], 1982. — 26p ; 21cm. — (Discussion paper / Exeter Research Group, ISSN 0143-6716 ; 9)
Cover title
ISBN 0-907021-04-2 (pbk) : Unpriced
B82-28899

The **House** of Lords : general information / [prepared by David Beamish on behalf of the House of Lords Information Office]. — [4th ed.]. — London : House of Lords Information Office, 1980. — 10p ; 30cm. — (House of Lords factsheets ; no.4)
Previous ed.: 1978. — Bibliography: p8-9
Unpriced (pbk) B82-21354

328.41'071 — Great Britain. *Parliament. House of Lords.* **Reform**
Scottish Young Conservatives. House of Lords reform. — Edinburgh (11 Atholl Crescent, Edinburgh EH3 8HG) : Scottish Young Conservatives, 1981. — 10p ; 30cm
Unpriced (unbound) B82-31780

328.41'071 — Great Britain. *Parliament. House of Lords.* **Reform,** *1850-1970*
House of Lords reform: 1850-1970 / [prepared by Francis Hawkings on behalf of the House of Lords Information Office]. — 2nd ed. — London : House of Lords Information Office, 1979. — 7p ; 30cm. — (House of Lords factsheets ; no.1)
Cover title. — Previous ed.: 1978. — Bibliography: p6-7
Unpriced (pbk) B82-21353

328.41'072'0207 — Great Britain. *Parliament. House of Commons* — *Humour*
Hoggart, Simon. Back on the House. — London : Robson, Nov.1982. — [160]p
ISBN 0-86051-194-4 : £4.95 : CIP entry
B82-26345

Hoggart, Simon. On the house / Simon Hoggart ; illustrated by John Jensen. — London : Robson, 1981. — 155p : ill ; 22cm
ISBN 0-86051-158-8 : £4.95 : CIP rev.
B81-27452

328.41'073 — Great Britain. *Parliament. House of Commons.* **Members**
Mitchell, Austin. Westminster man. — London : Thames Methuen, Oct.1982. — [176]p
ISBN 0-423-00380-1 : £6.95 : CIP entry
B82-24024

328.41'073 — Great Britain. *Parliament. House of Commons.* **Members** — *For children*
Bowler, Jane Elizabeth. A day with an M.P. / Jane Elizabeth Bowler and Julian Roup. — Hove : Wayland, 1981. — 55p : ill,ports ; 23cm. — (A day in the life)
Bibliography: p55
ISBN 0-85340-951-x : £3.25 B82-16424

328.41'073 — Great Britain. *Parliament. House of Commons.* **Members. Role,** *1945-1981*
Rose, Richard, *1933-*. British MPs : a bite as well as a bark? / by Richard Rose. — Glasgow (McCance Building, 16 Richmond St., Glasgow, G1 1XQ) : Centre for the Study of Public Policy, University of Strathclyde, 1982. — 40p ; 30cm. — (Studies in public policy, ISSN 0140-8240 ; no.98)
Unpriced (pbk) B82-39728

328.41'073 — Great Britain. *Parliament. House of Lords.* **Members** — *Lists*
Great Britain. *Parliament. House of Lords.* Roll of the Lords spiritual and temporal. — London : H.M.S.O., 1981. — 52p ; 25cm
Includes index
ISBN 0-10-400182-8 (unbound) : £3.80
B82-11386

328.41'0731 — Great Britain. *Parliament. House of Commons.* **Private members. Interests**
Judge, David. Backbench specialisation in the House of Commons / David Judge. — London : Heinemann Educational, 1981. — vii,243p ; 23cm
Bibliography: p221-232. — Includes index
ISBN 0-435-83450-9 : £16.50 : CIP rev.
B81-27958

328.41'0734 — Wales. Parliamentary representation, *1800-1979*
James, Arnold J.. Wales at Westminster : a history of the parliamentary representation of Wales 1800-1979 / Arnold J. James, John E. Thomas. — Llandysul : Gomer, 1981. — xv,284p,[8]leaves of plates : col.maps ; 22cm
Bibliography: p283-284
ISBN 0-85088-684-8 : £9.75 B82-10277

328.41'07657 — Great Britain. Select committees. Performance, *1979-1980*
Davies, Anne, *19---*. Reformed select committees : the first years / Anne Davies. — London (4 Cambridge Terrace NW1 4JL) : Outer Circle Policy Unit, 1980. — 66,xip ; 30cm
Bibliography: pviii-xi
£2.50 (spiral) B82-17622

328.41'07658 — Great Britain. *Parliament. House of Lords. Select Committee on the European Communities*
The **House** of Lords and the European Communities / [prepared by Jeremy Maule with members of the Overseas and European Office on behalf of the House of Lords Information Office]. — 3rd ed. — London : House of Lords Information Office, 1979. — 12p ; 30cm. — (House of Lords factsheets ; no.2)
Previous ed.: 1978. — Bibliography: p10-12
Unpriced (pbk) B82-21352

328.41'077 — Great Britain. Legislation

Miers, David R.. Legislation. — London : Sweet and Maxwell, Nov.1982. — [200]p
ISBN 0-421-27110-8 (cased) : £19.25 : CIP entry
ISBN 0-421-27120-5 (pbk) : £11.50
B82-27529

328.41'078 — Great Britain. *Parliament. House of Commons.* Members. Lobbying by public — *Manuals*

Lobbying your member of Parliament / Educational Centres Association. — London (Chequer St., Bunhill Row, EC1Y 8PL) : ECA, [1982]. — [3]p ; 21cm. — (ECA advisory leaflet ; no.8)
Unpriced (unbound) B82-39512

328.416'0734 — Northern Ireland. Parliamentary representation

Northern Ireland representation at Westminster / [The Electoral Reform Society]. — London (6, Chancel St, SE1 0UX) : The Society, 1979. — 9p : 1map ; 30cm. — (ERS ; 111)
Unpriced (unbound) B82-05877

328.42'071'09 — England and Wales. *Parliament. House of Lords, 1547-1558*

Graves, Michael A. R.. The House of Lords in the Parliaments of Edward VI and Mary I : an institutional study / Michael A.R. Graves. — Cambridge : Cambridge University Press, 1981. — viii,321p ; 23cm
Bibliography: p294-299. — Includes index
ISBN 0-521-23678-9 : £22.50 : CIP rev.
B81-34007

328.42'072 — England and Wales. *Parliament. House of Commons, 1642 — Correspondence, diaries, etc.*

The **Private** journals of the Long Parliament : 3 January to 5 March 1642 / edited by Willson H. Coates, Anne Steele Young, Vernon F. Snow. — New Haven ; London : Yale University Press, c1982. — xxxix,581p : ill ; 24cm
Includes index
ISBN 0-300-02545-9 : Unpriced : CIP rev.
B82-13476

328.42'073 — England. Local authorities. Councillors. Conduct

Danger zones for councillors / by Michael Holdsworth and others ; edited by Geoffrey Smith and Crispin Derby from articles first printed in Local government chronicle. — London : BKT Publications, [1981?]. — 32p ; 21cm
ISBN 0-904677-17-6 (pbk) : £3.50 B82-11239

328.42'073'0922 — England and Wales. *Parliament. House of Commons.* Members, *1558-1603 — Biographies*

The **House** of Commons 1558-1603 / [edited by] P.W. Hasler. — London : Published for the History of Parliament Trust by H.M.S.O., 1981. — 2v. : maps ; 25cm. — (The History of Parliament)
Three maps (folded leaves) in pocket. — Includes index
ISBN 0-11-887501-9 : £95.00 B82-13788

328.42'09 — England and Wales. *Parliament, 1621-1629*

Russell, Conrad. Parliaments and English politics 1621-1629 / by Conrad Russell. — Oxford : Clarendon, 1979 (1982 [printing]). — xxi,453p ; 22cm
Includes index
ISBN 0-19-822691-8 (pbk) : £9.95 : CIP rev.
B82-00193

328.42'09 — England. Parliaments, *ca 1377-ca 1465*

Roskell, J. S.. Parliament and politics in late medieval England. — London (35 Gloucester Ave., NW1 7AX) : Hambledon Press, Dec.1981. — (History series ; 7)
Vol.1. — 1v.
ISBN 0-9506882-8-2 : £18.00 : CIP entry
ISBN 0-9506882-7-4 (set) : £40.00 B81-31523

Roskell, J. S.. Parliament and politics in late medieval England. — London (35 Gloucester Ave., NW1 7AX) : Hambledon Press, Dec.1981. — (History series ; 8)
Vol.2. — [370]p
ISBN 0-9506882-9-0 : £22.00 : CIP entry
ISBN 0-9506882-7-4 (set) : £40.00 B81-31522

328.425'4'005 — Leicestershire. *County Council — Serials*

Leicestershire. *County Council*. Annual report / Leicestershire County Council. — 1980/81-. — [Leicester] ([County Hall, Glenfield, Leicester LE3 8RA]) : [The Council], [1981]-. — v. : ill ; 30cm
ISSN 0263-3000 = Annual report - Leicestershire County Council : £2.00
B82-22662

328.425'74'005 — Oxford. *City Council — Serials*

Oxford. *City Council*. Annual report / City of Oxford. — 1980-81-. — Oxford (City Treasurer, [City Chambers] Queen St., Oxford [OX1 1EN]) : [Oxford City Council], [1981]-. — v. ; 30cm
ISSN 0262-5431 = Annual report - City of Oxford : £1.00 B82-05226

328.73'073 — United States. *Congress. Senate.* Republican Party *(United States)* members, *1861-1865*

Bogue, Allan G.. The earnest men : Republicans of the Civil War Senate / Allan G. Bogue. — Ithaca ; London : Cornell University Press, c1981. — 369p : ill ; 24cm
Includes index
ISBN 0-8014-1357-5 : Unpriced B82-16922

328.73'0775 — United States. *Congress. House of Representatives.* Members. Voting behaviour. Econometric models

Kau, James B.. Congressmen, constituents and contributors : determinants of roll call voting in the House of Representatives / James B. Kau, Paul H. Rubin with contributions from R. Carter Hill, Donald C. Keenan. — Boston [Mass.] ; London : Martinus Nijhoff, c1982. — ix,160p ; 24cm. — (Studies in public choice)
Bibliography: p145-150. — Includes index
ISBN 0-89838-070-7 : Unpriced B82-10553

330 — ECONOMICS

330 — Applied economics

Seddon, Edmund. Applied economics / Edmund Seddon, J.D.S. Appleton. — 3rd ed. — Plymouth : Macdonald & Evans, 1981. — xii,372p : ill ; 18cm. — (The M & E handbook series)
Previous ed.: 1978. — Bibliography: p352-356. — Includes index
ISBN 0-7121-0177-2 (pbk) : £4.25 B82-07280

330 — Capitalist societies

Miliband, Ralph. The state in capitalist society. — London : Quartet Books, Mar.1982. — [262]p
Originally published: London : Weidenfeld and Nicolson, 1969
ISBN 0-7043-3082-2 (pbk) : £2.50 : CIP entry
B82-02644

330 — Economics

Aboyade, Ojetunji. Integrated economics. — London : Addison-Wesley, Jan.1983. — [512]p
ISBN 0-201-14068-3 (cased) : £16.50 : CIP entry
ISBN 0-201-14067-5 (pbk) : £9.50 B82-33493

al-Qadhdhāfī, Mu'ammar. The green book / Muammar al-Qadhafi. — London : Martin Brian & O'Keeffe
Pt.1: The solution of the problem of democracy : 'the authority of the people'. — 1976. — 32,48p : ill ; 19cm
Added t.p. in Arabic. — English and Arabic text
ISBN 0-85616-410-0 (pbk) : Unpriced
Primary classification 320 B82-21787

Cairncross, *Sir* Alec. Introduction to economics. — 6th ed. / Sir Alec Cairncross and Peter Sinclair. — London : Butterworths, 1982. — x,466p : ill ; 25cm
Previous ed.: 1973. — Includes index
ISBN 0-408-71056-x : Unpriced : CIP rev.
ISBN 0-408-71055-1 (pbk) : Unpriced
B81-31717

Galbraith, John Kenneth. The Galbraith reader : from the works of John Kenneth Galbraith / selected and arranged with a commentary by the editors of Gambit. — Harmondsworth : Penguin, 1980, c1977. — xvi,523p ; 18cm. — (Pelican books)
Originally published: Ipswich, Mass. : Gambit, 1977 ; London : Deutsch, 1979. — Includes index
ISBN 0-14-022174-3 (pbk) : £2.95 B82-16948

Goodwin, R. M.. Essays in economic dynamics / R.M. Goodwin. — London : Macmillan, 1982. — xi,220p : ill ; 23cm
Includes index
ISBN 0-333-29094-1 : £20.00 B82-38776

Gwartney, James D.. Essentials of economics / James D. Gwartney, Richard Stroup, J.R. Clark. — New York ; London : Academic Press, c1982. — xv,436p : ill,ports ; 25cm
Bibliography: p431-436. — Includes index
ISBN 0-12-311030-0 (pbk) : £10.00
B82-29968

Hardwick, Philip. An introduction to modern economics / Philip Hardwick, Bahadur Khan, John Langmead. — London : Longman, 1982. — xiii,498p : ill ; 25cm
Includes index
ISBN 0-582-44051-3 (pbk) : £6.95 : CIP rev.
B81-08846

Harvey, J.. Mastering economics / J. Harvey. — London : Macmillan, 1982. — 352p : ill ; 23cm. — (Macmillan master series)
Includes index
ISBN 0-333-31287-2 (cased) : £8.95 : CIP rev.
ISBN 0-333-30477-2 (pbk) : Unpriced
B81-26722

Illich, Ivan. Vernacular gender. — London : Marion Boyars, Apr.1982. — [128]p
ISBN 0-7145-2757-2 (cased) : £6.95 : CIP entry
ISBN 0-7145-2758-0 (pbk) : £3.50 B82-04504

Kempner, Thomas. The economic environment / by Thomas Kempner. — Major revision. — [Henley-on-Thames] : [Administrative Staff College] Henley, 1982. — 109p : ill ; 30cm
Cover title. — Previous ed.: 1981
£5.00 (pbk) B82-30189

McCarty, Marilu Hurt. Dollars and sense : an introduction to economics / Marilu Hurt McCarty. — 2nd ed. — Glenview ; London : Scott, Foresman, c1979. — 288p : ill(some col.) ; 23cm
Previous ed.: 1976. — Includes bibliographies and index
ISBN 0-673-15230-8 (pbk) : £11.00
B82-40998

Marschak, Jacob. Economic information, decision and prediction : selected essays / Jacob Marschak. — Dordrecht ; London : Reidel. — (Theory and decision library ; v.7)
Vol.1
Pt.1: Economics of decision. — c1974. — xviii,389p : ill ; 23cm
Includes bibliographies and index
ISBN 90-277-0544-5 (cased) : Unpriced
ISBN 90-277-1195-x (pbk) : Unpriced
B82-19938

Modern economic analysis. — London : Butterworth, Sept.1982
2. — [280]p
ISBN 0-408-10771-5 (cased) : £9.95 : CIP entry
ISBN 0-408-10772-3 (pbk) : £5.95 B82-18751

Robinson, Joan. Collected economic papers [of] Joan Robinson. — Oxford : Blackwell
General index. — 1980. — iv,60p ; 23cm
ISBN 0-631-12491-8 : £4.95 : CIP rev.
B80-05805

Scott, Robert Haney. Principles of economics / Robert Haney Scott, Nic Nigro. — New York : Macmillan ; London : Collier Macmillan, c1982. — xiv,882p : ill ; 26cm
Includes index
ISBN 0-02-408360-7 : £7.95 B82-39389

330 — Economics *continuation*

Sen, Amartya. Choice, welfare and measurement. — Oxford : Blackwell, Sept.1982. — [432]p
ISBN 0-631-12914-6 : £17.50 : CIP entry
B82-20283

Smith, Alasdair. A mathematical introduction to economics. — Oxford : Blackwell, Sept.1982. — [320]p
ISBN 0-631-12888-3 (cased) : £15.00 : CIP entry
ISBN 0-631-12976-6 (pbk) : £6.95 B82-20281

Stigler, George J.. The economist as preacher. — Oxford : Blackwell, Nov.1982. — [272]p
ISBN 0-631-13235-x (pbk) : £15.00 : CIP entry
B82-27977

Tobin, James. Essays in economics : theory and policy / James Tobin. — Cambridge, Mass. ; London : MIT, c1982. — x,685p : ill ; 24cm. — (The Papers of James Tobin ; v.3)
Includes index
ISBN 0-262-20042-2 : £31.50 B82-37522

Twelve contemporary economists / edited by J.R. Shackleton and Gareth Locksley. — London : Macmillan, 1981. — ix,263p : ill ; 23cm
Includes bibliographies and index
ISBN 0-333-29084-4 : £15.00 B82-10633

Wardle, H. T.. Introductory economics : a comprehensive study text / H.T. Wardle. — Exeter : Wheaton, 1982. — 144p : ill ; 30cm
Includes index
ISBN 0-08-024146-8 (pbk) : £3.50 B82-36495

Weidenaar, Dennis J.. Economics : an introduction to the world around you / Dennis J. Weidenaar, Emanuel T. Weiler. — 2nd ed. — Reading, Mass. ; London : Addison-Wesley, c1979. — xiii,498p : ill ; 23cm. — (Addison-Wesley series in economics)
Previous ed.: 1976. — Includes index
ISBN 0-201-08517-8 (pbk) : Unpriced
B82-27985

Welch, Patrick J.. Economics : theory & practice / Patrick J. Welch, Gerry F. Welch. — Chicago ; London : Dryden, c1982. — xvi,527p : ill(some col.),2col.maps,ports ; 24cm
Includes bibliographies and index
ISBN 0-03-055626-0 (pbk) : £12.50
B82-15365

Wonnacott, Paul. Economics / Paul Wonnacott, Ronald Wonnacott. — 2nd ed. — New York ; London : McGraw-Hill, c1982. — xl,858p : ill (some col.),port ; 25cm
Previous ed.: 1979. — Text and ports on lining papers. — Includes index
ISBN 0-07-071595-5 : £18.95 B82-22733

330 — Economics — *Conference proceedings*

Advances in economic theory. — Oxford : Blackwell, June 1982. — [300]p
Conference papers
ISBN 0-631-13081-0 : £20.00 : CIP entry
B82-09456

330 — Economics. Evolutionary aspects

Boulding, Kenneth E.. Evolutionary economics / Kenneth E. Boulding. — Beverly Hills ; London : Sage, c1981. — 200p : ill ; 23cm
Includes index
ISBN 0-8039-1648-5 (cased) : Unpriced
ISBN 0-8039-1649-3 (pbk) : £6.50 B82-07907

330 — Economics — *For Australian students*

Lipsey, Richard G.. Positive economics for Australian students / Richard G. Lipsey, Paul C. Langley, Dennis M. Mahoney. — London : Weidenfeld and Nicolson, c1981. — xviii,850p : ill ; 24cm
Based on An introduction to positive economics / Richard G. Lipsey. — 5th ed., 1979. — Includes bibliographies and index
ISBN 0-297-77972-9 (pbk) : £12.50
B82-02867

330 — Economics — *For Irish students*

McQuillan, Dominic. Economics today / Dominic McQuillan ; [diagrams Tommy McCann]. — Dublin : Educational Company, 1980. — vii,319p : ill ; 21cm
Includes index
Unpriced (pbk) B82-02550

330 — Economics — *For Nigerian students*

Adebo-Lawal, S.. Economics for Nigeria / S. Adebo-Lawal. — London : Cassell, 1982. — viii,35lp : ill ; 22cm
Includes index
ISBN 0-304-30609-6 (pbk) : £6.50 B82-31655

330 — Economics — *For schools*

Harbury, C .D.. Descriptive economics / Colin Harbury. — 6th ed. — London : Pitman, 1981. — xi,286p : ill,maps ; 23cm
Previous ed.: 1976. — Includes index
ISBN 0-273-01733-0 (pbk) : Unpriced
B82-24884

Harvey, J.. Intermediate economics. — 4th ed. — Basingstoke : Macmillan Education, July 1982. — [512]p
Previous ed.: 1976
ISBN 0-333-32895-7 (pbk) : £4.95 : CIP entry
B82-12274

Hobday, Ian. A first course in economics. — London : Arnold, Nov.1982. — [224]p
ISBN 0-7131-0801-0 (pbk) : £3.95 : CIP entry
B82-27945

330 — Economics — *For West African students*

Nwankwo, G. O.. Basic economics : for West African students / G.O. Nwankwo. — 2nd ed. — Cambridge : Cambridge University Press, 1982. — viii,263p : ill ; 23cm
Previous ed.: 1977
ISBN 0-521-28625-5 (pbk) : £3.85 B82-31121

330 — Economics — *Humanist viewpoints*

Pick, U.. Economics with a human face / U. Pick. — Croydon (3 Cheyne Court, Canning Rd., Croydon CR0 6QB) : U. Pick, [1981?]. — 21leaves : ill ; 30cm
Cover title
Unpriced (spiral) B82-08558

330 — Economics — *Islamic viewpoints*

aş-Şadr, Muḥammad Bāqir. Islam and schools of economics / [Muhammad Baqir Al Sadr]. — Karachi : Islamic Seminary Pakistan ; London (284 Kilburn High Rd., NW6 2DB) : Islamic Seminary [distributor], 1980. — 160p ; 21cm
Translation of: Al-madresah al-Islamiah
Unpriced (pbk) B82-14441

330 — Economics — *Marxist viewpoints*

Horvat, Branko. The political economy of socialism : a Marxist social theory / Branko Horvat. — Oxford : Robertson, 1982. — xx,671p : ill ; 24cm
Includes index
ISBN 0-85520-477-x : £25.00 : CIP rev.
B81-33827

330 — Economics *related to* **sociology**

Economics and sociology : towards an integration / edited by T. Huppes. — Boston [Mass.] ; London : Kluwer, c1976 (1982 [printing]). — vii,178p ; 24cm
ISBN 0-89838-093-6 : Unpriced
Also classified at 301 B82-24573

330 — Economics. Role of altruism

Collard, David. Altruism and economy. — Oxford : Martin Robertson, Apr.1981. — [220]p
Originally published: 1978
ISBN 0-85520-381-1 (pbk) : £4.95 : CIP entry
B81-07418

330 — Persons. Time. Allocation. Economic aspects

Sharp, Clifford. The economics of time / Clifford Sharp. — Oxford : Robertson, 1981. — viii,231p : ill ; 24cm
Bibliography: p221-226. — Includes index
ISBN 0-85520-162-2 : £15.00 : CIP rev.
B81-13750

330'.01 — Economics — *Philosophical perspectives*

Caldwell, Bruce J.. Beyond positivism. — London : Allen & Unwin, Jan.1983. — [288]p
ISBN 0-04-330327-7 : £15.00 : CIP entry
B82-33597

Gasparini, Nino. The vitanomic explanation / Nino Gasparini. — London (14 Melrose Gardens, W6) : Intellectus, c1982. — i,107p ; 21cm
£2.95 (pbk) B82-27489

330'.01 — Man. Rational economic expectations. Econometric models

Rational expectations and econometric practice / edited by Robert E. Lucas, Jr. and Thomas J. Sargent. — London : Allen & Unwin, 1981. — xl,689p : ill ; 24cm
Includes bibliographies
ISBN 0-04-339018-8 (cased) : Unpriced
ISBN 0-04-339019-6 (pbk) : Unpriced
B82-14470

Snell, A.. Rational forecasts from non-rational models / A. Snell. — Coventry : Department of Economics, University of Warwick, 1981. — 35,[8]p ; 31cm. — (Warwick economic research papers ; no.194)
Paper presented at the Econometric Society European Meeting in 1981. — Bibliography: p [8]
Unpriced (pbk) B82-11378

330'.01'51 — Economics. Applications of control theory

. Non-price control / edited by János Kornai and Béla Martos ; [translation from Hungarian by Gy Hajdú] ; [translation revised by P.G. Hare]. — Amsterdam ; Oxford : Excerpta Medica, 1981. — 334p : ill ; 23cm. — (Contributions to economic analysis ; v.133)
Bibliography: p321-325. — Includes index
ISBN 0-444-85486-x : £19.75 B82-08567

330'.01'51 — Economics. Mathematics

Cassels, J. W. S.. Economics for mathematicians / J.W.S. Cassels. — Cambridge : Cambridge University Press, 1981. — xi,145p : ill ; 22cm. — (London Mathematical Society lecture note series, ISSN 0076-0552 ; 62)
Includes bibliographies and index
ISBN 0-521-28614-x (pbk) : Unpriced
B82-28969

Handbook of mathematical economics / edited by Kenneth J. Arrow and Michael D. Intriligator. — Amsterdam ; Oxford : North-Holland. — (Handbooks in economics ; bk.1)
Vol.1. — 1981. — xvii,378p : ill ; 25cm
Includes bibliographies and index
ISBN 0-444-86126-2 : £21.65
ISBN 0-444-86054-1 (set) B82-00696

330'.01'5192 — Economics. Stochastic methods

Malliaris, A. G.. Stochastic methods in economics and finance / A.G. Malliaris with a foreword and contributions by W.A. Brock. — Amsterdam ; Oxford : North-Holland Publishing, c1982. — xv,303p : ill ; 23cm. — (Advanced textbooks in economics)
Bibliography: p279-293. — Includes index
ISBN 0-444-86201-3 : Unpriced B82-14599

330'.01'5193 — Economics. Game theory — *Conference proceedings*

Seminar on Game Theory and Mathematical Economic *(1980 : Bonn and Hagen)*. Game theory and mathematical economics : proceedings of the Seminar on Game Theory and Mathematical Economics, Bonn/Hagen, 7-10 October, 1980 / Managing editors O. Moeschlin, D. Pallaschke. — Amsterdam ; Oxford : North-Holland, c1981. — x,463p : ill ; 23cm
Includes bibliographies and index
ISBN 0-444-86296-x : £29.85 B82-09908

330'.01'5193 — Economics. Positional games

Krass, Iosif A.. The theory of positional games : with applications in economics / Iosif A. Krass, Shawkat M. Hammoudeh. — New York ; London : Academic Press, 1981. — xii,221p : ill ; 24cm. — (Economic theory, econometrics, and mathematical economics)
Bibliography: p213-215. — Includes index
ISBN 0-12-425920-0 : £24.60 B82-16315

330′.01′8 — Economics. Methodology

Boland, Lawrence A.. The foundations of economic method. — London : Allen & Unwin, Sept.1982. — 1v.
ISBN 0-04-330328-5 (cased) : £15.00 : CIP entry
ISBN 0-04-330329-3 (pbk) : £5.95 B82-19079

Mises, Ludwig von. Epistemological problems of economics / by Ludwig von Mises ; translated by George Reisman. — New York ; London : New York University Press, 1981, c1976. — xxxi,239p ; 24cm. — (Institute for Humane Studies series in economic theory)
Translation of: Grundprobleme der Nationalökonomie. — Originally published: Menlo Park : Institute for Humane Studies, 1976. — Includes index
ISBN 0-8147-8757-6 (cased) : £14.90
ISBN 0-8147-8758-4 (pbk) : £5.20 B82-38256

330′.024624 — Economics — *For construction*

Seddon, V. J.. Economics for the construction industry checkbook / V.J. Seddon, G.B.J. Atkinson. — London : Butterworths, 1982. — vi,137p : ill ; 20cm. — (Butterworths technical and scientific checkbooks)
Includes index
ISBN 0-408-00666-8 (cased) : £7.95 : CIP rev.
ISBN 0-408-00655-2 (pbk) : Unpriced B81-31424

330′.024658 — Economics — *For businessmen*

Bates, James. Business economics. — Rev. ed. — Oxford : Blackwell, Nov.1982. — [350]p
Previous ed.: 1976
ISBN 0-631-13146-9 (cased) : £15.00 : CIP entry
ISBN 0-631-13147-7 (pbk) : £6.95 B82-26573

330′.024658 — Economics — *For management*

Reekie, W. Duncan. Managerial economics. — 2nd ed. — Deddington : Philip Allan, Aug.1982. — [448]p
Previous ed.: 1975
ISBN 0-86003-045-8 (cased) : £20.00 : CIP entry
ISBN 0-86003-140-3 (pbk) : £9.95 B82-23840

330′.028 — Discrete econometric models

Structural analysis of discrete data with econometric applications / edited by Charles F. Manski and Daniel McFadden. — Cambridge, Mass. ; London : Harvard University Press, 1981. — xxv,477p : ill ; 24cm
Includes bibliographies and index
ISBN 0-262-13159-5 : £21.00 B82-13735

330′.028 — Econometric models

Klein, Lawrence R.. Econometric models as guides for decision-making / Lawrence R. Klein ; discussants Robert A. Kavesh, M. Ishaq Nadiri, Gary Wenglowski. — New York : Free Press ; London : Collier Macmillan, c1981. — 75p ; 22cm. — (The Charles C. Moskowitz memorial lectures ; no.22)
ISBN 0-02-917430-9 : Unpriced B82-33161

Qualitative and quantitative mathematical economics / edited by J.H.P. Paelinck. — The Hague ; London : Nijhoff, 1982. — x,266p : ill,1map,1port ; 25cm. — (Advanced studies in theoretical and applied econometrics ; v.1)
ISBN 90-247-2623-9 : Unpriced
ISBN 90-247-2622-0 (series) B82-40764

330′.028 — Econometric models — *Conference proceedings*

Economic modelling in theory and practice : proceedings of a Franco-Dutch conference held at Tilburg University, April 1979 / sponsored by the French Embassy at The Hague and the Office For International Relations of Tilburg University ; edited by Joseph Plasmans. — Hague ; London : Nijhoff, 1982. — xiii,232p : ill,1map ; 25cm
Includes bibliographies and index
ISBN 90-247-2553-4 : Unpriced B82-20799

330′.028 — Econometrics

Introduction to the theory and practice of econometrics / George G. Judge ... [et al.]. — New York ; Chichester : Wiley, c1982. — xxix,839p ; 24cm. — (Wiley series in probability and mathematical statistics)
Includes index
ISBN 0-471-08277-5 : £23.65 B82-27761

Katz, David A.. Econometric theory and applications / David A. Katz. — Englewood Cliffs ; London : Prentice-Hall, c1982. — viii,280p : ill ; 24cm
Bibliography: p273-275. — Includes index
ISBN 0-13-223313-4 : £18.70 B82-27561

Mayes, David G.. Applications of econometrics / David G. Mayes. — Englewood Cliffs ; London : Prentice-Hall, c1981. — xi,418p : ill ; 23cm
Includes bibliographies and index
ISBN 0-13-039180-8 (pbk) : £8.95 : CIP rev. B81-12912

330′.028 — Econometrics — *Festschriften*

Proceedings of the Econometric Society European Meeting 1979 : selected econometric papers in memory of Stefan Valavanis / editor E.G. Charatsis. — Amsterdam ; Oxford : North-Holland, 1981. — xv,444p : ill ; 23cm. — (Contributions to economic analysis ; 138)
Includes bibliographies and index
ISBN 0-444-86184-x : £48.93 B82-13429

Quantitative economics and development : essays in memory of Ta-Chung Liu / edited by L.R. Klein, M. Nerlove, S.C. Tsiang. — New York ; London : Academic Press, 1980. — xix,346p : ill ; 24cm. — (Economic theory, econometrics, and mathematical economics)
Includes bibliographies
ISBN 0-12-413350-9 : £27.80 B82-10062

330′.028 — Econometrics — *Serials*

Advances in econometrics : a research annual. — Vol.1 (1982)-. — Greenwich, Conn. ; London : JAI, 1982-. — v. : ill ; 24cm
Unpriced B82-33860

330′.028 — Economics. Disequilibria

Hey, John D.. Economics in disequilibrium / John D. Hey. — Oxford : Martin Robertson, 1981. — 271p : ill ; 24cm
Bibliography: p255-263. — Includes index
ISBN 0-85520-399-4 : £17.50 : CIP rev. B81-16894

Iwai, Katsuhito. Disequilibrium dynamics : a theoretical analysis of inflation and unemployment / Katsuhito Iwai. — New Haven ; London : Yale University Press, c1981. — xix,314p : ill ; 25cm. — (Cowles Foundation for Research in Economics at Yale University ; Monograph 27)
Bibliography: p299-307. — Includes index
ISBN 0-300-02556-4 : Unpriced : CIP rev. B81-32083

330′.028 — Soviet Union. Econometrics

New trends in Soviet economics / edited by Martin Cave, Alistair McAuley and Judith Thornton. — New York : Sharpe ; London : Eurospan [[distributor]], c1982. — x,412p : ill ; 24cm
Translated from the Russian
ISBN 0-87332-206-1 : £29.95 B82-36675

330′.028542 — Econometric models — *Programs*

Addis, Graham. The Broadwater economics simulations / Graham Addis. — Wilmslow : Sigma Technical Press, c1982. — 1sound cassette + 1 booklet ; in container 22x18x3cm
ISBN 0-905104-16-1 : £25.00 B82-34747

330′.03 — Economics — *Polyglot dictionaries*

Nasr, Z.. The dictionary of economics and commerce : English, French, Arabic = 'Anāsir li-mu' ǧam igtiṣādī wat-tiǧārī 'arabī / Z. Nasr. — London : Macmillan, 1980, c1979. — xiii,212p ; 29cm
ISBN 0-333-23109-0 : £12.95 : CIP rev. B79-17307

330′.03′21 — Economics — *Encyclopaedias*

Encyclopedia of economics / Douglas Greenwald, editor in chief. — New York ; London : McGraw-Hill, c1982. — xxxiii,1070p : ill ; 25cm
Includes bibliographies and index
ISBN 0-07-024367-0 : £37.50 B82-15988

330′.03′21 — Economics — *Encyclopaedias — For non-English speaking students*

Adam, J. H.. Longman dictionary of business English / J. H. Adam. — Harlow : Longman, 1982. — xiii,492p ; 23cm
ISBN 0-582-55552-3 : £5.95 B82-24104

330′.05 — Economics — *Serials*

Contributions to political economy. — Vol.1 (Mar. 1982)-. — London : Published for the Cambridge Political Economy Society by Academic Press, 1982-. — v. : ill ; 24cm
Annual
ISSN 0277-5921 = Contributions to political economy : £7.50 B82-32164

Research in political economy : an annual compilation of research. — Vol.1 (1977)-. — Greenwich, Conn. : JAI Press ; London (3 Henrietta St., WC2E 8LU) : Distributed by JAICON Press, 1977-. — v. ; 24cm
ISSN 0161-7230 = Research in political economy : £22.85 B82-02361

330′.05 — Economics. Serials: Review of economic studies, *1959-1981 — Indexes*

Rees, Hedley. The Review of economic studies : index to volumes 26-48, 1959-1981. — Clevedon (Bank House, 8a Hill Road, Clevedon, Avon BS21 7HH) : Tieto, July 1982. — [175]p
ISBN 0-905028-08-2 (pbk) : £15.00 : CIP entry B82-20791

330′.05 — Economics — *Socialist viewpoints — Serials*

Socialist economic review. — 1982. — London : Merlin Press, June 1982. — [300]p
ISBN 0-85036-285-7 (pbk) : £4.95 : CIP entry B82-14947

330′.0724 — Economic analysis. Quantitative methods

New quantitative techniques for economic analysis / edited by Giorgio P. Szegö. — New York ; London : Academic Press, 1982. — xiv,319p : ill ; 24cm. — (Economic theory, econometrics and mathematical economics)
ISBN 0-12-680760-4 : £32.80 B82-34854

330′.0724 — Economic conditions. Models

Meadows, Donella H.. Groping in the dark : the first decade of global modelling / Donella Meadows, John Richardson, Gerhart Bruckmann. — Chichester : Wiley, c1982. — xxiii,311p : ill ; 24cm
Includes index
ISBN 0-471-10027-7 (pbk) : £11.00 : CIP rev. B81-36236

330′.0724 — Economics. Applications of spatial models

Paelinck, J. H. P.. Formal spatial economic analysis. — Aldershot : Gower, Nov.1982. — [388]p. — (Studies in spatial analysis)
ISBN 0-566-00477-1 : £15.00 : CIP entry B82-26545

330′.0724 — Economics. Invariance. Analysis. Applications of Lie groups

Satō, Ryūzō. Theory of technical change and economic invariance : application of Lie groups / Ryuzo Sato. — New York ; London : Academic Press, 1981. — xv,439p : ill ; 24cm. — (Economic theory, econometrics, and mathematical economics)
Includes bibliographies and index
ISBN 0-12-619460-2 : £37.00 B82-10288

330′.0724 — Economics. Linear models

Dubbelman, C.. Disturbances in the linear model, estimation and hypothesis testing / C. Dubbelman. — Boston [Mass.] ; London : Kluwer, c1978 (1982 [printing]). — 108p : ill ; 24cm
Bibliography: p107-108. — Includes index
ISBN 0-89838-094-4 : Unpriced B82-25214

330'.0724 — Experimental economics — *Serials*

Research in experimental economics : a research annual. — Vol.1 (1979)-. — Greenwich, Conn. : JAI Press ; London (3 Henrietta St., WC2E 8LU) : Distributed by JAICON Press, 1979-. — v. : ill ; 24cm
Supplement: Research in experimental economics. Supplement
ISSN 0193-2306 = Research in experimental economics : £26.20 B82-02366

Research in experimental economics : a research annual. Supplement. — Vol.1 (1980)-. — Greenwich, Conn. : JAI Press ; London (3 Henrietta St., WC2E 8LU) : Distributed by JAICON Press, 1980-. — v. ; 24cm
Supplement to: Research in experimental economics
£22.85 B82-02367

330'.076 — Economics — *Questions & answers*

Gwartney, James D.. Instructor's manual and test bank for Essentials of economics / by James D. Gwartney, Richard Stroup, Jeffrey R. Clark. — New York : London : Academic Press, c1982. — viii,472p : ill ; 23cm
ISBN 0-12-311033-5 (pbk) : £2.00 B82-30128

Harbury, C. D.. Workbook in introductory economics / by Colin Harbury. — 3rd ed. — Oxford : Pergamon, 1982. — xiii,157p : ill,forms ; 28cm
Previous ed.: 1974
ISBN 0-08-027442-0 (pbk) : £3.50 : CIP rev. B82-00290

Marcis, John G.. Test bank for Introductory economics and Introductory macroeconomics and Introductory microeconomics by Michael Veseth / by John G. Marcis and Michael Veseth. — New York ; London : Academic Press, c1981. — vii,280p : ill ; 24cm
ISBN 0-12-719567-x (pbk) : £2.40 B82-29976

330'.076 — Economics — *Questions & answers — For schools*

Livesey, Frank. Objective tests in A level economics with answers. — London : Hodder and Stoughton, Sept.1982. — [160]p
ISBN 0-340-32732-4 (pbk) : £2.35 : CIP entry B82-25911

Maile, Roger. A textbook of questions and answers in A level economics. — London : Bell & Hyman, Sept.1982. — [256]p
ISBN 0-7135-1324-1 (pbk) : £5.95 : CIP entry B82-25060

Marder, K. B.. Stimulus questions for 'O' level economics / K.B. Marder and L.P. Alderson. — Oxford : Oxford University Press, 1981. — 48p : ill,3maps
ISBN 0-19-913272-0 (pbk) : £1.25 B82-04324

Oliver, J. M.. Data response questions in 'A' level economics / J.M. Oliver. — 2nd ed. — London : Heinemann Educational, 1982. — iv,59p ; 21cm
Previous ed.: 1976
ISBN 0-435-33921-4 (pbk) : £1.50 B82-15275

Thomas, D. J.. Economics. — London : Bell & Hyman, Sept.1981. — [96]p
ISBN 0-7135-1286-5 (pbk) : £1.50 : CIP entry B81-22523

Watts, Michael, *1943-*. Worked examples in data response questions for A Level economics / Michael Watts and Matthew Glew. — 2nd ed. — London : Heinemann Educational, 1982. — 108p : ill ; 22cm
Previous ed.: 1977
ISBN 0-435-33950-8 (pbk) : £1.60 B82-39931

330'.076 — England. Secondary schools. Curriculum subjects: Economics. G.C.E. (A level) examinations — *Comparative studies*

Report of the inter-board cross-moderation study in economics at Advanced Level, 1979 / The Associated Examining Board for the General Certificate of Education. — Aldershot (Wellington House, Aldershot, Hants. GU11 1BQ) : The Board, c1981. — 11p ; 24cm
Unpriced (pbk) B82-09149

330'.09'023 — Economics, *ca 1270-ca 1480*

Fryde, E. B.. Studies in medieval trade and finance. — London : Hambledon, Dec.1982. — [430]p. — (History series ; 13)
ISBN 0-907628-10-9 : £24.00 : CIP entry B82-30748

330'.09'04 — Economics, *1945-1980*

Bauer, P. T.. Equality, the Third World and economic delusion. — London : Methuen, Dec.1982. — [304]p
Originally published: London : Weidenfeld and Nicolson, 1981
ISBN 0-416-34230-2 (pbk) : £5.95 : CIP entry B82-29761

330'.092'2 — Economics, *1700-1981 — Biographies*

Blaug, Mark. Who's who in economics : a biographical dictionary 1700-1980. — Brighton : Wheatsheaf Books, Dec.1982. — [1600]p
ISBN 0-7108-0125-4 : £50.00 : CIP entry B82-30044

330'092'4 — Economics. List, Friedrich — *Biographies*

Henderson, W. O.. Friedrich List. — London : Cass, Mar.1982. — [296]p
ISBN 0-7146-3161-2 : £14.50 : CIP entry B82-01216

330'.0942 — Great Britain. Economics. Influence of Oxford Economic Society, *1886-1900*

Kadish, Alan. The Oxford economists in the late nineteenth century. — Oxford : Clarendon Press, July 1982. — [400]p. — (Oxford historical monographs)
ISBN 0-19-821886-9 : £19.50 : CIP entry B82-12546

330.1 — ECONOMICS. SYSTEMS AND THEORIES

330.1 — Economics. Theories

Breit, William. The academic scribblers / William Breit, Roger L. Ransom. — Rev. ed. — Chicago ; London : Dryden, c1982. — xiii,274p : ill,ports ; 24cm
Previous ed.: New York : Holt, Rinehart and Winston, 1971. — Includes index
ISBN 0-03-051236-0 (pbk) : £7.50 B82-15359

Duijn, Jacob van. The long wave in economic life. — London : Allen and Unwin, Oct.1982. — [240]p
ISBN 0-04-330330-7 (cased) : £16.00 : CIP entry
ISBN 0-04-330331-5 (pbk) : £6.50 B82-23089

Harcourt, G. C.. The social science imperialists / G.C. Harcourt ; edited by Prue Kerr. — London : Routledge & Kegan Paul, 1982. — vii,423p : ill ; 23cm
Bibliography: p394-416. — Includes index
ISBN 0-7100-9064-1 : £25.00 B82-33288

Hausman, Daniel M.. Capital, profits, and prices : an essay in the philosophy of economics / Daniel M. Hausman. — New York ; Guildford : Columbia University Press, 1981. — 253p : ill ; 24cm
Bibliography: p227-244. — Includes index
ISBN 0-231-05090-9 : £16.85 B82-19581

Hicks, John, *1904-*. Money, interest and wages / John Hicks. — Oxford : Blackwell, 1982. — xiii,351p : ill ; 24cm. — (Collected essays on economic theory ; v.2)
Includes index
ISBN 0-631-12537-x : Unpriced : CIP rev. B82-09453

Levine, David P.. Economic theory / David P. Levine. — London : Routledge & Kegan Paul
Vol.2: The system of economic relations as a whole. — 1981. — xi,318p ; 23cm
Includes index
ISBN 0-7100-0948-8 : £15.00 B82-05449

Nevin, Edward. Textbook of economic analysis. — 5th ed. — London : Macmillan, June 1981. — [544]p
Previous ed.: London : Macmillan, 1976
ISBN 0-333-31318-6 (pbk) : £2.95 : CIP entry B81-13789

Robinson, Joan. Economic philosophy / Joan Robinson. — Harmondsworth : Penguin, 1964, c1962 (1981 [printing]). — 140p ; 18cm. — (Pelican books)
Originally published: London : Watts, 1962. — Includes index
ISBN 0-14-020653-1 (pbk) : £1.35 B82-08149

330.1 — Economics. Theories, *1900-1981*

Stein, Jerome L.. Monetarist, Keynesian and new classical economics. — Oxford : Basil Blackwell, Sept.1982. — [224]p
ISBN 0-631-12908-1 : £12.50 : CIP entry B82-20292

330.1 — Economics. Theories, *ca 1840-1980*

Hutchison, T. W.. The politics and philosophy of economics : Marxians, Keynesians and Austrians / T.W. Hutchison. — Oxford : Blackwell, 1981. — x,310p ; 24cm
Includes bibliographies and index
ISBN 0-631-12517-5 : £15.00 : CIP rev. B81-14876

330.1 — Economics. Theories — *Early works*

Menger, Carl. Principles of economics / by Carl Menger ; translated by James Dingwall and Bert F. Hoselitz ; with an introduction by F.A. Hayek. — New York ; London : New York University Press, 1981. — 328p ; 24cm. — (The Institute of Humane Studies series in economic theory)
Translation of: Grundsätze der Volkswirthschaftslehre. — Bibliography: p11. — Includes index
ISBN 0-8147-5380-9 (cased) : £14.90
ISBN 0-8147-5381-7 (pbk) : £5.20 B82-35940

330.1 — Economics. Theories of Hobson, J.A.

Allett, John. New liberalism : the political economy of J.A. Hobson / John Allett. — Toronto ; London : University of Toronto Press, c1981. — 275p ; 24cm
Bibliography: p263-269. — Includes index
ISBN 0-8020-5558-3 : Unpriced B82-27779

330.1 — Economics. Theories of Marshall, Alfred — *Critical studies*

Alfred Marshall : critical assessments. — London : Croom Helm, Dec.1981. — 4v.([1456]p)
ISBN 0-7099-2705-3 : £200.00 : CIP entry B81-31432

330.1 — Economics. Theories of Wicksell, Knut — *Conference proceedings*

The **Theoretical** contributions of Knut Wicksell / edited by Steinar Strøm and Björn Thalberg. — London : Macmillan, 1979. — 151p : ill ; 24cm
Conference papers. — Includes bibliographies
ISBN 0-333-25345-0 : £15.00 : CIP rev. B79-18991

330.1 — Economics. Theories, *to 1979*

Cole, Ken. Why economists disagree : the political economy of economics. — London : Longman, Nov.1982. — [320]p
ISBN 0-582-29546-7 (pbk) : £7.95 : CIP entry B82-26527

330.12'2 — Capitalism

Shenfield, Arthur. Myth and reality in economic systems / Arthur Shenfield. — London (50, Westminster Mansions, Little Smith St., SW1P 3DQ) : Adam Smith Institute, c1981. — 60p ; 23cm
£1.50 (pbk) B82-24677

330.12'2 — Capitalism *expounded by* theories of value in economics of Marx, Karl

Weeks, John. Capital and exploitation / by John Weeks. — London : Edward Arnold, 1981. — x,223p ; 23cm
Includes index
ISBN 0-7131-6350-x (cased) : Unpriced : CIP rev.
ISBN 0-7131-6351-8 (pbk) : £4.95 B81-30385

330.12'2 — Capitalism — *Marxist viewpoints*

Harvey, David. The limits to capital. — Oxford : Basil Blackwell, Apr.1982. — [416]p
ISBN 0-631-12968-5 : £15.00 : CIP entry B82-04585

330.12'2 — Capitalism — *Marxist viewpoints continuation*

Uno, Kōzō. Principles of political economy : theory of a purely capitalist society / Kōzō Uno ; translated from the Japanese by Thomas T. Sekine. — Brighton : Harvester, 1980. — xxviii,224p : ill ; 24cm. — ([Marxist theory and contemporary capitalism] ; [no.24])
Translation of: Keizai genron. — Bibliography: p167-168. — Includes index
ISBN 0-85527-635-5 : £25.00 : CIP rev. B80-09107

330.12'2 — Capitalism — *Socialist viewpoints*

Bray, Jeremy. Producation, purpose and structure. — London : Pinter, Sept.1982. — [150]p
ISBN 0-86187-263-0 : £8.95 : CIP entry B82-21547

Tomlinson, Jim. The unequal struggle?. — London : Methuen, Oct.1982. — [192]p
ISBN 0-416-33150-5 (cased) : £8.95 : CIP entry
ISBN 0-416-33160-2 (pbk) : £3.95 B82-23977

330.12'2 — Capitalism. Theories — *Marxist viewpoints*

Fine, Ben. Theories of the capitalist economy / Ben Fine. — London : Edward Arnold, 1982. — 142p : ill ; 22cm
Bibliography: p135-137. — Includes index
ISBN 0-7131-6357-7 (pbk) : £5.95 : CIP rev. B81-33839

330.12'2 — Capitalism. Theories of Marxists, *to 1978*

Jessop, Bob. The capitalist state : Marxist theories and methods / Bob Jessop. — Oxford : Robertson, 1982. — xvi,296p ; 24cm
Bibliography: p260-281. — Includes index
ISBN 0-85520-269-6 (cased) : £17.00 : CIP rev.
ISBN 0-85520-268-8 (pbk) : £5.95 B81-35853

330.12'2 — Free economies. Theories

Hahn, F. H.. Reflections on the invisible hand / Frank Hahn. — Coventry : Department of Economics, University of Warwick, [1981]. — 27p ; 31cm. — (Warwick economic research papers ; no.196)
Text of the Fred Hirsch Memorial Lecture presented at the University of Warwick on the 5th November, 1981
Unpriced (pbk) B82-11381

330.12'2 — Open economies. Dynamics. Analysis

Aoki, Masanao. Dynamic analysis of open economies / Masanao Aoki. — New York ; London : Academic Press, 1981. — xxvi,341p : ill ; 24cm
Bibliography: p327-333. — Includes index
ISBN 0-12-058940-0 : £26.20 B82-10056

330.12'2'09 — Capitalism. Theories, *to 1981*

Maddison, Angus. Phases of capitalist development. — Oxford : Oxford University Press, July 1982. — [235]p
ISBN 0-19-828450-0 (cased) : £15.00 : CIP entry
ISBN 0-19-828451-9 (pbk) : £5.95 B82-13227

330.12'2'09 — Capitalism, *to 1980*

Schumpeter's vision. — Eastbourne : Praeger, Sept.1981. — [224]p
ISBN 0-03-060276-9 : £5.95 : CIP entry B81-25128

330.12'2'0903 — Capitalism, *1600-1978 — Conference proceedings*

The **World-system** of capitalism : past and present / edited by Walter L. Goldfrank. — Beverly Hills ; London : Sage, c1979. — 312p : 1map ; 23cm. — (Political economy of the world-system annuals ; v.2)
Includes index
ISBN 0-8039-1105-x (cased) : Unpriced
ISBN 0-8039-1106-8 (pbk) : Unpriced B82-17840

330.12'2'0922 — Capitalism. Theories of Weber, Max *compared with* **theories of Marx, Karl**

Löwith, Karl. Max Weber and Karl Marx / Karl Löwith ; edited with an introduction by Tom Bottomore and William Outhwaite ; translated by Hans Fantel. — London : Allen & Unwin, 1982. — 112p ; 23cm. — (Controversies in sociology ; 12)
Translated from the German. — Bibliography: p108-110. — Includes index
ISBN 0-04-301142-x (cased) : Unpriced : CIP rev.
ISBN 0-04-301143-8 (pbk) : Unpriced B82-15624

330.12'2'09492 — Netherlands. Capitalism, *1580-1800 — Conference proceedings*

Dutch capitalism and world capitalism = Capitalisme hollandais et capitalisme mondial / publié sous la direction de Maurice Aymard. — Cambridge : Cambridge University Press, 1982. — viii,312p : ill,1map ; 24cm. — (Studies in modern capitalism = Etudes sur le capitalisme moderne)
Conference papers. — Includes bibliographies
ISBN 0-521-23812-9 : £25.00 : CIP rev. B82-14489

330.12'2'09625 — Sudan. Maiurno. Capitalism, *to 1980.* **Socioeconomic aspects**

Duffield, Mark R.. Maiurno : capitalism & rural life in Sudan / Mark R. Duffield. — London : Ithaca, 1981. — vii,212p : ill ; 23cm. — (Ithaca Press Sudan studies ; no.5)
Bibliography: p200-212
ISBN 0-903729-79-2 : Unpriced B82-33281

330.12'2'0994 — Australia. Capitalism, *1900-1980*

Butlin, N. G.. Government and capitalism. — London : Allen & Unwin, Apr.1982. — [376]p
ISBN 0-86861-187-5 : £18.00 : CIP entry B82-05768

330.12'6 — Mixed economies — *Conference proceedings*

British Association for the Advancement of Science. *Section F (Economics). Meeting (1980 : Salford).* The mixed economy : proceedings of Section F (Economics) of the British Association for the Advancement of Science, Salford 1980 / edited by Lord Roll of Ipsden. — London : Macmillan, 1982. — xiii,233p : ill ; 23cm
Includes bibliographies and index
ISBN 0-333-31540-5 : £20.00 B82-32226

330.12'6 — Mixed economies. Theories of Galbraith, John Kenneth & Towney, R. H.

Reisman, David. State and welfare : Tawney, Galbraith and Adam Smith / David Reisman. — London : Macmillan, 1982. — vii,254p ; 23cm
Includes index
ISBN 0-333-31917-6 : Unpriced B82-28685

330.15'3 — Economics. Classical theory *related to* **Marxism** — *Festschriften*

Classical and Marxian political economy : essays in honour of Ronald L. Meek / edited by Ian Bradley and Michael Howard. — London : Macmillan, 1982. — xiv,300p : ill,1port ; 23cm
Includes bibliographies and index
ISBN 0-333-27027-4 (cased) : £15.00
ISBN 0-333-32199-5 (pbk) : Unpriced
Also classified at 335.4 B82-21620

330.15'3 — Economics. Classical theory — *Texts*

Smith, Adam, *1723-1790.* The wealth of nations : books I-III / Adam Smith ; with an introduction by Andrew Skinner. — Repr. with revisions. — Harmondsworth : Penguin, 1979, c1974 (1982 [printing]). — 537p ; 19cm
Previous ed.: i.e. 1st repr. with revisions. 1974. — Bibliography: p521-522. — Includes index
ISBN 0-14-043208-6 (pbk) : £2.95 B82-18150

330.15'3 — Economics. Smith, Adam, *1723-1790 — Biographies*

Campbell, R. H.. Adam Smith / R.H. Campbell and A.S. Skinner. — London : Croom Helm, c1982. — 231p ; 23cm
Includes index
ISBN 0-7099-0729-x : £12.95 : CIP rev. B82-04464

330.15'3 — Economics. Theories of Malthus, T.R.

Thompson, N. W.. Malthus and the problems of economic development / N.W. Thompson. — [Swansea] : Centre for Development Studies, University College of Swansea, 1982, c1981. — 10p ; 22cm. — (Occasional paper / Centre for Development Studies, University College of Swansea, ISSN 0114-9494 ; no.15)
Text on inside covers
ISBN 0-86094-105-1 (pbk) : Unpriced B82-27474

330.15'3 — Economics. Theories of Mill, John Stuart. Influence of theories of sociology of Auguste Comte

Weinberg, Adelaide. The influence of Auguste Comte on the economics of John Stuart Mill / by Adelaide Weinberg. — London (77 Marlborough Mansions, Cannon Hill, NW6 1JT) : E.G. Weinberg, c1982. — 406p ; 29cm
Bibliography: p395-406
£8.50 (pbk) B82-18892

330.15'5 — Economics. Theories of Samuelson, Paul A.

Samuelson and neoclassical economics / edited by George R. Feiwel. — Boston, Mass ; London : Kluwer, c1982. — xiii,358p : ill ; 24cm. — (Recent economic thought)
Includes bibliographies
ISBN 0-89838-069-3 : Unpriced B82-20796

330.15'5 — Social economics

Gordon, Alan. Economics and social policy. — Oxford : Robertson, Sept.1982. — [224]p
ISBN 0-85520-527-x (cased) : £16.50 : CIP entry
ISBN 0-85520-528-8 (pbk) : £5.50 B82-20841

330.15'5 — Welfare economics

Just, Richard E.. Applied welfare economics and public policy / Richard E. Just, Darell L. Hueth, Andrew Schmitz. — Englewood Cliffs ; London : Prentice-Hall, c1982. — xviii,491p : ill ; 24cm
Bibliography: p474-484. — Includes index
ISBN 0-13-043398-5 : £26.20 B82-28154

Mishan, E. J.. Introduction to political economy / E.J. Mishan. — London : Hutchinson, 1982. — 270p : ill ; 23cm
Bibliography: p258-264. — Includes index
ISBN 0-09-145390-9 (cased) : £15.00 : CIP rev.
ISBN 0-09-145391-7 (pbk) : £5.50 B81-22552

Osmani, Siddiqur Rahman. Economic inequality and group welfare : a theory of comparision with application to Bangladesh / Siddiqur Rahman Osmani. — Oxford : Clarendon, 1982. — viii,179p : ill ; 23cm
Bibliography: p170-175. — Includes index
ISBN 0-19-828425-x : £15.00 : CIP rev. B82-10454

330.15'6 — Economics. Keynes, John Maynard — *Critical studies*

John Maynard Keynes. — London : Croom Helm, Sept.1982. — 4v. — (The Croom Helm critical assessment of leading economists)
ISBN 0-7099-2729-0 : £200.00 : CIP entry B82-20021

330.15'6 — Economics. Theories of Keynes, John Maynard — *Critical studies*

Coddington, Alan. Keynesian economics. — London : Allen & Unwin, Jan.1983. — [144]p
ISBN 0-04-330334-x : £9.95 : CIP entry B82-34092

Milgate, M.. Capital and employment. — London : Academic Press, Jan.1983. — [210]p. — (Studies in political economy ; 1)
ISBN 0-12-496250-5 : CIP entry B82-33467

Patinkin, Don. Anticipations of the General Theory?. — Oxford : Blackwell, July 1982. — [272]p
ISBN 0-631-13156-6 : £12.50 : CIP entry B82-12993

330.15′6 — Economics. Theories of Keynes, John Maynard — *Texts*

Keynes, John Maynard. The collected writings of John Maynard Keynes. — London : Macmillan for the Royal Economic Society
Vol.19: Activities 1922-1929, the return to gold and industrial policy / edited by Donald Moggridge. — c1981. — 2v.(xiv,923p,[1]leaf of plates) : 1port ; 25cm
Includes index
ISBN 0-333-10727-6 : £36.00 : CIP rev. B80-07247

Keynes, John Maynard. The collected writings of John Maynard Keynes. — London : Macmillan : Cambridge University Press for the Royal Economic Society
Vol.20: Activities 1929-1931 : rethinking employment and unemployment policies / edited by Donald Moggridge. — c1981. — xii,668p : 1port ; 25cm
Includes index
ISBN 0-333-10735-7 : Unpriced B82-10098

Keynes, John Maynard. The collected writings of John Maynard Keynes. — London : Macmillan for the Royal Economic Society
Vol.21: Activities 1931-1939, world crises and policies in Britain and America / edited by Donald Moggridge. — c1982. — xiii,632p,[1] leaf of plates : 2ports ; 24cm
Includes index
ISBN 0-333-10728-4 : Unpriced B82-32231

Keynes, John Maynard. The collected writings of John Maynard Keynes. — London : Macmillan Cambridge University Press for the Royal Economic Society
Vol.25: Activities 1940-1944 : shaping the post-war world : the Clearing Union / edited by Donald Moggridge. — c1980. — xiv,522p,[1]leaf of plates : 2ports ; 24cm
Includes index
ISBN 0-333-15658-7 : £15.00 : CIP rev. B79-22227

Keynes, John Maynard. The collected writings of John Maynard Keynes. — London : Macmillan Cambridge University Press for the Royal Economic Society
Vol.27: Activities 1940-1946 : shaping the post-war world : employment and commodities / edited by Donald Moggridge. — c1980. — xiii,539p,[1]leaf of plate : 1port ; 24cm
Includes index
ISBN 0-333-24174-6 : £15.00 : CIP rev. B80-07248

330.15′7 — Economics. Jevons, W. Stanley — *Correspondence, diaries, etc.*

Jevons, W. Stanley. Papers and correspondence of William Stanley Jevons. — London : Macmillan in association with the Royal Economic Society
Vol.5: Papers on political economy / edited by R.D. Collison Black. — 1981. — xiii,357p ; 25cm
Includes index
ISBN 0-333-19979-0 : £20.00 B82-06692

330.15′7 — Economics. Theories of Austrian School

Taylor, Thomas C.. The fundamentals of Austrian economics / by Thomas C. Taylor. — 2nd ed. — [London] : Adam Smith Institute in association with the Carl Menger Society, [1981?]. — 68p ; 22cm
Previous ed.: Washington, D.C. : Cato Institute, 1980. — Includes bibliographies
ISBN 0-906517-15-x (pbk) : £1.50 B82-16617

330.15′7 — Economics. Theories of Schumpeter, Joseph Alois — *Critical studies*

Schumpeterian economics. — Eastbourne : Praeger, Oct.1982. — [176]p
ISBN 0-03-062766-4 : £9.95 : CIP entry B82-23084

330′.17 — Europe. Private property, *1835-1980*

Grossi, Paolo. An alternative to private property : collective property in the juridical consciousness of the nineteenth century / Paolo Grossi ; translated by Lydia G. Cochrane. — Chicago ; London : University of Chicago Press, 1981. — xv,344p ; 24cm
Translation of: Un altro modo di possedere. — Includes index
ISBN 0-226-31002-7 : £23.80 B82-13671

330′.17′0924 — Property. Theories of Locke, John

Tully, James. A discourse on property. — Cambridge : Cambridge University Press, Oct.1982. — [194]p
Originally published: 1980
ISBN 0-521-27140-1 (pbk) : £4.95 : CIP entry B82-40318

330.9 — ECONOMIC CONDITIONS

330.9 — Capitalist countries. Economic conditions. Political aspects

The **Impact** of parties : politics and policies in democratic capitalist states. — London : Sage Publications, Mar.1982. — [410]p
ISBN 0-8039-9787-6 : £17.00 : CIP entry B82-00377

330.9 — Capitalist countries. Economic policies — *Marxist viewpoints*

Present-day non-Marxist political economy : a critical analysis. — Moscow : Progress ; [London] : distributed by Central, c1981. — 574p ; 19cm
Translation of: Sovremennaia nemarksistskaia politėkonomiia
ISBN 0-7147-1740-1 : £3.95 B82-29293

330.9 — Economic conditions. Geographical aspects

Economic geography. — London : Longman, Feb.1983. — [336]p. — (Longman business education series)
ISBN 0-582-41220-x (pbk) : £5.95 : CIP entry B82-38678

Knowles, R.. Economic and social geography made simple. — 4th (revised) ed. — London : Heinemann, Jan.1983. — [336]p. — (Made simple books)
Originally published: London : W.H. Allen, 1981
ISBN 0-434-98478-7 (pbk) : £2.95 : CIP entry B82-34582

330.9 — Economic conditions — *History* — *Serials*

Research in economic history : an annual compilation of research. — Vol.1 (1976)-. — Greenwich, Conn. : JAI Press ; London (3 Henrietta St., WC2E 8LU) : Distributed by JAICON Press, 1976-. — v. ; 24cm
ISSN 0363-3268 = Research in economic history : £24.50 B82-02365

Research in economic history. Supplement. — Vol.1 (1977)-. — Greenwich, Conn. : JAI Press ; London (3 Henrietta St., WC2E 8LU) : Distributed by JAICON Press, 1977-. — v. ; 24cm
Supplement to: Research in economic history £24.50 B82-02364

330.9 — Economic development

Ascent and decline in the world-system / edited by Edward Friedman. — Beverly Hills ; London : Sage, c1982. — 303p : ill ; 23cm. — (Political economy of the world-system annuals ; v.5)
Includes bibliographies
ISBN 0-8039-1829-1 (cased) : Unpriced
ISBN 0-8039-1830-5 (pbk) : Unpriced B82-38223

Dialogue on Development II *(Conference : 1982 : Panchgani)*. Right side up : a fresh look at development : report on Dialogue on Development II, Panchgani, India, January 1982. — Bombay : Niketu Iralu on behalf of Moral Re-Armament ; London (54 Lyford Rd, SW18 3JJ) : Grosvenor Books [distributor], [1982]. — 21p : ill,ports ; 23cm
Cover title
Unpriced (unbound) B82-34973

Gilder, George F.. Wealth & poverty / George Gilder. — London : Buchan & Enright, 1982, c1981. — xxiii,292p ; 24cm
Originally published: New York : Basic Books, 1981. — Bibliography: p276-282. — Includes index
ISBN 0-907675-01-8 : £8.50 B82-22053

Olson, Mancur. The rise and decline of nations. — London : Yale University Press, Oct.1982. — [287]p
ISBN 0-300-02307-3 : £8.95 : CIP entry B82-35192

330.9 — Economic development — *Comparative studies*

Whynes, David K.. Comparative economic development. — London : Butterworth Scientific, Dec.1982. — [360]p. — (Butterworths advanced economics texts)
ISBN 0-408-10683-2 (cased) : £20.00 : CIP entry
ISBN 0-408-10682-4 (pbk) : £8.95 B82-29787

330.9 — Economic development. Ecological aspects

Singh, Narindar. Economics and the crisis of ecology / Narindar Singh. — 2nd ed. — Delhi ; Oxford : Oxford University Press, 1978, c1976. — xii,181p ; 22cm
Previous ed.: 1976. — Bibliography: p177. — Includes index
ISBN 0-19-561078-4 (pbk) : £0.95 B82-11637

Tolba, Mostafa Kamal. Development without destruction : evolving environmental perceptions / Mostafa Kamal Tolba. — Dublin : Tycooly, 1982. — viii, 197p ; 25cm. — (Natural resources and the environment series)
Includes index
ISBN 0-907567-22-3 (cased) : Unpriced
ISBN 0-907567-23-1 (pbk) : Unpriced B82-32265

330.9 — Economic development — *Festschriften*

The **Theory** and experience of economic development. — London : Allen and Unwin, Aug.1982. — [416]p
ISBN 0-04-330323-4 : £22.50 : CIP entry B82-15626

330.9 — Economic development. Geographical factors

Chisholm, Michael. Modern world development : a geographical perspective / Michael Chisholm. — London : Hutchinson, 1982. — 216p : ill ; 23cm
Bibliography: p195-207. — Includes index
ISBN 0-09-141380-x (cased) : Unpriced : CIP rev.
ISBN 0-09-141381-8 (pbk) : £4.95 B82-07247

330.9 — Economic development. Inequalities

Laidlaw, Kenneth. Fractured world. — London : Ash & Grant, Oct.1981. — [176]p
ISBN 0-904069-47-8 : £6.95 : CIP entry B81-28005

330.9 — Economic development. Inequalities. Alleviation. Independent Commission on International Development Issues. North-South, a programme for survival — *Critical studies*

Beyond Brandt : an alternative strategy for survival / Third World First. — Oxford (232 Cowley Rd., Oxford OX4 1UH) : Third World First, [1982]. — 16p : ill ; 30cm
Cover title. — Originally published: 1981?. — Text on inside covers
£0.60 (pbk) B82-41023

Towards one world? : international responses to the Brandt Report / edited by the Friedrich Ebert Foundation. — London : Temple Smith, 1981. — 381p ; 22cm
ISBN 0-85117-218-0 (pbk) : £5.95 : CIP rev. B81-31188

330.9 — Economic development. Inequalities. Alleviation. Role of Great Britain — *Inquiry reports*

Great Britain. *Parliament. House of Commons. Foreign Affairs Committee*. The Mexico Summit : the British Government's role in the light of the Brandt Commission Report : fifth report from the Foreign Affairs Committee, Session 1980-81, together with part of the proceedings of the Committee relating to the report ; and the minutes of evidence taken before the Committee on 5 August 1980 and before the Sub-Committee on 28 October, 4 and 11 November 1980 in the last Session, and on 5, 17 and 31 March 1981 with appendices. — London : H.M.S.O.. — ([HC] ; 211-II)
Vol.2: Minutes of evidence and appendices. — 1981. — ix,246p : 1ill ; 25cm
ISBN 0-10-008771-x (pbk) : £9.05 B82-00028

330.9 — Economic development. Inequalities. Attitudes of John Paul II, *Pope*

McCormack, Arthur. The Third World : the teaching of Pope John Paul II / Arthur McCormack. — London : Catholic Truth Society, 1982. — 16p ; 18cm
ISBN 0-85183-496-5 (pbk) : £0.40 B82-30174

330.9 — Economic development. Political aspects

Gregory, C. A.. Gifts and commodities. — London : Academic Press, Sept.1982. — [250] p. — (Studies in political economy ; 2)
ISBN 0-12-301460-3 (cased) : CIP entry
ISBN 0-12-301462-x (pbk) : Unpriced B82-19163

330.9 — Economic development — *Sociological perspectives*

Nieuwenhuijze, C. A. O. van. Development begins at home. — Oxford : Pergamon, July 1982. — [320]p
ISBN 0-08-027415-3 : £15.00 : CIP entry B82-12415

330.9 — Economic policies

Kaldor, Nicholas. Essays on economic policy / Nicholas Kaldor. — London : Duckworth. — (Collected economic essays / by Nicholas Kaldor)
2. — 1964 (1980 [printing])
4: Policies for international stability ; 5. Country studies. — xxii,320p ; 23cm
Includes index
ISBN 0-7156-0114-8 : £20.00 : CIP rev. B80-12266

330.9 — Economic policies. Influence of uncertainty

Shultz, George P.. Risk, uncertainty and foreign economic policy / by George P. Shultz. — London (12 Upper Belgrave St., SW1X 8BA) : David Davies Memorial Institute of International Studies, [1981]. — 10p ; 24cm. — (Annual memorial lecture / David Davies Memorial Institute of International Studies ; 1981)
£1.00 (pbk) B82-12053

330.9 — Economics. Development studies — *Festschriften*

Approaches to development studies. — Aldershot : Gower, Dec.1982. — [360]p
ISBN 0-566-00529-8 : £15.00 : CIP entry B82-30051

330.9 — Industrialised countries. Economic policies — *Conference proceedings*

The **Political** economy of new and old industrial countries / edited by Christopher Saunders. — London : Butterworths, 1981. — ix,325p : ill ; 25cm. — (Butterworths studies in international political economy)
Conference papers. — Includes index
ISBN 0-408-10774-x : Unpriced : CIP rev. B81-04202

330.9 — Regional economics

Ghali, Moheb A.. Empirical explorations in regional growth / Moheb A. Ghali in collaboration with Masayuki Akiyama, Junichi Fujiwara. — Boston, Mass. ; London : Nijhoff, c1981. — xv,164p : ill ; 24cm. — (Studies in applied regional science)
Bibliography: p159-160. — Includes index
ISBN 0-89838-059-6 : Unpriced B82-03455

Richardson, Harry W.. Regional and urban economics / Harry W. Richardson. — London : Pitman, 1979, c1978. — 416p : ill ; 23cm
Originally published: Harmondsworth : Penguin, 1978. — Bibliography: p376-403. — Includes index
ISBN 0-273-01461-7 : Unpriced B82-01754

330.9′005 — Economic conditions. Newspapers: Financial times — *Indexes*

Annual index to the Financial times. — 1981-. — London : Financial Times Business Information, 1981-. — v. ; 31cm
ISSN 0263-6891 = Annual index to the Financial times : Unpriced B82-29059

330.9′00724 — Economic policies. Econometric models

Preston, A. J.. The theory of economic policy : statics and dynamics / A.J. Preston, A.R. Pagan. — Cambridge : Cambridge University Press, 1982. — xii,392p : ill ; 24cm
Bibliography: p383-387. — Includes index
ISBN 0-521-23366-6 : £27.50 : CIP rev. B82-12004

330.9′034 — Economic development. Effects of populism, *ca 1800-1981*

Kitching, Gavin. Development and underdevelopment in historical perspective. — London : Methuen, May 1982. — [256]p. — (Development and underdevelopment)
ISBN 0-416-73130-9 (cased) : £10.50 : CIP entry
ISBN 0-416-73140-6 (pbk) : £5.95 B82-06759

330.9′04 — Economic policies. Influence of economic theories, *1900-1981*

Balogh, Thomas. The irrelevance of conventional economics / Thomas Balogh. — London : Weidenfeld and Nicolson, c1982. — ix,262p ; 23cm
Includes index
ISBN 0-297-78028-x : £16.50 B82-16430

330.9′047 — Economic conditions, *ca 1970-1980 — Marxist viewpoints*

Mandel, Ernest. The second slump : a Marxist analysis of recession in the seventies / Ernest Mandel ; translated by Jon Rothschild. — London : Verso, 1980, c1978. — 226p : ill ; 21cm
Translation of: Ende der Krise oder Krise ohne Ende?. — Originally published: London : NLB, 1978. — Includes index
ISBN 0-86091-012-1 (cased) : Unpriced
ISBN 0-86091-728-2 (pbk) : £2.95 B82-39323

330.9′048 — Economic conditions. International political aspects

Tumlir, Jan. The contribution of economics to international disorder / by Jan Tumlir. — London : Published for the Harry G. Johnson Memorial Fund by the Trade Policy Research Centre, 1981. — v,14p ; 22cm. — (Harry G. Johnson Memorial Lecture, ISSN 0262-2890 ; no.2)
ISBN 0-900842-59-8 (pbk) : £1.00 B82-14891

330.9′048 — Economic conditions. Political aspects

Simpson, David. The political economy of growth. — Oxford : Blackwell, Jan.1983. — [112]p
ISBN 0-631-10871-8 : £6.95 : CIP entry B82-32511

330.9′048 — Economic conditions — *Serials*

Economic handbook of the world. — 1981-. — New York ; London : Published for the Center for Social Analysis of the State University of New York at Binghamton by McGraw-Hill, 1981-. — v. : maps ; 29cm
Annual. — Maps on lining papers
ISSN 0275-5874 = Economic handbook of the world : Unpriced B82-20885

330.9′048 — Economic development — *Serials*

International development abstracts. — 1982/1-. — Norwich : Geo Abstracts, 1982-. — v. ; 21cm
Six issues yearly
ISSN 0262-0855 = International development abstracts : £20.00 per year B82-28108

330.9′048 — World. Economic conditions

Beenstock, Michael. The world economy in transition. — London : Allen and Unwin, Feb.1983. — [240]p
ISBN 0-04-339033-1 : £12.50 : CIP entry B82-36445

330.9′048′0724 — Economic conditions. Mathematical models

Dayal, Ram. An integrated system of world models : with separate models for economic growth, population and labour force, energy, food and agriculture, machinery and equipment and raw materials / Ram Dayal. — Amsterdam ; Oxford : North-Holland, c1981. — xviii,398p : ill ; 23cm. — (North-Holland systems and control series ; v.2)
Includes bibliographies
ISBN 0-444-86272-2 : Unpriced B82-01647

330.9171′7 — Communist developing countries. Politico-economic systems

Revolutionary socialist development in the third world. — Brighton : Harvester, Feb.1983. — [240]p
ISBN 0-7108-0220-x (cased) : £22.50 : CIP entry
ISBN 0-7108-0225-0 (pbk) : £8.95 B82-38900

330.9171′7 — Sovet ėkonomicheskoĭ vzaimopomoshchi countries. Economic conditions — *Statistics — Serials*

Comecon data / edited by the Vienna Institute for Comparative Economic Studies (Wiener Institut für Internationale Wirtschaftsvergleiche). — 1979-. — London : Macmillan, 1980-. — v. ; 21cm
Annual. — English edition of: RGW in Zahlen. — No issue published for 1980
ISSN 0263-3701 = Comecon data : £15.00 B82-18542

330.9172′2 — Developed countries. Economic conditions. Implications of economic conditions of developing countries

Wionczek, Miguel S.. Some key issues for the world periphery : selected essays / by Miguel S. Wionczek. — Oxford : Pergamon, 1982. — xiv,432p ; 24cm
Includes bibliographies and index
ISBN 0-08-025783-6 : £37.50 : CIP rev. B81-31726

330.9172′4 — Communist developing countries. Politico-economic systems

The **New** communist Third World : an essay in political economy / edited by Peter Wiles. — London : Croom Helm, c1982. — 392p ; 23cm
Bibliography: p378-386. — Includes index
ISBN 0-7099-2709-6 : £15.95 : CIP rev. B81-31167

330.9172′4 — Developing countries. Economic conditions

Hoogvelt, Ankie M. M.. The Third World in global development / Ankie M.M. Hoogvelt. — London : Macmillan, 1982. — xii,260p ; 23cm
Includes index
ISBN 0-333-27681-7 (cased) : Unpriced
ISBN 0-333-27682-5 (pbk) : Unpriced B82-34917

Sinclair, Stuart. The Third World economic handbook. — London : Euromonitor, Sept.1982. — [224]p
ISBN 0-903706-85-7 : £27.50 : CIP entry B82-20659

330.9172′4 — Developing countries. Economic conditions — *For schools*

Tames, Richard. Emergent nations : strategies for development / Richard Tames. — London : Blackie, 1981. — 72p : ill ; 21cm. — (Crossroads)
Bibliography: p67-71
ISBN 0-216-91066-8 (pbk) : £1.75 B82-09658

330.9172′4 — Developing countries. Economic development

Bagchi, Amiya Kumar. The political economy of underdevelopment / Amiya Kumar Bagchi. — Cambridge : Cambridge University Press, 1982. — viii,280p ; 23cm. — (Modern Cambridge economics)
Bibliography: p254-276. — Includes index
ISBN 0-521-24024-7 (cased) : £20.00 : CIP rev.
ISBN 0-521-28404-x (pbk) : £7.50 B82-07956

De Silva, S. B. D. The political economy of underdevelopment / S.B.D. de Silva. — London : Routledge & Kegan Paul, in association with the Institute of Southeast Asian Studies, Singapore, 1982. — viii,645,14p ; 23cm. — (International library of sociology)
Includes index
ISBN 0-7100-0469-9 : £20.00 B82-28429

Guernier, Maurice. Third world, three quarters of the world. — Oxford : Pergamon, Oct.1981. — [192]p
Translation of: Tiers-monde, trois quarts du monde
ISBN 0-08-027065-4 (cased) : £8.70 : CIP entry
ISBN 0-08-027066-2 (pbk) : £4.40 B81-31946

330.9172'4 — Developing countries. Economic development *continuation*

Rural development. — London : Hutchinson Education, Sept.1982. — [352]p
ISBN 0-09-144790-9 (cased) : £12.00 : CIP entry
ISBN 0-09-144791-7 (pbk) : £5.50 B82-19103

Small is beautiful : simple aids for world development. — London (PO Box No.1, SW9 8BH) : Christian Aid, 1978. — 7p : ill ; 30cm
Unpriced (unbound) B82-40865

Streeten, Paul. First things first : meeting basic human needs in the developing countries / Paul Streeten with Shahid Javed Burki ... [et al.]. — New York ; Oxford : Published for the World Bank [by] Oxford University Press, c1981. — xii,206p : ill ; 24cm
Bibliography: p193-199. — Includes index
ISBN 0-19-520368-2 (cased) : £10.00
ISBN 0-19-520369-0 (pbk) : £3.95 B82-34512

The **Struggle** for development. — Chichester : Wiley, Jan.1983. — [400]p
ISBN 0-471-10152-4 : £13.00 : CIP entry
B82-34613

330.9172'4 — Developing countries. Economic development. Applications of systems theory — *Conference proceedings*

System approach for development : third IFAC/IFIP/IFORS Conference Rabat, Morocco, 24-27 November 1980 / editors N. [i.e.M] Najim and Y.M. Abdel-Fattah. — Oxford : Published for the International Federation of Automatic Control by Pergamon, 1981, c1980. — lxxxv,592p : ill ; 31cm. — (IFAC proceedings series)
Includes bibliographies
ISBN 0-08-025670-8 : £54.00 B82-03886

330.9172'4 — Developing countries. Economic development — *Case studies*

Balassa, Bela. Development strategies in semi-industrial economies / Bela Balassa in association with Julio Berlinski ... [et al.]. — Baltimore ; London : Published for the World Bank [by] Johns Hopkins University Press, c1982. — xiii,394p ; 29cm. — (A World Bank research publication)
Includes index
ISBN 0-8018-2569-5 : Unpriced B82-36051

Case studies in development economics / edited by Peter Maunder ; [written by] Vincent Cable ... [et al.]. — London : Published by Heinemann Educational on behalf of the Economics Association, 1982. — vi,138p : 2maps ; 20cm. — (Case studies in economic analysis ; 8)
ISBN 0-435-33937-0 (pbk) : £3.95 : CIP rev.
B81-22593

330.9172'4 — Developing countries. Economic development. Effects of capitalism, *to 1969 — Marxist viewpoints*

Frank, André Gunder. On capitalist underdevelopment / André Gunder Frank. — Bombay ; Oxford : Oxford University Press, 1975 (1979 [printing]). — x,113p ; 22cm
Bibliography: p111-113
ISBN 0-19-560475-x (pbk) : £1.25 B82-16810

330.9172'4 — Developing countries. Economic development — *Proposals*

The **Challenge** of development in the eighties. — Oxford : Pergamon, Mar.1982. — [143]p
ISBN 0-08-027410-2 : £7.95 : CIP entry
B82-05374

330.9172'4 — Developing countries. Economic development. Role of developed countries

Global strategy for growth : a report on north-south issues / Lord McFadzean of Kelvinside ... [et al.]. — London : Trade Policy Research Centre, 1981. — xii,100p ; 19cm. — (Special report, ISSN 0262-141x ; no.1)
Text on inside cover. — Bibliography: p89-97
ISBN 0-900842-55-5 (pbk) : £2.00 B82-18700

330.9172'4 — Developing countries. Economic development — *Serials*

[Newsletter *(University College of Swansea. Centre for Development Studies)*]. Newsletter / Centre for Development Studies. — No.1 (Jan. 1980)-. — Swansea (University College of Swansea, Singleton Pk, Swansea SA2 8PP) : The Centre, 1980-. — v. : ill,ports ; 21cm
Quarterly. — No.1 issued for internal circulation only. — Description based on: No.5 (Dec. 1981)
ISSN 0263-2489 = Newsletter - Centre for Development Studies, University College of Swansea, University of Wales : Unpriced
B82-20876

330.9172'4 — Developing countries. Economic development — *Socialist viewpoints*

Neo-Marxist theories of development. — London : Croom Helm, Jan.1983. — [240]p
ISBN 0-7099-1641-8 : £9.95 : CIP entry
B82-40306

330.9172'4 — Developing countries. Rural regions. Economic development. Policies of governments

Das Gupta, Jyotirindra. Authority, priority and human development / Jyotirindra Das Gupta. — Delhi ; London : Oxford University Press, 1981. — viii,118p ; 23cm
Includes index
ISBN 0-19-561391-0 : £5.50 B82-39965

330.9173'2 — Urban economics

Miyao, Takahiro. Dynamic analysis of the urban economy / Takahiro Miyao. — New York ; London : Academic Press, 1981. — xv,188p : ill ; 24cm. — (Studies in urban economics)
Includes bibliographies and index
ISBN 0-12-501150-4 : £16.00 B82-02065

330.9173'2'05 — Urban regions. Economic conditions — *Serials*

Research in urban economics : a research annual. — Vol.1 (1981)-. — Greenwich, Conn. : JAI Press ; London (3 Henrietta St., WC2E 8LU) : Distributed by JAICON Press, 1981-. — v. : ill ; 24cm
£24.50 B82-02345

330.9173'4 — Rural regions. Economic development — *Serials*

[Bulletin *(Reading Rural Development Communications)*]. Bulletin / Reading Rural Development Communications. — 1 (1977)-. — Reading (University of Reading, Agricultural Extension and Rural Development Centre, London Road, Reading RG1 5AQ) : Reading Rural Development Communications, 1977-. — ill ; 30cm
Irregular. — Description based on: 11 (Oct. 1980)
ISSN 0261-0914 = Bulletin - Reading Rural Development Communications : £4.00 per year
B82-29056

330.917'4927 — Arab countries. Economic conditions

Amin, Samir. The Arab economy today. — London : Zed Press, Oct.1981. — [96]p
Translation of: L'économie arabe contemporaine
ISBN 0-86232-081-x : £9.95 : CIP entry
B81-27467

330.917'4927 — Arab countries. Economic conditions — *Comparative studies*

Sayigh, Yusif A.. The Arab economy : past performance and future prospects / Yusif A. Sayigh. — Oxford : Oxford University Press, 1982. — ix,175p : 1map ; 23cm
ISBN 0-19-877188-6 : £7.50 : CIP rev.
B81-35902

330.9'174927 — Arab countries. Economic development — *Conference proceedings*

Arab resources. — London : Croom Helm, Nov.1982. — [320]p
Conference papers
ISBN 0-7099-0727-3 (pbk) : £13.95 : CIP entry
B82-28748

330.917'4927'005 — Arab countries. Economic conditions — *For British businessmen — Serials*

[Directory *(Arab-British Chamber of Commerce)*] . Directory / Arab-British Chamber of Commerce. — 1981-. — London (P.O. Box 4BL, 42 Berkeley Sq., W1A 4BL) : The Chamber, 1981-. — v. : ill,ports ; 31cm
Annual. — Text in English and Arabic
ISSN 0262-7094 = Directory - Arab-British Chamber of Commerce : Unpriced B82-07627

330.917'7 — Organisation for Economic Co-operation and Development countries. Economic conditions

Anell, Lars. Recession, the Western economics and the changing world order. — London : Pinter, June 1981. — [230]p
ISBN 0-903804-94-8 : £12.50 : CIP entry
B81-11951

330.917'7 — Organisation for Economic Co-operation and Development countries. Economic conditions — *Forecasts*

The **World** economy in the 1980s : featuring : USA, Canada, Japan, West Germany, France, Italy, United Kingdom. — London : E.I.U. ; Philadelphia : Wharton, c1981. — 92p : ill ; 30cm. — (An EIU-Wharton EFA publication)
Unpriced (pbk) B82-00772

330.9'181'2 — Western world. Economic conditions, *to 1982*

Kahn, Herman. The coming boom. — London : Hutchinson, Feb.1983. — [240]p
ISBN 0-09-150970-x : £7.95 : CIP entry
B82-36560

330.9182'1 — Western world. Economic conditions, *1400-1800*

Braudel, Fernand. Afterthoughts on material civilization and capitalism / Fernand Braudel ; translated by Patricia M. Ranum. — Baltimore ; London : Johns Hopkins University Press, 1977 (1979 [printing]). — xi,120p : ill ; 21cm. — (The Johns Hopkins symposia in comparative history ; 7)
Translation from the French
ISBN 0-8018-2217-3 (pbk) : £3.00 B82-28514

330.9182'1 — Western world. Economic conditions, *1945-1980.* **Psychological aspects**

Maital, Shlomo. Minds, markets and money : psychological foundations of economic behavior / Shlomo Maital. — New York : Basic ; London : Harper & Row, c1982. — x,310p : ill ; 22cm
Includes index
ISBN 0-06-338001-3 : Unpriced B82-35140

330.9182'1 — Western world. Economic policies. Econometric models

Elkan, Peter G.. The new model economy : economic inventions for the rest of the century / by Peter G. Elkan. — Oxford : Pergamon, 1982. — xi,145p,[2]p of plates ; 22cm
Includes index
ISBN 0-08-028112-5 : £8.75 : CIP rev.
B81-35944

330.9182'1 — Western world. Economic policies. Formulation. Influence of economic theories, *1960-1981*

Shonfield, Andrew. The use of public power. — Oxford : Oxford University Press, Oct.1982. — [240]p
ISBN 0-19-215357-9 : £9.95 : CIP entry
B82-23659

330.937'06 — Ancient Rome. Economic conditions, *B.C.31-A.D.476*

Duncan-Jones, Richard. The economy of the Roman Empire. — 2nd ed. — Cambridge : Cambridge University Press, Aug.1982. — [448]p
Previous ed.: 1974
ISBN 0-521-24970-8 (cased) : £25.00 : CIP entry
ISBN 0-521-28793-6 (pbk) : £9.50 B82-15878

330.94 — Europe. Economic conditions, *500-*
The **Cambridge** economic history of Europe. — Cambridge : Cambridge University Press
Vol.7: The industrial economies : capital, labour, and enterprise / edited by Peter Mathias and M.M. Postan. — 1978 (1982 [printing]). — 2v. : ill ; 23cm
Includes bibliographies and index
ISBN 0-521-28800-2 (pbk) : Unpriced
ISBN 0-521-28801-0 (part 2) : £12.50
B82-32088

330.94 — European Community countries. Economic conditions — *Conference proceedings*
European business forum : finance investment and trade : Rome, 10 & 11 December, 1981 : speakers papers / sponsored by The Financial Times ... [et al.]. — [London] ([Minster House, Arthur St., EC4R 9AX]) : [Financial Times Ltd.], [1981?]. — 98p : ill ; 30cm. — (Financial Times conferences)
Text in English and Italian. — Cover title
Unpriced (pbk) B82-22469

330.94 — European Community countries. Economic conditions — *Serials* — *For British businessmen*
The **Directors** guide to the EEC economies : the current background to business with forecasts a year ahead / the Henley Centre for Forecasting. — July 1979-. — London (2 Tudor St., Blackfriars, EC4Y 0AA) : The Centre, 1979-. — v. : ill,maps ; 22cm
Monthly. — Description based on: Nov. 1979 issue
ISSN 0263-2721 = Directors guide to the EEC economies : £79.00 per year B82-28863

330.94 — European Community countries. Economic policies
Hu, Yau-su. Europe under stress : convergence and divergence in the European Community / Yau-su Hu. — London : Published for The Royal Institute of International Affairs by Butterworths, 1981. — xi,120p ; 24cm. — (Butterworths European studies)
Includes index
ISBN 0-408-10808-8 : Unpriced : CIP rev.
B81-20474

330.94 — European Community countries. Regional economic development
Keeble, David. The influence of peripheral and central locations on the relative development of regions : final report / by David Keeble, Peter L. Owens and Chris Thompson ; joint sponsors: Commission of The European Communities Directorate-General for Regional Policy, and United Kingdom Department of Industry. — Cambridge : Department of Geography, University of Cambridge, 1981. — iv,277p : ill,maps ; 30cm
Bibliography: p201-210
ISBN 0-11-513575-8 (pbk) : £11.95
B82-31335

330.94 — South-eastern Europe. Economic conditions, *1600-1800*
McGowan, Bruce. Economic life in Ottoman Europe : taxation, trade and the struggle for land, 1600-1800 / Bruce McGowan. — Cambridge : Cambridge University Press, 1981. — xii,226p : ill,maps ; 24cm. — (Studies in modern capitalism = Études sur le capitalisme moderne)
Includes index
ISBN 0-521-24208-8 : £20.00 : CIP rev.
B81-39255

330.94'01 — Europe. Economic conditions, *1000-1700*
Cipolla, Carlo M.. Before the industrial revolution : European society and economy, 1000-1700 / Carlo M. Cipolla. — 2nd ed. — London : Methuen, 1981, c1980. — xiv,352p : ill,maps ; 22cm
Previous ed.: 1976. — Bibliography: p309-336. — Includes index
ISBN 0-416-74920-8 (cased) : Unpriced
ISBN 0-416-74930-5 (pbk) : £5.50 B82-12183

330.94'01 — Western Europe. Economic conditions, *400-1100*
Latouche, Robert. The birth of western economy. — London : Methuen, Oct.1981. — [368]p. — (Methuen library reprints)
Translation of: Les origines de l'économie occidentale. — Originally published: 1961
ISBN 0-416-32090-2 : £18.00 : CIP entry
B81-27959

330.94'01 — Western Europe. Economic conditions, *600-1000* — *Sources of data: Antiquities*
Hodges, Richard, *1952-*. Dark age economics : the origins of towns and trade : A.D. 600-1000 / Richard Hodges. — London : Duckworth, 1982. — x,230p : maps,plans ; 26cm
Bibliography: p211-223. — Includes index
ISBN 0-7156-1531-9 : £24.00 B82-23506

330.94'022 — Europe. Economic conditions, *1500-1800*
An **Introduction** to the sources of European economic history 1500-1800. — London : Methuen. — (University paperbacks)
Vol.1: Western Europe / edited by Charles Wilson and Geoffrey Parker. — 1980, c1977. — xxxii,256p : ill ; 22cm
Originally published: London : Weidenfeld and Nicolson, 1977. — Includes index
ISBN 0-416-74210-6 (pbk) : £3.95 : CIP rev.
B80-08632

330.94'055 — Western Europe. Economic conditions. Information sources
Sources of European economic information. — 4th ed. — Aldershot : Gower, Aug.1982. — 2v.
Previous ed.: 1980 / by Cambridge Information and Research Services
ISBN 0-566-02322-9 : £45.00 : CIP entry
B82-16644

330.94'0555 — Western Europe. Economic conditions, *1950-1970*
The **European** economy. — Oxford : Oxford University Press, Oct.1982. — [650]p
ISBN 0-19-877118-5 (cased) : £20.00 : CIP entry
ISBN 0-19-877119-3 (pbk) : £9.95 B82-23699

330.94'0558 — Western Europe. Economic conditions
Europe's economy in crisis / edited by Ralf Dahrendorf ; preface by Gaston Thorn. — London : Weidenfeld and Nicolson, 1982. — xii,274p ; 23cm
Translation of: Trendwende. — Includes index
ISBN 0-297-78078-6 : £15.00 B82-37192

330.94'0558 — Western Europe. Economic conditions. Information sources
Sources of European economic information. — 3rd ed. / compiled by Cambridge Information and Research Services Ltd ; editors Andrew Buckley, Christopher Swain. — Farnborough, Hants : Gower, c1980. — x,316p ; 31cm
Previous ed.: 1977
ISBN 0-566-02150-1 : £37.50 : CIP rev.
B80-07249

330.941'07 — Great Britain. Economic conditions, *1700-1977*
The **economic** history of Britain since 1700 / edited by Roderick Floud and Donald McCloskey. — Cambridge : Cambridge University Press
Vol.1: 1700-1860. — 1981. — xv,323p : ill ; 24cm
Bibliography: p276-292. — Includes index
ISBN 0-521-23166-3 (cased) : £25.00 : CIP rev.
ISBN 0-521-29842-3 (pbk) : £7.95 B81-22550

The **economic** history of Britain since 1700 / edited by Roderick Floud and Donald McCloskey. — Cambridge : Cambridge University Press
Vol.2: 1860 to the 1970s. — 1981. — xvii,485p : ill ; 24cm
Bibliography: p417-443. — Includes index
ISBN 0-521-23167-1 (cased) : £30.00
ISBN 0-521-29843-1 (pbk) : £9.95 B82-02680

330.941'07 — Great Britain. Economic conditions, *1760-1973*
Business, banking and urban history : essays in honour of S.G. Checkland / edited by Anthony Slaven and Derek H. Aldcroft ; foreword by Sir Alec K. Cairncross. — Edinburgh : Donald, c1982. — xiv,235p,leaf of plate : 1map,1port ; 24cm
Bibliography: p233-235
ISBN 0-85976-083-9 : £15.00 B82-37593

330.941'081 — Great Britain. Economic conditions, *1837-1901*
Crouzet, François. The Victorian economy / François Crouzet ; translated by Anthony Forster. — London : Methuen, 1982. — xiii,430p ; 24cm
Translation of: L'Economie de la Grande Bretagne victorienne. — Bibliography: p423-424. — Includes index
ISBN 0-416-31110-5 (cased) : Unpriced : CIP rev.
ISBN 0-416-31120-2 (pbk) : Unpriced
B82-00301

330.941'081 — Great Britain. Economic conditions, *ca 1880-1980.* **Political aspects**
Gamble, Andrew. Britain in decline : economic policy, political strategy and the British state / Andrew Gamble. — London : Macmillan, 1981. — xxi,279p ; 21cm
Includes index
ISBN 0-333-22056-0 (cased) : Unpriced
ISBN 0-333-22057-9 (pbk) : Unpriced
B82-06638

330.941'081 — Great Britain. Economic development, *1856-1973*
Matthews, R. C. O.. British economic growth 1856-1973. — Oxford : Clarendon Press, Apr.1982. — [760]p. — (Studies of economic growth in industrial countries)
ISBN 0-19-828453-5 : £40.00 : CIP entry
B82-06025

330.941'081 — Great Britain. Economic policies, *1870-1945*
Tomlinson, Jim. Problems of British economic policy, 1870-1945. — London : Methuen, June 1981. — [155]p
ISBN 0-416-30430-3 : £8.50 : CIP entry
ISBN 0-416-30440-0 (pbk) : £4.25 B81-10458

330.941'082 — Great Britain. Economic development. Policies of government, *1870-1980* — *Communist Party of Britain viewpoints*
The **Economics** of genocide. — London (155, Fortress Rd, NW5) : Communist Party of Britain (Marxist-Leninist), [1982?]. — 3v. : ill ; 21cm
Bibliography: p16 (pt.1)
Unpriced (pbk) B82-19723

330.941'082 — Great Britain. Economic policies, *1911-1981* — *Festschriften*
Changing perceptions of economic policy : essays in honour of the seventieth birthday of Sir Alec Cairncross / edited by Frances Cairncross. — London : Methuen, 1981. — xii,276p ; 22cm
Includes index
ISBN 0-416-31550-x : £11.95 : CIP rev.
B81-27374

330.941'082 — Great Britain. Regional economic development, *1919-1979*
Law, Christopher M.. British regional development since World War 1. — London : Methuen, Nov.1981. — [272]p
Originally published: 1980
ISBN 0-416-32310-3 (pbk) : £4.95 : CIP entry
B81-30554

330.941'082 — Great Britain. Regional economic development. Policies of government, *1930-1975*
Green, W.. Regional problems and policies / W. Green, D. Clough. — London : Holt, Rinehart and Winston, c1982. — 143p : ill ; 22cm
Bibliography: p130-140. — Includes index
ISBN 0-03-910351-x (pbk) : £2.95 : CIP rev.
B82-11995

330.941'083 — Great Britain. Economic policies. Formulation. Influence of Keynes, John Maynard, *1913-1946*
Keynes Seminar *(5th : 1980 : University of Kent at Canterbury)*. Keynes as a policy adviser : the fifth Keynes Seminar held at the University of Kent at Canterbury, 1980 / edited by A.P. Thirlwall. — London : Macmillan, 1982. — xiv,182p : ports ; 23cm
Includes index
ISBN 0-333-32197-9 : £15.00 B82-38780

330.941'085 — Great Britain. Economic conditions, *1950-1980*

Eatwell, John. Whatever happended to Britain? : the economics of decline / John Eatwell. — London : Duckworth, 1982. — 168p : ill ; 23cm
Bibliography: p165-166. — Includes index
ISBN 0-7156-1643-9 (cased) : £9.95 : CIP rev.
ISBN 0-7156-1639-0 (pbk) : Unpriced
ISBN 0-563-16545-6 (cased (BBC))
ISBN 0-563-16544-8 (pbk (BBC)) B82-05410

330.941'085 — Great Britain. Economic development, *1930-1970*

The **Managed** economy. — Oxford : Oxford University Press, Dec.1982. — [260]p
ISBN 0-19-828290-7 (cased) : £15.00 : CIP entry
ISBN 0-19-828289-3 (pbk) : £6.95 B82-29625

330.941'085 — Great Britain. Economic policies, *1945-1981*

Pollard, Sidney. The wasting of the British economy : British economic policy 1945 to the present / Sidney Pollard. — London : Croom Helm, c1982. — 197p : ill ; 22cm
Includes index
ISBN 0-7099-2019-9 : £11.95 : CIP rev.
B81-33891

330.941'0856 — Great Britain. Economic development, *1960-1977*

Medlik, S.. Britain : workshop or service centre to the world? / S. Medlik. — [Guildford] ([Guildford, Surrey GU2 5XH]) : [University of Surrey], [1977?]. — 26p : ill ; 21cm. — (University of Surrey university lecture)
Cover title
Unpriced (pbk) B82-26658

330.941'0857 — Great Britain. Economic conditions, *1967-1980*

Black, John, *1931-*. The economics of modern Britain. — 3rd ed. — Oxford : Robertson, Sept.1982. — [302]p
Previous ed.: 1980
ISBN 0-85520-529-6 (cased) : £15.00 : CIP entry
ISBN 0-85520-530-x (pbk) : £5.95 B82-19822

330.941'0857 — Great Britain. Economic conditions, *1976-1981*

Townsend, Alan R.. The impact of recession. — London : Croom Helm, Nov.1982. — [192]p
ISBN 0-7099-2417-8 : £12.95 : CIP entry
B82-27941

330.941'0857 — Great Britain. Economic policies

Sartorius, Michael. The simple man's guide to national prosperity. — Porthmadoc (28f South Snowdon Quay, Porthmadoc, Gwynedd LL49 9ND) : Andreas, Sept.1981. — 1v.
ISBN 0-905539-01-x (pbk) : £3.00 : CIP entry
B81-22585

330.941'0857 — Great Britain. Economic policies, *1970-1974*

Holmes, Martin, *1954-*. Political pressure and economic policy : British government 1970-1974 / Martin Holmes. — London : Butterworth Scientific, 1982. — 164p ; 25cm
Bibliography: p156-160. — Includes index
ISBN 0-408-10830-4 : £15.00 : CIP rev.
B82-04038

330.941'0857 — Great Britain. Economic policies, *1970-1979*

Ball, R. J.. Money and employment / R.J. Ball. — London : Macmillan, 1982. — x,246p : ill ; 23cm
Bibliography: p235-237. — Includes index
ISBN 0-333-28795-9 (cased) : £15.00
ISBN 0-333-28796-7 (pbk) : Unpriced
B82-28393

330.941'0857 — Great Britain. Economic policies, *1970-1982*

Carter, *Sir* **Charles,** *1919-*. Policies for a constrained economy. — London : Heinemann Educational, Oct.1982. — [256]p. — (Policy Studies Institute series)
ISBN 0-435-84260-9 : £13.50 : CIP entry
B82-25924

330.941'0857 — Great Britain. Economic policies, *1979-1981*

Could do better : contrasting assessments of the economic progress and prospects of the Thatcher government at mid-term / Michael Beenstock ... [et al.]. — London : Institute of Economic Affairs, 1982. — 108p : ill ; 22cm. — (Occasional paper special / IEA, ISSN 0073-909x ; 62)
ISBN 0-255-36150-5 (pbk) : £2.80 B82-24638

330.941'0858 — Great Britain. Economic conditions

Britain's economy under strain : a series of ten macroeconomic briefs. — London : The Economist, [c1982]. — 21p : col.ill,col.maps ; 27cm
Cover title
ISBN 0-00-197418-1 (pbk) : £2.50 B82-31753

Brown, Leonard Louis. The British disease / Leonard Louis Brown. — [London] ([9, Grove Park, E11 2DN]) : L.L. Brown, c1982. — 163columns ; 21x29cm
Cover title. — Text on inside cover. — Includes index
Unpriced (pbk) B82-28671

Cairncross, Frances. The Guardian guide to the economy / Frances Cairncross and Phil Keeley. — London : Methuen, 1981. — viii,150p : ill ; 21cm
Bibliography: p145-149. — Includes index
ISBN 0-416-32560-2 (cased) : Unpriced : CIP rev.
ISBN 0-416-32570-x (pbk) : £2.50
ISBN 0-423-50940-3 (limp) : £1.95 B81-28000

Cameron, M. A.. Kindling a purpose : economics : brake or throttle? / by M.A. Cameron. — [Haywards Heath] ([22 Jireh Court, Perrymount Rd, Haywards Heath, W. Sussex RH16 3BH]) : [M.A. Cameron], [1982]. — 59,viiip ; 21cm
Cover title
Unpriced (pbk) B82-38246

Chandler, Geoffrey, *1922-*. The reindustrialisation of Britain / by Geoffrey Chandler. — Sheffield (c/o Hon. Sec., Sheffield City Polytechnic, Pond St., Sheffield S1 1WB) : Association of Colleges for Further and Higher Education, [1982]. — 9p ; 21cm
Paper from Annual General Meeting of ACFHE, Thursday and Friday 25 and 26 February 1982, The Institution of Electrical Engineers, Savoy Pl., London WC2. — Cover title
£0.75 (pbk) B82-36021

Dunnett, Andrew. Understanding the economy. — London : Longman, Nov.1982. — [172]p
ISBN 0-582-44646-5 (pbk) : £4.95 : CIP entry
B82-26537

Humphreys, R. G.. A fresh look at current economic problems / by R.G. Humphreys. — Herne Bay (47 William St., Herne Bay, Kent CT6 5NR) : Piranha Prints, c1982. — iv,144p : ill ; 22cm
£2.50 (pbk) B82-34671

Khamis, Chris. The U.K. economy : a review of performance and forecasts / Chris Khamis. — Watford (Letchmore Heath, Watford WD2 8DQ) : I.G.D., c1982. — 80p : ill ; 30cm
£20.00 (spiral) B82-27488

Maycock, Richard. Break the deadlock : a proposal for solving Britain's economic problems, and criticism of socialist and Marxist theories. — Halifax (12 Palatine Chambers, Market St., Halifax HX1 1RW) : Heigham Press, Aug.1982. — [240]p
ISBN 0-946154-00-7 (cased) : £9.95 : CIP entry
ISBN 0-946154-01-5 (pbk) : £3.50
Also classified at 335.4'12'0924 B82-25746

Sandford, Cedric. The economic structure / Cedric Sandford. — London : Longman, 1982. — x,113p : 1ill ; 20cm. — (Aspects of modern sociology. The social structure of modern Britain)
Bibliography: p107-108. — Includes index
ISBN 0-582-29544-0 (pbk) : £2.95 : CIP rev.
B82-20257

The **United** Kingdom economy / the National Institute of Economic and Social Research. — 5th ed. / contributors F.T. Blackaby ... [et al.]. — London : Published on behalf of the Commission of the European Communities by Heinemann Educational, 1982. — vi,102p ; 20cm. — (Studies in the British economy)
Previous ed.: 1979. — Includes index
ISBN 0-435-84587-x (pbk) : £1.95 B82-39936

330.941'0858 — Great Britain. Economic conditions, *1981-1983*

Khamis, Chris. The U.K. economy : a review of performance and forecasts / Chris Khamis. — Watford : IGD, c1982. — 64p ; 30cm
Unpriced (spiral) B82-23117

330.941'0858 — Great Britain. Economic conditions. Cooperation between government & trade unions — *Proposals*

Trades Union Congress. The economy, the government and trade union responsibilities : joint statement / by the TUC and the government. — London : H.M.S.O., 1979. — 19p ; 25cm
ISBN 0-11-360862-4 (unbound) : £0.40
B82-13674

330.941'0858 — Great Britain. Economic conditions — *Forecasts*

Holden, K.. Modelling the UK economy. — Oxford : Robertson, Oct.1982. — [220]p
ISBN 0-85520-519-9 (cased) : £15.00 : CIP entry
ISBN 0-85520-520-2 (pbk) : £5.95 B82-24111

The **UK** economy in the 1980s : projections and strategic assessments for business planners and investors. — London : Economist Intelligence Unit
1981 report. — c1981. — 30,77p : ill ; 30cm
Unpriced (spiral) B82-32694

The **UK** economy in the 1980's : projections and strategic assessments for business planners and investors. — London : Economist Intelligence Unit
Update to 1981 report. — c1981. — 37,[86]p ; 30cm
Unpriced (spiral) B82-32695

330.941'0858 — Great Britain. Economic conditions — *Forecasts* — *For investors*

How to survive the coming left wing government. — [Great Britain] : Chartsearch, 1981. — 33leaves : ill ; 31cm
Unpriced (pbk) B82-21424

330.941'0858 — Great Britain. Economic conditions — *Liberal Party viewpoints*

Saunders, James H.. Economics — the ecology of man / James H. Saunders. — Hythe (21 Fisher Close, Hythe, Kent, CT21 6AB) : New Creation Enterprises, [1982]. — 18p ; 21cm. — (The Orpington initiative ; pamphlet no.3)
£1.00 (pbk) B82-30657

330.941'0858 — Great Britain. Economic conditions. Policies of government — *Proposals*

Eaton, John, *1909-*. An alternative economic strategy for the labour movement / John Eaton, Michael Barratt Brown and Ken Coates. — Nottingham (45 Gamble St., Nottingham) : Published by the Spokesman for the Institute for Workers' Control, [1980]. — 12p ; 21cm. — (Spokesman pamphlet ; no.47)
£0.20 (pbk) B82-16891

330.941'0858 — Great Britain. Economic conditions. Political aspects

Meacher, Michael. Socialism with a human face : the political economy of Britain in the 1980s / Michael Meacher. — London : Allen & Unwin, 1982. — xvi,295p ; 23cm
Includes index
ISBN 0-04-320150-4 : Unpriced : CIP rev.
B82-00275

330.941'0858 — Great Britain. Economic conditions — *Trade union viewpoints*

Iron and Steel Trades Confederation. What is the future? : steel-rail-coal. — [Great Britain] : [S.n.], 1981 (Reading : CWS Printers). — 12p ; 21cm
Cover title. — "An Alternative Policy from the ISTC, NUM and NUR". — p.1
Unpriced (pbk) B82-11240

330.941'0858 — Great Britain. Economic development — *Forecasts — Serials*

Economic indicators, forecasts for company planning. — No.18 (Jan. 1982)-. — London (42 Colebrooke Row, N1 8AF) : Staniland Hall Associates, 1982-. — v. ; 21x30cm
Quarterly
ISSN 0263-7065 = Economic indicators, forecasts for company planning : Unpriced
B82-40058

330.941'0858 — Great Britain. Economic policies

The **1982** budget / edited by John Kay. — Oxford : Blackwell, 1982. — 147p : ill ; 22cm
ISBN 0-631-13153-1 (cased) : Unpriced
ISBN 0-631-13154-x (pbk) : Unpriced
B82-35823

What sort of society?. — Oxford : Martin Robertson, Sept.1982. — [250]p
ISBN 0-85520-523-7 (cased) : £15.00 : CIP entry
ISBN 0-85520-524-5 (pbk) : £4.95
Also classified at 361.6'1'0941 B82-20204

330.941'0858 — Great Britain. Economic policies. Implications of macroeconomic theories

Cross, Rod. Economic theory and policy in the UK : an outline and assessment of the controversies / Rod Cross. — Oxford : Robertson, 1982. — ix,223p : ill ; 22cm
Bibliography: p209-218. — Includes index
ISBN 0-85520-408-7 (cased) : £17.50 : CIP rev.
ISBN 0-85520-407-9 (pbk) : £5.95 B82-04802

330.941'0858 — Great Britain. Economic policies — *Inquiry reports*

Great Britain. *Parliament. House of Commons. Treasury and Civil Service Committee.* First report from the Treasury and Civil Service Committee : session 1981-82 : the government's economic policy autumn review together with the proceedings of the Committee, minutes of evidence and appendices. — London : H.M.S.O., [1981]. — 36p ; 25cm. — ([HC] ; 28)
ISBN 0-10-202882-6 (pbk) : £3.95 B82-14316

330.941'0858 — Great Britain. Economic policies — *Liberal Party viewpoints*

Finnie, Ross. The alternative economic strategy / Ross Finnie. — Edinburgh (2 Atholl Pl., Edinburgh) : Scottish Liberal Club, [1982?]. — 23p ; 21cm
Cover title
£0.50 (pbk) B82-24388

330.941'0858 — Great Britain. Economic policies — *Proposals*

Agenda for Britain / C.D. Cohen (editor). — Oxford : Philip Allan, 1982. — 2 : v.,ill ; 23cm
Includes bibliographies and index
ISBN 0-86003-034-2 (cased) : Unpriced : CIP rev.
ISBN 0-86003-132-2 (pbk) : £6.95 (v.2) : £10.00
ISBN 0-86003-138-1 (pbk) : £4.95 B81-39224

Williams, Shirley, *1930-*. Technology, employment and change / Shirley Williams. — Cambridge : Cambridge University Press, 1980. — 20p ; 19cm. — (The Rede lecture ; 1980)
Cover title
ISBN 0-521-28434-1 (pbk) : £1.40 B82-38838

330.941'0858 — Great Britain. Economic policies - *Socialist viewpoints*

Holland, Stuart. Strategy for socialism. — 2nd ed. — Nottingham : Spokesman, May 1981. — [100]p
Previous ed.: 1975
ISBN 0-85124-313-4 (cased) : £6.00 : CIP entry
ISBN 0-85124-314-2 (pbk) : £2.00 B81-07474

330.941'0858 — Great Britain. Regional economic development. Policies of government — *Selsdon Group viewpoints*

Bruce-Gardyne, Jock. An end to the Whitehall dole / Jock Bruce-Gardyne. — [London] ([170 Sloane St., SW1X 9QG]) : Selsdon Group, [1975?]. — 8p ; 23cm. — (Selsdon Group policy series ; no.3)
Cover title. — Text on inside cover
£0.50 (pbk) B82-07141

330.941'0858'05 — Great Britain. Economic conditions — *Forecasts — For business firms — Serials*

[Economic outlook *(Hoare Govett Ltd.)*].
Economic outlook : a monthy analysis of the British economy. — [197-]-. — London (319 High Holborn WC1V 7PB) : Hoare Govett, [197-]-. — v. : ill ; 30cm
Decription based on: 14th Aug. 1981
ISSN 0262-7698 = Economic outlook (Hoare Govett Ltd.) : Unpriced B82-07635

330.941'0858'05 — Great Britain. Economic conditions — *Forecasts — Serials*

UK economic prospect / the Economist Intelligence Unit. — No.1 (May 1982)-. — London : The Unit, 1982-. — v. : ill ; 30cm
Quarterly
ISSN 0262-8988 = UK economic prospect : Unpriced B82-31712

330.941'0858'0724 — Great Britain. Economic conditions. Econometric models

Coutts, K. J.. CEPG model of the UK economy technical manual. — 7th ed / by K.J. Coutts, T.F. Cripps and M. Anyadike-Danes. — Cambridge (Sidgwick Avenue, Cambridge, CB3 9DE) : University of Cambridge, Department of Applied Economics, 1981. — [102]p ; 30cm
Includes index
£4.50 (pbk) B82-03449

330.9411'085 — Scotland. Economic development, *1954-1978*

Lythe, Charlotte. The renaissance of the Scottish economy?. — London : Allen & Unwin, Nov.1982. — [256]p
ISBN 0-04-339032-3 : £8.95 : CIP entry
B82-27810

330.9411'0858 — Scotland. Economic conditions. Forecasting. Econometric models — *Serials*

The **Development** of a medium term model for Scotland. — 1-. — Glasgow (100 Montrose St., Glasgow G4 0LZ) : Fraser of Allander Institute for Research on the Scottish Economy, University of Strathclyde, 1982-. — v. : ill ; 21cm. — (Research monograph / Fraser of Allander Institute)
Annual
ISSN 0263-5445 = Development of a medium term model for Scotland : £3.00 B82-27656

330.9411'50858'05 — Scotland. Highland Region. Economic development — *Serials*

Highland focus : the bulletin of the Development Department of the Highland Regional Council. — Vol.1 (Apr. 1976)-. — Inverness (Regional Buildings, Glenurquhart Rd, Inverness IV3 5NX) : The Department, 1976-. — v. : ill,ports ; 30cm
Six issues yearly. — Suspended Sept. 1976-Sept. 1978. — Description based on: Vol.2, no.14 (Mar. 1981)
ISSN 0262-3331 = Highland focus : Unpriced
B82-03393

330.9413'10858'05 — Scotland. Central Region. Economic policies — *Serials*

Central Region economic review. — 1977-. — Stirling (Viewforth, Stirling [FK8 2ET]) : Planning Department, Central Regional Council, 1978-. — v. ; 30cm
Annual. — Description based on: 1978 issue
ISSN 0261-0981 = Central Region economic review : Unpriced B82-15769

330.9415'0821 — Ireland. Economic development, *ca 1915*

A. E.. The national being : some thoughts on an Irish polity / by A.E.. — Blackrock : Irish Academic Press, c1982. — 176p ; 22cm. — (Cooperative studies ; 2)
Originally published: Dublin : Maunsel, 1916
ISBN 0-7165-0336-0 (pbk) : £3.50 B82-29757

330.9417'0824 — Ireland *(Republic).* **Economic conditions,** *1972-1981*

Bacon, Peter, *1953-*. The Irish economy : policy and performance 1972-1981 / Peter Bacon, Joe Durkan, Jim O'Leary. — Dublin : Economic and Social Research Institute, c1982. — 123p,[3]folded leaves of plates : ill ; 22cm
Bibliography: p122-123
ISBN 0-7070-0051-3 (pbk) : £7.50 (Irish) (special rate for students £3.75 (Irish))
B82-40452

330.9417'0824 — Ireland *(Republic).* **Economic infrastructure** — *Forecasts — Conference proceedings*

Infrastructure : finance, employment, organisation : proceedings of a colloquy, Kilkea Castle, 1982. — Dublin : An Foras Forbartha, [1982]. — vii,80p : ill ; 30cm. — (Ireland in the year 2000)
£3.00 (pbk) B82-32044

330.9417'0824'0212 — Ireland *(Republic).* **Economic conditions** — *Statistics — For marketing*

Nabney, Peter. Marketing opportunities in Eire / [researched and compiled by Peter Nabney]. — London : Euromonitor, 1982. — 232p ; 30cm
ISBN 0-903706-75-x (spiral) : £135.00
B82-29182

330.942'07 — England. Economic development, *ca 1700-ca 1800*

McKendrick, Neil. The birth of a consumer society : the commercialization of eighteenth century England. — London : Europa, May 1982. — [300]p
ISBN 0-905118-00-6 : £19.50 : CIP entry
B82-07699

330.9426'180858 — Norfolk. Great Yarmouth. Economic conditions — *Serials*

Great Yarmouth port and industry handbook. — 1981-. — Downham Market (Bank Chambers, Downham Market, Norfolk PE38 9BU) : Charter Publications, [1980], c1979-. — v. : ill(some col.),maps(some col.) ; 24cm
Annual. — Description based on: 1982
ISSN 0260-9517 = Great Yarmouth port and industry handbook : £2.50 B82-15167

330.9426'44 — Suffolk. Bury St Edmunds. Economic development, *1290-1539*

Gottfried, Robert S.. Bury St. Edmunds and the urban crisis : 1290-1539 / Robert S. Gottfried. — Princeton ; Guildford : Princeton University Press, c1982. — xvi,313p : ill,maps ; 25cm
Bibliography: p291-306. — Includes index
ISBN 0-691-05340-5 : £19.40 B82-24309

330.9427'0858 — North-west England. Regional economic development

North Rhine-Westphalia — North West England : regional development in action : edited conference papers. — [London] : Anglo-German Foundation for the Study of Industrial Society, [c1980]. — 2v. : ill,maps ; 30cm
Cover title
ISBN 0-905492-21-8 (pbk) : Unpriced
ISBN 0-905492-20-x (v.2) : £1.50
Also classified at 330.943'550878 B82-01288

330.9427'0858'05 — Northern England. Regional economic development — *Serials*

Northern economic review / Centre for Urban and Regional Development Studies at the University of Newcastle upon Tyne. — No.1 (Nov. 1981)-. — Newcastle upon Tyne (Newcastle upon Tyne NE1 7RU) : The Centre, 1981-. — v. : ill,maps ; 21cm
Quarterly
ISSN 0262-0383 = Northern economic review : £6.00 per year B82-11829

330.9427'507 — Merseyside *(Metropolitan County).* **Economic development,** *1750-1960*

Marriner, Sheila. The economic and social development of Merseyside / Sheila Marriner. — London : Croom Helm, c1982. — viii,176p : ill,1map ; 23cm. — (Croom Helm series on the regional economic history of Britain)
Bibliography: p168-172. — Includes index
ISBN 0-7099-0260-3 : £12.95 : CIP rev.
B82-06514

330.9427'5081 — Merseyside *(Metropolitan County).* **Economic conditions,** *ca 1800-1982*

Commerce, industry and transport : studies in economic change on Merseyside. — Liverpool : Liverpool University Press, Feb.1983. — [264]p
ISBN 0-85323-374-8 : £15.00 : CIP entry
B82-39598

330.9429'40858 — South Wales. Urban regions. Economic development. Role of British government
Cooke, P. N.. Urban redevelopment and the local state : the case of South Wales / by Philip Cooke. — Cardiff (King Edward VII Av, Cardiff, CF1 3NU, Wales) : Dept. of Town Planning, University of Wales, Institute of Science and Technology, 1981. — iiileaves,32p ; 30cm. — (Papers in planning research ; 28)
Bibliography: p28.30
Unpriced (pbk) B82-25636

330.943'084 — Germany. Rural regions. Economic conditions, *1890-1907.* **Attitudes of Sozialdemokratische Partei Deutschlands**
Hussain, Athar. Marxism and the agrarian question / Athar Hussain, Keith Tribe. — London : Macmillan, 1981. — 2v. ; 23cm
Includes bibliographies and index
ISBN 0-333-24143-6 : Unpriced : CIP rev.
ISBN 0-333-28675-8 (v.2) : £15.00
Also classified at 330.947'08 B80-35745

330.943'086 — Germany. Nationalsozialistische Deutsche Arbeiter-Partei. *Schutzstaffel.* **Economic policies,** *to 1945 — Personal observations*
Speer, Albert. The slave state : Heinrich Himmler's masterplan for SS supremacy / Albert Speer ; translation by Joachim Neugroschel. — London : Weidenfeld and Nicolson, c1981. — xiv,384p ; 24cm
Translated from the German. — Includes index
ISBN 0-297-78013-1 : £10.95 B82-02178

330.943'0878 — West Germany. Economic conditions
West Germany. — London (41 Lothbury, EC2P 2BP) : National Westminster Bank, 1982. — [4]p ; 30cm. — (The National Westminster Bank overseas economic report series)
Unpriced (unbound) B82-21789

330.943'0878'0212 — West Germany. Economic conditions *— Statistics — For marketing*
Marketing opportunities in West Germany. — [London] : Euromonitor, [1982?]. — 235p ; 30cm
£195.00 (spiral) B82-29181

330.9431'0878 — East Germany. Economic conditions
German Democratic Republic : an economic report. — London (41 Lothbury, EC2P 2BP) : National Westminster Bank, 1981. — [4]p ; 30cm. — (The National Westminster Bank overseas economic report series)
Unpriced (unbound) B82-14830

330.943'550878 — West Germany. North Rhine-Westphalia. Regional economic development
North Rhine-Westphalia — North West England : regional development in action : edited conference papers. — [London] : Anglo-German Foundation for the Study of Industrial Society, [c1980]. — 2v. : ill,maps ; 30cm
Cover title
ISBN 0-905492-21-8 (pbk) : Unpriced
ISBN 0-905492-20-x (v.2) : £1.50
Primary classification 330.9427'0858
B82-01288

330.9436'053 — Austria. Economic conditions
Austria : an economic report. — London (41 Lothbury, EC2P 2BP) : National Westminster Bank, 1981. — [4]p ; 30cm. — (The National Westminster Bank overseas economic report series)
Unpriced (unbound) B82-14727

330.9437'043 — Czechoslovakia. Economic conditions
Czechoslovakia : an economic report. — London (41 Lothbury, EC2P 2BP) : National Westminster Bank, 1981. — [4]p ; 30cm. — (The National Westminster Bank overseas economic report series)
Unpriced (unbound) B82-14826

330.9438'055 — Poland. Economic conditions
Poland : an economic report. — London (41 Lothbury, EC2P 2BP) : National Westminster Bank, 1981. — [4]p ; 30cm. — (The National Westminster Bank overseas economic report series)
Unpriced (unbound) B82-14807

330.9439'053 — Hungary. Economic conditions
Hungary : an economic report. — London (41 Lothbury, EC2P 2BP) : National Westminster Bank, 1981. — [4]p ; 30cm. — (The National Westminster Bank overseas economic report series)
Unpriced (unbound) B82-14834

330.944'082 — France. Economic development, *1945-1981*
Hough, J. R.. The French economy. — London : Croom Helm, Aug.1982. — [224]p
ISBN 0-7099-1219-6 : £13.95 : CIP entry
B82-15905

330.944'0838 — France. Economic conditions
France : an economic report. — London (41 Lothbury, EC2P 2BP) : National Westminster Bank, 1981. — [4]p ; 30cm. — (The National Westminster Bank overseas economic report series)
Unpriced (unbound) B82-14829

330.944'0838 — France. Economic policies. Political aspects *— Conference proceedings*
France in the troubled world economy / [edited by] Stephen S. Cohen, Peter A. Gourevitch. — London : Butterworth Scientific, 1982. — 199p : 1ill ; 24cm. — (Butterworths studies in international political economy)
Conference papers. — Includes index
ISBN 0-408-10787-1 : Unpriced : CIP rev.
B82-01970

330.944'1063 — Urban regions. Economic change *— Study regions: New South Wales. Sydney*
Why cities change. — London : Allen & Unwin, Nov.1982. — [304]p
ISBN 0-86861-252-9 : £18.00 : CIP entry
B82-26087

330.944'64 — France. La Rochelle. Economic conditions, *1700-1790*
Clark, John G.. La Rochelle and the Atlantic economy during the eighteenth century / John G. Clark. — Baltimore ; London : Johns Hopkins University Press, c1981. — xiv,286p : ill,1map,1plan ; 24cm
Includes index
ISBN 0-8018-2529-6 : Unpriced B82-16924

330.944'84 — France. Clermont-de-Lodève. Economic conditions, *1633-1789*
Thomson, J. K. J.. Clermont-de-Lodève : 1633-1789 : fluctuations in the prosperity of a Languedocian cloth-making town / J.K.J. Thomson. — Cambridge : Cambridge University Press, 1982. — xii,502p : ill,2facsims,maps,2plans ; 24cm
Bibliography: p467-479. — Includes index
ISBN 0-521-23951-6 : £32.50 : CIP rev.
B82-26235

330.945'52 — Italy. Pescia. Economic conditions, *1500-1600*
Brown, Judith C.. In the shadow of Florence : provincial society in Renaissance Pescia / Judith C. Brown. — New York ; Oxford : Oxford University Press, 1982. — xxv,244p : ill,maps ; 23cm
Includes appendix in Italian. — Bibliography: p227-238. — Includes index
ISBN 0-19-502993-3 : £19.50 B82-34506

330.945'7092 — Southern Italy. Regional economic development, *1950-1980*
Mountjoy, Alan B.. The Mezzogiorno / Alan B. Mountjoy. — 2nd ed. — Oxford : Oxford University Press, 1982. — 48p : ill,col.maps ; 25cm. — (Problem regions of Europe)
Previous ed.: 1973. — Bibliography: p47. — Includes index
ISBN 0-19-913289-5 (pbk) : £2.50 B82-33075

330.945'85 — Malta. Economic conditions
Malta : an economic report. — London (41 Lothbury, EC2P 2BP) : National Westminster Bank, 1981. — [4]p : 2maps(some col.) ; 30cm. — (The National Westminster Bank overseas economic report series)
Unpriced (unbound) B82-14800

330.946'082 — Spain. Economic conditions, *1939-1981.* **Political aspects**
Lieberman, Sima. The contemporary Spanish economy : a historical perspective / Sima Lieberman. — London : Allen & Unwin, 1982. — xii,378p : ill ; 23cm
Bibliography: p360-365. — Includes index
ISBN 0-04-339026-9 : Unpriced : CIP rev.
B81-35927

330.946'083 — Spain. Economic conditions
Spain : an economic report. — London (41 Lothbury, EC2P 2BP) : National Westminster Bank, 1982. — [4]p ; 30cm. — (The National Westminster Bank overseas economic report series)
Unpriced (unbound) B82-25251

330.946'083 — Spain. Economic conditions — *Forecasts*
Spain : economic prospects to 1985. — London : Economist Intelligence Unit, 1981. — 58p ; 30cm. — (ETU special report ; no.114)
Unpriced (pbk) B82-11660

330.9469'044 — Portugal. Economic conditions
Portugal : an economic report. — London (41 Lothbury, EC2P 2BP) : National Westminster Bank, 1980. — [4]p ; 30cm. — (The National Westminster Bank overseas economic report series)
Unpriced (unbound) B82-14843

330.9469'044 — Portugal. Economic conditions, *1974-1980.* **Political aspects**
Morrison, Rodney J.. Portugal : revolutionary change in an open economy / Rodney J. Morrison. — Boston, Mass. : Auburn House ; London : distributed by Eurospan, c1981. — xvi,184p ; 25cm
Bibliography: p171-176. — Includes index
ISBN 0-86569-077-4 : £16.25 B82-13421

330.9469'044'0212 — Portugal. Economic conditions *— Statistics — For marketing*
Marketing opportunities in Portugal. — London : Euromonitor, [1981]. — 143p ; 30cm
ISBN 0-903706-58-x (pbk) : £75.00
B82-29180

330.947 — Eastern Europe & Soviet Union. Economic conditions, *1970-1980*
The **East** European economies in the 1970s / edited by Alec Nove, Hans-Hermann Höhmann, Gertraud Seidenstecher. — London : Butterworths, 1982. — xiv,353p : ill ; 24cm. — (Butterworths studies in international political economy)
Includes bibliographies and index
ISBN 0-408-10762-6 : Unpriced : CIP rev.
B81-31181

330.9'47 — Eastern Europe. Economic conditions
Crisis in the East European economy. — London : Croom Helm, Oct.1982. — [160]p
ISBN 0-7099-0826-1 : £10.95 : CIP entry
B82-23190

330.947 — Eastern Europe. Economic conditions
Krejčí, Jaroslav. National income and outlay in Czechoslovakia, Poland and Yugoslavia / Jaroslav Krejčí. — London : Macmillan, 1982. — viii,122p ; 23cm
Bibliography: p118-119. — Includes index
ISBN 0-333-26661-7 : Unpriced B82-39992

330.947'08 — Russia. Rural regions. Economic conditions, *1861-1930.* **Attitudes of Marxists**
Hussain, Athar. Marxism and the agrarian question / Athar Hussain, Keith Tribe. — London : Macmillan, 1981. — 2v. ; 23cm
Includes bibliographies and index
ISBN 0-333-24143-6 : Unpriced : CIP rev.
ISBN 0-333-28675-8 (v.2) : £15.00
Primary classification 330.943'084 B80-35745

330.947'084 — Eastern Europe. Economic conditions, *1919-1975*
The **Economic** history of Eastern Europe 1919-1975. — Oxford : Clarendon, May 1982
Vol.1: Economic structure and performance between the two wars. — [576]p
ISBN 0-19-828444-6 : £25.00 : CIP entry
B82-07518

330.947'084 — Soviet Union. Economic conditions, *1917-1980*

Millar, James R.. The ABCs of Soviet socialism / James R. Millar. — Urbana ; London : University of Illinois Press, c1981. — xvi,215p ; 24cm
Includes bibliographies and index
ISBN 0-252-00845-6 (cased) : £12.25
ISBN 0-252-00872-3 (pbk) : £4.55 B82-05708

Munting, Roger. The economic development of the USSR / Roger Munting. — London : Croom Helm, c1982. — 228p : 1map ; 23cm. — (Croom Helm series on the contemporary economic history of Europe)
Bibliography: p213-224. — Includes index
ISBN 0-85664-876-0 (cased) : £13.95 : CIP rev.
ISBN 0-7099-1740-6 (pbk) : Unpriced
B82-04810

Nove, Alec. An economic history of the U.S.S.R. / Alec Nove. — Harmondsworth : Penguin, 1972, c1969 (1980 [printing]). — 429p ; 20cm. — (Pelican books)
Originally published: London : Allen Lane, 1969. — Bibliography: p401-403. — Includes index
ISBN 0-14-021403-8 (pbk) : £2.95 B82-37245

330.947'084 — Soviet Union. Economic development, *1913-1967*

Hutchings, Raymond. Soviet economic development. — 2nd ed. — Oxford : Basil Blackwell, Oct.1982. — [368]p
Previous ed.: 1971
ISBN 0-631-12559-0 (cased) : £15.00 : CIP entry
ISBN 0-631-12795-x (pbk) : £5.95 B82-23175

330.947'085 — Soviet Union. Economic conditions. Geographical aspects, *1950-1973*

Mellor, Roy E. H.. The Soviet Union and its geographical problems / Roy E.H. Mellor. — London : Macmillan, 1982. — xii,207p : maps ; 25cm
Bibliography: p197-200. — Includes index
ISBN 0-333-27662-0 (cased) : £12.50
ISBN 0-333-27663-9 (pbk) : Unpriced
B82-32381

330.947'0853 — Soviet Union. Economic conditions

Perlo, Victor. Dynamic stability : the Soviet economy today / Victor and Ellen Perlo. — Moscow : Progress ; [London] : distributed by Central, c1980. — 343p,[32]p of plates : ill,2maps,ports ; 21cm. — (Impressions of the USSR)
ISBN 0-7147-1765-7 : £3.95 B82-37039

USSR : an economic report. — London (41 Lothbury, EC2P 2BP) : National Westminster Bank, 1981. — [4]p ; 30cm. — (The National Westminster Bank overseas report series)
Unpriced (unbound) B82-14809

330.947'0853 — Soviet Union. Economic development

Soviet economy today : with guidelines for the economic and social development of the USSR for 1981-1985 and for the period ending in 1990 / prepared by Novosti Press Agency Publishing House, Moscow. — London : Aldwych, 1981. — viii,356p ; 22cm. — (European studies ; no.9)
Includes index
ISBN 0-86172-023-7 : £26.50 B82-31087

330.9481'048 — Norway. Economic conditions

Norway : an economic report. — London (41 Lothbury, EC2P 2BP) : National Westminster Bank, 1981. — [4]p ; 30cm. — (The National Westminster Bank overseas economic report series)
Unpriced (unbound) B82-14803

330.9485'058 — Sweden. Economic conditions

Sweden : an economic report. — London (41 Lothbury, EC2P 2BP) : National Westminster Bank, 1981. — [4]p ; 30cm. — (The National Westminster Bank overseas economic report series)
Unpriced (unbound) B82-14837

330.9485'058 — Sweden. Economic conditions. Political aspects

Sweden : choices for economic and social policy in the 1980s / edited by Bengt Rydén and Villy Bergström. — London : Allen & Unwin, 1982. — x,257p : ill ; 23cm
Revised and up-updated English version of Vägval i Svensk politik. — Includes index
ISBN 0-04-339027-7 : Unpriced : CIP rev.
B82-00891

330.94897'033 — Finland. Economic conditions

Finland : an economic report. — London (41 Lothbury, EC2P 2BP) : National Westminster Bank, 1981. — [4]p ; 30cm. — (The National Westminster Bank overseas economic report series)
Unpriced (unbound) B82-14828

330.9492'073 — Netherlands. Economic conditions

Netherlands : an economic report. — London (41 Lothbury, EC2P 2BP) : National Westminster Bank, 1981. — [4]p ; 30cm. — (The National Westminster Bank overseas economic report series)
Unpriced (unbound) B82-14801

330.9493'043 — Belgium & Luxembourg. Economic conditions

Belgium and Luxembourg : an economic report. — London (41 Lothbury, EC2P 2BP) : National Westminster Bank, 1981. — [4]p ; 30cm. — (The National Westminster Bank overseas economic report series)
Unpriced (unbound) B82-14730

330.9494'073 — Switzerland. Economic conditions

Switzerland : an economic report. — London (41 Lothbury, EC2P 2BP) : National Westminster Bank, 1980. — [4]p ; 30cm. — (The National Westminster Bank overseas economic report series)
Unpriced (unbound) B82-14842

330.9495'076 — Greece. Economic conditions

Greece : an economic report. — London (41 Lothbury, EC2P 2BP) : National Westminster Bank, 1981. — [4]p ; 30cm. — (The National Westminster Bank overseas economic report series)
Unpriced (unbound) B82-14832

330.94965'03 — Albania. Economic development, *1945-1978*

Schnytzer, Adi. Stalinist economic strategy in practice. — Oxford : Oxford University Press, Sept.1982. — [180]p. — (Economies of the world)
ISBN 0-19-877125-8 : £15.00 : CIP entry
B82-18980

330.9497'02 — Yugoslavia. Economic conditions, *1918-1981*

Singleton, Fred. The economy of Yugoslavia / Fred Singleton and Bernard Carter. — London : Croom Helm, c1982. — 279p : ill,maps ; 23cm. — (Croom Helm series on the contemporary economic history of Europe)
Bibliography: p262-272. — Includes index
ISBN 0-7099-2342-2 : £19.95 : CIP rev.
B82-04471

330.9497'023 — Yugoslavia. Economic conditions

Stojanović, Radmila. The functions of the Yugoslav economy. — Nottingham : Spokesman, Nov.1982. — [276]p
ISBN 0-85124-364-9 : £18.50 : CIP entry
B82-37489

Yugoslavia : an economic report. — London (41 Lothbury, EC2P 2BP) : National Westminster Bank, 1981. — [4]p ; 30cm. — (The National Westminster Bank overseas report series)
Unpriced (unbound) B82-14811

Yugoslavia : an economic report. — London : National Westminster Bank, 1982. — 1folded sheet([4]p) ; 30cm
Unpriced B82-24385

330.9497'703 — Bulgaria. Economic conditions

Bulgaria : an economic report. — London (41 Lothbury, EC2P 2BP) : National Westminster Bank, 1981. — [4]p ; 30cm. — (The National Westminster Bank overseas economic report series)
Unpriced (unbound) B82-14733

330.9498'03 — Romania. Economic conditions

Romania : an economic report. — London (41 Lothbury, EC2P 2BP) : National Westminster Bank, 1981. — [4]p ; 30cm. — (The National Westminster Bank overseas economic report series)
Unpriced (unbound) B82-14835

330.95'0428 — East & South-east Asia. Economic conditions

Hofheinz, Roy. The Eastasia edge / Roy Hofheinz, Jr., Kent E. Calder. — New York : Basic ; London : Harper & Row, c1982. — ix,296p : ill,2maps ; 25cm
Maps on lining papers. — Includes index
ISBN 0-06-338000-5 : Unpriced B82-35141

330.95'0428'05 — Asia. Economic conditions — *For British businessmen — Serials*

Asia & Pacific. — 1981-. — Saffron Walden : World of Information, c1980-. — v. : ill,maps,ports ; 27cm
Annual. — Continues: Asia and Pacific annual review
ISSN 0262-5407 = Asia & Pacific : Unpriced
Also classified at 330.99'005 B82-15775

330.951'05 — China. Economic policies, *ca 1960-1981*

The **Chinese** economic reforms. — London : Croom Helm, Oct.1982. — [354]p
ISBN 0-7099-1022-3 : £15.95 : CIP entry
B82-25930

330.951'05 — China. Rural regions. Economic development, *1949-1979*

Wertheim, W.. Production, equality and participation in rural China. — London : Zed Press, Dec.1982. — [192]p
ISBN 0-86232-123-9 (pbk) : £5.95 : CIP entry
B82-30593

330.951'057 — China. Economic development, *1976-1981*

China's new development strategy / edited by Jack Gray and Gordon White. — London : Academic Press, 1982. — x,341p ; 24cm
Includes index
ISBN 0-12-296840-9 : £12.20 : CIP rev.
B81-36067

330.951'058 — China. Economic conditions

China : an economic report. — London (41 Lothbury, EC2P 2BP) : National Westminster Bank, 1981. — [4]p : 2maps(some col.) ; 30cm. — (The National Westminster Bank overseas economic report series)
Unpriced (unbound) B82-14824

330.951'058'0212 — China. Economic conditions — *Statistics — For marketing*

The **People's** Republic of China. — Aldershot : Gower, Feb.1983. — [150]p. — (The Markets of Asia/Pacific)
ISBN 0-566-02316-4 (pbk) : £25.00 : CIP entry
B82-38721

330.951'24905 — Taiwan. Economic conditions

Taiwan : an economic report. — London (41 Lothbury, EC2P 2BP) : National Westminster Bank, 1981. — [4]p : 2col.maps ; 30cm. — (The National Westminster Bank overseas economic report series)
Unpriced (unbound) B82-14838

330.951'2505 — Hong Kong. Economic conditions

The **Business** environment in Hong Kong / edited by David G. Lethbridge ; contributors Edward K.Y. Chen ... [et al.]. — Hong Kong ; Oxford : Oxford University Press, 1980. — xix,271p ; 26cm
Includes bibliographies and index
ISBN 0-19-580423-6 (corrected) : Unpriced
ISBN 0-19-580424-4 (pbk) : Unpriced
B82-37937

330.951'2505 — Hong Kong. Economic conditions *continuation*

Hong Kong : an economic report. — London (41 Lothbury, EC2P 2BP) : National Westminster Bank, 1981. — 1folded sheet([6]p) : maps(some col.) ; 30cm. — (The National Westminster Bank overseas economic report series)
Unpriced B82-14833

330.9519'5043 — South Korea. Economic conditions

Republic of Korea : an economic report. — London (41 Lothbury, EC2P 2BP) : National Westminster Bank, 1981. — 1folded sheet([6]p) : 2maps(some col.) ; 30cm. — (The National Westminster Bank overseas economic report series)
Unpriced B82-14815

330.9519'5043'05 — South Korea. Economic conditions — *Serials* — *For British exporters*

Korea in focus : newsletter of the Korea Trade Advisory Group. — No.1 (Jan.-Mar. 1981)-. — London (1 Victoria St., SW1H 0ET) : British Overseas Trade Board, 1981-. — v. : maps ; 30cm
Quarterly
ISSN 0262-3072 = Korea in focus : Unpriced
B82-14774

330.952'04 — Japan. Economic conditions, *1945-1980*

Braddon, Russell. A clock striking. — London : Collins, Feb.1983. — [256]p
ISBN 0-00-216393-4 : £9.95 : CIP entry
B82-40880

330.952'048 — Japan. Economic conditions

Japan : an economic report. — London (41 Lothbury, EC2P 2BP) : National Westminster Bank, 1981. — [4]p ; 30cm. — (The National Westminster Bank overseas economic report series)
Unpriced (unbound) B82-14821

330.952'048'0212 — Japan. Economic conditions — *Statistics* — *For marketing*

Japan. — Aldershot : Gower, Nov.1982. — [150] p. — (The Markets of Asia/Pacific)
ISBN 0-566-02315-6 (pbk) : £25.00 : CIP entry
B82-29071

330.953'57053 — United Arab Emirates. Economic conditions

United Arab Emirates : an economic report. — London (41 Lothbury, EC2P 2BP) : National Westminster Bank, 1981. — [4]p : 2maps(some col.) ; 30cm. — (The National Westminster Bank overseas report series)
Unpriced (unbound) B82-14808

330.953'57053'05 — United Arab Emirates. Economic conditions — *Serials*

[Silhouette *(London)***]**. Silhouette : the quarterly magazine of the Abu Dhabi Sheraton Hotel. — No.1 (Winter 1981/1982)-. — London (13A Hillgate St., W8 7SP) : Hillgate Publications for the Hotel, 1981-. — v. : ill(some col.),ports ; 30cm
ISSN 0262-6640 = Silhouette (London) : Unpriced B82-18509

330.953'6053'05 — Arabia. Gulf States. Economic conditions — *Serials*

The **Arab** Gulf journal. — Vol.1, no.1 (Oct. 1981)-. — London (98 Roebuck House, Stag Place, SW1E 5AA) : MD Research and Services Ltd., 1981-. — v. ; 25cm
Two issues yearly
ISSN 0261-5150 = Arab Gulf journal : £24.00 per year B82-11157

330.953'65053 — Bahrain. Economic conditions

Bahrain : an economic report. — London (41 Lothbury, EC2P 2BP) : National Westminster Bank, 1981. — [4]p : 2maps ; 30cm. — (The National Westminster Bank overseas economic report series)
Unpriced (unbound) B82-14729

330.953'67053 — Kuwait. Economic conditions

El Mallakh, Ragaei. The absorptive capacity of Kuwait : domestic and international perspectives / Ragaei El Mallakh, Jacob K. Atta. — Lexington, Mass. : Lexington Books ; [Aldershot] : Gower [distributor], 1981. — xviii,204p : ill ; 24cm
Bibliography: p193-196. — Includes index
ISBN 0-669-04541-1 : £15.00 B82-14746

Kuwait : an economic report. — London (41 Lothbury, EC2P 2BP) : National Westminster Bank, 1981. — [4]p : 2col.maps ; 30cm. — (The National Westminster Bank overseas economic report series)
Unpriced (unbound) B82-14823

330.953'67053 — Kuwait. Economic development. Role of science & technology — *Conference proceedings*

Symposium on Science and Technology for Development in Kuwait *(1978 : Kuwait Institute for Scientific Research)*. Proceedings of the Symposium on Science and Technology for Development in Kuwait / editors Kazem Behbehani, Maurice Girgis, M.S. Marzouk. — [Kuwait] : Kuwait Institute for Scientific Research ; London : Longman, 1981. — xvi,291p : ill,1map ; 23cm
ISBN 0-582-78325-9 : £29.00 : CIP rev.
B81-28085

330.953'8 — Saudi Arabia. Medina. Economic conditions. Geographical factors

Makki, M. S.. Medina, Saudi Arabia : a geographical analysis of the City and region / M.S. Makki. — [Amersham] : Avebury, 1982. — xiv,231p : ill,maps ; 23cm
Bibliography: p226-231
ISBN 0-86127-301-x (cased) : Unpriced : CIP rev.
ISBN 0-86127-304-4 (pbk) : Unpriced
B81-31642

330.953'8053 — Saudi Arabia. Economic conditions

Saudi Arabia / an economic report. — London (41 Lothbury, EC2P 2BP) : National Westminster Bank, 1982. — 1folded sheet([6]p) : 2maps(1 col.) ; 30cm. — (National Westminster Bank overseas economic report series)
Unpriced B82-19472

330.9'53'8053 — Saudi Arabia. Economic conditions — *Conference proceedings* — *For British businessmen*

Focus on Saudi Arabia : proceedings of a one-day conference held on 28 April 1982 by the Arab-British Chamber of Commerce, 42 Berkeley Square, London W1A 4BL. — London (P.O. Box 4BL, 42 Berkeley Square, W1A 4BL) : Arab-British Chamber of Commerce, c1982. — 52p : ill,ports ; 30cm. — (Focus report, ISSN 0260-700x) (An Arab-British Chamber of Commerce publication)
Unpriced (pbk) B82-40199

330.953'8053 — Saudi Arabia. Economic conditions — *For businessmen*

Saudi Arabia : keys to business success / edited by Kevin R. Corcoran. — London : McGraw-Hill, c1981. — xiii,225p : ill,1map,forms ; 24cm
Bibliography: p219-220. — Includes index
ISBN 0-07-084567-0 : £15.00 : CIP rev.
B81-24603

330.953'8053 — Saudi Arabia. Economic development

Saudi Arabia : energy, developmental planning and industrialization / edited by Ragaei El Mallakh, Dorothea H. El Mallakh. — Lexington, Mass. : Lexington Books ; [Aldershot] : Gower [[distributor]], 1982. — xiii,204p : ill ; 24cm
Includes index
ISBN 0-669-04801-1 : £16.50 B82-36672

330.953'8053 — Saudi Arabia. Economic development, *1960-1981*

Barker, Paul, *1953-*. Saudi Arabia : the development dilemma / by Paul Barker. — London : Economist Intelligence Unit, c1982. — 92p : ill,col.maps ; 30cm. — (EIU special report ; no.116)
Unpriced (pbk) B82-19912

El Mallakh, Ragaei. Saudi Arabia : rush to development : profile of an energy economy and investment / Ragaei El Mallakh. — London : Croom Helm, c1982. — 472p : ill,maps ; 22cm
Bibliography: p453-459. — Includes index
ISBN 0-7099-0905-5 : £16.95 : CIP rev.
B81-30534

330.954 — India. Economic conditions, *ca 1200-ca 1970*

The **Cambridge** economic history of India. — Cambridge : Cambridge University Press, Oct.1982
Vol.2: c. 1757-c. 1970. — [1078]p
ISBN 0-521-22802-6 : £60.00 : CIP entry
B82-29383

330.954'02 — India. Economic conditions, *ca 1200-ca 1950*

The **Cambridge** economic history of India / edited by Tapan Raychaudhuri and Irfan Habib. — Cambridge : Cambridge University Press
Vol.1: c1200-c.1750. — 1982. — xvi,543p : maps ; 24cm
Bibliography: p506-535. — Includes index
ISBN 0-521-22692-9 : £42.50 : CIP rev.
B82-12677

330.954'03 — India. Economic development. Effects of British colonial administration, *1800-1914*

Charlesworth, Neil. British rule and the Indian economy 1800-1914 / prepared for the Economic History Society by Neil Charlesworth. — London : Macmillan, 1982. — 91p : 1map ; 22cm. — (Studies in economic and social history)
Bibliography: p74-88. — Includes index
ISBN 0-333-27966-2 (pbk) : Unpriced
B82-19298

330.954'052 — India *(Republic)*. **Economic conditions**

India : an economic report. — London (41 Lothbury, EC2P 2BP) : National Westminster Bank, 1981. — 1folded sheet([6]p) : 2maps (some col.) ; 30cm. — (The National Westminster Bank overseas economic report series)
Unpriced B82-14816

330.954'82 — India *(Republic)*. **Tamil Nadu** *(State)*. **Rural regions. Economic conditions,** *1880-1955*

Baker, Christopher John. An Indian rural economy 1880-1955. — Oxford : Oxford University Press, Jan.1982. — [550]p
ISBN 0-19-821572-x : £30.00 : CIP entry
B81-34378

330.9549'105 — Pakistan. Economic conditions

Pakistan : an economic report. — London (41 Lothbury, EC2P 2BP) : National Westminster Bank, 1981. — 1folded sheet([6]p) : 2maps (some col.) ; 30cm. — (The National Westminster Bank overseas economic report series)
Unpriced B82-14804

330.955'054 — Iran. Economic conditions

Iran : an economic report. — London (41 Lothbury, EC2P 2BP) : National Westminster Bank, 1981. — [4]p : 2maps(some col.) ; 30cm. — (The National Westminster Bank overseas economic report series)
Unpriced (unbound) B82-14818

330.956'04'07 — Middle East. Economic conditions. Information sources — *Directories*

Sources of African and Middle-Eastern economic information / edited by Euan Blauvelt and Jennifer Durlacher. — Aldershot : Gower, c1982. — 2v. ; 31cm
Includes index
ISBN 0-566-02321-0 : Unpriced : CIP rev.
ISBN 0-566-02278-8 (v.1) : Unpriced
ISBN 0-566-02279-6 (v.2) : Unpriced
Primary classification 330.96'0328'07
B81-18148

330.9561'02 — Turkey. Economic conditions. Political aspects, *1920-1980 — Socialist viewpoints*

Berberoglu, Berch. Turkey in crisis : from state capitalism to neo-colonialism / Berch Berberoglu. — London : Zed, 1982. — iv,149p : ill,1map ; 23cm. — ([Middle East series]) Bibliography: p133-142. — Includes index
ISBN 0-905762-56-8 (cased) : Unpriced : CIP rev.
ISBN 0-905762-61-4 (pbk) : £3.95 B81-18060

330.9561'038 — Turkey. Economic conditions

Turkey : an economic report. — London (41 Lothbury, EC2P 2BP) : National Westminster Bank, 1981. — 1folded sheet([6]p) : 2maps (some col.) ; 30cm. — (The National Westminster Bank overseas economic report series)
Unpriced B82-14840

Turkey : an economic report. — London (41 Lothbury, EC2P 2BP) : National Westminster Bank, 1982. — 1folded sheet([6]p) : 2maps (some col.) ; 30cm. — (The National Westminster Bank overseas economic report series)
Unpriced (unbound) B82-25250

330.9567'043 — Iraq. Economic conditions

Iraq : an economic report. — London (41 Lothbury, EC2P 2BP) : National Westminster Bank, 1981. — [4]p : maps(some col.) ; 30cm. — (The National Westminster Bank overseas economic report series)
Unpriced (unbound) B82-14819

330.9567'043 — Iraq. Economic conditions — *Forecasts*

Iraq : a new market in region of turmoil. — London : Economist Intelligence Unit, 1980. — 105p : ill ; 30cm. — (EIU special report ; no.88)
£50.00 (pbk) B82-13858

330.95694'054 — Israel. Economic conditions

Israel : an economic report. — London (41 Lothbury, EC2P 2BP) : National Westminster Bank, 1981. — [4]p : 2maps(some col.) ; 30cm. — (The National Westminster Bank overseas economic report series)
Unpriced (unbound) B82-14820

330.95695 — Jordan. Jordan Valley. Economic development, *1970-1980*

Khouri, Rami. The Jordan Valley : life and society below sea level / written and photographed by Rami G. Khouri. — London : Longman published in association with the Jordan Valley Authority, 1981. — 238p : ill (some col.),maps ; 23cm
Bibliography: p228-231. — Includes index
ISBN 0-582-78318-6 : £12.50 : CIP rev.
B81-21491

330.95695'044 — Jordan. Economic conditions

Jordan : an economic report. — London (41 Lothbury, EC2P 2BP) : National Westminster Bank, 1981. — [4]p : 2maps(some col.) ; 30cm. — (The National Westminster Bank overseas economic report series)
Unpriced (unbound) B82-14822

330.95695'044 — Jordan. Economic development

Jordan : the Five Year Plan for economic and social development, 1981-1985 : a summary of development prospects and priorities and of opportunities in Jordan for British firms. — London (33, Bury St., SW1Y 6AX) : Committee for Middle East Trade, 1982. — vi,50p : 1 map ; 30cm. — (A COMET report)
£5.00 (spiral) B82-31578

330.9593'044 — Thailand. Economic conditions

Thailand : an economic report. — London (41 Lothbury, EC2P 2BP) : National Westminster Bank, 1981. — 2folded sheet([6]p) : 2col.maps ; 30cm. — (The National Westminster Bank overseas economic report series)
Unpriced B82-14839

330.9593'044'0212 — Thailand. Economic conditions *— Statistics — For marketing*

Thailand / the Asia Pacific Centre. — Aldershot : Gower, 1981. — xiii,141p : 1map ; 31cm. — (The Markets of Asia/Pacific)
Includes index
ISBN 0-566-02305-9 : Unpriced : CIP rev.
B81-14931

330.9595'053 — Malaysia. Economic conditions

Malaysia : an economic report. — London (41 Lothbury, EC2P 2BP) : National Westminster Bank, 1981. — 1folded sheet([6]p) : 2maps (some col.) ; 30cm. — (The National Westminster Bank overseas economic report series)
Unpriced B82-14799

330.9595'053'0212 — Malaysia. Economic conditions *— Statistics — For marketing*

Malaysia / the Asia Pacific Centre. — Aldershot : Gower, c1981. — xiv,151p : 1map ; 31cm. — (The Markets of Asia/Pacific)
ISBN 0-566-02304-0 : Unpriced : CIP rev.
B81-14933

330.9595'705 — Singapore. Economic conditions

Singapore : an economic report. — London (41 Lothbury, EC2P 2BP) : National Westminster Bank, 1980. — 1folded sheet([6]p) : 2col.maps ; 30cm. — (The National Westminster Bank overseas economic report series)
Unpriced B82-14844

330.9595'705'0212 — Singapore. Economic conditions *— Statistics — Marketing (for)*

Singapore / the Asia Pacific Centre. — Aldershot : Gower, c1981. — xii,165p : 2maps ; 31cm. — (The Markets of Asia/Pacific)
Includes index
ISBN 0-566-02303-2 : Unpriced : CIP rev.
B81-14934

330.9598'036 — Indonesia. Economic conditions, *ca 1960-1980*

The **Indonesian** economy during the Soeharto era / edited by Anne Booth and Peter McCawley. — Kuala Lumpur ; Oxford : Oxford University Press, 1981. — xxv,329p : ill,1map ; 26cm. — (East Asian social science monographs)
Includes index
ISBN 0-19-580477-5 (cased) : £22.00
ISBN 0-19-580484-8 (pbk) : Unpriced
B82-25871

330.9598'037'0212 — Indonesia. Economic conditions *— Statistics — For marketing*

Indonesia / the Asia Pacific Centre. — Aldershot : Gower, c1981. — xi,126p : 1map ; 31cm. — (The Markets of Asia/Pacific)
Includes index
ISBN 0-566-02306-7 : Unpriced : CIP rev.
B81-14932

330.9598'038 — Indonesia. Economic conditions

Indonesia : an economic report. — London (41 Lothbury, EC2P 2BP) : National Westminster Bank, 1981. — 1folded sheet([6]p) : 2maps (some col.) ; 30cm. — (The National Westminster Bank overseas economic report series)
Unpriced B82-14817

330.9599'046 — Philippines. Economic conditions

The **Philippines** : an economic report. — London (41 Lothbury, EC2P 2BP) : National Westminster Bank, 1980. — [4]p ; 30cm. — (The National Westminster Bank overseas economic report series)
Unpriced (unbound) B82-14806

330.96 — Africa. Economic conditions, *to ca 1930*

Wickins, P. L.. An economic history of Africa : from the earliest times to partition / P.L. Wickins. — Cape Town ; Oxford : Oxford University Press, 1981, c1980. — 323p : ill,maps ; 23cm
Includes bibliographies and index
ISBN 0-19-570192-5 : £16.00 B82-08292

330.96 — Africa. Economic development, *to 1980*

Onoh, J. K.. Money and banking in Africa. — London : Longman, Jan.1983. — [253]p
ISBN 0-582-64439-9 (cased) : £15.00 : CIP entry
ISBN 0-582-64336-8 (pbk) : £5.00 B82-32472

330.96'0328'07 — Africa. Economic conditions. Information sources *— Directories*

Sources of African and Middle-Eastern economic information / edited by Euan Blauvelt and Jennifer Durlacher. — Aldershot : Gower, c1982. — 2v. ; 31cm
Includes index
ISBN 0-566-02321-0 : Unpriced : CIP rev.
ISBN 0-566-02278-8 (v.1) : Unpriced
ISBN 0-566-02279-6 (v.2) : Unpriced
Also classified at 330.956'04'07 B81-18148

330.961'204 — Libya. Economic conditions

Libya : an economic report. — London (41 Lothbury, EC2P 2BP) : National Westminster Bank, 1981. — [4]p : 2maps(some col.) ; 30cm. — (The National Westminster Bank overseas economic report series)
Unpriced (unbound) B82-14798

The **Socialist** People's Libyan Arab Jamahiriya, the socio-economic transformation plan 1981-1985 : a summary of development prospects and priorities and of opportunities for British firms. — London (33 Bury St, SW1Y 6AX) : Committee for Middle East Trade, 1982. — 67p : ill,maps ; 30cm. — (Special report / COMET)
Bibliography: p66-67
£8.00 (spiral) B82-38974

330.961'204 — Libya. Economic development, *1952-1980*

Libya since independence. — London : Croom Helm, Sept.1982. — [224]p
ISBN 0-7099-0519-x : £12.95 : CIP entry
B82-21093

330.962'053 — Egypt. Urban regions. Economic development, *1952-1972*

Abdel-Fadil, Mahmoud. The political economy of Nasserism : a study in employment and income distribution policies in urban Egypt 1952-1972 / Mahmoud Abdel-Fadil. — Cambridge : Cambridge University Press, 1980. — xii,140p : ill ; 24cm. — (Occasional paper / University of Cambridge Department of Applied Economics, ISSN 0306-7890 ; 52)
Bibliography: p135-140
ISBN 0-521-22313-x (cased) : £12.50 : CIP rev.
ISBN 0-521-29446-0 (pbk) : £6.50 B80-25252

330.962'054 — Egypt. Economic conditions, *1970-1981*

Egypt : an economic report. — London (41 Lothbury, EC2P 2BP) : National Westminster Bank, 1981. — [4]p : 2maps(some col.) ; 30cm. — (The National Westminster Bank overseas economic report series)
Unpriced (unbound) B82-14827

330.965'05 — Algeria. Economic conditions

Algeria : an economic report. — London (41 Lothbury, EC2P 2BP) : National Westminster Bank, 1981. — [4]p : 2maps ; 30cm. — (The National Westminster Bank overseas economic report series)
Unpriced (unbound) B82-14725

330.965'05 — Algeria. Economic conditions *— For British exporters*

Algeria : the giant market of North Africa. — London : Economist Intellingence Unit, 1982. — 103p : ill,maps(some col.) ; 30cm. — (EIU special report ; no.119)
Unpriced (pbk) B82-22009

330.966 — West Africa. Economic conditions *— For West African students*

Anderson, David J.. Economics of West Africa / David J. Anderson. — Rev. ed. — London : Macmillan, 1981. — ix,342p : ill ; 22cm
Previous ed.: 1977. — Includes index
ISBN 0-333-32333-5 (pbk) : Unpriced
B82-06887

330.966 — West Africa. Economic conditions. Geographical aspects

Onyemelukwe, J. O. C.. Economic geography of West Africa. — Harlow : Longman, Jan.1983. — [208]p
ISBN 0-582-64671-5 (cased) : CIP entry
ISBN 0-582-64672-3 (pbk) : £5.00 B82-32473

330.966'0097541 — West Africa. French speaking countries. Economic conditions — *For British businessmen*

Clifford, Paul. Francophone West Africa : Cameroon, Gabon, Ivory Coast †, Guinea, Senegal, Benin, Togo / by Metra Consulting. — London : Metra Consulting Group, c1982. — i,347p : maps ; 30cm. — (Business opportunities in the 1980s)
Prepared by Paul Clifford
ISBN 0-902231-31-6 (spiral) : Unpriced
B82-36370

330.9667'05 — Ghana. Economic conditions

Ghana : an economic report. — London (41 Lothbury, EC2P 2BP) : National Westminster Bank, 1981. — [4]p : 2maps(some col.) ; 30cm. — (The National Westminster Bank overseas economic report series)
Unpriced (unbound) B82-14831

330.9669'05 — Nigeria. Economic conditions

Nigeria : an economic report. — London (41 Lothbury, EC2P 2BP) : National Westminster Bank, 1982. — 1folded sheet([6]p) : 2maps (1col.) ; 30x63cm folded to 30x21cm. — (National Westminster Bank overseas economic report series)
Unpriced B82-22482

330.9669'05 — Nigeria. Economic conditions — *For British businessmen*

Nigeria : business opportunities in the 1980s / by Metra Consulting. — London : Metra Consulting, c1981. — 220p ; 30cm
ISBN 0-902231-30-8 (spiral) : Unpriced
B82-16391

330.9669'05 — Nigeria. Economic conditions — *Forecasts*

Stevens, Christopher, *1948-*. Nigeria : economic prospects to 1985 : after the oil glut / by Christopher Stevens. — London : Economist Intelligence Unit, 1982. — 98p : 1col.map ; 30cm. — (EIU special report ; no.123)
Unpriced (pbk) B82-32019

330.9669'05 — Nigeria. Economic conditions — *Marxist viewpoints*

Path to Nigerian development / edited by Okwudiba Nnoli. — Dakar : Codesria ; London : Distributed by Codesria in conjunction with Zed, 1981. — viii,264p ; 22cm
Includes index
ISBN 0-86232-021-6 (pbk) : £4.95 B82-01769

330.9669'05 — Nigeria. Economic development, *1860-1960*

Onimode, Bade. Imperialism and underdevelopment in Nigeria. — London : Zed Press, Oct.1982. — [256]p
ISBN 0-86232-108-5 : £14.95 : CIP entry
B82-24584

330.9669'05'0212 — Nigeria. Economic conditions — *Statistics*

Maclean, Ian, *1930-*. Statistical guide to the Nigerian market / Ian Maclean & Guy Arnold. — London : Kogan Page, c1978. — 127p : 1ill,1map ; 30cm. — (Kogan Page special report)
ISBN 0-85038-107-x : £25.00 B82-24375

330.967 — Africa south of the Sahara. Economic conditions. Geographical aspects

African perspectives : an exchange of essays on the economic geography of nine African states / assembled and organized by Harm de Blij, Esmond Martin ; assisted by Ali Memon. — New York ; London : Methuen, c1981. — xxiii,264p : ill,maps ; 24cm
Includes bibliographies and index
ISBN 0-416-60231-2 : £12.95 B82-17593

330.9676 — East Africa. Economic development. Role of overseas higher education

Maliyamkono, T. L.. Higher education and development in Eastern Africa. — London : Heinemann Educational, May 1982. — [324]p
ISBN 0-435-89580-x : £15.00 : CIP entry
B82-09292

330.9676'204 — Developing countries. Economic development. Environmental aspects — *Study regions: Kenya*

Bartelmus, Peter. Economic development and the human environment : a study of impacts and repercussions with particular reference to Kenya / Peter Bartelmus. — München ; London : Weltforum, c1980. — viii,184p : ill ; 21cm. — (IFO-Studien zur Entwicklungsforschung ; Nr.8)
Includes index
ISBN 3-8039-0188-x : Unpriced B82-31842

330.9676'204 — Kenya. Economic conditions

Kenya : an economic report. — London (41 Lothbury, EC2P 2BP) : National Westminster Bank, 1981. — 1folded sheet([6]p) : 2maps (some col.) ; 30cm. — (The National Westminster Bank overseas economic report series)
Unpriced B82-14814

Papers on the Kenyan economy. — London : Heinemann Educational, June 1982. — [384]p. — (Studies in the economics of Africa ; 12)
ISBN 0-435-97385-1 : £15.00 : CIP entry
B82-14067

330.9678 — Tanzania. Economic conditions, *1800-1980.* **Political aspects**

Coulson, Andrew. Tanzania : a political economy / by Andrew Coulson. — Oxford : Clarendon, 1982. — xiv,394p : maps ; 22cm
Bibliography: p351-381. — Includes index
ISBN 0-19-828292-3 (cased) : £15.00 : CIP rev.
ISBN 0-19-828293-1 (pbk) : £6.95 B82-01109

330.9678'04 — Tanzania. Economic conditions

Tanzania : an economic report. — London (41 Lothbury, EC2P 2BP) : National Westminster Bank, 1980. — [4]p ; 30cm. — (The National Westminster Bank overseas economic report series)
Unpriced (unbound) B82-14841

Tanzania : an economic report. — London (41 Lothbury, EC2P 2BP) : National Westminster Bank, 1982. — [4]p : 2maps(some col.) ; 30cm. — (National Westminster Bank overseas economic report series)
Unpriced (unbound) B82-31394

330.968 — South Africa. Economic development, *1860-1980*

Nattrass, Jill. The South African economy : its growth and change / Jill Nattrass. — Cape Town ; Oxford : Oxford University Press, 1981. — xx,328p : ill,3maps ; 22cm
Bibliography: p311-320. — Includes index
ISBN 0-19-570194-1 : £11.50 B82-00999

330.968'04 — South Africa. Economic conditions, *1870-1930*

Industrialisation and social change in South Africa. — London : Longman, Aug.1982. — [368]p
ISBN 0-582-64338-4 (cased) : £9.95 : CIP entry
ISBN 0-582-64337-6 (pbk) : £4.50 B82-15896

330.968'063 — South Africa. Economic conditions

South Africa : an economic report. — London (41 Lothbury, EC2P 2BP) : National Westminster Bank, 1981. — [4]p ; 30cm. — (The National Westminster Bank overseas economic report series)
Unpriced (unbound) B82-14836

330.968'063 — South Africa. Economic conditions — *For businessmen*

Freer, P. A.. South Africa : business prospects re-assessed / by P.A. Freer and D. Samson. — London : Economist Intelligence Unit, 1982. — 107p,[2]p of plates : ill,1col.map ; 30cm. — (EIU special report ; no.126)
Text on inside back cover
Unpriced (pbk) B82-31975

330.968'063'05 — Southern Africa. Economic conditions — *Serials*

Quarterly economic review of Namibia, Botswana, Lesotho, Swaziland. — 1st quarter 1982-. — London : Economist Intelligence Unit, 1982-. — v. ; 30cm
Continues in part: Quarterly economic review of Southern Africa, Republic of South Africa, Namibia, Botswana, Lesotho, Swaziland
ISSN 0144-896X = Quarterly economic review of Namibia, Botswana, Lesotho, Swaziland : £45.00 for 4 quarterly issues and annual supplement B82-36707

330.9682'204 — South Africa. Transvaal. Witwatersrand, *1886-1914.* **Socioeconomic aspects**

Van Onselen, C.. Studies in the social and economic history of the Witwatersrand 1886-1914. — London : Longman, Oct.1982
Vol.1: New Babylon. — [320]p
ISBN 0-582-64382-1 (cased) : £15.00 : CIP entry
ISBN 0-582-64383-x (pbk) : £5.50 B82-23360

Van Onselen, C.. Studies in the social and economic history of the Witwatersrand 1886-1914. — London : Longman, Oct.1982
Vol.2: New Nineveh. — [320]p
ISBN 0-582-64384-8 (cased) : £15.00 : CIP entry
ISBN 0-582-64385-6 (pbk) : £5.50 B82-23361

330.9687 — South Africa. Pondoland. Economic conditions, *1860-1930.* **Political aspects**

Beinart, William. The political economy of Pondoland 1860-1930. — Cambridge : Cambridge University Press, Sept.1982. — [230]p. — (African studies series ; 33)
ISBN 0-521-24393-9 : £20.00 : CIP entry
B82-29362

330.968'7 — South Africa. Transkei. Economic conditions, *to 1980*

Southall, Roger. South Africa's Transkei : the political economy of an 'independent' Bantustan. — London : Heinemann Educational, June 1982. — [320]p
ISBN 0-435-96621-9 (pbk) : £6.50 : CIP entry
B82-09727

330.96891'04 — Zimbabwe. Economic conditions

Zimbabwe : an economic report. — London (41 Lothbury, EC2P 2BP) : National Westminster Bank, 1981. — [4]p : 2col.maps ; 30cm. — (The National Westminster Bank overseas economic report series)
Unpriced (unbound) B82-14813

Zimbabwe's first five years : economic prospects following independence. — London (Spencer House, 27 St. James's Place, SW1A 1NT) : Economist Intelligence Unit, 1981. — 125p,[1]p of plates : 1map ; 30cm. — (EIU special report ; no.111)
Unpriced (pbk) B82-08680

330.96894 — Africa. Developing countries. Rural regions. Economic development. Projects — *Study examples: Kaputa Joint Development Project*

MacDonald, John J.. The theory and practice of integrated rural development / John J. MacDonald. — [Manchester] : [Dept. of Adult and Higher Education, University of Manchester], 1981. — iv,124p ; 21cm. — (Manchester monographs ; 19)
Bibliography: p119-124
ISBN 0-903717-28-x (pbk) : Unpriced
B82-21048

330.96894'04 — Zambia. Economic conditions

Zambia : an economic report. — London (41 Lothbury, EC2P 2BP) : National Westminster Bank, 1981. — [4]p : 2maps(some col.) ; 30cm. — (The National Westminster Bank overseas economic report series)
Unpriced (unbound) B82-14812

330.971'0646 — Canada. Economic conditions

Canada : an economic report. — London (41 Lothbury, EC2P 2BP) : National Westminster Bank, 1981. — [4]p ; 30cm. — (The National Westminster Bank overseas economic report series)
Unpriced (unbound) B82-14732

330.971'0646 — Canada. Economic conditions, *1968-1979*
Canada. — London (41 Lothbury, EC2P 2BP) : National Westminster Bank, 1982. — [4]p ; 30cm. — (The National Westminster Bank overseas economic report series)
Unpriced (unbound) B82-21788

330.972'082 — Mexico. Economic policies, *1935-1975*
Thompson, John K.. Inflation, financial markets, and economic development : the experience of Mexico / by John K. Thompson ; foreword by Raúl Martínez Ostos. — Greenwich, Conn. : Jai Press ; London : distributed by Jaicon Press, c1979. — xx,239p : ill ; 24cm. — (Contemporary studies in economic and financial analysis ; v.16)
Bibliography: p220-239
ISBN 0-89232-084-2 : £21.10 B82-02014

330.972'0833 — Mexico. Economic conditions — *For marketing*
Mexico : a market assessment / Scottish Council Research Institute. — Edinburgh (23 Chester St., Edinburgh EH3 7ET) : The Institute, 1981. — i,35leaves ; 31cm
£10.00 (spiral) B82-01932

330.972'0833 — Mexico. Economic development — *Forecasts*
Best, Brinsley. Mexico : the next ten years / by Brinsley Best. — London : Euromoney, c1981. — 154p : ill,maps ; 30cm. — (A Euromoney special study) (Euromoney country risk report)
ISBN 0-903121-21-2 (spiral) : Unpriced B82-20739

330.97296 — Bahamas. Economic conditions
Bahamas : an economic report. — London (41 Lothbury, EC2P 2BP) : National Westminster Bank, 1981. — [4]p ; 30cm. — (The National Westminster Bank overseas economic report series)
Unpriced (unbound)
Also classified at 330.97299 B82-14728

330.97299 — Bermuda. Economic conditions
Bahamas : an economic report. — London (41 Lothbury, EC2P 2BP) : National Westminster Bank, 1981. — [4]p ; 30cm. — (The National Westminster Bank overseas economic report series)
Unpriced (unbound)
Primary classification 330.97296 B82-14728

330.973 — United States. Economic conditions, *to 1981*
Puth, Robert C.. American economic history / Robert C. Puth. — Chicago ; London : Dryden, c1982. — 485p : ill,maps,facsims ; 24cm
Includes bibliographies and index
ISBN 0-03-050556-9 : £15.95 B82-20712

330.973 — United States. Economic development. Role of federal courts, *1815-1972*
Freyer, Tony Allan. Forums of order : the Federal Courts and business in American history / by Tony Allan Freyer. — Greenwich, Conn. : Jai ; London : distributed by Jaicon, c1979. — xxii,187p : 2facsims ; 24cm. — (Industrial development and the social fabric ; v.1)
Bibliography: p177-187
£20.00 B82-08951

330.973'08'08996073 — United States. Negroes. Economic conditions, *1865-1980*
Harris, William H. (William Hamilton), *1944-*. The harder we run : black workers since the Civil War / William H. Harris. — New York ; Oxford : Oxford University Press, 1982. — ix,259p : ill,maps ; 21cm
Bibliography: p227-240. — Includes index
ISBN 0-19-502940-2 (cased) : Unpriced
ISBN 0-19-502941-0 (pbk) : £3.95 B82-31503

330.973'092 — United States. Economic conditions, *1970-1981*
Magdoff, Harry. The deepening crisis of U.S. capitalism / by Harry Magdoff and Paul M. Sweezy. — New York ; London : Monthly Review, 1981. — 219p : ill ; 21cm
ISBN 0-85345-573-2 (cased) : £8.65
ISBN 0-85345-574-0 (pbk) : Unpriced B82-15225

330.973'092 — United States. Economic policies, *ca 1960-1978 — Festschriften*
Economics in the public service : papers in honor of Walter W. Heller / edited by Joseph A. Pechman and N.J. Simler. — New York ; London : Norton, c1982. — 253p : 2ill ; 22cm
ISBN 0-393-01512-2 : Unpriced B82-37046

330.973'0927 — United States. Economic conditions
Peterson, Wallace C.. Our overloaded economy : inflation, unemployment, and the crises in American capitalism / Wallace C. Peterson. — New York : Sharpe ; London : distributed by Eurospan, c1982. — xvi,240p : 1ill ; 24cm
ISBN 0-87332-187-1 : £10.50 B82-26733

Solomon, Ezra. Beyond the turning point : the U.S. economy in the 1980s / Ezra Solomon. — Oxford : Freeman, c1982. — ix,157p : ill,1port ; 24cm
Originally published: Stanford : Stanford Alumni Association, 1981. — Bibliography: p144-146. — Includes index
ISBN 0-7167-1390-x (cased) : £10.40
ISBN 0-7167-1391-8 (pbk) : Unpriced B82-34389

330.973'0927 — United States. Economic policies, *1930-1982*
Minsky, Hyman. Inflation, recession and economic policy. — Brighton : Harvester Press, Nov.1982. — [304]p
ISBN 0-7108-0174-2 : £22.50 : CIP entry B82-27928

330.973'0927 — United States. Economic policies. Evaluation. Use of control groups
Ferber, Robert. Social experimentation and economic policy / Robert Ferber, Werner Z. Hirsch. — Cambridge : Cambridge University Press, 1982. — xii,251p : ill ; 22cm. — (Cambridge surveys of economic literature)
Bibliography: p234-241. — Includes index
ISBN 0-521-24185-5 (cased) : £17.50
ISBN 0-521-28507-0 (pbk) : £6.95 B82-18920

330.974'043 — New England. Economic development. Role of higher education
Business and academia : partners in New England's economic renewal / editors John C. Hoy, Melvin H. Bernstein. — Hanover, N.H. ; London : Published for New England Board of Higher Education by University Press of New England, 1981. — xii,160p ; 23cm. — (A Futures of New England book)
ISBN 0-87451-197-6 : Unpriced B82-28095

330.975'041 — United States. Southern states. Economic conditions, *1865-1900*
Market institutions and economic progress in the New South 1865-1900 : essays stimulated by one kind of freedom : the economic consequence of emancipation / edited by Gary M. Walton, James F. Shepherd. — New York ; London : Academic Press, 1981. — xii,162p : ill ; 24cm
Bibliography: p155-162
ISBN 0-12-733920-5 : £11.00 B82-21255

330.977'02 — United States. Mid-West region. Economic development, *1840-1857*
Abbott, Carl. Boosters and businessmen : popular economic thought and urban growth in the antebellum Middle West / Carl Abbott. — Westport ; London : Greenwood Press, 1981. — xii,266p : maps ; 22cm. — (Contributions in American studies ; no.53)
Bibliography: p227-258. — Includes index
ISBN 0-313-22562-1 : Unpriced B82-18026

330.98 — South America. Andes. Agricultural communities. Peasants. Economic conditions
Ecology and exchange in the Andes. — Cambridge : Cambridge University Press, Dec.1982. — [236]p. — (Cambridge studies in social anthropology ; 41)
ISBN 0-521-23950-8 : £25.00 : CIP entry B82-29397

330.98 — Western South America. Economic conditions — *For British businessmen*
Blakemore, Harold. Pacific South America : Chile, Colombia, Ecuador, Peru / by Metra Consulting and International Joint Ventures. — London : Metra Consulting Group, 1981. — ii,341p : maps ; 30cm. — (Business opportunities in the 1980s)
Prepared by Harold Blakemore and Paul Clifford
ISBN 0-902231-32-4 (spiral) : Unpriced B82-36371

330.98'003 — Latin America. Economic development. International political aspects
Economic issues and political conflict. — London : Butterworth Scientific, Aug.1982. — [256]p. — (Butterworths studies in international political economy)
ISBN 0-408-10807-x : £18.00 : CIP entry B82-17199

330.98'0038 — Latin America. Economic conditions — *For businessmen*
A **study** of the Latin American economies : their structure and outlook into the 1980s. — London : Economist Intelligence Unit. — (An EIU multi-client project)
Vol.1: Central America. — c1979. — 353p ; 30cm
Unpriced (spiral) B82-11567

330.98'0038'05 — Latin America. Economic conditions — *Spanish texts — Serials*
América Latina. Informe económico. — IE-81-01 (31 de jul. de 1981)-. — Londres [London] (90 Cowcross St., EC1M 6BL) : Latin American Newsletters Ltd, 1981-. — v. ; 30cm
Weekly. — Continues in part: América Latina informe semanal
ISSN 0261-3735 = América Latina. Informe económico : Unpriced B82-14782

330.98'0038'05 — South America. Economic conditions — *For British businessmen — Serials*
The **South** America file. — [198-?]-. — [Richmond, Surrey] ([165 Lower Mortlake Rd, Richmond, Surrey]) : South America Marketing and Business Advisors, [198-?]-. — v. ; 30cm
Six issues yearly. — Description based on: June and July 1981
£65.00 per year B82-26149

330.981'063 — Brazil. Economic conditions
Brazil : an economic report. — London (41 Lothbury, EC2P 2BP) : National Westminster Bank, 1981. — 1folded sheet([6p]) : 2maps ; 30cm. — (The National Westminster Bank overseas economic report series)
Unpriced (unbound) B82-14731

330.983'0647 — Chile. Economic conditions
Chile : an economic report. — London (41 Lothbury, EC2P 2BP) : National Westminster Bank, 1981. — [4]p : 2maps ; 30cm. — (The National Westminster Bank overseas economic report series)
Unpriced (unbound) B82-14734

330.985'0633 — Peru. Economic conditions
Peru : an economic report. — London (41 Lothbury, EC2P 2BP) : National Westminster Bank, 1981. — [4]p : 2maps(some col.) ; 30cm. — (The National Westminster Bank overseas economic report series)
Unpriced (unbound) B82-14805

330.9861'0632 — Colombia. Economic conditions
Colombia : an economic report. — London (41 Lothbury, EC2P 2BP) : National Westminster Bank, 1981. — [4]p : 2col.maps ; 30cm. — (The National Westminster Bank overseas economic report series)
Unpriced (unbound) B82-14825

330.987'0632 — Venezuela. Economic development, *1935-1975.* **Political aspects**
Allen, Loring. Venezuelan economic development : a politico-economic analysis / by Loring Allen. — Greenwich, Conn. : Jai ; London : distributed by Jaicon, c1977. — xviii,310p ; 24cm. — (Contemporary studies in economic and financial analysis ; v.7)
Bibliography: p259-267. — Includes index
ISBN 0-89232-011-7 : £21.10 B82-05929

330.987′0633 — Venezuela. Economic conditions

Venezuela : an economic report. — London (41 Lothbury, EC2P 2BP) : National Westminster Bank, 1981. — [4]p : 2maps(some col.) ; 30cm. — (The National Westminster Bank overseas report series)
Unpriced (unbound) B82-14810

330.9895′06 — Uruguay. Economic conditions, *1870-1981*

Finch, M. H. J.. A political economy of Uruguay since 1870 / M.H.J. Finch. — London : Macmillan, 1981. — xiii,339p : ill,1map ; 23cm
Bibliography: p310-328. — Includes index
ISBN 0-333-27852-6 : £25.00 B82-06651

330.99′005 — Pacific islands. Economic conditions — *For British businessmen — Serials*

Asia & Pacific. — 1981-. — Saffron Walden : World of Information, c1980-. — v. : ill,maps,ports ; 27cm
Annual. — Continues: Asia and Pacific annual review
ISSN 0262-5407 = Asia & Pacific : Unpriced
Primary classification 330.95′0428′05
B82-15775

330.9931′038 — New Zealand. Economic conditions

New Zealand : an economic report. — London (41 Lothbury, EC2P 2BP) : National Westminster Bank, 1980. — [4]p ; 30cm. — (The National Westminster Bank overseas economic report series)
Unpriced (unbound) B82-14802

330.9931′038 — New Zealand. Economic conditions — *For British businessmen*

New Zealand : an economic report. — London (41 Lothbury, EC2P 2BP) : National Westminster Bank, 1982. — [4]p ; 30cm. — (The National Westminster Bank overseas economic report series)
Unpriced (unbound) B82-25783

330.994′06 — Australia. Economic policies

Surveys of Australian economics. — London : Allen and Unwin
Vol.3. — Jan.1983. — [272]p
ISBN 0-86861-005-4 : £18.00 : CIP entry
B82-33236

330.994′063 — Australia. Economic conditions

Australia : an economic report. — London (41 Lothbury, EC2P 2BP) : National Westminster Bank, 1981. — [4]p ; 30cm. — (The National Westminster Bank overseas economic report series)
Unpriced (unbound) B82-14726

330.994′063 — Australia. Economic conditions — *Serials*

State of play. — 2. — London : Allen and Unwin, June 1982. — [176]p
ISBN 0-86861-116-6 (pbk) : £5.95 : CIP entry
B82-10259

330.994′063 — Australia. Economic policies. International economic aspects

Wealth, poverty and survival. — London : Allen & Unwin, Feb.1983. — [240]p
ISBN 0-86861-141-7 : £18.00 : CIP entry
B82-39830

330.994′063′0212 — Australia. Economic conditions — *Statistics — For marketing*

Australia. — Aldershot : Gower, Aug.1982. — [150]p. — (The Markets of Asia/Pacific)
ISBN 0-566-02312-1 (pbk) : £25.00 : CIP entry
B82-28457

330.994′063′0724 — Australia. Economic conditions. Econometric models

ORANI : a multisectoral model of the Australian economy / Peter B. Dixon ... [et al.]. — Amsterdam ; Oxford : North-Holland, 1982. — xvi,372p : ill ; 23cm. — (Contributions to economic analysis ; 142)
Bibliography: p355-362. — Includes index
ISBN 0-444-86294-3 : Unpriced B82-34478

331 — LABOUR ECONOMICS

331 — Great Britain. Offices. Personnel. Effects of automation

Staff attitudes and aptitudes / Urwick Nexos. — Slough : Urwick Nexos Limited, [1981?]. — ii,[47]leaves : ill ; 30cm. — (Managing office automation) (Urwick Nexos report series ; 3)
Bibliography: p46
ISBN 0-907535-03-8 (pbk) : Unpriced
B82-05204

331 — Industrial relations

International handbook of industrial relations : contemporary developments and research / edited by Albert A. Blum. — London : Aldwych, 1981. — xiv,698p : ill ; 25cm
Includes bibliographies and index
ISBN 0-86172-010-5 : £34.50 B82-30927

331 — Industrial relations. Applications of behavioural sciences — *Conference proceedings*

The **Behavioural** sciences and industrial relations : some problems of integration : proceedings of a Foundation for Management Education Conference held at the Administrative Staff College, Henley, 4-6 July, 1980 / edited by Andrew Thomson and Malcolm Warner. — Aldershot : Gower, c1981. — ix,202p : ill ; 23cm
Bibliography: p189-202
ISBN 0-566-00383-x : Unpriced : CIP rev.
B81-14874

331′.01′12 — Industrial democracy

Edwards, Robert, *1905-*. Industrial democracy / by Robert Edwards. — [Birmingham] : [University of Birmingham], c1982. — 11p ; 20cm. — (The Ernest Bader lecture)
Cover title. — Text on inside cover
ISBN 0-7044-0594-6 (pbk) : Unpriced
B82-28137

331′.01′120941 — Great Britain. Industrial democracy — *Conference proceedings*

Industrial relations & democracy. — Chelmsford (3 Lucas Ave., Chelmsford, Essex CM2 9JJ) : Chelmer Management Consultancy, Aug.1982. — [80]p
Conference papers
ISBN 0-946144-00-1 (pbk) : £5.00 : CIP entry
B82-25745

331′.01′120941 — Great Britain. Industrial democracy — *Proposals*

Economic planning & industrial democracy : the framework for full employment : report to the 1982 TUC Congress and Labour Party Conference / TUC-Labour Party Liaison Committee. — London : Labour Party, [1982]. — 35p ; 30cm
ISBN 0-86117-092-x (unbound) : £1.00
B82-41139

331′.01′1209497 — Yugoslavia. Industrial democracy, *to 1977*

Seibel, Hans Dieter. Self-management in Yugoslavia and the developing world / Hans Dieter Seibel and Ukandi G. Damachi. — London : Macmillan, 1982. — vii,316p ; 23cm
Bibliography: p298-306. — Includes index
ISBN 0-333-27433-4 : Unpriced B82-39991

331′.041027073 — United States. Libraries. Industrial relations

O′Reilly, Robert C.. Librarianship and labor relations : employment under union contracts / Robert C. O′Reilly and Marjorie I. O′Reilly. — Westport, Conn. ; London : Greenwood Press, 1981. — xiv,191p : ill ; 25cm. — (Contributions in librarianship and information science, ISSN 0084-9243 ; no.35)
Bibliography: p183-188. — Includes index
ISBN 0-313-22485-4 : Unpriced B82-02144

331′.04107212 — London *(City)*. Fleet Street. National newspaper publishing industries. Industrial relations. Effects of automation, *1975-1979*

Martin, Roderick. New technology and industrial relations in Fleet Street / Roderick Martin. — Oxford : Clarendon Press, 1981. — xii,367p ; 23cm
Includes index
ISBN 0-19-827243-x : £17.50 : CIP rev.
B81-31454

331′.0413621′0941 — Great Britain. Health services. Industrial relations

Industrial relations and health services / edited by Amarjit Singh Sethi and Stuart J. Dimmock. — London : Croom Helm, c1982. — 370p : ill ; 23cm
Includes index
ISBN 0-7099-0379-0 : £15.95 : CIP rev.
Also classified at 331′.0413621′097 B81-31168

331′.0413621′097 — North America. Health services. Industrial relations

Industrial relations and health services / edited by Amarjit Singh Sethi and Stuart J. Dimmock. — London : Croom Helm, c1982. — 370p : ill ; 23cm
Includes index
ISBN 0-7099-0379-0 : £15.95 : CIP rev.
Primary classification 331′.0413621′0941
B81-31168

331′.042 — Engineering industries. Industrial relations, *1939-1945*

Croucher, Richard. Engineers at war. — London : Merlin Press, Mar.1982. — [400]p
ISBN 0-85036-270-9 (cased) : £10.00 : CIP entry
ISBN 0-85036-271-7 (pbk) : £4.80 B82-09203

331′.0422334′0941 — Great Britain. Coal industries. Industrial relations, *to 1981*

Allen, V. L.. The militancy of British miners / V.L. Allen. — Shipley : Moor, 1981. — xix,337p : ill,facsims,ports ; 23cm
Includes index
ISBN 0-907698-00-x (cased) : Unpriced
ISBN 0-907698-01-8 (pbk) : Unpriced
B82-07566

331′.0422334′0941469 — Scotland. Strathclyde Region. Shotts. Coal industries. Industrial relations, *1919-1960*

Duncan, Robert, *1948-*. Shotts miners : conflicts and struggles, 1919-1960 / by Robert Duncan and Shotts History Workshop. — Motherwell : Motherwell District Libraries, 1982. — 31p,[8] leaves of plates : ill,1facsim,2maps ; 21cm
Bibliography: p30-31
Unpriced (corrected : pbk) B82-38091

331′.0422334′097544 — Southern West Virginia. Coal industries. Miners. Industrial relations, *1880-1922*

Corbin, David Alan. Life, work, and rebellion in the coal fields : the southern West Virginia miners 1880-1922 / David Alan Corbin. — Urbana ; London : University of Illinois Press, c1981. — xix,294p ; 24cm
Bibliography: p259-278. — Includes index
ISBN 0-252-00850-2 (cased) : Unpriced
ISBN 0-252-00895-2 (pbk) : £8.75 B82-13566

331′.0422354′094291 — North Wales. Slate quarrying industries. Industrial relations, *1874-1922*

Jones, R. Merfyn. The North Wales quarrymen, 1874-1922. — Cardiff : University of Wales Press, Nov.1982. — [368]p
Originally published: 1981
ISBN 0-7083-0829-5 (pbk) : £5.95 : CIP entry
B82-27975

331′.047′0941 — Great Britain. Manufacturing industries. Industrial relations

Marsh, Arthur. Employee relations policy and decision making. — Aldershot : Gower, Oct.1982. — [150]p
ISBN 0-566-00540-9 (pbk) : £12.50 : CIP entry
B82-23337

331′.047721′094276 — Lancashire. Cotton manufacturing industries. Industrial relations. Role of employers′ associations, *1890-1939*

McIvor, Arthur. Cotton employers′ organisation and labour relations strategy 1890-1939 / Arthur McIvor. — London (32 Wells St., W1P 3FG) : Polytechnic of Central London, School of Social Sciences and Business Studies, 1982. — 52p : 1map ; 30cm. — (Research working paper ; no.19)
Cover title
Unpriced (spiral) B82-40942

331'.06'041 — Great Britain. Industrial relations. Christian organisations: Industrial Christian Fellowship, *to 1929*

Studdert-Kennedy, Gerald. Dog-collar democracy : the Industrial Christian Fellowship 1919-1929 / Gerald Studdert-Kennedy. — London : Macmillan, 1982. — xv,228p[8]p of plates : ill,ports ; 23cm
Bibliography: p212-215. — Includes index
ISBN 0-333-29190-5 : £20.00 B82-20949

331'.07'041 — Great Britain. Industrial relations. Information sources

Guide to sources of information / [IDS]. — London : Incomes Data Services, 1982. — 74p ; 25cm
Includes index
Unpriced (pbk) B82-21591

331'.0722 — Great Britain. Industrial relations — *Case studies*

Purcell, John. Good industrial relations : theory and practice / John Purcell. — London : Macmillan, 1981. — xix,260p : ill ; 23cm
Bibliography: p249-255. — Includes index
ISBN 0-333-26114-3 : £15.00 B82-10830

331'.0722 — Industrial relations — *Case studies*

Hawkins, Kevin. Case studies in industrial relations practice. — London : Kogan Page, Mar.1982. — [220]p
ISBN 0-85038-418-4 : £11.50 : CIP entry B82-01560

331'.0941 — Great Britain. Industrial relations

Edwards, P. K.. The social organisation of industrial conflict. — Oxford : Blackwell, Sept.1982. — [352]p. — (Warwick studies in industrial relations)
ISBN 0-631-13127-2 : £18.00 : CIP entry B82-20286

Industrial relations handbook / Advisory, Conciliation and Arbitration Service. — London : H.M.S.O., 1980. — 354p ; 21cm
Includes index
ISBN 0-11-700960-1 (pbk) : £5.00 B82-16633

Jackson, Michael P.. Industrial relations. — 2nd ed. — London : Croom Helm, June 1982. — [288]p
Previous ed.: 1978
ISBN 0-7099-1417-2 : £3.95 : CIP entry B82-19273

James, Mike, *1937-*. A true and fair view : employee relations learning resource material for managers and supervisors / [written by Mike James] ; [illustrations by Bert Caine]. — Watford : Engineering Industry Training Board, 1981. — 1v(loose-leaf) : ill ; 30cm + 1 sound cassette
At head of title: EITB
ISBN 0-85083-526-7 : Unpriced B82-23572

The **Seventh** Industrial Relations Conference : London 29 & 30 April, 1982 : speakers papers. — [London] : [Financial Times Conference Organisation], 1982. — 88p ; 30cm. — (A Financial Times conference)
Unpriced (pbk) B82-36816

331'.0941 — Great Britain. Industrial relations, *1800-1900*

A History of British industrial relations 1875-1914 / edited by Chris Wrigley. — Brighton : Harvester, 1982. — xv,269p ; 23cm
Includes index
ISBN 0-7108-0316-8 : £25.00 : CIP rev. B82-12152

331'.0941 — Great Britain. Industrial relations, *1955-1977*

Mason, Keith. Front seat : a summing up of 22 years reporting on industry / by Keith Mason. — Sherwood (27 Wimbledon Rd., Sherwood, Nottingham) : K. 7ason, 1981. — 210p ; 21cm
Includes index
ISBN 0-9507933-0-2 (pbk) : £2.50 B82-03511

331'.0941 — Great Britain. Industrial relations, *1960-1979*

Strinanti, Dominic. Capitalism, the state and industrial relations. — London : Croom Helm, Sept.1982. — [256]p
ISBN 0-85664-996-1 : £12.95 : CIP entry B82-21397

331'.0941 — Great Britain. Industrial relations. Effects of industries. Innovation *compared with* **effects of innovation on industrial relations in West Germany**

The **Approach** to industrial change in Britain and Germany : a comparative study of workplace industrial relations and manpower policies in British and West German enterprises / by Eric Jacobs ... [et al.]. — London : Anglo-German Foundation for the Study of Industrial Society, 1978. — xix,136p ; 23cm. — (Series B ; 0179)
ISBN 0-905492-06-4 : £10.00
Also classified at 331'.0943 B82-01282

331'.0941 — Great Britain. Industrial relations — *Encyclopaedias*

Marsh, Arthur. Concise encyclopedia of industrial relations / Arthur Marsh. — Farnborough : Gower, 1979 (1981 [printing]). — 423p ; 23cm
Bibliography: p355-423
ISBN 0-566-02095-5 : Unpriced : CIP rev. B78-32770

331'.0941 — Great Britain. Industrial relations. Policies of government, *1893-1981*

Wigham, Eric. Strikes and the government 1893-1981 / Eric Wigham. — 2nd ed. — London : Macmillan, 1982. — viii,248p : ill ; 23cm
Previous ed.: published as Strikes and the government 1893-1974. 1976. — Includes index
ISBN 0-333-32302-5 : £20.00 B82-20950

331'.09415 — Ireland. Industrial relations

Industrial relations in practice / edited by Hugh M. Pollock. — Dublin : O'Brien Press, 1981. — 160p ; 22cm. — (Issues in industrial relations ; 1)
ISBN 0-86278-008-x (cased) : Unpriced : CIP rev.
ISBN 0-86278-009-8 (pbk) : Unpriced B81-21600

331'.09417 — Ireland *(Republic).* **Industrial relations,** *to 1980*

O'Hara, Bernard J.. The evolution of Irish industrial relations law and practice / by Bernard J. O'Hara. — Tallaght, Co. Dublin : Folens, c1981. — 146p ; 25cm
Bibliography: p140-145. — Includes index
Unpriced (pbk) B82-07709

331'.0943 — West Germany. Industrial relations. Effects of innovation *compared with* **effects of innovation on industrial relations in Great Britain**

The **Approach** to industrial change in Britain and Germany : a comparative study of workplace industrial relations and manpower policies in British and West German enterprises / by Eric Jacobs ... [et al.]. — London : Anglo-German Foundation for the Study of Industrial Society, 1978. — xix,136p ; 23cm. — (Series B ; 0179)
ISBN 0-905492-06-4 : £10.00
Primary classification 331'.0941 B82-01282

331'.0951'25 — Hong Kong. Industrial relations

England, Joe. Industrial relations and law in Hong Kong : an extensively rewritten version of Chinese labour under British rule / Joe England and John Rear. — Hong Kong ; Oxford : Oxford University Press, 1981. — xviii,421p,[8]p of plates : ill ; 26cm. — (East Asian social science monographs)
Includes index
ISBN 0-19-580479-1 (cased) : £18.50
ISBN 0-19-580494-5 (pbk) : Unpriced B82-27298

331'.0952 — Japan. Industries. Industrial relations

Reform of industrial relations. — Dublin : O'Brien Press, Sept.1982. — [160]p. — (Issues in industrial relations, ISSN 0332-1991 ; 2)
ISBN 0-86278-026-8 (cased) : £8.00 : CIP entry
ISBN 0-86278-027-6 (pbk) : £4.50 B82-29146

331'.0954 — India *(Republic).* **Industrial relations**

Ramaswamy, E. A.. Industry and labour : an introduction / E.A. Ramaswamy and Uma Ramaswamy. — Delhi ; Oxford : Oxford University Press, 1981. — viii,284p ; 22cm
Includes index
ISBN 0-19-561350-3 (pbk) : £3.95 B82-31567

331'.0973 — United States. Employment. Labour

Reynolds, Lloyd G.. Labor economics and labor relations / Lloyd G. Reynolds. — Englewood Cliffs ; London : Prentice-Hall, c1982. — xiv,625p : ill ; 24cm
Previous ed.: 1978. — Includes bibliographies and index
ISBN 0-13-517680-8 : £17.20 B82-23237

331'.0973 — United States. Employment. Labour, *1820-1980*

Gordon, David M.. Segmented work, divided workers : the historical transformation of labor in the United States / David M. Gordon, Richard Edwards, Michael Reich. — Cambridge : Cambridge University Press, 1982. — xii,228p : ill ; 24cm
Bibliography: p263-281. — Includes index
ISBN 0-521-23721-1 (cased) : £20.00
ISBN 0-521-28921-1 (pbk) : £6.50 B82-34881

331'.0973 — United States. Industrial relations

Mills, Daniel Quinn. Labor-management relations / Daniel Quinn Mills. — 2nd ed. — New York ; London : McGraw-Hill, c1982. — xix,595,[38]p : ill ; 25cm. — (McGraw-Hill series in management)
Previous ed.: 1978. — Includes bibliographies and index
ISBN 0-07-042419-5 : £17.50 B82-28051

New directions in labor economics and industrial relations / edited by Michael J. Carter and William H. Leahy. — Notre Dame ; London : University of Notre Dame Press, c 1981. — xxi,214p : ill ; 22cm
ISBN 0-268-01458-2 (cased) : £11.90
ISBN 0-268-01459-0 (pbk) : £4.90 B82-13109

331'.0983 — Chile. Industrial relations, *1973-1979*

Falabella, Gonzalo. Labour in Chile under the junta, 1973-1979 / by Gonzalo Falabella. — London : University of London, Institute of Latin American Studies, [1982?]. — 60p ; 25cm. — (Working papers / University of London. Institute of Latin American Studies, ISSN 0142-1875 ; 4)
English text, folded sheet in Spanish. — Text on inside covers. — Folded sheet attached to inside back cover
ISBN 0-901145-39-4 (pbk) : £1.25 B82-23380

331'.0994 — Australia. Industrial relations

Niland, John. Industrial relations in Australia. — London : Allen & Unwin, Jan.1982. — [340]p
ISBN 0-86861-330-4 : £18.00 : CIP entry B81-33709

331.1 — LABOUR FORCE AND MARKET

331.11'05 — Manpower — *Serials*

Research in human capital and development : a research annual. — Vol.1 (1979)-. — Greenwich, Conn. : JAI Press ; London (3 Henrietta St., WC2E 8LU) : Distributed by JAICON Press, 1979-. — v. ; 24cm
Supplement: Research in human capital and development. Supplement
ISSN 0194-3960 = Research in human capital and development : £24.50 B82-02352

Research in human capital and development : a research annual. Supplement. — Vol.1 (1981)-. — Greenwich, Conn. : JAI Press ; London (3 Henrietta St., WC2E 8LU) : Distributed by JAICON Press, 1981-. — v. : ill ; 24cm
Supplement to: Research in human capital and development
£26.95 B82-02353

331.11'0724 — Organisations. Manpower planning. Mathematical models

Verhoeven, C. J.. Techniques in corporate manpower planning : methods and applications / C.J. Verhoeven. — Boston, [Mass.] ; London : Kluwer-Nijhoff, c1982. — xii,186p : ill ; 24cm. — (International series in management science/operations research)
Bibliography: p179-184. — Includes index
ISBN 0-89838-072-3 : Unpriced B82-27299

331.11'0941 — Great Britain. Industries. Manpower. Economic aspects

Bowers, John. Labour hoarding in British industry. — Oxford : Blackwell, Sept.1982. — [176]p. — (Warwick studies in industrial relations)
ISBN 0-631-13128-0 : £12.50 : CIP entry
B82-20287

331.11'0941 — Great Britain. Manpower — *Statistics*

McIlwee, Terry. Personnel management in context : manpower statistics supplement. — Buckden (45 Park Rd., Buckden, Cambs PE18 9SL) : Elm Publications, Oct.1982. — [36]p
ISBN 0-9505828-9-1 (unbound) : £2.90 : CIP entry B82-29416

331.11'09411'35 — Scotland. Shetland. Manpower

Shetland manpower study. — Edinburgh : Manpower Services Commission, Office for Scotland, 1981. — 86p in various pagings : ill,1map ; 30cm
ISBN 0-905932-64-1 (pbk) : Unpriced
B82-04950

331.11'09422'6 — West Sussex. Business firms. Personnel, *1980*

Report on the 1980 survey of employers in West Sussex / West Sussex County Council. — Chichester : County Planning Officer, [1981?]. — 46p : 1form ; 30cm
ISBN 0-86260-024-3 (spiral) : Unpriced
B82-05018

331.11'0967'905 — Mozambique. Manpower. Sociopolitical aspects

First, Ruth. Black gold : the Mozambican miner, proletarian and peasant. — Brighton : Harvester Press, Dec.1982. — [272]p. — (Harvester studies in African political economy ; 3)
ISBN 0-7108-0314-1 : £18.95 : CIP entry
B82-30083

331.11'0988'1 — Guyana. Personnel, *1880-1905*

Rodney, Walter. A history of the Guyanese working people, 1881-1905 / Walter Rodney ; [foreword by George Lamming]. — Kingston, Jamaica ; London : Heinemann Educational, 1981. — xxv,282p : ill,maps,ports ; 23cm
Bibliography: p265-274. — Includes index
ISBN 0-435-98760-7 (pbk) : £5.90 B82-09827

331.11'422 — Engineering industries. Personnel. Maintenance skills. Effects of technological change

Maintenance skills in the engineering industry : the influence of technological change / a report prepared for the Engineering Industry Training Board by Peter Senker ... [et al.]. — Watford : EITB, c1981. — 58p ; 30cm. — (EITB occasional paper ; 8)
Bibliography: p54-55. — Includes index
ISBN 0-85083-520-8 (pbk) : Unpriced
B82-06134

331.11'423 — England. Polytechnic leavers. First employment, *1980 — Statistics*

First destinations of polytechnic students qualifying in 1980 : a statistical report on those obtaining first degrees and higher diplomas by full-time and sandwich course study / Polytechnic Careers Advisers Statistics Working Party. — London (309 Regent St., W1R 7PE) : Committee of Directors of Polytechnics, [1981?]. — xi,224p ; 30cm
£7.50 (spiral) B82-05810

331.11'734 — Agricultural industries. Bonded employment — *Anti-Slavery Society viewpoints*

Ennew, Judith. Debt bondage — a survey / Judith Ennew. — London : Anti-Slavery Society, 1981. — 85p ; 21cm. — (Human rights series report ; no.1)
Bibliography: p72-85
ISBN 0-900918-14-4 (pbk) : £1.50 B82-09086

331.11'8 — Personnel. Productivity

Macarov, David. Worker productivity : myths and reality / David Macarov. — Beverly Hills ; London : Sage, c1982. — 223p ; 23cm. — (Sage library of social research ; v.137)
Bibliography: p195-209. — Includes index
ISBN 0-8039-1774-0 (cased) : Unpriced (pbk) : Unpriced B82-26267

331.11'9042 — Great Britain. Public sector. Manpower *compared with* public sector manpower in Australia, *1950-1975*

Stanford, J. D.. The growth of public sector employment in Australia and the United Kingdom / by J.D. Stanford & P.M. Jackson. — Glasgow (McCance Building, 16 Richmond St., Glasgow, G1 1XQ) : Centre for the Study of Public Policy, University of Strathclyde, 1982. — 33p : ill ; 30cm. — (Studies in public policy, ISSN 0140-8240 ; no.99)
Bibliography: p24-25
Unpriced (pbk) B82-39727

331.11'9102'0941 — Great Britain. Information services & libraries. Manpower planning. Effects of technological development. Forecasting

Wight, Tony. A discourse on issues : an exploratory study of the implications of information technology for U.K. library and information work manpower planning / Tony Wight. — London : Aslib Research & Consultancy Division, 1980. — iii,190p : ill ; 30cm. — (British Library research and development report ; no.5656)
ISBN 0-85142-152-0 (spiral) : Unpriced
B82-14473

331.11'913621'09411 — Scotland. National health services. Personnel — *Statistics — Serials*

National manpower statistics / Information Services Division, Scottish Health Service, Common Services Agency. — [19—]-. — Edinburgh (Trinity Park House, South Trinity Rd., Edinburgh EH5 3SQ) : The Division, [19—]-. — v. ; 30cm
Description based on: 1981 issue
ISSN 0263-8916 = National manpower statistics : Unpriced B82-33870

331.11'9162131'0941 — Great Britain. Electricity supply industries. Manpower. Substitution of capital. Effects of energy demand. Econometric models

Westoby, Richard. Factor substitution and complementarity in energy : a case study of the U.K. electricity industry / by Richard Westoby and Alistair McGuire. — [Aberdeen] : [University of Aberdeen Department of Political Economy], [1981]. — 14leaves : ill ; 30cm. — (Discussion paper / University of Aberdeen Department of Political Economy, ISSN 0143-4543 ; 81-15)
Bibliography: leaf 14
Unpriced (pbk) B82-08385

331.11'9162131'0942 — England. Electricity generation industries. Manpower. Substitution of capital. Effects of energy demand. Econometric models

McGuire, Alistair. Factor input substitution in nuclear and fossil-fuelled electricity generation in England and Wales / by Ali McGuire and Richard Westoby. — Aberdeen : University of Aberdeen, Department of Political Economy, [1982]. — 11leaves ; 30cm. — (Discussion paper / University of Aberdeen. Department of Political Economy ; no.82-03)
Bibliography: leaf 11
Unpriced (pbk) B82-25304

331.12 — Labour market. Segmentation. Socioeconomic aspects — *Conference proceedings*

International Working Party on Labour Market Segmentation. *Conference (2nd : 1980 : Freie Universität)*. The dynamics of labour market segmentation / [Second Conference of the International Working Party on Labour Market Segmentation held at the Freie Universität, West Berlin, 7 to 11 July, 1980] ; edited by Frank Wilkinson. — London : Academic Press, 1981. — xvi,308p : ill ; 23cm
Bibliography: p291-308
ISBN 0-12-752080-5 (pbk) : £12.60 : CIP rev.
B81-14872

331.12'042 — Great Britain. Job creation programmes

Great Britain. *Department of Employment*. Employment Committee, session 1980-81 : employment creation memorandum / by the Department of Employment. — London : H.M.S.O., [1981]. — 46p ; 25cm. — ([HC] ; 443)
ISBN 0-10-244381-5 (unbound) : £3.40
B82-13826

Jackson, Michael P.. British work creation programmes / Michael P. Jackson, Victor J.B. Hanby. — Aldershot : Gower, c1982. — vii,87p ; 30cm
Bibliography: p87
ISBN 0-566-00523-9 (pbk) : Unpriced : CIP rev. B82-09732

331.12'042 — Great Britain. *Manpower Services Commission*. Programmes — *Serials*

MSC special programmes news. — Oct. 1981-. — London (166 High Holborn, WC1V 6PB) : Manpower Services Commission, 1981-. — v. : ill,ports ; 30cm
Six issues yearly. — Merger of: Actions (London); and, Network (London : 1977)
ISSN 0262-4621 = MSC special programmes news : Unpriced B82-05741

331.12'042 — Great Britain. Unemployed persons. Employment. Programmes. Great Britain. *Manpower Services Commission*

Grover, Richard. Work and the community : a report on the Manpower Services Commission's programmes for the unemployed / by Richard Grover with Stephen Hopwood, Trevor Davison and Rosemary Allen. — London : Bedford Square Press/NCVO, 1980. — x,54p ; 30cm
Bibliography: p53-54
ISBN 0-7199-1053-6 (pbk) : £2.75 B82-17508

331.12'042 — Wales. Employment. Generation. Role of Welsh Development Agency. Great Britain. *Parliament. House of Commons. Committee on Welsh Affairs*. Role of the Welsh Office and associated bodies in developing employment opportunities in Wales — *Critical studies*

Great Britain. Government observations upon the first report from the Committee on Welsh Affairs. — London : H.M.S.O., [1980]. — 25p ; 25cm. — (Cmnd. ; 8085)
ISBN 0-10-180850-x (unbound) : £2.40
B82-15135

331.12'042'091724 — Developing countries. Manpower. Supply & demand. Policies of governments — *Comparative studies*

Squire, Lyn. Employment policy in developing countries : a survey of issues and evidence / Lyn Squire. — New York ; Oxford : Published for the World Bank [by] Oxford University Press, c1981. — xiii,229p ; 25cm. — (A World Bank research publication)
Bibliography: p207-221. — Includes index
ISBN 0-19-520266-x (cased) : £11.50
ISBN 0-19-520267-8 (pbk) : Unpriced
B82-27296

331.12'05 — Labour market — *Serials*

Research in labor economics : an annual compilation of research. — Vol.1 (1977)-. — Greenwich, Conn. : JAI Press ; London (3 Henrietta St., WC2E 8LU) : Distributed by JAICON Press, 1977-. — v. ; 24cm
Supplement: Research in labor economics. Supplement
ISSN 0147-9121 = Research in labor economics : £26.20 B82-03434

Research in labor economics : a research annual. Supplement. — Vol.1 (1979)-. — Greenwich, Conn. : JAI Press ; London (3 Henrietta St., WC2E 8LU) : Distributed by JAICON Press, 1979-. — v. : ill ; 24cm
Supplement to: Research in labor economics
ISSN 0194-3057 = Research in labor economics. Supplement : £26.20 B82-03435

331.12'0941 — Great Britain. Labour market

The **Economics** of labour. — London : Butterworths, Sept.1982. — [384]p
ISBN 0-408-10827-4 (cased) : £14.00 : CIP entry
ISBN 0-408-10826-6 (pbk) : £6.95 B82-19215

331.12'0941 — Great Britain. Labour market, *1973-1977*

Labour force survey 1973, 1975 and 1977 : a survey conducted by OPCS, the General Register Office for Scotland and the Department of Finance in Northern Ireland on behalf of the Department of Employment and the European Community. — London : H.M.S.O., 1980. — iii,59p : ill,maps,forms ; 30cm. — (Series LFS ; no.1)
ISBN 0-11-690736-3 (pbk) : £5.60 B82-18623

331.12′0941 — Great Britain. Labour market. Effects of taxation
Taxation and labour supply. — London : Allen & Unwin, Sept.1981. — [304]p
ISBN 0-04-336073-4 : £18.50 : CIP entry
B81-20139

331.12′09429′71 — Mid Glamorgan. Bridgend. Labour market. Effects of Ford Motor Company
Jenkins, D. (Delvyn). Labour market effects of the Ford Motor Company′s new Bridgend plant / D. Jenkins. — [London] : [Manpower Services Commission, Manpower Intelligence and Planning], 1981. — 1v.(various pagings) : ill ; 30cm
Cover title: The Ford Bridgend report
ISBN 0-905932-69-2 (pbk) : Unpriced
B82-11171

331.1′2′0973 — United States. Labour market — *Conference proceedings*
Studies in labor markets / edited by Sherwin Rosen. — Chicago ; London : University of Chicago Press, 1981. — ix,395p : ill ; 24cm. — (A Conference report / Universities-National Bureau Committee for Economic Research ; no.31)
Conference papers. — Bibliography: p385-386. — Includes index
ISBN 0-226-72628-2 : £23.80 B82-20717

331.12′3161897′00973 — United States. Geriatricians. Supply & demand — *Forecasts*
Geriatrics in the United States : manpower projectins and training considerations / Robert L. Kane ... [et al.]. — Lexington, Mass. : Lexington Books ; [Aldershot] : Gower [distributor], c1981. — xx,186p : ill,1facsim ; 24cm
Bibliography: p169-176. — Includes index
ISBN 0-669-04386-9 : £13.50 B82-07871

331.12′5 — Great Britain. Employment. Effects of technological innovation
Rothwell, Roy. Technical change and employment / Roy Rothwell and Walter Zegveld ; foreword by Christopher Freeman. — London : Pinter, 1979. — ix,178p : ill ; 23cm
Bibliography: p171-173. — Includes index
ISBN 0-903804-55-7 : £12.50 B82-29254

331.12′5 — Israel. Kibbutzim. Overseas employment — *Practical information — For British personnel*
Bedford, John, *19---.* Kibbutz volunteer / John Bedford. — 2nd ed. — Oxford : Vacation Work, c1980. — 129p : 2maps ; 22cm
Previous ed.: 1978
ISBN 0-901205-81-8 (cased) : £4.50
ISBN 0-901205-73-7 (pbk) : £2.95 B82-12950

331.12′5 — Overseas employment — *Practical information — For British personnel*
Dodd, Philips, *1957-***The Directory** of jobs & careers abroad. — 5th ed. / edited by Philip Dodd. — Oxford : Vacation Work, 1982. — xi,284p ; 23cm
Previous ed.: 1979
ISBN 0-907638-12-0 : £9.50 B82-14466

Golzen, Godfrey. Working abroad : the Daily telegraph guide to working and living overseas. — 5th ed. — London : Kogan Page, Feb.1982. — [320]p
Previous ed.: 1981
ISBN 0-85038-500-8 (cased) : £9.25 : CIP entry
ISBN 0-85038-501-6 (pbk) : £4.95 B82-00151

Golzen, Godfrey. Working abroad. — 6th ed. — London : Kogan Page, Feb.1983. — [320]p
Previous ed.: 1982
ISBN 0-85038-616-0 (cased) : £9.95 : CIP entry
ISBN 0-85038-617-9 (pbk) : £5.95 B82-39280

331.12′5′0724 — Employment. Effects of technological change. Econometric models
Cooper, C. M.. Employment, economics and technology : the impact of technological change on the labour market / C.M. Cooper, J.A. Clark. — Brighton : Wheatsheaf, 1982. — 146p : ill ; 23cm
Bibliography: p142-146
ISBN 0-7108-0157-2 : £16.95 : CIP rev.
B82-12150

331.12′5′091724 — Developing countries. Employment. Effects of foreign trade
Trade and employment in developing countries. — Chicago ; London : University of Chicago Press
2: Factor supply and substitution / edited by Anne O. Krueger. — 1982. — xv,265p : ill ; 24cm
Includes bibliographies and index
ISBN 0-226-45493-2 : Unpriced B82-35312

331.12′5′091734 — Rural regions. Employment. Economic aspects
Hodge, Ian. Rural employment : trends, options and choices / Ian Hodge and Martin Whitby. — London : Methuen, 1981. — viii,262p : ill,1map ; 23cm
Bibliography: p245-256. — Includes index
ISBN 0-416-73080-9 : £13.50 : CIP rev.
B81-31709

331.12′5′094 — European Community countries. Employment. Local projects — *Serials*
Initiatives : the journal of the Centre for Employment Initiatives. — Issue 1 (May 1982)-. — London (5 Tavistock Place, WC1H 9SS) : The Centre, 1982-. — v. : ill ; 30cm
Quarterly
ISSN 0263-0001 = Initiatives : Unpriced
B82-36713

331.12′5′0941 — Great Britain. Employment
Shankland, Graeme. Our secret economy : the response of the informal economy to the rise of mass unemployment / Graeme Shankland. — London : Anglo-German Foundation for the Study of Industrial Society, c1980. — v,69p : ill ; 21cm
ISBN 0-905492-27-7 (pbk) : £2.90 B82-01284

331.12′5′0941 — Great Britain. Employment. Effects of microprocessors — *Liberal Party viewpoints*
Whitehead, J. L.. The new technology and unemployment / by J.L. Whitehead. — Edinburgh (2 Atholl Pl., Edinburgh) : Scottish Liberal Club, [1982?]. — 21 : ill ; 21cm
Cover title
£0.50 (pbk) B82-24393

331.12′5′0941 — Great Britain. Employment. Effects of technological innovation
Benson, Ian. New technology and industrial change. — London : Kogan Page, June 1982. — [220]p
ISBN 0-85038-284-x : £10.00 : CIP entry
B82-09840

331.12′5′0941 — Great Britain. Employment. Effects of technological innovation — *For women*
Huws, Ursula. Your job in the 80′s : a woman′s guide to new technology : Ursula Huws for Leeds TUCRIC. — London : Pluto, 1982. — 127p : ill ; 20cm
ISBN 0-86104-365-0 (pbk) : £2.50 B82-23773

331.12′5′0941 — Great Britain. Employment — *For school leavers*
Cannings, Barrie. The school leavers′ book / [Barrie Cannings]. — York : Longman, 1982. — 48p : ill,facsims,forms ; 23cm
Cover title. — Text on inside covers
ISBN 0-582-39678-6 (pbk) : £1.00 B82-33145

Shiach, Don. Language for work / Don Shiach. — Walton-on-Thames : Nelson, 1982. — 121p : ill(some col.),facsims ; 25cm
ISBN 0-17-433301-3 (pbk) : Unpriced
B82-26908

'Young worker'. — 2nd ed. — London (57 Chalton St., NW1 1HU) : British Youth Council, [1982?]. — 1portfolio : ill ; 32cm
Previous ed.: 197-?
Unpriced B82-35697

331.12′5′0941 — Great Britain. Employment. Regional variations
Fothergill, Stephen. Unequal growth : urban and regional employment change in the UK / Stephen Fothergill and Graham Gudgin. — London : Heinemann Educational, 1982. — xiii,210p : ill,2maps ; 23cm
Bibliography: p200-201. — Includes index
ISBN 0-435-84370-2 (cased) : £13.50 : CIP rev.
ISBN 0-435-84371-0 (pbk) : Unpriced
B81-23781

331.12′5′09421 — London. Employment. Projects — *Lists*
Employment projects in London / a directory compiled by LVSC Information Service and London Community Work Service. — [London] : [LVSC Information Service], 1982. — [18]p ; 30cm
Includes index
Unpriced (unbound) B82-22528

331.12′5′094235 — Devon. Rural regions. Employment
The **Development** of rural employment opportunities in Devon / compiled by George Bennett ; supervised by David Baker. — [Exeter] ([Amory Building, The Cattle Market, Marsh Barton Rd., Exeter EX2 8LH]) : Devon Federation of Young Farmers Clubs, [1980]. — 92p : 1ill,maps ; 30cm
Cover title
Unpriced (pbk) B82-19344

331.12′5′094237 — Cornwall. Employment — *Conference proceedings*
Industrial change in Cornwall : proceedings of a seminar on the collection and the analysis of data / edited by Gareth Shaw and Allan M. Williams. — [Plymouth] ([Derriford Rd., Plymouth, PL6 8BH]) : College of St. Mark & St. John, c1981. — ii,56p : ill,2forms ; 30cm. — (South west papers in geography ; 1)
Unpriced (pbk) B82-26508

331.12′5′094253 — Lincolnshire. Employment — *Practical information — Serials*
Lincolnshire information. Employment / Director of Highways & Planning, Lincolnshire County Council. — 1981-. — Lincoln (County Offices, Lincoln) : The Council, 1981-. — v. : ill,maps ; 21cm
Annual
ISSN 0262-1452 = Lincolnshire information. Employment : Unpriced B82-09676

331.12′5′09426752 — Essex. Chelmsford. Employment — *For environment planning*
Employment topic report : Chelmsford town centre district plan. — Chelmsford : Chelmsford Borough Council, 1980. — 40p,[4] folded leaves of plates : ill,maps ; 30cm
Unpriced (pbk) B82-08725

331.12′5′09427 — Northern England. Employment — *Forecasts*
Changing trends in occupations in the northern region. — Newcastle upon Tyne : Manpower Services Commission, Northern Region Manpower Intelligence Unit, [1982]. — 24p in various pagings : 1form ; 30cm
ISBN 0-905932-38-2 (pbk) : Unpriced
B82-23766

331.12′5′0942735 — Greater Manchester *(Metropolitan County).* **Tameside** *(District).* **Employment. Effects of technological change. Regional economic analysis**
Coombs, R.. Regional analysis of the impact of technical change on employment / R. Coombs and K. Green. — Manchester (P.O. Box 88, Manchester M60 1QD) : Department of Management Sciences, University of Manchester Institute of Science and Technology, 1982. — 16leaves ; 31cm. — (Occasional paper / Department of Management Sciences, University of Manchester Institute of Science and Technology ; no.8204)
Unpriced (pbk) B82-27236

331.1′25′09481 — Norway. Employment. Effects of computer systems
Computerisation of working life. — Chichester : Ellis Horwood, Feb.1983. — [145]p. — (Ellis Horwood series on computers and their applications)
ISBN 0-85312-584-8 : £15.00 : CIP entry
B82-37638

331.12′5′0952 — Japan. Employment *related to* **education**
Bowman, Mary Jean. Educational choice and labor markets in Japan / Mary Jean Bowman with the collaboration of Hideo Ikeda and Yesumasa Tomoda. — Chicago ; London : University of Chicago Press, c1981. — xvii,367p : ill,1map ; 24cm
Bibliography: p347-356. — Includes index
ISBN 0-226-06923-0 : £11.40
Primary classification 370′.952 B82-09576

331.12'51647944128 — Scotland. Hotel industries. Personnel. Employment. Estimation. Mathematical models — *Study regions: Scotland. Tayside Region. Pitlochry*

Hughes, C. George. Estimating employment in hotels and guest houses : a case study of Pitlochry / C. George Hughes. — Edinburgh (20 Chambers St., Edinburgh EH1 1JZ) : Department of Urban Design and Regional Planning, Edinburgh University, 1980. — 41p : forms,21cm. — (Occasional paper / Tourism Planning Study ; 1)
Bibliography: p41
Unpriced (pbk) B82-25951

331.12'516479541 — Great Britain. Catering industries. Employment. Attitudes of public

Ellis, Paul, *1948-*. The image of hotel and catering work : a report on three surveys / Paul Ellis. — Wembley : Hotel and Catering Industry Training Board, 1981. — 152p : ill,forms ; 29cm. — (HCITB research report)
ISBN 0-7033-0018-0 (pbk) : £5.00 B82-19116

331.12'521381'09411 — Scotland. Electronics industries. Electronics graduate personnel. Supply & demand — *Proposals*

Davis, L. E.. Electronics manpower for Scotland in the 1980's / by L.E. Davis and J.H. Collins, paper prepared for Scottish Council Development & Industry, Industrial Committee. — [Edinburgh] ([1 Castle St, Edinburgh, EH2 3AJ]) : [Scottish Council Development & Industry Industrial Committee], 1981. — 13leaves : ill ; 30cm
Unpriced (unbound) B82-35108

331.12'577'00943 — Industrialised countries. Manufacturing industries. Employment. Effects of industrialisation in developing countries — *Study regions: West Germany — Study examples: Textile industries*

Fröbel, Folker. The new international division of labour : structural unemployment in industrialised countries and industrialisation in developing countries / Folker Fröbel, Jürgen Heinrichs and Otto Kreye ; translated by Pete Burgess. — Cambridge : Cambridge University Press, 1980 (1981 [printing]). — xiv,407p : ill ; 23cm. — (Studies in modern capitalism = Études sur le capitalisme moderne)
Translation of: Die neue internationale Arbeitsteilung
ISBN 0-521-28720-0 (pbk) : £9.50 B82-08319

331.12'6 — Scotland. Hospitals. Nurses. Personnel turnover, *1968-1978*

Farmer, P. J.. Hospital nursing trends in Scotland / P.J. Farmer. — Edinburgh (Trinity Park House, South Trinity Rd, Edinburgh EH5 3SQ) : Information Services Division, Scottish Health Service Common Services Agency, [1982?]. — 12p : ill ; 30cm. — (Occasional papers ; 5)
Unpriced (unbound) B82-40982

331.12'7 — Great Britain. Construction industries. Personnel. Mobility — *Inquiry reports*

Marsh, Alan. Labour mobility in the construction industry / Alan Marsh and Patrick Heady with Jill Matheson. — London : H.M.S.O., 1981. — vi.91p ; 30cm
At head of title: Office of Population Censuses and Surveys. Social Survey Division
ISBN 0-11-690780-0 (pbk) : £12.00
B82-16794

331.12'7 — Personnel. Mobility. Economic aspects

Mueller, Charles F.. The economics of labor migration : a behavioral analysis / Charles F. Mueller. — New York ; London : Academic Press, c1982. — xii,199p ; 24cm. — (Studies in urban economics)
Bibliography: p185-191. — Includes index
ISBN 0-12-509580-5 : £14.60 B82-30142

331.12'791 — Guyana. Economic development. Effects of emigration of professional personnel

Boodhoo, Martin J.. The impact of brain drain on development : a case-study of Guyana / by Martin J. Boodhoo and Ahamad Baksh ; with research support from T.A. Pooran Singh and L.P. Rajrup. — Georgetown, Guyana : Ahamad Baksh Trust Fund ; Manchester (21 Parkville Rd., Manchester M20 9TX) : International Trading Agency [[distributor]], [1981?]. — xv,235p : forms ; 21cm
£4.00 (pbk) B82-01257

331.12'7971271 — Northern Canada. Mining communities. Personnel. Emigration — *Study regions: Manitoba. Thompson*

Smith, Geoffrey C.. Images of northern Canadian resource communities and the problem of out-migration / Geoffrey C. Smith & Paul F. Raths. — Birmingham : Department of Geography, University of Birmingham, 1980. — 23p : 1map ; 30cm. — (Working paper series / University of Birmingham. Department of Geography ; 7)
Bibliography: p19-20
ISBN 0-7044-0562-8 (pbk) : £0.40 B82-23554

331.12'8 — Great Britain. State employment services. Role of employers & trade unions *compared with* **role of employers & trade unions in state employment services in West Germany**

Carruthers, B. J.. Labour market services in Britain and Germany : employer and trade union participation / by B.J. Carruthers. — [London] : Anglo-German Foundation for the Study of Industrial Society, [c1979]. — 52p ; 30cm. — (Monograph series / Anglo-German Foundation for the Study of Industrial Society)
ISBN 0-905492-16-1 (pbk) : £2.50 B82-16404

331.12'9163 — Great Britain. Agricultural industries. Farms. Managers. Supply, *1970-1974*

Errington, A. J.. The supply of farm managers — past, present and future : an information paper / prepared by A.J. Errington ; for a conference on agricultural business management education and training, National Agricultural Centre, Kenilworth, 25th-26th March 1975. — [Beckenham] ([32 Beckenham Rd., Beckenham, Kent BR3 4PB]) : Research Department, Agricultural Training Board, 1975. — 12p : ill ; 30cm. — (Information paper / ATB ; [1])
Unpriced (pbk) B82-06090

331.13 — United States. Ph.D. graduates. Underemployment

Underemployed Ph.D.'s / Lewis C. Solomon ... [et al.]. — Lexington, Mass. : Lexington Books, c1981 ; [Aldershot] : Gower [distributor], 1982. — xvii,350p : ill ; 24cm
Bibliography: p329-333. — Includes index
ISBN 0-669-04482-2 : 23.50 B82-18039

331.13'3 — Northern Ireland. Secondary schools. Head teachers. Appointment. Sex discrimination by local education authorities

Clarke, M. T.. Men, women and post-primary principalship in Northern Ireland, 1978 / M.T. Clarke. — Belfast (Information Centre, Lindsay House, Callender St., Belfast BT1 5DT) : Equal Opportunities Commission for Northern Ireland, 1978. — 14p ; 30cm
£0.50 (pbk) B82-20135

331.13'3'0941 — Great Britain. Employment. Equality of opportunity — *Codes of conduct*

Great Britain. *Equal Opportunities Commission*. Code of practice : equal opportunity policies, procedures and practices in employment : revised consultative draft. — Manchester : Equal Opportunities Commission, 1982. — 19p ; 21cm
ISBN 0-905829-55-7 (pbk) : Unpriced
B82-36800

331.13'3'0973 — United States. Social minorities. Employment. Equality of opportunity

Wainwright, David, *1941-*. Learning from Uncle Sam : equal employment opportunities programme / by David Wainwright. — London (37a Gray's Inn Rd., WC1X 8PP) : Runnymede Trust, 1980. — 34p : 1ill ; 30cm. — (Industrial unit briefing paper ; no.3)
£1.50 (pbk) B82-41129

331.13'7 — Great Britain. Unemployed persons. Self-help — *Manuals*

Dauncey, Guy. The unemployment handbook / by Guy Dauncey. — 2nd ed. — Cambridge : National Extension College, 1982. — viii,153p : ill ; 21cm. — (NEC practical guides)
Previous ed.: 1981. — Text inside back cover. — Bibliography: p153. — Includes index
ISBN 0-86082-220-6 (pbk) : Unpriced
B82-40272

Nathan, Robert, *1949-*. How to survive unemployment : creative alternatives / Robert Nathan, Michel Syrett. — [London] : Institute of Personnel Management, 1981. — xii,308p ; 19cm
Includes index
ISBN 0-85292-303-1 (pbk) : £2.50 : CIP rev.
B81-31108

331.13'7 — Unemployment

Artis, Michael. The unemployment problem : by Michael Artis. — Stockport ([c/o P.K. Berry, C.I.S. Building, Miller St, Manchester M60 0AL]) : Manchester Statistical Society, [1979?]. — 16p : ill ; 21cm
At head of title: Manchester Statistical Society. — Text on inside cover
£2.00 (pbk) B82-02707

Jahoda, Marie. Employment and unemployment : a social-psychological analysis. — Cambridge : Cambridge University Press, Oct.1982. — [120] p. — (The Psychology of social issues ; 1)
ISBN 0-521-24294-0 (cased) : £10.50 : CIP entry
ISBN 0-521-28586-0 (pbk) : £3.95 B82-29377

Merritt, Giles. World out of work / Giles Merritt. — London : Collins, 1982. — 228p ; 20cm
Includes index
ISBN 0-00-216634-8 (pbk) : £2.50 : CIP rev.
B82-10563

331.13'7 — Unemployment *related to* **inflation**

Meade, J. E.. Wage-fixing / James E. Meade. — London : Allen & Unwin, 1982. — 233p : ill ; 22cm. — (Stagflation ; v.1)
Includes index
ISBN 0-04-339023-4 (cased) : Unpriced : CIP rev.
ISBN 0-04-339024-2 (pbk) : Unpriced
Also classified at 332.4'1 B81-33917

331.13'7'019 — Unemployed persons. Psychological aspects

Hayes, John. Understanding the unemployed. — London : Tavistock, July 1981. — [192]p
ISBN 0-422-77820-6 (cased) : £7.95 : CIP entry
ISBN 0-422-77830-3 (pbk) : £3.50 B81-14865

331.13'7'0724 — Unemployment. Mathematical models

Unemployment : macro and micro explanations / edited by Lars Matthiessen and Steinar Strøm. — London : Macmillan, 1981, c1980. — 183p : ill ; 25cm
Originally published: in The Scandinavian Journal of Economics, Vol.82, 1980, No.2. — Includes bibliographies
ISBN 0-333-31357-7 : £15.00 B82-10632

331.13'781 — Professional personnel. Unemployment. Psychological aspects

Kaufman, H. G.. Professionals in search of work : coping with the stress of job loss and underemployment / H.G. Kaufman ; foreword by Jerome M. Rosow. — New York ; Chichester : Wiley, c1982. — xviii,359p : ill ; 24cm
Bibliography: p311-335. — Includes index
ISBN 0-471-46069-9 : Unpriced B82-38316

331.13'78691'0942936 — Clwyd. Shotton. Iron & steel industries: Shotton Steel Works. Personnel. Redundancy

Chakravarty, S. P.. Redundancy at Shotton : the place of steel / S.P. Chakravarty, D.R. Jones, R.R. MacKay. — Mold : Clwyd County Council, 1981. — 46p : ill ; 30cm
ISBN 0-904444-64-3 (pbk) : Unpriced
B82-06883

331.13'7924 — Scotland. Unemployment. Personal adjustment — *Correspondence, diaries, etc*

Brown, Elaine. Grounded / Elaine Brown. — Tring : Lion, 1982. — 192p ; 18cm. — (A Lion paperback)
ISBN 0-85648-429-6 (pbk) : £1.50 B82-21037

331.13'794 — European Community countries. Unemployment

Unemployment : the European perspective / edited by Angus Maddison and Bote S. Wilpstra. — London : Croom Helm, c1982. — 180p : ill ; 25cm
Includes bibliographies
ISBN 0-7099-1739-2 : £12.95 : CIP rev. B82-08447

331.13'7941 — Great Britain. Unemployed persons — *Case studies*

Marsden, Dennis. Workless : an exploration of the social contract between society and the worker / Dennis Marsden. — Rev. and enl. ed. — London : Croom Helm, c1982. — 275p : ill ; 22cm
Previous ed.: Harmondsworth : Penguin, 1975
ISBN 0-7099-1723-6 (pbk) : £6.95 : CIP rev. B81-31169

331.13'7941 — Great Britain. Unemployment

Crick, Bernard. Unemployment. — London : Methuen, July 1981. — [150]p
ISBN 0-416-32470-3 (pbk) : £2.50 : CIP entry B81-14976

Daniel, W. W.. The nature of current unemployment / by W.W. Daniel. — London : British-North American Research Association, 1981. — iv,40p : 1ill ; 21cm. — (Occasional paper / BNARA ; 6)
£1.50 (pbk) B82-13488

Gillespie, Andrew. Unemployment trends in the current recession : industrial and spatial restructuring / by Andrew Gillespie and David Owen. — [Newcastle upon Tyne] : University of Newcastle upon Tyne. Centre for Urban and Regional Development Studies, 1981. — [24]p ; 30cm. — (Discussion paper, ISSN 0140-6515 ; no.39)
Subtitle: Paper presented at the 21st European Congress of the Regional Science Association, Barcelona, 25-28 August 1981 and also at the Department of Industry Research Staff Conference, University of Durham, 1 October, 1981. — Bibliography: p19-20
Unpriced (unbound) B82-27740

Jarratt, *Sir* Alex. Is unemployment here to stay? / Sir Alex Jarrett [i.e. Jarratt]. — [Birmingham] : [University of Birmingham], [1981]. — 13p ; 21cm. — (Josiah Mason memorial lecture ; 1981)
Cover title
ISBN 0-7044-0582-2 (pbk) : Unpriced B82-12119

Jordan, Bill, *1941-*. Mass unemployment and the future of Britain / Bill Jordan. — Oxford : Blackwell, 1982. — 250p : ill ; 22cm
Includes index
ISBN 0-631-13092-6 (cased) : Unpriced : CIP rev.
ISBN 0-631-13092-4 (pbk) : £4.95 B82-05398

Massey, Doreen B.. The anatomy of job loss : the how, why and where of employment decline / Doreen Massey and Richard Meegan. — London : Methuen, 1982. — viii,258p : ill,2maps ; 23cm
Bibliography: p239-248. — Includes index
ISBN 0-416-32350-2 (cased) : Unpriced : CIP rev.
ISBN 0-416-32360-x (pbk) : Unpriced B82-06505

331.13'7941 — Great Britain. Unemployment, *1979-1981 — Labour Party (Great Britain) viewpoints*

Britain on the dole : unemployment and the socialist alternative / the Labour Party. — London : Labour Party, 1982. — 23p : ill,ports ; 30cm
ISBN 0-86117-088-1 (unbound) : £0.60 B82-17375

331.13'7941 — Great Britain. Unemployment — *Child Poverty Action Group viewpoints*

Unemployment : who pays the price? / edited by Louie Burghes and Ruth Lister. — London : Child Poverty Action Group, 1981. — 116p : ill ; 21cm. — (Poverty pamphlet ; 53)
ISBN 0-903963-49-3 (pbk) : £2.40 B82-16180

331.13'7941 — Great Britain. Unemployment. Implications of theories of economics

Miller, Robert, *1947-*. What price unemployment? : an alternative approach / Robert Miller and John B. Wood. — London : Institute of Economic Affairs, 1982. — 80p ; 22cm. — (Hobart paper, ISSN 0073-2818 ; 92)
Bibliography: p77-78
ISBN 0-255-36149-1 (pbk) : £1.80 B82-23376

331.13'7941 — Great Britain. Unemployment. Policies of companies

Company responses to unemployment : a report by the Social Affairs Directorate. — London (Centre Point, 103 New Oxford St., WC2A 1DU) : Confederation of British Industry, 1981. — 35p ; 21x22cm
Bibliography: p34-35
£3.00 (pbk) B82-11897

331.13'7941 — Great Britain. Unemployment. Policies of local government

Needham, Barrie. Choosing the right policy instruments. — Aldershot : Gower, Dec.1982. — [200]p
ISBN 0-566-00608-1 : £12.50 : CIP entry
Also classified at 331.13'79492 B82-30056

331.13'7941 — Great Britain. Unemployment — *Practical information*

Kay, Isabel. Your hopeful future : how to live well financially, medically and emotionally during retirement, unemployment or disablement / Isabel and Ernest Kay. — London : Macdonald, 1982. — 192p ; 23cm
Bibliography: p186-188. — Includes index
ISBN 0-356-08604-6 (cased) : £7.95
ISBN 0-356-08605-4 (pbk) : Unpriced
Primary classification 362.4'0941 B82-37218

Stanway, Roger H.. Redundancy and beyond / by Roger Stanway and Chris Neill ; illustrated by Chris Neill. — Alderley Edge : Orwell House,, [1982?]. — [82]p : ill,1map ; 30cm
Bibliography: p65-69
ISBN 0-907921-00-0 (pbk) : Unpriced B82-16591

331.13'7941 — Great Britain. Unemployment — *Selsdon Group viewpoints*

Minford, Patrick. The problem of unemployment / Patrick Minford. — [London] ([170 Sloane St., SW1X 9QG]) : [Selsdon Group], [c1981]. — 15p ; 21cm. — (Selsdon Group policy series ; no.5)
Cover title
£1.00 (pbk) B82-05176

Minford, Patrick. The problem of unemployment / Patrick Minford. — London (170 Sloane St., SW1X 9QG) : Selsdon Group, [c1981]. — 15p : ill ; 21cm. — (Selsdon Group policy series ; no.5)
Cover title
£1.00 (pbk) B82-07140

331.13'7941 — Great Britain. Unemployment — *Trades Union Congress viewpoints*

Fighting closures. — Nottingham : Spokesman, Dec.1982. — [100]p
ISBN 0-85124-361-4 (cased) : £2.50 : CIP entry
ISBN 0-85124-362-2 (pbk) B82-32306

331.13'7941'024362 — Great Britain. Unemployment — *For Christian welfare work*

Our parish and unemployment : pastoral guidelines for parishes and local groups on making a positive response to the needs of the unemployed / FSA. — London (106 Clapham Rd, SW9 0JX) : Family and Social Action, 1981. — 40p : ill ; 21cm
£0.50 (pbk) B82-14536

331.13'79417 — Ireland *(Republic).* **Unemployment**

Walsh, Brendan M.. The unemployment problem in Ireland : background analysis and planning options / B.M. Walsh. — [Dublin] ([27 Merrion Sq, Dublin 2]) : Published by Kincora for the European League for Economic Co-operation and the Irish Council of the European Movement, [1978]. — 98p : ill ; 21cm
Unpriced (pbk) B82-27864

331.13'7942991 — Gwent. Newport. Unemployment. Social aspects

Miller, Joe. Situation vacant : the social consequences of unemployment in a Welsh town / by Joe Miller ; afterword by Community Projects Foundation. — London : Community Projects Foundation, c1982. — iv,96p ; 30cm
Text on inside covers. — Bibliography: p78-81
ISBN 0-902406-20-5 : £1.50 B82-39068

331.13'7943 — West Germany. Unemployment. Policies of government

Reyher, Lutz. Employment policy alternatives to unemployment in the Federal Republic of Germany : issues, effects on the labour market and costs / by Lutz Reyher, Martin Koller and Eugen Spitznagel ; English translation by Eileen Martin. — London : Anglo-German Foundation for the Study of Industrial Society, c1980. — 222p : ill ; 28cm
Translation from the German. — Bibliography: p212-222
ISBN 0-905492-28-5 (pbk) : £7.00 B82-01289

331.13'79492 — Netherlands. Unemployment. Policies of local government

Needham, Barrie. Choosing the right policy instruments. — Aldershot : Gower, Dec.1982. — [200]p
ISBN 0-566-00608-1 : £12.50 : CIP entry
Primary classification 331.13'7941 B82-30056

331.2 — WORKERS. CONDITIONS OF EMPLOYMENT

331.2 — Great Britain. Home employment. Conditions of service — *Inquiry reports*

Great Britain. *Parliament. House of Commons. Employment Committee.* First report from the Employment Committee, session 1981-82 : homeworking : together with the proceedings of the committee. — London : H.M.S.O., [1981]. — viiip ; 25cm. — ([HC] ; 39)
ISBN 0-10-203982-8 (unbound) : £1.15 B82-16059

331.2'0413321'0941 — Great Britain. Financial institutions. Personnel. Effects of technological innovation — *Trade union viewpoints*

Lombard in the eighties : an alternative view. — [London] ([Sheffield House, 17 Hillside, Wimbledon, London SW19 4NL]) : BIFU, [1982?]. — 8p ; 21cm
Cover title. — Ill on inside cover
Unpriced (pbk) B82-30384

Microtechnology : a programme for action. — [London] (Sheffield House, 17 Hillside, Wimbledon, SW19) : BIFU, [1982?]. — 34p : ill ; 21cm
Unpriced (pbk) B82-30385

331.2'04133212'0941 — Great Britain. Commercial banks: National Westminster Bank. Personnel. Effects of technological innovation — *Trade union viewpoints*

Beyond 1984 : a perspective of the impact of new technology and working procedures in National Westminster Bank. — London (Sheffield House, 17 Hillside, Wimbledon, SW19) : BIFU, 1981. — 8p : ill ; 21cm
Unpriced (pbk) B82-30386

331.2'0413711'009417 — Ireland *(Republic).* **Teachers. Conditions of service**

Irish National Teachers' Organisation. An introduction to the Irish National Teachers' Organisation and primary teaching. — [Dublin] : The organisation, [1982]. — 16p ; 22cm + 1 sheet(21x29cm folded to 21x15cm)
Cover title
Unpriced (pbk)
Primary classification 331.88'113711'009417 B82-25027

331.2'041385 — Great Britain. Railway services: British Rail. Footplate personnel. Conditions of service — *Inquiry reports*

Advisory Conciliation and Arbitration Service. Committee of inquiry report and recommendation on a dispute between British Railways Board and the Associated Society of Locomotive Engineers and Firemen. — [London] (Cleveland House, Page St., SW1P 4ND) : ACAS, 1982. — 38leaves ; 30cm
Cover title
Unpriced (pbk) B82-25287

331.2′0941 — Great Britain. Personnel. Conditions of service — *Serials*

LRD book of wage rates, hours and holidays / Labour Research Department. — 1981-. — London (78 Blackfriars Rd, SE1 8HF) : LRD Publications, 1981-. — v. ; 30cm
Annual
ISSN 0262-3447 = LRD book of wage rates, hours and holidays : £2.00 (£10.00 to non labour movement or educational bodies)
B82-05225

331.2′1 — Great Britain. Wage bargaining

Willman, Paul. Fairness, collective bargaining, and incomes policy / by Paul Willman. — Oxford : Clarendon, 1982. — x,197p : ill,plans ; 22cm
Bibliography: p189-194. — Includes index
ISBN 0-19-827252-9 : £15.00 : CIP rev.
B82-01087

331.2′1 — Personnel. Remuneration

Davidmann, M.. Work and pay, incomes and differentials, employer, employee and community / M. Davidmann. — [Stanmore] : Social Organisation Ltd., [c1981]. — 27leaves : ill ; 30cm. — (Community leadership and management)
ISBN 0-85192-018-7 (pbk) : £2.90 B82-17853

Harrop, David. World paychecks : who makes what, where, and why / by David Harrop. — London : Muller, c1982. — xvi,176p ; 22cm
Includes index
ISBN 0-584-11033-2 (pbk) : £3.95 : CIP rev.
B82-17961

331.2′1 — Scotland. Personnel: Debtors. Remuneration. Arrestment by employers

Connor, Anne. Arrestments of wages and salaries : a review of employers′ involvement / by Anne Connor. — Edinburgh (New St Andrews House, Edinburgh EH1 3SZ) : Central Research Unit, 1980. — v,13p ; 30cm. — (Central Research Unit papers) (Research report for the Scottish Law Commission ; no.4)
Unpriced (spiral) B82-02089

331.2′1′09417 — Ireland *(Republic)*. **Remuneration. Attitudes of personnel**

Whelan, Christopher T.. Employment conditions and job satisfaction : the distribution, perception and evaluation of job rewards / Christopher T. Whelan. — Dublin : Economic and Social Research Institute, 1980. — ix,171p : ill ; 25cm. — (Paper / Economic and Social Research Institute ; no.101)
Bibliography: p136-141
ISBN 0-7070-0034-3 (pbk) : £5.50 (Irish) (£2.75 for students)
Also classified at 658.31′422′09417 B82-41045

331.2′15 — Great Britain. Civil service. Personnel. Remuneration. Determination — *Inquiry reports*

Great Britain. *Committee of Inquiry into Civil Service Pay*. Inquiry into Civil Service pay : report of an inquiry into the principles and the system by which the remuneration of the non-industrial Civil Service should be determined : chairman: Sir John Megaw. — London : H.M.S.O., [1982]. — 2v. : ill ; 25cm. — (Cmnd. ; 8590)
Report of the Committee of Inquiry into Civil Service Pay. — Includes index
ISBN 0-10-185900-7 (pbk) : Unpriced
ISBN 0-10-185901-5 (v.2) : £9.35 B82-35144

331.2′15 — Great Britain. Civil service. Personnel. Remuneration. Determination — *Proposals*

Annexes to evidence to Inquiry into Civil Service Pay / Local Authorities′ Conditions of Service Advisory Board. — [London] : [The Board], 1981. — 138p in various pagings : ill ; 30cm
Cover title
ISBN 0-905677-03-x (pbk) : £5.00
ISBN 0-905677-01-3 (set) : Unpriced
B82-11202

331.2′15 — Great Britain. Civil service. Personnel. Remuneration. Determination. Proposals

How much are public servants worth?. — Oxford : Blackwell, Oct.1982. — [160]p
ISBN 0-631-13251-1 (pbk) : £7.50 : CIP entry
B82-29078

331.2′15 — Great Britain. Civil service. Personnel. Remuneration. Determination — *Proposals*

Roberts, Geoffrey. Evidence to the Inquiry into Civil Service Pay / prepared by Geoffrey Roberts. — [London] : [Local Authorities′ Conditions of Service Advisory Board], 1981. — 29p : facsims ; 30cm
At head of title: Local Authorities Conditions of Service Advisory Board
ISBN 0-905677-02-1 (pbk) : £2.50
ISBN 0-905677-01-3 (set) : Unpriced
B82-11201

331.2′15 — Great Britain. Industries. Low-income personnel. Remuneration. Determination. Wages councils. Performance, *1979-1980*

Crine, Simon. Pickpocketing the low paid / Simon Crine. — London : Low pay Unit, 1980. — 20p ; 21cm. — (Low pay report ; 1)
Cover title
£0.75 (pbk) B82-14636

331.2′15 — Great Britain. Industries. Personnel. Remuneration. Determination. Wages councils

Labour market structure, industrial organisation and low pay. — Cambridge : Cambridge University Press, Sept.1982. — [165]p. — (Occasional papers / University of Cambridge. Department of Applied Economics ; no.54)
ISBN 0-521-24579-6 : £12.50 : CIP entry
B82-25501

331.2′15 — Great Britain. New towns. Development corporations. Personnel. Remuneration. Determination — *Inquiry reports*

Great Britain. *Standing Commission on Pay Comparability*. New towns staff / Standing Commission on Pay Comparability. — London : H.M.S.O., [1980]. — 18p ; 25cm. — (Report ; no.12)
ISBN 0-10-181090-3 (unbound) : £2.10
B82-13679

331.2′15′0994 — Australia. Remuneration. Indexation, *1975-1981*

Plowman, David. Wage indexation. — London : Allen and Unwin, Jan.1982. — [192]p
ISBN 0-86861-363-0 : £10.00 : CIP entry
B81-34785

331.2′16 — Great Britain. Manual personnel. Remuneration — *Case studies*

White, Michael. Payment systems in Britain. — Farnborough : Gower, Oct.1981. — [120]p
ISBN 0-566-02294-x : £12.50 : CIP entry
B81-25826

331.2′16 — Remuneration. Payment. Methods — *Proposals*

Cashless pay : alternatives to cash in payment of wages / Central Policy Review Staff. — London : H.M.S.O., 1981. — 22p ; 21cm
ISBN 0-11-630820-6 (pbk) : £2.10 B82-32952

Non-cash payment of wages. — London (Broadway House, Tothill St., SW1H 9NQ) : Engineering Employers′ Federation, [1982?]. — 21p ; 30cm
£5.00 (£2.00 to members) (unbound)
B82-28821

331.2′164 — Great Britain. Profit sharing - *Conference proceedings*

Planning employee share schemes. — Farnborough : Gower, 1981. — [60]p. — (Gower executive report)
Conference papers
ISBN 0-566-03024-1 : £18.50 : CIP entry
B81-11945

331.2′164′0941 — Great Britain. Companies. Personnel. Remuneration. Incentive schemes — *For management*

Employee benefits and incentive rewards / chief editor Martin Paterson. — London : Oyez, 1980. — 1v.(loose-leaf) : ill ; 26cm
Unpriced
Also classified at 331.25′5′0941 B82-22475

331.2′166 — Great Britain. Sick personnel. Remuneration — *For hotel & catering industries*

Statutory sick pay : a self help training guide. — Wembley : Hotel and Catering Industry Training Board, 1982. — 1v.(6pieces) : forms ; 32cm
Includes flow charts, quiz, sample documentation, user′s cards / OHP masters and cassette tape, with transcript
ISBN 0-7033-0029-6 : Unpriced B82-40870

331.2′166 — Great Britain. Sick personnel. Remuneration. Policies of government — *Disability Alliance viewpoints*

Disability Alliance. Compensating employers for statutory sick pay : the Disability Alliance′s response to a DHSS consultative document. — London (1 Cambridge Terrace, NW1 4JL) : The Alliance, 1981. — 11p ; 30cm
£0.50 (pbk) B82-02870

331.2′2′0941 — Great Britain. Industries. Personnel. Remuneration. Relativities, *1959-1975*

Newlands, David. The causes of changes in relative earnings among U.K. industries 1959-1975 / by David Newlands and Andrew Tylecote. — [Aberdeen] : University of Aberdeen Department of Political Economy, 1981. — 20leaves ; 30cm. — (Discussion paper ; no.81-12)
Bibliography: leaves 19-20
Unpriced (pbk) B82-02424

331.2′2′0941 — Great Britain. Personnel. Remuneration. Relativities — *Inquiry reports*

Great Britain. *Standing Commission on Pay Comparability*. General report / Standing Commission on Pay Comparability ; Chairman H.A. Clegg. — London : H.M.S.O., [1980?]. — v,51p ; 25cm. — (Cmnd. ; 7995) (Report ; no.9)
ISBN 0-10-179950-0 (unbound) : £2.50
B82-24693

331.2′3 — Great Britain. Personnel. Remuneration. Guarantee payments. Limits

Great Britain. *Department of Employment*. Limits on guarantee payments : a report / by the Secretary of State for Employment. — London : H.M.S.O., [1980]. — 2p ; 25cm. — ([HC] ; 6)
ISBN 0-10-200681-4 (unbound) : £0.70
B82-16067

331.2′3′0941 — Great Britain. Personnel. Remuneration. Guarantee payments. Agreements — *Collections*

Guaranteed week agreements. — London : Incomes Data Services, 1981. — 62p ; 21cm. — (IDS handbook series ; no.20)
£5.00 (£3.50 to subscribers) (pbk) B82-02873

331.25′2 — Great Britain. Companies. Controlling directories. Self-administered superannuation schemes

Pointon, G. N.. Small self-administered pension schemes for controlling directors / G.N. Pointon and W.W. Huggins ; edited by Nigel Eastaway. — London : Current Account, 1979. — 81p ; 30cm. — (Current account special report)
ISBN 0-906840-16-3 (spiral) : Unpriced
B82-06674

Small self-invested pension schemes for controlling directors. — [London?] : Pointon York ; [Leicester] : [Current Account] [[distributor]], c1979. — 10p ; 18x26cm. — (Current account mini reports)
ISBN 0-906840-02-3 (spiral) : Unpriced
B82-06676

331.2′52 — Great Britain. Local authorities. Personnel. Superannuation schemes

Richards, J. C.. Knight′s employee′s guide to local government superannuation. — 7th ed. — Croydon : Charles Knight, Apr.1982. — [64]p
Previous ed.: 1974
ISBN 0-85314-309-9 (pbk) : £1.25 : CIP entry
B82-16205

331.25′2 — Great Britain. Occupational superannuation benefits. Payment. Methods

Pension payment methods : a survey / [Pensions Research Accountants Group]. — Sunbury on Thames : Published for the Pensions Research Accountants Group by CARL Communications, c1982. — 36p : ill,forms ; 21cm
ISBN 0-907653-02-2 (pbk) : £2.75 B82-39867

331.25′2 — Great Britain. Occupational superannuation schemes. Information. Disclosure to members — *Proposals*

National Association of Pension Funds. Information to members of pension schemes : code of practice. — Croydon (Prudential Hse., Wellesley Rd., Croydon CR9 9XY) : National Association of Pension Funds, 1980. — 15p ; 21cm
Unpriced (pbk) B82-28494

331.25′2 — Great Britain. Occupational superannuation schemes. Management. Participation of members

Member participation in pension schemes : a guide to good practice / the National Association of Pension Funds. — [Croydon] : The Association, c1982. — 7p ; 21cm
ISBN 0-905796-19-5 (unbound) : £1.35 (£0.90 to members) B82-25626

331.25′2 — Great Britain. Self-employed persons. Superannuation schemes

Daniel, Mark. Pensions for the self-employed / Mark Daniel. — [London] : Sunday Telegraph, 1981. — 80p : ill ; 21cm
£1.75 (pbk) B82-08782

331.25′2′094 — Western Europe. Occupational superannuation schemes

Callund, David. Employee benefits in Europe / David Callund. — 4th ed. / editor Melvin Nightingale. — London : Callund & Co., 1981. — 1v.(loose-leaf) ; 25cm
Previous ed.: 1978
ISBN 0-905607-02-3 : Unpriced
Primary classification 368.4′0094 B82-12793

331.25′2′0941 — Great Britain. Occupational superannuation schemes

Lander, Max. Occupational pension schemes in the U.K. / by Max Lander. — Stockport ([c/o P.K. Berry, C.I.S. Building, Miller St, Manchester M60 0AL]) : Manchester Statistical Society, [1979?]. — 32p : ill ; 21cm
At head of title: Manchester Statistical Society. — Text on inside cover
£2.00 (pbk) B82-02708

331.25′2′0941 — Great Britain. Occupational superannuation schemes — *Conference proceedings*

Pensions Conference *(7th : 1982 : London).* The Seventh Pensions Conference : London February 3 and 4 1982 : speakers papers. — [London] ([Minster House, Arthur St., EC4R 9AX]) : [Financial Times Conference Organisation], [1982?]. — 122p ; 30cm. — (A Financial times conference)
Cover title
Unpriced (pbk) B82-23822

331.25′2′0941 — Great Britain. Occupational superannuation schemes — *For personnel*

TUC guide to occupational pension schemes. — London : TUC, 1981. — 111p ; 21cm
Includes index
£1.00 (pbk) B82-20325

331.25′2′0941 — Great Britain. Superannuation schemes

Young, Michael, *1932-.* Accounting for pensions / Michael Young and Nigel Buchanan ; cartoons by Holland. — Cambridge : Woodhead-Faulkner, 1981. — xi,211p : ill,facsims,2forms ; 23cm
Includes index
ISBN 0-85941-124-9 : £12.50 B82-13540

331.25′2′0941 — Great Britain. Superannuation schemes — *For company directors*

The **Director's** guide to pensions 1981 / edited by George Bull. — New version. — London (116 Pall Mall, SW1Y 5ED) : Institute of Directors, 1981. — 88p : ill ; 21cm
Previous ed.: Sunbury-on-Thames : Quartermaine House Ltd. for the Institute of Directors, 1978
£2.00 (pbk) B82-01927

331.25′29 — England. Schools. Teachers. Superannuation schemes

Your pensions : a booklet for teachers about to retire. — 4th ed. — London : National Union of Teachers, [1982?]. — 36p : 1form ; 21cm
Cover title
Unpriced (pbk) B82-25603

331.25′29 — England. Teachers. Dependants. Financial assistance. Provision by teachers' superannuation schemes. Sex discrimination

The **Dependency** element in teachers' pensions / National Union of Teachers. — [London] ([Hamilton House, Mabledon Place, WC1H 9BD]) : [National Union of Teachers], [1981]. — 7p ; 21cm
Unpriced (unbound) B82-19751

331.25′29 — Great Britain. Public bodies. Personnel. Superannuation benefits

Evidence presented by a study group of the Centre for Policy Studies to the inquiry set up by the Prime Minister into the value of pensions. — London (8 Wilfred St., SW1E 6PL) : Centre for Policy Studies, 1980. — 30p ; 30cm
Unpriced (unbound) B82-23436

331.25′5 — Companies. Shareholding by personnel

Wilken, Folkert. The liberation of capital / Folkert Wilken ; translated by David Green. — London : Allen & Unwin, 1982. — xxiv,294p ; 23cm
Translation of: Das Kapital. — Bibliography: p285-287. — Includes index
ISBN 0-04-334005-9 : £12.00 : CIP rev. B81-01845

331.25′5 — Great Britain. Company cars. Leasing. Financial aspects

Car leasing and lease broking. — [London?] : Pointon York ; [Leicester] : [Current Account] [[distributor]], c1979. — 15p ; 18x26cm. — (Current account mini reports)
ISBN 0-906840-12-0 (spiral) : Unpriced B82-06677

331.25′5′0941 — Great Britain. Companies. Personnel. Fringe benefits — *For management*

Employee benefits and incentive rewards / chief editor Martin Paterson. — London : Oyez, 1980. — 1v.(loose-leaf) : ill ; 26cm
Unpriced
Primary classification 331.2′164′0941 B82-22475

331.25′7 — Great Britain. Trade unions. Members. Activities. Time off. Permission by employers — *Rules*

Guide to time-off arrangements / [IDS]. — London (140 Great Portland St., W.1) : Incomes Data Services, 1981. — 92p ; 25cm
Includes index
Unpriced (pbk) B82-09131

331.25′7 — Job sharing

Job-sharing : improving the quality and availability of part-time work. — Manchester : Equal Opportunities Commission, 1981. — 34p ; 21cm. — (Alternative working arrangements ; 1)
ISBN 0-905829-45-x (pbk) : Unpriced B82-05162

331.25′7 — Job sharing & work sharing. Economic aspects

Meltz, Noah M.. Sharing the work : an analysis of the issues in worksharing and jobsharing / Noah M. Meltz, Frank Reid, and Gerald S. Swartz. — Toronto ; London : University of Toronto Press, c1981. — viii,90p : ill ; 22cm
Bibliography: p89-90
ISBN 0-8020-2383-5 (pbk) : £5.25 B82-13936

331.25′7′0941 — Great Britain. Working hours

Working time in Britain : the effects of changes in pattern and duration in selected industries / Trade Union Research Unit, Ruskin College, Oxford ; ... financed by the Anglo-German Foundation for the Study of Industrial Society as part of its programme of study of social and economic policy issues. — London : [The foundation], c1981. — xix,317p : ill ; 21cm
ISBN 0-905492-32-3 (pbk) : £15.00 B82-16336

331.25′7′0943 — West Germany. Working hours

Bolle, M.. Working time in West Germany : the effects of changes in pattern and duration / M. Bolle, U. Fischer, B. Strümpel ; English translation by Eileen Martin ; ... financed by the Anglo-German Foundation for the Study of Industrial Society as part of its programme of study of social and economic policy issues. — London : [The foundation], c1981. — xviii,200p : ill ; 21cm
Translation from the German
ISBN 0-905492-34-x (pbk) : £10.00 B82-16337

331.25′72 — Flexible working hours

Nollen, Stanley D.. New work schedules in practice : managing time in a changing society / Stanley D. Nollen. — New York ; London : Van Nostrand Reinhold, c1982. — xvi,281p : ill ; 24cm. — (Van Nostrand Reinhold/Work in America Institute series)
Includes index
ISBN 0-442-26899-8 : £16.10 B82-14302

331.25′76 — Great Britain. Personnel. Paid leave, *1973-1980*

Holiday entitlement and (long) holiday-taking 1973-1980 / prepared by English Tourist Board Research Department, Mrs. P. King and NOP Market Research Ltd. — London (4 Grosvenor Gardens SW1W 3DU) : Planning & Research Services Branch, English Tourist Board, 1981. — 28,[16]leaves : ill ; 30cm
£3.00 (spiral) B82-21486

331.25′762 — Great Britain. Personnel. Short term sick leave. Certification

Employee self-certification of short-term sickness absence. — London (Broadway House, Tothill St., SW1H 9NQ) : Engineering Employers' Federation, [1982?]. — [20]p ; 30cm
£5.00(£2.00 to members) (unbound) B82-28820

Self-certification : the LRD guide. — London : LRD Publications, 1982. — 14p : ill,forms ; 21cm
ISBN 0-900508-51-5 (unbound) : £0.30 B82-40284

331.25′762 — Great Britain. Personnel. Short term sick leave. Certification — *Serials*

Sick pay bulletin. — Issue no.1 (Mar. 1982)-. — London : Incomes Data Services, 1982-. — v. : forms ; 30cm. — (IDS studies)
Monthly. — Running title: IDS sick pay bulletin
ISSN 0263-9157 = Sick pay bulletin : Unpriced B82-36706

331.25′763 — Great Britain. Personnel. Parental leave — *Equal Pay and Opportunity Campaign viewpoints*

Work and parenthood : a guide for negotiators. — London (59 Canonbury Park North, N1) : Equal Pay and Opportunity Campaign, 1978. — 23p ; 21cm
Unpriced (pbk) B82-23119

331.25′92 — Great Britain. Agricultural industries. Industrial training

Apprenticeship and craft training scheme. — [Beckenham] ([32 Beckenham Rd, Beckenham, Kent BR3 4PB]) : Agricultural Training Board on behalf of the Joint Working Party on Careers Literature, c1981. — 1folded sheet(6p) : 1ill ; 21cm
Unpriced (unbound) B82-19444

331.25'92 — Great Britain. Hospitals. Chefs. Training — *Inquiry reports*

Report on a review of the national trainee scheme for cooks in hospitals / National Health Service National Staff Committee for Accommodation Catering and Other Support Services Staff. — [Great Britain] : [The Committee], 1979. — 10p ; 30cm
Unpriced (pbk) B82-23716

331.25'92 — Great Britain. Polymer industries. Industrial training

Powell, P. C.. The needs for education and training in the British polymer and polymer-using industries : a pilot study / P.C. Powell. — London : Polymer Engineering Directorate, [1981]. — 26p ; 30cm
Unpriced (pbk) B82-31334

331.25'92 — Ireland *(Republic).* **Agricultural industries. Industrial training** — *Inquiry reports*

Report of the ACOT expert group on agricultural education and training. — Blackrock : ACOT, 1981. — xi,171p : ill,1map ; 21cm
ISBN 0-907816-00-2 (pbk) : £4.00
Primary classification 630'.7'11417 B82-08856

331.25'92 — United States. Hotel & catering industries. Industrial training

A Study of vocational and industrial training within the United States of America. — Wembley : HCITB, c1981. — 58p : ill,forms ; 30cm
ISBN 0-7033-0012-1 (pbk) : £3.00 B82-05451

331.25'92'09421 — London. Industries. Personnel. Training. Implications of microelectronics — *Inquiry reports*

Training for microtechnology / report of the Employment Working Party. — London (1-11 Hoxton St., N1 4NL) : Inner City Unit, 1981. — [18]p ; 30cm
At head of title: Hackney Islington Partnership
Unpriced (pbk) B82-36004

331.2'8133212'0942 — England. Clearing banks. Personnel. Remuneration — *Proposals*

The **1982** pay claim. — London (Sheffield House, 17 Hillside, Wimbledon, SW19 4NL) : BIFU, [1982?]. — 9p ; 21cm
Unpriced (unbound) B82-30388

331.2'813341'0941 — Great Britain. Housing associations. Personnel. Remuneration

NFHA salaries guide — 1980. — London : National Federation of Housing Associations, [1981?]. — 85p : ill ; 30cm. — (A Briefing note ; no.2)
ISBN 0-86297-001-6 (spiral) : Unpriced
B82-13810

331.2'81355345 — British military forces. Dentists. Remuneration — *Proposals*

Review Body on Armed Forces Pay. Service medical and dental officers : supplement to eleventh report 1982 / Review Body on Armed Forces Pay. — London : H.M.S.O., [1982]. — iii,14p ; 25cm. — (Cmnd. ; 8573)
ISBN 0-10-185730-6 (unbound) : £2.55
B82-37377

331.2'813811'0941 — Great Britain. Retail trades. Low-income personnel. Remuneration

Crine, Simon. Shopworkers' low wages / Simon Crine. — London (9 Poland St., W1V 3DG) : Low Pay Unit, 1982. — 20p ; 21cm. — (Low pay report ; 10)
Cover title. — Text on inside covers
£0.85 (pbk) B82-29563

331.2'81385'0941 — Great Britain. Railway services: British Rail. Low-income personnel

Owen, Tim. Wrong side of the tracks : low pay in British Rail / Tim Owen. — London (9 Poland St., W1V 3DG) : Low Pay Unit, [1980]. — 24p ; 21cm. — (Pamphlet / Low Pay Unit ; no.14)
Cover title
£0.90 (pbk) B82-16397

331.2'813875 — Ships. Crews. Remuneration — *Conference proceedings*

Lloyd's World of Shipping in Hong Kong *(Conference : 1981).* Is ITF right? : Lloyd's World of Shipping in Hong Kong October 12-16 1981. — [London] : [Lloyds of London Press], [1982?]. — 1v.(various pagings) : ill ; 31cm
ISBN 0-907432-19-0 : Unpriced B82-31133

331.2'816467242'0941 — Great Britain. Hairdressers. Low pay. Alleviation — *Proposals*

Crine, Simon. A cut below the rest : hairdressers' low wages / Simon Crine. — [London] ([9, Poland St., W1V 3DG]) : Low Pay Unit, 1982. — 16p ; 21cm. — (Low pay report ; 9)
Cover title
£0.75 (pbk) B82-34248

331.2'816584'00973 — United States. Companies. Executives. Remuneration

Ellig, Bruce R.. Executive compensation : a total pay perspective / Bruce R. Ellig. — New York ; London : McGraw-Hill, c1982. — viii,343p : ill ; 24cm
Includes index
ISBN 0-07-019144-1 : £17.50 B82-02517

331.2'81658422'0941 — Great Britain. Companies. Directors & chief executives. Remuneration — *Serials*

Rewarding management. — 1982. — Aldershot : Gower, Oct.1981. — [100]p
ISBN 0-566-02327-x : £15.00 : CIP entry
B81-31104

Rewarding management. — 1983. — Farnborough : Gower. — [135]p
ISBN 0-566-02399-7 (pbk) : £17.50 : CIP entry
ISSN 0263-7391 B82-28458

331.2'8178'0880621 — English court music. Musicians. Remuneration, *1660-1685* — *Lists*

Lists of payments to the King's musick in the reign of Charles II (1660-1685) / transcribed and edited by Andrew Ashbee. — Snodland : A. Ashbee, 1981. — xiv,129p ; 22cm
ISBN 0-9507207-1-2 (pbk) : Unpriced
B82-24791

331.2'8223422'0968 — South Africa. Gold mining industries. Miners. Low pay, *1886-1906*

Levy, Norman. The foundations of the South African cheap labour system / Norman Levy. — London : Routledge & Kegan Paul, 1982. — xv,367p ; 23cm. — (International library of sociology)
Bibliography: p349-357. — Includes index
ISBN 0-7100-0909-7 : £15.95 B82-39526

331.2'83'09411 — Scotland. Agricutural industries. Personnel. Remuneration

Wages structure : including a chart of educational opportunities. — Scottish ed. — Rev. — [Beckenham] ([32 Beckenham Rd, Beckenham, Kent BR3 4PB]) : Agricultural Training Board on behalf of the Joint Working Party on Careers Literature, 1982. — [4]p : 1col.ill ; 21cm. — (Careers in agriculture horticulture and poultry husbandry) (Suplementary leaflet)
Unpriced (unbound) B82-19443

331.2'83'0942 — England. Agricultural industries. Personnel. Remuneration

Wages structure : including a chart of educational opportunies. — England and Wales ed. — Rev. — [Beckenham] ([32 Beckenham Rd, Beckenham, Kent BR3 4PB]) : Agricultural Training Board on behalf of the Joint Working Party on Careers Literature, 1980. — [4]p : 1col.ill ; 21cm. — (Careers in agriculture horticulture and poultry husbandry) (Supplementary leaflet)
Unpriced (unbound) B82-19449

331.2'94 — Europe. Personnel. Remuneration *related to* **prices,** *1400-1965*

Brown, Henry Phelps. A perspective of wages and prices / Henry Phelps Brown and Sheila V. Hopkins. — London : Methuen, 1981. — xvii,214p : ill ; 24cm
ISBN 0-416-31950-5 : £11.95 : CIP rev.
Also classified at 338.5'2'094 B81-27348

331.2'94 — European Community countries. Personnel. Remuneration

Seidel, Bernhard. Wage policy and European integration. — Aldershot : Gower, Feb.1983. — [246]p
Translation of: Tarifpolitik und europäische Integration
ISBN 0-566-00357-0 : £15.00 : CIP entry
B82-38717

331.2'941 — Great Britain. High-income personal. Remuneration — *Serials*

[Monthly review of salaries and benefits *(Incomes Data Services. Top Pay Unit)].* Monthly review of salaries and benefits / IDS Top Pay Unit. — Review 8 (Oct. 1981)-. — London (140 Great Portland St., W1) : Incomes Data Services, 1981-. — v. ; 29cm
Continues: Review (Incomes Data Services. Top Pay Unit)
ISSN 0262-7361 = Monthly review of salaries and benefits - IDS Top Pay Unit : £45.00 per year B82-12475

331.2'941 — Great Britain. Personnel. Low pay

Duncan, Colin. Low pay — its causes, and the post-war trade union response / Colin Duncan. — Colchester : Research Studies, c1981. — xv,159p : ill ; 24cm. — (Social policy research monographs series ; 3)
Bibliography: p139-149. — Includes index
ISBN 0-471-10052-8 : £17.50 : CIP rev.
B81-30555

331.3 — WORKERS. SPECIAL AGE GROUPS

331.3'1'097292 — Jamaica. Children. Employment

Ennew, Judith. Child labour in Jamaica : general review / Judith Ennew and Pansy Young. — London : Anti-Slavery Society, 1981. — 75p : ill,1map ; 21cm. — (Child labour series ; report no.6)
ISBN 0-900918-11-x (pbk) : £1.50 B82-25642

331.3'4'0941 — Great Britain. Unemployed young persons. Employment. Projects: Community Industry

Murray, Chris. Youth unemployment : a socio-psychological study of disadvantaged 16-19 year-olds / C. Murray. — Windsor : NFER, 1978. — 258p : ill ; 22cm
Includes bibliographies and index
ISBN 0-85633-172-4 (pbk) : £6.00 B82-00938

Shanks, Kenneth. After Community Industry — : a follow up survey of young employees / Kenneth Shanks. — [London] ([14 Stratford Place, London W1N 9AF]) : [Community Industry], [1982]. — 105,[39]p : forms ; 30cm. — (Research and planning paper / Community Industry ; no.2)
Unpriced (spiral) B82-34153

331.3'4'09416 — Northern Ireland. Young persons, 16-19 years. Employment — *Practical information* — *For youth work*

Young people without work : an information pack for those working with young people / prepared by the Standing Conference of Youth Organisations in Northern Ireland. — Belfast : SCOYO, 1981. — 16p : ill ; 30cm
ISBN 0-906797-08-x (unbound) : Unpriced
B82-00099

331.3'4'0942719 — Cheshire. Warrington. School leavers. Employment, *1971-1980*

Evans, G. J.. The labour market for school-leavers in Warrington / G.J. Evans, P. Mitchell. — [London] : Manpower Services Commission, Manpower Intelligence and Planning Division, 1981. — 1v.(various pagings) : ill ; 30cm
Bibliography: p9.4
ISBN 0-905932-74-9 (pbk) : Unpriced
B82-11172

331.3'4'0942732 — Greater Manchester. Ordsall. Young persons. Employment

Marshall, Graham. Young people and the labour market : a case study / Graham Marshall and Dan Finn [of the] William Temple Foundation, Manchester Business School, Manchester, M15 6PB. — London (2 Marsham St, SW1P 3EB) : Inner Cities Directorate, Department of the Environment, 1981. — iv,68p : forms ; 30cm. — (Inner cities research programme ; 5)
£3.75 (pbk) B82-32676

331.3'4'0973 — United States. School leavers. First employment. Projects

Rist, Ray C.. Earning and learning : youth unemployment, policies and regions / Ray C. Rist ; with Mary Agnes Hamilton ... [et al.]. — Beverly Hills ; London : Sage, c1981. — 221p : ill ; 22cm. — (Sage library of social research ; v.134)
Bibliography: p211-215. — Includes index
ISBN 0-8039-1743-0 (cased) : Unpriced
ISBN 0-8039-1744-9 (pbk) : Unpriced
B82-21919

331.3'412042 — East Cornwall. Unemployed young persons. Employment. Programmes: Youth Opportunities Programme. Work Experience on Employers' Premises. Attitudes of unemployed young persons

Working for experience : a study of WEEP and unemployed young people in East Cornwall. — London (57 Chalton St., NW1 1HU) : Into Work, [1982?]. — 33p : ill ; 30cm
Unpriced (pbk) B82-38461

331.3'412042 — Great Britain. Unemployed young persons. Employment. Programmes: Youth Opportunities Programme — *Case studies*

I'll stay here if I can / [edited by Sue Ashby]. — Cambridge : National Extension College, c1981. — 14p + tutors notes([4]p ; 30cm) : ill,ports ; 30cm
Title page: Basic Skills Unit
ISBN 0-86082-219-2 (pbk) : £0.90 B82-38999

Williamson, Howard. Chance would be a fine thing / Howard Williamson. — Leicester : National Youth Bureau, 1981. — 17p ; 30cm. — (National Youth Bureau research report ; no.2)
"Produced jointly by MSC and NYB"
ISBN 0-86155-043-9 (pbk) : £1.00 B82-06098

331.3'4133'094167 — Belfast. School leavers: Boys. Employment. Equality of opportunity. Social aspects

Cormack, R. J.. Into work? : young school leavers and the structure of opportunity in Belfast / R.J. Cormack, R.D. Osborne, W.T. Thompson. — Belfast (Lindsay House, Callender St., Belfast) : Fair Employment Agency, 1980. — 66p : maps ; 30cm. — (Research paper ; 5)
At head of title: Fair Employment Agency for Northern Ireland. — Bibliography: p65-66
£2.00 (pbk) B82-18618

331.3'41377'0941 — Great Britain. Unemployed young persons. Counselling. Projects: Just the Job *(Project)*

Bradley, Jo. Just the Job : a mass media project for the unemployed / Jo Bradley. — Cambridge : International Extension College, 1982. — iv,46p : ill,maps ; 30cm
Bibliography: p46
ISBN 0-903632-23-3 (pbk) : Unpriced
B82-36034

331.3'4137941 — Great Britain. Young persons. Unemployment

Youth unemployment and the bridge from school to work / edited for the Acton Society by John Grimond. — London : Anglo-German Foundation for the Study of Industrial Society, c1979. — v,51p ; 21cm
ISBN 0-905492-23-4 (pbk) : £3.50 B82-01281

Youth unemployment conference, 9th May 1981. — [London] ([57 Chalton St., NW1 1HU]) : British Youth Council, [1981?]. — [32]p ; 30cm
Unpriced (unbound) B82-35696

331.3'41379411 — Scotland. Young persons. Unemployment

Youth unemployment : some key questions? / D. Bell ... [et al.]. — Edinburgh (Economics Dept, Heriot-Watt University, Grossmarket, Edinburgh) : Scottish Centre of Political Economy, [1981?]. — 38p : ill ; 21cm. — (A SCOPE publication)
Unpriced (pbk) B82-26607

331.3'41379421 — South-east London. Unemployment. Attitudes of unemployed young persons

In and out of the programme : a study of unemployed young people in South London / Into Work South London. — [London] ([57 Chalton St., NW1 1HU]) : [Into Work], [1982?]. — 51p : ill ; 30cm
£1.00 (pbk) B82-38462

An **Uncertain** age : a report on the education, training and employment of a group of 18-20 year olds facing employment problems in South London. — London (57 Chalton St., NW1 1HU) : Into Work, 1981. — 73p ; 21cm
Unpriced (pbk) B82-38463

331.3'413794237 — East Cornwall. Unemployment. Attitudes of unemployed young persons

Looking for an opening : a study of unemployed young people in East Cornwall / Into Work East Cornwall. — London (57 Chalton St., NW1 1HU) : Into Work, [1982?]. — 24p : 1map ; 30cm
Text on inside cover
Unpriced (pbk) B82-38460

331.3'4137942879 — Tyne and Wear *(Metropolitan County)*. **North Tyneside** *(District)*. **Unemployment. Attitudes of unemployed young persons**

Jobless : a study of unemployed young people in North Tyneside / Into Work North Tyneside. — London (57 Chalton St., NW1 1HU) : Into Work, [1982]. — 47p : ill,1map ; 30cm
£1.00 (pbk) B82-38459

331.3'4137973 — United States. Adolescents. Unemployment

The **Youth** labor market problem : its nature, causes and consequences / edited by Richard B. Freeman and David A. Wise. — Chicago ; London : University of Chicago Press, 1982. — ix,555p : ill ; 24cm. — (A National Bureau of Economic Research conference report)
Includes bibliographies and index
ISBN 0-226-26161-1 : Unpriced B82-35316

331.3'42592 — Great Britain. Unemployed young persons. Training. Programmes: New Training Initiative

Morrison, Ian, *1940-*. Perspectives on the new training initiative / by Ian Morrison and Harry Salmon. — Birmingham : Department of Community & Youth Work, Westhill College, 1982. — 16p ; 30cm. — (Papers on community and youth work ; no.1)
Cover title
ISBN 0-9502706-1-x (pbk) : Unpriced
B82-35602

331.3'42592 — Great Britain. Unemployed young persons. Training — *Proposals*

Great Britain. *Department of Employment*. A new training initiative : a programme for action / Department of Employment. — London : H.M.S.O., 1981. — 14p ; 25cm. — (Cmnd. ; 8455)
ISBN 0-10-184550-2 (unbound) : £1.90
B82-13809

331.3'42592'09411 — Scotland. Young persons. Industrial training. Great Britain. *Parliament. House of Commons. Committee on Scottish Affairs.* **First report ... session 1981-82** — *Critical studies*

Great Britain. First special report from the Committee on Scottish Affairs, session 1981-82 : youth unemployment and training : the Government's reply to the Committee's First report of session 1981-82. — London : H.M.S.O., 1982. — 15p ; 25cm. — ([HC] ; 184)
ISBN 0-10-218482-8 (unbound) : £1.90
B82-21609

331.3'42592'09411 — Scotland. Young persons. Industrial training — *Inquiry reports*

Great Britain. *Parliament. House of Commons. Committee on Scottish Affairs.* First report from the Committee on Scottish Affairs : session 1981-82 : youth unemployment and training. — London : H.M.S.O.. — ([HC] ; 96-1)
Vol.1: Report, proceedings of the Committee and index. — 1981. — lxviii ; 25cm
At head of title: House of Commons. — Includes index
ISBN 0-10-271982-9 (pbk) : £4.35 B82-13300

Great Britain. *Parliament. House of Commons. Committee on Scottish Affairs.* First report from the Committee on Scottish Affairs : session 1981-82 : youth unemployment and training. — London : H.M.S.O.
Vol.2: Minutes of evidence and appendices. — [1981?]. — vi,510p ; 25cm. — ([HC] ; 96-II)
ISBN 0-10-271682-x (pbk) : £13.65
B82-26359

331.3'459'0941 — Great Britain. Handicapped school leavers. Employment

Walker, Alan, *1949-*. Unqualified and underemployed : handicapped young people and the labour market / Alan Walker. — London : Macmillan, 1982. — x,214p : ill ; 23cm. — (National Children's Bureau series)
Includes index
ISBN 0-333-32189-8 (cased) : Unpriced
ISBN 0-333-32190-1 (pbk) : Unpriced
B82-16154

331.3'4624110421 — London. Homeless single young persons: Scots. Employment. Provision — *Proposals*

Young Scots in London : (second report, 1978). — London (New Horizon Youth Centre, 1 Macklin St., W.C.2) : The Scots Group, [1978]. — 14p : 1map ; 30cm
Cover title
£0.30 (pbk)
Primary classification 362.7'9791630421
B82-10309

331.3'94'0941 — Great Britain. Persons, 40 years-. Employment

Cooper, Cary L. After forty : the time for achievement? / edited by Cary L. Cooper and Derek P. Torrington. — Chichester : Wiley, c1981. — vii,211p : ill ; 24cm
Includes bibliographies and index
ISBN 0-471-28043-7 : £9.75 : CIP rev.
B81-31827

331.4 — WOMEN WORKERS

331.4 — United States. Negro women. Employment

Wallace, Phyllis A.. Black women in the labour force / Phyllis A. Wallace with Linda Datcher and Julianne Malveaux. — Cambridge, Mass. ; London : M.I.T., 1980. — xv,163p : ill ; 21cm
Bibliography: p144-157. — Includes index
ISBN 0-262-23103-4 : £10.50 B82-39734

331.4 — Women. Occupations. Choice. Theories

Holland, Janet. Work and women : a review of explanations for the maintenance and reproduction of sexual divisions / Janet Holland ; foreword by Basil Bernstein. — 2nd ed. — London : University of London Institute of Education, 1981. — 61p ; 20cm. — (Bedford Way papers, ISSN 0261-0078 ; 6)
Previous ed.: Stockholm : Stockholm Institute of Education, 1980. — Bibliography: p50-61
ISBN 0-85473-119-9 (pbk) : £1.95 B82-27688

331.4'092'6 — England. Factories. Women personnel. Working life — *Case studies*

Pollert, Anna. Girls, wives, factory lives / Anna Pollert. — London : Macmillan, 1981. — xviii,251p : ill ; 23cm
Bibliography: p244-251
ISBN 0-333-29177-8 (cased) : Unpriced
ISBN 0-333-29178-6 (pbk) : Unpriced
B82-08200

331.4'0941 — Great Britain. Women. Employment

Sanders, Deidre. Kitchen sink, or swim? : women in the eighties : the choices / Deidre Sanders with Jane Reed. — Harmondsworth : Penguin, 1982. — 278p : ill ; 19cm. — (Pelican books)
Includes index
ISBN 0-14-022438-6 (pbk) : £2.50 B82-33155

Work, women and the labour market / edited by Jackie West. — London : Routledge & Kegan Paul, 1982. — xi,187p ; 22cm
Bibliography: p173-180. — Includes index
ISBN 0-7100-0970-4 (pbk) : £4.95 B82-13466

331.4'0941 — Great Britain. Women. Employment, *1950-1974*

Joshi, Heather. Female labour supply in post-war Britain : a cohort approach / by Heather Joshi, Richard Layard and Susan Owen. — [London] : Centre for Labour Economics, London School of Economics, 1981. — 96p : ill ; 21cm. — (Discussion paper ; no.79)
Cover title. — Bibliography: p95-96
(pbk) B82-36209

331.4'0941 — Great Britain. Women. Employment. Discrimination by society

A **Woman's** right to work : the case for positive action / [Denny Fitzpatrick et al.]. — 2nd ed. — London : Published for Social Challenge by Cardinal Enterprises, [1982?]. — 32p : ill ; 22cm. — (A Socialist challenge pamphlet)
Previous ed.: London : International Marxist Group, 1980. — Text on inside front cover
ISBN 0-85612-313-7 (pbk) : £0.60 B82-38912

331.4'0941 — Great Britain. Women. Employment. Effects of word processing systems

Information technology in the office : the impact on women's jobs / Communications Studies and Planning Ltd. — Manchester : Equal Opportunities Commission, 1980. — 90,[16]p : ill,1form ; 30cm
ISBN 0-905829-34-4 (pbk) : Unpriced
B82-29211

Women and word processors : an EPOC survey. — London (59 Canonbury Park North, N.1.) : Equal Pay and Opportunity Campaign, 1980. — 4p ; 30cm
Unpriced (unbound) B82-11899

331.4'0941 — Great Britain. Women personnel. Trade unions — *Conference proceedings*

TUC Women's Advisory Committee. Women workers 1981 / [report for 1980-81 of the TUC Women's Advisory Committee and report of the 51st TUC Women's Conference March 1981]. — London : TUC Publications, 1981. — 111p ; 21cm
£3.00 (pbk) B82-27458

331.4'0941 — Great Britain. Women personnel. Working life, *1600-1700*

Clark, Alice. Working life of women in the seventeenth century / Alice Clark. — London : Routledge and Kegan Paul, 1982. — xliii,328p ; 22cm
Originally published: London : Routledge, 1919. — Text on inside cover. — Bibliography: p309-319. — Includes index
ISBN 0-7100-9045-5 (pbk) : £4.50 B82-37240

331.4'0941 — Great Britain. Women. Trade unionism

Beale, J.. Getting it together : women as trade unionists. — London : Pluto Press, Sept.1982. — [128]p. — (Arguments for socialism)
ISBN 0-86104-500-9 (pbk) : £2.50 : CIP entry
B82-22437

331.4'097292 — Developing countries. Urban regions. Women. Employment. Socioeconomic aspects — *Study regions: Jamaica. Kingston*

Standing, Guy. Unemployment and female labour : a study of labour supply in Kingston, Jamaica : a study prepared for the International Labour Office within the framework of the World Employment Programme with the financial support of the United Nations Fund for Population Activities / Guy Standing. — London : Macmillan, 1981. — xii,365p ; 23cm
Bibliography: p339-357. — Includes index
ISBN 0-333-32282-7 : £15.00 B82-10831

331.4'0973 — United States. Women. Employment, *1907-1928* — *Illustrations*

Hine, Lewis W.. Women at work : 153 photographs / by Lewis W. Hine ; edited by Jonathan L. Doherty. — Rochester, N.Y. : George Eastman House in association with Dover ; London : Constable, 1981. — 117p : chiefly ill ; 28cm
ISBN 0-486-24154-8 (pbk) : £4.50 B82-18046

331.4'0973 — United States. Women personnel, *to 1981*

Kessler-Harris, Alice. Out to work : a history of wage-earning women in the United States / Alice Kessler-Harris. — New York ; Oxford : Oxford University Press, 1982. — xvi,400p : ill,ports ; 24cm
Includes index
ISBN 0-19-503024-9 : £14.00 B82-40541

Matthaei, Julie A.. An economic history of women in America. — Brighton : Harvester, Nov.1982. — [362]p
ISBN 0-7108-0474-1 : £18.95 : CIP entry
B82-30294

331.4'133 — Bedfordshire. Luton. Household electric equipment industries: Electrolux Limited. Women. Employment. Discrimination

Report on the findings of the formal investigation into Electrolux Limited at Luton / Equal Opportunities Commission. — Manchester : The Commission, 1980. — 52,[25]p ; 31cm
£2.00 (spiral) B82-31329

331.4'133 — England. Women lawyers. Equality of opportunity

Women in the legal services : evidence submitted by the Equal Opportunities Commission to the Royal Commission on Legal Services. — [Manchester] : [Equal Opportunities Commission], 1978. — 66p : 1form ; 30cm
Unpriced (pbk) B82-20738

331.4'133'09 — Women. Employment. Equality of opportunity, *to 1979*

Lewenhak, Sheila. Women and work / Sheila Lewenhak ; consultant editor Heather Gordon Cremonesi. — London : Macmillan in association with Fontana Paperbacks, 1980. — 286p ; 23cm
Includes index
ISBN 0-333-29112-3 : £12.00 B82-39713

331.4'133'0941 — Great Britain. Women. Employment. Equality of opportunity — *Conference proceedings*

Practical approaches to women's career development : a report on the conference at St Hugh's, Oxford on 16-17 September 1981 / edited Cary L. Cooper ; [co-sponsors] Brunel Management Programme ... [et al.]. — Sheffield (Moorfoot, Sheffield S1 4PQ) : Training Services Manpower Services Commission, 1982. — 112p : ill,ports ; 30cm
Unpriced (pbk) B82-38443

331.4'133'0941 — Great Britain. Women. Employment. Equality of opportunity — *National Joint Committee of Working Women's Organisations viewpoints*

Women's right to work. — [Great Britain] : National Joint Committee of Working Women's Organisations, [1981?]. — [20]p : 1ill ; 21cm
Bibliography: p[19]
£0.35 (pbk) B82-05511

331.4'21 — Great Britain. Women personnel. Low pay

Glucklich, Pauline. Women : work and wages / Pauline Glucklich, Mandy Snell. — [London] : Low Pay Unit, [1982]. — 32p ; 21cm. — (Discussion series / Low Pay Unit ; no.2)
Unpriced (unbound) B82-27574

331.4'813321'0941 — Great Britain. Banking. Women. Employment. Equality of opportunity

Banking Insurance and Finance Union. *Equal Opportunities Committee*. Equality for women : proposals for positive action : report and recommendations of the Equal Opportunities Committee of the Banking Insurance & Finance Union. — London (Sheffield House, 17 Hillside, SW19) : BIFU, [1982?]. — 28p ; 21cm
Unpriced (pbk) B82-27852

331.4'813321'0941 — Great Britain. Financial institutions. Women personnel. Working conditions

Women in banking and finance. — Esher (Sheffield House, Portsmouth Rd., Esher, Surrey) : Banking Insurance and Finance Union, 1982?. — 7p ; 21cm
Unpriced (unbound) B82-30395

331.4'8163'0941 — Great Britain. Agricultural industries. Women personnel

Gasson, Ruth. The role of women in British agriculture / Ruth Gasson. — [Ashford, Kent] : Wye College, 1980. — 72p : 1form ; 21cm
Bibliography: p57-58
Unpriced (pbk) B82-27668

331.4'829234'0924 — England. Cars components industries. Assembly lines. Women manual personnel. Working conditions, *1977-1978* — *Personal observations*

Cavendish, Ruth. Women on the line / Ruth Cavendish. — London : Routledge & Kegan Paul, 1982. — ix,172p : 1ill ; 22cm
ISBN 0-7100-0987-9 (pbk) : £5.95 B82-13469

331.5 — WORKERS. CATEGORIES BY SOCIAL AND ECONOMIC STATUS

331.5'44 — Gambia. Groundnut industries. Migrant personnel

Swindell, Kenneth. The strange farmers of the Gambia : a study in the redistribution of African population / Kenneth Swindell. — [Swansea] : Centre for Development Studies, University College of Swansea, 1981, c1982. — viii,112p : ill,maps ; 21cm. — (Monograph / Centre for Development Studies, University College of Swansea, ISSN 0114-9486 ; 15)
Text on inside covers
ISBN 0-86094-100-0 (pbk) : Unpriced
B82-27473

331.5'44'096762 — Kenya. Migrant personnel, *1895-1975*

Stichter, Sharon. Migrant labour in Kenya : capitalism and African response, 1895-1975 / Sharon Stichter. — Harlow : Longman, 1982. — xiii,210p : 1map ; 23cm
Bibliography: p186-198. — Includes index
ISBN 0-582-64326-0 (pbk) : £6.95 B82-18333

331.5'44'098 — Latin American. Migrant personnel

State policies and migration : studies in Latin America and the Caribbean / edited by Peter Peek and Guy Standing. — London : Croom Helm, c1982. — 403p : ill,maps ; 23cm. — ([An ILO-WEP study])
'A study prepared for the International Labour Office within the framework of the World Employment Programme with the financial support of the United Nations Fund for Population Activities. — Includes bibliographies and index
ISBN 0-7099-2028-8 : £14.95 : CIP rev.
B82-06516

331.5'5 — Chimney sweeping services. Apprentices, *to ca 1875*

Strange, Kathleen. The climbing boys. — London : Allison & Busby, Sept.1981. — [160]p
ISBN 0-85031-431-3 : £6.95 : CIP entry
B81-25113

331.5'5 — Great Britain. Training Opportunities Scheme trainees. Employment

The **Post** training employment experience of TOPS trainees / Economics and Statistics Section, Training Opportunities Directorate, Manpower Services Commission. — London : Manpower Intelligence and Planning, Manpower Services Commission, 1982. — 39p ; 29cm
ISBN 0-905932-35-8 (pbk) : Unpriced
B82-17321

331.5'9 — Great Britain. Epileptics. Employment

Epilepsy and getting a job / [British Epilepsy Association]. — Wokingham ([Crowthorne House, Bigshotte, New Wokingham Rd., Wokingham, Berks. RG11 3AY]) : British Epilepsy Association, [1982?]. — 5p ; 21cm. — (Action for epilepsy)
Cover title
Unpriced (pbk) B82-37565

331.5'9 — Great Britain. Mentally handicapped persons. Employment

Whelan, Edward. Getting to work / by Edward Whelan & Barbara Speake. — London : Souvenir, 1981. — 249p,[8]p of plates : ill ; 22cm. — (Human horizons series) (A Condor book)
Bibliography: p226-239
ISBN 0-285-64918-3 (cased) : £6.95
ISBN 0-285-64919-1 (pbk) : £4.95 B82-05519

331.5'9 — Great Britain. Physically handicapped persons. Employment. Equality of opportunity. Quota scheme — *Disability Alliance viewpoints*
Disability Alliance. The MSC's review of the quota scheme for the employment of disabled people / comments by the Disability Alliance. — London (Star St., W2 1QB) : Disability Alliance, 1981. — 39p ; 30cm
£1.00 (pbk) B82-13723

331.5'9'0941 — Great Britain. Handicapped persons. Employment
Occupational disability : the approaches of government, industry and the universities / edited by W.T. Singleton and L.M. Debney. — Lancaster : MTP, 1982. — xi,307p : ill ; 24cm
Includes bibliographies and index
ISBN 0-85200-433-8 : £19.95 : CIP rev.
B81-36997

331.5'9'0941 — Great Britain. Handicapped persons. Employment — *For employers*
Employers' guide to disabilities / edited by Melvyn Kettle, Bert Massie. — London : Published for the IYDP Committee (England) by the Royal Association for Disability and Rehabilitation, c1982. — 1v.(loose leaf) : ill ; 23cm
ISBN 0-900270-26-8 : £4.50 B82-17886

331.6 — WORKERS. CATEGORIES BY RACIAL, ETHNIC, NATIONAL ORIGIN

331.6 — Great Britain. Industries. Coloured personnel. Racial discrimination — *Workers Against Racism viewpoints*
Workers Against Racism. Cleansing our ranks : a platform for anti-racist trade unionists / Workers Against Racism. — [London] ([c/o WAR, BM RCT, WC1N 3XX]) : Junius, c1981. — 11p : ill,facsims ; 21cm
Cover title
£0.20 (pbk) B82-12859

331.6'0941 — Great Britain. Ethnic minorities. Employment. Discrimination by employers
Discrimination and disadvantange in employment : the experience of black workers : a reader / edited by Peter Braham, Ed Rhodes and Michael Pearn. — London : Harper & Row, in association with the Open University Press, c1981. — 403p : ill ; 22cm. — (Open University set book)
Includes index
ISBN 0-06-318193-2 (cased) : Unpriced : CIP rev.
ISBN 0-06-318194-0 (pbk) : Unpriced
B81-33972

331.6'2 — Western Europe. Foreign personnel. Employment. Policies of governments
Miller, Mark J.. Administering foreign-worker programs : lessons from Europe / Mark J. Miller, Philip L. Martin. — Lexington, Mass. : Lexington Books ; [Aldershot] : Gower [distributor], 1982. — xviii,194p : ill ; 24cm
Includes index
ISBN 0-669-05227-2 : £17.00 B82-36086

331.6'2'0941 — Great Britain. Immigrant personnel. Racial discrimination — *Case studies*
Torrington, Derek. Management and the multi-racial work force : case studies in employment practice. — Aldershot : Gower, Nov.1982. — [124]p
ISBN 0-566-00585-9 : £12.50 : CIP entry
B82-26548

331.6'2'41 — Expatriate British personnel. Conditions of service — *For British employers*
Rayman, John. Expatriate compensation and benefits. — London : Kogan Page, Jan.1983. — [300]p
ISBN 0-85038-613-6 : £25.00 : CIP entry
B82-39299

331.6'2'4101724 — Developing countries. British personnel. Employment
Why not serve overseas?. — [Glasgow] ([Abercrombie House, Eaglesham Road, East Kilbride, Glasgow G75 8EA]) : Overseas Development Administration, [1982]. — 12p : ill ; 21cm
Cover title. — Ill on inside covers
Unpriced (pbk) B82-37683

331.6'2'4107 — North America. British colonies. British immigrant indentured personnel. Economic conditions, *1650-1780*
Galenson, David W.. White servitude in colonial America : an economic analysis / David W. Galenson. — Cambridge : Cambridge University Press, 1981. — xii,291p ; 23cm
Bibliography: p279-283. — Includes index
ISBN 0-521-23686-x : £22.50
Also classified at 331.6'2'410729 B82-19409

331.6'2'410729 — West Indies. British colonies. British immigrant indentured personnel. Economic conditions, *1650-1780*
Galenson, David W.. White servitude in colonial America : an economic analysis / David W. Galenson. — Cambridge : Cambridge University Press, 1981. — xii,291p ; 23cm
Bibliography: p279-283. — Includes index
ISBN 0-521-23686-x : £22.50
Primary classification 331.6'2'4107 B82-19409

331.7 — LABOUR ECONOMICS OF SPECIAL OCCUPATIONS

331.7'0012 — Great Britain. Occupations. Classification schemes: Standard Industrial Classification — *Indexes*
Indexes to the Standard industrial classification revised 1980 / Central Statistical Office. — London : H.M.S.O., 1981. — 188p ; 28cm
ISBN 0-11-620001-4 (pbk) : £12.95
B82-10956

331.7'0022'2 — Occupations — *Illustrations* — *For children*
Daniels, Meg. What people do. — London : Blackie, Feb.1982. — [12]p. — (Blackie concertina books)
ISBN 0-216-91128-1 : £0.95 : CIP entry
B81-36027

People you see / Walt Disney Productions. — Bristol : Purnell, 1975 (1982 [printing]). — [24]p : chiefly col.ill ; 25cm. — (Disney colour library)
ISBN 0-361-03251-x : Unpriced B82-25230

331.7'02 — European Community countries. Spare-time occupations
Alden, Jeremy. An analysis of second jobs in the European Economic Community / by Jeremy Alden and Richard Spooner. — Cardiff (King Edward VII Ave., Cardiff CF1 3NU) : Dept. of Town Planning, University of Wales Institute of Science and Technology, 1981. — xii,161p : ill ; 30cm. — (Papers in planning research ; 35)
Unpriced (pbk) B82-26832

331.7'02 — Spare-time occupations — *Manuals*
Farrell, Peter. Spare-time income. — London : Kogan Page, Aug.1982. — [180]p
ISBN 0-85038-587-3 : £6.95 : CIP entry
B82-22793

331.7'02 — United States. Careers. Information. Organisation & management
Fredrickson, Ronald H.. Career information / Ronald H. Fredrickson. — Englewood Cliffs ; London : Prentice-Hall, c1982. — vi,333p : ill,forms ; 24cm
Bibliography: p281-308. — Includes index
ISBN 0-13-114744-7 : £16.45 B82-20050

331.7'02'07041 — Great Britain. Careers. Information sources. Sex discrimination
A **Guide** to equal treatment of the sexes in careers materials : an "equal opportunities in education" guide. — Manchester : Equal Opportunities Commission, [1980?]. — 10p ; 21cm
Bibliography: p9-10
ISBN 0-905829-32-8 (pbk) : Unpriced
B82-30844

331.7'02'0941 — Great Britain. Careers. Choice — *For school leavers*
Ridgway, Bill. What are you going to do?. — London : Edward Arnold, Sept.1982. — [48]p
ISBN 0-7131-0650-6 (pbk) : £1.75 : CIP entry
B82-20029

331.7'02'0941 — Great Britain. Careers. Choice — *Manuals*
Faulder, Carolyn. Cosmopolitan's careers guide / by Carolyn Faulder ; research by Nikki Henriques. — London : National Magazine, 1979. — 260p ; 22cm
Bibliography: p259-260. — Includes index
£4.25 (pbk) B82-28829

331.7'02'0941 — Great Britain. Occupations — *Career guides*
Allsop, Kathleen. Earning a living. — Rev. ed. / Kathleen Allsop and Margaret Leiper. — Aylesbury : Ginn, 1980. — 128p : ill ; 23cm. — (Social education series)
Previous ed.: 1971
ISBN 0-602-22527-2 (pbk) : Unpriced
B82-39863

331.7'02'0941 — Great Britain. Occupations — *Career guides* — *For girls*
Menon, Kalyani. First steps to a career / Kalyani Menon. — New ed., rev. — London : Shepheard-Walwyn, c1981. — xvi,155p : ill ; 25cm
Previous ed.: i.e. new ed. 1975. — Includes index
ISBN 0-85683-054-2 (cased) : £6.95
ISBN 0-85683-055-0 (pbk) : Unpriced
B82-12883

331.7'02'09417 — Ireland *(Republic).* **Occupations** — *Career guides* — *For school leavers*
Murphy, Christina. Careers & living / by Christina Murphy ; careers consultants Richard Keane and Liam Dinneen. — Dublin : Irish Times, 1981. — 171p : ports ; 25cm
Reprinted from The Irish times
ISBN 0-907011-04-7 : £10.00 B82-29836

331.7'020942 — England. Residential institutions for children. School leavers. Career guides
Burgess, Charles. In care and into work. — London : Tavistock Publications, July 1981. — [192]p. — (Residential social work ; P216)
ISBN 0-422-77640-8 (cased) : £8.00 : CIP entry
ISBN 0-422-77650-5 (pbk) : £3.50 B81-13472

331.7'02'097 — North America. Careers. Planning & development
Williams, Richard S.. Career management & career planning : a study of North American practice / Richard Williams. — London : H.M.S.O., 1981. — viii,158p ; 25cm
Includes index
ISBN 0-11-630438-3 (pbk) : £6.50 B82-05110

331.7'02'0973 — United States. Young persons, 16-21 years. Careers guidance
Otto, Luther B.. Design for a study of entry into careers / Luther B. Otto, Vaughn R.A. Call, Kenneth I. Spenner. — Lexington, Mass. : Lexington Books, c1981 ; [Aldershot] : Gower [distributor], 1982. — xvi,233p : ill,forms ; 24cm. — (Entry into careers series ; v.1)
Bibliography: p107-120. — Includes index
ISBN 0-669-03643-9 : £14.00 B82-21165

331.7'023'0941 — Great Britain. Occupations — *Career guides* — *For school leavers*
Job ideas / [Careers & Occupational Information Centre]. — [London] : [Manpower Services Commission], [1982]. — iv,113p ; 30cm
Cover title. — Includes index
ISBN 0-86110-223-1 (pbk) : Unpriced
B82-40358

331.7'023'0941 — Great Britain. Occupations — *Career guides* — *For school leavers in Home Counties & South-east England* — *Serials*
Opportunities. — 1983/84. — London : New Opportunity Press, Dec.1982
South ed. — [195]p
ISBN 0-86263-032-0 (pbk) : £5.95 : CIP entry
B82-37497

331.7'023'0941 — Great Britain. Occupations — *Career guides* — *For school leavers in Midlands of England* — *Serials*
Opportunities. — Midlands ed. — 1982. — London : New Opportunity Press, Jan.1982. — [336]p
ISBN 0-86263-024-x (pbk) : £4.50 : CIP entry
B82-02473

331.7'023'0941 — Great Britain. Occupations — *Career guides — For school leavers in Midlands of England — Serials* *continuation*

Opportunities. — 1983/84. — London : New Opportunity Press, Dec.1982
Midlands ed. — [195]p
ISBN 0-86263-034-7 (pbk) : £4.95 : CIP entry
B82-37495

331.7'023'0941 — Great Britain. Occupations — *Career guides — For school leavers in North-east England — Serials*

Opportunities. — 1983/84. — London : New Opportunity Press, Dec.1982
North ed. — [195]p
ISBN 0-86263-033-9 (pbk) : £4.95 : CIP entry
B82-37496

331.7'023'0941 — Great Britain. Occupations — *Career guides — For school leavers in Northern England — Serials*

Opportunities. — North ed. — 1982. — London : New Opportunity Press, Jan.1982. — [336]p
ISBN 0-86263-025-8 (pbk) : £4.50 : CIP entry
B82-02474

331.7'023'0941 — Great Britain. Occupations — *Career guides — For school leavers in Scotland — Serials*

Opportunities. — Scotland ed. — 1982. — London : New Opportunity Press, Jan.1982. — [272]p
ISBN 0-86263-026-6 (pbk) : £4.50 : CIP entry
B82-02475

Opportunities. — 1983/84. — London : New Opportunity Press, Dec.1982
Scotland ed. — [195]p
ISBN 0-86263-035-5 (pbk) : £4.95 : CIP entry
B82-37500

331.7'023'0941 — Great Britain. Occupations — *Career guides — For school leavers in Southern England — Serials*

Opportunities. — South ed. — 1982. — London : New Opportunity Press, Jan.1982. — [416]p
ISBN 0-86263-023-1 (pbk) : £5.50 : CIP entry
B82-02472

331.7'023'0941 — Great Britain. Occupations — *Career guides — Serials*

The **Careers** adviser's handbook. — 1982. — London : New Opportunity Press, Feb.1982. — [506]p
ISBN 0-86263-022-3 (pbk) : £7.95 : CIP entry
B82-09202

331.7'12'0601 — Commonwealth countries. Professions. Organisations: Commonwealth Foundation, *to 1980*

Chadwick, John, *1915-*. The unofficial Commonwealth : the story of the Commonwealth Foundation 1965-1980 / John Chadwick. — London : Allen & Unwin, 1982. — xvi,266p ; 23cm
Bibliography: p255-257. — Includes index
ISBN 0-04-341021-9 : £15.00 : CIP rev.
B82-10574

331.7'61385'0941 — Great Britain. Railway services: London and North Eastern Railway. Personnel

Grafton, Peter. Men of the LNER / Peter Grafton. — London : Allen & Unwin, 1982. — 84p : ill ; 23cm. — (Steam past)
Includes index
ISBN 0-04-385085-5 : Unpriced : CIP rev.
B81-25106

331.7'616479541 — Great Britain. Small licensed premises. Personnel. Employment — *For licensees*

Employing people in the licensed trade : a licensed trade self-help guide from the small business service of the Hotel and Catering Industry Training Board. — Wembley : Hotel and Catering Industry Training Board, 1982. — 97p : ill ; 21cm
ISBN 0-7033-0015-6 (pbk) : £2.00 B82-17335

331.7'61719'09411 — Scotland. Countryside rangers. Grants from Countryside Commission for Scotland

Grants for countryside ranger services. — Redgorton : Countryside Commission for Scotland, 1982. — 4p ; 20cm
ISBN 0-902226-57-6 (pbk) : Unpriced
B82-33047

331.7'63318'09599 — Philippines. Rice production industries. Farms. Labourers. Socioeconomic aspects

Aguilar, Filomeno. Landlessness and hired labour in Philippine rice farms / Filomeno Aguilar, Jr.. — Swansea : Centre for Development Studies, University College of Swansea, 1981. — 66p ; 21cm. — (Monograph, ISSN 0114-9486 ; 14)
Bibliography: p62-66
ISBN 0-86094-096-9 (pbk) : Unpriced
B82-27923

331.7'9 — Great Britain. Outdoor occupations — *Career guides*

Humphries, Judith. Careers working outdoors / Judith Humphries. — London : Kogan Page, 1982. — 121p ; 19cm
ISBN 0-85038-516-4 (cased) : Unpriced : CIP rev.
ISBN 0-85038-517-2 (pbk) : £2.50 B82-00147

331.8 — TRADE UNIONS AND COLLECTIVE BARGAINING

331.87 — Great Britain. Public bodies. Manual personnel. Trade unions: National Union of Public Employees. Organisation structure — *Proposals*

National Union of Public Employees. NUPE reorganisation : an Executive Council discussion document on Union structure / National Union of Public Employees. — London : NUPE, 1981 (1982 [printing]). — [13]p ; 21cm
Cover title
ISBN 0-907334-12-1 (pbk) : Unpriced
B82-16727

331.87'2 — Great Britain. White-collar personnel. Trade unions. Branches. Activities. Participation of members — *Study examples: National and Local Government Officers Association. Sheffield Branch*

Nicholson, Nigel. The dynamics of white collar unionism : a study of local union participation / Nigel Nicholson, Gill Ursell, Paul Blyton. — London : Academic Press, 1981. — xiii,268p : ill,forms ; 24cm. — (Organizational and occupational psychology)
Bibliography: p251-259. — Includes index
ISBN 0-12-518020-9 : £15.40 : CIP rev.
B81-30296

331.87'33 — Facilities for shop stewards

Trades Union Congress. Facilities for shop stewards / a statement of policy issued by the Trades Union Congress. — Repr. with further amendments. — London : Trades Union Congress, 1980. — 11p ; 21cm
Previous ed.: i.e. repr., with amendments. 1978
£0.20 (pbk) B82-03774

331.87'33 — Great Britain. Engineering industries. Industrial relations. Role of shop stewards, *1914-1972*

Frow, Edmund. Engineering struggles : episodes in the story of the shop stewards' movement / Edmund & Ruth Frow. — [Manchester] : [Working Class Movement Library], [1982]. — 496p : ill,facsims,ports ; 22cm
Bibliography: p478-487. — Includes index
ISBN 0-906932-45-9 (pbk) : Unpriced
B82-35087

331.88 — TRADE UNIONS

331.88 — Great Britain. Staff associations

Great Britain. *Certification Office for Trade Unions and Employers' Associations.* Staff associations : supplement to the annual report of the Certification Officer 1979. — London (Cleland Hse., Page St., SW1P 4NO) : Certification Office for Trade Unions and Employers' Associations, 1981. — 52p ; 22cm
Unpriced (pbk) B82-27738

331.88 — Industrialised countries. Trade unions

Trade unions in the developed economies / edited by E. Owen Smith. — London : Croom Helm, c1981. — 218p : ill ; 23cm
Includes bibliographies and index
ISBN 0-7099-1907-7 : £12.95 : CIP rev.
B81-16370

331.88 — Trade unions

Jackson, Michael P.. Trade unions / Michael P. Jackson. — London : Longman, 1982. — vii,197p ; 20cm
Bibliography: p181-192. — Includes index
ISBN 0-582-29580-7 (pbk) : £3.50 : CIP rev.
B81-31370

331.88'025'41 — Great Britain. Trade unions — *Directories*

Eaton, Jack. The trade union directory : a guide to all TUC unions / Jack Eaton and Colin Gill. — London : Pluto, 1981. — xii,323p ; 20cm. — (Pluto Press workers' handbooks)
ISBN 0-86104-350-2 (pbk) : £6.95 B82-20698

331.88'06'041 — Great Britain. Trade unions. Organisations: General Federation of Trade Unions, *1899-1981*

Prochaska, Alice. History of the General Federation of Trade Unions, 1899-1980. — London : Allen & Unwin, Oct.1982. — [288]p
ISBN 0-04-331087-7 : £15.00 : CIP entry
B82-23090

331.88'06'041 — Great Britain. Trade unions. Organisations: Trades Union Congress. Decision making

Trade unions, national politics and economic management : a comparative study of the TUC and the DGB / Jon Clark ... [et al.]. — London : Anglo-German Foundation for the Study of Industrial Society, c1980. — 133p ; 21cm
Bibliography: p133
ISBN 0-905492-24-2 (pbk) : £5.50
Also classified at 331.88'06'043 B82-01285

331.88'06'041 — Great Britain. Trade unions. Organisations: Trades Union Congress — *Inquiry reports*

Trades Union Congress. *General Council.* TUC development programme : a special report by the General Council to the 1981 Congress following a review of the TUC's organisation, structure and services. — London : TUC, 1981. — 15p ; 24cm
£0.50 (unbound) B82-20326

331.88'06'043 — West Germany. Trade unions. Organisations: Deutscher Gewerkschaftsbund. Decision making

Trade unions, national politics and economic management : a comparative study of the TUC and the DGB / Jon Clark ... [et al.]. — London : Anglo-German Foundation for the Study of Industrial Society, c1980. — 133p ; 21cm
Bibliography: p133
ISBN 0-905492-24-2 (pbk) : £5.50
Primary classification 331.88'06'041
B82-01285

331.88'06'044 — France. Trade unions. Organisations: Confédération générale du travail. Relations with Parti communiste français, *to 1981*

Ross, George. Workers and communists in France : from Popular Front to Eurocommunism / George Ross. — Berkeley ; London : University of California Press, c1982. — xvi,357p ; 25cm
Bibliography: p337-347. — Includes index
ISBN 0-520-04075-9 : £22.50
Primary classification 324.244'075 B82-31178

331.88'07'041 — Great Britain. Trade unions. Members. Education

Is knowledge power? : problems and practice in trade union education / edited by Tom Schuller. — Aberdeen : Aberdeen People's Press, [1981?]. — 143p ; 21cm
ISBN 0-906074-18-5 (cased) : £6.50
ISBN 0-906074-19-3 (pbk) : £3.50 B82-13581

331.88'092'4 — Great Britain. Trade unionism. Tillett, Ben, *1887-1921* — *Biographies*
Schneer, Jonathan. Ben Tillett. — London : Croom Helm, Oct.1982. — [224]p
ISBN 0-7099-2341-4 : £12.95 : CIP entry
B82-23194

331.88'092'4 — Poland. Trade unions: Solidarność, *1980-1981* — *Personal observations*
Taylor, John, *19---*. Five months with Solidarity : a first-hand report from inside Hotel Morski, Gdansk / John Taylor. — London : Wildwood House, 1981. — 123p : 1map ; 20cm. — (A Wildwood special)
ISBN 0-7045-0463-4 (pbk) : £2.95 : CIP rev.
B81-36987

331.88'092'4 — Poland. Trade unions: Solidarność, *1980-1981*. Wał esa, Lech — *Personal observations — Collections*
The **Book** of Lech Wałęsa / introduced by Neal Ascherson. — Harmondsworth : Penguin, 1982. — 203p ; 20cm
Translation of: Wałęsa. — Translated by: Celina Wieniewska, Jacek Laskowski, Bolesław Taborski
ISBN 0-14-006376-5 (pbk) : £2.50 B82-24680

The **Book** of Lech Wałęsa / introduced by Neal Ascherson. — [London] : Allen Lane, 1982. — 203p ; 23cm
Translation of: Wałęsa. — Translated by: Celina Wieniewska, Jacek Laskowski, Bolesław Taborski
ISBN 0-7139-1506-4 : £8.95 B82-20818

331.88'094 — European Community countries. Trade unions
Chapman, Tom. Has the trade union movement a place in Europe? : based on an address given by Tom Chapman ... at a seminar held at St Edmund Hall, Oxford in August 1981 ... — Exeter (7 Cathedral Close, Exeter, Devon EX1 1EZ) : European-Atlantic Movement, [1982?]. — 16p ; 21cm
Cover title. — Bibliography: p14
Unpriced (pbk) B82-35506

331.88'0941 — Great Britain. Trade unionism
Coates, Ken. Trade unions in Britain / Ken Coates and Tony Topham. — Nottingham : Spokesman, 1980. — xii,385p ; 23cm
Bibliography: p370-378. — Includes index
ISBN 0-85124-293-6 (cased) : £14.50
ISBN 0-85124-294-4 (pbk) : Unpriced
B82-14586

331.88'0941 — Great Britain. Trade unions
Williamson, Hugh, *1943-*. The trade unions / by Hugh Williamson. — 6th ed. — London : Heinemann Educational, 1981. — viii,150p : ill ; 20cm. — (Studies in the British economy)
Previous ed.: 1979. — Bibliography: p143-145. — Includes index
ISBN 0-435-84584-5 (pbk) : £2.50 : CIP rev.
B81-28814

331.88'0941 — Great Britain. Trade unions. Policies of Conservative Party — *Labour Research Department viewpoints*
New Tory attack on union rights. — London : LRD Publications, 1981. — 19p : ill ; 21cm
Cover title. — Text, ill on inside covers
ISBN 0-900508-47-7 (pbk) : £0.40 B82-11592

331.88'0941 — Great Britain. Trade unions. Relations with government, *1964-1979*
Barnes, Denis. Governments and trade unions : the British experience, 1964-79 / Denis Barnes and Eileen Reid. — London : Heinemann Educational, 1980 (1982 [printing]). — xiii,242p ; 22cm
At head of title: Policy Studies Institute. — Bibliography: p229-230. — Includes index
ISBN 0-435-83046-5 (pbk) : £6.50 B82-20423

331.88'0941 — Great Britain. Trade unions. Role
The **Role** of the trade unions. — London : Granada, 1980. — 94p ; 18cm. — (The Granada Guildhall lectures ; 1980)
Contents: Industrial relations / by James Prior — Towards a constitutional settlement / by Tony Benn — The democratic bargain / by Lionel Murray
ISBN 0-586-05386-7 (pbk) : £1.00 B82-24568

331.88'09415 — Ireland. Trade unions, *1890-1914*
Keogh, Dermot. The rise of the Irish working class. — Belfast : Appleton Press, Apr.1982. — [280]p
ISBN 0-904651-75-4 : £12.00 : CIP entry
B82-06533

331.88'09417 — Ireland *(Republic)*. Trade unions: Irish Transport and General Workers' Union, *1909-1923*
Greaves, C. Desmond. The Irish Transport and General Workers' Union : the formative years 1909-1923 / C. Desmond Greaves. — Dublin : Gill and Macmillan for the Irish Transport and General Workers' Union, 1982. — ix,363p ; 22cm
Includes index
ISBN 0-7171-1253-5 (cased) : Unpriced
ISBN 0-7171-1199-7 (pbk) : £6.00 B82-35955

331.88'09423'93 — Avon. Bristol. Trade unions, *1860-1914*
Atkinson, Brian. Trade unions in Bristol / Brian Atkinson. — [Bristol] : Bristol Branch of the Historical Association, 1982. — 28p,[4]p of plates : ill,facsims,ports ; 22cm. — (Bristol Branch of the Historical Association local history pamphlets ; 51)
Cover title
ISBN 0-901388-27-0 : £0.80 B82-40938

331.88'0943 — Germany. Trade unions, *1869-1933*
Moses, John A.. Trade unionism in Germany from Bismarck to Hitler 1869-1933 / John A. Moses. — London : Prior, c1982. — 2v. ; 24cm
Bibliography: p159-551. — Includes index
ISBN 0-86043-450-8 : £25.00 : CIP rev.
ISBN 0-86043-483-4 (v.2) B81-27441

331.88'09438 — Poland. Trade unions. NSZZ "Solidarność" — *Personal observations*
Dobbs, Michael. Poland, Solidarity, Walesa. — Oxford : Pergamon, Aug.1981. — [128]p
ISBN 0-08-028147-8 : £7.50 : CIP entry
B81-23893

331.88'09438 — Poland. Trade unions: Solidarity, *to 1981*
MacShane, Denis. Solidarity. — Nottingham : Spokesman, Aug.1981. — [150]p
ISBN 0-85124-319-3 (cased) : CIP entry
ISBN 0-85124-318-5 (pbk) B81-20649

331.88'09438 — Poland. Trade unions: Solidarność — *Serials*
P.S.C. news : Polish Solidarity Campaign newsletter. — No.1 (1981)-. — London (18 Mervyn Rd, W.5) : Polish Solidarity Campaign, 1981-. — v. : ill,maps,ports ; 30cm
Six issues yearly. — Description based on: No.2 (May 1981)
ISSN 0263-6875 = P.S.C. news : £0.20
B82-29060

331.88'0944 — France. Economic policies. Influence of trade unions, *1945-1980*
Lange, Peter. Unions, change and crisis. — London : Allen & Unwin, Oct.1982. — [304]p. — (Harvard Center For European Studies Project on European Trade Union Responses to Economic Crisis ; v.1)
ISBN 0-04-331088-5 : £20.00 : CIP entry
Also classified at 331.88'0945 B82-23091

331.88'0945 — Italy. Economic policies. Influence of trade unions, *1945-1980*
Lange, Peter. Unions, change and crisis. — London : Allen & Unwin, Oct.1982. — [304]p. — (Harvard Center For European Studies Project on European Trade Union Responses to Economic Crisis ; v.1)
ISBN 0-04-331088-5 : £20.00 : CIP entry
Primary classification 331.88'0944 B82-23091

331.88'0947 — Soviet Union. Trade unions, *1957-1980*
Ruble, Blair A.. Soviet trade unions : their development in the 1970s / Blair A. Ruble. — Cambridge : Cambridge University Press, 1981. — xii,190p ; 23cm. — (Soviet and East European studies)
Bibliography: p167-180. — Includes index
ISBN 0-521-23704-1 : £16.00 B82-02780

331.88'097298'3 — Trinidad and Tobago. Trade unionism, *to 1982*
Ramdin, Ron. From chattel slave to wage earner : a history of trade unionism in Trinidad and Tobago / Ron Ramdin. — London : Martin Brian & O'Keaffe, 1982. — 314p ; 22cm
Bibliography: p299-304. — Includes index
ISBN 0-85616-241-8 (pbk) : £8.95 B82-35699

331.88'0973 — United States. Trade unions, *to 1978*
Brody, David. Workers in industrial America : essays on the twentieth century struggle / David Brody. — New York ; Oxford : Oxford University Press, 1980. — ix,257p ; 21cm
ISBN 0-19-502490-7 (cased) : Unpriced
B82-05421

331.88'09761 — Alabama. Trade unions, *to 1980*
Taft, Philip. Organizing Dixie : Alabama workers in the industrial era / Philip Taft ; revised and edited by Gary M. Fink ; foreword by Higdon C. Roberts Jr. — Westport, Conn. ; London : Greenwood Press, 1981. — xxv,228p : 1port ; 25cm. — (Contributions in labor history, ISSN 0146-3608 ; no.9)
Bibliography: p211-215. — Includes index
ISBN 0-313-21447-6 : Unpriced B82-02734

331.88'113321'0941 — Great Britain. Financial institutions. Trade unions: Banking Insurance and Finance Union
A **guide** to the union. — London (Sheffield House, 17 Hillside, London SW19) : Banking Insurance and Finance Union, [1982]. — 8p ; 21cm
Cover title
Unpriced (pbk) B82-30390

The **Merger** : your questions answered. — [London] ([Sheffield House, 17 Hillside, SW19 4NL]) : The Scottish Equitable Staff Association with The Banking Insurance and Finance Union, [1982?]. — [12]p ; 21cm
Unpriced (unbound) B82-30393

The **Union** for building society staff. — [London] ([Sheffield House, 17 Hillside, Wimbledon SW19 4NL]) : BIFU, [1982?]. — 1folded sheet (6p) : 1ill ; 23cm
Unpriced B82-30391

Why BIFU?. — [London] ([Sheffield House, 17 Hillside, Wimbledon SW19 4NL]) : [BIFU], [1982?]. — [12]p : col.ill ; 21cm
Unpriced (unbound) B82-30392

331.88'1133212'0942 — England. Clearing banks. Trade unions: Banking Insurance and Finance Union. *English Clearing Banks Section — Regulations*
Banking Insurance and Finance Union *(English Clearing Banks Section)*. Constitution and rules of the Clearing Banks section of BIFU. — Esher (Sheffield House, Portsmouth Rd., Esher, Surrey) : Banking Insurance & Finance Union, [1980?]. — 9p ; 21cm
Cover title
Unpriced (pbk) B82-30394

331.88'113711'009417 — Ireland *(Republic)*. Teachers. Trade unions: Irish National Teachers' Organisation
Irish National Teachers' Organisation. An introduction to the Irish National Teachers' Organisation and primary teaching. — [Dublin] : The organisation, [1982]. — 16p ; 22cm + 1 sheet(21x29cm folded to 21x15cm)
Cover title
Unpriced (pbk)
Also classified at 331.2'0413711'009417
B82-25027

331.88'113711'00942 — England. Teachers. Trade unions: National Union of Teachers
In your new job. — [London] : [National Union of Teachers], [1982]. — 8p : 1form ; 15x21cm
Cover title
Unpriced (pbk) B82-36424

National Union of Teachers. Student teachers — this is your union. — [London] ([Hamilton House, Mabledon Place, WC1H 9BD]) : [National Union of Teachers], [1981]. — 11p : 1port ; 22cm
Unpriced (unbound) B82-04522

331.88′113711′00942 — England. Teachers. Trade unions: National Union of Teachers — *Regulations*

National Union of Teachers. Rules. — London (Hamilton House, Mabledon Place, WC1H 9BD) : Natioal Union of Teachers, 1981. — 40p ; 22cm
Cover title. — Includes index
Unpriced (pbk) B82-04523

331.88′11385′0941 — Great Britain. Railway services. Trade unions: National Union of Railwaymen, *to 1980*

Bagwell, Philip S.. The railwaymen : the history of the National Union of Railwaymen / by Philip S. Bagwell. — London : Allen & Unwin
Vol.2: The Beeching era and after. — 1982. — xxiv,459p,16p of plates : ill,3maps,ports ; 23cm
Bibliography: p445-448. — Includes index
ISBN 0-04-331084-2 : Unpriced : CIP rev. B81-33920

331.88′12′000941 — Great Britain. Engineering industries. Trade unions: Amalgamated Union of Engineering Workers. Policies — *Left-wing political viewpoints*

What's gone wrong in engineering? : the case for change in the AUEW. — London : 265a Seven Sisters Rd., N.14 : The Charter, [1981]. — 39p : ill,ports,21cm. — (Engineers charter pamphlet)
£0.15 (pbk) B82-22210

331.88′12′000941 — Great Britain. Engineering industries. Trade unions: Amalgamated Union of Engineering Workers, *to 1981*

Frow, Edmund. Democracy in the engineering union / Edmund and Ruth Frow and Ernie Roberts. — [Nottingham] : [Institute for Workers' Control], [1982?]. — 16p ; 22cm. — (IWC pamphlet ; no.81)
Cover title
£0.50 (pbk) B82-29562

331.88′12184′0941 — Great Britain. Boilermaking industries. Trade unions: Boilermakers' Society, *to 1981*

Mortimer, J. E.. History of the Boilermakers' Society. — London : Allen & Unwin
2: 1906-1939. — Nov.1982. — [392]p
ISBN 0-04-331085-0 : £20.00 : CIP entry B82-27805

331.88′122′0924 — Scotland. Mining industries. Trade unions: Scottish Miners' Union. McDonald, Alexander — *Biographies*

Wilson, Gordon M.. Alexander McDonald : leader of the miners. — Aberdeen : Aberdeen University Press, May 1982. — [272]p
ISBN 0-08-028455-8 : £18.00 : CIP entry B82-07243

331.88′122334′0924 — Great Britain. Coal industries. Trade unions: National Union of Mineworkers. Gormley, Joe — *Biographies*

Gormley, Joe. Battered cherub : the autobiography of Joe Gormley. — London : Hamilton, 1982. — 216p,[16]p of plates : ill,ports ; 24cm
Includes index
ISBN 0-241-10754-7 : £7.95 : CIP rev. B82-04307

331.88′122334′0941 — Great Britain. Coal industries. Trade unions: National Union of Mineworkers, *1939-1946*

Arnot, R. Page. The miners : one union, one industry : a history of the National Union of Mineworkers : 1939-46 / by R. Page Arnot. — London : Allen & Unwin, 1979. — xiv,212p,[12]p of plates : ill,1map,ports ; 24cm
Includes index
ISBN 0-04-331074-5 : £15.00 : CIP rev. B78-35917

331.88′124′0941 — Great Britain. Construction industries. Trade unions

Howie, Will. Trade unions in construction / Will Howie. — London : Telford, 1981. — 30p ; 15x21cm. — (ICE works construction guides)
Bibliography: p30
ISBN 0-7277-0092-8 (pbk) : £2.00 B82-15393

331.88′13′09426 — East Anglia. Agricultural industries. Trade unionism. Role of Methodists, *1872-1896*

Scotland, Nigel. Methodism and the revolt of the field : a study of the Methodist contribution to agricultural trade unionism in East Anglia 1872-96 / Nigel Scotland. — Gloucester : Sutton, 1981. — 296p : ill,ports ; 23cm
Bibliography: p267-289. — Includes index
ISBN 0-904387-46-1 : Unpriced B82-25380

331.88′6′0973 — United States. Trade unions: Industrial Workers of the World, *to 1936*

At the point of production : the local history of the I.W.W. / edited by Joseph R. Conlin. — Westport ; London : Greenwood Press, 1981. — viii,329p ; 25cm. — (Contributions in labor history, ISSN 0146-3608 ; no.10)
Bibliography: p237-318. — Includes index
ISBN 0-313-22046-8 : Unpriced B82-18022

331.88′92 — Western world. Industries. Closed shops

Hanson, Charles. The closed shop : a comparative study in public policy and trade union security in Britain, the USA and West Germany / Charles Hanson, Sheila Jackson, Douglas Miller. — Aldershot : Gower, c1982. — x,264p ; 23cm
Bibliography: p238-252. — Includes index
ISBN 0-566-00414-3 : Unpriced : CIP rev. B81-34284

331.89 — COLLECTIVE BARGAINING AND DISPUTES

331.89′041368′00941 — Great Britain. Insurance companies: Phoenix Assurance. Industrial relations. Disputes — *Trade union viewpoints*

The **Dispute** : a report on events leading to the Union's current dispute with Phoenix Assurance Group. — London (Sheffield House, 17 Hillside, Wimbledon, SW19 4NL) : BIFU, [1982?]. — 13p ; 21cm
Unpriced (unbound) B82-30389

331.89′04137812′0973 — United States. Higher education institutions. Collective bargaining by teachers, *1960-1980*

Faculty and teacher bargaining : the impact of unions on education / edited by George W. Angell. — Lexington, Mass. : Lexington Books ; [Aldershot] : Gower [distributor], 1981. — x,114p ; 24cm
Includes index
ISBN 0-669-04360-5 : £11.00 B82-00396

331.89′041796357′0973 — United States. Baseball. Collective bargaining, *to 1981*

Dworkin, James B.. Owners versus players : baseball and collective bargaining / James B. Dworkin. — Boston, Mass. : Auburn House ; London : distributed by Eurospan, c1981. — xiv,306p : ill ; 24cm
Includes index
ISBN 0-86569-072-3 : £14.95 B82-08668

331.89′0941 — Great Britain. Collective bargaining

Basnett, David. The future of collective bargaining / David Basnett. — London : Fabian Society, 1982. — 14p ; 21cm. — (Fabian tract, ISSN 0307-7535 ; 481)
ISBN 0-7163-0481-3 (unbound) : £1.50 B82-32349

331.89′0941 — Great Britain. Collective bargaining *— For trade unionism — Serials*

Bargaining report. — 1 (Mar./Apr. 1979)-. — London : LRD Publications, 1979-. — v. ; 30cm
Six issues yearly. — Description based on: 2 (May/June 1979)
ISSN 0143-2680 = Bargaining report : £8.00 per year B82-19879

331.89′25′0941 — Great Britain. Political strikes: General Strike, *1926*

Hallas, Duncan. Days of hope : the General Strike of 1926 / by Duncan Hallas and Chris Harman. — London : Produced and distributed for the SWP by Socialists Unlimited, 1981. — 36p ; 21cm. — (International socialism reprint ; no.6)
Originally published: as two articles in International Socialism Journal, issues 48 (June/July 1977) and 88 (May 1976)
ISBN 0-905998-25-1 (unbound) : £0.65 B82-24443

331.89′26 — Great Britain. Industries. Redundancy. Protest by personnel: Sit-ins & work-ins

Coates, Ken. Work-ins, sit-ins and industrial democracy. — Nottingham : Spokesman, May 1981. — [160]p
ISBN 0-85124-277-4 (cased) : £6.25 : CIP entry
ISBN 0-85124-278-2 (pbk) : £2.50 B81-08837

331.89′2813871′094167 — Belfast. Dockers. Industrial relations. Strikes, *1907*

O'Hare, Fergus. The divine gospel of discontent : story of the Belfast dockers and carters strike 1907 / by Fergus O'Hare. — Belfast (Avoca Park, Andersonstown, Belfast) : Connolly Bookshop, [1981?]. — 32p : ill,ports ; 31cm
Cover title
£1.00 B82-11617

331.89′2822334′0941443 — Scotland. Strathclyde Region. Glasgow. Govan & Tollcross. Coal industries. Miners. Industrial relations. Strikes, *1842*

Duncan, Robert, *1948-*. Conflict and crisis : Monkland's miners and general strike 1842 / by Robert Duncan. — [Airdrie] : [Library Services Dept.], [1982?]. — 32p : 1ill,1map,1port ; 21cm
Cover title
ISBN 0-946120-01-3 (pbk) : Unpriced B82-35627

331.89′282383′094382 — Poland. Gdansk. Dockyards: Stocznia Gdańska im. Lenina. Political strikes

Polet, Robert. The Polish summer : worker's victories and popular non-violent civilian defence / by Robert Polet. — London (55 Dawes St., SE17 1EL) : WRI, 1981. — 43p ; 21cm
Translation from the French. — Text on inside cover
Unpriced (pbk) B82-19045

331.89′282383′094382 — Poland. Gdańsk. Dockyards: Stocznia Gdańska im. Lenina. Political strikes, *1980 — Russian texts*

Gdansk 1980 : fotografii. — London : Overseas Publications Interchange, 1981. — 63p : chiefly ill,ports ; 30cm
Translation of: Gdańsk 1980. — Title page transliterated
ISBN 0-903868-38-5 (pbk) : £5.00 B82-22176

331.89′28873′0977534 — Wisconsin. Marinette. Knitwear industries: Marinette Knitting Mills. Industrial relations. Strikes, *1951*

Karsh, Bernard. Diary of a strike / Bernard Karsh. — 2nd ed. — Urbana ; London : University of Illinois Press, 1982. — xv,177p ; 23cm. — (An Illini book)
Previous ed.: Urbana : University of Illinois Press, 1958. — Bibliography: p169-171. — Includes index
ISBN 0-252-00914-2 (pbk) : £4.20 B82-19493

331.89′2968 — Southern Africa. Negro personnel. Industrial relations. Strikes, *1980-1981 — Socialist Workers' Party viewpoints*

Rogers, John, *1952-*. Striking against apartheid : new moves in the struggle for Southern Africa / by John Rogers. — London : Produced and distributed for the SWP by Socialists Unlimited, 1982. — 30p : ill,1map ; 21cm. — (A Socialist Workers Party pamphlet)
ISBN 0-905998-30-8 (unbound) : £0.65 B82-24442

332 — FINANCE

332 — Euro-currency markets

The **Foreign** exchange and Eurocurrency markets. — Rev. — London (10 Lombard St., EC3V 9AT) : Bank Education Service, 1980. — 22p : ill,facsims ; 21cm. — (Study booklet series ; 13)
Unpriced (pbk)
Primary classification 332.4′5 B82-16269

332 — Euromarkets *— Conference proceedings*

Finanical Times Conference Organisation. The Euromarkets in 1982 : London 9 and 10 February : speakers papers / Financial Times Conference Organisation. — London (Minster House, Arthur Street, EC4R 9AX) : Financial Times Conference Organisation, 1982. — 105p : ill ; 30cm. — (Financial Times conferences)
Unpriced (unbound) B82-24672

332 — Finance

Financial economics : essays in honour of Paul Cootner / edited by William F. Sharpe, Cathryn M. Cootner. — Englewood Cliffs ; London : Prentice-Hall, c1982. — vii,264p : ill ; 25cm
Includes bibliographies
ISBN 0-13-315291-x : £20.00 B82-37733

Financial handbook. — 5th ed. / edited by Edward I. Altman ; associate editor Mary Jane McKinney. — New York ; Chichester : Wiley, c1981. — 1387p in various pagings : ill,1maps ; 25cm
Previous ed.: / edited by Jules I. Bogen. 1967. — Includes bibliographies and index
ISBN 0-471-07727-5 : £35.00 B82-08721

James, Simon. Pears guide to money and investment / by Simon James ; with additional chapters by John Black ... [et al.] ; general editor Chris Cook. — London : Pelham, 1982. — 233p : ill ; 25cm
Includes index
ISBN 0-7207-1370-6 : £9.50 B82-32980

Johnson, Ivan C.. Money and banking : a market-oriented approach / Ivan C. Johnson, William W. Roberts. — Chicago ; London : Dryden, c1982. — x,659p : ill,maps,ports ; 25cm
Includes bibliographies and index
ISBN 0-03-057157-x : £15.95 B82-16902

Smith, Adam, *1930-*. Paper money / Adam Smith. — London : Macdonald, 1982, c1981. — 335p : ill ; 23cm
Originally published: Boston, Mass. : G.K. Hall, 1981. — Bibliography: p319-322. — Includes index
ISBN 0-356-08573-2 : £8.95 B82-16944

Smith, Adam, *1930-*. Paper money / Adam Smith. — London : Futura, 1982, c1981. — 339p ; 18cm
Originally published: Boston, Mass. : G.K. Hall, 1981 ; London : Macdonald, 1982. — Bibliography: p321-325. — Includes index
ISBN 0-7088-2163-4 (pbk) : £1.95 B82-40565

332 — Finance — *For banking*

Checkley, P.. Applied economics / by P. Checkley. — Northwick (15 Constance Rd, Northwick, Worcs. WR3 7NF) : Northwick Publishers, c1980. — 204p in various pagings : ill ; 30cm. — (Personal course for bankers)
ISBN 0-907135-02-1 (pbk) : Unpriced
B82-00073

332 — Financial markets

Geisst, Charles R.. A guide to the financial markets / Charles R. Geisst. — London : Macmillan, 1982. — xv,144p : ill ; 23cm
Includes bibliographies and index
ISBN 0-333-30919-7 : £15.00 B82-20906

332 — International capital markets & international money markets

Kemp, L. J.. A guide to world money and capital markets / L.J. Kemp. — London : McGraw-Hill, c1981. — x,648p : ill ; 26cm
Includes index
ISBN 0-07-084566-2 : £40.00 : CIP rev.
B81-20192

332 — United States. Capital markets

Stapleton, Richard C.. Capital market equilibrium and corporate financial decisions / by Richard C. Stapleton, M.G. Subrahmanyam ; foreword by Jan Mossin. — Greenwich, Conn. : Jai Press ; London (3 Henrietta St., WC2E 8LU) : Distributed by Jaicon Press, c1980. — xviii,165p : ill ; 24cm. — (Contemporary studies in economic and financial analysis ; v.13)
Bibliography: p159-162. — Includes index
ISBN 0-89232-054-0 : £20.60 B82-02258

332′.023′41 — Great Britain. Finance — *Career guides — For graduates*

The **DOG** guide to accountancy & finance / [editor Iris Rosier]. — [London] : [VNU Business Publications], [1981?]. — 52p : ill ; 25cm
Cover title
ISBN 0-86271-017-0 (corrected : pbk) : Unpriced
Also classified at 657′.023′41 B82-05187

332.024 — Personal finance — *Manuals*

Clarke, Ted. Funding your future : part of the 'O' Level course in family economics / by Ted Clarke. — Cambridge : National Extension College, c1982. — vi,78p : 2ill,facsims,forms ; 21cm. — (National Extension College correspondence texts ; course no.HS26) (Managing your money)
ISBN 0-86082-292-3 (pbk) : Unpriced
ISBN 0-86082-297-4 (set) : Unpriced
B82-38356

Tolfree, W. Reay. Money : the facts of life / W. Reay Tolfree. — 7th ed. — Cambridge : Martin Books in association with Lloyds Bank, 1982. — 88p : ill ; 18cm
Previous ed.: 1981. — Includes index
ISBN 0-85941-207-5 (pbk) : £0.95 B82-36346

332.024 — Personal income — *Manuals — For children*

Eldin, Peter. The millionaire's handbook / Peter Eldin ; with drawings by Roger Smith. — London : Armada, 1982. — 128p : ill ; 18cm
ISBN 0-00-691947-2 (pbk) : £0.85 B82-31647

332.024′0028′5424 — Personal finance. Applications of programs written in Basic language

Goldsmith, W. B.. BASIC programs for home financial management / W.B. Goldsmith, Jr.. — Englewood Cliffs ; London : Prentice-Hall, c1981. — vi,314p : ill ; 29cm. — (A Spectrum book)
ISBN 0-13-066522-3 (cased) : Unpriced
ISBN 0-13-066514-2 (pbk) : £9.70 B82-16846

332.024′00941 — Great Britain. Personal finance — *Manuals*

Laidler, Michael. The money spinner system / Michael Laidler. — Durham : Paragon, c1982. — 24p ; 30cm
Accounts sheets in inside back pocket
ISBN 0-946177-00-7 : Unpriced B82-40007

Living with inflation. — 3rd ed. — Havant : Mason
Previous ed.: 1981
2: A simple guide to saving money — profitably and tax efficiently / [Julian Gibbs, Diana Wright]. — c1982. — 48p : ill ; 22cm
Includes index
ISBN 0-85937-288-x (pbk) : £1.25 : CIP rev.
B82-14960

The **Money** jungle. — [Mold] : County Money Management Association, [1982?]. — 83p : ill ; 21cm
ISBN 0-907880-00-2 (pbk) : £1.65 B82-28543

332.024′00941 — Great Britain. Personal finance — *Practical information*

The **Which?** book of money. — 2nd ed. — London : Consumers' Association and Hodder & Stoughton, c1981. — 240p : ill(some col.),1col.map,2facsims ; 26cm
Previous ed.: 1980. — Includes index
ISBN 0-340-27193-0 : £9.95 B82-02588

332.024′00941 — Great Britain. Personal finance — *Serials*

The **Money** observer. — No.1 (Oct. 1979)-. — [London] ([8 St. Andrews Hill, H1 EC4]) : The Observer, 1979-. — v. : ill ; 30cm
Monthly
ISSN 0263-7669 = Money observer : Unpriced
B82-33862

332.024′00973 — United States. Personal finance — *Manuals*

Brownstone, David M.. Personal financial survival : a guide for the 1980s and beyond / David M. Brownstone Jacques Sartisky. — New York ; Chichester : Wiley, c1981. — vii,364p : ill ; 24cm
Bibliography: p326-353. — Includes index
ISBN 0-471-05588-3 : £12.95 B82-05127

Raphaelson, Elliot. Planning your financial future : tax shelters, annuities, IRAs, Keoghs, stocks and other investment or retirement opportunities / Elliot Raphaelson. — New York ; Chichester : Wiley, c1982. — xi,239p ; 24cm
Includes index
ISBN 0-471-08134-5 : £14.75 B82-21802

332.024′01 — Great Britain. Retirement. Financial provision — *Practical information*

Assersohn, Roy. Express money book of prosperous retirement. — London : Quartet Books, Jan.1982. — [128]p
ISBN 0-7043-3397-x (pbk) : £2.50 : CIP entry
B81-40249

332.024′01 — Great Britain. Retirement. Financial provision — *Practical information — For self-employed persons*

Self-employed pensions handbook / editor Janet Walford ; editorial assistant Eileen Power. — 5th ed. — London : Financial Times Business Publishing, c1982. — 247p ; 24cm
Previous ed.: 1981
ISBN 0-902101-15-3 (pbk) : Unpriced
B82-23375

332.024′02 — Scotland. Debtors. Socioeconomic aspects

Adler, Michael. The origins and consequences of default : an examination of the impact of diligence (summary) / by Michael Adler and Edward Wozniak. — Edinburgh (New St Andrews House, Edinburgh EH1 3SZ) : Central Research Unit, 1981. — viii,71p : ill ; 30cm. — (Central Research Unit papers) (Research report for the Scottish Law Commission ; no.5)
Unpriced (spiral) B82-02092

332.024′042 — Great Britain. Personal finance — *Practical information — For women*

Faulds-Wood, Lynn. Cosmopolitan's money guide / Lynn Faulds-Wood. — London : Ebury, 1982. — 158p : ill ; 22cm
Bibliography: p156. — Includes index
ISBN 0-85223-224-1 : £6.95 B82-31173

332′.024′042 — Great Britain. Personal finance — *Practical information — For women*

McKenzie, Heather. Lady watch your money / by Heather McKenzie. — London : Clare, c1980. — 167p : ill ; 23cm
ISBN 0-906549-05-1 : £5.95 B82-11631

332.024′613′0973 — United States. Personal finance — *For nursing*

A **Financial** guide for nurses : investing in yourself and others / Dorothy J. del Bueno, editor. — Boston, [Mass.] ; Oxford : Blackwell Scientific, c1981. — x,224p : ill ; 24cm
Bibliography: p211-212
ISBN 0-86542-007-6 : £10.50 B82-13573

332′.03′21 — Finance — *Encyclopaedias*

Rosenberg, Jerry M.. Dictionary of banking and finance / Jerry M. Rosenberg. — New York ; Chichester : Wiley, c1982. — xiii,690p : ill ; 27cm
ISBN 0-471-08096-9 : £18.50 B82-28143

332′.0415 — Manufacturing industries. Capital. Use

Capital utilization in manufacturing : Columbia, Israel, Malaysia, and the Philippines / Romeo M. Bautista ... [et al.]. — New York ; Oxford : Published for the World Bank [by] Oxford University Press, c1981. — xiv,274p : ill,1form ; 25cm. — (A World Bank research publication)
Bibliography: p261-268. — Includes index
ISBN 0-19-520268-6 : £15.00 B82-31565

332′.0415′096 — Africa. Developing countries. Capital. Accumulation

Pol′shikov, P. I.. Capital accumulation and economic growth in developing Africa / P. Polshikov. — Moscow : Progress ; [London] : distributed by Central, c1981. — 206p ; 21cm. — (Problems of the developing countries)
Translation of: Nakoplenie i ėkonomicheskiĭ rost v razvivai͡ushchikhsi͡a stranakh Afriki
ISBN 0-7147-1738-x : £3.50 B82-29294

332'.042 — International finance

Miller, Norman C. (Norman Calvin). International reserves, exchange rates, and developing-country finance / edited by Norman C. Miller. — [Lexington, Mass.] : Lexington Books ; [Aldershot] : Gower [distributor], 1982. — xii,160p ; 24cm
ISBN 0-669-04856-9 : £15.50 B82-35427

Stewart, Frances. International financial cooperation : a framework for change. — London : Frances Pinter, Mar.1982. — [210]p
ISBN 0-86187-231-2 (cased) : £13.00 : CIP entry
ISBN 0-86187-232-0 (pbk) : £4.95 B82-06056

332'.042'05 — International finance — *Serials*

IFL Association newsletter / International Finance and Leasing Association. — No.16 (July 1980)-. — London (55 St. James's St., SW1A 1LF) : The Association, 1980-. — v. : ill,ports ; 28cm
Irregular. — Continues: ICU newsletter
ISSN 0262-4485 = IFL Association newsletter : Unpriced B82-02386

Journal of international money and finance. — Vol.1, no.1 (Apr. 1982)-. — Guildford : Butterworth, 1982-. — v. : ill ; 25cm
Three issues yearly
ISSN 0261-5606 = Journal of international money and finance : £12.50 per year (£30.00 to libraries) B82-36708

332'.042'0904 — International finance. Effects of economic policies of United States, *1945-1980*

De Saint Phalle, Thibaut. Trade, inflation, and the dollar / Thibaut de Saint Phalle. — New York ; Oxford : Oxford University Press, 1981. — 418p : ill ; 24cm
Bibliography: p387-406. — Includes index
ISBN 0-19-502970-4 : £14.95 B82-16079

332'.042'09041 — International finance, *1918-1923*

Silverman, Dan P.. Reconstructing Europe after the Great War / Dan P. Silverman. — Cambridge, Mass. ; London : Harvard University Press, 1982. — vii,347p ; 25cm
Bibliography: p339. — Includes index
ISBN 0-674-75025-x : £17.50 B82-34322

332'.05 — Finance — *Serials*

Research in finance : a research annual. — Vol.1 (1979)-. — Greenwich, Conn. : JAI Press ; London (3 Henrietta St., WC2E 8LU) : Distributed by JAICON Press, 1979-. — v. ; 24cm
ISSN 0196-3821 = Research in finance : £24.50 B82-02360

332'.09172'4 — Developing countries. Finance

Drake, P. J.. Money, finance and development. — Oxford : Robertson, June 1982. — [256]p
Originally published: 1980
ISBN 0-85520-513-x (pbk) : £6.50 : CIP entry B82-12166

332'.0917'4927 — Arab countries. Finance

Arab financial markets / edited by Peter Field and Alan Moore. — London : Euromoney Publications, c1981. — 164p : ill ; 30cm
ISBN 0-903121-25-5 (pbk) : Unpriced B82-15009

332'.0941 — Great Britain. Finance

Bain, A. D.. The economics of the financial system / A.D. Bain. — Oxford : Martin Robertson, 1981. — xi,292p : ill ; 23cm
Includes index
ISBN 0-85520-451-6 (cased) : Unpriced : CIP rev.
ISBN 0-85520-452-4 (pbk) : £6.95 B81-30179

Carter, H. (Howard). Applied economics in banking and finance / H. Carter and I. Partington. — 2nd ed. — Oxford : Oxford University Press, 1981. — x,390p : ill ; 23cm
Previous ed.: 1979. — Bibliography: p375. — Includes index
ISBN 0-19-877171-1 (cased) : Unpriced : CIP rev.
ISBN 0-19-877172-x (pbk) : Unpriced B81-26690

332'.0941 — Great Britain. Finance. Recession, *to 1981*

Factors underlying the recent recession / Bank of England. — London : Economics Division, Bank of England, c1981. — 93p : ill ; 30cm. — (Papers presented to the Panel of Academic Consultants, ISSN 0143-4691 ; no.15)
ISBN 0-903312-41-7 (pbk) : Unpriced B82-03987

332'.09669 — Nigeria. Finance, *to 1980*

Okigbo, P. N. C.. Nigeria's financial system / P.N.C. Okigbo. — Harlow : Longman, 1981. — xii,288p : 1ill ; 24cm
Includes index
ISBN 0-582-59733-1 (cased) : £14.50 : CIP rev.
ISBN 0-582-59732-3 (pbk) : Unpriced B82-18361

332'.0971 — Canada. Finance

Neave, Edwin H.. Canada's financial system / Edwin H. Neave. — Toronto ; Chichester : Wiley, c1981. — xiii,402p : ill ; 23cm
Includes bibliographies and index
ISBN 0-471-79926-2 (cased) : Unpriced
ISBN 0-471-79927-0 (pbk) : Unpriced B82-38448

332'.0973 — United States. Finance

Auerbach, Robert D.. Money, banking and financial markets / Robert D. Auerbach. — New York : Macmillan ; London : Collier Macmillan, c1982. — viii,498p : ill,1map,1form ; 26cm
Includes index
ISBN 0-02-304670-8 : £13.95 B82-19514

Mayo, Herbert. Finance / Herbert B. Mayo. — Chicago ; London : Dryden, c1982. — 608p : ill,facsims ; 25cm
Includes bibliographies and index
ISBN 0-03-059572-x (corrected) : £15.95 B82-18324

Prager, Jonas. Fundamentals of money, banking and financial institutions / Jonas Prager. — Cambridge, [Mass.] ; London : Harper & Row, c1982. — xiv,664p : ill ; 25cm
Includes bibliographies and index
ISBN 0-06-045253-6 : Unpriced B82-34017

Thomas, Lloyd B.. Money, banking and economic activity / Lloyd B. Thomas, Jr. — 2nd ed. — Englewood Cliffs ; London : Prentice-Hall, c1982. — xxii,618p : ill ; 25cm
Previous ed.: 1979. — Includes bibliographies and index
ISBN 0-13-599985-5 : £17.20 B82-31912

332.1 — BANKS AND BANKING

332.1 — Banking

Studies in retail banking. — [London] ([392 Goldhawk Road, W6 0SB]) : Retail Banker International, [1982]. — 70p : ill,ports ; 30cm
Articles reprinted from Retail Banker International, June-Nov. 1981. — Cover title. — Text and ill on inside cover
Unpriced (pbk) B82-29512

332.1 — Financial institutions. Competition & regulation

Competition and regulation in financial markets / edited by Albert Verheirstraeten. — London : Macmillan, 1981. — xxiii,282p ; 23cm
Includes bibliographies and index
ISBN 0-333-29388-6 : £20.00 B82-06654

332.1 — Great Britain. Automated banking

Jones, David, *1936 Nov.17-*. Easy money / David Jones. — Newbury : Scope, 1982. — 173p ; 22cm
ISBN 0-906619-11-4 : £7.50 : CIP rev. B82-10894

332.1 — Great Britain. Banks. Forms — *For personal customers*

Cards : forms & documents. — London (10 Lombard St., EC3V 9AT) : Banking Information Service, [1982?]. — 12p : ill(some col.),forms ; 25cm
Unpriced (pbk) B82-16274

332.1 — Great Britain. Financial institutions. Applications of microelectronic devices — *Trade union viewpoints*

Banking Insurance and Finance Union. New technology in banking, insurance and finance / BIFU. — London (17 Hillside, SW19 4NL) : Banking Insurance and Finance Union, [1982]. — 32p : ill,1port ; 30cm
£1.00 (free to members) (pbk) B82-36033

332.1 — Hong Kong dollar market — *Forecasts*

Prospects for the Hong Kong dollar. — London : International Forecasting Group, Henley Centre for forecasting, 1981. — 88p : ill ; 30cm
Unpriced (spiral) B82-01270

332.1'023'41 — Great Britain. Banking — *Career guides*

Banking / [written, designed and produced by SGS Education]. — Walton on Thames : Nelson, 1982. — 15p : ill ; 28cm. — (Career profiles ; 26)
ISBN 0-17-438367-3 (unbound) : Unpriced B82-27850

Moss, Stephen. Careers in banking / Stephen Moss. — London : Kogan Page, 1981. — 112p : ill,2forms ; 19cm
Bibliography: p108-110
ISBN 0-85038-482-6 (cased) : Unpriced : CIP rev.
ISBN 0-85038-483-4 (pbk) : £2.20 B81-30199

332.1'025'41 — Great Britain. Banks — *Directories* — *Serials*

British banking directory : institutions authorised under the 1979 Banking Act. — 1982-. — London : Financial Times Business Pub., 1982-. — v. : ill ; 21cm
ISSN 0264-0376 = British banking directory : Unpriced B82-38541

332.1'028'54 — Banking. Applications of digital computer systems

Banks and computers. — Rev. ed. — London (10 Lombard St., EC3V 9AT) : BES, 1980. — 15p : ill(some col.),1col.map ; 21cm. — (Study booklet series ; 11)
Cover title. — Text on inside covers
Unpriced (pbk) B82-16261

332.1'028'54 — Great Britain. Banking. Applications of digital computer systems

The **Banks** and information technology / [edited by Geoffrey Cooke]. — London (10 Lombard St., EC3V 9AR) : Banking Information Service, [1982]. — [21]p : ill(some col.),1facsim,1port ; 30cm
Cover title. — Text on inside cover
Unpriced (pbk) B82-41035

332.1'068'4 — United States. Banks. Directors. Duties

The **Bank** director's handbook / Edwin E. Cox ... [et al.] with the participation of Charles J. Thayer. — Boston, Mass. : Auburn House ; London : distributed by Eurospan, c1981. — xviii,217p : ill ; 25cm
Includes index
ISBN 0-86569-056-1 : £16.25 B82-13422

332.1'0917'4927 — Arab countries. Banking — *Serials*

Arab banking & finance = al-Māl wa-l-maṣārif. — Vol.1, no.1 (Apr. 1982)-. — London (21 John St., WC1N 2BP) : Middle East Economic Digest, 1982-. — ill(some col.),maps(some col.),ports(some col.) ; 28cm
Monthly. — Text in English, some summaries in Arabic
ISSN 0263-693X = Arab banking & finance : Unpriced B82-30486

332.1'094 — European Community countries. Banking. Regulation

The **Regulation** of banks in the member states of the EEC / edited by Jane Welch for the British Bankers Association. — 2nd ed. — The Hague ; London : Nijhoff ; London : Graham & Trotman [distributor], 1981. — viii,277p ; 25cm
Previous ed.: 1978. — Includes index
ISBN 90-247-2573-9 : Unpriced B82-05490

332.1′0941 — Great Britain. Banking

Doyle, E. P.. Practice of banking / E.P. Doyle. — 3rd ed. / revised by J.E. Kelly. — Plymouth : Macdonald & Evans, 1981. — xvi,380p ; 18cm. — (The M & E handbook series)
Previous ed.: 1972. — Includes index
ISBN 0-7121-1755-5 (pbk) : £3.95 B82-07279

Evans, Simon, *1940-*. Banking and payment systems / ... prepared by Simon Evans. — [Brighton] : [Retail Management Development Programme], [1982]. — 123p : ill ; 30cm. — (Retail management handbook ; 3)
ISBN 0-907923-02-x (pbk) : Unpriced
Also classified at 332.7′6′0941 B82-29832

Holden, J. Milnes. The law and practice of banking / J. Milnes Holden. — London : Pitman
Vol.1: Banker and customer. — 3rd ed. — 1982, c1974. — lviii,470p : ill ; 23cm
Previous ed.: 1974. — Includes index
ISBN 0-273-01761-6 : Unpriced : CIP rev. B81-31462

Holden, J. Milnes. The law and practice of banking / J. Milnes Holden. — London : Pitman
Vol.2: Securities for bankers′ advances. — 6th ed. — 1980. — xliii,459p ; 23cm
Previous ed.: 1971. — Includes index
ISBN 0-273-01422-6 : £9.95 B82-30617

Perry, F. E.. The elements of banking / F.E. Perry. — 3rd ed. — London : Methuen, in association with the Institute of Bankers, 1981. — xi,436p : ill ; 20cm
Previous ed.: 1977. — Includes index
ISBN 0-416-32080-5 (pbk) : £5.25 : CIP rev. B81-23785

332.1′0941 — Great Britain. Banking, ***1870-1970***

Bali, Ghila. Concentration in British banking 1870-1920 / Ghila Bali and Forrest Capie. — London (Northampton Sq., EC1V 0HB) : Centre for Banking & International Finance, City University, 1982. — 20p : ill ; 31cm. — ([Monetary history discussion paper series] ; no.4)
Report from the SSRC research project Monetary History of the U.K. 1870-1970
Unpriced (spiral) B82-25363

332.1′0941 — Great Britain. Banking, ***1960-1975***

Reid, Margaret, *1925-*. Secondary banking crises, 1973-75 : its causes and course / Margaret Reid. — London : Macmillan, 1982. — ix,219p ; 23cm
Includes index
ISBN 0-333-28376-7 : £20.00 B82-32341

332.1′0941 — Great Britain. Banking — ***For schools***

Ferguson, Cindy. Understanding banking / Cindy Ferguson, Rosemary Wells. — London : Bank Education Service
Bk.1: Money is our business. — [1981?]. — 27p : ill,forms ; 21cm
ISBN 0-904096-73-4 (pbk) : Unpriced B82-16275

Ferguson, Cindy. Understanding banking / Cindy Ferguson, Rosemary Wells. — London : Bank Education Service
Bk.2: Using your bank. — 1981. — 42p : ill,forms ; 21cm
ISBN 0-904096-74-2 (pbk) : Unpriced B82-16276

Ferguson, Cindy. Understanding banking / Cindy Ferguson, Rosemary Wells. — London : Bank Education Service
Bk.3: At your service. — [1981?]. — 25p : ill,forms,1map ; 21cm
ISBN 0-904096-78-5 (pbk) : Unpriced B82-16277

332.1′0941 — Great Britain. Banks — ***For consumers***

Duncan, John, *1936-*. How to manage your bank manager / John Duncan. — Newton Abbot : David & Charles, c1982. — 80p : ill ; 22cm. — (The making and managing series)
Includes index
ISBN 0-7153-8237-3 : £3.95 : CIP rev. B82-04871

332.1′0941 — Great Britain. Financial institutions. Public ownership — ***Socialist viewpoints***

Minns, R.. Take over the city. — London : Pluto Press, Sept.1982. — [128]p. — (Arguments for socialism)
ISBN 0-86104-502-5 (pbk) : £2.54 : CIP entry B82-21743

332.1′09417 — Ireland ***(Republic).*** **Banking —** ***Sinn Féin The Workers′ Party viewpoints***

The **Banks** / Research Section, Department of Economic Affairs Sinn Féin The Workers′ Party ; introduction by Eamonn Smullen. — Dublin : Repsol, 1978. — 60p ; 18cm. — (Studies in political economy)
Orginally published: 1976
ISBN 0-86064-005-1 (pbk) : £0.76 B82-17002

332.1′0942 — England. Banking, ***to 1975***

A **History** of banking. — Rev. — London (10 Lombard St., EC3V 9AT) : BES, 1975 (1980 [printing]). — 19p ; 21cm. — (Study booklet series ; 6)
Cover title. — Text on inside cover
Unpriced (pbk) B82-16262

332.1′09421′2 — London ***(City).*** **Financial institutions**

Ritchie, Nicholas. What goes on in the city? / Nicholas Ritchie. — 3rd ed. — Cambridge : Woodhead-Faulkner in association with Lloyds Bank, 1981. — 88p : ill,1map,forms,1port ; 21cm
Previous ed.: 1978. — Bibliography: p84-85
ISBN 0-85941-155-9 (cased) : Unpriced
ISBN 0-85941-156-7 (pbk) : £1.75 B82-13539

332.1′09421′2 — London ***(City).*** **Financial institutions & money markets**

Shaw, E. R.. The London money market / E.R. Shaw. — 3rd ed. — London : Heinemann, 1981. — xiv,267p : ill ; 22cm
Previous ed.: 1975. — Bibliography: p259-261. — Includes index
ISBN 0-434-91833-4 (pbk) : £7.50 B82-05118

332.1′09421′2 — London ***(City).*** **Money markets**

The **City** of London and its markets. — Rev. — London (10 Lombard St., EC3V 9AT) : BES, 1975 (1980 [printing]). — 29p : ill,1map ; 21cm. — (Study booklet series ; 12)
Cover title. — Text on inside covers
Unpriced (pbk) B82-16270

332.1′09494 — Switzerland. Banking, ***to 1981***

Faith, Nicholas. Safety in numbers : the mysterious world of Swiss banking / Nicholas Faith. — London : Hamish Hamilton, 1982. — viii,368p ; 23cm
Includes index
ISBN 0-241-10743-1 : £9.95 : CIP rev. B82-09976

332.1′09494 — Switzerland. Financial institutions — ***Socialist viewpoints***

Ziegler, Jean. Switzerland exposed / Jean Ziegler ; translated from the French by Rosemary Sheed Middleton. — London : Allison & Busby, 1978. — 173p ; 21cm
Translation of: Une Suisse au-dessus de tout soupçon. — Includes index
ISBN 0-85031-351-1 (cased) : Unpriced
ISBN 0-85031-247-7
Primary classification 320.9494 B82-15001

332.1′0952 — Japan. Banking

Prindl, Andreas R.. Japanese finance : a guide to banking in Japan / Andreas R. Prindl. — Chichester : Wiley, c1981. — xii,137p ; 24cm
Bibliography: p131-134. — Includes index
ISBN 0-471-09982-1 : £8.95 : CIP rev. B81-31831

332.1′0952 — Japan. Financial institutions

Japanese banking and capital markets. — London : Financial Times Business, c1981. — 119p ; 30cm. — (A Banker Research Unit report)
ISBN 0-902998-44-7 (spiral) : Unpriced B82-10921

332.1′0959 — South-east Asia. Financial institutions

Lee, Sheng-yi. Financial structures and monetary policies in Southeast Asia / S.Y. Lee, Y.C. Jao. — London : Macmillan, 1982. — xiv,338p : ill ; 23cm
Includes index
ISBN 0-333-28617-0 (cased) : Unpriced
ISBN 0-333-28618-9 (pbk) : Unpriced B82-17783

332.1′09669 — Nigeria. Financial institutions

Ojo, Ade T.. Banking & finance in Nigeria / Ade T. Ojo & ′Wole Adewunmi. — Leighton Buzzard : Burn, [1982]. — xx,316p : 2ill ; 21cm
Includes bibliographies and index
ISBN 0-907721-02-8 (pbk) : Unpriced B82-19895

332.1′09669 — Nigeria. Rural regions. Banking

Rural banking in Nigeria. — London : Longman, Jan.1983. — [128]p
ISBN 0-582-64419-4 (pbk) : £3.95 : CIP entry B82-32471

332.1′0973 — United States. Financial institutions

Campbell, Tim S.. Financial institutions, markets, and economic activity / Tim S. Campbell. — New York ; London : McGraw-Hill, c1982. — xviii,604p : ill ; 24cm. — (McGraw-Hill series in finance)
Includes bibliographies and index
ISBN 0-07-009691-0 : £16.50 B82-16340

332.1′097671 — Islamic countries. Banking

Siddiqi, Muhammad Nejatullah. Issues in Islamic banking. — Leicester : Islamic Foundation, Nov.1982. — [152]p. — (Islamic economics series ; 4)
ISBN 0-86037-118-2 (cased) : £4.95 : CIP entry
ISBN 0-86037-117-4 (pbk) : £2.75 B82-33356

332.1′2 — Capatalist countries. Monetary systems. Role of commercial banks

Banking systems abroad : the role of the large deposit banks in the financial systems of Germany, France, Italy, the Netherlands, Switzerland, Sweden, Japan and the United States / [contributors Dimitri Vittas (editor) ... et al.]. — London (32 City Rd., EC1Y 1AA) : IBRO, [1981]. — 347p ; 30cm
Cover title. — Bibliography: p343-347
Unpriced (spiral) B82-16279

332.1′2 — Commercial banking — ***Forecasts — Conference proceedings***

Retail Banking *(Conference : 1981 : London).* Retail Banking : a vital market for the 1980′s : London, November 30 & December 1, 1981 : speakers papers. — [London] : [Financial Times Conference Organisation], [1981]. — 136p ; 30cm. — (Financial Times conferences)
Unpriced (unbound) B82-16956

332.1′2′0941 — Great Britain. Clearing banks

The **Clearing** system. — Rev. — London (10 Lombard St., EC3V 9AT) : BES, 1980. — 14p : ill(some col.),1facsim ; 21cm. — (Study booklet series ; 4)
Unpriced (unbound) B82-16266

332.1′2′0941 — Great Britain. Commercial banks: Lloyds Bank, ***1918-1969***

Winton, J. R.. Lloyds Bank, 1918-1969 / J.R. Winton. — Oxford : Oxford University Press, 1982. — viii,210p,12p of plates : ill,ports ; 22cm
Includes index
ISBN 0-19-920125-0 : £15.00 : CIP rev. B82-03098

332.1′2′0941 — Great Britain. Commercial banks: Lloyds Bank. Social responsibility

Lloyds Bank. Lloyds Bank in the community. — London (71 Lombard St., EC3P 3BS) : The Bank, [1982?]. — 11p : ill(some col.),ports (some col.) ; 20x21cm
Unpriced (pbk) B82-25243

332.1′2′0942 — England. Commercial banks

Role of the banks. — Rev. — London (10 Lombard St., EC3V 9AT) : BES, 1980. — 12p ; 21cm. — (Study booklet series ; 1)
Cover title. — Text on inside cover
Unpriced (pbk) B82-16267

332.1'2'0973 — United States. Commercial banks. Failure

Sinkey, Joseph F.. Problem and failed institutions in the commercial banking industry / by Joseph F. Sinkey, Jr. — Greenwich, Conn. : Jai Press ; London (3 Henrietta St., WC2E 8LU) : Distributed by Jaicon Press, c1979. — xxix,287p : ill,2forms ; 24cm. — (Contemporary studies in economic and financial analysis ; v.4)
Bibliography: p275-282. — Includes index
ISBN 0-89232-005-2 : £22.85 B82-02081

332.1'5 — International banking — *Conference proceedings*

World banking : London 14 & 15 December, 1981 : speakers papers. — [London] : [Financial Times Conference Organisation], [1982]. — 116p ; 30cm. — (Financial Times conferences)
Unpriced (pbk) B82-21920

332.1'5 — International banking — *For children*

McKee, Robert. International banking / Robert McKee. — Hove : Wayland, 1981. — 71p : ill,1port ; 24cm. — (People, politics and powers)
Bibliography: p70. — Includes index
ISBN 0-85340-830-0 : £4.50 B82-06545

332.1'5 — Lending by banks. Country risks. Mathematical models

Abassi, Boulem. Country risk : a model of economic performance related to debt servicing capacity / by B. Abassi and R.J. Taffler. — London : [City University Business School], c1982. — 30leaves : ill ; 30cm. — (Working paper series / City University Business School, ISSN 0140-1041 ; no.36)
Bibliography: leaves 26-30
Unpriced (pbk) B82-21199

332.1'5 — Syndicated Euro-credit markets — *Statistics* — *Serials*

Euromoney syndication guide : the complete data service on syndicated loans and Eurobonds. — Jan. 1981-. — London (Nestor House, Playhouse Yard, EC4V 5EX) : Euromoney Publications, 1981-. — v. ; 30cm
Monthly. — Cumulation of: Euromoney syndication guide. Weekly fact sheet. — Continues: Euromoney syndication service
ISSN 0260-6747 = Euromoney syndication guide : Unpriced
Also classified at 336.3'435 B82-08455

332.1'5'09 — International banking, *ca 1800-1976*

Born, Karl Erich. International banking in the 19th and 20th centuries. — Leamington Spa (24, Binswood Ave., Leamington Spa CV32 5SQ) : Berg Publishers, Jan.1983. — [350]p
Translation of: Geld und Banken im 19. und 20. Jahrhundert
ISBN 0-907582-03-6 (cased) : £19.00 : CIP entry
ISBN 0-907582-04-4 (pbk) : £6.95 B82-33370

332.1'5'09 — International banking, *to 1980*

Sampson, Anthony. The money lenders / Anthony Sampson. — London : Hodder and Stoughton, 1981. — 336p ; 24cm
Includes index
ISBN 0-340-25719-9 : £7.95 : CIP rev. B81-20594

Sampson, Anthony. The money lenders. — London, Hodder and Stoughton, Sept.1982. — [560]p. — (Coronet books)
Originally published: 1981
ISBN 0-340-28771-3 (pbk) : £2.50 : CIP entry B82-15754

332.1'52 — International Monetary Fund — *Fabian viewpoints*

Butler, Nick. The IMF : time for reform / [Nick Butler]. — London : Fabian Society, 1982. — 29p ; 22cm. — (Young Fabian pamphlet ; 50)
ISBN 0-7163-2050-9 (pbk) : £0.85 B82-14611

332.1'53 — International development agencies. Development projects. Tendering — *Conference proceedings*

Bidding for projects financed by international lending agencies. — Aldershot : Gower, Oct.1982. — [300]p
ISBN 0-566-03033-0 (pbk) : £35.00 : CIP entry B82-28459

332.1'534 — European Investment Bank

Lewenhak, Sheila. The role of the European Investment Bank / Sheila Lewenhak. — London : Croom Helm, c1982. — 288p : ill,maps ; 23cm
Includes index
ISBN 0-7099-1613-2 : £13.95 : CIP rev. B82-03115

332.1'54'0941 — Great Britain. Foreign trade. Role of banks

Banks and overseas trade. — Rev. — London (10 Lombard St., EC3V 9AT) : BES, 1980. — 16p : 1form,1map ; 21cm. — (Study booklet series ; 8)
Cover title. — Text on inside cover
Unpriced (pbk) B82-16271

332.1'6 — United States. Commercial banks. Mergers. Effects of regulation. Mathematical models

Oldfield, George S.. Implications of regulation on bank expansion : a simulation analysis / by George S. Oldfield, Jr. — Greenwich, Conn. : Jai ; London : distributed by Jaicon, c1979. — ix,133p : ill ; 24cm. — (Contemporary studies in economic and financial analysis ; v.10)
Bibliography: p127-129. — Includes index
ISBN 0-89232-015-x : £19.50 B82-05920

332.1'753'0941 — Great Britain. Banks. Lending. Control

Competition and credit control. — London (10 Lombard St., EC3V 9AT) : BES, 1979. — 15p,[2]leaves ; 21cm. — (Study booklet series ; 14)
Cover title. — Bibliography: p.15
Unpriced (pbk) B82-16268

332.1'753'0941 — Great Britain. Lending by banks

Borrowing from a bank. — Rev. — London (10 Lombard St., EC3V 9AT) : BES, 1980. — 16p ; 21cm. — (Study booklet series ; 5)
Cover title. — Text on inside cover
Unpriced (pbk) B82-16257

332.1'754 — United States. Capital investment by commercial banks. Risks. Management

Risk and capital adequacy in commercial banks / edited by Sherman J. Maisel. — Chicago ; London : University of Chicago Press, 1981. — x,436p ; 24cm. — (A National Bureau of Economic Research monograph)
Bibliography: p409-423. — Includes index
ISBN 0-226-50281-3 : £29.40 B82-13916

332.1'754 — United States. Investments: Securities. Investment by commercial banks. Regulation

Securities activities of commercial banks / edited by Arnold W. Sametz. — Lexington, Mass. : Lexington Books ; [Aldershot] : Gower [distributor], 1981. — ix,191p ; 24cm
Includes index
ISBN 0-669-04031-2 : £14.50 B82-00399

332.1'754'0941 — Great Britain. Industries. Investment by banks

Vittas, Dimitri. Bank lending and industrial investment : a response to recent criticisms / Dimitri Vittas, Roger Brown. — London (10 Lombard St., EC3V 9AR) : Banking Information Service, 1982. — 82p ; 30cm
Unpriced (spiral) B82-21895

332.1'78 — Direct debits

An **Introduction** to direct debiting. — London (10 Lombard St., EC3V 9AT) : Banking Information Service, 1982. — 11p ; 21cm
Unpriced (pbk) B82-16273

332.1'78 — Great Britain. Banks. Giro services. Automation

Automation of the Bank Giro Credit system. — London (10 Lombard St., EC3V 9AR) : Banking Informatoin Service, [1981]. — 7p : ill,forms ; 30cm
Cover title
Unpriced (pbk) B82-16283

332.2 — SPECIALISED BANKING INSTITUTIONS

332.2'1'09 — Savings banks, *to 1980*

Fairlamb, David. Savings and co-operative banking / [by David Fairlamb and Jenny Ireland]. — London : Financial Times Business, c1981. — 255p ; 21cm. — (A Banker Research Unit survey)
ISBN 0-902998-45-5 : Unpriced
Also classified at 334'.2'09 B82-12089

332.3 — CREDIT AND LOAN INSTITUTIONS

332.3'2 — Great Britain. Building societies. Savings schemes

Save as you earn : a building society scheme for regular savers : scheme 3 (second issue). — [London] ([34 Park St., W1Y 3PF]) : Building Societies Association, 1980. — 1folded sheet([4] p) ; 23cm
Unpriced B82-36388

332.3'2'094 — European Community countries. Building societies — *Serials*

BSA European bulletin : an occasional bulletin from the Building Societies Association. — No.1 (1981)-. — London (34 Park St., W1Y 3PF) : The Association, 1981-. — v. : ports ; 30cm
Description based on: No.2 (July 1981)
ISSN 0261-6386 = BSA European bulletin : Unpriced B82-11136

332.3'2'0941 — Great Britain. Building societies

Boleat, Mark. The building society industry. — London : Allen & Unwin, Sept.1982. — [224]p
ISBN 0-04-332086-4 (cased) : £16.00 : CIP entry
ISBN 0-04-332087-2 (pbk) : £6.95 B82-19080

Facts about building societies. — London (34 Park St., W1Y 3PF) : Building Societies Association, 1981. — 1folded sheet([6]p) : ill ; 20cm
Unpriced B82-36387

Gough, T. J.. The economics of building societies / T.J. Gough. — London : Macmillan, 1982. — viii,173p : ill ; 23cm
Includes index
ISBN 0-333-30029-7 : £20.00 B82-20916

332.3'2'0941 — Great Britain. Building societies, *1974-1979*

Studies in building society activity 1974-79. — London (34 Park St., W1Y 3PF) : Building Societies Association, 1980. — iii,204p : ill,1map ; 31cm
Bibliography: p162-163
Unpriced (spiral) B82-26660

332.3'2'0941 — Great Britain. Building societies. Branches — *Statistics* — *Serials*

Hillier Parker survey of building society branches / Hillier Parker Reseach. — No.1-no.4. — London (77 Grosvenor St., W1A 2BT) : Hillier Parker May & Rowden, 1976-1979. — 4v. : ill ; 30cm
Annual. — Continued by: Survey of building society branches. — Description based on: No.4
ISSN 0261-0027 = Hillier Parker survey of building society branches : £5.00 B82-22692

Survey of building society branches. — No.5 (Oct. 1980)-. — London (77 Grosvenor St., W1A 2BT) : Research Department, Hillier Parker May & Rowden, 1980-. — v. : ill ; 30cm
Annual. — Continues: Hillier Parker survey of building society branches. — Description based on: No.6 (Sept. 1981)
ISSN 0263-2071 = Survey of building society branches : £5.00 B82-18497

332.3'2'0941 — Great Britain. Building societies — *Serials*

Building societies in ... — 1979-. — London (34 Park St., W1Y 3PF) : Building Societies Association, 1980-. — v. ; 21cm
Annual. — Description based on: 1980 issue
ISSN 0261-6408 = Building societies : Unpriced B82-11149

332.3′2′0941 — Great Britain. Building societies — *Serials* *continuation*

Building society news : a monthly newsletter from the Building Societies Association. — Vol.1, no.1 (Apr. 1981)-. — London (34 Park St, W1Y 3PF) : The Association, 1981-. — v. : ports ; 30cm
Continues: Building society affairs. — Description based on: Vol.2, no.6 (June 1982)
ISSN 0261-5304 = Building society news : Unpriced B82-40035

332.3′2′0941 — Great Britain. Building societies — *Statistics*

A **Compendium** of building society statistics / [Building Societies Association]. — 4th ed. — London : Building Societies Association, [1982]. — ii,123p ; 30cm
Previous ed.: 1980. — Includes index
ISBN 0-903277-28-x (spiral) : Unpriced B82-41017

332.3′2′0941 — Great Britain. Building societies — *Statistics — Serials*

BSA bulletin. — 1979-. — London (34 Park St., W1Y 3PF) : The Building Societies Association, 1979-. — v. ; 30cm
Quarterly. — Continues: Facts and figures (Building Societies Association). — Description based on: No.27 (July 1981)
ISSN 0261-6394 = BSA bulletin : Unpriced B82-11135

332.3′2′0941 — Great Britain. Building societies, *to 1980*

Davies, Glyn, *1919-*. Building societies and their branches : a regional economic survey / by Glyn Davies with Martin J. Davies. — London (Burgon St., EC4V 5DP) : Franey, 1981. — xiv,429p : ill,maps,1form ; 22cm
Includes index
Unpriced B82-09263

332.3′2′0941 — Great Britain. Personal finance. Savings. Use of building society accounts — *Statistics*

Savings facts. — London (34 Park St., W1Y 3PF) : Building Societies Association, 1981. — 1folded sheet(([6]p)) : ill ; 20cm
Unpriced B82-35502

332.4 — MONEY

332.4 — Monetarism

Desai, Meghnad. Testing monetarism. — London : Frances Pinter, Dec.1981. — [288]p
ISBN 0-903804-77-8 : £15.00 : CIP entry B81-40256

Kaldor, Nicholas. The scourge of monetarism / Nicholas Kaldor. — Oxford : Oxford University Press, 1982. — xiv,114p : ill ; 22cm
Includes index
ISBN 0-19-877187-8 (pbk) : £2.95 : CIP rev. B82-09217

Laidler, David E. W.. Monetarist perspectives. — Oxford : Philip Allan, Mar.1982. — [240]p
ISBN 0-86003-042-3 : £12.50 : CIP entry B82-05751

332.4 — Monetary system

Gale, Douglas. Money : in equilibrium / Douglas Gale. — Welwyn : Nisbet, 1982. — ix,349p ; 23cm. — (The Cambridge economic handbooks)
Bibliography: p341-346. — Includes index
ISBN 0-7202-0317-1 (cased) : £19.50
ISBN 0-7207-0316-3 (pbk) : £8.95 B82-14295

332.4 — Monetary systems

Auernheimer, Leonardo. The essentials of money and banking / Leonardo Auernheimer, Robert B. Ekelund, Jr. — New York ; Chichester : Wiley, c1982. — xiv,445p : ill,maps ; 24cm
Includes index
ISBN 0-471-02103-2 : £17.70 B82-13622

332.4 — Money

Davis, William, *1933-*. Money in the 1980s : how to make it, how to keep it : William Davis. — London : Weidenfeld and Nicolson, 1981. — 183p ; 23cm
Includes index
ISBN 0-297-77923-0 : £6.95 B82-01630

Your money and mine. — Rev. — [London] ([10 Lombard St., EC3V 9AT]) : BES, 1978. — 16p : ill(some col.) ; 21cm. — (Study booklet series ; 9)
Cover title. — Text, ill on inside covers
Unpriced (pbk) B82-16258

332.4′01 — Monetary system. Theories — *Readings*

Dow, Sheila C.. Money matters : a Keynesian approach to monetary economics. — Oxford : Martin Robertson, May 1982. — [290]p
ISBN 0-85520-484-2 (cased) : £15.00 : CIP entry
ISBN 0-85520-485-0 (pbk) : £5.95 B82-07034

332.4′04 — Bank of England dollars & tokens, *1797-1816*

Kelly, E. M.. Spanish dollars and silver tokens : an account of the issues of the Bank of England 1797-1816 / by E.M. Kelly. — London : Spink, 1976. — 151p,8p of plates : ill,1facsim ; 26cm
Bibliography: p149-151. — Includes index
Unpriced B82-17156

332.4′042 — Shillings, *to 1981.* **Social aspects**

Mays, James O'Donald. The splendid shilling : a social history of an engaging coin / James O'Donald Mays. — Ringwood : New Forest Leaves, c1982. — 186p,[1]leaf of plates : ill (some col.),1map,ports ; 25cm
Bibliography: p170. — Includes index
ISBN 0-907956-00-9 : £7.95 : CIP rev. B82-09213

332.4′042′0287 — London *(City).* **Gold & silver industries & trades. Guilds: Worshipful Company of Goldsmiths. Exhibits: Items associated with Trial of the Pyx,** *to 1982 — Catalogues*

Challis, C. E.. Seven centuries of the Trial of the Pyx / [catalogue compiled by C.E. Challis, G.P. Dyer]. — [London] ([Goldsmiths' Hall, Foster La., EC2V 6BN]) : [Worshipful Company of Goldsmiths], [1982]. — 13p ; 30cm
Catalogue of an exhibition held at Goldsmiths' Hall, 1982
£0.75 (pbk) B82-22271

332.4′042′0941 — Great Britain. Coinage, *1868-1914*

Capie, Forrest. Total coin and coin in circulation in the U.K., 1868-1914 / Forrest Capie and Alan Webber. — London (Northampton Sq., EC1 0HB) : Centre for Banking & International Finance, City University, 1981. — 33leaves : 1ill ; 31cm. — (Monetary history discussion paper series ; no.2)
Report from the SRC research project Monetary History of the U.K. 1870-1970
Unpriced (spiral) B82-25362

332.4′0724 — Monetary system. Econometric models

Beenstock, Michael. An aggregate monetary model of the world economy / by M. Beenstock and G.R. Dicks. — [London] : [City University Business School], c1981. — 28,[11] leaves : ill ; 30cm. — (Working paper series / the City University Business School, ISSN 0140-1041 ; no.29)
Unpriced (pbk) B82-11549

332.4′092′4 — Monetary system. Theories of Keynes, John Maynard

Gilbert, J. C.. Keynes's impact on monetary economics / J. C. Gilbert. — London : Butterworth Scientific, c1982. — viii,280p ; 24cm
Bibliography: p255. — Includes index
ISBN 0-408-10718-9 : £17.50 : CIP rev. B82-01715

332.4′1 — Economic development. Effects of inflation — *Conference proceedings*

Development in an inflationary world : proceedings of the 1979 Pinhas Sapir Conference, the Pinhas Sapir Center for Development, Tel Aviv University 17-19 June 1979 / edited by M. June Flanders, Assaf Razin. — New York ; London : Academic Press, 1981. — xxii,492p : ill,1port ; 24cm. — (Economic theory, econometrics, and mathematical economics)
Includes bibliographies and index
ISBN 0-12-259750-8 : £36.40 B82-02206

332.4′1 — Finance. Inflation

Hahn, F. H.. Money and inflation / Frank Hahn. — Oxford : Blackwell, 1982. — xii,116p : ill ; 23cm. — (Mitsui lectures in inflation)
Bibliography: p111-114. — Includes index
ISBN 0-631-12917-0 : Unpriced : CIP rev. B81-30173

Hudson, John. Inflation. — London : Allen and Unwin, Feb.1982. — [176]p
ISBN 0-04-339025-0 : £13.95 : CIP entry B81-35926

McCulloch, J. Huston. Money and inflation : a monetarist approach / J. Huston McCulloch. — 2nd ed. — New York ; London : Academic Press, c1982. — xii,115p : ill ; 23cm
Previous ed.: c1975. — Includes index
ISBN 0-12-483051-x (pbk) : £3.20 B82-25710

Slawson, W. David. The new inflation : the collapse of free markets / W. David Slawson. — Princeton ; Guildford : Princeton University Press, c1981. — xi,424p ; 23cm
Includes index
ISBN 0-691-04229-2 : £11.70 B82-14539

332.4′1 — Finance. Inflation. Expectation. Econometric models

Lahiri, Kajal. The econometrics of inflationary expectations / Kajal Lahiri. — Amsterdam ; Oxford : North-Holland, 1981. — xxii,250p ; 25cm. — (Studies in monetary economics ; v.7)
Bibliography: p229-244. — Includes index
ISBN 0-444-86208-0 : Unpriced B82-06107

332.4′1 — Finance. Inflation *related to* **unemployment**

Meade, J. E.. Wage-fixing / James E. Meade. — London : Allen & Unwin, 1982. — 233p : ill ; 22cm. — (Stagflation ; v.1)
Includes index
ISBN 0-04-339023-4 (cased) : Unpriced : CIP rev.
ISBN 0-04-339024-2 (pbk) : Unpriced
Primary classification 331.13′7 B81-33917

332.4′1′01 — Finance. Inflation. Theories

Jackman, Richard. The economics of inflation. — 2nd ed. / Richard Jackman, Charles Mulvey and James Trevithick. — Oxford : Robertson, 1981. — viii,211p : ill ; 24cm
Previous ed.: / by James Anthony Trevithick & Charles Mulvey. 1975. — Bibliography: p194-203. — Includes index
ISBN 0-85520-410-9 (cased) : Unpriced : CIP rev.
ISBN 0-85520-411-7 (pbk) : £5.95 B81-23821

332.4′1′0941 — Great Britain. Finance. Inflation — *Selsdon Group viewpoints*

Bourlet, James. Step by step against inflation / by James Bourlet & Michael Roots ; foreword by John Biffen. — [London] ([170 Sloane St., SW1X 9QG]) : Selsdon Group, [1974]. — iv,12p : 1ill ; 22cm. — (Selsdon policy series ; no.1)
Cover title. — Ill on inside cover
£0.40 (pbk) B82-07142

332.4′1′0941 — Great Britain. Finance. Inflation — *Social Democratic Party viewpoints*

Layard, Richard. More jobs, less inflation. — London : Grant McIntyre, Aug.1982. — [100]p
ISBN 0-86216-090-1 (cased) : £9.95 : CIP entry
ISBN 0-86216-092-8 (pbk) : £2.95 B82-20657

332.4′1′0973 — United States. Finance. Core inflation

Eckstein, Otto. Core inflation / Otto Eckstein. — Englewood Cliffs ; London : Prentice-Hall, c1981. — v,121p : ill ; 24cm
Bibliography: p114-116. — Includes index
ISBN 0-13-172643-9 (cased) : Unpriced
ISBN 0-13-172635-8 (pbk) : £5.95 B82-00091

332.4′1′0973 — United States. Finance. Inflation. Control. Policies of government, *1933-1980*

Dougherty, Thomas J.. Controlling the new inflation / Thomas J. Dougherty. — Lexington, Mass. : Lexington Books ; [Aldershot] : Gower [distributor], 1982, c1981. — xvii,171p : ill ; 24cm
Includes index
ISBN 0-669-04512-8 : £12.50 B82-08993

332.4'1'0973 — United States. Finance. Inflation. Control. Role of incomes policy

Weintraub, Sidney, *1914-*. Our stagflation malaise : ending inflation and unemployment / Sidney Weintraub. — Westport, Conn. ; London : Quorum, 1981. — xv,214p : ill ; 25cm
Includes index
ISBN 0-89930-005-7 : £16.95 B82-18364

332.4'5 — Europe. Euro-dollar market

Hogan, W. P.. The incredible Eurodollar / W.P. Hogan and I.F. Pearce. — London : Allen & Unwin, 1982. — viii,144p : 1ill ; 23cm
Includes bibliographies and index
ISBN 0-04-332081-3 : Unpriced : CIP rev. B82-00893

Kane, Daniel R.. The Euro-dollar market and the years of crisis. — London : Croom Helm, Nov.1982. — [208]p
ISBN 0-7099-1522-5 : £12.95 : CIP entry B82-26707

332.4'5 — Foreign exchange

Brown, Brendan. The forward market in foreign exchange. — London : Croom Helm, Jan.1983. — [192]p
ISBN 0-7099-0667-6 : £12.95 : CIP entry B82-32547

The **Foreign** exchange and Eurocurrency markets. — Rev. — London (10 Lombard St., EC3V 9AT) : Bank Education Service, 1980. — 22p : ill,facsims ; 21cm. — (Study booklet series ; 13)
Unpriced (pbk)
Also classified at 332 B82-16269

Whiting, D. P.. Finance of international trade / D. P. Whiting. — 4th ed. — Plymouth : Macdonald and Evans, 1981. — ix,278p : ill,facsims,forms ; 22cm
Previous ed.: published as Finance of foreign trade and foreign exchange. 1976. — Includes index
ISBN 0-7121-0637-5 (pbk) : £4.95
Also classified at 382 B82-01913

332.4'5 — Foreign exchange. Risks. Management

Lassen, Richard. Currency management / Richard Lassen. — Cambridge : Woodhead-Faulkner, 1982. — viii,158p : ill ; 23cm
Bibliography: p153. — Includes index
ISBN 0-85941-154-0 : £10.75 B82-25307

332.4'5 — International monetary system

Dam, Kenneth W.. The rules of the game : reform and evolution in the international monetary system / Kenneth W. Dam. — Chicago ; London : University of Chicago Press, 1982. — xviii,382p ; 24cm
Bibliography: p345-361. — Includes index
ISBN 0-226-13499-7 : Unpriced B82-35066

Davidson, Paul, *1930-*. International money and the real world / Paul Davidson. — London : Macmillan, 1982. — xi,312p ; 23cm
Includes index
ISBN 0-333-28993-5 (cased) : Unpriced
ISBN 0-333-32621-0 (pbk) : Unpriced B82-25550

332.4'5 — International monetary system, *1944-1980*

Brett, E. A.. International money and capitalist crisis. — London : Heinemann Educational, May 1982. — [272]p
ISBN 0-435-84081-9 (cased) : £13.50 : CIP entry
ISBN 0-435-84083-5 (pbk) : £6.50 B82-06820

332.4'5 — International monetary system, *1945-1980*

Recent developments in the international monetary system. — Rev. — London (10 Lombard St., EC3V 9AT) : BES, 1979. — 33p : ill ; 21cm. — (Study booklet series ; 15)
Unpriced (unbound) B82-16263

332.4'5 — International monetary system, *1945-1981*

Solomon, Robert. The international monetary system, 1945-1981 / Robert Solomon. — Updated and expanded ed. — New York ; London : Harper & Row, c1982. — xvi,432p ; 24cm
Previous ed.: published as The international monetary system, 1945-1976. 1977. — Includes index
ISBN 0-06-015004-1 : Unpriced B82-38732

Tew, Brian. The evolution of the international monetary system, 1945-81 / Brian Tew. — 2nd ed. — London : Hutchinson, 1982. — 250p : ill ; 22cm. — (Hutchinson university library)
Previous ed.: published as The evolution of the international monetary system, 1945-77. 1977. — Bibliography: p245-246. — Includes index
ISBN 0-09-145911-7 (pbk) : £5.95 : CIP rev. B81-34474

332.4'5 — International monetary system, *1970-1980*

Parboni, Riccardo. The dollar and its rivals : recession, inflation and international finance / Riccardo Parboni ; translated by Jon Rothschild. — London : NLB, 1981. — 207p ; 23cm
Translation of: Finanza e crisi internazionale
ISBN 0-86091-046-6 (cased) : £10.00 : CIP rev.
ISBN 0-86019-744-4 (pbk) : Unpriced B81-30148

332.4'5 — International monetary system. Composite reserves

Dreyer, Jacob S.. Composite reserve assets in the international monetary system / by Jacob S. Dreyer. — Greenwich, Conn. : Jai ; London : distributed by Jaicon, c1977. — xvi,191p : ill ; 24cm. — (Contemporary studies in economic and financial analysis ; v.2)
Bibliography: p183-186. — Includes index
ISBN 0-89232-003-6 : £21.10 B82-05926

332.4'5'02465 — Foreign exchange — *For companies*

Heywood, John, *1940-*. Foreign exchange and the corporate treasurer / John Heywood. — 3rd ed., rev. and extended. — London : Black, 1981. — viii,193p : ill ; 23cm
Previous ed.: 1979. — Bibliography: p189. — Includes index
ISBN 0-7136-2185-0 : £8.95 : CIP rev. B81-30360

332.4'56 — Foreign exchange. Flexible rates: Crawling pegs — *Conference proceedings*

Exchange rate rules : the theory, performance and prospects of the crawling peg / edited by John Williamson ; proceedings of a conference sponsored by the Ford Foundation, the Assosiação Nacional de Centros de Pós Graduação em Economia and the Pontifícia Universidade Católica do Rio de Janeiro, held in Rio de Janeiro. — London : Macmillan, 1981. — xxi,410p : ill ; 24cm
Includes bibliographies and index
ISBN 0-333-28057-1 : £25.00 B82-06701

332.4'56 — International monetary system. Foreign exchange. Rates. Changes. Forecasting

Levich, Richard M.. The international money market : an assessment of forecasting techniques and market efficiency / by Richard M. Levich ; foreword by Robert Z. Aliber. — Greenwich, Conn. : Jai ; London : distributed by Jaicon, c1979. — xvii,193p : ill ; 24cm. — (Contemporary studies in economic and financial analysis ; v.22)
Bibliography: p176-180. — Includes index
ISBN 0-89232-109-1 : £20.00 B82-05928

332.4'56'0212 — Foreign exchange. Rates — *Tables — Serials*

[**Currency** *(London)*]. Currency : the weekly report. — Vol.1, no.1 (19 Mar. 1979)-. — London (37 St. Andrews Hill, EC4V 5DD) : Chart Analysis, 1979-. — v. : charts ; 25x34cm
Description based on: Vol.3, no.32 (19 Oct. 1981)
ISSN 0262-7124 = Currency (London) : £500.00 per year B82-08456

Financial Times monthly currency statistics. — [No.1]-. — London : Financial Times, [1982]-. — v. ; 22x30cm
ISSN 0264-0279 = Financial Times monthly currency statistics : Unpriced B82-40059

332.4'56'05 — Foreign exchange. Rates. Changes — *Forecasts — Serials*

Currency forecasting Asia / Institute for International Research. — Issue 81-1 (Nov. 1981)-. — London (70 Warren St., W1P 5PA) : The Institute, 1981-. — v. : ill ; 28cm
Monthly
ISSN 0261-7900 = Currency forecasting Asia : Unpriced B82-15160

332.4'56'05 — Foreign exchange. Rates — *Forecasts — Serials*

Exchange rate movements ... year book / the Henley Centre of Forecasting. — 1981-. — London (2 Tudor St., Blackfriars EC4Y 0AA) : The Centre, 1981-. — v. ; 30cm
ISSN 0262-7663 = Exchange rate movements ... year book : Unpriced B82-07637

332.4'564'0941 — Great Britain. Foreign exchange. Rates. Control. Role of government

Exchange rate policy for the U.K. / CBI. — London (Centre Point, 103 New Oxford St, WC1A 1DU) : Confederation of British Industry, 1982. — 56p : ill ; 30cm
£2.50 (pbk) B82-28783

332.4'566'09174927 — Arab countries. Monetary systems. Integration — *Conference proceedings*

Arab monetary integration : issues and prerequisites / [proceedings of a seminar held in Abu Dhabi, on 24-27 November 1980, organised by the Centre for Arab Unity Studies and the Arab Monetary Fund] ; edited by Khair el-Din Haseeb and Samir Makdisi. — London : Croom Helm, [1981?]. — 475p : ill ; 23cm
Includes index
ISBN 0-7099-0712-5 : £19.95 : CIP rev. B81-31063

332.4'566'094 — European Community. Monetary systems: European Monetary System

European monetary union : progress and prospects / edited by M.T. Sumner and G. Zis. — London : Macmillan, 1982. — xv,266p : ill ; 23cm
Includes bibliographies and index
ISBN 0-333-30470-5 : £20.00 B82-38781

332.4'566094 — European Community. Monetary systems: European Monetary System

Ludlow, Peter. The making of the European monetary system : a case study of the politics of the European Community / Peter Ludlow. — London : Butterworths, 1982. — xii,319p ; 24cm. — (Butterworths European studies)
Includes index
ISBN 0-408-10728-6 : £15.00 : CIP rev. B82-09196

332.4'566'094 — European Community. Monetary systems: European Monetary System *related to* **international monetary system**

Zis, George. E.M.S. : a framework for international monetary reform and the reduction of inflation / by G. Zis. — [Salford] : Department of Economics, University of Salford, [1982]. — 21leaves ; 30cm. — (Salford papers in economics ; 82-1)
Unpriced (spiral) B82-20481

332.4'6 — Monetary policies

Currie, David A.. Monetarist policies and neo-Keynesian alternatives / D. Curris. — London : Thames Polytechnic, 1981. — 14p ; 22cm. — (Thames papers in political economy)
Text on inside cover. — Bibliography: on inside cover
ISBN 0-902169-16-5 (pbk) : Unpriced B82-06352

Meier, Gerald M.. Problems of a world monetary order / Gerald M. Meier. — 2nd ed. — New York ; Oxford : Oxford University Press, 1982. — xiv,343p : ill ; 23cm
Previous ed.: 1974. — Includes bibliographies
ISBN 0-19-503010-9 (pbk) : £5.95 B82-34509

332.4'6'942496 — West Midlands *(Metropolitan County).* **Birmingham. Mints: Birmingham Mint,** *1850-1980*

Sweeny, James O.. A numismatic history of the Birmingham Mint. — Birmingham (Icknield St., Birmingham B18 6RX) : Birmingham Mint, Oct.1981. — [256]p
ISBN 0-9507594-0-6 : £10.95 : CIP entry B81-25744

332.4'91821 — Western world. Monetary policies

King, Kenneth, *1944-*. US monetary policy and European responses in the 1980s / Kenneth King. — London : Royal Institute of International Affairs : Routledge & Kegan Paul, 1982. — 54p ; 22cm. — (Chatham House papers, ISSN 0143-5795 ; 16)
ISBN 0-7100-9337-3 (pbk) : £3.95 B82-38763

332.4'941 — Great Britain. Government. Policies. Role of monetarism

Ford, J. L.. Monetary aggregates and economic policy / J.L. Ford. — [Birmingham] : University of Birmingham, 1982. — 13p ; 21cm
'An inaugural lecture as delivered in the University of Birmingham on 1 December 1981' — inside cover. — Cover title
ISBN 0-7044-0591-1 (pbk) : Unpriced B82-16733

332.4'941 — Great Britain. Monetary policies

The **Framework** of the United Kingdom monetary policy. — London : Heinemann Educational, June 1982. — [384]p
ISBN 0-435-84466-0 (pbk) : £14.50 : CIP entry
ISBN 0-435-84464-4 (pbk) : £5.95 B82-09726

332.4'941 — Great Britain. Monetary policies — *Inquiry reports*

Great Britain. *Parliament. House of Commons. Treasury and Civil Service Committee.* Memoranda on monetary policy : Treasury and Civil Service Committee, session 1979-80. — London : H.M.S.O., [1980]
Vol.2. — v,77p : ill ; 25cm. — ([HC] ; 720-II)
ISBN 0-10-029969-5 (pbk) : £4.20 B82-15134

332.4'941 — Great Britain. Money supply. Control

Congdon, Tim. Monetary control in Britain / Tim Congdon. — London : Macmillan, 1982. — xi,139p ; 23cm
Includes index
ISBN 0-333-26831-8 : Unpriced B82-28528

Harrington, Richard, *1942-*. The money supply : the case for its control : presented 7th November 1978 / by Richard Harrington. — Stockport : Manchester Statistical Society, [1979?]. — 12p ; 20cm
At head of title: Manchester Statistical Society. — Text on inside cover
£1.80 (pbk) B82-00395

332.4'941 — Great Britain. Money supply. Control, *1970-1981*

Gowland, David. Controlling the money supply / David Gowland. — London : Croom Helm, c1982. — 215p : ill ; 22cm
Bibliography: p198-206. — Includes index
ISBN 0-7099-1105-x (cased) : £12.95 : CIP rev.
ISBN 0-7099-1116-5 (pbk) : Unpriced B81-37556

332.4'941 — Great Britain. Money supply. Control, *1971-1981*

Brown, Roger, *1948-*. Monetary control in Britain 1971-1981 / [prepared by Roger Brown]. — London (10 Lombard St., EC3V 9AT) : Banking Information Service, 1981. — 20p ; 21cm
Cover title. — Text on inside cover
Unpriced (pbk) B82-16278

332.4'942 — English banknotes & coinage. Circulation

The **Movement** of notes and coins. — [Rev.]. — London (10 Lombard St., EC3V 9AT) : BES, [1976]. — 8p : ill(some col.) ; 21cm. — (Study booklet series ; 3)
Cover title. — Text, ill on inside covers
Unpriced (pbk) B82-16259

332.4'9463 — Castile *(Kingdom).* **Monetary system,** *1390-1480.* **Political aspects**

Mackay, Angus. Money, prices and politics in fifteenth-century Castile / Angus Mackay. — London : Royal Historical Society, 1981. — xi,184p : ill,3maps ; 23cm. — (Royal Historical Society studies in history series ; no.28)
Bibliography: p173-176. — Includes index
ISBN 0-901050-82-2 : £8.85 (to members of the Society) B82-24503

332.4'973 — United States. Monetary policies

Siegel, Barry N.. Money, banking and the economy : a monetarist view / Barry N. Siegel. — New York ; London : Academic Press, c1982. — xv,541p : ill ; 25cm
Includes bibliographies and index
ISBN 0-12-641420-3 : £13.20 B82-29695

Wallich, Henry C.. Monetary policy and practice : a view from the Federal Reserve Board / Henry C. Wallich. — [Lexington, Mass.] : Lexington Books ; [Aldershot] : Gower [distributor], 1982. — xx,395p ; 24cm
Includes index
ISBN 0-669-04712-0 : £17.50 B82-27880

332.4'973 — United States. Monetary system

Siegel, Barry N.. Instructor's manual for Money, banking, and the economy : a monetarist view / by Barry N. Siegel. — New York ; London : Academic Press, c1982. — iv,67p ; 24cm
ISBN 0-12-641421-1 (pbk) : £2.40 B82-29987

332.6 — INVESTMENT

332.6 — Investment

Bourne, N.. Investment / [N. Bourne]. — 5th ed. — [London] : Pitman in co-operation with Michael Benn & Associates, 1981. — 128p ; 10x16cm. — (Pitman revision cards)
Previous ed.: 1979. — Includes index
ISBN 0-904096-88-2 (spiral) : Unpriced B82-01668

Chilver, Joseph. Investment : a student-centred approach / Joseph Chilver. — London : Macmillan, 1982. — x,216p : ill,forms ; 25cm
Includes index
ISBN 0-333-29415-7 (cased) : £15.00
ISBN 0-333-29416-5 (pbk) : Unpriced B82-38792

332.6 — Investment — *For expatriate British personnel*

The **Expatriate's** guide to savings and investment / [edited by Jessica Stone] ; [editorial assistant Alison Lucas]. — London : Financial Times Business, c1980. — lxxii,168p ; 30cm
ISBN 0-901369-52-7 (pbk) : Unpriced B82-28409

332.6 — Investments

Reilly, Frank K.. Investments / Frank K. Reilly. — Chicago ; London : Dryden, c1982. — 693p : col.ill,facsims,ports ; 25cm
Includes bibliographies and index
ISBN 0-03-056712-2 : £16.95 B82-16908

332.6'028'54 — Investment. Analysis. Applications of digital computer systems

Riley, William B.. Guide to computer-assisted investment analysis / William B. Riley, Jr., Austin H. Montgomery, Jr. — New York ; London : McGraw-Hill, c1982. — xiv,303p : ill,facsims ; 25cm. — (McGraw-Hill finance guide series)
Includes bibliographies and index
ISBN 0-07-052916-7 (cased) : £12.95
ISBN 0-07-052917-5 (pbk) : Unpriced B82-27151

332.6'05 — Investment — *For expatriate British personnel — Serials*

The **expatriate's** guide to savings and investment. — [No.1]-. — London : Financial Times Business Pub., 1980-. — v. ; 30cm
Annual. — Description based on: 1981/82 issue
ISSN 0263-1229 = Expatriate's guide to savings and investment : Unpriced B82-18488

332.6'0941 — Great Britain. Investment

Winfield, R. G.. Success in investment / R.G. Winfield and S.J. Curry ; consultant editor Peter Roots. — 2nd ed. — London : Murray, 1981. — xvi,365p : ill,forms ; 22cm. — (Success studybooks)
Previous ed.: / by Peter Roots. 1974. — Bibliography: p351-352. — Includes index
ISBN 0-7195-3839-4 (pbk) : £3.95 : CIP rev. B81-28113

332.6'0973 — United States. Investment

Christy, George A.. Introduction to investments / George A. Christy, John C. Clendenin. — 8th ed. — New York ; London : McGraw-Hill, c1982. — viii,805p : ill ; 24cm. — (McGraw-Hill series in finance)
Previous ed.: 1978. — Includes bibliographies and index
ISBN 0-07-010833-1 : £17.50 B82-16339

332.6'0973 — United States. Investment. Portfolios. Management

Ahlers, David M.. A new look at portfolio management / by David M. Ahlers ; foreword by Kalman J. Cohen. — Greenwich, Conn. : Jai ; London : distributed by Jaicon, c1977. — xvi,201p : ill ; 24cm. — (Contemporary studies in economic and financial analysis ; v.5)
Bibliography: p182-186. — Includes index
ISBN 0-89232-012-5 : £21.10 B82-05923

332.63 — Capital investment. Effects of financial incentives

Sumner, Michael T.. Criteria for efficient capital allocation / M.T. Sumner. — [Salford] : Department of Economics, University of Salford, [1982]. — 14,4leaves ; 30cm. — (Salford papers in economics ; 82-2)
Bibliography: leaf14
Unpriced (spiral) B82-20480

332.6'3 — Gold. Investment

Craig, Malcolm. Making money from gold. — Kingsclere (3 Sandford House, Kingsclere, Newbury, Berkshire RG15 8PA) : Scope, June 1982. — [100]p
ISBN 0-906619-12-2 : £7.50 : CIP entry B82-10895

332.63 — Great Britain. Venture capital investment

Venture capital. — [London?] : Pointon York ; [Leicester] : [Current Account] [[distributor]], c1979. — 18p ; 18x26cm. — (Current account mini reports)
Bibliography: p16-17
ISBN 0-906840-11-2 (spiral) : Unpriced B82-06680

332.63 — Investments: Maps

Antique maps. — [London?] : Pointon York ; [Leicester] : [Current Account] [[distributor]], c1979. — 12p ; 18x26cm. — (Current account mini reports)
Bibliography: p11-12
ISBN 0-906840-09-0 (spiral) : Unpriced B82-06686

332.63 — Precious metalware & jewellery. Valuation — *Manuals*

Morton, Henry A.. Your gold and silver : an easy guide to appraising hosehold objects, coins, heirlooms and jewelry / Henry A. Morton. — New York : Macmillan ; London : Collier Macmillan, c1981. — xv,127p : ill,facsims ; 21cm
Includes index
ISBN 0-02-077410-9 (pbk) : £3.95 B82-00980

332.6'3 — Strategic metals. Investment

Robbins, Peter. Investing in strategic metals. — London : Kogan Page, Dec.1981. — [224]p
ISBN 0-85038-522-9 (cased) : £15.00 : CIP entry
ISBN 0-85038-522-9 (pbk) : £5.95 B81-30887

332.63'22 — Egypt. Canals. Companies: Suez Canal Company. Shares. Purchase by British government, *1875*

Rothschild, Nathaniel Mayer Victor Rothschild, *Baron*. 'You have it, Madam' : the purchase, in 1875, of Suez Canal shares by Disraeli and Baron Lionel de Rothschild / by Lord Rothschild. — London ([P.O. Box 185, New Court, St. Swithin's La., EC4P 4DU]) : [N.M Rothschild], 1980. — 62p,[1]leaf of plates : 1geneal,table,1port ; 28cm
Includes index
Unpriced (pbk) B82-35256

332.63'22 — Great Britain. Companies. Shares. Marketing

Fanning, David. Marketing company shares / David Fanning. — Aldershot : Gower, c1982. — xiii,270p : forms ; 23cm
Bibliography: p261-262. — Includes index
ISBN 0-566-02174-9 : Unpriced : CIP rev. B81-31654

332.63'22 — United States. Companies. Shares. Investment. Risks. Effects of growth of companies. Mathematical models

Fewings, David R.. Corporate growth and common stock risk / by David R. Fewings ; foreword by Myron Gordon. — Greenwich, Conn. : Jai Press ; London : distributed by Jaicon Press, c1979. — xvi,146p ; 24cm. — (Contemporary studies in economic and financial analysis ; v.12)
Includes index
ISBN 0-89232-053-2 : £20.00 B82-02015

332.63'221 — Australia & United States. Stocks & shares. Dividends. Reinvestment

Skully, Michael T.. Divided reinvestment plan : improving shareholder relations while raising new equity / by Michael T. Skully. — Caterham : Australiana, 1981. — 41 leaves : ill,1form ; 30cm
ISBN 0-909162-17-4 (spiral) : Unpriced B82-22540

332.63'221 — Stocks & shares. Dividends & prices. Analysis. Applications of econometrics

Fogler, H. Russell. Financial econometrics : for researchers in finance and accounting / H. Russell Fogler, Sundaram Ganapathy. — Englewood Cliffs ; London : Prentice-Hall, c1982. — xii,212p : ill ; 24cm
Bibliography: p192-197. — Includes index
ISBN 0-13-315887-x : £12.70 B82-20072

332.63'23 — Investments: International bonds

Fisher, Frederick G.. International bonds / by Frederick G. Fisher, III. — London : Euromoney Publications, c1981. — 199p : ill ; 30cm
Bibliography: p195. — Includes index
ISBN 0-903121-22-0 (pbk) : Unpriced B82-15010

332.63'233'0973 — United States. Municipal bond markets

Bierwag, Gerald O.. The primary market for municipal debt : bidding rules and the cost of long-term borrowing / by Gerald O. Bierwag ; foreword by George G. Kaufman. — Greenwich, Conn. : Jai Press ; London : Distributed by Jaicon Press, c1981. — xxiv,241p : ill ; 24cm. — (Contemporary studies in economic and financial analysis ; v.29)
Bibliography: p235-237. — Includes index
ISBN 0-89232-167-9 : Unpriced B82-33523

Efficiency in the municipal bond market : the use of tax exempt financing for 'private' purposes / edited by George G. Kaufman. — Greenwich, Conn. ; London : Jai Press, c1981. — xvi,277p : ill ; 24cm. — (Contemporary studies in economic and financial analysis ; v.30)
Conference papers. — Includes bibliographies and index
ISBN 0-89232-168-7 : Unpriced B82-33524

332.63'24'0724 — United States. Real property. Investment. Mathematical models — *For estate agency*

Dilmore, Gene. Quantitative techniques in real-estate counseling / Gene Dilmore. — Lexington, Mass. : Lexington Books, c1981 ; [Aldershot] : Gower [distributor], 1982. — xii,256p : ill ; 24cm. — (Lexington Books special series in real estate and urban land economics)
Includes bibliographies and index
ISBN 0-669-98251-2 : £19.50 B82-21170

332.63'24'0941 — Great Britain. Investments: Real property. Valuation

Enever, Nigel. The valuation of property investments / by Nigel Enever. — 2nd ed. — London : Estates Gazette, 1981. — 212p ; 22cm
Previous ed.: 1977. — Includes bibliographies and index
£7.50 (pbk) B82-05575

332.63'24'0946 — Spain. Real property. Investment by Britons

Property in Spain. — [London?] : Pointon York ; [Leicester] : [Current Account] [[distributor]], c1979. — 9p ; 18x26cm. — (Current account mini reports)
Bibliography: p9
ISBN 0-906840-13-9 (spiral) : Unpriced B82-06678

332.63'24'0973 — United States. Investments: Real property. Transfer

McMullen, Charles W.. Selling real estate investments on land contract / Charles W. McMullen. — New York ; Chichester : Wiley, c1982. — xii,102p ; 23cm. — (Real estate for professional practitioners)
Includes index
ISBN 0-471-08527-8 (pbk) : £14.75 B82-28077

Walters, David W.. Real estate exchanges / David W. Walters. — New York ; Chichester : Wiley, c1982. — xv,205p : ill ; 29cm. — (Real estate for professional practitioners)
Includes index
ISBN 0-471-08083-7 : £22.00 B82-15403

332.63'24'099441 — New South Wales. Sydney. Real property. Investment, *ca 1960-1981*

Daly, M. T.. Sydney boom, Sydney bust. — London : Allen & Unwin, Apr.1982. — [224]p
ISBN 0-86861-156-5 : £15.00 : CIP entry B82-06532

332.63'243 — United States. Private residential property. Investment

Vidger, Leonard P.. Borrowing and lending on residential property : fundamentals for homeowners, investors and students / Leonard P. Vidger. — Lexington, Mass. : Lexington Books ; [Aldershot] : Gower [distributor], 1982, c1981. — xvi,285p : ill,forms ; 24cm. — (Lexington Books special series in real estate and urban land economics)
Includes index
ISBN 0-669-01643-8 : Unpriced B82-14757

332.63'27 — Great Britain. Unit trusts. Accounts — *Inquiry reports*

Unit Trust Association. Unit trust accounts / joint working party report by the Unit Trust Association and Companies Division, Department of Trade. — Repr. with amendments. — London : Department of Trade, 1981. — 28p ; 30cm
Originally published: 1981
£1.00 (pbk) B82-40100

332.63'28 — Commodities. Investment. Portfolio analysis — *Tables*

Barnes, Robert M.. Commodity portfolio performance handbook / Robert M. Barnes. — New York ; London : Van Nostrand Reinhold, c1982. — 392p : ill ; 26cm
ISBN 0-442-26290-6 : £51.00 B82-08233

332.63'28 — Futures commodity markets. Commodities. Prices. Analysis. Cyclical indicators

Bernstein, Jacob. The handbook of commodity cycles : a window on time / Jacob Bernstein. — New York ; Chichester : Wiley, c1982. — xiv,383p : ill ; 27cm
Bibliography: p377-380. — Includes index
ISBN 0-471-08197-3 : £31.50 B82-18935

332.64 — Great Britain. Unquoted shares markets

Secondary markets in unquoted shares. — [London?] : Pointon York ; [Leicester] : [Current Account] [[distributor]], c1979. — 10p ; 18x26cm. — (Current account mini reports)
Bibliography: p10
ISBN 0-906840-06-6 (spiral) : Unpriced B82-06684

332.64'2 — Stock markets. Analysis

Keane, Simon. Stock market efficiency. — Deddington : Philip Allan, Jan.1983. — [192]p
ISBN 0-86003-519-0 (cased) : £10.00 : CIP entry
ISBN 0-86003-619-7 (pbk) : £4.95 B82-40911

332.64'24 — European Community countries. Stock markets

Stonham, Paul. Major stock markets of Europe. — Aldershot : Gower, June 1982. — [250]p
ISBN 0-566-00379-1 : £12.50 : CIP entry B82-09729

332.64'241 — Great Britain. Stock markets — *For investment*

Cummings, Gordon. Investors guide to the stock market / Gordon Cummings. — 2nd ed. — London : Financial Times Business Publishing, c1981. — v,174p ; 24cm
Previous ed.: 1979?. — Includes index
ISBN 0-902101-11-0 (pbk) : Unpriced B82-15219

332.64'241 — Great Britain. Stock markets — *For private investment*

Stapley, Neil F.. The stock market : a guide for the private investor / Neil F. Stapley. — London : McAnally, Montgomery & Co, 1981. — x,116p : ill ; 21cm
Includes index
ISBN 0-9507721-0-0 (pbk) : £2.50 B82-03568

332.64'2411 — Scotland. Stock exchanges. Stockbroking, *1700-1914*

Michie, R. C.. Money, mania and markets : investment, company formation and the Stock Exchange in nineteenth-century Scotland / R.C. Michie. — Edinburgh, Donald, c1981. — ix,287p ; 24cm
Bibliography: p270-283. — Includes index
ISBN 0-85976-070-7 : £18.00 B82-01501

332.64'24212 — London *(City)*. **Stock exchanges** — *For children*

Althea. The Stock Exchange / by Althea ; illustrated by Chris Evans. — Cambridge : Published by Dinosaur for the Council of The Stock Exchange in Great Britain and Ireland, c1982. — 32p : col.ill ; 16x19cm
ISBN 0-85122-323-0 (cased) : Unpriced
ISBN 0-85122-322-2 (pbk) : Unpriced B82-32075

332.64'2421'2 — London *(City)*. **Stock exchanges: Stock Exchange** *(London)*. **Indices,** *1945-1979*

Ellinger, A. G.. A post-war history of the stock market / A.G. Ellinger and T.H. Stewart. — Cambridge : Woodhead-Faulkner in association with Investment Research, 1980. — 80p : ill ; 22cm
Includes index
ISBN 0-85941-153-2 : £9.25 B82-25388

332.64'273 — United States. Securities markets

Garbade, Kenneth D.. Securities markets / Kenneth Garbade. — New York ; London : McGraw-Hill, c1982. — xii,532p : ill ; 24cm. — (McGraw-Hill series in finance)
Bibliography: p503-527. — Includes index
ISBN 0-07-022780-2 : £16.75 B82-16290

332.64′273 — United States. Securities markets *continuation*
Impending changes for securities markets : what role for the exchanges? / edited by Ernest Bloch and Robert A. Schwartz. — Greenwich, Conn. : Jai ; London : distributed by Jaicon, c1979. — xxxix,240p : ill ; 24cm. — (Contemporary studies in economic and financial analysis ; v.14)
Includes bibliographies and index
ISBN 0-89232-081-8 : £21.10 B82-05927

332.64′273 — United States. Securities markets. Conflict of interests
Abuse on Wall Street : conflicts of interest in the securities markets : report to the Twentieth Century Fund Steering Committee on Conflicts of Interest in the Securities Markets. — Westport ; London : Quorum, 1980. — xv,621p : ill ; 25cm. — (A Twentieth Century Fund report)
Includes index
ISBN 0-89930-001-4 : Unpriced B82-14984

332.64′4 — Commodity markets
Guide to world commodity markets. — 3rd ed. / consultant editor John Parry. — London : Kogan Page, 1982. — 393p : ill,1map ; 24cm
Previous ed.: 1979. — Includes index
ISBN 0-85038-411-7 : £20.00 : CIP rev. B82-12825

332.64′4 — Gold markets. Trading
Sarnoff, Paul. Trading in gold / Paul Sarnoff. — Cambridge : Woodhead-Faulkner, 1980. — viii,128p : ill,facsims ; 24cm
Includes index
ISBN 0-85941-111-7 : £9.25 B82-25834

332.64′4 — Great Britain. Futures commodity markets. Investment. Syndicates
Commodity futures-trading syndicates. — [London?] : Pointon York ; [Leicester] : [Current Account] [[distributor]], c1979. — 13p ; 18x26cm. — (Current account mini reports)
ISBN 0-906840-08-2 (spiral) : Unpriced B82-06681

332.64′4 — Primary commodity markets. Stabilisation
Hallwood, Paul. Stabilization of international commodity markets / by Paul Hallwood. — Greenwich, Conn. : Jai Press ; London (3 Henrietta St., WC2E 8LU) : Distributed by Jaicon Press, c1979. — xv,230p : ill ; 24cm. — (Contemporary studies in economic and financial analysis ; v.18)
Includes index
ISBN 0-89232-086-9 : £20.60 B82-02112

332.64′4′05 — Commodity markets — *Serials*
Barclays commodities survey. — 1979-. — London (54 Lombard St., EC3P 3AH) : Barclays Bank Group Economics Department, 1979-. — v. : ill ; 30cm
Quarterly. — Description based on: 18th Nov. 1981
ISSN 0260-261x = Barclays commodities survey : Unpriced B82-13420

332.64′5 — Silver. Speculation, *1979-1980*
Fay, Stephen. The great silver bubble / Stephen Fay. — London : Hodder and Stoughton, 1982. — 275p,[4]p of plates : ports ; 24cm
Bibliography: p266-267. — Includes index
ISBN 0-340-28370-x : £8.95 : CIP rev. B82-06731

332.64′52 — Europe. Stock markets. Traded options — *For investors*
Chamberlain, Geoffrey. Trading in options : an investor′s guide to making high profits in the traded options market / Geoffrey Chamberlain. — Cambridge : Woodhead-Faulkner, 1981. — x,149p : ill ; 24cm
Includes index
ISBN 0-85941-168-0 : £9.75 B82-26919

Chamberlain, Geoffrey, *1941-*. Trading in options : an investor′s guide to making high profits in the traded options market / Geoffrey Chamberlain. — 2nd ed. — Cambridge : Woodhead-Faulkner, 1982. — vi,153p : ill ; 25cm
Previous ed.: 1981. — Includes index
ISBN 0-85941-218-0 : £10.75 B82-38156

332.64′52 — United States. Stock markets. Options — *For investors*
Bookstaber, Richard M.. Option pricing and strategies in investing / Richard M. Bookstaber. — Reading, Mass. ; London : Addison-Wesley, c1981. — x,222p : ill ; 25cm
Bibliography: p219-222
ISBN 0-201-00123-3 : £13.95 B82-37944

332.66′095 — Far East. Merchant banking
Skully, Michael T.. Merchant banking in the Far East / by Michael T. Skully. — 2nd ed. — London : Financial Times Business Publishing, c1980. — 474p ; 23cm
ISBN 0-902998-27-7 : Unpriced B82-28495

332.6′7154′0941 — Great Britain. Investment by financial institutions
Plender, John. That′s the way the money goes : the financial institutions and the nation′s savings / John Plender. — London : Deutsch, 1982. — 224p ; 22cm
Includes index
ISBN 0-233-97398-2 : £8.95 : CIP rev. B81-31075

332.6′722 — United States. Small firms. Venture capital investment. Sources
Silver, A. David. Up front financing : the entrepreneur′s guide / A. David Silver. — New York ; Chichester : Wiley, c1982. — xi,245p ; 24cm. — (Wiley series on small business management)
Inlcudes index
ISBN 0-471-86386-6 : £12.50 B82-32724

332.6′7252′09429 — Wales. Industries. Investment by Welsh Development Agency — *Inquiry reports*
Great Britain. *Parliament. House of Commons. Committee of Public Accounts.* Thirty-third report from the Committee of Public Accounts : together with the proceedings of the committee, the minutes of evidence and appendices : session 1979-80 : Welsh Office, Welsh Development Agency : financial duties, industrial investments, appraisal of investment opportunities and monitoring of investment, investment in P. Leiner and Sons Limited. — London : H.M.S.O., [1980]. — 24p ; 25cm. — (HC ; 782)
ISBN 0-10-027829-9 (pbk) : £2.80 B82-09926

332.6′7253 — Great Britain. Housing associations. Private investment — *Proposals*
National Federation of Housing Associations. Private finance for housing associations : an NFHA paper intended to stimulate debate. — [London] ([30-32 Southampton St., WC2E 7HE]) : [National Federation of Housing Associations], 1981. — 41p ; 30cm. — (A Briefing note ; 4)
Unpriced (spiral) B82-08678

332.6′7254 — Great Britain. Investment by companies. Profitability. Mathematical models
Jenkinson, N. H.. Investment, profitability and the valuation ratio / by N.H. Jenkinson. — London : Economics Division, Bank of England, c1981. — 63p : ill ; 30cm. — (Discussion paper / Bank of England, ISSN 0142-6753 ; no.17)
Bibliography: p60-63
ISBN 0-903312-39-5 (pbk) : Unpriced B82-03852

332.6′7254 — Great Britain. Occupational superannuation schemes. Funds. Investment. Portfolio analysis
Measurement of investment performance for U.K. Pension funds. — Sunbury on Thames : Published for the Pensions Research Accountants Group by CARL Communications, c1981. — 48p : ill,forms ; 21cm. — (A PRAG publication)
ISBN 0-907653-01-4 (pbk) : Unpriced B82-26601

332.6′7254 — Great Britain. Occupational superannuation schemes. Funds. Investments: Insurance policies. Valuation — *For accounting*
Valuing insurance policies for accounts purposes / Pensions Research Accountants Group. — [s.l.] : The Group, c1981. — 15p ; 21cm. — (Notes on pensions ; no.10)
ISBN 0-907110-01-0 (pbk) : Unpriced B82-04224

332.6′73 — Foreign investment. Country risks
O′Leary, Michael K.. Political risk in thirty countries / by Michael K. O′Leary and William D. Coplin. — London : Euromoney Publications, c1981. — 210p : ill ; 30cm. — (A Euromoney special study)
Bibliography: p205-210
ISBN 0-903121-23-9 (spiral) : Unpriced B82-15008

332.6′73 — Foreign investment. Country risks. Assessment
Assessing country risk / edited by Richard Ensor. — London : Euromoney, c1981. — 172p : ill ; 30cm
ISBN 0-903121-20-4 (pbk) : Unpriced B82-22045

332.6′73′025538 — Saudi Arabia. Investors — *Directories*
Carter, J. R. L.. Investors in Saudi Arabia : a reference to private investment / J.R.L. Carter. — London : Scorpion, 1981. — 452p : 1geneal.table ; 29cm
Geneal.table (1 folded sheet) attached to lining paper. — Bibliography: p428. — Includes index
ISBN 0-905906-32-2 : £75.00 B82-13590

332.6′73′091724 — Developing countries. Capital investment by foreign investors
Hazari, Bharat R.. Colonialism : and foreign ownership of capital : a trade theorist′s view / Bharat R. Hazari. — London : Croom Helm, c1982. — 108p : ill ; 23cm
Includes bibliographies and index
ISBN 0-7099-1241-2 : £10.95 : CIP rev. B82-12012

332.6′73′09411 — Scotland. Investment by foreign investors — *Inquiry reports*
Great Britain. *Parliament. House of Commons. Committee on Scottish Affairs.* Second report from the Committee on Scottish Affairs, session 1979-80 : inward investment. — London : H.M.S.O., [1980]
Vol.1: Report, proceedings of the committee and index. — v,58p ; 25cm. — ([HC] ; 769-I)
Includes index
ISBN 0-10-008999-2 (pbk) : £3.90 B82-10958

Great Britain. *Parliament. House of Commons. Committee on Scottish Affairs.* Second report from the Committee on Scottish Affairs, session 1979-80 : inward investment. — London : H.M.S.O., [1980]
Vol.2: Minutes of evidence and appendices. — iv,378p ; 25cm. — ([HC] ; 769-II)
ISBN 0-10-008959-3 (pbk) : £10.60 B82-10959

332.6′7314 — Foreign investment by multinational companies
Parry, Thomas G.. The multinational enterprise : international investment and host-country impacts / by Thomas G. Parry. — Greenwich, Conn. : Jai Press ; London (3 Henrietta St., WC2E 8LU) : Distributed by Jaicon Press, c1980. — xiv,172p : ill ; 24cm. — (Contemporary studies in economic and financial analysis ; v.20)
Bibliography: p159-168. — Includes index
ISBN 0-89232-092-3 : £20.60 B82-02075

332.6′7314 — Foreign investment by multinational companies from developing companies
Multinationals from developing countries / edited by Krishna Kumar, Maxwell G. McLeod. — Lexington, Mass. : Lexington Books, c1981 ; [Aldershot] : Gower publishing [distributor], 1982. — xxv,211p : ill ; 24cm
Includes bibliographies and index
ISBN 0-669-04113-0 : £16.00 B82-08153

332.6′734′073 — United States. Foreign capital investment by European investors, *to 1917*
Buckley, Peter J.. European direct investment in the U.S.A. before World War I / Peter J. Buckley and Brian R. Roberts. — London : Macmillan, 1982. — xiv,157p ; 23cm
Bibliography: p140-146. — Includes index
ISBN 0-333-29079-8 : £15.00 B82-20907

332.6'7341 — Foreign capital investment by British investors, *1850-1914*
Edelstein, Michael. Overseas investment in the age of high imperialism. — London : Methuen, Nov.1982. — [388]p
ISBN 0-416-34730-4 : £22.50 : CIP entry B82-28736

332.6'7341 — Foreign investment by British companies
Investment abroad and jobs at home. — London (103 New Oxford St, WC1A 1DU) : Confederation of British Industry, 1980. — 39p ; 20x21cm
Bibliography: p38-39
£7.50 (pbk) B82-41027

332.6'78 — Investment — *Manuals*
Craig, Malcolm. Investing to survive the 80s : inside information for businessmen and investors / Malcolm Craig. — Rev. and updated ed. — London : Corgi, 1981. — 200p : ill ; 18cm
Previous ed.: London : Scope, 1980. — Includes index
ISBN 0-552-11896-6 (pbk) : £1.50 B82-10211

Rowlatt, James. A guide to saving and investment / James Rowlatt. — Rev. ed. — London : Pan, 1981. — 267p : ill ; 20cm. — (Pan information)
Previous ed.: 1979. — Includes index
ISBN 0-330-25841-9 (pbk) : £2.50 B82-03481

332.6'78'0941 — Great Britain. Investment — *Manuals — For expatriate Indians*
Singh, K. K. (Krishan Kumar). Money does grow on trees / by K.K.Singh ; foreword by I.P. Singh. — London : Park, 1981. — 116p : ill,forms ; 21cm
Includes index
ISBN 0-9507708-0-9 (pbk) : £3.50
Primary classification 332.6'78'0954 B82-05318

332.6'78'0941 — Great Britain. Private investment — *Manuals*
Living with inflation. — Winter ed. — Havant : Mason
Previous ed.: 1981
1: A simple guide to lump sum investment. — Dec.1981. — [64]p
ISBN 0-85937-280-4 (pbk) : £1.25 : CIP entry B82-00181

Living with inflation. — Winter ed. — Havant, Mason
Previous ed.: 1982
1: A simple guide to lump sum investment. — Oct.1982. — [64]p
ISBN 0-85937-292-8 (pbk) : £1.25 : CIP entry B82-36328

332.6'78'0941 — Great Britain. Private investment — *Manuals — Serials*
Investment opportunities : an independent monthly guide to investment alternatives. — 1-. — London (42 New Broad St., EC2) : Leasing Report Ltd, 1980-. — v. ; 21cm
Continues: Leasing report. — Description based on: 21
ISSN 0262-4257 = Investment opportunities : £40.00 per year B82-04077

332.6'78'0954 — India *(Republic).* **Investment** — *Manuals — For expatriate Indians*
Singh, K. K. (Krishan Kumar). Money does grow on trees / by K.K.Singh ; foreword by I.P. Singh. — London : Park, 1981. — 116p : ill,forms ; 21cm
Includes index
ISBN 0-9507708-0-9 (pbk) : £3.50
Also classified at 332.6'78'0941 B82-05318

332.7 — CREDIT

332.7 — Economic incentives: Deposits
Bohm, Peter. Deposit-refund system : theory and applications to environmental, conservation and consumer policy / Peter Bohm. — Baltimore ; London : Published for Resources for the Future by the Johns Hopkins University Press, c1981. — xiv,175p : ill ; 24cm
Includes index
ISBN 0-8018-2706-x : Unpriced B82-17368

332.7'2'0941 — Great Britain. Building societies. Mortgage schemes
Building societies and house-purchase. — 3rd ed. — London : Building Societies Association, 1982. — ii,35p ; 21cm
Previous ed.: 1981. — Bibliography: p32-33
ISBN 0-903277-26-3 (pbk) : Unpriced B82-35499

Hints for home buyers. — London (34 Park St., W1Y 3PF) : Building Societies Association, 1982. — 1folded sheet(([6])p) ; 20cm
Unpriced B82-35500

332.7'2'0941 — Great Britain. Mortgages — *Tables*
Mortgage repayment tables. — London (34 Park St., W1Y 3PF) : Building Societies Association, [1982?]. — 51p ; 22cm
Unpriced (pbk) B82-35503

332.7'22'0285424 — Mortgage payments. Calculations. Applications of Sinclair ZX81 microcomputer systems — *Programs*
Bluston, H. S.. Applications of the ZX81 microcomputer : a simple program for computing mortgage repayment schedules, with total interest and time needed for repayment calculations / H.S. Bluston. — Bedford (24 Elm Close, Bedford MK41 8BZ) : Energy Consultancy, 1982. — 3p ; 30cm
Unpriced (unbound) B82-21771

332.7'22'0941 — Great Britain. Residences. Purchase by prospective occupiers. Financial assistance. Loans from building societies — *Statistics*
Housing facts. — London (34 Park St., W1Y 3PF) : Building Societies Association, 1981. — 1folded sheet(([6]p)) : 1ill ; 20cm
Unpriced B82-35501

332.7'42 — Great Britain. Export credit
Edwards, H. (Herbert). Export credit : the effective and profitable management of export credit and finance / H. Edwards. — Wantage : Shaws Linton, 1980. — xvii,362p : ill,1map,forms ; 23cm
Includes index
ISBN 0-906653-02-9 : Unpriced B82-28201

332.7'43 — Great Britain. Pawnbroking, *to 1981*
Hudson, Kenneth. Pawnbroking : an aspect of British social history / Kenneth Hudson. — London : Bodley Head, 1982. — 168p,[16]p of plates : ill,facsims,ports ; 23cm
Bibliography: p160-161. — Includes index
ISBN 0-370-30447-0 : £7.95 : CIP rev. B81-36372

332.7'43 — Great Britain. Trading check services — *Inquiry reports*
Trading check franchise and financial services : a report on the supply of trading check franchise and financial services in the United Kingdom / the Monopolies and Mergers Commission. — London : H.M.S.O., [1981]. — v,125p : ill,forms ; 25cm. — ([HC] ; 62)
Includes index
ISBN 0-10-242181-1 (pbk) : £5.70 B82-11947

332.7'43 — Great Britain. Women. Consumer credit
Howe, Elspeth Rosamund Morton, *Lady.* Women and credit / by Lady Howe. — Manchester : Equal Opportunities Commission, [1978?]. — 24p ; 21cm
Speech given at the 1978 National Conference of the Institute of Credit Management at the Hilton Hotel, London, on 15th March 1978
Unpriced (pbk) B82-30845

332.7'5 — Companies. Insolvency
Totty, Peter. Corporate insolvency. — London : McGraw-Hill, June 1982. — [148]p
ISBN 0-07-084582-4 : £12.95 : CIP entry B82-11286

332.7'6 — Cheques
How to handle cheques. — Rev. — London (10 Lombard St., EC3V 9AT) : BES, 1977 (1980 [printing]). — 9p : ill,forms ; 21cm. — (Study booklet series ; 2)
Cover title. — Text on inside cover
Unpriced (pbk) B82-16260

332.7'6 — Great Britain. Cheques
The **Life** story of a cheque. — London (10 Lombard St., EC3V 9AT) : Bank Education Service, [1978?]. — [20]p : col.ill ; 8x21cm
Unpriced (unbound) B82-16272

332.7'6'0941 — Great Britain. Money transmission services
Evans, Simon, *1940-.* Banking and payment systems / ... prepared by Simon Evans. — [Brighton] : [Retail Management Development Programme], [1982]. — 123p : ill ; 30cm. — (Retail management handbook ; 3)
ISBN 0-907923-02-x (pbk) : Unpriced
Primary classification 332.1'0941 B82-29832

332.8 — INTEREST AND DISCOUNT

332.8'2 — Floating rate notes
Ugeux, Georges. Floating rate notes / by Georges Ugeux ; preface by Michael von Clemm. — London : Euromoney, c1981. — xi,152p : ill ; 30cm
Bibliography: p152
ISBN 0-903121-18-2 (pbk) : Unpriced B82-20736

332.8'2'0212 — Finance. Interest. Calculation — *Tables — For schools*
Mathematics of finance tables. — Cheltenham : Stanley Thornes, Aug.1982. — [48]p. — (Mathematics towards relevance ; 5)
ISBN 0-85950-379-8 (pbk) : £1.50 : CIP entry B82-19280

333 — LAND ECONOMICS

333'.007'11171241 — Commonwealth countries. Land economists. Professional education
Commonwealth Association of Surveying and Land Economy. Education for surveying and land economy / Commonwealth Association of Surveying and Land Economy. — 3rd ed. — London : The Association, 1982. — 32p ; 30cm + Appendix B(p33-38; 30cm)
Cover title. — Previous ed.: 1977. — Text on inside cover
ISBN 0-903577-24-0 (pbk) : £3.00
Primary classification 526.9'07'11171241 B82-22897

333.1 — PUBLIC LAND

333.1 — England. Real property. Effects of public works. Compensation. Determination. Mathematical models
Ham, Roger. Road traffic disamenity and compensation / by Roger Ham. — [Sheffield] : Sheffield City Polytechnic, Department of Urban and Regional Studies, 1981. — 33p ; 30cm. — (Working papers in urban and regional studies ; no.3)
Bibliography: p31-33
ISBN 0-903761-39-4 (pbk) : Unpriced B82-11743

333.1'09423'7 — Cornwall. Crown lands. Land tenure, *1649-1650 — Early works*
The **Parliamentary** survey of the Duchy of Cornwall / edited with an introduction by Norman J.G. Pounds. — [Exeter] ([c/o Devon and Exeter Institution, 7 The Close, Exeter]) : [Devon and Cornwall Record Society]. — (New series / Devon & Cornwall Record Society ; v.25)
Pt.1: (Austell Prior — Saltash). — 1982. — xxiv,130p,2folded leaves of plates : 2maps ; 25cm
Unpriced (pbk) B82-25336

333.1'0973 — United States. Public land. Land use
Wyant, William K.. Westward in Eden : the public lands and the conservation movement / by William K. Wyant. — Berkeley ; London : University of California Press, 1982. — xiii,536p : ill,ports ; 24cm
Bibliography: p499-517. — Includes index
ISBN 0-520-04377-4 : £18.50 B82-31098

333.1′1 — England. Local authority housing. Sale. Implications. Great Britain. *Parliament. House of Commons. Environment Committee.* **Second report ... session 1980-81** — *Critical studies*
Great Britain. *Department of the Environment.* Council house sales : the government's reply to the Second report from the Environment Committee, session 1980-81, HC 366 / Department of the Environment. — London : H.M.S.O., [1981]. — 12p ; 25cm. — (Cmnd. ; 8377)
ISBN 0-10-183770-4 (unbound) : £1.90
B82-03334

333.1′1 — England. Local authority housing. Shared purchase
Allen, Patrick, *1953-*. Shared ownership : a stepping stone to home ownership : report on a survey of local authority shared ownership schemes / Patrick Allen. — London : H.M.S.O., 1982. — ii,53p ; 30cm
ISBN 0-11-751619-8 (pbk) : £4.30 B82-38442

333.1′1′094115 — Scotland. Highlands. Annexed estates, *1745-1785*
Smith, Annette M.. Jacobite estates of the Forty-five / Annette M. Smith. — Edinburgh : John Donald, c1982. — vii,288p : 2maps ; 25cm
Bibliography: p267-272. — Includes index
ISBN 0-85976-079-0 : £15.00 B82-24415

333.2 — COMMON LAND

333.2 — South Humberside. Enclosures, *1737-1865*
Russell, Eleanor. Landscape changes in South Humberside : the enclosures of thirty-seven parishes / by Eleanor and Rex C. Russell. — Hull : Humberside Leisure Services, 1982. — 159p : maps ; 30cm
ISBN 0-904451-17-8 (pbk) : Unpriced
B82-37619

333.2 — Surrey. Epsom. Common land: Epsom Common, *to 1980*
Epsom Common / The Epsom Common Association ; [editors: Janet Glover and Ted Dowman]. — Croydon (294 High St, Croydon, Surrey, CRO 1NG) : Living History, c1981. — 64p : ill,maps ; 21cm. — (Local guide ; no.5)
Cover title. — Text on inside covers. — Bibliography: inside back cover. — Includes index
£1.10 (pbk) B82-03307

333.3 — PRIVATE LAND

333.3′092′4 — Land. Ownership. Theories of Mill, John Stuart
Martin, David E.. John Stuart Mill and the land question / David Martin. — Hull : University of Hull, 1981. — 61p ; 22cm. — (Occasional papers in economic and social history, ISSN 0078-3013 ; no.9)
Bibliography: p44-45. — Includes index
ISBN 0-85958-431-3 (pbk) : £3.95 B82-19758

333.3′0941 — Great Britain. Land. Ownership
Bracewell-Milnes, Barry. Land and heritage : the public interest in personal ownership / Barry Bracewell-Milnes. — London : Institute of Economic Affairs, 1982. — 118p ; 22cm. — (Hobart paper, ISSN 0073-2818 ; 93)
Bibliography: p118
ISBN 0-255-36151-3 (pbk) : £3.00 B82-33255

333.3′1′4115 — Scotland. Highlands. Estates. Clearances, *ca 1770-1860*
Prebble, John. The Highland clearances / John Prebble. — Harmondsworth : Penguin in association with Secker & Warburg, 1969, c1963 (1982 [printing]). — 336p : 2maps ; 18cm
Originally published: London : Secker & Warburg, 1963. — Bibliography: p315-319. — Includes index
ISBN 0-14-002837-4 (pbk) : £2.25 B82-25837

333.3′2′0942 — England. Real property. Ownership, *1870-1914.* **Political aspects**
Offer, Avner. Property and politics 1870-1914 : landownership, law, ideology and urban development in England / Avner Offer. — Cambridge : Cambridge University Press, 1981. — xviii,445p : ill,maps,facsims ; 24cm
Bibliography: p407-428. — Includes index
ISBN 0-521-22414-4 : £27.50 : CIP rev.
B81-25884

333.3′22′0941 — Great Britain. Manors — *History — Serials*
The **Bulletin** of the Manorial Society of Great Britain. — Royal Wedding ed.-. — London (c/o Mr R. Smith, 65 Belmont Hill, SE13 5AX) : The Society, [1981]-. — v. : ill,ports ; 22cm
Quarterly
ISSN 0261-1368 = Bulletin of the Manorial Society of Great Britain : Free to Society members only B82-22674

333.3′22′0942 — England. Ecclesiastical estates: Estates of Abbaye aux Dames, Caen, *ca 1100-ca 1300 — Cartularies*
Charters and custumals of the Abbey of Holy Trinity, Caen. — Oxford : Oxford University Press for the British Academy, May 1982. — [194]p. — (Records of social and economic history. New series ; v.4)
ISBN 0-19-726009-8 : £12.50 : CIP entry
B82-12899

333.3′22′0942 — England. Episcopal estates. Ownership, *1580-1664.* **Political aspects**
Gentles, I. J.. Confiscation and restoration : the Archbishopric estates and the Civil War / by I.J. Gentles and W.J. Sheils. — [York] : [Borthwick Institute of Historical Research], 1981. — 53p : 1map ; 21cm. — (Borthwick papers ; no.59)
£1.00 (pbk) B82-13825

333.3′22′0942641 — Suffolk. Blythburgh. Priories: Blythburgh Priory. Ecclesiastical estates — *Cartularies*
Blythburgh Priory cartulary. — Woodbridge : Published by Boydall & Brewer for the Suffolk Records Society
Pt.1 / edited by Christopher Harper-Bill. — 1980. — 135p : 1map,geneal.tables ; 24cm. — (Suffolk charters ; 2)
English and Latin text. — Bibliography: 11-12th preliminary pages
ISBN 0-85115-128-0 : £12.50 : CIP rev.
B80-06313

333.3′22′0942644 — Suffolk. Stoke-by-Clare. Priories: Stoke by Clare Priory. Ecclesiastical estates — *Cartularies*
Stoke by Clare Cartulary : BL Cotton Appx.xxi / edited by Christopher Harper-Bill and Richard Mortimer. — Woodbridge : Published by Boydell & Brewer for the Suffolk Records Society. — (Suffolk charters ; 4)
Pt.1. — 1982. — x,150p ; 25cm
English and Latin text
ISBN 0-85115-165-5 : Unpriced : CIP rev.
B82-12159

333.3′22′094267 — Essex. Knights of Malta. Estates, *to 1442 — Cartularies*
The **Cartulary** of the Knights of St. John of Jerusalem in England : Essex. — Oxford : Oxford University Press, Aug.1982. — [618]p. — (Records of social and economic history ; 4)
ISBN 0-19-725996-0 : £60.00 : CIP entry
B82-15679

333.3′23 — Scotland. Family property. Ownership — *Inquiry reports*
Manners, A. J.. Family property in Scotland : an enquiry carried out on behalf of the Scottish Law Commission by the Social Survey Division of the Office of Population Censuses and Surveys in 1979 / A.J. Manners, I. Rauta. — London : H.M.S.O., 1981. — iv,45p : forms ; 30cm
ISBN 0-11-690779-7 (pbk) : £8.50 B82-16795

333.3′23 — Scotland. Rural regions. Private land. Access by public. Agreements — *Proposals*
Access agreements. — Redgorton : Countryside Commission for Scotland, 1982. — 11p ; 20cm
Previous ed.: 1971?
ISBN 0-902226-61-4 (pbk) : Unpriced
B82-33042

333.3′23′09415 — Ireland. Land tenure. Political aspects, *1840-1981*
Crotty, Raymond. The Irish land question and sectarian violence / Raymond Crotty. — [Ilford] : Economic and Social Research Association, 1981. — iv,15p ; 30cm. — (Centenary essay ; no.4)
ISBN 0-903980-05-3 (pbk) : Unpriced
B82-09170

Ireland : land, politics and people / edited by P.J. Drudy. — Cambridge : Cambridge University Press, 1982. — viii,331p : ill,maps ; 23cm. — (Irish studies ; 2)
Includes index
ISBN 0-521-24577-x : £25.00 : CIP rev.
B82-15826

333.3′23′09416 — Northern Ireland. Fishing industries & trades. Guilds: Worshipful Company of Fishmongers. Estates, *to 1918*
Curl, James Stevens. The history, architecture, and planning of the estates of the Fishmongers' Company in Ulster / by James Stevens Curl. — [Belfast] ([c/o The Secretary, 181a Stranmillis Rd., Belfast 9]) : Ulster Architectural Heritage Society, 1981. — 76p : ill,maps,plans,1port ; 21cm
Bibliography: p73-74
Unpriced B82-08506

333.3′23′0942 — England. Country estates, *to 1980*
Clemenson, Heather A.. English country houses and landed estates / Heather A. Clemenson. — London : Croom Helm, c1982. — 244p : ill,maps ; 23cm. — (Croom Helm historical geography series)
Includes index
ISBN 0-85664-987-2 : £15.95 : CIP rev.
B81-27966

333.3′23′0942784 — Cumbria. Estates. Lowther Estates. Archives, *1693-1698 — Collections*
Lowther, *Sir* **John**. The correspondence of Sir John Lowther of Whitehaven, 1693-1698. — Oxford : Oxford University Press for the British Academy, Dec.1982. — [816]p. — (Records of social and economic history. New series ; 7)
ISBN 0-19-726016-0 : £43.00 : CIP entry
B82-29895

333.3′23′0942821 — South Yorkshire *(Metropolitan County).* **Sheffield. Estates,** *1581 — Accounts*
Sheffield in 1581 / [edited by] David Postler. — Sheffield : Sheffield City Libraries, 1981. — 42p ; 31cm
ISBN 0-900660-79-1 (pbk) : Unpriced
B82-08142

333.3′23′097235 — Mexico. Guadalajara region. Haciendas, *1675-1820*
Van Young, Eric. Hacienda and market in eighteenth-century Mexico : the rural economy of the Guadalajara region, 1675-1820 / Eric Van Young. — Berkeley ; London : University of California Press, c1981. — xvi,388p : ill,2maps ; 25cm
Bibliography: p363-378. — Includes index
ISBN 0-520-04161-5 : Unpriced B82-22602

333.33 — REAL PROPERTY

333.33 — Real property. Development & management. Role of chartered surveyors
Royal Institution of Chartered Surveyors. International property : the chartered surveyor = Immobilier international = La propriedad internacional. — London (c/o Secretary General, 12, Great George St., SW1P 3AD) : Royal Institution of Chartered Surveyors, [1981]. — 21,[9]p : ill ; 30cm
English text with French, Spanish and Arabic translation. — Added t.p. in Arabic
£3.00 (pbk) B82-08048

333.33′03′21 — Real property — *Encyclopaedias*
Brownstone, David M.. The VNR real estate dictionary / David M. Brownstone, Irene M. Franck. — New York ; London : Van Nostrand Reinhold, c1981. — vi,335p ; 24cm. — (A Hudson Group book)
ISBN 0-442-25856-9 : £16.10 B82-00751

333.33′068′8 — Estate agency. Salesmanship — *Manuals*
Lumley, James E. A.. Real estate psychology : the dynamics of successful selling / James E.A. Lumley. — New York ; Chichester : Wiley, c1981. — xxiv,221p ; 24cm. — (Real estate for professional practitioners, ISSN 0190-1087)
Bibliography: p205-211. — Includes index
ISBN 0-471-09610-5 : £11.80 B82-07791

333.33'0924 — Great Britain. Estate agency. Gresswell, Fred — *Biographies*

Gresswell, Fred. Bright boots. — 2nd ed. — Newton Abbot : David & Charles, Nov.1982. — [232]p
Previous ed.: London : Hale, 1956
ISBN 0-7153-8400-7 : £8.95 : CIP entry
B82-26401

333.33'0942 — England. Estate agency — *Manuals*

Mepham, John, *1929-*. Your own estate agency / John Mepham. — 2nd ed. — London : Malcolm Stewart Books, 1982. — 96p ; 25cm. — (Kingfisher business guides)
Previous ed.: 1979. — Includes index
ISBN 0-904132-59-5 (pbk) : £4.50 B82-32342

333.33'0942 — England. Real property. Management — *For business firms*

Business property handbook / compiled by the Boisot Waters Cohen Partnership. — Aldershot : Gower, c1982. — x,534p : ill,plans ; 31cm
Bibliography: p499-510. — Includes index
ISBN 0-566-02157-9 : Unpriced : CIP rev.
B81-16881

333.33'0973 — United States. Real property — *Serials*

Research in real estate : a research annual. — Vol.1 (1982)-. — Greenwich, Conn. ; London : JAI Press, 1982-. — v. : ill ; 24cm
Unpriced B82-31725

333.33'2'02854 — Great Britain. Real property. Valuation. Applications of pocket electronic calculators — *Manuals*

Bowcock, Philip. Valuing with a pocket calculator. — Oxford : Technical Press, May 1982. — [100]p
ISBN 0-291-39490-6 (pbk) : £15.00 : CIP entry
B82-07422

333.33'2'0942 — England. Real property. Independent valuation surveying — *Manuals*

Royal Institution of Chartered Surveyors. Guidance notes for surveyors acting as arbitrators or as independent valuers / Royal Institution of Chartered Surveyors. — London : The Institution, c1981. — 26p ; 30cm
Includes index
ISBN 0-85406-145-2 (pbk) : £4.20 (£3.50 to members)
Primary classification 333.33'8 B82-02419

333.33'2'0942 — England. Real property. Valuation

Millington, A. F.. An introduction to property valuation / by A.F. Millington. — 2nd ed. — London (151 Wardour St., W1V 4BN) : Estates Gazette, 1982. — vii,188p ; 22cm
Previous ed.: 1975. — Includes index
£6.50 (pbk) B82-26909

333.33'22'0941 — Great Britain. Real property market — *Serials*

Property trends / Strutt & Parker. — Issue 1-. — London (13 Hill St., W1X 8DL) : Commercial Department, Strutt & Parker, [1979]-. — v. : ill ; 30cm
Irregular. — Description based on: Issue 5
ISSN 0262-8007 = Property trends : Unpriced
B82-09071

333.33'3 — Real property. Direct-mail marketing — *Manuals*

Lumley, James E. A.. How to sell real estate by using direct mail / James E.A. Lumley. — 2nd ed. — New York ; Chichester : Wiley, c1982. — xx,229p : ill,forms ; 29cm. — (Real estate for professional practitioners)
Previous ed.: 197-?. — Includes index
ISBN 0-471-86163-4 : £23.25 B82-36678

333.33'3'0942 — England. Real property. Sale. Standard conditions — *Critical studies*

Wilkinson, H. W.. The standard conditions of sale of land : a commentary on the Law Society and National General Conditions of Sale of Land / H.W. Wilkinson. — 3rd ed. — London : Oyez Longman, 1982. — xvii,260p ; 20cm
Previous ed.: 1974. — Includes index
ISBN 0-85120-646-8 : Unpriced B82-40494

333.33'3'0942 — England. Real property. Sale. Standard conditions: National Conditions of Sale — *Commentaries*

Aldridge, Trevor M.. Guide to National conditions of sale : (20th edition) / Trevor M. Aldridge. — London : Oyez, c1981. — iv,17p ; 26x11cm
ISBN 0-85120-620-4 (pbk) : Unpriced
B82-11927

333.33'5 — Scotland. Highlands. Crofters. Eviction, *1746-1886*

Richards, Eric. A history of the Highland clearances : agrarian transformation and the evictions 1746-1886 / Eric Richards. — London : Croom Helm, c1982. — 532p : maps ; 23cm
Bibliography: p506-521. — Includes index
ISBN 0-85664-496-x : £12.95 : CIP rev.
B81-33775

333.33'5'0941641 — Strabane *(District)*. **Agricultural land. Settlement,** *1600-1641*

The **Plantation** in Ulster in Strabane Barony, Co. Tyrone c.1600-41 / Strabane Local History Group ; organised R.J. Hunter. — [Londonderry] ([Londonderry]) : New University of Ulster, Institute of Continuing Education, 1982. — vii,61p : 1facsim,maps,plans ; 30cm. — (Local history series / New University of Ulster. Institute of Continuing Education ; no.1)
Bibliography: p61
£1.25 (pbk) B82-40443

333.33'5'095412 — India *(Republic)*. **Bihar. Agricultural land. Land tenure. Reform,** *to 1981*

Agrarian movements in twentieth century Bihar (India). — London : Cass, June 1982. — [160]p
ISBN 0-7146-3216-3 : £13.50 : CIP entry
B82-12922

333.33'5'096811 — Botswana. Land tenure. Reform

Land reform in the making : tradition, public policy and ideology in Botswana / edited by Richard P. Werbner. — London : Collings, 1982. — xv,162p : maps ; 25cm
Includes bibliographies
ISBN 0-86036-186-1 (pbk) : Unpriced
B82-37450

333.33'6 — Great Britain. Industrial premises. Rents — *Forecasts* — *Serials*

A **Forecast** of industrial rents. — No.1 (Apr. 1982)-. — London (77 Grosvenor St., W1A 2BT) : Research Department, Hillier Parker May & Rowden, 1982-. — v. : ill ; 30cm
Annual
ISSN 0263-6557 = Forecast of industrial rents : Unpriced B82-28864

333.33'6 — Great Britain. Industrial premises. Rents. Geographical aspects — *Serials*

Industrial rent contours. — Nov. 1980-. — London (77 Grosvenor St., W1A 2BT) : Research Department, Hillier Parker May & Rowden, 1980-. — v. : ill,maps ; 30cm
Irregular
ISSN 0263-0699 = Industrial rent contours : Unpriced B82-15161

333.33'7 — England. Towns. Burgage land, *1100-1500* — *Study regions: West Midlands*

Slater, T. R.. The analysis of burgages in medieval towns / T.R. Slater. — Birmingham : Department of Geography, University of Birmingham, 1980. — 14p : maps ; 30cm. — (Working paper series / University of Birmingham. Department of Geography ; 4)
ISBN 0-7044-0559-8 (pbk) : £0.40 B82-23555

333.33'7 — Great Britain. Single persons. Rented residences. Shared tenancies

Single person shared housing : planning permission & environmental health standards for homes and hostels. — London (30 Southampton St., WC2E 7HE) : National Federation of Housing Associations, 1980. — 26p : ill ; 30cm. — (NFHA special project guide ; no.4)
Bibliography: p26
Unpriced (pbk) B82-27684

333.33'7 — London. Lambeth *(London Borough)*. **Effra site. Proposed sale by government** — *Inquiry reports*

Great Britain. *Parliament. House of Commons. Committee of Public Accounts.* Thirty-second report from the Committee of Public Accounts : together with the proceedings of the committee, the minutes of evidence and appendices : session 1979-80 : H.M. Treasury, Department of Industry, Department of Energy, private finance for nationalised industries and publicly owned companies, H.M. Treasury, supplementary estimates, Property Services Agency, disposal of the Effra site, Vauxhall. — London : H.M.S.O., [1980]. — xix,26p ; 25cm. — ([HC] ; 781)
ISBN 0-10-027819-1 (pbk) : £3.10
Primary classification 338.941'02 B82-09508

333.33'7'097 — North America. Urban regions. Real property. Prices

Sands, Gary. Land/office business : land and housing prices in rapidly growing metropolitan areas / Gary Sands. — Lexington, Mass. : Lexington Books ; [Aldershot] : Gower [distributor], 1982. — xvi,153p : ill,plans ; 24cm
Bibliography: p137-148. — Includes index
ISBN 0-669-04859-3 : £15.00 B82-28663

333.33'8 — England. Residences. Removal — *Practical information* — *For retired persons*

Gordon, Lorna. Moving home in retirement? / Lorna Gordon, Rose Moreno. — London (189A Old Brompton Rd., SW5 0AR) : SHAC, [1982?]. — 44p : ill ; 21cm
Unpriced (pbk) B82-23368

333.33'8 — England. Residences. Rents. Assessment by rent assessment panels. Procedure — *Inquiry reports*

Great Britain. *Working Party on Rent Assessment Panel Procedures.* Working Party on Rent Assessment Panel Procedures : report. — London : D.O.E., 1981. — 26p,A-Gleaves : forms ; 30cm
Unpriced (unbound) B82-34002

333.33'8 — England. Residences. Rents. Disputes. Arbitration. Procedure — *For surveying*

Royal Institution of Chartered Surveyors. Guidance notes for surveyors acting as arbitrators or as independent valuers / Royal Institution of Chartered Surveyors. — London : The Institution, c1981. — 26p ; 30cm
Includes index
ISBN 0-85406-145-2 (pbk) : £4.20 (£3.50 to members)
Also classified at 333.33'2'0942 B82-02419

333.33'8 — Great Britain. Expensive residences. Purchase. Financing

Financing the purchase of a high priced home. — [London?] : Pointon York ; [Leicester] : [Current Account] [[distributor]], c1979. — 9p ; 18x26cm. — (Current accout mini reports)
ISBN 0-906840-10-4 (spiral) : Unpriced
B82-09118

Top mortgages. — London : published for the British Insurance Brokers' Association by Current Account, c1979. — 12p ; 18x26cm. — (B.I.B.A. mini reports)
ISBN 0-906840-33-3 (corrected : spiral) : Unpriced
ISBN 0-906840-10-4 B82-09119

333.33'8 — Great Britain. Houses. Purchase. Financial aspects

Blay's guide to house purchase finance / editors I.S. Grant, D.A.W. Black. — Chalfont St. Peter : Blay's Guides, [1981]. — 1v.((loose-leaf)) ; 22cm
ISBN 0-907914-00-4 : Unpriced B82-13979

333.33'8 — Great Britain. Local authority housing. Rents & rates. Proposed increases, *1981-1982* — *Socialist viewpoints*

Dunnipace, Phyllis. No cuts, no rates or rent rises! / Phyllis Dunnipace, Rob Jones. — London (P.O. Box 50, N.1) : Cardinal Enterprises, 1981. — 14p : ill,1port ; 21cm. — (Socialist challenge pamphlet)
£0.25 (unbound)
Primary classification 336.3'9'0941 B82-16958

333.33'8 — Great Britain. Offices. Buildings — *Statistics — Serials*

Survey of office market activity. — No.1 (Sept. 1981)-. — London (77 Grosvenor St., W1A 2BT) : Research Department, Hillier Parker May & Rowden, 1981-. — v. ; 30cm
Two issues yearly
ISSN 0262-5539 = Survey of office market activity : Unpriced B82-05218

333.33'8 — Great Britain. Private residential property. Management by chartered surveyors. Duties

The **Responsibilities** of residential managing agents / prepared by the General Practice Division, The Royal Institution of Chartered Surveyors. — London : Published on behalf of the Royal Institution of Chartered Surveyors by Surveyors Publications, c1981. — [8]p ; 21x10cm. — (A Practice note / Royal Institution of Chartered Surveyors)
Text on inside cover
ISBN 0-85406-159-2 (pbk) : £2.30 (£2.00 to members of the Institution) B82-09378

333.33'8 — Residences. Selling — *Manuals — For owners*

O'Callaghan, John J.. How to sell your house : without an estate agent / John J. O'Callaghan. — Expanded ed. — London : Collins, 1982. — 80p : ill,1form ; 18cm
Previous ed.: Castletown : Sales Dynamics, 1980
ISBN 0-00-434271-2 (pbk) : £1.25 B82-28933

333.33'8'0941 — Great Britain. Residences. Purchase by first time buyers

More first time buyers. — London (Market Planning Division, Nationwide Building Society, New Oxford House, High Holburn, WCIV 6PW) : Nationwide Building Society, 1981. — 4p : ill ; 30cm
Unpriced (unbound) B82-31396

333.33'8'0941 — Great Britain. Residences. Purchase — *Manuals*

James, Simon, *19---*. A place of your own : how to preserve your sanity while setting up home / Simon James ; illustrations by Honeysett. — London : Hutchinson, 1982. — 159p : ill ; 22cm
At head of title: Ideal home. — Includes index
ISBN 0-09-147901-0 (pbk) : £3.95 : CIP rev. B82-09275

333.33'8'0941 — Great Britain. Urban regions. Rented accommodation. Landlords & tenants. Socioeconomic aspects, *1838-1918*

Englander, David. Landlord and tenant in urban Britain, 1838-1918. — Oxford : Clarendon Press, Jan.1983. — [450]p
ISBN 0-19-822680-2 : £19.50 : CIP entry B82-37671

333.33'8'0942 — England. Residences. Purchase & sale — *Manuals*

Giles, Marjorie. Buying and selling a house or flat : in England and Wales / Marjorie Giles. — Ed. with amendments. — London : Pan, 1981. — 159p : ill ; 18cm. — (Pan information)
Previous ed.: published as Buying & selling a house in England and Wales. Cambridge : National Extension College, 1978
ISBN 0-330-26242-4 (pbk) : £1.75 B82-04260

333.33'9 — United States. Continental shelf. Natural gas deposits & petroleum deposits. Prospecting & exploitation. Leases. Bidding by offshore natural gas & petroleum industries

Ramsey, James B. (James Bernard). Bidding and oil leases / by James B. Ramsey ; foreword by John C. Sawhill. — Greenwich, Conn. : Jai Press ; London : distributed by Jaicon Press, c1980. — xxi,202p : ill ; 24cm. — (Contemporary studies in economic and financial analysis ; v.25)
Bibliography: p185-196. — Includes index
ISBN 0-89232-148-2 : £21.10 B82-06139

333.3'8 — Great Britain. Real property. Development. Proposals. Environmental impact analysis

A **Manual** for the assessment of major development proposals : report / prepared for the Scottish Development Department, The Department of the Environment and The Welsh Office by the Project Appraisal for Development Control Research Team, Aberdeen University, Department of Geography ; B.D. Clark ... [et al.]. — London : H.M.S.O., 1981. — viii,250p : ill ; 30cm
Includes bibliographies
ISBN 0-11-751503-5 (pbk) : £22.00 B82-05030

333.3'8 — Turks and Caicos Islands. Hotels. Development. Great Britain. *Parliament. House of Commons. Foreign Affairs Committee.* **Third report ... session 1980-81 —** *Critical studies*

Great Britain. Turks and Caicos Islands : hotel development : (Third report from the Foreign Affairs Committee of the House of Commons, session 1980-81) / observations by the Government. — London : H.M.S.O., [1981]. — 6p ; 25cm. — (Cmnd. ; 8386)
ISBN 0-10-183860-3 (unbound) : £1.15 B82-14646

333.3'8 — Turks and Caicos Islands. Hotels. Development — *Inquiry reports*

Great Britain. *Parliament. House of Commons. Foreign Affairs Committee.* Third report from the Foreign Affairs Committee, session 1980-81 : Turks and Caicos Islands : hotel development : together with part of the proceedings of the Committee relating to the report ; and the minutes of evidence taken before the Overseas Development Sub-Committee on 25 November and 16 December 1980, and 13 January 1981, with appendices. — London : H.M.S.O.
Vol.1: Report and minutes of proceedings. — [1981]. — xxxiiip : 1map ; 25cm. — ([HC] ; 26-I)
ISBN 0-10-008471-0 (pbk) : £3.20 B82-03417

333.3'8 — United States. Real property. Development. Projects. Feasibility studies — *Manuals*

Barrett, G. Vincent. How to conduct and analyze real estate market and feasibility studies / G. Vincent Barrett, John P. Blair. — New York ; London : Van Nostrand Reinhold, c1982. — xvii,322p : ill,1map,plans ; 24cm
Includes bibliographies and index
ISBN 0-442-22568-7 : £21.00 B82-02859

333.5 — LAND. TENANCY

333.5'3'09417 — Ireland *(Republic).* **Privately rented residences. Tenancies**

Private rented. — Dublin (Capuchin Friary, Church St., Dublin 7) : Threshold, June 1982. — [160]p
ISBN 0-946135-00-2 (pbk) : £4.00 : CIP entry B82-21111

333.7 — NATURAL RESOURCES

333.7 — Developing countries. Renewable natural resources. Management. Environmental aspects

Ruddle, Kenneth. Renewable natural resources and the environment : pressing problems in the developing world / by Kenneth Ruddle and Walther Manshard. — Dublin : Published for the United Nations University by Tycooly International, 1981. — xiii,396p : ill,maps ; 25cm. — (Natural resources and the environment series ; v.2)
Includes bibliographies and index
ISBN 0-907567-01-0 (cased) : Unpriced
ISBN 0-907567-06-1 (pbk) : Unpriced B82-29730

333.7 — Environment

Birch, Charles. The liberation of life : from the cell to the community / Charles Birch, John B. Cobb, Jr. — Cambridge : Cambridge University Press, 1981. — ix,363p ; 24cm
Bibliography: p332-343. — Includes index
ISBN 0-521-23787-4 : £17.50 : CIP rev. B81-31283

Maclean, Kenneth. World environmental problems / Kenneth Maclean and Norman Thomson. — Edinburgh : Bartholomew, 1981. — 67p : ill(some col.),col.maps ; 30cm
Text, ill on inside covers
ISBN 0-7028-0376-6 (pbk) : Unpriced
ISBN 0-7157-2023-6 (Holmes McDougall) : Unpriced B82-03468

Watt, Kenneth E. F.. Understanding the environment / Kenneth E.F. Watt. — Boston, Mass. ; London : Allyn and Bacon, c1982. — xv,431p : ill ; 25cm
Includes bibliographies and index
ISBN 0-205-07265-8 : £22.95 B82-31685

333.7 — Environment — *Conference proceedings*

Resources, environment and the future / edited by W.B. Fisher and P.W. Kent. — London : 11, Arlington St., SW1A 1RD : German Academic Exchange Service, 1982. — viii,522columns,[2]leaves of plates : ill,1map ; 20x30cm
Conference papers. — Includes bibliographies and index
Unpriced (pbk) B82-28692

333.7 — Environment. Economic aspects

Dasgupta, Partha. The control of resources. — Oxford : Blackwell, June 1982. — [272]p
ISBN 0-631-12935-9 (cased) : £15.00 : CIP entry
ISBN 0-631-13086-1 (pbk) : £5.95 B82-10861

333.7 — Environment — *For technicians*

Smith, B. J.. Environmental science. — London : Longman, Dec.1982. — [416]p. — (Longman technician series. Construction and civil engineering)
ISBN 0-582-41620-5 (pbk) : £7.50 : CIP entry B82-30064

333.7 — Environment. Management. Economic aspects

Lowe, J. F.. The economics of environmental management / Julian Lowe, David Lewis. — Deddington : Philip Allan, 1980. — viii,344p : ill ; 23cm
Includes index
ISBN 0-86003-027-x (cased) : £13.00
ISBN 0-86003-126-8 (pbk) : £6.50 B82-21347

333.7 — Environment. Management. Systems analysis — *Conference proceedings*

IFIP WG7.1 Working Conference on Environmental Systems Analysis and Management *(1981 : Rome)*. Environmental systems analysis and management : proceedings of the IFIP WG7.1 Working Conference on Environmental Systems Analysis and Management, Rome, Italy, 28-30 September 1981 / edited by S. Rinaldi. — Amsterdam ; Oxford : North-Holland, 1982. — xii,828p : ill,maps ; 23cm
Includes bibliographies
ISBN 0-444-86406-7 : Unpriced B82-39973

333.7 — Environment. Pollution. Economic aspects

Siebert, Horst. The political economy of environmental protection / by Horst Siebert, Ariane Berthoin Antal. — Greenwich, Conn. : Jai Press ; London (3 Henrietta St., WC2E 8LU) : Distributed by Jaicon Press, c1979. — xii,195p : ill ; 24cm. — (Contemporary studies in economic and financial analysis ; v.24)
Bibliography: p187-191. — Includes index
ISBN 0-89232-116-4 : £20.00 B82-02103

333.7 — Environmental change, *1972-1982*

The **World** environment 1972-1982 : a report / by the United Nations Environment Programme ; edited by Martin W. Holdgate, Mohammed Kassas, Gilbert F. White with the assistance of David Spurgeon ; study co-ordinator Essam El-Hinnawi. — Dublin : Published for the United Nations Environment Programme by Tycooly International, 1982. — xxxii,637p : ill,maps ; 25cm. — (Natural resources and the environment series ; v.8)
Includes bibliographies and index
ISBN 0-907567-13-4 (cased) : Unpriced
ISBN 0-907567-14-2 (pbk) : Unpriced B82-29727

333.7 — Environmental studies — *For schools*
Johnson, Roger, *1946-*. Environmental science / Roger Johnson and Peter Morrell. — Glasgow : Blackie, 1982. — 186p : ill,maps ; 25cm
Includes index
ISBN 0-216-91151-6 (pbk) : £5.25 B82-32419

333.7 — European Community countries. Environment. Effects of cleaning materials
Environmental Resources Ltd. Cleaning and conditioning agents : their impact on the environment in the EEC : a report prepared for the Directorate General for Industrial and Technological Affairs and for the Environment and Consumer Protection Services of the European Communities by Environmental Resources Ltd. — London : Graham & Trotman for the Commission of the European Communities, 1978, c1977. — 138p : ill ; 30cm
ISBN 0-86010-108-8 (pbk) : £15.00
B82-12116

333.7 — Land use. Planning. Implications of ecology
Selman, Paul H.. Ecology and planning. — London : George Godwin, Apr.1981. — [160]p
ISBN 0-7114-5555-4 : £9.50 : CIP entry
B81-07476

333.7 — Natural resources. Exploitation — *For schools*
Bryant, Lee, *1945-*. Using the earth / Lee Bryant, Raymond Pask. — Richmond, Victoria ; London : Heinemann Educational, 1982. — 132p : ill(some col.),col.maps,col.plans ; 26cm
Includes index
ISBN 0-435-34680-6 (pbk) : £3.50 B82-40626

333.7 — Natural resources — *For schools*
Ghaye, Tony. Resources. — London : Macmillan Education, Feb.1983. — [96]p. — (Discovering geography)
ISBN 0-333-28404-6 (pbk) : £2.35 : CIP entry
B82-37860

333.7 — Natural resources. Management. Applications of aerial photography
Paine, David P.. Aerial photography and image interpretation for resource management / David P. Paine. — New York ; Chichester : Wiley, c1981. — xii,571p,[8]p of plates : ill (some col.),maps ; 24cm
Includes index
ISBN 0-471-01857-0 : £22.15 B82-08722

333.7 — Natural resources. Remote sensing. British organisations — *Directories*
Remote sensing of earth resources : UK groups and individuals engaged in remote sensing with a brief account of their activities and facilities. — 5th ed. / compiled and edited by Elizabeth J. Lindsay on behalf of the Department of Industy. — London : Department of Industry, 1981. — v,386p ; 30cm
Previous ed.: 1979. — Includes index
£15.00 (pbk) B82-24676

333.7 — Unrenewable natural resources. Econometric models
Marks, Robert. Non renewable resources and disequilibrium macrodynamics / Robert Marks. — New York ; London : Garland, 1979. — xii,335p : ill ; 24cm
Includes index
ISBN 0-8240-4053-8 : Unpriced B82-23727

333.7'022'2 — Environment — *Illustrations*
Aldridge, Don. The monster book of environmental education / Don Aldridge. — Norwich : Geo, 1981. — [144]p : col.ill ; 16x22cm
Also available in French
Unpriced B82-11477

333.7'023 — Occupations involving the environment — *Career guides*
Careers in the environment. — Rev. ed. — Reading (School of Education, University of Reading, London Road, Reading RG1 5AQ) : Council for Environmental Education, Feb.1982. — [44]p
Previous ed. published as: Careers for environmentalists, 1977
ISBN 0-906711-04-5 (pbk) : £1.00 : CIP entry
B82-02484

333.7'0246 — Environmental studies — *For technicians*
Pritchard, M. D. W.. Environmental science 4 checkbook. — London : Butterworth, Sept.1982. — [224]p
ISBN 0-408-00663-3 (cased) : £6.95 : CIP entry
ISBN 0-408-00608-0 (pbk) : £3.95 B82-19213

333.7'028'51 — Environmental studies. Applications of systems analysis
Wilson, A. G.. Geography and the environment : systems analytical methods / A.G. Wilson. — Chichester : Wiley, c1981. — xv,297p : ill,maps ; 24cm
Bibliography: p278-283. — Includes index
ISBN 0-471-27956-0 (cased) : £15.50 : CIP rev.
ISBN 0-471-27957-9 (pbk) : Unpriced
B81-30482

333.7'05 — National resources. Management — *Serials*
Resource management and optimization : an international journal. — Vol.1, no.1 (1980)-. — Chur ; London : Harwood Academic Publishers, 1980-. — v. ; 23cm
Quarterly
ISSN 0142-2391 = Resource management and optimization : Unpriced B82-06795

333.7'07'104233 — Dorset. Schools. Curriculum subjects: Environmental studies. Projects: East Dorset Purbeck Project
Bailey, K. V.. Past, present, future : an account of an environmental education project carried out in the Purbeck district of East Dorset, 1980-81 / by K.V. Bailey. — Bexhill-on-Sea : Heritage Education Group, 1982. — 36p : ill,3maps ; 21cm
Maps on inside covers
ISBN 0-900849-38-x (pbk) : Unpriced
B82-36855

333.7'07'1042612 — Norfolk. Schools. Curriculum subjects: Environmental studies. Information sources — *Serials*
Environmental resources directory / Norfolk County Council Planning Department. — 1982-. — Norwich (c/o J.M. Shaw, County Planning Officer, County Hall, Martineau La., Norwich NR1 2DH) : The Council, 1982-. — v. ; 21cm
Annual
ISSN 0263-6948 = Environmental resources directory : £0.60 B82-30479

333.7'07'1042654 — Cambridgeshire. Huntingdon *(District)*. **Schools. Curriculum subjects: Environmental studies** — *For teaching*
Environmental education in Huntingdon District : a teachers manual. — Huntingdon (Pathfinder House, St. Mary's St., Huntingdon, Cambs. PE18 6TN) : Huntingdon District Council, Planning Department, 1982. — 17p : ill,maps ; 30cm
Bibliography: p12
Unpriced (pbk) B82-33162

333.7'07'1242 — England. Secondary schools. Curriculum subjects: Environmental studies. Curriculum. Development. Projects
Adams, Eileen. Art and the built environment : a teacher's approach / Eileen Adams and Colin Ward. — Harlow : Published for the Schools Council by Longman, 1982. — 160p : ill,maps,plans ; 30cm
Bibliography: p160
ISBN 0-582-36195-8 (pbk) : £8.95 B82-36955

333.7'072 — Environment. Policies. Econometric models
Siebert, Horst. Economics of the environment / Horst Siebert. — Lexington, Mass. : Lexington Books ; [Aldershot] : Gower [distributor], 1981. — xii,230p : ill ; 24cm
Bibliography: p213-224. — Includes index
ISBN 0-669-03693-5 : £15.00 B82-00843

333.7'072 — Environmental studies. Research. Methodology
Environmental science methods / edited by Robin Haynes. — London : Chapman and Hall, 1982. — x,404p : ill,maps ; 25cm
Includes bibliographies and index
ISBN 0-412-23280-4 (cased) : Unpriced : CIP rev.
ISBN 0-412-23290-1 (pbk) : Unpriced
B81-31731

333.7'0720417 — Ireland *(Republic)*. **Environment. Research projects** — *Lists*
Directory of environmental research in Ireland / compiled by Maureen Conroy. — Dublin : An Foras Forbartha, 1981. — 50p ; 30cm
Includes index
ISBN 0-906120-48-9 (pbk) : £3.00 B82-15381

333.7'072042511 — Derbyshire. Castleton. Field study centres: Losehill Hall
Burrell, Theo. Losehill Hall : Peak National Park Study Centre / [text Theo Burrell and Geoff Cooper ; [photographs Peak Park staff and Mike Williams) ; [illustrations Mike Goodwin and John Sewell] ; [maps Di Tranter and Trevor Bolton]. — Bakewell : Peak Park Joint Planning Board, c1982. — 19p : col.ill,2col.maps ; 20x21cm
Cover title. — Text and col. map inside cover
ISBN 0-901428-96-5 (pbk) : Unpriced
B82-30842

333.7'0724 — Natural resources. Econometric models
Explorations in natural resource economics / V. Kerry Smith and John V. Krutilla, editors. — Baltimore ; London : Published for Resources for the Future by Johns Hopkins University Press, c1982. — xiii,352p : ill ; 24cm
Includes bibliographies and index
ISBN 0-8018-2713-2 : £26.25 B82-34342

333.7'0724 — Natural resources. Exploitation. Econometric models
Fisher, Anthony C.. Resource and environmental economics / Anthony C. Fisher. — Cambridge : Cambridge University Press, 1981. — xv,284p : ill ; 22cm. — (Cambridge surveys of economic literature)
Bibliography: p241-275. — Includes index
ISBN 0-521-24306-8 (cased) : £20.00
ISBN 0-521-28594-1 (pbk) : £6.95 B82-18057

333.7'076 — Environment — *Questions & answers*
Watt, Kenneth E. F.. Instructor's manual to accompany Understanding the environment / prepared by Kenneth E.F. Watt. — Boston ; London : Allyn and Bacon, c1982. — 133p ; 24cm
ISBN 0-205-07266-6 (pbk) : Unpriced
B82-28380

333.7'092'4 — Natural resources. Exploitation. Theories of Schauberger, Viktor
Alexandersson, Olof. Living water : Viktor Schauberger and the secrets of natural energy / by Olof Alexandersson ; translated by Kit and Charles Zweigbergk. — Wellingborough : Turnstone, 1982. — 160p : ill ; 22cm
Translation of: Levande vattnet. —
Bibliography: p156-158. — Includes index
ISBN 0-85500-112-7 (pbk) : £4.95 : CIP rev.
B81-14952

333.7'0941 — Great Britain. Environment. Attitudes of residents
The **Neighbourhood**. — London : National Consumer Council, 1982. — 56p ; 29cm
"The survey was carried out for the National Consumer Council by Research Services Limited. This paper was written for us by Lindsey Etchell"
ISBN 0-905653-41-6 (pbk) : £1.00 B82-28966

333.7'0941 — Great Britain. Environment — *For schools*
Lovett, Patricia. The environment / Patricia Lovett. — London : Batsford Academic and Educational, 1982. — 72p : ill,maps ; 26cm. — (Living today)
Includes index
ISBN 0-7134-3580-1 : £5.95 B82-30751

333.7'09417 — Ireland *(Republic)*. **Environment. Interpretation** — *Conference proceedings*
Interpretation : understanding our surroundings : proceedings of the seminar held at Malahide, Co. Dublin, on 10th/11th April 1981. — Dublin (Fitzwilton House, Wilton Place, Dublin 2) : Forás Éireann, 1981. — 43p ; 30cm
Sponsored by the Carnegie United Kingdom Trust. — Bibliography: p42-43
Unpriced (pbk) B82-13329

333.7'0951 — China. Environment — *Conference proceedings*

The Environment : Chinese and American views / [proceedings of the world's first joint U.S.-China symposium sponsored by the Ohio Academy of Science with the cooperation of the Association of American Geographers, the Ford Foundation and the National Science Foundation, Wingspread Conference Center, the Johnson Foundation, Racine, Wisconsin, October 13-14, 1978] ; edited by Laurence J.C. Ma and Allen G. Noble. — New York ; London : Published for the Ohio Academy of Science by Methuen, 1981. — xiii,397p : ill,maps ; 24cm
Conference papers. — Includes bibliographies and index
ISBN 0-416-32050-3 : £16.50 : CIP rev.
Primary classification 333.7'0973 B81-13755

333.7'0973 — United States. Environment — *Conference proceedings*

The Environment : Chinese and American views / [proceedings of the world's first joint U.S.-China symposium sponsored by the Ohio Academy of Science with the cooperation of the Association of American Geographers, the Ford Foundation and the National Science Foundation, Wingspread Conference Center, the Johnson Foundation, Racine, Wisconsin, October 13-14, 1978] ; edited by Laurence J.C. Ma and Allen G. Noble. — New York ; London : Published for the Ohio Academy of Science by Methuen, 1981. — xiii,397p : ill,maps ; 24cm
Conference papers. — Includes bibliographies and index
ISBN 0-416-32050-3 : £16.50 : CIP rev.
Also classified at 333.7'0951 B81-13755

333.7'0973 — United States. Environment. Interpretation. Techniques

Interpreting the environment / [edited by] Grant W. Sharpe. — 2nd ed. — New York ; Chichester : Wiley, c1982. — xvi,694p : ill ; 24cm
Previous ed.: 1976. — Includes bibliographies and index
ISBN 0-471-09007-7 : £19.20 B82-18213

333.7'0973 — United States. Environment. Policies of government

Environmental policy formation : the impact of values, ideology and standards / edited by Dean E. Mann. — Lexington : Lexington Books, c1981 ; [Aldershot] : Gower [distributor], 1982. — xi,244p ; 24cm. — (Policy Studies Organization series)
Includes index
ISBN 0-669-03518-1 : £19.50 B82-18262

333.7'0979 — South-western United States. Natural resources. Exploitation. Environmental aspects

Kneese, Allen V.. The Southwest under stress : national resource development issues in a regional setting / Allen V. Kneese and F. Lee Brown with contributions by Frederick R. Anderson ... [et al.]. — Baltimore ; London : Published for Resources for the Future by Johns Hopkins University Press, c1981. — xv,268p : ill,maps ; 27cm
Ill on lining papers. — Includes index
ISBN 0-8018-2707-8 (cased) : £21.00
ISBN 0-8018-2708-6 (pbk) : Unpriced B82-11907

333.7'09798 — United States. Natural resources. Exploitation. Policies of government — *Study regions: Alaska*

Young, Oran R.. Natural resources and the state : the political economy of resource management / Oran R. Young. — Berkeley ; London : University of California Press, c1981. — xi,227p : ill ; 23cm. — (Studies in international political economy)
Includes index
ISBN 0-520-04285-9 : £13.75 B82-06999

333.7'1 — Environmental impact analysis — *Conference proceedings*

Environmental impact assessment : proceedings of a seminar of the United Nations Economic Commission for Europe, Villach, Austria, September 1979. — Oxford : Published for the United Nations by Pergamon, 1981. — xxxv,335p ; 26cm
Includes one contribution in French
ISBN 0-08-024445-9 : £23.00 : CIP rev. B81-10001

333.7'1 — Scotland. Lothian Region. Torness Point region. Electricity transmission equipment: Proposed 400 kV overhead lines. Environmental aspects

Torness power station : review of alternative routes for 400KV lines : report of the Working Party. — Edinburgh (12 St. Giles St., Edinburgh, EH1 1TU) : Dept. of Physical Planning, Lothian Regional Council, 1981. — 23p,[8]folded leaves of plates : ill,maps ; 30cm
Unpriced (pbk) B82-14428

333.7'1'091724 — Environment. Evaluation. Socioeconomic aspects — *Study regions: Developing countries*

Cooper, Charles. Economic evaluation and the environment : a methodological discussion with particular reference to developing countries / Charles Cooper ; sponsored by the United Nations Environment Programme under a programme of conceptual and methodological studies in the field of environment and development. — London : Hodder and Stoughton, 1981. — vii,161p : ill ; 24cm
Bibliography: p154-158. — Includes index
ISBN 0-340-26555-8 (pbk) : £8.00 : CIP rev. B81-13492

333.7'1'0941 — Great Britain. Environment planning. Environmental impact analysis

Environmental impact assessment : third informal seminar 17th October 1978 : environmental impact considerations at the level of planning policy : summary of prepared contributions. — [Birmingham] : University of Birmingham, Dept. of Transportation & Environmental Planning, [1978?]. — 25leaves ; 30cm. — (Departmental publications / University of Birmingham, Department of Transportation and Environmental Planning ; no.58)
ISBN 0-7044-0619-5 (spiral) : Unpriced B82-26377

333.7'1'09411 — Scotland. Environment planning. Environmental impact analysis — *Conference proceedings*

Environmental impact studies : less haste more speed : proceedings of the one day symposium at the Scottish Development Agency, Glasgow, Tuesday 28th October, 1980 / edited by Graham C. Barrow. — Glasgow (90 Mitchell St., Glasgow G1 3NL) : Anderson Semens Houston, 1980. — 97p : ill ; 30cm
Unpriced (pbk) B82-14285

333.7'13 — Natural resources. Substitution. Mathematical models

Modeling and measuring natural resource substitution / edited by Ernst R. Berndt, Barry C. Field. — Cambridge [Mass.] ; London : MIT Press, c1981. — 314p ; 24cm
Bibliography: p290-305
ISBN 0-262-06078-7 : £24.50 B82-21690

333.7'13'09485 — Natural resources. Depletion — *Study regions: Sweden*

Resources, society and the future : a report / prepared for the Swedish Secretariat for Futures Studies by Tomas Bertelman ... [et al.] ; translated from the Swedish by Roger G. Tanner. — Oxford : Pergamon, 1980. — viii,198p : ill,1map ; 26cm
Includes index
ISBN 0-08-023266-3 (cased) : £15.00 : CIP rev.
ISBN 0-08-023267-1 (pbk) : £7.50 B79-27067

333.7'2 — Energy resources. Conservation — *Conference proceedings*

Energy modelling studies and conservation : proceedings of a seminar of the United Nations Economic Commission for Europe, Washington, D.C., 24-28 March 1980. — Oxford : Published for the United Nations by Pergamon, 1982. — xxxiv,689p : ill,maps ; 26cm
Includes 2 papers in French. — Includes bibliographies
ISBN 0-08-027416-1 : £47.50 : CIP rev.
Primary classification 333.79'16'0724 B81-22566

333.7'2 — Environment. Conservation

Allen, Robert, *1942-*. How to save the world : strategy for world conservation / Robert Allen ; [based on the World Conservation Strategy prepared by the International Union for Conservation of Nature and Natural Resources (IUCN), with the advice, co-operation and financial assistance of the United Nations Environment Programme (UNEP) and the World Wildlife Fund]. — London : Corgi, 1982, c1980. — 176p : ill ; 18cm
Originally published: London : Kogan Page, 1980
ISBN 0-552-11992-x (pbk) : £1.25 B82-37810

Hackett, Brian. Landscape conservation / by Brian Hackett. — Chichester : Packard, 1980. — 111p : ill ; 25cm
Bibliography: p106-108. — Includes index
ISBN 0-906527-06-6 : Unpriced B82-08131

333.7'2 — Natural resources. Conservation

Gabor, Dennis. Beyond the age of waste : a report to the Club of Rome / D. Gabor and U. Colombo with A. King and R. Galli. — 2nd ed. — Oxford : Pergamon, 1981. — xviii,239p : ill,2maps ; 21cm. — (Pergamon international library)
Translation of: Oltre L'età dello spreco. — Previous ed.: 1978. — Includes index
ISBN 0-08-027303-3 (cased) : Unpriced
ISBN 0-08-027304-1 (pbk) : £8.00 B82-02408

333.7'2'02341 — Great Britain. Environment. Conservation — *Career guides*

McCormick, John. Careers in conservation. — London : Kogan Page, Sept.1982. — [100]p
ISBN 0-85038-561-x (cased) : £6.95 : CIP entry
ISBN 0-85038-562-8 (pbk) : £2.50 B82-29136

333.7'2'02851 — Environment. Conservation. Applications of systems analysis

Haith, Douglas A.. Environmental systems optimization / Douglas A. Haith. — New York ; Chichester : Wiley, c1982. — xii,306p : ill ; 25cm
Includes bibliographies and index
ISBN 0-471-08287-2 : £18.55 B82-12297

333.7'2'05 — Environment. Conservation — *Serials*

ENDS yearbook / Environmental Data Services Ltd. — 1981/82-. — London (Orchard House, 14 Great Smith St., SW1P 3BU) : ENDS, [1982]-. — v. : ports ; 21cm
ISSN 0263-1571 = ENDS yearbook : Unpriced B82-18718

333.7'2'06041 — Great Britain. Environment. Conservation. Organisations: Ecological Parks Trust — *Serials*

Ecological Parks Trust. Report / Ecological Parks Trust. — 1st (Feb. 1981)-. — London (c/o The Linnean Society, Burlington House, W1V OLQ) : The Trust, 1981-. — v. ; 21cm
Annual
ISSN 0263-130X = Report - Ecological Parks Trust : Unpriced B82-17245

333.7'2'06042178 — London. Bromley *(London Borough)*. **Environment. Conservation. Organisations: Environment Bromley** — *Serials*

Environment Bromley. En. Bro. : information from Environment Bromley. — No.1 (Feb. 1981)-. — [London] ([c/o Mr. P. Daniell, 300 Baring Rd, Lee SE12]) : Environment Bromley, 1981-. — v. ; 21cm
Monthly. — Description based on: No.3 (Apr. 1981)
ISSN 0262-7442 = En. Bro. : Unpriced B82-14269

333.7'2'060422165 — Surrey. Dorking region. Environment. Conservation. Organisations: Dorking and Leith Hill District Preservation Society, *to 1980*

Mercer, E. D. Fifty years of conservation / [written by E.D. Mercer] ; [drawings by K. Dodson]. — [Dorking] ([c/o Hon. Sec., 87 Parkway, Dorking, Surrey]) : Dorking and Leith Hill District Preservation Society, c1980. — 24p : ill ; 22cm
Cover title
£0.50 (pbk) B82-02865

333.7'2'0924 — Great Britain. Environment. Conservation. Hill, Octavia — *Biographies*

Boyd, Nancy. Josephine Butler, Octavia Hill, Florence Nightingale : three Victorian women who changed their world / Nancy Boyd. — London : Macmillan, 1982. — xviii,276p ; 23cm
Bibliography: p263-270. — Includes index
ISBN 0-333-30057-2 : £15.00
Primary classification 610.73'092'4 B82-28832

333.7'2'0941 — Great Britain. Environment. Conservation

Conservation / edited by Wendy Pettigrew. — Sevenoaks : Hodder and Stoughton, 1982. — 179p : ill,maps ; 20cm. — (Teach yourself books)
Includes bibliographies and index
ISBN 0-340-26821-2 (pbk) : £2.50 : CIP rev.
B82-03809

333.7'2'0941 — Great Britain. Environment. Conservation — *Proposals*

Programme Organising Committee. Earth's survival : a conservation and development programme for the UK. — [London] (c/o Nature Conservancy Council, 19-20 Belgrave Sq., SW1X 8PY) : Programme Organising Committee, 1981. — 6p ; 30cm. — (World Conservation Strategy — the UK dimension ; report no.1)
ISBN 0-86139-152-7 (pbk) : Unpriced
B82-25621

333.7'2'0941 — Great Britain. Environment. Conservation. Residential projects — *Lists* — *For volunteers*

Summer tasks. — Reading (10-14 Duke St., Reading, Berks. RG1 4RU) : National Conservation Corps, 1981. — 31p : ill ; 21cm
Unpriced (unbound) B82-12124

333.7'2'0941 — Great Britain. Environment. Conservation — *Serials*

Green drum : the paper for people who care. — No.39 (Winter 1981-2)-. — Birmingham (18 Cofton Lake Rd., Birmingham 45) : Bromsgrove Conservation Society, [1981]-. — v. : ill ; 41cm
Quarterly. — Continues: Good earth
ISSN 0263-0095 = Green drum : £1.48 per year B82-13409

333.7'2'094124 — Scotland. Highland Region. Cairngorms. Environment. Conservation — *Proposals*

Curry-Lindahl, Kai. The future of the Cairngorms / by Kai Curry-Lindahl, Adam Watson, R. Drennan Watson ; illustrated by Keith Brockie ; designed by Jenny Watson. — Aberdeen : North East Mountain Trust, 1982. — 47p : ill,1map ; 21cm
ISBN 0-9508186-0-7 (pbk) : Unpriced
B82-39709

333.7'2'094235 — Devon. Environment. Conservation

Nature conservation in Devon : an introduction to the conservation of wildlife and wildplaces of the county. — Rev. ed. — Exeter : Devon County Council, 1982. — 55p : ill,maps ; 21cm
Previous ed.: 1977
ISBN 0-86114-370-1 (pbk) : £0.40 B82-35764

333.7'2'0942396 — Avon. Long Ashton. Environment. Conservation

Evans, David, *1935-*. Long Ashton : a case for conservation / text and maps by David Evans ; drawings by Patrick Collins. — Long Ashton (c/o Secretary, 174 Long Ashton Rd., Long Ashton, Avon) : SCALA, 1979. — [18]p : ill,maps ; 30x42cm
Text and ill on inside cover
£1.00 (pbk) B82-23714

333.7'2'09426752 — Essex. Chelmsford. Environment. Conservation — *For environment planning*

Conservation & townscape topic report : Chelmsford town centre district plan. — Chelmsford : Chelmsford Borough Council, 1981. — 17p,8leaves of plates(some folded) : maps ; 30cm
Unpriced (pbk) B82-08729

333.73 — Developing countries. Arid regions. Irrigation. Socioeconomic aspects

Hazlewood, Arthur. Irrigation economics in poor countries. — Oxford : Pergamon, July 1982. — [150]p
ISBN 0-08-027451-x : £12.50 : CIP entry
B82-21076

333.73 — Great Britain. Land disturbed by quarrying. Reclamation. Ecological aspects — *Conference proceedings*

Ecology of quarries : the importance of natural vegetation / edited by B.N.K. Davis. — Huntingdon : Institute of Terrestrial Ecology, 1982. — 76p : ill ; 30cm. — (ITE symposium ; no.11)
Subtitle: Proceedings of a workshop held at Monks Wood Experimental Station 23-24 February 1981. — At head of title: Natural Environment Research Council. — Includes bibliographies
ISBN 0-904282-59-7 (pbk) : Unpriced
B82-27739

333.73 — Ireland *(Republic).* **Natural resources: Peat. Exploitation**

Morgan, B. J. W.. Bord na Mona Irish Peat Development Authority : report of a visit to the Republic of Ireland 9-10 March 1981 / by B.J.W. Morgan. — [London] : ADAS, 1982. — 15p : 1ill,1map ; 30cm
Cover title
Unpriced (pbk) B82-21805

333.73 — Land use. Evaluation

McRae, S. G.. Land evaluation / S.G. McRae, C.P. Burnham. — Oxford : Clarendon Press, 1981. — viii,239p : ill,maps ; 23cm. — (Monographs on soil survey) (Oxford science publications)
Bibliography: p201-229. — Includes index
ISBN 0-19-854518-5 : £10.00 : CIP rev.
B81-31456

333.73'0942 — England. Land use. Mapping — *For teaching*

Patterns on the map : land utilisation survey maps as resources for teaching and learning. — Sheffield : Geographical Association
1: Introductory handbook / Alice Coleman and Simon Catling. — c1982. — iv,46p : ill,maps ; 30cm
Bibliography: p45
ISBN 0-900395-71-0 (pbk) : Unpriced
B82-28971

Patterns on the map : land utilisation survey maps as resources for teaching and learning. — Sheffield : Geographical Association
2: Plymouth and Merthyr Tydfil / Alice Coleman ... [et al.]. — c1982. — iv,100p : ill,maps ; 30cm
Includes bibliographies
ISBN 0-900395-72-9 (pbk) : Unpriced
B82-28972

Patterns on the map : land utilisation survey maps as resources for teaching and learning. — Sheffield : Geographical Association
3: Leeds and Rosedale / Alice Coleman, John Bale, Michael Hewitt. — c1982. — iv,96p : ill,maps ; 30cm
Includes bibliographies
ISBN 0-900395-73-7 (pbk) : Unpriced
B82-28973

Patterns on the map : land utilisation survey maps as resources for teaching and learning. — Sheffield : Geographical Association
4: Sevenoaks and Gravesend / Alice Coleman, Inga Feaver, Raymond Pask. — c1982. — iv,90p : ill,maps ; 30cm
Includes bibliographies
ISBN 0-900395-74-5 (pbk) : Unpriced
B82-28974

333.73'0942 — England. Land use. Planning

Hall, John M.. The geography of planning decisions / John M. Hall. — Oxford : Oxford University Press, 1982. — 62p : maps ; 21cm. — (Theory and practice in geography)
Bibliography: p58-62. — Includes index
ISBN 0-19-874034-4 (pbk) : £2.50 : CIP rev.
B81-33902

333.73'0947 — Soviet Union. Land use. Planning

Shaw, Denis J. B.. Problems of land use and development in the USSR / Denis J.B. Shaw. — Birmingham : Department of Geography, University of Birmingham, 1980. — 14p ; 30cm. — (Working paper series / University of Birmingham. Department of Geography ; 5)
ISBN 0-7044-0560-1 (pbk) : £0.40 B82-23556

333.73'09941 — Western Australia. Catchment areas. Land use. Planning. Applications of systems analysis

On rational grounds : systems analysis in catchment land use planning / edited by David Bennett and John F. Thomas. — Amsterdam ; Oxford : Elsevier Scientific, 1982. — xxxii,362p : ill,maps(some col.) ; 25cm. — (Development in landscape management and urban planning ; 4)
Map on folded sheet in pocket. — Includes bibliographies and index
ISBN 0-444-42056-8 : £40.51 : CIP rev.
B82-00192

333.73'13 — Land use

Symons, Leslie. The land use challenge : eastern and western responses : inaugural lecture delivered at the college on 9th March 1982 / by Leslie Symons. — Swansea : University College Swansea, 1982. — 40p : ill,3maps ; 21cm
Bibliography: p37-40
ISBN 0-86076-028-6 (pbk) : Unpriced
B82-24314

333.73'13'072042 — England. Land use. Research & development by Land and Water Service

Land use, conservation and land economics 1980. — Alnwick : MAFF (Publications), c1982. — vi,39p ; 21cm. — (Research and development reports / ADAS, Land Service)
Cover title
£1.25 (pbk) B82-23828

333.73'13'0941 — Great Britain. Land use

Best, Robin H.. Land use and living space / Robin H. Best. — London : Methuen, 1981. — xxi,197p : ill,maps ; 23cm
Includes index
ISBN 0-416-73760-9 (cased) : £10.50 : CIP rev.
ISBN 0-416-73770-6 (pbk) : Unpriced
B81-31746

333.73'15'094227 — South Hampshire. Land. Development — *Forecasts*

South Hampshire land development study, 1980 / [reported to the Planning & Transportation Committee of the County Council, 24th November 1982]. — Winchester (The Castle, Winchester) : County Planning Department, 1980. — 19p : ill,1map ; 30cm. — (Strategic planning paper / Hampshire County Council ; no.8)
Cover title
£0.75 (pbk) B82-38209

333.73'17 — Derbyshire. Kinder Scout. Access. Restrictions. Protests by walkers, *1932*

Rothman, Benny. The 1932 Kinder trespass : a personal view of the Kinder Scout mass trespass / by Benny Rothman. — Altrincham : Willow Publishing, 1982. — 48p : ill,3maps,facsims,ports ; 24cm
ISBN 0-9506043-7-2 (pbk) : Unpriced
B82-26854

333.73'17 — England. Peak District. Private land. Access by public, *to 1981*

Rickwood, Pat. The story of access in the Peak District / Pat Rickwood ; foreword Tom Stephenson. — Bakewell : Peak Park Joint Planning Board, c1982. — 19p : ill,col.maps,ports ; 21cm. — (A Peak National Park publication)
Cover title. — Text and ill inside covers. — Bibliography: p19
ISBN 0-901428-98-1 (pbk) : Unpriced
B82-30841

333.74'0913 — Tropical regions. Rangeland. Management

Range and wildlife management in the tropics. — London : Longman, Oct.1982. — [240]p. — (Intermediate tropical agriculture series)
ISBN 0-582-60896-1 (pbk) : £3.95 : CIP entry
B82-25182

333.75 — Great Britain. Natural resources: Broad-leaved forests. Management — *Conference proceedings*
Broadleaves in Britain. — Edinburgh : Institute of Chartered Foresters, July 1982. — [253]p
Conference proceedings
ISBN 0-907284-02-7 : £8.00 : CIP entry
B82-17236

333.75 — Natural resources: Tropical hardwood
Tropical hardwood utilization : practice and prospects / book editor Roelof A.A. Oldeman ; section editors R.G. Fontaine ... [et al.]. — The Hague ; London : Nijhoff, 1982. — xviii,584p : ill ; 25cm. — (Forestry sciences)
Bibliography: p577-580. — Includes subject index
ISBN 90-247-2581-x : Unpriced B82-35973

333.75'09182'2 — Mediterranean region. Deforestation, *to 1980*
Thirgood, J. V.. Man and the Mediterranean forest : a history of resource depletion / J.V. Thirgood. — London : Academic, 1981. — x,194p : maps ; 24cm
Bibliography: p173-182. — Includes index
ISBN 0-12-687250-3 : £12.00 : CIP rev.
B81-13485

333.75'0941 — Great Britain. Natural resources: Forests. Management. Decision making
Williams, M. R. W.. Decision-making in forest management / M.R.W. Williams. — Chichester : Research Studies, c1981. — xviii,143p : ill ; 24cm. — (Forestry research studies series ; 1)
Bibliography: p139. — Includes index
ISBN 0-471-10097-8 : £11.80 : CIP rev.
B81-30285

333.75'0941 — Great Britain. Woodlands. Conservation & management
Peterken, G. F.. Woodland conservation and management / G.F. Peterken. — London : Chapman and Hall, 1981. — xv,328p : ill,maps,plans ; 26cm
Bibliography: p310-318. — Includes index
ISBN 0-412-12820-9 : £25.00 : CIP rev.
B81-31265

333.75'0941 — Great Britain. Woodlands. Conservation & management. Policies of Great Britain. *Forestry Commission*
Great Britain. *Forestry Commission.* The Forestry Commission & conservation. — Edinburgh : The Commission, 1980. — 12p : col.ill ; 21cm. — (Policy and procedure paper ; no.4)
ISBN 0-85538-077-2 (pbk) : Unpriced
B82-15521

333.75'09426'74 — Essex. Loughton. Epping Forest. Exploitation, *1630-1884*
Pratt, Barbara. The loppers of Loughton / Barbara Pratt. — Loughton (57 Smarts La., Loughton, Essex IG10 4BU) : Barbara Pratt Publications, c1981. — 14p,[5]p of plates (1fold.) : ill,ports,1geneal.table ; 21cm
ISBN 0-9507871-0-8 (pbk) : £0.75 B82-08141

333.75'13'0941 — Great Britain. Land use. Implications of afforestation
Afforestation : the case against expansion. — London (1 Wandsworth Rd, SW8 2LJ) : Ramblers' Association, [1980]. — 15p : ill ; 23cm. — (Brief for the countryside ; no.7)
£0.45 (unbound) B82-38408

Royal Institution of Chartered Surveyors. Forestry and land use. — [London] : Royal Institution of Chartered Surveyors, 1982. — 16p ; 30cm
Report of a working party of the Institution
Unpriced (pbk) B82-25361

333.75'13'0942547 — Leicestershire. Charnwood Forest. Land use, *43-1980*
Charnwood Forest : a changing landscape / editor John Crocker. — [Loughborough] : Loughborough Naturalists' Club, c1981. — 184p : ill,maps,1facsim ; 25x32cm
Maps on lining papers. — Limited ed. of 1,000 numbered copies. — Bibliography: p176-178. — Includes index
ISBN 0-905837-10-x : £15.00 B82-08069

333.76'0941 — Great Britain. Rural regions. Land use. Management. Implications of field sports
Piddington, Helen R.. Land management for shooting and fishing : a study of practice on farms and estates in Great Britain during 1971-76 / Helen R. Piddington. — [Cambridge] : University of Cambridge Department of Land Economy, 1981. — 131p : ill,1map ; 22cm. — (Occasional paper ; no.13)
Bibliography: p127-131
Unpriced B82-14889

333.76'0942 — England. Fields, *to 1974*
Taylor, Christopher, *1935-*. Fields in the English landscape / by Christopher Taylor. — London : Dent, 1975 (1982 [printing]). — 174p,[8]p of plates : ill,maps ; 22cm. — (Archaeology in the field series)
Bibliography: p165. — Includes index
ISBN 0-460-02232-6 (pbk) : £4.95 B82-26171

333.76'0944 — France. Rural regions. Land use, *1815-1914*
Clout, Hugh. The land of France 1815-1914. — London : Allen & Unwin, Nov.1982. — [176]p. — (The London research series in geography ; 1)
ISBN 0-04-911003-9 : £12.95 : CIP entry
B82-27186

333.76'11'0973 — United States. Agricultural land. Availability
The **Cropland** crisis : myth or reality? / Pierre R. Crosson, editor. — Baltimore ; London : Published for Resources for the Future by the Johns Hopkins University Press, c1982. — xxiii,250p : ill,1map ; 24cm
Includes index
ISBN 0-8018-2816-3 (cased) : £20.75
ISBN 0-8018-2817-1 (pbk) : Unpriced
B82-39776

333.76'13'09411 — Scotland. Rural regions. Land use. Information systems — *Proposals*
Rural land use information systems : report on a pilot project, Scotland. — [Edinburgh] ([New St. Andrew's House, Edinburgh EH1 3SZ]) : [Scottish Development Department Central Research Unit], 1980. — ii,72p ; 30cm
Cover title
£2.00 (spiral) B82-35110

333.76'13'0942264 — West Sussex. Brinsbury region. Agricultural land use, landscape conservation & nature conservation. Interrelationships
Farming and wildlife study 1980 / Sussex Farming and Wildlife Advisory Group and West Sussex College of Agriculture and Horticulture, Brinsbury. — Chichester (County Hall, Chichester, W. Sussex, PO19 1RQ) : West Sussex County Council, [1981]. — 18p : ill,maps ; 30cm
Unpriced (pbk) B82-04948

333.76'13'0942581 — Hertfordshire. North Hertfordshire *(District).* **Rural regions. Land use** — *For environment planning*
The **Countryside** of North Hertfordshire : its land uses and landscapes / [North Hertfordshire District Council]. — [Letchworth] ([Council Offices, Gernon Rd., Letchworth, Herts. SG6 3JF]) : [The Council], 1978. — iii,35p : col.maps ; 30cm. — (North Hertfordshire district plan. Topic studies)
£0.60 (pbk) B82-11579

333.76'13'0967825 — Tanzania. North Mkata Plain. Land use
Pitblado, J. Roger. The North Mkata Plain, Tanzania : a study of land capability and land tenure / J. Roger Pitblado. — Toronto ; London : Published for the University of Toronto, Dept. of Geography by the University of Toronto Press, c1981. — viii,178p,[6]p of plates : ill,maps ; 23cm. — (Research publications / University of Toronto. Department of Geography ; 16)
Bibliography: p167-178
ISBN 0-8020-3378-4 (pbk) : £6.00 B82-22620

333.76'16'0941 — Great Britain. Countryside. Conservation
Reynolds, Kev. The Spur book of countryside conservation / Kev Reynolds. — Edinburgh : Spurbooks, c1982. — 64p : ill ; 19cm. — (A Spurbooks venture guide)
ISBN 0-7157-2104-6 (pbk) : £1.25 B82-22945

333.76'16'0942 — England. Countryside. Conservation
The **Country** code book. — Cheltenham (John Dower House, Crescent Place, Cheltenham, Gloucestershire GL50 3RA) : Countryside Commission, [1982?]. — 24p : col.ill ; 19cm
Cover title. — Ill on inside back cover
Unpriced (pbk) B82-23825

Harrison, Fraser. Strange land : the countryside : myth and reality / Fraser Harrison. — London : Sidgwick & Jackson, 1982. — 133p ; 24cm
ISBN 0-283-98838-x (cased) : £7.95
ISBN 0-283-98861-4 (pbk) : £5.95 B82-14687

333.76'16'094283 — Humberside. Rural regions. Environment. Conservation — *Proposals*
Gill, David, *1927-*. Conservation : the rural landscape / David Gill. — [Beverley] ([c/o Director of Planning, Manor Rd, Beverley, N. Humberside HU17 7BX]) : Humberside County Council, 1981. — 15p ; 30cm
Cover title
£1.25 (spiral) B82-09964

333.77 — Dorset. Sites available for industries — *Serials*
[Land for industrial development *(Dorchester)***].** Land for industrial development / Dorset Planning Officers' Panel. — Mar. 1981-. — [Dorchester] ([c/o Planning Department, County Hall, Dorchester, Dorset DT1 1XJ]) : The Panel, 1981-. — v. : maps ; 30cm
Annual
ISSN 0262-7191 = Land for industrial development (Dorchester) : £5.00 B82-09678

333.77 — England. Industrial estates — *Directories*
English Industrial Estates Corporation. Trade index / The English Industrial Estates Corporation. — Gateshead : English Industrial Estates Corporation, 1981. — 43p ; 21cm
£2.50 (pbk) B82-12746

333.77 — Essex. Chelmsford. Offices. Development — *For environment planning*
Offices topic report : Chelmsford town centre district plan. — Chelmsford : Chelmsford Borough Council, 1980. — 35p,6folded leaves of plates : maps ; 30cm
Unpriced (pbk) B82-08728

333.77 — Great Britain. Commercial property
Daniels, Clive. UK commercial and industrial property into the 1980s / by Clive Daniels. — London : Economist Intelligence Unit, 1981. — 177p : ill ; 30cm. — (EIU special report ; no.107)
Bibliography: p173-174
Unpriced (pbk) B82-02574

333.77 — Great Britain. Urban regions. Inner areas. Residential areas. Environment. Quality
Roberts, Patricia, *1945- Aug.21-*. The quality of the residential environment in the inner city / Patricia Roberts. — London : Department of Town Planning, Polytechnic of the South Bank, c1981. — 51leaves ; 30cm. — (Occasional paper, ISSN 0143-4888 ; OP3/81)
Bibliography: leaves 48-51
ISBN 0-905267-20-6 (spiral) : £2.00
B82-02418

333.77 — London. Camden *(London Borough).* **Offices & warehouses. Development** — *Proposals* — *For environment planning*
A **Plan** for Camden : London Borough of Camden District Plan : proposals for the alteration of the written statement : policies for offices and warehousing. — [London] ([Camden Town Hall, Euston Rd., WC1H 8EQ]) : [Department of Planning and Communications], 1982. — 16p ; 30cm
Unpriced (unbound) B82-34492

333.77 — Norfolk. Norwich region. Housing land. Planning. Participation of public
Norwich area housing land : report on public consultation / [Norfolk County Council]. — Norwich (County Planning Office, County Hall, Martineau La., Norwich NR1 2DH) : Norfolk County Council, 1981. — 24,[63]p : 1form ; 30cm
£1.00 (pbk) B82-14033

333.77 — Norfolk. Norwich region. Housing land — *Proposals*
Norfolk structure plan : Norwich area housing land : proposed alterations : explanatory memorandum / Norfolk County Council. — [Norwich] ([County Planning Office, County Hall, Martineau La., Norwich NR1 2DH]) : [Norfolk County Council], 1981. — 13p : 1map ; 30cm
Cover title
£0.20 (pbk) B82-14032

333.77 — Scotland. Highland Region. Sites available for industries — *Practical information*
Development opportunities in industry : Highland Region of Scotland. — [Inverness] ([Regional Buildings, Glenurquhart Rd., Inverness IV3 5NX]) : Highland Regional Council, Development Department, [1982?]. — 67p : maps ; 31cm
Unpriced (spiral) B82-21663

333.77 — Urban regions. Land use. Planning
Bryant, C. R.. The city's countryside. — London : Longman, Sept.1982. — [272]p
ISBN 0-582-30045-2 (pbk) : £7.95 : CIP entry B82-20260

333.77 — West Sussex. Land for residential development
Land available for residential development at 1st July 1981 : West Sussex structure plan. — Chichester : West Sussex County Council, 1981. — [67]p : ill,maps(some col.) ; 30cm
Unpriced (spiral) B82-11959

333.77'13 — Urban regions. Land use. Planning
Chapin, F. Stuart. Hypothetical city exercise : workbook to accompany Urban land use planning, third edition / F. Stuart Chapin, Jr., and Edward J. Kaiser. — Urbana ; London : University of Illinois Press, c1979. — 140p : maps,chiefly forms ; 28cm
ISBN 0-252-00791-3 (pbk) : £4.90 B82-09667

333.77'16'06041 — Great Britain. Urban regions. Environment. Conservation. Promotion. Projects: European Campaign for Urban Renaissance — *Conference proceedings*
Whose town is it anyway? : proceedings of the conference held to review the progress of the European Campaign for Urban Renaissance in Britain / [organized by the] Department of the Environment ; technical editor Alun Sylvester-Evans, assisted by John Zetter, Derek Kerr and Mike Etkind. — London : H.M.S.O., 1982. — 80p : ill,1map ; 24cm
Ill on inside covers
ISBN 0-11-751602-3 (pbk) : £7.50 B82-23760

333.77'16'0941 — Great Britain. Urban regions. Environment. Conservation. Promotion. Projects: European Campaign for Urban Renaissance. Demonstration projects
Demonstration projects in the United Kingdom / European Campaign for Urban Renaissance. — London (Becker House, Room 635, 1 Lambeth Place Rd., SE1 7ER) : Department of the Environment, 1980. — 79p : ill,1map ; 30cm
Unpriced (sprial) B82-22449

333.7'8 — Recreation facilities. Geographical aspects
Smith, Stephen. Recreation geography. — London : Longman, Oct.1982. — [224]p. — (Themes in resource management)
ISBN 0-582-30050-9 (pbk) : £5.95 : CIP entry B82-24731

333.78 — Recreation facilities. Geographical aspects — *For schools*
Martin, Fred. Leisure / Fred Martin and Aubrey Whittle. — London : Hutchinson, 1982. — 128p : ill,maps,facsims,plans ; 24cm. — (Core geography)
Maps on inside covers
ISBN 0-09-144451-9 (pbk) : Unpriced : CIP rev. B81-28830

333.78'0941 — Great Britain. Recreation facilities. Management
Torkildsen, George. Leisure and recreation management. — London : Chapman and Hall, Dec.1982. — [400]p
ISBN 0-419-11740-7 (pbk) : £8.00 : CIP entry B82-29775

333.78'09411 — Scotland. Country parks. Management — *Proposals*
Management plans for country parks : a guide to their preparation. — Rev. — Redgorton : Countryside Commission for Scotland, 1982. — 10p ; 20cm
Previous ed.: 1980?
ISBN 0-902226-51-7 (pbk) : Unpriced B82-33043

333.78'09411 — Scotland. Rural regions. Outdoor recreation facilities. Testing. Projects
Product Testing and Demonstration Project : final report. — Perth : Countryside Commission for Scotland, 1980. — 27p : ill,1map ; 30cm
Unpriced (pbk) B82-35053

333.78'09413'2 — Scotland. Lothian Region. Leisure facilities & recreation facilities. Provision — *Proposals*
Leisure strategy : consultative draft / Lothian Regional Council, Department of Leisure Services. — [Edinburgh] ([40 Torphichen St., Edinburgh EH3 8JJ]) : [Lothian Regional Council, Leisure Services]
1: Urban recreation. — 1981. — 92leaves,[18] leaves of plates(some folded) : maps ; 30cm
Cover title
Unpriced (pbk) B82-20740

Leisure strategy : consultative draft / Lothian Regional Council, Department of Leisure Services. — [Edinburgh] ([40 Torphichen St., Edinburgh EH3 8JJ]) : [Lothian Regional Council, Leisure Services]
2: Countryside recreation. — 1981. — 88leaves : maps ; 30cm
Cover title
Unpriced (pbk) B82-20742

Leisure strategy : consultative draft / Lothian Regional Council, Department of Leisure Services. — [Edinburgh] ([40 Torphichen St., Edinburgh EH2 8JJ]) : [Lothian Regional Council, Leisure Services]
3: The arts. — 1981. — 67leaves : 1map ; 30cm
Cover title
Unpriced (pbk) B82-20741

333.78'09421'33 — London. Hammersmith and Fulham *(London Borough)*. Avonmore & Coningham. Recreation facilities
Noble, Paul. Recreational needs : facilities and organisations. — [London] ([Town Hall, King St., Hammersmith W6 9JU]) : Hammersmith & Fulham, 1981. — [64]p : maps ; 30cm. — (Research report ; 51)
Written by Paul Noble and Sue Williams
Unpriced (pbk) B82-06131

333.78'09421'33 — London. Hammersmith and Fulham *(London Borough)*. Avonmore & Coningham. Recreation facilities — *Proposals*
Noble, Paul. Recreational needs : a survey of children and young people : the main findings and conclusions. — [London] ([Town Hall, King St., Hammersmith W6 9JU]) : Hammersmith & Fulham, 1981. — [176]p : maps,forms ; 30cm. — (Research report ; 49)
Produced by Paul Noble and Sue Williams
Unpriced (pbk) B82-06130

333.78'09423'56 — Devon. Exeter. Recreation land
Casual recreation in Exeter. — Exeter : Exeter City Council, Planning Department, 1979. — [10]p : ill,maps ; 30cm
ISBN 0-86114-221-7 (unbound) : Unpriced B82-40959

333.78'09425 — England. East Midlands. Recreation facilities — *Proposals*
Regional Council for Sport and Recreation, East Midlands. Towards a regional strategy / the Regional Council for Sport and Recreation, East Midlands. — Nottingham (26 Musters Rd., West Bridgford, Nottingham NG2 7PL) : The Sports Council
Cover title
Issues report 3: Water-based recreation. — 1981. — 64p : 1col.map ; 30cm
£2.00 (spiral) B82-15264

Sport and recreation in the East Midlands : a regional strategy for the '80s / [prepared by the Regional Council for Sports and Recreation]. — Nottingham (26 Munster Rd., West Bridgford, Nottingham NG2 7PL) : Sports Council, East Midland Region, 1981. — 59p : 1map ; 21x30cm
Cover title. — Text on inside cover
£3.00 (spiral) B82-08001

333.78'09426'752 — Essex. Chelmsford. Leisure facilities & recreation facilities. Provision — *For environment planning*
Recreation and leisure topic report : Chelmsford town centre district plan. — Chelmsford : Chelmsford Borough Council, 1981. — 34p,6folded leaves of plates : maps ; 30cm
Unpriced (pbk) B82-08731

333.78'0973 — United States. Recreation land. Land use. Planning
Guiding land use decisions : planning and management for forests and recreation / edited by David W. Countryman, Denise M. Sofranko. — Baltimore ; London : Johns Hopkins University Press, c1982. — ix,251p : ill ; 24cm
Includes bibliographies and index
ISBN 0-8018-2650-0 : £15.00 B82-39777

333.78'158'09411 — Scotland. Landscape conservation & provision of outdoor recreation facilities in rural regions. Grants from Countryside Commission for Scotland
Countryside grants to private and voluntary bodies, individuals and public bodies other than local authorities. — Redgorton : Countryside Commission for Scotland, 1982. — 4p ; 20cm
ISBN 0-902226-56-8 (pbk) : Unpriced B82-33048

333.78'158'09411 — Scotland. Local authorities. Grants from Countryside Commission for Scotland: Grants for landscape conservation & provision of outdoor recreation facilities in rural regions
Countryside grants to local authorities. — Redgorton : Countryside Commission for Scotland, 1982. — 10p ; 20cm
ISBN 0-902226-59-2 (pbk) : Unpriced B82-33046

333.78'2 — Wilderness
Wilderness / edited by Vance Martin. — Moray : Findhorn, 1982. — 215p,[8]p of plates : ill (some col.),ports ; 24cm
ISBN 0-906191-61-0 (pbk) : £3.95 B82-27777

333.78'3'0942 — England. National parks. Management. Sociopolitical aspects
MacEwen, Ann. National parks : conservation or cosmetics? / Ann and Malcolm MacEwen. — London : Allen & Unwin, 1982. — xxii,314p : ill,maps ; 24cm. — (The Resource management series ; 5)
Bibliography: p287-297. — Includes index
ISBN 0-04-719003-5 (cased) : Unpriced : CIP rev.
ISBN 0-04-719004-3 (pbk) : £8.50 B81-33908

333.78'3'0942178 — London. Bromley *(London Borough)*. Parks: Crystal Palace Park. Development — *Proposals*
The Crystal Palace Museum and Park restoration project. — [London] ([84, Anerley Rd., Crystal Palace S.E.19]) : Crystal Palace Foundation, [1981]. — 1portfolio : ill,1facsim,plans ; 31cm
£2.00
Also classified at 760'.0444 B82-05576

333.78'4 — Great Britain. Coastal regions. Environment. Conservation — *Manuals*
The Coast and us : care and enjoyment / produced by the Council for Environmental Education for the English Tourist Board promotion Maritime England. — Reading (London Rd., Reading, RG1 5AQ) : Council for Environmental Education, School of Education, University of Reading, [1982?]. — 7pamphlets : ill(some col.),col.maps ; 22cm
£0.30 B82-28694

333.78'4 — Great Britain. Rural regions. Recreation facilities. Policies of Great Britain. *Forestry Commission*

Great Britain. *Forestry Commission.* The Forestry Commission & recreation. — Edinburgh : The Commission, [1980]. — 8p : col.ill ; 21cm. — (Policy and procedure paper ; no.2)
ISBN 0-85538-075-6 (pbk) : Unpriced B82-15520

333.78'4 — Scotland. Highland Region. Cairngorms. Environment. Effects of proposed development of ski slopes

Environmental impact study : proposed expansion of downhill skiing facilities at Coire an t'Sneachda, Coire an Lochain and Lurchers Gully, Cairngorm : survey and description of development proposals / [prepared by A.S.H. for the Cairngorm Chairlift Company]. — Glasgow (90 Mitchell St., Glasgow) : Anderson Semens Houston, 1981. — 27,17leaves,[24] leaves of plates : maps ; 30x42cm
Includes bibliographies
£20.00 (pbk) B82-01895

333.78'4'0941 — Great Britain. Water recreation facilities

Recreation : water and land / editor Bernard J. Dangerfield ; compiled ... by the Institution of Water Engineers and Scientists ; with a foreword by the Duke of Edinburgh. — London : The Institution, 1981. — xvi,336p,[16]p of plates : ill,maps ; 23cm. — (Water practice manuals ; 2)
Includes index
ISBN 0-901427-11-x : Unpriced B82-00427

333.78'4'0941423 — Scotland. Strathclyde Region. Oban. Water recreation facilities — *Proposals*

Oban marine centre : a proposal for tourism development / [The Highlands and Islands Development Board and Argyll and Bute District Council]. — [Argyll] ([Kilmory, Lochgilphead, Argyll PA31 8RT]) : [Argyll & Bute District Council, Department of Tourism, Leisure & Recreation], [1981]. — 14p : ill,maps ; 30cm
Unpriced (unbound) B82-26634

333.78'4'094226 — West Sussex. Water recreation facilities — *Proposals*

West Sussex. *County Council.* Water recreation in West Sussex : interim policies / West Sussex County Council. — [Chichester] : [West Sussex County Council], 1981. — 7p ; 30cm
Cover title
ISBN 0-86260-027-8 (spiral) : Unpriced B82-13797

333.79 — Energy resources

Bondi, *Sir* **Hermann.** Global energy considerations / Sir Hermann Bondi. — [Swansea] : Centre for Development Studies, University College of Swansea, 1982, c1981. — 7p ; 22cm. — (Occasional paper / Centre for Development Studies, University College of Swansea, ISSN 0114-9494 ; no.14)
Text on inside covers
ISBN 0-86094-104-3 (pbk) : Unpriced B82-27475

Energy. — Aldershot : Gower, Dec.1982. — [96]p
ISBN 0-566-00612-x : £10.00 : CIP entry B82-30315

Frazer, Frank. Discovering energy / by Frank Frazer. — Harlow : Longman, 1982, c1981. — 96p : ill(some col.),col.maps ; 27cm
Includes index
ISBN 0-582-25058-7 : £6.95 : CIP rev. B82-08444

Schumacher, E. F.. Schumacher on energy : speeches and writings of E.F. Schumacher / edited by Geoffrey Kirk. — London : Cape, 1982. — xvii,212p ; 23cm
Includes index
ISBN 0-224-01965-1 : £7.95 : CIP rev. B81-40273

333.79 — Energy resources — *Conference proceedings*

Energy systems analysis : international conference, 7th-11th October 1979, Dublin, Ireland : proceedings of the International Conference, held in Dublin, 9-11th October 1979 / edited by R. Kavanagh ; [the conference was jointly organized by the Commission of the European Communities Directorate-General Research, Science and Education, Brussels and the National Board for Science and Technology, Dublin, Ireland]. — Dordrecht ; London : Reidel, c1980. — xvi,678p : ill ; 24cm
Includes a chapter in French. — At head of title: Commission of the European Communities. — Bibliography: p618-620
ISBN 90-277-1111-9 : Unpriced B82-40486

International Conference on Energy Use Management *(3rd : 1981 : West Berlin).* Beyond the energy crisis. — Oxford : Pergamon, Nov.1981. — 3v.[(2500p.)]
Conference papers
ISBN 0-08-027589-3 : £175.00 : CIP entry B81-30287

333.79 — Energy resources. Economic aspects — *Conference proceedings*

Institute of Petroleum. *Conference (1981 : Cambridge).* Energy resources and finance : uncertainties and opportunities : proceedings of the Institute of Petroleum 1981 Annual Conference, Cambridge, UK. — London : Heyden on behalf of the Institute of Petroleum, London, c1982. — ix,67p : ill ; 25cm
ISBN 0-85501-664-7 : £19.00 : CIP rev. B82-03124

333.79 — Energy resources — *For schools*

Loraine, John A.. Energy policies around the world / John A. Loraine. — Glasgow : Blackie, 1982. — 67p : ill,1map ; 21cm. — (Crossroads)
Bibliography: p67
ISBN 0-216-91169-9 (pbk) : £1.75 B82-29240

333.79 — Energy resources. Policies of governments — *Comparative studies* — *Conference proceedings*

Oil or industry? : energy, industrialisation and economic policy in Canada, Mexico, the Netherlands, Norway and the United Kingdom / edited by Terry Barker, Vladimir Brailovsky. — London : Academic, 1981. — xiii,315p : ill ; 24cm
Conference papers. — Includes bibliographies and index
ISBN 0-12-078620-6 : £15.80 : CIP rev. B81-26789

333.79 — Energy resources. Political aspects — *Conference proceedings*

The **Hazards** of the international energy crisis : studies of the coming struggle for energy and strategic raw materials / edited by David Carlton and Carlo Schaerf. — London : Macmillan, 1982. — xviii,206p : ill,1map ; 23cm
Conference papers. — Includes index
ISBN 0-333-27206-4 : £20.00 B82-32222

333.79 — Energy resources. Social aspects — *Conference proceedings*

Mankind and energy. — Oxford : Elsevier Scientific, Dec.1981. — [700]p. — (Studies in environmental science ; 16)
Conference papers
ISBN 0-444-99715-6 : £60.00 : CIP entry B81-33861

333.79 — Renewable energy resources

Renewable sources of energy and the environment / Essam El-Hinnawi and Asit K. Biswas editors. — Dublin : Tycooly, 1981. — 219p : ill ; 26cm. — (Natural resources and the environment series ; v.6)
Includes bibliographies
ISBN 0-907567-05-3 (cased) : Unpriced
ISBN 0-907567-10-x (pbk) : Unpriced B82-08008

333.79 — Western world. Energy resources. Cooperation

Kohl, Wilfred L.. Western energy co-operation. — Aldershot : Gower, Dec.1982. — [96]p
ISBN 0-566-00611-1 : £10.00 : CIP entry B82-30314

333.79'0212 — Energy resources — *Statistics* — *Serials*

BP statistical review of world energy. — 1981-. — London : British Petroleum, [1982]-. — v. : col.ill,col.maps ; 30cm
Annual. — Continues: BP statistical review of the world oil industry
ISSN 0263-9815 = BP statistical review of world energy : Unpriced B82-40074

333.79'025 — Energy resources — *Directories*

World directory of energy information. — Aldershot : Gower
Vol.2: Middle East, Africa and Asia/Pacific. — July 1982. — [340]p
ISBN 0-566-02374-1 : £35.00 : CIP entry B82-12974

333.79'03 — Energy resources — *Polyglot dictionaries*

The **Multilingual** energy dictionary / Alan Isaacs, editor. — London : Muller, c1981. — 284p ; 26cm
ISBN 0-584-95568-5 : £10.95 B82-00790

333.79'05 — Energy resources. Economic aspects — *Serials*

Advances in the economics of energy and resources : a research annual. — Vol.1 (1979)-. — Greenwich, Conn. : JAI Press ; London (3 Henrietta St., WC2E 8LU) : Distributed by JAICON Press, 1979-. — v. ; 24cm
ISSN 0192-558x = Advances in the economics of energy and resources : £24.50 B82-02371

333.79'05 — Energy resources — *Serials*

Energy exploration & exploitation. — Vol.1, no.1-. — London : Graham & Trotman, [1981]-. — v. : ill,maps ; 25cm
Quarterly
ISSN 0144-5987 = Energy exploration & exploitation : £37.00 per year B82-20882

333.79'07204 — European Community countries. Energy resources. Research

Commission of the European Communities. Energy research and development programme : second status report (1975-1978). — The Hague ; London : Nijhoff, 1979. — 2v.(1055p) ; 25cm
ISBN 90-247-2220-9 : Unpriced
ISBN 90-247-2240-3 (v.1) : Unpriced
ISBN 90-247-2241-1 (v.2) : Unpriced B82-30127

333.79'072041 — Great Britain. Energy resources. Research projects — *Lists*

Furnival, J.. Energy : a register / compiled for the Department of Energy by J. Furnival with contributions from J. Foster and Susan E. Owens. — London : Social Science Research Council
Pt.2: Energy resources in the social sciences / compiled by Susan E. Owens. — 1980. — [430]p ; 30cm
Pt.2 has title Energy. — Includes bibliographies and index
ISBN 0-86226-005-1 (pbk) : £7.50 B82-36197

333.79'072041 — Great Britain. Renewable energy resources. Research & development

Conroy, Czech. Eclipse of the sun? : the future of renewable energy research in Britain / by Czech Conroy, Michael Flood, David Gordon. — London (377 City Rd, EC1V 1NA) : Friends of the Earth, 1982. — [18]p ; 30cm. — (Friends of the Earth energy paper ; no.5)
ISBN 0-905966-29-5 (pbk) : £1.95 B82-31977

333.79'072041 — Great Britain. Renewable energy resources. Research & development — *Serials*

RE news : renewable energy R & D / UK Department of Energy. — Issue 1 (June 1979)-. — Harwell (Building 156, AERE Harwell, Didcot, Oxon. OX11 0RA) : Energy Technology Support Unit for the Department, 1979-. — v. : ill ; 30cm
Irregular. — Description based on: Issue 5 (June 1981)
ISSN 0262-2556 = RE news : Unpriced B82-04911

333.79'072073 — United States. Energy resources. Research & development. Policies of government

Hunt, V. Daniel. Handbook of energy technology : trends and perspectives / V. Daniel Hunt. — New York ; London : Van Nostrand, c1982. — xii,1018p : ill ; 26cm
Bibliography: p982-986. — Includes index
ISBN 0-442-22555-5 : £50.15 B82-16326

333.79'072073 — United States. Energy resources. Research organisations — *Directories* — *Serials*

Energy research programs / edited by Jaques Cattell Press. — 1st ed. (1980)-. — New York ; London : R.R. Bowker, 1980-. — v. ; 29cm
Continues: Industrial research laboratories of the United States
£49.50 B82-11807

333.79'0724 — Energy resources. Ecological aspects. Mathematical models — *Conference proceedings*

Energy and ecological modelling : proceedings of a symposium held from 20 to 23 April 1981 at Louisville, Kentucky / sponsored by the International Society for Ecological Modelling (ISEM) in cooperation with Ecological Society of America ... [et al.] ; edited by W.J. Mitsch and R.W. Bosserman and J.M. Klopatek. — Amsterdam ; Oxford : Elsevier Scientific, 1981. — 839p : ill,maps ; 25cm. — (Developments in environmental modelling ; 1)
Includes bibliographies
ISBN 0-444-99731-8 : Unpriced B82-19624

333.79'0724 — Energy resources. Models

Lakshmanan, T. R.. Systems and models for energy and environmental analysis. — Aldershot : Gower, Feb.1983. — [244]p
ISBN 0-566-00558-1 : £20.00 : CIP entry B82-40903

333.79'0724 — Great Britain. Energy resources. Policies of government. Econometric models

Basu, Dipak R.. Future energy policies for the UK : an optimal control approach / Dipak R. Basu. — London : Macmillan, 1981. — xii,164p : ill ; 23cm
Includes bibliographies and index
ISBN 0-333-31277-5 : £20.00 B82-06657

333.79'09172'4 — Developing countries. Energy resources — *Conference proceedings*

Energy and environment in the developing countries / edited by Manas Chatterji. — Chichester : Wiley, c1981. — xii,357p : ill ; 24cm
Conference papers. — Includes bibliographies and index
ISBN 0-471-27993-5 : £19.00 : CIP rev. B81-33803

333.79'094 — Western Europe. Energy resources. Policies. Effects of shortages of petroleum — *Conference proceedings*

The **European** transition from oil : societal impacts and constraints on energy policy / [based on the Proceedings of the 49th Nobel Symposium held by the International Institute for Energy and Human Ecology (Beijer Institute), Royal Swedish Academy of Sciences, Stockholm, Sweden from 20-25 April, 1980] ; edited by Gordon T. Goodman, Lars A. Kristoferson and Jack M. Hollander. — London : Academic Press, 1981. — xvi,338p : ill ; 24cm
Includes bibliographies and index
ISBN 0-12-290420-6 : £20.60 : CIP rev. B81-18039

333.79'0941 — Great Britain. Energy resources. Management — *Conference proceedings*

Energy Management & Waste Heat Reovery Conference *(1980 : London)*. Energy Management & Waste Heat Recovery Conference : 25 and 26 March 1980 : Waldorf Hotel, London WC2 / [sponsored by the Institution of Plant Engineers] ; [organised by Conference Communication]. — [London?] ([138 Buckingham Palace Rd., SW1W 9SG?]) : [Institution of Plant Engineers?], [1980?]. — 132p in various pagings : ill ; 30cm
Unpriced (spiral)
Also classified at 621.402 B82-09410

333.79'0941 — Great Britain. Energy resources. Policies of government, *1945-1982*

Pearce, David, *19---*. United Kingdom energy policy : an historical overview, 1945-1982 / by David Pearce. — [Aberdeen] : [University of Aberdeen, Department of Political Economy], [1982]. — 64p : ill ; 31cm. — (Discussion paper / University of Aberdeen. Department of Political Economy ; 82-02)
Unpriced (pbk) B82-23263

333.79'09411 — Scotland. Energy resources — *Forecasts* — *Conference proceedings*

Energy in the '90s : proceedings of a conference sponsored by the Highlands and Islands Development Board and the Royal Society of Edinburgh, Aviemore, Scotland, 24-26 September 1980 / edited by Sir Kenneth Blaxter. — [Inverness] : Highlands and Islands Development Board in association with Royal Society of Edinburgh, c1980. — ix,108p : ill,1map ; 21cm
ISBN 0-902347-69-1 (pbk) : £8.00 B82-05051

333.79'0947 — Eastern Europe & Soviet Union. Energy resources. Political aspects

Stern, Jonathan P.. East European energy and East-West trade in energy / Jonathan P. Stern. — London : Policy Studies Institute, c1982. — 94p ; 21cm. — (Energy paper / British Institutes' Joint Energy Policy Programme ; no.1)
ISBN 0-85374-205-7 (pbk) : £4.50 B82-29574

333.79'0947 — Eastern Europe & Soviet Union. Energy resources — *Serials*

Quarterly energy review. USSR & Eastern Europe. Annual supplement. — 1981-. — London : Economist Intelligence Unit, 1981-. — v. ; 30cm
Supplement to: Quarterly energy review. USSR & Eastern Europe
ISSN 0262-3366 = Quarterly energy review. USSR & Eastern Europe. Annual supplement (corrected) : £20.00 B82-02392

333.79'0956 — Middle East. Alternative energy resources

Perera, Judith. Solar and other alternative energy in the Middle East / by Judith Perera. — London (Spencer House, 27 St James's Place, SW1A 1NT) : Economist Intelligence Unit, 1981. — 90p : col.ill,2maps ; 30cm. — (EIU special report ; no.108)
Unpriced (pbk) B82-05160

333.79'0956 — Middle East. Energy resources — *Serials*

Quarterly energy review. Middle East. Annual supplement. — 1981-. — London : Economist Intelligence Unit, 1981-. — v. ; 30cm
Supplement to: Quarterly energy review. Middle East
ISSN 0262-2149 = Quarterly energy review. Middle East. Annual supplement : £20.00 B82-03404

333.79'0973 — United States. Energy resources

Stephenson, Richard M.. Living with tomorrow : a factual look at America's resources / Richard M. Stephenson. — New York ; Chichester : Wiley, c1981. — vii,280p : ill ; 24cm
Bibliography: p269-270. — Includes index
ISBN 0-471-09457-9 : £16.75 B82-13388

333.79'0973 — United States. Energy resources. Economic aspects

Uri, Noel D.. Dimensions of energy economics / by Noel D. Uri. — Greenwich, Conn. : Jai Press ; London : Distributed by Jaicon Press, c1981. — xvi,176p : ill ; 24cm. — (Contemporary studies in economic and financial analysis ; v.32)
Includes index
ISBN 0-89232-226-8 : Unpriced B82-33525

333.79'0973 — United States. Energy resources. Policies

Energy, economics, and the environment : toward a comprehensive perspective / edited by Gregory A. Daneke. — [Lexington, Mass.] : Lexington Books ; [Aldershot] : Gower [distributor], 1982. — xviii,283p ; 24cm
ISBN 0-669-04717-1 : £19.50 B82-32258

Landsberg, Hans H.. High energy costs : uneven, unfair, unavoidable? / Hans H. Landsberg and Joseph M. Dukert. — Baltimore ; London : Published for Resources for the Future by Johns Hopkins University Press, c1981. — xiii,104p : ill,2maps ; 23x24cm
Includes index
ISBN 0-8018-2781-7 (cased) : £9.25
ISBN 0-8018-2782-5 (pbk) : Unpriced B82-34348

333.79'0973 — United States. Energy resources. Policies of government. Environmental aspects — *Conference proceedings*

Environment, energy, public policy : toward a rational future / edited by Regina S. Axelrod. — Lexington, Mass. : Lexington Books ; [Aldershot] : Gower [distributor], 1981. — xiv,175p : ill,1map ; 24cm
Conference papers. — Includes index
ISBN 0-669-03460-6 : £12.00 B82-00397

333.79'11'091734 — Rural regions. Energy supply — *Conference proceedings*

Energy for rural and island communities II : proceedings of the Second International Conference, held at Inverness, Scotland, 1-4 September 1981 / edited by John Twidell ; sponsored and assisted by U.N.E.S.C.O. ... [et al.]. — Oxford : Pergamon, 1982. — x,427p : ill,maps ; 26cm
Includes bibliographies and index
ISBN 0-08-027606-7 : £25.00 : CIP rev. B82-05375

333.79'12 — Energy resources — *Forecasts*

Energy-present and future options. — Chichester : Wiley
Vol.1 / edited by David Merrick and Richard Marshall. — c1981. — ix,340p,[2],leaves of plates : ill,maps ; 24cm
Includes index
ISBN 0-471-27922-6 : £21.00 : CIP rev. B81-19177

333.79'12 — Energy resources — *Forecasts* — *Conference proceedings*

Long-term energy resources : an international conference / sponsored by the United Nations Institute for Training and Research (UNITAR) and Petro-Canada in cooperation with United Nations Development Programme ... [et al.] November 26-December 7, 1979, Montreal, Quebec, Canada ; Joseph Barnea scientific secretary ; R.F. Meyer editor ; J.C. Olson associate editor. — Boston [Mass.] ; London : Pitman, c1981. — 3v.(lxiii,2111p) : ill,charts,maps ; 25cm
Includes bibliographies and index
ISBN 0-273-08534-4 : Unpriced B82-10847

333.79'12 — Energy. Supply & demand

Hedley, Don. World energy : the facts and the future / Don Hedley. — London : Euromonitor, 1981. — 368p : ill,maps ; 23cm
Bibliography: p367-368
ISBN 0-903706-60-1 : £15.00 B82-11859

333.79'12 — Energy. Supply & demand — *Forecasts*

An **Efficient** energy future. — London : Butterworths
Pt.1. — Feb.1983. — [600]p
ISBN 0-408-01328-1 : £25.00 : CIP entry B82-38291

Energy supply-demand integrations to the year 2000 : global and national studies : third technical report of the Workshop on Alternative Energy Strategies (WAES) / Paul S. Basile, editor ; Carroll L. Wilson, WAES projects director. — Cambridge, Mass. ; London : MIT Press, c1977 (1978 [printing]). — xiv,706p : ill ; 29cm
ISBN 0-262-23083-6 : £28.00 B82-35062

333.79'12'018 — Great Britain. Urban regions. Energy. Supply & demand. Spatial analysis

Beaumont, John R.. Future cities : spatial analysis of energy issues / John R. Beaumont and Paul Keys. — Chichester : Research Studies Press, c1982. — xviii,198p : ill ; 24cm. — (Geography and public policy research studies series ; 3)
Bibliography: p183-193. — Includes index
ISBN 0-471-10451-5 : £18.50 : CIP rev. B82-14230

333.79'12'05 — Energy. Supply & demand — *Serials*

Energy economist : an international analysis. — Nov. 1981-. — London (10 Cannon St., EC4P 4BY) : Financial Times Business Information, 1981-. — v. ; 30cm
Monthly
ISSN 0262-7108 = Energy economist : £150 per year B82-08454

333.79'12'0724 — Great Britain. Energy. Demand. Mathematical models

Littlechild, S. C.. Energy strategies for the UK. — London : Allen & Unwin, Oct.1982. — [256]p
ISBN 0-04-339029-3 : £15.00 : CIP entry B82-23086

Westoby, Richard. Price elasticities for energy inputs in the UK domestic and industrial sectors under conditions of non-neutral technical change / by Richard Westoby. — Aberdeen : University of Aberdeen, Department of Political Economy, [1981]. — 25leaves ; 30cm. — (Discussion paper / University of Aberdeen Department of Political Economy ; no.81-13)
Bibliography: leaves 24-25
Unpriced (pbk) B82-05826

333.79'12'0724 — United States. Energy resources. Supply & demand. Forecasting. Mathematical models

DeSouza, Glenn R.. Energy policy and forecasting : economic, financial and technological dimensions / Glenn R. DeSouza. — Lexington, Mass. : Lexington Books ; Aldershot : Gower [distributor], 1982, c1981. — xv,218p : ill ; 24cm
Bibliography: p197-209. — Includes index
ISBN 0-669-03614-5 : £16.50 B82-08997

333.79'12'094 — Europe. Energy. Supply & demand — *Forecasts*

Ray, George. European energy prospects to 1990 / George Ray and Colin Robinson. — London (42, Colebrooke Row., N1 8AF) : Staniland Hall Associates, 1982. — 121p ; 21x30cm
Unpriced (cased) B82-24396

333.79'12'0941 — Great Britain. Energy. Supply & demand — *Forecasts*

Forecasts of demand for energy and electricity. — Dorchester : Planning Department, Dorset County Council, 1981. — 20p ; 21cm. — (Nuclear power stations ; information paper no.3)
Cover title. — Text on inside cover
ISBN 0-85216-298-7 (pbk) : Unpriced B82-12741

333.79'12'0941 — Great Britain. Energy. Supply & demand — *Liberal Party viewpoints*

Bruce, Malcolm. Putting energy to work / by Malcolm Bruce. — Edinburgh (2 Atholl Pl., Edinburgh) : Scottish Liberal Club, [1982?]. — 20p ; 21cm
Cover title
£0.50 (pbk) B82-24387

333.79'12'0973 — United States. Energy. Demand. Elasticity. Econometric models

Bohi, Douglas R.. Analyzing demand behavior : a study of energy elasticities / Douglas R. Bohi. — Baltimore ; London : Published for Resources for the Future by the Johns Hopkins University Press, c1981. — xiv,177p ; 24cm
Bibliography: p165-172. — Includes index
ISBN 0-8018-2705-1 : Unpriced B82-16914

333.79'12'174927 — Arab countries. Energy resources - *Forecasts*

Arab energy. — Oxford : Pergamon, Apr.1981. — [250]p
ISBN 0-08-027581-8 : £21.00 : CIP entry B81-04200

333.79'13 — Environment. Effects of exploitation of energy resources

The **Environmental** impacts of production and use of energy : an assessment / prepared by the United Nations Environment Programme ; Essam E. El-Hinnawi, study director. — Dublin : Published for the United Nations Environment Programme by the Tycooly Press, c1981. — 322p : ill 25cm. — (Natural resources and the environment series ; v.1)
Includes bibliographies
ISBN 0-907567-00-2 : Unpriced B82-05557

333.79'13'094249 — West Midlands *(Metropolitan County)*. **Energy. Consumption,** *1951-1974*

Borg, Neville. Energy usage and activity in the West Midlands 1951-1974 / Neville Borg. — Birmingham : Department of Transportation & Environmental Planning, University of Birmingham, 1981. — 2v. : ill,maps ; 30cm. — (Departmental publications / Department of Transportation & Environmental Planning, University of Birmingham ; no.57)
ISBN 0-7044-0573-3 (pbk) : Unpriced B82-26625

333.79'13'096651 — Developing countries. Energy. Consumption by man — *Study regions: Gambia*

Haswell, Margaret. Energy for subsistence / Margaret Haswell. — London : Macmillan, 1981. — xii,100p : ill ; 23cm
Bibliography: p92-94. — Includes index
ISBN 0-333-28734-7 : £15.00 B82-06642

333.79'16 — Energy resources. Conservation

The **Energy** debate. — Croydon : Benn, Nov.1982. — [160]p
ISBN 0-85459-087-0 : £10.00 : CIP entry B82-28756

333.79'16 — Energy resources. Conservation — *Conference proceedings*

Energy, money, materials and engineering. — Oxford : Pergamon, Dec.1982. — [475]p. — (Institution of Chemical Engineers symposium series ; 78)
Conference papers
ISBN 0-08-028774-3 : £36.00 : CIP entry B82-32279

333.79'16 — Energy resources. Conservation. Environmental aspects

National perspectives on management of energy/environment systems. — Chichester : Wiley, Dec.1982. — [320]p. — (Wiley IIASA international series on applied systems analysis ; 11)
ISBN 0-471-10022-6 : £22.00 : CIP entry B82-30812

333.79'16 — Energy resources. Conservation. Implications of use of lead in motor vehicle petrol. Mathematical models

Price, Brian. Lead in petrol : an energy analysis / by Brian Price. — London : Friends of the Earth, c1982. — 12p ; 30cm
ISBN 0-905966-27-9 (pbk) : £1.00 B82-20098

333.79'16'0321 — Energy resources. Conservation — *Dictionaries*

Kut, David. Illustrated dictionary of applied energy conservation. — London : Kogan Page, Oct.1982. — [350]p
ISBN 0-85038-577-6 : £30.00 : CIP entry B82-24262

333.79'16'05 — Energy resources. Conservation — *Serials*

Energy action bulletin / Neighbourhood Energy Action. — Issue 1 (Dec. 1981)-. — Newcastle upon Tyne (81 Jesmond Rd, Newcastle upon Tyne NE2 1NH) : Energy Inform, 1981-. — v. : ill ; 30cm
Quarterly
ISSN 0262-5296 = Energy action bulletin : £7.00 per year B82-18490

333.79'16'0724 — Energy resources. Conservation. Models — *Conference proceedings*

Energy modelling studies and conservation : proceedings of a seminar of the United Nations Economic Commission for Europe, Washington, D.C., 24-28 March 1980. — Oxford : Published for the United Nations by Pergamon, 1982. — xxxiv,689p : ill,maps ; 26cm
Includes 2 papers in French. — Includes bibliographies
ISBN 0-08-027416-1 : £47.50 : CIP rev.
Also classified at 333.7'2 B81-22566

333.79'16'091732 — Urban regions. Energy resources. Conservation — *For children*

Moorcraft, Colin. Homes & cities / Colin Moorcraft. — London : Watts, 1982. — 38p : col.ill,col.maps,1port ; 30cm. — (Energy)
Includes index
ISBN 0-85166-941-7 : £3.99 B82-25328

333.79'16'0973 — United States. Energy resources. Conservation

Hunt, V. Daniel. Handbook of conservation and solar energy : trends and perspectives / V. Daniel Hunt. — New York ; London : Van Nostrand Reinhold, c1982. — xix,385p : ill,3maps ; 26cm
Bibliography: p373-375. — Includes index
ISBN 0-442-20056-0 : £33.60 B82-38591

Ross, Marc H.. Our energy : regaining control : a strategy for economic revival through redesign in energy use / Marc H. Ross, Robert H. Williams. — New York ; London : McGraw-Hill, c1981. — vii,354p : ill ; 25cm
Includes index
ISBN 0-07-053894-8 : £14.95 B82-25218

333.79'17 — Great Britain. Industries. Energy supply. Pricing. Policies of government. Great Britain. *Parliament House of Commons. Select Committee on Energy.* **Second report ... session 1980-81** — *Critical studies*

Great Britain. *Parliament. House of Commons. Select Committee on Energy.* First special report from the Select Committee on Energy, session 1981-82 : Government observations on the Second report of the Committee, session 1980-81 (industrial energy pricing policy). — London : H.M.S.O., 1982. — xip ; 25cm. — (HC ; 169)
ISBN 0-10-216982-9 (unbound) : £1.50 B82-22033

333.79'24 — Nuclear power. Attitudes of trade unions

Dalton, Les K.. Trade unions and nuclear power : an international survey / Les K. Dalton. — Nottingham (Bertrand Russell House, Gamble Street, Nottingham, NG7 4ET) : Spokesman for the Bertrand Russell Peace Foundation and the Socialist Environment and Resources Association, [1979]. — 25p ; 21cm. — (Spokesman pamphlet ; no.70)
£0.50 (unbound) B82-17675

333.79'24 — Nuclear power. Policies of governments, *to 1980*

Pringle, Peter, *1940-*. The nuclear barons / Peter Pringle & James Spigelman. — London : Joseph, 1982, c1981. — xii,578p ; 24cm
Originally published: New York : Holt, Rinehart & Winston, 1981. — Bibliography: p449-465. — Includes index
ISBN 0-7181-2061-2 : £12.95 B82-11323

333.79'24 — Nuclear power. Political aspects

Moss, Norman. The politics of uranium / Norman Moss. — London : Deutsch, 1981. — vii,239p ; 22cm
Bibliography: p226-228. — Includes index
ISBN 0-233-97397-4 (pbk) : £4.95 B82-04521

333.79'24 — Nuclear power. Political aspects — *Conference proceedings*

Missiles, reactors and civil liberties : against the nuclear state / ed. Gari Donn. — Glasgow : Scottish Council for Civil Liberties, [1982]. — 44p : 3maps ; 21cm
Conference papers
ISBN 0-906502-04-7 (pbk) : £1.40 B82-26849

333.79′24′091722 — Developing countries. Social conditions. Effects of use of nuclear power by developed countries

Nuclear links : the chain-reaction of energy arms and underdevelopment / edited by Adi Cooper ... [et al.]. — [Oxford] ([232 Cowley Rd., Oxford OX4 1UH]) : [Third World First], [1982?]. — 32p : ill ; 30cm
Cover title. — Text on inside covers
£0.50 (pbk) B82-41024

333.79′24′09485 — Sweden. Nuclear power, *1979-1980*. Political aspects

Little, P. Mark. The nuclear power issue in Swedish politics (March 1979-March 1980) / P. Mark Little. — [Hull] : University of Hull, Department of Politics, 1982. — 39p : ill ; 30cm. — (Hull papers in politics, ISSN 0142-7377 ; no.27)
Unpriced (pbk) B82-38226

333.79′24′0973 — United States. Nuclear power. Policies of government, *1974-1977*

Brenner, Michael J.. Nuclear power and non-proliferation : the remaking of U.S. policy / Michael J. Brenner. — Cambridge : Cambridge University Press, 1981. — xi,324p ; 24cm
Includes index
ISBN 0-521-23517-0 : £20.00 B82-02678

333.8 — SUBSURFACE RESOURCES

333.8′2 — Energy resources: Fossil fuels. Exploration. Economic aspects

The **economics** of exploration for energy resources / [edited] by James B. Ramsey. — Greenwich, Conn. ; London : Jai Press, c1981. — xix,342p : ill,1map ; 24cm. — (Contemporary studies in economic and financial analysis ; v.26)
Includes bibliographies and index
ISBN 0-89232-159-8 : Unpriced B82-33668

333.8′212 — Fuel resources: Hydrocarbons. Supply & demand — *Conference proceedings*

World hydrocarbon markets. — Oxford : Pergamon, Sept.1982. — [225]p
Conference papers
ISBN 0-08-029962-8 : £20.00 : CIP entry B82-25165

333.8′22 — Fuel resources: Coal

Grainger, L.. Coal utilisation : technology, economics and policy / L. Grainger and J. Gibson. — London : Graham & Trotman, 1981. — xxii,503p : ill,1map ; 25cm
Bibliography: p489-496. — Includes index
ISBN 0-86010-266-1 : £18.00 : CIP rev. B81-28143

James, Peter, *1953-*. The future of coal / Peter James. — London : Macmillan, 1982. — xxiii,271p : ill,maps ; 23cm
Includes index
ISBN 0-333-30731-3 : £20.00 B82-32219

Tsai, Shirley Cheng. Fundamentals of coal beneficiation and utilization. — Oxford : Elsevier Scientific, Apr.1982. — [400]p. — (Coal science and technology ; v.2)
ISBN 0-444-42082-7 : CIP entry B82-14049

333.8′22′0321 — Fuel resources: coal — *Encyclopaedias*

Todd, Arthur H. J.. Lexicon of terms relating to the assessment and classification of coal resources. — London : Graham & Trotman, Aug.1982. — [176]p
ISBN 0-86010-403-6 : £25.00 : CIP entry B82-21742

333.8′22′0941 — Great Britain. Coal. Production. Environmental aspects

Coal and the environment / Commission on Energy and the Environment. — London : H.M.S.O., 1981. — xv,257p [12]p of plates : ill,maps ; 30cm
Bibliography: p238-241. — Includes index
ISBN 0-11-751585-x (pbk) : £23.00
Also classified at 333.8′2213′0941 B82-14337

333.8′2213′0941 — Great Britain. Coal. Use. Environmental aspects

Coal and the environment / Commission on Energy and the Environment. — London : H.M.S.O., 1981. — xv,257p [12]p of plates : ill,maps ; 30cm
Bibliography: p238-241. — Includes index
ISBN 0-11-751585-x (pbk) : £23.00
Primary classification 333.8′22′0941 B82-14337

333.8′23 — Developing countries. Natural gas & petroleum deposits. Prospecting & exploitation — *Conference proceedings*

Petroleum exploration strategies in developing countries. — London : Graham and Trotman, Jan.1982. — [240]p
Conference papers
ISBN 0-86010-346-3 : £15.00 : CIP entry B82-00172

333.8′23′0916336 — North Sea. Buchan oil field. Natural gas deposits & petroleum deposits. Exploitation by British Petroleum Company

The **Buchan** oilfield. — London (Britannic House, Moor La., E.C.2) : BP Petroleum Development Limited, [1981]. — 7p : ill(some col.),1col.map ; 30cm
Col. ill on inside covers
Unpriced (pbk) B82-39908

333.8′23′0916336 — North Sea. East Shetland oil field. Natural gas deposits & petroleum deposits. Exploitation by British Petroleum Company

Shetland and oil development : the oilfields in the East Shetland basin and the terminal at Sullom Voe. — London ([Britannic House, Moor La., E.C.2]) : BP Petroleum Development Limited, 1981. — 8p : ill(some col.),1col.map ; 30cm
Text and ill on inside covers
Unpriced (pbk) B82-39907

Sullom Voe terminal and the East Shetland oilfields / [compiled by Derek Lamb]. — Lerwick (1 Mounthooly St., P.O. Box 16, Lerwick, Shetland) : Oil Industry in Shetland, [1978]. — 16p : ill,maps(some col.),1port ; 30cm
Cover title: Oil in Shetland. — Col. map and ill on inside covers
Unpriced (pbk) B82-39906

333.8′23′0916336 — North Sea. Magnus oil field. Natural gas deposits & petroleum deposits. Exploitation by British Petroleum Company

The **Magnus** oilfield. — London (Britannic House, Moor La., E.C.2) : BP Petroleum Development Limited, 1982. — 17p : ill(some col.),2col.maps ; 30cm
Ill and text on inside covers
Unpriced (pbk) B82-39909

333.8′23′0916336 — North Sea. Natural gas & petroleum deposits. Exploitation

North Sea oil & gas / UK offshore Operators Association. — London (192 Sloane St, SW1X 9QX) : The Association, [1981?]. — 31p : col.ill,2maps ; 30cm
Cover title
Unpriced (pbk) B82-26587

333.8′23′0916336 — North Sea. Natural gas deposits & petroleum deposits. Exploitation by British Petroleum Company

BP and Britain′s oil. — London (Britannic House, Moor La., E.C.2) : British Petroleum Company, Public Affairs and Information Department, [1978]. — 39p : ill(some col.),maps(some col.) ; 30cm
Ill and col. map on inside covers
Unpriced (pbk) B82-39905

The **Offshore** search. — London (Britannic House, Moor La., E.C.2) : British Petroleum Company, [1977]. — 8p : ill(some col.),2col.maps ; 30cm
Cover title. — Text and ill on inside covers
Unpriced (pbk) B82-39904

333.8′23′094 — North-western Europe. Continental shelf. Natural gas & petroleum deposits. Exploitation — *Serials*

North West European continental shelf oil & gas field development survey. — [Jan. 1981]-[July 1981]. — [Inverkeithing] ([20 Burleigh Cres., Inverkeithing, Fife KY11 1DQ]) : [Institute of Petroleum], 1981-1981. — 1v. ; 30cm
Two issues yearly. — Supplement to: Petroluem review (London : 1968). — Continued by: North West Europe offshore development survey
ISSN 0263-2500 = North West European continental shelf oil & gas field development survey : Unpriced B82-22657

333.8′23′09415 — Ireland. Offshore natural gas & petroleum deposits. Exploitation — *Sinn Féin The Workers′ Party viewpoints*

The **Great** Irish oil and gas robbery : a case study of monopoly capital / Research Section, Department of Economic Affairs, Sinn Fein The Workers′ Party. — Rev. ed. — Dublin : Repsol, 1977. — 120p : ill,1map,facsims ; 18cm. — (Studies in political economy)
Previous ed.: 1974. — Bibliography: p120
ISBN 0-86064-006-x (pbk) : £1.84 B82-17005

333.8′23′094227 — Hampshire. Natural gas deposits & petroleum deposits. Exploitation. Policies of Hampshire. *County Council*

Oil and gas exploration and exploitation in Hampshire. — Winchester (The Castle, Winchester) : County Planning Department, [1982?]. — 17p,1leaf of plate : 1map ; 30cm. — (Strategic planning paper / Hampshire County Council ; no.9)
Unpriced (unbound) B82-38213

333.8′232′0916336 — North Sea. Petroleum deposits. Exploitation. Environmental aspects — *Conference proceedings*

International Conference on Oil and the Environment *(1980 : University of Edinburgh)*. Onshore impacts of offshore oil / [proceedings of the International Conference on Oil and the Environment, Scotland 1980, held in the Pollock Halls, University of Edinburgh, 28 September-1 October] ; edited by William J. Cairns and Patrick M. Rogers. — London : Applied Science, c1981. — xvii,319p : ill,maps ; 23cm
Includes bibliographies and index
ISBN 0-85334-974-6 : £24.00 : CIP rev. B81-20161

333.8′232′0916336 — North Sea. Petroleum deposits. Exploitation. Policies of British & Norwegian governments

Noreng, Øystein. The oil industry and government strategy in the North Sea / Øystein Noreng. — London : Croom Helm, c1980. — 268p : ill,2maps ; 23cm
Includes index
ISBN 0-85664-850-7 : £14.95 : CIP rev. B80-09116

333.8′232′094233 — Dorset. Petroleum deposits. Exploitation, *to 1981*

Sherry, Desmond. Oil in Dorset / by D. Sherry. — 3rd ed. (rev.). — Bournemouth : Teachers′ Centre, 1981. — 10p ; 22cm. — (Bournemouth local studies publications ; no.641)
Previous ed.: 1980. — Text on inside cover. — Bibliography: inside back cover
ISBN 0-906287-38-3 (pbk) : £0.25 B82-12388

333.8′2321′095357 — United Arab Emirates. Petroleum deposits. Exploitation. Concessions, *1939-1981*

Al-Otaiba, Mana Saeed. The petroleum concession agreements of the United Arab Emirates 1939-1981. — London : Croom Helm Vol.1: 1939-1971. — Jan.1982. — [176]p
ISBN 0-7099-1915-8 : CIP entry B81-38840

333.8′23211 — Fuel resources: Petroleum. Stockpiling

International oil supplies and stockpiling : national policies, commercial practices and emergency uses : conference proceedings, Hamburg, September 17 and 18, 1981 / edited by Edward N. Krapels. — London : Economist Intelligence Unit, c1982. — 71p : ill,1col.map ; 30cm
Unpriced (pbk) B82-17326

333.8′23212 — Fuel resources: Petroleum. Supply & demand. Forecasting

Odell, Peter R.. The future of oil. — 2nd ed. — London : Kogan Page, Jan.1983. — [200]p
Previous ed.: 1980
ISBN 0-85038-625-x : £10.95 : CIP entry
B82-35187

333.8′23213′0941 — Great Britain. Petroleum. Consumption. Management

Institute of Petroleum. *Conference (1978 : London).* The effective use of petroleum : proceedings of the Institute of Petroleum 1978 Annual Conference London, England. — London : Heyden on behalf of the institute, c1979. — xiii,265p : ill ; 25cm
ISBN 0-85501-324-9 : Unpriced
Primary classification 333.8′23216′0941
B82-05130

333.8′23216′0941 — Great Britain. Petroleum. Conservation. Management

Institute of Petroleum. *Conference (1978 : London).* The effective use of petroleum : proceedings of the Institute of Petroleum 1978 Annual Conference London, England. — London : Heyden on behalf of the institute, c1979. — xiii,265p : ill ; 25cm
ISBN 0-85501-324-9 : Unpriced
Also classified at 333.8′23213′0941 B82-05130

333.8′5 — Bedfordshire. Oxford clay deposits. Exploitation. Policies of Bedfordshire. *County Council — Proposals*

Bedfordshire. *County Council.* Oxford clay : subject plan : draft consultation : April 1982. — Bedford ([County Hall, Bedford MK2 9AP]) : [Bedfordshire County Council], [1982]. — 112p : maps ; 30cm
Unpriced (pbk) B82-36019

333.8′5 — Hampshire. Sand deposits & gravel deposits. Exploitation *— For environment planning*

Hampshire minerals local plan : excluding hydrocarbons / background reports. — Winchester (The Castle, Winchester) : Hampshire County Council, 1982. — 72p in various pagings + 5 maps(60x42cm folded to 20x14cm) : maps(some col.) ; 30cm
Maps in pocket
Unpriced (pbk) B82-38210

333.8′5 — Mineral deposits. Exploitation. Economic aspects

Callot, F.. World production and consumption of minerals in 1978 / by F. Callot. — London : Mining Journal, 1981. — vi,109p : ill ; 28cm
Translated from the French
ISBN 0-900117-25-7 (pbk) : Unpriced
B82-00085

333.8′5 — Mineral resources. Exploitation. Management *— Conference proceedings*

National and international management of mineral resources : proceedings of a joint meeting of the Institution of Mining and Metallurgy, The Society of Mining Engineers of AIME and the Metallurgical Society of Aime held in London from 27 to 30 May, 1980 / edited by Michael J. Jones. — London : The Institution of Mining and Metallurgy, c1981. — viii,350p : ill,charts,maps ; 30cm
Includes index
ISBN 0-900488-58-1 (pbk) : Unpriced
B82-15425

333.8′5 — Natural resources. Scarcity *— Study examples: Mercury*

Roxbourgh, Nigel. Policy responses to resource depletion : the case of mercury / by Nigel Roxburgh. — Greenwich, Conn. : Jai Press ; London (3 Henrietta St., WC2E 8LU) : Distributed by Jaicon Press, c1980. — xv,219p,[1]folded leaf of plate : ill ; 24cm. — (Contemporary studies in economic and financial analysis ; v.21)
Includes index
ISBN 0-89232-093-1 : £20.60 B82-02074

333.8′5 — Natural resources: Uranium. Supply & demand *— Forecasts*

The **Balance** of supply and demand 1978-1990. — Edenbridge : Mining Journal Books, 1979. — ix,61p : ill ; 23cm
ISBN 0-900117-19-2 (pbk) : Unpriced
B82-17285

333.8′5 — Oceans. Bed. Manganese nodules

Assessment of manganese nodule resources : the data and the methodologies. — London : Graham & Trotman, Mar.1982. — [88]p. — (Seabed minerals series ; v.1)
ISBN 0-86010-347-1 : £12.00 : CIP entry
B82-06529

333.8′5′09174927 — Arab countries. Mineral resources

Habashi, F.. Mineral resources of the Arab countries / F. Habashi and F.A. Bassyouni. — 2nd ed. — London : Chemecon, 1982. — 60p,[39]p of plates : ill,maps(some col.) ; 31cm
Previous ed.: Quebec : Research Group in Energy and Natural Resources, Laval University, 198?. — Bibliography: p57-59
ISBN 0-902777-54-8 : Unpriced B82-31343

333.8′5′0941 — Great Britain. Mineral resources. Exploitation. Political aspects

Robert, Peter W.. Mineral resources in regional and strategic planning / Peter W. Roberts and Tim Shaw. — Aldershot : Gower, c1982. — 165p ; 23cm
Bibliography: p150-160. — Includes index
ISBN 0-566-00395-3 : Unpriced : CIP rev.
B82-03621

333.8′5′094227 — Hampshire. Mineral deposits. Exploitation *— Proposals — For environment planning*

Hampshire minerals local plan : excluding hydrocarbons : consultation draft. — Winchester (The Castle, Winchester, [SO23 8UJ]) : Hampshire County Council, 1982. — 62p : ill,maps(some col.) ; 30cm
Five maps on 5 folded sheets in pocket
Unpriced (pbk) B82-37958

333.8′5′094229 — Berkshire. Mineral deposits. Exploitation. Policies of Berkshire. *County Council — Proposals*

Minerals subject plan : proposals to meet the justifiable demand for minerals and rehabilitation of workings. — [Reading] ([Shire Hall, Shinfield Park, Reading, Berks.]) : [Berkshire County Council], [1982?]. — 99p : ill(some col.) ; 30cm + 2col.maps(2sheets ; 62x80cm folded to 31x20cm)
£2.50 (spiral) B82-22542

333.8′5′094259 — Buckinghamshire. Mineral deposits. Exploitation *— Proposals — For structure planning*

Buckinghamshire. *County Council.* Mineral subject plan : proposed modifications / Buckinghamshire County Council. — Aylesbury : [The Council], 1981. — 17p ; 21x30cm
Cover title
ISBN 0-86059-275-8 (pbk) : £0.25 B82-10622

Buckinghamshire. *County Council.* Proposed alterations — minerals — matters to be included and explanatory memorandum : County structure plan / Buckinghamshire County Council. — Aylesbury : [The Council], 1981. — 5p ; 21x30cm + map(85x92cm folded to 29x23cm)
ISBN 0-86059-280-4 (pbk) : £0.25 B82-10621

333.8′5′0968 — Southern Africa. Mineral resources. Exploitation. International economic aspects — *Conference proceedings*

Southern African Metals & Minerals in a World Context *(Conference : 1981 : Johannesburg).* Proceedings of the Southern African Metals & Minerals in a World Context conference : held at the Carlton Hotel, Johannesburg, S. Africa on 11th and 12th May, 1981 / organized and jointly sponsored by Metal Bulletin Congresses Limited and Metals & Minerals Research Services Limited ; edited by Trevor Tarring and Wynford Davies. — Worcester Park : Metal Bulletin Congresses Limited, c1981. — 207p in various pagings : ill,maps ; 30cm
ISBN 0-900542-61-6 (pbk) : £30.00
B82-16731

333.8′5′0973 — Mineral resources. Foreign relations of United States. Policies of government, *1914-1978*

Eckes, Alfred E.. The United States and the global struggle for minerals / Alfred E. Eckes, Jr.. — Austin ; London : University of Texas Press, c1979 (1980 printing). — xi,353p ; 24cm
Bibliography: p309-335. — Includes index
ISBN 0-292-78506-2 (cased) : Unpriced
ISBN 0-292-78511-9 (pbk) : £6.30 B82-00402

333.8′8′0979499 — California. Imperial County. Energy resources: Geothermal energy. Exploitation. Social aspects

Butler, Edgar W.. Geothermal energy development : problems and prospects in the Imperial Valley of California / Edgar W. Butler and James B. Pick. — New York ; London : Plenum, c1982. — xix,361p : ill,forms,maps ; 24cm
Bibliography: 341-352. — Includes index
ISBN 0-306-40772-8 : Unpriced B82-30350

333.9 — WATER, AIR, SPACE RESOURCES

333.91 — Natural resources: Water. Management *— Conference proceedings*

Lakes and water management : proceedings of the 30 years jubilee symposium of the Finnish Limnological Society, held in Helsinki, Finland, 22-23 September 1980 / edited by V. Ilmavirta, R.I. Jones and P.-E. Persson. — The Hague ; London : Junk, 1982. — ix,222p : ill,maps ; 27cm. — (Developments in hydrobiology ; 7)
"Reprinted from Hydrobiologia, Vol.86, no.1/2 (1982)". — Includes bibliographies
ISBN 90-619-3758-2 : Unpriced
Also classified at 574.5′26322′094897
B82-19407

333.91 — Natural resources: Water. Management. Risk-benefit analysis *— Conference proceedings*

Engineering Foundation Conference on Risk/Benefit Analysis in Water Resources Planning and Management *(1980 : Pacific Grove, Calif.).* Risk/benefit analysis in water resources planning and management / edited by Yacov Y. Haimes ; [proceedings of an UCOWR-sponsored Engineering Foundation Conference on Risk/Benefit Analysis in Water Resources Planning and Management held at the Asilomar Conference Grounds, Pacific Grove, California, September 21-26, 1980]. — New York ; London : Plenum, c1981. — xi,291p : ill,1map ; 26cm
Includes index
ISBN 0-306-40884-8 : Unpriced B82-20987

333.9′1 — Urban regions. Natural resources: Water. Ecological aspects *— Conference proceedings*

Role of water in urban ecology. — Oxford : Elsevier Scientific, July 1982. — [280]p. — (Developments in landscape management and urban planning ; 5)
Conference papers
ISBN 0-444-42078-9 : CIP entry B82-25099

333.91′0028′54404 — Water resource systems. Control & forecasting. Applications of real time computer systems *— Conference proceedings*

Real-time forecasting/control of water resource systems : selected papers from an IIASA workshop, October 18-21, 1976 / edited by Eric F. Wood with the assistance of András Szöllösi-Nagy. — Oxford : Pergamon, 1980. — ix,330p : ill ; 26cm. — (IIASA proceedings series ; v.8)
Includes bibliographies and index
ISBN 0-08-024486-6 : £24.00 : CIP rev.
B79-36212

333.91′0091724 — Developing countries. Natural resources: Water. Exploitation. Social aspects — *Conference proceedings*

Water and society : conflicts in development / edited by Carl Widstrand. — Oxford : Pergamon. — (Water development, supply and management ; v.8)
Pt.2: Water conflicts and research priorities / Malin Falkenmark ... [et al.]. — 1980. — viii,199p : ill,maps ; 26cm
Bibliography: p177-199
ISBN 0-08-023422-4 : £17.50 : CIP rev.
B80-18617

333.91′00962′3 — Egypt. Aswan. Natural resources: Water. Management. Mathematical models

Whittington, Dale. Water management models in practice. — Oxford : Elsevier Scientific, Feb.1983. — [400]p. — (Developments in environmental modelling ; v.2)
ISBN 0-444-42156-4 : CIP entry B82-37635

333.91′09428′81 — Northumberland. Kielder region. Natural resources: Water. Reservoirs: Kielder Water

Kielder Water : the commemorative handbook / Northumbrian Water. — London (Publicity House, Streatham Hill, SW2 4TR) : Burrow, [1982]. — 32p : ill(some col.),2maps ; 30cm
Unpriced (pbk) B82-37386

333.91′16′096 — Africa. Rural regions. Natural resources: Water. Conservation. Intermediate technology

Nissen-Petersen, Erik. Rain catchment and water supply in rural Africa. — London : Hodder and Stoughton, Sept.1982. — [128]p
ISBN 0-340-28429-3 (pbk) : £3.25 : CIP entry B82-20627

333.91′23 — Great Britain. Natural resources: Water. Use by industries. Conservation — *Conference proceedings*

Industrial water economy : EFCE event no. 268 / organised by the South Western Branch of the Institution of Chemical Engineers in Exeter, 23-24 September 1981 ; symposium organising committee C.S.H. Munro ... [et al.]. — Rugby : Institution of Chemical Engineers, c1981. — 216p : ill ; 22cm. — (EFCE publication series ; no.24) (Institution of Chemical Engineers symposium series ; no.67)
ISBN 0-85295-142-6 : Unpriced B82-04458

333.91′63′0942545 — Leicestershire. Rutland *(District).* **Natural resources: Water. Reservoirs: Rutland Water,** *to 1981 — Conference proceedings*

Rutland water : decade of change : proceedings of the conference held in Leicester, U.K. 1-3 April 1981 / edited by David M. Harper and John A. Bullock. — Hague ; London : Junk, 1982. — viii,232p : ill,maps ; 27cm. — (Developments in hydrobiology ; 8)
Reprinted from Hydrobiologia, v.88 no.1/2 (1982). — Includes bibliographies
ISBN 90-619-3759-0 : Unpriced B82-30371

333.91′64 — Washington *(State).* **Puget Sound. Economic development,** *1853-1977.* **Environmental aspects**

Chasan, Daniel Jack. The water link : a history of Puget Sound as a resource / Daniel Jack Chasan. — [Seattle] : Washington Sea Grant Program, University of Washington ; Seattle ; London : Distributed by University of Washington Press, 1981. — xi,179p : ill,maps,3facsims,ports ; 23cm. — (Puget Sound Books)
Includes index
ISBN 0-295-95782-4 (pbk) : £6.30 B82-19492

333.91′7 — Scotland. Highland Region. Beaches. Management

Highland beach management project, 1977-79 : final report. — [Redgorton] : Countryside Commission for Scotland, [1980]. — 51p : ill,3maps ; 30cm
Map and text on inside cover
ISBN 0-902226-50-9 (pbk) : Unpriced B82-30490

333.95 — BIOLOGICAL RESOURCES

333.95′6 — Fisheries. Resources. Management. Ecological aspects

Pitcher, Tony J.. Fisheries ecology / Tony J. Pitcher and Paul J.B. Hart. — London : Croom Helm, c1982. — 414p : ill ; 23cm
Bibliography: p378-402. — Includes index
ISBN 0-85664-894-9 : £16.95 : CIP rev. B81-31653

333.95′6 — Marine fish. Exploitation

Connell, J. J.. Trends in fish utilization / J.J. Connell and R. Hardy. — Farnham : Fishing News, c1982. — x,103p : ill ; 22cm. — (A Buckland Foundation book)
Bibliography: p100-101. — Includes index
ISBN 0-85238-120-4 (pbk) : £6.00 : CIP rev. B81-35894

333.95′617 — Oceans. Fisheries. Resources. Exploitation. Optimisation. Mathematical models

Laevastu, Taivo. Marine fisheries ecosystem : its quantitative evaluation and management / Taivo Laevastu and Herbert A. Larkins. — Farnham : Fishing News, c1981. — xiv,162p : ill,charts ; 26cm
Bibliography: p146-148. — Includes index
ISBN 0-85238-116-6 : £15.50 : CIP rev. B81-21547

334 — COOPERATIVES

334′.0941 — Great Britain. Cooperative movements. Development *— Proposals*

Clarke, Peter, *1949-.* Towards a united co-operative movement / by Peter Clarke. — [Manchester] : Co-operative Union on behalf of the Co-operative Party, 1981. — 50p ; 21cm
Unpriced (pbk) B82-15372

334′.0941 — Great Britain. Cooperative societies — *For children*

Langley, Andrew. The Co-op / Andrew Langley. — Hove : Wayland, 1982. — 64p : ill ; 22cm. — (In the High Street)
Bibliography: p62. — Includes index
ISBN 0-85340-985-4 : £4.25 B82-39794

334′.0941 — Great Britain. Cooperative societies. Organisation structure *— Proposals*

Albery, Nicholas. Co-op year 2000 : the nuts & bolts of caring & sharing / ideas for encouraging innovation within Co-operative Retail Societies : a report for submission to the Boards of Societies / by Nicholas Albery. — London (18 Victoria Park Sq., E2) : N. Albery, 1979. — 32leaves ; 30cm
Unpriced (unbound) B82-40955

334′.0941 — Great Britain. Rural regions. Cooperatives. Organisation *— Manuals*

Rural resettlement handbook. — 2nd ed. — Oxford (5 Crown St., Oxford OX4 1QG) : Rural Resettlement Group, 1979. — 218p : ill ; 21cm
Previous ed.: 1978?
ISBN 0-9506663-0-0 (pbk) : £1.80 B82-32762

334′.0944 — France. Cooperative movements. Development. Role of government

The Social economy : Mitterrand′s co-operative programme / commentary and translations by W.P. Watkins ; with a foreword by Harold Campbell. — London : Co-operative Party for the Co-operative Union, [1981]. — 23p : 2ports ; 21cm. — (Co-operative briefing)
£0.40 (unbound) B82-15374

334′.0971 — Canada. Rural regions. Economic development. Role of cooperatives

Clarke, Roger, *1948-.* Our own resources : cooperatives and community economic development in rural Canada / by Roger Clarke. — Langholm (Langholm, Dumfriesshire, DG13 0HL) : The Arkleton Trust, c1981. — 76p ; 21cm
Bibliography: p73-74
£2.50 (pbk) B82-20662

334.1 — BUILDING AND HOUSING COOPERATIVES

334′.1 — Great Britain. Housing associations. Committees. Members. Duties *— Manuals*

Improving performance : some thoughts for members of housing association committees : a report from the NFHA Working Party of Committee Membership. — London : National Federation of Housing Associations, 1981. — 6,4p ; 30cm
ISBN 0-86297-052-0 (pbk) : Unpriced B82-11315

334′.1 — Great Britain. Housing associations. Financial assistance by Housing Corporation — *Inquiry reports*

Great Britain. *Parliament. House of Commons. Committee of Public Accounts.* Twenty-third report from the Committee of Public Accounts : together with the proceedings of the committee, the minutes of evidence and an appendix : session 1979-80 : Department of the Environment, Housing Corporation : housing associations and the Housing Corporation, advances to Housing Corporation and housing associations. — London : H.M.S.O., [1980]. — xvi,32p ; 25cm. — ([HC] ; 741)
ISBN 0-10-027419-6 (pbk) : £4.00 B82-09505

334′.1 — Great Britain. Local authority housing. Tenants′ management cooperatives *— Case studies*

Matthews, Alison. Management cooperatives : the early stages / Alison Matthews. — London : H.M.S.O., 1981. — iv,34p ; 30cm
At head of cover title: Department of the Environment
ISBN 0-11-750019-4 (pbk) : £1.95 B82-00665

334′.1′02541 — Great Britain. Housing associations *— Directories — Serials*

National Federation of Housing Associations. Housing associations year book / National Federation of Housing Associations. — 1981/82-. — [London] ([30 Southampton St., WC2E 7HE]) : The Federation, [1981]-. — v. : ill ; 30cm
ISSN 0262-9844 = Housing associations year book : Unpriced B82-13417

334′.1′02854 — Great Britain. Housing associations. Applications of digital computer systems

Briefing note on computer systems for housing associations. — London : National Federation of Housing Associations, 1981. — 90p : ill ; 30cm. — (A Briefing note ; no.3)
ISBN 0-86297-002-4 (pbk) : Unpriced B82-13811

334′.1′068 — Great Britain. Housing associations. Commissioning agreements with architects

Commissioning agreements for architects. — London : National Federation of Housing Associations, [1981?]. — 29p ; 30cm. — (A Briefing note ; no.1)
ISBN 0-86297-000-8 (pbk) : Unpriced B82-13812

334′.1′0683 — Great Britain. Housing associations. Personnel management

Housing associations : a personnel handbook / [written by members of NFHA staff under the direction of the Federation′s Personnel and Organisation Committee]. — London : National Federation of Housing Associations, 1981. — 168p : forms ; 30cm
Bibliography: p160. — Includes index
ISBN 0-86297-037-7 (pbk) : Unpriced B82-11573

334′.1′0924 — Nottinghamshire. Nottingham. Registered housing associations: Family First Trust, *to 1975 — Personal observations*

Johns, Ruth I.. Life goes on / [Ruth I. Johns]. — Warwick : Unknown Publisher, c1982. — viii,184p : ill ; 21cm
ISBN 0-907895-00-x (pbk) : £3.75 B82-24859

334′.1′0941 — Great Britain. Housing associations. Membership

Membership of housing associations and their committees / National Federation of Housing Associations. — London : The Federation, 1981. — 34p ; 30cm
ISBN 0-86297-051-2 (pbk) : £1.00 B82-11316

334′.1′0941 — Great Britain. Housing cooperatives. Organisation *— Manuals*

Eno, Sarah. The collective housing handbook. — Castle Douglas : Laurieston Hall Publications, Dec.1982. — [150]p
ISBN 0-9508315-1-4 (pbk) : £13.50 : CIP entry B82-37492

334'.1'0941 — Great Britain. Housing cooperatives — *Serials*
[Scoop *(London : 1977)*]. Scoop : SCD's housing co-op magazine. — No.1 (Aug. 1977)-no.25 (Mar. 1982). — London (209 Clapham Rd, SW9 0QH) : Society for Co-operative Dwellings, 1977-1982. — 25v. : ill ; 30cm
Six issues yearly. — Continued by: Scoop broadsheet. — Index to no.1-12 in no.13. — Description based on: No.23 (Aug. 1981)
ISSN 0262-4605 = Scoop (London. 1977) : £2.50 per year B82-05231

334'.1'0941 — Great Britain. Self build housing societies
Stead, Peter, *1922-*. Self-build housing groups and co-operatives : ideas in practice : a report / by Peter Stead. — London : Anglo-German Foundation for the Study of Industrial Society, c1979. — xiv,79p : ill,plans ; 21cm
Bibliography: p70-74
ISBN 0-905492-19-6 (pbk) : £3.50 B82-01280

334'.1'0942 — England. Housing associations: Sutton Housing Trust, *to 1981*
Sutton Housing Trust. The Sutton Housing Trust : its foundation and history / by Harold Butcher and Ian Butcher. — [Tring] ([Sutton Court, Tring, Herts. HP23 5BB]) : [Sutton Housing Trust], 1982. — 87p : ill,ports ; 24cm
Cover title
Unpriced (pbk) B82-31893

334'.1'097447 — Massachusetts. Brookline. Housing condominiums
Dinkelspiel, John R.. Condominiums : the effects of conversion on a community / John R. Dinkelspiel, Joel Uchenick, Herbert L. Selesnick. — Boston, Mass. : Auburn House ; London : distributed by Eurospan, c1981. — xv,203p : ill,1map ; 24cm
Includes index
ISBN 0-86569-059-6 : £14.95 B82-08669

334.2 — BANKING AND CREDIT COOPERATIVES

334'.2'09 — Cooperative banks, *to 1980*
Fairlamb, David. Savings and co-operative banking / [by David Fairlamb and Jenny Ireland]. — London : Financial Times Business, c1981. — 255p ; 21cm. — (A Banker Research Unit survey)
ISBN 0-902998-45-5 : Unpriced
Primary classification 332.2'1'09 B82-12089

334.5 — CONSUMERS' COOPERATIVES

334'.5 — European Community countries. Agricultural products. Cooperative marketing
Foxall, Gordon R.. Co-operative marketing in European agriculture / Gordon Foxall. — Aldershot : Gower, c1982. — xi,101p ; 23cm
Bibliography: p96-101
ISBN 0-566-00512-3 : Unpriced : CIP rev. B81-36216

334.6 — PRODUCTION COOPERATIVES

334'.6'0722 — Workers' cooperatives — *Case studies*
The **Performance** of labour-managed firms / edited by Frank H. Stephen. — London : Macmillan, 1982. — xv,280p : ill ; 23cm
Bibliography: p265-274. — Includes index
ISBN 0-333-30096-3 : Unpriced B82-33847

334'.6'0941 — Great Britain. Industrial cooperatives, *to 1980*
Industrial co-operatives : the way ahead?. — Leicester (8 St. Martins, Leicester LE1 5DD) : Leicestershire Small Firms Centre, [1982?]. — 26p ; 21cm
Conference papers. — Editor: R.E. Parr. — Bibliography: p26
£0.50 (pbk) B82-19129

334'.6'094661 — Spain. Mondragon. Industrial cooperatives
Thomas, Henk. Mondragon : an economic analysis / Henk Thomas and Chris Logan. — London : Published in co-operation with the Institute of Social Studies at The Hague [by] Allen & Unwin, 1982. — viii,218p : ill ; 25cm
Bibliography: p203-210. — Includes index
ISBN 0-04-334006-7 : Unpriced : CIP rev. B81-33919

334'.6'097199 — Canada. Arctic. Eskimos. Industrial cooperatives, *1959-1979*
Iglauer, Edith. [The New people]. Inuit journey / by Edith Iglauer. — Seattle ; London : University of Washington Press, c1979. — xiii,240p ; 22cm
Originally published: Garden City : Doubleday ; London : Cape, 1966
ISBN 0-295-95650-x (pbk) : £4.90 B82-19766

334'.683 — Agricultural cooperatives
Sargent, Malcolm. Agricultural co-operation. — Aldershot : Gower, May 1982. — [166]p
ISBN 0-566-00460-7 : £15.00 : CIP entry B82-06851

334'.683'091724 — Developing countries. Agricultural cooperatives
Dooren, Pierre J. van. Co-operatives for developing countries : objectives, policies and practices / by Pierre J. van Dooren ; translated from the Dutch by Russell Lawson with Alette Konijnenbelt. — Oxford : Plunkett Foundation for Co-operative Studies, c1982. — ix,251p ; 21cm. — (Plunkett development series, ISSN 0143-8484 ; 4)
Translation of: Cooperaties voor ontwikkelingslanden. — Bibliography: p225-241. — Includes index
ISBN 0-85042-048-2 (pbk) : Unpriced B82-39629

334'.683'09415 — Ireland. Agriculture. Cooperation, *to 1900*
O'Dowd, Anne. Meitheal : a study of co-operative labour in rural Ireland / Anne O'Dowd. — Dublin : Comhairle Bhéaloideas Éireann, 1981. — 181p : ill,maps ; 23cm
Bibliography: p178-181
ISBN 0-906426-06-5 : Unpriced B82-21447

334'.68392'05 — Fishing cooperatives — *Serials*
Co-operative fishermen's bulletin — / International Co-operative Alliance. — No.1 (1980)-. — London (11 Upper Grosvenor St., W1X 9PA) : ICA, 1980-. — v. ; 30cm
Quarterly. — Description based on: No.2 (May 1981)
ISSN 0144-4484 = Co-operative fishermen's bulletin : Unpriced B82-10361

334.7 — BENEFIT SOCIETIES

334'.7'0941 — Great Britain. Friendly societies — *Serials*
Registry of Friendly Societies. Report of the Chief Registrar : incorporating the report of the Industrial Assurance Commissioner / Registry of Friendly Societies. — 1979-. — London : H.M.S.O., 1980-. — v. ; 25cm
Annual. — Merger of: Registry of Friendly Societies. Report of the Chief Registrar of Friendly Societies. Part 1, Friendly societies, industrial assurance companies and general; Registry of Friendly Societies. Report of the Chief Registrar of Friendly Societies. Part 2, Building societies; and, Registry of Friendly Societies. Report of the Chief Registrar of Friendly Societies. Part 3, Industrial and provident societies
ISSN 0263-4058 = Report of the Chief Registrar - Registry of Friendly Societies : £4.50 B82-19868

335 — SOCIALISM AND RELATED SYSTEMS

335 — Economics. Radical theories, *1900-1981*
McFarlane, Bruce. Radical economics / Bruce McFarlane. — London : Croom Helm, c1982. — 233p ; 23cm
Includes index
ISBN 0-7099-1733-3 : £14.95 : CIP rev. B82-01213

335 — Socialism
Bahro, Rudolf. Socialism and survival : articles, essays and talks 1979-1982. — London (PO Box 247, N15 6RW) : Heretic Books, Oct.1982. — [160]p
Translation of: Elemente einer neuen Politik
ISBN 0-946097-02-x (cased) : £6.95 : CIP entry
ISBN 0-946097-00-3 (pbk) : £3.50 B82-24607

Marković, Mihailo. Democratic socialism : theory and practice / Mihailo Marković. — Brighton : Harvester, 1982. — xvi,215p ; 23cm
Includes index
ISBN 0-7108-0387-7 : £18.95 : CIP rev. B82-00339

335 — Socialism — *Anarchist viewpoints*
Bakunin, M. A.. A critique of state socialism / by Michael Bakunin ; with drawings by Richard Warren. — Orkney (Over the Water, Sanday, Orkney, KW17 2BL) : Cienfuegos, [1981]. — 44p : ill ; 30cm
£0.75 (pbk) B82-02585

335 — Socialism — *Soviet viewpoints*
Socialism as a social system / [editors in chief: T.M. Jaroszewski, P.A. Ignatovsky] ; [translated from the Russian by Lenina Ilitskaya]. — Moscow : Progress ; [London] : distributed by Central Books, c1981. — 448p ; 18cm. — (Practice, problems and prospects of socialism)
Translation of: Sotsialisticheskiĭ stroĭ kak obshchestvennaiā
ISBN 0-7147-1709-6 (pbk) : £2.25 B82-19608

335 — Socialist movements. Role of women's movements — *Feminist viewpoints — Serials*
Beyond the Fragments bulletin. — No.1 (Jan. 1981)-. — [London] ([c/o Ms J. Meadows, 27 Stepney Green, E1]) : [Beyond the Fragments], 1981-. — v. : ill ; 21cm
Irregular
ISSN 0262-639x = Beyond the Fragments bulletin : £0.30 per issue B82-06780

335'.005 — Socialism — *Serials*
Socialist register. — 1982. — Manchester : Merlin Press. — [240]p
ISBN 0-85036-292-x (cased) : £8.50 : CIP entry
ISBN 0-85036-293-8 (pbk) : £4.50 B82-32299

335'.0088042 — Europe. Socialist feminists, *ca 1880-1980*
European women on the Left : socialism, feminism and the problems faced by political women, 1880 to the present / edited by Jane Slaughter and Robert Kern. — Westport, Conn. ; London : Greenwood Press, 1981. — vi,245p ; 22cm. — (Contributions in women's studies, ISSN 0147-104x ; no.24)
Bibliography: p221-232. — Includes index
ISBN 0-313-22543-5 : £20.95 B82-18369

335'.0088042 — United States. Socialist movements. Role of women, *1900-1980*
Flawed liberation : socialism and feminism / edited by Sally M. Miller. — Westport, Conn. ; London : Greenwood Press, 1981. — xxiii,214p : ill,ports ; 25cm. — (Contributions in women's studies, ISSN 0147-104x ; no.19)
Bibliography: p197-205. — Includes index
ISBN 0-313-21401-8 : £20.95 B82-18182

335'.0088042 — United States. Women's socialist movements, *1870-1920*
Buhle, Mari Jo. Women and American socialism, 1870-1920 / Mari Jo Buhle. — Urbana ; London : University of Illinois Press, c1981. — xix,344p,[14]p of plates : ill,ports ; 24cm. — (The Working class in American history)
Includes index
ISBN 0-252-00873-1 : £15.40 B82-12777

335'.009 — Socialism, *to 1979 — Trotskyist viewpoints*
Cliff, Tony. Neither Washington nor Moscow : essays on revolutionary socialism / Tony Cliff. — London : Bookmarks, 1982. — 285p : ill ; 22cm
ISBN 0-906224-06-3 (pbk) : £3.95 B82-26788

335'.009 — Socialism, *to 1980 — Marxist viewpoints*
Dunayevskaya, Raya. Marxism and freedom, from 1776 until today. — 5th ed. — Brighton : Harvester Press, Mar.1982. — [378]p
Previous ed.: London : Pluto Press, 1975
ISBN 0-7108-0368-0 (pbk) : £6.50 : CIP entry B82-10854

335′.009 — Socialism, *to 1981*

Lerner, Warren. A history of socialism and communism in modern times : theorists, activists and humanists / Warren Lerner. — Englewood Cliffs ; London : Prentice-Hall, c1982. — xii,253p ; 23cm
Bibliography: p244. — Includes index
ISBN 0-13-392183-2 (pbk) : £7.45 B82-20051

335′.009171′7 — Communist countries. Socialism, *to 1980*

Medvedev, Roĭ A.. Leninism and western socialism / Roy Medvedev ; translated by A.D.P. Briggs. — London : Verso, 1981. — 310p ; 23cm
Translation from the Russian. — Includes index
ISBN 0-86091-042-3 (cased) : Unpriced : CIP rev.
ISBN 0-86091-739-8 (pbk) : Unpriced
B81-27900

335′.0094 — Europe. Socialism

Hampton, Christopher, *1929-*. Socialism in a crippled world / Christopher Hampton. — Harmondsworth : Penguin, 1981. — 352p ; 20cm. — (Pelican books)
Bibliography: p322-325. — Includes index
ISBN 0-14-022370-3 (pbk) : £4.95 B82-07297

335′.0094 — Europe. Socialism — *Marxist viewpoints*

Szabó, Ervin. Socialism and social science : selected writings of Ervin Szabó (1877-1918) / edited by György Litván and János M. Bak. — London : Routledge & Kegan Paul, 1982. — vii,215p ; 23cm
Translated from the Hungarian and German. — Includes index
ISBN 0-7100-9007-2 : £11.95 B82-23256

335′.0094 — Europe. Socialism *related to* **nationalism,** *1848-1940*

Talmon, J. L.. The myth of the nation and the vision of revolution : the origins of ideological polarisation in the twentieth century / J.L. Talmon. — London : Secker & Warburg, 1981, c1980. — xviii,632p ; 24cm
Includes index
ISBN 0-436-51399-4 : £15.00
Primary classification 320.5′4′094 B82-02607

335′.00941 — Great Britain. Socialism — *Serials*

Calder voice : Calderdale′s socialist journal. — No.1 (Feb. 1977)-. — [Sowerby Bridge] ([c/o A. Graham, 4 Upper Gaukroger, Sowerby New Rd, Sowerby Bridge, W. Yorkshire]) : [Independent Labour Publications], 1977-. — v. : ill ; 30cm
Monthly. — Description based on: No.50 (May 1981)
ISSN 0262-723x = Calder voice : £1.80 per year B82-11142

335′.00941 — Great Britain. Socialism — *Socialist Workers′ Party viewpoints*

Foot, Paul. Three letters to a Bennite from Paul Foot / cartoons by Phil Evans. — London : Socialist Workers Party, 1982. — 30p : ill ; 21cm. — (A Socialist Workers Party pamphlet)
ISBN 0-905998-29-4 (unbound) : £0.50
B82-24444

335′.00947 — Eastern Europe & Soviet Union. Socialism

Wilczynski, J.. The economics of socialism : principles governing the operation of the centrally planned economies under the new system / by J. Wilczynski. — 4th ed. — London : Allen and Unwin, 1982. — xviii,238p ; 22cm. — (Studies in economics ; 2)
Previous ed.: 1977. — Bibliography: p226-233. — Includes index
ISBN 0-04-335044-5 (pbk) : Unpriced : CIP rev. B82-03711

335′.00947 — Eastern Europe & Soviet Union. Socialism. Economic aspects — *Festschriften*

Economic welfare and the economics of Soviet socialism : essays in honor of Abram Bergson / edited by Steven Rosefielde. — Cambridge : Cambridge University Press, 1981. — xii,340p : ill,1port ; 24cm
Bibliography: p334-337. — Includes index
ISBN 0-521-23273-2 : £25.00 B82-15279

335′.0096 — Africa. Socialism

Babu, Abdul Rahman Mohamed. African socialism or socialist Africa? / Abdul Rahman Mohamed Babu. — London : Zed, 1981. — xv,174p ; 23cm. — (Africa series)
ISBN 0-905762-19-3 : £16.95 : CIP rev.
B81-18059

335′.009669 — Nigeria. Socialism

Madunagu, Edwin. Problems of socialism. — London : Zed Press, Oct.1981. — [144]p
ISBN 0-86232-027-5 (pbk) : £4.95 : CIP entry
B81-28806

335′.009676′2 — Africa. Socialism, *1960-1977* — *Study regions: Kenya*

Mohiddin, Ahmed. African socialism in two countries / Ahmed Mohiddin. — London : Croom Helm, c1981. — 231p ; 23cm
Includes index
ISBN 0-7099-1702-3 : £12.50 : CIP rev.
Also classified at 335′.009678 B80-34635

335′.009678 — Africa. Socialism, *1960-1977* — *Study regions: Tanzania*

Mohiddin, Ahmed. African socialism in two countries / Ahmed Mohiddin. — London : Croom Helm, c1981. — 231p ; 23cm
Includes index
ISBN 0-7099-1702-3 : £12.50 : CIP rev.
Primary classification 335′.009676′2
B80-34635

335′.009678 — Tanzania. Socialism, *1967-1977*

Resnick, Idrian N.. The long transition : building socialism in Tanzania / Idrain N. Resnick. — New York ; London : Monthly Review, c1981. — 304p ; 21cm
Includes index
ISBN 0-85345-554-6 (cased) : £10.00
ISBN 0-85345-555-4 (pbk) : Unpriced
B82-14166

335′.00973 — United States. Socialism. Bellamy, Edward. Looking backward — *Critical studies*

Lipow, Arthur. Authoritarian socialism in America : Edward Bellamy & the nationalist movement / Arthur Lipow. — Berkeley ; London : University of California Press, c1982. — xii,315p ; 25cm
Bibliography: p289-297. — Includes index
ISBN 0-520-04005-8 : £21.50 B82-37063

335′.1′0922 — Great Britain. Labour movements, *1790-* — *Biographies*

Dictionary of Labour biography. — London : Macmillan, 1982
Includes bibliographies and index. — Consolidated list of names vols 1-6
Vol.6 / edited by Joyce M. Bellamy and John Saville. — xxxi,309p ; 24cm
ISBN 0-333-24095-2 : £25.00 B82-20940

335′.1092′4 — Great Britain. Labour movements. Spence, Thomas — *Critical studies*

Thomas Spence. — Nottingham : Spokesman, Oct.1981. — [150]p. — (Socialist classics ; no.2)
ISBN 0-85124-315-0 : £35.00 : CIP entry
B81-28045

335′.1′0941 — Great Britain. Labour movements, *1867-1974*

Hinton, James. Labour and socialism. — Brighton : Harvester Press, Jan.1983. — [224]p
ISBN 0-7108-0154-8 : £18.95 : CIP entry
B82-32555

335′.1′0941 — Great Britain. Labour movements, *1918-1931*

Wrigley, Chris. The British Labour Movement in the decade after the First World War : conference papers / by Chris Wrigley, Margaret Morris and Alan Deacon ; edited by Chris Wrigley. — Loughborough : Department of Economics, Loughborough University, 1979. — iii,54p ; 21cm
Unpriced (pbk) B82-40429

335′.1′0941 — Great Britain. Labour movements, *to 1980* — *Socialist viewpoints*

The **Forward** march of labour halted? / edited by Martin Jacques, Francis Mulhern ; [contributors] Eric Hobsbawm ... [et al.]. — London : NLB in association with Marxism Today, 1981. — 182p ; 23cm
ISBN 0-86091-041-5 (cased) : £8.50 : CIP rev.
ISBN 0-86091-737-1 (pbk) : Unpriced
B81-10430

335′.14′0924 — Great Britain. Socialism. Cole, Margaret — *Biographies*

Margaret Cole 1893-1980 / editor Betty Vernon. — London : Fabian Society, 1982. — 19p ; 22cm. — (Fabian tract, ISSN 0307-7535 ; 482)
Cover title
ISBN 0-7163-0482-1 (pbk) : £1.50 B82-40833

335′.14′0924 — Great Britain. Socialism. Webb, Beatrice, *1873-1892* — *Correspondence, diaries, etc.*

Webb, Beatrice. The diary of Beatrice Webb. — London : Virago
1: 1873-1892. — Oct.1982. — [416]p
ISBN 0-86068-209-9 : £15.00 : CIP entry
B82-24146

335′.2′088042 — France. Women′s socialist movements, *1876-1979*

Sowerwine, Charles. Sisters or citizens? : women and socialism in France since 1876 / Charles Sowerwine. — Cambridge : Cambridge University Press, 1982. — xx,248p ; 24cm
Bibliography: p235-241. — Includes index
ISBN 0-521-23484-0 : £15.00 : CIP rev.
B81-39253

335′.3′0922 — United States. Labour movements, *1930-1980* — *Personal observations* — *Collections*

Rank and file : personal histories by working-class organizers / edited by Alice and Staughton Lynd. — [2nd ed.]. — Princeton ; Guildford : Princeton University Press, 1981. — ix,296p : ill,ports ; 22cm
Previous ed.: Boston : Beacon Press, 1973
ISBN 0-691-09393-8 (cased) : Unpriced
ISBN 0-691-02825-7 (pbk) : £4.95 B82-13392

335′.3′0973 — United States. Labour movements, *1862-1872*

Montgomery, David. Beyond equality : labor and the radical Republicans 1862-1872 : with a bibliographical afterword / David Montgomery. — Urbana ; London : University of Illinois Press, 1981, c1967. — xi,535p ; 21cm
Originally published: New York : Knopf, 1967. — Bibliography: p470-580. — Includes index
ISBN 0-252-00869-3 (pbk) : £7.00 B82-09666

335.4 — MARXISM

335.4 — Marxism

Continuity and change in Marxism. — Brighton : Harvester Press, Dec.1982. — [256]p
ISBN 0-7108-0375-3 : CIP entry B82-30082

Marx and Marxisms / edited by G.H.R. Parkinson. — Cambridge : Cambridge University Press, c1982. — vi,267p ; 24cm. — (Royal Institute of Philosophy lecture series ; 14)
Includes index
ISBN 0-521-28904-1 (pbk) : Unpriced : CIP rev. B82-25770

The **Myth** of Marxism. — London : Wessex Study Group, 1982. — 32p ; 22cm
Bibliography: p32
ISBN 0-9508039-0-1 (pbk) : £0.90 B82-32670

Worsley, Peter. Marx and Marxism. — Chichester : Ellis Horwood, Dec.1981. — [128] p. — (Key sociologists series)
ISBN 0-85312-348-9 : £6.50 : CIP entry
B81-31377

335.4 — Marxism — *Anarchist viewpoints*

Graham, Marcus. Marxism & a free society / Marcus Graham. — 2nd ed. — Sanday : Cienfuegos, 1981. — 16p ; 22cm
Cover title. — Previous ed.: Sanday : Simian Publications, 1976
ISBN 0-904564-13-4 (pbk) : £0.50 B82-08518

335.4 — Marxism — *Early works*

Lenin, V. I.. Karl Marx ; Frederick Engels / Lenin. — Moscow : Progress, 1966 (1978 printing) ; [London] : Distributed by Central Book. — 55p ; 21cm
Translated from the Russian. — Includes index
£0.30 (pbk) B82-34680

335.4 — Marxism *related to* **Christianity**

Christianity & Marxism. — Exeter : Paternoster Press, Apr.1982. — [144]p
ISBN 0-85364-289-3 (pbk) : £3.20 : CIP entry
Primary classification 200 B82-05745

335.4 — Marxism *related to* **classical theory of economics** — *Festschriften*

Classical and Marxian political economy : essays in honour of Ronald L. Meek / edited by Ian Bradley and Michael Howard. — London : Macmillan, 1982. — xiv,300p : ill,1port ; 23cm
Includes bibliographies and index
ISBN 0-333-27027-4 (cased) : £15.00
ISBN 0-333-32199-5 (pbk) : Unpriced
Primary classification 330.15'3 B82-21620

335.4 — Marxism *related to* **feminism** — *Socialist viewpoints*

Women and revolution : a discussion of the unhappy marriage of marxism and feminism / edited by Lydia Sargent. — London : Pluto, 1981. — xxxi,373p ; 21cm
ISBN 0-86104-340-5 (pbk) : £3.95
Also classified at 305.4'2 B82-20689

335.4 — Marxist economics

Junankar, P. N.. Marx's economics / P.N. Junankar. — Oxford : Philip Allan, 1982. — x,166p : ill ; 23cm
Bibliography: p154-163. — Includes index
ISBN 0-86003-026-1 (cased) : £10.00 : CIP rev.
ISBN 0-86003-125-x (pbk) : £4.95 B82-05749

Krause, Ulrich. Money and abstract labour. — London : Verso Editions, Mar.1982. — [192]p
Translation of: Geld und abstrakte Arbeit
ISBN 0-86091-049-0 (cased) : £12.00 : CIP entry
ISBN 0-86091-749-5 (pbk) : £5.00 B82-02638

Nove, Alec. The economics of feasible socialism. — London : Allen and Unwin, Feb.1983. — [272]p
ISBN 0-04-335048-8 (cased) : £12.50 : CIP entry
ISBN 0-04-335049-6 (pbk) : £4.95 B82-36443

335.4 — United States. Universities. Marxism

The **Left** academy : Marxist scholarship on American campuses / edited by Bertell Ollman and Edward Vernoff. — New York ; London : McGraw-Hill, c1982. — vii,290p ; 21cm
Includes bibliographies and index
ISBN 0-07-047552-0 (pbk) : £6.95 B82-24556

335.4'01 — Marxism. Theories

Callinicos, Alex. Is there a future for Marxism? / Alex Callinicos. — London : Macmillan, 1982. — ix,263p ; 23cm
Includes index
ISBN 0-333-28477-1 (cased) : £15.00
ISBN 0-333-28479-8 (pbk) : Unpriced B82-20917

335.4'09 — Marxism. Theories, *to 1978*

The **history** of Marxism. — Brighton : Harvester Press
Vol.1: Marxism in Marx's day / edited by Eric J. Hobsbawm. — 1982. — xxiv,349p ; 25cm
Translation of: Storia del marxismo. Vol.1. Il marxismo ai tempi di Marx. — Includes index
ISBN 0-7108-0054-1 : £30.00 : CIP rev. B81-24616

335.4'092'2 — Economics. Marx, Karl & Engels, Friedrich — *Correspondence, diaries, etc.*

Marx, Karl. The Marx-Engels correspondence : the personal letters, 1844-1877 / a selection edited by Fritz J. Raddatz ; translated from the German by Ewald Osers. — London : Weidenfeld and Nicolson, 1981, 1980. — 174p ; 23cm
Translated from the German. — Includes index
ISBN 0-297-77994-x : £9.95 B82-04936

335.4'092'2 — Marxism. Marx *(Family)* — *Correspondence, diaries, etc.*

Longuet, Jenny Marx. The daughters of Karl Marx : family correspondence 1866-1898 / commentary and notes by Olga Meier ; translated and adapted by Faith Evans ; introduction by Sheila Rowbotham. — London : Deutsch, 1982. — xl,342p,[8]p of plates : ill,1facsim,1geneal.table,ports ; 25cm
Translation of: Les filles de Karl Marx. — Includes index
ISBN 0-233-97337-0 : £14.95 B82-29961

335.4'092'4 — Economics. Marx, Karl — *Critical studies*

Wolfson, Murray. Marx : economist, philosopher, Jew : steps in the development of a doctrine / Murray Wolfson. — London : Macmillan, 1982. — xx,279p ; 23cm
Includes index
ISBN 0-333-23999-7 : £20.00 B82-28681

335.4'092'4 — Economics. Marx, Karl. Local associations: London

Briggs, Asa. Marx in London : an illustrated guide / Asa Briggs with John Dekker and John Mair. — London : British Broadcasting Corporation, 1982. — 96p : ill,facsims,1geneal.table,maps,ports ; 23cm
Map on inside covers. — Includes index
ISBN 0-563-20076-6 (pbk) : £2.95 B82-35100

335.4'092'4 — Germany. Marxism. Luxemburg, Rosa — *Correspondence, diaries, etc.*

Luxemburg, Rosa. Comrade and lover : Rosa Luxemburg's letters to Leo Jogiches / edited and translated by Elżbieta Ettinger. — London : Pluto, 1981. — xxxiv,206p : ill,ports ; 20cm
Translation from the Polish. — Includes index
ISBN 0-86104-347-2 (pbk) : £3.95 B82-20695

335.4'092'4 — Marxism. Theories of Gramsci, Antonio

Salamini, Leonardo. The sociology of political praxis : an introduction to Gramsci's theory / Leonardo Salamini. — London : Routledge & Kegan Paul, 1981. — 258p ; 23cm
Bibliography: p242-249. — Includes index
ISBN 0-7100-0928-3 : £12.50 B82-06005

335.4'092'4 — Marxism. Theories of Luxemburg, Rosa

Bronner, Stephen Eric. A revolutionary for our times : Rosa Luxemburg / Stephen Eric Bronner. — London : Pluto, 1981. — 130p ; 19cm. — (Pluto ideas in prograss : Marxism and radical social thought)
Includes index
ISBN 0-86104-348-0 (pbk) : £2.95 B82-20686

335.4'094 — Western Europe. Marxism

Jacoby, Russell. Dialectic of defeat : contours of Western Marxism / Russell Jacoby. — Cambridge : Cambridge University Press, 1981. — x,202p ; 24cm
Includes index
ISBN 0-521-23915-x : £15.00 B82-13752

335.4'0943 — Europe. German speaking countries. Marxism. Relations with Christianity, *1870-1970*

Bentley, James. Between Marx and Christ : the dialogue in German-speaking Europe 1870-1970 / James Bentley. — London : Verso, 1982. — xi,191p ; 21cm
Bibliography: p166-185. — Includes index
ISBN 0-86091-048-2 (cased) : £12.00 : CIP rev.
ISBN 0-89091-748-7 (pbk) : Unpriced
Primary classification 261.2'1 B82-01576

335.4'0944 — France. Marxism

Kelly, Michael. Modern French Marxism. — Oxford : Blackwell, Oct.1982. — [256]p
ISBN 0-631-13202-3 : £12.00 : CIP entry B82-23172

335.4'112 — Marxism. Dialectical materialism

Lenin, V. I.. On the question of dialectics : a collection / Lenin. — Moscow : Progress, 1980 ; [London] : Distributed by Central Books. — 126p : 1ports ; 21cm
Translation of: K voprosu o dialektike. — Includes index
£0.60 (pbk) B82-34679

Oĭzerman, T.. Dialectical materialism and the history of philosophy : essays on the history of philosophy / Theodore Oizerman ; [translated from the Russian by Dmitri Beliavsky]. — Moscow : Progress ; [London] : Distributed by Central Books, c1982. — 286p ; 21cm
Translation of: Dialekticheskiĭ materializm i istoriîa filosofii. — Includes index
ISBN 0-7147-1756-8 : £4.95 B82-40116

335.4'112 — Marxism. Dialectical materialism — *Philosophical perspectives*

Sartre, Jean-Paul. Critique of dialectical reason. — London : Verso/NLB, Oct.1982. — 1v.
Translation of: Critique de la raison dialectique. — Originally published: London : NLB, 1976
ISBN 0-86091-757-6 (pbk) : £6.95 : CIP entry B82-28599

335.4'119 — Marxism. Historical materialism

Giddens, Anthony. A contemporary critique of historical materialism / Anthony Giddens. — London : Macmillan. — (Contemporary social theory)
Vol.1: Power, property and the state. — 1981. — 294p : ill ; 23cm
Includes index
ISBN 0-333-30971-5 (cased) : £12.95
ISBN 0-333-30972-3 (pbk) : Unpriced B82-10806

Schmidt, Alfred, *1931-*. History and structure : an essay on Hegelian-Marxist and structuralist theories of history / Alfred Schmidt ; translated by Jeffrey Herf. — Cambridge, Mass. ; London : MIT Press, c1981. — xxvi,146p ; 22cm. — (Studies in contemporary German social thought)
Translation of: Geschichte und Struktur. — Includes index
ISBN 0-262-19198-9 : £10.85 B82-20107

335.4'12 — Economics. Theories of Marx, Karl & Engels, Friedrich — *Texts*

Collected works / Karl Marx, Frederick Engels. — London : Lawrence & Wishart
Vol.17: Marx and Engels : 1859-60. — 1981. — xxvi,678p,[1]folded leaf of plates : 2col.maps,facsims ; 23cm
Includes index
ISBN 0-85315-438-4 : £5.00 B82-10970

Marx, Karl. Collected works / Karl Marx, Frederick Engels. — London : Lawrence & Wishart
Vol.14: Marx and Engels 1855-56. — 1980. — xxxii,832p,[3]folded leaves of plates : 1chart,col.maps ; 23cm
Includes index
ISBN 0-85315-435-x : £5.00 B82-14986

335.4'12 — Economics. Theories of Marx, Karl — *Texts*

Marx, Karl. Capital : a critique of political economy / Karl Marx. — Harmondsworth : Penguin in association with New Left review
Translation of: Das Kapital. — Bibliography: p1050-1065. — Includes index
Vol.3 / introduced by Ernest Mandel ; translated by David Fernbach. — 1981. — 1086p ; 20cm
ISBN 0-14-022116-6 (pbk) : £6.95 B82-07294

335.4'12 — Economics. Value. Theories

Hodgson, Geoff. Capitalism, value and exploitation. — Oxford : Martin Robertson, Sept.1981. — [220]p
ISBN 0-85520-414-1 : £12.50 : CIP entry B81-23822

335.4'12 — Marxist economics. Implications of theories of economics of Sraffa, Piero

Steedman, Ian. Marx after Sraffa / Ian Steedman. — London : Verso, 1981. — 218p : ill ; 21cm
Originally published: London : NLB, 1977. — Includes index
ISBN 0-86091-747-9 (pbk) : £3.50 : CIP rev. B81-30149

335.4′12′0924 — Economics. Theories of Marx, Karl — *Critical studies*
Maycock, Richard. Break the deadlock : a proposal for solving Britain's economic problems, and criticism of socialist and Marxist theories. — Halifax (12 Palatine Chambers, Market St., Halifax HX1 1RW) : Heigham Press, Aug.1982. — [240]p
ISBN 0-946154-00-7 (cased) : £9.95 : CIP entry
ISBN 0-946154-01-5 (pbk) : £3.50
Primary classification 330.941′0858
B82-25746

Vygodskiĭ, V. S.. The economic substantiation of the theory of socialism / Vitaly Vygodsky ; [translated from the Russian by Jane Sayer]. — Moscow : Progress ; [London] : Distributed by Central, c1981. — 277p ; 21cm
Translation of: Ėkonomicheskoe obosnovanie teorii nauchnogo kommunizma. — Includes index
ISBN 0-7147-1705-3 : £3.25 B82-29281

335.43 — Stalinism
Stalinism. — London : Temple Smith, June 1982. — [400]p
ISBN 0-85117-223-7 : £15.00 : CIP entry
B82-12843

335.43′05 — Communism — *Serials*
The **Leninist** : communist theoretical journal. — No.1 (Winter 1981/2)-. — London (P.O. Box 429, N.W.11) : Leninist Publications, 1981-. — v. ; 30cm
Quarterly
ISSN 0262-1649 = Leninist : £5.00 per year
B82-27649

335.43′09 — Communism, *1920-1981*
Coates, Ken. Heresies. — Nottingham : Spokesman, Nov.1982. — [100]p
ISBN 0-85124-355-x (cased) : CIP entry
ISBN 0-85124-356-8 (pbk) B82-32862

335.43′092′4 — England. Communism. Brown, Isabel — *Biographies*
Hill, May. Red roses for Isabel / by May Hill. — London (Box 202, 75 Farringdon Rd., EC1M 3JX) : M. Hill, c1982. — 110p,[16]p of plates : ill,ports ; 21cm
£1.50 (pbk) B82-31744

335.43′092′4 — Soviet Union. Communism. Sverdlov, ÎAkov Mikhaĭlovich — *Biographies*
Sverdlova, K.. Yakov Sverdlov / K. Sverdlova ; [translated from the Russian by Liv Tudge]. — Moscow : Progress ; London : distributed by Central Books, c1981. — 135p, [16]p of plates : ill,ports ; 21cm
Translation of: ÎAkov Mikhaĭlovich Sverdlov
ISBN 0-7147-1687-1 : £2.25 B82-20108

335.43′094 — Eurocommunism — *Conference proceedings*
Eurocommunism : the ideological and political-theoretical foundations / edited by George Schwab. — London : Aldwych, 1981. — xxvi,325p : ill ; 22cm. — (European studies ; no.7)
Conference proceedings. — Includes index
ISBN 0-86172-019-9 : £23.95 B82-31088

335.43′0947 — Eastern Europe. Communism
Fehér, Ferenc. Dictatorship over needs. — Oxford : Blackwell, Nov.1982. — [300]p
ISBN 0-631-13184-1 : £15.00 : CIP entry
B82-27976

335.43′095483 — India *(Republic)*. **Kerala. Communism,** *1946-1980*
Nossiter, T. J.. Communism in Kerala. — London : C. Hurst, Dec.1982. — [416]p
ISBN 0-905838-35-1 : £18.50 : CIP entry
B82-32878

335.43′0973 — United States. Labour movements. Communism, *1919-1949*
Levenstein, Harvey A.. Communism, anticommunism, and the CIO / Harvey A. Levenstein. — Westport, Conn. ; London : Greenwood Press, 1981. — xii,364p ; 24cm. — (Contributions in American history, ISSN 0084-9219 ; no.91)
Bibliography: p341-349. — Includes index
ISBN 0-313-22072-7 : Unpriced B82-01949

335.43′3′0924 — Trotskyism. Theories of Posadas, J.
Resolution by the Posadist IV International on the first anniversary of the death of J. Posadas : 14th May 1982. — London (24 Cranbourn St, WC2) : IV International Publications, [1982]. — 34p ; 21cm
At head of title: Revolutionary Workers Party (Trotskyist) : British Section of the IV International (Posadist). — Cover title
Unpriced (pbk) B82-40459

335.5 — STATE SOCIALISM AND SOCIAL DEMOCRACY

335.5′09497 — Yugoslavia. Socialism
Kardelj, Edvard. Democracy and socialism / Edvard Kardelj ; translated by Margot and Bosko Milosavljević. — London : Summerfield, c1978. — 244p ; 22cm
Translated from the Serbian
Unpriced B82-23617

335.6 — NATIONAL SOCIALISM

335.6 — Great Britain. Anti-fascism — *Serials*
Anti Nazi news. — Issue 01 (1980)-. — Birmingham (224 Digbeth High St., Birmingham 12) : Birmingham Anti Nazi League, 1980-. — v. : ill ; 30cm
Description based on: Issue 02 (Aug. 1980)
ISSN 0262-771x = Anti Nazi news : £0.15 per issue B82-08462

335.6 — National socialism — *National socialist viewpoints*
Jordan, Colin. National socialism : world creed for the 1980s / by Colin Jordan. — Harrogate : Gothic Ripples, c1981. — 13p ; 22cm
ISBN 0-907847-00-5 (unbound) : £0.25
B82-20930

335.6′09′04 — Fascism, *1920-1980*
Wilkinson, Paul. The new fascists / Paul Wilkinson. — London : Grant McIntyre, 1981. — 179p,[12]p of plates : ill,facsims,ports ; 23cm
Bibliography: p171-175. — Includes index
ISBN 0-86216-060-x : £7.95 : CIP rev.
B81-30309

335.6′094 — Europe. Fascism, *1919-1945*
Robinson, R. A. H.. Fascism in Europe, 1919-1945 / R.A.H. Robinson. — London : Historical Association, 1981. — 34p : ill ; 22cm. — (Appreciations in history ; no.8)
Bibliography: p32-34
ISBN 0-85278-243-8 (pbk) : Unpriced
B82-23228

335.6′094 — Europe. Fascism, *to 1980*
Fascism in Europe / edited by S.J. Woolf. — London : Methuen, 1981. — 408p ; 22cm
Previous ed.: published as European fascism : London : Weidenfeld & Nicolson, 1968. — Bibliography: p387-402. — Includes index
ISBN 0-416-30230-0 (cased) : Unpriced : CIP rev.
ISBN 0-416-30240-8 (pbk) : £5.95 B81-25839

335.6′0971 — Canada. National socialism, *1920-1942*
Wagner, Jonathan F.. Brothers beyond the sea : national socialism in Canada / by Jonathan F. Wagner. — Waterloo, Ont. : Wilfrid Laurier University Press ; Gerrards Cross : Distributed by Smythe, c1981. — xxiii,163p : ill,1facsim,ports ; 24cm
Bibliography: p151-159. — Includes index
ISBN 0-88920-096-3 : Unpriced B82-19626

335.8 — SYNDICALISM, ANARCHISM, ETC

335′.82′0924 — Anarcho-syndicalism. Witkop-Rocker, Milly — *Personal observations*
Rocker, Rudolf. Milly Witkop/Rocker / by Rudolf Rocker. — Sanday : Cienfuego Press, [1981]. — [24]p : ill ; 18cm
Originally published: Great Britain : s.n., 1956
£0.50 (unbound) B82-20995

335′.83 — Anarchism
Buffo! : a short anthology of political pranks and anarchic buffoonery / [compiled and edited by Larry Law]. — London : Spectacular Times, [1982]. — [26]p : ill ; 21cm
ISBN 0-907837-02-6 (unbound) : Unpriced
B82-37931

Taylor, Michael. Community, anarchy and liberty. — Cambridge : Cambridge University Press, Aug.1982. — [184]p
ISBN 0-521-24621-0 (cased) : £14.00 : CIP entry
ISBN 0-521-27014-6 (pbk) : £4.95 B82-15876

335′.83′09 — Anarchism, *to 1980*
Barclay, Harold. People without government. — London : Kahn & Averill, Sept.1982. — [160]p
ISBN 0-900707-75-5 (pbk) : £5.75 : CIP entry
B82-25731

335′.83′0924 — Japan. Anarchism. Ōsugi, Sakae — *Biographies*
Stanley, Thomas A.. Ōsugi Sakae anarchist in Taishō Japan : the creativity of the ego / Thomas A. Stanley. — Cambridge, Mass. : Council on East Asian Studies, Harvard University ; Cambridge, Mass. ; London : Distributed by Harvard University Press, 1982. — xviii,232p : 1port ; 24cm. — (Harvard East Asian monographs ; 102)
Bibliography: p205-220. — Includes index
ISBN 0-674-64493-x : £14.00 B82-40495

335′.83′0977311 — Illinois. Chicago. Anarchist movements, *1886*
De Cleyre, Voltairine. The first Mayday : the Haymarket speeches 1895-1910 / by Voltairine de Cleyre ; with an introduction, notes and bibliography by Paul Avrich. — Sanday : Cienfuegos, 1980. — ii,53p,[8]p of plates : ill,1facsim,ports ; 22cm
Ports on inside cover. — Bibliography: p51
ISBN 0-904564-35-5 (pbk) : £1.00 : CIP rev.
B80-02347

335.9 — SOCIALIST AND ANARCHIST COMMUNITIES

335′.941693′0924 — Donegal *(County)*. **Burtonport. Alternative communities: Atlantis** *(Alternative community)* — *Personal observations*
James, Jenny. They call us the screamers : the history of Atlantis Primal Therapy Commune, Burtonport, Co. Donegal / Jenny James. — Firle : Caliban, c1980. — 184p ; 23cm
ISBN 0-904573-27-3 : £7.00 B82-30159

335′.9423592 — Devon. Dartington. Utopian communities: Dartington Hall Trust, *to 1974*
Young, Michael. The Elmhirsts of Dartington : the creation of an Utopian community / Michael Young. — London : Routledge & Kegan Paul, 1982. — x,581p,[16]p of plates : ill,geneal.tables,ports ; 24cm
ISBN 0-7100-9051-x : £15.00 B82-31390

335′.942579 — Oxfordshire. Ipsden. Communes: Braziers Park School of Integrative Social Research, *to 1972*
Glaister, Dorothy. Braziers : a personal story / by Dorothy Glaister. — Rev. and repr. — Oxford (Braziers Park, Ipsden, Oxford OX9 6AN) : Braziers Park School of Integrative Social Research, 1981. — 16p ; 19cm
Cover title. — Previous ed.: i.e. rev. ed. 1973
£1.50 (pbk) B82-09469

335′.95694 — Israel. Kibbutzim. Organisation structure — *Case studies*
Lieblich, Amia. Kibbutz Makom : report from an Israeli kibbutz / by Amia Lieblich. — London : Deutsch, 1982, c1981. — xxvi,318p ; 24cm
ISBN 0-233-97457-1 : £9.95 B82-16075

335′.9712 — Western Canada. Utopian communities, *1885-1914*
Rasporich, Anthony. The vanishing West : utopian settlements in Western Canada 1885-1914 / by Anthony Rasporich. — [London] ([Canada House, Trafalgar Sq. SW1Y 5BJ]) : [Canadian High Commission], [1979?]. — 28p. — (Canada House lecture series ; no.7)
Cover title. — At head of title: Canada
Unpriced (pbk) B82-35983

335′.973′0321 — United States. Utopian communities, *to 1979 — Encyclopaedias*
Fogarty, Robert S.. Dictionary of American communal and utopian history / Robert S. Fogarty. — Westport ; London : Greenwood Press, 1980. — xxvi,271p ; 25cm
Bibliography: p247-253. — Includes index
ISBN 0-313-21347-x : Unpriced B82-15057

335′.976229 — Mississippi. Davis Bend. Negro utopian communities, *1827-ca 1875*
Hermann, Janet Sharp. The pursuit of a dream / Janet Sharp Hermann. — New York ; Oxford : Oxford University Press, 1981. — xi,290p,[4]p of plates : ill,maps,ports ; 22cm
Maps on lining papers. — Bibliography: p275-282. — Includes index
ISBN 0-19-502887-2 : £10.50
Also classified at 335′.976243 B82-00505

335′.976243 — Mississippi. Mound Bayou. Negro Utopian communities, *1877-1922*
Hermann, Janet Sharp. The pursuit of a dream / Janet Sharp Hermann. — New York ; Oxford : Oxford University Press, 1981. — xi,290p,[4]p of plates : ill,maps,ports ; 22cm
Maps on lining papers. — Bibliography: p275-282. — Includes index
ISBN 0-19-502887-2 : £10.50
Primary classification 335′.976229 B82-00505

336 — PUBLIC FINANCE

336′.014′1724 — Developing countries. Local government. Finance
Financing regional government. — Chichester : Wiley, Feb.1983. — [220]p. — (Public administration in developing countries)
ISBN 0-471-10356-x : £10.00 : CIP entry B82-38704

336′.014′41 — Great Britain. Local government. Finance
Bailey, S. J. (Stephen James). Local government finance and macroeconomic policy : an aspect of central-local relationships / S.J. Bailey. — Glasgow (North Hanover Place, Glasgow G4 0BA) : PARU, Department of Social Sciences, Glasgow College of Technology, 1982. — 25p ; 30cm. — (Discussion paper / Glasgow College of Technology. Policy Analysis Research Unit ; no.10)
Bibliography: p22-25
Unpriced (pbk) B82-33003

Fiscal stress in cities. — Cambridge : Cambridge University Press, Oct.1982. — [246]p
ISBN 0-521-24607-5 : £17.50 : CIP entry B82-40323

336′.014′41 — Great Britain. Local government. Finance. Effects of grants by government to local authorities
Topham, Neville. The incidence of grants-in-aid / Neville Topham. — [Salford] : Department of Economics, University of Salford, [1982]. — 16,4 leaves ; 30cm. — (Salford papers in economics ; 82-3)
Unpriced (spiral) B82-20479

336′.014′41 — Great Britain. Local government. Finance. Reform — *Proposals*
Tunley, Philip. Local income tax and local government reform / Philip Tunley. — London (Duncan House, High St, E15 2JB) : NELPCO, [1981?]. — 49p : ill ; 30cm. — (CIS commentary series ; no.16)
ISBN 0-901987-41-7 (spiral) : Unpriced B82-05878

336′.014′4110212 — Scotland. Local government. Finance — *Statistics — Serials*
Scottish local government financial statistics / the Scottish Office. — 1975-76 to 1977-78-. — Edinburgh : H.M.S.O., 1981-. — v. ; 30cm
Annual. — Continues: Local finacial returns, Scotland
ISSN 0262-7426 = Scottish local government financial statistics : £10.00 B82-14272

336′.014′42 — England. Local government. Finance — *For district councillors*
Aughton, Henry. Local government finance / by Henry Aughton. — Chichester : Rose, 1980. — 50p ; 21cm
Previous ed.: published as Local government finance for district councillors. 1973
ISBN 0-85992-205-7 (pbk) : £3.85 B82-34710

336′.09181′2 — Western world. Public finance. Applications of economic analysis
Peacock, Alan, *1922-*. The economic analysis of government, and related themes. — Oxford : Robertson, June 1982. — [258]p
Originally published: 1979
ISBN 0-85520-514-8 (pbk) : £6.50 : CIP entry B82-12849

336.1 — PUBLIC FINANCE. NON-TAX REVENUES

336′.185 — England. Rates. Supplementation. Block grants from government — *Statistics — Serials*
Block grant indicators. — 1981-82-. — Beverley : Society of County Treasurers in association with Society of Metropolitan Treasurers [and] Association of District Council Treasurers, 1981-. — v. ; 30cm
Annual. — Continues: Rate support grant statistics
ISSN 0261-7609 = Block grant indicators : £5.00 B82-26133

336′.185 — England. Rates. Supplementation from government
Bennett, R. J.. Central grants to local governments. — Cambridge : Cambridge University Press, Nov.1982. — [351]p. — (Cambridge geographical studies ; 17)
ISBN 0-521-24908-2 : £24.00 : CIP entry B82-29387

336′.185 — England. Rates. Supplementation. Grants from government — *Proposals*
Great Britain. *Department of the Environment*. Local government finance (England) : the rate support grant report (England) 1980 : report by the Secretary of State for the Environment and the Minister of Transport under section 60 of the Local Government Planning and Land Act 1980. — London : H.M.S.O., [1980]. — 66p ; 25cm. — ([HC] ; 56)
ISBN 0-10-205681-1 (unbound) : £4.20 B82-15132

Great Britain. *Department of the Environment*. Local government finance (England and Wales) : the Rate Support Grant (Increase) Order 1980 / Department of the Environment, Department of Transport. — London : H.M.S.O., [1980]. — 9p ; 25cm. — ([HC] ; 57)
ISBN 0-10-205781-8 (unbound) : £1.40 B82-01243

Great Britain. *Department of the Environment*. Local government finance (England and Wales) : the Rate Support Grant (Increase) (No.2) Order 1980 / Department of the Environment, Department of Transport. — London : H.M.S.O., [1980]. — 11p ; 25cm. — ([HC] ; 58)
ISBN 0-10-205881-4 (unbound) : £1.40 B82-01244

336′.185 — Grants economics — *Conference proceedings*
The **Grants** economy and collective consumption : proceedings of a conference held by the International Economic Association at Cambridge, England / edited by R.C.O. Matthews and G.B. Stafford. — London : Macmillan, 1982. — xvi,338p ; 22cm
Includes index
ISBN 0-333-28600-6 : Unpriced B82-32932

336′.185 — Scotland. Rates. Supplementation. Grants from government — *Proposals*
Great Britain. *Scottish Office*. The Rate Support Grant (Scotland) Order 1980 : report by the Secretary of State under section 3 and 4 of the Local Government (Scotland) Act 1966. — Edinburgh : H.M.S.O., [1981]. — 12p ; 25cm. — ([HC] ; 63)
ISBN 0-10-206381-8 (unbound) : £1.70 B82-16061

336′.185 — Wales. Rates. Grants from government — *Proposals*
Great Britain. *Welsh Office*. Local government finance (Wales) : the Welsh Rate Support Grant report 1980 / Welsh Office. — London : H.M.S.O., [1980]. — 44p : ill ; 25cm. — ([HC] ; 52)
ISBN 0-10-205281-6 (unbound) : £3.00 B82-01245

336.2 — PUBLIC FINANCE. TAXATION

336.2 — Great Britain. Capital. Taxation — *Selsdon Group viewpoints*
Bracewell-Milnes, Barry. Killing the goose : taxes on capital are taxes on capitalism / Barry Bracewell-Milnes. — [London] ([170 Sloane St., SW1X 9QG]) : Selsdon Group, [1974]. — 15p ; 22cm. — (Selsdon policy series ; no.2)
£0.50 (pbk) B82-07139

336.2 — Great Britain. Capital. Taxation — *Society for Individual Freedom viewpoints*
Bracewell-Milnes, Barry. Freedom under siege : capital taxation and political conformity / Barry Bracewell-Milnes. — [London] : Society for Individual Freedom, [1981?]. — [25]p ; 21cm
ISBN 0-9504470-0-5 (pbk) : £1.00 (£0.75 to members of SIF) B82-08002

336.2 — Great Britain. National heritage assets. Taxation
The **National** heritage : U.K. taxation guide. — London : Binder Hamlyn, [1982]. — 19p ; 21cm
Cover title
Unpriced (pbk) B82-27841

336.2 — Taxation
Kaldor, Nicholas. Reports on taxation / Nicholas Kaldor. — London : Duckworth. — (Collected economic essays / by Nicholas Kaldor)
2: Reports to foreign governments. — 1980. — xvi,356p ; 23cm
ISBN 0-7156-0911-4 : £20.00 : CIP rev. B80-11779

Lewis, Alan. The psychology of taxation. — Oxford : Robertson, Sept.1982. — [220]p
ISBN 0-85520-412-5 (cased) : £12.00 : CIP entry
ISBN 0-85520-413-3 (pbk) : £5.50 B82-20838

336.2′0094 — Western Europe. Taxation
Pocket guide to European individual taxes. — 5th ed. — London (1 Surrey St., WC2R 2PS) : Arthur Andersen & Co, 1982. — 93p ; 21x10cm
Previous ed.: 198-?
Unpriced (pbk) B82-32405

336.2′00941 — Great Britain. Economic inequality. Effects of taxation
Apps, Patricia. A theory of inequality and taxation / Patricia Apps. — Cambridge : Cambridge University Press, 1981. — x,132p : ill ; 24cm
Bibliography: p123-128. — Includes index
ISBN 0-521-23437-9 : £16.50 : CIP rev. B82-07959

336.2′00941 — Great Britain. Taxation
Bracewell-Milnes, Barry. The taxation of industry : fiscal barriers to the creation of wealth / Barry Bracewell-Milnes. — London : Panopticum, 1981. — 183p ; 25cm
ISBN 0-907256-06-6 : Unpriced B82-28379

Great Britain. *Board of Inland Revenue*. Inland Revenue official tax guides / compiled by Oyez editorial staff. — London : Oyez, c1982. — 1v.(loose-leaf) ; 26cm
Includes index
ISBN 0-85120-617-4 : Unpriced B82-27082

336.2′00941 — Great Britain. Taxation — *Encyclopaedias*
Hart, Gerry. Dictionary of taxation / by Gerry Hart ; consultant B.E.V. Sabine. — London : Butterworths, 1981. — v,236p ; 23cm. — (Butterworths professional dictionaries series)
ISBN 0-406-52159-x (cased) : £14.00
ISBN 0-406-52160-3 (pbk) : Unpriced B82-05444

336.2′00941 — Great Britain. Taxation — *For small firms — Serials*
SBB tax news. — 1-10/80-. — London (32 Smith Sq., SW1) : Conservative Small Business Bureau, 1980-. — v. ; 30cm
Monthly. — Data extracted from: Tax file. — Index published in every Jan. issue
ISSN 0263-3817 = SBB tax news : Free to SBB subscribers only B82-24752

336.2′00941 — Great Britain. Taxation — *Labour Party (Great Britain) viewpoints*

Taxation : a Labour Party discussion document. — [London] : The Party, [1981]. — 54p ; 21cm. — (Socialism in the 80s)
Cover title
ISBN 0-86117-085-7 (pbk) : £1.00 B82-05512

336.2′00941 — Great Britain. Taxation — *Serials*

British master tax guide. — 1982-83. — Bicester (Telford Rd., Bicester, Oxfordshire OX6 0XD) : 6 CCH Editions, Aug.1982. — [800]p
ISBN 0-86325-004-1 (pbk) : £17.00 : CIP entry B82-25756

Tax facts and tables. — 1981/82-. — London : Oyez Pub., 1981-. — v. ; 25cm
Annual. — Continues: Tax facts (London)
ISSN 0262-7388 = Tax facts and tables : £5.95 B82-13406

Tax insight : practical advice for the businessman and his professional adviser. — Jan. 1982-. — Woking (P.O. Box 2, Woking, Surrey) : Templegate Press, 1982-. — v. : ill,ports ; 25cm
Monthly. — Description based on: Feb. 1982
ISSN 0263-9076 = Tax insight : £36.00 per year B82-38536

336.2′00941 — Great Britain. Taxation — *Tables — Serials*

Five year tax tables : tax rates and reliefs ; National Insurance contributions and main social security benefits. — 1976/77 to 1980/81-. — London : Fourmat, 1980-. — v. ; 30cm. — (Lawyers costs & fees series ; 8)
Irregular
ISSN 0262-6187 = Five year tax tables : £1.10 B82-06815

Tolley′s tax data. — 1981-82-. — Croydon : Tolley Publishing Co., 1981-. — v. ; 21x30cm
Annual
ISSN 0262-4583 = Tolley′s tax data : £2.75 B82-05229

336.2′00942 — England. Taxation — *For executors & trustees*

Mellows, Anthony R.. Taxation for executors and trustees / by Anthony R. Mellows. — 5th ed. — London : Butterworths, 1981. — xxxiv,428p ; 23cm
Previous ed.: 1976. — Includes index
ISBN 0-406-62395-3 : £15.00 B82-05259

336.2′0095 — Asia. Taxation

Platt, C. J.. Tax systems of Africa, Asia and the Middle East : a guide for business and the professions / C.J. Platt. — Aldershot : Gower, c1982. — xxii,240p ; 22cm
ISBN 0-566-02335-0 (pbk) : Unpriced : CIP rev.
Also classified at 336.2′0096 ; 336.2′00956 B82-00199

336.2′00956 — Middle East. Taxation

Askari, Hossein. Taxation and tax policies in the Middle East. — London : Butterworths Scientific, July 1982. — [352]p. — (Butterworths studies in international political economy)
ISBN 0-408-10832-0 : £25.00 : CIP entry B82-12324

Platt, C. J.. Tax systems of Africa, Asia and the Middle East : a guide for business and the professions / C.J. Platt. — Aldershot : Gower, c1982. — xxii,240p ; 22cm
ISBN 0-566-02335-0 (pbk) : Unpriced : CIP rev.
Primary classification 336.2′0095 B82-00199

336.2′0096 — Africa. Taxation

Platt, C. J.. Tax systems of Africa, Asia and the Middle East : a guide for business and the professions / C.J. Platt. — Aldershot : Gower, c1982. — xxii,240p ; 22cm
ISBN 0-566-02335-0 (pbk) : Unpriced : CIP rev.
Primary classification 336.2′0095 B82-00199

336.2′00973 — United States. Taxation

Sommerfeld, Ray M.. An introduction to taxation / Ray M. Sommerfeld, Hershel M. Anderson, Horace R. Brock. — 1982 ed. — New York ; London : Harcourt Brace Jovanovich, c1981. — 1v.(various pagings) : ill,forms ; 29cm
Previous ed.: 1980. — Includes index
ISBN 0-15-546317-9 : Unpriced B82-33673

336.2′013′73 — United States. States. Taxation

Hale, Lloyd S.. State tax liability and compliance manual. — New York ; Chichester : Wiley
1982 supplement / Lloyd S. Hale, Ruth Goran. — c1982. — iii,82p ; 23cm
Includes index
ISBN 0-471-87564-3 (pbk) : Unpriced B82-37962

336.2′014′41 — Great Britain. Local taxation — *Proposals*

Alternatives to domestic rates / presented to Parliament by the Secretary of State for the Environment, the Secretary of State for Scotland, and the Secretary of State for Wales ... — London : H.M.S.O., [1981]. — 81p : ill ; 25cm. — (Cmnd. ; 8449)
ISBN 0-10-184490-5 (pbk) : £4.75 B82-12491

336.2′06 — Tax havens

Doggart, Caroline. Tax havens and their uses, 1981 / by Caroline Doggart. — London : Economist Intelligence Unit, 1981. — 138p : col.ill ; 30cm. — (EIU special report ; no.105)
Previous ed.: published as Tax havens and their uses. 1979. — Includes index
Unpriced (pbk) B82-00821

336.2′07 — United States. Railway services. Taxation

Thompson, Dennis L.. Taxation of American railroads : a policy analysis / Dennis L. Thompson with the assistance of John Barth, Raymond Garthner and Steven Sours. — Westport ; London : Greenwood, 1981. — xvi,186p ; 25cm. — (Contributions in economics and economic history ; no.34)
Bibliography: p179-182. — Includes index
ISBN 0-313-22248-7 : Unpriced B82-02003

336.2′07 — United States. Small firms. Taxation

Lane, Marc J.. Taxation for small business / Marc J. Lane. — 2nd ed. — New York ; Chichester : Wiley, c1982. — xii,284p : ill,facsims,forms ; 22cm
Previous ed.: 1980. — Includes index
ISBN 0-471-86774-8 : £18.00 B82-32706

336.2′07′0941 — Great Britain. Business firms. Taxation

Going into business. — [London] ([1 Surrey St, WC2R 2PS]) : Arthur Andersen & Co., 1982. — 69p : 1facsim,1col.map ; 21cm
Unpriced (pbk) B82-34571

336.2′07′0941 — Great Britain. Business firms. Taxation — *For management*

Walters, R. M.. Managing tax in your business / Robert Walters. — London : Business Books, 1982. — vi,226p : 1ill ; 23cm
Bibliography: p219-220. — Includes index
ISBN 0-09-147350-0 : Unpriced : CIP rev. B82-10414

336.22 — Derbyshire. Hearth tax, *1662-1670.* **Taxpayers** — *Lists*

Derbyshire hearth tax assessments 1662-70 / edited by David G. Edwards ; with an introduction incorporating material by the late C.A.F. Meekings. — Chesterfield : Derbyshire Record Society, 1982. — lxxv,225p,[4]p of plates : ill,maps ; 22cm. — (Derbyshire Record Society ; v. 8)
Includes index
ISBN 0-9505940-9-1 : £15.00 B82-31548

336.22 — Great Britain. Development land tax

Hardman, J. Philip. Development land tax / by J. Philip Hardman. — 2nd ed. / with examples by Iain P.A. Stitt and A. David W. Bertram. — London : Institute of Chartered Accountants in England and Wales, 1981. — xxviii,277p : ill ; 21cm. — (Chartac taxation guides)
Previous ed.: 1976. — Includes index
ISBN 0-85291-312-5 (pbk) : Unpriced B82-12105

Maas, Robert W.. Development land tax / by Robert W. Maas. — 4th ed. — Croydon : Tolley, 1982. — xiii,244p ; 23cm
Previous ed.: 1981. — Includes index
ISBN 0-85459-056-0 (pbk) : £10.50 B82-30691

336.2′2′0942 — England. Local authorities. Rates. Information — *Proposals*

Explaining the Local Authority Rate Bill : publication of rate demands and supporting information by local authorities : code of practice / issued by the Secretary of State for the Environment and the Secretary of State for Wales in agreement with the Consultative Council on Local Government Finance. — London : H.M.S.O., 1980. — 10p ; 21cm
ISBN 0-11-751500-0 (pbk) : Unpriced B82-17176

336.22′0942143 — London. Islington *(London Borough).* **Rates. Proposed increases. Attitudes of residents**

Market Opinion and Research International. Public attitudes to rates and council spending in Islington : January-February 1982 : research study conducted for London Borough of Islington / by Market and Opinion Research International Ltd. — London (Town Hall, Upper St., N1 2UD) : London Borough of Islington, 1982. — 38p : forms ; 30cm
Cover title
£12.00 (pbk)
Also classified at 336.3′9′0942143 B82-26492

336.22′0973 — United States. Real property. Investment. Taxation — *For British investors*

Investing in U.S. real property : a guide to the tax implications for the U.K. investor ... / Touche Ross & Co. — [London] : [Touche Ross & Co.], c1981. — 53p ; 30cm
Unpriced (pbk) B82-11595

336.22′2 — Great Britain. Urban regions. Land. Value. Taxation, *1880-1980*

Prest, A. R.. The taxation of urban land / A.R. Prest. — Manchester : Manchester University Press, c1981. — 207p ; 23cm
Bibliography: p190-201. — Includes index
ISBN 0-7190-0817-4 : £19.50 : CIP rev. B81-23752

336.2′3′094227 — Hampshire. Personal property. Taxation. Lay subsidy rolls, *1586* — *Texts*

The **Hampshire** lay subsidy rolls, 1586 : with the city of Winchester assessment of a fifteenth and tenth, 1585 / edited by C.R. Davey. — [Winchester] : Hampshire County Council, 1981. — xi,180p,[2]leaves of plates (some folded) : 1map,1facsim ; 23cm. — (Hampshire record series ; v.4)
Includes index
ISBN 0-906680-01-8 : Unpriced B82-11322

336.2′3′094233 — Dorset. Personal property. Taxation. Lay subsidy rolls, *1523-1593* — *Texts*

Dorset Tudor subsidies : granted in 1523, 1543, 1593 / edited ... by T.L. Stoate. — Bristol (Lower Court, Almondsbury, Bristol) : T.L. Stoate, c1982. — xxiv,256p ; 30cm
Bibliography: pxii. — Includes index
Unpriced B82-16580

336.24 — Great Britain. Charities. Donations by deeds of covenant. Taxation

Norton, Michael. Covenants. — 2nd ed. — London : Directory of Social Change, Jan.1983. — [128]p
Previous ed.: 1980
ISBN 0-907164-08-0 (pbk) : £3.95 : CIP entry B82-36306

336.24′0941 — Great Britain. Income tax

Thornton, Richard, *19---*. The Daily Telegraph guide to income tax. — Completely updated ed., prepared by Richard Thornton / revised by David B. Genders. — London : Collins, 1982. — 111p : 1form ; 20cm
Previous ed.: 1981
ISBN 0-00-434190-2 (pbk) : £1.95 B82-23941

Toch, Henry. Income tax : including corporation tax and capital gains tax / Henry Toch. — 12th ed. — Plymouth : Macdonald and Evans, 1981. — xi,218p ; 19cm. — (The M & E handbook series)
Previous ed.: 1979. — Includes index
ISBN 0-7121-0967-6 (pbk) : £3.75 B82-00721

336.24′17 — Great Britain. Private companies. Shareholders. Taxation

The Private company shareholder : U.K. taxation guide. — [London] : Binder Hamlyn, [1982]. — 18p ; 21cm
Cover title
Unpriced (pbk) B82-27842

336.24′2 — Expatriate British personnel. Taxation in Great Britain

United Kingdom taxation of British nationals working overseas. — [London] ([1 Little New St EC4A 3TR]) : Touche Ross, c1982. — v,33p ; 21cm. — (Touche Ross tax guide)
Unpriced (pbk) B82-31952

336.24′2 — Great Britain. Foreign personnel. Taxation

United Kingdom taxation of foreign nationals working in Britain. — London (1 Little New St EC4A 3TR) : Touche Ross, c1982. — 37p ; 21cm. — (Touche Ross tax guide)
Unpriced (pbk) B82-31953

336.24′2′0941 — Great Britain. Personal income tax — *For executives*

Tax for executives. — London (1 Surrey St., WC2R 2PS) : Arthur Andersen & Co., c1981. — 52p ; 21cm
Private circulation (pbk) B82-13202

336.24′216 — Great Britain. Building societies. Mortgages. Interest. Taxation. Allowances

Taxation and the building society borrower 1982/83. — London (34 Park St., W1Y 3PF) : Building Societies Association, [1982?]. — 1folded sheet([6]p) ; 21cm
Unpriced B82-36390

336.24′26 — Great Britain. Building societies. Investments. Interest. Taxation

Taxation and the building society investor 1982/83. — London (34 Park St., W1Y 3PF) : Building Societies Association, [1982?]. — 1folded sheet([6]p) ; 21cm
Unpriced B82-36389

336.24′3 — Great Britain. Business firms. Stock. Taxation. Allowances — *Serials*

Key to the new stock relief. — Finance Act 1981 ed.-. — [London] : [Taxation Pub. Co.], [1981]-. — v. ; 22cm. — (Taxation master key service)
ISSN 0262-7477 = Key to the new stock relief : £6.00 B82-15145

336.24′3 — Great Britain. Capital gains tax

Cox, Christopher. Capital gains tax on businesses / by Christopher Cox and Harry J. Ross. — London : Sweet & Maxwell, 1982. — xviii,221p,[1]folded leaf of plates : 1ill ; 23cm
Includes index
ISBN 0-421-28230-4 : £18.00 : CIP rev. B82-00295

336.24′3 — Great Britain. Family firms. Tranfer by owners to relatives. Taxation

Thornhill, A. R.. Passing down the family business : solving the tax problems : a specially commissioned report / by A.R. Thornhill and Robert Venables. — [London] : Oyez, [c1981]. — vi,34leaves ; 30cm. — (Oyez intelligence reports)
ISBN 0-85120-536-4 (spiral) : Unpriced B82-00034

336.24′3′0941 — Great Britain. Companies. Taxation

Moullin, Mavis. A guide to the taxation of companies / Mavis Moullin and John Sargent. — London : McGraw-Hill, c1982. — 1v.(loose-leaf) ; 30cm
Includes index
ISBN 0-07-084545-x : £35.00 B82-22483

336.24′3′0941 — Great Britain. Companies. Taxation *compared with* **taxation of companies in West Germany**

Wiseman, Jack. Comparative aspects of the taxaton of business in the United Kingdom and Germany / by Jack Wiseman. — London : Anglo-German Foundation for the Study of Industrial Society, c1980. — 149p : ill ; 22cm
ISBN 0-905492-22-6 : £8.50
Also classified at 336.24′3′0943 B82-01311

336.24′3′0941 — Great Britain. Corporation tax

Guide to UK corporation tax. — London : Arthur Andersen & Co., c1981. — 64p : 1form ; 21cm
Private circulation (pbk) B82-13203

Pritchard, W. E.. Corporation tax / W.E. Pritchard. — 6th ed. — Stockport : Polytech, 1981. — [124]p ; 21x27cm
Previous ed.: 197-. — Includes index
ISBN 0-85505-060-8 (pbk) : £4.50 B82-18396

Rowes, Peter. Corporation tax / by Peter Rowes. — St. Helier : Guild Press, [1981?]. — iv,201p ; 21cm. — (Ready reference series)
Includes index
ISBN 0-907342-01-9 (pbk) : £12.00 B82-02851

Topple, B. S.. Corporation tax / B.S. Topple. — 5th ed. — Plymouth : Macdonald and Evans, 1981. — viii,227p : ill ; 18cm. — (The M & E handbook series)
Previous ed.: 1979. — Includes index
ISBN 0-7121-0467-4 (pbk) : £4.50 B82-03567

336.24′3′0943 — West Germany. Companies. Taxation *compared with* **taxation of companies in Great Britain**

Wiseman, Jack. Comparative aspects of the taxaton of business in the United Kingdom and Germany / by Jack Wiseman. — London : Anglo-German Foundation for the Study of Industrial Society, c1980. — 149p : ill ; 22cm
ISBN 0-905492-22-6 : £8.50
Primary classification 336.24′3′0941 B82-01311

336.24′315 — Great Britain. Business firms. Stock. Taxation. Allowances. Reform — *Proposals*

Stock relief proposals. — [London] ([8 St Bride St., EC4A 4DA]) : Binder Hamlyn-BDO, 1980. — 7p ; 30cm
Unpriced (pbk) B82-23430

Stock relief proposals. — London (227 Strand, WC2R 1BZ) : Binder Hamlyn Fry & Co., c1980. — 10p ; 30cm. — (Executive guide ; BHF 779)
£1.50 (Free to clients) (unbound) B82-23431

336.24′315′0941 — Great Britain. Corporation tax. Reform — *Proposals*

Great Britain. *Treasury*. Corporation tax. — London : H.M.S.O., [1982]. — viii,153p : 3col.ill ; 25cm. — (Cmnd. ; 8456)
"Presented to Parliament by the Chancellor of the Exchequer"
ISBN 0-10-184560-x (pbk) : £7.10 B82-14315

336.2′76 — Great Britain. Capital transfer tax

Eastaway, Nigel. Principles of capital transfer tax / N.A. Eastaway. — London : HFL, c1979. — xi,266p : forms ; 22cm
Includes index
ISBN 0-372-30017-0 (pbk) : £4.95 B82-16307

336.2′76 — Great Britain. Capital transfer tax. Abolition — *Proposals*

Bracewell-Milnes, Barry. A fairer tax on transfers? / Barry Bracewell-Milnes. — London ([181, Sumatra Road, N.W.6]) : [Selsdon Group], [1981?]. — 23leaves ; 30cm. — (Selson brief ; no.2)
£0.35 (unbound) B82-08019

Bracewell-Milnes, Barry. A tax for the axe : the case for abolishing tax on capital transfers / Barry Bracewell-Milnes. — London (71, Fleet St., EC4) : CUT, the taxpayer Union, 1979. — iii,10leaves ; 30cm
Unpriced (pbk) B82-08018

336.2′76 — Great Britain. Capital transfer tax — *For agricultural industries*

Capital transfer tax : a guide for farmers. — Rev. — [Edinburgh] ([West Mains Rd., Edinburgh EH9 3JG]) : [East of Scotland College of Agriculture], 1981. — 13p ; 21cm. — (Publication, ISSN 0308-5708 ; 84)
Cover title. — Previous ed.: 1979
Unpriced (pbk) B82-10319

336.2′786797′094 — European Community countries. Tobacco products. Taxation

Kay, J. A.. The structure of the tobacco taxes in the European Community. — London : Institute for Fiscal Studies, Sept.1982. — [50]p. — (IFS report series ; 1)
ISBN 0-902992-29-5 (pbk) : £5.00 : CIP entry B82-30330

336.2′94 — Nigeria. Direct taxation

Ola, Christopher S.. Nigerian taxation : Christopher S. Ola. — 2nd ed. — Leighton Buzzard : Burn, 1981. — ix,99p ; 30cm
Previous ed.: 1980
ISBN 0-907721-00-1 (pbk) : £7.00 B82-03881

336.2′94 — Nigeria. Direct taxation — *Questions & answers*

Ola, Christopher S.. Examples & answers on Nigerian taxation / Christopher S. Ola. — Leighton Buzzard : Burn, 1981. — vii,71p ; 30cm
ISBN 0-907721-01-x (pbk) : £5.00 B82-03880

336.3 — PUBLIC FINANCE. PUBLIC DEBT AND EXPENDITURE

336.3′4′0941 — Great Britain. National Debt. Reduction by trust funds

Great Britain. *Treasury*. National debt : papers relative to the position as at 31st March 1980, of certain funds left in trust for the reduction of the National Debt. — London : H.M.S.O., 1982. — [4]p ; 25cm. — (Cmnd. ; 8468)
ISBN 0-10-184680-0 (unbound) : £0.70 B82-21804

336.3′4′0941 — Great Britain. Public sector borrowing requirement

Peacock, Alan, *1922-*. The public sector borrowing requirement / by Alan Peacock and G.K. Shaw. — Buckingham : University College at Buckingham, c1981. — 27p : ill ; 21cm. — (Occasional papers in economics ; no.1)
Ill on inside covers. — Bibliography: p25
ISBN 0-907805-00-0 (pbk) : £2.00 B82-10979

336.3′435 — Euro-bond market — *Statistics* — *Serials*

Euromoney syndication guide : the complete data service on syndicated loans and Eurobonds. — Jan. 1981-. — London (Nestor House, Playhouse Yard, EC4V 5EX) : Euromoney Publications, 1981-. — v. ; 30cm
Monthly. — Cumulation of: Euromoney syndication guide. Weekly fact sheet. — Continues: Euromoney syndication service
ISSN 0260-6747 = Euromoney syndication guide : Unpriced
Primary classification 332.1′5 B82-08455

336.3′63 — Great Britain. Public sector borrowing requirement. Interest rates. Econometric models

Beenstock, Michael. Debt management, interest rates and the money supply in the United Kingdom / by Michael Beenstock and Patrick Willcocks. — [London] : [City University Business School], c1981. — 21,[9]leaves : ill ; 30cm. — (Working paper series / the City University Business School, ISSN 0140-1041 ; no.28)
Unpriced (pbk) B82-11550

336.3′9′0941 — Great Britain. *Foreign and Commonwealth Oficee.* **Expenditure. Great Britain.** *Parliament. House of Commons. Foreign Affairs Committee.* **Fourth report ... session 1980-81** — *Critical studies*

Great Britain. *Foreign and Commonwealth Office*. Fourth report from the Foreign Affairs Committee, session 1980-81 : supply estimates 1981-82 (class II, votes 1,2,3,5 and 6) : observations by the Secretary of State for Foreign and Commonwealth Affairs, the Secretary of State for the Environment and the Chief Secretary to the Treasury. — London : H.M.S.O., [1981]. — 9p ; 25cm. — (Miscellaneous ; no.20 (1981)) (Cmnd. ; 8366)
ISBN 0-10-183660-0 (unbound) : £1.50 B82-02315

336.3'9'0941 — Great Britain. Government. Expenditure, *1946-1982*

Pliatzky, Leo. Getting and spending : public expenditure, employment and inflation / Leo Pliatzky. — Oxford : Blackwell, 1982. — viii232p : ill ; 24cm. — (Mainstream series)
Includes index
ISBN 0-631-12907-3 : £12.00 : CIP rev.
B82-01220

336.3'9'0941 — Great Britain. Government. Expenditure — *Inquiry reports*

Great Britain. *Parliament. House of Commons. Treasury and Civil Service Committee.* Fifth report from the Treasury and Civil Service Committee, session 1981-82 : the Government's expenditure plans 1982-83 to 1984-85 : together with the proceedings of the Committee, the minutes of evidence and appendices. — London : H.M.S.O., 1982. — 43p ; 25cm. — ([HC] ; 316)
ISBN 0-10-231682-1 (pbk) : £4.35 B82-27583

336.3'9'0941 — Great Britain. Government. Expenditure. Proposed reduction, *1981-1982 — Socialist viewpoints*

Dunnipace, Phyllis. No cuts, no rates or rent rises! / Phyllis Dunnipace, Rob Jones. — London (P.O. Box 50, N.1) : Cardinal Enterprises, 1981. — 14p : ill,1port ; 21cm. — (Socialist challenge pamphlet)
£0.25 (unbound)
Also classified at 333.33'8 B82-16958

336.3'9'0941 — Great Britain. *Parliament. House of Commons. Committee of Public Accounts.* **Reports** — *Critical studies*

Great Britain. *Treasury*. Treasury minute on the eighth to thirteenth reports from the Committee of Public Accounts, session 1979-80. — London : H.M.S.O., [1980]. — ii,5p ; 25cm. — (Cmnd. ; 8067)
ISBN 0-10-180670-1 (unbound) : £1.10
B82-14712

Great Britain. *Treasury*. Treasury minute on the fifteenth to thirty-fifth reports from the Committee of Public Accounts, session 1979-80 : and table of contents of all Treasury minutes on reports from the session. — London : H.M.S.O., [1981]. — 30p ; 25cm. — (Cmnd. ; 8125)
ISBN 0-10-181250-7 (unbound) : £2.40
B82-15133

Great Britain. *Treasury*. Treasury minute on the first, third to sixth and eighth to seventeenth reports from the Committee of Public Accounts, session 1980-81 : and table of contents of all Treasury minutes on reports from the session. — London : H.M.S.O., [1981]. — 21p ; 25cm. — (Cmnd. ; 8413)
Cover title
ISBN 0-10-184130-2 (pbk) : £2.30 B82-11544

Great Britain. *Treasury*. Treasury minute on the first to fifth reports from the Committee of Public Accounts, session 1981-82. — London : H.M.S.O., [1982?]. — ii,2p ; 25cm. — (Cmnd. ; 8536)
ISBN 0-10-185360-2 (unbound) : £0.70
B82-24694

336.3'9'0941 — Great Britain. Public bodies. Expenditure. Great Britain. *Parliament. House of Commons. Treasury and Civil Service Committee.* **Sixth report ... session 1980-81** — *Critical studies*

Great Britain. *Treasury*. First special report from the Treasury and Civil Service Committee, session 1980-81 : the form of the estimates : observations by HM Treasury on the sixth report from the committee in session 1980-81, HC 325. — London : H.M.S.O., [1981]. — ivp ; 25cm. — ([HC] ; 495)
ISBN 0-10-249581-5 (unbound) : £0.70
B82-11537

336.3'9'09411 — Scotland. Local authorities. Capital expenditure. Control by government of Great Britain — *Convention of Scottish Local Authorities viewpoints*

A Time to listen — a time to speak out : central/local government relationships. — [Edinburgh] ([16 Moray Place, Edinburgh, EH3 6BL]) : Convention of Scottish Local Authorities, 1982. — 40p ; 21cm
£1.00 (pbk) B82-22536

336.3'9'09416 — Northern Ireland. Government. Expenditure. Fourteenth report ... session 1979-80 — *Critical studies*

Great Britain. *Department of Finance for Northern Ireland*. Memorandum on the 14th report from the Committee of Public Accounts, session 1979-80 / Northern Ireland Department of Finance. — London : H.M.S.O., [1980]. — 5p ; 25cm. — (Cmnd. ; 8066)
ISBN 0-10-180660-4 (unbound) : £1.10
B82-14717

336.3'9'0942143 — Islington. *Council.* **Expenditure. Proposed reduction. Attitudes of residents**

Market Opinion and Research International. Public attitudes to rates and council spending in Islington : January-February 1982 : research study conducted for London Borough of Islington / by Market and Opinion Research International Ltd. — London (Town Hall, Upper St., N1 2UD) : London Borough of Islington, 1982. — 38p : forms ; 30cm
Cover title
£12.00 (pbk)
Primary classification 336.22'0942143
B82-26492

336.3'9'0973 — United States. Government. Expenditure, *1974-1980*

Ippolito, Dennis S.. Congressional spending / Dennis S. Ippolito. — Ithaca ; London : Cornell University Press, c1981. — 286p : ill ; 22cm. — (A Twentieth Century Fund report)
Includes index
ISBN 0-8014-1463-6 (cased) : Unpriced
ISBN 0-8014-9230-0 (pbk) : Unpriced
B82-16921

336.4/9 — PUBLIC FINANCE. GEOGRAPHICAL TREATMENT

336.41 — Great Britain. Public finance

Brown, C. V.. Public sector economics. — 2nd ed. — Oxford : Robertson, Sept.1982. — [472]p
Previous ed.: 1978
ISBN 0-85520-525-3 (cased) : £22.00 : CIP entry
ISBN 0-85520-526-1 (pbk) : £9.95 B82-22815

336.41'05 — Great Britain. Public finance — *Serials*

Public money : [policy journal of the public sector]. — Vol.1, no.1 (June 1981)-. — [London] : [CIPFA], 1981-. — v. : ill ; 30cm
Quarterly
ISSN 0261-1252 = Public money : £46.00 per year B82-12474

336.41'0722 — Great Britain. Public finance — *Case studies*

Case studies in public sector economics / edited by Peter Maunder ; [written by] David Greenaway ... [et al.]. — London : Published by Heinemann Educational on behalf of the Economics Association, 1982. — 140p : ill ; 20cm. — (Case studies in economic analysis ; 9)
ISBN 0-435-33939-7 (pbk) : £3.95 : CIP rev.
B81-13506

336.411 — Scotland. Public finance

Government spending in Scotland : a critical appraisal / editor Margaret Cuthbert. — Edinburgh : Harris in association with SCOPE, 1982. — 247p ; 22cm
ISBN 0-86228-050-8 (cased) : £7.95
ISBN 0-86228-051-6 (pbk) : £3.95 B82-29339

336.414'1'05 — Strathclyde. *Regional Council* — *Accounts — Serials*

Strathclyde. *Regional Council*. Strathclyde's finances / Strathclyde Regional Council. — 1978/79-. — [Glasgow] ([20 India St., Glasgow G2 4PF]) : Finance Department, [1980]-. — v. : col.ill,ports ; 30cm
Annual
ISSN 0263-3760 = Strathclyde's finances : Unpriced B82-19878

336.423'5'0212 — Devon. *County Council.* **Finance** — *Statistics — Serials*

Devon. *County Council*. Devon finance. — 1979/1980. — [Exeter] ([County Hall, Topsham Rd, Exeter EX2 4QD]) : [The Council], 1980. — 1v. ; 21x31cm
Continued by: Devon. County Council. Report and accounts. — Only one issue published under this title
£1.00 B82-12457

336.424'1'05 — Gloucestershire. *County Council.* **Finance** — *Serials*

Gloucestershire. *County Council*. Financial report / Gloucestershire County Council. — 1980-81-. — [Gloucester] ([c/o County Treasurer, Shire Hall, Quayside Wing, Gloucester GL1 2TJ]) : The Council, [1981]-. — v. ; 30cm
Annual
ISSN 0262-5148 = Financial report - Gloucestershire County Council : Unpriced
B82-04893

336.428'43 — North Yorkshire. York. Local government, *1396-1500 — Accounts — Latin texts*

York. York City Chamberlain's account rolls 1396-1500 / edited by R.B. Dobson. — Durham (Durham DH1 3EQ) : Surtees Society, 1980. — xlii,236p ; 23cm. — (The Publications of the Surtees Society ; v.192)
English and Latin text. — Includes index
Unpriced B82-22451

336.44 — France. Public finance. Policies of government. Political aspects, *1589-1661*

Bonney, Richard. The king's debts : finance and politics in France 1589-1661 / Richard Bonney. — Oxford : Clarendon, 1981. — xviii,344p ; 23cm
Bibliography: p326-335. — Includes index
ISBN 0-19-822563-6 : £22.50 : CIP rev.
B81-26704

337 — INTERNATIONAL ECONOMICS

337 — Economic relations

Corden, W. M.. Inflation, exchange rates, and the world economy : lectures on international monetary economics / by W.M. Corden. — 2nd ed. — Oxford : Clarendon Press, 1981. — viii,174p : ill ; 23cm
Previous ed.: 1977. — Includes index
ISBN 0-19-877169-x (cased) : Unpriced : CIP rev.
ISBN 0-19-877170-3 (pbk) : Unpriced
B81-11940

337 — Economic relations — *Conference proceedings*

World system structure : continuity and change / edited by W. Ladd Hollist and James N. Rosenau. — Beverly Hills ; London : Sage, c1981. — 320p : ill ; 23cm. — (Sage focus editions ; 37)
Conference papers. — Bibliography: p301-317
ISBN 0-8039-1629-9 (cased) : Unpriced
ISBN 0-8039-1630-2 (pbk) : £6.50 B82-11698

337 — Economic relations. International political aspects

Camps, Miriam. Collective management : the reform of global economic organizations / Miriam Camps with the collaboration of Catherine Gwin. — New York ; London : McGraw-Hill, c1981. — xxiii,371p ; 24cm. — (1980s Project/Council on Foreign Relations)
Bibliography: p353-359. — Includes index
ISBN 0-07-009708-9 (cased) : £12.95
ISBN 0-07-009709-7 (pbk) : Unpriced
B82-22227

337 — Industrialised countries. Economic policies. International economic aspects

National industrial strategies and the world economy / edited by John Pinder. — Totow : Allanheld, Osmun ; London : Croom Helm, 1982. — ix,302p : ill ; 24cm. — (An Atlantic Institute for International Affairs Research volume)
Includes index
ISBN 0-7099-2010-5 : £17.95 B82-33640

337'.09'034 — Economic relations, *1820-1980*

Kenwood, A. G.. Growth of the international economy 1820-1980. — London : Allen & Unwin, Dec.1982. — [320]p
ISBN 0-04-330332-3 : £6.95 : CIP entry
B82-29862

337'.09'04 — Economic relations, *1945-1980.* **International political aspects**
Spero, Joan Edelman. The politics of international economic relations / Joan Edelman Spero. — 2nd ed. — London : Allen & Unwin, 1982, c1981. — x,374p ; 22cm
Originally published: New York : St. Martin's Press, 1981. — Bibliography: p337-363. — Includes index
ISBN 0-04-382035-2 (pbk) : Unpriced : CIP rev. B81-33913

337'.09171'3 — Western bloc countries. Economic relations with communist countries, *1945-1977*
Levinson, Charles. Vodka Cola / Charles Levinson. — Horsham (c/o Biblias, Glenside, Partridge Green, Horsham, W. Sussex RH13 8LD) : C. Levinson, 1980, c1979. — 328p ; 24cm
Translation of: Vodka Cola. — Originally published: London : Gordon and Cremonesi, 1978. — Includes index
ISBN 0-9507313-1-5 (pbk) : Unpriced
Primary classification 337'.09171'7 B82-37984

337'.09171'7 — Communist countries. Economic relations with Western bloc countries, *1945-1977*
Levinson, Charles. Vodka Cola / Charles Levinson. — Horsham (c/o Biblias, Glenside, Partridge Green, Horsham, W. Sussex RH13 8LD) : C. Levinson, 1980, c1979. — 328p ; 24cm
Translation of: Vodka Cola. — Originally published: London : Gordon and Cremonesi, 1978. — Includes index
ISBN 0-9507313-1-5 (pbk) : Unpriced
Also classified at 337'.09171'3 B82-37984

337'.09172'2 — Developed countries. Economic relations with developing countries
East-West-South : economic interactions between three worlds / edited by Christopher T. Saunders. — London : Macmillan, 1981. — x,382p ; 25cm. — (East-West European economic interaction : Workshop papers ; v.6)
Includes index
ISBN 0-333-31870-6 : £20.00
Also classified at 337'.09172'4 B82-06699

Heath, Edward. Third Hoover address : delivered at the University of Strathclyde Glasgow / Edward Heath. — [Glasgow] ([George St., Glasgow G1 1XW]) : [University of Strathclyde], 1980. — 24p ; 22cm
Unpriced (pbk)
Primary classification 337'.09172'4 B82-02543

Marcussen, Henrik Secher. The internationalization of capital. — London : Zed Press, Mar.1982. — [176]p
ISBN 0-905762-90-8 : £16.95 : CIP entry
Primary classification 337'.09172'4 B82-02636

Portes, Alejandro. Labor, class and the international system / Alejandro Portes, John Walton. — New York ; London : Academic, 1981. — xi,230p ; 24cm. — (Studies in social discontinuity)
Bibliography: p199-219. — Includes index
ISBN 0-12-562020-9 : £13.00
Primary classification 337'.09172'4 B82-02008

Rich country interests and Third World development. — London : Croom Helm, June 1982. — [416]p
ISBN 0-7099-1306-0 : £14.95 : CIP entry
Primary classification 337'.09172'4 B82-09588

Singer, H. W.. Rich and poor countries / Hans W. Singer and Javed A. Ansari. — 3rd ed. — London : Allen & Unwin, 1982. — 270p : 1ill ; 22cm. — (Studies in economics ; 12)
Previous ed.: 1978. — Includes index
ISBN 0-04-330321-8 (pbk) : Unpriced : CIP rev.
Also classified at 337'.09172'4 B81-28764

337'.09172'4 — Developing countries. Economic relations with developed countries
East-West-South : economic interactions between three worlds / edited by Christopher T. Saunders. — London : Macmillan, 1981. — x,382p ; 25cm. — (East-West European economic interaction : Workshop papers ; v.6)
Includes index
ISBN 0-333-31870-6 : £20.00
Primary classification 337'.09172'2 B82-06699

Heath, Edward. Third Hoover address : delivered at the University of Strathclyde Glasgow / Edward Heath. — [Glasgow] ([George St., Glasgow G1 1XW]) : [University of Strathclyde], 1980. — 24p ; 22cm
Unpriced (pbk)
Also classified at 337'.09172'2 B82-02543

Marcussen, Henrik Secher. The internationalization of capital. — London : Zed Press, Mar.1982. — [176]p
ISBN 0-905762-90-8 : £16.95 : CIP entry
Also classified at 337'.09172'2 B82-02636

Portes, Alejandro. Labor, class and the international system / Alejandro Portes, John Walton. — New York ; London : Academic, 1981. — xi,230p ; 24cm. — (Studies in social discontinuity)
Bibliography: p199-219. — Includes index
ISBN 0-12-562020-9 : £13.00
Also classified at 337'.09172'2 B82-02008

Rich country interests and Third World development. — London : Croom Helm, June 1982. — [416]p
ISBN 0-7099-1306-0 : £14.95 : CIP entry
Also classified at 337'.09172'2 B82-09588

Singer, H. W.. Rich and poor countries / Hans W. Singer and Javed A. Ansari. — 3rd ed. — London : Allen & Unwin, 1982. — 270p : 1ill ; 22cm. — (Studies in economics ; 12)
Previous ed.: 1978. — Includes index
ISBN 0-04-330321-8 (pbk) : Unpriced : CIP rev.
Primary classification 337'.09172'2 B81-28764

337'.09172'4 — Developing countries. Economic relations with European Economic Community — *Serials*
EEC and the Third World. — 2. — London : Hodder and Stoughton, Feb.1982. — [192]p
ISBN 0-340-27772-6 (pbk) : £5.95 : CIP entry
ISSN 0261-3484
Primary classification 337.1'42 B81-40247

337'.094 — European Economic Community. Economic relations with Japan, *1959-1981*
Rothacher, Albrecht. Economic diplomacy between the European Community and Japan 1959-1981. — Aldershot : Gower, Dec.1982. — [380]p
ISBN 0-566-00532-8 : £15.00 : CIP entry
Also classified at 337'.0952 B82-30052

337'.0952 — Japan. Economic relations with European Economic Community, *1959-1981*
Rothacher, Albrecht. Economic diplomacy between the European Community and Japan 1959-1981. — Aldershot : Gower, Dec.1982. — [380]p
ISBN 0-566-00532-8 : £15.00 : CIP entry
Primary classification 337'.094 B82-30052

337.1'42 — European Community countries. Integration
Building Europe : Britain's partners in the EEC / edited by Carol and Kenneth J. Twitchett. — London : Europa, 1981. — xviii,262p ; 24cm
Bibliography: p237-254. — Includes index
ISBN 0-905118-61-8 : £16.00 : CIP rev. B81-13850

Contemporary perspectives on European integration : attitudes, nongovernmental behaviour, and collective decision making / edited by Leon Hurwitz. — London : Aldwych, 1980. — xx,292p : ill ; 25cm. — (European studies ; no.4)
Includes index
ISBN 0-86172-012-1 : £19.95 B82-30929

Taylor, Paul. The limits of European integration. — London : Croom Helm, Jan.1983. — [336]p
ISBN 0-7099-2423-2 : £14.95 : CIP entry B82-35210

337.1'42 — European Community countries. International economic cooperation
The **Collaboration** of nations : a study of European economic policy / edited by Douglas Dosser, David Gowland and Keith Hartley. — Oxford : Martin Robertson, 1982. — x,252p : ill ; 24cm
Bibliography: p233-242. — Includes index
ISBN 0-85520-389-7 (cased) : £19.50 : CIP rev.
ISBN 0-85520-395-1 (pbk) : £8.50 B81-22583

337.1'42 — European Community. Role of Great Britain — *Conference proceedings*
Britain in Europe / edited by William Wallace. — London : Heinemann, 1980. — x,213p : 1ill ; 23cm. — (Joint studies in public policy ; 1)
Conference papers. — Includes index
ISBN 0-435-83919-5 (cased) : £10.50 : CIP rev.
ISBN 0-435-83920-9 (pbk£4.95) B80-12758

337.1'42 — European Community. Role of Wales
Richard, Ivor. Wales and Europe — a new perspective / Ivor Richard. — London : British Broadcasting Corporation, 1981. — 23p ; 19cm
'Broadcast on Radio Wales and Radio Cymru, 24 November 1981 at 7.50pm'
ISBN 0-563-20064-2 (pbk) : £0.75 B82-09466

337.1'42 — European Economic Community. Economic relations with developing countries — *Serials*
EEC and the Third World. — 2. — London : Hodder and Stoughton, Feb.1982. — [192]p
ISBN 0-340-27772-6 (pbk) : £5.95 : CIP entry
ISSN 0261-3484
Also classified at 337'.09172'4 B81-40247

337.1'42 — European Economic Community. Economic relations with Japan
Japan and Western Europe. — London : Pinter, Aug.1982. — [240]p
ISBN 0-86187-252-5 : £16.50 : CIP entry
Primary classification 337.5204 B82-17930

337.1'42 — European Economic Community. Economic relations with New Zealand, *1973-1981*
Lodge, Juliet. The Economic Community and New Zealand. — London : Francis Pinter, Apr.1982. — [256]p
ISBN 0-86187-215-0 : £15.00 : CIP entry
Also classified at 337.93104 B82-14928

337.1'42 — European Economic Community. Enlargement
The **Second** enlargement of the EEC : the integration of unequal partners / edited by Dudley Seers and Constantine Vaitsos with the assistance of Marja-Liisa Kiljunen. — London : Macmillan, 1982. — xx,275p ; 23cm. — (Studies in the integration of Western Europe)
Includes index
ISBN 0-333-29189-1 : Unpriced B82-33849

337.1'42 — European Economic Community. Entry of Great Britain — *For children*
Crane, Peggy. Towards European unity / Peggy Crane. — Hove : Wayland, 1981. — 71p : ill,maps,ports ; 24cm. — (People, politics and powers)
Bibliography: p70. — Includes index
ISBN 0-85340-673-1 : £4.50 B82-06548

337.1'42 — European Economic Community. Entry of Spain & Portugal. Economic aspects — *Confederation of British Industry viewpoints*
Enlargement of the European Community to include Spain and Portugal : report of a CBI working party. — London : Confederation of British Industry, 1981. — 39p ; 30cm
£2.00 (pbk) B82-00948

337.1'42 — Western European countries. Integration, *1945-1950*
Lipgens, Walter. A history of European integration / by Walter Lipgens. — Oxford : Clarendon
Translation of: Die Anfänge der europäischen Einigungspolitik 1945-1950
Vol.1: The formation of the European unity movement / with contributions by Wilfried Loth and Alan Milward ; translated from the German by P.S. Falla and A.J. Ryder. — 1982. — xvi,723p ; 24cm
Includes index
ISBN 0-19-822587-3 : £48.00 : CIP rev. B81-31450

337.41073 — Great Britain. Economic relations with United States, *1942-1949*

Clarke, *Sir* **Richard**, *1910-*. Anglo-American economic collaboration in war and peace 1942-1949 / by Sir Richard Clarke ; edited by Sir Alec Cairncross. — Oxford : Clarendon, 1982. — xxiii,215p ; 24cm
ISBN 0-19-828439-x : Unpriced : CIP rev.
Also classified at 337.73041 B81-33859

337.52 — Japan. Economic relations

Ozawa, Terutomo. Multinationalism, Japanese style : the political economy of outward dependency / Terutomo Ozawa. — Princeton, N.J. ; Guildford : Princeton University Press, 1979 (1982 [printing]). — xxiii,289p ; 22cm
Bibliography: p263-275. — Includes index
ISBN 0-691-00367-x (pbk) : Unpriced
B82-38417

337.5204 — Japan. Economic relations with European Economic Community

Japan and Western Europe. — London : Pinter, Aug.1982. — [240]p
ISBN 0-86187-252-5 : £16.50 : CIP entry
Also classified at 337.1'42 B82-17930

337.52073 — Japan. Economic relations with United States

Coping with U.S.-Japanese economic conflicts / edited by I.M. Destler, Hideo Sato. — Lexington, Mass. : Lexington Books ; [Aldershot] : Gower [distributor], 1982. — viii,293p : ill ; 24cm
Includes bibliographies
ISBN 0-669-05144-6 : £18.50
Primary classification 337.73052 B82-36670

337.67'9'068 — South Mozambique. Economic relations with South Africa, *1875-1980*

Katzenellenbogen, Simon E.. South Africa and southern Mozambique : labour, railways and trade in the making of a relationship / Simon E. Katzenellenbogen. — Manchester : Manchester University Press, c1982. — 178p : 1map ; 23cm
Bibliography: p164-171. — Includes index
ISBN 0-7190-0853-0 : £18.50 : CIP rev.
Also classified at 337.68067'9 B81-33830

337.68067'9 — South Africa. Economic relations with Southern Mozambique, *1875-1980*

Katzenellenbogen, Simon E.. South Africa and southern Mozambique : labour, railways and trade in the making of a relationship / Simon E. Katzenellenbogen. — Manchester : Manchester University Press, c1982. — 178p : 1map ; 23cm
Bibliography: p164-171. — Includes index
ISBN 0-7190-0853-0 : £18.50 : CIP rev.
Primary classification 337.67'9'068 B81-33830

337.73 — United States. Economic relations, *1970-1980*

Bergsten, C. Fred. The world economy in the 1980s : selected papers of C. Fred Bergsten, 1980 / C. Fred Bergsten. — Lexington : Lexington Books, c1981 ; [Aldershot] : Gower [distributor], 1982. — x,178p ; 24cm
Includes index
ISBN 0-669-04658-2 : £13.50 B82-18258

337.73041 — United States. Economic relations with Great Britain, *1942-1949*

Clarke, *Sir* **Richard**, *1910-*. Anglo-American economic collaboration in war and peace 1942-1949 / by Sir Richard Clarke ; edited by Sir Alec Cairncross. — Oxford : Clarendon, 1982. — xxiii,215p ; 24cm
ISBN 0-19-828439-x : Unpriced : CIP rev.
Primary classification 337.41073 B81-33859

337.73052 — United States. Economic relations with Japan

Coping with U.S.-Japanese economic conflicts / edited by I.M. Destler, Hideo Sato. — Lexington, Mass. : Lexington Books ; [Aldershot] : Gower [distributor], 1982. — viii,293p : ill ; 24cm
Includes bibliographies
ISBN 0-669-05144-6 : £18.50
Also classified at 337.52073 B82-36670

337.8 — Latin America. Economic policies. International economic aspects

Latin America and the new international economic order / edited by Ricardo Ffrench-Davis and Ernesto Tironi. — Oxford : Macmillan in association with St. Anthony's College, Oxford, 1982. — xv,254p : 1ill ; 23cm. — (St Antony's/Macmillan series)
Includes bibliographies and index
ISBN 0-333-30074-2 : Unpriced B82-31690

337.93104 — New Zealand. Economic relations with European Economic Community, *1973-1981*

Lodge, Juliet. The Economic Community and New Zealand. — London : Francis Pinter, Apr.1982. — [256]p
ISBN 0-86187-215-0 : £15.00 : CIP entry
Primary classification 337.1'42 B82-14928

338 — ECONOMICS. PRODUCTION, INDUSTRIES

338 — Industries — *For schools*

Hogarth, Alasdair J.. Understanding industry. — London : Arnold, Nov.1982. — [64]p
ISBN 0-7131-0813-4 (pbk) : £1.50 : CIP entry
B82-27943

Price, Nigel. Industry. — London : Edward Arnold, Nov.1982. — [64]p. — (Foundation geography)
ISBN 0-7131-0664-6 (pbk) : £2.00 : CIP entry
B82-27954

338 — International industrial cooperation — *German texts*

Pollak, Christian. Neue Formen internationaler Unterneh-menszusammenarbeit ohne Kapitalbeteiligung / von Christian Pollak. — München ; London : Weltforum Verlag, 1982. — v,161p ; 21cm. — (IFO-Studien zur Entwicklungsforschung ; 10)
At head of title: IFO-Institut für Wirtschaftsforschung, München. —
Bibliography: p152-161
ISBN 3-8039-0224-x : Unpriced B82-21654

338 — Nationalised industries

Welsh, Frank. The profit of the state : nationalised industries and public enterprises. — London : Temple Smith, Aug.1982. — [240]p
ISBN 0-85117-225-3 : £10.00 : CIP entry
B82-18480

338 — Production

Leake, Andrew. Consumption and production. — London : Macmillan, Feb.1982. — [48]p. — (Casebooks on economic theory)
ISBN 0-333-27988-3 (pbk) : £1.25 : CIP entry
B81-35951

338'.0025'4267 — Essex. Industrial estates. Industries — *Directories*

Enterprise in Essex : industrial estate directory. — Chelmsford (c/o Employment Promotion Officer, County Hall, Chelmsford CM1 1LF) : Essex County Council, c1981. — [178]p : maps ; 30cm
Unpriced (spiral) B82-29478

338'.0025'4281 — Yorkshire. Industries — *Directories*

The **Yorkshire** & Humberside company guide : manufacturing and construction industries / Yorkshire & Humberside Development Association. — [2nd ed.]. — Halifax : Metro, 1981. — 312p : ill,1port ; 30cm
Previous ed.: 1976
ISBN 0-907884-00-8 (pbk) : Unpriced
B82-20537

338'.003 — Industries — *Polyglot dictionaries*

Logie, Gordon. Glossary of employment and industry : English-French-Italian-Dutch-German-Swedish / Gordon Logie. — Amsterdam ; Oxford : Elsevier Scientific, 1982. — xxix,290p ; 23cm. — (International planning glossaries ; 3)
Bibliography: p287-288. — Includes index
ISBN 0-444-42064-9 : £28.78 : CIP rev.
B82-05396

338'.007 — Avon. Industries & trades. Information sources — *Lists* — *For small firms*

Sources of advice for smaller firms in Avon / Avon County Council. — Bristol : Avon County Public Relations and Publicity Department, [1982]. — 38p ; 15x22cm
Bibliography: p38
ISBN 0-86063-141-9 (pbk) : £0.50 B82-29847

338'.01 — Factors of production

Leake, Andrew. Factor markets. — London : Macmillan Education, Feb.1982. — [48]p. — (Casebooks on economic theory)
ISBN 0-333-27989-1 (pbk) : £1.25 : CIP entry
B81-35949

338'.01 — Factors of production: Capital & labour. Optimisation. Mathematical models

Murphy, Phil. A simple model of optimal capital and labour accumulation for the competitive firm under conditions of uncertainty and risk aversion / by Phil Murphy. — Aberdeen : University of Aberdeen Department of Political Economy, [1981]. — 19p ; 30cm. — (Discussion paper / University of Aberdeen Department of Political Economy ; no.81-14)
Bibliography: leaf 19
Unpriced (pbk) B82-05823

338'.02 — South-east Asia. Consumer goods. Supply & demand. Forecasts — *Conference proceedings*

Marketing trends in the Asia Pacific region : economic forecasts and consumer developments : Indonesia, Malaysia, Hong Kong, the Philippines, Singapore, Thailand / the Asia Pacific Centre. — Aldershot : Gower, [1981?]. — ix,221p ; 31cm
Conference papers
ISBN 0-566-02361-x : Unpriced : CIP rev.
B81-36215

338'.04 — Entrepreneurship

Casson, Mark. Unemployment. — Oxford : Martin Robertson, Oct.1981. — [250]p
ISBN 0-85520-306-4 (cased) : £12.50 : CIP entry
ISBN 0-85520-439-7 (pbk) : £3.75 B81-27400

338'.04'0924 — England. Entrepreneurship. Goldsmith, *Sir* **Jame** — *Biographies*

Wansell, Geoffrey. Sir James Goldsmith / Geoffrey Wansell. — [London] : Fontana, 1982. — 222p,[8]p of plates : ill,ports ; 18cm
Includes index
ISBN 0-00-636503-5 (pbk) : £1.95 B82-26519

338'.04'0941 — Great Britain. Entrepreneurship, *ca 1700-1870*

Honeyman, Katrina. Origins of enterprise : business leadership in the industrial revolution. — Manchester : Manchester University Press, Nov.1982. — [224]p
ISBN 0-7190-0873-5 : £15.00 : CIP entry
B82-26402

338'.06 — Great Britain. Industries. Effects of microelectronic devices — *Trade union viewpoints*

TUC Education. The chip at work : a discussion book on the new technology / TUC Education. — London : TUC, 1981. — 38p : ill ; 30cm
Cover title. — Bibliography: p36-37
Unpriced (pbk) B82-24078

338'.06 — Great Britain. Industries. Innovation

Carey, *Sir* **Peter**. Towards industrial innovation / by Sir Peter Carey. — Sheffield (c/o Hon. Sec. Sheffield City Polytechnic, Pond St., Sheffield S1 1WB) : Association of Colleges for Further and Higher Education, [1982]. — 11p ; 21cm
Conference paper from ACFHE annual general meeting, 25-26 Februrary 1982
£0.75 (unbound) B82-24394

338'.06 — Great Britain. Industries. Innovation. Effects of regional economic development

Thwaites, A. T.. Some evidence of regional variations in the innovation and diffusion of industrial products and processes within British manufacturing industry / by Alfred Thwaites. — [Newcastle upon Tyne] : [University of Newcastle upon Tyne. Centre for Urban and Regional Development Studies], 1981. — [22]p ; 30cm. — (Discussion paper, ISSN 0140-6515 ; no.40)
Bibliography: p21-22
Unpriced (unbound) B82-27745

338'.06 — Great Britain. Industries. Innovation. Statistical analysis

Regional and urban perspectives on industrial innovation : applications of logit and cluster analysis to industrial survey data / by N. Alderman ... [et al.]. — [Newcastle upon Tyne] : University of Newcastle upon Tyne. Centre for Urban and Regional Development Studies, 1982. — 41p ; 30cm. — (Discussion paper, ISSN 0140-6515 ; no.42)
Subtitle: Papers given at a joint meeting of the Urban and Quantitative Study Groups, 14-15 Sept., Woolton Hall, Manchester. — Bibliography: p41
Unpriced (unbound) B82-27744

338'.06 — Great Britain. Industries. Technological innovation

Great Britain. The Government response to the ACARD report on information technology. — [London] ([Ashdown House Library, 123 Victoria St., SW1E 6RB]) : Department of Industry, 1981. — [9]p ; 30cm
Unpriced (unbound) B82-38332

Technology, putting it to work : opportunities, prospects, problems. — London (103 New Oxford St. WC1A 1DU) : Confederation of British Industry, 1982. — 47p ; 30cm
£5.00 (pbk) B82-41140

338'.06 — Great Britain. Industries. Technological innovation, *1945-1980*

Science and technology indicators for the UK : innovations in Britain since 1945 / by J. Townsend ... [et al.]. — Brighton : Science Policy Reseach Unit, University of Sussex, c1981. — v,129p ; 30cm. — (SPRU occasional paper series ; no.16)
ISBN 0-903622-17-3 (spiral) : Unpriced B82-21196

338'.06 — Great Britain. Industries. Technological innovation. Socioeconomic aspects

Wilkinson, Barry. The shopfloor politics of new technology. — London : Heinemann Educational, Dec.1982. — [144]p
ISBN 0-435-82950-5 (cased) : £14.50 : CIP entry
ISBN 0-435-82051-3 (pbk) : £5.95 B82-36133

338'.06 — Great Britain. Industries. Technological innovation. Socioeconomic aspects, *1815-1848*

Berg, Maxine. The machinery question and the making of political economy 1815-1848 / Maxine Berg. — Cambridge : Cambridge University Press, 1980 (1982 [printing]). — x,379p : ill ; 23cm
Bibliography: p343-366. — Includes index
ISBN 0-521-28759-6 (pbk) : £8.95 : CIP rev. B82-07961

338'.06 — Great Britain. Technological innovation. Economic aspects

Technical innovation and British economic performance / Science Policy Research Unit, Sussex ; edited by Keith Pavitt. — London : Macmillan, 1980 (1982 [printing]). — x,353p : ill ; 22cm
Includes bibliographies and index
ISBN 0-333-33381-0 (pbk) : £8.95 B82-38786

338'.06 — Industries. Applications of microprocessor systems

Baldwin, J. N. W.. Microprocessors for industry. — London : Butterworths, Mar.1982. — [144]p
ISBN 0-408-00517-3 : £7.50 : CIP entry B82-00922

338'.06 — Industries. Applications of microprocessors

Microprocessors in industry : selected papers. — Manchester : NCC, 1981. — 270p : ill ; 21cm
Bibliography: p265
ISBN 0-85012-322-4 (pbk) : Unpriced : CIP rev. B81-18045

338'.06 — Industries. Microelectronic devices. Implications

The **Impact** of microelectronics / Technology Policy Unit, University of Aston, Birmingham ; prepared by J.R. Bessant ... [et al.] ; foreword by Ernest Braun. — London : Pinter, 1981. — 174p : ill ; 22cm
Bibliography: p137-174
ISBN 0-903804-71-9 : Unpriced B82-02115

338'.06 — Industries. Production. Standards

Tucker, Spencer A.. Production standards for profit planning / Spencer A. Tucker, Thomas H. Lennon. — New York ; London : Van Nostrand Reinhold, c1982. — xvi,193p : ill,forms ; 28cm
Includes index
ISBN 0-442-88016-2 : £29.35 B82-18928

338'.06 — Industries. Productivity — *Comparative studies*

Smith, A. D.. International industrial productivity. — Cambridge : Cambridge University Press, Nov.1982. — [170]p. — (Occasional papers / National Institute of Economic and Social Research ; 34)
ISBN 0-521-24901-5 : £13.50 : CIP entry B82-29386

338'.06 — Soviet Union. Industries. Role of technological innovation

Industrial innovation in the Soviet Union / edited by Ronald Amann and Julian Cooper. — New Haven ; London : Yale University Press, 1982. — xxix,526p : ill ; 26cm
Includes index
ISBN 0-300-02772-9 : Unpriced : CIP rev. B82-21367

338'.06 — Technological innovation. Influence of market structure. Economic aspects

Kamien, Morton I.. Market structure and innovation / Morton I. Kamien and Nancy L. Schwartz. — Cambridge : Cambridge University Press, c1982. — xi,241p ; 22cm. — (Cambridge surveys of economic literature)
Bibliography: p224-235. — Includes index
ISBN 0-521-22190-0 : £17.50
ISBN 0-521-29385-5 (pbk) : £6.95 B82-22196

338'.06'094 — Western Europe. Industrialisation. Role of engineers, *1800-1930*

Ahlström, Göran. Engineers and industrial growth : higher technical education and the engineering profession during the nineteenth and early twentieth centuries : France, Germany, Sweden and England / Göran Ahlström. — London : Croom Helm, c1982. — 118p ; 23cm
Bibliography: p109-116. — Includes index
ISBN 0-7099-0506-8 : £10.95 : CIP rev. B81-34310

338'.06'0941 — Great Britain. Industries. Productivity, *1850-1914 related to* **development of state education,** *1850-1914*

Where did we go wrong? : industrial performance, education and the economy in Victorian Britain / edited and introduced by Gordon Roderick and Michael Stephens. — Lewes (Falmer House, Barcombe, Lewes, Sussex BN8 5DL) : Falmer Press, 1981. — 262p : ill ; 24cm. — ([Politics and education series])
Includes index
ISBN 0-905273-11-7 : Unpriced
Also classified at 379.41 B82-02431

338'.06'0941 — Great Britain. Industries. Productivity, *1870-1980 related to* **development of state education,** *1870-1980*

The **British** malaise : industrial performance, education & training in Britain today / edited and introduced by Gordon Roderick and Michael Stephens. — Barcombe : Falmer, 1982. — viii,173p : ill ; 24cm. — ([Politics and education series])
Includes index
ISBN 0-905273-21-4 : Unpriced
Also classified at 379.41 B82-17182

338'.06'0941 — Great Britain. Industries. Productivity. Attitudes of personnel, managers & trade unions

Productivity : the British perspective / conducted in Great Britain by Louis Harris International. — [Milton Keynes] ([499 Silbury Boulevard, Milton Keynes MK9 2LA]) : Sentry Insurance Group [UK] Limited, 1981. — 24p ; 30cm. — (A Sentry study)
Cover title
Unpriced (pbk) B82-25953

338'.06'0947 — Soviet Union. Technological development. Economic aspects

Kheĭnman, S. A.. Scientific and technical revolution : economic aspects / S.A. Heinman ; [translated from the Russian by Yu. Sdobnikov]. — Moscow : Progress, 1981 ; [London] : Distributed by Central Books. — 341p ; 21cm
Translation of: Ekonomicheskie aspekty nauchno-tekhnicheskoĭ revolíutsii
ISBN 0-7147-1761-4 : £3.95 B82-39307

338.09 — Industries. Geographical aspects — *For schools*

Huggett, Richard. Industry / Richard Huggett & Iain Meyer. — London : Harper & Row, 1981. — 184p : ill,maps ; 25cm. — (Geography ; bk.3)
ISBN 0-06-318164-9 (pbk) : £4.95 B82-27324

338.09171'3 — Western bloc countries. Industrial cooperation with communist countries

Paliwoda, Stanley J.. Industrial cooperation : theory and practice, with special reference to the East-West context / S.J. Paliwoda. — Manchester (P.O. Box 88, Manchester M60 1QD) : Department of Management Sciences, University of Manchester Institute of Science and Technology, 1982. — 26leaves ; 31cm. — (Occasional paper / Department of Management Sciences, University of Manchester Institute of Science and Technology ; no.8202)
Unpriced (pbk)
Also classified at 338.09171'7 B82-27240

338.09171'7 — Communist countries. Industrial cooperation with Western bloc countries

Paliwoda, Stanley J.. Industrial cooperation : theory and practice, with special reference to the East-West context / S.J. Paliwoda. — Manchester (P.O. Box 88, Manchester M60 1QD) : Department of Management Sciences, University of Manchester Institute of Science and Technology, 1982. — 26leaves ; 31cm. — (Occasional paper / Department of Management Sciences, University of Manchester Institute of Science and Technology ; no.8202)
Unpriced (pbk)
Primary classification 338.09171'3 B82-27240

338.09172'4 — Developing countries. Industrialisation

Mountjoy, Alan B.. Industrialization and developing countries / Alan B. Mountjoy. — 5th ed. — London : Hutchinson, 1982. — 256p : ill,maps ; 22cm. — (Hutchinson university library)
Previous ed.: 1975. — Bibliography: p243-246. — Includes index
ISBN 0-09-146801-9 (pbk) : £4.95 : CIP rev. B82-03743

338.09172'4 — Developing countries. Industries — *For schools*

Massingham, Bryan. Cities and industry in the developing world / Bryan Massingham. — London : Edward Arnold, 1981. — 64p : ill,maps ; 24cm. — (Patterns of development)
ISBN 0-7131-0455-4 (pbk) : £2.25 : CIP rev.
Primary classification 307.7'6'091724 B81-23832

338.09172'4 — Newly industrialising countries. Industrial development

Turner, Louis. The newly industrializing countries : trade and adjustment / Louis Turner and Neil McMullen with Colin I. Bradford, Jr ... [et al.]. — London : Published for the Royal Institution of International Affairs by Allen & Unwin, 1982. — xi,290p ; 24cm
Bibliography: p271-284. — Includes index
ISBN 0-04-382036-0 : Unpriced : CIP rev. B82-15641

338.094 — Europe. Industrial development — *Serials*

Industry, commerce, development. — Vol.1, no.1 (Mar. 1982)-. — Bradford : MCB (Industrial Development) on behalf of the Association of Industrial Development Officers, 1982-. — v. : ill,ports ; 30cm
Monthly. — Merger of: European industrial and commercial review; and, Industrial development officer
ISSN 0262-7620 = Industry, commerce, development : £25.00 per year (free to members of the Association) B82-24762

338.094 — Europe. Industrialisation, *1780-1914 — Comparative studies*

Trebilcock, Clive. The industrialization of the continental powers 1780-1914 / Clive Trebilcock. — London : Longman, 1981. — xvi, : maps ; 24cm
Bibliography: p454-474. — Includes index
ISBN 0-582-49119-3 (cased) : Unpriced : CIP rev.
ISBN 0-582-49120-7 (pbk) : £7.50 B80-25316

338.094 — Europe. Industrialisation, *1800-1900 — For children — Irish texts*

Matthys, Robert. Fás na tionsclaíochta sa naoú céad déag / Robert Matthys ; Ghislaine Joos a mhaisigh ; Peadar Ó Casaide a rinne an leagan Gaeilge. — Baile Átha Cliath : Oifig an tSoláthair, c1981. — 26p : ill(some col.) ; 23cm. — (Leabhair staire le léaraidí)
Unpriced B82-19590

338'.094 — Western Europe. Industrialisation, *1790-1914.* **Attitudes of Scandinavian, Mediterranean & Eastern European countries**

Berend, I.. The European periphery and industrialization 1780-1914. — Cambridge : Cambridge University Press, Nov.1982. — [176]p. — (Studies in modern capitalism = Etudes sur le capitalisme moderne, ISSN 0144-2333)
ISBN 0-521-24210-x : £17.50 : CIP entry B82-29394

338.0941 — Great Britain. Industrial development, *1740-1900 — For schools*

Nichol, Jon. Developing Britain 1740-1900 : the agrarian, transport and industrial revolutions / Jon Nichol. — Oxford : Blackwell, 1981. — 64p : ill,maps,facsims,plans ; 30cm. — (Evidence in history)
Text on back cover
ISBN 0-631-93350-6 (pbk) : Unpriced B82-24205

338.0941 — Great Britain. Industrialisation, *1760-1837 — For schools*

Farnworth, Warren. Industrial Britain. — London : Bell & Hyman, Oct.1981. — [80]p. — (History around us)
ISBN 0-7135-1289-x (pbk) : £3.95 : CIP entry B81-25722

338.0941 — Great Britain. Industries

Braddeley, J. M.. Understanding industry. — 2nd ed. — London : Butterworth Scientific, Feb.1983. — [136]p
Previous ed.: 1980
ISBN 0-408-10860-6 (pbk) : £3.25 : CIP entry B82-38282

Morrell, James. The regeneration of British industry / by James Morrell and James Bellini. — London (2/4 Tudor St., E.C.4) : Henley Centre for Forecasting, [1981]. — 231p : ill ; 30cm
Unpriced (spiral) B82-02511

338.0941 — Great Britain. Industries & trades — *Statistics — Serials — For marketing*

The **A-Z** of UK marketing data. — 1982 (2nd ed.). — London : Euromonitor, July 1982. — [256]p
Previous ed.: 1980
ISBN 0-903706-83-0 (pbk) : £22.50 : CIP entry B82-20658

338.0941 — Great Britain. Industries, *1000-1500.* **Sources of evidence: Antiquities**

Medieval industry / edited by D.W. Crossley. — London : Council for British Archaeology, 1981. — vii,156p : ill,maps ; 30cm. — (Research report, ISSN 0589-9036 ; no.40)
Includes bibliographies and index
ISBN 0-906780-07-1 (pbk) : Unpriced : CIP rev. B81-28204

338.0941 — Great Britain. Industries, *1500-1939*

Musson, A. E.. The growth of British industry / A.E. Musson. — London : Batsford, 1978 (1981 [printing]). — 396p ; 22cm
Bibliography: p359-387. — Includes index
ISBN 0-7134-1243-7 (pbk) : £7.95 B82-01686

338.0941 — Great Britain. Industries — *Liberal Party viewpoints*

Saunders, James H.. Redeveloping British industry / James H. Saunders. — Hythe (21 Fisher Close, Hythe, Kent, CT21 6AB) : New Creation Enterprises, [1982]. — 21p ; 21cm. — (The Orpington initiative ; pamphlet no.4)
£1.00 (pbk) B82-30658

338.0941 — Great Britain. Industries. Resources. Allocation *compared with* **allocation of resources in West German industries**

Cox, Joan G.. Growth, innovation and employment : an Anglo-German comparison / by Joan G. Cox with Herbert Kriegbaum. — London : Anglo-German Foundation for the Study of Industrial Society, c1980. — vi,77p : ill ; 21cm
ISBN 0-905492-31-5 (pbk) : £3.50
Also classified at 338'.0943 B82-34557

338.0941 — Great Britain. Nationalised industries

Redwood, John. Controlling public industries / John Redwood and John Hatch. — Oxford : Basil Blackwell, 1982. — vi,169p : ill ; 24cm
Includes index
ISBN 0-631-13017-9 (cased) : Unpriced : CIP rev.
ISBN 0-631-13078-0 (pbk) : Unpriced B82-09459

338.0941 — Great Britain. Nationalised industries. Attitudes of consumers

The **Nationalised** industries / ... survey carried out for the National Consumer Council by Research Services Limited. — London : The Council, 1981. — 28p ; 30cm. — (Occasional paper ; [2])
ISBN 0-905653-34-3 (pbk) : Unpriced B82-01508

338.0941 — Great Britain. Nationalised industries. Consumer protection services

Consumers' interests and the nationalised industries — a consultative document / Department of Trade. — London : The Department, 1981. — 42p : 3maps ; 30cm
Unpriced (pbk) B82-40101

Memorandum in response to the Department of Trade's consultative document "Consumers' interest and the nationalised industries" / Electricity Consumers' Council. — London (119 Marylebone Rd., NW1 5PY) : The Council, 1982. — 25leaves ; 30cm
£1.00 (spiral) B82-30835

338.0941 — Great Britain. Nationalised industries. Privatisation

Labour Research Department. Public or private : the case against privatisation / Labour Research Department]. — London : LRD Publications, 1982. — 37p : ill ; 21cm
Cover title
ISBN 0-900508-50-7 (pbk) : £0.70
Also classified at 363'.0941 B82-36864

338.0941 — Great Britain. Nationalised industries. Shares. Sale — *Inquiry reports*

Great Britain. *Parliament. House of Commons. Committee of Public Accounts.* Tenth report from the Committee of Public Accounts : together with the proceedings of the committee, minutes of evidence and appendices, session 1981-82 : Department of Industry : sale of shares in British aerospace; sale of Government shareholdings in other publicly owned companies and in British Petroleum Ltd; postponement of payments. — London : H.M.S.O., 1982. — 18p ; 25cm. — ([HC] ; 189)
ISBN 0-10-218982-x (pbk) : £3.40 B82-27582

338.09417 — Ireland *(Republic).* **Industries & trades —** *Serials*

[**Success** *(Dun Laoghaire)*]. Success. — Apr. 1982-. — Dun Laoghaire (6c Kill Ave., Kill O' The Grange, Dun Laoghaire, Co. Dublin) : Success Publications, 1982-. — v. : ill(some col.),ports(some col.) ; 28cm
Monthly. — Description based on: June 1982
£9.60 per year B82-32138

338.09425'74 — Oxfordshire. Oxford Airport region. Industrial development — *Proposals*

Consultation on possible development : Oxford Airport / Oxford City Council. — [Oxford] ([109 St. Aldate's, Oxford OX1 1DX]) : [City Architect and Planning Officer], [1981?]. — [5]p : 1ill ; 30cm
Unpriced (unbound) B82-05019

338.09428'1 — West Yorkshire *(Metropolitan County).* **Industrial development,** *1500-1830*

Thornes, R. C. N.. West Yorkshire : a noble scene of industry : the development of the county 1500 to 1830 / by R.C.N. Thornes. — [Wakefield] : West Yorkshire Metropolitan County Council, c1981. — x,59p : ill,maps ; 30cm
Bibliography: p57-59
ISBN 0-86181-002-3 (pbk) : £2.50 B82-07573

338'.09428'1 — Yorkshire. Industries — *Serials*

Business in Yorkshire. — Vol.1, no.1 (Feb. 1982)-. — Chesterfield (Penmore House, Hasland Rd, Chesterfield S41 0SJ) : Direct Business Communications, 1982-. — v. : ill,ports ; 30cm
Monthly
ISSN 0263-1067 = Business in Yorkshire : £6.00 per year B82-18725

338.09429'63 — Dyfed. Saundersfoot. Industrial development, *1750-1950*

Price, M. R. C.. Industrial Saundersfoot / M.R.C. Price. — Llandysul : Gomer Press, 1982. — 237p,[57]p of plates : ill,facsims,maps,plans,ports ; 22cm
ISBN 0-85088-866-2 : £7.95 B82-28308

338'.0943 — West Germany. Industries. Resources. Allocation *compared with* **allocation of resources in British industries**

Cox, Joan G.. Growth, innovation and employment : an Anglo-German comparison / by Joan G. Cox with Herbert Kriegbaum. — London : Anglo-German Foundation for the Study of Industrial Society, c1980. — vi,77p : ill ; 21cm
ISBN 0-905492-31-5 (pbk) : £3.50
Primary classification 338.0941 B82-34557

338.0946 — Spain. Business enterprise — *For foreign businessmen*

Blackshaw, Ian S.. Doing business in Spain / Ian S. Blackshaw. — London : Oyez, 1980. — xi,198p ; 25cm
Includes index
ISBN 0-85120-449-x : Unpriced B82-06204

338.0951 — China. Industrial development, *1976-1981*

Tung, Rosalie L.. Chinese industrial society after Mao / Rosalie L. Tung. — Lexington, Mass. : Lexington Books ; [Aldershot] : Gower [distributor], 1982. — xvi,357p ; 24cm
Bibliography: p275-278. — Includes index
ISBN 0-669-04565-9 : £19.50 B82-36673

338.0952 — Japan. Business enterprise, *1600-1980*

Hirschmeier, Johannes. The development of Japanese business : 1600-1980 / Johannes Hirschmeier and Tsunehiko Yui. — 2nd ed. — London : Allen & Unwin, 1981. — 406p ; 22cm
Previous ed.: 1975. — Includes index
ISBN 0-04-330322-6 (pbk) : Unpriced : CIP rev. B81-31529

338.0952 — Japan. Industrial development *compared with* **industrial development in United States,** *ca 1950-1981*

Baranson, Jack. The Japanese challenge to U.S. industry / Jack Baranson. — Lexington, Mass. : Lexington Books ; [Aldershot] : Gower [distributor], 1982, c1981. — xvi,188p ; 24cm
Bibliography: p173-179. — Includes index
ISBN 0-669-04402-4 : £15.50
Also classified at 338.0973 B82-18409

338.0952 — Japan. Industrial development. Role of Japanese culture

Morishima, Michio. Why has Japan 'succeeded'? : Western technology and the Japanese ethos / Michio Morishima. — Cambridge : Cambridge University Press, 1982. — xi,207p : 1map ; 24cm
Includes index
ISBN 0-521-24494-3 : £12.50 : CIP rev. B82-07955

338.0952 — Japan. Industries — *For Western businessmen*

Saso, Mary. Japanese industry : how to compete and how to cooperate / by Mary Saso. — London : Economist Intelligence Unit, 1981. — 116p : ill ; 30cm. — (EIU special report ; no.110)
Unpriced (pbk) B82-05822

338′.0953′57 — United Arab Emirates. Sharjah. Industries & trades

Sharjah. — Liverpool (Fowlers Building, Victoria St., Liverpool L2 5QA) : Journal of Commerce & Shipping Telegraph (1980) Ltd., 1982. — 55p : ill(some col.),map,ports(some col.) ; 30cm. — (A Journal of commerce special publication)
Unpriced (pbk) B82-32988

338′.09567 — Iraq. Nationalised industries — *Lists*

Iraq : departments and state organisations / Middle East Branch, Department of Trade. — London (1 Victoria St., SW1H 0ET) : The Branch, 1982. — 67p in various pagings ; 21cm
Unpriced (unbound) B82-33373

338.096 — Africa. Industrialisation, *to 1980 — Conference proceedings*

Industry and accumulation in Africa / edited by Martin Fransman. — London : Heinemann, 1982. — 438p : ill ; 23cm. — (Studies in the economics of Africa)
Bibliography: p416-431. — Includes index
ISBN 0-435-97139-5 (cased) : £15.00 : CIP rev.
ISBN 0-435-97140-9 (pbk) : Unpriced
B81-34501

338.09669′2 — Nigeria. Ife. Industries & trades, *1200-1700.* **Archaeological sources: Jewellery**

Willett, Frank. Baubles, bangles and beads : trade contacts of mediaeval Ife / Frank Willett. — [Edinburgh] ([Adam Ferguson Building, 40 George Square, Edinburgh, EH8 9LL]) : [Centre of African Studies, University of Edinburgh], [1977]. — 31p : ill,1map ; 21cm. — (Thirteenth Melville J. Herskovits memorial lecture)
Cover title. — Bibliography: p29-31
Unpriced (pbk) B82-20664

338.0972 — Mexico. Industries — *For British businessmen*

Mexico : 5th to 12th September, 1981. — Birmingham (PO Box 360, 75 Harborne Rd, Birmingham B15 3DH) : Birmingham Chamber of Industry and Commerce, [1981?]. — 13p ; 30cm. — (Mission report)
Unpriced (unbound) B82-11740

338.0973 — United States. Industrial development *compared with* **industrial development in Japan,** *ca 1950-1981*

Baranson, Jack. The Japanese challenge to U.S. industry / Jack Baranson. — Lexington, Mass. : Lexington Books ; [Aldershot] : Gower [distributor], 1982, c1981. — xvi,188p ; 24cm
Bibliography: p173-179. — Includes index
ISBN 0-669-04402-4 : £15.50
Primary classification 338.0952 B82-18409

338.0973 — United States. Industrialisation. Role of families, *1838-1936 — Sources of data: Amoskeag Manufacturing Company*

Hareven, Tamara K.. Family time and industrial time : the relationship between the family and work in a New England industrial community / Tamara K. Hareven. — Cambridge : Cambridge University Press, 1982. — xviii,474p : ill,facsims,1map ; 24cm. — (Interdisciplinary perspectives on modern history)
Bibliography: p434-455. — Includes index
ISBN 0-521-23094-2 : £25.00
ISBN 0-521-28914-9 (pbk) : £9.95 B82-31125

338.0973 — United States. Industries

Caves, Richard. American industry : structure, conduct, performance / Richard Caves. — 5th ed. — Englewood Cliffs ; London : Prentice-Hall, c1982. — x,127p : ill ; 24cm. — (Foundations of modern economics series)
Previous ed.: 1977. — Bibliography: p119-120. — Includes index
ISBN 0-13-027656-1 (pbk) : £8.75 B82-38574

The **Reindustrialization** of America : by the Business week team, Seymour Zucker ... [et al.]. — New York ; London : McGraw-Hill, c1982. — v,200p : ill ; 24cm
Based on a Business week report, June 1980. — Includes index
ISBN 0-07-009324-5 : £11.50 B82-14174

The **Structure** of American industry / [edited by] Walter Adams. — 6th ed. — New York : Macmillan ; London : Collier Macmillan, c1982. — xi,513p : ill ; 24cm
Previous ed.: 1977. — Includes bibliographies and index
ISBN 0-02-300800-8 (pbk) : £10.95
B82-29748

338.0973 — United States. Industries, *1929-1964.* **Effects of theories of economics of Keynes, John Maynard**

Collins, Robert M.. The business response to Keynes, 1929-1964 / Robert M. Collins. — New York ; Guildford : Columbia University Press, 1981. — xii,293p ; 24cm. — (Contemporary American history series)
Bibliography: p267-281. — Includes index
ISBN 0-231-04486-0 : £16.95 B82-10817

338.0981 — Brazil. Industrial development, *1975-1979*

Tyler, William G.. The Brazilian industrial economy / William G. Tyler. — Lexington, Mass. : Lexington Books, c1981 ; [Aldershot] : Gower [distributor], 1982. — xvii,152p : ill ; 24cm
Bibliography: p143-150. — Includes index
ISBN 0-669-03448-7 : £13.50 B82-11321

338′.0994 — Australia. Industries. Economic aspects

Industrial economics. — London : Allen and Unwin, Jan.1982. — [500]p
ISBN 0-86861-060-7 : £7.50 : CIP entry
B81-34782

338.1 — AGRICULTURAL INDUSTRIES

338.1 — Agricultural industries — *Conference proceedings*

International Conference of Agricultural Economists *(17th : 1979 : Banff, Alberta)*. The rural challenge : contributed papers read at the 17th International Conference of Agricultural Economists / edited by Margot A. Bellamy and Bruce L. Greenshields. — Aldershot : Gower, c1981. — xii,329p : ill ; 22cm. — (IAAE occasional paper ; no.2)
′International Association of Agricultural Economists′. — Includes bibliographies and index
ISBN 0-566-00472-0 (pbk) : Unpriced : CIP rev. B81-30969

338.1 — Agricultural industries — *For schools*

Grierson, Ian. Farming. — London : Edward Arnold, Nov.1982. — [64]p. — (Foundation geography)
ISBN 0-7131-0666-2 (pbk) : £2.00 : CIP entry
B82-27956

Jones, Barbara, *1942 July 4-*. Food, farming and famine / Barbara Jones, Richard Wales. — Walton-on-Thames : Nelson for the Schools Council, 1982. — 48p : ill(some col.),maps (some col.) ; 28cm. — (Geography and change)
ISBN 0-17-434183-0 (pbk) : Unpriced
B82-29550

338.1 — Agricultural industries — *Socialist viewpoints*

Clutterbuck, C.. More than we can chew. — London : Pluto Press, Sept.1982. — [128]p. — (Arguments for socialism)
ISBN 0-86104-501-7 (pbk) : £2.50 : CIP entry
B82-21992

338.1 — Part-time agricultural industries

Thear, Katie. Part-time farming. — London : Ward Lock, Oct.1982. — [192]p
ISBN 0-7063-5932-1 : £7.95 : CIP entry
B82-23183

338.1′028′54 — Agricultural industries. Applications of digital computer systems

Rehman, T.. Computers in farming : millstone or milestone? / by T. Rehman and R.J. Esslemont. — Reading : Farm Management Unit, University of Reading, 1981. — vii,70p : ill ; 30cm. — (Study ; no.1)
Includes bibliographies
ISBN 0-7049-0244-3 (pbk) : £2.50 B82-03892

338.1′06′0417 — Ireland *(Republic).* **Agricultural industries. Development. Organisations: Council for Development in Agriculture**

Council for Development in Agriculture. An Chomhairle Oiliúna Talmhaíochta : a tionscnaíodh ag An Taoiseach Cathal Ó hEochaidh, TD ar 16 Iúil 1980 ag Coláiste Uí Mhaoiliosa, Baile Átha An Rí, Co. na Gaillimhe = was inaugurated by An Taoiseach Charles J. Haughey, TD on 16th July 1980 at Mellowes Agricultural College, Athenry, Co. Galway / [ACOT]. — Blackrock (Frascati Rd., Blackrock, Co. Dublin) : [ACOT], [1981?]. — 20p : col.ill,maps(some col.),ports ; 18x23cm
Unpriced (pbk) B82-05191

338.1′06′0417 — North-western Ireland *(Republic).* **Agricultural industries. Development. Organisations: Council for Development in Agriculture**

Council for Development in Agriculture. North West Region / ACOT. — Sligo (5 Castle St., Sligo) : [ACOT], [1981?]. — 12p : ill,2maps (some col.),ports ; 21cm
Cover title
Unpriced (pbk) B82-05198

338.1′06′0418 — Ireland *(Republic).* **Leinster. Agricultural industries. Development. Organisations: Council for Development in Agriculture**

Council for Development in Agriculture. Midland and East Region / ACOT. — Newcastle, [Co. Dublin] (Headquarters, Lyons Estate, Newcastle, Co. Dublin) : [ACOT], [1981?]. — [16]p : ill,2maps(some col.),ports ; 22cm
Unpriced (unbound) B82-05196

338.1′06′0418 — South-eastern Ireland *(Republic).* **Agricultural industries. Development. Organisations: Council for Development in Agriculture**

Council for Development in Agriculture. ACOT : An Chomhairle Oiliúna Talmhaíochta = Council for Development in Agriculture. — Piltown (Kildalton Agricultural and Horticultural College, Piltown, Co. Kilkenny) : [ACOT], [1981?]. — 11p : ill,2maps,ports ; 17x23cm
Cover title. — Text, port on inside cover
Unpriced (pbk) B82-05199

338.1′06′0419 — Ireland *(Republic).* **South-western Munster. Agriculture industries. Development. Organisations: Council for Development in Agriculture**

Council for Development in Agriculture. South West Region / ACOT. — Fermoy (Ashe Quay, Fermoy, Co. Cork) : [ACOT], [1981?]. — [16]p : ill,2maps(some col.),ports ; 21cm
Unpriced (unbound) B82-05197

338.1′068′1 — Agricultural industries. Farms. Financial management

Warren, Martyn F.. Financial management for farmers : the basic techniques of ′money farming′. — London : Hutchinson Educational, June 1982. — [352]p
ISBN 0-09-148930-x (cased) : £10.00 : CIP entry
ISBN 0-09-148931-8 (pbk) : £5.95 B82-10609

338.1′0724 — Agricultural industries. Decision making. Mathematical models

Planning and decision in agribusiness. — Oxford : Elsevier Scientific, Jan.1983. — [374]p. — (Developments in agricultural economics ; 1)
ISBN 0-444-42134-3 : CIP entry B82-33339

338.1′09 — Agricultural industries, *to 1981*

Grigg, David, *1934-*. The dynamics of agricultural change : the historical experience / David Grigg. — London : Hutchinson, 1982. — 260p : ill,maps ; 23cm
Includes index
ISBN 0-09-147790-5 (cased) : £12.00 : CIP rev.
ISBN 0-09-147791-3 (pbk) : £5.95 B82-19105

338.1'09172'2 — Developed countries. Agricultural industries
Hill, Brian E.. An economic analysis of agriculture / B.E. Hill and K.A. Ingersent. — 2nd ed. — London : Heinemann, 1982. — viii,355p : ill ; 22cm
Previous ed.: 1977. — Includes index
ISBN 0-435-84409-1 (pbk) : £7.50 B82-24035

338.1'09172'4 — Developing countries. Agricultural industries. Economic development
Buchanan, Anne. Food, poverty, power. — Nottingham : Spokesman, Dec.1982. — [120]p
ISBN 0-85124-351-7 (cased) : £12.50 : CIP entry
ISBN 0-85124-352-5 (pbk) : £2.95 B82-32305

338.1'09172'4 — Developing countries. Agricultural industries. Economic development. Projects
Benjamin, McDonald P.. Investment projects in agriculture : principles and case studies / McDonald P. Benjamin. — Harlow : Longman, 1981. — xxiii,297p : ill ; 24cm
Includes index
ISBN 0-582-64306-6 (corrected) : £29.95 : CIP rev.
ISBN 0-582-64306-8 B81-23757

338.1'09172'4 — Developing countries. Agricultural industries — *For schools*
Price, Gillian. Population and food resources in the developing world. — London : Edward Arnold, Sept.1982. — [64]p. — (Patterns of development ; 5)
ISBN 0-7131-0454-6 (pbk) : £2.25 : CIP entry
Primary classification 304.6'09172'4
B82-20028

338.1'09172'4 — Developing countries. Rural regions. Agricultural industries. Development. Role of urban food markets
Epstein, T. Scarlett. Urban food marketing and third world rural development : the structure of producer-seller markets / T. Scarlett Epstein. — London : Published in association with the Research Center for South West Pacific Studies, La Trobe University [by] Croom Helm, c1982. — 260p : ill,forms,maps,plans ; 23cm
Bibliography: p255-260
ISBN 0-7099-0911-x : £13.95 : CIP rev.
B82-04466

338.1'094 — Europe. Agricultural industries, *to ca 1914.* **Historiography**
Fussell, G. E.. Agricultural history in Great Britain and Europe before 1914. — London (35 Palace Court, W2 4LS) : Pindar Press, Oct.1981. — [128]p
ISBN 0-907132-04-9 : £15.00 : CIP entry
B81-27995

338.1'094 — Western Europe. Agricultural industries, *1880-1980*
Tracy, Michael. Agriculture in Western Europe : challenge and response 1880-1980. — 2nd ed. — London : Granada, May 1982. — [432]p
Previous ed.: London : Cape, 1964
ISBN 0-246-11446-0 : £12.00 : CIP entry
B82-09284

338.1'0941 — Great Britain. Agricultural industries
Agriculture in Britain / [prepared by Reference Division, Central Office of Information]. — 2nd ed. — London : H.M.S.O., 1980. — 59p ; 21cm. — (Central Office of Information reference pamphlet ; 43)
Previous ed.: 1977. — Bibliography: p58-59
ISBN 0-11-701007-3 (pbk) : £3.60 B82-15518

Haines, Michael. Introduction to farming systems. — London : Longman, July 1981. — [180]p
ISBN 0-582-45081-0 (pbk) : £6.95 : CIP entry
B81-22680

338.1'0941 — Great Britain. Agricultural industries — *Conference proceedings*
Forestry & farming in upland Britain : selected papers presented at the British Association for the Advancement of Science, 1979. — Edinburgh : Forestry Commission, c1980. — 244p : ill ; 22cm. — (Occasional paper ; no.6)
Cover title. — Includes bibliographies
ISBN 0-85538-083-7 (spiral) : £3.00
B82-38453

338.1'0941 — Great Britain. Agricultural industries. Development *compared with* **agricultural development in West Germany,** *1967-1980*
The **Development** of agriculture in Germany and the UK. — Ashford, Kent : Wye College. — (Miscellaneous study, ISSN 0306-1345 ; no.5)
4: A comparison of output, structure and productivity. — c1981. — vi,48p : ill ; 30cm
At head of title: Centre for European Agricultural Studies
ISBN 0-905378-18-0 (pbk) : £5.75
Also classified at 338.1'0943 B82-03988

338.1'0941 — Great Britain. Agricultural industries — *Forecasts — Conference proceedings*
The **Outlook** for agriculture 1982 and beyond : proceedings of a conference held on 8 and 9 October 1981 at the Skean Dhu Hotel, Dyce, Aberdeen / Chairmen James Davidson, Sylvester Campbell ; edited by B.J. Revell. — Aberdeen (581, King St., Aberdeen, AB9 1UD) : School of Agriculture, Aberdeen, 1982. — iv,111p : ill ; 30cm
£5.00 (spiral) B82-17457

338.1'0941 — Great Britain. Agricultural industries. Forecasts: Food from our own resources — *Critical studies*
Body, Richard. No way to feed a nation / Richard Body. — [London] ([170 Sloane St., SW1X 9QG]) : Selsdon Group, [1975?]. — 16p ; 23cm. — (A selsdon Group viewpoint series ; no.1)
Cover title
£0.50 (pbk) B82-07143

338.1'0941 — Great Britain. Agricultural industries — *Statistics*
Statistical handbook of U.K. agriculture / by Denis K. Britton ... [et al.]. — Ashford, Kent : Wye College, Agricultural Economics Unit, 1980. — vii,135p ; 30cm
Bibliography: p133-135
ISBN 0-901859-91-5 (spiral) : Unpriced
B82-35363

338.1'09411 — Scotland. Agricultural industries — *Statistics — Serials*
Economic report on Scottish agriculture : (incorporating Scottish agricultural economics and Agricultural statistics, Scotland) / Department of Agriculture and Fisheries for Scotland. — 1980-. — Edinburgh : H.M.S.O., 1981-. — v. ; 25cm
Annual. — Merger of: Scottish agricultural economics ; and, Agricultural statistics. Scotland
ISSN 0262-9135 = Economic report on Scottish agriculture : £6.80 B82-12463

338.1'09416 — Northern Ireland. Agricultural industries — *Serials*
Great Britain. *Department of Agriculture for Northern Ireland. Economics and Statistics Division*. Northern Ireland farm business planning handbook. — 1977-1978. — Belfast (Dundonald House, Belfast BT4 3SB) : Economics and Statistics Division, Department of Agriculture, N.I., 1977-1978. — 2v. ; 30cm
Annual. — Only two issues published. — Description based on: 1978
Unpriced B82-12456

338.1'09417 — Ireland *(Republic).* **Agricultural industries** — *Serials*
[The Farmer *(Dublin)***]**. The Farmer. — Vol.1, no.1 (Mar. 1979)-v.4 (1982). — Dublin (50 Fitzwilliam Square West, Dublin 2) : Baggot Pub., 1979-1982. — 34v. : ill(some col.),maps (some col.),ports(some col.) ; 30cm
Monthly. — Cover title from Vol.3, no.6 (Aug. 1981): The Farmer magazine (Dublin). — Continued by: Practical farmer
£0.40 B82-28861

The **Practical** farmer : the monthly journal for Ireland's farmers : incorporating the Farmer magazine. — Vol.1, no.1 (May 1982)-. — Dublin (50 Fitzwilliam Square West, Dublin 2) : Baggot Publishing, 1982-. — v. : ill(some col.),ports ; 33cm
Continues: Farmer (Dublin)
£12.00 per year B82-28858

338.1'0942 — England. Agricultural industries, *ca 1350-1870*
Agricultural improvement : medieval and modern / edited by Walter Minchinton. — [Exeter] : University of Exeter, 1981. — vii,137p : ill,1map ; 21cm. — (Exeter papers in economic history ; no.14)
ISBN 0-85989-142-9 (pbk) : Unpriced
B82-09801

338.1'09423'5 — Devon. Agricultural industries
Rosenthall, Pamela. Agricultural production and marketing in Cornwall and Devon : recent trends and possible developments / Pamela Rosenthall. — [Exeter] : University of Exeter Agricultural Economics Unit, 1981. — 72p : ill,maps ; 30cm. — (Report ; no.212)

£2.50 (pbk)
Also classified at 338.1'09423'7 B82-01507

338.1'09423'7 — Cornwall. Agricultural industries
Rosenthall, Pamela. Agricultural production and marketing in Cornwall and Devon : recent trends and possible developments / Pamela Rosenthall. — [Exeter] : University of Exeter Agricultural Economics Unit, 1981. — 72p : ill,maps ; 30cm. — (Report ; no.212)

£2.50 (pbk)
Primary classification 338.1'09423'5
B82-01507

338.1'09424'8 — Warwickshire. Agricultural industries, *1349-1520*
Dyer, Christopher. Warwickshire farming 1349-c.1520 : preparations for agricultural revolution / by Christopher Dyer. — Oxford : Dugdale Society, 1981. — 41p : 1map ; 25cm. — (Dugdale Society occasional papers ; no.27)
ISBN 0-85220-057-9 (pbk) : Unpriced
B82-03854

338.1'09425'13 — Derbyshire. Outseats. Agricultural industries. Farms, *1200-1800*
Meredith, Rosamond. Farms and families of Hathersage Outseats : from the 13th to the 19th century / by Rosamond Meredith. — Sheffield : [c/o Sheffield City Libraries]
Pt.1: Nether Hirst, North Lees, Brookfield, Green's House and Cowclose Farm. — 1981. — 28p : ill ; 25cm
Cover title. — Map on inside covers
ISBN 0-9507815-0-9 (pbk) : £1.40 B82-06884

338.1'0943 — West Germany. Agricultural industries. Development *compared with* **agricultural development in Great Britain,** *1967-1980*
The **Development** of agriculture in Germany and the UK. — Ashford, Kent : Wye College. — (Miscellaneous study, ISSN 0306-1345 ; no.5)
4: A comparison of output, structure and productivity. — c1981. — vi,48p : ill ; 30cm
At head of title: Centre for European Agricultural Studies
ISBN 0-905378-18-0 (pbk) : £5.75
Primary classification 338.1'0941 B82-03988

338.1'09495 — Greece. Agricultural industries — *For British exporters*
The **Market** for farm inputs, consultancy and agro-industrial projects in Greece. — London (35 Belgrave Square, SW1X 8QN) : BAEC, 1981. — iv,48p : ill,1map ; 30cm
Cover title: A report on Greece for agricultural exporters
£10.00 (pbk) B82-11353

338.1'0953'8 — Saudi Arabia. Agricultural industries — *For British exporters*
Davies, Piers. Prospects for agricultural and project business in the kingdom of Saudi Arabia / prepared by Piers Davies. — London (35 Belgrave Square, SW1X 8QN) : BAEC, 1981. — iv,51p : 1map ; 30cm
Cover title: A report on Saudi Arabia for agricultural exports
£15.00 (pbk) B82-11355

338.1'09549'2 — Bangladesh. Agricultural economics
De Vylder, Stefan. Agriculture in chains. — London : Zed Press, Mar.1982. — [192]p
ISBN 0-86232-041-0 : £16.95 : CIP entry
B82-02637

338.1'0956 — Middle East. Agricultural industries — *Serials*

Middle East agribusiness. — Vol.1 no.1 (Oct./Nov. 1981)-. — Redhill (2 Queensway, Redhill, Surrey RH1 1QS) : International Trade Publications, 1981-. — v. : ill(some col.),maps,ports ; 30cm
Six issues yearly. — Text in English, some Arabic translations
ISSN 0262-592X = Middle East agribusiness : £15.00 per year B82-17259

338.1'095645 — Cyprus. Part-time agricultural industries

Pearce, Richard, *1944-*. Part-time farming in Cyprus : a pilot study / Richard Pearce. — [Reading] : University of Reading, Department of Agricultural Economics & Management, 1981. — 93p : maps ; 30cm. — (Development study ; no.21)
Cover title
ISBN 0-7049-0697-x (pbk) : £2.00 B82-02713

338.1'095695 — East Jordan. Agricultural industries. Economic development. Effects of migration of personnel

Seccombe, Ian J.. Manpower and migration : the effects of international labour migration on agricultural development in the East Jordan Valley 1973-1980 / by Ian J. Seccombe. — [Durham] ([Old Shire Hall, Durham DH1 2HP]) : University of Durham, Centre for Middle Eastern and Islamic Studies, c1981. — viii,110p : ill,maps ; 21cm. — (Occasional papers series, ISSN 0307-0654 ; no.11)
Bibliography: p105-109
Unpriced (pbk) B82-14475

338.1'096 — Africa. Agricultural industries. Economic development

Levi, John. Economics of African agriculture / John Levi and Michael Havinden. — Harlow : Longman, 1982. — vii,175p : ill,maps ; 24cm
Includes index
ISBN 0-582-64147-0 (cased) : Unpriced : CIP rev.
ISBN 0-582-64148-9 (pbk) : £3.95 B82-01123

338.1'0962 — Egypt. Agricultural industries — *For British exporters*

Davies, Piers. A report on agriculture in Egypt / prepared by Piers Davies. — London (35 Belgrave Square, SW1X 8QN) : BAEC, c1981. — iv,51p ; 30cm : 1map
Cover title: A report on Egypt for agricultural exporters
£20.00 (pbk) B82-11356

338.1'0966 — West Africa. Agricultural industries. Economic development

Hart, Keith. The political economy of West African agriculture / Keith Hart. — Cambridge : Cambridge University Press, 1982. — ix,226p : 1map ; 24cm. — (Cambridge studies in social anthropology ; 43)
Bibliography: p174-207. — Includes index
ISBN 0-521-24073-5 (cased) : £19.00
ISBN 0-521-28423-6 (pbk) : £7.50 B82-34879

338.1'0966'4 — Sierra Leone. Agricultural industries

Gleave, M. B.. Agricultural development in Sierra Leone : some basic patterns / M.B. Gleave. — Salford : University of Salford, Department of Geography, 1978. — 26p,[6]p of plates : maps ; 30cm. — (Discussion papers in geography / University of Salford. Department of Geography ; no.6)
Bibliography: p26
£0.50 (pbk) B82-36204

338.1'09669 — Nigeria. Agricultural industries — *For British exporters*

A Report on the agricultural industry and the market for UK farm inputs in Nigeria. — London (35 Belgrave Square, SW1X 8QN) : BAEC, 1981. — 63p : 1map ; 30cm
Cover title: A report on Nigeria for agricultural exporters
£15.00 (pbk) B82-11354

338.1'0967'21 — Gabon. Agricultural industries — *For British exporters*

A Report on the current state of the agricultural industry and the developing market for farm inputs in Gabon. — London (35 Belgrave Sq., SW1X 8QN) : BAEC, 1981. — ii,23p : 1map ; 30cm
Cover title: A report on Gabon for agricultural exporters
£8.00 (pbk) B82-11357

338.1'09688 — Namibia. Agricultural industries, *to 1981*

Moorsom, Roger. Agriculture. — London : Catholic Institute for International Relations, Oct.1982. — [100]p. — (A Future for Namibia ; 2)
ISBN 0-904393-85-2 (pbk) : £2.95 : CIP entry B82-30574

338.1'0973 — United States. Agricultural economics

Sjo, John. Economics for agriculturalists : a beginning text in agricultural economics / by John Sjo. — New York ; Chichester : Wiley, c1976. — xii,232p : ill,1map ; 24cm
Includes bibliographies and index
ISBN 0-471-87003-x : £13.50 B82-30381

338.1'0973 — United States. Agricultural industries

Cramer, Gail L.. Agricultural economics and agribusiness / Gail L. Cramer, Clarence W. Jensen. — 2nd ed. — New York ; Chichester : Wiley, c1982. — xiii,465p : ill,maps,ports ; 24cm
Previous ed.: 1979. — Bibliography: p448-449. — Includes index
ISBN 0-471-09393-9 : Unpriced B82-19711

338.1'0973 — United States. Agricultural industries. Influence of Communist Party of the United States, *1920-1960*

Dyson, Lowell K.. Red harvest : the Communist Party and American farmers / Lowell K. Dyson. — Lincoln [Neb.] ; London : University of Nebraska Press, c1982. — xii,259p ; 23cm
Bibliography: p243-247. — Includes index
ISBN 0-8032-1659-9 : £13.50 B82-40409

338.1'0975 — United States. Southern states. Economic development. Role of Northern states cotton planters, *1862-1876*

Powell, Lawrence N.. New masters. — London : Yale University Press, July 1982. — [267]p. — (Yale historical publications. Miscellany ; 124)
ISBN 0-300-02882-2 (pbk) : £6.00 : CIP entry B82-22780

338.1'098 — Latin America. Agricultural industries. Development, *1940-1980*

De Janvry, Alain. The agrarian question and reformism in Latin America / Alain de Janvry. — Baltimore, Md. ; London : Johns Hopkins University Press, c1981. — xvi,311p : ill ; 24cm. — (Johns Hopkins studies in development)
Bibliography: p303-306. — Includes index
ISBN 0-8018-2531-8 (cased) : Unpriced
ISBN 0-8018-2532-6 (pbk) : Unpriced B82-28094

338.1'0981'3 — North-east Brazil. Agricultural industries

Kutcher, Gary P.. The agricultural economy of northeast Brazil / Gary P. Kutcher and Pasquale L. Scandizzo. — Baltimore ; London : Published for the World Bank [by] Johns Hopkins University Press, c1981. — xiv,217p : ill,1map ; 25cm. — (A World Bank research publication)
Bibliography: p259-264. — Includes index
ISBN 0-8018-2581-4 : £18.75 B82-31174

338.1'3 — Warwickshire. Burton Dassett. Agriculture. Temple, Peter, *ca 1517-1578, 1543-1553* — *Accounts*

Alcock, N. W.. Warwickshire grazier and London skinner 1532-1555 : the account book of Peter Temple and Thomas Heritage / N.W. Alcock. — London : Published for the British Academy by the Oxford University Press, c1981. — xix.281p,6p of plates : ill,maps,facsims,1port,geneal.tables ; 26cm. — (Records of social and economic history. New series ; 4)
Bibliography: pxix. — Includes index
ISBN 0-19-726008-x : £29.00 : CIP rev.
Also classified at 380.1'4567731'0924 B81-31448

338.1'3'094 — European Community countries. Agricultural industries. Financial assistance

Schemes of assistance to farmers in less favoured areas of the EEC : background paper for 1982 Arkleton Seminar on institutional approaches to rural development in Europe. — Langholm (Langholm, Dumfriesshire, DG13 0HL) : Arkleton Trust, c1982. — 68p ; 30cm
Includes bibliographies
£2.75 (pbk) B82-37959

338.1'3'094111 — Northern Scotland. Agricultural industries. Farms. Income — *Statistics*

Isaacs, R. J.. Farm incomes in the north of Scotland 1976/77 to 1978/79 / by R.J. Isaacs. — Aberdeen ([581 King St., Aberdeen AB9 1UD]) : North of Scotland College of Agriculture, Agricultural Economics Division, 1980. — 73p : 1map ; 30cm. — (Financial report, ISSN 0308-728x ; no.77)
£2.50 (pbk) B82-35361

338.1'36686 — Pets: Birds. Breeding. Financial aspects

Clear, Val. Making money with birds / Val Clear. — Neptune, N.J. ; Reigate : T.F.H., c1981. — 189p : ill(some col.) ; 21cm
Ill on lining papers. — Includes index
ISBN 0-87666-825-2 : £4.95 B82-10815

338.1'371'09423 — South-west England. Milk. Production. Economic aspects

Milk production : an economic survey in south west England 1980/81 / [University of Exeter Agricultural Economics Unit]. — Exeter (Lafrowda House, St German's Rd., Exeter EX4 6TL) : The Unit, 1981. — 29p : 1ill ; 30cm. — (Report, ISSN 0531-5344 ; no.214)
£1.50 (pbk) B82-14474

338.1'37141'094 — European Community countries. Milk. Prices — *Comparative studies*

Keane, Michael. A comparison of producer milk prices in EEC countries / Michael Keane and Eamonn Pitt. — Dublin : Marketing Department, Economics and Rural Welfare Research Centre, 1981. — 130p ; 20cm
ISBN 0-905442-58-x (pbk) : Unpriced B82-20682

338.1'381 — Developing countries. Bee-keeping. Development projects. Grants. Agencies — *Directories*

International Bee Research Association. Sources of grant-aid for apicultural development. — Gerrards Cross : International Bee Research Association, Apr.1982. — [12]p. — (Source materials for apiculture ; no.6)
ISBN 0-86098-116-9 (pbk) : £1.00 : CIP entry B82-16202

338.1'6 — Great Britain. Agricultural industries. Application of microprocessors — *Conference proceedings*

Reading University Agricultural Club. *Conference (14th : 1980)*. Microprocessors in agriculture, will farming have its' [sic] chips? : proceedings of the fourteenth Annual Conference of the Reading University Agricultural Club, 1980 / edited by G. Palmer. — Reading : The Club, 1980. — 39p : 1ill ; 30cm
Includes bibliographies
ISBN 0-7049-0308-3 (corrected pbk) : Unpriced B82-35055

338.1'6 — Great Britain. Agricultural industries. Farms. Livestock. Productivity. Mathematical models

Livestock units handbook / ADAS. — Pinner : Ministry of Agriculture, Fisheries and Food, 1980. — 22p ; 22cm. — (Booklet / Ministry of Agriculture, Fisheries and Food ; 2267)
Cover title
Unpriced (pbk) B82-15572

338.1'6 — Great Britain. Agricultural industries. Farms. Planning. Applications of digital computer systems

Farm planning by computer / Ministry of Agriculture, Fisheries and Food. — 2nd ed. — London : H.M.S.O., 1979 (1980 [printing]). — 139p : ill,forms ; 25cm. — (Reference book ; 419)
ISBN 0-11-240314-x (pbk) : £5.75 B82-17817

338.1′6 — Great Britain. Broad-leaved woodlands. Trees. Cultivation. Economic analysis

Pryor, S. N.. An economic analysis of silvicultural options for broadleaved woodland / by S.N. Pryor. — [Oxford] : Commonwealth Forestry Institute, University of Oxford, 1982. — 2v(viii,120;xi,116p) : ill ; 30cm. — (CFI occasional papers, ISSN 0141-8181 ; no.19)
Vol.2 by R. Lorrain-Smith. — Includes bibliographies
ISBN 0-85074-041-x (pbk) : Unpriced
ISBN 0-85074-042-8 (v.2) B82-36909

338.1′6 — Scotland. Highlands & Islands. Livestock production industries. Crofting. Efficiency. Improvement — *Inquiry reports*

Great Britain. *Parliament. House of Commons. Committee of Public Accounts.* Seventeenth report from the Committee of Public Accounts : together with the proceedings of the committee and the minutes of evidence : session 1979-80 : Ministry of Agriculture, Fisheries and Food, Department of Agriculture and Fisheries for Scotland, Intervention Board for Agricultural Produce : export levy debts, livestock improvement schemes for crofters, Thames tidal defences. — London : H.M.S.O., [1980]. — xvi,48p ; 25cm. — ([HC] ; 683)
Includes index
ISBN 0-10-268380-8 (pbk) : £4.65
Primary classification 382′.41′0941 B82-09507

338.1′6 — Tropical regions. Crops. Intensive production

Beets, Willen C.. Multiple cropping and tropical farming systems. — Aldershot : Gower, Sept.1982. — [172]p
ISBN 0-566-00567-0 : £11.50 : CIP entry B82-18756

338.1′61 — Agricultural industries. Applications of digital computer systems

IFIP TC5 Working Conference on Food Production and Agricultural Engineering *(1981 : Havana).* Computer applications in food production and agricultural engineering : proceedings of the IFIP TC5 Working Conference on Food Production and Agricultural Engineering, Havana, Cuba, 26-30 October 1981 / edited by Róbert E. Kálmán and Jesús Martínez ; [sponsored by United Nations Educational, Scientific and Cultural Organization]. — Amsterdam ; Oxford : North-Holland, 1982. — xi,334p : ill ; 23cm
Includes bibliographies
ISBN 0-444-86382-6 : £21.20
Also classified at 338.4′5664 B82-39845

IFIP TC5 Working Conference on Food Production and Agricultural Engineering *(1981 : Havana).* Computer applications in food production and agricultural engineering : proceedings of the IFIP TC5 Working Conference on Food Production and Agricultural Engineering, Havana, Cuba, 26-30 October 1981 / edited by Róbert E. Kálmán and Jesús Martínez ; [sponsored by United Nations Educational, Scientific and Cultural Organization]. — Amsterdam ; Oxford : North-Holland, 1982. — xi,334p : ill ; 23cm
Includes bibliographies
ISBN 0-444-86384-2 : £21.10
Also classified at 338.4′5664 B82-39845

338.1′61 — Agricultural industries. Applications of microcomputer systems

Butterworth, K. (Keith). Microcomputer developments : report of a visit to Tasmania and Australia November/December 1981 / K. Butterworth. — [London] ([Great Westminster House, Horseferry Rd., SW1P 2AE]) : ADAS, [1982]. — 21p ; 30cm
Cover title
Unpriced (pbk) B82-40879

338.1′61 — Agricultural industries. Mechanisation — *Conference proceedings*

Shipway, G. P.. 27th Session of the FAO-ECE Working Party on Mechanization of Agriculture : report of a visit to Switzerland, 26-29 October 1981 / G.P. Shipway. — [London] ([Great Westminster House, Horseferry Rd., SW1P 2AE]) : ADAS, 1982. — 10p ; 30cm
Cover title. — At head of title: Ministry of Agriculture, Fisheries and Food. — Text on inside cover
Unpriced (pbk) B82-24281

338.1′61′095492 — Bangladesh. Agricultural industries. Mechanisation

Farm power in Bangladesh. — [Reading] : Department of Agricultural Economics and Management, University of Reading
Vol.1: A comparative analysis of animal and mechanical farm power in Bangladesh. — 1981. — iv,248p : ill,1map ; 30cm. — (Development study / University of Reading Department of Agricultural Economics & Management ; no.19)
Bibliography: p245-248
ISBN 0-7049-0695-3 (pbk) : £2.00 B82-11246

Farm power in Bangladesh. — [Reading] : Department of Agricultural Economics and Management, University of Reading. — (Development study / Department of Agricultural Economics and Management, University of Reading ; no.20)
Vol.2 / by H. Mettrick [and] by P. James. — 1981. — 145p : ill ; 30cm
Includes bibliographies. — Contents: Some aspects of the economics of animal power / by H. Mettrick. — Mechanisation and institutions in Noakhaki / by P. James
ISBN 0-7049-0696-1 (pbk) : £2.00 B82-21610

338.1′62 — India (*Republic*). Andhra Pradesh. Irrigation projects

Ali, Syed Hashim. Practical experience of irrigation reform, Andhra Pradesh, India / by Syed Hashim Ali. — Brighton : Institute of Development Studies, 1980. — 17p ; 21cm. — (Discussion paper, ISSN 0308-5864 ; 153)
£0.60 (pbk) B82-32255

338.1′62 — Ireland (*Republic*). Agricultural land. Drainage. Economic aspects

Bruton, Richard. Land drainage policy in Ireland / Richard Bruton and Frank J. Convery. — Dublin : Economic and Social Research Institute, 1982. — 93p : ill,2maps ; 22cm. — (Policy research series ; no.4)
Previous ed.: lll82-83
ISBN 0-7070-0049-1 (pbk) : £4.00 (Irish) (£2.00 (Irish) for students) B82-38930

338.1′62 — Jordan. Wadi Dhuleil. Irrigation projects: Wadi Dhuleil Project, *to 1974*

Clayton, Eric. Wadi Dhuleil, Jordan : an ex-post evaluation / [Eric Clayton, Ian Carruthers, Fahd Hamawi]. — London : Agrarian Development Unit, Wye College, University of London, 1974. — vii,74,[34]p ; 31cm. — (Occasional paper / Wye College. Agrarian Development Unit ; no.1)
£2.00 (spiral) B82-20240

338.1′62 — Nigeria. Northern states. Livestock. Trypanosomiasis. Vectors: Tsetse flies. Control. Costs & benefits

The Social and economic implications of trypanosomiasis control : a study of its impact on livestock production and rural development in Northern Nigeria / S.N.H. Putt ... [et al.]. — Reading : Veterinary Epidemiology and Economics Research Unit, University of Reading, 1980. — xx,549p : ill,maps ; 30cm
Bibliography: p526-549
ISBN 0-7049-0243-5 (pbk) : £20.00 B82-03450

338.1′7310482 — England. Cereals industries. Break crops, *1977-1978 — Statistics*

Burns, Susan M.. Combine harvested non-cereal crop survey : 1977 & 1978 / Susan M. Burns. — Reading : University of Reading, Department of Agricultural Economics and Management, 1980. — 68p : 1ill ; 30cm. — (Agricultural enterprise studies in England & Wales. Economics report, ISSN 0306-8900 ; no.73)
ISBN 0-7049-0689-9 (pbk) : £1.00 B82-36246

338.1′731′0941 — Great Britain. Cereals. Production. Economic aspects

Davidson, J. G.. Cereals 1979/80 : a study of cereal production and marketing in the United Kingdom / J.G. Davidson. — Cambridge (16-21 Silver Street, Cambridge CB3 9EL) : Agricultural Economics Unit, Department of Land Economy, [1982?]. — 46p ; 30cm. — (Agricultural enterprise studies in England and Wales. Economic report ; no.83)
At head of title: University of Cambridge
£3.00 (pbk) B82-40646

338.1′731′09417 — Ireland (*Republic*). Cereals industries & trades — *Serials*

Market intelligence bulletin / Cereals Authority of Ireland Ltd. — No.1 (Aug. 1981)-. — [Ireland] : [The Authority] ; Dublin (19 Sandymount Ave., Dublin 4) : An Foras Talúntais [distributor], 1981-. — v. : ill ; 25cm
Compiled for: the Cereals Authority of Ireland Ltd. by An Foras Talúntais
Unpriced B82-05738

338.1′7315′0973 — United States. Maize production industries, *to 1970*

Hardeman, Nicholas P.. Shucks, shocks, and hominy blocks : corn as a way of life in pioneer America / Nicholas P. Hardeman ; drawings by Linda M. Steele. — Baton Rouge ; London : Louisiana State University Press, c1981. — xii,271p : ill,1map ; 24cm
Bibliography: p249-264. — Includes index
ISBN 0-8071-0793-x : £14.00 B82-09771

338.1′7316′09416 — Northern Ireland. Barley production industries

Economic features of barley production in Northern Ireland 1979. — Belfast (Dundonald House, Belfast BT4 3SB) : Economics and Statistics Division, Dept. of Agriculture, N.I., [1980]. — 73p ; 30cm. — (Studies in agricultural economics)
Cover title
Unpriced (pbk) B82-34137

338.1′73491′094 — Western Europe. Potato industries

Young, N. A.. The European potato industry : a descriptive account of the potato sectors of the member states of the EEC-10, Spain and Portugal / N.A. Young. — Ashford, Kent : Wye College, 1981. — 157p : 11maps ; 30cm
At head of title: Potato Marketing Board. — Bibliography: p134-136
Unpriced (pbk) B82-23765

338.1′73491′094 — Western Europe. Potato industries — *Statistics*

Dadson, R. J.. Handbook of EEC potato statistics : including states applying for membership / compiled by R.J. Dadson. — London : 50 Hans Crescent, Knightsbridge, SW1X 0NB : Potato Marketing Board, [1981]. — 1v.(loose-leaf) ; 21cm
Unpriced (pbk) B82-25300

338.1′73491′09495 — Greece. Potato industries & trades

Varnham, K. B.. Greek potato production / K.B. Varnham. — London (50 Hans Cres., SW1X 0NB) : Potato Marketing Board, 1981. — 51p : maps ; 21cm. — (James E. Rennie awards ; report no.10)
Unpriced (pbk) B82-05828

338.1′7361′097291 — Cuba. Sugarcane industries, *1959-1980*

Pollitt, Brian H.. Revolution and the mode of production in the sugar-cane sector of the Cuban economy, 1959-1980 : some preliminary findings / by Brian H. Pollitt. — [Glasgow] ([Glasgow G12 8QH]) : Institute of Latin American Studies, University of Glasgow, 1981. — 14p ; 30cm. — (Occasional papers, ISSN 0305-8647 ; no.35)
Cover title
Unpriced (pbk) B82-06336

338.1′75′0941 — Great Britain. Horticultural industries — *Serials*

Commercial grower weekly : the week′s market prices and trends at a glance. — Tuesday 8th Sept. 1981-Mar. 1982. — Tonbridge : Benn, 1981-1982. — v. : ill ; 22cm
Absorbed by: Nurseryman & garden centre
ISSN 0262-3765 = Commercial grower weekly : £20.00 per year B82-02335

338.1′7535′094237 — Cornwall. Cauliflower industries & trades, *ca 1970-1980*

Leat, P. M. K.. Economic aspects of Cornish winter cauliflower / Philip M.K. Leat. — Exeter (Lafrowda House, St German′s Rd, Exeter EX4 6TL) : Agricultural Economics Unit, 1982. — 23p : ill ; 30cm. — (Report / University of Exeter. Agricultural Economics Unit, ISSN 0531-5344 ; no.215)
£1.50 (pbk) B82-19776

338.1′758′0941 — Great Britain. Mushroom industries
Hinton, Lynn. Mushrooms in Britain and Ireland : an economic study / by Lynn Hinton. — [Cambridge] : Agricultural Economics Unit, Department of Land Economy, Cambridge University, 1982. — 25p ; 30cm. — (Occasional papers ; no.25)
£5.00 (pbk) B82-37373

338.1′76′00941 — Great Britain. Livestock production industries
Kempster, Tony. Carcase evaluation in livestock breeding, production and marketing. — London : Granada, Sept.1982. — [320]p
ISBN 0-246-11509-2 : £20.00 : CIP entry B82-18742

338.1′762′00722 — United States. Western states. Cattle industries & trades. Historiography
Walker, Don D.. Clio′s cowboys : studies in the historiography of the cattle trade / by Don D. Walker. — Lincoln [Neb.] ; London : University of Nebraska Press, c1981. — xxi,210p ; 23cm
Includes index
ISBN 0-8032-4713-3 : £9.80 B82-09767

338.1′762083 — North Yorkshire. Hambleton Hills. Cattle trades. Droving, *1600-1900*
Arnold, Denis V.. Scottish cattle droving and the Hambleton drove road / Denis V. Arnold. — [Northallerton] ([1, Belle Vue Cottages, Osmotherley, Northallerton, N. Yorks. DL6 3PR]) : [D.V. Arnold], 1982. — 16p : ill,1map ; 21cm
Cover title. — Bibliography: p16
£0.80 (pbk) B82-32643

338.1′76213 — Livestock: Beef cattle. Winter feeding. Economic aspects. Sumulations. Applications of digital computer systems
A **Computer** program for simulation and budgeting of beef fattening systems. — Belfast (Dundonald House, Belfast BT4 3SB) : Economic & Statistics Division, Department of Agriculture, N.I., [1978]. — 46p ; 30cm. — (Agricultural economics paper ; 2)
Cover title
Unpriced (pbk) B82-36247

338.1′76213′094 — European Community countries. Beef cattle industries — *Conference proceedings*
The **Future** of beef production in the European Community : a seminar in the EEC programme of coordination of research on beef production and land use, organised by M. Bonsembiante and P. Susmel, with J.C. Bowman as conference chairman, at Abano Teme, Italy, November 13-17, 1978 : sponsored by the Commission of the European Communities, Directorate General for Agriculture, Coordination of Agricultural Research / edited by J.C. Bowman, P. Susmel. — The Hague ; London : Nijhoff for the Commission of European Communities, 1979. — x,653p : ill,maps ; 25cm. — (Current topics in veterinary medicine and animal science ; v.5)
Includes bibliographies
ISBN 90-247-2234-9 : Unpriced B82-12874

338.1′76213′09417 — Ireland *(Republic).* **Beef cattle industries**
Nobel, J. R.. Report on EEC seminar on beef production from different dairy breeds and dairy beef crosses, France and Republic of Ireland, April 1981 / J.R. Nobel. — [Pinner] ([Tolcarne Drive, Pinner, Middx HA5 2DT]) : ADAS, [1981]. — 24p ; 30cm
Cover title
Unpriced (pbk)
Primary classification 338′.1′76213′0944
B82-03317

338.1′76213′0942 — England. Beef cattle industries — *Statistics*
Dench, J. A. L.. A national beef survey : a random sample economic study of lowland beef production in 1978-9 together with some results from a structure survey of beef production carried out in 1976 / J.A.L. Dench and R.L. Vaughan. — [Reading] : [University of Reading, Department of Agricultural Economics & Management], 1981. — 88p ; 30cm. — (Agricultural enterprise studies in England and Wales. Economic report, ISSN 0306-8900 ; no.78)
At head of title: University of Reading Department of Agricultural Economics
ISBN 0-7049-0693-7 (pbk) : £1.00 B82-11247

338′.1′76213′0944 — France. Beef cattle industries
Nobel, J. R.. Report on EEC seminar on beef production from different dairy breeds and dairy beef crosses, France and Republic of Ireland, April 1981 / J.R. Nobel. — [Pinner] ([Tolcarne Drive, Pinner, Middx HA5 2DT]) : ADAS, [1981]. — 24p ; 30cm
Cover title
Unpriced (pbk)
Also classified at 338.1′76213′09417
B82-03317

338.1′76294 — Scotland. Red deer industries
Jarvie, Elizabeth. The red deer industry : finance and employment (1978-9) : a survey report / by Elizabeth Jarvie. — Edinburgh : Scottish Landowner′s Federation, [1981?]. — 49,xixp : ill,1map,forms ; 23cm
Cover title
Unpriced (pbk) B82-08486

338.1′76313′09411 — Western Scotland. Hilly regions. Livestock: Lambs. Production, *1979.* **Economic aspects**
McGregor, I. M.. Hillfarms : profitability and prospects : (1979 lamb crop year) / I.M. McGregor. — Ayr (Oswald Hall, Auchincruive, Ayr KA6 5HW) : West of Scotland Agriculture College, Economics Division, 1981. — 34p ; 30cm. — (FPI ; no.5)
Cover title
Unpriced (pbk) B82-34402

338.1′77 — Dairy industries & trades
Parry, D. R.. Report on 65th annual sessions of the International Dairy Federation, Torremolinos, Spain 5-9 October 1981 / D.R. Parry. — [London] ([Great Westminster House, Horseferry Rd., SW1P 2AE]) : ADAS, 1982. — 11p ; 30cm
Cover title
Unpriced (pbk) B82-18705

338.1′77′03 — Dairy industries & trades — *Polyglot dictionaries*
Dictionary of dairy terminology. — Oxford : Elsevier Scientific, Dec.1982. — [250]p
ISBN 0-444-42101-7 : CIP entry B82-29808

338.1′8′096 — Africa. Agricultural industries. Role of multinational companies. Economic aspects
Dinham, Barbara. Agribusiness in Africa. — London (258 Pentonville Rd., N1 9JY) : Earth Resources Research, Nov.1982. — 1v.
ISBN 0-946281-00-9 (pbk) : £4.95 : CIP entry B82-31325

338.1′81 — Developing countries. Agricultural products. Prices. Policies of governments
Tolley, George S.. Agricultural price policies and the developing countries / George S. Tolley, Vinod Thomas, Chung Ming Wong. — Baltimore ; London : Published for the World Bank [by] Johns Hopkins University Press, c1982. — xii,242p : ill ; 25cm. — (A World Bank publication)
Includes index
ISBN 0-8018-2704-3 : £18.75 B82-31175

338.1′81 — European Community countries. Agricultural industries. Policies of European Economic Community: Common Agricultural Policy
The **Costs** of the common agricultural policy / Allan E. Buckwell ... [et al.]. — London : Croom Helm, c1982. — 184p : ill ; 23cm
Includes index
ISBN 0-7099-0671-4 : £12.95 : CIP rev. B82-02628

Pearce, Joan. The common agricultural policy : prospects for change / Joan Pearce. — [London] : Royal Institute of International Affairs, 1981. — 122p ; 22cm. — (Chatham House papers, ISSN 0143-5795)
ISBN 0-7100-9069-2 (pbk) : £3.95 B82-09168

338.1′81 — European Community countries. Agricultural industries. Policies of European Economic Community: Common Agricultural Policy. Reform — *Forecasts*
Josling, T. E.. Options for farm policy in the European Community / T.E. Josling, Mark Langworthy and Scott Pearson. — London : Trade Policy Research Centre, 1981. — xii,84p ; 19cm. — (Thames essay, ISSN 0306-6991 ; no.27)
ISBN 0-900842-52-0 (pbk) : £3.00 B82-08339

338.1′841 — Great Britain. *Ministry of Agriculture, Fisheries and Food.* **Expenditure. Great Britain.** *Parliament. House of Commons. Agriculture Committee.* **Second report ... session 1980-81** — *Critical studies*
Great Britain. *Ministry of Agriculture, Fisheries and Food.* Third special report from the Agriculture Committee session 1980-81 : supply estimates 1981-82, class III, votes 2, 3, 5 and 7 : observations by the Minister of Agriculture, Fisheries and Food on the second report from the Agriculture Committee 1980-81 (HC (1980-81) 361). — London : H.M.S.O., [1981]. — iiip ; 25cm. — ([HC] ; 475)
ISBN 0-10-247581-4 (unbound) : £0.70 B82-11540

338.1′8411 — Scotland. Agricultural industries. Effects of Common Agricultural Policy of the European Economic Community
Royal Institution of Chartered Surveyors. *Scottish Branch.* Working party report on European Economic Community Common Agricultural Policy : an initial appraisal of its impact on agriculture and the rural social infrastructure in Scotland / the Scottish Branch of the Royal Institution of Chartered Surveyors. — Edinburgh (7 Manor Place, Edinburgh, EH3 7DN) : The Branch, 1981. — 12p : 1map ; 30cm
Cover title
Unpriced (pbk) B82-08243

338.1′8425′3 — Lincolnshire. Peasant communities. Agricultural industries, *ca 1500-1914*
Thirsk, Joan. English peasant farming. — London : Methuen, Oct.1981. — [368]p. — (Methuen library reprints)
Originally published: London : Routledge & Kegan Paul, 1957
ISBN 0-416-30530-x : £18.50 : CIP entry B81-25726

338.1′867 — Africa. Tropical regions. Agricultural industries. Policies of government
Bates, Robert H.. Markets and states in tropical Africa : the political basis of agricultural policies / Robert H. Bates. — Berkeley ; London : University of California Press, c1981. — xi,178p : ill ; 21cm. — (California series on social choice and political economy)
Bibliography: p147-166. — Includes index
ISBN 0-520-04253-0 : £10.50 B82-06997

338.1′872 — Mexico. Agricultural industries. Policies of government, *1980*
Redclift, Michael. Development policymaking in Mexico : the SAM / Michael Redclift. — London : University of London, Institute of Latin American Studies, [1982?]. — 12,vp ; 25cm. — (Working papers / University of London. Institute of Latin American Studies, ISSN 0142-1875 ; 6)
ISBN 0-901145-45-9 (pbk) : £1.25 B82-23377

338.1′87249 — Mexico. Morelos *(State).* **Highlands. Agricultural industries,** *1800-1980.* **Political aspects**
Peña, Guillermo de la. A legacy of promises : agriculture, politics and ritual in the Morelos highlands of Mexico / Guillermo de la Peña. — Manchester : Manchester University Press, c1982. — ix,289p : ill,1map ; 24cm. — (Manchester Latin American studies)
Bibliography: p271-283. — Includes index
ISBN 0-7190-0766-6 : £25.00 B82-24511

338.1′9 — Energy resources. Conservation by food production industries — *Conference proceedings*
International Seminar on Energy Conservation and the Use of Renewable Energies in the Bio-Industries *(2nd : 1982 : Oxford).* Energy conservation and use of renewable energies in the bio-industries 2. — Oxford : Pergamon, Sept.1982. — [750]p. — (Advances in the biosciences ; 42/43)
ISBN 0-08-029781-1 : £75.00 : CIP entry B82-22799

338.1′9′05 — Food production industries — *Serials*
Food production. — Issue no.1 (June 1982)-. — London (161 Greenwich High Rd, SE10 8JA) : Dewberry Publication Services, 1982-. — v. : ill ; 31cm
Monthly
ISSN 0264-0260 = Food production : £25.00 per year B82-40062

338.1'9'51 — China. Food production industries
Croll, Elisabeth. The family rice bowl : food and the domestic economy in China. — London : Zed Press, Dec.1982. — [400]p
ISBN 0-86232-124-7 (cased) : £20.00 : CIP entry
ISBN 0-86232-125-5 (pbk) : £7.95 B82-30592

338.1'9'56 — Middle Eastern countries. Food supply. Political aspects
Weinbaum, Marvin G.. Food, development, and politics in the Middle East / Marvin G. Weinbaum. — Boulder : Westview ; London : Croom Helm, 1982. — xii,205p : ill ; 24cm. — (Westview's special studies on the Middle East)
Bibliography: p181-189. — Includes index
ISBN 0-7099-2726-6 : £13.95 B82-31739

338.1'9'6 — Africa. Developing countries. Food supply. Foreign assistance by developed countries — *Case studies — French texts*
Blogg, Keith. Family London / [Keith Blogg]. — London : London Transport, 1982. — 63p : col.ill,col.maps,1port ; 21x10cm. — (A Visitor's London guide)
Text and ill on inside covers
ISBN 0-85329-112-8 (pbk) : £0.99 B82-39549

338.2 — ECONOMICS OF MINERAL PRODUCTS

338.2'0212 — Minerals industries & trades — *Statistics*
World mineral statistics 1975-79 : production, exports, imports / compiled by C.D.G. Black ... [et al.]. — London : H.M.S.O., 1981. — iv,261p ; 30cm
At head of title: Institute of Geological Sciences
ISBN 0-11-884158-0 (pbk) : £15.50
B82-02744

338.2'068 — Mining industries. Management
Sloan, Douglas A.. Operational mine management. — London : Chapman and Hall, Dec.1982. — [350]p
ISBN 0-412-24070-x : £25.00 : CIP entry
B82-29779

338.2'0941 — Great Britain. Mining industries, *to 1981*
Memoirs of the Northern Mine Research Society 1980-1982. — Sheffield (41 Windsor Walk, South Anston, Sheffield S31 7EL) : Northern Mine Research Society, [1982]. — 122p : ill,maps,plans ; 30cm. — (British mining, ISSN 0308-2199 ; no.19)
Unpriced (pbk) B82-28627

338'.2'0942 — England. Mining industries, *to 1670 — Early works — Facsimiles*
Pettus, *Sir* John. Fodinae Regales, or, The history, laws and places of the chief mines and mineral works in England, Wales, and the English Pale in Ireland : as also of the mint and mony with a clavis explaining some difficult words relating to mines, &c. / by Sir John Pettus. — [London] : [Institution of Mining and Metallurgy], [1982]. — 108p,[1]leaf of plates : coat of arms,1port ; 26cm
Facsim of: 1st ed. London : H. L. and R. B. for T. Basset, 1670. — Limited ed. of 600 copies in slip case
£15.00 B82-17689

338.2'09423'7 — Cornwall. Mining industries — *History*
Jenkin, A. K. Hamilton. Mines and miners of Cornwall / A.K. Hamilton Jenkin. — Bracknell : Forge
6: Around Gwennap. — 1981, c1963. — 60p,[1]folded leaf of plates : ill,maps ; 22cm
Originally published: Truro : Truro Bookshop, 1963. — Includes index
Unpriced (pbk) B82-01899

338.2'095 — Asia. Metals mining industries — *Conference proceedings*
Asian Mining '81 *(Conference : Singapore)*. Asian mining '81 : papers presented at the Asian Mining '81 conference organised by the Institution of Mining and Metallurgy and held in Singapore from 23 to 25 November, 1981. — [London] : Institution of Mining and Metallurgy, 1981. — vi,311p : ill,maps,plans ; 30cm
ISBN 0-900488-61-1 (pbk) : Unpriced
B82-16008

338.2'0951 — China. Metals mining industries
Report of the Institution of Mining and Metallurgy mission to China, 14-30 October 1979. — [London] : Institution of Mining and Metallurgy, 1980. — iv,28p : 1map ; 30cm
£25.00 (£10.00 to members) (unbound)
B82-16006

338.2'3 — Mining industries. Financial management
Wanless, R. M.. Finance for mine management. — London : Chapman and Hall, Dec.1982. — [180]p
ISBN 0-412-24060-2 : £18.00 : CIP entry
B82-29778

338.2'3 — Petroleum. Pricing. Role of Organization of the Petroleum Exporting Countries, *1960-1980*
Kemp, Alexander G.. The medium and long term behaviour of crude oil and petroleum product prices with special reference to the role of OPEC : paper presented at Third European Petroleum and Gas Conference, Amsterdam, 5-7 April, 1982 / by Alexander G. Kemp. — [Aberdeen] : [University of Aberdeen, Department of Political Economy], [1982]. — 34leaves : ill ; 31cm. — (Discussion paper / University of Aberdeen, Department of Political Economy, ISSN 0143-4543 ; 82-04)
Includes bibliographies
Unpriced (pbk) B82-28136

338.2'3 — Petroleum. Production & pricing. Policies of Organisation of the Petroleum Exporting Countries. International aspects
OPEC behavior and world oil prices. — London : Allen & Unwin, Nov.1982. — [256]p
ISBN 0-04-338102-2 (cased) : £15.00 : CIP entry
ISBN 0-04-338103-0 (pbk) : £5.95 B82-27809

338.2'3 — Petroleum. Production & pricing. Policies of Organization of the Petroleum Exporting Countries. International aspects
The **Challenge** of energy / edited by Mohammad W. Khouja. — London : Longman, 1981. — vi,127p ; 22cm. — (Energy resources and policies of the Middle East and North Africa)
ISBN 0-582-78335-6 (pbk) : £4.50 : CIP rev.
B81-31180

338.2'3 — Petroleum. Production & pricing. Policies of Organization of the Petroleum Exporting Countries. International aspects — *Spanish texts*
[The Challenge of energy. *Spanish*]. El reto de la energia : programas de actuacion en curso / editado por Mohammad W. Khouja. — Londres : Longman, 1981. — 139p ; 22cm. — (Recursos energeticos y programas de actuacion en Oriente Medio y Africa del Norte)
Translation from the English
ISBN 0-582-78333-x (pbk) : £6.95 B82-10852

338.2'3 — Petroluem. Production & pricing. Policies of Organisation of the Petroleum Exporting Countries. International aspects — *Japanese texts*
[The Challenge of energy. *Japanese*]. Enerugī no chōsen : enerugī seisaku no keisei / Mohamadd · W · Hōja = The challenge of energy : policies in the making / edited by Mohamad W. Khoja. — London : Ronguman, 1981. — 113p ; 22cm. — (Chūtō · Kita-Afurika no enerugī shigen to enerugī seisaku = Energy resources and policies of the Middle East and North Africa)
Translation from the English
ISBN 0-582-78334-8 (pbk) : £6.95 B82-10851

338.2'3 — United States. Petroleum. Prices. Control by government
Kalt, Joseph P.. The economics and politics of oil price regulations : federal policy in the post-embargo era / Joseph P. Kalt. — Cambridge, Mass. ; London : MIT Press, c1981. — ix,327p : ill ; 24cm. — (MIT Press series on the regulation of economic activity)
Bibliography: p307-316. — Includes index
ISBN 0-262-11079-2 : £24.50 B82-09578

338.2'3 — Western world. Petroleum. Prices. Increases by petroleum exporting countries. International political aspects
Badger, Daniel. Oil supply and price : what went right in 1980? / Daniel Badger and Robert Belgrave. — London : Policy Studies Institute, c1982. — p95-148 : ill ; 21cm. — (Energy paper / British Institutes' Joint Energy Policy Programme ; no.2)
Text on inside covers
ISBN 0-85374-207-3 (pbk) : £4.50 B82-32715

338.2'6 — Great Britain. Offshore natural gas & petroleum industries. Electronic equipment
Bedwell, Charles. Opportunities for electronics companies in offshore oil and gas complexes : a paper prepared for Tayside Region Industrial Office / by Charles Bedwell. — [Dundee] ([Tayside Regional Council, Tayside House, Dundee DD1 3RB]) : [The Office], [1982?]. — [8]p ; 30cm
Cover title
Unpriced (pbk) B82-16351

338.2'724 — Coal industries & trades
The **Economics** of coal. — London : Roskill Information Services, 1981. — 450,[160]p : ill,maps ; 30cm
ISBN 0-86214-196-6 (pbk) : Unpriced
B82-13773

338.2'724 — Coal industries. Environmental aspects
Gibson, J.. Coal and the environment. — Northwood : Science Reviews, July 1981. — [60]p
ISBN 0-905927-60-5 (pbk) : £1.75 : CIP entry
B81-20576

338.2'724'0941 — Great Britain. Coal industries, *1870-1946*
Griffin, A. R.. The collier / A.R. Griffin. — Princes Risborough : Shire, 1982. — 32p : ill,1map ; 21cm. — (Shire album ; 82)
Bibliography: p32
ISBN 0-85263-590-7 (pbk) : £0.95 B82-31143

338.2'724'0941 — Great Britain. Coal industries, *to 1981*
Anderson, D. (Donald). Coal : a pictorial history of the British coal industry / D. Anderson. — Newton Abbot : David & Charles, c1982. — 96p : ill,facsims,ports ; 25cm
ISBN 0-7153-8242-x : £4.95 : CIP rev.
B82-01173

338.2'724'0941 — Great Britain. Coal industries, *to 1981.* **Political aspects**
Hall, Tony, *1951-*. King Coal : miners, coal and Britain's industrial future / Tony Hall. — Harmondsworth : Penguin, 1981. — 278p ; 18cm. — (Pelican books)
Bibliography: p269-271. — Includes index
ISBN 0-14-022253-7 (pbk) : £2.25 B82-07284

338.2'724'094252 — Nottinghamshire. Coal industries, *1881-1981*
Griffin, A. R.. The Nottinghamshire coalfield 1881-1981. — Ashbourne : Moorland Publishing, Dec.1981. — [96]p
ISBN 0-86190-046-4 : £5.95 : CIP entry
B81-38835

338.2'724'0942732 — Greater Manchester *(Metropolitan County)*. Worsley. Coal industries, *1760-1900*
Atkinson, Glen. The canal duke's collieries : Worsley 1760-1900 / by Glen Atkinson. — Swinton : Neil Richardson, [1982?]. — 52p : ill,maps,ports ; 30cm
Cover title
ISBN 0-9506257-7-9 (pbk) : £3.50 B82-35289

338.2'724'094287 — Tyne and Wear *(Metropolitan County)*. Opencast coal mining industries — *Proposals*
Proposed ten year rolling programme for opencast coal extraction in Tyne and Wear County 1982-1992 : a consultation document. — Newcastle upon Tyne : Tyne and Wear County Council, 1982. — 16,12p : maps ; 30cm
Unpriced (pbk) B82-40450

338.2′728′06041 — Great Britain. Offshore natural gas & petroleum industries. Organisations: UK Offshore Operators Association
UK Offshore Operators Association. UK Offshore Operators Association. — London (192 Sloane St, SW1X 9QX) : The Association, [1980?]. — 16p : col.ill,2maps ; 30cm
Cover title
Unpriced (pbk) B82-26592

338.2′728′0916336 — North Sea. Natural gas & petroleum industries — *For schools*
Glen, Ann. North Sea oil and gas / by Ann Glen. — London : Heinemann Educational, 1982. — 66p : ill,maps ; 19x21cm. — (Contemporary Scotland ; 11)
ISBN 0-435-34188-x (pbk) : £2.25 : CIP rev. B82-04065

338.2′728′0941 — Great Britain. Offshore natural gas & petroleum industries — *Serials*
Offshore oil & gas yearbook : UK & continental Europe. — 4th ed. (1981-82). — London : Kogan Page, Dec.1981. — [400]p
ISBN 0-85038-498-2 : £45.00 : CIP entry B81-33866

338.2′728′094227 — Hampshire. Offshore natural gas & petroleum industries — *For environment planning*
Off-shore oil and gas. — Winchester : Hampshire County Council, County Planning Department, 1982. — 9,[20]p : 1map ; 30cm. — (Strategic planning paper / Hampshire. County Council ; no.11)
ISBN 0-900908-73-4 (pbk) : £0.50 B82-29571

338.2′728′0947 — Soviet Union. Natural gas & petroleum industries — *Forecasts*
Wilson, David, *1947 Mar.5-*. Soviet oil & gas to 1990 / by David Wilson. — London : Economist Intelligence Unit, 1980. — 138p : 1col.map ; 30cm. — (EIU special report ; no.90)
Bibliography: p137-138
£60.00 (pbk) B82-35359

338.2′7282 — Petroleum industries & trades. International economic aspects
Taher, Abdulhady Hassan. Energy : a global outlook : the case for effective international co-operation / Abdulhady Hassan Taher. — Oxford : Pergamon, 1982. — xvii,388p,[12] leaves of plates : ill(some col.),1port ; 26cm. — (Pergamon international library)
Bibliography: p374-380. — Includes index
ISBN 0-08-027292-4 (cased) : Unpriced
ISBN 0-08-027293-2 (pbk) : £8.95 B82-18919

338.2′7282 — Scotland. Highland Region. Caithness *(District)*. **Services for North Sea petroleum industries**
Caithness. — Inverness : Highland Regional Council, [1981?]. — 1portfolio : ill,maps ; 22cm
Unpriced B82-07346

338.2′7282 — Scotland. Tayside Region. Services for offshore petroleum industries — *Directories*
Tayside offshore oil register / Tayside Region Industrial Office. — [Dundee] ([Tayside Regional Council, Tayside House, Dundee DD1 3RB]) : [The Office], [1982?]. — 36p : ill,3maps,1plan ; 30cm
Cover title
Unpriced (pbk) B82-16350

338.2′7′28205 — Petroleum industries — *Serials*
Oil and gas international yearbook. — 1982. — London : Longman, Jan.1982. — [694]p
ISBN 0-582-90310-6 : £40.00 : CIP entry B81-34574

338.2′7282′05 — Petroleum producing countries. Petroleum industries. International political aspects — *Serials*
International oil politics : the monthly analysis of political and commercial developments in the major oil producing countries. — Issue no.1 (Sept. 1981)-issue no.3 (Nov.1981). — Great Waldingfield (Rectory Rd, Great Waldingfield, Sudbury, Sufolk CO10 0TL) : The Centre for Legal & Business Information in association with Géopolitique du pétrole, 1981-1981. — 3v. ; 30cm
Monthly. — Translation of: Géopolitique du pétrole. — Only three issues published
Unpriced B82-05740

338.2′7′28209174927 — Arab countries. Petroleum industries
Sayigh, Yusif A.. Arab oil policies. — London : Croom Helm, Dec.1982. — [288]p
ISBN 0-7099-2374-0 : £11.95 : CIP entry B82-30808

338.2′7282′0972 — Mexico. Petroleum industries & trades. Foreign relations between Mexico & United States — *Conference proceedings*
U.S.-Mexican energy relationships : realities and prospects / edited by Jerry R. Ladman, Deborah J. Baldwin, Elihu Bergman. — Lexington, Mass. : Lexington Books, c1981 ; [Aldershot] : Gower publishing [distributor], 1982. — xvii,237p : ill,maps ; 24cm
Conference papers. — Bibliography: p221-226. — Includes index
ISBN 0-669-04398-2 (cased) : £17.50
ISBN 0-669-04399-0 (pbk) : Unpriced B82-08159

338.2′7282′0973 — United States. Petroleum industries & trades. Policies of government, *to 1980*
Shaffer, Ed. Oil and the American empire. — London : Croom Helm, Nov.1982. — [288]p
ISBN 0-7099-2366-x : £13.95 : CIP entry B82-27940

338.2′7282′098 — Latin America. Petroleum industries
Philip, George D. E.. Oil and politics in Latin America : nationalist movements and state companies / George Philip. — Cambridge : Cambridge University Press, 1982. — xviii,577p : maps ; 22cm. — (Cambridge Latin American studies ; 40)
Bibliography: p553-569. — Includes index
ISBN 0-521-23865-x : £37.50 : CIP rev. B82-11519

338.2′73 — Iron ores. Supply & demand — *Forecasts*
Iron ore and the demand for crude steel to 2000. — London : Roskill Information Services, 1982. — xii,284,80,7p : ill ; 30cm
ISBN 0-86214-214-8 (pbk) : Unpriced B82-35789

338.2′73′0942545 — Leicestershire. Cottesmore region. Iron ore quarrying industries, *to 1980*
Ironstone quarrying in the Cottesmore area : a brief, illustrated history of ironstone quarrying activity in the Cottesmore, Burley and Exton Park area of Rutland. — Cottesmore : Rutland Railway Museum, 1981. — 16p : ill,1map ; 22cm
ISBN 0-9506723-1-9 (pbk) : Unpriced B82-11245

338.2′74′094235 — Devon. Metals mining industries, *to 1973*
Jenkin, A. K. Hamilton. Mines of Devon : north and east of Dartmoor / A.K. Hamilton Jenkin. — Exeter : Devon Library Services, 1981. — xi,226p : ill,maps ; 30cm
Includes index
ISBN 0-86114-317-5 : Unpriced B82-22732

338.2′743′0724 — Chile. Copper mining industries. Economic models
Lasaga, Manuel. The copper industry in the Chilean economy : an econometric analysis / Manuel Lasaga. — Lexington : Lexington Books, c1981 ; [Aldershot] : Gower [distributor], 1982. — xi,198p ; 24cm. — (The Wharton econometric studies series)
Bibliography: p189-193. — Includes index
ISBN 0-669-04543-8 : £18.50 B82-18257

338.2′743′0942374 — Cornwall. Northern Caradon *(District)*. **Copper mining industries,** *1837-1914*
Trivett, Robert. An industry of the past / Robert Trivett. — [Plymouth] ([Tavistock Place, Plymouth PL4 8AT]) : Plymouth College of Art and Design, c1981. — 30p : ill,2maps ; 21cm
Unpriced (pbk) B82-24389

338.2′7453′09669 — Nigeria. Tin mining industries, *to 1979*
Freund, Bill. Capital and labour in the Nigerian tin mines / Bill Freund. — Harlow : Longman, 1981. — ix,266p : maps ; 22cm. — (Ibadan history series)
Bibliography: p236-257. — Includes index
ISBN 0-582-64333-3 : £17.50 B82-05207

338.2′74926 — Bauxite & aluminium industries & trades — *Conference proceedings*
International Conference on Bauxite *(1980 : Jamaica)*. Towards increased co-operation in bauxite development / proceedings of the International Conference on Bauxite, Ochos Rios, Jamaica, December 9-11, 1980. — Worcester Park : Published for the International Bauxite Association by Metal Bulletin PLC, 1981. — 180p : ill,maps ; 30cm
ISBN 0-900542-59-4 (pbk) : £30.00 B82-05367

338.2′75 — England. Aggregates industries — *Statistics*
Great Britain. *Department of the Environment*. Collation of the results of the 1977 survey / regional aggregate working parties. — [London] : Dept of the Environment, 1980. — 93p : ill,maps ; 30cm
£2.80 (pbk) B82-36818

338.2′761 — Dorset. Ball clay mining industries
Ball clay in Dorset : a consultative document. — Dorchester, [Dorset] : [Dorset County Council Planning Department], 1982. — 27p,[11]leaves of plates : ill(some col.),maps ; 30cm
ISBN 0-85216-307-x (pbk) : £1.25 B82-31779

338.2′782 — Diamonds industries & trades
Schumach, Murray. The diamond people / Murray Schumach. — New York ; London : Norton, c1981. — 255p : ill ; 22cm
ISBN 0-393-01404-5 : £9.25 B82-32730

338.3 — ECONOMICS OF PRIMARY INDUSTRIES(OTHER THAN AGRICULTURE AND MINERALS)

338.3′713′094281 — Yorkshire. Fish farming industries, *to ca 1320*
McDonnell, J.. Inland fisheries in medieval Yorkshire 1066-1300 / by J. McDonnell. — [York] (St. Anthony′s Hall, Peasholme Green, York YO1 2PW) : [Borthwick Institute of Historical Research], 1981. — 42p : 1ill,maps,1facsim ; 21cm. — (Borthwick papers ; no.60)
£1.00 (pbk) B82-13818

338.3′727 — Iceland. Coastal waters. Trawling by British trawlers, *1956-1975*. **Political aspects**
Jónsson, Hannes. Friends in conflict : the Anglo-Icelandic cod wars and the law of the sea / Hannes Jónsson. — London : Hurst, 1982. — xi,240p : ill,maps,ports ; 23cm
Bibliography: p225-233. — Includes index
ISBN 0-905838-78-5 : £16.50 : CIP rev. B82-12173

338.3′727′0942375 — Cornwall. Newlyn. Fishing industries, *1881-1981*
100 years of fishing. — [Penzance] : [Newlyn Orion], [1981?]. — 8leaves,3p : ill ; 30cm
Produced to accompany an exhibition by Newlyn Orion, 1981. — Cover title
Unpriced (pbk) B82-05965

338.3′72′735 — Great Britain. Herring. British catches. Trophies: Prunier Herring Trophy, *1936-1966*
Hawkins, Leslie W. G.. The Prunier Herring Trophy 1936-1966. — Lowestoft (52 Salisbury Rd., Lowestoft, Suffolk, NR33 0HE) : Port of Lowestoft Research Society, Dec.1982. — [80]p
ISBN 0-9505311-1-1 (pbk) : £2.25 : CIP entry B82-34102

338.4 — ECONOMICS OF SECONDARY INDUSTRIES

338.4 — Great Britain. Business service industries
Marshall, J. N.. Corporate organisation of the business service sector / by J.N. Marshall. — [Newcastle upon Tyne] : University of Newcastle upon Tyne. Centre for Urban and Regional Development Studies, 1982. — 28p ; 30cm. — (Discussion paper, ISSN 0140-6515 ; no.43)
Bibliography: p28
Unpriced (unbound) B82-27743

338.4 — Service industries — *Geographical perspectives*

Daniels, P. W.. Service industries : growth and location. — Cambridge : Cambridge University Press, Sept.1982. — [94]p. — (Cambridge topics in geography. 2nd series)
ISBN 0-521-23730-0 (cased) : £6.95 : CIP entry
ISBN 0-521-28185-7 (pbk) : £3.25 B82-26233

338.4'068'4 — United States. Service industries. Management. Operations research

Fitzsimmons, James A.. Service operations management / James A. Fitzsimmons, Robert S. Sullivan. — New York ; London : McGraw-Hill, c1982. — xiv,449p : ill ; 24cm. — (McGraw-Hill series in quantitative methods for management)
Includes bibliographies and index
ISBN 0-07-021215-5 : £18.95 B82-25265

338.4'0941 — Great Britain. Regional planning. Policies of government. Implications of service industries

McEnery, J. H.. Manufacturing two nations : the sociological trap created by the bias of British regional policy against service industry / J.H. McEnery. — London : Institute of Economic Affairs, 1981. — 47p ; 22cm. — (Research monographs / Institute of Economic Affairs, ISSN 0073-9103 ; 36)
ISBN 0-255-36147-5 (pbk) : £1.50 B82-02028

338.4'3 — Great Britain. Research & development by industries. Financial assistance by government

Product and process research & development support : guidance notes for applicants seeking financial assistance for industrial research and development / Department of Industry. — Rev. — London ([Electronics Applications Division, Department of Industry, 29 Bressenden Place, SW1E 4DT]) : Department of Industry, 1982. — 12p : forms ; 30cm
Previous ed.: 1980. — Summary applications form for financial assistance ([7]p) as insert
Unpriced (pbk) B82-38326

338.4'3002 — Non-fiction: Academic books: Books with British imprints. Prices — *Statistics*

Cooper, Alan, *1948-*. Average prices of British academic books 1981 / Alan Cooper and Marilyn Hart. — Loughborough ([Department of Library and Information Studies, Loughborough University of Technology, Leicestershire]) : Centre for Library and Information Management, c1982. — 11p ; 30cm. — (Report / CLAIM, ISSN 0261-0302 ; 12)
ISBN 0-904924-35-1 (pbk) : £7.00 B82-32802

338.4'30274411 — Scotland. Public libraries — *Accounts — Serials*

Public library expenditure in Scotland. — 1982-83-. — Glasgow : Scottish Library Association, [1982]-. — v. ; 30x21cm
Annual
ISSN 0263-9181 = Public library expenditure in Scotland : Unpriced B82-38499

338.4'3069 — South-east England. Voluntary museums. Finance. Sources

Sources of funds and of help for small museums / Area Museums Service for S.E. England. — London : National Council for Voluntary Organisations, 1981?. — [9]p ; 30cm
Unpriced (unbound) B82-05430

338.4'30705'0941 — Great Britain. Book publishing industries. Companies. Finance — *Statistics — Serials*

Book publishing. — [1979]-. — London : Jordan & Sons (Surveys) Ltd, 1979-. — v. ; 30cm
Annual. — Description based on: [1980] issue
ISSN 0263-2454 = Book publishing : £60.00 B82-18533

338.4'3070595'0941 — Great Britain. *Her Majesty's Stationery Office.* **Trading operations** — *Inquiry reports*

Great Britain. *Parliament. House of Commons. Committee of Public Accounts.* Sixteenth report from the Committee of Public Accounts : together with the proceedings of the committee and minutes of evidence and appendices : session 1980-81 : Her Majesty's Stationery Office : trading operations. — London : H.M.S.O., [1981]. — xi,24p ; 25cm. — ([HC] ; 370)
ISBN 0-10-237081-8 (pbk) : £3.20 B82-05636

338.4'3072'0212 — Great Britain. Newspaper publishing industries. Companies. Finance — *Statistics — Serials*

The **British** newspaper industry. — [1978]-. — London : Jordan & Sons (Surveys) Ltd, 1978-. — v. ; 30cm
Issued every two years
ISSN 0263-2462 = British newspaper industry : £30.00 B82-18537

338.4'33'0072041 — Great Britain. Social sciences. Research. Financing

Williams, Frances, *19---*. The 'cuts' and social research : an interim report / [Frances Williams]. — London (35 Northampton St., EC1V 0AX) : Social Research Association, 1980. — 15leaves ; 30cm
Unpriced (unbound) B82-35001

338.4'33'0072041 — Social sciences. Research. Financial assistance by Great Britain. *Social Science Research Council* — *Inquiry reports*

Great Britain. *Parliament. House of Commons. Committee of Public Accounts.* Thirty-fourth report from the Committee of Public Accounts : together with the proceedings of the committee, the minutes of evidence and an appendix : session 1979-80 : Department of Education and Science, University Grants Committee, Social Science Research Council : assessment of universities grant needs, research and training in the social sciences. — London : H.M.S.O., [1980]. — 26p ; 25cm. — ([HC] ; 783)
ISBN 0-10-027839-6 (pbk) : £4.00
Primary classification 379.1'214'0941
B82-09925

338.4'3361941 — Great Britain. Social services. Expenditure. Great Britain. *Parliament. House of Commons. Social Services Committee.* **Third report ... session 1980-81** — *Critical studies*

Great Britain. *Department of Health and Social Security.* Public expenditure on the social services : reply by the government to the third report of the Select Committee on Social Services, session 1980-81. — London : H.M.S.O., 1981. — 9p ; 24cm. — (Cmnd. ; 8464)
At head of title: Department of Health and Social Security
ISBN 0-10-184640-1 (unbound) : £1.50
B82-13298

338.4'3361941 — Great Britain. Welfare services. Expenditure by government

Public expenditure and social policy : an examination of social spending and social priorities / edited by Alan Walker. — London : Heinemann Educational, 1982. — xii,212p : ill ; 23cm
Bibliography: p195-206. — Includes index
ISBN 0-435-82905-x (cased) : £14.50 : CIP rev.
ISBN 0-435-82906-8 (pbk) : £7.50 B82-04067

338.4'3361971 — Canada. Welfare services. Subsidies

Krashinsky, Michael. User charges in the social services : an economic theory of need and inability / Michael Krashinsky. — Toronto ; London : Published for the Ontario Economic Council by University of Toronto Press, c1981. — vii,162p ; 22cm. — (Ontario Economic Council research studies, ISSN 0708-3688 ; 22)
Bibliography: p159-162
ISBN 0-8020-3381-4 (pbk) : Unpriced
B82-27904

338.4'33621 — Great Britain. Health services. Capital

Review of health capital : a discussion document on the role of capital in the provision of health services / [Department of Health and Social Security]. — London (Alexander Fleming House, Elephant and Castle, SE1 6BY) : The Department, 1979. — 127p : ill ; 30cm
Unpriced (unbound) B82-40960

338.4'33621'0941 — Great Britain. Health authorities. Finance

Sharples, M.. Health authority financing / M. Sharples. — [Manchester] : Health Services Management Unit, Department of Social Administration, University of Manchester, 1982. — 28leaves : ill,forms ; 30cm. — (Working paper series, ISSN 0141-2647 ; no.62)
Unpriced (pbk) B82-38225

338.4'33621'0941 — Great Britain. Health services. Cost-benefit analysis

Pentol, Ann. Cost-benefit analysis : theory and practice in the health field / Ann Pentol. — Manchester (Manchester Business School, Booth Street West, Manchester M15 6PB) : Health Services Management Unit, University of Manchester. — (Working paper series / University of Manchester. Health Services Management Unit, ISSN 0141-2647 ; no.50)
Part 1: Theory and application. — 1981. — i,79leaves ; 30cm
£2.00 (pbk)
Also classified at 338.4'336219819'00941
B82-05611

Pentol, Ann. Cost benefit analysis : theory and practice in the health field / Ann Pentol. — Manchester (Manchester Business School, Booth Street West, Manchester M15 6PB) : Health Services Management Unit, University of Manchester. — (Working paper series / University of Manchester. Health Services Management Unit, ISSN 0141-2647 ; no.51)
Part 2: Case study. — 1981. — 63,[16]leaves ; 30cm
£2.00 (pbk)
Also classified at 338.4'336219819'00941
B82-05612

338.4'33621'0941 — Great Britain. National health services. Costs. Control — *Inquiry reports*

Great Britain. *Parliament. House of Commons. Committee of Public Accounts.* Twenty-fifth report from the Committee of Public Accounts : together with the proceedings of the committee, the minutes of evidence and appendices : session 1979-80 : Department of Health & Social Security, Scottish Home and Health Department, Welsh Office : cost control of pharmaceutical prescribing in the National Health Service, banking arrangements in the National Health Service, the Royal Hospital for Sick Children, Glasgow. — London : H.M.S.O., [1980]. — xviii,61p ; 25cm. — ([HC] ; 764)
ISBN 0-10-027649-0 (pbk) : £4.90
Also classified at 690'.557 B82-09501

338.4'33621'0941 — Great Britain. National health services. Finance

Chester, T. E.. Financing the National Health Service / T.E. Chester & D.E. Allen. — [Manchester] : [Health Services Management Unit, University of Manchester], 1982. — 41p ; 31cm. — (Working paper series ; no.61)
Unpriced (pbk) B82-30880

338.4'33621'0941 — Great Britain. National health services. Patients: Foreign visitors. Charges — *Inquiry reports*

Great Britain. *Parliament. House of Commons. Home Affairs Committee.* Third report from the Home Affairs Committee, Session 1981-82 : NHS charges for overseas visitors : together with the proceedings of the committee, the minutes of evidence and appendices. — London : H.M.S.O., [1982]. — xxv,79p ; 25cm. — ([H.C.] ; 121)
ISBN 0-10-212182-6 (pbk) : £6.05 B82-31678

338.4'336216'0973 — United States. Nursing homes. Patients: Old persons. Long-term care. Finance by Medicaid Programme, *1973-1977*

Buchanan, Robert J.. Health-care finance : an analysis of cost and utilization issues / Robert J. Buchanan. — Lexington, Mass. : Lexington Books ; [Aldershot] : Gower [distributor], 1981. — xv,174p ; 24cm
Bibliography: p169-172. — Includes index
ISBN 0-669-04035-5 : £12.50 B82-00557

338.4'336219819'00941 — Great Britain. Women with mastectomies. Counselling. Cost-benefit analysis

Pentol, Ann. Cost-benefit analysis : theory and practice in the health field / Ann Pentol. — Manchester (Manchester Business School, Booth Street West, Manchester M15 6PB) : Health Services Management Unit, University of Manchester. — (Working paper series / University of Manchester. Health Services Management Unit, ISSN 0141-2647 ; no.50)
Part 1: Theory and application. — 1981. — i,79leaves ; 30cm
£2.00 (pbk)
Primary classification 338.4'33621'0941
B82-05611

338.4′336219819′00941 — Great Britain. Women with mastectomies. Counselling. Cost-benefit analysis *continuation*

Pentol, Ann. Cost benefit analysis : theory and practice in the health field / Ann Pentol. — Manchester (Manchester Business School, Booth Street West, Manchester M15 6PB) : Health Services Management Unit, University of Manchester. — (Working paper series / University of Manchester. Health Services Management Unit, ISSN 0141-2647 ; no.51)
Part 2: Case study. — 1981. — 63,[16]leaves ; 30cm
£2.00 (pbk)
Primary classification 338.4′33621′0941
B82-05612

338.4′33626′0941 — Great Britain. Old persons. Care. Costs

Wright, K. G.. Costing care : the cost of alternative patterns of care for the elderly / K.G. Wright, J.A. Cairns, M.C. Snell. — [Sheffield] : [University of Sheffield Joint Unit for Social Services Research], c1981. — ii,56p : ill ; 21cm. — (Social services monographs)
ISBN 0-907484-01-8 (pbk) : Unpriced
B82-11566

338.4′33635′0941 — Great Britain. Housing. Expenditure by government. Distribution — *Inquiry reports*

Great Britain. *Parliament. House of Commons. Environment Committee.* First report from the Environment Committee, session 1979-80 : enquiry into implications of government′s expenditure plans 1980-81 to 1983-84 for the housing policies of the Department of the Environment : together with the proceedings of the committee, the minutes of evidence and appendices. — London : H.S.M.O., [1980]. — xxiii,78p ; 25cm. — (HC ; 714) (HC ; 578-i)
ISBN 0-10-027149-9 (pbk) : £5.10 B82-10968

338.4′33635′0941 — Great Britain. Housing. Finance

Housing & the economy : a priority for reform. — London : Shelter, 1982. — 22p : ill ; 30cm
ISBN 0-901242-61-6 (pbk) : £2.00 B82-35334

338.4′33635′0941 — Great Britain. Housing. Finance. Reform — *Proposals*

Goss, Sue. What price housing? : a review of housing subsidies and proposals for reform / Sue Goss, Stewart Lansley. — London (189 Old Brompton Rd., SW5 OAR) : SHAC, 1981. — 34p : ill ; 30cm. — (1981 research report ; 4)
£2.50 (pbk) B82-08503

338.4′33637′0722 — England. Local authorities. Environmental services. Pricing — *Case studies*

Service provision and pricing in local government : studies in local environmental services / [commissioned by the Department of the Environment from Coopers & Lybrand Associates Limited]. — London : H.M.S.O., 1981. — xi,272p,[24]p : ill ; 30cm
Bibliography: p[24]
ISBN 0-11-751587-6 (pbk) : Unpriced
Primary classification 363.7′056′0722
B82-11174

338.4′336373926′0973 — United States. Air. Pollution. Control. Cost-benefit analysis

Halvorsen, Robert. Benefit-cost analysis of air-pollution control / Robert Halvorsen, Michael G. Ruby. — Lexington, Mass. : Lexington Books, c1981 ; [Aldershot] : Gower [distributor], 1982. — xv,264p : ill ; 24cm
Bibliography: p237-256. — Includes index
ISBN 0-669-02647-6 : £18.50 B82-12106

338.4′35′072041 — Science. Research in British universities. Finance — *Inquiry reports*

Joint Working Party on the Support of University Scientific Research. Report of a Joint Working Party on the Support of University Scientific Research. — London : H.M.S.O., c1982. — v,53p : ill ; 25cm. — (Cmnd. ; 8567)
At head of title: Advisory Board for the Research Councils, University Grants Committee
ISBN 0-10-185670-9 (pbk) : £4.35 B82-31969

338.4′3616′00973 — United States. Man. Diseases & injuries. Costs — *Comparative studies*

Hartunian, Nelson S.. The incidence and economic costs of major health impairments : a comparative analysis of cancer, motor vehicle injuries, coronary heart disease, and stroke / Nelson S. Hartunian, Charles N. Smart, Mark S. Thompson. — Lexington, Mass. : Lexington Books ; [Aldershot] : Gower [distributor], 1981. — xxiv,420p : ill ; 24cm. — (An Insurance Institute for Highway Safety book)
Bibliography: p379-406. — Includes index
ISBN 0-669-03975-6 : £29.50 B82-04780

338.4′362 — Engineering. Decision making. Use of cost-benefit analysis

Collier, Courtland A.. Engineering cost analysis / Courtland A. Collier, William B. Ledbetter. — New York ; London : Harper & Row, c1982. — xvi,528p : ill ; 25cm
Includes index
ISBN 0-06-041329-8 : £18.95 B82-28711

338.4′362′000941 — Great Britain. Engineering industries. Financial assistance by government

Flexible manufacturing systems scheme : (notes for the guidance of applicants). — [London] ([Room 420, 123 Ashdown House, SW1E 6RB]) : Department of Industry, 1982. — 17p ; 30cm
Cover title
Unpriced (pbk) B82-38337

Small engineering firms investment scheme : (notes for the guidance of applicants). — [Brimingham] ([West Midland Regional Office, Ladywood House, Stephenson St., Birmingham B2 4DT]) : Department of Industry, 1982. — [11]p ; 30cm
Unpriced (unbound) B82-38336

338.4′362131 — England. Energy intensive industries. Electricity supply. Charges

England, Glyn. Helping large power users : a talk by Glyn England, chairman of the Central Electricity Generating Board, to the Rotary Club of London on 27 January 1982. — London (Press and Publicity Office, Sudbury House, 15 Newgate St., EC1A 7AU) : Central Electricity Generating Board, 1982. — 6p : 1port ; 21cm
Cover title. — Text and port on inside cover
Unpriced (pbk) B82-21049

338.4′362131 — Great Britain. Industries. Electricity supply. Charges

Windett, A. S.. Reducing the cost of electricity supply for the industrial and commercial purchaser / A.S. Windett. — 3rd ed. — Aldershot : Gower, 1982, c1980. — xiv,129p : ill ; 30cm
Previous ed.: 1980
ISBN 0-566-03032-2 (pbk) : Unpriced : CIP rev. B82-03110

338.4′362131 — Great Britain. Residences. Electricity supply. Charges

The **Structure** of the domestic unrestricted tariff. — [London] : Electricity Consumers Council, 1981. — 9,2leaves ; 30cm. — (Information paper / Electricity Consumers′ Council ; 8)
Unpriced (pbk) B82-14653

338.4′362131′0942 — England. Bulk electricity supply. Charges

Review of the structure of the bulk supplying tariff : the Electricity Supply Industry in England and Wales. — [London] : Electricity Counil, 1981. — 28leaves ; 30cm
Cover title
Unpriced (spiral) B82-25301

338.4′362131′0959 — South-east Asia. Electricity supply. Pricing

Munasinghe, Mohan. Electricity pricing : theory and case studies / Mohan Munasinghe and Jeremy J. Warford. — Baltimore ; London : Published for the World Bank [by] the Johns Hopkins University Press, c1982. — xviii,381p : ill,maps ; 25cm. — (A World Bank publication)
Bibliography: p368-373. — Includes index
ISBN 0-8018-2703-5 : £17.00 B82-34982

338.4′36213121 — Great Britain. Nuclear power stations. Costs *compared with* **costs of coal-fired & oil-fired power stations**

Comparative costs of generating electricity by nuclear and other fuels. — [Dorchester] : Planning Department, Dorset County Council, 1981. — 16p ; 21cm. — (Nuclear power stations ; information paper no.4)
Cover title
ISBN 0-85216-299-5 (pbk) : Unpriced
B82-12744

338.4′36213125′09413 — Southern Scotland. Electricity supply industries: South of Scotland Electricity Board. Nuclear power stations. Costs

Cheap electrickery? : the real cost of nuclear power in Scotland : a report / by the Scottish Consumer Campaign Against Nuclear Power. — [Edinburgh] ([37 West Nicholson St. Edinburgh EH8 9DD]) : Scottish Consumer Campaign, [1982?]. — 42p ; 21cm
Cover title. — Text on inside cover
£1.50 (pbk) B82-27127

338.4′3621381′0941 — Great Britain. Electronics industries. Companies. Finance — *Statistics — Serials*

Britain′s top 500 electronic companies. — [1979]-. — London : Jordan & Sons (Surveys) Ltd, 1979-. — v. ; 30cm
Issued every two years
ISSN 0263-2446 = Britain′s top 500 electronic companies : £40.00 B82-18536

338.4′36216 — Pumps. Costs — *Conference proceedings*

Pump Manufacturers Association. *Technical Conference (5th : 1977 : University of Bath).* ′Pump costs′ : papers presented at the Fifth Technical Conference of the British Pump Manufacturers′ Association : conference held at University of Bath 19th-21st April 1977. — Bedford : BHRA Fluid Engineering, c1977. — vi,266p : ill ; 30cm
Accompanied by ″Standards for pump makers and users : Third Technical Conference of the BPMA, 1973″ (2 microfiche in pocket ; 11x16cm)
ISBN 0-900983-68-x (pbk) : Unpriced
B82-31361

338.4′3623 — Military equipment. Expenditure by governments

The **Cost** of arms / Peace Force Scotland. — Kirkcaldy (The Lantern House, Olympia Arcade, Kirkcaldy, KY1 1QF) : Peace Force Scotland, [1982]. — [4]p : ill ; 21cm. — (Fact sheet ; 1)
Bibliography: p4
Unpriced (unbound) B82-27588

338.4′36234′0941 — Great Britain. Armaments industries. Financial aspects — *Statistics*

The **British** defence industry / market overview by J.O.G. Paton. — London : Jordan & Sons (Surveys), c1981. — xxiii,72p ; 30cm. — (A Jordan survey)
ISBN 0-85938-152-8 (pbk) : Unpriced
B82-06393

338.4′3624′0941 — Great Britain. Construction industries. Prices. Indices

Tysoe, Brian A.. Construction cost and price indices : description and use / Brian A. Tysoe. — London : Spon, 1981. — 213p : ill ; 24cm
Bibliography: p205. — Includes index
ISBN 0-419-11930-2 : £9.50 B82-38856

338.4′362576′0941 — Great Britain. Roads. Maintenance. Expenditure — *British Road Federation viewpoints*

Road maintenance : the decline of Britain′s roads. — [London] ([388-396 Oxford St., W1N 9HE]) : British Road Federation, [1982]. — 16p ; 30cm
Cover title
Unpriced (pbk) B82-23373

338.4'362742 — London. Flood barriers: Thames Barrier. Construction. Costs — *Inquiry reports*

Great Britain. *Parliament. House of Commons. Committee of Public Accounts*. Seventeenth report from the Committee of Public Accounts : together with the proceedings of the committee and the minutes of evidence : session 1979-80 : Ministry of Agriculture, Fisheries and Food, Department of Agriculture and Fisheries for Scotland, Intervention Board for Agricultural Produce : export levy debts, livestock improvement schemes for crofters, Thames tidal defences. — London : H.M.S.O., [1980]. — xvi,48p ; 25cm. — ([HC] ; 683)
Includes index
ISBN 0-10-268380-8 (pbk) : £4.65
Primary classification 382'.41'0941 B82-09507

338.4'3629 — Great Britain. Cars. Prices compared with prices of cars in Belgium

Ashworth, M. H.. Differentials between car prices in the United Kingdom and Belgium. — London : Institute for Fiscal Studies, Sept.1982. — [50]p
ISBN 0-902992-31-7 (pbk) : £5.00 : CIP entry B82-30328

338.4'3629133349 — Great Britain. Concorde aeroplanes. Expenditure by government — *Inquiry reports*

Great Britain. *Parliament. House of Commons. Industry and Trade Committee*. Second report from the Industry and Trade Committee, session 1981-82 : Concorde : together with the proceedings of the Committee relating to the report, the minutes of evidence and appendices. — London : H.M.S.O., 1982. — 30p ; 25cm. — ([HC] ; 193)
At head of title: House of Commons
ISBN 0-10-219382-7 (pbk) : £3.20 B82-23225

338.4'36292222'0973 — United States. Car industries. Finance, *1970-1981*

Lowry, A. T.. Financial assessment of the U.S. automotive industry / by A.T. Lowry & Scott Laing. — London : Economist Intelligence Unit, 1982. — 167p ; 30cm. — (EIU special report ; no.118)
Unpriced (pbk) B82-23831

338.4'366'00941 — Great Britain. Chemical industries. Companies. Finance — *Statistics — Serials*

The **British** chemical industry. — [1978]-. — London : Jordan & Sons (surveys) Ltd, 1978-. — v. ; 30cm
Issued every two years
ISSN 0263-2438 = British chemical industry : £37.50 B82-18532

338.4'36862'0941 — Great Britain. Printing industries. Companies. Finance — *Statistics*

Britains top 300 printing companies. — London : Jordan & Sons (Surveys), c1982. — xi,17,[15] leaves ; 30cm. — (A Jordan survey)
Includes index
ISBN 0-85938-163-3 (pbk) : Unpriced B82-40595

338.4'369083'0941 — Great Britain. Houses. Construction. Costs

Simpson, Barry J.. Site costs in housing development. — London : Construction Press, Jan.1983. — [176]p
ISBN 0-582-30515-2 (pbk) : £9.95 : CIP entry B82-32465

338.4'3692 — Buildings. Dimensional coordination. Costs & benefits

Goodacre, Peter. Cost factors of dimensional co-ordination : report of a Science Research Council project 1976-1980 / Peter Goodacre with J.R. Kelly, T.C. Cornick. — Reading : College of Estate Management, 1981. — 79p : ill ; 21cm. — (Studies in construction economy ; 3)
Bibliography: p77-79
ISBN 0-902132-66-0 (pbk) : Unpriced B82-17181

338.4'374 — Drawings. Auction prices — *Lists*

The **ASI** art market survey 1975-1978 / edited by Richard Hislop. — Weybridge : Art Sales Index, 1979. — 132p : ill ; 21x30cm
ISBN 0-903872-08-0 (pbk) : Unpriced
Primary classification 338.4'375 B82-08535

338.4'37451 — Antiques, *1800-1875*. **Auction prices**

Popular antiques and their values 1800-1875 / compiled and edited by Tony Curtis. — Galashiels : Lyle, c1981. — 127p : chiefly ill ; 22cm
Includes index
ISBN 0-86248-026-4 (pbk) : £2.50 B82-08173

338.4'37451 — Antiques, *1875-1950*. **Auction prices**

Popular antiques and their values 1875-1950 / compiled and edited by Tony Curtis. — Galashiels : Lyle, c1981. — 128p : chiefly ill ; 22cm
Includes index
ISBN 0-86248-027-2 (pbk) : £2.50 B82-08174

338.4'37451'0941 — Antiques. Auction prices — *Lists — Serials*

Millers antiques price guide. — [1980]-. — Tenterden : M.J.M. Publications ; [London] : [Mitchell Beazley] [distributor], 1979-. — v. : chiefly ill,facsims,ports ; 29cm
Annual. — Spine title: Millers guide
ISSN 0262-1851 = Millers antiques price guide : £8.95 B82-01069

338.4'375 — Paintings, *1900-1980*. **Auction prices** — *Lists*

1970-1980 auction prices of impressionist and 20th century artists / edited by Richard Hislop. — Weybridge : Art Sales Index, 1981. — 2v.(1322p,[24]p of plates) : ill,ports ; 30cm
ISBN 0-903872-12-9 : Unpriced B82-14999

338.4'375 — Paintings. Auction prices — *Lists*

The **ASI** art market survey 1975-1978 / edited by Richard Hislop. — Weybridge : Art Sales Index, 1979. — 132p : ill ; 21x30cm
ISBN 0-903872-08-0 (pbk) : Unpriced
Also classified at 338.4'374 B82-08535

338.4'375'05 — Paintings. Auction prices — *Serials*

Pictura times. — Issue 1 (Dec. 4th 1981)-. — Uckfield (68 Newtown High St., Uckfield, Sussex TN22 5DE) : Thoughtfield Ltd, 1981-. — v. : ill ; 44cm
Fortnightly
ISSN 0263-4694 = Pictura times : £24.00 per year B82-26155

338.4'5 — Great Britain. Public bodies. Efficiency

Chapman, Leslie. Waste away / Leslie Chapman. — London : Chatto & Windus, 1982. — 216p ; 23cm
Includes index
ISBN 0-7011-2629-9 : £7.95 : CIP rev. B82-04707

338.4'562'000941 — Great Britain. Engineering industries. Productivity

A **Pilot** study of performance and productivity in the UK engineering industry. — London (Broadcasting House, Tothill St., SW1 H9NQ) : Engineering Employers' Federation, 1979. — 59p : ill ; 21cm
Cover title
£5.00 (£2.00 to EEF members) (pbk) B82-37072

338.4'5664 — Food processing industries. Applications of digital computer systems

IFIP TC5 Working Conference on Food Production and Agricultural Engineering *(1981 : Havana)*. Computer applications in food production and agricultural engineering : proceedings of the IFIP TC5 Working Conference on Food Production and Agricultural Engineering, Havana, Cuba, 26-30 October 1981 / edited by Róbert E. Kálmán and Jesús Martínez ; [sponsored by United Nations Educational, Scientific and Cultural Organization]. — Amsterdam ; Oxford : North-Holland, 1982. — xi,334p : ill ; 23cm
Includes bibliographies
ISBN 0-444-86382-6 : £21.20
Primary classification 338.1'61 B82-39845

IFIP TC5 Working Conference on Food Production and Agricultural Engineering *(1981 : Havana)*. Computer applications in food production and agricultural engineering : proceedings of the IFIP TC5 Working Conference on Food Production and Agricultural Engineering, Havana, Cuba, 26-30 October 1981 / edited by Róbert E. Kálmán and Jesús Martínez ; [sponsored by United Nations Educational, Scientific and Cultural Organization]. — Amsterdam ; Oxford : North-Holland, 1982. — xi,334p : ill ; 23cm
Includes bibliographies
ISBN 0-444-86384-2 : £21.10
Primary classification 338.1'61 B82-39845

338.4'566862'091724 — Developing countries. Technology transfer from developed countries — *Study examples: Fertiliser industries*

Ghatak, Subrata. Technology transfer to developing countries : the case of the fertilizer industry / by Subrata Ghatak in collaboration with Derek Deadman, Christine Eadie. — Greenwich, Conn. : Jai Press ; London (3 Henrietta St., WC2E 8LU) : Distributed by Jaicon Press, c1981. — xix,181p : ill ; 24cm. — (Contemporary studies in economic and financial analysis ; v.27)
Includes index
ISBN 0-89232-160-1 : £21.50 B82-02079

338.4'567 — Manufacturing industries. Applications of microprocessors

Kochhar, A. K.. Microprocessors and their manufacturing applications. — London : Edward Arnold, Nov.1982. — [328]p
ISBN 0-7131-3470-4 (pbk) : £12.00 : CIP entry B82-27959

338.4'567'05 — Manufacturing industries. Applications of digital computer systems — *Serials*

CadCam international. — Sept. 1981-. — London (43 St John St., EC1M 4AN) : Woodpecker Publications, 1981-. — v. : ill,ports ; 30cm
Monthly
ISSN 0261-6920 = CadCam international : £18.00 per year
Also classified at 745.4'028'54 B82-05221

338.4'567'091724 — Developing countries. Manufacturing industries. Applications of digital computer systems — *Conference proceedings*

IFIP WG5.2 Working Conference on CAD/CAM as a Basis for the Development of Technology in Developing Nations *(1981 : Sao Paulo)*. CAD/CAM as a basis for the development of technology in developing nations : proceedings of the IFIP WG5.2 Working Conference on CAD/CAM as a Basis for the Development of Technology in Developing Nations, Sao Paulo, Brazil, October 21-23, 1981 / [sponsored by IFIP Working Group 5.2, Computer-Aided Design, International Federation for Information Processing and SUCESU Society of Computer and Subsidiary Equipment Users] ; edited by José L. Encarnaçao, Oswaldo F.F. Torres and Ernest A. Warman. — Amsterdam ; Oxford : North-Holland, c1981. — xii,437p : ill,maps ; 23cm
Includes index
ISBN 0-444-86320-6 : £38.14
Primary classification 620'.00425'02854 B82-18326

338.4'567'0941 — Great Britain. Manufacturing industries. Productivity *compared with* **productivity of manufacturing industries in West Germany & United States,** *1945-1980*

Prais, S. J.. Productivity and industrial structure : a statistical study of manufacturing industry in Britain, Germany and the United States / by S.J. Prais with the collaboration of Anne Daly, Daniel T. Jones, Karin Wagner. — Cambridge : Cambridge University Press, 1981. — xix,401p : ill ; 24cm. — (Economic and social studies ; 33)
Bibliography: p379-390. — Includes index
ISBN 0-521-24189-8 : £20.00 : CIP rev.
Also classified at 338.4'567'0943 ; 338.4'567'0973 B82-01357

338.4′567′0941 — Great Britain. Manufacturing industries. Use of microprocessor systems. Feasibility studies

MAPCON. Guidelines for feasibility study grants. — 2nd ed. — Stevenage (Warren Spring Laboratory, Department of Industry, P.O. Box 20, Gunnels Wood Rd., Stevenage, Herts. SG1 2BX) : MAPCON, 1980. — 21p ; 30cm
Previous ed.: 197-?
Unpriced (pbk) B82-38367

338.4′567′0943 — West Germany. Manufacturing industries. Productivity *compared with* productivity of manufacturing industries in Great Britain, *1945-1980*

Prais, S. J.. Productivity and industrial structure : a statistical study of manufacturing industry in Britain, Germany and the United States / by S.J. Prais with the collaboration of Anne Daly, Daniel T. Jones, Karin Wagner. — Cambridge : Cambridge University Press, 1981. — xix,401p : ill ; 24cm. — (Economic and social studies ; 33)
Bibliography: p379-390. — Includes index
ISBN 0-521-24189-8 : £20.00 : CIP rev.
Primary classification 338.4′567′0941
B82-01357

338.4′567′0973 — United States. Manufacturing industries. Productivity *compared with* productivity of manufacturing industries in Great Britain, *1945-1980*

Prais, S. J.. Productivity and industrial structure : a statistical study of manufacturing industry in Britain, Germany and the United States / by S.J. Prais with the collaboration of Anne Daly, Daniel T. Jones, Karin Wagner. — Cambridge : Cambridge University Press, 1981. — xix,401p : ill ; 24cm. — (Economic and social studies ; 33)
Bibliography: p379-390. — Includes index
ISBN 0-521-24189-8 : £20.00 : CIP rev.
Primary classification 338.4′567′0941
B82-01357

338.4′56752′091724 — Developing countries. Leather. Production. Techniques. Economic aspects

Huq, M. M.. Choice of technique in leather manufacture / M.M. Huq and H. Aragaw. — Edinburgh : Scottish Academic Press, 1981. — xviii,115p ; 25cm. — (David Livingstone Institute series on choice of technique in developing countries ; v.4)
Bibliography: p101-102. — Includes index
ISBN 0-7073-0301-x (cased) : Unpriced
ISBN 0-7073-0303-6 (pbk) : £7.50 B82-03514

338.4′567731′09429 — Wales. Wool industries. Technological development, *to 1981*

Jenkins, J. Geraint. From fleece to fabric : the technological history of the Welsh woollen industry / J. Geraint Jenkins. — Llandysul : Gomer, 1981. — 37p : ill ; 22cm
ISBN 0-85088-785-2 (pbk) : £0.95 B82-10704

338.4′700163 — Automated information processing systems. Economic factors

The **Economics** of information processing / Robert Goldberg. Harold Lorin. — New York ; Chichester : Wiley, c1982. — 2 : ill ; 29cm
ISBN 0-471-09206-1 : Unpriced
ISBN 0-471-09767-5 (v.2) : £18.50 B82-25450

338.4′700164′0941 — Great Britain. Computer services industries

The **British** computer services industry / industrial commentary by Joseph F. Roth. — London : Jordan & Sons (Surveys), c1981. — xxxiv,81p : ill ; 30cm. — (A Jordan survey)
ISBN 0-85938-151-x (pbk) : Unpriced
B82-14413

338.4′70016425 — Digital computer systems. Software. Design. Economic aspects

Boehm, Barry W.. Software engineering economics / Barry W. Boehm. — Englewood Cliffs ; London : Prentice-Hall, c1981. — xxvii,767p : ill ; 25cm
Bibliography: p733-749. — Includes index
ISBN 0-13-822122-7 : £24.40 B82-14457

338.4′70705′0941 — Great Britain. Book publishing industries — *Statistics*

Book publishers. — 10th ed. — London : Inter Company Comparisons, [c1980]. — 35p ; 21x30cm. — (ICC financial survey)
ISBN 0-86191-142-3 (pbk) : Unpriced
B82-24675

Book publishing / industry commentary by Michael R. Johnston. — London : Jordan & Sons (Surveys), c1982. — xx,76p ; 30cm. — (A Jordan survey)
ISBN 0-85938-159-5 (pbk) : Unpriced
B82-33997

338.4′70705′09421 — London. Printing & publishing industries, *ca 1800-1870* — *Directories*

Brown, Philip A. H.. London publishers and printers c.1800-1870. — London : British Library, Reference Division Publications, Dec.1982. — [233]p
ISBN 0-7123-0012-0 : £15.00 : CIP entry
B82-30198

338.4′70705′0973 — United States. Book publishing industries — *Serials*

U.S. book publishing yearbook and directory. — 1979-80-. — White Plains, N.Y. ; London (3 Henrietta St., WC2 8LU) : Knowledge Industry Publications, 1979-. — v. ; 28cm
Descripton based on: 1980-81 issue
ISSN 0193-6417 = U.S. book publishing yearbook and directory : Unpriced B82-13405

338.4′7072 — Great Britain. National newspaper publishing industries

Jenkins, Simon, *1943-*. Newspapers through the looking-glass : presented 10th February 1981 / by Simon Jenkins. — Manchester (C.I.S. Building, Miller St., Manchester M60 3AL) : Manchester Statistical Society, [1981?]. — 12p ; 21cm
£2.00 (pbk) B82-11621

338.4′7072′0212 — Great Britain. Newspaper publishing industries — *Statistics*

The **British** newspaper industry / market overview by Derek Terrington. — London : Jordan & Sons (Surveys), c1981. — 73p ; 30cm. — (A Jordan survey)
ISBN 0-85938-149-8 (pbk) : Unpriced
B82-07137

338.4′7072′05 — Great Britain. Newspaper publishing industries — *Serials*

[Newstime *(London)*]. Newstime : monthly journal of the Newspaper Society. — Vol.1, no.1 (Oct. 1981)-. — London (6 Carmelite St., EC4Y 0BL) : The Society, 1981-. — v. : ill,ports ; 30cm
Merger of: Newspaper Society news ; Newspaper sales ; and, Talking points (London : 1947)
ISSN 0262-6373 = Newstime (London) : £10.00 per year (Free to Society members)
B82-06172

338.4′73441 — Great Britain. Legal services

Law in the balance : legal services in the 1980s / edited by Philip A. Thomas. — Oxford : Robertson, 1982. — x,245p ; 23cm. — (Law in society series)
Includes bibliographies and index
ISBN 0-85520-444-3 (cased) : £18.50 : CIP rev.
ISBN 0-85520-482-6 (pbk) : £6.50 B81-30178

338.4′7361 — Welfare services. Economic aspects

Wilson, Thomas, *1916-*. The political economy of the welfare state / Thomas Wilson and Dorothy J. Wilson. — London : Allen & Unwin, 1982. — ix,223p ; 23cm. — (Studies in economics ; 19)
Bibliography: p209-218. — Includes index
ISBN 0-04-336077-7 (cased) : Unpriced : CIP rev.
ISBN 0-04-336078-5 (pbk) : Unpriced
B82-15631

338.4′7361941 — Great Britain. Welfare services. Economic aspects

Seldon, Arthur. Wither the welfare state / Arthur Seldon. — London : Institute of Economic Affairs, 1981. — 49p ; 22cm. — (Occasional paper / Institute of Economic Affairs, ISSN 0073-909x ; 60)
Bibliography: p49
ISBN 0-255-36146-7 (pbk) : £1.50 B82-00441

338.4′73621′05 — Health services. Economic aspects — *Serials*

Research in health economics : a research annual. — Vol.1 (1979)-. — Greenwich, Conn. : JAI Press ; London (3 Henrietta St., WC2E 8LU) : Distributed by JAICON Press, 1979-. — v. ; 24cm
£24.50 B82-02368

338.4′73621′091724 — Developing countries. Health services. Economic aspects

Health links / Third World First ; contributors Lesley Doyal ... [et al.] ; edited by Gill Alcock and Hilary Scannell. — Oxford (232 Cowley Rd., Oxford OX4 1UH) : Third World First, [1982?]. — 32p : ill ; 30cm
Cover title. — Text on inside covers
£0.80 (pbk) B82-41025

338.4′73621′0973 — United States. Health services. Economic aspects

Economics and health care / edited by John B. McKinlay. — Cambridge, Mass. ; London : MIT Press,, c1981. — xvi,547p ; 24cm. — (Milbank reader ; 1)
Bibliography: p524-534. — Includes index
ISBN 0-262-13176-5 (cased) : £15.75
ISBN 0-262-63077-x (pbk) : Unpriced
B82-23725

Health care consumers, professionals, and organizations / edited by John B. McKinlay. — Cambridge, Mass. ; London : MIT Press, c1981. — xiii,444p ; 24cm. — (Milbank reader ; 2)
Includes bibliographies and index
ISBN 0-262-13177-3 (corrected cased) : £15.75
ISBN 0-262-63078-8 (pbk) : Unpriced
B82-23786

338.4′73621′0973 — United States. Health services. Economic aspects — *Serials*

Advances in health economics and health services research : a research annual. — Vol.2 (1981)-. — Greenwich, Conn. ; London : JAI, 1981-. — v. : ill ; 24cm
Continues: Research in health economics
Unpriced B82-33859

338.4′736211′0974 — United States. Hospitals. Administration. Economic aspects — *Study regions: New England*

Barocci, Thomas A.. Non-profit hospitals : their structure, human resources, and economic importance / Thomas A. Barocci. — Boston, Mass. : Auburn House ; London : distributed by Eurospan, c1981. — xix,232p : ill,forms ; 25cm
Bibliography: p209-220. — Includes index
ISBN 0-86569-054-5 : £15.75 B82-13427

338.4′7362197581 — Great Britain. National health services: Hip prosthesis services. Economic aspects

Hip replacement and the NHS. — London : Office of Health Economics, c1982. — 56p : col.ill ; 21cm. — (Studies of current health problems, ISSN 0473-8837 ; 21)
Bibliography: p54
£1.00 (pbk) B82-25623

338.4′7363 — Urban regions. Public amenties. Economic aspects

The **Economics** of urban amenities / edited by Douglas B. Diamond, Jr, George S. Tolley. — New York ; London : Academic Press, 1982. — xiii,226p : ill ; 24cm. — (Studies in urban economics)
Includes bibliographies and index
ISBN 0-12-214840-1 : £19.60 B82-38385

338.4′73635 — Housing. Economic aspects

Maclennan, Duncan. Housing economics. — London : Longman, Feb.1982. — [220]p
ISBN 0-582-44381-4 (pbk) : £6.95 : CIP entry
B81-36018

338.4′73644′0973 — United States. Crime. Prevention. Economic aspects

Phillips, Llad. The economics of crime control / Llad Phillips, Harold L. Votey. — Beverly Hill ; London : Sage, c1981. — 312p : ill ; 22cm. — (Sage library of social research ; v.132)
Bibliography: p297-305. — Includes index
ISBN 0-8039-1715-5 (cased) : Unpriced
ISBN 0-8039-1716-3 (pbk) : Unpriced
B82-21917

338.4'737133 — Teaching aids: Audiovisual materials. Economic aspects

Wagner, Leslie. The economics of educational media / Leslie Wagner. — London : Macmillan, 1982. — x,162p ; 23cm
Bibliography: p152-157. — Includes index
ISBN 0-333-31690-8 : £20.00 B82-39745

338.4'76046 — Waste material recycling industries

Vogler, Jon. Work from waste : recycling wastes to create employment / by Jon Vogler. — London : Intermediate Technology, c1981. — xiv,396p : ill,forms ; 22cm
Bibliography: p379-382. — Includes index
ISBN 0-903031-79-5 (pbk) : £6.50 B82-18337

338.4'76151'091811 — Eastern hemisphere. Pharmaceutical industries — *Serials*

IMS monitor report. Asia, Africa and Australasia. — Jan. 1976-Oct. 1981. — London (229 High Holborn, WC1V 7DA) : IMSWORLD, 1976-1981. — 24v. ; 30cm
Quarterly. — Merged with: IMS monitor report. Europe; and, IMS monitor report. Americas, to become: IMS monitor report. International. — Description based on: Jan. 1978 issue
ISSN 0140-4725 = IMS monitor report. Asia, Africa and Australasia : Unpriced B82-18728

338.4'76151'094 — Europe. Pharmaceutical industries — *Serials*

IMS monitor report. Europe. — Jan. 1976-Oct. 1981. — London (229 High Holborn, WC1V 7DA) : IMSWORLD, 1976-1981. — 24v. ; 30cm
Quarterly. — Merged with: IMS monitor report. Americas; and, IMS monitor report. Asia, Africa and Australasia, to become: IMS monitor report. International. — Description based on: Jan. 1978 issue
ISSN 0140-4741 = IMS monitor report. Europe : Unpriced B82-18726

338.4'76151'0941 — Great Britain. Pharmaceutical industries, *1950-1979*

The **Pharmaceutical** industry and the nation's health. — 11th ed. — London (12 Whitehall, SW1A 2DY) : Association of the British Pharmaceutical Industry, 1982. — 48p : col.ill ; 21x10cm
Cover title. — Previous ed.: 1978
Unpriced (pbk) B82-39065

338.4'76151'097 — America. Pharmaceutical industries — *Serials*

IMS monitor report. Americas. — Jan. 1976-Oct. 1981. — London (229 High Holborn, WC1V 7DA) : IMSWORLD, 1976-1981. — 24v. ; 30cm
Quarterly. — Merged with: IMS monitor report. Europe; and, IMS monitor report. Asia, Africa and Australasia, to become: IMS monitor report. International. — Description based on: Jan. 1978 issue
ISSN 0140-4733 = IMS monitor report. Americas : Unpriced B82-18727

338.4'762'0006041 — Great Britain. Engineering industries & trades. Organisations: Engineering Industries Association — *Regulations*

Engineering Industries Association. Constitution / Engineering Industries Association. — London : [The Association], 1980. — 8p ; 21cm
Unpriced (pbk) B82-24378

338.4'762'0006041 — Great Britain. Engineering industries & trades. Organisations: Engineering Industries Association, *to 1981*

Engineering Industries Association. Born in strife and survived : a brief history of the Association / by Eric Ford. — London : Engineering Industries Association, [1982]. — [16]p ; 25cm
Unpriced (pbk) B82-24383

338.4'7621042'05 — Energy industries — *Serials*

[Reference book & buyers' guide *(Energy Business Centre)*]. Reference book & buyers' guide / the Energy Business Centre. — 1982-. — London (86 Edgware Rd, W2 2YW) : Published for the Centre by Sterling Publications, 1982-. — v. : ill,maps,ports ; 30cm
Annual
ISSN 0261-7633 = Reference book & buyers' guide - Energy Business Centre : Unpriced B82-29061

338.4'7621'0941 — Great Britain. Mechanical engineering industries. Forecasts. Engineering Employers' Federation. *Short Term Trends Working Party.* **Mechanical engineering industry short term trends** — *Critical studies* — *Serials*

Engineering Employers' Federation. *Short Term Trends Working Party.* Mechanical engineering short term trends. Supplement / Engineering Employers' Federation [Short Term Trends Working Party]. — No.4 (Feb. 1981)-. — [London] ([Broadway House, Tothill St., SW1H 9HQ]) : [The Federation], 1981-. — v. : ill ; 30cm
Two issues yearly. — Continues: Engineering Employers' Federation. Short Term Trends Working Party. Mechanical engineering industry short term trends. Supplement. — Supplement to: Engineering Employers' Federation. Short Term Trends Working Party. Mechanical engineering industry short term trends
ISSN 0262-186x = Mechanical engineering short term trends. Supplement : £35.00 per year with Mechanical engineering industry short term trends (£14.00 to EEF members) B82-01071

338.4'7621'0941 — Great Britain. Mechanical engineering industries — *Forecasts* — *Serials*

Engineering Employers' Federation. *Short Term Trends Working Party.* Mechanical engineering industry short term trends / Engineering Employers' Federation. — Aug. 1978-. — London (Broadway House, Tothill St., SW1H 9HW) : The Federation, 1978-. — v. : ill ; 30cm
Three issues yearly (1978-1979), quarterly (1980-). — Represents the views of: the Short Term Trends Working Party. — Continues: National Economic Development Council. Economic Development Committee for Mechanical Engineering. Short Term Trends Working Party. Short term trends. — Supplement: Engineering Employers' Federation. Short Term Trends Working Party. Mechanical engineering short term trends. Supplement. — Description based on: Nov. 1980
ISSN 0143-2605 = Mechanical engineering industry short term trends : £35.00 per year (£14.00 to EEF members) B82-01072

338.4'76212'094 — Western Europe. Hydraulic equipment industries — *Statistics*

A **Market** studies report on air pumps, compressors and hydraulic equipment : a study of this important industry in Belgium, Denmark, France, West Germany, Italy, The Netherlands, Sweden and the United Kingdom. — London : Market Studies International, c1982. — 85p : ill(some col.) ; 30cm
Text in English and several other languages
ISBN 0-86191-921-1 (pbk) : £98.00
Primary classification 338.4'762151'094 B82-30040

338.4'762131'0941 — Great Britain. Electricity supply industries

Electricity supply in the United Kingdom : organisation and development, 30 September 1980. — 4th ed. — London : Electricity Council, 1980. — 71p : ill,maps ; 30cm
Previous ed.: 1978
ISBN 0-85188-082-7 (pbk) : Unpriced B82-35938

338.4'762131'0941 — Great Britain. Electricity supply industries, *1947-1962*

Hannah, Leslie. Engineers, managers and politicians : the first fifteen years of nationalised electricity supply in Britain / Leslie Hannah ; research by Margaret Ackrill ... [et al.]. — London : Macmillan, 1982. — xiii,336p : 1ill,1map ; 23cm
Includes index
ISBN 0-333-22087-0 : £15.00 B82-39741

338.4'762131'0941 — Great Britain. Electricity supply industries, *to 1981*

Gordon, Bob. One hundred years of electricity supply 1881-1981 : a brief account of some aspects of growth and development over the past century / by Bob Gordon. — Hove (Grand Ave., Hove, East Sussex BN3 2LS) : South Eastern Electricity Board, [1981]. — 83p : ill,maps,ports ; 21cm. — (A Milne Museum booklet)
At head of title: Milne Museum. — Bibliography: p83
Unpriced (pbk) B82-11208

338.4'762131'0942393 — Avon. Bristol. Electricity supply industries, *1863-1948*

Lamb, Peter G.. Electricity in Bristol 1863-1948 / by Peter G. Lamb. — Bristol (74 Bell Barn Rd., Stoke Bishop, Bristol [BS9 2DG]) : Bristol Branch of the Historical Association, 1981. — 34p : ill,1port ; 21cm. — (Local history pamphlets / Bristol Branch of the Historical Association ; 48)
Cover title
£0.60 (pbk) B82-00040

338.4'7621315'094 — Western Europe. Capacitor industries

Profile of European capacitor manufacturers. — Luton : Mackintosh Publications, 1980. — iv,91p : 1ill ; 30cm
ISBN 0-904705-25-0 (pbk) : £180.00 B82-32197

338.4'7621381'09415 — Ireland. Electronics industries — *Serials*

Electronics report. — Vol.1, no.1 (Nov. 1981)-. — Loughlinstown (Birchdale, Cherrywood Rd, Loughlinstown, Co. Dublin) : Computer Publications of Ireland, 1981-. — v. : ill,ports ; 30cm
Monthly
Unpriced B82-11831

338.4'7621381'0952 — Japan. Electronics industries

Bownas, Geoffrey. Japan's strategy for the 1980's : in industrial electrical & electronic equipment / report by G. Bownas. — London (8 Leicester St., WC2H 7BN) : British Electrical and Allied Manufacturers' Association, c1981. — 82,[43] leaves : 1ill ; 30cm
Cover title
£30.00 (spiral) B82-35528

338.4'762138151'0941 — Great Britain. Electronic components industries — *Conference proceedings*

ECIF seminar at Electronics 79 : components of assessed quality — the contribution of the UK industry, 20th-22nd November 1979, Pillar Hall, Olympia. — [London] ([7/8 Savile Row, W1X 1AF]) : [Electronic Components Industry Federation], c1978. — 150p : ill ; 30cm
Unpriced (pbk) B82-08244

338.4'76213893'0941 — Great Britain. Sound recording & reproduction equipment industries & trades — *Statistics*

The **Audio** report 1981. — London : Euromonitor Publications, 1981. — 57p ; 30cm
ISBN 0-903706-71-7 (spiral) : Unpriced B82-11889

338.4'762144'0973 — United States. Energy sources: Geothermal energy. Economic aspects

Blair, Peter D.. Geothermal energy : investment decisions and commercial development / Peter D. Blair, Thomas A.V. Cassel, Robert H. Edelstein. — New York ; Chichester : Wiley, c1982. — x,184p : ill,2maps ; 24cm. — (Alternate energy)
Bibliography: p172-180. — Includes index
ISBN 0-471-08063-2 : £25.70 B82-32704

338.4'762147'0973 — United States. Solar energy. Economic aspects

Walton, A. L.. The solar alternative : an economic perspective / A.L. Walton, E.H. Warren, Jr.. — Englewood Cliffs ; London : Prentice-Hall, c1982. — xiv,173p : ill,1map ; 23cm
Includes index
ISBN 0-13-822262-2 (pbk) : £6.95 B82-22235

338.4'762148'0944 — France. Nuclear power industries

Sweet, Colin. A study of nuclear power in France / by Colin Sweet. — [London] : Polytechnic of the South Bank, 1981. — 76p : ill ; 30cm. — (Energy paper ; no.2)
Unpriced (pbk) B82-03315

338.4′762151′094 — Western Europe. Compressors industries — *Statistics*

A **Market** studies report on air pumps, compressors and hydraulic equipment : a study of this important industry in Belgium, Denmark, France, West Germany, Italy, The Netherlands, Sweden and the United Kingdom. — London : Market Studies International, c1982. — 85p : ill(some col.) ; 30cm
Text in English and several other languages
ISBN 0-86191-921-1 (pbk) : £98.00
Also classified at 338.4′76212′094 B82-30040

338.4′762156′094 — Western Europe. Refrigeration equipment industries & trades — *Statistics*

A **Market** studies report on refrigeration equipment in Europe : a study of the European industry in Belgium, Denmark, France, West Germany, Italy, The Netherlands, Spain and the United Kingdom. — London (81 City Rd., EC1) : Inter Company Comparisons, c1981. — 83p : ill(some col.) ; 30cm. — (Market studies)
ISBN 0-86191-909-2 (pbk) : Unpriced
B82-07770

338.4′76218 — Great Britain. Mechanical power transmission equipment industries

Power transmission reference guide 1980-1981. — 5th ed. — London (120 Wigmore St, W1) : Engineers′ Digest, [1981?]. — 104p : ill(some col.) ; 30cm
Previous ed.: 197-
Unpriced (pbk) B82-25857

338.4′7621824′094 — Western Europe. Springs manufacturing industries & trades — *Statistics*

A **Market** studies report on springs and wire : a study of the wire products industry in Belgium, France, West Germany, Italy, The Netherlands, Sweden, Switzerland and the United Kingdom. — London (81 City Rd., EC1) : Inter Company Comparisons. — (Market studies)
Vol.1: Ferrous. — [1981]. — 82p : ill(some col.) ; 30cm
ISBN 0-86191-907-6 (pbk) : Unpriced
Primary classification 338.4′7671842′094
B82-07766

A **Market** studies report on springs and wire : a study of the European wire products industry in Belgium, France, West Germany, Italy, The Netherlands, Sweden, Switzerland and the United Kingdom. — London (81 City Rd., EC1) : Inter Company Comparisons. — (Market studies)
Vol.2: Non-ferrous. — [1981]. — 77p : ill(some col.) ; 30cm
ISBN 0-86191-908-4 (pbk) : Unpriced
Primary classification 338.4′7671842′094
B82-07767

338.4′762186′094 — Western Europe. Mechanical handling equipment industries & trades — *Statistics*

A **Market** studies report on the mechanical handling equipment industry in Europe : a study of this important industry in Belgium, Denmark, France, West Germany, Italy, The Netherlands, Sweden and the United Kingdom. — London (81 City Rd., EC1) : Inter Company Comparisons, c1981. — 90p : ill ; 30cm. — (Market studies)
ISBN 0-86191-916-5 (pbk) : Unpriced
B82-07771

338.4′7621863 — Western Europe. Industrial trucks industries — *Statistics*

A **Market** studies report on fork lift, industrial trucks and trailers : a study of this important industrial sector in Belgium, Denmark, France, West Germany, Italy, The Netherlands, Sweden and the United Kingdom. — London : Market Studies International, c1982. — 77p : ill(some col.) ; 30cm
Text in English and several other languages
ISBN 0-86191-925-4 (pbk) : £98.00
B82-30039

338.4′76218672′094 — Western Europe. Pipes & tubes industries & trades — *Statistics*
A **Market** studies report on tubes and pipes : a study of the European industry in Belgium, France, West Germany, Italy, The Netherlands and the United Kingdom. — London (81 City Rd., EC1) : Inter Company Comparisons. — (Market studies)
Vol.1: (Ferrous). — c1981. — 75p : ill,(some col.) ; 30cm
ISBN 0-86191-912-2 (pbk) : Unpriced
B82-07772

A **Market** studies report on tubes and pipes : a study of the European industry in Belgium, Denmark, France, West Germany, Italy, The Netherlands, Sweden and the United Kingdom. — London (81 City Rd., EC1) : Inter Company Comparisons. — (Market studies)
Vol.2: (Non-ferrous and plastic). — c1981. — 76p : ill ; 30cm
ISBN 0-86191-911-4 (pbk) : Unpriced
B82-07773

338.4′762188′094 — Western Europe. Engineering components industries & trades: Fastenings industries & trades — *Statistics*
A **Market** studies report on industrial fasteners in Europe : a study of the European wire products industry in Belgium, France, West Germany, The Netherlands, Italy, Sweden, Switzerland, the United Kingdom. — London (81 City Rd., EC1) : Inter Company Comparisons, [1981]. — 79p : ill(some col.) ; 30cm. — (Market studies)
ISBN 0-86191-906-8 (pbk) : Unpriced
B82-07768

338.4′762193 — Great Britain. Saws industries & trades — *Statistics* — *Serials*
ICC financial survey. Saw manufacturers & distributors. — 1st ed.-. — London : Inter Company Comparisons, 1980-. — v. ; 21x30cm
Annual. — Description based on: 2nd ed.
ISSN 0263-9564 = ICC financial survey. Saw manufacturers & distributors : Unpriced
B82-38524

338.4′7623′091724 — Developing coutries. Military equipment industries. Effects of multinational companies in military equipment industries
Tuomi, Helena. Transnational corporations, armaments and development / Helena Tuomi and Raimo Väyrynen. — Aldershot : Gower, 1982. — xv,312p ; 23cm
Originally published: Tampere : Tampere Peace Research Institute, 1980
ISBN 0-566-00506-9 : Unpriced : CIP rev.
Also classified at 355′.009172′4 B81-36217

338.4′76234′09034 — Armaments industries, *1800-1979*
War, business and world military-industrial complexes / edited by Benjamin Franklin Cooling. — Port Washington ; London : National University Publications, 1981. — 217p ; 22cm
Bibliography: p209-212. — Includes index
ISBN 0-8046-9276-9 : £16.65 B82-17550

338.4′76234′0941 — Great Britain. Armaments industries
War lords : CIS report : the UK arms industry. — [London] ([9 Poland St., W1]) : [Counter Information Services], [1982]. — 32p : ill,1map. — (Anti-report ; no.31)
Cover title. — Text and ill on inside covers. — Bibliography: p32
£0.95 (pbk) B82-26626

338.4′7623441 — United States. Weapons manufacturers: Knives manufacturers
Lewis, Jack. The Gun Digest book of knives. — 2nd ed. / by Jack Lewis and Roger Combs. — London : Arms and Armour, c1982. — 288p : ill,ports ; 28cm
Previous ed.: / B.R. Hughes and Jack Lewis. Northfield, Ill. : Digest Books, 1973
ISBN 0-910676-37-2 (pbk) : Unpriced
B82-28411

338.4′7′624 — Construction industries. Economic aspects
Shutt, R. C.. Economics for the construction industry. — London : Longman, May 1982. — [224]p. — (Longman technician series. Construction and civil engineering)
ISBN 0-582-41214-5 : £6.50 : CIP entry
B82-10761

338.4′7624′05 — Construction industries — *Forecasts* — *Serials*
Construction market planner : the monthly digest of world construction trends. — [Vol.1, no.1] (Feb. 1982)-. — London (Wheatsheaf House, Carmelite St., EC4Y OAX) : Olsenhurst, 1982-. — v. ; 30cm
ISSN 0263-6999 = Construction market planner : £95.00 per year B82-31711

338.4′7624′09567 — Iraq. Construction industries — *For British businessmen*
Frith, Dennis E.. New priorities and developments in the construction market in Saudi Arabia and Iraq / Dennis E. Frith. — London : Graham & Trotman, 1978. — 125p : 1map ; 30cm
ISBN 0-86010-135-5 (pbk) : £95.00
Primary classification 338.4′7627′09538
B82-13320

338.4′762581′0941162 — Scotland. Highland Region. Caithness *(District)*. **Paving flags industries & trades,** *to 1980*
Omand, Donald, *1936-*. The flagstone industry of Caithness / by Donald Omand and John Porter. — [Aberdeen] : Department of Geography, University of Aberdeen, 1981. — 19p,[17]p of plates : ill,1map,facsims,1port,1geneal.table ; 29cm. — (O′Dell memorial monograph, ISSN 0141-1454 ; no.10)
Bibliography: p17
Unpriced (pbk) B82-19914

338.4′7627′09538 — Saudi Arabia. Construction industries — *For British businessmen*
Frith, Dennis E.. New priorities and developments in the construction market in Saudi Arabia and Iraq / Dennis E. Frith. — London : Graham & Trotman, 1978. — 125p : 1map ; 30cm
ISBN 0-86010-135-5 (pbk) : £95.00
Also classified at 338.4′7624′09567 B82-13320

338.4′762798 — Great Britain. Offshore structures. Decommissioning — *Conference proceedings*
Decommissioning offshore structures : June 9, 1981, London : conference transcript / edited by Catherine O′Keeffe. — [London] : Scientific and Technical Studies, [1981]. — iii,72p : ill ; 30cm
ISBN 0-9505774-5-6 (pbk) : £23.00
B82-05671

338.4′7628 — Africa. Water industries — *Serials*
African water and sewage. — Vol.1, no.1 (Mar. 1982)-. — Redhill (2 Queensway, Redhill, Surrey RH1 1QS) : Fuel & Metallurgical Journals, 1982-. — v. : ill(some col.),maps ; 30cm
Quarterly. — Text in English, French summaries
ISSN 0262-6411 = African water and sewage : £17.00 per year B82-28123

338.4′7628 — Great Britain. Water industries — *Serials*
Water bulletin : journal of the water industry. — No.1 (2 Apr. 1982)-. — London : National Water Council, 1982-. — v. : ill,ports ; 30cm
Weekly. — Merger of: Water (London : 1974); and, Bulletin (National Water Council)
ISSN 0262-9909 = Water bulletin : £45.00 per year B82-32161

338.4′76291 — Aerospace industries — *Forecasts* — *Conference proceedings*
Aerospace into the eighties and beyond : London, August 26, 27 & 28, 1980 : speakers papers / sponsors Financial Times, The Royal Aeronautical Society. — London (Minster House, Arthur Street, EC4R 9AX) : Financial Times Ltd, [1980?]. — 202p : ill,maps ; 30cm
Cover title
Unpriced (pbk) B82-07066

338.4′762913′00973 — United States. Aircraft industries, *to 1980*
Bluestone, Barry. Aircraft industry dynamics : an analysis of competition, capital and labor / Barry Bluestone, Peter Jordan, Mark Sullivan. — Boston, Mass. : Auburn House ; London : distributed by Eurospan, c1981. — xv,208p : ill ; 25cm
Bibliography: p192-197. — Includes index
ISBN 0-86569-053-7 : £16.25 B82-13423

338.4'762913'09422145 — Surrey. Brooklands. Aircraft industries, *1907-1981*
Johnson, Howard, *1916-*. Wings over Brooklands : the story of the birthplace of British aviation / Howard Johnson ; with a foreword by Sir Thomas Sopuith. — Weybridge : Whittet, 1981. — 157p : ill,maps,2facsims,ports ; 26cm
Bibliography: p153. — Includes index
ISBN 0-905483-20-0 : £8.95 : CIP rev.
ISBN 0-905483-21-9 (pbk) : £4.95
Primary classification 629.13'09422'145
B81-27990

338.4'7629133349 — United States. Supersonic passenger aeroplanes. Development. Policies of government. Influence of public opinion
Horwitch, Mel. Clipped wings : the American SST conflict / Mel Horwitch. — Cambridge, Mass. ; London : MIT, c1982. — x,473p : ill,ports ; 24cm
Includes index
ISBN 0-262-08115-6 : £17.50 B82-37514

338.4'76292 — Western Europe. Motor vehicle components industries — *Statistics*
A **Market** studies report on the motor components industry in Europe : a study of this major industry in Belgium, Denmark, France, West Germany, Italy, The Netherlands, Sweden and the United Kingdom / Market Studies International. — London : Inter Company Comparisons, c1981. — 100p : ill (some col.) ; 30cm
Includes bibliographies
ISBN 0-86191-913-0 (pbk) : Unpriced
B82-21287

338.4'76292222 — Car industries & trades — *Conference proceedings*
World Motor Conference *(4th : 1982 : Geneva).* The Fourth World Motor Conference : Geneva 1 & 2 March 1982 : speakers papers / sponsored by Financial Times, Booz.Allen & Hamilton. — London (Minister House, Arthur St., EC4R 9AX) : Financial Times Conference Organisation, [1982]. — 122p : ill ; 30cm. — (Financial Times conferences)
Cover title
Unpriced (pbk) B82-25784

338.4'76292222 — Car industries, *to 1982*
Sinclair, Stewart. The world car : the future of the automobile industry. — London : Euromonitor, Nov.1982. — [220]p
ISBN 0-903706-91-1 : £38.00 : CIP entry
B82-33363

338.4'76292222'09415 — Ireland. Car industries, *to 1981*
Moore, John S. (John Shaw). Motor makers in Ireland. — Belfast : Blackstaff Press, June 1982. — [192]p
ISBN 0-85640-264-8 (cased) : £14.95 : CIP entry B82-14966

338.4'7629225 — Western Europe. Agricultural tractors industries & trades — *Statistics*
A **Market** studies report on agricultural tractors in Europe : a study of the European agricultural machinery industry in Austria, France, West Germany, The Netherlands, Italy, Sweden and the United Kingdom. — London (81 City Rd., EC1) : Inter Company Comparisons, [1981]. — 89p : ill(some col.) ; 30cm. — (Market studies)
ISBN 0-86191-905-x (pbk) : Unpriced
B82-07774

338.4'762926'0941 — Great Britain. Motor vehicle bodywork industries — *Statistics — Serials*
ICC financial survey. Motor body builders & engineers. — 1st ed.-. — London : Inter Company Comparisons, [197-]-. — v. ; 21x30cm
Annual. — Description based on: 5th ed.
ISSN 0263-9556 = ICC financial survey. Motor body builders & engineers : Unpriced
B82-38527

338.4'7629892 — Industrial robot industries & trade — *Serials*
Robot news international. — Vol.1, no.1 (Oct. 1981)-. — Bedford (35 High St., Kempston, Bedford MK42 7BT) : Industrial Newsletters and IFS (Publications), 1981-. — v. : ill ; 30cm
Monthly
ISSN 0262-1460 = Robot news international : £115.00 for first 15 months B82-10115

338.4'7641'0941 — Great Britain. Food & drinks industries & trades
Hillier, Maurice C.. The grocery world moving into the 1980s : some implications for training in food, drink and tobacco companies arising from developments in the grocery trade / Maurice C. Hillier. — Gloucester (Barton House, Barton St., Gloucester GL1 1QQ) : Food, Drink and Tobacco Industry Training Board, 1980. — [42]p : ill ; 30cm
Bibliography: p42
£2.00 (pbk) B82-26491

338.4'76413'0094 — Western Europe. Food industries & trades — *Statistics — Serials*
Food markets in Western Europe. — 1981-. — London : Euromonitor Publications, 1981-. — v. ; 30cm
ISSN 0262-334x = Food markets in Western Europe : Unpriced B82-02389

338.4'76413'00941 — Great Britain. Food industries & trades — *Serials*
Food quarterly : a quarterly note on the UK food retailing and manufacturing industries. — [June?] 1979-. — London (319 High Holborn, WC1V 7PB) : Hoare Govett, 1979-. — v. : ill ; 30cm
Description based on: July 1981
ISSN 0262-768x = Food quarterly : Unpriced
B82-07636

338.4'764672 — Beauty care industries & trades
Coleman, Vernon. Face values : how the beauty industry affects you / Vernon Coleman with Margaret Coleman ; foreword by Miriam Stoppard. — London : Pan, 1981. — xvi,288p ; 20cm
Includes index
ISBN 0-330-26506-7 (pbk) : £1.95 B82-11642

338.4'7647944101'0212 — Great Britain. Hotel industries — *Statistics — Serials*
The **British** hotel industry. — [1980]-. — London : Jordan & Sons (Surveys) Ltd, 1980-. — v. ; 30cm
Issued every two years
ISSN 0263-368X = British hotel industry : £60.00 B82-19874

338.4'76479541'05 — Great Britain. Catering industries — *Serials*
[Catering *(London)*]. Catering. — Vol.1, no.1 (Feb. 1981)-. — London (161 Greenwich High Rd, SE10 8JA) : Dewberry Publication Services, 1981-. — v. : ill(some col.),ports (some col.) ; 30cm
Monthly. — Description based on: Vol.2, no.8 (Aug. 1982)
ISSN 0264-0562 = Catering (London) : £30.00 per year B82-40054

CMA year book / the Catering Managers' Association of Great Britain. — [19—]-. — Eastbourne : John Offord Publications, [19—]-. — v. : ill,ports ; 21cm
Annual. — Description based on: 1980 issue
ISSN 0143-7933 = CMA year book (corrected) : Unpriced B82-28134

338.4'76485 — Great Britain. Cleaning maintenance services — *Statistics — Serials*
Contract cleaners : an industry sector analysis. — 1st ed.-. — London : ICC Business Ratios, [1981]-. — v. ; 30cm. — (ICC business ratio report)
Annual
ISSN 0261-7765 = ICC business ratio report. Contract cleaners : £80.00 B82-04081

338.4'76591 — Advertising. Economic aspects
Chiplin, Brian. Economics of advertising. — 2nd ed. / Brian Chiplin and Brian Sturgess ; under the editorial direction of J.H. Dunning. — London : Holt, Rinehart and Winston with the Advertising Association, c1981. — xii,145p : ill ; 25cm
Previous ed.: / by Economists Advisory Group. 1967. — Includes bibliographies and index
ISBN 0-03-910315-3 : £12.50 : CIP rev.
B81-22694

338.4'76591 — Economic conditions. Effects of advertising
Albion, Mark S.. The advertising controversy : evidence on the economic effects of advertising / Mark S. Albion, Paul W. Farris. — Boston, Mass. : Auburn House ; London : Eurospan [distributor], c1981. — xxi,226p : ill ; 24cm
Bibliography: p201-217. — Includes index
ISBN 0-86569-057-x : £16.25 B82-23217

338.4'76592'094 — Europe. Public relations industries — *Serials*
Eurocomment : magazine of the Eurocom public relations and communications group. — New Year 1982-. — London (21 Buckingham St., WC2N 6EF) : The Eurocom Group, 1982-. — v. : ill,facsim,ports ; 29cm
Annual
ISSN 0263-6654 = Eurocomment : Unpriced
B82-28876

338.4'766 — Chemical industries — *Conference proceedings*
The **Chemical** industry / editors D.H. Sharp and T.F. West. — Chichester : Published for the Society of Chemical Industry, London by Ellis Horwood, 1982. — 643p : ill,1port ; 24cm
Conference papers. — Includes index
ISBN 0-85312-388-8 : £37.50 : CIP rev.
B81-35019

Opportunities and constraints : Eurochem 80 / organised by the Institution of Chemical Engineers in conjunction with the Eurochem 80 exhibition at the National Exhibition Centre, Birmingham, 24-26 June, 1980. — Rugby : Institution of Chemical Engineers, c1980. — 463p in various pagings : ill ; 22cm. — (EFCE event ; no.239) (EFCE publication series ; no.14)
Conference papers
ISBN 0-85295-123-x : £18.00 B82-38650

338.4'766'006042753 — Merseyside *(Metropolitan County).* **Liverpool. Chemical industries. Organisations: Society of Chemical Industry.** *Liverpool Section, 1881-1981*
Society of Chemical Industry. Centennial history of the Liverpool Section, Society of Chemical Industry 1881-1981 / by D.W. Broad. — London : The Society, 1981. — 144,lip : ill,1map,facsims,ports ; 25cm
Ill on lining papers. — Bibliography: pxl-xli. — Includes index
ISBN 0-901001-73-2 : Unpriced B82-24893

338.4'766'00941 — Great Britain. Chemical industries — *Serials*
[Manufacturing chemist *(London : 1981)*]. Manufacturing chemist : incorporating Chemical age. — Vol.52, no.9 (Sept. 1981)-. — London (30 Calderwood St., Woolwich, SE18 6QH) : Morgan-Grampian, 1981-. — v. : ill ; 29cm
Monthly. — Merger of: Manufacturing chemist and aerosol news ; and, Chemical age (London : 1974)
ISSN 0262-4230 = Manufacturing chemist (London. 1981) (corrected) : £25.00 per year
B82-03394

338.4'766'00941 — Great Britain. Chemical industries — *Statistics*
The **British** chemical industry. — London : Jordan & Sons (Surveys) Ltd, c1981. — xix,77p ; 30cm. — (A Jordan survey)
ISBN 0-85938-150-1 (pbk) : Unpriced
B82-05366

338.4'766'00952 — Japan. Chemical industries — *Statistics*
Chemfacts : Japan / Chemical Data Services. — Sutton : IPC Industrial Press, 1981. — vi,196p : maps ; 30cm
ISBN 0-617-00250-9 (pbk) : £70.00
B82-17707

338.4'7660297'0973 — United States. Electrochemical industries, *1880-1910*
Trescott, Martha Moore. The rise of the American electrochemicals industry, 1880-1910 : studies in the American technological environment / Martha Moore Trescott. — Westport, Conn. ; London : Greenwood Press, 1981. — xxxviii,391p : ill,ports ; 25cm. — (Contributions in economics and economic history ; no.38)
Bibliography: p365-379. — Includes index
ISBN 0-313-20766-6 : £33.75 B82-18188

338.4'76610382 — Sodium sulphate industries & trades — *Statistics*

Statistical supplement, 1981 to The economics of cobalt (third edition 1979). — London : Roskill Information Services, c1981. — 112p in various pagings ; 30cm
ISBN 0-86214-201-6 (pbk) : Unpriced
B82-20705

338.4'76611 — Silicon carbide, silicon nitride & sialon industries & trades

The **Economics** of silicon ceramics : silicon carbide, silicon nitride and the sialons. — London : Roskill Information Services, 1981. — vi,69,[18]p ; 30cm
ISBN 0-86214-197-4 (pbk) : Unpriced
B82-13775

338.4'766142 — Fluorite industries & trades — *Statistics*

Statistical supplement 1981 to The Economics of flourspar third edition 1979. — London : Roskill Information Services, c1981. — 73,A61p ; 30cm. — (Roskill reports on metals & minerals)
ISBN 0-86214-198-2 (pbk) : Unpriced
B82-13774

338.4'766142 — Iodine industries & trades

The **Economics** of iodine. — 3rd ed. — London : Roskill Information Services, 1982. — iv,61,A1-A15 ; 30cm
Previous ed.: 197-?
ISBN 0-86214-927-4 (pbk) : Unpriced
B82-24686

338.4'766143 — Bentonite industries & trades — *Statistics*

Statistical supplement 1982 to the Economics of bentonite, fuller's earth and allied clays, third edition 1979. — London : Roskill Information Services, 1982. — 49,A1-A24p ; 30cm. — (Roskill reports on metals & minerals)
ISBN 0-86214-202-4 (pbk) : Unpriced
B82-24681

338.4'766143 — Mica industries & trades

The **Economics** of mica. — 3rd ed. — London : Roskill Information Services, c1982. — 96,[142]p ; 30cm
Previous ed.: 1977
ISBN 0-86214-209-1 (pbk) : Unpriced
B82-31673

338.4'766143 — Perlite industries & trades

The **Economics** of perlite. — 3rd ed. — London : Roskill Information Services, 1981. — 101p ; 29cm
Previous ed.: 1977
ISBN 0-86214-925-8 (pbk) : Unpriced
B82-21613

338.4'766143 — Phosphate industries & trades

The **Economics** of phosphate rock. — London : Roskill Information Services, 1982. — v,145,[68]p ; 30cm
ISBN 0-86214-926-6 (pbk) : Unpriced
B82-22581

338.4'766143 — Vermiculite industries & trades

The **Economics** of vermiculite. — 3rd ed. — London : Roskill Information Services, 1982. — v,82p ; 30cm
Previous ed.: 1977
Unpriced (pbk)
B82-21612

338.4'7661804'05 — Petrochemicals industries — *Serials*

World petrochemicals. — No.1 (30 Apr. 1982)-. — London (10 Cannon St., EC4P 4BY) : Financial Times Business Information, 1982-. — v. ; 30cm
Fortnightly
ISSN 0263-9122 = World petrochemicals : Unpriced
B82-32372

338.4'76631'0941 — Great Britain. Alcoholic drinks industries & trades — *Statistics*

Alcoholic drinks 1980 : a Euromonitor leisure report / researched, compiled and published by Euromonitor Publications. — London : Euromonitor Publications, [1980?]. — 177leaves ; 30cm
Unpriced (pbk)
B82-20130

The **British** beers, wines and spirits industry / industry commentary by Robert Tiltscher. — London : Jordan & Sons (Surveys) Ltd, c1982. — lxv,[114]p ; 30cm
ISBN 0-85938-166-8 (pbk) : Unpriced
B82-39637

338.4'76632 — Wines industries

Great vineyards and winemakers / consultant editor Serena Sutcliffe ; [other contributors Robert Barton-Clegg ... [et al.]] ; [the photographers Jon Wyand ... [et al.]]. — London : Macdonald, 1982, c1981. — 256p : ill (some col.),col.maps,facsims(some col.),ports (some col.) ; 31cm. — (A QED book)
Originally published: New York : Routledge, 1981. — Includes index
ISBN 0-354-04699-3 : £13.95
B82-10025

338.4'76633'0942733 — Greater Manchester *(Metropolitan County).* **Manchester. Brewing industries,** *ca 1850-1940*

Gall, Alan. Manchester breweries of times gone by / Alan Gall. — Swinton : N. Richardson, 1982
2. — 20p : ill,facsims,maps,ports ; 29cm
Cover title. — Text on inside covers
ISBN 0-9506257-4-4 (pbk) : £1.00
B82-25559

338.4'76633'0942821 — South Yorkshire *(Metropolitan County).* **Sheffield. Brewing industries,** *1850-1950*

Parry, Dave. Bygone breweries of Sheffield : a summary of the brewing trade in the city 100 years ago / by Dave Parry, Don Parry and Alan Walker. — Manchester : Richardson, [1981?]. — 27p : ill,maps,facsims ; 30cm
ISBN 0-9506257-1-x (unbound) : £1.50
B82-19900

338.4'76635'00941 — Great Britain. Alcoholic drinks industries. Distilleries — *Statistics* — *Serials*

The **British** distilling industry. — [1980]-. — London : Jordan & Sons (Surveys) Ltd, 1980-. — v. ; 30cm
Issued every two years
ISSN 0263-3698 = British distilling industry : £75.00
B82-19871

338.4'766352'09411 — Scotland. Whisky industries & trades, *to 1980*

Cooper, Derek. The whisky roads of Scotland. — London : Jill Norman, Oct.1981. — [196]p
ISBN 0-906908-21-3 : £7.95 : CIP entry
B81-27459

338.4'766352'09411 — Scotland. Whisky industries, *to 1981*

Brander, Michael. Scotch whisky / Michael Brander ; drawings by Richard Hook. — Edinburgh : Spurbooks, c1982. — 64p : ill ; 19cm. — (Introducing Scotland)
Bibliography: p63. — Includes index
ISBN 0-7157-2078-3 (pbk) : £1.25
B82-20595

338.4'76636'0941 — Great Britain. Soft drinks industries — *Statistics*

Britain's soft drinks industry. — London : Jordan & Sons (Surveys), c1981. — xvi,70p ; 30cm. — (A Jordan survey)
ISBN 0-85938-154-4 (pbk) : Unpriced
B82-22260

The **Soft** drinks report. — London : Euromonitor Publications, 1981. — 67p ; 30cm
ISBN 0-903706-63-6 (pbk) : Unpriced
B82-11887

338.4'766401'0941 — Great Britain. Food ingredients industries — *Statistics*

Food ingredients : an industry sector analysis. — 2nd ed. — London : ICC Business Ratios, [1982?]. — [68]p ; 30cm. — (ICC business ratio report)
Previous ed.: 1979
ISBN 0-86261-080-x (pbk) : Unpriced
B82-15457

338.4'766402852'0941 — Great Britain. Chilled food industries & trades — *Serials*

Chilled foods. — Vol.1, no.1 (Mar. 1982)-. — Redhill (2 Queensway, Redhill, Surrey RH1 1QS) : Retail Journals, 1982-. — v. : ill,ports ; 30cm
Monthly
ISSN 0262-7566 = Chilled foods : £14.00 per year
B82-28128

338.4'766402853'094 — Western Europe. Frozen food industries — *Statistics*

A **Market** studies report on the frozen food. — London : Inter Company Comparisons, c1982. — 2v : ill ; 30cm
Unpriced (pbk)
ISBN 0-86191-917-3 (v.1) : Unpriced
B82-21479

338.4'76643 — Oilseeds crushing industries — *Conference proceedings*

International Association of Seed Crushers. *Amsterdam Congress (1979).* International Association of Seed Crushers : Amsterdam Congress, June 6th-8th, 1979 / J.E.Th.M. Randag, chairman. — London (8 Salisbury Sq., EC4P 4AN) : [The Association], [1980?]. — 128p : ill ; 30cm
Includes a contribution in French
Unpriced (pbk)
B82-35935

International Association of Seed Crushers. *Dakar Congress (1980).* International Association of Seed Crushers : Dakar Congress, April 15th-17th, 1980 / J.E.Th.M. Randag, Chairman. — London (8 Salisbury Sq, EC4P 4AN) : [The Association], [1980]. — 135p : ill ; 30cm
Includes contributions in French
Unpriced (pbk)
B82-41104

338.4'76646 — Great Britain. Convenience food industries & trades — *Statistics*

Goldman, Michael. The convenience foods report / [by Michael Goldman]. — London : Euromonitor Publications, 1981. — 121p : 2maps,1form ; 30cm
ISBN 0-903706-69-5 (pbk) : Unpriced
B82-11888

338.4'76646 — Snacks industries & trades — *Serials*

SMM : snackfood manufacture and marketing. — Vol.1, no.1 (Summer 1981)-. — London (22 Methuen Park, N10 2JS) : J.G. Kennedy & Co., 1981-. — v. : ill,ports ; 30cm
Quarterly
ISSN 0262-2580 = SMM. Snackfood manufacture and marketing : £10.00 per year
B82-11827

338.4'766476'0941 — Great Britain. Feedingstuffs industries — *Statistics*

British animal & pet food manufacturers / industry commentary by David Lang. — London : Jordan & Sons (Surveys) Ltd, c1982. — xxviii,71p : ill ; 30cm. — (A Jordan survey)
ISBN 0-85938-153-6 (pbk) : Unpriced
B82-16134

338.4'766492'09417 — Ireland *(Republic).* **Beef products industries & trades & beef products packaging industries**

Development study of the Irish beef packing and processing industries / a report prepared for the Industrial Development Authority by Coopers & Lybrand Associates. — Dublin : IDA Ireland, c1977. — 133p : ill ; 25cm
ISBN 0-902647-17-2 (pbk) : £3.60
B82-14651

338.4'766494'0941 — Great Britain. Fish processing industries — *Statistics* — *Serials*

Report on the census of production. Fish processing / Department of Industry, Business Statistics Office. — 1980-. — London, H.M.S.O., 1982-. — v. ; 30cm. — (Business monitor)
Annual. — Continues in part: Report on the census of production. Bacon curing, meat and fish products
ISSN 0263-659X = Report on the census of production. Fish processing : £3.25
B82-28872

338.4′766553′0976 — United States. Gulf coast. Petroleum refining industries, *to ca 1970*

Pratt, Joseph A.. The growth of a refining region / Joseph A. Pratt. — Greenwich, Conn. : Jai Press ; London : distributed by Jaicon Press, c1980. — xvi,297p : ill ; 24cm. — (Industrial development and the social fabric ; v.4)
Bibliography: p273-282. — Includes index
ISBN 0-89232-090-7 : £21.10 B82-02011

338.4′76657′0212 — Natural gas industries — *Statistics*

L′Industrie du gaz dans le monde : les informations technico-économiques de l'Institut français du pétrole = The gas industry in the world : technico-economic data from the Institut français du petrole / [réalisé par] = [compiled by] M. Valais, M. Hiegel. — 3e éd. — Paris : Technip, c1977 ; London : Distributed by Graham & Trotman. — iva,258ap : ill,maps ; 30cm
Text in French and English. — Previous ed.: 1975
ISBN 2-7108-0336-4 (pbk) : Unpriced
B82-00761

338.4′76657′0941 — Great Britain. Gas industries *— For schools — Serials*

North Thames education bulletin / North Thames Gas. — Issue no.1 (Sept. 1977)-. — Staines (North Thames House, London Rd., Staines, Middx TW18 4AE) : Public Relations Department, North Thames Gas, 1977-. — v. : ill ; 30cm
Three issues yearly. — Description based on: Issue no.11 (Sept. 1981)
ISSN 0262-8627 = North Thames education bulletin : Unpriced B82-10112

338.4′76657′0942527 — Nottinghamshire. Nottingham. Gas industries, *1818-1949*

Roberts, D. E.. The Nottingham gas undertaking 1818-1949 / prepared for Emgas by D.E. Roberts. — Leicester : East Midlands Gas, 1980. — 54p : ill,1map,ports ; 21cm. — (Studies in East Midlands gas history)
Bibliography: p53-54
ISBN 0-9506339-2-5 (pbk) : £0.75 B82-35954

338.4′76657′0942542 — Leicestershire. Leicester. Gas industries, *1821-1921*

Roberts, D. E.. The Leicester gas undertaking 1821-1921 / prepared for Emgas by D.E. Roberts. — Leicester (De Montfort St., Leicester) : East Midlands Gas, 1978. — 50p : ill,2facsims,2ports ; 21cm. — (Studies in East Midlands gas history)
Bibliography: p49-50
£0.60 (pbk) B82-35953

338.4′76661′05 — Flat glass industries — *Serials*

Flat glass international. — No.1 (Sept. 1981)-. — Epping (129 High St., Epping, Essex CM16 4AG) : Glass and Glass Technology Ltd., 1981-. — v. : ill,ports ; 30cm
Monthly
ISSN 0262-3315 = Flat glass international : £12.00 per year B82-02385

338.4′76661′0941 — Great Britain. Glass industries, *to 1981*

Dodsworth, Roger. Glass and glassmaking / Roger Dodsworth. — Princes Risborough : Shire, 1982. — 32p : ill ; 21cm. — (Shire album ; 83)
Bibliography: p32
ISBN 0-85263-585-0 (pbk) : £0.95 B82-31141

338.4′76661′09415 — Ireland. Glass industries, *1745-1835*

Warren, Phelps. Irish glass : Waterford, Cork, Belfast in the age of exuberance / Phelps Warren. — 2nd ed. — London : Faber and Faber, 1981. — 264p,[4]p of plates : ill(some col.) ; 26cm. — (Faber monographs on glass)
Previous ed. 1970. — Ill on lining papers. — Bibliography: p255-256. — Includes index
ISBN 0-571-18028-0 : £25.00 : CIP rev.
B81-21467

338.4′76661′094287 — Tyne and Wear *(Metropolitan County).* **Wearside. Glass industries,** *to 1978*

Glassmaking on Wearside. — [Newcastle upon Tyne] ([Sandyford House, Newcastle upon Tyne NE2 1ED]) : Tyne and Wear County Council, 1979. — 40p : ill(some col.) ; 21cm. — (The Glass industry of Tyne and Wear ; pt.1)
Cover title. — Text, ill on inside covers
Unpriced (pbk) B82-01037

338.4′76666′0937 — Ancient Rome. Provinces. Pottery industries

Peacock, D. P. S.. Pottery in the Roman world. — London : Longman, Sept.1982. — [256]p
ISBN 0-582-49127-4 : £19.00 : CIP entry
B82-20270

338.4′76666′0942971 — Mid Glamorgan. Ewenny region. Pottery industries, *to 1981*

Lewis, J. M.. The Ewenny potteries / by J.M. Lewis. — Cardiff : Amgueddfa Genedlaethol Cymru, 1982. — x,126p : ill(some col.),2geneal.tables,maps,2plans ; 25cm
Bibliography: p69. — Includes index
ISBN 0-7200-0250-8 (pbk) : £7.75 B82-30550

338.4′76667 — Refractories industries. Raw materials

Raw materials for the refractories industry / edited by B.M. Coope and E.M. Dickson. — London : Metal Bulletin, 1981. — 178p : ill ; 30cm. — (An Industrial Minerals consumer survey)
ISBN 0-900542-60-8 (pbk) : £14.50
B82-02496

338.4′7666737′0942651 — Cambridgeshire. Peterborough region. Fletton bricks industries, *to 1980*

Hillier, Richard. Clay that burns : a history of the fletton brick industry / Richard Hillier. — [London] : [London Brick Company], [1981]. — 100p : ill,col.maps,facsims,plans,ports ; 25cm
Bibliography: p97. — Includes index
ISBN 0-9507802-0-0 : £3.50 B82-11960

338.4′7666893′05 — Concrete industries & trades *— Serials*

Concrete works international. — Vol.1, no.1 (Jan. 1982)-. — London : Eyre & Spottiswoode, 1982-. — v. : ill ; 30cm
Monthly. — Continues: Precast concrete
ISSN 0262-4761 = Concrete works international : £15.00 per year B82-18489

338.4′766694′094 — European Community countries. Cement industries. Policies of governments

Bianchi, Patrizio. Public and private control in mass power industry : the cement industry cases / by Patrizio Bianchi. — The Hague ; London : Nijhoff, 1982. — xi,138p : ill,maps ; 25cm. — (Studies in industrial organisation ; v.3)
Includes index
ISBN 90-247-2603-4 : Unpriced B82-40146

338.4′7667 — Great Britain. Household chemicals industries & trades — *Statistics*

U.K. household chemical markets 1980. — London : Euromonitor Publications, 1980. — 70leaves ; 30cm
£45.00 (pbk) B82-21481

338.4′7667 — Great Britain. Household chemicals industries — *Statistics — Serials*

Report on the census of production. Specialised chemical products mainly for household and office use / Department of Industry, Business Statistics Office. — 1980-. — London : H.M.S.O., 1982-. — v. ; 30cm. — (Business monitor)
Annual
ISSN 0263-6573 = Report on the census of production. Specialised chemical products mainly for household and office use : £3.25
B82-28870

338.4′76684 — Plastics industries. Effects of demand for video software

Scott, P.. The video software market for plastics / P. Scott. — Shrewsbury (Shawbury, Shrewsbury, Shropshire, SY4 4NR) : RAPRA, [1981]. — 49p ; 30cm. — (Business report ; no.2)
Unpriced (pbk) B82-19756

338.4′76684′0941 — Great Britain. Plastics processing industries — *Statistics — Serials*

Report on the census of production. Processing of plastics / Department of Industry, Business Statistics Office. — 1980-. — London : H.M.S.O., 1982-. — v. ; 30cm. — (Business monitor)
Annual
ISSN 0263-6581 = Report on the census of production. Processing of plastics : £3.25
B82-28869

338.4′7668494′05 — Reinforced plastic industries — *Serials*

IRPI : international reinforced plastics industry. — Vol.1, no.1 (Sept. 1981)-. — Slough (48 Wellington St., Slough SL1 1UB) : Channel Publications, 1981-. — v. : ill,ports ; 30cm
Monthly
ISSN 0261-5487 = IRPI. International reinforced plastics industry : £12.00 per year
B82-06181

338.4′76685 — Great Britain. Cosmetics & toiletries industries & trades — *Statistics — Serials*

U.K. cosmetics & toiletries census. — 1981-. — London : Euromonitor, 1981-. — v. ; 30cm
Issued every two years
ISSN 0263-2055 = U.K. cosmetics & toiletries census : Unpriced B82-18496

338.4′766855 — Cosmetics industries & trades — *For children*

Mattock, Kate. Cosmetics / Kate Mattock. — London : Evans, 1982. — 48p : ill(some col.) ; 21cm. — (Talking shop)
ISBN 0-237-29255-6 (pbk) : Unpriced
B82-16623

338.4′766855 — Great Britain. Men′s toiletries industries & trades — *Statistics*

Mens toiletries and shaving markets 1978 / [compiled by Euromonitor Publications]. — [London] ([P.O. Box 115, Russell Sq., WC1B 5DL]) : Euromonitor Publications, [c1979]. — 43leaves ; 30cm
£55.00 (pbk)
Also classified at 338.4′76885 B82-18611

338.4′7669 — Nonferrous metals industries & trades

Robbins, Peter. Guide to non-ferrous metals and their markets. — 3rd ed. — London : Kogan Page, Feb.1982. — [215]p
Previous ed.: 1980
ISBN 0-85038-524-5 : £20.00 : CIP entry
B82-04694

338.4′7669 — Nonferrous metals industries & trades, *to 1980*

Müller-Ohlsen, Lotte. Non-ferrous metals : their role in industrial development / Lotte Müller-Ohlsen. — Cambridge : Woodhead-Faulkner in association with Metallgesellschaft AG, 1981. — xiii,297p : ill ; 24cm
Translation of: Die Weltmetallwirtschaft im industriellen Entwicklungsprozeß. — Bibliography: p291-297
ISBN 0-85941-190-7 : £15.00 B82-06382

338.4′7669 — South-east Asia. Nonferrous metals industries

Non-ferrous fabricating industries in South East Asia. — London : E.I.U., 1981. — 92p ; 30cm. — (EIU special report ; no.112)
Unpriced (pbk) B82-15213

338.4′7669′0212 — Metals industries — *Statistics*

Roskill′s metals databook. — 3rd ed. — London : Roskill Information Services, 1982. — 283p ; 30cm
Previous ed.: 1980. — Includes index
ISBN 0-86214-203-2 (pbk) : Unpriced
B82-17338

338.4'7669'042 — Great Britain. Scrap metal industries — *Statistics*
The **Scrap** metal processing industry. — London : Jordan Dataquest, c1978. — xxii,84p ; 30cm. — (Dataquest survey)
ISBN 0-85938-092-0 (pbk) : Unpriced
B82-20140

338.4'7'66910941 — Great Britain. Iron & steel industries, *to 1980*
Docherty, Charles. Steel and steelworkers. — London : Heinemann Educational, May 1982. — [224]p
ISBN 0-435-82196-2 : £14.50 : CIP entry
B82-06819

338.4'7669142 — Steel industries
Wilshire, B.. Technological and economic trends in the steel industries. — Swansea : Pineridge Press, Dec.1982. — [320]p
ISBN 0-906674-21-2 : £38.00 : CIP entry
B82-37493

338.4'766922 — Gold industries & trades. Economic aspects — *Conference proceedings*
World Conference on Gold. The gold problem. — Oxford : Oxford University Press, Oct.1982. — [250]p
ISBN 0-19-920130-7 : £20.00 : CIP entry
B82-36126

338.4'766922'0904 — Gold industries & trades, *ca 1850-1980*
Green, Timothy. The new world of gold : the inside story of the mines, the markets, the politics, the investors / Timothy Green. — London : Weidenfeld and Nicolson, 1982, c1981. — xxvi,260p : maps ; 23cm
Includes index
ISBN 0-297-78037-9 : £7.95 B82-17274

338.4'76692931 — Uranium industries — *Forecasts*
Uranium and plutonium, and the growth of nuclear power 1980 to 2030. — London : Roskill Information Services, c1981. — x,260,[98]p ; 30cm. — (Uranium 2)
ISBN 0-86214-192-3 (pbk) : Unpriced
B82-00109

338.4'76692931'05 — Uranium industries & trades. International political aspects — *Serials*
KIITG : keep it in the ground : international stop uranium mining news letter. — Nr.1 (1979)-. — Amsterdam ; Oxford (34 Cowley Rd, Oxford) : WISE, 1979-. — v. : ill ; 21cm
Ten issues yearly. — Description based on: Nr.21 (Apr. 1982)
Unpriced B82-28110

338.4'76693 — Copper industries & trades
Mezger, Dorothea. Copper in the world economy / by Dorothea Mezger ; translated by Pete Burgess. — London : Heinemann Educational, 1980. — 282p ; 21cm
Translation of: Das Beispiel Kupfer. — Bibliography: p255-273. — Includes index
ISBN 0-435-84480-6 : £9.50 : CIP rev.
B79-33999

338.4'76693'096894 — Zambia. Economic development. Role of copper industries & trades. Econometric models
Obidegwu, Chukwuma F.. Copper and Zambia : an econometric analysis / Chukwuma F. Obidegwu, Mudziviri Nziramasanga. — Lexington, Mass. : Lexington Books, c1981 ; [Aldershot] : Gower [distributor], 1982. — xvii,221p : ill ; 24cm. — (The Wharton econometric studies series)
Includes index
ISBN 0-669-04659-0 : £18.50 B82-21163

338.4'76694'0904 — Lead industries & trades, *1950-1978*
The **Changing** lead market. — London (2 Lindsey St., EC1A 9HN) : Rayner-Harwill, c1979. — iii,42p : ill ; 31cm
Cover title
Unpriced (spiral) B82-35813

338.4'766952 — Zinc industries & trades
Gupta, Satyadev. The world zinc industry / Satyadev Gupta. — Lexington : Lexington Books ; [Aldershot] : Gower [distributor], c1982. — xiii,203p : ill ; 24cm
Bibliography: p191-194. — Includes index
ISBN 0-669-04587-x : £18.50 B82-24411

338.4'76696 — Tin industries & trades
Robertson, W.. Tin : its production and marketing. — London : Croom Helm, July 1982. — [192]p. — (Croom Helm commodity series)
ISBN 0-7099-2202-7 : £14.95 : CIP entry
B82-16228

338.4'7669725 — Barytes industries & trades — *Statistics*
Statistical supplement 1982 to the Economics of barytes (3rd ed. 1979). — London : Roskill Information Services, c1982. — 51,A34p ; 30cm. — (Roskill reports on metals & minerals)
Previous ed.: published as statistical supplement to Barytes second edition 1976. 1977
ISBN 0-86214-211-3 (pbk) : Unpriced
B82-31672

338.4'7669725 — Calcium industries & trades
The **Economics** of calcium metal. — London : Roskill Information Services, 1982. — 63,A3p ; 30cm
ISBN 0-86214-207-5 (pbk) : Unpriced
B82-25106

338.4'7669725 — Lithium industries & trades — *Statistics*
Statistical supplement 1982 to The economics of lithium, 3rd ed., 1979. — London : Roskill Information Services, c1982. — 59,A26p ; 30cm. — (Roskill reports on metals & minerals)
ISBN 0-86214-210-5 (pbk) : Unpriced
B82-27575

338.4'766973'0212 — Ferro-alloys industries — *Statistics*
Pariser, Heinz H.. Ferro alloy statistics : production, imports, exports and consumption of ferro-alloys / Heinz H. Pariser. — Worcester Park : Metal Bulletin
Vol.1: Ferro-manganese, silicon-manganese, ferro-silicon, ferro-chromium. — c1981. — vii,425p ; 30cm
ISBN 3-9800635-0-x (pbk) : Unpriced
B82-31668

Pariser, Heinz H.. Ferro alloy statistics : production, imports, exports and consumption of ferro-alloys / Heinz H. Pariser. — Worcester Park : Metal Bulletin
Vol.2: Nickel, tungsten, cobalt, molybdenum. — c1981. — vi,343p ; 30cm
ISBN 3-9800635-1-8 (pbk) : Unpriced
B82-31669

Pariser, Heinz H.. Ferro alloy statistics : production, imports, exports and consumption of ferro-alloys / Heinz H. Pariser. — Worcester Park : Metal Bulletin
Vol.3: Silicon metal, ferro silicon chromium, ferro aluminium, ferro niobium, ferro titanium, ferro vanadium. — c1981. — 195p ; 30cm
ISBN 3-9800635-2-6 (pbk) : Unpriced
B82-31670

338.4'7669732 — Manganese industries & trades
The **Economics** of manganese. — 3rd ed. — London : Roskill Information Service, 1982. — vii,226,[168]p ; 30cm
Previous ed.: 1978
ISBN 0-86214-212-1 (pbk) : Unpriced
B82-35788

338.4'7669733 — Cobalt industries & trades — *Statistics*
Statistical supplement, 1982 to The economics of sodium sulphate (third edition 1979). — London (2, Clapham Rd., SW9 0JA) : Roskill Information Services, 1982. — 80p in various pagings ; 30cm
Unpriced (pbk) B82-20704

338.4'76697332 — Nickel industries & trades
Buchanan, D. L.. Nickel : a commodity review / D.L. Buchanan. — London : Institution of Mining and Metallurgy, c1982. — 28p : maps ; 30cm. — (Occasional papers of the Institution of Mining and Metallurgy, ISSN 0262-527x ; paper 1)
Unpriced (pbk) B82-34123

338.4'7669734 — Chromium industries & trades
The **Economics** of chromium. — 4th ed. — London : Roskill Information Services, c1982. — 359p,[210]p ; 30cm
Previous ed.: 1978
ISBN 0-86214-208-3 (pbk) : Unpriced
B82-31674

338.4'7669734 — Tungsten industries & trades
The **Economics** of tungsten. — 4th ed. — London : Roskill Information Services, 1981. — vii,327,[143]p : ill,maps ; 30cm
Previous ed.: 1977
ISBN 0-86214-200-8 (pbk) : Unpriced
B82-14892

338.4'766975 — Arsenic industries & trades — *Statistics*
The **Economics** of arsenic. — 4th ed. — London : Roskill Information Services, 1982. — 134p in various pagings : 1map ; 30cm
Previous ed.: 1977
ISBN 0-86214-205-9 (pbk) : Unpriced
B82-24687

338.4'767 — Great Britain. Giftware industries & trades — *Statistics* — *Serials*
The **Giftware** industry : an industry sector analysis. — 2nd ed.-. — London : ICC Business Ratios, [1981]-. — v. ; 30cm. — (ICC business ratio report)
Annual. — Continues: Giftware
ISSN 0261-8338 = ICC business ratio report. The giftware industry : £80.00 B82-04079

338.4'767'09 — Manufacturing industries. Geographical aspects — *For schools*
Horsfall, David. Manufacturing industry / David Horsfall. — Oxford : Blackwell, 1982. — 63p : ill,maps,facsims ; 30cm. — (Geography applied)
Bibliography: p63. — Includes index
ISBN 0-631-12693-7 (pbk) : Unpriced
ISBN 0-631-12651-1 (school ed.) : Unpriced
B82-24206

338.4'767'0941 — Great Britain. Manufacturing industries. Decline
Blackaby, F. T.. Deindustrialisation : presented 13th January, 1981 / by Frank Blackaby. — Manchester (c/o P.K. Berry, C.I.S. Building, Miller St., Manchester, M60 0AL) : Manchester Statistical Society, [1981?]. — 11p ; 20cm
Cover title. — Text on inside covers
£2.00 (pbk) B82-18056

338.4'767'09417 — Ireland *(Republic)*. **Manufacturing industries,** *to 1980*
O'Hagan, J. W.. The evolution of manufacturing industry in Ireland : a report commissioned by the Confederation of Irish Industry in June 1980 / John W. O'Hagan, Kyran P. McStay. — Dublin : Helicon : Educational Company of Ireland [distributor], 1981. — 63p ; 22cm
Bibliography: p51-53
Unpriced (pbk) B82-04355

338.4'76712'094131 — Scotland. Central Region. Foundry industries
The **Foundry** industry in Central Region : a short report on the current situation in the foundry industry generally, with a review of the future prospects of the industry within Central Region. — Stirling (Viewforth, Stirling FK8 2ET) : Planning Department, Central Regional Council, 1980. — [17]leaves ; 30cm
Unpriced (spiral) B82-15453

338.4'7671842'094 — Western Europe. Wire products industreis & trades — *Statistics*
A **Market** studies report on springs and wire : a study of the European wire products industry in Belgium, France, West Germany, Italy, The Netherlands, Sweden, Switzerland and the United Kingdom. — London (81 City Rd., EC1) : Inter Company Comparisons. — (Market studies)
Vol.2: Non-ferrous. — [1981]. — 77p : ill(some col.) ; 30cm
ISBN 0-86191-908-4 (pbk) : Unpriced
Also classified at 338.4'7621824'094
B82-07767

338.4′7671842′094 — Western Europe. Wire products industries & trades — *Statistics*

A **Market** studies report on springs and wire : a study of the wire products industry in Belgium, France, West Germany, Italy, The Netherlands, Sweden, Switzerland and the United Kingdom. — London (81 City Rd., EC1) : Inter Company Comparisons. — (Market studies)
Vol.1: Ferrous. — [1981]. — 82p : ill(some col.) ; 30cm
ISBN 0-86191-907-6 (pbk) : Unpriced
Also classified at 338.4′7621824′094
B82-07766

338.4′76752′0942542 — Leicestershire. Leicester. Leather working industries, *1200-1500.* **Archaeological investigation**

Allin, Clare E.. The medieval leather industry in Leicester / by Clare E. Allin. — [Leicester] : Leicestershire County Council, 1981. — 30p : ill,2maps,1facsim ; 30cm. — (Archaeological reports series / Leicestershire Museums, Art Galleries and Records Service ; no.3)
Bibliography: p1
ISBN 0-85022-100-5 (pbk) : Unpriced
B82-14656

338.4′7676′094 — Europe. Pulp & paper industries — *Conference proceedings*

European Pulp & Paper in the 80′s *(1982 : Helsinki)*. European pulp & paper in the 80′s : Helsinki : 17 & 18 March 1982 / [speakers papers] ; sponsors Financial Times, Helsingin Sanomat. — London (Minster House, Arthur St, EC4R 9AX) : Financial Times Conference Organisation, [1982]. — 125p : ill,maps ; 30cm
Unpriced (pbk) B82-28310

338.4′7676′0941 — Great Britain. Pulp, paper & boards industries — *Statistics* — *Serials*

Report on the census of production. Pulp, paper and board / Department of Industry, Business Statistics Office. — 1980-. — London : H.M.S.O., 1982-. — v. ; 30cm. — (Business monitor)
Annual. — Continues: Report on the census of production. Paper and board
ISSN 0263-6611 = Report on the census of production. Pulp, paper and board : £3.25
B82-28871

338.4′76762′0212 — Paper industries. Statistics. Information sources — *Lists*

Handbook of statistical sources / project team: J. Borstnik, C.J.E. Cross, M.R. Forsyth ; Pira Internal advisory group : B.W. Blunden ... [et al.] ; external advisory group : P. Brown ... [et al.]. — Leatherhead (Randalls Rd., Leatherhead, Surrey KT22 7RU) : Pira, 1978. — vii leaves,216p ; 30cm
Unpriced (spiral) B82-39663

338.4′7677′005 — Textile industries — *Serials*

Textile horizons : the international magazine of the Textile Institute. — Vol.1, no.1 (Sept. 1981)-. — Manchester (10 Blackfriars St., Manchester M3 5DR) : The Institute, 1981-. — v. : ill,ports ; 30cm
Monthly. — Continues: Textile Institute and industry
ISSN 0260-6518 = Textile horizons : Unpriced
B82-06165

338.4′7677′0091812 — Western world. Textile industries

Shepherd, Geoffrey, *1943-*. Textile-industry adjustment in developed countries / by Geoffrey Shepherd. — London : Trade Policy Research Centre, 1981. — x,58p ; 19cm. — (Thames essay, ISSN 0306-6991 ; no.30)
ISBN 0-900842-57-1 (pbk) : £2.00 B82-12515

338.4′7677′0094 — Europe. Textile industries, *1400-1600* — *Festschriften*

Cloth and clothing in medieval Europe. — London : Heinemann Educational, Feb.1982. — [448]p. — (Pasold studies in textile history ; 2)
ISBN 0-435-32382-2 : £15.00 : CIP entry
B81-35691

338.4′7677′00941 — Great Britain. Textile industries — *Statistics* — *Serials*

Report on the census of production. Miscellaneous textiles / Department of Industry, Business Statistics Office. — 1980-. — London : H.M.S.O., 1982-. — v. ; 30cm. — (Business monitor)
Annual. — Continues in part: Report on the census of production. Other textile industries
ISSN 0263-6603 = Report on the census of production. Miscellaneous textiles : £3.25
B82-28868

338.4′7677′00941 — Great Britain. Textile industries, *to 1980* — *For schools*

Hale, Don. Textiles. — London : Edward Arnold, Sept.1981. — [32]p. — (People and progress)
ISBN 0-7131-0587-9 (pbk) : £1.50 : CIP entry
B81-22516

338.4′7677′00942511 — England. South Pennines. Textile industries, *to 1980*

Murtagh, Maria. Fabric of the Pennines / [written and designed by Maria Murtagh]. — Hebden Bridge : Pennine Heritage Network, c1982. — 1folded sheet : ill(some col.),1map ; 59x21cm folded to 21x15cm
ISBN 0-907613-06-3 : Unpriced B82-37740

338.4′7677′00942648 — Suffolk. Lavenham. Textile industries, *to 1930*

Dymond, David. Lavenham : 700 years of textile making / David Dymond & Alec Betterton. — Woodbridge : Boydell, 1982. — vi,121p : ill,maps ; 24cm
Includes index
ISBN 0-85115-164-7 (pbk) : £8.95 : CIP rev.
B82-09209

338.4′7677′0094281 — West Yorkshire *(Metropolitan County).* **Textile industries & trades,** *1800-1830*

Freeman, M. J. (Michael John), *1950-*. A perspective on the geography of English internal trade during the Industrial Revolution : the trading economy of the textile district of Yorkshire West Riding circa 1800 / M.J. Freeman. — Oxford (Mansfield Rd., Oxford OX1 3TB) : School of Geography [University of Oxford], 1982. — 36p : ill,maps ; 22cm. — (Research paper / School of Geography, University of Oxford ; 29)
Text on inside cover
Unpriced (pbk) B82-29567

338.4′7677028242′09415 — Ireland. Hand loom weaving industries, *to 1979*

Sutton, E. F.. Weaving : the Irish inheritance / E.F. Sutton. — Dublin (4 Dublin Rd, Stillorgan, County Dublin) : Dalton, 1980. — 64p : ill(some col.),ports(some col.) ; 23cm
Unpriced (pbk) B82-37455

338.4′76771164′0941298 — Scotland. Fife Region. Dunfermline. Linen industries, *to 1933*

Dunfermline linen : an outline history. — [Dunfermline] ([Central Library, Abbot St., Dunfermline]) : Dunfermline District Libraries, 1977. — 7p ; 30cm
Cover title. — Bibliography: p7
Unpriced (pbk) B82-08890

338.4′767713′094127 — Scotland. Tayside Region. Dundee. Jute textile industries, *1960-1977*

Howe, W. Stewart. The Dundee textiles industry, 1960-1977. — Aberdeen : Aberdeen University Press, June 1982. — [192]p
ISBN 0-08-028454-x : £12.00 : CIP entry
B82-11999

338.4′767731′094 — European Community countries. Wool textile industries — *Inquiry reports*

An **Investigation** into the woollen and worsted sector of the textile & garment making industries in the United Kingdom, France, Germany and Italy / prepared by Werner International for the Department of Industry Chemicals and Textile Division. — London : Department of Industry, 1981. — 317p : ill ; 30cm
ISBN 0-85605-303-1 (pbk) : £60.00
B82-23800

338.4′767731′0941 — Great Britain. Wool textile industries, *1770-1914*

Jenkins, David. The British wool textile industry. — London : Heinemann, Apr.1982. — [384]p. — (Pasold studies in textile history ; 3)
ISBN 0-435-32469-1 : £17.50 : CIP entry
B82-04064

338.4′767731′0941 — Great Britain. Wool textile industries, *to 1981*

Aspin, Chris. The woollen industry / Chris Aspin. — Princes Risborough : Shire, 1982. — 32p : ill,1coat of arms,facsims,1map ; 21cm. — (Shire album ; 81)
ISBN 0-85263-598-2 (pbk) : £0.95 B82-39395

338.4′767731′094281 — West Yorkshire *(Metropolitan County).* **Wool textile industries,** *1972-1976*

Hardill, Irene. Components of employment change in the West Yorkshire woollen textile industry, 1972-1976 / by Irene Hardill. — [Newcastle upon Tyne] : University of Newcastle upon Tyne. Centre for Urban and Regional Development Studies, 1982. — 38p : ill,3maps ; 30cm. — (Discussion paper, ISSN 0140-6515 ; no.44)
Bibliography: p35-38
Unpriced (unbound) B82-27741

338.4′767731′0942819 — West Yorkshire *(Metropolitan County).* **Leeds. Wool textile industries,** *to 1980*

Nelson, Barbara. The woollen industry of Leeds / by Barbara Nelson ; illustrated by David Thornton. — Leeds : D. & J. Thornton, c1980. — 48p : ill,maps,ports ; 21cm. — (The Local library series)
Bibliography: p2
ISBN 0-907339-01-8 (pbk) : £1.00 B82-16530

338.4′767731′09429 — Wales. Wool industries & trades, *to 1981*

Williams-Davies, John. Welsh sheep and their wool / John Williams-Davies. — Llandysul : Gomer, 1981. — 74p : ill ; 22cm
Bibliography: p73-74
ISBN 0-85088-964-2 (pbk) : £1.25
Primary classification 636.3′2 B82-10705

338.4′76773164′0942 — England. Wool fabrics industries, *1200-1400*

Bridbury, A. R.. Medieval English clothmaking : an economic survey / A.R. Bridbury. — London : Heinemann Educational, 1982. — xiii,125p : 2ill,1map ; 23cm. — ([Pasold studies in textile history])
Includes index
ISBN 0-435-32138-2 : £9.50 : CIP rev.
B82-04063

338.4′767739′0951 — China. Silk industries, *1842-1937*

Li, Lillian M.. China′s silk trade : traditional industry in the modern world 1842-1937 / Lillian M. Li. — Cambridge, Mass. ; London : Council on East Asian Studies, Harvard University ; Cambridge, Mass. ; London : Distributed by Harvard University Press, 1981. — xv,288p : ill ; 24cm. — (Harvard East Asian monographs ; 97)
Bibliography: p249-269. — Includes index
ISBN 0-674-11962-2 : £10.50 B82-03875

338.4′7677391242′0942716 — Cheshire. Macclesfield. Silk weaving industries, *to 1980*

Macclesfield silk heritage / produced by the members of the Silk Heritage Project ; editor Mary Hampson. — Macclesfield ([c/o Macclesfield Borough Council, Services and Information Centre, P.O. Box 44, Town Hall, Macclesfield]) : The Project, 1980. — 24p : ill,1map,2ports ; 27cm
Unpriced (pbk) B82-22741

Macclesfield silk heritage / editor, Mary Hampson ; designer, Maria Murtagh ; produced by members of the Silk Heritage Project, Macclesfield 1980. — 2nd ed. — [Macclesfield] ([Macclesfield Sunday School, P.O. Box 67, Macclesfield, Cheshire, SK11 6US]) : [Friends of Macclesfield Silk Heritage], 1982. — 24p : ill,1map,1port ; 30cm
Previous ed.: Macclesfield : Macclesfield Borough Council, Services and Information Centre, 1980
Unpriced (pbk) B82-39639

338.4'767754 — Great Britain. Straw planting industries, *to 1930*
Davis, Jean, *1925-*. Straw plait / Jean Davis. — Princes Risborough : Shire, 1981. — 32p : ill,facsims,ports ; 21cm. — (Shire album ; 78)
Bibliography: p32
ISBN 0-85263-580-x (pbk) : £0.95 B82-31137

338.4'7677643'0941 — Great Britain. Carpet industries & trades — *Statistics*
Carpet manufacturers & wholesale distributors. — 10th ed. — London : Inter Company Comparisons, [c1980]. — 13p ; 21x30cm. — (ICC financial survey)
ISBN 0-86191-192-x (pbk) : Unpriced B82-24674

338.4'7677653'0942527 — Nottinghamshire. Nottingham. Lace industries, *to 1980*
Lowe, David, *1946-*. The city of lace / by David Lowe and Jack Richards. — [Nottingham] : Nottingham Lace Centre, c1982. — iv,90p : ill,ports ; 21cm
Text on inside covers
ISBN 0-9508126-0-9 (pbk) : Unpriced B82-32893

338.4'76782'094 — Europe. Rubber industries & trades — *Serials*
Rubber industry Europe : a confidential service of news, trends, analysis and interpretation. — Vol.1, no.1 (Apr. 1982)-. — Wallington (31 Alington Grove, Wallington, Surrey SM6 9NH) : Techline Industrial Data Services, 1982-. — v. ; 30cm
Monthly
ISSN 0263-8886 = Rubber industry Europe : £75.00 per year B82-33872

338.4'76797 — Tobacco industries & trades — *Forecasts*
Tucker, David. Tobacco : an international perspective. — London : Euromonitor, Oct.1982. — [224]p
ISBN 0-903706-86-5 : £35.00 : CIP entry B82-24614

338.4'76797'0973 — United States. Tobacco industries & trades
The **Tobacco** industry in transition : policies for the 1980s / edited by William R. Finger. — Lexington, Mass. : Lexington Books, c1981 ; [Aldershot] : Gower [distributor], 1982. — xii,339p : ill ; 24cm. — (A North Caroline Center for Public Policy Research book)
Includes index
ISBN 0-669-04552-7 : £17.50 B82-21166

338.4'768 — Hertfordshire. Hitchin. Rural industries & trades, *to 1981*
Hitchin als Landgemeinde = Hitchin, communauté rurale = Hitchin as a rural community. — [Hitchen] ([Museum & Art Gallery, Paynes Park, Hitchin]) : [North Hertfordshire Museums], [1978]. — 12p : ill,1maps ; 30cm
Text in German, French and English. — Cover title. — Text and map on inside covers
Unpriced (pbk) B82-11210

338.4'768'094 — Western Europe. Rural industries & trades, *1600-1850*
Kriedte, Peter. Industrialization before industrialization : rural industry in the genesis of capitalism / Peter Kriedte, Hans Medick, Jürgen Schlumbohm ; translated by Beate Schempp ; with contributions from Herbert Kisch and Franklin F. Mendels. — Cambridge : Cambridge University Press, 1981. — xi,335p : ill,1maps ; 24cm. — (Past and present publications) (Studies in modern capitalism)
Translation of: Industrialisierung vor der Industrialisierung. — Includes index
ISBN 0-521-23809-9 (cased) : £25.00 : CIP rev.
ISBN 0-521-28228-4 (pbk) : £7.95 B81-38816

338.4'7681418'094 — Western Europe. Photographic equipment industries — *Statistics*
A **Market** data report on photographic and cinematographic equipment : a study of this important industry in Belgium, France, West Germany, Italy, Japan, The Netherlands, Sweden, the United Kingdom and the USA. — London : Market Studies International, c1982. — 98p : ill(some col.) ; 30cm
Text in English and several other languages
ISBN 0-86191-926-2 (spiral) : £98.00
Also classified at 338.4'777853'028 B82-30038

338.4'7681418'0941 — Great Britain. Photographic equipment industries & trades — *Statistics — Serials*
The **Photography** report. — 1982 ed.-. — London : Euromonitor Publications, 1982-. — v. ; 30cm
Continues: Euromonitor report on UK photographic market
ISSN 0263-4872 = Photography report : Unpriced B82-28118

338.4'768175'094 — Western Europe. Scientific instruments industries — *Statistics*
A **Market** data report on scientifc instruments and equipment : a study of this important specialised technology industry sector in Belgium, Denmark, France, West Germany, Italy, The Netherlands, Sweden and the United Kingdom. — London : Market Studies International, c1982. — 101p : ill(some col.) ; 30cm
Text in English and several other languages
ISBN 0-86191-924-6 (pbk) : £150.00 B82-30037

338.4'7681761'094 — Western Europe. Medical equipment industries & trades — *Statistics*
A **Market** studies report on medical and dental equipment in Europe / Market Studies International. — London : Inter Company Comparisons, c1982. — 78p : ill(some col.) ; 30cm. — (Market studies ; 20)
English text, table headings in several languages
ISBN 0-86191-920-3 (pbk) : Unpriced B82-16181

338.4'76817631 — Western Europe. Harvesting & threshing machinery industries and trades — *Statistics*
A **Market** studies report on harvesting and threshing machinery in Europe : a study of the European agricultural industry in Austria, Belgium, France, West Germany, The Netherlands, Italy, Sweden and the United Kingdom. — London (81 City Rd., EC1) : Inter Company Comparisons, [1981]. — 99p : ill(some col.) ; 30cm. — (Market studies)
ISBN 0-86191-904-1 (pbk) : Unpriced B82-07764

338.4'76817631 — Western Europe. Soil preparation machinery industries & trades — *Statistics*
A **Market** studies report on soil preparation machinery in Europe : a study of the European agricultural machinery industry in Austria, Belgium, France, West Germany, The Netherlands, Italy, Sweden and the United Kingdom. — London (81 City Rd., EC1) : Inter Company Comparisons, [1981]. — 95p : ill(some col.) ; 30cm. — (Market studies)
ISBN 0-86191-903-3 (pbk) : Unpriced B82-07765

338.4'768408'0941 — Great Britain. Do-it-yourself industries & trades — *Statistics*
The **D.I.Y.** industry : an industry sector analysis. — 2nd ed.-. — London : ICC Business Ratios, [1981]-. — v. ; 30cm. — (ICC business ratio report)
Annual. — Continues: Home improvement & D.I.Y.
ISSN 0261-7811 = ICC business ratio report. The D.I.Y. industry : £80.00 B82-04080

338.4'768408'0941 — Great Britain. Do-it-yourself industries & trades — *Statistics — Serials — For marketing*
The **Do-it-yourself** report. — 1982 ed.-. — London : Euromonitor, 1982-. — v. : maps ; 30cm
Irregular. — Continues: D.I.Y. and home improvements
ISSN 0263-5437 = Do-it-yourself report : Unpriced B82-27657

338.4'7686'05 — Book industries & trades — *Serials*
Book world advertiser. — Vol.1 (1981)-. — London : Fudge & Co. Ltd, 1981-. — v. : ill,facsims,maps,ports ; 30cm
Fortnightly. — Description based on: Vol.1, no.12 (Mar. 25th 1982)
ISSN 0262-298X = Book world advertiser : £11.85 per year B82-32159

338.4'7686'0941 — Great Britain. Book industries & trades, *1700-1899 — Conference proceedings*
Development of the English book trade, 1700-1899 / edited by Robin Myers and Michael Harris. — Oxford : Oxford Polytechnic Press, 1981. — xii,172p : 1port ; 21cm. — (Publishing pathways series)
Conference papers. — Includes bibliographies
ISBN 0-902692-26-7 (pbk) : £5.50 B82-11559

338.4'7686'0942753 — Merseyside *(Metropolitan County)*. **Liverpool. Book industries & trades,** *to 1805 — Lists*
The **Book** trade in Liverpool to 1805 : a directory / compiled by members of the Liverpool Bibliographical Society ; edited by M.R. Perkin. — Liverpool : The Bibliographical Society, 1981. — x,35p ; 30cm. — (Occasional Publications ; 1)
Bibliography: piv-ix
ISBN 0-905000-05-6 (spiral) : £2.00 (£1.50 to members of the Liverpool Bibliographical Society) B82-35979

338.4'7686'0973 — United States. Book industries & trades, *to 1932*
Winterich, John T.. Early American books & printing / by John T. Winterich. — New York : Dover ; London : Constable, 1981. — vii,252p,[8]p of plates : ill,facsims ; 22cm
Originally published: Boston : Houghton, Mifflin, 1935. — Includes index
ISBN 0-486-24171-8 (pbk) : £3.40 B82-18193

338.4'76862 — Printing industries
Marshall, Alan. Changing the word : the printing industry in transition. — London : Comedia, Jan.1983. — [176]p
ISBN 0-906890-10-1 (cased) : £9.50 : CIP entry
ISBN 0-906890-11-x (pbk) : £3.50 B82-40300

338.4'7687'0941 — Great Britain. Clothing industries & trades — *Serials*
Apparel international : the journal of the Clothing and Footwear Institute. — Vol.1, no.1 (Jan. 1982)-. — Purley (51 Hillcrest Rd, Purley, Surrey CR2 2JF) : Piel-Caru Pub., 1982-. — v. : ill,ports ; 30cm
Monthly. — Continues: Clothing and footwear journal
ISSN 0263-1008 = Apparel international : £16.00 per year B82-15774

338.4'76885 — Great Britain. Men's shaving equipment industries & trades — *Statistics*
Mens toiletries and shaving markets 1978 / [compiled by Euromonitor Publications]. — [London] ([P.O. Box 115, Russell Sq., WC1B 5DL]) : Euromonitor Publications, [c1979]. — 43leaves ; 30cm
£55.00 (pbk)
Primary classification 338.4'766855 B82-18611

338.4'76887 — Great Britain. Coin slot recreational machinery industries & trades — *Manuals*
Amis, Martin. Invasion of the space invaders. — London : Hutchinson, June 1982. — [128]p
ISBN 0-09-147841-3 (pbk) : £4.95 : CIP entry B82-16475

338.4'76887'0941 — Great Britain. Toy industries & trades & games equipment industries & trades — *Statistics*
Toys and games 1980 : a Euromonitor leisure report. — London : Euromonitor Publications, [1980?]. — 76p ; 30cm
£45.00 (pbk) B82-20131

338.4'76887472'0941 — Great Britain. Billiards equipment industries & trades, *to 1980*
Billiards & snooker : a trade history / compiled by J.R. Mitchell. — [England] : British Sports and Allied Industries Federation, [198-]. — 97p : ill ; 24cm
ISBN 0-9507422-0-1 (pbk) : Unpriced B82-18040

338.4'768876'0941 — Great Britain. Sports equipment industries & trades — *Statistics*
Sports goods 1980. — London : Euromonitor Publications, [1980?]. — 45p ; 30cm
Cover title: Sports equipment
£45.00 (pbk) B82-20129

338.4'76888'0941 — Great Britain. Packaging industries — *Forecasts*
Mills, Rowena. Cost and availability of packaging in the UK to 1985 / by Rowena Mills. — Shortened and updated version. — London : Economist Intelligence Unit, 1981. — 112p : ill ; 30cm. — (EIU special report ; no.113)
Previous ed.: published as Packaging in the 1980s. 1979. — Text on inside covers
Unpriced (pbk) B82-12730

338.4'76888'0941 — Great Britain. Packaging industries — *Serials*
The **Packaging** report. — 1982-. — London (18 Doughty St., WC1N 2PN) : Euromonitor Publications, 1982-. — v. ; 30cm
ISSN 0263-6913 = Packaging report : Unpriced B82-30485

338.4'769 — Building industries
Rebuild. — Chichester : Wiley, Oct.1982. — [320]p. — (Properties of materials safety and environmental factors)
ISBN 0-471-10173-7 : £17.50 : CIP entry B82-23324

Stone, P. A.. Building economy. — 3rd ed. — Oxford : Pergamon, Aug.1982. — [250]p. — (Pergamon international library)
Previous ed.: 1976
ISBN 0-08-028677-1 (cased) : £22.50 : CIP entry
ISBN 0-08-028678-x (pbk) : £6.95 B82-15657

338.4'769'00941 — Great Britain. Building industries, *1815-1979*
Powell, C. G.. An economic history of the British building industry 1815-1979 / C.G. Powell. — London : Methuen, 1982, c1980. — ix,211p,[16]p of plates : ill,1plan ; 24cm
Originally published: London : Architectural Press, 1980. — Includes index
ISBN 0-416-32010-4 (pbk) : £4.95 : CIP rev. B81-34400

338.4'769'00941 — Great Britain. Direct labour organisations
Langford, D. A.. Direct labour organisations in the construction industry. — Aldershot : Gower, July 1982. — [148]p
ISBN 0-566-00542-5 : £12.50 : CIP entry B82-14237

338.4'769'00942 — England. Direct labour organisations. Implications of Local Government Planning and Land Act 1980
Elliott, D. A.. Direct labour organisations : implications of the Local Government Planning and Land Act 1980 / D.A. Elliott. — Ascot : Chartered Institute of Building, [1982]. — 22p ; 30cm. — (Occasional paper / Chartered Institute of Building ; no.26)
ISBN 0-906600-54-5 (pbk) : Unpriced : CIP rev. B82-06062

338.4'76901823'05 — Windows industries & trades — *Serials*
Window industries : incorporating Double glazing. — Jan. 1982-. — Watford (177 Hagden La., Watford WD1 8LW) : Comprint Ltd., 1982-. — v. : ill ; 30cm
Six issues yearly. — Continues: Double glazing
ISSN 0263-1784 = Window industries : £9.25 per year B82-18503

338.4'769083 — Great Britain. House building industries — *Statistics*
Housebuilders : an industry sector analysis. — 4th ed. — London : ICC Business Ratios, [1981]. — [58]p : ill ; 30cm. — (ICC business ratio report)
Previous ed.: [1980?]
ISBN 0-86261-175-x (pbk) : £80.00 B82-31146

338.4'7691 — Great Britain. Building materials supply industries & trades — *Serials*
Builders & timber merchants : the business journal for building supplies distribution. — Vol.63, no.785 (Mar. 8 1982)-. — Tonbridge : Benn Publications, 1982-. — v. : ill,ports ; 30cm
Fortnightly. — Continues: Builders & home improvement merchants journal. — Description based on: Vol.63, no.786 (Mar. 22, 1982)
ISSN 0262-6063 = Builders & timber merchant : £18.00 per year B82-26150

338.4'7693832 — Great Britain. Domestic thermal insulation industries & trades
The **Private** sector home insulation market / P.N. Chesters ... [et al.]. — Manchester : Manchester Business School, [1981?]. — 70p : ill ; 30cm. — (Research report, ISSN 0306-5227. Market position series / Centre for Business Research)
At head of title: Centre for Business Research
Unpriced (spiral) B82-14894

338.4'7693832 — Great Britain. Roof insulation industries & trades — *Serials*
Roofing, cladding & insulation. — Mar. 1980-. — Stanford-le-Hope (One Grover Walk, Corringham Town Centre, Stanford-le-Hope, Essex SS17 7LU) : Patey Doyle (Publishing) Ltd, 1980-. — v. : ill ; 31cm
Ten issues yearly. — Description based on: July/Aug. 1981
ISSN 0262-4575 = Roofing, cladding & insulation : £20.00 per year B82-04903

338.4'76961'06041 — Great Britain. Plumbing industries. Organisations: Institute of Plumbing — *Directories — Serials*
Institute of Plumbing. Business directory of registered plumbers : compiled from the Register of plumbers of the Institute of Plumbing. — 3rd ed.-. — Hornchurch (Scottish Mutual House, North St., Hornchurch, Essex RM11 1RU) : The Institute, [1980]-. — v. ; 21cm
Annual. — Continues: Institute of Plumbing. Business directory of plumbers
ISSN 0260-4612 = Business directory of registered plumbers : Unpriced B82-11139

338.4'7697'00094 — Western Europe. Air conditioning, heating & ventilation equipment industries & trades — *Statistics*
A **Market** studies report on heating and ventilation equipment in Europe : a study of the European industry in Belgium, Denmark, France, West Germany, Italy, The Netherlands, Spain and the United Kingdom. — London (81 City Rd., EC1) : Inter Company Comparisons, c1981. — 83p : ill ; 30cm. — (Market studies)
ISBN 0-86191-910-6 (pbk) : Unpriced B82-07769

338.4'773927'0941 — Great Britain. Jewellery industries & trades — *Statistics*
Jewellery / [compiled by Euromonitor Publications Ltd.]. — [London] : [Euromonitor], [1978?]. — 27leaves ; 29cm
£32.00 (pbk) B82-19342

338.4'7747 — Interior design services — *For clients*
Turner, William, *19---*. How to work with an interior designer / by William Turner. — New York : Whitney Library of Design ; London : Architectural Press, 1981. — 160p : ill,plans ; 26cm
Includes index
ISBN 0-85139-851-0 : £12.95 B82-17681

338.4'777853'028 — Western Europe. Cinematographic equipment industries — *Statistics*
A **Market** data report on photographic and cinematographic equipment : a study of this important industry in Belgium, France, West Germany, Italy, Japan, The Netherlands, Sweden, the United Kingdom and the USA. — London : Market Studies International, c1982. — 98p : ill(some col.) ; 30cm
Text in English and several other languages
ISBN 0-86191-926-2 (spiral) : £98.00
Primary classification 338.4'7681418'094 B82-30038

338.4'77785992 — Great Britain. Videorecording equipment industries — *Statistics*
Aspects of video : a report on the UK market for video recorders. — London (18 Doughty St., WC1N 2PN) : Euromonitor Publications, c1981. — 60,[18]leaves ; 30cm
Unpriced (spiral) B82-11890

338.4'778991 — London. Westminster *(London Borough)*. **Abbey Road. EMI recording studios,** *to 1981*
Southall, Brian. Abbey Road. — Cambridge : Patrick Stephens, Sept.1982. — [250]p
ISBN 0-85059-601-7 : £6.95 : CIP entry B82-20491

338.4'779'00941 — Great Britain. Leisure industries & trades — *Statistics*
The **U.K.** leisure market 1980. — London : Euromonitor Publications, [1980?]. — 133leaves ; 30cm
£85.00 (pbk) B82-20128

338.4'779202 — Great Britain. Theatrical accessories industries, *1883-1884 — Early works*
Victorian theatrical trades : articles from the Stage 1883-1884 / edited by Michael R. Booth. — London : Society for Theatre Research, [1981]. — ix,56p ; 18cm
ISBN 0-85430-032-5 (pbk) : £3.00 (£2.00 to members of the Society) B82-17408

338.4'7792029'541 — Great Britain. Theatre industries *Directories — Serials*
British theatre directory. — 1982. — Eastbourne : John Offord, July 1982. — [600]p
ISBN 0-903931-50-8 : £10.25 : CIP entry B82-17955

338.4'7792'06041 — Great Britain. Theatre. Management. Organisations: Theatrical Management Association — *Serials*
Theatrical Management Association. Yearbook and diary / Theatrical Management Association, incorporating the Council of Regional Theatre and the Association of Touring and Producing Managers. — 1982-. — London (Bedford Chambers, The Piazza, Covent Garden, WC2E 8HQ) : The Association, 1982 [i.e. 1981]-. — v. : ill,ports ; 30cm
Cover title: TMA year book & diary
ISSN 0262-737x = Yearbook and diary - Theatrical Management Association : £2.25 B82-13407

338.4'7796357'0973 — United States. Baseball. Economic aspects
Markham, Jesse W.. Baseball economics and public policy / Jesse W. Markham, Paul V. Teplitz. — Lexington, Mass. : Lexington Books, c1981 ; [Aldershot] : Gower [distributor], 1982. — xiv,179p : ill,2maps ; 24cm
Bibliography: p169-173. — Includes index
ISBN 0-669-03607-2 : £16.00 B82-14752

338.4'791 — British tourism — *Forecasts*
Forecasts of tourism by British residents 1980-1985 / prepared for the English Tourist Board by Pannell Kerr Forster Associates and the English Tourist Board Socio-Economic Research Unit. — London (4 Grosvenor Gardens SW1W 3DU) : Planning and Research Services Branch, English Tourist Board, 1981. — 10leaves ; 30cm
£2.00 (spiral) B82-21485

338.4'791 — Tourism
Prosser, Robert. Tourism / Robert Prosser. — Walton-on-Thames : Nelson for the Schools Council, 1982. — 48p : ill(some col.),maps (some col.) ; 28cm. — (Geography and change)
ISBN 0-17-434181-4 (pbk) : Unpriced B82-29549

338.4'791 — Tourism. Socioeconomic aspects
Mathieson, Alister. Tourism. — London : Longman, Oct.1982. — [224]p
ISBN 0-582-30061-4 (pbk) : £5.95 : CIP entry B82-24732

338.4'791 — Tourist industries. Planning. Geographical aspects
Pearce, Douglas G.. Tourist development / Douglas G. Pearce. — London : Longman, 1981. — 112p : ill,maps,plans ; 24cm. — (Topics in applied geography)
Bibliography: p104-110. — Includes index
ISBN 0-582-30053-3 (pbk) : £3.95 : CIP rev. B81-34325

338.4'791'0688 — Tourism. Marketing
Senior, Robert. The world travel market. — London : Euromonitor, Aug.1982. — [270]p
ISBN 0-903706-67-9 : £35.00 : CIP entry B82-18592

338.4'791091724 — Developing countries. Economic conditions. Effects of tourism

Archer, Brian. Tourism in the third world : some economic considerations / B.H. Archer. — [Guildford] ([Guildford, Surrey GU2 5XH]) : [University of Surrey], [1979?]. — 31p : ill ; 21cm. — (University of Surrey inaugural lecture)
Cover title
Unpriced (pbk) B82-26646

338.4'79141'007 — Great Britain. Tourism. Information services — *Serials*

British tourism yearbook. — 1982-. — Sutton (Quadrant House, Sutton, Surrey SU2 5AS) : IPC Consumer Industries Press in association with the Tourism Society, 1981-. — v. : ill,ports ; 28cm
Continues: Tourism Society. Handbook and members list
ISSN 0262-0308 = British tourism yearbook : £7.50 per year B82-12467

338.4'7914131 — Scotland. Central Region. Tourism. Planning — *Proposals*

Central Region. *Department of Planning.* Revised STARPS strategy for Central Region / prepared by the Planning Department, Central Regional Council, in consultation with Clackmannan, Falkirk and Stirling District Councils. — [Stirling] ([Viewforth, Stirling FK8 2ET]) : [Central Regional Council], [1981?]. — 35p ; 30cm
Unpriced (unbound)
Primary classification 711'.558'094131
B82-15462

338.4'791416'005 — Northern Ireland. Tourist industries — *Serials*

[Travel & leisure *(Belfast)*]. Travel & leisure. — Vol.1, no.1 (July 1981)-. — Belfast (101 University St., Belfast BT7 1HP) : Travel & Leisure, 1981-. — v. : ill,maps,ports ; 30cm
Monthly
ISSN 0262-3439 = Travel & leisure (Belfast) : £6.50 per year B82-04892

338.4'79142 — England. Tourist boards

Montague, Michael. The official tourist board structure in England : based on an address by Michael Montague to the members of the North West Tourist Board. — London : English Tourist Board, [1981]. — 3leaves ; 30cm
Unpriced (pbk) B82-05824

338.4'791421'00212 — London. Tourism — *Statistics* — *Serials*

[Research *(English Tourist Board)*. **London]**. Research / English Tourist Board. London. — 1977-. — London (4 Grosvenor Gardens, SW1W 0DU) : The Board, 1978-. — v. : maps ; 30cm
Annual. — Continues: Tourism regional fact sheets. London. — Description based on: 1980
ISSN 0262-6241 = Research - English Tourist Board. London : Unpriced B82-06801

338.4'791422 — Central Southern England. Tourism — *Statistics* — *Serials*

[Research *(English Tourist Board)*. **Southern]**. Research / English Tourist Board. Southern. — 1977-. — London (4 Grosvenor Gardens, SW1W 0DU) : The Board, 1978-. — v. : maps ; 30cm
Annual. — Continues: Tourism regional fact sheets. Southern. — Description based on: 1980
ISSN 0262-6314 = Research - English Tourist Board. Southern : Unpriced B82-06798

338.4'791422'00212 — South-east England. Tourism — *Statistics* — *Serials*

[Research *(English Tourist Board)*. **South East]**. Research / English Tourist Board. South East. — 1977-. — London (4 Grosvenor Gardens, SW1W 0DU) : The Board, 1978-. — v. : maps ; 30cm
Annual. — Continues: Tourism regional fact sheets. South East. — Description based on: 1980
ISSN 0262-6276 = Research - English Tourist Board. South East : Unpriced B82-06804

338.4'791423'00212 — South-west England. Tourism — *Statistics* — *Serials*

[Research *(English Tourist Board)*. **West Country]**. Research / English Tourist Board. West Country. — 1977-. — London (4 Grosvenor Gardens, SW1W 0DU) : The Board, 1978-. — v. : maps ; 30cm
Annual. — Continues: Tourism regional fact sheets. West Country. — Description based on: 1980
ISSN 0262-6292 = Research - English Tourist Board. West Country : Unpriced B82-06803

338.4'791424'00212 — England. West Midlands. Tourism — *Statistics* — *Serials*

[Research *(English Tourist Board)*. **Heart of England]**. Research / English Tourist Board. Heart of England. — 1977-. — London (4 Grosvenor Gardens, SW1W 0DU) : The Board, 1978-. — v. : maps ; 30cm
Annual. — Continues: Tourism regional fact sheets. Heart of England. — Description based on: 1980
ISSN 0262-6233 = Research - English Tourist Board. Heart of England : Unpriced
B82-06800

338.4'791425 — England. Southern East Midlands. Tourism — *Statistics* — *Serials*

[Research *(English Tourist Board)*. **Thames and Chilterns]**. Research / English Tourist Board. Thames and Chilterns. — 1977-. — London (4 Grosvenor Gardens, SW1W 0DU) : The Board, 1978-. — v. : maps ; 30cm
Annual. — Continues: Tourism regional fact sheets. Thames and Chilterns. — Description based on: 1980
ISSN 0262-6284 = Research - English Tourist Board. Thames and Chilterns : Unpriced
B82-06799

338.4'791425'00212 — England. East Midlands. Tourism — *Statistics* — *Serials*

[Research *(English Tourist Board)*. **East Midlands]**. Research / English Tourist Board. East Midlands. — 1977-. — London (4 Grosvenor Gardens, SW1W 0DU) : The Board, 1978-. — v. : maps ; 30cm
Annual. — Continues: Tourism regional fact sheets. East Midlands. — Description based on: 1980
ISSN 0262-6225 = Research - English Tourist Board. East Midlands : Unpriced B82-06806

338.4'791426'00212 — East Anglia. Tourism — *Statistics* — *Serials*

[Research *(English Tourist Board)*. **East Anglia]**. Research / English Tourist Board. East Anglia. — 1977-. — London (4 Grosvenor Gardens, SW1W 0DU) : The Board, 1978-. — v. : maps ; 30cm
Annual. — Continues: Tourism regional fact sheets. East Anglia. — Description based on: 1980
ISSN 0262-6217 = Research - English Tourist Board. East Anglia : Unpriced B82-06805

338.4'791427'00212 — North-west England. Tourism — *Statistics* — *Serials*

[Research *(English Tourist Board)*. **North West]**. Research / English Tourist Board. North West. — 1977-. — London (4 Grosvenor Gardens, SW1W 0DU) : The Board, 1978-. — v. : maps ; 30cm
Annual. — Continues: Tourism regional fact sheets. North West. — Description based on: 1980
ISSN 0262-625x = Research - English Tourist Board. North West : Unpriced B82-06808

338.4'7914278'00212 — Cumbria. Tourism — *Statistics* — *Serials*

[Research *(English Tourist Board)*. **Cumbria]**. Research / English Tourist Board. Cumbria. — 1977-. — London (4 Grosvenor Gardens, SW1W 0DU) : The Board, 1978-. — v. : maps ; 30cm
Annual. — Continues: Tourism regional fact sheets. Cumbria. — Description based on: 1980
ISSN 0262-6209 = Research - English Tourist Board. Cumbria : Unpriced B82-06802

338.4'791428'00212 — North-east England. Tourism — *Statistics* — *Serials*

[Research *(English Tourist Board)*. **Northumbria]**. Research / English Tourist Board. Northumbria. — 1977-. — London (4 Grosvenor Gardens, SW1W 0DU) : The Board, 1978-. — v. : maps ; 30cm
Annual. — Continues: Tourism regional fact sheets. Northumbria. — Description based on: 1980
ISSN 0262-6268 = Research - English Tourist Board. Northumbria : Unpriced B82-06807

338.4'7914281'00212 — Yorkshire. Tourism — *Statistics* — *Serials*

[Research *(English Tourist Board)*. **Yorkshire and Humberside]**. Research / English Tourist Board. Yorkshire and Humberside. — 1977-. — London (4 Grosvenor Gardens, SW1W 0DU) : The Board, 1978-. — v. : maps ; 30cm
Annual. — Continues: Tourism regional fact sheets. Yorkshire and Humberside. — Description based on: 1980
ISSN 0262-6306 = Research - English Tourist Board. Yorkshire and Humberside : Unpriced
B82-06809

338.4'7914585 — Malta. Tourism, *to 1980*
Oglethorpe, Miles. Maltese development issues / Miles Oglethorpe. — [Glasgow] : University of Glasgow, Department of Geography, 1982. — i,150p : ill,maps ; 30cm. — (Occasional papers / Geography Department Glasgow University ; no.8)
Unpriced (spiral)
Also classified at 628.1'0945'85 B82-27873

338.4'791729 — Caribbean countries. Tourist industries — *For Caribbean students*
Sealey, Neil E.. Tourism in the Caribbean. — London : Hodder and Stoughton, Dec.1982. — [64]p
ISBN 0-340-27881-1 (pbk) : £1.95 : CIP entry
B82-29641

338.5 — PRODUCTION ECONOMICS

338.5 — Economics. Markets. Effects of government policies
Leake, Andrew. Government and markets. — London : Macmillan Education, Feb.1982. — [48]p. — (Casebooks in economic theory)
ISBN 0-333-27990-5 (pbk) : £1.25 : CIP entry
B81-35950

338.5 — Governments. Microeconomic policies
Hartley, Keith. Micro-economic policy / Keith Hartley and Clem Tisdell. — Chichester : Wiley, c1981. — xiv,410p : ill ; 24cm
Includes bibliographies and index
ISBN 0-471-28026-7 (cased) : £18.50 : CIP rev.
ISBN 0-471-28027-5 (pbk) : Unpriced
B81-34645

338.5 — Microeconomics
Douglas, Evan J.. Intermediate microeconomic analysis : theory and applications / Evan J. Douglas. — Englewood Cliffs ; London : Prentice-Hall, c1982. — xviii,508p : ill ; 25cm
Includes bibliographies and index
ISBN 0-13-470708-7 : £16.45 B82-28157

Leftwich, Richard H.. The price system and resource allocation. — 8th ed. / Richard H. Leftwich, Ross D. Eckert. — Chicago ; London : Dryden, c1982. — 591p : ill ; 25cm
Previous ed.: 1979. — Includes bibliographies and index
ISBN 0-03-059367-0 (cased) : Unpriced
ISBN 4-8337-0085-9 (pbk) : Unpriced
B82-20602

List, Friedrich. The national system of political economy 1837. — London : Cass, Apr.1982. — [208]p
Translation of: Das nationale System der politischen Oekonomie
ISBN 0-7146-3206-6 : £15.00 : CIP entry
B82-04506

Microeconomics : selected readings / edited by Edwin Mansfield. — 3rd ed. — New York ; London : Norton, c1979. — xiv,677p : ill ; 24cm
Previous ed.: 1975
ISBN 0-393-95015-8 : £5.50 B82-13865

338.5 — Microeconomics *continuation*

Microeconomics : selected readings / edited by Edwin Mansfield. — 4th ed. — New York ; London : Norton, c1982. — xii,555p : ill ; 24cm
Previous ed.: 1979?
ISBN 0-393-95208-8 (pbk) : £8.75 B82-39347

Miller, Roger LeRoy. Economics today : the micro view / Roger LeRoy Miller. — 4th ed. — New York ; London : Harper & Row, c1982. — xv,487p : ill ; 28cm
Previous ed.: 1979. — Includes index
ISBN 0-06-044491-6 (pbk) : Unpriced B82-22535

Tisdell, C. A.. Microeconomics of markets / C.A. Tisdell. — Brisbane ; Chichester : Wiley, 1982. — xi,626p : col.ill ; 25cm
Includes bibliographies and index
ISBN 0-471-33383-2 (pbk) : £10.80 B82-37203

Wonnacott, Paul. [Economics. Selections]. An introduction to microeconomics / Paul Wonnacott, Ronald Wonnacott. — 2nd ed. — New York ; London : McGraw-Hill, c1982. — xxx,552p : ill(some col.),maps(some col.),ports ; 24cm
Previous ed.: 1979. — Includes index. — Includes chapters 1-6 and 19-37 of Economics. 2nd ed. 1982
ISBN 0-07-071583-1 (pbk) : Unpriced B82-27571

338.5 — Microeconomics — *Irish texts*

Heilbroner, Robert L.. [Understanding microeconomics. Irish]. An mhicraecnamaíocht / Robert L. Heilbroner, Lester C. Thurow ; Diarmaid Ó Cearbhaill a d'aistrigh. — [Baile Átha Cliath] : Oifig an tSoláthair, 1981. — 254p : ill ; 24cm
Includes index
Unpriced (pbk) B82-30874

338.5'024658 — Microeconomics — *For business management*

Blair, Roger. Microeconomics for managerial decision making / Roger D. Blair, Lawrence W. Kenny. — New York ; London : McGraw-Hill, c1982. — xiv,447p : ill ; 25cm
Includes bibliographies and index
ISBN 0-07-005800-8 : £16.75 B82-21466

338.5'077 — Microeconomics — *Programmed instructions*

Lumsden, Keith. Microeconomics : a programmed book / Keith Lumsden, Richard Attiyeh, George Leland Bach. — 4th ed. — Englewood Cliffs ; London : Prentice-Hall, c1982. — ix,262p : ill ; 23cm
Previous ed.: 1974
ISBN 0-13-581397-2 (pbk) : £8.20 B82-16843

338.5'1'01 — Costs. Theories

L.S.E. essays on cost / edited by J.M. Buchanan and G.F. Thirlby. — New York ; London : New York University Press, 1981, c1973. — 290p ; 24cm. — (The Institute for Humane Studies series in economic theory)
Originally published: London : Weidenfeld and Nicolson, 1973. — Includes index
ISBN 0-8147-1034-4 : £14.90
ISBN 0-8147-1035-2 (pbk) : £5.20 B82-35939

338.5'144 — Industries. Economies of scale — *Conference proceedings*

Scale in production systems / John A. Buzacott ... [et al.] editors. — Oxford : Pergamon, c1982. — x,249p : ill ; 26cm. — (IIASA proceedings series ; 15)
Conference papers. — Includes bibliographies
ISBN 0-08-028725-5 : £25.00 : CIP rev. B82-02439

338.5'2 — Commodities. Prices

Two studies of commodity price behaviour. — London : Economics Division, Bank of England, c1981. — 70p : ill ; 30cm. — (Discussion paper / Bank of England, ISSN 0142-6753 ; no.18)
Includes bibliographies. — Contents: Inter-relationships between commodity prices / by J.L. Hedges — Short-run pricing behaviour in commodity markets / by C.A. Enoch
ISBN 0-903312-43-3 (pbk) : Unpriced B82-13776

338.5'2 — Primary commodities. Prices. Stabilisation

Newbery, David M. G.. The theory of commodity price stabilization : a study in the economics of risk / David M.G. Newbery and Joseph E. Stiglitz. — Oxford : Clarendon, 1981. — xv,462p : ill ; 25cm
Bibliography: p446-451. — Includes index
ISBN 0-19-828417-9 (cased) : £19.95 : CIP rev.
ISBN 0-19-828438-1 (pbk) : Unpriced B81-16858

338.5'2 — Primary commodities. Prices. Stabilisation. Funds: Common Fund for Commodities

Laidlaw, Ken. Fund for the future : UNCTAD's common fund for commodities / Ken Laidlaw, Roy Laishley ; prepared by Development Press Services in collaboration with the UNCTAD Information Unit. — Plumpton Green : Development Press Services, 1980. — 48p : ill ; 21cm
ISBN 0-9507373-0-5 (pbk) : Unpriced B82-24656

338.5'2'01 — Prices. Theories

Friedman, Milton. Prices of money and goods across frontiers : the pound and the dollar over a century / by Milton Friedman. — London : Published for the Harry G. Johnson Memorial Fund by the Trade Policy Research Centre, 1980. — viii,15p : ill ; 22cm. — (Harry G. Johnson Memorial Lecture, ISSN 0262-2890 ; no.1)
ISBN 0-900842-58-x (pbk) : £1.00 B82-30186

338.5'2'0724 — Commodities. Prices. Forecasting. Mathematical models

Barnes, Robert M.. Commodity profits through trend trading : a price model and strategies / Robert M. Barnes. — New York ; Chichester : Wiley, c1982. — ix,276p : ill ; 25cm
Bibliography: p265-273. — Includes index
ISBN 0-471-08515-4 : £25.00 B82-26266

338.5'2'094 — Europe. Prices *related to* **remuneration of personnel**, *1400-1965*

Brown, Henry Phelps. A perspective of wages and prices / Henry Phelps Brown and Sheila V. Hopkins. — London : Methuen, 1981. — xvii,214p : ill ; 24cm
ISBN 0-416-31950-5 : £11.95 : CIP rev.
Primary classification 331.2'94 B81-27348

338.5'21 — Supply. Effects of economic policies. Econometric models — *Conference proceedings*

The **Supply-side** effects of economic policy / edited by Laurence H. Meyer. — Boston ; London : Kluwer, c1981. — xi,266p : ill ; 24cm. — (Economic policy conference series)
Conference proceedings. — Includes bibliographies
ISBN 0-89838-088-x : Unpriced B82-17289

338.5'22 — Free markets. Legal aspects

Courts and free markets. — Oxford : Clarendon Press
Vol.2. — Feb.1982. — [380]p
ISBN 0-19-825392-3 : £25.00 : CIP entry B81-38328

338.5'4 — Economic crises

Financial crises : theory, history and policy / edited by Charles P. Kindleberger and Jean-Pierre Laffargue. — Cambridge : Cambridge University Press, 1982. — ix,301p : ill ; 24cm
Includes bibliographies and index
ISBN 0-521-24380-7 : £22.50 B82-40076

338.5'42 — Trade cycles. Analysis — *Conference proceedings*

CIRET Conference *(15th : 1981 : Athens)*. Business cycle surveys. — Aldershot : Gower, July 1982. — [500]p
ISBN 0-566-00439-9 : £20.00 : CIP entry B82-12971

338.5'44 — Business firms. Economic forecasting

Bails, Dale G.. Business fluctuations : forecasting techniques and applications / Dale G. Bails, Larry C. Peppers. — Englewood Cliffs ; London : Prentice-Hall, c1982. — xiv,482p : ill ; 24cm
Includes bibliographies and index
ISBN 0-13-098400-0 : £18.70 B82-16718

Profit forecasts. — Aldershot : Gower, Aug.1982. — [250]p
ISBN 0-566-02207-9 : £17.50 : CIP entry B82-15883

338.5'44 — Business firms. Social forecasting

Social forecasting for company planning / edited by Brian C. Twiss. — London : Macmillan, 1982. — xxv,310p : ill ; 23cm
Includes index
ISBN 0-333-27076-2 : £25.00 B82-20909

338.5'44'025 — Economic forecasting. Organisations — *Directories*

World index of economic forecasts : industrial tendency surveys and development plans / edited by George Cyriax. — 2nd ed. — Aldershot : Gower, c1981. — xvi,378p : ill ; 31cm
Previous ed.: 1978. — Includes index
ISBN 0-566-02199-4 : Unpriced : CIP rev. B81-14882

338.5'44'0941 — Great Britain. Economic forecasting

Bruce-Gardyne, Jock. The future of economic forecasting / by Jock Bruce-Gardyne. — Stockport ([c/o P.K. Berry, C.I.S. Building, Miller St, Manchester M60 0AL]) : Manchester Statistical Society, [1981?]. — 9p ; 21cm
At head of title: Manchester Statistical Society. — Text on inside cover
£2.030 (pbk) B82-02711

338.5'442 — Business firms. Forecastings. Methods

Lewis, C. D.. Industrial and business forecasting methods : a practical guide to exponential smoothing and curve fitting / Colin D. Lewis. — London : Butterworth Scientific, 1982. — 143p : ill ; 23cm
Includes bibliographies and index
ISBN 0-408-00559-9 : Unpriced : CIP rev. B81-39222

338.5'442 — United States. Economic forecasting. Dynamic econometric models

Hunt, Lacy H.. Dynamics of forecasting financial cycles : theory, technique and implementation / by Lacy H. Hunt ; foreword by Robert A. Kavesh. — Greenwich, Conn. : Jai Press ; London : distributed by Jaicon Press, c1976. — xxiv,296p : ill ; 24cm. — (Contemporary studies in economic and financial analysis ; v.1)
Bibliography: p286-289. — Includes index
ISBN 0-89232-002-8 : £21.10 B82-02013

338.6 — ECONOMICS. ORGANISATION OF PRODUCTION

338.6 — Business firms. Management. Control by personnel. Economic aspects

Ireland, Norman J.. The economics of labour-managed enterprises. — London : Croom Helm, May 1982. — [232]p
ISBN 0-7099-1303-6 (cased) : £13.95 : CIP entry
ISBN 0-7089-1304-4 (pbk) : £7.95 B82-11278

338.6 — Chile. Industries. Management. Control by personnel. Economic aspects, *1970-1973* — *Socialist viewpoints*

Espinosa, Juan G.. Economic democracy : workers' participation in Chilean industry 1970-1973 / Juan G. Espinosa, Andrew S. Zimbalist. — Updated student ed. — New York ; London : Academic Press, c1981. — xix,211p : ill ; 23cm. — (Studies in social discontinuity)
Previous ed.: 1978. — Bibliography: p195-207. — Includes index
ISBN 0-12-242751-3 (pbk) : £6.40 B82-15536

338.6 — Great Britain. Industries. Management. Control by personnel. Economic aspects — *Socialist viewpoints*

Scargill, Arthur. The myth of workers' control / Arthur Scargill and Peggy Kahn. — [Leeds] : University of Leeds and University of Nottingham, c1980. — v,22p ; 21cm. — (Occasional papers in industrial relations)
£1.00 (pbk) B82-16034

338.6 — Great Britain. Management. Control by personnel

Bodington, Stephen. The cutting edge of socialism : working people against transnational capital / Stephen Bodington. — Nottingham : Spokesman, 1982. — 87p ; 22cm
ISBN 0-85124-332-0 (pbk) : £1.95 B82-14694

338.6 — Industries. Economic systems — *Comparative studies*

Buck, Trevor. Comparative industrial systems : industry under capitalism, central planning and self-management / Trevor Buck. — London : Macmillan, 1982. — xi,177p : ill ; 23cm
Bibliography: p159-169. — Includes index
ISBN 0-333-31113-2 (cased) : Unpriced
ISBN 0-333-31114-0 (pbk) : Unpriced
B82-20923

338.6′041 — Great Britain. Industries. Financial assistance by clearing banks

The **Banks** and industry : some recent developments : memorandum for the NEDC Committee on Finance for Industry by The Committee of London Clearing Bankers. — London (10 Lombard St., EC3V 9AR) : Banking Information Service, [1981]. — 21p ; 30cm
Cover title
Unpriced (pbk) B82-16280

338.6′041′0941 — Great Britain. Business firms. Finance

Davies, Brinley. Business finance and the City of London / by Brinley Davies. — 3rd ed. — London : Heinemann Educational, 1982. — 156p : ill ; 20cm. — (Studies in the British economy)
Previous ed.: 1979. — Bibliography: p147-150. — Includes index
ISBN 0-435-84349-4 (pbk) : £2.95 B82-40169

Ogley, Brian. Business finance / Brian Ogley. — London : Longman, 1981. — x,543p ; 22cm
Bibliography: p530-532. — Includes index
ISBN 0-582-29573-4 (pbk) : £7.95 : CIP rev.
B82-00212

338.6′041′0941 — Great Britain. Industries & trades. Finance, *1976-1979* **—** *Statistics*

Industrial performance analysis : a financial analysis of U.K. industry & commerce. — 6th ed. — London : Business Ratio Division of Inter Company Comparisons, c1981. — xix,135p : ill ; 30cm
Previous ed.: 1979
ISBN 0-86261-058-3 (pbk) : £20.00
B82-10989

338.6′041′0941 — Great Britain. Industries. Finance, *1918-1976*

Taylor, Michael, *1946-*. The geographical implications of the supply of funds for industry : an historical perspective / by Michael Taylor and Nigel Thrift. — [Newcastle upon Tyne] : University of Newcastle upon Tyne. Centre for Urban and Regional Development Studies, 1982. — 47p : ill ; 30cm. — (Discussion paper, ISSN 0140-6515 ; no.45)
Bibliography: p6
Unpriced (unbound) B82-27746

Thomas, W. A.. The finance of British industry, 1918-1976 / W.A. Thomas. — London : Metheun, 1982, c1978. — x,351p : ill ; 24cm
Originally published: 1978. — Bibliography: p339-344. — Includes index
ISBN 0-416-34300-7 (pbk) : Unpriced : CIP rev. B82-12336

338.6′042 — Business firms. Location. Socioeconomic aspects

Taylor, Michael, *1946-*. Organisation, location and political economy : towards a geography of business organisations / by Michael Taylor and Nigel Thrift. — [Newcastle upon Tyne] : University of Newcastle upon Tyne, Centre for Urban and Regional Development Studies, 1981. — 64p : ill ; 30cm. — (Discussion paper / University of Newcastle upon Tyne. Centre for Urban and Regional Development Studies, ISSN 0140-6515 ; no.38)
Bibliography: p54-64
Unpriced (pbk) B82-11668

338.6′042 — Great Britain. Offices. Relocation — *Practical information — Serials*

Business location handbook. — 2nd ed. (1982/83)-. — Northampton : Beacon Pub., [1982]-. — v. : ill,maps ; 25cm
Annual. — Continues: UK business relocation handbook
ISSN 0261-796X = Business location handbook : £15.00 B82-40072

The **U.K.** business relocation handbook. — 1981. — Weston Favell (Jubilee House, Billing Brook Rd, Weston Favell, Northampton NN3 4NW) : Parrish-Rogers International, 1981. — 1v. : ill,maps ; 25cm
Continued by: Business location handbook. — Only one issue published
£15.00 B82-05232

338.6′042 — Great Britain. Regional economic development. Role of advance factories

Slowe, Peter M.. The advance factory in regional development / Peter M. Slowe. — Aldershot : Gower, c1981. — xiii,271p : ill,1map,forms ; 23cm
Bibliography: p241-271
ISBN 0-566-00437-2 : Unpriced : CIP rev.
B81-23886

338.6′042 — Industries. Location

Norman, George. Economies of scale, transport costs, and location / George Norman. — Boston, Mass. ; London : Nijhoff, c1979. — xv,205p : ill,maps ; 24cm. — (Studies in applied regional science ; 16)
Bibliography: p190-194. — Includes index
ISBN 0-89838-017-0 : Unpriced B82-37772

338.6′042 — Scotland. Grampian Region. Banff and Buchan *(District)*. **Petrochemicals industries. Location. Planning —** *Proposals*

Contingency plan for petrochemical industries. — Aberdeen (Woodhill House, Ashgrove Road West, Aberdeen) : Grampian Regional Council, 1980. — 20p : ill,maps ; 30cm
Unpriced (spiral) B82-26737

338.6′042 — Scotland. Relocation of offices of government departments from England. Great Britain. *Parliament. House of Commons. Committee on Scottish Affairs.* **First report. Session 1980-81 —** *Critical studies*

Great Britain. Third special report from the Committee on Scottish Affairs, session 1980-81 : dispersal of Civil Service jobs to Scotland : the Government′s reply to the Committee′s first report of session 1980-81. — London : H.M.S.O., [1981]. — 11p ; 25cm. — ([HC] ; 347)
ISBN 0-10-234781-6 (pbk) : £1.40 B82-04934

338.6′042′01 — Industries. Location. Theories — *Conference proceedings*

Industrial location : alternative frameworks / edited by Doreen Massey, W.I. Morrison. — London : Centre for Environmental Studies, [1974?]. — 136p : ill,maps ; 30cm. — (Conference paper / Centre for Environmental Studies ; 15)
″Proceedings of a workshop held at CES in December 1974″. — Includes bibliographies
£2.00 (pbk) B82-08894

338.6′042′018 — Industries. Location. Analysis. Methodology

Marshall, J. N.. Social theory and industrial location / J.N. Marshall. — Birmingham : Department of Geography, University of Birmingham, 1980. — 15p : ill ; 30cm. — (Working paper series / University of Birmingham. Department of Geography ; no.9)
Bibliography: p11-15
ISBN 0-7044-0564-4 (pbk) : £0.40 B82-23553

338.6′042′0941 — Great Britain. Industries. Location. Geographical aspects

Taylor, Michael. Industrial organisation and location. — Cambridge : Cambridge University Press, Oct.1982. — [225]p. — (Cambridge geographical studies)
ISBN 0-521-24671-7 : £24.00 : CIP entry
B82-25504

338.6′042′0942837 — Humberside. Hull. Industries. Location

Hull industrial location and freight transport study : final summary report / prepared by the Economist Intelligence Unit Ltd. — [London] ([2 Marsham St., SW1P 3EB]) : Inner Cities Directorate (3), 1979. — 30p : 1map ; 30cm
£0.60 (pbk) B82-35921

338.6′042′0952 — Japan. Industries. Location

An **Industrial** geography of Japan / edited by Kiyoji Murata ; associate editor Isamu Ota. — London : Bell & Hyman, 1980. — 205p : ill,maps ; 23cm. — ([Advanced economic geographies])
Includes index
ISBN 0-7135-1625-9 : £11.50 : CIP rev.
B80-08133

338.6′042′098 — Andean Group countries. Industries. Location. Mathematical models

Wengel, Jan ter. Allocation of industry in the Andean Common Market / Jan ter Wengel. — Boston, Mass. ; London : Nijhoff, c1980. — xi,177p ; 24cm. — (Studies in development and planning ; 11)
Bibliography: p173-177
ISBN 0-89838-020-0 : Unpriced B82-04232

338.6′046 — Division of labour. Theories of Marx, Karl

Rattansi, Ali. Marx and the division of labour / Ali Rattansi. — London : Macmillan, 1982. — xv,251p ; 23cm. — (Contemporary social theory)
Bibliography: p225-234. — Includes index
ISBN 0-333-28555-7 (cased) : £15.00
ISBN 0-333-28556-5 (pbk) : Unpriced
B82-39151

338.6′048 — Business firms. Competition

Demsetz, Harold. Economic, legal, and political dimensions of competition / Harold Demsetz. — Amsterdam ; Oxford : North-Holland, 1982. — 125p ; 20cm. — (Professor Dr. F. De Vries lectures in economics ; v.4)
ISBN 0-444-86442-3 (pbk) : Unpriced
B82-38184

338.6′048 — Petroleum industries & trades. Competition. Mathematical models

Salant, Stephen W.. Imperfect competition in the world oil market : a computerized Nash-Cournot model / Stephen W. Salant. — Lexington : Lexington Books ; [Aldershot] : Gower [distributor], c1982. — xx,169p : ill ; 24cm
Bibliography: p163-166. — Includes index
ISBN 0-669-04344-3 : £18.50 B82-24412

338.6′048′0941 — Great Britain. Manufacturing industries. Competitiveness. Effects of change in working hours

The **Effects** of changes in working time on competitiveness / PA International Management Consultants ; ... financed by the Anglo-German Foundation for the Study of Industrial Society as part of its programme of study of social and economic policy issues. — London : [The foundation], c1981. — xviii,86p : ill ; 21cm
ISBN 0-905492-33-1 (pbk) : £8.00 B82-16335

338.6′048′0973 — United States. Industries. Competitiveness. Improvement — *Proposals*

Bolling, Richard. America′s competitive edge : how to get our country moving again / Richard Bolling, John Bowles. — New York ; London : McGraw-Hill, c1982. — xv,272p : ill ; 24cm
Includes index
ISBN 0-07-006438-5 : £10.50 B82-02284

338.6′1′095491 — Pakistan. Industrial development. Role of private enterprise, *1960-1970*

Amjad, Rashid. Private industrial investment in Pakistan, 1960-1970. — Cambridge : Cambridge University Press, Oct.1982. — [248] p. — (Cambridge South Asian studies ; 26)
ISBN 0-521-23261-9 : £25.00 : CIP entry
B82-29384

338.6'2'094 — European Community countries. Public enterprise

Osborn, Harold. Public enterprises in the UK and the EEC : now and in the future / Harold Osborn. — [London] ([Holloway, N7 8DB]) : Polytechnic of North London, 1979. — 71p in various pagings ; 30cm
Unpriced (spiral) B82-21433

338.6'2'094 — European Community countries. Public enterprises

Public enterprise in the European Economic Community : CEEP review 1981 / [prepared by the British Airports Authority on behalf of the British Section of CEEP]. — London : British Section of CEEP, 1981. — 358p ; 30cm
Unpriced (spiral) B82-01040

338.6'32 — London *(City)*. Freemen. Guilds: Guild of Freemen of the City of London, *to 1981*

Dyer, Colin F. W.. The Guild of Freemen of the City of London : a record of its formation and history / by Colin Dyer. — London : Guild of Freemen of the City of London, [1982?]. — ix,192p,[4]p of plates : ill(some col.),coats of arms(some col.),facsims(some col.),plans,ports ; 28cm
Includes index
Unpriced B82-24045

338.6'32 — London *(City)*. Transport services. Guilds: Worshipful Company of Carmen of London, *to 1980*

Bennett, Eric. The Worshipful Company of Carmen of London / Eric Bennett. — New ed. — Buckingham : Barracuda for the Company, 1982. — 244p : ill,facsims,ports ; 23cm
Previous ed.: Folkestone : Dawson, 1961. — Ill on lining papers. — Includes index
ISBN 0-86023-168-2 : Unpriced B82-39700

338.6'32'094212 — London *(City)*. Guilds

Doolittle, I. G.. The City of London and its livery companies. — Dorchester (36 Fore St., Evershot, Dorchester, Dorset DT2 0JW) : Gavin Press, Nov.1982. — [208]p
ISBN 0-905868-11-0 : £12.50 : CIP entry B82-31319

338.6'32'094212 — London *(City)*. Guilds, *to 1982*

Hope, Valerie. The freedom : the past and present of the livery, guilds and City of London / Valerie Hope, Clive Birch, Gilbert Torry assisted by Carolyn Birch ; foreword by Sir Christopher Leaver. — Buckingham : Barracuda, 1982. — 288p : ill,coats of arms,facsims,maps,music,plans,ports ; 27cm
Bibliography: p261-266. — Includes index
ISBN 0-86023-136-4 : £15.00 B82-39789

338.6'42 — Europe. Agricultural industries. Smallholdings — *Conference proceedings*

Small farming and the rural community : proceedings of a conference organised by the Smallfarmers' Association of the U.K. and held at the Department of Agriculture and Horticulture, University of Reading in March 1981 / edited by B.J. Marshall and R.B. Tranter. — Reading : Centre for Agricultural Strategy, University of Reading, 1982. — 48p ; 21cm. — (CAS paper, ISSN 0141-1330 ; 11)
Bibliography: p27
Unpriced (pbk) B82-29620

338.6'42 — Great Britain. Rural regions. Hotel & catering industries. Small firms — *Practical information*

Small business information pack. — 2nd ed., repr. in rev. format. — Wembley : Hotel and Catering Industry Training Board, 1982. — 42p : 1map ; 30cm
Previous ed.: 1980. — Bibliography: p23-29
ISBN 0-7033-0025-3 (spiral) : £1.00 B82-38439

338.6'42 — Great Britain. Services for small firms

Helping small firms start up and grow : common services and technological support : final report / Department of Industry, Shell UK Limited. — London : H.M.S.O., 1982. — 88p in various pagings ; 30cm
ISBN 0-11-513606-1 (pbk) : £5.40 B82-31236

338.6'42 — Great Britain. Small firms. Advisory services & information services

Collins, John, *19---*. A study paper on sources of advice and information for small businesses in the United Kingdom / presented at the conference organised by the United Kingdom Small Business Management Education Association on Wednesday 9th May 1979 held at the London Graduate School of Business Studies ; by John Collins and Alan Murtagh. — Bristol : Bristol Polytechnic, South West Regional Management Centre, 1979. — 48,[18]p : forms ; 30cm
Bibliography: p66
ISBN 0-904951-03-0 (unbound) : Unpriced B82-27483

338.6'42 — Great Britain. Small firms. Financial assistance by clearing banks

The **Banks** and small firms. — London (10 Lombard St., EC3V 9AR) : Banking Information Service, [1981]. — 13p ; 30cm
Cover title
Unpriced (pbk) B82-16281

338.6'42 — Small firms

Stimulating small firms. — Aldershot : Gower, Dec.1982. — [280]p
ISBN 0-566-00513-1 : £12.50 : CIP entry B82-30050

338.6'42 — Small firms. Entrepreneurship

Farrell, Peter. Buying a business. — London : Kogan Page, Feb.1983. — [160]p
ISBN 0-85038-634-9 (cased) : £7.95 : CIP entry
ISBN 0-85038-635-7 (pbk) : £3.95 B82-39281

Sweeney, G. P.. New entrepreneurship and the smaller firm / by G.P. Sweeney ; with a foreword by Albert Shapero. — Dublin : Institute for Industrial Research and Standards, c1981. — v,97p ; 21cm
Bibliography: p93-97
ISBN 0-900450-61-4 : £3.25 B82-24297

338'.6'42'06041 — Great Britain. Small firms. Organisations

Which voice? : a guide to organisations representing small firms. — [Leicester] : Leicestershire Small Firms Centre, [1982?]. — 39p ; 21cm
Cover title
£0.50 (pbk) B82-18895

338.6'42'06041 — Great Britain. Small firms. Owners. Counselling by Small Firms Service — *Inquiry reports*

The **Value** of the counselling activity of the Small Firms Service : report for the Department of Industry by Research Associates Ltd. — London : Department of Industry, 1981. — 40p : forms ; 30cm
£15.00 (pbk) B82-05432

338.6'42'0924 — Poultry production industries. Small scale production — *Personal observations*

MacDonald, Betty. The egg and I. — Bath : Chivers, Sept.1982. — [240]p. — (A New Portway book)
Originally published: London : Hammond, 1946
ISBN 0-86220-510-7 : £4.95 : CIP entry B82-19840

338.6'42'0941 — Great Britain. New small firms — *Case studies*

Birley, Sue. New enterprises. — London : Croom Helm, Aug.1982. — [192]p
ISBN 0-7099-0614-5 (cased) : £12.95 : CIP entry
ISBN 0-7099-0680-3 (pbk) : £6.95 B82-24341

338.6'42'0941 — Great Britain. Regional development. Role of new small firms

Storey, D. J.. Entrepreneurship and the new firm. — London : Croom Helm, Aug.1982. — [224]p
ISBN 0-7099-2347-3 : £15.95 : CIP entry B82-15909

338.6'42'0941 — Great Britain. Small firms — *Conference proceedings*

Bolton ten years on : perspectives on a decade of small business research. — Aldershot : Gower, Nov.1982. — [214]p
Conference papers
ISBN 0-566-00587-5 : £12.50 : CIP entry B82-26549

338.6'42'0941 — Great Britain. Small firms. Economic aspects

Smaller firms in the economy 1981 : a position and policy progress report. — [London] ([Centre Point, 103 New Oxford St, WC1A IDU]) : CBI, 1981. — 79p : ill ; 30cm
Unpriced (pbk) B82-04942

338.6'42'0942357 — Devon. Honiton. Small firms, *1961-1980*

Glyn-Jones, Anne. Small firms in a country town / by Anne Glyn-Jones. — Exeter : Devon County Council, c1982. — 79p : forms ; 21cm
ISBN 0-85989-138-0 (pbk) : £3.00 B82-24645

338.6'42'095412 — India *(Republic)*. Ranchi. Small scale industries. Development. Role of Birla Institute of Technology

Carr, Marilyn. Developing small-scale industries in India : an integrated approach : the experience of the Birla Institute of Technology's small industry scheme / by Marilyn Carr. — London : Intermediate Technology Publications, 1981. — 87p : ill,1map ; 26cm
Bibliography: p87
ISBN 0-903031-81-7 (pbk) : Unpriced B82-18289

338.6'44'0941 — Great Britain. Big business. Political aspects

Utton, M. A.. The political economy of big business. — Oxford : Martin Robertson, Feb.1982. — [220]p
ISBN 0-85520-409-5 : £12.50 : CIP entry B81-35704

338.6'44'0973 — United States. Big business. Regulation by government, *to ca 1980*

Regulations in perspective : historical essays / Thomas K. McCraw ; Morton Keller ... [et al.]. — Boston : Division of Research Graduate School of Business Administration Harvard University ; London : Harvard University Press [distributor], 1981. — ix,246p : ill ; 25cm
ISBN 0-87584-121-x : £10.50 B82-17778

338.7 — INDUSTRIAL ENTERPRISE. ORGANISATIONS AND THEIR STRUCTURE

338.7 — Business enterprise

The **Business** environment. — London : Edward Arnold, June 1982. — [384]p
ISBN 0-7131-0726-x (pbk) : £6.50 : CIP entry B82-12014

338.7 — Business firms

Beardshaw, John. The organisation in its environment / John Beardshaw, David Palfreman. — 2nd ed. — Plymouth : Macdonald and Evans, 1982. — xvi,655p : ill ; 22cm. — (The M & E BECBook series)
Previous ed.: 1979. — Includes index
ISBN 0-7121-1541-2 (pbk) : £7.25 B82-36224

338.7 — Society. Role of business firms

Burden, Tom. Business in society : consensus and conflict / Tom Burden, Reg Chapman, Richard Stead. — London : Butterworths, 1981. — xi,260p : ill ; 25cm
Includes index
ISBN 0-408-10693-x (cased) : Unpriced
ISBN 0-408-10694-8 (pbk) : Unpriced B82-00553

338.7 — United States. Business firms. Growth. Restriction

Baysinger, Barry D.. Barriers to corporate growth / Barry D. Baysinger, Roger E. Meiners, Carl P. Zeithaml. — Lexington, Mass. : Lexington Books ; [Aldershot] : Gower [distrbutor], c1981. — xi,132p : ill ; 24cm
Bibliography: p115-125. — Includes index
ISBN 0-669-04323-0 : £11.00 B82-04746

338.7 — United States. Family firms
Alcorn, Pat B.. Success and survival in the family-owned business / Pat B. Alcorn. — New York ; London : McGraw-Hill, c1982. — x,253p : ill ; 24cm
Includes index
ISBN 0-07-000961-9 : £12.95 B82-02285

338.7′01 — Business firms. Theories
Monthoux, Pierre Guillet de. Action and existence : anarchism for business administration. — Chichester : Wiley, Feb.1983. — [288]p
Translation from the Swedish
ISBN 0-471-10217-2 : £17.50 : CIP entry B82-38277

338.7′05 — Business enterprise — *Serials*
Accountants′ & administrators′ handbook. — 1982-. — London : Gee & Co., 1982-. — v. ; 21cm
Annual. — Continues: Handbook for accountants and administrators
ISSN 0263-0974 = Accountants′ & administrators′ handbook : £10.50 B82-15767

338.7′076 — Business enterprise — *Questions & answers — For Irish students*
Business organisation 1981 (Ordinary and Higher Level). — [Dublin] : Folens Solutions / John O′Connor. — [1981?]. — 156p ; 25cm
Cover title
£0.50 (pbk) B82-18015

338.7′09171′7 — Communist countries. Industries. Organisation structure. Politico-economic aspects
Holmes, Leslie. The policy process in communist states : politics and industrial administration / Leslie Holmes ; foreword by Roger E. Kanet. — Beverly Hills ; London : Sage, c1981. — 320p : ill ; 22cm. — (Sage library of social research ; v.127)
Bibliography: p291-309. — Includes index
ISBN 0-8039-1646-9 (cased) : Unpriced
ISBN 0-8039-1647-7 (pbk) : £6.50 B82-07900

338.7′0973 — United States. Business firms
Clarkson, Kenneth W.. Industrial organization : theory, evidence, and public policy / Kenneth W. Clarkson, Roger LeRoy Miller. — New York ; London : McGraw-Hill, c1982. — ix,518p : ill ; 25cm
Includes index
ISBN 0-07-042036-x : £16.75 B82-22766

338.7′4 — Great Britain. Private companies — *Statistics — Serials*
Britain′s top 2000 private companies. — 1980-. — London : Jordan & Sons, 1980-. — v. ; 30cm
Annual. — Continues: Britain′s top 1000 private companies
ISSN 0263-3671 = Britain′s top 2000 private companies : £18.00 B82-19873

338.7′4 — United States. Large companies. Control by government
Millstein, Ira M.. The limits of corporate power : existing constraints on the exercise of corporate discretion / Ira M. Millstein, Salem M. Katsh. — New York : Macmillan ; London : Collier Macmillan, c1981. — xx,265p : ill ; 25cm. — (Studies of the modern corporation)
Includes index
ISBN 0-02-921490-4 : £12.50 B82-00981

338.7′4′025174927 — Arab countries. Companies — *Directories — Serials*
Major companies of the Arab world. — 1982. — London : Graham & Trotman, Nov.1981. — [800]p
ISBN 0-86010-330-7 (cased) : £67.00 : CIP entry
ISBN 0-86010-329-3 (pbk) : £60.00 B81-33631

338.7′4′0254 — Europe. Companies — *Directories — Serials*
Major companies of Europe. Vol.1, companies in the European Economic Community. — 1982. — London : Graham and Trotman, Jan.1982. — [700]p
ISBN 0-86010-320-x (cased) : £67.00 : CIP entry
ISBN 0-86010-319-6 (pbk) : £60.00 B82-04711

Major companies of Europe. Vol.2, companies in Western Europe outside the European Economic Community. — 1982. — London : Graham and Trotman, Jan.1982. — [200]p
ISBN 0-86010-322-6 (cased) : £32.00 : CIP entry
ISBN 0-86010-321-8 (pbk) : £25.00 B82-04712

338.7′4′02541 — Great Britain. Companies — *Directories — For careers*
The **Good** job guide : the Daily telegraph guide to employment opportunities and key employers. — 6th ed. — London : New Opportunity Press, Dec.1981. — 1v.
Previous ed.: 1980
ISBN 0-86263-011-8 (cased) : £8.95 : CIP entry
ISBN 0-86263-010-x (pbk) : £3.95 B82-00173

338.7′4′025669 — Nigeria. Companies — *Directories — Serials*
Major companies of Nigeria. — 1982. — London : Graham & Trotman, Sept.1981. — [284]p
ISBN 0-86010-304-8 (cased) : £42.00 : CIP entry
ISBN 0-86010-305-6 (pbk) : £35.00 B81-28144

338.7′4′02572 — Mexico. Companies — *Directories — Serials*
Major companies of Argentina, Brazil, Mexico & Venezuela. — 1982. — London : Graham & Trotman, Oct.1981. — [470]p
ISBN 0-86010-328-5 (cased) : £67.00 : CIP entry
ISBN 0-86010-327-7 (pbk) : £60.00
Primary classification 338.7′4′02582 B81-31184

338.7′4′02581 — Brazil. Companies — *Directories — Serials*
Major companies of Argentina, Brazil, Mexico & Venezuela. — 1982. — London : Graham & Trotman, Oct.1981. — [470]p
ISBN 0-86010-328-5 (cased) : £67.00 : CIP entry
ISBN 0-86010-327-7 (pbk) : £60.00
Primary classification 338.7′4′02582 B81-31184

338.7′4′02582 — Argentina. Companies — *Directories — Serials*
Major companies of Argentina, Brazil, Mexico & Venezuela. — 1982. — London : Graham & Trotman, Oct.1981. — [470]p
ISBN 0-86010-328-5 (cased) : £67.00 : CIP entry
ISBN 0-86010-327-7 (pbk) : £60.00
Also classified at 338.7′4′02581 ; 338.7′4′02572 ; 338.7′4′02587 B81-31184

338.7′4′02587 — Venezuela. Companies — *Directories — Serials*
Major companies of Argentina, Brazil, Mexico & Venezuela. — 1982. — London : Graham & Trotman, Oct.1981. — [470]p
ISBN 0-86010-328-5 (cased) : £67.00 : CIP entry
ISBN 0-86010-327-7 (pbk) : £60.00
Primary classification 338.7′4′02582 B81-31184

338.7′4′094 — European Community countries. Limited companies
Limited liability and the corporation / edited by Tony Orhnial. — London : Croom Helm, 1982. — 223p : ill ; 23cm
Includes bibliographies
ISBN 0-7099-0515-7 : £12.95 : CIP rev. B82-05403

338.7′4′0941 — Great Britain. Companies. Trading operations — *Inquiry reports*
Blofeld, John, *1932-*. Fourth City and Commercial Investment Trust Limited (section 164), Excelads Limited (section 164), Systematic Tooling Limited (section 165(b)), Cambramain Limited (section 165(b)) : investigations under section 164 and 165(b) of the Companies Act 1948 : report / by John Blofeld, and Brian Currie. — London : H.M.S.O., 1981. — 330,[204]p : ill,facsims ; 30cm
At head of title: Department of Trade
ISBN 0-11-513493-x (pbk) : £22.00 B82-17857

338.7′4′09411 — Scotland. Community firms — *Serials*
[CBS newsletter *(Glasgow)*]. CBS newsletter. — Issue no.1 (Sept. 1981)-. — [Glasgow] ([4th Floor, 266 Clyde St., Glasgow G1 4JH]) : Community Business Scotland, 1981-. — v. ; 30cm
ISSN 0262-7159 = CBS newsletter (Glasgow) : Unpriced B82-09691

338.7′4′09595 — Malaysia. Large companies. Ownership
Lim, Mah Hui. Ownership and control of the one hundred largest corporations in Malaysia / Lim Mah Hui. — Kuala Lumpur ; Oxford : Oxford University Press, 1981. — xiii,190p : ill ; 26cm. — (East Asian social science monographs)
Bibliography: p173-180. — Includes index
ISBN 0-19-580458-9 (cased) : £18.50
ISBN 0-19-580454-6 (pbk) : Unpriced B82-11568

338.7′6′0941441 — Scotland. Strathclyde Region. Paisley. Local authority housing estate: Ferguslie Park. Community firms: Flagstone Enterprises
Flagstone Enterprises Limited : the setting up of a community business in a housing estate in the West of Scotland. — Paisley (High St., Paisley, PA1 2BE) : Paisley College of Technology, Local Government Unit, 1982. — iv,51p ; 30cm. — (Working paper / Paisley College of Technology. Local Government Unit ; no.12)
£1.50 (spiral) B82-38934

338.7′6100164′02541 — Great Britain. Computer services industries — *Directories*
Computing market-place : a directory of computing services and software supplies for word processors, micros, minis and mainframes / edited by BIS-Pedder Associates Limited. — Aldershot : Gower with Computing Services Association, c1981. — vii,501p : ill,1port ; 30cm
Includes index
ISBN 0-566-03401-8 (pbk) : Unpriced : CIP rev. B81-37541

338.7′6100164′0941 — Great Britain. Computer industries: International Computer Ltd. Financial assistance by government — *Inquiry reports*
Great Britain. *Parliament. House of Commons. Committee of Public Accounts.* First report from the Committee of Public Accounts : together with the proceedings of the committee and minutes of evidence : session 1981-82 : government financial assistance for International Computers Ltd. — London : H.M.S.O., [1981]. — xi,29p ; 25cm. — ([HC] ; 17)
ISBN 0-10-201782-4 (pbk) : £4.25 B82-16055

338.7′610705′025 — Publishing industries — *Directories*
Publishers′ international directory. — 8th ed. / edited by Michael Zils. — London : Library Association, 1979. — xiii,798p ; 31cm. — (Handbook of international documentation and information ; v.7)
English text, English and German preface and suggestions for use. — Previous ed.: 1977
ISBN 0-85365-991-5 : £50.00 (£40.00 to members of the L.A.) : CIP rev. B79-27108

338.7′610705′025171241 — Commonwealth countries. Publishing industries — *Directories — Serials*
Cassell and Publishers Association directory of publishing. — 1982. — London : Cassell, Oct.1982. — [400]p
ISBN 0-304-30913-3 (pbk) : £14.95 : CIP entry B82-23113

338.7′610705′02573 — United States. Publishing industries & trades — *Directories*
Sheppard, R.. American publishers and their addresses. — Beckenham : Trigon Press, Aug.1982. — [64]p
ISBN 0-904929-10-8 (pbk) : £3.50 : CIP entry B82-26711

338.7′61′07050942 — Great Britain. Publishing industries: Nonesuch Press, *to 1980*
Dreyfus, John. A history of the Nonesuch Press. — London : Nonesuch Press, Nov.1981. — [320]p
ISBN 0-370-30397-0 : £95.00 : CIP entry B81-30515

338.7′610705′0973 — United States. Book publishing industries: John Wiley & Sons, *to 1982*

Moore, John Hammond. Wiley : one hundred and seventy five years of publishing / writer John Hammond Moore ; editor A. Wayne Anderson. — New York ; Chichester : Wiley, c1982. — 279p : ill,facsims,2maps,ports ; 24cm
Text on inside covers. — Bibliography: p266-267. — Includes index
ISBN 0-471-86082-4 : Unpriced B82-39649

338.7′610705′097471 — United States. Publishing industries: Appleton-Century-Crofts, Inc., *to 1980*

Wolfe, Gerard R.. The house of Appleton : the history of a publishing house and its relationship to the cultural, social, and political events that helped shape the destiny of New York city / by Gerard R. Wolfe. — Metuchen, N.J. ; London : Scarecrow, 1981. — xviii,450p : ill,1map,facsims,ports ; 25cm
Bibliography: p418-427. — Includes index
ISBN 0-8108-1432-3 : £14.00 B82-03954

338.7′610705794′0942 — England. Music printing & publishing industries: Novello & Company, *to 1980*

Hurd, Michael. Vincent Novello : — and company / Michael Hurd. — London : Granada, 1981. — 163p,[8]p of plates : ill,facsims,ports ; 24cm
Bibliography: p152. — Includes index
ISBN 0-246-11733-8 : £9.95 B82-09826

338.7′61071 — United States. Newspaper publishing industries. Owners, *ca 1830-1981*

Brendon, Piers. The life and death of the press barons. — London : Secker & Warburg, Oct.1982. — [279]p
ISBN 0-436-06811-7 : £12.50 : CIP entry
Primary classification 338.7′61072 B82-25518

338.7′61072 — Great Britain. Newspaper publishing industries. Owners, *ca 1830-1981*

Brendon, Piers. The life and death of the press barons. — London : Secker & Warburg, Oct.1982. — [279]p
ISBN 0-436-06811-7 : £12.50 : CIP entry
Also classified at 338.7′61071 B82-25518

338.7′6136344′0924 — Prostitution. Madams: Payne, Cynthia — *Biographies*

Bailey, Paul. An English madam. — London : Cape, Nov.1982. — [176]p
ISBN 0-224-02037-4 : £7.50 : CIP entry
B82-26218

338.7′61367′0924 — Clubs. Management. Lownes, Victor — *Biographies*

Lownes, Victor. Playboy extraordinary. — London : Granada, Sept.1982. — [224]p
ISBN 0-246-11793-1 : £7.95 : CIP entry
B82-25154

338.7′616151″025 — Pharmaceutical industries — *Directories*

World directory of pharmaceutical manufacturers. — 2nd ed. — London : IMSWORLD, 1978. — 299p ; 30cm
Previous ed.: 197-?
ISBN 0-906184-00-2 (pbk) : Unpriced
B82-39335

338.7′6164794′028 — Great Britain. Hotel equipment industries & trades — *Directories — Serials*

Caterer & hotelkeeper directory & buyers guide. — 3rd ed. (1982)-. — Sutton (Quadrant House, The Quadrant, Sutton, Surrey SM2 5AS) : IPC Consumer Industries Press, [1981]-. — v. ; 30cm
Issued every two years. — Continues: Caterer & hotelkeeper buyers′ guide
ISSN 0262-9801 = Caterer & hotelkeeper directory & buyers guide : £6.50
Also classified at 338.7′6164795′028
B82-13418

338.7′6164795′028 — Great Britain. Catering equipment industries & trades — *Directories — Serials*

Caterer & hotelkeeper directory & buyers guide. — 3rd ed. (1982)-. — Sutton (Quadrant House, The Quadrant, Sutton, Surrey SM2 5AS) : IPC Consumer Industries Press, [1981]-. — v. ; 30cm
Issued every two years. — Continues: Caterer & hotelkeeper buyers′ guide
ISSN 0262-9801 = Caterer & hotelkeeper directory & buyers guide : £6.50
Primary classification 338.7′6164794′028
B82-13418

338.7′6164795′0924 — Wales. Public houses. Management — *Personal observations*

Green, Martin, *1932-*. A year in the drink / Martin Green. — [London] : Fontana, 1982. — 186p ; 18cm
ISBN 0-00-636488-8 (pbk) : £1.75 B82-29520

338.7′61657′0941 — Great Britain. Accountancy. Partnerships: Touche Ross & Co., *to 1981*

Touche Ross & Co.. Touche Ross & Co. 1899-1981 : the origins and growth of the United Kingdom firm / Archibald B. Richards. — London (1 Little New St., EC4A 3TR) : Touche Ross & Co., c1981. — xiii,145p : ill,facsims,ports ; 24cm
Unpriced B82-12189

338.7′61657′0941 — Great Britain. Accountancy firms: Ernest & Whinney, *to 1980*

Jones, Edgar. Accountancy and the British economy 1840-1980 : the evolution of Ernst & Whinney / Edgar Jones ; introduction by Peter Mathias. — London : Batsford, 1981. — 288p,[16]p of plates : ill,facsims,ports ; 23cm
Bibliography: p271-281. — Includes index
ISBN 0-7134-3776-6 : £10.00 B82-14094

338.7′616592′025 — Public relations industries — *Directories — Serials*

The **Public** relations year book. — 1981-. — [London] : Financial Times Business Pub., 1980-. — v. : ill,ports ; 30cm
Absorbed: Public Relations Consultants Association. Register of members, 1980. — Published in co-operation with: Public Relations Consultants Association. — Description based on: 1982 issue
ISSN 0262-9534 = Public relations year book : Unpriced B82-12458

338.7′617′00924 — Italy. Florence. Arts. Patronage. Rucellai, Giovanni — *Biographies*

Giovanni Rucellai ed il suo Zibaldone. — London : Warburg Institute, University of London. — (Studies of the Warburg Institute ; v.24, II)
2: A Florentine patrician and his palace / studies by F.W. Kent ... [et al.] ; with an introduction by Nicolai Rubinstein. — 1981. — xiv,258p,[66]p of plates : ill,plans,2geneal.tables ; 30cm
Includes three chapters and documentary material in Italian. — Includes index
ISBN 0-85481-057-9 : £35.00
Also classified at 945′.51 B82-09051

338.7′617365′094215 — London. Tower Hamlets *(London Borough).* **Stone monuments industries: J. Samuel & Son,** *to 1981*

J. Samuel & Son. J. Samuel & Son : a short history. — London (40 Raven Row, Mile End, E1 2EH) : [J. Samuel & Son], [1982?]. — [12]p : ill,ports ; 22x10cm
Unpriced (unbound) B82-37172

338.7′6178042′0924 — Great Britain. Pop music industries, *1960-1970 — Personal observations*

Napier-Bell, Simon. You don′t have to say you love me / Simon Napier-Bell. — Sevenoaks : New English Library, 1982. — 178p,[8]p of plates : ill,ports ; 18cm
ISBN 0-450-05504-3 (pbk) : £1.50 : CIP rev.
B82-15809

338.7′6178991′0924 — Great Britain. Music recording industries. Culshaw, John — *Biographies*

Culshaw, John. Putting the record straight : the autobiography of John Culshaw. — London : Secker & Warburg, 1981. — 362p ; 23cm
Includes index
ISBN 0-436-11802-5 : £8.50 : CIP rev.
B81-32087

338.7′6178991′0941 — Great Britain. Music recording & reproduction industries: EMI, *to 1981*

Miller, Russell. The incredible music machine. — London : Quartet, Oct.1982. — [288]p
ISBN 0-7043-2324-9 : £12.50 : CIP entry
B82-29079

338.7′6179633463′0924 — Association football. Clubs. Management. Docherty, Tommy — *Biographies*

Docherty, Tommy. Call the Doc / Tommy Docherty with the assistance of Derek Henderson. — London : Hamlyn, 1981. — 192p : ports ; 23cm
ISBN 0-600-34672-2 : £5.95 B82-11703

338.7′6179633463′0924 — Association football. Clubs. Management. Robson, Bobby — *Biographies*

Robson, Bobby. Time on the grass / Bobby Robson. — London : Barker, [1982]. — xi,180p,[16]p of plates : ill,ports ; 23cm
ISBN 0-213-16845-6 : £6.50 B82-40717

338.7′6179633463′0924 — England. Association football. Clubs: Chelsea Football Club. Management, *1970-1982 — Personal observations*

Mears, Brian. Chelsea : the real story / Brian Mears. — London : Pelham, 1982. — 175p,[16]p of plates : ill,ports ; 23cm
ISBN 0-7207-1425-7 : £7.95 : CIP rev.
B82-20390

338.7′619141′00924 — Great Britain. Tourist industries. Entrepreneurship. Butlin, *Sir* **Billy** — *Biographies*

Butlin, *Sir* **Billy**. The Billy Butlin story : ‘a showman to the end’ / Sir Billy Butlin with Peter Dacre. — London : Robson, 1982. — 287p,[8]p of plates : ill,ports ; 23cm
ISBN 0-86051-168-5 : £7.50 : CIP rev.
B82-07051

338.7′620 — England. Engineering industries. Tenders & contracts

Pike, Andrew. Engineering tenders, sales and contracts : standard forms and procedures. — London : Spon, Dec.1982. — [600]p
ISBN 0-419-12530-2 : £22.50 : CIP entry
B82-29793

338.7′62′0002541 — Great Britain. Engineering industries — *Directories — Serials*

Dial industry. Metals, metal working, mechanical engineering, shipbuilding, aerospace, marine & vehicle industries. — 1982-. — [East Grinstead] ([Windsor Court, East Grinstead, W. Sussex RH19 1XA]) : [IPC Business Press Information Services Ltd], 1982-. — v. : maps ; 30cm
Annual
ISSN 0263-1628 = Dial industry. Metals, metal working, mechanical engineering, shipbuilding, aerospace, marine & vehicle industries : Unpriced B82-20884

338.7′62′000254125 — Scotland. Tayside Region. Engineering industries — *Directories*

Tayside engineering register / Tayside Region Industrial Office. — [Dundee] ([Tayside Regional Council, Tayside House, Dundee DD1 3RB]) : [The Office], [1982?]. — 47p : ill ; 30cm
Cover title
Unpriced (pbk) B82-16353

338.7′62′00025424 — England. Midlands. Engineering industries — *Directories — Serials*

Engineering Industries Association. *Midlands Region*. Members′ capacity & plant list / Engineering Industries Association Midlands Region. — Ed.1 (1980)-. — [Birmingham] ([190 Broad St., Birmingham B15 1EA]) : The Association′s Midlands Region, 1980-. — v. : ill ; 21cm
Three editions yearly. — Description based on: Ed.6 (Apr. 1982)
ISSN 0263-578X = Members′ capacity & plant list - Engineering Industries Association. Midlands Region : Unpriced B82-28130

338.7′62′000941 — Great Britain. Engineering industries: John Brown and Company, *to 1980*

Mensforth, Eric. Family engineers. — London : Ward Lock, Nov.1981. — [160]p
ISBN 0-7063-6170-9 (cased) : £9.95 : CIP entry
ISBN 0-7063-6171-7 (pbk) : £7.95 B81-30298

338.7′62086 — Marine safety equipment industries & trades — *Directories — Serials*

International marine safety directory. — 1982-. — Redhill (2 Queensway, Redhill, Surrey RH1 1QS) : Fuel & Metallurgical Journals, 1982-. — v. : ill(some col.) ; 21cm
ISSN 0263-7618 = International marine safety directory : Unpriced B82-32357

338.7′62131′0942 — England. Electricity generation & transmission industries: Central Electricity Generating Board

England, Glyn. Electricity production and transmission in a changing world / Glyn England. — London : Central Electricity Generating Board, 1982. — 16p : col.ill,1col.port ; 30cm
Cover title
ISBN 0-902543-65-2 (pbk) : Unpriced
B82-23767

338.7′62131934′0941 — Great Britain. Insulated electric cables industries: Callender′s *(Firm), to 1945*

BICC. Callender′s : 1882-1945 / R.M. Morgan. — Prescot ([P.O. Box 1, Prescot, Merseyside L34 5SZ]) : BICC plc, [c1982]. — ix,256p : ill,1facsim,1geneal.table,maps,1plan ; 26cm
Bibliography: p247. — Includes index
£9.50 B82-28502

338.7′62138′0941 — Great Britain. Telecommunication equipment industries: Standard Telephones and Cables Limited, *to 1982*

Young, Peter. Power of speech : a history of Standard Telephones and Cables 1883-1983. — London : Allen & Unwin, Nov.1982. — [224]p
ISBN 0-04-382039-5 : £8.95 : CIP entry
B82-27816

338.7′6213817′02541 — Great Britain. Microelectronic industries — *Directories*

Directory of custom microelectronics. — [London] ([MAP Information Centre, Room 524, Dean Bradley House, Horseferry Rd., SW1P 4AG]) : Electronics Applications Division, Department of Industry, 1981. — 32p ; 30cm
Cover title
Unpriced (pbk) B82-38330

338.7′622 — Mining industries: Rio Tinto Company, *to 1954*

Harvey, Charles E.. The Rio Tinto Company : an economic history of a leading international mining concern : 1873-1954 / by Charles E. Harvey. — Penzance : Alison Hodge, 1981. — xiv,390p : ill,maps ; 22cm
Bibliography: p373-381. — Includes index
ISBN 0-906720-03-6 : £25.00 B82-05546

338.7′622338 — Natural gas & petroleum drilling rigs industries: Delta Drilling Company, *to 1980*

Presley, James. Never in doubt : a history of Delta Drilling Company / James Presley. — Houston ; London : Gulf, c1981. — xiii,543p,[32]p of plates : ill(some col.),facsims,ports(some col.) ; 24cm
Bibliography: p522-530. — Includes index
ISBN 0-87201-581-5 : Unpriced B82-29166

338.7′6223382′02516336 — North Sea. Petroleum industries — *Directories — For investors*

Davis, Jonathan. Investing in North Sea oil / Jonathan Davis. — [London] : Sunday Telegraph, 1981. — 60p : ill,maps ; 21cm
ISBN 0-901684-63-5 (pbk) : £1.75 B82-08780

338.7′6223382′0941 — Great Britain. Petroleum industries: British National Oil Corporation. Finance — *Inquiry reports*

Great Britain. *Parliament. House of Commons. Committee of Public Accounts.* Fourth report from the Committee of Public Accounts : together with the proceedings of the committee, minutes of evidence and an appendix : session 1981-82 : Department of Energy : financial control of BNOC; advances to the British Gas Corporation. — London : H.M.S.O., [1981]. — xi,15p ; 25cm. — ([HC] ; 30)
ISBN 0-10-203082-0 (pbk) : £2.80
Also classified at 338.7′6657′0941 B82-16052

338.7′6223382′0941 — Great Britain. Petroleum industries: British Petroleum Company, *to 1980*

Ferrier, R. W.. The history of the British Petroleum Company. — Cambridge : Cambridge University Press
Vol.1: The developing years 1901-1932. — Oct.1982. — [672]p
ISBN 0-521-24647-4 : £35.00 : CIP entry
B82-26247

338.7′6223382′0973 — United States. Petroleum industries & trades. Political aspects — *Study examples: Sun Oil Company, 1876-1945*

Giebelhaus, August W.. Business and government in the oil industry : a case study of Sun Oil, 1876-1945 / by August W. Giebelhaus. — Greenwich, Conn. : Jai Press ; London (3 Henrietta St., WC2E 8LU) : Distributed by Jaicon Press, c1980. — xvi,332p : ill,ports ; 24cm. — (Industrial development and the social fabric ; v.5)
Bibliography: p307-320. — Includes index
ISBN 0-89232-089-3 : £22.55 B82-02080

338.7′62382′002541 — Great Britain. Shipbuilding industries — *Directories*

Shipping. — Great Missenden : Data Research Group, [1982]. — 39,115,67p ; 30cm
Cover title. — Includes index
ISBN 0-86099-350-7 (pbk) : Unpriced
Also classified at 381′.4562386′02541 ; 387.5′025′41 B82-24688

338.7′62382′00922 — Lancashire. Lancaster. Shipbuilding industries. Brockbank *(Family), 1700-1850*

Kennerley, Eija. The Brockbanks of Lancaster : the story of an 18th century shipbuilding firm / by Eija Kennerley. — [Lancaster] ([Old Town Hall, Market Sq., Lancaster) : [Lancaster Museum], 1981. — 27p ; 30cm. — (A Lancaster Museum monograph)
Cover title
Unpriced (pbk) B82-09552

338.7′62382′00941 — Great Britain. Shipbuilding industries: British Shipbuilders — *Inquiry reports*

Great Britain. *Parliament. House of Commons. Industry and Trade Committee.* First report from the Industry and Trade Committee, session 1981-82 : British Shipbuilders : together with the proceedings of the Committee relating to the report, the minutes of evidence and appendices. — London : H.M.S.O., 1982. — xviii,157p,1folded leaf : ill ; 25cm. — ([HC] ; 192)
At head of title: House of Commons. — Includes the text of HC 81
ISBN 0-10-219282-0 (pbk) : £7.00 B82-23224

338.7′624183414′02541 — Great Britian. Precast concrete structural components industries & trades — *Directories — Serials*

British Precast Concrete Federation. Directory of precast concrete products of British Precast Concrete Federation members. — 1981-. — Leicester (60 Charles St., Leicester LE1 1FB) : The Federation, 1981-. — v. : maps ; 30cm
Annual
ISSN 0260-9703 = Directory of precast concrete products of British Precast Concrete Federation members : Unpriced B82-06171

338.7′62′5260942712 — Cheshire. Crewe. Locomotive industries: British Rail Engineering, *to 1981*

Reed, Brian. Crewe locomotive works and its men. — Newton Abbot : David & Charles, Nov.1982. — [240]p
ISBN 0-7153-8228-4 : £10.95 : CIP entry
B82-26395

338.7′62′5260942733 — Great Manchester *(Metropolitan County).* **Gorton. Locomotive industries: Beyer Peacock and Company,** *1855-1966*

Hills, R. L.. Beyer, Peacock : locomotive builders of Gorton, Manchester. — Manchester (97 Grosvenor St., Manchester M1 7HF) : North Western Museum of Science and Industry, June 1982. — [12]p
ISBN 0-9505790-4-1 (pbk) : £0.75 : CIP entry
B82-25747

338.7′6281′094287 — Tyne and Wear *(Metropolitan County).* **Water supply industries: Newcastle and Gateshead Water Company,** *to 1978*

Newcastle and Gateshead Water Company. Water to Tyneside : a history of the Newcastle and Gateshead Water Company / by Robert William Rennison. — [Newcastle upon Tyne] : The Company, c1979. — xx,361p : ill,maps,facsims,ports ; 24cm
Bibliography: p349-354. — Includes index
ISBN 0-9506547-0-1 : £9.25
Also classified at 338.7′6281′094288
B82-08222

338.7′6281′094288 — Northumberland. Water supply industries: Newcastle and Gateshead Water Company, *to 1978*

Newcastle and Gateshead Water Company. Water to Tyneside : a history of the Newcastle and Gateshead Water Company / by Robert William Rennison. — [Newcastle upon Tyne] : The Company, c1979. — xx,361p : ill,maps,facsims,ports ; 24cm
Bibliography: p349-354. — Includes index
ISBN 0-9506547-0-1 : £9.25
Primary classification 338.7′6281′094287
B82-08222

338.7′6291′0941 — Great Britain. Aerospace engineering industries: Lucas Aerospace. Diversification. Proposals: Lucas Aerospace Combine Shop Stewards Committee. Lucas Aerospace alternative corporate plan, *to 1980*

Wainwright, Hilary. The Lucas struggle. — London : Allison & Busby, Oct.1981. — [192]p
ISBN 0-85031-429-1 (cased) : £7.95 : CIP entry
ISBN 0-85031-430-5 (pbk) : £2.95 B81-28002

338.7′62913′00254 — Europe. Aeronautical engineering industries. Directories — *Serials*

Flight international directory of European aviation : incorporating Who′s who in European aviation. — 1982-. — Sutton (Quadrant House, The Quadrant, Sutton, Surrey SM2 5AS) : IPC Transport Press, 1982-. — v. : ill,maps ; 22cm
Annual. — Spine title: Directory of European aviation
ISSN 0263-7006 = Flight international directory of European aviation : £20.00
B82-31716

338.7′629133352′02541 — Helicopter industries & trades — *Directories — Serials*

Hereford′s helicopter world. — Vol.1, no.1 (Summer/Autumn 1981)-. — London (25 Elystan Place, SW3 3JY) : Hereford Press, 1981-. — v. : ill ; 30cm
Two issues yearly
ISSN 0262-6365 = Hereford′s helicopter world (corrected) : £35.00 per year B82-06168

338.7′62913435 — Great Britain. Aircraft engines industries: Rolls-Royce. Financial assistance by government — *Inquiry reports*

Great Britain. *Parliament. House of Commons. Committee of Public Accounts.* Thirtieth report from the Committee of Public Accounts : together with the proceedings of the committee, the minutes of evidence and appendices : session 1979-80 : Department of Industry, National Enterprise Board, Rolls Royce Limited : future role of the National Enterprise Board, monitoring of the National Enterprise Board′s investments, Rolls-Royce Limited. — London : H.M.S.O., [1980]. — xxiv,62p ; 25cm. — ([HC] ; 779)
ISBN 0-10-027799-3 (pbk) : £5.20
Also classified at 354.410082 B82-09928

338.7'6292'0924 — Great Britain. Motor vehicle industries: BL Limited. Management, *1977-1980 — Personal observations*

Edwardes, *Sir Michael, 1930-*. The management of change / Sir Michael Edwardes. — Egham (Park House, Wick Rd., Egham, Surrey TW20 0HW) : Maurice Lubbock Memorial Fund, c1981. — 22p ; 21cm. — (The Second Lubbock lecture on management)
£0.50 (pbk) B82-01692

338.7'6292222'0924 — Italy. Car industries. Ferrari, Enzo — *Biographies*

Casucci, Piero. Enzo Ferrari : 50 years of greatness / Piero Casucci ; [translated by Simon Pleasance]. — Yeovil : Haynes, 1982. — 167p : ill(some col.),1facsim,ports ; 27cm. — (A Foulis motoring book)
Translation of: Enzo Ferrari. — Bibliography: p167. — Includes index
ISBN 0-85429-327-2 : £8.95 B82-35326

338.7'6292222'0924 — United States. Car industries. Ford, Henry, *1863-1947 — Biographies — For children*

Stoney, Barbara. Henry Ford : the motor man / by Barbara Stoney. — London : Hodder and Stoughton, 1981. — 128p : ill,1facsim,ports ; 24cm. — (Twentieth century people)
For adolescents. — Includes index
ISBN 0-340-25913-2 : £5.50 : CIP rev.
B81-27985

338.7'6292222'0941 — Great Britain. Car industries: Rover-British Leyland UK Limited, *to 1980*

Robson, Graham. The Rover story / Graham Robson. — 2nd ed. — Cambridge : Stephens, 1981. — 185p : ill,ports ; 25cm
Previous ed.: 1977. — Includes index
ISBN 0-85059-543-6 : £9.95 : CIP rev.
B81-28018

338.7'6292222'0973 — United States. Car industries: Nissan Motor Corporation in U.S.A., *to 1980*

Rae, John B.. Nissan-Datsun : a history of Nissan Motor Corporation in U.S.A. 1960-1980 / John B. Rae. — New York ; London : McGraw-Hill, c1982. — xii,331p,[16]p of plates : ill,1facsim,ports ; 24cm
Bibliography: p305-309. — Includes index
ISBN 0-07-051112-8 : £14.95 B82-28052

338.7'629228'0942 — England. Racing car industries: Williams Grand Prix Engineering, *to 1981*

Nye, Doug. Racers : the inside story of Williams Grand Prix Engineering / Doug Nye ; general editor David McDonough. — London : Barker, c1982. — ix,173p,[8]p of plates : ill(some col.),ports(some col.) ; 23x27cm
Ill on lining papers
ISBN 0-213-16815-4 : £10.95 B82-14577

338.7'62982 — Great Britain. Vending machine industtries & trades — *Serials*

Vending today : a staff & welfare publication. — [Vol.1, no.1] (Feb. 1981)-. — Sutton : IPC Business Press, 1981-. — v. : ill(some col.),ports ; 29cm
Quarterly
ISSN 0261-4138 = Vending today : £1.00 per issue B82-23592

338.7'63'02541 — Great Britain. Farms offering pick-your-own produce — *Directories — Serials*

Farm fresh. — 1982. — London (124 Cornwall Rd, S.E.1) : Grant Jarvis, May 1982. — [176]p
ISBN 0-907741-01-0 (pbk) : £1.25 : CIP entry
B82-11107

338.7'63'0924 — New Zealand. Agricultural industries — *Personal observations*

Savage, M. J.. Report of an exchange year in New Zealand 1980-1981 / by M.J. Savage. — [London] ([Great Westminster House, Horseferry Rd., SW1P 2AE]) : ADAS, [1981]. — 10p : 1ill ; 30cm
Cover title
Unpriced (pbk) B82-11662

338.7'635'028 — Great Britain. Garden supplies industries & trades — *Directories — Serials*

The **Gardening** handbook. — 1st ed.-. — Northampton : Beacon, 1982-. — v. : ill ; 25cm
Annual
ISSN 0261-7951 = Gardening handbook : £5.95 B82-40063

338.7'639544'09798 — Alaska. King crab fishing industries: Wakefield Seafoods, *to 1970*

Blackford, Mansel G.. Pioneering a modern small business : Wakefield Seafoods and the Alaskan frontier / by Mansel G. Blackford. — Greenwich, Conn. : Jai ; London : distributed by Jaicon, c1979. — xx,210p : ill,2maps ; 24cm. — (Industrial development and the social fabric ; v.6)
Bibliography: p201-206. — Includes index
ISBN 0-89232-088-5 : £20.60 B82-05177

338.7'641'02541 — Great Britain. Food & drinks industries — *Directories — For careers guidance*

Where to ask about careers in the food, drink and tobacco industries / [Food, Drink and Tobacco Industry Training Board]. — 3rd ed. — Gloucester (Barton House, Barton St., Gloucester GL1 1QQ) : The Board, 1981. — 20p : ill ; 21cm
Cover title
Unpriced (pbk)
Also classified at 338.7'6797'02541 B82-17323

338.7'6413'00941 — Great Britain. Food industries: Peek Foods Limited — *Inquiry reports*

Hamilton, Adrian W.. Peek Foods Limited : investigation under section 165(b) of the Companies Act 1948 : report / by Adrian W. Hamilton and Peter W. Foss [for the] Department of Trade. — London : H.M.S.O., 1981. — iv,230,[100]p : facsims,forms ; 30cm
ISBN 0-11-513490-5 (pbk) : £16.00
B82-11891

338.7'66'00257 — America. Chemical industries — *Directories*

The **Americas** / Chemical Data Services. — 2nd ed. — Sutton : Chemical Data Services, 1981. — iii,244p ; 30cm. — (Chemical company profiles)
Previous ed.: 1978. — Includes index
ISBN 0-617-00430-7 (pbk) : £55.00
B82-12209

338.7'66028'0941 — Great Britain. Chemical engineering industries: Hoechst UK

Hoechst UK. Hoechst in the UK. — Hounslow (Hoechst House, 50 Salisbury Rd., Hounslow, Middx TW4 6JH) : Hoechst, c1981. — 24p : col.ill ; 30cm
Cover title
Unpriced (pbk) B82-40863

338.7'660281 — Great Britain. Chemical engineering plant construction industries: A.P.V. Company, *to 1980*

Dummett, G. A.. From little acorns : a history of The A.P.V. Company Limited / G.A. Dummett. — London : Hutchinson Benham, 1981. — xiv,247p,[14]p of plates : ill,ports ; 24cm
Includes index
ISBN 0-09-146370-x : £12.00 B82-08364

338.7'6606'0254 — Europe. Industrial biology industries — *Directories*

Biotechnology Europe / a special report from IMSWORLD Publications. — London (37 Queen Sq., WC1N 3BL) : IMSWORLD, 1981. — [126]p ; 30cm
Unpriced (spiral) B82-09745

338.7'6606'02573 — United States. Industrial biology industries — *Directories*

Biotechnology USA. — London : IMSWORLD, 1981. — [142]p
Unpriced (spiral) B82-11352

338.7'661'00941 — Great Britain. Industrial chemicals industries: Ciba-Geigy Plastics and Additives Company. *Industrial Chemicals Division — Serials*

ICD pipe line : Industrial Chemicals Division news and comment / Ciba-Geigy. — Nov. 1981-. — [Manchester] ([Tenax Rd, Trafford Park, Manchester M17 1WT]) : Public Relations Department, Industrial Chemicals Division, Ciba-Geigy Plastics and Additives Co., 1981-. — v. : ill,ports ; 38cm
Continues: Trafford telegraph
ISSN 0262-0405 = ICD pipe line : Unpriced
B82-08457

338.7'6632'00254 — Europe. Wines industries & wines agents allowing visits — *Directories*

Hogg, Anthony. Guide to visiting vineyards / Anthony Hogg. — Rev. ed. — London : Joseph, 1981 (1982 [printing]). — 229p : ill,maps ; 21cm
Previous ed.: 1976. — Includes index
ISBN 0-7181-2181-3 (pbk) : £5.50 B82-36943

338.7'6633'02541 — Great Britain. Brewing industries, *1900-1980 — Directories*

Barber, Norman, *1932-*. Where have all the breweries gone? : a directory of British brewery companies / compiled by Norman Barber. — Swinton (375 Chorley Rd., Swinton M27 2AY) : Neil Richardson in association with the Campaign for Real Ale, [1981?]. — 49p : ill ; 30cm
Includes index
£3.50 (unbound) B82-03245

338.7'6633'0942527 — Nottinghamshire. Kimberley. Brewing industries: Hardys & Hansons PLC, *to 1982*

Bruce, George, *1910-*. Kemberley ale : the story of Hardys & Hansons, Kimberley 1832-1982 / by George Bruce. — London : Melland, c1982. — 128p : ill(some col.),facsims,ports ; 24cm
Ill on lining papers
ISBN 0-9500730-9-1 : £8.00 B82-38340

338.7'6633'0942733 — Greater Manchester *(Metropolitan County).* **Manchester. Brewing industries: Whitbread Chesters Brewery Company,** *to 1981*

Cowen, Frank. A history of Chesters Brewery Company / by Frank Cowen. — [Swinton] : [Neil Richardson], [c1982]. — 44p : ill,facsims,maps ; 30cm
Cover title. — Text on inside covers. — Includes index
ISBN 0-907511-01-5 (pbk) : £2.00 B82-39746

338.7'6633'0942753 — Merseyside *(Metropolitan County).* **Liverpool. Brewing industries: Higsons Brewery,** *to 1980*

Higsons Brewery. Higsons Brewery : 1780-1980. — Liverpool ([46 The Albany, Old Hall Street, Liverpool L3 9EG]) : Kershaw Press Services, [1981]. — 50p : ill,facsims,ports ; 21x22cm
Facsims on inside covers
Unpriced (pbk) B82-22479

338.7'664153'0924 — Great Britain. Confectionery industries. Rowntree, Joseph — *Biographies*

Vernon, Anne. A Quaker business man : the life of Joesph Rowntree 1836-1925 / Anne Vernon. — York : William Sessions, 1982. — 207,[8]p of plates : ill,1geneal.table,ports ; 21cm
Originally published: London : Allen & Unwin, 1958. — Includes index
ISBN 0-900657-63-4 (pbk) : Unpriced
B82-27125

338.7'6655'025 — Petroleum industries — *Directories — Serials*

Financial times who's who in world oil and gas. — 1982/83. — London : Longman, July 1982. — [570]p. — (Financial times international year books : information to business)
ISBN 0-582-90313-0 : £32.00 : CIP entry
ISSN 0141-3236
Also classified at 338.7'6657'025 B82-22775

338.7'6657'025 — Gas industries — *Directories — Serials*

Financial times who's who in world oil and gas. — 1982/83. — London : Longman, July 1982. — [570]p. — (Financial times international year books : information to business)
ISBN 0-582-90313-0 : £32.00 : CIP entry
ISSN 0141-3236
Primary classification 338.7'6655'025
B82-22775

338.7′6657′0941 — Dorset. Purbeck *(District).* Oil fields: Wytch Farm oil field. Assets of British Gas Corporation. Sale — *Inquiry reports*

Great Britain. *Parliament. House of Commons. Select Committee on Energy.* First report from the Select Committee on Energy : together with appendices and minutes of proceedings : session 1981-82 : the disposal of the British Gas Corporation's interest in the Wytch Farm oil-field. — London : H.M.S.O., [1982]. — xxxip ; 25cm. — (HC ; 138)
ISBN 0-10-213882-6 (pbk) : £2.80 B82-20573

338.7′6657′0941 — Great Britain. Gas industries: British Gas Corporation. Financial assistance. Loans from government — *Inquiry reports*

Great Britain. *Parliament. House of Commons. Committee of Public Accounts.* Fourth report from the Committee of Public Accounts : together with the proceedings of the committee, minutes of evidence and an appendix : session 1981-82 : Department of Energy : financial control of BNOC; advances to the British Gas Corporation. — London : H.M.S.O., [1981]. — xi,15p ; 25cm. — ([HC] ; 30)
ISBN 0-10-203082-0 (pbk) : £2.80
Primary classification 338.7′6223382′0941
B82-16052

338.7′6666′0942233 — Kent. Faversham. Pottery industries: Boughton Pottery, *to 1957*

Welland, L. G.. Boughton Pottery / by L.G. Welland. — Faversham : Faversham Society, 1982. — iv,32p : ill,1map,1plan,1geneal.table ; 26cm. — (Faversham papers, ISSN 0014-892x ; no.18)
ISBN 0-900532-30-0 (pbk) : Unpriced
B82-25360

338.7′6666′0942876 — Tyne and Wear *(Metropolitan County).* Newcastle upon Tyne. Pottery industries: C. T. Maling and Sons, *to 1963*

Maling : a Tyneside pottery. — [Newcastle Upon Tyne] : Tyne and Wear County Council Museums, [1981]. — 72p : ill(some col.),2ports ; 20x21cm
Bibliography: p72
ISBN 0-905974-05-0 (pbk) : Unpriced
B82-05566

338.7′666737′0924 — Kent. Murston. Bricks industries. Smeed, George

Perks, Richard-Hugh. George Bargebrick Esquire : the story of George Smeed, the brick and cement king / by Richard-Hugh Perks. — Rainham : Meresborough, 1981. — 64p : ill,1geneal.table,1map,1plan,ports ; 30cm
Text on inside cover. — Bibliography: p64
ISBN 0-905270-47-9 (pbk) : £2.95 B82-36017

338.7′66862′025 — Fertiliser industries — *Directories*

World directory of fertilizer products. — 5th ed. / editor: C. Wahba. — London : British Sulphur Corporation, 1981. — xxi,125p : ill (some col.) ; 31cm
Previous ed.: / British Sulphur Corporation Limited. 1977
ISBN 0-902777-46-7 : Unpriced B82-15443

338.7′669 — Minor metals industries & trades — *Directories*

World minor metals survey. — 2nd ed. / edited by Norman Connell. — Worcester Park : Metal Bulletin, c1981. — 118p ; 30cm
Previous ed.: 1977
ISBN 0-900542-63-2 (pbk) : £15.00
B82-16730

338.7′669′042 — Western world. Scrap metals industries — *Directories* — *Serials*

European & North American scrap directory. — 1st ed. (1981)-. — Worcester Park (Park House, Park Terrace, Worcester Park, Surrey KT4 7HY) : Metal Bulletin Books Ltd, 1981-. — v. ; 23cm
Every 3-4 years. — Continues: European scrap directory
ISSN 0261-426X = European & North American scrap directory : £35.00 B82-20881

338.7′6691′0941 — Great Britain. Iron & steel industries: British Steel Corporation. Financial management, *to 1980*

Bryer, R. A.. Accounting for British Steel : a financial analysis of the failure of the British Steel Corporation 1967-80, and who was to blame / R.A. Bryer, T.J. Brignall, A.R. Maunders. — Aldershot : Gower, c1982. — xv,303p : ill ; 23cm
Bibliography: p281-284. — Includes index
ISBN 0-566-00531-x : Unpriced : CIP rev.
B82-01547

338.7′6691′0941 — Great Britain. Iron & steel industries: British Steel Corporation — *Inquiry reports*

Great Britain. *Parliament. House of Commons. Industry and Trade Committee.* Fourth report from the Industry and Trade Committee, session 1981-82 : British Steel Corporation : together with the proceedings of the Committee relating to the report, the minutes of evidence and appendix. — London : H.M.S.O., 1982. — vi,41p ; 25cm. — ([HC] ; 308) ([HC] ; 6-i and ii)
ISBN 0-10-230882-9 (pbk) : Unpriced
B82-27584

338.7′6691′0941 — Great Britain. Iron & steel industries: British Steel Corporation, *to 1981*

Cottrell, Elizabeth. The giant with feet of clay : the British steel industry 1945-1981 / by Elizabeth Cottrell. — London : Centre for Policy Studies, 1981. — vi,222p : ill,maps ; 30cm
Bibliography: p219-222
ISBN 0-905880-40-4 (pbk) : £25.00
B82-16955

338.7′67′02541 — Great Britain. Manufacturing industries allowing visits — *Directories*

Lansbury, Angela. See Britain at work : a whole world of fascinating visits to craft workshops and factories / [by Angela Lansbury]. — 3rd (completely rev.) ed. — Watford : Exley, 1981. — 224p : ill(some col.),col.maps ; 22cm
Previous ed.: 1978. — Includes index
ISBN 0-905521-56-0 (cased) : £6.50
ISBN 0-905521-54-4 (pbk) : Unpriced
B82-29724

338.7′67′0254125 — Scotland. Tayside Region. Manufacturing industries — *Directories*

Tayside manufacturers register / Tayside Region Industrial Office. — [Dundee] ([Tayside Regional Council, Tayside House, Dundee DD1 3RB]) : [The office], [1982?]. — 15p ; 30cm
Cover title
Unpriced (pbk) B82-16346

338.7′674′0941 — Great Britain. Timber industries: J. Alsford Limited, *to 1982*

Beaver, Patrick. The Alsford tradition : a century of quality timber 1882-1982 / by Patrick Beaver. — London : Melland, 1982. — 100p : ill(some col.),facsims,ports(some col.) ; 24cm
ISBN 0-907929-00-1 : £7.50 B82-26296

338.7′676183 — Somerset. Street. Leatherboard manufacturing industries: Avalon Leatherboard Company, *to 1967*

Avalon Leatherboard Company. Bowlingreen Mill : a centenary history / Michael McGarvie. — vi,153p,[8]p of plates : ill(some col.),facsims,1geneal.table,maps(some col.),1plan,ports ; 25cm
Includes index
Unpriced (pbk) B82-36343

338.7′6762′0941 — Great Britain. Paper manufacturing industries: Bowater Corporation, *to 1980*

Reader, W. J.. Bowater : a history / W.J. Reader ; research by Rachel Lawrence ... [et al.] ; general adviser Robert Knight. — Cambridge : Cambridge University Press, 1981. — xv,426p : ill,2facsims,1plan,port ; 26cm
Bibliography: p402-406. — Includes index
ISBN 0-521-24165-0 : £25.00 : CIP rev.
B81-31263

338.7′676284 — France. Laboratory paper manufacturing industries: Whatman LabSales — *French texts* — *Serials*

Allo ferrières. — Issues 1-. — [Maidstone] ([Maidstone, Kent ME14 1BR]) : Whatman LabSales, Whatman Reeve Angel Group, [1980]-. — v. : ill,ports ; 81x28cm folded to 21x28cm
Quarterly
ISSN 0144-8226 = Allo ferrieres : Unpriced
B82-06793

338.7′67731′0941 — Great Britain. Wool industries. Organisations: British Wool Marketing Board — *Serials*

British Wool Marketing Board. Report and accounts 30 April ... / British Wool Marketing Board. — 1977-. — Bradford (Oak Mills, Clayton, Bradford, W. Yorkshire BD14 6JD) : The Board, [1977]-. — v. : col.ill ; 30cm
Annual. — Continues: British Wool Marketing Board. Annual report and accounts 30 April ... — Description based on: 1981
ISSN 0262-1932 = Report and accounts - British Wool Marketing Board : Unpriced
B82-01073

338.7′677653′0942561 — Bedfordshire. Bedford. Lace industries: C.& T. Lester, *1820-1905*

Buck, Anne. Thomas Lester, his lace and the East Midlands industry 1820-1905 / Anne Buck. — Bedford : Ruth Bean, 1981. — x,108p : ill,1port ; 29cm
Bibliography: p106. — Includes index
ISBN 0-903585-09-x : Unpriced B82-02181

338.7′6797′02541 — Great Britain. Tobacco industries — *Directories* — *For careers guidance*

Where to ask about careers in the food, drink and tobacco industries / [Food, Drink and Tobacco Industry Training Board]. — 3rd ed. — Gloucester (Barton House, Barton St., Gloucester GL1 1QQ) : The Board, 1981. — 20p : ill ; 21cm
Cover title
Unpriced (pbk)
Primary classification 338.7′641′02541
B82-17323

338.7′681418′02541 — Great Britain. Photographic equipment industries & trades — *Directories* — *Serials*

Professional photographer directory of photographic equipment and services. — 1981-. — [Croydon] ([P.O. Box 109, Maclaren House, 19 Scarbrook Rd, Croydon CR9 1QH]) : [Maclaren Publishers Ltd], 1981-. — v. ; 30cm
Annual. — Continues: Industrial & commercial photographer directory of photographic equipment and services. — Supplement to: Professional photographer
ISSN 0263-3159 = Professional Photographer directory of photographic equipment and services : Unpriced B82-19883

338.7′6841′00254 — Western Europe. Furniture industries equipment industries — *Directories* — *Serials*

ASFI. Directory of members and buyers guide / Association of Suppliers to the Furniture Industry Limited. — 1982-. — Oxted : Magnum Publications, [1981]-. — v. : ill,ports ; 30cm
Includes text in German, French, Spanish and Italian. — Spine title: ASFI directory of members and buyers guide
ISSN 0262-9607 = Directory of members and buyers guide - ASFI : Unpriced B82-13412

338.7′686′0256 — Africa. Book industries & trades — *Directories*

The **African** book world and press : a directory / edited by Hans M. Zell = Répertoire du livre et de la presse en Afrique / editée par Hans M. Zell. — 2nd ed. = 2e éd. — London : Zell, 1980. — xxiv,244p : ill ; 31cm
English and French text. — Previous ed.: 1977
ISBN 0-905450-06-x : £35.00 : CIP rev.
Primary classification 027′.0025′6 B80-21286

338.7′6862′094212 — London *(City).* Printing industries: Long Shop, *1523-1624*

Avis, F. C.. The 16. century Long Shop printing office in the Poultry / F.C. Avis. — London : Glenview, c1982. — 72p : ill,3maps,1plan ; 23cm
Limited ed. of 250 numbered copies. — Includes index
ISBN 0-211-26853-4 : Unpriced B82-28990

338.7′68643′02541 — Great Britain. Microform services — *Directories*

Directory of commercial microfilm services in the United Kingdom / National Reprographic Centre for documentation. — 5th ed. / compiled by Tony Hendley. — Hertford : NRCd, 1980. — 39p ; 30cm
Previous ed.: 1976
ISBN 0-85267-181-4 (spiral) : Unpriced B82-35929

338.7′688765′025 — Expedition equipment industries & trades — *Directories*

Wesley-Smith, Shane. Equipment and services directory for expeditions / compiled by Shane Wesley-Smith. — London (Royal Geographical Society, 1 Kensington Gore, SW7 2AR) : Expedition Advisory Centre, [1981?]. — 19p ; 21cm
Cover title. — Bibliography: p19
Unpriced (spiral) B82-11733

338.7′697 — Merseyside *(Metropolitan County).* **Kirkby. Air conditioning equipment industries & heating radiators industries: KME,** *to 1979*

Eccles, Tony. Under new managment : the story of Britain′s largest worker cooperative - its successes and failures / Tony Eccles. — London : Pan, 1981. — 416p ; 18cm. — (Pan business / industrial relations) (Pan original)
Bibliography: p407-410. — Includes index
ISBN 0-330-26285-8 (pbk) : £2.95 B82-01597

338.7′697′04502541 — Great Britain. Electric heating equipment industries & trades — *Directories — Serials*

Electroheat equipment suppliers directory. — 1981-. — London (30 Millbank, SW1P 4RD) : British National Committee for Electroheat, 1981-. — v. ; 30cm
Irregular
ISSN 0262-3323 = Electroheat equipment suppliers directory : Unpriced B82-02387

338.8 — INDUSTRIAL ENTERPRISE. COMBINATIONS, MONOPOLIES, MERGERS, MULTINATIONAL COMPANIES

338.8′042′0943 — West Germany. Multidivisioanl companies. Econometric models

Cable, John. American innovation abroad : the multidivisional hypothesis in West Germany / by John Cable and Manfred J. Dirrheimer. — Coventry : Department of Economics, University of Warwick, [1981?]. — 31p ; 31cm. — (Warwick economic research papers ; no.195)
Bibliography: p29-31
Unpriced (pbk) B82-11377

338.8′2 — Capitalist countries. Economic development. Effects of monopolies

Cowling, Keith. Monopoly capitalism / Keith Cowling. — London : Macmillan, 1982. — 200p ; 23cm. — (Radical economics)
Bibliography: p183-194. — Includes index
ISBN 0-333-29204-9 (cased) : Unpriced
ISBN 0-333-29205-7 (pbk) : Unpriced B82-20922

338.8′2′0941 — Great Britain. Monopolies — *For schools*

Pass, C. L.. Monopoly. — 2nd ed. / C.L. Pass, J.R. Sparkes. — London : Heinemann Educational, 1980. — 166p : ill ; 20cm. — (Studies in the British economy)
Previous ed.: / by Derek Lee, Vivian S. Anthony and Allen Skuse. 1968. — Includes index
ISBN 0-435-84582-9 (pbk) : £2.95 : CIP rev. B80-03562

338.8′261072821 — South Yorkshire *(Metropolitan County).* **Sheffield. Newspaper publishing industries: Sheffield Newspapers. Fair trading practice** — *Inquiry reports*

Great Britain. *Office of Fair Trading.* A report by the Director General of Fair Trading on an investigation under section 3 of the Competition Act 1980 : Sheffield Newspapers Limited. — [London] ([Field House, Breams Buildings, EC4]) : Office of Fair Trading, 1981. — 72p ; 30cm
Unpriced (spiral) B82-21428

338.8′26292 — Great Britain. Car components industries & wholesale car components trades. Monopolies — *Inquiry reports*

Great Britain. *Monopolies and Mergers Commission.* Car parts : a report on the matter of the existence or the possible existence of a complex monopoly situation in relation to the wholesale supply of motor car parts in the United Kingdom / The Monopolies and Mergers Commission. — London : H.M.S.O., 1982. — vii,86p ; 25cm. — (H.C. ; 318)
Includes index
ISBN 0-10-231882-4 (pbk) : £5.65 B82-29616

338.8′2629277 — Great Britain. Commercial vehicle refrigeration equipment industries: Petter Refrigeration. Fair trading practice — *Inquiry reports*

Petter Refrigeration Limited : a report by the Director General of Fair Trading on an investigation under Section 3 of the Competition Act 1980. — [London] ([Field House, Bream′s Buildings, EC4A 1PR]) : Office of Fair Trading, 1981. — 56p ; 30cm
Unpriced (spiral) B82-05571

338.8′26649′00973 — United States. Meat trades. Oligopolies, *1800-1912*

Yeager, Mary. Competition and regulation : the develoment of oligopoly in the meat packing industry / by Mary Yeager. — Greenwich, Conn. : Jai Press ; London (3 Henrietta St., WC2E 8LU) : Distributed by Jaicon Press, c1981. — xxvi,296p : ill,maps,plans ; 24cm. — (Industrial development and the social fabric ; v.2)
Bibliography: p263-283. — Includes index
ISBN 0-89232-058-3 : £21.95 B82-02077

338.8′2666893 — Great Britian. Ready-mixed concrete industries. Monopolies — *Inquiry reports*

Great Britain. *Monopolies and Mergers Commission.* Ready mixed concrete : a report on the supply in the United Kingdon of ready mixed concrete / the Monopolies and Mergers Commission. — London : H.M.S.O., 1981. — v,53p ; 25cm. — (Cmnd. ; 8354)
Includes index
ISBN 0-10-183540-x (pbk) : £4.35 B82-00026

338.8′2677′009 — Textile industries. Oligopolies, *to 1981*

Clairmonte, Frederick. The world in their web : dynamics of textile multinationals / Frederick Clairmonte and John Cavanagh. — London : Zed, c1981. — xix,278p ; 23cm. — (Imperialism series)
Bibliography: p257-270. — Includes index
ISBN 0-905762-95-9 : £17.95 : CIP rev. B81-19212

338.8′26843′0941 — Great Britain. Furnishing textile industries: Arthur Sanderson & Sons. Fair trading practice — *Inquiry reports*

A **Report** by the Director General of Fair Trading on an investigation under section 3 of the Competition Act 1980 : Arthur Sanderson & Sons Limited. — [London] ([Field House, Breams Buildings, EC4]) : Office of Fair Trading, 1981. — 53p ; 30cm
Unpriced (spiral) B82-05494

338.8′3′0973 — United States. Companies. Mergers & take-overs

Mergers and acquisitions : current problems in perspective / edited by Michael Keenan, Lawrence J. White. — Lexington, Mass. : Lexington Books ; [Aldershot] : Gower [distributor], 1982. — vi,355p : ill ; 24cm
Includes bibliographies
ISBN 0-669-04719-8 : £23.50 B82-36674

338.8′361072 — Great Britain. Newspaper publishing industries: Benham Newspapers & St Regis International. Mergers with Reed International — *Inquiry reports*

Great Britain. *Monopolies and Mergers Commission.* Benham Newspapers Ltd, St Regis International Ltd and Reed International PLC : a report on the proposed transfer of eight newspapers owned by Benham Newspapers Ltd and of eleven newspapers owned by St Regis International Ltd to Reed International PLC ... / the Monopolies and Mergers Commission. — London : H.M.S.O., [1982]. — v,47p : 1map ; 25cm. — (HC ; 402)
ISBN 0-10-240282-5 (pbk) : £4.35 B82-35980

338.8′36107292991 — Gwent. Newport. Newspaper publishing industries: South Wales Argus (Holdings). Mergers with Express Newspapers Limited — *Inquiry reports*

Great Britain. *Monopolies and Mergers Commission.* South Wales Argus (Holdings) Ltd and Express Newspapers Ltd : a report on the proposed transfer of three newspapers owned by South Wales Argus (Holdings) Ltd to Express Newspapers Ltd / Monopolies and Mergers Commission. — London : H.M.S.O., [1981]. — 40p ; 25cm. — (Cmnd. ; 8385)
ISBN 0-10-183850-6 (pbk) : £3.55 B82-03636

338.8′36133212′0941 — Great Britain. Commercial banks: Royal Bank of Scotland Group. Mergers with Standard Chartered Bank — *Inquiry reports*

Great Britain. *Monopolies and Mergers Commission.* The Hongkong and Shanghai Banking Corporation, Standard Chartered Bank Limited, The Royal Bank of Scotland Group Limited : a report on the proposed mergers / the Monopolies and Mergers Commission. — London : H.M.S.O., [1982]. — v,104p ; 25cm. — (Cmnd. ; 8472)
ISBN 0-10-184720-3 (pbk) : £5.45
Primary classification 338.9′36133212′0941 B82-15214

338.8′362 — Great Britain. Engineering components industries: BTR PLC. Mergers with Serck PLC — *Inquiry reports*

Great Britain. *Monopolies and Mergers Commission.* BTR Limited and Serck Limited : a report on the merger. — London : H.M.S.O., 1982. — v,56p : ill ; 25cm. — ([HC] ; 392)
At head of title: The Monopolies and Mergers Commission
ISBN 0-10-239282-x (pbk) : £4.80 B82-32498

338.8′3621042′0973 — United States. Energy industries: Enserch Corporation. Mergers with Davy Corporation — *Inquiry reports*

Great Britain. *Monopolies and Mergers Commission.* Enserch Corporation and Davy Corporation Limited : a report on the proposed merger / the Monopolies and Mergers Commission. — London : H.M.S.O., 1981. — vi,85p ; 25cm. — (Cmnd. ; 8360)
ISBN 0-10-183600-7 (pbk) : £5.10 B82-00025

338.8′6′0941 — Great Britain. Holding companies: Cornhill Consolidated Group — *Inquiry reports*

Calcutt, David, *1930-.* Cornhill Consolidated Group Limited (in liquidation) : investigation under section 165 (b) of Companies Act 1948 : report / by David Calcutt and John Whinney. — London : H.M.S.O., 1980. — 302,[92]p : ill ; 30cm
At head of title: Department of Trade
ISBN 0-11-513246-5 (pbk) : £16.00 B82-21614

338.8′6′0941 — Great Britain. Holding companies: Gilgate Holdings, Raybourne Group, Calomefern Limited & Desadean Properties — *Inquiry reports*

Morritt, R. A.. Gilgate Holdings Limited, Raybourne Group Limited, Calomefern Limited, Desadean Properties Limited : investigation under Section 165(b) of the Companies Act 1948 / report by R.A. Morritt and P.L. Ainger. — London : Her Majesty′s Stationery Office, 1981. — ca.780p ; 30cm
At head of title: Department of Trade
ISBN 0-11-513485-9 (pbk) : £23.00 B82-00559

338.8′6′0941 — Great Britain. Holding companies: Orbit Holdings Limited — *Inquiry reports*

Evans, Anthony H. M.. Orbit Holdings Limited : investigation under section 165(b) of the Companies Act 1948 : report / by Anthony H.M. Evans and R. Hugh Morcom. — London : H.M.S.O., 1981. — 107,[108]p ; 30cm
At head of title: Department of Trade
ISBN 0-11-513542-1 (pbk) : £12.50 B82-14403

338.8'6'0941 — Great Britain. Holding companies: Robert Jenkins (Holdings), *to 1981*

Robert Jenkins (Holdings). Jenkins of Rotherham 1856-1981 : 125 years of industrial history. — 2nd ed. / by Eric N. Simons and E.M. Sessions. — [York] : Sessions in association with Robert Jenkins and Company 1856-1968 and Robert Jenkins (Holdings) 1969-1981, 1981. — viii,120p,[8]p of plates : ill(some col.),1col.coat of arms,2facsims,1geneal.table,plans,ports(some col.) ; 25cm
Previous ed.: Rotherham : R. Jenkins, 1956. — Includes index
ISBN 0-900657-62-6 (cased) : Unpriced
ISBN 0-900657-60-x (pbk) : Unpriced
B82-25687

338.8'6'0941 — Great Britain. Holding companies: Saint Piran Limited — *Inquiry reports*

Godfrey, G. M.. Saint Piran Limited : investigation under section 165(b) and section 172 of the Companies Act 1948 : interim report / by G.M. Godfrey and A.J. Hardcastle. — London : H.M.S.O., 1980. — 36p ; 30cm
At head of title: Department of Trade
ISBN 0-11-513247-3 (pbk) : £5.40 B82-19394

338.8'8 — Companies. International joint ventures

Walmsley, John. Handbook of international joint ventures. — London : Graham & Trotman, June 1982. — [170]p
ISBN 0-86010-369-2 : £25.00 : CIP entry
B82-20784

338.8'8 — International business enterprise

Handbook of international business / edited by Ingo Walter ; associate editor Tracy Murray. — New York ; Chichester : Wiley, c1982. — 1v. in various pagings : ill ; 24cm. — (A Ronald Press publication)
Text on lining papers. — Includes bibliographies and index
ISBN 0-471-07949-9 : £39.50 B82-30271

338.8'8 — Multinational companies

The **Geography** of multinationals. — London : Croom Helm, June 1982. — [352]p. — (Croom Helm series in geography and environment)
ISBN 0-7099-2403-8 : £19.95 : CIP entry
B82-09594

Madsen, Axel. Private power : multinational corporations for the survival of our planet / Axel Madsen. — [London] : Abacus, 1981, c1980. — 258p ; 20cm
Originally published: New York : Morrow, 1980. — Bibliography: p245-246. — Includes index
ISBN 0-349-12274-1 (pbk) : £2.50 B82-08370

A **Multinational** look at the transnational corporation : an international collection of academic and corporate views on the future of transnational enterprise / edited by Michael T. Skully. — Sydney : Dryden ; Caterham : Australiana, 1978. — iv,278p : 2ill ; 27cm
ISBN 0-909162-04-2 : Unpriced B82-39128

New theories of the multinational enterprise. — London : Croom Helm, Sept.1982. — [288]p
ISBN 0-7099-2224-8 : £14.95 : CIP entry
B82-20767

338.8'8 — Multinational companies. Concentration

Grunberg, Leon. Failed multinational ventures : the political economy of international divestments / Leon Grunberg. — Lexington, Mass. : Lexington Books, c1981 ; [Aldershot] : Gower publishing [distributor], 1982. — xi,176p ; 24cm
Bibliography: p161-167. — Includes index
ISBN 0-669-04032-0 : £15.00 B82-08158

338.8'8 — Multinational companies. Economic aspects

The **New** international economy. — London : Sage, Jan.1982. — [320]p
ISBN 0-8039-9792-2 : £12.50 : CIP entry
B81-33842

338.8'8 — Multinational companies. Effects of flexible foreign exchange rates

Blin, John M.. Flexible exchange rates and international business / by John M. Blin, Stuart I. Greenbaum, Donald P. Jacobs ... in collaboration with the J.L. Kellogg Graduate School of Management, Northwestern University. — [London] : British-North American Committee, 1981. — xi,99p : ill ; 22cm
ISBN 0-89068-058-2 (pbk) : £3.00 B82-14345

338.8'8 — Multinational companies. Organisation structure

The **Management** of headquarters-subsidiary relationships in multinational corporations / edited by Lars Otterbeck. — Aldershot : Gower, c1981. — ix,343p : ill ; 23cm
Includes bibliographies
ISBN 0-566-00484-4 : Unpriced : CIP rev.
B81-21535

338.8'8 — Multinational companies. Political aspects

Robinson, John. Multinationals and political control. — Aldershot : Gower, Feb.1983. — [510]p
ISBN 0-566-00394-5 : £25.00 : CIP entry
B82-38718

338.8'8'05 — International business enterprise — *Serials*

Research in international business and finance : an annual compilation of research. — Vol.1 (1979)-. — Greenwich, Conn. : JAI Press ; London (3 Henrietta St., WC2E 8LU) : Distributed by JAICON Press, 1979-. — v. : ill ; 24cm
ISSN 0275-5319 = Research in international business and finance : £26.20 B82-02338

338.8'84 — Multinational companies: Lonrho Limited. Mergers with House of Fraser — *Inquiry reports*

Great Britain. *Monopolies and Mergers Commission*. Lonrho Limited and House of Fraser Limited : a report on the proposed merger. — London : H.M.S.O., 1981. — v,93p : 1map ; 25cm. — ([HC] ; 73)
At head of title: The Monopolies and Mergers Commission
ISBN 0-10-207382-1 (pbk) : £5.45 B82-11607

338.8'84 — Multinational companies. Restrictive practices

Competition in international business : law and policy on restrictive practices / edited by Oscar Schachter and Robert Hellawell. — New York ; Guildford : Columbia University Press, 1981. — ix,441p : ill ; 24cm
Includes index
ISBN 0-231-05220-0 : £21.10 B82-10647

338.8'87 — Chile. Nitrate industries. British companies, *1880-1914*

Fernandez, Manuel A.. Technology and British nitrate enterprises in Chile, 1880-1914 / by Manuel A. Fernandez. — [Glasgow] ([Glasgow G12 8QH]) : Institute of Latin American Studies, University of Glasgow, 1981. — 18p ; 30cm. — (Occasional papers, ISSN 0305-8647 ; no.34)
Cover title
Unpriced (pbk) B82-06344

338.8'87 — Developing countries. Economic conditions. Effects of multinational aluminium companies

Graham, Ronald. The aluminium industry and the Third World. — London : Zed Press, Sept.1982. — [288]p
ISBN 0-86232-057-7 : £16.95 : CIP entry
B82-20184

338.8'87 — Developing countries. Economic conditions. Effects of multinational pharmaceutical companies

Muller, Mike. The health of nations : a north-south investigation / by Mike Muller. — London : Faber, 1982. — 255p ; 23cm
Includes index
ISBN 0-571-11888-7 (cased) : £7.95 : CIP rev.
ISBN 0-571-11956-5 (pbk) : Unpriced
B82-06039

338.8'87 — Developing countries. Economic development. Role of diversified multinational companies — *Study examples: Electric equipment industries — Study regions: Brazil*

Newfarmer, Richard. Transnational conglomerates and the economics of dependent development : a case study of the international electrical oligopoly and Brazil's electrical industry / by Richard Newfarmer. — Greenwich, Conn. : Jai ; London : distributed by Jaicon, c1980. — xx,442p : ill ; 24cm. — (Contemporary studies in economic and financial analysis ; v.23)
Bibliography: p403-419. — Includes index
ISBN 0-89232-110-5 : £24.50 B82-05925

338.8'87 — Developing countries. Multinational pharmaceutical companies. Accountability

Medawar, Charles. Drug diplomacy. — London (9 Poland St., W1V 3DG) : Social Audit, Mar.1982. — [150]p
ISBN 0-9503392-9-6 (pbk) : £2.95 : CIP entry
B82-08409

338.8'87 — Petroleum industries. Multinational companies — *Statistics — For investment*

Lilley, Peter. Major oil companies / Peter Lilley, Jonquil Lowe. — London (Bow Bells House, Bread St, EC4M 9EL) : W. Greenwell & Co., 1982. — 1v.(loose-leaf) ; 35cm
£250.00 B82-31011

338.8'87 — Semiconductor industries. Multinational companies. Oligopolistic competition. Role of technological innovation. Economic aspects

Sciberras, Edmond. Multinational electronics companies and national economic policies / by Edmond Sciberras ; foreword by C. Freeman. — Greenwich, Conn. : Jai ; London : distributed by Jaicon, c1977. — xx,328p : ill,1map ; 24cm. — (Contemporary studies in economic and financial analysis ; v.6)
Bibliography: p313-318. — Includes index
ISBN 0-89232-016-8 : £22.85 B82-05924

338.8'884 — European Community countries. Public opinion on multinational companies

Who's afraid of the multinationals? : a survey of European opinion on multinational corporations / Georges Peninou ... [et al.]. — Farnborough, Hants. : Saxon House, 1978 (1979 [printing]). — 207p : ill ; 23cm
ISBN 0-566-00219-1 : Unpriced : CIP rev.
B78-13294

338.8'8841 — Great Britain. Foreign companies. Finance — *Statistics — Serials*

Britain's top 1000 foreign-owned companies. — 1979-. — London : Jordan & Sons (Surveys) Ltd, 1979-. — v. ; 30cm
Annual
ISSN 0263-242x = Britain's top 1000 foreign-owned companies : £15.00 B82-18534

338.8'88411 — Scotland. Economic conditions. Effects of multinational companies, *1961-1981*

Hood, Neil. Multinationals in retreat : the Scottish experience / by Neil Hood and Stephen Young. — Edinburgh : Edinburgh University Press, c1982. — xi,193p : ill ; 24cm. — (Scottish industrial policy series ; 1)
Includes index
ISBN 0-85224-428-2 (pbk) : £10.00 : CIP rev.
B82-10882

338.8'88538 — Saudi Arabia. Saudi Arabian companies. Joint ventures with British companies — *For British businessmen*

Emerson, E. C.. Prospects and procedures for establishing a joint venture in Saudi Arabia : a report prepared for COMET / by E.C. Emerson. — London : 33 Bury St., SW1Y 6AX : Committee for Middle East Trade, 1981. — v,50p : ill,1map ; 30cm
£5.00 (spiral) B82-20196

Walmsley, J.. Joint ventures in Saudi Arabia / J. Walmsley. — London : Graham & Trotman, 1979. — xiii,170p : 1ill,forms ; 23cm
Includes index
ISBN 0-86010-166-5 : £25.00 B82-14136

338.8'886762 — Kenya. Economic conditions. Effects of multinational companies
Langdon, Steven W.. Multinational corporations in the political economy of Kenya / Steven W. Langdon. — London : Macmillan, 1981. — vii,229p : ill,maps ; 23cm
Bibliography: p214-223. — Includes index
ISBN 0-333-27757-0 : £20.00 B82-06640

338.8'8873 — United States. Multinational companies. Policies. Environmental factors
Gladwin, Thomas N.. Environment, planning and the multinational corporation / by Thomas N. Gladwin ; foreword by Maurice F. Strong. — Greenwich, Conn. : Jai Press ; London : distributed by Jaicon Press, c1977. — xix,295p : ill ; 24cm. — (Contemporary studies in economic and financial analysis ; v.8)
Bibliography: p276-286. — Includes index
ISBN 0-89232-014-1 : £21.10 B82-02017

338.8'8952'041 — Great Britain. Japanese industries & trades
The **Japanese** presence in Britain / [editor Reginald Cudlipp]. — London (342 Grand Buildings, Trafalgar Sq., W.C.2) : Produced for the Japan Information Centre by the Anglo-Japanese Economic Institute, 1981. — 36p : ill,ports ; 24cm
Cover title
Unpriced (pbk) B82-03572

338.9 — ECONOMIC PLANNING

338.9 — Regional economic planning. Applications of input-output analysis
Clay, Pat. Frogs and toads / Pat and Helen Clay. — London : A. & C. Black, 1981. — 25p : col.ill ; 22cm. — (Nature in close-up ; 13)
Includes index
ISBN 0-7136-2152-4 : £3.50 : CIP rev. B81-22529

Mulhearn, Chris. Input-output analysis : a review of some regional aspects / Chris Mulhearn. — London : Department of Town Planning, Polytechnic of the South Bank, c1981. — 33leaves ; 30cm. — (Occasional paper, ISSN 0143-4888 ; OP4/81)
Bibliography: leaves 31-33
ISBN 0-905267-21-4 (spiral) : £2.00 B82-02420

338.9 — Small states. Economic planning. Effects of size — *Conference proceedings*
Problems and policies in small economies / edited by B. Jalan. — London : Croom Helm, c1982. — 275p : ill ; 23cm
Conference papers. — Includes bibliographies and index
ISBN 0-7099-1410-5 : £10.95 : CIP rev. B82-00166

338.9 — State. Economic aspects
Whynes, David K.. The economic theory of the state. — Oxford : Robertson, June 1982. — [252]p
Originally published: 1981
ISBN 0-85520-512-1 (pbk) : £5.95 : CIP entry B82-12165

338.9'009171'7 — Communist countries. Economic planning
Socialist models of development. — Oxford : Pergamon, Apr.1982. — [239]p
ISBN 0-08-027921-x : £17.50 : CIP entry B82-09268

338.91 — Technology transfer, *to 1914*
Kenwood, A. G.. Technological diffusion and industrialisation before 1914 / A.G. Kenwood and A.L. Lougheed. — London : Croom Helm, c1982. — 216p : ill ; 23cm
Originally published: New York : St. Martin's Press, 1982. — Includes bibliographies and index
ISBN 0-7099-1508-x : £13.95 : CIP rev. B81-31427

338.91'09172'4 — Developing countries. Development projects. Financing
Harvey, Charles. Analysis of project finance in developing countries. — London : Heinemann Educational, Feb.1983. — [192]p
ISBN 0-435-84390-7 (cased) : £14.00 : CIP entry
ISBN 0-435-84391-5 (pbk) : £5.95 B82-38303

338.91'09172'4 — Developing countries. Economic development. Financial assistance by commercial banks — *Conference proceedings*
International Finance for Development *(Conference : 1981 : London)*. International Finance for Development : London, 1 & 2 December, 1981 : speakers papers. — [London] : [Financial Times Conference Organisation], [1981]. — 94p ; 30cm. — (Financial Times seminars)
Unpriced (unbound) B82-16957

338.91'09172'4 — Developing countries. Technology transfer from developed countries. Role of industries — *Conference proceedings*
World Congress of Engineers and Architects in Israel *(5th : 1979 : Israel)*. Industrial development and technology transfer. — London : George Godwin, Sept.1981. — [152] p. — (International forum series)
ISBN 0-7114-5729-8 : £12.00 : CIP entry B81-23854

338.91'1722'01724 — Developing countries. Foreign assistance by developed countries
McNeill, Desmond. The contradictions of foreign aid / Desmond McNeill. — London : Croom Helm, c1981. — 114p ; 23cm
Includes index
ISBN 0-7099-1713-9 : £10.95 : CIP rev. B81-21504

338.91'172'4 — Developing countries. Economic development. Financial assistance by developed countries
Development financing. — London : Frances Pinter, Mar.1982. — [210]p
ISBN 0-86187-237-1 : £16.50 : CIP entry B82-06057

338.91'172'401722 — Developing countries. Economic development. Foreign assistance by developed countries. Theories
Dependency theory. — London : Pinter, June 1981. — [220]p
ISBN 0-903804-84-0 : £13.50 : CIP entry B81-10425

338.91'1724'01722 — Developing countries. Technology transfer from developed countries
Emmanuel, Arghiri. Appropriate or underdeveloped technology?. — Chichester : Wiley, Sept.1982. — [190]p. — (Wiley/IRM series on multinationals)
Translation of: Technologie appropriée ou technologie sous-développée?
ISBN 0-471-10467-1 : £11.00 : CIP entry B82-19530

338.91'177 — Developing countries. Economic development. Financial assistance by Organisation of the Petroleum Exporting Countries
Shihata, Ibrahim F. I.. The other face of OPEC : financial assistance to the Third World. — London : Longman, June 1982. — [320]p. — (Energy resources and policies of the Middle East and North Africa)
ISBN 0-582-78336-4 (pbk) : £5.95 : CIP entry B82-11765

338.914 — European Community countries. Industries. Grants from European Community
Bentley, Philip. State and community aids to European industry. — Orpington (6 Stanbrook House, Orchard Grove, Orpington, Kent BR6 0SR) : European Business Publications, Sept.1982. — [180]p. — (European business reports ; no.3)
ISBN 0-907027-06-7 : £23.00 : CIP entry B82-26091

338.91'4 — European Community. Enlargement — *European Democratic Group viewpoints*
From nine to twelve : the enlargement of the Community. — London : Published by Conservative Political Centre on behalf of the European Democratic Group, [1980]. — 52p ; 21cm
Bibliography: p52
ISBN 0-85070-651-3 (pbk) : £1.95 B82-17064

338.91'41 — Economic development. Inequalities. Alleviation. Role of British government. Great Britain. *Parliament. House of Commons. Foreign Affairs Committee.* **Mexico summit** — *Critical studies*
Great Britain. Relations with developing countries : Government reply to the Mexico summit — the British Government's role in the light of the Brandt Commission report, the fifth report from the Foreign Affairs Committee in the session 1980-81. — London : H.M.S.O., [1981]. — 13p ; 25cm. — (Miscellaneous ; no.21 (1981))
ISBN 0-10-183690-2 (unbound) : £1.90 B82-02750

338.91'41'01724 — British colonies. Economic development. Financial assistance by British government, *1924-1971*
Morgan, D. J. (David John). The official history of colonial development / D.J. Morgan. — London : Macmillan, 1980. — 5v. ; 24cm
Includes index
ISBN 0-333-28800-9 : £85.00
ISBN 0-333-26224-7 (v.1) : £20.00
ISBN 0-333-26230-1 (v.2) : £20.00
ISBN 0-333-26232-8 (v.3) : £20.00
ISBN 0-333-26233-6 (v.4) : £20.00
ISBN 0-333-26234-4 (v.5) : £20.00 B82-27094

338.91'41'01724 — Developing countries. Foreign assistance by Great Britain
Aid policy and the work of Overseas Development Administration : a briefing paper / produced by Information Dept. Overseas Development Administration. — London (Eland House, Stag Pl., S.W.1) : [Overseas Development Administration], [1982?]. — [12]p ; 21cm
Unpriced (pbk) B82-37681

338.91'41'01724 — Economic development. Financial assistance by Commonwealth Development Corporation. Projects
Partners in development : finance plus management / Commonwealth Development Corporation. — London (33 Hill St., W1A 3AR) : The Corporation, 1981. — 25p : col.ill ; 26cm
Cover title
Unpriced (pbk) B82-16792

338.91'41'06891 — Zimbabwe. Economic development. Foreign assistance by Great Britain. Great Britain. *Parliament. House of Commons. Foreign Affairs Committee.* **Sixth report ... session 1980-81** — *Critical studies*
Great Britain. *Parliament. House of Commons. Foreign Affairs Committee.* Sixth report from the Foreign Affairs Committee of the House of Commons, session 1980-81 : Zimbabwe : the role of British aid in the economic development of Zimbabwe : observations by the Government. — London : H.M.S.O., 1981. — 11p ; 25cm. — (Cmnd. ; 8438)
ISBN 0-10-184380-1 (unbound) : £1.50 B82-11385

338.91'41'06891 — Zimbabwe. Economic development. Foreign assistance by Great Britain — *Inquiry reports*
Great Britain. *Parliament. House of Commons. Foreign Affairs Committee.* Sixth report from the Foreign Affairs Committee, session 1980-81 : Zimbabwe : the role of British aid in the economic development of Zimbabwe : together with part of the proceedings of the committee relating to the report ; and the minutes of evidence taken before the Overseas Development Sub-Committee on 27 January, 3 March, 14 April and 5 May 1981, with appendices. — London : H.M.S.O., [1981]. — lv,220p : 1map ; 25cm. — ([HC] ; 117)
ISBN 0-10-211781-0 (pbk) : £9.05 B82-05635

338.91'494'01724 — Developing countries. Economic development. Financial assistance by Switzerland. Political aspects — *German texts*
Schrötter, Dieter, *Freiherr von*. Schweizerische Entwicklungspolitik in der direkten Demokratie / Dieter Freiherr von Schrötter. — München ; London : Weltforum, c1981. — viii,284p : ill,1map,facsims ; 22cm. — (Materialien zu Entwicklung und Politik ; 20)
At head of title: Arnold-Bergstraesser-Institut. — Bibliography: p238-259
ISBN 3-8039-0192-8 : Unpriced B82-10528

338.91′54 — India *(Republic).* **Exports: Technology**

Lall, Sanjaya. Developing countries as exporters of technology : a first look at the Indian experience / Sanjaya Lall. — London : Macmillan, 1982. — viii,134p ; 23cm
Bibliography: p126-130. — Includes index
ISBN 0-333-28844-0 : £15.00 B82-38809

338.91′73′051 — China. Foreign assistance by United States, *1949-1950 — Inquiry reports*

Economic assistance to China and Korea 1949-50 / with an introduction by Richard D. Challener. — New York ; London : Garland, 1979. — xi,v,289p,[2]p of plates : ill,map ; 24cm. — (The Legislative origins of American foreign policy) (The Senate Foreign Relations Committee historical series)
Originally published: Washington : U.S. Govt. Printing Office, 1974
ISBN 0-8240-3036-2 : Unpriced
Also classified at 338.91′73′0519 B82-19606

338.91′73′0519 — Korea. Foreign assistance by United States, *1949-1950 — Inquiry reports*

Economic assistance to China and Korea 1949-50 / with an introduction by Richard D. Challener. — New York ; London : Garland, 1979. — xi,v,289p,[2]p of plates : ill,map ; 24cm. — (The Legislative origins of American foreign policy) (The Senate Foreign Relations Committee historical series)
Originally published: Washington : U.S. Govt. Printing Office, 1974
ISBN 0-8240-3036-2 : Unpriced
Primary classification 338.91′73′051
B82-19606

338.9′36133212′0941 — Great Britain. Commercial banks: Royal Bank of Scotland Group. Mergers with Hongkong and Shanghai Banking Corporation *— Inquiry reports*

Great Britain. *Monopolies and Mergers Commission*. The Hongkong and Shanghai Banking Corporation, Standard Chartered Bank Limited, The Royal Bank of Scotland Group Limited : a report on the proposed mergers / the Monopolies and Mergers Commission. — London : H.M.S.O., [1982]. — v,104p ; 25cm. — (Cmnd. ; 8472)
ISBN 0-10-184720-3 (pbk) : £5.45
Also classified at 338.8′36133212′0941
B82-15214

338.94 — European Community countries. Industrial development agencies *— Comparative studies*

Regional development agencies in Europe. — Aldershot : Gower, Nov.1982. — [460]p
ISBN 0-566-00589-1 : £17.50 : CIP entry
B82-26550

338.94 — European Community countries. Industries. Policies. Effects on European integration

Franzmeyer, Fritz. Approaches to industrial policy within the EC and its impact on European integration. — Aldershot : Gower, Aug.1982. — [200]p
Translation and revision of: Industrielle Strukturprobleme und sektorale Strukturpolitik in der Europaischen Gemeinschaft
ISBN 0-566-00358-9 : £12.50 : CIP entry
B82-16643

338.94 — European Community countries. Industries. Policies of governments

Price, Victoria Curzon. Industrial policies in the European Community / Victoria Curzon Price. — London : Macmillan for the Trade Policy Research Centre, 1981. — xvi,141p ; 23cm. — (World economic issues)
Bibliography: p132-135. — Includes index
ISBN 0-333-31911-7 : £15.00 B82-10812

338.941 — Great Britain. Economic planning, *1905-1915*

French, David. British economic and strategic planning 1905-1915 / David French. — London : Allen & Unwin, 1982. — x,191p ; 23cm
Bibliography: p180-187. — Includes index
ISBN 0-04-942174-3 : Unpriced : CIP rev.
B81-35942

338.941 — Great Britain. Enterprise zones

Enterprise zones in the UK : views on potential : April 1981. — [Preston] ([Vernon St., Moor Lane, Preston PR1 3PQ]) : Building Design Partnership, [1982?]. — 38leaves : maps(some col.) ; 30cm. — (BDP research report)
Unpriced (spiral) B82-25611

Rodrigues, David. Zoning in on enterprise : A businessman′s guide to the enterprise zones. — London : Kogan Page, Jan.1982. — [120]p
ISBN 0-85038-530-x (pbk) : £10.00 : CIP entry
B82-00148

338.941 — Great Britain. Government. Relations with industries

Coombes, David. Representative government and economic power / David Coombes. — London : Heinemann, 1982. — 208p ; 22cm
At head of title: Policy Studies Institute. — Bibliography: p193-201. — Includes index
ISBN 0-435-83180-1 (cased) : £15.00 : CIP rev.
ISBN 0-435-83181-x (pbk) : £6.95 B82-01959

338.941 — Great Britain. Industries. Planning — *Conference proceedings*

Planning for industry : papers from a conference held at Cambridge September 1979 / organised by the Bar Council, the Law Society and the Royal Institution of Chartered Surveyors. — London : Sweet & Maxwell, 1980. — v,78p ; 25cm. — (Journal of planning and environment law occasional papers)
ISBN 0-421-27140-x (pbk) : £10.00 : CIP rev.
B80-10519

338.941 — Great Britain. Industries. Policies of government

Allies or adversaries? : perspectives on government and industry in Britain. — London : Royal Institute of Public Administration, 1981. — 86p ; 21cm
ISBN 0-900628-24-3 (pbk) : £4.95 B82-08051

338.941 — Great Britain. Industries. Policies of government, *1945-1980*

Peacock, Alan, *1922-*. Structural economic policies in West Germany and the United Kingdom / by Alan Peacock in collaboration with Rob Grant ... [et al.]. — London : Anglo-German Foundation for the Study of Industrial Society, c1980. — iv,128p : ill ; 31cm
Includes bibliographies
ISBN 0-905492-26-9 : £15.00
Also classified at 338.943 B82-01287

338.941 — Great Britain. Industries. Policies of government, *1972-1979*

Grant, Wyn. The political economy of industrial policy / Wyn Grant. — London : Butterworths, 1982. — xii,160p ; 24cm
Bibliography: p149-151. — Includes index
ISBN 0-408-10765-0 : Unpriced : CIP rev.
B81-33877

338.941 — Great Britain. Industries. Policies of government, *1974-1979*

Coates, David. Capital and state in Britain : the industrial policy of the Labour Government 1974-1979 / by David Coates. — [Hull] : University of Hull, Department of Politics, 1981. — 28p ; 30cm. — (Hull papers in politics, ISSN 0142-7377 ; no.24)
Unpriced (pbk) B82-11379

338.941 — Great Britain. Nationalised industries. Finance. Great Britain. *Parliament. House of Commons. Treasury and Civil Service Committee.* **Eighth report ... session 1980-81** *— Critical studies*

Great Britain. *Treasury*. Second special report from the Treasury and Civil Service Committee, session 1980-81 : financing of the nationalised industries : observations by HM Treasury on the eighth report from the committee in session 1980-81, HC 348. — London : H.M.S.O., [1981]. — vip ; 25cm. — ([HC] ; 496)
ISBN 0-10-249681-1 (unbound) : £1.15
B82-11542

338.941′02 — Great Britain. Industries. Financial assistance by government

Financial assistance for industry and commerce in the United Kingdom / prepared by Peat, Marwick, Mitchell & Co.. — Rev. ed. — London : Peat, Marwick, Mitchell & Co., c1981. — 96p : col.maps ; 21cm
Previous ed.: 1977
Unpriced (pbk) B82-01380

Grant, R. M.. Appraising selective financial assistance to industry : a review of experiences in the United Kingdom, Sweden and West Germany / by R.M. Grant. — London ([Basinghall St, EC2V 5AH]) : Gresham College, c1982. — 36p ; 30cm. — (Working paper / City University. Business School, ISSN 0140-1041 ; no.39)
Unpriced (pbk)
Also classified at 338.9485′02 ; 338.943′02
B82-32207

338.941′02 — Great Britain. Nationalised industries. Financial assistance by private enterprise *— Inquiry reports*

Great Britain. *Parliament. House of Commons. Committee of Public Accounts*. Thirty-second report from the Committee of Public Accounts : together with the proceedings of the committee, the minutes of evidence and appendices : session 1979-80 : H.M. Treasury, Department of Industry, Department of Energy, private finance for nationalised industries and publicly owned companies, H.M. Treasury, supplementary estimates, Property Services Agency, disposal of the Effra site, Vauxhall. — London : H.M.S.O., [1980]. — xix,26p ; 25cm. — ([HC] ; 781)
ISBN 0-10-027819-1 (pbk) : £3.10
Also classified at 333.33′7 B82-09508

338.941′02 — Great Britain. Regional economic development. Financial incentives of government *— For businessmen*

Incentives for industry in the areas for expansion : special development areas, development areas, intermediate areas, Northern Ireland. — [London] : Department of Industry, 1981. — 61p : 2col.maps ; 21cm
Unpriced (pbk) B82-38371

338.9411 — Scotland. Industrial development. Planning *— Proposals*

Industrial change in Scotland : an agenda for progress. — Edinburgh (23 Chester St., Edinburgh, EH3 7ET) : Scottish Council, Development and Industry, 1981. — 36p ; 30cm
Unpriced (spiral) B82-41128

338.9411 — Scotland. Nationalised industries. Influence of Great Britain. *Scottish Office*

Laing, James F.. The Scottish Office and nationalised industries / by James F. Laing. — London : Acton Society Trust, [1982]. — 16p ; 21cm. — (Acton Society Trust occasional papers ; 1)
Cover title. — At head of title: Nationalised Industries Project
ISBN 0-85000-018-1 (pbk) : £1.00 B82-37965

338.9411′02 — Scotland. Economic development. Financial assistance. Sources

Financial resources for economic development : Scotland. — Glasgow : Planning Exchange, c1980. — 1v.(loose-leaf) ; 27cm
Includes index
ISBN 0-905011-17-1 : Unpriced B82-17515

338.9411′502 — Scotland. Highland Region. Industrial development. Financial assistance. Sources

Regional assistance guide. — [Inverness] : [Highland Regional Council], [1981?]. — 29p ; 30cm
Cover title
Unpriced (spiral) B82-07348

338.9429'4 — South Wales. Industrial development. Planning

Cooke, P. N.. The industrial restructuring of South Wales : the career of a state managed region / by P.N. Cooke and Gareth Rees. — Cardiff (King Edward VII Av, Cardiff, CF1 3NU, Wales) : Dept. of Town Planning, University of Wales, Institute of Science and Technology, 1981. — iiileaves,21p ; 30cm. — (Papers in planning research ; 25)
Bibliography: p17-19
Unpriced (pbk) B82-25635

338.943 — West Germany. Industries. Policies of government, *1945-1980*

Peacock, Alan, *1922-*. Structural economic policies in West Germany and the United Kingdom / by Alan Peacock in collaboration with Rob Grant ... [et al.]. — London : Anglo-German Foundation for the Study of Industrial Society, c1980. — iv,128p : ill ; 31cm
Includes bibliographies
ISBN 0-905492-26-9 : £15.00
Primary classification 338.941 B82-01287

338.943'02 — West Germany. Industries. Financial assistance by government

Grant, R. M.. Appraising selective financial assistance to industry : a review of experiences in the United Kingdom, Sweden and West Germany / by R.M. Grant. — London ([Basinghall St, EC2V 5AH]) : Gresham College, c1982. — 36p ; 30cm. — (Working paper / City University. Business School, ISSN 0140-1041 ; no.39)
Unpriced (pbk)
Primary classification 338.941'02 B82-32207

338.944 — France. Economic planning, *ca 1960-1982*

Estrin, Saul. French planning in theory and practice. — London : Allen & Unwin, Nov.1982. — [224]p
ISBN 0-04-339028-5 : £14.95 : CIP entry B82-26208

338.947 — Soviet Union. Economic development. Policies of Kommunisticheskaîa partiîa Sovetskogo Soîuza

Tikhonov, N. A.. Guidelines for the economic and social development of the USSR for 1981-1985 and for the period ending in 1990 : report by Comrade N.A. Tikhonov, chairman of the Council of Ministers of the USSR, to the 26th Congress of the Communist Party of the Soviet Union : February 27, 1981. — Moscow : Novosti ; [London] : Distributed by Central, 1981. — 61p ; 20cm
Translation of: Osnovnye napravleniîa ėkonomicheskogo i sotsial'nogo razvitiîa SSSR na 1981-1985 gody i na period do 1990 goda
ISBN 0-7147-1647-2 (pbk) : £0.30 B82-29279

338.9485'02 — Sweden. Industries. Financial assistance by government

Grant, R. M.. Appraising selective financial assistance to industry : a review of experiences in the United Kingdom, Sweden and West Germany / by R.M. Grant. — London ([Basinghall St, EC2V 5AH]) : Gresham College, c1982. — 36p ; 30cm. — (Working paper / City University. Business School, ISSN 0140-1041 ; no.39)
Unpriced (pbk)
Primary classification 338.941'02 B82-32207

338.9492 — Regional economic planning. Applications of imput-output analysis — *Study regions: Netherlands*

Oosterhaven, Jan. Interregional input-output analysis and Dutch regional policy problems / Jan Oosterhaven. — Aldershot : Gower, c1981. — xiii,209p : ill,1map ; 23cm
Bibliography: p181-189. — Includes index
ISBN 0-566-00521-2 : Unpriced : CIP rev. B81-34283

338.953'8 — Saudi Arabia. Economic planning

Looney, Robert E.. Saudi Arabia's development potential : application of an Islamic growth model / Robert E. Looney. — Lexington, Mass. : Lexington ; [Aldershot] : Gower [distributor], c1982. — xvii,358p ; 24cm
Bibliography: p339-351. — Includes index
ISBN 0-669-03083-x : £25.00 B82-31789

338.972 — Mexico. Industrial development. Planning

Mexico : National Industrial Development Plan. — London : Graham & Trotman, 1979. — 2 : v.,ill,maps ; 30cm
Translated from the Spanish
ISBN 0-86010-182-9 (pbk) : £30.00
ISBN 0-86010-187-8 (v.2) : Unpriced B82-38971

338.973 — United States. Government. Relations with business firms

Dominguez, George S.. Government relations : a handbook for developing and conducting the company program / George S. Dominguez. — New York ; Chichester : Wiley, c1982. — xv,420p : ill,facsims ; 25cm
Bibliography: p417. — Includes index
ISBN 0-471-06421-1 : £25.75 B82-27722

338.973 — United States. Industries. Policies of government. Effects of regional economic planning

Regional dimensions of industrial policy / edited by Michael E. Bell, Paul S. Lande. — Lexington, Mass. : Lexington Books ; [Aldershot] : Gower [distributor], 1982. — ix,204p : ill,1map ; 24cm
Includes bibliographies and index
ISBN 0-669-04491-1 : £17.00 B82-32407

338.973 — United States. Industries. Regulation

Instead of regulation : alternatives to Federal regulatory agencies / edited by Robert W. Poole, Jr.. — Lexington, Mass. : Lexington Books : [Aldershot], Gower [distributor], 1982. — xi,404p : ill ; 24cm
Includes index
ISBN 0-669-04585-3 : £18.50 B82-24918

338.973 — United States. Industries. Regulation by government

Breyer, Stephen. Regulation and its reform / Stephen Breyer. — Cambridge, Mass. ; London : Harvard University Press, 1982. — xii,472p : ill ; 25cm
Bibliography: p382-385. — Includes index
ISBN 0-674-75375-5 : Unpriced B82-27087

The **Limits** of government regulation / edited by James F. Gatti ; with a foreword by Malcolm F. Severance. — New York ; London : Academic Press, 1981. — xxi,186p : ill ; 24cm
ISBN 0-12-277620-8 (cased) : £16.20
ISBN 0-12-277622-4 (pbk) : Unpriced B82-10145

338.973 — United States. Industries. Regulation — *Conference proceedings*

Studies in public regulation / edited by Gary Fromm. — Cambridge, Mass. ; London : MIT Press, c1981. — 393p : ill ; 24cm. — (MIT Press series on the regulation of economic activity ; 4)
Conference papers. — Includes bibliographies and index
ISBN 0-262-06074-4 : £31.50 B82-09579

338.995'3 — Papua New Guinea. Economic planning, *1974-1980.* **Financial aspects**

Allan, Bill. Planning, policy analysis and public spending : theory and the Papua New Guinea practice / Bill Allan and Keith Hinchliffe. — Aldershot : Gower, c1982. — viii,159p : ill ; 23cm
Bibliography: p151-155. — Includes index
ISBN 0-566-00496-8 : Unpriced : CIP rev. B81-36218

339 — MACROECONOMICS, CONSUMPTION, ETC

339 — Macroeconomics

Chick, Victoria. Macroeconomics after Keynes. — Deddington : Philip Allan, Oct.1982. — [384]p
ISBN 0-86003-021-0 (cased) : £20.00 : CIP entry
ISBN 0-86003-122-5 (pbk) : £9.95 B82-29409

Demand management, supply constraints and inflation / edited by M.J. Artis ... [et al.]. — Manchester : Manchester University Press, c1982. — x,294p : ill ; 22cm
Bibliography: p275-286. — Includes index
ISBN 0-7190-0846-8 (cased) : Unpriced : CIP rev.
ISBN 0-7190-0881-6 (pbk) : £6.50 B81-30956

Essays in fiscal and monetary policy. — Oxford : Oxford University Press, Sept.1981. — [256]p
ISBN 0-19-829001-2 : £15.00 : CIP entry B81-21634

Gapinski, James H.. Macroeconomic theory : statics, dynamics and policy / James H. Gapinski. — New York ; London : McGraw-Hill, c1982. — xi,432p : ill ; 25cm. — (Economics handbook series)
Includes index
ISBN 0-07-022765-9 : £18.25 B82-29497

Hadjimichalakis, Michael G.. Modern macro-economics : an intermediate text / Michael G. Hadjimichalakis. — Englewood Cliffs ; London : Prentice-Hall, c1982. — xvi,670p : ill ; 25cm
Includes bibliographies and index
ISBN 0-13-595074-0 : £15.45 B82-16721

Johnson, Karen, *1945-*. Instructor's manual for Wallace Peterson, Income, employment and economic growth, Fourth edition / by Karen Johnson. — New York ; London : Norton, [1982]. — 252p : ill ; 26cm
ISBN 0-393-95038-7 (pbk) : £2.25 B82-37047

Kornai, János. Growth, shortage and efficiency. — Oxford : Blackwell, Oct.1981. — [128]p. — (Yrjö Jahnsson lectures)
ISBN 0-631-12787-9 : £7.95 : CIP entry B81-28068

Leake, Andrew. Macroeconomics. — London : Macmillan, July 1981. — [48]p
ISBN 0-333-27991-3 (pbk) : £1.25 : CIP entry B81-16351

Miller, Roger LeRoy. Economics today : the macro view / Roger LeRoy Miller. — New York ; London : Harper & Row, c1982. — xv,492p : ill ; 28cm
Previous ed.: 1979. — Includes index
ISBN 0-06-044492-4 (pbk) : Unpriced B82-19417

Nagatani, Keizo. Macroeconomic dynamics / Keizo Nagatani. — Cambridge : Cambridge University Press, 1981. — x,245p : ill ; 24cm
Bibliography: p237-242. — Includes index
ISBN 0-521-23515-4 (cased) : £20.00
ISBN 0-521-28015-x (pbk) : £7.95 B82-21363

Sawyer, Malcolm C.. Macro-economics in question : the Keynesian-monetarist orthodoxies and the Kaleckian alternative / Malcolm C. Sawyer. — Brighton : Wheatsheaf, 1982. — xiii,190p : ill ; 23cm
Bibliography: p175-187. — Includes index
ISBN 0-7108-0140-8 (cased) : £18.95 : CIP rev.
ISBN 0-7108-0172-6 (pbk) : Unpriced B82-06519

Vane, Howard R.. An introduction to macroeconomic policy / Howard R. Vane and John L. Thompson. — Brighton : Wheatsheaf, 1982. — x,317p : ill ; 23cm
Bibliography: p312-314. — Includes index
ISBN 0-7108-0130-0 (cased) : £20.00 : CIP rev.
ISBN 0-7108-0135-1 (pbk) : Unpriced B82-02660

Wonnacott, Paul. [Economics. Selections]. An introduction to macroeconomics / Paul Wonnacott, Ronald Wonnacott. — 2nd ed. — New York ; London : McGraw-Hill, c1982. — xxii,448p : ill(some col.),col.maps,ports ; 24cm
Previous ed.: 1979. — Includes index. — Selection of chapters from Economics. 2nd ed. 1982
ISBN 0-07-071582-3 (pbk) : £11.50 B82-27572

339′.072041 — Macroeconomics. Research projects supported by Great Britain. *Social Science Research Council*

Macro-economic research in the United Kingdom : the report of a Social Science Research Council sub-committee. — London : SSRC, c1981. — 44p ; 30cm
ISBN 0-86226-027-2 (pbk) : £2.00 B82-05704

339′.0724 — Macroeconomics. Econometric models

Large-scale macro-econometric models : theory and practice / edited by J. Kmenta and J.B. Ramsey. — Amsterdam ; Oxford : Excerpta Medica, 1981. — xiii,462p : ill ; 23cm. — (Contributions to economic analysis ; v.141)
Includes bibliographies
ISBN 0-444-86295-1 : £21.54 B82-08568

339′.0724 — Macroeconomics. Econometric models. Assessment — *Conference proceedings*

Evaluating the reliability of macro-economic models. — Chichester : Wiley, Sept.1982. — [350]p
Conference proceedings
ISBN 0-471-10150-8 : £18.00 : CIP entry B82-19523

339′.0724 — Macroeconomics. Mathematical models

Dadaîan, V. S.. Macroeconomic models / V.S. Dadayan ; [translated from the Russian by Paul Medow]. — Moscow : Progress, 1981 ; [London] : Distributed by Central Books. — 207p : ill ; 25cm
Translation of: Makroėkonomicheskie modeli
ISBN 0-7147-1757-6 : £5.95 B82-39314

339′.07′7 — Macroeconomics — *Programmed instructions*

Attiyeh, Richard. Macroeconomics : a programmed book / Richard Attiyeh, Keith Lumsden, George Leland Bach. — 6th ed. — Englewood Cliffs ; London : Prentice-Hall, c1982. — iii,235p : ill ; 23cm
Previous ed.: 1974
ISBN 0-13-542704-5 (pbk) : £8.20 B82-16994

339′.09182′1 — Western world. Macroeconomic policies

Perkins, J. O. N.. Unemployment, inflation and new macroeconomic policy / J.O.N. Perkins. — London : Macmillan, 1982. — xi,136p ; 23cm
Bibliography: p132-133. — Includes index
ISBN 0-333-32115-4 (cased) : £15.00
ISBN 0-333-32116-2 (pbk) : Unpriced B82-38779

339′.0941 — Great Britain. Macroeconomic policies

Peston, M. H.. The British economy : an elementary macroeconomic perspective / M.H. Peston. — Oxford : Philip Allan, 1982. — 172p : ill ; 23cm
Includes index
ISBN 0-86003-115-2 (cased) : £8.00 : CIP rev.
ISBN 0-86003-014-8 (pbk) : Unpriced B82-17911

Sayer, Stuart. An introduction to macroeconomic policy / Stuart Sayer. — London : Butterworth Scientific, 1982. — x,274p : ill ; 22cm
Bibliography: p259-263. — Includes index
ISBN 0-408-10779-0 (pbk) : Unpriced : CIP rev. B82-14083

339.2′0724 — Income. Distribution. Econometric models

Pasinetti, Luigi L.. Growth and income distribution : essays in economic theory / Luigi L. Pasinetti. — Cambridge : Cambridge University Press, 1974 (1979 [printing]). — x,151p : ill ; 22cm
Includes index
ISBN 0-521-20474-7 (pbk) : £3.95
Also classified at 339.5′0724 B82-26840

339.2′09172′4 — Developing countries. Income. Distribution

Bigsten, Arne. Income distribution and development. — London : Heinemann Educational, Jan.1983. — [208]p
ISBN 0-435-84086-x (cased) : £14.50 : CIP entry
ISBN 0-435-84087-8 (pbk) : £5.95 B82-36134

339.2′09172′4 — Developing countries. Income. Distribution. Equalisation. Economic aspects

Griffin, Keith. The transition to egalitarian development : economic policies for structural change in the Third World / Keith Griffin and Jeffrey James. — London : Macmillan, 1981. — ix,128p ; 23cm
Includes index
ISBN 0-333-30989-8 : £15.00 B82-06653

339.2′094 — European Community countries. Income. Distribution. Inequalities

Saunders, Christopher, *1907-*. Pay inequalities in the European Community / Christopher Saunders, David Marsden. — London : Butterworths in association with the Sussex European Research Centre, University of Sussex, 1981. — xiv,369p : ill ; 25cm
Includes index
ISBN 0-408-10727-8 : Unpriced : CIP rev. B81-23906

339.2′0941 — Great Britain. Wealth. Distribution — *Labour Research Department viewpoints*

Unfair shares : rich and poor in Britain today. — London : LRD, 1981. — 35p : ill ; 21cm
ISBN 0-900508-45-0 (pbk) : £0.65 B82-06888

339.2′0973 — United States. Wealth. Distribution. Attitudes of society

Hochschild, Jennifer L.. What's fair? : American beliefs about distributive justice / Jennifer L. Hochschild. — Cambridge, Mass. ; London : Harvard University Press, 1981. — 345p : ill ; 24cm
Includes index
ISBN 0-674-95086-0 : £15.75 B82-17779

339.2′2 — Great Britain. Families. Income, *1950-1981*

Piachaud, David. Family incomes since the war / David Piachaud. — London : Study Commission on the Family, c1982. — 20p ; 21cm. — (Occasional paper / Study Commission on the Family ; no.9)
ISBN 0-907051-16-2 (pbk) : £1.50 B82-40978

339.2′3′091724 — Developing countries. Economic conditions. Input-output analysis

Bulmer-Thomas, V.. Input-output analysis in developing countries. — Chichester : Wiley, Oct.1982. — [304]p
ISBN 0-471-10149-4 : £15.00 : CIP entry B82-24725

339.2′3′0947 — Soviet Union. Economic conditions. Input-output analysis

Soviet economy. — London : Allen and Unwin, Feb.1983. — [496]p
ISBN 0-04-335045-3 : £27.50 : CIP entry B82-36444

339.3′01 — Macroeconomics. Theories

Parkin, Michael. Modern macroeconomics : Michael Parkin & Robin Bade. — Deddington : Philip Allan, 1982. — xxi,597p : ill ; 26cm
Includes index
ISBN 0-86003-047-4 (cased) : £20.00 : CIP rev.
ISBN 0-86003-142-x (pbk) : £9.95 B82-14952

Peston, M. H.. Theory of macroeconomic policy / M.H. Peston. — 2nd ed. — Oxford : Philip Allan, 1982. — 279p : ill ; 23cm
Previous ed.: 1974. — Bibliography: p273-277. — Includes index
ISBN 0-86003-038-5 (cased) : £18.00 : CIP rev.
ISBN 0-86003-136-5 (pbk) : £8.95 B82-12830

339.3′01 — Macroeconomics. Theories. Role of econometric models of rational economic expectations

Begg, David K. H.. The rational expectations revolution in macroeconomics : theories and evidence / David K.H. Begg. — Oxford : Philip Allan, 1982. — xii,291p : ill ; 22cm
Bibliography: p266-284. — Includes index
ISBN 0-86003-044-x (cased) : £16.00 : CIP rev.
ISBN 0-86003-130-6 (pbk) : £7.95 B81-39246

339.3′01′51955 — Macroeconomics. Time series. Analysis. Econometric models

Mills, T. C.. Unobserved components, signal extraction and relationships between macroeconomic time series / by T.C. Mills. — London : Economics Division, Bank of England, c1981. — 31p : ill ; 30cm. — (Discussion paper / Bank of England, ISSN 0142-6753 ; no.19)
Bibliography: p30-31
ISBN 0-903312-44-1 (pbk) : Unpriced B82-12516

339.3′09′043 — Macroeconomics. Theories, *1927-1937*

Hansson, Björn A.. The Stockholm school and the development of dynamic method / Björn A. Hansson. — London : Croom Helm, c1982. — 286p ; 23cm
Bibliography: p257-269. — Includes index
ISBN 0-7099-1225-0 : £13.95 : CIP rev. B81-31103

339.3′1 — Gross national product — *Comparative studies*

Kravis, Irving B.. World product and income : international comparisons of real gross product / produced by the Statistical Office of the United Nations and the World Bank ; Irving B. Kravis, Alan Heston, Robert Summers in collaboration with Alicia R. Civitello ... [et al.]. — Baltimore ; London : Published for the World Bank [by] Johns Hopkins University Press, c1982. — x,388p : ill ; 29cm. — (United Nations International Comparison Project ; phase 3)
Statistics also available on computer tape. — Bibliography: p375-379. — Includes index
ISBN 0-8018-2359-5 (cased) : Unpriced
ISBN 0-8018-2360-9 (pbk) : Unpriced B82-34350

339.4′1 — Cost-benefit analysis

Mishan, E. J.. Cost benefit analysis. — 3rd ed. — London : Allen and Unwin, Aug.1982. — [384]p
Previous ed.: 1975
ISBN 0-04-338099-9 : £7.95 : CIP entry B82-15632

339.4′2′024658 — Cost of living — *Statistics* — *For British businessmen*

Financial Times business travel costs. — London : Financial Times Publishing, 1981. — xvi,207p ; 30cm
ISBN 0-902101-02-1 (pbk) : Unpriced B82-05120

339.4′2′0880816 — Great Britain. Handicapped persons. Cost of living

Durward, Lyn. That's the way the money goes : the extra cost of living with disability / Lyn Durward. — London (1 Cambridge Terrace, NW1 4JL) : Disability Alliance, 1981. — 52p : ill ; 21cm
£0.90 (pbk) B82-02841

339.4′7 — Consumer behaviour. Economic aspects — *Festschriften*

Essays in the theory and measurement of consumer behaviour : in honour of Sir Richard Stone / edited by Angus Deaton. — Cambridge : Cambridge University Press, 1981. — viii,344p : ill ; 24cm
Bibliography: p325-337. — Includes index
ISBN 0-521-22565-5 : £25.00 : CIP rev. B81-19168

339.4′7 — Consumer behaviour. Effects of economic growth, *1800-1980* — *Conference proceedings*

Consumer behaviour and economic growth in the modern economy / edited by Henri Baudet and Henk van der Meulen. — London : Croom Helm, c1982. — 283p : ill ; 23cm
Conference proceedings
ISBN 0-7099-0646-3 : £14.95 : CIP rev. B82-06515

339.4′7 — South-east Hampshire. Consumers. Expenditure, *1980-1981*

Hallsworth, A. G.. Patterns of change in consumer expenditure in south-east Hampshire 1980-81 / A.G. Hallsworth. — Portsmouth ([Buckingham Building, Lion Terrace, Portsmouth, Hants. PO1 3HE]) : Portsmouth Polytechnic, Department of Geography, 1982. — i,77leaves : 1form,1map,1plan ; 30cm
Unpriced (spiral) B82-31105

339.4′7′07 — Supply & demand. Information sources — *Lists* — *For marketing*

Blauvelt, Euan. World sources of market information. — Aldershot : Gower, May 1982
Vol.2: Africa/Middle East. — [300]p
ISBN 0-566-02180-3 : £35.00 : CIP entry
B82-06854

World sources of market information. — Farnborough, Hants. : Gower, Apr.1981
Vol.1: Asia/Pacific. — [300]p
ISBN 0-566-02179-x : £35.00 : CIP entry
B81-03157

World sources of market information. — Aldershot : Gower
Vol.3. — Sept.1982. — [600]p
ISBN 0-566-02355-5 : £30.00 : CIP entry
B82-19546

339.4′7′0724 — Consumer goods. Consumption. Econometric models

Theil, Henri. International consumption comparisons : a system-wide approach / by Henri Theil and Frederick E. Suhm ; with an appendix by James F. Meisner. — Amsterdam ; Oxford : North-Holland, 1981. — xv,200p ; 22cm. — (Studies in mathematical and managerial economics ; 30)
Bibliography: p194-197. — Includes index
ISBN 0-444-86312-5 : £27.60 B82-15174

339.4′7′0941 — Great Britain. Consumer goods. Consumption, *1850-1914*

Fraser, W. Hamish. The coming of the mass market 1850-1914 / Wittamish Fraser. — London : Macmillan, 1981. — x,268p,16p of plates : ill,1facsim ; 23cm
Bibliography: p259-260. — Includes index
ISBN 0-333-31033-0 (cased) : Unpriced
ISBN 0-333-31034-9 (pbk) : Unpriced
Also classified at 381′.1′0941 B82-14866

339.4′7′0944 — France. Consumer behaviour, *1860-ca 1900* — *Sociological perspectives*

Williams, Rosalind H.. Dream worlds : mass consumption in late nineteenth-century France / Rosalind H. Williams. — Berkeley ; London : University of California Press, c1982. — xii,451p,[24]p of plates : ill,1port ; 24cm
Bibliography: p427-429. — Includes index
ISBN 0-520-04355-3 : £22.25 B82-34357

339.4′80015543 — Great Britain. Sound tape recordings. Supply & demand

A Study of the United Kingdom market for blank and pre-recorded audio cassettes, cartridges and tapes. — London : Economist Intelligence Unit, c1978. — 212p ; 30cm. — (An E.I.U. multi-client project)
Private circulation (spiral)
Primary classification 339.4′8621389324
B82-08218

339.4′8002′0941 — Great Britain. Booksellers. Stock: Books. Supply & demand

Lost book sales : a nationwide survey of book buyers and their bookshop purchases. — [London] : Book Marketing Council of the Publishers Association, 1980. — 51leaves in various foliations : 7forms ; 30cm
ISBN 0-901690-68-6 (spiral) : £10.00 (£5.00 to members of the Booksellers Association or Publishers Association)
ISBN 0-85386-068-8 (Publishers Association)
B82-34311

339.4′83635′0724 — Housing. Supply & demand. Econometric models

Modelling housing market search / edited by W.A.V. Clark. — London : Croom Helm, c1982. — 244p : ill,1map ; 23cm. — (Croom Helm series in geography and environment)
Includes bibliographies and index
ISBN 0-7099-0726-5 : £13.95 : CIP rev.
B82-09178

339.4′83635′09426752 — Essex. Chelmsford. Housing. Demand — *For environment planning*

Population and housing topic report : Chelmsford town centre district plan. — Chelmsford : Chelmsford Borough Council, 1980. — 53p,4folded leaves of plates : ill,maps ; 30cm
Unpriced (pbk) B82-08727

339.4′86213825 — Teletex systems. Demand — *Forecasts*

The **Future** of text communications : the impact of teletex. — Luton : Mackintosh Publications, 1980. — viii,88p : ill ; 30cm. — (A Mackintosh monitor report)
ISBN 0-904705-23-4 (pbk) : £195.00
B82-32250

339.4′8621389324 — Great Britain. Sound magnetic tapes. Supply & demand

A Study of the United Kingdom market for blank and pre-recorded audio cassettes, cartridges and tapes. — London : Economist Intelligence Unit, c1978. — 212p ; 30cm. — (An E.I.U. multi-client project)
Private circulation (spiral)
Also classified at 339.4′80015543 B82-08218

339.4′862138933 — Western Europe. Record players. Demand — *Forecasts*

European audio equipment and media markets : (disc based audio equipment). — Luton : Mackintosh Publications, 1980. — xii,192p : ill ; 30cm. — (A Mackintosh monitor report)
ISBN 0-904705-31-5 (pbk) : £200.00
B82-36226

339.4′86214025 — Great Britain. Heat pumps. Supply & demand — *Forecasts*

Heat pumps in the UK : an illustrated overview of heat-pump prospects and developments in the UK / W.M. Currie ... [et al.]. — Didcot : Energy Technology Support Unit, [1981]. — 26p : ill ; 30cm. — (ETSU note ; N-2/81)
Unpriced (spiral) B82-10969

339.4′86292272′0941 — Great Britain. Retail bicycle trades. Supply. Policies of TI Raleigh Industries & TI Raleigh — *Inquiry reports*

Great Britain. *Monopolies and Mergers Commission*. Bicycles : a report on the application by TI Raleigh Indutries Limited and TI Raleigh Limited of certain criteria for determining whether to supply bicycles to retail outlets / the Monopolies and Mergers Commission. — London : H.M.S.O., [1981]. — v,48p ; 25cm. — (HC ; 67)
ISBN 0-10-206782-1 (pbk) : £3.95 B82-12492

339.4′86371′0941 — Great Britain. Milk. Supply & demand. Effects of prices

Jones, George. The effect of milk prices on the dairy herd and milk supply in the United Kingdom and Ireland / George Jones. — [Oxford] : IAE, [1982?]. — 58p ; 30cm
Cover title. — Bibliography: p49-51
Unpriced (pbk) B82-28690

339.4′86372′094 — European Community countries. Butter. Demand

Pitt, Eamonn. Factors affecting demand for butter and margarine in the European Community / Eamonn Pitt. — Dublin : Marketing Department, Economics and Rural Welfare Research Centre, 1981. — iv,125p : ill,maps ; 20cm
ISBN 0-905442-50-4 (pbk) : £3.00
Also classified at 339.4′866432′094 B82-20683

339.4′8639541 — Europe. North American lobsters. Supply & demand

Milligan, Ian. The markets for lobster in Europe with reference to North American production / Ian Milligan, Robert Mounce. — Edinburgh (10 Young St., Edinburgh EH2 4JQ) : Fishery Economics Research Unit, Sea Fish Industry Authority, 1981. — 51p : ill ; 30cm. — (Occasional paper series, ISSN 0309-605x ; no.4)
Cover title
Unpriced (spiral) B82-13027

339.4′8641392′0941 — Great Britain. Food: Fish. Consumption — *Statistics* — *Serials*

Household fish consumption in Great Britain / Sea Fish Industry Authority, Fishery Economics Research Unit. — Quarter ended June 1981-. — Edinburgh (10 Young St., Edinburgh EH2 4JQ) : The Authority, 1981-. — v. : ill,maps ; 30cm
ISSN 0262-3269 = Household fish consumption in Great Britain : Unpriced
B82-14776

339.4′86512 — Western Europe. Electronic office equipment. Demand — *Forecasts*

Electronic office equipment : European market trends to 1983. — Luton : Mackintosh Publications, 1980. — vi,96p : ill ; 30cm. — (A Mackintosh monitor report)
ISBN 0-904705-22-6 (pbk) : £225.00
B82-32254

339.4′866262 — Coal. Supply & demand — *Forecasts* — *Conference proceedings*

Financial Times Conference Organisation. World coal markets : London, 20 & 21 January 1982 in association with International Coal Report : speakers papers. — London (Minster House, Arthur Street, EC4R 9AX) : Financial Times Conference Organisation, 1982. — 177p : ill,maps ; 30cm. — (Financial Times conferences)
Unpriced (pbk) B82-24673

339.4′866432′094 — European Community countries. Margarine. Demand

Pitt, Eamonn. Factors affecting demand for butter and margarine in the European Community / Eamonn Pitt. — Dublin : Marketing Department, Economics and Rural Welfare Research Centre, 1981. — iv,125p : ill,maps ; 20cm
ISBN 0-905442-50-4 (pbk) : £3.00
Primary classification 339.4′86372′094
B82-20683

339.4′869054′0941 — Great Britain. Industrial buildings. Supply & demand

Small workshops scheme : survey of the effect of the 100% industrial buildings allowance / Department of Industry. — [London] : [The Department], [1982]. — 10p : 1ill ; 30cm
Cover title
Unpriced (pbk) B82-40097

339.4′8695 — Great Britain. Buildings. Roofs. Concrete tiles. Supply — *Inquiry reports*

Great Britain. *Monopolies and Mergers Commission*. Concrete roofing tiles : a report on the supply in the United Kingdom of concrete roofing tiles. — London : H.M.S.O., 1981. — vi,154p : ill,1map ; 25cm
At head of title: The Monopolies and Mergers Commission
ISBN 0-10-201282-2 (pbk) : £7.00 B82-08682

339.4′869707′0941 — Great Britain. Buildings. Heating equipment. Supply & demand

Radiators and other heat emitters. — [Bracknell] : Statistics and Forecasting Unit, [Building Services Research and Information Association], 1981. — vii,113leaves : ill ; 30cm. — (BSRIA market profile)
ISBN 0-86022-175-x (spiral) : Unpriced
B82-29623

339.4′869707′0941 — Great Britain. Residences. Heating equipment. Supply & demand

Hudson, Mark. Domestic appliances in the UK : market structure, suppliers and future prospects / by Mark Hudson. — London : Economist Intelligence Unit, 1982. — 118p : ill(some col.) ; 30cm. — (EIU special report ; no.117)
Includes index
Unpriced (pbk) B82-18701

339.4′8796′0941 — Great Britain. Sports facilities. Demand

The **Next** ten years : sport in the community. — [London] : The Sports Council, 1982. — 52p : ill(some col.),col.maps,1port ; 30cm
ISBN 0-906577-19-5 (pbk) : £2.00 B82-38440

339.5 — Economic growth

Guha, Ashok S.. An evolutionary view of economic growth / Ashok S. Guha. — Oxford : Clarendon, 1981. — 139p ; 23cm
Bibliography: p133-139
ISBN 0-19-828431-4 : £8.95 : CIP rev.
B81-34385

339.5 — Economic growth. Equilibrium theory

Derviş, Kemal. General equilibrium models for development policy / Kemal Derviş, Jaime De Melo, Sherman Robinson ; with a foreword by Hollis Chenery. — Cambridge : Cambridge University Press, 1982. — xviii,526p : ill ; 24cm. — (A World Bank research publication)
Bibliography: p504-514. — Includes index
ISBN 0-521-24490-0 (cased) : £20.00
ISBN 0-521-27030-8 (pbk) : £9.95 B82-34351

339.5 — Economic growth. Policies of governments. Social aspects

Atkinson, A. B.. Social justice and public policy. — Brighton : Wheatsheaf Books, July 1982. — [550]p
ISBN 0-7108-0134-3 : £40.00 : CIP entry B82-13011

339.5 — Economic growth. Social aspects

Zolotas, Xenophon. Economic growth and declining social welfare / Xenophon Zolotas. — New York ; London : New York University Press, 1981. — xiv,199p : ill ; 24cm
Includes index
ISBN 0-8147-9658-3 : £11.15 B82-36367

339.5'0724 — Economic growth. Econometric models

Pasinetti, Luigi L.. Growth and income distribution : essays in economic theory / Luigi L. Pasinetti. — Cambridge : Cambridge University Press, 1974 (1979 [printing]). — x,151p : ill ; 22cm
Includes index
ISBN 0-521-20474-7 (pbk) : £3.95
Primary classification 339.2'0724 B82-26840

339.5'09172'4 — Developing countries. Economic conditions. Stabilisation. Role of International Monetary Fund, *1960-1980*

Killick, Tony. The impact of IMF stabilisation programmes in developing countries / Tony Killick. — London : Overseas Development Institute, 1982. — 40p : 1ill ; 30cm. — (ODI working paper ; no.7)
Bibliography: p39-40
ISBN 0-85003-081-1 (pbk) : Unpriced B82-35793

339.5'09172'4 — Developing countries. Economic growth. Role of capitalism, *to 1963*

Frank, André Gunder. On capitalist underdevelopment / Andre Gunder Frank. — Bombay ; Oxford : Oxford University Press, 1975 (1979 [printing]). — x,113p ; 22cm
Bibliography: p111-113
ISBN 0-19-560475-x (pbk) : Unpriced B82-25119

339.5'0941 — Great Britain. Economic growth *compared with* economic growth of Germany, *1850-1914*

Saul, S. B.. Industrialisation and de-industrialisation? : the interaction of the German and British economies before the first World War / by S.B. Saul. — London ([42, Russell Sq., WC1]) : German Historical Institute, [1980?]. — 32p ; 22cm. — (The 1979 annual lecture)
Unpriced (pbk)
Also classified at 339.5'0943 B82-08681

339.5'0941 — Great Britain. Employment. Subsidies by government: Temporary Employment Subsidy. Effectiveness

Deakin, B. M.. Effects of the Temporary Employment Subsidy / B.M. Deakin and C.F. Pratten. — Cambridge : Cambridge University Press, 1982. — xvi,236p : ill,forms ; 25cm. — (Occasional paper / University of Cambridge Department of Applied Economics ; 53)
ISBN 0-521-24358-0 : £15.00 : CIP rev. B81-39211

339.5'0941 — Great Britain. Incomes policy

Incomes policy / edited by Robin E.J. Charter, Andrew Dean and Robert Elliott. — Oxford : Clarendon Press, 1981. — viii,228p : ill ; 22cm
Includes bibliographies and index
ISBN 0-19-877145-2 (cased) : £15.00 : CIP rev.
ISBN 0-19-877146-0 (pbk) : Unpriced B81-23889

339.5'0943 — Germany. Economic growth *compared with* economic growth of Great Britain, *1850-1914*

Saul, S. B.. Industrialisation and de-industrialisation? : the interaction of the German and British economies before the first World War / by S.B. Saul. — London ([42, Russell Sq., WC1]) : German Historical Institute, [1980?]. — 32p ; 22cm. — (The 1979 annual lecture)
Unpriced (pbk)
Primary classification 339.5'0941 B82-08681

339.5'09519'5 — South Korea. Economic growth, *1945-1975*

Kim, Kwang Suk. Growth and structural transformation / Kwang Suk Kim and Michael Roemer. — [Cambridge, Mass.] : Council on East Asian Studies, Harvard University ; Cambridge, Mass. ; London : Distributed by Harvard University Press, 1979. — xxiv,195p : ill,1map ; 24cm. — (Studies in the modernization of the Republic of Korea, 1945-1975) (Harvard East Asian monographs ; 86)
Bibliography: p177-183. — Includes index
ISBN 0-674-36475-9 : £10.50 B82-22635

339.5'09598 — Indonesia. Economic conditions. Stabilisation. Role of International Monetary Fund, *1966-70*

Sutton, Mary. Indonesia 1966-70 : economic management and the role of the IMF / Mary Sutton. — London : Overseas Development Institute, 1982. — 59p : 1ill ; 30cm. — (ODI working paper ; no.8)
Bibliography: p58-59
ISBN 0-85003-082-x (pbk) : Unpriced B82-35794

339.5'0966'83 — Benin *(People's Republic)*. Economic growth, *1640-1960*

Manning, Patrick. Slavery, colonialism and economic growth in Dahomey, 1640-1960 / Patrick Manning. — Cambridge : Cambridge University Press, 1982. — xvii,446p ; 24cm. — (African studies series ; 30)
Bibliography: p415-434. — Includes index
ISBN 0-521-23544-8 : Unpriced : CIP rev. B82-01750

339.5'09676'2 — Kenya. Economic conditions. Stabilisation. Role of International Monetary Fund, *1970-1980*

Killick, Tony. The IMF and economic management in Kenya / Tony Killick. — [London] : [Overseas Development Institute], 1981. — 62p ; 30cm. — (ODI working paper ; no.4)
Bibliography: p61-62
ISBN 0-85003-078-1 (pbk) : Unpriced B82-17834

339.5'098 — Latin America. Economic conditions. Stabilisation. Policies of governments, *1970-1979*

Sutton, Mary. The costs and benefits of stabilisation programmes : some Latin American experiences / Mary Sutton. — [London] : [Overseas Development Institute], 1981. — 51p ; 30cm. — (ODI working paper ; no.3)
Bibliography: p50-51
ISBN 0-85003-077-3 (pbk) : Unpriced B82-17833

340 — LAW

340 — Law

Rutherford, L. A.. Introduction to law. — London : Sweet & Maxwell, Sept.1982. — [350]p
ISBN 0-421-29380-2 (pbk) : £15.95 : CIP entry B82-19666

340 — Law. Information systems — *Conference proceedings*

Artificial intelligence and legal information systems : edited versions of selected papers from the international conference on 'Logic, Informatics, Law', Florence, Italy, April 1981 / editor: Constantino Ciampi ; Deontic logic, computational linguistics and legal information systems : edited versions of selected papers from the international conference on 'Logic, Informatics, Law', Florence, Italy, April 1981 / editor: Antonio A. Martino. — Amsterdam ; Oxford : North-Holland, 1982. — 2v. : ill ; 24cm
Bibliography: p409-442. — Includes indexes
ISBN 0-444-86413-x : £25.00
ISBN 0-444-86414-8 (v.1) : £25.00 B82-38185

340 — Law — *Marxist viewpoints*

Collins, Hugh. Marxism and law / Hugh Collins. — Oxford : Clarendon, 1982. — viii,159p ; 23cm. — (Marxist introductions)
Bibliography: p150-155. — Includes index
ISBN 0-19-876093-0 : £8.95 : CIP rev. B82-18970

ÎAvich, L. S.. The general theory of law : social and philosophical problems / L.S. Jawitsch ; translated from the Russian by H. Campbell Creighton. — Moscow : Progress Publishers ; [London] : Distributed by Central Books, 1981. — 293p ; 21cm
Translation of: Obshchaîa teoriîa prava
ISBN 0-7147-1680-4 : £2.50 B82-06708

Marxism and law / edited by Piers Beirne, Richard Quinney. — New York ; Chichester : Wiley, c1982. — xiv,381p ; 24cm
Includes bibliographies and index
ISBN 0-471-08758-0 (pbk) : £10.20 B82-28142

340'.023 — Legal profession

Kime's international law handbook : brief facts about legal practice in most of the countries of the world / editor James M. Matthews ; research and compilation Roderick N. Matthews. — London : Kime's International Law Directory, 1981. — 266p ; 18cm
ISBN 0-900503-14-9 (pbk) : £8.75 B82-04353

340'.023'41 — Great Britain. Legal profession — *Career guides*

Usher, Elizabeth. Careers in the law. — London : Kogan Page, Feb.1982. — [100]p
ISBN 0-85038-518-0 (cased) : £5.95 : CIP entry
ISBN 0-85038-519-9 (pbk) : £2.50 B82-00152

340'.023'42 — England. Legal profession

Introduction to legal practice / edited by Grenfell Huddy ; foreword by Jack I.H. Jacob. — London : Sweet & Maxwell in association with the Institute of Legal Executives
v.1. — c1982. — xv,296p ; 25cm
Includes index
ISBN 0-421-29290-3 (pbk) : £14.50 : CIP rev. B82-14365

340'.028'54 — Law. Applications of digital computer systems — *Conference proceedings*

Lawyers in the eighties : proceedings of the conference held by Society for Computers and Law in York from 3rd to 6th July 1980 / Conference Organising Committee, Richard Morgan ... [et al.]. — Abingdon : [The Society], [1980]. — 70p : ill ; 30cm
Cover title
ISBN 0-906122-04-x (spiral) : £15.00 (£10.00 to members of the Society for Computers and Law) B82-32205

340'.03'21 — Law. Terminology — *Thesauri*

Burton, William C.. Legal thesaurus / Williams C. Burton. — New York : Macmillan ; London : Collier Macmillan, c1980. — xii,1058p ; 26cm
ISBN 0-02-691000-4 : Unpriced B82-16585

340'.05 — Law — *For law students in London — Serials*

Wig & gavel : the official magazine of the London law students. — Vol.1, issue 1 (Dec. 1980)-. — [London] ([c/o Mr S Baker, Faculty of Law, King's College, Strand, WC2]) : [s.n.], 1980-. — v. : ill ; 30cm
Three issues yearly
ISSN 0263-2063 = Wig & gavel : Unpriced B82-18498

340'.06'0421 — London. Inns of Court, *to 1800* — *Early works — Facsimiles*

Ireland, Samuel. Picturesque views with an historical account of the Inns of Court in London and Westminster. — London (45 Blackfriars Rd., SE1 8N2) : Kudos Publications, Jan.1982. — [255]p
Facsim of 1800 ed.: London : R. Faulder & J. Egerton
ISBN 0-906293-01-4 : £75.00 : CIP entry B82-06061

340'.07'1142 — England. Higher education institutions. Curriculum subjects: Law. Degree courses — *Conference proceedings*

Law in higher education : into the 1980's : proceedings of a special Association of Law Teachers conference held at Bristol Polytechnic, 8-10 February 1980 / edited by Michael Slade. — Stoke on Trent (c/o The Treasurer, Association of Law Teachers, North Staffordshire Polytechnic, Brindley Building, Leek Rd., Stoke on Trent ST4 2DE) : Published on behalf of The Association of Law Teachers, [1980?]. — 176p ; 30cm
Cover title
£2.00 (pbk) B82-25601

340'.07'114223 — Kent. Legal executives. Professional education

Horne, John N.. Legal education survey 1978 / John N. Horne. — [Hampton] ([51 High St., Hampton, Middx. TW12 2SX]) : Edmund Plowden Trust, 1979. — 31p ; 22cm
£1.50 (pbk) B82-31666

340'.07'1173 — United States. Higher education institutions. Curriculum subjects: Law. Teaching — *Conference proceedings*

Legal education and lawyer competency : curricula for change / Fernand N. Dutile, editor. — Notre Dame ; London : University of Notre Dame Press, c1981. — viii,155p ; 21cm
Conference proceedings
ISBN 0-268-01264-4 : £10.50 B82-19499

340'.09171'241 — Commonwealth countries. Common law countries. Law — *Encyclopaedias*

Words and phrases legally defined. — London : Butterworths
Supplement. — 2nd ed. / under the general editorship of John B. Saunders. — 1981. — 269p ; 25cm
ISBN 0-406-08051-8 (pbk) : Unpriced B82-09166

340.1 — LAW. PHILOSOPHY AND THEORY

340'.1 — Jurisprudence

Christie, George C.. Law, norms and authority / George C. Christie. — London : Duckworth, 1982. — x,181p ; 23cm
Includes index
ISBN 0-7156-1593-9 : £18.00 : CIP rev. B81-36225

340'.1 — Law — *Philosophical perspectives*

MacCormick, Neil. Legal right and social democracy. — Oxford : Clarendon Press, Nov.1982. — [256]p
ISBN 0-19-825385-0 : £17.50 : CIP entry B82-26877

340'.1 — Law. Theories

Torrance, Thomas F.. Juridical law and physical law : toward a realist foundation for human law / by Thomas F. Torrance ; with a foreword by Her Majesty's Advocate for Scotland. — Edinburgh : Scottish Academic Press, 1982. — xii,70p ; 20cm
Includes index
ISBN 0-7073-0314-1 (pbk) : £2.25 B82-32406

340'.109 — Law. Theories of Austin, John

Morison, W. L.. John Austin. — London : E. Arnold, Sept.1982. — [192]p. — (Jurists)
ISBN 0-7131-6359-3 (cased) : £11.00 : CIP entry
ISBN 0-7131-6360-7 (pbk) : £5.50 B82-20041

340'.109 — Law. Theories of Ulpian — *Critical studies*

Honoré, Tony. Ulpian. — Oxford : Clarendon, July 1982. — [400]p
ISBN 0-19-825358-3 : £30.00 : CIP entry B82-12550

340'.112 — Law. Ethical aspects

Ethics, eonomics, and the law / edited by J. Roland Pennock and John W. Chapman. — New York ; London : New York University Press, 1982. — xix,323p ; 22cm. — (Nomos ; 24)
Includes index
ISBN 0-8147-6583-1 : £18.60
Primary classification 340'.115 B82-38250

340'.112 — Law *related to* **morals** — *Philosophical perspectives*

Bentham, Jeremy. An introduction to the principles of morals and legislation. — London : Methuen, July 1982. — [384]p
Originally published: London : Athlone Press, 1970
ISBN 0-416-31910-6 (pbk) : £6.95 : CIP entry B82-12331

340'.115 — Law. Economic aspects

The **Economic** approach to law / edited by Paul Burrows, Cento G. Veljanovski. — London : Butterworths, 1981. — xi,343p : ill ; 25cm
Includes bibliographies and index
ISBN 0-408-10686-7 (cased) : £21.00 : CIP rev.
ISBN 0-408-10685-9 (pbk) : £8.95 B81-16929

Ethics, eonomics, and the law / edited by J. Roland Pennock and John W. Chapman. — New York ; London : New York University Press, 1982. — xix,323p ; 22cm. — (Nomos ; 24)
Includes index
ISBN 0-8147-6583-1 : £18.60
Also classified at 340'.112 B82-38250

340'.115 — Law. Economic aspects — *Serials*

Research in law and economics : a research annual. — Vol.1 (1979)-. — Greenwich, Conn. : JAI Press ; London (3 Henrietta St., WC2E 8LU) : Distributed by JAICON Press, 1979-. — v. : ill ; 24cm
Supplement: Research in law and economics. Supplement
ISSN 0193-5895 = Research in law and economics : £22.85 B82-02343

Research in law and economics : a research annual. Supplement. — Vol.1 (1980)-. — Greenwich, Conn. : JAI Press ; London (3 Henrietta St., WC2E 8LU) : Distributed by JAICON Press, 1980-. — v. ; 24cm
Supplement to: Research in law and economics
£24.50 B82-02344

340'.115 — Law — *Sociological perspectives*

Aubert, Vilhelm. In search of law. — Oxford : Martin Robertson, Sept.1982. — [224]p. — (Law in society)
ISBN 0-85520-491-5 : £12.50 : CIP entry B82-20843

340'.115 — Rules — *Study examples: Law. Rules*

Twining, William. How to do things with rules : a primer of interpretation / William Twining, David Miers. — 2nd ed. — London : Weidenfeld and Nicolson, 1982. — xx,387p ; 22cm. — (Law in context)
Previous ed.: 1976
ISBN 0-297-78083-2 (cased) : Unpriced
ISBN 0-297-78084-0 (pbk) : £8.95 B82-35842

340'.115 — United States. Deviance. Social control. Legal aspects — *Sociological perspectives*

Law and deviance / edited by H. Laurence Ross. — Beverly Hills ; London : Sage, c1981. — 278p : ill ; 23cm. — (Sage annual reviews of studies in deviance ; v.5)
Includes bibliographies
ISBN 0-8039-1650-7 (cased) : Unpriced
ISBN 0-8039-1651-5 (pbk) : Unpriced B82-08575

340'.115'05 — Law — *Sociological perspectives — Serials*

Research in law and sociology : an annual compilation of research. — Vol.1 (1978)-. — Greenwich, Conn. : JAI Press ; London (3 Henrietta St., WC2E 8LU) : Distributed by JAICON Press, 1978-. — v. ; 24cm
ISSN 0163-6588 = Research in law and sociology : £22.85 B82-02357

340'.115'0942 — England. Law. Social aspects, *1600-1800 — Case studies*

An **Ungovernable** people. — London : Hutchinson Education, Feb.1983. — [400]p
Originally published: 1980
ISBN 0-09-138201-7 (pbk) : £6.95 : CIP entry B82-36453

340'.23 — England. Legal profession, *ca 1800-1899*

Duman, Daniel. The English and colonial bar in the nineteenth century. — London : Croom Helm, Oct.1982. — [256]p
ISBN 0-85664-468-4 : £13.95 : CIP entry B82-27201

340.3 — LAW REFORM

340'.3'0941 — Great Britain. Law. Statutes. Reform — *Proposals*

Great Britain. *Law Commission*. Statute law revision : tenth report : draft Statute Law (Repeals) Bill / the Law Commission and the Scottish Law Commission. — London : H.M.S.O., [1980]. — ii,70p ; 25cm. — (Law Com. ; no.106) (Scot. Law Com. ; no.63)
ISBN 0-10-180890-9 (pbk) : £4.20 B82-14713

340'.3'0942 — England. Law. Reform. Role of Great Britain. *Law Commission — Conference proceedings*

Law reform : summary of the proceedings of a seminar at the Civil Service College on 8-10 October 1980. — Ascot (Sunningdale Park, Ascot, Berks. SL5 0QE) : Civil Service College, 1980. — iv,25p ; 30cm. — (C.S.C. working paper ; no.26)
Unpriced (unbound) B82-18602

340'.3'0952 — Japan. Law. Reform, *1867-1882*

Ch'en, Paul Heng-chao. The formation of the early Meiji legal order : the Japanese code of 1871 and its Chinese foundation / by Paul Heng-Chao Ch'en. — Oxford : Oxford University Press, 1981. — xxii,204p ; 23cm. — (London oriental series ; v.35)
Bibliography: p187-190. — Includes index
ISBN 0-19-713601-x : £12.00 : CIP rev. B81-31742

340.5 — SYSTEMS OF LAW

340.5'5 — Europe. Law, *1000-1500*

Ullmann, Walter. Jurisprudence in the Middle Ages : collected studies / Walter Ullmann. — London : Variorum, 1980. — 390p in various pagings : ill,1port ; 24cm. — (Collected studies series ; CS 120)
Includes one chapter in German. — Facsim reprints. — Includes index
ISBN 0-86078-065-1 : £22.00 : CIP rev. B80-17605

340.5'9 — Islamic law

Islamic practical laws : prepared and published by the Islamic Seminary for the educational program of the World Shi'a Muslim Organization New York / translated and organized by Sh. Muhammad Sarwar. — 2nd rev. ed. — New York : Islamic Seminary ; London : Islamic Seminary Publications, 1980. — a-h,390p ; 22cm
Previous ed.: [s.l.] : [s.n.], 197-?
Unpriced (pbk) B82-12727

Murad, Khurram. Sharī'ah : the way to God / Khurram Murad. — Leicester : Islamic Foundation, c1981. — 24p ; 21cm
ISBN 0-86037-098-4 (pbk) : Unpriced : CIP rev. B81-28050

Murad, Khurram. Sharī'ah : the way of justice / Khurram Murad. — Leicester : Islamic Foundation, c1981. — 20p ; 21cm
ISBN 0-86037-099-2 (pbk) : Unpriced : CIP rev. B81-28368

Schacht, Joseph. An introduction to Islamic law. — Oxford : Clarendon Press, July 1982. — [312]p
Originally published: 1964
ISBN 0-19-825473-3 (pbk) : £8.95 : CIP entry B82-22788

340.9 — CONFLICT OF LAWS

340.9 — Conflict of laws

Lipstein, K.. Principles of the conflict of laws, national and international / by K. Lipstein. — The Hague ; London : Nijhoff, 1981. — xii,144p : 1port ; 23cm
Rev. ed.: of The general principles of private international law. v.135 (1972-1) of the Collected courses. The Hague Academy of International Law. — Bibliography: p127-128. — Includes index
ISBN 90-247-2544-5 (pbk) : Unpriced
B82-03456

Private international law : cases and materials. — London (10 Wandon Rd, SW6 2JF) : Laureate Press, Oct.1982. — [320]p
ISBN 0-907392-04-0 (cased) : CIP entry
ISBN 0-907392-05-9 (pbk) : £16.95
B82-26092

340.9 — Conflict of laws — *Treaties — Collections*

Hague Conference on Private International Law. Recueil des conventions / Conférence de la Haye de droit international privé = Collection of conventions (1951-1980) / Hague Conference on Private International Law. — [The Hague] : Permanent Bureau of the Hague Conference on Private International Law ; [London] : [Butterworth] [distributor], [1981]. — 313p ; 25x12cm
Parallel French and English text
ISBN 90-621-5051-9 (pbk) : Unpriced
B82-13020

340.9 — England. Conflict of laws with foreign countries. English law

Dicey, A. V.. Dicey and Morris on the conflict of laws. — 10th ed. / under the general editorship of J.H.C. Morris, with specialist editors. — London : Stevens, 1980. — 2v.(cxl,1351p) ; 26cm
Previous ed.: 1973. — Bibliography: p cxxxix-cxl. — Includes index
ISBN 0-420-45690-2 (corrected : pbk) : £70.00 : CIP rev.
B80-12283

340.9 — England. Conflict of laws with foreign countries. Limitation of actions. English law. Reform — *Proposals*

Great Britain. *Law Commission.* Classification of limitation in private international law : report on a reference under section 3(1)(e) of the Law Commission Act 1965 / the Law Commission. — London : H.M.S.O., [1982]. — v,59p ; 25cm. — (Law Com. ; no.114)
ISBN 0-10-185700-4 (pbk) : £4.80 B82-32823

340.9′16 — Marriage. Conflict of laws

Pålsson, Lennart. Marriage in comparative conflict of laws : substantive conditions / Lennart Pålsson. — The Hague ; London : Nijhoff, 1981. — lxxvi,388p ; 25cm
Includes index
ISBN 90-247-2548-8 : Unpriced B82-03862

340.9′2′094 — European Community countries. Contracts. Conflict of laws with other European Community countries — *Treaties*

[Convention on the Law applicable to Contractual Obligations *(1980)***].** Convention on the Law applicable to Contractual Obligations : with protocol and joint declarations : Rome, 19 June 1980. — London : H.M.S.O., 1982. — 15p ; 25cm. — (Miscellaneous ; no.5 (1980)) (Cmnd. ; 8489)
ISBN 0-10-184890-0 (unbound) : £1.90
B82-21608

340.9′2′094 — European Community countries. Contracts. Conflict of laws with other European Community countries. Treaties: Convention on the Law Applicable to Contractual Obligations — *Critical studies*

Contract conflicts : the EEC Convention on the Law Applicable to Contractual Obligations : a comparative study / edited by P.M. North. — Amsterdam ; Oxford : North-Holland, 1982. — xviii,401p ; 23cm
ISBN 0-444-86446-6 : £24.26 B82-38186

341 — INTERNATIONAL LAW

341 — International law

Akehurst, Michael, *1940-*. A modern introduction to international law / Michael Akehurst. — 4th ed. — London : Allen and Unwin, 1982. — 304p ; 25cm
Previous ed.: 1977. — Includes bibliographies and index
ISBN 0-04-341019-7 (cased) : Unpriced : CIP rev.
ISBN 0-04-341020-0 (pbk) : Unpriced
B82-07226

341 — International law — *Conference proceedings*

International law teaching and practice / edited by Bin Cheng. — London : Stevens, 1982. — xxix,287p ; 25cm
Conference papers. — Includes index
ISBN 0-420-46350-x : £23.00 : CIP rev.
B82-10502

341 — International law — *Documents*

Brownlie, Ian. Basic documents in international law. — 3rd ed. — Oxford : Clarendon Press, Feb.1983. — [336]p
Previous ed.: 1972
ISBN 0-19-876158-9 (cased) : £14.00 : CIP entry
ISBN 0-19-876159-7 (pbk) : £8.95 B82-39272

341′.05 — International law — *Serials*

The **British** year book of international law. — 51st (1980). — Oxford : Clarendon, Dec.1981. — [420]p
ISBN 0-19-825386-9 : £35.00 : CIP entry
B81-31739

341′.07 — International law. Teaching

Lachs, Manfred. The teacher in international law : (teachings and teachers) / Manfred Lachs. — The Hague ; London : Nijhoff, 1982. — 236p ; 25cm
Bibliography: p211-225. — Includes index
ISBN 90-247-2566-6 : Unpriced B82-25211

341′.094 — European Community. Law. Secondary legislation — *Inquiry reports*

Great Britain. *Parliament. House of Commons. Select Committee on European Legislation, &c.* . Eighth report from the Select Committee on European Legislation, &c., together with the proceedings of the Committee, session 1981-82 : documents considered by the Committee. — London : H.M.S.O., 1982. — 13p ; 25cm. — (HC 21-viii)
ISBN 0-10-280282-3 (unbound) : £1.90
B82-20701

Great Britain. *Parliament. House of Commons. Select Committee on European Legislation, &c.* . Eleventh report from the Select Committee on European Legislation, &c. : together with the proceedings of the committee : session 1980-1981 : documents considered by the committee including: shipping safety and pollution prevention (8480/80), oil pollution at sea: community information system (8479/80), annual economic report 1980-81. — London : H.M.S.O., [1981]. — 20p ; 25cm. — (HC ; 32-xi)
ISBN 0-10-280481-8 (unbound) : £2.10
B82-09929

Great Britain. *Parliament. House of Commons. Select Committee on European Legislation, &c.* . First report from the Select Committee on European Legislation, &c. : together with the proceedings of the committee : session 1980-81 : documents considered by the committee including: food aid (9175/80), flavourings in food (7605/80), excise harmonisation: alcoholic beverages (7854/80), trade in endangered species (9150/80), asbestos (9953/80), 1981 budget: letter of amendment (10479/80), 1981 budget: amendments and modifications by European Parliament, organisation of the market in fishery products (11392/80), annual economic report, 1980-81 (10444/80). — London : H.M.S.O., [1980]. — 30p ; 25cm. — (HC ; 32-i)
ISBN 0-10-270481-3 (unbound) : £2.40
B82-09931

Great Britain. *Parliament. House of Commons. Select Committee on European Legislation, &c.* . First special report from the Select Committee on European Legislation, &c., session 1980-81 : annual review of the work of the committee. — London : H.M.S.O., [1980]. — 5p ; 25cm. — (HC ; 50)
ISBN 0-10-205081-3 (unbound) : £1.10
B82-10334

Great Britain. *Parliament. House of Commons. Select Committee on European Legislation, &c.* . Forty-fifth report from the Select Committee on European Legislation, &c. : together with the proceedings of the committee : session 1979-80 : documents considered by the committee including : regional development fund (9263/80), aid to shipbuilding (9866/80). — London : H.M.S.O., [1980]. — 17p ; 25cm. — (HC ; 159-xlv)
ISBN 0-10-029939-3 (unbound) : £2.10
B82-10332

Great Britain. *Parliament. House of Commons. Select Committee on European Legislation, &c.* . Forty-first report from the Select Committee on European Legislation, &c. : together with the proceedings of the committee : session 1979-80 : documents considered by the committee including : right of residence (8475/80), community labour market policy (6861/80). — London : H.M.S.O., [1980]. — 14p ; 25cm. — (HC ; 159-xli)
ISBN 0-10-009309-4 (unbound) : £1.70
B82-10336

Great Britain. *Parliament. House of Commons. Select Committee on European Legislation, &c.* . Forty-fourth report from the Select Committee on European Legislation, &c. : together with the minutes of the evidence taken on 4th November 1980 : session 1979-80 : draft general budget of the European communities for 1981. — London : H.M.S.O., [1980]. — viii,13p ; 25cm. — (HC ; 159-xliv) (HC ; 255-v)
ISBN 0-10-029789-7 (unbound) : £3.00
B82-10335

Great Britain. *Parliament. House of Commons. Select Committee on European Legislation, &c.* . Forty-second report from the Select Committee on European Legislation, &c. : together with the proceedings of the committee : session 1979-80 : documents considered by the committee including : restriction of investment aids for milk and pig production (9280/80), fisheries: allocation and distribution of quotas (9336/80) (10090/80), organisation of the market in fishery products (9917/80), steel industry: crisis measures. — London : H.M.S.O., [1980]. — 21p ; 25cm. — (HC ; 159-xlii)
ISBN 0-10-009479-1 (unbound) : £2.10
B82-10337

Great Britain. *Parliament. House of Commons. Select Committee on European Legislation, &c.* . Forty-sixth report from the Select Committee on European Legislation, &c. : together with the proceedings of the committee : session 1979-80 : documents considered by the committee including : social measures in the steel industry (10179/80), aid to shipyard workers (9198/80), regional development fund (10220/80), distribution of fish catches 1980 (9336/80), (10722/80). — London : H.M.S.O., [1980]. — 17p ; 25cm. — (HC ; 159-xlvi)
ISBN 0-10-029749-8 (unbound) : £2.10
B82-10333

Great Britain. *Parliament. House of Commons. Select Committee on European Legislation, &c.* . Fourth report from the Select Committee on European Legislation, &c. : together with the proceedings of the committee : session 1980-81 : documents considered by the committee including: social measures in the steel industry (10879/80), energy labelling (7298/80), newsprint: duty-free quota, STABEX (10988/80) (10920/80). — London : H.M.S.O., [1981]. — 22p ; 25cm. — (HC ; 32-iv)
ISBN 0-10-271181-x (unbound) : £2.10
B82-09933

341′.094 — European Community. Law. Secondary legislation — *Inquiry reports* *continuation*

Great Britain. *Parliament. House of Commons. Select Committee on European Legislation, &c.* Fourth report from the Select Committee on European Legislation, &c : together with the proceedings of the Committee : session 1981-82 : documents considered by the Committee including: community information systems (8467/81), annual economic report (10077/81). — London : H.M.S.O., 1981. — 29p ; 25cm
ISBN 0-10-271882-2 (unbound) : £2.65
B82-12634

Great Britain. *Parliament. House of Commons. Select Committee on European Legislation, &c.* . Second report from the Select Committee on European Legislation, &c. : together with the proceedings of the committee : session 1980-81 : documents considered by the committee including: right of residence (10651/80), hormones: use in domestic animals (10994/80), sugar regime (10009/80), European Development Fund (10987/80), newsprint: duty-free quota. — London : H.M.S.O., [1980]. — 20p ; 25cm. — (HC ; 32-ii)
ISBN 0-10-270781-2 (unbound) : £2.10
B82-09932

Great Britain. *Parliament. House of Commons. Select Committee on European Legislation, &c.* . Third report from the Select Committee on European Legislation, &c. : together with the proceedings of the committee : session 1981-82 : documents considered by the committee including : fish prices 1982 (10710/81). — London : H.M.S.O., [1981]. — 20p ; 25cm. — (HC ; 21-iii)
ISBN 0-10-271082-1 (unbound) : £2.30
B82-16056

Great Britain. *Parliament. House of Commons. Select Committee on European Legislation, &c.* . Third report from the Select Committee on European Legislation, &c., session 1980-81 : round-up of outstanding debates. — London : H.M.S.O., [1980]. — 14p ; 25cm. — ([HC] ; 32-iii)
ISBN 0-10-270881-9 (unbound) : £1.70
B82-09934

Great Britain. *Parliament. House of Commons. Select Committee on European Legislation, &c.* . Thirty-second report from the Select Committee on European Legislation, &c. : together with the proceedings of the Committee : session 1980-81 : documents considered by the Committee including: foodstuffs : claims (6498/81). — London : H.M.S.O., [1981]. — 15p ; 25cm. — (HC ; 32-xxxii)
ISBN 0-10-008741-8 (unbound) : £1.90
B82-02313

Great Britain. *Parliament. House of Commons. Select Committee on European Legislation, &c.* . Thirty-third report from the Select Committee on European Legislation, &c. : together with the proceedings of the committee, session 1980-81 : documents considered by the committee including: Fisheries: total allowable catches 1981 (8696/81), Fish quotas 1981 (8695/81), Keeping laying hens in cages (8832/81), Member states′ quotas for Swedish and Faroese waters, 1981 (9631/81), Catch quotas for member states in north Norwegian waters (9743/81), Fishery agreement with Norway 1981 (8598/81). — London : H.M.S.O., [1981]. — 30p ; 25cm. — (HC ; 32-xxxiii)
ISBN 0-10-009171-7 (unbound) : £2.65
B82-11545

Great Britain. *Parliament. House of Commons. Select Committee on European Legislation, &c.* . Twelfth report from the Select Committee on European Legislation, &c. : together with the proceedings of the committee : session 1980-81 : documents considered by the committee including: environmental impact assessment (7972/80), excise duty on cigarettes (8449/80), excise duty on cigarettes: high tar surcharge (4074/81), ceramic research (7445/79) (8978/80), fisheries conservation: sprat fishing, fisheries: total allowable catches 1981, fish quotas 1981. — London : H.M.S.O., [1981]. — 25p ; 25cm. — (HC ; 32-xii)
ISBN 0-10-281181-4 (unbound) : £2.40
B82-09930

341′.094 — European Community. Law — *Serials — For British businessmen*

E.E.C. information services : the advisory service for business enquiries about EEC directives, regulations, agreements or documents. — Issue no.1 (1st quarter 1982)-. — Sudbury (Rectory Rd, Great Waldingfield, Sudbury, Suffolk CO10 0TL) : Centre for Legal & Business Information, 1982-. — v. ; 30cm
Quarterly
ISSN 0262-9380 = E.E.C. information services : Unpriced B82-15165

341′.094 — European Economic Community. Law

Parry, Anthony. EEC Law. — 2nd ed. / by Anthony Parry and James Dinnage. — London : Sweet & Maxwell, 1981. — lvi,531p ; 25cm
Previous ed.: 1973. — Includes index
ISBN 0-421-26090-4 (cased) : £25.00 : CIP rev.
ISBN 0-421-26100-5 (pbk) : £16.00
B81-23772

341.2 — INTERNATIONAL LEGAL ORGANISATIONS

341.2 — International organisations. International law

Bowett, D. W.. The law of international institutions / D.W. Bowett. — 4th ed. — London : Published under the auspices of the London Institute for World Affairs by Stevens & Sons, 1982. — xv,431p ; 23cm
Previous ed.: 1975. — Includes index
ISBN 0-420-46010-1 (cased) : £19.00 : CIP rev.
ISBN 0-420-46020-9 (pbk) : £12.50
B82-15790

341.2 — International organisations — *Regulations*

International organization and integration : annotated basic documents and descriptive directory of international organizations and arrangements. — The Hague ; London : Nijhoff
Vol.1.A. — 2nd rev. ed. / board of editors P.J.G. Kapteyn ... [et al.] ; with a foreword by Louis B. Sohn. — c1981. — 1v.(various pagings) ; 25cm
Previous ed.: 1968. — "Table of members of organizations and of parties to conventions and treaties" (2 folded sheets) as inserts. — Includes index
ISBN 90-247-2579-8 : Unpriced
ISBN 90-247-2578-x (set) : Unpriced
B82-12083

International organization and integration : annotated basic documents and descriptive directory of international organizations and arrangements. — 2nd rev. ed. / Board of editors P.J.G. Kapteyn ... [et al.] ; with a foreword by Louis B. Sohn. — The Hague ; London : Nijhoff
Previous ed.: / editors H.F. van Panhuys ... et al. — Deventer : Kluwer, 1968
Vol.2A. — c1982. — 1v.(various pagings) : ill ; 25cm
Ebvelope containing replacement pages for Vol.1.A, sheet of tabular data and erratum sheet for Vol.2.A, as inserts. — Includes index
ISBN 90-247-2587-9 : Unpriced B82-29465

341.2′09172′4 — Developing countries. Intergovernmental organisations

Williams, Gwyneth. Third-World political organizations : a review of developments / Gwyneth Williams. — London : Macmillan, 1981. — xiii,133p ; 23cm
Bibliography: p126-127. — Includes index
ISBN 0-333-28202-7 : £12.00 B82-10634

341.23′09 — United Nations — *History*

Luard, Evan. A history of the United Nations / Evan Luard. — London : Macmillan
Vol.1: The years of Western domination, 1945-1955. — 1982. — viii,404p ; 23cm
Includes index
ISBN 0-333-24389-7 : Unpriced B82-33845

341.23′2 — United Nations. Specialised agencies. Role of politics

Ameri, Houshang. Politics and process in the specialized agencies of the United Nations. — Aldershot : Gower, Nov.1982. — [296]p
ISBN 0-566-00538-7 : £15.00 : CIP entry
B82-26546

341.24′09171′7 — Sovet ėkonomicheskoĭ vzaimopomoshchi, *to 1979*

The **Council** for Mutual Economic Assistance, 30 years. — Moscow : CMEA Secretariat Economic Information Department ; [London] : Distributed by Central Books, 1979. — 93p,[24]p of plates : ill(some col.),col.maps,ports ; 21cm
Translation of: Sovet ėkonomicheskoĭ vzaimopomoshchi 30 let
ISBN 0-7147-1676-6 : £1.95 B82-06703

341.24′22 — European Community

About Europe. — Luxembourg ; London (20 Kensington Palace Gardens, W8 6QQ) : Office for Official Publications of the European Communities, [1982?]. — 22p : ill(some col.) ; 20cm
Cover title. — Text and ill on inside covers
Unpriced (pbk) B82-30855

341.24′22 — European Community. Organisation structure

Foakes, Joanne S.. Tolley′s European Community institutions / Joanne S. Foakes. — Croydon : Tolley, c1982. — xv,83p : ill,1map ; 23cm
ISBN 0-85459-060-9 (pbk) : £4.50 B82-32891

341.24′22 — European Community. Political aspects

Daltrop, Anne. Politics and the European Community / Anne Daltrop. — Harlow : Longman, 1982. — x,166p : maps ; 21cm. — (Political realities)
Bibliography: p158-162. — Includes index
ISBN 0-582-35302-5 (cased) : Unpriced
ISBN 0-582-35303-3 (pbk) : £2.75 B82-30903

341.24′22 — European Community. Reform. Role of Great Britain

Rutherford, Malcolm. Can we save the Common Market? / Malcolm Rutherford. — Oxford : Blackwell, 1981. — 115p ; 23cm. — (Mainstream series)
Includes index
ISBN 0-631-12933-2 : £7.95 : CIP rev.
B81-30172

341.24′22 — European Court — *Cases — Serials*

European Court of Justice reporter : a digest of all decisions and opinions of the European Court of Justice. — 1, pt.1 (Jan. 1982)-. — Oxford (25 Beaumont St., Oxford OX1 2NP) : ESC Pub. Ltd., 1982-. — v. ; 30cm
Eleven issues yearly. — Cumulative index in each issue
ISSN 0262-5156 = European Court of Justice reporter : £90.00 per year B82-22695

341.24′22 — European Economic Community — *For schools*

Ibanes. Europe and the EEC. — London : Hart-Davis Educational, Sept.1982. — [64]p. — (Signposts series)
Translation of: L′Europe
ISBN 0-247-13222-5 : £3.95 : CIP entry
B82-18867

341.24′22 — European Economic Community — *Socialist viewpoints*

Out of crisis. — Nottingham : Spokesman, Jan.1983. — [160]p. — (European socialist thought) (Spokesman university paperback ; 39)
ISBN 0-85124-354-1 (pbk) : £2.50 : CIP entry
B82-33105

341.24′22 — European Parliament

Scalingi, Paula. The European Parliament : the three-decade search for a united Europe / Paula Scalingi. — London : Aldwych, 1980. — x,221p ; 22cm
Bibliography: p201-215. — Includes index
ISBN 0-86172-006-7 : £14.95 B82-31086

341.24′22 — European Parliament, *to 1980.* **European Democratic Group members**

The **First** year : July 1979-July 1980 : report from the European Parliament / by the European Democratic Group. — [London] ([2 Queen Anne′s Gate, SW1H 9AA]) : The Group, [1980]. — 47p ; 21cm
Cover title
Unpriced (pbk) B82-17143

341.24′22′024354 — European Community — *For local authorities in Scotland*

Aitken, C. P.. Scottish local authorities and their involvement with the European Economic Community / C.P. Aitken. — Stirling (12 Clarendon Place, Stirling FK8 2QW) : C.P. Aitken, 1981. — 108,[34]p ; 30cm
£7.00 (pbk) B82-10618

341.24′22′024354 — European Community — *Serials — For local authorities in Great Britain*

European information service / British Sections, International Union of Local Authorities [and] Council of European Municipalities. — No.1 (26 June 1978)-. — London (26 Old Queen St., SW1H 9HP) : The Sections, 1978-. — v. ; 30cm
Monthly. — Description based on: No.21 (8 May 1981)
ISSN 0261-2747 = European information service : £10.00 per year B82-02388

341.24′22′0321 — European Community — *Encyclopaedias*

Morris, Brian, *1941-*. The European Community : the practical guide for business and government / Brian Morris, Peggy Crane, Klaus Boehm. — London : Macmillan, 1981. — xiii,303p ; 23cm
Includes index
ISBN 0-333-26205-0 : Unpriced B82-14867

341.24′22′05 — European Economic Community — *For executives — Serials*

Fideurop European commentary. — No.1 (Dec. 1981)-. — Frankfurt am Main ; London (1 Little New St., EC4A 3TR) : Fideurop SA, 1981-. — v. ; 30cm
Quarterly
Unpriced B82-12460

341.24′22′05 — European Parliament — *Serials*

European Parliament digest. — No.1 (Nov. 1979)-no.16 (Mar. 1982). — London (2 Queen Anne's Gate, SW1) : European Parliament Information Office, 1979-1982. — 16v. ; 30cm
Description based on: No.12 (Feb.-Mar. 1981)
Unpriced B82-15772

341.24′22′09 — European Economic Community, *to 1980 — Polish texts*

Grodzicki, Bogusław. Wspólnota Europejska : przewodnik dokumentalny / pod redakcją Bogusława Grodzickiego i Jana Pomiana ; teksty tłumaczyła Halina Carroll-Najder. — Londyn : Polonia Book Fund, 1982. — 238p ; x22cm
Includes index
ISBN 0-902352-20-2 (pbk) : £4.50 B82-32389

341.24′22′09047 — European Community, *1979*

Developments in the European Communities January-December 1979. — London : H.M.S.O., [1980]. — iv,47p ; 25cm. — (European Communities ; no.5 (1980)) (Cmnd. ; 7780)
ISBN 0-10-177800-7 (unbound) : £2.50 B82-14716

341.24′22′09047 — European Economic Community, *1976-1978*

Cooney, John. The EEC in crisis / John Cooney. — [Dublin] : Dublin University Press, 1979. — 236p ; 21cm
£1.95 (pbk) B82-34672

341.24′22′09048 — European Community, *1981*

Developments in the European Community July-December 1981. — London : H.M.S.O., [1982]. — 71p ; 25cm. — (European Communities ; no.13 (1982)) (Cmnd. ; 8525)
ISBN 0-10-185250-9 (pbk) : £4.35 B82-25139

341.24′77 — Central Treaty Organization. Dissolution — *Treaties between Great Britain & Turkey*

Great Britain. [Treaties, etc. Turkey, 1979 Oct.2]. Exchange of notes between the Government of the United Kingdom of Great Britain and Northern Ireland and the Government of the Republic of Turkey terminating the Pact of Mutual Co-operation signed at Baghdad on 24 February 1955 and the Agreement on the Status of the Central Treaty Organization, National Representatives and International Staff signed at Ankara on 9 November 1960, Ankara, 2 and 4 October 1979. — London : H.M.S.O., [1980]. — 3p ; 25cm. — (Treaty series ; no.85 (1980)) (Cmnd. ; 8065)
ISBN 0-10-180650-7 (unbound) : £0.70 B82-02895

341.24′9 — Organization of African Unity, *to 1980*

Mbuyinga, Elenga. Pan-Africanism or neo-colonialism. — London : Zed Press, Jan.1982. — [240]p
ISBN 0-86232-076-3 (cased) : £16.95 : CIP entry
ISBN 0-86232-013-5 (pbk) : £4.95 B81-37538

341.26 — Anguilla. Government. British law — *Statues*

Great Britain. [Anguilla Act 1980]. Anguilla Act 1980 : Elizabeth II, 1980, chapter 67. — London : H.M.S.O., [1980]. — 1sheet ; 25x16cm
ISBN 0-10-546780-4 : £0.30 B82-09249

341.3 — RELATIONS BETWEEN STATES. DIPLOMACY AND TREATIES

341.3 — Foreign relations. International legal aspects

Fawcett, J. E. S.. Law and power in international relations / James Fawcett. — London : Faber and Faber, 1982. — 140p ; 23cm
ISBN 0-571-10537-8 : £9.50 : CIP rev. B82-07847

341.3′3 — Diplomatic service

Feltham, R. G.. Diplomatic handbook. — 4th ed. — London : Longman, Feb.1983. — [160]p
Previous ed.: 1980
ISBN 0-582-49339-0 (pbk) : £4.95 : CIP entry B82-38857

341.3′7′09034 — Treaties, *1850-1980 — Critical studies*

Degenhardt, Henry W.. Treaties and alliances of the world / compiled and written by Henry W. Degenhardt. — 3rd ed. — Harlow : Longman, 1981. — ix,409p : maps ; 26cm. — (A Keesing's reference publication)
Previous ed.: 1974. — Includes index
ISBN 0-582-90250-9 : £27.00 : CIP rev. B81-27998

341.4 — JURISDICTION AND JURISDICTIONAL RELATIONS OF STATES

341.4′09 — Territorial claims. Disputes, *to 1981*

Day, A. J.. Border and territorial disputes. — London : Longman, July 1982. — [450]p. — (Keesing's reference publications)
ISBN 0-582-90251-7 : £30.00 : CIP entry B82-14380

341.4′2 — Antarctic. International law

Auburn, F. M.. Antarctic law and politics / F.M. Auburn. — London : Hurst, c1982. — xx,361p : ill,maps ; 23cm
Bibliography: p337-356. — Includes index
ISBN 0-905838-39-4 : £17.50 : CIP rev. B81-33875

341.4′2 — Falklands Islands. Sovereignty. Disputes between Great Britain & Argentina. Settlement — *Proposals*

Dent, M. J.. The dispute over Falklands/Malvinas, the road to an honourable and lasting peace : the opportunity to work out a new political category : a study of the political skills needed in peacemaking / by M.J. Dent. — Keele : Dark Horse, 1982. — 16p ; 21cm
ISBN 0-906128-01-3 (pbk) : £1.20 B82-29834

341.4′2 — Mexico. Frontiers with United States. Geopolitical aspects

House, John W.. Frontier on the Rio Grande. — Oxford : Clarendon Press, July 1982. — [300] p. — (Oxford research studies in geography)
ISBN 0-19-823237-3 : £15.00 : CIP entry B82-14360

341.4′42 — International rivers. International law

The **Legal** regime of international rivers and lakes = Le régime juridique des fleuves et des lacs internationaux / edited by Ralph Zacklin, Lucius Caflisch ; with Gerald Graham, Haritini Dipla. — The Hague ; London : Nijhoff, 1981. — xiv,414p : ill,maps ; 25cm
ISBN 90-247-2565-8 : Unpriced
Also classified at 341.4′44 B82-03861

341.4′44 — International lakes. International law

The **Legal** regime of international rivers and lakes = Le régime juridique des fleuves et des lacs internationaux / edited by Ralph Zacklin, Lucius Caflisch ; with Gerald Graham, Haritini Dipla. — The Hague ; London : Nijhoff, 1981. — xiv,414p : ill,maps ; 25cm
ISBN 90-247-2565-8 : Unpriced
Primary classification 341.4′42 B82-03861

341.4′5 — Oceans. International law

Mangone, Gerard J.. Law for the world ocean / by Gerard J. Mangone. — London : Stevens, 1981. — ii,313p ; 19cm. — (Tagore Law lectures)
Bibliography: p292-300. — Includes index
ISBN 0-421-28480-3 : £12.00 B82-00080

O'Connell, D. P.. The international law of the sea. — Oxford : Clarendon, Sept.1982
Vol.1. — [520]p
ISBN 0-19-825346-x : £40.00 : CIP entry B82-18995

341.4′7 — Outer space. International law

Forkosch, Morris D.. Outer space and legal liability / Morris D. Forkosch. — The Hague ; London : Nijhoff, 1982. — xvi,290p : ill ; 25cm
Bibliography: p267-270. — Includes index
ISBN 90-247-2582-8 : Unpriced B82-40148

341.4′81 — Developing countries. Human rights. Implications of economic development. Legal aspects — *Conference proceedings*

Development, human rights and the rule of law : report of a conference held in The Hague on 27 April-1 May 1981 / convened by the International Commission of Jurists. — Oxford : Pergamon, 1981. — vi,237p ; 23cm
ISBN 0-08-028921-5 (cased) : Unpriced : CIP rev.
ISBN 0-08-028951-7 (pbk) : £3.75 B81-31955

341.4′81 — European Commission of Human Rights. Recognition by Great Britain — *Treaties between Great Britain & European Commission of Human Rights*

Great Britain. *Foreign and Commonwealth Office* . Declarations by the Government of the United Kingdom of Great Britain and Northern Ireland, in respect of the United Kingdom and certain overseas territories, prolonging the period of recognition or acceptance of the competence of the European Commission of Human Rights to receive individual petitions; and the period of recognition as compulsory of the Jurisdiction of the European Court of Human Rights : Strasbourg, 1 December 1980, 19 August and 4 December 1981. — London : H.M.S.O., 1982. — 7p ; 25cm. — (Treaty series ; no.11 (1982)) (Cmnd. ; 8488)
ISBN 0-10-184880-3 (unbound) : £1.15 B82-23226

341.4′81 — Human rights. International law

McKean, Warwick A.. Equality and discrimination under international law. — Oxford : Clarendon, Feb.1983. — [392]p
ISBN 0-19-825311-7 : £30.00 : CIP entry B82-36598

341.4'81 — Human rights. International law — *Collections*

Basic documents on human rights / edited by Ian Brownlie. — 2nd ed. — Oxford : Clarendon Press, 1981. — x,505p ; 24cm
Previous ed.: 1971. — Includes index
ISBN 0-19-876124-4 (cased) : £22.50 : CIP rev.
ISBN 0-19-876125-2 (pbk) : Unpriced
B80-38886

The **International** law of human rights. — Oxford : Clarendon, Dec.1982. — [600]p
ISBN 0-19-876096-5 : £35.00 : CIP entry
B82-32287

341.4'81 — Human rights. International legal aspects

Robertson, A. H.. Human rights in the world. — 2nd ed. — Manchester : Manchester University Press, June 1982. — [224]p
Previous ed.: 1972
ISBN 0-7190-0863-8 : £15.00 : CIP entry
B82-09632

341.4'81 — Human rights. Treaties: International Covenant on Civil and Political Rights — *Critical studies*

The **International** Bill of Rights : the covenant on civil and political rights / Louis Henkin editor. — New York ; Guildford : Columbia University Press, 1981. — x,523p ; 24cm
Includes index
ISBN 0-231-05180-8 : £24.60 B82-10944

341.4'81 — Western Europe. Human rights. International law. Treaties: European Convention for the Protection of Human Rights and Fundamental Freedoms. Procedure, *ca 1960-1980 — Case studies*

Morrisson, Clovis C.. The dynamics of development in the European Human Rights Convention system / Clovis C. Morrisson, Jr.. — The Hague ; London : Nijhoff, 1981. — xii,176p ; 24cm
ISBN 90-247-2546-1 : Unpriced B82-00481

341.4'84 — Double taxation — *Treaties between Great Britain & Australia*

Australia. [Treaties, etc. Great Britain, 1967 Dec.7. Protocols, etc. 1980 Jan.29]. Protocol between the Government of the United Kingdom of Great Brtain and Northern Ireland and the Government of the Commonwealth of Australia amending the Agreement for the avoidance of double taxation and the prevention of fiscal evasion with respect to taxes on income and capital gains, signed at Canberra on 7 December 1967 : Canberra, 29 January 1980. — London : H.M.S.O., [1981]. — 3p ; 25cm. — (Treaty series ; no.82 (1981)) (Cmnd. ; 8415)
ISBN 0-10-184150-7 (unbound) : £0.70
B82-10963

341.4'84 — Double taxation — *Treaties between Great Britain & Bangladesh*

Bangladesh. [Treaties, etc. Great Britain, 1979 Aug.8]. Convention between the Government of the United Kingdom of Great Britain and Northern Ireland and the Government of the People's Republic of Bangladesh for the avoidance of double taxation and the prevention of fiscal evasion with respect to taxes on income and capital gains : Dacca, 8 August, 1979. — London : H.M.S.O., [1980]. — 18p ; 25cm. — (Treaty series ; no.80 (1980)) (Cmnd. ; 8043)
" ... previously published as Bangladesh No.1 (1979), Cmnd. 7741"
ISBN 0-10-180430-x (unbound) : £2.10
B82-11417

341.4'84 — Double taxation — *Treaties between Great Britain & Canada*

Canada. [Treaties, etc. Great Britain, 1978 Sept.8. Protocols, etc., 1980 Apr.15]. Protocol amending the convention between the Government of the United Kingdom of Great Britain and Northern Ireland and the Government of Canada for the avoidance of double taxation and the prevention of fiscal evasion with respect to taxes on income and capital gains, signed at London on 8 September 1978 : Ottawa, 15 April 1980. — London : H.M.S.O., [1980]. — 5p ; 25cm. — (Canada ; no.1 (1980)) (Cmnd. ; 8024)
ISBN 0-10-180240-4 (unbound) : £1.10
B82-11452

341.4'84 — Double taxation — *Treaties between Great Britain & Cyprus*

Cyprus. [Treaties, etc. Great Britain, 1974 June 20. Protocols, etc. 1980 Apr.2]. Protocol between the Government of the United Kingdom of Great Britain and Northern Ireland and the Government of the Republic of Cyprus amending the convention for the avoidance of double taxation and the prevention of fiscal evasion with respect to taxes on income, signed in Nicosia on 20 June 1974, Nicosia, 2 April 1980. — London : H.M.S.O., [1980]. — 3p ; 25cm. — (Cyprus ; no.1 (1980)) (Cmnd. ; 8035)
ISBN 0-10-180350-8 (unbound) : £0.70
B82-01237

341.4'84 — Double taxation — *Treaties between Great Britain & Egypt*

Egypt. [Treaties, etc. Great Britain, 1977 Apr.25]. Convention between the Government of the United Kingdom of Great Britain and Northern Ireland and the Government of the Arab Republic of Egypt for the avoidance of double taxation and the prevention of fiscal evasion with respect to taxes on income and capital gains : Cairo, 25 April 1977. — London : H.M.S.O., [1980]. — 19p ; 25cm. — (Treaty series ; no.81 (1980)) (Cmnd. ; 8044)
" ... previously published as Egypt No.1 (1978), Cmnd. 7087
ISBN 0-10-180440-7 (unbound) : £2.10
B82-11422

341.4'84 — Double taxation — *Treaties between Great Britain & India (Republic)*

Great Britain. [Treaties, etc. India, 1981 Apr.16]. Convention between the Government of the United Kingdom of Great Britain and Northern Ireland and the Government of India for the avoidance of double taxation and the prevention of fiscal evasion with respect to taxes on income and capital gains : New Delhi, 16 April 1981. — London : H.M.S.O., [1982]. — 77p ; 25cm. — (Treaty series ; no.2 (1982)) (Cmnd. ; 8442)
Parallel English and Hindi text
ISBN 0-10-184420-4 (pbk) : £4.75 B82-15216

341.4'84 — Double taxation. Treaties between Great Britain & Ireland (Republic): Great Britain. Treaties, etc. Ireland, 1976 June 2 — *Critical studies*

Forbes, Michael J.. Ireland-UK Tax Treaty : evening lecture / speaker Michael J. Forbes. — [London] ([29 Lincolns Inn Fields, WC2A 3FE]) : Association of Certified Accountants, Irish Region, [1978?]. — 23leaves ; 30cm
Cover title
Unpriced (pbk) B82-25854

341.4'84 — Double taxation — *Treaties between Great Britain & Luxembourg*

Great Britain. [Treaties, etc. Luxembourg, 1967 May 24. Protocols, etc., 1978 July 18]. Protocol amending the convention between the United Kingdom of Great Britain and Northern Ireland and the Grand Duchy of Luxembourg for the avoidance of double taxation and the prevention of fiscal evasion with respect to taxes on income and on capital, signed at London on 24 May 1967 : London, 18 July 1978. — London : H.M.S.O., [1980]. — 11p ; 25cm. — (Treaty series ; no.83 (1980)) (Cmnd. ; 8060)
" ... previously published as Luxembourg No.1 (1978), Cmnd. 7358"
ISBN 0-10-180600-0 (unbound) : £1.40
B82-11423

341.4'84 — Double taxation — *Treaties between Great Britain & Mauritius*

Great Britain. [Treaties, etc. Mauritius, 1981 Feb.11]. Convention between the Government of the United Kingdom of Great Britain and Northern Ireland and the Government of Mauritius for the avoidance of double taxation and the prevention of fiscal evasion with respect to taxes on income and capital gains : London, 11 Feburary 1981. — London : H.M.S.O., [1981]. — 22p ; 25cm. — (Treaty series ; no.81 (1981)) (Cmnd. ; 8406)
ISBN 0-10-184060-8 (unbound) : £2.30
B82-10729

341.4'84 — Double taxation — *Treaties between Great Britain & Netherlands*

Great Britain. [Treaties, etc. Netherlands, 1979 Dec.11]. Convention between the United Kingdom of Great Britain and Northern Ireland and the Kingdom of the Netherlands for the avoidance of double taxation and the prevention of fiscal evasion with respect to taxes on estates of deceased persons and inheritances and on gifts : The Hague, 11 December 1979. — London : H.M.S.O., [1980]. — 24p ; 25cm. — (Treaty series ; no.77 (1980)) (Cmnd. ; 8020)
English and Dutch text. — " ... previously published as Netherlands No.1 (1980), Cmnd. 7860"
ISBN 0-10-180200-5 (unbound) : £2.40
B82-11449

341.4'84 — Double taxation — *Treaties between Great Britain & Sweden*

Great Britain. [Treaties, etc. Sweden, 1980 Oct.8]. Convention between the Government of the United Kingdom of Great Britain and Northern Ireland and the Government of the Kingdom of Sweden for the avoidance of double taxation and the prevention of fiscal evasion with respect to taxes on estates of deceased persons and inheritances and on gifts : Stockholm, 8 October 1980. — London : H.M.S.O., [1981]. — 21p ; 25cm. — (Cmnd. ; 8361) (Treaty series ; no.66 (1981))
English and Swedish text. — Originally published: as Sweden no.1 (1981), Cmnd.8122
ISBN 0-10-183610-4 (unbound) : £2.30
B82-02751

341.4'84 — Double taxation — *Treaties between Great Britain & Thailand*

Great Britain. [Treaties, etc. Thailand, 1981 Feb.18]. Convention between the Government of the United Kingdom of Great Britain and Northern Ireland and the Government of the Kingdom of Thailand for the avoidance of double taxation and the prevention of fiscal evasion with respect to taxes on income, Bangkok, 18 February 1981. — London : H.M.S.O., [1982]. — 49p ; 25cm. — (Cmnd. ; 8426) (Treaty series ; no.1 (1982))
English and Thai text
ISBN 0-10-184260-0 (unbound) : £3.85
B82-14612

341.4'84 — Double taxation — *Treaties between Great Britain & United States*

Great Britain. [Treaties, etc. United States, 1975 Dec.31]. Convention between the Government of the United Kingdom of Great Britain and Northern Ireland and the Government of the United States of America for the avoidance of double taxation and the prevention of fiscal evasion with respect to taxes on income and capital gains : London, 31 December 1975 ; with, Amending exchange of notes : London, 13 April 1976 ; and, Three protocols : London, 26 August 1976, 31 March 1977 and 15 March 1979. — London : H.M.S.O., [1980]. — 37p ; 25cm. — (Treaty series ; no.76 (1980)) (Cmnd. ; 8019)
"The Convention and Exchange of Notes were previously published as United States No. 2 (1976), Cmnd. 6508 and the protocols as United States No.2 (1976), Cmnd. 6642, United States No.3 (1977), Cmnd. 6867 and United States No.3 (1979), Cmnd. 7611"
ISBN 0-10-180190-4 (unbound) : £2.70
B82-11454

341.5 — DISPUTES BETWEEN STATES

341.5 — Arab countries. Conflict with Israel. International legal aspects

Stone, Julius. Israel and Palestine : assault on the law of nations / Julius Stone. — Baltimore ; London : Johns Hopkins University Press, c1981. — xiii,223p : maps ; 24cm
Includes index
ISBN 0-8018-2535-0 : £12.25 B82-02223

341.5'2 — Disputes. Settlement. International law. Interim protection

Elkind, Jerome B.. Interim protection : a functional approach / Jerome B. Elkind. — The Hague ; London : Nijhoff, 1981. — xxiv,287p ; 25cm
Bibliography: p263-266. — Includes index
ISBN 90-247-2539-9 : Unpriced B82-03453

341.5′8 — Italy. International economic sanctions. Role of Great Britain & Greece, *1934-1936*

Barros, James. Britain, Greece and the politics of sanctions. — London : Swift, Dec.1982. — [256]p. — (Studies in history ; 33)
ISBN 0-901050-86-5 : £17.50 : CIP entry
B82-35216

341.5′8 — United Nations. Peace keeping operations, *to 1979*

Higgins, Rosalyn. United Nations peacekeeping : documents and commentary / Rosalyn Higgins. — Oxford : Issued under the auspices of the Royal Institute of International Affairs [by] Oxford University
Bibliography: p408-411. — Includes index
4: Europe 1946-1979. — 1981. — xii,419p : 1map ; 24cm
ISBN 0-19-218322-2 : £40.00 : CIP rev.
B80-23094

341.6 — LAW OF WAR

341.6 — Iran. Wars with Iraq, *1980-*. **Legal aspects**

Amin, S. H.. The Iran-Iraq war : legal implications. — Glasgow (165 Roebank St., Glasgow G31 3EG) : S.H. Amin, June 1982. — [110]p
ISBN 0-946124-00-0 (pbk) : £12.95 : CIP entry
B82-21952

341.6′09 — War. International law, *1856-1981 — Treaties*

Documents on the laws of war. — Oxford : Clarendon Press, Dec.1981. — [432]p
ISBN 0-19-876117-1 (cased) : £18.50 : CIP entry
ISBN 0-19-876118-x (pbk) : £10.95
B81-33860

341.6′09 — War. International law, *to 1977*

Best, Geoffrey. Humanity in warfare. — London : Methuen, Jan.1983. — [424]p. — (University paperbacks)
Originally published: London : Weidenfeld and Nicolson, 1980
ISBN 0-416-34810-6 (pbk) : £5.95 : CIP entry
B82-34572

341.6′7 — Great Britain. Enemy property. Administration, *1939-1965*

McKenzie, A. W.. The treatment of enemy property in the United Kingdom during and after the Second World War / by A.W. McKenzie. — [Chislehurst] : A.W. McKenzie, c1981. — 62p ; 21cm
Bibliography: p52. — Includes index
ISBN 0-9507837-0-6 (pbk) : £3.50 B82-11575

341.6′7 — War victims. Human rights. International law

Bothe, Michael. New rules for victims of armed conflicts : commentary on the two 1977 protocols additional to the Geneva Conventions of 1949 / by Michael Bothe, Karl Josef Partsch, Waldemar A. Solf with the collaboration of Martin Eaton. — The Hague ; London : Nijhoff, 1982. — xxi,746p : ill,forms ; 25cm
Bibliography: p707-716. — Includes index
ISBN 90-247-2537-2 : Unpriced B82-30623

341.6′9 — German war criminals. Prosecution. Policies of Allied countries

Bower, Tom. Blind eye to murder : Britain, America and the purging of Nazi Germany : a pledge betrayed / Tom Bower. — London : Deutsch, 1981. — 501p,12p of plates : ill,facsims,ports ; 23cm
Includes index
ISBN 0-233-97292-7 : Unpriced B82-21357

341.6′9 — German war criminals. Trials, *1944-1945 — National Socialist viewpoints*

Harwood, Richard. Nuremberg and other war crimes trials : a new look / by Richard Harwood. — Ladbroke : Historical Review, c1978. — 69p : ill,ports ; 29cm. — (Historical fact ; no.2)
Bibliography: p69
ISBN 0-9505505-3-1 (unbound) : £0.75
B82-04329

341.6′9 — War crimes: Rape. International law

Khushalani, Yougindra. Dignity and honour of women as basic and fundamental human rights / by Yougindra Khushalani. — The Hague ; London : Nijhoff, 1982. — 153p ; 25cm
ISBN 90-247-2585-2 : Unpriced B82-34777

341.6′9 — West Germany. Nuremberg. German war criminals. Trials, *1945-1946*

Rassinier, Paul. The real Eichmann trial, or, The incorrigible victors / by Paul Rassinier. — Southam : Historical Review Press, c1979. — 170p : ports ; 22cm
Translation of: Le véritable procès Eichmann. — Originally published: 1976
ISBN 0-9505505-5-8 (pbk) : Unpriced
B82-04403

341.7 — INTERNATIONAL COOPERATION. LEGAL ASPECTS

341.7′2 — Civil defence. International law

Jakovljević, Boško. New international status of civil defence : as an instrument for strengthening the protection of human rights / Boško Jakovljević. — The Hague ; London : Nijhoff, 1982. — 142p : ill,forms ; 25cm. — (Teneat lex gladium ; no.5)
Includes Article 61 in French. — Includes index
ISBN 90-247-2567-4 (pbk) : Unpriced
B82-21453

341.7′2 — West Germany. North Atlantic Treaty Organization military forces — *Treaties*

Agreement to amend the protocol of signature to the agreement of 3 August 1959 to supplement the agreement between the parties to the North Atlantic Treaty regarding the status of their forces with respect to foreign forces stationed in the Federal Republic of Germany as amended by the agreement of 21 October 1971 : Bonn 18 May 1981. — London : H.M.S.O., [1981]. — 3p ; 25cm. — (Miscellaneous ; no.22 (1981)) (Cmnd. ; 8371)
ISBN 0-10-183710-0 (unbound) : £0.70
B82-02747

341.7′22 — West Germany. British military forces — *Treaties between Great Britain & West Germany*

Germany *(Federal Republic)*. [Treaties, etc. Great Britain, 1982 Feb.16]. Exchange of notes between the Government of the United Kingdom of Great Britain and Northern Ireland and the Government of the Federal Republic of Germany constituting an administrative agreement under article 71, paragraph 4, of the agreement to supplement the agreement between the parties to the North Atlantic Treaty regarding the status of their forces with respect to foreign forces stationed in the Federal Republic of Germany : Bonn, 16 February 1982. — London : H.M.S.O., [1982]. — 5p ; 25cm. — (Cmnd. ; 8562)
English and German text
ISBN 0-10-185620-2 (pbk) : £1.25 B82-32828

341.7′28 — Belize. British military forces — *Treaties between Great Britain & Belize*

Great Britain. [Treaties, etc. Belize, 1981 Dec.1]. Exchange of notes between the Government of the United Kingdom of Great Britain and Northern Ireland and the Government of Belize concerning the continuing presence in Belize after independence of United Kingdom armed forces, Belmopan, 1 December 1981. — London : H.M.S.O., 1982. — 13p ; 25cm. — (Cmnd. ; 8520) (Treaty series ; no.17 (1982))
ISBN 0-10-185200-2 (unbound) : £1.90
B82-27587

341.7′28 — Singapore. British military forces — *Treaties between Great Britain & Singapore*

Great Britain. [Treaties, etc. Singapore, 1971 Dec.1. Protocols, etc., 1978 July 26]. Exchange of notes between the Government of the United Kingdom of Great Britain and Northern Ireland and the Government of Singapore further amending the Agreement regarding Assistance for the Armed Forces of Singapore and the Arrangements for a United Kingdom Force in Singapore of 1 December 1971, as amended by the exchange of notes of 26 July 1978 : Singapore, 10 June 1981. — London : H.M.S.O., [1981]. — 3p ; 25cm. — (Treaty series ; no.76 (1981)) (Cmnd. ; 8391)
ISBN 0-10-183910-3 (unbound) : £0.70
B82-06095

341.7′28 — Trident I nuclear weapons systems. Acquisition by Great Britain — *Treaties between Great Britain & United States*

The **British** strategic nuclear force, July 1980 : text of letters exchanged between the Prime Minister and the President of the United States and between the Secretary of State for Defence and the United States Secretary of Defense. — London : H.M.S.O., [1981]. — 3p ; 25cm. — (Cmnd. ; 7979)
ISBN 0-10-179790-7 (unbound) : £0.50
B82-13673

341.7′33 — Military resources: Conventional weapons. Prohibition — *Treaties*

[Convention on Prohibitions or Restrictions on the Use of certain Conventional Weapons which may be deemed to be excessively injurious or to have indiscriminate effects *(1981)*]. Convention on Prohibitions or Restrictions on the Use of certain Conventional Weapons which may be deemed to be excessively injurious or to have indiscriminate effects (with annexed protocols), New York, 10 April 1981-10 April 1982. — London : H.M.S.O., [1981]. — 19p ; 25cm. — (Miscellaneous ; no.23 (1981)) (Cmnd. ; 8370)
ISBN 0-10-183700-3 (unbound) : £2.30
B82-03336

341.7′5 — Britons. Debts of Czechoslovakia. Settlement — *Treaties between Great Britain & Czechoslovakia*

Czechoslovakia. [Treaties, etc. Great Britain, 1982 Jan.29]. Agreement between the Government of the United Kingdom of Great Britain and Northern Ireland and the Government of the Czechoslovak Socialist Republic on the settlement of certain outstanding claims and financial issues : Prague, 29 January 1982 : with amending exchange of notes : Prague, 2 February 1982. — London : H.M.S.O., [1982]. — 23p ; 25cm. — (Treaty series ; no.21 (1982)) (Cmnd. ; 8557)
English and Czech text
ISBN 0-10-185570-2 (pbk) : £2.55 B82-32827

341.7′5 — Economic relations. International legal aspects

VerLoren van Themaat, Pieter. The changing structure of international economic law : a contribution of legal history, of comparative law and of general legal theory to the debate on a new international economic order / by Pieter VerLoren van Themaat. — The Hague ; London : Nijhoff, 1981. — xxv,395 ; 25cm
ISBN 90-247-2540-2 : Unpriced B82-00478

341.7′5′0614 — Brazil. Economic relations with European Economic Community — *Treaties between Brazil & European Economic Community*

Brazil. [Treaties, etc. European Economic Community, 1980 Sept.18]. Framework agreement for co-operation between the European Economic Community and the Federative Republic of Brazil ; and, Exchange of letters on sea transport. and, Protocol concerning commercial and economic co-operation between the European Coal and Steel Community and the Federative Republic of Brazil : Brussels, 18 September 1980. — London : H.M.S.O., 1982. — 11p ; 25cm. — (Cmnd. ; 8485) (European Communities ; no.4 (1982))
ISBN 0-10-184850-1 (unbound) : £1.50
B82-22032

341.7′5′0614 — European Economic Community. Entry of Greece — *Treaties between Cyprus & European Economic Community*

Cyprus. [Treaties, etc. European Economic Community, 1972 Dec.19. Protocols, etc. 1980 Dec.12]. Protocol to the agreement establishing an association between the European Economic Community and the Republic of Cyprus consequent on the accession of the Hellenic Republic to the Community, Brussels, 12 December 1980. — London : H.M.S.O., [1981]. — 27p ; 25cm. — (European communities ; no.60(1981)) (Cmnd. ; 8378)
ISBN 0-10-183730-5 (unbound) : £2.65
B82-03335

341.7'5'0614 — European Economic Community. Entry of Greece — *Treaties between European Economic Community & Spain*

European Economic Community. [Treaties, etc., 1970 June 29. Protocols, etc., 1980 Dec.12]. Protocol to the agreement between the European Economic Community and Spain consequent on the accession of the Hellenic Republic to the Community : Brussels, 12 December 1980. — London : H.M.S.O., [1982]. — 31p ; 25cm. — (Cmnd. ; 8452) (European Communities ; no.1 (1982))
ISBN 0-10-184520-0 (unbound) : £2.65 B82-20562

341.7'5'0614 — European Economic Community. Entry of Greece — *Treaties between Jordan & European Economic Community*

European Economic Community. [Treaties, etc. Jordan 1977 Jan. 18. Protocols, etc., 1980 Dec.12]. Additional protocol to the Co-operation Agreement between the European Economic Community and the Hashemite Kingdom of Jordan consequent on the accession of the Hellenic Republic to the Community. and, Additional protocol to the Agreement between the member states of the European Coal and Steel Community and the Hashemite Kingdom of Jordan consequent on the accession of the Hellenic Republic to the Community : Brussels, 12 December 1980. — London : H.M.S.O., 1982. — 30p ; 25cm. — (Cmnd. ; 8483) (European Communities ; no.6 (1982))
ISBN 0-10-184830-7 (unbound) : £2.65 B82-22034

341.7'5'0614 — India *(Republic).* **Economic relations with European Economic Community** — *Treaties between European Economic Community & India (Republic)*

European Economic Community. [Treaties, etc. India, 1981 June 23]. Agreement on commercial and economic co-operation between the European Economic Community and India and Protocol concerning commercial and economic co-operation between the European Coal and Steel Community and India, Luxembourg, 23 June 1981. — London : H.M.S.O., 1982. — 11p ; 25cm
£1.50 (unbound) B82-27585

341.7'51 — Postal orders. Exchange — *Treaties between Great Britain & Japan*

Great Britain. [Treaties, etc. Japan, 1981 Feb.13]. Agreement for the exchange of postal payment orders between the United Kingdom of Great Britain and Northern Ireland and Japan : Tokyo, 13 February 1981. — London : H.M.S.O., [1981]. — 11p ; 25cm. — (Cmnd. ; 8396)
English and Japanese text
ISBN 0-10-183960-x (unbound) : £1.50 B82-11547

341.7'52'02664105332 — Foreign investment — *Treaties between Great Britain & Yemen (Arab Republic)*

Great Britain. [Treaties, etc. Yemen Arab Republic, 1982 Feb.25]. Agreement between the Government of the United Kingdom of Great Britain and Northern Ireland and the Government of the Yemen Arab Republic for the promotion and protection of investments : Sana'a, 25 February 1982. — London : H.M.S.O., 1982. — 7p ; 25cm. — (Cmnd. ; 8559) (Yemen Arab Republic ; no.1 (1982))
ISBN 0-10-185590-7 (unbound) : £1.25 B82-32500

341.7'52'02664105492 — Channel Islands & Isle of Man. Extension of treaties on foreign investment between Great Britain & Bangladesh — *Treaties between Great Britain & Bangladesh*

Bangladesh. [Treaties, etc. Great Britain, 1981 Aug.31]. Exchange of notes between the Government of the United Kingdom of Great Britain and Northern Ireland and the Government of the People's Republic of Bangladesh concerning the extension to the Bailiwicks of Jersey and Guernsey and the Isle of Man of the agreement for the promotion and protection of investments, signed at London on 19 June 1980 : Dacca, 31 August 1981/21 January 1982. — London : H.M.S.O., [1982]. — 30p ; 25cm. — (Treaty series ; no.23 (1982)) (Cmnd. ; 8563)
ISBN 0-10-185630-x (pbk) : £0.75 B82-32830

341.7'52'02664105695 — Channel Islands & Isle of Man. Extension of treaties on foreign investment between Great Britain & Jordan — *Treaties between Great Britain & Jordan*

Great Britain. [Treaties, etc. Jordan, 1979 Oct.10. Protocols, etc. 1981 June 2]. Exchange of notes between the Government of the United Kingdom of Great Britain and Northern Ireland and the Government of the Hashemite Kingdom of Jordan concerning the extension to the Bailiwicks of Jersey and Guernsey and the Isle of Man of the agreement for the promotion and protection of investments, signed at Amman on 10 October 1979, Amman, 2/14 June 1981. — London : H.M.S.O., [1981]. — 3p ; 25cm. — (Treaty series ; no.73 (1981)) (Cmnd. ; 8383)
ISBN 0-10-183830-1 (unbound) : £0.70 B82-03337

341.7'52'0266410595 — Foreign investment — *Treaties between Great Britain & Malaysia*

Great Britain. [Treaties, etc. Malaysia, 1981 May 21]. Agreement between the Government of the United Kingdom of Great Britain and Northern Ireland and the Government of Malaysia for the promotion and protection of investments : London, 21 May 1981. — London : H.M.S.O., 1981. — 7p ; 25cm. — (Cmnd. ; 8269) (Malaysia ; no.1 (1981))
£1.10 (unbound) B82-34122

341.7'52'0266410664 — Foreign investment — *Treaties between Great Britain & Sierra Leone*

Great Britain. [Treaties, etc. Sierra Leone, 1981 Dec.8]. Agreement between the Government of the United Kingdom of Great Britain and the Northern Ireland and the Government of the Republic of Sierra Leone for the promotion and protection of investments, Freetown, 8 December 1981. — London : H.M.S.O., [1982]. — 7p ; 25cm. — (Cmnd. ; 8501) (Sierra Leone ; no.1 (1982))
ISBN 0-10-185010-7 (unbound) : £1.15 B82-31679

341.7'52'0266410953 — Foreign investment — *Treaties between Great Britain & Papua New Guinea*

Great Britain. [Treaties, etc. Papua New Guinea, 1981 May 14]. Agreement between the government of the United Kingdom of Great Britain and Northern Ireland and the government of the Independent State of Papua New Guinea for the promotion and protection of investments : London, 14 May 1981. — London : H.M.S.O., [1982]. — 7p ; 25cm. — (Treaty series ; no.15 (1982)) (Cmnd. ; 8506)
" ... previously published as Papua New Guinea No.1 (1981) Cmnd. 8307"
ISBN 0-10-185060-3 (unbound) : £1.15 B82-25144

341.7'53 — European Community countries. Free markets. European Economic Community law

Courts and free markets : perspectives from the United States and Europe / edited by Terrance Sandalow and Eric Stein. — Oxford : Clarendon
Vol.1. — 1982. — xxxix,271p ; 24cm
ISBN 0-19-825366-4 : £20.00 : CIP rev.
Primary classification 347.303'723 B81-36968

341.7'53 — European Community countries. Industries. Competition. European Economic Community law

Kerse, C. S.. EEC antitrust procedure. — London (4 Bloomsbury Sq., WC1A 2RL) : European Law Centre, May 1981. — [320]p
ISBN 0-907451-03-9 : £34.00 : CIP entry B81-14779

Kerse, C. S.. EEC antitrust procedure. — London (4 Bloomsbury Sq., WC1A 2RL) : European Law Centre
Supplement 1982. — Oct.1982. — [56]p
ISBN 0-907451-06-3 (pbk) : £6.00 : CIP entry B82-33211

Korah, Valentine. An introductory guide to EEC competition law and practice / Valentine Korah. — 2nd ed. — Oxford : ESC, 1981. — xxii,160p ; 22cm
Previous ed.: 1978. — Bibliography: p134-136. — Includes index
ISBN 0-906214-08-4 (pbk) : Unpriced : CIP rev. B81-21580

341.7'54 — Britons. Commercial transactions with Poles. Debts of Poles. Repayment — *Treaties between Great Britain & Poland*

Great Britain. [Treaties, etc. Poland, 1981 July 2]. Agreement between the Government of the United Kingdom of Great Britain and Northern Ireland and the Government of the Polish People's Republic on certain commercial debts : Warsaw, 2 July 1981. — London : H.M.S.O., [1981]. — 6p ; 25cm. — (Treaty series ; no.68 (1981)) (Cmnd. ; 8374)
ISBN 0-10-183740-2 (unbound) : £1.15 B82-03637

341.7'54 — Foreign trade in primary commodities. International legal aspects

Atimomo, Emiko. Law and diplomacy in commodity economics : a study of techniques, co-operation and conflict in international public policy issues / Emiko Atimomo ; preface by Pierre Vellas. — London : Macmillan, 1981. — xix,384p ; 23cm
Bibliography: p363-371. — Includes index
ISBN 0-333-27745-7 : £30.00 B82-06869

Khan, Kabir-ur-Rahman. The law and organisation of international commodity agreements / Kabir-ur-Rahman Khan. — The Hague ; London : Nijhoff, 1982. — xxv,416p ; 25cm
Bibliography: p395-400. — Includes index
ISBN 90-247-2554-2 : Unpriced B82-37031

341.7'54 — Foreign trade. International law

McGovern, Edmond. International trade regulation. — Exeter : Globefield Press, Nov.1982. — [500]p
ISBN 0-9508463-0-9 : £20.00 : CIP entry B82-36170

341.7'54'0265 — European Economic Community. Foreign trade, *to 1981* — *Treaties*

Oliver, Peter. Free movement of goods in the EEC. — London : European Law Centre, June 1982. — [285]p
ISBN 0-907451-05-5 : £34.00 : CIP entry B82-16493

341.7'54'0265 — European Economic Community. Foreign trade with Yugoslavia — *Treaties between European Economic Community & Yugoslavia*

European Economic Community. [Treaties, etc. Yugoslavia, 1980 May 6]. Interim agreement between the European Economic Community and the Socialist Federal Republic of Yugoslavia on trade and trade co-operation : (with Final Act) : Brussels, 6 May 1980. — London : H.M.S.O., [1981]. — 109p : forms ; 25cm. — (Cmnd. ; 8120) (European Communities ; no.1 (1981))
ISBN 0-10-181200-0 (pbk) : £4.90 B82-00434

341.7'543 — Developed countries. Foreign trade with developing countries. Policies of developed countries: Generalised Systems of Preferences. Legal aspects

Yusuf, Abdulqawi. Legal aspects of trade preferences for developing states : a study in the influence of development needs on the evolution of international law / by Abdulqawi Yusuf. — The Hague ; London : Nijhoff, 1982. — xx,185p ; 25cm
Bibliography: p169-181. — Includes index
ISBN 90-247-2583-6 : Unpriced B82-32403

341.7'5471311'0265 — Foreign trade in wheat — *Treaties*

[International Wheat Agreement *(1971). Protocols, etc. 1979 Apr.25*]. Protocols for the fifth extension of the Wheat Trade Convention and Food Aid Convention constituting the International Wheat Agreement 1971 : Washington, 25 April-16 May 1979. — London : H.M.S.O., [1980]. — 19p ; 25cm. — (Treaty series ; no.75 (1980)) (Cmnd. ; 8016)
"... previously published as Miscellaneous No.16 (1979), Cmnd. 7593"
ISBN 0-10-180160-2 (unbound) : £2.10 B82-12757

341.7′5471373′0265 — Foreign trade in coffee — *Treaties*

[International Coffee Agreement *(1976). Protocols, etc., 1981 Sept.25*]. Resolution to extend the International Coffee Agreement 1976 : approved at the thirty-sixth session of the International Coffee Council on 25 September 1981. — London : H.M.S.O., 1982. — [4]p ; 25cm. — (Miscellaneous ; no.9 (1982)) (Cmnd. ; 8503)
ISBN 0-10-185030-1 (Unbound) : £0.70
B82-21814

[International Coffee Agreement *(1976). Protocols, etc., 1982 July 2*]. Resolution to amend the resolution to extend the International Coffee Agreement 1976 : approved at the thirty-seventh session of the International Coffee Council on 2 July 1982. — London : H.M.S.O., 1982. — [4]p ; 25cm. — (Miscellaneous ; no.15 (1982)) (Cmnd. ; 8605)
ISBN 0-10-186050-1 (unbound) : £0.75
B82-39377

341.7′54714′026640561 — European Community countries. Imports from Turkey: Fruit. Import duties — *Treaties between European Economic Community & Turkey*

European Economic Community. [Treaties, etc. Turkey, 1981 Jan.20]. Agreement in the form of an exchange of letters between the European Economic Community and the Republic of Turkey concerning Article 3(3) of Decision no.1/80 of the Association Council : Brussels, 20 Jan. 1981. — London : H.M.S.O., 1982. — 3p ; 25cm. — (Cmnd. ; 8482) (European Communities ; no.5 (1982))
ISBN 0-10-184820-x (unbound) : £0.70
Primary classification 341.7′54715′0266140561
B82-22030

341.7′54715′0266140561 — European Community countries. Imports from Turkey: Vegetables. Import duties — *Treaties between European Economic Community & Turkey*

European Economic Community. [Treaties, etc. Turkey, 1981 Jan.20]. Agreement in the form of an exchange of letters between the European Economic Community and the Republic of Turkey concerning Article 3(3) of Decision no.1/80 of the Association Council : Brussels, 20 Jan. 1981. — London : H.M.S.O., 1982. — 3p ; 25cm. — (Cmnd. ; 8482) (European Communities ; no.5 (1982))
ISBN 0-10-184820-x (unbound) : £0.70
Also classified at 341.7′54714′026640561
B82-22030

341.7′54715642′0265 — European Community countries. Imports from Portugal: Preserved tomatoes — *Treaties between European Economic Community & Portugal*

European Economic Community. [Treaties, etc. Portugal, 1981 Apr.24]. Agreement in the form of an exchange of letters between the European Economic Community and the Portuguese Republic regarding prepared or preserved tomatoes falling within subheading 20.02C of the Common Customs Tariff, Brussels, 24 April 1981. — London : H.M.S.O., [1981]. — 3p ; 25cm. — (European communities ; no.61 (1981)) (Cmnd. ; 8378)
ISBN 0-10-183780-1 (unbound) : £0.70
B82-03338

341.7′54716313′0265 — European Community countries. Imports from Argentina: Lamb & mutton — *Treaties between European Economic Community & Argentina*

Argentina. Arrangement in the form of an exchange of letters between the European Economic Community and the Argentine Republic on trade in mutton and lamb, Brussels, 17 October 1980. — London : H.M.S.O., 1981. — 5p ; 25cm. — (European Communities ; no.71 (1981)) (Cmnd. ; 8433)
ISBN 0-10-184330-5 (unbound) : £1.15
B82-11604

341.7′54716313′0265 — European Community countries. Imports from Uruguay: Lamb & mutton — *Treaties between European Economic Community & Uruguay*
European Economic Community. [Treaties, etc. Uruguay, 1980 Oct.17]. Arrangement in the form of an exchange of letters between the European Economic Community and the Eastern Republic of Uruguay on trade in mutton and lamb : Brussels, 17 October 1980. — London : H.M.S.O., [1981]. — 6p ; 25cm. — (European Communities ; no.69 (1981)) (Cmnd. ; 8409)
ISBN 0-10-184090-x (unbound) : £1.15
Also classified at 341.7′547163913′0265
B82-11348

341.7′54716313′0265 — European Community countries. Imports from Yugoslavia: Mutton — *Treaties between European Economic Community & Yugoslavia*
European Economic Community. [Treaties, etc. Yugoslavia, 1981 May 8]. Exchanges of letters between the European Economic Community and the Socialist Federal Republic of Yugoslavia on trade in the sheepmeat and goatmeat sector : Brussels, 8 May 1981. — London : H.M.S.O., [1981]. — 7p ; 25cm. — (European Communities ; no.68 (1981)) (Cmnd. ; 8408)
ISBN 0-10-184080-2 (unbound) : £1.15
Also classified at 341.7′547163913′0265
B82-11347

341.7′54716313′026640436 — European Community countries. Imports from Austria: Lamb & mutton — *Treaties between European Community & Austria*
Austria. [Treaties, etc. European Economic Community, 1981 July 10]. Arrangement in the form ofan exchange of letters between the European Economic Community and the Republic of Austria on trade in mutton, lamb and goatmeat and exchange of letters relevant to clause 2 of the arragnement Brussels, 10 July 1981. — London : H.M.S.O., [1982]. — 7p ; 25cm. — (European Communities ; no.11 (1982)) (Cmnd. ; 8498)
ISBN 0-10-184980-x (unbound) : £1.15
Also classified at 341.7′547163913′026640436
B82-25146

341.7′54716313′026640439 — European Community countries. Imports from Hungary: Mutton — *Treaties between European Economic Community & Hungary*
European Economic Community. [Treaties, etc. Hungary, 1981 July 10]. Exchange of letters between the European Economic Community and the People′s Republic of Hungary on trade in the sheepmeat and goatmeat sector : Geneva, 10 July 1981. — London : H.M.S.O., 1982. — 7p ; 25cm. — (Cmnd. ; 8484) (European Communities ; no.7 (1982))
ISBN 0-10-184840-4 (unbound) : £1.15
Also classified at 341.7′547163913′02664039
B82-22035

341.7′54716313′0266404912 — European Community countries. Imports from Iceland: Mutton — *Treaties between European Economic Community & Iceland*
European Economic Community. [Treaties, etc. Iceland, 1981 May 15]. Arrangement in the form of an exchange of letters between the European Economic Community and the Republic of Iceland on trade in sheepmeat and goatmeat and exchange of letters relevant to clause 2 of the arrangement : Brussels, 15 May 1981. — London : H.M.S.O., 1982. — 6p ; 25cm. — (Cmnd. ; 8492) (European Communities ; no.9 (1982))
ISBN 0-10-184920-6 (unbound) : £1.15
Also classified at 341.7′547163913′0266404912
B82-21860

341.7′547163913′0265 — European Community countries. Imports from Uruguay: Goatmeat — *Treaties between European Economic Community & Uruguay*
European Economic Community. [Treaties, etc. Uruguay, 1980 Oct.17]. Arrangement in the form of an exchange of letters between the European Economic Community and the Eastern Republic of Uruguay on trade in mutton and lamb : Brussels, 17 October 1980. — London : H.M.S.O., [1981]. — 6p ; 25cm. — (European Communities ; no.69 (1981)) (Cmnd. ; 8409)
ISBN 0-10-184090-x (unbound) : £1.15
Primary classification 341.7′54716313′0265
B82-11348

341.7′547163913′0265 — European Community countries. Imports from Yugoslavia: Goatmeat — *Treaties between European Economic Community & Yugoslavia*

European Economic Community. [Treaties, etc. Yugoslavia, 1981 May 8]. Exchanges of letters between the European Economic Community and the Socialist Federal Republic of Yugoslavia on trade in the sheepmeat and goatmeat sector : Brussels, 8 May 1981. — London : H.M.S.O., [1981]. — 7p ; 25cm. — (European Communities ; no.68 (1981)) (Cmnd. ; 8408)
ISBN 0-10-184080-2 (unbound) : £1.15
Primary classification 341.7′54716313′0265
B82-11347

341.7′547163913′02664039 — European Community countries. Imports from Hungary: Goatmeat — *Treaties between European Economic Community & Hungary*

European Economic Community. [Treaties, etc. Hungary, 1981 July 10]. Exchange of letters between the European Economic Community and the People′s Republic of Hungary on trade in the sheepmeat and goatmeat sector : Geneva, 10 July 1981. — London : H.M.S.O., 1982. — 7p ; 25cm. — (Cmnd. ; 8484) (European Communities ; no.7 (1982))
ISBN 0-10-184840-4 (unbound) : £1.15
Primary classification 341.7′54716313′026640439
B82-22035

341.7′547163913′026640436 — European Community countries. Imports from Austria: Goatmeat — *Treaties between European Community & Austria*

Austria. [Treaties, etc. European Economic Community, 1981 July 10]. Arrangement in the form ofan exchange of letters between the European Economic Community and the Republic of Austria on trade in mutton, lamb and goatmeat and exchange of letters relevant to clause 2 of the arragnement Brussels, 10 July 1981. — London : H.M.S.O., [1982]. — 7p ; 25cm. — (European Communities ; no.11 (1982)) (Cmnd. ; 8498)
ISBN 0-10-184980-x (unbound) : £1.15
Primary classification 341.7′54716313′026640436
B82-25146

341.7′547163913′0266404912 — European Community countries. Imports from Iceland: Goatmeat — *Treaties between European Economic Community & Iceland*

European Economic Community. [Treaties, etc. Iceland, 1981 May 15]. Arrangement in the form of an exchange of letters between the European Economic Community and the Republic of Iceland on trade in sheepmeat and goatmeat and exchange of letters relevant to clause 2 of the arrangement : Brussels, 15 May 1981. — London : H.M.S.O., 1982. — 6p ; 25cm. — (Cmnd. ; 8492) (European Communities ; no.9 (1982))
ISBN 0-10-184920-6 (unbound) : £1.15
Primary classification 341.7′54716313′0266404912
B82-21860

341.7′547224 — European Coal and Steel Community. Revenue. Contributions — *Treaties*

Decision of the representatives of the governments of the member states of the European Coal and Steel Community, meeting within Council, allocating to that Community supplementary revenue for 1981 : Brussels, 7 December 1981. — London : H.M.S.O., [1982]. — 3p ; 25cm. — (Treaty series ; no.12 (1982))
ISBN 0-10-184900-1 (unbound) : £0.70
B82-20565

341.7′5472453′0265 — Foreign trade in tin — *Treaties*

[Sixth International Tin Agreement *(1981)*]. Sixth International Tin Agreement : New York, 3 August 1981 to 30 April 1982. — London : H.M.S.O., [1982]. — 54p ; 25cm. — (Cmnd. ; 8546)
ISBN 0-10-185460-9 (unbound) : £4.20
B82-27234

341.7′54756292′0265 — Portugal. Imports from European Community countries: Motor vehicles — *Treaties between European Economic Community & Portugal*

European Economic Community. [Treaties, etc. Portugal, 1972 July 22. Protocols, etc. 1979 December 19]. Supplementary protocol to the agreement between the European Economic Community and the Portuguese Republic with protocol on imports of motor vehicles, final act and exchanges of letters : Brussels, 19 December 1979. — London : H.M.S.O., [1980]. — 27p ; 25cm. — (European Communities ; no.38 (1980)) (Cmnd. ; 8026)
ISBN 0-10-180260-9 (unbound) : £2.40
B82-12760

341.7′5475664362′0265 — European Community countries. Imports from Algeria: Olive oil. Import duties — *Treaties between Algeria & European Economic Community*

Algeria. [Treaties, etc. European Economic Community, 1981 Dec.16]. Agreement in the form of an exchange of letters between the European Economic Community and the Democratic and Popular Republic of Algeria fixing the additional amount to be deducted from the levy on imports into the Community of untreated olive oil, originating in Algeria, for the period from 1 November 1981 to 31 October 1982 : Brussels, 16 December 1981. — London : H.M.S.O., [1982]. — 3p ; 25cm. — (European Communities ; no.27(1982)) (Cmnd. ; 8580)
ISBN 0-10-185800-0 (unbound) : £0.75
B82-40837

341.7′5475664362′0265 — European Community countries. Imports from Morocco: Olive oil. Import duties — *Treaties between European Economic Community & Morocco*

European Economic Community. [Treaties, etc. Morocco, 1981 Dec.16]. Agreement in the form of an exchange of letters between the European Economic Community and the Kingdom of Morocco fixing the additional amount to be deducted from the levy on imports into the Community of untreated olive oil, originating in Morocco, for a period from 1 November 1987 to 31 October 1982 : Brussels, 16 December 1981. — London : H.M.S.O., 1982. — 3p ; 25cm. — (European Communities ; no.25 (1982)) (Cmnd. ; 8578)
ISBN 0-10-185780-2 (unbound) : £0.75
B82-39985

341.7′5475664362′0265 — European Community countries. Imports from Turkey: Olive oil. Import duties — *Treaties between European Economic Community & Turkey*

European Economic Community. [Treaties, etc. Turkey, 1982 Dec.21]. Agreement in the form of an exchange of letters between the European Economic Community and Turkey fixing the additional amount to be deducted from the levy on imports into the Community of untreated olive oil, originating in Turkey, for the period 1 November 1981 to 31 October 1982 : Brussels, 21 December 1981. — London : H.M.S.O., [1982]. — 3p ; 25cm. — (European Communities ; no.22(1982)) (Cmnd. ; 8583)
ISBN 0-10-185830-2 (unbound) : £0.75
B82-40836

341.7′5475664362′0265 — Foreign trade in olive oil — *Treaties*

[International Olive Oil Agreement *(1979)***]**. International Olive Oil Agreement, 1979 : Madrid, 1 July-16 November 1979. — London : H.M.S.O., [1980]. — v,24p ; 25cm. — (Miscellaneous ; no.26 (1980)) (Cmnd. ; 8101)
ISBN 0-10-181010-5 (unbound) : £2.40
B82-11420

341.7′54756648 — European Community countries. Imports from Algeria: Preserved fruit salads — *Treaties between Algeria & European Economic Community*

Algeria. [Treaties, etc. European Economic Community, 1981 Dec.16]. Agreement in the form of an exchange of letters between the European Economic Community and the Democratic and Popular Republic of Algeria concerning the import into the Community of preserved fruit salads originating in Algeria : Brussels, 16 December 1981. — London : H.M.S.O., [1982]. — 3p ; 25cm. — (European Communities ; no.26(1982))
ISBN 0-10-185810-8 (unbound) : £0.75
B82-40838

341.7′54756648 — European Community countries. Imports from Israel: Preserved fruit salads — *Treaties between European Economic Community & Israel*

European Economic Community. [Treaties, etc. Israel, 1981 Dec.30]. Agreement in the form of an exchange of letters relating to Article 9 of Protocol no.1 to the agreement between the European Economic Community and the State of Israel concerning the importation into the Community of preserved fruit salads originating in Israel (1982) : Brussels, 30 December 1981. — London : H.M.S.O., [1982]. — 3p ; 25cm. — (European Communities ; no.23(1982)) (Cmnd. ; 8582)
ISBN 0-10-185820-5 (unbound) : £0.75
B82-40839

341.7′54756648 — European Community countries. Imports from Morocco: Preserved fruit salads — *Treaties between European Economic Community & Morocco*

European Economic Community. [Treaties, etc. Morocco, 1981 Dec.16]. Agreement in the form of an exchange of letters between the European Economic Community and the Kingdom of Morocco concerning the import into the Community of preserved fruit salads originating in Morocco : Brussels, 16 December 1981. — London : H.M.S.O., 1982. — 3p ; 25cm. — (European Communities ; no.24 (1982)) (Cmnd. ; 8579)
ISBN 0-10-185790-x (unbound) : £0.75
B82-39986

341.7′54756648 — European Community countries. Imports from Tunisia: Preserved fruit salads — *Treaties between European Economic Community & Tunisia*

European Economic Community. [Treaties, etc. Tunisia, 1981 Dec.18]. Agreement in the form of an exchange of letters between the European Economic Community and the Tunisian Republic concerning the import into the Community of preserved fruit salads originating in Tunisia : Brussels, 18 December 1981. — London : H.M.S.O., 1982. — 3p ; 25cm. — (Cmnd. ; 8585) (European Communities ; no.28 (1982))
ISBN 0-10-185850-7 (unbound) : £0.75
B82-39517

341.7′547566538′0265 — Petroleum products. Foreign trade between Norway & European Community countries — *Treaties between Norway & European Economic Community*

European Economic Community. [Treaties, etc. Norway, 1973 May 14. Protocols, etc. 1981 Mar.27]. Agreement in the form of an exchange of letters derogating further from Article 1 of Protocol No.3 to the agreement between the European Economic Community and the Kingdom of Norway : Brussels, 27 March 1981. — London : H.M.S.O., [1981]. — 3p ; 25cm. — (European communities ; no.49 (1981)) (Cmnd. ; 8347)
ISBN 0-10-183470-5 (unbound) : £0.70
B82-02805

341.7′5475665538′0265 — European Community countries. Imports from Portugal: Petroleum products — *Treaties between European Economic Community & Portugal*

European Economic Community. [Treaties, etc. Portugal, 1972 July 22,. Protocols, etc. 1981 Mar.20]. Agreement in the form of an exchange of letters derogating further from Article 1 of Protocol no.3 to the agreement between the European Economic Community and the Portuguese Republic, Brussels, 20 March 1981. — London : H.M.S.O., 1981. — 3p ; 25cm. — (European communities ; no.52 (1981)) (Cmnd. ; 8349)
ISBN 0-10-183490-x (unbound) : £0.70
B82-00027

341.7′547567628 — Great Britain. Imports from Finland: Paper products. Import duties — *Treaties between European Economic Community & Finland*

European Economic Community. [Treaties, etc. Finland, 1973 Oct.5. Protocols, etc. 1980 Apr.18]. Agreement in the form of an exchange of letters rectifying certain duty-free quotas opened by the United Kingdom in accordance with protocol no.1 to the free trade agreement between the European Economic Community and Finland, Brussels, 18 April 1980. — London : H.M.S.O., [1980]. — 3p ; 25cm. — (European communities ; no.39 (1980)) (Cmnd. ; 8028)
ISBN 0-10-180280-3 (unbound) : £0.70
B82-01241

European Economic Community. [Treaties, etc. Finland, 1973 Oct.5. Protocols, etc., 1981 Oct.1]. Agreement in the form of an exchange of letters amending certain Zero-Duty tariff quotas opened by the United Kindon for 1981 in accordance with Protocol No.1 of the Agreement between the European Economic Community and the Republic of Finland : Brussels, 1 October 1981. — London : H.M.S.O., 1982. — 3p ; 25cm. — (Cmnd. ; 8493) (European Communities ; no.10 (1982))
ISBN 0-10-184930-3 (unbound) : £0.70
B82-21859

341.7′547567628 — Great Britain. Imports from Norway: Paper products. Import duties — *Treaties between European Economic Community & Norway*

European Economic Community. [Treaties, etc. Norway, 1973 May 14. Protocols, etc. 1980 Apr.29]. Agreement in the form of an exchange of letters rectifying certain duty-free quotas opened by the United Kingdom in accordance with protocol no.1 to the free trade agreement between the European Economic Community and Norway, Brussels, 29 April 1980. — London : H.M.S.O., [1980]. — 2p ; 25cm. — (European communities ; no.40 (1980)) (Cmnd. ; 8029)
ISBN 0-10-180290-0 (unbound) : £0.70
B82-01236

341.7′5475676288′0265 — Great Britain. Imports from Sweden: Paperboard. Import duties — *Treaties between European Economic Community & Sweden*

European Economic Community. [Treaties, etc. Sweden, 1972 July 22. Protocols, etc., 1980 June 16]. Agreement in the form of an exchange of letters rectifying certain duty-free quotas opened by the United Kingdom in accordance with protocol no.1 to the Free Trade Agreement between the European Economic Community and the Kingdom of Sweden : Brussels, 16 June 1980. — London : H.M.S.O., [1980]. — 3p ; 25cm. — (European Communities ; no.46 (1980)) (Cmnd. ; 8055)
ISBN 0-10-180550-0 (unbound) : £0.70
B82-11453

341.7′54756770286′0265 — European Community countries. Imports from Colombia: Textile products — *Treaties between Colombia & European Economic Community*

Colombia. [Treaties, etc. European Economic Community, 1981 Feb.25]. Agreement between the European Economic Community and the Republic of Colombia on trade in textile products (with exchange of letters and declaration by the European Economic Community) : Brussels, 25 February 1981. — London : H.M.S.O., [1982]. — 38p ; 25cm. — (European communities ; no.2 (1982)) (Cmnd. ; 8466)
ISBN 0-10-184660-6 (unbound) : £3.05
B82-18671

341.7′54756770286′0265 — European Community countries. Imports from Egypt: Textile products — *Treaties between Egypt & European Economic Community*

Egypt. [Treaties, etc. European Economic Community, 1980 Nov.24]. Agreement between the European Economic Community and the Arab Rebublic of Egypt on trade in textile products, Brussels, 24 November 1980. — London : H.M.S.O., [1981]. — 38p ; 25cm. — (European communities ; no.65 (1981)) (Cmnd. ; 8397)
ISBN 0-10-183970-7 (unbound) : £3.05
B82-09561

341.7′54756770286′0265 — European Community countries. Imports from India *(Republic)*: **Textile products** — *Treaties between European Economic Community & India (Republic)*

European Economic Community. [Treaties, etc. India, 1981 Feb.17]. Agreement between the European Economic Community and the Republic of India on trade in textile products, Brussels, 17 February 1981. — London : H.M.S.O., 1981. — 42p ; 25cm. — (Cmnd. ; 8394) (European communities ; no.64(1981))
ISBN 0-10-183940-5 (pbk) : £3.40 B82-08338

341.7′54756770286′0265 — European Community countries. Imports from Malaysia: Textile products — *Treaties between European Economic Community & Malaysia*

European Economic Community. [Treaties, etc. Malaysia, 1981 June 17]. Agreement between the European Economic Community and Malaysia on trade in textile products : Brussels, 17 June 1981. — London : H.M.S.O., 1982. — 39p ; 25cm. — (Cmnd. ; 8568) (European Communities ; no.21 (1982))
ISBN 0-10-185680-6 (pbk) : £3.40 B82-39375

341.7′54756770286′0265 — European Community countries. Imports from Romania: Textile products — *Treaties between European Economic Community & Romania*

European Economic Community. [Treaties, etc. Romania, 1980 Nov.27]. Agreement between the European Economic Community and the Socialist Republic of Romania on trade in textile products : Brussels, 27 November 1980. — London : H.M.S.O., [1981]. — 43p : forms ; 25cm. — (European communities ; no.66 (1981)) (Cmnd. ; 8407)
ISBN 0-10-184070-5 (pbk) : £3.40 B82-09806

European Economic Community. [Treaties, etc. Romania, 1980 Nov.27]. Agreement in the form of an exchange of letters between the European Economic Community and the Socialist Republic of Romania : Brussels, 27 November 1980. — London : H.M.S.O., [1981]. — 6p ; 25cm. — (European Communities ; no.67 (1981)) (Cmnd. ; 8416)
ISBN 0-10-184160-4 (unbound) : £1.15
B82-11346

341.7′54756770286′0265 — European Community countries. Imports from Yugoslavia: Textile products — *Treaties between European Economic Community & Yugoslavia*

European Economic Community. [Treaties, etc. Yugoslavia, 1981 May 8]. Agreement between the European Economic Community and the Socialist Federative Republic of Yugoslavia on trade in textile products : Brussels, 8 May 1981. — London : H.M.S.O., [1981]. — 42p : forms ; 25cm. — (European communities ; no.63 (1981)) (Cmnd. ; 8392)
ISBN 0-10-183920-0 (unbound) : £3.40
B82-06094

341.7′55 — North Sea. Natural gas deposits. Murchison Field Reservoir. Exploitation — *Treaties between Great Britain & Norway*

Great Britain. [Treaties, etc. Norway, 1979 Oct.16. Protocols, etc., 1981 Oct.22]. Agreement supplementary to the Agreement of 16 October 1979 between the Government of the United Kingdom of Great Britain and Northern Ireland and the Government of the Kingdom of Norway : relating to the exploitation of the Murchison Field Reservoir and the offtake of petroleum therefrom : Oslo, 22 October 1981. — London : H.M.S.O., 1982. — 9p ; 25cm. — (Cmnd. ; 8577) (Treaty series ; no.25 (1982))
Text in English and Norwegian
ISBN 0-10-185770-5 (unbound) : £1.65
B82-39516

341.7′55 — Nuclear materials. Handling. Safety measures — *Treaties*

[Convention on the Physical Protection of Nuclear Material *(1980)*]. Convention on the Physical Protection of Nuclear Material : opened for signature at the headquarters of the International Atomic Energy Authority in Vienna and at the headquarters of the United Nations in New York on 3 March 1980. — London : H.M.S.O., [1980]. — 15p ; 25cm. — (Miscellaneous ; no.27 (1980)) (Cmnd. ; 8112)
ISBN 0-10-181120-9 (unbound) : £1.70
B82-12759

341.7′55 — Nuclear materials. Transfer — *Treaties between Great Britain & Switzerland*

Great Britain. [Treaties, etc. Switzerland, 1981 July 13]. Exchange of notes between the Government of the United Kingdom of Great Britain and Northern Ireland and the Government of the Swiss Confederation concerning the safeguards and assurances relating to a transfer of nuclear material from the United Kingdom to Switzerland, Berne, 13/15 July 1981. — London : H.M.S.O., [1981]. — 3p ; 25cm. — (Treaty series ; no.79 (1981)) (Cmnd. ; 8400)
ISBN 0-10-184000-4 (unbound) : £0.70
B82-09562

341.7′56 — Austria. International freight transport: Transport between European Community countries & Greece or Turkey. Customs procedures — *Treaties between Austria & European Economic Community*

Austria. [Treaties, etc. European Economic Community, 1972 Nov.30. Protocols, etc. 1980 Dec.30]. Agreement in the form of an exchange of letters relating to the amendment of the agreement between the European Economic Community and the Republic of Austria on the simplification of formalities in respect of goods traded between the European Economic Community, on the one hand, and Greece and Turkey, on the other hand, when the said goods are forwarded from Austria : Brussels, 30 December 1980. — London : H.M.S.O., [1981]. — 11p : 1form ; 25cm. — (European communities ; no.56 (1981)) (Cmnd. ; 8362)
ISBN 0-10-183620-1 (unbound) : £1.50
B82-02753

341.7′56 — Austria. International freight transport: Transport between European Community countries. Customs procedures — *Treaties between Austria & European Economic Community*

Austria. [Treaties, etc. European Economic Community, 1972 Nov.30. Protocols, etc., 1980 June 23]. Agreement in the form of an exchange of letters on the amendment of the agreement between the European Economic Community and the Repubic of Austria on the application of the rules on Community transit : Brussels, 23 June 1980. — London : H.M.S.O., [1980]. — 3p ; 25cm. — (European Communities ; no.43 (1980)) (Cmnd. ; 8052)
ISBN 0-10-180520-9 (unbound) : £0.70
B82-11451

341.7′56 — Austria. International freight transport: Transport between European Community countries. Customs procedures. Treaties. Texts in Modern Greek — *Treaties between Austria & European Economic Community*

Austria. [Treaties, etc., 1977 July 12. Protocols, etc., 1981 Sept.18]. Agreement on the text in the Greek language of the agreement between the European Economic Community, the Swiss Confederation and the Rebublic of Austria on the extension of the application of the rules on community transit : Brussels, 18 September 1981. — London : H.M.S.O., [1982]. — 3p ; 25cm. — (European Communities ; no.8 (1982)) (Cmnd. ; 8481)
ISBN 0-10-184810-2 (unbound) : £0.70
Also classified at 341.7′56 B82-20563

341.7′56 — Colombia. Steel bridges. Construction equipment. Financial assistance. Loans from Great Britain — *Treaties between Great Britain & Colombia*

Colombia. [Treaties, etc. Great Britain, 1981 Dec.16]. Exchange of notes concerning a loan by the Government of the United Kingdom of Great Britain and Northern Ireland to the Government of the Republic of Colombia (United Kingdom-Colombia Loan (no.1) 1981) : Bogota, 16 December 1981. — London : H.M.S.O., [1982]. — 16p ; 25cm. — (Cmnd. ; 8542)
Text in English and Spanish
ISBN 0-10-185420-x (unbound) : £2.55
B82-27235

341.7′56 — Freight containers. Safety measures — *Treaties*

[International Convention for Safe Containers *(1972). Protocols, etc. 1981?*]. Amendments to annex 1 of the International Convention for Safe Containers, 1972. — London : H.M.S.O., [1981]. — 3p ; 25cm. — (Treaty series ; no.93 (1981)) (Cmnd. ; 8445)
ISBN 0-10-184450-6 (unbound) : £0.70
B82-12498

341.7′56 — Switzerland. International freight transport: Transport between European Community countries. Customs procedures — *Treaties between European Economic Community & Switzerland*

European Economic Community. [Treaties, etc. Switzerland, 1972 Nov.23. Protocols, etc. 1980 June 23]. Agreement in the form of an exchange of letters on the amendment of the agreement between the European Economic Community and the Swiss Confederation on the application of the rules on Community transit : Brussels, 23 June 1980. — London : H.M.S.O., [1980]. — 3p ; 25cm. — (European Communities ; no.44 (1980)) (Cmnd. ; 8053)
ISBN 0-10-180530-6 (unbound) : £0.70
B82-11450

341.7′56 — Switzerland. International freight transport: Transport between European Community countries. Customs procedures. Treaties. Texts in Modern Greek — *Treaties between European Economic Community & Switzerland*

Austria. [Treaties, etc., 1977 July 12. Protocols, etc., 1981 Sept.18]. Agreement on the text in the Greek language of the agreement between the European Economic Community, the Swiss Confederation and the Rebublic of Austria on the extension of the application of the rules on community transit : Brussels, 18 September 1981. — London : H.M.S.O., [1982]. — 3p ; 25cm. — (European Communities ; no.8 (1982)) (Cmnd. ; 8481)
ISBN 0-10-184810-2 (unbound) : £0.70
Primary classification 341.7′56 B82-20563

341.7′565 — Austria. Coal & steel. International rail freight transport: Transport between European Community countries. Charges — *Treaties between European Coal and Steel Community & Austria*

Austria. [Treaties, etc. European Coal and Steel Community, 1957 July 26. Protocols, etc. 1981 Apr.2]. Second supplementary protocol to the agreement of 26 July 1957 between the governments of the member states of the European Coal and Steel Community and the High Authority of the European Coal and Steel Community, of the one part, and the Austrian Federal Government, of the other part, on the introduction of through international railway tariffs for the carriage of coal and steel through the territory of the Republic of Austria : Brussels, 2 April 1981. — London : H.M.S.O., [1981]. — 3p ; 25cm. — (European Communities ; no.70 (1981)) (Cmnd. ; 8417)
ISBN 0-10-184170-1 (unbound) : £0.70
B82-13347

341.7′565 — Switzerland. Coal & steel. International rail freight transport: Transport between European Community countries. Charges — *Treaties between European Coal and Steel Community & Switzerland*

Second supplementary protocol in the agreement of 28 July 1956 on the introduction of through international railway tariffs for the carriage of coal and steel through Swiss territory : Brussels, 2 April 1981. — London : H.M.S.O., [1981]. — 3p ; 25cm. — (European communities ; no.57 (1981)) (Cmnd. ; 8368)
ISBN 0-10-183630-9 (unbound) : £0.70
B82-02748

341.7′565′0265 — International railway services — *Treaties*

[Convention concerning International Carriage by Rail *(1980)*]. Convention concerning International Carriage by Rail (COTIF) : Berne, 9 May 1980. — London : H.M.S.O., [1982]. — 194p ; 25cm. — (Miscellaneous ; no.11 (1982)) (Cmnd. ; 8535)
Parallel French text and English translation
ISBN 0-10-185350-5 (pbk) : £7.65 B82-28138

341.7'566 — Inter-Governmental Maritime Consultative Organization. Privileges. Accordance by Great Britain — *Treaties between Great Britain & Inter-Governmental Maritime Consultative Organization*

Great Britain. *Foreign and Commonwealth Office* . [Treaties, etc. Inter-Governmental Maritime Consultative Organization, 1968 Nov.28. Protocols, etc., 1982 Jan.20]. Exchange of notes between the Government of the United Kingdom of Great Britain and Northern Ireland and the Inter-Governmental Maritime Consultative Organization further amending the Agreement regarding the headquarters of the Organization, signed at London on 28 November 1968 : London, 20 January 1982. — London : H.M.S.O., 1982. — 5p ; 25cm. — (Cmnd. ; 8495) (Miscellaneous ; no.7 (1982))
ISBN 0-10-184950-8 (unbound) : £1.15
B82-23227

341.7'566'09 — Shipping. International law, *to 1981*

Gold, Edgar. Maritime transport : the evolution of international marine policy and shipping law / Edgar Gold. — Lexington, Mass. : Lexington Books ; [Aldershot] : Gower [distributor], 1981. — xxi,425p ; 24cm
Bibliography: p377-409. — Includes index
ISBN 0-669-04338-9 : £21.50 B82-04779

341.7'5664 — European Commission of the Danube. Assets — *Treaties*

Agreement between the European Commission of the Danube and the Government of the French Republic, the Italian Republic, the United Kingdom of Great Britain and Northern Ireland and the Hellenic Republic (with declaration and agreement with the Government of the Socialist Republic of Romania), Rome, 23 April 1977 .... — London : H.M.S.O., [1981]. — 13p ; 25cm. — (Treaty series ; no.74 (1981)) (Cmnd. ; 8384)
French and English text. — 'The agreement ws previously published as Miscellaneous No.4 (1978), Cmnd.7116
ISBN 0-10-183840-9 (unbound) : £1.90
B82-04554

341.7'5666 — Europe. Rhine River. Shipping. Navigation — *Treaties*

[Revised Convention for Rhine Navigation *(1868). Protocols, etc., 1979 Oct.17*]. Additional protocol no.2 to the Revised Convention for Rhine Navigation of 17 October 1868, as amended on 20 November 1963 with protocol of signature : Strasbourg, 17 October 1979. — London : H.M.S.O., [1981]. — 9p ; 25cm. — (Miscellaneous ; no.16 (1981)) (Cmnd. ; 8309)
French text and English translation
ISBN 0-10-183090-4 (pbk) : £1.50 B82-06096

341.7'5666 — Ships. Collisions. Prevention — *Treaties*

[International Regulations for Preventing Collisions at Sea *(1972). Protocols, etc. 1981 Nov.19*]. Resolution to amend the International Regulations for Preventing Collisions at Sea, 1972 : adopted by the twelfth session of the Assembly of the Inter-Governmental Maritime Consultative Organization on 19 November 1981. — London : H.M.S.O., 1982. — 10p ; 25cm. — (Miscellaneous ; no.8 (1982)) (Cmnd. ; 8500)
ISBN 0-10-185000-x (unbound) : £1.50
B82-21813

341.7'5668 — Bills of lading. International law

Mitchelhill, Alan. Bills of lading : law and practice / Alan Mitchelhill. — London : Chapman and Hall, 1982. — x,127p : forms ; 31cm
Includes index
ISBN 0-412-23960-4 (cased) : Unpriced : CIP rev.
ISBN 0-412-23940-x (pbk) : Unpriced
B82-06745

341.7'567 — Air services. Double taxation — *Treaties between Great Britain & China*

China. [Treaties, etc. Great Britain, 1981 Mar.10]. Agreement between the Government of the United Kingdom of Great Britain and Northern Ireland and the Government of the People's Republic of China for the reciprocal avoidance of double taxation on revenues arising from the business of air transport : Beijing (Peking), 10 March 1981. — London : H.M.S.O., [1982]. — 7p ; 25cm. — (Treaty series ; no.7 (1982)) (Cmnd. ; 8462)
English text with Chinese translation
ISBN 0-10-184620-7 (unbound) : £1.15
B82-18673

341.7'5678'0266410593 — Air services — *Treaties between Great Britain & Thailand*

Great Britain. [Treaties, etc. Thailand, 1950 Nov.10. Protocols, etc., 1980 May 22]. Exchange of notes between the Government of the United Kingdom of Great Britain and Northern Ireland and the Government of the Kingdom of Thailand further amending the schedule to the Agreement for air services of 10 November 1950 : Bangkok, 22 May/30 June 1980. — London : H.M.S.O., [1980]. — 3p ; 25cm. — (Treaty series ; no.82 (1980)) (Cmnd. ; 8051)
ISBN 0-10-180510-1 (unbound) : £0.70
B82-11421

341.7'5678'02664106711 — Air services — *Treaties between Great Britain & Cameroon*

Great Britain. [Treaties, etc. Cameroon, 1981 Sept.11]. Agreement between the Government of the United Kingdon of Great Britain and Northern Ireland and the Government of the United Republic of Cameroon relating to air services, Yasundé, 11 September 1981. — London : H.M.S.O., 1981. — 13p ; 25cm. — (Cmnd. ; 8428) (Cameroon ; no.1 (1981))
ISBN 0-10-184280-5 (unbound) : £1.90
B82-13296

341.7'5678'0266410678 — Air services — *Treaties between Great Britain & Tanzania*

Great Britain. [Treaties, etc. Tanzania, 1980 July 1]. Agreement between the Government of the United Kingdom of Great Britain and Northern Ireland and the Government of the United Republic of Tanzania for air services between and beyond their respective territories : Dar-es-Salaam, 1 July 1980. — London : H.M.S.O., 1981. — 10p ; 25cm. — (Treaty series ; no.91 (1981)) (Cmnd. ; 8441)
Originally published: 1981
ISBN 0-10-184410-7 (unbound) : £1.50
B82-12635

341.7'5678'02664106891 — Air services — *Treaties between Great Britain & Zimbabwe*

Great Britain. [Treaties, etc. Zimbabwe, 1981 Aug.19]. Agreement between the Government of the United Kingdom of Great Britain and Northern Ireland and the Government of the Republic of Zimbabwe for air services between and beyond their respective territories, London, 19 August 1981. — London : H.M.S.O., [1981]. — 11p ; 25cm. — (Treaty series ; no.80 (1981)) (Cmnd. ; 8399)
ISBN 0-10-183990-1 (unbound) : £1.50
B82-09563

341.7'5678'02664106982 — Air services — *Treaties between Great Britain & Mauritius*

Great Britain. [Treaties, etc. Mauritius, 1973 July 12. Protocols, etc. 1981 July 31]. Exchange of notes between the Government of the United Kingdom of Great Britain and Northern Ireland and the Government of Mauritius revising the route schedule annexed to the Agreement for air services between their respective territories, signed at Port Louis on 12 July 1973 : Port Louis, 31 July/10 August 1981. — London : H.M.S.O., [1981]. — 3p ; 25cm. — (Treaty series ; no.85 (1981)) (Cmnd. ; 8425)
ISBN 0-10-184250-3 (unbound) : £0.70
B82-12493

341.7'568 — Europe. International road transport services. Crews — *Treaties*

Great Britain. Proposed amendments to articles 3, 6, 10, 11, 12 and 14 of the European Agreement concerning the Work of Crews of Vehicles engaged in International Road Transport (AETR), done at Geneva on 1 July 1970. — London : H.M.S.O., 1982. — 3p ; 25cm. — (Cmnd. ; 8572) (Miscellaneous ; no.14 (1982))
ISBN 0-10-185720-9 (unbound) : £0.75
B82-39378

341.7'56883'02664105645 — International road freight transport services — *Treaties between Great Britain & Cyprus*

Cyprus. [Treaties, etc. Great Britain, 1980 Sept.9]. Agreement between the Government of the United Kingdom of Great Britain and Northern Ireland and the Government of the Republic of Cyprus on the international carriage of goods by road : London 9 September 1980. — London : H.M.S.O., 1981. — 6p ; 25cm. — (Treaty series ; no.92 (1981)) (Cmnd. ; 8440)
ISBN 0-10-184400-x (unbound) : £1.15
B82-12636

341.7'57 — Communication. International law

Ploman, Edward W.. International law governing communications and information. — London : Pinter, May 1982. — [420]p
ISBN 0-86187-204-5 : £25.00 : CIP entry
B82-11984

341.7'577 — Amateur radio stations. Licensing — *Treaties between Great Britain & Spain*

Great Britain. [Treaties, etc. Spain, 1981 Oct.1]. Exchange of notes between the Government of the United Kingdom of Great Britain and Northern Ireland and the Government of Spain concerning the reciprocal granting of licences to amateur radio operators : Madrid, 5 May and 1 October 1981. — London : H.M.S.O., [1982]. — 3p ; 25cm. — (Cmnd. ; 8458) (Treaty series ; no.5 (1982))
ISBN 0-10-184580-4 (unbound) : £0.70
B82-20561

341.7'577 — International Telecommunications Satellite Organization. Privileges — *Treaties*

[Protocol on INTELSAT Privileges, Exemptions and Immunities *(1978)*]. Protocol on INTELSAT Privileges, Exemptions and Immunities : Washington, 19 May-20 November 1978. — London : H.M.S.O., [1981]. — 11p ; 25cm. — (Treaty series ; no.2 (1981)) (Cmnd. ; 8103)
'... previously published in Miscellaneous No.31 (1978), Cmnd. 7385'
ISBN 0-10-181030-x (unbound) : £1.40
B82-13820

341.7'577 — Maritime communications satellites — *Treaties*

Final act of the diplomatic conference for the conclusion of a protocol on the privileges and immunities of the International Maritime Satellite Organization (INMARSAT) with text of the protocol : London, 17 November 1981. — London : H.M.S.O., [1982]. — 14p ; 25cm. — (Miscellaneous ; no.6 (1982)) (Cmnd. ; 8497)
ISBN 0-10-184970-2 (unbound) : £1.90
B82-25142

341.7'58 — Austria & European Community countries. Wines. Designations of origin. Protection — *Treaties between Austria & European Economic Community*

Austria. [Treaties, etc. European Economic Community, 1981 Oct.21]. Agreement between the European Economic Community and the Republic of Austria on the control and reciprocal protection of quality wines and certain wines bearing a geographical ascription : Brussels, 21 October 1981. — London : H.M.S.O., [1982]. — 54p ; 25cm. — (European Communities ; no.19 (1982)) (Cmnd. ; 8556)
ISBN 0-10-185560-5 (pbk) : £4.20 B82-32831

341.7′58 — Plants. New varieties. Protection — *Treaties*

[International Convention for the Protection of New Varieties of Plants *(1961). Protocols, etc. 1972 Nov.10]*. Additional act of November 10 1972 amending the International Convention for the Protection of New Varieties of Plants, Geneva, 10 November 1972-1 April 1973. — London : H.M.S.O., [1980]. — 9p ; 25cm. — (Treaty series ; no.79 (1980)) (Cmnd. ; 8036)
French and English text. — "The Additional Act was previously published as Miscellaneous No.4 (1974), Cmnd. 5758"
ISBN 0-10-180360-5 (unbound) : £1.40
B82-01238

341.7′582 — European Community countries. Music. Sound recordings. Copyright. European Economic Community law

Davies, Gillian. The piracy of phonograms. — Oxford (25 Beaumont St., Oxford OX1 2NP) : ESC Publishing, July 1981. — [120]p
ISBN 0-906214-07-6 (pbk) : £15.00 : CIP entry
B81-21583

341.7′586 — International patent depositary organisations. Deposits: Microorganisms. International recognition — *Treaties*

[Budapest Treaty on the International Recognition of the Deposit of Microorganisms for the Purposes of Patent Procedure *(1981). Protocols, etc. 1981 Jan.20]*. Amendments to the regulations under the Budapest Treaty on the International Recognition of the Deposit of Microorganisms for the Purposes of Patent Procedure adopted by the Assembly of the Union for the International Recognition of the Deposit of Microorganisms for the Purposes of Patent Procedure (Budapest Union) : on January 20, 1981. — London : H.M.S.O., [1981]. — 7p ; 25cm. — (Treaty series ; no.67 (1981)) (Cmnd. ; 8364)
£1.15 (unbound) B82-05574

341.7′586′0265 — European patents. Registration — *Treaties*

Convention on the grant of European patents : (European Patent Convention) with related documents : Munich, 5 October 1973. — [Rev. ed.]. — London : H.M.S.O., [1982]. — xii,152p ; 25cm. — (Treaty series ; no.16 (1982)) (Cmnd. ; 8510)
Previous ed.: 1978
ISBN 0-10-185100-6 (pbk) : £7.00 B82-25341

341.7′586′0265 — Patents. International recognition — *Treaties*

[Patent Co-operation Treaty *(1970). Protocols, etc., 1981 July 3]*. Amendments to the regulations under the Patent Co-operation Treaty done at Washington 19 June 1970, adopted by the Assembly of the International Patent Co-operation Union on 3 July 1981. — London : H.M.S.O., [1982]. — 3p ; 25cm. — (Treaty series ; no.13 (1982)) (Cmnd. ; 8502)
ISBN 0-10-185020-4 (unbound) : £0.70
B82-25143

[Patent Cooperation Treaty *(1970). Protocols, etc. 1980 June 16]*. Amendments to the regulations under the Patent Cooperation Treaty done at Washington 19 June 1970, adopted by the Assembly of the International Patent Cooperation Union on June 16 1980. — London : H.M.S.O., [1980]. — 21p ; 25cm. — (Treaty series ; no.92 (1980)) (Cmnd. ; 8078)
ISBN 0-10-180780-5 (unbound) : £2.10
B82-01240

341.7′586′0265 — Western Europe. Patents — *Treaties*

[Convention on the Unification of Certain Points of Substantive Law on Patents for Invention *(1963)]*. Convention on the Unification of Certain Points of Substantive Law on Patents for Invention : Strasbourg, 27 November 1963. — London : H.M.S.O., [1980]. — 7p ; 25cm. — (Treaty series ; no.70 (1980)) (Cmnd. ; 8002)
"... previously published as Miscellaneous No.15 (1964), Cmnd. 2362"
ISBN 0-10-180020-7 (unbound) : £1.00
B82-11416

341.7′59 — Developing countries. Food supply. Foreign assistance. Grants from Western bloc countries: Grants of wheat — *Treaties*

Final act of the conference to establish the text of the Food Aid Convention, 1980. With Food Aid Convention, 1980 : Washington, 11 March to 30 April 1980. — London : H.M.S.O., [1980]. — 13p ; 25cm. — (Miscellaneous ; no.20 (1980)) (Cmnd. ; 8009)
ISBN 0-10-180090-8 (unbound) : £1.25
B82-11447

341.7′59 — Economic development. International law

Rivero B., Oswaldo de. New economic order and international development law / by Oswaldo de Rivero B. — Oxford : Pergamon, 1980. — xvi,141p ; 22cm
Bibliography: p137-138. — Includes index
ISBN 0-08-024706-7 : £8.00 : CIP rev.
B79-34756

341.7′59 — Jordan. Economic development. Financial assistance. Loans from Great Britain — *Treaties between Great Britain & Jordan*

Great Britain. [Treaties, etc. Jordan, 1982 March 14]. Exchange of notes concerning a loan by the Government of the United Kingdom of Great Britain and Northern Ireland to the Government of the Hashemite Kingdom of Jordan (The United Kingdom/Jordan Loan 1982) : Amman, 14 March 1982. — London : H.M.S.O., [1982]. — 3p ; 25cm. — (Treaty series ; no.28(1982)) (Cmnd. ; 8593)
ISBN 0-10-185930-9 (unbound) : £0.75
B82-40840

341.7′59 — Portugal. Economic development. Grants from European Economic Community — *Treaties between European Economic Community & Portugal*

European Economic Community. [Treaties, etc. Portugal, 1980 Dec.3]. Agreement in the form of an exchange of letters between the European Economic Community and the Portuguese Republic concerning the implementation of pre-accession aid for Portugal : Brussels, 3 December 1980. — London : H.M.S.O., [1982]. — 6p ; 25cm. — (European Communities ; no.12 (1982)) (Cmnd. ; 8499)
ISBN 0-10-184990-7 (unbound) : £1.15
B82-25147

341.7′59 — Turkey. Economic development. Financial assistance. Loans from Great Britain — *Treaties between Great Britain & Turkey*

Great Britain. [Treaties, etc. Turkey, 1981 July 20]. Exchange of notes concerning a loan by the government of the United Kingdom of Great Britain and Northern Ireland to the government of the Republic of Turkey (the United Kindom/Turkey programme loan 1981) : Ankara 20 July 1981. — London : H.M.S.O., [1982]. — 6p ; 25cm. — (Treaty series ; no.4 (1982)) (Cmnd. ; 8448)
ISBN 0-10-184480-8 (unbound) : £1.15
B82-16556

341.7′59 — United Nations. *Relief and Works Agency for Palestine Refugees.* **Grants from European Economic Community: Grants for food supply —** *Treaties*

European Economic Community. [Treaties, etc. United Nations Relief and Works Agency for Palestine Refugees, 1980 May 21]. Convention between the European Economic Community and the United Nations Relief and Works Agency for Palestine Refugees (UNRWA) concerning aid to refugees in the countries of the Near East for 1979 and 1980 : Brussels, 21 May 1980. — London : H.M.S.O., [1980]. — 5p ; 25cm. — (European Communities ; no.45 (1980)) (Cmnd. ; 8054)
ISBN 0-10-180540-3 (unbound) : £1.10
B82-12766

341.7′59′0265 — European Community countries. Social cooperation with Yugoslavia — *Treaties between European Economic Community & Yugoslavia*

European Economic Community. [Treaties, etc. Yugoslavia, 1980, Apr.2]. Co-operation agreement between the European Economic Community and the Socialist Federal Republic of Yugoslavia (with final act). And Agreement between the member states of the European Coal and Steel Community and the Socialist Federal Republic of Yugoslavia (with final act) : Belgrade, 2 April 1980. — London : H.M.S.O., [1980]. — 132p : forms ; 25cm. — (European Communities ; no.52 (1980)) (Cmnd. ; 8088)
ISBN 0-10-180880-1 (pbk) : £5.70 B82-11446

341.7′6 — Great Britain. Social security contributions by personnel of Western European Union. Exemption by Great Britain — *Treaties between Great Britain & Western Union*

Great Britain. [Treaties, etc. Western European Union, 1981 Sept.8]. Exchange of notes between the Government of the United Kingdom of Great Britain and Northern Ireland and the Western European Union concerning the application of social security provisions to Western European Union officials : London, 8 September 1981. — London : H.M.S.O., [1981]. — 3p ; 25cm. — (Miscellaneous ; no.24 (1981)) (Cmnd. ; 8398)
ISBN 0-10-183980-4 (unbound) : £0.70
B82-06340

341.7′6 — Industrial injuries benefits. International agreements: International Labour Conference *(66th session : 1980 : Geneva).* **Policies of British government —** *Proposals*

Great Britain. International labour conference : proposed action by Her Majesty's Government in the United Kingdom of Great Britain and Northern Ireland on a recommendation adopted at, and an amendment to a convention considered at the 66th (1980) session of the International Labour Conference. — London : H.M.S.O., 1981. — 28p ; 25cm. — (Cmnd. ; 8457)
ISBN 0-10-184570-7 (unbound) : £2.65
Primary classification 341.7′63 B82-13821

341.7′6 — Social security benefits — *Treaties between Great Britain & Finland*

Finland. [Treaties, etc. Great Britain, 1978 Dec.12. Protocols, etc. 1980 Mar.21]. Protocol between the Government of the United Kingdom of Great Britain and Northern Ireland and the Government of the Republic of Finland, amending the convention on Social Security signed at London on 12 December 1978, London, 21 March 1980. — London : H.M.S.O., [1980]. — 3p ; 25cm. — (Finland ; no.1 (1980)) (Cmnd. ; 8113)
ISBN 0-10-181130-6 (unbound) : £0.70
B82-01242

341.7′6 — Social security benefits — *Treaties between Great Britain & Mauritius*

Great Britain. [Treaties, etc. Mauritius, 1981 Aug.24]. Exchange of notes between the Government of the United Kingdom of Great Britain and Northern Ireland and the Government of Mauritius concerning the provisional application from 1 November 1981 of the convention on social security signed at Port Louis, on 22 April 1981 : Port Louis, 24 August and 8 October 1981. — London : H.M.S.O., [1981]. — 3p ; 25cm. — (Treaty series ; no.90 (1981)) (Cmnd. ; 8434)
ISBN 0-10-184340-2 (unbound) : £0.70
B82-12494

Great Britain. [Treaties, etc. Mauritius, 1981 Aug.24]. Convention on social security between the Government of the United Kingdom of Great Britain and Northern Ireland and the Government of Mauritius, Port Louis, 22 April 1981 : with exchange of notes covering the provisional application of the convention from 1 November 1981, Port Louis, 24 August and 8 October 1981. — London : H.M.S.O., 1982. — 22p ; 25cm. — (Cmnd. ; 8584) (Treaty series ; no.26 (1982))
ISBN 0-10-185840-x (unbound) : £2.55
B82-39376

341.7'6 — Western Europe. Social security — *Treaties*

[European Convention on Social and Medical Assistance *(1953). Protocols, etc., 1981 June 10-Dec.21*]. Amendments to annexes I, II and III to the European Convention on Social and Medical Assistance, signed at Paris on 11 December 1953. — London : H.M.S.O., [1982]. — 3p ; 25cm. — (Treaty series ; no.14 (1982)) (Cmnd. ; 8505)
ISBN 0-10-185050-6 (unbound) : £0.70
B82-25145

341.7'62 — Crops. Protection — *Treaties*

[International Plant Protection Convention *(1979)*]. Revised text of the International Plant Protection Convention, signed at Rome on 6 December 1951. — London : H.M.S.O., [1981]. — 11p : 2forms ; 25cm. — (Cmnd. ; 8108)
ISBN 0-10-181080-6 (unbound) : £1.40
B82-11415

341.7'62 — Foreign trade in organisms in danger of extinction — *Treaties*

[Convention on International Trade in Endangered Species of Wild Fauna and Flora *(1973). Protocols, etc. 1981 Mar.8*]. Revised appendices I, II and III to the Convention on International Trade in Endangered Species of Wild Fauna and Flora : done at Washington on 3 March 1973. — London : H.M.S.O., [1981]. — 30p ; 25cm. — (Treaty series ; no.77 (1981)) (Cmnd. ; 8395)
ISBN 0-10-183950-2 (unbound) : £2.65
B82-11546

341.7'622 — Baltic Sea. Salmon. Reproduction. Promotion — *Treaties between European Economic Community & Sweden*

European Economic Community. [Treaties, etc. Sweden, 1979 Nov.21]. Agreement between the European Economic Community and the Government of Sweden on certain measures for the purpose of promoting the reproduction of salmon in the Baltic Sea and agreement in the form of two exchanges of letters : Brussels, 21 November 1979. — London : H.M.S.O., [1980]. — 6p ; 25cm. — (European Communities ; no.49 (1980)) (Cmnd. ; 8057)
ISBN 0-10-180570-5 (unbound) : £1.10
B82-12764

European Economic Community. [Treaties, etc. Sweden, 1980 July 3]. Agreement in the form of an exchange of letters applying in 1980 the agreement between the European Economic Community and the Government of Sweden on certain measures for the purpose of promoting the reproduction of salmon in the Baltic Sea : Brussels, 3 July 1980. — London : H.M.S.O., [1980]. — 3p ; 25cm. — (European Communities ; no.51 (1980)) (Cmnd. ; 8059)
ISBN 0-10-180590-x (unbound) : £0.70
B82-12765

341.7'622 — International Whaling Commission. Privileges. Accordance by Great Britain — *Treaties between Great Britain & International Whaling Commission*

Great Britain. [Treaties, etc. International Whaling Commission, 1975 Aug.21. Protocols, etc. 1981 Aug.7]. Exchange of notes between the Government of the United Kingdom of Great Britain and Northern Ireland and The International Whaling Commission amending The Headquarters Agreement, signed at London on 21 August 1975, London/Cambridge 7 August 1981. — London : H.M.S.O., [1981]. — 3p ; 25cm. — (Treaty series ; no.75 (1981)) (Cmnd. ; 8387)
ISBN 0-10-183870-0 (unbound) : £0.70
B82-04555

341.7'622 — Northeast Atlantic Fisheries Commission. Establishment — *Treaties*

[Convention on Future Multilateral Co-operation in North-East Atlantic Fisheries. *1980 Nov.18*]. Convention on Future Multilateral Co-operation in North-East Atlantic Fisheries : London, 18 November 1980-28 February 1981. — London : H.M.S.O., [1982]. — 13p ; 25cm. — (Miscellaneous ; no.2 (1982)) (Cmnd. ; 8474)
ISBN 0-10-184740-8 (unbound) : £1.90
B82-18672

341.7'622'0265 — Guinea-Bissau. Coastal waters. Fishing by European Community ships. Regulation — *Treaties between European Economic Community & Guinea-Bissau*

European Economic Community. [Treaties, etc. Guinea-Bissau, 1980 Feb.27]. Agreement between the European Economic Community and the Government of the Republic of Guinea-Bissau on fishing off the coast of Guinea-Bissau ; and, Agreements in the form of exchanges of letters between the Government of the Republic of Guinea Bissau and the European Economic Community on Fishing off the coast of Guinea-Bissau and on the provisional application thereof : Brussels, 27 February 1980. — London : H.M.S.O., [1980]. — 17p : 2forms ; 25cm. — (European Communities ; no.34 (1980)) (Cmnd. ; 7993)
ISBN 0-10-179930-6 (unbound) : £1.50
B82-12761

341.7'622'0265 — North Sea. Fishing. Restrictions — *Treaties between Norway & European Economic Community*

European Economic Community. [Treaties, etc. Norway, 1981 May 11]. Agreement in the form of an exchange of letters establishing fishing arrangements between the European Economic Community and the Kingdom of Norway : Brussels, 11 May 1981. — London : H.M.S.O., [1981]. — 7p ; 25cm. — (European communities ; no.62 (1981)) (Cmnd. ; 8390)
ISBN 0-10-183900-6 (unbound) : £1.15
B82-06097

341.7'622'0265 — Norway. Coastal waters. Fisheries. Management — *Treaties between Norway & European Economic Community*

European Economic Community. [Treaties, etc. Norway, 1980 Feb.27]. Agreement on fisheries between the European Economic Community and the Kingdom of Norway (with oral declarations) : Brussels, 27 February 1980. — London : H.M.S.O., [1980]. — 7p ; 25cm. — (European Communities ; no.50 (1980)) (Cmnd. ; 8058)
ISBN 0-10-180580-2 (unbound) : £1.10
B82-12763

341.7'63 — Botswana. British personnel. Conditions of service — *Treaties between Great Britain & Botswana*

Botswana. [Treaties, etc. Great Britain, 1976. Protocols, etc, 1981 Mar.19]. Exchange of notes between the Government of the United Kingdom of Great Britain and Northern Ireland and the Government of Botswana amending and extending the British Expatriates Supplementation (Botswana) Agreement 1976, as amended (British Expatriates Supplementation (Botswana) Agreement 1976-1981) : Gaborone, 19 March 1981. — London : H.M.S.O., [1981]. — 3p ; 25cm. — (Treaty series ; no.72 (1981)) (Cmnd. ; 8382)
ISBN 0-10-183820-4 (unbound) : £0.70
B82-04208

341.7'63 — Gambia. British personnel. Conditions of service — *Treaties between Great Britain & Gambia*

Gambia. [Treaties, etc. Great Britain, 1976 Mar.9. Protocols, etc., 1980 Mar.3]. Exchange of notes between the Government of the United Kingdom of Great Britain and Northern Ireland and the Government of the Republic of the Gambia amending the British Expatriates Supplementation (The Gambia) Agreement, 1976 : (The British Supplementation (The Gambia) Agreement 1976 Amendment 1979) : Banjul, 3 and 4 March 1980. — London : H.M.S.O., [1980]. — 3p ; 25cm. — (Treaty series ; no.67 (1980)) (Cmnd. ; 7999)
ISBN 0-10-179990-x (unbound) : £0.50
B82-12758

341.7'63 — Lesotho. British personnel. Conditions of service — *Treaties between Great Britain & Lesotho*

Great Britain. [Treaties, etc. Lesotho, 1976 Aug.2. Protocols, etc. 1981 Aug.20]. Exchange of notes between the Government of the United Kingdom of Great Britain and Northern Ireland and the Government of the Kindom of Lesotho further amending the British Expatriates Supplementation (Lesotho) Agreement 1976/81 : (The British Expatriates Supplementation (Lesotho) Agreement 1981, Amendment 1981) : Maseru, 20 August/30 September 1981. — London : H.M.S.O., [1982]. — 3p ; 24cm. — (Treaty series ; no.9 (1982)) (Cmnd. ; 8478)
ISBN 0-10-184780-7 (unbound) : £0.70
B82-20568

341.7'63 — Old personnel. Employment. International agreements: International Labour Conference *(66th session : 1980 : Geneva).* **Policies of British government —** *Proposals*

Great Britain. International labour conference : proposed action by Her Majesty's Government in the United Kingdom of Great Britain and Northern Ireland on a recommendation adopted at, and an amendment to a convention considered at the 66th (1980) session of the International Labour Conference. — London : H.M.S.O., 1981. — 28p ; 25cm. — (Cmnd. ; 8457)
ISBN 0-10-184570-7 (unbound) : £2.65
Also classified at 341.7'6 B82-13821

341.7'63 — States. Law. Incorporation of international law — *Study examples: Employment. Treaties*

Leary, Virginia A.. International labour conventions and national law : the effectiveness of the automatic incorporation of treaties in national legal systems / Virginia A. Leary. — The Hague ; London : Nijhoff, 1982. — xiv,191p ; 25cm
Bibliography: p171-179. — Includes index
ISBN 90-247-2551-8 : Unpriced B82-21459

341.7'63 — Swaziland. British personnel. Conditions of service — *Treaties between Great Britain & Swaziland*

Great Britain. [Treaties, etc. Swaziland, 1976 June 3. Protocols, etc. 1981 Mar. 23 and 25]. Exchange of notes between the Government of the United Kingdom of Great Britain and Northern Ireland and the Government of the Kingdom of Swaziland amending and extending the British Expatriates Supplementation (Swaziland) Agreement 1976 as amended in 1977 : (British Expatriates Supplementation (Swaziland) Agreement 1976/81) : Mbabane, 23 and 25 March 1981. — London : H.M.S.O., [1981]. — 3p ; 25cm. — (Treaty series ; no.69 (1981)) (Cmnd. ; 8379)
ISBN 0-10-183790-9 (unbound) : £0.70
B82-06484

341.7'632 — Botswana. Civil service. British personnel. Conditions of service — *Treaties between Great Britain & Botswana*

Botswana. [Treaties, etc., Great Britain, 1970. Protocols, etc., 1981 Mar.19]. Exchange of notes between the Government of the United Kingdom of Great Britain and Northern Ireland and the Government of Botswana amending and extending the Overseas Service (Botswana) Continuance Agreement 1970-76 (Overseas Service (Botswana) Agreement 1970-81) : Gaborone, 19 March 1981. — London : H.M.S.O., [1981]. — 3p ; 25cm. — (Treaty series ; no.71 (1981)) (Cmnd. ; 8381)
ISBN 0-10-183810-7 (unbound) : £0.70
B82-04207

341.7'632 — Freight transport services. Personnel. Working conditions. International agreements. Policies of British government — *Proposals*

Great Britain. International Labour Conference : proposed action by Her Majesty's Government in the United Kingdom of Great Britain and Northern Ireland on two conventions and two recommendations adopted at the 65th session (1979) of the International Labour Conference and a convention adopted at the 55th (Maritime) session (1970) of the International Labour Conference. — London : H.M.S.O., [1980]. — 44p ; 25cm. — (Cmnd. ; 8118)
Includes the texts of the conventions
ISBN 0-10-181180-2 (unbound) : £3.00
B82-11012

341.7′632 — Malawi. Civil service. British personnel. Conditions of service — *Treaties between Great Britain & Malawi*

Great Britain. [Treaties etc. Malawi, 1972 Jan.11. Protocols, etc. 1981 Mar.27]. Exchange of notes between the Government of the United Kingdom of Great Britain and Northern Ireland and the Government of Malawi constituting the Overseas Service (Malawi) Agreement 1971/1981, Lilongwe, 27 and 31 March 1981. — London : H.M.S.O., 1981. — 3p ; 25cm. — (Treaty series ; no.84 (1981)) (Cmnd. ; 8423)
ISBN 0-10-184230-9 (unbound) : £0.70
B82-11605

341.7′632 — Swaziland. Civil service. British personnel. Conditions of service — *Treaties between Great Britain & Swaziland*

Great Britain. [Treaties, etc. Swaziland, 1976. Protocols, etc., 1981 Mar.25]. Exchange of notes between the Government of the United Kingdom of Great Britain and Northern Ireland and the Government of the Kingdom of Swaziland amending and extending the Overseas Service (Swaziland) Agreement 1976 (Overseas Service (Swaziland) Agreement 1976-81) : Mbabane, 23 and 25 March 1981. — London : H.M.S.O., [1981]. — 3p ; 25cm. — (Treaty series ; no.70 (1981)) (Cmnd. ; 8380)
ISBN 0-10-183800-x (unbound) : £0.70
B82-04206

341.7′632 — Zambia. Civil service. British personnel. Conditions of service — *Treaties between Great Britain & Zambia*

Great Britain. [Treaties, etc. Zambia, 1981 Mar.19/Aug.14]. Exchange of notes between the Government of the United Kingdom of Great Britain and Northern Ireland and the Government of the Republic of Zambia constituting the Overseas Service (Zambia) Agreement 1981 : Lusaka 19 March/14 August 1981. — London : H.M.S.O., 1981. — 5p ; 25cm. — (Treaty series ; no.89 (1981)) (Cmnd. ; 8432)
ISBN 0-10-184320-8 (unbound) : £1.15
B82-12637

341.7′636 — Malawi. British personnel. Remuneration — *Treaties between Great Britain & Malawi*

Great Britain. [Treaties, etc. Malawi, 1971 Mar.27. Protocols, etc. 1981 Mar.27]. Exchange of notes between the Government of the United Kingdom of Great Britain and Northern Ireland and the Government of Malawi constituting the British Expatriates Supplementation (Malawi) Agreement 1971/81, Lilongwe, 27 and 31 March 1981. — London : H.M.S.O., 1981. — 3p ; 25cm. — (Treaty series ; no.83 (1981)) (Cmnd. ; 8419)
ISBN 0-10-184190-6 (unbound) : £0.70
B82-11606

341.7′636 — Malawi. Civil service. British personnel. Superannuation — *Treaties between Great Britain & Malawi*

Great Britain. [Treaties, etc. Malawi, 1975 Nov.26]. Agreement between the Government of the United Kingdom of Great Britain and Northern Ireland and the Government of Malawi concerning public officers′ pensions : (Public Officers′ Pensions (Malawi) Agreement 1975) : Llilongwe, 26 November 1975. — London : H.M.S.O., [1981]. — 7p ; 25cm. — (Treaty series ; no.87 (1981)) (Cmnd. ; 8430)
ISBN 0-10-184300-3 (unbound) : £1.15
B82-12495

341.7′636′02664109681 — Kiribati. British personnel. Remuneration — *Treaties between Great Britain & Kiribati*

Great Britain. [Treaties, etc. Kiribati, 1981 Feb.27]. Exchange of notes between the Government of the United Kingdom of Great Britain and Northern Ireland and the Government of the Republic of Kiribati constituting the British Expatriates′ Supplementation (Kiribati) Agreement 1980, Tarawa, 11 December 1980 / 27 February 1981. — London : H.M.S.O., [1981]. — 3p ; 25cm. — (Cmnd. ; 8324) (Treaty series ; no.S7 (1981))
ISBN 0-10-183240-0 (unbound) : £0.70
B82-01620

341.7′65 — Firearms. Proof marks. International recognition — *Treaties*

[Convention for the Reciprocal Recognition of Proof Marks of Small-Arms *(1969)*]. Convention for the Reciprocal Recognition of Proof Marks of Small-Arms, Brussels, 1 July 1969. — London : H.M.S.O., [1980]. — 25p : ill ; 25cm. — (Treaty series ; no.84 (1980)) (Cmnd. ; 8063)
French and English text. — ″The convention was previously published as Miscellaneous No.2 (1975), Cmnd. 5942″
ISBN 0-10-180630-2 (unbound) : £2.40
B82-01239

341.7′65 — Medicine. Cooperation between Great Britain & Egypt — *Treaties between Great Britain & Egypt*

Egypt. [Treaties, etc. Great Britain, 1981 Apr.26]. Agreement between the Government of the United Kingdom of Great Britain and Northern Ireland and the Government of the Arab Republic of Egypt on co-operation in the field of medicine and public health : Cairo, 26 April 1981. — London : H.M.S.O., [1981]. — 6p ; 25cm. — (Treaty series ; no.86 (1981)) (Cmnd. ; 8429)
Text in English and Arabic
ISBN 0-10-184290-2 (unbound) : £1.15
B82-12496

341.7′65′0265 — Public health. International law — *Treaties*

[International Health Regulations (1969). *Protocols, etc. 1981 May 20*]. Additional regulations amending the International Health Regulations (1969), as amended, in particular with respect to Articles 1, 7, 18, 19 and 47 : Geneva, 20 May 1981. — London : H.M.S.O., [1982]. — 3p ; 25cm. — (Treaty series ; no.19 (1982)) (Cmnd. ; 8544)
ISBN 0-10-185440-4 (unbound) : £0.75
B82-28139

341.7′67 — European Community countries. European Schools. European Baccalaureate examinations — *Treaties*

[Statute of the European School *(1957). Protocols, etc., 1978, June 19*]. Agreement amending the annex to the Statute of the European School laying down the regulations for the European Baccalaureate : Luxembourg, 19 June 1978. — London : H.M.S.O., [1981]. — 10p ; 23cm. — (Treaty series ; no.1 (1981)) (Cmnd. ; 8083)
″... previously published as European Communities No.44 (1978), Cmnd. 7363″
ISBN 0-10-180830-5 (unbound) : £1.40
B82-11418

341.7′67 — Sweden. Information retrieval systems. Networks. Interconnection of EURONET — *Treaties between European Economic Community & Sweden*

European Economic Community. [Treaties, etc. Sweden, 1981 Dec.18]. Co-operation agreement between the European Economic Community and the Kingdom of Sweden on the interconnection of the community network for data transmission (EURONET) and the Swedish data network for information retrieval purposes : Brussels, 18 December 1981. — London : H.M.S.O., [1982]. — 7p ; 25cm. — (European Communities ; no.20 (1982)) (Cmnd. ; 8565)
ISBN 0-10-185650-4 (pbk) : £1.25 B82-32829

341.7′67 — West Germany. Munich. European Patent Organisation. Personnel. Children. European Schools. Organisation — *Treaties*

[Statute of the European School *(1957). Protocols, etc., 1975 Dec.15*]. Supplementary protocol to the protocol of 13 April 1962 on the setting-up of European schools (with protocol of provisional application) : Luxembourg, 15 December 1975. — London : H.M.S.O., [1981]. — 6p ; 25cm. — (Treaty series ; no.3 (1981)) (Cmnd. ; 8104)
″... previously published as European Communities No.17 (1976), Cmnd. 6549″
ISBN 0-10-181040-7 (unbound) : £1.10
B82-11419

341.7′672 — Western Europe. International law. Information. Dissemination — *Treaties*

[European Convention on Information on Foreign Law *(1968). Protocols, etc., 1978 Mar.15*]. Additional protocol to the European Convention on Information on Foreign Law : Strasbourg, 15 March 1978. — London : H.M.S.O., [1981]. — 6p ; 25cm. — (Treaty series ; no.88 (1981)) (Cmnd. ; 8431)
Originally published: as Miscellaneous no.5 (1981), Cmnd. 8149
ISBN 0-10-184310-0 (unbound) : £1.15
B82-12499

341.7′6753 — France. Grenoble. Very high flux neutron reactors. Construction & operation. Organisations: Institut Max von Laue-Paul Langevin. Participation of Great Britain. *Science Research Council — Treaties between Great Britain, France & West Germany*

France. Second protocol to the convention of 19 January 1967, as amended by the protocol of 6 July 1971, between the Government of the French Republic and the Government of the Federal Republic of Germany on the construction and operation of a very high flux reactor, as further amended by the agreement of 19 July 1974 between the above-mentioned two governments and the Government of the United Kingdom of Great Britain and Northern Ireland concerning that governments accession to the convention, and by the protocol of 27 July 1976 between the above-mentioned three governments : London, 9 December 1981. — London : H.M.S.O., [1982]. — 3p ; 25cm. — (Treaty series ; no.10 1982)) (Cmnd. ; 8480)
ISBN 0-10-184800-5 (unbound) : £0.70
B82-20569

341.7′6754 — European Community countries. Food. Processing. Effects. Research — *Treaties*

European Economic Community. [Treaties, etc. 1980 Mar.27]. Community-COST concertation agreement on a concerted action project on the effects of processing on the physical properties of foodstuffs (COST project 90) : Brussels, 27 March 1980. — London : H.M.S.O., [1980]. — 10p ; 25cm. — (European Communities ; no.33 (1980)) (Cmnd. ; 7990)
ISBN 0-10-179900-4 (unbound) : £1.25
B82-12762

341.7′6755 — Meteorological satellites: Meteosat. Use — *Treaties*

[Arrangement between certain member states of the European Space Research Organisation and the European Space Research Organisation concerning the execution of a meteorological satellite programme. *Protocols, etc. 1975 Dec.17*] **Amendments** to the Protocol concerning the exploitation of a preoperational meteorological satellite (METEOSAT) of 17 December 1975. — London : H.M.S.O., 1982. — 7p ; 25cm. — (Treaty series ; no.24 (1982)) (Cmnd. ; 8564)
ISBN 0-10-185640-7 (unbound) : £1.25
B82-35097

341.7′6755 — North Atlantic Ocean. Weather stations. Organisation — *Treaties*

[Agreement for Joint Financing of North Atlantic Ocean Stations *(1974). Protocols, etc., 1981 June 30*]. Amendment to Annex I of the Agreement for Joint Financing of North Atlantic Ocean Stations. — London : H.M.S.O., [1982]. — 3p ; 25cm. — (Miscellaneous ; no.4 (1982)) (Cmnd. ; 8459)
ISBN 0-10-184590-1 (unbound) : £0.70
B82-20567

341.7′6757 — Commonwealth Agricultural Bureaux. Privileges. Accordance by Great Britain — *Treaties between Great Britain and Commonwealth Agricultural Bureaux*

Commonwealth Agricultural Bureaux. [Treaties, etc. Great Britain]. Draft headquarters agreement between the Government of the United Kindom of Great Britain and Northern Ireland and the Commonwealth Agricultural Bureaux. — London : H.M.S.O., 1982. — 7p ; 25cm. — (Miscellaneous ; no.10) (Cmnd. ; 8509)
ISBN 0-10-185090-5 (unbound) : £1.15
B82-25114

341.7′6757 — European Community countries. Water. Pollutants: Microorganisms. Research — *Treaties*

[Community-COST Concertation Agreement on a Concerted Action Project in the Field of Analysis of Organic Micro-Pollutants in Water (COST project 64b bis) *(1980)***]**. Community COST concertation Agreement on a Concerted Action Project in the Field of Analysis of Organic Micro-Pollutants in Water (COST project 64b bis) : Brussels, 27 March 1980. — London : H.M.S.O., [1980]. — 10p ; 25cm. — (European Communities ; no.30 (1980)) (Cmnd. ; 7973)
ISBN 0-10-179730-3 (unbound) : £1.25
B82-11448

341.7′75 — United States. Imports: Narcotics. Importing by British ships. Prevention — *Treaties*

Great Britain. [Treaties, etc. United States, 1981 Nov.13]. Exchange of notes between the Government of the United Kingdom of Great Britain and Northern Ireland and the Government of the United States of America concerning co-operation in the suppression of the unlawful importation of narcotic drugs into the United States : London, 13 November 1981. — London : H.M.S.O., 1982. — [4]p ; 25cm. — (Treaty series ; no.8 (1982)) (Cmnd. ; 8470)
ISBN 0-10-184700-9 (unbound) : £0.70
B82-16579

341.7′75′0904 — Drug abuse. International control, *1909-1980.* **Legal aspects**

Chatterjee, S. K.. Legal aspects of international drug control / S.K. Chatterjee. — The Hague ; London : Nijhoff, 1981. — xxiv,587p ; 25cm
Bibliography: p547-555. — Includes index
ISBN 90-247-2556-9 : Unpriced B82-00476

341.7′8 — Arbitration agreements. Awards. International recognition. Treaties: Convention on the Recognition and Enforcement of Foreign Arbitral Awards — *Critical studies*

Berg, Albert Jan van den. The New York arbitration convention of 1958 : towards a uniform judicial interpretation / Albert Jan van den Berg. — Antwerp ; London : Kluwer Law and Taxation, 1981. — xv,466p ; 25cm
At head of title: T.M.C. Asser Institute-The Hague. — Bibliography: p440-450. — Includes index
ISBN 90-654-4035-6 : Unpriced B82-10554

341.7′8 — European Court. Judicial powers — *Cases*

Bebr, Gerhard. Development of judicial control of the European Communities / Gerhard Bebr. — The Hague ; London : Nijhoff, 1981. — xviii,882p ; 25cm
Bibliography: p719-808. — Includes index
ISBN 90-247-2541-0 : Unpriced B82-03863

342 — COMPARATIVE LAW

342′.0094 — Europe. Law — *Serials*

Yearbook of European law. — 1 (1981). — Oxford : Clarendon Press, Nov.1982. — [550]p
ISBN 0-19-825384-2 : £40.00 : CIP entry
ISSN 0263-3264 B82-35226

342′.05 — Law — *Comparative studies — Serials*

Comparative law yearbook / issued by the Center for International Legal Studies. — Vol.1 (1977)-. — The Hague ; London : Martinus Nijhoff, 1978-. — v. ; 25cm
Published: Alphen aan den Rijn : Sijthoff & Noordhoff, 1978-1980
Unpriced B82-22681

342.2′29′094 — Western Europe. Constitutional law. Theories, *1150-1650*

Tierney, Brian. Religion, law, and the growth of constitutional thought 1150-1650 / Brian Tierney. — Cambridge : Cambridge University Press, 1982. — xi,114p ; 23cm. — (The Wiles Lectures given at the Queen′s University of Belfast)
Bibliography: p109-114
ISBN 0-521-23495-6 : £12.50 : CIP rev.
B81-39208

342.3′32 — Money. Law
Mann, F. A.. The legal aspect of money : with special reference to comparative private and public international law / by F.A. Mann. — 4th ed. — Oxford : Clarendon, 1982. — lvi,602p ; 25cm
Previous ed.: Oxford : Oxford University Press, 1971. — Bibliography: pliv. — Includes index
ISBN 0-19-825367-2 : £35.00 : CIP rev.
B82-01085

342.34 — Tax avoidance. Social aspects
Bracewell-Milnes, Barry. Tax avoidance and evasion : the individual and society / Barry Bracewell-Milnes. — London : Panopticum, 1979, c1980 (1980 [printing]). — 120p ; 21cm
Bibliography: p119-120
ISBN 0-9504138-4-4 : Unpriced
Also classified at 364.1′33 B82-08126

342.34′09182′1 — Western world. Tax avoidance
Bawly, Dan. The subterranean economy / Dan Bawly. — New York ; London : McGraw-Hill, c1982. — xv,187p ; 24cm
Includes index
ISBN 0-07-004153-9 : £15.50
Primary classification 342.5′233 B82-24416

342.35′5 — European Community countries. International services. Value-added tax. Law — *French texts*
Kaiser, François. La taxe sur la valeur ajoutée et les prestations de services internationales : étude de droit comparé et de droit communautaire / François Kaiser. — Deventer ; London : Kluwer, 1981. — 233p ; 24cm
Bibliography: p195-218
ISBN 90-654-4029-1 : Unpriced B82-10139

342.3′71′094 — European Community countries. Consumer protection. Law — *Comparative studies — French texts*
Reich, Norbert. Le droit de la consommation dans les pays membres de la CEE : une analyse comparative : une étude préparée pour la Commission de la Communauté Européenne / Norbert Reich, Hans-W. Micklitz. — New York ; London : Van Nostrand Reinhold, c1981. — xiv,231p ; 24cm
Includes index
ISBN 0-442-30412-9 : £1.50 B82-07878

342.3′72 — Industries. Competition. Conflict of laws
Canenbley, Cornelis. Enforcing antitrust against foreign enterprises : procedural problems in the extraterritorial application of antitrust laws : report submitted to Committee C - Antitrust Law and Monopolies during the IBA Berlin Conference, August 1980 / general rapporteur Cornelis Canenbley with the assistance of Amanda Dalton. — Deventer ; London : Kluwer, 1981. — xiii,125p : 1facsim ; 25cm
ISBN 90-654-4014-3 : Unpriced B82-11199

Jones, Kelvin. Law and economy. — London : Academic Press, Jan.1983. — [280]p. — (Law, state and society series)
ISBN 0-12-390040-9 : CIP entry B82-33466

342.3′96 — Freight transport. Shipping. Law — *Conference proceedings*
Lloyd′s World of Shipping in Hong Kong *(Conference : 1981)*. Ocean carriers rights and liabilities : Lloyd′s World of Shipping in Hong Kong October 12-16 1981. — [London] : [Lloyd′s of London Press], [1982?]. — 1v.(various pagings) ; 31cm
ISBN 0-907432-18-2 : Unpriced B82-31130

342.3′97 — Aviation. Law
Essays in air law / edited by Arnold Kean. — The Hague ; London : Nijhoff, 1982. — xvi,369p ; 25cm
Includes index
ISBN 90-247-2543-7 : Unpriced B82-30625

342.3′97 — Aviation. Law — *Conference proceedings*
International Aviation Law Seminar *(1981 : Tobago)*. International Aviation Law Seminar : the Mount Irvine Bay Hotel, Tobago, West Indies March 16, 17, 18, 19, 1981 / organised by Lloyd′s of London Press ; sponsored by the Royal Aeronautical Society. — London : Lloyd′s of London Press, [1982?]. — 349p ; 31cm
ISBN 0-907432-27-1 : Unpriced B82-31129

342.4′12596′094 — European Community countries. Personnel. Dismissal. Law — *Comparative studies*

Honoré, Tony. The quest for security : employees, tenants, wives / by Tony Honoré. — London : Stevens, 1982. — xiv,128p ; 19cm. — (The Hamlyn lectures ; 34th series)
Includes index
ISBN 0-420-46410-7 (cased) : £12.00 : CIP rev.
ISBN 0-420-46420-4 (pbk) : £5.80
Also classified at 342.61′66′094 ; 342.64′32′094
B82-06766

342.4′533′094 — Europe. Firearms, *to 1890.* **Law**

Historical firearms in Europe : law and the collector, shooter and historian : proceedings of the Symposium held at the National Army Museum, London, October 1980. — London : Historical Breechloading Smallarms Association, [1982]. — 92,iip ; 30cm
ISBN 0-9508178-0-5 (spiral) : £3.50
B82-34488

342.5′233 — Western world. Tax evasion

Bawly, Dan. The subterranean economy / Dan Bawly. — New York ; London : McGraw-Hill, c1982. — xv,187p ; 24cm
Includes index
ISBN 0-07-004153-9 : £15.50
Also classified at 342.34′09182′1 B82-24416

342.5′2523′0904 — Murder. Trials, *1892-1972*

Jones, Elwyn, *1923-*. [On trial]. Death trials : seven intriguing cases of capital crime / Elwyn Jones ; introduction by Lord Elwyn-Jones. — London : W.H. Allen, 1981. — 160p : ill ; 18cm. — (A Star book)
Originally published: London : Macdonald and Jane′s, 1978
ISBN 0-352-30686-6 (pbk) : £1.25 B82-11713

342.5′56 — Criminal courts. Defendants. Rights — *Comparative studies*

Human rights in criminal procedure : a comparative study / edited by J.A. Andrews. — The Hague ; London : Nijhoff, 1982. — 451p ; 25cm. — (United Kingdom comparative law series)
ISBN 90-247-2552-6 : Unpriced B82-35975

342.5′77 — Criminal law. Justice. Administration. Discretion

Pattenden, Rosemary. The judge, discretion, and the criminal trial. — Oxford : Clarendon Press, 1982. — [300]p
ISBN 0-19-825373-7 : £20.00 : CIP entry
B82-10452

342.5′773 — Capital punishment. Judicial review — *Comparative studies*

Pannick, David. Judicial review of the death penalty / David Pannick. — London : Duckworth, 1982. — 245p ; 23cm
Includes index
ISBN 0-7156-1594-7 : £18.00 : CIP rev.
B82-04876

342.61′66′094 — European Community countries. Divorce. Financial settlements & maintenance orders. Law — *Comparative studies*

Honoré, Tony. The quest for security : employees, tenants, wives / by Tony Honoré. — London : Stevens, 1982. — xiv,128p ; 19cm. — (The Hamlyn lectures ; 34th series)
Includes index
ISBN 0-420-46410-7 (cased) : £12.00 : CIP rev.
ISBN 0-420-46420-4 (pbk) : £5.80
Primary classification 342.4′12596′094
B82-06766

342.63′094 — Europe. Torts. Law

Lawson, F. H.. Tortious liability for unintentional harm in the Common law and the Civil law. — Cambridge : Cambridge University Press. — (Cambridge studies in international and comparative law. New series)
Vol.1: Study. — Sept.1982. — [239]p
ISBN 0-521-23585-5 (cased) : £25.00 : CIP entry
ISBN 0-521-27209-2 (pbk) : £12.50
B82-29364

342.63'094 — Europe. Torts. Law *continuation*

Lawson, F. H.. Tortious liability for unintentional harm in the Common law and the Civil law. — Cambridge : Cambridge University Press. — (Cambridge studies in international and comparative law. New series)
Vol.2: Texts. — Aug.1982. — 1v.
ISBN 0-521-23586-3 (cased) : £25.00 : CIP entry
ISBN 0-521-27210-6 (pbk) : £12.50 B82-29353

342.64 — Computer systems. Law

Tapper, Colin. Computer law / Colin Tapper. — 2nd ed. — London : Longman, 1982. — xxvi,221p ; 22cm. — (Business data processing)
Previous ed.: 1978. — Bibliography: p211-214. — Includes index
ISBN 0-582-49702-7 : £10.50 : CIP rev. B82-18362

342.64'32'094 — European Community countries. Rented residences. Tenants. Eviction. Law — *Comparative studies*

Honoré, Tony. The quest for security : employees, tenants, wives / by Tony Honoré. — London : Stevens, 1982. — xiv,128p ; 19cm. — (The Hamlyn lectures ; 34th series)
Includes index
ISBN 0-420-46410-7 (cased) : £12.00 : CIP rev.
ISBN 0-420-46420-4 (pbk) : £5.80
Primary classification 342.4'12596'094
B82-06766

342.64'685 — Mineral resources. Exploitation. Legal aspects — *Conference proceedings*

. Legal and institutional arrangements in minerals developments : a study based on an international workshop organised in Berlin (West) in August 1980 by the Department of Technical Co-operation for Development, United Nations, and the Development Policy Forum of the German Foundation for International Development. — London : Mining Journal Books, 1982. — xi,224p : ill ; 23cm
ISBN 0-900117-29-x (pbk) : Unpriced
B82-25872

342.64'8 — Capitalist countries. Inventions by personnel. Law — *Case studies*

Employees' inventions : a comparative study / edited by Jeremy Phillips. — Sunderland : Fernsway, 1981. — 212p : ill ; 21cm
ISBN 0-9507626-0-1 (pbk) : Unpriced
B82-12963

342.64'82 — Digital computer systems. Programs. Copyright. Law

The **Legal** protection of computer software / edited by Lawrence Perry and Hugh Brett. — Oxford : ESC, 1981. — xiv,197p : ill ; 22cm
ISBN 0-906214-06-8 (pbk) : Unpriced
B82-08215

342.65'4 — Wills, *to 1978 — Collections*

Menchin, Robert S.. Where there's a will / Robert S. Menchin. — London : Corgi, 1981, c1979. — 169p : ill ; 18cm
Originally published: London : F. Muller, 1980
ISBN 0-552-11861-3 (pbk) : £1.25 B82-10212

342.6'668 — France, Great Britain & West Germany. Companies. Groups. Law — *Comparative studies*

Wooldridge, Frank. Groups of companies : the law and pactice in Britain, France and Germany / by Frank Wooldridge. — London : Institute of Advanced Legal Studies (University of London), 1981. — xxvi,159p ; 21cm
ISBN 0-901190-26-8 (pbk) : Unpriced
B82-17369

342.6'682 — Eastern Europe. Western companies. Joint ventures with Eastern European companies. Legal aspects

Legal aspects of joint ventures in Eastern Europe / edited Dennis Campbell. — Deventer ; London : Kluwer, 1981. — 133p ; 25cm
Includes index
ISBN 90-654-4034-8 : Unpriced B82-10136

342.6'92 — Companies. Shares. Insider trading. Law

Rider, Barry Alexander K.. The regulation of insider trading / Barry Alexander K. Rider and H. Leigh Ffrench. — London : Macmillan, 1979. — xvi,474p ; 29cm. — (British Institute of Securities laws)
Includes index
ISBN 0-333-23842-7 : £50.00 : CIP rev.
B79-12803

342.7 — Justice. Administration

The **Politics** of informal justice / edited by Richard L. Abel. — New York ; London : Academic Press. — (Studies on law and social control)
Vol.1: The American experience. — c1982. — ix,335p ; 24cm
Includes bibliographies and index
ISBN 0-12-041501-1 : £19.60 B82-30143

The **Politics** of informal justice / edited by Richard L. Abel. — New York ; London : Academic Press. — (Studies on law and social control)
Vol.2: Comparative studies. — c1982. — x,338p : ill,1map ; 24cm
Includes bibliographies and index
ISBN 0-12-041502-x : £19.60 B82-30144

342.7'16 — Law courts. Interpreters. Role

Channan, Omkar Nath. The role of the court interpreter / by Omkar Nath Channan ; with a foreword by the Lord Hailsham of St Marylebone. — London : Shaw, 1982. — 44p ; 22cm
ISBN 0-7219-0920-5 (pbk) : Unpriced
B82-27456

342.7'5'019 — Law courts. Procedure. Psychological aspects

The **Psychology** of the courtroom / edited by Norbert L. Kerr, Robert M. Bray. — New York ; London : Academic Press, 1982. — xiii,370p : ill ; 24cm
Includes bibliographies and index
ISBN 0-12-404920-6 : £19.60 B82-30107

342.7'7'0903 — Trials, *1526-1973*

Comyn, James. Lost causes. — London : Secker and Warburg, Sept.1982. — [160]p
ISBN 0-436-10581-0 : £7.50 : CIP entry
B82-22424

343 — LAW. ANCIENT WORLD

343.7 — Ancient Rome. Law

Curzon, L. B.. Roman law / L.B. Curzon. — Plymouth : Macdonald and Evans, 1966 (1981 [printing]). — xiii,223p : ill ; 18cm. — (The M. & E. handbook series)
Includes index
ISBN 0-7121-1853-5 (pbk) : £4.50 B82-00797

343.7 — Ancient Rome. Law. Making, *193-305*

Honoré, Tony. Emperors and lawyers / Tony Honoré. — London : Duckworth, 1981. — xv,190p ; 26cm
Bibliography: p183-187. — Includes index
ISBN 0-7156-1449-5 : Unpriced B82-00562

343.805'252 — Ancient Greece. Homicide. Law

Gagarin, Michael. Drakon and early Athenian homicide law / Michael Gagarin. — New Haven ; London : Yale University Press, c1981. — xvii,175p ; 22cm. — (Yale classical monographs ; 3)
Includes index. — Includes the Greek text and English translation of Drakon's law
ISBN 0-300-02627-7 : Unpriced : CIP rev.
B81-35027

343.8'5022 — Athenian Empire. Constitution. Athenaion politeia — *Commentaries*

Rhodes, P. J.. A commentary on the Aristotelian Athenaion politeia : by P.J. Rhodes. — Oxford : Clarendon, 1981. — xiii,795p : 1map,1plan ; 23cm
Bibliography: p739-763. — Includes index
ISBN 0-19-814004-5 : £45.00 : CIP rev.
B82-01088

344.1 — LAW. GREAT BRITAIN

344.1'001'9 — Great Britain. Law. Applications of psychology — *Conference proceedings*

Law and psychology : papers presented at SSRC law and psychology conferences 1979-1980 / edited by Sally Lloyd-Bostock. — Oxford : SSRC Centre for Socio-legal Studies, Wolfson College, 1982. — viii,165p ; 21cm
Includes bibliographies
ISBN 0-86226-075-2 (pbk) : Unpriced
B82-34564

344.1'007 — Great Britain. Law. Study techniques — *Manuals*

Williams, Glanville. Learning the law / by Glanville Williams. — 11th ed. — London : Stevens, 1982. — viii,241p ; 19cm
Previous ed.: 1978. — Includes index
ISBN 0-420-46290-2 (cased) : Unpriced : CIP rev.
ISBN 0-420-46300-3 (pbk) : £3.55 B82-07973

344.102'29 — Great Britain. Constitution, *1970-1980.* **Political aspects**

Norton, Philip. The constitution in flux. — Oxford : Martin Robertson, Sept.1982. — [250]p
ISBN 0-85520-521-0 (cased) : £15.00 : CIP entry
ISBN 0-85520-522-9 (pbk) : £4.95 B82-20842

344.102'66 — Great Britain. Public administration. Decision making. Judicial review

De Smith, S. A.. De Smith's judicial review of administrative action / by the late S.A. De Smith. — 4th ed. / by J.M. Evans. — London : Stevens, 1980. — lxviii,626p ; 26cm
Previous ed.: 1973. — Includes index
ISBN 0-420-45400-4 : £24.00 : CIP rev.
B80-01559

344.102'68 — Great Britain. Premises. Entry. Powers of government inspectors

An **Inspector** at the door : an index of officials who can demand rights of entry. — London : Adam Smith Institute, 1979. — 70p : ill ; 21cm
ISBN 0-906517-04-4 (pbk) : £2.00 B82-10822

344.102'82 — Great Britain. Immigration. Entry controls. Law — *For advice centres*

You don't have to be a lawyer to help someone being threatened with immediate arrest, detention or expulsion under the Immigration Act : a practical guide for advice workers (including lawyers!) and anyone else wanting to help the victims of immigration control. — Manchester (593 Stockport Rd., Longsight, Manchester) : Manchester Law Centre, [1982?]. — 56p : ill,facsims ; 21cm. — (Manchester Law Centre immigration handbook ; no.4)
£1.00 (pbk) B82-17760

344.102'82 — Great Britain. Immigration. Law — *Regulations*

Statement of changes in immigration rules. — London : H.M.S.O., [1980]. — iii,37p ; 25cm. — ([HC] ; 394)
ISBN 0-10-239480-6 (unbound) : £2.25
B82-13675

344.102'83 — British nationality. Law: British Nationality Act 1981 — *Critical studies*

Fransman, Laurie. British nationality law and the 1981 Act / by Laurie Fransman ; in consultation with Mithu Ghosh. — London : Fourmat, 1982. — xv,129p : ill,forms ; 22cm. — (Lawyers practice and procedure series)
ISBN 0-906840-48-1 (pbk) : £6.25 B82-21229

Stanbrook, Ivor. British nationality : the new law / by Ivor Stanbrook. — London : Clement, 1982. — xxiii,213p ; 23cm
Includes text of the act
ISBN 0-907027-02-4 : £9.50 : CIP rev.
B81-38848

344.102'83'02633 — British nationality. Law — *Statutes — Texts with commentaries*

Great Britain. [British Nationality Act 1981]. The new nationality law / Ian A. Macdonald and Nicholas Blake. — London : Butterworths, 1982. — 208p ; 26cm
Includes index
ISBN 0-406-28280-3 : Unpriced B82-31643

344.102'83'02633 — British nationality. Law — *Statutes — Texts with commentaries*

continuation

Great Britain. [British Nationality Act 1981]. British Nationality Act 1981 / with annotations by M.D.A. Freeman. — London : Sweet & Maxwell, 1982. — [92]p ; 25cm. — (Current Law statutes reprints)
ISBN 0-421-30060-4 (pbk) : £5.00 B82-31644

344.102'85 — Great Britain. Citizens. Rights

Morby, Grainne. Know how : to find out your rights / Grainne Morby. — London : Pluto, 1982. — 188p ; 20cm
Includes index
ISBN 0-86104-359-6 (pbk) : £3.95 : CIP rev.
B82-14927

344.102'85 — Great Britain. Civil rights. Law

Stevens, I. N.. The protection of liberty. — Oxford : Blackwell, Oct.1982. — [256]p
ISBN 0-631-12944-8 (cased) : £12.00 : CIP entry
ISBN 0-631-13176-0 (pbk) : £4.95 B82-23167

344.102'858 — Great Britain. Privacy. Encroachment by computer systems. Control. Law — *Proposals*

Great Britain. Data protection : the Government's proposals for legislation. — London : H.M.S.O., [1982]. — 23p ; 25cm. — (Cmnd. ; 8539)
At head of title: Home Office
ISBN 0-10-185390-4 (unbound) : £2.30
B82-25342

344.102'87 — Great Britain. Racial discrimination & sex discrimination. Law

Malone, Michael, *1943-*. A practical guide to discrimination law / Michael Malone. — London : Grant McIntyre, 1981. — xviii,273p ; 22cm
Includes index
£9.95 (pbk) B82-20996

344.102'88 — Great Britain. Government liability. Law

Harlow, Carol. Compensation and government torts. — London : Sweet and Maxwell, Nov.1982. — [130]p. — (Modern legal studies)
ISBN 0-421-29250-4 (cased) : £11.50 : CIP entry
ISBN 0-421-29260-1 (pbk) : £7.50 B82-28281

344.103'0967 — Great Britain. Shipping. Laytime. Law

Summerskill, Michael Brynmor. Laytime. — 3rd ed. — London : Stevens, May 1982. — [300]p
Previous ed.: 1973
ISBN 0-420-46210-4 : £36.00 : CIP entry
B82-06765

344.103'14 — Great Britain. *Army. Ulster Defence Regiment.* **Medals: Medal for Long Service and Good Conduct (Ulster Defence Regiment). Law** *— Prerogative instruments*

Great Britain. The Medal for Long Service and Good Conduct (Ulster Defence Regiment) : royal warrant. — London : H.M.S.O., 1982. — 3p ; 25cm. — (Cmnd. ; 8604)
ISBN 0-10-186040-4 (unbound) : £0.75
B82-39382

344.103'14 — Great Britain. *Army. Ulster Defence Regiment.* **Part-time soldiers. Medals: Ulster Defence Regiment Medal. Law —** *Prerogative instruments*

Great Britain. The Ulster Defence Regiment Medal : royal warrant. — London : H.M.S.O., 1982. — [4]p ; 25cm
ISBN 0-10-186030-7 (unbound) : £0.75
B82-39383

344.103'14 — Great Britain. *Royal Navy.* **Officers,** *1660-1900.* **Conduct. Law —** *Statutes — Collections*

Articles of War : the statutes which governed our fighting navies 1661, 1749, 1886 / by N.A.M. Rodger. — Homewell : Mason, c1982. — 62p : ill ; 22cm
Bibliography: p62. — Includes the texts of The Articles of War 1661, The Articles of War 1749 and the Naval Discipline Act 1866
ISBN 0-85937-275-8 : £6.95 : CIP rev.
B82-03382

344.103'34 — Great Britain. Government. Finance. Consolidated Fund. Law — *Statutes*

Great Britain. [Consolidated Fund (No.2) Act 1980]. Consolidated Fund (No.2) Act 1980 : Elizabeth II, 1980, chapter 68. — London : H.M.S.O., [1980]. — 1sheet ; 25x16cm
ISBN 0-10-546880-0 : £0.30 B82-09251

344.1034 — Great Britain. Business firms. Stock & work in progress. Taxation. Tax concessions. Law: Finance Act 1981 — *Critical studies*

Gammie, Malcolm. Stock relief : the new system explained / Malcolm Gammie and David Williams. — London : Oyez, 1981. — xiv,202p ; 21cm. — (The Oyez practical tax series)
Includes index
ISBN 0-85120-585-2 (pbk) : Unpriced
B82-11023

344.1034 — Great Britain. Tax avoidance. Law

Ashton, R. K.. Anti-avoidance legislation / R.K. Ashton. — London : Butterworths, 1981. — xvii,255p ; 22cm
Includes index
ISBN 0-406-11140-5 (pbk) : Unpriced
B82-13019

344.103'4 — Great Britain. Tax avoidance — *Manuals*

Potter, D. C.. Potter and Monroe's tax planning with precedents. — 9th ed. — London : Sweet & Maxwell, Dec.1982. — [400]p
Previous ed.: 1978
ISBN 0-421-29180-x : £42.00 : CIP entry
B82-29767

344.1034 — Great Britain. Tax avoidance. Use of wills. Legal aspects

Venables, Robert. Tax planning through wills (with precedents) / by Robert Venables, Andrew R. Thornhill, A. Michael Jepson. — London : Butterworths, 1981. — xxvi,203p ; 26cm
Includes index
ISBN 0-406-39660-4 : Unpriced B82-13980

344.1034 — Great Britain. Taxation. Law

Pinson, Barry. Pinson on revenue law : comprising income tax, capital gains tax, development land tax, corporation tax, capital transfer tax, value added tax, stamp duties, tax planning / by Barry Pinson. — 14th ed. / sections on value added tax and development land tax by John Gardiner. — London : Sweet & Maxwell, 1981. — lxiii,719p ; 25cm
Previous ed.: 1980. — Includes index
ISBN 0-421-29050-1 (cased) : £32.00 : CIP rev.
ISBN 0-421-29060-9 (pbk) : £17.75
B81-31174

Pinson, Barry. Pinson on revenue law. — 15th ed. — London : Sweet and Maxwell, Oct.1982. — [700]p
Previous ed.: 1981
ISBN 0-421-30500-2 (cased) : £32.00 : CIP entry
ISBN 0-421-30510-x (pbk) : £20.00
B82-25186

Tiley, John. Revenue law / John Tiley. — 3nd ed. — London : Butterworths, 1981. — lvi,873,28p ; 25cm
Previous ed.: 1978. — Bibliography: pxv. — Includes index
ISBN 0-406-66595-8 : Unpriced
ISBN 0-406-66596-6 (pbk) : Unpriced
B82-13976

344.1034 — Great Britain. Taxation. Law — *For tax avoidance*

Sunday telegraph 101 ways of saving tax '82 : the book everyone needs! Income tax, corporation tax, capital gains tax and VAT / Touche Ross & Co.. — London : Sunday Telegraph, 1982. — 134p ; 18cm
Spine title: 101 Ways of saving tax '82
ISBN 0-901684-75-9 (pbk) : £2.50 B82-31738

344.1034 — Great Britain. Taxation. Law. Great Britain. *Parliament. House of Commons.* **Finance Bill. Session 1981-82 —** *Critical studies*

Dean, P. R.. The Budget and Finance Bill 1982 / P.R. Dean. — [Guildford] ([Braboeuf Manor, St. Catherines, Guildford, Surrey, GU3 1HA]) : [The College of Law], [1982]. — 24p ; 22cm. — (Crash course lecture / The College of Law, ISSN 0309-2771 ; 1982)
Cover title
£1.50 (pbk) B82-40239

Great Britain. *Parliament. House of Commons. Treasury and Civil Service Committee.* Fourth report from the Treasury and Civil Service Committee, session 1981-82 : the 1982 Budget : together with the proceedings of the Committee, the minutes of evidence and appendices. — London : H.M.S.O., 1982. — xxv,85p : 1ill ; 25cm. — ([HC] ; 270)
ISBN 0-10-227082-1 (pbk) : £7.35 B82-26848

344.1034 — Great Britain. Taxation. Law. Great Britain. *Parliament. House of Commons.* **Finance Bill. Session 1982-83 —** *Critical studies*

Cowdrey, M. R.. The Budget 1982 / by M.R. Cowdrey and R.E. Holloway. — Nottingham (145 Derby Rd., Nottingham NG7 1NE) : Holloway, Cowdrey & Co., [1982]. — 10,vileaves ; 30cm
£1.50 (spiral) B82-22038

344.1034 — Great Britain. Taxation. Law. Reform — *Proposals*

Kay, J. A.. Tax reform — problems and possibilities / by John Kay. — Stockport ([c/o P.K. Berry, C.I.S. Building, Miller St, Manchester M60 0AL]) : Manchester Statistical Society, [1980?]. — 11p ; 21cm
At head of title: Manchester Statistical Society. — Text on inside cover
£2.00 (pbk) B82-02710

344.1034'0212 — Great Britain. Direct taxation. Law — *Algorithms — Serials*

Tolley's tax cards. — 1981/82-. — Croydon : Tolley Pub. Co., 1981-. — v. ; 30cm
Annual. — Continues: Marchmont tax cards
ISSN 0263-4481 = Tolley's tax cards : £7.95
B82-24756

344.1034'02632 — Great Britain. Taxation. Law — *Statutes — Collections*

Sweet & Maxwell's tax statutes / edited by Sweet & Maxwell's Legal Editorial Staff ; advisory editors, Julian Farrand, Geoffrey Morse, David Williams ; Scottish editor, Robert Burgess. — London : Sweet & Maxwell, 1980. — ix,400p : ill ; 25cm
Includes index
ISBN 0-421-27070-5 (cased) : £15.75 : CIP rev.
ISBN 0-421-27080-2 (pbk) : £11.00
B80-29345

344.1034'02633 — Great Britain. Taxation. Law — *Statutes — Texts with commentaries*

British tax legislation, 1982-83. — Bicester (Telford Rd., Bicester, Oxfordshire OX6 0XD) : CCH Editions
Vol.1: Income and corporation taxes. — Aug.1982. — [1700]p
ISBN 0-86325-005-x (pbk) : £16.00 : CIP entry
B82-25937

British tax legislation, 1982-83. — Bicester (Telford Rd., Bicester, Oxfordshire OX6 0XD) : CCH Editions
Vol.2: Capital taxes. — Aug.1982. — [650]p
ISBN 0-86325-006-8 (pbk) : £14.50 : CIP entry
B82-25936

344.1034'0264 — Great Britain. Taxation. Law — *Cases — Serials*

Current tax intelligence. — 1981-. — London : Sweet & Maxwell, 1982-. — v. ; 25cm
Annual
ISSN 0263-6042 = Current tax intelligence : £6.00 B82-28865

344.1034'05 — Great Britain. Taxation. Law — *Serials*

Current tax intelligence. — 1981. — London : Sweet & Maxwell, Mar.1982. — [180]p
ISBN 0-421-29910-x (cased) : £9.00 : CIP entry
ISBN 0-421-29920-7 (pbk) : £6.00 B82-05393

344.1034′05 — Great Britain. Taxation. Law — *Serials* *continuation*
Law & tax review. — Vol.1, no.1 (Mar. 1982)-. — London : Oyez Longman, 1982-. — v. ; 26cm
Monthly
ISSN 0262-7647 = Law & tax review : Unpriced B82-26144

344.1035′2′0880655 — Great Britain. Married couples. Taxation. Law. Reform — *Proposals*
The **Taxation** of husband and wife. — London : H.M.S.O., [1980]. — 73p ; 25cm. — (Cmnd. ; 8093)
ISBN 0-10-180930-1 (pbk) : £4.20 B82-14641

344.1035′245 — Great Britain. Capital gains tax. Law
Di Palma, Vera. Capital gains tax / Vera Di Palma. — 5th ed. — Plymouth : Macdonald and Evans, 1981. — viii,208p ; 19cm. — (The M & E handbook series)
Previous ed.: 1977. — Includes index
ISBN 0-7121-0460-7 (pbk) : £4.50 B82-01914

Sumption, Anthony. Capital gains tax / by Anthony Sumption assisted by John Risby, Giles Clarke. — London : Butterworths, 1981. — 1v.(loose-leaf) ; 26cm
Includes index
ISBN 0-406-53882-4 : Unpriced B82-08925

Whiteman, Peter G.. Whiteman and Wheatcroft on capital gains tax. — 3rd ed. / by Peter G. Whiteman and Stephen Allcock ... [et al.]. — London : Sweet & Maxwell, 1980. — xxxix,688p ; 26cm. — (British tax encyclopedia, ISSN 0141-9633)
Previous ed.: 1973. — Includes index
ISBN 0-421-24770-3 : Unpriced : CIP rev. B80-35862

344.1035′3 — Great Britain. Capital transfer tax. Law
Ind, Ronald C.. Capital transfer tax / Ronald C. Ind. — 2nd ed. / revised by Martyn H. Jones. — Plymouth : Macdonald and Evans, 1981. — x,326p : ill,facsims ; 18cm. — (The M & E handbook series)
Previous ed.: 1977. — Includes index
ISBN 0-7121-0392-9 (pbk) : £4.95 B82-05075

344.1035′3 — Great Britain. Capital transfer tax. Tax avoidance
Capital tax planning : (with will precedents). — Guildford : College of Law, c1982. — vii,115p ; 22cm. — (College of Law lectures, ISSN 0309-3166)
With "Supplement: draft clauses on discretionary trusts" (7 folded leaves) as insert
£4.80 (pbk) B82-22005

344.1035′5 — Great Britain. Value-added tax. Law — *For tax avoidance*
Mainprice, H. H.. A practical guide to VAT planning / H.H. Mainprice. — London : Financial Times Business Publishing, c1981. — viii,187p ; 24cm
Includes index
ISBN 0-902101-06-4 : Unpriced B82-03333

344.1035′582282′02633 — Great Britain. Petroleum revenue tax. Law — *Statutes — Texts with commentaries*
United Kingdom oil and gas tax legislation 1981 / edited and annotated by Anne G. Lavies, J. Gordon McClure. — Woking : Tax & Financial Planning Ltd, 1981. — iv,209p ; 23cm
ISBN 0-86010-367-6 (pbk) : Unpriced B82-08294

344.1035′7 — Great Britain. Stamp duties. Law
Sergeant, E. G.. Sergeant and Sims on stamp duties and capital duty. — 8th ed. / B.J. Sims ; assistant editors E.M.E. Sims, R.D. Fulton ; consultant editor A.K. Tavaré. — London : Butterworths, 1982. — li,681p : forms ; 26cm. — (Butterworths modern text books)
Previous ed.: 1977. — Includes index
ISBN 0-406-37035-4 : Unpriced B82-33670

344.1036′2 — Great Britain. Farmers & landowners. Taxation. Law
Stanley, Oliver. Taxation of farmers and landowners / by Oliver Stanley. — London : Butterworths, 1981. — xv,354p ; 22cm
Includes index
ISBN 0-406-38390-1 (pbk) : Unpriced B82-05830

344.1036′2 — Great Britain. Personal taxation. Liability of taxpayers. Implications of residence. Law
Piper, Geoffrey S. F.. Residence and domicile : for United Kingdom tax purposes / by Geoffrey S.F. Piper and Walter B. Deadman. — St. Helier : Guild, [1982?]. — ii,134p ; 21cm. — (Ready reference series)
Includes index
ISBN 0-907342-02-7 (pbk) : £12.00 B82-14009

344.1036′6 — Great Britain. Banks. Profits. Taxation. Law: Great Britain. *Parliament. House of Commons.* Finance Bill. Session 1980-81 — *Critical studies*
The **Case** against the banking levy. — London (10 Lombard St., EC3V 9AR) : Banking Information Service, [1981]. — 11p : 1ill ; 30cm
Cover title
Unpriced (pbk) B82-16282

344.1036′6 — Great Britain. Offshore natural gas & petroleum industries. Taxation. Law
Hayllar, R. F.. UK taxation of offshore oil and gas. — 2nd ed. / R.F. Hayllar, R.M. Rouse. — London : Butterworths, 1980. — 1v.(loose-leaf) : forms ; 26cm
Previous ed.: 1977. — Includes index
ISBN 0-406-22067-0 : £30.00 B82-17514

344.1036′7 — Great Britain. Companies. Taxation. Law. Reform — *Proposals*
Confederation of British Industry. *Taxation Committee*. A technical taxation bill : the CBI's proposals / report by CBI Taxation Committee. — London : Confederation of British Industry, 1981. — 20p ; 30cm
£2.00 (pbk) B82-07868

Institute for Fiscal Studies. *Working Party on Company Residence, Tax Havens and Upstream Loans*. Report of the IFS Working Part on Company Residence, Tax Havens and Upstream Loans. — London : Institute for Fiscal Studies, Sept.1982. — [48]p
ISBN 0-902992-30-9 (pbk) : £5.00 : CIP entry B82-30329

344.1036′8 — Great Britain. Business firms. Stock. Taxation. Allowances. Law: Finance Act 1981
Stock relief : the November 1980 proposals. — London (6 Long La., EC1A 9DP) : Chalmers, Impey, [1980]. — 8p ; 21cm
Unpriced (pbk) B82-21926

344.1036′8 — Great Britain. Business firms. Stock. Taxation. Law: Finance Act 1981 — *Critical studies*
Saunders, Glyn. Tolley's stock relief / by Glyn Saunders. — Croydon : Tolley, c1981. — ix,49p ; 23cm. — (A Benn Group Publication)
Includes index
ISBN 0-85459-052-8 (pbk) : £3.50 B82-14424

344.1036′8 — Great Britain. Capital allowances. Law
Pickerill, R. J.. Capital allowance in law and practice / by R.J. Pickerill. — 2nd ed. / the section on mines and oil wells is contributed by G.D. Swaine. — London : Institute of Chartered Accountants in England and Wales, 1981. — xix,307p : 1map ; 21cm. — (Chartac taxation guides)
Previous ed.: 1977. — Includes index
ISBN 0-85291-307-9 (pbk) : Unpriced B82-08928

344.1036′8 — Great Britain. Family firms. Taxation. Law
White, Peter, *1944 Nov.28-*. Law and tax for the family company / by Peter White. — London : Oyez, c1982. — xxii,224p : plans ; 23cm. — (Law & tax series)
Includes index
ISBN 0-85120-614-x (pbk) : Unpriced B82-20681

344.103′7 — Great Britain. Economic policies. Legal aspects
Bowles, Roger A.. Law and the economy. — Oxford : Martin Robertson, Sept.1982. — [250]p
ISBN 0-85520-465-6 (cased) : £12.50 : CIP entry
ISBN 0-85520-474-5 (pbk) : £5.50 B82-20203

344.103′71 — Great Britain. Consumer protection. Law
Encyclopedia of consumer law / general editor W.H. Thomas ; Scottish editor Matthew G. Clarke. — London : Sweet & Maxwell, 1980. — 1v.(loose-leaf) ; 26cm
Includes index
ISBN 0-421-25320-7 : £78.00 B82-17516

Harvey, Brian W.. The law of consumer protection and fair trading / Brian W. Harvey. — 2nd ed. — London : Butterworths, 1982. — xxviii,424p ; 23cm
Previous ed.: 1978. — Bibliography: p391-396. — Includes index
ISBN 0-406-22260-6 (cased) : £19.50
ISBN 0-406-22261-4 (pbk) : Unpriced B82-34906

344.103′71 — Great Britain. Consumer services. Law. Reform — *Proposals*
Lantin, Barbara. Service please : services and the law : a consumer view / prepared for the National Consumer Council by Barbara Lantin and Geoffrey Woodroffe. — London : National Consumer Council, c1981. — 35p ; 30cm
ISBN 0-905653-38-6 (pbk) : Unpriced B82-07273

344.103′72′0269 — Great Britain. Fair trading practice. Decisions of Great Britain. *Department of Trade.* Appeals — *Manuals*
Great Britain. *Department of Trade*. Consumer Credit Act 1974, guide on appeals from licensing determinations of the Director General of Fair Trading / Department of Trade. — London : The Department, 1981. — 7p : 1ill,1form ; 30cm
Unpriced (pbk) B82-40096

344.103′748′02633 — Foreign assistance by Great Britain. Law — *Statutes*
Great Britain. [Overseas Development and Co-operation Act 1980]. Overseas Development and Co-operation Act 1980 : chapter 63. — London : H.M.S.O., [1980]. — ii,21p ; 25cm
ISBN 0-10-546380-9 (unbound) : £2.10 B82-09256

344.103′75 — Great Britain. Aerosol containers. Law: Aerosol Dispensers (EEC Requirements) Regulations 1977 — *Critical studies*
A Guide to the Aerosol Directive (75/324/EEC-20 May 1975) and the Aerosol Dispensers (EEC Requirements) Regulations 1977 (Statutory Instrument 1977 No.1140) 1980. — London (93 Albert Embankment, SE1 7TU) : British Aerosol Manufacturers' Association, 1980. — 23p ; 25cm
Statutory instrument (7p.) in pocket
£3.00 (pbk) B82-13322

344.103′75 — Great Britain. Weights & measures. Law — *For packaging industries*
Code of practical guidance for packers and importers : Weights and Measures Act 1979 / Department of Trade. — Issue no.1. — London : H.M.S.O., 1979. — 87p : ill ; 30cm
ISBN 0-11-512922-7 (pbk) : £3.50 B82-18625

344.103′772′05 — Great Britain. Continental shelf. Offshore natural gas & petroleum industries. Law — *Serials*
United Kingdom offshore legislation guide. — 2nd ed. (1981). — London : Kogan Page, Nov.1981. — [240]p
ISBN 0-85038-499-0 (pbk) : £30.00 : CIP entry B81-33640

344.103'78624 — Great Britain. Construction. Contracts. Claims

Wood, R. D. (Reginald Douglas). Supplement to Building and civil engineering claims (second edition) : supplement - chapters 8 & 9 dealing with the J.C.T. 1980 edition of the Standard form of building contract / by R.D. Wood. — London : Estates Gazette, 1981. — ix,229p : ill ; 22cm
Bibliography: p229
£11.00 (pbk) B82-03260

344.103'786413'005 — Great Britain. Food industries & trades. Law — *Serials*

Food law monthly : the advisory service for the food, drug and cosmetics industries. — Vol.1, issue no.1 (Oct. 1981)-. — Great Waldingfield (Rectory Rd, Great Waldingfield, Sudbury, Suffolk CO10 0TL) : Monitor Press, 1981-. — v. ; 30cm
ISSN 0262-0030 = Food law monthly : Unpriced B82-04908

344.103'78'690 — Great Britain. Buildings. Construction. Contracts. Conditions — *Critical studies*

Turner, Dennis F.. Building contracts. — 4th ed. — London : Godwin, Dec.1982. — [400]p
Previous ed.: 1977
ISBN 0-7114-5656-9 : CIP entry B82-30197

344.103'7872892 — Great Britain. Agricultural industries. Farms. Buildings. Environment planning. Law

Weller, John B.. Agricultural buildings planning and allied controls / by John Weller ; commissioned and funded by the Social Science Research Council. — Edinburgh : Capital Planning Information, 1981. — 59p ; 21x30cm. — (Planning reviews ; no.2)
Bibliography: p57-59
ISBN 0-906011-12-4 (pbk) : £3.00 : CIP rev. B81-26686

344.103'8'05 — Great Britain. Trading. Law — *Serials — For businessmen*

Trading law. — Vol.1, no.1-. — [Chichester] ([Little London, Chichester, Sussex]) : Barry Rose Law Periodicals, [1981]-. — v. ; 24cm
Eight issues yearly
ISSN 0262-9240 = Trading law : £32.00 per year B82-11823

344.103'82 — Great Britain. Consumer credit. Advertising. Requirements: Truth. Law

Karpinski, Jan. Truth in lending / by Jan Karpinski. — London : Current Account, 1980. — x,80p ; 30cm. — (Current account special report)
ISBN 0-906840-31-7 (spiral) : Unpriced B82-06675

344.103'925 — Great Britain. Commercial nuclear power. Legal aspects — *Conference proceedings*

Commercial nuclear power / legal and constitutional issues : contributions to a conference held at Imperial College of Science and Technology / edited by Richard Macrory ; with a foreword by the Lord Flowers. — London : Imperial College Centre for Environmental Technology, 1982. — 69p ; 22cm
ISBN 0-9507744-0-5 (pbk) : Unpriced B82-24213

344.103'925 — Great Britain. Nuclear power stations. Construction & operation. Regulation

Controls on the building and running of nuclear power stations. — [Dorchester] : Planning Department, Dorset County Council, 1981. — 8p : 1ill ; 21cm. — (Nuclear power stations ; information paper no.1)
Cover title
ISBN 0-85216-296-0 (pbk) : Unpriced B82-12743

344.103'94 — Great Britain. Road traffic. Law

Chiswell, P. G.. Road traffic offences / P.G. Chiswell. — [Guildford] ([Braboeuf Manor, St. Catherines, Guildford, Surrey, GU3 1HA]) : [The College of Law], [1982]. — 25p ; 22cm. — (Crash course lecture / The College of Law, ISSN 0309-2771 ; 1982)
Cover title
£1.50 (pbk) B82-40240

Sloan, Kenneth. The law relating to traffic / by Kenneth Sloan. — London : Police Review Publishing, [1981]. — x,265p ; 14cm. — (A Police Review publication)
Includes index
ISBN 0-85164-992-0 (pbk) : Unpriced B82-21592

344.103'944 — Great Britain. Heavy commercial vehicles. Law

Summers, Dennis, *1929-*. HGV law guide / Dennis Summers. — London : Butterworths, 1981. — 92p : ill,2forms ; 23cm
Includes index
ISBN 0-408-00569-6 : Unpriced : CIP rev. B81-23951

344.103'944 — Great Britain. Traction engines. Law

Tew, David. Traction engines and the law / David Tew. — [Leicester] : National Traction Engine Club, 1981 ; Comberton (60 Harbour Avenue, Comberton, Cambs. CB3 7DD) : Distributed by NTEC Sales. — 43p : ill,facsims ; 21cm
ISBN 0-905818-03-2 (pbk) : Unpriced B82-03266

344.103'946 — Great Britain. Commercial vehicles. Operation. Law — *Questions & answers — For road transport services*

CPC questions & answers / edited and published by Commercial motor in association with Avis Truck Leasing and Rental. — [Great Britain] : Commercial Motor, [1980?]. — 54p : ill ; 21cm
£1.00 (unbounmd) B82-13879

344.103'946 — Great Britain. Dangerous materials for transport by road. Safety aspects. Statutory regulations

Great Britain. *Health and Safety Executive.* A guide to the Dangerous Substances (Conveyance by Road in Road Tankers and Road Tank Containers) Regulations 1981. — London : H.M.S.O., Dec.1981. — [50]p. — (HS(R))
ISBN 0-11-883476-2 : CIP entry B81-38852

344.103'946 — Great Britain. Motor vehicles. Driving. Legal aspects

Thompson, B. A.. Professional driver's guide / by B.A. Thompson. — 6th ed. — New Malden : Croner, 1982. — 190p : ill ; 17cm
Previous ed.: 1979
ISBN 0-900319-28-3 : Unpriced B82-26501

344.103'9483 — Great Britain. Road freight transport. Law — *Serials*

The **Transport** manager's handbook. — 12th ed. (1982). — London : Kogan Page, Dec.1981. — [500]p
ISBN 0-85038-492-3 : £13.50 : CIP entry B81-33865

The **Transport** manager's handbook. — 13th ed. (1983). — London : Kogan Page, Oct.1982. — [800]p
ISBN 0-85038-555-5 : £14.50 : CIP entry
ISSN 0306-9435 B82-24741

344.103'96 — Merchant shipping. British law — *For British shipmasters*

Hopkins, F. N.. Business and law for the shipmaster / by F.N. Hopkins. — 6th ed., rev. by G.G. Watkins. — Glasgow : Brown, Son & Ferguson, 1982. — xii,908p : ill,facsims,forms ; 22cm
Previous ed.: 1979. — Includes index
ISBN 0-85174-434-6 : £24.00 B82-37036

344.103'968 — Great Britain. Freight transport. Shipping. Law

Carver, Thomas Gilbert. Carver's carriage by sea. — 13th ed. — London : Stevens, Apr.1982. — 2v.. — (British shipping laws)
Previous ed.:1971
ISBN 0-420-45110-2 : £12.00 : CIP entry B82-04055

344.103'968 — Great Britain. Freight transport. Shipping. Law — *Cases*

Casebook on carriage by sea / [compiled] by E.R. Hardy Ivamy. — 4th ed. — London : Lloyd's of London, 1979. — xxiii,148p ; 26cm
Previous ed.: 1977. — Includes index
ISBN 0-904093-72-7 : Unpriced B82-22019

344.103'978'02633 — Great Britain. Air services. Law — *Statutes*

Great Britain. [Civil Aviation Act 1980]. Civil Aviation Act 1980 : chapter 60. — London : H.M.S.O., [1980]. — ii,30p ; 25cm
ISBN 0-10-546080-x (unbound) : £2.40 B82-09253

344.103'9945 — Great Britain. Commercial broadcasting services. Law — *Statutes*

Great Britain. [Broadcasting Act 1980]. Broadcasting Act 1980 : chapter 64. — London : H.M.S.O., [1980]. — iii,39p ; 25cm
ISBN 0-10-546480-5 (unbound) : £3.00 B82-09254

344.104'1 — Great Britain. Employment. Labour. Law

Drake, Charles D.. Labour law / by Charles D. Drake. — 3rd ed. — London : Sweet & Maxwell, 1981. — 278p ; 23cm. — (Concise college texts)
Previous ed.: 1973. — Includes index
ISBN 0-421-28100-6 (cased) : Unpriced : CIP rev.
ISBN 0-421-28110-3 (pbk) : £7.50 B81-13471

344.104'1'0269 — Great Britain. Industrial tribunals. Jurisdiction

Howell, Arthur H.. The industrial tribunal : a guide to the jurisdiction of industrial tribunals within the provisions of the following Acts : The Employment Act 1975, The Employment Protection (Consolidation) Act 1978, The Employment Act 1980, The Equal Pay Act 1970, The Sex Discrimination Act 1975, The Race Relations Act 1976 / Arthur H. Howell. — Chichester : Barry Rose, c1981. — [38]p ; 26cm
Cover title
ISBN 0-85992-218-9 (spiral) : £7.75 B82-10063

344.104'1125 — Great Britain. Employment. Law

Birtles, Bill. Your rights at work : a practical guide. — 2nd ed., completely rev. / Bill Birtles and Patricia Hewitt ; cartoons by Liz Mackie. — London : National Council for Civil Liberties, 1980. — 95p : ill ; 21cm. — (NCCL know your rights handbooks ; 2)
Previous ed.: i.e. rev. ed. 1979. — Includes index
ISBN 0-901108-88-x (pbk) : £1.50 B82-13180

Fleeman, R. K.. Employment law : a guide / R.K. Fleeman, R.J. Rhodes. — 9th ed. — [Sutton Coldfield] ([34-36 Streetly Lane, Four Oaks, Sutton Coldfield, West Midlands B74 4TU]) : Fleeman Coper, [1981]. — 62p ; 21cm
Cover title. — Previous ed.: 197-?. — Includes index
Unpriced (pbk) B82-19973

Hepple, B. A.. Employment law / Hepple & O'Higgins. — 4th ed. / by B.A. Hepple. — London : Sweet & Maxwell, 1981. — lvii,430p ; 25cm
Previous ed.: 1979. — Bibliography: p401-402. — Includes index
ISBN 0-421-28830-2 (pbk) : £13.25 : CIP rev. B81-31172

Janner, Greville. Janner's consolidated compendium of employment law / Greville Janner ; cartoons by Tobi. — London : Business Books, 1982. — xiii,508p : ill ; 31cm
Includes index
ISBN 0-09-147340-3 : Unpriced : CIP rev. B82-04122

Snow, R. F.. Employment law and industrial relations / R.F. Snow. — [Guildford] ([Braboeuf Manor, St. Catherines, Guildford, Surrey, GU3 1HA]) : [The College of Law], [1982]. — 19p ; 22cm. — (Crash course lecture / The College of Law, ISSN 0309-2771 ; 1982)
Cover title
£1.50 (pbk) B82-40236

344.104'1125 — Great Britain. Employment. Law: Employment Act 1980 — *Critical studies*

Lewis, J. R. (John Royston). Striking a balance? : employment law after the 1980 Act / Roy Lewis and Bob Simpson. — Oxford : Martin Robertson, 1981. — ix,269p : ill ; 22cm
Includes index
ISBN 0-85520-442-7 (cased) : Unpriced : CIP rev.
ISBN 0-85520-443-5 (pbk) : £4.95 B81-27426

344.104'1125 — Great Britain. Employment. Law: Employment Protection (Consolidation) Act 1978 — *Commentaries*

Henderson, Joan. A guide to the Employment Protection (Consolidation) Act 1978 : individual rights of employees / by Joan Henderson. — London : Industrial Society, 1978 (1979 [printing]). — 47p ; 22cm
ISBN 0-85290-170-4 (pbk) : £1.50 B82-17400

344.104'1125'024055 — Great Britain. Employment. Law — *For young personnel*

Jordon, Julian. Workfacts for young workers / Julian Jordon. — Rev. ed. / prepared by Johanna Fawkes. — Cambridge : Basic Skills Unit, c1981. — 40p : ill,forms ; 21cm
Previous ed.: 197-?. — Bibliography: p38
ISBN 0-86082-205-2 (pbk) : Unpriced B82-38996

344.104'1125'02462 — Great Britain. Employment. Law — *For engineering industries*

EEF employment guide. — London (Broadway House, Tothill Street, SW1H 9NQ) : Engineering Employers' Federation, c1981. — 1v.(loose-leaf) : ill ; 32cm
Unpriced B82-07067

344.104'1125'024658 — Great Britain. Employment. Law — *For management*

Engaging an employee ; Disciplinary and grievance procedures ; Industrial tribunals. — [London] : Fourmat, [1979]. — 1portfolio : forms ; 32cm. — (Employment law practice guides)
ISBN 0-906840-00-7 : £6.95 B82-05857

Field, David, *1945-*. Inside employment law : a guide for managers / David Field. — London : Pan, 1982. — 266p ; 18cm. — (Pan business/law)
Includes index
ISBN 0-330-26647-0 (pbk) : £2.50 B82-23286

Lewis, David. Essentials of employment law. — London : Institute of Personnel Management, Jan.1983. — [250]p
ISBN 0-85292-295-7 (pbk) : £13.95 : CIP entry B82-33108

344.104'1133 — Great Britain. Employment. Equality of opportunity. Law — *For employers*

Guidance on equal opportunity policies & practices in employment. — Manchester : Equal Opportunities Commission, [1981?]. — 19p ; 21cm
ISBN 0-905829-03-4 (pbk) : Unpriced B82-23797

344.104'12 — Great Britain. Personnel. Conditions of service. Law

Labour Research Department. Terms of employment and how to control them / Labour Research Department. — London : LRD Publications, 1981. — 63p : ill ; 21cm. — (Bargaining and the law)
ISBN 0-900508-46-9 (pbk) : £0.90 B82-13607

344.104'12041651 — Great Britain. Offices. Working conditions. Law. Offices, Shops and Railway Premises Act 1963 — *Critical studies*

A Guide to the 1963 OSRP Act. — London : H.M.S.O., 1979. — vi,36p ; 22cm. — (HS(R4) 4)
At head of title: Health and Safety Executive. — Previous ed.: i.e. 2nd ed. published as the Offices, Shops and Railway Premises Act, a general guide / prepared by the Department of Employment, 1971
ISBN 0-11-883243-3 (pbk) : £0.75 : CIP rev.
Also classified at 344.104'1204165887
B79-10137

344.104'1204165887 — Great Britain. Shops. Working conditions. Law. Offices, Shops and Railway Premises Act 1963 — *Critical studies*

A Guide to the 1963 OSRP Act. — London : H.M.S.O., 1979. — vi,36p ; 22cm. — (HS(R4) 4)
At head of title: Health and Safety Executive. — Previous ed.: i.e. 2nd ed. published as the Offices, Shops and Railway Premises Act, a general guide / prepared by the Department of Employment, 1971
ISBN 0-11-883243-3 (pbk) : £0.75 : CIP rev.
Primary classification 344.104'12041651
B79-10137

344.104'121 — Great Britain. Sick personnel. Remuneration. Law

Janner, Greville. Janner's guide to the law of sick pay and absenteeism. — London : Business Books, Nov.1982. — [320]p
ISBN 0-09-149790-6 : £20.00 : CIP entry B82-30577

344.104'12166 — Great Britain. Sick personnel. Remuneration. Law

Statutory sick pay in the UK : a summary of the legislation. — Chichester (Metropolitan House, Northgate, Chichester, W. Sussex PO19 1BE) : MPA, c1982. — 5p ; 30cm
Unpriced (unbound) B82-40280

344.104'1255 — Great Britain. Employment. Termination. Payments. Calculation. Law

Fox, Ronald D.. Payments on termination of employment : calculation and taxation / Ronald D. Fox. — London : Oyez, 1981. — viii,31p ; 22cm
ISBN 0-85120-608-5 (pbk) : Unpriced B82-03053

344.104'12596 — Great Britain. Business firms. Personnel. Rights. Effects of transfer of business firms. Law — *Statutory instruments — Texts with commentaries*

Great Britain. [Transfer of Undertakings (Protection of Employment) Regulations 1981]. Transfer of employment : the Transfer of Undertakings (Protection of Employment) Regulations 1981 / with annotations by Paul Davies and Mark Freedland. — London : Sweet & Maxwell, 1982. — [31]p ; 25cm
ISBN 0-421-30230-5 (pbk) : £3.45 B82-28503

344.104'12596 — Great Britain. Personnel. Dismissal. Law

Napier, B. W.. Comparative dismissal law / B.W. Napier, J.-C. Javillier and P. Verge. — London : Croom Helm, c1982. — 175p ; 23cm
ISBN 0-7099-1808-9 : £12.50 : CIP rev.
Also classified at 344.404'12596 B82-05404

Ream, Betty. Unfair dismissal / Betty Ream. — Rev. — London : Industrial Society, 1978. — 27p ; 22cm
Previous ed.: 1976
ISBN 0-85290-175-5 (pbk) : £1.50 B82-16019

344.104'13425922 — Great Britain. Apprentices. Rights. Law

A Guide for apprentices. — Edinburgh (132 Lauriston Place, Edinburgh) : Citizens Rights Office, [1982]. — 6p ; 21cm
Unpriced (unbound) B82-35135

344.104'1421 — Great Britain. Women personnel. Remuneration. Law. Enforcement. Role of Great Britain. *Central Arbitration Committee*

Harris, John, *1934-*. Has discrimination been eliminated in collective agreements? : the Central Arbitration Committee and equal pay / John Harris and Helen Snider. — London (32 Wells St, W1P 3FG) : Polytechnic of Central London School of Social Sciences and Business Studies, 1982. — 30p ; 30cm. — (Research working paper / Polytechnic of Central London, School of Social Sciences and Business Studies ; no.16)
Cover title
£2.00 (spiral) B82-27448

344.104'1769 — Great Britain. Building industries. Performance. Improvement. Organisations: National Building Agency. Professional personnel. Indemnification by Great Britain. *Department of the Environment — Proposals*

Great Britain. *Department of the Environment.* Minute dated 12 March 1982 relating to an indemnity to be given by the Secretary of State for the Environment in favour of employees and former employees of the National Building Agency. — London : H.M.S.O, [1982]. — [3]p ; 25cm. — (Cmnd. ; 8524)
ISBN 0-10-185240-1 (unbound) : £0.70 B82-23265

344.104'188 — Great Britain. Trade unions. Law. Reform. Great Britain. *Department of Employment.* **Trade union immunities** — *Critical studies*

Great Britain. *Parliament. House of Commons. Employment Committee.* Second report from the Employment Committee : session 1980-81 : the legal immunities of trade unions and other related matters : the green paper on trade union immunities : together with the proceedings of the Committee, minutes of evidence taken before the Committee on 8 April, 6 May, 3 June and 1, 7 and 8 July 1981, and appendices. — London : H.M.S.O., [1981?]. — xiv,345p ; 25cm. — ([HC] ; 282)
ISBN 0-10-228281-1 (pbk) : £10.35 B82-14479

344.104'188 — Great Britain. Trade unions. Law. Reform. Great Britain. *Department of Employment.* **Trade union immunities. Criticism. Great Britain.** *Parliament. House of Commons. Employment Committee.* **Second report ... session 1980-81** — *Critical studies*

Great Britain. *Parliament. House of Commons. Employment Committee.* First special report from the Employment Committee, session 1981-82 : the legal immunities of trade unions and other related matters : the Green Paper on trade union immunities : observations by the Secretary of State for Employment on the Second report of the Committee in session 1980-81. — London : H.M.S.O., [1982]. — xivp ; 25cm. — ([HC] ; 85)
ISBN 0-10-208582-x (pbk) : £2.05 B82-22029

344'.104'188 — Great Britain. Trade unions. Law. Reform — *Proposals*

Centre for policy Studies. *Trade Union Reform Committee.* Liberties and liabilities : the case for trade union reform : a report of the Trade Union Reform Committee. — London : Centre for Policy Studies, 1980. — viii,57p ; 30cm
ISBN 0-905880-32-3 (pbk) : £3.55 B82-17612

344.104'188 — Great Britain. Trade unions. Law. Reform. Proposals — *Communist Party of Great Britain viewpoints*

Costello, Mick. Tebbit's Bill — kill it! / by Mick Costello. — London : Communist Party, 1982. — 18p ; 21cm. — (A Communist Party pamphlet)
ISBN 0-86224-017-4 (unbound) : £0.40 B82-25708

344.104'188 — Great Britain. Trade unions. Law. Reform. Proposals. Great Britain. *Parliament. House of Commons. Employment Committee.* **Second report ... session 1979-80** — *Critical studies*

Great Britain. *Department of Employment.* Second special report from the Employment Committee, session 1979-80 : the legal immunities of trade unions and other related matters — draft codes of practice on picketing and the closed shop : observations by the Secretary of State for Employment on the second report of the committee in session 1979-80. — London : H.M.S.O., [1980]. — 7p ; 25cm. — ([HC] ; 848)
ISBN 0-10-028489-2 (unbound) : £1.10 B82-10329

344.104'18927 — Great Britain. Industrial relations. Picketing. Law — *For trade unionism*

Picketing : a trade unionist's guide / Labour Research Department. — London : LRD Publications, 1976. — 12p ; 19cm
£0.20 (unbound) B82-02737

344.104'2 — Great Britain. Social security benefits. Increase. Law. Statutory instruments. Drafts. Financial aspects — *Inquiry reports*

Great Britain. *Government Actuary.* Report by the Government Actuary on the draft of the social security benefits up-rating order 1982. — London : H.M.S.O., [1982]. — 5p ; 25cm. — (Cmnd. ; 8588)
ISBN 0-10-185880-9 (unbound) : £1.25
B82-37376

344.104'2 — Great Britain. Social security benefits. Law. Statutory instruments. Drafts — *Inquiry reports*

Great Britain. *National Insurance Advisory Committee.* The Social Security (Overlapping Benefits) Amendment Regulations 1980 (S.I. 1980 no.1927) : report of the National Insurance Advisory Committee in accordance with section 139(3) of the Social Security Act 1975 preceded by a statement made by the Secretary of State for Social Services in accordance with section 10(4) of the Social Security Act 1980. — London : H.M.S.O., [1980]. — 2p ; 25cm. — (Cmnd. ; 8116)
ISBN 0-10-181160-8 (unbound) : £0.70
B82-13677

Great Britain. *Social Security Advisory Committee.* The Social Security (Unemployment, Sickness and Invalidity Benefit and Credits) Amendment Regulations 1982 (S.I. 1982 no.96) : report of the Social Security Advisory Committee in accordance with section 10(3) of the Social Security Act 1980 preceded by a statement made by the Secretary of State for Social Services in accordance with section 10(4) of that act. — London : H.M.S.O., 1982. — 10p ; 25cm. — (Cmnd. ; 8486)
ISBN 0-10-184860-9 (unbound) : £1.50
B82-20566

Great Britain. *Social Security Advisory Committee.* The Supplementary Benefit (Requirements and Resources) Amendment Regulations 1982 (SI1982 no.[ ].) and the Supplementary Benefit (Miscellaneous Amendments) Regulations 1982 (SI1982 no.[ ].) : Report of the Social Security Advisory Committee in accordance with Section 10(3) of the Social Security Act 1980 preceded by a statement made by the Secretary of State for Social Services in accordance with section 10(4) of that Act. — London : H.M.S.O., [1982]. — 20p ; 25cm
ISBN 0-10-185980-5 (unbound) : £2.55
B82-35148

344.104'2 — Great Britain. Social security contributions. Law — *For employers*

Booth, Neil D.. Social security contributions / Neil D. Booth. — London : Butterworths, 1982. — xxviii,204p ; 25cm
Includes index
ISBN 0-406-12899-5 (pbk) : £8.00 B82-24406

344.104'2 — Great Britain. Social security contributions. Law. Great Britain. *Parliament. House of Commons.* **Social Security (Contributions) Bill. Session 1981-1982. Financial aspects**

Great Britain. *Government Actuary.* Social Security (Contributions) Bill 1981 : report by the Government Actuary on the financial provisions of the bill. — London : H.M.S.O., [1981]. — 10p ; 25cm. — (Cmnd. ; 8443)
At head of title: Department of Health and Social Security
ISBN 0-10-184430-1 (unbound) : £1.80
B82-13777

344.104'2 — Great Britain. Social security contributions. Law. Statutes. Drafts. Financial aspects

Great Britain. *Government Actuary.* Social Security (Contributions) Bill 1980 : report by the Government Actuary on the financial provisions of the bill. — London : H.M.S.O., [1980]. — 10p ; 25cm. — (Cmnd. ; 8091)
At head of title: Department of Health and Social Security
ISBN 0-10-180910-7 (unbound) : £1.80
B82-16063

344.104'2 — Great Britain. Social security contributions. Law. Statutory instruments. Drafts — *Inquiry reports*

Great Britain. *National Insurance Advisory Committee.* The Social Security (Contributions) Amendment Regulations 1980 (S.I. 1980 no. 1975) : report of the National Insurance Advisory Committee in accordance with section 139(3) of the Social Security Act 1975 preceded by a statement made by the Secretary of State for Social Services in accordance with section 10(4) of the Social Security Act 1980. — London : H.M.S.O., [1981]. — 13p ; 25cm. — (Cmnd. ; 8117)
ISBN 0-10-181170-5 (unbound) : £1.70
B82-13676

344.104'2 — Great Britain. Social security. Law

Williams, David W.. Social security taxation. — London : Sweet and Maxwell, Oct.1982. — [350]p
ISBN 0-421-26230-3 : £25.00 : CIP entry
B82-24002

344.104'2 — Great Britain. Supplementary benefits. Law

Levin, Jennifer. A guide to supplementary benefit law. — 3rd ed. / by Jenny Levin. — London : Legal Action Group, [1981]. — 136p : 1form ; 21cm. — (Law and practice guides, ISSN 0307-3483 ; no.3)
Cover title. — Previous ed.: 1978. — Bibliography: p7-9. — Includes index
£3.85 (pbk) B82-05587

344.104'2'02632 — Great Britain. Supplementary benefits. Law — *Statutes & statutory instruments — Collections*

Great Britain. The law relating to supplementary benefits and family income supplements : the statutes, regulations and orders as now in force / Department of Health and Social Security, Supplementary Benefits Commission ; editor (supplementary benefits) E.O.F. Stocker, editor (family incomes supplements) P.C. Nilsson. — Consolidated ed. — London : H.M.S.O., 1977 (1979 [printing]). — 1v.(loose-leaf) ; 32cm
"Amended up to and including Supplement No. 9"
ISBN 0-11-760625-1 : £11.50 B82-19387

344.104'2'0264 — Great Britain. Supplementary benefits. Law — *Cases*

Decisions of the courts relating to supplementary benefits and family income supplements legislation / Department of Health and Social Security. — London : H.M.S.O., 1980. — 1v.(loose-leaf) ; 23cm
ISBN 0-11-760675-8 : £12.50 B82-19388

344.104'20269 — Great Britain. Supplementary benefit appeal tribunals. Procedure

Supplementary Benefits Appeal Tribunals : a guide to procedure / Department of Health and Social Security. — Rev. [ed.]. — London : H.M.S.O., 1982. — vi,60p : forms ; 21cm
Previous ed.: 1977
ISBN 0-11-760844-0 (pbk) : £2.00 B82-32996

344.104'2'0883875 — Great Britain. Shipping services. Personnel: Sailors. Social security contributions. Law. Statutory instruments. Drafts — *Inquiry reports*

The **Social** Security (Contributions) (Mariners) Amendment Regulations 1982 : report of the Social Security Advisory Committee in accordance with Section 10(3) of the Social Security Act 1980 preceded by a statement made by the Secretary of State for Social Services in accordance with Section 10(4) of that Act. — London : H.M.S.O., 1982. — 9p ; 25cm. — (Cmnd. ; 8477)
ISBN 0-10-184770-x (unbound) : £1.50
B82-19139

344.104'21 — Great Britain. Industrial injuries benefits. Law. Reform — *Proposals*

Great Britain. *Department of Health and Social Security.* Social Security Act 1975 : reform of the industrial injuries scheme / presented to Parliament by the Secretary of State for Social Services ... — London : H.M.S.O., 1981. — iv,30p ; 25cm. — (Cmnd. ; 8402)
At head of title: Department of Health and Social Security
ISBN 0-10-184020-9 (unbound) : £3.05
B82-08340

344.104'21 — Great Britain. Industrial injuries. Compensation. Law. Reform. Great Britain. *Department of Health and Social Security.* **Reform of the industrial injuries scheme** — *Critical studies*

Disability Alliance. Reforming the industrial injuries scheme the wrong priorities / the Disability Alliance's response to the Government's white paper on The reform of the industrial injuries scheme. — London (21 Star St., W2 1QB) : Disability Alliance, 1982. — 16p ; 30cm
£0.50 (pbk) B82-31345

344.104'22 — Great Britain. Sick personnel. Social security benefits. Law. Statutory instruments. Drafts — *Inquiry reports*

Great Britain. *Social Security Advisory Committee.* The Social Security (Medical Evidence, Claims and Payments) Amendment Regulations 1982 (S.I. 1982 No.699.) / report of the Social Security Advisory Committee in accordance with Section 10(3) of the Social Security Act 1980 preceded by a statement made by the Secretary of State for Social Services in accordance with Section 10(4) of that Act. — London : HMSO, 1982. — 8p ; 25cm. — (Cmnd. ; 8560)
ISBN 0-10-185600-8 (unbound) : £1.65
B82-31363

344.104'23 — Great Britain. Judiciary. Superannuation schemes. Law. Reform — *Inquiry reports*

Great Britain. *Parliament. Joint Committee on Consolidation Bills.* Consolidation bills 1980-81 : second report of the Joint Committee on Consolidation Bills : being a report upon the Judicial Pensions Bill (H.L.). — London : H.M.S.O., [1980]. — 1 : sheet ; 25x16cm. — (H.L. ; 36) (H.C. ; 75)
ISBN 0-10-403681-8 : £0.30 B82-16069

344.104'23'088343 — Great Britain. Judges. State superannuation benefits. Law. Great Britain. *Parliament. House of Lords.* **Judicial Pensions Bill (H.L.). Session 1980-81** — *Critical studies*

Great Britain. *Law Commission.* Judicial Pensions Bill : report on the consolidation of certain enactments relating to pensions and other benefits payable in respect of service in judicial office / the Law Commission and the Scottish Law Commission. — London : H.M.S.O., [1980]. — 11p ; 25cm. — (Law. Com. ; no.105) (Scot. Law Com. ; no.62) (Cmnd. ; 8097)
ISBN 0-10-180970-0 (unbound) : £1.70
B82-15138

344.104'24 — Great Britain. Unemployment benefits. Disallowances. Law. Statutory instruments. Drafts — *Critical studies*

Great Britain. *National Insurance Advisory Committee.* Social Security (Claims and Payments) Amendment Regulations 1980 (S.I. 1980 no. 1943) : report of the National Insurance Advisory Committee in accordance with section 139(3) of the Social Security Act 1975 preceded by a statement made by the Secretary of State for Social Services in accordance with section 10(4) of the Social Security Act 1980. — London : H.M.S.O., [1980]. — 3p ; 25cm. — ([HC] ; 76)
ISBN 0-10-207681-2 (unbound) : £0.70
B82-14141

344.104'3211 — Great Britain. Health authorities. Law

Kloss, D. M.. Health service law / D.M. Kloss. — Manchester (Manchester Business School, Booth St. West, Manchester M15 6PB) : Health Services Management Unit, Department of Social Administration, University of Manchester, 1981. — 22leaves ; 30cm. — (Working paper series, ISSN 0141-2647 ; no.47)
Unpriced (pbk) B82-26621

344.104'32795 — Great Britain. Children. Care. Law: Children Act 1975 — *For welfare work*

The **Saga** of the McKay family : a Scottish practice guide to the Children Act 1975. — London : Association of British Adoption & Fostering Agencies, 1977. — x,63p ; 32cm
Bibliography: piii
£2.00 (pbk) B82-34822

344.104′328282 — Great Britain. Child benefits. Law. Statutory instruments. Drafts — *Inquiry reports*

Great Britain. *Social Security Advisory Committee*. The child benefit (claims and payments) amendment regulations 1981 (S.I. 1981 no.1772) : report of the Social Security Advisory Committee in accordance with Section 10(3) of the Social Security Act 1980 preceded by a statement made by the Secretary of State for Social Services in accordance with Section 10(4) of that Act. — London : H.M.S.O., 1981. — 7p ; 25cm. — (Cmnd. ; 8453)
ISBN 0-10-184530-8 (unbound) : £1.15 B82-12639

Great Britain. *Social Security Advisory Committee*. Child benefit (general) amendment regulations 1982 (s.i. 1982 no.470) : report of the Social Security Advisory Committee in accordance with section 10(3) of the Social Security Act 1980 preceded by a statement made by the Secretary of State for Social Services in accordance with section 10(7) of that Act. — London : H.M.S.O., [1982]. — 10p ; 25cm
ISBN 0-10-185860-4 (unbound) : £1.95 B82-40842

344.104′41 — Great Britain. Medicine. Law

Taylor, J. Leahy. The doctor and the law. — 2nd ed. — London : Pitman, Dec.1982. — [244]p
Previous ed.: 1970
ISBN 0-272-79680-8 (pbk) : £9.95 : CIP entry B82-29637

344.104′41 — Great Britain. Medicine. Legal aspects

Legal issues in medicine / edited by Sheila A.M. McLean. — Aldershot : Gower, c1981. — xiv,219p ; 23cm
ISBN 0-566-00428-3 : Unpriced : CIP rev. B81-22595

344.104′413 — Great Britain. Dental profession. Law

Seear, John. Law and ethics in dentistry / John Seear. — 2nd ed. / with a foreword by Paul Bramley. — Bristol : John Wright, 1981. — vii,251p : ill ; 22cm. — (A Dental practitioner handbook ; 19)
Previous ed.: 1975. — Includes index
ISBN 0-7236-0588-2 (pbk) : Unpriced : CIP rev. B81-26692

344.104′4233 — Great Britain. Controlled drugs. Law

West, W. T.. Drugs law / W.T. West. — Chichester : Rose, 1982. — xiii,93p ; 22cm
Includes index
ISBN 0-85992-228-6 (pbk) : £12.00 B82-21464

344.104′4233 — Great Britain. Controlled drugs. Law. Reform. Proposals. Advisory Council on the Misuse of Drugs. Report on a review of the classification of controlled drugs — *Legalise Cannabis Campaign viewpoints*

Legalise Cannabis Campaign. Trash rehashed : commentary on the report of the Advisory Council on the Misuse of Drugs : 'Review of the classification of Drugs and Penalties under Schedules 2 and 4 of the Misuse of Drugs Act 1976' / Legalise Cannabis Campaign. — London : Legalise Cannabis Campaign, 1979. — 46p,1folded leaf of plates : ill ; 22cm
Text on inside covers
ISBN 0-906497-01-9 (pbk) : £0.95 B82-02687

344.104′463 — Great Britain. Environment. Pollution. Law

McLoughlin, J.. The law and practice relating to pollution control in the United Kingdom. — 2nd ed. — London : Graham and Trotman, Dec.1982. — [200]p
Previous ed.: 1976
ISBN 0-86010-306-4 (cased) : £18.00 : CIP entry
ISBN 0-86010-440-0 (pbk) : £9.00 B82-33355

344.104′46342′09 — Great Britain. Atmosphere. Pollution. Legal aspects, *1820-1980*

Ashby, Eric. The politics of clean air / Eric Ashby and Mary Anderson. — Oxford : Clarendon, 1981. — viii,178p ; 24cm. — (Monographs on science, technology, and society)
Includes index
ISBN 0-19-858330-3 : £15.00 : CIP rev. B81-26740

344.104′465 — Great Britain. Construction. Safety measures. Law. Statutes & statutory instruments — *Digests*

Construction regulations handbook : formerly the Building regulations handbook, and the Building & construction regulations handbook : a comprehensive guide to the safety, health and welfare requirements for building operations and works of engineering construction. — 11th ed. — Birmingham : RoSPA, 1982. — 48p ; 28cm
Previous ed.: 1975. — Includes index
ISBN 0-900635-58-4 : £6.60 : (£4.40 to members) B82-40844

344.104′465 — Great Britain. Construction. Sites. Safety measures. Law. Statutory regulations

The **Supervisor's** guide to the construction regulations : an abridged pocket edition of the Construction regulations handbook : providing a guide to all safety legislation affecting building operations and works of engineering construction. — Metric ed. — Birmingham : Royal Society for the Prevention of Accidents, 1980. — 45p ; 18cm
Previous ed.: 1966. — Includes index
ISBN 0-900635-33-9 (pbk) : £1.38 (£0.92 to members) B82-13341

344.104′465 — Great Britain. *Health and Safety Executive.* **Notification of accidents in workplaces. Law**

The **Notification** of accidents and dangerous occurrences / Health and Safety Executive. — London : H.M.S.O., 1980. — iii,43p : forms ; 21cm. — (Health and safety series booklet ; HS (R)5)
ISBN 0-11-883413-4 (pbk) : £1.50 B82-16635

344.104′465 — Great Britain. Industrial health & industrial safety. Law

Rowe, Peter. Health and safety / Peter Rowe. — London : Sweet & Maxwell, 1980. — vi,89p ; 18cm. — (Law at work)
Includes index
ISBN 0-421-27250-3 (pbk) : £1.95 : CIP rev. B80-20406

344.104′465 — Great Britain. Industrial health & industrial safety. Law: Health and Safety at Work etc. Act 1974 — *Commentaries*

A **Guide** to the HSW Act / Health and Safety Executive. — London : H.M.S.O., 1980. — 43p,[2] folded leaves of plates : 2forms ; 21cm. — (Health and safety series booklet ; HS(R)6)
ISBN 0-11-883264-6 (pbk) : £2.75 : CIP rev. B80-06835

344.104′465 — Great Britain. Industrial health & industrial safety. Law: Health and Safety at Work etc. Act 1974 — *Critical studies*

The **Act** outlined : Health and Safety at Work etc. Act 1974. — [London] : Health & Safety Commission, [1982?]. — 15p ; 21cm. — (HSC ; 2)
Unpriced (unbound) B82-40285

Drake, Charles. Health and Safety at Work law. — London : Sweet and Maxwell, Dec.1982. — [300]p
ISBN 0-421-28620-2 (cased) : £27.00 : CIP entry
ISBN 0-421-28630-x (pbk) : £20.00 B82-32290

Selwyn, Norman M.. Law of health and safety at work / Norman Selwyn. — London : Butterworths, 1982. — xxviii,354p ; 22cm
Includes index
ISBN 0-406-66750-0 (pbk) : Unpriced B82-23051

344.104′465 — Great Britain. Industrial health & industrial safety. Law: Health and Safety at Work etc. Act 1974 — *For distributive trades*

Don't forget HASAWA : a guide to the Health and Safety at Work Act 1974. — Manchester (MacLaren House, Talbot Rd., Stretford, Manchester M32 0FP) : Distributive Industry Training Board, 1976. — 23p : ill ; 22cm
Bibliography: p20-23
£0.35 (unbound) B82-12117

344.104′465 — Great Britain. Industrial health & industrial safety. Law. Health and Safety at Work etc. Act 1974 — *For employers*

Janner, Greville. Janner's Compendium of health and safety law. — 3rd ed. / Greville Janner ; cartoons by Tobi. — London : Business Books, 1982. — xxiv,648p : ill ; 23cm
Previous ed.: published as The employer's guide to the law on health, safety and welfare at work, under the name Ewan Mitchell. 1977. — Includes index
ISBN 0-09-147400-0 : Unpriced : CIP rev. B82-09201

344.104′465 — Great Britain. Industrial health & industrial safety. Law: Health and Safety at Work etc. Act 1974 — *For management*

Howells, Richard. The Health and Safety at Work Act. — 2nd ed. — London : Institute of Personnel Management, Aug.1982. — [258]p
Previous ed.: 1975
ISBN 0-85292-310-4 (pbk) : £7.50 : CIP entry B82-29030

344.104′465 — Great Britain. Industrial health & industrial safety. Law. Health and Safety at Work etc. Act 1974. Implementation

Quayle, V. J.. Health and safety enforcement : a guide to the enforcement provisions of the Health and Safety at Work etc. Act 1974 / by V.J. Quayle. — London : Shaw & Sons, 1980. — 47p : 1form ; 22cm. — (The Shaway guides ; no.3)
ISBN 0-7219-0872-1 (pbk) : Unpriced B82-39118

344.104′465 — Great Britain. Industrial health & industrial safety. Law — *Trade union viewpoints*

Beaumont, P. B.. Safety legislation : the trade union response / P.B. Beaumont. — [Leeds] : University of Leeds and the University of Nottingham in association with the Institute of Personnel Management, c1979. — iv,32p ; 21cm. — (Occasional papers in industrial relations ; 4)
Bibliography: p32
ISBN 0-85292-267-1 (pbk) : £2.00 B82-15063

344.104′465 — Great Britain. Safety representatives & safety committees. Law: Safety Representatives and Safety Committees Regulations 1977 — *Critical studies*

Safety representatives and safety committees : a guide to Health and Safety Commission's Regulations, Code of Practice and Guidance notes. — London : Engineering Employers' Federation, 1978. — 19p ; 21cm + 1 pamphlet (8p ; 21cm)
£1.00 (£0.50 to members) (pbk) B82-05111

344.104′472 — Great Britain. Offshore natural gas & petroleum industries offshore structures. Safety measures. Law

The **Offshore** installation manager's handbook : a guide to OIM responsibilities as defined by law. — 8th ed. — Aylesbury (Kingfisher House, Walton St., Aylesbury, Bucks.) : Petroleum Industry Training Board, 1980. — 149p in various pagings : forms ; 30cm
Previous ed.: 1979. — Includes index
£12.00 (pbk) B82-13344

The **Offshore** installation manager's handbook : a guide to OIM responsibilities as defined by law / Petroleum Industry Training Board. — 9th ed. — Aylesbury (Kingfisher House, Walton St., Aylesbury, Bucks. HP21 7TQ) : The Board, 1981. — 121p in various pagings : forms ; 30cm
Previous ed.: 198-. — Includes index
Unpriced (pbk) B82-05641

344.104'472 — Great Britain. Toxic agricultural chemicals. Use. Safety measures. Law — *Proposals*

Draft proposals for poisonous substances in agriculture regulations. — London : H.M.S.O., 1980. — 18p ; 30cm. — (Consultative document / Health and Safety Commission)
ISBN 0-11-883412-6 (pbk) : £2.00 B82-20452

344.104'472 — Great Britain. Woodworking machines. Safety measures. Regulations: Woodworking Machines Regulations 1974 - *Critical studies*

Woodworking machines : guide to the 1974 regulations. — London : Health & Safety Executive, July 1981. — [20]p. — (HS(R))
Originally published: / Department of Employment. 1974
ISBN 0-11-883437-1 (pbk) : CIP entry B81-15823

344.104'53 — Great Britain. Public order. Law

Brownlie, Ian. Brownlie's law of public order and national security. — 2nd ed. / Michael Supperstone. — London : Butterworths, 1981. — lvii,415p ; 26cm
Previous ed.: published as The law relating to public order. 1968. — Includes index
ISBN 0-406-13701-3 : Unpriced
Also classified at 344.105'231 B82-02950

344.104'63635 — Great Britain. Housing. Law: Housing Act 1980 — *For housing associations*

The **Housing** Act 1980 : a guide for housing associations / [National Federation of Housing Associations]. — London : The Federation, 1980. — 88p : 1ill ; 30cm
Unpriced (pbk) B82-02020

344.104'636358 — Great Britain. Homeless persons. Housing. Provision. Powers of local authorities. Law: Housing (Homeless Persons) Act 1977. Implementation — *For homeless persons*

Homeless? : know your rights. — New & rev. ed. — London : SHAC, 1982. — 11p ; 21cm
Cover title. — Previous ed.: 1981
Unpriced (pbk) B82-35083

344.104'636358 — Great Britain. Local authority housing. Law: Housing Act 1980 — *Critical studies*

Schifferes, Steve. The tenants' charter : the Housing Act 1980 : a guide to the provisions of the Housing Act 1980 which affect public sector tenants / compiled by Steve Schifferes and Steve Hilditch. — London : Shelter, c1981. — 30p ; 21cm
ISBN 0-901242-57-8 (pbk) : £1.50 B82-09490

344.104'636358'02648 — Great Britain. Homeless persons. Housing. Provision. Powers of local authorities. Law. Cases, *1977-1981 — Digests*

Smythe, John. Homelessness : a digest of court decisions. — London : Shelter National Housing Aid Trust, May 1982. — [54]p
ISBN 0-86265-004-6 (unbound) : £6.00 : CIP entry B82-14931

344.104'74 — Great Britain. Adult education. Provision. Law. Reform

Changing the legislation. — London (Chequer Centre, Chequer St, Bunhill Row, EC1Y 8PL) : Educational Centres Association, 1981. — [3] leaves ; 27cm
Unpriced (unbound) B82-29223

344.104'99 — Great Britain. Sports & games. Law

Grayson, Edward. Sport and the law / by Edward Grayson. — [London] : Sunday Telegraph, c1978. — 78p : ill ; 21cm
Includes index
£1.00 (pbk) B82-09495

344.105'231 — Great Britain. National security. Law

Brownlie, Ian. Brownlie's law of public order and national security. — 2nd ed. / Michael Supperstone. — London : Butterworths, 1981. — lvii,415p ; 26cm
Previous ed.: published as The law relating to public order. 1968. — Includes index
ISBN 0-406-13701-3 : Unpriced
Primary classification 344.104'53 B82-02950

344.105'233 — Great Britain. Tax evasion

Heertje, Arnold. The black economy / Arnold Heertje, Margaret Allen and Harry Cohen. — London : Pan, 1982. — 158p : ill ; 18cm
Translated and revised version of: Het officieuze circuit. — Includes index
ISBN 0-330-26765-5 (pbk) : £1.95 B82-23283

344.105'253 — Great Britain. Homosexuality. Law

Crane, Paul. Gays and the law. — London : Pluto Press, Oct.1982. — [256]p
ISBN 0-86104-386-3 (pbk) : £4.95 : CIP entry B82-25740

344.105'2536 — Great Britain. Male homosexuality. Law

Amin, S. H.. The law and homosexuality. — Glasgow (165 Roebank St., Glasgow G31 3EG) : S.H. Amin, June 1982. — [112]p
ISBN 0-946124-04-3 (pbk) : £7.50 : CIP entry B82-21951

344.106'24 — Great Britain. Employment. Contracts. Law

Continuity of employment. — London (140 Great Portland St, W1) : Incomes Data Services, 1982. — 58p ; 21cm. — (IDS handbook series ; no.22)
Includes index
£5.00 (pbk) B82-36206

Employment contracts. — [London] ([140 Gt. Portland St. W.1]) : [Incomes Data Services], 1981. — 124p ; 21cm. — (IDS handbook series ; no.21)
Previous ed.: 1976. — Includes index
Unpriced (pbk) B82-05608

Suter, Erich. Contracts at work / Erich Suter. — London : Institute of Personnel Management, 1982. — x,276p ; 22cm
Includes index
ISBN 0-85292-297-3 (pbk) : £13.95 : CIP rev. B82-12846

344.1063'2 — Great Britain. Accountants. Negligence. Liability. Law

Pockson, Jonathan R. H. H.. Accountant's professional negligence : developments in legal liability / Jonathan R.H.H. Pockson. — London : Macmillan, 1982. — xxi,212p : ill ; 23cm
Bibliography: p192-208. — Includes index
ISBN 0-333-27845-3 : £25.00
Also classified at 347.3063'2 B82-20938

344.1063'82 — Great Britain. Products. Defects. Liability of manufacturers & retailers. Law

Dangerous goods : a DITB guide to product safety and liability. — Stretford : Distributive Industry Training Board, 1981. — 23p : 1map,1form ; 21cm
Cover title. — Bibliography: p22
ISBN 0-903416-27-1 (pbk) : Unpriced B82-17429

Miller, C. J.. Product liability & safety encyclopaedia / C.J. Miller. — London : Butterworths, 1979. — 1v.(loose-leaf) ; 26cm
ISBN 0-406-29629-4 : Unpriced B82-17297

344.1064'3'09 — Great Britain. Real property. Law, *to 1977*

Sydenham, Angela. Land law lecture notes / Angela Sydenham. — London : Polytechnic of North London Students' Union, 1981. — 224p : ill ; 21cm
Cover title. — Bibliography: p221-222
ISBN 0-906513-01-4 (pbk) : £3.00 B82-03510

344.1064'34 — Great Britain. Group homes & hostels. Licences & tenancies. Law

Tenancies & licences for homes & hostels. — Rev. — London (169 Clapham Rd., SW9 0PU) : National Association for the Care & Resettlement of Offenders, 1982. — 20p ; 30cm. — (NFHA special project guide ; no.5)
Previous ed.: published as Rights of residents in hostels and similar accommodation. London : NACRO, 19--. — Bibliography: p20
Unpriced (pbk) B82-27685

344.1064'34 — Great Britain. Housing associations. Tenancy agreements. Law

The **Housing** Act 1980 : a guide to tenancy agreements / [National Federation of Housing Associations]. — London : The Federation, 1980. — iii,26p ; 30cm
ISBN 0-86297-021-0 (pbk) : Unpriced B82-02022

344.1064'34 — Great Britain. Housing associations. Tenants. Consultation. Law

The **Housing** Act 1980 : a guide to tenant consultation / [National Federation of Housing Associations]. — London : The Federation, 1980. — iv,31p ; 30cm
Unpriced (pbk) B82-02021

344.1064'34 — Great Britain. Housing associations. Tenants. Information. Provision. Law

The **Housing** Act 1980 : a guide to tenants' information / [National Federation of Housing Associations]. — London : The Federation, 1980. — 52p ; 30cm
ISBN 0-86297-016-4 (pbk) : Unpriced B82-02023

344.1064'344'02633 — Great Britain. Rented residences. Tenancies. Law — *Statutes*

Great Britain. [Rent Act 1977]. The Rent Act 1977 : revised / edited by Lorna K. Newton ; with an introduction by Trevor M. Aldridge. — London : Oyez, c1981. — xvi,135p ; 24cm
Complete text of the Rent Act 1977, revised to incorporate amendments made by the Housing Act 1980. — Includes index
ISBN 0-85120-613-1 (pbk) : Unpriced B82-00031

344.1064'37 — Great Britain. Estate agency. Law. Estate Agents Act 1979 — *Critical studies*

Murdoch, J. R.. The Estate Agents Act 1979 / J.R. Murdoch. — 2nd ed. — London : Estates Gazette, 1982. — xv,160p ; 22cm
Previous ed.: 1979. — Includes index. — Includes the text of the Act
£7.60 (pbk) B82-30547

344.1064'8 — Great Britain. Inventions by personnel. Law: Patents Act 1977 — *Critical studies*

Phillips, Jeremy. Employees' inventions in the United Kingdom. — Oxford (25 Beaumont St., Oxford OX1 2NP) : ESC Publishing, Mar.1982. — [186]p
ISBN 0-906214-11-4 (pbk) : £9.50 : CIP entry B82-07835

344.1064'82 — Copyright documents: Serials with British imprints. Photoreproduction — *Codes of conduct*

Periodical Publishers Association. Photocopying from periodicals : a code of fair practice / PPA. — London : Periodical Publishers Association, 1980. — 8p ; 30cm
Unpriced (unbound) B82-25954

344.1064'82 — Great Britain. Copyright. Law

Copinger, W. A.. Copinger and Skone James on Copyright : including international copyright : with the statutes and orders relating thereto and forms and precedents : also related forms of protection. — 12th ed. / by E.P. Skone James, John F. Mummery, J.E. Rayner James ; copyright law of the U.S.A. Alan Latman ; taxation Stephen Silman. — London : Sweet & Maxwell, 1980. — lxxii,1196p ; 26cm
Previous ed.: 1971. — Includes index
ISBN 0-421-25880-2 : £70.00 B82-12118

McFarlane, Gavin. A practical introduction to copyright / Gavin McFarlane. — London : McGraw-Hill, c1982. — xiv,235p ; 26cm. — (Business law series)
Includes index
ISBN 0-07-084569-7 : £14.00 : CIP rev. B81-24602

344.1064'82'0242 — Great Britain. Copyright. Law — *For Christians*

Thorn, Eric A.. Caution — copyright! / Eric A. Thorn. — Maidstone : Third Day Enterprises, 1981. — 14p : ill ; 21cm
ISBN 0-9505912-5-4 (pbk) : £0.95 B82-09648

344.1064′82′0242 — Great Britain. Copyright. Law — *For Christians* *continuation*
Thorn, Eric A.. Caution — copyright! / Eric A. Thorn. — 2nd ed. — Maidstone : Third Day Enterprises, 1982. — 15p : ill ; 21cm
Previous ed.: 1981
ISBN 0-9505912-7-0 (pbk) : Unpriced
B82-31019

344.1064′86 — Great Britain. Patents. Law
Terrell, Thomas. Terrell on the law of patents. — 13th ed. — London : Sweet & Maxwell, May 1982. — [730]p
Previous ed.: 1971
ISBN 0-421-24900-5 : £40.00 : CIP entry
B82-06769

344.1064′86 — Great Britain. Patents. Licensing — *Forms*
Standard clauses in a licensing agreement. — 2nd ed. — Havant : K. Mason, Oct.1981. — [47]p
Previous ed.: 1970
ISBN 0-85937-114-x (pbk) : £7.50 : CIP entry
B81-31097

344.1064′86′024574 — Great Britain. Patents. Law — *For biology*
Crespi, R. S.. Patenting in the biological sciences : a practical guide for research scientists in biotechnology and the pharmaceutical and agrochemical industries / R.S. Crespi. — Chichester : Wiley, c1982. — 211p : ill ; 24cm
Includes index
ISBN 0-471-10151-6 : £16.00 : CIP rev.
B82-19524

344.1064′86′02633 — Great Britain. Patents. Law — *Statutes — Texts with commentaries*
C.I.P.A. guide to the Patents Act 1977 / by the Chartered Institute of Patent Agents. — London : Sweet & Maxwell
3rd cumulative supplement : up to date to September 1, 1981. — 1982. — vii,135p : 1form ; 25cm
Includes index
ISBN 0-421-29530-9 (pbk) : Unpriced
ISBN 0-421-26260-5 B82-21605

344.1064′88′024658 — Great Britain. Trade marks. Law — *For businessmen*
Michaels, Amanda. A practical guide to trade marks / Amanda Michaels. — Oxford : ESC Publishing, 1982. — xxi,226p : ill ; 22cm
Bibliography: p145-146. — Includes index
ISBN 0-906214-12-2 (cased) : Unpriced : CIP rev.
ISBN 0-906214-09-2 (pbk) : Unpriced
B81-31952

344.1065′4 — Great Britain. Wills. Law
Theobald, *Sir* Henry Studdy. Theobald on wills. — 14th ed. — London : Sweet & Maxwell, Aug.1982. — [850]p. — (Property and conveyancing library ; no.3)
Previous ed.: 1971
ISBN 0-420-45250-8 : £70.00 : CIP entry
B82-19661

344.106′6 — Great Britain. Organisations. Law — *For business studies*
Buchanan, Robert. The organisation in the legal environment. — Cheltenham : Stanley Thornes, June 1982. — [256]p
ISBN 0-85950-305-4 (pbk) : £2.95 : CIP entry
B82-10224

344.106′63 — Great Britain. Accounting. Law
Carr, J. Graham. Accountancy law and practice manual / J. Graham Carr. — Farnborough, Hants. : Gower Press, 1978. — 1v.(loose-leaf) ; 26cm
ISBN 0-566-02090-4 : £41.00 : CIP rev.
B78-31315

344.106′64 — Great Britain. Charities. Law
Norton, Michael. A guide to the benefits of charitable status. — London : Directory of Social Change, Jan.1983. — [160]p
ISBN 0-907164-09-9 (pbk) : £4.95 : CIP entry
B82-33368

Phillips, Andrew, *1939-*. Charitable status. — 2nd ed. — London : Inter-Action, July 1982. — [80]p
Previous ed: 1980
ISBN 0-904571-39-4 (pbk) : £3.00 : CIP entry
B82-17988

344.106′652 — Great Britain. Small firms. Law
Chesterman, Michael R.. Small businesses. — 2nd ed. — London : Sweet and Maxwell, Jan.1983. — [270]p
Previous ed.: 1977
ISBN 0-421-28600-8 (cased) : £17.80 : CIP entry
ISBN 0-421-28610-5 (pbk) : £9.50 B82-34577

Clayton, Patrica E.. Law for the small business / Pat Clayton. — 2nd rev. ed. — London : Kogan Page, 1981. — 224p ; 22cm
Previous ed.: published as Law for the small businessman. London : Marchmont Publications, 1979. — Bibliography: p206-207. — Includes index
ISBN 0-85038-472-9 (cased) : Unpriced : CIP rev.
ISBN 0-85038-486-9 (pbk) : £4.95 B81-21578

Clayton, Patricia E.. Law for the small business. — 3rd ed. — London : Kogan Page, Nov.1982. — [200]p
Previous ed.: 1981
ISBN 0-85038-606-3 (cased) : £9.95 : CIP entry
ISBN 0-85038-607-1 (pbk) : £5.50 B82-32301

344.106′66 — Great Britain. Companies. Law
Butterworths company law handbook / edited by Keith Walmsley. — 3rd ed. — London : Butterworths, 1982. — viii,891,24p ; 25cm
Previous ed.: 1980. — Includes index
ISBN 0-406-14312-9 (pbk) : £13.95
B82-23052

Magnus, S. W.. Companies : law and practice : supplement to fifth edition / S.W. Magnus, M. Estrin. — London : Butterworths, 1981. — xvii,A396p ; 25cm
Includes index
ISBN 0-406-28527-6 (pbk) : Unpriced
B82-05150

Roundell, Francis. Company law in a nutshell / Francis Roundell. — 2nd ed. — London : Sweet & Maxwell, 1982. — vi,89p ; 18cm. — (New nutshells)
Previous ed.: 1980. — Includes index
ISBN 0-421-29640-2 (pbk) : £1.95 : CIP rev.
B82-15792

Schmitthoff, Clive M.. Palmer′s company law : fourth cumulative supplement to volume 1 of the twenty-second edition : uptodate to July 1, 1980 / by Clive M. Schmitthoff in collaboration with Paul L. Davies ... [et al.]. — London : Stevens, 1980. — [202]p ; 24cm
ISBN 0-420-46150-7 (pbk) : Unpriced
B82-17623

Thomas, Colin. Company law / Colin Thomas. — [London] : Hodder & Stoughton, c1982. — 238p ; 20cm. — (Teach yourself books)
ISBN 0-340-26820-4 (pbk) : £2.95 : CIP rev.
B82-12258

344.106′66 — Great Britain. Companies. Law: Companies Act 1980 — *Critical studies*
Joffe, Victor. The Companies Act 1980 : a practical guide / Victor Joffe, assisted by Andrew Hochhauser. — London : Oyez, 1980. — [329]p ; 22cm
Includes index
ISBN 0-85120-467-8 (pbk) : Unpriced
B82-18426

344.106′66 — Great Britain. Companies. Law: Companies Act 1981 — *Critical studies*
The **Companies** Act 1981 handbook / edited by Alan Hardcastle and Michael Renshall. — London : Institute of Chartered Accountants in England and Wales, 1981. — xxv,230p ; 22cm
Includes index. — Includes the text of the Act
ISBN 0-85291-303-6 (pbk) : Unpriced
B82-23887

Godfrey, M.. The Companies Act 1981 and the small family company / M. Godfrey. — [Guildford] ([Braboeuf Manor, St. Catherines, Guildford, Surrey, GU3 1HA]) : [The College of Law], [1982]. — 21p ; 22cm. — (Crash course lecture / The College of Law, ISSN 0309-2771 ; 1982)
Cover title
£1.50 (pbk) B82-40233

344.106′66 — Great Britain. Companies. Law: Companies Act 1981 — *Critical studies*
Guide to the Companies Act 1981. — [London] (1 Surrey Street, WC2R 2PS) : Arthur Anderson & Co., 1982. — 103p ; 21cm
Unpriced (pbk) B82-19363

344.106′66 — Great Britain. Companies. Law: Companies Act 1981 — *Critical studies*
McMonnies, Peter N.. The Companies Act 1981 : a practical guide / Peter N. McMonnies. — London : Oyez, 1982. — viii,184p ; 22cm
Includes index
ISBN 0-85120-609-3 (pbk) : Unpriced
B82-16428

344.106′66 — Great Britain. Companies. Law — *For company directors*
Bourne, Nicholas. Duties and responsibilities of British company directors. — Bicester (c/o Telford Road, Bicester OX6 0XD) : CCH Editions, Apr.1982. — [130]p
ISBN 0-86325-000-9 (pbk) : £10.50 : CIP entry
B82-14389

344.106′66 — Great Britain. Companies. Law — *Texts with commentaries*
Palmer, *Sir* Francis Beaufort. Palmer′s company law. — 23rd ed. — London : Stevens
Previous ed.: 1976
Vol.1: The treatise. — Nov.1981. — [1250]p
ISBN 0-420-45760-7 : CIP entry B81-31246

344.106′66′02632 — Great Britain. Companies. Law — *Statutes — Collections*
Great Britain. [Companies acts]. Companies Acts: Table A 1856-1981 / edited by R.W. Ramage. — London : Butterworths, 1982. — xviii,160p ; 22cm
Includes text from the Companies acts
ISBN 0-406-35123-6 : Unpriced B82-18291

344.106′66′02632 — Great Britain. Companies. Law — *Statutes — Collections — Texts with commentaries*
Wrenbury, Henry Burton Buckley, *Baron*. Buckley on the Companies Acts / by the late Lord Wrenbury. — 14th ed. / by G. Brian Parker and Martin Buckley ; consultant editor, Sir Raymond Walton. — London : Butterworths, 1981. — 2v.(2336p in various pagings) : forms ; 26cm
Previous ed.: 1957. — Includes index
ISBN 0-406-14104-5 : Unpriced
ISBN 0-406-14103-7 (v.1)
ISBN 0-406-14105-3 (v.2) B82-12745

344.106′66′02633 — Great Britain. Companies. Law — *Statutes — Texts with commentaries*
Great Britain. [Companies Act 1981]. The Companies Act 1981 / with annotations by Geoffrey Morse ... [et al.]. — London : Sweet & Maxwell, 1982. — vii,[212]p ; 25cm. — (Current law statutes reprints)
Includes index. — Includes the text of the Act
ISBN 0-421-29320-9 (pbk) : £7.75 B82-22478

Schmitthoff, Clive M.. The Companies Act 1980 / by Clive M. Schmitthoff. — London : London Chamber of Commerce and Industry, 1981. — x,191p ; 30cm. — (Books for business)
Includes index. — Includes the text of the Act
ISBN 0-901902-53-5 (spiral) : Unpriced
B82-13800

344.106′66′0264 — Great Britain. Companies. Law — *Cases*
Oliver, M. C.. Cases in company law / M.C. Oliver. — 3rd ed. — Plymouth : Macdonald and Evans, 1982. — xv,396p ; 19cm. — (The M & E casebook series)
Previous ed.: 1976. — Includes index
ISBN 0-7121-0466-6 (pbk) : £4.95 B82-19416

344.106′662 — Great Britain. Companies. Organisation. Legal aspects. Costs — *Tables — Serials*
[Companies *(London : 1980)***]**. Companies : fees and duties. — [1st ed.]-. — London : Fourmat, 1980-. — v. ; 30cm. — (Lawyers costs & fees series ; 7)
Irregular
ISSN 0262-6179 = Companies (London. 1980) : £1.10
Also classified at 344.106′78 B82-10348

344.106′664 — Great Britain. Companies. Directors. Duties. Law

Mitchell, Philip L.R.. Director′s duties and insider dealing / Philip L.R. Mitchell. — London : Butterworths, 1982. — xxiv,268p ; 22cm
Includes index
ISBN 0-406-29580-8 (pbk) : Unpriced B82-23050

344.106′664 — Great Britain. Companies. Published accounts. Law

Jones, Frank H.. Accounting requirements for companies / by Frank H. Jones. — 12th ed. / revised by Desmond Goch. — St. Albans (36 Lattimore Rd., St. Albans, Herts. AL1 3XP) : Barkeley, c1980. — 48p ; 21cm
Previous ed.: 1977. — Includes index
£2.50 (pbk) B82-41026

344.106′664 — Great Britain. Company secretaryship — *Manuals*

Handbook of company administration. — 4th ed. / edited by Keith Walmsley in collaboration with John Birds. — Bristol : Published under the authority of the Institute of Chartered Secretaries and Administrators [by] Jordon & Sons, 1981. — xvi,318p ; 21cm
Previous ed.: / by A. Harding Boulton in collaboration with J.E. Neill. 1977. — Includes index
ISBN 0-85308-065-8 (pbk) : £6.00 B82-00730

344.106′664 — Great Britain. Company secretaryship — *Questions & answers*

Taylor, Raymond J.. How to pass examinations in company secretarial practice and law / Raymond J. Taylor. — London : Cassell, 1982. — xi,115p ; 22cm
Includes index
ISBN 0-304-30928-1 (pbk) : £3.95 B82-31654

344.106′6648 — Great Britain. Companies. Accounts. Law

Companies accounts check list / Peat, Marwick, Mitchell & Co.. — Croydon : Tolley, c1981. — 1v.(loose-leaf) ; 30cm
ISBN 0-85459-050-1 (unbound) : £3.00 B82-13279

Stilling, P. J.. Company accounting requirements : a practical guide / P.J. Stilling and R.A. Wyld. — London : Oyez, 1981. — 78p ; 24cm
ISBN 0-85120-619-0 (pbk) : Unpriced B82-16429

344.106′7 — Great Britain. Commercial law

Affley, G. M.. Business law / G.M. Affley. — Plymouth : Macdonald and Evans, 1982. — xxiv,258p : forms ; 22cm. — (The M & E BECbook series)
Includes index
ISBN 0-7121-0261-2 (pbk) : £4.50 B82-25386

Meinhardt, Peter. Company law in Great Britain. — Aldershot : Gower, Nov.1982. — [300]p
ISBN 0-566-02389-x : £15.00 : CIP entry B82-26553

344.106′72 — Great Britain. Goods. Title. Retention. Law

Parris, John. Retention of title on the sale of goods. — London : Granada, Apr.1982. — [192]p
ISBN 0-246-11612-9 : £15.00 : CIP entry B82-04318

344.106′73 — Great Britain. Consumer credit. Law: Consumer Credit Act 1974 — *Critical studies*

Meston, Dougall Meston, *Baron*. Guide to the Consumer Credit Act 1974 / by Lord Meston. — Chichester : Rose, 1982. — 112p ; 22cm
ISBN 0-85992-310-x (pbk) : £10.50 B82-29273

344.106′74 — Great Britain. Loans. Securities. Law

Goode, R. M.. Legal problems of credit and security. — London : Sweet and Maxwell, Nov.1982. — [128]p
ISBN 0-421-30270-4 (pbk) : £10.00 : CIP entry B82-28282

344.106′78 — Great Britain. Companies. Liquidation & receivership. Legal aspects. Costs — *Tables* — *Serials*

[Companies *(London : 1980)*]. Companies : fees and duties. — [1st ed.]-. — London : Fourmat, 1980-. — v. ; 30cm. — (Lawyers costs & fees series ; 7)
Irregular
ISSN 0262-6179 = Companies (London. 1980) : £1.10
Primary classification 344.106′662 B82-10348

344.106′82 — Great Britain. Banking. Law

Palfreman, David. The law of banking / David Palfreman. — 2nd ed. — Plymouth : Macdonald and Evans, 1982. — xvi,319p ; 18cm. — (M & E handbook series)
Previous ed.: 1980. — Includes index
ISBN 0-7121-1258-8 (pbk) : £3.95 B82-17544

344.106′86′00264 — Great Britain. Insurance. Law — *Cases* — *Serials*

Insurance law reports. — Vol.1-. — Harlow : Godwin, 1982-. — v. ; 24cm
Three issues yearly
ISSN 0263-6964 = Insurance law reports : £13.50 per issue B82-31707

344.106′8622 — Shipping. Insurance in Great Britain. Law

Arnould, *Sir* Joseph. Arnould′s law of marine insurance and average. — 16th ed. / by Sir Michael J. Mustill and Jonathan C.B. Gilman. — London : Stevens, 1981. — 2v.(lxxv,1242p) ; 26cm. — (British shipping laws)
Previous ed.: 1961. — Includes index
ISBN 0-420-44500-5 : £95.00 : CIP rev. B81-25313

344.108′25 — Great Britain. Law. Statutory instruments. Great Britain. *Parliament. Joint Committee on Statutory Instruments.* Sixth report ... session 1981-82 — *Critical studies*

Great Britain. Government response to the sixth report of the Joint Committee on Statutory Instruments : (session 1981-82). — London : H.M.S.O., 1982. — 5p ; 25cm. — (Cmnd. ; 8600)
ISBN 0-10-186000-5 (unbound) : £1.25 B82-39380

344.108′25 — Great Britain. Law. Statutory instruments — *Inquiry reports*

Great Britain. *Parliament. House of Commons. Select Committee on Statutory Instruments.* Fortieth report from the Select Committee on Statutory Instruments, session 1979-80. — London : H.M.S.O., [1980]. — 5p ; 25cm. — ([HC] ; 147-xliv)
ISBN 0-10-029899-0 (unbound) : £1.10 B82-10962

Great Britain. *Parliament. House of Commons. Select Committee on Statutory Instruments.* Fourth report from the Select Committee on Statutory Instruments, session 1981-82. — London : H.M.S.O., 1982. — [4]p ; 25cm. — (HC ; 16-iv)
ISBN 0-10-276582-0 (unbound) : £0.70 B82-20702

Great Britain. *Parliament. House of Commons. Select Committee on Statutory Instruments.* House of Commons twelfth report from the Select Committee on Statutory Instruments : session 1981-82. — London : H.M.S.O., [1982]. — 3p ; 25cm. — ([HC] 16-xiv)
ISBN 0-10-294482-2 (unbound) : £0.75 B82-25343

344.11 — LAW. SCOTLAND

344.11 — Scotland. Law

General principles of Scots law / [CII Tuition Service]. — [London] ([20 Aldermanbury, EC2V 7HY]) : The Service, [1980?]. — x,140p ; 19cm. — (Study course / Chartered Insurance Institute Tuition Service ; IC301c)
Bibliography: pvi. — Includes index
Unpriced (pbk) B82-21699

Marshall, Enid A.. General principles of Scots law / by Enid A. Marshall. — 4th ed. — Edinburgh : Green, 1982. — xxiv,584p ; 22cm. — (Concise college texts)
Previous ed.: 1978. — Includes bibliographies and index
ISBN 0-414-00681-x (pbk) : Unpriced B82-36671

344.1103′78 — Scotland. Pipelines. Law

Commercial pipelines. — Edinburgh ([Room 5/93, New St. Andrew′s House, Edinburgh EH1 3SZ]) : [Scottish Development Department], 1980. — 15p ; 30cm. — (Planning advice note, ISSN 0141-514x ; 25)
At head of title: Scottish Development Department
Unpriced (unbound) B82-17310

344.1103′7864795 — Scotland. Licensed premises. Licensing. Law

Knight, Ian. Scottish licensing laws : a survey carried out on behalf of the Scottish Home and Health Department / Ian Knight, Paul Wilson. — London : H.M.S.O., 1980. — x,95p : ill,1map,forms ; 30cm
At head of title: Office of Population Censuses and Surveys, Social Survey Division
ISBN 0-11-690745-2 (pbk) : £8.60 B82-17327

344.1103′7869 — Scotland. Buildings. Construction. Law: Building Standards (Scotland) Regulations 1971-1979 — *Critical studies*

Building Standards (Scotland) Regulations 1971-1979 : explanatory memorandum / Scottish Development Department. — London : H.M.S.O., 1980
Part J: Resistance to the transmission of heat Section 2: Buildings other than houses and chalets. — 26p : ill ; 30cm
ISBN 0-11-491635-7 (pbk) : £2.50 B82-20453

344.1104′94 — Scotland. Listed buildings. Law — *For surveying*

Buildings of special historic or architectural interest / prepared by the Planning and Development Division of the Scottish Branch of the Royal Institution of Chartered Surveyors. — Edinburgh : [The Institution], 1980. — 9p ; 30cm. — (Planning practice note (Scotland) ; no.2)
Unpriced (pbk) B82-05170

344.1105′024362 — Scotland. Criminal law - *For welfare work*

Moore, George. Social work and criminal law in Scotland. — Aberdeen : Aberdeen University Press, Apr.1981. — [224]p
ISBN 0-08-025731-3 : £7.50 : CIP entry B81-04354

344.1105′0264 — Scotland. Criminal law — *Cases* — *Serials*

Scottish criminal case reports. — Sept. 1981-. — Edinburgh (P.O. Box 75, 26 Drumsheugh Gardens, Edinburgh EH3 7YR) : Law Society of Scotland, 1981-. — v. ; 25cm
ISSN 0263-2381 = Scottish criminal case reports : Unpriced B82-22668

344.1105′247 — Scotland. Motoring offences. Fixed penalties. Law. Reform — *Proposals*

Great Britain. *Committee on Alternatives to Prosecution.* The motorist and fixed penalties / first report by the Committee on Alternatives to Prosecution appointed by the Secretary of State for Scotland and the Lord Advocate ; (chairman: Lord Stewart). — Edinburgh : H.M.S.O., 1980. — 117p : forms ; 25cm. — (Cmnd. ; 8027)
ISBN 0-10-180270-6 (pbk) : £5.30 B82-14637

344.1105′2523′0924 — Scotland. Strathclyde Region. Ayr. Ross, Rachel. Murder. Trial of Meehan, Patrick

Hunter, John Oswald Mair Hunter, *Lord*. Report of inquiry into the whole circumstances of the murder of Mrs. Rachel Ross at Ayr in July 1969, and the action taken by the police, the Crown Office and the Scottish Home and Health Department relating to that case both before and after the trial of Mr. Patrick Meehan / by the Lord Hunter. — Edinburgh : H.M.S.O., 1982. — 4v. : ill,facsims ; 25cm. — ([HC] ; 444)
ISBN 0-10-244482-x (pbk) : £47.00 B82-38324

344.1105'2536 — Scotland. Incest. Law. Reform — *Proposals*

Scottish Law Commission. The law of incest in Scotland : report of a reference under Section 3 (1)(e) of the Law Commissions Act 1965 / Scottish Law Commission. — Edinburgh : H.M.S.O., 1981. — vii,74p ; 25cm. — (Scot. Law Com. ; no.69) (Cmnd. ; 8422)
ISBN 0-10-184220-1 (pbk) : £4.80 B82-13817

344.1105'5'02633 — Scotland. Criminal law. Justice. Administration. Procedure. Law — *Statutes*

Great Britain. [Criminal Justice (Scotland) Act 1980]. Criminal Justice (Scotland) Act 1980 : chapter 62. — London : H.M.S.O., [1980]. — iv,108p ; 25cm
Cover title
ISBN 0-10-546280-2 (pbk) : £4.90 B82-09247

344.1105'772 — Scotland. Criminal courts. Sentencing

Nicholson, C. G. B.. The law and practice of sentencing in Scotland / C.G.B. Nicholson. — Edinburgh : W. Green, 1981. — xxxi,274p ; 22cm
Includes index
ISBN 0-414-00684-4 (pbk) : Unpriced
B82-10521

344.1105'8 — Scotland. Children's hearings

Asquith, Stewart. Children and justice. — Edinburgh : Edinburgh University Press, Dec.1982. — [200]p
ISBN 0-85224-429-0 (cased) : £10.00 : CIP entry
ISBN 0-85224-466-5 (pbk) : Unpriced
B82-36154

344.1105'87'094141 — Scotland. Strathclyde Region. Children's hearings — *Inquiry reports*

Are we listening? / report of an officer/member working group of Strathclyde Regional Council on the children's hearing system. — [Glasgow] ([Melrose House, 19 Cadogan St., Glasgow G2 GHR]) : Strathclyde Regional Council, [1982?]. — vi,96p : ill ; 30cm
Ill on inside covers
Unpriced (pbk) B82-24439

344.1106 — Scotland. Private law

Walker, David M.. Principles of Scottish private law. — 3rd ed. — Oxford : Clarendon Press
Previous ed.: 1975
Vol.1. — Sept.1982. — [550]p
ISBN 0-19-876132-5 : £25.00 : CIP entry
B82-18975

Walker, David M. (David Maxwell). Principles of Scottish private law. — 3rd ed. — Oxford : Clarendon Press, Feb.1983. — [520]p
Previous ed.: 1975
ISBN 0-19-876135-x : £25.00 : CIP entry
B82-37865

Walker, David M. (David Maxwell). Principles of Scottish private law. — 3rd ed. — Oxford : Clarendon
Previous ed.: 1975
Vol.2. — Dec.1982. — [680]p
ISBN 0-19-876133-3 : £25.00 : CIP entry
B82-29629

Walker, David M. (David Maxwell). Principles of Scottish private law. — 3rd ed. — Oxford : Clarendon Press
Previous ed.: 1975
Vol.3
Bk.5: Law of property. — Jan.1983. — [640]p
ISBN 0-19-876134-1 : £25.00 : CIP entry
B82-33492

344.11061'66 — Scotland. Divorce. Financial settlements & maintenance orders. Law. Reform — *Proposals*

Scottish Law Commission. Family law, report on aliment and financial provision / Scottish Law Commission. — Edinburgh : H.M.S.O., [1981]. — x,239p : ill ; 25cm. — ([H.C.] ; 2) (Scot. Law Com. ; no.67)
ISBN 0-10-200282-7 (pbk) : £8.40 B82-06345

344.11061'78 — Scotland. Step-children. Adoption. Law

Step-children and adoption : information for parents and step-parents in Scotland. — London (11 Southwark St, SE1 1RQ) : Association of British Adoption & Fostering Agencies, c1980. — 1folded sheet([6]p) ; 21cm
Unpriced B82-37721

344.11063 — Scotland. Torts. Law

Walker, David M. (David Maxwell). The law of delict in Scotland / by David M. Walker. — 2nd ed., rev. — Edinburgh : Published under the auspices of the Scottish Universities Law Institute [by] W. Green, 1981. — cxli,1111p ; 26cm
Previous ed.: 1966. — Includes index
ISBN 0-414-00669-0 : Unpriced B82-08687

344.11064 — Scotland. Matrimonial homes. Occupancy. Law: Matrimonial Homes (Family Protection) (Scotland) Act 1981 — *Critical studies*

Nichols, David Ian. The Matrimonial Homes (Family Protection) (Scotland) Act 1981 / by D.I. Nichols and M.C. Meston. — Edinburgh : W. Green, 1982. — vii,68p : 1ill ; 25cm
Includes index
ISBN 0-414-00687-9 (pbk) : Unpriced
B82-26355

344.11064'3 — Scotland. Dangerous buildings. Law — *For residents*

MacInnes, Neil, *1950-*. Homes in danger : a guide to dangerous building orders in Scotland / [written by Neil MacInnes]. — London : Community Projects Foundation, c1981. — 23p : ill ; 21cm
Cover title. — Text on inside covers
ISBN 0-902406-19-1 (pbk) : Unpriced
B82-39067

344.11064'5 — Scotland. Environment planning. Law — *For surveying*

Planning policy, planning applications and enforcement of planning control / prepared by the Planning and Development Division of the Scottish Branch of the Royal Institution of Chartered Surveyors. — Edinburgh : [The Institution], 1979. — 61p ; 30cm. — (Planning practice note (Scotland) ; no.1)
Bibliography: p60
Unpriced (pbk) B82-05169

344.11065'4'0240664 — Scotland. Wills. Composition — *For homosexuals*

Trouble with — making a will : a free gay guide to making a will in Scotland, published by the Scottish Homosexual Rights Group. — Edinburgh (58a Broughton St., Edinburgh EH1) : SHRG, [1981?]. — 4p ; 21cm
Unpriced (unbound) B82-11626

344.1106'72 — Scotland. Goods. Sale. Law. Reform — *Proposals*

Scottish Consumer Council. Scottish Consumer Council's review of the law of sale of goods in Scotland / prepared ... by Gerry Maher. — Glasgow : Scottish Consumer Council, 1981. — 23leaves ; 30cm
ISBN 0-907067-08-5 (pbk) : £1.00 B82-12878

344.1106'77 — Scotland. Debtors. Poinded goods. Warrant sale. Law

Connor, Anne. The characteristics of warrant sales / by Anne Connor. — Edinburgh (New St Andrews House, Edinburgh EH1 3SZ) : Central Research Unit, 1980. — vi,25p ; 30cm. — (Central Research Unit papers) (Research report for the Scottish Law Commission ; no.2)
Unpriced (spiral) B82-02090

344.1106'77 — Scotland. Debts. Law

Wilson, W. A. (William Adam). The law of Scotland relating to debt / W.A. Wilson. — Edinburgh : W. Green, 1982. — lxxvii,380p ; 22cm
Includes index
ISBN 0-414-00682-8 (pbk) : Unpriced
B82-22209

344.1106'77'0264 — Scotland. Debts. Payment. Enforcement. Law. Cases

Doig, Barbara. The nature and scale of diligence / by Barbara Doig. — Edinburgh (New St Andrews House, Edinburgh EH1 3SZ) : Central Research Unit, 1980. — vii,31p : ill,1form ; 30cm. — (Central Research Unit papers) (Research report for the Scottish Law Commission ; no.1)
Unpriced (spiral) B82-02094

344.1106'77'0269 — Scotland. Debts. Payment. Enforcement by sheriff courts

Doig, Barbara. Debt recovery through the Scottish sheriff courts / by Barbara Doig. — Edinburgh (New St Andrews House, Edinburgh EH1 3SZ) : Central Research Unit, 1980. — ix,56p : ill,forms ; 30cm. — (Central Research Unit papers) (Research report for the Scottish Law Commission ; no.3)
Unpriced (spiral) B82-02093

344.1106'78 — Scotland. Bankruptcy. Law. Reform — *Proposals*

Scottish Law Commission. Report on bankruptcy and related aspects of insolvency and liquidation / Scottish Law Commission. — Edinburgh : H.M.S.O., 1982. — xv,597p ; 25cm. — (Scot. Law Com. ; no.68) ([HC] ; 176)
ISBN 0-10-217682-5 (pbk) : £14.90
B82-21808

344.1107 — Scotland. Legal system

The **Legal** system of Scotland / [prepared by members of the legal staffs of the Scottish Law Commission and of the Office of the Solicitor to the Secretary of State for Scotland]. — 3rd ed. — Edinburgh : Published for the Scottish Office by H.M.S.O., 1981. — iv,50p ; 21cm
Previous ed.: 1977. — Bibliography: p49-50
ISBN 0-11-491747-7 (pbk) : £3.50 B82-08802

Walker, David M. (David Maxwell). The Scottish legal system : an introduction to the study of Scots law / by David M. Walker. — 5th ed., rev. — Edinburgh : Green, 1981. — xlv,543p : ill ; 23cm
Previous ed.: 1976. — Includes bibliographies and index
ISBN 0-414-00683-6 : Unpriced B82-03471

344.1107'212 — Scotland. Sheriff courts. Administration — *Inquiry reports*

Great Britain. *Committee on the Administration of Sheriffdoms by Full-Time Sheriffs Principal*. Administration of sheriffdoms : report by the Committee on the Administration of Sheriffdoms by Full-Time Sheriffs Principal appointed by the Secretary of State for Scotland / (chairman: Lord Greive). — Edinburgh : H.M.S.O., [1982]. — v,28p ; 25cm. — (Cmnd. ; 8548)
At head of title: Scottish Courts Administration
ISBN 0-10-185480-3 (pbk) : £3.60 B82-32822

344.1107'212 — Scotland. Sheriff courts. Facilities

Gilmore, Sheila. Waiting for justice : an SCC survey of facilities in Scotland's Sheriff Courts : results and recommendations by Sheila Gilmore. — Glasgow : Scottish Consumer Council, 1981. — 44,A1-A6p,[11]leaves : forms ; 30cm
ISBN 0-907067-06-9 (pbk) : £1.50 B82-06397

344.1107'2136 — Scotland. Sheriff officers. Duties — *Manuals*

Maher, Gerry. A textbook of diligence / by G. Maher. — [Glasgow] ([2 Allander Walk, Cumbernauld, Glasgow G67 1DR]) : Society of Messengers-at-Arms and Sheriff Officers, c1981. — 183p ; 22cm
Unpriced (pbk)
Also classified at 344.1107'2336 B82-24854

344.1107'2336 — Great Britain. *Court of Session*. Messengers-at-arms. Duties — *Manuals*

Maher, Gerry. A textbook of diligence / by G. Maher. — [Glasgow] ([2 Allander Walk, Cumbernauld, Glasgow G67 1DR]) : Society of Messengers-at-Arms and Sheriff Officers, c1981. — 183p ; 22cm
Unpriced (pbk)
Primary classification 344.1107'2136
B82-24854

344.1108′22 — Scotland. Law, *1153-1424 — Statutes — Collections*

Regesta regum Scottorum. — Edinburgh : Edinburgh University Press
Vol.6: The acts of David II, King of Scots 1329-1371. — Mar.1982. — [576]p
ISBN 0-85224-395-2 : £25.00 : CIP entry
B82-01729

344.1108′6 — Scotland. Law — *Encyclopaedias*

Beaton, John Angus. Scots law : terms and expressions / John Angus Beaton. — Edinburgh : W. Green, 1982. — 116p ; 22cm
ISBN 0-414-00691-7 (pbk) : Unpriced
B82-32761

344.15 — LAW. IRELAND

344.1508′46 — Ireland. Law. Cases — *Digests*

Ryan, Edward F.. Notes of Irish cases : reported in the Irish reports, the Northern Ireland reports, and the Irish law times reports 1969-1978 / compiled by Edward F. Ryan. — Cork : Cork University Press, 1982. — xxii,76p ; 23cm
Includes index
ISBN 0-902561-21-9 : Unpriced B82-37976

344.16 — LAW. NORTHERN IRELAND

344.1602′2 — Northern Ireland. Constitution

The **Constitution** of Northern Ireland : problems and prospects / edited by David Watt. — London : Heinemann, 1981. — 227p : maps ; 23cm. — (Joint studies in public policy ; 4)
Includes index
ISBN 0-435-83807-5 (corrected : cased) : £15.00 : CIP rev.
ISBN 0-435-83807-5
ISBN 0-435-83920-9
ISBN 0-435-83808-3 (pbk) : Unpriced
B81-34726

344.1604′44 — Northern Ireland. Mentally ill persons. Treatment. Law — *Inquiry reports*

Northern Ireland Review Committee on Mental Health Legislation. Northern Ireland Review Committee on Mental Health Legislation. — Belfast : H.M.S.O., 1981. — v,65p : ill ; 25cm
ISBN 0-337-07218-3 (pbk) : £3.90 B82-13806

344.1604′522 — Northern Ireland. Police. Medals: Royal Ulster Constabulary Service Medal. Law — *Prerogative instrument*

Great Britain. The Royal Ulster Constabulary service medal. — London : H.M.S.O., 1982. — 1sheet ; 25cm. — (Cmnd. ; 8602)
ISBN 0-10-186020-x : £0.35 B82-39381

344.1604′533′02633 — Northern Ireland. Firearms. Control. Law — *Statutes*

Great Britain. Firearms Act (Northern Ireland) 1969. — Reprint to 1977. — Belfast : H.M.S.O., 1977. — 42p ; 25cm
Previous ed.: 1969
ISBN 0-337-37450-3 (pbk) : £0.85 B82-09927

344.1607′2 — Northern Ireland. County courts. Small claims. Procedure — *Manuals*

Greer, Desmond S.. Small claims : the new procedure in Northern Ireland / by D.S. Greer. — Belfast : Faculty of Law, Queen′s University, Belfast, 1979. — 54p : forms ; 21cm. — (The Law in action)
£0.60 (pbk) B82-40432

344.1608′22 — Northern Ireland. Law — *Statutes — Collections*

Northern Ireland. [Laws, etc.]. The statutes revised : Northern Ireland. — 2nd ed. — Belfast : H.M.S.O.
Previous ed.: 197-?
Vol.1: Acts of the Northern Ireland Parliament 1921-1949. — 1982. — 1v.(loose-leaf) ; 26cm
Includes index
ISBN 0-337-23365-9 : Unpriced
ISBN 0-337-23364-0 (set) : Unpriced
B82-32191

Northern Ireland. [Laws, etc.]. The statutes revised : Northern Ireland. — 2nd ed. — Belfast : H.M.S.O.
Previous ed.: 197-?
Vol.2: Acts of the Northern Ireland Parliament 1950-1959. — 1982. — 1v.(loose-leaf) ; 26cm
Includes index
ISBN 0-337-23366-7 : Unpriced
ISBN 0-337-23364-0 (set) : Unpriced
B82-32192

Northern Ireland. [Laws, etc.]. The statutes revised : Northern Ireland. — 2nd ed. — Belfast : H.M.S.O.
Previous ed.: 197-?
Vol.3: Acts of the Northern Ireland Parliament 1960-1963. — 1982. — 1v.(loose-leaf) : forms ; 26cm
Includes index
ISBN 0-337-23367-5 : Unpriced
ISBN 0-337-23364-0 (set) : Unpriced
B82-32193

Northern Ireland. [Laws, etc.]. The statutes revised : Northern Ireland. — 2nd ed. — Belfast : H.M.S.O.
Previous ed.: 197-?
Vol.4: Acts of the Northern Ireland Parliament 1964-1966. — 1982. — 1v.(loose-leaf) ; 26cm
Includes index
ISBN 0-337-23368-3 : Unpriced
ISBN 0-337-23364-0 (set) : Unpriced
B82-32194

Northern Ireland. [Laws, etc.]. The statutes revised : Northern Ireland. — 2nd ed. — Belfast : H.M.S.O.
Previous ed.: 197-?
Vol.5: Acts of the Northern Ireland Parliament 1967-1969. — 1982. — 1v.(loose-leaf) ; 26cm
Includes index
ISBN 0-337-23369-1 : Unpriced
ISBN 0-337-23364-0 (set) : Unpriced
B82-32195

Northern Ireland. [Laws, etc.]. The statutes revised : Northern Ireland. — 2nd ed. — Belfast : H.M.S.O.
Previous ed.: 197-?
Vol.6: Acts of the Northern Ireland Parliament 1970-1972. — 1982. — 1v.(loose-leaf) ; 26cm
Includes index
ISBN 0-337-23370-5 : Unpriced
ISBN 0-337-23364-0 (set) : Unpriced
B82-32196

344.1608′25 — Northern Ireland. Law. Statutory instruments. Drafts — *Inquiry reports*

Great Britain. *Parliament. Joint Committee on Consolidation Bills*. Consolidation bills 1980-81 : first report of the Joint Committee on Consolidation Bills : being a report upon the Draft Firearms (Northern Ireland) Order 1980, Draft Clean Air (Northern Ireland) Order 1980, Draft Road Traffic (Northern Ireland) Order 1980, Draft Judgments Enforcement (Northern Ireland) Order 1981. — London : H.M.S.O., [1980]. — 1sheet ; 25x16cm. — (H.L. ; 35) (H.C. ; 74)
ISBN 0-10-403581-1 : £0.30 B82-16066

344.17 — LAW. IRELAND(REPUBLIC)

344.17′0092′4 — Ireland *(Republic)*. **Law. Duffy, George Gavan** — *Biographies*

Golding, G. M.. George Gavan Duffy 1882-1951 : a legal biography / G.M. Golding. — Blackrock : Irish Academic Press, c1982. — xvi,224p,[1]leaf of plates : 1port ; 22cm
Bibliography: p209-214. — Includes index
ISBN 0-7165-0078-7 (cased) : £15.00
ISBN 0-7165-0207-0 (pbk) : Unpriced
B82-29754

344.1702′853 — Ireland *(Republic)*. **Freedom of information. Law** — *Proposals*

Irish Council for Civil Liberties. Proposals for a freedom of information act and an open meetings (public bodies) act. — Dublin (Liberty Hall, Dublin 1) : Irish Council for Civil Liberties, 1981. — 14p ; 21cm. — (ICCL Report ; no.13)
£0.50 (pbk) B82-18192

344.1704′1125 — Ireland *(Republic)*. **Employment. Law**

Employment legislation / FUE. — 2nd ed. — Dublin (Baggot Bridge House, 84-86 Lower Baggot Street, Dublin 2) : Research and Information Division, Federated Union of Employers, 1980. — 123p ; 21cm
Cover title. — Previous ed.: 1977
Unpriced (pbk) B82-15433

344.1704′120413711 — Ireland *(Republic)*. **Schools. Teachers. Conditions of service. Law**

McCarthy, Charles. Freedom and obligation under the law / Charles McCarthy and David Dillon. — [Dublin?] : [Irish National Teachers′ Organisation], [1981?]. — vii,64p ; 30cm
At head of title: The Irish National Teachers′ Organisation
Unpriced (pbk) B82-29556

344.1704′463 — Ireland *(Republic)*. **Environment. Pollution. Law**

Scannell, Yvonne. The law and practice relating to pollution control in Ireland. — 2nd ed. — London : Graham and Trotman, Dec.1982. — [200]p
Previous ed.: 1976
ISBN 0-86010-313-7 : £18.00 : CIP entry
B82-34061

344.1705′0264 — Ireland *(Republic)*. **Criminal law** — *Cases*

Findlay, Mark. A casebook of Irish criminal law / by Mark Findlay and Barry McAuley. — Dublin : Precedent, 1981. — xi,447p ; 25cm
ISBN 0-907806-00-7 (pbk) : Unpriced
B82-11075

344.1706′2 — Ireland *(Republic)*. **Contracts. Law**

Clark, Robert, *19---*. Contract / by Robert Clark. — London : Sweet & Maxwell, 1982. — xxxviii,241p ; 22cm. — (Irish law texts)
Includes index
ISBN 0-421-28540-0 (pbk) : £6.50 : CIP rev.
B82-07107

344.1706′7 — Ireland *(Republic)*. **Commercial law**

O′Malley, Liam. Business law / by Liam O′Malley. — London : Sweet & Maxwell, 1982. — xxxii,222p ; 22cm. — (Irish law texts)
Includes index
ISBN 0-421-28500-1 (pbk) : £6.50 : CIP rev.
B82-07974

344.1707 — Ireland *(Republic)*. **Justice. Administration. Law**

Delany, V. T. H.. The administration of justice in Ireland / V.T.H. Delany. — 4th ed., edited by Charles Lysaght. — Dublin : Institute of Public Administration, 1975 (1981 [printing]). — vi,105p : ill ; 22cm
Previous ed.: / edited by Vincent Grogan. 1970. — Bibliography: p100-101. — Includes index
ISBN 0-902173-64-2 (pbk) : £3.96 B82-25124

344.1708′4′05 — Ireland *(Republic)*. **Law** — *Cases — Serials*

Irish law reports monthly : incorporating Irish Law times. — Vol.1, no.1 (1981)-. — Blackrock (c/o Irish Academic Press, Kill La., Blackrock, County Dublin) : Round Hall Press, 1981-. — v. ; 22cm
Continues: Irish law times and solicitors′ journal
Unpriced B82-06778

344.2 — LAW. ENGLAND

344.2 — England. Law

Atiyah, P. S.. Law and modern society. — Oxford : Oxford University Press, Jan.1983. — [240]p. — (OPUS)
ISBN 0-19-219166-7 : £9.95 : CIP entry
B82-33477

Conniff, Chris. The law in your hands : a self-help law pack / Chris Conniff and Steve Williams. — Cambridge : National Extension College, 1980. — v,186p ; 21cm
″Linked to the BBC TV series ‘Wainwright′s law’″
ISBN 0-86082-181-1 (pbk) : Unpriced
B82-41029

344.2 — England. Law *continuation*

Halsbury, Hardinge Stanley Giffard, *Earl of.* Halsbury's Laws of England. — 4th ed. / [editor in chief] Lord Hailsham of St Marylebone. — London : Butterworths
Previous ed.: published in 43 vols. 1952-1964
Vol.27. — 1981. — 866p ; 26cm
Includes index
ISBN 0-406-03427-3 : Unpriced
ISBN 0-406-03547-4 (deluxe) : unpriced
ISBN 0-406-03400-1 (set) : unpriced
ISBN 0-406-06520-2 (set deluxe) : unpriced B82-05105

Marsh, S. B.. Outlines of English law. — 3rd ed. — London : McGraw-Hill, Aug.1982. — [304]p
Previous ed.: 1978
ISBN 0-07-084655-3 (pbk) : £4.95 : CIP entry B82-21962

Pritchard, John, *19---*. The Penguin guide to the law / John Pritchard. — London : Penguin, 1982. — 957p ; 21cm
Includes index
ISBN 0-14-051102-4 (pbk) : £6.95 B82-41151

Pritchard, John, *1949-*. The Penguin guide to the law / John Pritchard. — London : Allen Lane, 1982. — 957p : ill,forms ; 22cm
Includes index
ISBN 0-7139-1356-8 : £14.95 B82-38197

Smith, Kenneth, *1910-1966*. English law. — 7th ed. — London : Pitman, Sept.1982. — [838]p
Previous ed.: 1979
ISBN 0-273-01829-9 (pbk) : £8.50 : CIP entry B82-18872

344.2 — England. Law — *Early works*

Fortescue, *Sir* **John**. De laudibus legum Anglie / Sir John Fortescue. De republica Anglorum / Sir Thomas Smith. — New York ; London : Garland, 1979. — 1v.(various pagings) ; 23cm. — (Classics of English legal history in the modern era)
De laudibus legum Anglie: parallel Latin text and English translation. — De republica Anglorum : Middle English text. — Facsims. of: De laudibus legum Anglie — Cambridge : Cambridge University Press, 1942 ; De republica Anglorum — Cambridge : Cambridge University Press, 1906. — Includes index
ISBN 0-8240-3065-6 : Unpriced B82-05863

344.2 — England. Law — *For schools*

Brown, W. J.. 'O' level law / by W.J. Brown. — 2nd ed. — London : Sweet & Maxwell, 1982. — xiv,227p : ill ; 22cm. — (Concise college texts)
Previous ed.: 1978. — Includes index
ISBN 0-421-28060-3 (cased) : Unpriced : CIP rev.
ISBN 0-421-28070-0 (pbk) : £4.75 B82-06771

Drewry, Gavin. Law, justice and politics / Gavin Drewry. — 2nd ed. — Harlow : Longman, 1981. — x,182p : ill,1map ; 20cm. — (Political realities)
Previous ed.: 1975. — Bibliography: p173-176. — Includes index
ISBN 0-582-35329-7 (pbk) : £2.95 B82-18360

Edmunds, Judith. Rights, responsibilities and the law / Judith Edmunds. — Walton-on-Thames : Nelson, 1982. — 125p : ill,ports ; 28cm
Includes index
ISBN 0-17-438190-5 (pbk) : Unpriced B82-30359

Jones, Barry, *1922-*. "A" Level law / Barry Jones. — Plymouth : Macdonald & Evans, 1981. — xxii,213p ; 19cm. — (The M & E handbook series)
Bibliography: p201. — Includes index
ISBN 0-7121-0160-8 (pbk) : £2.95 B82-01036

Scott, D. M. M.. 'O' Level English law / by D.M.M. Scott. — 4th ed. — London : Butterworths, 1981. — xvi,269p,[6]p of plates : ill,2maps,facsims,ports ; 23cm
Previous ed.: 1976. — Includes index
ISBN 0-406-65305-4 : Unpriced B82-08924

344.2'0023 — England. Barristers. Role

Cecil, Henry. Brief to counsel / by Henry Cecil ; illustrated by Edward Ardizzone. — 3rd ed. / revised and edited by Edgar Dennis Smith ; with a foreword by Lord Edmund-Davies. — Chichester : Rose, 1982. — 204p : ill ; 21cm
Previous ed.: i.e. New ed. London : Joseph, 1972. — Includes index
Unpriced B82-34711

344.2'0023 — England. Solicitorship

The **Solicitor's** practice / editor Peter H.M. Soar. — London : Butterworths
1. — 1981. — 1v.(loose-leaf) ; 26cm
ISBN 0-406-37353-1 (unbound) : Unpriced B82-11741

344.2'0024097 — England. Law — *For journalism*

McNae, L. C. J.. Essential law for journalists. — 8th ed. — London : Granada, June 1982. — [208]p
Previous ed.: 1979
ISBN 0-246-11730-3 : £6.95 : CIP entry B82-09987

344.2'0024362 — England. Law — *For welfare work*

Alcock, Pete. Welfare law and order : a critical introduction to law for social workers / Pete Alcock and Phil Harris. — London : Macmillan, 1982. — xvi,219p ; 23cm. — (Critical texts in social work and the welfare state)
Bibliography: p207-213. — Includes index
ISBN 0-333-29490-4 (cased) : £12.95
ISBN 0-333-29491-2 (pbk) : Unpriced B82-38812

344.2'0068 — England. Solicitorship. Private practice. Management — *Manuals*

Shurman, Laurence. The practical skills of the solicitor : a handbook of working techniques / Laurence Shurman. — London : Oyez, c1981. — xii,124p ; 22cm
Bibliography: p123-124
ISBN 0-85120-610-7 (pbk) : Unpriced B82-03051

344.2'009 — England. Law, *ca 1200-ca 1700*

Plucknett, T. F. T.. Studies in English legal history. — London : Hambledon, Jan.1983. — [350]p. — (History series ; 14)
ISBN 0-907628-11-7 : £24.00 : CIP entry B82-33244

344.2'0092'4 — England. Law. Razzall, Leonard Humphrey — *Biographies*

Razzall, Leonard Humphrey. A man of law's tale : an autobiography / by Leonard Humphrey Razzall. — London : Razzalls Riverside Books, 1982. — 30p : ill,ports ; 24cm
ISBN 0-9508082-0-2 (pbk) : Unpriced B82-37595

344.2'0092'4 — England. Law. Skelhorn, *Sir* **Norman** — *Biographies*

Skelhorn, *Sir* **Norman**. Public prosecutor : the memoirs of Sir Norman Skelhorn. — London : Harrap, 1981. — 207p,[16]p of plates : ill,ports ; 24cm
Includes index
ISBN 0-245-53763-5 : £10.50 B82-08922

344.2'0092'4 — England. Law. Woolfe, Geoffrey — *Biographies*

Woolfe, Geoffrey. The unloved profession / Geoffrey Woolfe. — Bognor Regis : New Horizon, c1982. — 183p ; 22cm
ISBN 0-86116-859-3 : £5.75 B82-22235

344.2'0092'4 — England. Solicitors: Lewis, *Sir* **George Henry** — *Biographies*

Juxon, John. Lewis and Lewis. — London : Collins, Jan.1983. — [256]p
ISBN 0-00-216476-0 : £12.95 : CIP entry B82-35202

344.202 — England. Constitutional law — *Early works* — *Facsimiles*

The **Judgement** of whole kingdoms and nations / Sir John Somers. Lex constitutionis / Giles Jacob. — New York ; London : Garland, 1979. — 71,xiv,360p ; 23cm. — (Classics of English legal history in the modern era)
Facsims of: The judgement of whole kingdoms and nations / variously attributed to Daniel Defoe, Sir John Somers and John Dunton. London : T. Harrison, 1710 and Lex constitutionis, or, The gentleman's law. London : E. Nutt and R. Gosling, 1719
ISBN 0-8240-3068-0 : Unpriced B82-18890

344.202'418 — England. Powers of search & powers of seizure. Law

Polyviou, Polyvios G.. Search and seizure : constitutional and common law. — London : Duckworth, June 1982. — [392]p
ISBN 0-7156-1592-0 : £28.00 : CIP entry
Also classified at 347.302'418 B82-09627

344.202'6 — England. Administrative law

Foulkes, David, *1924-*. Administrative law / David Foulkes. — 5th ed. — London : Butterworths, 1982. — xxxii,460p ; 26cm
Previous ed.: published as Introduction to administrative law, 1976. — Includes index
ISBN 0-406-58407-9 : Unpriced
ISBN 0-406-58408-7 (pbk) : Unpriced B82-37678

Wade, H. W. R.. Administrative law. — 5th ed. — Oxford : Clarendon Press, Oct.1982. — [900]p
Previous ed.: 1977
ISBN 0-19-876138-4 (cased) : £25.00 : CIP entry
ISBN 0-19-876139-2 (pbk) : £17.50 B82-23698

Yardley, D. C. M.. Principles of administrative law / D.C.M. Yardley. — London : Butterworths, 1981. — xx,238p ; 23cm
Includes index
ISBN 0-406-68991-1 (cased) : Unpriced
ISBN 0-406-68990-3 (pbk) : Unpriced B82-09798

344.202'62 — England. Monarchy. Law — *Early works* — *Facsimiles*

Toland, John, *1670-1722*. Anglia Libera / John Toland. A treatise of the rights of the crown / William Noy. concerning 'Nullum tempus occurit regi' / Granville Sharp. On the King's power of granting pardons / Heneage Finch. — New York ; London : Garland, 1979. — 1v.(various pagings) ; 19cm. — (Classics of English legal history in the modern era)
Facsimile editions
ISBN 0-8240-3170-9 : Unpriced B82-11014

344.202'7 — England. Local authorities. Members. Elections. Law — *For election agents*

Conduct of local elections (England and Wales) : Greater London, London Borough, County, District. — 10th ed. — London : Labour Party, 1982. — 64p ; 21cm
Previous ed.: 1973. — Includes index
£1.20 (pbk) B82-29325

344.202'85 — England. Citizens. Rights. Law. England and Wales. *Convention.* **Declaration of Rights** — *Critical studies*

Schwoerer, Lois G.. The Declaration of Rights, 1689 / Lois G. Schwoerer. — Baltimore ; London : Johns Hopkins University Press, c1981. — xv,391p : ill,facsims,ports ; 24cm
Bibliography: p369-379. — Includes index
ISBN 0-8018-2430-3 : £18.50 B82-11908

344.202'85 — England. Civil rights. Law

Street, Harry. Freedom, the individual and the law / H. Street. — 5th ed. — Harmondsworth : Penguin, c1982. — 352p ; 20cm
Previous ed.: 1977. — Includes index
ISBN 0-14-020646-9 (pbk) : £3.50 B82-20317

344.202'85 — England. Civil rights. Law — *Early works — Facsimiles*

Jacob, Giles. The laws of liberty and property / Giles Jacob. A letter concerning libels / John Almon. On the nature of civil liberty / Richard Price. — New York ; London : Garland, 1979. — 1v.(various pagings) ; 23cm. — (Classics of English legal history in the modern era)
Facsims of: The laws of liberty and property / Giles Jacob. 2nd ed. London : J. Cooper, 1734 — A letter concerning libels, warrants, seizure of papers, and security for the peace / the Father of Candor [i.e. John Alman]. 3rd ed. London : J. Almon, 1765 — Observations on the nature of civil liberty, the principles of government, and the justice and policy of the War with America / by Richard Price. London : T. Cadell, 1776
ISBN 0-8240-3155-5 : Unpriced B82-31270

344.202'85'0321 — England. Citizens. Rights — *Encyclopaedias*

You and your rights : an A to Z guide to the law / Reader's Digest. — 4th ed. — London : Reader's Digest Association, c1982. — 751p : ill(some col.),facsims,forms ; 27cm
Previous ed.: 1981. — Facism on lining papers. — Includes index
£13.95 B82-10278

344.202'87 — England. Precedence. Law

Squibb, G. D.. Precedence in England and Wales / G.D. Squibb. — Oxford : Clarendon Press, 1981. — xviii,139p ; 23cm
Bibliography: p126-130. — Includes index
ISBN 0-19-825389-3 : £12.50 : CIP rev. B81-33643

344.202'87 — England. Young persons. Law — *Law — For youth work*

Enfranchisement : young people and the law : an information pack for youth workers / [... compiled by the Youth Work Unit]. — Leicester : The Unit, NYB, 1981. — 1v.(loose-leaf) : ill ; 31cm
Bibliography: 8p
ISBN 0-86155-047-1 (pbk) : £3.50 B82-06135

344.202'9 — England. Local government. Law

Cross, C. A.. Principles of local government law / by C.A. Cross. — 6th ed. — London : Sweet & Maxwell, 1981. — xc,719p ; 22cm
Previous ed.: 1974. — Includes index
ISBN 0-421-24860-2 (cased) : £19.00 : CIP rev.
ISBN 0-421-24870-x (pbk) : £13.00 B80-10977

344.202'9 — England. Local government. Law: Local Government Planning and Land Act 1980 — *Critical studies*

Gillon, Steve. The Local Government, Planning and Land Act 1980 : a layman's guide / Steve Gillon, Marc Dorfman, Andy Moye. — [London] ([17 Carlton House Terrace, SW1Y 5AS]) : TCPA, Planning Aid Unit, [1982?]. — 31p ; 30cm
Cover title
£1.00 (pbk) B82-39769

344.202'9'02633 — England. Local government. Law — *Statutes*

Great Britain. [Local Government, Planning and Land Act 1980]. Local Government, Planning and Land Act 1980 : chapter 65. — London : H.M.S.O., [1980]. — xii,330p ; 25cm
Cover title
ISBN 0-10-546580-1 (pbk) : £9.30 B82-09248

344.203'34 — England. Local authorities. Accounts. Auditing. Law

Jones, Reginald. Local government audit law / by Reginald Jones. — London : H.M.S.O., 1981. — xxxvii,380p ; 26cm
Includes index
ISBN 0-11-751486-1 : £15.00 B82-08604

344.2034 — England. Taxation. Law — *Early works — Facsimiles*

Hakewill, William. Against the pretended power of impositions / William Hakewill. The question concerning impositions / Sir John Davies. — New York ; London : Garland, 1979. — 142,166p ; 19cm. — (Classics of English legal history in the modern era)
Against the pretended power of impositions. Facsim. of: ed. published as The libertie of the subject. London : printed by R.H., 1641 — The question concerning impositions. Facsim. of : ed. published London : printed by S.G. for H. Twyford, 1656
ISBN 0-8240-3094-x : Unpriced B82-14680

344.2035'4 — England. Rates. Law — *Statutes — Collections*

Great Britain. [General Rate Act]. The text of the General Rate Acts (1967 to 1978) / introduced and edited by H. Howard Karslake. — London (115 Ebury Street, Belgravia, SW1W 9QT) : Rating and Valuation Associaton, 1979. — xxvii,343p ; 22cm
£8.50 (pbk) B82-40975

344.203'7 — England. Premises. Licensing. Law

Underhill, Michael. The licensing guide / Michael Underhill. — 8th ed. — London : Oyez Longman, 1982. — x,117p ; 22cm. — (Oyez Longman practice notes)
Previous ed.: 1979. — Includes index
ISBN 0-85120-588-7 (pbk) : Unpriced B82-33144

344.203'7752 — Gloucestershire. Forest of Dean. Coal industries. Customary rights, *1788-1888*. Law

Fisher, Chris. Custom, work and market capitalism : the Forest of Dean colliers, 1788-1888 / Chris Fisher. — London : Croom Helm, c1981. — xvi,203p : 1map ; 23cm
Bibliography: p194-200. — Includes index
ISBN 0-7099-1001-0 : £12.95 B82-07144

344.203'78624 — England. Civil engineering. Contracts. Law

Haswell, Charles K.. Civil engineering contracts : practice and procedure / Charles K. Haswell, Douglas S. de Silva. — London : Butterworths Scientific, 1982. — xii,221p : ill ; 23cm
Bibliography: p214. — Includes index
ISBN 0-408-00526-2 : Unpriced : CIP rev. B82-06741

344.203'78624 — England. Construction. Contracts. Disputes. Litigation. Procedure

Elliott, Robert Fenwick. Building contract litigation / Robert Fenwick Elliott. — London : Oyez : c1981. — xvii,186p ; 22cm
Includes index
ISBN 0-85120-601-8 (pbk) : Unpriced B82-04944

344.203'78624 — England. Construction. Contracts. Law

Keating, Donald. Building contracts : including a commentary on the JCT standard form of building contract / Donald Keating. — 4th ed. / with a commentary on I.C.E. conditions of contract by John Uff. — London : Sweet & Maxwell
Previous ed.: published as Law and practice of building contracts. 1969
1st Suppl. / prepared by the Author and Anthony May, John Uff. — 1982. — 142p ; 26cm : 1form
ISBN 0-421-29560-0 : £15.00 : CIP rev. B82-11502

344.203'78624 — England. Law — *For construction industries*

Galbraith, Anne. Building law 4 checkbook / Anne Galbraith. — London : Butterworth Scientific, 1982. — vi,130p : 1ill ; 20cm. — (Butterworths technical and scientific checkbooks. Level 4)
Includes index
ISBN 0-408-00677-3 (cased) : Unpriced : CIP rev.
ISBN 0-408-00583-1 (pbk) : Unpriced B82-04033

344.203'78624'0264 — England. Construction industries. Law — *Cases*

Building law reports / edited by Humphrey Lloyd and Colin Reese. — London : George Godwin
Vol.18: Theme supervision and certification. — 1982. — vi,184p ; 24cm
Includes index
ISBN 0-7114-5716-6 : Unpriced B82-34024

344.203'78624'0264 — England. Construction industries. Law. — *Cases — Serials*

Building law reports. — Vol.19. — London : Godwin, Apr.1982. — [128]p
ISBN 0-7114-5759-x : £13.50 : CIP entry B82-11262

344.203'78624'0264 — England. Construction industries. Law — *Cases — Serials*

Building law reports. — Vol.20. — London : Godwin, July 1982. — [128]p
ISBN 0-7114-5760-3 : £13.50 : CIP entry B82-13132

344.203'78624'05 — England. Construction industries. Law — *Cases — Serials*

Building law reports. — Vol.21. — London : Godwin, Sept.1982. — [128]p
ISBN 0-7114-5761-1 : £13.50 : CIP entry B82-20025

344.203'786479542 — England. Catering industries. Law

Richards, Margaret, *1932-*. Legal aspects of the hotel and catering industry / Margaret Richards and S.W. Stewart. — 2nd ed, Repr. with minor additions. — London : Bell & Hyman, 1982. — xxi,266p ; 22cm
Previous ed.: i.e. 2nd ed. 1979. — Includes index
ISBN 0-7135-1176-1 (pbk) : £6.95 : CIP rev. B81-34723

344.203'7869 — England. Buildings. Construction. Law: Building Regulations 1976 — *Critical studies*

Elder, A. J.. Guide to the Building Regulations, 1976 / A.J. Elder. — 7th ed. — London : Architectural Press, 1981. — 231p : ill,plans ; 30cm
Previous ed.: 1979. — Bibliography: p227. — Includes index
ISBN 0-85139-850-2 : £7.95 B82-17682

344.203'7869 — England. Buildings. Construction. Law: Building (Second Amendment) Regulations 1981 — *Texts with commentaries*

Great Britain. [Building Regulations 1981]. The Building (Second Amendment) Regulations 1981 in detail : (a supplement to the Building Regulations 1976 in detail) / John Stephenson. — London : Northwood, 1982. — 46p : ill ; 30cm
ISBN 0-7198-2910-0 (pbk) : Unpriced B82-37999

344.203'7869 — England. Buildings. Construction. Legal aspects — *For architectural design*

Stephenson, John. Building development controls. — London : Construction Press, Nov.1982. — [288]p
ISBN 0-582-30512-8 : £15.00 : CIP entry B82-26571

344.203'7869 — England. Buildings. Construction - *Statutory instruments - Texts with commentaries*

Whyte, W. S.. The Building Regulations explained and illustrated for residential buildings. — 5th ed. (metric). — London : Granada, July 1981. — 1v.
This ed. originally published: Crosby Lockwood Staples, 1978
ISBN 0-246-11611-0 (pbk) : £5.95 : CIP entry B81-13906

344.203'78'690 — England. Construction industries. Law

Uff, John. Construction law. — 3rd ed. — London : Sweet & Maxwell, Sept.1981. — [250]p. — (Concise college texts)
Previous ed.: 1978
ISBN 0-421-28300-9 (cased) : £12.75 : CIP entry B81-21576

344.203′7869′002636 — England. Buildings. Construction — *Statutory instruments — Texts with commentaries*

Whyte, W. S.. The buildings regulations. — 6th ed. — London : Granada, Aug.1982. — [316]p
Previous ed.: 1981
ISBN 0-246-11931-4 : £8.95 : CIP entry
B82-16465

344.203′929 — England. Electricity supply. Law

A **Guide** to questions of law and practice in relation to electricity consumers in England and Wales. — 2nd ed. — London : Electricity Consumers′ Council, 1981. — 53,2leaves ; 30cm
Previous ed.: [197-?]. — Includes index
£1.50 (spiral) B82-04949

344.203′932 — England. Freight transport. Law

Ridley, Jasper. The law of the carriage of goods by land, sea and air / by Jasper Ridley. — 6th ed. / edited by Geoffrey Whitehead. — London : Shaw, 1982. — xlviii,328p : 2forms ; 22cm
Previous ed.: 1978. — Includes index
ISBN 0-7219-0622-2 (pbk) : £9.50 B82-38851

344.203′94 — England. Road traffic. Law — *For motoring*

Wickerson, John. The motorist and the law / John Wickerson. — 2nd ed. — London : Oyez, 1982. — viii,129p ; 20cm. — (It′s your law)
Previous ed.: 1975. — Includes index
ISBN 0-85120-477-5 (cased) : Unpriced
ISBN 0-85120-478-3 (pbk) : Unpriced
B82-16426

344.203′94′0243632 — England. Road traffic. Law — *For police*

Wilson, Gordon, *1947-*. The traffic officer′s companion : a practical handbook of road traffic law / by Gordon Wilson. — London : Police Review Publication, c1982. — 161p : ill ; 19cm
Includes index
ISBN 0-85164-995-5 (pbk) : £2.75 B82-23401

344.203′942 — England. Private roads. Maintenance by county councils. Law — *For residents*

The **Making** up of private streets : a brief guide / West Sussex County Council. — [Chichester] : [The Council], [1981?]. — [8]p : ill ; 21cm
Cover title
ISBN 0-86260-020-0 (pbk) : Unpriced
B82-01465

344.203′942 — England. Rights of way. Law

Garner, J. F.. Rights of way and access to the countryside / J.F. Garner. — 4th ed. — London : Oyez Longman, 1982. — xi,122p ; 22cm. — (Oyez Longman practice notes)
Previous ed.: 1974. — Includes index
ISBN 0-85120-466-x (pbk) : Unpriced
B82-27098

344.203′942′02633 — England. Highways. Law — *Statutes*

Great Britain. [Highways Act 1980]. Highways Act 1980 : chapter 66. — London : H.M.S.O., [1980]. — xvii,358p ; 25cm
Cover title
ISBN 0-10-546680-8 (pbk) : £9.30 B82-09252

344.203′9483 — England. International road freight transport. Law

Clarke, Malcolm A.. International carriage of goods by road : CMR / by Malcolm A. Clarke. — London : Stevens, 1982. — xxvi,212p ; 26cm
Appendix in French. — Includes index
ISBN 0-420-46490-5 : £19.50 : CIP rev.
B82-06767

344.203′96 — Shipping. English law

Hill, Christopher, *19---*. Maritime law / Christopher Hill. — London : Pitman, 1981. — xxi,394p : forms ; 24cm
Includes index
ISBN 0-273-01593-1 : Unpriced B82-06202

344.203′968 — England. Maritime liens. Law

Thomas, D. R.. Maritime liens / by D.R. Thomas. — London : Stevens, 1980. — xlix,397p : forms ; 26cm. — (British shipping laws ; v.14)
Includes index
ISBN 0-420-46050-0 : £35.00 B82-16166

344.203′998 — England. Law — *For journalism*

McNae, L. C. J.. Essential law for journalists / L.C.J. McNae. — 8th ed. / revised and edited by Walter Greenwood and Tom Welsh. — London : Butterworths, 1982. — x,191p ; 22cm
Previous ed.: 1979. — Bibliography: p180-182. — Includes index
ISBN 0-406-77280-0 (pbk) : Unpriced
B82-38393

344.204′1 — England. Employment. Labour. Law

Wright, M.. Labour law / M. Wright. — 3rd ed. — Plymouth : Macdonald and Evans, 1981. — xviii,190p ; 19cm. — (The M & E handbook series)
Previous ed.: 1979. — Bibliography: p174. — Includes index
ISBN 0-7121-1257-x (pbk) : £3.75 B82-01912

344.204′1 — England. Hotel & catering industries. Industrial relations. Law — *For management*

Employee relations : a comprehensive guide. — 4th ed. — Wembley : Hotel and Catering Industry Training Board, 1981. — 92p : ill,1map,forms ; 21cm
Previous ed.: 1978. — Includes index
ISBN 0-7033-0010-5 (pbk) : Unpriced
B82-05050

344.204′1′0269 — England. Industrial tribunals. Procedure

Mulhern, John. The industrial tribunal : a practical guide to employment law and tribunal procedure / by John Mulhern and Ian McLean. — Chichester : Rose, 1982. — 280p : forms ; 23cm
Includes index
ISBN 0-85992-224-3 : £19.50 B82-24307

344.204′1425763 — England. Women teachers. Maternity rights. Law

Maternity provisions for women teachers / NUT. — [London] ([Hamilton House, Mabledon Place, WC1H 9BD]) : National Union of Teachers, 1981. — 20p ; 21cm
Cover title
Unpriced (pbk) B82-19754

344.204′317 — England. Fund raising. Law

Finney, Jarlath. Gaming, lotteries, fundraising and the law. — London : Sweet and Maxwell, Nov.1982. — [220]p
ISBN 0-421-29980-0 (pbk) : £25.00 : CIP entry
Primary classification 344.204′542 B82-27530

344.204′322 — England. Mental health services. Law

Whitehead, Tony. Mental illness and the law / Tony Whitehead. — Oxford : Basil Blackwell, 1982. — viii,181p : forms ; 23cm
Includes index
ISBN 0-631-12721-6 (cased) : Unpriced : CIP rev.
ISBN 0-631-12615-5 (pbk) : Unpriced
B81-09499

344.204′3258′0924 — England. Poverty relief. Law. Reform. Theories of Bentham, Jeremy

Bahmueller, Charles F.. The National Charity Company : Jeremy Bentham′s silent revolution / Charles F. Bahmueller. — Berkeley ; London : University of California Press, c1981. — xi,272p ; 24cm
Includes index
ISBN 0-520-03796-0 : £17.50 B82-13757

344.204′327 — England. Child care services. Law

Slomnicka, B. I.. Law of child care / B.I. Slomnicka. — Plymouth : MacDonald and Evans, 1982. — xlvi,415p : ill,forms ; 23cm
Includes index
ISBN 0-7121-1252-9 : £9.95 B82-30678

344.204′3273 — England. Local authorities. Child care services. Children. Committal. Procedure. Legal aspects

Hilgendorf, Linden. Social workers and solicitors in child care cases / by Linden Hilgendorf with the assistance of Deborah Holland, Barrie Irving, Diana Schlaefli. — London : H.M.S.O., 1981. — ix,150p ; 25cm
At head of title: Department of Health and Social Security. — Bibliography: p150
ISBN 0-11-320769-7 (cased) : £7.50
ISBN 0-11-320759-x (pbk) : £3.95 B82-11204

344.204′32732 — England. Children in care. Law

Holden, Alan S.. Children in care : the Association of Directors of Social Services guide to personal social services legislation / Alan S. Holden. — Leamington Spa : Comyn, 1980. — 231p : 1form ; 21cm
Includes index
ISBN 0-907267-00-9 (pbk) : £4.95 B82-36978

344.204′32795 — England. Children. Care. Law

Rawstrom, Diana. Child care law : a summary of the law in England and Wales / Diana Rawstrom. — Rev. and repr. — [London] : British Agencies for Adoption & Fostering, 1981, c1980. — 38p ; 21cm. — (Practice series, ISSN 0260-0803 ; 3)
Bibliography: p28
ISBN 0-903534-30-4 (pbk) : £1.00 B82-11746

344.204′32795 — England. Children. Care. Law — *For welfare work*

Dingwall, Robert. Care proceedings : a practical guide for social workers, health visitors and others / Robert Dingwall and John Eekelaar. — Oxford : Basil Blackwell, 1982. — viii,140p ; 23cm
Bibliography: p135-136. — Includes index
ISBN 0-631-12756-9 (cased) : Unpriced : CIP rev.
ISBN 0-631-12757-7 (pbk) : Unpriced
B82-04588

344.204′32828 — England. Welfare benefits for separated persons. Law

Low income families and the divorce practitioner / by Graham Beecher ... [et al.]. — Guildford : College of Law, c1982. — vi,98p : forms ; 22cm. — (College of Law lectures, ISSN 0309-3166)
£4.00 (pbk) B82-22004

344.204′41 — England. Health services. Medical personnel. Law

Whincup, Michael. Legal aspects of medical and nursing service : a guide to employment rights and practitioners′ duties / Michael H. Whincup. — 3rd ed. (enl.). — Beckenham : Ravenswood, 1982. — 160p ; 22cm. — (Studies in law and practice for health service management ; v.5)
Previous ed.: 1978. — Includes index
ISBN 0-901812-48-x (cased) : Unpriced
ISBN 0-901812-47-1 (pbk) : Unpriced
B82-25257

344.204′44 — England. Man. Mental illness. Law — *Early works — Facsimiles*

Brydall, John. Non compos mentis / John Brydall. A treatise on the law of idiocy and lunacy / Anthony Highmore. — New York ; London : Garland, 1979. — 1v.(various pagings) ; 19cm. — (Classics of English legal history in the modern era)
Non compos mentis: facsim of: 1st ed. : London : Atkins, 1700 ; A treatise on the law of idiocy and lunacy: facsim of: 1st ed. : London : Butterworth, 1807
ISBN 0-8240-3095-8 : Unpriced B82-11015

344.204′44 — England. Mental health. Law. Great Britain. *Parliament. House of Lords.* **Mental Health (Amendment) Bill. Session 1981-82** — *Critical studies*

Gostin, Larry O.. The great debate : reform of the mental health legislation in England and Wales. — London (22 Harley St., W.1) : Mind, [1982]. — 1folded sheet([6]p) ; 29cm
Prepared by Larry O. Gostin
£0.15 B82-20936

344.204'44 — England. Mental health. Law. Reform — *Proposals*

Reform of mental health legislation / Department of Health and Social Security ... [et al.]. — London : H.M.S.O., [1981]. — 26p ; 25cm. — (Cmnd. ; 8405)
Cover title
ISBN 0-10-184050-0 (pbk) : £2.65 B82-11536

344.204'45 — England. Disposal of the dead. Law

Davies, M. R. Russell. The law of burial, cremation and exhumation / by M.R. Russell Davies. — 5th ed. / with a foreword by Lord Greenwood of Rossendale. — London : Shaw, 1982. — lii,244p ; 22cm
Previous ed.: 1974. — Includes index
ISBN 0-7219-0063-1 (pbk) : Unpriced
B82-38854

344.204'4632 — England. Environment. Pollution. Control. Legal aspects

Richardson, Genevra. Policing pollution. — Oxford : Clarendon, Dec.1982. — [224]p. — (Oxford socio-legal studies)
ISBN 0-19-827510-2 (cased) : £15.00 : CIP entry
ISBN 0-19-827512-9 (pbk) : £6.95 B82-31287

344.204'542 — England. Lotteries. Law

Finney, Jarlath. Gaming, lotteries, fundraising and the law. — London : Sweet and Maxwell, Nov.1982. — [220]p
ISBN 0-421-29980-0 (pbk) : £25.00 : CIP entry
Also classified at 344.204'317 B82-27530

344.204'63635 — England. Homeless persons. Housing. Provision. Responsibility of local authorities. Disputes between local authorities. Law — *Cases*

Housing (Homeless Persons) Act, 1977, digest of referees decisions / London Boroughs Association. — [London] : [The Association]
Addendum 1: Case nos.26-43, revised index. — 1982. — [20]p ; 30cm
Includes index
£0.75 (unbound) B82-39540

Housing (Homeless Persons) Act, 1977 referrals under section 5 : the local authority agreement and digest of referees' decisions for England and Wales / London Boroughs Association. — London : The Association, 1980. — 7,[33]p ; 32cm
ISBN 0-7168-1174-x (pbk) : Unpriced
B82-22452

344.204'63635 — England. Housing. Law

Cutting, Marion. A housing rights handbook / Marion Cutting. — Updated and expanded version. — Dorchester : Prism, 1979. — 385p : forms ; 21cm
Originally published: Harmondsworth : Penguin, 1979. — Includes index
ISBN 0-904727-92-0 : £7.50 B82-15226

Lomnicki, A. J.. Housing, tenancy and planning law made simple / A.J. Lomnicki. — London : Heinemann, 1981. — xiii,242p ; 23cm. — (Made simple books)
Includes index
ISBN 0-434-98481-7 (cased) : £5.95
ISBN 0-434-98487-6 (pbk) : £2.95
Also classified at 344.2064'344 ; 344.2064'5
B82-02506

344.204'63635 — England. Local authority housing. Law — *For tenants*

Hoath, David C.. Council housing / by David C. Hoath. — 2nd ed. — London : Sweet & Maxwell, 1982. — xxvii,223p ; 18cm. — (Modern legal studies)
Previous ed.: 1978. — Includes index
ISBN 0-421-27610-x (cased) : Unpriced : CIP rev.
ISBN 0-421-27620-7 (pbk) : £6.95 B82-10508

344.204'63635'0264 — England. Housing. Law. Cases — *Serials*

Housing law reports. — Vol.4. — London : Godwin, Nov.1982. — [128]p
ISBN 0-7114-5767-0 : £13.50 : CIP entry
B82-27968

344.204'63635'0264 — England. Housing. Law — *Cases* — *Serials*

Housing law reports. — Vol.1-. — Harlow : Godwin, [1982]-. — v. ; 24cm
Quarterly
ISSN 0263-7537 = Housing law reports : Unpriced B82-32139

344.204'7 — England. Education. Law

Taylor, George, *1900-*. The law of education : first supplement to eighth edition / by George Taylor and John B. Saunders. — London : Butterworths, 1980. — xi,A147p ; 25cm
ISBN 0-406-39642-6 (pbk) : £11.00
B82-18598

344.204'7 — England. Schools. Administration. Legal aspects

County and voluntary schools. — 6th ed., completely rev. / written by Kenneth Brooksbank ... [et al.] on behalf of the Society of Education Officers ; with a foreword by Lord Alexander of Potterhill. — [Harlow] : Councils and Education Press, c1982. — vii,197p : 1plan ; 23cm
Previous ed.: 1977. — Includes index
ISBN 0-900313-40-4 : £9.95 : CIP rev.
B82-10887

344.204'7 — England. Schools. Governing boards. Members: Teachers. Election & role. Law: Education Act 1980 — *Critical studies* — *For teachers*

Teacher governors : guidelines on the Education Act 1980 : new arrangements concerning school government ; election and role of teacher governors. — [London] : National Union of Teachers, [1982?]. — 30p ; 21cm
Cover title. — Text on inside cover. — Bibliography: p20-21
£0.50 (pbk) B82-24625

344.204'94 — England. Listed buildings. Law

Suddards, Roger W.. Listed buildings : the law and practice / by Roger W. Suddards ; with a foreword by Sir Desmond Heap. — London : Sweet & Maxwell, 1982. — xxxiii,343p : ill ; 23cm
Includes index
ISBN 0-421-27710-6 : £27.00 : CIP rev.
B82-10669

344.205 — England. Criminal law

Sweet & Maxwell's criminal law statutes. — London : Sweet and Maxwell, Sept.1982. — [120]p
ISBN 0-421-30300-x (cased) : £9.00 : CIP entry
ISBN 0-421-30310-7 (pbk) : £6.00 B82-21973

344.205'0243632 — England. Criminal law — *For police*

Baker, E. R.. Criminal law. — 6th ed. / by E.R. Baker and F.B. Dodge. — London : Butterworths, 1980. — x,250p ; 19cm. — (Police promotion handbooks ; 1)
Previous ed.: 1978. — Includes index
ISBN 0-406-84121-7 (pbk) : £4.50 B82-17498

344.205'0264 — England. Criminal law — *Cases*

Dobson, A. P.. Cases and statutes on criminal law. — 2nd ed. / by A.P. Dobson. — London : Sweet & Maxwell, 1981. — xix,146p ; 22cm. — (Concise college casenotes)
Previous ed.: / by John C.N. Slater. 1973. — Includes index
ISBN 0-421-24810-6 (pbk) : £6.50 : CIP rev.
B81-31708

Elliott, D. W.. Elliott and Wood's casebook in criminal law. — 4th ed. — London : Sweet and Maxwell, Oct.1982. — [720]p
Previous ed.: 1974
ISBN 0-421-27740-8 (cased) : £28.00 : CIP entry
ISBN 0-421-27750-5 (pbk) : £18.50
B82-24004

344.205'02648 — England. Criminal law — *Cases* — *Digests*

Bingham, Richard. The modern cases and statutes on crown court crime / by Richard Bingham. — Chichester : Rose, 1982
2nd cumulative supplement: containing cases and statutes as reported down to March 30, 1982. — [132]p ; 24cm
ISBN 0-85992-311-8 (pbk) : Unpriced
B82-31223

344.205'02648 — England. Criminal law. Cases in assize courts in Home Counties, *1558-1625* — *Digests*

Calendar of assize records / edited by J.S. Cockburn. — London : H.M.S.O.
Elizabeth I. — 1980. — vii,724p ; 26cm
Includes index
ISBN 0-11-440103-9 : £60.00 B82-19389

Calendar of assize records / edited by J.S. Cockburn. — London : H.M.S.O.
Essex indictments : James 1. — 1981. — vii,370p ; 26cm
Includes index
ISBN 0-11-440116-0 : £45.00 B82-34397

344.205'1 — England. Criminal courts. Procedure

Hampton, Celia. Criminal procedure / Celia Hampton. — 3rd ed. — London : Sweet & Maxwell, 1982. — lxi,472p ; 22cm
Previous ed.: 1977. — Includes index
ISBN 0-421-28660-1 (cased) : Unpriced : CIP rev.
ISBN 0-421-28670-9 (pbk) : £8.95 B82-01120

344.205'1 — England. Prosecuting solicitors' departments

The **Prosecution** system. — London : H.M.S.O., 1980. — v,104p : ill ; 25cm. — (Research studies ; no.11 and no.12)
At head of title: Royal Commission on Criminal Procedure. — Contents: Survey of prosecuting solicitors' departments / Mollie Weatheritt in collaboration with Joan MacNaughton — Organisational implications of change / David R. Kaye with the assistance of R.L. Redman and G.J. Brennand
ISBN 0-11-730130-2 (pbk) : £4.50 B82-16043

344.205'12 — England. Criminal law. Jurisdiction of magistrates' courts

Harris, Brian, *1932-*. The criminal jurisdiction of magistrates / by Brian Harris. — 8th ed. — Chichester : Rose
Previous ed.: published in 1 vol. 1979
Binding over. — 1982. — 10p ; 25cm
Includes index
ISBN 0-85992-315-0 (pbk) : £2.85 B82-30995

Harris, Brian, *1932-*. The criminal jurisdiction of magistrates / by Brian Harris. — 8th ed. — Chichester : Rose
Previous ed.: in 1v. 1979. — Also available in 1v
Common offences and disqualification. — 1982. — 98p ; 25cm
Includes index
ISBN 0-85992-301-0 (pbk) : £8.50 B82-22446

Harris, Brian, *1932-*. The criminal jurisdiction of magistrates / by Brian Harris. — 8th ed. — Chichester : Rose
Previous ed.: in 1v. 1979. — Also available in 1v
Magistrates and their courts. — 1982. — 29p ; 25cm
Includes index
ISBN 0-85992-300-2 (pbk) : £3.25 B82-22445

Harris, Brian, *1932-*. The criminal jurisdiction of magistrates / by Brian Harris. — 8th ed. — Chichester : Rose
Previous ed.: in 1v. 1979. — Also available in 1v.
Trial and sentencing. — [1982?]. — 57p ; 25cm
Includes index
Unpriced (pbk) B82-38956

344.205'12 — England. Magistrates' courts. Contested trials. Prosecution

Vennard, Julie. Contested trials in magistrates' courts : the case for the prosecution / Julie Vennard with the assistance of Karen Williams. — London : H.M.S.O., 1980. — vi,26p ; 25cm. — (Research study)
At head of title: Commission on Criminal Procedure. — Bibliography: p26
ISBN 0-11-730125-6 (pbk) : £2.40 B82-16048

344.205′12 — England. Magistrates′ courts — *Forms & precedents*
A **Handbook** of cautions, oaths and recognizances, etc. : for use in the Magistrates′ Courts. — 10th ed. / [compiled] by Wilfred Helme. — London : Shaw & Sons, c1981. — [34]p ; 14x21cm
Cover title. — Previous ed.: by Frank Shannon. 1979
ISBN 0-7219-0473-4 (spiral) : Unpriced
B82-17426

344.205′12 — England. Magistrates′ courts. Jurisdiction
Jones, Colin E.. An elementary introduction to the work of a magistrates′ court / by Colin E. Jones. — 3rd ed. — Chichester : Rose, c1982. — ix,27p ; 21cm
Previous ed.: 1974
ISBN 0-85992-303-7 (pbk) : £3.25 B82-41075

344.205′12 — England. Magistrates′ courts. Procedure
Moiser, C. H.. Practice and procedure in magistrates′ courts / by C.H. Moiser. — London : Fourmat, 1982. — xii,175p ; 22cm. — (Lawyers practice and procedure series)
Includes index
ISBN 0-906840-50-3 (pbk) : £8.95 B82-33435

344.205′14 — Great Britain. ***Crown Court.*** **Defendants. Confession**
Baldwin, John, *1945-*. Confessions in Crown Court trials / John Baldwin and Michael McConville. — London : H.M.S.O., 1980. — vii,39p : ill ; 25cm. — (Research study ; no.5)
At head of title: Royal Commission on Criminal Procedure. — Bibliography: p37-39
ISBN 0-11-730124-8 (pbk) : £3.00 B82-16046

344.205′2 — England. Conspiracy. Law, *to 1980.* **Political aspects**
Spicer, Robert. Conspiracy : law, class and society / Robert Spicer. — London : Lawrence and Wishart, 1981. — 190p ; 23cm
Bibliography: p178-184. — Includes index
ISBN 0-85315-548-8 : £7.50 B82-03058

344.205′231 — England. Treason. Trials, *1945-1960*
West, Rebecca. The meaning of treason / Rebecca West. — [New] ed. / with a new introduction by the author. — London : Virago, 1982. — xi,439p ; 20cm
Previous ed.: Harmondsworth : Penguin, 1965. — Includes index
ISBN 0-86068-256-0 (pbk) : £4.50 : CIP rev.
Also classified at 347.305′231 B81-40235

344.205234 — England. Contempt of court. Law
Arlidge, Anthony. The law of contempt. — London : Sweet & Maxwell, Nov.1982. — [440]p
ISBN 0-421-25920-5 : £30.00 : CIP entry
B82-28737

344.205′234 — London *(City).* **Perjury. Trials,** *1754* — *Cases*
Phillips, Pauline L.. ′Upon my word, I am no scholar′ / by Pauline L. Phillips. — [Edmonton] : [Edmonton Hundred Historical Society], 1982. — 12p : 1ill,1map,1plan ; 30cm. — (Occasional paper / Edmonton Hundred Historical Society ; no.44)
Conference paper
ISBN 0-902922-40-8 (pbk) : £0.70 B82-25338

344.205′243 — Shropshire. Shrewsbury. Building industries. Industrial relations. Picketing. Intimidation. Conspiracy. Trial of Shrewsbury Six, *1972*
Warren, Des. The key to my cell / by Des Warren. — London : New Park, 1982. — 319p : ill,facsims,ports ; 21cm
Includes index
ISBN 0-86151-022-4 (pbk) : £3.00 B82-31007

344.205′2523′0924 — London. Drummond, Edward. Murder. Trial of McNaughtan, Daniel
Moran, Richard. Knowing right from wrong : the insanity defense of Daniel McNaughtan / Richard Moran. — New York : Free Press ; London : Collier Macmillan, c1981. — xiii,234p : 1facsim,1port ; 25cm
Bibliography: p213-224. — Includes index
ISBN 0-02-921890-x : £9.95 B82-18011

344.205′2523′0924 — Suffolk. Peasenhall. Harsent, Rose. Murder. Trial of Gardiner, William
Packer, Edwin. The Peasenhall murder / Edwin Packer ; illustrated by Julie Ann Noad. — Yoxford : Yoxford Publications, 1980. — 54p : ill,1map,2ports ; 22cm
Bibliography: p54
ISBN 0-907265-01-4 (pbk) : £1.00 B82-19896

344.205′262 — England. Theft. Law. Theft Act 1968 & Theft Act 1978 — *Critical studies*
Griew, Edward. The Theft Acts 1968 and 1978 / by Edward Griew. — 4th ed. — London : Sweet & Maxwell, 1982. — xxix,240p ; 25cm
Previous ed.: 1978. — Includes index. — Includes the texts of The Theft Act 1968 and The Theft Act 1978
ISBN 0-421-28640-7 (cased) : Unpriced : CIP rev.
ISBN 0-421-28650-4 (pbk) : £9.50 B82-04056

344.205′274 — England. Obscenity. Law — *Inquiry reports*
Great Britain. *Committee on Obscenity and Film Censorship.* Obscenity and film censorship : an abridgement of the Williams report / edited by Bernard Williams. — Cambridge : Cambridge University Press, 1981. — x,166p ; 24cm
Full ed.: published as Report of the Committee on Obscenity and Film censorship. London : H.M.S.O., 1979
ISBN 0-521-24267-3 (cased) : £12.50 : CIP rev.
ISBN 0-521-28565-8 (pbk) : £4.95 B81-31240

344.205′5 — England. Criminal courts. Procedure
Archbold, John Frederick. Pleading, evidence, & practice in criminal cases. — 41st ed. — London : Sweet and Maxwell, Oct.1982. — [2500]p
Previous ed.: 1979
ISBN 0-421-27170-1 (cased) : £50.00 : CIP entry
ISBN 0-421-27330-5 (unbound) : £64.00
B82-24003

344.205′5 — England. Criminal law. Procedure. Reform — *Proposals*
National Council for Civil Liberties. Submission of the National Council for Civil Liberties to the Royal Commission on Criminal Procedure. — London : National Council for Civil Liberties, 1979. — 60p in various pagings ; 30cm
£3.00 (pbk) B82-07370

National Council for Civil Liberties. Submission of the National Council for Civil Liberties to the Royal Commission on Criminal Procedure. — London : National Council for Civil Liberties, 1979. — [62]p ; 30cm
£3.00 (unbound) B82-37769

344.205′5042 — England. Offenders. Non-police prosecution
Lidstone, K. W.. Prosecutions by private individuals and non-police agencies / K.W. Lidstone, Russell Hogg and Frank Sutcliffe in collaboration with A.E. Bottoms and Monica A. Walker. — London : H.M.S.O., 1980. — xi,236p ; 25cm. — (Research study ; no.10)
At head of title: Royal Commission on Criminal Procedure. — Bibliography: p201-203
ISBN 0-11-730129-9 (pbk) : £6.90 B82-16045

344.205′5042 — England. Offenders. Prosecution. Procedure
McConville, Michael. Courts, prosecution, and conviction / by Michael McConville and John Baldwin. — Oxford : Clarendon, 1981. — 232p : 2ill ; 23cm
Bibliography: p213-226. — Includes index
ISBN 0-19-825355-9 : £12.00 : CIP rev.
B81-13871

344.205′5042 — England. Offenders. Prosecution. Procedure — *Inquiry reports*
Great Britain. *Royal Commission on Criminal Procedure.* The investigation and prosecution of criminal offences in England and Wales : the law and procedure / the Royal Commission on Criminal Procedure ; Chairman: Sir Cyril Philips. — London : H.M.S.O., [1981]. — vii,229p ; 25cm. — (Cmnd. ; 8092-1)
ISBN 0-10-180921-2 (pbk) : £7.50
Primary classification 344.205′52 B82-16058

Great Britain. *Royal Commission on Criminal Procedure.* Report / the Royal Commission on Criminal Procedure ; chairman: Sir Cyril Philips. — London : H.M.S.O., [1981]. — xiii,240p ; 25cm. — (Cmnd. ; 8092)
Includes index
ISBN 0-10-180920-4 (pbk) : £7.50
Primary classification 344.205′52 B82-16057

344.205′5044 — England. Criminal courts. Cases. Defence — *For solicitors*
Morton, James. Defending : the solicitor′s practical guide / by James Morton. — London : Beattie, 1981. — x,85p ; 22cm
ISBN 0-907591-01-9 (pbk) : Unpriced
B82-17162

344.205′52 — England. Criminal investigation. Law — *Inquiry reports*
Great Britain. *Royal Commission on Criminal Procedure.* The investigation and prosecution of criminal offences in England and Wales : the law and procedure / the Royal Commission on Criminal Procedure ; Chairman: Sir Cyril Philips. — London : H.M.S.O., [1981]. — vii,229p ; 25cm. — (Cmnd. ; 8092-1)
ISBN 0-10-180921-2 (pbk) : £7.50
Also classified at 344.205′5042 B82-16058

Great Britain. *Royal Commission on Criminal Procedure.* Report / the Royal Commission on Criminal Procedure ; chairman: Sir Cyril Philips. — London : H.M.S.O., [1981]. — xiii,240p ; 25cm. — (Cmnd. ; 8092)
Includes index
ISBN 0-10-180920-4 (pbk) : £7.50
Also classified at 344.205′5042 B82-16057

344.205′56 — England. Suspects. Rights — *Bengali texts*
Puliśa o āpanāra adhikāra = Your rights and the police : Bengali. — [London] ([186 Kings Cross Rd., WC1X 9DE]) : Cobden Trust and National Council for Civil Liberties, [1982?]. — [30]p ; 22cm
Cover title. — Bengali title transliterated
Unpriced (pbk) B82-32666

344.205′56 — England. Suspects. Rights — *Gujerati texts*
Āpanā hakka ane polīsa vishe mārgadarśikā = Your rights and the police : Gujerati. — [London] ([186 Kings Cross Rd., WC1X 9DE]) : Cobden Trust and National Council for Civil Liberties, [1982]. — [16]p ; 21cm
Cover title. — Gujerati title transliterated
Unpriced (pbk) B82-32667

344.205′56 — England. Suspects. Rights — *Hindi texts*
Apake adhikāra aura pulisa = Your rights and the police : Hindi. — [London] ([186 Kings Cross Rd., WC1X 9DE]) : Cobden Trust and National Council for Liberties, [1982?]. — 20p ; 22cm
Cover title. — Hindi title transliterated
Unpriced (pbk) B82-32668

344.205′56 — England. Suspects. Rights — *Punjabi texts*
Pulisa ate tuhāde hakka = Your rights and the police : Punjabi. — [London] ([186 Kings Cross Rd., WC1X 9DE]) : Cobden Trust and National Council for Civil Liberties, [1982?]. — 17p ; 21cm
Cover title. — Punjabi title transliterated. — Text on inside cover
Unpriced (pbk) B82-32669

344.205′6 — England. Criminal law. Cases. Proof — *For police*
Calligan, Stewart. Points to prove / Stewart Calligan. — London : Police Review, c1981. — xvii,184p ; 14cm
ISBN 0-85164-991-2 (pbk) : Unpriced
B82-05237

344.205′6′0243632 — England. Criminal courts. Evidence. Law — *For police*
Baker, E. R.. Criminal evidence and procedure / by E.R. Baker and F.B. Dodge. — 7th ed. — London : Butterworths, 1981. — xii,228p : ill ; 19cm. — (Police promotion handbooks ; 2)
Previous ed.: 1979. — Includes index
ISBN 0-406-84131-4 (pbk) : Unpriced
B82-09799

344.205'6'02632 — England. Criminal courts. Evidence — *Statutes — Collections*

Carter, P. B. (Peter Basil). Cases and statutes on evidence : being based upon Cockle's cases and statutes on evidence / by P.B. Carter. — London : Sweet & Maxwell, 1981. — lviii,864p ; 26cm
Includes index
ISBN 0-421-20320-x (cased) : £28.00 : CIP rev.
ISBN 0-421-20330-7 (pbk) : £15.00
Primary classification 344.205'6'0264
B81-28821

344.205'6'0264 — England. Criminal courts. Evidence. Law — *Cases*

Carter, P. B. (Peter Basil). Cases and statutes on evidence : being based upon Cockle's cases and statutes on evidence / by P.B. Carter. — London : Sweet & Maxwell, 1981. — lviii,864p ; 26cm
Includes index
ISBN 0-421-20320-x (cased) : £28.00 : CIP rev.
ISBN 0-421-20330-7 (pbk) : £15.00
Also classified at 344.205'6'02632 B81-28821

344.205'72 — England. Criminal law. Charges. Use *compared with* **use of summonses**

Gemmill, R. Arrest, charge and summons : current practice and resource implications / R. Gemmill and R.F. Morgan-Giles. — London : H.M.S.O., 1980. — ix,70p : ill,2forms ; 25cm. — (Research study ; no.9)
At head of title: Royal Commission on Criminal Procedure
ISBN 0-11-730128-0 (pbk) : £3.90 B82-16047

344.205'75 — England. Criminal courts. Juries. Rights & duties — *Manuals*

Robertson, Geoffrey. The people's court. — London : Quartet Books, May 1982. — 1v.
ISBN 0-7043-2328-1 : £8.95 : CIP entry
B82-13496

344.205'77 — England. Criminal courts. Social inquiry reports

Shaw, Roger. Who uses social inquiry reports? : a study of the social inquiry reports outside the courts and their influence upon decisions / Roger Shaw. — [Cambridge] ([7 West Rd., Cambridge, CB3 9DT]) : [Institute of Criminology], [1981]. — 61p : 2forms ; 22cm. — (Occasional papers / University of Cambridge. Institute of Criminology ; no.7)
Bibliography: p59-61
Unpriced (pbk) B82-31150

344.205'772 — England. Criminal courts. Sentencing

Thomas, D. A. Current sentencing practice / David Thomas. — London : Sweet & Maxwell, 1982. — 1v.(loose-leaf) ; 25cm
Includes index
ISBN 0-421-25740-7 : £65.00 B82-37229

344.205'772 — England. Criminal courts. Sentencing — *Conference proceedings*

The **Future** of sentencing. — [Cambridge] : University of Cambridge, Institute of Criminology, 1982. — 82p ; 21cm. — (Occasional paper ; no.8)
Conference papers
Unpriced (pbk) B82-40980

344.205'773 — England. Imprisonment. Law — *Statutes*

Great Britain. [Imprisonment (Temporary Provisions) Act 1980]. Imprisonment (Temporary Provisions) Act 1980 : chapter 57. — London : H.M.S.O., [1980]. — 7p ; 25cm
Cover title
ISBN 0-10-545780-9 (pbk) : £1.40 B82-09255

344.205'8 — England. Juvenile courts. Procedure

Pain, Kenneth W. Practice and procedure in juvenile courts / by Kenneth W. Pain. — London : Fourmat, 1982. — xiii,149p : forms ; 22cm. — (Lawyers practice and procedure series)
Includes index
ISBN 0-906840-49-x (pbk) : £7.95 B82-33430

344.205'8 — London. Young offenders. Prosecution & cautions by Metropolitan Police

Oliver, Ian Thomas. The Metropolitan Police approach to the prosecution of juvenile offenders / Ian Thomas Oliver. — London : Peel, 1978. — ix,169p ; 22cm
Bibliography: p165-166
ISBN 0-85164-980-7 (pbk) : Unpriced
B82-05136

344.205'87 — England. Young offenders. Punishment. Law. Reform — *Proposals*

Great Britain. *Home Office.* Young offenders / Home Office, Welsh Office, Department of Health and Social Security. — London : H.M.S.O., [1980]. — 17p ; 25cm. — (Cmnd. ; 8045)
ISBN 0-10-180450-4 (unbound) : £1.70
B82-14715

344.206'04 — England. Law. Equity

Hanbury, Harold Greville. Modern equity / by Harold Greville Hanbury. — 11th ed. / by Ronald Harling Maudsley and Jill E. Martin. — London : Stevens, 1981. — cvi,796p ; 25cm
Previous ed.: 1976. — Includes index
ISBN 0-420-46130-2 (cased) : £27.50 : CIP rev.
ISBN 0-420-46140-x (pbk) : £16.50
B81-25315

Snell, Edmund Henry Turner. Snell's Principles of equity. — 28th ed. / by P.V. Baker and P.St.J. Langan. — London : Sweet & Maxwell, 1982. — clv,703p ; 25cm
Previous ed.: 1973. — Includes index
ISBN 0-421-25020-8 : Unpriced : CIP rev.
B82-06768

344.2061'5 — England. Families. Law

Bromley, P. M. Family law / P.M. Bromley. — 6th ed. — London : Butterworths, 1981. — xlix,703p ; 26cm
Previous ed.: 1976. — Includes index
ISBN 0-406-56010-2 (cased) : Unpriced
ISBN 0-406-56011-0 (pbkUnpriced)
B82-01009

Cretney, S. M. Family law / Stephen Cretney. — London : Teach Yourself Books, 1982. — vi,196p ; 20cm
Bibliography: p191-192. — Includes index
ISBN 0-340-26823-9 (pbk) : £2.50 : CIP rev.
B82-03811

Grant, Brian, *1917-*. Family law. — 4th ed. — London : Sweet & Maxwell, Oct.1982. — [160] p. — (Concise college texts)
Previous ed.: 1977
ISBN 0-421-30240-2 (cased) : £20.00 : CIP entry
ISBN 0-421-28280-0 (pbk) : £10.50
B82-25080

344.2061'5 — England. Families. Violence. Injunctions. Law: Domestic Violence and Matrimonial Proceedings Act 1976. Procedure — *For battered women*

Coote, Anna. Battered women and the new law / Anna Coote and Tess Gill ; foreword Jo Richardson ; drawings Jo Nesbitt. — Rev. and extended ed. — London : Inter-Action Inprint, 1979. — 40p : ill,1form ; 21cm. — (Inter-Action guide ; 1)
Previous ed.: 1977. — Bibliography: p37-40
ISBN 0-904571-19-x (pbk) : £0.85 B82-11564

344.2061'5'02632 — England. Families. Law — *Statutes — Collections*

Sweet & Maxwell's family law statutes. — 3rd ed / advisory editor Olive M. Stone, assistant editor Jenny Bough. — London : Sweet & Maxwell, 1981. — xiii,549p ; 25cm
Previous ed.: 1976. — Includes index
ISBN 0-421-28080-8 (cased) : £15.50 : CIP rev.
ISBN 0-421-28090-5 (pbk) : £12.65
B81-16405

344.2061'6 — England. Cohabiting persons. Law

Dyer, Clare. Living together / Clare Dyer and Marcel Berlins. — London : Hamlyn Paperbacks, 1982. — 208p ; 18cm
Includes index
ISBN 0-600-20450-2 (pbk) : £1.50 B82-07931

344.2061'6 — England. Cohabiting persons. Law — *For women*

The **Cohabitation** handbook : a women's guide to the law / Anne Bottomley ... [et al.]. — London : Pluto, 1981. — 236p ; 20cm
Includes index
ISBN 0-86104-329-4 (pbk) : £3.95 B82-20692

344.2061'66 — England. Divorce. Financial aspects. Law. Reform — *Proposals*

Great Britain. *Law Commission.* Family law : the financial consequences of divorce : the basic policy : a discussion paper / the Law Commission. — London : H.M.S.O., [1980]. — 57p : ill ; 25cm. — (Law Com. ; no.103)
ISBN 0-10-180410-5 (pbk) : £3.70 B82-14714

344.2061'66 — England. Divorce. Financial settlements & maintenance orders. Law. Reform. Great Britain. *Law Commission.* **Financial consequences of divorce** — *Critical studies*

Great Britain. *Law Commission.* The financial consequences of divorce : the response to the Law Commission's discussion paper, and recommendations on the policy of the law / The Law Commission. — London : H.M.S.O., [1981]. — iii,23p ; 25cm. — (Family law) (Law Com. ; no.112) ([HC] ; 68)
ISBN 0-10-206882-8 (unbound) : £2.80
B82-12500

344.2061'66 — England. Divorce. Law

Griffiths, L. R. H. Divorce 1982 / L.R.H. Griffiths. — [Guildford] ([Braboeuf Manor, St. Catherines, Guildford, Surrey, GU3 1HA]) : [The College of Law], [1982]. — 19p ; 22cm. — (Crash course lecture / The College of Law, ISSN 0309-2771 ; 1982)
Cover title
£1.50 (pbk) B82-40231

Rayden, William. Rayden's law and practice in divorce and family matters in the High Court, County Courts and Magistrates' Courts. — 13th ed. / editor in chief Joseph Jackson ; editors ... [others]. — London : Butterworths
Cover title: Rayden on divorce
2nd cumulative supplement. — 1981. — xxvii,B642p : forms ; 25cm
ISBN 0-406-35169-4 (pbk) : Unpriced
B82-02572

344.2061'66 — England. Foreign divorce. Financial settlements & maintenance orders. Law. Reform — *Proposals*

Great Britain. *Law Commission.* Family law : financial relief after foreign divorce / the Law Commission. — London : H.M.S.O., 1980. — v,83p ; 21cm. — (Working paper ; no.77)
ISBN 0-11-730157-4 (pbk) : £4.20 B82-14644

344.2061'66 — England. Matrimonial causes. Law

Chiswell, P. G. Marriage breakdown / by P.G. Chiswell. — [London] ([27 Chancery La., W.C.2.]) : College of Law, c1980. — 16p ; 22cm. — (College of Law refresher lecture, ISSN 0140-9735 ; 1979)
£1.20 (pbk) B82-16399

344.2061'66'0269 — England. Matrimonal causes. Law. Cases. Costs — *Tables*

Biggs, A. K. Fees in matrimonial proceedings / [by A.K. Biggs]. — London (25 Bedford Row, WC1R 4HE) : Fourmat, c1980. — 1folded sheet ; 30x32cm folded to 30x11cm. — (Lawyers cost & fees series ; 9)
£1.40 B82-05859

344.2061'66'0269 — England. Matrimonial causes. Law. Cases. Costs — *Tables — Serials*

Costs in matrimonial causes. — June 1979-. — London : Fourmat, 1979-. — v. ; 30cm. — (Lawyers costs & fees series ; 2)
Irregular
ISSN 0262-6128 = Costs in matrimonial causes : £1.10 B82-06813

344.2061'66'0269 — England. Matrimonial causes. Procedure of county courts & Great Britain. *High Court of Justice. Family Division*

Biggs, A. K. Matrimonial proceedings / by A.K. Biggs. — London : Fourmat, 1980. — xi,99p ; 22cm. — (Lawyers practice and procedure series)
Includes index
ISBN 0-906840-20-1 (pbk) : £5.95 B82-06625

344.2061′66′0269 — England. Matrimonial causes. Procedure of county courts & Great Britain. *High Court of Justice. Family Division* *continuation*

Humphreys, Thomas S.. Humphreys′ notes on matrimonial causes proceeding in county courts and district registries. — 15th ed. / Hugh C. Collins. — London : Oyez, 1981. — xi,246p ; 22cm. — (Oyez practitioner series. Practice and procedure)
Previous ed.: 1979. — Includes index
ISBN 0-85120-604-2 (pbk) : Unpriced
B82-11021

344.2061′66′0269 — England. Matrimonial causes. Procedure of magistrates′ courts

Strachan, Billy. Matrimonial proceedings in magistrates courts : the Domestic Proceedings and Magistrates′ Court Act 1978 / Billy Strachan ; with a foreword by Lord McGregor of Durris. — London : Sweet & Maxwell, 1982. — xxvii,169p ; 22cm
Includes index
ISBN 0-421-28970-8 (pbk) : £10.75 : CIP rev.
B81-31539

344.2061′66′0924 — England. Divorce. Law — *Personal observations*

Grant, Brian, *1917-*. Conciliation & divorce : a father′s letters to his daughter / Brian Grant. — Chichester : Barry Rose, c1981. — 48p ; 23cm
ISBN 0-85992-306-1 (pbk) : £3.85 B82-03482

344.2061′78 — England. Step-children. Adoption. Law

Step-children and adoption : information for parents and step-parents following divorce. — London (11 Southwark St, SE1 1RQ) : British Agencies for Adoption and Fostering, 1980. — 1folded sheet([5]p) ; 21cm
Originally published: London : ABAFA, 1977
Unpriced B82-37716

344.2061′78′02632 — England. Children. Adoption. Law — *Statutes — Collections*

Great Britain. [Laws, etc.]. Adoption ′82 : the Association of Directors of Social Services guide to personal social services legislation / [edited by] Alan S. Holden. — Durham : Comyn, 1982. — xiv,82p : forms ; 21cm
ISBN 0-907267-02-5 (pbk) : £3.25 B82-38361

344.2061′8 — England. Wards of court. Law

Levy, Allan. Wardship proceedings / Allan Levy. — London : Oyez Longman, c1982. — xvi,122p : forms ; 22cm. — (Oyez Longman practice notes ; 21)
Includes index
ISBN 0-85120-636-0 (pbk) : Unpriced
B82-29723

344.2062 — England. Contracts. Law

Cheshire, G. C.. Cheshire and Fifoot′s law of contract. — 10th ed. / M.P. Furmston ; historical introduction A.W.B. Simpson. — London : Butterworths, 1981. — xliv,636p ; 26cm
Previous ed.: 1976. — Includes index
ISBN 0-406-56531-7 (cased) : Unpriced
ISBN 0-406-56532-5 (pbk) : Unpriced
B82-02202

Davies, F. R.. Contract / by F.R. Davies. — 4th ed. — London : Sweet & Maxwell, 1981. — xxii,213p ; 23cm. — (Concise college texts)
Previous ed.: 1977. — Includes index
ISBN 0-421-27550-2 (cased) : Unpriced : CIP rev.
ISBN 0-421-27560-x (pbk) : £3.95 B81-09964

344.2062′0264 — England. Contracts. Law — *Cases*

Smith, J. C.. A casebook on contract / by J.C. Smith and the late J.A.C. Thomas. — 7th ed. — London : Sweet & Maxwell, 1982. — xxxi,604p ; 24cm
Previous ed.: 1977. — Includes index
ISBN 0-421-28320-3 (cased) : Unpriced : CIP rev.
ISBN 0-421-28330-0 (pbk) : £12.95
B82-03105

344.206′2′076 — England. Contracts. Law — *Questions & answers*

Leal, A. R.. Objective tests in contract law / A.R. Leal, N. Coleman. — London : Longman, 1980. — 98p ; 20cm. — (Longman objective tests series)
ISBN 0-582-41572-1 (pbk) : £1.95 : CIP rev.
B80-05833

344.206′22 — England. Contracts. Exemption clauses. Law

Yates, David. Exclusion clauses in contracts. — 2nd ed. — London : Sweet and Maxwell, Sept.1982. — [350]p. — (Modern legal studies)
Previous ed.: 1978
ISBN 0-421-28680-6 (cased) : £9.50 : CIP entry
ISBN 0-421-28690-3 (pbk) : £7.00 B82-22422

344.2063 — England. Torts. Law

Clerk, John Frederic. Clerk & Lindsell on torts. — 15th ed. / [general editor R.W.M. Dias]. — London : Sweet & Maxwell, 1982. — cclxiv,1417p ; 26cm. — (The Common law library ; no.3)
Previous ed.: / general editors Sir Arthur L. Armitage and R.W.M. Dias. 1975. — Includes index
ISBN 0-421-26250-8 : £65.00 : CIP rev.
B81-39252

Salmond, *Sir* **John**. Salmond and Heuston on the law of torts. — 18th ed. / by R.F.V. Heuston and R.S. Chambers. — London : Sweet & Maxwell, 1981. — ci,588p ; 24cm
Previous ed.: 1977. — Includes index
ISBN 0-421-28700-4 (cased) : £19.00 : CIP rev.
ISBN 0-421-28710-1 (pbk) : £14.50
B81-31171

344.2063′076 — England. Torts. Law — *Questions & answers*

Leal, A. R.. Objective tests in tort / A.R. Leal, N. Coleman. — London : Longman, 1981. — 91p ; 20cm. — (Longman objective tests series)
ISBN 0-582-41187-4 (pbk) : £1.95 B82-02899

344.2063′2 — England. Professional personnel. Negligence. Law

Dugdale, A. M.. Professional negligence / A.M. Dugdale, K.M. Stanton. — London : Butterworths, 1982. — xlii,400p ; 26cm
Includes index
ISBN 0-406-17910-7 : Unpriced B82-32748

Jackson, Rupert M.. Professional negligence / by Rupert M. Jackson and John L. Powell. — London : Sweet & Maxwell, 1982. — xxxvii,352p ; 25cm
Includes index
ISBN 0-421-26480-2 : £25.00 : CIP rev.
B82-12917

Underwood, Ashley. Professional negligence / by Ashley Underwood and Stephen Holt. — London : Fourmat, 1981. — xv,96p ; 23cm
Also available as pbk. ed. — Includes index
ISBN 0-906840-36-8 : £9.50 B82-06621

344.2063′22 — England. Accidents. Personal injuries. Damages. Claims. Law

Personal injury claims. — Guildford (Braboeuf Manor, St. Catherines, Guildford, Surrey GU3 1HA) : College of Law, c1981. — vii,88p ; 22cm. — (College of Law lectures, ISSN 0309-3166)
£4.50 (pbk) B82-11339

344.2063′23 — England. Accident victims. Personal injuries. Damages. Claims. Law

Personal injury claims. — Guildford : College of Law, c1981. — vii,88p ; 22cm. — (College of Law lectures, ISSN 0309-3166)
£4.50 (pbk) B82-22003

344.2063′23 — England. Death. Damages. Rights of dependants. Law

Harmer, C. G.. Damages for personal injury and death / by Caroline Harmer. — [Guildford] ([Braboeuf Manor, St. Catherines, Guildford, Surrey]) : College of Law, c1980. — 16p ; 22cm. — (Crash course lecture / College of Law, ISSN 0309-2771 ; 1980)
£1.20 (pbk)
Primary classification 344.2063′23 B82-13784

344.2063′23 — England. Personal injuries. Damages. Law

Harmer, C. G.. Damages for personal injury and death / by Caroline Harmer. — [Guildford] ([Braboeuf Manor, St. Catherines, Guildford, Surrey]) : College of Law, c1980. — 16p ; 22cm. — (Crash course lecture / College of Law, ISSN 0309-2771 ; 1980)
£1.20 (pbk)
Also classified at 344.2063′23 B82-13784

344.2063′23 — England. Personal injuries. Damages. Limitations of actions. Law

Todd, Stephen. Limitation periods in personal injury claims / by Stephen Todd. — London : Sweet & Maxwell, 1982. — xxii,131p ; 23cm
Includes index
ISBN 0-421-28590-7 : £13.00 : CIP rev.
B82-11762

344.2063′23′0269 — England. Accidents. Personal injuries. Damages. Claims. Law. Procedure

Goldrein, Ian S.. Key to personal injury practice and compensation / Ian S. Goldrein, Margaret R. de Haas. — London : Oyez, c1981. — 25p ; 20x11cm
ISBN 0-85120-615-8 (pbk) : Unpriced
B82-04100

344.2063′3 — England. Confidential information. Misuse. Law. Reform — *Proposals*

Great Britain. *Law Commission*. Breach of confidence : report on a reference under section 3(1)(e) of the Law Commissions Act 1965. — London : H.M.S.O., [1981]. — 239p ; 25cm. — (Cmnd. ; 8388) (Law Com. ; no.110)
ISBN 0-10-183880-8 (unbound) : £8.35
B82-05871

344.2063′4 — England. Defamation. Law

Gatley, John Clement Carpenter. Gatley on libel and slander. — 8th ed. / by Philip Lewis ; consulting editor J.E. Previte ; precedents editor R.W. Ground ; indexer M.G. Bloch. — London : Sweet & Maxwell, 1981. — cxxxvii,751p ; 26cm. — (The Common law library ; no.8)
Previous ed.: 1979. — Includes index
ISBN 0-421-24340-6 : £60.00 : CIP rev.
B81-31173

344.2063′4 — England. Defamation. Law. Cases, *1550-1730.* **Social aspects —** *Sources of data: Church of England. Province of York. Ecclesiastical courts*

Sharpe, J. A.. Defamation and sexual slander in early modern England : the church courts at York / by J.A. Sharpe. — York (St Anthony′s Hall, Peasholme Green, York Y01 2PW) : University of York, Borthwick Institute of Historical Research, [1980?]. — 36p ; 21cm. — (Borthwick papers ; no.58)
£1.00 (pbk) B82-17504

344.2063′6 — England. Buildings. Defects. Cilvil liability. Law

Holyoak, J. H.. Civil liability for defective premises / J.H. Holyoak, David K. Allen. — London : Butterworths, 1982. — xxvii,278p ; 26cm
Includes index
ISBN 0-406-23340-3 : Unpriced B82-31637

344.206′36 — England. Buildings. Defects. Liability. Law

Speaight, Anthony. The law of defective premises. — London : Pitman, July 1982. — [219]p
ISBN 0-273-01770-5 : £15.00 : CIP entry
B82-12271

344.2063′6 — England. Buildings. Design & construction. Negligence. Law

Cornes, David L.. Design liability in the construction industry. — London : Granada, Nov.1982. — [208]p
ISBN 0-246-11865-2 : £15.00 : CIP entry
B82-28727

344.2063′6 — England. Nuisances. Law

Buckley, R. A.. The law of nuisance / R.A. Buckley. — London : Butterworths, 1981. — xxxv,181p ; 26cm
Includes index
ISBN 0-406-14110-x : Unpriced B82-12036

344.2063'6 — England. Nuisances. Law *continuation*

Macrory, Richard. Nuisance / Richard Macrory. — London : Oyez Longman, c1982. — xiv,114p ; 22cm. — (Oyez Longman practice notes)
Includes index
ISBN 0-85120-624-7 (pbk) : Unpriced
B82-20811

344.2063'8 — England. Strict liability. Legal aspects

Leigh, L. H.. Strict and vicarious liability. — London : Sweet & Maxwell, Dec.1982. — [100] p. — (Modern legal studies)
ISBN 0-421-26760-7 (cased) : £11.95 : CIP entry
ISBN 0-421-26770-4 (pbk) : £6.95 B82-29765

344.2064 — England. Matrimonial homes. Law

Marriage breakdown and the matrimonial home. — Guildford (Braboeuf Manor, St. Catherines, Guildford, Surrey GU3 1HA) : The College of Law, [1982]. — 90p ; 22cm. — (College of Law lectures, ISSN 0309-3166)
£4.50 (pbk) B82-40242

344.2064'02632 — England. Property. Law — *Statutes — Collections*

[Property acts]. Sweet & Maxwell's property statutes. — 4th ed. — London : Sweet and Maxwell, Oct.1982. — [540]p
Previous ed.: 1977
ISBN 0-421-28810-8 (cased) : £20.00 : CIP entry
ISBN 0-421-28820-5 (pbk) : £12.25
B82-24005

344.2064'0264 — England. Matrimonial property. Apportionment on divorce. Law — *Cases*

Rakusen, Michael L.. Distribution of matrimonial assets on divorce / Michael L. Rakusen, D. Peter Hunt. — 2nd ed. — London : Butterworths, 1982. — xxii,375p ; 26cm
Previous ed.: 1979. — Includes index
ISBN 0-406-35101-5 : Unpriced B82-22266

344.2064'3 — England. Flats. Law

Aldridge, Trevor M.. The law of flats / Trevor M. Aldridge. — London : Oyez Longman, c1982. — xxii,208p ; 24cm. — (Oyez Longman practitioner series. Property and conveyancing)
Includes index
ISBN 0-85120-625-5 (pbk) : Unpriced
B82-27073

344.2064'3 — England. Leasehold real property. Law

Aldridge, Trevor M.. Leasehold law / Trevor M. Aldridge. — [London] : Oyez, c1980. — 3v.(loose-leaf) ; 26cm
Includes index
ISBN 0-85120-471-6 : Unpriced
ISBN 0-85120-494-5 (v.1) : Unpriced
ISBN 0-85120-495-3 (v.2) : Unpriced
ISBN 0-85120-496-1 (v.3) : Unpriced
B82-22472

344.2064'3 — England. Neighbouring land. Access. Rights of landowners. Law — *Proposals*

Great Britain. *Law Commission*. Rights of access to neighbouring land / the Law Commission. — London : H.M.S.O., 1980. — v,70p ; 21cm. — (Working paper ; no.78)
ISBN 0-11-730158-2 (pbk) : £3.90 B82-14645

344.2064'3 — England. Real property. Law

Curzon, L. B.. Land law / L.B. Curzon. — 4th ed. — Plymouth : Macdonald and Evans, 1982. — xxviii,292p : ill,1form ; 18cm. — (The M & E handbook series)
Previous ed.: 1979. — Bibliography: p277-278. — Includes index
ISBN 0-7121-1259-6 (pbk) : £4.75 B82-33762

Harwood, Michael. Modern English land law. — 2nd ed. — London : Sweet & Maxwell, Aug.1982. — [500]p
Previous ed. published as: English land law. 1975
ISBN 0-421-27890-0 (cased) : £22.00 : CIP entry
ISBN 0-421-27900-1 (pbk) : £16.25
B82-15791

Lawson, F. H.. The law of property. — 2nd ed. — Oxford : Clarendon Press, Sept.1982. — [200]p. — (Clarendon law series)
Previous ed. published as: Introduction to the law of property. 1958
ISBN 0-19-876128-7 (cased) : £15.00 : CIP entry
ISBN 0-19-876129-5 (pbk) : £6.95 B82-18969

Megarry, *Sir* Robert. Megarry's manual of the law of real property. — 6th ed. — London : Stevens, Aug.1982. — [600]p
Previous ed.: 1975
ISBN 0-420-46330-5 (cased) : £19.50 : CIP entry
ISBN 0-420-46340-2 (pbk) : £11.50
B82-21757

344.2064'3 — England. Residences. Law

Aldridge, Trevor M.. Questions of law : homes : buying, selling, owning, renting / Trevor M. Aldridge. — [Feltham] : Hamlyn Paperbacks, 1982. — 208p ; 18cm
Bibliography: p203-204. — Includes index
ISBN 0-600-20552-5 (pbk) : £1.50 B82-30544

344.2064'32 — England. Land. Boundaries. Law

Aldridge, Trevor M.. Boundaries, walls and fences / Trevor M. Aldridge. — 5th ed. — London : Oyez Longman, 1982. — vii,75p ; 22cm
Previous ed: 1978. — Includes index
ISBN 0-85120-664-6 (pbk) : Unpriced
B82-34656

344.2064'32 — England. Privately rented residences. Maintenance & repair. Liability of landlords. Enforcement by tenants — *Manuals*

Your rights to repairs : a guide for private and housing association tenants. — London (189a Old Brompton Rd., SW5) : SHAC, c1981. — 32p ; 21cm
Unpriced (pbk) B82-01651

344.2064'32 — England. Real property. Reversion. Law. Reform — *Proposals*

Great Britain. *Law Commission*. Property law : rights of reverter : report on a reference under section 3(1) (e) of the Law Commissions Act 1965 / the Law Commission. — London : H.M.S.O., [1981]. — vi,52p ; 25cm. — (Law Com. ; no.111) (Cmnd. ; 8410)
ISBN 0-10-184100-0 (pbk) : £4.00 B82-11538

344.2064'32 — England. Rented residences. Tenants. Eviction. Law — *For tenants*

Private tenants : protection from eviction. — New and rev. ed. — London (189a Old Brompton Rd., SW5) : SHAC, c1981. — 23p ; 21cm
Previous ed.: 1978
Unpriced (pbk) B82-01654

344.2064'34 — England. Freehold real property. Restrictive covenants. Law

Preston, Cecil Herbert Sansome. Preston and Newsom's restrictive covenants affecting freehold land. — 7th ed. — London : Sweet & Maxwell, Dec.1982. — [350]p
Previous ed.: 1976
ISBN 0-421-28490-0 : £32.00 : CIP entry
B82-29766

344.2064'34 — England. Tenancies. Law

Donell, R. A.. Landlord and tenant up-to-date / R.A. Donell. — [Guildford] ([Braboeuf Manor, St. Catherines, Guildford, Surrey, GU3 1HA]) : [The College of Law], [1982]. — 20p ; 22cm. — (Crash course lecture / The College of Law, ISSN 0309-2771 ; 1982)
Cover title
£1.50 (pbk) B82-40234

Hill, H. A.. Hill and Redman's law of landlord and tenant. — 17th ed. / general editor Michael Barnes ; specialist editors Joseph Harper ... [et al.]. — London : Butterworth, 1982. — 2v.(xiii,2933,202p) : forms ; 26cm
Previous ed.: 1976. — Includes index
ISBN 0-406-22711-x (cased) : Unpriced
ISBN 0-406-22712-8 (v.1)
ISBN 0-406-22713-6 (v.2) B82-25461

344.2064'34'0269 — England. Rented residences. Tenancy agreements. Law — *Forms & precedents*

New tenancy agreements : a model for landlords and tenants based on the Housing Act 1980. — London : National Consumer Council, 1981. — 23p ; 21cm
Cover title
ISBN 0-905653-37-8 (pbk) : Unpriced
B82-08169

344.2064'344 — England. Premises. Rents. Reviews. Law

Bernstein, Ronald. Handbook of rent review / Ronald Bernstein and Kirk Reynolds ; consultant editor on valuation and arbitration practice J.C. Hill. — London : Sweet & Maxwell in collaboration with the Royal Institution of Chartered Surveyors, 1981. — 1v.(loose-leaf) ; 32cm
Includes index
ISBN 0-421-27980-x : Unpriced B82-02819

344.2064'344 — England. Premises. Rents. Reviews. Law — *Cases — Serials*

Rent review. — Vol.1, pt.1 (July 1981)-. — London (88 Baker St., W1) : Henry Stewart Publications, 1981-. — v. ; 22cm
Quarterly
ISSN 0260-907x = Rent review : £40.00 per year B82-17239

344.2064'344 — England. Rented residences. Tenancies. Law

Butterworths landlord and tenant handbook / edited by LEXIS editorial staff ; consulting editor David Lloyd Evans. — London : Butterworths, 1982. — vii,793,9p ; 25cm
Includes index
ISBN 0-406-25370-6 (pbk) : Unpriced
B82-34366

Lomnicki, A. J.. Housing, tenancy and planning law made simple / A.J. Lomnicki. — London : Heinemann, 1981. — xiii,242p ; 23cm. — (Made simple books)
Includes index
ISBN 0-434-98481-7 (cased) : £5.95
ISBN 0-434-98487-6 (pbk) : £2.95
Primary classification 344.204'63635
B82-02506

Male, J. M.. Landlord and tenant / J.M. Male. — Plymouth : Macdonald and Evans, 1982. — xviii,284p ; 19cm. — (M & E handbook series)
Includes index
ISBN 0-7121-1251-0 (pbk) : £3.95 B82-16248

Yates, David, *1946-*. Landlord and tenant law / David Yates and A.J. Hawkins. — London : Sweet & Maxwell, 1981. — lxxxi,622p ; 24cm
Includes index
ISBN 0-421-26210-9 (cased) : £26.00
ISBN 0-421-26220-6 (pbk) : £14.50
B82-03201

344.2064'344'02633 — England. Rented residences. Tenancies. Law — *Statutes — Texts with commentaries*

Farrand, J. T.. Rent acts and regulations amended and annotated. — 2nd ed. / by Julian T. Farrand and Andrew Arden. — London : Sweet & Maxwell, 1981. — xl,435p : forms ; 26cm
Previous ed.: published as The Rent Act 1977. The protection from Eviction Act 1977. 1978
ISBN 0-421-28220-7 : £16.50 : CIP rev.
B81-23769

344.2064'346 — West Midlands *(Metropolitan County)*. Birmingham. Saltley. Leasehold houses. Leases. Enfranchisement. Rights of leaseholders. Enforcement

Leasehold loopholes. — Oxford : Birmingham Community Development Project Research Team, 1978. — 36p : ill,facsims,maps ; 26cm. — (Birmingham Community Development Project final report ; 5)
ISBN 0-9505516-8-6 (pbk) : £1.25 B82-40529

344.2064'348 — England. Agricultural holdings. Law

Densham, H. A. C.. Scammell and Densham's Law of agricultural holdings : first supplement to sixth edition / H.A.C. Densham. — London : Butterworths, 1980. — x,49p ; 25cm
ISBN 0-406-36811-2 (pbk) : £3.50 B82-22740

344.2064′362 — England. Real property. Acquisition by Christian church. Law. Statutes, *1279-1500*

Raban, Sandra. Mortmain legislation and the English church 1279-1500 / Sandra Raban. — Cambridge : Cambridge University Press, 1982. — xiii,216p ; 23cm. — (Cambridge studies in medieval life and thought. 3rd series ; v.17)
Bibliography: p195-204. — Includes index
ISBN 0-521-24233-9 : £25.00 : CIP rev. B82-20202

344.2064′38 — England. Freehold real property. Conveyancing. Costs — *Tables* — *Serials*

Conveyancing. Fees and duties on sale of freehold. — [1st ed.]-. — London : Fourmat, 1979-. — v. ; 30cm. — (Lawyers costs & fees series ; 5)
Irregular
ISSN 0262-6152 = Conveyancing. Fees and duties on sale of freehold : £1.10 B82-06811

344.2064′38 — England. Freehold real property. Conveyancing — *Manuals*

Newman, Phyllis E.. Conveyancing of freehold property / by Phyllis E. Newman. — London : Fourmat, 1980. — xii,53p ; 22cm. — (Lawyers practice and procedure series)
Includes index
ISBN 0-906840-25-2 (pbk) : £3.95 B82-06622

344.2064′38 — England. Houses. Conveyancing — *Amateurs′ manuals*

Bradshaw, Joseph. Bradshaw′s DIY guide to changing home ownership into joint or intended heir′s names / Joseph Bradshaw. — Leamington Spa : Castle, c1982. — 22p ; 30cm
ISBN 0-9507170-2-9 (pbk) : £5.00 B82-27487

344.2064′38 — England. Leasehold real property. Conveyancing. Costs — *Tables* — *Serials*

Conveyancing. Fees and duties on dealings with leaseholds. — [1st ed.]-. — London : Fourmat, 1980-. — v. ; 30cm. — (Lawyers costs & fees series ; 6)
Irregular
ISSN 0262-6160 = Conveyancing. Fees and duties on dealings with leaseholds : £1.10 B82-06812

344.2064′38 — England. Leasehold real property. Conveyancing — *Manuals*

Newman, Phyllis E.. Conveyancing of leasehold property / by Phyllis E. Newman. — London : Fourmat, 1982. — xii,84p ; 22cm. — (Lawyers practice and procedure series)
Includes index
ISBN 0-906840-51-1 (pbk) : £5.95 B82-38920

344.2064′38 — England. Local land charges. Inquiries before contract. Standard forms — *Commentaries*

Aldridge, Trevor M.. Guide to enquiries of local authorities (1982 edition) : enquiries of District Councils: form Con 29A England and Wales (excluding London) : enquiries of local authorities: form 29D (London only) / Trevor M. Aldridge. — London : Oyez Longman, c1982. — 15p ; 26x11cm
ISBN 0-85120-645-x (pbk) : Unpriced B82-36348

344.2064′38 — England. Matrimonial homes. Conveyancing on divorce

Hartley, William M.. Matrimonial conveyancing : a draftsman′s handbook / William M. Hartley. — London : Oyez, c1981. — xiii,130p ; 24cm
Includes index
ISBN 0-85120-603-4 (pbk) : Unpriced B82-11020

344.2064′38 — England. Real property. Conveyancing — *Amateurs′ manuals* — *For sitting tenants of rented residences*

Bradshaw, Joseph. Bradshaw′s guide to conveyancing for sitting tenants / Joseph Bradshaw. — Leamington Spa : Castle, c1981. — 127p : 1map,forms ; 21cm
Includes index
ISBN 0-9507170-1-0 (pbk) : £2.50 B82-05016

344.2064′38 — England. Real property. Conveyancing. Law

Donell, R. A.. Gibson′s conveyancing : supplement to the twenty-first edition : the Housing Act 1980 / by R.A. Donell and J.A. Treleaven. — London : Law Notes Lending Library, 1982. — 36p ; 25cm
Includes index
£1.50 (pbk) B82-21283

Farrand, J. T.. Contract and conveyance / J.T. Farrand. — 3rd ed. — London : Oyez, 1980. — lxiii,340p ; 24cm
Previous ed.: 1973. — Includes index
ISBN 0-85120-439-2 (pbk) : Unpriced B82-18332

Holbrook, R. G.. Conveyancing 1982 / R.G. Holbrook. — [Guildford] ([Braboeuf Manor, St. Catherines, Guildford, Surrey, GU3 1HA]) : [The College of Law], [1982]. — 13p ; 22cm. — (Crash course lecture / The College of Law, ISSN 0309-2771 ; 1982)
Cover title
£1.50 (pbk) B82-40237

Moeran, Edward. Practical conveyancing : a system of working for solicitors / Edward Moeran. — 8th ed. — London : Oyez, 1981. — xii,244p ; 22cm. — (Oyez practice notes ; 44)
Previous ed.: 1979. — Includes index
ISBN 0-85120-591-7 (pbk) : Unpriced B82-03050

344.206′438 — England. Real property. Conveyancing — *Manuals*

Ruoff, Theodore B. F.. Concise land registration practice. — 3rd ed. — London : Sweet & Maxwell, Dec.1982. — [290]p
Previous ed.: 1967
ISBN 0-421-28770-5 : £21.00 : CIP entry B82-30832

344.2064′38 — England. Real property. Title. Registration. Procedure

Wontner, John Joseph. Wontner′s guide to land registry practice. — 14th ed. / P.J. Timothy. — London : Oyez Longman, 1982. — xii,235p ; 22cm
Previous ed.: / by F. Quickfall. 1979. — Includes index
ISBN 0-85120-647-6 (pbk) : Unpriced B82-33143

344.2064′4 — England. Residences. Conversion, extension or improvement. Planning permission. Law — *For householders*

Planning permission : a guide for householders / [prepared by the Department of the Environment, the Welsh Office and the Central Office of Information]. — [London] : [H.M.S.O.], [1981]. — 20p ; 18cm
Cover title
Unpriced (pbk) B82-40591

344.2064′5 — England. Environment planning. Law

Grant, Malcolm, *19---*. Planning law handbook / by Malcolm Grant. — London : Sweet & Maxwell, 1981. — xxx,488p ; 25cm
ISBN 0-421-28570-2 (pbk) : £12.50 : CIP rev. B81-25857

Heap, *Sir* **Desmond**. An outline of planning law. — 8th ed. — London : Sweet & Maxwell, Apr.1982. — [400]p
Previous ed.: 1978
ISBN 0-421-29540-6 (cased) : £22.00 : CIP entry
ISBN 0-421-29550-3 (pbk) : £18.00 B82-04057

Lomnicki, A. J.. Housing, tenancy and planning law made simple / A.J. Lomnicki. — London : Heinemann, 1981. — xiii,242p ; 23cm. — (Made simple books)
Includes index
ISBN 0-434-98481-7 (cased) : £5.95
ISBN 0-434-98487-6 (pbk) : £2.95
Primary classification 344.204′63635 B82-02506

Telling, A. E.. Planning law and procedure / A.E. Telling. — 6th ed. — London : Butterworths, 1982. — xxix,321p ; 23cm
Previous ed.: 1977. — Includes index
ISBN 0-406-66509-5 (cased) : Unpriced
ISBN 0-406-66520-6 (pbk) : Unpriced B82-34905

Williams, Anne, *1951 Feb.14-*. Town and country planning law / Anne Williams. — Plymouth : Macdonald and Evans, 1981. — x,117p ; 19cm. — (The M & E handbook series)
Includes index
ISBN 0-7121-2031-9 (pbk) : £2.95 B82-04768

344.206′45 — England. Town planning. Law

Grant, Malcolm. Urban planning law. — London : Sweet and Maxwell, Oct.1982. — [550]p
ISBN 0-421-24120-9 (cased) : £20.00 : CIP entry
ISBN 0-421-24130-6 (pbk) : £17.00 B82-24001

344.2064′691 — England. Natural resources: Water. Law

Wisdom, A. S.. The law and management of water resources and supply / by A.S. Wisdom and J.L.G. Skeet. — London : Shaw & Sons, 1981. — xxx,275p ; 22cm
Includes index
ISBN 0-7219-0910-8 (pbk) : Unpriced B82-12109

344.2064′6954′09 — England. Game animals. Law, *1671-1831.* **Social aspects**

Munsche, P. B.. Gentlemen and poachers : the English game laws 1671-1831 / P.B. Munsche. — Cambridge : Cambridge University Press, 1981. — ix,255p : ill,2ports ; 24cm
Bibliography: p233-249. — Includes index
ISBN 0-521-23284-8 : £18.50 : CIP rev. B81-31828

344.2065′2 — England. Probate. Law

Biggs, A. K.. Probate practice and procedure / by A.K. Biggs and A.P. Rogers. — London : Fourmat, 1980. — xiii,157p : forms ; 22cm. — (Lawyers practice and procedure series)
Includes index
ISBN 0-906840-26-0 (pbk) : £6.95 B82-06623

344.2065′2 — England. Probate. Law — *Tables* — *Serials*

Probate : probate fees, intestacy tables, capital transfer tax scales. — [1st ed.]. — London : Fourmat, 1979-. — v. ; 30cm. — (Lawyers costs & fees series ; 3)
Irregular. — Description based on: 2nd ed.
ISSN 0262-6136 = Probate : £1.40 B82-06817

344.2065′2 — England. Succession. Law

Curzon, L. B.. Law of succession / L.B. Curzon. — Plymouth : Macdonald and Evans, 1981. — xxxiii,233p ; 19cm. — (The M & E handbook series)
Previous ed.: 1976. — Bibliography: p218. — Includes index
ISBN 0-7121-1256-1 (pbk) : £4.50 B82-00724

William, *Sir* **E. V.**. Williams, Mortimer and Sunnucks on executors, administrators and probate / by J.H.G. Sunnucks, J.G. Ross Martyn, K.M. Garnett. — London : Stevens & Sons, 1982. — clxxxviii,1157p ; 26cm. — (Property and conveyancing library ; no.10)
′Being the 16th edition of Williams on Executors and the 4th edition of Mortimer on Probate′. — Includes index
ISBN 0-420-45500-0 : £75.00 : CIP rev. B81-31707

344.2065′4 — England. Wills. Composition

Pettitt, D. M.. The will draftsman′s handbook / D.M. Pettitt. — 2nd ed. — London : Oyez, 1982. — xx,219p ; 24cm
Previous ed.: 1978. — Includes index
ISBN 0-85120-611-5 (pbk) : Unpriced B82-16427

344.2065'9 — England. Trusts. Administration — *Manuals*

Sladen, Michael. Practical trust administration / Michael Sladen. — London : Europa Supplement to the first edition. — 1980. — 30p ; 24cm
ISBN 0-905118-58-8 (unbound) : Unpriced
B82-24390

344.2065'9 — England. Trusts. Law

Brindley, L. P. K.. Settlements and will trusts : (with special reference to the new CTT regime for discretionary trusts) / L.P.K. Brindley. — [Guildford] ([Braboeuf Manor, St. Catherines, Guildford, Surrey, GU3 1HA]) : [The College of Law], [1982]. — 23p ; 22cm. — (Crash course lecture / The College of Law, ISSN 0309-2771 ; 1982)
Cover title
£1.50 (pbk)
B82-40232

Riddall, J. G.. The law of trusts / J.G. Riddall. — 2nd ed. — London : Butterworths, 1982. — xxxi,371p ; 26cm
Previous ed.: 1977. — Includes index
ISBN 0-406-64837-9 (cased) : £16.50
ISBN 0-406-64838-7 (pbk) : Unpriced
B82-34907

344.206'6 — England. Clubs. Law

Josling, J. F.. The law of clubs : with a note on unincorporated associations / J.F. Josling, Lionel Alexander. — 4th ed. — London : Oyez, 1981. — xl,235p ; 24cm. — (Oyez practitioner series. Practice and procedure)
Previous ed.: 1975. — Includes index
ISBN 0-85120-582-8 (pbk) : Unpriced
B82-03052

344.206'63 — England. Law — *For accountancy*

Card, Richard. Law for accountancy students / by Richard Card and Jennifer James. — 2nd ed. — London : Butterworths, 1982. — xl,547p ; 25cm
Previous ed.: 1978. — Includes index
ISBN 0-406-70882-7 (pbk) : Unpriced
B82-38389

Leal, A. R.. Essential law for accountancy students / A.R. Leal. — London : Edward Arnold, 1982. — viii,278p : ill,forms ; 22cm
Includes index
ISBN 0-7131-0605-0 (pbk) : £5.95 : CIP rev.
B81-33905

344.206'6626 — England. Private companies. Acquisition. Law

Knight, W. J. L.. The acquisition of private companies / W.J.L. Knight. — 3rd ed. — London : Oyez Longman, 1982. — xviii,228p : ill ; 23cm
Previous ed.: 1979. — Includes index
Unpriced
B82-30501

344.206'682 — England. Professions. Partnerships. Law

Godfrey, M.. Professional partnerships / by Michael Godfrey, Cardine Harmer, Dai Jones. — Guildford : College of Law, c1982. — viii,93p ; 22cm. — (College of Law lectures, ISSN 0309-3166)
£4.00 (pbk)
B82-22007

344.206'7 — England. Commercial law

Business law / Michael G. Butler (editor) ; Neil Hamilton, Neil Lucas. — Stockport : Polytech Publishers, 1982. — 186p : ill ; 22cm
Includes index
ISBN 0-85505-062-4 (pbk) : £3.60
B82-32765

Hamblin, C.. Introduction to commercial law / by C. Hamblin and F.B. Wright. — 2nd ed. — London : Sweet & Maxwell, 1982. — xxiii,302p ; 22cm. — (Concise college texts)
Previous ed.: published as ONC-OND commercial law. 1976. — Includes index
ISBN 0-421-30260-7 (cased) : Unpriced : CIP rev.
ISBN 0-421-28510-9 (pbk) : £6.50
B82-10509

Smith, Kenneth, *1910-1966.* Mercantile law / Kenneth Smith, Denis Keenan. — 5th ed. / by Denis Keenan. — London : Pitman, 1982. — xiii,753p : ill ; 22cm
Previous ed.: 1977. — Includes index
ISBN 0-273-01769-1 (pbk) : Unpriced : CIP rev.
B82-03795

344.206'72 — England. Goods. Sale. Law

Atiyah, P. S.. The sale of goods / P.S. Atiyah. — 6th ed. — London : Pitman, 1980 (1982 [printing]). — xxxvii,423p ; 22cm
Previous ed.: 1975. — Includes index
ISBN 0-273-01612-1 (cased) : Unpriced
ISBN 0-273-01448-x (pbk) : Unpriced
B82-26736

Soulsby, J.. Sale of goods / John Soulsby. — London : Anderson Keenan, 1981. — vii,109p ; 24cm. — (Law unit)
Includes index
ISBN 0-906501-18-0 (pbk) : £3.70
B82-29472

344.206'72 — England. Goods. Supply. Contracts. Implied terms. Law

Woodroffe, Geoffrey F.. Supply of goods and services — the new law. — London : Sweet & Maxwell, Sept.1982. — [100]p
ISBN 0-421-30200-3 (pbk) : £10.00 : CIP entry
B82-20755

344.206'72'0264 — England. Goods. Sale. Law — *Cases*

Adams, John, *1939-.* Cases and materials on sale of goods / John Adams. — London : Croom Helm, c1982. — 174p ; 21cm. — (Croom Helm study guides to commercial law)
Includes index
ISBN 0-7099-0509-2 (pbk) : £6.95 : CIP rev.
B81-34312

344.206'74 — England. Finance. Personal sureties. Law

Rowlatt, *Sir* **Sidney Arthur Taylor.** Rowlatt on the law of principal and surety. — 4th ed. / by David G.M. Marks and Gabriel S. Moss ; with a foreword by Sir Alan Mocatta. — London : Sweet & Maxwell, 1982. — liv,289p : 1port ; 26cm
Previous ed.: Published as The law of principal and surety. 1936. — Includes index
ISBN 0-421-26240-0 : £24.00 : CIP rev.
B81-31245

344.206'77 — England. Debts. Collection. Law

Theunissen, Andrew. A guide to successful debt collecting / Andrew Theunissen. — Bristol : Rose-Jordan, c1982. — xii,147p : forms ; 21cm
Includes index
ISBN 0-907313-02-7 (pbk) : £4.00
B82-22250

344.206'77 — England. Foreign debts. Payment. Law. Reform — *Proposals*

Great Britain. *Law Commission.* Private international law foreign money liabilities / the Law Commission. — London : H.M.S.O., 1981. — ix,195p ; 21cm. — (Working paper / Law Commission ; no.80)
ISBN 0-11-730160-4 (pbk) : £7.00
B82-05462

344.206'78 — England. Bankruptcy. Law

Redmond, P. W. D.. Bankruptcy law / P.W.D. Redmond. — 8th ed. / revised by I.M. McCallum. — Plymouth : Macdonald and Evans, 1981. — xii,163p ; 19cm. — (The M & E handbook series)
Previous ed.: 1973. — Includes index
ISBN 0-7121-0264-7 (pbk) : £2.95
B82-01911

344.206'78 — England. Companies. Liquidation. Receivership. Procedure — *Conference proceedings*

Liquidation and bankruptcy : aspects of conveyancing. — Aldershot : Gower, May 1982. — [52]p
Conference papers
ISBN 0-566-03035-7 : £25.00 : CIP entry
B82-16512

344.206'78 — England. Insolvency. Law — *Inquiry reports*

Great Britain. Insolvency law and practice : report of the Review Committee / chairman Sir Kenneth Cork. — London : H.M.S.O., [1982]. — xvi,460p ; 25cm. — (Cmnd. ; 8558)
ISBN 0-10-185580-x (pbk) : £13.35
B82-31970

344.206'82 — England. Banking. Law

Encyclopaedia of banking law / general editor P.J. Cresswell ; editors W.J.L. Blair, G.J.S. Hill, P.R. Wood ; consulting editor on consumer credit R.M. Goode. — London : Butterworths, 1982. — 2v(loose-leaf) : ill ; 26cm
Includes index
ISBN 0-406-56983-5 : Unpriced
B82-30000

344.206'86 — England. Insurance companies. Disclosure of information: Disclosure by insured persons. Law. Reform — *Proposals*

Great Britain. *Law Commisssion.* Insurance law : non-disclosure and breach of warranty : report on a reference under section 3(1) (e) of the Law Commissions Act 1965 / the Law Commission. — London : H.M.S.O., [1980]. — vii,165p ; 25cm. — (Law Com. ; no.104)
ISBN 0-10-180640-x (pbk) : £6.20
Also classified at 344.206'86
B82-14711

344.206'86 — England. Insurance. Law

Birds, John. Modern insurance law / by John Birds. — London : Sweet & Maxwell, 1982. — xxxviii,357p ; 22cm
Includes index
ISBN 0-421-27760-2 (cased) : Unpriced : CIP rev.
ISBN 0-421-27770-x (pbk) : £10.50
B81-34394

MacGillivray, E. J.. MacGillivray & Parkington on insurance law : relating to all risks other than marine. — 7th ed. / general editor Michael Parkington ; assistant general editor Anthony O'Dowd ; book 1 [edited by] Nicholas Legh-Jones ; book 2 [edited by] Andrew Longmore. — London : Sweet & Maxwell, 1981. — cxxiv,1028p ; 26cm
Previous ed.: 1975. — Includes index
ISBN 0-421-25310-x : £65.00
B82-05057

344.206'86 — England. Insurance. Warranties. Law. Reform — *Proposals*

Great Britain. *Law Commisssion.* Insurance law : non-disclosure and breach of warranty : report on a reference under section 3(1) (e) of the Law Commissions Act 1965 / the Law Commission. — London : H.M.S.O., [1980]. — vii,165p ; 25cm. — (Law Com. ; no.104)
ISBN 0-10-180640-x (pbk) : £6.20
Primary classification 344.206'86
B82-14711

344.206'86'0264 — England. Insurance. Law — *Cases — Serials*

Insurance law reports. — Vol.2. — London : Godwin, July 1982. — [128]p
ISBN 0-7114-5771-9 : £13.50 : CIP entry
B82-13266

Insurance law reports. — Vol.3. — London : Godwin, Oct.1982. — [128]p
ISBN 0-7114-5772-7 : £13.50 : CIP entry
B82-23210

344.207 — England. Legal system

Eddey, K. J.. The English legal system / by K.J. Eddey. — 3rd ed. — London : Sweet & Maxwell, 1982. — xv,191p : 1ill ; 22cm. — (Concise college texts)
Previous ed.: 1977. — Bibliography: p185-186. — Includes index
ISBN 0-421-27570-7 (cased) : Unpriced : CIP rev.
ISBN 0-421-27580-4 (pbk) : £5.95
B82-06770

Stott, Vanessa. English legal system / Vanessa Stott. — London : Anderson Keenan, 1981. — viii,87p ; 24cm. — (Law unit)
Includes index
ISBN 0-906501-20-2 (pbk) : £3.40
B82-29471

344.207 — England. Legal system. Reform — *Proposals*

Tench, David. Towards a middle system of law / David Tench. — London : Consumers' Association, c1981. — 73p ; 21cm
Includes index
ISBN 0-85202-214-x (pbk) : Unpriced
ISBN 0-340-28163-4
B82-39933

344.207′09 — England. Legal system, *to ca 1900*

Curzon, L.B.. English legal history / L.B. Curzon. — 2nd ed. — Plymouth : Macdonald & Evans, 1979. — xii,335p ; 18cm. — (The M & E handbook series)
Previous ed.: 1968. — Bibliography: p323-324. — Includes index
ISBN 0-7121-0578-6 (pbk) : £3.25 B82-07281

344.207′14 — England. Judges, *1727-1875*

Duman, Daniel. The judicial bench in England 1727-1875 : the reshaping of a professional elite / Daniel Duman. — London : Royal Historical Society, 1982. — x,208p : 1ill ; 23cm. — (Royal Historical Society studies in history series ; no.29)
Bibliography: p190-199. — Includes index
ISBN 0-901050-80-6 : £8.87 B82-38921

344.207′14 — England. Lord Chief Justices, *to 1981*

Mockler, Anthony. Lions under the throne. — London : Muller, Jan.1983. — [416]p
ISBN 0-584-10437-5 : £15.95 : CIP entry
B82-32508

344.207′16 — England. Coroners. Role

The **Work** of the coroner : some questions answered / [prepared for Home Office by the Central Office of Information]. — [London] : [Home Office], 1981. — 1folded sheet ; 21cm. — (A Home Office guide)
Unpriced B82-33374

344.207′16 — England. Justices of the Peace. Bias. Law

Stevens, R. D. S.. Bias and impartiality in magistrates′ courts / R.D.S. Stevens. — Chichester : Rose, 1982. — xvii,105p ; 22cm
Includes index
ISBN 0-85992-231-6 (pbk) : £6.80 B82-21461

344.207′2′0942453 — Shropshire. Market Drayton. Manorial courts, *1545-1727*

Rowley, N.. Drayton court leet : introduction to the bye-laws, 1547-1727 / N. Rowley. — [Shrewsbury] ([′Blue Gates′, Weston Lullingfields, Shrewsbury, SY4 2AA]) : N. Rowley, 1981. — 7leaves ; 30cm
Cover title
£0.30 (pbk) B82-00737

344.207′21 — England. County courts. Cases. Costs — *Tables* — *Serials*

County Court costs & fees. — [1st ed.]-. — London : Fourmat, 1979-. — v. ; 30cm. — (Lawyers costs & fees series ; 1)
Irregular. — Description based on: 3rd ed.
ISSN 0262-611x = County Court costs & fees : £1.40 B82-06814

344.207′21 — England. County courts. Procedure

Civil litigation now : the new County Court jurisdiction. — Guildford : College of Law, c1982. — vi,79p : ill ; 22cm. — (College of Law lectures, ISSN 0309-3166)
£3.60 (pbk) B82-22006

Deighan, Maurice. County court practice and procedure / by Maurice Deighan. — London : Fourmat, 1980. — xv,125p ; 22cm. — (Lawyers practice and procedure series)
Includes index
ISBN 0-906840-29-5 (pbk) : £5.95 B82-06624

Deighan, Maurice. County court practice and procedure / by Maurice Deighan. — 2nd ed. — London : Fourmat, 1982. — xiii,151p ; 22cm. — (Lawyers practice and procedure series)
Previous ed.: 1980. — Includes index
ISBN 0-906840-56-2 (pbk) : £8.95 B82-38919

Williams, Emlyn. ABC guide to the practice of the County Court. — London : Sweet & Maxwell, Dec.1982. — [150]p
ISBN 0-421-30210-0 (pbk) : £9.75 : CIP entry
B82-32291

344.207′21′09 — England. County courts, *1150-1350*

Palmer, Robert C.. The county courts of medieval England, 1150-1350 / Robert C. Palmer. — Princeton, N.J. ; Guildford : Princeton University Press, c1982. — xvii,360p ; 25cm
Bibliography: p335-344. — Includes index
ISBN 0-691-05341-3 : £24.70 B82-37592

344.207′25 — England. Civil law. Cases. Procedure of Great Britain. *High Court of Justice*

Casson, D. B.. Modern developments in the law of civil procedure. — London : Sweet and Maxwell, Aug.1982. — [112]p
ISBN 0-421-29000-5 (pbk) : £5.00 : CIP entry
B82-17200

Odgers, William Blake. Odgers′ principles of pleading and practice in civil actions in the High Court of Justice. — 22nd ed. / by D.B. Casson and I.H. Dennis. — London : Stevens, 1981. — lix,565p ; 22cm
Previous ed.: 1975. — Includes index
ISBN 0-420-45710-0 (pbk) : £13.50 : CIP rev.
B81-25314

344.207′29 — Great Britain. *Supreme Court of Judicature.* **Cases. Costs** — *Tables* — *Serials*

Supreme Court costs & fees : Queen′s Bench Division fees & fixed costs ; Court of Appeal fees. — [1st ed.]. — London : Fourmat, 1979-. — 1v. ; 30cm. — (Lawyers costs & fees series ; 4)
Continued by: Supreme Court fees & fixed costs. — Only one issue published under this title
£1.10 B82-06816

Supreme Court fees & fixed costs. — 2nd ed.-. — London : Fourmat, 1980-. — v. ; 30cm. — (Lawyers costs & fees series ; 4)
Irregular. — Continues: Supreme Court costs & fees
ISSN 0262-6144 = Supreme Court fees & fixed costs : £1.40 B82-06810

344.207′29 — Great Britain. *Supreme Court of Judicature.* **Procedure**

Fage, John. Supreme Court practice and procedure / by John Fage. — London : Fourmat, 1980. — xii,116p : forms ; 22cm. — (Lawyers practice and procedure series)
Includes index
ISBN 0-906840-22-8 (pbk) : £5.95 B82-06626

Fage, John. Supreme Court practice and procedure / by John Fage. — 2nd ed. — London : Fourmat, 1981. — x,121p ; 22cm. — (Lawyers practice and procedure series)
Previous ed.: 1980. — Includes index
ISBN 0-906840-45-7 (pbk) : £6.25 B82-34014

344.207′29′02633 — Great Britain. *Supreme Court of Judicature.* **Law** — *Statutes* — *Texts with commentaries*

Great Britain. *Supreme Court of Judicature.* The Supreme Court Act 1981 / with annotations by Robin White. — London : Sweet & Maxwell, 1981. — ca.150p ; 25cm. — (Current law statutes reprints)
ISBN 0-421-29410-8 (pbk) : £6.85 B82-15368

344.207′29′0321 — Great Britain. *Supreme Court of Judicature.* **Procedure** — *Encyclopaedias*

Williams, Emlyn, *1946-*. ABC guide to the practice of the Supreme Court / by Emlyn Williams. — 40th ed. — London : Sweet & Maxwell, 1981. — viii,207p ; 19cm
Previous ed.: 1978
ISBN 0-421-27700-9 : £7.75 : CIP rev.
B82-03649

344.207′29′05 — Great Britain. *Supreme Court of Judicature.* **Procedure** — *Serials*

Great Britain. *Supreme Court of Judicature.* The Supreme Court practice. — 1982. — London : Sweet & Maxwell, Sept.1981. — 2v. [(1900;1600p.)]
ISBN 0-421-27200-7 : £110.00 : CIP entry
B81-28155

344.207′5 — England. Civil courts. Procedure

Hill, R. N.. High Court or County Court? : recent and prospective changes in civil litigation / R.N. Hill. — [Guildford] ([Braboeuf Manor, St. Catherines, Guildford, Surrey, GU3 1HA]) : [The College of Law], [1982]. — 24p ; 22cm. — (Crash course lecture / The College of Law, ISSN 0309-2771 ; 1982)
Cover title
£1.50 (pbk) B82-40238

344.207′5 — England. Civil law. Procedure

Jacob, *Sir* **Jack I. H.**. The reform of civil procedural law and other essays in civil procedure. — London : Sweet & Maxwell, Sept.1982. — [350]p
ISBN 0-421-30110-4 : £22.50 : CIP entry
B82-20754

344.207′5 — England. Law. Procedure

Witchell, Rowland G.. Practice and procedure / by Rowland G. Witchell. — 7th ed. / editors Rowland G. Witchell ... [et al.]. — London : Oyez
Previous ed.: 1976-1977
Vol.1: County courts and magistrates′ courts. — 1979. — x,150p ; 22cm
Includes index
ISBN 0-85120-428-7 (pbk) : Unpriced
B82-05251

344.207′5′05 — England. Civil law. Procedure — *Serials*

Civil justice quarterly. — Vol.1 (Jan. 1982)-. — London : Sweet & Maxwell in association with the Institute of Judicial Administration at the University of Birmingham, 1982-. — v. ; 25cm
ISSN 0261-9261 = Civil justice quarterly : £35.00 per year B82-22672

344.207′5′05 — England. Litigation. Procedure — *Serials*

Litigation : a journal of contentious business. — Vol.1, no.1-. — Chichester (Little London, Chichester, West Sussex PO19 1PG) : Barry Rose Law Periodicals, [1981]-. — v. ; 21cm
Eight issues yearly. — Description based on: Vol.1, no.2
ISSN 0263-2160 = Litigation : Unpriced
B82-19846

344.207′52 — England. Limitation of actions. Law

Cooklin, A.. Limitation and other time limit problems / A. Cooklin. — [Guildford] ([Braboeuf Manor, St. Catherines, Guildford, Surrey, GU3 1HA]) : [The College of Law], [1982]. — 17p ; 22cm. — (Crash course lecture / The College of Law, ISSN 0309-2771 ; 1982)
Cover title
£1.50 (pbk) B82-40235

Josling, J. F.. Periods of limitation : with practical notes / J.F. Josling. — 5th ed. — London : Oyez, c1981. — viii,113p ; 22cm. — (Oyez practice notes)
Previous ed.: 1973. — Includes index
ISBN 0-85120-589-5 (pbk) : Unpriced
B82-06201

344.207′55 — England. Civil law. Procedure — *Forms & precedents*

Atkin, James Richard Atkin, *Baron*. Atkin′s encyclopaedia of court forms in civil proceedings. — 2nd ed. / by the late Lord Evershed and other lawyers. — London : Butterworths
Vol.10: Companies (winding-up proceedings). — 1981 issue / [consulting editor Ingrid Persadsingh, editor Andrew Marshall]. — 1981. — xxii,449p ; 26cm
Previous ed.: published as Vol.11, 1971. — Includes index
ISBN 0-406-01071-4 : Unpriced
ISBN 0-406-01020-x (set) : Unpriced
B82-13794

344.207'55 — England. Civil law. Procedure — *Forms & precedents* *continuation*

Atkin, James Richard Atkin, *Baron*. Atkin's encyclopaedia of court forms in civil proceedings. — 2nd ed. / by the late Lord Evershed and other lawyers. — London : Butterworths
Previous ed.: published as Encyclopaedia of court forms and precedents in civil proceedings, 1961-1971
Vol.11: Consumer credit. — 1981 issue / [edited by Andrew Marshall]. — c1981. — xxiii,220p ; 26cm
Includes index
ISBN 0-406-01076-5 : Unpriced
ISBN 0-406-01020-x (set) : Unpriced
B82-02880

The **Encyclopaedia** of forms and precedents other than court forms. — London : Butterworths
Cumulative noter-up, 1980 / managing editor L.G. Jory assisted by G.D. Dann and B. Russell Davis. — c1980. — 1492,60,25p ; 26cm
Includes index
ISBN 0-406-02302-6 : Unpriced B82-23801

The **Encyclopaedia** of forms and precedents other than court forms. — London : Butterworths
Cumulative noter-up, 1981 / managing editor L.G. Jory, assisted by G.D. Dann. — c1981. — 1678,61,29p ; 26cm
Includes index
ISBN 0-406-02303-4 : Unpriced B82-13795

344.207'6 — England. Law courts. Evidence. Law

Phipson, Sidney Lovell. Phipson on evidence. — 13th ed. — London : Sweet and Maxwell, Nov.1982. — [1000]p. — (The Common law library ; no.10)
Previous ed.: 1976
ISBN 0-421-26990-1 : £60.00 : CIP entry
B82-28279

344.207'6 — England. Law courts. Evidence. Provision by digital computers

Kelman, Alistair. The computer in court. — Aldershot : Gower, May 1982. — [120]p
ISBN 0-566-03419-0 : £12.50 : CIP entry
B82-07845

344.207'72 — England. Civil law. Cases. Documents. Discovery & inspection. Law *compared with* **law of discovery & inspection of documents in American civil cases**

Levine, Julius Byron. Discovery : a comparison between English and American civil discovery law with reform proposals / Julius Byron Levine. — Oxford : Clarendon, 1982. — xl,208p ; 23cm
Bibliography: p154-160. — Includes index
ISBN 0-19-825368-0 : £16.00 : CIP rev.
Also classified at 347.307'72 B81-31740

344.207'77 — England. Writs. Law — *French texts — Early works — Facsimiles*

Theloall, Simon. Le digest des briefs originals et des choses concernant eux / Simon Theloall. — New York ; London : Garland, 1979. — 239p ; 29cm. — (Classics of English legal history in the modern era)
French text, English introduction. — Facsim of: 1st ed. London : Atkins, 1687
ISBN 0-8240-3182-2 : Unpriced B82-15183

344.207'8 — England. Law. Appeals. Procedure

Price, David, *1954-*. Appeals / by David Price. — London : Fourmat, 1982. — xii,439p : forms ; 22cm. — (Lawyers practice and procedure series)
Includes index
ISBN 0-906840-42-2 (pbk) : £12.95
B82-13332

344.2079 — England. Arbitration. Law

Russell, Francis. Russell on the law of arbitration. — 20th ed. — London : Stevens, Jan.1983. — [650]p
Previous ed.: 1979
ISBN 0-420-46380-1 : £38.00 : CIP entry
B82-34576

344.208'22 — England. Law — *Statutes — Collections*

Great Britain. [Laws, etc]. Halsbury's statutes of England. — 3rd ed. — London : Butterworths
Cumulative supplement
Pt. 1. — 1981
Vols.1-25: Action—public authorities. — 2145p in various pagings ; 26cm
ISBN 0-406-04311-6 : Unpriced
ISBN 0-406-04312-4 (set) : Unpriced
B82-02928

Great Britain. [Laws, etc]. Halsbury's statutes of England. — 3rd ed. — London : Butterworths
Cumulative supplement
Pt.2. — 1981
Vols.26-39: Public health—wills and European supplement. — 1741p in various pagings ; 26cm
ISBN 0-409-04313-3 : Unpriced
ISBN 0-406-04312-4 (set) : Unpriced
B82-02929

344.208'25 — England. Law — *Statutory instruments — Collections*

Great Britain. Halsbury's statutory instruments : being a companion work to Halsbury's statutes of England / prepared by Butterworth's legal editorial staff. — London : Butterworths, 1981
Vol.9: Fire services, fisheries, food and drugs, forestry, friendly societies and industrial assurance, gaming and wagering
5th re-issue. — vi,396p ; 26cm
Includes index
ISBN 0-406-04593-3 : Unpriced
ISBN 0-406-04500-3 (set) : Unpriced
B82-14793

344.208'25 — England. Royal proclamations, *1603-1714 — Collections*

England and Wales. *Sovereign*. Stuart royal proclamations. — Oxford : Clarendon Press
Vol.2: Royal proclamations of King Charles I, 1625-1646. — Jan.1983. — [1200]p
ISBN 0-19-822466-4 : £65.00 : CIP entry
B82-33490

344.208'6 — England. Law — *Encyclopaedias*

Stroud, Frederick. Stroud's judicial dictionary of words and phrases. — 4th ed. / by John S. James. — London : Sweet & Maxwell
Previous ed.: 1951-1953
2nd cumulative suppl. — 1982. — viii,210p ; 26cm
ISBN 0-421-27920-6 : £12.00 : CIP rev.
B82-09735

344.21064'3 — Inner London. Party walls. Law

Party wall legislation and procedure. — London : Published on behalf of The Royal Institution of Chartered Surveyors by Surveyors Publications, c1982. — 36p : ill,forms ; 30cm
ISBN 0-85406-171-1 (pbk) : Unpriced
B82-38172

344.23'4034 — Channel Islands. Taxation. Law

Tolley's taxation in the Channel Islands and Isle of Man 1982 / [edited by] David Harrington. — Croydon : Tolley, c1982. — viii,176p ; 23cm
Text on inside cover
ISBN 0-85459-064-1 (pbk) : £6.95
Also classified at 344.27'9034 B82-39782

344.23'4206166 — Guernsey. Married persons. Separation & divorce. Law

Marshall, Michael, *19---*. Divorce and separation law in Guernsey, Alderney and Sark / by Michael Marshall. — [Petit Bot] ([Manor Hotel, Petit Bot, Guernsey]) : M. Marshall, 1980. — 12p ; 21cm. — (Family law series)
Cover title
Unpriced (pbk) B82-29327

344.23'420822 — Guernsey. Law — *Statutes — Collections*

Marshall, Michael, *1928-*. A small handbook of Guernsey law / by Michael Marshall. — [Petit Bot] ([Manor Hotel, Petit Bot, Guernsey]) : M. Marshall, 1981. — 15p ; 22cm. — (Family law series)
Cover title
Unpriced (pbk) B82-27472

344.27'9034 — Isle of Man. Taxation. Law

Tolley's taxation in the Channel Islands and Isle of Man 1982 / [edited by] David Harrington. — Croydon : Tolley, c1982. — viii,176p ; 23cm
Text on inside cover
ISBN 0-85459-064-1 (pbk) : £6.95
Primary classification 344.23'4034 B82-39782

344.27'90686 — Isle of Man. Insurance companies. Law

Starting an insurance operation in the Isle of Man / Peat, Marwick, Mitchell & Co.. — Douglas (17 Circular Rd, Douglas, Isle of Man) : PMM, 1982. — 28p ; 21cm
Unpriced (pbk) B82-26603

344.3/9 — LAW. EUROPEAN COUNTRIES(OTHER THAN GREAT BRITAIN AND IRELAND)

344.302'29 — Holy Roman Empire. Constitution, *ca 1500-ca 1800*. **Influence of Neostoicism**

Oestreich, Gerhard. Neostoicism and the early modern state / Gerhard Oestreich ; edited by Brigitta Oestreich and H.G. Koenigsberger ; translated by David McLintock. — Cambridge : Cambridge University Press, 1982. — viii,280p ; 24cm. — (Cambridge studies in early modern history)
Translation of: Geist und Gestalt des frühmodernen Staates. — Bibliography: p272-273. — Includes index
ISBN 0-521-24202-9 : £25.00 : CIP rev.
B82-21721

344.303'71 — West Germany. Consumer protection. Law

Reich, Norbert. Consumer legislation in the Federal Republic of Germany : a study prepared for the EC Commission / Norbert Reich, Hans-W. Micklitz ; translation: Diplomierter Dolmetcher Sabine Geis. — New York ; London : Van Nostrand Reinhold, c1981. — xxii,383p ; 25cm. — (Consumer legislation in the EC countries)
Translation of: Verbraucherschutzrecht in der Bundesrepublik Deutschland. — Includes index
ISBN 0-442-30421-8 : £15.00 B82-09758

344.303'71 — West Germany. Consumer protection. Law — *German texts*

Reich, Norbert. Verbraucherschutzrecht in der Bundesrepublik Deutschland : eine Studie im Auftrage der EG Kommission / Norbert Reich, Hans-W. Micklitz. — New York ; London : Van Nostrand Reinhold, c1980. — xix,410p ; 24cm. — (Verbraucherschutzrecht in den EG-Staaten)
Includes index
ISBN 0-442-30419-6 : £15.00 B82-41032

344.304'463 — West Germany. Environment. Pollution. Law

Salzwedel, Jürgen. The law and practice relating to pollution control in the Federal Republic of Germany. — 2nd ed. — London : Graham and Trotman, Dec.1982. — [200]p
Previous ed.: 1976 / by Heinhard Steiger and Otto Kimminich
ISBN 0-86010-308-0 : £18.00 : CIP entry
B82-34056

344.306 — West Germany. Private law

Horn, Norbert. German private and commercial law : an introduction / by Norbert Horn, Hein Kötz and Hans G. Leser ; translated by Tony Weir. — Oxford : Clarendon, 1982. — xvi,355p ; 22cm
Translation from the German. — Bibliography: p332-334. — Includes index
ISBN 0-19-825382-6 (cased) : £16.50 : CIP rev.
ISBN 0-19-825383-4 (pbk) : Unpriced
B81-33901

344.403'71 — France. Consumer protection. Law

Calais-Auloy, J.. Consumer legislation in France : a study prepared for the EC Commission / by J. Calais-Auloy with the collaboration of H. Bricks ... [et al.] ; translated from the French by Michael Corkery. — New York ; London : Van Nostrand Reinhold, c1981. — xi,192p : ill ; 24cm. — (Consumer legislation in the EC countries)
Includes index
ISBN 0-442-30415-3 : £15.00 B82-30958

344.404′12596 — France. Personnel. Dismissal. Law
Napier, B. W.. Comparative dismissal law / B.W. Napier, J.-C. Javillier and P. Verge. — London : Croom Helm, c1982. — 175p ; 23cm
ISBN 0-7099-1808-9 : £12.50 : CIP rev.
Primary classification 344.104′12596
B82-05404

344.404′463 — France. Environment. Pollution. Law
Despax, Michel. The law and practice relating to pollution control in France. — 2nd ed. — London : Graham and Trotman, Dec.1982. — [200]p
Previous ed.: 1976
ISBN 0-86010-307-2 : £18.00 : CIP entry
B82-34055

344.405′231 — France. Treason. Law, *1328-1494*
Cuttler, S. H.. The law of treason and treason trials in later medieval France / S.H. Cuttler. — Cambridge : Cambridge University Press, 1981. — x,272p ; 23cm. — (Cambridge studies in medieval life and thought. 3rd series ; v.16)
Bibliography: p245-262. — Includes index
ISBN 0-521-23968-0 : £25.00 : CIP rev.
B81-36949

344.405′2523′0924 — Paris. Calmette, Gaston. Murder. Trial of Caillaux, Henriette
Shankland, Peter. Death of an editor : the Caillaux drama / Peter Shankland ; foreword by Sir Michael Havers. — London : Kimber, 1981. — 223p,[14]p of plates : ill,ports ; 25cm
Bibliography: p210-212. — Includes index
ISBN 0-7183-0248-6 : £9.75 B82-06068

344.406′2 — France. Contracts. Law
Nicholas, Barry. French law of contract / Barry Nicholas. — London : Butterworths, 1982. — xxxviii,253p ; 22cm
Includes index
ISBN 0-406-63096-8 (cased) : Unpriced
ISBN 0-406-63095-x (pbk) : Unpriced
B82-38729

344.407′1 — France. Law courts. Reform, *1500-1789*
Carey, John A.. Judicial reform in France before the revolution of 1789 / John A. Carey. — Cambridge, Mass. ; London : Harvard University Press, 1981. — xii,162p : ill,ports ; 25cm. — (Harvard historical studies ; v.99)
Bibliography: p151-158. — Includes index
ISBN 0-674-48878-4 : £15.75 B82-27088

344.407′2 — France. English persons. Law. Cases in France. *Parlement (Paris), 1420-1436 — Collections — French texts*
English suits before the Parlement of Paris : 1420-1436 / edited for the Royal Historical Society by C.T. Allmand and C.A.J. Armstrong. — London : The Society, 1982. — 328p ; 23cm. — (Camden fourth series ; v.26)
French and Latin text, English introduction and notes. — Includes index
ISBN 0-86193-095-9 : Unpriced B82-40554

344.4′463′094 — European Community countries. Environment. Pollution. Law — *Comparative studies*
McLoughlin, J.. The law and practice relating to pollution control in the member states of the European Community. — 2nd ed. — London : Graham and Trotman, Dec.1982. — [545]p
Previous ed.: 1976
ISBN 0-86010-315-3 : £18.00 : CIP entry
B82-34063

344.503′71 — Italy. Consumer protection. Law
Ghidini, Gustavo. Consumer legislation in Italy : a study prepared for the EC Commission / [by] Gustavo Ghidini. — New York ; London : Van Nostrand Reinhold, c1980. — xiv,107p ; 24cm. — (Consumer legislation in the EC countries)
Includes index
ISBN 0-442-30426-9 : £15.00 B82-40810

344.504′463 — Italy. Environment. Pollution. Law
Guttieres, Mario. The law and practice relating to pollution control in Italy. — 2nd ed. — London : Graham and Trotman, Dec.1982. — [200]p
Previous ed.: by / P. Dell′Anno. 1976
ISBN 0-86010-309-9 : £18.00 : CIP entry
B82-34057

344.505′288 — Italy. Friuli. Heresy. Trials of Menocchio
Ginzburg, Carlo. The cheese and the worms : the cosmos of a sixteenth-century miller / Carlo Ginzburg ; translated by John and Anne Tedeschi. — London : Routledge & Kegan Paul, 1980 (1981 [printing]). — xxvii,177p : ill ; 24cm
Translation of: Il formaggio e i vermi. — Includes index
ISBN 0-7100-0960-7 (pbk) : £3.95 B82-27048

344.7′0092′4 — Russia. Law. Cruzenberg, O. O. — *Biographies*
Gruzenberg, O. O.. Yesterday: memoirs of a Russian-Jewish lawyer / O.O. Gruzenberg ; edited and with an introduction by Don C. Rawson ; translated by Don C. Rawson and Tatiana Tipton. — Berkeley ; London : University of California Press, c1981. — xxix,235p : 1map,1port ; 23cm
Translation of: Vchera. — Bibliography: p223-229. — Includes index
ISBN 0-520-04264-6 : £19.25 B82-12185

344.702′29 — Soviet Union. Constitutions, *1918-1977*
Unger, Aryeh L.. Constitutional development in the USSR. — London : Methuen, Aug.1981. — [320]p
ISBN 0-416-71680-6 (cased) : £15.00 : CIP entry
ISBN 0-416-71690-3 (pbk) : £7.50 B81-16403

344.703′2 — Soviet Union. Public property. Legal aspects
Khalfina, R. O.. State property in the USSR : legal aspects / R. Khalfina ; [translated from the Russian by Yuri Sdobnikov]. — Moscow : Progress Publishers, 1980 ; [London] : Distributed by Central Books. — 168p ; 20cm. — (Progress books about the USSR)
Translation of: Pravo gosudarstvennoĭ sobstvennosti v SSSR
ISBN 0-7147-1639-1 (pbk) : £0.95 B82-02535

344.8505′5042 — Sweden. Offenders. Prosecution. Procedure
Leigh, L. H.. The management of the prosecution process in Denmark, Sweden and the Netherlands / L.H. Leigh & J.E. Hall Williams. — Leamington Spa : James Hall in association with the London School of Economics and Political Science, 1981. — 86p ; 21cm
Bibliography: p85-86
ISBN 0-907471-01-3 (pbk) : £5.50 : CIP rev.
Also classified at 344.8905′5042 ; 344.9205′5042 B81-31239

344.8904′463 — Denmark. Environment. Pollution. Law
Jensen, C. H.. The law and practice relating to pollution control in Denmark. — 2nd ed. — London : Graham and Trotman, Dec.1982. — [200]p
Previous ed.: 1976
ISBN 0-86010-312-9 : £18.00 : CIP entry
B82-34060

344.8905′5042 — Denmark. Offenders. Prosecution. Procedure
Leigh, L. H.. The management of the prosecution process in Denmark, Sweden and the Netherlands / L.H. Leigh & J.E. Hall Williams. — Leamington Spa : James Hall in association with the London School of Economics and Political Science, 1981. — 86p ; 21cm
Bibliography: p85-86
ISBN 0-907471-01-3 (pbk) : £5.50 : CIP rev.
Primary classification 344.8505′5042
B81-31239

344.9204′463 — Netherlands. Environment. Pollution. Law
Environmental Resources Ltd.. The law and practice relating to pollution control in the Netherlands. — 2nd ed. — London : Graham and Trotman, Dec.1982. — [200]p
Previous ed.: 1976 / by J.J. de Graeff
ISBN 0-86010-311-0 : £18.00 : CIP entry
B82-34059

344.9205′5042 — Netherlands. Offenders. Prosecution. Procedure
Leigh, L. H.. The management of the prosecution process in Denmark, Sweden and the Netherlands / L.H. Leigh & J.E. Hall Williams. — Leamington Spa : James Hall in association with the London School of Economics and Political Science, 1981. — 86p ; 21cm
Bibliography: p85-86
ISBN 0-907471-01-3 (pbk) : £5.50 : CIP rev.
Primary classification 344.8505′5042
B81-31239

344.9303′71 — Belgium & Luxembourg. Consumer protection. Law
Fontaine, M.. Consumer legislation in Belgium and Luxemburg : a study prepared for the EC Commission / M. Fontaine, Th. Bourgoignie ; translated from French by Michael Corkery. — Wokingham : Van Nostrand Reinhold (UK), c1982. — xvi,229p ; 24cm. — (Consumer legislation in the EC countries)
Translation of: Droit de la consommation en Belgique et au Luxembourg. — Includes index
ISBN 0-442-30418-8 : £15.00 B82-38593

344.9304′463 — Belgium. Environment. Pollution. Law
Suetens, L. P.. The law and practice relating to pollution control in Belgium and Luxembourg. — 2nd ed. — London : Graham and Trotman, Dec.1982. — [200]p
Previous ed.: 1976 / by J.M. Didier and Associates
ISBN 0-86010-310-2 : £18.00 : CIP entry
Also classified at 344.93504′463 B82-34058

344.93504′463 — Luxembourg. Environment. Pollution. Law
Suetens, L. P.. The law and practice relating to pollution control in Belgium and Luxembourg. — 2nd ed. — London : Graham and Trotman, Dec.1982. — [200]p
Previous ed.: 1976 / by J.M. Didier and Associates
ISBN 0-86010-310-2 : £18.00 : CIP entry
Primary classification 344.9304′463
B82-34058

344.9503′96 — Greece. Shipping. Law
Greece. [Kōdix Idiōtikou Nautikou Dikaiou. English]. The Greek Code of Private Maritime Law / Theodoros B. Karatzas and Nigel P. Ready. — The Hague ; London : Nijhoff, 1982. — viii,98p ; 25cm
Includes index
ISBN 90-247-2586-0 : Unpriced B82-28044

344.9504′463 — Greece. Environment. Pollution. Law
Timagenis, J.. The law and practice relating to pollution control in Greece. — 2nd ed. — London : Graham and Trotman, Dec.1982. — [200]p
Previous ed.: 1976
ISBN 0-86010-314-5 : £18.00 : CIP entry
B82-34062

345 — LAW. ASIA

345.105′02632 — China. Criminal law — *Penal codes*
China. [Chung-hua jen min kung ho kus hsing (1980)]. The criminal code of the People′s Republic of China / translated and with an introduction by Chin Kim. — Littleton, Colo. : Rothman ; London : Sweet & Maxwell, 1982. — xiii,74p ; 23cm. — (The American series of foreign penal codes ; 25)
Translated from the Chinese
ISBN 0-421-30010-8 : £25.00 B82-36833

345.107′09 — China. Legal system, *ca 1911-ca 1980*
Brady, James P.. Justice and politics in People′s China. — London : Academic Press, Dec.1982. — [300]p. — (Law, state and society series)
ISBN 0-12-124750-3 : CIP entry B82-29874

345.1′250615 — Hong Kong. Families. Law
Pegg, Leonard. Family law in Hong Kong / Leonard Pegg. — London : Butterworths, 1981. — xxii,183p ; 23cm. — (Hong Kong law series)
Includes index
ISBN 0-406-66760-8 : £12.50 B82-09049

345.1′2506438 — Hong Kong. Real property. Conveyancing. Law
Bramwell, Hartley. Conveyancing in Hong Kong / Hartley Bramwell. — London : Butterworths, 1981. — xxvii,403p ; 23cm. — (Hong Kong law series)
Includes index
ISBN 0-406-66210-x : £21.00 B82-09048

345.1′73 — Mongolia *(People's Republic).* **Law**
Butler, William E.. The Mongolian legal system : contemporary legislation and documentation / W.E. Butler ; translations from Mongolian A.J. Nathanson, translations from Russian W.E. Butler. — The Hague ; London : Nijhoff, 1982. — xxiii,995p : forms ; 25cm. — (Studies on socialist legal systems)
Bibliography: p969-990
ISBN 90-247-2685-9 : Unpriced B82-40172

345.3′53067′02632 — Oman. Commercial law — *Statutes — Collections*
Oman. [Laws, etc.]. Oman company and business law / edited by M.A. Nafa. — London : Arab Consultants, c1978. — 268p ; 22cm
ISBN 0-905413-04-0 : £35.00 B82-22738

345.3′67034′02632 — Kuwait. Taxation. Law — *Statutes — Collections*
Kuwait. [Business laws of Kuwait. Selections]. Tax laws of Kuwait : selected texts reprinted from Business laws of Kuwait / translated by N.H. Karam. — London : Graham & Trotman, 1979. — 44p ; 24cm
Translated from the Arabic
ISBN 0-86010-140-1 (pbk) : £10.00
B82-35408

345.3′67067′02633 — Kuwait. Commercial law — *Statutes — Collections*
Business laws of Kuwait / translated from Arabic into English by Nicola H. Karam. — London : Graham & Trotman. — (Middle East business law series)
Vol.1. — 3rd ed. — 1981. — 1v.(loose-leaf) ; 25cm + Supplements
Previous ed.: 1980. — Includes index
ISBN 0-86010-275-0 (unbound) : Unpriced
B82-18016

345.3′8067 — Saudi Arabia. Commercial law
Lerrick, Alison. Saudi business and labour law. — London : Graham & Trotman, June 1982. — [295]p
ISBN 0-86010-391-9 : £70.00 : CIP entry
B82-20785

345.506′7 — Iran. Commercial law — *For businessmen*
Amin, S. H.. Trading with Iran. — Glasgow (165 Roebank St., Glasgow G31 3EG) : S.H. Amin, Aug.1982. — [312]p
ISBN 0-946124-02-7 (pbk) : £36.00 : CIP entry
B82-21972

345.5′37067′02632 — United Arab Emirates. Commercial law — *Statutes — Collections*
United Arab Emirates. Business laws of the United Arab Emirates / translated from Arabic into English by Marjorie J. Hall ; with an introductory essay by Richard L. Moxon. — 3rd ed. — London : Graham & Trotman, 1981. — 2v.(loose-leaf) ; 25cm
Previous ed.: published in 1 vol. 1980. — Includes index
ISBN 0-86010-277-7 : Unpriced
ISBN 0-86010-300-5 (v.2) B82-25364

346 — LAW. AFRICA

346.207′1 — Egypt. Mixed courts, *to 1949*
Maakad, Adib. General principles of the Egyptian mixed courts. — London : Laureate Press, Nov.1981. — [500]p
Translation of: Notions générales sur les juridictions mixtes d'Egypte
ISBN 0-907612-00-8 : £30.00 : CIP entry
B81-33632

346.6′3037 — Senegal. Banjal. Economic change, *1900-1975.* **Legal aspects**
Snyder, Francis G.. Capitalism and legal change : an African transformation / Francis G. Snyder. — New York ; London : Academic Press, c1981. — xiv,334p : ill,1map ; 24cm. — (Studies on law and social control)
Bibliography: p305-320. — Includes index
ISBN 0-12-654220-1 : £19.60 B82-12301

346.6902′23 — Nigeria. Constitution, *1979 — Texts with commentaries*
Nigeria. [Constitution of the Federal Republic of Nigeria 1979]. The constitution of the Federal Rebublic of Nigeria 1979 : with annotations / by Jadesola O. Akande. — London : Sweet & Maxwell, 1982. — 277p ; 22cm
Includes index
ISBN 0-421-28940-6 (cased) : Unpriced: CIP rev. B82-14058

346.6902′29 — Nigeria. Constitution, *ca 1900-1979*
Nwabueze, B. O.. A constitution history of Nigeria. — London : C. Hurst, Oct.1982. — [272]p
ISBN 0-905838-79-3 : £12.50 : CIP entry
B82-36293

346.69′05 — Nigeria. Southern States. Criminal law
Aguda, T. Akinola. The criminal law and procedure of the southern states of Nigeria. — 3rd ed. — London : Sweet & Maxwell, Dec.1981. — [1000]p. — (Nigerian practice library)
Previous ed.: published as Brett and McLean's The criminal law and procedure of the six southern states of Nigeria / by C.O. Madarikan and T. Akinola Aguda. 1974
ISBN 0-421-24920-x : £75.00 : CIP entry
B81-31745

346.6905′0264 — Nigeria. Criminal law — *Cases — Serials*
The **Nigerian** criminal reports. — Vol.1 (1980)-. — Oxford (c/o Dr. A. Milner, Trinity College, Oxford) : The African Law Reports, 1981-. — v. ; 24cm
Annual
ISSN 0262-4737 = Nigerian criminal reports : Unpriced B82-04072

346.6906′3 — Nigeria. Torts. Law
Kodilinye, Gilbert. Introduction to the Nigerian law of torts. — London : Sweet and Maxwell, Sept.1982. — [320]p
ISBN 0-421-29150-8 (pbk) : £15.00 : CIP entry
B82-19664

346.6906′7 — Nigeria. Commercial law
Ezejiofor, Gaius. Nigerian business law. — London : Sweet and Maxwell, Sept.1982. — [360]p
ISBN 0-421-30120-1 (cased) : £25.00 : CIP entry
ISBN 0-421-29230-x (pbk) : £16.00
B82-19668

Orojo, J. Olakunle. Nigerian commercial law and practice. — London : Sweet & Maxwell, Sept.1982. — 2v. ([1200]p.). — (Nigerian practice library)
ISBN 0-421-29170-2 : £65.00 : CIP entry
B82-19665

346.6908′48 — Nigeria. Law. Cases — *Indexes*
Jegede, Oluremi. All Nigeria law reports index 1961-1970. — London : Sweet & Maxwell, Sept.1982. — [250]p
ISBN 0-421-30070-1 : £30.00 : CIP entry
B82-24349

346.802′3 — South Africa. Constitution. Reform — *Proposals*
Van Zyl Slabbert, F.. South Africa's options : strategies for sharing power / F. Van Zyl Slabbert and David Welsh. — Cape Town : David Philip ; London : Collings, 1979. — 196p ; 22cm
Bibliography: p184-193. — Includes index
ISBN 0-86036-117-9 (cased) : Unpriced (pbk) : Unpriced B82-08373

347 — LAW. NORTH AMERICA

347.1′009 — Canada. Law — *History*
Essays in the history of Canadian law. — Toronto ; London : Published for the Osgoode Society by University of Toronto Press
Vol.1 / edited by David H. Flaherty. — c1981. — xvi,428p ; 23cm
Includes index
ISBN 0-8020-3382-2 : Unpriced B82-27147

347.102′3 — Canada. Constitution. Law: British North America Acts. Reform. Role of Great Britain. *Parliament.* **Great Britain.** *Parliament. House of Commons. Foreign Affairs Committee.* **First report ... session 1980-81** — *Critical studies*
Great Britain. *Foreign and Commonwealth Office*. First report from the Foreign Affairs Committee, session 1980-81 : British North America acts : the role of Parliament / observations by the Secretary of State for Foreign and Commonwealth Affairs. — London : H.M.S.O., [1981]. — 6p ; 25cm. — (Miscellaneous ; no.26 (1981)) (Cmnd. ; 8450)
ISBN 0-10-184500-6 (unbound) : £1.15
B82-16054

347.104′92 — Canada. Public libraries. Law
Bewley, Lois M.. Public library legislation in Canada : a review and evaluation / by Lois M. Bewley. — London : Vine, 1981. — v,44,[166]p ; 28cm. — (Occasional paper / Dalhousie University Libraries and Dalhousie University. School of Library Service, ISSN 0318-7403 ; 26)
Bibliography: p43-44
ISBN 0-7703-0166-5 (pbk) : Unpriced
B82-19477

347.298′3082 — Trinidad and Tobago *(Republic).* **Law** — *Statutes & secondary legislation — Collections*
The **Laws** of Trinidad and Tobago. — Rev. ed. — Trinidad and Tobago : Government of Trinidad and Tobago ; London : Sweet and Maxwell [distributor]
[Vol.17]: Index / compiled by A.R. Hewitt. — 1981. — 1v.(loose-leaf) ; 26cm
Unpriced B82-33029

347.3′009 — United States. Law, *to 1977*
Law in the American Revolution and the revolution in the law : a collection of review essays on American legal history / edited by Hendrik Hartog. — New York ; London : New York University Press, 1981. — xiii,264p ; 24cm. — (New York University School of Law series in legal history ; 3) (Linden studies in the historiography of American law)
Includes index
ISBN 0-8147-3413-8 : £17.00 B82-36366

347.3′0092′4 — United States. Law. Hamilton, Alexander, *1757-1804 — Correspondence, diaries, etc.*
Hamilton, Alexander, *1757-1804*. The law practice of Alexander Hamilton : documents and commentary. — New York ; London : Published under the auspices of the William Nelson Cromwell Foundation by Columbia University Press
Vol.5 / editors Julius Goebel, Jr. and Joseph H. Smith ; associate editors Winnifred Bowers ... [et al.]. — 1981. — xiv,754p ; 24cm
Includes index
ISBN 0-231-08929-5 : £52.00 B82-17717

347.3′0092′4 — United States. Law. Pisar, Samuel — *Biographies*
Pisar, Samuel. Of blood and hope / Sammuel Pisar. — London : Cassell, 1980. — 316p : ill,ports ; 24cm
Translation from the Polish
ISBN 0-304-30737-8 : £7.95 B82-04945

347.302 — United States. Constitutional law
Corwin, Edward S.. Corwin & Peltason's Understanding the Constitution. — 9th ed. / J.W. Peltason. — New York ; London : Holt, Rinehart and Winston, c1982. — xii,283p ; 24cm
Previous ed.: 1979. — Includes index
ISBN 0-03-060126-6 (pbk) : £10.50
B82-29501

Corwin, Edward S.. Corwin on the Constitution / edited with an introduction and an epilogue by Richard Loss. — Ithaca ; London : Cornell University Press
Vol.1: The foundations of American constitutional and political thought, the powers of Congress, and the President's power of removal. — 1981. — 392p ; 25cm
Includes index
ISBN 0-8014-1381-8 : Unpriced B82-17012

347.302′2 — United States. Constitution

The **American** founding : politics, statesmanship and the constitution / edited by Ralph A. Rossum and Gary L. McDowell. — Port Washington ; London : National University Publications, 1981. — 190p ; 23cm
Includes index
ISBN 0-8046-9283-1 : £14.85 B82-08696

347.302′412 — United States. Territorial expansion, *to 1962.* **Law. Cases**

Kerr, James Edward. The insular cases : the role of the Judiciary in American expansionism / James Edward Kerr. — Port Washington ; London : National University, 1982. — viii,131p ; 22cm. — (Multi-disciplinary studies in the law)
Bibliography: p126-128. — Includes index
ISBN 0-8046-9287-4 : £14.00 B82-31915

347.302′418 — United States. Powers of search & powers of seizure. Law

Polyviou, Polyvios G.. Search and seizure : constitutional and common law. — London : Duckworth, June 1982. — [392]p
ISBN 0-7156-1592-0 : £28.00 : CIP entry
Primary classification 344.202′418 B82-09627

347.302′664 — United States. Litigation by government agencies, *1933-1939*

Irons, Peter H.. The new deal lawyers / by Peter H. Irons. — Princeton ; Guildford : Princeton University Press, c1982. — xiv,351p ; 24cm
Bibliography: p333-340. — Includes index
ISBN 0-691-04688-3 : £13.80 B82-34988

347.302′85 — United States. Civil rights. Legal aspects

Abraham, Henry J.. Freedom and the court : civil rights and liberties in the United States / Henry J. Abraham. — 4th ed. — New York ; Oxford : Oxford University Press, 1982. — xvi,443p ; 21cm
Previous ed.: 1977. — Bibliography: p403-410. — Includes index
ISBN 0-19-502960-7 (cased) : Unpriced
ISBN 0-19-502961-5 (pbk) : £7.95 B82-37009

Perry, Michael J.. The constitution, the courts and human rights. — London : Yale University Press, Nov.1982. — [288]p
ISBN 0-300-02745-1 : £18.50 : CIP entry
B82-40336

347.302′853 — United States. Freedom of speech. Law

Haiman, Franklyn S.. Speech and law in a free society / Franklyn S. Haiman. — Chicago ; London : University of Chicago Press, 1981. — x,499p ; 24cm
Includes index
ISBN 0-226-31213-5 : £13.50 B82-22275

Schauer, Frederick. Free speech : a philosophical enquiry. — Cambridge : Cambridge University Press, Oct.1982. — [237]p
ISBN 0-521-24340-8 (pbk) : £20.00 : CIP entry
ISBN 0-521-28617-4 (pbk) : £6.50 B82-29378

347.302′87 — United States. Children. Law — *Serials*

Advances in law and child development : a research annual. — Vol.1 (1982)-. — Greenwich, Conn. ; London : JAI, 1982-. — v. ; 24cm
Unpriced B82-38535

347.3034 — United States. Tax avoidance — *Manuals*

Steiner, Barry R.. Perfectly legal : 275 foolproof methods for paying less taxes / Barry R. Steiner and David W. Kennedy. — New York ; Chichester : Wiley, c1982. — xvii,201p : facsims,forms ; 29cm
ISBN 0-471-08420-4 : £9.60 B82-25451

347.3035′3 — United States. Inheritance taxes. Tax avoidance

Whitney, Victor P.. The essentials of estate planning : Victor P. Whitney. — New York ; London : Van Nostrand, 1981, c1979. — 256p ; 22cm
Originally published as How to beat the money-grabbers. New Rochelle : Arlington, 1979. — Includes index
ISBN 0-442-29055-1 (pbk) : £6.75 B82-16330

347.3036′6 — United States. Taxation. Liability of organisations. Exemption. Law

Galloway, Joseph M.. The unrelated business income tax / Joseph M. Galloway. — New York ; Chichester : Wiley, c1982. — xiii,186p : ill,2forms ; 24cm. — (The Wiley/Ronald series in professional accounting and business)
Includes index
ISBN 0-471-09916-3 : £25.00 B82-34340

Hopkins, Bruce R.. The law of tax-exempt organizations : Bruce R. Hopkins. — 3rd ed. — New York ; Chichester : Wiley
1982 supplement. — 1982. — vi,105p ; 23cm
Unpriced (pbk) B82-37961

347.303′7 — United States. Industries. Regulation. Law. Reform

Baram, Michael S.. Alternatives to regulation : managing risks to health, safety and the envirnonment / Michael S. Baram with Kevin McAllister and the assistance of Larry Dufault ... [et al.]. — [Lexington, Mass.] : Lexington Books ; [Aldershot] : Gower [distributor], c1982. — ix,245p ; 23cm
Includes index
ISBN 0-669-04666-3 : £18.50 B82-25101

347.303′72 — United States. Industries. Competition. Law

Armentano, Dominick T.. Antitrust and monopoly : anatomy of a policy failure / Dominick T. Armentano. — New York ; Chichester : Wiley, c1982. — xi,292p ; 24cm
Includes index
ISBN 0-471-09931-7 (cased) : £17.00
ISBN 0-471-09930-9 (pbk) : Unpriced
B82-27721

Erickson, Myron L.. Antitrust and trade regulation : cases and materials / Myron L. Erickson, Thomas W. Dunfee, Frank F. Gibson. — New York ; Chichester : Wiley, c1977. — xv,430p : facsims ; 23cm
Includes index
ISBN 0-471-87014-5 (pbk) : £14.00
B82-34741

347.303′723 — United States. Free markets. Law

Courts and free markets : perspectives from the United States and Europe / edited by Terrance Sandalow and Eric Stein. — Oxford : Clarendon
Vol.1. — 1982. — xxxix,271p ; 24cm
ISBN 0-19-825366-4 : £20.00 : CIP rev.
Also classified at 341.7′53 B81-36968

347.303′7864794 — United States. Hotel industries. Law — *For management*

Sherry, John H.. The Laws of innkeepers : for hotels, motels, restaurants and clubs / John H. Sherry. — Rev. ed. / John E.H. Sherry. — Ithaca ; London : Cornell University Press, 1981. — xvi,674p : 3forms ; 25cm
Previous ed.: 1972. — Bibliography: p645-651. — Includes index
ISBN 0-8014-1421-0 : Unpriced
Also classified at 347.303′7864795 B82-16982

347.303′7864795 — United States. Catering industries. Law — *For management*

Sherry, John H.. The Laws of innkeepers : for hotels, motels, restaurants and clubs / John H. Sherry. — Rev. ed. / John E.H. Sherry. — Ithaca ; London : Cornell University Press, 1981. — xvi,674p : 3forms ; 25cm
Previous ed.: 1972. — Bibliography: p645-651. — Includes index
ISBN 0-8014-1421-0 : Unpriced
Primary classification 347.303′7864794
B82-16982

347.303′8 — United States. Commodity markets. Regulation. Law

Friedman, Howard M.. Securities and commodities enforcement : criminal prosecutions and civil injunctions / Howard M. Friedman. — Lexington, Mass. : Lexington Books ; [Aldershot] : Gower [distributor], 1981. — xiii,238p ; 24cm
Includes index
ISBN 0-669-03617-x : £21.50
Primary classification 347.306′926 B82-06205

347.303′967 — United States. Ships. Towing by tugs. Law

Parks, Alex L.. The law of tug, tow, and pilotage. — 2nd ed. — London : Chapman and Hall, Nov.1982. — [1354]p
Previous ed.: Cambridge, Md. : Cornell Maritime Press, 1971
ISBN 0-412-25020-9 : £50.00 : CIP entry
B82-27206

347.303′99 — United States. Mass media. Law

Overbeck, Wayne. Major principles of media law / Wayne Overbeck and Rick D. Pullen. — New York ; London : Holt, Rinehart and Winston, c1982. — xx,354p ; 24cm
ISBN 0-03-058293-8 : £14.50 B82-25412

347.304′3 — United States. Welfare benefits. Administration. Law

Cofer, M. Donna Price. Administering public assistance : a constitutional and administrative perspective / M. Donna Price Cofer. — Port Washington, N.Y. ; London : National University Publications : Kennikat, 1982. — 118p ; 22cm. — (Multidisciplinary studies in law and jurisprudence)
Bibliography: p111-112. — Includes index
ISBN 0-8046-9298-x : Unpriced B82-31902

347.304′414 — United States. Medicine. Nursing. Law

Murchison, Irene. Legal accountability in the nursing process / Irene Murchison, Thomas S. Nichols, Rachel Hanson. — 2nd ed. — St. Louis, Mo. ; London : Mosby, 1982. — xv,188p : ill ; 23cm
Previous ed.: 1978. — Includes index
ISBN 0-8016-3604-3 (pbk) : £8.50 B82-31863

347.304′42 — United States. Motor vehicles. Safety measures. Law

Lambert, John, *1949-*. Motor vehicle safety standards and product liability in the USA / by John Lambert. — London : Economist Intelligence Unit, 1982. — 131p : ill ; 29cm. — (EIU special report ; no.121)
Unpriced (pbk) B82-25007

347.304′44 — United States. Mental health services. Patients. Rights. Law — *Conference proceedings*

Wyatt v. Stickney : retrospect and prospect / [proceedings of a conference on the rights of mental patients at the University of Alabama Ferguson Center, University, Alabama, September 25-26, 1980] ; edited by L. Ralph Jones, Richard R. Parlour. — New York ; London : Grune & Stratton, c1981. — xvii,245p ; 24cm
Includes index
ISBN 0-8089-1422-7 : Unpriced B82-11561

347.304′46 — United States. Environment. Conservation. Legal aspects

Mandelker, Daniel R.. Environment and equity : a regulatory challenge / Daniel R. Mandelker. — New York ; London : McGraw-Hill, c1981. — xiii,162p ; 25cm. — (Regulation of American business and industry)
Includes index
ISBN 0-07-039864-x : £17.45 B82-07447

347.304′462 — United States. Dangerous waste material. Law

Mallow, Alex. Hazardous waste regulations : an interpretive guide / Alex Mallow. — New York ; London : Van Nostrand Reinhold, c1981. — viii,403p : ill,forms ; 29cm
Includes index. — Includes the text of the Resource Conservation and Recovery Act (RCRA) as amended by the Quiet Communities Act of 1978
ISBN 0-442-21935-0 : £34.00 B82-00748

347.304′465 — United States. Industrial health & industrial safety. Law: Occupational Safety and Health Act of 1970 — *For design*

Hopf, Peter S.. Designer′s guide to OSHA : a practical design guide to the Occupational Safety and Health Act for architects, engineers and builders / Peter S. Hopf. — 2nd ed. — New York ; London : McGraw-Hill, c1982. — viii,301p : ill,plans ; 29cm. — (Architectural Record series book)
Previous ed.: 1974. — Includes index. — Includes the text of the Act
ISBN 0-07-030317-7 : £27.95 B82-23892

347.304'48 — United States. Population. Policies of government. Legal aspects

Barnett, Larry D.. Population policy and the U.S. Constitution / Larry D. Barnett ; with a foreword by Kurt W. Back. — The Hague ; London : Kluwer Nijhoff, c1982. — xviii,183p : ill ; 24cm. — (Kluwer Nijhoff studies in human issues)
Includes index
ISBN 0-89838-082-0 : Unpriced B82-35974

347.304'7 — United States. Schools. Law

Valente, William D.. Law in the schools / William D. Valente. — Columbus, Ohio ; London : Merrill, c1980. — xvii,556p ; 26cm
Includes index
ISBN 0-675-08165-3 : £14.25 B82-25670

347.304'798 — United States. Schools. Desegregation. Decisions of United States. *Supreme Court, 1954-1978*

Wilkinson, J. Harvie. From Brown to Bakke : the Supreme Court and school integration, 1954-1978 / J. Harvie Wilkinson III. — New York ; Oxford : Oxford University Press, 1979. — viii,368p : 1facsim ; 24cm
Includes index
ISBN 0-19-502567-9 : £11.50 B82-25893

347.304'92 — United States. Libraries. Administration. Law

Ladenson, Alex. Library law and legislation in the United States / Alex Ladenson. — Metuchen ; London : Scarecrow, 1982. — x,191p ; 22cm. — (Scarecrow library administration series ; no.1)
Includes index
ISBN 0-8108-1513-3 : £11.60 B82-31806

347.305'06 — United States. Criminal courts. Evidence. Presentation & evaluation

Bennett, W. Lance. Reconstructing reality in the courtroom. — London : Tavistock, Sept.1981. — [180]p
ISBN 0-422-77840-0 : £8.25 : CIP entry B81-22474

347.305'231 — United States. Treason. Trials, *1945-1960*

West, Rebecca. The meaning of treason / Rebecca West. — [New] ed. / with a new introduction by the author. — London : Virago, 1982. — xi,439p ; 20cm
Previous ed.: Harmondsworth : Penguin, 1965. — Includes index
ISBN 0-86068-256-0 (pbk) : £4.50 : CIP rev.
Primary classification 344.205'231 B81-40235

347.305'2532 — United States. Crimes: Rape. Law

Marsh, Jeanne C.. Rape and the limits of law reform / Jeanne C. Marsh, Alison Geist, Nathan Caplan. — Boston, Mass. : Auburn House ; London : Eurospan [distributor], c1982. — xix,171p : ill,forms ; 25cm
Includes index
ISBN 0-86569-083-9 : Unpriced B82-39783

347.305'5042 — United States. Offenders. Prosecution. Procedure

Nissman, David M.. The prosecution function / David M. Nissman, Ed Hagen. — [Lexington, Mass.] : Lexington Books ; [Aldershot] : Gower [distributor], c1982. — xi,203p ; 24cm
Includes index
ISBN 0-669-04591-8 : £16.50 B82-25104

347.305'72 — United States. Criminal courts. Defendants. Pre-trial release

Feeney, Floyd. The police and pretrial release / Floyd Feeney ; foreword by Edward L. Barrett, Jr. — [Lexington, Mass.] : Lexington Books ; [Aldershot] : Gower [distributor], 1982. — xviii,211p ; 24cm
ISBN 0-669-03597-1 : £17.50 B82-35426

347.3063'2 — United States. Accountants. Negligence. Liability. Law

Pockson, Jonathan R. H. H.. Accountant's professional negligence : developments in legal liability / Jonathan R.H.H. Pockson. — London : Macmillan, 1982. — xxi,212p : ill ; 23cm
Bibliography: p192-208. — Includes index
ISBN 0-333-27845-3 : £25.00
Primary classification 344.1063'2 B82-20938

347.3064'32 — United States. Land. Boundaries. Law

Brown, Curtis M.. Evidence and procedures for boundary location. — 2nd ed. / Curtis M. Brown, Walter G. Robillard, Donald A. Wilson. — New York ; Chichester : Wiley, c1981. — xi,450p : ill ; 24cm
Previous ed.: 1962. — Includes index
ISBN 0-471-08382-8 : £29.00 B82-11630

347.3064'67923 — United States. Solar energy. Legal aspects

Legal aspects of solar energy / edited by John H. Minan, William H. Lawrence. — Lexington, [Mass.] : Lexington Books ; [Aldershot] : Gower [distributor], 1982, c1981. — xiii,231p : ill ; 24cm
ISBN 0-669-03761-3 : £18.50 B82-11712

347.306'652 — United States. Small firms. Contracts. Legal aspects — *Manuals*

Adams, Paul, *1936-*. The complete legal guide for your small business / Paul Adams. — New York ; Chichester : Wiley, c1982. — xx,218p : forms ; 24cm. — (Small business management series, ISSN 0271-6054)
Bibliography: p213. — Includes index
ISBN 0-471-09436-6 : Unpriced B82-19651

347.306'7 — United States. Commercial law

Dunfee, Thomas W.. Modern business law : an introduction to government and business / Thomas W. Dunfee, Frank F. Gibson. — 2nd ed. — New York ; Chichester : Wiley, c1977. — xii,257p ; 23cm
Previous ed.: Columbus, Ohio : Grid, 1973. — Includes index
ISBN 0-471-87016-1 (pbk) : £10.10 B82-34743

Howell, Rate A.. Business law / Rate A. Howell, John R. Allison, N.T. Henley. — 2nd alternate ed. — Chicago ; London : Dryden, c1982. — xxii,931p : ill ; 25cm
Previous ed.: 1978. — Includes index
ISBN 0-03-059742-0 : £18.95 B82-27388

347.306'7 — United States. Commercial law — *For executives*

Corley, Robert N.. Fundamentals of business law. — 3rd ed. / Robert N. Corley, Eric M. Holmes, William J. Robert. — Englewood Cliffs ; London : Prentice-Hall, c1982. — xviii,749p : ill,forms ; 25cm. — (A Special projects book)
Previous ed.: 1978. — Includes index
ISBN 0-13-332189-4 : £15.75 B82-16984

347.306'7'076 — United States. Commercial law — *Questions & answers*

Grimes, Ellen. How to prepare for the business law section of the C.P.A. examination / Ellen Grimes ; editor-in-chief Caryl Ann Russell. — New York ; London : McGraw-Hill, c1978. — 169p ; 28cm. — (A Trafalgar House book)
ISBN 0-07-024827-3 (pbk) : £7.45 B82-24801

Person, Samuel. Business law / Samuel Person, Daniel Wolinsky ; technical editor Robert Beekman. — Chicago ; London : Dryden, c1982. — xix,169p : forms ; 28cm. — (CPA exam supplement)
ISBN 0-03-059796-x (corrected : pbk) : £6.95 B82-19058

347.306'926 — United States. Securities markets. Regulation. Law

Friedman, Howard M.. Securities and commodities enforcement : criminal prosecutions and civil injunctions / Howard M. Friedman. — Lexington, Mass. : Lexington Books ; [Aldershot] : Gower [distributor], 1981. — xiii,238p ; 24cm
Includes index
ISBN 0-669-03617-x : £21.50
Also classified at 347.303'8 B82-06205

347.307 — United States. Legal system. Attitudes of students at Kent State University. Effects of legal proceedings relating to shooting of students at Kent State University, *1970*

Hensley, Thomas R.. The Kent State incident : impact of judicial process on public attitudes / Thomas R. Hensley with James J. Best ... [et al.]. — Westport, Conn. ; London : Greenwood Press, 1981. — xiv,281p : ill,forms ; 22cm. — (Contributions in political science, ISSN 0147-1066 ; no.56)
Bibliography: p271-276. — Includes index
ISBN 0-313-21220-1 : Unpriced B82-01944

347.307'09 — United States. Legal system, *1908-1940*

Johnson, John W. (John William). American legal culture, 1908-1940 / John W. Johnson. — Westport ; London : Greenwood, 1981. — x,185p ; 22cm. — (Contributions in legal studies, ISSN 0147-1074 ; no.16)
Bibliography: p165-173. — Includes index
ISBN 0-313-22337-8 : Unpriced B82-02004

347.307'1 — United States. Government. Role of law courts

Governing through courts / edited by Richard A. L. Gambitta, Marlynn L. May, James C. Foster. — Beverly Hills ; London : Sage, c1981. — 319p : 2ill ; 22cm. — (Sage focus editions ; 40)
Includes index
ISBN 0-8039-1719-8 (cased) : Unpriced
ISBN 0-8039-1720-1 (pbk) : £6.50 B82-21512

Neely, Richard. How courts govern America / Richard Neely. — New Haven ; London : Yale, c1981. — xvii,233p ; 24cm
Includes index
ISBN 0-300-02589-0 : Unpriced : CIP rev. B81-30242

347.307'12 — United States. Federal courts. Jurisdiction

Freyer, Tony Allan. Harmony & dissonance : the Swift & Erie cases in American federalism / Tony Freyer. — New York ; London : New York University Press, 1981. — xv,190p ; 24cm. — (New York University School of Law series in legal history ; 4) (Linden studies in American legal history)
Includes index
ISBN 0-8147-2568-6 : £16.70 B82-35944

347.307'202 — United States. Federal courts. Judicial powers. Political aspects

Radcliffe, James E.. The case-or-controversy provision / James E. Radcliffe. — University Park ; London : Pennsylvania State University Press, c1978. — 285p ; 24cm
Bibliography: p268-274. — Includes index
ISBN 0-271-00509-2 : £11.50 B82-27553

347.307'26'09 — United States. *Supreme Court, 1969-1975*

Woodward, Bob. The brethren : inside the Supreme Court. — London : Hodder & Stoughton, Nov.1981. — [576]p. — (Coronet books)
Originally published: London : Secker & Warburg, 1980
ISBN 0-340-26781-x (pbk) : £1.95 : CIP entry B81-30137

347.307'26'09 — United States. *Supreme Court — History*

History of the Supreme Court of the United States. — New York : Macmillan ; London : Collier Macmillan
Vol.2: Foundations of Power : John Marshall, 1801-15. — c1981. — xiv,687p,[24]p of plates : ill,ports ; 25cm
At head of title: The Oliver Wendell Holmes Devise. — Pt.1 / by George Lee Haskins — Pt.2 / by Herbert A. Johnson. — Includes index
ISBN 0-02-541360-0 : £35.00 B82-18003

347.307'2634'0924 — United States. *Supreme Court.* Judges: Brandeis, Louis D. — *Biographies*

Gal, Allon. Brandeis of Boston / Allon Gal. — Cambridge, Mass. ; London : Harvard University Press, 1980. — xi,271p ; 25cm
Bibliography: p209-217. — Includes index
ISBN 0-674-08043-2 : £11.55 B82-26810

347.307′67 — United States. Law courts. Expert evidence — *Manuals — For accountancy*
Dykeman, Francis C.. Forensic accounting : the accountant as expert witness / Francis C. Dykeman. — New York ; Chichester : Wiley, c1982. — ix,236p ; 23cm
Includes index
ISBN 0-471-08395-x : £27.00 B82-18204

347.307′72 — United States. Civil law. Cases. Documents. Discovery & inspection. Law *compared with* **law of discovery & inspection of documents in English civil cases**
Levine, Julius Byron. Discovery : a comparison between English and American civil discovery law with reform proposals / Julius Byron Levine. — Oxford : Clarendon, 1982. — xl,208p ; 23cm
Bibliography: p154-160. — Includes index
ISBN 0-19-825368-0 : £16.00 : CIP rev.
Primary classification 344.207′72 B81-31740

347.308′04 — United States. Law. Codification, *1776-1860*
Cook, Charles M.. The American codification movement : a study of antebellum legal reform / Charles M. Cook. — Westport ; London : Greenwood Press, 1981. — xi,234p ; 25cm. — (Contributions in legal studies ; no.14)
Bibliography: p215-228. — Includes index
ISBN 0-313-21314-3 : Unpriced B82-18019

347.308′2 — United States. Law. Statutes
Hurst, James Willard. Dealing with statutes / James Willard Hurst. — New York ; Guildford : Columbia University Press, 1982. — 140p ; 24cm
Bibliography: p127-132. — Includes index
ISBN 0-231-05390-8 : £10.50 B82-19569

347.308′22 — United States. Law. Statutes
Calabresi, Guido. A common law for the age of statutes / Guido Calabresi. — Cambridge, Mass. ; London : Harvard University Press, 1982. — 319p ; 24cm. — (Oliver Wendell Holmes lectures)
Bibliography: p300-309. — Includes index
ISBN 0-674-14604-2 : Unpriced B82-27089

347.308′28 — United States. States. Law. Statutes. Subject indexes — *Lists*
Foster, Lynn, *1952-*. Subject compilations of state laws : research guide and annotated bibliography / Lynn Foster and Carol Boast. — Westport, Conn. ; London : Greenwood, 1981. — xi,473p ; 24cm
Includes index
ISBN 0-313-21255-4 : Unpriced B82-02616

347.4402 — Massachusetts. Constitutional law — *Early works*
Massachusetts. *Governor (1770-1774 : Hutchinson)*. The briefs of the American Revolution : constitutional arguments between Thomas Hutchinson, Governor of Massachusetts Bay, and James Bowdoin for the Council and John Adams of the House of Representatives / edited by John Phillip Reid. — New York ; London : New York University Press, 1981. — 194p ; 24cm. — (New York University School of Law series in legal history ; 1) (Linden studies in American constitutional history)
Bibliography: p167-173. — Includes index
ISBN 0-8147-7384-2 : £16.75 B82-36365

347.4405′2523′0922 — Massachusetts. Boston. Murder. Trial of Sacco, Nicola & Vanzetti, Bartolomeo
Jackson, Brian, *1932-*. The black flag : a look at the strange case of Nicola Sacco and Bartolomeo Vanzetti / Brian Jackson. — Boston, Mass. ; London : Routledge & Kegan Paul, 1981. — xiv,208p ; 25cm
Bibliography: p197-202. — Includes index
ISBN 0-7100-0897-x : £6.95 B82-05332

347.4705′2523′0924 — New York *(State)*. **Tarnower, Herman. Murder. Trial of Harris, Jean**
Trilling, Diana. Mrs Harris : the death of the Scarsdale diet doctor / Diana Trilling. — London : Hamilton, 1982, c1981. — 341p ; 25cm
Originally published: New York : Harcourt Brace Jovanovich, 1981
ISBN 0-241-10822-5 : £8.95 : CIP rev. B82-04315

347.47061′8 — New York *(City)*. **Vanderbilt, Gloria,** *1924-*. **Custody. Petition by Vanderbilt, Gloria,** *1904-1965, 1934*
Goldsmith, Barbara. Little Gloria — happy at last / Barbara Goldsmith. — London : Pan in association with Macmillan, 1981, c1980. — xvii,587p,[12]p of plates : 1facsim,ports ; 18cm
Originally published: New York : Knopf, 1980 ; London : Macmillan, 1980. — Bibliography: p555-568. — Includes index
ISBN 0-330-26411-7 (pbk) : £1.95 B82-04248

347.8064′32 — United States. Western states. North American Indians. Agricultural land. Land tenure. Law: General Allotment Act of 1887. Operation, *to 1934*
Carlson, Leonard A.. Indians, bureaucrats, and land : the Dawes Act and the decline of Indian farming / Leonard A. Carlson. — Westport, Conn. ; London : Greenwood, 1981. — xii,219p : ill ; 24cm. — (Contributions in economics and economic history ; no.36)
Bibliography: p207-212. — Includes index
ISBN 0-313-22533-8 : Unpriced B82-02617

349 — LAW. OCEANIA, ATLANTIC OCEAN ISLANDS, POLAR REGIONS, ETC

349.403′71 — Australia. Consumers. Rights
Goldring, John. Consumers or victims?. — London : Allen & Unwin, Apr.1982. — [176]p
ISBN 0-86861-012-7 : £15.00 : CIP entry B82-05766

349.4061′3 — Queensland. Australian aborigines. Legal status
Nettheim, Garth. Victims of the law. — London : Allen & Unwin, Jan.1982. — [216]p
ISBN 0-86861-395-9 : £17.95 : CIP entry B81-34636

350 — PUBLIC ADMINISTRATION

350 — Public administration. Information systems — *Conference proceedings*
Information systems in public administration : and their role in economic and social development : proceedings of an international seminar held in Chamrousse, France, 17-23, June, 1979 / organized by the Data for Development International Association under the auspices of the United Nations Educational, Scientific and Cultural Organization and the International Federation for Information Processing ; edited by David Eade, John Hodgson. — Amsterdam ; Oxford : North-Holland, c1981. — xiii,475p : ill ; 23cm
ISBN 0-444-86275-7 : £17.95 B82-08566

350′.00092′4 — Great Britain. Public administration. Cook, Pat, *19---* — *Biographies*
Cook, Pat, *1920-*. Ombudsman : an autobiography / by Pat Cook. — London : BKT, 1981. — 155p ; 22cm
ISBN 0-904677-19-2 : £6.95 B82-31412

350′.000941 — Great Britain. Public administration — *For business studies*
Sallis, E. J.. The machinery of government : an introduction to public administration / Edward Sallis. — London : Holt, Rinehart and Winston, c1982. — x,262p : ill,maps ; 22cm
Bibliography: p253-258. — Includes index
ISBN 0-03-910368-4 (pbk) : Unpriced : CIP rev. B82-10691

350′.0009669 — Nigeria. Public administration
Adamolekun, Ladipo. Public administration : a Nigerian and comparative perspective. — London : Longman, Dec.1982. — [224]p
ISBN 0-582-64349-x (pbk) : £3.95 : CIP entry B82-30067

350′.000973 — United States. Public administration
Doing public administration : exercises, essays and cases / [editor] Nicholas Henry. — 2nd ed. — Boston, Mass. ; London : Allyn and Bacon, c1982. — x,388p : ill,forms ; 28cm
Previous ed.: 1978. — Includes bibliographies
ISBN 0-205-07648-3 (pbk) : Unpriced B82-27112

Garson, G. David. Public administration : concepts, readings, skills / G. David Garson, J. Oliver Williams. — Boston, Mass. ; London : Allyn and Bacon, c1982. — viii,472p : ill ; 25cm
Includes bibliographies and index
ISBN 0-205-07562-2 : £18.95 B82-03085

350′.001 — Bureaucracy
Jackson, Peter McLeod. The political economy of bureaucracy. — Oxford : Philip Allan, Oct.1981. — [296]p
ISBN 0-86003-024-5 : £12.50 : CIP entry B81-31949

351 — CENTRAL GOVERNMENT ADMINISTRATION

351 — Governments — *Comparative studies*
Blandel, Jean. World governments. — London : Sage Publications, Aug.1982. — [246]p. — (Political executives in comparative perspective. a cross-national empirical study ; v.2)
ISBN 0-8039-9776-0 (cased) : £15.00 : CIP entry
ISBN 0-8039-9777-9 (pbk) : £5.95 B82-15850

351′.000966 — West Africa. Governments — *For West African students*
Oyeneye, Ibeyimi. West African government for O-level / Ibeyimi Oyeneye. — Harlow : Longman, 1981. — xiv,191p : ill,maps,ports ; 24cm
Includes index
ISBN 0-582-60958-5 (pbk) : £2.35 B82-12363

351.003′73′096 — Government. Role of law courts — *Study regions: Africa. English speaking countries*
Amissah, A. N. E.. The contribution of the courts to government. — Oxford : Clarendon Press, July 1981. — [385]p
ISBN 0-19-825356-7 : £22.50 : CIP entry B81-19197

351.004′094 — Europe. Government departments. Names — *Lists — For cataloguing*
List of uniform headings for higher legislative and ministerial bodies in European countries / compiled by the USSR Cataloguing Committee. — 2nd ed. rev. — London : IFLA International Office for UBC, 1979. — x,53p ; 30cm
English introduction, text in various languages. — Previous ed.: London : IFLA Committee on Cataloguing, 1975. — Includes index
ISBN 0-903043-23-8 (pbk) : £8.00 : CIP rev.
Also classified at 328′.3′094 B79-34030

351.004′096 — Africa. Government departments. Names — *Lists — For cataloguing*
African legislative and ministerial bodies : list of Uniform headings for higher legislative and ministerial bodies in African countries / compiled by the IFLA International Office for UBC in association with the African Standing Conference on Bibliographic Control. — London : The Office, 1980. — viii,37p ; 30cm
English and French text with one chapter in parallel French and Kirundi. — Includes index
ISBN 0-903043-25-4 (pbk) : £6.00 : CIP rev.
Also classified at 328′.3′096 B80-12296

351.007′2 — Western World. Governments. Policies. Formulation. Role of politicians *compared with* **role of civil servants** — *Comparative studies*
Aberbach, Joel D.. Bureaucrats and politicians in Western democracies / Joel D. Aberbach, Robert D. Putnam, Bert A. Rockman with the collaboration of Thomas J. Anton, Samuel J. Eldersveld, Ronald Inglehart. — Cambridge, Mass. ; London : Harvard University Press, 1981. — xii,308p : ill ; 24cm
Includes index
ISBN 0-674-08625-2 : £20.65 B82-11873

351.007′2′05 — Governments. Policies — *Serials*
Journal of public policy. — Vol.1, pt.1 (Feb. 1981)-. — Cambridge : Cambridge University Press, 1981-. — v. ; 24cm
Quarterly
ISSN 0143-814X = Journal of public policy : £30.00 per year (£15.00 for individuals) B82-20875

351.007'2'094 — European Community countries. Governments. Policies. Harmonisation

Harmonisation in the EEC / edited by Carol Cosgrove Twitchett. — London : Macmillan, 1981. — vii,144p ; 23cm
Conference proceedings. — Includes index
ISBN 0-333-26131-3 : £20.00 B82-03908

351.007'25 — Governments. Policies. Decision-making

Hogwood, Brian W.. Policy dynamics. — Brighton : Wheatsheaf Books, Oct.1982. — [320]p
ISBN 0-7108-0177-7 : £22.50 : CIP entry B82-25765

351.009 — Governments. Agents in Great Britain: Crown Agents for Overseas Governments and Administrations — *Inquiry reports*

Report of the tribunal appointed to inquire into certain issues arising out of the operations of the Crown Agents as financiers on own account in the years 1967-74. — London : H.M.S.O., [1982?]. — xi,604p ; 25cm. — (HL ; 149) (HC ; 364)
Includes index
ISBN 0-10-414982-5 (pbk) : £16.35 B82-29615

351.01 — Foreign ministries

The **Times** survey of foreign ministries of the world / selected and edited by Zara Steiner. — London : Times Books, c1982. — 624p,[2]p of folded leaves : ill ; 24cm
Includes bibliographies and index
ISBN 0-7230-0245-2 : £40.00 : CIP rev. B82-00379

351.71'45 — Western world. Official secrets. Disclosure. Policies of governments

Robertson, K. G.. Public secrets : a study in the development of government secrecy / K.G. Robertson. — London : Macmillan, 1982. — x,216p ; 23cm
Includes index
ISBN 0-333-32008-5 : £15.00 B82-32376

351.72'32 — Governments. Performance auditing

Brown, Richard E.. Auditing performance in government : concept and cases / Richard E. Brown, Thomas P. Gallagher, Meredith C. Williams. — New York ; Chichester : Wiley, c1982. — xii,298p : ill ; 24cm
Includes index
ISBN 0-471-08188-4 : £25.50 B82-37200

351.89'2'0941 — Great Britain. Foreign diplomats — *Illustrations — Serials*

At the Court of St. James's. — 1981. — London (58 Theobalds Rd, WC1) : Diplomatist Associates, [1981]. — 100p
£10.00 B82-03411

351.9'1'091821 — Western world. Governments. Complaints by public. Procedure

Hurwitz, Leon. The state as defendant : governmental accountability and the redress of individual grievances / Leon Hurwitz. — London : Aldwych, 1981. — xvii,211p ; 24cm. — (Studies in human rights ; no.2)
Bibliography: p197-203. — Includes index
ISBN 0-86172-017-2 : £18.50 B82-30922

352 — LOCAL GOVERNMENT

352 — Local government. Political aspects — *Comparative studies*

Schulz, Ann. Local politics and nation-states : case studies in politics and policy / Ann Schulz. — Santa Barbara ; Oxford : Clio, c1979. — xii,234p : ill,maps ; 24cm. — (Studies in international and comparative politics ; 12)
Includes index
ISBN 0-87436-289-x : £14.25 B82-27404

352'.00023'41 — Great Britain. Local government — *Career guides*

Crabtree, J. W.. Working in a town hall / by J.W. Crabtree ; photography by Chris Fairclough. — Hove : Wayland, 1982. — 94p : ill,ports ; 25cm. — (People at work)
Includes index
ISBN 0-85340-927-7 : £4.95 B82-34832

Taylor, Felicity. Careers in local government / Felicity Taylor. — London : Kogan Page, 1981. — 96p : ill ; 18cm
ISBN 0-85038-437-0 (cased) : Unpriced : CIP rev.
ISBN 0-85038-438-9 (pbk) : £2.50 B81-30638

352'.00028'54 — United States. Local government. Applications of digital computer systems

Computers and politics : high technology in American local governments / James N. Danziger ... [et al.]. — New York ; Guildford : Columbia University Press, 1982. — xv,280p ; 24cm
Bibliography: p265-276. — Includes index
ISBN 0-231-04888-2 : £18.00 B82-21496

352'.00028'5404 — Great Britain. Local government. Applications of microcomputer systems

A **Study** of the local government computer environment. — London : LAMSAC, 1980. — 137p : ill ; 30cm. — (Micro computing in local government ; element 2)
£3.00 (spiral) B82-11049

352'.0004725'0941 — Great Britain. Local authorities. Decision making. Influence of public — *Manuals*

Influencing your local council / Educational Centres Association. — London (Chequer St., Bunhill Row, EC1Y 8PL) : ECA, [1982]. — 1sheet ; 21x45cm folded to 21x15cm. — (ECA advisory leaflet ; no.9)
Unpriced B82-39514

352'.0004725'0941 — Great Britain. Local authorities. Decision making. Participation of public

Public participation in local services / Noel Boaden ... [et al.]. — London : Longman, 1982. — 194p ; 20cm
Bibliography: p180-186. — Includes index
ISBN 0-582-29562-9 (pbk) : £3.50 : CIP rev. B82-20258

352'.000473 — Ireland *(Republic)*. Local government. Reform — *Proposals*

Tierney, Myles, *1935-*. The parish pump : a study of democratic efficiency and local government in Ireland / Myles Tierney ; foreword by Basil Chubb. — Dublin : Able Press, c1982. — 126p ; 21cm : maps
ISBN 0-906281-03-2 (pbk) : Unpriced B82-16965

352'.000473 — Local government. Reorganisation — *Comparative studies*

International handbook on local government reorganization : contemporary developments / edited by Donald C. Rowat. — London : Aldwych, 1980. — xv,626p : ill ; 25cm
Bibliography: p605-610. — Includes index
ISBN 0-86172-008-3 : £34.50 B82-31083

352'.0005 — Local government — *Serials*

IULA/CEM news. — Autumn 1980--. — London (26 Old St., SW1H 9HP) : IULA/CEM British Sections, 1980-. — v. : ports ; 30cm
Quarterly. — Continues: Municipal world. — Description based on: Spring 1981 issue
ISSN 0261-2739 = IULA/CEM news : Unpriced B82-31705

352'.002 — France. Nice. Local government. Corruption

Greene, Graham. J'accuse — Nice, the darker side. — London : Bodley, Apr.1982. — [32]p
English and French text
ISBN 0-370-30930-8 (pbk) : £0.95 : CIP entry B82-11266

352'.002 — Great Britain. Local government. Corruption, *ca 1955-1972:* Poulson case

Fitzwalter, Raymond. Web of corruption : the story of J.G.L. Poulson and T. Dan Smith / Raymond Fitzwalter and David Taylor. — London : Granada, 1981. — 282p,[8]p of plates : ports ; 25cm
Includes index
ISBN 0-246-10915-7 : £12.50 B82-09234

352'.0051'00942 — England. Local authorities. Personnel management

Fowler, Alan. Personnel management in local government / Alan Fowler. — 2nd ed. — London : Institute of Personnel Management, 1980. — 307p ; 22cm
Previous ed.: 1975. — Bibliography: p304. — Includes index
ISBN 0-85292-270-1 (pbk) : £7.95 : CIP rev. B80-19678

352'.0054 — Great Britain. Local authorities. Personnel. Effects of technological innovation — *National Union of Public Employees viewpoints*

Danger : new technology at work. — London : National Union of Public Employees, 1982. — 12p : ill ; 22cm
Cover title. — Text on inside cover
ISBN 0-907334-13-x (pbk) : Unpriced B82-21341

352'.0072'071041 — Great Britain. Educational institutions. Curriculum subjects: Urban regions. Local government — *Conference proceedings*

Education for urban governance : a report on the CES conference. — London : Centre for Environmemtal Studies, 1974. — 101p : ill ; 30cm. — (Conference paper / Centre for Environmental Studies ; 10)
£0.50 (pbk) B82-08895

352'.0072'09429 — Wales. Community councils. Boundaries — *Proposals*

Local Government Boundary Commission for Wales. Special community review / Local Government Boundary Commission for Wales = Arolwg cymdeithas arbennig / Comisiwn Ffiniau Llywodraeth Leol i Gymru. — [Cardiff] ([Queens Court, Plymouth St., Cardiff CF1 4DA]) : [The Commission]
Parallel Welsh and English text. — Map (1 folded sheet) in pocket
Report and proposals for District of Montgomery = Adroddiad a chynigion ar gyfer Dosbarth Trefaldwyn. — [1981?]. — 347p : 1col.map ; 30cm
(spiral) B82-29565

Local Government Boundary Commission for Wales. Special community review / Local Government Boundary Commission for Wales = Arolwg cymdeithas arbennig / Comisiwn Fffiniau Llywodraeth Leol i Gymru. — [Cardiff] ([Queens Court, Plymouth St., Cardiff CF1 4DA]) : [The Commission]
Report and proposals for District of Rhymney Valley = Adroddiad a chynigion ar gyfer Dosbarth Dyffryn Rhymni. — [1981?]. — 111p : 1col.map ; 30cm
Parallel Welsh and English text. — Map on folded sheet in pocket
Unpriced (spiral) B82-06300

Special community review / Local Government Boundary Commission for Wales = Arolwg cymdeithas arbennig / Comisiwn Ffiniau Llywodraeth Leol i Gymru. — [Cardiff] ([The Hayes, Cardiff CF1 1JW]) : [H.M.S.O.]
Report and proposals for Borough of Blaenau Gwent = Adroddiad a chynigion ar gyfer Bwrdeistref Blaenau Gwent. — [1982]. — 79p : 1col.map ; 30cm
Parallel Welsh and English text. — Map on folded sheet in pocket
Unpriced (spiral) B82-34249

Special community review / Local Government Boundary Commission for Wales = Arolwg cymdeithas arbennig / Comisiwn Ffiniau Llywodraeth Leol i Gymru. — [Cardiff] ([The Hayes, Cardiff CF1 1JW]) : [H.M.S.O.]
Report and proposals for Borough of Torfaen = Adroddiad a chynigion ar gyfer Bwrdeistref Torfaen. — [1982]. — 107p,1folded leaf of plates : col.maps ; 30cm
Parallel Welsh and English text. — Map on folded sheet in pocket
Unpriced (spiral) B82-34250

Special community review / Local Government Boundary Commission for Wales = Arolwg cymdeithas arbennig. — [Cardiff] ([The Hayes, Cardiff CF1 1JW]) : [H.M.S.O.]
Parallel Welsh and English texts
Report and proposals for District of Ceredigion = Adroddiad a chynigion ar gyfer Dosbarth Ceredigion. — [1982]. — 429p : 1col.map ; 30cm
Map of folded sheet in pocket
Unpriced (spiral) B82-21044

352'.00722'0947 — Russia. Rural regions. Local government, *to 1917 — Conference proceedings*

The **Zemstvo** in Russia : an experiment in local self-government / edited by Terence Emmons and Wayne S. Vucinich. — Cambridge : Cambridge University Press, 1982. — xii,452p ; 24cm
Includes index
ISBN 0-521-23416-6 : £25.00 B82-29933

352'.00724'0942 — England. Cities. Local government, *1837-1901*

Municipal reform and the industrial city / edited by Derek Fraser. — [Leicester] : Leicester University Press, 1982. — x,165p : ill ; 24cm. — (Themes in urban history)
Includes bibliographies and index
ISBN 0-7185-1176-x : £12.00 : CIP rev. B82-09628

352'.0073 — England. District councils. Officers: District secretaries. Organisations: Association of District Secretaries — *Serials*

[Bulletin *(Association of District Secretaries)***]**. Bulletin / Association of District Secretaries. — Ed. no.1 (July 1982)-. — Chippenham (North Wiltshire District Council, Monkton Park, Chippenham, Wilts. SN15 1ER) : B.J. Quoroll, 1982-. — v. ; 30cm
Quarterly. — Continues: A.D.S. journal
ISSN 0263-4562 = Bulletin - Association of District Secretaries : Unpriced B82-40073

352'.0073 — Gloucestershire. Cotswold *(District).* **Parish boundaries** — *Proposals*

Cotswold. *District Council.* Parish boundary review / draft recommendations of Cotswold District Council [to the] Local Government Boundary Commission for England. — [Cirencester] ([5 Dyer St, Cirencester, Gloucestershire]) : [Cotswold District Council], [1982?]. — 54p ; 21cm
Cover title
Unpriced (pbk) B82-26987

352'.0073'0942 — England. Regional government

Regional government in England / edited by Brian W. Hogwood, Michael Keating. — Oxford : Clarendon Press, 1982. — x,277p : ill,maps ; 23cm
Includes index
ISBN 0-19-827434-3 : £18.50 : CIP rev. B82-03095

352'.0073'09429 — Wales. District councils. Wards — *Proposals*

Local Government Boundary Commission for Wales. Review of district electoral arrangements / Local Government Boundary Commission for Wales = Arolwg o drefniadau'r etholiadau dosbarth / Comisiwn Ffiniau Llywodraeth Leol i Gymru. — [Cardiff] ([Queens Court, Plymouth St., Cardiff CF1 4DA]) : [The Commission]
Parallel Welsh and English text
Report and proposals for Borough of Vale of Glamorgan = Adroddiad a chynigion ar gyfer Bwrdeistref Bro Morgannwy. — [1982]. — 27p ; 30cm
Unpriced (unbound) B82-23550

Local Government Boundary Commission for Wales. Review of district electoral arrangements / Local Government Boundary Commission for Wales = Arolwg o drefniadau'r etholiadau dosbarth / Comisiwn Ffiniau Llywodraeth Leol i Gymru. — [Cardiff] ([Queens Court, Plymouth St., Cardiff CF1 4DA]) : [The Commission]
Parallel Welsh and English text
Report and proposals for City of Cardiff = Adroddiad a chynigion ar gyfer Dinas Caerdydd. — [1982]. — 19p ; 30cm
Unpriced (unbound) B82-23551

Review of district electoral arrangements / Local Government Boundary Commission for Wales = Arolwg o drefniadau'r etholiadau dosbarth / Comisiwn Ffiniau Llywodraeth Leol i Gymru. — [Cardiff] ([The Hayes, Cardiff CF1 1JW]) : [H.M.S.O.]
Parallel Welsh and English texts
Report and proposals for Borough of Neath = Adroddiad a chynigion ar gyfer Bwrdeistref Nedd. — [1982]. — [27]p ; 30cm
Unpriced (unbound) B82-21043

Review of district electoral arrangements draft proposals / Local Government Boundary Commission for Wales = Arolwg o drefniadau'r etholiadau dosbarth cynigion drafft / Comisiwn Ffiniau Llywodraeth Leol i Gymru. — [Cardiff] ([The Hayes, Cardiff. CF1 1JW]) : [H.M.S.O]
Cover title
Borough of Arfon = Bwrdeistref Arfon. — [1981]. — 15,[14]p ; 30cm
Parallel Welsh text and English translation
Unpriced (pbk) B82-04379

Review of district electoral arrangements draft proposals / Local Government Boundary Commission for Wales = Arolwg o drefniadau'r etholiadau dosbarth cynigion drafft / Comisiwn Ffiniau Llywodraeth Leol i Gymru. — [Cardiff] ([The Hayes, Cardiff. CF1 1JW]) : [H.M.S.O]
Borough of Cynon Valley = Bwrdeistref Cwm Cynon. — [1981]. — 15,[10]p ; 30cm
Parallel Welsh text and English translation
Unpriced (pbk) B82-04378

Review of district electoral arrangements draft proposals / Local Government Boundary Commission for Wales = Arolwg o drefniadau'r etholiadau dosbarth cynigion drafft / Comisiwn Ffiniau Llywodraeth Leol i Gymru. — [Cardiff] ([The Hayes, Cardiff. CF1 1JW]) : [H.M.S.O]
Borough of Merthyr Tydfil = Bwrdeistref Merthyr Tudful. — [1981]. — 11,[8]p ; 30cm
Parallel Welsh text and English translation
Unpriced (pbk) B82-04383

Review of district electoral arrangements draft proposals / Local Government Boundary Commission for Wales = Arolwg o drefniadau'r etholiadau dosbarth cynigion drafft / Comisiwn Ffiniau Llywodraeth Leol i Gymru. — [Cardiff] ([The Hayes, Cardiff. CF1 1JW]) : [H.M.S.O]
Borough of Neath = Bwrdeistref Nedd. — [1981]. — 17,[6]p ; 30cm
Parallel Welsh text and English translation
Unpriced (pbk) B82-04381

Review of district electoral arrangements draft proposals / Local Government Boundary Commission for Wales = Arolwg o drefniadau'r etholiadau dosbarth cynigion drafft / Comisiwn Ffiniau Llywodraeth Leol i Gymru. — [Cardiff] ([The Hayes, Cardiff. CF1 1JW]) : [H.M.S.O]
Borough of Newport = Bwrdeistref Casnewydd. — [1981]. — 11,[12]p ; 30cm
Parallel Welsh text and English translation
Unpriced (pbk) B82-04385

Review of district electoral arrangements draft proposals / Local Government Boundary Commission for Wales = Arolwg o drefniadau'r etholiadau dosbarth cynigion drafft / Comisiwn Ffiniau Llywodraeth Leol i Gymru. — [Cardiff] ([The Hayes, Cardiff. CF1 1JW]) : [H.M.S.O]
Borough of Rhuddlan = Bwrdeistref Rhuddlan. — [1981]. — 15,[6]p ; 30cm
Parallel Welsh text and English translation
Unpriced (pbk) B82-04377

Review of district electoral arrangements draft proposals / Local Government Boundary Commission for Wales = Arolwg o drefniadau'r etholiadau dosbarth cynigion drafft / Comisiwn Ffiniau Llywodraeth Leol i Gymru. — [Cardiff] ([The Hayes, Cardiff. CF1 1JW]) : [H.M.S.O]
Borough of Vale of Glamorgan = Bwrdeistref Bro Morgannwg. — [1981]. — 19,[8]p ; 30cm
Parallel Welsh text and English translation
Unpriced (pbk) B82-04382

Review of district electoral arrangements draft proposals / Local Government Boundary Commission for Wales = Arolwg o drefniadau'r etholiadau dosbarth cynigion drafft / Comisiwn Ffiniau Llywodraeth Leol i Gymru. — [Cardiff] ([The Hayes, Cardiff. CF1 1JW]) : [H.M.S.O]
City of Cardiff = Dinas Caerdydd. — [1981]. — 17,[10]p ; 30cm
Parallel Welsh text and English translation
Unpriced (pbk) B82-04380

Review of district electoral arrangements draft proposals / Local Government Boundary Commission for Wales = Arolwg o drefniadau'r etholiadau dosbarth cynigion drafft / Comisiwn Ffiniau Llywodraeth Leol i Gymru. — [Cardiff] ([The Hayes, Cardiff. CF1 1JW]) : [H.M.S.O]
District of Radnor = Dosbarth Maesyfed. — [1981]. — 9,[14]p ; 30cm
Parallel Welsh text and English translation
Unpriced (pbk) B82-04384

352'.008'09 — Mayors. Role, *to 1981*

Johns, W. P.. Mr Mayor / W.P. Johns. — London : Hale, 1982. — 192p,[12]p of plates : ill,1coat of arms,ports ; 23cm
Includes index
ISBN 0-7091-9366-1 : £8.50 B82-14622

352'.008'0941 — Great Britain. Urban regions. Local government, *1776-1914*

Patricians, power and politics in nineteenth-century towns. — Leicester : Leicester University Press, Sept.1982. — [240]p. — (Themes in urban history)
ISBN 0-7185-1193-x : £20.00 : CIP entry B82-19845

352.041 — Great Britain. Local government

Alexander, Alan, *1943-*. Local government in Britain since reorganisation / Alan Alexander. — London : Allen & Unwin, c1982. — ix,191p ; 22cm. — (The New local government series ; no.23)
Bibliography: p179-187. — Includes index
ISBN 0-04-352100-2 (cased) : Unpriced : CIP rev.
ISBN 0-04-352101-0 (pbk) : Unpriced B82-10610

Elcock, Howard. Local government : politicians, professionals and the public in local authorities / Howard Elcock with a chapter by Michael Wheaton. — London : Methuen, 1982. — xi,330p : ill,maps ; 23cm
Includes index
ISBN 0-416-85750-7 (cased) : Unpriced : CIP rev.
ISBN 0-416-33170-x (pbk) : Unpriced B82-10507

Henney, Alex. Inside local government. — London (10 Archway Close, N19 3TD) : Sinclair Browne, June 1982. — [192]p
ISBN 0-86300-014-2 (cased) : £8.95 : CIP entry
ISBN 0-86300-015-0 (pbk) : £3.50 B82-10257

352.041 — Great Britain. Local government — *For schools*

Allsop, Kathleen. Local and central government / Kathleen Allsop. — 3rd ed. / revised by Tom Brennan. — London : Hutchinson, 1982. — 128p : ill,facsims,maps,2plans,ports ; 24cm
Previous ed.: 1978
ISBN 0-09-147011-0 (pbk) : Unpriced : CIP rev.
Also classified at 354.41 B82-04120

352.041 — Great Britain. Local government. Political aspects, *1945-1981*

Alexander, Alan. The politics of local government in the United Kingdom. — London : Longman, Nov.1982. — [144]p
ISBN 0-582-29541-6 (pbk) : £3.95 : CIP entry B82-26526

352.0417 — Ireland *(Republic).* **Local government**

Roche, Desmond. Local government in Ireland / Desmond Roche. — Dublin : Institute of Public Administration, 1982. — x,391p ; 22cm
Bibliography: p355-368. — Includes index
ISBN 0-906980-06-2 (pbk) : Unpriced : CIP rev. B81-30637

352.042 — England. Local authorities. Management — *Conference proceedings*

Local authorities — austerity management : conference proceedings Eastbourne 23-26 March 1981. — London : Local Authorities Management Services and Computer Committee, 1981. — 94p : ill,ports ; 30cm
Cover title
ISBN 0-85497-124-6 (pbk) : £6.00 B82-03792

352.042 — England. Local authorities. Organisation structure

Patterns of management in local government. — Oxford : Robertson, June 1982. — [192]p. — (Government and administration series)
Originally published: 1980
ISBN 0-85520-245-9 (pbk) : £5.95 : CIP entry
B82-12162

352.042 — England. Local government

Jefferies, Roger. Tackling the town hall : a local authority handbook / Roger Jefferies. — London : Routledge & Kegan Paul, 1982. — xii,289p ; 22cm
Bibliography: p284-286. — Includes index
ISBN 0-7100-9031-5 (pbk) : £5.95 B82-39013

Richards, Peter G.. The local government system. — London : Allen and Unwin, Oct.1982. — [208]p. — (The New local government series ; no.5)
ISBN 0-04-352104-5 (cased) : £14.95 : CIP entry
ISBN 0-04-352105-3 (pbk) : £5.95 B82-23092

352.042 — England. Local government. Economic aspects

Town hall power or Whitehall pawn? : local autonomy, local revenue, misuse of welfare as power base, deficiencies of research, ineffectiveness of social work, economics of politics and bureaucracy, saving local government / David King ... [et al.] ; introduction by the seminar chairman Arthur Seldon. — London : Institute of Economic Affairs, 1980. — xiii,154p ; 21cm. — (IEA readings, ISSN 0305-814x ; 25)
Conference proceedings
ISBN 0-255-36135-1 (pbk) : Unpriced
B82-21924

352.042 — England. Local government — *For schools*

Van der Molen, Frank. Local government / Frank van der Molen & Kay Hammond. — Harlow : Longman, 1981. — 46p : ill,maps ; 24cm. — (Longman social science studies. Series 2)
Bibliography: p46
ISBN 0-582-22306-7 (pbk) : £1.45 B82-08907

352.0421'092'4 — Greater London Council. Administration, *1965-1981 — Personal observations*

Cutler, Horace. The Cutler files / Horace Cutler. — London : Weidenfeld and Nicolson, 1982. — v,183p : ill,1map ; 23cm
ISBN 0-297-78017-4 : £6.95 B82-17276

352.0421'2'0924 — London *(City)*. Lord mayors: White, *Sir* Thomas, *1492-1567 — Biographies*

Briscoe, A. Daly. A Marian Lord Mayor : Sir Thomas White / by A. Daly Briscoe ; foreword by William Serjeant. — Ipswich : East Anglian Magazine, c1982. — 112p : ill,3maps,1coat of arms,ports ; 21cm
Bibliography: p102-103. — Includes index
ISBN 0-900227-59-1 (pbk) : £3.50 B82-25665

352.0421'83'05 — Hillingdon. *Council.* Services — *Serials*

Hillingdon. *Council.* Annual report / London Borough of Hillingdon. — 1979-80-. — [Uxbridge] ([Civic Centre, High St., Uxbridge, Middx UB8 1UW]) : [Hillingdon Council], [1980]-. — v. : ill,maps ; 30cm
Spine title: London Borough of Hillingdon annual report
ISSN 0263-161X = Annual report - London Borough of Hillingdon : Unpriced B82-20883

352.0422'5'05 — East Sussex. *County Council — Serials*

East Sussex. *County Council.* Annual report & financial statement / East Sussex County Council. — 1979-1980-. — Lewes (County Hall, Lewes, East Sussex) : County Planning Department, East Sussex County Council, 1980-. — v. : ill,map ; 30cm
Description based on: 1980-1981 issue
ISSN 0263-9165 = Annual report & financial statement - East Sussex County Council : Unpriced B82-38504

352.0422'57 — East Sussex. Lewes. Local government, *to 1981*

Lewes. *Town Council.* Town of Lewes : 1881-1981 : centenary meeting of Lewes Town Council and presentations to Maurice S. Breese and James Taylor to commemorate their admission as Honorary Freeman 9th November 1981 : order of proceedings / with an historical introduction by the Mayor Graham J. Mayhew. — [Lewes] ([The Mayor's Parlour, Town Hall, Lewes, East Sussex BN7 2DQ]) : [The Council], [1981]. — [18]p ; 30cm
Unpriced (pbk) B82-05489

352.0422'57 — Lancashire. Urban regions. Local government, *1830-1880*

Garrard, John. Leadership and power in Victorian industrial towns 1830-80. — Manchester : Manchester University Press, Dec.1982. — [256]p
ISBN 0-7190-0897-2 : £16.50 : CIP entry
B82-30218

352.0422'9 — Berkshire. *County Council, to 1974*

Davies, Ellis Roger. A history of the first Berkshire County Council / by Ellis Roger Davies. — [Reading] : Berkshire County Secretariat, [1981]. — [427]p : ill,1map,ports ; 29cm
Includes index
£10.00 (pbk) B82-08645

352.0424'1 — Gloucestershire. *County Council.* Services — *Statistics*

Gloucestershire. *County Council.* Gloucestershire trends : 1980-1981. — Gloucester : Gloucestershire County Council, 1981. — 19p : 1col.map ; 21cm
Text and map on inside covers. — Cover title
Unpriced (pbk) B82-06367

352.0425'21 — Nottinghamshire. Clayworth. Local government. Parish records, *1674-1714 — Texts*

Coming into line : local government in Clayworth 1674-1714 / edited by Alan Rogers. — [Nottingham] : [Centre for Local History, University of Nottingham], [c1979]. — xxiii,170p : ill ; 20cm. — (Record series / University of Nottingham. Centre for Local History)
Includes index
£1.50 (pbk) B82-17007

352.0425'74 — Oxford. Boundaries. Extension — *Proposals*

A Consultation paper on a possible boundary review. — Oxford ([St. Aldate's Chambers, Oxford OX1 1DS]) : [Oxford City Council], 1981. — 25p : maps ; 21cm
At head of title: City of Oxford. — Map (48x30cm folded to 15x11cm) as insert
Unpriced (pbk) B82-12125

352.0425'9 — Buckinghamshire. *County Council.* Services — *Practical information*

Buckinghamshire. *County Council.* A-Z guide to Buckinghamshire County Council's services. — Aylesbury : Buckinghamshire County Council, 1981. — 39p : 3maps,1plan ; 21cm
Cover title
ISBN 0-86059-193-x (pbk) : £1.00 B82-02893

352.0426'4'05 — Suffolk. *County Council — Serials*

Suffolk. *County Council.* Annual report and accounts / Suffolk County Council. — 1980-81-. — [Ipswich] ([Central Library, Northgate St., Ipswich IP1 3DE]) : [The Council], [1981]-. — v. : ill,maps ; 21x30cm
ISSN 0263-3175 = Annual report and accounts - Suffolk County Council : Unpriced
B82-23580

352.0427'6 — Lancashire. Justices of the peace. Proceedings, *1578-1694 — Early works*

Proceedings of the Lancashire Justices of the Peace at the Sherrif's table during assizes week, 1578-1694 / edited by B.W. Quintrell. — [Chester] : [Record Society of Lancashire and Cheshire], 1981. — viii,215p ; 24cm. — (The Record Society of Lancashire and Cheshire ; v.121)
Includes index
ISBN 0-902593-11-0 : Unpriced B82-12396

352.0427'63 — Lancashire. Rossendale *(District)*. Local government, *to 1982*

Elliot, Jon, *1911-*. Local government in Rossendale : an outline history / Jon Elliott. — [Rawtenstall] ([Rawtenstall, Rossendale, Lancs. BB4 6RE]) : Rossendale Museum, 1982. — 21p ; 16x22cm
£0.50 (pbk) B82-18336

352.0428'49 — North Yorkshire. Rudby. Local government, *1600-1900*

Hastings, R. P.. Rudby-in-Cleveland local government and society c.1600-1900 / by R.P. Hastings. — Hutton Rudby (3 Linden Cres., Hutton Rudby, [N. Yorks TS15 0HU]) : Hutton Rudby and District Local History Society, c1981. — 28,[11]p : ill,facsims ; 30cm
Unpriced (pbk) B82-04097

352.0429'7 — Mid Glamorgan. *County Council — Serials*

Mid Glamorgan. *County Council.* Annual report and financial statement : year ended 31st March / Mid Glamorgan County Council. — 1981-. — Cardiff (County Hall, Cardiff [CF1 3NE]) : The Council, 1981-. — v. : ill,maps ; 21x30cm
ISSN 0262-7418 = Annual report and financial statement - Mid Glamorgan County Council : Unpriced B82-14243

352.0429'82 — West Glamorgan. Swansea. Freemen, *1760-1981 — Lists*

Alban, J. R.. Calendar of Swansea freemen's records from 1760 / J.R. Alban. — Swansea (Chief Executive and Town Clerk's Dept, Guildhall, Swansea SA1 4PE) : Swansea City Council, 1982. — v,86p : 2facsims ; 30cm
Includes index
Unpriced (pbk) B82-40253

352.0429'82'0922 — West Glamorgan. Swansea. Mayors, *to 1981 — Lists*

Portreeves and mayors of Swansea. — Swansea (Guildhall, Swansea SA1 4PE) : Swansea City Council, c1982. — 11p ; 21cm
Cover title
Unpriced (pbk) B82-24391

352.073 — United States. Local government

Grant, Daniel R.. State and local government in America / Daniel R. Grant, H.C. Nixon. — 4th ed. — Boston, Mass. ; London : Allyn and Bacon, c1982. — x,502p : ill,maps ; 25cm
Previous ed.: 1975. — Includes bibliographies and index
ISBN 0-205-07705-6 : £19.95
Primary classification 353.9 B82-22025

352.0747'1 — New York *(City)*. Local government. Personnel management. Political aspects

Rich, Wilbur C.. The politics of urban personnel policy : reformers, politicians, and bureaucrats / Wilbur C. Rich. — Port Washington ; London : National University Publications : Kennikat, 1982. — ix,178p : ill ; 22cm. — (Interdisciplinary urban series)
Includes index
ISBN 0-8046-9290-4 : £15.70 B82-24797

352.1'0942 — England. Local government. Financial management

Rose, Richard, *1933-*. Incrementalism or instability? : managing local government fiscal systems in a turbulent time / by Richard Rose & Edward C. Page. — Glasgow (University of Strathclyde, Glasgow G1 1XQ) : Centre for the Study of Public Policy, 1981. — ii,33p ; 30cm. — (Studies in public policy, ISSN 0140-8240 ; no.88)
£1.50 (pbk) B82-00822

352.1'09427'1 — Cheshire. Local government. Financial management, *1272-1377*

Booth, P. H. W.. The financial administration of the lordship and county of Chester : 1272-1377 / by P.H.W. Booth. — Manchester : Published for the [Chetham] Society by Manchester University Press, 1981. — xii,207p : 1map ; 23cm. — (Remains historical and literary connected with the palatine counties of Lancaster and Chester. 3rd series ; v.28)
Bibliography: p177-190. — Includes index
ISBN 0-7190-1337-2 : £16.50 : CIP rev.
B81-10455

352.1′0973 — United States. Local government. Financial management — *Case studies*

Levine, Charles H.. The politics of retrenchment : how local governments manage fiscal stress / Charles H. Levine, Irene S. Rubin, George G. Wolohojian. — Beverly Hills ; London : Sage, c1981. — 224p : ill ; 23cm. — (Sage library of social research ; v.130)
Includes bibliographies and index
ISBN 0-8039-1688-4 (cased) : Unpriced
ISBN 0-8039-1689-2 (pbk) : £6.50 B82-11697

352.1′633 — England. Local authority buildings. Maintenance. Planning

Terotechnology and the maintenance of local authority buildings. — London : Local Authorities Management Services and Computer Committee, 1981. — 50p : ill ; 30cm
ISBN 0-85497-125-4 (pbk) : £5.00 B82-03793

352.1′635′0942 — England. Local authorities. Supplies departments. Information systems

Thursfield, P.. Supplies information systems in local government : an introduction to the modular scheme / P. Thursfield, J.G. Eary. — Reading (201 Kings Rd., Reading RG1 4LH) : Local Government Operational Research Unit, Royal Institute of Public Administration, 1979. — 15p : ill ; 30cm. — (Report / Royal Institute of Public Administration. Local Government Operational Research Unit ; no.C279/1)
Text on inside back cover
£4.00 (pbk) B82-17510

352.1′642′09423 — South-west England. Local authorities. Communication

Hathway, Tony. Communication patterns in local authorities / a study prepared for British Telecom ; Tony Hathway, Debra Lawson, Barry Hutton. — Bristol : Department of Town and Country Planning, Bristol Polytechnic, 1981. — [95]p : ill ; 21x30cm
Unpriced (pbk) B82-31240

352.1′71 — England. Local authority housing. Accounting — *Manuals*

Housing subsidies and accounting manual / Department of the Environment, the Welsh Office. — 1981 ed. — London : H.M.S.O., 1982. — i,78p ; 30cm
Previous ed.: 1975. — Includes index
ISBN 0-11-751612-0 (pbk) : £4.50
Primary classification 363.5′8 B82-23761

352.4′09421 — London. District health authorities. Boundaries — *Proposals*

London Advisory Group. District health authorities in London : report to the Secretary of State for Social Services / London Advisory Group. — [London] ([Alexander Fleming House, Elephant and Castle, SE1 6BY]) : [Department of Health and Social Security], 1981. — 15p ; 30cm
Unpriced (unbound) B82-40106

352.4′09426′5 — Cambridgeshire. Area health authorities: Cambridgeshire Area Health Authority (Teaching). Information services — *Proposals*

Smith, S. E.. Cambridgeshire area information service research project final report 1979-1982 : a joint research project with Cambridgeshire Area Health Authority (Teaching) and Cambridgeshire County Council, County Libraries Department / S.E. Smith. — Cambridge : Cambridge Area Health Authority (Teaching), 1982. — 45,A48p : ill ; 30cm
Cover title. — Bibliography: p43-45
ISBN 0-9507983-0-4 (spiral) : Unpriced : CIP rev. B82-11101

352.6′1′09422 — England. Thames River Basin. Regional water authorities: Thames Water Authority — *Statistics* — *Serials*

Thames Water Authority. Thames Water operational assets / collated and prepared by Central Information Unit, Planning Directorate, [Thames Water Authority]. — 1980-. — Reading (Nugent House, Vastern Rd, Reading, Berks) : [The Authority], [1980]-. — v. ; 30cm
Irregular. — Continues in part: Thames Water Authority. Thames Water statistics
ISSN 0263-3930 = Thames Water operational assets (corrected) : Unpriced B82-19872

352.7′5′09423592 — Great Britain. Rural regions. Local authority housing. Management — *Study regions: Devon. South Hams (District)*

Phillips, David R.. Rural housing and the public sector / David R. Phillips and Allan M. Williams. — Aldershot : Gower, c1982. — viii,174p : ill,maps ; 23cm
Bibliography: p163-172. — Includes index
ISBN 0-566-00456-9 : Unpriced : CIP rev. B82-06850

352.94′2′094275 — Merseyside *(Metropolitan County)*. **Economic development. Organisations: Merseyside Development Corporation**

Merseyside Development Corporation : information for community and voluntary organisations. — Liverpool (14 Castle St., Liverpool L2 ONJ) : Liverpool Council for Voluntary Service, 1982. — 9p : maps ; 30cm
£0.50 (unbound) B82-22959

352.94′2′094275 — Merseyside *(Metropolitan County)*. **Economic development. Organisations: Merseyside Development Corporation. Gifts of office equipment by Great Britain.** *Department of the Environment* — *Proposals*

Great Britain. *Treasury*. Treasury minute dated 19 March 1982 relative to the transfer, free of charge, of works to office buildings and office equipment to the Merseyside Development Corporation. — London : H.M.S.O., [1982]. — 1sheet ; 25x16cm. — (Cmnd. ; 8527)
ISBN 0-10-185270-3 : £0.30 B82-25137

352.94′4′0941 — Great Britain. Local authorities. Social service departments. Organisation structure

Kakabadse, Andrew. Culture of the social services / Andrew Kakabadse. — Aldershot : Gower, c1982. — xi,199p : ill,1form ; 23cm
Bibliography: p171-175. — Includes index
ISBN 0-566-00366-x : Unpriced : CIP rev. B81-34285

352.94′4′0942 — England. Local authorities. Social services departments. Organisation

Hallett, Christine. The personal social services in local government / Christine Hallett. — London : Allen & Unwin, 1982. — 125p ; 23cm. — (Studies in the personal social services ; 6)
Bibliography: p113-119. — Includes index
ISBN 0-04-362048-5 (cased) : Unpriced : CIP rev.
ISBN 0-04-362049-3 (pbk) : Unpriced B82-15635

352.9′6′0942 — England. Environment planning. Policies of local authorities. Investigation — *Manuals* — *For surveying*

Investigations of a local authority′s planning policies and proposals : a check list for practitioners / prepared by the Planning & Development Division, the Royal Institution of Chartered Surveyors. — London : Published on behalf of The Institution by Surveyors Publications, c1981. — 6p : ill ; 30cm. — (A Practice note, ISSN 0141-1462)
ISBN 0-85406-163-0 (unbound) : £2.50 B82-08054

353 — FEDERAL AND STATE ADMINISTRATIVE STRUCTURE. UNITED STATES

353 — United States. Government

Krasner, Michael A.. American government : structure and process / Michael A. Krasner, Stephen G. Chaberski. — 2nd ed. — New York : Macmillan ; London : Collier Macmillan, c1982. — ix,358p : ill ; 21cm
Previous ed.: 1977. — Includes bibliographies and index
ISBN 0-02-366270-0 (pbk) : Unpriced B82-35270

353 — United States. Government. Relations with press

Juergens, George. News from the White House : the presidential-press relationship in the progressive era / George Juergens. — Chicago ; London : University of Chicago Press, c1981. — x,338p,[12]p of plates : ill,ports ; 24cm
Bibliography: p309-324. — Includes index
ISBN 0-226-41472-8 : £17.50 B82-29484

353′.0009 — United States. Government, *1877-1920*

Skowronek, Stephen. Building a new American state : the expansion of national administrative capacities, 1877-1920 / Stephen Skowronek. — Cambridge : Cambridge University Press, 1982. — x,389p ; 24cm
Bibliography: p353-374. — Includes index
ISBN 0-521-23022-5 (cased) : £25.00
ISBN 0-521-28865-7 (pbk) : Unpriced B82-39938

353.001′3 — United States. Government. Officials. Appointment, *1945-1981.* **Political aspects**

Mackenzie, G. Calvin. The politics of presidential appointments / G. Calvin Mackenzie. — New York : Free Press ; London : Collier Macmillan, c1981. — xxi,298p : 1ill ; 25cm
Includes index
ISBN 0-02-919670-1 : £13.95 B82-30026

353.006′09 — United States. Civil service, *to 1981*

Mosher, Frederick C.. Democracy and the public service / Frederick C. Mosher. — 2nd ed. — New York ; Oxford : Oxford University Press, 1982. — xvi,251p : 1ill ; 21cm
Previous ed.: 1968. — Includes index
ISBN 0-19-503018-4 (pbk) : £5.95 B82-41063

353.0072′2 — United States. Government. Budgeting

Public budgeting : program planning and implementation / edited by Fremont J. Lyden, Ernest G. Miller. — 4th ed. — Englewood Cliffs ; London : Prentice-Hall, c1982. — xiii,410p : ill ; 23cm
Previous ed.: Chicago : Rand McNally, 1978
ISBN 0-13-737403-8 (pbk) : £11.20 B82-35165

353.0072′232 — United States. Government. Expenditure. Control. Role of bureaucracy

Peirce, William Spangar. Bureaucratic failure and public expenditure / William Spangar Peirce. — New York ; London : Academic Press, 1981. — xii,319p ; 24cm. — (Quantitative studies in social relations)
Bibliography: p299-307. — Includes index
ISBN 0-12-550220-6 : £19.60 B82-10048

353.0087′22043 — United States. Electricity supply industries. Regulation by government

Anderson, Douglas D.. Regulatory politics and electric utilities : a case study in political economy / Douglas D. Anderson. — Boston, Mass. : Auburn House ; London : distributed by Eurospan, c1981. — xv,191p : ill ; 25cm
Includes index
ISBN 0-86569-058-8 : £15.75 B82-13426

353.0087′3 — United States. *Postal Service.* **Management**

Tierney, John T.. Postal reorganization : managing the public′s business / John T. Tierney. — Boston, Mass. : Auburn House ; London : distributed by Eurospan, 1981. — xix,191p ; 25cm
Includes index
ISBN 0-86569-061-8 : Unpriced B82-13533

353.0087′77 — United States. Air services. Regulation by government, *to 1980*

Airline deregulation : the early experience / John R. Meyer and Clinton V. Oster, Jr, editors ; [contributions by] John R. Meyer ... [et al.]. — Boston, Mass. : Auburn House ; London : distributed by Eurospan, c1981. — xx,287p : ill ; 25cm
Includes index
ISBN 0-86569-078-2 : £16.25 B82-13245

353′.01 — United States. Government. Bureaucracy

Yates, Douglas. Bureaucratic democracy : the search for democracy and efficiency in American government / Douglas Yates. — Cambridge, Mass. ; London : Harvard University Press, 1982. — viii,224p : ill ; 24cm
Includes index
ISBN 0-674-08611-2 : £12.95 B82-36048

353.03′1 — United States. Presidents. Integrity

Bailey, Thomas A.. Presidential saints and sinners / Thomas A. Bailey. — New York : Free Press ; London : Collier Macmillan, c1981. — viii,304p : ports ; 25cm
Ports on lining papers. — Bibliography: p287-291. — Includes index
ISBN 0-02-901330-5 : £12.95 B82-18903

353.03′18′0904 — United States. Vice presidency, *1953-1980*
Goldstein, Joel K.. The modern American vice presidency : the transformation of a political institution / Joel K. Goldstein. — Princeton ; Guildford : Princeton University Press, c1982. — xii,409p ; 22cm
Bibliography: p379-396. — Includes index
ISBN 0-691-07636-7 (cased) : £19.80
ISBN 0-691-02208-9 (pbk) : Unpriced
B82-31197

353.03′2 — United States. Presidency. Powers
The **Tethered** presidency : congressional restraints on executive power / edited by Thomas M. Frank. — New York ; London : New York University Press, 1981. — xiii,299p ; 24cm
ISBN 0-8147-2567-8 : £21.20 B82-35947

353.03′2 — United States. Presidents. Social policies. Implementation, *1961-1980*
Light, Paul Charles. The president′s agenda : domestic policy choice from Kennedy to Carter (with notes on Ronald Reagan) / Paul Charles Light. — Baltimore, Md. ; London : Johns Hopkins University Press, c1982. — ix,246p ; 24cm
Bibliography: p239-241. — Includes index
ISBN 0-8018-2657-8 : Unpriced B82-28093

353.03′22 — United States. Presidency. Powers. Political aspects, *to 1981*
Kessler, Frank. The dilemmas of presidential leadership : of caretakers and kings / Frank Kessler. — Englewood Cliffs ; London : Prentice-Hall, c1982. — xii,404p : ill ; 23cm
Includes index
ISBN 0-13-214593-6 (pbk) : £8.95 B82-20546

353.03′4 — United States. Government. Policies. Effects of succession of rulers *compared with* **effects of succession of rulers on government policies in Soviet Union**
Bunce, Valerie. Do new leaders make a difference? : executive succession and public policy under capitalism and socialism / Valerie Bunce. — Princeton ; Guildford : Princeton University Press, c1981. — xiii,296p ; 23cm
Bibliography: p261-291. — Includes index
ISBN 0-691-07631-6 (cased) : £15.80
ISBN 0-691-02205-4 (pbk) : £4.95
Also classified at 354.4703′4 B82-00726

353′.072 — United States. Government. Policies. Public opinion in Great Britain, *1932-1938*
Dizikes, John. Britain, Roosevelt and the New Deal : British opinion 1932-1938 / John Dizikes. — New York ; London : Garland, 1979. — iv,330p ; 24cm. — (Modern American history)
Bibliography: p316-323. — Includes index
ISBN 0-8240-3631-x : Unpriced B82-18910

353′.072′05 — United States. Government. Policies — *Serials*
Research in public policy analysis and management. — Vol.1 (1981)-. — Greenwich, Conn. ; London : JAI Press, 1981-. — v. : ill ; 24cm
Annual. — 'Official publication of the Association for Public Policy Analysis and Management'. — Description based on: Vol.2 (1981)
Unpriced B82-31726

353′.0725 — United States. Government. Policies. Decision making
Quade, E. S.. Analysis for public decisions / E.S. Quade. — 2nd ed. — New York ; Oxford : North-Holland, c1982. — xii,380p : ill,1form,1port ; 24cm
Previous ed.: New York : American Elsevier ; London : Elsevier, 1975. — Bibliography: p359-371. — Includes index
ISBN 0-444-00665-6 : £22.93 B82-34295

353′.0725 — United States. Government. Policies. Decision making. Analysis
Public policy and public choice / Douglas W. Rae and Theodore J. Eismeier, editors. — Beverly Hills ; London : Sage, c1979. — 284p : ill ; 23cm. — (Sage yearbooks in politics and public policy ; v.6)
Includes bibliographies
ISBN 0-8039-0725-7 (cased) : £17.00
ISBN 0-8039-7026-5 (pbk) : Unpriced
B82-05990

353′.0725 — United States. Government. Policies. Decision making — *Case studies*
Cases in public policy-making / James E. Anderson, editor. — 2nd ed. — New York ; London : Holt, Rinehart and Winston, c1982. — xi,281p ; 24cm
Previous ed.: New York : Praeger, 1976. — Bibliography: p275-281
ISBN 0-03-058208-3 (pbk) : £9.95 B82-14553

353′.073 — United States. Government. Executive branches. Reorganisation, *1963-1969*
Redford, Emmette S.. Organizing the executive branch : the Johnson presidency / Emmette S. Redford and Marlan Blissett. — Chicago ; London : University of Chicago Press, 1981. — x,277p ; 24cm. — (An Administrative history of the Johnson presidency)
Includes index
ISBN 0-226-70675-3 : £14.70 B82-13668

353.9 — United States. State governments
Grant, Daniel R.. State and local government in America / Daniel R. Grant, H.C. Nixon. — 4th ed. — Boston, Mass. ; London : Allyn and Bacon, c1982. — x,502p : ill,maps ; 25cm
Previous ed.: 1975. — Includes bibliographies and index
ISBN 0-205-07705-6 : £19.95
Also classified at 352.073 B82-22025

353.9′292 — United States. State governments. Effects of policies of government
The **Nationalization** of state government / edited by Jerome J. Hanus. — Lexington, Mass. : Lexington Books ; [Aldershot] : Gower [distrbutor], c1981. — xiii,169p ; 24cm
Includes index
ISBN 0-669-04334-6 : £14.00 B82-04748

354 — CENTRAL ADMINISTRATIVE STRUCTURE(OTHER THAN UNITED STATES)

354.41 — Great Britain. Government
Birch, Anthony H.. The British system of government. — 5th ed. — London : Allen and Unwin, Feb.1982. — [304]p. — (Minerva series of students′ handbooks ; no.20)
Previous ed.: 1980
ISBN 0-04-320149-0 (pbk) : £4.95 : CIP entry
B81-35925

Birch, Anthony H.. The British system of government. — 6th ed. — London : Allen & Unwin, Nov.1982. — [304]p. — (The Minerva series of students′ handbooks ; no.20)
Previous ed.: 1982
ISBN 0-04-320154-7 (pbk) : £4.95 : CIP entry
B82-27807

Brennan, Tom. Politics and government in Britain. — 2nd ed. — Cambridge : Cambridge University Press, Oct.1982. — [442]p
Previous ed.: 1972
ISBN 0-521-28600-x (pbk) : £6.25 : CIP entry
B82-26253

354.41 — Great Britain. Government — *Fabian viewpoints*
Making government work / editor David Lipsey. — London : Fabian Society, 1982. — 23p ; 22cm. — (Fabian tract, ISSN 0307-7535 ; 480)
ISBN 0-7163-0480-5 (pbk) : £1.50 B82-26631

354.41 — Great Britain. Government — *For schools*
Allsop, Kathleen. Local and central government / Kathleen Allsop. — 3rd ed. / revised by Tom Brennan. — London : Hutchinson, 1982. — 128p : ill,facsims,maps,2plans,ports ; 24cm
Previous ed.: 1978
ISBN 0-09-147011-0 (pbk) : Unpriced : CIP rev.
Primary classification 352.041 B82-04120

354.41′000722 — Great Britain. Government. Policies. Implementation — *Case studies*
Policy and action : essays on the implementation of public policy / edited by Susan Barrett and Colin Fudge. — London : Methuen, 1981. — x,308p : ill ; 25cm
Bibliography: p279-297. — Includes index
ISBN 0-416-30670-5 (cased) : Unpriced : CIP rev.
ISBN 0-416-30680-2 (pbk) : £7.95 B81-30159

354.41′0009 — England. Government, *1485-1603* — *Early works*
Smith, *Sir* **Thomas**. De republica Anglorum. — Cambridge : Cambridge University Press, Aug.1982. — [164]p. — (Cambridge studies in the history and theory of politics)
Originally published: London : H. Midleton for G. Seton, 1583
ISBN 0-521-24109-x : £19.50 : CIP entry
B82-21727

354.41′0009 — Great Britain. Government, *1914-1919*
War and the state : the transformation of British government 1914-1919 / edited by Kathleen Burk. — London : Allen & Unwin, 1982. — 189p ; 23cm
Includes index
ISBN 0-04-940065-7 : £12.50 : CIP rev.
B82-10588

354.41′0009 — Great Britain. Government, *1945-1980*
Rose, Richard, *1933-*. The growth of government in the United Kingdom since 1945 : a programme of research / by Richard Rose. — Glasgow (16 Richmond St., Glasgow G1 1XQ) : University of Strathclyde, 1981. — 34p ; 30cm. — (Studies in public policy, ISSN 0140-8240 ; no.94)
Bibliography: p30-34
Unpriced (pbk) B82-12869

354.41′0009 — Great Britain. Government, *1945-1981*
Rose, Richard, *1933-*. United Kingdom facts / Richard Rose and Ian McAllister. — London : Macmillan, 1982. — x,168p ; 26cm
Includes index
ISBN 0-333-25341-8 : £30.00 : CIP rev.
B80-12736

354.41′0009 — Great Britain. Government. Changes, *1945-1980*
Punnett, R. M.. Alternating governments : the inefficient secret of British politics / by R.M. Punnett. — Glasgow : Centre for the Study of Public Policy, University of Strathclyde, 1981. — 44p : 1ill ; 30cm. — (Studies in public policy, ISSN 0140-8240 ; no.93)
Unpriced (pbk) B82-11248

354.41001 — Great Britain. Civil service. Personnel: Scientists. Personnel management. Great Britain. *Civil Service Department. Management Committee for the Science Group.* **Review of the Scientific Civil Service 1980** — *Critical studies*
Great Britain. The Government response to the Review of the Scientific Civil Service (Cmnd 8032). — London : Civil Service Department, c1981. — 6p ; 30cm
Cover title
ISBN 0-7115-0034-7 (pbk) : Unpriced
B82-35632

354.41001 — Great Britain. Civil service. Personnel: Scientists. Personnel management — *Inquiry reports*
Great Britain. *Civil Service Department. Management Committee for the Science Group.* Review of the Scientific Civil Service (1980) : report of a working group of the Management Committee for the Science Group (CSD). — London : H.M.S.O., [1980]. — viii,137p : ill ; 25cm. — (Cmnd. ; 8032)
Bibliography: p69-70
ISBN 0-10-180320-6 (pbk) : £6.10 B82-02577

354.41001′232 — Great Britain. Civil service. Personnel. Remuneration
Great Britain. *Civil Service Department.* Civil Service pay : factual background memorandum on the non-industrial Home Civil Service : submitted to the Enquiry into Non-Industrial Civil Service Pay under the chairmanship of the Rt. Hon. Sir John Megaw / Civil Service Department. — London : H.M.S.O., c1981. — iii,88p ; 30cm + booklet(13leaves ; 30cm)
ISBN 0-11-630447-2 (pbk) : £4.80 B82-33379

354.41001′232 — Great Britain. Public bodies. Senior personnel. Remuneration — *Proposals*
Review Body on Top Salaries. Fifth report on top salaries / [Review Body on Top Salaries] ; chairman: Lord Plowden. — London : H.M.S.O., [1982]. — iv,96p ; 25cm. — (Report / Review Body on Top Salaries ; no.18)
ISBN 0-10-185520-6 (pbk) : £7.25 B82-32825

354.41001′322 — Great Britain. Quangos. Ministerially appointed women personnel
Investigation into the numbers of women appointed to public bodies : report no.4. — Manchester (Overseas House, Quary St., Manchester M3 3HN) : Equal Opportunities Commission, 1981. — ii,14p ; 25cm
Unpriced (pbk) B82-00664

354.41001′5 — Great Britain. Civil service. Personnel. Training. Organisations: Civil Service College. Charges
Attendance charges for Civil Service College courses : a scrutiny of the possibility of charging for attendance at some courses at the Civil Service College. — London : Civil Service Department, 1980. — ii,41p ; 30cm. — (CSD Rayner review)
ISBN 0-7115-0032-0 (spiral) : £1.00 B82-36922

354.41′0022 — Great Britain. Government. Ministers, *to 1981* **—** *Lists*
Pickrill, D. A.. Ministers of the crown / D.A. Pickrill. — London : Routledge & Kegan Paul, 1981. — viii,135p ; 24cm. — (Routledge direct editions)
ISBN 0-7100-0916-x : £7.95 : CIP rev. B81-33893

354.41004 — Great Britain. Civil service. Senior personnel. Organisation structure
Chain of command review : the open structure : report of a team led by Sir Geoffrey Wardale. — London : Civil Service Department, 1981. — 37,[13]p ; 30cm
ISBN 0-7115-0038-x (spiral) : £1.50 B82-33378

354.41005 — Great Britain. Civil service. Superannuation schemes: Principal Civil Service Pension Scheme — *For personnel*
Civil service pensions explained : a guide to the benefits of the Principal Civil Service Pension Scheme and to the arrangement for increasing pensions under the Pensions (Increase) Act 1971 (as amended) / [Civil Service Department]. — 2nd ed. — London : H.M.S.O. [for] Her Majesty′s Treasury, 1982. — 54p ; 21cm
At head of title: Civil Service Pension Scheme. — Previous ed.: 1976
ISBN 0-11-630449-9 (pbk) : £3.75 B82-32960

354.41006 — Great Britain. Civil service
Young, Hugo. No, minister / by Hugo Young and Anne Sloman. — London : British Broadcasting Corporation, c1982. — 112p ; 23cm
Includes index
ISBN 0-563-20056-1 (cased) : £4.75
ISBN 0-563-20105-3 (pbk) : £2.50 B82-35302

354.41006′023 — Great Britain. Civil service — *Career guides — For graduates*
Accept society′s challenge : administrative careers for graduates in the Civil Service / [prepared by the Civil Service Commission and the Central Office of Information]. — London : H.M.S.O., 1981. — [24]p : col.ill,col.ports ; 23cm
Supersedes Administration trainees in the Civil Service
ISBN 0-903741-64-4 (unbound) : Unpriced B82-32953

354.410061 — Great Britain. *Colonial Office.* **Policies,** *1945-1966.* **Effects of World War 2**
Lee, Martin. The Colonial Office, war and redevelopment policy. — London : Maurice Temple Smith, Jan.1982. — [320]p
ISBN 0-85117-221-0 : £15.00 : CIP entry B81-33831

354.410071′2 — Great Britain. Purchasing by government departments — *Inquiry reports*
Great Britain. *Parliament. House of Commons. Committee of Public Accounts.* Third report from the Committee of Public Accounts : together with the proceedings of the committee, minutes of evidence and an appendix : session 1981-82 : HM Treasury, Civil Service Department, Department of Industry : introduction of a new general policy for public purchasing. — London : H.M.S.O., [1981]. — ix,9p ; 25cm. — ([HC] ; 29)
ISBN 0-10-202982-2 (pbk) : £2.45 B82-16053

354.410071′4 — Great Britain. Civil service. Office practices. Information systems. Technological development
Information technology : the challenge of the 80s / [prepared by Urwick Nexos Limited]. — [Sunningdale] ([Sunningdale Peak, Ascot, Berks.]) : Civil Service College, [1982?]. — 63p : ill ; 30cm
Cover title
Unpriced (spiral) B82-33399

354.410071′44 — British government forms — *Inquiry reports*
Administrative forms in Government. — London : H.M.S.O., 1982. — 13p ; 25cm. — (Cmnd. ; 8504)
ISBN 0-10-185040-9 (unbound) : £2.30 B82-23223

Forms under control : a report / by the Management and Personnel Office [written by] M.H. Grant ... [et al.]. — [London] : Management and Personnel Office, 1982. — 85p : ill,forms ; 30cm
ISBN 0-7115-0040-1 (spiral) : Unpriced B82-33377

Rayner, *Sir* **Derek.** Review of administration forms : report to the Prime Minister / by Sir Derek Rayner. — [London] ([Whitehall, SW1A 2AZ]) : [Central Management Library, Management and Personnel Office], 1982. — 23,[34]p : forms ; 30cm
Cover title
£2.00 (spiral) B82-35630

354.410071′45 — Great Britain. Official secrets. Disclosure. D notices. Great Britain. *Parliament. House of Commons. Defence Committee.* **Third report ... session 1979-80 —** *Critical studies*
Great Britain. *Ministry of Defence.* Third report from the Defence Committee : the D notice system : observations presented by the Secretary of State for Defence [on] House of Commons paper 773 session 1979-80. — London : H.M.S.O., [1981]. — 1sheet ; 25x16cm. — (Cmnd. ; 8129)
ISBN 0-10-181290-6 : £0.30 B82-16065

354.410071′45 — Great Britain. Official secrets. Disclosure. D notices — *Inquiry reports*
Great Britain. *Parliament. House of Commons. Defence Committee.* Third report from the Defence Committee, session 1979-80 : the D notice system : together with the minutes of proceedings of the committee relating to the report, part of the minutes of evidence taken before the committee on 11 and 17 June and 8, 15 and 22 July, and appendices. — [London] : H.M.S.O., [1980]. — xxiii,150p ; 25cm. — (HC ; 773) ([HC] ; 640 i-v)
ISBN 0-10-027739-x (pbk) : £6.90 B82-10955

354.410072′441′02854 — Great Britain. Personal income tax. PAYE. Assessment. Applications of digital computer systems
Butcher, John. The big steal : the computerisation of PAYE assessment / John Butcher, Philip Virgo. — London (240 High Holborn, WC1V 7DT) : Bow, [1980]. — [4]p ; 30cm. — (A Bow paper)
£2.50 (unbound) B82-21927

354.410072′53 — Great Britain. Local authorities. Grants from government. Equalisation. King, David N.. Defence of equalising grants to local authorities — *Critical studies*
Barnett, R. R.. A critique of a defence of equalising grants to local authorities / R.R. Barnett, N. Topham. — [Salford] : [Department of Economics, University of Salford], [1982]. — 11,4leaves ; 30cm. — (Salford papers in economics ; 82-4)
Bibliography: leaf11
Unpriced (spiral) B82-20478

354.410074 — Great Britain. Police. Complaints by public. Administration — *Inquiry reports*
Great Britain. *Parliament. House of Commons. Home Affairs Committee.* Fourth report from the Home Affairs Committee, session 1981-82 : police complaints procedures. — London : H.M.S.O.. — (HC98-I)
Vol.1: Report with minutes of proceedings. — 1982. — xlii ; 25cm
ISBN 0-10-008082-0 (pbk) : £3.95 B82-31967

Great Britain. *Parliament. House of Commons. Home Affairs Committee.* Fourth report from the Home Affairs Committee, session 1981-82 : police complaints procedures. — London : H.M.S.O.. — (HC 98-II)
Vol.2: Evidence and appendices. — 1982. — vii,326p ; 25cm
ISBN 0-10-008092-8 (pbk) : £12.40 B82-31968

354.410081′4 — Great Britain. *Commission for Racial Equality* **—** *Inquiry reports*
Great Britain. *Parliament. House of Commons. Home Affairs Committee.* First report from the Home Affairs Committee, session 1981-82 : Commission for Racial Equality. — London : H.M.S.O., [1981]
Vol.1: Report with minutes of proceedings. — lvp ; 25cm. — (HC ; 46-1)
ISBN 0-10-270882-7 (unbound) : £3.95 B82-16049

Great Britain. *Parliament. House of Commons. Home Affairs Committee.* First report from the Home Affairs Committee, session 1981-82 : Commission for Racial Equality. — London : H.M.S.O., [1981]
Vol.2: Evidence and appendices. — v,257p ; 25cm. — (HC ; 46-II)
ISBN 0-10-270282-9 (pbk) : £9.05 B82-16050

354.410081′4 — Great Britain. *Commission for Racial Equality.* **Inquiry reports. Great Britain.** *Parliament. House of Commons. Home Affairs Committee.* **"First report ... session 1981-82" —** *Critical studies*
Great Britain. The Government reply to the First report from the Home Affairs Committee, session 1981-82, HC 46-I : Commission for Racial Equality. — London : H.M.S.O., 1982. — 15p ; 25cm. — (Cmnd. ; 8547)
ISBN 0-10-185470-6 (unbound) : £2.10 B82-27586

354.410081′9 — Great Britain. Government departments. Research organisations. Support services. Financial management
Great Britain. *Management and Personnel Office.* Review of support services in research and development and allied scientific establishments : report to the Prime Minister / Management and Personnel Office. — [London] : The Office, 1982. — 57p : ill ; 30cm
Cover title
ISBN 0-7115-0047-9 (pbk) : £3.50 B82-40108

354.410082 — Great Britain. Public enterprise. Organisations: National Enterprise Board — *Inquiry reports*
Great Britain. *Parliament. House of Commons. Committee of Public Accounts.* Thirtieth report from the Committee of Public Accounts : together with the proceedings of the committee, the minutes of evidence and appendices : session 1979-80 : Department of Industry, National Enterprise Board, Rolls Royce Limited : future role of the National Enterprise Board, monitoring of the National Enterprise Board′s investments, Rolls-Royce Limited. — London : H.M.S.O., [1980]. — xxiv,62p ; 25cm. — ([HC] ; 779)
ISBN 0-10-027799-3 (pbk) : £5.20
Primary classification 338.7′62913435 B82-09928

354.410082′1 — Standards committees. British government representatives. Role
Great Britain. *Department of Trade. Metrology, Quality Assurance, Safety and Standards Division.* Guidelines for government representatives on standards committees / [prepared by Metrology, Quality Assurance, Safety and Standards Division (MQS Division) of the Department of Trade]. — Rev. ed. — London : The Department, 1981. — iii,22p ; 21cm
Previous ed.: 1979
Unpriced (pbk) B82-40098

354.410082′338 — Great Britain. *Forestry Commission.* **Objectives**
Great Britain. *Forestry Commission.* The Forestry Commission′s objectives. — Edinburgh : The Commission, 1980. — 12p : col.ill ; 21cm. — (Policy and procedure paper ; no.1)
ISBN 0-85538-074-8 (pbk) : Unpriced B82-15522

354.410082'38 — Great Britain. *Department of Energy. Economic and Statistics Division.* **Expenditure. Reduction** — *Proposals*

Great Britain. *Department of Energy.* Rayner scrutiny : economic and statistical services in the Department of Energy / Department of Energy. — [London] ([Thames House South, Millbank SW1P 4QJ]) : [The Department], [1981]. — 3v ; 30cm
£4.00 (spiral) B82-01887

354.410082'5 — Great Britain. Consumer credit. Provision. Licences — *Serials*

Consumer credit bulletin / Office of Fair Trading. — No.1 (9 June 1976)-. — London (Government Buildings, Bromyard Ave., Acton, W3 7BB) : Consumer Credit Licensing Branch, Office of Fair Trading, 1976-. — v. ; 30cm
Weekly
ISSN 0143-9529 = Consumer credit bulletin : £50.00 per year B82-19877

354.410083'3 — Great Britain. *Employment Service Division*

The **General** employment service in Great Britain : report of the ESD Rayner Scrutiny, 1982 / Bryan Winkett ... [et al.]. — [Sheffield] ([Room W915, Moorfoot, Sheffield S1 4PQ]) : Manpower Services Commission, 1982. — [243]p : 1map ; 30cm
Cover title
Unpriced (pbk) B82-35520

354.410083'3 — Great Britain. *Manpower Services Commission.* **Corporate planning,** *1980-1984.* **Great Britain.** *Parliament. House of Commons. Employment Committee.* **First report ... session 1979-80** — *Critical studies*

Great Britain. First special report from the Employment Committee, session 1979-80 : the Manpower Services Commission's corporate plan 1980-84 : observations by the government and Manpower Services Commission on the first report of the committee in session 1979-80. — London : H.M.S.O., [1980]. — 10p ; 25cm. — ([HC] ; 817)
ISBN 0-10-028179-6 (unbound) : £1.40 B82-10328

354.410084 — Great Britain. *Department of Health and Social Security.* **Staffing. Great Britain.** *Parliament. House of Commons. Committee of Public Accounts.* **Third report ... session 1981-82** — *Critical studies*

Great Britain. *Treasury.* Treasury minute on the sixth report from the Committee of Public accounts session 1981-82. — London : H.M.S.O., 1982. — 4p ; 25cm. — (Cmnd. ; 8620)
ISBN 0-10-186200-8 (unbound) : £1.25 B82-38221

354.410084'1 — Great Britain. *Health Service Commissioner.* **Reports. Reports: Great Britain.** *Parliament. House of Commons. Select Committee on the Parliamentary Commissioner for Administration.* **Reports** — *Critical studies*

Great Britain. *Parliament. House of Commons. Select Committee on the Parliamentary Commissioner for Administration.* First special report from the Select Committee on the Parliamentary Commissioner for Administration, session 1979-80 : departmental observations on second report of session 1978-79 — reports of the Health Service Commissioner. — London : H.M.S.O., [1980]. — 4p ; 25cm. — ([HC] ; 405)
ISBN 0-10-240580-8 (unbound) : £0.50 B82-10960

354.410085'5 — Great Britain. Government. Scientific advice. Supply. Great Britain. *Parliament. House of Lords. Select Committee on Science and Technology.* **Science and government** — *Critical studies*

Great Britain. Science and government : Government observations on the first report of the House of Lords Select Committee on Science and Technology (session 1981-82). — London : H.M.S.O., [1982]. — 9p ; 25cm. — (Cmnd. ; 8591)
ISBN 0-10-185910-4 (unbound) : £1.65 B82-40841

354.410085'6 — Great Britain. Inventions. Development. Organisations: National Research Development Corporation. Accounts — *Inquiry reports*

Great Britain. *Parliament. House of Commons. Committee of Public Accounts.* Twenty-first report from the Committee of Public Accounts : together with the proceedings of the committee and the minutes of evidence : session 1979-80 : Department of Industry, National Research Development Corporation : National Research Development Corporation accounts, 1978-79. — London : H.M.S.O., [1980]. — ix,9p ; 25cm. — ([HC] ; 739)
ISBN 0-10-027399-8 (pbk) : £2.25 B82-09502

354.410086'5 — Great Britain. Houses. Improvement. Grants from government

Hawkins, Nigel. Housing grants. — London : Kogan Page, Jan.1982. — [200]p
ISBN 0-85038-541-5 (pbk) : £3.95 : CIP entry B82-00153

354.41009'1 — Great Briain. *Parliamentary Commissioner for Administration.* **Role** — *Personal observations*

Clothier, C. M.. The Ombudsman — jurisdiction, powers and practice / by C.M. Clothier. — Stockport ([c/o P.K. Berry, C.I.S. Building, Miller St, Manchester M60 0AL]) : Manchester Statistical Society, [1980?]. — 16p : ill ; 21cm
At head of title: Manchester Statistical Society. — Text on inside cover
£2.00 (pbk) B82-02709

354.41009'1 — Great Britain. *Parliamentary Commissioner for Administration.* **Jurisdiction** — *Inquiry reports*

Great Britain. *Parliament. House of Commons. Select Committee on the Parliamentary Commissioner for Administration.* Select Committee on the Parliamentary Commissioner for Administration : fourth report : session 1979-80 : the jurisdiction of the Parliamentary Commissioner : together with the proceedings of the committee relating to the report and the minutes of evidence taken on 13 and 20 May and 8 July, 1980. — London : H.M.S.O., [1980]. — xv,42p ; 25cm. — ([HC] ; 593)
ISBN 0-10-259380-9 (pbk) : £4.40 B82-10961

354.41'01 — Great Britain. Bureaucracy. Attitudes of consumers

Bureaucracies : ... survey was carried out for the National Consumer Council by Research Services Limited. — London : National Consumer Council, 1981. — 30p ; 30cm
ISBN 0-905653-39-4 (unbound) : £1.00 B82-17835

354.41'01'0207 — Great Britain. Bureaucracy — *Humour*

Fishall, R. T.. Bureaucrats : how to annoy them! / R.T. Fishall ; drawings by William Rushton. — London : Sidgwick & Jackson, 1981. — 92p : ill ; 20cm
Includes index
ISBN 0-283-98785-5 : £2.80 B82-02508

354.4103 — Great Britain. Government agencies & government departments — *Directories* — *For offshore engineering industries*

Offshore operations handbook : a guide to communications with Government departments and agencies. — 2nd ed. — Aylesbury (Kingfisher House, Walton St., Aylesbury, Bucks.) : Petroleum Industry Training Board, 1982. — 54p : 1map ; 30cm
Previous ed.: published as Offshore operator's handbook. 1981. — Includes index
Unpriced (pbk) B82-40864

354.4103 — Great Britain. Government departments. Information. Disclosure

Michael, James. The politics of secrecy / James Michael. — Harmondsworth : Penguin, 1982. — 240p ; 20cm
Bibliography: p225-229. — Includes index
ISBN 0-14-022060-7 (pbk) : £2.50 B82-18148

354.4103'12 — Great Britain. Monarchy

Packard, Jerrold M.. The Queen and her court : a guide to the British monarchy today / Jerrold M. Packard. — London : Robson, 1981. — 234p,[12]p of plates : ill,1coat of arms,plans,ports ; 24cm
Bibliography: p222-225. — Includes index
ISBN 0-86051-144-8 : £7.50 B82-28994

354.41062 — Great Britain. *Exchequer and Audit Department.* **Role** — *Inquiry reports*

Great Britain. *Parliament. House of Commons. Committee of Public Accounts.* Role of the Comptroller and Auditor General / Committee of Public Accounts. — London : H.M.S.O., [1980]
Appendices to the minutes of evidence
Vol.1. — 95p ; 25cm. — ([HC] ; 653 iii)
ISBN 0-10-009409-0 (pbk) : £4.70 B82-15129

354.41062'092'4 — Great Britain. *Treasury, 1974-1979* — *Personal observations*

Barnett, Joel. Inside the Treasury / Joel Barnett. — London : Deutsch, 1982. — 200p ; 24cm
Includes index
ISBN 0-233-97394-x : £8.95 B82-16077

354.41063 — Great Britain. *Scottish Office.* **Role**

Keating, Michael, *1950-.* The Scottish Office in the United Kingdom policy network / Michael Keating and Arthur Midwinter. — Glasgow (University of Strathclyde, Glasgow, G1 1XQ) : Centre for the Study of Public Policy, c1981. — ii,24p : 1ill ; 30cm. — (Studies in public policy, ISSN 0140-8240 ; no.96)
Unpriced (pbk) B82-12870

354.41063 — Great Britain. *Welsh Office.* **Organisation**

Thomas, Ian C.. The creation of the Welsh Office : conflicting purposes in institutional change / by Ian C. Thomas. — Glasgow (University of Strathclyde, Glasgow G1 1XQ) : Centre for the Study of Public Policy, 1981. — iv,80p : 1map ; 30cm. — (Studies in public policy, ISSN 0140-8240 ; no.91)
Bibliography: p76-80
Unpriced (pbk) B82-06968

354.41063'09 — Great Britain. *Home Office, 1848-1914*

Pellew, Jill. The Home Office 1848-1914 : from clerks to bureaucrats / Jill Pellew. — London : Heinemann, 1982. — xi,271p ; 22cm
Bibliography: p225-233. — Includes index
ISBN 0-435-32685-6 : £12.50 : CIP rev. B82-00925

354.41063'09 — Great Britain. *Home Office, to 1982*

Great Britain. *Home Office.* Calendar of events : the Home Office : 1782-1982. — [London] ([Queen Anne's Gate, SW1H 9AT]) : [Home Office], [1982]. — [8]p ; 30cm
Unpriced (unbound) B82-40596

Great Britain. *Home Office.* Home Office 1782-1982 : to commemorate the bicentenary of the Home Office. — London : Home Office, 1981. — 48p : ill(some col.),ports ; 30cm
Text and ill on inside covers
ISBN 0-86252-005-3 (pbk) : Unpriced B82-23820

354.41068 — Great Britain. *Department of the Environment (central).* **Non-staff running costs**

Joubert, C. J. P.. Report on Rayner study of non-staff running costs in the Department of the Environment (central) / C.J.P. Joubert, H.C.S. Derwent. — [London] ([2 Marsham St., SW1P 3EB]) : Department of the Environment, 1981. — 2v. : ill,forms ; 30cm
Cover title
£22.00 (pbk) B82-35519

354.41068 — Great Britain. *Department of the Environment. West Midlands Regional Office* — *Inquiry reports*

Great Britain. *Parliament. House of Commons. Environment Committee.* First report from the Environment Committee, session 1980-81 : the Department of the Environment and the West Midlands region : together with the proceedings of the committee. — London : H.M.S.O., 1980. — vip ; 25cm. — (HC ; 60)
ISBN 0-10-206081-9 (unbound) : £1.10 B82-12767

354.410685′1 — Great Britain. *Department of Education and Science.* **Senior personnel** — *Directoriese*

Great Britain. *Department of Education and Science.* List of senior staff and their responsibilities. — London (Elizabeth House, York Rd, SE1 7PH) : Department of Education and Science, 1982. — 42p ; 21cm
Cover title
Unpriced (pbk) B82-25299

354.4107′2 — Great Britain. Government. Policies — *Forecasts*

Hood, Christopher, *1947-*. The future of United Kingdom politics : a probabilistic analysis / by Christopher Hood. — Glasgow (University of Strathclyde, Glasgow G1 1XQ) : Centre for the Study of Public Policy, 1981. — ii,20p ; 30cm. — (Studies in public policy, ISSN 0140-8240 ; no.90)
Bibliography: p20
£1.50 (pbk) B82-00817

354.4107′2 — Great Britain. Government. Policies. Formulation *compared with* **formulation of government policies in France**

Ashford, Douglas E.. British dogmatism and French pragmatism : central-local policymaking in the Welfare State / Douglas E. Ashford. — London : Allen & Unwin, 1982. — xvii,406p : ill ; 23cm. — (The New local government series ; no.22)
Includes index
ISBN 0-04-352096-0 : Unpriced : CIP rev.
Also classified at 354.4407′2 B81-28785

354′.4107′22 — Great Britain. Government departments. Administration. Use of computer systems & telecommunication systems. Advisory services: Central Computer and Telecommunications Agency, *to 1980*

Hearson, P.. The Central Computer and Telecommunications Agency — its role and functions / [P. Hearson]. — [London] ([Whitehall, SW1A 2AZ]) : Civil Service Department, 1981. — 5p ; 30cm
Unpriced (unbound) B82-00873

354.4107′3 — Great Britain. Government departments. Management. Operations research — *Career guides*

Operational research : an opportunity for scientists in management & administration. — London (Whitehall, SW1A 2AZ) : Civil Service Department, 1981. — [12]p : 2ill ; 21cm
Cover title
Unpriced (pbk) B82-33380

354.4107′3 — Great Britain. Government. Organisational change, *1950-1979*

Fry, Geoffrey K.. The administrative ′revolution′ in Whitehall : a study of the politics of administrative change in British central government since the 1950s / G.K. Fry. — London : Croom Helm, c1981. — 217p ; 23cm
Bibliography: p183-207. — Includes index
ISBN 0-7099-1010-x : £11.95 : CIP rev. B81-30984

354.4108′2 — Northern Ireland. Devolution of powers of British government — *Proposals*

Great Britain. Northern Ireland : a framework for devolution. — London : H.M.S.O., [1982]. — 17p ; 25cm. — (Cmnd. ; 8541)
Cover title
ISBN 0-10-185410-2 (pbk) : £2.30 B82-25140

354.4109 — Great Britain. Quangos

Holland, Philip, *1917 Mar.14-*. Quango, quango, quango, : the full dossier on patronage in Britain / Philip Holland. — [London] : Adam Smith Institute, [1981?]. — 9p,[1]concertina folded leaf ; 22cm
ISBN 0-906517-02-8 (pbk) : £2.00 B82-18884

Quangos in Britain : government and the networks of public policy-making / edited by Anthony Barker. — London : Macmillan, 1982. — xiii,250p : ill ; 23cm
Bibliography: p232-241. — Includes index
ISBN 0-333-29468-8 : £20.00 B82-28679

354.4109′0212 — Great Britain. Quangos — *Statistics — Serials*

Non-departmental public bodies : facts and figures / Civil Service Department. — 1980-. — London : H.M.S.O., 1981-. — v. ; 25cm
Annual
£4.70 B82-14788

354.4110082 — Scotland. Economic development. Organisations: Scottish Development Agency. Accounts — *Inquiry reports*

Great Britain. *Parliament. House of Commons. Committee of Public Accounts.* Eighteenth report from the Committee of Public Accounts : together with the proceedings of the committee, the minutes of evidence and appendices : session 1979-80 : Scottish Development Agency, Scottish Economic Planning Department : Scottish Development Agency accounts, 1976-77, 1977-78 and 1978-79. — London : H.M.S.O., [1980]. — xv,16p ; 25cm. — ([HC] ; 736)
ISBN 0-10-027369-6 (pbk) : £2.50 B82-09503

354.4110082 — Scotland. Highlands & Islands. Economic development. Organisations: Highlands and Islands Development Board. Role

Geddes, Mike. The role of the state in regional development : the Highlands and Islands Development Board / Mike Geddes. — London : Department of Town Planning, Polytechnic of the South Bank, c1981. — 18leaves ; 30cm. — (Occasional paper, ISSN 0143-4888 ; OP2/81)
ISBN 0-905267-19-2 (spiral) : £2.00 B82-02423

354.4110082′09 — Scotland. Highlands & Islands. Economic development. Organisations: Highlands and Islands Development Board, *to 1981*

Grassie, James. Highland experiment. — Aberdeen : Aberdeen University Press, Oct.1982. — [144]p
ISBN 0-08-025765-8 (cased) : £10.00 : CIP entry
ISBN 0-08-028473-6 (pbk) : £6.00 B82-24949

354.416′0009 — Northern Ireland. Government, *1972-1981*

Wallace, Martin. British government in Northern Ireland : from devolution to direct rule / Martin Wallace. — Newton Abbot : David & Charles, c1982. — 192p : 1map ; 23cm
Bibliography: p182-187. — Includes index
ISBN 0-7153-8153-9 : £6.95 : CIP rev. B81-35821

354.4170072′4 — Ireland. *Revenue Commissioners, to 1977*

Réamonn, Seán. History of the Revenue Commissioners / Seán Réamonn. — Dublin : Institute of Public Administration, 1981. — xii,385p : ill,ports ; 23cm
Spine title: The revenue commissioners. — Bibliography: p356-369. — Includes index
ISBN 0-902173-99-5 : £14.96 B82-08702

354.4170082 — Ireland *(Republic).* **Industrial development. Organisations: Industrial Development Authority. Policies,** *1978-1982*

IDA industrial plan 1978-82. — Dublin : IDA Ireland, 1979. — 77p : ill,maps ; 30cm
Unpriced (pbk) B82-36646

354.420082′2 — Dyfed. Aberystwyth. Mints: Aberystwyth Mint, *to 1667*

Boon, George C.. Cardiganshire silver and the Aberystwyth Mint in peace & war / by George C. Boon. — Cardiff : National Museum of Wales, 1981. — xiii,287p,[3]leaves of plates (some folded) : ill(some col.),maps,coat of arms,facsims,1plan,ports ; 26cm
Bibliography: p145-150. — Includes index
ISBN 0-7200-0240-0 : Unpriced B82-11335

354.4203′12 — England. Monarchy. Relations with local communities, *1400-1500*

The Crown and local communities : in England and France in the fifteenth century / edited by J.R.L. Highfield and Robin Jeffs. — Gloucester : Sutton, 1981. — 192p ; 23cm
Includes index
ISBN 0-904387-67-4 (cased) : £8.95 : CIP rev.
ISBN 0-904387-79-8 (pbk)
Also classified at 354.4403′12 B81-30175

354.4207′2′09 — England. Government. Policies, *1572-1588*

MacCaffrey, Wallace T.. Queen Elizabeth and the making of policy, 1572-1588 : by Wallace T. MacCaffrey. — Princeton, N.J. ; Guildford : Princeton University Press, 1981. — 530p ; 23cm
Bibliography: p511-520. — Includes index
ISBN 0-691-05324-3 (cased) : £28.20
ISBN 0-691-10112-4 (pbk) : £10.80 B82-02435

354.429008 — Wales. Grants. Eligibility of citizens — *Practical information*

Can you take it for granted? : a guide to grants. — Cardiff (Oxford House, Hills St., Cardiff CF1 2DR) : Welsh Consumer Council, [1981?]. — 1portfolio : 1map ; 22cm
Unpriced B82-15340

354.4290082 — Wales. Economic development. Organisations: Welsh Development Agency, *to 1981*

Welsh Development Agency. The first five years : 1 January 1976 to 31 March 1981 / Welsh Development Agency. — Pontypridd (Treforest Industrial Estate, Pontypridd, Mid Glamorgan CF37 5UT) : Welsh Development Agency, [1981]. — 24p : ill(some col.),col.maps,facsims,ports ; 30cm
Also available in Welsh as Y pum mlynedd cyntaf
ISBN 0-9503406-5-0 (pbk) : Unpriced B82-00667

354.4290082 — Wales. Economic development. Organisations: Welsh Development Agency, *to 1981 — Welsh texts*

Welsh Development Agency. Y pum mlynedd cyntaf : I Ionawr 1976 tan 31 Mawrth 1981 / Awdurdod Datblygu Cymru. — Pontypridd (Treforest Industrial Estate, Pontypridd, Mid Glamorgan CF37 5UT) : Awdurdod Datblygu Cymru, [1981]. — 24p : ill(some col.),col.maps,facsims,ports ; 30cm
Also available in English as The first five years
ISBN 0-9503406-6-9 (pbk) : Unpriced B82-00668

354.4290082′325 — Wales. Water authorities: Welsh Water Authority. Capital expenditure — *Statistics — Serials*

Welsh Water Authority. Capital expenditure programme ; Capital design schedule / Welsh Water Authority. — [No.1]-. — [Brecon] ([Cambrian Way, Brecon, Powys LO3 7HP]) : [The Authority], 1980-. — v. ; 21x30cm
Annual. — Continues: Welsh National Water Development Authority. Capital expenditure programme
ISSN 0143-9022 = Capital expenditure programme ... . Capital design schedule ... - Welsh Water Authority : Unpriced B82-19885

354.43 — West Germany. Government

Johnson, Nevil. State and government in the Federal Republic of Germany. — 2nd ed. — Oxford : Pergamon, Feb.1983. — [240]p. — (Governments of western Europe)
Previous ed.: published as Government in the Federal Republic of Germany. 1973
ISBN 0-08-030188-6 (cased) : £17.50 : CIP entry
ISBN 0-08-030190-8 (pbk) : £8.75 B82-36468

354.430072′2 — West Germany. Government. Budgeting. Effects of macroeconomic policies

Knott, Jack H.. Managing the German economy : budgetary politics in a federal state / Jack H. Knott. — Lexington, Mass. : Lexington Books, c1981 ; [Aldershot] : Gower [distributor], 1982. — xviii,215p : ill ; 24cm
Bibliography: p203-210. — Includes index
ISBN 0-669-04401-6 : £16.50 B82-11320

354.4403′12 — France. Monarchy. Relations with local communities, *1400-1500*

The Crown and local communities : in England and France in the fifteenth century / edited by J.R.L. Highfield and Robin Jeffs. — Gloucester : Sutton, 1981. — 192p ; 23cm
Includes index
ISBN 0-904387-67-4 (cased) : £8.95 : CIP rev.
ISBN 0-904387-79-8 (pbk)
Primary classification 354.4203′12 B81-30175

354.4407′2 — France. Government. Policies. Formulation *compared with* **formulation of government policies in Great Britain**

Ashford, Douglas E.. British dogmatism and French pragmatism : central-local policymaking in the Welfare State / Douglas E. Ashford. — London : Allen & Unwin, 1982. — xvii,406p : ill ; 23cm. — (The New local government series ; no.22)
Includes index
ISBN 0-04-352096-0 : Unpriced : CIP rev.
Primary classification 354.4107′2 B81-28785

354.470072′2′09 — Soviet Union. Government. Budgeting, *1940-1978*

Birman, Igor. Secret incomes of the Soviet state budget / Igor Birman. — The Hague ; London : Nijhoff, 1981. — xv,315p ; 25cm
Bibliography: p295-308. — Includes index
ISBN 90-247-2550-x : Unpriced B82-06117

354.4703′4 — Soviet Union. Government. Policies. Effects of succession of rulers *compared with* **effects of succession of rulers on government policies in United States**

Bunce, Valerie. Do new leaders make a difference? : executive succession and public policy under capitalism and socialism / Valerie Bunce. — Princeton ; Guildford : Princeton University Press, c1981. — xiii,296p ; 23cm
Bibliography: p261-291. — Includes index
ISBN 0-691-07631-6 (cased) : £15.80
ISBN 0-691-02205-4 (pbk) : £4.95
Primary classification 353.03′4 B82-00726

354.4707′25 — Soviet Union. Government. Policies. Decision making, *1950-1980*

Löwenhardt, John. Decision making in Soviet politics / by John Löwenhardt. — London : Macmillan, 1981. — x,238p ; 25cm
Bibliography: p227-235. — Includes index
ISBN 0-333-32281-9 : £15.00 B82-10828

354.51′1401 — China. Shandong *(Province).* **Government. Bureaucracy,** *1500-1600*

Littrup, Leif. Subbureaucratic government in China in Ming times : a study of Shandong Province in the sixteenth century / Leif Littrup. — Oslo : Universitetsforlaget ; London : Global Book Resources [distributor], c1981. — 224p ; 23cm. — (Instituttet for sammenlignende kulturforskning. Serie B. Skrifter ; 64)
At head of title: Instituttet for Sammenlignende Kulturforskning. — Bibliography: p209-217. — Includes index
ISBN 82-00-09531-2 : £12.90 B82-37803

354.520072′46 — Japan. Imports. Customs procedures — *For British businessmen*

Further opening of the Japanese market : import testing procedures simplified : the handling of complaints. — London (342 Grand Buildings, Traflagar Square, WC2) : Anglo-Japanese Economic Institute, [1982]. — [8p] ; 24cm
Unpriced (unbound) B82-26487

354.595′1006 — Peninsular Malaysia. Civil service. British personnel, *1867-1942*

Heussler, Robert. British rule in Malaya : the Malayan Civil Service and its predecessors, 1867-1942 / Robert Heussler. — Oxford : Clio Press, 1981. — xx,356p : 1map ; 25cm
Bibliography: p337-339. — Includes index
ISBN 0-903450-49-6 : £22.50 B82-02739

354.6207′2′09 — Egypt. Government. Policies, *1971-1980 — Left-wing political viewpoints*

Makhlouf, Fawzeya. Four questions asked by Baheya in Egypt / by Fawzeya Makhlouf. — [London] (21, Brookfield Park NW5 1ES) : [The Committee for Peace, Democracy and Development in Egypt], [1980]. — 63p : ill ; 21cm
Cover title
£1.50 (pbk) B82-26746

354.6690072′2 — Nigeria. Government. Budgeting

Obinna, O. E.. An introduction to Nigerian budget policy. — London : Allen & Unwin, Aug.1982. — [208]p
ISBN 0-04-336076-9 : £4.95 : CIP entry B82-15630

354.94′01 — Australia. Public administration. Bureaucracy. Reform

Hawker, Geoffrey. Who's master, who's servant? : reforming bureaucracy / Geoffrey Hawker. — Sydney ; Londn : Allen & Unwin, 1981. — x,100p : ill ; 23cm
Bibliography: p95. — Includes index
ISBN 0-86861-075-5 (cased) : Unpriced
ISBN 0-86861-083-6 (pbk) : Unpriced B82-05544

354.940681′8 — Australia. *Department of Urban and Regional Development, 1972-1977*

Lloyd, C. J.. Innovation and reaction : the life and death of the Federal Department of Urban and Regional Development. — London : Allen and Unwin, Mar.1982. — [198]p
ISBN 0-86861-394-0 (cased) : £14.95 : CIP entry
ISBN 0-86861-003-8 (pbk) : £5.95 B82-12888

355 — MILITARY FORCES

355 — Armies

Weeks, John. Armies of the world / compiled by John Weeks. — London : Jane's, 1981. — 224p : ill ; 12x19cm. — (Jane's pocket book)
ISBN 0-7106-0149-2 : £5.95 B82-07916

355 — Military science

Dunnigan, James F.. How to make war. — London : Arms and Armour, Sept.1982. — [448]p
Originally published: New York : Morrow, 1982
ISBN 0-85368-539-8 : £8.95 : CIP entry B82-20834

355′.005 — Military forces — *Serials*

RUSI and Brassey's defence yearbook. — 1982. — London : Pergamon, Nov.1981. — [360]p
ISBN 0-08-027039-5 (cased) : £10.00 : CIP entry
ISBN 0-08-027040-9 (pbk) : £10.00 B81-28761

355′.009 — Soldiers, *B.C.334-ca 1980*

Young, Peter, *1915-.* The fighting man : from Alexander the Great's army to the present day / Peter Young ; introduction by Haim Laskov. — London : Orbis, c1981. — 238p : ill(some col.),ports(some col.) ; 30cm
Includes index
ISBN 0-85613-025-7 : Unpriced B82-01480

355′.009 — Warfare. Geographical aspects

O'Sullivan, Patrick. The geography of warfare. — London : Croom Helm, Nov.1982. — [160]p
ISBN 0-7099-1918-2 : £12.95 : CIP entry B82-27938

355′.009′021 — Armies, *600-1066*

Heath, Ian. Armies of the Dark Ages 600-1066 : organization, tactics, dress and weapons / by Ian Heath. — 2nd ed. — [Goring by Sea] ([75, Ardingly Drive, Goring by Sea, Sussex]) : Wargames Research Group, 1980. — 128p : ill,2maps ; 26cm
Bibliography: p126-128
Unpriced B82-21306

355′.009171′241 — Commonwealth military forces — *Abbreviations*

Scott, B. K. C.. Dictionary of military abbreviations : British-Empire-Commonwealth / by B.K.C. Scott. — Hastings : Tamarisk, 1982. — 117p ; 21cm
ISBN 0-907221-01-7 (pbk) : £4.00 B82-24872

355′.009172′4 — Developing countries. Military self-reliance. Achievement. Role of multinational companies in military equipment industries

Tuomi, Helena. Transnational corporations, armaments and development / Helena Tuomi and Raimo Väyrynen. — Aldershot : Gower, 1982. — xv,312p ; 23cm
Originally published: Tampere : Tampere Peace Research Institute, 1980
ISBN 0-566-00506-9 : Unpriced : CIP rev.
Primary classification 338.4′7623′091724 B81-36217

355′.0093 — Mediterranean region. Military forces, *ca B.C.100-A.D.600*

Barker, Phil. The armies and enemies of Imperial Rome : organization, tactics, dress and weapons / by Phil Barker ; drawings by Ian Heath. — [Goring by Sea] ([75, Ardingly Drive, Goring by Sea, Sussex]) : Wargames Research Group, 1981. — 146p : ill ; 26cm
Previous ed.: 197-?. — Bibliography: p3
Unpriced
Primary classification 355′.00936 B82-21305

355′.00936 — Europe. Military forces, *ca B.C.100-A.D.600*

Barker, Phil. The armies and enemies of Imperial Rome : organization, tactics, dress and weapons / by Phil Barker ; drawings by Ian Heath. — [Goring by Sea] ([75, Ardingly Drive, Goring by Sea, Sussex]) : Wargames Research Group, 1981. — 146p : ill ; 26cm
Previous ed.: 197-?. — Bibliography: p3
Unpriced
Also classified at 355′.0093 B82-21305

355′.00937 — Ancient Roman armies, *117-337*

Simkins, Michael. The Roman army from Hadrian to Constantine / text by Michael Simkins ; colour plates by Ronald Embleton. — London : Osprey, 1979 (1981 [printing]). — 40p,A-Hp of plates : ill(some col.),2maps,plans ; 25cm. — (Men-at-arms series ; 93)
English text, English, French and German captions to plates. — Bibliography: p2
ISBN 0-85045-333-x (pbk) : Unpriced B82-10730

355′.00937 — Ancient Rome. Military forces. Terminology — *Encyclopaedias*

Graham, Frank, *1913-.* Dictionary of Roman military terms / by Frank Graham. — Newcastle upon Tyne : F. Graham, c1981. — 32p : ill,2plans ; 22cm
ISBN 0-85983-166-3 (pbk) : £0.70 B82-03938

355′.00937 — Great Britain. Ancient Roman armies

Holder, Paul A.. The Roman army in Britain / P.A. Holder. — London : Batsford, 1982. — 173p,[16]p of plates : ill,maps,plans,ports ; 25cm
Bibliography: p156-162. — Includes index
ISBN 0-7134-3629-8 : £9.95 : CIP rev. B82-01209

355′.00937 — Punic Wars. Armies, *to B.C.146*

Wise, Terence. Armies of the Carthaginian wars 265-146BC / text by Terence Wise ; colour plates by Richard Hook. — London : Osprey, 1982. — 40p,A-H p of plates : ill(some col.),maps,1plan,ports ; 25cm. — (Men-at-arms series ; 121)
English text, with notes on the plates in French and German. — Bibliography: p39
ISBN 0-85045-430-1 (pbk) : Unpriced B82-37337

355′.0094 — European armies, *1480-1650*

Gush, George. Renaissance armies 1480-1650. — 2nd ed. — Cambridge : Patrick Stephens, May 1982. — [128]p
Previous ed.: 1975
ISBN 0-85059-604-1 : £7.95 : CIP entry B82-07613

355′.0094 — European armies, *1648-1789*

Childs, John. Armies and warfare of Europe 1648-1789. — Manchester : Manchester University Press, June 1982. — [208]p
ISBN 0-7190-0880-8 : £14.50 : CIP entry B82-09633

355.00941 — British military forces. Portrayal by mass media

Hooper, Alan. The military and the media. — Aldershot : Gower, Nov.1982. — [200]p
ISBN 0-566-00610-3 : £13.50 : CIP entry B82-31296

355′.00941 — Great Britain. *Army, 1793-1815*

Fox, Kenneth O.. Making life possible : a study of military aid to the civil power in Regency England / Kenneth O. Fox ; with a foreword by Peter Young. — [Great Britain?] : [K.O. Fox], 1982 (Kineton : Roundwood). — viii,259p ; 22cm
Bibliography: p196-200. — Includes index
Unpriced (pbk) B82-39781

355'.00941 — Great Britain. *Army, 1945-1980*

Gander, Terry. Encyclopaedia of the modern British army. — 2nd ed. — Cambridge : Patrick Stephens, June 1982. — [280]p
Previous ed.: 1980
ISBN 0-85059-577-0 : £16.95 : CIP entry B82-09844

355'.009411 — Scotland. Military forces, *1639-1651*

Reid, Stuart. Scots armies of the Civil War, 1639-1651 / Stuart Reid ; with central illustrations by Hawk Norton. — Leigh-on-Sea (59 Leighton Ave., Leigh-on-Sea, Essex) : Partizan Press, 1982. — 50p,[4]p of plates : ill,coats of arms,2maps ; 22cm
£1.95 (pbk) B82-38939

355'.00943 — Germany. *Heer, 1933-1945*

Seaton, Albert. The German army 1933-45 / Albert Seaton. — London : Weidenfeld and Nicolson, c1982. — xxiv,310p : 7maps ; 25cm
Bibliography: p283-292. — Includes index
ISBN 0-297-78032-8 : £16.50 B82-10978

355'.00943 — Germany. Nationalsozialistische Deutsche Arbeiter-Partei. *Waffenschutzstaffel, to 1945*

Mollo, Andrew. To the death's head true / Andrew Mollo. — [London] : Thames-Methuen, 1982. — ix,131p,[16]p of plates : ill,1facsim,ports ; 20cm
Bibliography: p124-126. — Includes index
ISBN 0-423-00060-8 (pbk) : £1.50 B82-33876

Quarrie, Bruce. Hitler's samurai : the Waffen SS in action. — Cambridge : Stephens, Feb.1983. — [160]p
ISBN 0-85059-572-x : £9.95 : CIP entry B82-39470

355'.00947 — Soviet military forces

Soviet war power / edited by Ray Bonds. — London : Corgi, 1982, c1980. — 282p : ill (some col.),ports ; 24cm
Originally published: London : Salamander, 1980
ISBN 0-552-98201-6 (pbk) : £4.95 B82-18691

355'.00947 — Soviet military forces. Control systems

Hemsley, John, *1935-*. Soviet troop control : the role of command technology in the Soviet military system / John Hemsley. — Oxford : Brassey's, 1982. — xxvi,276p,[24]p of plates : ill,maps,ports ; 24cm. — (Battlefield weapons systems and technology series)
Bibliography: p231-244. — Includes index
ISBN 0-08-027008-5 : £25.00 : CIP rev. B82-07990

355'.00947 — Union of Soviet Socialist Republics. *Armiia*

Suvorov, Viktor. Inside the Soviet army. — London : Hamilton, Sept.1982. — [320]p
ISBN 0-241-10889-6 : £9.95 : CIP entry B82-18740

355'.00947 — Union of Soviet Socialist Republics. *Armiia, 1956-1980*

Suvorov, Viktor. The liberators. — London : H. Hamilton, Sept.1981. — [224]p
ISBN 0-241-10675-3 : £8.95 : CIP entry B81-20118

Suvorov, Viktor. The liberators. — London : New English Library, Jan.1983. — [288]p
Originally published: London : Hamilton, 1981
ISBN 0-450-05546-9 (pbk) : £1.75 : CIP entry B82-36142

355'.009495 — Byzantine Empire armies, *886-1118*

Heath, Ian. Byzantine armies 886-1118 / text by Ian Heath ; colour plates by Angus McBride. — London : Osprey, 1979 (1981 [printing]). — 40p,A-H p of plates : ill(some col.),2maps,ports ; 25cm. — (Men-at-arms series ; 89)
English text, with notes on the plates in French and German
ISBN 0-85045-306-2 (pbk) : £3.50 B82-37334

355'.009495 — Byzantine Empire. Armies, *ca 400-ca 1200*

Kaegi, Walter Emil. Army, society and religion in Byzantium. — London : Variorum, Sept.1982. — [320]p. — (Collected studies series ; CS162)
ISBN 0-86078-110-0 : £26.00 : CIP entry B82-21404

355'.00952 — Japan. Socialism, *ca 1860-1918*

Crump, John. The origins of socialist thought in Japan. — London : Croom Helm, Nov.1982. — [416]p
ISBN 0-7099-0739-7 : £15.95 : CIP entry B82-30581

355'.00954 — Great Britain. *Army. Indian Army, to 1947*

Mollo, Boris. The Indian Army / by Boris Mollo. — Poole : Blandford, 1981. — 191p : ill (some col.),ports(some col.) ; 26cm
Bibliography: p189-191
ISBN 0-7137-1074-8 : £10.50 : CIP rev. B81-28017

355'.02 — War

The Correlates of war. — New York : Free Press ; London : Collier Macmillan
1: Research origins and rationale / edited by J. David Singer. — c1979. — xix,405p : ill ; 25cm
Bibliography: p363-394. — Includes index
ISBN 0-02-928960-2 : £11.95 B82-35621

355'.02 — War. Role of religions. Symbolism

Aho, James Alfred. Religious mythology and the art of war : comparative religious symbolisms of military violence / James A. Aho. — London : Aldwych, 1981. — xv,258p : maps ; 22cm
Bibliography: p227-240. — Includes index
ISBN 0-86172-020-2 : £19.95 B82-30923

355'.02 — Warfare

Lider, Theodore. Military theory. — Aldershot : Gower, Oct.1982. — [460]p. — (Swedish studies in international relations ; 12)
ISBN 0-566-00485-2 : £17.50 : CIP entry B82-23335

355'.02 — Warfare — *Early works*

Clausewitz, Carl von. On war / Carl von Clausewitz ; edited with an introduction by Anatol Rapoport. — [Abridged version]. — Harmondsworth : Penguin, 1968 (1982 [printing]). — 460p ; 19cm. — (Penguin classics)
Translation of: Vom Kriege. — Translated by J.J. Graham. — Originally published: London : Routledge & Kegan Paul, 1908. —
Bibliography: p433-437. — Includes index
ISBN 0-14-044427-0 (pbk) : £2.95 B82-37814

Sun Zi. The art of war / by Sun Tzu ; edited and foreword by James Clavell. — London : Hodder and Stoughton, 1981. — 95p ; 22cm
Translated from the Chinese
ISBN 0-340-27604-5 (pbk) : £3.95 : CIP rev. B81-30548

355'.02 — Warfare. Rules

Glover, Michael, *1922-*. The velvet glove : the decline and fall of moderation in war. — London : Hodder and Stoughton, Nov.1982. — [288]p
ISBN 0-340-26643-0 : £9.95 : CIP entry B82-27349

355'.02'0724 — War. Mathematical models

Bueno de Mesquita, Bruce. The war trap / Bruce Bueno de Mesquita. — New Haven ; London : Yale University Press, c1981. — xii,223p : ill ; 22cm
Bibliography: p211-215. — Includes index
ISBN 0-300-02558-0 : Unpriced : CIP rev. B81-31944

355'.02'09 — Warfare, *1000-1980*

McNeil, William. The pursuit of power. — Oxford : Blackwell, Sept.1982. — [410]p
ISBN 0-631-13134-5 : £9.95 : CIP entry B82-20289

355'.02'09 — Warfare, *ca 1450-ca 1631*

Hale, John Rigby. Renaissance war studies. — London (35 Gloucester Ave., NW1 7AX) : Hambledon Press, Sept.1982. — [624]p. — (History series ; no.11)
ISBN 0-907628-02-8 : £28.00 : CIP entry B82-21582

355'.02'09 — Warfare — *History* — *Serials*

Born in battle magazine. — No.1-. — Köln : Eshel ; West Drayton (Tavistock Rd, West Drayton, Middx UB7 7QE) : Distributed by COMAG, 1978-. — v. : ill(some col.),maps,ports ; 27cm
Quarterly. — Description based on: No.16
£1.40 per issue B82-09065

355'.02'09 — Warfare, *to 1980*

Dupuy, Trevor N. The evolution of weapons and warfare / by Trevor N. Dupuy. — London : Jane's, 1982, c1980. — 350p : ill,2maps ; 24cm
Includes index
ISBN 0-7106-0123-9 : £8.95 B82-16138

355'.02'0903 — Warfare, *1618-1815*

Koch, H. W.. The rise of modern warfare : 1618-1815 : H.W. Koch. — London : Hamlyn, 1981. — 256p : ill(some col.),maps,facsims,ports(some col.) ; 32cm
Includes index
ISBN 0-600-34165-8 : £7.95 B82-02720

355'.02'094 — Europe. Warfare, *1830-1945*

Pearton, Maurice. The knowledgeable state : diplomacy, war and technology since 1830 / Maurice Pearton. — [London] : Burnett, 1982. — 287p ; 25cm
Bibliography: p262-272. — Includes index
ISBN 0-09-147230-x : £12.95 : CIP rev. B82-09272

355'.0213 — Militarism & anti-militarism — *Socialist viewpoints*

Shaw, Martin, *1947-*. Socialism & militarism / Martin Shaw. — Nottingham (Bertrand Russell House, Gamble Street, Nottingham, NG7 4ET) : Bertrand Russell Peace Foundation, [1981]. — 33p ; 21cm. — (Spokesman pamphlet ; no.74)
Title on first page: Socialism against war
£0.75 (unbound) B82-17665

355'.0213'09 — Militarism, *to 1979*

Berghahn, Volker R.. Militarism : the history of an international debate 1861-1979 / Volker R. Berghahn. — Leamington Spa : Berg, 1981. — 132p ; 23cm
Bibliography: p125-128. — Includes index
ISBN 0-907582-01-x : £8.95 : CIP rev. B81-31060

355'.0217 — Great Britain. Nuclear warfare by Soviet Union. Effects — *Forecasts*

Clarke, Magnus. The nuclear destruction of Britain / Magnus Clarke. — London : Croom Helm, c1982. — 291p ; 23cm
Bibliography: p280-285. — Includes index
ISBN 0-7099-0458-4 : £11.95 : CIP rev. B81-24655

355'.0217 — Nuclear warfare

Humphrey, Nicholas. Four minutes to midnight / Nicholas Humphrey. — London : BBC, 1981. — 19p : ill,1facsim ; 21cm. — (The Bronowski memorial lecture ; October 1981)
ISBN 0-563-20048-0 (pbk) : £1.25 B82-07940

McEwan, Ian. Or shall we die?. — London : Cape, Feb.1983. — [48]p
ISBN 0-224-02947-9 B82-37836

Martin, Laurence. The two-edged sword : armed force in the modern world : the Reith lectures 1981 / Laurence Martin. — London : Weidenfeld and Nicolson, c1982. — xii,108p ; 33cm
Bibliography: p107-108
ISBN 0-297-78139-1 : £5.95 B82-21289

Nuclear strategies / Peace Force Scotland. — Kirkcaldy (The Lantern House, Olympia Arcade, Kirkcaldy, KY1 1QF) : Peace Force Scotland, [1982]. — [4]p : ill ; 21cm. — (Fact sheet ; 3)
Bibliography: p4
Unpriced (unbound) B82-27590

355'.0217 — Nuclear warfare. Attitudes of Marxists — *Conference proceedings*

World Congress of Philosophy. *Special Colloquium (15th : 1973 : Varna)*. Soviet Marxism and nuclear war : an international debate : from the proceedings of the special Colloquium of the XVth World Congress of Philosophy / edited with an introduction by John Somerville. — London : Aldwych, 1981. — xii,166p ; 22cm. — (Studies in human rights ; no.3)
Includes index
ISBN 0-86172-021-0 : £19.95 B82-31089

355'.0217 — Nuclear warfare. Control

Ball, Desmond. Can nuclear war be controlled? / by Desmond Ball. — London : International Institute for Strategic Studies, 1981. — iii,51p ; 25cm. — (Adelphi papers, ISSN 0567-932x ; no.169)
Cover title. — Text on inside cover
ISBN 0-86079-051-7 (pbk) : £2.00 B82-06091

Luzin, N. P.. Nuclear strategy and common sense / Nikolai Luzin ; [translated from the Russian by Dmitri Belyavsky and David Fidlon]. — Moscow : Progress ; [London] : Distributed by Central, c1981. — 350p ; 18cm
Translation of: ĪAdernaīa strategiīa i zdravyĭ smysl. — Includes index
ISBN 0-7147-1725-8 : £2.25 B82-29278

355'.0217 — Nuclear warfare. Deterrence

Ruston, Roger. Nuclear deterrence, right or wrong? : a study of the morality of nuclear deterrence / prepared for the Commission for International Justice and Peace of England and Wales as a contribution to discussion ; Roger Ruston. — Abbots Langley : Catholic Information Service, c1981. — 80p ; 21cm
Bibliography: p20
ISBN 0-905241-09-6 (pbk) : £1.25 B82-39079

355'.0217 — Nuclear warfare. Deterrence — *Bertrand Russell Peace Foundation viewpoints*

Coates, Ken. Deterrence : why we must think again / Ken Coates. — Nottingham (Bertrand Russell House, Gamble Street, Nottingham, NG7 4ET) : Bertrand Russell Peace Foundation, [1981]. — 11p ; 21cm. — (Spokesman pamphlet ; no.76)
£0.30 (unbound) B82-17667

355'.0217 — Nuclear warfare. Deterrence — *Conference proceedings*

International Standing Conference on Conflict and Peace Studies *(2nd : 1981 : Danbury Park, Essex)***Nuclear** deterrence. — Tunbridge Wells : Castle House Publications, May 1982. — [256]p
ISBN 0-7194-0079-1 : £15.00 : CIP entry B82-14390

Nuclear attack : civil defence. — Oxford : Pergamon, Oct.1982. — [225]p
Conference papers
ISBN 0-08-027041-7 (cased) : £11.50 : CIP entry
ISBN 0-08-027042-5 (pbk) : £4.95 B82-32843

355'.0217 — Nuclear warfare. Effects — *Forecasts*

Greene, Felix. Let there be a world : a call for an end to the arms race / Felix Greene. — Rev. ed. — London : Gollancz, 1982. — 64p : ill,1map,3ports ; 25cm
Cover title. — Previous ed.: Palo Alto : Fulton, 1963
ISBN 0-575-03136-0 (pbk) : £1.95 : CIP rev. B82-06234

Nuclear radiation in warfare / Stockholm International Peace Research Institute. — London : Taylor & Francis, 1981. — xvii,149p : ill ; 24cm
Includes index
ISBN 0-85066-217-6 : £9.50 : CIP rev. B81-18056

Nuclear war. — Oxford : Pergamon, Sept.1982. — [100]p
ISBN 0-08-028175-3 (cased) : £7.50 : CIP entry
ISBN 0-08-028176-1 (pbk) : £2.50 B82-28436

Schell, Jonathan. The fate of the earth / Jonathan Schell. — London : Cape, 1982. — 244p ; 23cm
Originally published: in The New Yorker. — Includes index
ISBN 0-224-02064-1 : £7.95 : CIP rev. B82-14362

Schell, Jonathan. The fate of the earth / Jonathan Schell. — London : Picador in association with Cape, 1982. — 244p ; 20cm
Originally published: in The New Yorker. — Includes index
ISBN 0-330-26915-1 (pbk) : £1.95 B82-31201

Zuckerman, Solly Zuckerman, *Baron*. Nuclear illusion and reality / Solly Zuckerman. — London : Collins, 1982. — 154p ; 22cm
Includes index
ISBN 0-00-216555-4 (cased) : Unpriced : CIP rev.
ISBN 0-00-216554-6 (pbk) : £4.95 B81-34583

355'.0217 — Nuclear warfare. Effects — *Study regions: London — Forecasts*

London after the bomb : what a nuclear attack really means / Owen Greene ... [et al.]. — Oxford : Oxford University Press, 1982. — x,142p : ill,maps ; 18cm
Bibliography: p135. — Includes index
ISBN 0-19-285123-3 (pbk) : £1.95 : CIP rev. B82-18992

355'.0217 — Nuclear warfare — *Forecasts*

Rogers, Paul, *1943-*. As lambs to the slaughter : the facts about nuclear war / Paul Rogers, Malcolm Dando, Peter van den Dungen ; illustrated by Richard Wilson. — London : Arrow Books in association with Ecoropa, 1981. — 289p : ill,2maps ; 18cm. — (An Ecoropa report)
ISBN 0-09-927270-9 (pbk) : £1.75 B82-04627

355'.0217 — Nuclear warfare. Limits. Theories, *1945-1980*

Clark, Ian. Limited nuclear war. — Oxford : Martin Robertson, Mar.1982. — [256]p
ISBN 0-85520-483-4 : £12.50 : CIP entry B82-01140

355'.0217 — Nuclear weapons. Proliferation

Nuclear proliferation : breaking the chain / edited by George H. Quester. — Madison, Wis. ; London : University of Wisconsin Press, 1981. — ix,245p ; 21cm
Includes index
ISBN 0-299-08600-3 (cased) : Unpriced
ISBN 0-299-08604-6 (pbk) : £4.90 B82-05710

355'.0217 — Nuclear weapons. Proliferation. Implications of use of nuclear power

Durie, Sheila. Fuelling the nuclear arms race : the links between nuclear power and nuclear weapons / Sheila Durie and Rob Edwards. — London : Pluto, 1982. — 159p : ill,1map ; 20cm. — (Militarism, state and society)
Bibliography: p112-113. — Includes index
ISBN 0-86104-372-3 (pbk) : £2.95 B82-31745

Nuclear power and the non-proliferation issue / British Nuclear Forum. — London (1 St. Alban's St., SW1Y 4SL) : BNF, 1978. — [10]p : 2ill ; 21cm
Unpriced (unbound) B82-24857

355'.0217 — Nuclear weapons. Proliferation — *Socialist Workers' Party viewpoints*

Binns, Peter. Missile madness : the weapons systems & how they threaten your life / by Peter Binns. — London : Produced and distributed for the SWP by Socialists Unlimited, 1981. — 39p : ill,ports ; 21cm. — (A Socialist Workers Party pamphlet)
Previous ed.: 1980
ISBN 0-905998-26-x (unbound) : £0.60 B82-24441

355'.0217 — Scotland. Nuclear warfare. Targets

Target Scotland. — Kirkcaldy (The Lantern House, Olympia Arcade, Kirkcaldy KY1 1QF) : Peace Force Scotland Publications, 1982. — 1sheet : ill ; 42x30cm folded to 21x15cm
Unpriced B82-28378

355'.02184 — Africa. Guerrilla warfare, *to 1980*

Davidson, Basil. The people's cause : a history of guerrillas in Africa / Basil Davidson. — London : Longman, 1981. — xi,210p : ill,maps,plans ; 24cm. — (Longman studies in African history)
Includes index
ISBN 0-582-64680-4 (cased) : £13.95 : CIP rev.
ISBN 0-582-64681-2 (pbk) : £4.95 B81-34557

355'.02184 — Spain. Urban guerrilla warfare. Facerías, José Lluis — *Biographies*

Téllez, Antonio. Facerías. — Sanday (Over the Water, Sanday, Orkney KW17 2BL) : Cienfuegos Press, Apr.1982. — [366]p
Translation of: Facerías
ISBN 0-904564-48-7 : £8.00 : CIP entry B82-05773

355'.027'01 — War. Causes. Theories

Howard, Michael, *1922-*. The causes of war and other essays. — London : Temple Smith, Sept.1982. — [190]p
ISBN 0-85117-222-9 : £10.00 : CIP entry B82-20778

355'.028 — Wars. Termination. Role of United Nations, *1946-1964*

Bailey, Sydney D.. How wars end : the United Nations and the termination of armed conflicts, 1946-1964. — Oxford : Clarendon Press
Vol.1. — Oct.1982. — [400]p
ISBN 0-19-827424-6 : £35.00 : CIP entry B82-23692

Bailey, Sydney D.. How wars end : the United Nations and the termination of armed conflicts, 1946-1964. — Oxford : Clarendon
Vol.2. — Oct.1982. — [720]p
ISBN 0-19-827462-9 : £45.00 : CIP entry B82-23693

355'.031'091821 — North Atlantic Tready Organization countries. Security

Flynn, Gregory. The internal fabric of Western security / Gregory Flynn with Josef Joffe ... [et al.]. — Totowa : Allanheld, Osmun ; London : Croom Helm, 1981. — xiii,250p ; 24cm. — (An Atlantic Institute for International Affairs research volume)
Includes index
ISBN 0-7099-1007-x : £15.95
ISBN 0-86598-039-x (U.S.) B82-07149

355'.031'091821 — North Atlantic Treaty Organization

Ireland, Timothy P.. Creating the entangling alliance : the origins of the North Atlantic Treaty Organization / Timothy P. Ireland. — London : Aldwych, 1981. — x,245p ; 22cm. — (European studies ; no.6)
Bibliography: p229-233. — Includes index
ISBN 0-86172-018-0 : £19.95 B82-30930

355'.031'091821 — North Atlantic Treaty Organization. Role of France, *to 1980*

Harrison, Michael M.. The reluctant ally : France and Atlantic security / Michael M. Harrison. — Baltimore ; London : John Hopkins University Press, c1981. — xiii,304p ; 24cm
Bibliography: p273-293. — Includes index
ISBN 0-8018-2474-5 : £16.75 B82-02228

355'.0332 — Military power. International political aspects

Estimating foreign military power / edited by Philip Towle. — London : Croom Helm, c1982. — 276p : maps ; 23cm
Includes index
ISBN 0-7099-0434-7 : £13.95 : CIP rev. B81-30348

355'.0335 — Military policies

The **Defense** policies of nations : a comparative study / edited by Douglas J. Murray and Paul R. Viotti. — Baltimore ; London : Johns Hopkins University Press, c1982. — xvi,525p : ill,maps ; 26cm
Includes bibliographies and index
ISBN 0-8018-2636-5 (cased) : £26.25
ISBN 0-8018-2637-3 (pbk) : Unpriced B82-34349

355'.0335 — Military policies. Economic aspects
Kennedy, Gavin. Defense economics. — London : Duckworth, Jan.1983. — [248]p
ISBN 0-7156-1687-0 : £15.00 : CIP entry
B82-35222

355'.0335 — Nuclear weapons. Policies of governments — *Socialist viewpoints*
Exterminism and cold war. — London : Verso, May 1982. — [352]p
ISBN 0-86091-051-2 (cased) : £15.00 : CIP entry
ISBN 0-86091-746-0 (pbk) : £4.95 B82-12909

355'.0335'1713 — Western bloc countries. Military policies
Churchill, Winston S. (Winston Spencer), *1940-*. Defending the West. — London : Maurice Temple Smith, Sept.1981. — [224]p
ISBN 0-85117-210-5 : £8.95 : CIP entry
B81-28496

355'.0335'41 — Great Britain. Military policies, *1960-1980*
Chichester, Michael. The uncertain ally : British defence policy 1960-1990 / Michael Chichester and John Wilkinson. — Aldershot : Gower, c1982. — xvii,246p ; 23cm
Includes index
ISBN 0-566-00534-4 : Unpriced : CIP rev.
B82-06852

355'.0335'41 — Great Britain. Military policies — *Liberal Party viewpoints*
Saunders, James H.. Defence or madness / James H. Saunders. — Hythe (21 Fisher Close, Hythe, Kent, CT21 6AB) : New Creation Enterprises, [1982]. — 18p ; 21cm. — (The Orpington initiative ; pamphlet no.5)
£1.00 (pbk) B82-30659

355'.0335'41 — Great Britain. Nuclear weapons. Policies of government
McMahan, Jeff. British nuclear weapons. — London : Junction Books, Nov.1981. — [224]p
ISBN 0-86245-047-0 (cased) : £9.95: CIP entry
ISBN 0-86245-049-7 (pbk) : £3.95 B81-30631

355'.0335'41 — Great Britain. Nuclear weapons. Policies of government — *Christian viewpoints*
The **Future** of the British nuclear deterrent / a report to the British Council of Churches by the Council on Christian Approaches to Defence and Disarmament. — London (2 Eaton Gate, S.W.1) : British Council of Churches, [c1979]. — iv,20p ; 21cm
"The Division of International Affairs of the British Council of Churches". — Bibliography: p19-20
ISBN 0-85169-073-4 (unbound) : £1.00
B82-36774

355'.0335'47 — Developing countries — *Military policies of Soviet Union, 1920-1981*
Katz, Mark N.. The Third World in Soviet military thought / Mark N. Katz. — London : Croom Helm, c1982. — 188p ; 23cm
Bibliography: p168-183. — Includes index
ISBN 0-7099-1516-0 : £10.95 : CIP rev.
B82-04468

355'.0335'47 — Soviet Union. Military policies
Soviet military thinking / edited by Derek Leebaert. — London : Allen & Unwin, 1981. — xii,300p ; 24cm
Includes index
ISBN 0-04-355014-2 (cased) : Unpriced : CIP rev.
ISBN 0-04-355016-9 (pbk) : Unpriced
B81-25143

Ustinov, D. F.. Serving the homeland and the cause of communism. — Oxford : Pergamon, Dec.1982. — [96]p
ISBN 0-08-028174-5 : £15.00 : CIP entry
B82-39259

355'.0335'73 — United States. Military policies
Whence the threat to peace. — Moscow : USSR Ministry of Defense ; [London] : Distributed by Central, 1982. — 77p : ill(some col.),col.maps,1col.plan ; 26cm
Translated from the Russian
ISBN 0-7147-1727-4 (pbk) : £1.50 B82-29282

355'.0335'73 — United States. Nuclear weapons. Policies of government, *1946-1976*
Mandelbaum, Michael. The nuclear question : the United States and nuclear weapons, 1946-1976 / Michael Mandelbaum. — Cambridge : Cambridge University Press, 1979 (1981 [printing]). — x,277p ; 23cm
Includes index
ISBN 0-521-29614-5 (pbk) : £5.50 B82-04565

355'.0335'94 — Australia. Military policies
Strategy & defence. — London : Allen & Unwin, Jan.1983. — [400]p
ISBN 0-86861-316-9 : £18.00 : CIP entry
B82-33234

355.1 — MILITARY LIFE

355.1'092'4 — Far East. Great Britain. *Army.* **Soldiers. Army life** — *Personal observations*
Zolman, P. A.. Soldier in the East / P.A. Zolman. — Bognor Regis : New Horizon, c1982. — 52p : ill ; 21cm
ISBN 0-86116-072-x : £3.25 B82-32661

355.1'092'4 — Great Britain. *Army.* **Soldiers. Army life,** *1850-1870* — *Personal observations*
Bodell, James. A soldier's view of empire : the reminiscences of James Bodell, 1831-92 / edited by Keith Sinclair. — London : Bodley Head, 1982. — 215p,[12]p of plates : ill,facsims,ports ; 23cm
ISBN 0-370-30224-9 : £7.95 : CIP rev.
B82-10476

355.1'342 — Great Britain. *Army. Special Reserve.* **Awards of medals: Special Reserve Long Service and Good Conduct Medal** — *Lists*
Tamplin, J. M. A.. The special reserve and good conduct medal / J.M.A. Tamplin. — London : Spink, c1979. — 40p : ill,1facsim ; 21cm. — (Spink medal booklets ; no.3)
Cover title
Unpriced (pbk) B82-35605

355.1'342 — Great Britain. *Army. Volunteer Force.* **Decorations: Volunteer Long Service Medal**
Tamplin, J. M. A.. The Volunteer Long Service Medal / J.M.A. Tamplin. — London : Spink, c1980. — 48p : ill,ports ; 21cm. — (Spink medal booklets)
Cover title
Unpriced (pbk) B82-32679

355.1'4 — Great Britain. *Army.* **Badges,** *1820-1960* — *Illustrations*
Wilkinson, Frederick. Badges of the British Army 1820-1960 : an illustrated reference guide for collectors / by F. Wilkinson. — 5th ed. with price guide supplement. — London : Arms and Armour, 1982. — [74]p : chiefly ill ; 23cm
Previous ed.: 1980. — Bibliography: 1p. — Includes index
ISBN 0-85368-188-0 : £4.95 B82-28414

355.1'4 — Great Britain. *Army.* **Headgear. Badges,** *to 1978*
Kipling, Arthur L.. Head-dress badges of the British army / Arthur L. Kipling and Hugh L. King. — London : Muller
Vol.2: From the end of the Great War to the present day. — 1979. — x,242p : ill ; 28cm
Includes index
ISBN 0-584-10949-0 : Unpriced : CIP rev.
B79-23169

355.1'4 — Military forces. Elite units. Uniforms
Thompson, Leroy. Uniforms of the elite forces / Leroy Thompson ; illustrated by Michael Chappell. — Poole : Blandford Press, 1982. — 121p,[8]p of plates : ill(some col.) ; 20cm. — (Blandford colour series)
ISBN 0-7137-1259-7 : £4.95 : CIP rev.
B82-12015

355.1'4'0903 — Military forces. Uniforms, *1700-1937*
Knötel, Herbert. Uniforms of the world : a compendium of army, navy and air force uniforms : 1700-1937 : revised, brought up to date and enlarged by Herbert Knötel, Jr. and Herbert Sieg / with 1,600 illustrations of uniforms by Richard Knötel and Herbert Knötel, Jr ; translated from the 1956 edition by Ronald G. Ball. — London : Arms and Armour, 1980. — xii,483p : ill ; 27cm
Translation of: Handbuch der Uniformkunde. 3 Aufl.
ISBN 0-85368-313-1 : £14.95 : CIP rev.
B80-04118

355.1'4'094 — Europe. Military forces. Uniforms, *700-1500*
Funcken, Liliane. The age of chivalry / Lilian and Fred Funcken. — London : Ward Lock. — (Arms and uniforms)
Pt.1: The 8th to the 15th century : helmets and mail, tournaments and heraldic bearings, bows and crossbows. — 1980. — 102p : ill(some col.) ; 25cm
Includes index
ISBN 0-7063-5808-2 : £6.95 : CIP rev.
Also classified at 623'.094 B80-04120

Funcken, Liliane. The age of chivalry / Liliane and Fred Funcken. — London : Ward Lock. — (Arms and uniforms)
Translation of: Le costume, l'armure et les armes au temps de la chevalerie
Pt.3: The Renaissance : arms, horses and tournaments ; helmets and armour ; tactics and artillery. — 1982. — 104p : col.ill,col.ports ; 25cm
Ill on lining papers. — Includes index
ISBN 0-7063-5937-2 : £7.95 : CIP rev.
Also classified at 623'.094 B81-37566

355.1'4'0941 — Great Britain. *Army.* **Uniforms,** *1890*
Walton, P. S.. Simkin's soldiers : the British Army in 1890 / P.S. Walton. — Dorking : Victorian Military Society, c1981. — (Special publication / Victorian Military Society ; v.5)
Vol.1: The cavalry and the Royal Artillery with a special section on the Royal Marines / with a foreword by Sir Michael Gow. — 94p,[18]leaves of plates : ill(some col.) ; 21cm
ISBN 0-9506885-1-7 (pbk) : Unpriced
B82-26498

355.1'4'0941 — Great Britain. *Army.* **Uniforms,** *to ca 1900* — *Illustrations*
Simkin, Richard. Richard Simkin's uniforms of the British army. — Exeter : Webb & Bower
Vol.1: The cavalry regiments. — Nov.1982. — [224]p
ISBN 0-906671-13-2 : £9.95 : CIP entry
B82-32320

355.1'4'0943 — Prussia. *Armee.* **Uniforms,** *1830* — *Illustrations*
Elsholtz, L.. Full-colour uniforms of the Prussian Army : 72 plates from the year 1830 / L. Sachse & Co.. — New York : Dover ; London : Constable, 1981. — [7]p,72p of plates : chiefly ill(some col.),1facsim ; 30cm
Translation of: Das preussische Heer / gezeichnet und lithographirt von L. Elzholz, C. Rechlin, J. Schulz
ISBN 0-486-24085-1 (pbk) : £7.50 B82-05283

355.1'5'094 — European armies. Flags, *1792-1815*
Wise, Terence. Flags of the Napoleonic wars / text by Terence Wise ; colour plates by Guido Rosignoli ; line drawings by William Walker. — London : Osprey. — (Men-at-arms series ; 115)
3: Colours, standards and guidons of Anhalt, Kleve-Berg, Brunswick, Denmark, Finland, Hanover, Hesse, the Netherlands, Mecklenburg, Nassau, Portugal, Reuss, Spain, Sweden, Switzerland & Westphalia. — 1981. — 40p,A-Hp of plates : ill(some col.) ; 25cm
ISBN 0-85045-410-7 (pbk) : £2.95 B82-05040

355.2 — MILITARY RESOURCES

355.2'0968 — South Africa. Military resources

Crocker, Chester A.. South Africa's defense posture : coping with vulnerability / Chester A. Crocker ; foreword by Michael A. Samuels. — Beverly Hills ; London : Sage, c1981. — 104p ; 22cm. — (The Washington papers ; vol.IX,84)
'The Center for Strategic and International Studies'. — Bibliography: p103-104
ISBN 0-8039-1685-x (pbk) : Unpriced B82-08574

355.2'2'02541 — British military forces. Personnel — *Directories — Serials*

British defence directory : the quarterly, updated, computerised directory of service & civilian personnel in the Ministry of Defence, Royal Navy, Army, Royal Air Force & NATO command (British component) ... — Vol.1, no.1 (Mar. 1982)-. — Oxford : Brassey's Defence Publishers, 1982-. — v. ; 30cm
£150.00 per year B82-23588

355.22'3'0973 — American military forces. Personnel. Recruitment

Military service in the United States. — Englewood Cliffs ; London : Prentice-Hall, c1982. — viii,226p ; 20cm. — (Spectrum book)
At head of title: The American Assembly, Columbia University. — Includes index
ISBN 0-13-583062-1 (cased) : £11.20
ISBN 0-13-583054-0 (pbk) : Unpriced B82-28825

355.2'232 — Hampshire. Portsmouth. Great Britain. *Ministry of Defence.* **Training centres: Portsmouth Dockyard Apprentice Training Centre. Leasing to Hampshire.** *County Council* — *Proposals*

Great Britain. *Treasury.* Treasury minute dated 18 June 1982 concerning the granting of a conditional lease to the Hampshire County Council at a peppercorn rent of the Portsmouth Dockyard Apprentice Training Centre. — London : H.M.S.O., 1982. — [2]p ; 25cm. — (Cmnd. ; 8574)
ISBN 0-10-185740-3 (unbound) : £0.35 B82-37510

355.2'24 — Conscientious objection

Conscription and conscientious objection : a brief survey. — London (55 Dawes Street, SE 17 1EL) : War Resisters' International, 1981. — [36]p ; 30cm
Includes survey questions in French and German
Unpriced (unbound) B82-19746

355.3 — MILITARY ORGANISATION

355.3'1'0941 — Great Britain. *Army.* *Household Division*

Edgeworth, Anthony. The guards / photographed by Anthony Edgeworth ; written by John de St. Jorre. — London : Aurum, c1981. — 255p : chiefly col.ill,col.ports ; 31cm
ISBN 0-906053-25-0 : £12.95 B82-31368

355.3'1'0954016 — Great Britain *Foreign and Commonwealth Office* **Libraries: India Office Library and Records. Stock:Archives of India Office** *Military Department - Lists*

Farrington, Anthony. Guide to the records of the India Office Military Department. — London : India Office Library and Records, May 1981. — 1v.
ISBN 0-903359-30-8 : CIP entry B81-07462

355.3'31 — Military forces. Generals. Incompetence, *1854-1945.* **Psychological aspects**

Dixon, Norman F.. On the psychology of military incompetence / Norman Dixon ; with a foreword by Shelford Bidwell. — London : Futura, 1979, c1976. — 447p ; 20cm
Originally published: London : Cape, 1976. — Bibliography: p424-439. — Includes index
ISBN 0-7088-1482-4 (pbk) : £2.50 B82-32982

355.3'31'0924 — France. *Armée.* **Ney, Michel** — *Biographies*

Horricks, Raymond. Marshal Ney : the romance and the real / Raymond Horricks. — Tunbridge Wells : Midas, 1982. — xv,283p,[16]p of plates : ill,1facsim,ports ; 25cm
Includes index
ISBN 0-85936-276-0 : £12.50 B82-32505

355.3'31'0924 — Germany. *Heer.* **Rommel, Erwin** — *Biographies*

Rutherford, Ward. The biography of field marshal Erwin Rommel / Ward Rutherford. — London : Hamlyn, 1981. — 165p : ill(some col.),maps,(some col.),ports(some col.) ; 30cm. — (A Bison book)
Includes index
ISBN 0-600-34179-8 : £5.95 B82-19926

355.3'31'0924 — Great Britain. *Army.* **Alanbrooke, Alan Brooke,** *Viscount* — *Biographies*

Fraser, *Sir* **David,** *1920-*. Alanbrooke / David Fraser ; with a prologue and epilogue by Arthur Bryant. — London : Collins, 1982. — 604p,[8]p of plates : ill,ports ; 24cm
Includes index
ISBN 0-00-216360-8 : £12.95 : CIP rev. B81-34582

355.3'31'0924 — Great Britain. *Army.* **Auchinleck,** *Sir* **Claude** — *Biographies*

Warner, Philip. Auchinleck : the lonely soldier / Philip Warner. — London : Buchan & Enright, 1981. — xii,288p,[16]p of plates : ill,maps,ports ; 24cm
Ill on lining papers. — Bibliography: p277-279. — Includes index
ISBN 0-907675-00-x : £10.50 B82-05363

Warner, Philip. Auchinleck : the lonely soldier / Philip Warner. — London : Sphere Books, 1982. — xvi,365p : ill,maps,ports ; 18cm
Originally published: London : Buchan & Enright, 1981. — Bibliography: p354-356. — Includes index
ISBN 0-7221-8905-2 (pbk) : £2.25 B82-37361

355.3'31'0924 — Great Britain. *Army.* **French,** *Sir* **John** — *Biographies*

Holmes, Richard, *1946-*. The little field-marshall : Sir John French / Richard Holmes. — London : Cape, 1981. — xii,427p,[12]p of plates : ill,maps,ports ; 23cm
Bibliography: p409-416. — Includes index
ISBN 0-224-01575-3 : £12.50 : CIP rev. B81-27334

355.3'31'0924 — Great Britain. *Army.* **Montgomery of Alamein, Bernard Law Montgomery,** *Viscount* — *Biographies*

Hamilton, Nigel, *1944-*. Monty / Nigel Hamilton. — [Feltham] : Hamlyn Paperbacks, 1982, c1981. — xix,876p,[32]p of plates : ill,facsims,plans,ports ; 20cm
Originally published: London : Hamilton, 1981. — Bibliography: p849-854. — Includes index
ISBN 0-600-20595-9 (pbk) : £4.95 B82-29673

355.3'31'0924 — Poland. *Wojsko.* **Sikorski, Władysław,** *1939-1943* — *Biographies*

General Sikorski : Premier, Naczelny Wodz = Prime Minister, Commander in Chief / photographs selected by Regina Opman = Regina Opman wybor fotografii / text, Bohdan Wroński = Bohdan Wroński tekst / designed by Juliusz L. Englert = Juliusz L. Englert oprawa graficzna. — [London] : Instytut Polski i Muzeum im. Gen Sikorskiego w Londynie, 1981. — 130p : ill,1map,facsims,ports ; 30cm
Parallel Polish text and English translation. — Ill on inside cover. — Includes index
ISBN 0-902508-09-1 (pbk) : £8.00 B82-07540

355.3'31'0924 — United States. *Army.* **Collins, J. Lawton** — *Biographies*

Collins, J. Lawton. Lightning Joe : an autobiography / by J. Lawton Collins. — Baton Rouge ; London : Louisiana State University, c1979. — xvii,462p : ill,maps,ports ; 24cm
Bibliography: p445-448. — Includes index
ISBN 0-8071-0499-x : £18.75 B82-38559

355.3'31'0924 — United States. *Army.* **MacArthur, Douglas** — *Biographies*

Mayer, S. L.. The biography of General of the Army, Douglas MacArthur / S.L. Mayer. — London : Hamlyn, 1981. — 167p : ill(some col.),maps(some col.),ports(some col.) ; 31cm
Includes index
ISBN 0-600-34180-1 : £5.95 B82-02722

355.3'31'0924 — United States. *Army.* **Marshall, George C.** — *Biographies*

Mosley, Leonard. Marshall, organizer of victory. — London : Methuen, Oct.1982. — [608]p
ISBN 0-413-50260-0 : £10.00 : CIP entry B82-25528

355.3'31'0924 — United States. *Army.* **Marshall, George Catlett** — *Correspondence, diaries, etc.*

Marshall, George Catlett. The papers of George Catlett Marshall. — Baltimore ; London : Johns Hopkins University Press
Vol.1: "The Soldierly Spirit", December 1880-June 1939 / Larry I. Bland, editor ; Sharon R. Ritenour, assistant editor. — 1981. — xxx,742p : ill,maps,facsims,ports,1geneal.table ; 24cm
Includes index
ISBN 0-8018-2552-0 : Unpriced B82-22601

355.3'31'0924 — United States. *Army.* **Patton, George S.** — *Biographies*

Hogg, Ian V.. The biography of General George S. Patton / Ian V. Hogg. — London : Hamlyn, 1982. — 160p : ill,maps,ports ; 30cm. — (A Bison book)
Includes index
ISBN 0-86124-082-0 (pbk) : £6.95 B82-40633

355.3'31'0924 — United States. Custer, George A. — *Correspondence, diaries, etc.*

Custer, George A.. Nomad : George A. Custer in Turf, field and farm / edited by Brian W. Dippie. — Austin ; London : University of Texas Press, c1980. — xvii,174p : ill,1map,2ports ; 26cm
Includes index
ISBN 0-292-75519-8 : £16.80 B82-34347

355.3'32'08996073 — United States. *Army.* **Negro officers,** *to 1941*

Patton, Gerald W.. War and race : the black officer in the American military, 1915-1941 / Gerald W. Patton. — Westport, Conn. ; London : Greenwood Press, 1981. — x,214p ; 22cm. — (Contributions in Afro-American and African studies, ISSN 0069-9624 ; no.62)
Bibliography: p187-201. — Includes index
ISBN 0-313-22176-6 : £18.95 B82-18371

355.3'41 — Germany. *Heer.* *Légion des volontaires français.* **Postal services,** *1941-1944*

Reader, R. E.. The Legion of French Volunteers 1941-44 / by R.E. Reader ; edited by C.S. Holder. — [Great Britain] : France & Colonies Philatelic Society of Great Britain (Banbury : Kemble), c1981. — 23p : ill,1map,facsims ; 20cm. — (F.C.P.S. brochure ; no.4)
Bibliography: p23
Unpriced (pbk) B82-15295

355.3'41 — Great Britain. Military forces. Canteens: Naafi, *to 1981*

Cole, Howard N.. Naafi in uniform / Howard N. Cole. — [London] ([Naafi Public Relations, Imperial Court, Kennington La., SE11 5QX]) : NCS/EFI Old Comrades Association, c1982. — 198p,[16]p of plates : ill,ports ; 22cm
Unpriced B82-38168

355.3'41 — Paraguay. Chaco region. Military postal services, *1932-1935*

Shepherd, A.. Postal history of the Chaco War / by A. Shepherd. — Halifax (3 Willowfield Rd., Halifax HX2 7JN) : A. Shepherd
Pt.2: Bolivia. — c1981. — 35p : ill,maps,facsims ; 30cm
Bibliography: p2
Unpriced (pbk) B82-11730

355.3′41 — South Africa. British military postal services, *1899-1902 — Readings from contemporary sources*

The **Post** Office militant 1899-1902 : the Anglo Boer war / selected and edited by A.G.M. Batten. — Woking (Brackenber, Wych Hill Way, Woking, England) : A.G.M. Batten, 1981. — 155p : ill,facsims,ports ; 21cm
Articles originally published in St. Martin′s-le-Grand, the staff magazine of the Post Office
Unpriced (pbk) B82-08624

355.3′46 — South Africa. Commonwealth military forces. Personnel. Entertaining by SAWAS, *1939-1947*

Book of thanks, 1980 : SAWAS 1939-1947 / editor E.A.S. Bailey ; assistant editor for historical research J.D.R. Haslett ; assistant editors A.E. Sutcliff, Douglas Clifford. — Ardgour : E.A.S. Bailey, 1981. — 127p : ill (some col.),charts,ports ; 30cm
Limited ed. of 700 numbered copies, nos. 1-5 bound in leather, nos. 1-50 signed by the sponsors. — Includes index
ISBN 0-9507481-0-2 : £16.00 B82-13312

355.3′52′0941 — West Germany. British military forces. Great Britain. *Parliament. House of Commons. Defence Committee.* **First report ... session 1981-82** *— Critical studies*

Allied forces in Germany : first report from the Defence Committee : observations / presented by the Secretary of State for Defence. — London : H.M.S.O., 1982. — 4p ; 25cm. — (Cmnd. ; 8571) (House of Commons paper ; HC 93)
ISBN 0-10-185710-1 (unbound) : £1.25 B82-31973

355.4 — MILITARY OPERATIONS

355.4′09494 — Military operations by Swiss military forces, *1300-1500*

Miller, Douglas. The Swiss at war 1300-1500. text by Douglas Miller and G.A. Embleton / colour plates by G.A. Embleton. — London : Osprey, 1979 (1981 [printing]). — 40p,A-Hp of plates : ill(some col.),1maps ; 25cm. — (Men-at-arms series ; 94)
English text, English, French and German captions to plates. — Bibliography: p2
ISBN 0-85045-334-8 (pbk) : Unpriced B82-10735

355.4′0994 — Army operations by Australia. *Army, 1899-1975*

Laffin, John. The Australian army at war 1899-1975 / text by John Laffin ; colour plates by Mike Chappell. — London : Osprey, 1982. — 40p,A-H p of plates : ill(some col.),ports ; 25cm. — (Men-at-arms series ; 123)
English text, with notes on the plates in French and German
ISBN 0-85045-418-2 (pbk) : Unpriced B82-37336

355.4′2 — Military operations, *to 1981.* **Applications of deception**

Military deception and strategic surprise. — London : Cass, June 1982. — [200]p
ISBN 0-7146-3202-3 : £15.00 : CIP entry B82-16486

355.4′307′091812 — Soviet Union. Nuclear warfare by Western world. Strategy

Menaul, Stewart. Changing concepts of nuclear war / Stewart Menaul. — London (12 Golden Sq., W1R 3AF) : Institute for the Study of Conflict, 1980. — 15p ; 30cm + summary (1sheet; 30cm). — (Conflict studies, ISSN 0069-8792 ; no.125)
Cover title
£2.00 (pbk) B82-16403

355.6 — MILITARY ADMINISTRATION

355.6 — American military forces. Leadership

Buck, James H.. Military leadership / James H. Buck and Lawrence J. Korb. — Beverly Hills ; London : Sage, c1981. — 270p ; 22cm. — (Sage research progress series on war, revolution, and peacekeeping ; v.10)
Bibliography: p249-263. — Includes index
ISBN 0-8039-1679-5 (cased) : Unpriced
ISBN 0-8039-1680-9 (pbk) : £7.50 B82-17076

355.6′213 — Portugal. Government. Gifts of British military equipment by British government — *Proposals*

Great Britain. *Treasury.* Copy of a Treasury minute dated 4 November 1981 concering the gift of military equipment to the Government of Portugal. — London : H.M.S.O., [1981]. — 1sheet ; 25x16cm. — (Cmnd. ; 8403)
ISBN 0-10-184030-6 : £0.30 B82-06343

355.6′22 — Avon. Bristol. Castles: Bristol Castle. Constables, *1221-1303 — Accounts*

Accounts of the constables of Bristol Castle : in the thirteenth and early fourteenth centuries / edited by Margaret Sharp. — [Bristol] : Printed for the Bristol Record Society, 1982. — lxiii,128p ; 24cm. — (Bristol Record Society′s publications, ISSN 0305-8730 ; v.34)
Includes some documents in Latin. — Bibliography: p97-110. — Includes index
Unpriced B82-40553

355.6′22 — Britain military forces. Expenditure by government. Great Britain. *Parliament. House of Commons. Defence Committee.* **Second report ... session 1980-81** *— Critical studies*

Great Britain. Second special report from the Defence Committee, session 1980-81 : statement on the defence estimates 1981 : government observations on the second report of the committee. — London : H.M.S.O., [1981]. — ivp ; 25cm. — ([HC] ; 461)
ISBN 0-10-246181-3 (unbound) : £0.70 B82-02314

355.7 — MILITARY ESTABLISHMENTS

355′.7′0941 — Great Britain. Christian Socialist Movement, *to 1910*

Colloms, Brenda. Victorian visionaries / Brenda Colloms. — London : Constable, 1982. — 284p : ports ; 23cm
Bibliography: p275-276. — Includes index
ISBN 0-09-463370-3 : £12.50 B82-31073

355.7′09411′4 — Scotland. Western Isles. Military bases

Islands at risk / editor: Frank Thompson. — [Stornoway] : Keep NATO Out and Hebrides Against Nuclear Dumping, 1980. — 59p : ill,1map,1plan ; 21cm
AL: Mar.29, Frank George
ISBN 0-9507215-0-6 (pbk) : £1.00 B82-16959

355.7′09411′4 — Scotland. Western Isles. St Kilda. Military bases

Spackman, R. A.. Soldiers on St. Kilda : a chronicle of military involvement on the islands of St. Kilda, the furthest Hebrides / R.A. Spackman. — Balivanich (Benbecula, Western Isles) : Uist Community Press, 1982. — 56p : ill,1map ; 21x30cm
Unpriced (pbk) B82-40533

355.8 — MILITARY EQUIPMENT AND SUPPLIES

355.8′09 — Militaria, *to 1975 — Collectors′ guides*

Curtis, Tony, *1939-.* Militaria / compiled by Tony Curtis. — Galashiels : Lyle, c1982. — 126p : ill ; 17cm. — (Antiques and their values)
Includes index
ISBN 0-86248-036-1 : £2.50 B82-28677

355.8′2 — Military equipment: Weapons. Proliferation

The **Arms** race and arms control / SIPRI. — London : Taylor & Francis, 1982. — xiii,242p : ill,maps ; 19cm
Includes index
ISBN 0-85066-232-x (pbk) : £3.95 : CIP rev.
Also classified at 327.1′74 B82-21752

355.8′2 — Military operations. Military equipment: Weapons - *Forecasts*

Baker, David. The shape of wars to come. — Cambridge : Patrick Stephens, Sept.1981. — [176]p
ISBN 0-85059-483-9 : £9.95 : CIP entry B81-20132

355.8′2′0904 — Military equipment: Weapons. Proliferation, *to 1918-1980*

Headicar, Richard. The arms race / Richard Headicar. — Hove : Wayland, 1981. — 72p : ill,ports ; 24cm. — (People, politics and powers)
Bibliography: p70. — Includes index
ISBN 0-85340-824-6 : £4.50 B82-03878

355.8′2′0904 — Military resources: Weapons, *1945-1981*

Kaldor, Mary. The baroque arsenal / Mary Kaldor. — London : Deutsch, 1982, c1981. — 294p ; 23cm
Bibliography: p255-284. — Includes index
ISBN 0-233-97388-5 : £7.95 B82-11314

355.8′2′091724 — Developing countries. Military equipment: Weapons. Acquisition. International political aspects *— German texts*

Brzoska, Michael. Rüstung und Dritte Welt : zum Stand der Forschung / Michael Brzoska. — München ; London : Weltforum Verlag, c1981. — x,209p : ill ; 21cm. — (Weltwirtschaft und internationale Beziehungen ; 25)
German text
ISBN 3-8039-0197-9 (pbk) : Unpriced B82-12224

356 — FOOT FORCES

356′.11′0941 — Great Britain. *Army. Duke of Cornwall′s Light Infantry, to 1980*

Salusbury-Trelawny, P. M.. The Duke of Cornwall′s Light Infantry (32nd and 46th) / written by P.M. Salusbury-Trelawny ; photography by Glen Forster. — [Bodmin] ([The Keep, The Barracks, Bodmin, Cornwall]) : Trustees of the DCLI Museum, 1981. — 15p : ill(some col.) ; 15x21cm
Unpriced (pbk) B82-16161

356′.11′0941 — Great Britain. *Army.* **Infantry regiments,** *1790-1815*

Fosten, Bryan. Wellington′s infantry / text and colour plates by Bryan Fosten. — London : Osprey. — (Men-at-arms series ; 114)
Notes in French and German
1. — London : Osprey. — 40p,A-Hp of plates : ill(some col.) ; 25cm. — (Men-at-arms series ; 114)
Notes in French and German
ISBN 0-85045-395-x (pbk) : £2.95 B82-05038

356′.11′0941 — Great Britain. *Army.* **Rifle volunteer corps,** *1859-1908*

Westlake, Ray. The rifle volunteers : the history of the rifle volunteers 1859-1908 / Ray Westlake. — Chippenham : Picton, 1982. — xviii,173p,[32]p of plates : ill,ports ; 22cm
Bibliography: p173
ISBN 0-902633-79-1 : £9.95 B82-28658

356′.11′0941 — West Germany. Army. Royal Green Jackets. Battalion, 2nd Great Britain. Army life *— For children*

Fairclough, Chris. A day with a soldier / Chris Fairclough. — Hove : Wayland, 1981. — 55p : ill ; 24cm. — (A Day in the life)
Bibliography: p55
ISBN 0-85340-837-8 : £3.25 B82-06541

356′.166 — Airborne forces

Weeks, John. The airborne soldier. — Poole : Blandford Press, Apr.1982. — [192]p
ISBN 0-7137-0918-9 : CIP entry B82-04862

356′.166′0904 — Military operations by airborne forces, *1940-1977*

Airborne operations : an illustrated history of the battles, tactics and equipment of the world′s airborne forces. — London : Salamander, 1978 (1982 [printing]). — 221p : ill(some col.),col.maps ; 31cm
Includes index
ISBN 0-86101-122-8 (pbk) : £4.95 B82-22557

356′.167′0941 — Great Britain. *Army. Special Air Service Regiment, to 1980*

Shortt, James G.. The Special Air Service : and Royal Marines Special Boat Squadron / text by James G. Shortt ; colour plates by Angus McBride. — London : Osprey, 1981. — 40p,A-Hp of plates : ill(some col.),ports ; 25cm. — (Men-at-arms series ; 116)
Notes in French and German
ISBN 0-85045-396-8 (pbk) : £2.95 B82-05039

356'.167'0941 — Great Britain. *Army. Special Air Service Regiment, to 1982*

Geraghty, Tony. This is the SAS : a pictorial history of the Special Air Service Regiment / Tony Geraghty. — London : Arms and Armour Press, 1982. — 156p : ill(some col.),1facsim,ports ; 30cm
Ill on lining papers. — Bibliography: p156
ISBN 0-85368-522-3 : £9.95 : CIP rev.
B82-24108

356'.186 — Great Britain. *Army.* **Infantry. Uniforms,** *1660-1980*

Barthorp, Michael. British infantry uniforms since 1660. — Poole : Blandford Press, Oct.1982. — [160]p
ISBN 0-7137-1127-2 : £10.95 : CIP entry
B82-25091

357 — MOUNTED FORCES

357'.1'0941 — Great Britain. *Army.* **Heavy cavalry,** *ca 1790-1815*

Foster, Bryan. Wellington's heavy cavalry. — London : Osprey, Nov.1982. — [40]p. — (Men-at-arms series ; 130)
ISBN 0-85045-474-3 (pbk) : £3.50 : CIP entry
B82-26421

357'.1'0941 — Great Britain. *Army. Scottish Horse, to 1956*

Campbell-Preston, R. M. T.. The Scottish Horse 1900-1956 / by R.M.T. Campbell Preston. — [Fort William] ([c/o Nevisport Ltd., Fort William, Inverness]) : [R.M.T. Campbell-Preston], [1982]?. — 64p : ill,maps,ports ; 21cm
Unpriced (pbk) B82-25014

357'.1'0944 — France. *Armée. Légion de la Vistule, 1808-1814 — Polish texts*

Kirkor, Stanisław. Legia Nadwiślańska : 1808-1814 / Stanisław Kirkor. — Londyn [London] : Oficyna Poetow i Malarzy, 1981. — 621p,[24]p of plates : ill,maps ; 22cm
Polish text, French summary. — Includes index
Unpriced (pbk) B82-06612

357'.1'0954 — India. *Army.* **Cavalry regiments,** *1857-1914*

Harris, R. G.. Bengal Cavalry Regiments 1857-1914 / text by R.G. Harris ; colour plates by Chris Warner. — London : Osprey, 1979. — 40p,A-Hp of plates : ill(some col.),ports ; 25cm. — (Men-at-arms series)
English text, English, French and German captions to plates
ISBN 0-85045-308-9 (pbk) : Unpriced
B82-10739

357'.188 — Great Britain. *Army. Westmorland and Cumberland Yeomanry.* **Uniforms,** *to 1914*

Barlow, L.. Westmorland and Cumberland Yeomanry / by L. Barlow and R.J. Smith ; illustrations by R.J. Marrion. — [Aldershot] : Robert Ogilby Trust, [1982?]. — 20p : ill,ports ; 25cm. — (The Uniforms of the British Yeomanry Force 1794-1914 ; 4)
Cover title. — Ill, text on covers
ISBN 0-85936-285-x (pbk) : £2.00 B82-38822

358.1 — ARTILLERY, MISSILE AND ARMOURED FORCES

358'.1'0941 — Army operations by Great Britain. *Army, 1904-1945.* **Artillery. Tactics**

Bidwell, Shelford. Fire-power : British army weapons and theories of war 1904-1945 / by Shelford Bidwell and Dominick Graham. — London : Allan & Unwin, 1982. — xvi,327p ; 24cm
Bibliography: p309-320. — Includes index
ISBN 0-04-942176-x : Unpriced : CIP rev.
B82-10589

358'.17 — Antiballistic missile systems, *1980-*

Antiballistic missile defence in the 1980s. — London : Cass, Jan.1983. — [144]p. — (Arms control, ISSN 0144-0381 ; v.3, no.2)
ISBN 0-7146-3207-4 : £15.00 : CIP entry
B82-37646

358'.17 — Strategic nuclear weapon systems

Constant, James N.. Fundamentals of strategic weapons : offense and defense systems / James N. Constant. — The Hague ; London : Nijhoff, 1981. — 2v. : ill,maps,plans ; 22cm
Includes index
ISBN 90-247-2545-3 : Unpriced B82-02730

358'.17'0941 — Great Britain. Strategic nuclear weapon systems. Policies of government — *Inquiry reports*

Great Britain. *Parliament. House of Commons. Defence Committee.* First special report from the Defence Committee, session 1981-82 : strategic nuclear weapons policy : together with the minutes of evidence taken before the Committee on 17 March, and appendices. — London : H.M.S.O., 1982. — iv,31p ; 25cm. — (HC 266) (HC 266-I)
ISBN 0-10-226682-4 (pbk) : £4.25 B82-31971

358'.1754'0973 — MX intercontinental ballistic missile systems. Policies of United States government

Scoville, Herbert. MX : prescription for disaster / Herbert Scoville, Jr. — Cambridge, Mass. ; London : MIT Press, c1981. — xi,231p : ill,maps ; 21cm
Includes index
ISBN 0-262-19199-7 (cased) : £10.50
ISBN 0-262-69077-2 (pbk) : Unpriced
B82-21007

358'.18 — Anti-tank warfare

Simpkin, Richard. Antitank : an airmechanized response to armored threats in the 90s / Richard E. Simpkin. — Oxford : Brassey's, 1982. — xv,320p,[21]p of plates : ill,1map ; 25cm
Map on lining papers. — Bibliography: p297-305. — Includes index
ISBN 0-08-027036-0 : £22.50 : CIP rev.
B81-28810

358'.18 — Army operations by armoured combat vehicles, *to 1973:* **Centurion tanks**

Dunstan, Simon. The Centurion tank in battle / text by Simon Dunstan ; colour plates by Peter Sarson, Tony Bryan and David E. Smith. — London : Osprey, 1981. — 40p,A-Hp of plates : ill(some col.),1port ; 25cm. — (Vanguard series ; 22)
ISBN 0-85045-398-4 (pbk) : £2.95 B82-05031

358.2 — MILITARY FORCES. ENGINEERS

358'.2'0941 — Great Britain. *Army. Engineer and Railway Staff Corps, to 1980*

Great Britain. *Army. Engineer and Railway Staff Corps.* All rank and no file : a history of the Engineer and Railway Staff Corps RE : supplement 1966-1980 / by C.E.C. Townsend. — Purley (Royal Oak House, Brighton Road, Purley, Surrey) : The Engineer & Railway Staff Corps, 1981. — vi,26p ; 22cm
Unpriced (pbk) B82-07059

358.3 — MILITARY TECHNICAL FORCES

358'.3 — Biological & chemical warfare, *to 1981*

Harris, Robert, *1957-.* A higher form of killing : the secret story of gas and germ warfare / Robert Harris and Jeremy Paxman. — London : Chatto & Windus, 1982. — xii,274p ; 23cm
Includes index
ISBN 0-7011-2585-3 : £9.95 : CIP rev.
B82-01195

358'.34 — Chemical weapons

Chemical weapons / Peace Force Scotland. — Kirkcaldy (The Lantern House, Olympia Arcade, Kirkcaldy, KY1 1QF) : Peace Force Scotland, [1982]. — [4]p : ill ; 21cm. — (Fact sheet ; 5)
Bibliography: p4
Unpriced (unbound) B82-27592

358'.38 — Biological warfare

Germ warfare / Peace Force Scotland. — Kirkcaldy (The Lantern House, Olympia Arcade, Kirkcaldy, KY1 1QF) : Peace Force Scotland, [1982]. — [4]p : ill ; 21cm. — (Fact sheet ; 6)
Bibliography: p4
Unpriced (unbound) B82-27593

358'.39 — Nuclear weapons

Brown, Neville. An unbreakable nuclear stalemate / discussion paper by Neville Brown. — Windsor (5 High St., Windsor) : Council for Arms Control, 1982. — 18p ; 30cm
Cover title
Unpriced (pbk) B82-37099

Nuclear arsenal / Peace Force Scotland. — Kirkcaldy (The Lantern House, Olympia Arcade, Kirkcaldy, KY1 1QF) : Peace Force Scotland, [1982]. — [4]p : ill ; 21cm. — (Fact sheet ; 2)
Bibliography: p4
Unpriced (unbound) B82-27589

358'.39 — Nuclear weapons. Proliferation — *Conference proceedings*

The Nuclear arms race : control or catastrophe?. — London : Frances Pinter, Feb.1982. — [250]p
Conference papers
ISBN 0-86187-229-0 : £12.50 : CIP entry
B81-40254

358'.39'0941 — Great Britain. Nuclear weapons

The Nuclear numbers game : understanding the statistics behind the bombs / Radical Statistics Nuclear Disarmament Group. — London : Radical Statistics, c1982. — 93p : ill,maps ; 21cm. — (Publication ; no.8)
Bibliography: p91
ISBN 0-906081-04-1 (pbk) : £1.50 B82-19128

358'.39'0941425 — Scotland. Strathclyde Region. Faslane region. Nuclear weapons. Attitudes of public

Macdonald, Iain O.. Faslane — facts & feelings / by Iain O. Macdonald. — Edinburgh (121 George St., Edinburgh, EH2 4YN) : Religion and Technology Project, Church of Scotland Home Mission Committee, [1982?]. — iv,41p : ill,maps ; 21cm. — (A Study of people's knowledge and attitudes)
Cover title
£1.25 (pbk) B82-27774

358.4 — AIR FORCES

358.4'009 — Air warfare, *to 1978*

Aerial warfare : an illustrated history / foreword by Adolf Galland ; edited by Anthony Robinson. — London : Orbis, 1982. — 384p : ill(some col.),col.maps,ports ; 30cm
Includes index
ISBN 0-85613-261-6 : £12.50 B82-33387

358.4'00941 — Great Britain. *Royal Air Force, to 1981*

Donne, Michael. Per ardua ad astra : seventy years of the RFC & the RAF / Michael Donne & Cynthia Fowler. — London : Muller, 1982. — 191p : ill(some col.),2facsims,ports ; 28cm
Bibliography: p189. — Includes index
ISBN 0-584-11022-7 : £12.95 : CIP rev.
B82-06512

Mason, R. A.. The Royal Air Force : today and tomorrow / R.A. Mason. — London : Ian Allan, 1982. — 144p,[4]p of plates : ill(some col.),ports ; 30cm
Includes index
ISBN 0-7110-1176-1 : £9.95 B82-25647

358.4'00941 — Great Britain. *Royal Navy. Fleet Air Arm, to 1980*

Longstaff, Reginald. The Fleet Air Arm : a pictorial history / Reginald Longstaff. — London : Hale, 1981. — 256p : ill ; 24cm
Bibliography: p249. — Includes index
ISBN 0-7091-9141-3 : £9.95 B82-04183

358.4'00941'07402187 — London. Barnet *(London Borough).* **Museums: Royal Air Force Museum** *— Serials*

The Flying M / Friends of the Royal Air Force Museum. — Vol.5, no.2 (1980)-. — [London] ([Hendon, NW9 5LL]) : The Friends, 1980-. — v. : ill ; 21cm
Continues: Newsletter (Royal Air Force Museum. Friends of the Royal Air Force Museum). — Description based on: Vol.5, no.3 (Jan. 1981)
ISSN 0262-8201 = Flying M : Free to Friends of the Museum B82-09682

358.4'00943 — Germany. *Luftwaffe, 1933-1945*
Great Britain. *Air Ministry*. The rise and fall of the German Air Force, 1933-1945. — London : Arms and Armour, Oct.1982. — [452]p
ISBN 0-85368-560-6 : £17.95 : CIP entry
B82-27200

358.4'00943 — Germany. *Luftwaffe, 1933-1945 — Illustrations*
The **Luftwaffe** 1933-1945. — London : Arms and Armour. — (Warbirds illustrated ; 5)
Vol.3. — June 1982. — [68]p
ISBN 0-85368-513-4 (pbk) : £3.95 : CIP entry
B82-10213

The **Luftwaffe** 1933-1945. — London : Arms and Armour
Vol.4. — June 1982. — [68]p
ISBN 0-85368-514-2 (pbk) : £3.95 : CIP entry
B82-10214

358.4'00973 — United States. *Air Force. Strategic Air Command, to 1981*
Peacock, Lindsay T.. Strategic Air Command. — London : Arms and Armour, Feb.1983. — [68] p. — (Warbirds illustrated ; 9)
ISBN 0-85368-547-9 (pbk) : £3.95 : CIP entry
B82-39595

358.4'114 — Great Britain. *Royal Air Force.* **Squadrons. Badges**
Tanner, John, *1927-*. Twenty-five great badges / by John Tanner ; foreword by His Royal Highness The Prince Philip, Duke of Edinburgh ; illustrations by J.D. Middleton. — [Hendon] : Royal Air Force Museum, [c1981]. — 32p : ill ; 21cm
ISBN 0-9504788-4-9 (pbk) : Unpriced
B82-03850

358.4'1332'0924 — Great Britain. *Royal Air Force.* **Bader,** *Sir* **Douglas** — *Biographies*
Lucas, Laddie. Flying colours : the epic story of Douglas Bader / Laddie Lucas. — London : Hutchinson, 1981. — 303p,[16]p of plates : ill,1facsim,ports ; 24cm
Includes index
ISBN 0-09-146470-6 : £8.95 : CIP rev.
B81-30304

358.4'1332'0924 — Great Britain. *Royal Air Force.* **Officers,** *1943-1966 — Personal observations*
Careless, John. Trenchard's Brat / John Careless. — Bognor Regis : New Horizon, c1982. — 179p,[10]p of plates : ill ; 21cm
ISBN 0-86116-673-6 : £5.25 B82-13400

358.4'17'0941 — Great Britain. Great Britain. *Royal Air Force.* **Aerodromes,** *to 1981*
Action stations. — Cambridge : Stephens
4: Military airfields of Yorkshire / Bruce Barrymore Halpenny. — 1982. — 216p : ill,maps,ports ; 24cm
Ill on lining papers. — Includes index
ISBN 0-85059-532-0 : £8.95 : CIP rev.
B82-01450

Ashworth, Christopher. Action stations. — Cambridge : Patrick Stephens
5: Military airfields of the South-west. — Oct.1982. — [256]p
ISBN 0-85059-510-x : £9.95 : CIP entry
B82-24268

358.4'17'0942449 — Hereford and Worcester. Pershore. Aerodromes: Pershore RAF Station, *to 1981*
Warren, Glyn. RAF Pershore : a history / Glyn Warren. — Newport Pagnell : Enthusiasts for G. Warren, c1982. — 59p : ill,facsims,1plan ; 21cm
ISBN 0-907700-05-5 (pbk) : Unpriced
B82-35322

358.4'17'0942497 — West Midlands *(Metropolitan County).* **Castle Bromwich: Castle Bromwich Aerodrome,** *to 1945*
Newell, M. D.. Castle Bromwich : its airfield and aircraft factory / M.D. Newell. — Newport Pagnell : Enthusiasts Publications for M.D. Newell, c1982. — 21p : ill ; 21cm
Bibliography: p21
ISBN 0-907700-06-3 (pbk) : Unpriced
B82-21615

358.4'2'0973 — Air operations by United States. *Army Air Force, to 1953.* **B29 Boeing aeroplanes**
Pimlott, John, *1948-*. B-29 superfortress / John Pimlott. — London : Arms and Armour, 1980. — 64p : ill(some col.),ports(some col.) ; 29cm. — (A bison book) ([War planes in colour] ; 2)
Bibliography: p64
ISBN 0-85368-095-7 : £2.95 : CIP rev.
B80-17617

358.4'3'0941 — Air operations by Great Britain. *Royal Air Force. Fighter Command, 1936-1968*
Bowyer, Chaz. Fighter Command 1936-1968 / Chaz Bowyer. — London : Sphere, 1981, c1980. — 242p,[8]p of plates : ill,ports ; 18cm
Originally published: London : Dent, 1980. — Bibliography: p235-237. — Includes index
ISBN 0-7221-1808-2 (pbk) : £1.75 B82-02173

358.4'3'0941 — Great Britain. *Royal Air Force Regiment, to 1981*
Great Britain. *Royal Air Force Regiment*. The Royal Air Force Regiment : a short history. — [4th ed]. — [London] : [Ministry of Defence], [1982]. — 108p : ill(some col.),1coat of arms,ports(some col.) ; 25cm
40th anniversary ed. — Cover title. — Previous ed.: 1974. — Includes index
Unpriced (pbk) B82-27453

358.4'5'0941 — Great Britain. *Royal Air Force.* **Reconnaissance squadrons. Air operations,** *to 1981*
Rawlings, John D. R.. Coastal support and special squadrons of the RAF and their aircraft / John D.R. Rawlings. — London : Jane's, 1982. — 270p : ill ; 29cm
Includes index
ISBN 0-7106-0187-5 : £17.50 B82-40586

359 — NAVAL FORCES

359'.009163'84 — Eastern Mediterranean Sea. Naval warfare, *1559-1863*
Anderson, Roger Charles. Naval wars in the Levant 1559-1863. — Liverpool : Liverpool University Press, Apr.1981. — [640]p
Originally published: 1952
ISBN 0-85323-112-5 : £10.00 : CIP entry
Also classified at 359'.009163'89 B81-10494

359'.009163'89 — Black Sea. Naval warfare, *1559-1863*
Anderson, Roger Charles. Naval wars in the Levant 1559-1863. — Liverpool : Liverpool University Press, Apr.1981. — [640]p
Originally published: 1952
ISBN 0-85323-112-5 : £10.00 : CIP entry
Primary classification 359'.009163'84
B81-10494

359'.0092'2 — Great Britain. *Royal Navy.* **Involvement of royal families,** *1901-1981*
Winton, John. Captains and kings : the Royal Family and the Royal Navy 1901-1981 / by John Winton. — Denbigh : Bluejacket, c1981. — 114p : ill,ports ; 21cm
Includes index
ISBN 0-907001-01-7 (pbk) : £1.95 B82-12086

359'.00941 — Great Britain. *Royal Navy*
Beaver, Paul. Encyclopaedia of the modern Royal Navy. — Cambridge : Stephens, Nov.1982. — [360]p
ISBN 0-85059-560-6 : £17.95 : CIP entry
B82-26425

Hill, J. R.. The Royal Navy : today and tomorrow / J.R. Hill. — London : Ian Allan, 1981. — 144p : ill(some col.),maps,ports ; 30cm
Bibliography: p143. — Includes index
ISBN 0-7110-1168-0 : £9.95 B82-11222

359'.00941 — Great Britain. *Royal Navy, 1793-1815 — For schools*
Brownlee, Walter. The navy that beat Napoleon / Walter Brownlee. — Cambridge : Cambridge University Press, 1980. — 48p : ill,1facsim,maps,plans,3ports ; 21x22cm. — (Cambridge introduction to the history of mankind. Topic book)
ISBN 0-521-22145-5 (pbk) : £1.95 B82-38820

359'.00941 — Great Britain. *Royal Navy, 1830-1870*
White, Colin. The end of the sailing Navy / Colin White ; foreword by Sir Terence Lewin. — London : Mason, c1981. — 161p : ill,1facsim,1plan,ports ; 17x25cm. — (Victoria's navy)
Ill on lining papers. — Bibliography: p161
ISBN 0-85937-224-3 : £9.95 : CIP rev.
B80-19136

359'.00941 — Great Britain. *Royal Navy, 1946-1982*
Wettern, Desmond. The decline of British seapower / Desmond Wettern. — London : Jane's, 1982. — 452p,[32]p of plates : ill,1map,1port ; 25cm
Includes index
ISBN 0-7106-0043-7 : £17.50 B82-35416

359'.00941 — Great Britain. *Royal Navy, ca 1850-1981*
Hill-Norton, Peter Hill-Norton, *Baron*. Sea power / Lord-Hill Norton and John Dekker. — London : Faber and Faber, 1982. — 192p : ill ; 25cm
Includes index
ISBN 0-571-11890-9 : £7.50 : CIP rev.
B81-36978

359'.00941 — Great Britain. *Royal Navy, to 1980*
Clark, Gregory, *1916-*. Britain's naval heritage / Gregory Clark. — London : H.M.S.O., 1981. — 131p,[16]p of plates : ill,ports ; 23cm
Includes index
ISBN 0-11-290365-7 (cased) : £7.95
ISBN 0-11-290346-0 (pbk) : £3.95 B82-05510

359'.009931 — New Zealand. *Royal New Zealand Navy, to 1981*
Howard, Grant. The navy in New Zealand : an illustrated history / Grant Howard. — London : Jane's, 1982, c1981. — 170p : ill,maps,facsims,ports ; cm
Includes index
ISBN 0-7106-0171-9 : £9.95 B82-04765

359'.03'0924 — Great Britain. Naval policies. Historiography. Corbett, Julian S. — *Biographies*
Schurman, Donald M.. Julian S. Corbett, 1854-1922 : historian of British maritime policy from Drake to Jellicoe / Donald M. Schurman. — London : Royal Historical Society, 1981. — x,216p ; 22cm. — (Royal Historical Society studies in history series ; no.26)
Bibliography: p202-203. — Includes index
ISBN 0-901050-59-8 : £9.87 B82-08497

359.1'0941 — Great Britain. *Royal Navy.* **Naval life,** *ca 1770-1805*
Pope, Dudley. Life in Nelson's navy / by Dudley Pope. — London : Allen & Unwin, 1981. — ix,279p : ill ; 22cm
Bibliography: p265-273. — Includes index
ISBN 0-04-359008-x : Unpriced B82-29313

359.1'0941 — Great Britain. *Royal Navy.* **Sailors. Naval life,** *1900-1939*
Carew, Anthony. The lower deck of the Royal Navy : 1900-1939 : the Invergordon mutiny in perspective / Anthony Carew. — Manchester : Manchester University Press, c1981. — xx,269p : ill,ports ; 24cm
Bibliography: p257-263. — Includes index
ISBN 0-7190-0841-7 : £19.50 : CIP rev.
B81-21508

359.1'334 — Great Britain. *Royal Navy.* **Sailing vessels: Bounty** *(Ship).* **Mutiny**
Nordoff, Charles. Mutiny on the Bounty. — Bath : Chivers, Sept.1982. — [424]p. — (A New Portway book)
Originally published: London : Chapman and Hall, 1933
ISBN 0-86220-511-5 : £6.95 : CIP entry
B82-21995

359.1'334 — Great Britain. *Royal Navy.* **Sailing vessels: Bounty** *(Ship).* **Mutiny —** *Correspondence, diaries, etc.*

Bligh, William. An account of the mutiny on HMS Bounty / William Bligh ; edited by Robert Bowman. — Gloucester : Sutton, 1981. — 158p : ill,maps,1port ; 26cm
Includes index
ISBN 0-904387-47-x (cased) : Unpriced : CIP rev.
ISBN 0-422-21390-5 (pbk) : £12.70 B80-31227

Bligh, William. The mutiny on board H.M.S. Bounty 1789 / by William Bligh. — Guildford : Pageminster Press in association with Argot Press & Mitchell Beazley, 1981. — xi,[192]p : ill ; 34cm
Facsim. of: part of the Admiralty copy of Bligh's log, reference ADM 55/151
ISBN 0-86134-032-9 : £13.95 B82-33654

359.1'334 — Great Britain. *Royal Navy.* **Sailing vessels: Bounty** *(Ship).* **Mutiny —** *Early works*

Barrow, *Sir* John. The mutiny of the Bounty. — Horsham (9 Queen St., Horsham, West Sussex, RH13 5AA) : Russel Sharp, Oct.1981. — [216]p
ISBN 0-907722-00-8 : £8.95 : CIP entry B81-28824

Bligh, William. An account of the mutiny on H.M.S. Bounty. — Gloucester : Alan Sutton, Mar.1982. — [162]p
Originally published: 1980
ISBN 0-86299-005-x (pbk) : £4.95 : CIP entry B82-08412

359.1'334'0924 — Great Britain. *Royal Navy.* **Sailing vessels: Bounty** *(Ship).* **Mutiny. Christian, Fletcher —** *Biographies*

Christian, Glynn. Fragile paradise. — London : Hamilton, Sept.1982. — [256]p
ISBN 0-241-10757-1 : £12.95 : CIP entry B82-18837

359.1'34 — Great Britain. *Royal Navy.* **Rum issue,** *to 1970*

Pack, J.. Nelson's blood. — Havant : Kenneth Mason, Oct.1982. — [160]p
ISBN 0-85937-279-0 : £9.95 : CIP entry B82-24122

359.1'342 — Great Britain. *Royal Navy.* **Awards of medals,** *1793-1840:* **Naval General Service Medal** *— Lists*

Douglas-Morris, Kenneth. The Naval General Service Medal roll 1793-1840. — London (10 Chancellor House, Hyde Park Gate, S.W.7) : The author, Sept.1982. — [416]p
Limited ed. of 250 numbered copies signed by the author
ISBN 0-9507971-0-3 : £180.00 : CIP entry B82-21741

359.1'6 — England. Solent. Naval reviews, *1935-1977 — Illustrations*

Ransome-Wallis, P.. The Royal Naval reviews 1935-1977 / P. Ransome-Wallis. — London : Ian Allan, 1982. — 144p : chiefly ill ; 30cm
Bibliography: p4. — Includes index
ISBN 0-7110-1166-4 : £9.95 B82-34781

359.3'252 — Battleships. Sinking, *1855-1955*

Woodward, David, *1909-*. Sunk! : how the great battleships were lost / by David Woodward. — London : Allen & Unwin, 1982. — 153p,[8]p of plates : ill ; 24cm
Includes index
ISBN 0-04-359009-8 : £8.95 : CIP rev. B82-15634

359.3'253'0943 — Naval operations by Germany. *Kriegsmarine, 1895-1945.* **Commerce raiders: Auxiliary cruisers**

Schmalenbach, Paul. German raiders : a history of auxiliary cruisers of the German navy 1895-1945 / Paul Schmalenbach. — Cambridge : Stephens, 1979. — 144p : ill,facsims,ports ; 25cm
Translation of: Die deutschen Hilfskreuzer 1895-1945. — Bibliography: p142. — Includes index
ISBN 0-85059-351-4 : £8.95 : CIP rev. B79-25660

359.3'257'09 — Naval operations to 1945 submarines

Poolman, Kenneth. Periscope depth : submarines at war / Kenneth Poolman. — London : Kimber, 1981. — 199p,[16]p of plates : ill,ports ; 25cm
Bibliography: p177-179. — Includes index
ISBN 0-7183-0158-7 : £8.95 B82-06614

359.3'31'0924 — Great Britain. *Royal Navy.* **Nelson, Horatio Nelson,** *Viscount — Biographies*

Edgington, Harry. Nelson : the hero — and the lover / Harry Edgington. — Feltham : Hamlyn Paperbacks, 1981. — 207p,[4]p of plates : ports ; 18cm
ISBN 0-600-20144-9 (pbk) : £1.50 B82-04692

359.3'31'0924 — Great Britain. *Royal Navy.* **Nelson, Horatio Nelson,** *Viscount — Serials*

The **Nelson** dispatch : journal of the Nelson Society. — Vol.1, pt.1 (Jan. 1982)-. — Norwich (43 King St., Norwich, Norfolk) : B.B. & Co., 1982-. — v. : ports ; 21cm
Quarterly. — Description based on: Vol.1, pt.2 (Apr. 1982)
ISSN 0262-8198 = Nelson dispatch : £5.00 per year B82-30481

359.3'31'0924 — Great Britain. *Royal Navy.* **Richmond,** *Sir* **Herbert —** *Biographies*

Hunt, Barry D.. Sailor-scholar : Admiral Sir Herbert Richmond 1871-1946 / Barry D. Hunt. — Waterloo, Ont. : Wilfred Laurier University Press ; Gerrards Cross : distributed by Smythe, c1982. — xii,259p ; 24cm
Bibliography: p238-248. — Includes index
ISBN 0-88920-104-8 : Unpriced B82-33132

359.3'32'0924 — Germany. *Kriegsmarine.* **Kretschmer, Otto,** *1939-1947 — Biographies*

Robertson, Terence. [The Golden horseshoe]. Night raider of the Atlantic : (formerly The golden horseshoe) / by Terence Robertson ; preface by Sir George Creasy. — London : Evans Bros., c1955 (1981 [printing]). — xiii,210p,[16]p of plates : ill,ports ; 22cm
Includes index
ISBN 0-237-45549-8 (pbk) : £6.25 : CIP rev. B80-25398

359.4'09 — Naval operations. Role of British royal families, *1327-1981*

Thomas, David. Royal admirals 1327-1981. — London : Deutsch, June 1982. — [272]p
ISBN 0-233-97427-x : £12.95 : CIP entry B82-10703

359.4'09'03 — Naval operations, *1481-1978*

Padfield, Peter. Tide of empires : decisive naval campaigns in the rise of the west / Peter Padfield. — London : Routledge & Kegan Paul
Vol.2: 1654-1763. — 1982. — ix,270p,[16]p of plates : ill,maps,ports ; 23cm
Ill on lining papers. — Bibliography: p253-264. — Includes index
ISBN 0-7100-9215-6 : £12.50 B82-30552

359.4'3'09 — Navies. Strategy, *to 1979*

Till, Geoffrey. Maritime strategy and the nuclear age / Geoffrey Till with contributions from John Hattendorf ... [et al.]. — London : Macmillan, 1982. — x,274p ; 23cm
Bibliography: p254-265. — Includes index
ISBN 0-333-26109-7 : £20.00 B82-28686

359.6'22'0942 — England. *Royal Navy, 1422-1427 — Accounts*

Soper, William. The navy of the Lancastrian Kings : accounts and inventories of William Soper, Keeper of the King's Ships, 1422-1427 / edited by Susan Rose. — London : Published by Allen & Unwin for the Navy Records Society, 1982. — 288p,[1]leaf of plates : 1facsim ; 23cm. — (Publications of the Navy Records Society ; v.123)
Includes index
ISBN 0-04-942175-1 : Unpriced : CIP rev. B82-12425

359.7 — Mediterranean region. British naval bases, *to 1980*

Hughes, Quentin. Britain in the Mediterranean & the defence of her naval stations / by Quentin Hughes. — Liverpool : Penpaled, 1981. — 235p,[16]leaves of plates : ill,maps,plans ; 30cm
Text on inside cover. — Bibliography: p230-232. — Includes index
ISBN 0-907809-00-6 (pbk) : Unpriced B82-13554

359.9'6'0941 — Great Britain. *Royal Marines, to 1980*

Ladd, James. Royal Marine Commando / James D. Ladd ; foreword by Sir Steuart R. Pringle. — London : Hamlyn, c1982. — 176p : ill(some col.),facsims,2maps,ports(some col.) ; 31cm
Bibliography: p173. — Includes index
ISBN 0-600-34203-4 : £6.95 B82-32414

Moulton, J. L.. The Royal Marines / by J.L. Moulton. — Rev ed. — Southsea : Royal Marines Museum, 1981. — vi,153p,[16]p of plates : ill,ports ; 22cm
Previous ed.: London : Cooper, 1972. — Bibliography: p149-153
ISBN 0-9505235-1-8 (cased) : Unpriced
ISBN 0-9505235-2-6 (pbk) : Unpriced B82-08016

359.9'81 — Great Britain. Polaris ballistic missile systems. Improvement. Programmes: Chevaline programme. Expenditure by Great Britain. *Ministry of Defence, 1972-1981 — Inquiry reports*

Great Britain. *Parliament. House of Commons. Committee of Public Accounts.* Ninth report from the Committee of Public Accounts, session 1981-82 : Ministry of Defence, Chevaline improvement to the Polaris missile system : together with the proceedings of the Committee, minutes of evidence and appendices. — London : H.M.S.O., 1982. — xiii,31p ; 25cm. — ([HC] ; 269)
ISBN 0-10-226982-3 (pbk) : £3.95 B82-26846

361 — SOCIAL PROBLEMS AND SOCIAL WELFARE

361 — Urban regions. Welfare work

Davis, Martin. The essential social worker. — London : Heinemann Educational, Apr.1981. — [256]p. — (Community care handbooks)
ISBN 0-435-82267-5 (cased) : £12.50 : CIP entry
ISBN 0-435-82268-3 (pbk) : £4.95 B81-04313

361 — Welfare services

Golding, Peter. Images of welfare. — Oxford : Robertson, Jan.1982. — [224]p. — (Aspects of social policy)
ISBN 0-85520-447-8 (cased) : £10.00 : CIP entry
ISBN 0-85520-448-6 (pbk) : £3.95 B81-33777

361'.0025'41 — Great Britain. Welfare services — *Directories*

Sunday times self-help directory. — 2nd ed. — London : Granada, Apr.1982. — [320]p
Previous ed.: London : Times Newspapers, 1975
ISBN 0-246-11304-9 (pbk) : £3.95 : CIP entry
Also classified at 016.61 B82-04317

361'.0025'41 — Great Britain. Welfare services — *Directories — Serials*

Social services yearbook. — 1982/83. — London : Longman, Sept.1982. — [928]p. — (Longman community information guides)
ISBN 0-900313-71-4 : £22.00 : CIP entry
ISSN 0307-093x B82-21996

361'.0025'4245 — Shropshire. Social services — *Directories*

Social services in Shropshire / [Shropshire County Council Social Services Department]. — rev. ed. — Shrewsbury (Shire Hall, Abbey Foregate, Shrewsbury SY2 6ND) : [The Department], 1981. — 22p ; 21cm
Cover title. — Previous ed.: 1979
Unpriced (pbk) B82-40588

361'.0025'4293 — Clwyd. Social services — *Directories*

Who can help? : a directory of help and advice agencies / [Clwyd Information Providers Steering Group] ; [Eddie Hughes editor]. — [Mold] : [The Group], [1981]. — 1v.(loose-leaf) ; 30cm
Includes index
ISBN 0-904444-59-7 (unbound) : Unpriced
B82-02860

361'.006'042 — England. Personal welfare services. Organisations: Personal Social Services Council, *to 1980*

PSSC : Personal Social Services Council 1973-1980 : the case-history of an Advisory Non-Governmental Organization / [prepared by Raymond T. Clarke with Malcolm L. Johnson, Colleen Shambrook and Lewis E. Waddilove]. — [London] : [National Institute for Social Work], c1981. — 67p ; 21cm
Cover title. — Text on inside covers
ISBN 0-902789-23-6 (pbk) : Unpriced
B82-06270

361'.007'041 — Great Britain. Social services. Information sources

Streatfield, David. Social work : an information sourcebook : a guide to publications and other information sources / by David Streatfield. — Edinburgh : Capital Planning Information, 1982. — 165p ; 21cm. — (CPI sourcebooks ; no.2)
Includes index
ISBN 0-906011-16-7 (pbk) : Unpriced : CIP rev.
B82-12852

361'.007'1141 — Great Britain. Welfare workers. Professional education. Curriculum subjects: Welfare services. Cooperation with national health services — *Conference proceedings*

Symposium on Interprofessional Learning *(1979 : University of Nottingham)*. Education for co-operation in health and social work : papers from the Symposium on Interprofessional Learning, University of Nottingham, July 1979 / [organized by] Central Council for Education and Training in Social Work ... [et al.] ; edited by Hugh England. — London : Journal of the Royal College of General Practitioners, [1980]. — 31p : ill ; 29cm. — (Occasional paper ; 14)
Bibliography: p31
ISBN 0-85084-075-9 (pbk) : £3.00
Also classified at 610'.7'1141
B82-40678

361'.007'1141 — Great Britain. Welfare workers. Professional education — *Serials*

Social work education : a journal for education and training in local authority, probation and allied personal social services. — Vol.1, no.1 (Autumn 1981)-. — London (Hamilton House, Mabledon Pl., WC1H 9BD) : Joint University Council, Social Work Education Committee, Royal Institute of Public Administration, 1981-. — v. ; 30cm
ISSN 0261-5479 = Social work education : £8.00 per year (£6.00 to individuals)
B82-19855

361'.007'1142132 — London. Westminster *(London Borough)*. **Universities. Colleges: London School of Economics and Political Science. Curriculum subjects: Social administration. Ex-students,** *1949-1973*

Changing course : a follow-up study of students taking the certificate and diploma in social administration at the London School of Economics, 1949-1973 / Kit Russell ... [et al.]. — London : London School of Economics and Political Science, 1981. — xii,308p ; 22cm
Bibliography: p307-308
ISBN 0-85328-076-2 (pbk) : £3.00
B82-03513

361'.0072 — Social services. Evaluation research — *Conference proceedings*

Crane, John A.. The evaluation of social policies / John A. Crane. — Boston, Mass. ; London : Kluwer Nijhoff, c1982. — x,221p : ill ; 24cm. — (International series in social welfare)
Bibliography: p205-212. — Includes index
ISBN 0-89838-075-8 : Unpriced
B82-31278

Evaluative research in social care : papers from a workshop on recent trends in evaluative research in social work and the social services, May 1980 / edited by E. Matilda Goldberg and Naomi Connelly. — London : Heinemann Educational, 1981. — 320p : ill,1form ; 23cm
At head of title: Policy Studies Institute. — Includes bibliographies and index
ISBN 0-435-83351-0 (cased) : £15.00 : CIP rev.
ISBN 0-435-83352-9 (pbk) : Unpriced
B81-15900

361'.0072 — Social services. Evaluation research. Methodology

Bloom, Martin. Evaluating practice : guidelines for the accountable professional / Martin Bloom, Joel Fischer. — Englewood Cliffs ; London : Prentice-Hall, c1982. — xi,512p : ill,forms ; 24cm
Bibliography: p487-498. — Inlcudes index
ISBN 0-13-292318-1 : £18.70
B82-31820

361'.0072 — Welfare work. Research. Methodology

Reid, William J.. Research in social work / William J. Reid and Audrey D. Smith. — New York ; Guildford : Columbia University Press, 1981. — xi,417p : ill ; 24cm
Bibliography: p388-404. — Includes index
ISBN 0-231-04700-2 : £14.05
B82-10653

361'.00723 — Great Britain. Social surveys, *to 1980*

Kent, Raymond A.. A history of British empirical sociology / Raymond A. Kent. — Aldershot : Gower, c1981. — viii,228p ; 23cm
Bibliography: p205-220. — Includes index
ISBN 0-566-00415-1 (cased) : Unpriced : CIP rev.
ISBN 0-566-00520-4 (pbk) : Unpriced
B81-28071

361'.00723 — Social surveys. Methodology

Theories and methods in rural community studies . — Oxford : Pergamon, Oct.1982. — [304]p
ISBN 0-08-025813-1 : £19.50 : CIP entry
B82-28434

361'.00723 — Social surveys. Methodology — *Serials*

Survey methodology bulletin / [Social Survey Division, Office of Population Censuses and Surveys]. — No.1 (Dec. 1977). — London ([St Catherine's House, 10 Kingsway, WC2B 6JP]) : [The Division], 1977-. — v. ; 30cm
Quarterly. — Primarily designed as a house journal for: Social Survey Division staff. — Issued by: Methodology Unit, Social Survey Division, Office of Population Censuses and Surveys, 1977-1979. — Description based on: No.12 (Apr. 1981)
ISSN 0263-158X = Survey methodology bulletin : Unpriced
B82-18717

361'.00723 — Social surveys. Questionnaires. Design & interpretation

Belson, William A.. The design and understanding of survey questions / William A. Belson. — Aldershot : Gower, c1981. — viii,399p ; 24cm
Appendix (3 microfiches) in pocket
ISBN 0-566-00420-8 : Unpriced
B82-17821

361'.00723 — Social surveys. Responses. Effects of interviewing

Response behaviour in the survey-interview. — London : Academic Press, July 1982. — [400]p
ISBN 0-12-712050-5 : CIP entry
B82-12529

361'.00723 — Social surveys. Responses. Effects of interviewing & questionnaires

Schuman, Howard. Questions and answers in attitude surveys : experiments on question form, wording, and context / Howard Schuman, Stanley Presser. — New York ; London : Academic Press, 1981. — xii,370p : ill ; 24cm. — (Quantitative studies in social relations)
Bibliography: p351-362. — Includes index
ISBN 0-12-631350-4 : £19.60
B82-18685

361'.00723 — Social surveys. Sampling — *Conference proceedings*

International Symposium on Survey Sampling *(1980 : Ottawa)*. Current topics in survey sampling : [proceedings of the International Symposium on Survey Sampling held in Ottawa, Canada, May 7-9, 1980] / edited by D. Krewski, R. Platek, J.N.K. Rao. — New York ; London : Academic Press, 1981. — xv,509p : ill,maps ; 24cm
Includes bibliographies
ISBN 0-12-426280-5 : £19.60
B82-30014

361'.05 — Great Britain. Residential care

Davis, Ann, *1948-*. The residential solution : state alternatives to family care / Ann Davis. — London : Tavistock Publications, 1981. — viii,150p ; 22cm. — (Tavistock library of social work practice ; SSP 222)
Bibliography: p140-145. — Includes index
ISBN 0-422-77320-4 (cased) : Unpriced : CIP rev.
ISBN 0-422-77330-1 (pbk) : £3.75
B81-21629

361'.05 — Great Britain. Residential care — *For welfare work*

Davis, Leonard, *1931-*. Residential care : a community resource / Leonard Davis. — London : Heinemann Educational, 1982. — 118p ; 22cm. — (Community care practice handbooks ; 8)
Includes index
ISBN 0-435-82264-0 (pbk) : £2.95 : CIP rev.
B81-35696

361'.05 — Great Britain. Residential institutions. Inmates. Discharge

Brearley, Paul. Leaving residential care. — London : Tavistock, Nov.1982. — [208]p. — (Residential social work)
ISBN 0-422-77920-2 (cased) : £8.00 : CIP entry
ISBN 0-422-77930-x (pbk) : £3.95
B82-27509

361'.05 — Scotland. Public. Financial assistance by local anthorities — *For welfare work*

Strathclyde. *Social Work Department*. Provision of financial assistance : policy and procedures handbook : section 12 and local promotional use of section 10, Social Work (Scotland) Act 1968 / Social Work Department. — [Rev. ed.]. — [Glasgow] : Strathclyde Regional Council, 1980. — 86p : forms ; 30cm
Cover title. — Previous ed.: 1978. — Text on inside cover
Unpriced (pbk)
B82-25262

361'.06 — Clwyd. Alyn and Deeside *(District)*. **Community advisory services & community information services. Provision. Implications of unemployment**

Astbury, Raymond. A survey of information, advice and counselling providers in North-East Clwyd, February-September 1981 / by Raymond Astbury. — [Mold] : Clwyd Information Providers Steering Group, c1982. — 24p ; 22cm
ISBN 0-904444-77-5 (pbk) : £0.75
B82-40519

361'.06 — Great Britain. Community information services

Bunch, Allan. Community information services : their origin, scope and development / Allan Bunch. — London : Bingley, 1982. — viii,168p ; 23cm
Includes index
ISBN 0-85157-318-5 : Unpriced : CIP rev.
B82-01166

361'.06 — Greater Manchester *(Metropolitan County)*. **Manchester. Moss Side. Community advice centres: Moss Side Family Advice Centre,** *to 1978*

The FAC book : a history of the Moss Side Family Advice Centre. — Manchester : Youth Development Trust, c1981. — iv,77p : ill,maps ; 25cm
Cover title
ISBN 0-903178-04-4 (pbk) : Unpriced
B82-00625

361′.06 — Lancashire. Central Lancashire New Town. Advice centres — *Directories*

Enquire within : a directory of advice-giving agencies in the Central Lancashire New Town area covering the districts of Preston, Chorley, and South Ribble. — Preston : Lancashire Library, 1981. — xi,68p : 1map ; 30cm
Includes index
ISBN 0-902228-42-0 (spiral) : Unpriced
B82-03934

361′.06 — West Midlands *(Metropolitan County).* **Birmingham. Community information services. Videotex services: Prestel. Use**

Sullivan, Catherine, *19---*. Local community information on Prestel : use of the Birmingham local information file / Catherine Sullivan, David Oliver. — London : Aslib Research & Consultancy Division, 1981. — iii,28leaves,[4]p of plates : forms ; 30cm. — (British Library research and development report ; no.5693)
ISBN 0-85142-158-x (spiral) : £5.00
B82-27578

361.1 — SOCIAL PROBLEMS

361.1 — Social problems

Liazos, Alexander. People first : an introduction to social problems / Alexander Liazos. — Boston ; London : Allyn and Bacon, c1982. — x,437p ; 24cm
Bibliography: p399-425. — Includes index
ISBN 0-205-07646-7 (pbk) : Unpriced
B82-26939

361.1′09173′2 — Cities. Social problems. Geographical aspects

Herbert, David, *1935-*. Social problems and the city: a geographic view : inaugural lecture delivered at the College on 27 October 1981 / by David T. Herbert. — Swansea : University College of Swansea, 1981. — 45p : ill,maps ; 21cm
Bibliography: p44-45
ISBN 0-86076-025-1 (pbk) : Unpriced
B82-06193

361.1′09181′2 — Western world. Cities. Inner areas. Social problems

Advanced industrialization and the inner cities / edited by Gail Garfield Schwartz. — Lexington : Lexington Books, c1981 ; [Aldershot] : Gower [distributor], 1982. — x,173p ; 24cm. — (Urban roundtable series)
Bibliography: p161-165. — Includes index
ISBN 0-669-03512-2 : £16.00 B82-18254

361.1′0941 — Great Britain. Social problems. Committees of inquiry. Proposals. Implementation by Great Britain. *Home Office — Inquiry reports*

Great Britain. *Parliament. House of Commons. Home Affairs Committee.* First report from the Home Affairs Committee, session 1980-81 : Home Office reports : report together with the proceedings of the committee and appendix. — London : H.M.S.O., [1980]. — xiip ; 25cm. — (HC ; 23)
ISBN 0-10-202381-6 (unbound) : £1.40
B82-11424

361.1′0941 — Great Britain. Social problems — *Practical information — For Christian welfare work*

Jackson, Ruth, *1932-*. Battered clergy wives / Ruth Jackson. — Bognor Regis : New Horizon, c1982. — 72p ; 21cm
ISBN 0-86116-595-0 : £3.25
Also classified at 248.4′83043 B82-09560

361.3 — SOCIAL WORK

361.3 — Great Britain. Social services. Professional personnel. Role

Wilding, Paul. Professional power and social welfare / Paul Wilding. — London : Routledge & Kegan Paul, 1982. — x,169p ; 22cm. — (Radical social policy)
Bibliography: p150-163. — Includes index
ISBN 0-7100-0885-6 (pbk) : £4.50 B82-12941

361.3 — Great Britain. Welfare services. Risks. Management

Brearley, C. Paul. Risk and social work / C. Paul Brearley. — London : Routledge & Kegan Paul, 1982. — x,175p ; 22cm. — (Hazards and helping)
Bibliography: p160-169. — Includes index
ISBN 0-7100-0999-2 (pbk) : £5.50 B82-20429

361.3 — Residential welfare work. Management

Middle management in residential social work. — London : Residential Care Association, 1982. — 54p ; 30cm. — (RCA publications)
At head of title: The Ollerton Report
ISBN 0-901244-08-2 (pbk) : Unpriced
B82-24208

361.3 — Residential welfare work — *Questions & answers*

Douglas, Robin. Developing residential practice : five role play and simulation exercises : for staff in residential settings / Robin Douglas, Chris Payne. — London : National Institute for Social Work, 1981. — 1v.(loose-leaf) : ill ; 30cm
Includes bibliographies
ISBN 0-902789-21-x (pbk) : £4.50 B82-05317

361.3 — Welfare work

Northen, Helen. Clinical social work / by Helen Northen. — New York ; Guildford : Columbia University Press, 1982. — xii,369p ; 24cm
Bibliography: p333-360. — Includes index
ISBN 0-231-03800-3 : £12.30 B82-19502

Rees, Stuart. Verdicts on social work / Stuart Rees and Alison Wallace. — London : Edward Arnold, 1982. — vii,192p ; 22cm
Bibliography: p169-186. — Includes index
ISBN 0-7131-6279-1 (pbk) : £5.95 : CIP rev.
B82-06918

Theory and practice in social work. — Oxford : Basil Blackwell, Apr.1982. — [250]p
ISBN 0-631-12653-8 (cased) : £12.50 : CIP entry
ISBN 0-631-12709-7 (pbk) : £5.95 B82-04584

361.3 — Welfare work — *Conference proceedings*

National Conference on Social Welfare. *Forum (108th : 1981 : San Francisco).* The social welfare forum, 1981 : official proceedings, 108th annual forum, National Conference on Social Welfare, San Francisco, California, June 7-10, 1981. — New York ; Guildford : published for the National Conference on Social Welfare by Columbia University Press, 1982. — xiv,244p,1leaf of plates : 1port ; 24cm
Includes index
ISBN 0-231-05486-6 (cased) : £19.80
ISBN 0-231-05487-4 (pbk) : Unpriced
B82-28064

361.3′01 — Welfare work — *Philosophical perspectives*

Wilkes, Ruth. Social work with undervalued groups / Ruth Wilkes. — London : Tavistock Publications, 1981. — viii,141p ; 22cm. — (Tavistock library of social work practice ; SSP 218)
Bibliography: p125-129. — Includes index
ISBN 0-422-77100-7 (cased) : Unpriced : CIP rev.
ISBN 0-422-77110-4 (pbk) : £3.75 B81-21557

361.3′01 — Welfare work. Theories

Theories of practice in social work / edited by Pauline Hardiker and Mary Barker. — London : Academic Press, 1981. — ix,313p ; 24cm
Bibliography: p271-303. — Includes index
ISBN 0-12-324780-2 : £12.40 : CIP rev.
B81-36065

361.3′068 — Great Britain. Welfare work. Management

Bamford, Terry. Managing social work. — London : Tavistock, Jan.1983. — [180]p. — (Tavistock library of social work practice)
ISBN 0-422-77960-1 (cased) : £9.50 : CIP entry
ISBN 0-422-77970-9 (pbk) : £4.50 B82-34579

361.3′07′1142132 — London. Westminster *(London Borough).* **Universities. Colleges: London School of Economics and Political Science. Curriculum subjects: Welfare work. Courses: Carnegie Course,** *1954-1958*

Hartshorn, Alma E.. Milestone in education for social work : the Carnegie experiment 1954-1958 / Alma E. Hartshorn. — Dunfermline : Carnegie United Kingdom Trust, 1982. — xviii,145p ; 21cm
Bibliography: p130-134. — Includes index
ISBN 0-900259-02-7 (pbk) : £5.95 B82-34867

361.3′0722 — Great Britain. Welfare work — *Case studies*

Leighton, Neil. Rights and responsibilities : discussion of moral dimensions in social work / Neil Leighton, Richard Stalley, David Watson. — London : Heinemann Educational, 1982. — vi,62p ; 22cm. — (Community care practice handbooks ; 11)
Bibliography: p60-62
ISBN 0-435-82515-1 (pbk) : £2.95 : CIP rev.
B82-08107

361.3′0941 — Great Britain. Welfare work

Community care. — Oxford : Robertson, Sept.1982. — [224]p. — (Aspects of social policy series)
ISBN 0-85520-455-9 (cased) : £12.50 : CIP entry
ISBN 0-85520-456-7 (pbk) : £4.95 B82-20839

Murgatroyd, Stephen. Coping with crisis. — London : Harper & Row, July 1982. — [220]p
ISBN 0-06-318228-9 (cased) : £7.95 : CIP entry
ISBN 0-06-318229-7 (pbk) : £4.95 B82-12446

Walton, Ronald G.. Social work 2000. — London : Longman, Sept.1982. — [128]p
ISBN 0-582-29622-6 (pbk) : £3.50 : CIP entry
B82-22426

361′.3′0941 — Great Britain. Welfare work, *1950-1975*

Younghusband, Eileen. Social work in Britain, 1950-1975 : a follow-up study / Eileen Younghusband. — London : Allan & Unwin. — 1978
Vol.2. — 311p ; 25cm
Bibliography: p285-306. — Includes index
ISBN 0-04-360044-1 : £15.00 : CIP rev.
B78-27250

361.3′0941 — Great Britain. Welfare work, *to 1980*

Younghusband, Eileen. The newest profession : a short history of social work / Eileen Younghusband. — Sutton : Community care, 1981. — 46p : ill,1port ; 21cm
Bibliography: p38
ISBN 0-617-00363-7 (pbk) : £2.50 B82-08391

361.3′0942 — England. Welfare work

Sainsbury, Eric. Social work in focus : clients′ and social workers′ perceptions in long-term social work / Eric Sainsbury, Stephen Nixon and David Phillips. — London : Routledge & Kegan Paul, 1982. — x,205,14p ; 22cm. — (Library of social work)
Bibliography: p196-198. — Includes index
ISBN 0-7100-9068-4 (pbk) : £4.95 B82-35276

361.3′2 — Great Britain. Welfare workers. Accountability

Fletcher, Harry, *1947-*. No accountability, no redress : the powers of social workers and the rights of parents / a social worker′s view — Harry Fletcher, a barrister′s view — Joanna Dodson. — London (255 Kentish Town Rd., NW5 2LX) : One Parent Families, 1982. — 10p ; 10cm
£0.60 (unbound) B82-32071

361.3′23 — Counselling

Hansen, James C.. Counseling : theory and process / James C. Hansen, Richard R. Stevic, Richard W. Warner, Jr.. — 3rd ed. — Boston ; London : Allyn and Bacon, c1982. — 473p : ill ; 25cm
Previous ed.: 1977. — Includes bibliographies and index
ISBN 0-205-07640-8 : Unpriced B82-26934

361.3′23 — Counselling *continuation*

O′Leary, Eleanor. The psychology of counselling / Eleanor O′Leary. — Cork : Cork University Press, 1982. — 109p ; 21cm
Bibliography: p91-108. — Includes index
ISBN 0-902561-22-7 (pbk) : Unpriced
B82-38171

Priestley, Philip. Learning to help. — London : Tavistock, Jan.1983. — [200]p
ISBN 0-422-77470-7 (cased) : £12.50 : CIP entry
ISBN 0-422-77480-4 (pbk) : £5.95 B82-34578

Skills in social and educational caring. — Aldershot : Gower, July 1982. — [164]p
ISBN 0-566-00385-6 : £12.00 : CIP entry
B82-14236

361.3′23 — Counselling. Techniques. Effectiveness

Counseling on personal decisions : theory and research on short-term helping relationships / edited by Irving L. Janis. — New Haven, Conn. ; London : Yale University Press, c1982. — ix,409p ; 25cm
Bibliography: p385-401. — Includes index
ISBN 0-300-02484-3 : £24.50 : CIP rev.
B82-01317

361.3′23 — Counselling. Use of astrology

Rose, Christina. Astrological counselling. — Wellingborough : Aquarian Press, Nov.1982. — [128]p
ISBN 0-85030-301-x (pbk) : £3.95 : CIP entry
B82-26413

361.3′23′0941 — Great Britain. Counselling

Counselling in Britain : a reader / edited by A.W. Bolger. — London : Batsford Academic, 1982. — 320p ; 22cm
Bibliography: p311-312. — Includes index
ISBN 0-7134-3702-2 (pbk) : £7.95 : CIP rev.
B82-04491

361.3′7′0880816 — Great Britain. Voluntary welfare work by physically handicapped persons

Disabled people as volunteers. — Berkhamsted (29 Lower King′s Rd., Berkhamsted, Herts. HP4 2AB) : Volunteer Centre, [1981?]. — 1portfolio ; 34cm
£1.50 B82-04423

361.3′7′0941 — Great Britain. Voluntary welfare work

Gundrey, Elizabeth. Sparing time : the observer guide to helping others / Elizabeth Gundry. — London : Unwin, 1981. — 161p : ill ; 18cm
ISBN 0-04-361044-7 (pbk) : £2.25 B82-28918

361.3′7′09411 — Scotland. Voluntary welfare services. Welfare workers

Miller, Pat. Key employees of voluntary organisations in Scotland, 1979 / by Pat Miller. — Edinburgh (43 Jeffrey St., Edinburgh EH1 1DN) : Social Work Services Group, [1978]. — 48p : ill ; 30cm
Unpriced (spiral) B82-20134

361.4 — SOCIAL GROUP WORK

361.4′068′3 — Great Britain. Welfare work. Team-work. Supervision

Payne, Chris. Developing supervision of teams in field and residential social work / Chris Payne, Tony Scott. — London : National Institute for Social Work, 1982. — 58p : ill ; 29cm. — (Papers / National Institute for Social Work ; no.12)
Cover title. — Bibliography: p56-58
ISBN 0-902789-24-4 (pbk) : £4.00 B82-25008

361.4′0941 — Great Britain. Welfare services. Intake teams

Buckle, Joanna. Intake teams / Joanna Buckle. — London : Tavistock, 1981. — viii,213p ; 23cm. — (Tavistock library of social work practice)
Bibliography: p202-206. — Includes index
ISBN 0-422-77300-x (cased) : £9.50 : CIP rev.
ISBN 0-422-77310-7 (pbk) : Unpriced
B81-21558

361.4′0941 — Great Britain. Welfare work. Team-work

Payne, Malcolm, *1947-*. Working in teams / Malcolm Payne. — London : Macmillan, 1982. — viii,146p ; 23cm. — (Practical social work)
Bibliography: p136-141. — Includes index
ISBN 0-333-30886-7 (cased) : Unpriced
ISBN 0-333-30887-5 (pbk) : Unpriced
B82-25395

361.4′0973 — United States. Welfare work: Group work, *to 1980*

Reid, Kenneth E.. From character building to social treatment : the history of the use of groups in social work / Kenneth E. Reid. — Westport ; London : Greenwood, 1981. — xviii,249p : ill ; 22cm
Bibliography: p235-242. — Includes index
ISBN 0-313-22016-6 : Unpriced B82-01526

361.6 — PUBLIC SOCIAL WELFARE

361.6 — Social development — *Marxist viewpoints*

Momdzhīan, Kh. N.. Landmarks in history : the Marxist doctrine of socio-economic formations / Kh. Momjan ; [translated from the Russian by G. Sdobnikova]. — Moscow : Progress ; [London] : Distributed by Central, 1980. — 247p ; 21cm
Translation of: Vekhi istorii
£2.95 B82-21634

361.6′1′094585 — Malta. Government. Social policies, *1972-1980*

Kaim-Caudle, P. R.. Malta 1720-1980 : an evaluation of social policy / P.R. Kaim-Caudle. — [Durham] ([Elvet Hill, Durham, DH1 3TR]) : University of Durham, Centre for Middle Eastern and Islamic Studies, c1981. — 28p ; 21cm. — (Occasional papers series, ISSN 0307-0654 ; no.10)
Bibliography: p28
Unpriced (pbk) B82-08679

361.6′03′21 — Social development — *Encyclopaedias*

Glossary of development terminology / [prepared by the Research Unit of the Irish Commission for Justice and Peace]. — Dublin (11 Ely Place, Dublin 2) : CONGOOD, 1980. — 8p ; 30cm
Cover title
£0.20 (pbk) B82-09473

361.6′05 — Social planning - *Serials*

Progress in planning. — Vol.13. — Oxford : Pergamon, July 1981. — [178]p
ISBN 0-08-028398-5 : £25.00 : CIP entry
B81-15853

361.6′05 — Social planning — *Serials*

Progress in planning. — Vol.14. — Oxford : Pergamon, Nov.1981. — [310]p
ISBN 0-08-028432-9 : £24.00 : CIP entry
B81-31084

Progress in planning. — Vol.15. — Oxford : Pergamon, Nov.1981. — [264]p
ISBN 0-08-028433-7 : £24.00 : CIP entry
B81-31085

361.6′0941 — Great Britain. Public welfare services, *to 1981* — *For schools* — *Welsh texts*

Price, Emyr. Y wladwriaeth les / paratowyd ... gan Broject Defnyddiau ac Adnoddau y Swyddfa Gymreig, yn yr Adran Addysg, Coleg Prifysgol Cymru, Aberystwyth ; cyfarwyddwr Carl Dodson ... ; awdur ... Emyr Price ... — Caerdydd : Gwasg Prifysgol Cymru, 1982. — ii,26p : ill,facsims,1plan ; 30cm. — (Hanes)
ISBN 0-7083-0821-x (pbk) : Unpriced : CIP rev.
B82-13484

361.6′0941 — Great Britain. Social services. Policies of government

Cawson, Alan. Corporatism and welfare. — London : Heinemann Educational, Mar.1982. — [160]p. — (Studies in social policy and welfare ; 17)
ISBN 0-435-82136-9 (cased) : £13.50 : CIP entry
ISBN 0-435-82137-7 (pbk) : £6.50 B82-02646

361.6′0941 — Great Britain. Welfare benefits

Lister, Ruth. Welfare benefits / by Ruth Lister. — London : Sweet and Maxwell, 1981. — xxvi,284p ; 22cm. — (Social work and law)
Bibliography: p251. — Includes index
ISBN 0-421-24960-9 (pbk) : £8.00 : CIP rev.
B81-25294

361.6′09411 — Scotland. Urban aid programmes, *to 1980* — *Conference proceedings*

The **Urban** aid programme in Scotland : proceedings of a one day seminar / Keith Hayton (editor). — Glasgow (Bourdon Building, 177 Renfrew St, Glasgow G3) : Glasgow School of Art, Dept. of Planning, 1981. — 35leaves ; 30cm. — (Occasional papers / Glasgow School of Art, Department of Planning ; no.6)
Unpriced (spiral) B82-25855

361.6′09427 — North-west England. Regional development *compared with* **regional development of North Rhine-Westphalia**

Bowden, Phyllis. North Rhine Westphalia: North West England : regional development in action / by Phyllis Bowden. — London : Anglo-German Foundation for the Study of Industrial Society, c1979. — xv,119p : maps ; 21cm
ISBN 0-905492-17-x (pbk) : £7.95
Also classified at 361.6′0943′55 B82-17063

361.6′09428′76 — Tyne and Wear *(Metropolitan County).* **Newcastle upon Tyne. Byker. Community development projects: Byker Community Development Project,** *to 1978*

Hampton, William. The Byker Community Development Project, 1974-1978 / William Hampton and Iris Walkland. — Newcastle (MEA House, Ellison Pl., Newcastle upon Tyne NE1 8XS) : Newcastle upon Tyne Council for Voluntary Service, c1980. — 77p ; 30cm
£2.00 (pbk) B82-25956

361.6′09429 — Wales. Regional planning. Political aspects

Clavel, Pierre. Opposition planning in Wales and Appalachia. — Cardiff : University of Wales Press, Dec.1982. — [256]p
ISBN 0-7083-0832-5 : £12.95 : CIP entry
Also classified at 361.6′0974 B82-30831

361.6′0943′55 — West Germany. North Rhine-Westphalia. Regional development *compared with* **regional development of North-west England**

Bowden, Phyllis. North Rhine Westphalia: North West England : regional development in action / by Phyllis Bowden. — London : Anglo-German Foundation for the Study of Industrial Society, c1979. — xv,119p : maps ; 21cm
ISBN 0-905492-17-x (pbk) : £7.95
Primary classification 361.6′09427 B82-17063

361.6′0974 — United States. Appalachian region. Regional planning. Political aspects

Clavel, Pierre. Opposition planning in Wales and Appalachia. — Cardiff : University of Wales Press, Dec.1982. — [256]p
ISBN 0-7083-0832-5 : £12.95 : CIP entry
Primary classification 361.6′09429 B82-30831

361.6′1 — Coastal regions. Regional planning

United Nations. *Ocean Economics and Technology Branch.* Coastal area management and development. — Oxford : Pergamon, Oct.1982. — [184]p
ISBN 0-08-023393-7 : £20.00 : CIP entry
B82-25166

361.6′1 — Policy studies

Hogwood, Brian W.. The policy orientation / Brian W. Hogwood and Lewis A. Gunn. — Glasgow (16 Richmond St., Glasgow G1 1XQ) : Centre for the Study of Public Policy, University of Strathclyde, [1981]. — 28p : 1ill ; 21cm. — (Policy analysis teaching package ; PAT 1.0)
Cover title. — Bibliography: p26
Unpriced (pbk) B82-01622

361.6′1 — Regional planning — *Conference proceedings*

Planning theory. — Oxford : Pergamon, July 1982. — [330]p. — (Urban and regional planning series)
Conference papers
ISBN 0-08-027449-8 : £24.00 : CIP entry
B82-17928

361.6′1 — Social planning

Critical readings in planning theory. — Oxford : Pergamon, June 1982. — [260]p. — (Urban and regional planning series ; v.27) (Pergamon international library)
ISBN 0-08-024681-8 (cased) : £13.50 : CIP entry
ISBN 0-08-024680-x (pbk) : £7.50 B82-10592

Progress in resource management and environmental planning. — Chichester : Wiley
Vol.3. — Oct.1981. — [320]p
ISBN 0-471-27968-4 : £15.00 : CIP entry
B81-28846

361.6′1 — Social services. Policies. Evaluation

Evaluating and optimizing public policy / edited by Dennis J. Palumbo, Stephen B. Fawcett, Paula Wright. — Lexington, Mass. : Lexington Books ; [Aldershot] : Gower [distributor], 1981. — xv,223p ; 24cm
Includes bibliographies and index
ISBN 0-669-04306-0 : Unpriced B82-06400

361.6′1′018 — Policy analysis. Methodology

House, Peter W.. The art of public policy analysis : the arena of regulations and resources / Peter W. House. — Beverly Hills ; London : Sage, c1982. — 296p ; 22cm. — (Sage library of social research ; v.135)
Bibliography: p289-295
ISBN 0-8039-1764-3 (cased) : Unpriced
ISBN 0-8039-1765-1 (pbk) : Unpriced
B82-25549

361.6′1′05 — Social planning — *Serials*

Progress in planning. — Vol.16. — Oxford : Pergamon, Jan.1982. — [246]p
ISBN 0-08-029080-9 (pbk) : £24.00 : CIP entry
B81-38299

Progress in planning. — 17. — Oxford : Pergamon, July 1982. — [272]p
ISBN 0-08-029701-3 : £28.00 : CIP entry
B82-17927

361.6′1′072 — Social planning. Evaluation

Rossi, Peter H.. Evaluation : a systematic approach / Peter H. Rossi, Howard E. Freeman with the collaboration of Sonia Rosenbaum. — 2nd ed. — Beverly Hills ; London : Sage, c1982. — 351p : ill ; 24cm
Previous ed.: 1979. — Bibliography: p331-344. — Includes index
ISBN 0-8039-1784-8 : £12.50 B82-24074

361.6′1′0722 — United States. Social policies. Implementation by government agencies — *Case studies*

Implementing public policy / edited by Dennis J. Palumbo, Marvin A. Harder. — Lexington, Mass. : Lexington Books ; [Aldershot] : Gower [distributor], 1981. — xvi,168p : ill ; 24cm. — (Policy Studies Organization series)
Includes bibliographies and index
ISBN 0-669-04305-2 : £12.50 B82-00841

361.6′1′0724 — United States. Government. Social policies. Microeconometric models — *Conference proceedings*

Microeconomic simulation models for public policy analysis : a 1978 conference sponsored by the Institute for Research on Poverty, Mathematica Policy Research, Inc., The National Science Foundation / edited by Robert H. Haveman, Kevin Hollenbeck. — New York ; London : Academic Press, 1980. — (Institute for Research on Poverty monograph series)
Vol.2: Sectoral, regional, and general equilibrium models. — xxx,285p : ill ; 24cm
Bibliography: p267-282. — Includes index
ISBN 0-12-333202-8 : £16.60 B82-06538

361.6′1′091724 — Developing countries. Social planning

Conyers, Diana. An introduction to social planning in the Third World / Diana Conyers. — Chichester : Wiley, c1982. — xii,224p : ill,maps ; 24cm. — (Social development in the Third World)
Includes bibliographies and index
ISBN 0-471-10043-9 (cased) : Unpriced : CIP rev.
ISBN 0-471-10044-7 (pbk) : Unpriced
B82-01102

Hardiman, Margaret. The social dimensions of development : social policy and planning in the Third World. — Chichester : Wiley, Aug.1982. — [320]p
ISBN 0-471-10184-2 (cased) : £14.50 : CIP entry
ISBN 0-471-10193-1 (pbk) : £7.00 B82-22796

Planning processes in developing countries : techniques and achievements / edited by Wade D. Cook, Tillo E. Kuhn. — Amsterdam ; Oxford : North-Holland, 1982. — vi,416p : ill,maps ; 25cm. — (TIMS studies in the management sciences ; v.17)
ISBN 0-444-86344-3 : £31.65 B82-27162

361.6′1′0941 — Great Britain. Social policies

What sort of society?. — Oxford : Martin Robertson, Sept.1982. — [250]p
ISBN 0-85520-523-7 (cased) : £15.00 : CIP entry
ISBN 0-85520-524-5 (pbk) : £4.95
Primary classification 330.941′0858
B82-20204

361.6′1′0941 — Great Britain. Social policies. Decision making. Applications of social sciences research

Bulmer, Martin. The uses of social research : social investigation in public policy-making / Martin Bulmer. — London : Allen & Unwin, 1982. — xvi,184p : ill ; 23cm. — (Contemporary social research series ; 3)
Bibliography: p168-180. — Includes index
ISBN 0-04-312011-3 (cased) : Unpriced : CIP rev.
ISBN 0-04-312012-1 (pbk) : Unpriced
B82-07224

361.6′1′0941 — Great Britain. Social services. Policies of government

Webb, Adrian. Whither state welfare? : policy and implementation in the personal social services 1979-80 / Adrian Webb, Gerald Wistow. — London : Royal Institute of Public Administration, 1982. — 93p : 1ill ; 21cm. — (RIPA Studies ; 8)
ISBN 0-900628-25-1 (pbk) : £2.95 B82-35988

361.6′1′09417 — Ireland *(Republic)*. **Social planning. Technological aspects** — *Conference proceedings*

Technology and the infrastructure : Ireland in the Year 2000 : proceedings of a colloquy, Kilkea Castle, April 1981. — Dublin : An Foras Forbartha, 1981. — v,85p : ill,4forms ; 30cm. — (Ireland in the year 2000)
ISBN 0-906120-51-9 (pbk) : £3.00 B82-15375

361.6′1′0942185 — London. Brent *(London Borough)*. **Social planning. Policies of Brent. Council** — *Serials*

Brent. *Chief Executive′s Office*. Cross council review / Chief Executive′s Office. — 1981-. — [London] ([Town Hall, Forty La., Wembley Park, HA9 9HD]) : London Borough of Brent, 1981-. — v. ; 30cm
Annual
ISSN 0263-0133 = Cross council review - London Borough of Brent. Chief Executive′s Office : Unpriced B82-13401

361.6′1′095694 — Israel. Social planning

Can planning replace politics? : the Israeli experience / edited by Raphaella Bilski ... [et al.]. — The Hague ; London : Nijhoff, c1980. — 337p : ill ; 25cm. — (The Van Leer Jerusalem Foundation series)
ISBN 90-247-2324-8 : Unpriced B82-40807

361.6′1′0973 — United States. Government. Social policies. Effectiveness. Evaluation

Judd, Charles M.. Estimating the effects of social interventions / Charles M. Judd and David A. Kenny. — Cambridge : Cambridge University Press, 1981. — xii,243p : ill ; 24cm
Bibliography: p230-238. — Includes index
ISBN 0-521-22975-8 : £19.50
ISBN 0-521-29755-9 (pbk) : £6.95 B82-08355

Models for analysis of social policy : an introduction / Ron Haskins and James J. Gallagher, editors. — Norwood, N.J. : Ablex ; London (3 Henrietta St., WC2E 8LU) : Eurospan [distributor], c1981. — xvii,238p : ill ; 24cm. — (Advances in child and family policy ; v.1)
Includes bibliographies and index
ISBN 0-89391-084-8 : £16.95 B82-27695

361.6′1′0973 — United States. Regional planning, *to 1981*

The **American** planner. — London : Methuen, Jan.1983. — [450]p
ISBN 0-416-33360-5 : £15.00 : CIP entry
B82-34451

361.6′1′09811 — Brazil. Amazon River Basin. Social development. Effects of Transamazônica highway

Smith, Nigel J. H.. Rainforest corridors : the transamazon colonization scheme / Nigel J.H. Smith. — Berkeley ; London : University of California Press, c1982. — xvii,248p : ill,maps ; 23cm
Bibliography: p201-227. — Includes index
ISBN 0-520-04497-5 : £21.50 B82-40211

361.6′14 — Great Britain. Welfare rights — *Serials*

Rights worker news. — Feb. 1981-. — Edinburgh (132 Lauriston Place, Edinburgh) : Citizens Rights Office, 1981-. — v. ; 30cm
Six issues yearly. — Continues: CRO newsletter. — Description based on: Issue no.25
ISSN 0262-9658 = Rights worker news : Unpriced B82-30482

361.6′8′0973 — United States. Public welfare services. Policies of government. Reform — *Conference proceedings*

Welfare reform in America : perspectives and prospects / Paul M. Sommers, editor. — Boston, [Mass.] ; London : Kluwer-Nijhoff, c1982. — viii,254p : ill,1map ; 24cm. — (Middlebury Conference series on economic issues)
Conference papers. — Includes bibliographies
ISBN 0-89838-079-0 : Unpriced B82-27295

361.7 — PRIVATE SOCIAL WELFARE

361.7 — Great Britain. Voluntary community work by retired persons — *Personal observations*

Bornat, Joanna. Have you heard — / [written by Joanna Bornat]. — [London] : Help the Aged Education Department in association with London Voluntary Service Council, [1982?]. — 19p : ill(some col.),ports ; 25cm
ISBN 0-905852-12-5 (unbound) : Unpriced
B82-40561

361.7 — Scotland. Lothian Region. Community work by secondary school students. Projects

Low, Isabelle. Organising school-based community service : a practical guide for teachers and others interested in developing community service activities for school pupils / [written by Isabelle Low]. — Edinburgh (5 Leamington Terrace, Edinburgh, EH10 4JW) : Lothian Group, Association for Community Service in Education, 1980. — 54p : ill ; 30cm
Cover title. — In a folder
Unpriced (pbk) B82-25242

361.7′025 — Voluntary welfare services — *Directories*

Nineham, Gillian. The international directory of voluntary work. — 2nd ed. / Gillian Nineham and David Woodworth. — Oxford : Vacation Work, 1982. — viii,173p ; 23cm
Previous ed.: 1979. — Includes index
ISBN 0-907638-00-7 : £6.50 B82-14461

361.7'06'0416 — Northern Ireland. Voluntary welfare work. Organisations — *For youth work*

Partnership : the role of voluntary organisations in relation to the Education and Library Boards : a discussion paper. — Belfast : Standing Conference of Youth Organisations in Northern Ireland, [1979]. — 16leaves ; 30cm. — (Occasional paper / [Standing Conference of Youth Organisations in Northern Ireland] ; no.3)
Cover title
ISBN 0-906797-00-4 (spiral) : £0.50
B82-00097

361.7'06'042356 — Devon. Exeter. Councils for voluntary service: Exeter Council for Voluntary Service, *1968-1981*

Grundy, Martin H.. Looking back - and forward : an address by the retiring General Secretary, Martin H. Grundy to the Executive Committee, 7th April 1981. — Exeter (1 Wynards, Magdalen St., Exeter EX2 4HX) : ExVos, [1981]. — 9p ; 22cm
Unpriced (pbk) B82-05935

361.7'0941 — Great Britain. Charities. Fund raising — *Manuals*

Industrial sponsorship and joint promotions. — London (9 Mansfield Place, NW3 1HS) : Directory of Social Change, Nov.1981. — [128]p
ISBN 0-907164-07-2 (pbk) : £2.95 : CIP entry
B81-33623

Raising money from government. — London (9 Mansfield Place, NW3 1HS) : Directory of Social Change, Nov.1981. — [144]p
ISBN 0-907164-06-4 (pbk) : £2.95 : CIP entry
B81-33626

Raising money from industry. — London (9 Mansfield Place, NW3 1HS) : Directory of Social Change, Nov.1981. — [128]p
ISBN 0-907164-05-6 (pbk) : £2.95 : CIP entry
B81-33625

Raising money from trusts. — London (9 Mansfield Place, NW3 1HS) : Directory of Social Change, Nov.1981. — [128]p
ISBN 0-907164-04-8 (pbk) : £2.95 : CIP entry
B81-33624

361.7'0941 — Great Britain. Voluntary work — *Practical information — For young persons*

Volunteering to help others — and yourself. — [Edinburgh] ([4 Queensferry St., Edinburgh EH2 4PA]) : Scottish Community Education Centre, [1981]. — 12p : ill ; 21cm
Cover title. — Text on inside covers
Unpriced (pbk) B82-00628

361.7'09411 — Scotland. Tenants' associations & residents' associations

Wilson, Monica. Tenants associated : a survey of tenants groups in Scotland / written by Monica Wilson. — [Glasgow] : Scottish Consumer Council, [1981]. — iv,67p ; 21cm
ISBN 0-907067-07-7 (pbk) : £1.50 B82-22894

361.7'09414'43 — Scotland. Strathclyde Region. Glasgow. Tenants' associations & residents' associations — *Directories*

Directory of community groups : Glasgow. — [Glasgow] : TPAS, [1982?]. — 43p : 1ill ; 30cm
ISBN 0-903589-65-6 (unbound) : £0.40
B82-35578

361.7'4'0924 — England. Philanthropy. Edwards, John Passmore — *Biographies*

Best, R. S.. The life and good works of John Passmore Edwards / by R.S. Best ; with an appendix by Peter Laws and illustrations and cover design by C.M. Pellow. — Redruth : Truran, 1982. — 48p : ill,1port ; 21cm
Bibliography: p46
ISBN 0-907566-18-9 (pbk) : Unpriced
B82-35324

361.7'5 — Church Army. Welfare work — *Case studies*

Lynch, Donald. Action stations : Church Army officers at work / by Donald Lynch. — Wallingford : Gem, c1981. — 101p : ill,ports ; 20cm
ISBN 0-906802-03-2 (pbk) : £1.85 B82-37076

361.7'5 — England. Catholic welfare services — *Directories — Serials*

Catholic welfare services, England/Wales. — 1981-. — Abingdon (1a Stert St., Abingdon, Oxon. OX14 3JF) : Social Welfare Commission, [1981]-. — v. ; 30cm
£1.50 B82-23586

361.7'63'0973 — United States. Non-profit making organisations. Donations. Effects of taxation

Hopkins, Bruce R.. Charitable giving and tax-exempt organizations : the impact of the 1981 Tax Act / Bruce R. Hopkins. — New York ; Chichester, Wiley, c1982. — xi,166p ; 22cm
ISBN 0-471-86736-5 : £21.75 B82-26473

361.7'632 — Charities. Fund raising — *Manuals*

Feek, Warren. Hitting the right notes : information on applying for funds / Warren Feek. — Leicester : National Youth Bureau, 1982. — 22p : ill ; 30cm. — (Talk about management ; 2)
Cover title. — Text on inside cover
ISBN 0-86155-056-0 (pbk) : £1.20 B82-38227

361.7'632 — Grant making charities. Decision making

Feek, Warren. Can you credit it? : grant-givers' views on funding applications / Warren Feek. — Leicester : National Youth Bureau, 1982. — 20p : ill ; 30cm. — (Talk about management ; 3)
Cover title. — Text on inside cover
ISBN 0-86155-057-9 (pbk) : £1.20 B82-38222

361.7'632'0681 — Great Britain. Charities. Financial management — *Conference proceedings*

Charities Aid Foundation. Charity conference report : charity finance : prospects, opportunities and management : Drapers' Hall, London, 4th November 1981. — Tonbridge : Charities Aid Foundation, [1981]. — 46p ; 21cm
ISBN 0-904757-13-7 (pbk) : £2.50 B82-25023

361.7'632'0942 — England. Charities: Sir James Reckitt Charity, *to 1979*

Sir James Reckitt Charity. A history of the Sir James Reckitt Charity 1921-1979 / B.N. Reckitt. — [Withernsea] ([32 Louville Ave., Withernsea, N. Humberside HU19 2PB]) : [Trustees of the Sir James Reckitt Charity], 1981. — 53p,[6]leaves of plates : ill,ports(some col.),geneal.tables ; 22cm
Bibliography: p40. — Includes index
Private circulation B82-07535

361.7'634'09411 — Scotland. Voluntary welfare services: British Red Cross Society. *Scottish Branch — Serials*

Scottish Red Cross news. — Issue no.1 (Nov. 1981)-. — [Glasgow] ([Alexandra House, 204 Bath St., Glasgow G2 4HL]) : Appeals & Publicity Dept, Scottish Branch, British Red Cross Society, 1981-. — v. : ill,maps ports ; 43cm
Continues: Spectrum (Glasgow)
ISSN 0263-1504 = Scottish Red Cross news : Unpriced B82-19857

361.8 — COMMUNITY SOCIAL WELFARE

361.8 — Community action groups. Leadership — *Manuals*

Kahn, Si. Organizing : a guide for grassroots leaders / Si Kahn. — New York ; London : McGraw-Hill, 1982. — xi,387p ; 21cm
Includes index
ISBN 0-07-033215-0 (cased) : £9.95
ISBN 0-07-033199-5 (pbk) : Unpriced
B82-16378

361.8 — Community work

Social & community work in a multiracial society . — London : Harper and Row, Jan.1982. — [336]p
ISBN 0-06-318197-5 (cased) : £9.95 : CIP entry
ISBN 0-06-318198-3 (pbk) : £5.95 B81-33968

361.8 — Community work. Organisation — *Manuals*

Twelvetrees, Alan. Community work / Alan Twelvetrees. — London : Macmillan, 1982. — vii,137p ; 22cm. — (Practical social work)
Bibliography: p129-134. — Includes index
ISBN 0-333-30900-6 (cased) : Unpriced
ISBN 0-333-30901-4 (pbk) : Unpriced
B82-24539

361.8'07'1241 — Great Britain. Secondary schools. Curriculum subjects: Community work

Scrimshaw, Peter. Community service, social education and the curriculum / Peter Scrimshaw. — London : Hodder and Stoughton, 1981. — 85p ; 25cm
Bibliography: p83-85
ISBN 0-340-24450-x (pbk) : £3.95 : CIP rev.
B81-26741

361.8'0722 — Great Britain. Community work — *Case studies*

Community work : case studies / edited by Gary Craig. — 2nd ed. — [London] ([Colombo Street Centre, 22 Colombo St, SE1 8DP]) : [Association of Community Workers], [1980?]. — 47p ; 30cm
Cover title. — Previous ed.: 1974
Unpriced (pbk) B82-08247

361.8'0941 — Great Britain. Community action groups. Organisation — *Manuals*

Smith, Mark, *19---*. Organise! : a guide to practical politics for youth and community groups / [Mark Smith]. — Leicester : National Association of Youth Clubs, 1981. — 71p : ill,form ; 30cm
Includes bibliographies and index
ISBN 0-907095-07-0 (pbk) : Unpriced
B82-09962

361.8'0941 — Great Britain. Community work. Management committees

Feek, Warren. Management committees : practising community control / Warren Feek. — [Leicester] : [National Youth Bureau], [1982]. — 20p : ill ; 30cm. — (Talk about management ; 1)
Cover title
ISBN 0-86155-053-6 (pbk) : £1.00 B82-38228

361.8'0941 — Great Britain. Community work — *Manuals*

The Community workers' skills manual / the Association of Community Workers. — 2nd ed. — London (Colombo Street Centre, 22 Colombo St, SE1 8DP) : The Association, 1981, c1979. — viii,95p : ill ; 26cm
Cover title
£3.00 (pbk) B82-08246

361.8'0941 — Great Britain. Community work. Organisations: Community Projects Foundation. Projects — *Case studies*

Community works. — London : Community Projects Foundation
1 / editor: Michaela Dungate ; authors: Colin & Mog Ball, Stewart & Susan Seale. — 1980. — xi,156p : ill,1map,2plans ; 21cm
Contents: School's out! / by Colin & Mog Ball — Clarence rules, OK? / by Colin & Mog Ball — Street action / by Stewart & Susan Seale
ISBN 0-902406-17-5 (pbk) : £2.50 B82-20986

361.8'0941'43 — Scotland. Strathclyde Region. Glasgow. Community work

Bryant, Barbara. Change and conflict. — Aberdeen : Aberdeen University Press, Dec.1982. — [240]p
ISBN 0-08-028475-2 (cased) : £11.00 : CIP entry
ISBN 0-08-028480-9 (pbk) : £6.00 B82-32278

361.8'09416 — Northern Ireland. Community work — *Conference proceedings*

Community work in a divided society / [compiled by Hugh Frazer]. — Belfast : Farset Co-operative Press, c1981. — 56p ; 22cm. — (Community action in Northern Ireland ; v.1, no.1)
Conference papers
ISBN 0-9504292-2-8 (pbk) : £2.00 B82-21413

361.8'094167 — Belfast. Shankhill. Community action

Wiener, Ron. The rape & plunder of the Shankill : community action : the Belfast experience / by Ron Wiener ; with a postscript by Jackie Redpath. — 2nd ed. — Belfast : Farset Co-operative Press, 1980. — 176p,[8]p of plates : ill,facsims,maps,plans ; 21cm
Previous ed.: Belfast : Notaems Press, 1978
ISBN 0-9504292-0-1 (pbk) : £3.00 B82-25229

361.8'09422'56 — East Sussex. Brighton. Community action groups — *Serials*

Community information bulletin / Brighton Council for Voluntary Service. — 1979-. — Brighton (c/o Brighton Voluntary Service Centre, 17 Ditchling Rise, Brighton BN1 4QL) : The Council, 1979-. — v. : ill ; 30cm
Six issues yearly. — Description based : 16 (Apr. 1982)
ISSN 0263-0494 = Community information bulletin : £4.00 per year B82-29048

361.8'094239 — Avon. Community action — *Serials*

Field fare : the quarterly magazine of Avon Community Council. — No.1 (May 1981)-. — Bristol (209 Redland Rd, Bristol BS6 6YU) : Avon Community Council, 1981-. — v. : ill ; 30cm
ISSN 0263-984X = Field fare : £3.00 per year B82-40033

361.9 — SOCIAL SERVICES. HISTORICAL AND GEOGRAPHICAL TREATMENT

361'.941 — Great Britain. Social administration

Brown, Muriel. Introduction to social administration in Britain. — 5th ed. — London : Hutchinson Education, Mar.1982. — [288]p
Previous ed.: 1977
ISBN 0-09-146660-1 (cased) : £10.00 : CIP entry
ISBN 0-09-146661-x (pbk) : £4.95 B82-00267

361.941 — Great Britain. Social services. Implications of estimates of government expenditure, *1980-1981.* **Great Britain.** *Parliament. House of Commons. Social Services Committee.* **Government's white papers on public expenditure, the social services** — *Critical studies*

Great Britain. *Department of Health and Social Security.* The government's white papers on public expenditure : the social services : reply by the government to the third report from the Social Services Committee, Session 1979-80 / Department of Health and Social Security. — London : H.M.S.O., [1980]. — 15p ; 25cm. — (Cmnd. ; 8086)
ISBN 0-10-180860-7 (unbound) : £2.10 B82-16068

361'.941 — Great Britain. Welfare services

Social welfare in Britain / [prepared for British Information Services by the Central Office of Information]. — London : Central Office of Information, Publication Division Reference Services, 1980. — 35p ; 21cm
Bibliography: p34-35
Unpriced (pbk) B82-16113

361'.941 — Great Britain. Welfare services, *1962-1974*

Cooper, Joan. The creation of the British personal social services 1962-1974. — London : Heinemann Educational, Dec.1982. — [224]p. — (Studies in social policy and welfare)
ISBN 0-435-82188-1 : £14.50 : CIP entry B82-29770

361'.941 — Great Britain. Welfare services. Policies of government, *1900-1950* — *For schools*

Wood, Sydney. The British welfare state 1900-1950 / Sydney Wood. — Cambridge : Cambridge University Press, 1982. — 47p : ill,maps,3facsims,1plan,ports ; 21cm. — (Cambridge introduction to the history of mankind)
ISBN 0-521-22843-3 (pbk) : £1.95 : CIP rev. B81-32529

361'.941'05 — Great Britain. Social services — *Serials*

[Journal *(Social Services Research Group (England))*]. Journal / Social Services Research Group. — No.1 (Oct. 1977)-. — Carlisle (c/o W.D. Gwynne, Social Services Dept., Cumbria County Council, Geltsdale, The Plains, Wetheral, Carlisle, Cumbria CA4 8LF) : The Group, 1977-. — v. ; 30cm
Irregular. — Description based on: No.12 (Sept. 1981)
ISSN 0144-0640 = Journal - Social Services Research Group : Free to Group members B82-05217

361'.9411 — Scotland. Social services. Cooperation with primary schools

Bruce, Nigel. Interagency cooperation in the primary school : the social work/education interface / Nigel Bruce ; report on research sponsored by the Scottish Education Department and the Social Work Services Group. — [Edinburgh] ([Dept. of Social Administration, University of Edinburgh, 23 Buccleuch Place, Edinburgh EH8 9LN]) : [N. Bruce], 1982. — 192p ; 21cm
Cover title. — Bibliography: p187-190. — Includes index
£2.00 (pbk)
Primary classification 372.9411 B82-32925

361'.9411'0246181 — Scotland. Welfare services — *For midwifery*

Social and statistical facts for student midwives / members of the Education Advisory Group of the Scottish Board of the Royal College of Midwives. — London : Pitman, 1982. — viii,88p : ill,forms,maps ; 23cm
Bibliography: p86-88
ISBN 0-272-79648-4 (pbk) : Unpriced : CIP rev. B82-07415

361'.94127'05 — Scotland. Tayside Region. Dundee region. Welfare services — *Serials*

DASS newsletter. — June/July 1979-. — Dundee (1 High St., Dundee DD1 1TE) : Dundee Association for Social Service, 1979-. — v. : facsims ; 30cm
Six issues yearly. — Continues: DASS. — Supplements accompany some issues. — Description based on: Issue no.38 (Nov./Dec. 1981)
ISSN 0262-6705 = DASS newsletter : Unpriced B82-23600

361'.942581 — Hertfordshire. North Hertfordshire *(District).* **Social services** — *For environment planning*

Social & community facilities topic study / [North Hertfordshire District Council]. — [Letchworth] ([Council Offices, Gernon Rd., Letchworth, Herts. SG6 3JF]) : [The Council], 1978. — 15p : 1map ; 30cm. — (North Hertfordshire district plan. Topic studies)
£0.30 (pbk) B82-11580

361'.9426752 — Essex. Chelmsford. Social services — *For environment planning*

Joint topic reports : education, social and community services, public utilities and resources : Chelmsford town centre district plan. — Chelmsford : Chelmsford Borough Council, 1980. — 37p,5folded leaves of plates : maps ; 30cm
Unpriced (pbk) B82-08724

361'.973 — United States. Social services

Social welfare in society / George T. Martin, Jr and Mayer N. Zald, editors. — New York ; Guildford : Columbia University Press, 1981. — xi,600p : ill ; 24cm
Bibliography: p539-572. — Includes index
ISBN 0-231-04922-6 (cased) : £21.60
ISBN 0-231-04923-4 (pbk) : £10.80 B82-05617

361'.973 — United States. Welfare services

Helping networks and human services / Charles Froland ... [et al.] ; foreword by Alice H. Collins. — Beverly Hills ; London : Sage, c1981. — 200p : ill ; 21cm. — (Sage library of social research ; v.128)
Bibliography: p193-198
ISBN 0-8039-1625-6 (cased) : Unpriced
ISBN 0-8039-1626-4 (pbk) : £6.50 B82-17077

Segalman, Ralph. Poverty in America : the welfare dilemma / Ralph Segalman, Asoke Basu. — Westport, Conn. ; London : Greenwood Press, 1981. — xvi,418p ; 25cm. — (Contributions in sociology, ISSN 0084-9278 ; no.39)
Bibliography: p377-397. — Includes index
ISBN 0-313-20751-8 : £26.75 B82-18186

Spindler, Arthur. Public welfare / Arthur Spindler. — New York ; London : Human Sciences, c1979. — 513p : ill,2maps ; 24cm
Includes index
ISBN 0-87705-325-1 : Unpriced B82-24171

361'.973 — United States. Welfare services, *1930-1980*

Patterson, James T.. The welfare state in America, 1930-1980 / James T. Patterson. — Durham : British Association for American Studies, 1981. — 43p : ill ; 22cm. — (BAAS pamphlets in American studies ; 7)
Bibliography: p37-39
ISBN 0-9504601-7-6 (pbk) : Unpriced B82-12023

361'.973 — United States. Welfare services. Organisation

Azarnoff, Roy S.. Delivering human services / Roy S. Azarnoff, Jerome S. Seliger. — Englewood Cliffs ; London : Prentice-Hall, c1982. — xv,252p : ill,forms ; 24cm
Includes index
ISBN 0-13-198317-2 : £14.20 B82-20122

362 — SOCIAL WELFARE. PROBLEMS AND SERVICES

362'.042 — Great Britain. Socially disadvantaged persons. Transmitted deprivation

Coffield, Frank. Cycles of deprivation : an inaugural lecture / by Frank Coffield. — [Durham] : University of Durham, 1982. — 23p : ill,geneal.tables ; 22cm
Bibliography: p22-23
£0.60 (pbk) B82-31108

362'.042'05 — Social problems — *Serials*

Research in social problems and public policy : a research annual. — Vol.1 (1979)-. — Greenwich, Conn. : JAI Press ; London (3 Henrietta St., WC2E 8LU) : Distributed by JAICON Press, 1979-. — v. ; 24cm
ISSN 0196-1152 = Research in social problems and public policy : £22.85 B82-02340

362'.0425'019 — Social problems. Alleviation. Applications of attribution theory

Attribution theory and research : conceptual, developmental and social dimensions. — London : Academic Press, Jan.1983. — [460]p. — (European monographs in social psychology ; no.32)
ISBN 0-12-380980-0 : CIP entry B82-33463

362.1 — WELFARE SERVICES FOR THE PHYSICALLY ILL

362.1 — England. Health services. Distribution. Inequalities. Social aspects

Whitelegg, John. Inequalities in health care. — Retford (16 Whitehall Rd., Retford, Notts.) : Straw Barnes Press, Oct.1982. — [170]p
ISBN 0-946307-00-8 (pbk) : £6.95 : CIP entry B82-31328

362.1 — England. National health services. Patients. Transport — *Inquiry reports*

Patient transport services / a report of a working party. — Sheffield (Public Relations Office, Trent Regional Health Authority, Old Fulwood Rd, Sheffield) : Trent Regional Health Authority on behalf of the National Health Service, 1981. — 123p ; 21cm
£3.00 (pbk) B82-02120

362.1 — Great Britain. Medical services. Regional planning teams

Mullen, Penelope. Survey of planning teams : methodology and basic results / Penelope Mullen, Kate Murray Sykes, William E. Kearns. — [Birmingham] : University of Birmingham, Health Services Management Centre, 1981. — 29,[15]p : ill,facsims,forms ; 21cm. — (Occasional paper ; 29)
ISBN 0-7044-0521-0 (pbk) : Unpriced
B82-17713

362.1 — Great Britain. Private health services — *Directories — Serials*

The **Directory** of private hospitals & health services. — 1983. — London : Longman, Jan.1983. — [750]p
ISBN 0-582-90356-4 : £20.00 : CIP entry
Also classified at 362.1'1 B82-39296

362.1 — Great Britain. Private medical services — *Communist Party of Great Britain viewpoints*

Iliffe, Steve. Condition critical : the case against private medicine / by Steve Iliffe. — London : Communist Party of Great Britain, 1982. — 40p : ill,1map,facsims ; 21cm. — (A Communist Party pamphlet)
Text on inside covers
ISBN 0-86224-016-6 (pbk) : £0.50 B82-21776

362.1 — Great Britain. Private medical services — *Socialist viewpoints*

Fightback *(Campaign)*. Going private : the case against private medicine / [Fightback and the Politics of Health Group]. — London : [Fightback], [1981?]. — 46p : ill ; 26cm
Cover title. — Text on inside covers. — Bibliography: p46
ISBN 0-907840-00-0 (pbk) : £0.70 B82-12781

362.1 — Health services

World health environmental surveys / [HERMES]. — London : IMSWORLD, 1978. — 390p in various pagings ; 30cm
ISBN 0-906184-02-9 (pbk) : Unpriced
B82-11554

362.1 — Man. Diseases. Aetiology. Theories — *Anthropological perspectives*

Murdock, George Peter. Theories of illness : a world survey / George Peter Murdock. — Pittsburgh : University of Pittsburgh Press ; London : Feffer and Simons, c1980. — xv,127p ; 22cm
Includes bibliographies and index
ISBN 0-8229-3428-0 : Unpriced B82-23745

362.1 — Medical technology. Social aspects

Technology and the future of health care / edited by John B. McKinlay. — Cambridge, Mass. ; London : MIT, c1982. — xiv,454p : ill ; 24cm. — (Milbank reader ; 8)
Includes bibliographies and index
ISBN 0-262-13183-8 (cased) : £14.00
ISBN 0-262-63084-2 (pbk) : Unpriced
B82-37517

362.1 — Medicine. Social aspects

Cockerham, William C.. Medical sociology / William C. Cockerham. — 2nd ed. — Englewood Cliffs ; London : Prentice-Hall, c1982. — x,356p ; 24cm. — (Prentice-Hall series in sociology)
Previous ed.: 1978. — Bibliography: p317-346. — Includes index
ISBN 0-13-573410-x : £15.70 B82-16708

Inglis, Brian. The diseases of civilisation / Brian Inglis. — London : Hodder and Stoughton, 1981. — xi,371p ; 24cm
Bibliography: p340-358. — Includes index
ISBN 0-340-21717-0 : £10.95 : CIP rev.
B81-17532

McKeown, Thomas. The role of medicine : dream, mirage or nemesis? / Thomas McKeown. — London : Nuffield Provincial Hospitals Trust, 1976. — xv,180p : ill ; 23cm. — (The Rock Carling Fellowship ; 1976)
ISBN 0-900574-24-0 : £3.25 B82-25658

362.1 — Sick persons. Visiting — *For Christians*

Autton, Norman. A handbook of sick visiting / by Norman Autton. — London : Mowbray, 1981. — viii,162p ; 18cm
Bibliography: p156-157. — Includes index
ISBN 0-264-66779-4 (pbk) : £3.50 : CIP rev.
B81-30635

362.1'028'54 — England. National health services. Applications of digital computer systems

A **Time** for decision? : computing policy and practice in the NHS : four papers / S.I. Herbert ... [et al.]. — London : Nuffield Provincial Hospitals Trust, c1982. — vi,100,[40]p : ill ; 22cm
Bibliography: 7p
ISBN 0-904956-23-7 (pbk) : Unpriced
B82-25653

362.1'042 — Man. Health. Social aspects

Keywood, Olive. Personal and community health / Olive Keywood. — Oxford : Blackwell Scientific, 1982. — viii,263p : ill ; 22cm
Bibliography: p245-246. — Includes index
ISBN 0-632-00807-5 (pbk) : £4.00 : CIP rev.
B82-11972

362.1'0422 — Medical services. Risks

Weitz, Martin. Health shock / Martin Weitz. — rev. ed. — Feltham : Hamlyn, 1982. — 343p : ill ; 18cm
Previous ed.: Newton Abbot : David and Charles, 1980. — Includes index
ISBN 0-600-20441-3 (pbk) : £1.75 B82-14161

362.1'0425 — Christian medical missions

McGilvray, James C.. The quest for health and wholeness / James C. McGilvray. — Tübingen : German Institute for Medical Missions ; [Oxford] : Distributed by Becket Publications, 1981. — xvi,118p ; 21cm
Bibliography: p117-118
ISBN 0-7289-0014-9 (pbk) : Unpriced
B82-34796

362.1'0425 — Community medicine — *Serials*

Recent advances in community medicine. — No.2. — Edinburgh : Churchill Livingstone, Oct.1981. — [212]p
ISBN 0-443-02357-3 : £15.00 : CIP entry
ISSN 0144-1256 B81-25317

362.1'0425 — England. Community health councils

Mental handicap and the Community Health Council : report of the conference held at Lea Castle Hospital, Wolverley near Kidderminster, on Thursday, 25th September, 1975 / [papers presented by G.B. Simon, Brian Watkin, Peggy Jay]. — Kidderminster (Wolverhampton Rd., Kidderminster, Worcs.) : Institute of Mental Subnormality, 1976. — 32p ; 21cm. — (IMS conference proceedings)
£1.00 (pbk) B82-35268

362.1'0425 — England. Community primary health services. Volunteers. Role, *1978-1980* **—** *Case studies*

Volunteers in primary health care. — Berkhamsted : Volunteer Centre, 1981. — 22p ; 22cm
Contents: Medway Health District : the voluntary services co-ordinator / Kaye Davidson — The Milson Road Project / Ian Morcroft
ISBN 0-904647-15-3 (pbk) : £1.00 B82-04328

362.1'0425 — General practice

Morrell, David Cameron. An introduction to primary medical care / D.C. Morrell. — 2nd ed. — Edinburgh : Churchill Livingstone, 1981. — vii,130p : ill ; 22cm. — (Churchill Livingstone medical text)
Previous ed.: 1976. — Includes index
ISBN 0-443-02459-6 (pbk) : £3.25 : CIP rev.
B81-32014

362.1'0425 — General practice. Delegation

Bowling, Ann. Delegation in general practice. — London : Tavistock Publications, Sept.1981. — [256]p
ISBN 0-422-77490-1 : £10.50 : CIP entry
B81-22473

362.1'0425 — General practice. Role of welfare workers — *Sociological perspectives*

Social work and primary health care. — London : Academic Press, Aug.1982. — [370]p
ISBN 0-12-174740-9 : CIP entry B82-19249

362.1'0425 — Great Britain. Community health services. Great Britain. *Department of Health and Social Security.* **Care in the community —** *Trade union viewpoints*

Wilson, Eric. Care in the community : COHSE's response to the consultative paper / Eric Wilson, Albert Spanswick. — Banstead (Glen House, High St., Banstead, Surrey, SM7 2LH) : Confederation of Health Service Employees, 1981. — 22p ; 21cm
Text on inside cover
£0.75 (pbk) B82-28055

362.1'0425 — Great Britain. National health services. Districts. Administration

Nichol, D. K.. Problems of integration at the district and unit levels / D.K. Nichol. — Manchester (Manchester Business School, Booth Street West, Manchester M15 6PB) : Health Services Management Unit, University of Manchester, 1981. — 11leaves ; 30cm. — (Working paper series / University of Manchester. Health Services Management Unit, ISSN 0141-2647 ; no.49)
At head of title: Fourth International Seminar for Administrators, University of Toronto, May 1981
£2.00 (pbk) B82-05614

362.1'0425 — Patients. Rehabilitation

Mattingly, Stephen. Rehabilitation today in Great Britain. — 2nd ed. — London : Update Publications, Sept.1981. — [182]p
Previous ed.: 1977
ISBN 0-906141-34-6 (pbk) : £7.00 : CIP entry
B81-24626

362.1'0425 — Sick persons. Community care — *For welfare work*

Halliburton, Primrose. Get help : a guide for social workers to the management of illness in the community / Primrose Halliburton and Kate Quelch. — London : Tavistock, 1981. — 142p ; 24cm
Bibliography: p132
ISBN 0-422-77560-6 (cased) : Unpriced : CIP rev.
ISBN 0-422-77570-3 (pbk) : £2.95 B81-31744

362.1'0425 — United States. Health maintenance organisations

Health maintenance organisations / edited by John B. McKinlay. — Cambridge, Mass. ; London : MIT, c1981. — xiv,452p : ill ; 24cm. — (Milbank readers ; 5)
Includes bibliographies and index
ISBN 0-262-13180-3 (cased) : £14.00
ISBN 0-262-63081-8 (pbk) : Unpriced
B82-35668

362.1'04256 — Great Britain. Medicine. Nursing. Counselling

Tschudin, Verena. Counselling skills for nurses / Verena Tschudin ; with a foreword by Gaynor Nurse. — London : Baillière Tindall, 1982. — xii,140p : ill ; 21cm
Bibliography: p133-136. — Includes index
ISBN 0-7020-0909-1 (pbk) : £5.00 : CIP rev.
B82-04622

362.1'05 — Health services for families — *Serials*

Advances in international maternal and child health. — Vol.1-. — Oxford : Oxford University Press, 1981-. — v. ; 25cm
Annual
ISSN 0262-8244 = Advances in international maternal and child health : £15.00 B82-09681

362.1'05 — Health services — *Sociological perspectives — Serials*

Research in the sociology of health care : a research annual. — Vol.1 (1980)-. — Greenwich, Conn. : JAI Press ; London (3 Henrietta St., WC2E 8LU) : Distributed by JAICON Press, 1980-. — v. ; 24cm
£26.20 B82-02336

362.1'05 — Health services — *Sociological perspectives* — *Serials* continuation
Research in the sociology of health care. Supplement. — 1 (1981)-. — Greenwich, Conn. : JAI Press ; London (3 Henrietta St., WC2E 8LU) : Distributed by JAICON Press, 1981-. — v. ; 24cm
Supplement to: Research in the sociology of health care
£21.95 B82-02337

362.1'068 — Great Britain. National health services. Decision making
Lee, Kenneth, *1944-*. Policy-making and planning in the health sector / Kenneth Lee and Anne Mills. — London : Croom Helm, c1982. — 201p : ill ; 23cm
Bibliography: p187-197. — Includes index
ISBN 0-85664-965-1 : £13.95 : CIP rev. B82-04811

362.1'068'1 — Great Britain. National health services. Financial management — *Inquiry reports*
Great Britain. *Parliament. House of Commons. Committee of Public Accounts.* Seventeenth report from the Committee of Public Accounts : together with the proceedings of the committee, minutes of evidence and appendices : session 1980-81 : financial control and accountability in the National Health Service. — London : H.M.S.O., [1981]. — xxv,118p ; 25cm. — ([HC] ; 255)
ISBN 0-10-225581-4 (pbk) : £7.25 B82-05637

362.1'068'4 — Great Britain. National health services. Management. Teams
Nichol, Brian. The team development process for health service administrators / Brian Nichol. — Manchester (Manchester Business School, Booth Street West, Manchester M15 6PB) : Health Services Management Unit, University of Manchester, [1981]. — 12,4leaves ; 30cm. — (Working paper series / Health Services Management Unit, Department of Social Administration, University of Manchester, ISSN 0141-2647 ; no.57)
£2.00 (pbk) B82-05586

362.1'07'11411 — Scotland. National health services. Administrators. Training schemes: National Administrative Training Scheme, *1956-1981*
Scottish Health Service National Administrative Training Scheme : the first twenty five years 1956-1981 / [edited and produced by G.H. France]. — [Edinburgh] ([Crewe Rd. South, Edinburgh, EH4 2LF]) : [Management Education and Training Division], [1981]. — 21p ; 30cm
Cover title
Unpriced (pbk) B82-04943

362.1'09 — Paramedical services, *to 1980*
Macdonald, E. M.. World-wide conquests of disabilities : the history, development and present functions of the remedial services / E.M. Macdonald ; foreword by Hugh J. Glanville. — London : Baillière Tindall, 1981. — 299p ; 22cm
Bibliography: p281-284. — Includes index
ISBN 0-7020-0832-x (pbk) : £8.50 : CIP rev. B80-24301

362.1'09172'4 — Developing countries. Health services. Development. Effects of capitalism
Imperialism, health and medicine / edited by Vicente Navarro. — London : Pluto, 1982. — 285p ; 22cm. — (The Politics of health)
ISBN 0-86104-375-8 (pbk) : £6.95 B82-23774

362.1'0941 — Great Britain. Health services. Administration. Applications of organisation theory
Warmington, Allan. Organisation theory and health service administration / Allan Warmington. — Manchester (Manchester Business School, Booth Street West, Manchester M15 6PB) : Health Services Management Unit, University of Manchester, 1981. — 53leaves ; 30cm. — (Working paper series / University of Manchester Health Services Management Unit, ISSN 0141-2647 ; no.48)
Bibliography: leaves 51-53
£2.00 (pbk) B82-05613

362.1'0941 — Great Britain. Health services — *Serials*
THS : the Times health supplement. — No.1 (Friday 30 Oct. 1981)-. — London : Times Newspapers, 1981-. — v. : ill,ports ; 40cm
Weekly. — Supplement to: The Times
ISSN 0262-0782 = THS. Times health supplement : £0.45 per issue B82-14773

362.1'0941 — Great Britain. National health services
Mixed communications : four essays / Charles Fletcher ... [et al.] ; edited by Gordon McLachlan. — Oxford : Published for the Nuffield Provincial Hospital Trust by the Oxford University Press, c1979. — viii,126p ; 22cm. — (Problems and progress in medical care)
ISBN 0-19-721224-7 (pbk) : £4.50 B82-05023

NHS handbook. — Birmingham (Park House, 40 Edgbaston Park Rd, Edgbaston, Birmingham B15 2RT) : National Association of Health Authorities in England and Wales, [1981?]. — 1v.(loose-leaf) ; 32cm
First supplement to previous NHS handbook, 1980. — Includes bibliographies and index
Unpriced (spiral) B82-27244

362.1'0941 — Great Britain. National health services. Complaints by public
Great Britain. *Health Service Commissioner.* First report for session 1980-81 : selected investigations completed April-September 1980 / Health Service Commissioner. — London : H.M.S.O., [1980]. — 217p ; 25cm. — ([HC] ; 1)
ISBN 0-10-200181-2 (pbk) : £6.90 B82-15130

Great Britain. *Health Service Commissioner.* First report for session 1981-82 : selected investigations completed April-September 1981 / Health Service Commissioner. — London : H.M.S.O., [1981]. — 214p ; 25cm. — (HC ; 9)
ISBN 0-10-200982-1 (pbk) : £7.70 B82-10967

362.1'0941 — Great Britain. National health services. Planning
Tallis, P. A.. Planning in the National Health Service / P.A. Tallis. — Manchester (Manchester Business School, Booth St. West, Manchester M15 6PB) : Health Services Management Unit, Department of Social Administration, University of Manchester, 1981. — 40leaves ; 30cm. — (Working paper series, ISSN 0141-2647)
Unpriced (pbk) B82-26618

362.1'0941 — Great Britain. National health services. Reorganisation
Chaplin, N. W.. Getting it right? : the 1982 reorganisation of the National Health Service / Norman Chaplin. — London, Institute of Health Service Administrators, 1981. — 40p ; 21cm. — (Management series ; 3)
ISBN 0-901003-26-3 (pbk) : Unpriced B82-34994

Confederation of Health Service Employees. NHS reorganisation : a local negotiators guide / compiled by the Confederation of Health Service Employees for branch officers involved in negotiating new management structures and services under the 1982 reorganisation of the National Health Service. — [Banstead] ([Glen House, High Street, Banstead, Surrey SM7 2LH]) : COHSE, c1982. — 24p ; 24cm
Unpriced (pbk) B82-33638

362.1'0941 — Great Britain. National health services — *Socialist viewpoints*
Thunhurst, C. It makes you sick. — London : Pluto Press, Sept.1982. — [128]p. — (Arguments for socialism)
ISBN 0-86104-503-3 (pbk) : £2.50 : CIP entry B82-21744

362.1'0941 — Great Britain. Primary health services
Pritchard, Peter. Manual of primary health care : its nature and organization / Peter Pritchard. — 2nd ed. — Oxford : Oxford University Press, 1981. — viii,209p : ill ; 22cm. — (Oxford medical publications)
Previous ed.: 1978. — Bibliography: p195-203. — Includes index
ISBN 0-19-261355-3 (pbk) : £6.95 : CIP rev. B81-30530

362.1'0941 — Great Britain. Primary health services — *Inquiry reports*
Ritchie, Jane. Access to primary health care : an enquiry carried out on behalf of the United Kingdom health departments / Jane Ritchie, Ann Jacoby, Margaret Bone ; [for the] Office of Population Censuses and Surveys, Social Survey Division. — London : H.M.S.O., 1981. — vi,183p : 2ill,2forms ; 30cm
ISBN 0-11-690767-3 (pbk) : £12.50 B82-13829

362.1'09411 — Scotland. Health services — *Inquiry reports*
Scottish Health Service Planning Council. Scottish Health Authorities priorities for the eighties : a report / by the Scottish Health Service Planning Council. — [London] : H.M.S.O., 1980. — ix,103p : 2ill ; 21cm
At head of title: Scottish Home and Health Department
ISBN 0-11-491689-6 (pbk) : £4.80 B82-14638

362.1'09411 — Scotland. Health services — *Statistics* — *Serials*
[Advance tables *(Scottish Health Service. Common Services Agency. Information Services Division)*]. Advance tables / Scottish Health Service, Common Services Agency, Information Services Division. — Issue no.1 (June 1981)-. — Edinburgh (Trinity Park House, South Trinity Rd, Edinburgh EH5 3SQ) : The Division, 1981-. — v. ; 30cm
ISSN 0263-8096 = Advance tables - Scottish Health Service. Common Services Agency. Information Services Division : Unpriced B82-36697

S.H.A.R.E. tables. — [197-]-. — Edinburgh (Trinity Park House, South Trinity Rd, Edinburgh EH5 3SQ) : Information Services Division, Scottish Health Service Common Services Agency, [197-]-. — v. ; 30cm
Annual. — Description based on: 1979/80 issue
ISSN 0263-8789 = S.H.A.R.E. tables : Unpriced B82-36703

362.1'09411 — Scotland. National health services. Patients. Rights
Wootton, Hilary. Patients' rights : a guide to the rights and responsibilities of patients and doctors in the NHS / [researched and written by Hilary Wootton, Petra Griffiths and Beti Wyn Thomas] ; [edited by Brian Guthrie] ; [illustrations by Christine Roche]. — [Glasgow] : Scottish Consumer Council, [1982]. — 37p : ill ; 30x14cm
Cover title. — Text on inside covers. — Bibliography: p36. — Includes index
ISBN 0-905653-46-7 (pbk) : Unpriced B82-41002

362.1'09414'1 — Scotland. Strathclyde Region. Health services — *Statistics* — *Serials*
Argyll & Clyde Health Board. Annual Statistical report / Argyll & Clyde Health Board. — 1980-. — [Paisley] ([Gilmour House, Paisley, Renfrew PA1 1DU]) : The Board, [1981]-. — v. ; 21x30cm
Continues: Argyll & Clyde Health Board. Annual Statistics & C.A.M.O.'s report
ISSN 0262-7434 = Annual statistical report - Argyll & Clyde Health Board : Unpriced B82-14273

362.1'0942 — England. Medicine, *1100-1154*. **Social aspects**
Kealey, Edward J.. Medieval medicus : a social history of Anglo-Norman medicine / by Edward J. Kealey. — Baltimore ; London : Johns Hopkins University Press, c1981. — x,211p : ill,facsims ; 24cm
Bibliography: p163-186. — Includes index
ISBN 0-8018-2533-4 : £11.50 B82-02224

362.1'0942 — England. National health services. Development — *Proposals* — *Conference proceedings*
The **Promotion** of innovation in health care : the case for development agencies in the NHS : a report of, and commentary upon, a conference held at the King's Fund Centre on Wednesday, 28 October 1981 / by Chris Ham and Laurie McMahon. — London (126 Albert St., NW1 7NF) : King's Fund Centre, 1982. — 26p ; 30cm
Text on inside cover
£1.00 (spiral) B82-39047

362.1'09421 — London. National health services
Chronic and critical : the long crisis in London's everyday health care : a discussion document commissioned by Community Health Councils in London / researched by Nick Davidson. — [London] : [Community Health Councils in London], [1980]. — 23p : ill ; 26cm
ISBN 0-9507307-0-x (pbk) : £0.35 B82-25037

362.1'09428'37 — Humberside. Hull. Public health services, *1298-1974*
Patrick, George. A plague on you, sir! : a community road to health / compiled by George Patrick. — Hull : G. Patrick, c1981. — vii,335p,16p of plates : ill,1facsim,ports ; 24cm
Includes index
ISBN 0-9507868-0-2 : £8.50 B82-17790

362.1'0973 — United States. Health services. Evaluation
Program evaluation in the health fields / edited by Herbert C. Schulberg, Frank Baker. — New York ; London : Human Sciences
Vol.2. — c1979. — xvi,467p : ill ; 24cm
Includes index
ISBN 0-87705-012-0 : Unpriced B82-24165

362.1'0973 — United States. Health services. Planning
Health services research, planning and change / edited by John B. McKinlay. — Cambridge, Mass. ; London : MIT, c1981. — xiv,393p : ill ; 24cm. — (Milbank reader ; 4)
Includes bibliographies and index
ISBN 0-262-13179-x (cased) : £14.00
ISBN 0-262-63080-x (pbk) : Unpriced B82-35669

362.1'0973 — United States. Health services. Political aspects
Politics and health care / edited by John B. McKinlay. — Cambridge, Mass. ; London : MIT, c1981. — xiii,363p ; 24cm. — (Milbank reader ; 6)
Includes bibliographies and index
ISBN 0-262-13181-1 (cased) : £14.00
ISBN 0-262-63082-6 (pbk) : Unpriced B82-37518

362.1'0973 — United States. Health services. Resources. Allocation — *Conference proceedings*
Allocating health resources for the aged and disabled : technology versus politics / edited by Robert Morris. — Lexington, Mass. : Lexington Books ; [Aldershot] : Gower [distrbutor], c1981. — vi,153p : ill ; 24cm
Conference proceedings. — Includes bibliographies and index
ISBN 0-669-04329-x : £12.00 B82-04750

362.1'0973 — United States. Holistic health services
Tubesing, Donald A.. Wholistic health : a whole-person approach to primary health care / Donald A. Tubesing. — New York ; London : Human Sciences, c1979. — 232p : ill,1form ; 22cm
Includes index
ISBN 0-87705-370-7 : £19.25 B82-21463

362.1'0973 — United States. Rural regions. Health services
Wallack, Stanley S.. Rural medicine : obstacles and solutions for self-sufficiency / Stanley S. Wallack, Sandra E. Kretz. — Lexington, [Mass.] : Lexington Books ; [Aldershot] : Gower [distributor], 1982, c1981. — xv,184p : ill ; 24cm. — (University Health Policy Consortium series)
Bibliography: p173-177. — Includes index
ISBN 0-669-03691-9 : £16.00 B82-11707

362.1'1 — Great Britain. Independent hospitals — *Directories* — *Serials*
The **Directory** of private hospitals & health services. — 1983. — London : Longman, Jan.1983. — [750]p
ISBN 0-582-90356-4 : £20.00 : CIP entry
Primary classification 362.1 B82-39296

362.1'1 — Hospitals — *For children*
Milburn, Constance. The hospital / Constance Milburn ; illustrated by David T. Gray. — [Glasgow] : Blackie, [1981]. — 32p : col.ill ; 22cm
Includes index
ISBN 0-216-91037-4 (pbk) : £0.95 B82-05312

362.1'1 — Hospitals. Patients. Stress. Alleviation. Role of sensory information — *For nursing*
Distress reduction through sensory preparation / CURN Project ; principal investigator Jo Anne Horsley ; director Joyce Crane ; the protocol manuscript ... prepared by Margaret A. Reynolds, Karen B. Haller. — New York ; London : Grune & Stratton, c1981. — xvii,108p : ill,forms ; 23cm. — (Using research to improve nursing practice)
Bibliography: p99-100. — Includes index
ISBN 0-8089-1400-6 (spiral) : £7.60 B82-18678

Pain : deliberative nursing interventions / CURN project ; principal investigator Jo Anne Horsley ; director Joyce Crane ; the protocol manuscript ... prepared by Margaret A. Reynolds. — New York ; London : Grune & Stratton, c1982. — xvii,140p : ill ; 23cm. — (Using research to improve nursing practice)
Includes bibliographies and index
ISBN 0-8089-1401-4 (spiral) : Unpriced B82-35737

362.1'1'02341 — Great Britain. Hospitals — *Career guides*
Storr, S. D.. Working in a hospital / S.D. Storr ; photography by Tim Humphrey. — Hove : Wayland, 1982. — 94p : ill,ports ; 25cm. — (People at work)
Includes index
ISBN 0-85340-926-9 : £4.95 B82-39792

362.1'1'0604239 — Avon. Leagues of hospital friends, *to 1981*
Avon leagues of hospital friends : a record of achievements 1948-1981. — [Bristol] ([c/o C. Bishop, 11 Avon Way, Stoke Bishop, Bristol BS9 1SJ]) : [Avon County Association of Leagues of Hospital Friends], [1981]. — 32p,1leaf of plates : 1facsim ; 30cm
Cover title
£0.19 (pbk) B82-04569

362.1'1'068 — Great Britain. Hospitals. Wards. Management. Role of ward sisters
Matthews, Arline. In charge of the ward / Arline Matthews. — Oxford : Blackwell Scientific, 1982. — xi,209p : ill ; 22cm
Bibliography: p199-202. — Includes index
ISBN 0-632-00829-6 (pbk) : £5.50 : CIP rev. B82-12011

362.1'1'068 — Hospitals. Commissioning
Millard, Graham. Commissioning hospital buildings / by Graham Millard ; foreword by John Hoare. — 3rd ed. — London : King Edward's Hospital Fund for London, 1981. — 131p : ill,facsims,2col.plans,forms ; 30cm. — (A King's Fund guide)
Previous ed.: 1975. — Bibliography: p126-127. — Includes index
ISBN 0-900889-87-x (pbk) : Unpriced B82-07760

362.1'1'068 — United States. Hospitals. Management
Smalley, Harold E.. Hospital management engineering : a guide to the improvement of hospital management systems. — [Rev. version] / Harold E. Smalley. — Englewood Cliffs ; London : Prentice-Hall, c1982. — xxvi,453p : ill,forms,plans,ports ; 24cm. — (Prentice-Hall international series in industrial and systems engineering)
Previous ed.: published as Hospital industrial engineering. New York : Reinhold, 1966. — Includes bibliographies and index
ISBN 0-13-394775-0 : £20.95 B82-28162

362.1'1'0681 — United States. Hospitals. Administration. Costs. Control. Role of government
Joskow, Paul L.. Controlling hospital costs : the role of government regulation / Paul L. Joskow. — Cambridge, Mass. ; London : MIT, c1981. — 211p : ill ; 24cm. — (MIT Press series in health and public policy ; 2)
Bibliography: p193-205. — Includes index
ISBN 0-262-10024-x : £17.50 B82-21013

362.1'1'0924 — Tanzania. Tanganyika. Hospitals. Hospital life, *ca 1940-ca 1950* — *Personal observations*
White, Paul, *1910-*. Lion hunter. — Exeter : Paternoster, Oct.1982. — [260]p
ISBN 0-85364-349-0 (pbk) : £2.60 : CIP entry B82-24746

362.1'1'094 — European Community countries. Hospitals. Statistics

Workshop on Hospital Statistics for Population-Based Health Care and Epidemiology : Role of the Minimum Basic Data Set *(1981 : Brussels)*. Hospital statistics in Europe : proceedings of Workshop on Hospital Statistics for Population-Based Health Care and Epidemiology : Role of the Minimum Basic Data Set, held in Brussels, Belgium, 9-11 September 1981 under the sponsorship of the Commission of the European Communities (CEC) ... [et al.] / edited by P.M. Lambert and F.H. Roger. — Amsterdam ; Oxford : North-Holland for the Commission of the European Communities, 1982. — x,200p : ill ; 23cm
ISBN 0-444-86383-4 : Unpriced B82-39972

362.1'1'0941 — Great Britain. Hospitals. Patients. Care. Cultural factors

Sampson, A. C. M.. The neglected ethic : cultural and religious factors in the care of patients / A.C.M. Sampson. — London : McGraw-Hill, c1982. — xiv,112p : ill ; 23cm. — (The McGraw-Hill nursing studies series)
Bibliography: p108-109. — Includes index
ISBN 0-07-084645-6 (pbk) : Unpriced : CIP rev. B81-34488

362.1'1'0942142 — London. Camden *(London Borough)*. **Hospitals: National Hospitals for Nervous Diseases,** *to 1982*

Robinson, Geoffrey A.. The National Hospitals for Nervous Diseases 1948-1982. — London (National Hospitals for Nervous Diseases, Queen Sq., WC1) : The Board of Governors, Dec.1982. — [128]p
ISBN 0-9508268-0-4 : £4.00 : CIP entry B82-30749

362.1'1'0942144 — London. Hackney *(London Borough)*. **Hospitals: Bearstead Memorial Hospital. Leasing by Great Britain.** *Department of Health and Social Security:* **Leasing to Central Council for Jewish Social Services** — *Proposals*

Great Britain. *Treasury*. Treasury minute dated 23rd November 1981 relative to the leasing at a nominal rent of Bearstead Memorial Hospital to the Central Council for Jewish Social Services. — London : H.M.S.O., [1981]. — 1sheet ; 25x16cm. — (Cmnd. ; 8404)
ISBN 0-10-184040-3 : £0.30 B82-09805

362.1'1'094215 — London. Tower Hamlets *(London Borough)*. **Bethnal Green. Hospitals: Military Mission Hospital,** *to 1981*

Thompson, Phyllis, *1906-*. No bronze statue : a living documentary of the Mildmay Mission Hospital / Phyllis Thompson. — Eastbourne : Kingsway, 1982. — 192p ; 18cm
Originally published: London : Word Books, 1972
ISBN 0-86065-187-8 (pbk) : £1.75 B82-36018

362.1'1'0942193 — London. Merton *(London Borough)*. **District general hospitals: Nelson Hospital,** *to 1980*

Deas, Frank. Origin, growth and development of The Nelson Hospital, Merton : (one of the smaller general hospitals) / Frank Deas with additional notes by D.I. Deas. — London (c/o The Borough Librarian, Merton Libraries Department, Merton Cottage, Church Path, Merton Park, SW19 3HH) : Merton Library Service, c1981. — 14p : ill,1plan,1port ; 21cm
£0.75 (pbk) B82-14666

362.1'1'0942454 — Shropshire. Shrewsbury. Hospitals: Royal Salop Infirmary, *to 1977*

Royal Salop Infirmary. In retrospect : a short history of the Royal Salop Infirmary / by Margaret Keeling-Roberts. — Wem ([The Crescent, Wem, Salop]) : J. and M. Keeling-Roberts, c1981. — xvii,102p,xxxivp of plates : ill,coats of arms,facsims,ports ; 21cm
Bibliography: p95. — Includes index
ISBN 0-9507849-0-7 (pbk) : £4.50 B82-14575

362.1′1′0942583 — Hertfordshire. Bishop′s Stortford. Hospitals: Rye Street Hospital *(Bishop′s Stortford).* **Leasing by Great Britain.** *Department of Health and Social Security:* **Leasing to Save the Children Fund** — *Proposals*

Great Britain. *Treasury.* Treasury minute dated 22 December 1981 relative to the leasing at a nominal rental of the Rye Street Hospital, Bishop′s Stortford, Hertfordshire to the Save the Children Fund. — London : H.M.S.O., 1981. — 1sheet ; 25cm
£0.30 B82-13822

362.1′1′099431 — Queensland. Brisbane. Hospitals: Mater Public Hospital *(Brisbane), to 1978*

Summers, H. J. (Harold James). They crossed the river : the founding of the Mater Misericordiae Hospital, Brisbane, by the Sisters of Mercy / H.J. Summers. — [St Lucia] : University of Queensland Press ; Hemel Hempstead : Distributed by Prentice-Hall, c1979. — 242p : ill(some col.),1map,ports(some col.) ; 22cm
Includes index
ISBN 0-7022-1357-8 : £10.75 B82-07151

362.1′2′094141 — Scotland. Strathclyde Region. Health centres. Welfare work

Social work in health centres : results of a survey undertaken in eleven health centres in Strathclyde / Strathclyde Regional Council, Social Work Department. — [Glasgow] : Strathclyde Regional Council, 1981. — 27p ; 30cm
Cover title. — Bibliography: p27
Unpriced (pbk) B82-25259

362.1′2′0942 — England. Day care centres for adults — *Statistics*

Edwards, Carol. The data of day care / by Carol Edwards and Jan Carter. — [London] ([5 Tavistock Place WC1H 9SS]) : National Institute for Social Work, 1980. — 3v.(270leaves) ; 30cm
Cover title
£11.00 (spiral) B82-10310

362.1′2′0942164 — London. Southwark *(London Borough).* **Health centres: Pioneer Health Centre,** *to 1946*

Biologists in search of material : an interim report on the work of the Pioneer Health Centre, Peckham / edited by G. Scott Williamson and I.H. Pearse. — 2nd ed. — [Edinburgh] : Scottish Academic Press, 1982. — 107p,iip of plates : ill,3plans ; 20cm
Previous ed.: London : Faber, 1938. — Includes index
ISBN 0-7073-0319-2 (pbk) : Unpriced B82-30669

362.1′4 — Great Britain. District nursing services — *Directories* — *Serials*

Handbook of community nursing (district nursing). — 1980. — Newcastle-under-Lyme (5 The Crescent, Pilkington Ave., Westlands, Newcastle-under-Lyme, Staffs. ST5 3RB) : J.L. Gee, R.C. Gee, 1980, c1978. — 1v. ; 21cm
Continued by: Handbook of community nursing. — Only one issue published
£1.00 B82-10358

362.1′4 — Hospitals. Discharged patients. Community care

Rehabilitation within the community. — London : Faber, Oct.1982. — [208]p
ISBN 0-571-11901-8 (pbk) : £3.50 : CIP entry B82-23338

362.1′4 — Scotland. District nursing services — *Statistics* — *Serials*

Community nursing statistics. — [197-?]-. — Edinburgh (Trinity Park House, South Trinity Rd, Edinburgh EH5 3SQ) : Information Services Division, Scottish Health Service Common Services Agency, [197-?]-. — v. ; 21x30cm
Annual. — Description based on: 1977 issue
ISSN 0263-8770 = Community nursing statistics : Unpriced B82-36698

362.1′4 — Sick persons. Home care

St. John Ambulance. Caring for the sick. — London (9 Henrietta St., WC2E 8PS) : Dorling Kindersley, Sept.1982. — [176]p
ISBN 0-86318-002-7 (cased) : £5.95 : CIP entry
ISBN 0-86318-003-5 (pbk) : £3.95 B82-21564

362.1′4′0715 — Great Britain. Health visitors. Lifelong education

Council for the Education and Training of Health Visitors. Report on continuing education for health visitors. — London : Council for the Education and Training of Health Visitors, 1981. — 12p : 1ill ; 21cm
Bibliography: p11
Unpriced (pbk) B82-28501

362.1′4′0941 — Great Britain. Health visiting

Health visiting : principles in practice. — London : Council for the Education and Training of Health Visitors, 1982. — 111p : ill ; 21cm
Includes bibliographies
ISBN 0-906144-03-5 (pbk) : £1.50 B82-27727

Health visiting. — 2nd ed. — London : Baillière Tindall, Feb.1983. — [352]p
Previous ed.: 1977
ISBN 0-7020-0981-4 (pbk) : £8.75 : CIP entry B82-38872

Robinson, Jane. An evaluation of health visiting / Jane Robinson. — London : Council for the Education and Training of Health Visitors, 1982. — vii,99p : ill ; 21cm
ISBN 0-906144-04-3 (pbk) : £2.00 B82-27728

362.1′4′0941 — Great Britain. Home help services

Hedley, Rodney. Home help : key issues in service provision / Rodney Hedley, Alison Norman. — London : Centre for Policy on Ageing, 1982. — iv,42p ; 30cm. — (CPA reports ; 1)
Bibliography: p42
ISBN 0-904139-28-x (pbk) : £3.50 B82-34637

Managing at home : a report on domiciliary supportive services provided by the health and social services and by voluntary organisations for patients/clients and their families : including research submitted to the Royal Commission of the National Health Service. — London : Consumers′ Association, 1978. — 80p ; 30cm. — (A Which? campaign report)
Unpriced (spiral) B82-26777

362.1′4′09416 — Northern Ireland. Health visiting

Orr, Jean. Health visiting in focus : a consumer view of health visiting in Northern Ireland / Jean Orr. — London : Royal College of Nursing, c1980. — 98p : 2forms ; 22cm
Bibliography: p90-98
ISBN 0-902606-62-x (pbk) : Unpriced B82-14619

362.1′72 — General practice

Common dilemmas in family medicine. — Lancaster : MTP Press, June 1982. — [480]p
ISBN 0-85200-470-2 : £15.00 : CIP entry B82-17953

Drury, M.. Whole person medicine / M. Drury. — [Birmingham] : University of Birmingham, 1982. — 14p ; 21cm
′An inaugural lecture delivered in the University of Birmingham on 17 November 1981′. — Cover title
ISBN 0-7044-0588-1 (pbk) : Unpriced B82-27480

General practice / edited by Eric Gambrill. — London : Heinemann Medical, 1982. — x,364p : ill ; 23cm. — (Tutorials in postgraduate medicine)
Includes index
ISBN 0-433-11120-8 : £17.50 B82-25387

The Nature of general family practice. — Lancaster : MTP Press, Dec.1982. — [650]p
ISBN 0-85200-489-3 : £20.00 : CIP entry B82-32308

362.1′72 — Patients. Care by general practitioners. Quality. Assessment

Fabb, W. E.. The assessment of clinical competence in general family practice. — Lancaster : MTP Press, Oct.1982. — [200]p
ISBN 0-85200-490-7 : £14.50 : CIP entry B82-29025

362.1′72′02854 — General practice. Applications of digital computer systems — *Conference proceedings*

Computers and the general practitioner / [proceedings of the GP-Info Symposium, London 1980] ; general editors Alastair Malcolm and John Poyser. — Oxford : Published for the Royal College of General Practitioners by Pergamon, 1982. — xi,124p : ill,facsims,forms ; 24cm
Includes bibliographies
ISBN 0-08-026865-x : £10.00 : CIP rev. B81-31067

362.1′72′02854 — Great Britain. General practice. Applications of digital computer systems — *Serials*

Computer update. — Vol.1, no.1 (Apr./May 1982)-. — [London] : [Update Publications], 1982-. — v. : ill(some col.),ports ; 29cm
Six issue yearly
ISSN 0262-9690 = Computer update : £6.00 per year B82-27639

362.1′72′0941 — Great Britain. General practice. Preventive medicine

Preventive medicine in general practice. — Oxford : Oxford University Press, Feb.1983. — [250]p. — (Oxford general practice series ; 3) (Oxford medical publications)
ISBN 0-19-261299-9 (pbk) : £9.95 : CIP entry B82-36585

362.1′72′0941 — Great Britain. General practice, *to 1981*

Gibson, *Sir* **Ronald,** *1909-.* The family doctor : his life and history / Sir Ronald Gibson. — London : Published in association with Pulse [by] Allen & Unwin, 1981. — xv,214p,[16]p of plates : ill,1coat of arms,ports ; 23cm
Includes index
ISBN 0-04-610017-2 : Unpriced : CIP rev. B81-28789

362.1′72′0941 — Great Britain. General practitioners — *Case studies* — *For children*

Bowler, Jane Elizabeth. A day with a doctor / Jane Elizabeth Bowler and Christine Day. — Hove : Wayland, 1982. — 55p : ill,ports ; 24cm. — (A Day in the life)
Bibliography: p55
ISBN 0-85340-898-x : £3.25 B82-18434

362.1′72′0941 — Great Britain. Urban regions. Inner areas. General practice

Bolden, K. J.. Inner cities / K.J. Bolden. — London : Royal College of General Practitioners, 1981. — 13p ; 28cm. — (Occasional paper / Royal College of General Practitioners ; 19)
Bibliography: p13
£3.00 (pbk) B82-18278

362.1′72′0942 — England. General practice — *Stories, anecdotes*

Hamilton, Andrew, *1916-.* Sorry to bother you doctor / Andrew Hamilton. — Tring : Lion, 1982. — 172p ; 18cm. — (A Lion paperback)
ISBN 0-85648-332-x (pbk) : £1.50 B82-38756

362.1′72′0947 — Russia *(RSFSR).* **Health services. Physicians,** *1856-1905*

Frieden, Nancy Mandelker. Russian physicians in an era of reform and revolution, 1856-1905 / Nancy Mandelker Frieden. — Princeton ; Guildford : Princeton University Press, c1981. — xvii,378p : ill,ports ; 25cm
Bibliography: p351-369. — Includes index
£22.80 B82-24911

362.1′73′0941 — Great Britain. National health services. Nurses. Accountability

Accountability in nursing : the report of a seminar for Fellows of the Royal College of Nursing held at Leeds Castle, Kent, 15-18 April 1980. — [London] ([Henrietta Pl., W1M 0AB]) : [Royal College of Nursing], c1980. — 56p : ill ; 21cm
Unpriced (pbk) B82-28328

362.1'73'0941 — Great Brtain. Nursing services, *1900-1981*

Nursing, midwifery and health visiting since 1900 / edited by Peta Allan and Moya Jolley ; with a foreword by Catherine M. Hall. — London : Faber, 1982. — 316p : ill ; 23cm
Includes bibliographies and index
ISBN 0-571-11839-9 (cased) : £7.95 : CIP rev.
ISBN 0-571-11840-2 (pbk) : Unpriced
B82-06862

362.1'74 — Hospitals. Special-care facilities. Design

Hospital special-care facilities : planning for user needs / edited by Harold Laufman. — New York ; London : Academic Press, 1981. — xxvi,533p : ill,plans ; 24cm. — (Clinical engineering series)
Conference papers. — Includes bibliographies and index
ISBN 0-12-437740-8 : £32.80 B82-02205

362.1'75 — Hospices — *Conference proceedings*

Hospice : the living idea / edited by Cicely Saunders, Dorothy H. Summers, Neville Teller. — London : Edward Arnold, 1981. — x,198p : ill ; 23cm
Conference papers. — Includes bibliographies and index
ISBN 0-7131-4398-3 (pbk) : £5.50 : CIP rev.
B81-30595

362.1'75 — Terminally ill patients. Care

McKerrow, Margaret M.. A time to care : a study in terminal illness / by Margaret M. McKerrow. — [Torquay] ([Rowcroft House, Avenue Rd., Torquay, Devon TQ2 5LS]) : [Torbay & South Devon Hospice], 1982
Book 2: Relatives. — 28p ; 21cm
Unpriced (pbk) B82-24997

362.1'75 — Terminally ill persons. Care

The **Dying** patient : the medical management of incurable and terminal illness / edited by Eric Wilkes. — Lancaster : MTP, 1982. — xii,336p : ill ; 25cm
Includes bibliographies and index
ISBN 0-85200-339-0 : £18.50 : CIP rev.
B81-21545

362.1'75'0926 — Death. Attitudes of terminally ill persons — *Case studies*

Kübler-Ross, Elisabeth. Living with death and dying / Elisabeth Kübler-Ross. — London : Souvenir, 1982, c1981. — x,181p,[8]p of plates : ill(some col.) ; 23cm
Includes one chapter by Gregg M. Furth, and one chapter by Martha Pearse Elliott. — Originally published: New York : Macmillan, 1981
ISBN 0-285-64958-2 (cased) : £7.95
ISBN 0-285-64957-4 (pbk) : £5.95 B82-20545

Saunders, Cicely. Living with dying. — Oxford : Oxford University Press, Jan.1983. — [64]p. — (Oxford medical publications)
ISBN 0-19-261404-5 (pbk) : £4.95 : CIP entry
B82-33481

362.1'75'0941 — Great Britain. Welfare work with terminally ill persons

Smith, Carole R.. Social work with the dying and bereaved / Carole R. Smith. — London : Macmillan, 1982. — vi,149p ; 23cm. — (Practical social work)
Bibliography: p137-146. — Includes index
ISBN 0-333-30894-8 (cased) : £10.00
ISBN 0-333-30895-6 (pbk) : Unpriced
Also classified at 362.8 B82-21618

362.1'77 — Scotland. Hospitals. Clinical chemistry laboratories — *Statistics* — *Serials*

Laboratory statistics. Clinical chemistry. — [197-?]-. — Edinburgh (Trinity Park House, South Trinity Rd, Edinburgh EH5 3SQ) : Information Services Division, Scottish Health Service Common Services Agency, [197-?]-. — v. ; 30cm
Annual. — Description based on: 1981 issue
ISSN 0263-8797 = Laboratory statistics. Clinical chemistry : Unpriced B82-36701

362.1'77 — Scotland. Hospitals. Haematology laboratories — *Statistics* — *Serials*

Laboratory statistics. Haematology. — [197-?]-. — Edinburgh (Trinity Park House, South Trinity Rd, Edinburgh EH5 3SQ) : Information Services Division, Scottish Health Service Common Services Agency, [197-?]-. — v. ; 30cm
Annual. — Description based on: 1981 issue
ISSN 0263-8800 = Laboratory statistics. Haematology : Unpriced B82-36702

362.1'77 — Scotland. Hospitals. Medical microbiology laboratories — *Statistics* — *Serials*

Laboratory statistics. Microbiology. — [197-?]-. — Edinburgh (Trinity Park House, South Trinity Rd, Edinburgh EH5 3SQ) : Information Services Division, Scottish Health Service Common Services Agency, [197-?]-. — v. ; 30cm
Annual. — Description based on: 1981 issue
ISSN 0263-8819 = Laboratory statistics. Microbiology : Unpriced B82-36700

362.1'77 — Scotland. Hospitals. Pathology laboratories — *Statistics* — *Serials*

Laboratory statistics. Pathology. — [197-?]-. — Edinburgh (Trinity Park House, South Trinity Rd, Edinburgh EH5 3SQ) : Information Services Division, Scottish Health Service Common Services Agency, [197-?]-. — v. ; 30cm
Annual. — Description based on: 1981 issue
ISSN 0263-8827 = Laboratory statistics. Pathology : Unpriced B82-36699

362.1'78 — Hospitals. Respiratory therapy services. Management

McLaughlin, Arthur J.. Organization and management for respiratory therapists / Arthur J. McLaughlin, Jr.. — St. Louis ; London : Mosby, 1979. — ix,159p : ill,plans,forms ; 22cm
Includes bibliographies and index
ISBN 0-8016-3311-7 (pbk) : Unpriced
B82-24779

362.1'783 — Tissue banks

Klen, R.. Biological principles of tissue banking. — Oxford : Pergamon, June 1982. — [273]p
ISBN 0-08-024413-0 : £30.00 : CIP entry
B82-11996

362.1'8 — Ambulance services — *For children*

Bowler, Jane Elizabeth. A day with an ambulanceman / Jane Elizabeth Bowler and Christine Day. — Hove : Wayland, 1982. — 55p : ill ; 24cm. — (A Day in the life)
Bibliography: p55
ISBN 0-85340-968-4 : £3.25 B82-33432

362.1'8 — London. Ambulance services, *1973-1981* — *Personal observations*

McCoy, Glen. Ambulance! / Glen McCoy. — Newton Abbot : David & Charles, c1982. — 183p : ill ; 23cm
Includes index
ISBN 0-7153-8182-2 : £6.95 : CIP rev.
B82-04868

362.1'8 — United States. Hospitals. Casualty departments. Management — *Manuals*

MacDonald, Jeffrey R.. Department of emergency medicine guideline manual : policies and procedures / Jeffrey R. MacDonald, Pat Kinder. — St. Louis ; London : Mosby, 1979. — xii,329p : ill,forms,2plans ; 26cm
Bibliography: p317. — Includes index
ISBN 0-8016-3054-1 (pbk) : £21-00
B82-24774

362.1'8'02541 — Great Britain. Emergency medical services — *Directories* — *Serials* — *For general practice*

GP guide to emergency services. — 1981-. — London (5a Warwick St., W1R 5RA) : Asgard Pub. Co., 1981-. — v. : forms,maps ; 21cm
Annual
ISSN 0262-1010 = GP guide to emergency services : £3.50 B82-10360

362.1'96123 — Man. Heart. Coronary diseases. Personal adjustment

Back to normal : advice and encouragement for someone who has had a heart attack. — Rev. and repr. — London (57 Gloucester Place, W1H 4DH) : British Heart Foundation, 1981. — 8 : 1ill ; 18cm. — (Heart research series ; no.1)
Cover title. — Previous ed.: 1980?
Unpriced (pbk) B82-40602

362.1'96462 — Adolescents. Diabetes. Personal adjustment — *Practical information*

Farquhar, J. W.. Diabetes in your teens. — Edinburgh : Churchill Livingstone, Apr.1982. — [136]p. — (Churchill Livingstone patient handbook ; 10)
ISBN 0-443-02220-8 (pbk) : £1.50 : CIP entry
B82-03581

362.1'96462 — Man. Diabetes. Personal adjustment — *Personal observations*

Stritch, Elaine. Am I blue?. — London : Granada, Aug.1982. — [128]p
ISBN 0-246-11592-0 : £4.50 : CIP entry
B82-28445

362.1'965 — Man. Skin. Diseases. Personal adjustment

Orton, Christine. Learning to live with skin disorders / Christine Orton. — London : Souvenir, 1981. — 197p : ill ; 22cm. — (Human horizons series)
Bibliography: p190-191. — Includes index
ISBN 0-285-64945-0 (cased) : £6.95
ISBN 0-285-64946-9 (pbk) : £4.95 B82-04940

362.1'96722'00924 — Rheumatoid arthritics — *Personal observations*

Floyd, Peter G.. Peace and calm in thee we find : my Lord knows the way through the wilderness : an autobiographical sketch / by Peter G. Floyd. — Ilkeston : Moorley's, c1982. — 40p ; 22cm
ISBN 0-86071-150-1 (pbk) : £0.75 B82-31377

Joseph, Marie. One step at a time / Marie Joseph. — London : Arrow, 1982. — 168p ; 18cm
Originally published: London : Heinemann, 1976
ISBN 0-09-928810-9 (pbk) : £1.50 B82-32915

362.1'968 — Neurological patients. Rehabilitation

Rehabilitation of the neurological patient / [edited by] L.S. Illis, E.M. Sedgwick, H.J. Glanville ; with a foreword by Baroness Masham of Ilton. — Oxford : Blackwell Scientific, 1982. — xii,424p : ill,forms ; 24cm
Includes bibliographies and index
ISBN 0-632-00595-5 : £22.50 : CIP rev.
B82-06944

362.1'9681 — Stroke patients. Care

Rose, F. Clifford. Stroke : the facts / F. Clifford Rose, Rudy Capildeo ; with a foreword by Sir Peter Medawar. — Oxford : Oxford University Press, 1981 (1982 [printing]). — 145p,[8]p of plates : ill ; 20cm
Includes index
ISBN 0-19-286029-1 (pbk) : £2.95 : CIP rev.
B82-15678

362.1'9681 — Stroke patients. Rehabilitation — *Manuals*

Johnstone, Margaret. The stroke patient : principles of rehabilitation / Margaret Johnstone ; illustrated by Estrid Barton ; foreword by Bernard Isaacs. — 2nd ed. — Edinburgh : Churchill Livingstone, 1982. — 91p : ill ; 24cm
Previous ed.: 1976. — Includes index
ISBN 0-443-02544-4 (pbk) : £3.75 B82-38473

362.1'96834 — Man. Multiple sclerosis. Personal adjustment

Dowie, Robin— Learning to live with MS / Robin Dowie, Robert Povey, Gillian Whitley ; foreword by Bryan Matthews ; illustrations by Keith Lovet Watson. — [London] : Multiple Sclerosis Society of Great Britain and Northern Ireland, 1981. — 70p : ill ; 15x22cm
Bibliography: p64-65
ISBN 0-9507171-2-6 (spiral) : Unpriced
B82-05665

362.1'96835'00924 — Poliomyelitis victims. Twistington Higgins, Elizabeth — *Biographies*
Alexander, Marc. The dance goes on : the life and art of Elizabeth Twistington Higgins / by Marc Alexander ; with a foreword by HRH Prince Philip, Duke of Edinbrugh. — Kingsley : Leader, [1982?]. — 143p : ill(some col.),ports (some col.) ; 31cm
ISBN 0-907159-00-1 : £5.95 B82-19123

362.1'96853'005 — Epileptics — *Serials*
Epilepsy now!. — 1 (Spring '81)-. — Wokingham (New Wokingham Rd, Wokingham, Berks. [RG11 3AY]) : British Epilepsy Association, 1981-. — v. : ill,ports ; 30cm
Irregular. — Newsletter of: British Epilepsy Association. — Continues: Epilepsy news
ISSN 0262-5474 = Epilepsy now! : £0.20 per issue (Free to BEA members) B82-06784

362.1'96853'00941 — Great Britain. Man. Epilepsy. Personal adjustment — *Practical information*
McGovern, Shelagh. The epilepsy handbook / Shelagh McGovern. — London : Sheldon, 1982. — viii,104p ; 22cm. — (Overcoming common problems)
Bibliography: p103. — Includes index
ISBN 0-85969-331-7 (pbk) : £3.95 B82-11334

362.1'96994'00924 — Cancer victims — *Personal observations*
Allwood, Martin. Death was in my body / by Martin Allwood ; with a preface by Conrad Arensberg. — Mullsjö : Anglo-American Center ; Addingham-Ilkley 'Casita', (Springfield Mount, Addingham-Ilkley) : Keth Laycock [distributor], 1980. — 111p ; 21cm
ISBN 91-85412-18-x (pbk) : Unpriced B82-20611

Cook, Stephani. Second life / Stephani Cook. — London : Joseph, 1982, c1981. — 376p ; 23cm
Originally published: New York : Simon and Schuster, 1981
ISBN 0-7181-2104-x : £8.95 B82-15191

362.1'96994'00942733 — Great Britain *(Metropolitan County).* **Manchester. Hospitals: Christie Hospital and Holt Radium Institute. Computerised axial tomography scanners. Fund raising projects: Pat Seed Appeal Fund,** *to 1979*
Seed, Pat. One day at a time / by Pat Seed. — Large print ed. — Bolton-by-Bowland : Magna, 1980, c1979. — 492p ; 23cm
Originally published: London : Heinemann, 1979. — Published in large print
ISBN 0-86009-232-1 : £6.75 : CIP rev. B79-36248

362.1'9699449'00924 — United States. Breast cancer victims — *Personal observations*
Graham, Jory. In the company of others. — London : Gollancz, Jan.1983. — [192]p
ISBN 0-575-03205-7 (cased) : £6.95 : CIP entry
ISBN 0-575-03206-5 (pbk) : £3.95 B82-32455

362.1'971028'0924 — Great Britain. Road accident victims: Children. Severe injuries. Recovery — *Personal observations — Correspondence, diaries, etc.*
Collins, Joan, *1933-*. Katy : a fight for life / Joan Collins. — London : Gollancz, 1982. — 156p,[24]p of plates : ports ; 22cm
ISBN 0-575-03111-5 : £5.95 : CIP rev. B82-06935

362.1'9711 — West Sussex. East Grinstead. Hospitals: Queen Victoria Hospital *(East Grinstead).* **Ward 3. Ex-patients: Royal Air Force aircrew with burns: Guinea Pig Club** — *Biographies*
Williams, Peter, *1933-*. McIndoe's army : the injured airman who faced the world / Peter Williams and Ted Harrison. — Leicester : Charnwood, 1981, c1979. — 222p : ill ; 23cm
Originally published: London : Pelham, 1979. — Published in large print
ISBN 0-7089-8016-3 : £4.50 B82-10097

Williams, Peter, *1933-*. McIndoe's army : the injured airmen who faced the world / Peter Williams and Ted Harrison. — London : Sphere, 1981, c1979. — xi,179p,[8]p of plates : ill,ports ; 18cm
Originally published: London : Pelham, 1979. — Bibliography: p168. — Includes index
ISBN 0-7221-4488-1 (pbk) : £1.50 B82-07082

362.1'973'00941 — Great Britain. Hospitals. Orthopaedic patients. Admission & outpatient treatment. Waiting lists — *Inquiry reports*
Orthopaedic services : waiting time for out-patient appointments and in-patient treatment : report of a Working Party to the Secretary of State for Social Services. — London : H.M.S.O., 1981. — x,84p : ill ; 25cm
At head of title: Department of Health and Social Security
ISBN 0-11-320754-9 (pbk) : £4.95 B82-00705

362.1'975541 — Ileostomists. Self-help — *Manuals*
Schindler, Margaret. Living with a colostomy : reassuring advice on returning to normal life after a colostomy operation / by Margaret Schindler. — Wellingborough : Thorsons, 1981. — 128p : ill ; 22cm
Includes index
ISBN 0-7225-0680-5 (cased) : Unpriced : CIP rev.
ISBN 0-7225-0681-3 (pbk) : £3.50
Primary classification 362.1'975547 B81-30447

362.1'975547 — Colostomists. Self-help — *Manuals*
Schindler, Margaret. Living with a colostomy : reassuring advice on returning to normal life after a colostomy operation / by Margaret Schindler. — Wellingborough : Thorsons, 1981. — 128p : ill ; 22cm
Includes index
ISBN 0-7225-0680-5 (cased) : Unpriced : CIP rev.
ISBN 0-7225-0681-3 (pbk) : £3.50
Also classified at 362.1'975541 B81-30447

362.1'976'0068 — Great Britain. Dental services. Practices. Management — *Manuals*
Crosthwaite, David W.. A handbook of dental practice management / David W. Crosthwaite. — Edinburgh : Churchill Livingstone, 1982. — 117p : ill,forms ; 22cm. — (Churchill Livingstone dental series)
Includes bibliographies and index
ISBN 0-443-01989-4 (pbk) : £4.95 : CIP rev. B82-01961

362.1'976'00941 — Great Britain. Dental health services
Cowell, Colin R.. Promoting dental health / by Colin R. Cowell and Aubrey Sheiham. — London : King Edward's Hospital Fund for London, c1981. — xiv, 129p ; 24cm
Bibliography: p112-122. — Includes index
ISBN 0-900889-83-7 : Unpriced : CIP rev. B81-28803

362.1'9795 — Man. Organs & tissues. Transplantation. Social aspects
Scott, Russell, *19---*. The body as property / Russell Scott. — London : Allen Lane, 1981. — x,274p ; 24cm
Includes index
ISBN 0-7139-1321-5 : £7.95 B82-00928

362.1'982 — Wales. Medicine. Social aspects — *Study examples: Harry, Dassy. Unnatural childbirth, 1701 — Welsh texts*
Jenkins, Geraint H.. Geni plentyn ym 1701 : profiad 'rhyfeddol' Dassy Harry / Geraint H. Jenkins. — [Cardiff] : Amgueddfa Werin Cymru, 1981. — 14p : ill,1facsim ; 23cm
A lecture delivered at the Welsh Folk Musuem's Easter School, April 1979
ISBN 0-85485-051-1 (pbk) : Unpriced B82-21937

362.1'982'0094134 — Edinburgh. Maternity health services — *Practical information — For pregnant women*
Having a baby in Edinburgh : a guide to Edinburgh's maternity hospitals / written ... by the Edinburgh Health Council ; [illustrations by Judith Allan]. — Edinburgh (29 Castle Terrace, Edinburgh) : The Council, 1981. — 29p : ill ; 21cm
Bibliography: p27
Unpriced (pbk) B82-11207

362.1'982'00941835 — Dublin. Maternity hospitals: Coombe Lying-in Hospital, *to 1976*
Coombe Lying-In Hospital. The Coombe Lying-In Hospital, Dublin, 1826-1976 : souvenir programme. — [Dublin] : [The Hospital], [1976]. — [20]p : ill,2ports ; 22cm
Cover title
Unpriced (pbk) B82-15437

362.1'982'0096683 — Benin *(People's Republic).* **Maternity health services. Use by Bariba. Cultural factors**
Sargent, Carolyn Fishel. The cultural context of therapeutic choice : obstetrical care decisions among the Bariba of Benin / by Carolyn Fishel Sargent. — Dordrecht ; London : Reidel, c1982. — xii,192p : ill,1map,1port ; 25cm. — (Culture, illness and healing ; v.3)
Bibliography: p178-185. — Includes index
ISBN 90-277-1344-8 : Unpriced B82-25213

362.1'9892 — Children. Hospitalisation — *For children*
Althea. Going into hospital / by Althea ; illustrated by Maureen Galvani. — Cambridge : Dinosaur, c1981. — [25]p : col.ill ; 16x19cm. — (Dinosaur's Althea books)
ISBN 0-85122-309-5 (cased) : Unpriced
ISBN 0-85122-069-x (pbk) : Unpriced B82-31829

362.1'9892 — Chronically sick children. Care. Psychosocial aspects — *For parents*
McCollum, Audrey T.. The chronically ill child : a guide for parents and professionals / Audrey T. McCollum. — Rev. and enl. ed. — New Haven ; London : Yale University Press, c1981. — x,273p ; 24cm
Previous ed.: published as Coping with prolonged health impairment in your child. Boston, Mass. : Little, Brown, 1975. — Includes index
ISBN 0-300-02764-8 (cased) : £17.50 : CIP rev.
ISBN 0-300-02782-6 (pbk) : Unpriced B81-35892

362.1'9892 — Hospitals. Patients: Children. Care — *For children*
Wade, Barrie. Linda goes to hospital / Barrie Wade ; photographs by Chris Fairclough. — London : A. & C. Black, c1981. — 25p : col.ill ; 22cm
Bibliography: p25
ISBN 0-7136-2154-0 : £3.50 : CIP rev. B81-24680

362.1'9892 — Hospitals. Patients: Children. Psychological aspects
Goodall, Janet. Suffering in childhood : the 1979 Barnardo lecture / Janet Goodall. — London : Christian Medical Fellowship, 1980. — 24p : ill,1port ; 21cm
ISBN 0-906747-04-x (pbk) : £0.75 B82-17146

362.1'98928'0973 — United States. Neurologically handicapped children. Care
Prensky, Arthur L.. Care of the neurologically handicapped child : a book for parents and professionals / Arthur L. Prensky, Helen Stein Palkes with contribution by Suzanne Busch ... [et al.]. — New York ; Oxford : Oxford University Press, 1982. — xv,331p : ill ; 24cm
Includes bibliographies and index
ISBN 0-19-502917-8 : £18.50 B82-26515

362.1'9892994'00924 — Children: Cancer victims — *Personal observations*
Phillips, Carolyn E.. Michelle / Carolyn E. Phillips. — London : Hodder and Stoughton, 1982. — 156p,[16]p of plates : ill,ports ; 18cm
ISBN 0-340-27894-3 (pbk) : £1.50 : CIP rev. B82-03820

Vianney, Gina. Martin : the true story of a boy's fight against cancer / by Gina Vianney. — London : Mowbray, 1982. — 187p ; 18cm
Originally published: Alton : Redemptorist, 1974
ISBN 0-264-66876-6 (pbk) : £1.75 B82-41082

362.1'989299419'00924 — Leukaemic children — *Personal observations*
Murton, Mary. Gerry / by Mary Murton with Mary Kerr. — Edinburgh : Saint Andrew Press, 1982. — vii,83p,[8]p of plates : ill,1map,ports ; 20cm
ISBN 0-7152-0496-3 (pbk) : £2.50 B82-20612

362.1'989299481'00924 — Terminally ill children: Brain cancer victims — *Personal observations*
Chambers, Ruth. A miracle for Jason? / Ruth Chambers. — London : Catholic Truth Society, 1980. — 40p ; 19cm
ISBN 0-85183-361-6 (pbk) : £0.35 B82-19336

362.1′9897′00941 — Great Britain. Health services for old persons

Establishing a geriatric service / edited by Davis Coakley. — London : Croom Helm, c1982. — 235p : ill,1map ; 23cm
Includes bibliographies and index
ISBN 0-7099-0700-1 : £14.95 : CIP rev. B81-34313

362.1′9897′009411 — Scotland. General hospitals. In-patients: Old persons — *Statistics*

Bed use by the elderly. — Edinburgh (Trinity Park House, South Trinity Rd, Edinburgh EH5 3SQ) : Information Services Division, Scottish Health Service Common Services Agency, [1982?]. — 9p : ill ; 30cm. — (Occasional papers ; no.3)
Cover title
Unpriced (pbk) B82-40985

362.2 — WELFARE SERVICES FOR THE MENTALLY ILL

362.2 — Attempted suicides. Treatment

Hawton, Keith. Attempted suicide. — Oxford : Oxford University Press, Oct.1982. — [150]p. — (Oxford medical publications)
ISBN 0-19-261289-1 (pbk) : £6.95 : CIP entry B82-23663

362.2 — Autistic children. Care

Everard, Peggie. Involuntary strangers : autism : the problems faced by parents / by Peggie Everard. — London : Clare, c1980. — vi,238p ; 22cm
Bibliography: p231-234. — Includes index
ISBN 0-906549-10-8 : £5.95 B82-21946

362.2 — Great Britain. Voluntary welfare services for suicidal persons: Samaritans, *to 1980* — *For schools*

Constant, Audrey. Someone to talk to : the story of Chad Varah and the Samaritans / Audrey Constant. — Exeter : Religious Education Press, 1981. — 29p : ill ; 21cm. — (Faith in action series)
Bibliography: p28
ISBN 0-08-026418-2 (pbk) : £0.65
ISBN 0-08-026417-4 (pbk) : Unpriced (non-net) B82-12068

362.2 — Man. Anti-social behaviour. Treatment

The Treatment of antisocial syndromes / edited by Willaim H. Reid. — New York ; London : Van Nostrand Reinhold, c1981. — xvi,269p ; 24cm
Includes index
ISBN 0-442-25630-2 : £15.75 B82-14006

362.2 — Psychotic persons: Manic depressives — *Personal observations*

Myerscough, Graham. I'm not a bloody label! / Graham Myerscough. — Southsea : Issness, 1981. — 157p ; 20cm
ISBN 0-9507907-0-2 (pbk) : £2.50 B82-12936

362.2 — Schizophrenics. Community treatment — *Case studies*

Korer, Jacky. Not the same as you? : the social situation of 190 schizophrenics living in the community / [Jacky Korer]. — London (The Groupwork Centre, 21A Kingsland High St., Dalston, E8) : Psychiatric Rehabilitation Association, [1981?]. — 24p : ill ; 30cm
Cover title. — Bibliography: p24
Unpriced (pbk) B82-03448

362.2 — Suicide. Durkheim, Emile. Suicide, *Le* — *Critical studies*

Taylor, Steve. Durkheim and the study of suicide / Steve Taylor. — London : Macmillan, 1982. — xii,249p ; 23cm. — (Contemporary social theory)
Bibliography: p236-244. — Includes index
ISBN 0-333-28645-6 (cased) : Unpriced
ISBN 0-333-28646-4 (pbk) : Unpriced B82-38772

362.2 — United States. Mental health services for ethnic minorities

Cross-cultural psychiatry / edited by Albert Gaw. — Boston, Mass. ; Bristol : John Wright, 1982. — xvii,366p ; 24cm
Includes bibliographies and index
ISBN 0-88416-338-5 : Unpriced B82-16124

362.2 — United States. Young persons, 13-19 years. Suicide. Psychosocial aspects

Giovacchini, Peter L. The urge to die : why young people commit suicide / Peter Giovacchini. — New York : Macmillan ; London : Collier Macmillan, c1981. — viii,216p ; 22cm
Bibliography: p193-195
ISBN 0-02-543440-3 : £7.95 B82-00979

362.2 — Women. Stress. Social aspects

Lives in stress : women and depression / edited by Deborah Belle ; forword by Jessie Bernard. — Beverly Hills ; London : Sage, c1982. — 246p : ill ; 23cm
Includes bibliographies
ISBN 0-8039-1768-6 (cased) : Unpriced
ISBN 0-8039-1769-4 (pbk) : £6.50 B82-25199

362.2′025′4127 — Scotland. Tayside Region. Dundee *(District)*. Community mental health services — *Directories*

Good practices in mental health : in the Dundee district. — [Dundee] ([Castlehill House, 1 High St., Dundee, DD1 1TE]) : Dundee Association for Social Service, 1981. — v,66p ; 30cm. — (An International Hospital Federation project)
Cover title
Unpriced (pbk) B82-28842

362.2′025′4257 — Oxfordshire. Community mental health services — *Directories*

Good practices in mental health. — Rev. version / Oxford Mental Health Association. — [Oxford] : [The Association], 1982. — 97p in various pagings ; 30cm
Cover title. — Previous ed.: 1980. — Includes index
£2.50 (pbk) B82-32055

362.2′025′42615 — Norfolk. Norwich. Community mental health services — *Directories*

Good practices in mental health : an International Hospital Federation report. — [England?] : [The Federation], 1980 ; Norwich (Drayton High Rd, Norwich NR6 5BE) : Hellesdon Hospital Sector Administrator [distributor]. — 83p : 1ill ; 21cm
Cover title
£0.60 (spiral) B82-11553

362.2′042 — United States. Community mental health services. Applications of social networks

Social networks and social support / edited by Benjamin H. Gottlieb. — Beverly Hills ; London : Sage, c1981. — 304p ; 22cm. — (Sage studies in community mental health ; v.4)
Includes bibliographies
ISBN 0-8039-1669-8 (cased) : Unpriced
ISBN 0-8039-1670-1 (pbk) : Unpriced B82-21863

362.2′0425 — Mentally disordered persons. Rehabilitation

Taylor, C. M. Returning to mental health / C.M. Taylor. — Cheltenham : Stanley Thornes, 1981. — xiv,144p ; 23cm
Bibliography: p134-138. — Includes index
ISBN 0-85950-307-0 : £4.95 : CIP rev. B81-19207

362.2′0425 — Mentally ill persons. Treatment

Neuman, Fredric. Caring : home treatment for the emotionally disturbed / by Fredric Neuman. — Wellingborough : Turnstone, 1982, c1980. — vi,245p ; 22cm
Originally published: New York : Dial, 1980. — Bibliography: p239-245
ISBN 0-85500-168-2 (pbk) : Unpriced : CIP rev. B81-35854

362.2′0425 — Patients with mental disorders. Rehabilitation

Rehabilitation in psychiatric practice. — London : Pitman, June 1982. — [228]p
ISBN 0-272-79647-6 (pbk) : £14.95 : CIP entry B82-09992

362.2′0425 — Scotland. Mental health officers. Duties. Performance

Functions of mental health officers : notes for local authorities on their responsibilities regarding the functions of mental health officers under the Mental Health (Scotland) Act 1960. — [Edinburgh] ([43 Jeffrey St., Edinburgh EH1 1DN]) : Social Work Services Group, [1980]. — 31p ; 21cm. — (Notes for local authorities)
Unpriced (pbk) B82-32992

Social workers as mental health officers : summary of research findings. — [Edinburgh] ([c/o Social Work Services Group, 43 Jeffrey St., Edinburgh EH1 1DN]) : Central Research Unit, [1980]. — 7p ; 21cm
"A Summary of the Scottish Office Central Research Unit Study of Social Workers as Mental Health Officers" — cover
Unpriced (pbk) B82-32991

362.2′0425 — Suicide. Prevention. Psychosocial aspects

New trends in suicide prevention / volume editors J. Wilmotte, J. Mendlewicz. — Basel ; London : Karger, 1982. — 103p : ill ; 24cm. — (Bibliotheca psychiatrica ; no.162)
Includes bibliographies and index
ISBN 3-8055-3430-2 (pbk) : Unpriced B82-34290

362.2′0425 — United States. Chronically mentally ill persons. Rehabilitation

Krauss, Judith Belliveau. The chronically ill psychiatric patient and the community / Judith Belliveau Krauss, Ann Tomaino Slavinsky. — Boston, [Mass.] ; Oxford : Blackwell Scientific, c1982. — ix,376p ; 24cm
Includes bibliographies and index
ISBN 0-86542-006-8 : £14.50 B82-32699

362.2′0425 — United States. Psychiatric patients. Rehabilitation — *Sociological perspectives*

Estroff, Sue E.. Making it crazy : an ethnography of psychiatric clients in an American community / Sue E. Estroff ; foreword by H. Richard Lamb. — Berkeley ; London : University of California Press, c1981. — xxi,328p : 1map ; 24cm
Bibliography: p289-317. — Includes index
ISBN 0-520-03963-7 : £14.00 B82-02226

362.2′0425 — United States. Rural regions. Mental health services. Psychologists. Training

Training professionals for rural health / edited by H.A. Dengerink and H.J. Cross. — Lincoln [Neb.] ; London : University of Nebraska Press, c1982. — 135p : ill ; 24cm
Includes bibliographies
ISBN 0-8032-1660-2 : Unpriced B82-37233

362.2′0425′0941 — Great Britain. Mentally disordered persons. Care — *For welfare work*

Wilder, John, *1927-*. An aid to community care / by John Wilder. — Rev. — London : Psychiatric Rehabilitation Association, 1980. — 183p : ill,1form ; 21cm
Previous ed.: 1978. — Includes index
ISBN 0-900980-12-5 (pbk) : £4.00 B82-00129

362.2′0425′0941 — Great Britain. Psychiatric services. Attitudes of patients

Brandon, David. Voices of experience : consumer perspectives of psychiatric treatment / David Brandon. — [London] : [MIND], [1981]. — 36p ; 21cm
Cover title. — Text on inside cover
ISBN 0-900557-48-6 (pbk) : £1.30 B82-08523

362.2′0425′0941 — Great Britain. Welfare work with mentally disordered persons

Hudson, Barbara L.. Social work with psychiatric patients / Barbara L. Hudson. — London : Macmillan, 1982. — xi,218p ; 23cm
Bibliography: p181-184, 189-205. — Includes index
ISBN 0-333-26685-4 (cased) : £12.50
ISBN 0-333-26686-2 (pbk) : Unpriced B82-38791

362.2'0425'0941 — Great Britain. Welfare work with mentally disordered persons — *Manuals — For volunteers*

Brandon, David. The trick of being ordinary : notes for volunteers & students / David Brandon. — London : MIND, c1982. — 19p : ill ; 21cm. — (MIND publications)
Bibliography: p19
ISBN 0-900557-51-6 (pbk) : £0.85 B82-20724

362.2'0425'09411 — Scotland. Mentally disordered patients. Care — *Inquiry reports*

Mental Welfare Commission for Scotland. Does the patient come first? : an account of the work of the Mental Welfare Commission for Scotland between 1975 and 1980 / the Mental Welfare Commission for Scotland. — Edinburgh : H.M.S.O., 1981. — 54p ; 25cm
ISBN 0-11-491978-x (pbk) : £4.00 B82-06337

362.2'04256 — United States. Mental health education

Ketterer, Richard F.. Consultation and education in mental health : problems and prospects / Richard F. Ketterer. — Beverly Hills ; London : Sage, c1981. — 245p : ill ; 22cm. — (Sage series in community mental health ; v.3)
Bibliography: p235-244
ISBN 0-8039-1638-8 (cased) : Unpriced
ISBN 0-8039-1639-6 (pbk) : Unpriced
B82-08572

362.2'072073 — United States. Walfare work with mentally ill persons. Research

Scheirer, Mary Ann. Program implementation : the organizational context / Mary Ann Scheirer. — Beverly Hills ; London : Sage, c1981. — 232p : forms ; 23cm. — (Contemporary evaluation research ; 5)
Bibliography: p225-231
ISBN 0-8039-1540-3 : Unpriced B82-07781

362.2'088054 — Mental health services for children

Today's priorities in mental health : children and families : needs, rights and action / editors, Stuart H. Fine, Robert Krell, Tsung-yi Lin ; associate editors, Morton Beiser, David S. Freeman, Richard Nann ; contributing staff, Roberta Beiser, Nora Curiston, Ann McCarthy. — Dordrecht ; London : Reidel, c1981. — xi,251p ; 25cm. — (Priority issues in mental health ; v.1)
Conference papers. — Includes bibliographies and index
ISBN 90-277-1148-8 : Unpriced B82-35799

362.2'0941 — Great Britain. Community mental health services

Local services for mentally handicapped people : the community team, the community unit and the role and function of the community nurse, social worker and some other members of the CMHT / edited by: G.B. Simon ; foreword by: Peter Mittler. — Kidderminster : British Institute of Mental Handicap, 1981. — 87p : ill ; 22cm
Bibliography: p78-82
ISBN 0-906054-31-1 (cased) : Unpriced
ISBN 0-906054-30-3 (pbk) : £4.85 B82-40094

362.2'0941 — Great Britain. Mental health — *Serials*

The **Mental** health year book. — 1981/82-. — London : MIND, c1981-. — v. ; 21cm
ISSN 0262-5423 = Mental health year book : Unpriced B82-05224

362.2'09716 — Nova Scotia. Community mental health services, *to 1981*

Leighton, Alexander H.. Caring for mentally ill people : psychological and social barriers in historical context / Alexander H. Leighton. — Cambridge : Cambridge University Press, 1982. — x,277p ; 24cm
Includes index
ISBN 0-521-23415-8 (cased) : £20.00
ISBN 0-521-28816-9 (pbk) : £7.50 B82-29928

362.2'0973 — United States. Community mental health services

Levine, Murray. The history and politics of community health / Murray Levine. — New York ; Oxford : Oxford University Press, 1981. — 232p ; 22cm
Bibliography: p207-222. — Includes index
ISBN 0-19-502955-0 (cased) : £11.00
ISBN 0-19-502956-9 (pbk) : Unpriced
B82-31568

362.2'0973 — United States. Medicine. Psychiatry. Social aspects — *Conference proceedings*

Psychiatry in crisis / edited by Richard C.W. Hall. — Lancaster : MTP, c1982. — 148p ; 24cm
Includes bibliographies and index
ISBN 0-85200-576-8 : £11.75 B82-17279

362.2'0973 — United States. Mental health services. Evaluation

Innovative approaches to mental health evaluation / edited by Gerald J. Stahler, William R. Tash. — New York ; London : Academic Press, c1982. — xvi,394p : ill ; 24cm
Includes bibliographies and index
ISBN 0-12-663020-8 : £21.60 B82-30136

362.2'0973 — United States. Mental health services. Political aspects

Castel, Robert. The psychiatric society / Robert Castel, Françoise Castel, and Anne Lovell ; translated by Arthur Goldhammer. — New York ; Guildford : Columbia University Press, 1982. — xxiii,358p : ill ; 24cm. — (European perspectives)
Translation of: La société psychiatrique avancée. — Includes index
ISBN 0-231-05244-8 : £18.00 B82-28061

362.2'1 — Scotland. Mental illness hospitals. Patients. Compulsory admission. Procedure — *For mental health officers*

Social work practice in formal admissions : notes for mental health officers on social work practice in formal admission procedures under the Mental Health (Scotland) Act 1960. — [Edinburgh] ([43 Jeffrey St., Edinburgh EH1 1DN]) : Social Work Services Group, [1980]. — 37p ; 21cm. — (Notes for mental health officers)
Unpriced (pbk) B82-32993

362.2'1'0941 — Great Britain. Mental illness hospitals. Patients. Care. Complaints by nurses

Beardshaw, Virginia. Conscientious objectors at work. — London (9 Poland St., W1V 3DG) : Social Audit, Sept.1981. — [90]p
ISBN 0-9503392-6-1 (pbk) : £3.50 : CIP entry
B81-28158

362.2'1'0941 — Great Britain. Psychiatric hospitals — *MIND viewpoints — Conference proceedings*

MIND. *Conference (1980).* The future of the mental hospitals : a report of MIND's 1980 Annual Conference. — London : MIND, c1981. — 75p ; 30cm
ISBN 0-900557-50-8 (pbk) : £2.20 B82-08529

362.2'1'094126 — Scotland. Tayside Region. Montrose. Mental illness hospitals: Sunnyside Royal Hospital, *to 1981*

Presly, A. S.. A Sunnyside chronicle : a history of Sunnyside Royal Hospital, produced for its bi-centenary / by A.S. Presly. — [Dundee] ([Thru' Tayside Health Board, Area Printing Department, 76 Brook St., Dundee D1 5BP]) : [The Hospital], [1981?]. — 57p : ill,facsims ; 21cm
Unpriced (pbk) B82-26480

362.2'1'0941486 — Scotland. Dumfries and Galloway Region. Dumfries. Psychiatric hospitals: Crichton Royal *(Hospital), 1937-1971*

Turner, George B.. Chronicle of Crichton Royal : 1937-1971 / by George B. Turner ; review of clinical services by Allan C. Tait. — [Dumfries] : [Dumfries and Galloway Health Board], [1980?]. — iv,282p,[30]p of plates : ill,1coat of arms,facsims,ports ; 25cm
Includes index
Unpriced B82-28537

362.2'1'0942 — England. Psychiatric hospitals — *Statistics*

The **Facilities** and services of mental illness and mental handicap hospitals in England 1976 / Department of Health and Social Security. — London : H.M.S.O., 1980. — viii,134p : ill ; 30cm. — (Statistical and research report series ; no.21)
Bibliography: p122
ISBN 0-11-320753-0 (pbk) : £9.00 B82-20456

362.2'1'0942298 — Berkshire. Crowthorne. Special hospitals: Broadmoor Special Hospital

Cohen, David, *1946-*. Broadmoor / David Cohen ; [edited by Felicity Grant]. — London : Psychology News Press, [1982?]. — 146p : ill ; 21cm
ISBN 0-907633-00-5 (cased) : £6.95
ISBN 0-907633-01-3 (pbk) : £3.95 B82-21326

362.2'1'09425895 — Hertfordshire. Shenley. Psychiatric hospitals: Harperbury Hospital, *to 1978*

Baranyay, Eileen. Fifty years of Harperbury Hospital 1928-1978 / Eileen Baranyay. — London : National Society for Mentally Handicapped Children and Adults, c1981. — 42p ; 21cm
£1.50 (pbk) B82-02724

362.2'1'09429 — Wales. Mental illness hospitals. In-patients — *Statistics — Serials*

Census of patients in mental illness hospitals and units / Welsh Office. — 31 Aug. 1979-. — Cardiff (Economic and Statistical Services (5c), Welsh Office, New Crown Building, Cathays Park, Cardiff CF1 3NQ) : The Office, 1979-. — v. ; 22x30cm
Issued every two years. — Description based on: 5 Apr. 1981 issue
ISSN 0262-7213 = Census of patients in mental illness hospitals and units : Unpriced
B82-09677

362.2'1'09714281 — Quebec *(Province)*. Montreal. Mentally disordered persons. Home care *compared with* hospitalisation

Home and hospital psychiatric treatment / Fred R. Fenton ... [et al.]. — London : Croom Helm, c1982. — 197p ; 22cm
Bibliography: p185-192. — Includes index
ISBN 0-7099-0350-2 : £12.95 : CIP rev.
B81-30349

362.2'2'0941 — Great Britain. Mentally ill persons. Day care — *MIND viewpoints — Conference proceedings*

New directions for psychiatric day services : a report of a MIND conference held in 1980. — London : MIND, c1981. — 104p : ill ; 30cm
ISBN 0-900557-49-4 (pbk) : £2.80 B82-08528

362.2'9 — Alcoholism & drug abuse — *Conference proceedings*

National Drug Abuse Conference *(5th : 1978 : Seattle)*. Drug dependence and alcoholism / [... proceedings of the 1978 National Drug Abuse Conference, held in Seattle, Washington, April 3-8, 1978] ; edited by Arnold J. Schecter. — New York ; London : Plenum
Includes bibliographies and index
Vol.1: Biomedical issues. — c1981. — xxviii,1342p : ill,1map ; 26cm
ISBN 0-306-40323-4 : Unpriced B82-05804

National Drug Abuse Conference *(5th : 1978 : Seattle)*. Drug dependence and alcoholism / [... proceedings of the 1978 National Drug Abuse Conference, held in Seattle, Washinton, April 3-8, 1978] ; edited by Arnold J. Schecter. — New York ; London : Plenum
Vol.2: Social and behavioral issues. — c1981. — xxii,1041p : ill ; 26cm
Includes bibliographies and index
ISBN 0-306-40324-2 : Unpriced B82-13995

362.2'9 — Alcoholism & drug addiction

Schlaadt, Richard G.. Drugs of choice : current perspectives on drug use / Richard G. Schlaadt, Peter T. Shannon. — Englewood Cliffs ; London : Prentice-Hall, c1982. — xvi,303p : ill ; 23cm
Includes index
ISBN 0-13-220772-9 (pbk) : £11.95
B82-31821

362.2'9'05 — Alcoholism & drug abuse — *Serials*

Advances in substance abuse : behavioral and biological research : a research annual. — Vol.1 (1980)-. — Greenwich, Conn. : JAI Press ; London (3 Henrietta St., WC2E 8LU) : Distributed by JAICON Press, 1980. — v. : ill ; 24cm
ISSN 0272-1740 = Advances in substance abuse. Behavioral and biological research : £26.20 B82-02347

362.2'9'0926 — United States. Alcoholism & drug abuse. Treatment — *Case studies*

Brill, Leon. The clinical treatment of substance abusers / Leon Brill. — New York : Free Press ; London : Collier Macmillan, c1981. — xviii,250p : 1form ; 25cm. — (Fields of practice series)
Includes index
ISBN 0-02-905160-6 : £10.95 B82-30020

362.2'9'0973 — United States. Alcoholism & drug abuse

Perspectives in alcohol and drug abuse : similarites and differences / edited by Joel Solomon, Kim A. Keeley. — Boston, Mass. ; Bristol : John Wright, 1982. — ix,259p : ill ; 24cm
Includes index
ISBN 0-88416-306-7 (pbk) : Unpriced B82-16126

362.2'92 — Alcoholics. Behaviour. Assessment. Questionnaires: Hilton Questionnaire

Hilton, Margaret R.. The Hilton questionnaire : a measure of drinking behaviour / Margaret R. Hilton. — Windsor : NFER-Nelson, c1982. — 2v. : 1ill,1forms ; 30cm
ISBN 0-7005-0477-x : Unpriced
ISBN 0-7005-0476-1 (Questionnaire) : (Sold in packs of 25) £2.50 B82-25463

362.2'92 — Alcoholics. Treatment: Controlled drinking

Heather, Nick. Controlled drinking. — London : Methuen, Oct.1981. — [350]p
ISBN 0-416-71970-8 : £19.50 : CIP entry B81-28083

362.2'92 — Alcoholism

Alcohol problems. — London : British Medical Association, c1982. — 59p : ill ; 30cm
ISBN 0-7279-0094-3 (pbk) : Unpriced B82-34793

Alcoholism : development, consequences and interventions / [edited by] Nada J. Estes, M. Edith Heinemann. — 2nd ed. — St. Louis ; London : Mosby, 1982. — x,385p : ill ; 24cm
Previous ed.: 1977. — Includes bibliographies and index
ISBN 0-8016-1500-3 (pbk) : £10.00 B82-31872

Glatt, Max. Alcoholism / Max Glatt ; foreword by the late Lord Rosenheim. — [1982 ed.]. — Sevenoaks : Teach Yourself Books, 1982. — xiii,553p ; 18cm. — (Care and welfare)
Previous ed.: 1975. — Bibliography: p536-538. — Includes index
ISBN 0-340-26817-4 (pbk) : £2.95 : CIP rev. B81-34127

362.2'92 — Alcoholism — *Conference proceedings*

ALC 80 International Conference *(1980 : Bath)*. Alcoholism : a modern perspective / proceedings of the ALC 80 International Conference held in Bath, England 20-24th September 1980 ; edited by P. Golding. — Lancaster : MTP, c1982. — xii,539p : ill ; 24cm
Includes index
ISBN 0-85200-409-5 : £29.95 : CIP rev. B81-30903

362.2'92 — Alcoholism. Psychosocial aspects — *Conference proceedings*

Currents in alcoholism / edited by Marc Galanter. — New York ; London : Grune & Stratton
Vol.8: Recent advances in research and treatment / managing editor Jeanette Mason ; associate editors Henri Begleiter ... [et al.]. — c1981. — xii,527p : ill ; 24cm
Includes index
ISBN 0-8089-1458-8 : £32.20
Primary classification 616.86'1 B82-27137

362.2'92'0321 — Alcoholism — *Encyclopaedias*

The **Encyclopedia** of alcoholism. — London : Library Association, Dec.1982. — [400]p
ISBN 0-85365-586-3 : £30.00 : CIP entry B82-30333

362.2'92'094 — Europe. Alcoholism — *Sociological perspectives*

Davies, Phil. Alcohol problems and alcohol control in Europe. — London : Croom Helm, July 1982. — [256]p
ISBN 0-7099-0816-4 : £12.95 : CIP entry B82-15925

362.2'92'0941 — Great Britain. Alcoholism. Psychosocial aspects — *For welfare work*

Hunt, Linda. Alcohol related problems / Linda Hunt. — London : Heinemann Educational, 1982. — 116p ; 22cm. — (Community care practice handbooks ; 7)
Bibliography: p108-112. — Includes index
ISBN 0-435-82450-3 (pbk) : £2.95 : CIP rev. B81-35692

362.2'92'0941 — Great Britain. Alcoholism. Role of family life

Alcohol and the family / edited by Jim Orford and Judith Harwin. — London : Croom Helm, c1982. — 295p : ill ; 23cm
Bibliography: p266-286. — Includes index
ISBN 0-7099-0473-8 : £14.95 : CIP rev. B81-34309

362.2'92'0973 — United States. Alcoholism

Royce, James E.. Alcohol problems and alcoholism : a comprehensive survey / James E. Royce. — New York : Free Press ; London : Collier Macmillan, c1981. — xiii,383p : ill ; 25cm
Bibliography: p335-372. — Includes index
ISBN 0-02-927540-7 : £13.95 B82-18008

362.2'927'0941 — Great Britain. Alcoholism. Prevention

Drinking sensibly : a discussion document / prepared by the Health Departments of Great Britain and Northern Ireland. — London : H.M.S.O., 1981. — 74p : ill ; 21cm. — (Prevention and health series)
At head of title: Department of Health and Social Security. — Bibliography: p71-73
ISBN 0-11-320775-1 (pbk) : £2.95 B82-17685

362.2'928'09411 — Scotland. Welfare services for alcoholics — *Inquiry reports*

Responding to alcohol-related problems in Scotland : report of the Working Party on Community Services for Alcoholics, appointed by the Professional and General Services Committee of the Scottish Council on Alcoholism. — [Edinburgh] ([49 York Place, Edinburgh EH1 3JD]) : The Council, [1980]. — 29p : 1ill ; 21cm
Unpriced (pbk) B82-31840

362.2'9286 — Alcoholics. Treatment — *Manuals* — *For welfare work*

Davies, Ian, *1946-*. Dealing with drink / Ian Davies and Duncan Raistrick. — London : British Broadcasting Corporation, 1981. — 256p : ill ; 19cm
Includes index
ISBN 0-563-16489-1 (pbk) : £4.25 B82-06449

362.2'93 — Drug abuse

Krivanek, Jara A.. Drug problems, people problems. — London : Allen and Unwin, Jan.1983. — [256]p
ISBN 0-86861-364-9 : £15.00 : CIP entry B82-33241

Substance abuse : clinical problems and perspectives / edited by Joyce H. Lowinson, Pedro Ruiz. — Baltimore ; London : Williams & Wilkins, c1981. — xxiii,885p : ill,1form ; 26cm
Includes bibliographies and index
ISBN 0-683-05210-1 : Unpriced B82-02593

362.2'93 — Heroin addiction

Trebach, Arnold S.. The heroin solution. — London : Yale University Press, Oct.1982. — [352]p
ISBN 0-300-02773-7 : £15.00 : CIP entry B82-35193

362.2'93'0941 — Great Britain. Heroin addiction, *1960-1980*

Stimson, Gerry V.. Heroin addiction : treatment and control in Britain / Gerry V. Stimson and Edna Oppenheimer. — London : Tavistock, 1982. — 267p ; 25cm
Bibliography: p253-256. — Includes index
ISBN 0-422-77890-7 : Unpriced : CIP rev. B82-19670

362.2'93'0942 — England. Opiates. Use, *ca 1800-1900*. **Social aspects**

Berridge, Virginia. Opium and the people : opiate use in nineteenth-century England / Virginia Berridge and Griffith Edwards. — London : Allen Lane, 1981. — xxx,369p,[4]p of plates : ill,facsims,ports ; 23cm
Bibliography: p327-348. — Includes index
ISBN 0-7139-0852-1 : £20.00 B82-07536

362.2'93'095 — East Asia, South Asia & South-east Asia. Drug abuse

Spencer, C. P.. Drug abuse in east Asia / C.P. Spencer, V. Navaratnam ; prepared for the National Drug Dependence Research Centre, University of Science Malaysia, Penang. — Kuala Lumpur ; Oxford : Oxford University Press, 1981. — 227p ; 26cm
Bibliography: p198-214. — Includes index
ISBN 0-19-580476-7 (cased) : £15.50
ISBN 0-19-580482-1 (pbk) : Unpriced B82-26513

362.2'93'0973 — United States. Opiate addiction, *to 1940*

Courtwright, David T.. Dark paradise : opiate addiction in America before 1940 / David T. Courtwright. — Cambridge, Mass. ; London : Harvard University Press, 1982. — 270p : ill ; 25cm
Bibliography: p225-263. — Includes index
ISBN 0-674-19261-3 : £14.00 B82-33390

362.2'938'088042 — Women. Drug addiction. Treatment

Cuskey, Walter R.. Female addiction : a longitudinal study / Walter R. Cuskey, Richard B. Wathey. — Lexington, Mass. : Lexington Books ; [Aldershot] : Gower [distributor], 1982. — xxi,169p : ill ; 24cm
Bibliography: p155-162. — Includes index
ISBN 0-669-04029-0 : £15.00 B82-28661

362.3 — WELFARE SERVICES FOR THE MENTALLY RETARDED

362.3 — Down's Syndrome children

Ludlow, J. R.. Down's syndrome : let's be positive : an approach to help Down's syndrome children reach their full potential / by J.R. Ludlow. — Birmingham (Quinborne Community Centre, Ridgacre Rd., Birmingham B32 2TW) : Down's Children's Association, South East Branch, c1980. — 54p : ill,forms ; 30cm
Bibliography: p54
£0.50 (spiral) B82-35048

362.3 — Down's syndrome children — *For parents*

Cunningham, Cliff. Down's syndrome : an introduction for parents / Cliff Cunningham. — London : Souvenir, 1982. — 187p,[24]p of plates : ill,ports ; 22cm. — (Human horizons series)
Bibliography: p178-181. — Includes index
ISBN 0-285-64930-2 (cased) : £6.95
ISBN 0-285-64931-0 (pbk) : £4.95 B82-27041

362.3 — Mentally handicapped persons

Chinn, Philip C.. Mental retardation : a life cycle approach / Philip C. Chinn, Clifford J. Drew, Don R. Logan. — 2nd ed. — St. Louis ; London : C.V. Mosby, 1979. — x,491p : ill ; 25cm
Previous ed.: 1975. — Includes bibliographies and index
ISBN 0-8016-0968-2 : £15.00 B82-33565

362.3 — Mentally handicapped persons. Self-advocacy

Williams, Paul, *1944-*. We can speak for ourselves : self-advocacy by mentally handicapped people / Paul Williams and Bonnie Shoultz. — London : Souvenir, 1982. — 245p,[16]p of plates : ill,ports ; 22cm. — (Human horizons series)
ISBN 0-285-64938-8 (cased) : £7.95
ISBN 0-285-64939-6 (pbk) : £5.95 B82-24882

362.3'088054 — Devon. Welfare services for mentally handicapped children — *For parents*
Help : for parents of mentally-handicapped children in Devon / Devon Area Health Authority, Devon Local Education Authority, Devon Social Services Department ; [photographs by Sue Currant]. — 2nd ed. — [Exeter] : [The Authorities], c1981. — 16p : ill ; 20x21cm
Previous ed.: 1975?
ISBN 0-86114-303-5 (pbk) : Unpriced
B82-19920

362.3'088054 — Kent. Gillingham & Rochester upon Medway ***(District).*** **Welfare services for mentally handicapped children** — *For parents of mentally handicapped children*
A **Helping** booklet : for families caring about mental handicap. — [Gillingham] ([c/o Community Health Administrator, Medway Hospital, Windmill Rd., Gillingham, Kent ME7 5NY]) : [Medway Health District], [1982?]. — 46p : ill ; 21cm
Includes index
Unpriced (pbk) B82-22880

362.3'088054 — Mentally handicapped children. Behaviour modification
Behaviour modification for the mentally handicapped / edited by William Yule and Janet Carr. — London : Croom Helm, c1980 (1982 [printing]). — 298p : ill,forms ; 22cm
Bibliography: p263-294. — Includes index
ISBN 0-7099-2902-1 (pbk) : £8.95 B82-26941

362.3'088054 — Mentally handicapped children. Care — *For parents*
Worthington, Ann. Coming to terms with mental handicap / Ann Worthington ; foreword by Brian Rix. — Huddersfield : Helena Press, 1982. — 194p ; 22cm
Bibliography: p181-190. — Includes index
ISBN 0-9507930-0-0 (pbk) : Unpriced : CIP rev. B82-04728

362.3'092'2 — Avon. Bristol. Mentally handicapped children — *Personal observations — Collections*
Tears and joy / [by parents of mentally handicapped children]. — Bristol : Bristol Broadsides, c1981. — 68p : ill,ports ; 22cm
ISBN 0-906944-11-2 (pbk) : £1.20 B82-10995

362.3'092'4 — United States. Mentally retarded persons — *Personal observations*
Bogdan, Robert. Inside out : the social meaning of mental retardation / Robert Bogdan and Steven J. Taylor. — Toronto ; London : University of Toronto Press, c1982. — xiv,231p ; 22cm
Bibliography: p227-231
ISBN 0-8020-2432-7 : Unpriced B82-27905

Monty, Shirlee. May's boy. — Oxford : Mowbray, Sept.1982. — [186]p
Originally published: Nashville : Nelson, 1981
ISBN 0-264-66878-2 (pbk) : £1.75 : CIP entry
B82-18868

362.3'0941 — Great Britain. Mentally handicapped persons
Clarke, David, *1940-.* Mentally handicapped people : living and learning / David Clarke ; with a foreword by Harry McCree. — London : Baillière Tindall, 1982. — xi,346p : ill,facsims,forms ; 24cm
Includes bibliographies and index
ISBN 0-7020-0894-x (pbk) : £12.50 : CIP rev.
B81-34300

362.3'0973 — United States. Mentally retarded persons
Gearheart, Bill R.. The trainable retarded : a foundations approach / Bill R. Gearheart, Freddie W. Litton. — 2nd ed. — St. Louis ; London : Mosby, 1979. — xi,290p : ill ; 27cm
Previous ed.: 1975. — Includes bibliographies and index
ISBN 0-8016-1761-8 : £13.50 B82-28890

362.3'53 — Residential welfare work with mentally handicapped persons
Tjosvold, Dean. Working with mentally handicapped persons in their residences / Dean Tjosvold, Mary M. Tjosvold. — New York : Free Press ; London : Collier Macmillan, c1981. — 232p : forms ; 25cm
Bibliography: p219-225. — Includes index
ISBN 0-02-932490-4 : £12.95 B82-30025

362.3'537 — Voluntary welfare work with mentally handicapped persons
Gathercole, C. E.. Leisure volunteer's guide : a supplement to the series Residential alternatives for adults who are mentally handicapped / by C.E. Gathercole. — Kidderminster : British Institute of Mental Handicap, 1981. — viii p ; 21cm
Cover title
ISBN 0-906054-54-0 (pbk) : £0.35 B82-40091

362.3'56'0941 — Great Britain. Mentally handicapped persons. Policies of government. Formulation
Donges, Gregory S.. Policymaking for the mentally handicapped / Gregory S. Donges. — Aldershot : Gower, c1982. — vi,138p ; 23cm
Bibliography: p136-138
ISBN 0-566-00514-x : Unpriced : CIP rev.
B82-06853

362.3'58'088054 — Great Britain. Mentally handicapped children. Community care — *Conference proceedings*
Family placements for mentally handicapped children : King's Fund College, Bayswater, 14th-16th May 1979 / organised jointly by the British Institute of Mental Handicap and the Association of British Adoption and Fostering Agencies. — Wolverhampton : British Institute of Mental Handicap, 1980. — i,66p ; 21cm
"Report of a residential workshop"
ISBN 0-906054-22-2 (pbk) : £3.50 B82-31147

362.3'8 — England. Mentally handicapped persons. Rehabilitation — *Conference proceedings*
Forms of rehabilitation for the mentally handicapped : proceedings of the conference held at Lea Castle Hospital, near Kidderminster, Wednesday, 2nd July, 1975 / [papers presented by J.G. Kendall ... et al.]. — Kidderminster (Wolverhampton Rd, Kidderminster, Worcs. DY10 3PP) : Institute of Mental Subnormality, 1977. — 44p ; 21cm. — (IMS conference proceedings)
Includes bibliographies
£1.00 (pbk) B82-35266

362.3'8 — Mentally handicapped persons. Care
Hallas, Charles H.. The care and training of the mentally handicapped : a manual for the caring professions / Charles H. Hallas, William I. Fraser, Ronald C. MacGillivray. — 7th ed. — Bristol : John Wright, 1982. — xii,409p : ill,2forms ; 22cm
Previous ed.: 1978. — Bibliography: p391-396. — Includes index
ISBN 0-7236-0624-2 (pbk) : Unpriced : CIP rev. B82-15929

362.3'8 — Welfare services for mentally handicapped persons — *Conference proceedings*
Parents, professionals and mentally handicapped people. — London : Croom Helm, Jan.1983. — [200]p
Conference papers
ISBN 0-7099-1750-3 : £11.95 : CIP entry
B82-33349

362.3'8'0941 — Great Britain. Mentally handicapped persons. Care
Mental handicap in the eighties / Joan Bicknell ... [et al.]. — London : National Society for Mentally Handicapped Children and Adults, c1981. — 16p ; 21cm
Cover title
ISBN 0-85537-066-1 (pbk) : £1.00 B82-00630

362.3'8'0941 — Great Britain. Services for mentally handicapped persons — *National Union of Public Employees viewpoints*
A **policy** for mental handicap care. — London : National Union of Public Employees, [1981]. — 20p : ill ; 21cm
Cover title
ISBN 0-907334-09-1 (pbk) : £0.25 B82-00629

362.3'8'0941 — Great Britain. Services for mentally handicapped persons. Planning — *Proposals*
Joint planning and utilisation of resources to meet the needs of the mentally handicapped : proceedings of the conference held at St. Margarets Hospital, Great Barr, Birmingham, on Thursday, 17th June, 1976 / [papers presented by Roger S. Tarver ... et al.]. — Kidderminster (Wolverhampton Rd., Kidderminster, Worcs. DY10 3PP) : Institute of Mental Subnormality, 1977. — 58p : ill ; 21cm. — (IMA conference proceedings)
£1.80 (pbk) B82-35267

362.3'8'0941 — Great Britain. Welfare services for mentally handicapped persons — *Conference proceedings*
Right from the start '81 : report of conference proceedings, 23 June 1981 / editor Victoria Shennan ; contributors Joan Bicknell ... [et al.] ; foreword Brian Rix. — London : MENCAP, c1981. — ii,44p ; 21cm
ISBN 0-85537-067-x (pbk) : £2.50 B82-10181

362.3'8'094132 — Scotland. Lothian Region. Services for mentally handicapped persons — *Practical information*
Help for mentally handicapped children and adults living in Lothian. — [Edinburgh] : Lothian Regional Council Department of Social Work, [1981?]. — ii,65p : ill,2maps ; 20cm
Cover title. — Maps on inside covers. — Includes index
Unpriced (spiral) B82-08301

362.3'8'09417 — Ireland ***(Republic).*** **Welfare services for mentally handicapped persons** — *For parents of mentally handicapped persons — Serials*
[Notes for parents *(National Association for the Mentally Handicapped of Ireland)*]. Notes for parents / National Association for the Mentally Handicapped of Ireland. — No.1-. — Dublin (5 Fitzwilliam Place, Dublin 2) : N.A.M.H.I., [197-?]-. — v. ; 22cm
Description based on: No.5
Unpriced B82-22660

362.3'85 — Mentally handicapped persons. Community residential care
Gathercole, C. E.. Residential alternatives : for adults who are mentally handicapped / C.E. Gathercole. — Kidderminster : British Institute of Mental Handicap, 1981. — 4v. : 1ill,forms ; 21cm
Includes bibliographies
ISBN 0-906054-50-8 (pbk) : Unpriced
ISBN 0-906054-51-6 (v.2) : £2.25
ISBN 0-906054-52-4 (v.3) : £2.25
ISBN 0-906054-53-2 (v.4) : £2.25 B82-40095

362.3'85 — Residential institutions for mentally handicapped persons: Arche ***(Association)***
The **Challenge** of l'Arche. — London : Darton Longman & Todd, Nov.1982. — [288]p
ISBN 0-232-51560-3 (pbk) : £6.95 : CIP entry
B82-26900

362.3'85'0942819 — West Yorkshire ***(Metropolitan County).*** **Leeds. Mental handicap hospitals: Meanwood Park Hospital,** ***to 1982***
Spencer, Douglas A.. Meanwood Park Hospital, Leeds : a history / Douglas A. Spencer. — Leeds : Leeds Area Health Authority (Teaching), 1982. — i,39p ; 30cm
Cover title
ISBN 0-946031-00-2 (pbk) : Unpriced
B82-22824

362.3'85'09429 — Wales. Mental handicap hospitals. In-patients — *Statistics — Serials*
Census of patients in mental handicap hospitals and units / Welsh Office. — 31 Aug. 1979-. — Cardiff (Economic and Statistical Services (5c), Welsh Office, New Crown Building, Cathays Park, Cardiff CF1 3NQ) : The Office, 1979-. — v. ; 22x30cm
Issued every two years. — Description based on: 5 Apr. 1981 issue
ISSN 0262-7205 = Census of patients in mental handicap hospitals and units : Unpriced
B82-09679

362.3′86 — Mentally handicapped persons. Social skills. Teaching — *Manuals*

Let′s go : book 2 : notes for parents, teachers and instructors to accompany the BBC television series on social skills. — London : British Broadcasting Corporation, [1981]. — 63p : ill ; 30cm
Cover title
ISBN 0-563-16461-1 (pbk) : £0.95 B82-40198

362.3′86 — Mentally retarded persons. Behaviour modification

Handbook of behavior modification with the mentally retarded / edited by Johnny L. Matson and John R. McCartney. — New York ; London : Plenum, c1981. — xvi,414p : ill ; 26cm. — (Applied clinical psychology)
Includes bibliographies and index
ISBN 0-306-40617-9 : Unpriced B82-14279

Perkins, E. A.. Helping the retarded : a systematic behavioural approach / E.A. Perkins, P.D. Taylor, A.C. Capie. — 2nd ed. — Kidderminster : British Institute of Mental Handicap, 1980. — 105p : ill ; 21cm
Previous ed.: 1976. — Text on inside cover
ISBN 0-906054-00-1 (pbk) : £3.95 B82-31194

362.4 — WELFARE SERVICES FOR THE PHYSICALLY HANDICAPPED

362.4 — Handicaped children. Interpersonal relationships with parents

Marshall, Margaret R.. Parents and the handicapped child : a guide for families. — London : MacRae, Sept.1982. — [160]p
ISBN 0-86203-102-8 : £6.25 : CIP entry
B82-21554

362.4 — Handicapped persons

Bloom, Freddy. Care to help / Freddy Bloom. — London : Clare, c1980. — 139p : ill ; 22cm
ISBN 0-906549-14-0 : £5.50 B82-11629

Davies, Brian Meredith. The disabled child and adult / Brian Meredith Davies. — London : Baillière Tindall, 1982. — viii,288p ; 24cm
Includes index
ISBN 0-7020-0863-x (pbk) : £8.50 : CIP rev.
B82-00227

Handicap in a social world / a reader edited by Ann Brechin, Penny Liddiard and John Swain. — Sevenoaks : Hodder and Stoughton in association with the Open University Press, 1981. — vii,344p : ill ; 22cm
Includes bibliographies and index
ISBN 0-340-27625-8 (pbk) : £6.95 : CIP rev.
B81-30130

The **Handicapped** person in the community. — Milton Keynes : Open University Press. — (A post experience and second level course)
At head of title: The Open University
Block 3 [pt.1]: What about the neighbours?. — 1982. — 112p : ill ; 30cm. — (P251 ; block 3 pt.1, 7 and 8)
Includes bibliographies. — Contents: Unit 7: Aiding human functioning — Unit 8: Mental handicap and integration
ISBN 0-335-00122-x (pbk) : Unpriced
B82-32218

The **Handicapped** person in the community. — Milton Keynes : Open University Press
At head of title: The Open University
Block 5: What next?. — 1982. — 142p : ill ; 30cm. — (P251 : block 5, units 13, 14 and 15)
Includes bibliographies. — Contents: Unit 13: The costs of disability and how they are met / prepared by Andrew Sackville and Jonathan Seagrave for the course team — Unit 14: Pressures for change / prepared by Ann Brechin for the course team — Unit 15: What next? / prepared by Mary Croxen for the course team
ISBN 0-335-00115-7 (pbk) : Unpriced
B82-38951

Thomas, David. The experience of handicap. — London : Methuen, July 1982. — [250]p. — (Education paperbacks)
ISBN 0-416-74710-8 (cased) : £8.50 : CIP entry
ISBN 0-416-74720-5 (pbk) : £3.95 B82-12337

362.4 — Physically handicapped persons. Social adjustment

Lindemann, James E.. Psychological and behavioral aspects of physical disability : a manual for health practitioners / James E. Lindemann ; with contributions by Robert D. Boyd ... [et al.] ; medical consultant Victor D. Menashe. — New York ; London : Plenum, c1981. — xxv,426p : 1ill ; 24cm
Includes bibliographies and index
ISBN 0-306-40776-0 : Unpriced B82-14756

362.4 — Scotland. Arts for handicapped persons. Organisations: Scottish Committee for Arts and Disability — *Serials*

SCAD newsheet / Scottish Committee for Arts and Disability. — [No.1]-. — Edinburgh (18 Claremont Cres., Edinburgh EH7 4QD) : The Committee, [1981]-. — v. ; 30cm
Quarterly
ISSN 0262-785x = SCAD newssheet : Unpriced B82-09675

362.4′028 — Great Britain. Equipment for physically handicapped persons — *Buyers′ guides*

Equipment for the disabled. — Oxford : Oxfordshire Area Health Authority (Teaching)
Outdoor transport. — 5th ed. / compiled E.R. Wilshere ; editors G.M. Cochrane, E.R. Wilshere. — 1982. — 42p : ill,1plan ; 30cm
Previous ed.: 1977. — Bibliography: p34. — Includes index
£3.30 (pbk) B82-22324

362.4′0453 — Physically handicapped persons. Rehabilitation. Role of welfare work

Rehabilitation services and the social work role : challenge for change / edited by J.A. Browne, Betty A. Kirlin, Susan Watt. — Baltimore ; London : Williams & Wilkins, c1981. — xxi,371p ; 24cm. — (Rehabilitation medicine library)
Includes index
ISBN 0-683-01091-3 : Unpriced B82-15515

362.4′0453′0942 — England. Handicapped persons. Social integration. Promotion. International Year of Disabled People *(England)*

Kates, Hilary. International year of Disabled People — a beginning, not an end — / [written and compiled by Hilary Kates, Linda Waller and Stephen Crampton]. — London : National Council For Voluntary Organisations, [1982?]. — 59p : ill,facsims,ports ; 15x21cm
Cover title
ISBN 0-7199-1079-x (pbk) : £1.00 B82-19364

362.4′0456′0941 — Great Britain. Handicapped persons. Policies of government — *Proposals*

Disability in Britain : a manifesto of rights / edited by Alan Walker and Peter Townsend. — Oxford : Robertson, 1981. — x,220p ; 23cm. — (Aspects of social policy)
Bibliography: p205-214. — Includes index
ISBN 0-85520-459-1 (cased) : Unpriced : CIP rev.
ISBN 0-85520-460-5 (pbk) : £3.50 B81-31062

362.4′0456′0941 — Great Britain. Public welfare services for handicapped persons, *to 1980*

Player, I. C.. The giant of disease : those disabled in 'wit or member' : Cassino Monastery sixth century A.D. to date / I.C. Player. — Braunton : Merlin, 1982. — 287p ; 22cm. — (The Five giants)
Bibliography: p286-287
ISBN 0-86303-008-4 : £7.00 B82-27718

362.4′048 — Physically handicapped persons. Rehabilitation

Brechin, Ann. Look at it this way : new perspectives in rehabilitation / by Ann Brechin and Penny Liddiard. — Sevenoaks : Hodder and Stoughton in association with the Open University Press, c1981. — ix,277p : ill ; 22cm
Includes index
ISBN 0-340-27632-0 (pbk) : £5.25 : CIP rev.
B81-32008

362.4′048 — Physically handicapped persons. Rehabilitation. Policies of governments — *Sociological perspectives*

Cross national rehabilitation policies : a sociological perspective / edited by Gary L. Albrecht. — London : Sage, c1981. — 282p : ill ; 23cm. — (Sage studies in international sociology ; 25)
Includes bibliographies
ISBN 0-8039-9793-0 : £15.50 : CIP rev.
B81-18096

362.4′048′02341 — Great Britain. Physically handicapped persons. Care — *Career guides*

Taylor, Judith. Careers working with the disabled. — London : Kogan Page, Jan.1983. — [100]p. — (Kogan Page careers series)
ISBN 0-85038-600-4 (cased) : £6.95 : CIP entry
ISBN 0-85038-601-2 (pbk) : £2.50 B82-35185

362.4′048′0254125 — Scotland. Tayside Region. Services for handicapped persons — *Directories*

Magowan, S. A.. Handicapped in Tayside : a directory of services for the handicapped / compiled by S.A. Magowan and Bernadette Barclay. — [Dundee] : University of Dundee, Dept. of Education, 1981. — 65p ; 22cm
Includes index
Unpriced (pbk) B82-38844

362.4′048′0941 — Great Britain. Welfare services for handicapped persons

Who can help you? / [text by members of Chailey Heritage staff]. — North Chailey (North Chailey, Lewes, Sussex) : Chailey Heritage, [1982?]. — 78p ; 21cm. — (Chailey Heritage information for independence ; 3)
Includes index
£0.40 (unbound) B82-36550

362.4′048′094141 — Scotland. Strathclyde Region. Social services for physically handicapped persons. Reform — *Proposals*

Strathclyde. *Member-Officer Group on Physical Handicap*. The cost of living in a hostile environment / report by a group of regional council members and officers on physical handicap in Strathclyde. — [Glasgow] : Strathclyde Regional Council, 1981. — 55p ; 30cm + 10 topic papers
At head of title of topic papers : Member-Officer Group on Physical Handicap
£2.50 (£1.00 per topic paper ; £12.50 set) (pbk)
B82-24679

362.4′048′0941443 — Scotland. Strathclyde Region. Cambuslang. Welfare services for handicapped persons

Legg, Gail. Action on handicap : a community research project on the handicapped and elderly / Gail Legg, Robert Stewart. — [Glasgow] : Strathclyde Regional Council, [1980?]. — 57p : forms ; 30cm
Cover title
Unpriced (pbk)
Also classified at 362.6′09414′43 B82-25263

362.4′0482′0941 — Great Britain. Physically handicapped persons. Mobility allowances. Increase — *Proposals*

Great Britain. *Department of Health and Social Security*. Uprating of mobility allowance : statement prepared pursuant to section 37A(4) of the Social Security Act 1975 as amended by section 3(2) of the Social Security Act 1979 / [Department of Health and Social Security]. — London : H.M.S.O., [1981]. — 2p ; 25cm. — ([HC] ; 408)
ISBN 0-10-240881-5 (unbound) : £0.70
B82-13828

Great Britain. *Department of Health and Social Security*. Uprating of mobility allowance : statement prepared pursuant to section 37A(4) of the Social Security Act 1975 as amended by section 3(2) of the Social Security Act 1979 : presented pursuant to c.14 1975 section 37A(4). — London : H.M.S.O., 1982. — 2p ; 25cm. — (HC ; 393)
ISBN 0-10-239382-6 (unbound) : £0.75
B82-32711

362.4'0483 — Great Britain. Handicapped persons. Activities: Arts — *Interviews*

The **Arts** and disabilities : a creative response to social handicap / edited by Geoffrey Lord. — Edinburgh : Macdonald, 1981. — 135p : ill,2ports ; 24cm
Includes bibliographies
ISBN 0-904265-62-5 (cased) : £6.95
ISBN 0-904265-61-7 (pbk) : £3.95 B82-18946

362.4'0483 — Great Britain. Physically handicapped persons. Residences. Adaptation

Lockhart, Terence. Housing adaptations for disabled people / Terence Lockhart. — London : Published for the Disabled Living Foundation by The Architectural Press, 1981. — xiv,130p : ill,plans ; 22cm
Bibliography: p128-130
ISBN 0-85139-331-4 (pbk) : £8.95 B82-00100

362.4'0485'0941 — Great Britain. Boarding houses for handicapped persons

At home in a boarding house : caring for elderly disabled or mentally disordered residents in boarding houses and similar settings / report of an independent working group ; [prepared by Raymond Clarke and Molly Stone]. — [London] : National Institute for Social Work, 1981. — 70p ; 22cm
Cover title. — Bibliography: p59-63
ISBN 0-902789-23-6 (pbk) : Unpriced
Also classified at 362.6'1'0941 B82-02686

362.4'0485'0942 — England. Local authorities. Residential institutions for handicapped persons, to 65 years — *Statistics*

Residential care of handicapped persons under the age of 65 in England and Wales : statements prepared pursuant to section 18(3) of the Chronically Sick and Disabled Persons Act 1970. — London : H.M.S.O., [1980]. — 2p ; 25cm. — (HC ; 654)
ISBN 0-10-265480-8 (unbound) : £0.50 B82-14142

Residential care of handicapped persons under the age of 65 in England and Wales : statements prepared pursuant to section 18(3) of The chronically sick and disabled persons Act 1970 / [statement by the Secretaty of State for Social Services and the Secretary of State for Wales]. — London : H.M.S.O., 1981. — [4]p ; 25cm. — (HC ; 83)
ISBN 0-10-208382-7 (unbound) : £0.70 B82-13297

362.4'05 — Handicapped persons — *Serials*

[Activity *(London : 1981)*]. Activity : celebrating International Year of Disabled People. — June 1981-. — [London] ([31 Mountgrove Rd, N5 2LX]) : [Ray's Bookshop], 1981-. — v. : ill,ports ; 30cm
Two issues yearly
ISSN 0262-7256 = Activity (London. 1981) : £0.20 per issue B82-11137

362.4'07'8 — Physically handicapped persons. Teaching aids: Microcomputer systems

Schofield, Julia M.. Microcomputer-based aid for the disabled / Julia M. Schofield. — London : Published by Heyden on behalf of the British Computer Society, c1981. — xii,116p : ill ; 24cm. — (Monographs in informatics)
Bibliography: p113-114. — Includes index
ISBN 0-85501-700-7 (pbk) : £12.00 : CIP rev. B81-30458

362.4'088054 — Great Britain. Handicapped children

Selfe, Lorna. Children with handicaps / Lorna Selfe and Lynn Stow. — [London] : Teach Yourself, 1981. — 247p ; 18cm. — (Care and welfare)
Bibliography: p213-227. — Includes index
ISBN 0-340-26819-0 (pbk) : £1.95 : CIP rev. B81-27390

362.4'088054 — Handicapped children

Handicaps in childhood / volume editor M. Manciaux. — Basel ; London : Karger, c1982. — vi,179p : ill ; 25cm. — (Child health and development ; v.1)
English and French text. — Bibliography: p170-179
ISBN 3-8055-2935-x : £26.50 B82-11590

362.4'088054 — Handicapped children. Activities: Movement. Teaching — *Manuals*

Hollis, Katy. Progress to standing : for children with severe physical and mental handicap / Katy Hollis ; illustrations: David Baird. — New ed. — Kidderminster : British Institute of Mental Handicap, 1980. — v,16p : ill ; 21cm
Previous ed.: 1977. — Bibliography: pv
ISBN 0-906054-16-8 (pbk) : £0.95 B82-31336

362.4'088054 — Handicapped children — *For teaching*

Wood, Grace E.. Handicapped children in the community. — Bristol : John Wright, Jan.1983. — [144]p
ISBN 0-7236-0675-7 (pbk) : £5.50 : CIP entry B82-40914

362.4'088054 — Handicapped children. Interpersonal relationships with adults. Communication

Newson, Elizabeth. Getting through to your handicapped child. — Cambridge : Cambridge University Press, Nov.1982. — [144]p
ISBN 0-521-27056-1 (pbk) : £3.95 : CIP entry B82-27537

362.4'088054 — Handicapped children. Lifting & carrying — *Manuals*

York-Moore, Rosemary. Management of the physically handicapped child : guidelines to lifting, carrying and seating / by Rosemary York-Moore and Pamela Stewart ; photographs P. Denys Stone, Pamela Stewart. — Kidderminster : British Institute of Mental Handicap, 1982. — ii,16p : ill ; 15x21cm. — (Pamphlet ; no.2)
Bibliography: p15
ISBN 0-906054-24-9 (pbk) : £1.50
Also classified at 684.1'3 B82-35264

362.4'088054 — London. Camden *(London Borough)*. **Services for handicapped children** — *Directories* — *For parents*

Help for the handicapped child. — [London] (Camden Town Hall, Euston Rd NW1) : London Borough of Camden, 1982. — 72p : ill ; 30cm
Cover title
Unpriced (pbk) B82-27853

362.4'092'2 — London. Brent *(London Borough)*. **Physically handicapped persons** — *Personal observations* — *Collections*

I am labelled disabled. — London : Brent Community Health Council, 1981. — 50p ; 21cm
Bibliography: p50
ISBN 0-9507520-1-0 (pbk) : Unpriced B82-25036

362.4'0941 — Great Britain. Handicapped persons

The **Handicapped** person in the community. — Milton Keynes : Open University Press, 1982
At head of title: The Open University
Block 1: What a handicap!. — 128p : ill ; 30cm. — (P251 ; block 1, 1,2,3)
Contents: Unit 1: Family circles — Unit 2: Disablement in society — Unit 3: The individual behind the statistics
ISBN 0-335-00100-9 (pbk) : Unpriced B82-24502

The **Handicapped** person in the community. — Milton Keynes : Open University Press. — (A Post-experience and second level course)
Block 4: What's to be done?. — 1981. — 71p : ill,1port ; 30cm. — (P251 ; Block 4. 11 and 12)
At head of title: The Open University. — Bibliography: 65-68. — Contents: Units 11/12: Adopting a life-style
ISBN 0-335-00121-1 (pbk) : Unpriced B82-04677

Topliss, Eda. Social responses to handicap / Eda Topliss. — London : Longman, 1982. — viii,190p ; 20cm. — (Social policy in modern Britain)
Bibliography: p184-186. — Includes index
ISBN 0-582-29538-6 (pbk) : £3.50 : CIP rev. B82-06922

Why? : what is the purpose of the International Year of Disabled Persons?. — Dublin (c/o Department of Health, Hawkins House, Dublin 2) : National Committee, International Year of Disabled Persons, 1981. — [20]p : ports ; 19x25cm
Unpriced (unbound) B82-21222

362.4'0941 — Great Britain. Handicapped persons — *Serials*

DIG around. — [No.1] (1981)-. — London (28 Commercial St., E1 6LR) : Disablement Income Group, 1981-. — v. : ill,ports ; 42cm
Quarterly. — Description based on: No.6 (May 1982)
ISSN 0263-6980 = DIG around : £0.08 B82-31710

362.4'0941 — Great Britain. Physical handicaps — *Practical information*

Kay, Isabel. Your hopeful future : how to live well financially, medically and emotionally during retirement, unemployment or disablement / Isabel and Ernest Kay. — London : Macdonald, 1982. — 192p ; 23cm
Bibliography: p186-188. — Includes index
ISBN 0-356-08604-6 (cased) : £7.95
ISBN 0-356-08605-4 (pbk) : Unpriced
Also classified at 646.7'9'0941 ; 331.13'7941 B82-37218

362.4'0941 — Great Britain. Physically handicapped persons. Attitudes of society

Dartington, T.. A life together : the distribution of attitudes around the disabled. — London : Tavistock, Dec.1981. — [148]p
ISBN 0-422-77900-8 (cased) : £6.50 : CIP entry
ISBN 0-422-77910-5 (pbk) : £3.50 B81-31630

362.4'0973 — United States. Handicapped persons

Cleland, Charles C.. Exceptionalities through the lifespan : an introduction / Charles C. Cleland / Jon D. Swartz. — New York : Macmillan ; London : Collier Macmillan, c1982. — xvi,464p : ill ; 27cm
Includes bibliographies and index
ISBN 0-02-322860-1 : Unpriced B82-35271

362.4'1'088054 — Soviet Union. Deaf-blind children

Meshcherīakov, A.. Awakening to life : forming behaviour and the mind in deaf-blind children / A. Meshcheryakov ; [translated from the Russian by Katherine Judelson]. — Moscow : Progress Publishers, 1979 ; [London] : Distributed by Central Books. — 349p : ill,ports ; 21cm
Translation of: Vozvrashchenie k zhizni. — Bibliography: p345-348. — Includes index
ISBN 0-7147-1661-8 : £3.95 B82-02704

362.4'1'0880565 — Partially sighted old persons

Marshall, G. H.. The ageing person who is or becomes partially sighted / G.H. Marshall. — [London] ([346 Kensington High Street, W14]) : [Disabled Living Foundation], [1981?]. — 7p ; 30cm
Unpriced (unbound) B82-03760

362.4'1'0924 — England. Spastic persons: Counsell, Alan — *Biography*

Counsell, Alan. So clear in my mind. — London : Hutchinson, Oct.1982. — [192]p
ISBN 0-09-149690-x : £6.95 : CIP entry B82-24968

362.4'1'0924 — Great Britain. Blind persons: Brace, Mike — *Biographies*

Brace, Mike. Where there's a will / Mike Brace. — London : Sphere, 1982, c1980. — 181,[8]p of plates : ill,ports ; 18cm
Originally published: London : Souvenir, 1980
ISBN 0-7221-1838-4 (pbk) : £1.75 B82-29173

362.4'1'0924 — Hong Kong. Blind persons: Ching, Lucy — *Biographies*

Ching, Lucy. One of the lucky ones / Lucy Ching ; with a foreword by Sheila Hocken. — London : Souvenir, 1982, c1980. — 287p,[8]p of plates : ill,1map,ports ; 23cm
Originally published: Hong Kong : Gulliver, 1980
ISBN 0-285-62522-5 : £7.50 B82-23927

362.4′1′0924 — Man. Sight. Recovery. Personal adjustment of blind persons — *Personal observations*

Hocken, Sheila. Emma V.I.P. / Sheila Hocken. — London : Sphere, 1981, c1980. — ix,181p,[8]p of plates : ill,ports ; 18cm
Originally published: London : Gollancz, 1980
ISBN 0-7221-4601-9 (pbk) : £1.25 B82-02175

362.4′1′0924 — Partially sighted persons: Monkhouse, June — *Biographies*

Monkhouse, June. Sight in the dark. — London : Hodder and Stoughton, May 1982. — [176]p. — (Coronet books)
Originally published: 1981
ISBN 0-340-27918-4 (pbk) : £1.10 : CIP entry B82-06726

Monkhouse, June. Sight in the dark. — Large print ed. — Long Preston : Magna Print, Dec.1982. — [336]p
Originally published: London : Hodder and Stoughton, 1981
ISBN 0-86009-452-9 : £5.50 : CIP entry B82-30729

362.4′18 — Deaf-blind children. Care

McInnes, John. Deaf-blind infants and children. — Milton Keynes : Open University, Sept.1982. — [304]p. — (Children with special needs)
ISBN 0-335-10185-2 : £11.95 : CIP entry B82-18829

362.4′18′0941 — Great Britain. Services for blind persons

Dobree, John H.. Blindness and visual handicap : the facts / John H. Dobree and Eric Boulter. — Oxford : Oxford University Press, 1982. — 241p,[12]p of plates : ill ; 23cm. — (Oxford medical publications)
Bibliography: p227-228. — Includes index
ISBN 0-19-261328-6 : £6.95 : CIP rev.
Primary classification 617.7′12 B82-11748

362.4′18′0941 — Great Britain. Welfare services for visually handicapped persons

Ford, Margaret, *1932-*. In touch : aids and services for blind and partially sighted people / Margaret Ford and Thena Heshel ; illustrations by Patricia Capon. — 3rd ed. — London : British Broadcasting Corporation, 1982. — 295p : ill ; 21cm
Previous ed.: i.e. rev. ed., 1977. — Includes index
ISBN 0-563-17907-4 (pbk) : £2.95 B82-23498

362.4′2 — Deaf persons. Social integration

The **Integration** and disintegration of the deaf in society / edited by George Montgomery. — [Edinburgh] : Scottish Workshop Publications, 1981. — xiiii,453p : ill,1facsim ; 21cm
Includes bibliographies
£3.50 (pbk) B82-31117

362.4′2′06041 — Great Britain. Welfare services for deaf persons: Royal National Institute for the Deaf

Royal National Institute for the Deaf. Into the eighties / the Royal National Institute for the Deaf. — London : The Institute, [1980?]. — 15p : ill(some col.),1port ; 21cm
Unpriced (pbk) B82-19936

362.4′2′088054 — Deaf children — *For parents*

Freeman, Roger D.. Can′t your child hear? : a guide for those who care about deaf children / by Roger D. Freeman, Clifton F. Carbin, Robert J. Boese ; sponsored by the International Association of Parents of the Deaf. — London : Croom Helm, 1981. — xxi,340p : ill ; 23cm
Originally published: Baltimore : University Park Press, 1981. — Bibliography: p313-333. — Includes index
ISBN 0-7099-1018-5 (pbk) : £9.95 : CIP rev. B81-25690

Stelle, Truman W.. A primer for parents with deaf children : aid understanding of early education and communication / by Truman W. Stelle. — [Edinburgh] : Scottish Workshop Publications, c1982. — 43p ; 21cm
Bibliography: p43
ISBN 0-9506538-1-0 (pbk) : £2.00 B82-28232

362.4′2′088054 — Hearing disordered children, to 5 years. Rehabilitation

Boothroyd, Arthur. Hearing impairments in young children / Arthur Boothroyd. — Englewood Cliffs ; London : Prentice Hall, c1982. — xvi,239p : ill,1form ; 24cm. — (Remediation of communication disorders series)
Bibliography: p226-229. — Includes index
ISBN 0-13-384701-2 : £14.95 B82-19945

362.4′2′0924 — Man. Deafness. Personal adjustment — *Personal observations*

Jack, Michael. Life among the dead / by Michael Jack ; foreword by Lord Coggan. — Luton : Cortney, 1981. — vii,72p : ill,ports ; 21cm
ISBN 0-904378-15-2 (pbk) : £2.50 B82-11949

362.4′28 — Hearing disordered persons. Rehabilitation

Davis, Julia M.. Rehabilitative audiology for children and adults / Julia M. Davis, Edward J. Hardick with a chapter by Dianne J. Van Tasell. — New York ; Chichester : Wiley, c1981. — ix,509p : ill ; 24cm
Includes bibliographies and index
ISBN 0-471-03560-2 : £16.25 B82-08622

Sanders, Derek A.. Aural rehabilitation : a management model / Derek A. Sanders. — 2nd ed. — Englewood Cliffs ; London : Prentice-Hall, c1982. — xiv,450p : ill ; 24cm
Previous ed.: 1971. — Includes bibliographies and index
ISBN 0-13-053215-0 : £16.45 B82-16990

362.4′28′0254259 — Buckinghamshire. Services for hearing disordered persons — *Directories*

A **Guide** to services for the hearing impaired in Buckinghamshire / [... produced by the British Deaf Association ; Departments of Bucks County Council ; and the Workers′ Educational Association, Berks, Bucks & Oxon District]. — [Aylesbury] : [County Reference Library] (Aylesbury : Central Printing Section, Buckinghamshire County Council), [1982]. — 35p ; 21cm
Cover title. — Includes index
ISBN 0-86059-179-4 (pbk) : Unpriced B82-14624

362.4′28′0880565 — Hearing disordered old persons. Rehabilitation. Projects

Nattrass, Susan. Sound sense : how local groups can help hard of hearing people / Susan Nattrass. — London (54 Knatchbull Rd., SE5) : Age Concern Greater London, 1982. — 38p : ill ; 30cm
£2.00 (pbk) B82-21423

362.4′28′09411 — Scotland. Services for deaf persons

Thomson, William, *1925-*. Hard of hearing? / [text William Thomson] ; [illustrated by I. Lesley Main]. — Hamilton (Board Office, 14, Beckford St., Hamilton, ML3 3TA) : Lanarkshire Health Board, [1982?]. — [16]p : ill(some col.) ; 22cm
Unpriced (unbound) B82-28237

362.4′3 — Leg amputees. Rehabilitation

Troup, Ian M.. Total care of the lower limb amputee / Ian M. Troup, Marjorie A. Wood. — London : Pitman, 1982. — 134p : ill ; 24cm
Bibliography: p131. — Includes index
ISBN 0-272-79641-7 : Unpriced : CIP rev. B81-35782

362.4′3′028 — Great Britain. Equipment for muscular dystrophic persons — *Buyers′ guides*

Harpin, Phillipa. With a little help : a guide to aids and adaptations for people with muscular dystrophy and allied neuro muscular diseases / written by Phillipa Harpin ; illustrated by T.M. Thackeray ; edited by Heather A. Russell. — London : Muscular Dystrophy Group of Great Britain, [1981?]. — 8v. : ill ; 21cm
Bibliography: p3-7(Vol.8). — Includes index
ISBN 0-903561-02-6 (spiral) : Unpriced B82-08713

362.4′3′0924 — Australia. Cerebral palsied children — *Personal observations*

Crossley, Rosemary. Annie′s coming out / Rosemary Crossley and Anne McDonald. — Harmondsworth : Penguin, 1982, c1980. — xiii,251p : ill ; 19cm. — (A Pelican book)
ISBN 0-14-022443-2 (pbk) : £2.25 B82-40773

362.4′3′0924 — Hydrocephalic babies — *Personal observations*

Baumgartner, Diane. Melissa. — London (Holy Trinity Church, Marylebone Rd., NW1 4DU) : Triangle, Sept.1982. — [112]p
ISBN 0-281-04010-9 (pbk) : £1.95 : CIP entry B82-18821

362.4′3′0924 — Ireland. Cerebral palsied children — *Personal observations*

Collins, Patricia. Mary : a mother′s story / Patricia Collins. — Loughton : Piatkus, c1980. — viii,243p,[8]p of plates : ports ; 21cm
ISBN 0-86188-115-x : £6.95 : CIP rev. B81-15852

362.4′3′0924 — Multiple sclerosis victims — *Personal observations*

Kidd, Pennie. I′m smiling as hard as I can / Pennie Kidd. — London : Mowbray, 1982, c1981. — 113p,[8]p of plates : ill(some col.),ports(some col.) ; 18cm. — (Mowbray′s popular Christian paperbacks)
ISBN 0-264-66846-4 (pbk) : £1.75 B82-15218

362.4′3′0924 — Myalgic encephalomyelitis victims — *Personal observations*

Jeffreys, Toni. The mile-high staircase. — London : Hodder and Stoughton, Sept.1982. — [216]p
ISBN 0-340-27990-7 : £8.95 : CIP entry B82-18797

362.4′3′0941 — Great Britain. Cerebral palsied adolescents & spina bifida adolescents. Social adjustment

Anderson, Elizabeth M.. Disability in adolescence. — London : Methuen, Oct.1982. — [340]p
ISBN 0-416-72730-1 (cased) : £14.95 : CIP entry
ISBN 0-416-72740-9 (pbk) : £6.95 B82-23984

362.4′38 — Amputees. Rehabilitation

Amputation surgery and rehabilitation : the Toronto experience / edited by John P. Kostuik ; co-editor for children Robert Gillespie. — New York ; Edinburgh : Churchill Livingstone, 1981. — xv,448p : ill,music,forms ; 26cm
Includes bibliographies and index
ISBN 0-443-08024-0 : £32.00
Primary classification 617′.58059 B82-16548

362.5 — WELFARE SERVICES FOR THE POOR

362.5 — London. Homeless single persons — *Interviews*

Biebuyck, Tony. Six discussion groups of single homeless people / by Tony Biebuyck, Madeline Drake. — [London] : Department of Environment, 1982. — 196p ; 30cm. — (Single and homeless working paper ; 4)
One of four working papers subsidiary to a study entitled: Single and homeless / M.M. Drake, M. O′Brien and T.G. Biebuyck. London : H.M.S.O., 1982. — Includes index
£9.15 (pbk) B82-32680

362.5 — Scotland. Consumers. Debts. Payment. Counselling organisations

Millar, Ann R.. Debt counselling : an assessment of the services and facilities available to consumer debtors in Scotland / by Ann R. Millar. — Edinburgh (New St Andrews House, Edinburgh EH1 3SZ) : Central Research Unit, 1980. — vii,83p : maps,forms ; 30cm. — (Central Research Unit papers) (Research report for the Scottish Law Commission ; no.7)
Unpriced (spiral) B82-02088

362.5 — Southern England. Homeless single persons. Social conditions — *Personal observations*

Biebuyck, Tony. A participant observation study of the single homeless / by Tony Biebuyck. — [London] : Department of Environment, 1982. — 98p ; 30cm. — (Single and homeless working paper ; 3)
One of four working papers subsidiary to a study entitled: Single and homeless / M.M. Drake, M. O'Brien and T.G. Biebuyck. London : H.M.S.O, 1982
£5.00 (pbk) B82-32681

362.5'56'0924 — Great Britain. Poverty relief. Policies of government, *1975-1980* — *Personal observations*

Donnison, David. The politics of poverty / David Donnison. — Oxford : Martin Robertson, 1982. — x,239p : ill ; 22cm
Bibliography: p233-234. — Includes index
ISBN 0-85520-480-x (cased) : Unpriced : CIP rev.
ISBN 0-85520-481-8 (pbk) : £3.50 B81-31000

362.5'56'09417 — Ireland *(Republic)*. **Poverty relief. Policies of government**

Joyce, Laraine. Poverty & social policy : the Irish national report presented to the Commission of the European Communities / compiled by Laraine Joyce and A. McCashin. — Dublin : Institute of Public Administration, 1982, c1981. — 156p : ill ; 30cm
Bibliography: p113-115
ISBN 0-906980-09-7 (pbk) : Unpriced
B82-18918

362.5'56'0973 — United States. Organisational change. Effects of government policies on poverty, *1960-1970*

Jacobs, Bruce. The political economy of organizational change : urban institutional response to the war on poverty / Bruce Jacobs. — New York ; London : Academic Press, c1981. — x,196p ; 24cm. — (Quantitative studies in social relations)
Includes index
ISBN 0-12-379660-1 : £13.00 B82-07553

362.5'56'0973 — United States. Poverty relief. Policies of government, *1900-1980*

Patterson, James T.. America's struggle against poverty 1900-1980 / James T. Patterson. — Cambridge, Mass. ; London : Harvard University Press, 1981. — ix,268p ; 25cm
Includes index
ISBN 0-674-03120-2 : £12.00 B82-11839

362.5'8'0941 — Great Britain. Poverty relief. Policies of government, *1961-1980*

Beckerman, Wilfred. Poverty and social security in Britain since 1961 / by Wilfred Beckerman and Stephen Clark. — Oxford : Oxford University Press for The Institute for Fiscal Studies, 1982. — ix,94p : ill ; 23cm
Includes index
ISBN 0-19-829004-7 : £7.95 : CIP rev.
B82-10441

362.5'8'094484 — France. Poverty relief, *1740-1815* — *Study regions: Montpellier region*

Jones, Colin. Charity and bienfaisance : the treatment of the poor in the Montpellier region 1740-1815. — Cambridge : Cambridge University Press, Nov.1982. — [317]p
ISBN 0-521-24593-1 : £25.00 : CIP entry
B82-40328

362.5'8'0954 — South Asia. Poverty. Alleviation. Role of irrigation of agricultural land — *Proposals*

Who gets a last resource? : the potential and challenge of lift irrigation for the rural poor / by IDS Study Seminar 88. — Brighton : Institute of Development Studies, 1980. — 13p ; 21cm. — (Discussion paper, ISSN 0308-5864 ; 156)
£0.60 (pbk) B82-35054

362.5'8'0973 — United States. Poverty relief. Policies of government

Levitan, Sar A.. Programs in aid of the poor for the 1980s / Sar A. Levitan. — 4th ed. — Baltimore ; London : Johns Hopkins University Press, 1980. — viii,159p : ill ; 21cm. — (Policy studies in employment and welfare ; no.1)
Previous ed.: 1976. — Includes bibliographies and index
ISBN 0-8018-2483-4 (cased) : £6.50
ISBN 0-8018-2484-2 (pbk) : £2.35 B82-15076

362.5'82 — United States. Income maintenance programmes

Income support : conceptual and policy issues / edited by Peter G. Brown, Conrad Johnson, Paul Vernier. — Totowa, N.J. : Rowman and Littlefield ; London : Distributed by Prior, 1981. — xiii,378p ; 25cm. — (Maryland studies in public philosophy)
Includes index
ISBN 0-8476-6969-6 : Unpriced B82-12102

362.5'85'0942 — England. Workhouses, *to 1930*

Crowther, M. A.. The workhouse system 1834-1929 : the history of an English social institution / M.A. Crowther. — London : Batsford Academic and Educational, 1981. — 305p : ill ; 23cm
Bibliography: p292-295. — Includes index
ISBN 0-7134-3671-9 : £17.50 B82-03473

362.6 — WELFARE SERVICES FOR OLD PEOPLE

362.6 — Old persons. Care — *Manuals*

Care of the long-stay elderly patient. — London : Croom Helm, Jan.1983. — [240]p
ISBN 0-7099-0809-1 (cased) : £12.95 : CIP entry
ISBN 0-7099-0820-2 (pbk) : £7.95 B82-32548

362.6 — Old persons. Long-term care. Requirements. Estimation — *Manuals*

Kane, Rosalie A.. Assessing the elderly : a practical guide to measurement / Rosalie A. Kane, Robert L. Kane. — [Lexington, Mass.] : Lexington Books ; [Aldershot] : Gower [distributor], 1982, c1981. — xvi,301p ; 24cm
Bibliography: p273-292. — Includes index
ISBN 0-669-04551-9 : £13.50 B82-08043

Values and long-term care / edited by Robert L. Kane, Rosalie A. Kane. — Lexington, Mass. : Lexington Books ; [Aldershot] : Gower [[distributor]], 1982. — xi,292p : ill ; 24cm
Includes bibliographies
ISBN 0-669-04685-x : Unpriced B82-36676

362.6 — Old persons. Policies of governments — *Proposals*

Selby, Philip, *1936-*. Aging 2000 : a challenge for society / Philip Selby, Mal Schechter in collaboration with Jean-Jacques Vollbrecht, Raymond Rigoni, Adrian Griffiths ; in consultation with United Nations Centre for Social Development and Humanitarian Affairs. — Lancaster : MTP, 1982. — 222p : ill ; 22cm
ISBN 0-85200-471-0 : Unpriced : CIP rev.
B82-19277

362.6 — West Midlands *(Metropolitan County)*. **Birmingham. Inner areas. Ethnic minorities. Old persons. Social problems**

Bhalla, Anil. Elders : of the minority ethnic groups / [authors Anil Bhalla, Ken Blakemore]. — Birmingham : AFFOR, 1981. — 59p : ill,1map,forms ; 21cm
Bibliography: p48
ISBN 0-907127-06-1 (pbk) : £1.00 : CIP rev.
B81-28321

362.6'025'42716 — Cheshire. Macclesfield *(District)*. **Welfare services for old persons** — *Directories*

Stoner, Sylvia D.. Services for the elderly in the Macclesfield district / compiled by Sylvia D. Stoner. — [Macclesfield] ([c/o Rehabilitation Unit, West Park Hospital, Macclesfield, Cheshire]) : B.A.S.E. East Cheshire Branch, 1981. — 20p ; 30cm
Cover title. — Includes index
Unpriced (pbk) B82-17631

362.6'06'041 — Great Britain. Welfare services for old persons. Organisations: Help the Aged, *to 1981*

Hudson, Kenneth. Help the Aged : twenty-one years of experiment and achievement / Kenneth Hudson. — London : Bodley Head, 1982. — 208p,[16]p of plates : ill,ports ; 23cm
Bibliography: p197-201. — Includes index
ISBN 0-370-30463-2 : £7.95 : CIP rev.
B82-18819

362.6'06'0411 — Scotland. Welfare services for old persons. Organisations: Age Concern Scotland — *Serials*

Adage. — No.1 (Apr./May 1982)-. — Edinburgh (33 Castle St., Edinburgh) : Age Concern Scotland, 1982-. — v. : ill,ports ; 30cm
Six issues yearly. — Also entitled: Age Concern Scotland newsletter (1982). — Continues: Age Concern Scotland newsletter (1974)
ISSN 0262-5962 = Adage : £1.50 per year
B82-33856

362.6'06'042 — England. Welfare services for old persons. Organisations: Age Concern. Policies

Age Concern England. The national policy / Age Concern. — [London?] : [Age Concern England?], [1982?]. — [17]p ; 30cm
Unpriced (pbk) B82-32989

Priorities for action / Age Concern Scotland. — Edinburgh (33 Castle St., Edinburgh EH2 3DN) : [Age Concern Scotland], [1982?]. — [3]p ; 22cm
Unpriced (unbound) B82-32798

362.6'0941 — Great Britain. Old persons. Care. Risks

Brearley, C. Paul. Risk and ageing / C. Paul Brearley with M.R.P. Hall ... [et al.]. — London : Routledge & Kegan Paul, 1982. — 149p ; 22cm. — (Hazards and helping)
Bibliography: p138-144. — Includes index
ISBN 0-7100-9080-3 (pbk) : £3.95 B82-35998

362.6'0941 — Great Britain. Old persons. Care. Role of families. Social aspects

Rossiter, Chris. Crisis or challenge? : family care, elderly people and social policy / Chris Rossiter and Malcolm Wicks. — London : Study Commission on the Family, c1982. — 102p : 1ill ; 21cm. — (Occasional paper)
ISBN 0-907051-15-4 (pbk) : £4.00 B82-41020

362.6'0941 — Great Britain. Social services for old persons

Goldberg, E. Mathilde. The effectiveness of social care for the elderly. — London : Heinemann Educational, Sept.1982. — [288]p. — (Policy studies institute series)
ISBN 0-435-83353-7 (cased) : £15.00 : CIP entry
ISBN 0-435-83354-5 (pbk) : £5.95 B82-25152

362.6'0941 — Great Britain. Welfare work with old persons

Mortimer, Eunice. Working with the elderly / Eunice Mortimer. — London : Heinemann Educational, 1982. — 90p ; 22cm. — (Community care practice handbooks ; 9)
Includes bibliographies and index
ISBN 0-435-82607-7 (pbk) : £2.95 : CIP rev.
B81-35693

362.6'09411 — Great Britain. Old persons. Care. Role of health visitors — *Study examples: Old women living alone* — *Study regions: Scotland*

Luker, Karen A.. Evaluating health visiting practice. — London : Royal College of Nursing, Sept.1982. — [98]p
ISBN 0-902606-70-0 (pbk) : £4.00 : CIP entry
B82-30567

362.6'09414'43 — Scotland. Strathclyde Region. Cambuslang. Welfare services for old persons

Legg, Gail. Action on handicap : a community research project on the handicapped and elderly / Gail Legg, Robert Stewart. — [Glasgow] : Strathclyde Regional Council, [1980?]. — 57p : forms ; 30cm
Cover title
Unpriced (pbk)
Primary classification 362.4'048'0941443
B82-25263

362.6'09421 — London. Welfare services for old persons

Snow, Tom. Services for old age : a growing crisis in London / Tom Snow. — Mitcham : Age Concern England, c1981. — 32p : ill ; 30cm. — (Age Concern England Research Unit publication)
Text on inside covers
ISBN 0-86242-008-3 (pbk) : Unpriced B82-36768

362.6'09421'65 — London. Lambeth *(London Borough)*. Welfare services for old persons

Services for the over sixties. — [Brixton] ([1-5 Acre Lane, Brixton SW2 5SD]) : Age Concern Lambeth, 1982. — 64p : 2maps ; 21cm
Cover title. — Includes index
Unpriced (pbk) B82-19897

362.6'1 — East Anglia. Day care centres for old persons

Day centres for the elderly in East Anglia / G. Fennell ... [et al.]. — Norwich : Centre for East Anglian Studies, University of East Anglia, 1981. — vii,227p : ill ; 24cm
Bibliography: p213-214
ISBN 0-906219-09-4 (cased) : Unpriced
ISBN 0-906219-08-6 (pbk) : Unpriced B82-11472

362.6'1 — Great Britain. Day care centres for old persons

Fennell, Graham. Good practice guide : day centres for the elderly / Graham Fennell and Moyra Sidell. — Norwich : Geo Abstracts for Centre for East Anglian Studies, University of East Anglia, c1982. — 32p : ill,2plans ; 30cm
Cover title. — Bibliography: p31
ISBN 0-906219-12-4 (pbk) : Unpriced B82-38953

362.6'1 — Residential homes for old persons. Inmates. Care — *For personnel*

Masters, Mike. Training for people who care : (senior staff pack) : training for staff employed in homes for the elderly through self-learning and group-learning techniques / developed by Mike Master with Social Services Training Section, Cheshire County Council. — Chester : Cheshire Social Services, 1981. — 1v.(loose-leaf) ; 35cm
ISBN 0-906768-02-0 : Unpriced B82-23272

362.6'1'0941 — Great Britain. Boarding houses for old persons

At home in a boarding house : caring for elderly disabled or mentally disordered residents in boarding houses and similar settings / report of an independent working group ; [prepared by Raymond Clarke and Molly Stone]. — [London] : National Institute for Social Work, 1981. — 70p ; 22cm
Cover title. — Bibliography: p59-63
ISBN 0-902789-23-6 (pbk) : Unpriced
Primary classification 362.4'0485'0941 B82-02686

362.6'1'0941 — Great Britain. Old persons. Community care — *Conference proceedings*

The **Care** and housing of the elderly in the community : a report of a seminar held at the University of Nottingham on 19-21 September 1979 / [edited by] Arthur J. Wilcocks [i.e. Willcocks]. — [Stafford] ([16, Hempits Grove, Acton Trussell, Stafford ST17 0SL]) : [Institute of Social Welfare], [1981?]. — 68p ; 21cm
£0.95 (pbk) B82-12390

362.6'1'0942498 — West Midlands *(Metropolitan County)*. Coventry. Old persons. Residential care

Approaches to the care of the elderly in Coventry / [DHSS Social Work Service, West Midlands Region, Development Group — Coventry Social Service Department]. — [London] ([Room B1104, Alexander Fleming House, SE1 6BY]) : Department of Health and Social Security, 1980. — 149p ; 30cm. — (A Development Group report)
Unpriced (pbk) B82-17688

362.6'1'0973 — United States. Old persons. Residential care

Bowker, Lee H.. Humanizing institutions for the aged / Lee H. Bowker. — Lexington, Mass. : Lexington Books ; [Aldershot] : Gower [distributor], 1982. — x,115p ; 24cm
Bibliography: p93-111. — Includes index
ISBN 0-669-05209-4 : £11.50 B82-36677

362.6'3 — England. Old persons. Residences. Adaptation

Welsh Nursing and Midwifery Committee. The home environment / Welsh Nursing and Midwifery Committee. — [Wales?] : [The Committee?], 1979. — 8p ; 21cm. — (Ageing and disablement, ISSN 0142-4890 ; 2)
ISBN 0-904251-30-6 (pbk) : Unpriced B82-16409

362.6'3 — United States. Old persons. Home care. Role of welfare services

Frankfather, Dwight L.. Family care of the elderly : public initiatives and private obligations / Dwight L. Frankfather, Michael J. Smith, Francis G. Caro. — Lexington : Lexington Books, c1981 ; [Aldershot] : Gower [distributor], 1982. — xvii,123p ; 24cm
Includes index
ISBN 0-669-03759-1 : £13.50 B82-19435

362.6'6 — Old persons. Counselling

Sherman, Edmund. Counseling the aging : an integrative approach / Edmund Sherman. — New York : Free Press ; London : Collier Macmillan, c1981. — ix,261p : ill ; 25cm
Bibliography: p245-254. — Includes index
ISBN 0-02-928810-x : £10.95 B82-30028

362.7 — WELFARE SERVICES FOR YOUNG PERSONS

362.7 — Children. Care — *Conference proceedings*

Eugenics Society. *Symposium (17th : 1980 : London)*. Changing patterns of child-bearing and child rearing : proceedings of the Seventeenth Annual Symposium of the Eugenics Society, London 1980 / edited by R. Chester, Peter Diggory, Margaret B. Sutherland. — London : Academic Press, 1981. — x,180p : ill ; 24cm
Includes bibliographies and index
ISBN 0-12-171660-0 : £10.80 : CIP rev.
Primary classification 618.3'2 B81-35915

362.7 — Great Britain. Welfare work with young persons leaving residential care

The **16+** Project : task centred work with young people leaving care / by Tony Sayer ... [et al.]. — Barkingside : Dr Barnardo's, c1982. — 76p ; 21cm. — (Barnardo social work proper ; no.15)
Bibliography: p75-76
Unpriced (pbk) B82-39374

362.7 — Scotland. Welfare services for children. Reporters. Referral of children — *Statistics*

Davidson, Kirsty. Children and the hearings : a longitudinal study of children referred to reporters / by Kirsty Davidson. — Edinburgh (Room 422, 43 Jeffery St., Edinburgh EH1 1DN) : Social Work Services Group, [1981?]. — 30p : ill,1form ; 30cm
Unpriced (spiral) B82-14407

362.7'023'41 — Great Britain. Occupations involving children — *Career guides*

Cullum, Margaret G.. Working with children. — London : Batford, Feb.1983. — [112]p
ISBN 0-7134-4463-0 : £5.95 : CIP entry B82-39425

362.7'023'41 — Great Britain. Welfare work with young persons — *Careers guides*

Working with young people / [written, designed and produced by SGS Education ; photographs by André Gordon : illustrations by John Plumb / careers adviser Brian Heap]. — Walton on Thames : Nelson, 1981. — 15p : ill,ports ; 28cm. — (Career profiles ; 27)
ISBN 0-17-438365-7 (unbound) : Unpriced B82-14312

362.7'042 — Great Britain. Adolescent girls. Personal problems. Advice, *1880-1882* — *Readings from contemporary sources*

Oh, no dear! : advice to girls a century ago. — Newton Abbot : David & Charles, Sept.1982. — [64]p
ISBN 0-7153-8330-2 (pbk) : £2.95 : CIP entry B82-20377

362.7'044 — Children. Abuse by adults. Cultural aspects — *Anthropological perspectives*

Child abuse and neglect : cross-cultural perspectives / edited by Jill E. Korbin ; with forewords by Robert B. Edgerton and C. Henry Kempe. — Berkeley ; London : University of California Press, c1981. — xiv,217p ; 24cm
Conference papers. — Includes bibliographies and index
ISBN 0-520-04432-0 : £13.00 B82-13756

362.7'044 — Children. Abuse by parents

Understanding child abuse / [written by] David N. Jones (editor) ... [et al.]. — [Sevenoaks] : Teach Yourself, 1982. — xix,299p ; 18cm
Bibliography: p277-293. — Includes index
ISBN 0-340-26818-2 (pbk) : £2.95 : CIP rev. B82-12257

362.7'044 — Children. Abuse by parents. Consequences

Lynch, M.. The consequences of child abuse. — London : Academic Press, Sept.1982. — [230]p
ISBN 0-12-460570-2 : CIP entry B82-19164

362.7'044 — Great Britain. Homeless single young persons, *1977-1980*

Drake, Madeline. Single and homeless / Madeline Drake, Maureen O'Brien, Tony Biebuyck. — London : H.M.S.O., 1981. — 130p ; 25cm
At head of title: Department of Environment. — Bibliography: p130-131
ISBN 0-11-751586-8 (pbk) : £9.50 B82-23385

362.7'044 — United States. Children. Sexual abuse by adults. Intervention by welfare services

Sgroi, Suzanne M.. Handbook of clinical intervention in child sexual abuse / Suzanne M. Sgroi. — Lexington, Mass. : Lexington Books : [Aldershot], Gower [distributor], 1982. — xi,387p : ill ; 24cm
Includes bibliographies and index
ISBN 0-669-04720-1 (pbk) : £21.00
ISBN 0-669-05213-2 (pbk) B82-24917

362.7'044 — United States. Welfare work with abused children & welfare work with neglected children — *Manuals*

Social work with abused and neglected children : a manual of interdisciplinary practice / edited by Kathleen Coulborn Faller. — New York : Free Press ; London : Collier Macmillan, c1981. — xiv,268p ; 25cm
Bibliography: p253-260. — Includes index
ISBN 0-02-910280-4 : Unpriced B82-33159

362.7'044'094 — Western Europe. Disadvantaged families. Children. Social conditions

Manciaux, Michel. Children of disadvantaged families / Michel Manciaux. — [Exeter] : University of Exeter, 1981, c1980. — 28p : ill ; 21cm. — (Greenwood lecture)
Bibliography: p28
ISBN 0-85989-147-x (pbk) : £0.75 B82-01693

362.7'07'1141 — Great Britain. Nursery nurses. Professional education. Organisations: National Nursery Examination Board — *National Union of Public Employees viewpoints*

National Union of Public Employees. NUPE, nursery nurses and the NNEB. — [London] : The National Union of Public Employees, 1981. — 16p ; 21cm
ISBN 0-907334-11-3 (pbk) : Unpriced B82-17283

362.7'0941 — Great Britain. Children. Care

Wendelken, Claire. Children in and out of care. — London : Heinemann Educational, Sept.1982. — [112]p. — (Community care practice handbooks ; 13)
ISBN 0-435-82926-2 (pbk) : £2.95 : CIP entry B82-29005

362.7'0941 — Great Britain. Welfare services for young persons. Policies of government

Davies, Bernard. Restructuring youth policies in Britain : the state we're in / Bernard Davies. — Leicester : National Youth Bureau, 1981. — 16p ; 30cm. — (Occasional paper / National Youth Bureau ; 21)
ISBN 0-86155-052-8 (pbk) : £0.90 B82-11667

362.7'1 — Great Britain. Working mothers. Children. After school care. Provision

Robinson, Ann, *1940-*. Latchkey schemes : a National Children's Bureau briefing paper / Ann Robinson. — London (8 Wakley St., EC1V 7QE) : Library & Information Service, National Children's Bureau, 1982. — 11p ; 30cm
Cover title
Unpriced (pbk) B82-29698

362.7'1 — Holiday play schemes. Organisation — *Manuals*

Duncanson, Jessie B.. Playschemes : a practical handbook / prepared by Jessie B. Duncanson ; illustrated by Elsie R. Lennox. — Glasgow (39 Hope St., Glasgow G2 6AE) : Fair Play for Children in Scotland, [1982?]. — [62]p : ill ; 30cm
Unpriced (pbk) B82-28815

The **Holiday** playscheme : a community project. — [Dublin] ([71, Lower Leeson St., Dublin 2]) : National Social Service Board, [1982?]. — 33p : ill ; 21cm
Bibliography: p30-33
Unpriced (unbound) B82-21285

362.7'1 — Merseyside *(Metropolitan County)*. **Birkenhead. Battered children: Brown, Paul Steven. Care,** *to 1976 — Inquiry reports*

Great Britain. *Committee of Inquiry into the Case of Paul Steven Brown.* The report of the Committee of Inquiry into the Case of Paul Steven Brown. — London : H.M.S.O., [1980]. — xv,108p : ill,1map ; 25cm. — (Cmnd. ; 8107)
At head of title: Department of Health and Social Security
ISBN 0-10-181070-9 (pbk) : £5.30 B82-16125

362.7'12 — Childminding — *For children*

Althea. My childminder / by Althea ; illustrated by Cynthia Pickard. — Cambridge : Dinosaur, c1981. — [25]p : col.ill ; 16x19cm. — (Dinosaur's Althea books)
ISBN 0-85122-325-7 (cased) : Unpriced
ISBN 0-85122-191-2 (pbk) : Unpriced B82-31830

362.7'12'05 — Pre-school children. Day care — *Serials*

Advances in early education and day care : a research annual. — Vol.1 (1980)-. — Greenwich, Conn. : JAI Press ; London (3 Henrietta St., WC2E 8LU) : Distributed by JAICON Press, 1980-. — v. ; 24cm
ISSN 0270-4021 = Advances in early education and day care : £21.75
Primary classification 372'.21'05 B82-03430

362.7'12'068 — United States. Day care centres for pre-school children. Organisation — *Manuals*

Administering day care and preschool programs / [edited by] Donald T. Streets. — Boston [Mass.] ; London : Allyn and Bacon, c1982. — xiii,355p : ill,forms ; 25cm
Includes bibliographies and index
ISBN 0-205-07556-8 : £13.95 B82-08544

362.7'12'0941 — Great Britain. Working mothers. Children. Day care. Provision

Great Britain. *Equal Opportunities Commission.* 'I want to work — but what about the kids?' : day care for young children and opportunities for working parents / a report prepared by the Equal Opportunities Commission. — Manchester : The Commission, 1978. — 24p ; 21cm
ISBN 0-905829-06-9 (pbk) : Unpriced B82-23794

362.7'12'0941 — Great Britain. Working mothers. Children. Day care. Provision — *Proposals*

Simpson, Robin. Day care for school age children : a report prepared for the Equal Opportunities Commission / Robin Simpson. — Manchester : Equal Opportunities Commission, 1978. — 25p ; 30cm
ISBN 0-905829-10-7 (pbk) : Unpriced B82-23799

362.7'12'0942 — England. Day care centres for pre-school children — *Case studies*

Mottershead, Peter. A survey of child care for pre-school children with working parents : costs and organisation : a report prepared for the Equal Opportunities Commission / Peter Mottershead. — Manchester (Overseas House, Quay St, Manchester, M3 3HN) : Equal Opportunities Commission, 1978. — 77p ; 30cm
Unpriced (pbk) B82-23798

362.7'12'0973 — United States. Children, to 5 years. Day care

Weiser, Margaret G.. Group care and education of infants and toddlers / Margaret G. Weiser. — St. Louis ; London : Mosby, 1982. — xii,331p : ill,facsims,forms,1port ; 25cm
Includes bibliographies and index
ISBN 0-8016-5538-2 : Unpriced B82-31876

362.7'12'0973 — United States. Working mothers. Children. Day care

Day care : scientific and social policy issues / edited by Edward F. Zigler, Edmund W. Gordon, under the auspices of the American Orthopsychiatric Association. — Boston, Mass. : Auburn House ; London : distributed by Eurospan, c1982. — xix,515p ; 25cm
Includes bibliographies and index
ISBN 0-86569-098-7 (cased) : £18.95
ISBN 0-86569-109-6 (pbk) : Unpriced B82-39750

362.7'3 — Scotland. Strathclyde Region. Children. Placement. Policies of Strathclyde. *Regional Council*

Policy and procedures for the Regional Resource Exchange : families for children / Strathclyde Regional Council Social Work Department. — [Glasgow] ([20 India St., Glasgow G2 4PF]) : Strathclyde Regional Council, 1980. — 30p,[15] leaves : 1facsim,forms ; 30cm
Unpriced (pbk) B82-25798

362.7'32 — Great Britain. Voluntary child care services — *Serials*

News about child care / National Council of Voluntary Child Care Organisations. — No.43 (May 1982)-. — London (c/o Thomas Coram Foundation, 40 Brunswick Sq., WC1N 1AZ) : R.T. Clarke on behalf of the Council, 1982-. — v. ; 30cm
Monthly. — Continues: News from NCVCCO
ISSN 0263-4856 = News about child care (corrected) : Unpriced B82-28117

362.7'32 — Residential homes for children. Small group units

Group care for children : concept and issues / edited by Frank Ainsworth and Leon C. Fulcher. — London : Tavistock Publications, 1981. — xvi,308p : ill ; 22cm
Includes bibliographies and index
ISBN 0-422-77290-9 (cased) : Unpriced : CIP rev.
ISBN 0-422-77850-8 (pbk) : £4.95 B81-31705

362.7'32 — Residential welfare work with children. Use of group therapy

Lennox, Daphne. Residential group therapy for children. — London : Tavistock, Nov.1982. — [208]p. — (Residential social work)
ISBN 0-422-77540-1 (cased) : £8.00 : CIP entry
ISBN 0-422-77550-9 (pbk) : £3.75 B82-27508

362.7'32 — Scotland. Strathclyde Region. Children in care. Rights of parents. Assumption by Strathclyde. *Regional Council*

Assumption of parental rights / Strathclyde Regional Council, Social Work Department. — [Glasgow] : [Strathclyde Regional Council], 1982. — 37leaves : forms ; 30cm
Cover title
Unpriced (pbk) B82-25261

Strathclyde's Children : 111 children whose parents are the Regional Council : a sample survey of cases in which the Regional Council took parental rights over children in its care during 1978. — [Glasgow] : Strathclyde Regional Council, 1980. — i,56p : ill,forms ; 30cm
Unpriced (pbk) B82-25260

362.7'32'0722 — London. Residential institutions for children — *Case studies*

Jacobs, Jerry. In the best interest of the child : an evaluation of assessment centers / by Jerry Jacobs. — Oxford : Pergamon, 1982. — vi,114p : 1ill,1plan,1form ; 22cm
ISBN 0-08-028108-7 : £7.95 : CIP rev. B82-00288

362.7'32'0941 — Great Britain. Children in care — *Practical informaiton — For parents*

Guide for parents with children in care : 101 questions and answers. — [Harlow] : [Parents Aid], [1982]. — 36p ; 20cm
ISBN 0-9507954-0-2 (pbk) : £0.40 B82-30172

362.7'32'0941 — Great Britain. Residential institutions for children. Discipline — *Inquiry reports*

Issues of control in residential child-care / Spencer Millham ... [et al.]. — London : H.M.S.O., 1981. — v,99p ; 25cm
At head of title: Department of Health and Social Security. — Bibliography: p76-99
ISBN 0-11-320756-5 (pbk) : £4.50 B82-00703

362.7'32'09411 — Scotland. Children in care — *Statistics*

Miller, Pat. A Longitudinal study of children in care / by Pat Miller. — Edinburgh (43 Jeffrey St., Edinburgh EH1 1DN) : Statistics Branch, Social Work Services Group, [1981?]. — 45p : ill,forms ; 30cm
Unpriced (spiral) B82-14412

362.7'32'094141 — Scotland. Strathclyde Region. Residential child care services. Conferences

Liveston, S. G.. The views of officers and children who attended the Speak Out Conference / S.G. Liveston. — [Glasgow] ([20 India St., Glasgow G2 4PF]) : Social Work Department, Strathclyde Regional Council, 1980. — 20p : ill ; 30cm
Unpriced (unbound) B82-25799

362.7'32'0941443 — Scotland. Strathclyde Region. Glasgow. Children in care. Projects: Barnardo New Families Project

Barnardo New Families Project. Barnardo New Families Project — Glasgow : the first two years / by Carol Lindsay Smith, Emmet Price. — Barking : Dr Barnardo's, c1981. — 64p : 4maps ; 21cm. — (Barnardo social work paper ; no.13)
Unpriced (pbk) B82-14181

362.7'32'0942142 — London. Camden *(London Borough)*. **Orphanages: Foundling Hospital** *(London), to 1789*

McClure, Ruth K.. Coram's children : the London Foundling Hospital in the eighteenth century / Ruth K. McClure. — New Haven ; London : Yale, 1981. — xiii,321p : ill,maps,facsims,1plan,1port,1geneal.table ; 24cm
Bibliography: p298-310. — Includes index
ISBN 0-300-02465-7 : Unpriced : CIP rev. B81-30247

362.7'32'0942191 — London. Croydon *(London Borough)*. **Purley. Orphanages: Reedham School,** *to 1980*

Rolph, Harry Edward. The home on the hill / by Harry Edward Rolph. — [Coulsdon] ([c/o 55 Brighton Rd, Coulsdon, Surrey, CR3 2BE]) : Reedham Old Scholars Association, [1981]. — 124p,[32]p of plates : ill,maps,facsims,ports ; 21cm
Unpriced (pbk) B82-04114

362.7'33 — Children. Foster care. Personal adjustment — *For welfare workers*

Fahlberg, Vera. Attachment and separation / [Vera Fahlberg]. — [London] : British Agencies for Adoption & Fostering, 1981. — 60p : ill,facsims,forms ; 21cm. — (Practice series, ISSN 0260-0803 ; 5)
Originally published: Lansing : Michigan Dept. of Social Services, 1979. — Bibliography: p60
ISBN 0-903534-37-1 (pbk) : £1.80 B82-11745

362.7′33 — Children. Foster care. Personal adjustment. Role of welfare workers

Fahlberg, Vera. Helping children when they must move / [Vera Fahlberg]. — [Great Britain] : British Agencies for Adoption & Fostering, 1981. — 101p : forms ; 21cm. — (Pactice series, ISSN 0260-0803 ; 6)
Originally published: Lansing : Michigan Department of Social Services, 1979
ISBN 0-903534-38-x (pbk) : £3.00 B82-14477

362.7′33 — Great Britain. Handicapped children. Foster care — *Conference proceedings*

Foster care of the disabled child. — London : National Foster Care Association, July 1982. — [112]p
Conference papers
ISBN 0-946015-00-7 (pbk) : £6.00 : CIP entry
B82-14930

362.7′33′071141 — Great Britain. Welfare workers. Professional education. Curriculum subjects: Welfare work with adopted children & fostered children — *For teaching*

Working with children who are joining new families. — London (11 Southwark St, SE1 1RQ) : British Agencies for Adoption & Fostering
Teacher′s handbook. — c1980. — 36p : ill ; 21cm
Originally published: London : ABAFA, 1977. — Text on inside covers
£1.00 (pbk) B82-37717

362.7′33′0941 — Great Britain. Children. Adoption & foster care

Meeting children′s needs through adoption and fostering. — Rev. ed. — London : British Agencies for Adoption & Fostering, 1980 (1982 [printing]). — [8]p ; 21cm
Previous ed.: 197-?
ISBN 0-903534-28-2 (unbound) : Unpriced
B82-37714

362.7′33′0941 — Great Britain. Children. Foster care

Fostering in the 70s and beyond : a descriptive analysis of the current scene. — London : Association of British Adoption & Fostering Agencies, 1977. — 8p ; 30cm
£0.25 (unbound) B82-34821

362.7′33′0941 — Great Britain. Welfare work with adopted children & fostered children

Working with children who are joining new families : training aid. — London : Association of British Adoption & Fostering Agencies, [1977] ([1980 printing]). — 63p : ill,facsims,forms,ports ; 30cm
Cover title. — Includes bibliographies
£3.50 (pbk) B82-34819

362.7′33′09421 — London. West Indian children. Adoption & foster care by West Indian families. Projects: Soul Kids

Soul Kids. *Steering Group*. Report of the steering group of the Soul Kids campaign : London 1975-1976. — London (4 Southampton Row, WC1B 4AA) : Association of British Adoption & Fostering Agencies on behalf of the Soul Kids Campaign, c1977. — 48p : ill,ports ; 21cm
£0.50 (pbk) B82-37713

362.7′33′0966 — West Africa. Children. Foster care

Goody, Esther N.. Parenthood and social reproduction : fostering and occupational roles in West Africa / Esther N. Goody. — Cambridge : Cambridge University Press, 1982. — xiii,348p : ill ; 24cm. — (Cambridge studies in social anthropology ; 35)
Bibliography: p333-340. — Includes index
ISBN 0-521-22721-6 : £25.00 : CIP rev.
B82-01358

362.7′34 — Children. Adoption

Fitzgerald, John. Building new families. — Oxford : Blackwell, Oct.1982. — [128]p. — (The Practice of social work ; 10)
ISBN 0-631-13148-5 (cased) : £12.50 : CIP entry
ISBN 0-631-13193-0 (pbk) : £4.95 B82-23168

362.7′34 — Children. Adoption — *For children*

Hasler, Joy. ′One of the family′ / Joy Hasler, Oonagh Hodges. — [London] ([Area Social Services Office 3, 10 Warwick Row, SW1E 5EP]) : [Westminster City Council], [1982]. — 16p : ill ; 15x21cm
Cover title
Unpriced (pbk) B82-28845

Stanford, James. So, you′re adopted! / James Stanford ; illustrated by Sylvia Woodcock-Clarke. — Edinburgh : Macdonald, c1981. — 47p : ill ; 24cm
ISBN 0-904265-53-6 : £2.95 B82-36093

Wagstaff, Sue. Wayne is adopted / Sue Wagstaff ; photographs by Chris Fairclough. — London : A. & C. Black, [1981]. — 25p : col.ill,1facsim ; 22cm
Bibliography: p25
ISBN 0-7136-2141-9 : £3.50 : CIP rev.
B81-26724

362.7′34 — Great Britain. Coloured children. Adoption by white parents

Gill, Owen. Adoption and race. — London : Batsford, Jan.1983. — [160]p. — (Child care policy and practice)
ISBN 0-7134-2023-5 (pbk) : £6.95 : CIP entry
B82-32594

Jackson, Barbara. Family experiences of inter-racial adoption / Barbara Jackson. — London (4 Southampton Row, WC1B 4AA) : The Association of British Adoption & Fostering Agencies, [198-?]. — 32p ; 21cm
Cover title. — Bibliography: p30-32
£0.60 (pbk) B82-37723

362.7′34 — United States. Children. Adoption. Suitability of families. Assessment

Hartman, Ann. Finding families : an ecological approach to family assessment in adoption / by Ann Hartman. — Beverly Hills ; London : Sage in cooperation with the North American Center on Adoption, Inc. and the Continuing Education Program in the Human Services of the University of Michigan School of Social Work, c1979. — 108p : ill ; 22cm. — (A Project CRAFT publication) (Sage human services guides ; v.7)
Bibliography: p107
ISBN 0-8039-1216-1 (pbk) : £4.00 B82-24071

362.7′34 — United States. Coloured adopted children. Interpersonal relationships with white parents — *Case studies*

Simon, Rita James. Transracial adoption : a follow-up / Rita J. Simon, Howard Altstein. — Lexington : Lexington Books, c1981 ; [Aldershot] : Gower [distributor], 1982. — xi,147p ; 24cm
Includes index
ISBN 0-669-04357-5 : £21.50 B82-14745

362.7′34′0941 — Great Britain. Children. Adoption

Adoption : some question answered. — Rev. — London (11 Southwark St, SE1 1RQ) : British Agencies for Adoption & Fostering, 1982. — [7]p : ill ; 21cm
Previous ed.: 1980
Unpriced (unbound) B82-37719

Adoption in the 70s : three papers comprising background briefing notes on the current adoption scene and reviews of recent studies in adoption practice. — London : Association of British Adoption & Fostering Agencies, 1976. — 16p ; 30cm
£0.30 (unbound) B82-34820

Adoption Resource Exchange. Working together : a guide to the policy procedure and practice of inter-agency adoption placements. — London : Adoption Resource Exchange, 1980. — 52p ; 22cm
Bibliography: p52
ISBN 0-9506807-0-2 (pbk) : Unpriced
B82-37715

Child from the past : information for people who placed a child for adoption years ago. — London (11 Southwark St, SE1 1RQ) : The Association of British Adoption & Fostering Agencies, [1982?]. — 1folded sheet([5]p) ; 21cm
Unpriced B82-37722

If you are adopted : answers to some questions you might like to ask. — London (11 Southwark St, SE1 1RQ) : British Agencies for Adoption & Fostering, [198-?]. — [4]p : ill ; 21cm
Unpriced (unbound) B82-37720

362.7′34′0941 — Great Britain. Children. Adoption — *For adoptive parents*

Rowe, Jane. Yours by choice : a guide for adoptive parents / Jane Rowe. — New ed. — London : Routledge & Kegan Paul, 1982. — xi,188p : ill ; 22cm
Previous ed.: i.e. rev. ed., 1969. — Bibliography: p184. — Includes index
ISBN 0-7100-9035-8 (pbk) : £3.95 B82-23260

Talking about origins : an open letter to adoptive parents. — Rev. — London (11 Southwark St, SE1 1RQ) : British Agencies for Adoption and Fostering, 1980 (1981 [printing]). — 1folded sheet([5]p) ; 21cm
Previous ed.: London : ABAFA, 1976
Unpriced B82-37718

362.7′34′0941 — Great Britain. Children. Adoption — *Practical information*

Adopting a child : a brief guide for prospective adopters. — 1982 ed. — London : British Agencies for Adoption & Fostering, 1982. — 24p ; 21cm
Previous ed.: 1981. — Includes index
ISBN 0-903534-39-8 (unbound) : £0.75
B82-15421

362.7′4 — England. Day care centres for maladjusted children — *Case studies*

Day units for children with emotional and behavioural difficulties / Neville Jones ... [et al.]. — Cardiff (c/o Treasurer, J.G. Visser, Department of Education, University College, P.O. Box 78, Cardiff CF1 1XL) : Association of Workers for Maladjusted Children and Therapeutic Education, [1981]. — 56p ; 25cm. — (Monograph ; 1)
Cover title. — Includes bibliographies
£2.00 (pbk) B82-33136

362.7′4 — Maladjusted children

Stott, Denis H.. Helping the maladjusted child / Denis H. Stott. — Milton Keynes : Open University Press, 1982. — viii,124p ; 24cm. — (Children with special needs)
Bibliography: p120. — Includes index
ISBN 0-335-10044-9 (cased) : £11.95 : CIP rev.
ISBN 0-335-10039-2 (pbk) : £4.95 B81-31087

362.7′4 — Maladjusted children. Short term residential care & treatment

The Evaluation and care of severely disturbed children and their families. — Lancaster : MTP, c1982. — xiv,126p : forms ; 26cm
Includes bibliographies and index
ISBN 0-85200-587-3 : Unpriced B82-37190

362.7′4 — Visually handicapped children — *For children*

Chapman, Elizabeth. Suzy. — London : Bodley Head, Oct.1981. — [32]p. — (Special situation picture books ; 7)
ISBN 0-370-30375-x : £3.25 : CIP entry
B81-25770

362.7′4′0926 — Australia. Victoria. Melbourne. Maladjusted children. Social problems — *Case studies*

What happens to children : the origins of violence / a collection of stories told by children who could not write them ; edited by Valerie Yule. — London : Angus & Robertson, 1979. — 168p : ill ; 24cm
Ill on lining papers
ISBN 0-207-14201-7 (cased) : £5.95
ISBN 0-207-13807-9 (pbk) : Unpriced
B82-05657

362.7′4′0973 — United States. Maladjusted children. Rehabilitation

Hobbs, Nicholas. The troubled and troubling child / Nicholas Hobbs. — San Francisco ; London : Jossey-Bass, 1982. — xxii,397p : ill ; 24cm. — (The Jossey-Bass social and behavioral science series)
Bibliography: p377-383. — Includes index
ISBN 0-87589-518-2 : Unpriced B82-32919

362.7'95 — United States. Divorced persons. Children. Custody

Divorce, child custody, and the family / by the Committee on the Family, Group for the Advancement of Psychiatry. — San Francisco ; London : Jossey-Bass, 1981, c1980. — xviii,180p ; 23cm. — (The Jossey-Bass social and behavioral science series)
Originally published: New York : Mental Health Materials Center, 1980. — Includes index
ISBN 0-910958-10-6 (pbk) : £7.95 B82-17051

Luepnitz, Deborah Anna. Child custody : a study of families after divorce / Deborah Anna Luepnitz. — Lexington, Mass. : Lexington ; [Aldershot] : Gower [distributor], c1982. — xiv,191p : 1ill ; 24cm
Bibliography: p183-187. — Includes index
ISBN 0-669-04365-6 : £15.00 B82-31797

362.7'95'02542356 — Devon. Exeter. Facilities for children — *Directories*

Out of the house : Exeter's guide for parents with young children. — [Exeter] : [Family Matters], c1980. — 60p : ill,1map ; 21cm
Includes index
ISBN 0-9507087-0-4 (pbk) : £0.80 B82-31074

362.7'95'0880694 — Great Britain. Socially disadvantaged children. Care

Holman, Robert, *1936-*. Inequality in child care / Robert Holman. — 2nd ed. — London (1 Macklin St., WC2B 5NH) : Child Poverty Action Group, 1980. — 48p ; 21cm. — (Poverty pamphlet ; 26)
Previous ed.: 1975
£1.00 (pbk) B82-24655

362.7'95'0880694 — Social services for socially disadvantaged children

Justice and troubled children around the world / edited with an introduction by V. Lorne Stewart. — New York ; London : New York University Press
Vol.2. — c1981. — xxiii,190p ; 22cm
Includes index
ISBN 0-8147-7817-8 : £13.00 B82-38253

Justice and troubled children around the world / edited with an introduction by V. Lorne Stewart. — New York ; London : New York University Press
Vol.3. — c1981. — xxi,230p ; 22cm
Includes index
ISBN 0-8147-7820-8 : £18.60 B82-38252

362.7'95'0942 — England. Local authorities. Services for children to 5 years. Coordination

Bradley, Martin. Coordination of services for children under five : final report of the research project presented to the Department of Education and Science and the Department of Health and Social Security by the project director / Martin Bradley. — Liverpool (Liverpool Institute of Higher Education, Stand Park Rd., Liverpool L16 9JD) : S. Katharine's College, 1981. — 137,[31]p ; 30cm
Unpriced (spiral) B82-03656

362.7'96'0941 — Great Britain. Welfare workers. Interpersonal relationships with adolescents

Crompton, Margaret. Adolescents and social workers. — London : Heinemann Educational, Sept.1982. — [96]p. — (Community care practice handbooks ; 12)
ISBN 0-435-82189-x (pbk) : £2.95 : CIP entry B82-21756

362.7'9791630421 — London. Homeless single young persons: Scots. Accommodation. Provision — *Proposals*

Young Scots in London : (second report, 1978). — London (New Horizon Youth Centre, 1 Macklin St., W.C.2) : The Scots Group, [1978]. — 14p : 1map ; 30cm
Cover title
£0.30 (pbk)
Also classified at 331.3'4624110421 B82-10309

362.8 — WELFARE SERVICES FOR FAMILIES, UNMARRIED MOTHERS, MINORITY GROUPS, ETC

362.8 — Great Britain. Welfare work with bereaved persons

Smith, Carole R.. Social work with the dying and bereaved / Carole R. Smith. — London : Macmillan, 1982. — vi,149p ; 23cm. — (Practical social work)
Bibliography: p137-146. — Includes index
ISBN 0-333-30894-8 (cased) : £10.00
ISBN 0-333-30895-6 (pbk) : Unpriced
Primary classification 362.1'75'0941 B82-21618

362.8'2 — Families with alcoholics. Self-help

Burr, Alison. Families and alcoholics / Alison Burr. — London : Constable, 1982. — 126p ; 23cm
Bibliography: p125-126
ISBN 0-09-464100-5 : £5.95 B82-27043

362.8'2 — Families with handicapped children

Philp, Mark. Children with disabilities and their families : a review of research / Mark Philp and Derek Duckworth. — Windsor : NFER-Nelson, 1982. — xii,131p ; 22cm
Bibliography: p111-124. — Includes index
ISBN 0-7005-0491-5 (pbk) : £6.95 B82-38152

362.8'2 — Families with mentally retarded children. Self-help groups — *Manuals*

Working towards independence : a manual for self-help groups for parents with difficult or special children and for workers in the community / [authors Stephen Chelms ... et al.] ; [illustrations Neil Clitheroe]. — London : West-Central, c1980. — 72p : ill ; 21cm
Bibliography: p72
ISBN 0-907378-00-5 (pbk) : £2.50 B82-15078

362.8'2 — Great Britain. Electricity supply & gas supply. Consumers: Low-income families. Debts. Payment — *Electricity Consumers' Council viewpoints*

Electricity Consumers' Council. Fuel debts, disconnections and the avoidance of hardship. — London : Electricity Consumers' Council, 1982. — 51p ; 30cm. — (Occasional paper / Electricity Consumers' Council ; 3)
£2.00 (spiral) B82-22002

362.8'2'0924 — Great Britain. Married men alcoholics. Interpersonal relationships with wives — *Personal observations*

Murray, Eva. My life with an alcoholic / Eva Murray. — Bognor Regis : New Horizon, c1982. — 22p ; 21cm
ISBN 0-86116-822-4 : £3.25 B82-13399

362.8'2'0924 — United States. Families with brain-damaged children. Personal problems — *Personal observations*

Kupfer, Fern. Before and after Zachariah. — London : Gollancz, Sept.1982. — [256]p
ISBN 0-575-03196-4 : £8.95 : CIP entry B82-18763

362.8'2'0941 — Great Britain. Single-parent families

Shiach, Don. One-parent families : a source book for schools / [compiled and written by Don Shiach and the Information Office of the National Council for One Parent Families]. — London : The Council, 1982. — 18p : ill ; 30cm
Bibliography: p17
ISBN 0-901582-45-x (unbound) : Unpriced B82-32073

362.8'2'0941 — Great Britain. Single parent families — *Practical information*

Davenport, Diana, *19---*. One parent families / Diana Davenport. — London : Sheldon, 1982, c1979. — 192p ; 20cm. — (Overcoming common problems)
Originally published: London : Pan, 1979. — Includes bibliographies and index
ISBN 0-85969-362-7 (pbk) : £2.50 B82-29726

362.8'2'09415 — Ireland. Single-parent families — *Manuals*

Clark, Clara. Coping alone / Clara Clark ; Northern Ireland section by Stella Mahon. — Dublin : Arlen House, 1982. — 192p : ill ; 18cm. — (Help yourself)
ISBN 0-905223-25-x (pbk) : £2.95 B82-39667

362.8'2'0973 — United States. Families with patients with coronary heart diseases. Personal problems — *Case studies*

Speedling, Edward. Heart attack : the family response at home and in the hospital. — London : Tavistock, July 1982. — [200]p
ISBN 0-422-77790-0 (cased) : £8.95 : CIP entry
ISBN 0-422-77800-1 (pbk) : £4.50 B82-12339

362.8'253 — Scotland. Strathclyde Region. Welfare work with families with pre-school children

Overton, Jennifer. Stepping stone projects : the first three years, 1978-1981 / Jennifer Overton. — Glasgow : Scottish Pre-School Playgroups Association, 1982. — vii,43p : ill ; 26cm
Text on inside cover
ISBN 0-907662-06-4 (pbk) : £1.50 B82-37987

362.8'254'0941 — Great Britain. Welfare services for socially disadvantaged families: Family groups

Cowan, Jim. People cope : family groups in action / Jim Cowan. — London : COPE, c1982. — 120p : ill ; 21cm
ISBN 0-907760-01-5 (pbk) : Unpriced : CIP rev. B82-13174

362.8'254'09421 — London. Welfare services for socially disadvantaged families: Family groups — *Correspondence, diaries, etc.*

A funny thing happened to me on the way to becoming a group leader : the diary of a family group leader. — London : COPE, 1981. — 92p : ill ; 21cm
Cover title
ISBN 0-907760-00-7 (pbk) : £1.75 : CIP rev. B81-31094

362.8'256'0941 — Great Britain. Families. Policies of government — *Proposals*

Craven, Edward. Family issues and public policy / Edward Craven, Lesley Rimmer and Malcolm Wicks. — [London] : Study Commission on the Family, c1982. — 46p ; 21cm. — (Occasional paper / Study Commission on the Family ; no.7)
ISBN 0-907051-09-x (unbound) : £2.25 B82-35238

362.8'28 — Great Britain. General practice. Family planning services — *Proposals*

Family planning : an exercise in preventive medicine : report of a sub-committee of the Royal College of General Practitioners' Working Party on Prevention. — London : The College, 1981. — vi,7p ; 28cm. — (Report from general practice ; 21)
Bibliography: p7
ISBN 0-85084-082-1 (pbk) : Unpriced B82-00421

362.8'28'0941 — Great Britain. Welfare services for families with handicapped children — *Conference proceedings*

Handicap in the family : sixty-eighth annual conference report, 1981, Wednesday 22nd July, University of Birmingham / [National Association for Maternal and Child Welfare]. — London (1 South Audley St., W1Y 6JS) : NAMCW, [1981?]. — 43p : 1port ; 21cm
£0.80 (pbk) B82-10724

362.8'28'09411 — Scotland. Social services for families with adopted children. Attitudes of families

Kerrane, Ailie. Adopting older and handicapped children : a consumer's view of the preparation, assessment, placement and post-placement support services / by Ailie Kerrane, Ailsa Hunter, Mary Lane. — Barkingside ([Tanners La., Barkingside, Ilford, Essex IG6 1QG]) : Dr. Barnardo's, c1980. — 139p : ill,maps,facsims,forms ; 21cm. — (Barnardo social work paper ; no.14)
Bibliography: p139
Unpriced (pbk) B82-08383

362.8′282 — Great Britain. Child benefits — *Proposals*

A Little pride and dignity : the importance of child benefit / edited by Jen McClelland. — London : Child Poverty Action Group, 1982. — 24p : 1ill ; 21cm. — (Poverty pamphlet ; 54)
Bibliography: p24
ISBN 0-903963-51-5 (pbk) : £0.90 B82-27444

362.8′282 — Scotland. Independent secondary schools. Students from low-income families. Tuition fees. Payment by Great Britain. *Scottish Education Department*

Assisted places : a new bursary scheme for the lower income families. — [Edinburgh] ([New St. Andrews House, Scotland EH1 3SY]) : Scottish Education Department, [1981?]. — 3p ; 30cm
Unpriced (unbound) B82-14319

362.8′282′06041 — Great Britain. Low-income families. Poverty relief. Organisations: Child Poverty Action Group, *1970-1979*

Field, Frank, *1942-*. Poverty and politics : the inside story of the CPAG campaigns in the 1970s / Frank Field. — London : Heinemann, 1982. — x,205p ; 23cm
Includes index
ISBN 0-435-82305-1 (cased) : £14.50 : CIP rev.
ISBN 0-435-82306-x (pbk) : Unpriced B82-03361

362.8′283 — Great Britain. Free school meals. Take-up — *Inquiry reports*

Wilson, Paul, *1949 Feb.10-*. Free school meals : a survey carried out on behalf of the Department of Education and Science / Paul Wilson. — [London] : Office of Population Census and Surveys, Social Survey Division, 1981. — 39p : ill,1form ; 30cm. — (Occasional paper ; 23) (SS 1131)
ISBN 0-906197-24-4 (pbk) : £2.00 B82-06335

362.8′286 — Marriage counselling

Brannen, Julia. Marriages in trouble. — London : Tavistock, Dec.1982. — [300]p
ISBN 0-422-78100-2 : £14.00 : CIP entry B82-29794

362.8′286 — Parents of handicapped children. Counselling

Nettles, Olwen. Counselling parents of children with handicaps / by Olwen Nettles. — Crawley (16 Parkfield Close, Gossops Green, Crawley, Sussex) : Tappenden, 1978, c1979 (1979 [printing]). — 56p ; 22cm
Cover title. — Text on inside covers
£1.65 (pbk) B82-34670

362.8′286 — Scotland. Marriage counselling, *1931-1981*

Haldane, J. D.. A celebration of marriage? Scotland 1931-81 : implications for marital counselling and therapy. — Aberdeen : Aberdeen University Press, Apr.1982. — [48]p
ISBN 0-08-028466-3 (pbk) : £1.50 : CIP entry B82-03739

362.8′286 — Welfare work. Family therapy — *Conference proceedings*

Models of family treatment / Eleanor Reardon Tolson and William J. Reid editors. — New York ; Guildford : Columbia University Press, 1981. — 365p ; 24cm
Conference papers. — Includes bibliographies and index
ISBN 0-231-04950-1 : £14.40 B82-05627

362.8′3 — Scotland. Battered women. Care & protection — *Practical information*

Women′s aid : a manual for local authorities. — Edinburgh (11 St Colme St., Edinburgh) : Scottish Women′s Aid, [1982?]. — 13[i.e.21]p ; 30cm
Includes bibliographies
£0.70 (pbk) B82-31119

362.8′3 — Scotland. Single mothers. Social conditions

Lamotte, Judith R.. The home that Jill built : a follow-up study of single mothers who set out to bring up their chilren on their own / Judith Lamotte in collaboration with Julie-Ann Macqueen. — Edinburgh : Scottish Council for Single Parents, c1981. — 53p ; 21cm
Cover title. — Sequel to: Single mothers / Angela Hopkinson. 1976. — Bibliography: p53
£1.50 (pbk) B82-24077

362.8′3 — United States. Battered wives. Psychosocial aspects

Pagelow, Mildred Daley. Woman-battering : victims and their experiences / Mildred Daley Pagelow ; foreword by Del Martin. — Beverly Hills ; London : Sage, c1981. — 288p ; 23cm. — (Sage library of social research ; v.129)
Bibliography: p275-287
ISBN 0-8039-1681-7 (cased) : Unpriced
ISBN 0-8039-1682-5 (pbk) : £6.50 B82-07902

362.8′4 — Immigrants. Resettlement. Psychological aspects — *Conference proceedings*

Uprooting and surviving : adaptation and resettlement of migrant families and children / edited by Richard C. Nann. — Dordrecht ; London : Reidel, c1982. — xvi,194p : ill,1map ; 25cm. — (Priority issues in mental health ; v.2)
Conference papers. — Includes bibliographies and index
ISBN 90-277-1339-1 : Unpriced B82-21452

362.8′4′007 — Great Britain. Welfare workers. Professional education. Curriculum subjects: Welfare work with ethnic minorities

Social work and ethnicity. — London : Allen & Unwin, Aug.1982. — [256]p. — (National Institute social services library ; no.43)
ISBN 0-04-362050-7 (cased) : £12.95 : CIP entry
ISBN 0-04-362051-5 (pbk) : £5.95 B82-15636

362.8′4′00941 — Great Britain. Local authorities. Welfare services for ethnic minorities — *Inquiry reports*

Multi-racial Britain : the Social services response : a working party report / Association of Directors of Social Services and the Commission for Racial Equality. — London : The Commission, 1978 (1980 [printing]). — 83p : forms ; 21cm
ISBN 0-902355-78-3 (pbk) : £1.00 B82-14410

362.8′4′00973 — United States. Welfare work with ethnic minorities

Social work practice with minorities / [edited by] David R. Burgest. — Metuchen ; London : Scarecrow, 1982. — 308p : 1ill ; 23cm
ISBN 0-8108-1476-5 : £13.20 B82-17420

362.8′5 — Great Britain. Industrial health services

Great Britain. *Health and Safety Executive.* Guidelines for occupational health services. — London : H.M.S.O., Feb.1982. — [30]p. — (HS(G)20)
ISBN 0-11-883625-0 (pbk) : CIP entry B82-03089

362.8′5 — Scotland. Social services for unemployed persons — *Directories*

Unemployment action : a selection of unemployment initiatives : an annotated directory of community based responses to unemployment. — [Edinburgh] ([4 Queensferry St. Edinburgh EH2 4PA]) : Unemployment Initiatives Service, Scottish Community Education Centre, [1982?]. — 42p ; 30cm
Cover title
Unpriced (pbk) B82-29256

362.8′7 — Great Britain. Vietnamese refugees. Resettlement — *Practical information — For young persons′ organisations*

A Guide for youth organisations wishing to work with Vietnamese refugees. — London (57 Chalton St., NW1 1HU) : British Youth Council, 1980. — 2,5p ; 30cm
Cover title
Unpriced (pbk) B82-38465

362.8′83′0942733 — Greater Manchester *(Metropolitan County).* **Voluntary welfare services for rape victims: Manchester Rape Crisis Line**

Manchester Rape Crisis Line. Report / Manchester Rape Crisis Line. — 1st (Mar. 1980-Dec. 1981)-. — Manchester (PO Box 336, Manchester M60 2BS) : [The Line], [1982]-. — v. ; 30cm
ISSN 0263-4732 = Report - Manchester Rape Crisis Line : £1.00 B82-26151

362.9 — SPECIALISED WELFARE SERVICES. HISTORICAL AND GEOGRAPHICAL TREATMENT

362′.92′4 — Great Britain. Social reform. Butler, Josephine — *Biographies*

Boyd, Nancy. Josephine Butler, Octavia Hill, Florence Nightingale : three Victorian women who changed their world / Nancy Boyd. — London : Macmillan, 1982. — xviii,276p ; 23cm
Bibliography: p263-270. — Includes index
ISBN 0-333-30057-2 : £15.00
Primary classification 610.73′092′4 B82-28832

363 — PUBLIC SAFETY, POLICE, HOUSING AND OTHER PUBLIC SERVICES

363 — Urban regions. Public services. Policies of local authorities. Political aspects

The Politics of urban public services / edited by Richard C. Rich. — Lexington, Mass. : Lexington ; [Aldershot] : Gower [distributor], c1982. — xv,249p : ill,2maps ; 24cm
Includes bibliographies and index
ISBN 0-669-03765-6 : £19.00 B82-31793

363′.025′42184 — London. Ealing *(London Borough).* **Public services —** *Directories*

The London Borough of Ealing information handbook / published by authority of the London Borough of Ealing. — 4th ed. — London : Burrow, [1982]. — 40p ; 21cm
Previous ed.: 1977
Unpriced (pbk) B82-37387

363′.0941 — Great Britain. Local authorities. Public services. Privatisation — *Trade union viewpoints*

Keep your council services public : say no to private contractors. — London : National Union of Public Employees, 1982. — 22p : ill ; 21cm. — (A NUPE pamphlet)
Cover title
ISBN 0-907334-16-4 (pbk) : £0.50 B82-27126

National Union of Public Employees. Defend direct labour. — London : NUPE, 1982. — 30p : ill,facsims,1form ; 21cm. — (A NUPE pamphlet)
Cover title. — Author: National Union of Public Employees
ISBN 0-907334-17-2 (pbk) : £0.50 B82-31920

363′.0941 — Great Britain. Public health

Clay, Henry M.. Clay′s handbook of environmental health. — 15th ed. / revised by W.H. Bassett and F.G. Davies. — London : H.K. Lewis, 1981. — viii,851p : ill ; 24cm
Previous ed.: 1977. — Includes bibliographies and index
ISBN 0-7186-0451-2 : £30.00 B82-08198

363′.0941 — Great Britain. Public services. Privatisation

Labour Research Department. Public or private : the case against privatisation / Labour Research Department]. — London : LRD Publications, 1982. — 37p : ill ; 21cm
Cover title
ISBN 0-900508-50-7 (pbk) : £0.70
Primary classification 338.0941 B82-36864

Privatisation?. — Nottingham : Spokesman, Nov.1982. — [120]p
ISBN 0-85124-359-2 (cased) : £12.50 : CIP entry
ISBN 0-85124-360-6 (pbk) : £3.50 B82-33354

363'.0941 — Great Britain. Urban regions. Public services. Political aspects — *Conference proceedings*

Institute of British Geographers. *Conference (1982 : Southampton)*. Public provision and urban politics : papers from the IGB Conference January 1982 / edited by Andrew Kirby and Stephen Pinch ; papers by Peter Saunders [... et al.]. — Reading : Department of Geography, University of Reading, 1982. — 95p ; 22cm. — (Geographical papers ; no.80)
Includes bibliographies
ISBN 0-7049-0671-6 (pbk) : Unpriced B82-30884

363'.09413'4 — Edinburgh. Public works, *1752* — *Proposals* — *Early works*

Elliot, *Sir* **Gilbert**. Proposals for carrying on certain public works in the city of Edinburgh. — Edinburgh : Harris, 1982. — 43p ; 23cm
Author: Sir Gilbert Elliot. — Facsim of ed. published: Edinburgh : [s.n.], 1752
ISBN 0-86228-003-6 : £12.50 B82-39927

363'.09422'5 — East Sussex. Public services. Administration areas

East Sussex boundaries / by Local Government Unit - County Library. — [Lewes] ([County Library, 44 St. Anne's Cres., Lewes, E. Sussex]) : [East Sussex County Council], 1982. — 38p : maps ; 30cm
Unpriced (unbound) B82-35814

363'.09428'37 — Humberside. Hull. Public health, *1847*

Report of the Sanitary Committee of the Hull Medical Society on the sanitary state of the town (1847) / with an introduction and illustrations by Stephen Bryant ; foreword & medical glossary by A.J. Shillitoe. — Hull (39, High St., Hull [N. Humberside]) : Bradley, 1977. — 37p,[9] leaves of plates : ill,1map,2ports ; 22cm
Limited ed. of 500 copies. — Bibliography: p34. — Includes index
£1.50 (pbk) B82-09374

363'.09775'95 — Wisconsin. Milwaukee. Public health, *1867-1930*

Leavitt, Judith Walzer. The healthiest city : Milwaukee and the politics of health reform / Judith Walzer Leavitt. — Princeton, N.J. ; Guildford : Princeton University Press, c1982. — xvii,294p : ill,maps ; 23cm
Bibliography: p275-279. — Includes index
ISBN 0-691-08298-7 : £15.90 B82-31586

363.1 — PUBLIC SAFETY SERVICES

363.1 — Great Britain. Science. Research. Safety aspects — *Inquiry reports*

Safety in research : report of a Royal Society study group, December 1981. — London : Royal Society, 1981. — 46p ; 21cm
Bibliography: p39-41
ISBN 0-85403-186-3 (pbk) : Unpriced B82-14996

363.1 — Safety — *For children*

Prowse, Dave. Play safe with the stars : a child's guide to safety / by Dave Prowse. — London : Proteus, 1981. — 64p : col.ill,music ; 28cm
ISBN 0-906071-53-4 : £3.25 B82-06977

363.1 — Technological development. Risks. Assessment

Lagadec, Patrick. Major technological risk. — Oxford : Pergamon, Oct.1982. — [450]p
Translation of: Le risque technologique majeur
ISBN 0-08-028913-4 : £30.00 : CIP entry B82-24958

363.1'1 — Great Britain. Laboratories. Safety aspects — *For technicians*

Clarke, B. P.. Safety and laboratory practice : level 1 / B.P. Clarke. — New York ; London : Van Nostrand Reinhold, 1981. — 157p : ill ; 23cm. — (Technical education courses)
With answers. — Includes index
ISBN 0-442-30402-1 (cased) : £8.00
ISBN 0-442-30404-8 (pbk) : £3.75 B82-09757

363.1'1 — Great Britain. Workplaces. Hazards. Identification

Alcock, P. A.. Safety inspections : the detection of hazards at work / by P.A. Alcock. — London : H.K. Lewis, 1982. — vi,156p : ill,forms ; 23cm
Includes index
ISBN 0-7186-0454-7 : £8.00 B82-20960

363.1'1 — Industrial health

Occupational hygiene : an introductory text / edited by H.A. Waldron and J.M. Harrington. — Oxford : Blackwell Scientific, 1980. — ix,424p : ill ; 24cm
Includes bibliographies and index
ISBN 0-632-00563-7 : £16.50 : CIP rev. B80-19781

Patty, Frank Arthur. Patty's industrial hygiene and toxicology. — New York ; Chichester, Wiley
Vol.2B: Toxicology. — 3rd rev. ed. / George D. Clayton, Florence E. Clayton, editors ; contributors D.M. Aviado ... [et al.]. — c1981. — xviii,p2879-3816 : ill ; 24cm
Previous ed.: New York ; London : Interscience, 1963. — Includes index
ISBN 0-471-07943-x : £45.00 B82-05819

363.1'1 — Industrial health. Hazards

Burgess, William A.. Recognition of health hazards in industry : a review of materials and processes / William A. Burgess. — New York ; Chichester : Wiley, c1981. — xiii,275p : ill ; 24cm
Includes index
ISBN 0-471-06339-8 : £20.35 B82-04433

363.1'1 — Industries. Explosions. Safety aspects

BEAMA/BASEEFA seminar on explosive atmospheres : Royal Lancaster Hotel, Thursday November 12 1981. — [London] ([8 Leicester St., WC2H 7BN]) : British Electrical and Allied Manufacturers' Association, [1981]. — [48]leaves ; 30cm
£15.00 (spiral) B82-35530

Explosion hazards and evaluation. — Oxford : Elsevier Scientific, July 1982. — [440]p. — (Fundamental studies in engineering ; 5)
ISBN 0-444-42094-0 : CIP entry B82-20757

363.1'1 — Industries. Safety. Risk-benefit analysis

High risk safety technology. — Chichester : Wiley, Oct.1982. — [648]p
ISBN 0-471-10153-2 : £25.00 : CIP entry B82-24726

363.1'1 — Netherlands. Rijnmond. Industries. Hazards. Analysis

Risk analysis of six potentially hazardous industrial objects in the Rijmond area : a pilot study : a report to the Rijmond Public Authority. — Dordrecht ; London : Reidel, c1982. — xx,793p : ill ; 24cm
Includes index
ISBN 90-277-1393-6 : Unpriced B82-23503

363.1'1'05 — Industrial health — *Serials*

Recent advances in occupational health. — No.1-. — Edinburgh : Churchill Livingstone, 1981-. — v. ; 24cm
ISSN 0261-1449 = Recent advances in occupational health : Unpriced B82-09672

363.1'1'078 — Great Britain. Hotel & catering industries. Personnel. Training. Curriculum subjects: Industrial health & industrial safety. Teaching aids — *Catalogues*

Source list of training aids in health and safety and hygiene. — 3rd ed. — Wembley : Hotel and Catering Industry Training Board, 1981. — 62p ; 30cm
Previous ed.: 1979
ISBN 0-7033-0013-x (pbk) : £3.00 B82-11931

363.1'1'0941 — Great Britain. Industrial health

Harrington, J. M.. Doctors at work / J.M. Harrington. — [Birmingham] : University of Birmingham, 1982. — 18p ; 21cm
Cover title
ISBN 0-7044-0593-8 (pbk) : Unpriced B82-31037

363.1'1'0941 — Great Britain. Industrial health & industrial safety — *For safety representatives*

Guide for BIFU safety representatives. — London (Sheffield House, 17 Hillside, Wimbledon, SW19 4NL) : The Banking Insurance & Finance Union, [1982?]. — 30p ; 21cm
Cover title
Unpriced (pbk) B82-30387

Safety skills programme for safety representatives / jointly developed by Food, Drink and Tobacco Industry Training Board and Manpower Services Commission (TWI Service). — Gloucester (Barton House, Barton St., Gloucester GL1 1QQ) : The Board, [1982?]. — 1v(loose-leaf) : ill(some col.) ; 32cm
Forty-eight 35mm colour slides in envelope, 69 sheets (handouts) in envelope, fold. sheet as inserts
£85.00 B82-23754

363.1'1'0941 — Great Britain. Industrial health & industrial safety — *For trade unionism*

Beaumont, P. B.. Safety at work and the unions. — London : Croom Helm, Nov.1982. — [208]p
ISBN 0-7099-0097-x : £12.95 : CIP entry B82-28745

363.1'1'0941 — Great Britain. Industrial health & industrial safety — *Questions & answers* — *For safety representatives*

Safety skills programme for safety representatives / jointly developed by Food, Drink and Tobacco Industry Training Board and Manpower Services Commission (TWI Service). — Gloucester (Barton House, Barton St., Gloucester GL1 1QQ) : The Board, [1982?]
Exercises. — 1v(loose-leaf) : ill ; 32cm
Sixty-five visual aids in envelope as insert
Unpriced B82-23757

363.1'1'0941 — Great Britain. Industrial health & industrial safety — *Serials*

Manufacturing and service industries. — 1980. — London : H.M.S.O., Jan.1982. — [100]p
ISBN 0-11-883457-6 (pbk) : CIP entry B81-34115

363.1'1'0941 — Great Britain. Industrial health & industrial safety - *Statistics*

Health and safety statistics. — 1978-79. — London : Health & Safety Executive, June 1981. — [60]p
ISBN 0-11-883438-x (pbk) : CIP entry B81-14822

363.1'1'0941 — Great Britain. Industrial safety — *Serials*

Industrial safety data file. — [Jan. 1982]-. — London : United Trade Press, [1982]-. — v. : ill ; 30cm
Monthly. — Continues: Industrial safety. — Revised index published every six months. — Description based on: Mar. 1982
ISSN 0262-3226 = Industrial safety data file : Unpriced B82-24769

363.1'1'0942678 — Essex. Thurrock *(District).* **Industries. Hazards** — *Inquiry reports*

Canvey : a second report : a summary of a review of potential hazards from operations in the Canvey Island/Thurrock area three years after publication of the Canvey Report / Health and Safety Executive. — London : H.M.S.O., 1981. — 18p : 1col.map ; 30cm
Map on folded leaf attached to inside cover
ISBN 0-11-883618-8 (pbk) : £2.50
Primary classification 363.1'1'09426792 B82-16798

363.1'1'09426792 — Essex. Canvey Island & Thurrock *(District).* **Industries. Hazards** — *Inquiry reports*

Canvey : a second report : a review of potential hazards from operations in the Canvey Island/Thurrock area three years after publication of the Canvey Report / Health and Safety Executive. — London : H.M.S.O., 1981. — vi,128p,[1]folded leaf of plates : 1col.map ; 30cm
Bibliography: p119-125
ISBN 0-11-883459-2 (pbk) : £7.00 B82-16797

363.1′1′09426792 — Essex. Canvey Island. Industries. Hazards — *Inquiry reports*

Canvey : a second report : a summary of a review of potential hazards from operations in the Canvey Island/Thurrock area three years after publication of the Canvey Report / Health and Safety Executive. — London : H.M.S.O., 1981. — 18p : 1col.map ; 30cm
Map on folded leaf attached to inside cover
ISBN 0-11-883618-8 (pbk) : £2.50
Also classified at 363.1′1′0942678 B82-16798

363.1′1′0973 — United States. Industrial health

Patty, Frank Arthur. Patty′s Industrial hygiene and toxicology. — 3rd rev. ed. / George D. Clayton, Florence E. Clayton editors. — New York ; Chichester : Wiley
Previous ed.: New York : London : Interscience, 1958
Vol.2C: Toxicology : with cumulative index for volume 2 / contributors B.D. Astill ... [et al.]. — c1982. — xx,p3847-5112 : ill ; 24cm
Includes index
ISBN 0-471-09258-4 : £75.00 B82-34749

363.1′12 — Industrial safety. Measurement

Tarrants, William E.. The measurement of safety performance / William E. Tarrants. — New York ; London : Pubblished under the auspices of the American Society of Safety Engineers [by] Garland STPM, c1980. — xv,414p : ill,forms ; 24cm. — (Garland safety management series)
Bibliography: p392-397. — Includes index. — Includes eight papers presented at a symposium held in Chicago on Sept.14-17, 1970
ISBN 0-8240-7170-0 : Unpriced B82-26809

363.1′16215 — Great Britain. Compressed air chambers. Industrial health & safety — *Standards*

Medical code of practice for work in compressed air. — 3rd ed. — London : Construction Industry Research and Information Association, c1982. — 52p : ill,forms ; 30cm. — (Report / CIRIA, ISSN 0305-408x ; 44)
Previous ed.: 1975
ISBN 0-86017-175-2 (pbk) : £20.00 B82-20472

363.1′163 — Industrial health. Hazards. Monitoring

Gill, Frank S.. Monitoring for health hazards at work / by Frank S. Gill and Indira Ashton ; foreword by Richard Warburton. — [Birmingham] : ROSPA, 1982. — xiv,155p : ill ; 21cm
Includes index
ISBN 0-86286-029-6 (pbk) : £8.50 : CIP rev. B82-11979

363.1′17 — United States. Workplaces. Accidents. Prevention

Heinrich, H. W.. Industrial accident prevention : a safety management approach / H.W. Heinrich, Dan Petersen, Nestor Roos. — 5th ed. — New York ; London : McGraw-Hill, c1980. — xii,468p : ill ; 24cm
Previous ed.: 1959. — Bibliography: p455-461. — Includes index
ISBN 0-07-028061-4 : £20.75 B82-25219

363.1′172 — Respiratory protective equipment

Respiratory protection : principles and applications / edited by Bryan Ballantyne and Paul H. Schwabe. — London : Chapman and Hall, 1981. — x,376p : ill ; 24cm
Includes bibliographies and index
ISBN 0-412-22750-9 : £20.00 B82-17598

363.1′172′0941 — Great Britain. Industries. Hazards. Control measures. Planning — *Conference proceedings*

Planning for major hazards : 30 October, 1981 London. — Leighton Buzzard : Scientific and Technical Studies, 1981. — ivleaves,74p ; 30cm
Conference papers
ISBN 0-9505774-8-0 (pbk) : £28.00 : CIP rev. B82-06536

363.1′175 — Industrial safety. Applications of microprocessors

Microprocessors. — London (11 Norwich St., EC4A 1AB) : Scientific and Technical Studies, July 1982. — [100]p
ISBN 0-907822-05-3 (pbk) : £29.50 : CIP entry B82-19294

363.1′175 — Man. Cancer. Pathogens: Chemicals. Safety measures

Great Britain. *Health and Safety Executive*. Carcinogens in the workplace : the views of the Health and Safety Executive on a strategy for control. — London : H.M.S.O., Nov.1981. — [8]p. — (Technical report ; no.1)
ISBN 0-11-883619-6 (pbk) : £1.00 : CIP entry B82-00156

363.1′1933378′0941 — Great Britain. Public open spaces. Industrial health & industrial safety

Weeding out danger : a NUPE health and safety handbook for parks, open spaces, playing fields and cemeteries staff. — London : National Union of Public Employees, 1982. — 76p : ill ; 21cm
Includes index
ISBN 0-907334-15-6 (pbk) : £0.50 B82-37925

363.1′19621042 — Energy industries. Hazards. Control measures

Young, R. E.. Control in hazardous environments / R.E. Young. — Stevenage : Peregrinus on behalf of the Institution of Electrical Engineers, c1982. — 111p : ill ; 23cm. — (IEE control engineering series ; 17)
Includes index
ISBN 0-906048-69-9 (pbk) : Unpriced : CIP rev. B82-02482

363.1′19622334′0941 — Great Britain. Coal mines. Industrial health & industrial safety — *Serials*

Health and safety. Mines / Health and Safety Executive. — 1979-. — London : H.M.S.O., 1980-. — v. : ill ; 30cm
Annual. — Continues: Health and safety. Coal mines ; and, in part, Health and safety. Quarries & mines other than coal
ISBN 0-11-883272-7 : £3.50 : CIP rev.
ISSN 0262-0316 = Health and safety. Mines B80-13839

363.1′19622334′0942976 — Mid Glamorgan. Senghenydd. Coal mines: Universal Colliery. Lancaster Pit. Accidents, *1913*

Brown, John H.. The valley of the shadow : an account of Britain′s worst mining disaster, the Senghenydd explosion / by John H. Brown. — Port Talbot : Alun Books, c1981. — 171p : ill,1map,1facsim,3plans,ports ; 21cm
Bibliography: p163-164. — Includes index
ISBN 0-907117-07-4 (cased) : £5.50
ISBN 0-907117-06-6 (pbk) : Unpriced B82-03488

363.1′19622338′0941 — Great Britain. Continental shelf. Offshore natural gas & petroleum industries. Safety aspects

Carson, W. G.. The other price of Britain′s oil : safety and control in the North Sea / W.G. Carson. — Oxford : Robertson, 1981, c1982. — xi,320p : ill ; 24cm
Includes index
ISBN 0-85520-392-7 (cased) : £15.00
ISBN 0-85520-393-5 (pbk) : £5.95 B82-24207

363.1′19622338′0941 — Great Britain. Continental shelf. Offshore natural gas & petroleum industries. Safety aspects — *Conference proceedings*

Certification and safety of offshore installations : May 11 and 12, 1981, London / edited by Catherine O′Keeffe. — [London] : Scientific and Technical Studies, [1981]. — iv,190p : ill ; 30cm
Conference papers
ISBN 0-9505774-4-8 (pbk) : £35.00 B82-05670

363.1′1962235′0941 — Great Britain. Quarries. Industrial health & industrial safety — *Serials*

Health and safety. Quarries / Health & Safety Executive. — 1979-. — London : H.M.S.O., 1980-. — v. : ill ; 30cm
Annual. — Continues in part: Health and safety. Quarries and mines other than coal
ISSN 0263-3094 = Health and safety. Quarries : £3.50 B82-18724

363.1′1962382′00941 — Great Britain. Shipbuilding industries. Industrial health & industrial safety, *1971-1978*

Great Britain. *Factory Inspectorate. Shipbuilding National Industry Group***Shipbuilding** and ship-repairing : health and safety 1971-1978. — London : H.M.S.O., 1980. — 28p : ill ; 30cm
At head of title: Health and Safety Executive
ISBN 0-11-883267-0 (pbk) : £2.50 : CIP rev. B80-10626

363.1′19641 — Great Britain. Food & drinks industries & trades. Safety measures, *1975-1980*

The **Drinks** industry 1975-1980. — London : H.M.S.O., Dec.1981. — [60]p
ISBN 0-11-883458-4 (pbk) : CIP entry B81-31376

363.1′19651 — Great Britain. Offices. Hazards

Craig, Marianne. Office workers′ survival handbook : a guide to fighting health hazards in the office / [Marianne Craig]. — London : BSSRS, c1981. — 200p : ill ; 21cm
Includes index
ISBN 0-9502541-5-0 (pbk) : Unpriced B82-32810

363.1′196679′0941 — Great Britain. Coatings industries. Industrial safety — *Serials*

Hazards, pollution & legislation in the coatings field : a quarterly bulletin published by the Paint Research Association. — Vol.1, no.1 (Mar. 1981)-. — Teddington (Waldegrave Rd., Teddington, Middx. TW11 8LD) : The Association, 1981-. — v. ; 21cm
Subject index published in the last issue of each year
ISSN 0262-7116 = Hazards, pollution & legislation in the coatings field (corrected) : £130.00 per year B82-08469

363.1′196712′0941 — Great Britain. Foundry industries. Industrial health & industrial safety, *1975-1978*

Foundries : health and safety 1975-78 / a report by HM Factory Inspectorate. — London : H.M.S.O., 1980. — 11p : ill ; 30cm
At head of title: Health & Safety Executive
ISBN 0-11-883277-8 (pbk) : £2.00 : CIP rev. B80-18754

363.1′19671842′0941 — Great Britain. Wire manufacturing & products industries. Industrial health & industrial safety, *1975-1980*

Wire, rope and cable : health and safety 1975-80 / Health & Safety Executive. — London : H.M.S.O., 1981. — 44p : ill,2maps ; 30cm
ISBN 0-11-883424-x (pbk) : £2.50 : CIP rev. B81-06059

363.1′196782′0941 — Great Britain. Rubber industries. Industrial health & industrial safety, *1976-1980*

Rubber : health and safety 1976-80 / Health & Safety Executive. — London : H.M.S.O., 1981. — 20p : ill ; 30cm
ISBN 0-11-883445-2 (pbk) : £2.50 B82-23548

363.1′2′0942837 — Humberside. Hull region. Transport. Accidents, *1837-1927*

Ulyatt, Michael E.. Five Hull tragedies : the Union steam packet explosion 1837, the whaler Diana′s dramatic voyage 1866-7, the Dogger Bank incident 1904, the R38 airship disaster 1921, the train disaster 1927 / by Michael E. Ulyatt. — Hull (39 High St., Hull, [N. Humberside]) : Bradley, 1977. — 28p : ill ; 21cm
Limited ed. of 500 copies
£1.00 B82-09373

363.1′22′0941 — Great Britain. Railways. Accidents — *History* — *Illustrations*

Trains in trouble : railway accidents in pictures. — St Day : Atlantic
Vol.1 / [compiled by] Arthur Trevena. — 1980 (1982 [printing]). — [48]p : ill ; 20cm
ISBN 0-906899-01-x (pbk) : £1.95 B82-37533

Trains in trouble : railway accidents in pictures. — St Day : Atlantic
Vol.2 / [compiled by] Arthur Trevena. — 1981. — [48]p : ill ; 20cm
ISBN 0-906899-03-6 (pbk) : £1.95 B82-37534

363.1'22'0941 — Great Britain. Railways. Accidents, *to 1980*

Rolt, L. T. C.. Red for danger : a history of railway accidents and railway safety / by L.T.C. Rolt. — 4th ed. / revised and with additional material by Geoffrey Kichenside. — Newton Abbot : David & Charles, 1982. — 308p,[8]p of plates : ill ; 23cm
Previous ed.: 1976. — Bibliography: p308. — Includes index
ISBN 0-7153-8362-0 : £6.50 : CIP rev.
B82-13072

363.1'2265'0941 — Great Britain. Railways. Accidents — *Inquiry reports*

Great Britain. *Department of the Environment for Northern Ireland.* Railway accident : report on the collision that occurred on 20th December 1978 at Lisburn Station : on the railway of the Northern Ireland Railways Company Limited / Department of the Environment for Northern Ireland. — Belfast : H.M.S.O., 1981. — 17p,[1]folded leaf of plates : 1map ; 30cm
ISBN 0-337-08171-9 (pbk) : £3.00 B82-13807

Great Britain. *Department of Transport.* Railway accident : report on the collision that occurred on 25th February 1979 between Hilsea and Fratton in the Southern Region, British Railways / Department of Transport. — London : H.M.S.O., 1980. — 13p : 1map,1plan ; 30cm
Map and plan on folded leaf attached to inside back cover
ISBN 0-11-550531-8 (pbk) : £2.70 B82-14146

Great Britain. *Department of Transport.* Railway accident : report of the derailment that occurred on 8th September 1978 at Waterloo Station in the Southern Region, British Railways / Department of Transport. — London : H.M.S.O., 1980. — 10p : plans ; 30cm
Plans on folded leaf attached to inside back cover
ISBN 0-11-550532-6 (unbound) : £2.70
B82-14147

Great Britain. *Department of Transport.* Railway accident : report on the accident that occurred on 20th April 1980 at Bushey / in the London Midland Region British Railways ; Department of Transport. — London : H.M.S.O., 1981. — 3p : 1map ; 30cm
ISBN 0-11-550553-9 (unbound) : £1.50
B82-04204

Great Britain. *Department of Transport.* Railway accident : report on the collision that occurred on 5th April 1981 at Kirby Cross in the Eastern Region, British Railways / Department of Transport. — London : H.M.S.O., 1981. — 4p : 1map,1plan ; 30cm
Cover title
ISBN 0-11-550556-3 (pbk) : £1.50 B82-11548

Great Britain. *Department of Transport.* Railway accident : report on the collision that occurred on 14th February 1979 at Chinley North Junction in the London Midland Region of British Railways / Department of Transport. — London : H.M.S.O., c1982. — 8p,[1]folded leaf of plates : ill ; 30cm
ISBN 0-11-550560-1 (pbk) : £2.40 B82-26380

Great Britain. *Department of Transport.* Railway accident : report on the collision that occurred on 12th March 1979 at Sheffield in the Eastern Region, British Railways / Department of Transport. — London : H.M.S.O., 1982. — 13p : 1map,1plan ; 30cm
ISBN 0-11-550562-8 (pbk) : £2.10 B82-32826

363.1'23'091631 — North Atlantic Ocean. Steam liners: Titanic *(Ship).* **Sinking,** *1912*

McCaughan, Michael. Titanic / Michael McCaughan. — [Holywood] ([Cultra Manor, Holywood, BT18 0EU, Co. Down]) : Ulster Folk & Transport Museum, 1982. — 32p : ill,plans ; 15x21cm
Unpriced (pbk) B82-28383

363.1'23'094234 — Channel Islands. Shipwrecks, *1859-1981*

Couling, David. Wrecked on the Channel Islands. — London : Stanford Maritime, June 1982. — [128]p
ISBN 0-540-07399-7 (pbk) : £4.95 : CIP entry
B82-16223

363.1'23'0942847 — North Yorkshire. Whitby Bay. Shipwrecks: Rohilla *(Ship), 1914*

Wilson, Ken. Wreck of the Rohilla. — Orpington (6 Stanbrook House, Orchard Grove, Orpington, Kent) : Clement, Oct.1982. — [100]p
ISBN 0-907027-08-3 (pbk) : £4.95 : CIP entry
B82-30610

363.1'2365 — Great Britain. Fishing boats. Capsizing — *Inquiry reports*

The **Merchant** Shipping Act 1894 : mfv Do It Again : report of Court no. S502 : formal investigation. — London : H.M.S.O., 1980. — 19p ; 30cm
ISBN 0-11-511662-1 (pbk) : £1.75 B82-18622

363.1'2381'0941 — Great Britain. Canoe life saving services — *Manuals*

The **Canoe** lifeguard manual. — 4th rev. ed. — Weybridge (Flexel House, 45-47 High St., Addlestone, Weybridge, Surrey KT15 1JV) : Corps of Canoe Lifeguards, 1980. — 8v. : ill,maps ; 21cm
Previous ed.: 1974
Unpriced (pbk) B82-22511

363.1'2381'0942532 — Lincolnshire. Skegness. Lifeboat services, *to 1977*

Major, F. S. W.. A century and a half of Skegness lifeboats : an account of Skegness Lifeboat Station / from the stories written and collected by the late F.S.W. Major. — Skegness (41 Lumley Rd., Skegness, Lincolnshire) : B.S. Major, c1977. — vii,74p : ill,1map,ports ; 21cm
Unpriced (pbk) B82-24195

363.1'2381'0942759 — Merseyside *(Metropolitan County).* **Formby. Lifeboat services,** *1776-1918*

Yorke, Barbara. Britain's first lifeboat station : at Formby, Merseyside 1776-1918 / by Barbara and Reginald Yorke. — Liverpool (3 Wicks La., Formby, Liverpool L37 3JE) : Alt Press, [1982?]. — 72p : ill,facsims,maps,port ; 22cm
Text and map on inside covers
ISBN 0-9508155-0-0 (pbk) : Unpriced
B82-35323

363.1'24 — DeHavilland Mosquito aeroplanes. Accidents, *1942-1964 — Chronologies*

Smith, David J. (David John), *1943-*. De Havilland Mosquito : crash log. — 2nd ed. (fully rev.) / compiled by David J. Smith. — Earl Shilton : Midland Counties Publications, c1980. — 48p : ill ; 21cm
Previous ed.: England? : Warplane Wreck Investigation Group. 1976
ISBN 0-904597-33-4 (pbk) : £2.50 B82-35021

363.1'24 — Handley Page Hampden aeroplanes. Accidents, *1939-1944 — Lists*

Roberts, Nicholas. Handley Page Hampden & Hereford : crash log / compiled by Nicholas Roberts. — Earl Shilton : Midland Counties Publications, c1980. — 56p : ill,1map ; 21cm
Map on inside cover. — Bibliography: p56
ISBN 0-904597-34-2 (pbk) : £2.50 B82-35020

363.1'2465 — Aircraft. Accidents — *Inquiry reports*

France. *Bureau enquêtes-accidents.* Beechcraft Super King Air 200 G-BGHR : report on the accident near Nantes, France, on 25 September 1979 : translation of the report / by the French Bureau enquêtes-accidents. — London : H.M.S.O., [1980]. — 19p,[5]leaves of plates : ill,charts ; 30cm. — (Aircraft accident report ; 9/80)
Translation from the French. — At head of title: Department of Trade, Accidents Investigation Branch
ISBN 0-11-513176-0 (pbk) : £3.60 B82-12489

Great Britain. *Accidents Investigation Branch.* Piper PA E 23 (Aztec) series 250 G-AYSF : report on the accident 7n.m. north east of Moffat Dumfriesshire, Scotland on 27 July 1976 : including the review before Mr C.E. Jauncey now the Hon. Lord Jauncey, Captain Duncan McIntosh OBE AFC, Pilot Assessor, and Mr John Barker, Engineer Assessor / Department of Trade, Accidents Investigation Branch. — London : H.M.S.O., c1979. — iii,36p : ill ; 30cm. — (Aircraft accident report ; 3/78)
ISBN 0-11-511819-5 (pbk) : £1.75 B82-19393

Great Britain. *Accidents Investigation Branch.* Report on the accident to Edgar Percival Prospector G-AOZO near Ashford Aerodrome, Kent, on 2 July 1980 / Department of Trade [Accidents Investigation Branch]. — London : H.M.S.O., 1981. — 17p ; 30cm. — (Aircraft accident report ; 6/81)
ISBN 0-11-513499-9 (pbk) : £2.90 B82-02714

Great Britain. *Accidents Investigation Branch.* Report on the accident to Pilatus PC-6/B2-H2 Turbo Porter G-BHCR at Peterborough (Sibson) Aerodrome, on 15 February 1981 / Department of Trade, Accidents Investigation Branch. — London : H.M.S.O., c1982. — 20p ; 30cm. — (Aircraft accident report ; 1/82)
ISBN 0-11-513505-7 (pbk) : £3.50 B82-26379

Great Britain. *Accidents Investigation Branch.* Report on the accident to Piper Aztec PA23-25OF G-BOST near Riplingham, North Humberside, on 21 January 1981 / Department of Trade [Accidents Investigation Branch]. — London : H.M.S.O., c1982. — 13p ; 30cm. — (Aircraft accident report ; 10/81)
ISBN 0-11-513503-0 (pbk) : £3.20 B82-14613

Great Britain. *Accidents Investigation Branch.* Report on the accident to Piper PA 38-112 Tomahawk G-BGGH at Wood Farm, Kiddington, Oxfordshire, on 27 May 1980 / Department of Trade [Accidents Investigation Branch]. — London : H.M.S.O., 1982. — 22p : ill ; 30cm. — (Aircraft accident report ; 11/81)
ISBN 0-11-513504-9 : £4.70 B82-20574

Great Britain. *Accidents Investigation Branch.* Report on the accident to Piper PA31 Navajo G-LCCO at Earl Stonham, Stowmarket, Suffolk, on 20 August 1980 / Department of Trade [Accidents Investigation Branch]. — London : H.M.S.O., 1981. — 14p : 2maps ; 30cm. — (Aircraft accident report ; 7/81)
ISBN 0-11-513500-6 (pbk) : £2.90 B82-05166

Report on the accident to BAe (Vickers) Viscount 708 G-ARBY near Ottery St Mary, Devon, on 17 July 1980 / [Department of Trade, Accidents Investigation Branch]. — London : H.M.S.O., [1981]. — 32p ; 30cm. — (Aircraft accident reort ; 9/81)
ISBN 0-11-513502-2 (pbk) : £4.20 B82-14317

Spain. *Civil Aviation Accident Commission.* Report on the accident to Boeing 727 G-BDAN on Tenerife, Canary Islands on 25 April 1980 : translation of the report produced by the Spanish Civil Aviation Accident Commission. — London : H.M.S.O., 1981. — iii,31,[14]p : ill ; 30cm. — (Aircraft accident report ; 8/81)
Translation from the Spanish
ISBN 0-11-513496-4 (pbk) : £5.40 B82-12490

363.1'2465'028 — Great Britain. Civil aircraft. Accidents. Investigation. Methods — *For police*

Memorandum on the investigation of civil air accidents / Accidents Investigation Branch, Department of Trade. — Rev. — London ([66 Victoria St, SW1E 6SJ]) : [The Branch], 1977 (1981 [printing]). — 25p : forms(some col.) ; 30cm. — (A1B note ; 1/71 (Revised))
Unpriced (pbk) B82-11944

363.1'2492 — Yugoslavia. Vrbovec. Passenger aeroplanes. Mid-air collisions, *1976*

Weston, Richard. Zagreb one four. — London : Granada, Aug.1982. — [208]p
ISBN 0-246-11185-2 : £8.95 : CIP entry
B82-17196

363.1'25 — Great Britain. Road transport services. Safety aspects

Road transport safety and security handbook. — London : Kogan Page, Mar.1982. — [200]p
ISBN 0-85038-417-6 : £11.95 : CIP entry
B82-01559

363.1'251 — Great Britain. Pedestrians. Accidents. Psychological factors

Pedestrian accidents / edited by Antony J. Chapman, Frances M. Wade and Hugh C. Foot. — Chichester : Wiley, c1982. — xii,354p : ill ; 24cm
Bibliography: p293-339. — Includes index
ISBN 0-471-10057-9 : £18.95 : CIP rev.
B82-09697

363.1'2565 — United States. Road traffic. Accidents. Investigation — *Manuals*

Clark, Warren E.. Traffic management and collision investigation / Warren E. Clark. — Englewood Cliffs ; London : Prentice-Hall, c1982. — xiv,332p : ill,1plan,forms ; 24cm. — (Prentice-Hall series in criminal justice)
Bibliography: p325-326. — Includes index
ISBN 0-13-926162-1 : £13.45 B82-20543

363.1'257'088054 — Pedestrians: Children. Accidents. Prevention — *For motorists*

Don't blame the children. — [Birmingham] ([Cannon House, The Priory, Queensway, Birmingham B4 6BS]) : RoSPA, [1982?]. — [8]p : ill(some col.) ; 21cm
Unpriced (unbound) B82-19422

363.1'2572 — Great Britain. Motor vehicles. Seat belts. Compulsory wearing — *Proposals*

Great Britain. *Department of Transport*. Compulsory seat belt wearing for adults and children in cars : proposals by the Secretary of State for Transport : presented to Parliament on 8th September 1981. — [London] ([2 Marsham St., SW1P 3EB]) : [Department of Transport], c1981. — 30p ; 30cm
Cover title
Unpriced (pbk) B82-38483

363.1'2572'09417 — Ireland *(Republic)*. Road traffic. Accidents. Reduction. Effects of compulsory wearing of motor vehicle seat belts

Hearne, R.. The initial impact of the safety-belt legislation in Ireland / R. Hearne. — Dublin : An Foras Forbartha, 1981. — 14p : ill ; 30cm. — (RS ; 255)
Text on inside cover
ISBN 0-906120-46-2 (spiral) : Unpriced
B82-15380

363.1'2575 — Road safety

Foot, Hugh C.. Road safety. — Eastbourne : Praeger, Aug.1981. — [196]p
ISBN 0-03-060054-5 : £12.50 : CIP entry
B81-18172

363.1'2575'0941 — Great Britain. Pedestrians. Road safety

Roads fit to walk on. — London (1 Wandsworth Rd, SW8 2LJ) : Ramblers' Association, [1978]. — 15p : ill ; 23cm. — (Brief for the countryside ; no.5)
£0.25 (unbound) B82-38409

363.1'3 — Domestic emergencies — *Amateurs' manuals*

Dealing with household emergencies / [edited by Edith Rudinger]. — London : Consumers' Association, c1982. — 162p : ill ; 21cm. — (A Consumer publication)
Includes index
ISBN 0-85202-206-9 (pbk) : Unpriced
ISBN 0-340-25909-4 (Hodder & Stoughton)
B82-16950

363.1'3 — Residential institutions. Health & safety — *For wardens*

Safety in group dwellings : a NUPE health and safety handbook for housing wardens. — London : National Union of Public Employees, 1982. — 31p : ill ; 15cm
ISBN 0-907334-14-8 (pbk) : £0.25 B82-31048

363.1'3'0941 — Great Britain. Residences. Safety — *For retired persons*

Safety in retirement / RoSPA. — 2nd rev. ed. — [Birmingham] : The Royal Society for the Prevention of Accidents, 1981. — [16]p : col.ill ; 21cm
ISBN 0-900635-56-8 (unbound) : £0.80
B82-11934

363.1'375 — Residences. Safety — *For children*

Purves, Marjory. Home safety / by Marjory Purves ; with illustrations by Carole Hughes ; and 'Simla' cartoon drawings by Keith Logan. — Loughborough : Ladybird, c1981. — 51p : col.ill ; 18cm. — (Series 819)
Text, ill on lining papers
ISBN 0-7214-0685-8 : £0.50 B82-06287

363.1'4 — Water recreations. Safety measures — *For children*

Birch, Robert. Water safety / by Robert Birch ; photographs by John Hemming ; illustrations by Kathy [i.e. Kathie] Layfield. — Loughborough : Ladybird, c1981. — 51p : col.ill ; 18cm. — (Series 819)
Text, ill on lining papers
ISBN 0-7214-0687-4 : £0.50 B82-06289

The **Water** safety book / with a foreword by Rolf Harris. — Birmingham (Cannon House, The Priory, Queensway, Birmingham B4 6BS) : Sponsored by DER on behalf of RoSPA, [1982?]. — 26p : col.ill ; 30cm
£0.40 (unbound) B82-25034

363.1'5 — Hospitals. Safety measures

Engineering a safe hospital environment / David L. Stoner ... [et al.]. — New York ; Chichester : Wiley, c1982. — xi,195p : ill ; 24cm. — (Biomedical engineering and health systems)
Includes bibliographies and index
ISBN 0-471-04494-6 : Unpriced B82-22830

363.1'79 — Chemical laboratories. Safety measures

Freeman, N. T.. Introduction to safety in the chemical laboratory. — London : Academic Press, Sept.1982. — [270]p
ISBN 0-12-267220-8 : CIP entry B82-19162

363.1'79 — Chemicals. Handling. Safety measures — *Manuals*

Frankel, Maurice. Chemical risk : a workers' guide to chemical hazards and data sheets / Maurice Frankel. — London : Pluto, 1982. — 96p : forms ; 20cm. — (Workers' handbooks)
Bibliography: p85-91. — Includes index
ISBN 0-86104-362-6 (pbk) : £1.95 B82-23772

363.1'79 — Dangerous chemicals. Regulation — *Serials*

ICR news : international chemicals regulatory news. — [No.1]-. — Oxford (256 Banbury Rd, Oxford OX2 7DH) : Elsevier International Bulletins in association with Springborn Management Consultants, [1982]-. — v. ; 30cm
ISSN 0263-2039 = ICR news : Unpriced
B82-27635

363.1'79 — England. Nuclear reactors. Spent fuels. Transport through London. Safety aspects

Carrying the can : report of the Working Party on the Transportation of Nuclear Spent Fuel through London. — London (3 Howard Rd, E17) : London Region Ecology Party, 1980. — 87p : 1ill,1map ; 21cm
At head of title: Ecology Party, North London Branch
£1.00 (pbk) B82-40479

363.1'79 — Great Britain. Electricity generation industries. Risks

Ferguson, R. A. D.. Comparative risks of electricity generating fuel systems in the UK / R.A.D. Ferguson ; undertaken by the Energy Centre, University of Newcastle upon Tyne. — Stevenage : Peregrinus, c1981. — 210p in various pagings : ill,1map ; 30cm
ISBN 0-906048-66-4 (pbk) : Unpriced : CIP rev. B81-34212

363.1'79 — Great Britain. Irradiated nuclear fuels. Transport. Safety aspects — *Proposals*

London Region Waste Transport Campaign. Transportation of irradiated fuel elements : report of the London Region Waste Transport Campaign to the London Boroughs Association General Purposes Committee — 15th September 1980. — London ([15 Klea Avenue SW4]) : [The Campaign], [1981?]. — 66p ; 26cm
Unpriced (unbound) B82-18882

363.1'79 — Great Britain. Nuclear power. Safety aspects. Policies of government. Great Britain. Government. Policies on safety aspects of nuclear power

Chicken, John C.. Nuclear power hazard control policy / by John C. Chicken. — Oxford : Pergamon, 1982. — x,272p : ill ; 24cm
Bibliography: p247-261. — Includes index
ISBN 0-08-023254-x (cased) : Unpriced : CIP rev.
ISBN 0-08-023255-8 (pbk) : £7.50 B81-32603

363.1'79 — Great Britain. Nuclear power stations. Safety aspects

Nuclear safety / British Nuclear Forum. — London (1 St. Alban's St., SW1Y 4SI) : BNF, 1978. — [14]p : ill ; 21cm
Unpriced (unbound) B82-24862

363.1'79 — Great Britain. Radioactive waste materials. Transport. Safety aspects

Nuclear info : transporting spent fuel. — London (1 St. Alban's St., SW1Y 4SL) : British Nuclear Forum, 1981. — 1folded sheet(6p) : ill (some col.) ; 21cm. — (A BNF publication)
Unpriced B82-24853

363.1'79 — Insulating materials. Ignition by electrostatics. Prevention

Great Britain. *Health and Safety Executive*. Electrostatic ignition hazards of insulating materials. — London : H.M.S.O., May 1982. — [15]p. — (Occasional paper / Great Britain. Health and Safety Executive ; 5)
ISBN 0-11-883629-3 (pbk) : CIP entry
B82-09280

363.1'79 — Ionising radiation. Protection of man: Protection by residences. Influence of building materials — *Technical data*

Protective qualities of buildings / Home Office Scientific Advisory Branch. — London : Home Office, 1981. — [44]p : ill ; 30cm
ISBN 0-86252-006-1 (unbound) : £2.10
B82-00931

363.1'79 — Ionising radiation. Safety aspects — *Serials*

Journal of the Society for Radiological Protection. — Vol.1, no.1 (Spring 1981)-. — [Gosport] ([c/o R.S. Iles, Institute of Naval Medicine, Alverstoke, Gosport, Hants. PO12 2DL]) : The Society, 1981-. — v. : ill,ports ; 25cm
Quarterly. — Description based on: Vol.2, no.2 (Summer 1982)
ISSN 0260-2814 = Journal of the Society for Radiological Protection : £15.00 per year (£25.00 to institutions and libraries)
B82-38513

363.1'79 — Ionising radiation. Safety measures — *Conference proceedings*

International Radiation Protection Society. *Congress (5th : 1980 : Jerusalem)*. Radiation protection : a systematic approach to safety : proceedings of the 5th Congress of the International Radiation Protection Society, Jerusalem, March 1980. — Oxford : Pergamon, 1980. — 2v.(xliii,1234p) : ill,maps ; 26cm
ISBN 0-08-025912-x : £89.00 : CIP rev.
B80-11898

363.1'79 — Nuclear power. Hazards

Murphy, Dervla. Race to the finish? : the nuclear stakes / Dervla Murphy. — London : John Murray, 1981. — 264p ; 22cm
Bibliography: p251-254. — Includes index
ISBN 0-7195-3884-x (cased) : £9.50 : CIP rev.
ISBN 0-7195-3890-4 (pbk) : £5.95 B81-28106

363.1'79 — Nuclear power industries. Risks. Management — *Conference proceedings*
Planning for rare events : nuclear accident preparedness and management : proceedings of an international workshop January 28-31, 1980 / John W. Lathrop, editor. — Oxford : Pergamon, 1981. — xi,268p : ill ; 26cm. — (IIASA proceedings series ; 14)
Includes bibliographies and index
ISBN 0-08-028703-4 : £27.50 : CIP rev. B81-32041

363.1'79 — Nuclear power industries. Risks. Mathematical models
McCormick, Norman J.. Reliability and risk analysis : methods and nuclear power applications / Norman J. McCormick. — New York ; London : Academic Press, 1981. — xii,446p : ill ; 24cm
Includes index
ISBN 0-12-482360-2 : Unpriced B82-02066

363.1'79 — Radioisotopes. Ionising radiation. Safety aspects
Hughes, Donald. Notes on ionising radiations. — Northwood : Science Reviews, Dec.1981. — [120]p. — (Occupational hygiene monographs, ISSN 0141-7568 ; 5)
ISBN 0-905927-80-x (pbk) : £5.00 : CIP entry B81-36996

363.1'79 — Scotland. Dumfries and Galloway. Mullwharchar. Radioactive waste materials. Disposal. Exploratory drilling. Public inquiries — *S.C.R.A.M. viewpoints*
Poison in our hills : the first inquiry on atomic waste burial. — Edinburgh : SCRAM, c1980. — 71p : ill,1map ; 21cm
ISBN 0-9507282-0-9 (pbk) : £1.80 B82-01519

363.1'79 — Suffolk. Sizewell. Proposed nuclear power stations. Safety aspects — *Conference proceedings*
Seminar on the Sizewell 'B' power station proposal : held at the Wolsey Theatre, Ipswich on 10th June, 1981 : report of proceedings / Suffolk County Council. — Ipswich : The Council, 1981. — 78p in various pagings ; 30cm
ISBN 0-86055-085-0 (pbk) : Unpriced
Also classified at 621.48'1 B82-01258

363.1'79 — Sweden. Radioactive waste materials. Disposal
Johansson, Thomas B.. Radioactive waste from nuclear power plants / Thomas B. Johansson and Peter Steen. — Berkeley ; London : University of California Press, c1981. — x,197p : ill ; 23cm
Includes index
ISBN 0-520-04199-2 : £11.25 B82-06981

363.1'79 — Tritium. Safety aspects
Martin, E. B. M.. Health physics aspects of tritium. — Northwood : Science Reviews, Dec.1981. — [120]p. — (Occupational hygiene monographs, ISSN 0141-7568 ; 6)
ISBN 0-905927-85-0 (pbk) : £5.00 : CIP entry B81-36994

363.1'79 — X-ray diffraction. Safety aspects
Martin, E. B. M.. A guide to the safe use of x-ray diffraction and spectrometry equipment. — Northwood : Science Reviews, Jan.1983. — [80]p. — (Occupational hygiene monographs, ISSN 0141-7568 ; 8)
ISBN 0-905927-11-7 (pbk) : £5.50 : CIP entry B82-37461

363.1'89 — Industries. Microprocessor systems. Safety aspects
Microprocessors in industry : safety implications of the uses of programmable electronic systems in factories. — London : H.M.S.O., 1981. — 18p ; 21cm. — (HSE occasional paper series ; OP2)
Bibliography: p17
ISBN 0-11-883429-0 (pbk) : £1.50 B82-04386

363.1'92 — Great Britain. Food. Additives: Artificial sweeteners — *Inquiry reports*
Great Britain. *Food Additives and Contaminants Committee*. Food Additives and Contaminants Committee report on the review of sweeteners in food. — London : H.M.S.O., 1982. — iii,61p ; 25cm. — (FAC/REP/34)
Cover title
ISBN 0-11-241211-4 (pbk) : £3.90 B82-25643

363.1'92 — Great Britain. Food. Additives: Bulking aids — *Inquiry reports*
Great Britain. *Food Additives and Contaminants Committee*. Food Additives and Contaminants Committee review of remaining classes of food additives used as ingredients in food : report on the review of bulking aids. — London : H.M.S.O., 1980. — iii,13p ; 25cm. — (FAC/REP ; 32)
ISBN 0-11-240870-2 (unbound) : £1.90 B82-14144

363.1'92 — Great Britain. Food. Additives: Modified starches — *Inquiry reports*
Great Britain. *Food Additives and Contaminants Committee*. Food Additives and Contaminants Committee report on modified starches. — London : H.M.S.O., 1980. — 39p ; 25cm. — (FAC/REP ; 31)
Bibliography: p21-26
ISBN 0-11-240871-0 (unbound) : £2.80 B82-14143

363.1'92 — Great Britain. Food. Contaminants: Mycotoxins — *Inquiry reports*
Steering Group on Food Surveillance. *Working Party on Mycotoxins*. Survey of mycotoxins in the United Kingdom : the fourth report of the Steering Group on Food Surveillance, the Working Party on Mycotoxins. — London : H.M.S.O., 1980. — iii,35p : ill ; 25cm. — (Food surveillance paper ; no.4)
Bibliography: p28-32
ISBN 0-11-241174-6 (pbk) : £3.30 B82-14145

363.1'92 — Great Britain. Food. Contamination by copper & zinc — *Inquiry reports*
Steering Group on Food Surveillance. *Working Party on the Monitoring of Foodstuffs for Heavy Metals*. Survey of copper and zinc in food : the fifth report of the Steering Group on Food Surveillance, the Working Party on the Monitoring of Foodstuffs for Heavy Metals. — London : H.M.S.O., 1981. — iv,50p ; 25cm. — (Food surveillance paper ; no.5)
ISBN 0-11-241199-1 (pbk) : £4.20 B82-13827

363.1'927 — Food. Hygiene — *Manuals*
Aberdeen food hygiene handbook. — London (Publicity House, Streatham Hill, SW2 4TR) : Pyramid Press, [1982?]. — 68p : ill ; 21cm
Unpriced (pbk) B82-37406

363.1'927'024642 — Food. Hygiene — *For catering industries*
Basic hygiene for people who handle food. — Wembley ([PO Box 18, Wembley, HA9 7AP]) : Hotel & Catering Industry Training Board, [1980]. — 1portfolio : ill ; 30cm
Also available in Urdu and Spanish versions
Unpriced (unbound) B82-00848

363.1'927'024642 — Food. Hygiene — *For catering industries — Spanish texts*
Higiene basica para gente que manipula alimentos : (traducción en ingles sito al otro lado de cada carte). — [Wembley] ([PO Box 18, Wembley, HA9 7AP]) : Hotel and Catering Industry Training Board, c1980. — 1portfolio : ill ; 30cm
Spanish text, English translation. — Also available in Urdu and English versions
Unpriced (unbound) B82-00847

363.1'927'024642 — Food. Hygiene — *For catering industries — Urdu texts*
Ashyā' khvurdanī ko chūne vāle logon ke li'e ṣafā'ī kebunyādī uṣūl : angrezī tarjamah har Kārḍ kī pusht par hai. — [Wembley] ([PO Box 18, Wembley, HA9 7AP]) : Hotel & Catering Industry Training Board, c1980. — 1portfolio : ill ; 30cm
Urdu text, English translation. — Also available in Spanish and English versions
Unpriced (unbound) B82-00846

363.1'927'024642 — United States. Food. Hygiene — *For catering industries — Manuals*
Longrée, Karla. Sanitary techniques in foodservice / Karla Longrée, Gertrude G. Blaker. — 2nd ed. — New York ; Chichester : Wiley, c1982. — xii,271p : ill,1facsim,1form ; 23cm
Previous ed.: 1971. — Includes bibliographies and index
ISBN 0-471-08820-x (pbk) : £11.95 B82-13991

363.1'927'0941 — Great Britain. Food. Hygiene — *For catering industries & retail food trades*
Davenport, John K.. Food hygiene in the catering and retail trades / John K. Davenport. — London : H.K. Lewis, 1982. — viii,214p : ill ; 24cm
Bibliography: p204-207. — Includes index
ISBN 0-7186-0456-3 : £10.00 B82-12872

363.1'946 — Drugs. Development. Regulation — *Conference proceedings*
NATO Advanced Study Institute on Drug Development, Regulatory Assessment, and Postmarketing Surveillance *(1980 : Erice)*. Drug development, regulatory assessment, and postmarketing surveillance / [proceedings of a NATO Advanced Study Institute on Drug Development, Regulatory Assessment, and Postmarketing Surveillance held October 2-13, 1980, in Erice, Sicily] ; edited by William M. Wardell and Giampaolo Velo with the assistance of Nancy M. Jarocha. — New York ; London : Plenum in cooperation with NATO Scientific Affairs Division, c1981. — x,356p : ill ; 26cm. — (NATO advanced study institutes series. Series A, Life sciences ; v.39)
Includes index
ISBN 0-306-40822-8 : Unpriced B82-06143

363.2 — POLICE

363.2 — Great Britain. Coloured persons. Relations with police — *Communist Party of Great Britain viewpoints*
Black & blue : racism and the police. — London : Communist Party, 1981. — 32p : ill ; 21cm. — (A Communist Party pamphlet)
ISBN 0-86224-013-1 (unbound) : £0.50 B82-08734

363.2 — United States. Criminal law. Enforcement
Contemporary issues in law enforcement / edited by James J. Fyfe. — Beverly Hills ; London : Sage in cooperation with the American Society of Criminology, c1981. — 168p : ill ; 22cm. — (Sage research progress series in criminology ; v.20)
Includes bibliographies
ISBN 0-8039-1692-2 (cased) : Unpriced
ISBN 0-8039-1693-0 (pbk) : £4.95 B82-17089

363.2'023'41 — Great Britain. Police — *Career guides*
Joss, Jean. Careers in the police force. — London : Kogan Page, Oct.1982. — [100]p
ISBN 0-85038-508-3 (cased) : £6.95 : CIP entry
ISBN 0-85038-509-1 (pbk) : £2.50 B82-23878

363.2'092'4 — London. Police: Metropolitan Police. Slipper, Jack — *Biographies*
Slipper, Jack. Slipper of the yard / Jack Slipper. — London : Sidgwick & Jackson, 1981. — 190p ; 18cm
Includes index
ISBN 0-283-98819-3 (pbk) : £1.50 B82-11177

363.2'092'4 — London. Southwark *(London Borough)*. **Police: Metropolitan Police,** *1952-1979 — Personal observations*
Cole, Harry. Policeman's patch / Harry Cole. — [London] : Fontana, 1982. — 220p ; 18cm
ISBN 0-00-636458-6 (pbk) : £1.50 B82-31648

363.2'0941 — Great Britain. Police
Whitaker, Ben. The police in society / Ben Whitaker ; foreword by Lord Scarman. — London : Sinclair Browne, 1982, c1979. — 351p : ill ; 22cm
Originally published: London : Eyre Methuen, 1979. — Bibliography: p334-343. — Includes index
ISBN 0-86300-018-5 (pbk) : £4.95 : CIP rev. B82-02635

363.2'0941 — Great Britain. Police — *For children*
Murdock, Hy. The police force / written by Hy Murdock ; photographs by Tim Clark. — Loughborough : Ladybird, c1982. — 51p : col.ill ; 18cm. — (People who help us)
ISBN 0-7214-0699-8 : £0.50 B82-17754

363.2'0941 — Great Britain. Police — *Serials*

Bramshill journal. — Vol.1 ([197-])-. — Liverpool (42 Stanley St., Liverpool L1 6AL) : M. & W. Publications (Liverpool) Ltd, [197-]-. — v. ; 24cm
Annual. — Journal of: Police Staff College. — Description based on: Vol.1,no.3 (Winter 1981-82)
ISSN 0263-8002 = Bramshill journal : Unpriced B82-32162

Police officer magazine. — No.1 (Dec. 1981)-. — [Great Dunmow] ([PO Box 273, Great Dunmow, Essex CM6 2RU]) : [Police Officer Magazine], 1981-. — v. : ill,ports ; 30cm
Monthly
ISSN 0263-3884 = Police officer magazine : £6.75 per year B82-28119

363.2'0941 — Great Britain. Police — *Sociological perspectives*

Baldwin, Robert. Police powers and politics. — London : Quartet, June 1982. — 1v.
ISBN 0-7043-2333-8 (cased) : £9.95 : CIP entry
ISBN 0-7043-3412-7 (pbk) : £3.95 B82-12836

363.2'0942 — England. Police

Brogden, M.. The police. — London : Academic Press, Dec.1982. — [320]p. — (Law, state and society series)
ISBN 0-12-135180-7 : CIP entry B82-29875

363.2'09421 — London. Police: Metropolitan Police. Policies — *Proposals*

Policing London : the policing aspects of Lord Scarman's report on the Brixton disorders. — London ([The County Hall, SE1 7PB]) : Greater London Council, 1982. — 32p ; 30cm
Includes index
Unpriced (pbk) B82-38853

363.2'09421'65 — London. Lambeth *(London Borough)*. Police — *ALARM viewpoints*

A Cause for ALARM : a study of policing in Lambeth. — [London] ([506 Brixton Rd., S.W.9]) : [ALARM], [1982?]. — 32p : ill ; 21cm
Unpriced (pbk) B82-23568

363.2'09429'54 — Powys. Radnor *(District)*. Police: Radnorshire Constabulary, *to 1948*

Maddox, W. C.. A history of the Radnorshire Constabulary / W.C. Maddox. — [Llandrindod Wells] ([Wynberg, Dyffryn Rd., Llandrindod Wells, Powys, LD1 6AN]) : Radnorshire Society, 1959 (1981 [printing]). — 85p,[4]p of plates : ill,1port ; 21cm
£2.00 (pbk) B82-27268

363.2'0944'59 — France. Auvergne. Criminal law. Enforcement, *1720-1790*

Cameron, Iain A.. Crime and repression in the Auvergne and the Guyenne 1720-1790 / Iain A. Cameron. — Cambridge : Cambridge University Press, 1981. — xvi,283p : maps ; 24cm
Bibliography: p265-274. — Includes index
ISBN 0-521-23882-x : £18.50 : CIP rev.
Also classified at 363.2'0944'7 B81-32597

363.2'0944'7 — France. Guyenne. Criminal law. Justice. Enforcement, *1720-1790*

Cameron, Iain A.. Crime and repression in the Auvergne and the Guyenne 1720-1790 / Iain A. Cameron. — Cambridge : Cambridge University Press, 1981. — xvi,283p : maps ; 24cm
Bibliography: p265-274. — Includes index
ISBN 0-521-23882-x : £18.50 : CIP rev.
Primary classification 363.2'0944'59 B81-32597

363.2'0952 — Japan. Police

Ames, Walter L.. Police and community in Japan / Walter L. Ames. — Berkeley ; London : University of California Press, c1981. — xvi,247p : ill,1map,1facsim,2plans,1port ; 24cm
Bibliography: p233-237. — Includes index
ISBN 0-520-04070-8 : £15.75 B82-02235

363.2'0971 — Canada. Police: Royal Canadian Mounted Police. Alleged illegal methods

Fidler, Richard. RCMP, the real subversives / by Richard Fidler. — [Toronto] : Vanguard ; London : Pathfinder [[distributor]], c1978. — 95p : ill ; 22cm
Bibliography: p95
ISBN 0-88758-036-x (cased) : Unpriced
ISBN 0-88758-037-8 (pbk) : £1.95 B82-09954

363.2'0972 — Mexico. Society. Role of police, *1800-1910*

Vanderwood, Paul J.. Disorder and progress : bandits, police, and Mexican development / Paul J. Vanderwood. — Lincoln [Neb.] ; London : University of Nebraska Press, 1981. — xix,264p,[24]p of plates : ill,maps,ports ; 22cm. — (A Bison book)
Bibliography: p225-258. — Includes index
ISBN 0-8032-4651-x (cased) : Unpriced
ISBN 0-8032-9600-2 (Unpriced)
Also classified at 364.1'55'0972 B82-02050

363.2'0973 — United States. Police

Cooper, John L.. You can hear them knocking : a study in the policing of America / John L. Cooper. — Port Washington ; London : National University Publications : Kennikat, 1981. — 121p ; 23cm. — (Multi-disciplinary studies in the law)
Includes index
ISBN 0-8046-9285-8 : £12.30 B82-12282

Managing police work : issues and analysis / edited by Jack R. Greene. — Beverly Hills ; London : Sage in cooperation with the Academy of Criminal Justice Sciences, c1982. — 160p : ill ; 23cm. — (Perspectives in criminal justice ; 4)
Includes bibliographies
ISBN 0-8039-1787-2 (cased) : Unpriced
ISBN 0-8039-1788-0 (pbk) : Unpriced B82-26269

363.2'3'0973 — United States. Rural regions. Law. Enforcement — *Manuals*

Bristow, Allen P.. Rural law enforcement / Allen P. Bristow. — Boston, Mass. ; London : Allyn and Bacon, c1982. — vi,202p : ill ; 22cm. — (The Allyn and Bacon criminal justice series)
Includes index
ISBN 0-205-07366-2 (pbk) : Unpriced B82-27681

363.2'32'0971 — Canada. Police. Patrols

Ericson, Richard V.. Reproducing order : a study of police patrol work / Richard V. Ericson. — Toronto ; London : Published in association with the Centre of Criminology, University of Toronto, by University of Toronto Press, c1982. — xii,243p ; 24cm. — (Canadian studies in criminology)
Bibliography: p225-236. — Includes index
ISBN 0-8020-5569-9 (cased) : Unpriced
ISBN 0-8020-6475-2 (pbk) : £9.90 B82-35663

363.2'332 — United States. Police. Highway patrols. Insignia, *1917-1978*

Cole, Roy. The State Police and Highway Patrol patches of the United States / Roy Cole ; design Steve Marriott ; illustrations Roy Cole — Mike Rumble ; additional illustration Paul Harrison ; additional information John Emmett ... [et al.]. — [Harrogate] ([c/o Ralph B. Lindley, 12 Kendal Rd., Harrogate. N. Yorks. HG1 4SH]) : Police Insignia Collectors Association of Great Britain, c1982. — 24p : ill ; 21x30cm
Unpriced (pbk) B82-22259

363.2'5 — England. Suspects. Interrogation by police

Police interrogation. — London : H.M.S.O., 1980. — v,99p ; 25cm. — (Research studies ; no.3 and no.4)
At head of title: Royal Commission on Criminal Procedure. — Includes bibliographies. — Contents: Review of literature / Pauline Morris — An observational study in four police stations / Paul Softley with the assistance of David Brown et al.
ISBN 0-11-730123-x (pbk) : £4.50 B82-16042

363.2'5 — England. Suspects. Interrogation by police. Psychological aspects

Police interrogation. — London : H.M.S.O., 1980. — vii,153p : ill ; 25cm. — (Research studies ; no.1 and no.2)
At head of title: Royal Commission on Criminal Procedure. — Bibliography: p66-74. — Contents: The psychological approach / Barrie Irving and Linden Hilgendorf — A case study of current practice / Barrie Irving with the assistance of Linden Hilgendorf
ISBN 0-11-730122-1 (pbk) : £5.70 B82-16044

363.2'5 — England. Suspects. Interrogation of police

Softley, Paul. Police interrogation : an observational study in four police stations / by Paul Softley with the assistance of David Brown ... [et al.]. — London : H.M.S.O., 1980. — vii,63p : 1form ; 25cm. — (A Home Office Research Unit report) (Home office research study ; no.61)
Bibliography: p63
ISBN 0-11-340701-7 (pbk) : £3.90 B82-14642

363.2'501'9 — Crimes. Witnesses — *Psychological perspectives*

Evaluating witness evidence. — Chichester : Wiley, Dec.1982. — [350]p
ISBN 0-471-10463-9 : £16.00 : CIP entry B82-30828

363.2'5'0973 — United States. Criminal investigation — *Manuals*

Criminal and civil investigation handbook / Joseph J. Grau editor in chief with the assistance of Ben Jacobson ; foreword by Joseph McNamara. — New York ; London : McGraw-Hill, c1981. — xxv,1100p in various pagings : ill,forms ; 24cm
Includes index
ISBN 0-07-024130-9 : £36.50 B82-24555

363.2'58 — Great Britain. Criminals. Identification — *Psychological perspectives*

Shepherd, John W.. Identification evidence. — Aberdeen : Aberdeen University Press, June 1982. — [164]p
ISBN 0-08-028441-8 : £12.50 : CIP entry B82-11287

363.2'83'0924 — South Africa. *Bureau of State Security, 1963-1979* — *Personal observations*

Winter, Gordon. Inside BOSS : South Africa's secret police / Gordon Winter. — London : Allen Lane, 1981. — 640p ; 21cm
Includes index
ISBN 0-7139-1391-6 : £7.95 B82-03202

Winter, Gordon, *1934-*. Inside BOSS : South Africa's secret police / Gordon Winter. — Harmondsworth : Penguin, 1981. — 640p ; 20cm
Includes index
ISBN 0-14-005751-x (pbk) : £3.95 B82-03203

363.2'89 — Great Britain. Private security services — *Statistics*

British security companies / industry commentary by A.T. Lowry. — London : Jordan & Sons (Surveys), c1982. — xxii,65p ; 30cm. — (A Jordan survey)
ISBN 0-85938-162-5 (pbk) : Unpriced B82-34000

363.2'89 — Great Britain. Private security services — *Statistics* — *Serials*

British security companies. — [1978]-. — London : Jordan & Sons (Surveys) Ltd., 1978-. — v. ; 30cm
Issued every two years. — Description based on: [1980] issue
ISSN 0263-3655 = British security companies : £69.00 B82-18721

363.3 — PUBLIC ORDER, DISASTER, FIRE SERVICES, ETC

363.3'48 — United States. Natural disasters. Evacuation of communities. Planning

Perry, Ronald W.. Evacuation planning in emergency management / Ronald W. Perry, Michael K. Lindell, Marjorie R. Greene. — Lexington : Lexington Books, c1981 ; [Aldershot] : Gower [distributor], 1982. — xiv,199p : ill,maps ; 24cm. — (The Battelle Human Affairs Research Centre series)
Bibliography: p181-196. — Includes index
ISBN 0-669-04650-7 : £18.50 B82-18259

363.3'48'0973 — United States. Disaster relief

Rossi, Peter H.. Natural hazards and public choice : the state and local politics of hazard mitigation / Peter H. Rossi, James D. Wright, Eleanor Weber-Burdin with the assistance of Marianne Pietras, William F. Diggins. — New York ; London : Academic Press, 1982. — xvi,337p : forms ; 24cm. — (Quantitative studies in social relations)
Bibliography: p336-337
ISBN 0-12-598220-8 : £19.60 B82-38387

363.3'49 — Natural disasters. Economic aspects

Sorkin, Alan L.. Economic aspects of natural hazards / Alan L. Sorkin. — Lexington : Lexington Books ; [Aldershot] : Gower [distributor], 1982. — xi,178p ; 24cm
Includes index
ISBN 0-669-03639-0 : £17.50 B82-32248

363.3'492 — Famines caused by drought, *1972*. Social aspects

Drought and man. — Oxford : Pergamon, Sept.1981
Vol.2: The constant catastrophe. — [304]p
ISBN 0-08-025824-7 : £23.25 : CIP entry B81-23883

363.3'497 — Riots. Control

Applegate, Rex. Riot control : material and techniques / Rex Applegate. — 2nd ed. — Boulder : Paladin Press ; London : Arms & Armour, 1981. — 332p : ill ; 24cm
Previous ed.: Harrisburg, Pa. : Stackpole Books, 1969. — Includes index
ISBN 0-85368-198-8 : Unpriced B82-01599

363.3'49875 — Nuclear warfare. Safety measures — *Manuals*

Goodwin, Peter. Nuclear war. — London (9 Henrietta St., W.C.2) : Ash and Grant, May 1981. — [128]p
ISBN 0-904069-43-5 : £4.95 : CIP entry B81-07589

363.3'49883'09492 — Netherlands. Famines caused by war, *1944-1945*. Relief by allies

Zee, Henri van der. The hunger winter : occupied Holland 1944-5. — London : Jill Norman and Hobhouse, Apr.1982. — [224]p
ISBN 0-906908-71-x : £9.95 : CIP entry B82-05785

363.3'5 — Nuclear warfare. Safety measures — *Manuals*

Tyrrell, Ivan. The survival option. — London : Cape, Oct.1982. — [232]p
ISBN 0-224-02059-5 : £7.95 : CIP entry B82-24362

363.3'5'0941 — Great Britain. Civil defence

'Civil defence' / Peace Force Scotland. — Kirkcaldy (The Lantern House, Olympia Arcade, Kirkcaldy, KY1 1QF) : Peace Force Scotland, [1982]. — [4]p : ill ; 21cm. — (Fact sheet ; 7)
Bibliography: p4
Unpriced (unbound) B82-27594

363.3'5'0941 — Great Britain. Civil defence. Policies of government

Campbell, Duncan. War plan '82. — London : Burnett Books, Sept.1982. — [192]p
ISBN 0-09-150671-9 : £3.95 : CIP entry B82-21736

363.3'5'0941 — Great Britain. Civil defence. Policies of government — *Campaign for Nuclear Disarmament viewpoints*

Bolsover, Phil. Civil defence : the cruellest confidence trick / by Phil Bolsover. — London : Campaign for Nuclear Disarmament, 1982. — 64p : ill,1map,2facsims ; 21cm
ISBN 0-907321-02-x (pbk) : £0.80 B82-28959

Bolsover, Philip. Civil defence : the cruellest confidence trick / by Philip Bolsover. — [London] ([11 Goodwin St., N4 3HQ]) : The Campaign for Nuclear Disarmament, [1982?]. — 23p ; 21cm
Cover title
£0.40 (pbk) B82-21846

363.3'5'0941 — Great Britain. Civil defence. Policies of government — *Labour Party (Great Britain) viewpoints*

Labour Party, *Great Britain, National Executive Committee*. Civil defence, home defence and emergency planning / National Executive Committee. — London (150 Walworth Rd., SE17 1JT) : Labour Party, 1981. — 6p ; 30cm. — (Advice note ; no.6)
£0.20 (unbound) B82-01694

363.3'71 — Great Britain. Fire vandalism — *Inquiry reports*

Great Britain. *Working Party on Fires Caused by Vandalism*. Report of Home Office Working Party on Fires Caused by Vandalism. — [London] : Home Office, 1980. — 36p ; 21cm
Unpriced (pbk) B82-16629

363.3'78'0941 — Great Britain. Fire brigades — *For children*

Dodds, Irene. The fire service / written by Irene Dodds ; photographs by Tim Clark. — Loughborough : Ladybird, c1982. — 51p : col.ill ; 18cm. — (People who help us)
ISBN 0-7214-0700-5 : £0.50 B82-17752

363.3'79 — Great Britain. Chemical engineering plants. Fires — *Conference proceedings*

The **Recognition** and reduction of ignition hazards in the chemical industry, 12 November 1981 London. — [London] : Scientific and Technical Studies, c1982. — iv,leaves,120p : ill ; 30cm
Conference papers
ISBN 0-9505774-9-9 (pbk) : Unpriced : CIP rev. B82-10853

363.3'79 — Towns. Fires — *For children*

Morris, Neil. Fire in the town. — London : Hodder & Stoughton Children's Books, Feb.1983. — [32]p. — (Story facts)
ISBN 0-340-28613-x : £1.95 : CIP entry B82-38051

363.4 — SERVICES FOR CONTROL OF PUBLIC MORALS

363.4'2 — Great Britain. Local authority lotteries — *Conference proceedings*

Local authority lotteries : papers from a seminar held in the University of Birmingham on 30th November 1977 / edited by A.J. Veal. — Birmingham : Centre for Urban and Regional Studies, University of Birmingham, 1979. — 49p ; 30cm. — (Conference and seminar papers ; no.5)
ISBN 0-7044-0335-8 (pbk) : £1.40 B82-11400

363.4'4'0942 — England. Prostitution

McLeod, Eileen. Women working : prostitution now. — London : Croom Helm, July 1982. — [192]p
ISBN 0-7099-1717-1 : £10.95 : CIP entry B82-12933

363.4'4'0973 — United States. Prostitution — *Early works — Facsimiles*

Roe, Clifford. The great war on white slavery / Clifford Roe. — New York ; London : Garland, 1979. — 448p,[32]p of plates : ill,facsims,ports ; 23cm. — (Prostitution)
Facsim of: 1st ed. U.S. : C. Roe, 1911
ISBN 0-8240-9712-2 : Unpriced B82-26822

363.4'6'0942 — England. Abortion — *Serials*

Abortion review. — No.1 (Oct./Nov. 1981)-. — London (27 Mortimer St., W1N 7RJ) : Birth Control Trust, 1981-. — v. ; 30cm
Six issues yearly. — Statistics sheet accompanies No.1
ISSN 0262-7299 = Abortion review : £3.00 per year B82-11836

363.4'7 — Pornography — *Feminist viewpoints*

Faust, Beatrice. Women, sex & pornography / Beatrice Faust. — Harmondsworth : Penguin, 1981, c1980, 1982 [printing]. — 200p,[32]p of plates : ill ; 18cm. — (Pelican books)
Originally published: London : Melbourne House, 1980. — Includes index
ISBN 0-14-022393-2 (pbk) : £1.95 B82-22496

Faust, Beatrice. Women, sex, and pornography / by Beatrice Faust. — London : Melbourne House, 1980. — 200p,[32]p of plates : ill ; 22cm
Includes index
ISBN 0-86161-006-7 : £8.95 B82-10180

363.4'7 — Pornography. Social aspects

Dworkin, Andrea. Pornography : men possessing women / Andrea Dworkin. — London : Women's Press, 1981. — 304p ; 21cm
Originally published: New York : Perigee, 1981. — Bibliography: p239-285. — Includes index
ISBN 0-7043-3876-9 (pbk) : £4.75 : CIP rev. B81-28064

Griffin, Susan. Pornography and silence : culture's revenge against nature / Susan Griffin. — London : Women's Press, 1981. — ix,277p ; 21cm
Originally published: New York : Harper & Row, 1981. — Bibliography: p266
ISBN 0-7043-3877-7 (pbk) : £4.75 : CIP rev. B81-99999

The **Influence** of pornography on behaviour. — London : Academic Press, Oct.1982. — [340]p
ISBN 0-12-767850-6 : CIP entry B82-27195

363.5 — HOUSING

363.5 — England. Homeless persons. Accommodation. Provision by local authorities — *Statistics — Serials*

Homelessness statistics. Actuals / CIPFA Statistical Information Service. — 1978-79-. — London : Chartered Institute of Public Finance and Accountancy, 1980-. — v. ; 30cm
Annual. — Description based on: 1980-81 issue
ISSN 0144-4514 = Homelessness statistics. Actuals : £6.00 B82-32153

363.5 — Great Britain. Squatting, *to 1980*

Squatting : the real story / written by Nick Anning ... [et al.] ; designed by Caroline Lwin ; illustrated by Andy Milburn ; edited by Nick Wates and Christian Wolmar ; compiled by Nick Wates. — London : Bay Leaf, 1980. — 240p : ill(some col.),1map,facsims, ports ; 22x26cm
Bibliography: p236-237. — Includes index
ISBN 0-9507259-0-0 (cased) : £11.50
ISBN 0-9507259-1-9 (pbk) : £4.90 B82-24276

363.5 — Housing — *Comparative studies*

World housing. — London (Market Planning Division, Nationwide Building Society, New Oxford House, High Holburn, WC1V 6PW) : Nationwide Building Society, 1980. — 1folded sheet(6p) : maps ; 30cm
Unpriced B82-31395

363.5 — Nottinghamshire. Nottingham. Inner areas. Private housing. Development

Private housing development process : a case study / D.C. Nicholls ... [et. al. of the] University of Cambridge Department of Land Economy, 19 Silver Street, Cambridge, CB3 9EP. — London (2 Marsham St,SW1P 3EB) : Inner Cities Directorate, Department of the Environment, c1981. — iii,124p,[10]p of plates : ill,forms,2maps ; 30cm. — (Inner cities research programme ; 4)
£4.35 (pbk) B82-32678

363.5 — Urban regions. Housing. Self-help

Self help housing : a critique / edited by Peter M. Ward. — London : Mansell, 1982. — viii,296p : ill,maps,plans ; 24cm
Bibliography: p279-291. — Includes index
ISBN 0-7201-1636-8 : £19.00 : CIP rev. B82-00168

363.5′068′1 — London. Westminster *(London Borough).* **Maida Vale. Housing estates: Maida Vale Estate. Financial management**

Furbey, Robert. Renting the Vale : housing and the Church Commisssioners / Robert Furbey and David Skinner. — [Sheffield] : [Department of Urban and Regional Studies, Sheffield City Polytechnic], 1980. — 17leaves ; 30cm. — (Occasional papers in urban and regional studies ; no.1)
ISBN 0-903761-38-6 (pbk) : Unpriced B82-22031

363.5′0722 — South-east England. Housing — *Case studies*

Public housing, private development : a collection of case studies / [edited by] David Crouch, Stephen Musgrave. — [Chelmsford] : Chelmer Institute, 1980. — 48,viip,[4]leaves of plates : ill,1plan ; 30cm. — (Chelmer working papers in environmental planning ; no.5)
Cover title
£1.30 (pbk) B82-20237

363.5′0724 — United States. Urban regions. Housing market *related to* **mobility of population. Mathematical models**

Pollakowski, Henry O.. Urban housing markets and residential location / Henry O. Pollakowski. — Lexington, Mass. : Lexington ; [Aldershot] : Gower [distributor], c1982. — xvii,141p : ill ; 24cm
Bibliography: p129-137. — Includes index
ISBN 0-669-02773-1 : £15.00
Primary classification 307′.2′0724 B82-31792

363.5′092′4 — Northern Ireland. Housing. Planning, *1969-1981* — *Personal observations*

Brett, C. E. B.. Architectural schizophrenia / by C.E.B. Brett. — [Belfast] ([181a Stranmillis Rd., Belfast 9]) : Ulster Architectural Heritage Society, 1981. — 24p : ill ; 26cm
£1.60 (pbk) B82-09133

363.5′0941 — Great Britain. Housing, *1945-1981*

Short, John R.. Housing in Britain. — London : Methuen, Dec.1982. — [250]p
ISBN 0-416-74280-7 (cased) : £11.00 : CIP entry
ISBN 0-416-74290-4 (pbk) : £6.00 B82-29764

363.5′0941 — Great Britain. Housing — *For schools*

Fyson, Nance Lui. Homes and housing / Nance Lui Fyson. — London : Batsford Academic and Educational, 1982. — 72p : ill ; 26cm. — (Living today)
Includes index
ISBN 0-7134-3578-x : £5.95 B82-30752

A **Roof** over your head. — London (57 Chalton St., NW1 1HU) : British Youth Council, [1982?]. — 1portfolio : ill ; 40cm
Unpriced B82-35703

363.5′0941 — Great Britain. Housing — *Serials*

The **SNHAT** news bulletin. — No.1-. — London (157 Waterloo Rd, SE1) : Shelter National Housing Aid Trust, 1979-. — v. ; 30cm
Five issues yearly. — Description based on: No.14
ISSN 0262-4885 = SNHAT news bulletin : Unpriced B82-04921

363.5′0941 — Great Britain. Housing — *Shelter viewpoints*

Build homes build hope : a report on Britain′s mounting housing crisis. — London : Shelter, 1981. — 28p : ill,ports ; 30cm
ISBN 0-901242-60-8 (unbound) : £2.00 B82-11958

363.5′0941 — Great Britain. Rural regions. Housing

Rural housing : hidden problems and possible solutions : the report of a National Federation of Housing Associations working party. — London : The Federation, [1981]. — 28p : ill ; 30cm
ISBN 0-86297-053-9 (pbk) : £2.75 B82-11317

363.5′0941 — Great Britain. Rural regions. Housing. Planning

Clark, G.. Housing and planning in the countryside. — Chichester : Wiley, May 1982. — [300]p. — (Geography and public policy research studies series ; v.2)
ISBN 0-471-10212-1 : £18.00 : CIP entry B82-06837

363.5′09411 — Scotland. Housing

Clark, David, *1946-*. Who cares? : a report on Scotland′s neglected housing problems / by David Clark. — Aberdeen (c/o Aberdeen People′s Press, 163 King St., Aberdeen) : Scottish Federation of Housing Associations, [1981?]. — 19p : ill,1map,ports ; 30cm
Cover title
£1.00 (pbk) B82-25281

Dible, James. Residential renewal in Scottish cities : a report for the Scottish Development Department / study team, James Dible, Judith Webster. — Edinburgh (40 Melville St. Edinburgh, EH3 7UG) : National Building Agency, 1981. — 137p : ill,maps,plans ; 30cm
Bibliography: p136-137
Unpriced (spiral) B82-35109

363.5′09412′35 — Scotland. Grampian Region. Aberdeen. Housing — *Serials*

Aberdeen *(Grampian). District Council.* Housing plan / City of Aberdeen District Council. — 1978-83-. — [Aberdeen] ([City of Aberdeen, Department of Law and Administration, Town House, Aberdeen AB9 1AQ]) : [The Council], [1978?]. — v. ; 30cm
Annual. — Description based on: 1980-1985
ISSN 0263-3132 = Housing plan - City of Aberdeen District Council : Unpriced B82-19884

363.5′09412′7 — Scotland. Tayside Region. Dundee *(District).* **Housing** — *Proposals*

Dundee. *District Council.* The City of Dundee District Council housing plan 1981-1986 (No.4). — Dundee (7 Castle St., Dundee) : [The Council], 1981. — iv,112p,[23]p ; 30cm
Unpriced (pbk) B82-12956

Dundee. *District Council.* The City of Dundee District Council housing plan 1982-1987 (No.5). — Dundee (7 Castle St., Dundee) : [The Council], 1981. — 155p ; 30cm
Includes index
Unpriced (pbk) B82-12955

363.5′09413′3 — Scotland. Lothian Region. West Lothian *(District).* **Housing. Planning** — *Proposals*

West Lothian. *Department of Physical Planning.* Housing for special needs in West Lothian / West Lothian District Council, Department of Physical Planning : Department of Housing Services. — [Linlithgow] ([Old County Buildings, Linlithgow EH49 7EZ]) : [The Council], 1982. — iii,25leaves ; 30cm
Cover title
Unpriced (pbk) B82-38995

363.5′09413′95 — Scotland. Borders Region. Berwickshire *(District).* **Housing. Planning** — *Proposals* — *Serials*

Berwickshire. *District Council.* Housing plan / Berwickshire District Council. — 1977-. — Duns (Council Offices, 8 Newtown St., Duns, Berwickshire TD11 3DU) : The Council, [1977]-. — v. : maps ; 30cm
Annual
ISSN 0262-7337 = Housing plan - Berwickshire District Council : Unpriced B82-12454

363.5′09414′83 — Scotland. Dumfries and Galloway Region. Annandale and Eskdale *(District).* **Housing** — *Serials*

Annandale and Eskdale. *District Council.* Housing plan / Annandale and Eskdale District Council. — 1977-. — [Annan] ([District Council Chambers, High St., Annan]) : [The Council], 1977-. — v. : maps ; 30cm
Annual
ISSN 0262-916x = Housing plan - Annandale and Eskdale District Council : Unpriced B82-14274

363.5′0942496 — Urban regions. Housing market *related to* **mobility of population** — *Study regions: West Midlands (Metropolitan County). Birmingham*

Ford, Robert G.. Intra-urban migration and British housing submarkets / by Robert G. Ford and Geoffrey C. Smith. — [Birmingham] : [Department of Geography, University of Birmingham], 1979. — 82p : ill,1map ; 30cm. — (Occasional publication / Department of Geography ; no.9)
Cover title. — Bibliography: p79-82
£1.00 (corrected : pbk)
Primary classification 307′.2′0942496 B82-02399

363.5′09425′79 — Oxfordshire. Littlemore. Blackbird Leys region. Housing. Planning — *Proposals*

Consultation on possible development : South of Blackbird Leys & Littlemore / Oxford City Council. — [Oxford] ([109 St. Aldate′s, Oxford OX1 1DX]) : [City Architect and Planning Officer], [1981?]. — [21]p : maps ; 30cm
Unpriced (unbound) B82-05020

363.5′09425′81 — Hertfordshire. North Hertfordshire *(District).* **Housing** — *For environment planning*

Housing topic study / [North Hertfordshire District Council]. — [Letchworth] ([Council Offices, Gernon Rd., Letchworth, Herts. SG6 3JF]) : [The Council], 1978. — ii,45p : ill,2maps ; 30cm. — (North Hertfordshire district plan. topic studies)
£0.65 (pbk) B82-08889

363.5′09426′13 — Norfolk. King′s Lynn and West Norfolk *(District).* **Villages. Housing** — *Proposals*

Village development guidelines / Borough Council of King′s Lynn and West Norfolk. — [King′s Lynn] ([King′s Court, Chapel St., King′s Lynn PE30 1EX]) : [Borough Council of King′s Lynn and West Norfolk], [1981]. — [256]p(22 folded) : plans ; 30cm
Unpriced (spiral) B82-12953

363.5′09429 — Wales. Housing — *Statistics* — *Serials*

Welsh housing statistics / Welsh Office = Ystadegau tai Cymru / y Swyddfa Gymreig. — [No.1]-. — [Cardiff] ([Crown Building, Cathays Park, Cardiff CF1 3NQ]) : [Economic and Statistical Services Division, Welsh Office], [197-]-. — v. ; 30cm
Annual. — Description based on: 1981 issue
ISSN 0262-8333 = Welsh housing statistics : £2.00 B82-32146

363.5′0964′6 — Morocco. Marrakesh. Urban regions. Housing

Schwerdtfeger, Friedrich W.. Traditional housing in African cities : a comparative study of houses in Zaria, Ibadan, and Marrakech / Friedrich W. Schwerdtfeger. — Chichester : Wiley, c1982. — xl,480p : ill,maps,plans ; 26cm
Bibliography: p467-475. — Includes index
ISBN 0-471-27953-6 : £23.00 : CIP rev.
Primary classification 363.5′09669′2 B81-30978

363.5′09669′2 — Nigeria. Ibadan. Urban regions. Housing

Schwerdtfeger, Friedrich W.. Traditional housing in African cities : a comparative study of houses in Zaria, Ibadan, and Marrakech / Friedrich W. Schwerdtfeger. — Chichester : Wiley, c1982. — xl,480p : ill,maps,plans ; 26cm
Bibliography: p467-475. — Includes index
ISBN 0-471-27953-6 : £23.00 : CIP rev.
Also classified at 363.5′09669′5 ; 363.5′0964′6 B81-30978

363.5'09669'5 — Nigeria. Zaria. Urban regions. Housing

Schwerdtfeger, Friedrich W.. Traditional housing in African cities : a comparative study of houses in Zaria, Ibadan, and Marrakech / Friedrich W. Schwerdtfeger. — Chichester : Wiley, c1982. — xl,480p : ill,maps,plans ; 26cm
Bibliography: p467-475. — Includes index
ISBN 0-471-27953-6 : £23.00 : CIP rev.
Primary classification 363.5'09669'2
B81-30978

363.5'1 — Tunisia. Tunis. Residences. Location. Socioeconomic aspects

The **Socio-professional** characteristics of the residents of central Tunis / Habib Abichou ... [et al]. — [Glasgow] : Department of Geography, University of Glasgow, 1981. — iii,57p : ill,maps ; 30cm. — (Occasional papers / Geography Department Glasgow University ; no.7)
Includes summary in French. — Bibliography: p56
Unpriced (spiral) B82-27869

363.5'56'094 — Europe. Housing. Policies of governments

Donnison, David. Housing policy / David Donnison and Clare Ungerson. — Harmondsworth : Penguin, 1982. — 314p ; 20cm. — (Penguin education)
Bibliography: p295-296. — Includes index
ISBN 0-14-080454-4 (pbk) : £3.95 B82-33148

363.5'56'0941 — Great Britain. Housing. Policies of government. Implications of proposed reduction of expenditure by government. Great Britain. *Parliament. House of Commons. Environment Committee.* First report ... session 1979-80 — *Critical studies*

Great Britain. Department of the Environment : the government's reply to the first report from the Environment Committee, session 1979-80, HC714. — London : H.M.S.O., [1980]. — 7p ; 25cm. — (Cmnd. ; 8105)
ISBN 0-10-181050-4 (pbk) : £1.10 B82-09250

363.5'56'09411 — Scotland. Housing action areas — *Inquiry reports*

Housing action areas : first report. — Edinburgh : Scottish Development Department, 1980. — 93p : ill ; 30cm
ISBN 0-11-491661-6 (pbk) : £5.10 B82-13346

363.5'56'095125 — Hong Kong. Housing. Policies of government

Keung, John. Government intervention and housing policy in Hong Kong : a structural analysis / by John Keung. — Cardiff (King Edward VII Av, Cardiff, CF1 3NU, Wales) : Dept. of Town Planning, University of Wales, Institute of Science and Technology, 1981. — ileaf,35p ; 30cm. — (Papers in planning research ; 30)
Unpriced (pbk) B82-25640

363.5'56'095645 — Cyprus. Housing. Policies of government. Effects of social change, *1960-1980*

Zetter, Roger. Housing policy and social change in Cyprus 1960-1980 : the reactions to political instability / Roger Zetter. — [Oxford] : [Oxford Polytechnic Department of Town Planning], 1981. — 54p ; 30cm. — (Working paper / Oxford Polytechnic Department of Town Planning ; no.56)
£1.80 (pbk) B82-09570

363.5'8 — England. Homeless single persons. Housing — *Manuals — For welfare work*

Access to permanent housing for single people : a guide to obtaining accommodation from councils & housing associations / produced by CHAR, Cyrenians, NACRO. — [London] ([27 John Adam St., WC2]) : [CHAR], 1980. — 52p : ill ; 30cm
Cover title
Unpriced (spiral) B82-14647

363.5'8 — England. Local authority housing. Subsidies — *Manuals*

Housing subsidies and accounting manual / Department of the Environment, the Welsh Office. — 1981 ed. — London : H.M.S.O., 1982. — i,78p ; 30cm
Previous ed.: 1975. — Includes index
ISBN 0-11-751612-0 (pbk) : £4.50
Also classified at 352.1'71 B82-23761

363.5'8 — Great Britain. Homeless single persons. Accommodation. Referral agencies — *Case studies*

Drake, Madeline. A study of the records of a national referral agency / by Madeline Drake, Caroline Francis. — [London] : Department of Environment, 1982. — 39p : ill,1form ; 30cm. — (Single and homeless working paper ; 1)
One of four working papers subsidiary to a study entitled: Single and homeless / M.M. Drake, M. O'Brien and T.G. Biebuyck. London : H.M.S.O, 1982
£3.25 (pbk) B82-32683

363.5'8 — Great Britain. Housing. Self-help

Goodchild, Barry. The application of self help to housing : a critique of self build and urban homesteading / Barry Goodchild. — [Sheffield] : Sheffield City Polytechnic, Department of Urban and Regional Studies, 1981. — 11leaves ; 30cm. — (Working papers in urban and regional studies ; no.1)
ISBN 0-903761-40-8 (pbk) : Unpriced
B82-11744

363.5'8 — Great Britain. Local authority housing

The **Future** of council housing / edited by John English. — London : Croom Helm, c1982. — 202p : ill ; 22cm
Includes index
ISBN 0-7099-0900-4 : £12.95 : CIP rev.
B81-34658

363.5'8 — Great Britain. Local authority housing. Policies of government. Decision making, *1945-1975*

Dunleavy, Patrick. The politics of mass housing in Britain, 1945-1975 : a study of corporate power and professional influence in the welfare state / Patrick Dunleavy. — Oxford : Clarendon, 1981. — xvi,447p : ill,maps ; 22cm
Bibliography: p409-436. — Includes index
ISBN 0-19-827426-2 : Unpriced B82-00998

363.5'8 — Great Britain. Public housing — *Labour Party (Great Britain) viewpoints*

A **Future** for public housing : a Labour Party discussion document. — [London] : The Party, [1981]. — 72p ; 21cm. — (Socialism in the 80s)
Cover title
ISBN 0-86117-070-9 (pbk) : £1.00 B82-05513

363.5'8 — Housing. Policies

McGuire, Chester C.. International housing policies : a comparative analysis / Chester C. McGuire. — Lexington, Mass. : Lexington Books ; [Aldershot] : Gower [distrbutor], c1981. — xv,251p : ill ; 24cm
Includes bibliographies and index
ISBN 0-669-04385-0 : £16.00 B82-04744

363.5'8 — London. East End. Night shelters for homeless persons — *Case studies*

Drake, Madeline. A study of an East End night shelter / by Madeline Drake, Maureen O'Brien. — [London] : Department of Environment, 1982. — 36p ; 30cm. — (Single and homeless working paper ; 2)
One of four working papers subsidiary to a study entitled: Single and homeless / M.M. Drake, M. O'Brien and T.G. Biebuyck. London : H.M.S.O, 1982
£2.40 (pbk) B82-32682

363.5'8 — Scotland. Local authority housing. Allocation & transfer

Great Britain. *Scottish Housing Advisory Committee*. Allocation and transfer of council houses : report by a subcommittee of the Scottish Housing Advisory Committee / Scottish Development Department. — Edinburgh : H.M.S.O., 1980. — 92p ; 21cm
ISBN 0-11-491670-5 (pbk) : £3.75 B82-16412

363.5'8 — Scotland. Local authority housing. Financial assistance by government — *Proposals*

Great Britain. *Scottish Office*. The Housing Support Grant (Scotland) Variation (No.2) Order 1981 : report by the Secretary of State for Scotland under section 1(6), in connection with a variation order made under section 3, of the Housing (Financial Provisions) (Scotland) Act 1978. — Edinburgh : H.M.S.O., [1981]. — 10p ; 25cm. — ([HC] ; 92)
ISBN 0-10-209281-8 (uubound) : £1.75
B82-16064

Great Britain. *Scottish Office*. The Housing Support Grant (Scotland) Variation Order 1981 : report by the Secretary of State for Scotland under section 1(6), in connection with a variation order made under section 3, of the Housing (Financial Provisions) (Scotland) Act 1978. — Edinburgh : H.M.S.O., [1981]. — 10p ; 25cm. — ([HC] ; 91)
ISBN 0-10-209181-1 (unbound) : £1.75
B82-16062

363.5'8'0941 — Great Britain. Housing. Provision. Participation of public

Bristow, David. Participation in housing. — [Oxford] : [Oxford Polytechnic, Department of Town Planning]. — (Working paper / Oxford Polytechnic Department of Town Planning ; no.58)
No.2: The legal and administrative framework / papers by David Bristow, Bob Greenstreet, Harold Campbell ; edited by Nabeel Hamdi and Bob Greenstreet. — 1981. — iv,103p : ill ; 30cm
Includes bibliographies
£3.20 (pbk) B82-25109

Hamdi, Nabeel. Participation in housing. — [Oxford] : [Oxford Polytechnic, Department of Town Planning]. — (Working paper / Oxford Polytechnic Department of Town Planning ; no.59)
No.3: Two case studies / papers by Nebeel Hamdi and Rod Hackney ; edited by Nebeel Hamdi and Bob Greenstreet. — 1982. — 71p : ill,plans ; 30cm
£2.50 (pbk) B82-25110

Participation in housing. — [Oxford] : [Oxford Polytechnic Department of Town Planning]. — (Working Paper / Oxford Polytechnic Department of Town Planning ; no.57)
No.1: Theory and implementation / papers by John Habraken ... [et al.] ; edited by Nabeel Hamdi and Bob Greenstreet. — 1981. — x,58p ; 30cm
£3.20 (pbk) B82-09568

363.5'8'0941 — Great Britain. Housing. Provision. Special projects. Cooperation between housing associations & voluntary organisations

Special projects : a guide for voluntary organisations working with housing associations. — Rev. — London (30 Southampton St., WC2E 7HE) : National Federation of Housing Associations, 1981. — 23p : ill ; 30cm. — (NFHA special project guide ; no.1)
Cover title. — Bibliography: p23
£0.50 (pbk) B82-27682

Wurtzburg, Rosemary. Special projects and joint funding arrangements / by Rosemary Wurtzburg ; illustrations by Alan Bailey. — London (30 Southampton St., WC2R 7HE) : National Federation of Housing Associations, 1978. — 63p : ill,forms ; 30cm. — (Special project guide ; no.2)
£1.00 (pbk) B82-27683

363.5'9 — Cardiff. Homeless single persons. Housing

Turning the key : a model housing policy for Cardiff's single people. — Cardiff (90 St. Mary St., Cardiff) : Cardiff Cyrenians, 1980. — 18p : ill ; 30cm
Cover title
£1.50 (pbk) B82-17683

363.5'9 — Cornwall. Tin mining industries & copper mining industries. Miners. Housing, *1750-1900*

Chesher, Veronica. Industrial housing in the tin & copper mining areas of Cornwall, later 18th & 19th centuries / [Veronica Chesher]. — [Truro] : Trevithick Society, c1981. — 26p : ill,plans ; 30cm
Cover title. — Originally published: as part of the Society's Newsletter No.23. 1978
ISBN 0-904040-18-6 (pbk) : Unpriced
B82-00626

363.5′9 — Gloucestershire. Gloucester. Homeless single young coloured persons. Housing

Cowen, Harry. The hidden homeless : a report of a survey on homelessness and housing amongst single young Blacks in Gloucester / Harry Cowen with Richard Lording. — Gloucester (15 Brunswick Rd, Gloucester GL1 1HG) : Gloucester Community Relations Council, 1982. — 54p : ill ; 21cm
Unpriced (pbk) B82-40283

363.5′9 — Great Britain. Mentally handicapped persons. Housing — *Case studies*

Heginbothan, Christopher. Housing projects for mentally handicapped people / Christopher Heginbotham. — London : Centre on Environment for the Handicapped, 1981. — 30p : ill,plans ; 30cm
Bibliography: p30
ISBN 0-903976-06-4 (spiral) : £2.00 B82-07378

363.5′9 — Great Britain. Single persons. Housing

Single person shared housing : notes on housing management & design / National Federation of Housing Associations. — London (30-32 Southampton St., WC2E 7HE) : The Federation, 1981. — 21,[12]p : ill,plans ; 30cm. — (NFHA special project guide ; no.7)
Cover title. — Bibliography: p33
£1.50 (pbk) B82-22028

363.5′9 — Great Britain. Suburbs. Old persons. Housing — *Study regions: West Midlands (Metropolitan County). Birmingham. Hall Green*

Rose, Edgar A.. Growing old in a suburb. — Aldershot : Gower, Dec.1982. — [104]p
ISBN 0-566-00586-7 : £12.50 : CIP entry B82-30054

363.5′9 — London. Hostels for homeless single persons

Hostels for the single homeless in London / GLC/LBA Joint Working Party on Provision in London for People Without a Settled Way of Living. — London : London Boroughs Association, 1981. — 37p : ill ; 30cm
ISBN 0-7168-1223-1 (pbk) : £2.00 B82-04425

363.5′9 — London. Southwark *(London Borough)*. **Young persons. Housing. Needs** — *Inquiry reports*

The **housing** needs of Southwark′s young people : a report from the Consortium Young Single Housing Group. — London : South East London Consortium, 1980. — 55p ; 30cm
£2.00 (pbk) B82-22190

363.5′9 — Scotland. Grampian Region. Aberdeen *(District)*. **Single persons. Housing**

Buchanan, Glen. Aberdeen district report : an assessment of the accommodation experiences, needs and preferences of single people in Aberdeen district / by Glen Buchanan and Barbara Balmer. — Edinburgh : Scottish Council for Single Homeless, 1981. — ix,58p : ill ; 29cm
At head of title: Scottish Council for Single Homeless. — Single Person Accommodation Needs Project
ISBN 0-907050-04-2 (pbk) : £1.50 (£1.00 to members of the Scottish Council for Single Homeless) B82-23537

363.5′9 — Scotland. Single persons. Accommodation. Planning

Currie, Hector. Single initiatives II : a discussion paper on planning approval and definition problems in single person housing / by Hector Currie ; illustrated by Sebastian Tombs. — Edinburgh : Scottish Council for Single Homeless, 1981. — iv,43p : ill ; 29cm
Sequel to Single initiatives I, a study of single person and special needs housing by housing associations, published 1980
ISBN 0-907050-03-4 (pbk) : £1.60 (£1.30 to members of the Scottish Council for Single Homeless) B82-23532

363.5′9 — Scotland. Single young persons. Housing

Housing and young single people : information pack : for teachers, youth workers and careers staff. — [Edinburgh?] : British Youth Council (Scotland), 1981. — 1portfolio : ill ; 32cm
Includes bibliographies
£1.20 B82-27883

363.5′9 — Scotland. Strathclyde Region. Cunninghame *(District)*. **Single persons. Housing**

Buchanan, Glen. Cunninghame district report : an assessment of the accommodation experiences, needs and preferences of single people in Cunninghame district / by Glen Buchanan and Barbara Balmer. — Edinburgh : Scottish Council for Single Homeless, 1981. — x,70p : ill ; 29cm
At head of title: Scottish Council for Single Homeless. — Single Person Accommodation Needs Project
ISBN 0-907050-05-0 (pbk) : £1.50 (£1.00 to members of the Scottish Council for Single Homeless) B82-23534

363.5′9 — Scotland. Strathclyde Region. East Kilbride *(District)*. **Single persons. Housing**

Buchanan, Glen. East Kilbride district report : an assessment of the accommodation experiences, needs and preferences of single people in East Kilbride district / by Glen Buchanan and Barbara Balmer. — Edinburgh : Scottish Council for Single Homeless, 1981. — ix,65p : ill ; 29cm
At head of title: Scottish Council for Single Homeless. — Single Person Accommodation Needs Project
ISBN 0-907050-06-9 (pbk) : £1.50 (£1.00 to members of the Scottish Council for Single Homeless) B82-23533

363.5′9 — Scotland. Strathclyde Region. Kyle and Carrick *(District)*. **Single persons. Housing**

Buchanan, Glen. Kyle and Carrick district report : an assessment of the accommodation experiences, needs and preferences of single people in Kyle and Carrick district / by Glen Buchanan and Barbara Balmer. — Edinburgh : Scottish Council for Single Homeless, 1981. — ix,59p : ill ; 29cm
At head of title: Scottish Council for Single Homeless. — Single Person Accommodation Needs Project
ISBN 0-907050-07-7 (pbk) : £1.50 (£1.00 to members of the Scottish Council for Single Homeless) B82-23536

363.5′9 — Scotland. Strathclyde Region. Motherwell *(District)*. **Single persons. Housing**

Buchanan, Glen. Motherwell district report : an assessment of the accommodation experiences, needs and preferences of single people in Motherwell district / by Glen Buchanan and Barbara Balmer. — Edinburgh : Scottish Council for Single Homeless, 1981. — xi,68p : ill ; 29cm
At head of title: Scottish Council for Single Homeless. — Single Person Accommodation Needs Project
ISBN 0-907050-08-5 (pbk) : £1.50 (£1.00 to members of the Scottish Council for Single Homeless) B82-23535

363.5′9 — Western Europe & North America. Old persons. Housing

Heumann, Leonard. Housing for the elderly. — London : Croom Helm, Sept.1982. — [224]p
ISBN 0-7099-1234-x : £12.95 : CIP entry B82-20643

363.5′9 — Women. Housing. Social change

Building for women / edited by Suzanne Keller. — Lexington : Lexington Books, c1981 ; [Aldershot] : Gower [distributor], 1982. — xii,221p : ill,plans ; 24cm
Includes index
ISBN 0-669-04368-0 : £18.50 B82-18255

363.6 — PUBLIC UTILITY SERVICES

363.6′0942 — England. Urban regions. Inner areas. Public utilities

Bishop, D.. Underground services in the inner city / D. Bishop, G. Blundell and B. Curtis [of the] Centre for Advanced Land Use Studies, College of Estate Management, Whiteknights, Reading, RG6 2AW. — London (2 Marsham St, SW1) : Inner Cities Directorate, Department of the Environment, c1980. — 92p : plans ; 30cm. — (Inner cities research programme ; 3)
£3.00 (pbk) B82-32677

363.6′09425′81 — Hertfordshire. North Hertfordshire *(District)*. **Public utilities** — *For environment planning*

Utility services topic study / [North Hertfordshire District Council]. — [Letchworth] ([Council Offices, Gernon Rd., Letchworth, Herts. SG6 3JF]) : [The Council], 1978. — ii leaves,20p : ill,col.maps ; 30cm. — (North Hertfordshire district plan. topic studies)
£0.40 (pbk) B82-08888

363.6′1′0979494 — California. Los Angeles. Water supply systems. Development, *1900-1981*

Kahrl, William L.. Water and power : the conflict over Los Angeles′ water supply in the Owens Valley / William L. Kahrl. — Berkeley ; London : University of California Press, c1982. — xii,583p,[8]p of plates : ill,maps,ports ; 24cm
Bibliography: p545-574. — Includes index
ISBN 0-520-04431-2 : Unpriced B82-36873

363.6′9 — Buildings of historical importance. Conservation

Feilden, Bernard M.. Conservation of historic buildings / Bernard M. Feilden. — London : Butterworth Scientific, 1982. — x,472p : ill,charts,plans ; 31cm. — (Technical studies in the arts, archaeology and architecture)
Bibliography: p445-462. — Includes index
ISBN 0-408-10782-0 : Unpriced : CIP rev. B82-02447

Fitch, James Marston. Historic preservation : curatorial management of the built world / James Marston Fitch. — New York ; London : McGraw-Hill, c1982. — xii,433p : ill ; 25cm
Includes index
ISBN 0-07-021121-3 : £26.50 B82-25215

363.6′9 — Devon. Exeter. Listed buildings

Listed buildings in Exeter. — Exeter : Exeter City Council, Planning Department, [197-?]. — [7]p : ill ; 30cm
ISBN 0-86114-183-0 (unbound) : Unpriced B82-40958

363.6′9 — Great Britain. Listed buildings — *Lists*

Clark, Iain. The best buildings in Britain : a catalogue of grade 1 buildings and grade A churches in England, category A buildings in Scotland and Western Isles, grade 1 buildings and grade A churches in Wales / compiled by Iain Clark, Clive Aslet and Louise Nicholson ; edited by Roger Coppen ... [et al.]. — London (3 Park Sq West, NW1) : Save Britain′s Heritage, c1980. — viii,87p ; 30cm
Unpriced (pbk) B82-36648

363.6′9 — Southern England. Royal dockyards. Buildings of historical importance. Conservation — *Proposals*

Ancient Monuments Board for England. The Royal Dockyards : a unique survival / report prepared by a panel of the Ancient Monuments Board for England, May 1981. — London ([2 Marsham St, SW1P 3EB]) : Ancient Monuments Directorate, [1981]. — 18p,3folded leaves of plates : 3col.plans ; 22x30cm
Unpriced (spiral) B82-35112

363.6′9′060411 — Scotland. Buildings of historical importance. Organisations: National Trust for Scotland — *Serials*

National Trust for Scotland. News / the National Trust for Scotland. — Mar. 1981-. — Edinburgh (5 Charlotte Sq., Edinburgh EH2 4DU) : The Trust, 1981-. — v. : ill,ports ; 30cm
Three issues yearly. — Continues: National Trust for Scotland. News letter. — Description based on: June 1982
ISSN 0263-8452 = News - National Trust for Scotland : Unpriced
Primary classification 719′.06′0411 B82-32368

363.6′9′094133 — Scotland. Lothian Region. West Lothian *(District)*. **Buildings of historical importance. Conservation**

Thinking about conservation / [West Lothian District Council, Department of Physical Planning]. — [Linlithgow] ([Old County Buildings, High St., Linlithgow, W. Lothian EH9 7EX]) : The Department
1: A short guide to the protection of old buildings. — [1982?]. — [9]p ; 21cm
Unpriced (unbound) B82-39864

363.6′9′094133 — Scotland. Lothian Region. West Lothian *(District)*. Buildings of historical importance. Conservation *continuation*

Thinking about conservation / [West Lothian District Council, Department of Physical Planning]. — [Linlithgow] ([Old County Buildings, High St., Linlithgow, W. Lothian EH9 7EX]) : The Department
2: Conservation grants. — [1982?]. — [5]p ; 21cm
Unpriced (unbound) B82-39865

363.6′9′0942 — England. Ruins. Preservation

Thompson, M. W. (Michael Welman). Ruins : their preservation and display / M.W. Thompson. — London : British Museum Publications, c1981. — 104p : ill,plans ; 24cm. — (A Colonnade book)
Includes index
ISBN 0-7141-8034-3 : £6.95 B82-30907

363.6′9′0942 — Great Britain. Buildings of historical importance. Administration. Policies of government — *Proposals*

Great Britain. *Department of the Environment*. The way forward : organisation of ancient monuments and historic buildings in England / Department of the Environment. — London : H.M.S.O., 1982. — 41p ; 21cm
ISBN 0-11-751624-4 (pbk) : £3.55 B82-35111

363.6′9′094212 — London *(City)*. Buildings of historical importance. Conservation

Save the city : a conservation study of the City of London / prepared by David Lloyd (general editor), Jennifer Freeman, Jane Fawcett. — [London] ([55, Great Ormond St., WC1N 3JA]) : Society for the Protection of Ancient Buildings, 1976 (1979 [printing]). — xiv,196p : ill,maps ; 30cm
Includes index
£6.00 (pbk) B82-10919

363.6′9′094235 — Devon. Buildings of historical importance. Conservation

Devon′s heritage : buildings and landscape : a collection of essays on the conservation of Devon′s environment / produced and edited by Peter Beacham ... [et al.]. — Exeter : County Planning Department, Devon County Council, 1982. — 87p : ill ; 25cm
Text on inside cover. — Bibliography: p87
ISBN 0-86114-356-6 (pbk) : £2.00 B82-24878

363.6′9′0942865 — Durham *(County)*. Durham. Buildings of historical importance. Conservation — *Practical information*

Caring for historic buildings : a general guide based on experience in the City of Durham. — [Durham] ([City Planning Office, Byland Lodge, Hawthorn Terrace, Durham DH1 4TD]) : [City of Durham], c1977. — [24]p : ill,1map ; 29cm
Bibliography: p23
£0.50 (pbk) B82-35031

363.7 — ENVIRONMENTAL PROBLEMS AND SERVICES

363.7 — Buildings. Hygiene — *Encyclopaedias*

Lucas, Colin M.. Hygiene in buildings : a guide to health, hygiene and industrial cleaning / Colin M. Lucas. — East Grinstead : Rentokil, 1982. — 303p,[41]p of plates : ill(some col.) ; 24cm. — (The Rentokil library)
ISBN 0-906564-04-2 : £15.00 B82-21938

363.7 — Urban regions. Environment. Hazards. Perception by residents *compared with* **perception of environmental hazards by town planners** — *Study regions: Ontario. Windsor*

Smith, Geoffrey C.. Urban environmental hazard cognition and concern / by Geoffrey C. Smith. — [Birmingham] : [Department of Geography, University of Birmingham], 1976. — 55p : maps ; 30cm. — (Occasional publication / Department of Geography, University of Birmingham ; no.3)
Bibliography: p53-55
ISBN 0-7044-0354-4 (pbk) : £0.50 B82-04263

363.7′056′0722 — England. Local authorities. Environmental services. Provision — *Case studies*

Service provision and pricing in local government : studies in local environmental services / [commissioned by the Department of the Environment from Coopers & Lybrand Associates Limited]. — London : H.M.S.O., 1981. — xi,272p,[24]p : ill ; 30cm
Bibliography: p[24]
ISBN 0-11-751587-6 (pbk) : Unpriced
Also classified at 338.4′33637′0722 B82-11174

363.7′294′09411 — Scotland. Physically handicapped persons′ public conveniences — *Lists*

Richardson, Ruth. A guide to public toilets in Scotland accessible to people in wheelchairs / [compiled by Ruth Richardson]. — Rev. ed. — Edinburgh : Scottish Council on Disability, 1981. — i,59p : ill ; 21cm
Cover title. — Previous ed.: 1979
ISBN 0-903589-54-0 (pbk) : £0.25 B82-14331

363.7′3 — Environment. Pollution

Carson, Rachel. Silent spring / Rachel Carson ; introduction by Lord Shackleton ; preface by Julian Huxley. — Harmondsworth : Penguin in association with Hamilton, 1965 (1982 [printing]). — 317p ; 18cm. — (A Pelican book)
Originally published: Boston, Mass. : Houghton Mifflin, 1962 ; London : Hamilton, 1963. — Includes index
ISBN 0-14-022404-1 (pbk) : £2.50 B82-40775

363.7′303 — Atmosphere. Pollution. Control measures - *English-Russian dictionaries*

Milovanov, E. L.. English-Russian dictionary of environmental control. — Oxford : Pergamon, Apr.1981. — [368]p
Originally published: Moscow : Russkiĭ Îazyk, 1980
ISBN 0-08-023576-x : £20.00 : CIP entry B81-09981

363.7′3′0724 — Environment. Pollution. Experiments — *For schools*

Palmer, Ernest J.. Pollution / Ernest J. Palmer. — St. Albans : Published for the Schools Council by Hart-Davis Educational, 1979. — 32p : ill ; 21cm
Cover title
ISBN 0-247-12910-0 (pbk) : Unpriced B82-24630

363.7′3′09417 — Ireland *(Republic)*. Environment. Pollution — *Irish texts*

Ó Ceallacháin, C. N.. Truailliú ar Éirinn? : cuntas ar thruailliú na timpeallachta / le C.N. Ó Ceallachain. — Baile Atha Cliath : Oifig an tSolathair, 1980. — 141p : ill,3maps ; 21cm
Bibliography: p138-141
Unpriced (pbk) B82-24033

363.7′31 — Great Britain. Coal. Use by industries. Public health aspects

Study of coal / evidence by the HSE to the Commission on Energy and the Environment concerning public health and amenity in the external environment. — London : H.M.S.O., 1980. — iii,43p : 2ill ; 30cm. — (HSE report)
At head of title: Health & Safety Commission
ISBN 0-11-883276-x (pbk) : £3.00 : CIP rev. B80-19783

363.7′32 — Space. Pollution. Hazards

Detrimental activities in space. — Oxford : Pergamon, June 1982. — [164]p. — (Advances in space research ; v.2, no.3)
ISBN 0-08-029694-7 (pbk) : £10.00 : CIP entry B82-17906

363.7′36 — Environment. Pollution. Control. Economic aspects

Sandbach, Francis. Principles of pollution control / Francis Sandbach. — London : Longman, 1982. — xvi,174p : ill,1map ; 24cm. — (Themes in resource management)
Bibliography: p160-171. — Includes index
ISBN 0-582-30042-8 (pbk) : £5.95 : CIP rev. B82-09447

363.7′38 — Environment. Pollution by heavy metals — *Conference proceedings*

Heavy metals in northern England : environmental and biological aspects / edited by P.J. Say and B.A. Whitton. — Durham : Department of Botany, University of Durham, 1981. — x,198p,[1]leaf of plates : ill,maps ; 30cm
Conference papers. — Includes bibliographies and index
ISBN 0-903569-01-9 (pbk) : £3.00 B82-28693

363.7′38 — Great Britain. Environment. Gamma radiation. Dosage. Measurement

Spiers, F. W.. A guide to the measurement of environmental gamma-ray dose rate / by F.W. Spiers, J.A.B. Gibson, I.M.G. Thompson. — Teddington : published on behalf of the British Committee on Radiation Units and Measurements by the National Physical Laboratory, c1981. — x,107p : ill ; 30cm
Bibliography: p99-107
ISBN 0-9504496-7-9 (pbk) : Unpriced B82-05722

363.7′382′05 — Environment. Pollution by petroleum — *Serials*

Oil & petrochemical pollution. — Vol.1, no.1-. — London : Graham & Trotman, 1982-. — v. : ill,maps ; 25cm
Quarterly
ISSN 0143-7127 = Oil & petrochemical pollution : £35.00 per year B82-40039

363.7′382′094 — European Community countries. Environment. Pollution by petroleum. Control

Measures to combat oil pollution : the improvement of oil spill response within the European Economic Community : a report prepared by the International Tanker Owners Pollution Federation Limited for the Environment and Consumer Protection Service of the Commission of the European Communities. — London : Graham & Trotman for the Commission, 1980. — 294p : maps ; 30cm
Bibliography: p293-294
ISBN 0-86010-250-5 (pbk) : £12.50 B82-35937

363.7′384 — Carbon dioxide. Environmental aspects

Carbon dioxide review. — Oxford : Oxford University Press, Apr.1982. — [440]p
ISBN 0-19-855368-4 (pbk) : £15.00 : CIP entry B82-13492

363.7′384 — Chemicals. Environmental impact analysis

Environmental risk analysis for chemicals / edited by Richard A. Conway. — New York ; London : Van Nostrand Reinhold, c1982. — xxiv,558p : ill ; 24cm. — (Van Nostrand Reinhold environmental engineering series)
Includes index
ISBN 0-442-21650-5 : £31.90 B82-08232

363.7′384 — Environment. Pollution by cadmium

Cadmium in the environment / edited by Jerome O. Nriagu. — New York ; Chichester : Wiley. — (Environmental science and technology)
Pt.2: Health effects. — c1981. — xii,908p : ill ; 24cm
Includes bibliographies index
ISBN 0-471-05884-x : £85.00 B82-13389

363.7′384 — Environment. Pollution by lead

Kollerstrom, Nick. Lead on the brain. — London : Wildwood House, June 1982. — [128]p. — (Wildwood specials)
ISBN 0-7045-0476-6 (pbk) : £1.25 : CIP entry B82-14943

363.7′384 — Great Britain. Environment. Pollutants: Lead. Reduction. Economic aspects

Fellowship of Engineering. *Working Party on Lead*. ″Reduction of lead in the environment — energy, technology, and cost″ : Fellowship of Engineering report of a Working Party on Lead. — London (2 Little Smith St., SW1P 3DL) : The Fellowship, 1981. — 33p ; 30cm
Unpriced (pbk) B82-08239

363.7′384 — Great Britain. Man. Health. Effects of cadmium environmental pollutants — *Inquiry reports*

Great Britain. *Central Directorate on Environmental Pollution.* Cadmium in the environment and its significance to man : an inter-departmental report / Department of the Environment, Central Directorate on Environmental Pollution [et al.]. — London : H.M.S.O., 1980. — xi,64p : 1ill ; 25cm. — (Pollution paper ; no.17(1980))
Bibliography: p58-64
ISBN 0-11-751475-6 (pbk) : £3.50 B82-14643

363.7′384 — Man. Health. Hazards: Chemicals

Hazard assessment of chemicals : current developments. — New York ; London : Academic Press
Vol.1 / edited by Jitendra Saxena, Farley Fisher. — 1981. — xii,461p : ill ; 24cm
Includes bibliographies and index
ISBN 0-12-312401-8 : £32.80 B82-30141

363.7′387 — Coal. Combustion. Environmental aspects

Environmental implications for expanded coal utilization. — Oxford : Pergamon, July 1982. — [208]p
ISBN 0-08-028734-4 : £25.00 : CIP entry B82-12403

363.7′392 — Atmosphere. Pollen. Measurement

Frankland, A. W.. Making the pollen count count. — Oxford (52 New Inn Hall St., Oxford OX1 2BS) : Medicine Publishing Foundation, Mar.1982. — [12]p
ISBN 0-906817-24-2 (pbk) : £2.00 : CIP entry B82-14194

363.7′392 — Atmosphere. Pollutants: Particulate carbon — *Conference proceedings*

Particulate carbon : atmospheric life cycle / [proceedings of an international symposium on partiulate carbon - atmospheric life cycle, held October 13-14, 1980, at the General Motors Research Laboratories, Warren, Michigan] ; edited by George T. Wolff and Richard L. Klimisch. — New York ; London : Plenum, 1982. — x,411p : ill ; 26cm
Includes index
ISBN 0-306-40918-6 : Unpriced B82-22015

363.7′392 — Atmosphere. Pollutants: Sulphur compounds — *Conference proceedings*

Sulphur emissions and the environment : international symposium : London 8, 9, 10 May 1979. — London : Society of Chemical Industry Water and Environment Group, 1979. — 2v.(iii,520p) : ill ; 31cm
Cover title
Unpriced (spiral) B82-31243

363.7′392 — Atmosphere. Pollutants: Sulphur dioxide. Diffusion. Mathematical models

Nochumson, David H.. Models for the long distance transport of atmospheric sulfur oxides / David H. Nochumson. — New York ; London : Garland, 1979. — 453 in various pagings : ill,maps ; 24cm. — (Outstanding dissertations on energy)
ISBN 0-8240-3992-0 : Unpriced B82-10722

363.7′392 — Atmosphere. Pollutants: Sulphur dioxide. Effects

Effects of SO2 and its derivatives on health and ecology / report of a working group sponsored by the International Electric Research Exchange ; represented by the Electric Power Research Institute ... [et al.]. — [Leatherhead] ([c/o Central Electricity Generating Board, Central Electrical Research Laboratories, Leatherhead, Surrey, KT22 7SE]) : [International Electric Research Exchange], 1981. — 2v.(various pagings) : ill ; 30cm + 1 preface and executive summary(2,5p; 30cm) + 1 technical summary (2,19p; 30cm)
Unpriced (spiral) B82-31393

363.7′392 — Atmosphere. Pollution by coat-fired power stations. Control. Mathematical models

Mendelsohn, Robert O.. Towards efficient regulation of air pollution from coal-fired power plants / Robert O. Mendelsohn. — New York ; London : Garland, 1979. — ix,194p : ill ; 24cm
Includes bibliographies
ISBN 0-8240-4055-4 : Unpriced B82-14148

363.7′392 — Atmosphere. Pollution by nitrogen oxides — *Conference proceedings*

Air pollution by nitrogen oxides. — Oxford : Elsevier, Sept.1982. — [300]p. — (Studies in environmental science ; 21)
Conference papers
ISBN 0-444-42127-0 : CIP entry
ISBN 0-444-41696-x (set) B82-29006

363.7′392 — Atmosphere. Pollution — *Conference proceedings*

Atmospheric pollution 1982 : proceedings of the 15th International Colloquium, UNESCO Building, Paris, France, May 4-7, 1982 organised by the Institut national de recherche chimique appliquée, Vert-le-Petit, France, in association with the Commission on Atmopheric Environment of the International Union of Pure and Applied Chemistry (IUPAC) ... [et al.] / edited by Michel M. Benarie. — Amsterdam ; Oxford : Elsevier Scientific, 1982. — xi,404p : ill,maps ; 25cm. — (Studies in environmental science ; v.20)
Papers published as special issue of Science of the total environment, vol.23, 1982. — Includes index
ISBN 0-444-42083-5 : £40.43 : CIP rev. B82-14048

363.7′392′0724 — Atmosphere. Pollution. Simulations: Models — *Conference proceedings*

International Technical Meeting on Air Pollution Modeling and its Application *(11th : 1980 : Amsterdam).* Air pollution modeling and its application I / [proceedings of the Eleventh International Technical Meeting on Air Pollution Modeling and its Application, held November 24-27, 1980, in Amsterdam, The Netherlands] ; edited by C. de Wispelaere. — New York ; London : Published in cooperation with NATO Committee on the Challenges of Modern Society [by] Plenum, c1981. — xiii,747p : ill,maps ; 26cm. — (NATO challenges of modern society ; v.1)
Includes bibliographies and index
ISBN 0-306-40820-1 : Unpriced B82-05445

363.7′392′0941 — Great Britain. Atmosphere. Pollution — *Serials*

Health and safety. Industrial air pollution. — 1980. — London : H.M.S.O., Jan.1982. — 1v.
ISBN 0-11-883623-4 (pbk) : CIP entry B82-02441

363.7′39263 — Atmosphere. Pollution. Biological monitoring. Use of plants

Manning, William J.. Biomonitoring air pollutants with plants / William J. Manning and William A. Feder. — London : Applied Science, c1980. — x,142p : ill ; 23cm. — (Pollution monitoring series)
Bibliography: p134-135. — Includes index
ISBN 0-85334-916-9 : £11.00 : CIP rev. B80-18319

363.7′394 — Drinking water. Odours. Effects of aquatic herbicides. Assessment

Arthey, V. D.. A proposed procedure for the determination of the threshold odour concentrations of herbicides in water : a paper presented at the conference 'Aquatic Weeds and Their Control' / organised by the Association of Applied Biologists Weed Group in conjunction with the Association of Drainage Authorities and the National Water Council, Oxford, 8th April, 1981 ; by V.D. Arthey and D.H. Lyon. — Chipping Camden (Chipping Camden, Gloucestershire GL55 6LD) : Campden Food Preservation Research Association, 1981. — 5p ; 30cm. — (Reprint ; no.202)
Conference paper
Unpriced (pbk) B82-14797

363.7′394 — Water. Pollution - *Conference proceedings*

Water pollution research and development. — Oxford : Pergamon, June 1981. — [1073]p
Conference papers
ISBN 0-08-026025-x : £85.00 : CIP entry B81-16860

363.7′3946 — United States. Natural resources: Water. Pollution by industrial waste materials. Control. Role of charges for disposal

Hudson, James F.. Pollution-pricing : industrial response to wastewater charges / James F. Hudson, Elizabeth E. Lake, Donald S. Grossman. — Lexington, Mass. : Lexington Books ; Aldershot : Gower [distributor], 1982, c1981. — xix,212p : ill,1map,plans ; 24cm
Bibliography: p199-203. — Includes index
ISBN 0-669-04033-9 : £16.50 B82-08992

363.7′39463 — Ireland *(Republic).* **Rivers. Pollution. Biological monitoring,** *1971-1979*

Clabby, K. J.. The national survey of Irish rivers : a review of biological monitoring 1971-1979 / K.J. Clabby. — [Dublin] ([St. Martin's House, Waterloo Rd., Dublin 4]) : Water Resources Division, An Foras Forbartha, 1981. — xiv,322p : ill,maps ; 30cm. — (WR ; R12)
Bibliography: p289-291. — Includes index
£10.00 (spiral) B82-15382

363.7′43 — Industries. Personnel. Hearing disorders. Prevention

Hearing protection in industry. — London : Croom Helm, Apr.1981. — [400]p
ISBN 0-7099-0501-7 : £19.95 : CIP entry B81-07445

363.7′46 — Great Britain. Rural regions. Motor vehicles. Noise. Control

Curbing the noise invasion. — London (1 Wandsworth Rd, SW8 2LJ) : Ramblers' Association, [1979]. — 11p : ill ; 23cm. (Brief for the countryside ; no.6)
£0.30 (unbound) B82-38407

363.7′46′0942863 — Great Britain. Urban regions. Noise. Reduction. Participation of public — *Study regions: Durham (County). Darlington*

Noise Advisory Council. The Darlington quiet town experiment : September 1976-September 1978 : report by a working group of the Council / Noise Advisory Council. — London : H.M.S.O., 1981. — vii,71p : ill,maps(some col.),facsims,1port ; 30cm + 5fold. sheets in pocket(ill)
ISBN 0-11-751526-4 (pbk) : £8.50 B82-07268

363.7′5 — England. Local authority cemeteries — *Statistics — Serials*

Cemeteries statistics ... actuals / CIPFA Statistical Information Service. — 1980-81. — London : Chartered Institute of Public Finance and Accountancy, 1981. — 1v. ; 30cm
Annual. — Only one issue published under this title
ISSN 0260-9959 = Cemeteries statistics ... actuals : £6.00 B82-22678

363.8 — FOOD SUPPLY

363.8 — Africa. Famines — *Conference proceedings*

Famine in Africa : proceedings of the conference of a Working Group on Famine in Africa, held at Kinshasa, Zaire, in January 1980 / editor James P. Carter. — Oxford : Pergamon, 1982. — xvi,35p ; 23cm
ISBN 0-08-027998-8 (pbk) : £5.00 : CIP rev. B82-02624

363.8 — Africa. Famines — *Conference proceedings — French texts*

La Famine en Afrique : rapports de Conférence d'un Groupe de Travail sur la Famine en Afrique à Kinshasa au Zaïre en janvier 1980 / editeur James P. Carter. — Oxford : Pergamon, 1982. — xvi,42p ; 23cm
ISBN 0-08-028885-5 (pbk) : Unpriced : CIP rev. B82-05379

363.8′56 — Food supply. Policies of governments

Food politics : the regional conflict / edited by David N. Balaam and Michael J. Carey. — Totowa : Allanheld, Osmun ; London : Croom Helm, 1981. — ix,246p : ill ; 25cm
Includes index
ISBN 0-7099-0631-5 : £16.95
ISBN 0-916672-52-2 (U.S.) B82-07148

363.8'8 — Developing countries. Food supply. Foreign assistance by developed countries

Jackson, Tony, *1945 Nov.26-*. Against the grain : the dilemma of project food aid / by Tony Jackson with Deborah Eade. — [Oxford] : [Oxfam], [1982]. — vi,132p : ill ; 22cm
Bibliography: p127-132
ISBN 0-85598-063-x (pbk) : £4.50 B82-39676

363.8'8 — Developing countries. Food supply. Foreign assistance by Western bloc countries. Political aspects

Cathie, John. The political economy of food aid / John Cathie. — Aldershot : Gower, c1982. — ix,190p ; 23cm
Bibliography: p158-177. — Includes index
ISBN 0-566-00509-3 : Unpriced : CIP rev.
B82-03622

364 — CRIMINOLOGY

364 — Crime & punishment — ***Sociological perspectives***

Christie, Nils. Limits to pain. — Oxford : Martin Robertson, Oct.1981. — [144]p
ISBN 0-85520-476-1 (cased) : £8.95 : CIP entry
ISBN 0-85520-475-3 (pbk) : £3.95 B81-31100

364 — Crime. Social aspects — ***Marxist viewpoints***

Crime and social justice / Tony Platt and Paul Takagi. — London : Macmillan, 1981. — vi,219p : ill ; 22cm. — (Critical criminology series)
Includes bibliographies and index. — Contains articles originally published in the periodical 'Crime and social justice'
ISBN 0-333-28260-4 (cased) : £12.95 : CIP rev.
ISBN 0-333-28261-2 (pbk) : Unpriced
B80-18648

364 — Crime. Strategy

Laver, Michael. The crime game. — Oxford : Robertson, Oct.1982. — [176]p
ISBN 0-85520-561-x (cased) : £10.00 : CIP entry
ISBN 0-85520-562-8 (pbk) : £4.95 B82-24112

364 — Criminology

Developments in the study of criminal behaviour. — Chichester : Wiley
Vol.1: The prevention and control of offending. — Dec.1982. — [240]p
ISBN 0-471-10176-1 : £14.95 : CIP entry
B82-30814

Gibbons, Don C.. Society, crime and criminal behavior / Don C. Gibbons. — 4th ed. — Englewood Cliffs, N.J. ; London : Prentice-Hall, c1982. — xii,560p : ill,1map ; 25cm
Previous ed.: published as Society, crime and criminal careers. 1977. — Includes index
ISBN 0-13-820118-8 : Unpriced B82-28347

Hall Williams, J. E.. Criminology and criminal justice / by J.E. Hall Williams. — London : Butterworths, 1982, c1981. — xvii,266p : ill,1map ; 23cm
Bibliography: p243-254. — Includes index
ISBN 0-406-59320-5 (cased) : Unpriced
ISBN 0-406-59321-3 (pbk) : Unpriced
B82-28566

364 — Criminology — ***Festschriften***

The Mad, the bad and the different : essays in honor of Simon Dinitz / edited by Israel L. Barak-Glantz, C. Ronald Huff. — Lexington, Mass. : Lexington Books, c1981 ; [Aldershot] : Gower [distributor], 1982. — xxiv,280p : ill,1port ; 24cm
Includes index
ISBN 0-669-03997-7 : £18.00 B82-21162

364'.042 — Crime. Spatial aspects

Davidson, R. N.. Crime and environment / R.N. Davidson. — London : Croom Helm, c1981. — 189p ; 23cm. — (Croom Helm series in geography and environment)
Bibliography: p171-185. — Includes index
ISBN 0-7099-0803-2 : £11.95 : CIP rev.
B81-25712

364'.042'0973 — United States. Crime. Spatial aspects

Crime spillover / edited by Simon Hakim and George F. Rengert. — Beverly Hills ; London : Sage in cooperation with the American Society of Criminology, c1981. — 151p : ill ; 22cm. — (Sage research progress series in criminology ; v.23)
Includes bibliographies
ISBN 0-8039-1698-1 (cased) : Unpriced
ISBN 0-8039-1699-x (pbk) : £4.95 B82-17087

364'.0724 — Crime. Mathematical models

Models in quantitative criminology / edited by James Alan Fox. — New York ; London : Academic Press, 1981. — xviii,190p : ill ; 24cm. — (Quantitative studies in social relations)
Includes bibliographies and index
ISBN 0-12-263950-2 : £16.20 B82-07554

364.1 — CRIMES

364.1'06'07471 — New York ***(City).*** **Organised crimes,** ***1930-1950***

Block, Alan A.. East side-West side : organizing crime in New York 1930-1950 / Alan Block. — Cardiff : University College Cardiff Press, 1980. — 265p : ill,maps(some col.),ports ; 23cm. — (British journal of law and society series)
Includes index
ISBN 0-901426-99-7 : Unpriced B82-28243

Block, Alan A.. East side-West side. — Cardiff : University College Cardiff Press. — [274]p. — (British journal of law and society series)
ISBN 0-906449-46-4 (pbk) : £4.95 : CIP entry
B82-25947

364.1'066'0942821 — South Yorkshire ***(Metropolitan County).*** **Sheffield. Gangsters,** ***1923-1929***

Bean, J. P.. The Sheffield gang wars / J.P. Bean. — Sheffield : D. & D., 1981. — 136p,[8]p of plates : ill,1map,ports ; 21cm
Includes index
ISBN 0-9507645-0-7 (pbk) : £2.50 B82-00556

364.1'092'4 — London. Gangsters: Richardson, Charles, ***1934- — Biographies***

Parker, Robert, *1947-*. Rough justice / Robert Parker. — [London] : Fontana, 1981. — 352p,[8]p of plates : ill,ports ; 18cm
Includes index
ISBN 0-00-636354-7 (pbk) : £1.95 B82-05079

364.1'092'4 — United States. Mafia. Fratianno, Jimmy — ***Biographies***

Demaris, Ovid. The last Mafioso : the treacherous world of Jimmy Fratianno / Ovid Demaris. — London : Corgi, 1981. — xi,565p : ill,ports ; 18cm
Includes index
ISBN 0-552-11917-2 (pbk) : £1.95 B82-24932

364.1'092'4 — United States. Mafia. Lansky, Meyer — ***Biographies***

Eisenberg, Dennis. Meyer Lansky : mogul of the mob / Dennis Eisenberg, Uri Dan, Eli Landau. — [London] : Corgi, 1980, c1979. — 391p : facsims ; 18cm
Originally published: New York : Paddington Press, 1979
ISBN 0-552-11587-8 (pbk) : £1.75 B82-19467

364.1'09414'43 — Scotland. Strathclyde Region. Glasgow. Crimes, ***1855-1977***

Forbes, George. Such bad company : the story of Glasgow criminality / George Forbes and Paddy Meehan. — Edinburgh : Harris, 1982. — 274p,[12]p of plates : ill,ports ; 23cm
ISBN 0-86228-042-7 : £9.50 B82-26731

364.1'31 — Jerusalem. Hotels: King David Hotel. Bombing by Jewish terrorists, ***1946***

Clarke, Thurston. By blood and fire / Thurston Clarke. — London : Arrow, 1982, c1981. — 346p : ill,maps,1plan ; 18cm
Originally published: London : Hutchinson, 1981. — Bibliography: p331-336. — Includes index
ISBN 0-09-928430-8 (pbk) : £1.95 B82-36076

364.1'31 — Political crimes

Turk, Austin T.. Political criminality : the defiance and defense of authority / Austin T. Turk. — Beverly Hills ; London : Sage, c1982. — 232p ; 22cm. — (Sage library of social research ; v.136)
Bibliography: p211-223. — Includes index
ISBN 0-8039-1772-4 (cased) : Unpriced
ISBN 0-8039-1773-2 (pbk) : Unpriced
B82-25548

364.1'31 — Soviet Union. Dissidents, ***1956-1975 — Biographies***

Boer, S. P. de. Biographical dictionary of dissidents in the Soviet Union, 1956-1975 / compiled and edited by S.P. de Boer, E.J. Driessen and H.L. Verhaar. — The Hague ; London : Nijhoff, 1982. — xviii,679p ; 25cm
Bibliography: 667-679
ISBN 90-247-2538-0 : Unpriced B82-35970

364.1'31 — Soviet Union. Dissidents: Azbel, Mark Ya. — ***Biographies***

Azbel, Mark Ya.. Refusenik : trapped in the Soviet Union / Mark Ya. Azbel ; edited by Grace Pierce Forbes. — London : Hamish Hamilton, 1982, c1981. — xiii,513,[16]p of plates : ill,ports ; 24cm
Originally published: Boston,[Mass.] : Houghton Mifflin, 1981. — Includes index
ISBN 0-241-10633-8 : £12.50 B82-15095

364.1'323'0973 — United States. Politics. Watergate affair

Muzzio, Douglas. Watergate games : strategies, choices, outcomes / Douglas Muzzio. — New York ; London : New York University Press, 1982. — x,205p : ill ; 24cm
Bibliography: p185-195. — Includes index
ISBN 0-8147-5384-1 : £13.30 B82-35946

Woodward, Bob. All the president's men. — London : Hodder & Stoughton, Nov.1981. — [352]p. — (Coronet books)
Originally published: London : Quartet, 1974
ISBN 0-340-26780-1 (pbk) : £1.75 : CIP entry
B81-30126

364.1'33 — Down ***(District).*** **Strangford Lough. Smuggling,** ***ca 1800***

Lyttle, W. G.. Daft Eddie, or, The smugglers of Strangford Lough / by W.G. Lyttle. — Newcastle, Co. Down : Mourne Observer Press, 1979. — 86p : ill,ports ; 26cm
Daft Eddie originally published: in the North Down Herald, and later in book form ca.1890. — Includes a new appendix, researched by W.H. Carson and D.J. Hawthorne, originally published in the Mourne Observer
£3.50 B82-18404

364.1'33 — Tax evasion. Social aspects

Bracewell-Milnes, Barry. Tax avoidance and evasion : the individual and society / Barry Bracewell-Milnes. — London : Panopticum, 1979, c1980 (1980 [printing]). — 120p ; 21cm
Bibliography: p119-120
ISBN 0-9504138-4-4 : Unpriced
Primary classification 342.34 B82-08126

364.1'47 — England. Motoring offences — ***Statistics — Serials***

Offences relating to motor vehicles England and Wales / Home Office. — 1979-. — London : H.M.S.O., 1980-. — v. ; 25cm
Annual. — Continues: Offences relating to motor vehicles
ISSN 0263-3949 = Offences relating to motor vehicles England and Wales : £6.70
B82-19866

364.1'5 — West Germany. Crimes against the person by mentally disordered persons

Häfner, H.. Crimes of violence by mentally abnormal offenders : a psychiatric and epidemiological study in the Federal German Republic / H. Häfner, W. Böker in collaboration with H. Immich ... [et al.] ; foreword by T.C.N. Gibbens ; translated by Helen Marshall. — Cambridge : Cambridge University Press, 1982. — xv,384p : ill ; 24cm
Translation of: Gewalttaten Geistesgestörter. — Bibliography: p350-364. — Includes index
ISBN 0-521-24136-7 : £20.00 : CIP rev.
B82-08420

364.1′5′0973 — United States. Crimes of violence — *Sociological perspectives*

Criminal violence / edited by Marvin E. Wolfgang, Neil Alan Weiner. — Beverly Hills ; London : Sage, c1982. — 350p : ill ; 22cm
Includes bibliographies
ISBN 0-8039-1800-3 (cased) : Unpriced
ISBN 0-8039-1801-1 (pbk) : £8.95 B82-38160

364.1′5′09943 — Queensland. Australian aboriginal reservations. Crimes of violence — *Sociological perspectives*

Wilson, Paul R.. Black death, white hands. — London : Allen & Unwin, Nov.1982. — [160]p
ISBN 0-86861-300-2 : £12.95 : CIP entry B82-26088

364.1′51 — Genocide. International political aspects

Kuper, Leo. International action against genocide / by Leo Kuper. — London : 36 Craven St., WC2N 5NG : Minority Rights Group, 1982. — 17p ; 30cm. — (Report / Minority Rights Group, ISSN 0305-6252 ; no.53)
£1.20 (pbk) B82-26620

364.1′51′0904 — Genocide, *ca 1900-1980*

Kuper, Leo. Genocide : its political use in the twentieth century / Leo Kuper. — New Haven ; London : Yale University Press, 1982, c1981. — 255p ; 22cm
Originally published: Harmondsworth : Penguin, 1981. — Bibliography: p221-236. — Includes index
ISBN 0-300-02795-8 : £10.50 : CIP rev. B82-13448

364.1′522 — Suicide — *Sociobiological perspectives*

deCatanzaro, Denys. Suicide and self-damaging behavior : a sociobiological perspective / Denys deCatanzaro. — New York ; London : Academic Press, 1981. — x,246p ; 23cm. — (Personality and psychopathology ; 28)
Bibliography: p215-234. — Includes index
ISBN 0-12-163880-4 : £16.00 B82-29970

364.1′522′0977865 — Missouri. St Louis region. Suicide — *Case studies*

Robins, Eli. The final months : a study of the lives of 134 persons who committed suicide / Eli Robins. — New York ; Oxford : Oxford University Press, 1981. — xvc,437p ; 24cm
Includes index
ISBN 0-19-502911-9 : Unpriced B82-13635

364.1′523 — England. Infanticide, *1558-1803*

Hoffer, Peter C.. Murdering mothers : infanticide in England and New England 1558-1803 / Peter C. Hoffer and N.E.H. Hull. — New York ; London : New York University Press, 1981. — xxii,211p : ill ; 24cm. — (New York University School of Law series in legal history ; 2) (Linden studies in Anglo-American legal history)
Includes index
ISBN 0-8147-3412-x : £16.70
Also classified at 364.1′523 B82-38255

364.1′523 — Murder by doctors, *1850-1954*

Camp, John. One hundred years of medical murder / John Camp. — London : Bodley Head, 1982. — 220p ; 23cm
ISBN 0-370-30354-7 : £6.95 : CIP rev. B82-06735

364.1′523 — Murderers, *1800-1866.* **Residences**

Harte, Glynn Boyd. Murderers′ cottages : a garden of residences of notorious criminals / gather′d & new drawn by Glynn Boyd Harte. — London (28 Ifield Rd., S.W.10) : Warren Editions, 1976. — [21]p : col.ill ; 14cm
Limited ed. of 500 copies
Unpriced (pbk) B82-32685

364.1′523 — New England. Infanticide, *1558-1803*

Hoffer, Peter C.. Murdering mothers : infanticide in England and New England 1558-1803 / Peter C. Hoffer and N.E.H. Hull. — New York ; London : New York University Press, 1981. — xxii,211p : ill ; 24cm. — (New York University School of Law series in legal history ; 2) (Linden studies in Anglo-American legal history)
Includes index
ISBN 0-8147-3412-x : £16.70
Primary classification 364.1′523 B82-38255

364.1′523′088042 — Great Britain. Women murderers

Gaute, J. H. H.. Lady killers. — Large print ed. — Bath : Chivers, Jan.1983. — [280]p. — (A Lythway book)
Originally published: London : Granada, 1980
ISBN 0-85119-885-6 : £6.90 : CIP entry B82-33099

364.1′523′09046 — Murder, *1959-1980* — *Case studies*

Dunning, John. Strange deaths / John Dunning. — London : Hamlyn Paperbacks, 1981. — 240p ; 18cm
ISBN 0-600-20405-7 (pbk) : £1.35 B82-07932

364.1′523′0922 — England. Edward V, *King of England* **& Richard,** *Duke of York.* **Murder**

Williamson, Audrey, *1913-*. The mystery of the princes : an investigation into a supposed murder / Audrey Williamson. — Dursley : Sutton, 1978. — 215p,[14]p of plates : ill,2facsims,1plan,ports ; 22cm
Bibliography: p200-205. — Includes index
ISBN 0-904387-28-3 : £6.95 B82-25353

364.1′523′0922 — Kansas. Holcomb. Clutter *(Family).* **Murder by Hickock, Dick & Smith, Perry,** *1928-1965*

Capote, Truman. In cold blood : a true account of a multiple murder and its consequences / Truman Capote. — London : Sphere, 1981, c1965. — 335p ; 18cm
Originally published: New York : Random House, 1965 ; London : H. Hamilton, 1966
ISBN 0-7221-2288-8 (pbk) : £1.95 B82-08757

364.1′523′0922 — Scotland. Tayside Region. Perth. Gowrie, John Ruthven, *Earl of* **& Ruthven, Alexander. Murder,** *1600*

Ruthven-Finlayson, Arthur. Alexander Ruthven and the Gowrie mystery : a chronicle of events / Major & Mrs. Arthur Ruthven-Finlayson. — Bognor Regis : New Horizon, c1982. — 48p,[8]p of plates : ill ; 21cm
Bibliography: p48
ISBN 0-86116-455-5 : £3.25 B82-13972

364.1′523′0922 — Women murderers — *Biographies*

Gaute, J. H. H.. Lady killers. — Bath : Chivers, Nov.1982. — [192]p. — (Firecrest books)
Originally published: London : Granada, 1980
ISBN 0-85997-502-9 : £5.95 : CIP entry B82-26334

364.1′523′0924 — California. Tulare County. Ashlock, Bill. Murder by Walker, G. Daniel

Barthel, Joan. A death in California / Joan Barthel. — London : Allen Lane, 1982, c1981. — xii,370p ; 23cm
Originally published: New York : Congdon & Lattès, 1981
ISBN 0-7139-1472-6 : £7.95 B82-21134

364.1′523′0924 — France. Murderers: Petiot, Marcel — *Biographies*

Grombach, John V.. The great liquidator / John V. Grombach. — London : Sphere, 1982, c1981. — xvi,408p,[8]p of plates : ill,1plan,ports ; 18cm
Originally published: Garden City, N.Y. : Doubleday, 1981
ISBN 0-7221-4120-3 (pbk) : £1.95 B82-11200

364.1′523′0924 — Great Britain. Murderers: Adams, Peter. Interpersonal relationships with Adams, Shirley — *Personal observations*

Adams, Peter. Knockback. — London : Duckworth, Oct.1982. — [200]p
ISBN 0-7156-1677-3 : £6.95 : CIP entry
Also classified at 792′.028′0924 B82-28574

364.1′523′0924 — London. Murderers: Evans, Timothy — *Biographies*

Kennedy, Ludovic. Ten Rillington Place. — Bath : Chivers, Sept.1982. — [320]p. — (A New Portway book)
Originally published: London : Gollancz, 1961
ISBN 0-86220-509-3 : £5.95 : CIP entry B82-19839

364.1′523′0924 — Scotland. Highland Region. Appin. Campbell, Colin, *d.1752.* **Murder**

MacDonald, Màiri. The Appin mystery : fact and folklore / compiled and illustrated by Màiri MacDonald. — [Scotland] : [West Highland Publications], [1982]. — 24p : ill,1map ; 22cm. — (West Highland series ; no.1)
Ill on inside cover
Unpriced (pbk) B82-35792

364.1′523′0942 — England. Murder, *1870-1970* — *Case studies*

Honeycombe, Gordon. The murders of the Black Museum : 1870-1970 / Gordon Honeycombe. — London : Hutchinson, 1982. — xiv,296p : ill,facsims,maps,ports ; 27cm
Bibliography: p289. — Includes index
ISBN 0-09-147610-0 : £9.95 : CIP rev. B82-09273

364.1′523′0973 — United States. Murder, *1778-1977* — *Case studies*

Nash, Jay Robert. Murder, America : homicide in the United States from the Revolution to the present / by Jay Robert Nash. — London : Harrap, 1981, c1980. — 479p : ill,ports ; 24cm
Originally published: New York : Simon and Schuster, 1980. — Bibliography: p447-467. — Includes index
ISBN 0-245-53764-3 : £9.95 B82-01814

364.1′524′0924 — Germany. Hitler, Adolf. Attempted assassination, *1944*

Galante, Pierre. Hitler lives — : and the generals die / Pierre Galante with Eugène Silianoff ; translated from the French by Mark Howson and Cary Ryan. — London : Sidgwick & Jackson, 1982, c1981. — x,274p,[16]p of plates : ill,maps,2facsims,ports ; 25cm
Translation of: Hitler est-il mort?. — Originally published as: Operation Valkyrie. New York : Harper & Row, 1981. — Bibliography: p265-266. — Includes index
ISBN 0-283-98672-7 : £8.95 B82-14021

364.1′524′0924 — United States. Kennedy, John F.. Assassination

Kurtz, Michael L.. Crime of the century : the Kennedy assassination from a historian′s perspective / by Michael L. Kurtz. — Brighton : Harvester Press, c1982. — xi,291p : ill,1plan,1port ; 23cm
Originally published: Knoxville : University of Tennessee Press, 1982. — Bibliography: p263-281. — Includes index
ISBN 0-7108-0471-7 : £12.95 B82-21360

Lifton, David S.. Best evidence : disguise and deception in the assassination of John F. Kennedy / David S. Lifton. — New York : Macmillan ; London : Collier Macmillan, c1980. — xix,747p,[24]p of plates : ill,facsims,ports ; 25cm
Includes index
ISBN 0-02-571870-3 : £9.95 B82-26390

364.1′532 — England. Crimes: Rape

Toner, Barbara. The facts of rape / Barbara Toner. — Rev ed. — London : Arrow, 1982. — 272p ; 18cm
Previous ed.: London : Hutchinson ; Arrow, 1977
ISBN 0-09-929070-7 (pbk) : £1.75 B82-31202

364.1′534 — White slave trade. Role of Jews, *1880-1939*

Bristow, Edward J.. Prostitution and slavery : the Jewish fight against white slavery 1880-1939. — Oxford : Clarendon, Nov.1982. — [350]p
ISBN 0-19-822588-1 : £15.00 : CIP entry B82-26871

364.1′54 — United States. Children. Kidnapping by parents

Agopian, Michael W.. Parental child-stealing / Michael W. Agopian. — Lexington, Mass. : Lexington Books ; Aldershot : Gower [[distributor]], 1982, c1981. — xix,146p : facsims,forms ; 24cm
Bibliography: p135-142. — Includes index
ISBN 0-669-04152-1 : £12.00 B82-08998

364.1′54′0942132 — London. Westminster *(London Borough).* Embassies: Iran. *Sifārat (Great Britain).* Persons. Taking as hostages by Mahealdin Al Naser Martyr Group — *Personal observations*

Cramer, Chris. Hostage / by Chris Cramer and Sim Harris. — London : Clare, c1982. — 213p ; 23cm
ISBN 0-906549-25-6 (cased) : £6.95
ISBN 0-906549-26-4 (pbk) : Unpriced
B82-33846

364.1′55′0924 — Scotland. Outlaws: MacGregor, Rob Roy — *Biographies*

Murray, W. H.. Rob Roy MacGregor. — Glasgow : Drew, Sept.1982. — [288]p
ISBN 0-904002-98-5 : £9.95 : CIP entry
B82-20660

364.1′55′0972 — Mexico. Society. Role of outlaws, *ca 1800-1910*

Vanderwood, Paul J.. Disorder and progress : bandits, police, and Mexican development / Paul J. Vanderwood. — Lincoln [Neb.] ; London : University of Nebraska Press, 1981. — xix,264p,[24]p of plates : ill,maps,ports ; 22cm. — (A Bison book)
Bibliography: p225-258. — Includes index
ISBN 0-8032-4651-x (cased) : Unpriced
ISBN 0-8032-9600-2 (Unpriced)
Primary classification 363.2′0972 B82-02050

364.1′555 — Great Britain. Coloured persons. Assault by white persons — *Inquiry reports*

Great Britain. *Parliament. House of Commons. Home Affairs Committee.* Second report from the Home Affairs Committee, session 1981-82 : racial attacks : together with the minutes of evidence taken before the Sub-Committee on Race Relations and Immigration of Monday, 14 December, 1981. — London : H.M.S.O., 1982. — 31p ; 25cm. — (HC ; 106)
ISBN 0-10-210682-7 (pbk) : £3.50 B82-20703

364.1′5554′072 — Battered women. Research

The Existing research into battered women. — [Leeds] ([18 Park Row, Leeds LS1 5JA]) : National Women's Aid Federation, [1976?]. — 20p ; 21cm
£0.20 (pbk) B82-16395

364.1′62 — Durham. Weardale. Poaching, *1818*

Egglestone, William Morley. The bonny moorhen, or, The battle of Stanhope : a sketch of an encounter between the Weardale poachers and the gamekeepers : with ballad / by William Morley Egglestone. — Whitley Bay : Strong Words, 1979. — 14p ; 21cm
Originally published: Great Britain : s.n., 1880?
£0.30 (pbk) B82-31961

364.1′62 — England. Pennines. Poaching — *Personal observations*

Fawcett, Dick. Pennine poacher : nocturnal exploits in the Dales recounted / by 'Rabbity Dick' (Richard Fawcett). — Clapham : Dalesman, 1982. — 72p : ill ; 21cm
ISBN 0-85206-678-3 (pbk) : £1.75 B82-31381

364.1′62 — England. Poaching — *Personal observations*

Plummer, David Brian. Rogues and running dogs / D. Brian Plummer. — Rev. and reset ed. — Woodbridge : Boydell, 1982. — 142p : ill ; 23cm
Previous ed.: Lichfield : Tabard Press, 1978
ISBN 0-85115-166-3 : £7.95 : CIP rev.
B82-10856

364.1′62 — England. Residences. Burglary — *Study regions: Southern East Midlands*

Maguire, Mike. Burglary in a dwelling : the offence, the offender and the victim / Mike Maguire in collaboration with Trevor Bennett. — London : Heinemann, 1982. — ix,204p : ill ; 23cm. — (Cambridge studies in criminology ; 49) (Heinemann library of criminology and penal reform)
Bibliography: p194-199. — Includes index
ISBN 0-435-82567-4 : £13.50 : CIP rev.
B82-12342

364.1′62 — France. Nice. Banks: Société générale. Robbery, *1976* — *Personal observations*

Spaggiari, Albert. [Les égouts du paradis. English]. The sewers of gold / Albert Spaggiari ; translated by Martin Sokolinsky. — London : Granada, 1979 (1981 [printing]). — 226p,[16]p of plates : ill,ports ; 18cm
Translation of: Les égouts du paradis
ISBN 0-586-04971-1 (pbk) : £1.50 B82-23510

364.1′62 — Germany. Government assets. Theft, *1945*

Sayer, Ian. Nazi gold. — London : Granada, Sept.1982. — [350]p
ISBN 0-246-11767-2 : £8.95 : CIP entry
B82-18860

364.1′62 — Great Britain. Crimes: Fiddling — *Sociological perspectives*

Mars, Gerald. Cheats at work. — London : Allen & Unwin, Nov.1982. — [256]p
ISBN 0-04-301151-9 : £8.95 : CIP entry
B82-27802

364.1′62 — Norfolk. Poaching — *Personal observations*

King of the Norfolk poachers. I walked by night : being the life and history of the King of the Norfolk poachers / written by himself ; edited by Lilias Rider Haggard ; illustrated by Edward Seago. — Oxford : Oxford University Press, 1982, c1974. — xi,184p : ill ; 20cm. — (Oxford paperbacks)
Originally published: London : Nicholson and Watson, 1935
ISBN 0-19-281311-0 (pbk) : £2.95 : CIP rev.
B82-04166

364.1′62 — North Staffordshire. Poaching, *ca 1920-1970* — *Personal observations*

Bedson, G.. The notorious poacher : memoirs of an old poacher / by G. Bedson ('Grandad'). — Hindhead : Saiga, c1981. — xii,141p : ill ; 24cm. — (Field sports library)
ISBN 0-904558-97-5 : £7.50 B82-08707

364.1′63 — England. Commercial fraud. Control

Leigh, L. H.. The control of commercial fraud / L.H. Leigh. — London : Heinemann, 1982. — xii,339p ; 23cm. — (Cambridge studies in criminology ; 45)
Bibliography: p315-326p. — Includes index
ISBN 0-435-82519-4 : £16.50 : CIP rev.
B81-07483

364.1′63 — England. Long-firm fraud, *1945-1980*

Levi, Michael. The phantom capitalists : the organisation and control of long-firm fraud / by Michael Levi. — London : Heinemann, 1981. — 346p : ill ; 23cm. — (Cambridge studies in criminology ; 44)
Bibliography: p335-341. — Includes index
ISBN 0-435-82520-8 : £16.50 : CIP rev.
B81-16414

364.1′63 — Great Britain. Computer fraud

Computer fraud survey. — [Bristol] ([29 Broad St., Bristol BS1 2EX]) : Local Government Audit Inspectorate, 1981. — 34p : 1form ; 30cm
Unpriced (pbk) B82-17855

364.1′63 — International maritime fraud

Ellen, Eric. International maritime fraud / by Eric Ellen, and Donald Campbell. — London : Sweet & Maxwell, 1981. — viii,174p : ill,forms ; 22cm
Bibliography: p160. — Includes index
ISBN 0-421-27150-7 (pbk) : £8.00 : CIP rev.
B81-25858

364.1′68 — White-collar crime

White-collar and economic crime : multidiscipinary and cross-national perspectives / edited by Peter Wickman, Timothy Dailey. — Lexington : Lexington Books ; [Aldershot] : Gower [distributor], c1982. — xviii,285p : ill ; 24cm
Conference papers. — Includes bibliographies and index
ISBN 0-669-04665-5 : £18.00 B82-24410

364.1′68′0973 — United States. White-collar crime

White-collar crime : an agenda for research / edited by Herbert Edelhertz, Thomas D. Overcast. — Lexington, Mass. : Lexington Books ; [Aldershot] : Gower [distributor], c1982. — viii,235p : 1form ; 24cm. — (The Battelle Human Affairs Research Centers series)
Bibliography: p205-224. — Includes index
ISBN 0-669-04649-3 : £13.00 B82-28772

364.1′68′0973 — United States. White-collar crimes

Ermann, M. David. Corporate deviance / M. David Ermann, Richard J. Lundman. — New York ; London : Holt, Rinehart and Winston, c1982. — xiii,198p ; 24cm
Bibliography: p179-192. — Includes index
ISBN 0-03-044386-5 (pbk) : £8.95 B82-15346

364.2 — CAUSES OF CRIME AND DELINQUENCY

364.2′2 — Crime. Geographical factors

Environmental criminology / edited by Paul J. Brantingham, Patricia L. Brantingham. — Beverly Hills ; London : Sage, c1981. — 264p : ill ; 22cm. — (Sage focus editions ; 39)
Bibliography: p247-262
ISBN 0-8039-1677-9 (cased) : Unpriced
ISBN 0-8039-1678-7 (pbk) : £6.50 B82-24894

364.2′4 — Crime. Role of consumption of alcoholic drinks

Drinking and crime. — London : Tavistock Publications, Oct.1981. — [350]p. — (The Guilford alcohol studies series)
ISBN 0-422-78080-4 : £18.00 : CIP entry
B81-26698

364.2′5 — United States. Crime. Role of drug abuse

Criminal justice and drugs : the unresolved connection / edited by James C. Weissman and Robert L. DuPont. — Port Washington ; London : National University Publications : Kennikat, 1982. — xii,204p ; 22cm. — (Multi-disciplinary studies in the law)
Bibliography: p202-204
ISBN 0-8046-9291-2 : £23.75 B82-24795

364.2′56 — Guyana. Crime. Racial factors

Jones, Howard, *1918-.* Crime, race and culture : a study in a developing country / Howard Jones. — Chichester : Wiley, c1981. — xv,184p ; 24cm
Bibliography: p175-179. — Index
ISBN 0-471-27996-x : £12.75 : CIP rev.
B81-34560

364.3 — CRIMINALS

364.3 — Man. Criminal behaviour

Developments in the study of criminal behaviour. — Chichester : Wiley, Jan.1983
Vol.2: Violence. — [250]p
ISBN 0-471-10373-x : £15.00 : CIP entry
B82-34616

364.3 — Man. Criminal behaviour. Prediction. Applications of graphology

Marne, Patricia. Crime and sex in handwriting / Patricia Marne. — London : Constable, 1981. — 150p : ill,facsims ; 23cm
Bibliography: p150
ISBN 0-09-464320-2 : £6.95
Also classified at 155.3 B82-06383

364.3 — Offenders. Psychological aspects

Abnormal offenders, delinquency, and the criminal justice system / edited by John Gunn and David P. Farrington. — Chichester : Wiley, c1982. — ix,384p : ill ; 24cm. — (Wiley series on current research in forensic psychiatry and psychology)
Includes bibliographies and indexes
ISBN 0-471-28047-x : Unpriced : CIP rev.
B81-36200

364.3′08921094 — Australia. British criminals. Social conditions, *1788-1890*

Sweeney, Christopher. Transported : in place of death : convicts in Australia / Christopher Sweeney. — South Melbourne ; London : Macmillan, 1981. — xiv,185p : ill,facsims,ports ; 23cm
Bibliography: p174-178. — Includes index
ISBN 0-333-33751-4 : £9.95 B82-32334

364.3'092'4 — United States. Crimes. Abbott, Jack Henry — *Biographies*
Abbott, Jack Henry. In the belly of the beast / Jack Henry Abbott. — London : Arrow, 1982, c1981. — xvi,166p ; 18cm
Originally published: New York : Random House, 1981
ISBN 0-09-928140-6 (pbk) : £1.50 B82-37538

364.3'6 — Juvenile delinquency. Psychosocial aspects
Stott, Denis H.. Delinquency : the problem and its prevention / by Denis Stott. — London : Batsford, 1982. — 345p ; 23cm
Bibliography: p325-333. — Includes index
ISBN 0-7134-4196-8 (pbk) : £9.95 B82-36001

364.3'6 — Juvenile delinquency — *Sociological perspectives*
Sociology of delinquency current issues / edited by Gary F. Jensen. — Beverly Hills ; London : Published in cooperation with the American Society of Criminology [by] Sage, c1981. — 144p ; 22cm. — (Sage research progress series in criminology ; v.22)
Includes bibliographies
ISBN 0-8039-1696-5 (cased) : Unpriced
ISBN 0-8039-1697-3 (pbk) : £4.95 B82-18958

364.3'6 — Oral history. Special subjects: Juvenile delinquency
Bennett, James. Oral history and delinquency : the rhetoric of criminology / James Bennett. — Chicago ; London : University of Chicago Press, 1981. — xv,363p ; 24cm
Bibliography: p335-351. — Includes index
ISBN 0-226-04245-6 : £19.95 B82-17773

364.3'6'01 — Juvenile delinquency. Theories
Vulnerabilities to delinquency / edited by Dorothy Otnow Lewis. — Lancaster : MTP, c1981. — 327p : ill ; 24cm
Includes bibliographies and index
ISBN 0-85200-563-6 : £24.50 B82-02828

364.3'6'05 — Juvenile delinquency — *Serials*
Orchard Lodge studies of deviancy : a forum for debate regarding issues concerning troublesome adolescents. — Vol.1, no.1 (Autumn 1981)-. — London (William Booth Rd, Anerley, SE20 8BG) : Orchard Lodge Regional Resource Centre, 1981-. — v. ; 30cm
Irregular
ISSN 0261-9296 = Orchard Lodge studies of deviancy : £2.00 per issue B82-10110

364.3'6'0941 — Great Britain. Juvenile delinquency
West, D. J.. Delinquency : its roots, careers and prospects / D.J. West. — London : Heinemann Educational, 1982. — 186p : 2ill ; 23cm. — (Cambridge studies in criminology ; 50) (The Heinemann library of criminology and penal reform)
Bibliography: p172-181. — Includes index
ISBN 0-435-82932-7 (cased) : £13.50 : CIP rev.
ISBN 0-435-82933-5 (pbk) : Unpriced B82-01957

364.3'6'0942876 — Tyne and Wear *(Metropolitan County)*. Newcastle upon Tyne. Scotswood region. Juvenile delinquency
Frisch, Monica. Young people in trouble : a survey of needs and resources in Scotland and W. Newcastle / by Monica Frisch. — Newcastle upon Tyne (MEA House, Ellison Pl., Newcastle upon Tyne NE1 8XS) : Newcastle upon Tyne Council for Voluntary Service, c1981. — 84p : ill,maps ; 30cm
Cover title
£3.00 (pbk) B82-25957

364.3'6'0973 — United States. Juvenile delinquency
Juvenile delinquency : a book of readings / [selected and edited by] Rose Giallombardo. — 4th ed. — New York ; Chichester : Wiley, c1982. — viii,591p : ill ; 24cm
Previous ed.: 1976. — Includes bibliographies
ISBN 0-471-08344-5 (pbk) : £11.00 B82-26470

364.3'7'0973 — United States. Condemned prisoners — *Interviews*
Magee, Doug. Slow coming dark. — London : Quartet, Jan.1982. — [192]p
Originally published: New York : Pilgrim Press, 1980
ISBN 0-7043-2318-4 : CIP entry B81-34643

364.3'74 — Women. Criminal behaviour. Theories
Leonard, Eileen B.. Women, crime and society : a critique of theoretical criminology / Eileen B. Leonard. — New York ; London : Longman, c1982. — xvi,208p ; 24cm
Bibliography: p195-204. — Includes index
ISBN 0-582-28288-8 (cased) : Unpriced
ISBN 0-582-28289-6 (pbk) : £6.95 B82-34753

364.3'74'0973 — United States. Women offenders
Comparing female and male offenders / edited by Marguerite Q. Warren. — Beverly Hills ; London : Sage in cooperation with the American Society of Criminology, c1981. — 141p : ill ; 22cm. — (Sage research progress series in criminology ; v.21)
Includes bibliographies
ISBN 0-8039-1695-7 (cased) : Unpriced
ISBN 0-8039-1694-9 (pbk) : £4.95 B82-17088

364.4 — CRIME PREVENTION

364.4 — Great Britain. Crime. Prevention. Effects of imprisonment of offenders
Brody, Stephen. Taking offenders out of circulation / by Stephen Brody and Roger Tarling. — London : H.M.S.O., 1980. — v,42p ; 25cm. — (A Home Office Research Unit report) (Home Office research study ; no.64)
Bibliography: p38-42
ISBN 0-11-340704-1 (pbk) : £3.00 B82-14639

364.4 — Great Britain. Crimes. Prevention. Role of publicity
Riley, D. (David). Crime prevention publicity : an assessment / by D. Riley and P. Mayhew. — London : H.M.S.O., 1980. — v,43p : ill ; 25cm. — (A Home Office Research Unit report) (Home Office research study ; no.63)
Bibliography: p40-43
ISBN 0-11-340703-3 (pbk) : £3.30 B82-14640

364.4'0942 — England. Crime. Prevention. Social aspects
Designing out crime / edited by R.V.G. Clarke and P. Mayhew ; [for the] Home Office Research Unit. — London : H.M.S.O., 1980. — viii,182p : ill ; 25cm
Bibliography: p163-171. — Includes indexes
ISBN 0-11-340732-7 (pbk) : £6.95 B82-16413

364.4'4 — Great Britain. Violent criminals. Social control
Dangerousness : problems of assessment and prediction. — London : Allen & Unwin, Nov.1982. — [176]p
ISBN 0-04-364021-4 : £15.00 : CIP entry B82-26210

364.6 — PUNISHMENT OF CRIME

364.6 — Netherlands. Delinquents. Treatment — *Conference proceedings*
Involuntary institutionalization, changing concepts in the treatment of delinquency : proceedings of a workshop held on the occasion of the 25th anniversary of the Dr. Henri van der Hoeven Kliniek, Utrecht, The Netherlands, on April 15, 1980 / editors J.T.T.M. Feldbrugge and Y.A. Werdmüller von Elgg. — Amsterdam ; Oxford : Excerpta Medica, 1981. — xiv,106p : 1ill ; 25cm. — (International congress series ; no.562)
ISBN 90-219-0507-8 : Unpriced B82-06108

364.6 — Traffic offences. Drivers. Diversion programmes
Canagarayar, J. K.. Diversion of traffic offenders / by J.K. Canagarayar ; with a foreword by J.W. Mohr. — Singapore : Malayan Law Journal ; [London] : [Sweet & Maxwell], 1981. — xi,229p ; 22cm
Bibliography: p219-229
ISBN 9-9717001-5-8 : £12.50 B82-21262

364.6 — United States. Offenders. Corrective treatment
Johnston, Norman, *1921-*. Legal process and corrections / Norman Johnston, Leonard D. Savitz. — New York ; Chichester : Wiley, c1982. — viii,352p : ill ; 24cm
Includes bibliographies
ISBN 0-471-08337-2 (pbk) : £8.00
Primary classification 364'.973 B82-18065

364.6'088055 — Welfare work with young offenders
Collins, Stephen. Social work with young offenders / Stephen Collins, David Behan. — London : Butterworths, 1981. — xii,148p ; 22cm
Bibliography: p140-144. — Includes index
ISBN 0-406-55690-3 (pbk) : £4.95 B82-08855

364.6'2'0942 — England. Prisoners. Parole — *Howard League for Penal Reform viewpoints*
Howard League for Penal Reform. Freedom on licence : the development of parole and proposals for reform : report of a Howard League Working Party under the chairmanship of Professor the Lord McGregor of Durris ... — Sunbury : Quartermaine House, 1981. — xxvi,70p ; 22cm
Bibliography: p70
ISBN 0-905898-14-1 (pbk) : £4.25 B82-11311

364.6'2'0973 — United States. Prisoners. Parole
Cavender, Gray. Parole : a critical analysis / Gray Cavender. — Port Washington ; London : National University, 1982. — 109p ; 22cm
Bibliography: p94-106. — Includes index
ISBN 0-8046-9296-3 : £14.00 B82-31914

364.6'3 — Hampshire. Hostels for offenders
Fisher, Roy. Authority or freedom? : probation hostels for adults. — Aldershot : Gower, Jan.1983. — [224]p
ISBN 0-566-00593-x : £12.50 : CIP entry B82-32439

364.6'3'0942 — England. Probation services
Assist and befriend or direct and control : a report on probation services in Poland and England / edited by John Harper ... [et al.]. — London : North East London Polytechnic, c1982. — iii,211p ; 21cm
Cover title. — At head of title: North East London Polytechnic. Department of Applied Social Sciences
ISBN 0-901987-50-6 (pbk) : £2.50
Also classified at 364.6'3'09438 B82-24296

364.6'3'09438 — Poland. Probation services
Assist and befriend or direct and control : a report on probation services in Poland and England / edited by John Harper ... [et al.]. — London : North East London Polytechnic, c1982. — iii,211p ; 21cm
Cover title. — At head of title: North East London Polytechnic. Department of Applied Social Sciences
ISBN 0-901987-50-6 (pbk) : £2.50
Primary classification 364.6'3'0942 B82-24296

364.6'6'0973 — United States. Capital punishment
The Death penalty in America / edited by Hugo Adam Bedau. — 3rd ed. — New York ; Oxford : Oxford University Press, 1982. — xiii,424p : ill ; 24cm
Previous ed.: Chicago : Aldine Pub. Co., 1968. — Bibliography: p383-406. — Includes index
ISBN 0-19-502986-0 (cased) : £21.50
ISBN 0-19-502987-9 (pbk) : Unpriced B82-37364

364.6'8 — England. Offenders. Community service orders
Pease, Ken. Community service order : a first decade of promise / a review undertaken by Ken Pease on behalf of the Howard League for Penal Reform. — [London] ([169 Clapham Rd, SW6 0PU][Howard League for Penal Reform]), 1981. — ix,76p ; 21cm
Bibliography: p66-70
£1.75 (pbk) B82-29222

364.6'8 — London. Hounslow *(London Borough)*. Juvenile delinquency. Intermediate treatment. Role of voluntary organisations
Locke, Trevor. The involvement of the voluntary sector in intermediate treatment in Hounslow / written by Trevor Locke. — Leicester : National Youth Bureau, 1981. — 10leaves ; 30cm. — (Intermediate treatment field reports)
Unpriced (pbk) B82-05719

364.6′8 — London. Southwark *(London Borough)*. Juvenile delinquency. Intermediate treatment. Role of voluntary organisations

Locke, Trevor. The involvement of the voluntary sector in intermediate treatment in Southwark / written by Trevor Locke. — Leicester : National Youth Bureau, 1981. — 17leaves ; 30cm. — (Intermediate treatment field reports)
Unpriced (pbk) B82-05720

364.6′8 — South Yorkshire *(Metropolitan County)*. Doncaster. Juvenile delinquency. Intermediate treatment. Role of voluntary organisations

Locke, Trevor. The involvement of the voluntary sector in intermediate treatment in Doncaster / written by Trevor Locke. — Leicester : National Youth Bureau, 1981. — 10leaves ; 30cm ; pbk. — (Intermediate treatment field reports)
Unpriced B82-05721

364.8 — DISCHARGED PRISONERS

364.8′09428′6 — Durham *(County)*. Discharged prisoners. Aftercare services, *1882-1982*

Cranfield, Ruth E. G.. One hundred years of prisoners' aid in County Durham : 1882-1982 / Ruth E.G. Cranfield. — Durham (19, Old Elvet, Durham DH1 3HL) : North Eastern Prison After Care Society, 1982. — 34p ; 21cm
Cover title
Unpriced (pbk) B82-20096

364.9 — CRIMINOLOGY. HISTORICAL AND GEOGRAPHICAL TREATMENT

364′.91724 — Developing countries. Crime & punishment

Crime, justice and underdevelopment / edited by Colin Sumner. — London : Heinemann, 1982. — xvi,345p ; 23cm. — (Cambridge studies in criminology ; 46)
Bibliography: p312-331. — Includes index
ISBN 0-435-82888-6 : £19.50 : CIP rev.
B81-23768

364′.91732 — Urban regions. Crime. Geographical aspects

Herbert, David, *1935-*. The geography of urban crime / David T. Herbert. — London : Longman, 1982. — xii,120p : ill,maps ; 24cm. — (Topics in applied geography)
Bibliography: p113-118. — Includes index
ISBN 0-582-30046-0 (pbk) : £4.95 : CIP rev.
B81-34558

364′.924 — London. Crime, *1915-1935* — *Personal observations*

Benney, Mark. Low company : describing the evolution of a burglar / by Mark Benney. — Horsham : Caliban, 1981. — 350p ; 21cm
Originally published: London : P. Davies, 1936
ISBN 0-904573-18-4 : £12.00 B82-38249

364.941 — Great Britain. Crime & punishment

Prins, Herschel. Criminal behaviour. — 2nd ed. — London : Tavistock, Oct.1982. — [320]p
Previous ed.: London : Pitman, 1973
ISBN 0-422-77680-7 (cased) : £11.00 : CIP entry
ISBN 0-422-77690-4 (pbk) : £4.95 B82-24010

364′.941 — Great Britain. Crime & punishment, *1800-1900*

Jones, David, *1941-*. Crime, protest, community and police in nineteenth-century Britain / David Jones. — London : Routledge & Kegan Paul, 1982. — xi,247p : ill,2maps ; 23cm
Bibliography: p236-242. — Includes index
ISBN 0-7100-9008-0 : £14.95 B82-16361

364′.941 — Great Britain. Crime & punishment — *Sociological perspectives*

Issues in crime and society / [D335 Course Team]. — Milton Keynes : Open University Press. — (Social sciences : a third level course)
At head of title: The Open University
Block 1: Talking about crime : notions of crime and justice / prepared for the Course Team by John Muncie. — 1981. — 48p : ill,facsims,ports ; 30cm. — (D335 ; 1)
Bibliography: p47-48
ISBN 0-335-12110-1 (pbk) : Unpriced
B82-21210

Issues in crime and society / [D335 Course Team]. — Milton Keynes : Open University Press. — (Social sciences : a third level course)
At head of title: The Open University
Block 2: Law and disorder : histories of crime and justice. — 1981. — 151p : ill,facsims,ports ; 30cm. — (D335 ; 2,[1-3])
Includes bibliographies. — Contents: Part 1: Introduction to block 2 — Part 2: Custom and law, law and crime as historical processes — Part 3: Intervention, regulation and surveillance
ISBN 0-335-12111-x (pbk) : Unpriced
B82-21209

Issues in crime and society / [D335 Course Team]. — Milton Keynes : Open University Press. — (Social sciences : a third level course)
At head of title: The Open University
Block 2: Law and disorder : histories of crime and justice. — 1982. — 80p : ill,ports ; 30cm. — (D335 ; 2,(4-5))
Inlcudes bibliographies. — Contents: Part 4: Youth and the reforming zeal — Part 5: Policing society, policing crime
ISBN 0-335-12112-8 (pbk) : Unpriced
B82-32211

Issues in crime and society / [DS335 Course Team]. — Milton Keynes : Open University Press. — (Social sciences : a third level course)
At head of title: The Open University
Block 3: Thinking about crime : theories of crime and justice. — 1982. — 88p : ill,maps ; 30cm. — (D335 ; 3 (1-4))
Includes bibliographies. — Contents: Study guide 1: Individual deviance — Study guide 2: Moral development and the family — Study guide 3: The person and group reality — Study guide 4: Footprints on the sand
ISBN 0-335-12113-6 (pbk) : Unpriced
B82-32210

Issues in crime and society / [D335 Course Team]. — Milton Keynes : Open University Press. — (Social sciences : a third level course)
At head of title: The Open University
Block 4: The anatomy of crime and justice. — 1982. — 119p : ill,facsims,1map ; 30cm. — (D335 ; 4(1-4))
Includes bibliographies. — Contents: Part 1: The police — Part 2: The courts — Part 3: The prisons — Part 4: Criminal justice in Scotland
ISBN 0-335-12114-4 (pbk) : Unpriced
B82-34535

364′.941 — Great Britain. Crime, *1800-1830*

Low, Donald A.. Thieves' kitchen : the Regency underworld / Donald A. Low. — London : Dent, 1982. — vii,192p,[16]p of plates : ill,1map,1facsim,ports ; 24cm
Bibliography: p185-187. — Includes index
ISBN 0-460-04438-9 : £8.95 : CIP rev.
B81-34511

364′.941 — Great Britain. Crime, *to 1980*

Crime and society : readings in history and theory / compiled by Mike Fitzgerald, Gregor McLennan and Jennie Pawson. — London : Routledge & Kegan Paul in association with Open University Press, 1981. — vii,504p ; 22cm. — (An Open University set book)
Includes bibliographies and index
ISBN 0-7100-0944-5 (pbk) : £8.95 : CIP rev.
B81-31640

364′.941′0723 — Great Britain. Crime. Data. Statistical analysis

Anderton, C. James. Crime in perspective : presented 12th December, 1978 / by C. James Anderton. — Stockport : Manchester Statistical Society, [1979?]. — 24p ; 20cm
At head of title: Manchester Statistical Society. — Text on inside cover
£2.00 (pbk) B82-02528

364′.942 — England. Crime & punishment, *1939-1945*

Smithies, Edward. Crime in wartime : a social history of crime in World War II / by Edward Smithies. — London : Allen & Unwin, 1982. — 219p ; 23cm
Includes index
ISBN 0-04-364020-6 : Unpriced : CIP rev.
B81-33916

364′.942 — England. Criminal law. Justice. Adminstration. Policies of government, *1945-1980 — Socialist viewpoints*

Taylor, Ian, *1944-*. Law and order : arguments for socialism / Ian Taylor. — London : Macmillan, 1981. — xxii,234p ; 22cm
Bibliography: p224-234
ISBN 0-333-21442-0 (cased) : Unpriced
ISBN 0-333-21444-7 (pbk) : Unpriced
B82-16304

364′.942′0212 — England. Crime — *Statistics*

Criminal statistics, England and Wales, supplementary tables 1980. — London : Home Office, [1981?]. — 4v. ; 21x30cm
Cover title. — At head of title: Home Office
ISBN 0-86252-013-4 (pbk) : Unpriced
ISBN 0-86252-014-2 (v.2) : £12.75
ISBN 0-86252-015-0 (v.3) : £18.75
ISBN 0-86252-016-2 (v.4) : £9.75 B82-06965

364′.94251 — Derbyshire. Crime & punishment, *1760-1830*

Power, E. G.. Hanged for a sheep : crime and punishment in bygone Derbyshire / E.G. Power. — Cromford : Scarthin, [1981]. — 79p : ill,facsims ; 21cm
Bibliography: p79
ISBN 0-907758-00-2 (pbk) : £1.65 B82-16951

364′.94436 — France. Paris. Crime & punishment, *1789-1799*

Wills, Antoinette. Crime and punishment in revolutionary Paris / Antoinette Wills. — Westport ; London : Greenwood, 1981. — xxi,227p : ill,2maps ; 22cm. — (Contributions in legal studies, ISSN 0147-1074 ; no.15)
Bibliography: p207-215. — Includes index
ISBN 0-313-21494-8 : Unpriced B82-02005

364′.973 — United States. Crime & punishment

Reid, Sue Titus. Crime and criminology / Sue Titus Reid. — 3rd ed. — New York ; London : Holt, Rinehart and Winston, c1982. — xiv,689p : ill ; 24cm
Previous ed.: 1979. — Includes bibliographies and index
ISBN 0-03-059248-8 : £16.50 B82-15363

364′.973 — United States. Crime — *Sociological perspectives*

Savitz, Leonard. Contemporary criminology / Leonard D. Savitz, Norman Johnston. — New York ; Chichester : Wiley, c1982. — viii,379p : 1map ; 23cm
ISBN 0-471-08336-4 (pbk) : £8.85 B82-21535

364′.973 — United States. Criminal law. Justice. Administration

Conrad, John P.. Justice and consequences / John P. Conrad. — Lexington, Mass. : Lexington Books ; [Aldershot] : Gower [distrbutor], c1981. — xv,175p ; 24cm
Includes index
ISBN 0-669-02190-3 : £12.00 B82-04747

Johnston, Norman, *1921-*. Legal process and corrections / Norman Johnston, Leonard D. Savitz. — New York ; Chichester : Wiley, c1982. — viii,352p : ill ; 24cm
Includes bibliographies
ISBN 0-471-08337-2 (pbk) : £8.00
Also classified at 364.6 B82-18065

364′.973 — United States. Criminal law. Justice. Administration. Effects of intelligence operations by Federal Bureau of Investigation

Amnesty International. Proposal for a commission of inquiry into the effect of domestic intelligence activities on criminal trials in the United States of America. — London : Amnesty International, 1981. — iii,141p ; 30cm
Cover title
ISBN 0-86210-038-0 (pbk) : Unpriced
B82-21324

364′.973 — United States. Criminal law. Justice. Administration. Evaluation

Evaluation and criminal justice policy / edited by Ronald Roesch and Raymond R. Corrado. — Beverly Hills ; London : Sage in cooperation with the American Society of Criminology, c1981. — 160p : ill ; 22cm. — (Sage research progress series in criminology ; v.19)
Includes bibliographies
ISBN 0-8039-1690-6 (cased) : Unpriced
ISBN 0-8039-1691-4 (pbk) : £4.95 B82-17086

364'.973 — United States. Criminal law. Justice. Administration. Participation of community action groups

Neighborhood justice : assessment of an emerging idea / [edited by] Roman Tomasic, Malcolm M. Feeley. — New York ; London : Longman, c1982. — xviii,286p ; 24cm
Bibliography: p249-275. — Includes index
ISBN 0-582-28253-5 : Unpriced B82-33646

364'.973 — United States. Society. Effects of crime

Reaction to crime / Dan A. Lewis, editor. — Beverly Hills ; London : Sage, c1981. — 253p : ill ; 22cm. — (Sage criminal justice system annuals ; v.16)
Includes bibliographies
ISBN 0-8039-1702-3 (cased) : Unpriced B82-21862

364'.973'019 — United States. Criminal law. Justice. Administration — *Psychological perspectives*

The **Criminal** justice system : a social psychological analysis / edited by Vladimir J. Konečni and Ebbe B. Ebbesen. — Oxford : Freeman, c1982. — xiv,418p : ill ; 25cm
Includes bibliographies and index
ISBN 0-7167-1312-8 (cased) : £14.80
ISBN 0-7167-1313-6 (pbk) : £10.40 B82-35949

365 — DETENTION INSTITUTIONS

365'.068 — Unted States. Prisons. Administration

McGee, Richard A.. Prisons and politics / Richard A. McGee. — Lexington, [Mass.] : Lexington Books, 1981 ; [Aldershot] : Gower [distributor], 1982. — xiv,161p ; 24cm
Bibliography: p157. — Includes index
ISBN 0-669-04527-6 : £14.50 B82-11706

365'.33 — United States & Western Europe. Maximum-security prisons — *Conference proceedings*

Confinement in maximum custody : new last-resort prisons in the United States and Western Europe / edited by David A. Ward, Kenneth F. Schoen. — Lexington, Mass. : Lexington Books ; [Aldershot] : Gower [distrbutor], c1981. — xiii,206p : ill ; 24cm
Conference proceedings. — Includes index
ISBN 0-669-02799-5 : £14.50 B82-04749

365'.34 — Tasmania. Port Arthur. Penal colonies

Weidenhofer, Maggie. Port Arthur : a place of misery / Maggie Weidenhofer. — Melbourne ; Oxford : Oxford University Press, 1981. — 145p : ill(some col.),facsims,map,plan,ports ; 20x26cm
Ill. on lining papers. — Bibliography: p138-139. — Includes index
ISBN 0-19-554323-8 : Unpriced B82-40525

365'.4 — Great Britain. Prisoners: Informers & sex offenders. Segregation

Priestley, Philip. Community of scapegoats : the segregation of sex offenders and informers in prisons / by Philip Priestley. — Oxford : Pergamon, 1980. — vii,155p : ill ; 22cm
Bibliography: p147-149. — Includes index
ISBN 0-08-025231-1 : £10.00 : CIP rev. B80-23141

365'.4'0926 — England. Irish prisoners. Prison life, *1976-1979 — Case studies*

Special category 'A' : Irish political prisoners in England : a account of prison life in England based on the experiences of Irish Republican John Higgins, imprisoned between 1976 and 1979. — Dublin (5, Blessington St., Dublin) : Sinn Fein POW Department, 1980. — 100p : ill,1map,ports ; 22cm
Ill on inside covers
Unpriced (pbk) B82-02051

365'.42 — Edinburgh. List D boys' schools: Dr Guthrie's Boys' School. Curriculum. Development

Broadening the curriculum in a list D school : a descriptive account of an experiment in curriculum development / [edited by] Clive Foster. — Edinburgh (Moray House, College of Education, Holyrood Rd., Edinburgh EH8 8AQ) : Scottish Curriculum Development Service - Edinburgh Centre, c1981. — iii,29p ; 30cm
Cover title. — Text on inside covers
£0.50 (pbk) B82-25108

365'.42 — Juvenile delinquents: Girls. Residential care

Ackland, John W.. Girls in care. — Aldershot : Gower, July 1982. — [180]p
ISBN 0-566-00511-5 : £11.50 : CIP entry B82-12973

365'.44 — Great Britain. White-collar men prisoners. Prison life

Breed, Bryan. White collar bird / by Bryan Breed. — London : Clare, c1979. — 159p ; 23cm
ISBN 0-906549-02-7 : £5.95 B82-00826

365'.44'0924 — United States. Male prisoners. Prison life — *Personal observations*

Abbott, Jack Henry. In the belly of the beast : letters from prison / Jack Henry Abbott ; with an introduction by Norman Mailer. — London : Hutchinson, 1982, c1981. — xvi,166p ; 23cm
Originally published: New York : Random House, 1981
ISBN 0-09-147330-6 : £6.95 : CIP rev. B81-39221

365'.45 — Chile. Political prisoners: Horman, Charles. Execution

Hauser, Thomas. Missing / Thomas Hauser. — Harmondsworth : Penguin, 1982, c1978. — 253p ; 19cm
Originally published: New York : Harcourt Brace Jovanovich, 1978
ISBN 0-14-006453-2 (pbk) : £1.75 B82-31207

365'.45 — China. Political prisoners. Political education, *1949-1979 — Case studies*

Fyfield, J. A.. Re-educating Chinese anti-communists / J.A. Fyfield. — London : Croom Helm, c1982. — 117p ; 23cm
Bibliography: p105-108. — Includes index
ISBN 0-7099-1017-7 : £10.95 : CIP rev. B81-30535

365.4'5 — Soviet Union. Jewish dissidents. Detention

The **Increased** arrests of Soviet Jews in 1981. — London (11 Hertford St., W1Y 7DX) : IJA, 1981. — 6p ; 24cm. — (Research report / Institute of Jewish Affairs ; no.21)
Unpriced (unbound) B82-27693

365'.45 — Soviet Union. Political prisoners: Christians — *Lists*

Soviet Christian prisoner list 1981. — Orange : SSRC ; Keston (Heathfield Rd., Keston, Kent BR2 6BA) : Keston College, c1981. — 59p ; 21cm
Unpriced (pbk) B82-35829

Soviet Christian prisoner list 1982 update. — Keston (Heathfield Rd., Keston, Kent BR2 6BA) : Keston College, [1982]. — 27p ; 22cm
£1.00 (unbound) B82-35830

365'.45'0924 — Argentina. Political prisoners, *1977-1979 — Personal observations*

Timerman, Jacobo. Prisoner without a name, cell without a number / Jacobo Timerman ; translated from the Spanish by Toby Talbot. — Harmondsworth : Penguin, 1982, c1981. — viii,164p ; 19cm
Translation of: Preso sin nombre, celda sin numero. — Originally published: London : Weidenfeld & Nicolson, 1981
ISBN 0-14-006164-9 (pbk) : £1.25 B82-31206

365'.45'0924 — East Germany. Political prisoners: Bahro, Rudolf

The **Case** of Rudolf Bahro : a Socialist in an East German prison. — Nottingham (Bertrand Russell House, Gamble Street, Nottingham, NG7 4ET) : Bertrand Russell Peace Foundation, [1979]. — 22p ; 21cm. — (Spokesman pamphlet ; no.66)
£0.40 B82-17669

365'.45'0924 — Romania. Political prisoners. Prison life, *ca 1945-ca 1955 — Personal observations*

Valéry, Nicole. Prisoner, rejoice / Nicole Valéry ; translated from the French by Tony and Jane Collins. — London : Hodder and Stoughton, 1982. — 238p ; 18cm. — (Hodder Christian paperbacks)
Translation of: Bénie sois-tu, prison
ISBN 0-340-27157-4 (pbk) : £1.95 : CIP rev. B82-12259

365'.45'0924 — South Africa. Pretoria. Political prisoners, *1964-1971 — Personal observations*

Lewin, Hugh. Bandiet : seven years in a South African prison / Hugh Lewin. — London : Heinemann, 1981, c1974. — 228p ; 19cm. — (African writers series)
Originally published: London : Barrie and Jenkins, 1974
ISBN 0-435-90251-2 (pbk) : £1.95 B82-09153

365'.45'0924 — South Africa. Robben Island. Political prisoners. Prison life, *1963-1973 — Personal observations*

Prisoner 885/63. Island in chains : ten years on Robben Island / Prisoner 885/63 ; as told by Indres Naidoo to Albie Sacks. — Harmondsworth : Penguin, 1982. — 278p ; 18cm
ISBN 0-14-006053-7 (pbk) : £1.95 B82-22085

365'.45'0924 — Soviet Union. Polish political prisoners. Prison life, *1939-1942 — Personal observations*

Kmiecik, Jerzy. Growing up in the Gulag. — London : Quartet, Sept.1982. — [320]p
ISBN 0-7043-2321-4 : £10.95 : CIP entry B82-21979

365'.45'0926 — Political prisoners — *Case studies*

Prisoners of conscience. — London : Amnesty International, 1981. — 42p : ill,ports ; 30cm. — (An Amnesty International report)
ISBN 0-86210-037-2 (pbk) : Unpriced B82-08060

365'.45'0946 — Spain. Political prisoners. Torture

Report of an Amnesty International mission to Spain, 3-28 October 1979. — London : Amnesty International, c1980. — ii,64p ; 30cm
English text, appendices in Spanish
ISBN 0-86210-022-4 (pbk) : Unpriced B82-16343

365'.45'0947 — Russia. Labour camps. Political prisoners. Prison life — *Russian texts*

Maksimovich, Matveĭ. Nevol'nye sravneni͡ia : dokumenty vospominani͡ia vstrechi / Matveĭ Maksimovich. — London : Overseas Publications Interchange, 1982. — 158p ; 19cm
Russian text. — Added t.p. in English
ISBN 0-903868-43-1 : Unpriced B82-38924

365'.45'09497 — Yugoslavia. Political prisoners

Yugoslavia : prisoners of conscience. — London : Amnesty International Publications, 1982. — 47p : ill,ports ; 30cm. — (An Amnesty International report)
Cover title
ISBN 0-86210-043-7 (pbk) : Unpriced B82-23120

365'.45'0964 — Morocco. Political prisoners. Treatment

Amnesty International. Report on Amnesty International mission to the Kingdom of Morocco : 10-13 February 1981. — London : Amnesty International, 1982. — vi,74p ; 29cm
ISBN 0-86210-046-1 (pbk) : Unpriced B82-30168

365'.45'097285 — Nicaragua. Political prisoners, *1979-1980*

Report of the Amnesty International missions to the Republic of Nicaragua, August 1979, January 1980 and August 1980 : including memoranda exchanged between the government and Amnesty International. — London : Amnesty International, 1982. — 73p ; 30cm
Translation from the Spanish
ISBN 0-86210-047-x (unbound) : Unpriced B82-34706

365.5 — Great Britain. Round Tables — *Serials*

Tabler : the official journal of the National Association of Round Tables of Great Britain and Ireland. — Vol.53, no.1 (Autumn 1981)-. — London (15 Park Rd, NW1 6XN) : The Association, 1981-. — v. : ill,maps,ports ; 30cm
Quarterly. — Continues: News and views (National Association of Round Tables of Great Britain and Ireland). — Description based on: Vol.53, no.3 (Spring 1982)
ISSN 0263-3825 = Tabler : Unpriced B82-23594

365'.6 — Great Britain. Borstals. Inmates: Ethnic minorities

Fludger, Neil. Ethnic minorities in borstal / by Neil Fludger. — London : Home Office, Prison Department, Directorate of Psychological Services, 1981. — 47leaves : ill ; 30cm. — (Directorate of Psychological Services papers, ISSN 0262-3293 ; no.1)
ISBN 0-86252-030-4 (pbk) : Unpriced
B82-25878

365'.6'0924 — Thailand. British prisoners, *1976-1980 — Personal observations*

Nightingale, Rita. Freed for life. — London : Marshall, Morgan & Scott, Mar.1982. — [192]p
ISBN 0-551-00921-7 (pbk) : £1.60 : CIP entry
B82-01156

365'.64 — Lisburn *(District).* **Prisons: Maze Prison. Detainees** *— Information on Ireland viewpoints*

Curtis, Liz. The H blocks : an indictment of British prison policy in the North of Ireland / text by Liz Curtis ; graphics by Jack Clafferty and the Committee to Unsell the War. — London : Information on Ireland, 1981. — 30p : ill(some col.) ; 21cm
Bibliography: p28
ISBN 0-9507381-1-5 (unbound) : £0.40
B82-13461

The H blocks : the new internment / [written and produced by the United Troops Out Movement (Central London Branch)]. — London (1 North End Road, London W14) : Information on Ireland, [1980]. — 1sheet : ill ; 89x63cm folded to 32x23cm
Includes bibliography
£0.10 B82-13463

H-Blocks : the truth : a reply to H.M. Government / foreword by Ernie Roberts. — London : Information on Ireland, [1980]. — [12]p : ill,ports ; 30cm
ISBN 0-9507381-0-7 (unbound) : £0.30
B82-13462

365'.641 — Armagh *(County).* **Prisons: Armagh Prison. Administration. Protest by Provisional IRA women prisoners,** *1979-1980*

D'Arcy, Margaretta. Tell them everything : a sojourn in the prison of Her Majesty Queen Elizabeth II at Ard Macha (Armagh) / Margaretta D'Arcy. — London : Pluto, 1981. — 127p ; 20cm
ISBN 0-86104-349-9 (pbk) : £1.95 B82-20690

365'.641 — California. San Francisco Bay. Alcatraz. Prisons: Alcatraz Federal Penitentiary. Prisoners. Attempted escapes, *1946*

Bruce, J. Campbell. Escape from Alcatraz / J. Campbell Bruce. — Rev. ed. — London : Futura, 1979, c1976 (1980 [printing]). — 217p ; 18cm
ISBN 0-7088-1692-4 (pbk) : £0.95 B82-35509

365'.643 — Great Britain. Prisoners. Communication with society

Communications in prison : a short guide. — [London] : [Home Office Library], [1982?]. — 14p : ill ; 21cm
Text and ill on inside covers
ISBN 0-86252-019-3 (pbk) : £0.05 B82-33999

365'.643 — Great Britain. Prisoners. Communication with society *— Proposals*

Standing order 5. — London : Home Office, [1981]. — 18p ; 30cm
Cover title
ISBN 0-86252-020-7 (pbk) : £1.00 B82-36819

365'.643 — Great Britain. Prisons. Adjudication

Smith, David, *19---.* Board of visitor adjudications / David Smith, Claire Austin and John Ditchfield. — London : Home Office, c1981. — v,45p ; 30cm. — (Research Unit paper ; 3)
Bibliography: p40
ISBN 0-86252-004-5 (pbk) : Unpriced
B82-39646

365'.65'0973 — United States. Prison industries

Funke, Gail S.. Assets and liabilities of correctional industries / Gail S. Funke, Billy L. Wayson, Neal Miller. — Lexington, Mass. : Lexington ; [Aldershot] : Gower [distributor], c1982. — xi,159p ; 24cm
Bibliography: p145-150. — Includes index
ISBN 0-669-04542-x : £15.00 B82-31796

365'.66 — England. Prisoners. Education

Prison education in England and Wales / edited by W. Forster. — Leicester : National Institute of Adult Education (England and Wales), 1981. — 140p ; 21cm
ISBN 0-900559-44-6 (pbk) : Unpriced : CIP rev. B82-01346

365'.7'0924 — England. Prisons. Reform. Fry, Elizabeth *— Biographies — For schools*

Hanks, Geoffrey. Friend of prisoners : the story of Elizabeth Fry / Geoffrey Hanks. — Exeter : Religious Education Press, 1981. — 30p : ill,1plan,ports ; 21cm. — (Faith in action series)
Bibliography: p29-30
ISBN 0-08-026413-1 (pbk) : £0.65
ISBN 0-08-026412-3 (pbk) : Unpriced (non net)
B82-12067

365'.7'0941 — Great Britain. Penal system. Reform *— Proposals*

Wright, Martin, *1930-.* Making good : prisons, punishment and beyond / Martin Wright ; foreword by Barbara Wootton. — [London] : Burnett, 1982. — 316p : ill ; 23cm
Bibliography: p271-292. — Includes index
ISBN 0-09-147220-2 (cased) : Unpriced : CIP rev.
ISBN 0-09-147221-0 (pbk) : £5.95 B82-09271

365'.941 — England. Prisons. Overcrowding — *Inquiry reports*

Parliamentary All-Party Penal Affairs Group. Too many prisoners : an examination of ways of reducing the prison population / Parliamentary All-Party Penal Affairs Group. — Chichester : Rose, 1980. — 56p ; 21cm
ISBN 0-85992-194-8 (pbk) : £4.00 B82-12379

365'.941 — Great Britain. Prisons

Fitzgerald, Mike. British prisons / Mike Fitzgerald and Joe Sim. — 2nd ed. — Oxford : Basil Blackwell, 1982. — 182p ; 23cm
Previous ed.: 1979. — Bibliography: p167-170. — Includes index
ISBN 0-631-12529-9 (cased) : Unpriced : CIP rev.
ISBN 0-631-12606-6 (pbk) : Unpriced
B81-22625

365'.941 — Great Britain. Prisons. Buildings. Construction. Policies *— Howard League for Penal Reform viewpoints*

Rutherford, Andrew, *1940-.* No more prison building / Andrew Rutherford and Rod Morgan on behalf of the Howard League for Penal Reform. — London (169 Clapham Rd, SW9 0PU) : The League, 1981. — 8p ; 30cm
Cover title
£0.50 (pbk) B82-04570

365'.941 — Great Britain. Prisons *— Labour Party (Great Britain) viewpoints*

Prisons. — London : Labour Party, 1982. — 15p ; 21cm. — (Socialism in the 80s) (A Labour Party discussion document)
ISBN 0-86117-090-3 (pbk) : £0.40 B82-25029

365'.941165 — Scotland. Highland Region. Dornoch. Prisons: Dornoch Town Jail, *to 1880*

Town Jail Craft Centre *(Dornoch).* Town Jail Craft Centre : a brief history. — Dornoch (Cathedral Sq., Dornoch, Sutherland) : The Centre, [1970?] (1981 [printing]). — [28]p : ill ; 21cm
Cover title. — Author: T.R. Hart
£0.50 (pbk) B82-26745

365'.941619 — Lisburn *(District).* **Prisons: Maze Prison. H Block. Prisoners. Political status. Campaigns by prisoners**

Coogan, Tim Pat. On the blanket : the H Block story / Tim Pat Coogan. — Dublin : Ward River, 1980. — xii,271p ; 18cm
ISBN 0-907085-01-6 (pbk) : £2.50 B82-29722

365'.94167 — Belfast. Prisons: Crumlin Road Prison. Prison life *— Christian viewpoints*

Jardine, David. In jail with Jesus / by David Jardine. — Belfast : Christian Journals, 1978. — 150p ; 18cm
ISBN 0-904302-52-0 (pbk) : £1.50 B82-18601

365'.942 — England. Dangerous criminals. Imprisonment

Floud, Jean. Dangerousness and criminal justice / Jean Floud and Warren Young. — London : Heinemann, 1981. — xvii,228p ; 23cm. — (Cambridge studies in criminology ; 47)
At head of title : Howard League for Penal Reform. — Bibliography: p203-221. — Includes index
ISBN 0-435-82307-8 : £14.50 : CIP rev.
B81-31843

365'.942 — England. Prisons. Great Britain. *Parliament. House of Commons. Home Affairs Committee.* **Fourth report ... session 1980-81 —** *Critical studies*

Great Britain. The prison service : the government reply to the fourth report from the Home Affairs Committee, session 1980-1981 HC412. — London : H.M.S.O., 1981. — 20p ; 25cm. — (Cmnd. ; 8446)
ISBN 0-10-184460-3 (unbound) : £2.30
B82-13299

365'.942133 — London. Hammersmith and Fulham *(London Borough).* **Prisons: Wormwood Scrubs Prison. Prisoners. Riots,** *1979 — Inquiry reports*

Great Britain. *Home Office.* Home Office statement on the background, circumstances and action subsequently taken relative to the disturbance in 'D' wing at H.M. Prison Wormwood Scrubs on 31 August 1979 ; together with the Report of an Inquiry by the Regional Director of the South East Region of the Prison Department. — London : H.M.S.O., 1982. — 63p,[12]p of plates : ill,1plan ; 25cm. — (HC ; 199)
ISBN 0-10-219982-5 (pbk) : £5.45 B82-21861

365'.942678 — Essex. Grays. North Stifford. Boys' community home schools: Ardale *(Community Home with Education)*

Mayers, Michael O.. The hard-core delinquent : an experiment in control and care in a community home with education / Michael O. Mayers. — Farnborough, Hants. : Saxon House, c1980. — ix,198p : ill ; 23cm
Bibliography: p188-192. — Includes index
ISBN 0-566-00318-x : Unpriced : CIP rev.
B80-03580

365'.944 — France. Prisons, *1810-1885*

O'Brien, Patricia. The promise of punishment : prisons in nineteenth-century France / Patricia O'Brien. — Princeton ; Guildford : Princeton University Press, c1982. — xiii,330p : ill ; 23cm
Bibliography: p305-324. — Includes index
ISBN 0-691-05339-1 : £20.10 B82-24562

365'.946'89 — Gibraltar. Prisons: Moorish Castle Prison. Social conditions

Blom-Cooper, Jane. A prison 1000 years old : a report on the Moorish Castle Prison, Gibraltar / by Jane Blom-Cooper on behalf of the Howard League for Penal Reform. — London (169 Clapham Rd, SW9 0PU) : Howard League for Penal Reform, 1982. — iii,44p ; 21cm
Cover title
Unpriced (pbk) B82-29221

365'.973 — United States. Prisons

Sherman, Michael. Imprisonment in America : choosing the future / Michael Sherman and Gordon Hawkins. — Chicago ; London : University of Chicago Press, 1981. — xi,146p : ill ; 24cm. — (Studies in crime and justice)
Includes index
ISBN 0-226-75279-8 : £12.00 B82-22277

366 — ASSOCIATIONS

366'.00945'51 — Italy. Florence. Confraternities, *1250-1600*

Weissman, Ronald F. E.. Ritual brotherhood in renaissance Florence / Ronald F.E. Weissman. — New York ; London : Academic Press, c1982. — xiii,254p : ill ; 24cm. — (Population and social structure)
Includes index
ISBN 0-12-744480-7 : £18.20 B82-30011

366'.08995105951 — Peninsular Malaysia. Chinese secret societies — *Sociological perspectives*
Fong, Mak Lau. The sociology of secret societies : a study of Chinese secret societies in Singapore and Peninsular Malaysia / Mak Lau Fong. — Kuala Lumpur ; Oxford : Oxford University Press, 1981. — ix,178p : ill,maps ; 26cm. — (East Asian social science monographs)
Includes some appendixes in Chinese. — Bibliography: p160-169. — Includes index
ISBN 0-19-580471-6 : £17.00
Also classified at 366'.08995105957
B82-11571

366'.08995105957 — Singapore. Chinese secret societies — *Sociological perspectives*
Fong, Mak Lau. The sociology of secret societies : a study of Chinese secret societies in Singapore and Peninsular Malaysia / Mak Lau Fong. — Kuala Lumpur ; Oxford : Oxford University Press, 1981. — ix,178p : ill,maps ; 26cm. — (East Asian social science monographs)
Includes some appendixes in Chinese. — Bibliography: p160-169. — Includes index
ISBN 0-19-580471-6 : £17.00
Primary classification 366'.08995105951
B82-11571

366'.1 — Freemasonary
Carr, Harry. The Freemason at work. — 6th revised ed. — Shepperton : A. Lewis, May 1981. — 1v.
Previous ed.: London : The author, 1976
ISBN 0-85318-126-8 : £6.95 : CIP entry
B81-06053

366'.1 — Freemasonry — *Christian viewpoints*
Lawrence, John, *1947-*. Freemasonry — a way of salvation? / by John Lawrence. — Bramcote : Grove, 1982. — 25p ; 21cm. — (Grove pastoral series, ISSN 0144-171x ; no.10)
Text on inside cover
ISBN 0-907536-23-9 (pbk) : £0.70 B82-33256

366.1 — Freemasonry. Symbolism
Dyer, Colin F. W.. Symbolism in craft freemasonry. — Shepperton : A. Lewis, Jan.1983. — [192]p
Originally published: 1976
ISBN 0-85318-130-6 (pbk) : £4.95 : CIP entry
B82-32858

366'.1 — London. Freemasons: Freemasons. *Emulation Lodge of Improvement* — *Rites*
Emulation second degree ritual. — London : Lewis Masonic, c1981. — 127p ; 14cm
ISBN 0-85318-127-6 : Unpriced B82-12359

The **Installing** master's guide. — 6th ed. — London : Lewis Masonic, c1981. — 94p ; 14cm
Previous ed.: 1970
ISBN 0-85318-117-9 : Unpriced B82-12358

366'.1'0321 — Freemasonry — *Encyclopaedias*
Pick, Fred L.. The Freemason's pocket reference book. — 3rd ed. — London : Muller, Jan.1983. — [448]p
Previous ed.: 1965
ISBN 0-584-11040-5 : £7.95 : CIP entry
B82-32510

366'.1'09 — Freemasonry, *to 1982*
Pick, Fred Lomax. The pocket history of Freemasonry. — 7th ed. — London : Muller, Jan.1983. — [352]p
Previous ed.: 1977
ISBN 0-584-11039-1 : £7.95 : CIP entry
B82-32854

366'.1'0924 — England. Freemasonry. Dunckerley, Thomas — *Biographies*
Chudley, Ron. The incredible Brother Thomas Dunckerley / Ron Chudley. — Exmouth (2 Hartley Rd., Exmouth EX8 2SG) : [R. Chudley], 1981. — 150p,[24]p of plates : ill,1coat of arms,facsims,ports ; 25cm
Bibliography: p150
Unpriced (pbk) B82-11619

366'.1'0924 — England. Freemasons. Dunckerley, Thomas — *Biographies*
Chudley, Ron. Thomas Dunckerley. — Shepperton : A. Lewis, Sept.1982. — [188]p
ISBN 0-85318-129-2 : £6.95 : CIP entry
B82-23859

366'.1'0942 — England. Freemasonry. Orders & degrees
Jackson, Keith B.. Beyond the craft / Keith B. Jackson. — 2nd and rev. ed. — Shepperton : Lewis Masonic, 1982, c1980. — 90p : ill,1port ; 19cm
ISBN 0-85318-128-4 (pbk) : Unpriced
B82-24649

367 — SOCIAL CLUBS

367'.068 — Great Britain. Social clubs. Management — *Manuals*
A **Handbook** of social club management. — Manchester (St. Jame's House, Charlotte St., Manchester M1 4DZ) : PA Management Consultants, Oct.1981. — [240]p
ISBN 0-902453-09-2 (pbk) : £11.95 : CIP entry
B81-32089

367'.942132 — London. Westminster *(London Borough)*. **Social clubs: East India, Devonshire, Sports and Public Schools Club,** *to 1981*
East India, Devonshire, Sports and Public Schools Club. Foursome in St. James's : the story of the East India, Devonshire, Sports and Public Schools Club / by Denys Forrest. — London (16 St. James's Sq., S.W.1) : East India, Devonshire, Sports and Public Schools Club, 1982. — xiii,207p,[25]p of plates : ill,plans,ports ; 23cm
Bibliography: p194. — Includes index
£10.00 B82-37234

367'.94215 — London. Tower Hamlets *(London Borough)*. **Working men's clubs: Jewish Working Men's Club & Institute,** *1874-1912*
Pollins, Harold. A history of the Jewish Working Mens Club & Institute 1874-1912 / Harold Pollins. — Oxford (Ruskin College, Oxford OX1 2HE) : Ruskin College Library, 1981. — 41p ; 26cm. — (Ruskin College Library occasional publications ; no.2)
Bibliography: p40-41
£2.00 (pbk) B82-07351

368 — INSURANCE

368 — Business firms. Insurance — *Conference proceedings*
Choosing and using an insurance market : report of a conference on how to reduce costs, minimise risks and improve settlements / contributors J.M. Seatter ... [et al.]. — Aldershot : Gower, c1981. — viii,82p ; 30cm. — (Gower executive report)
ISBN 0-566-03025-x (pbk) : Unpriced : CIP rev. B81-22678

368 — Captive insurance companies
Bawcutt, P. A.. Captive insurance companies : establishment, operation and management / P.A. Bawcutt. — Cambridge : Woodhead-Faulkner, 1982. — xii,235p : ill ; 25cm
Bibliography: p231-232. — Includes index
ISBN 0-85941-077-3 : £15.00 B82-17588

368 — Captive insurance companies — *Serials*
Captive insurance company review. — [No.1]-. — London (181 Queen Victoria St., EC4V 4DD) : Foresight Publications, [1981]-. — v. ; 30cm
Monthly
ISSN 0262-7701 = Captive insurance company review : £55.00 per year B82-08464

368 — Insurance
Dorfman, Mark S.. Introduction to insurance / Mark S. Dorfman. — 2nd ed. — Englewood Cliffs, N.J. ; London : Prentice-Hall, c1982. — xxi,421p : ill,forms ; 25cm. — (Prentice-Hall series in security and insurance)
Previous ed.: 1978. — Includes bibliographies and index
ISBN 0-13-485367-9 : Unpriced B82-28345

368 — Tax havens. Captive insurance companies. Organisation
Captive insurance companies in offshore tax havens. — [London?] : Pointon York ; [Leicester] : [Current Account] [[distributor]], c1979. — 14p : ; 18x26cm. — (Current account mini reports)
Bibliography: p13-14
ISBN 0-906840-01-5 (spiral) : Unpriced
B82-06682

368'.0023'41 — Great Britain. Insurance — *Career guides*
Insurance / [written, designed and produced by SGS Education]. — Walton on Thames : Nelson, 1982. — 15p : ill ; 28cm. — (Career profiles ; 25)
ISBN 0-17-438366-5 (unbound) : Unpriced
B82-27849

Verner, Jordan. Careers in insurance / Jordan Verner. — London : Kogan Page, 1982. — 124p : ill,1form ; 18cm
Bibliography: p119-120
ISBN 0-85038-474-5 (cased) : Unpriced : CIP rev.
ISBN 0-85038-475-3 (pbk) : £2.50 B81-40252

368'.0025 — Insurance companies — *Directories* — *Serials*
Financial times world insurance year book. — 1982/83. — London : Longman, Sept.1982. — [470]p. — (Financial times international year books : information to business)
ISBN 0-582-90312-2 : £39.00 : CIP entry
ISSN 0309-751x B82-22806

368'.0028'5404 — Great Britain. Insurance companies. Applications of microcomputer systems
Curran, Susan. New technology and insurance / Susan Curran. — London : Fourmat, 1980. — vi,106p ; 22cm
Bibliography: p99-101. — Includes index
ISBN 0-906840-24-4 (pbk) : Unpriced
B82-06620

368'.005 — Insurance — *Serials*
Policy holder insurance news. — Vol.99, no.27 (July 10 1981). — London : Kluwer, 1981-. — v. : ill,ports ; 30cm
Weekly. — Continues: Policy holder insurance journal
ISSN 0262-4281 = Policy holder insurance news (corrected) : £35.00 per year B82-03395

368'.0068'4 — Great Britain. Insurance companies. Corporate planning
Corporate planning in the insurance industry / report by Advanced Study Group No. 213 of the Insurance Institute of London. — London : The Institute, 1982. — 49p ; 21cm
Text on inside cover. — Bibliography: p49
ISBN 0-900493-62-3 (pbk) : Unpriced
B82-39511

368'.012 — Reinsurance
Kiln, Robert. Reinsurance in practice / by Robert Kiln. — London : Witherby, 1981. — x,330p ; 23cm
Includes index
ISBN 0-900886-55-2 : £21.00 B82-09660

368'.012 — Reinsurance. Implications of inflation
Neave, J. A. S.. Inflation and the reinsurer : a luncheon talk by J.A.S. Neave C.B.E., J.P., to the Toronto Chapter of the Society of Fellows on Wednesday, 17th March, 1982. — [London] ([Moorfields House, Moorfields, London EC2Y 9AL]) : [Mercantile and General Reinsurance Company], c1982. — [11]p ; 21cm
Unpriced (pbk) B82-32990

368'.012'094212 — Great Britain. Underwriting. Organisations: Corporation of Lloyd's
Moore, John. Inside Lloyds of London. — London (10 Archway Close, N19 3TD) : Sinclair Browne, Apr.1982. — [192]p
ISBN 0-86300-009-6 : £12.50 : CIP entry
B82-04703

368'.014'0924 — Dorset & Hampshire. Insurance. Claims — *Personal observations*
Mitchell, Reginald. [Truth will out]. Amusing tales from Hampshire and Dorset / by Reginald Mitchell. — Sherborne : Dorset Publishing, 1979 (1980 [printing]). — 94p ; 22cm
Includes index
ISBN 0-902129-41-4 (pbk) : £1.50 B82-09238

368.2 — TRANSPORT INSURANCE

368.2 — Cargo handling. Insurance

Cargo handlers : liabilities & insurance / by John Sandys Dawes ... [et al.]. — London : Published and distributed on behalf of Technical Committee of the United Kingdom section of ICHCA by the ICHCA Central Office, c1982. — 73p : ill ; 30cm. — (Briefing pamphlet, ISSN 0143-2834 ; 5)
ISBN 0-906297-22-2 (pbk) : £15.00 (£7.50 to members) B82-34247

368.2′2 — Shipping. Insurance — *Conference proceedings*

Salvage, general average and marine insurance / sponsored by Ernest Robert Lindley & Sons B.V. ; organised by Lloyd′s of London Press Ltd. — [London] : [Lloyd′s of London], [1982?]. — 1v.(various foliations) ; 31cm. — (Europort ′81 conferences)
ISBN 0-907432-17-4 : Unpriced B82-31131

368.2′2012 — Shipping. Reinsurance

Brown, Robert H. (Robert Henry), *1921-*. Marine reinsurance / by Robert H. Brown and Peter B. Reed. — London : Witherby, 1981. — xi,343p : forms ; 23cm
Includes index
ISBN 0-900886-61-7 : £21.00 B82-11913

368.2′2012 — Shipping. Reinsurance — *Encyclopaedias*

Brown, Robert H. (Robert Henry), *1921-*. Marine reinsurance terms and abbreviations / by Robert H. Brown. — London : Witherby, 1981. — 32p ; 21cm
ISBN 0-900886-58-7 (pbk) : £1.50 B82-08328

368.2′2014′0942 — Shipping: Insurance in England. Claims

Goodacre, J. Kenneth. Marine insurance claims / by J. Kenneth Goodacre. — 2nd ed. — London : Witherby, c1981. — liv,1015p,[12]p of plates : ill,1facsim ; 23cm. — (Monument series)
Previous ed.: 1974. — Includes index
ISBN 0-900886-53-6 : £35.00 B82-14744

Marine claims (hull) for indemnity : the Eugenides Foundation, Athens, April 29/30, 1982. — [London] : [Lloyd′s of London Press], [1982]. — [139]leaves : forms ; 31cm
Conference papers
ISBN 0-907432-40-9 : Unpriced B82-37328

368.3 — INSURANCE AGAINST DEATH, OLD AGE, ILLNESS, INJURY

368.3′2′00941 — Great Britain. Life assurance

Trimm, Leonard H.. Life assurance and financial planning / by Leonard H. Trimm, with contributions by Peter M. Smith and Brian M. Evans. — London : Financial Times Business, c1981. — vi,316p : 2forms ; 24cm
Includes index
ISBN 0-902101-07-2 : Unpriced B82-12088

368.3′2′00941 — Great Britain. Life assurance companies: Friends′ Provident Life Office, *to 1982*

Tregoning David. Friends of life : Friends′ Provident Life Office 1832-1982 / David Tregoning & Hugh Cockerell. — London : Melland, c1982. — 196p : ill(some col.),facsims,ports(some col.) ; 26cm
Facsims on lining papers. — Includes index
ISBN 0-9500730-8-3 : £8.50 B82-26294

368.4 — NATIONAL INSURANCE

368.4 — Great Britain. Supplementary benefits. Violent claimants. Visiting. Procedure — *Proposals*

Review of visiting procedures : report of a working party. — [London] ([Alexander Fleming House, Elephant and Castle, SE1 6BY]) : [Department of Health and Social Security], 1981. — 11p in various pagings ; 30cm
Unpriced (unbound) B82-40107

368.4′0088054 — Great Britain. Children. Social security benefits — *Child Poverty Action Group viewpoints*

Piachaud, David. Children and poverty / by David Piachaud. — London : Child Poverty Action Group, 1981. — 29p ; 21cm. — (Poverty research series ; 9)
ISBN 0-903963-50-7 (pbk) : £0.90 B82-12734

368.4′0094 — Western Europe. Personnel. Social security benefits

Callund, David. Employee benefits in Europe / David Callund. — 4th ed. / editor Melvin Nightingale. — London : Callund & Co., 1981. — 1v.(loose-leaf) ; 25cm
Previous ed.: 1978
ISBN 0-905607-02-3 : Unpriced
Also classified at 331.25′2′094 B82-12793

368.4′0094 — Western Europe. Social security, *1881-1981*

The **Evolution** of social insurance, 1881-1981. — London : Frances Pinter, Apr.1982. — [500]p
ISBN 0-86187-242-8 : £20.00 : CIP entry B82-11098

368.4′00941 — Great Britain. Handicapped married women. Social security benefits. Provision. Discrimination

Behind closed doors : a report on the public response to an advertising campaign about discrimination against married women in certain social security benefits. — Manchester : Equal Opportunities Commission, [1981?]. — 30p ; 21cm
ISBN 0-905829-50-6 (pbk) : Unpriced B82-14333

368.4′00941 — Great Britain. Handicapped persons, to 65 years. Social security benefits — *Practical information*

Benefits for handicapped people of working age / [Greater London Association for the Disabled]. — London (1 Thorpe Close, W10 5XL) : Greater London Association for the Disabled, 1981. — [4]p ; 30cm
£2.50 for 50 copies (unbound) B82-14221

368.4′00941 — Great Britain. Non-means tested social security benefits — *Manuals* — *For claimants*

Rowland, Mark. Rights guide to non-means-tested social security benefits. — 4th ed. / Mark Rowland. — London (1 Macklin St., WC2B 5NH) : Child Poverty Action Group, 1981. — 160p ; 21cm
Previous ed.: 1980. — Includes index
£2.00 (pbk) B82-26608

368.4′00941 — Great Britain. Social security benefits

Bennett, Frances. Your social security : know your rights : the questions and the answers / Frances Bennett. — Harmondsworth : Penguin, 1982. — 363p ; 18cm
Includes index
ISBN 0-14-022385-1 (pbk) : £1.95 B82-40951

368.4′00941 — Great Britain. Social security benefits, *1982* — *For trade unionism*

State benefits 1982 : a guide for trade unionists. — London : LRD, 1982. — 34p ; 21cm
Text on inside covers
ISBN 0-900508-48-5 (pbk) : £0.60 B82-19428

368.4′00941 — Great Britain. Social security benefits. Administration. Great Britain. *Parliament. House of Commons. Social Services Committee.* **First report ... session 1979-80** — *Critical studies*

Great Britain. *Department of Health and Social Security.* Reply to the first report from the Social Services Committee on arrangements for paying social security benefits / Department of Health and Social Security. — London : H.M.S.O., [1980]. — 60p : ill ; 25cm. — (CMND ; 8106)
ISBN 0-10-181060-1 (pbk) : £4.20 B82-15136

368.4′00941 — Great Britain. Social security benefits — *For welfare work*

Cohen, Ruth. Welfare rights / Ruth Cohen and Andrée Rushton. — London : Heinemann Educational, 1982. — 117p ; 22cm. — (Community care practice handbooks ; 10)
Bibliography: p111-112. — Includes index
ISBN 0-435-82175-x (pbk) : £2.95 : CIP rev. B81-35695

368.4′00941 — Great Britain. Social security — *Labour (Great Britain) viewpoints*

Social security : a Labour Party discussion document. — [London] : The Party, [1981]. — 51p : 1ill ; 21cm. — (Socialism in the 80s)
Cover title
ISBN 0-86117-082-2 (pbk) : £1.00 B82-05514

368.4′00941 — Great Britain. Supplementary benefits — *For claimants*

TUC guide to supplementary benefits. — London : TUC, 1981. — 79p ; 21cm
£0.75 (pbk) B82-20327

368.4′00941 — Great Britain. Supplementary benefits. Policies of government

Nixon, Jaqi. The review of the supplementary benefit scheme : a case study / Jaqi Nixon. — Ascot (Sunningdale Park, Ascot, Berks, SL5 0QE) : Civil Service College, 1980. — 17p ; 30cm. — (C.S.C. working paper ; no.25)
Cover title. — Bibliography: p17
Unpriced (pbk) B82-16402

368.4′00941 — Great Britain. Women. Social security benefits — *Socialist viewpoints*

Women and social security. — London (296 Bethnal Green Rd., E2) : The Federation of Claimants Union, [1982?]. — 28p : ill ; 29cm
Unpriced (unbound) B82-26169

368.4′00973 — United States. Social security

Turnbull, John G.. Economic and social security : social insurance and other approaches. — 5th ed. / C. Arthur Williams, Jr, John G. Turnbull, Earl F. Cheit. — New York ; Chichester : Wiley, c1982. — vii,608p ; 24cm
Previous ed.: New York : Ronald Press, 1973. — Includes bibliographies and index
ISBN 0-471-08409-3 : £17.70 B82-28941

368.4′014′0941423 — Scotland. Strathclyde Region. Colonsay & Tiree. Supplementary benefits. Claims, *1978-1981*

The **Case** for an island cost of living addition for DHSS claimants. — [Glasgow] ([20 India St., Glasgow G2 4PF]) : Strathclyde Regional Council, [1981]. — [7]p ; 34cm
Unpriced (unbound) B82-24789

368.4′015′0941 — Great Britain. Social security benefits. Administration. Costs — *Inquiry reports*

Great Britain. *Parliament. House of Commons. Committee of Public Accounts.* Twenty-sixth report from the Committee of Public Accounts : together with the proceedings of the committee, the minutes of evidence and appendices : session 1979-80 : Department of Health & Social Security, Government Actuary : social security benefits, costs of administration, estimated and statistical accounting. — London : H.M.S.O., [1980]. — x,32p ; 25cm. — ([HC] ; 765)
ISBN 0-10-027659-8 (pbk) : £4.00 B82-09506

368.4′015′0973 — United States. Social security. Finance — *Conference proceedings*

Social security financing / edited by Felicity Skidmore. — Cambridge, Mass. ; London : MIT Press, c1981. — xiii,295p : ill ; 24cm
Conference papers. — Includes bibliographies and index
ISBN 0-262-19196-2 : £21.00 B82-09577

368.4′1 — Great Britain. Industries. Personnel. Fingers. Vibration induced white finger. Industrial injuries benefits. Provision — *Inquiry reports*

Vibration white finger : report by the Industrial Injuries Advisory Council in accordance with Section 141 of the Social Security Act 1975 on the question whether, having regard to those sections of the Council′s 1975 report on vibration syndrome relating to vibration white finger and to the new evidence on that condition which has since come forward, vibration white finger should be prescribed under the act. — London : H.M.S.O., [1981]. — 15p ; 25cm
ISBN 0-10-183500-0 (unbound) : £1.90 B82-02754

368.4'1 — Personnel with industrial diseases. Compensation — *Inquiry reports*

Industrial Injuries Advisory Council. Industrial diseases : a review of the schedule and question of individual proof : report by the Industrial Injuries Advisory Council on the questions whether adjustments should be made in the terms of prescription of the diseases prescribed in Part I of Schedule I to the Social Security (Industrial Injuries) (Prescribed Diseases) Regulations 1980 and whether compensation should be extended to any individual claimant who can show that his disease is occupational in origin and a particular risk of his occupation. — London : H.M.S.O., [1981]. — 76p ; 25cm. — (Cmnd. ; 8393)
ISBN 0-10-183930-8 (unbound) : £4.75
B82-05869

368.4'2 — Great Britain. Handicapped persons. Supplementary benefits

Stowell, Richard. Disabled people on supplementary benefit : interim report / Richard Stowell. — Oxford : Centre for Socio-Legal Studies ; [London] : Social Science Research Council, 1980. — 145p : ill,forms ; 21cm. — (Research study / Centre for Socio-Legal Studies ; no.3)
ISBN 0-86226-065-5 (pbk) : Unpriced
B82-35003

368.4'24'00941 — Great Britain. National insurance benefits: Maternity grants. Great Britain. *Department of Health and Social Security*. **Fresh look at maternity benefits** — *Critical studies*

Institute of Personnel Management. A fresh look at maternity benefits : comments of the Institute of Personnel Management on the DHSS consultative document. — London (IPM House, Camp Road, Wimbledon, SW19 4UW) : The Institute, 1980. — 7p : ill ; 30cm
Unpriced B82-26633

368.4'24'00941 — Great Britain. Unmarried pregnant women. Social security benefits

Single and pregnant : a guide to benefits. — [London] ([255 Kentish Town Rd., NW5 2LX]) : One Parent Families, 1982. — 24p ; 21cm
£0.60 (pbk) B82-32070

368.4'3'00941 — Great Britain. Handicapped persons, 65 years-. Social security benefits — *Practical information*

Benefits for handicapped people of pension age / [Greater London Association for the Disabled]. — London (1 Thorpe Close, W10 5XL) : Greater London Association for the Disabled, 1981. — [4]p ; 30cm
£2.50 for 50 copies (unbound) B82-14422

368.4'3'00941 — Great Britain. State superannuation schemes

Creedy, John, *1949-*. State pensions in Britain / John Creedy. — Cambridge : Cambridge University Press, 1982. — ix,102p : ill ; 24cm. — (Occasional papers / The National Institute of Economic and Social Research ; 33)
Includes index
ISBN 0-521-24519-2 : £10.50 : CIP rev.
B82-11480

368.4'3'00941 — Great Britain. State superannuation schemes. Contracting-out by members of occupational superannuation schemes. Financial aspects — *Inquiry reports*

Great Britain. *Department of Health and Social Security*. Occupational pension schemes review of certain contracting-out terms : report by the Secretary of State for Social Services by command of Her Majesty March 1982. — London : H.M.S.O., 1982. — 5p ; 25cm. — (Cmnd. ; 8518)
ISBN 0-10-185180-4 (unbound) : £1.15
B82-23830

Great Britain. *Government Actuary*. Occupational pension schemes review of certain contracting-out terms : reports by the Government Actuary in accordance with sections 28 and 46 of the Social Security Pensions Act 1975. — London : H.M.S.O., 1982. — 21p ; 25cm. — (Cmnd. ; 8516)
ISBN 0-10-185160-x (unbound) : £2.30
B82-23829

368.5 — ACCIDENT INSURANCE

368.5 — England. Professional liability insurance

Jess, Digby Charles. A guide to the insurance of professional negligence risks / Digby Charles Jess. — London : Butterworths, 1982. — xxiv,239p ; 21cm
Includes index
ISBN 0-406-25710-8 (pbk) : Unpriced
B82-38731

368.5 — Great Britain. Travel agencies & tour operators. Liability insurance

Airey, D. W.. Travel agents and tour operators liability and its insurance in Great Britain / D.W. Airey, R.G. Bamford. — [Guildford] : [Department of Hotel, Catering and Tourism Management, University of Surrey GU2 5XH], [1981]. — ii,61p ; 22cm
Cover title. — Bibliography: p60-61
ISBN 0-902116-01-0 (pbk) : Unpriced
B82-04438

368.8 — INSURANCE. MISCELLANEOUS TYPES

368.8'15'00941 — Great Britain. Business firms. Consequential loss insurance

Hibbitt, Tony. A new approach to consequential loss insurance / by Tony Hibbitt. — London (20 Aldermanbury, EC2V 7HY) : Chartered Insurance Institute, c1982. — 18p : 2forms ; 26cm
Unpriced (pbk) B82-28245

Riley, Denis, *1905-*. Consequential loss and business interruption insurances and claims / by Denis Riley. — 5th ed. — London : Sweet & Maxwell, 1981. — x,499columns,15p ; 26cm
Previous ed.: 1977. — Includes index
ISBN 0-421-28780-2 : £27.50 : CIP rev.
B81-34968

368.8'4 — Contractors. Performance bonds

Performance bonds. — [London?] : Pointon York ; [Leicester] : [Current Account] [[distributor]], c1979. — 9p ; 18x26cm. — (Current account mini reports)
ISBN 0-906840-07-4 (spiral) : Unpriced
B82-06685

368.8'5 — Great Britain. *Export Credits Guarantee Department*

Great Britain. *Export Credits Guarantee Department*. ECGD services : the services of the British Government's Export Credits Guarantee Department : credit insurance, investment insurance, support for bank finance / [prepared by the Exports Credit Guarantee Department and the Central Office of Information]. — Rev. — [London] ([P.O. Box 272, Aldermanbury House, Aldermanbury, EC2P 2EL]) : [The Department], 1979. — 64p : ill,1map ; 24cm
Includes index
Unpriced (pbk) B82-05492

368.8'5 — Great Britain. *Export Credits Guarantee Department* — *Inquiry reports*

Great Britain. *Parliament. House of Commons. Committee of Public Accounts*. Twenty-second report from the Committee of Public Accounts : together with the proceedings of the committee, the minutes of evidence and appendices : session 1979-80 : Export Credits Guarantee Department : special guarantees scheme : operation of the tender to contract scheme, export credit insurance and guarantees for goods manufactured outside the United Kingdom. — London : H.M.S.O., [1980]. — xiv,23p ; 25cm. — ([HC] ; 740)
ISBN 0-10-027409-9 (pbk) : £2.80 B82-09500

368.8'5 — Great Britain. *Export Credits Guarantee Department* — *Practical information*

Great Britain. *Export Credits Guarantee Department*. ECGD : your questions answered / [prepared by the Export Credits Guarantee Department and the Central Office of Information]. — [London] ([PO Box 272, Aldermanbury House, Aldermanbury, EC2P 2EL]) : The Department, [1980]. — 8p ; 21cm
Cover title. — Text on inside covers
Unpriced (pbk) B82-05493

368.9 — INSURANCE. HISTORICAL AND GEOGRAPHICAL TREATMENT

368'.941 — Great Britain. Insurance

Allen, Margaret, *1933-*. A guide to insurance / Margaret Allen. — London : Pan, 1982. — 175p : facsims ; 20cm
Includes index
ISBN 0-330-26538-5 (pbk) : £1.95 B82-15208

Cockerell, H. A. L.. What goes on in insurance? / Hugh Cockerell. — Cambridge : Woodhead-Faulkner, in association with the British Insurance Brokers' Association, 1982. — 95p : ill,2facsims,1plan ; 22cm
Bibliography: p89-90
ISBN 0-85941-160-5 (cased) : £5.75
ISBN 0-85941-161-3 (pbk) : £2.75 B82-38155

368'.941'0212 — Great Britain. Non-life insurance — *Statistics*

Composite insurance commentary : the non-life insurance market in the United Kingdom. — London (Bow Bells House, Bread St., EC4M 9EL) : W. Greenwell & Co., 1981. — 33leaves ; 22x23cm. — (Financial shares service)
£75.00 (unbound) B82-13586

368'.941'025 — Great Britain. Insurance companies — *Directories* — *Serials*

Insurance register. — 1982-. — [London] ([42 New Bond St., EC2M 1QY]) : City Financial Business Publications, 1982-. — v. ; 29cm
Annual
ISSN 0261-555X = Insurance register : Unpriced B82-36714

368'.941'05 — Great Britain. Insurance — *Serials*

The **Insuror** / Institute of Insurance Consultants. — Vol.1, ed.1 (June 1980)-. — Hitchin (90 Tilehouse St., Hitchin, Herts.) : The Institute, 1980-. — v. : ill,ports ; 30cm
Four issues yearly. — Continues: Newsletter (Institute of Insurance Consultants). — Description based on: Vol.2, ed.2 (Nov. 1981)
ISSN 0262-6497 = Insuror : Unpriced
B82-15141

368'.941'068 — Great Britain. Insurance companies. Management

A **Selection** of papers on management services topics (1978-1981). — London : Insurance Institute of London, 1982. — 64p ; 21cm. — (Booklet / Insurance Institute of London ; no.3)
Cover title
ISBN 0-900493-61-5 (pbk) : £2.50 B82-34291

368'.973 — United States. Insurance

Vaughan, Emmett J.. Fundamentals of risk and insurance. — 3rd ed / Emmett J. Vaughan. — New York ; Chichester : Wiley, c1982. — 673p : ill,forms ; 25cm
Previous ed.: 1978. — Includes index
ISBN 0-471-09951-1 : £19.60 B82-26496

369.4 — YOUTH ORGANISATIONS

369.4 — Great Britain. Youth councils

Denham, John. A democratic voice? : the changing role of youth councils / John Denham & Martin Notley. — Leicester : National Youth Bureau, 1982. — 107p : ill ; 21cm
ISBN 0-86155-054-4 (pbk) : £2.50 B82-32958

369.4 — Great Britain. Youth councils: British Youth Council. Relations with Eastern European young persons' organisations, *1976-1981*

Stanley, Nigel. BYC and Eastern Europe : a report of the relations between the British Youth Council and the youth organisations of Eastern Europe since 1976 / by Nigel Stanley. — London (57 Chalton St., NW1 1HU) : British Youth Council, 1981. — 20p : ill,col.maps ; 30cm
Text on inside cover
Unpriced (pbk) B82-38456

369.4'025'416 — Northern Ireland. Young persons' organisations — *Directories*

Northern Ireland youth service directory. — Belfast : Standing Conference of Youth Organisations in Northern Ireland, 1979. — 1v.(loose-leaf) ; 32cm
ISBN 0-906797-03-9 : Unpriced B82-04099

369.4′0941 — Great Britain. Youth movements. Organisations: British Youth Council. Branches. Organisations

Starting a local youth council. — Pilot ed. — [London] ([Local Youth Affairs Dept., British Youth Council, 57 Chalton St., NW1 1HU]) : Local Youth Councils Development Project, [198-]. — [25]leaves ; 30cm
£1.00 (pbk) B82-35513

369.4′0941 — Great Britain. Youth movements. Organisations: British Youth Council — *Serials*

British Youth Council. Annual report / British Youth Council. — ′77-′78-. — London (57 Chalton St., NW1 1HU) : The Council, 1978-. — v. : ill,ports ; 21cm
Description based on: ′80-′81 issue
ISSN 0263-8932 = Annual report - British Youth Council : Unpriced B82-33873

369.4′0941 — Great Britain. Youth movements. Role of young persons

British Youth Council. Putting the 'youth' in the youth service : BYC evidence to the review group on the youth service. — London (57 Chalton St., NW1) : British Youth Council, [1982?]. — [19]p in various pagings ; 30cm
£0.50 (unbound) B82-35512

369.42′06′041 — Great Britain. Boys′ clubs. Organisations: National Association of Boys′ Clubs — *Conference proceedings*

Operation 5 : an opportunity for members to voice opinions on matters that concern them : Sheffield University, September 1981, report and recommendations / National Association of Boys′ Clubs. — London (24 Highbury Grove, N5 2EA) : The association, 1981. — 1folded sheet(6p) : ill,ports ; 30x21cm
Conference report
Unpriced B82-23279

369.43 — Cub scouts. Activities. Planning — *Manuals*

Barrow, Jean. A pack scouter′s activity book / by Jean Barrow. — Rev. ed.. — Glasgow : Brown, Son & Ferguson, c1981. — vii,149p : ill ; 18cm
Previous ed.: i.e. 2nd ed. 1978
ISBN 0-85174-415-x (pbk) : £4.00 B82-02586

369.43′0941 — Great Britain. Boys′ organisations: Scout Association — *Regulations*

Scout Association. The policy, organisation and rules of the Scout Association. — 3rd ed
Pt.2: Training. — London : The Association. — 1982, c1977. — 304p : ill ; 18cm
Previous ed.: 1980?
ISBN 0-85165-169-0 (pbk) : £1.75 B82-31375

369.43′09438 — Poland. Scouting — *Polish texts*

Szczęsny, Wojciech Bogusław. W kręgu wspomnień harcerskiej piosenki / Wojciech Bogusław Szczęsny. — London : Veritas Foundation Publication Centre, [198-]. — 168p ; 21cm
Unpriced (pbk) B82-12176

369.46′3 — Brownie Guides. Activities — *Manuals*

The **Brownie** Guide handbook / illustrated by Jennetta Vise. — 3rd ed., rev.. — London (17 Buckingham Palace Rd., SW1W 0PT) : Girl Guides Association, 1980 (1981 [printing]). — 189p : col.ill,music ; 22cm
Includes index
£0.95 (pbk) B82-28247

369.46′3 — Great Britain. Girl Guides & Brownie Guides. Activities connected with woodlands — *Manuals*

Morton, Brenda. The woodland book for Guides and Brownies / by Brenda Morton ; with drawings by Juliet Renny. — Glasgow : Published in collaboration with the Girl Guides Association [by] Brown, Son & Ferguson, 1972 (1982 [printing]). — vii,121p : ill,forms ; 19cm
Includes index
ISBN 0-85174-256-4 (pbk) : Unpriced B82-32486

369.46′3′09 — Girl Guides, *to 1979*

History notes. — [London] ([17-19 Buckingham Palace Rd., SW1W 0PT]) : [Girl Guides Association], 1980. — 31p : music ; 15x22cm
Bibliography: p29
£0.50 (pbk) B82-26362

370 — EDUCATION

370 — Education

Aspects of education : selected papers from the Dartington Conference / edited by Mark Braham. — Chichester : Wiley, c1982. — xxvi,215p : ill ; 24cm
Includes bibliographies and index
ISBN 0-471-28019-4 (cased) : £26.00 : CIP rev.
ISBN 0-471-28022-4 (pbk) : Unpriced B82-04853

Loukes, Harold. Education. — Oxford : Martin Robertson, Jan.1983. — [152]p
ISBN 0-85520-598-9 (cased) : £12.50 : CIP entry
ISBN 0-85520-599-7 (pbk) : £4.95 B82-33113

370 — Education — *Festschriften*

A **Volume** of essays for Elizabeth Halsall / compiled and edited by Colin Brock and Raymond Ryba on behalf of the University of Hull Department and Institute of Educational Studies and the British Comparative Education Society. — Hull : University of Hull Institute of Education, 1980. — 163p : ill ; 21cm. — (Aspects of education ; no.22)
Includes index
ISBN 0-85958-208-6 (pbk) : Unpriced B82-40860

370 — Education. Implications of 'North-South, a programme for survival' — *Conference proceedings*

North-south debate : the educational implications of the Brandt report : the proceedings of a conference held at the University of Bristol School of Education, Bristol, UK, convened between 5 and 7 January 1981, and organized by the centre for overseas studies / edited by Roger M. Garrett. — Windsor : NFER-Nelson, c1981. — 165p ; 30cm
Includes bibliographies
ISBN 0-85633-228-3 (pbk) : £8.50 B82-05263

370 — Education. Innovation

Adams, Raymond S.. The process of educational innovation : an international perspective / Raymond S. Adams with David Chen. — London : Kogan Page, 1981. — xi,284p : ill,plans ; 22cm
At head of title: International Institute for Educational Planning. — Bibliography: p283-284
ISBN 0-85038-511-3 (pbk) : Unpriced : CIP rev. B81-31086

370 — Education. Role of critical thought

McPeck, John E.. Critical thinking and education / John E. McPeck. — Oxford : Robertson, 1981. — 170p : ill ; 23cm. — (Issues and ideas in education series)
Bibliography: p163-167. — Includes index
ISBN 0-85520-383-8 (cased) : Unpriced : CIP rev.
ISBN 0-85520-384-6 (pbk) : £4.50 B81-04291

370 — Education. Role of language

Language perspectives : papers from the Educational review / edited by Barrie Wade. — London : Heinemann Educational, 1982. — 193p ; 22cm
Bibliography: p185-193
ISBN 0-435-10910-3 (pbk) : £4.95 : CIP rev. B81-34503

370 — Education — *Soviet viewpoints*

Lunacharskiĭ, A. V.. On education : selected articles and speeches / Anatoli Lunacharsky ; [translated from the Russian by Ruth English]. — Moscow : Progress ; [London] : distributed by Central Books, c1981. — 328p ; 21cm
Translation of: Ob obrazovanii i vospitanii. — Includes index
ISBN 0-7147-1706-1 : £3.50 B82-19610

370 — Educational systems. Development — *Sociological perspectives*

The **Sociology** of educational expansion. — London : Sage Publications, Sept.1982. — [324] p. — (Sage studies in international sociology ; 27)
ISBN 0-8039-9773-6 : £15.50 : CIP entry B82-20484

370 — Multicultural societies. Education

Bullivant, Brian M.. The pluralist dilemma in education : six case studies / Brian M. Bullivant. — Sydney ; London : Allen & Unwin, 1981. — xi,267p ; 23cm
Bibliography: p245-264. — Includes index
ISBN 0-86861-266-9 : Unpriced B82-01224

The **School** in the multicultural society : a reader / edited by Alan James and Robert Jeffcoate. — London : Harper & Row in association with the Open University Press, c1981. — xiii,309p ; 22cm. — (Open University set book)
Includes index
ISBN 0-06-318195-9 (cased) : Unpriced : CIP rev.
ISBN 0-06-318196-7 (pbk) : Unpriced B81-33970

370′.1 — Children. Education. Theories, *1861-1862*

Tolstoĭ, L. N.. Tolstoy on education. — London : Athlone Press, Nov.1981. — [328]p
ISBN 0-485-11198-5 : £18.00 : CIP entry B81-30559

370′.1 — Education. Applications of theories of liberty

Strike, Kenneth. Liberty and learning. — Oxford : Robertson, Dec.1981. — [224]p. — (Issues and ideas in education series)
ISBN 0-85520-431-1 (cased) : £10.00 : CIP entry
ISBN 0-85520-432-x (pbk) : £3.95 B81-31649

370′.1 — Education — *Philosophical perspectives*

Barrow, Robin. An introduction to philosophy of education. — 2nd ed. — London : Methuen, Oct.1982. — [216]p
Previous ed.: 1975
ISBN 0-416-30330-7 (cased) : £8.50 : CIP entry
ISBN 0-416-30340-4 (pbk) : £3.95 B82-24490

Kleinig, John. Philosophical issues in education / John Kleinig. — London : Croom Helm, c1982. — 306p ; 23cm
Bibliography: p269-294. — Includes index
ISBN 0-7099-1517-9 (cased) : £12.95 : CIP rev.
ISBN 0-7099-1518-7 (pbk) : Unpriced B82-04469

Moore, T. W.. Philosophy of education : an introduction / T.W. Moore. — London : Routledge & Kegan Paul, 1982. — xi,142p ; 22cm. — (International library of the philosophy of education)
Bibliography: p138-139. — Includes index
ISBN 0-7100-9192-3 (pbk) : £3.95 B82-39520

Power, Edward J.. Philosophy of education : studies in philosophies, schooling and educational policies / Edward J. Power. — Englewood Cliffs ; London : Prentice-Hall, c1982. — xiii,385p ; 24cm
Bibliography: p367-375. — Includes index
ISBN 0-13-663252-1 : £14.95 B82-16699

370′.1 — Education — *Philosophical perspectives — For Nigerian students*

Akinpelu, J. A.. An introduction to philosophy of education / J.A. Akinpelu. — London : Macmillan, 1981. — xi,252p ; 22cm. — (Studies in Nigerian education series)
Includes bibliographies and index
ISBN 0-333-30696-1 (pbk) : Unpriced B82-06871

370′.1 — Education. Role of arts. Aristotle. 'Politics' — *Critical studies*

Lord, Carnes. Education and culture in the political thought of Aristotle / by Carnes Lord. — Ithaca ; London : Cornell University Press, 1982. — 226p ; 23cm
Bibliography: p221-223. — Includes index
ISBN 0-8014-1412-1 : £13.25 B82-36991

370′.1 — Education. Theories of Mason, Charlotte M.

King, Jenny. Charlotte Mason reviewed : a philosophy of education / Jenny King. — Ilfracombe : Stockwell, 1981. — 61p ; 19cm
ISBN 0-7223-1519-8 (pbk) : £2.10 B82-12284

370.11 — Education. Objectives
White, John, *1934-*. The aims of education restated / John White. — London : Routledge & Kegan Paul, 1982. — xi,177p ; 23cm
Bibliography: p173-174. — Includes index
ISBN 0-7100-0941-0 (cased) : £8.95
ISBN 0-7100-0998-4 (pbk) : £4.95 B82-16880

370.11'14 — Children. Moral education — *For parents*
Peters, R. S.. Moral development and moral education. — London : Allen & Unwin, Oct.1981. — [192]p. — (Unwin education books)
ISBN 0-04-370107-8 (pbk) : £4.50 : CIP entry B81-26787

370.11'3 — Great Britain. Schools. Cooperation with industries
Jamieson, Ian. Schools and industry. — London : Methuen Educational, Nov.1982. — [256]p. — (Schools Council working papers ; 73)
ISBN 0-423-51070-3 (pbk) : £6.95 : CIP entry B82-29127

370.11'3 — Great Britain. Schools. Cooperation with industries. Organisations — *Directories*
Schools and industry : a guide to schools-industry links / [Bank Education Service ... et al.]. — [London] : [Department of Industry, Industry/Education Unit], [1982?]. — 16p ; 21cm
Cover title. — Text on covers
Unpriced (pbk) B82-38481

370.11'3 — Vocational education. Supervision
Bjorkquist, David C.. Supervision in vocational education : management of human resources / David C. Bjorkquist. — Boston ; London : Allyn and Bacon, c1982. — x,238p : ill ; 25cm
Includes bibliographies and index
ISBN 0-205-07357-3 : £16.95 B82-09812

370.11'3'0942 — England. Vocational education *compared with* **vocational education in West Germany**
The **Anglo-German** report / edited by Jean Finlayson, David Parkes and Russ Russell. — Bristol : Further Education Staff College, 1979. — 85p : 2ill ; 30cm. — (Comparative papers in further education, ISSN 0143-327x ; no.2)
Conference papers
£2.25 (pbk)
Also classified at 370.11'3'0943 B82-24182

370.11'3'0942 — England. Vocational education. Participation of employers
Wray, Monika Jamieson. Employer involvement in schemes of unified vocational preparation / Monika Jamieson Wray, Sheelagh Hill, John Collobear. — Windsor : NFER-Nelson, 1982. — vi,152p ; 22cm
ISBN 0-7005-0492-3 (pbk) : £7.95 B82-38151

370.11'3'0943 — West Germany. Vocational education
Andrews, Philippa. The German vocational educational system / by Philippa Andrews, Russ Russell, and John Whybrow. — Bristol : Further Education Staff College, 1979. — 36p : ill ; 30cm. — (Comparative papers in further education, ISSN 0143-327x ; no.4)
Bibliography: p34
Unpriced (pbk) B82-24184

370.11'3'0943 — West Germany. Vocational education, *1945-1973*
Taylor, M. E.. Education and work in the Federal Republic of Germany / by M.E. Taylor. — London : Anglo-German Foundation for the Study of Industrial Society, [c1981]. — x,349p ; 21cm
Bibliography: p331-349
ISBN 0-905492-36-6 (pbk) : £9.50 B82-17847

370.11'3'0943 — West Germany. Vocational education *compared with* **vocational education in England**
The **Anglo-German** report / edited by Jean Finlayson, David Parkes and Russ Russell. — Bristol : Further Education Staff College, 1979. — 85p : 2ill ; 30cm. — (Comparative papers in further education, ISSN 0143-327x ; no.2)
Conference papers
£2.25 (pbk)
Primary classification 370.11'3'0942 B82-24182

370.11'3'0973 — United States. Vocational education
Jobs and training in the 1980s : vocational policy and the labor market / edited by Peter B. Doeringer, Bruce Vermeulen. — Boston, Mass. ; London : Nijhoff, c1981. — viii,206p ; 24cm. — (Boston studies in applied economics. Series on labor and employment)
ISBN 0-89838-062-6 : Unpriced B82-02726

370.11'3'0973 — United States. Vocational education. Management
Finch, Curtis R.. Administering and supervising occupational education / Curtis R. Finch, Robert L. McGough. — Englewood Cliffs ; London : Prentice-Hall, c1982. — xv,302p : ill ; 25cm
Includes bibliographies and index
ISBN 0-13-004838-0 : £13.45 B82-21679

370.11'4 — Children. Moral education
Straughan, Roger. Can we teach children to be good?. — London : Allen & Unwin, Nov.1982. — [128]p. — (Introductory studies in philosophy of education)
ISBN 0-04-370120-5 (cased) : £7.50 : CIP entry
ISBN 0-04-370121-3 (pbk) : £3.50 B82-27813

370.11'4 — Schools. Moral & social education. Teaching
McPhail, Peter. Social and moral education / Peter McPhail. — Oxford : Basil Blackwell, 1982. — viii,205p : ill ; 23cm. — (Theory and practice in education ; 4)
Bibliography: p195-198. — Includes index
ISBN 0-631-12792-5 (cased) : Unpriced : CIP rev.
ISBN 0-631-12947-2 (pbk) : Unpriced B82-04591

370.11'4 — Schools. Moral education — *For teaching*
Ward, Lionel O.. The ethical dimension of the school curriculum. — Swansea (Hendrefoilan, Swansea, SA2 7NB) : University College of Swansea, Faculty of Education, May 1982. — 1v.
ISBN 0-900944-17-x (pbk) : £3.00 : CIP entry B82-19282

370.11'4 — Schools. Moral education — *Philosophical perspectives*
Straughan, Roger. 'I ought to, but —' : a philosophical approach to the problem of weakness of will in education / Roger Straughan. — Windsor : NFER/Nelson, 1982. — 235p ; 22cm
Bibliography: p227-232. — Includes index
ISBN 0-85633-235-6 (pbk) : £10.95 B82-25345

370.11'4'072041 — Great Britain. Schools. Moral education. Research
Wilson, John, *1928-*. Discipline and moral education : a survey of public opinion and understanding / John Wilson. — Windsor : NFER-Nelson, 1981. — viii,137p ; 22cm
Bibliography: p136-137. — Includes index
ISBN 0-85633-233-x (pbk) : £10.95
Also classified at 371.5'072041 B82-10711

370.11'5 — England. Schools. Students. Social development. Assessment
Personal and social development. — [London] ([Dept. of Education and Science, 2/11 Elizabeth House, York Rd., London SE1 7PH]) : Assessment of Performance Unit, [1981?]. — 24p : 1ill ; 30cm
Cover title
Unpriced (pbk) B82-30917

370.11'5 — Great Britain. Schools. Curriculum subjects: World studies
Richardson, Robin. Culture, race and peace : tasks and tensions in the classroom : this paper was originally given as a lecture at the Atlantic College Peace Education Conference in June 1981 / Robin Richardson. — Lancaster : S. Martin's College, c1982. — 15p : 2ill,1form ; 30cm. — (Occasional paper / Centre for Peace Studies ; no.2)
Unpriced (spiral) B82-38842

370.11'5 — Schools. Curriculum subjects: World studies. Teaching
Teaching world studies. — London : Longman, Sept.1982. — [240]p
ISBN 0-582-49711-6 (pbk) : £5.95 : CIP entry B82-20272

370.15 — Children. Education — *Psychoanalytical perspectives*
Gammage, Philip. Children and schooling. — London : Allen & Unwin, Aug.1982. — [240]p. — (Unwin education books)
ISBN 0-04-370117-5 (cased) : £15.00 : CIP entry
ISBN 0-04-370118-3 (pbk) : £5.50 B82-15638

370.15 — Education. Role of self-image
Burns, R. B.. Self-concept development and education / Robert B. Burns. — London : Holt, Rinehart and Winston, c1982. — xii,441p : ill ; 25cm. — (Holt education)
Bibliography: p405-433. — Includes index
ISBN 0-03-910354-4 (pbk) : £6.95 : CIP rev. B82-06020

370.15 — Educational psychology
The **Handbook** of school psychology / Cecil R. Reynolds, Terry B. Gutkin, editors. — New York ; Chichester : Wiley, c1982. — xviii,1284,30p : ill ; 26cm
Bibliography: p1173-1284. — Includes index
ISBN 0-471-05869-6 : £39.20 B82-27734

Quicke, J. C.. The cautious expert : a social analysis of developments in the practice of educational psychology. — Milton Keynes : Open University Press, Aug.1982. — [192]p
ISBN 0-335-10110-0 : CIP entry B82-25513

Stone, David R.. Educational psychology : the development of teaching skills / David R. Stone, Elwin C. Nielsen. — New York ; London : Harper & Row, c1982. — xxii,401p : ill,forms ; 24cm
Includes bibliographies and index
ISBN 0-06-046448-8 (pbk) : £9.50 B82-26281

370.15'2 — Knowledge. Acquisition. Role of education
Brownhill, R. J.. Education and the nature of knowledge. — London : Croom Helm, Dec.1982. — [128]p. — (New patterns of learning series)
ISBN 0-7099-0654-4 : £11.95 : CIP entry B82-21412

370.15'23 — Education. Applications of learning theories
Travers, Robert M. W.. Essentials of learning : the new cognitive learning for students of education / Robert M.W. Travers. — 5th ed. — New York : Macmillan ; London : Collier Macmillan, c1982. — xvii,570p : ill ; 24cm
Previous ed.: 1977. — Bibliography: p521-548. — Includes index
ISBN 0-02-421390-x : Unpriced B82-26386

370.15'23 — Great Britain. Learning by school students. Role of use of language in schools
Richmond, John. The resources of classroom language. — London : Edward Arnold, June 1982. — [128]p. — (Explorations in language study)
ISBN 0-7131-6234-1 (pbk) : £3.95 : CIP entry B82-12921

370.15'23 — Great Britain. Learning by secondary school students, 11-16 years. Role of oral communication with other students
Learning through talking 11-16 : the report of the Schools Council/Avon Education Authority Language Development Project based at Weston Teachers' Centre (1975-77). — London : Evans, 1979. — 138p : ill ; 21cm. — (Schools Council working paper, ISSN 0533-1668 ; 64)
Bibliography: p134-135
ISBN 0-423-50710-9 (pbk) : £5.25 : CIP rev. B79-31660

370.15'23 — Learning by school students — *For teaching*

Biggs, John B.. The process of learning / John B. Biggs, Ross Telfer. — Sydney ; London : Prentice-Hall, c1981. — 539p : ill,facsims,forms ; 22cm
Bibliography: p498-525. — Includes index
ISBN 0-7248-1001-3 (pbk) : £10.35
B82-29168

370.15'23 — Learning by school students. Role of use of language in schools

Chilver, Peter. Learning and language in the classroom. — Oxford : Pergamon, Aug.1982. — [110]p
ISBN 0-08-026777-7 : £8.00 : CIP entry
B82-15655

370.15'23 — Learning by students

Biggs, John B.. Evaluating the quality of learning : the SOLO taxonomy (Structure of the Observed Learning Outcome) / John B. Biggs, Kevin F. Collis. — New York ; London : Academic Press, 1982. — xiii,245p : ill,1map ; 24cm. — (Educational psychology)
Bibliography: p237-242. — Includes index
ISBN 0-12-097550-5 : £17.60 B82-30140

370.15'23'019 — Learning by school students

Psychological aspects of learning and teaching. — London : Croom Helm, Nov.1982. — [224]p
ISBN 0-7099-0460-6 : £14.95 : CIP entry
Also classified at 371.1'02'019 B82-29012

370.15'3 — Education. Role of interpersonal relationships

Salomon, Gavriel. Communication and education : social and psychological interactions / Gavriel Salomon. — Beverly Hills ; London : Sage, c1981. — 271p : ill ; 23cm. — (People and communications ; v.13)
Bibliography: p241-258. — Includes index
ISBN 0-8039-1717-1 (cased) : Unpriced
ISBN 0-8039-1718-x (pbk) : £6.50 B82-11696

370.19 — Education — *Anthropological perspectives*

Musgrove, Frank, *1922-*. Education and anthropology : other cultures and the teacher / Frank Musgrove. — Chichester : Wiley, c1982. — vi,193p ; 24cm
Includes bibliographies and index
ISBN 0-471-10143-5 : £13.50 : CIP rev.
B82-11299

370.19 — Education. Social aspects

Cultural and economic reproduction in education : essays on class, ideology and the state / [edited by] Michael W. Apple. — London : Routledge & Kegan Paul, 1982. — x,362p : ill ; 22cm. — (Routledge education books)
Includes bibliographies and index
ISBN 0-7100-0845-7 (cased) : £9.95
ISBN 0-7100-0846-5 (pbk) : £7.95 B82-24902

370.19 — Education — *Sociological perspectives*

Society, education and the state. — Milton Keynes : Open University Press. — (Educational studies : a third level course)
At head of title: The Open University
Block 2: Education and national development. — 1981. — 128p : ill ; 30cm. — (E353 ; block 2, (units 5-7))
Includes bibliographies. — Contents: Unit 5: Education and 'development' — Unit 6: Education systems in an international context — Unit 7: Education and production in socialist countries
ISBN 0-335-13057-7 (pbk) : Unpriced
B82-04762

Society, education and the state. — Milton Keynes : Open University Press, 1981. — (Educational studies : a third level course) (E353 ; block 3, (units 8-9))
Block 3: The politics of cultural production. — 108p : ill,ports ; 30cm
At head of title: The Open University. — Includes bibliographies. — Contents: Unit 8 : Ideology, politics and curriculum — Unit 9 : Popular culture, class and schooling
ISBN 0-335-13058-5 (pbk) : Unpriced
B82-14893

370.19 — Education — *Sociological perspectives* — *Conference proceedings*

Schools, teachers & teaching / edited and introduced by Len Barton and Stephen Walker. — Lewes : Falmer Press, 1981. — 358p ; 24cm. — (Politics and education series)
Conference papers. — Includes bibliographies and index
ISBN 0-905273-23-0 (cased) : Unpriced
ISBN 0-905273-22-2 (pbk) : Unpriced
B82-12629

370.19 — Schools — *Sociological perspectives*

Tyler, William. The sociology of the school : a review / by William Tyler. — Herne Bay : W.B. Tyler, c1982. — 77p ; 22cm
'Commissioned by the Social Science Research Council'. — Bibliography: p66-77
ISBN 0-9508202-0-2 (pbk) : Unpriced
B82-40020

370.19 — Sociology of education

The Social sciences in educational studies : a selective guide to the literature / edited by Anthony Hartnett. — London : Heinemann Educational, 1982. — 294p ; 23cm
Includes bibliographies
ISBN 0-435-80409-x : £12.50 : CIP rev.
B82-01956

370.19'05 — Education — *Sociological perspectives* — *Serials*

Research in sociology of education and socialization : a research annual. — Vol.1 (1980)-. — Greenwich, Conn. : JAI Press ; London (3 Henrietta St., WC2E 8LU) : Distributed by JAICON Press, 1980-. — v. ; 24cm
ISSN 0197-5080 = Research in sociology of education and socialization B82-02341

370.19'0941 — Great Britain. Education. Social aspects, *1850-1900*

New approaches to the study of popular education, 1851-1902 / edited by Roy Lowe. — Leicester (4, Marydene Drive, Evington, Leicester, LE5 6HD) : [History of Education Society], 1979. — 67p : ill,maps ; 21cm. — (Occasional publication / History of Education Society ; no.4)
Unpriced (pbk) B82-40430

370.19'0941 — Great Britain. Education. Sociopolitical aspects

Race, class and education. — London : Croom Helm, Jan.1983. — [256]p
ISBN 0-7099-0683-8 (cased) : £27.95 : CIP entry
ISBN 0-7099-0684-6 (pbk) : £14.95
B82-33347

Salter, Brian. Education, politics and the State : the theory and practice of educational change / Brian Salter & Ted Tapper. — London : McIntyre, 1981. — viii,264p : 1ill ; 20cm
Bibliography: p236-254. — Includes index
ISBN 0-86216-075-8 (cased) : £14.95 : CIP rev.
ISBN 0-86216-076-6 (pbk) : £5.95 B81-30512

370.19'0973 — United States. Education — *Anthropological perspectives*

Doing the ethnography of schooling : educational anthropology in action / edited by George Spindler. — New York ; London : Holt, Rinehart and Winston, c1982. — viii,504p : ill,ports ; 24cm
Includes bibliographies and index
ISBN 0-03-059039-6 : £15.95 B82-15356

370.19'0973 — United States. Education. Implications of psychosocial aspects of power

Nyberg, David. Power over power : what power means in ordinary life, how it is related to acting freely, and what it can contribute to a renovated ethics of education / David Nyberg. — Ithaca ; London : Cornell University Press, c1981. — 200p ; 23cm
Bibliography: p188-195. — Includes index
ISBN 0-8014-1414-8 : £10.50 B82-11910

370.19'3 — Education. Sociopolitical aspects — *Marxist viewpoints*

Sarup, Madan. Education, state and crisis : a Marxist perspective / Madan Sarup. — London : Routledge & Kegan Paul, 1982. — xiii,137p ; 22cm. — (Routledge education books)
Includes index
ISBN 0-7100-0956-9 (cased) : £8.95
ISBN 0-7100-0959-3 (pbk) : £4.95 B82-20532

370.19'3'096 — Africa. Social development. Role of education

Thompson, A. R.. Education and development in Africa : an introduction to the study of the role education may play in national development intended primarily for teachers in training and in service / A.R. Thompson. — London : Macmillan, 1981. — viii,358p : ill ; 23cm
Bibliography: p339-353. — Includes index
ISBN 0-333-30018-1 (cased) : £14.00
ISBN 0-333-30020-3 (pbk) : Unpriced
B82-00573

370.19'31'09411 — Scotland. Local communities. Relations with schools

Scottish Council for Community Education. Report on the discussion paper — "The community school in Scotland" / Scottish Council for Community Education. — Edinburgh (New St., Andrews House, St. James Centre, Edinburgh EH1 3SX) : The Council, 1982. — 12p ; 21cm
Text on cover
Unpriced (pbk) B82-31047

370.19'31'0973 — United States. Schools. Role of communities

Gittell, Marilyn. Limits to citizen participation : the decline of community organizations / Marilyn Gittell with Bruce Hoffacker ... [et. al.]. — Beverly Hills ; London : Sage, 1980. — 280p ; 23cm. — (Sage library of social research ; v.109)
Bibliography: p265-273
ISBN 0-8039-1478-4 (cased) : Unpriced
ISBN 0-8039-1479-2 (pbk) : Unpriced
B82-32675

370.19'34 — India *(Republic)*. **Education. Implications of language**

Pattanayak, D. P.. Multilingualism and mother-tongue education / D.P. Pattanayak ; with a foreword and an essay by Ivan Illich. — Delhi ; Oxford : Oxford University Press, 1981. — xvii,185p ; 23cm
Includes index
ISBN 0-19-561304-x : £7.95 B82-37004

370.19'342 — Iraq. Baghdad. Islamic education, *1000-1100*

Makdisi, George. The rise of colleges : institutions of learning in Islam and the West / George Makdisi. — Edinburgh : Edinburgh University Press, 1981. — xiv,377p ; 22cm
Bibliography: p345-354. — Includes index
ISBN 0-85224-375-8 : £20.00 : CIP rev.
B81-35895

370.19'342 — Massachusetts. Boston. Schools. Students. Busing, *to 1980*

Buell, Emmett H.. School desegregation and defended neighborhoods : the Boston controversy / Emmett H. Buell, Jr. with Richard A. Brisbin, Jr. — Lexington, Mass. : Lexington Books ; [Aldershot] : Gower [[distributor]], c1982. — xiv,202p : ill,1map ; 24cm. — (Lexington Books politics of education series)
Includes index
ISBN 0-669-02646-8 : £16.50 B82-24989

370.19'342 — United States. Schools. Desegregation

Chesler, Mark A.. Making desegregation work : a professional's guide to effecting change / Mark A. Chesler, Bunyan I. Bryant, James E. Crowfoot. — Beverly Hills ; London : Published in cooperation with the Continuing Education Program in the Human Services of the University of Michigan School of Social Work [by] Sage, c1981. — 184p : ill ; 22cm. — (A Sage human services guide ; 23)
Includes bibliographies
ISBN 0-8039-1725-2 (pbk) : Unpriced
B82-21515

370.19′342 — United States. Schools. Desegregation *continuation*

Effective school desegregation : equity, quality and feasibility / edited by Willis D. Hawley. — Beverly Hills ; London : Sage, c1981. — 311p ; 22cm. — (Sage focus editions ; 42)
Includes bibliographies
ISBN 0-8039-1455-5 (cased) : Unpriced
ISBN 0-8039-1456-3 (pbk) : £6.50 B82-21513

370.19′342′0942 — England. Schools. Race relations — *National Union of Teachers viewpoints*

National Union of Teachers. Combatting racialism in schools : a Union policy statement: guidance for members / [Working party on Multi-ethnic Education of the National Union of Teachers]. — [London] ([Hamilton House, Mabledon Place, WC1H 9BD]) : [National Union of Teachers], 1981. — 12p ; 21cm
Cover title
Unpriced (pbk) B82-19749

370.19′345 — Schools. Sexism

Stanworth, Michelle. Gender and schooling. — London : Hutchinson Education, Jan.1983. — [64]p. — (Explorations in feminism)
ISBN 0-09-151161-5 (pbk) : £1.95 : CIP entry B82-33459

370.19′346′0973 — United States. Rural regions. Education. Projects: Rural Experimental Schools Program

Rosenblum, Sheila. Stability and change : innovation in an educational context / Sheila Rosenblum and Karen Seashore Louis with the assistance of Nancy Brigham and Robert E. Herriott. — New York ; London : Plenum, c1981. — xvii,352p : ill,forms ; 24cm. — (Environment, development, and public policy. Public policy and social services)
Bibliography: p279-287. — Includes index
ISBN 0-306-40665-9 : Unpriced B82-02032

370.19′4 — Community education

Poster, Cyril. Community education : its development and management / Cyril Poster. — London : Heinemann Educational, 1982. — viii,184p : ill ; 23cm. — (Heinemann organization in schools series)
Includes index
ISBN 0-435-80641-6 : £9.95 : CIP rev. B81-28167

370.19′4′091724 — Developing countries. Community education — *Conference proceedings*

The **Integration** of school and community learning in developing countries : a report of a workshop organised by the Department of Education in Developing Countries, March 1982 / edited by Roger Barnard. — London : Department of Education in Developing Countries, University of London Institute of Education, 1982. — iv,90p ; 30cm
Includes bibliographies
ISBN 0-85473-131-8 (spiral) : Unpriced B82-36514

370.19′4′0941 — Great Britain. Community education — *Serials*

Community education network. — Vol.1, no.1 (Sept. 1981)-. — Coventry (Briton Rd, Coventry CV2 4LF) : C.E.D.C., 1981-. — v. : ill,ports ; 44cm
Monthly
ISSN 0262-706x = Community education network : £3.00 per year for 2 copies per month B82-06775

370.19′4′09411 — Scotland. Community education

Horobin, J. C.. Community education statistics : a report commissioned by the Council / research director J.C. Horobin ; research assistant Pamela Waterston. — [St. Andrews] : Department of Adult Education and Extra-Mural Studies, University of St. Andrews, 1980. — 154p : ill,forms ; 21cm
At head of title: Scottish Council for Community Education. — Bibliography: p112
Unpriced (pbk) B82-28223

370.19′5 — Comparative education

Comparative education / Philip G. Altbach, Robert F. Arnove, Gail P. Kelly editors. — New York : Macmillan ; London : Collier Macmillan, c1982. — ix,533p : ill ; 25cm
ISBN 0-02-301920-4 : £8.95 B82-26388

Comparative research on education. — Oxford : Pergamon, June 1982. — [281]p
ISBN 0-08-027934-1 : £17.50 : CIP entry B82-14220

370.19′6′0941 — Great Britain. Multicultural education

Phillips-Bell, M.. Issues and resources. — Birmingham : AFFOR, Oct.1982. — [72]p
ISBN 0-907127-10-x (pbk) : £1.00 : CIP entry B82-31323

Ruddell, D.. Race relations teaching pack. — Birmingham : AFFOR, Sept.1982. — [60]p
ISBN 0-907127-08-8 : £4.99 : CIP entry B82-31321

370.19′62 — Northern Ireland. Young persons. International exchange visits. Organisation — *Practical information — For youth work*

Hope, Roger. Getting away : a handbook for organising international holidays and exchanges for young people / prepared by Roger Hope and Arthur Dempster. — Belfast : Standing Conference of Youth Organisations in Northern Ireland, 1980. — 38p : forms ; 30cm
Cover title
ISBN 0-906797-06-3 (spiral) : Unpriced
Primary classification 910′.2′02 B82-00098

370′.25′41 — Great Britain. Education — *Directories — Serials*

Education year book. — 1983. — London : Longman, Dec.1982. — [1016]p. — (Longman community information guides)
ISBN 0-900313-73-0 : £23.00 : CIP entry
ISSN 0143-5469 B82-30737

370′.28′5404 — Education. Applications of microcomputer systems

Maddison, Alan. Microcomputers in the classroom / Alan Maddison. — London : Hodder and Stoughton, c1982. — 189p : ill ; 24cm
Bibliography: p176-177. — Includes index
ISBN 0-340-27688-6 (pbk) : £3.95 : CIP rev. B82-14512

Microcomputers in education / editor I.C.H. Smith. — Chichester : Horwood, 1982. — 212p : ill ; 24cm. — (Ellis Horwoood series in computers and their applications ; 16)
Includes bibliographies and index
ISBN 0-85312-424-8 : £16.50 : CIP rev.
ISBN 0-470-27319-4 (Halsted) B82-00186

370′.3′21 — Education — *Encyclopaedias*

Rowntree, Derek. A dictionary of education / Derek Rowntree. — London : Harper & Row, 1981. — viii,354p ; 22cm
ISBN 0-06-318157-6 : Unpriced : CIP rev. B81-28193

370′.5 — Education — *Serials*

World yearbook of education. — 1981. — London : Kogan Page, July 1981. — [400]p
ISBN 0-85038-457-5 : £13.95 : CIP entry B81-19216

World yearbook of education. — 1982-1983. — London : Kogan Page, Dec.1982. — [350]p
ISBN 0-85038-565-2 : £15.95 : CIP entry
ISSN 0084-2508 B82-32300

370′.7′1 — Teachers. Professional education

Advanced study for teachers : the role in professional development of higher degree and diploma courses in education / edited by Robin J. Alexander and James W. Ellis. — Guildford : Teacher Education Study Group, Society for Research into Higher Education, 1981. — xii,129p : ill ; 21cm
Bibliography: p125-127
ISBN 0-9506737-2-2 (pbk) : Unpriced B82-15250

Changing priorities in teacher education. — London : Croom Helm, Aug.1982. — [240]p
ISBN 0-7099-1130-0 : £12.95 : CIP entry B82-20769

Wragg, E. C.. A review of research in teacher education / E.C. Wragg. — Windsor : NFER-Nelson, 1982. — 104p ; 22cm
Bibliography: p82-104
ISBN 0-85633-247-x (pbk) : £3.95 B82-31651

370′.7′10917671 — Islamic countries. Teachers. Professional education

Curriculum and teacher education / edited by Muhammad Hamid Al-Afendi and Nabi Ahmed Baloch. — London : Hodder and Stoughton, 1980. — viii,212p ; 24cm. — (Islamic education series)
ISBN 0-340-23609-4 : £5.50 : CIP rev.
Primary classification 375 B80-04731

370′.7′10941 — Great Britain. Teachers. Professional education — *National Association of Teachers in Further and Higher Education viewpoints*

National Association of Teachers in Further and Higher Education. Teacher education : a policy statement / NATFHE. — London (Hamilton House, Mabledon Place, WC1H 9BH) : NATFHE, 1978. — 23p ; 21cm
Cover title
£0.35 (pbk) B82-14405

370′.7′109416 — Northern Ireland. Teachers. Professional education

Higher Education Review Group for Northern Ireland. The future structure of teacher education in Northern Ireland : an interim report of the Higher Education Review Group for Northern Ireland chairman Sir Henry Chilver. — Belfast : H.M.S.O., 1980. — 69p : ill ; 24cm
ISBN 0-337-04112-1 (unbound) : £3.00 B82-14140

370′.7′1240942 — England. Further education institutions & higher education institutions. Teachers. Professional education — *National Association of Teachers in Further and Higher Education viewpoints*

National Association of Teachers in Further and Higher Education. The education and training of teachers for further and higher education : a policy statement / NATFHE. — [London] : [National Association of Teachers in Further and Higher Education], 1978. — 20p ; 21cm
Cover title
£0.35 (£0.25 to members of the Association) (pbk) B82-08494

370′.7′30942561 — Bedfordshire. Bedford. Colleges of higher education: Bedford College of Higher Education, *to 1982*

Smart, Richard. Bedford training college : 1882-1982 : a history of a Froebel college and its schools / Richard Smart ; foreword by Christopher Fry. — Bedford : Bedford Training College Publication Committee, 1982. — xv,178p : ill,1coat of arms,facsims,1map,ports ; 21cm
Bibliography: p173. — Includes index
ISBN 0-9507967-0-0 (pbk) : £4.50 B82-32777

370′.7′30942659 — Cambridgeshire. Cambridge. Universities: University of Cambridge. *Department of Education, to 1939*

Searby, Peter. The training of teachers in Cambridge University : the first sixty years, 1879-1939 / Peter Searby. — [Cambridge] (Brookside Resources Centre, Cambridge) : Cambridge University Department of Education, 1982. — 45p : 1facsim,ports ; 22cm
Unpriced (pbk) B82-35287

370′.7′30942713 — Cheshire. Alsager. Colleges of higher education: Crewe and Alsager College of Higher Education, *to 1977*

Doherty, Geoffrey D. C.. A marriage of convenience : a case study of the amalgamation of Crewe and Alsager Colleges of Education / Geoffrey D.C. Doherty ; illustrations by Peter Welton. — [Alsager] ([Alsager, Cheshire ST7 2HL]) : Crewe & Alsager College of Higher Education, [c1981]. — 91p : ill ; 21cm
Cover title. — Bibliography: p91
Unpriced (pbk) B82-00707

370'.7'320941 — Great Britain. Teachers. Professional education. Diploma of Higher Education courses: Council for National Academic Awards courses — *Regulations*

Council for National Academic Awards. Principles and regulations for the award of the Council's first degrees and Diploma of Higher Education / Council for National Academic Awards. — London (344 Gray's Inn Rd., WC1X 8BP) : C.N.A.A., 1979. — 48p ; 30cm
Includes index
Unpriced (pbk)
Also classified at 378'.1552'0941 B82-32775

370'.7'320942 — England. Higher education institutions. Curriculum subjects: Education. Degree courses — *National Union of Teachers viewpoints*

National Union of Teachers. Initial and in-service BEd degrees : a policy statement issued by the National Union of Teachers. — [London] ([Hamilton House, Mabledon Place, WC1H 9BD]) : [NUT], [1981]. — 23p ; 15x21cm
£0.50 (unbound) B82-04526

370'.7'320942 — England. Teachers. Professional education. B.Ed. courses

McNamara, David. The B.Ed. degree and its future : being the report of a research project sponsored by the Department of Education and Science and conducted at the University of Lancaster 1979-1981 / by D.R. McNamara and A.M. Ross. — Lancaster : School of Education, University of Lancaster, 1982. — vi,193p : ill,forms ; 21cm
Bibliography: p82-83
ISBN 0-901699-85-3 (pbk) : Unpriced B82-21588

370'.7'320942 — England. Teachers. Professional education. Diploma of Higher Education courses: Council for National Academic Awards courses

Council for National Academic Awards. Diploma of Higher Education / CNAA. — London (344 Grays Inn Rd., WC1X 8BP) : Council for National Academic Awards, 1980. — 27p ; 21cm
Cover title
Unpriced (pbk) B82-32772

370'.7'320942 — England. Teachers. Professional education. Postgraduate Certificate of Education courses

PGCE in the public sector. — London (Room 2/11, Elizabeth House, York Rd., SE1 7PH) : Department of Education and Science, 1980. — [19]p : ill ; 21cm. — (An HMI discussion paper)
Unpriced (pbk) B82-19335

370'.7'33 — Teachers. Professional education. Teaching practice — *Manuals*

Heywood, John, *1930-*. Pitfalls and planning in student teaching / John Heywood. — London : Kogan Page, 1982. — 200p : ill ; 22cm
Bibliography: p193. — Includes index
ISBN 0-85038-554-7 (pbk) : £8.95 : CIP rev. B82-17979

370'.7'330941 — Great Britain. Teachers. Professional education. B.Ed. courses. Teaching practice

McCulloch, Myra. School experience in initial B. Ed./B. Ed. Hons degrees validated by the Council for National Academic Awards : a report of the research project carried out between 1 August 1977 and 31 July 1979 under the aegis of the School Experience Sub-Committee and with the guidance of the Research Project Steering Committee / Myra McCulloch. — London (344 Gray's Inn Rd., WC1X 8BP) : Council for National Academic Awards, 1980. — 136p : forms ; 30cm
Bibliography: p130-136
Unpriced (pbk) B82-20239

370'.7'330942 — England. Teachers. Professional education. Teaching practice

Teaching practice : a brief guide to teaching practice / prepared for teaching students by the National Union of Teachers. — [London] ([Hamilton House, Mabledon Place, WC1H 9BD]) : [National Union of Teachers], [1981?]. — 16p ; 21cm
Unpriced (unbound) B82-04524

Teaching practice and the probationary years. — London : Edward Arnold, July 1982. — [96]p. — (Teaching matters)
ISBN 0-7131-0723-5 (pbk) : £3.50 : CIP entry B82-17920

370'.74'02819 — West Yorkshire *(Metropolitan County)*. **Leeds. Museums: Museum of the History of Education. Stock** — *Catalogues*

Museum of the History of Education. Museum of the History of Education : catalogue / edited by P.H.J.H. Gosden and W.B. Stephens. — Leeds (Museum of the History of Education, Parkinson Court, The University, Leeds LS2 9JT) : University of Leeds, 1979. — 98p,[4]p of plates : ill ; 20cm
Unpriced (pbk) B82-24295

370'.7'8 — Education. Research. Qualitative methods

Bogdan, Robert C.. Qualitative research for education : an introduction to theory and methods / Robert C. Bogdan and Sari Knopp Biklen. — Boston, Mass. ; London : Allyn and Bacon, c1982. — xv,253p : ill,ports ; 25cm
Bibliography: p235-246. — Includes index
ISBN 0-205-07695-5 : £19.95 B82-22024

370'.7'80416 — Northern Ireland. Education. Research — *Serials*

NICER bulletin. — No.16 (Jan. 1982)-. — Belfast (52 Malone Rd, Belfast BT9 5BS) : Northern Ireland Council for Educational Research, Queen's University of Belfast, 1982-. — v. ; 30cm
Annual. — Continues: Information bulletin (Northern Ireland Council for Educational Research)
ISSN 0262-8163 = NICER bulletin : Unpriced B82-28855

370'.7'8073 — United States. Education. Research. Results. Applications — *For teaching*

Borg, Walter R.. Applying educational research : a practical guide for teachers / Walter R. Borg. — New York ; London : Longman, c1981. — viii,327p : ill,forms ; 25cm
Includes bibliographies and index
ISBN 0-582-28145-8 : £9.95 B82-02902

370.9 — EDUCATION. HISTORICAL AND GEOGRAPHICAL TREATMENT

370'.9 — Education, *to 1980* — *For children*

Ross, Alistair. Going to school. — London : A. & C. Black, Sept.1982. — [64]p. — (Beans)
ISBN 0-7136-2240-7 : £3.50 : CIP entry B82-20360

370'.9'04 — Education, *1955-1979*

Twenty-five years of educational practice and theory 1955-1979 : International review of education jubilee volume / edited by Leo Fernig and James Bowen. — The Hague ; London : Nijhoff, 1980. — vi,358p : ill ; 25cm
English text, English, French and German summaries. — Reprinted from IRE, vol.XXV (1979), nos.2-3. — Includes bibliographies and index
ISBN 90-247-2284-5 : Unpriced B82-41048

370'.9171'241 — Commonwealth countries. Informal education — *Conference proceedings*

Commonwealth Conference on Non-Formal Education for Development *(1979 : New Delhi)*. Mobilizing human resources : report of the Commonwealth Conference on Non-formal Education for Development, New Delhi, 22 January-2 February 1979. — London : Commonwealth Secretariat, c1979. — viii,94p ; 29cm
ISBN 0-85092-168-6 (pbk) : £2.00 B82-05431

370'.9172'4 — Developing countries. Education. Influence of developed countries

Education in the Third World. — London : Croom Helm, Aug.1982. — [256]p
ISBN 0-7099-2749-5 : £13.95 : CIP entry B82-17934

370'.9172'4 — Developing countries. Education — *Serials*

EDC occasional papers. — No.1 (Oct. 1981)-. — London : University of London, Institute of Education, 1981-. — v. ; 30cm
Irregular
ISSN 0262-7396 = EDC occasional papers : Unpriced B82-13404

370'.918'2 — Western world. Education, *ca 1530-*

Bowen, James. A history of Western education. — London : Methuen, June 1981
Vol.3: The modern West : Europe and the New World. — [560]p
ISBN 0-416-16130-8 (cased) : £17.50 : CIP entry
ISBN 0-416-85160-6 (pbk) : £7.95 B81-09993

370'.918'21 — Caribbean region. Education

Murray, R. N.. Foundations of education in the Caribbean. — London : Hodder and Stoughton, Feb.1983. — [128]p. — (Caribbean education series)
ISBN 0-340-32423-6 : £2.95 : CIP entry B82-38024

370'.92'2 — Education — *Biographies*

International who's who in education. — 2nd ed. / editorial director Ernest Kay. — Cambridge : International Who's Who in Education, 1981. — ix,490p ; 25cm
Previous ed.: published as Who's who in education. London : Business Books, 1974
ISBN 0-900332-56-5 : Unpriced B82-15246

370'.92'4 — Great Britain. Education. Woodward, Nathaniel — *Biographies*

Wylie, John A. H.. Nathaniel Woodard : educator of the middle classes / John A.H. Wylie. — Hove (9 Brunswick Sq., Hove, E. Sussex BN3 1EN) : Chichester Diocesan Fund and Board of Finance, [1981?]. — 10p : 1port ; 22cm
Bibliography: p9-10
Unpriced (unbound) B82-05247

370'.94 — European Community countries. Educational systems

The **Educational** systems in the European Community : a guide / edited by Lionel Elvin. — Windsor : NFER-Nelson, c1981. — 270p : ill (some col.) ; 25cm
Edited in cooperation with the Commission of the European Communities, Directorate-General for Research, Science and Education. — Includes bibliographies
ISBN 0-85633-223-2 (pbk) : £9.95 B82-12855

370'.941 — Great Britain. Education

Contemporary issues in education / [The E200 Course Team]. — Milton Keynes : Open University Press. — (Educational studies : a second level course)
At head of title: The Open University
Block 3: Control and choice in education
12: Post-secondary education : access and control / prepared by Ian McNay and Tim Horton for the Course Team. — 1981. — 47p : ill ; 30cm. — (E200 ; [block 3, unit 12])
Bibliography: p44-45
ISBN 0-335-13011-9 (pbk) : Unpriced B82-04758

Contemporary issues in education / [The E200 Course Team]. — Milton Keynes : Open University Press. — (Educational studies : a second level course)
At head of title: The Open University
Block 4: Educational standards
17: Schools and deviance / prepared by Peter Woods for the Course Team. — 1981. — 48p : ill ; 30cm. — (E200 ; [block 4, unit 17])
Bibliography: p44-45
ISBN 0-335-13016-x (pbk) : Unpriced B82-04757

370'.941 — Great Britain. Education
continuation

Contemporary issues in education / [The E200 Course Team]. — Milton Keynes : Open University Press. — (Educational studies : a second level course)
At head of title: The Open University
Block 4: Educational standards
Introduction to Block 4 / prepared by Peter Barnes for the Course Team ; 15: Approaches to teaching / prepared by Robert Bell for the Course Team. — 1981. — 56p : ill ; 30cm. — (E200 ; [block 4, unit 15])
Bibliography: p54
ISBN 0-335-13014-3 (pbk) : Unpriced
B82-04756

Contemporary issues in education / [The E200 Course Team]. — Milton Keynes : Open University Press. — (Educational studies : a second level course)
At head of title: The Open University
Block 5: The family as educator : adult life
22: Marriage and parenthood / prepared by Peter Woods for the Course Team. — 1981. — 44p : ill ; 30cm. — (E200 ; [block 5, unit 22])
Bibliography: p40-41
ISBN 0-335-13021-6 (pbk) : Unpriced
B82-04754

Contemporary issues in education / [The E200 Course Team]. — Milton Keynes : Open University Press. — (Educational studies : a second level course)
At head of title: The Open University
Block 5: The family as educator : adult life
23: The family and later life / prepared by Peter Townsend for the Course Team. — 1981. — 44p : ill ; 30cm. — (E200 ; [block 5, unit 23])
Bibliography: p42-44
ISBN 0-335-13022-4 (pbk) : Unpriced
B82-04755

Contemporary issues in education / [The E200 Course Team]. — Milton Keynes : Open University Press. — (Educational studies : a second level course)
At head of title: The Open University
Block 6: Work, leisure and learning
24: Careers and work cultures / prepared by Peter Woods for the Course Team. — 1981. — 44p : ill ; 30cm. — (E200 ; [block 6, unit 24])
Bibliography: p41-43
ISBN 0-335-13023-2 (pbk) : Unpriced
B82-04752

Contemporary issues in education / [The E200 Course Team]. — Milton Keynes : Open University Press. — (Educational studies : a second level course)
At head of title: The Open University
Block 6: Work, leisure and learning
25: The division of labour by gender / prepared by Ann Oakley for the Course Team. — 1981. — 40p : ill ; 30cm. — (E200 ; [block 6, unit 25])
Bibliography: p36-40
ISBN 0-335-13024-0 (pbk) : Unpriced
B82-04753

Contemporary issues in education / [The E200 Course Team]. — Milton Keynes : Open University Press. — (Educational studies : a second level course)
At head of title: The Open University
Block 6: Work, leisure and learning
26: Leisure, work and education / prepared by Kenneth Roberts for the Course Team. — 1981. — 39p : ill ; 30cm. — (E200 ; [block 6, unit 26])
Bibliography: p36-37
ISBN 0-335-13025-9 (pbk) : Unpriced
B82-04751

Contemporary issues in education / [The E200 Course Team]. — Milton Keynes : Open University Press. — (Educational studies : a second level course)
At head of title: The Open University
Block 7: Education and the future. — 1981. — (E200 ; block 7, unit 28)
28: Visions of the future / prepared by Aldwyn Cooper for the Course Team. — 34p : ill ; 30cm
Bibliography: p32-33
ISBN 0-335-13027-5 (pbk) : Unpriced
B82-15036

Contemporary issues in education / [The E200 Course Team]. — Milton Keynes : Open University Press. — (Educational studies : a second level course)
At head of title: The Open University
Block 7: Education and the future. — 1981. — (E200 ; block 7, unit 29)
29: Computers, communications and learning / prepared by Aldwyn Cooper and Fred Lockwood for the Course Team. — 28p : ill,ports ; 30cm
Bibliography: p21
ISBN 0-335-13028-3 (pbk) : Unpriced
B82-15037

Contemporary issues in education / [The E200 Course Team]. — Milton Keynes : Open University Press. — (Educational studies : a second level course)
At head of title: The Open University
Block 7: Education and the future. — 1981. — (E200 ; block 7, unit 30)
30: The future of educational institutions : the case for recurrent education / prepared by Nick Small and Ian McNay for the Course Team. — 32p : ill ; 30cm
Bibliography: p31-32
ISBN 0-335-13029-1 (pbk) : Unpriced
B82-15038

Hoggart, Richard. An English temper : essays on education, culture and communications / Richard Hoggart. — London : Chatto & Windus, 1982. — 207p ; 23cm
Includes index
ISBN 0-7011-2581-0 : £9.50 : CIP rev.
Also classified at 941.085'6 B82-01194

The **Study** of education : a collection of inaugural lectures / edited by Peter Gordon. — London : Woburn Press. — (The Woburn education series)
Includes bibliographies
Vol.2: The last decade. — 1980. — xxii,325p : ill ; 23cm
ISBN 0-7130-0171-2 (corrected : cased) : £18.00
ISBN 0-7130-4006-8 (pbk) : £8.50 B82-07874

370'.941 — Great Britain. Education. Equality of opportunity

Great Britain. *Equal Opportunities Commission*. Sex discrimination and equality of opportunity in primary and secondary schools / Equal Opportunities Commission (Education and Training Section). — [Manchester] : [Equal Opportunities Commission], 1979. — 19p ; 31cm
Unpriced (pbk) B82-38492

Lodge, Paul. Educational policy and educational inequality / Paul Lodge, Tessa Blackstone. — Oxford : Robertson, 1982. — xiii,256p ; 23cm
Bibliography: p249-253. — Includes index
ISBN 0-85520-192-4 : £16.00 : CIP rev.
B82-07033

Mortimore, Jo. Disadvantage and education / Jo Mortimore and Tessa Blackstone. — London : Heinemann Educational, 1982. — 216p ; 22cm. — (Studies in deprivation and disadvantage ; 4)
Bibliography: p185-204. — Includes index
ISBN 0-435-82608-5 (cased) : £12.50 : CIP rev.
ISBN 0-435-82609-3 (pbk) : £6.50 B82-05394

370'.941 — Great Britain. Education — *Liberal Party viewpoints*

Saunders, James H.. Eliminating Britain's educational anachronisms / James H. Saunders. — Hythe (21 Fisher Close, Hythe, Kent, CT21 6AB) : New Creation Enterprises, [1982]. — 15p ; 21cm. — (The Orpington initiative ; pamphlet no.2)
£1.00 (pbk) B82-30656

370'.9411 — Scotland. Education

Choice, compulsion and cost / Scottish Education Department. — Edinburgh : H.M.S.O., 1980. — 60p ; 21cm. — (Occasional papers)
Includes bibliographies
ISBN 0-11-491688-8 (pbk) : £3.60 B82-16630

370'.9417 — Ireland *(Republic)*. **Education**

Ireland/Eire. — London (The British Council, 10 Spring Gardens, SW1A 2BN) : National Equivalence Information Centre, 1982. — 3p ; 30cm
Unpriced (unbound) B82-34721

370'.9417 — Ireland *(Republic)*. **Education,** *1800-1980*

Coolahan, John. Irish education : its history and structure / John Coolahan. — Dublin : Institute of Public Administration, 1981. — xi,329p ; 23cm
Bibliography: p301-321. — Includes index
ISBN 0-906980-03-8 : £9.90 : CIP rev.
B81-22579

370'.9417 — Ireland *(Republic)*. **Education** — *Serials*

Irish educational studies. — Vol.1 (1981)-. — Dublin (c/o J. Coolahan, Education Department, University College, Dublin 4) : Educational Studies Association of Ireland, 1981-. — v. : ill ; 21cm
Annual. — Includes one chapter in Irish. — Continues: Proceedings of annual education conference of the Educational Studies Association of Ireland
£6.00 (£4.00 to members) B82-38534

370'.942 — England. Education

Dent, H. C.. Education in England and Wales / H.C. Dent. — 2nd ed. — London : Hodder and Stoughton, 1982. — 187p ; 24cm
Previous ed.: i.e. Rev. ed. 1977. — Includes bibliographies and index
ISBN 0-340-26300-8 (pbk) : £4.50 : CIP rev.
B82-01145

370'.942 — England. Education, *1500-1800*

O'Day, Rosemary. Education and society 1500-1800. — London : Longman, Oct.1982. — [336]p. — (Themes in British social history)
ISBN 0-582-48917-2 (cased) : £12.00 : CIP entry
ISBN 0-582-48918-0 (pbk) : £5.95 B82-25072

370'.942 — England. Education, *1911-1920*

Sherington, Geoffrey. English education, social change and war 1911-20 / Geoffrey Sherington. — Manchester : Manchester University Press, c1981. — xiii,194p : ill,1port ; 23cm
Bibliography: p183-188. — Includes index
ISBN 0-7190-0840-9 : £14.50 : CIP rev.
B81-25831

370'.942 — England. Education, *to 1981*

Aldrich, Richard. An introduction to the history of education. — London : Hodder and Stoughton, July 1982. — [192]p. — (Studies in teaching and learning)
ISBN 0-340-26293-1 (pbk) : £3.65 : CIP entry
B82-12726

370'.9431 — East Germany. Education

German Democratic Republic. — London (The British Council, 10 Spring Gardens, SW1A 2BN) : National Equivalence Information Centre, 1982. — 3p ; 30cm
Unpriced (unbound) B82-34715

370'.9437 — Czechoslovakia. Education

Czechoslovakia. — London (10 Spring Gardens, SW1A 2BN) : National Equivalence Information Centre, The British Council, 1981. — 5p ; 30cm
Unpriced (unbound) B82-22285

370'.9439 — Hungary. Education

Hungary. — London (10 Spring Gardens, SW1A 2BN) : National Equivalence Information Centre, The British Council, 1981. — 4p ; 30cm
Unpriced (unbound) B82-22284

370'.945 — Italy. Education

Italy. — London (The British Council, 10 Spring Gardens, SW1A 2BN) : National Equivalence Information Centre, 1982. — 3p ; 30cm
Unpriced (unbound) B82-34720

370'.945'85 — Malta. Education

Malta. — London (10 Spring Gardens, SW1A 2BN) : National Equivalence Information Centre, the British Council, 1981. — 6p ; 30cm
Unpriced (unbound) B82-20469

370'.947 — Soviet Union. Education

Soviet education in the 1980s. — London : Croom Helm, Nov.1982. — [288]p
ISBN 0-7099-2429-1 : £14.95 : CIP entry
B82-27942

370'.9485 — Sweden. Education, *to 1981*

Boucher, Leon. Tradition and change in Swedish education / by Leon Boucher. — Oxford : Pergamon, 1982. — xiv,264p : ill,maps ; 22cm. — (International studies in education and social change)
Bibliography: p247-264
ISBN 0-08-025240-0 : £12.75 : CIP rev. B82-03732

370'.94897 — Finland. Education

Finland. — London (10 Spring Gardens, SW1A 2BN) : National Equivalence Information Centre, The British Council, 1981. — 7p ; 30cm
Unpriced (unbound) B82-22287

370'.9491'2 — Ireland. Education

Iceland. — London (10 Spring Gardens, SW1A 2BN) : National Equivalence Information Centre, The British Council, 1981. — 4p ; 30cm
Unpriced (unbound) B82-22289

370'.9492 — Netherlands. Education

Netherlands. — London (10 Spring Gardens, SW1A 2BN) : National Equivalence Information Centre, the British Council, 1981. — 9p ; 30cm
Unpriced (unbound) B82-01474

370'.951'27 — China. Canton. Education, *1960-1980*

Unger, Jonathan. Education under Mao : class and competition in Canton schools, 1960-1980 / Jonathan Unger. — New York ; Guildford, Surrey : Columbia University Press, 1982. — xii,308p ; 24cm. — (Studies of the East Asian Institute)
Bibliography: p299-301. — Includes index
ISBN 0-231-05298-7 : £17.85 B82-36483

370'.952 — Japan. Education *related to* **employment**

Bowman, Mary Jean. Educational choice and labor markets in Japan / Mary Jean Bowman with the collaboration of Hideo Ikeda and Yesumasa Tomoda. — Chicago ; London : University of Chicago Press, c1981. — xvii,367p : ill,1map ; 24cm
Bibliography: p347-356. — Includes index
ISBN 0-226-06923-0 : £11.40
Also classified at 331.12'5'0952 B82-09576

370'.953'35 — Yemen *(People's Democratic Republic).* **Education**

People's Democratic Republic of Yemen/South Yemen. — London (10 Spring Gardens, SW1A 2BN) : National Equivalence Information Centre, The British Council, 1981. — 3p ; 30cm
Unpriced (unbound) B82-22301

370'.953'65 — Bahrain. Education

Bahrain. — London (The British Council, 10 Spring Gardens, SW1A 2BN) : National Equivalence Information Centre, 1982. — 3p ; 30cm
Unpriced (unbound) B82-34713

370'.95691 — Syria. Education

Syria. — London (10 Spring Gardens, SW1A 2BN) : National Equivalence Information Centre, The British Council, 1981. — 4p ; 30cm
Unpriced (unbound) B82-22298

370'.95695 — Jordan. Education

Jordan. — London (10 Spring Gardens, SW1A 2BN) : National Equivalence Information Centre, The British Council, 1981. — 5p ; 30cm
Unpriced (unbound) B82-22295

370'.95695 — Jordan. West Bank. Education

West Bank. — London (10 Spring Gardens, SW1A 2BN) : National Equivalence Information Centre, The British Council, 1981. — 3p ; 30cm
Unpriced (unbound) B82-22300

370'.96 — Africa. Education

Education in Africa : a comparative survey / edited by A. Babs Fafunwa, J.U. Aisiku. — London : Allen & Unwin, c1982. — 270p : 1map ; 22cm
Map on inside cover. — Includes index
ISBN 0-04-370113-2 (pbk) : Unpriced : CIP rev. B82-03717

370'.9629 — Southern Sudan. Education, *1899-1964*

Sanderson, Lilian Passmore. Education, religion & politics in Southern Sudan 1899-1964 / by Lilian Passmore Sanderson and Neville Sanderson. — London : Ithaca, 1981. — vi,511p,[6]p of plates : 3maps ; 23cm. — (Ithaca Press Sudan studies ; no.4)
Bibliography: p462-482. — Includes index
ISBN 0-903729-63-6 : Unpriced B82-33287

370'.963 — Ethiopia. Education

Ethiopia. — London (10 Spring Gardens, SW1A 2BN) : National Equivalence Information Centre, The British Council, 1981. — 4p ; 30cm
Unpriced (unbound) B82-22294

370'.966'25 — Upper Volta. Education

Upper Volta. — London (10 Spring Gardens, SW1A 2BN) : National Equivalence Information Centre, the British Council, 1981. — 3p ; 30cm
Unpriced (unbound) B82-20575

370'.966'26 — Niger. Education

Niger. — London (10 Spring Gardens, SW1A 2BN) : National Equivalence Information Centre, the British Council, 1981. — 3p ; 30cm
Unpriced (unbound) B82-20577

370'.966'4 — Sierra Leone. Education

Sierra Leone. — London (10 Spring Gardens, SW1A 2BN) : National Equivalence Information Centre, the British Council, 1981. — 3p ; 30cm
Unpriced (unbound) B82-20578

370'.966'51 — Gambia. Education

Gambia. — London (10 Spring Gardens, SW1A 2BN) : National Equivalence Information Centre, the British Council, 1981. — 2p ; 30cm
Unpriced (unbound) B82-20466

370'.9666'2 — Liberia. Education

Liberia. — London (10 Spring Gardens, SW1A 2BN) : National Equivalence Information Centre, the British Council, 1981. — 3p ; 30cm
Unpriced (unbound) B82-20461

370'.9666'8 — Ivory Coast. Education

Ivory Coast. — London (10 Spring Gardens, SW1A 2BN) : National Equivalence Information Centre, the British Council, 1981. — 3p ; 30cm
Unpriced (unbound) B82-20465

370'.9669'5 — Nigeria. Northern states. Education, *to 1981*

Ozigi, Albert. Education in Northern Nigeria / Albert Ozigi, Lawrence Ocho. — London : Allen & Unwin, 1981. — x,143p : ill,1map ; 22cm
Bibliography: p136-137. — Includes index
ISBN 0-04-372036-6 (pbk) : Unpriced : CIP rev. B81-33914

370'.967'21 — Gabon. Education

Gabon. — London (The British Council, 10 Spring Gardens, SW1A 2BN) : National Equivalence Information Centre, 1982. — 3p ; 30cm
Unpriced (unbound) B82-34714

370'.967'24 — Congo. Education

Congo. — London (The British Council, 10 Spring Gardens, SW1A 2BN) : National Equivalence Information Centre, 1982. — 3p ; 30cm
Unpriced (unbound) B82-34718

370'.967'3 — Angola. Education

Angola. — London (The British Council, 10 Spring Gardens, SW1A 2BN) : National Equivalence Information Centre, 1982. — 3p ; 30cm
Unpriced (unbound) B82-34719

370'.967'41 — Central African Republic. Education

Central African Republic. — London (10 Spring Gdns. SW1A 2BN) : National Equivalence Information Centre, British Council, 1981. — 3p ; 30cm
Unpriced (unbound) B82-19586

370'.9675'1 — Zaire. Education

Zaire. — London (10 Spring Gardens, SW1A 2BN) : National Equivalence Information Centre, the British Council, 1981. — 4p ; 30cm
Unpriced (unbound) B82-20582

370'.9676'2 — Kenya. Education

Kenya. — London (10 Spring Gardens, SW1A 2BN) : National Equivalence Information Centre, the British Council, 1981. — 6p ; 30cm
Unpriced (unbound) B82-20460

370'.9678'1 — Tanzania. Zanzibar. Education

Zanzibar/Tanzania. — London (10 Spring Gardens, SW1A 2BN) : National Equivalence Information Centre, The British Council, 1981. — 2p ; 30cm
Unpriced (unbound) B82-22296

370'.9678'2 — Tanzania. Tanganyika. Education

Tanzania/Tanganyika. — London (10 Spring Gardens, SW1A 2BN) : National Equivalence Information Centre, The British Council, 1981. — 4p ; 30cm
Unpriced (unbound) B82-22297

370'.96894 — Zambia. Education

Zambia. — London (10 Spring Gardens, SW1A 2BN) : National Equivalence Information Centre, the British Council, 1981. — 5p ; 30cm
Unpriced (unbound) B82-20579

370'.969'82 — Mauritius. Education

Mauritius. — London (10 Spring Gardens, SW1A 2BN) : National Equivalence Information Centre, The British Council, 1981. — 3p ; 30cm
Unpriced (unbound) B82-22286

370'.97281 — Guatemala. Education

Guatemala. — London (10 Spring Gardens, SW1A 2BN) : National Equivalence Information Centre, the British Council, 1981. — 3p ; 30cm
Unpriced (unbound) B82-20468

370'.97282 — Belize. Education

Belize/British Honduras. — London (The British Council, 10 Spring Gardens, SW1A 2BN) : National Equivalence Information Centre, 1982. — 3p ; 30cm
Unpriced (unbound) B82-34717

370'.97283 — Honduras. Education

Honduras. — London (The British Council, 10 Spring Gardens, SW1A 2BN) : National Equivalence Information Centre, 1982. — 3p ; 30cm
Unpriced (unbound) B82-34712

370'.97285 — Nicaragua. Education

Nicaragua. — London (10 Spring Gardens, SW1A 2BN) : National Equivalence Information Centre, the British Council, 1981. — 2p ; 30cm
Unpriced (unbound) B82-20581

370'.97286 — Costa Rica. Education

Costa Rica. — London (10 Spring Gardens, SW1A 2BN) : National Equivalence Information Centre, the British Council, 1981. — 5p ; 30cm
Unpriced (unbound) B82-20463

370'.97287 — Panama. Education

Panama. — London (10 Spring Gardens, SW1A 2BN) : National Equivalence Information Centre, The British Council, 1981. — 3p ; 30cm
Unpriced (unbound) B82-22293

370'.97291 — Cuba. Education

Cuba. — London (10 Spring Gardens, SW1A 2BN) : National Equivalence Information Centre, the British Council, 1981. — 3p ; 30cm
Unpriced (unbound) B82-20462

370′.97295 — Puerto Rico. Education

Puerto Rico. — London (10 Spring Gardens, SW1A 2BN) : National Equivalence Information Centre, the British Council, 1981. — 2p ; 30cm
Unpriced (unbound) B82-20580

370′.97296 — Bahamas. Education. Role of Methodist Church, *1790-1975*

Williams, Colbert V.. The Methodist contribution to education in the Bahamas. — Gloucester : Alan Sutton, Oct.1982. — [256]p
ISBN 0-86299-027-0 : £16.00 : CIP entry B82-23874

370′.97298′1 — Barbados. Education

Barbados. — London (10 Spring Gardens, SW1A 2BN) : National Equivalence Information Centre, the British Council, 1981. — 3p ; 30cm
Unpriced (unbound) B82-20464

370′.97298′3 — Trinidad and Tobago. Education

Trinidad and Tobago. — London (10 Spring Gardens, SW1A 2BN) : National Equivalence Information Centre, the British Council, 1981. — 3p ; 30cm
Unpriced (unbound) B82-20576

370′.973 — United States. Education

Introduction to the foundations of American education / James A. Johnson ... [et al.]. — 5th ed. — Boston ; London : Allyn and Bacon, c1982. — xiv,482p : ill(some col.),1facsim ; 25cm
Previous ed.: 1979. — Text on lining papers. — Includes bibliographies and index
ISBN 0-205-07631-9 : Unpriced B82-26936

370′.973 — United States. Education — *For teaching*

Bloom, Benjamin S.. All our children learning : a primer for parents, teachers and other educators / Benjamin S. Bloom. — New York ; London : McGraw-Hill, c1981 (1982 [printing]). — xii,275p ; 23cm
Includes bibliographies and index
ISBN 0-07-006121-1 (pbk) : £5.50 B82-29495

370′.984 — Bolivia. Education

Bolivia. — London (10 Spring Gardens, SW1A 2BN) : National Equivalence Information Centre, The British Council, 1981. — 5p ; 30cm
Unpriced (unbound) B82-22290

370′.987 — Venezuela. Education

Venezuela. — London (10 Spring Gardens, SW1A 2BN) : National Equivalence Information Centre, The British Council, 1981. — 5p ; 30cm
Unpriced (unbound) B82-22292

370′.988′1 — Guyana. Education

Guyana. — London (10 Spring Gardens, SW1A 2BN) : National Equivalence Information Centre, the British Council, 1981. — 3p ; 30cm
Unpriced (unbound) B82-20467

370′.9892 — Paraguay. Education

Paraguay. — London (10 Spring Gardens, SW1A 2BN) : National Equivalence Information Centre, The British Council, 1981. — 4p ; 30cm
Unpriced (unbound) B82-22288

370′.9895 — Uruguay. Education

Uruguay. — London (10 Spring Gardens, SW1A 2BN) : National Equivalence Information Centre, The British Council, 1981. — 3p ; 30cm
Unpriced (unbound) B82-22291

370′.993′4 — Vanuatu. Education

Vanuatu/New Hebrides. — London (10 Spring Gardens, SW1A 2BN) : National Equivalence Information Centre, The British Council, 1981. — 4p ; 30cm
Unpriced (unbound) B82-22299

370′.994 — Australia. Education, *to 1980*

Barcan, Alan. A history of Australian education / Alan Barcan. — Melbourne ; London : Oxford University Press, 1980. — vii,415p : ill,1map,1facsim,1port ; 23cm
Includes index
ISBN 0-19-554251-7 (cased) : £19.00
ISBN 0-19-554229-0 (pbk) : Unpriced B82-08293

370′.996′11 — Fiji. Education

Fiji. — London (The British Council, 10 Spring Gardens, SW1A 2BN) : National Equivalence Information Centre, 1982. — 3p ; 30cm
Unpriced (unbound) B82-34716

371 — SCHOOLS

371 — England. Schools. Prospectuses. Preparation — *Manuals*

Taylor, Felicity. ACE school prospectus planning kit : a guide to help schools provide information for parents and students / compiled for the Advisory Centre for Education by Felicity Taylor. — London : The Centre, c1980. — 32p : ill ; 30cm
Cover title. — Text on inside covers
ISBN 0-900029-55-2 (pbk) : Unpriced B82-33031

371′.006′042 — England. Schools. Organisations: Schools Council — *Proposals*

Trenaman, Nancy. Review of the Schools Council / report from Nancy Trenaman ... to the Secretaries of State for Education and Science and for Wales and to the Local Authority Associations. — [London] : Department of Education and Science, 1981. — 48p,[26]p ; 30cm
Cover title
Unpriced (pbk) B82-17334

371′.00941 — Great Britain. Schools. Choice by parents

Midwinter, Eric. Education choice thoughts : a discussion of the pros and cons of parental choice of school / written by Eric Midwinter for the Advisory Centre for Education. — London : The Advisory Centre, 1980. — 18p ; 21cm. — (An ACE handbook)
ISBN 0-900029-51-x (pbk) : £1.00 B82-32796

Taylor, Felicity. Choosing a school : how to get information : what questions to ask / written for the Advisory Centre for Education by Felicity Taylor. — 2nd rev. ed. — London : The Centre, 1981. — 56p : ill,1form ; 21cm. — (An ACE handbook)
Previous ed.: 1975. — Bibliography: p51-52
ISBN 0-900029-58-7 (pbk) : Unpriced B82-33167

371′.009413′1 — Scotland. Central Region. Schools — *Statistics — Serials*

Central Region. *Department of Education*. Central Region schools' capacity study / Central Regional Council, Departments of Education and Planning. — 1976/77 to 1982/83-. — [Stirling] ([Viewforth, Stirling FK8 2ET]) : [The Council], 1977-. — v. : ill ; 21x30cm
Annual. — Description based on: 1979/80 issue
ISSN 0261-1015 = Central Region schools' capacity study : Unpriced B82-14786

371′.009413′4 — Edinburgh. Calton Hill region. Schools, *to 1976*

In the shadow of Calton Hill. — [Edinburgh] ([8A Great King St., Edinburgh]) : [John Dickie], 1977. — 26p : ill,1map ; 21cm
Unpriced (pbk) B82-23606

371′.00942 — England. Schools

Sallis, Joan. The school in its setting : a guide to the education service for school governors, teachers, students and parent groups / written by Joan Sallis for the Advisory Centre for Education. — 2nd rev. ed. — London : The Advisory Centre, 1980. — 30p : ill ; 21cm. — (An ACE handbook)
Previous ed.: 1980. — Includes index
ISBN 0-900029-53-6 (pbk) : £1.00 B82-32797

371′.00942 — England. Schools — *Statistics — Serials*

Statistics of schools. — Jan. 1980-. — Darlington (Room 027, Mowden Hall, Staindrop Rd, Darlington DL3 9BG) : Department of Education and Science. Statistics Branch, 1981-. — v. ; 30cm
Annual. — Continues: Statistics of Education. Vol.1, Schools
ISSN 0263-7847 = Statistics of schools : Unpriced B82-32351

371′.00973 — United States. Schools. Choice by parents

Family choice in schooling : issues and dilemmas / edited by Michael E. Manley-Casimir. — Lexington, Mass : Lexington Books ; [Aldershot] : Gower [distributor], c1982. — xiii,210p ; 24cm
ISBN 0-669-04546-2 : £16.50 B82-28769

371′.00973 — United States. Schools. Education. Innovation

Improving schools : using what we know / edited by Rolf Lehming, Michael Kane. — Beverly Hills ; London : Sage, c1981. — 312p : ill ; 23cm. — (Sage focus editions ; 29)
Bibliography: p287-310
ISBN 0-8039-1623-x (cased) : Unpriced
ISBN 0-8039-1624-8 (pbk) : £6.50 B82-07905

Sarason, Seymour B.. The culture of the school and the problem of change / Seymour B. Sarason. — 2nd ed. — Boston, [Mass.] ; London : Allyn and Bacon, c1982. — ix,311p ; 24cm
Previous ed.: 1971. — Bibliography: p299-305. — Includes index
ISBN 0-205-07700-5 (pbk) : Unpriced B82-27100

371′.00994 — Australia. Schools. Social aspects

Making the difference : schools, families and social division. — London : Allen & Unwin, Apr.1982. — [224]p
ISBN 0-86861-124-7 : £15.00 : CIP entry B82-05767

371′.01′0973 — United States. State schools

Maeroff, Gene I.. Don't blame the kids : the trouble with America's public schools / Gene I. Maeroff. — New York ; London : McGraw-Hill, c1982. — xii,260p ; 24cm
Includes index
ISBN 0-07-039465-2 : £11.50 B82-16380

371′.02′02541 — Great Britain. Independent schools — *Directories*

Schools — private. — Great Missenden : Data Research Group, [1981]. — 183p ; 30cm
Cover title
ISBN 0-86099-349-3 (pbk) : Unpriced B82-24689

371′.02′025427 — Northern England. Independent schools — *Directories*

A **Guide** to independent schools in Northern England and North Wales / ISIS (North). — [York] ([9 Minster Yard, York YO1 2HH]) : ISIS (North), 1981. — 72p : 1col.map ; 21cm
Map (29x32cm folded to 14x17cm) as insert
Unpriced (pbk) B82-03848

371′.03′0942 — England. Community schools — *National Union of Teachers viewpoints*

National Union of Teachers. Community schools : a Union view / a policy statement by the National Union of Teachers. — [London] ([Hamilton House, Mabledon Place, WC1H 9BD]) : [National Union of Teachers], [1981]. — 21p ; 30cm
Cover title
Unpriced (pbk) B82-19752

371′.04 — England. Free schools — *Proposals*

A **Case** for alternative schools within the maintained System. — London : Advisory Centre for Education, [1982?]. — 10p ; 21cm
Bibliography: p10
ISBN 0-900029-60-9 (pbk) : Unpriced B82-32795

371.1 — TEACHING AND TEACHING PERSONNEL

371.1'0092'4 — Soviet Union. Teaching — *Personal observations*

Shatskiĭ, S. T.. A teacher's experience : a collection / Stanislav Shatsky ; [translated from the Russian by Catherine Judelson] ; [compiled and commented by D.J. Latishina] ; [preface by N.P. Kuzin]. — Moscow : Progress ; [London] : distributed by Central, c1981. — 341p : 1port ; 20cm
Translation of: Opyt pedagoga. — Includes index
ISBN 0-7147-1739-8 : £3.95 B82-29709

371.1'0092'4 — Ukraine. Pavlysh. Teaching, *1945-1970* — *Personal observations*

Sukhomlinskiĭ, V. A.. To children I give my heart / Vasily Sukhomlinsky ; [translated from the Russian by Holly Smith]. — Moscow : Progress ; [London] : Distributed by Central Books, c1981. — 436p ; 18cm
Translation of: Serdtse otdaiu detiam
ISBN 0-7147-1748-7 : £3.50 B82-40117

371.1'02 — Capitalist countries. Schools. Teaching — *Marxist viewpoints*

Harris, Kevin. Teachers and classes : a Marxist analysis / Kevin Harris. — London : Routledge & Kegan Paul, 1982. — ix,173p : ill ; 22cm. — (Routledge education books)
Bibliography: p162-167. — Includes index
ISBN 0-7100-0865-1 (pbk) : £4.95 B82-12940

371.1'02 — Schools. Teachers. Interpersonal relationships with students. Psychological aspects

Rogers, Colin, *1936-*. A social psychology of schooling : the expectancy process / Colin Rogers. — London : Routledge & Kegan Pual, 1982. — xi,198p : ill ; 23cm. — (Routledge education books)
Bibliography: p178-192. — Includes index
ISBN 0-7100-9012-9 (cased) : £9.75
ISBN 0-7100-9013-7 (pbk) : £5.95 B82-26595

371.1'02 — Schools. Teaching

Doing teaching : the practical management of classrooms / edited by G.C.F. Payne and E.C. Cuff. — London : Batsford, 1982. — xi,193p : plans ; 22cm
Bibliography: p187-189. — Includes index
ISBN 0-7134-4380-4 (pbk) : £5.95 : CIP rev. B82-15827

Teacher learning / edited by Gwyneth Dow ; with contributions from Rory Barnes ... [et al.]. — London : Routledge & Kegan Paul, 1982. — x,185p : ill,2forms ; 22cm. — (Routledge education books)
Includes index
ISBN 0-7100-9020-x (pbk) : £5.95 B82-32504

371.1'02 — Schools. Teaching — *Manuals*

Honeyford, R.. Starting teaching / R. Honeyford. — London : Croom Helm, c1982. — 178p ; 23cm
Bibliography: p176. — Includes index
ISBN 0-7099-1226-9 (cased) : £10.95 : CIP rev.
ISBN 0-7099-1227-7 (pbk) : Unpriced B81-33895

371.1'02 — Teaching

Combs, Arthur W.. A personal approach to teaching : beliefs that make a difference / Arthur W. Combs. — Boston ; London : Allyn and Bacon, c1982. — x,194p ; 21cm
Includes bibliographies and index
ISBN 0-205-07643-2 (pbk) : £9.95 B82-17097

371.1'02 — Teaching — *Manuals*

Elliott-Kemp, John. The effective teacher : a person-centred devlopment guide / John Elliott-Kemp, Carl Rogers. — Sheffield : PAVIC Publications, c1982. — 42p : ill ; 30cm. — (Gems ; 10)
Cover title. — Includes bibliographies
ISBN 0-903761-83-1 (spiral) : Unpriced B82-39035

Perrott, Elizabeth. Effective teaching. — London : Longman, Jan.1983. — [192]p
ISBN 0-582-49712-4 (pbk) : £3.95 : CIP entry B82-32468

Waterhouse, Philip. Managing the learning process. — London : McGraw-Hill, Jan.1983. — [224]p. — (McGraw-Hill series for teachers)
ISBN 0-07-084136-5 (pbk) : £5.25 : CIP entry B82-33601

371.1'02'01 — Teaching — *Philosophical perspectives*

Cohen, Brenda. Means and ends in education. — London : Allen & Unwin, Nov.1982. — [128]p
ISBN 0-04-370122-1 (cased) : £8.50 : CIP entry
ISBN 0-04-370123-x (pbk) : £3.50 B82-27814

371.1'02'019 — Teaching. Psychological aspects

Gowin. Educating / D. Bob Gowin. — Ithaca ; London : Cornell University Press, c1981. — 210p : ill ; 23cm
Bibliography: p203-205. — Includes index
ISBN 0-8014-1418-0 : Unpriced B82-16915

Psychological aspects of learning and teaching. — London : Croom Helm, Nov.1982. — [224]p
ISBN 0-7099-0460-6 : £14.95 : CIP entry
Primary classification 370.15'23'019 B82-29012

371.1'02'02341 — Great Britain. Teaching — *Career guides*

Teaching / [written, designed and produced by SGS Education ; photographs by André Gordon ; illustrations by Barrie Thorpe and John Plumb ; careers adviser Brian Heap]. — Walton on Thames : Nelson, 1981. — 15p : ill,ports ; 28cm. — (Career profiles ; 23)
ISBN 0-17-438362-2 (unbound) : Unpriced B82-14313

371.1'02'05 — Schools. Teaching. Applications of behavioural sciences — *Serials*

Behavioural approaches with children : the quarterly journal of the Association for Behavioural Approaches with Children. — Vol.5, no.2 (June 1981)-. — Hartlepool (c/o S. Winter, County Psychological Service, Burn Valley Centre, Elwick Rd, Hartlepool, Cleveland) : The Association, 1981-. — v. ; 21cm
Continues: Behaviour modification with children
ISSN 0262-4109 = Behavioural approaches with children : Unpriced B82-15766

371.1'02'0966 — West Africa. Teaching — *Manuals*

Robinson, Adjai. Principles and practice of teaching / Adjai Robinson. — London : Allen & Unwin, 1980. — 160p : ill,forms ; 20cm
Includes index
ISBN 0-04-370098-5 (pbk) : £2.50 : CIP rev. B80-18206

371.1'02'09669 — Nigeria. Schools. Teaching

Bello, Joseph Y.. Basic principles of teaching / Joseph Y. Bello (Chief). — Ibadan : Spectrum ; Chichester : Wiley, c1981. — xiii,169p : ill ; 24cm. — (Education in Africa)
Bibliography: p165-166. — Includes index
ISBN 0-471-27979-x (cased) : £9.00 : CIP rev.
ISBN 0-471-27981-1 (pbk) : Unpriced B81-28042

371.1'02'0973 — United States. Schools. Teaching

Grant, Carl A.. Bringing teaching to life : an introduction to education / Carl A. Grant. — Boston ; London : Allyn and Bacon, c1982. — xx,504p : ill(some col.) ; 25cm + Instructor's manual(113p ; 24cm)
Includes index
ISBN 0-205-07635-1 : Unpriced
ISBN 0-205-07636-x (instructor's manual) B82-26940

371.1'02'0973 — United States. Schools. Teaching — *Manuals*

Hoover, Kenneth H.. The professional teacher's handbook : a guide for improving instruction in today's middle and secondary schools / Kenneth H. Hoover. — Boston, Mass. ; London : Allyn and Bacon, c1982. — xiv,672p : ill ; 24cm
Previous ed.: 1976. — Includes index
ISBN 0-205-07724-2 : Unpriced B82-28518

371.1'022 — Schools. Teachers. Communication with students

Communicating in the classroom : a guide for subject teachers on the more effective use of reading, writing and talk / contributing editor Clive Sutton. — London : Hodder and Stoughton, c1981. — 121p : ill ; 25cm
Includes bibliographies
ISBN 0-340-26659-7 (pbk) : £3.95 B82-05548

Communication in the classroom : original essays / edited by Larry L. Barker. — Englewood Cliffs ; London : Prentice-Hall, c1982. — xviii,174p : ill ; 24cm
Includes bibliographies and index
ISBN 0-13-153551-x : £10.45 B82-21695

371.1'024 — Children. Classroom behaviour. Behaviour modification

Harrop, Alex. Behaviour modification in the classroom. — London : Hodder & Stoughton, Feb.1983. — [160]p
ISBN 0-340-28172-3 (pbk) : £3.45 : CIP entry B82-38044

371.1'024 — Classroom behaviour

Dreikurs, Rudolf. Maintaining sanity in the classroom : classroom management techniques / the late Rudolf Dreikurs, Bernice Bronia Grunwald, Floy Childers Pepper. — 2nd ed. — New York ; London : Harper & Row, c1982. — xii,353p : 1ill ; 24cm
Previous ed.: 1971. — Includes bibliographies and index
ISBN 0-06-041761-7 (pbk) : Unpriced B82-08631

371.1'024 — Schools. Classrooms. Discipline — *For teaching*

Wragg, E. C.. Class management and control : a teaching skills workbook / E.C. Wragg. — Basingstoke : Macmillan Education, 1981. — 79p : forms ; 30cm. — (DES teacher education project focus books)
Text on inside cover. — Bibliography: p79
ISBN 0-333-31656-8 (pbk) : Unpriced B82-10092

371.1'04'0951 — China. Society. Role of teachers. Political aspects, *1949-1980*

White, Gordon, *1942-*. Party and professionals : the political role of teachers in contemporary China / Gordon White. — Armonk, N.Y. : Sharpe ; London : distributed by Eurospan, c1981. — x,361p ; 24cm
ISBN 0-87332-188-x : £17.00 B82-17303

371.1'22'0973 — United States. Trainers. Training

Grabowski, Stanley M.. Preparing educators of adults / Stanley M. Grabowski and associates. — San Francisco ; London : Jossey-Bass, 1981. — xix,164p : ill ; 24cm. — (The AEA handbook series in adult education) (The Jossey-Bass series in higher education)
Bibliography: p139-156. — Includes index
ISBN 0-87589-509-3 : £13.75 B82-17052

371.1'46 — Schools. Teachers. In-service training

Morant, Roland W.. In-service education within the school / Roland W. Morant. — London : Allen & Unwin, 1981. — x,125p : ill ; 23cm. — (Unwin education books)
Includes index
ISBN 0-04-370111-6 (cased) : £10.00 : CIP rev.
ISBN 0-04-370112-4 (pbk) : Unpriced B81-33915

Rudduck, Jean. Making the most of the short in-service course. — London : Methuen Educational, Dec.1981. — [160]p. — (Schools Council working paper, ISSN 0533-1668 ; 71)
ISBN 0-423-50850-4 (pbk) : £5.75 : CIP entry B81-31701

371.1'46'0941 — Great Britain. Schools. Teachers. In-service training

Bolam, Ray. School-focussed in-service training. — London : Heinemann Educational, June 1982. — [256]p. — (Organization in schools series)
ISBN 0-435-80090-6 : £9.95 : CIP entry B82-09725

371.1′46′0941 — Great Britain. Schools. Teachers. In-service training *continuation*

In-service : the teacher and the school / edited by Carol Donoughue with Sue Ball, Bob Glaister and Geoffrey Hand for the Open University Centre for Continuing Education (INSET). — London : Kogan Page in association with the Open University Press, 1981. — 256p : ill ; 22cm. — (An Open University set book)
Includes bibliographies
ISBN 0-85038-497-4 (pbk) : £9.75 : CIP rev.
B81-30888

Initial in-service training for teachers. — London : Croom Helm, Oct.1982. — [144]p
ISBN 0-7099-1248-x : £11.95 : CIP entry
B82-25734

Neville, Clive. Development and use of materials for in-service training of teachers. — London : Council for Educational Technology, Oct.1982. — [80]p. — (Working paper, ISSN 0307-9571 ; 21)
ISBN 0-86184-073-9 (pbk) : £5.50 : CIP entry
B82-33357

371.1′46′0942 — England. Teachers. In-service training — *National Union of Teachers viewpoints*

National Union of Teachers. The importance of in-service education in the professional development of teachers / NUT. — [London] ([Hamilton House, Mabledon Place, WC1H 9BD]) : [National Union of Teachers], 1981. — 17p ; 21cm
Cover title
£0.50 (pbk) B82-19750

371.1′46′094217 — South-west Outer London. Schools. Teachers. In-service training. Attitudes of head teachers

Lomax, P. (Pamela). Headteachers' perspectives on INSET / P. Lomax ad B. McDonald. — Kingston upon Thames (Kingston Polytechnic, Gipsy Hill Centre, Kingston Hill, Kingston upon Thames, Surrey KT2 7LB) : INSET Research Project, [1979]. — 18p : 1form ; 30cm. — (Working paper / KINPOL INSET Project)
Cover title
Unpriced (pbk)
Also classified at 371.1′46′094221 B82-02290

371.1′46′0942195 — London. Richmond upon Thames *(London Borough).* **Teachers. In-service training. Attitudes of teachers**

Lomax, P. (Pamela). Richmond teachers' perspectives on INSET / P. Lomax, B. McDonald and P.J. Murphy ; preface by S.T. Lewis. — Kingston upon Thames (Kingston Polytechnic, Gipsy Hill Centre, Kingston Hill, Kingston upon Thames, Surrey KT2 7LB) : INSET Research Project, [1981]. — 16p ; 30cm. — (Working paper / KINPOL INSET Project ; 2/81)
Cover title
Unpriced (pbk) B82-02291

371.1′46′094221 — Surrey. Schools. Teachers. In-service training. Attitudes of head teachers

Lomax, P. (Pamela). Headteachers' perspectives on INSET / P. Lomax ad B. McDonald. — Kingston upon Thames (Kingston Polytechnic, Gipsy Hill Centre, Kingston Hill, Kingston upon Thames, Surrey KT2 7LB) : INSET Research Project, [1979]. — 18p : 1form ; 30cm. — (Working paper / KINPOL INSET Project)
Cover title
Unpriced (pbk)
Primary classification 371.1′46′094217
B82-02290

371.2 — SCHOOL ADMINISTRATION

371.2 — Educational institutions. Management

The **Management** of educational institutions : theory, research and consultancy / edited by H.L. Gray. — Lewes, Falmer, 1982. — iv,294p : ill,2forms ; 24cm. — (Curriculum series for teachers)
Includes bibliographies and index
ISBN 0-905273-25-7 (cased) : £11.95
ISBN 0-905273-24-9 (pbk) : £6.95 B82-26914

371.2 — England. Schools. Evaluation

Smith, Kevin R.. Developments towards formalised processes for school self-evaluation / by Kevin R. Smith. — [Sheffield] : Sheffield City Polytechnic Department of Education Management, 1980. — 30leaves ; 20cm. — (Sheffield papers in education management ; no.18)
ISBN 0-903761-33-5 (pbk) : Unpriced
B82-03247

371.2 — United States. Schools. Administrators. Sex roles

Educational policy and management : sex differentials / edited by Patricia A. Schmuck, W.W. Charters, Jr, Richard O. Carlson. — New York ; London : Academic Press, 1981. — xiv,337p ; 24cm. — (Educational psychology)
Includes bibliographies and index
ISBN 0-12-627350-2 : £17.60 B82-15540

371.2′00941 — Great Britain. Schools. Administration

Barry, C. H.. Running a school / C.H. Barry and F. Tye. — 2nd ed. — London : Temple Smith, 1975 (1979 [printing]). — 247p ; 22cm. — (Teaching in practice)
Previous ed.: 1972. — Bibliography: p239-247
ISBN 0-85117-190-7 (pbk) : £3.75 B82-07852

371.2′00941 — Great Britain. Schools. Management

Management and the school. — Milton Keynes : Open University Press. — (Educational studies : a third level course)
At head of title: The Open University
Management and the school : using the literature / prepared by Sheila Dale for the course team. — 1981. — 32p : ill ; 30cm. — (E323)
Unpriced (pbk) B82-11344

371.2′009669 — Nigeria. Schools. Administration

Musaazi, J. C. S.. The theory and practice of educational administration / J.C.S. Musaazi. — London : Macmillan Nigeria, 1982. — 274p : ill ; 22cm. — (Studies in Nigerian education)
Includes bibliographies and index
ISBN 0-333-31489-1 (pbk) : £5.95 B82-32335

371.2′01 — Education. Personnel management

Rebore, Ronald W.. Personnel administration in education : a management approach / Ronald W. Rebore. — Englewood Cliffs ; London : Prentice-Hall, c1982. — x,358p : ill ; 24cm
Bibliography: p350-351. — Includes index
ISBN 0-13-657742-3 : £17.20 B82-35161

371.2′012′0924 — Suffolk. Leiston. Boarding schools: Summerhill School. Neill, A. S. — *Correspondence, diaries, etc.*

Reich, Wilhelm. Record of a friendship : the correspondence between Wilhelm Reich and A.S. Neill : 1936-1957 / edited, and with an introduction, by Beverley R. Placzek. — London : Gollancz, 1982, c1981. — xviii,429p : 1port ; 24cm
Originally published: New York : Farrar, Straus, Giroux, 1981. — Includes index
ISBN 0-575-03054-2 : £12.50
Primary classification 150.19′52′0924
B82-10195

371.2′012′0942 — England. Schools. Headmasters

Blackburn, Keith. Head of house, head of year. — London : Heinemann Educational, Jan.1983. — [256]p. — (Organization in schools)
ISBN 0-435-80081-7 : £9.50 : CIP entry
B82-32851

371.2′04 — Great Britain. Educational institutions. Self-evaluation

James, Mary. A first review and register of school and college initiated self-evaluation activities, in the United Kingdom / by Mary James with the assistance of Leseley Holly. — Milton Keynes : Educational Evaluation and Accountability Research Group, Faculty of Educational Studies, The Open University, 1982. — iii,113p : 1facsim,2maps ; 30cm
Bibliography: p97-98
ISBN 0-335-10112-7 (spiral) : £1.50
B82-41131

371.2′06′0973 — United States. Schools. Financial management

Burrup, Percy E.. Financing education in a climate of change. — 3rd ed. / Percy E. Burrup, Vern Brimley, Jr. — Boston, [Mass.] ; London : Allyn and Bacon, c1982. — vii,424p : ill ; 25cm
Previous ed.: 1977. — Includes bibliographies and index
ISBN 0-205-07748-x : Unpriced B82-23518

371.2′07 — England. Schools. Effectiveness. Self-assessment

Adelman, Clem. The self-evaluating institution. — London : Methuen, Nov.1982. — [220]p
ISBN 0-416-32740-0 (cased) : £9.95 : CIP entry
ISBN 0-416-32750-8 (pbk) : £4.95 B82-28288

371.2′1 — Distance study institutions. Students. Admission

Friedman, H. Zvi. The admission system in distance teaching institutions / by H. Zvi Friedman. — Milton Keynes (Walton Hall, Milton Keynes MK7 6AA) : Open University Distance Education Research Group, 1981. — 35p : ill ; 25cm. — (DERG papers ; no.2)
Cover title
£1.50 (pbk) B82-06690

371.2′16′094259 — Buckinghamshire. Schools. Students. Admission, *1982-1983* — *For parents*

Buckinghamshire. *Education Department.* Admissions to schools 1982-83 : information for parents / Buckinghamshire County Council Education Department. — [Aylesbury] : [The Department], [1981?]. — 40p ; 21cm
Cover title
ISBN 0-86059-225-1 (pbk) : Unpriced
B82-01935

371.2′52 — Great Britain. Schools. Mixed ability groups. Teaching

Mixed ability teaching / edited by Margaret Sands and Trevor Kerry. — London : Croom Helm, c1982. — 125p : ill ; 23cm
Bibliography: p120-121. — Includes index
ISBN 0-7099-2315-5 : £9.95 : CIP rev.
B81-25716

371.2′6′013 — United States. Educational institutions. Students. Tests. Bias. Detection. Methodology — *Conference proceedings*

Handbook of methods for detecting test bias / edited by Ronald A. Berk. — Baltimore ; London : Johns Hopkins University Press, c1982. — x,325p : ill,forms ; 24cm
Conference papers. — Includes bibliographies and index
ISBN 0-8018-2662-4 : Unpriced B82-36046

371.2′64 — Education. Attainment tests. Design

Gronlund, Norman E.. Constructing achievement tests / Norman E. Gronlund. — 3rd ed. — Englewood Cliffs ; London : Prentice-Hall, c1982. — x,148p : ill ; 23cm
Previous ed.: 1977. — Includes index
ISBN 0-13-169151-1 (pbk) : £9.70 B82-16697

371.2′64 — Great Britain. Educational institutions. Students. Continuous assessment. Tests

Ashworth, A. E.. Testing for continuous assessment : a handbook for teachers in schools and colleges / A.E. Ashworth. — London : Evans, 1982. — vii,136p : ill ; 22cm
ISBN 0-237-50516-9 (pbk) : Unpriced
B82-13398

371.2′64 — Schools. Students. Academic achievement. Assessment

Issues in evaluation and accountability / edited by Colin Lacey and Denis Lawton. — London : Methuen, 1981. — x,248p ; 21cm
Includes bibliographies and index
ISBN 0-416-74740-x (cased) : £9.95 : CIP rev.
ISBN 0-416-74750-7 (pbk) : Unpriced
B81-30553

371.2′64 — Schools. Students. Academic achievement. Assessment — *For teaching*

Black, Harry. Keeping track of teaching : assessment in the modern classroom / Harry Black and Patricia Broadfoot. — London : Routledge & Kegan Paul, 1982. — x,154p : forms ; 22cm. — (Routledge education books)
Includes index
ISBN 0-7100-9017-x (pbk) : £5.95 B82-39703

371.2′64 — Students. Academic achievement. Assessment
The **Rise** and fall of national test scores / edited by Gilbert R. Austin, Herbert Garber. — New York ; London : Academic Press, c1982. — xvii,270p : ill ; 24cm. — (Educational psychology)
Includes bibliographies and index
ISBN 0-12-068580-9 : £15.20 B82-29690

371.2′64 — Students. Academic achievement. Assessment. Criterion-referenced tests
Roid, Gale H.. A technology for test-item writing / Gale H. Roid, Thomas M. Haladyna. — New York ; London : Academic Press, 1982. — xii,247p : ill ; 24cm. — (The Educational technology series)
Includes bibliographies and index
ISBN 0-12-593250-2 : £16.60 B82-30016

371.2′64 — Students. Academic achievement. Assessment. Tests. Standardisation. Effects — *Study regions: Ireland (Republic)*
Kellaghan, Thomas. The effects of standardized testing / Thomas Kellaghan, George F. Madaus, Peter W. Airasian. — Boston, Mass. ; London : Kluwer-Nijhoff, c1982. — xiii,284p : ill ; 24cm. — (Evaluation in education and human services)
Bibliography: p263-273. — Includes index
ISBN 0-89838-076-6 : Unpriced B82-19406

371.2′64′0973 — United States. Schools. Students. Academic achievement
Garbarino, James. Successful schools and competent students / James Garbarino with the assistance of C. Elliott Asp. — Lexington, Mass. : Lexington Books, c1981 ; [Aldershot] : Gower [distributor], 1982. — iv,170p ; 24cm
Includes index
ISBN 0-669-04526-8 : £15.00 B82-14750

371.2′7′0942 — England. Schools. Students. Performance. Assessment — *Serials*
APU newsletter / Assessment of Performance Unit. — No.1 (Spring 1982)-. — London (Elizabeth House, York Rd, SE1 7PH) : APU, 1982-. — v. : ports ; 30cm
Two issues yearly
ISSN 0262-8910 = APU newsletter : Unpriced B82-26143

371.3 — TEACHING METHODS

371.3 — Canary Islands. Distance study institutions: Radio ECCA *(Canary Islands)*
Espina Cepeda, Luis. Radio ECCA : a distance learning system in the Canary Islands / by Luis Espina Cepeda ; translated by Geoffrey Pucci ; edited by Keith Harry. — [Milton Keynes] ([Walton Hall, Milton Keynes MK7 6AA]) : Open University, Distance Education Research Group, 1982. — 59p : ill,forms ; 25cm. — (DERG papers ; no.5)
Translated from the Spanish. Appendices in Spanish. — Cover title. — Form on inside cover. — Bibliography: p25-26
Unpriced (pbk) B82-23445

371.3 — Great Britain. Schools. Teaching. Explanation — *Manuals*
Brown, George, *1935-*. Explanations and explaining : a teaching skills workbook / George Brown, Neville Hatton. — Basingstoke : Macmillan Education, 1982. — 63p : ill,forms ; 30cm. — (DES teacher education project focus books)
Bibliography: p62
ISBN 0-333-31660-6 (unbound) : £1.95 B82-32337

371.3 — Lesotho. Distance study institutions: Lesotho Distance Teaching Centre, *to 1980*
Murphy, Paud. The Lesotho distance teaching centre : five years' learning / Paud Murphy. — Cambridge : International Extension College, 1981. — 86p : 1map ; 21cm. — (IEC broadsheets on distance learning ; no.16)
ISBN 0-903632-19-5 (pbk) : Unpriced B82-34635

371.3 — Schools. Teaching methods
Elbaz, Freema. The teacher's practical knowledge. — London : Croom Helm, Nov.1982. — [256]p. — (Croom Helm curriculum policy and research series)
ISBN 0-7099-0910-1 : £12.95 : CIP entry B82-27204

371.3 — Teaching methods — *Manuals*
Walklin, L.. Instructional techniques and practice. — Cheltenham : Stanley Thornes, Sept.1982. — [420]p
ISBN 0-85950-344-5 (pbk) : £7.50 : CIP entry B82-20846

371.3 — Teaching methods: Role-playing
Lewis, Roger, *1944-*. Using role play : an introductory guide / [written by Roger Lewis and John Mee]. — Cambridge : Basic Skills Unit, c1981. — 40p : ill ; 21cm
Bibliography: p40
ISBN 0-86082-206-0 (pbk) : Unpriced B82-38998

371.3′028′12 — Great Britain. Education. Examinations. Techniques — *Manuals*
Coles, M.. How to study and pass exams / M. Coles, C. White. — [Glasgow] : Collins Educational, [1982]. — [64]p : ill,facsims,maps ; 30cm. — (Collins revision aids)
Cover title
ISBN 0-00-197255-3 (pbk) : £1.50
ISBN 0-00-327784-4 (non-net ed.) : Unpriced B82-32061

371.3′028′12 — Schools. Students. Study techniques. Teaching — *Manuals*
Bragstad, Bernice Jensen. A guidebook for teaching study skills and motivation / Bernice Jensen Bragstad, Sharyn Mueller Stumpf. — Boston, Mass. ; London : Allyn and Bacon, c1982. — xiii,312p : ill,1form ; 28cm. — (A Guidebook for teaching series)
Includes bibliographies
ISBN 0-205-07737-4 (pbk) : Unpriced B82-28517

Starting to teach study skills. — London : Edward Arnold, July 1982. — [96]p
ISBN 0-7131-0744-8 (pbk) : £3.50 : CIP entry B82-17913

371.3′028′12 — Study techniques — *Manuals*
Ashman, Sandra. Study and learn : a self-help guide for students / Sandra Ashman, Alan George. — London : Heinemann, 1982. — x,228p : ill ; 22cm
Includes index
ISBN 0-434-90080-x (pbk) : £4.95 B82-36875

Burgen, A. D.. How to study : a practical guide / A.D. Burgen. — London : Harrap, 1982. — 48p : ill ; 18cm
ISBN 0-245-53887-9 (pbk) : £0.95 B82-37446

Freeman, Richard, *1943-*. Mastering study skills / R. Freeman. — [London] : Macmillan, 1982. — 87p : ill ; 23cm. — (Macmillan master series)
ISBN 0-333-31298-8 (cased) : £5.95
ISBN 0-333-30448-9 (pbk) : Unpriced B82-17112

Rowntree, Derek. Learn how to study : a programmed introduction to better study techniques / Derek Rowntree. — 2nd ed. — London : Macdonald, 1976 (1982 [printing]). — ix,158p : ill ; 18cm
Previous ed.: 1970. — Bibliography: p154-156. — Includes index
ISBN 0-354-04009-x (pbk) : £1.25 B82-26843

Sullivan, Tony. Studying / by Tony Sullivan. — Cambridge : National Extension College, c1979. — 54p : ill ; 21cm. — (Studying skills series) (National Extension College course ; no.ED17)
ISBN 0-86082-166-8 (pbk) : Unpriced B82-40821

371.3′028′12 — Study techniques — *Questions & answers — For children*
Milward, Charles. Basic study skills / Charles Milward. — London : Macmillan Education. — (A Macmillan teach and test book)
Teacher's book. — 1981. — 64p : ill,maps,1form ; 26cm
Cover title
ISBN 0-333-29379-7 (pbk) : £1.95 B82-01939

371.3′028′14 — Schools. Students. Study techniques *- For teaching*
Hamblin, D.. Teaching study skills. — Oxford : Blackwell, May 1981. — [176]p
ISBN 0-631-12533-7 (pbk) : CIP entry B81-08931

371.3′07′8 — Educational technology — *Conference proceedings*
Aspects of educational technology. — London : Kogan Page
Conference papers
Vol.15: Distance learning and evaluation. — Dec.1981. — [336]p
ISBN 0-85038-494-x : £14.95 : CIP entry
ISSN 0141-5956 B81-34224

Educational technology twenty years on / edited for the Association for Educational and Training Technology by G. Terry Page and Quentin A. Whitlock. — London : Kogan Page, 1979. — 361p : ill ; 24cm. — (Aspects of educational technology, ISSN 0141-5956 ; v.13)
Conference proceedings. — Includes index
ISBN 0-85038-247-5 : Unpriced B82-33302

371.3′07′8 — Educational technology — *Serials*
International yearbook of educational and instructional technology. — 1982-83. — London : Kogan Page, Mar.1982. — [450]p
ISBN 0-85038-550-4 : £16.50 : CIP entry
ISSN 0307-9732 B82-06050

371.3′07′8 — Great Britain. Educational technology. Organisations: Council for Educational Technology for the United Kingdom *— Serials*
Annual report for the year October-September. — 1981-1982. — London : Council for Educational Technology for the United Kingdom, Dec.1982. — [128]p
ISBN 0-86184-100-x (pbk) : CIP entry
ISSN 0307-921x B82-37643

371.3′07′8 — Great Britain. Schools. Teaching support services. Management
Secondary comprehensive, middle and primary schools / based on an investigation by Gerald Collier ; edited by Norman Willis. — London : Council for Educational Technology, 1981. — 48p ; 21cm. — (Teaching & learning support services ; 3)
ISBN 0-86184-039-9 (pbk) : £4.50 : CIP rev. B81-35870

371.3′2 — Great Britain. Educational institutions. Books. Supply
The **Supply** of books to schools and colleges / [report of the committee of enquiry convened by the Booksellers Association and the Publishers Association under the chairmanship of the Baroness David to consider all aspects of the supply of books to schools and colleges]. — London : Booksellers Association, 1981. — 112p : ill ; 21cm
Bibliography: p73-74. — Includes index
ISBN 0-85386-073-4 (pbk) : Unpriced B82-02916

371.3′3 — Education. Role of mass media — *Serials*
MED : media in education and development : a journal of the British Council. — Vol.14 no.4 (Dec. 1981)-. — Stevenage : Peter Peregrinus for the British Council, 1981-. — v. : ill,maps ; 30cm
Quarterly. — Continues: Educational broadcasting international
ISSN 0262-0251 = MED. Media in education and development : £14.00 per year (£18.00 to libraries) B82-14785

371.3′3 — Scotland. Schools. Use of British educational broadcasting services
'School broadcasting in Scottish schools' : report of the Inter-College Research Project on School Broadcasting / A. Macintyre et al.. — [Glasgow] ([Southbrae Drive, Glasgow G13 1PP]) : Jordanhill College of Education, 1981. — vi,52p ; 30cm
At head of title: National Inter-College Committee on Educational Research
Unpriced (spiral) B82-25249

371.3′3 — Teaching aids: Aduiovisual equipment & audiovisual materials

Audio visual aids in training. — Manchester : Marylebone, 1982. — 64p : ports ; 22cm
Selection of articles from The training officer. — Text on inside cover
ISBN 0-946136-00-9 (pbk) : Unpriced
B82-38464

Heinich, Robert. Instructional media and the new technologies of instruction / Robert Heinich, Michael Molenda, James D. Russell. — New York ; Chichester : Wiley, c1982. — xiv,375p : ill(some col.),ports ; 29cm
Bibliography: p346-350. — Includes index
ISBN 0-471-36893-8 : £13.50 B82-18215

371.3′3 — Teaching aids: Audiovisual equipment

Audio visual and micro-computer handbook. — 3rd ed. — London : Kogan Page, Oct.1982. — [150]p
Previous ed. published as: Audio visual handbook. 1981
ISBN 0-85038-546-6 (pbk) : £11.95 : CIP entry
Also classified at 371.3′9445 B82-26052

371.3′3 — Teaching aids: Audiovisual equipment — *Lists*

Audio visual and video equipment survey. — [London] ([National Audio-visual Aids Centre, Paxton Place, Gipsy Rd., SE27 9SR]) : EFVA, 1981. — 40p : ill ; 30cm
Cover title
Unpriced (pbk) B82-11399

371.3′3 — Teaching aids: Games — *Catalogues*

Jordanhill College of Education. *Audio-Visual Library.* Games and simulations : a list of A-V materials for students and teachers / compiled by George Geddes. — 3rd ed. — Glasgow (76 Southbrae Drive, Glasgow, G13 1PP) : Jordanhill College of Education Library, 1982. — iii,19p ; 21cm. — (Audio visual bibliographies ; no.4)
Previous ed.: 197-?. — Text on inside cover
£0.25 (pbk) B82-35146

371.3′3′0212 — Teaching aids: Audiovisual equipment — *Technical data* **—** *Serials*

[Technical report *(Training & Educational Systems Testing Bureau)***].** Technical report / TEST Bureau. — May 1981-. — London (Vauxhall School, Vauxhall St., SE11 5LG), 1981-. — v. : ill ; 30cm
Six issues yearly. — Continues: Technical report (International Council for Educational Media)
ISSN 0261-2364 = Technical report - TEST Bureau : Unpriced B82-18510

371.3′32 — Education. Teaching methods: Drama

Drama and the whole curriculum / edited by Jon Nixon. — London, 1982. — 200p ; 22cm
Bibliography: p193-197. — Includes index
ISBN 0-09-149251-3 (pbk) : Unpriced : CIP rev. B82-09419

371.3′32 — Great Britain. Secondary schools. Students. Study techniques — *For teaching*

Information skills in the secondary curriculum. — London : Methuen Educational, Sept.1981. — [60]p. — (Schools Council curriculum bulletin ; 9)
ISBN 0-423-50910-1 (pbk) : £4.00 : CIP entry
B81-22643

371.3′333 — Teaching aids: Sound cassette tape recordings — *For school libraries*

Greenhalgh, Michael. Audiocassettes : a guide to selection and management / Michael Greenhalgh. — [Great Britain] : School Library Association, 1982. — 27p ; 21cm. — (School Library Association guidelines ; 2)
Bibliography: p26-27
£2.00 (£1.50 to LA members) (pbk)
B82-19915

371.3′35 — England. Multiracial communities. Schools. Teaching aids: Visual arts

Projects and prospects : art in multicultural society. — Birmingham (Margeret St., Birmingham B3 3BX) : School of Art Education, Birmingham Polytechnic, [1981?]. — 70p,[4]leaves of plates : ill(some col.) ; 30cm
Conference papers. — Cover title
Unpriced (pbk) B82-04424

371.3′35 — Great Britain. Education. Applications of Prestel

Thompson, Vincent. PRESTEL and education : a report of a one-year trial / Vincent Thompson. — London : CET, 1981. — 29p ; 30cm
ISBN 0-86184-055-0 (pbk) : Unpriced
B82-05858

Thompson, Vincent. Videotex in education. — London : Council for Educational Technology, Nov.1982. — [54]p
ISBN 0-86184-072-0 (pbk) : £5.00 : CIP entry
B82-34088

371.3′358′05 — Education. Use of television — *Serials*

Journal of educational television : journal of the Educational Television Association. — Vol.8, no.1 (1982)-. — Abingdon (P.O. Box 25, Abingdon, Oxon OX14 1RW) : Carfax Pub. Co., 1982-. — v. : ill ; 25cm
Three issues yearly. — Continues: Journal of educational television and other media
ISSN 0260-7417 = Journal of educational television : Unpriced B82-24763

371.3′7 — Great Britain. Schools. Students. Questioning by teachers — *Manuals*

Kerry, Trevor. Effective questioning : a teaching skills workbook / Trevor Kerry. — Basingstoke : Macmillan Education, 1982. — [48]p : ill,forms ; 30cm. — (DES teacher education project focus books)
Bibliography: p48
ISBN 0-333-31659-2 (unbound) : £1.95
B82-32331

371.3′7 — Schools. Students. Questioning by teachers — *Manuals*

Kissock, Craig. A guide to questioning : classroom procedures for teachers / Craig Kissock and Peter T. Iyortsuun. — London : Macmillan, 1982. — ix,142p ; 22cm
Bibliography: p138-140. — Includes index
ISBN 0-333-31544-8 (pbk) : £3.95 B82-32382

371.3′8 — Northumberland. National parks: Northumberland National Park. Use by educational institutions

The **Educational** use of Northumberland National Park & countryside. — [Hexham] : Northumberland National Park & Countryside Committee, [1981?]. — 33,5p : ill,facsims,forms ; 30cm. — (Occasional paper ; no.3)
Bibliography: 1 leaf
ISBN 0-907632-01-7 (spiral) : Unpriced
B82-11951

371.3′8 — Oxfordshire. Secondary schools. Educational cruises, *1966-1976* **—** *Personal observations*

Russell, Mary B.. School at sea / Mary B. Russell. — Oxford : Positif, 1980. — 168p : ill,ports ; 22cm
ISBN 0-906894-02-6 (pbk) : £5.00 B82-28510

371.3′94 — Distance study. Tutoring

Lewis, Roger, *1944-.* How to tutor in an open-learning scheme : self-study version / Roger Lewis. — [London] : Council for Educational Technology, 1981. — 187p : ill,forms ; 22cm
ISBN 0-86184-050-x (spiral) : £8.00 : CIP rev.
B81-28976

Lewis, Roger, *1944-.* How to tutor in an open-learning scheme : group-study version / Roger Lewis. — [London] : Council for Educational Technology, 1981. — 191p : ill,forms ; 31cm
ISBN 0-86184-051-8 (pbk) : £15.00 : CIP rev.
B81-28969

371.3′94 — Educational institutions. Students. Individualised instruction. Organisation

Davies, W. J. K.. Alternatives to class teaching in schools and colleges / W.J.K. Davies. — London : Council for Educational Technology, 1980. — 239p : ill,forms ; 21cm. — (Guidelines, ISSN 0308-0323 ; 9)
Includes bibliographies
ISBN 0-86184-011-9 (pbk) : £12.00 : CIP rev.
B80-13760

371.3′94 — Schools. Students. Individualised instruction

Søvik, Nils. On individualized instruction : theories and research / Nils Søvik, Hans Magne Eikeland, Anders Lysne. — Oslo : Universitetsforlaget ; London : Global Book Resources [distributor], c1981. — 243p : ill ; 22cm
Includes bibliographies
ISBN 82-00-05802-6 (pbk) : £12.25
B82-11845

371.3′944 — Self-teaching. Teaching aids. Design & development — *For teaching*

Lewis, Roger, *1944-.* How to write self-study materials / Roger Lewis. — London : Council for Educational Technology, 1981. — 61p : ill ; 21cm. — (Guidelines, ISSN 0308-0323 ; 10)
ISBN 0-86184-036-4 (pbk) : £5.00 : CIP rev.
B81-32001

371.3′9445 — Computer assisted learning

Burke, Robert L.. CAI sourcebook / Robert L. Burke. — Englewood Cliffs ; London : Prentice-Hall, c1982. — 206p : ill,forms ; 24cm
Includes index
ISBN 0-13-110155-2 (cased) : £11.20
ISBN 0-13-110148-x (pbk) : Unpriced
B82-20057

Hawkridge, David G.. New information technology in education. — London : Croom Helm, Nov.1982. — [240]p
ISBN 0-7099-1231-5 : £11.95 : CIP entry
B82-27936

Intelligent tutoring systems / edited by D. Sleeman and J.S. Brown. — London : Academic Press, 1982. — xi,345p : ill ; 26cm. — (Computers and people series)
Includes bibliographies and index
ISBN 0-12-648680-8 : £19.20 : CIP rev.
B82-07491

Papert, Seymour. Mindstorms : children, computers, and powerful ideas / Seymour Papert. — Brighton : Harvester, 1980 (1982 [printing]). — viii,230p : ill ; 21cm
Includes index
ISBN 0-7108-0472-5 (pbk) : £3.95 B82-38145

Selected readings in computer-based learning / edited by Nick Rushby. — London : Kogan Page, 1981. — 234p : ill ; 23cm. — (AETT occasional publications ; no.5)
Bibliography: p222-234
ISBN 0-85038-473-7 : £10.95 : CIP rev.
B81-21542

371.3′9445 — Computer assisted learning — *Conference proceedings*

CAL 81 Symposium *(University of Leeds).* Computer assisted learning. — Oxford : Pergamon, Nov.1981. — [150]p
ISBN 0-08-028111-7 : £12.00 : CIP entry
B81-30288

371.3′9445 — Schools. Teaching aids: Electronic programmable toys

Meredith, M. D.. Bigtrak plus. — London : Council for Educational Technology, Oct.1982. — [120]p. — (Microelectronics Education Programme case study, ISSN 0262-5237 ; 3)
ISBN 0-86184-074-7 (pbk) : £4.50 : CIP entry
B82-32875

371.3′9445 — Schools. Teaching methods. Applications of computer systems

Rushby, Nick. An introduction to educational computing / Nicholas John Rushby. — London : Croom Helm, 1980, c1979. — 123p : ill ; 22cm
Bibliography: p108-112. — Includes index
ISBN 0-7099-2210-8 (pbk) : Unpriced
B82-38556

371.3′9445 — Teaching aids: Microcomputer systems

Audio visual and micro-computer handbook. — 3rd ed. — London : Kogan Page, Oct.1982. — [150]p
Previous ed. published as: Audio visual handbook. 1981
ISBN 0-85038-546-6 (pbk) : £11.95 : CIP entry
Primary classification 371.3′3 B82-26052

371.3'9445 — Teaching aids: Microcomputer systems *continuation*

Nash, Andrew. An introduction to microcomputers in teaching. — London : Hutchinson Education, Sept.1982. — [256]p
ISBN 0-09-149031-6 (pbk) : £5.95 : CIP entry
B82-19151

371.3'9445 — Teaching methods. Applications of computer systems — *Conference proceedings*

IFIP TC-3 World Conference on Computers in Education *(3rd : 1981 : Lausanne)*. Computers in education : proceedings of the IFIP TC-3 3rd World Conference on Computers in Education — WCCE81, Lausanne, Switzerland, July 27-31 1981 / edited by Bob Lewis, Donovan Tagg. — Amsterdam ; Oxford : North-Holland, c1981. — xviii,876p : ill ; 27cm
Includes index
ISBN 0-444-86255-2 : £44.68 B82-13456

371.3'9445 — Training. Applications of digital computer systems

Dean, Christopher. A handbook of computer-based training. — London : Kogan Page, Dec.1982. — [250]p
ISBN 0-85038-557-1 : £13.00 : CIP entry
B82-35184

371.3'9445'0941 — Great Britain. Schools. Teaching. Applications of microcomputer systems — *Serials*

Computers in schools : the journal of MUSE. — Vol.2, no.5 (Sept. 1979)-. — [Harlow] ([MUSE Information Office, Ilmington School, Ilmington Rd, Weoley Castle, Birmingham]) : [Longman], 1979-. — v. : ill ; 30cm
Five issues yearly. — Continues: MUSEletter
ISSN 0263-0982 = Computers in schools : £6.00 per year B82-15143

371.3'95 — Great Britain. Schools. Group teaching — *Manuals*

Kerry, Trevor. Handling classroom groups : a teaching skills workbook / Trevor Kerry, Margaret Sands. — Basingstoke : Macmillan Education, 1982. — 46p : 1ill,forms,plans ; 30cm. — (DES teacher education project focus books)
Bibliography: p45
ISBN 0-333-31661-4 (unbound) : £1.95
B82-32336

371.3'96 — Lecturing — *Manuals*

Brown, George, *1935-*. Lecturing and explaining / George Brown. — London : Methuen, 1978 (1980 [printing]). — ix,134p ; 24cm
Bibliography: p123-131. — Includes index
ISBN 0-416-70910-9 (cased) : Unpriced
ISBN 0-416-70920-6 (pbk) : Unpriced
B82-27493

371.3'97 — Teaching aids: Simulations — *Collections*

Watson, F. R.. Some exercises in simulation : (pupil materials) / F.R. Watson. — [Keele] : University of Keele, Institute of Education, 1980. — 41p in various pagings : ill ; 21x30cm
Unpriced (unbound) B82-36201

371.4 — EDUCATION. GUIDANCE AND COUNSELLING

371.4'0941 — Great Britain. Schools. Students. Counselling

Education and care. — London : Heinemann Educational, Jan.1983. — [288]p. — (Organization in schools)
ISBN 0-435-80642-4 : £12.50 : CIP entry
B82-32853

371.4'25 — Careers guidance

The **Career** adviser's handbook. — London : New Opportunity Press, Dec.1982. — [400]p
ISBN 0-86263-036-3 (pbk) : £8.95 : CIP entry
B82-34089

Healy, Charles C.. Career development : counseling through the life stages / Charles C. Healy. — Boston, Mass. ; London : Allyn and Bacon, c1982. — ix,662p : ill ; 25cm
Bibliography: p611-649. — Includes index
ISBN 0-205-07557-6 : £19.95 B82-11570

371.4'25 — Careers guidance. Applications of graphology

Hill, Barbara. Handwriting analysis as a guide to careers / Barbara Hill. — Sudbury : Spearman, 1982. — 147p : ill,facsims ; 23cm
ISBN 0-85435-474-3 : £4.50 B82-19487

371.4'25'072041 — Great Britain. Careers guidance. Research projects: Career Counselling Programme

Career development counselling : an experiment / MSC. — Sheffield (Moorfoot, Sheffield S1 4PQ) : Manpower Services Commission, 1982. — ii,20p ; 21cm
Unpriced (unbound) B82-38438

371.4'6 — Great Britain. Schools. Welfare work — *Serials*

The **Education** social worker / National Association of Social Workers in Education. — No.171 (Mar. 1977)-. — [Birmingham] ([c/o Mr D. Beer, 19 Moorside Rd, Yardley Wood, Birmingham B14 4HR]) : The Association, 1977-. — v. ; 21cm
Quarterly. — Continues: Education welfare officer. — Description based on: No.188 (Sept. 1981)
ISSN 0263-0664 = Education social worker : £2.50 per year (Free to Association members)
B82-15157

371.4'6 — United States. Schools. Welfare work

Hancock, Betsy Ledbetter. School social work / Betsy Ledbetter Hancock. — Englewood Cliffs ; London : Prentice-Hall, c1982. — viii,262p : ill ; 24cm. — (PH series in social work practice)
Includes bibliographies and index
ISBN 0-13-794453-5 : £14.95 B82-21698

371.5 — SCHOOL DISCIPLINE

371.5 — Schools. Discipline

Furtwengler, Willis J.. Improving school discipline : an administrator's guide / Willis J. Furtwengler, William Konnert. — Boston, Mass. ; London : Allyn and Bacon, c1982. — viii,268p : ill,forms ; 25cm
Includes index
ISBN 0-205-07757-9 : Unpriced B82-27308

371.5'072041 — Great Britain. Schools. Discipline. Research

Wilson, John, *1928-*. Discipline and moral education : a survey of public opinion and understanding / John Wilson. — Windsor : NFER-Nelson, 1981. — viii,137p ; 22cm
Bibliography: p136-137. — Includes index
ISBN 0-85633-233-x (pbk) : £10.95
Primary classification 370.11'4'072041
B82-10711

371.5'0973 — United States. Schools. Discipline. Role of justice

Bybee, Rodger W.. Violence, values, and justice in the schools / Rodger W. Bybee, E. Gordon Gee. — Boston ; London : Allyn and Bacon, c1982. — x,254p ; 25cm
Includes index
ISBN 0-205-07387-5 : £17.95 B82-14468

371.5'42'094 — Europe. Schools. Corporal punishment. Abolition

The **European** example : the abolition of corporal punishment in European schools. — Croydon (c/o Hon. Sec., 10 Lennox Gardens, Croydon, Surrey CRO 4HR) : Society of Teachers Opposed to Physical Punishment, [1981?]. — 28p ; 20cm
Cover title. — Bibliography: p28
Unpriced (pbk) B82-14281

371.5'42'0941 — Great Britain. Schools. Corporal punishment. Abolition

Abolition handbook : corporal punishment in schools / edited for STOPP, Society of Teachers Opposed to Physical Punishment, by Peter Newell. — [Croydon] ([c/o The Secretary, 10 Lennox Gardens, Croydon, Surrey CR0 4HR]) : [STOPP], [1981?]. — 40p : ill ; 21cm
Text on inside covers. — Bibliography: p38
£0.80 (pbk) B82-14280

371.5'42'0941 — Great Britain. Schools. Corporal punishment. Abolition — *Serials*

STOPP news / Society of Teachers Opposed to Physical Punishment. — Oct. 1979-. — Croydon (c/o C. Bagnall, 10 Lennox Gdns, Croydon, Surrey CR0 4HR) : The Society, 1979-. — v. ; 30cm
Six issues yearly. — Continues: Newsletter (Society of Teachers Opposed to Physical Punishment). — Description based on: Dec. 1981/Jan. 1982 issue
ISSN 0263-3787 = STOPP news : Unpriced
B82-23591

371.5'42'09411 — Scotland. Schools. Corporal punishment. Abolition

Making the change : a study of the process of the abolition of corporal punishment / C.E. Cumming ... [et al.]. — Dunton Green : Hodder and Stoughton for the Scottish Council for Research in Education, c1981. — viii,48p : 1ill,3forms ; 22cm. — (SCRE publication ; 76)
ISBN 0-340-28180-4 (cased) : Unpriced
ISBN 0-340-28175-8 (pbk) : £2.95 B82-11852

371.6 — SCHOOL BUILDINGS AND EQUIPMENT

371.6'7 — England. Schools. Applications of microelectronic devices. Programmes: Microelectronics Education Programme

Microelectronics education programme : the strategy. — Stanmore (Honeypot Lane, Canons Park, Stanmore HA7 1AZ) : Publications Despatch Centre, Department of Education and Science, [1981]. — 11p ; 30cm
Unpriced (unbound) B82-17328

371.6'7 — Schools. RML 380Z microcomputer systems. Programming — *Manuals*

Wells, Colin. Aspects of programming for teaching unit design and development. — London : Council for Educational Technology. — (Microelectronics education program information guide, ISSN 0262-2181 ; 2)
1: A practical course using the RML 380Z microcomputer. — Oct.1982. — [256]p
ISBN 0-86184-075-5 (pbk) : £20.00 : CIP entry
B82-32314

371.6'7 — Schools. Sinclair ZX80 & ZX81 microcomputer systemss — *Serials*

EZUG newsletter / Educational ZX80/1 Users' Group. — No.1 (Dec. 1980)-. — Birmingham ([c/o Eric Deeson, Highgate School, Balsall Heath Rd., Birmingham B12 9DS]) : Highgate School, 1980-. — v. : ill ; 30cm
ISSN 0262-0804 = EZUG newsletter : £2.50 per year B82-11820

371.7 — SCHOOL HEALTH AND SAFETY

371.7'0941 — Great Britain. Schools. Health & safety — *For school ancillary services*

School at work : a NUPE health and safety handbook for school ancillary staff. — [London] : National Union of Public Employees, 1981. — 32p : ill ; 16cm
ISBN 0-907334-08-3 (pbk) : £0.25 B82-00632

371.7'7'0941 — Great Britain. Educational institutions. Safety asapects — *For teachers* — *Serials*

Safety in education / Department of Education and Science. — Bull. no.1 (Nov. 1981)-. — London (Elizabeth House, York Rd, SE1 7PH) : The Department, 1981-. — v. : ill ; 30cm
Irregular
ISSN 0262-5229 = Safety in education : Unpriced B82-17242

371.9 — SPECIAL EDUCATION

371.9 — Children. Learning disorders

Devereux, Kathleen. Understanding learning difficulties. — Milton Keynes : Open University Press, Aug.1982. — 1v.. — (Children with special needs)
ISBN 0-335-10049-x (pbk) : CIP entry
B82-25932

371.9 — Children. Learning disorders — *Comparative studies*
Comparative reading and learning difficulties / edited by Lester Tarnopol, Muriel Tarnopol. — Lexington : Lexington Books, c1981 ; Aldershot : Gower [distributor], 1982. — xiii,562p : ill,facsims ; 24cm
Includes bibliographies and index
ISBN 0-669-04107-6 : £27.50 B82-18041

371.9 — Children. Learning disorders — *Serials*
Analysis and intervention in developmental disabilities. — Vol.1, no.1 (1981)-. — New York ; Oxford : Pergamon, 1981-. — v. ; 23cm
Quarterly
ISSN 0270-4684 = Analysis and intervention in developmental disabilities : Unpriced B82-07642

371.9 — Exceptional children. Assessment
Swanson, H. Lee. Educational and psychological assessment of exceptional children : theories, strategies, and applications / H. Lee Swanson, Billy L. Watson. — St. Louis, Mo. ; London : Mosby, 1982. — xvii,468p : ill,forms ; 25cm
Bibliography: p431-454. — Includes index
ISBN 0-8016-4842-4 : £14.00 B82-34467

371.9 — Great Britain. Handicapped young persons. Vocational preparation
Hutchinson, David, *1942-*. Work preparation for the handicapped / David Hutchinson. — London : Croom Helm, c1982. — 109p : ill,1plan,forms ; 25cm. — (Croom Helm special education series)
Bibliography: p105. — Includes index
ISBN 0-7099-0283-2 (pbk) : £6.95 : CIP rev. B81-31440

371.9 — Handicapped children. Education
Morgenstern, Franz. Teaching plans for handicapped children / Franz Morgenstern. — London : Methuen, 1981. — xi,196p : ill ; 22cm
Bibliography: p187-190. — Includes index
ISBN 0-416-73260-7 (cased) : Unpriced : CIP rev.
ISBN 0-416-73270-4 (pbk) : £3.95 B81-25296

371.9 — Handicapped children. Education. Behavioural aspects — *Personal observations*
Madge, Nicola. Ask the children : experiences of physical disability in the school years. — London : Batsford, Oct.1982. — [160]p
ISBN 0-7134-1896-6 : £5.95 : CIP entry B82-22988

371.9 — Special education
The **Nature** of special education : people, places and change : a reader / edited by Tony Booth and June Statham. — London : Croom Helm in association with the Open University Press, c1982. — 450p ; 22cm
Includes index
ISBN 0-7099-1910-7 (pbk) : £5.25 : CIP rev. B81-31430

Special education : policy, practices and social issues / edited by Len Barton and Sally Tomlinson. — London : Harper & Row, c1981. — 270p : ill ; 22cm. — (Harper education series)
Includes bibliographies and index
ISBN 0-06-318199-1 (cased) : Unpriced : CIP rev.
ISBN 0-06-318200-9 (pbk) : Unpriced B81-24623

371.9 — Special education — *Sociological perspectives*
Tomlinson, Sally. A sociology of special education / Sally Tomlinson. — London : Routledge & Kegan Paul, 1982. — 203p : ill ; 22cm
Bibliography: p186-198. — Includes index
ISBN 0-7100-0940-2 (cased) : £8.95
ISBN 0-7100-9003-x (pbk) : £4.50 B82-13772

371.9′042′0973 — United States. Special schools. Administration — *Manuals*
Mayer, C. Lamar. Educational administration and special education : a handbook for school administrators / C. Lamar Mayer. — Boston [Mass.] ; London : Allyn and Bacon, c1982. — xii,383p : ill,forms ; 25cm
Includes bibliographies and index
ISBN 0-205-07555-x : £16.50 B82-08543

371.9′043 — Great Britain. Handicapped pre-school children. Education. Portage system
Working together : portage in the U.K. / edited by R.J. Cameron. — Windsor : NFER-Nelson, 1982. — xii,178p : ill,forms,1map ; 22cm
Collection of papers presented at the first conference on portage in the U.K. held in Lymington, Hants. in August 1981. — Bibliography: p173-175
ISBN 0-85633-241-0 (pbk) : £5.95 B82-38150

371.9′043 — Handicapped children. Teaching
Riddick, Barbara. Toys and play for the handicapped child. — London : Croom Helm, July 1982. — [160]p. — (Croom Helm special education series)
ISBN 0-7099-0292-1 : £7.95 : CIP entry B82-16241

371.9′043 — Learning disordered children. Development. Assessment. Neuropsychological aspects
Neuropsychological assessment and the school-age child : issues and procedures / edited by George W. Hynd, John E. Obrzut. — New York ; London : Grune & Stratton, c1981. — xvi,422p : ill ; 24cm
Includes bibliographies and index
ISBN 0-8089-1381-6 : Unpriced B82-10556

371.9′043 — Learning disordered children. Teaching
Siegel, Ernest. Educating the learning disabled / Ernest Siegel, Ruth F. Gold ; with contributions by David Levinsky, Joan Lange Bildman. — New York : Macmillan ; London : Collier Macmillan, c1982. — xiv,384p : ill ; 25cm
Includes bibliographies and index
ISBN 0-02-410400-0 : Unpriced B82-35277

371.9′043 — Schools. Learning disordered children & deviant children. Teaching
Hammill, Donald D.. Teaching children with learning and behavior problems / Donald D. Hammill, Nettie R. Bartel. — 3rd ed. — Boston ; London : Allyn and Bacon, c1982. — vii,466p : ill ; 25cm
Previous ed.: 1978. — Bibliography: p435-466. — Includes index
ISBN 0-205-07678-5 (cased) : Unpriced
ISBN 0-205-07694-7 (pbk) B82-26938

371.9′043′0941 — Great Britain. Learning disordered children. Teaching
Ways and means 2 : children with learning difficulties : a resource book of aids, methods, materials and systems for use in all curriculum areas with less able children / co-ordinated by Ric Taylor [for] Somerset Education Authority. — Basingstoke : Globe Education, 1981. — ix,222p : ill,1form ; 30cm
Includes bibliographies
ISBN 0-333-29669-9 (pbk) : Unpriced B82-06633

371.9′043′0973 — United States. Handicapped children. Teaching
Hayden, Torey L.. Somebody else′s kids / Torey L. Hayden. — London : Souvenir, 1982, c1981. — 333p ; 23cm
Originally published: New York : G.P. Putnam′s Sons, 1981
ISBN 0-285-62537-3 : £7.95 B82-29848

Stephens, Thomas M.. Teaching mainstreamed students / Thomas M. Stephens, A. Edward Blackhurst, Larry A. Magliocca. — New York ; Chichester : Wiley, c1982. — x,380p : ill,forms,1plan ; 24cm
Includes bibliographies and index
ISBN 0-471-02479-1 (pbk) : £8.95 B82-36954

371.9′044 — Handicapped children. Physical education. Teaching
Miller, Arthur G. (Arthur George). Teaching physical activities to impaired youth : an approach to mainstreaming / Arthur G. Miller, James V. Sullivan. — New York ; Chichester : Wiley, c1982. — x,242p : ill,forms ; 24cm
Bibliography: p227-236. — List of films: p218-226. — Includes index
ISBN 0-471-08534-0 : Unpriced B82-23949

371.9′044 — Learning disordered children. Language skills. Development — *For teaching*
Wiig, Elisabeth Hemersam. Language assessment and intervention for the learning disabled / Elisabeth Hemersam Wiig, Eleanor Messing Semel. — Columbus [Ohio] ; London : Merrill, c1980. — x,451p : ill ; 27cm
Bibliography: p432-442. — Includes index
ISBN 0-675-08180-7 : £12.75 B82-26766

371.9′05 — Special education — *Serials*
Advances in special education : a research annual. — Vol.1 (1980)-. — Greenwich, Conn. : JAI Press ; London (3 Henrietta St., WC2E 8LU) : Distributed by JAICON Press, 1980-. — v. ; 24cm
ISSN 0270-4013 = Advances in special education : £22.85 B82-02372

371.9′072041 — Great Britain. Handicapped young persons, 14-19 years. Special education. Research
Bradley, Judy. Students with special needs in FE : a review of current and completed research relating to young people in the 14-19 age range with special educational needs : report of a project commissioned by FEU from the National Foundation for Educational Research / Judy Bradley and Seamus Hegarty. — [London] : [Further Education Curriculum Review and Development Unit], 1981. — 44p ; 30cm. — (Project report / Further Education Curriculum Review and Development Unit ; P.R.12)
Text on inside cover. — Bibliography: p33-44
ISBN 0-85522-095-3 (pbk) : Unpriced B82-05610

371.9′0941 — Great Britain. Handicapped children. Education — *National Association of Teachers in Further and Higher Education viewpoints*
National Association of Teachers in Further and Higher Education. Special educational needs : a response to the report of the Committee of Enquiry into the Education of Handicapped Children and Young People (Warnock report) / NATFHE. — London (Hamilton House, Mabledon Place, WC1H 9BH) : NATFHE, 1979. — 36p ; 21cm
Cover title
£0.50 (£0.35 to members) (pbk) B82-14406

371.9′0941 — Great Britain. Handicapped pre-school children. Education
Some of our children : the early education of children with special needs / Maurice Chazan ... [et al.]. — London : Open Books, 1980. — vii,260p ; 22cm
Bibliography: p252-256. — Includes index
ISBN 0-7291-0103-7 (pbk) : £5.95 B82-03258

371.9′0941 — Great Britain. Learning disordered children. Remedial education
Sewell, Geof. Reshaping remedial education. — London : Croom Helm, Sept.1982. — [140]p
ISBN 0-7099-2348-1 : £9.95 : CIP entry B82-20646

371.9′0941 — Great Britain. Special education
Brennan, W. K.. Changing special education / Wilfred K. Brennan. — Milton Keynes : Open University Press, 1982. — viii,119p ; 24cm. — (Children with special needs)
Bibliography: p114. — Includes index
ISBN 0-335-10046-5 (cased) : £11.95
ISBN 0-335-10045-7 (pbk) : £4.95 B82-22212

371.9′0941 — Great Britain. Special education — *Serials*
Great Britain. *Committee on Special Educational Needs.* News / the Committee on Special Educational Needs. — No.1 (Sept. 1981)-. — Glasgow (SCDS, Glasgow Centre, Jordanhill College of Education, 76 Southbrae Drive, Glasgow G13 1PP) : COSPEN, 1981-. — v. ; 30cm
Two issues yearly. — Also entitled: COSPEN news
ISSN 0262-2793 = News - Committee on Special Educational Needs : Unpriced B82-06789

371.9′0942 — England. Handicapped children. Special education — *National Union of Teachers viewpoints*
National Union of Teachers. Special education in ordinary schools / National Union of Teachers. — London : NUT, [1977?]. — 23p ; 21cm
£0.25 (unbound) B82-06598

371.9'0942 — England. Schools. Handicapped students. Integration into schools

Hegarty, Seamus. Integration in action : case studies in the integration of pupils with special needs / Seamus Hegarty and Keith Pocklington with Dorothy Lucas. — Windsor : NFER-Nelson, 1982. — viii,294p ; 22cm
Bibliography: 293-294
ISBN 0-85633-238-0 (pbk) : £10.95
B82-32659

371.9'0942 — England. Special education

Special needs in education / [E241 Course Team]. — Milton Keynes : Open University Press. — (Education studies : a second level course)
At head of title: The Open University
Unit 3: Family views / prepared by David Thomas and Will Swann for the Course Team. — 1982. — 39p : ill ; 30cm. — (E241 ; 3)
Bibliography: p38-39
ISBN 0-335-13121-2 (pbk) : Unpriced
B82-21193

Special needs in education / [E241 Course Team]. — Milton Keynes : Open University Press. — (Education studies : a second level course)
At head of title: The Open University
Unit 4: Education for adult life? / prepared by Richard Tomlinson for the Course Team. — 1982. — 36p : ill ; 30cm. — (E241 ; 4)
Bibliography: p35-36
ISBN 0-335-13120-4 (pbk) : Unpriced
B82-21192

Special needs in education / [E241 Course Team]. — Milton Keynes : Open University Press. — (Educational studies : a second level course)
At head of title: The Open University
Units 5/6: A special curriculum / prepared by Will Swann and Dennis Briggs for the Course Team. — 1982. — 75p : ill,maps ; 30cm. — (E241 ; 5/6)
Includes bibliographies
ISBN 0-335-13123-9 (pbk) : Unpriced
B82-32031

Special needs in education / [E241 Course Team]. — Milton Keynes : Open University Press. — (Educational studies : a second level course)
At head of title: The Open University
Unit 7: The professionals / prepared by Patricia Potts for the Course Team. — 1982. — 40p : ill ; 30cm. — (E241 ; 7)
Includes bibliographies
ISBN 0-335-13124-7 (pbk) : Unpriced
B82-32030

Special needs in education / [E241 Course Team]. — Milton Keynes : Open University Press. — (Educational studies : a second level course)
At head of title: The Open University
Unit 8: The powers that be / prepared by Andrew Sutton for the Course Team. — 1982. — 32p : ill ; 30cm. — (E241 ; 8)
Bibliography: p30
ISBN 0-335-13125-5 (pbk) : Unpriced
B82-32034

Special needs in education / [E241 Course Team]. — Milton Keynes : Open University Press. — (Educational studies : a second level course)
At head of title: The Open University
Unit 9: Origins / prepared by Patricia Potts for the Course Team. — 1982. — 42p : ill ; 30cm. — (E241 : 9)
Includes bibliographies
ISBN 0-335-13126-3 (pbk) : Unpriced
B82-36362

Special needs in education / [E241 Course Team]. — Milton Keynes : Open University Press. — (Educational studies : a second level course)
At head of title: The Open University
Unit 10: National perspectives / prepared by Tony Booth for the Course Team. — 1982. — 56p : ill ; 30cm. — (E241 ; 10)
Includes bibliographies
ISBN 0-335-13127-1 (pbk) : Unpriced
B82-32032

Special needs in education / [E241 Course Team]. — Milton Keynes : Open University Press. — (Educational studies : a second level course)
At head of title: The Open University
Unit 11: Biology and handicap / prepared by Patricia Potts for the Course Team. — 1982. — 40p : ill,facsims ; 30cm. — (E241 ; 11)
Bibliography: p39-40
ISBN 0-335-13128-x (pbk) : Unpriced
B82-34536

371.9'0973 — United States. Handicapped children. Education

Heron, Timothy E.. The educational consultant : helping professionals, parents and mainstreamed students / Timothy E. Heron, Kathleen C. Harris. — Boston, Mass. ; London : Allyn and Bacon, c1982. — xiii,332p : ill,1form ; 25cm
Includes bibliographies and index
ISBN 0-205-07726-9 : Unpriced B82-27303

371.9'0973 — United States. Language disordered & learning disordered pre-school children. Education

Bangs, Tina E.. Language and learning disorders of the preacademic child : with curriculum guide / Tina E. Bangs ; Anne Mauzy, co-author Chapters 8 and 9. — Englewood Cliffs ; London : Prentice-Hall, c1982. — x,293p : ill,forms ; 24cm
Previous ed.: New York : Appleton-Century-Crofts, 1968. — Bibliography: p276-285. — Includes index
ISBN 0-13-523001-2 : £14.95 B82-20074

371.9'0973 — United States. Schools. Handicapped students. Integration into schools

Children with cancer : mainstreaming and reintegration / edited by Jan van Eys. — Lancaster : M.T.P. Press, c1982. — viii,184p ; 24cm
Conference proceedings. — Includes index
ISBN 0-85200-607-1 : £11.25 B82-39874

371.9'0973 — United States. Special education

Hallahan, Daniel P.. Exceptional children : introduction to special education / Daniel P. Hallahan, James M. Kauffman. — 2nd ed. — London : Prentice-Hall, c1982. — xv,473p : ill ; 23cm. — (Prentice-Hall series special education)
Previous ed.: 1978. — Includes bibliographies and index
ISBN 0-13-294009-4 (pbk) : £8.95 B82-16705

Heward, William L.. Exceptional children : an introductory survey to special education / William L. Heward, Michael D. Orlansky. — Columbus ; London : Merrill, c1980. — xiii,461p : ill,ports ; 24cm
Bibliography: p415-436. — Includes index
ISBN 0-675-08179-3 : £11.95 B82-09792

371.91'0941 — Great Britain. Higher education institutions. Physically handicapped students — *Conference proceedings*

The **disabled** student in higher education : access and support : report of a conference for the International Year of Disabled People / edited by Richard Holmes and Francis Aprahamian. — Milton Keynes : Open University Press, 1981. — 64p ; 22cm
ISBN 0-335-10105-4 (pbk) : £2.50 B82-25689

371.91'2 — Deaf children. Education

Quigley, Stephen P.. The education of deaf children : issues, theory, and practice / Stephen P. Quigley, Robert E. Kretschmer. — London : Edward Arnold, 1982. — xii,127p ; 23cm
Bibliography: p111-122. — Includes index
ISBN 0-7131-6353-4 (pbk) : £9.50 : CIP rev.
B82-05407

371.91'4 — Education. Applications of research in dyslexia

Dyslexia research and its applications to education / edited by George Th. Pavlidis and T.R. Miles. — Chichester : Wiley, c1981. — xxi,307p : ill ; 24cm
Includes bibliographies and index
ISBN 0-471-27841-6 : £12.95 B82-05121

371.91'4 — Language disordered pre-school children. Remedial education

An **Interdisciplinary** language intervention program : for the moderately to profoundly language-retarded child / by Sol Adler ... [et al.]. — New York ; London : Grune & Stratton, c1980. — x,108leaves ; 28cm
Bibliography: p102-105
ISBN 0-8089-1301-8 (spiral) : £11.00
B82-35050

371.91'4 — Primary schools. Reading disordered students. Remedial teaching — *For teaching*

Webster, James. Reading matters. — London : McGraw-Hill, May 1982. — [208]p. — (McGraw-Hill series for teachers)
ISBN 0-07-084134-9 (pbk) : £5.25 : CIP entry
B82-09267

371.91'4 — Reading disordered children. Remedial education

Rubin, Dorothy. Diagnosis and correction in reading instruction / Dorothy Rubin. — New York ; London : Holt, Rinehart and Winston, c1982. — xiv,417p : ill ; 25cm
Includes index
ISBN 0-03-059292-5 : £17.95 B82-25825

371.91'4 — Reading disordered children. Remedial education — *For teaching*

McGinnis, Dorothy J.. Analyzing and treating reading problems / Dorothy J. McGinnis, Dorothy E. Smith. — New York : Macmillan ; London : Collier Macmillan, c1982. — xv,384p : ill,forms ; 25cm
Includes bibliographies and index
ISBN 0-02-379130-6 : Unpriced B82-33411

371.91'4 — Secondary schools. Reading disordered students. Remedial education — *For teaching*

Cassell, Christine. Teaching poor readers in the secondary school / Christine Cassell. — London : Croom Helm, c1982. — 73p : ill,forms ; 25cm. — (Croom Helm special education series)
Bibliography: p71-73
ISBN 0-7099-0294-8 (pbk) : £5.95 : CIP rev.
B81-34306

371.91'4 — Secondary schools. Reading disordered students. Remedial education. Use of phonics — *For teaching*

Gregory, Jill. Phonics. — London : J. Murray, Dec.1981. — [168]p
ISBN 0-7195-3851-3 (pbk) : £6.95 : CIP entry
B81-31532

371.92'0942 — England. Schools. Educationally subnormal children. Teaching — *Personal observations*

Day, Philip. "Bless yuo, my chilbern" [sic] : (a sort of autobiography) / by Philip Day ; illustarterd [i.e. illustrated] by Malclom [i.e. Malcolm] Green. — Bognor Regis : New Horizon, c1982. — 196p : ill ; 21cm
ISBN 0-86116-837-2 : £5.25 B82-31549

371.92'6 — England. Schools. Students of low academic achievement. Curriculum subjects: Mathematics. Teaching

Denvir, Brenda. Low attainers in mathematics 5-16. — London : Methuen Educational, June 1982. — [200]p. — (Schools Council working paper ; 72)
ISBN 0-423-51020-7 (pbk) : £5.95 : CIP entry
B82-09737

371.92'6 — Great Britain. Schools. Slow learning students. Curriculum

Planning effective progress : planning and implementing the curriculum for children with learning difficulties / edited by Mike Hinson and Martin Hughes. — Amersham : Hulton Educational in conjunction with the National Association for Remedial Education, 1982. — 242p : ill ; 24cm
Includes bibliographies and index
ISBN 0-7175-1007-7 (pbk) : Unpriced
B82-28236

371.92′6 — Secondary schools. Slow learning students. Teaching

Weber, Kenneth J.. The teacher is the key : a practical guide for teaching the adolescent with learning difficulties / Ken Weber. — Milton Keynes : Open University Press, 1982. — 166p : ill ; 24cm. — (Children with special needs)
ISBN 0-335-10175-5 (cased) : Unpriced : CIP rev.
ISBN 0-335-10047-3 (pbk) : Unpriced
B82-03102

371.92′63′0941 — Great Britain. Schools. Mixed ability groups. Slow learning students. Teaching — *Manuals*

Bell, Peter, *1924-*. Teaching slow learners : in mixed ability classes : a self-instructional handbook of strategies and suggestions for teachers / Peter Bell, Trevor Kerry. — Basingstoke : Macmillan Education, 1982. — 55p : 1ill,forms ; 30cm. — (DES teacher education project focus books)
Bibliography: p55
ISBN 0-333-31654-1 (unbound) : £1.95
B82-32330

371.92′64 — Great Britain. Secondary schools. Slow learning students. Curriculum subjects: History. Teaching

Cuthbert, M. (Mary). Foundation history / by M. Cuthbert, D. Morrison. — [Dundee] ([Gardyne Rd., Broughty Ferry, Dundee DD5 1NY]) : [Dundee College of Education], [1982?]. — [224]p : ill,facsims,forms ; 30cm
Cover title. — Bibliography: p91
Unpriced (pbk) B82-37399

371.92′8 — Great Britain. Educational institutions. Courses for mentally handicapped adults — *Directories*

Directory of educational courses for mentally handicapped adults / editor Victoria Shennan. — London : Royal Society for Mentally Handicapped Children and Adults, c1982. — vi,21p ; 21cm
Text on back inside cover
ISBN 0-85537-072-6 (pbk) : £3.95 B82-33442

371.92′8 — Mentally handicapped children. Teaching

In search of a curriculum : notes on the education of mentally handicapped children / by staff of Rectory Paddock School. — Sidcup : Wren, 1981. — 134p : ill ; 30cm
Bibliography: p127-133. — Includes index
ISBN 0-9507759-0-8 (pbk) : £5.00 B82-30836

371.92′8 — Mentally retarded children. Education. Curriculum

Radabaugh, Martha T.. Curriculum and methods for the mildly handicapped / Martha T. Radabaugh, Joseph F. Yukish. — Boston, [Mass.] ; London : Allyn and Bacon, c1982. — viii,259p : ill ; 24cm
Bibliography: p239-252. — Includes index
ISBN 0-205-07696-3 (spiral) : Unpriced
B82-23530

371.92′803 — Great Britain. Schools for mentally handicapped children. Teachers. In-service training. Curriculum subjects: Mentally handicapped children. Behaviour modification

Foxen, Tom. Training staff in behavioural methods : the EDY in-service course for mental handicap practitioners / Tom Foxen and Judith McBrien. — [Manchester] : Manchester University Press, [1981]
Cover title. — Bibliography: 1p
Trainee workbook. — x,82p : ill ; 30cm
ISBN 0-7190-0830-1 (spiral) : £6.50 : CIP rev.
ISBN 0-7190-0845-x (Instructor′s handbook) : £12.00 B81-28191

371.92′803 — Mentally retarded persons. Education. Behaviour modification — *For teaching*

Capie, A. C. M.. Teaching basic behavioural principles / A.C.M. Capie, P.D. Taylor, E.A. Perkins. — Kidderminster : British Institute of Mental Handicap, 1980. — 88p : 2forms ; 22cm
Bibliography: p85-86
ISBN 0-906054-20-6 (pbk) : £4.50 B82-40093

371.92′804 — Mentally handicapped persons. Curriculum subjects: Roads. Crossing. Teaching — *Manuals*

Taylor, P. D.. Crossing the road : a guide to teaching the mentally handicapped / by Peter D. Taylor and Paul Robinson ; prepared ... for the British Institute of Mental Handicap and Hereford and Worcester County Council Road Safety Unit. — Kidderminster : The Institute, 1979. — vi,41p ; 11x16cm
Bibliography: p41
ISBN 0-906054-12-5 (pbk) : £0.25 B82-40089

371.92′804 — Mentally handicapped persons. Education. Curriculum subjects: Music. Teaching

Wood, Miriam, *19---*. Music for living : enriching the lives of profoundly mentally handicapped people / Miriam Wood ; illustrations David Baird ; photographs James D. Gilford. — Kidderminster : British Institute of Mental Handicap, c1982. — 75p : ill ; 21cm
Bibliography: p69-72
ISBN 0-906054-47-8 (pbk) : £5.25 B82-39770

371.92′806′0973 — United States. Schools. Mentally handicapped students. Integration into schools

Strain, Phillip S.. Mainstreaming of children in schools : research and programmatic issues / Phillip S. Strain, Mary Margaret Kerr, with a contributed chapter by Ann P. Turnbull, Jan Blacher-Dixon. — New York ; London : Academic Press, 1981. — xii,218p ; 24cm. — (Educational psychology)
Includes index
ISBN 0-12-673460-7 : £13.00 B82-02068

371.92′84 — Severely mentally handicapped childen. Motor skills. Develoment. Teaching

Presland, John, *1935-*. Paths to mobility in ″special care″ : a guide to teaching gross motor skills to very handicapped children / John L. Presland ; illustrations, David Baird. — Kidderminster : British Institute of Mental Handicap, 1982. — 108p : ill,forms ; 24cm
Bibliography: p99-104
ISBN 0-906054-33-8 : £10.75 B82-29265

371.92′84 — Severely mentally handicapped children. Communication. Teaching

Williams, Chris, *1943-*. Towards teaching communication skills : a model for use with the profoundly and severely mentally handicapped / Chris Williams. — Rev. ed. — Kidderminster : British Institute of Mental Handicap, 1980. — 61p : ill ; 21cm
Cover title. — Previous ed.: published as A language development programme. Kidderminster : Institute of Mental Subnormality, 1973. — Bibliography: p61
ISBN 0-906054-23-0 (pbk) : £3.40 B82-34974

371.92′84 — Severely mentally handicapped children. Education. Curriculum. Development — *Conference proceedings*

Curriculum planning for the ESN(S) child. — Kidderminster : The Institute
Vol.1: A report of the first residential workshop in curriculum planning / organised by A.C.M. Capie and N.B. Crawford on behalf of the British Institute of Mental Handicap ; edited by N.B. Crawford. — 1980. — 79p : ill,2forms ; 21cm
ISBN 0-906054-21-4 (pbk) : £3.75 B82-40090

371.92′84 — Severely mentally handicapped children. Motor skills. Development. Teaching

The **Paths** to mobility checklist : objectives for teaching gross motor skills to ″special care″ children. — Kidderminster : BIMH, c1982. — 20p ; 30cm
For use with Paths to mobility in ″special care″ / John L. Presland
ISBN 0-906054-48-6 (unbound) : £0.75
B82-39767

371.92′84′0973 — United States. Severely mentally retarded children. Teaching — *Manuals*

Tawney, James W.. Programmed environments curriculum / James W. Tawney with Deborah Stevens Knapp, Carol Doehner O′Reilly, Sandra Sloan Pratt. — Columbus ; London : Merrill, 1979. — xiii,558 : ill ; 28cm
ISBN 0-675-08265-x (pbk) : £14.25
B82-03959

371.93 — London. Islington *(London Borough)*. **Experimental schools for habitual truants: Islington Intermediate Treatment Centre,** *to 1975* — *Personal observations*

Grunsell, Rob. [Born to be invisible]. Absent from school : the story of a truancy centre / Rob Grunsell. — London : Writers and Readers in association with Chameleon, 1980. — ix,117p ; 20cm
Originally published: Basingstoke : Macmillan, 1978. — Bibliography: p117
ISBN 0-906495-61-x (cased) : Unpriced
ISBN 0-906495-42-3 (pbk) : £1.95 B82-22251

371.94 — Boarding schools for maladjusted students. Students. Behaviour modification — *Case studies* — *Personal observations*

Barnes, Ronald, *1923-*. Miracles take longer / Ronald Barnes. — Bognor Regis : New Horizon, c1982. — 149p ; 22cm
£5.25 B82-10742

371.94 — Residential homes for children. Maladjusted children. Social learning

Brown, Barrie. Social learning practice in residential child care / by Barrie Brown and Marilyn Christie. — Oxford : Pergamon, 1981. — ix,187p : ill ; 21cm. — (Pergamon international library)
Bibliography: p127. — Includes index
ISBN 0-08-026779-3 (cased) : Unpriced : CIP rev.
ISBN 0-08-026778-5 (pbk) : £5.50 B81-13909

371.94 — Schools. Maladjusted students. Treatment

Help starts here : the maladjusted child in the ordinary school / Israel Kolvin ... [et al.]. — London : Tavistock, 1981. — xii,436p : ill ; 25cm
Bibliography: p385-423. — Includes index
ISBN 0-422-77380-8 : £25.00 : CIP rev.
B81-31706

371.94′0941 — Great Britain. Secondary schools. Maladjusted students. Behaviour

Tattum, Delwyn P.. Disruptive pupils in schools and units / Delwyn P. Tattum. — Chichester : Wiley, c1982. — 329p : ill ; 24cm
Bibliography: p309-320. — Includes index
ISBN 0-471-10157-5 : £13.95 B82-40417

371.94′0942 — England. Schools. Maladjusted students

Schools and disruptive pupils / David Galloway ... [et al.]. — London : Longman, 1982. — xvi,176p : ill ; 22cm
Bibliography: p162-173. — Includes index
ISBN 0-582-49707-8 (pbk) : £5.50 : CIP rev.
B82-15894

371.94′0973 — United States. Maladjusted children. Education

Swanson, H. Lee. Teaching strategies for children in conflict : curriculum, methods, and materials / H. Lee Swanson, Henry R. Reinert. — St. Louis, Mo. ; London : Mosby, 1979. — xv,358p : ill,forms ; 26cm
List of texts: p315-320. — Includes bibliographies and index
ISBN 0-8016-4106-3 (pbk) : Unpriced
B82-21894

371.95′0973 — United States. Gifted children. Education

Khatena, Joe. Educational psychology of the gifted / Joe Khatena. — New York ; Chichester : Wiley, c1982. — ix,480p : ill ; 24cm
Bibliography: p427-457. — Includes index
ISBN 0-471-05078-4 : £13.50 B82-16546

371.95′6′0941 — Great Britain. Schools. Mixed ability groups. Gifted students. Teaching — *Manuals*

Kerry, Trevor. Teaching bright pupils in mixed ability classes : a self-instructional handbook of strategies and suggestions for teachers / Trevor Kerry. — Basingstoke : Macmillan Education, 1981. — 62p : ill,forms ; 30cm. — (DES teacher education project focus books)
Bibliography: p62
ISBN 0-333-31658-4 (pbk) : Unpriced
B82-10094

371.96'7 — Developing countries. Rural regions. Poor children. Education. Effects of nutrition. Socioeconomic aspects — *Study regions: Guatemala*

Berkeley Project on Education and Nutrition. Malnourished children of the rural poor : the web of food, health, education, fertility, and agricultural production / [written by] Judith B. Balderston ... [et al.] ; with forewords by Charles S. Benson, Sheldon Margen. — Boston, Mass. : Auburn House ; London : distributed by Eurospan, c1981. — xix,204p : ill ; 25cm
Report of the Berkeley Project on Education and Nutrition. — Includes bibliographies and index
ISBN 0-86569-071-5 : £15.75 B82-13424

371.96'7 — England. Secondary schools. Disadvantaged students. Curriculum subjects: Geography. Projects: Schools Council Geography for the Young School Leaver Project

GYSL with the disadvantaged / edited by David Boardman. — Sheffield : The Geographical Association, c1981. — 80p : ill,maps,plans ; 30cm
ISBN 0-900395-69-9 (pbk) : £1.95(£1.25 to members) B82-03451

371.96'7 — England. Socially disadvantaged children. Compensatory education

Cox, T.. Disadvantaged eleven year olds. — Oxford : Pergamon, Jan.1983. — [140]p
ISBN 0-08-028911-8 : £9.90 : CIP entry B82-35198

371.96'7 — Great Britain. Schools. Disadvantaged students. Integration into schools

Hegarty, Seamus. Educating pupils with special needs in the ordinary school / Seamus Hegarty and Keith Pocklington with Dorothy Lucas. — Windsor : NFER-Nelson, 1981. — 555p ; 22cm
Bibliography: p534-540. — Includes index
ISBN 0-85633-234-8 (pbk) : £14.45 B82-10712

371.96'7'0924 — Hertfordshire. Hertford. Girls' charity schools: Christ's Hospital *(Hertford)*. **School life,** *1916-1925 — Personal observations*

Angus, Louie. Blue skirts into blue stockings, or, Recollections of Christ's Hospital / by Louie Angus. — London : Ian Allan, c1981. — 152p : ill(some col.),1col.coat of arms,1 plan ; 23cm
Ill on lining papers
ISBN 0-7110-1226-1 : £3.95 B82-11215

371.96'7'0941 — Great Britain. Socially disadvantaged children. Educational problems

Essen, Juliet. Continuities in childhood disadvantage. — London : Heinemann Educational, Sept.1982. — [272]p. — (SSRC/DHSS studies in deprivation and disadvantage ; 6)
ISBN 0-435-82283-7 : £13.50 : CIP entry B82-19676

371.96'7'0942376 — Cornwall. Camborne. Charity schools: Mrs Percival's Endowed School, *to 1876*

Thomas, Charles, *1928-*. Mrs Percival's endowed school at Penponds and Treslothan Camborne : 1761 to 1876 / Charles Thomas. — Redruth (Institute of Cornish Studies), 1982. — [32]p : ill,facsims,maps,ports ; 25cm
ISBN 0-903686-38-4 (pbk) : Unpriced B82-39558

371.96'75'0924 — England. Travelling theatre. Actors & actresses. Children. Home-based education — *Personal observations*

Kiddle, Catherine. What shall we do with the children? / Catherine Kiddle. — Barnstaple : Spindlewood, 1981. — 109p ; 23cm
ISBN 0-907349-05-6 : Unpriced : CIP rev. B81-28807

371.97 — Bilingual education

Issues in international bilingual education : the role of the vernacular / edited by Beverly Hartford and Albert Valdman and Charles R. Foster. — New York ; London : Plenum, c1982. — xiv,348p ; 24cm. — (Topics in language and linguistics)
Bibliography: p305-329. — Includes index
ISBN 0-306-40998-4 : Unpriced B82-31523

371.9'7 — Ethnic minorities. Education. Racial aspects

Talking chalk. — Birmingham : AFFOR, Sept.1982. — [60]p
ISBN 0-907127-09-6 (pbk) : £1.00 : CIP entry B82-31322

371.97 — Great Britain. Multiracial schools. Teaching

Saunders, Malcolm. Multicultural teaching : a guide for the classroom / Malcolm Saunders. — London : McGraw-Hill, c1982. — 156p : ill ; 22cm. — (McGraw-Hill series for students)
Bibliography: p145-152. — Includes index
ISBN 0-07-084133-0 (pbk) : £4.95 : CIP rev. B82-00914

371.97 — Great Britain. Multiracial schools. Teaching — *Conference proceedings*

Teaching in a multicultural society : the task for teacher education / edited by Maurice Craft. — Lewes : Falmer, 1981. — ix,192p ; 21cm. — (The Falmer Press monograph series)
Includes bibliographies and index
ISBN 0-905273-28-1 (pbk) : Unpriced B82-08303

371.97 — Great Britain. Multiracial schools. Teaching materials. Special subjects: Race

In black and white : guidelines for teachers on racial stereotyping in textbooks and learning materials. — London (Hamilton House, Mabledon Place, WC1) : National Union of Teachers, [1980]. — 11p ; 21cm
Bibliography: p10-11
£0.20 (unbound) B82-19748

371.97 — Great Britain. Multiracial schools. Teaching — *Serials*

Multiracial education. — Vol.9, no.1 (Autumn 1980)-. — London (745a Finchley Rd, NW11) : National Associaton for Multiracial Education, 1980-. — v. : ill,ports ; 24cm
Three issues yearly. — Continues: NAME. — Description based on: Vol.9, no.3 (Summer 1981)
ISSN 0260-0226 = Multiracial education : £8.00 per year B82-10352

371.97 — Great Britain. Schools. Ethnic minority students. Intelligence tests

Hegarty, Seamus. Able to learn? : the pursuit of culture-fair assessment / Seamus Hegarty and Dorothy Lucas. — Windsor : NFER, 1979. — 95p ; 22cm
Bibliography: p91-93. — Includes index
ISBN 0-85633-173-2 (pbk) : £4.00 B82-00084

371.97 — Muslims. Education. Social aspects

Education and society in the Muslim world. — London : Hodder & Stoughton, Mar.1982. — [144]p. — (Islamic education series)
ISBN 0-340-23610-8 : £6.95 : CIP entry B82-01838

371.97'00941 — Great Britain. Education. Attitudes of ethnic minority students

Together we learn? : submission by the British Youth Council to the Committee of Enquiry into the education of children from ethnic minority groups. — London (57 Chalton St., NW1 1HU) : British Youth Council, [1981]. — 24p ; 30cm
Cover title
Unpriced (pbk) B82-38457

371.97'00941 — Great Britain. Multiracial schools. Curriculum

Craft, Maurice. Education for diversity : the challenge of cultural pluralism / Maurice Craft. — [Nottingham] : [University of Nottingham School of Education], [1982]. — 24p ; 30cm
Unpriced (unbound) B82-36396

371.97'00941 — Great Britain. Schools. Ethnic minority students. Education

National Union of Teachers. Education for a multicultural society / evidence to the Swann Committee of Inquiry submitted by the National Union of Teachers. — London : National Union of Teachers, 1982. — 16p ; 21cm
Cover title. — Text on inside cover
£0.50 (pbk) B82-36422

Self-concept, achievement and multicultural education / edited by Gajendra K. Verma and Christopher Bagley. — London : Macmillan, 1982. — xxii,276p : ill ; 23cm
Bibliography: p240-264. — Includes index
ISBN 0-333-30944-8 : £20.00 B82-28527

371.97'00942 — England. Ethnic minorities. Adult education. Provision

Little, Alan, *1934-*. Adult education and the black communities / Alan Little, Richard Willey, Jagdish Gundara. — Leicester : ACACE, 1982. — vi,35p ; 21cm
ISBN 0-906436-16-8 (pbk) : £2.00 B82-39499

371.97'0941 — Great Britain. Multiracial education — *For teaching*

Race, migration and schooling / John Tierney ... [et al.]. — London : Holt, Rinehart and Winston, c1982. — xiii,202p ; 25cm
Bibliography: p161-176. — Includes index
ISBN 0-03-910362-5 (pbk) : £4.95 : CIP rev. B82-01533

371.97'0941 — Great Britain. Multiracial schools

Cohen, Louis. Multicultural classrooms. — London : Croom Helm, Nov.1982. — [240]p
ISBN 0-7099-0719-2 (cased) : £12.95 : CIP entry
ISBN 0-7099-0747-8 (pbk) : £5.95 B82-27934

371.97'0971 — Canada. Bilingual education

Swain, Merrill. Evaluating bilingual education. — Clevedon (8A Hill Rd, Clevedon, Avon BS21 7HH) : Multilingual Matters, Sept.1982. — [117]p. — (Multilingual matters ; 2)
ISBN 0-905028-10-4 (cased) : £8.90 : CIP entry
ISBN 0-905028-09-0 (pbk) : £3.90 B82-27211

371.97'51'041 — Great Britain. Schools. Italian speaking students. Education

Association of Teachers of Italian. Observations to the Committee of Inquiry into the Education of Children from Ethnic Minority Groups / Association of Teachers of Italian. — [Oxford] ([10 Bankside, Headington Quarry, Oxford OX3 8LT]) : Association of Teachers of Italian, 1982. — 7p ; 21cm
Unpriced (unbound) B82-38022

371.97'9166 — Wales. Bilingual secondary education. Projects: Cymraeg fel Ail Iaith yn yr Ysgol Uwchradd *(Project)*

Cymraeg fel Ail Iaith yn yr Ysgol Uwchradd *(Project)*. Llyfr yr athro : project addysg ddwyieithog (Ysgolion uwchradd) / [Cymraeg fel Ail Iaith yn yr Ysgol Uwchradd]. — London : Schools Council, c1981. — vi,162p : ill,maps ; 30cm
Bibliography: p143-149
ISBN 0-901681-59-8 (unbound) : Unpriced B82-20737

371.97'9275694 — Palestinian Arab refugees. Education. Role of United Nations. *Relief and Works Agency for Palestine Refugees*

UNRWA. — London (10 Spring Gardens, SW1A 2BN) : National Equivalence Information Centre, the British Council, 1981. — 2p ; 30cm
Unpriced (unbound) B82-20583

371.97'96073'075 — United States. Southern states. Negroes. Education, *1861-1870*

Morris, Robert C. (Robert Charles). Reading, 'riting, and reconstruction : the education of freedmen in the South 1861-1870 / Robert C. Morris. — Chicago ; London : University of Chicago Press, 1981. — xv,341p : ill,facsims,ports ; 23cm
Bibliography: p305-330. — Includes index
ISBN 0-226-53928-8 : £12.00 B82-20103

371.97'969729'041 — Great Britain. Schools. West Indian students. Education — *National Union of Teachers viewpoints*

The **Achievement** of West Indian pupils : Union evidence to the Rampton Committee of Enquiry into the education of children from ethnic minority groups. — [London] ([Hamilton House, Mabledon Place, WC1H 9BD]) : [National Union of Teachers], [1980]. — 14p ; 21cm
Cover title
£0.30 (pbk) B82-19753

371.97′969729′041 — Great Britain. Schools. West Indian students. Education. Research

Taylor, Monica J.. Caught between : a review of research into the education of pupils of West Indian origin / Monica J. Taylor. — Windsor : NFER, 1981. — xii,265p ; 22cm
Bibliography: p243-257. — Includes index
ISBN 0-85633-231-3 (pbk) : £9.95 B82-05250

372.1 — PRIMARY SCHOOLS

372.1′042202541 — Great Britain. Preparatory schools — *Directories — Serials*

Public & preparatory schools yearbook. — 1982. — London : A. & C. Black, Apr.1982. — [780]p
ISBN 0-7136-2182-6 (pbk) : £7.95 : CIP entry
Primary classification 373.2′22′02541
B82-04495

372.11′0092′4 — England. Preparatory schools. Teaching, *1919-1962 — Personal observations*

Campbell, P. J.. Refuge from fear / P.J. Campbell ; with a foreword by Lord David Cecil. — London : Hamilton, 1982. — x,128p ; 23cm
ISBN 0-241-10736-9 : £7.95 : CIP rev.
B81-36385

372.11′02 — West Africa. Primary schools. Teachers. Interpersonal relationships with students

Asiedu-Akrofi, K.. A living classroom. — London : Allen & Unwin, Oct.1981. — [128]p
ISBN 0-04-370110-8 (pbk) : £3.50 : CIP entry
B81-25868

372.11′02′0926 — Great Britain. Primary schools. Teachers — *Case studies — For children*

Fairclough, Chris. A day with a teacher / Chris Fairclough. — Hove : Wayland, 1982. — 55p : ill,ports ; 24cm. — (A day in the life)
Bibliography: p55
ISBN 0-85340-965-x : £3.25 B82-28023

372.11′02′09417 — Ireland *(Republic)*. Primary schools. Teaching — *Irish texts*

Lámhleabhar do stiúrthóirí naíonraí / an Comhchoiste Réamhscolaíochta igcomhar leis na Naíscoileanna Gaelacha. — [Baile Átha Cliath] ([37 Sr. an Mhóta Uacht., Baile Atha Cliath 2]) : Comhchoiste Réamhscolaíochta, 1979. — 72p : ill ; 21cm
Ill on inside covers
Unpriced (pbk) B82-30563

372.11′02′094252 — Nottinghamshire. Primary schools. Teaching — *Topics for discussion groups*

Bassey, Michael. Starters for staff discussion / Michael Bassey. — Nottingham (Clifton Hall, Clifton, Nottingham NG11 8NJ) : Trent Polytechnic Centre for Educational Research, 1980. — 2v. in 1 ; 30cm
Contents: V.1, Heads — V.2. Juniors — V.3 Infants
ISBN 0-907032-09-5 (spiral) : Unpriced
ISBN 0-907032-08-7 (V.2) : £0.40
ISBN 0-907032-07-9 (V.3) : £0.40 B82-20133

372.11′04′0941 — Great Britain. Primary schools. Teaching. Social aspects

Berlak, Ann. Dilemmas of schooling : teaching and social change / Ann & Harold Berlak. — London : Methuen, 1981. — x,299p : ill,1plan ; 21cm. — (Education paperbacks)
Bibliography: p276-292. — Includes index
ISBN 0-416-74140-1 (cased) : Unpriced : CIP rev.
ISBN 0-416-74110-x (pbk) : £4.95 B81-11965

372.12′00942 — England. Primary schools. Administration

Waters, Derek. Responsibility and promotion in the primary school. — London : Heinemann Educational, Oct.1982. — [228]p
ISBN 0-435-80915-6 : £9.50 : CIP entry
B82-23996

372.12′012′0942 — England. Primary schools. Head teachers. Role

Whitaker, Patrick. The primary head. — London : Heinemann Educational, Oct.1982. — [160]p
ISBN 0-435-80917-2 : £9.50 : CIP entry
B82-23998

372.13′0973 — United States. Primary schools. Teaching methods — *Manuals*

Hoover, Kenneth H.. A handbook for elementary school teachers / Kenneth H. Hoover, Paul M. Hollingsworth. — 3rd ed. — Boston [Mass.] ; London : Allyn and Bacon, c1982. — xiv,292p : ill,plans ; 24cm
Previous ed: 1978. — Includes index
ISBN 0-205-07630-0 (spiral) : £14.95
B82-25306

372.13′358′0941 — Great Britain. Children, to 7 years. Education. Use of television programmes — *For parents*

Using TV with young children. — [London] ([1 South Audley St., W1Y 6JS]) : [National Association for Maternal and Child Welfare], [1982?]. — 14p : ill ; 21cm
Unpriced (unbound) B82-22954

372.13′358′0942 — England. Infant schools. Teaching aids: Educational television programmes. Use

Choat, Ernest. Monograph of the dissemination meeting on teachers′ use of educational television in infants′ schools / Ernest Choat and Leslie A. Smith in collaboration with Harry Griffin and Dorothy Hobart. — London : [University of London Goldsmiths′ College], c1982. — 50p : ill ; 22cm
Unpriced (unbound) B82-32743

372.13′6 — Great Britain. Primary schools. Projects. Planning

Waters, Derek. Primary school projects : planning and development. — London : Heinemann Educational, Oct.1982. — [120]p
ISBN 0-435-80916-4 (pbk) : £3.95 : CIP entry
B82-23997

372.13′6′05 — Primary schools. Projects — *For teaching — Serials*

Junior education special. — No.1-. — Southam : Scholastic Publications (Magazines), 1982-. — v. : ill(some col.) ; 31cm
Six issues yearly. — Continues: Pictorial education special
ISSN 0262-7515 = Junior education special : £5.30 per year B82-22664

372.13′9445′094285 — Cleveland. Primary schools. Teaching. Applications of microcomputer systems — *Feasibility studies*

Informatics in primary education : a feasibility study of a collaborative research project / edited and co-ordinated by Gordon Bell ; [collaborating institutions, Teesside Polytechnic, Department of Educational Studies, Department of Computer Science, the Computer Centre ... [et al.]. — Middlesbrough (Flatts La., Middlesbrough, Cleveland TS6 0QS) : Teesside Polytechnic, Department of Educational Studies, 1981. — 109columns ; 21x30cm. — (Occasional studies in teacher applicable research)
Unpriced (pbk) B82-10024

372.16′7 — England. Primary schools. Microcomputer systems

Ellingham, David. Managing the microcomputer in the classroom / David Ellingham. — London : Council for Educational Technology on behalf of the Microelectronics Education Programme, 1982. — 34p : forms ; 22cm. — (Microelectronics Education Programme case study, ISSN 0262-5237 ; 1)
ISBN 0-86184-059-3 (pbk) : £2.75 : CIP rev.
B82-05754

. Five of the best : computer programs for primary school children / [edited by] Ron Jones. — London : Council for Educational Technology on behalf of the Microelectronics Education Programme, 1982. — 88p : ill ; 21cm. — (Microelectronics Education Programme case study, ISSN 0262-5237 ; 2)
ISBN 0-86184-058-5 (pbk) : £5.00 : CIP rev.
B82-11082

Jones, Richard, *1946-*. Microcomputers : their uses in primary schools / R. Jones. — London : Council for Educational Technology, 1980. — 111p : ill ; 30cm
ISBN 0-86184-031-3 (pbk) : Unpriced
B82-13337

Jones, Ron, *1933 Dec.30-*. Microcomputers in primary schools : a before-you-buy guide / R. Jones. — [London] : Council for Educational Technology on behalf of the Microelectronics Education Programme, 1982. — 58p : ill ; 21cm. — (Microelectronics Education Programme information guide, ISSN 0262-2181 ; 1)
ISBN 0-86184-057-7 (pbk) : £4.50 : CIP rev.
B82-05753

Microcomputers and children in the primary school / edited by Roy Garland. — Lewes : Falmer, 1982. — 225p ; 24cm
Includes index
ISBN 0-905273-33-8 (cased) : £10.25
ISBN 0-905273-32-x (pbk) : £5.50 B82-37751

372.18′092′6 — England. Primary schools. Students — *Case studies*

Mills, Richard W.. Classroom observation of primary school children : all in a day / Richard W. Mills. — London : Allen & Unwin, 1979. — x,219p : ill ; 23cm. — (Unwin education books)
Bibliography: p212-214. — Includes index
ISBN 0-04-372028-5 (cased) : £10.00 : CIP rev.
ISBN 0-04-372029-3 (pbk) : £4.50 B80-09153

372.18′0941 — Great Britain. Primary schools. School life, *1900-1945*

Parsley, Olive. Living and learning / Olive Parsley. — Woodbridge : O. Parsley, 1982. — 32p ; 19cm
ISBN 0-7223-1599-6 (pbk) : £0.82 B82-31778

372.18′1 — England. Primary schools. Students. Intellectual development — *Case studies*

Armstrong, Michael, *1934-*. Closely observed children : the diary of a primary classroom / Michael Armstrong. — London : Writers and Readers in association with Chameleon, c1980. — 207p : ill ; 21cm
ISBN 0-906495-04-0 (cased) : £5.95
ISBN 0-906495-21-0 (pbk) : Unpriced
B82-01375

372.18′2 — Devon. Primary schools. Students: Girls. Education. Equality of opportunity

Sex equality in education : curriculum in the primary school. — [Exeter] : Devon Education Department, 1981. — 32p ; 21cm
Bibliography: p30
ISBN 0-86114-283-7 (pbk) : Unpriced
B82-02195

372.19 — Children, 2-5 years. Education. Curriculum. Development

Robinson, Helen F.. Designing curriculum for early childhood / Helen F. Robinson, Sydney L. Schwartz. — Boston, Mass. ; London : Allyn and Bacon, c1982. — x,342p : ill,forms ; 25cm
Includes bibliographies and index
ISBN 0-205-07725-0 : Unpriced B82-28488

372.19 — Primary schools. Activities — *For children*

Althea. Starting school / by Althea ; illustrated by Maureen Galvani. — Over : Dinosaur, c1981. — [24]p : col.ill ; 16x19cm. — (Dinosaur′s Althea books)
ISBN 0-85122-302-8 (cased) : £2.25
ISBN 0-85122-096-7 (pbk) : Unpriced
B82-08274

372.19 — Primary schools. Activities — *For teaching*

Long, Jan. [Doing social studies]. Looking, making, displaying / by Jan Long ; [photographs by Robert Long]. — [Driffield] : [Studies in Education], 1980. — 69p : ill ; 18x23cm. — (New primary ideas)
Originally published: Melbourne, Vic. : Primary Education, 1979
ISBN 0-905484-28-2 (pbk) : £3.25 B82-14974

372.19'09416 — Northern Ireland. Primary schools. Curriculum. Development. Projects. Use

Sutherland, A. E.. Curriculum projects in primary schools : an investigation of project adoption and implementation in 185 Northern Ireland schools / by A.E. Sutherland. — [Belfast] : Northern Ireland Council for Educational Research, c1981. — xi,188p ; 30cm. — (Publications of the Northern Ireland Council for Educational Research ; 20)
Bibliography: p154-157
ISBN 0-903478-18-8 (pbk) : £6.00 B82-02861

372.19'0973 — United States. Primary schools. Curriculum

Ragan, William B.. Modern elementary curriculum. — 6th ed. / Gene D. Shepherd, William B. Ragan. — New York ; London : Holt, Rinehart and Winston, c1982. — xii,510p : ill ; 24cm
Previous ed.: 1977. — Includes bibliographies and index
ISBN 0-03-058324-1 : £17.50 B82-25370

372.2 — LEVELS OF PRIMARY EDUCATION

372'.21 — Children, to 6 years. Education — *For teaching*

Drakes, Ruth. Developments in early childhood education : a lecture / by Ruth Drakes. — Dublin : Irish National Teachers' Organisation, 1982. — 15p ; 21cm
Unpriced (unbound) B82-25025

372'.21'05 — Pre-school children. Education — *Serials*

Advances in early education and day care : a research annual. — Vol.1 (1980)-. — Greenwich, Conn. : JAI Press ; London (3 Henrietta St., WC2E 8LU) : Distributed by JAICON Press, 1980-. — v. ; 24cm
ISSN 0270-4021 = Advances in early education and day care : £21.75
Also classified at 362.7'12'05 B82-03430

372'.21'094 — Western Europe. Children, 3-8 years. Education — *Forecasts*

Van der Eyken, Willem. The education of three-to-eight year olds in Europe in the eighties / Willem van der Eyken ; a report commissioned by the Council of Europe for the standing conference of European ministers of education for their twelfth session, Lisbon, June 1981 and edited extracts of statements by representatives of states participating in the conference presented to the twelfth session. — Windsor : NFER-Nelson, 1982. — vi,168p ; 22cm
Bibliography: p164-168
ISBN 0-85633-237-2 (pbk) : £5.50 B82-38148

372'.21'0941 — Great Britain. Pre-school educational institutions. Students. Social adjustment

Blatchford, Peter. The first transition : home to pre-school : a report on the "Transition from Home to Pre-school" project / Peter Blatchford, Sandra Battle, Julia Mays. — Windsor : NFER-Nelson, 1982. — ix,181p : ill,forms ; 22cm
Bibliography: p178-181
ISBN 0-7005-0493-1 (pbk) : £6.95 B82-31653

372'.21'095694 — Israel. Pre-school children. Education. Programmes: Home Instruction Program for Preschool Youngsters

Lombard, Avima D.. Success begins at home : educational foundations for preschoolers / Avima D. Lomard. — Lexington, Mass. : Lexington Books, c1981 ; [Aldershot] : Gower [distributor], 1982. — xvii,150p : ill ; 24cm
Bibliography: p115-121. — Includes index
ISBN 0-669-04798-8 : £13.50 B82-21168

372'.21'0973 — United States. Pre-school children. Education

Decker, Celia Anita. Planning and administering early childhood programs / Celia Anita Decker, John R. Decker. — 2nd ed. — Columbus ; London : Merrill, c1980. — vii,471p : ill ; 25cm
Includes bibliographies and index
ISBN 0-675-08160-2 (pbk) : £9.75 B82-28540

372'.216 — Great Britain. Playgroups

Pre-school Playgroups Association. Playgroups in the eighties : opportunities for parents & children : a joint statement / by the Pre-school Playgroups Association (England and Wales), the Scottish Pre-school Playgroups Association, the Northern Ireland Pre-school Playgroups Association. — [London] ([Alfred House, Aveline St., SE11 5DH]) : [Pre-school Playgroups Association], [1980?]. — 1folded sheet ; 30cm
Unpriced (unbound) B82-23427

372'.216 — Great Britain. Playgroups. Organisation — *Manuals*

Henderson, Ann. Pre-school playgroups : a handbook / Ann Henderson and Joyce Lucas. — London : Allen & Unwin, 1981. — v,231p : ill,1form ; 23cm
Bibliography: p228. — Includes index
ISBN 0-04-372034-x (cased) : Unpriced : CIP rev.
ISBN 0-04-372035-8 (pbk) : Unpriced B81-30216

372'.216 — Great Britain. Playgroups. Organisations: Pre-school Playgroups Association

Facts & figures / PPA ; [prepared by Kath France ... et al.]. — [London] : [Pre-school Playgroups Association], 1981. — 30p : ill,1map ; 30cm
Cover title. — Text on inside cover. — "Facts & figures from the local information survey for Inner London", (1 sheet), as insert
ISBN 0-901755-45-1 (pbk) : £0.50 B82-32062

372'.216 — Mother & toddler groups. Organisation & management

Donoghue, Joyce. Running a mother and toddler group. — Hemel Hempstead : Allen & Unwin, Feb.1983. — 1v.
ISBN 0-04-649020-5 (cased) : £6.95 : CIP entry
ISBN 0-04-649021-3 (pbk) : £3.50 B82-36478

372'.216 — Scotland. Playgroups. Participation of secondary school students

Playgroups and secondary schools in Scotland. — [Clydebank] ([Miller Street School, Kilbowie Rd, Clydebank]) : Strathclyde Department of Education, Dunbarton Division, Curriculum Development Centre, 1982. — 54p : ill ; 30cm
Unpriced (spiral) B82-27438

372'.241 — Great Britain. Primary schools. Preparation of children — *For parents*

Basham, Margaret L.. Getting ready for school : a parents' guide / Margaret Basham. — Harlow : Longman, 1982. — 48p : ill ; 28cm
ISBN 0-582-25050-1 (pbk) : £1.95 B82-36087

372'.241'0941 — Great Britain. Infant schools. Students. Social adjustment

Cleave, Shirley. — And so to school : a study of continuity from pre-school to infant school / Shirley Cleave, Sandra Jowett, Margaret Bate. — Windsor : NFER-Nelson, 1982. — 216p : ill,plans ; 22cm
Report of the project 'Continuity of Children's Experience in the Years 3 to 8'. — Bibliography: p215-216
ISBN 0-85633-245-3 (pbk) : £5.90 B82-31652

372'.241'0942 — England. Children, 5-9 years. Education

Education 5-9 : an illustrative survey of 80 first schools in England / Department of Education and Science. — London : H.M.S.O., 1982. — 81p ; 25cm
Includes index
ISBN 0-11-270530-8 (pbk) : £3.50 B82-32994

372'.241'0942731 — Greater Manchester *(Metropolitan County)*. Timperley. Church of England infant schools, *1851-1981*

Pryor, Hazel. Church schools in Timperley 1851 to 1981 / by Hazel Pryor. — Altrincham (11, Thorley La., Timperley, Altrincham, Cheshire) : H. Pryor, c1982. — 15p ; 21cm
Cover title
£0.30 (pbk) B82-40621

372.3/8 — PRIMARY SCHOOL CURRICULUM

372.3'5 — Primary schools. Curriculum subjects: Science — *For teaching*

Finch, Irene. Science workshop 2 / Irene Finch. — Harlow : Longman, 1982. — 48p : col.ill ; 29cm
Text on inside covers
ISBN 0-582-18350-2 (pbk) : Unpriced B82-36237

Primary science guidelines. — [Chester] : [Cheshire County Council], [c1982]. — 32p : ill,plans ; 20x22cm
Cover title. — Bibliography: p32
ISBN 0-904431-03-7 (pbk) : Unpriced B82-38989

372.3'5044 — Primary schools. Curriculum subjects: Science. Teaching

Gega, Peter C.. Science in elementary education / Peter C. Gega. — 4th ed. — New York ; Chichester : Wiley, c1982. — xvii,600p : ill ; 26cm
Previous ed.: 1977. — Text and ill on lining papers. — Includes bibliographies and index
ISBN 0-471-09678-4 : £15.50 B82-26452

Schmidt, Victor E.. Teaching science with everyday things / Victor E. Schmidt, Verne N. Rockcastle. — 2nd ed. — New York ; London : McGraw-Hill, c1982. — xi,210p : ill ; 24cm
Previous ed.: 1968. — Bibliography: p201-204. — Includes index
ISBN 0-07-055355-6 (pbk) : £9.25 B82-16289

Starting primary science. — London : Edward Arnold, July 1982. — [96]p. — (Teaching matters)
ISBN 0-7131-0745-6 (pbk) : £3.50 : CIP entry B82-17914

372.3'5'0973 — United States. Primary schools. Curriculum subjects: Science — *For teaching*

Cain, Sandra E.. Sciencing : an involvement approach to elementary science methods / Sandra E. Cain and Jack M. Evans. — Columbus ; London : Merrill, c1979. — 322p : ill ; 26cm
Includes bibliographies and index
ISBN 0-675-08364-8 (pbk) : £8.95 B82-40484

372.3'57 — Pre-school children. Curriculum subjects: Natural history — *For teaching*

Goddard, Eileen. See the daisies feel the rain / written by Eileen Goddard with the help and advice of London Playgroup Course Tutors, her colleagues, Margaret Hanton, Bobby Jones and her husband ; illustrated by Trac Hilliard, Diana McGreachan and Celia Whittaker. — [London] : Greater London P.A.A. [Pre-School Playgroups Association], [1982?]. — 32p : ill ; 15x21cm
Text on inside cover
ISBN 0-901755-36-2 (pbk) : £0.75 B82-28787

372.3'57 — Primary schools. Curriculum subjects: Plants. Growth. Experiments — *For teaching*

McKinlay, Brian. Growing things : nature study ideas for the primary school / Brian McKinlay ; illustrated by Elizabeth Honey. — [Driffield] : Studies in Education, 1980. — 55p : ill ; 18x22cm
Originally published: Melbourne, Vic. : Primary Education, 1979
ISBN 0-905484-29-0 (pbk) : £2.95 B82-14975

372.3'7 — Primary schools. Curriculum subjects: Health education — *For teaching*

Jimmy on the road to super health : health education in the primary school : a health centre of interest for primary 6 and 7 / an education project funded by the Cancer Research Campaign. — [Glasgow] : [Department of Clinical Oncology, University of Glasgow], 1982. — 96p : ill,forms ; 30cm
Cover title
Unpriced (spiral) B82-29702

372.4 — Children. Reading skills. Teaching. Role of reading aloud

Arnold, Helen. Listening to children reading. — London : Hodder & Stoughton, Aug.1982. — [128]p. — (UKRA teaching of reading monographs)
ISBN 0-340-26298-2 (pbk) : £2.95 : CIP entry
B82-18565

372.4 — Children. Reading skills. Teaching. Use of music — *Manuals*

Wisbey, Audrey S.. Learn to sing to learn [to] read : a course book for parents and teachers / by Audrey Wisbey with Janet Thomas. — London : British Broadcasting Corporation, c1981. — 93p : ill,music ; 24cm
ISBN 0-563-17640-7 (pbk) : £3.25 B82-14537

372.4 — England. Children, 9 to 11 years. Reading skills. Teaching — *Case studies*

Neville, Mary H.. Towards independent reading / M.H. Neville and A.K. Pugh. — London : Heinemann, 1982. — ix,112p : ill ; 22cm
Bibliography: p100-108. — Includes index
ISBN 0-435-10722-4 (pbk) : £3.95 B82-24034

372.4 — Pre-school children. Reading skills. Teaching — *For parents*

Gold, Jacqueline. Talk your child into reading / Jacqueline Gold, J. Alan Evans. — [Ystrad] ([Old Lamb House, Ystrad, Rhondda, M. Glam.]) : J. Gold & J.A. Evans, 1981. — 42p : ill ; 22x31cm
ISBN 0-9507621-0-5 : £2.50 B82-07369

372.4 — Primary schools. Curriculum subjects: Reading

Francis, Hazel. Learning to read : literate behaviour and orthographic knowledge / by Hazel Francis. — London : Allen & Unwin, 1982. — x,173p : ill ; 22cm. — (Unwin education books)
Bibliography: p169-170. — Includes index
ISBN 0-04-372037-4 (cased) : Unpriced : CIP rev.
ISBN 0-04-372038-2 (pbk) : Unpriced
B82-10578

372.4 — Primary schools. Curriculum subjects: Reading. Teaching

Dechant, Emerald. Improving the teaching of reading / Emerald V. Dechant. — 3rd ed. — Englewood Cliffs ; London : Prentice-Hall, c1982. — xiv,492p : ill,2ports ; 25cm
Previous ed.: 1970. — Bibliography: p470-486. — Includes index
ISBN 0-13-453423-9 : £15.70 B82-31826

Rubin, Dorothy. A practical approach to teaching reading / Dorothy Rubin. — New York ; London : Holt, Rinehart and Winston, c1982. — xiv,397p : ill,facsims,forms ; 25cm
Includes bibliographies and index
ISBN 0-03-059103-1 : £14.95 B82-17015

372.4 — Primary schools. Students. Reading skills. Development. Role of parents — *For teaching*

Ervin, Jane. How to have a successful parents and reading program : a practical guide / [Jane Ervin]. — Boston, [Mass.] ; London : Allyn and Bacon, 1982. — x,246p : ill,forms ; 29cm
Bibliography: p173-175. — Includes index
ISBN 0-205-07715-3 (spiral) : Unpriced
B82-27062

372.4 — United States. Primary schools. Curriculum subjects: Reading skills. Teaching

Aulls, Mark W.. Developing readers in today's elementary school / Mark W. Aulls. — Boston, Mass. ; London : Allyn and Bacon, c1982. — xii,656p : ill ; 25cm
Includes bibliographies and index
ISBN 0-205-07722-6 : Unpriced B82-28491

Mangieri, John N.. Elementary reading : a comprehensive approach / John N. Mangieri, Lois A. Bader, James E. Walker. — New York ; London : McGraw-Hill, c1982. — xx,438p : ill,forms ; 25cm
Includes bibliographies and index
ISBN 0-07-039886-0 : £15.25 B82-22167

372.4'0973 — United States. Nursery schools. Curriculum subjects: Reading. Teaching — *Manuals*

Durkin, Dolores. Getting reading started / Dolores Durkin. — Boston [Mass.] ; London : Allyn and Bacon, c1982. — x,214p : ill ; 24cm
Includes bibliographies and index
ISBN 0-205-07559-2 (pbk) : £7.50 B82-08542

372.4'0973 — United States. Primary schools. Curriculum subjects: Reading. Teaching

Olson, Joanne P.. Learning to teach reading in the elementary school : utilizing a competency-based instructional system / Joanne P. Olson, Martha H. Dillner. — 2nd ed. — New York : Macmillan ; London : Collier Macmillan, c1982. — ix,598p : ill ; 26cm
Previous ed.: 1976. — Text on inside cover. — Bibliography: pi. — Includes index
ISBN 0-02-389300-1 (pbk) : £8.95 B82-26385

372.4'0973 — United States. Primary schools. Curriculum subjects: Reading. Teaching — *Manuals*

The **Teaching** of reading / Martha Dallmann ... [et al.]. — 6th ed. — New York ; London : Holt, Rinehart and Winston, c1982. — viii,456p : ill ; 25cm
Previous ed.: 1978. — Bibliography: p429-448. — Includes index
ISBN 0-03-059884-2 : £17.50 B82-25824

372.4'0973 — United States. Primary schools. Students. Reading skills. Teaching

Hafner, Lawrence E.. Teaching reading to children / Lawrence E. Hafner, Hayden B. Jolly. — 2nd ed. — New York : Macmillan ; London : Collier Macmillan, c1982. — x,436p : ill,forms ; 26cm
Previous ed.: published as Patterns of teaching reading in the elementary school. New York : Macmillan, 1972. — Includes bibliographies and index
ISBN 0-02-348780-1 (pbk) : £11.50
B82-39554

372.4'1'0941 — Great Britain. Primary schools. Students. Reading skills. Development. Teaching

Wray, David, *1950-*. Extending reading skills / David Wray. — [Lancaster] : Centre for Educational Research and Development, University of Lancaster, [1980?]. — 87p : ill ; 21cm
Bibliography: p85-87
ISBN 0-901699-67-5 (pbk) : £1.50 B82-17620

372.4'14 — Great Britain. Primary schools. Reading schemes: Basic reading scheme — *For teaching*

Tansley, A. E.. Basic reading : manual for "Racing to read", "Early to read", "Sound sense", "Listening to sounds" / A.E. Tansley. — 2nd rev. ed. — Leeds : E.J. Arnold, 1981, c1972. — 60p : 2ill ; 24cm
Previous ed. i.e. rev. ed.: 1976
ISBN 0-560-00961-5 (pbk) : Unpriced
B82-31918

372.4'14 — Great Britain. Primary schools. Reading schemes: Story chest reading scheme — *For teaching*

Teacher's notes for evaluation materials / with a commentary by Brenda Thompson. — Leeds : E.J. Arnold, c1982. — 21p ; 21cm
'For use with the Story chest evaluation pack' — Introducton. — Cover title
ISBN 0-560-08686-5 (pbk) : Unpriced
B82-32340

372.4'14 — Primary schools. Students. Reading skills. Teaching aids: Games

Root, Betty. 40 reading games to make and play / Betty Root ; contributions Diana Bentley, Wendy Body, Harry Piper. — London : Macmillan Education, 1982. — 95p : ill ; 30cm. — (The DIY series)
ISBN 0-333-31628-2 (spiral) : Unpriced
B82-39149

Spache, Evelyn B.. Reading activities for child involvement / Evelyn B. Spache. — 3rd ed. — Boston [Mass.] ; London : Allyn and Bacon, c1982. — viii,216p : ill ; 24cm
Previous ed.: 1976. — Includes index
ISBN 0-205-07605-x (cased) : Unpriced
ISBN 0-205-07634-3 (pbk) : Unpriced
B82-20539

372.6'044 — Primary schools. Students. Language skills. Development. Projects — *For teaching*

Long, Jan. Sparks! / Jan Long ; [photographs by Robert Long]. — [Duffield] : Studies in Education, 1980. — 72p : ill ; 18x23cm. — (New primary ideas)
Originally published: Melbourne, Vic. : Primary Education, 1979
ISBN 0-905484-24-x (pbk) : £3.25 B82-14973

372.6'044'0973 — United States. Primary schools. Students. Language skills. Teaching

Norton, Donna E.. The effective teaching of language arts / Donna E. Norton. — Columbus, Ohio ; London : Merrill, c1980. — viii,504p : ill,forms ; 26cm
Includes bibliographies and index
ISBN 0-675-08196-3 : £11.95 B82-25664

372.6'22'0287 — Children, to 10 years. Speech skills. Assessment

Tough, Joan. Listening to children talking : a guide to the appraisal of children's use of language / Joan Tough. — London : Ward Lock Educational in association with Drake Educational Associates, 1976 (1981 [printing]). — 174p : ill ; 24cm
At head of title: Schools Council Communication Skills in Early Childhood Project. — Bibliography: p170. — Includes index
Unpriced (cased) B82-13815

372.6'23 — Children, 7-13 years. Writing skills. Development — *Sociological perspectives*

Kress, Gunther. Learning to write / Gunther Kress. — London : Routledge & Kegan Paul, 1982. — xii,205p : ill ; 23cm
Bibliography: p196-200. — Includes index
ISBN 0-7100-9048-x (cased) : £10.95
ISBN 0-7100-9082-x (pbk) : £5.95 B82-26594

372.6'23 — Children. Writing skills. Development

Temple, Charles A.. The beginnings of writing / Charles A. Temple, Ruth G. Nathan, Nancy A. Burris. — Boston, [Mass.] ; London : Allyn and Bacon, c1982. — x,230p : ill ; 24cm
Bibliography: p217-218. — Includes index
ISBN 0-205-07679-3 (cased) : Unpriced
ISBN 0-205-07699-8 (pbk) : Unpriced
B82-27103

372.6'23 — Primary schools. Curriculum subjects: English language. Composition. Teaching

Language matters : writing / editorial board Norris Bentham ... [et al.] ; editor Ian Forsyth. — London (The Ebury Teachers' Centre, Sutherland St., SW1 4LD) : Centre for Language in Primary Education, [1982?]. — 23p : ill,2maps,facsims ; 20x21cm
Unpriced (pbk) B82-22465

372.6'59166 — Wales. Primary schools. Curriculum subjects: Welsh language. Listening comprehension

Development of assessment materials in the Welsh language : report on the survey of listening comprehension skills among 11-year-old pupils learning Welsh as a second language, 1980 / commissioned by the Welsh Office ; National Foundaton for Educational Research in England and Wales ; research team : Eurwen Price, Robat Rowell, Ann Jones ; statistician : Barry Sexton. — [Windsor] : National Foundation for Educational Research in England and Wales, [1980?]. — 59,ivp : ill ; 30cm
Unpriced (spiral) B82-31331

372.6'6 — Primary schools. Activities: Drama. Teaching

Davies, G. C.. Practical primary drama. — London : Heinemann Educational, Nov.1982. — [80]p
ISBN 0-435-18236-6 (pbk) : £2.25 : CIP entry
B82-30578

372.7 — Great Britain. Nursery & primary schools. Pupils: Girls. Mathematical skills

Walden, Rosie. Girls and mathematics : the early years : a review of literature and an account of original research / Rosie Walden and Valerie Walkerdine. — London : University of London Institute of Education, 1982. — 73p : 1ill ; 22cm. — (Bedford Way papers, ISSN 0261-0078 ; 8)
Bibliography: p66-73
ISBN 0-85473-124-5 (pbk) : £1.80 B82-17337

372.7 — Primary schools. Curriculum subjects: Mathematics — *For teaching*

Gerber, Harvey. Mathematics for elementary school teachers / Harvey Gerber. — Philadelphia ; London : Saunders College Publishing, c1982. — xi,542p : ill ; 25cm
Includes index
ISBN 0-03-058326-8 : Unpriced B82-30511

372.7'3044 — Primary schools. Curriculum subjects: Mathematics. Teaching

Elementary mathematical methods. — 2nd ed. / Donald D. Paige, Diane Thiessen, Margaret Wild. — New York ; Chichester : Wiley, c1982. — viii,413p : ill(some col.) ; 25cm
Previous ed.: 1978. — Includes bibliographies and index
ISBN 0-471-09063-8 : £14.15 B82-30697

372.7'3044 — Primary schools. Curriculum subjects: Mathematics. Teaching aids: Games

Williams, Margaret, *1933-*. 40 maths games to make and play : the early years / Margaret Williams and Heather Somerwill. — London : Macmillan Education, 1982. — 88p : ill ; 30cm. — (The DIY series)
List of games: p88
ISBN 0-333-31730-0 (spiral) : Unpriced B82-39148

372.7'3044 — Primary schools. Curriculum subjects: Mathematics. Teaching — *Manuals*

Biggs, Edith. Teaching mathematics 5 to 9. — London : McGraw-Hill, Jan.1983. — [304]p. — (McGraw-Hill series for teachers)
ISBN 0-07-084138-1 (pbk) : £4.95 : CIP entry B82-33602

Copeland, Richard W.. Mathematics and the elementary teacher / Richard W. Copeland. — 4th ed. — London : Macmillan, c1982. — viii,335p : ill,facsims,1plan ; 25cm
Previous ed.: Philadelphia : Saunders, 1976. — Includes index
ISBN 0-02-324830-0 : £7.95 B82-26289

Emery, W. J. Norman. Mathspan : a practical comprehensive guide to the what, why, how & when of teaching mathematics during the years 4 to 9 / by W.J. Norman Emery ; foreword by Peter Taylor. — Cardiff (67 Queen St., Cardiff CF1 4AY) : School Span
Bk.2: Moving forward with sixes and sevens. — c1980. — V,101p : ill,1port ; 21cm
Port & text on inside cover
ISBN 0-906743-01-x (pbk) : £2.50 B82-02404

Notes on mathematics in primary schools / by members of the Association of Teachers of Mathematics. — Nelson : The Association, 1979. — 340p : ill(some col.) ; 21cm
Originally published: Cambridge : Cambridge University Press, 1967. — Bibliography: p332-338. — Includes index
ISBN 0-900095-06-7 (pbk) : £3.60 B82-34499

372.7'3044'0941 — Great Britain. Primary schools. Curriculum subjects: Mathematics. Teaching — *Manuals*

Paling, D.. Teaching mathematics in primary schools / D. Paling. — Oxford : Oxford University Press, 1982. — 313p : ill ; 24cm. — (Oxford studies in education)
Includes index
ISBN 0-19-832539-8 (pbk) : £4.95 B82-31499

372.7'30442 — Pre-school children. Curriculum subjects: Mathematics. Teaching — *For parents*

Doman, Glenn. Teach your baby maths / Glenn Doman. — London : Pan, 1982, c1979. — 111p ; 18cm
Originally published: London : Cape, 1979
ISBN 0-330-26593-8 (pbk) : £1.50 B82-15209

372.8 — Great Britain. Primary schools. Christian religious education — *For teaching*

Religious education and the man-made world / [editor Susan E. Tompkins]. — London (2 Chester House, Pages Lane, N10 1PR) : Christian Education Movement, 1977. — 1portfolio : ill ; 30cm. — (CEM primary resource for religious education, ISSN 0308-4523 ; v.5 ; no.1)
Bibliography on inside covers of portfolio
Unpriced B82-40258

Religious education in primary schools / edited by Norman Richards. — London (130 City Rd., EC1V 2NJ) : Association of Christian Teachers, 1981. — 28p : 1ill ; 22cm
Cover title. — Bibliography: p28
Unpriced (pbk) B82-12486

372.8 — Great Britain. Primary schools. Curriculum subjects: Christian life. Neighbourliness. Teaching

Who is my neighbour / [editor Danny Sullivan]. — London (2 Chester House, Pages La., N10 1PR) : Christian Education Movement, c1982. — 23p : ill ; 26cm. — (CEM primary resource for religious education, ISSN 0308-4523)
Unpriced (pbk) B82-35096

372.8 — Great Britain. Primary schools. Curriculum subjects: Religion — *For teaching*

The **Primary** school and world community / [editor Danny Sullivan]. — London (2 Chester House, Pages La., N10 1PR) : Christian Education Movement, c1981. — 39p : ill ; 26cm. — (CEM primary resource for religious education, ISSN 0308-4523)
Cover title. — Text on inside cover
Unpriced (pbk) B82-08920

372.8 — Primary schools. Christian religious education. Teaching — *Manuals*

Christianity today / [editor Susan E. Tompkins]. — London (2 Chester House, Pages La, N10 1PR) : Christian Education Movement, c1977. — 35p : ill ; 26cm. — (Christianity ; 2) (CEM primary resource for religious education, ISSN 0308-4523)
Cover title. — Text on inside cover. — Includes bibliographies
£0.80 (pbk) B82-40969

372.8 — Primary schools. Curriculum subjects: Bible. Teaching

The **Bible** / [editor Susan E. Tompkins]. — London (2 Chester House, Pages Lane, N10 1PR) : Christian Education Movement, 1977. — 23p ; 26cm. — (Christianity ; 3) (CEM primary resource for religious education, ISSN 0308-4523)
This work is a special supplement to Jesus and Christianity today, volumes 1 and 2 in the Christianity series. — Cover title. — Text on inside cover. — Bibliography: p19-21
Unpriced (pbk) B82-40966

372.8 — Primary schools. Religious education

Mumford, Carol. Young children and religion. — London : E. Arnold, Oct.1982. — [88]p
ISBN 0-7131-0733-2 (pbk) : £1.00 : CIP entry B82-22986

372.8 — Primary schools. Religious education. Teaching

Beginnings / editor Danny Sullivan. — London (2, Chester House, Pages La, N10 1PR) : Christian Education Movement, c1979. — 16p : ill ; 26cm. — (CEM primary resource for religious education, ISSN 0308-4523)
Bibliography: p16
Unpriced (pbk) B82-40971

Myth / [editor Susan E. Tompkins]. — [2nd ed]. — London : Christian Education Movement, [1979?]. — 23p : ill ; 26cm. — (CEM primary resource for religious education)
Previous ed.: 1973. — Text on inside cover. — Bibliography: p22-23
ISBN 0-905022-25-4 (pbk) : Unpriced B82-40973

Religious education and environmental studies / [editor Susan E. Tompkins]. — [Rev. ed]. — London : Christian Education Movement, c1978. — 31p : ill ; 26cm. — (CEM primary resource for religious education)
Previous ed. published in 3 separate booklets entitled The world about us, Places in the community and People in the community, 1974-1975. — Includes bibliographies
ISBN 0-905022-34-3 (pbk) : Unpriced B82-40972

372.8'3 — Primary schools. Curriculum subjects: Environmental studies. Projects — *For teaching*

McQuillen, Brian. Mud, daisies and sparrows : exploring outdoor environments / Dawn Anderson, Brian McQuillen ; [photographs by Howard Birnstihl]. — [Driffield] : Studies in Education, 1980. — 71p : ill ; 18x23cm. — (New primary ideas)
Originally published: Melbourne, Vic. : Primary Education, 1979
ISBN 0-905484-22-3 (pbk) : £3.25 B82-14977

372.8'3044'0941 — Great Britain. Primary schools. Curriculum subjects: Social studies. Topics. Teaching methods

Gunning, Stella. Topic teaching in the primary school : teaching about society through topic work / Stella Gunning, Dennis Gunning and Jack Wilson. — London : Croom Helm, c1981. — 219p : ill ; 23cm
Bibliography: p214-217. — Includes index
ISBN 0-7099-0437-1 (cased) : £10.95 : CIP rev.
ISBN 0-7099-1118-1 (pbk) : Unpriced B81-21503

372.8'6 — Great Britain. Primary schools. Activities: Sports & games — *For teaching*

Castle, R. N.. Games teaching to children in the 7-11 age group : a scheme of work for teachers to assist in the planning of games lessons with the 7-11 year olds / compiled by R. N. Castle, G. Bancroft. — Ipswich : [Suffolk County Council], [1982]. — 135p : ill ; 30cm
Unpriced (spiral) B82-36652

372.8'6 — Primary schools. Curriculum subjects: Movement. Teaching

Gallahue, David L.. Developmental movement experiences for children / David L. Gallahue. — New York ; Chichester : Wiley, c1982. — xv,397p : ill ; 24cm
Includes bibliographies, lists of sound recordings and index
ISBN 0-471-08778-5 (pbk) : £12.45 B82-34744

372.8'6044'0973 — United States. Primary schools. Curriculum subjects: Physical education. Teaching

Werner, Peter H.. A movement approach to games for children / Peter H. Werner. — St. Louis ; London : Mosby, 1979. — xi,143p : ill ; 24cm
Bibliography: p138-139. — Includes index
ISBN 0-8016-5416-5 (pbk) : £8.00 B82-19324

372.8'7044 — Pre-school children. Curriculum subjects: Music. Teaching

Bayless, Kathleen M.. Music : a way of life for the young child / Kathleen M. Bayless, Marjorie E. Ramsey. — 2nd ed. — St. Louis ; London : Mosby, 1982. — xii,251p : ill,music ; 28cm
Previous ed.: 1978. — Includes bibliographies and index
ISBN 0-8016-0521-0 (pbk) : £10.00 B82-31908

372.8'7044 — Primary schools. Curriculum subjects: Music — *For teaching*

Johnston, Tom. Music with your project. — Aberdeen : Aberdeen University Press, Aug.1982. — [80]p
ISBN 0-08-025761-5 (pbk) : £4.50 : CIP entry B82-15654

372.8'73 — Children, to 5 years. Education. Musical activities — *For parents & for teaching*

Shephard, Margaret. Music with mum : fun with music for the under-5's at home and in groups / Margaret Shephard ; foreword by Avril Dankworth. — London : Unwin Paperbacks, 1982. — 87p : ill,music ; 20cm
ISBN 0-04-649014-0 (pbk) : £1.95 : CIP rev. B82-00924

372.8'9044'0942 — England. Primary schools. Curriculum subjects: History. Teaching

Blyth, Joan. History in primary schools : a practical approach for teachers of 5- to 11-year-old children / Joan E. Blyth. — London : McGraw-Hill, c1982. — x,226p : ill,facsims,forms ; 22cm. — (McGraw-Hill series for teachers)
Bibliography: p219-221. — Includes index
ISBN 0-07-084128-4 (pbk) : Unpriced : CIP rev. B81-22672

372.8′9044′0942 — England. Primary schools. Curriculum subjects: Local studies. Teaching

Prosser, Peter. The world on your doorstep : the teacher, the environment, and integrated studies / Peter Prosser. — London : McGraw-Hill, c1982. — ix,143p : ill ; 22cm. — (McGraw-Hill series for teachers)
Includes index
ISBN 0-07-084132-2 (pbk) : £5.25 : CIP rev. B82-00913

372.9 — PRIMARY EDUCATION. HISTORICAL AND GEOGRAPHICAL TREATMENT

372.941 — Great Britain. Preparatory schools

Marshall, Arthur. Whimpering in the rhododendrons. — London : Collins, Sept.1982. — [200]p
ISBN 0-00-216647-x : £5.95 : CIP entry B82-19069

372.941 — Great Britain. Primary education. Role of Wilderspin, Samuel, *1820-1866*

McCann, Phillip. Samuel Wilderspin and the infant school movement. — London : Croom Helm, Aug.1982. — [336]p
ISBN 0-7099-2903-x : £14.95 : CIP entry B82-22411

372.9411 — Scotland. Primary schools. Cooperation with social services

Bruce, Nigel. Interagency cooperation in the primary school : the social work/education interface / Nigel Bruce ; report on research sponsored by the Scottish Education Department and the Social Work Services Group. — [Edinburgh] ([Dept. of Social Administration, University of Edinburgh, 23 Buccleuch Place, Edinburgh EH8 9LN]) : [N. Bruce], 1982. — 192p ; 21cm
Cover title. — Bibliography: p187-190. — Includes index
£2.00 (pbk)
Also classified at 361′.9411 B82-32925

372.942 — England. Primary education

New directions in primary education / edited and introduced by Colin Richards. — Lewes : Falmer Press, 1982. — 310p : ill ; 25cm. — (New directions series)
Includes bibliographies and index
ISBN 0-905273-27-3 (cased) : £11.50
ISBN 0-905273-26-5 (pbk) : £6.95 B82-22204

372.942 — England. Primary education, *1840-1870*

Ball, Nancy. Educating the people. — London : Maurice Temple Smith, Jan.1983. — [250]p
ISBN 0-85117-227-x : £12.00 : CIP entry B82-33083

372.9422′375 — Kent. Boughton Monchelsea. Primary schools: Boughton Monchelsea School, *to 1963 — Correspondence, diaries, etc.*

Boughton Monchelsea School. Boughton Monchelsea School : log book extracts, 1863-1963. — 2nd ed. — [Boughton Monchelsea] : Boughton Monchelsea School, [1976?]. — [59]p ; 22cm
Edited by D.F. Tye. — Previous ed.: 1970
Unpriced (pbk) B82-27566

372.9422′375 — Kent. Boughton Monchelsea. Primary schools: Boughton Monchelsea School, *to 1980*

Tye, Denis. A village school : Boughton Monchelsea 1850-1970 / Denis Tye. — Sittingbourne : Prototype, [1982?]. — 140p : ill,facsims,2plans,ports ; 22cm
Facsims. on inside covers
ISBN 0-9508047-0-3 (pbk) : Unpriced B82-27766

372.9422′75 — Hampshire. Bramshaw. Primary schools: Bramshaw School, *to 1977*

Merson, Elizabeth. Once there was — the village school / written and illustrated by Elizabeth Merson. — Southampton : Cave, [1979]. — 104p : ill,2maps,1plan ; 25cm
Spine title: The village school
ISBN 0-86146-001-4 (pbk) : £2.00 B82-16531

372.9424′13 — Gloucestershire. Newnham. Boys′ preparatory schools: Brightlands School, *to 1982 — Personal observations*

Hardwicke, Glyn. Brightlands : the building of a school / by Glyn Hardwicke. — Braunton : Merlin Books on behalf of the Governors of Brightlands School, 1982. — 142p,[8]p of plates : ill,ports ; 22cm
Includes index
ISBN 0-86303-018-1 : Unpriced B82-41116

372.9425′76 — Oxfordshire. Abingdon. Primary schools: St. Edmund′s School, *to 1982*

Let′s celebrate 1982. — [Abingdon] : St. Edmund′s School, [1982?]. — 65p : ill ; 26cm
Cover title
Unpriced (pbk) B82-33643

372.9429′67 — Dyfed. Llanelli. Girls′ primary schools: Market Street Junior School *(Llanelli), to 1981 — Welsh texts*

Jones, Eluned. Eu ceiniogau prin / Eluned Jones. — Llandybie : C. Davies, c1982. — 157p : ill,facsims,ports ; 21cm
£2.50 (pbk) B82-24646

372.9429′68 — Dyfed. Esgerdawe. Junior schools: Ysgol Esgerdawe, *to 1959 — Welsh texts*

Williams, M. E. (Mary Eunice). Hanes Ysgol Esgerdawe / M.E. Williams. — Llandysul : Gwasg Gower, 1982. — 151p : ill,1map,ports ; 19cm
ISBN 0-85088-707-0 (pbk) : £3.75 B82-37025

372.959 — ASEAN countries. Primary education *— Comparative studies*

Schooling in the ASEAN region : primary and secondary education in Indonesia, Malaysia, the Philippines, Singapore and Thailand / edited by T. Neville Postlethwaite and R. Murray Thomas. — Oxford : Pergamon, 1980. — xviii,328p : ill,maps ; 22cm
Includes bibliographies and index
ISBN 0-08-024289-8 : £12.00 : CIP rev.
Also classified at 373.959 B80-06853

372.9669′5 — Nigeria. Kano *(State).* Primary education, *1976-1980*

Bray, Mark. Universal primary education in Nigeria : a study of Kano State / Mark Bray. — London : Routledge & Kegan Paul, 1981. — xxi,212p : ill,maps ; 22cm
Bibliography: p195-209. — Includes index
ISBN 0-7100-0933-x (pbk) : £5.50 B82-03312

372.994 — Australia. Primary schools

Bassett, G. W.. The modern primary school in Australia. — London : Allen & Unwin, Apr.1982. — [280]p. — (Classroom and curriculum in Australia ; no.5)
ISBN 0-86861-172-7 : £15.00 : CIP entry B82-05769

373 — SECONDARY EDUCATION

373′.01′1509411 — Scotland. Secondary schools. Social education

Social education : notes towards a definition / John MacBeath ... [et al.]. — [Glasgow] : Scottish Social Education Project, c1981. — 42p : ill ; 30cm
ISBN 0-903915-43-x (pbk) : £2.00 B82-25616

373′.01′1509411 — Scotland. Secondary schools. Social education. Role of geography

Geography and social education / Tweed Basin Geography Teachers′ Panel. — [Dalkeith] ([c/o Ian S. Gilchrist, Newbattle High School, 64 Easthouses Rd., Dalkeith]) : S.A.G.T., 1982. — 16p : ill ; 30cm. — (Occasional paper / Scottish Association of Geography Teachers)
Unpriced (pbk) B82-31220

373.1 — SECONDARY SCHOOLS

373.11′02 — Secondary schools. Teaching *— Manuals*

Teaching in the middle and secondary schools / [edited by] Joseph F. Callahan, Leonard H. Clark. — 2nd ed. — New York : Macmillan ; London : Collier Macmillan, c1982. — xi,443p : ill,forms ; 26cm
Previous ed.: published as Teaching in the secondary school. 1977. — Includes bibliographies
ISBN 0-02-318260-1 (pbk) : £11.75 B82-29745

373.11′02′0924 — Down *(County).* Downpatrick. Secondary schools: Down High School. Teaching, *1939-1965 — Personal observations*

Fowweather, Arthur. ′Up Down′ / by Arthur Fowweather ; illustrations and dust jacket by Rowel Friers ; foreword by Arthur Mitchell. — Newcastle, Co. Down : Mourne Observer Press, c1981. — 190p : ill,ports ; 23cm
£6.95 B82-21068

373.12′009429 — Wales. Comprehensive schools. Organisation structure

Comprehensive schools in Wales : aspects of organisation and the roles of senior staff / Welsh Office = Ysgolion cyfun yng Nghymru : agweddau ar drefniadaeth a rolau′r staff hŷn / Y Swyddfa Gymreig. — [Cardiff] : H.M.S.O., c1981. — iv,51p ; 25cm. — (Education issues = Materion addysg, ISSN 0141-4526 ; 3)
English and Welsh text
ISBN 0-904251-48-9 (pbk) : Unpriced B82-13831

373.12′012′0922 — Oxfordshire. Oxford. Boys′ public schools: Magdalen College School. Headmasters, *1800-1900*

Hare, Patrick. Victorian masters : a biographical essay on the nineteenth century headmasters of Magdalen College School, Oxford / Patrick Hare. — [Oxford] ([Oxford OX4 1DZ]) : [Magdalen College School], [1982?]. — 18p,[7]p of plates : ill,facsims,ports ; 30cm
Text on inside cover. — Bibliography: on inside cover
£1.00 (pbk) B82-21219

373.12′012′0924 — Avon. Bristol. Girls public schools: Badminton School. Baker, B.M. *— Biographies*

At Badminton with B.M.B. / by those who were there ; compiled and edited by Jean Storry. — Bristol : Badminton School, 1982. — viii,54p,[13]p of plates : ill,ports(some col.) ; 22cm
ISBN 0-9508005-0-3 (pbk) : Unpriced B82-27839

373.12′19′42 — England. Secondary schools. Students. Intake. Reduction *— Case studies*

Falling rolls in secondary schools / [edited by] Eric Briault and Frances Smith. — Windsor : NFER
Pt.2. — c1980. — 403p : ill ; 22cm
Conference papers
ISBN 0-85633-208-9 (pbk) : £9.95 B82-35622

373.12′52 — Great Britain. Secondary schools. Mixed ability groups. Teaching

Kerry, Trevor. Mixed ability teaching : in the early years of the secondary school : a teaching skills workbook / Trevor Kerry, Margaret Sands. — Basingstoke : Macmillan Education, 1982. — 46p : forms ; 30cm. — (DES teacher education project focus books)
Bibliography: p45
ISBN 0-333-31657-6 (unbound) : £1.95 B82-32332

373.12′52′0942 — England. Comprehensive schools. Mixed ability groups. Teaching

Mixed ability teaching : problems and possibilities / Margaret I. Reid ... [et al.]. — Windsor : NFER-Nelson, 1981. — xii,178p : ill ; 22cm
Bibliography: p172-173. — Includes index
ISBN 0-85633-232-1 (pbk) : £8.95 B82-09659

373.12′6 — Great Britain. Secondary schools. Graded examinations

Harrison, Andrew. Review of graded tests / Andrew Harrison. — London : Methuen Educational, 1982. — 94p ; 21cm. — (Schools Council examinations bulletin ; 41)
Bibliography: p53-58
ISBN 0-423-51040-1 (pbk) : Unpriced : CIP rev. B82-12340

373.12′62 — England. Secondary schools: C.S.E. examinations & G.C.E. (O level) examinations. Syllabuses. Multicultural aspects

Chalkley, Brian. Education for international understanding in the United Kingdom : a study of the syllabuses of the G.C.E. and C.S.E. examination boards to assess their international content / by Brian Chalkley. — London : Extramural Division, School of Oriental and African Studies, University of London, c1982. — iii,37p ; 30cm. — (Occasional papers / Extramural Division School of Oriental and African Studies University of London, ISSN 0261-5428 ; 2)
ISBN 0-7286-0094-3 (pbk) : Unpriced
B82-22367

373.12′62 — England. Secondary schools. G.C.E. (O level) examinations. Techniques — *Manuals*

Stevenson, B.. How to pass exams / by B. Stevenson. — London : Letts, 1982. — 95p : ill ; 19cm. — (Key facts. Learning aid)
Includes index
ISBN 0-85097-438-0 (pbk) : £1.25 B82-31589

373.12′62 — England. Secondary schools. Public examinations. Results. Publication

Publishing school examination results : a discussion / Ian Plewis .. [et al.]. — London : University of London Institute of Education, 1981. — 66p : ill ; 21cm. — (Bedford Way papers, ISSN 0261-0078 ; 5)
Includes bibliographies
ISBN 0-85473-116-4 (pbk) : £1.80 B82-08686

373.12′62′0942 — England. Secondary schools. Public examinations, ***1944-1964***

Fisher, Peter, *1942-*. External examinations in secondary schools in England and Wales 1944-1964 / by Peter Fisher. — [Leeds] ([23 Lyddon Terrace, Leeds LS2 9JT]) : Museum of the History of Education, University of Leeds, 1982. — iv,83p ; 22cm. — (Educational administration and history monograph, ISSN 0140-0428 ; no.11)
Unpriced (pbk) B82-36911

373.12′62′0942 — England. Secondary schools. Public examinations. Standards

Christie, T.. Defining public examination standards / T. Christie, G.M. Forrest. — Basingstoke : Macmillan Education, 1981. — ix,101p ; 24cm. — (Schools Council research studies)
Bibliography: p81-88. — Includes index
ISBN 0-333-31496-4 (pbk) : £4.95 : CIP rev.
B81-25694

373.12′64 — England. Secondary schools. Students 16 years-. Academic achievement. Assessment. Techniques

Tattersall, Kathleen. Differential examinations. — London : Methuen Educational, Jan.1983. — [80]p. — (Schools Council examination bulletin ; 42)
ISBN 0-423-51080-0 (pbk) : £3.95 : CIP entry
B82-34574

373.12′914′094259 — Buckinghamshire. Middle schools. Transfer of primary school students, ***1982*** **—** ***For parents***

Buckinghamshire. *Education Department*. Transfer from first to middle and combined schools September 1982 : information for parents / Buckinghamshire County Council Education Department. — [Aylesbury] : [The Department], [1981?]. — 17p ; 21cm
Cover title
ISBN 0-86059-235-9 (pbk) : Unpriced
B82-01934

373.12′914′094259 — Buckinghamshire. Secondary schools. Transfer of primary school students, 12 years — *For parents*

Buckinghamshire. *Education Department*. Transfer to secondary schools at 12+ September 1982 : information for parents / Buckinghamshire County Council Education Department. — [Aylesbury] : [The Department], [1981?]. — 31p ; 21cm
Cover title
ISBN 0-86059-230-8 (pbk) : Unpriced
B82-01933

373.13′0941 — Great Britain. Secondary schools. Teaching methods

Button, Leslie. Group tutoring for the form teacher : a developmental model : programmes and working papers / Leslie Button. — London : Hodder and Stoughton
1: Lower secondary school, years one and two. — 1981. — vi,185p : ill ; 25cm
Includes index
ISBN 0-340-26691-0 (pbk) : £5.25 : CIP rev.
B81-22646

Button, Leslie. Group tutoring for the form teacher. — London : Hodder & Stoughton, July 1982
2: Upper secondary school, years three, four and five. — [352]p
ISBN 0-340-26690-2 (pbk) : £9.50 : CIP entry
B82-17962

373.14′0941 — Great Britain. Secondary schools. Students. Counselling — *For teaching*

McGuiness, J. B.. Planned pastoral care : a guide for teachers / J.B. McGuiness. — London : McGraw-Hill, c1982. — viii,140p : ill ; 22cm. — (McGraw-Hill series for teachers)
Bibliography: p129-135. — Includes index
ISBN 0-07-084131-4 (pbk) : £4.95 : CIP rev.
B82-00912

373.14′25 — Great Britain. Adolescents, 17-19 years. Vocational preparation. Courses — *Proposals*

ABC in action : a report from an FEU/CGLI Working Party on the piloting of A Basis for Choice 1979-1981. — Stanmore : Further Education Curriculum Review and Development Unit, 1981. — [150]p : ill,facsims ; 30cm
ISBN 0-85522-099-6 (pbk) : Unpriced
B82-12732

373.14′25 — Great Britain. Secondary schools. Fifth forms. Students: Girls. Careers guidance. Sex discrimination — *Case studies*

Benett, Yves. Sidetracked? : a look at the careers advice given to fifth-form girls / Yves Benett and Dawn Carter. — Manchester : Equal Opportunities Commission, 1981. — 19p ; 20cm
ISBN 0-905829-48-4 (pbk) : Unpriced
B82-17319

373.1′425 — Great Britain. Secondary schools. Students. Work experience

Watts, A. G.. Work experience and schools. — London : Heinemann Educational, Oct.1982. — [272]p. — (Organization in schools series)
ISBN 0-435-80911-3 : £9.50 : CIP entry
B82-25529

373.14′25 — Great Britain. Young persons. Vocational preparation. Role of assessment of basic skills

The **Basic** skills analysis : how a checklist can help make the most of training opportunities. — [London] ([Selkirk House, High Holborn, WC1]) : Manpower Services Commission, [1981]. — 28p(8folded) : facsims ; 30cm
Checklist developed by Michael R. Freshwater
Unpriced (spiral) B82-03642

373.14′6 — England. Catholic comprehensive schools. Pastoral work

Pastoral care in comprehensive schools. — London (114 Mount St., W1Y 6AH) : National Council of Bishops and Religious, [1980]. — 6p ; 21cm
£0.10 (unbound) B82-13910

373.15′43′0942 — England. Secondary schools. Students. Suspension

Grunsell, Rob. Beyond control? : schools and suspension / Rob Grunsell. — London : Writers and Readers, in association with Chameleon, c1980. — 132p ; 21cm
ISBN 0-906495-22-9 (cased) : £4.95
ISBN 0-906495-23-7 (pbk) : Unpriced
B82-34553

373.16′2′0942576 — Oxfordshire. Abingdon. Boys′ public schools: Radley College. Buildings, ***1720-1900***

Cherniavsky, M. T.. Looking at Radley : an architectural & historical survey of the earlier buildings / M.T. Cherniavsky and A.E. Money. — [Abingdon] ([Abingdon, Oxon.]) : Radley College, [1981]. — 61p : ill(some col.),2ports ; 25cm
Unpriced (pbk) B82-02888

373.16′7 — Secondary schools. Applications of microcomputer systems — *Conference proceedings*

IFIP TC3 Working Conference on Microcomputers in Secondary Education *(1980 : Sèvres)*. Microcomputers in secondary education : proceedings of the IFIP TC3 Working Conference on microcomputers in secondary education, Sèvres, Paris, France 14-18 April 1980 / edited by E.D. Tagg. — Amsterdam ; Oxford : North-Holland Publishing, 1980. — x,152p : ill ; 23cm
Includes index
ISBN 0-444-86047-9 : £12.85 B82-14326

373.18 — Secondary schools. School life

The **Quality** of school life / edited by Joyce Levy Epstein ; foreword by Philip W. Jackson. — Lexington, Mass. : Lexington, c1981 ; [Aldershot] : Gower, 1982. — xii,298p : ill ; 24cm
Includes bibliographies and index
ISBN 0-669-03869-5 : £18.50 B82-08650

373.18′0941 — Great Britain. Secondary schools. Students. Effects of school life. Research reports: Fifteen thousand hours — *Critical studies*

'Fifteen thousand hours′ : secondary schools and their effect on children : a discussion / Barbara Tizard ... [et al.] ; with a response from the authors. — London : University of London Institute of Education, 1980. — 48p : ill ; 21cm. — (Bedford Way papers, ISSN 0261-0078)
Bibliography: p48
ISBN 0-85473-090-7 (pbk) : £1.50 B82-12397

373.18′0973 — United States. Suburbs. Secondary schools. Students — *Sociological perspectives*

Larkin, Ralph W.. Suburban youth in cultural crisis / Ralph W. Larkin. — New York ; Oxford : Oxford University Press, 1979 (1981 [printing]). — xi,259p ; 21cm
Bibliography: p247-252. — Includes index
ISBN 0-19-502523-7 (pbk) : £3.50 B82-00503

373.18′1′0951 — China. Secondary schools. Students. Political behaviour, ***1960-1980***

Shirk, Susan L.. Competitive comrades : career incentives and student strategies in China / Susan L. Shirk. — Berkeley ; London : University of California Press, c1982. — xiii,231p ; 25cm
Bibliography: p209-217. — Includes index
ISBN 0-520-04299-9 : £18.00 B82-40212

373.19′0942 — England. Secondary schools. Students, 11-16 years. Curriculum

Curriculum 11-16 : a review of progress / a joint study by HMI and five LEAs. — London : H.M.S.O., 1981. — vii,85p ; 25cm
At head of title: Department of Education and Science. — Includes index
ISBN 0-11-270533-2 (pbk) : £2.95 B82-17332

373.19′0942 — England. Secondary schools. Students, 14-16 years. Curriculum. Great Britain. *Parliament. House of Commons, Education, Science and Arts Committee.* **Second report ... session 1981-82** — *Critical studies*

. The Secondary school curriculum and examinations : initial Government observations on the Second report from the Education, Science and Arts Committee, session 1981-82. — London : H.M.S.O., 1982. — 14p ; 25cm. — (Cmnd. ; 8551)
ISBN 0-10-185510-9 (unbound) : £2.10
B82-31972

373.19'0942 — England. Secondary schools. Students, 14-16 years. Curriculum — *Inquiry reports*

Great Britain. *Parliament. House of Commons. Education, Science and Arts Committee.* Second report from the Education, Science and Arts Committee, session 1981-82 : the secondary school curriculum and examinations : with special reference to the 14 to 16 year old age group : together with part of the proceedings of the committee, the minutes of evidence and appendices. — London : H.M.S.O.
Vol.2: minutes of evidence. — [1982]. — x,589p ; 25cm. — ([HC] ; 116-II)
ISBN 0-10-275882-4 (pbk) : £15.30
B82-20570

Great Britain. *Parliament. House of Commons. Education, Science and Arts Committee.* Second report from the Education, Science and Arts Committee, session 1981-82 : the secondary school curriculum and examinations : with special reference to the 14 to 16 year old age group : together with part of the proceedings of the committee, the minutes of evidence and appendices. — London : H.M.S.O.
Vol.1: Report. — [1982]. — clip ; 25cm. — ([HC] ; 116-I)
ISBN 0-10-277882-5 (pbk) : 7.00 B82-20572

Great Britain. *Parliament. House of Commons. Education, Science and Arts Committee.* Second report from the Education, Science and Arts Committee, session 1981-82 : the secondary school curriculum and examinations, with special reference to the 14 to 16 year old age group : together with part of the proceedings of the committee, the minutes of evidence and appendices. — London : H.M.S.O.
Vol.3: Appendices. — 1981. — vii,[72]p ; 25cm. — ([HC] ; 116-III)
Includes bibliographies
ISBN 0-10-278582-1 (pbk) : £4.75 B82-20571

373.2 — SECONDARY SCHOOLS. SPECIAL TYPES AND LEVELS

373.2'22 — England. Boys' public schools. Resources. Implications of N level & F level courses — *Case studies*

Examinations at 18+ : resource implications of an N. and F. curriculum and examination structure in H.M.C. schools. — London (29 Gordon Sq., W.C.1.) : Headmasters' Conference, 1979. — 91p ; 21cm
£1.00 (pbk) B82-10985

373.2'22 — Great Britain. Boys' public schools. Cooperation with industries

Emms, David. H.M.C. schools and British industry : a personal enquiry / by David Emms. — [London] ([29 Gordon Sq., W.C.1]) : [Headmasters' Conference], 1981. — 68p ; 22cm. — (An H.M.C. discussion document)
Unpriced (pbk) B82-10982

373.2'22'02541 — Great Britain. Public schools — *Directories — Serials*

Public & preparatory schools yearbook. — 1982. — London : A. & C. Black, Apr.1982. — [780]p
ISBN 0-7136-2182-6 (pbk) : £7.95 : CIP entry
Also classified at 372.1'042202541 B82-04495

373.2'22'0941 — Great Britain. Public schools, *to 1980.* **Political aspects**

Armstrong, Albert. Public school power : also Oxford and Cambridge Universities : a historical study up to November 1980 / by Albert Armstrong. — Hatfield (13 White Lion House, Town Centre Hatfield, Herts.) : Armstrong Publications, [1981?]. — 84p ; 21cm
£2.00 (pbk) B82-07705

373.2'38 — England. Sixth forms. Courses

Dean, Judy. 17 plus : the new sixth form in schools and FE / Judy Dean and Andrew Steeds. — Windsor : NFER/Nelson, 1981. — vii,168p ; 22cm
Bibliography: p168
ISBN 0-85633-236-4 (pbk) : £6.75 B82-25348

373.2'38 — England. Sixth forms. N level & F level courses — *Headmasters' Conference viewpoints*

Examinations at 18+ : the N. and F. studies : comments submitted to the Schools Council in conjunction with the Headmasters' Conference publication on resource implications of the N and F curriculum and examination structure. — [London] ([29 Gordon Sq., W.C.1.]) : Headmasters' Conference, 1979. — 8p ; 21cm
Unpriced (pbk) B82-10984

373.2'38'0941 — Great Britain. Young persons, 16-18 years. Education — *Secondary Heads Association viewpoints*

On to eighteen : responses on educational opportunities from 16 to 18. — London : Secondary Heads Association, c1979. — 101p ; 21cm. — (Topics)
ISBN 0-906916-00-3 (pbk) : £1.00 B82-10184

373.2'38'0942 — England. Educational institutions. Students, 16-19 years. Education

Great Britain. *Department of Education and Science.* 17+ : a new qualification / Department of Education and Science, Welsh Office. — [London] : H.M.S.O., 1982. — 9p ; 25cm
ISBN 0-11-270307-0 (pbk) : £1.50 B82-32995

373.2'38'0942 — England. Sixth form colleges

Watkins, Peter. The sixth form college in practice. — London : Edward Arnold, Aug.1982. — [96]p. — (Teaching matters)
ISBN 0-7131-0730-8 (pbk) : £3.50 : CIP entry
B82-17933

373.2'38'0942 — England. Young persons, 16-19 years. Education — *Proposals*

National Association of Teachers in Further and Higher Education. Education and training for the 16-19s : a discussion paper / NATFHE. — [London] : [National Association of Teachers in Further and Higher Education], 1979. — 15p ; 21cm
Cover title
£0.35 (£0.25 to members of the Association) (pbk) B82-08496

National Union of Teachers. 16-19 : a joint policy statement on the education and training of the 16-19 age group / NUT, NATFHE. — [London] : NUT, 1981. — 8p ; 21cm
Cover title. — Text on inside cover
Unpriced (pbk) B82-06597

373.2'38'094281 — Yorkshire. Educational institutions. Students, 16-19 years. Full-time education — *Proposals*

16-19 full-time education : a regional response / Yorkshire & Humberside Council for Further Education. — Leeds (c/o The Secretary, Yorkshire & Humberside Council for Further Education, Bowling Green Terrace, Leeds, LS11 9SX) : Yorkshire & Humberside Association for Further & Higher Education, 1982. — 26p ; 30cm
Cover title. — Text on inside cover. — Bibliography: p22
£0.25 (pbk) B82-22037

373.2'5'0941 — Great Britain. Comprehensive schools. School life

Turner, Glen. The social world of the comprehensive school. — London : Croom Helm, Oct.1982. — [160]p
ISBN 0-7099-2424-0 : £11.95 : CIP entry
B82-23195

373.2'5'09411 — Scotland. Comprehensive schools. Curriculum. Choice

Ryrie, Alexander C.. Routes and results : a study of the later years of schooling / by Alexander C. Ryrie. — Dunton Green : Hodder and Stoughton for the Scottish Council for Research in Education, c1981. — 135p : 2ill ; 22cm. — (SCRE publication ; 75)
Bibliography: p129-132. — Includes index
ISBN 0-340-26714-3 (cased) : Unpriced
ISBN 0-340-26716-x (pbk) : £4.95 B82-11853

373.2'5'0942 — England. Comprehensive education

Hargreaves, David H.. The challenge for the comprehensive school : culture, curriculum and community / David H. Hargreaves. — London : Routledge & Kegan Paul, 1982. — x,243p ; 22cm
Includes index
ISBN 0-7100-0981-x (pbk) : £4.95 B82-23259

373.2'5'09429 — Wales. Comprehensive schools. Fourth forms & fifth forms

Years IV and V in comprehensive schools / Welsh Office = Blynddoedd IV a V yn yr ysgolion cyfun / Y Swyddfa Gymreig. — [Cardiff], 1981. — 101p ; 25cm. — (Education issues = Materion addysg, ISSN 0141-4526 ; 4)
ISBN 0-904251-52-7 (pbk) : Unpriced
B82-39980

373.2'5'09429 — Wales. Comprehensive schools. Students. Social adjustment

Pastoral care in the comprehensive schools of Wales / Welsh Office = Gofal bugeilol yn ysgolion cyfun Cymru / Y Swyddfa Gymreig. — [Cardiff] : H.M.S.O., 1982. — 44p ; 25cm. — (Education issues = Materion addysg, ISSN 0141-4526 ; 5)
ISBN 0-904251-58-6 (pbk) : Unpriced
B82-39979

373.3/9 — SECONDARY EDUCATION. HISTORICAL AND GEOGRAPHICAL TREATMENT

373.41 — England. Secondary education. Role of parents

Johnson, Daphne. Family and school. — London : Croom Helm, Dec.1982. — [192]p
ISBN 0-7099-2236-1 : £11.95 : CIP entry
B82-30807

373.41 — Great Britain. Compulsory secondary education. Reform — *Fabian viewpoints*

Kohn, Ray. Enforced leisure : enforced education / Ray Kohn. — London : Fabian Society, 1982. — 22p : ill ; 21cm. — (Fabian tract, ISSN 0307-7535 ; 479)
ISBN 0-7163-0479-1 (unbound) : £1.50
B82-22008

373.411'4 — Scotland. Western Isles. Barra, North Uist & South Uist. Secondary education — *Proposals*

Western Isles. *Islands Council.* Liniclate school / Comhairle Nan Eilean. — [Stornaway] ([Sandwick Rd., Stornaway PA87 2BW]) : [Comhairle Nan Eilean], [1977?]. — 24p : maps ; 30cm
Cover title
Unpriced (spiral) B82-14342

373.416'64 — Armagh *(District).* **Craigavon region. Secondary education,** *1966-1980*

McKernan, James. Transfer at 14 : a study of the Craigavon two-tier system as an organisational innovation in education / by James McKernan with the assistance of Mary Sandby-Thomas. — [Belfast] : Northern Ireland Council for Educational Research, 1981. — viii,112p : ill,3maps ; 30cm. — (Publications of the Northern Ireland Council for Educational Research ; 21)
Bibliography: p107-112
ISBN 0-903478-19-6 (pbk) : £4.00 B82-08049

373.418'35 — Dublin. Catholic boys' secondary schools: Belvedere College, *1832-1982* — *Personal observations*

Portraits : Belvedere College Dublin 1832-1982 / edited by John Bowman and Ronan O'Donoghue ; original photographs by Derek Speirs. — Dublin : Gill and Macmillan, 1982. — 162p : ill,facsims,ports ; 25cm
Ill on lining papers
ISBN 0-7171-1235-7 : £18.00 B82-31027

373.42 — England. Secondary education

Aspects of secondary education in England : a survey / by HM Inspectors of Schools. — London : H.M.S.O., 1979 (1980 [printing]). — viii,311p : ill,forms ; 2kcm
Includes index
ISBN 0-11-270498-0 (pbk) : Unpriced
B82-05026

373.421'42 — London. Camden *(London Borough).* **Boys' public schools: University College School,** *to 1980*

University College School. An angel without wings : the history of University College School 1830-1980 / by H.J.K. Usher, C.D. Black-Hawkins, G.J. Carrick ; Junior Branch by C.E.F. Smaggasgale, H.J. Byrom and M.E. Dean ; foreword by Lord Lloyd of Hampstead ; edited by G.G.H. Page. — [London] : University College School, 1981. — 114p : ill (some col.),facsims,plans,ports ; 24cm
Ill on inside covers
Unpriced (pbk) B82-11727

373.421'63 — London. Lewisham *(London Borough).* **Boys' public schools: Christ's College** *(Blackheath), to 1976*

Crombie, A. E. O.. A view of Christ's College, Blackheath / A.E.O. Crombie. — Gillingham : Meresborough, 1980. — 103p : ill,ports ; 22cm
ISBN 0-905270-22-3 : £6.95 B82-36972

373.422'735 — Hampshire. Winchester. Boys' public schools: Winchester College, *to 1982 — Festschriften*

Winchester College : sixth-centenary essays / edited by Roger Custance. — Oxford : Oxford University Press, 1982. — xxv,515p,[41]p of plates : ill,facsims,1map,ports ; 23cm
Includes index
ISBN 0-19-920103-x : £20.00 : CIP rev.
B82-07522

373.422'96 — Berkshire. Eton. Boys' public schools: Eton College, *to 1981*

Ollard, Richard. An English education : a perspective of Eton. — London : Collins, Sept.1982. — [256]p
ISBN 0-00-216495-7 : £9.95 : CIP entry
B82-19064

373.423'54 — Devon. Tiverton. Boys' boarding schools: Blundell's School, *1846-1882*

Jenkins, J. B.. The removal of Blundell's : town and gown in Tiverton 1846-1882 / J.B. Jenkins ; foreword by Sir John Palmer. — Tiverton : Blundell's School, c1982. — 86p,[18]p of plates : ill,facsims,1plan,ports ; 22cm
One folded sheet attached to inside cover. — Includes index
ISBN 0-9508217-0-5 (pbk) : Unpriced
B82-36088

373.423'96 — Avon. Winscombe. Independent secondary schools: Sidcot School. Ex-students. Organisations: Sidcot Old Scholars' Association, *1871-1971*

Roberts, Kathleen. Sidcot Old Scholars' Association 1871-1971 / by Kathleen Roberts. — Winscombe : The Association, c1982. — 160p : ill,1map,ports ; 21cm
ISBN 0-9507958-0-1 (pbk) : Unpriced
B82-25237

373.424'81 — Warwickshire. Polesworth. Comprehensive schools: Polesworth School, *to 1981*

Moss, L. S.. Changeful years unresting : Polesworth School 1881-1981 / by L.S. Moss. — Tamworth (Dordon Rd, Dordon, Tamworth, Staffs., B78 1QT) : Published by L.S. Moss on behalf of the Polesworth School Educational Fund, [1981]. — 80p : plans ; 30cm
Cover title
Unpriced (pbk) B82-08241

373.425'61 — Bedfordshire. Bedford. Boys' public schools: Bedford Modern School, *to 1980*

Underwood, Andrew. Bedford Modern School of the black & red / Andrew Underwood. — [Bedford] : [Bedford Modern School], c1981. — 288p : ill,1coat of arms,music,plans,ports ; 22cm
Includes index
ISBN 0-9507608-0-3 (cased) : Unpriced
ISBN 0-9507608-1-1 (pbk) : Unpriced
B82-10095

373.425'61 — Bedfordshire. Bedford. Girls' grammar schools: Dame Alice Harper School, *to 1982*

Dame Alice Harpur School. The history of the school : 1882 B.G.M.S. — D.A.H.S. 1982 / Constance M. Broadway & Esther I. Buss. — [Bedford] : [Dame Alice Harpur School], c1982. — 190p,16p of plates : ill,2facsims,1col.map,ports ; 22cm
Ill on lining papers
ISBN 0-9508060-0-5 : Unpriced B82-38431

373.425'71 — Oxfordshire. Burford. Comprehensive schools: Burford School, *1955-1980*

Glover, D. C.. Burford School 1955-1980 : a case study in the development of comprehensive education / D.C. Glover. — [Oxford] ([County Hall, Oxford]) : Oxfordshire County Council, 1980. — 70p ; 30cm
Cover title: Comprehensive education at Burford School. — At head of title: Oxfordshire County Council, Oxfordshire Education Committee
Unpriced (pbk) B82-29554

373.425'71'0924 — Oxfordshire. Burford. Comprehensive schools: Burford School, *1954-1979 — Personal observations*

Simpson, Anges. Burford School : memoirs : being the personal reminiscences of Miss Agnes Simpson, B.A., Head of History during the period 1954-1979 and giving an insight into life in a developing comprehensive school. — [Oxford] ([Oxford OX8 4PL]) : [Burford School], [1982?]. — 52p ; 28cm
Unpriced (pbk) B82-29555

373.425'76 — Oxfordshire. Abingdon. Secondary schools: Abingdon School *— Personal observations*

Willis, Donald. A song on a bugle blown. — Oxford (1A Abingdon Rd., Cumnor, Oxford OX2 9QN) : Kenton Books, Jan.1983. — [220]p
ISBN 0-9508503-0-6 (pbk) : £3.50 : CIP entry
B82-40929

373.425'8 — Hertfordshire. Secondary education

Secondary education in Hertfordshire / Hertfordshire County Council Education Committee. — Hertford (County Hall, Hertford [SG13 8DF]) : [The Committee], 1978. — 50p ; 21cm
Cover title
Unpriced (pbk) B82-08643

373.425'85 — Hertfordshire. Harpenden. Secondary schools: St George's School *(Harpenden), to 1982*

Weatherley, Pam. A history of St George's School, Harpenden / by Pam Weatherley. — Harpenden : St George's School Association of Parents & Staff, c1982. — 48p : ill,ports ; 21cm
ISBN 0-9508204-0-7 (pbk) : Unpriced
B82-38339

373.426'41 — Suffolk. Beccles. Boys' grammar schools: Fauconberge Grammar School, *to 1926*

Goodwyn, E. A.. The Fauconberge School, Beccles 1770-1926 / E.A. Goodwyn. — Beccles (c/o Bidnall's, 17 Blyburgate, Beccles, Suffolk NR34 9TB) : [E.A. Goodwyn], 1980. — 40p : ill,facsims,ports ; 21cm
Cover title. — Bibliography: p40
£1.20 (pbk) B82-31374

373.426'752 — Essex. Chelmsford. Girls' grammar schools: Chelmsford County High School, *to 1980*

Kenyon, Mary. A history of Chelmsford County High School / Mary Kenyon. — Chelmsford : Essex Libraries, 1982. — ii,112p : ill,ports ; 20cm
ISBN 0-903630-16-8 (pbk) : Unpriced
B82-30170

373.429 — Wales. Secondary education, *1889-1944*

Jones, Gareth Elwyn. Controls and conflicts in Welsh secondary education 1889-1944 / Gareth Elwyn Jones. — Cardiff : University of Wales Press, 1982. — x,248p ; 23cm
Bibliography: p200-211. — Includes index
ISBN 0-7083-0814-7 : £14.95 : CIP rev.
B82-14216

373.429 — Wales. Secondary schools

Planning for progress : a contribution to the debate on achievement in secondary schools / Welsh Office. — [Cardiff] : [Welsh Office], 1982. — 29p ; 30cm. — (HMI (Wales) occasional paper)
'Summary of considerations and conclusions' (5p) as insert
Unpriced (unbound) B82-23549

373.744'61 — Massachusetts. Boston. Multicultural societies. Secondary education

Baynes, R. D.. At the hub : secondary schools in multi-ethnic urban areas, Boston and Haringey / R.D. Baynes. — London : Extramural Division, School of Oriental and African Studies, University of London, c1982. — 40p ; 30cm. — (Occasional papers / Extramural Division School of Oriental and African Studies University of London, ISSN 0261-5428 ; 1)
Bibliography: p38-39
ISBN 0-7286-0090-0 (pbk) : Unpriced
B82-22369

373.959 — ASEAN countries. Secondary education *— Comparative studies*

Schooling in the ASEAN region : primary and secondary education in Indonesia, Malaysia, the Philippines, Singapore and Thailand / edited by T. Neville Postlethwaite and R. Murray Thomas. — Oxford : Pergamon, 1980. — xviii,328p : ill,maps ; 22cm
Includes bibliographies and index
ISBN 0-08-024289-8 : £12.00 : CIP rev.
Primary classification 372.959 B80-06853

374 — ADULT AND FURTHER EDUCATION

374 — Adult education *— Conference proceedings*

Policy and research in adult education : the First Nottingham International Colloquium, 1981 : papers given at the First Nottingham International Colloquium on Policy and Research in Adult Education held at the University of Nottingham in July 1981 / selected by Brian Harvey ... [et al.]. — [Nottingham] : Department of Adult Education, University of Nottingham, c1981. — 150p ; 20cm. — (Nottingham studies in the theory and practice of the education of adults)
ISBN 0-902031-60-0 (pbk) : Unpriced
B82-17071

374 — Adult education. Implications of sex differences

Berryman, Julia C.. Sex differences in behaviour : their relevance for adult educators / by Julia C. Berryman. — Nottingham : Department of Adult Education, University of Nottingham, c1981. — ii,27p ; 21cm. — (Adults ; 6)
Includes bibliographies
ISBN 0-902031-51-1 (pbk) : Unpriced
B82-17449

374 — England. Adult education. Advisory, information & counselling services

Advisory Council for Adult and Continuing Education. Links to learning : a report on educational information, advisory and counselling services for adults / ACACE. — Leicester : ACACE, c1979. — 70p ; 21cm. — (Report / Advisory Council for Adult and Continuing Education)
ISBN 0-906436-02-8 (pbk) : £1.50 B82-39500

374 — England. Colleges of further education. Technician Education Council courses. Curriculum. Development, *1974-1980*

Curriculum change : an evaluation of TEC programme development in colleges : the main findings. — [London] : [Further Education Curriculum Review and Development Unit, 1981. — x,127p : ill ; 30cm
ISBN 0-85522-096-1 (pbk) : Unpriced
B82-26591

374 — England. Further education institutions. Curriculum. Development. Organisations: Further Education Curriculum Review and Development Unit — *Serials*

Further Education Curriculum Review and Development Unit. Annual report / Further Education Curriculum Review and Development Unit. — 1977-78-. — London (Elizabeth House, York Rd, SE1 7PH) : The Unit, 1978-. — v. ; 30cm
Description based on: 1980-81 issue
ISSN 0263-1334 = Annual report - Further Education Curriculum Review and Development Unit : Unpriced B82-17251

374 — Great Britain. Adult education. Advisory, information & counselling services

Tilley, N. V.. Education advice service for adults. — London : British Library, Research and Development Dept., Nov.1982. — [53]p. — (Library and information research reports, ISSN 0263-1709 ; 8)
ISBN 0-7123-3011-9 (pbk) : CIP entry B82-35212

374 — Great Britain. Adult education. Advisory, information & counselling services — *Conference proceedings*

Educational information and guidance for adults / edited by Roger H. Mercer. — [Sheffield] : Sheffield City Polytechnic, Department of Education Management, 1981. — 106p ; 21cm. — (Sheffield papers in education management ; no.16)
ISBN 0-903761-31-9 (pbk) : £1.50 B82-03246

374 — Great Britain. Adult education institutions. Closure. Prevention — *Manuals*

If the axe threatens you. — [London] ([Chequer Centre, Chequer St., Bunhill Row, EC1Y 8PL]) : Educational Centres Association, [1982?]. — [4]p ; 21cm. — (ECA advisory leaflet ; no.1)
Unpriced (unbound) B82-29618

374 — Great Britain. Adult education institutions. Students' associations. Organisation — *Manuals*

A Members association, partnership in action / Educational Centres Association. — London (Chequer St., Bunhill Row, EC1Y 8PL) : ECA, [1982]. — 1sheet ; 21x45cm folded to 21x15cm. — (ECA advisory leaflet ; no.5)
Includes bibliography
Unpriced B82-39515

374 — Great Britain. Adult educational guidance services — *Directories*

Directory of educational guidance services for adults / compiled by the Educational Advisory Services Project ; funded by the British Library. — Rev. ed. — Leicester (196 De Montfort St, Leicester LE1 7GE) : Advisory Council for Adult and Continuing Education, 1982. — [8]p ; 21cm
Previous ed.: 1981
Unpriced (unbound) B82-39326

374 — Great Britain. Education. G.C.E. examinations. Adult external candidates — *Inquiry reports*

Butler, Linda. Adult external candidates for GCE examinations / by Linda Butler. — Leicester : ACACE, 1981. — iii,101p ; 30cm. — (Enquiry officer's report / Advisory Council for Adult and Continuing Education)
ISBN 0-906436-06-0 (pbk) : £2.50 B82-39324

374 — Great Britain. Further education institutions. Catering services

Cowell, F. M.. Catering in colleges / by F.M. Cowell. — Sheffield (c/o Hon Sec., Sheffield City Polytechnic, Pond St., Sheffield S1 1WB) : Association of Colleges for Further and Higher Education, [1982]. — 11p ; 21cm
Conference paper from ACFHE summer meeting, 11-12 June, 1981
£0.75 (unbound)
Primary classification 378'.19716'0941
B82-24395

374 — Great Britain. Further education institutions. Curriculum. Development

Curriculum development in further education : a collection of papers for in-service development groups / [edited by] John Russell and Jack Latcham. — 3rd ed. — [Bristol] ([Blagdon, Bristol, BS18 6RG]) : Further Education Staff College, Coombe Lodge, [1979?]. — 1v.(loose-leaf) : ill ; 33cm
Previous ed.: 1976?. — Includes bibliographies
Unpriced B82-35691

374 — Great Britain. Further education institutions. Examinations. Objective tests. Setting & marking

Ward, Christine. Preparing and using objective questions / Christine Ward. — Cheltenham : Thornes, 1981. — ix,240p : ill ; 23cm. — (ST (P) handbooks for further education)
Bibliography: p236. — Includes index
ISBN 0-85950-438-7 : £6.25 : CIP rev.
B81-20536

374 — Lifelong education

Continuing education for the post-industrial society. — Milton Keynes : Open University Press, Nov.1982. — [160]p
ISBN 0-335-10186-0 (pbk) : £5.95 : CIP entry
B82-33331

374 — Nonformal education

Townsend Coles, Edwin K.. Maverick of the education family : two essays in non-formal education / by Edwin K. Townsend Coles ; with an appendix by Pia Kjaer-Olsen. — Oxford : Pergamon, 1982. — xi,111p : ill,maps ; 24cm
Appendix, entitled Non-formal education, is a synthesis of part of the Botswana Natural Development Plan V. — Includes index
ISBN 0-08-025239-7 : £7.95 : CIP rev.
B82-07657

Wedemeyer, Charles A.. Learning at the back door : reflections on non-traditional learning in the lifespan / Charles A. Wedemeyer. — Madison ; London : University of Wisconsin Press, 1981. — xxviii,260p : ill ; 24cm
Bibliography: p243-250. — Includes index
ISBN 0-299-08560-0 : £13.65 B82-19649

374 — United States. Adult education. Advisory, information & counselling services

Heffernan, James M.. Educational and career services for adults / James M. Heffernan. — Lexington, Mass. : Lexington Books ; [Aldershot] : Gower [distributor], 1981. — xvi,272p ; 24cm
Bibliography: p255-266. — Includes index
ISBN 0-669-03440-1 : £15.50 B82-00400

374'.0025'41 — Great Britain. Colleges of further education — *Directories* — *Serials*

United Kingdom colleges of further education. — [1982]-. — Great Missenden : Data Research Group, 1982-. — v. ; 30cm
Annual. — Continues: United Kingdom technical colleges
ISSN 0263-8088 = United Kingdom colleges of further education : Unpriced B82-36695

374'.006'041 — Great Britain. Adult education. Organisations: Educational Centres Association

Educational Centres Association. The Educational Centres Association. — [London] ([Chequer Centre, Chequer St., Bunhill Row, EC1Y 8PL]) : Educational Centres Association, [1982?]. — 1folded sheet(6p) ; 21cm. — (ECA advisory leaflet ; no.2)
Unpriced B82-29227

Educational Centres Association. Why the Educational Centres Association?. — [London] ([Chequer Centre, Chequer St, Bunhill Row, EC1Y 8PL]) : [Educational Centres Association], [1982]. — [4]p : ill ; 21cm
Unpriced (unbound) B82-29225

374'.0068'3 — England. West Midlands. Colleges of further education. Staff development

Staff developments in further education : a series of lectures/discussions given by members of the West Midlands Regional Staff Development Network during the 1980-81 session / compiled by R.H. Herbert. — [Wolverhampton] : West Midlands Regional Advisory Council for Further Education, 1982. — 55p ; 30cm
Unpriced (pbk) B82-20607

374'.0072042 — England. Further education. Research — *Serials*

FERN journal / Further Education Research Network. — 1 (Autumn 1980)-. — [Leicester] ([c/o D.G. Rogers, Centre for Postgraduate Studies, Leicester Polytechnic, Scraptoft Campus, Scraptoft, Leicester LE7 9SU]) : FERN, 1980-. — v. : ill ; 30cm
Two issues yearly
ISSN 0260-5058 = FERN journal : Free to FERN members B82-09079

374'.00880696 — Scotland. Retired persons. Education

Retirement education in Scotland : a working party report. — Edinburgh (33 Castle St., Edinburgh EH2 3DN) : Age Concern Scotland, [1981?]. — 54p ; 21cm
Cover title
£0.80 (pbk) B82-32794

374'.012 — Great Britain. Adult literacy education, *1966-1977*

Charnley, A. H.. The concept of success in adult literacy / A.H. Charnley and H.A. Jones. — London : Adult Literacy & Basic Skills Unit, 1981, c1979. — iv,200p ; 21cm
Originally published: Cambridge : Huntinton, 1979
ISBN 0-906509-07-6 (pbk) : £4.00 B82-31699

374'.012 — Great Britain. Adult literacy education — *Personal observations*

Smith, Delroy. A second chance / by Delroy Smith. — London : Peckham Publishing Project, c1981. — 11p : ill ; 21cm
ISBN 0-906464-75-7 (pbk) : £0.50 B82-36423

374'.012 — Nottinghamshire. Nottingham region. Adult literacy education. Role of volunteers

Elsey, Barry. Voluntary tutors in adult literacy : a survey of adult literacy volunteers in the Nottingham area / Barry Elsey and Margaret Gibbs. — Nottingham : University of Nottingham, Department of Adult Education, 1981. — 67p : forms ; 21cm. — (Nottingham working papers in the education of adults ; 3)
Bibliography: p51
ISBN 0-902031-56-2 (pbk) : £2.20 B82-17453

374'.013 — Great Britain. Unemployed young persons, 16-18 years. Vocational preparation. Role of Youth Opportunities Programme community work projects

Scope for skills : vocational preparation in YOP community projects. — Edinburgh (4, Queensferry St., Edinburgh EH2 4PA) : Community Schemes Resource Unit, Scottish Community Education Centre, 1981. — 75p : forms ; 30cm
Unpriced (pbk) B82-14602

374'.013 — Great Britain. Unemployed young persons. Vocational preparation. Courses

Preparation for work in a multi-racial society. — London : Commission for Racial Equality, 1981. — pamphlets ; 32cm. — (Operation interchange)
ISBN 0-902355-95-3 : £1.00 B82-00682

374'.0143 — Great Britain. Youth Opportunities Programme trainees. Social education — *For management*

Spragg, Derrick. Learning in action : a framework for social education in the Youth Opportunities Programme / by Derrick Spragg. — Leicester : National Youth Bureau, 1981. — 37p : ill ; 30cm
Bibliography: p37
ISBN 0-86155-049-8 (unbound) : £1.70
B82-06138

374'.02 — Adult education. Distance study — *Conference proceedings*

Education of adults at a distance : based on the Conference on the Education of Adults at a Distance, organised by the Open University, England, in November 1979 / prologue by Michael J. Pentz ; commentary by Michael W. Neil. — London : Kogan Page in association with the Open University Press, 1981. — 270p : ill ; 22cm
Report of the Open University's Tenth Anniversary International Conference
ISBN 0-85038-415-x (pbk) : £9.95 : CIP rev.
B81-38847

374'.02 — Adult education. Distance study. Teaching

Jenkins, Janet. Materials for learning : how to teach adults at a distance / Janet Jenkins. — London : Routledge & Kegan Paul, 1981. — xii,209p : ill,1map,1form ; 24cm
Bibliography: p192-205. — Includes index
ISBN 0-7100-0808-2 (pbk) : £7.95 B82-00093

374'.02 — Adult education. Study techniques & teaching

Millard, Lesley. Adult learners : study skills and teaching methods / by Lesley Millard. — Nottingham : Department of Adult Education, University of Nottingham, c1981. — ii,26p ; 21cm. — (Adults ; 4)
Includes bibliographies
ISBN 0-902031-49-x (pbk) : Unpriced
B82-17450

374'.02 — Adults. Teaching. Implications of cognitive styles

Squires, Geoffrey. Cognitive styles and adult learning / by Geoffrey Squires. — Nottingham : Department of Adult Education, University of Nottingham, c1981. — ii,21p ; 21cm. — (Adults ; 3)
Includes bibliographies
ISBN 0-902031-48-1 (pbk) : £1.25 B82-17448

374'.02 — Europe. Adult basic education. Distance study. Teaching aids: Mass media — *Case studies*

Using the media for adult basic education / edited by Anthony Kaye and Keith Harry. — London : Croom Helm, c1982. — 255p : ill ; 23cm
Includes index
ISBN 0-7099-1506-3 : £12.95 B82-16354

374'.02 — Europe. Adult education. Distance study

Harry, Keith. The European experience of the use of mass media and distance methods for adult basic education / by Keith Harry, Anthony Kaye, Kevin Wilson. — Milton Keynes (Walton Hall, Milton Keynes MK7 6AA) : Open University Distance Education Research Group. — (DERG papers ; no.3a)
Vol.1: Main report. — 1981. — ii,101p : ill ; 25cm
At head of title: The Open University. — Bibliography: p95-97
Unpriced (pbk) B82-06689

Harry, Keith. The European experience of the use of mass media and distance methods for adult basic education / by Keith Harry, Anthony Kaye, Kevin Wilson. — [Milton Keynes] ([Walton Hall, Milton Keynes MK7 6AA]) : Open University Distance Education Research Group. — (DERG papers ; no.3b)
Vol.2: Appendices. — 1981. — ii,114p ; 25cm
Cover title. — Includes bibliographies
Unpriced (pbk) B82-06691

374'.02 — Great Britain. Adult education. Teaching methods

Wilson, John T. (John Thomas). Surviving the first lesson / [text by John T. Wilson] ; [illustrations by Valerie Harper]. — [London] ([Chequer Centre, Chequer St, Bunhill Row, EC1Y 8PL]) : Educational Centres Association, [1982]. — [12]p : ill ; 21cm. — (An E.C.A. booklet)
£0.10 (unbound) B82-29226

374'.02 — Great Britain. Further education. Educational technology — *Serials*

AVCET / Audio Visual Communication & Educational Technology (a section of NATFHE). — 1 (1976)-. — [London] ([c/o. NATFHE, Hamilton House, Mapledon Place, WC1]) : [The Section], 1978-. — v. ; 21cm
Annual. — Description based on: 2 (1977)
ISSN 0144-4603 = AVCET : Unpriced
Also classified at 378'.17'078 B82-14778

374'.02 — Great Britain. Further education institutions. Teaching support services. Management

Further education / based on an investigation by Gerald Collier ; edited by Norman Willis. — London : Council for Educational Technology, 1981. — 40p ; 21cm. — (Teaching & learning support services ; 2)
ISBN 0-86184-038-0 (pbk) : £4.50 : CIP rev.
B81-35871

374'.02 — Study techniques — *Manuals* — *For adult education*

Apps, Jerold W.. Study skills for adults returning to school / Jerold W. Apps. — 2nd ed. — New York ; London : McGraw-Hill, c1982. — xvi,200p : ill,facsims ; 23cm
Previous ed.: published as Study skills, for those adults returning to school, 1978. — Includes index
ISBN 0-07-002165-1 (pbk) : £6.95 B82-16379

374'.0880694 — Great Britain. Unemployed adults. Further education

Storrie, T. C.. Adult unemployed : a college perspective / by T.C. Storrie. — Sheffield, c/o Hon. Sec. Sheffield City Polytechnic, Pond St., Sheffield S1 1WB : Association of Colleges for Further and Higher Education, [1982]. — 10p ; 21cm
Paper from summer meeting of ACFHR, Bath June 10th & 11th 1982. — Cover title
£0.75 (pbk) B82-36020

374'.0973 — United States. Lifelong education

Barton, Paul. Worklife transitions : the adult learning connection / Paul Barton and The National Institute for Work and Learning ; foreword by Willard Wirtz. — New York ; London : McGraw-Hill, c1982. — xv,196p : 1ill ; 24cm
Includes index
ISBN 0-07-003974-7 : £11.50 B82-21157

374'.1'0941 — Great Britain. Further education. Self-teaching. Teaching aids. Provision

Clarke, John, *1922-*. Resource-based learning for higher and continuing education / John Clarke. — London : Croom Helm, c1982. — 211p : ill,plans,forms ; 23cm. — (New patterns of learning series)
Bibliography: p202-206. — Includes index
ISBN 0-7099-0705-2 : £11.95 : CIP rev.
Primary classification 378'.17944'0941
B81-30347

374'.1'09411 — Scotland. Self-teaching courses — *Lists*

Open learning opportunities in Scotland / S.I.A.E. ... [et al.]. — Glasgow : Scottish Council for Educational Technology, [1982]. — [68]p ; 20cm
ISBN 0-86011-048-6 (pbk) : Unpriced
B82-20679

374'.28'0941135 — Scotland. Shetland. Lerwick. Community centres: Islesburgh Community Centre

Islesburgh House : with Islesburgh Community Centre and Islesburgh (Garrison) Theatre. — Lerwick (Isleburgh House, Lerwick, Scotland) : Shetland Islands Council Leisure and Recreation Department, c1980. — 40p : ill,ports ; 28cm
Unpriced (pbk) B82-27862

374'.4 — Cambridgeshire. Cambridge. Correspondence colleges: National Extension College. Teaching by course tutors — *Manuals*

Lewis, Roger, *1944-*. How to tutor with NEC / by Roger Lewis. — [Cambridge] : National Extension College, c1981. — 36p : facsims,forms ; 21cm
ISBN 0-86082-304-0 (pbk) : Unpriced
B82-40270

374'.841835 — Dublin. Vocational education institutions: Liberties Vocational School

Liberties Vocational School, Bull Alley. — [Dublin] : CDVEC, [1979]. — [36]p : ill ; 21x30cm
Unpriced (pbk) B82-25952

374'.842 — England. Adult education. Accommodation

Prime use accommodation for adult education : an enquiry report / by Keith Percy ... [et al.] ; [for] ACACE. — Leicester : ACACE, [1982]. — 71p : 2ill ; 21cm. — (Report / Advisory Council for Adult and Continuing Education)
ISBN 0-906436-15-x (pbk) : £2.00 B82-39495

374'.842163 — London. Lewisham *(London Borough)*. **Universities. Colleges: Goldsmiths' College.** *School of Adult and Social Studies, to 1981*

Goldsmiths' College. *School of Adult and Social Studies*. Fifty years of adult studies : University of London Goldsmiths' College School of Adult and Social Studies Golden Jubilee 1931-1981. — London : University of London, [1981]. — 112p : ill,3facsims,2ports ; 21cm
Cover title. — Bibliography: p110-111
ISBN 0-901542-43-1 (pbk) : £2.50 B82-02883

374.9 — ADULT AND FURTHER EDUCATION. HISTORICAL AND GEOGRAPHICAL TREATMENT

374'.924 — Great Britain. Adult education. Peers, Robert — *Biographies*

Brown, Geoffrey F.. Robert Peers and the Department of Adult Education / Geoffrey F. Brown. — [Nottingham] : Department of Adult Education, University of Nottingham, c1981. — 20p ; 20cm
ISBN 0-902031-59-7 (pbk) : Unpriced
B82-17000

374'.941 — Great Britain. Adult education

Communist Party of Great Britain. *Education Sub-Committee*. Education for adults : a policy for defence and advance / issued for discussion by the Education Subcommittee of the Communist Party of Great Britain. — [London] : CPGB, [1982]. — 20p ; 22cm
Cover title. — Text on inside covers
ISBN 0-86224-018-2 (pbk) : £0.40 B82-31161

Legge, Derek. The education of adults in Britain / Derek Legge. — Milton Keynes : Open University Press, 1982. — xi,244p ; 24cm. — (The Open University Press series in adult and continuing education)
Bibliography: p223-225. — Includes index
ISBN 0-335-00267-6 : £12.95 : CIP rev.
B81-36981

374'.941 — Great Britain. Adult education, *1919* — *A inquiry reports* — *Early works*

Great Britain. *Ministry of Reconstruction. Adult Education Committee*. The 1919 report : the final and interim reports of the Adult Education Committee of the Ministry of Reconstruction 1918-1919 / reprinted with introductory essays by Harold Wiltshire, John Taylor, Bernard Jennings. — Nottingham : Department of Adult Education, University of Nottingham, 1980. — 157,vi,409p : maps ; 22cm
Includes index
ISBN 0-902031-45-7 : £15.00 B82-19933

374'.941 — Great Britain. Adult education, *1970-1979*

Woodhall, Maureen. The scope and costs of the education and training of adults in Britain : developments in the seventies / by Maureen Woodhall. — Leicester : ACACE, 1980. — iv,27p ; 21cm. — (Occasional paper / Advisory Council for Adult and Continuing Education ; 4)
ISBN 0-906436-05-2 (pbk) : £0.90 B82-39329

374'.941 — Great Britain. Adult education. Debates by Great Britain. *Parliament*

Education debates : House of Lords, 18th March, on education : House of Commons, 16th February, on adult education. — London (Chequer Centre, Chequer St, Bunhill Row, EC1Y 8PL) : Educational Centres Association, [1981]. — [3]leaves ; 30cm
Unpriced (unbound) B82-29224

374'.941 — Great Britain. Adult education — *For teaching*

Goodman, Sylvia J.. Mirror images / by Sylvia J. Goodman. — Bushey Heath (11 Linnet Close, Bushey Heath, Herts. WD2 1AX) : Fresh Start Centre, [1981?]. — [10]p ; 30cm
Cover title
Unpriced (pbk) B82-04109

374'.941 — Great Britain. Adult education — *Practical information*

Bell, Judith, *1930-*. Never too late to learn : the complete guide to adult education / Judith Bell, Gordon Roderick. — London : Longman, c1982. — viii,110p ; 20cm
Bibliography: p107. — Includes index
ISBN 0-582-49706-x (pbk) : £2.50 : CIP rev.
B82-00240

Pates, Andrew. Second chances. — 4th ed. — Cambridge (82 Castle St., Cambridge, CB3 0AJ) : Great Ouse Press
Previous ed.: 1982
1983. — Jan.1983. — [368]p
ISBN 0-907351-09-3 (pbk) : £4.95 : CIP entry
B82-37672

374'.941 — Great Britain. Further education institutions. Flexible study courses

Freeman, Richard, *1943-*. Flexi study : some questions answered / by Richard Freeman. — [Cambridge] : National Extension College, c1981. — 16p ; 21cm
ISBN 0-86082-240-0 (pbk) : Unpriced
B82-40273

374'.941 — Great Britain. Further education — *Serials*

Further education newsletter / the Economics Association. — No.1 (Apr. 1982)-. — Shifnal (c/o G.D. Podmore, 15 Manor Close, Shifnal, Shropshire TF11 9AJ) : The Association, 1982-. — v. ; 21cm
Two issues yearly
Unpriced B82-32168

374'.941 — Great Britian. Adult education, *1945-1980*

Rees, D. Ben. Preparation for crisis : adult education 1945-80 / D. Ben Rees. — Ormskirk : Hesketh, 1982. — ix,360p ; 21cm
Bibliography: p309-336. — Includes index
ISBN 0-905777-15-8 (pbk) : £12.50
B82-39636

374'.9411 — Scotland. Further education — *Conference proceedings*

Organising for Change *(Conference : 1981 : Glasgow)*. Report : Organising for Change : an educational workshop for senior personnel in the further education service in Scotland, 20-21 March 1981. — Glasgow : Jordanhill College of Education, School of Further Education, [1981?]. — 67p : 1ill ; 30cm
Cover title. — Text on inside cover. — Bibliography: p54
Unpriced (spiral) B82-26456

374'.9416 — Northern Ireland. Lifelong education. Role of universities — *Conference proceedings*

Groombridge, Brian, *1926-*. The universities and continuing education : into the 1990s / Brian Groombridge, Alan Rogers and others. — Londonderry : New University of Ulster Institute of Continuing Education, Magee University College, 1981. — 2,36p ; 30cm. — (The Magee papers ; 3)
Conference papers
ISBN 0-901229-33-4 (pbk) : Unpriced
B82-27866

374'.942 — England. Adult education. Provision

Advisory Council for Adult and Continuing Education. Protecting the future for adult education : a report on the issues affecting the present provision of adult general education / ACACE. — Leicester : ACACE, [1981]. — 64p ; 21cm. — (Report / Advisory Council for Adult and Continuing Education)
ISBN 0-906436-07-9 (pbk) : £1.50 B82-39493

Advisory Council for Adult and Continuing Education. A strategy for the basic education of adultsreport commissioned by the Secretary of State for Education and Science / ACACE. — Leicester : ACACE, 1979. — 107p ; 21cm. — (Report / Advisory Council for Adult and Continuing Education)
ISBN 0-906436-01-x (pbk) : £1.50 B82-39498

374'.942 — England. Further education

Russell, Russ. The FE system of England and Wales / by Russ Russell. — Bristol : Further Education Staff College, 1979. — 46p : ill ; 30cm. — (Comparative papers in further education, ISSN 0143-327x ; no.3)
Bibliography: p46
Unpriced (pbk) B82-24183

374'.942 — England. Lifelong education

Advisory Council for Adult and Continuing Education. Continuing education : from policies to practice : a report on the future development of a system of continuing education for adults in England and Wales / ACACE. — Leicester : ACACE, [c1982]. — ix,211p : ill ; 22cm. — (Report / Advisory Council for Adult and Continuing Education)
ISBN 0-906436-14-1 (pbk) : £2.50 B82-39494

374'.9421 — Inner London. Adult education, *1870-1980*

Devereux, W. A.. Adult education in Inner London 1870-1980 / W.A. Devereux. — London : Shepheard-Walwyn in collaboration with Inner London Education Authority, 1982. — x,342p,[16]p of plates : ill ; 25cm
Bibliography: p332-335. — Includes index
ISBN 0-85683-059-3 : £10.50 : CIP rev.
B82-04812

374'.942162 — London. Greenwich *(London Borough)*. **Continuing education, Role of Royal Arsenal Co-operative Society,** *1877-1957*

Attfield, John. With light of knowledge. — London : Journeyman Press, May 1981. — [160]p
ISBN 0-904526-67-4 (pbk) : £3.25 : CIP entry
B81-07915

374'.9492 — Netherlands. Further education institutions. Students, 16-19 years. Education

The **Netherlands:** 16-19 education. — Bristol : Further Education Staff College, 1979. — 53p : ill ; 30cm. — (Comparative papers in further education, ISSN 0143-327x ; no.1)
Bibliography: p53
Unpriced (pbk) B82-24181

374'.966 — West Africa. Adult education

Adult education in West Africa. — London : Allen & Unwin, Aug.1982. — [192]p
ISBN 0-04-374004-9 (cased) : £12.50 : CIP entry
ISBN 0-04-374005-7 (pbk) : £4.50 B82-15639

374'.973 — United States. Adult education

Solmon, Lewis C.. The characteristics and needs of adults in postsecondary education / Lewis C. Solmon, Joanne J. Gordon. — Lexington, Mass. : Lexington Books ; [Aldershot] : Gower [distrbutor], c1981. — xv,155p ; 24cm
Bibliography: p141-144. — Includes index
ISBN 0-669-04361-3 : £13.50 B82-04745

375 — CURRICULUM

375 — Islamic education. Curriculum

Curriculum and teacher education / edited by Muhammad Hamid Al-Afendi and Nabi Ahmed Baloch. — London : Hodder and Stoughton, 1980. — viii,212p ; 24cm. — (Islamic education series)
ISBN 0-340-23609-4 : £5.50 : CIP rev.
Also classified at 370'.7'10917671 B80-04731

375 — Schools. Curriculum

Kelly, A. V.. The curriculum : theory and practice / A.V. Kelly. — 2nd ed. — London : Harper & Row, c1982. — 269p ; 21cm
Previous ed.: 1977. — Bibliography: p248-259. — Includes index
ISBN 0-06-318217-3 (cased) : Unpriced : CIP rev.
ISBN 0-06-318218-1 (pbk) : Unpriced
B82-11285

375'.001 — Educational institutions. Curriculum. Design & development

Planning in the curriculum. — London : Hodder and Stoughton, Dec.1982. — [272]p
ISBN 0-340-28775-6 (pbk) : £4.95 : CIP entry
B82-29649

375'.001 — Great Britain. Schools. Curriculum. Planning. Applications of educational technology

Rowntree, Derek. Educational technology in curriculum development. — 2nd ed. — London : Harper & Row, June 1982. — [240]p
Previous ed.: 1974
ISBN 0-06-318169-x (cased) : £9.95 : CIP entry
ISBN 0-06-318170-3 (pbk) : £4.95 B82-11281

375'.001 — Schools. Curriculum. Development

Goodson, Ivor. School subjects and curriculum change. — London : Croom Helm, Sept.1982. — [192]p. — (Croom Helm curriculum policy and research series)
ISBN 0-7099-1104-1 : £12.95 : CIP entry
B82-20766

375'.001 — Schools. Curriculum. Innovation

Challenge and change in the curriculum. — London : Hodder and Stoughton, Dec.1982. — [256]p
ISBN 0-340-28774-8 (pbk) : £4.95 : CIP entry
B82-29648

375'.001 — Schools. Curriculum. Planning

Pope, Derek. The objectives model of curriculum planning and evaluation. — London : Council for Educational Technology, Apr.1982. — [80] p. — (Occasional papers / Council for Educational Technology ; 10)
ISBN 0-86184-070-4 : £5.50 : CIP entry
ISSN 0307-952x B82-13483

375'.001'0973 — United States. Schools. Curriculum. Development

Doll, Ronald C.. Curriculum improvement : decision making and process / Ronald C. Doll. — 5th ed. — Boston [Mass.] ; London : Allyn and Bacon, c1982. — xxi,466p ; 24cm
Previous ed.: 1978. — Includes bibliographies and index
ISBN 0-205-07558-4 : £17.25 B82-08539

375'.001'0973 — United States. Schools. Curriculum. Planning

Saylor, J. Galen. Curriculum planning for better teaching and learning. — 4th ed. / J. Galen Saylor, William M. Alexander, Arthur J. Lewis. — New York ; London : Holt, Rinehart and Winston, c1981. — xi,419p : ill ; 21cm
Previous ed.: published as Planning curriculum for schools. 1974. — Includes bibliographies and index
ISBN 4-8337-0103-0 (pbk) : £7.50
ISBN 0-03-048761-7 (U.S. college ed)
B82-31896

375'.006 — Schools. Curriculum. Evaluation

Curriculum in action : an approach to evaluation. — Milton Keynes : Open University Press. — (A continuing education course)
'This course was developed as a joint project of the Schools Council and the Open University'. — At head of title: The Open University
Block 3: The teacher and the curriculum / prepared by Patricia Ashton ... [et al.] for the Course Team. — 1980. — 77p in various pagings : ill,forms ; 21x30cm. — (P234 ; 3)
Contents: Unit 5: What did I do? — Unit 6: What did I learn? — Unit 7: What do I intend to do now?
ISBN 0-335-10012-0 (pbk) : Unpriced
B82-04644

Curriculum in action : an approach to evaluation. — Milton Keynes : Open University Press. — (A continuing education course)
'This course was developed as a joint project of the Schools Council and the Open University'. — At head of title: The Open University
Block 5: Observing classroom processes / prepared by David Middleton for the Course Team. — 1981. — 68p : ill ; 30cm. — (P234 ; 5)
Bibliography: p66-67
ISBN 0-335-10014-7 (pbk) : Unpriced
B82-04645

375'.006 — Schools. Curriculum. Evaluation *continuation*

Curriculum in action : an approach to evaluation. — Milton Keynes : Open University Press. — (A continuing education course)
'This course was developed as a joint project of the Schools Council and the Open University'. — At head of title: The Open University
Block 6: Measuring learning outcomes / prepared by Henry Macintosh, Desmond Nuttall and Phil Clift with assistance from John Bynner, for the Course Team. — 1981. — 143p : ill ; 30cm. — (P234 ; 6)
ISBN 0-335-10015-5 (pbk) : Unpriced
B82-04646

Curriculum in action : an approach to evaluation. — Milton Keynes : Open University Press. — (A continuing education course)
'This course was developed as a joint project of the Schools Council and the Open University'. — At head of title: The Open University
Block 7: Analysing curriculum materials / prepared by Robert McCormick for the Course Team. — 1981. — 79p : ill ; 30cm. — (P234 ; 7)
'Frameworks for analysing curriculum materials' (12p leaflet) as insert. — Bibliography: p77
ISBN 0-335-10016-3 (pbk) : Unpriced
B82-04647

Curriculum in action : an approach to evaluation. — Milton Keynes : Open University Press. — (A continuing education course)
'This course was developed as a joint project of the Schools Council and the Open University'. — At head of title: The Open University
Issues in methodology / prepared by John Bynner for the Course Team. — 1981. — 80p : ill,1port ; 30cm. — (P234 ; IM)
Bibliography: p79-80
ISBN 0-335-10018-x (pbk) : Unpriced
B82-04648

Curriculum in action : an approach to evaluation. — Milton Keynes : Open University Press. — (A continuing education course)
'This course was developed as a joint project of the Schools Council and the Open University'. — At head of title: The Open University
Parkside Community College / prepared by David Middleton for the Course Team. — 1981. — 60p : ill,ports ; 30cm. — (P234 ; PCC)
ISBN 0-335-10019-8 (pbk) : Unpriced
B82-04643

375'.006'0722 — United States. Schools. Curriculum. Reform — *Case studies*

Popkewitz, Thomas S.. The myth of educational reform : a study of school responses to a program of change / Thomas S. Popkewitz, B. Robert Tabachnick, Gary Wehlage. — Madison ; London : University of Wisconsin Press, 1982. — xi,209p ; 24cm
Bibliography: p195-201. — Includes index
ISBN 0-299-08840-5 : Unpriced B82-37422

375'.006'0941 — Great Britain. Educational institutions. Curriculum. Assessment & evaluation

Curriculum evaluation and assessment in educational institutions. — Milton Keynes : Open University Press. — (Educational studies : a third level course)
At head of title: The Open University
Block 1: Accountability and evaluation / part A and B prepared for the course team by Desmond L. Nuttall; part C by Desmond L. Nuttall and John Bynner. — 1982. — 83p : ill,forms,1port ; 30cm. — (E364 ; block 1)
Bibliography: p79-82
ISBN 0-335-13089-5 (pbk) : Unpriced
B82-21174

Curriculum evaluation and assessment in educational institutions. — Milton Keynes : Open University Press. — (Educational studies : a third level course)
At head of title: The Open University
Case study 1: An Oxfordshire School / prepared by Phil Clift for the course team. — 1982. — 38p : ill,facsims ; 30cm. — (E364 ; OS)
ISBN 0-335-13092-5 (pbk) : Unpriced
B82-21177

Curriculum evaluation and assessment in educational institutions. — Milton Keynes : Open University Press. — (Educational studies : a third level course)
At head of title: The Open University
Block 2: Approaches to evaluation. — 1982. — 52p : ill ; 30cm. — (E364 ; block 2, part 1)
Bibliography: p50. — Contents: Part 1: LEA-initiated schemes
ISBN 0-335-13090-9 (pbk) : Unpriced
B82-21175

Curriculum evaluation and assessment in educational institutions. — Milton Keynes : Open University Press. — (Educational studies : a third level course)
At head of title: The Open University
Block 2: Approaches to evaluation. — 1982. — 64p : ill,facsims ; 30cm. — (E364 ; block 2, part 2)
Bibliography: p62-63. — Contents: Part 2: Institutional self-evaluation
ISBN 0-335-13096-8 (pbk) : Unpriced
B82-21176

Curriculum evaluation and assessment in educational institutions. — Milton Keynes : Open University Press. — (Educational studies : a third level course)
At head of title: The Open University
Block 2: Approaches to evaluation. — 1982. — 52p ; 30cm. — (E364 ; block 2)
Bibliography: p50-51. — Contents: Part 4: Audited self-evaluation
ISBN 0-335-13097-6 (pbk) : Unpriced
B82-32001

Curriculum evaluation and assessment in educational institutions. — Milton Keynes : Open University Press. — (Educational studies : a third level course)
At head of title: The Open University
Case study 2: Stantonbury Campus / prepared by Bob Moon, Ann Shelton and Peter Green for the course team. — 1982. — 40p : ill ; 30cm. — (E364 ; SC)
Bibliography: p40
ISBN 0-335-13093-3 (pbk) : Unpriced
B82-21178

Curriculum evaluation and assessment in educational institutions. — Milton Keynes : Open University Press. — (Educational studies : a third level course)
At head of title: The Open University
Case study 3: The CNAA / prepared for the Course Team by Ian McNay and Robert McCormick, with a contribution from Peter Torode. — 1982. — 52p ; 30cm. — (E364 ; CNAA)
Bibliography: p51
ISBN 0-335-13094-1 (pbk) : Unpriced
B82-32002

Curriculum evaluation and assessment in educational institutions. — Milton Keynes : Open University Press. — (Educational studies : a third level course)
At head of title: The Open University
Case study 5: Great Barr School / prepared by Phil Clift, Barry Abel and Geoff Simpson for the course team. — 1982. — 30p ; 30cm. — (E364 : GBS)
Bibliography: p30
ISBN 0-335-13095-x (pbk) : Unpriced
B82-40649

Curriculum evaluation and assessment in educational institutions. — Milton Keynes : Open University Press. — (Educational studies : a third level course)
At head of title: The Open University
Block 6: Organization and use of evaluation / prepared by John Bynner, Robert McCormick and Desmond Nuttall for the course team. — 1982. — 59p : ill ; 30cm. — (E364 ; block 6)
Bibliography: p56-59
ISBN 0-335-13091-7 (pbk) : Unpriced
B82-40648

Curriculum evaluation and assessment in educational institutions. — Milton Keynes : Open University Press. — (Educational studies : a third level course)
At head of title: The Open University
Making more sense of examination results / prepared by John Gray for the course team. — 1982. — 23p : ill ; 30cm. — (E364 ; MMS)
Bibliography: p22
Unpriced (unbound) B82-40647

375'.0082'0941 — Great Britain. Schools. Curriculum. Multicultural aspects

Lynch, James. The multicultural curriculum. — London : Batsford, Feb.1983. — [160]p
ISBN 0-7134-4510-6 (pbk) : £6.95 : CIP entry
B82-39424

375'.00941 — Great Britain. Schools. Curriculum — *Serials*

Great Britain. *Consultative Committee on the Curriculum.* News / the Consultative Committee on the Curriculum. — No.2 (Feb. 1979)-. — Edinburgh (New St. Andrew's House, Edinburgh EH1 3SY) : The Committee, 1979-. — v. : ports ; 30cm
Irregular. — Also entitled: CCC news. — Continues: Great Britain. Consultative Committee on the Curriculum. Bulletin. — Description based on: No.8 (Mar. 1981)
ISSN 0263-4767 = News - Consultative Committee on the Curriculum : Unpriced
B82-27646

375'.00942 — England. Schools. Curriculum. Reform. Great Britain. *Department of Education and Science.* **'School curriculum'** — *Critical studies*

No, minister : a critique of the DES paper, The school curriculum / John White ... [et al.]. — London : University of London Institute of Education, c1981. — 55p ; 21cm. — (Bedford Way papers, ISSN 0261-0078 ; 4)
ISBN 0-85473-115-6 (pbk) : £1.50 B82-08685

376 — EDUCATION OF WOMEN

376 — Great Britain. Women. Further education

Stoney, Sheila M.. Further opportunities in focus : a study of bridging courses for women / by Sheila M. Stoney and Margaret I. Reid. — [London] ([39 York Rd., SE1 7PH]) : Further Education Curriculum Review and Development Unit, 1980. — vi,158p ; 30cm. — (Project report / Further Education Curriculum Review and Development Unit ; P.R.5)
Bibliography: p149-158
Unpriced (pbk) B82-20242

376'.63 — Great Britain. Girls' public schools — *Directories — Serials*

Girls schools yearbook. — 1982. — London : A. & C. Black, Apr.1982. — [450]p
ISBN 0-7136-2184-2 (pbk) : £5.95 : CIP entry
B82-04496

376'.63'0942 — England. Adolescent girls. Education, *1870-1920.* **Social aspects**

Dyhouse, Carol. Girls growing up in late Victorian and Edwardian England / Carol Dyhouse. — London : Routledge & Kegan Pual, 1981. — ix,224p ; 23cm. — (Studies in social history)
Includes index
ISBN 0-7100-0821-x : £8.95 B82-03270

376'.941 — England. Nonconformist independent girls' schools, *1830-1920*

Binfield, Clyde. Belmont's Portias : Victorian nonconformists and middle-class education for girls / by Clyde Binfield. — London : Dr. Williams's Trust, c1981. — 35p ; 22cm. — (Lecture / Friends of Dr. Williams's Library ; 35)
At head of title: Friends of Dr. Williams's Library
£0.80 (pbk) B82-03989

376'.942 — England. Female students. Education. Equality of opportunity — *Statistics*

Education of girls : a statistical analysis. — Manchester : Equal Opportunities Commission, 1981. — 27p ; 31cm
Unpriced (pbk) B82-31238

377 — SCHOOLS AND RELIGION

377'.1 — Great Britain. Primary schools. Morning assembly. Activities — *For teaching*

Junior assemblies / edited by Geraldine Witcher ; illustrations by Elizabeth Norman-Clarke. — London : Scripture Union, c1982. — 160p : ill ; 22cm
Includes bibliography
ISBN 0-85421-949-8 (pbk) : £2.95 B82-28225

377'.1 — Great Britain. Primary schools. Morning assembly — *Christian viewpoints*
Reflections on assembly / editor Danny Sullivan. — London (2 Chester House, Pages La., N10 1PR) : Christian Education Movement, c1981. — 29p : ill ; 26cm
Text on lining papers. — Includes bibliographies
Unpriced (pbk) B82-05138

377'.1 — Great Britain. Schools. Morning assembly
Hoffman, S. H.. Worship and education in schools and parish : a discussion paper / S.H. Hoffman. — [Rochester] : [Rochester Diocesan Board of Education], [1980]. — 13leaves ; 30cm
Unpriced (unbound) B82-36397

377'.1 — Great Britain. Schools. Morning assembly. Themes — *For schools*
Brooks, Michael, *19---*. Assemblies for seniors / Michael Brooks and Michael Cockett. — Leigh-on-Sea : Mayhew, 1977. — 76p ; 21cm
ISBN 0-905725-31-x (pbk) : £2.00 B82-01818

377'.1 — Middle schools. Morning assembly. Themes
Farncombe, Anne. Time for assembly : assemblies for 8-12s : with optional follow-up work for the class-room / Anne Farncombe. — Redhill : National Christian Education Council, 1980. — 127p : ill ; 21cm
Includes index
ISBN 0-7197-0263-1 (pbk) : £2.75 : CIP rev. B80-19714

377'.1 — Primary schools. Morning assembly. Activities — *For teaching*
Barratt, Sylvia. The tinder-box assembly book. — London : Black, Sept.1982. — [112]p
ISBN 0-7136-2169-9 (spiral) : £5.95 : CIP entry B82-21393

377'.1 — Primary schools. Morning assembly — *For teaching*
New approaches to the assembly / [editor Susan E. Tompkins]. — London (2 Chester House, Pages Lane, N10) : Christian Education Movement, c1976 (1978 [printing]). — 26p : music ; 26cm. — (CEM primary resource of religious education, ISSN 0308-4523)
Cover title. — Text and music on inside cover. — Includes bibliographies
Unpriced (pbk) B82-40965

377'.1 — Primary schools. Morning assembly. Poems & stories — *Anthologies*
Farncombe, Anne. Our turn for assembly : more assembly topics for 5-8s / Anne Farncombe. — Redhill : NCEC, 1981. — 128p ; 21cm
ISBN 0-7197-0311-5 (pbk) : £2.75 B82-08555

377'.1 — Primary schools. Morning assembly — *Prayers & readings*
Brimer, Sylvia. Themes for assembly / Sylvia Brimer. — Glasgow : Blackie, 1982. — 168p ; 25cm
ISBN 0-216-91164-8 (spiral) : £4.95 B82-22539

Worsnop, I. R.. Gather together : an assembly and story book for infant, first and junior schools / I.R. Worsnop. — Walton-on-Thames : Nelson, 1980. — 128p : ill ; 25cm
Includes index
ISBN 0-17-428031-9 (pbk) : Unpriced B82-40846

377'.1 — Schools. Morning assembly. Activities — *For teaching*
Smith, Harry, *1939-*. Assemblies : a resource book for junior and middle schools / Harry Smith. — London : Heinemann Educational, 1981. — x,245p ; 22cm
Includes bibliographies
ISBN 0-435-01830-2 : £4.95 : CIP rev. B81-23783

377'.1 — Schools. Morning assembly — *Prayers & readings*
Lloyd, R. H.. Acts of worship for assemblies / by R.H. Lloyd. — London : Mowbray, c1982. — xi,80p ; 22cm
Bibliography: p80
ISBN 0-264-66850-2 (pbk) : £2.50 B82-19122

Readings / chosen and edited by Denys Thompson. — Cambridge : Cambridge University Press, 1974 (1980 [printing]). — xxix,273p ; 23cm
Bibliography: p270. — Includes index
ISBN 0-521-29789-3 (pbk) : £5.50 B82-32324

377'.1 — Schools. Morning assembly. Themes
Lloyd, R. H.. Assembly themes / R.H. Lloyd. — [Exeter] : Religious Education, 1979. — 73p ; 21cm
ISBN 0-08-022887-9 (pbk) : £1.75 B82-16018

378 — HIGHER EDUCATION

378 — Great Britain. Hihger education institutions. Conferences, open days & visits — *Directories* — *For sixth formers*
Taylor, Felicity. Going places : how to find out about further education and training. — 2nd ed. — London : Kogan Page, Aug.1982. — 1v.
Previous ed.: 1981
ISBN 0-85038-574-1 (cased) : £8.95 : CIP entry
ISBN 0-85038-575-x (pbk) : £4.50 B82-17981

378 — Higher education — *Comparative studies*
World guide to higher education. — 2nd ed. — Epping : Bowker, Nov.1981. — [362]p
ISBN 0-85935-066-5 : CIP entry B81-30471

378'.0025 — Higher education institutions — *Directories*
International handbook of universities : and other institutions of higher education. — 8th ed. / [editor D.J. Aitken] ; [assistant editor Ann C.M. Taylor]. — London : Macmillan for the International Association of Universities, 1981. — 1205p ; 28cm
Previous ed.: joint editors H.M.R. Keyes, D.J. Aitken. 1978. — Includes index
ISBN 0-333-23869-9 : Unpriced B82-37932

378'.0025'73 — United States. Colleges — *Directories*
Cass, James. Comparative guide to American colleges : for students, parents, and counselors / by James Cass and Max Birnbaum. — 10th ed. — New York ; London : Harper & Row, c1981. — 778p ; 27cm
Previous ed.: 1979. — Includes index
ISBN 0-06-010711-1 (cased) : £17.50
ISBN 0-06-090896-3 (pbk) : Unpriced B82-21903

378'.006'0417 — Ireland *(Republic)*. **Higher education. Organisations: National Council for Educational Awards** — *Serials*
[Information *(National Council for Educational Awards)*]. Information / the National Council for Educational Awards = Faisnéis / Comhairle Náisúnta na gCáilíochtaí Oideachais. — Vol.1, no.1 (Nov. 1981)-. — Dublin (26 Mountjoy Sq., Dublin 1) : The Council, 1981-. — v. : ports ; 30cm
Three issues yearly. — Text mainly in English, but also in Irish
Unpriced B82-15760

378'.009 — Universities — *History* — *Serials*
History of universities. — Vol.2 (1982). — Amersham : Avebury Publishing, May 1982. — [240]p
ISBN 0-86127-052-5 : £20.00 : CIP entry
ISSN 0144-5138 B82-11111

378'.01 — Professional education
Jarvis, P.. Professional education. — London : Croom Helm, 1982. — [144]p. — (New patterns of learning series)
ISBN 0-7099-1409-1 : £11.95 : CIP entry B82-30043

378'.012'0973 — United States. Higher education institutions. Liberal education
Winter, David G.. A new case for the liberal arts / David G. Winter, David C. McClelland, Abigail J. Stewart. — San Francisco ; London : Jossey-Bass, 1981. — xxii,247p : ill ; 24cm. — (The Jossey-Bass series in higher education)
Bibliography: p219-235. — Includes index
ISBN 0-87589-502-6 : £14.75 B82-17050

378'.013 — Great Britain. Universities. Cooperation with industries
Universities and industry. — London (29 Tavistock Sq., WC1H 9EZ) : Committee of Vice-Chancellors and Principals of the Universities of the United Kingdom, 1981. — 64p ; 21cm
Bibliography: p64
Unpriced (pbk) B82-16253

378'.01'305 — British qualifications — *Serials*
British qualifications. — 12th ed. (1981). — London : Kogan Paul, Dec.1981. — [880]p
ISBN 0-85038-503-2 : £15.95 : CIP entry B81-33867

British qualifications. — 13th ed. (1982). — London : Kogan Page, Nov.1982. — [800]p
ISBN 0-85038-579-2 : £16.95 : CIP entry
ISSN 0141-5972 B82-26416

378'.02 — United States. Higher education institutions. Running costs. Management
Mingle, James R.. Challenges of retrenchment / James R. Mingle and associates. — San Francisco ; London : Jossey-Bass, 1981. — xx,394p ; 24cm. — (The Jossey-Bass series in higher education)
Bibliography: p354-380. — Includes index
ISBN 0-87589-507-7 : £12.25 B82-17049

378.1 — HIGHER EDUCATION. ORGANISATION AND ADMINISTRATION

378'.101 — United States. Higher education institutions. Autonomy, *1636-1820*
Herbst, Jurgen. From crisis to crisis : American college government 1636-1819 / Jurgen Herbst. — Cambridge, Mass. ; London : Harvard University Press, 1982. — xvi,301p ; 25cm
Includes index
ISBN 0-674-32345-9 : £17.50 B82-34321

378'.103 — Community education. Role of universities — *Case studies*
Towards the community university : case studies of innovation and community service / edited by David C.B. Teather. — London : Kogan Page, 1982. — 244p : ill,2forms ; 23cm
Includes bibliographies and index
ISBN 0-85038-496-6 : £12.50 : CIP rev. B82-04695

378'.103 — United States. Society. Role of universities
Bok, Derek. Beyond the ivory tower : social responsibilities of the modern university / Derek Bok. — Cambridge, Mass. ; London : Harvard University Press, 1982. — 318p ; 25cm
Includes index
ISBN 0-674-06899-8 : £11.20 B82-36045

378'.1056'0941 — Great Britain. Higher education institutions. Students. Selection. Bias — *Conference proceedings*
Society for Research into Higher Education. *Conference (17th : 1971 : Manchester Polytechnic)*. Is higher education fair? : papers presented to the 17th annual conference of the Society for Research into Higher Education / edited by David Warren Piper. — Guildford : The Society, 1981. — xvii,194p : ill ; 22cm
Bibliography: p172-194
ISBN 0-900868-82-1 (pbk) : £9.00(members £6.00) B82-24317

378'.107 — Great Britain. Higher education institutions. Education consultants
Boud, David. Educational development through consultancy / David Boud, Rod McDonald. — Guildford : Society for Research into Higher Education, 1981. — 54p ; 21cm. — (Research into higher education monographs ; 42)
Bibliography: p49-52. — Includes index
ISBN 0-900868-81-3 (pbk) : £6.00(members £4.00) B82-24321

378'.11'0973 — United States. Higher education institutions. Personnel management

Fortunato, Ray T.. Personnel administration in higher education / Ray T. Fortunato, D. Geneva Waddell. — San Francisco ; London : Jossey-Bass, 1981. — xxv,384p : ill,forms ; 24cm. — (The Jossey-Bass series in higher education)
Bibliography: p367-374. — Includes index
ISBN 0-87589-506-9 : £18.75 B82-17054

378'.111'0924 — United States. Negroes. Professional education. Washington, Booker T. — *Correspondence, diaries, etc.*

Washington, Booker T.. The Booker T. Washington papers. — Urbana ; London : University of Illinois Press
Bibliography: p623-625. — Includes index
Vol.10: 1909-11 / Louis R. Harlan and Raymond W. Smock editors ; Geraldine McTigue and Nan E. Woodruff assistant editors. — c1981. — xxvi,660p : 1facsim ; 25cm
ISBN 0-252-00800-6 : £19.25 B82-25795

378'.121 — Oxfordshire. Oxford. Universities: University of Oxford. Teachers. Professional status, *1800-1914*

Engel, A. J.. From clergyman to don. — Oxford : Clarendon Press, Jan.1983. — [350]p
ISBN 0-19-822606-3 : £22.50 : CIP entry B82-33488

378'.122 — United States. Higher education institutions. Teachers. Tenure

Chait, Richard P.. Beyond traditional tenure / Richard P. Chait, Andrew T. Ford. — San Francisco ; London : Jossey-Bass, 1982. — xxiii,291p ; 24cm. — (The Jossey-Bass series in higher education)
Bibliography: p273-279. — Includes index
ISBN 0-87589-519-0 : Unpriced B82-32917

378'.155'0704 — Europe. Universities. Administration. Personnel. Training

The **Training** of university administrators in Europe. — Aldershot : Gower, Aug.1982. — [144]p
ISBN 0-566-00522-0 : £10.50 : CIP entry B82-15879

378'.1552 — Great Britain. Sandwich courses — *For food industries & trades*

Sandwich training : what's in it for you?. — Gloucester (Barton House, Barton St., Gloucester GL1 1QQ) : Food, Drink and Tobacco Industry Training Board, [1978]. — 14p : ill ; 21cm
Cover title. — Text on inside covers
Unpriced (pbk) B82-27912

378'.1552 — United States. Higher education institutions. Part-time degree courses. Development

Providing access for adults to alternative college programs / edited by Ronald H. Miller. — [Metuchen] : Scarecrow Press for The Alliance ; Folkestone : Bailey Bros & Swinfen [[distributor]], 1981. — xii,117p ; 22cm. — (Alliance manual ; no.1)
Bibliography: p107-113. — Includes index
ISBN 0-8108-1467-6 (pbk) : £5.55 B82-12366

378'.1552'02541 — Great Britain. Council for National Academic Awards courses: First degree courses — *Directories — Serials*

Council for National Academic Awards. Directory of first degree and diploma of higher education courses / Council for National Academic Awards. — 1979-80-. — London (344 Gray's Inn Rd, WC1X 8BP) : The Council, 1979-. — v. ; 21cm
Annual. — Continues: Council for National Academic Awards. Directory of first degree courses. — Description based on: 1981-82 issue
ISSN 0262-5652 = Directory of first degree and diploma of higher education courses - Council for National Academic Awards : Unpriced B82-05744

378'.1552'0941 — Great Britain. Council for National Academic Awards courses: First degree courses — *Regulations*

Council for National Academic Awards. Principles and regulations for the award of the Council's first degrees and Diploma of Higher Education / Council for National Academic Awards. — London (344 Gray's Inn Rd., WC1X 8BP) : C.N.A.A., 1979. — 48p ; 30cm
Includes index
Unpriced (pbk)
Primary classification 370'.7'320941 B82-32775

378'.1552'0973 — United States. Higher education institutions. First degree courses. Design

Bergquist, William H.. Designing undergraduate education / William H. Bergquist, Ronald A. Gould, Elinor Miller Greenberg. — San Francisco ; London : Jossey-Bass, 1981. — xxii,332p : ill ; 24cm. — (The Jossey-Bass series in higher education)
Bibliography: p303-320. — Includes index
ISBN 0-87589-508-5 : £12.25 B82-17053

378'.1553'02541 — Great Britain. Council for National Academic Awards courses: Postgraduate courses — *Directories — Serials*

Council for National Academic Awards. Directory of postgraduate and post-experience courses / Council for National Academic Awards. — 1978-79-. — London (334 Gray's Inn Rd, WC1X 8BP) : The Council, 1978-. — v. ; 21cm
Annual. — Continues: Council for National Academic Awards. Directory of Postgraduate courses. — Description based on: 1981-82 issue
ISSN 0262-5679 = Directory of postgraduate and post-experience courses - Council for National Academic Awards : Unpriced B82-05743

378'.1553'0941 — Great Britain. Postgraduate education — *Inquiry reports*

Great Britain. *Working Party on Postgraduate Education.* Report of the Working Party on Postgraduate Education. — London : H.M.S.O., 1982. — 120p ; 25cm
At head of title: Advisory Board for the Research Councils
ISBN 0-10-185370-x (pbk) : £7.00 B82-25303

378'.1554'0941 — Great Britain. Adult education. Role of universities

Williams, I. M.. Continuity and change - the role of the university in the education of adults : inaugural lecture delivered at the College on 10 November, 1981 / by I.M. Williams. — [Swansea] : University College of Swansea, 1981. — 23p ; 21cm
ISBN 0-86076-026-x (pbk) : Unpriced B82-08603

378'.1554'0942 — England. Adult education. Provision. Role of universities, *1870-1900*

Marriott, Stuart. A backstairs to a degree : demands for an open university in late Victorian England / Stuart Marriott. — Leeds : Department of Adult Education and Extramural Studies, University of Leeds, 1981. — iv,107p ; 21cm. — (Leeds studies in adult and continuing education, ISSN 0261-1406)
ISBN 0-907644-00-7 (pbk) : Unpriced B82-05978

378'.1554'0942 — England. Universities. Extra-mural education, *1908-1958*

Blyth, John. English university adult education 1908-1958. — Manchester : Manchester University Press, Jan.1983. — [384]p
ISBN 0-7190-0903-0 : £15.00 : CIP entry B82-32621

378'.17 — Great Britain. Higher education institutions. Teaching aids: Games & simulations - *Conference proceedings*

Perspectives on academic gaming. — 6. — London : Kogan Page, July 1981. — [250]p
Conference papers
ISBN 0-85038-422-2 : £12.50 : CIP entry
ISSN 0141-5965 B81-15849

378'.17 — Universities. Distance study

The **Distance** teaching universities. — London : Croom Helm, Sept.1982. — [256]p
ISBN 0-7099-2230-2 : £12.95 : CIP entry B82-20645

Dodd, John, *1942-*. The credibility of distance education / by John Dodd. — Milton Keynes (Walton Hall, Milton Keynes, MK7 6AA) : Open University Education Research Group, 1981. — 14p ; 25cm. — (DERG papers ; no.1)
Cover title. — Text on inside cover
£1.00 (pbk) B82-07992

378'.17028 — Higher education institutions. Students. Learning skills

Wright, Jean. Learning to learn in higher education / Jean Wright. — London : Croom Helm, c1982. — 199p ; 23cm. — (New patterns of learning series)
Includes bibliographies and index
ISBN 0-7099-2744-4 : £12.95 : CIP rev. B82-09180

378'.17'02812 — Study techniques — *Manuals — For higher education institution students*

Wood, Nancy V.. College reading and study skills : a guide to improving academic communication / Nancy V. Wood. — 2nd ed. — New York ; London : Holt, Rinehart and Winston, c1982. — xiv,271p : ill,forms ; 24cm
Previous ed.: 1978. — Includes index
ISBN 0-03-058997-5 (pbk) : £7.50 B82-23312

378'.17'02812 — Study techniques — *Manuals — For non-English speaking students in higher education institutions in Great Britain*

Wallace, Michael J.. Study skills in English / Michael J. Wallace. — Cambridge : Cambridge University Press, c1980. — vi,218p ; 23cm
Bibliography: p218
ISBN 0-521-22110-2 (pbk) : £2.95 B82-39486

378'.17'02812096 — Study techniques — *Manuals — For students in African higher education institutions*

Montgomery, Michael. Study skills for colleges and universities in Africa. — London : Longman, July 1982. — [216]p
ISBN 0-582-64218-3 (pbk) : £3.00 : CIP entry B82-12931

378'.17'028120973 — Study techniques — *Manuals — For students in American higher education institutions*

Cohen, Elaine Landau. Discovering college reading, thinking and study skills : a Piagetian approach / Elaine Landau Cohen, Mary A. Poppino. — New York ; London : Holt, Rinehart and Winston, c1982. — xv,234p : ill ; 24cm
ISBN 0-03-058626-7 (pbk) : £8.50 B82-16911

378'.17'078 — Great Britain. Higher education. Educational technology — *Serials*

AVCET / Audio Visual Communication & Educational Technology (a section of NATFHE). — 1 (1976)-. — [London] ([c/o. NATFHE, Hamilton House, Mapledon Place, WC1]) : [The Section], 1978-. — v. ; 21cm
Annual. — Description based on: 2 (1977)
ISSN 0144-4603 = AVCET : Unpriced
Primary classification 374'.02 B82-14778

378'.17'078 — Great Britain. Higher education institutions. Teaching support services. Management

Higher education : task and activity details at professional and managerial levels / based on an investigation by Gerald Collier ; edited by Norman Willis. — London : Council for Educational Technology, 1981. — 39p ; 21cm. — (Teaching & learning support services ; 1)
ISBN 0-86184-037-2 (pbk) : £4.50 : CIP rev. B81-35872

378'.17078 — Great Britain. Polytechnics. Literacy resource centres. Provision

Powney, Janet. Survey of provision of literacy centres in polytechnics / by Janet Powney, Denis Vincent and Christine Groothues. — Chelmsford : Nelpress, 1981. — 37,[14]p : forms ; 30cm
Bibliography: p37
ISBN 0-901987-42-5 (pbk) : £3.00 B82-07856

378'.176 — Higher education institutions. Students. Research projects. Supervision

Howard, Keith. Management of a student research project. — Aldershot : Gower, Feb.1983. — [236]p
ISBN 0-566-00462-3 (cased) : £13.50 : CIP entry
ISBN 0-566-00613-8 (pbk) : £4.95 B82-38719

378'.178 — Higher education institutions. Students. Study service

Study service : an examination of community service as a method of study in higher education / edited for the Higher Education Foundation by Sinclair Goodlad. — Windsor : NFER-Nelson, 1982. — 250p : ill ; 22cm
Bibliography: p246-250
ISBN 0-85633-242-9 (pbk) : £8.95 B82-32655

378'.17944'0941 — Great Britain. Higher education. Self-teaching. Teaching aids. Provision

Clarke, John, *1922-*. Resource-based learning for higher and continuing education / John Clarke. — London : Croom Helm, c1982. — 211p : ill,plans,forms ; 23cm. — (New patterns of learning series)
Bibliography: p202-206. — Includes index
ISBN 0-7099-0705-2 : £11.95 : CIP rev.
Also classified at 374'.1'0941 B81-30347

378'.19716'0941 — Great Britain. Higher education institutions. Catering services

Cowell, F. M.. Catering in colleges / by F.M. Cowell. — Sheffield (c/o Hon Sec., Sheffield City Polytechnic, Pond St., Sheffield S1 1WB) : Association of Colleges for Further and Higher Education, [1982]. — 11p ; 21cm
Conference paper from ACFHE summer meeting, 11-12 June, 1981
£0.75 (unbound)
Also classified at 374 B82-24395

378'.198 — Great Britain. Higher education institutions. Students living away from home. Social life - *Practical information*

Jones, Graham. The TSB guide to student life away from home. — Newton Abbot : David & Charles, Aug.1981. — [192]p
ISBN 0-7153-8234-9 (pbk) : £3.95 : CIP entry B81-17499

378'.198'09425 — England. East Midlands. Higher education institutions. Students

Osborne, R. H.. A spatial survey of students in higher education in the East Midlands / by R.H. Osborne, F.H. Molyneux. — Nottingham : Department of Geography [and] School of Education, University of Nottingham, 1981. — xiv,332p : maps ; 30cm
ISBN 0-85358-024-3 (pbk) : Unpriced B82-31577

378'.1981 — North America. Higher education institutions. Students. Political behaviour *related to* **political beliefs,** *1968-1970 — Study examples: University of Alberta*

Sutherland, S. L.. Patterns of belief and action : measurement of student political activism / S.L. Sutherland. — Toronto ; London : University of Toronto Press, c1981. — xi,362p : ill ; 24cm
Bibliography: p301-347. — Includes index
ISBN 0-8020-5534-6 : £21.00 B82-13935

378'.1981 — United States. Higher education institutions. Students. Interpersonal relationships. Racial aspects

Willie, Charles Vert. The ivory and ebony towers : race relations and higher education / Charles Vert Willie. — Lexington, Mass. : Lexington Books, c1981 ; [Aldershot] : Gower [distributor], 1982. — xii,173p ; 24cm
Includes bibliographies and index
ISBN 0-669-04479-2 : £15.00 B82-11319

378'.1981'09046 — Students. Politics, *1960-1980*

Student politics : perspectives for the eighties / edited by Philip G. Altbach. — Metuchen, N.J. ; London : Scarecrow, 1981. — iv,272p ; 23cm
Includes bibliographies and index
ISBN 0-8108-1430-7 : £11.60 B82-05360

378'.1981'0941623 — Londonderry *(District).* **Londonderry. Adult education institutions: New University of Ulster.** *Institute of Continuing Education.* **Students. Attitudes**

Courtney, Sean. The Magee experiment : an analysis of adults in education / Sean Courtney. — Londonderry : Institute of Continuing Education, New University of Ulster, c1981. — vi,169p ; 29cm. — (The Magee papers ; 1)
Bibliography: p164-169
ISBN 0-901229-29-6 (pbk) : Unpriced B82-13107

378'.1982 — United States. Higher education institutions. Negro students

Black students in higher education : conditions and experiences in the 1970s / edited by Gail E. Thomas. — Westport, Conn. ; London : Greenwood Press, 1981. — xx,405p ; 25cm. — (Contributions to the study of education, ISSN 0196-707x ; no.1)
Conference papers. — Includes bibliographies and index
ISBN 0-313-22477-3 : Unpriced B82-02188

378'.1983'0941956 — Cork *(County).* **Cork** *(City).* **Universities. Colleges. Student unions: University College, Cork.** *Students' Union — Serials*

Demi-tasse. — Issue 1-. — [Cork] ([4 Carrigside, College Rd, Cork]) : [Students Union, University College, Cork], [1981]-. — v. : ill ; 30cm
Description based on: Issue 2
Unpriced B82-11132

378'.1983'0942132 — London. Westminster *(London Borough).* **Universities. Colleges. Student unions: Imperial College Union** — *Serials*

Fritz. — No.1 (Apr. 1982)-. — London (c/o The Felix Office, Imperial College Union, Prince Consort Rd, SW7) : Felix Club, 1982-. — v. : ill,ports ; 22cm
ISSN 0262-9879 = Fritz : Unpriced B82-36712

378'.199 — Great Britain. Degree courses. Validation — *Manuals*

Council for National Academic Awards. Guidance on the validation of courses which make significant use of resource-based learning / Council for National Academic Awards. — London (344 Gray's Inn Rd., WC1X 8BP) : CNAA, [1982]. — 21p ; 21cm
Unpriced (pbk) B82-40156

378'.199 — Great Britain. Degree courses. Validation. Organisations: Council for National Academic Awards

Council for National Academic Awards. The Council : its place in British higher education / Council for National Academic Awards. — London : The Council, 1979. — 71p : ill(some col.) ; 21cm
Unpriced (pbk) B82-20597

Council for National Academic Awards. Regulations and conditions for postgraduate courses of study leading to the award of the Council's Master's degrees and postgraduate diplomas / [Council for National Academic Awards]. — London (344 Gray's Inn Rd., WC1X 8BP) : CNAA, 1982. — 17p ; 20cm
Unpriced (unbound) B82-29204

378'.199 — Great Britain. Higher education institutions. Integrated studies — *Serials*

[Cross-currents *(Nottingham)***]**. Cross-currents : a journal of combined studies. — No.1 (1980)-. — [Nottingham] ([The Editors, Cross-currents, Trent Polytechnic, Clifton, Nottingham NG11 8NS]) : [S.n.], 1980-. — v. : ill ; 23cm
ISSN 0262-6861 = Cross-currents (Nottingham) : Unpriced B82-10359

378'.199'0941 — Great Britain. Higher education institutions. Courses. Development

Council for National Academic Awards. Developments in partnership in validation / council for National Academic Awards. — London (344 Gray's Inn Rd., WC1X 8BP) : CNAA, 1979. — 19p ; 30cm
Unpriced (pbk) B82-40157

Rowntree, Derek. Developing courses for students / Derek Rowntree. — London : McGraw-Hill, c1981. — 308p : ill ; 22cm. — (McGraw-Hill series for teachers)
Bibliography: p289-299. — Includes index
ISBN 0-07-084126-8 (pbk) : £4.95 : CIP rev. B81-15829

378.2 — HIGHER EDUCATION. ACADEMIC DEGREES

378'.24 — Great Britain. Higher education institutions. Council for National Academic Awards Ph. D. & M. Phil. degrees. Awarding

Council for National Academic Awards. Regulations for the award of the Council's degrees of Master of Philosophy and Doctor of Philosophy / Council for National Academic Awards. — London (344 Gray's Inn Rd., WC1X 8BP) : CNAA, 1978. — 39p ; 21cm
Unpriced (pbk) B82-40158

378'.241 — Great Britain. Council for National Academic Awards first degrees — *Rules*

Council for National Academic Awards. Regulations and conditions for the award of the Council's first degrees / Council for National Academic Awards. — London (344-354 Grays Inn Road, WC1X 8BP) : The Council, 1978. — [40]p ; 30cm
Unpriced (pbk) B82-33030

378'.241 — Great Britain. Part-time degree courses

Tight, Malcolm. Part-time degree level study in the United Kingdom : the report of an enquiry financed by the Advisory Council for Adult and Continuing Education, the Baring Foundation, Birkbeck College, University of London, Goldsmiths' College, University of London, the Guild of St George, London University Extra-Mural Studies Department / by Malcolm Tight. — Leicester : ACACE, c1982. — xiii,129p ; 21cm
ISBN 0-906436-13-3 (pbk) : £2.50 B82-39331

378'.28'0942574 — Oxfordshire. Oxford. Universities: University of Oxford. Academic costume

Venables, D. R.. Academic dress of the University of Oxford / D.R. Venables & R.E. Clifford. — 5th ed. — [Oxford] : [Oxford University Registry], 1979. — 38p : col.ill ; 21cm
Cover title. — Previous ed.: 1975
£0.75 (pbk) B82-11920

378.3 — HIGHER EDUCATION. STUDENT FINANCES

378.3 — Postgraduate courses. Awards — *Directories*

The **Grants** register. — London : Macmillan 1981-1983 / editor Craig Alan Lerner. — [7th ed.]. — 1980. — xxv,782p ; 25cm
Previous ed.: 1978. — Bibliography: p781-782. — Includes index
ISBN 0-333-25866-5 : £18.50 B82-35337

378.4/9 — HIGHER EDUCATION. HISTORICAL AND GEOGRAPHICAL TREATMENT

378.4 — Western Europe. Higher education

Deverell, John, *1939-*. European higher education : a review of some recent developments and their implications for C.N.A.A. and H.C.H.E. / John Deverell, John Salmon. — [London] ([344 Gray's Inn Rd., WC1X 8BP]) : [CNAA], 1979. — 77p ; 30cm
Unpriced (pbk) B82-40155

378.4 — Western Europe. Universities. Political aspects

Universities, politicians and bureaucrats : Europe and the United States / edited by Hans Daalder, Edward Shils. — Cambridge : Cambridge University Press, 1982. — viii,511p ; 24cm
ISBN 0-521-23673-8 : £37.50 : CIP rev. B81-36243

378.41 — Great Britain. Adults. Higher education

Jones, H. A. (Henry Arthur). Adult students and higher education. — [New ed.] / H.A. Jones and Katherine E. Williams. — Leicester : ACACE, c1979. — vi,64p ; 21cm. — (Occasional paper / Advisory Council for Adult and Continuing Education ; 3)
Previous ed.: published as Adult access to post-secondary education in the United Kingdom. London : Organisation for Economic Co-operation and Development, 1977
ISBN 0-906436-03-6 (pbk) : £1.50 B82-39330

378.41 — Great Britain. Higher education

Agenda for institutional change in higher education / Leslie Wagner (editor) ; [contributors] John Sizer ... [et al.]. — Guildford : Society for Research into Higher Education, 1982. — 200p : ill ; 21cm. — (Programme of study into the future of higher education ; 3) (Research into higher education monographs ; 45)
Conference papers. — Includes bibliographies
ISBN 0-900868-85-6 (pbk) : £6.00 B82-35291

Hewton, Eric. Rethinking educational change : a case for diplomacy / Eric Hewton. — Guildford : Society for Research into Higher Education, 1982. — 113p : ill ; 21cm. — (Research into higher education monographs ; 46)
Bibliography: p103-108. — Includes index
ISBN 0-900868-93-7 (pbk) : Unpriced
B82-35290

Hoggart, Richard. After expansion : a time for diversity : the universities into the 1990's : this paper is based on a lecture given to the annual conference of the American Association for Higher Education at Chicago on 20 March 1978 / Richard Hoggart. — Leicester : ACACE, c1978. — 12p ; 21cm. — (Occasional paper / Advisory Council for Adult and Continuing Education ; 1)
ISBN 0-906436-00-1 (pbk) : £0.50 B82-39327

378.41 — Great Britain. Higher education, *1800-1981*

Edwards, E. G.. Higher education for everyone. — Nottingham : Spokesman, July 1982. — [200]p
ISBN 0-85124-335-5 (cased) : £15.00 : CIP entry
ISBN 0-85124-345-2 (pbk) : £4.95 B82-15931

378.41 — Great Britain. Higher education. Access

Access to higher education / Oliver Fulton editor. — Guildford : Society for Research into Higher Education, 1981. — 202p : ill ; 21cm. — (Research into higher education monographs ; 44)
Includes bibliographies
ISBN 0-900868-89-9 (pbk) : £4.95 (members £3.30) B82-24322

378.41 — Great Britain. Higher education. Administration by local authorities. Advisory services: National Advisory Body for Local Authority Higher Education

Bevan, J. S.. The National Advisory Body for local authority higher education / by J.S. Bevan. — [Sheffield] ([c/o Hon. Sec., Sheffield City Polytechnic, Pond St., Sheffield S1 1WB]) : Association of Colleges for Further and Higher Education, [1982]. — 4p ; 21cm
Paper from Summer meeting of ACFHE, Bath, June 10th & 11th 1982. — Cover title
Unpriced (pbk) B82-37173

378.41 — Great Britain. Higher education — *Conference proceedings*

Society for Research into Higher Education. *Conference (16th : 1980)*. Higher education at the cross roads : research into higher education 1965-1995 : papers presented at the 16th annual conference of the Society for Research into Higher Education 1980 / edited by Robert Oxtoby. — Guildford : The Society, 1980. — 182p : ill ; 21cm. — (SRHE proceedings ; 3)
Includes bibliographies
ISBN 0-900868-80-5 (pbk) : £7.95(£5.30 to members) B82-03444

378.41 — Great Britain. Higher education. Effects of reduction in government expenditure — *Association of University Teachers viewpoints*

Universities at risk / Association of University Teachers. — London : AUT, 1980. — 9p ; 22cm
Cover title. — Text on inside cover
Unpriced (pbk) B82-21899

378.41 — Great Britain. Higher education. Effects of reduction in government expenditure — *Inquiry reports*

Great Britain. *Parliament. House of Commons. Education, Science and Arts Committee*. First report from the Education, Science and Arts Committee, session 1981-82 : expenditure cuts in higher education : the effects on the "Robbins principle" and on the universities : together with the minutes of proceedings relating to the report. — London : H.M.S.O., [1981]. — 7p ; 25cm. — ([HC] ; 82)
ISBN 0-10-020828-2 (unbound) : £1.15
B82-16051

378.41 — Great Britain. Higher education. Expectations of society

Silver, Harold. Expectations of higher education : some historical pointers / Harold Silver with the collaboration of Pamela Silver. — Reading : Brunel University, 1981. — 102p ; 30cm. — (Paper / Brunel University ; no.1)
Bibliography: p89-102
Unpriced (pbk) B82-12097

378.41 — Great Britain. Higher education — *For school leavers*

Dixon, David. Higher education : finding your way : a brief guide for school and college students / by David Dixon. — London : H.M.S.O., 1979 (1981 [printing]). — 32p : ill ; 21cm
Bibliography: p28-32
ISBN 0-11-270384-4 (pbk) : £0.50 B82-05589

378.41 — Great Britain. Higher education. Implications of labour market — *Conference proceedings*

Higher education and the labour market / Robert M. Lindley (editor), Laurence C. Hunter ... [et al.]. — Guildford : Society for Research into Higher Education, 1981. — 171p : ill ; 21cm. — (Programme of study into the future of higher education ; 1.1) (Research into higher education monographs)
Includes bibliographies
ISBN 0-900868-83-x (pbk) : £4.95 B82-07937

378.41 — Great Britain. Higher education institutions

David, Peter, *1951-*. Guide for applicants : universities, polytechnics, and colleges offering degree courses / written by Peter David for the Advisory Centre for Education. — 2nd ed. — London : The Advisory Centre, 1981. — 40p : ill ; 21cm. — (An ACE handbook)
Previous ed.: 1979. — Bibliography: p33-39
ISBN 0-900029-59-5 (pbk) : Unpriced
B82-33050

378.41 — Great Britain. Higher education institutions. Courses — *Directories — For foreign students*

Higher education in the United Kingdom. — 1982-84. — London : Longman, Aug.1982. — [308]p
ISBN 0-582-49713-2 (pbk) : £5.95 : CIP entry
B82-15895

378.41 — Great Britain. Universities

Dainton, *Sir* Frederick. British universities purposes, problems and pressures / Sir Frederick Dainton. — Cambridge : Cambridge University Press, 1982. — 20p ; 22cm. — (The Rede lecture ; 1981)
Cover title
ISBN 0-521-28954-8 (pbk) : £1.50 B82-30528

378.41 — Great Britain. Universities: Open University

Rumble, Greville. The Open University of the United Kingdom : an evaluation of an innovative experience in the democratisation of higher education / Greville Rumble. — [Milton Keynes] : Open University Distance Education Research Group, 1982. — 119p : ill,1map ; 30cm. — (DERG papers ; no.6)
Bibliography: p111-119
Unpriced (pbk) B82-35099

378.411 — Scotland. Higher education institutions. National Diploma courses. Attitudes of students

Freshwater, Susan. Student choice in Higher National Diploma courses / Susan Freshwater. — Edinburgh : Scottish Council for Research in Education, c1981. — vi,33p : forms ; 30cm
Bibliography: p22
ISBN 0-901116-31-9 (pbk) : Unpriced
B82-19361

378.411'01 — Scotland. Universities, *1800-1900* — *Philosophical perspectives*

Davie, George Elder. The democratic intellect : Scotland and her universities in the nineteenth century. — Edinburgh : Edinburgh University Press, Dec.1981. — [372]p
ISBN 0-85224-435-5 (pbk) : £15.00 : CIP entry
B81-39216

378.412'35 — Scotland. Grampian Region. Aberdeen. Universities: University of Aberdeen. Graduates, *1860-1970* — *Registers*

University of Aberdeen. Roll of the graduates of the University of Aberdeen 1956-1970 : with supplement 1860-1955. — Aberdeen : Aberdeen University Press, July 1982. — [800]p
ISBN 0-08-028469-8 : £45.00 : CIP entry
B82-12448

378.412'7 — Scotland. Tayside Region. Dundee. Universities: University of Dundee, *to 1981*

Southgate, Donald. University education in Dundee : a centenary history / Donald Southgate. — Edinburgh : Published for the University of Dundee by Edinburgh University Press, c1982. — xi,417p,[9]p of plates : ill,2plans,ports ; 24cm
Includes index
ISBN 0-85224-434-7 : £15.00 : CIP rev.
B82-04735

University education in Dundee 1881-1981 / compiled by Michael Shafe. — [Dundee] : University of Dundee, 1982. — vi,214p : ill (some col.),facsims(some col.),1plan,ports(some col.) ; 21x30cm
Includes index
Unpriced (pbk) B82-37949

378.412'92 — Scotland. Fife Region. St Andrews. Universities: University of St Andrews Rectors, *to 1981* — *Biographies*

Twiss, Greg. P.. Famous rectors of St. Andrews / by Greg. P. Twiss and Paul Chennell. — St. Andrews (52 Buchanan Gardens, St. Andrews, KY16 9LX) : Alvie, 1982. — 143p : ports ; 21cm
Bibliography: p138-139. — Includes index
Unpriced (pbk) B82-25385

378.412'92 — Scotland. Fife Region. St Andrews. Universities: University of St Andrews — *Serials*

[Newsletter *(University of St Andrews)*]. Newsletter / University of St Andrews. — No.1 (Feb. 1980)-. — [St Andrews] ([Public Relations Office, University of St Andrews, St Andrews, Fife KY16 9AJ]) : [The University], 1980-. — v. : ill,plans,ports ; 30cm
Ten issues yearly. — Continues: Staff news sheet (University of St Andrews)
ISSN 0262-5857 = Newsletter - University of St. Andrews : Unpriced B82-17256

378.418'35 — Dublin. Universities: Trinity College *(Dublin), to 1952*

McDowell, R. B.. Trinity College Dublin : 1592-1952 : an academic history / R.B. McDowell and D.A. Webb ; with a foreword by F.S.L. Lyons. — Cambridge : Cambridge University Press, 1982. — xxiii,580p : ill,1facsim,1plan,ports ; 24cm
Bibliography: p557-566. — Includes index
ISBN 0-521-23931-1 : £35.00 B82-31816

378.42 — England. Higher education. Administration. Reorganisation. Great Britain. *Department of Education and Science.* Higher education in England outside the universities — *Critical studies*

Pratt, John, *1945-*. Agenda for a central body : a response to the DES' consultative document on public sector higher education / John Pratt and Michael Locke with Jim Antia. — London : NELPCO, 1981. — 20p ; 30cm. — (CIS commentary ; no.21)
Bibliography: p20
ISBN 0-901987-43-3 (spiral) : Unpriced
B82-27446

378.42 — England. Higher education — *National Association of Teachers in Further and Higher Education viewpoints*

National Association of Teachers in Further and Higher Education. Higher education : a policy statement / NATFHE. — [London] : [National Association of Teachers in Further and Higher Education], 1978. — 35p ; 21cm
Cover title
£0.50 (£0.35 to members of the Association) (pbk) B82-08495

378.421′42 — London. Camden *(London Borough).* **Universities. Colleges: University College, London,** *to 1978*

University College, London. The world of University College London 1823-1978 / by Negley Harte and John North ; introduction by Lord Annan. — [London] : University College London, [1979?]. — 216p : ill(some col.),facsims,maps,plans,ports ; 25cm
Text, ill on inside covers
ISBN 0-902137-23-9 (pbk) : Unpriced B82-29210

378.423′56 — Devon. Exeter. Universities: University of Exeter, *to 1981*

Clapp, B. W.. The University of Exeter : a history / by B.W. Clapp. — [Exeter] : University of Exeter, 1982. — xiv,208p,[19]p of plates : ill,1facsim,maps,1plan,ports ; 22cm
Map on lining papers. — Bibliography: p191-194. — Includes index
ISBN 0-85989-133-x : Unpriced B82-31554

378.423′98 — Avon. Bath. Universities: University of Bath. Founding

Moore, G. H.. The University of Bath : the formative years 1949-1969 : a short history of the circumstances which led to the foundation of the University of Bath / by G.H. Moore. — Bath : Bath University Press, c1982. — 110p : ill,2coats of arms,ports ; 30cm
ISBN 0-86197-033-0 (pbk) : £5.00 B82-31205

378.425′74 — Oxfordshire. Oxford. Universities. Colleges: Exeter College, *to ca 1980*

Exeter College. Exeter College, Oxford / [illustrated by J.W. Thomas]. — Oxford : Thomas-Photos, [1982?]. — 24p : ill(some col.),1map,1col.facsim ; 24cm
Text on inside cover. — 1 folded sheet as insert
ISBN 0-9501337-4-4 (pbk) : Unpriced B82-24041

378.427′33 — Greater Manchester *(Metropolitan County).* **Manchester. Polytechnics: Manchester Polytechnic**

Many arts, many skills. — [Manchester] ([All Saints Building, Manchester, M15 6BH]) : Manchester Polytechnic, [1982?]. — 54p : ill (some col.),1col.plan,ports ; 24cm
Cover title. — Text and ill on inside covers
Unpriced (pbk) B82-40201

378.428′21 — South Yorkshire *(Metropolitan County).* **Sheffield. Universities: University of Sheffield,** *to 1980*

University of Sheffield. The University of Sheffield : an illustrated history / [written and compiled by Maureen Boylan and Gillian Riley]. — [Sheffield] : [University of Sheffield], [1981?]. — 40p : ill(some col.),facsims,ports ; 30cm
Text and ill on inside cover
ISBN 0-85426-028-5 (pbk) : Unpriced B82-08240

378.428′65 — Durham *(County).* **Durham. Universities. Colleges: University of Durham.** *St. Mary′s College, to 1981*

Doves & dons : a history of St. Mary′s College Durham : an account of the women′s hostel 1899-1920 and some impressions of later college life / edited by Marilyn Hird. — Rev. and enl. ed. — Durham : St. Mary′s College, 1982. — [104]p : ill,ports ; 22cm
Previous ed.: published as St. Mary′s College, 1899-1974. 1974. — Text on inside front cover
ISBN 0-9503216-1-3 (pbk) : Unpriced B82-35779

378.428′65 — Durham *(County).* **Durham. Universities: University of Durham. Founding**

Heesom, Alan. The founding of the University of Durham : [lecture] delivered in Elvet Riverside, Durham, 11 March 1982 / Alan Heesom. — [Durham] : Dean and Chapter of Durham, c1982. — 32p ; 21cm. — (Durham Cathedral lecture ; 1982)
ISBN 0-907078-13-3 (pbk) : Unpriced B82-27694

378.429′87′05 — Cardiff. Universities. Colleges: University College, Cardiff — *Serials*

Ex-communication. — No.1 (1982)-. — Cardiff ([c/o The Editor, Department of English, University College Cardiff, P.O. Box 78, Cardiff CF1 1XL]) : University College Cardiff, 1982-. — v. ; 21cm
Continues: Communication (Cardiff)
ISSN 0263-807X = Ex-communication : Unpriced B82-36692

378.62 — Egypt. Higher education. Implications of labour market

University education and the labour market in the Arab Republic of Egypt / by Bikas C. Sanyal ... [et al.]. — Oxford : Pergamon, 1982. — xx,266p : ill,forms ; 24cm
At head of title: Unesco ; International Institute for Educational Planning. — Bibliography: p265-266
ISBN 0-08-028123-0 (cased) : Unpriced : CIP rev.
ISBN 0-08-028122-2 (pbk) : £8.00 B82-14954

378.7286 — Costa Rica. Universities: Universidad Estatal a Distancia

Rumble, Greville. Costa Rica′s Universidad Estatal a Distancia : a case study / Greville Rumble. — Milton Keynes : Open University Distance Education Research Group, 1981. — 44p : ill,maps ; 25cm. — (DERG papers ; no.4)
Cover title. — Bibliography: p43-44
Unpriced (pbk) B82-21189

378.73 — United States. Higher education

Riesman, David. On higher education : the academic enterprise in an era of rising student consumerism / David Riesman. — San Francisco ; London : Jossey-Bass, 1981, c1980. — xxxiv,421p ; 24cm. — (The Carnegie Council series)
Bibliography: p381-399. — Includes index
ISBN 0-87589-484-4 : Unpriced B82-36801

378.742′3 — New Hampshire. Hanover. Colleges: Dartmouth College, *1881*

Tobias, Marilyn. Old Dartmouth on trial : the transformation of the academic community in nineteenth-century America / Marilyn Tobias. — New York ; London : New York University Press, 1982. — xii,249p : ill,ports ; 24cm. — (New York University series in education and socialization in American history)
Includes index
ISBN 0-8147-8168-3 : £26.00 B82-35945

378.749′67′0922 — New Jersey. Princeton. Universities: College of New Jersey. Graduates, *1776-1783 — Biographies*

Harrison, Richard A.. Princetonians 1776-1783 : a biographical dictionary / by Richard A. Harrison. — Princeton ; Guildford : Princeton University Press, 1981. — xli,498p : ports ; 25cm
Includes index
ISBN 0-691-05336-7 : £24.60 B82-11458

379 — EDUCATION AND THE STATE

379 — Education. Political aspects

Politics and educational change : an international survey / edited by Patricia Broadfoot, Colin Brock and Witold Tulasiewicz. — London : Croom Helm, c1981. — 227p ; 23cm
ISBN 0-7099-0655-2 : £10.95 B82-07145

379 — Education. Role of politics

Politics and education. — Oxford : Pergamon, Jan.1983. — [330]p
ISBN 0-08-028905-3 (cased) : £16.00 : CIP entry
ISBN 0-08-028904-5 (pbk) : £7.50 B82-33613

379.1/2 — PUBLIC EDUCATION

379.1′1′0942 — England. Schools. Finance

Knight, Brian. Managing school finance. — London : Heinemann Educational, Jan.1983. — [176]p. — (Organization in schools)
ISBN 0-435-80480-4 : £7.50 : CIP entry B82-32852

379.1′13 — England. Secondary schools & sixth form colleges. Students, 16-19 years. Education. Costing

Costing educational provision for the 16-19 age group / prepared for the Government and the Local Authority Associations by Arthur Young McClelland Moores. — [London] ([Elizabeth House, York Rd., SE1]) : [Department of Education & Science], [1982?]. — 39p : ill ; 30cm
Cover title
Unpriced (pbk) B82-23827

379.1′14′0941 — Great Britain. Further education institutions. Finance

Humphreys, D. A.. Financial control in further education / by D.A. Humphreys. — Sheffield (c/o Hon. Sec. Sheffield City Polytechnic, Pond St., Sheffield S1 1WB) : Association of Colleges for Further and Higher Education, [1982]. — 19p ; 21cm
Paper from Summer Meeting of ACFHE, Bath June 10th and 11th 1982. — Cover title
£0.75 (pbk) B82-36022

379.1′21′0941 — Great Britain. Education. Finance — *Conference proceedings*

Collective choice in education / edited by Mary Jean Bowman. — Boston, Mass. ; London : Kluwer-Nijhoff, 1982, c1981. — vi,272p : ill ; 24cm. — (Studies in public choice)
Conference papers. — ″Reprinted from Public choice. 36 (special issue, 3) 1982″ — T.p. verso. — Includes bibliographies
ISBN 0-89838-091-x : Unpriced
Also classified at 379.1′21′0973 B82-21460

379.1′21′0973 — United States. Education. Finance

Weaver, W. Timothy. The contest for educational resources : equity and reform in a meritocratic society / W. Timothy Weaver with contributions by Alan K. Gaynor, Barry M. Richmond, Ross Zerchykov. — Lexington, Mass. : Lexington ; [Aldershot] : Gower [distributor], c1982. — xv,188p : ill ; 24cm
Bibliography: p179-184. — Includes index
ISBN 0-669-04586-1 : £17.00 B82-31798

379.1′21′0973 — United States. Education. Finance — *Conference proceedings*

Collective choice in education / edited by Mary Jean Bowman. — Boston, Mass. ; London : Kluwer-Nijhoff, 1982, c1981. — vi,272p : ill ; 24cm. — (Studies in public choice)
Conference papers. — ″Reprinted from Public choice. 36 (special issue, 3) 1982″ — T.p. verso. — Includes bibliographies
ISBN 0-89838-091-x : Unpriced
Primary classification 379.1′21′0941 B82-21460

379.1′214′0941 — Great Britain. Universities. Finance — *Inquiry reports*

Great Britain. *Parliament. House of Commons. Committee of Public Accounts.* Eleventh report from the Committee of Public Accounts : together with the proceedings of the Committee, minutes of evidence and appendices : session 1981-82 : Department of Education and Science, University Grants Committee : assessment of universities grant needs, relaxation of control over university building projects by the University Grants Committee; excess of expenditure over grant. — London : H.M.S.O., [1982]. — xvi,47p ; 25cm. — ([H.C.] ; 175)
ISBN 0-10-217582-9 (pbk) : £4.65 B82-27233

379.1'214'0941 — Great Britain. Universities. Finance — *Inquiry reports* *continuation*

Great Britain. *Parliament. House of Commons. Committee of Public Accounts.* Thirty-fourth report from the Committee of Public Accounts : together with the proceedings of the committee, the minutes of evidence and an appendix : session 1979-80 : Department of Education and Science, University Grants Committee, Social Science Research Council : assessment of universities grant needs, research and training in the social sciences. — London : H.M.S.O., [1980]. — 26p ; 25cm. — ([HC] ; 783)
ISBN 0-10-027839-6 (pbk) : £4.00
Also classified at 338.4'33'0072041 B82-09925

379.1'22'0942561 — Bedfordshire. Bedford. Education. Effects of reduction of local education authorities' expenditure

What is happening to our schools? : the effect of budgetary cuts on education in the town of Bedford / a report by the Bedford and District Campaign for the Advancement of State Education. — [Bedford] ([84, Tyne Crescent, Bedford]) : [Bedford and District Campaign for the Advancement of State Education], 1980. — 6p ; 30cm
£0.40 (unbound) B82-29851

379.1'5 — England. Education. Accountability

Becker, Tony. Policies for educational accountability. — London : Heinemann Educational, Sept.1981. — [196]p. — (Organization in schools series)
ISBN 0-435-80060-4 : £8.50 : CIP entry
B81-22636

379.1'5 — Great Britain. Educational institutions. Accountability

Calling education to account : a reader / edited by Robert McCormick ... [et al.]. — London : Heinemann Educational in association with the Open University Press, 1982. — 376p : ill ; 22cm. — (Open University set book)
Includes bibliographies and index
ISBN 0-435-80629-7 (corrected : pbk) : £6.50 : CIP rev. B81-38292

379.1'5'0941 — Great Britain. Education. Administration — *Serials*

Educational management & administration : journal of the British Educational Management and Administration Society. — Vol.10, no.1 (Feb. 1982)-. — Harlow : Longman, 1982-. — v. : ill ; 25cm
Three issues yearly. — Continues: Educational administration
ISSN 0263-211x = Educational management & administration : £15.00 per year B82-38528

379.1'5'09669 — Nigeria. Education. Administration

Edem, D. A.. Introduction to educational administration in Nigeria / D.A. Edem. — Ibadan : Spectrum ; Chichester : Wiley, c1982. — xiv,143p ; 23cm. — (Education in Africa)
Bibliography: p136-138. — Includes index
ISBN 0-471-27984-6 (pbk) : Unpriced : CIP rev. B82-40502

379.1'5'0973 — United States. Education. Administration

Morphet, Edgar L.. Educational organization and administration : concepts, practices and issues / Edgar L. Morphet, Roe L. Johns, Theodore L. Reller. — 4th ed. — Englewood Cliffs ; London : Prentice-Hall, c1982. — x,422p : ill ; 24cm
Previous ed.: 1974. — Includes bibliographies and index
ISBN 0-13-236729-7 : £17.20 B82-16849

379.1'53'0942 — England. Local education authorities. Administration

Tomlinson, J. R. G.. The profession of education officer : past pluperfect, present tense, future conditional / by J.R.G. Tomlinson. — [Sheffield] : Department of Education Management, Sheffield City Polytechnic, 1982. — 26leaves ; 21cm. — (Sheffield papers in education management ; 25)
ISBN 0-903761-54-8 (pbk) : Unpriced
B82-38546

379.1'53'0942 — England. Local education authorities. Chief education officers. Role, *1972 compared with* **role,** *1980*

Bush, Tony. Directors of education. — London : Allen & Unwin, Aug.1982. — [208]p
ISBN 0-04-379001-1 (cased) : £12.50 : CIP entry
ISBN 0-04-379002-x (pbk) : £4.50 B82-15640

379.1'531'0942 — England. Schools. Administration by governing boards — *Manuals*

Sallis, Joan. The effective school governor : a guide to the practice of school government / written by Joan Sallis for the Advisory Centre for Education. — 2nd ed. — London : The Advisory Centre, 1982. — 31p : ill ; 21cm. — (An ACE handbook)
Previous ed.: 1980
ISBN 0-900029-65-x (pbk) : £1.00 B82-32800

Sallis, Joan. School governors : partnership in practice : an ACE guide to current arrangements for school government in all the local education authorities of England and Wales : including a summary of the recommendations of the Taylor report / written by Joan Sallis for the Advisory Centre for Education. — London : The Advisory Centre, 1979. — 28p : ill ; 21cm. — (An ACE handbook)
Bibliography: p28
ISBN 0-900029-49-8 (pbk) : £1.50 B82-32799

379.1'531'0942 — England. Schools. Governing boards & managing boards. Role — *Labour Party (Great Britain) viewpoints*

Labour Party, *Great Britain, National Executive Committee*. School governors / National Executive Committee. — London (150 Walworth Rd., SE17 1JT) : Labour Party, 1981. — 8p ; 30cm. — (Advice note ; no.9)
Unpriced (unbound) B82-01695

379.1'54 — Education. Evaluation

Holt, Maurice. Evaluating the evaluators / Maurice Holt. — London : Hodder and Stoughton, 1981. — 187p ; 22cm. — (Studies in teaching and learning)
Bibliography: p177-183. — Includes index
ISBN 0-340-27245-7 (pbk) : £3.45 : CIP rev.
B81-30248

Practising evaluation / edited by David Smetherham. — Driffield : Studies in Education, 1981. — 165p ; 22cm
Includes bibliographies
ISBN 0-905484-39-8 (cased) : £7.50
ISBN 0-905484-16-9 (pbk) : £3.95 B82-12937

Ruddock, Ralph. Evaluation : a consideration of principles and methods / Ralph Ruddock. — [Manchester] : [Dept. of Adult and Higher Education, University of Manchester], 1981. — vi,107p : ill ; 21cm. — (Manchester monographs ; 18)
Bibliography: p104-107
ISBN 0-903717-27-1 (pbk) : Unpriced
B82-21046

379.1'54 — Education. Evaluation — *Manuals*

Harris, N. D. C.. Signposts for evaluating : a resource pack / developed at the University of Bath, School of Education by N.D.C. Harris, C.D. Bell and J.E.H. Carter. — London : Council for Educational Technology with the Schools Council, 1981. — 1portfolio : ill ; 32cm
Includes bibliographies
ISBN 0-86184-054-2 : £15.00 : CIP rev.
B82-02470

379.1'54 — Education. Evaluation - *Serials*

Evaluation in education. — Vol.4. — Oxford : Pergamon, June 1981. — [361]p
ISBN 0-08-028404-3 : £27.00 : CIP entry
B81-16386

379.1'54 — Education. Policies. Formulation — *Case studies*

Howell, D. A.. Educational policy making. — London : Heinemann Educational, Dec.1982. — [136]p
ISBN 0-85473-130-x (pbk) : £4.50 : CIP entry
B82-39263

379.1'54 — England. Educational institutions. Accountability

Accountability in the English educational system / edited by Hugh Sockett. — London : Hodder and Stoughton, c1980. — 117p ; 22cm. — (Unibooks)
Bibliography: p112-117. — Includes index
ISBN 0-340-24459-3 (pbk) : £2.95 : CIP rev.
B79-29333

379.1'54 — Great Britain. Schools. Accountability

School accountability : The SSRC Cambridge Accountability Project / John Elliott ... [et al.]. — London : McIntyre, 1981. — xvii,247p : ill ; 20cm
Bibliography: p239-244. — Includes index
ISBN 0-86216-074-x (pbk) : £14.95 : CIP rev.
ISBN 0-86216-077-4 (pbk) : £5.95 B81-32588

379.1'54 — United States. Education. Evaluation

Improving educational evaluation methods : impact on policy / edited by Carol B. Aslanian. — Beverly Hills ; London : Published in cooperation with the Evaluation Research Society [by] Sage, c1981. — 151p : ill ; 22cm. — (Sage research progress series in evaluation ; v.11)
Includes bibliographies
ISBN 0-8039-1729-5 (cased) : Unpriced
ISBN 0-8039-1730-9 (pbk) : Unpriced
B82-21864

379.1'54'09411 — Scotland. Education. Planning. Reform — *Proposals*

Scotland, a half-educated nation / contributors Pat Clarke ... [et al.] ; illustrations Archibald McIntosh ; Joint editors David Jenkins, Ken Reid, Don Skinner. — Falkirk (Falkirk FK1 1YS) : Callendar Park College of Education, c1980. — 48p : ill ; 21cm
£0.25 (pbk) B82-17505

379.1'57 — Great Britain. Schools. Women teachers. Promotion. Discrimination

Promotion and the woman teacher. — [London] : NUT, 1980. — 75p ; 30cm
Bibliography: p56
ISBN 0-900560-66-5 (pbk) : Unpriced
B82-19043

379.1'57'0942 — England. Schools. Teachers. Selection & promotion — *Proposals*

National Union of Teachers. A fair way forward : NUT memorandum on appointment, promotion and career development. — [London] ([Hamilton House, Mabledon Place, WC1H 9BD]) : [National Union of Teachers], [1981]. — 31p ; 21cm
Cover title
£0.40 (pbk) B82-04525

379.3 — PRIVATE EDUCATION AND THE STATE

379.3'22'0942 — England. Independent secondary schools. Fees. Payment by local education authorities. Great Britain. *Department of Education and Science.* **Assisted Places Scheme** — *Labour Party (Great Britain) viewpoints*

Labour Party, *Great Britain, National Executive Committee*. The assisted places scheme / National Executive Committee. — London (150 Walworth Rd., SE17 1JT) : Labour Party, 1981. — 6p ; 30cm. — (Advice note ; no.4)
Unpriced (unbound) B82-01696

379.4/9 — EDUCATION AND THE STATE. HISTORICAL AND GEOGRAPHICAL TREATMENT

379.41 — Great Britain. Education. Policies of government

Contemporary education policy. — London : Croom Helm, Nov.1982. — [304]p
ISBN 0-7099-0512-2 : £8.95 : CIP entry
B82-28746

Great Britain. *Equal Opportunities Commission.* The effects of the government's financial policy on educational provision / comments by the Equal Opportunities Commission. — [Manchester] : [Equal Opportunities Commission], [1979?]. — 8leaves ; 30cm
Unpriced (pbk) B82-38491

379.41 — Great Britain. State education. Development, *1850-1914 related to* **industrial productivity,** *1850-1914*
Where did we go wrong? : industrial performance, education and the economy in Victorian Britain / edited and introduced by Gordon Roderick and Michael Stephens. — Lewes (Falmer House, Barcombe, Lewes, Sussex BN8 5DL) : Falmer Press, 1981. — 262p : ill ; 24cm. — ([Politics and education series])
Includes index
ISBN 0-905273-11-7 : Unpriced
Primary classification 338'.06'0941 B82-02431

379.41 — Great Britain. State education. Development, *1870-1980 related to* **industrial productivity,** *1870-1980*
The **British** malaise : industrial performance, education & training in Britain today / edited and introduced by Gordon Roderick and Michael Stephens. — Barcombe : Falmer, 1982. — viii,173p : ill ; 24cm. — ([Politics and education series])
Includes index
ISBN 0-905273-21-4 : Unpriced
Primary classification 338'.06'0941 B82-17182

379.47 — Soviet Union. Education. Policies, *1953-1980*
Matthews, Mervyn. Education in the Soviet Union : policies and institutions since Stalin / Mervyn Matthews. — London : Allen & Unwin, 1982. — xiv,225p ; 23cm
Bibliography: p214-222. — Includes index
ISBN 0-04-370114-0 : £15.00 : CIP rev.
B82-10576

379.7284 — El Salvador. Education. Repression by government, *1980-1981*
El Salvador : education and repression / World University Service ... [et al.]. — London : El Salvador Solidarity Campaign, [1981]. — 23p : ill,maps,facsims ; 30cm
Compiler: John Bevan
ISBN 0-9505721-9-5 (unbound) : £0.75
B82-08517

379.73 — United States. Education. Policies of government
Atkin, J. Myron. The government in the classroom : the ninth Sir John Adams lecture, delivered at the University of London Institute of Education on Thursday, 6 March 1980 / J. Myron Atkin. — London : University of London Institute of Education, 1980. — 24p ; 21cm. — (Ninth Sir John Adams lecture)
At head of title: University of London Institute of Education
ISBN 0-85473-089-3 (pbk) : £0.60 B82-12398

379.73 — United States. Education. Policies of state governments. Decision making
Mitchell, Douglas E.. Shaping legislative decisions : education policy and the social sciences / Douglas E. Mitchell. — Lexington, Mass. : Lexington Books, c1981 ; [Aldershot] : Gower [distributor], 1982. — xvi,201p : ill,1form ; 24cm. — (Lexington Books politics of education series)
Bibliography: p157-162. — Includes index
ISBN 0-669-04091-6 : £16.50 B82-14749

380.1 — TRADE

380.1 — Commerce
Jones, H. L.. Groundwork of commerce. — London : Edward Arnold
Book 1. — 7th ed. — Jan.1983. — [288]p
Previous ed.: 1977
ISBN 0-7131-0728-6 (pbk) : £3.50 : CIP entry
B82-32591

Lobley, Derek. Success in commerce / Derek Lobley. — 2nd ed. — London : Murray, 1982. — xii,254p : ill,forms ; 22cm
Previous ed.: 1975. — Bibliography: p250. — Includes index
ISBN 0-7195-3962-5 (pbk) : £2.95 B82-35600

Pitfield, Ronald R.. Mastering commerce / R.R. Pitfield. — [London] : Macmillan, 1982. — xviii,256p : ill ; 23cm. — (Macmillan master series)
Includes index
ISBN 0-333-31288-0 (cased) : £8.95
ISBN 0-333-30445-4 (pbk) : Unpriced
B82-17108

380.1 — Commerce — *For Asian students*
Li, Betsy. Certificate commerce / Betsy Li, Tan Sai Kim. — 2nd ed. — Singapore ; Oxford : Oxford University Press, 1981. — vi,106p : ill ; 25cm. — (Modern certificate guides) (Oxford in Asia)
Previous ed.: 1977?
ISBN 0-19-582813-5 (pbk) : £1.75 B82-35166

380.1 — Commerce — *For Caribbean students*
Waterman, Ivan L.. Principles of business for Caribbean examinations / Ivan L. Waterman. — [London] : Macmillan Caribbean, 1981. — viii,200p ; 22cm
Includes index
ISBN 0-333-30467-5 (pbk) : £2.25 B82-10832

380.1 — Commerce — *For Irish students*
McQuillan, Dominic. Complete commerce for students beginning business studies / Dominic McQuillan. — Dublin : Educational, 1982. — 360p : ill ; 22cm
Includes index
Unpriced (pbk) B82-35971

380.1 — Commerce — *For schools*
Gow, Marion. Role playing in commerce. — London : Arnold, Dec.1982. — [64]p
ISBN 0-7131-0827-4 (pbk) : £1.75 : CIP entry
B82-30202

Thomas, D. J. (Derek John). A first course in commerce / D.J. Thomas. — 5th ed. — London : Bell & Hyman, 1981. — viii,200p : ill,forms ; 21cm
Previous ed.: 1979. — Bibliography: p196. — Includes index
ISBN 0-7135-1074-9 (pbk) : Unpriced
B82-24509

Tomlin, Constance. Commerce in everyday life / Constance Tomlin. — Slough : University Tutorial Press, 1982. — 156p : ill,facsims,maps ; 25cm
Includes index
ISBN 0-7231-0828-5 (pbk) : £3.00 B82-35077

380.1 — Commerce — *For West African students*
Lawal, O. A.. Commerce today for West Africa. — London : Hodder and Stoughton, July 1982. — [176]p
ISBN 0-340-26437-3 (pbk) : £2.95 : CIP entry
B82-18462

Lobley, Derek. Success in commerce. — West African ed. / O.A. Lawal and Derek Lobley. — London : African University Press in association with Murray, 1982. — xii,240p : ill,forms ; 22cm
Previous ed.: 1976. — Includes index
ISBN 0-7195-3901-3 (pbk) : £2.80 : CIP rev.
B82-01139

380.1 — Marketing. Economic aspects
Leake, Andrew. Market analysis. — London : Macmillan, July 1981. — [48]p
ISBN 0-333-27987-5 (pbk) : £1.25 : CIP entry
B81-14941

380.1'025 — Chambers of commerce — *Directories*
Padget, J.. Chambers of commerce worldwide : a selected list / compiled by J. Padget and C.A. Ferreira. — London : London Chamber of Commerce and Industry, 1981. — 164p ; 30cm
Includes index
ISBN 0-901902-54-3 (pbk) : £10.00
B82-03655

380.1'025 — Products. Suppliers — *Directories — For tax-free retail trades — Serials*
International tax and duty free buyers' index. — 1980-. — London (Bremar House, Sale Place, W2) : London & Continental Advertising, 1980-. — v. : ill ; 30cm
Annual
ISSN 0262-7310 = International tax and duty free buyers' index : Unpriced B82-11797

International tax-free trader. Buyers guide & directory. — No.1 (1982)-. — Redhill (2 Queensway, Redhill, Surrey RH1 1QS) : International Trade Publications, 1982-. — v. : col.ill ; 30cm
Annual
ISSN 0263-5488 = International tax-free trader. Buyers guide & directory : £25.00
B82-28122

380.1'025'41 — Great Britain. Industries & trades — *Directories — For local authorities — Serials*
The **Local** authority specifiers' reference book and buyers' guide. — 1981-. — London (88 Edgware Rd, W2 2YW) : Sterling Publications for the District Council Technical Association, 1981-. — v. : ill ; 22cm
Annual. — Continues: Housing managers buyers guide
ISSN 0260-3756 = Local authority specifiers' reference book and buyers' guide : Unpriced
B82-05230

380.1'025'41 — Great Britain. Japanese industries & trades — *Directories*
Japanese addresses in Britain / The Anglo-Japanese Economic Institute. — London (342 Grand Buildings, Trafalgar Sq., WC2N 5HB) : The Institute, c1982. — 32p ; 21cm
Includes index
Unpriced (unbound) B82-40173

380.1'025'42737 — Greater Manchester *(Metropolitan County).* **Bolton. Industries & trades,** *1821-1853 — Directories — Facsimiles*
Four Bolton directories : 1821/2, 1836, 1843, 1853. — Manchester (375 Chorley Rd., Swinton, Manchester M27 2AY) : Neil Richardson, 1982. — 106p : ill ; 21cm
Cover title
ISBN 0-9506257-3-6 (pbk) : £2.50 B82-25024

380.1'025'42757 — Merseyside *(Metropolitan District).* **St Helens. Industries & trades** — *Directories*
St. Helens directory of manufacturing and related industries. — St. Helens ([c/o Central Library, Victoria Sq., St. Helens, WA10 1DY]) : St. Helens MBC, [1981]. — 1v.(loose-leaf)
Includes index
£5.00 (unbound) B82-14535

380.1'025'42812 — West Yorkshire *(Metropolitan County).* **Calderdale** *(District).* **Industries & trades** — *Directories*
Calderdale : products and services register. — London : Burrow, [1981]. — 108p ; 25cm
Includes index
Unpriced (pbk) B82-13326

Calderdale products and services register. — London (Publicity House, Streatham Hill, SW2 4TR) : Burrow, [1981]. — 108p : ill ; 25cm
£3.25 (pbk) B82-10988

380.1'025'4282 — South Yorkshire *(Metropolitan County).* **Industries & trades** — *Directories*
The **South** Yorkshire industrial & commercial directory / M.J. Thompson, County Planning Officer. — [Barnsley] ([County Hall, Barnsley, S. Yorkshire S70 2TN]) : South Yorkshire County Council, 1982. — 330p : ill,maps ; 30cm
Includes index
Unpriced (pbk) B82-39361

380.1'025'4285 — Cleveland. Industries & trades — *Directories*
Cleveland county : industrial & commercial register. — London : Burrow, [1981?]. — 136p : ill(some col.),maps ; 30cm
£1.00 (pbk) B82-14570

380.1'025'5 — Asia. Industries & trades — *Directories — Serials*
Owen's : trade directory & business travel guide. — 29th ed.-. — Bulle, Switzerland ; Alperton : Owen's Publications, 1982-. — v. : ill,maps ; 30cm
Annual. — Continues: Owen's commerce and travel and international register
Unpriced
Also classified at 380.1'025'6 B82-27658

380.1'025'6 — Africa. Industries & trades — *Directories — Serials*
Owen's : trade directory & business travel guide. — 29th ed.-. — Bulle, Switzerland ; Alperton : Owen's Publications, 1982-. — v. : ill,maps ; 30cm
Annual. — Continues: Owen's commerce and travel and international register
Unpriced
Primary classification 380.1'025'5 B82-27658

380.1'06'077311 — Chicago. *Board of Trade, to 1905*
Lurie, Jonathan. The Chicago Board of Trade 1859-1905 : the dynamics of self-regulation / by Jonathan Lurie. — Urbana ; London : University of Illinois Press, c1979. — xiv,234p : ill ; 24cm
Bibliography: p214-232
ISBN 0-252-00732-8 : Unpriced B82-16952

380.1'076 — Commerce — *Questions & answers — For East African students*
Anderson, David J.. Multiple choice tests in commerce for East Africa / D.J. Anderson and R.N. Gichira. — London : Macmillan, 1981. — v,98p ; 25cm
ISBN 0-333-30975-8 (pbk) : £1.25 B82-20899

Mukiibi, P.. O-level commerce for East Africa : questions and answers/objective tests / P. Mukiibi, A.B. Songok. — London : Longman, 1981. — 105p ; 22cm. — (Study for success)
ISBN 0-582-65529-3 (pbk) : £1.00 B82-11529

Rana, M. S.. Questions and answers in O level commerce / M.S. Rana, M.P.S. Rana. — London : Pitman, 1981. — 187p : forms ; 23cm
ISBN 0-273-01509-5 (pbk) : Unpriced B82-37423

380.1'076 — Commerce — *Questions & answers — For schools*
Curzon, L. B.. Objective tests in commerce / L.B. Curzon. — Estover : Macdonald & Evans, 1981. — viii,152p ; 19cm
ISBN 0-7121-1535-8 (pbk) : £2.25 B82-08507

380.1'076 — Commerce — *Questions & answers — For West African students*
Okolo, M. N.. Objective tests : commerce for West Africa / M.N. Okolo. — Harlow : Longman, 1980. — iv,124p : ill ; 22cm. — (Study of success)
ISBN 0-582-65052-6 (pbk) : £1.15 B82-02039

380.1'092'4 — Scotland. Shetland. Trade. Williamson, James, *1800-1872 — Biographies*
Johnson, Robert L.. A Shetland country merchant : being an account of the life and times of James Williamson of Mid Yell 1800-1872 / Robert L. Johnson. — [Shetland] : Shetland Publishing, 1979. — 63p : 1plan ; 22cm
ISBN 0-906736-02-1 (pbk) : £1.60 B82-08487

380.1'0934 — Pakistan. Harappa. Trade, *to B.C.1700*
Ratnagar, Shereen. Encounters : the westerly trade of the Harappa civilisation / Shereen Ratnagar. — Delhi ; Oxford : Oxford University Press, 1981. — xxi,294p : ill,col.maps ; 23cm
Maps on lining papers. — Bibliography: p255-286. — Includes index
ISBN 0-19-561253-1 : Unpriced B82-40542

380.1'0937 — Ancient Rome. Trade. Attitudes of society
D'Arms, John H.. Commerce and social standing in ancient Rome / John H. D'Arms. — Cambridge, Mass. ; London : Harvard University Press, 1981. — xviii,201p,[16]p of plates : ill,maps,plans ; 24cm
Bibliography: p182-194. — Includes index
ISBN 0-674-14475-9 : £12.00 B82-04447

380.1'0942 — England. European merchants, *1200-1350*
Lloyd, T. H.. Alien merchants in England in the high Middle Ages / T.H. Lloyd. — Brighton : Harvester, 1982. — 253p ; 23cm
Bibliography: p234-235. — Includes index
ISBN 0-7108-0066-5 : £18.95 : CIP rev. B82-12149

380.1'096891 — Zimbabwe. Manyika. Trade. Political aspects, *1575-1902*
Bhila, H. H. K.. Trade and politics in a Shona kingdom : the Manyika and their African and Portuguese neighbours 1575-1902 / H.H.K. Bhila. — Harlow : Longman, 1982. — xvi,291p ; 23cm. — (Studies in Zimbabwean history)
Bibliography: p263-284. — Includes index
ISBN 0-582-64354-6 (pbk) : £7.50 B82-34354

380.1'098 — Latin America. Commerce — *Spanish texts — Serials*
América Latina. Informe de mercados. — IM-81-01 (31 de jul. de 1981)-. — Londres [London] (90 Cowcross St., EC1M 6BL) : Latin American Newsletters Ltd, 1981-. — v. : maps ; 30cm
Fortnightly. — Continues in part: América Latina informe semanal
ISSN 0261-3751 = América Latina. Informe de mercados : Unpriced B82-14783

380.1'414'0941 — Great Britain. Fruit trades
Gill, A. H.. Supermarkets and the marketing of fresh fruit and vegetables / A.H. Gill. — [Reading] : University of Reading, Department of Agricultural Economics & Management, 1980. — 51p ; 30cm. — (Miscellaneous study ; no.69)
Summaries in French and German
ISBN 0-7049-0690-2 (pbk) : £2.00
Also classified at 380.1'415'0941 B82-36244

An **Introduction** to distributing fresh fruit, vegetables, potatoes and flowers. — London (308 Seven Sisters Rd., Finsbury Park, N4 2BN) : National Institute of Fresh Produce in association with the Food, Drink and Tobacco Industry Training Board, [1979]. — [20]p : ill ; 21cm
Cover title. — Text on inside covers
£0.60 (pbk)
Primary classification 380.1'415'0941 B82-27919

380.1'415'0941 — Great Britain. Vegetable trades
Gill, A. H.. Supermarkets and the marketing of fresh fruit and vegetables / A.H. Gill. — [Reading] : University of Reading, Department of Agricultural Economics & Management, 1980. — 51p ; 30cm. — (Miscellaneous study ; no.69)
Summaries in French and German
ISBN 0-7049-0690-2 (pbk) : £2.00
Primary classification 380.1'414'0941 B82-36244

An **Introduction** to distributing fresh fruit, vegetables, potatoes and flowers. — London (308 Seven Sisters Rd., Finsbury Park, N4 2BN) : National Institute of Fresh Produce in association with the Food, Drink and Tobacco Industry Training Board, [1979]. — [20]p : ill ; 21cm
Cover title. — Text on inside covers
£0.60 (pbk)
Also classified at 380.1'414'0941 B82-27919

380.1'4248 — Nickel trades
An **Introduction** to the nickel market. — London (2 Lindsey St., EC1A 9HN) : Rayner-Harwill, [1979]. — 19p : ill,maps ; 30cm
Cover title
Unpriced (spiral) B82-05310

380.1'437'094 — Europe. Fish & fish products. Marketing
The **Marketing** of fish and fishery products in Europe. — Edinburgh (10 Young St., Edinburgh EH2 4JQ) : Fishery Economics Research Unit, White Fish Authority
No.4: France / David I.A. Steel. — 1980. — 30p : ill,1map ; 30cm. — (F.E.R.U. occasional paper series, ISSN 0309-605x ; no.2)
Unpriced (spiral) B82-36248

380.1'45002'0212 — Book trades — *Statistics — Serials*
World book news : a monthly statistical digest of the world book trade. — Issue 1 (Sept. 1981)-. — London : Euromonitor Publications, 1981-. — v. ; 31cm
ISSN 0261-4391 = World book news : Unpriced B82-11828

380.1'45002'0941 — Great Britain. Book trades — *Statistics — Serials*
ICC financial survey. Book sellers. — 1st ed.-. — London : Inter Company Comparisons, [197-]-. — v. ; 21x30cm
Annual. — Description based on: 3rd ed.
ISSN 0263-9092 = ICC financial survey. Book sellers : Unpriced B82-38526

380.1'4562'0002541 — Great Britain. Engineering trades — *Directories*
Engineers merchants. — Great Missenden : Data Research Group, [1981]. — 97leaves ; 30cm
Cover title
ISBN 0-86099-345-0 (pbk) : Unpriced B82-24685

380.1'456213193702541 — Great Britain. Electric equipment. Insulating materials. Suppliers — *Directories*
EEIA guide to insulation. — London (8 Leicester St., WC2 7BN) : Electrical and Electronic Insulation Association, [1980?]. — 16p ; 30cm
Unpriced (free to members of the Association) (pbk) B82-35932

380.1'456292'0941 — Great Britain. Foreign motor vehicle trades — *Statistics*
Foreign vehicle distributor : an industry sector analysis. — 9th ed. — London : ICC Business Ratios, 1981. — [50]p : ill ; 30cm. — (ICC business ratio report)
Previous ed.: [1980?]
ISBN 0-86261-171-7 (pbk) : £80.00 B82-31145

380.1'456649'00941 — Great Britain. Meat. Marketing. Economic aspects — *Serials*
[**Newsletter** *(Great Britain. Meat and Livestock Commission. Marketing Services)*]. Newsletter / MLC Marketing Services. — No.14 (Mar. 1978)-. — Bletchley (PO Box 44, Queensway House, Bletchley MK2 2EF) : Meat and Livestock Commission, 1978-. — v. ; 30cm
Irregular. — Continues: MLC marketing newsletter. — Numbering irregular. — Description based on: No.18 (Dec.1978)
ISSN 0263-3310 = MLC newsletter. Marketing Services : Unpriced B82-28132

380.1'45674'093 — Ancient Mediterranean region. Timber trades
Meiggs, Russell. Trees and timber in the ancient Mediterranean world. — Oxford : Clarendon Press, Nov.1982. — [456]p
ISBN 0-19-814840-2 : £25.00 : CIP entry B82-26883

380.1'45674'0941464 — Scotland. Strathclyde Region. Ayr. Timber trades: Adam Wilson & Sons, *to 1979*
Adam Wilson & Sons. Adam Wilson & Sons : the history of a firm of timber merchants : founded 1856. — Ayr (Heathfield Rd., Ayr) : Adam Wilson & Sons Ltd, 1980. — 40p : ill,ports ; 21cm
Unpriced (pbk) B82-29241

380.1'45677'009533 — Yemen. Textile trades, *to 1970*
Baldry, John. Textiles in Yemen : historical references to trade and commerce in textiles in Yemen from antiquity to modern times / John Baldry. — London : British Museum, 1982. — 107p : ill,3maps ; 30cm. — (Occasional paper, ISSN 0142-4815 ; no.27)
ISBN 0-86159-027-9 (pbk) : Unpriced B82-31671

380.1'4567731'0924 — London. Wool trades. Heritage, Thomas, *1532-1540 — Accounts*
Alcock, N. W.. Warwickshire grazier and London skinner 1532-1555 : the account book of Peter Temple and Thomas Heritage / N.W. Alcock. — London : Published for the British Academy by the Oxford University Press, c1981. — xix.281p,6p of plates : ill,maps,facsims,1port,geneal.tables ; 26cm. — (Records of social and economic history. New series ; 4)
Bibliography: pxix. — Includes index
ISBN 0-19-726008-x : £29.00 : CIP rev.
Primary classification 338.1'3 B81-31448

380.1′45745′02341 — Great Britain. Antiques trades — *Career guides*
Johnson, Keith, *19---*. Careers in antiques and auctioneering. — London : Kogan Page, Feb.1983. — [100]p. — (Kogan Page careers series)
ISBN 0-85038-646-2 (cased) : £6.95 : CIP entry
ISBN 0-85038-647-0 (pbk) : £2.50
Also classified at 381′.1 B82-39282

380.1′45′745102541 — Great Britain. Antiques trades - *Directories*
Guide to the antique shops of Britain. — 1982. — Woodbridge : Antique Collectors′ Club, June 1981. — [1000]p
ISBN 0-907462-03-0 : £5.95 : CIP entry B81-16385

380.1′457451′0924 — Great Britain. Rural regions. Antiques trades — *Personal observations*
Austen, Peter. The country antique dealer : with a gazetteer of market towns and auctioneers in the United Kingdom / Peter Austen ; illustrations by Leslie Atkinson. — Newton Abbot : David & Charles, c1982. — 186p : ill ; 23cm
ISBN 0-7153-8223-3 : £6.95 : CIP rev. B81-33815

380.1′457451′09422 — Southern England. Antiques trades — *Serials*
LAPADA views. — Vol.2, no.2 (1979)-. — London (112 Brompton Rd, SW3 1JJ) : London and Provincial Antique Dealers′ Association, 1979-. — v. : ill ; 30cm
Quarterly. — Continues: News from LAPADA. — Description based on: Vol.3, no.8 (Summer 1982)
ISSN 0263-919X = LAPADA views : Unpriced B82-38500

380.5 — TRANSPORT

380.5 — Energy. Consumption by transport services — *For children*
Hamer, Mick. Transport / Mick Hamer. — London : Watts, 1982. — 38p : col.ill,col.maps,1port ; 30cm. — (Energy)
Includes index
ISBN 0-85166-942-5 : £3.99 B82-25327

380.5 — Transport. Choice. Mathematical models
New horizons in travel-behavior research / edited by Peter R. Stopher, Arnim H. Meyburg, Werner Brög. — Lexington, Mass. : Lexington Books, c1981 ; [Aldershot] : Gower [distributor], 1982. — xxxviii,744p : ill ; 24cm
Conference papers
ISBN 0-669-02850-9 : £29-50 B82-21161

380.5 — Transport — *Conference proceedings*
World Confernce on Transport Research *(1980 : London)*. Transport research for social and economic progress : proceedings of the World Conference on Transport Research, London 14-17 April 1980 / ... supported by the United Kingdom Government and held under the patronage of the OECD (Organisation for Economic Co-operation and Development) and the ECMT (European Conference of Ministers of Transport) ; edited by J. Stuart Yerrell. — Aldershot : Gower, c1981. — 4v.(xx,2726p) : ill,maps,1facsim ; 24cm
Includes twenty three chapters in French. — Includes bibliographies
ISBN 0-566-00504-2 : Unpriced : CIP rev.
ISBN 0-566-00443-7 (v.1) : Unpriced
ISBN 0-566-00444-5 (v.2) : Unpriced
ISBN 0-566-00445-3 (v.3) : Unpriced
ISBN 0-566-00446-1 (v.4) : Unpriced B82-18028

380.5 — Transport — *For children*
Welsh, Robert. The colour book of transport / Robert Welsh. — [London] : Octopus, [1982]. — 128p : col.ill ; 29cm
Ill on lining papers
ISBN 0-7064-1728-3 : £2.95 B82-24561

380.5 — Transport — *For schools*
Hayes, John. Transport. — London : Hutchinson Education, Nov.1982. — [32]p. — (Down to earth)
ISBN 0-09-149151-7 (pbk) : £0.80 : CIP entry B82-26901

Price, Nigel. Transport. — London : Edward Arnold, Nov.1982. — [64]p. — (Foundation geography)
ISBN 0-7131-0663-8 (pbk) : £2.00 : CIP entry B82-27953

Webber, Peter. Transport and movement / Peter Webber. — Basingstoke : Macmillan Education, 1982. — 84p : ill,maps,plans ; 25cm. — (Geography in focus)
Includes index
ISBN 0-333-28980-3 (pbk) : Unpriced : CIP rev. B82-03800

380.5 — Transport. Printed ephemera — *Collectors′ guides*
Anderson, Janice. Ephemera of travel and transport / Janice Anderson and Edmund Swinglehurst ; with an introduction by Maurice Rickards, founder of the Ephemera Society. — London : New Cavendish, 1981. — 96p : ill (some col.),facsims ; 29cm
Bibliography: p94. — Includes index
ISBN 0-904568-27-x : £7.95 B82-17564

380.5 — Transport services. Environmental aspects
Cohn, Louis F.. Environmental analysis of transportation systems / Louis F. Cohn, Gary R. McVoy. — New York ; Chichester : Wiley, c1982. — xii,374p : ill ; 29cm
Includes bibliographies and index
ISBN 0-471-08098-5 : £35.00 B82-30692

380.5′068 — Europe. Transport services. Management. Projects
May, Adolf D.. Transportation system management : TSM-type projects in six selected European countries / by Adolf D. May and Dick Westland. — London (29 Newman St., WIP 3PE) : Printerhall, 1979. — 30p ; 30cm
′First published as a supplement to the February 1979 issue of Traffic Engineering and Control′. — Bibliography: p25-30
Unpriced (pbk) B82-27482

380.5′068′4 — Transport services. Security measures — *Serials*
Port police international : aviation, marine and railroad security : the journal of the International Association of Airport and Seaport Police. — Jan. 1980-May 1980. — Downham Market (11 London Rd, Downham Market, Norfolk PE38 9BX) : Ryston Publications, 1980-1980. — 3v. : ill,ports ; 30cm
Six issues yearly. — Three issues only published. — Description based on: Mar. 1980
ISSN 0143-8077 = Port police international : £10.00 per year B82-09069

380.5′09′04 — Transport, *1900-1980* — *Interviews*
Transport pioneers of the twentieth century : interviews recorded by the Transport Trust / conducted by Sir Peter Allen ; and edited by Graham Robson. — Cambridge : Published for the trust by Stephens, 1981. — xiv,240p : ill,facsims,ports ; 30cm
Limited ed. of 1000 copies. — In slipcase
ISBN 0-85059-542-8 : Unpriced : CIP rev. B81-20131

380.5′0941 — Great Britain. Transport
Maltby, D.. Transport in the United Kingdom / D. Maltby, H.P. White. — London : Macmillan, 1982. — xii,207p : ill,maps ; 25cm
Includes index
ISBN 0-333-27826-7 (cased) : Unpriced
ISBN 0-333-27827-5 (pbk) : Unpriced B82-39995

380.5′0941 — Great Britain. Transport, *1600-1979* — *For schools*
Burrell, R. E. C.. Travel and transport / R.E.C. Burrell. — Exeter : Wheaton. — (The Making of the Industrial Revolution series ; bk.3)
1: Transport by muscle power. — 1980. — 106p : ill,maps,1plan,ports ; 21cm
ISBN 0-08-020576-3 (pbk) : £2.20 B82-13324

Burrell, R. E. C.. Travel and transport / R.E.C. Burrell. — Exeter : Wheaton. — (The Making of the Industrial Revolution series ; bk.4)
2: Transport by machine before 1914. — 1980. — 117p : ill,maps,1facsim,ports ; 21cm
ISBN 0-08-021398-7 (pbk) : £2.90 B82-13325

380.5′09411 — Scotland. Transport — *Liberal Party viewpoints*
Watson, Graham, *1956-*. Transport policy in Scotland : time for a rethink / by Graham Watson. — Edinburgh (2 Atholl Place, Edinburgh) : Printout Publications, [1980]. — 15p ; 21cm
Unpriced (pbk) B82-16529

380.5′09411′4 — Scotland. Western Isles Islands Area. Transport services — *Proposals*
Western Isles. *Islands Council*. Transport policies and programmes / Comhairle Nan Eilean. — [Stornaway] ([Sandwick Rd., Stornaway PA87 2BW]) : [Comhairle Nan Eilean], 1976. — 34p : ill ; 30cm
Unpriced (spiral) B82-14343

380.5′09412′5 — Scotland. Tayside Region. Transport — *Proposals* — *Serials*
Tayside. *Regional Council*. Transport policies and programmes / Tayside Regional Council. — 1976-81-. — [Dundee] ([28 Crichton St., Dundee DD1 3RA]) : The Council, [1981]-. — v. : maps ; 30cm
Annual. — Description based on: 1977-82 issue
ISSN 0264-035X = Transport policies and programmes - Tayside Regional Council : Unpriced B82-38509

380.5′09413 — Scotland. Central Lowlands. Transport, *ca 1700-1980* — *Readings from contemporary sources* — *For schools*
Transport 18th-20th centuries. — [Stirling] ([c/o D.M. Dickie, Local Studies Adviser, Viewforth, Stirling FK8 2ET]) : [Central Regional Educational Committee], [c1980]. — 88p,[10] leaves of plates : ill,1map,1facsim ; 21cm. — (Historical sources for Central Scotland ; 4)
Cover title. — Researched and edited by Lynda Wright. — Bibliography: p82-84
Unpriced (pbk) B82-03286

380.5′09414′7 — Scotland. Dumfries and Galloway Region. Transport — *Proposals*
Dumfries and Galloway. *Regional Council*. Dumfries and Galloway Regional Council transport policies and programme 1981-86. — Dumfries (Council Offices, English St., Dumfries DG1 2DD) : Dumfries and Galloway Regional Council, [1981]. — 29p ; 30cm
Unpriced (pbk) B82-03643

380.5′09422′9 — Berkshire. Public transport services — *Proposals* — *Serials*
Berkshire. *County Council*. Public transport plan / Royal County of Berkshire. — 1979-1980-. — [Reading] ([24 Westcote Rd., Reading, Berks.]) : The Council, 1979-. — v. : ill,plans ; 30cm
Annual. — Description based on: 1982-1983 issue
ISSN 0263-7634 = Public transport plan - Royal County of Berkshire : Unpriced B82-32170

380.5′09423′38 — Dorset. Bournemouth. Transport services — *History*
Ransom, W. P.. The story of Bournemouth Corporation transport / by W.P. Ransom. — Bournemouth (The Teachers′ Centre, 40 Lowther Rd., Bournemouth) : Bournemouth Local Studies Publications
Pt.1: The trams. — 1982. — 27p : ill ; 21cm
ISBN 0-906287-40-5 (pbk) : £0.60 B82-29247

380.5′09423′5 — Devon. Transport. Policies of Devon. *County Council.* **Implementation** — *Serials*
Devon. *County Engineer′s Department.* Transportation : topic report / County Engineer′s Department. — 1981-. — Exeter (County Hall, Topsham Rd., Exeter EX2 4QW) : Devon County Council, County Engineer′s Department, 1981-. — v. : ill,maps (chiefly col.) ; 30cm
Annual
ISSN 0261-2461 = Transportation topic report : £0.40 B82-10355

380.5′09423′9 — Avon. Transport — *Proposals*
Avon. *County Council*. Transport policies and programme : submission for 1980/81. — [Bristol] : Avon County Council, [1980?]. — 1v (various pagings) : ill(some col.),maps(some col.) ; 30cm
Cover title
ISBN 0-86063-072-2 (pbk) : Unpriced B82-40470

380.5'09425'11 — England. South Pennines. Transport, *to ca 1980*

Breakell, Bill. Pennine ways / [written and designed by Bill Breakell]. — Hebden Bridge : Pennine Heritage Network, c1982. — 1folded sheet : ill(some col.),3maps ; 59x21cm folded to 21x15cm
ISBN 0-907613-08-x : Unpriced B82-37734

380.5'09425'81 — Hertfordshire. North Hertfordshire *(District).* **Transport** — *For environment planning*

Transport topic study / [North Hertfordshire District Council]. — [Letchworth] ([Council Offices, Gernon Rd., Letchworth, Herts. SG6 3JF]) : [The Council], [1981?]. — 64p,[4]folded leaves of plates : maps ; 30cm. — (North Hertfordshire district plan. Topic studies)
£0.75 (pbk) B82-11578

380.5'09426'752 — Essex. Chelmsford. Transport — *For environment planning*

Transportation topic report : Chelmsford town centre district plan. — Chelmsford : Chelmsford Borough Council, 1981. — 37p,10leaves of plates(some folded) : maps ; 30cm
Unpriced (pbk) B82-08732

380.5'09427'3 — Greater Manchester *(Metropolitan County).* **Transport services,** *1900-1950*

Joyce, James, *1927-.* Roads & rails of Manchester 1900-1950 / J. Joyce. — London : Ian Allan, 1982. — 143p : ill,maps ; 24cm
Maps on lining papers. — Bibliography: p140. — Includes index
ISBN 0-7110-1174-5 : £7.95 B82-30638

380.5'09428'3 — Humberside. Public transport services — *Proposals*

Humberside. *County Council.* Public transport plan, 1982-1987 / Humberside County Council. — [Beverley] ([Manor Rd., Beverley HU17 7BX]) : Director of Planning, [1982]. — 13p,2folded leaves of plates : 2maps ; 30cm
Cover title
£2.00 (spiral) B82-34037

Public transport plan 1981-1986 / Humberside County Council. — [Beverley] ([Manor Rd., Beverley, N. Humberside, HU17 7BX]) : [The Council], 1981. — 26p,[4]leaves of plates(some col.) : maps(some col.) ; 30cm
Unpriced (spiral) B82-15229

380.5'094299 — Gwent. Transport services: Monmouthshire Railway and Canal Company, *to 1870*

Byles, Aubrey. The history of the Monmouthshire Railway and Canal Company. — Cwmbran (The Red Door, 13 Victoria St., Old Cwmbran, Cwmbran, Gwent NP44 3JS) : Village Publishing, May 1982. — [132]p
ISBN 0-946043-00-0 (pbk) : £2.95 : CIP entry B82-19295

380.5'22 — England. Public transport services. Planning. Participation of public — *Manuals*

Winfield, Richard. Public transport plans and all that / [written and designed by Richard Winfield]. — Cardiff (Oxford House, Hills Street, Cardiff CF1 2DR) : Welsh Consumer Council, [1981]. — 36p,[8]p of plates : forms ; 21cm
Unpriced (pbk) B82-09098

380.5'22'0880816 — Transport services for handicapped persons — *Serials*

Specialized transportation planning and practice : an international journal. — Vol.1, no.1 (1982)-. — New York ; London : Gordon and Breach, 1982-. — v. : ill ; 23cm
Quarterly
Unpriced B82-27643

380.5'22'0880816 — Transport services for physically handicapped persons

Lightfoot, Graham. "Getting there" : some recent developments in door-to-door transport for people with disabilities / [written by Graham Lightfoot]. — Manchester : ADAPT, 1982. — 24p : ill ; 30cm
Cover title. — Text, ill on inside covers. — Bibliography: p22
ISBN 0-946073-00-7 (pbk) : £0.50 B82-29489

380.5'22'0941 — Great Britain. Public transport

Public transport : ... survey carried out for the National Consumer Council / by Research Services Limited ; ... written ... by Jenny Potter. — London : National Consumer Council, c1982. — 58p : ill ; 30cm
ISBN 0-905653-53-x (unbound) : £1.00 B82-25040

380.5'22'09422792 — Hampshire. Portsmouth. Passenger transport services, *1840-1977*

Milton, A. F.. Portsmouth city transport 1840-1977 / A.F. Milton & L.T.A. Bern. — Rev. ed. — Portsmouth (45 Great Copse Drive, Leigh Park, Portsmouth PO9 5BZ) : A.F. Milton, [1979?]. — iv,140p : ill,maps ; 30cm
Previous ed.: 1977?. — Includes index
£1.65 (pbk) B82-11413

380.5'24 — International freight transport. Freight conferences, *to ca 1900*

Moore, K. A.. The early history of freight conferences : background and main developments until around 1900 / by K.A. Moore ; foreword by L.G. Hudson. — London : Trustees of the National Maritime Museum, 1981. — ix,73p : ill,facsims,ports ; 30cm. — (Maritime monographs and reports, ISSN 0307-8590 ; no.51)
ISBN 0-905555-58-9 (pbk) : Unpriced B82-11380

380.5'24'0942252 — East Sussex. Rye. Freight transport services: John Jempson & Son

Barker, Theo. The transport contractors of Rye : John Jempson and Son. — London : Athlone Press, Sept.1982. — [120]p
ISBN 0-485-11234-5 : £7.95 : CIP entry B82-19534

380.5'3 — United States. Rural regions. Transport services for poor persons

Maggied, Hal S.. Transportation for the poor : research in rural mobility / Hal S. Maggied ; foreword by William E. Bivens, III ; afterword by John S. Hassell, Jr. — Boston, [Mass.] ; London : Kluwer-Nijhoff, c1982. — xxvi,178p : ill,maps ; 24cm. — (Studies in applied regional science)
Bibliography: p149-165. — Includes index
ISBN 0-89838-081-2 : Unpriced B82-40161

380.5'9 — England. Public transport. Expenditure of local authorities — *Statistics* — *Serials*

Highways and transportation statistics. Estimates / CIPFA Statistical Information Service. — 1981-82-. — London : Chartered Institute of Public Finance and Accountancy, 1981-. — v. ; 30cm
Annual. — Continues: Highways and transportation statistics. Based on estimates
ISSN 0260-9894 = Highways and transportation statistics. Estimates : £6.00 B82-11133

380.5'9 — Transport. Economic aspects

Button, K. J.. Transport economics / K.J. Button. — London : Heinemann, 1982. — vii,295p : ill ; 23cm
Includes bibliographies and index
ISBN 0-435-84092-4 (cased) : £14.50 : CIP rev.
ISBN 0-435-84093-2 (pbk) : Unpriced B82-04069

380.5'9 — Transport. Effects of shortages of fuel resources — *Forecasts* — *Conference proceedings*

Transport and energy : proceedings of a conference held in London on 17-18 November 1980 and organized by the Institution of Civil Engineers in association with the Chartered Institute of Transport ... [et al.]. — London : Telford for the Institution, 1981. — 126p : ill ; 31cm
ISBN 0-7277-0125-8 : £14.00 B82-15389

380.5'9'0941 — Great Britain. Public transport. Economic aspects

Nash, C. A.. Economics of public transport / C.A. Nash. — London : Longman, 1982. — x,194p : ill ; 24cm. — (Modern economics)
Bibliography: p185-191. — Includes index
ISBN 0-582-44631-7 (pbk) : £6.95 : CIP rev. B81-37600

381 — DOMESTIC TRADE

381 — Great Britain. Distributive trades. Small firms. Applications of microelectronic devices

Computers in store : a DITB guide to new technology. — Manchester : Distributive Industry Training Board, [1981?]. — 32p : ill (some col.) ; 20cm. — (A DisTec aid)
Cover title. — Text on inside cover
ISBN 0-903416-26-3 (pbk) : Unpriced B82-17315

381 — Soviet Union. Black markets

Simis, Konstantin M.. USSR : secrets of a corrupt society. — London : Dent, Sept.1982. — [288]p
ISBN 0-460-04581-4 : £9.50 : CIP entry B82-20189

381'.068'4 — Distributive trades. Information processing systems

Processing information. — Manchester (MacLaren House, Talbot Rd., Manchester M32 0FP) : Distributive Industry Training Board, [1981?]. — 12leaves : 1ill ; 22cm. — (Clerical work control aids)
Cover title
Unpriced (spiral) B82-11173

381'.094 — European Community countries. Distributive trades, *1961-1981*

Dawson, John A.. Commercial distribution in Europe / John A. Dawson. — London : Croom Helm, c1982. — 244p : ill,maps ; 23cm
Bibliography: p217-238. — Includes index
ISBN 0-7099-0812-1 : £13.95 : CIP rev. B82-04465

381'.0941 — Great Britain. Distributive trades. Effects of technological change

Technology : the issues for the distributive trades / a report by the Working Party on Technology ; [prepared for publication by the National Economic Development Office on behalf of the Distributive Trades EDC]. — [London] : [Distributive Trades EDC, 1982. — 54p ; 30cm
ISBN 0-7292-0506-1 (pbk) : £3.00 B82-30489

381'.1 — Auctioneering firms — *Practical information* — *Directories*

Leab, Daniel J.. The auction companion / Daniel J. Leab and Katharine Kyes Leab. — London : Macmillan, 1981. — ix,490p ; 22cm
Includes index
ISBN 0-333-27059-2 : £9.95 B82-06641

381'.1 — Avon. Bristol. Cribbs Causeway. Hypermarkets: Carrefour Hypermarket *(Bristol).* **Use**

Carrefour : a study of a hypermarket and its effects. — Bristol : Avon County Planning Department, 1980. — [126]p : ill,maps ; 30cm
ISBN 0-86063-101-x (spiral) : £2.50 B82-35601

381'.1 — Great Britain. Auctioneers — *Career guides*

Johnson, Keith, *19---.* Careers in antiques and auctioneering. — London : Kogan Page, Feb.1983. — [100]p. — (Kogan Page careers series)
ISBN 0-85038-646-2 (cased) : £6.95 : CIP entry
ISBN 0-85038-647-0 (pbk) : £2.50
Primary classification 380.1'45745'02341 B82-39282

381'.1 — Great Britain. Cash and carry depots — *Statistics*

Cash and carry : an industry sector analysis. — 2nd ed. — London : ICC Business Ratios, c1981. — [70]p : ill ; 30cm. — (ICC Business Ratio report)
ISBN 0-86261-052-4 (pbk) : £80.00 B82-36651

381'.1 — Great Britain. Retail warehouses. Planning. Proposals. Inquiry reports

Gibbs, Anne. An analysis of retail warehouse planning inquiries / Anne Gibbs. — Reading : Unit for Retail Planning Information Limited, 1981. — 122p : 1ill ; 30cm. — (URPI report. U ; 22)
Unpriced (pbk) B82-09923

381′.1 — Great Britain. Supermarkets — *Statistics*
Supermarkets and superstores / industry commentary by Michael Goldman. — London : Jordan & Sons (Surveys), c1981. — xviii,70p ; 30cm
ISBN 0-85938-155-2 (pbk) : Unpriced B82-08532

381′.1 — Hampshire. Bedhampton. Hypermarkets: Havant Hypermarket. Use
Hallsworth, A. G.. Trading patterns of a free-standing hypermarket : Havant hypermarket / A.G. Hallsworth. — Portsmouth (Department of Geography, Lion Terrace, Portsmouth PO1 3HE) : Portsmouth Polytechnic, [1981?]. — 50leaves : ill,maps,1plan,1form ; 30cm
Unpriced (spiral) B82-08065

381′.1 — Hampshire. Waterlooville. Superstores: ASDA *(Superstore : Waterlooville).* **Use**
Hallsworth, A. G.. Trading patterns of a district centre superstore : ASDA Waterlooville / A.G. Hallsworth. — Portsmouth (Department of Geography, Lion Terrace, Portsmouth PO1 3HE) : Portsmouth Polytechnic, [1981?]. — 50leaves : ill,maps,1plan,1form ; 30cm
Unpriced (spiral) B82-08066

381′.1 — Shopping — *For children*
Garland, Sarah. Going shopping / Sarah Garland. — London : Bodley Head, 1982. — [30]p : col.ill ; 19cm
ISBN 0-370-30446-2 : £3.50 : CIP rev. B82-09288

381′.1′0212 — Great Britain. Retail trades. Census data. Census of Distribution 1971 *compared with* **Retailing Inquiry 1976**
Some characteristic differences between the retailing inquiry 1976 and the census of distribution for 1971 / [Business Statistics Office]. — Newport (Cardiff Rd., Newport, Gwent, NP1 1XG) : The Office, 1979. — 8p ; 21x30cm
Unpriced (unbound) B82-40956

381′.1′02541 — Great Britain. Department stores — *Directories*
Department stores. — Great Missenden : Data Research Group, [1982]. — 49leaves ; 30cm
Cover title
ISBN 0-86099-355-8 (pbk) : Unpriced B82-24684

381′.1′068 — Shopping centres. Management
Martin, P. G.. Shopping centre management. — London : Spon, Nov.1982. — [200]p
ISBN 0-419-11870-5 : £18.00 : CIP entry B82-28252

381′.1′0722 — Shopping areas. Visits by public. Mathematical models
Crouchley, R.. A general heterogeneous binary Markov model with an application to shopping behaviour / by R. Crouchley, A.R. Pickles, and R.B. Davies. — Cardiff (King Edward VII Ave., Cardiff CF1 3NU) : Dept. of Town Planning, University of Wales Institute of Science and Technology, 1981. — 16p ; 30cm. — (Papers in planning research ; 38)
Bibliography: p10-11
Unpriced (pbk) B82-26833

Crouchley, R.. State dependency and the market place / by R. Crouchley, A.R. Pickles and R.B. Davies. — Cardiff (King Edward VII Ave., Cardiff CF1 3NU) : Dept. of Town Planning, University of Wales Institute of Science and Technology, 1981. — i,18p ; 30cm. — (Papers in planning research ; 37)
Bibliography: p16
Unpriced (pbk) B82-26834

381′.1′0724 — Local shopping facilities. Effects of hypermarkets. Simulations — *For environment planning*
Guy, Clifford M.. The use of models and simulations methods in hypermarket impact studies / by Clifford M. Guy. — Cardiff (King Edward VII Av, Cardiff, CF1 3NU, Wales) : Dept. of Town Planning, University of Wales, Institute of Science and Technology, 1981. — ii,36p ; 30cm. — (Papers in planning research ; 27)
Bibliography: p31-34
Unpriced (pbk) B82-25638

381′.1′0941 — Great Britain. Department stores — *Statistics*
Goldman, Michael. British department stores / Market Overview by Michael Goldman. — London : Jordan & Sons (Surveys), c1978. — xi,66p ; 30cm. — (A Jordan survey)
£30.00 (pbk) B82-22193

381′.1′0941 — Great Britain. Retail trades, *1850-1914*
Fraser, W. Hamish. The coming of the mass market 1850-1914 / Wittamish Fraser. — London : Macmillan, 1981. — x,268p,16p of plates : ill,1facsim ; 23cm
Bibliography: p259-260. — Includes index
ISBN 0-333-31033-0 (cased) : Unpriced
ISBN 0-333-31034-9 (pbk) : Unpriced
Primary classification 339.4′7′0941 B82-14866

381′.1′0941 — Great Britain. Retail trades — *Forecasts*
Manufacturing and retailing in the 80′s : a zero sum game : a one day seminar and exclusive report Thursday 13 May 1982, Centrepoint, London / the Henley Centre for Forecasting. — London : Food Manufacturers′ Federation in association with Nielsen Marketing Research, [1982]. — viii,437p,1leaf of plates : ill,forms ; 30cm
Bibliography: p432-437
ISBN 0-9503970-9-1 (pbk) : Unpriced B82-31736

381′.1′0941 — Great Britain. Retail trades — *Serials*
Better business : official journal of the National Chamber of Trade. — Vol.1, issue 1 (Oct. 1981)-. — Reading (19 Blagrave St., Reading, [Berks.]) : Reading Newspaper Co., 1981-. — v. : ill ; 30cm
Monthly. — Continues: Intercom (Henley-on-Thames)
ISSN 0262-2513 = Better business : Free to Chamber members B82-05211

Goad directory of retailers′ requirements. — Summer 1982-. — Old Hatfield (Salisbury Sq., Old Hatfield, Herts. AL9 5BE) : Chas E. Goad, 1982-. — v. : ill(some col.),maps(some col.) ; 30cm
Three issues yearly
ISSN 0261-6874 = Goad directory of retailers′ requirements : Unpriced B82-32363

Large mixed retailing : the magazine of non-foods management. — Pilot issue (May 1982)-. — Tonbridge : Benn Publications, 1982-. — v. : ill(some col.),ports(some col.) ; 30cm
Monthly
ISSN 0263-4228 = Large mixed retailing : Unpriced B82-38506

381′.1′0941 — Great Britain. Retail trades — *Statistics*
Structure of retailing in the UK. — Brighton : Retail Management Development Programme, [1982?]. — 144p : ill ; 30cm. — (The Retail management handbooks ; 1)
ISBN 0-907923-00-3 (pbk) : Unpriced B82-31662

381′.1′0941 — Great Britain. Shopping. Attitudes of consumers
Shopping / ... survey was carried out for the National Consumer Council by Research Services Limited ; This paper was written for us by Barbara Lantin. — London : National Consumer Council, 1982, c1981. — 32p ; 30cm
ISBN 0-905653-40-8 (unbound) : Unpriced B82-17836

381′.1′0941 — Great Britain. Shopping centres — *Serials*
British shopping developments. Supplement. — 1979-. — London (77 Grosvenor St., W1A 2BT) : Hillier Parker May & Rowden, 1980-. — v. : ill ; 30cm
Annual. — Supplement to: British shopping developments
ISSN 0261-0035 = British shopping developments. Supplement : £1.00 B82-29053

381′.1′0941 — Great Britain. Urban regions. Shopping areas, *1880-1980*
Hudson, Kenneth. Behind the High Street / Kenneth Hudson. — London : Bodley Head, 1982. — 48p : ill,facsims ; 26cm
Includes index
ISBN 0-370-30394-6 : £3.95 : CIP rev. B82-03838

381′.1′094131 — Scotland. Central Region. Shopping facilities. Provision — *For environment planning*
Central Region. *Department of Planning.* Central Region interim shopping policy / Central Regional Council, Department of Planning. — [Stirling] ([Viewforth, Stirling FK8 2ET]) : The Council, 1978. — 34p : maps ; 30cm
Bibliography: p32-33
Unpriced (unbound) B82-15461

381′.1′0941312 — Scotland. Central Region. Stirling. Central areas. Retail trades, *ca 1970-1980*
Aitken, C. P.. Retailing change in Stirling town centre : a study of trends through the 1970′s. / C.P. Aitken. — Stirling (12 Clarendon Place, Stirling FK8 2QW) : C.P. Aitken. — 88p,[4]p of plates : maps ; 30cm
£6.00 (pbk) B82-08723

381′.1′094134 — Edinburgh. Shops — *Visitors′ guides*
Shopping in Edinburgh. — Edinburgh : Pastime, [1982]. — 104p : ill,maps ; 22cm
£0.50 (pbk) B82-35959

381′.1′0942 — England. Shops, *1830-1914*
Winstanley, Michael J.. Shops and shopkeepers 1830-1914. — Manchester : Manchester University Press, Feb.1983. — [224]p
ISBN 0-7190-0728-3 : £17.50 : CIP entry B82-39456

381′.1′09421 — London. Shops — *Visitors′ guides*
DuCann. A guide to London′s best shops / DuCann. — London : Virgin in association with London Transport, c1982. — 198p : ill,maps,1plan ; 20cm
Includes index
ISBN 0-907080-36-7 (pbk) : £1.95 B82-28014

381′.1′0942142 — London. Camden *(London Borough).* **Shopping facilities** — *Proposals* — *For environment planning*
A Plan for Camden : London Borough of Camden District Plan : proposals for the alteration of the written statement : policies for shopping. — [London] ([Camden Town Hall, Euston Rd., WC1H 8EQ]) : [Department of Planning and Communications], 1982. — 24p ; 30cm
Unpriced (unbound) B82-34491

381′.1′0942256 — East Sussex. Brighton. Shops, *1900-1930*
Griffiths, Neil. Shops book : Brighton 1900-1930 : shopkeepers and street traders in East Brighton, 1900-1930 / by Neil Griffiths. — Brighton (13 West Drive, Brighton BN2 2GD) : QueenSpark, [1981?]. — 71p : ill,2maps,ports ; 22cm. — (QueenSpark book ; 6)
£0.30 (pbk) B82-05686

381.1′09422′6 — West Sussex. Shopping facilities — *Proposals*
West Sussex. *County Council.* Shopping : interim policies. — Chichester : West Sussex County Council, 1982. — 9p ; 30cm
Cover title
ISBN 0-86260-033-2 (spiral) : Unpriced B82-28086

381′.1′094226 — West Sussex. Shopping — *For environmental planning*
Shopping study : technical report. — Chichester : West Sussex County Council, 1981. — vi,143p,[16]leaves of plates : ill,maps,plans ; 30cm
Cover title
ISBN 0-86260-026-x (spiral) : Unpriced B82-12660

381′.1′094227 — South Hampshire. Shopping. Policies of Hampshire. *County Council*
Hampshire. *County Council.* Shopping policies in South Hampshire / adopted by the County Council, December 1978. — [Winchester] ([The Castle, Winchester]) : [Hampshire County Council], [1978]. — 79p : 1ill,maps ; 30cm. — (Strategic planning paper / Hampshire County Council ; no.5)
£2.00 plus postage (pbk) B82-38208

381′.1′0942338 — Dorset. Bournemouth. Department stores: J. E. Beale Ltd, *to 1914*
J.E. Beale and the growth of Bournemouth. — Bournemouth (40 Lowther Rd., Bournemouth) : Bournemouth Local Studies Publications
Pt.3: Business expansion 1905-1914 / by J.F. Parsons. — 1982. — 62p : ill,facsims,1plan ; 21cm
ISBN 0-906287-34-0 (pbk) : £0.70 B82-29238

381′.1′0942581 — Hertfordshire. North Hertfordshire *(District).* **Shopping facilities** — *For environment planning*
Shopping topic study / [North Hertfordshire District Council]. — [Letchworth] ([Council Offices, Gernon Rd., Letchworth, Herts. SG6 3JF]) : [The Council], 1978. — 27p : 1col.map ; 30cm. — (North Hertfordshire district plan. Topic studies)
£0.50 (pbk) B82-11581

381′.1′09426752 — Essex. Chelmsford. Shopping facilities. Provision — *For environment planning*
Shopping topic report : Chelmsford town centre district plan. — Chelmsford : Chelmsford Borough Council, 1980. — 39p,7leaves of plates(some folded) : maps ; 30cm
Unpriced (pbk) B82-08726

381′.1′094287 — Tyne and Wear *(Metropolitan County).* **Retail bulky goods trades**
Bulky goods retailing in Tyne and Wear. — Newcastle upon Tyne (Sandyford House, Newcastle upon Tyne, NE2 1ED) : Tyne and Wear County Council, 1981. — 118p : ill,forms,maps ; 30cm
£10.00 (pbk) B82-39048

381.1′0944′36 — France. Paris. Department stores: Bon Marché, *to 1920*
Miller, Michael B.. The Bon Marché : bourgeois culture and the department store, 1869-1920 / Michael B. Miller. — London : Allen & Unwin, 1981. — xii,266p,[16]p of plates : ill,facsims ; 23cm
Bibliography: p245-257. — Includes index
ISBN 0-04-330316-1 : Unpriced : CIP rev.
B81-20140

381′.1′0973 — United States. Department stores. Economic aspects
The **Retail** revolution : market transformation, investment, and labor in the modern department store / Barry Bluestone ... [et al.]. — Boston, Mass. : Auburn House ; London : distributed by Eurospan, c1981. — xvi,160p : ill ; 24cm
Bibliography: p152-154. — Includes index
ISBN 0-86569-052-9 : £14.95 B82-08676

381′.12′0941 — Great Britain. Multiple shops: Marks & Spencer *(Firm)* — *For children*
Kent, Graeme. Marks & Spencer / Graeme Kent. — Hove : Wayland, 1982. — 64p : ill,1map,1coat of arms,ports ; 21cm. — (In the High Street)
Bibliography: p62. — Includes index
ISBN 0-85340-932-3 : £4.25 B82-28025

381′.14′0941 — Great Britain. Mail-order firms — *Forecasts*
The **Future** of mail order in Britain : a study / by Economists Advisory Group Ltd for the Post Office ; this report was prepared by Graham Bannock with the collaboration of John Arnold ... [et al.]. — London (54b Tottenham Court Rd., W1P 9RE) : The Group, 1979. — 98p ; 30cm
Unpriced (spiral) B82-35056

381′.18′09421 — London. Street markets — *Visitors' guides*
Perlmutter, Kevin. London street markets. — London : Wildwood House, Sept.1982. — [156]p
ISBN 0-7045-0462-6 (pbk) : £2.95 : CIP entry
B82-19644

381′.18′094267 — Essex. Markets, *to 1981*
Walker, Wendy. Essex markets and fairs / by Wendy Walker. — [Chelmsford] : Essex Record Office, 1981. — 44p : ill,maps,facsims ; 25cm. — (Essex Record Office publication ; no.83)
Bibliography: p44
ISBN 0-900360-59-3 (pbk) : Unpriced
Also classified at 394′.6′094267 B82-12052

381′.18′097274 — Mexico. Oaxaca *(State).* **Markets. Social aspects**
Malinowski, Bronislaw. Malinowski in Mexico : the economics of a Mexican market system / Bronislaw Malinowski and Julio de la Fuente ; edited and with an introduction by Susan Drucker-Brown. — London : Routledge & Kegan Paul, 1982. — xiii,217,14p,24p of plates : ill,maps ; 23cm. — (International library of anthropology)
Bibliography: p203-210. — Includes index
ISBN 0-7100-9197-4 : £12.50 B82-35999

381′.19 — Hungary. Black markets — *Personal observations*
Kenedi, János. Do it yourself : Hungary's hidden economy / János Kenedi. — London : Pluto, 1981. — 128p ; 20cm
Translation of the Hungarian
ISBN 0-86104-344-8 (pbk) : £2.95 B82-20694

381′.3 — Great Britain & United States. Business firms. Relations with consumers
Adamson, Colin, *1944-.* Consumers in business : how business has responded to the consumer interest : some case histories / by Colin Adamson. — London : National Consumer Council, c1982. — 42p ; 30cm
Cover title
ISBN 0-905653-51-3 (pbk) : Unpriced
B82-25042

381′.34′06041 — Great Britain. Consumer protection. Organisations — *Directories*
Consumer congress directory : a directory of organisation in the consumer movement in the UK. — 4th ed. — London : National Consumer Council, 1982. — 55p ; 22cm
Includes index
ISBN 0-905653-52-1 (pbk) : Unpriced
B82-25041

381′.34′0941 — Great Britain. Consumer protection — *For schools*
Stewart, Jean, *1945-.* The careful consumer / Jean Stewart ; illustrated by Dave Farris. — 3rd ed. — London : Heinemann Educational, 1982. — 95p : ill ; 25cm
Previous ed.: 1978. — Bibliography: p92. — Includes index
ISBN 0-435-42282-0 : Unpriced B82-14330

381′.34′0941 — Great Britain. Consumer protection — *Serials*
[Consumer education newsletter *(Cardiff)*].
Consumer education newsletter. — No.1 (1979)-. — Cardiff (8 St. Andrew's Place, Cardiff CF1 3BE) : Welsh Consumer Council, 1979-. — v. : ill ; 30cm
Three issues yearly. — Description based on: No.8 (June 1981)
ISSN 0261-7110 = Consumer education newsletter (Cardiff) : Unpriced B82-09075

381′.34′0941 — Great Britain. Consumer protection — *Welsh texts* — *Serials*
Cylchlythyr addysg defnyddwyr. — Rhif 1 (1979)-. — Caerdydd [Cardiff] (8 St. Andrew's Place, Caerdydd CF1 3BE) : Cyngor Defnyddwyr Cymru, 1979-. — v. : ill ; 30cm
Three issues yearly. — Welsh edition of: Consumer education newsletter (Cardiff). — Description based on: Rhif 8 (Meh. 1981)
ISSN 0261-7129 = Cylchlythyr addysg defnyddwyr : Unpriced B82-09074

381′.34′09411 — Scotland. Rural regions. Consumer protection
Mackay, G. A.. Consumer problems in rural areas / by G.A. Mackay and G. Laing. — [Glasgow] : Scottish Consumer Council, [1982?]. — vi,145p : 1map ; 21cm
ISBN 0-907067-10-7 (pbk) : Unpriced
B82-37684

381′.414′07 — Retail fruit trades. Industrial training
Basic training in retailing fresh produce. — London (308 Seven Sisters Rd., Finsbury Park, N4 2BN) : National Institute of Fresh Produce in association with the Food, Drink and Tobacco Industry Training Board, c1982. — 12p : ill ; 21cm. — (Trade management handbook ; no.2)
Cover title. — Text on inside covers
£2.00 (pbk)
Primary classification 381′.415′07 B82-27914

381′.414′0941 — Great Britain. Fruit. Retailing
Retailing fresh fruit, vegetables, potatoes and flowers. — London (308 Seven Sisters Rd., Finsbury Park, N4 2BN) : National Institute of Fresh Produce in association with the Food, Drink and Tobacco Industry Training Board, c1981. — 32p : ill ; 21cm
Cover title. — Text on inside covers
£2.00 (pbk)
Primary classification 381′.415′0941
B82-27916

381′.414′0941 — Great Britain. Fruit. Wholesaling
Wholesaling fresh fruit, vegetables, potatoes and flowers. — London (308 Seven Sisters Rd., Finsbury Park, N4 2BN) : National Institute of Fresh Produce in association with the Food, Drink and Tobacco Industry Training Board, c1980. — 32p : ill ; 21cm
Cover title. — Text on inside covers
£2.00 (pbk)
Primary classification 381′.415′0941
B82-27913

381′.415′02341 — Great Britain. Garden centres — *Career guides*
Working in a garden centre. — [Beckenham] : Agricultural Training Board on behalf of the Joint Working Party on Careers Literature, 1980. — [4]p : ill ; 21cm. — (Careers in horticulture)
Unpriced (unbound) B82-19773

381′.415′028 — Great Britain. Garden supplies trades. Mail-order firms — *Directories*
Montague, Joy. Shopping by post for gardeners / compiled by Joy Montague. — Watford : Exley, 1980. — 253p : ill ; 21cm
Includes index
ISBN 0-905521-33-1 (cased) : Unpriced : CIP rev.
ISBN 0-905521-34-x (pbk) : £3.95 B80-05274

381′.415′07 — Retail vegetable trades. Industrial training
Basic training in retailing fresh produce. — London (308 Seven Sisters Rd., Finsbury Park, N4 2BN) : National Institute of Fresh Produce in association with the Food, Drink and Tobacco Industry Training Board, c1982. — 12p : ill ; 21cm. — (Trade management handbook ; no.2)
Cover title. — Text on inside covers
£2.00 (pbk)
Also classified at 381′.414′07 B82-27914

381′.415′0941 — Great Britain. Vegetables. Retailing
Retailing fresh fruit, vegetables, potatoes and flowers. — London (308 Seven Sisters Rd., Finsbury Park, N4 2BN) : National Institute of Fresh Produce in association with the Food, Drink and Tobacco Industry Training Board, c1981. — 32p : ill ; 21cm
Cover title. — Text on inside covers
£2.00 (pbk)
Also classified at 381′.414′0941 B82-27916

381′.415′0941 — Great Britain. Vegetables. Wholesaling
Wholesaling fresh fruit, vegetables, potatoes and flowers. — London (308 Seven Sisters Rd., Finsbury Park, N4 2BN) : National Institute of Fresh Produce in association with the Food, Drink and Tobacco Industry Training Board, c1980. — 32p : ill ; 21cm
Cover title. — Text on inside covers
£2.00 (pbk)
Also classified at 381′.414′0941 B82-27913

381′.41525′0941 — Great Britain. Retail onion trades. Role of Breton onion-sellers, *1900-1979* — *Welsh texts*

Griffiths, Gwyn. Y Shonis olaf / Gwyn Griffiths. — Llandysul : Gwasg Gomer, 1981. — 185p : ill,1map,ports ; 18cm
Includes some poems in Breton with Welsh translations
ISBN 0-85088-864-6 (pbk) : £2.25 B82-02428

381′.45002 — Bookselling, *1700-1980* — *Conference proceedings*

Sale and distribution of books from 1700. — Oxford (Oxford Polytechnic, Headington, Oxford OX3 OB1) : Oxford Polytechnic Press, Aug.1982. — [165]p. — (Publishing pathways series ; 4)
Conference papers
ISBN 0-902692-27-5 (pbk) : £5.50 : CIP entry B82-17985

381′.45002 — Great Britain. Antiquarian booksellers & second-hand booksellers — *Directories — Serials*

Lewis, Roy Harley. The bookbrowser's guide to secondhand and antiquarian bookshops / Roy Harley Lewis. — 2nd ed. — Newton Abbot : David & Charles, c1982. — 256p ; 23cm
Previous ed.: 1975. — Includes index
ISBN 0-7153-8095-8 : £9.50 : CIP rev. B81-33818

381′.45002 — Great Britain. Specialist booksellers — *Dictionaries*

Marcan, Peter. Directory of specialist bookdealers in the United Kingdom handling mainly new books with appendices listing specialist directories of museums libraries and associations / Peter Marcan. — 2nd ed. — High Wycombe : [P. Marcan], 1982. — x,262p ; 21cm
Previous ed.: 1979. — Includes index
ISBN 0-9504211-3-8 (pbk) : £5.90 B82-31193

381′.45002′068 — Great Britain. Bookselling — *Manuals*

Knightley, M.. Your own bookshop / M. Knightley. — London : Malcolm Stewart, 1980. — 81p ; 25cm. — (Kingfisher business guides)
Includes index
ISBN 0-904132-54-4 (pbk) : £3.90 B82-15236

381′.45002′0942837 — Humberside. Hull. Booksellers, *to 1840*

Chilton, C. W.. Early Hull printers and booksellers : an account of the printing, bookselling and allied trades from their beginnings to 1840 / by C.W. Chilton. — [Kingston-upon-Hull] : Kingston-upon-Hull City Council, 1982. — 274,lxxxiii p ; 30cm
Map on inside cover. — Bibliography: p277-274. — Includes index
ISBN 0-904767-07-8 (spiral) : Unpriced
Also classified at 686.2′09428′37 B82-34756

381′.4562131042 — Great Britain. Retail electric recreation equipment trade — *Serials*

Relay : retailing electric leisure appliances. — Oct. 1981-. — London : Turret Press, 1981-. — v. : ill ; 28cm
Monthly. — Continues: Radio and electrical retailing
ISSN 0262-6357 = Relay : £16.00 per year B82-06169

381′.4562131042′02541 — Great Britain. Retail electric equipment trades — *Directories*

Electrical retailers. — Great Missenden : Data Research Group, [1981]. — 225p ; 30cm
Cover title
ISBN 0-86099-346-9 (pbk) : Unpriced B82-24690

381′.4562131042′02541 — Great Britain. Wholesale electric equipment trades — *Directories*

Electrical wholesalers. — Great Missenden : Data Research Group, [1982]. — 78leaves ; 30cm
Cover title
ISBN 0-86099-347-7 (pbk) : Unpriced B82-24682

381′.4562386′02541 — Great Britain. Ships' chandlers — *Directories*

Shipping. — Great Missenden : Data Research Group, [1982]. — 39,115,67p ; 30cm
Cover title. — Includes index
ISBN 0-86099-350-7 (pbk) : Unpriced
Primary classification 338.7′62382′002541 B82-24688

381′.456292′0922 — Hampshire. Motor vehicle trades: Wadham Brothers Motor Vehicle Distributors. Founders — *Biographies*

Young, A. F.. The founders of Wadham Brothers Motor Vechicle Distributors, Hampshire, 1905 onwards / by A.F. Young. — [Southampton] ([15 Bassett Court, Bassett Ave., Southampton S01 7DR]) : [R.R. Newitt], 1982. — 56p,[2] leaves of plates : ports ; 13x21cm
Unpriced (pbk) B82-25111

381′.456292222 — Great Britain. New cars. Purchase by motorists. Decision making. Evaluation. Applications of expectancy value theory

Towriss, John G.. The new car buyer : the determinants of choice / John G. Towriss. — Cranfield : Centre for Transport Studies, Cranfield Institute of Technology, 1981. — 95p : form ; 30cm. — (CTS report ; no.18)
Bibliography: p93-95
ISBN 0-902937-61-8 (spiral) : Unpriced B82-00815

381′.456292222 — Great Britain. Second-hand cars. Purchase — *Inquiry reports*

Consumer difficulties in the used-car sector : a report and recommendations made by the Director General of Fair Trading under section 2(3) of the Fair Trading Act 1973. — [London] ([Field House, Breams Buildings, EC4A 1PR]) : Office of Fair Trading, 1980. — 27p ; 30cm
Unpriced (pbk) B82-20238

381′.456359′0941 — Great Britain. Floristry — *Serials*

The **Florist's** news. — No.1 (1981)-. — Kingston (120 Lower Ham Rd, Kingston, Surrey) : Florist's News, 1981-. — v. : ill,ports ; 45cm
Three issues yearly. — Description based on: No.3 (Mar./Apr. 1982)
ISSN 0263-6670 = Florist's news : Unpriced B82-28875

381′.456413 — Great Britain. Fresh food trades — *Career guides*

Careers in the fresh produce industry. — London (308 Seven Sisters Rd., Finsbury Park, N4 2BN) : National Institute of Fresh Produce in association with the Food, Drink and Tobacco Industry Training Board, [1981]. — 1folded sheet([6]p) : ill ; 21cm
Unpriced B82-27922

381′.456413′007 — Great Britain. Retail grocery trades. Managers. Training

The **Training** of retail shop managers / [issued by the Food, Drink and Tobacco Industry Training Board]. — Croydon (Leon House, High St., Croydon, CR9 3NT) : [The Board], [1982?]. — 20p : col.ill,forms ; 30cm([4]p 28cm). — (Training recommendations ; no.1)
Cover title. — Text on inside cover
£0.60 (pbk) B82-24290

381′.456413′00941 — Great Britain. Grocery trades, *1970-1980*

The **Grocery** business 1970-1980 / prepared by the IGD Information Unit for the 1980 Annual Convention. — Watford (Letchmore Heath, Watford WD2 8DQ) : Institute of Grocery Distribution, c1980. — 56p : ill ; 30cm
Unpriced (pbk) B82-37304

381′.456413′0094127 — Scotland. Tayside Region. Dundee. Grocery trades, *1800-1950*

Hartwich, Veronica C.. Ale an' a'thing / Veronica C. Hartwich. — [Dundee] : Dundee Museums and Art Galleries, [c1981]. — 32p : ill,facsims,1plan ; 21cm
Bibliography: p32
ISBN 0-900344-47-4 (pbk) : Unpriced
Primary classification 381′.456631′094127 B82-08208

381′.456631′094127 — Scotland. Tayside Region. Dundee. Alcoholic drinks trades, *1800-1950*

Hartwich, Veronica C.. Ale an' a'thing / Veronica C. Hartwich. — [Dundee] : Dundee Museums and Art Galleries, [c1981]. — 32p : ill,facsims,1plan ; 21cm
Bibliography: p32
ISBN 0-900344-47-4 (pbk) : Unpriced
Also classified at 381′.456413′0094127 B82-08208

381′.456649′00941 — Great Britain. Meat trades — *Serials*

Trading outlook for butchers. — Dec. 1981-. — Bletchley (PO Box 44, Queensway House, Bletchley MK2 2EF) : Meat and Livestock Commission, 1981-. — v. : ill ; 30cm
Annual
ISSN 0263-2683 = Trading outlook for butchers : £5.00 B82-28116

381′.4566494 — Scotland. Tay River. Salmon trades. Richardson, John, *1760-1821* — *Biographies*

Haldane, A. R. B.. The Great Fishmonger of the Tay : John Richardson of Perth & Pitfour (1760-1821) / A.R.B. Haldane. — Dundee : Abertay Historical Society, 1981. — 64p : ill,1facsim ; 22cm. — (Abertay Historical Society publication ; no.21)
Unpriced (pbk) B82-05161

381′.4568382′0941 — Great Britain. Retail kitchen equipment trades — *Serials*

Kitchens : incorporating Retail newsletter. — 1978-. — London (30 Old Burlington St., W1X 2AE) : Troup Publications, 1978-. — v. : ill ; 29cm
Monthly. — Absorbed: Retail newsletter, 1980. — Description based on: Sept. 1981
ISSN 0260-1745 = Kitchens : £18.00 per year B82-06173

381′.45687′068 — Great Britain. Retail second-hand clothing trades. Small firms. Organisation — *Manuals*

Maynard, Julian. Your own dress agency : or nearly-new shop / Julian Maynard. — London : Malcolm Stewart, 1982. — 80p : ill,1plan,forms ; 25cm. — (Kingfisher business guides)
Includes index
ISBN 0-904132-57-9 (pbk) : £4.50 B82-17183

382 — FOREIGN TRADE

382 — Foreign trade

Hansson, Göte. Social clauses and international trade. — London : Croom Helm, Sept.1982. — [192]p
ISBN 0-7099-1244-7 : £14.95 : CIP entry B82-20644

Williams, Alex O.. International trade and investment : a managerial approach / Alex O. Williams. — New York ; Chichester : Wiley, c1982. — xvii,461p : ill ; 24cm
Includes index
ISBN 0-471-03293-x : Unpriced B82-38318

382 — Foreign trade. Finance

Whiting, D. P.. Finance of foreign trade / D.P. Whiting. — 5th ed. — Plymouth : Macdonald and Evans, 1981. — 171p : facsims ; 19cm. — (The M & E handbook series)
Previous ed.: 1977. — Includes index
ISBN 0-7121-0638-3 (pbk) : £2.75 B82-04769

Whiting, D. P.. Finance of international trade / D. P. Whiting. — 4th ed. — Plymouth : Macdonald and Evans, 1981. — ix,278p : ill,facsims,forms ; 22cm
Previous ed.: published as Finance of foreign trade and foreign exchange. 1976. — Includes index
ISBN 0-7121-0637-5 (pbk) : £4.95
Primary classification 332.4′5 B82-01913

382 — Nationalised industries. Foreign trade

State trading in international markets : theory and practice of industrialized and developing countries / edited by M.M. Kostecki. — London : Macmillan, 1982. — xv,308p : ill ; 22cm
Bibliography: p295-300. — Includes index
ISBN 0-333-30930-8 : £20.00 B82-20905

382′.09′04 — Foreign trade. Influence of technological innovation, *1945-1973*

Walker, William B.. Industrial innovation and international trading performance / by William B. Walker. — Greenwich, Conn. : Jai ; London : distributed by Jaicon, c1979. — xiv,122p : ill ; 24cm. — (Contemporary studies in economic and financial analysis ; v.15)
Bibliography: p115-118. — Includes index
ISBN 0-89232-083-4 : £18.85 B82-05921

382′.09171′3047 — Western bloc countries. Foreign trade with Eastern Europe. Policies of governments

Woolcock, Stephen. Western politics on East-West trade / Stephen Woolcock. — London : The Royal Institute of International Affairs : Routledge & Kegan Paul, 1982. — 86p ; 22cm. — (Chatham House papers, ISSN 0143-5795 ; 15)
ISBN 0-7100-9314-4 (pbk) : £3.95 : CIP rev.
Also classified at 382′.0947′01713 B82-12833

382′.09172′4 — Developing countries. Foreign trade

Frank, Isaiah. Trade policy issues of interest to the Third World / by Isaiah Frank. — London : Trade Policy Research Centre, 1981. — viii,68p ; 19cm. — (Thames essay, ISSN 0306-6991 ; no.29)
ISBN 0-900842-53-9 (pbk) : £2.00 B82-10727

382′.09172′4 — Developing countries. Industrialisation. Role of foreign trade

Ballance, Robert H.. The international economy and industrial development : the impact of trade and investment on the third world / Robert H. Ballance, Javed A. Ansari, Hans W. Singer. — Brighton : Wheatsheaf, 1982. — 326p : ill ; 23cm
Includes index
ISBN 0-7108-0129-7 : £22.50 : CIP rev.
B82-03116

382′.091821′041 — Caribbean countries. Foreign trade with Great Britain

Trade with the Caribbean / [Department of Trade]. — [London] : Department of Trade, 1981. — ii,23leaves : 1ill,1map ; 30cm
Unpriced (unbound)
Primary classification 382′.0941′01821
B82-40361

382′.0941 — Great Britain. Foreign trade — *Forecasts*

United Kingdom international freight forecasts to 1988 / Economics and Statistics Division, National Ports Council. — 4th ed. — London : National Ports Council, 1980
Previous ed.: published in 1v. as United Kingdom international trade 1980-1985. 1976
Vol.1: Foreign trade, commodities and countries. — 4th ed. — London : National Ports Council, 1980. — viii,250p : 1ill ; 30cm
Previous ed.: published in 1v. as United Kingdom international trade 1980-1985. 1976
ISBN 0-86073-046-8 (pbk) : £75.00
B82-36192

382′.0941 — Great Britain. Foreign trade. Role of foreign language skills — *Conference proceedings*

Does Britain need linguists? : language education and our trading future : papers given at an Export United conference held on May 19 1978 at the Royal Society of Arts under the joint sponsorship of the Society, the British Overseas Trade Board and the University of Surrey. — London (1 Victoria St, SW1H 0ET) : The Board, [1978]. — 57p : ill ; 30cm
£1.50 (pbk) B82-40961

382′.0941 — Great Britain. Seaborne foreign trade. Defence, *1914-1918 & 1939-1945*

Doughty, Martin. Merchant shipping and war. — London : Swift Printers, Aug.1982. — [218]p. — (Royal Historical Society studies in history series ; no.31)
ISBN 0-901050-83-0 : £15.75 : CIP entry
B82-17929

382′.0941′01821 — Great Britain. Foreign trade with Caribbean countries

Trade with the Caribbean / [Department of Trade]. — [London] : Department of Trade, 1981. — ii,23leaves : 1ill,1map ; 30cm
Unpriced (unbound)
Also classified at 382′.091821′041 B82-40361

382′.0941′047 — Great Britain. Foreign trade with Eastern Europe

Hill, Malcolm R.. East-West trade, industrial cooperation and technology transfer. — Aldershot : Gower, Jan.1983. — [236]p
ISBN 0-566-00591-3 : £15.00 : CIP entry
Also classified at 382′.0947′041 B82-32438

382′.0941′0492 — Great Britain. Foreign trade with Netherlands

90 years of Anglo-Dutch trade : special celebration supplement of In Touch / The Netherlands-British Chamber of Commerce ; [editor-in-chief Jim van de Worp]. — [Ashford, Kent] ([P.O. Box 22, Ashford, Kent]) : [The Netherlands-British Chamber of Commerce], [1982]. — 128p : ill,maps,ports ; 30cm
Cover title
Unpriced (pbk)
Also classified at 382′.09492′041 B82-21220

382′.0941′054 — Great Britain. Foreign trade with India *(Republic)*. **Effects of British entry into European Economic Community**

Anwar, S. A.. The European Community and Indo-British trade relations. — Aldershot : Gower, Jan.1983. — [162]p
ISBN 0-566-00574-3 : £12.50 : CIP entry
Primary classification 382′.0954′041
B82-32437

382′.0947′01713 — Eastern Europe. Foreign trade with Western bloc countries. Policies of governments of Western bloc countries

Woolcock, Stephen. Western politics on East-West trade / Stephen Woolcock. — London : The Royal Institute of International Affairs : Routledge & Kegan Paul, 1982. — 86p ; 22cm. — (Chatham House papers, ISSN 0143-5795 ; 15)
ISBN 0-7100-9314-4 (pbk) : £3.95 : CIP rev.
Primary classification 382′.09171′3047
B82-12833

382′.0947′041 — Eastern Europe. Foreign trade with Great Britain

Hill, Malcolm R.. East-West trade, industrial cooperation and technology transfer. — Aldershot : Gower, Jan.1983. — [236]p
ISBN 0-566-00591-3 : £15.00 : CIP entry
Primary classification 382′.0941′047
B82-32438

382′.09492′041 — Netherlands. Foreign trade with Great Britain

90 years of Anglo-Dutch trade : special celebration supplement of In Touch / The Netherlands-British Chamber of Commerce ; [editor-in-chief Jim van de Worp]. — [Ashford, Kent] ([P.O. Box 22, Ashford, Kent]) : [The Netherlands-British Chamber of Commerce], [1982]. — 128p : ill,maps,ports ; 30cm
Cover title
Unpriced (pbk)
Primary classification 382′.0941′0492
B82-21220

382′.0951′25 — Hong Kong. Foreign trade, *1800-1914*

Crisswell, Colin N.. The Taipans : Hong Kong′s merchant princes / Colin N. Crisswell. — Hong Kong ; Oxford : Oxford University Press, 1981. — x,249p,[32]p of plates : ill,ports ; 23cm
Bibliography: p233-235. — Includes index
ISBN 0-19-580495-3 : £13.00 B82-05634

382′.0952 — Japan. Foreign trade — *Forecasts*

Sinha, Radha. Japan′s options for the 1980s / Radha Sinha. — London : Croom Helm, c1982. — 269p ; 22cm
Bibliography: p252-263. — Includes index
ISBN 0-7099-2311-2 : £14.95 : CIP rev.
B81-35868

382′.0953′8 — Saudi Arabia. Foreign trade. Family firms

Carter, J. R. L.. Leading merchant families of Saudi Arabia / J.R.L. Carter. — [London] : Scorpion in association with the D.R. Llewellyn Group, 1979. — 190p : geneal.tables ; 27cm
Bibliography: p190
ISBN 0-905906-22-5 : £22.50 B82-08606

382′.0954′041 — India *(Republic)*. **Foreign trade with Great Britain. Effects of British entry into European Economic Community**

Anwar, S. A.. The European Community and Indo-British trade relations. — Aldershot : Gower, Jan.1983. — [162]p
ISBN 0-566-00574-3 : £12.50 : CIP entry
Also classified at 382′.0941′054 B82-32437

382′.09549′1 — Pakistan. Economic development. Role of foreign trade, *1947-1970*

Islam, Nurul. Foreign trade and economic controls in development : the case of United Pakistan / Nurul Islam. — New Haven ; London : Yale University Press, c1981. — xv, 271p ; 24cm. — (A publication of the Economic Growth Center, Yale University)
Includes index
ISBN 0-300-02535-1 : £22.75 : CIP rev.
B82-01318

382′.09675′1 — Zaire. Zaire River region. Foreign trade, *1500-1891*

Harms, Robert W.. River of wealth, river of sorrow : the central Zaire basin in the era of the slave and ivory trade, 1500-1891 / Robert W. Harms. — New Haven ; London : Yale, c1981. — xv,277p : ill,maps ; 22cm
Bibliography: p259-267. — Includes index
ISBN 0-300-02616-1 : Unpriced : CIP rev.
B81-30209

382′.0973 — United States. Foreign trade. Policies of government, *1953-1961*

Kaufman, Burton I.. Trade and aid : Eisenhower′s foreign economic policy 1953-1961 / Burton I. Kaufman. — Baltimore ; London : Johns Hopkins University Press, c1982. — xiv,279p ; 24cm. — (The Johns Hopkins University studies in historical and political science. One hundredth series (1982) ; 1)
Bibliography: p253-267. — Includes index
ISBN 0-8018-2623-3 : Unpriced B82-36871

382′.0976 — North America. Gulf of Mexico region. Seaborne foreign trade — *Conference proceedings*

U.S. Gulf Shipping Conference *(1981 : New Orleans Hilton Hotel)*. U.S. Gulf Shipping Conference : New Orleans Hilton Hotel, New Orleans 4-5 June 1981 / [edited by David Robinson]. — Colchester : Seatrade Conference, [1981]. — 156p : ill,2maps ; 30cm
Unpriced (pbk) B82-01495

382.1 — ECONOMIC RELATIONS

382.1 — Economic imperialism

Capitalism and colonial production. — London : Croom Helm, June 1982. — [208]p
ISBN 0-7099-0634-x : £11.95 : CIP entry
B82-11306

382.1′03′21 — Foreign trade — *Encyclopaedias*

Phillips, Janet, *1946-*. Dictionary of trading terms / Janet Phillips. — Old Hatfield : Broomhills, [1982]. — 69p ; 21cm
ISBN 0-9508002-0-1 (pbk) : £10.00
B82-31576

382.1′7 — Balance of payments

Davidmann, M.. Inflation, balance of payments and currency exchange rates, quality of government (national and local), standard of living and world-wide inequality, confrontation compared with co-operation / M. Davidmann. — [Stanmore] : Social Organisation Ltd., [c1981]. — 30 leaves : ill ; 30cm. — (Community leadership and management)
ISBN 0-85192-019-5 (pbk) : £2.90 B82-17852

382.1′7 — Foreign trade. Financing

Trade financing / co-ordinated by Charles J. Gmür. — London : Euromoney, c1981. — 190p : ill,1facsim,forms ; 30cm
Includes index
ISBN 0-903121-19-0 (pbk) : Unpriced
B82-20735

382.1′7 — Invisible exports — *Statistics*

Morgan, E. Victor. World invisible trade / prepared for the Committee on Invisible Exports by Economists Advisory Group Limited ; this report was prepared by E. Victor Morgan, Alan Doran and Nigel Hinton. — London (7th Floor, Stock Exchange, EC2N 1HH) : Committee on Invisible Exports, 1981 (1982 [printing]). — 19p ; 26cm
£6.00 (pbk) B82-35634

382.1′7′091724 — Developing countries. Balance of payments. Stabilisation. Policies of governments

Bird, Graham, *1947-*. Balance of payments stabilisation policy in developing countries / Graham Bird. — London : Overseas Development Institute, 1981. — 50p ; 30cm. — (ODI working paper ; no.5)
Bibliography: p47-50
ISBN 0-85003-080-3 (unbound) : Unpriced
B82-17339

382.1′7′091724 — Developing countries. Balance of payments. Stabilisation. Policies of International Monetary Fund

Killick, Tony. IMF stabilisation programmes / Tony Killick. — London : Overseas Development Institute, 1981. — 56p ; 30cm. — (ODI working paper ; no.6)
Bibliography: p55-56
ISBN 0-85003-079-x (unbound) : Unpriced
B82-17708

382.1′7′0941 — Great Britain. Balance of payments

The **Balance** of payments. — Rev. — London (10 Lombard St. EC3V 9AT) : BES, 1980. — 16p : ill ; 21cm. — (Study booklet series ; 7)
Cover title. — Text on inside covers
Unpriced (pbk) B82-16264

382.4 — FOREIGN TRADE. SPECIAL COMMODITIES AND SERVICES

382′.41′0941 — Great Britain. Exports: Agricultural products. Levies. Debts — *Inquiry reports*

Great Britain. *Parliament. House of Commons. Committee of Public Accounts.* Seventeenth report from the Committee of Public Accounts : together with the proceedings of the committee and the minutes of evidence : session 1979-80 : Ministry of Agriculture, Fisheries and Food, Department of Agriculture and Fisheries for Scotland, Intervention Board for Agricultural Produce : export levy debts, livestock improvement schemes for crofters, Thames tidal defences. — London : H.M.S.O., [1980]. — xvi,48p ; 25cm. — ([HC] ; 683)
Includes index
ISBN 0-10-268380-8 (pbk) : £4.65
Also classified at 338.1′6 ; 338.4′362742
B82-09507

382′.4131′0947 — Soviet Union. Supply of cereals from United States. Embargoes by United States, *1971-1980.* **Effectiveness**

Healy, Dermot. The grain weapon / by Dermot Healy. — Aberdeen (Edward Wright Building, Dunbar St., Aberdeen AB9 2TY) : Centre for Defence Studies, 1982. — 50p ; 30cm. — (Centrepieces ; no.1)
£2.50 (pbk) B82-25683

382′.41816′025 — Hive product importers — *Directories*

International Bee Research Association. Marketing bee products : addresses of importers and agents. — Gerrards Cross : International Bee Research Association, Apr.1982. — [10]p. — (Source materials for apiculture ; no.2)
ISBN 0-86098-112-6 (pbk) : £1.00 : CIP entry
B82-14045

382′.42282 — Organization of the Petroleum Exporting Countries — *Serials*

OPEC review : an energy and economic forum. — Vol.1, no.1 (1977)-. — Oxford : Pergamon on behalf of the Organization of the Petroleum Exporting Countries, 1977-. — v. ; 24cm
Quarterly. — Description based on: Vol.5, no.2 (Summer 1981)
Unpriced B82-08470

382′.42282 — Organization of the Petroleum Exporting Countries, *to 1980*

OPEC : twenty years and beyond / edited by Ragaei El Mallakh. — Boulder : Westview ; London : Croom Helm, 1982. — xxiii,270p : ill ; 23cm. — (Westview′s special studies in international economics and business)
Includes index
ISBN 0-7099-0904-7 : £14.95 B82-16118

382′.42282′0973 — United States. Imports: Petroleum. Policies of government

Conant, Melvin A.. The oil factor in US foreign policy, 1980-1990 / Melvin A. Conant. — Lexington, Mass. : Lexington ; [Aldershot] : Gower [distributor], c1982. — xvi,119p : 1map ; 24cm
Includes index
ISBN 0-669-04728-7 (cased) : £11.50
ISBN 0-669-05206-x (pbk) : Unpriced
B82-31794

382′.42282′0973 — United States. Imports: Petroleum. Policies of government, *1941-1947*

Stoff, Michael B.. Oil, war and American security. — London : Yale University Press, Feb.1982. — [262]p. — (Yale historical publications. Miscellany ; 125)
Originally published: 1980
ISBN 0-300-02841-5 (pbk) : £4.95 : CIP entry
B82-07092

382′.44 — Slave trade. Abolition — *Conference proceedings*

The **Abolition** of the Atlantic slave trade : origins and effects in Europe, Africa, and the Americas / edited by David Eltis and James Walvin with the collaboration of Svend E. Green-Pedersen ; and with an introduction by Stanley L. Engerman. — Madison ; London : University of Wisconsin Press, 1981. — xiii,314p : ill,maps ; 24cm
Conference papers. — Bibliography: p303-306. — Includes index
ISBN 0-299-08490-6 : £15.75 B82-19641

382′.44′0941 — Great Britain. Slave trade with Spanish America, *1700-1739*

Palmer, Colin A.. Human cargoes : the British slave trade to Spanish America, 1700-1739 / Colin Palmer. — Urbana ; London : University of Illinois Press, c1981. — xv,183p : 2maps ; 24cm. — (Blacks in the New World)
Bibliography: p171-177. — Includes index
ISBN 0-252-00846-4 : £13.65
Also classified at 382′.44′098 B82-05915

382′.44′098 — Spanish America. Slave trade with Great Britain, *1700-1739*

Palmer, Colin A.. Human cargoes : the British slave trade to Spanish America, 1700-1739 / Colin Palmer. — Urbana ; London : University of Illinois Press, c1981. — xv,183p : 2maps ; 24cm. — (Blacks in the New World)
Bibliography: p171-177. — Includes index
ISBN 0-252-00846-4 : £13.65
Primary classification 382′.44′0941 B82-05915

382′.45002 — Great Britain. Exports to France: Books. Supply & demand — *For British businessmen*

The **market** for British books in France / edited for the Book Promotion Department of the British Council by Doris Bendemann. — London : British Council, 1980. — 1v. in various pagings : ill,1map ; 29cm
ISBN 0-901618-32-2 (pbk) : £21.00
B82-36650

382′.45581 — North America. Exports to Great Britain: Plants

Grieve, Hilda. A transatlantic gardening friendship, 1694-1777 : the Kenneth Newton Memorial Lecture, 1980 / Hilda Grieve. — [Chelmsford] : Historical Association, Essex Branch, c1981. — 27p ; 22cm
Bibliography: p26-27
ISBN 0-9507779-0-0 (pbk) : Unpriced
B82-07470

382′.456234 — Developing countries. Economic conditions. Effects of foreign trade in military equipment with developed countries

Bombs for breakfast : how the arms trade reinforces a vicious cycle of impoverishment, repression and militarisation in the Third World. — 2nd ed. — [London] : Committee on Poverty and the Arms Trade, c1981. — 42p : ill ; 21cm
Previous ed.: 1978
ISBN 0-9506155-1-x (pbk) : £0.75 B82-03647

382′.456234 — Foreign trade in military equipment. Control measures

The **Sale** and transfer of conventional arms, arms systems and related technology / a report of a working party of the Council on Christian Approaches to Defence and Disarmament for the Division of International Affairs of the British Council of Churches and the Conference of British Missionary Societies. — [London] ([10 Eaton Gate, S.W.1]) : [BBC Publications], [1977]. — 20p ; 21cm
Cover title
£0.60 (pbk) B82-36772

382′.45634 — Military equipment trades: Weapons trades. International political aspects

Pierre, Andrew J.. The global politics of arms sales / Andrew J. Pierre. — Princeton, N.J. ; Guildford : Princeton University Press, c1982. — xvi,352p : ill ; 23cm. — (Council on foreign relations books)
Includes index
ISBN 0-691-07635-9 (cased) : £14.10
ISBN 0-691-02207-0 (pbk) : £4.20 B82-20216

382′.456686366 — Peru. Guano. Exporting by Antony Gibbs and Sons, *1820-1879*

Mathew, W. M.. The House of Gibbs and the Peruvian guano monopoly / W.M. Mathew. — London : Royal Historical Society, 1981. — xiii,281p ; 22cm. — (Royal Historical Society studies in history series ; no.25)
Bibliography: p254-263. — Includes index
ISBN 0-901050-61-x : £11.37 B82-08498

382′.4567 — India *(Republic).* **Exports to Middle East: Manufactured goods**

Thomas, Richard, *1938-*. India′s emergence as an industrial power : Middle Eastern contracts / Richard Thomas. — London : Hurst for the Royal Institute of International Affairs, 1982. — xiv,160p : ill ; 23cm
Bibliography: p149-152. — Includes index
ISBN 0-905838-56-4 : £11.50 B82-23735

382′.45691′0941 — Great Britain. Foreign trade in building materials

Building materials export opportunities and import substitution / [prepared for publication by the National Economic Development Office on behalf of the Building and Civil Engineering EDCs]. — London : NEDO, c1980. — x,145p : ill ; 30cm
ISBN 0-11-700911-3 (pbk) : £10.00
B82-38653

382.5 — IMPORTS

382′.5 — Great Britain. Imports. Demand. Income elasticity. Econometric models

Beenstock, Michael. UK imports and the international trading order / by Michael Beenstock and Peter Warburton. — London : [City University Business School], c1981. — 33leaves : ill ; 30cm. — (Working paper / City University Business School, ISSN 0140-1041 ; no.30)
Bibliography: leaves 28-29
Unpriced (pbk) B82-09571

382′.5 — Great Britain. Imports. Destinations — *Statistics*

Inland origins and destinations of U.K. international trade 1978 / Department of Transport, National Ports Council. — London : The Council, c1980. — 100p : 1ill ; 30cm
ISBN 0-86073-043-3 (pbk) : £35.00
Also classified at 382′.6 B82-35930

382'.5 — Import substitution

Ahmad, Jaleel. Import substitution, trade and development / by Jaleel Ahmad. — Greenwich, Conn. : Jai ; London : distributed by Jaicon, c1978. — viii,128p : ill ; 24cm. — (Contemporary studies in economic and financial analysis ; v.11)
Bibliography: p109-119. — Includes index
ISBN 0-89232-055-9 : £19.50 B82-05922

382'.53 — Imports. Large increases. Protection of states. Role of General Agreement on Tariffs and Trade *(Organization)* — *Proposals*

Lal, Deepak. Resurrection of the pauper-labour argument / by Deepak Lal. — London : Trade Policy Research Centre, 1981. — viii,74p ; 19cm. — (Thames essay, ISSN 0306-6991 ; no.28)
ISBN 0-900842-54-7 (pbk) : £2.00 B82-10728

382.6 — EXPORTS

382'.6 — Great Britain. Exporting by business firms. Videotex services: Europort — *Serials*

Europort update. — Issue 1 (July 1982)-. — London (15 Whitehall, SW1) : NVA Consultants, 1982-. — v. ; 30cm
Monthly
ISSN 0263-5925 = Europort update : Unpriced B82-40037

382'.6 — Great Britain. Exports. Origins — *Statistics*

Inland origins and destinations of U.K. international trade 1978 / Department of Transport, National Ports Council. — London : The Council, c1980. — 100p : 1ill ; 30cm
ISBN 0-86073-043-3 (pbk) : £35.00
Primary classification 382'.5 B82-35930

382'.6'0941 — Great Britain. Exports. Finance. Use of foreign currencies

Foreign currency : invoicing and export finance. — London (1 Victoria St, SW1H 0ET) : British Overseas Trade Board, 1981. — [12]p ; 26cm. — (BOTB occasional papers)
Unpriced (pbk) B82-14321

382'.6'0973 — United States. Exports. Political aspects, *1893-1921*

Becker, William H.. The dynamics of business-government relations : industry & exports 1893-1921 / William H. Becker. — Chicago ; London : University of Chicago Press, 1982. — xvi,240p ; 23cm
Bibliography: p223-235. — Includes index
ISBN 0-226-04121-2 (pbk) : Unpriced B82-35068

382.7 — TARIFF POLICIES

382.7'3'094 — European Community countries. Foreign trade with developing countries. Policies of European Economic Community: Generalized System of Preferences, *to 1979*

Borrmann, Axel. The EC's generalized system of preferences / by Axel Borrmann, Christine Borrmann, Manfred Stegger. — The Hague ; London : Nijhoff, 1981. — 276p ; 25cm
Bibliography: p265-276
ISBN 90-247-2547-x : Unpriced B82-00480

383 — POSTAL SERVICES

383'.125'0941 — Great Britain. Parcel post, *to 1980*

Mackay, James A.. The parcel post of the British Isles / by James A. Mackay. — Dumfries (11 Newall Terr., Dumfries DG1 1LN) : J. Mackay, c1982. — 232p : ill,facsims ; 30cm
£8.70 (pbk) B82-38401

383'.23'0944 — France. Postal services. Charges, *to 1906*

Smith, A. D.. The development of rates of postage (France) : an historical & analytical study / by A.D. Smith ; with an introduction by Herbert Samuel. — Rev. ed. / revised and abridged for the France & Colonies Philatelic Society by C.S. Holder. — Banbury : Kemble, 1980. — x,65p ; 21cm
Previous ed.: London : Allen & Unwin, 1917. — Bibliography: p63
ISBN 0-906835-04-6 (pbk) : Unpriced B82-15288

383'.24 — Israel. Postal services. Automation, *1925-1981*

Loebl, W. Y.. Postal mechanisation in the Holy Land 1925-1981 / W.Y. Loebl. — Rickmansworth : British Association of Palestine-Israel Philatelists, c1982. — 62p : ill,facsims,1map,1plan ; 30cm. — (Monograph)
ISBN 0-9505571-2-9 (pbk) : Unpriced B82-38914

383'.4941 — Great Britain. *Post Office* — *For children*

Kent, Graeme. The Post Office / Graeme Kent. — Hove : Wayland, 1982. — 64p : ill,1facsim,3ports ; 21cm. — (In the High Street)
Bibliography: p62. — Includes index
ISBN 0-85340-933-1 : £4.25 B82-28021

383'.4941 — Great Britain. *Post Office* — *Inquiry reports*

Great Britain. *Parliament. House of Commons. Industry and Trade Committee.* Fifth report from the Industry and Trade Committee, session 1981-82 : the Post Office : together with the proceedings of the Committee relating to the report, the minutes of evidence and appendices. — London : H.M.S.O., [1982]. — xxiii,142p ; 25cm. — ([H.C.] ; 343) ([H.C.] ; 241-i-iv)
ISBN 0-10-234382-9 (pbk) : £8.50 B82-31677

383'.4941 — Great Britain. Postal services — *For children*

Peacock, Frank. Let's go to the post office / Frank Peacock ; general editor Henry Pluckrose ; photography by G.W. Hales. — London : Watts, c1975 (1982 [printing]). — [30]p : ill(some col.) ; 22cm. — (Let's go series)
£2.99
ISBN 0-85166-555-1 B82-28622

383'.494251'05 — Derbyshire. Postal services — *History* — *Serials*

Derbyshire messenger : the magazine of the Derbyshire Postal History Society. — Vol.1, no.1 (Jan.-Mar. 1982)-. — Matlock (c/o Mr P. Moore, 164 Smedley St., Matlock, Derbyshire DE4 3JA) : The Society, 1982-. — v. ; 30cm
ISSN 0263-306X = Derbyshire messenger : Free to society members B82-22699

383'.49425'13 — Derbyshire. Matlock region. Postal services, *to 1981*

Wilson, H. S.. Postal history of Matlock and district / by H.S. Wilson. — [Matlock] ([163 Smedley St, Matlock, Derbyshire, DE4 3JA]) : The Derbyshire Postal History Society, [1982?]. — 93p : ill,facsims,maps ; 30cm
Bibliography: p93
Unpriced (pbk) B82-39681

383'.494414 — France. St Nazaire region. Postal services, *1944-1945*

Stuckey, Robert E.. The Saint Nazaire pocket : August 1944-May 1945 : the background, vignettes and postal history / by Robert E. Stuckey ; edited C.S. Holder. — [Great Britain] : France & Colonies Philatelic Society of Great Britain in association with Kemble, c1982. — 25p : ill,2maps,facsims ; 21cm. — (F.C.P.S. brochure ; no.5)
ISBN 0-906835-06-2 (pbk) : Unpriced B82-15296

383'.495951 — Peninsular Malaysia. Postal services — *History*

Proud, Edward B.. The postal history of British Malaya / by Edward B. Proud. — [Heathfield] ([Heathfield Towers, Heathfield, Sussex TN21 8PY]) : Proud-Bailey
Vol.1. — 1982. — 362p : ill,maps,facsims ; 26cm
Bibliography: p131
Unpriced B82-21593

383'.49973 — Tristan da Cunha. Postal services, *to 1979*

Crabb, George. The history and postal history of Tristan da Cunha / by George Crabb. — Epsom (Charlwood, Howard Ave., Ewell, Epsom, Surrey) : G. Crabb, 1980. — 347p : ill,maps,facsims,ports ; 31cm
Bibliography: p340-342
Unpriced (spiral)
Also classified at 997'.3 B82-08863

384 — TELECOMMUNICATION SERVICES

384 — Telecommunication services — *Conference proceedings*

World telecommunications : a Financial times conference, London, 16 & 17 November, 1981 : speakers papers. — [London] : [Financial Times Conference Organisation], [1981]. — 129p : ill ; 30cm
Cover title
Unpriced (pbk) B82-15992

384'.041 — Great Britain. Telecommunication services. Monopolies — *Proposals*

Great Britain. *Department of Industry*. The future of telecommunications in Britain / Department of Industry. — London : H.M.S.O., 1982. — 4p ; 25cm. — (Cmnd. ; 8610)
ISBN 0-10-186100-1 (unbound) : £1.25 B82-39379

384'.06541 — Great Britain. Telecommunication services: British Telecom

Corby, Michael E.. Telecomms users' handbook : the official manual of the Telecommunications Users' Association / M.E. Corby, E.J. Donohue, M.P.R. Hamer. — London : Telecommunications Press, 1982. — xv,362p : ill,maps,ports ; 30cm
Includes index
ISBN 0-907401-00-7 (pbk) : Unpriced B82-17695

Lane, J. E.. A guide to British Telecom services. — Manchester : NCC Publications, Apr.1982. — [60]p
ISBN 0-85012-373-9 (pbk) : £2.00 : CIP entry B82-12817

384'.065'41 — Great Britain. Telecommunication services: British Telecom — *Statistics* — *Serials*

British Telecom. Statistics / British Telecom. — 1980-. — London (Service and Performance Department, (SP1.2.1), 2 Gresham St., EC2V 7AG) : British Telecom, 1980-. — v. ; 30cm
Annual. — Continues: Great Britain. Post Office. Telecommunications Management Services Department. Telecommunications statistics. — Description based on: 1981 issue
ISSN 0262-379x = Statistics - British Telecom : £3.00 B82-03425

384'.0941 — Great Britain. Telecommunication services. Policies of government. Implications of British Telecommunications Act 1981

Centre for Policy Studies. Telecommunications in Britain : switching direction / Centre for Policy Studies. — London : [The Centre], c1982. — 53p : 1ill ; 30cm
Cover title. — Bibliography: p51-53
ISBN 0-905880-45-5 (pbk) : £2.50 B82-39799

384.54 — Broadcasting services — *Forecasts*

The **Future** of broadcasting : essays on authority, style and choice / edited by Richard Hoggart and Janet Morgan. — London : Macmillan, 1982. — x,166p ; 22cm
Includes index
ISBN 0-333-28848-3 : £20.00 B82-28652

Murphy, Brian. The world wired up. — London (9 Poland St., W.1) : Comedia, Jan.1983. — [160]p
ISBN 0-906890-25-x (cased) : £9.50 : CIP entry
ISBN 0-906890-24-1 (pbk) : £3.50 B82-40924

384.54 — Wales. Broadcasting services in Welsh. Great Britain. *Parliament. House of Commons. Committee on Welsh Affairs.* **Second report ... session 1980-81** — *Critical studies*

Great Britain. *Parliament. House of Commons. Committee on Welsh Affairs.* Second report from the Committee on Welsh Affairs session 1980-81 : broadcasting in the Welsh language and the implications for Welsh and non-Welsh speaking viewers and listeners : observations by the Secretary of State for the Home Department and the Secretary of State for Wales, the British Broadcasting Authority, the Independent Broadcasting Authority and the Welsh Fourth Channel Authority. — London : H.M.S.O., [1982]]. — 23p ; 25cm. — (Cmnd. ; 8469) (HC ; 448-1)
At head of title: Home Office, Welsh Office
ISBN 0-10-184690-8 (unbound) : £2.30
B82-16557

384.54 — Wales. Broadcasting services in Welsh — *Inquiry reports*

Great Britain. *Parliament. House of Commons. Committee on Welsh Affairs.* Second report from the Committee on Welsh Affairs : together with the proceedings of the committee thereon, the minutes of evidence and appendices : session 1980-81 : broadcasting in the Welsh language and the implications for Welsh and non-Welsh speaking viewers and listeners. — London : H.M.S.O., [1981]. — ([HC] ; 448-II)
Vol.2: Minutes of evidence and appendices. — xii,738p ; 25cm. — ([HC] ; 28-i-xvi) ([HC] ; 818 (session 1979-80))
ISBN 0-10-008861-9 (pbk) : £18.35
B82-05638

384.54'023'41 — Great Britain. Radio broadcasting — *Career guides*

Crimp, Susan. Careers in radio and television. — London : Kogan Page, Feb.1983. — [100]p. — (Kogan Page careers series)
ISBN 0-85038-628-4 (cased) : £6.95 : CIP entry
ISBN 0-85038-629-2 (pbk) : £2.50
Primary classification 384.55'4'02341
B82-39433

Keats, John, *19---*. Careers in radio / John Keats. — Northampton : Hamilton House, 1981. — 48p : maps ; 22cm. — (Careerscope ; 6)
Bibliography: p46-48
ISBN 0-906888-23-9 (pbk) : Unpriced
B82-12735

384.54'025'41 — Great Britain. Broadcasting services — *Directories — Serials*

PIMS media directory. — Jan. 1981-. — London (4 St John's Place, EC1M 4AH) : Press Information & Mailing Services, 1981-. — v. ; 26x31cm
Monthly. — Continues: PRADS media lists
ISSN 0261-5169 = PIMS media directory (corrected) : Unpriced
Primary classification 070'.025'41 B82-11810

384.54'025'41 — Great Britain. Radio broadcasting services — *Directories — Serials*

Radio directory : a twice yearly handbook to the UK radio industry. — Winter 1981/2-. — Northampton (Grooms Lane, Creaton, Northampton NN6 8NN) : Radio Month and Hamilton House Publishing, 1981-. — v. : ill,maps ; 30cm
Continues: Radio year
ISSN 0263-1318 = Radio directory : £4.50 per issue
B82-17250

384.54'0924 — Great Britain. Broadcasting services: British Broadcasting Corporation. Greene, *Sir* **Hugh** — *Biographies*

Tracey, Michael. A variety of lives. — London : Bodley Head, May 1982. — [304]p
ISBN 0-370-30026-2 : £8.95 : CIP entry
B82-06732

384.54'0941 — Great Britain. Broadcasting services

Howkins, John, *1945-*. New technologies, new policies? : a report for the Broadcasting Research Unit / John Howkins. — London : BFI, 1982. — ix,74p ; 21cm
ISBN 0-85170-128-0 (pbk) : Unpriced : CIP rev.
B82-16221

Paulu, Burton. Television and radio in the United Kingdom / Burton Paulu. — London : Macmillan, 1981. — xiv,476p ; 25cm
Bibliography: p449-465. — Includes index
ISBN 0-333-29346-0 : £25.00 B82-06648

384.54'0941 — Great Britain. Broadcasting services — *Forecasts*

Howard, George, *1920-*. Towards 1996 / the 1981 Wentworth lecture given by George Howard at Wentworth College, University of York, Friday 12 June 1981. — London : British Broadcasting Corporation, 1981. — 18p ; 21cm
Unpriced (pbk) B82-05669

384.54'0941 — Great Britain. Commercial broadcasting services: Independent Broadcasting Authority. Licences — *Texts*

Broadcasting : copy of the licence granted on the 22nd day of December 1981, by the Secretary of State for the Home Department to the Independent Broadcasting Authority. — London : H.M.S.O., [1982]. — 6p ; 25cm. — (Cmnd. ; 8467)
ISBN 0-10-184670-3 (unbound) : £1.15
B82-14478

384.54'09429 — Wales. Broadcasting services: British Broadcasting Corporation. *Welsh Region, to 1973*

Lucas, Rowland. The voice of a nation? : a concise account of the BBC in Wales 1923-1973 / Rowland Lucas. — Llandysul : Gomer, 1981. — 233p : ill,ports ; 22cm
ISBN 0-85088-745-3 : £6.75 B82-10265

384.54'43 — Educational broadcasting services

Hawkridge, David G.. Organizing educational broadcasting / David Hawkridge and John Robinson. — London : Croom Helm, 1982. — 302p : ill ; 23cm
Includes bibliographies and index
ISBN 0-7099-1216-1 : £10.95 : CIP rev.
B81-30537

384.54'43 — Great Britain. Broadcasting services: British Broadcasting Corporation. *External Services, to 1982*

British Broadcasting Corporation. *External Services. Publicity Unit.* Voice for the world : 50 years of broadcasting to the world : 1932-1982 : BBC / researched by Andrew Walker. — London : BBC External Services Publicity Unit, 1982. — 46p : ill(some col.),2col.maps,ports(some col.) ; 20x21cm
Ill on inside covers. — Includes index
ISBN 0-563-20103-7 (pbk) : £1.00 B82-38767

384.54'43 — Ireland *(Republic).* **Broadcasting services: Radio Telefís Eireann. Educational broadcasting services** — *Inquiry reports*

Radio Telefis Eireann. *Advisory Committee on Educational Broadcasting.* Report of Advisory Committee on Educational Broadcasting. — [Dublin] ([Dublin 4]) : Radio Telefis Eireann, [1979]. — 54p ; 21cm
Unpriced (pbk) B82-18609

384.54'52 — Great Britain. Community radio services

Partridge, Simon. Not the BBC/IBA : the case for community radio / by Simon Partridge. — London : Comedia, 1982. — 75p : ill,1facsim,1plan,ports ; 22cm. — (Comedia/Minority Press Group series ; no.8)
Bibliography: p75
ISBN 0-906890-17-9 (cased) : Unpriced
ISBN 0-906890-18-7 (pbk) : £1.95 B82-40855

384.54'52 — Great Britain. Local radio services — *Career guides*

Roberts, Geoffrey, *1936-*. Work in local radio! / Geoffrey Roberts ; [photographs by Martin White]. — [Bradford] ([Great Horton Rd., Bradford, W. Yorkshire BD7 1AY]) : [Bradford College], [1980]. — [14]p : ill,1map ; 30cm
Cover title. — Map on inside cover
£0.60 (pbk) B82-19340

384.54'56 — Great Britain. Broadcasting services. Direct broadcast satellite services — *Inquiry reports*

Direct broadcasting by satellite : report of a Home Office Study. — London : H.M.S.O., [1981]. — 100p : ill,maps ; 25cm
ISBN 0-11-340740-8 (pbk) : £4.50 B82-00433

384.54'56 — Western Europe. Direct satellite broadcasting services — *Forecasts*

Wels, I.. The prospects of direct television and radio broadcasting via satellites in the U.K. and Europe / by I. Wels. — London (33 Monmouth Rd, W2 4UT) : I. Wells [i.e. Wels], 1981. — 17p ; 22cm
£0.55 (£1.20 by post) (pbk) B82-21132

384.55'4 — Great Britain. Viewdata services: Prestel

Nicholson, Roger. The Prestel business / Roger Nicholson and Guy Consterdine. — London : Northwood, 1980. — 104p : ill ; 22cm
ISBN 0-7198-2601-2 : £4.95 B82-15204

384.55'4 — Television services — *For children*

Orton, Diana. Television / Diana Orton. — London : Evans, 1982. — 48p : ill(some col.) ; 21cm. — (Talking shop)
ISBN 0-237-29252-1 (pbk) : Unpriced
B82-16624

384.55'4 — Television services — *Forecasts*

The Third age of broadcasting. — London : Faber, Oct.1982. — [192]p
ISBN 0-571-11981-6 : £2.95 : CIP entry
B82-28476

384.55'4 — Viewdata services

Sigel, Efrem. Videotext : the coming revolution in home-office information retrieval / Efrem Sigel with Joseph Reizen, Colin McIntyre, Max Wilkinson. — White Plains, N.Y. : Knowledge Industry ; London : Eurospan [distributor], c1980. — 154p : ill ; 23cm. — (Communications library)
Includes index
ISBN 0-914236-41-5 : £19.95 B82-08805

Yeates, Robin. Which private viewdata system? : report of a one-day seminar held 2nd October 1981 / R. Yeates. — [London] ([33 Alfred Place, WC1E 7DP]) : London and South Eastern Library Region, 1981. — 5p ; 30cm. — (BL R and D report ; 5675)
Unpriced (unbound) B82-11340

384.55'4'02341 — Great Britain. Television broadcasting — *Career guides*

Crimp, Susan. Careers in radio and television. — London : Kogan Page, Feb.1983. — [100]p. — (Kogan Page careers series)
ISBN 0-85038-628-4 (cased) : £6.95 : CIP entry
ISBN 0-85038-629-2 (pbk) : £2.50
Also classified at 384.54'023'41 B82-39433

384.55'4'02341 — Great Britain. Television services — *Career guides*

Working in TV / [written, designed and produced by SGS Education]. — Walton on Thames : Nelson, 1981. — 15p : ill ; 28cm. — (Career profiles ; 22)
ISBN 0-17-438370-3 (unbound) : Unpriced
B82-27848

384.55'4'02541 — Great Britain. Television services — *Directories — Serials*

The TV directory : a twice yearly handbook to the UK television industry. — Summer 1982-. — Northampton : Hamilton House Pub., 1982-. — v. ; 30cm
ISSN 0263-9874 = TV directory : £5.00 per issue B82-40038

384.55'40941 — Great Britain. Commercial television services: Channel Four

What's this Channel Four?. — London (9 Poland St., W.1) : Comedia, Dec.1982. — [192]p
ISBN 0-906890-29-2 (cased) : £9.50 : CIP entry
ISBN 0-906890-28-4 (pbk) : £3.50 B82-40341

384.55'4'0941 — Great Britain. Commercial television services: Channel Four, *to 1982*

Lambert, Stephen. Channel Four. — London : BFI, Nov.1982. — [150]p
ISBN 0-85170-124-8 (pbk) : £3.95 : CIP entry
B82-29424

384.55′4′0941 — Great Britain. Commercial television services: Granada Television, *to 1981* *— Chronologies*
Granada Television. The Granada years 1956-1981. — Manchester (Manchester, M60 9EA) : Granada Television, [1981]. — 15p ; 20cm
Unpriced (pbk) B82-24658

384.55′4′0941 — Great Britain. Television services. Political aspects
Hood, Stuart. On television / Stuart Hood. — London : Pluto, 1980. — 120p ; 20cm
Bibliography: p119-120
ISBN 0-86104-328-6 (pbk) : £2.95 B82-15060

384.55′4′0973 — United States. Television services
DeLuca, Stuart M.. Television's transformation : the next 25 years / Stuart M. DeLuca. — San Diego : Barnes ; London : Tantivy, c1980. — 287p : ill ; 24cm
Includes index
ISBN 0-498-02474-1 : £5.95 B82-34049

384.55′4′0981 — Brazil. Television services: TV Globo *(Brazil)*
Brazilian television in context / edited by Richard Paterson. — [London] : British Film Institute, 1982. — 29p : 1map ; 21cm. — (A BFI TV projects publication)
Unpriced (pbk) B82-34976

384.55′43 — Great Britain. Videotape recordings. Production. Finance. Sources
Sources of funding for film/video making / compiled by Linda Wood. — London : [British Film Institute], 1981. — 45p ; 30cm. — (BFI information guide ; no.2)
Cover title. — At head of title: BFI library services
Unpriced (pbk)
Primary classification 384′.83 B82-06966

384.55′44′05 — Television services *— Serials*
TV market international. — Vol.1, no.1-. — London (72 Tottenham Court Rd., W1P 9PA) : Westway Publishing, [1981]-. — v. : ill,ports ; 30cm
Six issues yearly
ISSN 0263-2950 = TV market international : £25.00 per year B82-32174

384.6′028 — Telephones. Use. Techniques *— For school leavers*
Phoning. — Cambridge : Basic Skills Unit, [1980?]. — 24p : ill,2facsims ; 30cm
Based on What the hell are social and life skills? Unit 1. The telephone by Martin Good, Eileen Mathie and Andrew Pates. — Bibliography: p24
ISBN 0-86082-202-8 (pbk) : Unpriced B82-19934

384.6′48 — Great Britain. Videotex services: Prestel
Maynes, E. Scott. Prestel in use : a consumer view / by E. Scott Maynes. — London : National Consumer Council, 1982. — i,70p ; 30cm
ISBN 0-905653-45-9 (pbk) : Unpriced B82-31237

384.6′48 — Videotex services
Firth, R. J.. Viewdata. — Manchester : NCC, June 1982. — [64]p
ISBN 0-85012-382-8 (pbk) : £7.00 : CIP entry B82-18585

384.6′48 — Videotex services *— Conference proceedings*
Viewdata 82. — Northwood Hills : Online Publications, Oct.1982. — [500]p
ISBN 0-903796-90-2 (pbk) : £56.00 : CIP entry B82-30608

384.8 — CINEMA INDUSTRIES

384′.8 — Great Britain. Natural history film industries: Oxford Scientific Films Ltd, *to 1981*
Crowson, P. S.. Animals in focus : the business life of a natural history film unit / by P.S. Crowson ; foreword by Sir Peter Scott. — Horsham : Caliban, 1981. — ix,140p,[8]p of plates : ill(some col.) ; 24cm
Includes index
ISBN 0-904573-34-6 (cased) : Unpriced
ISBN 0-904573-95-1 (pbk) : £6.00 B82-05590

384′.8′0924 — California. Los Angeles. Hollywood. Cinema industries, *to 1979 — Personal observations*
Davis, Sammy. Hollywood in a suitcase / Sammy Davis, Jnr. — London : W.H. Allen, 1981, c1980. — 255p,[8]p of plates : ports ; 18cm. — (A Star book)
Originally published: London : Granada, 1980
ISBN 0-352-30965-2 (pbk) : £1.60 B82-03037

384′.8′0942184 — London. Ealing *(London Borough).* **Cinema industries: Ealing Studios,** *to 1960*
Perry, George, *1935-*. George Perry presents forever Ealing : a celebration of the great British film studio / with a foreword by Peter Ustinov. — London : Pavilion, 1981. — 200p : ill,ports ; 27cm
Bibliography: p194. — Includes index
ISBN 0-907516-06-8 : £8.95 : CIP rev. B81-25741

384′.8′0979494 — California. Los Angeles. Hollywood. Cinema industries: Mascot Pictures, *to 1935*
Tuska, Jon. The vanishing legion : a history of Mascot Pictures 1927-1935 / Jon Tuska. — Jefferson, N.C. ; London : McFarland, 1982. — viii,215p,[32]p of plates : ill,facsims,ports ; 24cm
Includes index
ISBN 0-89950-030-7 : £12.55 B82-24792

384′.8′0994 — Australia. Cinema industries, *ca 1920-ca 1940*
Tullock, John. Australian cinema : industry, narrative and meaning. — London : Allen & Unwin, Apr.1982. — [266]p. — (Studies in society)
ISBN 0-86861-140-9 : £15.00 : CIP entry
ISBN 0-86861-148-4 (pbk) : Unpriced B82-06263

384′.83 — Great Britain. Cinema films. Production. Finance. Sources
Sources of funding for film/video making / compiled by Linda Wood. — London : [British Film Institute], 1981. — 45p ; 30cm. — (BFI information guide ; no.2)
Cover title. — At head of title: BFI library services
Unpriced (pbk)
Also classified at 384.55′43 B82-06966

385 — RAILWAY TRANSPORT

385 — Great Britain. Railways. Electrification *— Inquiry reports*
Great Britain. *Parliament. House of Commons. Transport Committee.* Second report from the Transport Committee, session 1981-82 : main line railway electrification : together with the proceedings of the committee, minutes of evidence and appendices. — London : H.M.S.O., [1982]. — 2v.(lxviii,v,175p) ; 25cm. — ([HC] ; 317)
ISBN 0-10-296682-6 (pbk) : Unpriced
ISBN 0-10-296782-2 (v.2) : £8.50 B82-28626

385 — Great Britain. Railways. Electrification *— Proposals*
Railway electrification in Britain : the railway industry view. — London (9 Catherine Place, SW1E 6DX) : Railway Industry Association of Great Brtain, [1978?]. — 16p ; 21cm
Cover title
Unpriced (pbk) B82-12120

385 — London. Railways. Electrification, *1890-1923*
Moody, G. T.. London's electrifications 1890-1923 / by G.T. Moody. — [Sutton Coldfield] : Electric Railway Society, 1961, 1981 printing. — 14p ; 21cm
£0.25 (unbound) B82-34022

385 — Railway services
Allen, Geoffrey Freeman. Modern railways international review / G. Freeman Allen. — London : Ian Allan, 1981. — 160p : ill,2maps ; 30cm
ISBN 0-7110-1123-0 : £9.95 B82-01618

385 — United States. Railways. Electrification, *to 1968*
Bezilla, Michael. Electric traction on the Pennsylvania railroad 1895-1968 / Michael Bezilla. — University Park, Pa. ; London : Pennsylvania State University Press, c1980. — 233p : ill,maps,plans ; 24cm
Includes index
ISBN 0-271-00241-7 : Unpriced B82-34702

385′.025′41 — Great Britain. Railway services *— Directories*
Who's who in Britain's railway industry / edited by E.L. Cornwell. — London : Ian Allan, 1982. — 111p : ill ; 22cm
ISBN 0-7110-1182-6 : £7.95 B82-30644

385′.065′74 — United States. Eastern states. Railway services: Penn Central Transportation Company. Failure
Salsbury, Stephen. No way to run a railroad : the untold story of the Penn Central crisis / Stephen Salsbury. — New York ; London : McGraw-Hill, c1982. — xvii,363p : ill ; 24cm
Includes index
ISBN 0-07-054483-2 : £10.50 B82-09025

385′.09 — Railways, *to 1980 — For children*
Wood, Sydney. The railway revolution / Sydney Wood. — London : Macmillan Children's, 1981. — 96p : ill(some col.),2col.maps,ports (some col.) ; 30cm
Includes index
ISBN 0-333-31307-0 : £4.95 : CIP rev. B81-30273

385′.092′4 — England. Railway services: British Rail. *London Midland Region.* **Steam locomotives. Driving,** *to 1967 — Personal observations*
Cockman, F.G.. Midland engineman / by Horace Mann ; edited by F.G. Cockman. — [Bedford] ([8, Balmoral Avenue]) : [F.G. Cockman], 1981. — 40p : ill ; 21cm
Cover title. — Written by F.G. Cockman as if by Horace Mann
ISBN 0-9507872-0-5 (pbk) : £1.80 B82-12750

385′.092′4 — Great Britain. Railway services: British Rail. Steam locomotives. Firing & driving, *1944-1957 — Personal observations*
Johnson, 'Piccolo Pete'. Through the links at Crewe : more top link footplate memories / 'Piccolo Pete' Johnson. — Truro : Barton, [1981?]. — 124p : ill ; 21cm
ISBN 0-85153-378-7 (pbk) : £2.95 B82-10909

385′.092′4 — Great Britain. Railway services. Disused routes. Recreations: Walking *— Personal observations*
Davies, Hunter. A walk along the tracks / Hunter Davies. — London : Weidenfeld and Nicolson, 1982. — xii,196p,[8]p of plates : ill,maps,ports ; 23cm
Bibliography: p182-185. — Includes index
ISBN 0-297-78042-5 : £7.95 B82-20421

385′.092′4 — Great Britain. Railway services. Elliott, *Sir* **John,** *1898- — Biographies*
Elliot, *Sir* **John,** *1898-*. On and off the rails / Sir John Elliot in association with Michael Esau. — London : Allen & Unwin, 1982. — 123p : ill,facsims,ports ; 23cm. — (Steam past)
Includes index
ISBN 0-04-385089-8 : Unpriced : CIP rev. B82-10579

385′.092′4 — Railways, *1907-1980 — Personal observations*
Nock, O. S.. Line clear ahead : 75 years of ups and downs / O.S. Nock. — Cambridge : Stephens, 1982. — 217p : ill,maps,1facsim,ports ; 25cm
Ill on lining papers. — Bibliography: p212-215. — Includes index
ISBN 0-85059-545-2 : £8.95 : CIP rev. B82-04986

385′.092′4 — Scotland. Railway services, *1920-1965 — Personal observations*
Dunbar, A. G.. Fifty years with Scottish steam / Alan G. Dunbar and I.A. Glen. — Truro : Barton, [1982?]. — 112p : ill ; 22cm
ISBN 0-85153-427-9 (pbk) : £3.50 B82-35708

385'.092'4 — South-west England. Railway services: British Rail. Salisbury-Exeter line, *1955-1962 — Personal observations*
King, Donald. South West railwayman. — London : Allen & Unwin, Dec.1982. — [112]p
ISBN 0-04-385098-7 : £6.95 : CIP entry B82-29864

385'.092'4 — Wiltshire. Swindon. Railway services: Great Western Railway, *1923-1938 — Personal observations*
Mountford, Eric R.. Swindon GWR reminiscences / Eric R. Mountford. — Truro : Barton, [1982?]. — 112p : ill ; 22cm
ISBN 0-85153-438-4 (pbk) : £3.50 B82-35711

385'.0941 — Great Britain. Preserved standard gauge railways
Nock, O. S.. On steam. — London : Granada, July 1982. — [224]p
ISBN 0-246-11736-2 : £10.00 : CIP entry B82-12231

385'.0941 — Great Britain. Railway services, *1901-1910 — Readings from contemporary sources*
King Edward's railways : contemporary impressions from the Railway magazine / compiled by Tom Middlemass. — [Theydon Bois] : [Steamchest], [c1979]. — 96p,[8]p of plates : ill ; 21cm. — (A steamchest publication ; no.3)
Cover title
ISBN 0-906679-00-1 (pbk) : £1.70 B82-00095

385'.0941 — Great Britain. Railway services, *1920-1939.* **Social aspects**
Unwin, Philip. Travelling by train in the 'twenties and 'thirties / Philip Unwin. — London : Allen & Unwin, 1981. — xv,78p : ill,facsims ; 23cm. — (Steam past)
Includes index
ISBN 0-04-385086-3 : Unpriced : CIP rev. B81-15876

385'.0941 — Great Britain. Railway services, *1975-1979 — Illustrations*
Trains of thought. — London : Allen and Unwin, May 1981. — [128]p
ISBN 0-04-385081-2 : £9.95 : CIP entry B81-04205

385'.0941 — Great Britain. Railway services: British Rail, *1950-1970 — Correspondence, diaries, etc.*
Hondelink, E. R.. Switches & crossings / by E.R. Hondelink ; introduction by C.E.R. Sherrington ; edited by Roger Calvert. — Truro (15, The Parade, Truro, Cornwall) : [R. Calvert], 1981. — 83p : ill,maps,facsims,1port ; 30cm
£3.00 (pbk) B82-06874

385'.0941 — Great Britain. Railway services — *For children*
Peacock, Frank. Let's go to the railway station / Frank Peacock ; general editor Henry Pluckrose ; photography by G.W. Hales. — London : Watts, c1974 (1982 [printing]). — [36]p : col.ill ; 22cm. — (Let's go series)
ISBN 0-85166-356-7 : £2.99 B82-26837

385'.0941 — Great Britain. Railway services — *Illustrations — Serials*
Jane's railway year. — [1981]-. — London : Jane's Pub. Co., 1982-. — v. : ill ; 28cm
Annual
ISSN 0263-5224 = Jane's railway year : £6.95 B82-26134

385'.0941 — Great Britain. Railway services: London and North Eastern Railway, *to 1947*
Bonavia, Michael R.. A history of the LNER / Michael R. Bonavia. — London : Allen & Unwin
1: The early years, 1923-33. — 1982. — xii,90p : ill,1coat of arms,ports ; 23cm. — (Steam past)
Includes index
ISBN 0-04-385088-x : Unpriced : CIP rev. B82-03712

Bonavia, Michael R.. History of the LNER. — London : Allen & Unwin
2: Gresley and the streamlined high speed trains, 1934-39. — Sept.1982. — [112]p
ISBN 0-04-385094-4 : £6.95 : CIP entry B82-19081

385'.0941 — Great Britain. Railway services: London, Midland and Scottish Railway, *to 1947*
Nock, O. S.. A history of the LMS / O.S. Nock. — London : Allen & Unwin. — (Steam past)
Includes index
Vol.1: The first years, 1923-30. — 1982. — 94p : ill,1coat of arms,3ports ; 24cm
ISBN 0-04-385087-1 : Unpriced : CIP rev. B82-03710

385'.0941 — Great Britain. Railway services: London, Midland and Scottish Railway, *to 1948*
Nock, O. S.. A history of the LMS. — London : Allen & Unwin
Vol.2: The record breaking 'thirties', 1931-39. — Aug.1982. — [112]p
ISBN 0-04-385093-6 : £6.95 : CIP entry B82-15642

385'.0941 — Great Britain. Railway services — *Serials*
Rail enthusiast. — Apr./May 1981-. — Peterborough (Bushfield House, Orton Centre. Peterborough PE2 0UW) : EMAP National Publications, 1981-. — v. : ill(some col.) ; 30cm
Six issues yearly. — Description based on: Dec./Jan. 1982 issue
ISSN 0262-561x = Rail enthusiast : £5.40 per year B82-18521

385'.0941 — Great Britain. Railway services. Statistics. Information sources
Aldcroft, Derek H.. Rail transport / by Derek H. Aldcroft. Sea transport / by Derrick Mort. — Oxford : Published for the Royal Statistical Society and the Social Science Research Council by Pergamon, 1981. — xii,268p : forms ; 26cm. — (Reviews of United Kingdom statistical sources ; v.14)
Includes bibliographies and index
ISBN 0-08-026105-1 : £14.50 : CIP rev.
Also classified at 387.5'0941 B81-25849

385'.0941 — Great Britain. Railway services, *to 1947 — For children*
Harris, Sarah. Railways / Sarah Harris. — London : Batsford, 1982. — 48p : ill,facsims,2maps ; 26cm. — (Finding out about)
Bibliography: p47. — Includes index
ISBN 0-7134-4299-9 : £4.50 B82-41036

385'.0941 — Great Britain. Railway services, *to 1980*
The **Illustrated** history of British railways / foreword by Sir Peter Parker ; consultant editors Geoffrey Freeman Allen and Patrick Whitehouse. — London : Arthur Barker, c1981. — 224p : ill(some col.),maps(some col.),coats of arms(some col.),facsims(some col.),ports ; 25x32cm
Includes index
ISBN 0-213-16811-1 : £12.95 B82-02437

385'.0941 — Great Britain. Railway services, *to 1981.* **Social aspects**
Turnock, David. Railways in the British Isles. — London : A. & C. Black, Oct.1982. — [264]p
ISBN 0-7136-2281-4 : £12.00 : CIP entry B82-22992

385'.0941 — Great Britain. Railways, *1960-1980 — Illustrations*
Cavalier, Peter. Peter Cavalier : rail and steam. — Cambridge : Patrick Stephens, June 1982. — [128]p
ISBN 0-85059-575-4 : £7.95 : CIP entry B82-09843

385'.0941 — Great Britain. Railways. Preservation, *to 1980*
Body, Geoffrey. An illustrated history of preserved railways / Geoffrey Body. — Ashborne : Moorland, c1981. — 152p : ill ; 22cm
Includes index
ISBN 0-86190-018-9 : £6.95 : CIP rev. B81-08864

385'.0941 — Great Britain. Railways, *to 1900 — Readings from comtemporary sources*
The **Railway** age. — [Luton] ([Wardown Park, Luton, LU2 7HA]) : Luton Museum and Art Gallery, [1981]. — 67p : ill,facsims,maps ; 27x43cm
Cover title
Unpriced (pbk) B82-31232

385'.0941 — Great Britain. Railways, *to 1962*
Adley, Robert. The call of steam. — Poole : Blandford Press, July 1982. — [160]p
ISBN 0-7137-1274-0 : £10.95 : CIP entry B82-13518

385'.0941 — Great Britain. Railways, *to 1981 — For children*
Hale, Don. Railways. — London : Edward Arnold, Sept.1982. — [32]p. — (People and progress)
ISBN 0-7131-0609-3 (pbk) : £1.50 : CIP entry B82-19803

385'.09411 — Scotland. Railway services. Disused routes, *1930- — Illustrations*
Scotland's lost railways. — Edinburgh : Moorfoot
1: The Borders / edited by Iain R. Smith. — 1982. — [36]p : chiefly ill ; 23cm
ISBN 0-906606-05-5 (pbk) : Unpriced B82-33780

385'.09411 — Scotland. Railway services, *to 1980*
Smith, Alastair. Railways / Alastair Smith ; drawings by John Marshall. — Edinburgh : Spurbooks, c1982. — 64p : ill ; 19cm. — (Introducing Scotland)
Bibliography: p63. — Includes index
ISBN 0-7157-2077-5 (pbk) : £1.25 B82-20591

385'.09411'5 — Scotland. Highlands. Railway services: British Rail. *Scottish Region.* **West Highland line,** *to 1981*
McGregor, John A.. All stations to Mallaig! : the West Highland line since nationalisation / John A. McGregor. — Truro : Barton, [1982?]. — 112p : ill,1map ; 22cm
ISBN 0-85153-426-0 (pbk) : £3.50 B82-35709

385'.09412'1 — Scotland. Grampian Region. Railway services: Great North of Scotland Railway, *1880-1930 — Illustrations*
Great North memories : scenes of the North East's own railway. — Aberdeen : Great North of Scotland Railway Association
No.2. — c1981. — 47p : ill,1map,facsims,ports ; 21cm
ISBN 0-902343-02-5 (unbound) : Unpriced B82-08642

385'.09413'15 — Scotland. Central Region. Clackmannan *(District).* **Railway services. Projects: Alloa-Dollar Project**
A **Steam** railway for central Scotland / [the Scottish Railway Preservation Society]. — Scotland : The Society, [1982?]. — 6p : ill,1map,ports ; 30cm
Four folded sheets in pocket
£1.50 (pbk) B82-33567

385'.09416'5 — Down *(County).* **Railway services: Belfast & County Down Railway,** *to 1950*
Patterson, Edward M.. The Belfast & County Down railway / Edward M. Patterson. — Newton Abbot : David & Charles, c1982. — 48p : ill,1facsim,maps ; 25cm
Bibliography: p46
ISBN 0-7153-8306-x : £4.95 : CIP rev. B82-09624

385'.094169'3 — Donegal *(County).* **Railway services: Londonderry & Lough Swilly Railway,** *ca 1900-1948 — Illustrations*
The **Londonderry** & Lough Swilly Railway / [compiled by] J.I.C. Boyd. — Truro : Barton, [1981]. — 96p : chiefly ill,maps,facsims ; 23cm
Ill on lining papers
ISBN 0-85153-447-3 : £6.95 B82-12386

385'.0942 — England. Railway services: British Rail. *London Midland Region, ca 1930-1968 — Illustrations*
Conolly, W. Philip. London Midland main line cameraman. — London : Allen & Unwin, Nov.1982. — [128]p
ISBN 0-04-385099-5 : £9.95 : CIP entry B82-27185

385'.0942 — England. Railway services: British Rail. Northeast-Southwest route, *1971-1981 — Illustrations*
Chalcraft, John. NE/SW main line album / John Chalcraft. — London : Ian Allan, 1982. — 111p : ill ; 25cm
ISBN 0-7110-1172-9 : £5.95 B82-26196

385'.0942 — England. Railway services: British Rail. *Western Region.* **Great Western and Great Central joint line,** *to 1981*

Edwards, Dennis F.. The final link : a pictorial history of the Great Western & Great Central Joint Line — the last main line steam railway to be built in England and its effect upon the Chilterns and South Midlands / Dennis F. Edwards & Ron Pigram. — Tunbridge Wells : Midas, c1982. — 144p : ill,coats of arms,facsims,1map ; 30cm
Map, coats of arms on lining papers
ISBN 0-85936-280-9 : £8.50 B82-28197

385'.0942 — England. Railway services: Great Western Railway, *to 1947*

History of the Great Western Railway. — London : Ian Allan
Vol.1: 1833-1863 / E.T. MacDermot. — Rev. ed. / revised by C.R. Clinker. — 1964 (1982 [printing]). — xii,480p,[30]p of plates : ill,maps,plans,ports ; 24cm
Previous ed.: 1927. — Includes index
ISBN 0-7110-0411-0 : £14.95 B82-26955

History of the Great Western Railway. — London : Ian Allan
Vol.2: 1863-1921 / E.T. MacDermot. — Rev. ed. / revised by C.R. Clinker. — 1964 (1982 [printing]). — v,362p,[31]p of plates : ill,maps,facsims ; 24cm
Previous ed.: 1931. — Includes index
ISBN 0-7110-0412-9 : £9.95 B82-26956

History of the Great Western Railway. — London : Ian Allan
Vol.3: 1923-1947 / O.S. Nock. — 1967 (1982 [printing]). — xii,268p,[49]p of plates : ill,maps,ports ; 24cm
Bibliography: pvi. — Includes index
ISBN 0-7110-0304-1 : £9.95 B82-26957

385'.09421'6 — South London. Railway services: Surrey Iron Railway & Croydon, Merstham & Godstone Iron Railway, *to 1848*

Bayliss, Derek A.. Retracing the first public railway / Derek A. Bayliss. — Croydon (294 High St., Croydon, Surrey CRO 1NG) : Living History Publications, 1981. — 80p : ill,maps,facsims ; 21cm. — (Living History local guide ; no.4)
Cover title. — Text on inside covers. — Bibliography: p77-78. — Includes index
£1.70 (pbk) B82-03309

385'.09421'78 — London. Bromley *(London Borough).* **Railway services: British Rail.** *Southern Region.* **Hayes branch,** *to 1982*

Woodman, Trevor. The railway to Hayes : an historical review of the development of the railway and locality of Hayes, Kent / by Trevor Woodman. — [Bromley] : Hayes (Kent) Village Association, 1982. — 36p : ill,maps ; 21cm
Text on inside covers
ISBN 0-9508110-0-9 (pbk) : Unpriced B82-39939

385'.09422 — Central Southern England. Railway services: British Rail. *Western Region.* **Didcot, Newbury & Southampton branch,** *to 1966*

Karau, Paul. An illustrated history of the Didcot Newbury and Southampton Railway / by Paul Karau, Mike Parsons and Kevin Robertson. — Upper Bucklebury : Wild Swan, [1982?]. — vii,224p : chiefly ill,facsims,maps,plans,ports ; 28cm
ISBN 0-906867-04-5 : £11.50 B82-23526

385'.09422 — England. Thameas Valley. Railway services, *to 1980 — Illustrations*

Coles, C. R. L.. Railways through the Thames Valley / C.R.L. Coles. — London : Ian Allan, 1982. — 124p : ill,1map ; 24cm
Map on lining paper
ISBN 0-7110-1158-3 : £5.95 B82-17811

385'.09422 — England. Thames River Region. Railway services, *to 1980*

Christiansen, Rex. Thames and Severn / Rex Christiansen. — Newton Abbot : David & Charles, c1981. — 205p : ill,maps ; 23cm. — (A regional history of the railways of Great Britain ; v.13)
Map (folded sheet) attached to lining paper. — Bibliography: p195-197. — Includes index
ISBN 0-7153-8004-4 : £8.95 : CIP rev.
Also classified at 385'.09424 B81-30369

385'.09422 — South-east England. Railway services: London, Brighton & South Coast Railway, *to 1923 — Illustrations*

London Brighton & South Coast Railway album / [compiled by] Klaus Marx & John Minnis. — London : Ian Allan, 1982. — 112p : chiefly ill,maps,ports ; 24cm
Maps on lining papers
ISBN 0-7110-1187-7 : £5.95 B82-34783

385'.09422 — South-east England. Railway services, *to 1980*

White, H. P.. Southern England / by H.P. White. — 4th ed. — Newton Abbot : David & Charles, 1982. — ix,232p,[20]p of plates : ill,1facsim,maps ; 23cm. — (A Regional history of the railways of Great Britain ; v.2)
Previous ed.: 1969. — Map (1 folded sheet) attached to lining papers. — Bibliography: p222-225. — Includes index
ISBN 0-7153-8365-5 : £9.50 : CIP rev. B82-15841

385'.09422'56 — East Sussex. Brighton. Railway services, *to 1980*

Cooper, B. K. (Basil Knowlman). Rail centres : Brighton / B.K. Cooper. — London : Ian Allan, 1981. — 144p : ill,plans ; 24cm
Ill on lining papers
ISBN 0-7110-1155-9 : £6.95 B82-11217

385'.09423 — South-west England. Railway services: British Rail. *Western Region.* **Bath-Weymouth line,** *to 1981*

Maggs, Colin G.. The Bath to Weymouth line : including Westbury to Salisbury / Colin Maggs. — [Trowbridge] : Oakwood, 1982. — 74p,[18]p of plates : ill,1map ; 22cm. — (Locomotion papers ; no.138)
Bibliography: p74
ISBN 0-85361-289-7 (pbk) : £3.90 B82-40135

385'.09423 — South-west England. Railway services. Disused routes — *Walkers' guides*

Somerville, Christopher. Walking West Country railways / Christopher Somerville. — Newton Abbot : David & Charles, 1982. — 111p : ill,maps ; 22cm
Bibliography: p111
ISBN 0-7153-8143-1 : £3.95 : CIP rev. B82-01175

385'.09423 — South-west England. Railway services: Somerset & Dorset Joint Railway, *1950-1966*

MacDermott, Brian. PSL modellers' and enthusiasts' guide to the Somerset and Dorset Line. — Cambridge : Patrick Stephens, Aug.1982. — [100]p
ISBN 0-85059-586-x : £7.95 : CIP entry B82-16656

385'.09423 — South-west England. Railway services, *to 1887 — Early works*

Worth, R. Hansford. Early western railroads : an 1888 description of nine railway locations in South West England / by R. Hansford Worth. — Weston-super-Mare : Avon-AngliA, [1982?]. — 15p : ill ; 21cm. — (Avon-AngliA transport history series)
Cover title. — Reprinted from the transactions of the Plymouth Institution and Devon and Cornwall Natural History Society, 1887-8
ISBN 0-905466-46-2 (pbk) : Unpriced B82-26990

385'.09423'5 — Devon. Railway services, *to 1981*

Leigh, Chris. Rail routes in Devon & Cornwall / Chris Leigh. — London : Ian Allan, 1982. — 112p : ill,maps ; 25cm
ISBN 0-7110-1184-2 : £5.95
Also classified at 385'.09423'7 B82-26194

385'.09423'5 — South Devon. Railway services: British Rail. *Western Region.* **South Devon lines,** *to 1980*

Gregory, Roy, *1913-*. The South Devon Railway / Roy Gregory. — [Trowbridge] : Oakwood, 1982. — 123p : ill,facsims,maps ; 22cm. — (Oakwood library of railway history ; no.62)
ISBN 0-85361-286-2 (pbk) : £4.50 B82-30100

385'.09423'7 — Cornwall. Railway services: Cornwall Railway, *to 1846 — Early works*

Osler, Edward. History of the Cornwall Railway 1835-1846 / by Edward Osler. — Weston-super-Mare : Avon-Anglia, c1982. — 39p : ill,1map ; 21cm. — (Avon-Anglia transport history series)
ISBN 0-905466-48-9 (pbk) : £2.25 B82-41072

385'.09423'7 — Cornwall. Railway services, *to 1981*

Leigh, Chris. Rail routes in Devon & Cornwall / Chris Leigh. — London : Ian Allan, 1982. — 112p : ill,maps ; 25cm
ISBN 0-7110-1184-2 : £5.95
Primary classification 385'.09423'5 B82-26194

385'.09423'93 — Avon. Bristol. Railway services, *to 1980*

Maggs, Colin G.. Bristol / Colin Maggs. — London : Ian Allan, 1981. — 128p : ill,maps,1plan ; 24cm. — (Rail centres)
Bibliography: p128
ISBN 0-7110-1153-2 : £6.95 B82-07362

385'.09423'96 — Avon. Woodspring *(District).* **Railway services: Weston, Clevedon & Portishead Railway,** *to 1940*

Redwood, Christopher. The Weston, Clevedon and Portishead Railway : the detailed study of an independent light railway / by Christopher Redwood. — Weston-Super-Mare : Sequoia in association with Avon-Anglia, c1981. — 183p : ill,2maps,facsims,plans ; 22cm
Includes index
ISBN 0-905466-42-x : £9.95 B82-02856

385'.09424 — England. Severn River region. Railway services, *to 1980*

Christiansen, Rex. Thames and Severn / Rex Christiansen. — Newton Abbot : David & Charles, c1981. — 205p : ill,maps ; 23cm. — (A regional history of the railways of Great Britain ; v.13)
Map (folded sheet) attached to lining paper. — Bibliography: p195-197. — Includes index
ISBN 0-7153-8004-4 : £8.95 : CIP rev.
Primary classification 385'.09422 B81-30369

385'.09424 — England. West Midlands. Railway services: Birmingham and Derby Junction Railway, *to 1844*

Clinker, C. R.. The Birmingham and Derby Junction railway / by C.R. Clinker. — Weston-super-Mare : Avon-AngliA, c1982. — 24p : ill,1map ; 22cm. — (Avon-AngliA transport history series)
Text on inside cover
ISBN 0-905466-47-0 (pbk) : Unpriced B82-26989

385'.09424'17 — England. Cotswolds. Railway services, *to 1980*

Maggs, Colin G.. Railways of the Cotswolds / by Colin Maggs. — Cheltenham : Peter Nicholson, c1981. — 96p : ill,1map ; 23cm
Fold-out map attached to rear lining paper. — Bibliography: p95
ISBN 0-907036-07-4 : £4.50 B82-39332

385'.09424'43 — Hereford and Worcester. Redditch *(District).* **Railways,** *to 1979*

The **Redditch** railways : 1859-1979 / [edited by David R. Morgan] ; [with drawings by David G. Budgen]. — [Redditch] ([Peakman St., Redditch, Worcs.]) : Redditch College of Further Education, 1980. — 50p : ill,1col.map,facsims ; 30cm
Cover title. — Text on inside covers
Unpriced (pbk) B82-09411

385'.09424'5 — Shropshire. Railway services, *to 1960 — Illustrations*

Shropshire railways revisited / selected and edited by members of the Shropshire Railway Society. — Shrewsbury : Shropshire Libraries, 1982. — [82]p : chiefly ill,facsims,1map ; 17x22cm
ISBN 0-903802-20-1 (pbk) : £2.00 : CIP rev. B82-12172

385′.09424′54 — Shropshire. Railway services: Shropshire & Montgomeryshire Railway, *to 1960*
Turner, Keith. The Shropshire & Montgomeryshire light railway / Keith & Susan Turner. — Newton Abbot : David & Charles, c1982. — 48p : ill,1facsim,1map,1port ; 25cm
Bibliography: p48
ISBN 0-7153-8233-0 : £4.95 : CIP rev.
B82-13066

385′.09424′59 — Shropshire. Bridgnorth *(District).* **Railway services: Severn Valley Railway** — *Illustrations*
Riley, Steve. Moods of steam : photographs of the Severn Valley railway / by Steve Riley. — Worcester (112 Monarch Drive, Henwick Park, Worcester WR2 6EU) : S. Riley, [1982]. — [19]p : all ill ; 21cm
Unpriced (unbound) B82-40392

385′.09424′6 — Staffordshire. Railway services: British Rail. *London Midland Region.* **Uttoxeter branch,** *to 1957*
Jones, P.. The Stafford & Uttoxeter railway / P. Jones. — [Trowbridge] : Oakwood, [1981]. — 40p,[12]p of plates : ill,1map,1facsim,plans ; 22cm. — (Oakwood library of railway history)
Bibliography: p39
ISBN 0-85361-277-3 (pbk) : £1.80 B82-12942

385′.09425 — England. Railway services: British Rail. *London Midland Region.* **London — Wolverhampton line** — *Visitors′ guides*
Owen, Rh. W.. A guide to the London (Euston), Rugby, Coventry, Birmingham, Wolverhampton railway route : with historical details of towns served and route diagrams / author Rh.W. Owen. — Llanfyllin : Cledren, [1981?]. — 15p : ill,1map ; 14x21cm
ISBN 0-9506876-0-x (pbk) : Unpriced
B82-14600

385′.09425′1 — Derbyshire. Railway services: British Rail. *London Midland Region.* **Peak line,** *to 1981*
Stephenson, John M.. The Peak Line / John M. Stephenson. — [Trowbridge] : Oakwood, 1982. — 88p : ill,maps ; 22cm
ISBN 0-85361-282-x (pbk) : £3.00 B82-35580

385′.09425′11 — Derbyshire. Railway services: British Rail. *London Midland Region.* **Cromford and High Peak line,** *to 1981*
Marshall, John, *1922 May 1-*. The Cromford & High Peak Railway / John Marshall. — Newton Abbot : David & Charles, c1982. — 64p : ill,facsims,maps,1port ; 21cm
Includes index
ISBN 0-7153-8128-8 (pbk) : £2.95 : CIP rev.
B82-01176

385′.09426 — East Anglia. Railway services: British Rail. *Eastern Region.* **Midland and Great Northern Joint lines,** *to 1968* — *Illustrations*
M & GN in action / [compiled by] M.D. Beckett and P.R. Hemnell. — Norwich : Becknell, 1981. — 64p : chiefly ill,1map ; 24cm
ISBN 0-907087-04-3 (pbk) : £3.25 B82-11905

385′.09426 — East Anglia. Railway services: British Rail. *Eastern Region.* **Midland and Great Northern Joint lines,** *to 1980*
Rhodes, John, *19---*. The Midland & Great Northern Joint Railway / John Rhodes. — London : Ian Allan, 1982. — 128p : ill,maps,plans ; 25cm
Maps on lining papers
ISBN 0-7110-1145-1 : £7.95 B82-34785

385′.09426 — East Anglia. Railway services, *ca 1919-1982* — *Illustrations*
Swinger, Peter W.. Railway history in pictures : East Anglia. — Newton Abbot : David & Charles, Jan.1983. — [96]p
ISBN 0-7153-8205-5 (pbk) : £5.95 : CIP entry
B82-32606

385′.09426 — East Anglia. Railway services: Eastern Countries Railway, *1840* — *Regulations*
Signals and regulations : 20 December 1846. — Weston-super-Mare : Avon-Anglia, [1982?]. — [24]p : ill ; 15x22cm. — (Avon-Anglia transport history series)
Cover title. — Facsim of: ed. published. [Stratford] : Eastern Counties Railways, [1846?]
ISBN 0-905466-52-7 (pbk) : £1.60 B82-41071

385′.09426 — Eastern England. Railway services: British Rail. *Eastern Region, to 1979*
Allen, Geoffrey Freeman. The Eastern since 1948 / G. Freeman Allen. — London : Ian Allan, 1981. — 143p : ill,maps ; 30cm
Maps on lining papers
ISBN 0-7110-1106-0 : £9.95 B82-07368

The **Eastern** yesterday and today / [compiled by] G. Freeman Allen. — London : Ian Allan, 1982. — 62p : ill ; 24cm
ISBN 0-7110-1185-0 (pbk) : £1.95 B82-38010

385′.09426′1 — Norfolk. Railway services, *1955-1980*
Norfolk Railway Society. The Norfolk Railway Society : 1955-1980 / edited by R.S. Adderson, G.L. Kenworthy, D.C. Pearce. — Norwich (c/o J.C. Thomas, 12 Stafford Ave., New Costessey, Norwich NR5 0QF) : Norfolk Railway Society, c1981. — 26p,[12]p of plates : ill,maps ; 21cm
£2.35 (pbk) B82-25383

385′.09426′12 — Norfolk. Fakenham region. Railway services — *Serials*
[Blastpipe *(East Harling)***]**. The Blastpipe : magazine of the Fakenham and Dereham Railway Society. — No.1 (Spring 1981)-. — [East Harling] ([c/o I. Jowett, Market Place, East Harling, Norfolk NOR 12X]) : The Society, 1981-. — v. : ill ; 21cm
ISSN 0263-0125 = Blastpipe (East Harling) : £0.10 per issue B82-14263

385′.09426′12 — Norfolk. Sheringham. Railway services: North Norfolk Railway Co., *to 1981* — *Illustrations*
Fisher, Brian. North Norfolk Railway album / Brian Fisher. — Norwich : Becknell, 1981. — 32p : chiefly ill,2ports ; 24cm
ISBN 0-907087-05-1 (pbk) : £1.95 B82-11901

385′.09426′5 — Cambridgeshire. Railway services: British Rail. *Eastern Region.* **Ely-St Ives line,** *to 1958*
Paye, Peter. The Ely & St. Ives railway / P. Paye. — Trowbridge : Oakwood, 1982. — 36p,[8]p of plates : ill,maps ; 22cm. — (Locomotion papers ; no.136)
Bibliography: p36
ISBN 0-85361-272-2 (pbk) : £1.80 B82-25115

385′.09426′51 — Cambridgeshire. Peterborough *(District).* **Railway services: Nene Valley Railway International** — *Serials*
Nene steam : the magazine of Nene Valley Railway International. — No.1 (1979)-. — Peterborough (Wansford Station, Old Great North Rd, Stibbington, Peterborough PE8 6LR) : Peterborough Railway Society, 1979-. — v. : ill,ports ; 21cm
Three issues yearly. — Description based on: No. 5 (Winter 1980/81)
ISSN 0263-3345 = Nene steam : £0.25
B82-31730

385′.09426′7 — Essex. Railway services: British Rail. *Eastern Region.* **Bishop′s Stortford, Dunmow & Braintree Branch,** *to 1972*
Paye, Peter. The Bishop′s Stortford Dunmow & Braintree branch / by P. Paye. — Oxford : Oxford Publishing, c1981. — iv,209p : ill,1map,facsims,plans ; 21cm
Bibliography: piv
ISBN 0-86093-142-0 (pbk) : £4.50 B82-10064

385′.09426′756 — Essex. Railway services: British Rail. *Eastern Region.* **Southminster branch,** *to 1981*
Swindale, Dennis L.. Branch line to Southminster / Dennis L. Swindale. — Colchester (Chappel and Wakes Colne Station, Colchester, Essex) : Published jointly by the author and the Stour Valley Railway Preservation Society, [1981]. — 71p : ill,1map,1facsim,plans ; 21cm
£2.25 (pbk) B82-13946

385′.09427 — Northern England. Railway services: British Rail. *London Midland Region.* **Settle-Carlisle line,** *1967-1979* — *Illustrations*
Walton, Peter. Diesels over the Settle to Carlisle route / Peter Walton. — Oxford : Oxford Publishing, c1982. — [120]p : chiefly ill,plans,ports ; 28cm
ISBN 0-86093-119-6 : £6.95 B82-31351

385′.09427 — Northern England. Railway services: British Rail. *London Midland Region.* **Settle-Carlisle line,** *to 1981*
Mitchell, W. R. (William Reginald). Settle to Carlisle : a railway over the Pennines / by W.R. Mitchell and David Joy. — Clapham : Dalesman, 1982. — 88p : ill,1map,2ports ; 21cm
Bibliography: p88
ISBN 0-85206-677-5 (pbk) : £2.25 B82-31386

Steam on the Settle and Carlisle / compiled by David Joy. — Clapham : Dalesman, 1981. — 80p : ill ; 18x22cm. — (Dalesman heritage)
ISBN 0-85206-648-1 (pbk) : £3.25 B82-06073

385′.09428′1 — Yorkshire. Railway services, *to 1967* — *Illustrations*
Railways in Yorkshire. — Clapham, N. Yorkshire : Dalesman
1: West Riding / compiled by David Joy. — 2nd ed. — 1979. — 80p : chiefly ill,1map ; 18x22cm
Previous ed.: 1976. — Bibliography: p6-7
ISBN 0-85206-494-2 (pbk) : £2.25 B82-11009

385′.09428′12 — West Yorkshire *(Metropolitan County).* **Calderdale** *(District).* **Railway services: British Rail.** *London Midland Region.* **Rishworth Branch,** *to 1953*
Hodgson, John, *1920-*. The Rishworth Branch / [John Hodgson assisted by Trevor Sutcliffe]. — Sutton-in-Craven (26, The Hawthorns, Sutton-in-Craven, Nr. Keighley, W. Yorkshire, BD20 8Bp) : Published on behalf of the Lancashire & Yorkshire Railway Society by B.C. Lane, [1982?]. — 24p : ill,1map,plan ; 21cm. — (Branchlines of the L. & Y. R., ISSN 0261-7919 ; no.1)
Cover title. — Text, ill on inside covers
Unpriced (pbk) B82-27232

385′.09428′3 — North Humberside. Railway services, *to 1981*
Goode, C. T.. The railways of east Yorkshire / C.T. Goode. — [Salisbury] : Oakwood, c1981. — 92p : ill,maps,1facsim,1plan ; 22cm. — (Locomotion papers ; no.135)
ISBN 0-85361-280-3 (pbk) : £3.00 B82-19780

385′.09428′3 — Yorkshire. Railway services: Hull & Barnsley Railway, *to 1922*
The **Hull** & Barnsley Railway
Vol.2 / by A.L. Barnett ... [et al.] ; editor B. Hinchliffe. — Sheffield : Turntable, 1980. — 288p,[49]p of plates(1 folded) : ill,maps ; 23cm
Includes index
ISBN 0-902844-51-2 : £11.95 B82-38824

385′.09428′38 — Humberside. Holderness *(District).* **Railway services: Spurn Head Railway,** *to 1952*
Hartley, Kenneth E.. The Spurn Head railway / by Kenneth E. Hartley and Howard M. Frost. — [Withernseal] ([12 Seaside Rd., Withernsea, N. Humberside]) : [Lunart Productions], c1981. — 49p : ill,maps,plans,ports ; 23cm
Cover title. — New ed. — Previous ed.: Market Harborough : Industrial Railway Society, 1976. — Text on inside covers. — Bibliography: p49
ISBN 0-906971-05-5 (pbk) : £0.85 B82-20600

385′.09428′46 — North Yorkshire. North York Moors. Railway services: North Yorkshire Moors Railway, *to 1979* — *Illustrations*
North Yorkshire Moors Railway : a pictorial survey / compiled by Peter Williams and David Joy. — 2nd ed. — Clapham, North Yorkshire : Dalesman, 1979. — 80p : of ill ; 18x22cm
Previous ed.: 1977
ISBN 0-85206-534-5 (pbk) : £2.25 B82-14854

385′.09428′7 — Tyne and Wear *(Metropolitan County).* **Railway services: Tyne and Wear Metro System**
Metro. — [Newcastle upon Tyne] ([Central Research and Intelligence Unit, Sandyford House, Newcastle upon Tyne NE2 1ED]) : Tyne and Wear County Council in association with the Passenger Transport Executive, [1981]. — [28]p : ill(some col.),maps,ports ; 27cm
Text on inside cover
Unpriced (pbk) B82-18077

385'.09428'7 — Tyne and Wear *(Metropolitan County)*. **Railways,** *to 1980*
Warn, C. R.. Rails between Wear and Tyne / by C.R. Warn. — Newcastle upon Tyne : Frank Graham, [1982?]. — 96p : ill,maps,facsims,1port ; 22cm
Bibliography: p96
ISBN 0-85983-160-4 (pbk) : £3.00 B82-21837

385'.09429 — Wales. Railway services: Great Western Railway. *Central Wales Division, to 1947 — Illustrations*
Cambrian Railways album 2 / [compiled by] C.C. Green. — London : Ian Allan, 1981. — 112p : chiefly ill,facsims,1map,ports ; 24cm
Dedication and postscript in English and Welsh. — Bibliography: p6
ISBN 0-7110-1055-2 : £5.95 B82-40426

385'.09429 — Wales. Railway services, *to 1974*
Owen-Jones, Stuart. Railways of Wales / by Stuart Owen-Jones. — Cardiff : Amgueddfa Genedlaethol Cymru, 1981. — 48p : ill,1map,facsims,ports ; 21cm
Bibliography: p4
ISBN 0-7200-0248-6 (pbk) : £1.50 B82-27707

385'.09429'5 — England. Wye Valley. Railway services: British Rail. *Western Region.* **Wye Valley line,** *to 1964*
Handley, Brian. The Wye Valley Railway / Brian M. Handley. — [Tisbury] : Oakwood, 1982. — 34p,[8]p of plates : ill,maps ; 22cm. — (Locomotion papers ; no.137)
ISBN 0-85361-283-8 (pbk) : £1.80 B82-19917

385'.09429'82 — West Glamorgan. Mumbles. Railway services: Mumbles Railway, *to 1960 — Illustrations*
The **Mumbles** Railway : the world's first passenger railway : a selection of old photographs of the Swansea to Mumbles railway, commemorating the 175th anniversary of the world's first passenger railway journey from Swansea, to the village of Oystermouth on 25th March, 1807. — Swansea ([c/o Chairman], 5A Slade Rd., Newton, Swansea) : Mumbles Railway Society, 1981. — 32p : chiefly ill,facsims ; 17x22cm
Unpriced (pbk) B82-38925

385'.0951 — China. Railway services, *to 1980*
Cantlie, Kenneth. The railways of China / by Kenneth Cantlie. — London (31B Torrington Sq., W.C.1.) : China Society, 1981. — 48p : 1ill,1map ; 21cm. — (China Society occasional papers, ISSN 0306-6665 ; no.21)
Map on leaf attached to back cover
Unpriced (pbk) B82-12095

385'.0954 — India. Railways, *to 1914*
Satow, Michael. Railways of the Raj / Michael Satow & Ray Desmond ; with a foreword by Paul Theroux. — London : Scolar Press, 1980 (1982 [printing]). — 118p : ill(some col.),1map,facsims,ports ; 25x27cm
Bibliography: p50
ISBN 0-85967-658-7 (pbk) : £7.50 : CIP rev. B81-39230

385'.0956 — Middle East. Railway services, *to 1970*
Hughes, Hugh. Middle East railways / by Hugh Hughes. — Harrow : Continental Railway Circle, 1981. — 128p : ill,maps ; 24cm
ISBN 0-9503469-7-7 (pbk) : £3.90 B82-17645

385'.09675'18 — Zaire. Katanga. Railway services: Benguela Railway, *to 1981*
Scott Morgan, John. The Lobito route : a history of the Benguela Railway. — Manchester : North Western Museum of Science and Industry, Mar.1982. — 1v.
ISBN 0-9505790-5-x (pbk) : £0.75 : CIP entry B82-16197

385'.096891 — Zimbabwe. Railway services, *to 1981*
Croxton, Anthony H.. Railways of Zimbabwe. — New ed. — Newton Abbot : David & Charles, Aug.1982. — [316]p
Previous ed. published as: Railways of Rhodesia, 1973
ISBN 0-7153-8130-x : £7.95 : CIP entry
Primary classification 385'.096894 B82-15835

385'.096894 — Zambia. Railway services, *to 1981*
Croxton, Anthony H.. Railways of Zimbabwe. — New ed. — Newton Abbot : David & Charles, Aug.1982. — [316]p
Previous ed. published as: Railways of Rhodesia, 1973
ISBN 0-7153-8130-x : £7.95 : CIP entry
Also classified at 385'.096891 B82-15835

385'.0971 — Canada. Railway services, *to 1980 — Encyclopaedias*
Hubbard, Freeman. Encyclopedia of North American railroading : 150 years of railroading in the United States and Canada / Freeman Hubbard. — New York ; London : McGraw-Hill, c1981. — vi,377p : ill,maps,facsims,ports ; 29cm
Includes bibliographies and index
ISBN 0-07-030828-4 : £29.95
Primary classification 385'.0973 B82-02334

385'.0973 — United States. Railway services, *to 1980 — Encyclopaedias*
Hubbard, Freeman. Encyclopedia of North American railroading : 150 years of railroading in the United States and Canada / Freeman Hubbard. — New York ; London : McGraw-Hill, c1981. — vi,377p : ill,maps,facsims,ports ; 29cm
Includes bibliographies and index
ISBN 0-07-030828-4 : £29.95
Also classified at 385'.0971 B82-02334

385'.22 — Rail travel
Great railway journeys of the world / Michael Frayn ... [et al.]. — London : British Broadcasting Corporation, c1981. — 192p,[16]p of plates : ill(some col.),maps ; 22cm
Includes index
ISBN 0-563-17903-1 : £9.95 B82-01384

385'.22 — Rail travel, *to 1979*
A **Book** of railway journeys / compiled by Ludovic Kennedy. — London : Fontana, 1981, c1980. — 356p : ill,ports ; 20cm
Originally published: London : Collins, 1980
ISBN 0-00-636427-6 (pbk) : £2.95 B82-01940

385'.22 — United States. Railway freight transport services. Stowing away *— Practical information*
Leen, Daniel. The freighthopper's manual for North America : hoboing in the 1980s / Daniel Leen. — London : Travelaid, c1981. — 95p : ill,ports ; 22cm
Bibliography: p94-95
ISBN 0-902743-19-8 (pbk) : £1.95 B82-40531

385'.22'0941 — Great Britain. Railway passenger transport services. Unadvertised stations *— Lists*
Croughton, Godfrey. Private and untimetabled railway stations : halts and stopping places / Godfrey Croughton, R.W. Kidner, Alan Young. — [Trowbridge] : Oakwood, 1982. — 148p : ill,maps ; 22cm
ISBN 0-85361-281-1 (pbk) : £4.50 B82-39798

385'.22'09422 — South-east England. Railway passenger transport services *— Inquiry reports*
Great Britain. *Monopolies and Mergers Commission.* British Railways Board : London and South East commuter services : a report on rail passenger services supplied by the Board in the South East of England / the Monopolies and Mergers Commission. — London : H.M.S.O., [1980]. — xi,315p : ill ; 25cm. — (Cmnd. ; 8046)
ISBN 0-10-180460-1 (pbk) : £8.60 B82-14710

385'.262 — Railway passenger transport services. Fares. Tickets. Edmondson, Thomas *— Biographies*
Farr, Michael, *1938-*. Thomas Edmondson : transport ticket pioneer : 1792-1851 / by Michael Farr. — Weston-super-Mare : Avon-Anglia, 1982, c1979. — 8p,4p of plates : facsims ; 22cm
Cover title. — Originally published: Lancaster : Lancaster Museum, 1979
ISBN 0-905466-55-1 (pbk) : £0.65 B82-39752

385'.264'0941 — Great Britain. Railway freight transport services *— Illustrations*
Rhodes, Michael, *1960-*. Freight trains of British Rail / by Michael Rhodes. — Oxford : Oxford Publishing, [c1982]. — [88]p : chiefly ill ; 28cm
ISBN 0-86093-129-3 : £6.95 B82-35850

385'.312 — English Channel. Proposed underwater tunnels: Channel Tunnel *— Proposals*
Fixed Channel link : report of UK/French study group / Department of Transport. — London : H.M.S.O., [1982]. — 103p : ill,maps ; 25cm. — (Cmnd. ; 8561)
ISBN 0-10-185610-5 (pbk) : £6.40 B82-32821

385'.314 — Eastern England. Railway services: British Rail. *Eastern Region.* **Steam locomotive depots,** *1950-1965*
Bolger, Paul. BR steam motive power depots : ER / Paul Bolger. — London : Ian Allan, 1982. — 112p : ill,plans ; 23cm
Includes index
ISBN 0-7110-1193-1 : £6.95 B82-39785

385'.314 — England. Railway services: British Rail. Locomotives depots, *to 1970*
Forsythe, H. G.. Steam shed portrait / H.G. Forsythe. — St Day : Atlantic, 1981. — [48]p : ill,plans,ports ; 20cm
ISBN 0-906899-02-8 (pbk) : £1.95 B82-37531

385'.314 — England. Railway services: British Rail. *London Midland Region.* **Locomotive depots,** *1954-1968 — Illustrations*
London Midland steam on shed / compiled by '45562'. — Truro : Barton
2. — [1981?]. — 95p : chiefly ill,plans ; 23cm
ISBN 0-85153-435-x : £5.95 B82-11007

385'.314 — Great Britain. Railway services: London, Midland and Scottish Railway. Locomotive depots, *to 1947*
Hawkins, Chris. LMS engine sheds : their history and development / by Chris Hawkins & George Reeve. — Upper Bucklebury : Wild Swan. — v,258p : chiefly ill,1map,plans ; 28cm
ISBN 0-906867-05-3 : £14.50 B82-23522

385'.314'0942 — England. Railway services: Great Western Railway. Stations
Clark, R. H.. An historical survey of selected Great Western stations : layouts and illustrations / by R.H. Clark. — Oxford : Oxford Publishing
Text and maps on lining papers. — Includes bibliographies
Vol.3. — c1981. — 222p : ill,plans ; 32cm
ISBN 0-86093-111-0 : £9.90 B82-10069

385'.314'09421 — London. Railways. Stations, *to 1979 — Lists*
A **Chronology** of passenger stations in the Greater London area. — Croydon (73 Bardsley Close, Croydon, Surrey CRO 5PT) : A. Leonard, c1980. — [70]p ; 21cm
Bibliography: p[70]
£1.50 (pbk) B82-17393

385'.314'0942132 — London. Westminster *(London Borough)*. **Railways. Stations: Paddington Station,** *to 1981*
Vaughan, J. A. M.. This is Paddington / John Vaughan. — Shepperton : Ian Allan, 1982. — 55p : ill,maps ; 29cm
ISBN 0-7110-1114-1 (pbk) : £2.50 B82-26189

385'.314'0942733 — Greater Manchester *(Metropolitan County)*. **Manchester. Railways. Stations: Liverpool Road Station** *(Manchester), to 1900*
Fitzgerald, R. S.. Liverpool Road Station, Manchester : an historical and architectural survey / R.S. Fitzgerald. — Manchester : Manchester University Press in association with the Royal Commission on Historical Monuments and the Greater Manchester Council, 1980. — 64p : ill,plans ; 28cm. — (Royal Commission on Historical Monuments supplementary series ; 1)
Includes index
ISBN 0-7190-0765-8 (cased) : Unpriced : CIP rev.
ISBN 0-7190-0790-9 (pbk) : £5.90 B80-05855

385'.314'0942733 — Greater Manchester *(Metropolitan County)*. **Manchester. Railways. Stations: Liverpool Road Station** *(Manchester), to 1980*
Oldest in the world : the story of Liverpool Road Station, Manchester, 1830-1980 / C.E. Makepeace, editor. — Stockport : Liverpool Road Station Society, 1980. — 89p : ill,3plans,2ports ; 21cm
Bibliography: p87-89
ISBN 0-907172-01-6 (pbk) : £1.95 B82-35536

385'.316 — England. Railway services: British Rail. *Western Region.* **Signalling systems,** *1948-1958 — Personal observations*

Gasson, Harold. Signalling days : final reminiscences of a Great Western railwayman / by Harold Gasson. — Oxford : Oxford Publishing, c1981. — 119p,[16]p of plates : ill,facsims,forms ; 22cm
ISBN 0-86093-118-8 (pbk) : £3.95 B82-10065

385'.361'0941 — Great Britain. Railway services: British Rail. Standard classes steam locomotives. Allocations, *1957-1968 — Lists*

Hands, P. B.. The B.R. Standard 9F 2-10-0's / by P.B. Hands. — Solihull (190 Yoxall Rd., Shirley, Solihull, W. Midlands B90 3RN) : P.B. Hands, 1980. — 34p ; 21cm. — (What happened to steam ; v.12)
Text on inside covers
Unpriced (pbk) B82-02977

385'.361'0941 — Great Britain. Railway services: British Rail. Steam locomotives. Allocations, *1957-1968 — Lists*

Hands, P. B.. The B.R. Britannia's, Clan's, Duke and Class 5's 4-6-0s / by P.B. Hands. — Solihull (190 Yoxall Rd., Shirley, Solihull, W. Midlands B90 3RN) : P.B. Hands, 1980. — 34p ; 21cm. — (What happened to steam ; v.9)
Text on inside covers
£0.85 (pbk) B82-02980

385'.361'0941 — Great Britain. Railway services: London and North Eastern Railway. 4-6-0 steam locomotives. Allocations, *1957-1964 — Lists*

Hands, P. B.. The L.N.E.R. B16, B12, B2, & B17 4-6-0's / by P.B. Hands. — Solihull (190 Yoxall Rd., Shirley, Solihull, W. Midlands B90 3RN), 1981. — 26p ; 21cm. — (What happened to steam ; v.18)
Text on inside covers
Unpriced (pbk) B82-02978

385'.361'0941 — Great Britain. Railway services: London and North Eastern Railway. B1 class steam locomotives. Allocations, *1957-1967 — Lists*

Hands, P. B.. The L.N.E.R. B1 4-6-0's / by P.B. Hands. — Solihull (190 Yoxall Rd., Shirley, Solihull, W. Midlands B90 3RN) : P.B. Hands, 1981. — 54p ; 21cm. — (What happened to steam ; v.13)
Text on inside covers
Unpriced (pbk) B82-02973

385'.361'0941 — Great Britain. Railway services: London and North Eastern Railway. Pacific type steam locomotives. Allocations, *1957-1966 — Lists*

Hands, P. B.. The London North Eastern A4, A3, A1 & A2 Pacific Locomotives / by P.B. Hands. — Solihull (190 Yoxall Rd., Shirley, Solihull, W. Midlands B90 3RN) : P.B. Hands, 1980. — 30p ; 21cm. — (What happened to steam ; v.4)
Text on inside covers
£0.75 (pbk) B82-02979

385'.361'0941 — Great Britain. Railway services: London and North Eastern Railway. V2 class steam locomotives. Allocations, *1957-1966 — Lists*

Hands, P. B.. The London North Eastern V2's 2-6-2's / by P.B. Hands. — Solihull (190 Yoxall Rd., Shirley, Solihull, W. Midlands B90 3RN) : P.B. Hands, 1980. — 26p ; 21cm. — (What happened to steam ; v.8)
Text on inside covers
£0.60 (pbk) B82-02972

385'.361'0941 — Great Britain. Railway services: London, Midland and Scottish Railway. 8F 2-8-0 steam locomotives. Allocations, *1957-1968 — Lists*

Hands, P. B.. The L.M.S. 8F 2-8-0's & Somerset and Dorset 7F 2-8-0's / by P.B. Hands. — [Solihull] ([190 Yoxall Rd., Shirley, Solihull, West Midlands B90 3RN]) : [P.B. Hands], 1982. — 86p ; 21cm. — (What happened to steam ; v.28)
Unpriced (pbk)
Also classified at 385'.361'09423 B82-39763

385'.361'0941 — Great Britain. Railway services: London, Midland and Scottish Railway. Crab class steam locomotives & Stanier Crab steam locomotives. Allocations, *1957-1967 — Lists*

Hands, P. B.. The L.M.S. 'Crabs' & 'Stanier Crabs' nos.42700-944 and 42945-84 / by P.B. Hands. — Solihull (190 Yoxall Rd., Shirley, Solihull, W. Midlands B90 3RN) : P.B. Hands, 1981. — 42p ; 21cm. — (What happened to steam ; v.19)
Text on inside covers
Unpriced (pbk) B82-02964

385'.361'0941 — Great Britain. Railway services: London, Midland and Scottish Railway. Ivatt class steam locomotives. Allocations, *1957-1967 — Lists*

Hands, P. B.. The L.M.S. IVATT 2-6-0's nos.43000-161 & 46400-527 / by P.B. Hands. — Solihull (190 Yoxall Rd., Shirley, Solihull, W. Midlands B90 3RN) : P.B. Hands, 1981. — 42p ; 21cm. — (What happened to steam ; v.15)
Text on inside covers
Unpriced (pbk) B82-02965

385'.361'0941 — Great Britain. Railway services: London, Midland and Scottish Railway. Jubilee class steam locomotives. Allocations, *1957-1967 — Lists*

Hands, P. B.. The London Midland 'Jubilee's' 4-6-0's / by P.B. Hands. — Solihull (190 Yoxall Rd., Shirley, Solihull, W. Midlands B90 3RN) : P.B. Hands, 1980. — 30p ; 21cm. — (What happened to steam ; v.3)
Text on inside covers
£0.75 (pbk) B82-02981

385'.361'0941 — Great Britain. Railway services: London, Midland and Scottish Railway. Steam locomotives. Allocations, *1957-1965 — Lists*

Hands, P. B.. The London Midland Patriot, Royal Scot, Princess and Coronation classes / by P.B. Hands. — Solihull (190 Yoxall Rd., Shirley, Solihull, W. Midlands B90 3RN) : P.B. Hands, 1980 (1981 [printing]). — 30p ; 21cm. — (What happened to steam ; v.7)
Text on inside covers
£0.75 (pbk) B82-02982

385'.361'0942 — England. Railway services: Great Western Railway. 2-8-0 steam locomotives. Allocations, *1957-1965 — Lists*

Hands, P. B.. The Great Western 2-8-0s / by P.B. Hands. — Solihull (190 Yoxall Rd., Shirley, Solihull, W. Midlands B90 3RN) : P.B. Hands, 1980. — 24p ; 21cm. — (What happened to steam ; v.1)
Text on inside covers
£0.60 (pbk) B82-02971

385'.361'0942 — England. Railway services: Great Western Railway. 4-6-0 steam locomotives. Allocations, *1957-1966 — Lists*

Hands, P. B.. The Great Western Counties, Granges, Modified Halls and Manors 4-6-0's / by P.B. Hands. — Solihull (190 Yoxall Rd., Shirley, Solihull, W. Midlands B90 3RN) : P.B. Hands, 1980. — 34p ; 21cm. — (What happened to steam ; v.10)
Text on inside covers
£0.85 (pbk) B82-02974

385'.361'0942 — England. Railway services: Great Western Railway. 57xx 0-6-0 tank locomotives. Allocations, *1957-1968 — Lists*

Hands, P. B.. The Great Western 57xx 0-6-0 pannier tanks / by P.B. Hands. — [Solihull] ([190 Yoxall Rd., Shirley, Solihull, West Midlands B90 3RN]) : [P.B. Hands], 1982. — 94p ; 21cm. — (What happened to steam ; v.27)
Unpriced (pbk) B82-39764

385'.361'0942 — England. Railway services: Great Western Railway. 1400 class tank locomotives & 4500 class tank locomotives. Allocations, *1957-1965 — Lists*

Hands, P. B.. The Great Western 14XX 0-4-2 tanks & 45XX 2-6-2 tanks / by P.B. Hands. — Solihull (190 Yoxall Rd., Shirley, Solihull, W. Midlands B90 3RN) : P.B. Hands, 1981. — 30p ; 21cm. — (What happened to steam ; v.20)
Text on inside covers
Unpriced (pbk) B82-02967

385'.361'0942 — England. Railway services: Great Western Railway. Castle class steam locomotives & King class steam locomotives. Allocations, *1957-1964 — Lists*

Hands, P. B.. The Great Western Castles and Kings 4-6-0s / by P.B. Hands. — Solihull (190 Yoxall Rd., Shirley, Solihull, W. Midlands B90 3RN) : P.B. Hands, 1980. — 29p ; 21cm. — (What happened to steam ; v.2)
Text on inside covers
£0.75 (pbk) B82-02966

385'.361'0942 — England. Railway services: Great Western Railway. Dukedog clas steam locomotives & 4300 class steam locomotives. Allocations, *1957-1964 — Lists*

Hands, P. B.. The Great Western 43XX 2-6-0's & Dukedog 4-4-0's / by P.B. Hands. — Solihull (190 Yoxall Rd., Shirley, Solihull, W. Midlands B90 3RN) : P.B. Hands, 1981. — 30p ; 21cm. — (What happened to steam ; v.14)
Text on inside covers
Unpriced (pbk) B82-02975

385'.361'0942 — England. Railway services: Great Western Railway. Hall class steam locomotives. Allocations, *1957-1965 — Lists*

Hands, P. B.. The Great Western Halls 4-6-0s / by P.B. Hands. — Solihull (190 Yoxall Rd., Shirley, Solihull, W. Midlands B90 3RN) : P.B. Hands, 1980. — 34p ; 21cm. — (What happened to steam ; v.6)
Text on inside covers
£0.85 (pbk) B82-02976

385'.361'09422 — Southern England. Railway services: Southern Railway Company. 2-6-0 steam locomotives. Allocations, *1957-1966 — Lists*

Hands, P. B.. The Southern K, N, N1, U, U1, 2-6-0's & W 2-6-4 tanks / by P.B. Hands. — Solihull (190 Yoxall Rd., Shirley, Solihull, W. Midlands B90 3RN) : P.B. Hands, 1981. — 30p ; 21cm. — (What happened to steam ; v.16)
Text on inside covers
Unpriced (pbk) B82-02970

385'.361'09422 — Southern England. Railway services: Southern Railway Company. Merchant Navy class steam locomotives, Schools class steam locomotives & West Country and Battle of Britain class steam locomotives. Allocations, *1957-1967 — Lists*

Hands, P. B.. The Southern, West Country & Battle of Britain Merchant Navy & School's classes / by P.B. Hands. — Solihull (190 Yoxall Rd., Shirley, Solihull, W. Midlands B90 3RN) : P.B. Hands, 1980. — 30p ; 21cm. — (What happened to steam ; v.5)
Text on inside covers
£0.75 (pbk) B82-02969

385'.361'09422 — Southern England. Railway services: Southern Railway Company. Steam locomotives. Allocations, *1957-1965 — Lists*

Hands, P. B.. The Southern H15, N15, 'King Arthurs' S15 & 'Lord Nelson' 4-6-0's, G16 4-8-0 tanks, H16 4-6-2 tanks / by P.B. Hands. — Solihull (190 Yoxall Rd., Shirley, Solihull, W. Midlands B90 3RN) : P.B. Hands, 1980. — 26p ; 21cm. — (What happened to steam ; v.11)
Text on inside covers
Unpriced (pbk) B82-02968

385'.361'09423 — South-west England. Railway services: British Rail. Somerset & Dorset Joint line. 7F 2-8-0 steam locomotives. Allocations, *1957-1968 — Lists*

Hands, P. B.. The L.M.S. 8F 2-8-0's & Somerset and Dorset 7F 2-8-0's / by P.B. Hands. — [Solihull] ([190 Yoxall Rd., Shirley, Solihull, West Midlands B90 3RN]) : [P.B. Hands], 1982. — 86p ; 21cm. — (What happened to steam ; v.28)
Unpriced (pbk)
Primary classification 385'.361'0941
B82-39763

385'.5'02541 — Great Britain. Light railways — *Directories*

AAA guide to light railway and industrial preservation / edited by Geoffrey Body, Ian G. Body. — Weston-super-Mare : Avon-AngliA, c1982. — 52p : ill,1map ; 22cm
Cover title: Light railways transport and industrial presentation
ISBN 0-905466-45-4 (pbk) : £0.85
Also classified at 629.04'074'0941 B82-26988

385'.5'0941693 — Donegal *(County)*. Light railway services, *to 1959*

Patterson, Edward M.. The County Donegal railways / by Edward M. Patterson. — 3rd ed. — Newton Abbot : David & Charles, 1982. — 208p : ill,facsims,maps,plans ; 23cm
Previous ed.: 1969. — Bibliography: p200-201. — Includes index
ISBN 0-7153-8167-9 : £6.95 : CIP rev.
B82-09618

385'.5'0942825 — South Yorkshire *(Metropolitan County)*. Barnsley *(District)*. Light railway services: Dearne District Light Railways, *to 1936*

Denton, A. S.. D.D.L.R. : the story of the Dearne District Light Railways and competitors / by A.S. Denton. — Bromley : Omnibus Society, [1982?]. — 23p : ill,ports ; 26cm
ISBN 0-901307-35-1 (unbound) : £0.85
B82-29242

385'.509429'4 — Powys. Montgomery *(District)*. Narrow gauge railway services : Welshpool and Llanfair Railway, *1901-1973*

Cartwright, Ralph. The Welshpool & Llanfair light railway. — Newton Abbot : David & Charles, Apr.1981. — [208]p
Previous ed.: 1972
ISBN 0-7153-8151-2 : £6.50 : CIP entry
B81-06889

385'.52'0941 — Great Britain. Miniature railways & narrow-gauge railways, *to 1980*

Miniature railways past and present / [compiled by] Anthony J. Lambert. — Newton Abbot ; London : David & Charles, c1982. — 95p : all ill,ports ; 25cm
ISBN 0-7153-8109-1 : £5.95 : CIP rev.
B82-04867

385'.52'09429 — Wales. Narrow gauge railway services, *to 1977 — Illustrations*

The **Welsh** narrow gauge railway : a pictorial history / [compiled by] J.D.C.A. Prideaux. — 2nd ed. — Newton Abbot : David & Charles, 1982. — 96p : ill,facsims,1map ; 25cm
Previous ed.: 1976. — Bibliography: p96
ISBN 0-7153-8354-x : £5.95 B82-29328

385'.54 — Central Southern England. Industrial railway services. Locomotives

Industrial locomotives of Central Southern England / compiled by Roger Hateley. — Market Harborough : Industrial Railway Society, [1982?]. — xxxvii,146p,[84]p of plates : ill,maps ; 21cm. — (Handbook ; J)
ISBN 0-901096-41-5 (cased) : Unpriced
ISBN 0-901096-42-3 (pbk) : Unpriced
B82-31388

385'.54 — Great Britain. Railway services: British Rail. Diesel locomotives sold to industries, *1964-1980 — Lists*

Booth, A. J.. BR in industry : former British Railways diesel locomotives sold for industrial service / A.J. Booth. — 2nd ed. — Rotherham : Industrial Railway Society, 1981. — 32p,[24]p of plates : ill ; 21cm
Previous ed.: 1972
ISBN 0-901096-40-7 (pbk) : £1.20 B82-08733

385'.54'0942352 — North Devon. Ball clay mining industries. Industrial railway services, *to ca. 1970*

Messenger, Michael J.. North Devon Clay : the history of an industry and its transport / M.J. Messenger. — Truro : Twelveheads Press, 1982. — 104p : ill,maps,1facsim,1plan ; 24cm
Bibliography: p97-98. — Includes index
ISBN 0-906294-06-1 (cased) : Unpriced
ISBN 0-906294-07-x (pbk) : Unpriced
B82-18896

385'.54'0942956 — Powys. Brecknock *(District)*. Tramroads: Brecon Forest Tramroad, *to 1860*

Reynolds, P. R.. The Brecon Forest tramroad / P.R. Reynolds. — Swansea (12 Beaconsfield Way, Sketty, Swansea, SA2 9JR) : P.R. Reynolds, 1979. — 142p : ill,maps ; 21cm
Bibliography: p134-136. — Includes index
£2.40 (pbk) B82-11963

386 — INLAND WATERWAYS TRANSPORT, FERRY TRANSPORT

386'.0941 — Great Britain. Inland waterways

Gagg, J. C.. The observer's book of canals / John Gagg ; with photographs by the author and drawings by Robert Wilson. — London : Warne, 1982. — 192p,[8]p of plates : ill(some col.),maps,1port ; 15cm. — (The Observer's pocket series ; 95)
Bibliography: p182-183. — Includes index
ISBN 0-7232-1625-8 : £1.95 B82-22825

McKnight, Hugh. The Shell book of inland waterways / Hugh McKnight ; editorial adviser: Charles Hadfield. — 2nd ed. — Newton Abbot : David & Charles, c1981. — 493p,[16]p of plates : ill(some col.),maps,ports ; 23cm
Previous ed.: 1975. — Includes index
ISBN 0-7153-8239-x : £10.95 : CIP rev.
B81-21510

386'.09422 — Southern England. Inland waterways — *Illustrations*

Pratt, Derek. Southern inland waterways / Derek Pratt. — London : Ian Allan, 1982. — 202p : ill,maps ; 25cm
ISBN 0-7110-1225-3 : £8.95 B82-38013

386'.1 — North-western Europe. Ferry services: European Ferries. Mergers with Sealink UK Ltd — *Inquiry reports*

Great Britain. *Monopolies and Mergers Commission*. European Ferries Limited, Sealink Limited : a report on the proposed merger. — London : H.M.S.O., 1981. — vii,114p : maps ; 25cm. — ([HC] ; 65)
At head of title: The Monopolies and Mergers Commission
ISBN 0-10-206582-9 (pbk) : £5.85 B82-11608

386'.2245 — Great Britain. Inland waterway freight transport. Horse-drawn canal boats, *to 1981*

Smith, D. J. (Donald John). The horse on the cut : the story of the canal horses of Britain / Donald J. Smith. — Cambridge : Stephens, 1982. — 184p : ill,1map,music,ports ; 24cm
Ill on lining papers. — Bibliography: p180. — Includes index
ISBN 0-85059-514-2 : £8.95 : CIP rev.
B81-35837

386'.2245 — Inland waterway freight transport. Canal barges

Scarry, Huck. Travels on a barge : a sketchbook / by Huck Scarry ; illustrated by the author. — London : Collins, 1981. — 69p : ill ; 29cm
Translation of: Un voyage en péniche
ISBN 0-00-138368-x : £3.95 B82-28240

386'.244'0941 — Great Britain. Inland waterway freight transport — *Proposals*

Hill, Peter, *1943-*. Transport : the water way / [text by Peter Hill] ; [photography by Ken Kirkwood ... [et al.]. — London : British Waterways Board, 1982. — 25p : ill(some col.),2col.maps,2ports ; 30cm
ISBN 0-903218-25-9 (pbk) : £2.50 B82-30834

386'.244'0941 — Great Britain. Inland waterways. Freight transport — *Proposals*

British freight waterways today and tomorrow / compiled and edited by Mark Baldwin with an introduction by David Hilling. — London : Inland Waterways Association, 1980. — 64p : ill,maps ; 30cm
Maps on inside covers. — Bibliography: p59-61
ISBN 0-900970-08-1 (corrected : pbk) : £2.50
B82-12114

386'.35'09426 — England. Great Ouse River. Water traffic. Density

Carter, W. B.. The Great Ouse and its tributaries : a capacity and density study / prepared by W.B. Carter. — [Bedford] ([26 Bromham Rd, Bedford MK40 2QP]) : Eastern Council for Sport and Recreation
Addendum 3: Zone 1, The Great Ouse and its associated waterways. — 1979. — 12p : ill ; 30cm
Cover title
Unpriced (pbk) B82-40695

386'.4 — Canals — *For children*

Woodlander, David. Canals. — London : Black, Jan.1983. — [32]p. — (History explorers)
ISBN 0-7136-2275-x (cased) : £2.95 : CIP entry
ISBN 0-7136-2276-8 (pbk) : £1.45 B82-32598

386'.46'0924 — England. Canals — *Personal observations*

Bryce, Iris. Canals are my life / Iris Bryce. — Homewell : Mason, c1982. — 104p,[8]p of plates : ill,1map,2ports ; 23cm
Includes index
ISBN 0-85937-277-4 : £7.95 : CIP rev.
B82-19279

386'.46'0941 — Great Britain. Canals — *Personal observations*

Harrington, Illtyd. The romance of the canals. — London : Longman, Oct.1982. — [192]p. — (Longman travellers series)
ISBN 0-582-50291-8 : £7.95 : CIP entry
B82-23358

386'.46'094273 — Greater Manchester *(Metropolitan County)*. Canals, *1650-1868*

Malet, Hugh. Coal, cotton and canals : three studies in local canal history / by Hugh Malet. — Swinton (375 Chorley Rd., Swinton, M27 2AY) : N. Richardson, [1981?]. — [12]p : ill,1map,ports ; 30cm
Cover title. — Text on inside covers
£1.00 (pbk) B82-05309

386'.47'094271 — Greater Manchester *(Metropolitan County)*. Canals: Manchester Ship Canal, *1820-1981*

Owen, David. The Manchester Ship Canal. — Manchester : Manchester University Press, Feb.1983. — [160]p
ISBN 0-7190-0864-6 : £9.50 : CIP entry
B82-39457

386'.48'09422 — Southern England. Canals: Kennet and Avon Canal — *Illustrations*

The **Kennet** & Avon Canal in pictures from Bath to Reading / [compiled by the Kennet and Avon Canal Trust]. — Devizes (Membership Office, The Wharf, Couch La., Devizes SN10 1EB) : Kennet and Avon Canal Trust, 1980. — 45p : chiefly ill,1map,1facsim ; 26cm
ISBN 0-9501173-2-3 (pbk) : Unpriced
B82-17371

386'.48'09424 — England. West Midlands. Canals: Birmingham Canal Navigations — *Illustrations*

May, Robert, *1932-*. The BCN in pictures / compiled wholly from the photographs collected and taken by Robert May. — [Birmingham?] : Birmingham Canal Navigations Society, 1973, c1982 ([1982 printing]). — [36]p : ill,facsims,2maps,ports ; 21x30cm
Unpriced (pbk) B82-39761

386'.48'094249 — West Midlands *(Metropolitan County)*. Abandoned canals

Chester-Browne, Richard. The other sixty miles : a survey of the abandoned canals of Birmingham and the Black Country / Richard Chester-Browne. — Stafford ('Brades', Lower Penkridge Rd., Acton Trussell, Stafford) : Birmingham Canal Navigations Society, 1981. — [42]p : ill ; 30cm
Cover title. — Bibliography: p42
Unpriced (pbk) B82-41034

386'.48'0942719 — North-west England. Canals: Bridgewater Canal

The **Bridgewater** Canal handbook. — London : Burrow, [1981?]. — 40p : ill,2maps,1port ; 25cm
Unpriced (pbk) B82-14568

386'.6 — English Channel. Ferry services. Cargoes: Lorries. Drivers

Survey of cross channel lorry drivers at Dover : a report of the main findings. — [London] ([2 Marsham St., SW1P 3EB]) : Department of Transport, 1981. — 15p ; 30cm
Cover title
Unpriced (pbk) B82-38479

386'.6'0916336 — English Channel. Newhaven-Dieppe ferry services, *to 1980*
O'Mahoney, B. M. E.. Newhaven-Dieppe 1825-1980 : the history of an Anglo-French joint venture / B.M.E. O'Mahoney. — 2nd ed. — Stowmarket : Cappella, 1981, c1980. — 114p,[34]p of plates : ill,2maps,facsims ; 22cm
Previous ed.: Wetherden : B.M.E. O'Mahoney, 1980. — Bibliography: p104. — Includes index
ISBN 0-9507011-0-6 (pbk) : £5.40 B82-17434

386'.6'0941 — Europe. Ferry services: Sealink UK Ltd.
Haresnape, Brian. This is Sealink / Brian Haresnape. — London : Ian Allan, 1982. — 32p : chiefly ill,ports ; 30cm
ISBN 0-7110-1250-4 (pbk) : £1.00 B82-34784

386'.6'094233 — East Dorset. Ferry services, *to 1980*
Tully, A.. Ferries of East Dorset / A. Tully. — Bournemouth : Bournemouth Local Studies Publications, 1981. — 24p : ill,2maps ; 21cm
Bibliography: p24
ISBN 0-906287-37-5 (pbk) : £0.35 B82-03267

386'.6'09424 — England. Severn Estuary. Ferry services, *to 1966*
Jordan, Christopher. Severn enterprise : the story of the old and new passage ferries / Christopher Jordan. — Ilfracombe : Stockwell, 1977 (1982 [printing]). — 112p,[32]p : ill,facsims,maps,plans,ports ; 22cm
Plans on inside covers. — Bibliography: p106-107
ISBN 0-7223-1536-8 (pbk) : £2.75 B82-31756

386'.6'094585 — Malta. Malta-Gozo ferry services, *to 1981*
Somner, Graeme. Ferry Malta : IL-Vapuri ta Ghawdex / by Graeme Somner. — Kendal : World Ship Society, 1982. — 42p : ill,1map ; 21cm
ISBN 0-905617-19-3 (pbk) : Unpriced
B82-19629

386'.8'09422323 — Kent. Medway River. Ports — *Practical information — Serials*
Medway ports shipping handbook. — 1981-. — Downham Market (11 London Rd, Downham Market, Norfolk, PE38 9BX) : Charter Publications, 1981-. — v. : ill,maps ; 21cm
Annual
ISSN 0261-281x = Medway ports shipping handbook : £2.50 B82-09062

387.1 — PORTS

387.1 — Harbours — *For children*
Crews, Donald. Harbour. — London : Bodley Head, Oct.1982. — [32]p
ISBN 0-370-30937-5 : £4.50 : CIP entry
B82-24455

387.1'0941 — Great Britain. Ports — *Serials*
Ports : guide to the nineteen ports / British Transport Docks Board. — '82-. — Norfolk (Bank Chambers, Downham Market, Norfolk PE38 9BV) : Charter Publications, 1982-. — v. : ill,maps,ports ; 21cm
Spine title: BTDB ports
ISSN 0262-1630 = Ports : £3.00 B82-32148

387.1'0941 — Great Britain. Ports — *Statistics — Serials*
Port statistics / compiled by the Department of Transport from returns made by port authorities and undertakings. — 1980-. — London : Department of Transport ; London (1 New Oxford St., WC1A 1DZ) : British Ports Association [distributor], 1981-. — v. ; 30cm
Annual. — Continues in part: Annual digest of port statistics
ISSN 0263-9149 = Port statistics : £20.00 per issue B82-36705

387.1'09411'75 — Scotland. Highland Region. Inverness. Ports: Port of Inverness — *Practical information*
The Port of Inverness. — [Inverness] ([23 Academy St, Inverness, IV1 1JN]) : Trustees of the Harbour of Inverness, 1978. — [16]p : ill,col.maps ; 21cm
Free (pbk) B82-26606

387.1'09413'1 — Scotland. Firth of Forth. Ports — *Practical information*
The Forth ports : official handbook of the Forth Ports Authority. — London : Publicity House, Streatham Hill, SW2 4TR : Burrow, [1980]. — 120p : ill(some col.),2maps ; 25cm
Unpriced (pbk) B82-19470

387.1'09415 — Ireland. Ports — *Practical information — Serials*
Ireland ports & shipping handbook. — 1981-. — Downham Market (11 London Rd, Downham Market, Norfolk PE38 9BX) : Charter Publications, 1981-. — v. : ill ; 21cm
Annual
ISSN 0260-924x = Ireland ports & shipping handbook : £2.50 B82-11148

387.1'09422'352 — Kent. Dover. Harbours: Dover Harbour, *to 1978*
Hasenson, Alec. The history of Dover Harbour / Alec Hasenson. — London : Aurum, c1980. — 475p : ill,maps,plans ; 24cm
Bibliography: p470-472. — Includes index
ISBN 0-906053-17-x : £40.00 B82-17990

387.1'09423'4 — Channel Islands. Ports — *Serials*
Channel Islands shipping & transport handbook. — 1982-. — Downham Market (Bank Chambers, Downham Market, Norfolk PE38 9BU) : Charter Publications, 1982-. — v. : ill,maps ; 21cm
Issued every two years
ISSN 0263-2918 = Channel Islands shipping & transport handbook : £2.50 B82-40075

387.1'09423'93 — Avon. Bristol. Ports: Port of Bristol, *to 1981*
Shipsides, Frank. Bristol : maritime city / Frank Shipsides and Robert Wall. — Bristol : Redcliffe, 1981. — 144p,[12]p of plates : ill (some col.),1map,1coat of arms ; 26cm
Bibliography: p138-139. — Includes index
ISBN 0-905459-37-7 : £10.00 B82-13531

387.1'09427'69 — Lancashire. Lancaster. Ports: Port of Lancaster, *to 1981*
Wilkinson, Eric. The port of Lancaster / by Eric Wilkinson ; edited with additional material by Edith Tyson. — [Lancaster] ([Old Town Hall, Market Sq., Lancaster LA1 1HT]) : [Museum and Art Gallery], 1982. — 15p ; 30cm. — (A Lancaster Museum monograph)
Bibliography: p15
Unpriced (unbound) B82-26916

387.1'09428'33 — Humberside. Immingham. Ports: Immingham Dock — *Visitors' guides*
British Transport Docks Board. The Port of Grimsby and Immingham / [British Transport Docks Board]. — London : Burrow, [1981?]. — 88p,[2]p of plates : ill(some col.),maps,col.ports ; 25cm
Unpriced (pbk)
Also classified at 387.1'09428'34 B82-14569

387.1'09428'34 — Humberside. Grimsby. Ports: Grimsby Docks — *Visitors' guides*
British Transport Docks Board. The Port of Grimsby and Immingham / [British Transport Docks Board]. — London : Burrow, [1981?]. — 88p,[2]p of plates : ill(some col.),maps,col.ports ; 25cm
Unpriced (pbk)
Primary classification 387.1'09428'33
B82-14569

387.1'09428'35 — Humberside. Goole. Ports: Port of Goole — *Serials*
Goole port handbook. — 1982-. — Downham Market ([Bank Chambers, Downham Market, Norfolk PE38 9BU]) : Charter Publications, 1981-. — v. : ill,maps ; 21cm
Annual
ISSN 0262-1622 = Goole port handbook : £2.00 B82-13416

387.1'09428'37 — Humberside. Ports: Port of Hull — *Visitors' guides*
British Transport Docks Board. The port of Hull : official handbook / [British Transport Docks Board Hull]. — [Gloucester] : [British Publishing Company by authority of the British Transports Docks Board, Hull], [1982?]. — 80p : ill(some col.),maps(some col.) ; 25cm
Cover title
ISBN 0-7140-2038-9 (pbk) : Unpriced
B82-20308

387.1'5 — Hampshire. Southampton. Docks, *to 1930 — Early works — Facsimiles*
A Souvenir of Southampton Docks / Southern Railway. — [Southampton] ([c/o Dr. E.K. Lloyd, Faculty of Mathematical Studies, The University, Southampton SO9 5NH]) : [Southampton University Industrial Archaeology Group], 1982. — 32p : ill ; 26cm
Cover title. — Facsim of ed. published: London : Southern Railway Co., 1930?
Unpriced (pbk) B82-37767

387.2 — WATER TRANSPORT. SHIPS

387.2'0216 — Merchant ships — *Lists*
Hornsby, D. T.. Ocean ships. — [New ed.] / David Hornsby. — London : Ian Allan, 1982. — 255p : ill ; 23cm
Previous ed.: i.e. 6th, 1978. — Includes index
ISBN 0-7110-1150-8 : £6.95 B82-14463

387.2'245 — Eastern England. Coastal waters. Freight transport. Sailing barges, *to 1975*
Hazell, Martin. Sailing barges / Martin Hazell. — 2nd ed. — Princes Risborough : Shire, 1982. — 32p : ill,1map ; 21cm. — (Shire album ; 13)
Previous ed.: 1976. — Text, ill on inside covers. — Bibliography: p33
ISBN 0-85263-584-2 (pbk) : £0.95 B82-31144

387.2'4 — Scotland. Strathclyde Region. Clyde Estuary. Shipping. Steam coasters, *to 1980 — Lists*
Duckworth, Christian Leslie Dyce. Clyde river and other steamers / Christian Leslie Dyce Duckworth, Graham Easton Langmuir. — 3rd ed. — Glasgow : Brown, Son & Ferguson Supplement. — 1982. — x,55p : ill ; 22cm
ISBN 0-85174-421-4 (pbk) : £3.00 B82-22951

387.2'432 — Passenger transport. Shipping. Four-funneled steam liners, *to 1958*
Shaum, John H.. Majesty at sea : the four-stackers / by John H. Shaum Jr. & William H. Flayhart III. — Cambridge : Stephens, 1981. — 168p : ill(some col.),facsims,ports ; 32cm
Includes index
ISBN 0-85059-461-8 : £14.95 : CIP rev.
B81-25886

387.2'432 — Passenger transport. Shipping. Steam liners, *to 1981*
Braynard, Frank O.. Fifty famous liners / Frank O. Braynard & William H. Miller. — Cambridge : Stephens, 1982. — 233p : ill,facsims,1port ; 25cm
Facsims on lining papers. — Includes index
ISBN 0-85059-504-5 : £12.95 : CIP rev.
B82-04981

387.2'432'0924 — Passenger transport. Shipping. Steam liners. Sailing. Arnott, Robert H. — *Biographies*
Arnott, Robert H.. Captain of the Queen / Robert H. Arnott and Ronald L. Smith. — Sevenoaks : New English Library, 1982. — 331p,[16]p of plates : ill,ports ; 23cm
ISBN 0-450-04891-8 : £7.95 B82-40165

387.5 — OCEAN TRANSPORT

387.5 — Shipping
Branch, Alan E.. Economics of shipping practice and management / Alan E. Branch. — London : Chapman and Hall, 1982. — xii,242p : ill ; 23cm
Bibliography: p228. — Includes index
ISBN 0-412-23580-3 (cased) : Unpriced : CIP rev.
ISBN 0-412-16350-0 (pbk) : Unpriced
B81-14851

Branch, Alan E.. Elements of shipping / Alan E. Branch. — 5th ed. — London : Chapman and Hall, c1981. — xiii,391p : ill,plans ; 23cm
Previous ed.: 1977. — Includes index
ISBN 0-412-23700-8 (cased) : £12.50 : CIP rev.
ISBN 0-412-23710-5 (pbk) : Unpriced
B81-30441

387.5 — Shipping — *Conference proceedings*

East-West Shipping Conference *(1981 : Sofia).* East-West Shipping Conference / organised jointly by the Bulgarian Chamber of Commerce and Industry and Lloyd's of London Press. — [London] : [Lloyd's of London Press], [1982-?]. — 1v.(various foliations) ; 31cm
ISBN 0-907432-26-3 : Unpriced B82-32230

Lloyd's World of Shipping in Hong Kong *(Conference : 1981).* The challenge of change : Lloyd's World of Shipping in Hong Kong October 12-16 1981. — [London] : [Lloyd's of London Press], [1982?]. — 1v.(various foliations) : ill ; 31cm
ISBN 0-907432-21-2 : Unpriced B82-31132

387.5'025'41 — Great Britain. Shipping — *Directories*

Shipping. — Great Missenden : Data Research Group, [1982]. — 39,115,67p ; 30cm
Cover title. — Includes index
ISBN 0-86099-350-7 (pbk) : Unpriced
Primary classification 338.7'62382'002541
B82-24688

387.5'025'4212 — London *(City).* **Shipping services** — *Directories — Serials*

The **City** handbook : [guide to the shipping services of the City of London]. — 1979-. — Downham Market (11 London Rd., Downham Market, Norfolk PE38 9BX) : Charter Publications, 1979-. — v. : ill,maps ; 21cm
Annual. — Description based on: 1982
ISSN 0260-9290 = City handbook : £2.50
B82-10109

387.5'06'01 — International marine organisations

Bekīashev, K. A.. International marine organizations : essays on structure and activities / by Kamil A. Bekiashev and Vitali V. Serebriakov ; translated from Russian by Vitali V. Serebriakov. — The Hague ; London : Nijhoff, 1981. — xxii,578p ; 25cm
Translation of: Mezhdunarodnie morskie organizatsii. — Includes bibliographies and index
ISBN 90-247-2464-3 : Unpriced B82-04421

387.5'065'41 — Great Britain. Shipping services: P & O Company — *Correspondence, diaries, etc.*

Padfield, Peter. Beneath the house flag of the P & O / Peter Padfield. — London : Hutchinson, 1981. — 147p,[16]p of plates : ill,1facsim,2ports ; 24cm
Includes index
ISBN 0-09-145760-2 : £9.95 : CIP rev.
B81-20144

387.5'06541 — Great Britain. Shipping services: Royal Mail Shipping Group, *1902-1937*

Green, Edwin. A business of national importance. — London : Methuen, Nov.1982. — [280]p
ISBN 0-416-32220-4 : £15.00 : CIP entry
B82-28289

387.5'065'42987 — Cardiff. Shipping services: Evan Thomas, Radcliffe and Company, *to 1981*

Jenkins, J. Geraint. Evan Thomas Radcliffe : a Cardiff shipowning company / by J. Geraint Jenkins. — Cardiff : National Museum of Wales, 1982. — 92p : ill,1facsim,port ; 21cm
ISBN 0-7200-0247-8 (pbk) : £2.50 B82-32642

387.5'06542987 — Cardiff. Shipping services: Morel Limited, *to 1957*

Gibbs, John Morel. Morels of Cardiff : the history of a family shipping firm / by John Morel Gibbs. — Cardiff : Amgueddfa Genedlaethol Cymru, c1982. — 183p,[1]folded sheet : ill,1form,ports,2geneal.tables ; 21cm
Includes index
ISBN 0-7200-0246-x (pbk) : £4.00 B82-27708

387.5'09 — Shipping, *1400-1900 — Conference proceedings*

International Reunion for the History of Nautical Science and Hydrography *(3rd : 1979 : National Maritime Museum).* Five hundred years of nautical science 1400-1900 : proceedings of the Third International Reunion for the History of Nautical Science and Hydrography held at the National Maritime Museum, Greenwich 24-28 September 1979 / edited by Derek Howse. — London : National Maritime Museum, c1981. — xii,408p : ill,ports ; 30cm
Includes index
ISBN 0-905555-55-4 (pbk) : £11.00
B82-23370

387.5'09163'36 — English Channel. Shipping

Ireland, Bernard. The busy Channel / Bernard Ireland. — London : Ian Allan, 1981. — 144p : ill ; 24cm
ISBN 0-7110-1138-9 : £6.95 B82-07365

387.5'092'2 — Great Britain. Merchant shipping, *1917-1979 — Personal observations — Collections*

The **Seaman's** world : merchant seamen's reminiscences / selected and introduced by Ronald Hope. — London : Harrap in association with The Marine Society, 1982. — 142p ; 23cm
ISBN 0-245-53893-3 : £4.95 B82-28768

387.5'092'4 — Bristol Channel. Freight transport. Cargo ships: Sailing coasters, *1915-1930 — Personal observations*

Eglinton, Edmund. The last of the sailing coasters : reminiscences and observations of the days in the Severn trows, coasting ketches and schooners / Edmund Eglinton. — London : H.M.S.O., 1982. — 131p,[16]p of plates : ill,1map,ports ; 23cm. — ([Recollections])
ISBN 0-11-290336-3 : £4.95 B82-17767

387.5'092'4 — Devon. Appledore. Shipping. Slade, W. J. — *Biographies*

Slade, W. J.. Out of Appledore : the autobiography of a coasting shipmaster and ship owner in the last days of wooden sailing ships / W.J. Slade. — 4th ed. / edited and with a new preface by Basil Greenhill. — London : Conway Maritime, 1980. — xxi,124p,[13]leaves of plates : ill,ports ; 22cm
Previous ed.: 1974
ISBN 0-85177-026-6 (pbk) : £3.20 B82-14323

387.5'092'4 — East Anglia. Coastal waters. Freight transport. Sailing barges, *ca 1940-1965 — Personal observations*

Roberts, Bob. Breeze for a bargeman / by Bob Roberts. — Lavenham : Terence Dalton, 1981. — vii,134p : ill,ports ; 23cm
ISBN 0-86138-007-x (pbk) : £4.95 B82-09920

387.5'092'4 — Eastern England. Coastal waters. Sailing oyster smacks. Sailing, *1945-1980 — Personal observations*

Frost, Michael. Half a gale / Michael Frost. — Havant : Mason, c1981. — 128p : ill,3charts ; 22cm
ISBN 0-85937-263-4 : £5.95 : CIP rev.
B81-20637

387.5'092'4 — Merchant shipping. William, W. E. — *Biographies — Welsh texts*

Williams, W. E. (William Edward). Ar y bont / gan W.E. Williams. — [Denbigh] : Gwasg Gee, c1981. — 198p,[13]p of plates : ill,1port ; 19cm
£3.50 B82-13764

387.5'092'4 — Sailing ships. Sailing. Behenna, Richard — *Correspondence, diaries, etc.*

Behenna, Richard. A Victorian sailor's diary : Richard Behenna of Vergan, 1833-1898 / introduced, edited and annotated by R.B. Behenna. — Redruth : Institute of Cornish Studies, 1981. — 73p : ill,facsims ; 21cm
Bibliography: p67
ISBN 0-903686-35-x (pbk) : Unpriced
B82-16356

387.5'092'4 — Sailing ships. Sailing. Jones, Tristan — *Biographies*

Jones, Tristan. A steady trade. — London : Bodley Head, Oct.1982. — [256]p
ISBN 0-370-30472-1 : £6.95 : CIP entry
B82-24849

387.5'092'4 — Sailing ships. Sailing. Nelson, William Andrew — *Biographies*

Falkus, Hugh. Master of Cape Horn : the story of a square-rigger captain and his world : William Andrew Nelson 1839-1929 / by Hugh Falkus. — London : Gollancz, 1982. — 160p,[23]p of plates : ill(some col.),facsims,1map,ports ; 26cm
Map on lining papers. — Bibliography: p10
ISBN 0-575-03089-5 : £12.95 : CIP rev.
B82-10781

387.5'0941 — Great Britain. Shipping services. Statistics. Information sources

Aldcroft, Derek H.. Rail transport / by Derek H. Aldcroft. Sea transport / by Derrick Mort. — Oxford : Published for the Royal Statistical Society and the Social Science Research Council by Pergamon, 1981. — xii,268p : forms ; 26cm. — (Reviews of United Kingdom statistical sources ; v.14)
Includes bibliographies and index
ISBN 0-08-026105-1 : £14.50 : CIP rev.
Primary classification 385'.0941 B81-25849

387.5'0941 — Great Britain. Shipping, *to 1981*

Simper, Robert. Britain's maritime heritage / Robert Simper. — Newton Abbot : David & Charles, c1982. — 392p : ill(some col.),maps,1facsim ; 23cm
Bibliography: p382-384. — Includes index
ISBN 0-7153-8177-6 : £11.95 : CIP rev.
B81-35826

387.5'0941 — Great Britain. Steamship services: P. & A. Campbell Ltd, *1853-1980*

Hope, Iain. The Campbells of Kilmun : shipowners 1853-1980 / Iain Hope. — Johnstone ([Loanhead Transport Ltd., Boghouse, Brookfield], Johnstone, Renfrewshire [PA5 8UD]) : Aggregate Publications, c1981. — [88]p : ill,ports ; 21cm
Bibliography: p[85]-[88]
£1.80 (pbk) B82-00039

387.5'0942 — England, *to 1980.* **Maritime aspects**

Shea, Michael. Maritime England / Michael Shea. — [London] : Country Life in association with the English Tourist Board, 1981. — 208p : ill(some col.),3charts(some col.),ports(some col.) ; 31cm
Bibliography: p204. — Includes index
ISBN 0-600-36803-3 : £12.50 B82-04459

387.5'09422'52 — East Sussex. Rye. Shipping, *to 1974*

Collard, John A.. A maritime history of Rye / by John A. Collard. — Rye : J.A. Collard, 1978. — 153p,[3]folded leaves of plates : ill,charts,maps,facsims ; 25cm
Includes index
ISBN 0-9506276-1-5 (cased) : Unpriced
ISBN 0-9506276-0-7 (pbk) : Unpriced
B82-03447

387'.509423 — South-west England. Shipping, *ca 1790-ca 1930.* **Social aspects**

West Country maritime and social history : some essays / edited by Stephen Fisher. — [Exeter] : University of Exeter, 1980. — ix,159p : ill,maps,facsims,1port ; 30cm. — (Exeter papers in economic history ; no.13)
ISBN 0-85989-121-6 (pbk) : Unpriced
B82-19041

387.5'09428'3 — Humberside. Humber River. Shipping, *to 1978*

Humber shipping : a pictorial history / compiled by Michael E. Ulyatt & Edward W. Paget-Tomlinson. — Clapham, N. Yorkshire : Dalesman, 1979. — 80p : ill,1map ; 18cm
Bibliography: p78
ISBN 0-85206-488-8 (pbk) : £2.25 B82-03634

387.5'09429'21 — Gwynedd. Ynys Môn. Shipping, *1879 — Welsh texts*

Eames, Aled. Morwyr Môn gan mlynedd yn ôl, 1879 / gan Aled Eames. — [Caernarfon] : Cyngor Sir Gwynedd, Gwasanaeth Llyfrgell, c1982. — 21p ; 22cm. — (Cyfres darlithoedd Môn ; 5)
A lecture delivered at Moelfre Central Hall, Wed. 21 March 1979
ISBN 0-904852-24-5 (pbk) : £0.60 B82-21303

387.5'095 — Far East. Shipping — *Serials*

Far East shipping. — 1st ed. (1980/81)-. — Colchester (Fairfax House, Colchester CO1 1RJ) : Seatrade Publications, 1980-. — v. : ill,maps ; 29cm
Annual
ISSN 0144-8781 = Far East shipping : Unpriced B82-09076

387.5'098 — Latin America. Merchant shipping — *Conference proceedings*

Latin American Shipping Conference *(1981 : Rio de Janeiro).* Latin American Shipping Conference : Riocentro, Rio de Janeiro 13, 14, 15 October 1981 / [edited by David Robinson and Hazel Lloyd]. — Colchester (Fairfax House, Colchester CO1 1RJ) : Seatrade Conferences, [1982?]. — 149p : 1map ; 30cm
Unpriced (pbk) B82-18382

387.5'1 — Freight transport. Shipping. Economic aspects

Advances in maritime economics. — Cardiff : University College Cardiff Press, Oct.1982. — [294]p
Originally published: Cambridge : Cambridge University Press, 1977
ISBN 0-906449-47-2 : £12.00 : CIP entry B82-27217

387.5'1 — Gwynedd. Mawddach River. Freight transport. Shipping. Evans, David, *b. ca. 1825.* **Accounts,** *1846-1869*

Lloyd, Lewis. Sails on the Mawddach : the account books of David Evans, boatman / Lewis Lloyd. — Harlech (Cadair Owain, Llanfair, Harlech, Gwynedd) : L. Lloyd, c1981. — 48p : ill,1map,facsims ; 20x21cm. — (Maritime Merioneth ; 7)
Text and ill on inside covers
ISBN 0-9504022-1-4 (pbk) : £2.25 B82-09470

387.5'1 — Shipping services. Financial aspects — *Conference proceedings*

Seatrade Money and Ships Conference *(10th : 1982 : London).* Money & ships 1982 : transcript of the tenth Seatrade Money and Ships conference held at the Grosvenor House Hotel, 30 & 31 March 1982 / [edited by David Robinson and Hazel Lloyd]. — Colchester (Fairfax House, Colchester CO1 1RJ) : Seatrade, [1982]. — 146p : ill ; 30cm
Cover title
Unpriced (pbk) B82-35355

387.5'4044 — Merchant sailing ships. Naval life, *ca 1870-1926*

Greenhill, Basil. Seafaring under sail : the life of the merchant seaman / Basil Greenhill & Denis Stonham. — Cambridge : Stephens, 1981. — 184p : ill,ports ; 25cm
Ill on lining papers
ISBN 0-85059-466-9 : £9.95 : CIP rev. B81-30573

387.5'44 — Freight transport. Shipping — *Forecasts*

Review and outlook for the shipping market 1980-83. — London (Rodwell House, Middlesex St., E1 7HJ) : Terminal Operators, 1981. — v,44leaves : ill ; 30cm
£70.00 (spiral) B82-03985

387.5'44'072042 — Freight transport. Shipping. Research organisations: Lambert Brothers Shipping. *Studies and Projects Unit*

Lambert Brothers Shipping. *Studies and Projects Unit.* A statement of capability of the Studies and Projects Unit of Lambert Brothers Shipping Limited. — London (43 Worship St., EC2A 2LB) : The Unit, 1981. — 12 leaves ; 31cm
Unpriced (pbk) B82-01498

387.5'442 — Freight transport. Shipping. Containerisation — *Conference proceedings*

Container operations & shipping conference : in co-operation with the European Shippers' Councils [ESC], November 27/28/29th, 1979, RAI Congress Centre, Amsterdam. — [Great Britain] : CS Publications Conferences, 1979. — lv.(loose-leaf) : ill,maps,plans ; 24cm
Unpriced B82-05867

387.5'442 — Freight transport. Shipping. Deep sea roll on/roll off services

The **Status** of deep-sea ro/ro services / prepared by the Research Division, H.P. Drewry (Shipping Consultants). — London : Drewry, 1980. — 68p : ill(some col.) ; 30cm. — (An Economic study, ISSN 0307-4919 ; no.87)
£40.00 (pbk) B82-35931

387.5'442 — Freight transport. Shipping. Roll in/roll off services — *Conference proceedings*

RoRo 81 *(Conference : Hamburg).* RoRo 81 : Congress Centrum Hamburg, 30 June-2 July 1981. — Rickmansworth : BML Business Meetings, c1982. — xiii,353p : ill,maps,plans,ports ; 30cm
ISBN 0-904930-18-1 (pbk) : £50.00 B82-39031

387.5'448 — Steam coal. Freight transport. Shipping — *Forecasts*

The **Growth** of steam coal trade : a review and forecast of international trade in thermal coal and shipping requirements : 1980-90 / prepared by the Research Division H.P. Drewry (Shipping Consultants) Limited. — London (34 Brook St., W1Y 2LL) : [H.P. Drewry], c1980. — 138p : ill ; 30cm. — (Survey ; no.22) (HPD Shipping publications)
£95.00 (pbk) B82-40679

387.7 — AIR TRANSPORT

387.7 — Air transport — *For children*

Althea. Flying in an aeroplane / by Althea ; illustrated by Roger Phillippo. — Cambridge : Dinosaur, c1981. — [24]p : col.ill ; 16x19cm
ISBN 0-85122-313-3 (cased) : Unpriced
ISBN 0-85122-140-8 (pbk) : Unpriced B82-32074

387.7 — Airlines — *For children*

Methold, Ken. Airline / Ken Methold. — London : Evans, 1982. — 48p : ill(some col.) ; 21cm. — (Talking shop)
ISBN 0-237-29249-1 (pbk) : Unpriced B82-16622

387.7'023'41 — Great Britain. Civil aviation — *Career guides*

Brunn, Walter. Working as aircrew / Walter Brunn. — London : Batsford Academic and Educational, 1982. — 104p,[8]p of plates : ill ; 23cm. — (Careers series)
Includes index
ISBN 0-7134-4457-6 : £5.95 : CIP rev. B82-06953

387.7'05 — Air services — *Serials*

[Air travel & interline news *(Agents' edition)***].** Air travel & interline news. — Agents' ed. — Issue no.369 (Apr. 13 1981)-. — [Bexhill-on-Sea] ([P.O Box 1, Bexhill-on-Sea, Sussex]) : Interline News Ltd., 1981-. — v. : ill,ports ; 36cm
Twenty-two issues yearly. — Continues: Interline & air travel news (Agents' edition)
ISSN 0262-4249 = Air ravel & interline news. Agents' edition : £2.50 per year B82-03410

387.7'0973 — United States. Civil aviation

Taneja, Nawal K.. Airlines in transition / Nawal K. Taneja. — Lexington, Mass. : Lexington Books ; [Aldershot] : Gower [distributor], 1981. — xvii,247p : ill ; 24cm
Bibliography: p239-244. — Includes index
ISBN 0-669-04345-1 : £14.50 B82-00842

387.7'1 — Great Britain. Airlines — *Accounts*

Airlines passenger & freight / industrial commentary by Roy Allen. — London : Jordan & Sons (Surveys), c1982. — xxx,55p ; 30cm
ISBN 0-85938-158-7 (pbk) : Unpriced B82-28398

387.7'1'0973 — United States. American airlines. Economic aspects

Airline economics / edited by George W. James. — [Lexington, Mass.] : Lexington Books ; [Aldershot] : Gower [distributor], 1982. — xxx,316p : ill,maps ; 24cm
Includes index
ISBN 0-669-04909-3 : £25.00 B82-27878

387.7'12 — Europe. International air passenger transport services. Fares. Great Britain. *Parliament. House of Commons. Industry and Trade Committee.* **Fifth report ... session 1980-81** — *Critical studies*

Great Britain. Fourth special report from the Industry and Trade Committee, session 1980-81 : European air fares : observations by the government on the fifth report of the committee in session 1980-81. — London : H.M.S.O., [1981]. — xip ; 25cm. — ([HC] ; 472)
ISBN 0-10-247281-5 (unbound) : £1.50 B82-11543

387.7'333'0941 — Great Britain. Gliders — *Lists*

British gliders : a comprehensive listing of sailplane registrations and identities used in the U.K., 1930-1980 / edited by P.H. Butler. — 3rd ed. — Liverpool : Merseyside Aviation Society, 1980. — 102p : ill ; 21cm. — (A Merseyside Aviation Society publication)
Previous ed.: 1975. — Ill on inside covers
ISBN 0-902420-35-6 (pbk) : £3.90 B82-37919

387.7'334 — Civil aircraft. Registration. Index marks — *Lists* — *Serials*

Civil aircraft registrations. — 1982-. — London : Janes Pub. Co., 1982-. — v. : ill ; 19cm
Two issues yearly
ISSN 0263-1385 = Civil aircraft registrations : £1.50 per issue B82-18522

387.7'334'05 — Civil aircraft — *Lists* — *Serials*

[Archive *(Air-Britain)***].** Archive : the Air-Britain civil aviation historical quarterly. — 1980, no.1-. — [Nailsworth] ([c/o D. Partington, The Haven, Nympsfield Rd., Nailsworth, Glos.]) : [Air-Britain], 1980-. — v. : ill ; 30cm
Description based on: 1980, no.4
ISSN 0262-4923 = Archive (Altrincham) : Unpriced B82-09673

387.7'334'091822 — Mediterranean region. Civil aircraft — *Lists*

Civil aircraft register of Italy, Greece, Morocco, Monaco, Cyprus, Algeria, Malta. — 4th ed.. — [Brentwood] : LAAS International, 1981. — 43p : ill ; 21cm
Previous ed.: 1977. — Ill. on inside covers
ISBN 0-85075-055-5 (pbk) : Unpriced B82-06199

387.7'334'0941 — Great Britain. Civil aircraft — *Lists*

Hoddinott, R.. British civil aircraft register G-AHAA to G-AHZZ / compiled by R. Hoddinott. — [Brentwood] : LAAS International, 1982. — [20]p : ill ; 22cm
Ill on inside covers
ISBN 0-85075-056-3 (pbk) : Unpriced B82-30677

Hoddinott, R.. British civil aircraft register G-AIAA to G-AIZZ / compiled by R. Hoddinott. — [Brentwood] : LAAS International, 1981. — [20]p : ill ; 21cm
Ill. on inside covers
ISBN 0-85075-054-7 (pbk) : Unpriced B82-06198

Hoddinott, R.. British civil aircraft register G-BDAA to G-BDZZ / compiled by R. Hoddinott. — [Brentwood] : LAAS, 1979. — [20]p : ill ; 21cm
Ill on inside covers
ISBN 0-85075-037-7 (pbk) : Unpriced B82-06403

387.7'334'0944 — France. Civil aircraft — *Lists*

Civil aircraft register of France. — 9th ed. — [Brentwood] : LAAS International, 1981. — 135p : ill ; 21cm
Previous ed.: published as France. 1979. — Ill. on inside covers
ISBN 0-85075-051-2 (pbk) : Unpriced B82-06200

387.7'36 — Airports — *For children*

Barton, Byron. Airport. — London : MacRae, Oct.1982. — [32]p
ISBN 0-86203-111-7 : £4.95 : CIP entry B82-24589

387.7'36 — Airports — *For children*
continuation

Jay, Michael, *1946-*. Airports / Michael Jay and Mark Hewish. — London : Watts, 1982. — 32p : col.ill,1form ; 22cm. — (A First look book)
Includes index
ISBN 0-85166-953-0 : £2.99 B82-23300

Peacock, Frank. Let's go to the airport / Frank Peacock ; general editor Henry Pluckrose ; photography by G.W. Hales. — London : Watts, c1974 (1982 [printing]). — [36]p : col.ill ; 22cm. — (Let's go series)
ISBN 0-85166-518-7 : £2.99 B82-25841

387.7'36 — Airports. Planning. Political aspects

Feldman, Elliot J.. Technocracy versus democracy : the comparative politics of international airports / Elliot J. Feldman, Jerome Milch ; with a foreword by Theodore J. Lowi. — Boston : Auburn House ; London : Eurospan [[distributor]], c1982. — xlv,299p : ill,maps ; 25cm
Includes index
ISBN 0-86569-063-4 : £16.50 B82-23118

387.7'36'06041 — Great Britain. Airports. Administration. Organisations: British Airports Authority. Financial assistance by Great Britain. *Department of Trade — Inquiry reports*

Great Britain. *Parliament. House of Commons. Committee of Public Accounts.* Twentieth report from the Committee of Public Accounts : together with the proceedings of the committee, the minutes of evidence and appendices : session 1979-80 : Department of Trade : advances to the British Airports Authority. — London : H.M.S.O., [1980]. — xiii,24p ; 25cm. — ([HC] ; 738)
ISBN 0-10-027389-0 (pbk) : £2.85 B82-09504

387.7'36'0941 — Great Britain. Aerodromes — *Lists*

British Isles airfield guide / edited by P.H. Butler. — 9th ed. / map by M.C. McIvor. — Liverpool : Merseyside Aviation Society, 1981. — 32p : ill ; 22cm + 1col.map(44x58cm folded to 20x11cm). — (A Merseyside Aviation Society publication)
Previous ed.: 1978. — Map attached to inside back cover also available separately
ISBN 0-902420-37-2 (pbk) : £2.00
ISBN 0-902420-38-0 (map) : Unpriced
B82-12738

387.7'36'0941 — Great Britain. Airports. Regional planning — *Proposals*

Colvin, Michael. Airport UK : a policy for the UK's civil airports / Michael Colvin, Graham Bright, Christopher Thompson. — London : Centre for Policy Studies, 1982. — 64p ; 30cm
Maps on inside covers. — Bibliography: p46
ISBN 0-905880-44-7 (pbk) : £2.50 B82-40463

387.7'36'0942 — England. Airports: London Airport. Third site. Location — *Feasibility studies*

Bringing the third London airport down to earth : a two-part study / compiled by the Willingale Anti-Airport Group. — Ongar : Willingale Anti-Airport Group, [1979]. — 15leaves ; 30cm
Cover title: Assessment of Willingale as a possible site for the third London airport
ISBN 0-9506718-1-9 (spiral) : £1.50
B82-35925

387.7'36'0942191 — London. Croydon *(London Borough).* **Aerodromes: Croydon Aerodrome** — *History — Serials*

[Journal *(Croydon Airport Society)*]. Journal / Croydon Airport Society. — Issue 1 (1981)-. — [Carshalton] ([c/o Mr E. Sanders, 'Wychwood' Sunnymede Ave., Carshalton, Surrey]) : The Society, 1981-. — v. : ill ; 21cm
Quarterly
ISSN 0263-3043 = Journal - Croydon Airport Society : £0.20 per issue B82-22693

387.7'36'0942356 — Devon. Exeter. Airports: Exeter Airport

Exeter airport : handbook / issued by authority of Exeter Airport Ltd. — Wallington : Home Publishing, [1982?]. — 36p : ill,1map ; 21cm
Unpriced (pbk) B82-36029

387.7'36'0942548 — Leicestershire. Castle Donnington. Airports: East Midlands Airport — *Practical information*

East Midlands Airport / issued by the authority of the East Midlands Airport. — 7th ed. — Wallington : Home Publishing, [1982?]. — 72p : ill,1map,3ports ; 21cm
Unpriced (pbk) B82-24643

387.7'36'09426712 — Essex. Stansted Mountfitchet. Airports: Stansted Airport. Development. Proposals

The **Case** for the North : Stansted Airport-London public inquiry 1982 / North of England Regional Consortium. — Manchester (c/o J. Hetherington, PO Box KOI, Town Hall, Manchester M60 2LA) : City of Manchester Public Relations Office, [1982?]. — 1folded sheet([6]p) : col.ill,col.maps ; 30cm
Unpriced B82-36236

387'.7'36'0942733 — Greater Manchester *(Metropolitan County).* **Manchester. Airports: Manchester International Airport**

Britain's northern gateway / editor: Mike Kiddey ; assistant editor: David Tierney. — Bradford : M.C.B., [1982?]. — 44p : ill,2maps,plans(some col.) ; 30cm
Unpriced (pbk) B82-36030

387.7'362 — Essex. Stansted Mountfitchet. Airports: Stansted Airport. Railway services — *Proposals*

Great Britain. *Working Party on Rail Access to Stansted Airport.* Report of the Working Party on Rail Access to Stansted Airport. — [London] : Department of Transport, 1981. — 46p : ill,1map ; 30cm
Unpriced (pbk) B82-40105

387.7'362 — West Sussex. Crawley. Airports: Gatwick Airport. Second terminal. Development. Proposals — *Inquiry reports*

Second terminal, Gatwick and other works : report of the public enquiry 29 January-11 July 1980 / inspector, John Newey ; assessors, E.B. Haran, J.B. Veal ; secretary, Charles Nicholls. — London : H.M.S.O., 1981. — iii,178p + 6sheets(maps ; 27-35cm folded to 17x14cm) ; 29cm
Six maps on six sheets in pocket. — Includes index
ISBN 0-11-751540-x (pbk) : £15.00
B82-17322

387.7'4042 — Great Britain. Airports. Civil aeroplanes. Arrival & departure — *Lists — Serials*

Airport schedules : for airports in the U.K. and Ireland. — 1981-. — Hounslow (Noble Corner, Great West Rd, Hounslow, Middx TW5 0PA) : Airline Publications and Sales, [1981]-. — v. : ill ; 21cm
Annual. — Continues: UK and Ireland airport schedules
ISSN 0262-8384 = Airport schedules : £2.50
B82-10118

387.7'4'0688 — Air services. Marketing

Shaw, S.. Air transport : a marketing perspective. — London : Pitman, Oct.1981. — [288]p
ISBN 0-273-01760-8 (pbk) : £9.95 : CIP entry
B81-30255

387.7'42 — Air passenger transport services — *For children*

Wilson, Mike. Jet journey / authors Mike Wilson and Robin Scagell. — London : Marshall Cavendish, 1978. — 59p : col.ill ; 29cm. — (Woodpecker books)
Text on lining papers. — Includes index
ISBN 0-85685-336-4 : Unpriced B82-32413

387.7'42 — Europe. International air transport services. Fares — *Proposals*

The **New** EEC proposals for European air fares and transport services. — London (6 Stanbrook House, Orchard Grove, Orpington, Kent BR6 0SR) : European Business Publications, Dec.1981. — [88]p. — (European business reports ; no.2)
ISBN 0-907027-05-9 (unbound) : £26.00 : CIP entry B81-38295

387.7'42'0207 — Air travel — *Humour*

Parker, Cliff. How to avoid flying / Cliff Parker ; illustrated by Barry Robson. — Sevenoaks : New English Library, 1982. — 144p : ill ; 20cm
ISBN 0-450-05412-8 (pbk) : £1.50 : CIP rev.
B82-06824

387.7'42'05 — Air travel — *Practical information — Serials*

Hickmans' international air traveller. — [1982]-. — London : Mitchell Beazley, 1982-. — v. : ill,maps,plans ; 22cm
Annual. — Continues: Hickmans' world air travel guide
ISSN 0263-0966 = Hickmans international air traveller : £6.95 B82-15768

387.7'42'09 — Air travel, *to 1981*

A **Book** of air journeys. — London : Collins, Nov.1982. — [275]p
ISBN 0-00-216377-2 : £7.95 : CIP entry
B82-27792

387.7'42'0924 — Great Britain. International air passenger transport services. Laker, *Sir* **Freddie** — *Biographies*

Banks, Howard. The rise and fall of Freddie Laker. — London : Faber, Oct.1982. — [250]p
ISBN 0-571-11986-7 : £6.95 : CIP entry
B82-28473

387.7'44'025 — Air freight transport services — *Directories — Serials*

Airtrade air freight directory. — Apr. to Sept. 1979-. — [London] ([30 Old Burlington St., W1X 2AE]) : [Maclean Hunter Ltd.], 1979-. — v. ; 29cm
Two issues yearly. — Spine title: Air freight directory (London). — Description based on: Oct. 1981 to Mar. 1982 issue
ISSN 0262-6888 = Airtrade air freight directory : £5.00 per issue B82-10123

388 — LAND TRANSPORT

388 — Roads & road traffic. Environmental aspects

Watkins, L. H.. Environmental impact of roads and traffic / L.H. Watkins. — London : Applied Science Publishers, c1981. — viii,268p : ill,maps ; 24cm
Includes index
ISBN 0-85334-963-0 : £26.00 : CIP rev.
B81-17512

388.09172'2 — Developed countries. Industries — *For schools*

Butts, Peter. Resources and industry in the developed world / Peter Butts. — London : Edward Arnold, 1982. — 64p : ill,maps ; 24cm. — (Patterns of development)
ISBN 0-7131-0453-8 (pbk) : Unpriced : CIP rev. B81-23831

388.1 — ROADS

388.1 — Dorset. Roads. Networks — *For structure planning*

Definition of the strategic highway network : Dorset structure plan (excluding South East Dorset) / Structure Plan Team, Dorset County Council. — [Dorchester] : Dorset County Council, 1980. — ii,14p : maps ; 30cm. — (DSP.16)
ISBN 0-85216-276-6 (pbk) : Unpriced
B82-23442

388.1'0936 — Europe. Ancient Roman roads

Sitwell, N. H. H.. Roman roads of Europe / N.H.H. Sitwell. — London : Cassell, 1981. — 240p : ill(some col.),maps(some col.),col.ports ; 32cm
Ill on lining papers. — Bibliography: p221-229. — Includes index
ISBN 0-304-30075-6 : £14.95 B82-20416

388.1'09362'7393 — Greater Manchester *(Metropolitan County)*. Oldham region. Ancient Roman roads: Margary 712

Saddleworth seven one two : a survey of Roman road Margary 712 through the Oldham area undertaken by Bradford Grammar School Archaeological Society and the Saddleworth W.E.A. Archaeology Class / editor, Donald Haigh. — Bradford : Donald Haigh and the 712 Group, 1982. — 45p : ill,maps,1plan ; 21cm
Cover title. — Bibliography: p45
ISBN 0-9508232-0-1 (pbk) : £2.50 B82-41077

388.1'0941 — Great Britain. Roads & trackways, *to 1977*

Taylor, Christopher. Roads and tracks of Britain / Christopher Taylor. — London : Dent, 1979 (1982 [printing]). — xiv,210p,[8]p of plates : ill,maps ; 23cm
Includes index
ISBN 0-460-02233-4 (pbk) : £4.95 B82-23939

388.1'09422'7 — Hampshire. Trackways

Doherty, Jane. Ancient lanes and tracks / [written and produced in the Hampshire County Planning Department] ; [text by Jane Doherty] ; [designed and illustrated by Paul Jones]. — [Winchester] : [The Planning Department], 1981. — 25p : ill,maps ; 30cm. — (Hampshire's countryside heritage ; 1)
Bibliography: p25
ISBN 0-900908-69-6 (pbk) : £3.00 B82-37077

388.1'1 — Devon. Chudleigh. Roads: Bypasses. Effectiveness

The **Economic** performance of the Chudleigh bypass (A38), Devon : interim report. — London (Upper Grosvenor St, W1X 0AP) : Brian Colquhoun & Partners, 1977. — 49p : ill,maps ; 30cm
At head of title: Department of Transport, Economic[s] Highways and Freight Division
Unpriced (spiral) B82-40576

388.1'1 — England. Trunk roads. Cost-benefit analysis. Applications of digital computer systems. Programs: COBA program

Great Britain. *Department of Transport*. Getting the best roads for our money : the COBA method of appraisal. — [London] ([St. Christopher House, Southwark St., SE1]) : Dept. of Transport, [1982?]. — [32]p : ill ; 25cm
Cover title
Unpriced (pbk) B82-40594

388.1'1 — Great Britain. Roads. Construction & maintenance. Economic aspects — *Proposals*

Roth, Gabriel. Private road ahead / by Gabriel Roth and Eamonn Butler. — London : Adam Smith Institute, 1982. — 32p ; 21cm
ISBN 0-906517-19-2 (pbk) : £1.00 B82-33782

388.1'1 — Wales. Trunk roads. Construction & improvement. Economic aspects

M4-A55 study : the effects of major road investment schemes in Wales. — [Cardiff] : Welsh Office Planning Services, 1981. — iii,128p,[4]leaves of plates : maps ; 30cm
£4.95 (spiral) B82-33400

388.1'14 — Scotland. Grampian Region. Aberdeenshire. Turnpike roads

Patrick, John, *1931-*. The coming of turnpikes to Aberdeenshire / John Patrick ; illustrations adapted by Helen Patrick from a series of engravings by W.H. Pyne published with a commentary by G. Gray ... ; maps by Helen Patrick ; drawn by Martin Cooper. — [Aberdeen] ([Edward Wright Building, King's College, Old Aberdeen. AB9 2TY) : Centre for Scottish Studies], [1982?]. — 55p : ill,maps ; 21cm. — (Local history pamphlet series)
Unpriced (pbk) B82-31665

388.1'2 — Berkshire. Finchampstead. Public paths. Preservation

Shone, Brian. The Devil's Highway and Finchampstead's footpath and bridlepath network with the case for declaring Finchampstead a rural and recreational conservation area / by Brian Shone. — Finchampstead (The Paddock, Longwater La., Berks.) : B. Shone
Part 2: Representations to be submitted by Major Brian Shone ... at the public meeting ... to consider Wokingham District Council's draft plan for the 'rides' area. — [1981]. — p.43-90,[9]folded leaves of plates : ill,maps (some col.),facsims,ports ; 30cm
Cover title. — Originally published: 1979
£12.00 (pbk) B82-02920

Shone, Brian. The Devil's Highway and Finchampstead's footpath and bridlepath network with the case for declaring Finchampstead a rural and recreational conservation area / by Brian Shone. — Finchampstead (The Paddock, Longwater La., Berks.) : B. Shone
Part 2: Representations to be submitted by Major Brian Shone ... at the public meeting ... to consider Wokingham District Council's draft plan for the 'rides' area
£6.00 (pbk) B82-02921

388.1'2 — England. Cycleways. Conversion from disused railway routes — *Proposals*

Study of disused railways in England and Wales : potential cycle routes / a study for the Department of Transport by John Grimshaw and Associates. — London : H.M.S.O., 1982. — viii,88p : ill,maps(some col.),plans ; 30cm
Map (118x108cm folded to 24x17cm) in inside back pocket
ISBN 0-11-550558-x (pbk) : £11.50 B82-23821

Study of disused railways in England and Wales : potential cycle routes / a study for the Department of Transport by John Grimshaw & Associates. — London (2 Marsham St, SW1) : The Department, 1982
[Annex 1]: Manchester lines. — [63]p : ill,maps,plans ; 30cm
Text and ill on inside covers
£2.70 (spiral) B82-34265

Study of disused railways in England and Wales : potential cycle routes / a study for the Department of Transport by John Grimshaw & Associates. — London (2 Marsham St, SW1) : The Department, 1982
[Annex 2]: Swansea-Newport. — [58]p,[1] folded leaf : ill,maps,plans ; 30cm
Text and ill on inside covers
£2.70 (spiral) B82-34266

Study of disused railways in England and Wales : potential cycle routes / a study for the Department of Transport by John Grimshaw & Associates. — London (2 Marsham St, SW1) : The Department, 1982
[Annex 3]: Leeds to Wakefield & Barnsley. — [36]p : ill,maps,plans ; 30cm
Text and ill on inside covers
£2.70 (spiral) B82-34267

Study of disused railways in England and Wales : potential cycle routes / a study for the Department of Transport by John Grimshaw & Associates. — London (2 Marsham St, SW1) : The Department, 1982
[Annex 4]: Durham & Newcastle. — [44]p,[1] folded leaf : ill,maps,plans ; 30cm
Text and ill on inside covers
£2.70 (spiral) B82-34268

Study of disused railways in England and Wales : potential cycle routes / a study for the Department of Transport by John Grimshaw & Associates. — London (2 Marsham St, SW1) : The Department, 1982
[Annex 5]: Liverpool loop line. — [37]p : ill,maps,plans ; 30cm
Text and ill on inside covers
£2.70 (spiral) B82-34264

Study of disused railways in England and Wales : potential cycle routes / a study for the Department of Transport by John Grimshaw & Associates. — London (2 Marsham St, SW1) : The Department, 1982
[Annex 6]: Stoke on Trent loop line links. — [34]p : ill,maps,plans ; 30cm
Text and ill on inside covers
£2.70 (spiral) B82-34263

Study of disused railways in England and Wales : potential cycle routes / a study for the Department of Transport by John Grimshaw & Associates. — London (2 Marsham St, SW1) : The Department, 1982
[Annex 7]: Abergavenny to Newport. — [40]p : ill,maps,plans ; 30cm
Cover title: Newport to Abergavenny. — Text and ill on inside covers
£2.70 (spiral) B82-34269

Study of disused railways in England and Wales : potential cycle routes / a study for the Department of Transport by John Grimshaw & Associates. — London (2 Marsham St, SW1) : The Department, 1982
[Annex 8]: Hertfordshire lines. — [47]p : ill,maps,plans ; 30cm
Text and ill on inside covers
£2.70 (spiral) B82-34262

Study of disused railways in England and Wales : potential cycle routes / a study for the Department of Transport by John Grimshaw & Associates. — London (2 Marsham St, SW1) : The Department, 1982
[Annex 10]: Bristol Bridge to Yate. — [43]p : ill,maps,plans ; 30cm
Text on inside covers
£2.70 (spiral) B82-34270

Study of disused railways in England and Wales : potential cycle routes / a study for the Department of Transport by John Grimshaw & Associates. — London (2 Marsham St, SW1) : The Department, 1982
[Annex 12]: Lines in Derby & Burton upon Trent. — [43]p : ill,maps,plans ; 30cm
Text and ill on inside covers
£2.70 (spiral) B82-34261

Study of disused railways in England and Wales : potential cycle routes / a study for the Department of Transport by John Grimshaw & Associates. — London (2 Marsham St, SW1) : The Department, 1982
[Annex 13]: Nottingham lines. — [36]p : ill,maps,plans ; 30cm
Text and ill on inside covers
£2.70 (spiral) B82-34275

Study of disused railways in England and Wales : potential cycle routes / a study for the Department of Transport by John Grimshaw & Associates. — London (2 Marsham St, SW1) : The Department, 1982
[Annex 14]: Lancaster, Morecambe & Preston. — [41]p : ill,maps,plans ; 30cm
Text and ill on inside covers
£2.70 (spiral) B82-34274

Study of disused railways in England and Wales : potential cycle routes / a study for the Department of Transport by John Grimshaw & Associates. — London (2 Marsham St, SW1) : The Department, 1982
[Annex 15]: Gosport and Fareham. — [34]p : ill,maps,plans ; 30cm
Text and ill on inside covers
£2.70 (spiral) B82-34273

Study of disused railways in England and Wales : potential cycle routes / a study for the Department of Transport by John Grimshaw & Associates. — London (2 Marsham St, SW1) : The Department, 1982
[Annex 17]: London lines. — [58]p : ill,maps,plans ; 30cm
Text and ill on inside covers
£2.70 (spiral) B82-34271

388.1'2 — England. Cycleways. Conversion from disused railway routes — *Proposals*
continuation

Study of disused railways in England and Wales : potential cycle routes / a study for the Department of Transport by John Grimshaw & Associates. — London (2 Marsham St, SW1) : The Department, 1982
[Annex 18]: Leicester Great Central. — [38]p : ill,maps,plans ; 30cm
Text and ill on inside covers
£2.70 (spiral) B82-34272

Study of disused railways in England and Wales : potential cycle routes / a study for the Department of Transport by John Grimshaw & Associates. — London (2 Marsham St, SW1) : The Department, 1982
[Annex 21]: Kingston upon Hull. — [37]p : ill,maps,plans ; 30cm
Text and ill on inside covers
£2.70 (spiral) B82-34278

Study of disused railways in England and Wales : potential cycle routes / a study for the Department of Transport by John Grimshaw & Associates. — London (2 Marsham St, SW1) : The Department, 1982
[Annex 22]: Lincoln lines. — [37]p : ill,maps,plans ; 30cm
Text and ill on inside covers
£2.70 (spiral) B82-34280

Study of disused railways in England and Wales : potential cycle routes / a study for the Department of Transport by John Grimshaw & Associates. — London (2 Marsham St, SW1) : The Department, 1982
[Annex 23]: Birmingham to Wolverhampton & Kingswinford Branch. — [52]p : ill,maps,plans ; 30cm
Text and ill on inside covers
£2.70 (spiral) B82-34279

Study of disused railways in England and Wales : potential cycle routes / a study for the Department of Transport by John Grimshaw & Associates. — London (2 Marsham St, SW1) : The Department, 1982
[Annex 24]: Bodmin to Padstow. — [34]p : ill,maps,plans ; 30cm
Text and ill on inside covers
£2.70 (spiral) B82-34277

Study of disused railways in England and Wales : potential cycle routes / a study for the Department of Transport by John Grimshaw & Associates. — London (2 Marsham St, SW1) : The Department, 1982
[Annex 25]: Barnstaple to Ilfracombe. — [33]p : ill,maps,plans ; 30cm
Text and ill on inside covers
£2.70 (spiral) B82-34276

Study of disused railways in England and Wales : potential cycle routes / a study for the Department of Transport by John Grimshaw & Associates. — London (2 Marsham St., S.W.1) : Department of Transport, 1982
Text and ill on inside cover
[Annex no.26]: Plymouth to Dartmoor. — [37]p : ill,maps,plans ; 30cm
£2.70 (spiral) B82-38214

Study of disused railways in England and Wales : potential cycle routes / a study for the Department of Transport by John Grimshaw & Associates. — London (2 Marsham St., S.W.1) : Department of Transport, 1982
Text and ill on inside cover
[Annex no.28]: Poole to Brockenhurst. — [39]p : ill,maps,plans ; 30cm
£2.70 (spiral) B82-38217

Study of disused railways in England and Wales : potential cycle routes / a study for the Department of Transport by John Grimshaw & Associates. — London (2 Marsham St., S.W.1) : Department of Transport, 1982
Text and ill on inside cover
[Annex no.29]: Peasemarsh [i.e. Peasmarsh] Junction Guildford to Shoreham-by-Sea. — [41]p : ill,maps,plans ; 30cm
£2.70 (spiral) B82-38215

Study of disused railways in England and Wales : potential cycle routes / a study for the Department of Transport by John Grimshaw & Associates. — London (2 Marsham St., S.W.1) : Department of Transport, 1982
Text and ill on inside cover
[Annex no.30]: Cheltenham to Stratford on Avon. — [40]p : ill,maps,plans ; 30cm
£2.70 (spiral) B82-38216

Study of disused railways in England and Wales : potential cycle routes / a study for the Department of Transport by John Grimshaw & Associates. — London (2 Marsham St., S.W.1) : Department of Transport, 1982
Text and ill on inside cover
[Annex no.31]: Peak District lines. — [51]p : ill,maps,plans ; 30cm
£2.70 (spiral) B82-38220

Study of disused railways in England and Wales : potential cycle routes / a study for the Department of Transport by John Grimshaw & Associates. — London (2 Marsham St., S.W.1) : Department of Transport, 1982
Text and ill on inside cover
[Annex no.32]: Disused railway routes in Gwynedd. — [55]p : ill,maps,plans ; 30cm
£2.70 (spiral) B82-38219

Study of disused railways in England and Wales : potential cycle routes / a study for the Department of Transport by John Grimshaw & Associates. — London (2 Marsham St., S.W.1) : Department of Transport, 1982
Text and ill on inside cover
[Annex no.33]: Keswick-Penrith. — [37]p : ill,maps,plans ; 30cm
£2.70 (spiral) B82-38218

388.1'2 — England. Footpaths — *Proposals*

A **Policy** for footpaths. — London (1 Wandsworth Rd, SW8 2LJ) : Ramblers' Association, [1980?]. — 11p : col.ill,1col.map ; 23cm. — (Brief for the countryside ; no.8)
£0.50 (unbound) B82-38410

388.1'2 — England. Public paths

Parish and community councils and public paths. — London : Ramblers' Association, [1979?]. — 1folded sheet([6]p) ; 21cm
£0.10 B82-35150

Path clearance. — London : Ramblers' Association, 1979. — 1folded sheet([6]p) ; 21cm. — (Guidance note ; 3)
ISBN 0-900613-39-4 : £0.10 B82-35153

Path surveys. — London : Ramblers' Association, 1979. — 1folded sheet([6]p) ; 21cm. — (Guidance note ; 1)
ISBN 0-900613-37-8 : £0.10 B82-35151

Producing a path guide or map. — London : Ramblers' Association, 1979. — 1folded sheet ([6]p) ; 21cm. — (Guidance note ; 4)
ISBN 0-900613-40-8 : £0.10 B82-35152

388.1'2 — North Yorkshire. North York Moors. Stone causeways

Breakell, Bill. Stone causeways of the North York Moors / Bill Breakell. — Hebden Bridge : Footsteps Books, c1982. — 16p : ill,maps ; 21cm
Map, text on inside covers. — Bibliography: inside back cover
ISBN 0-9507991-0-6 (pbk) : Unpriced B82-38737

388.1'22 — California. Los Angeles region. Motorways

Brodsly, David. L.A. freeway : an appreciative essay / David Brodsly. — Berkeley, [Calif.] ; London : University of California Press, c1981. — 178p : ill,maps ; 23x29cm
Bibliography: p169-174. — Includes index
ISBN 0-520-04068-6 : Unpriced B82-28300

388.3 — ROAD TRANSPORT

388.3 — Great Britain. Road transport services. Consumers. Influence — *Conference proceedings*

Consumers in transport : proceedings of a conference held at Liverpool Polytechnic, 26th Ocotober 1981 / organised by (1) Department of Town and Country Planning, (2) the Merseyside Section of the Chartered Institute of Transport ; edited by Lewis Lesley. — [London] : Chartered Institute of Transport, 1981. — 65p : ill ; 30cm
ISBN 0-906442-08-7 (pbk) : Unpriced B82-14991

388.3 — Surrey. Motoring. Organisations: Automobile Association. Motorcycle patrols, *1959-1968* — *Personal observations*

Quinn, Paul. The yellow motorbike : the trials and tribulations of an AA road patrol / by Paul Quinn ; illustrations by Fünf. — Polegate : P. Quinn, c1982. — 136p : ill ; 21cm
ISBN 0-9507819-0-8 (pbk) : £1.90 B82-16148

388.3'14'0941 — Great Britain. Road traffic. Policies of government, *1945-1981*

Starkie, David. The motorway age : road traffic policies in post-war Britain / by David Starkie. — Oxford : Pergamon, 1982. — 175p : ill,maps ; 23cm. — (Urban and regional planning series ; v.28)
Includes index
ISBN 0-08-026091-8 (cased) : Unpriced : CIP rev.
ISBN 0-08-027924-4 (pbk) : £7.00 B82-12411

388.3'2 — Scotland. Borders Region. Public road transport services: Border Courier Service

Final monitoring report : Border Courier Service. — Newtown St. Boswells (Regional Headquarters, Newtown St. Boswells, Roxburghshire TD6 OSA) : Borders Regional Council, 1981. — 36p : ill(some col.) ; 30cm
Unpriced (pbk) B82-15422

388.3'2'02341 — Great Britain. Road transport services — *Career guides*

Lewis, David, *1948-*. Careers in road transport / David Lewis. — London : Kogan Page, 1982. — 135p ; 19cm
Bibliography: p123
ISBN 0-85038-548-2 (cased) : Unpriced : CIP rev.
ISBN 0-85038-549-0 (pbk) : £2.50 B82-14069

388.3'22'02341 — Great Britain. Bus services — *Career guides*

Working for a bus company / edited by Maurice Martin ; photography by Chris Fairclough. — Hove : Wayland, 1982. — 94p : ill,ports ; 25cm. — (People at work)
Includes index
ISBN 0-85340-975-7 : £4.95 B82-34827

388.3'22'0681 — England. Bus services. Companies. Financial information. Disclosure

Accounting for bus operations : a memorandum providing guidance to local authorities on information to be obtained from bus operators / Department of Transport, Welsh Office. — [London] : Department of Transport, 1981. — [20]p ; 30cm
Unpriced (unbound) B82-40356

Code of practice : publication of information by bus operators / Department of Transport, Welsh Office. — [London] : Department of Transport, 1981. — [10],7p ; 30cm
Unpriced (unbound) B82-40357

388.3'22'094 — Western Europe. International bus services & international coach services. Licensing

Taking a coach abroad. — [London] ([2 Marsham St., SW1P 3EB]) : Department of Transport, 1981. — 21p ; 22cm
Unpriced (pbk) B82-38485

388.3'22'0941 — Great Britain. Bus services, *1930-1939*

Millar, Alan. British buses of the thirties. — Cambridge : Patrick Stephens, Sept.1982. — [150]p
ISBN 0-85059-496-0 : £8.95 : CIP entry B82-20489

388.3′22′0941461 — Scotland. Strathclyde Region. Arran. Bus services, *to 1980*

Mitchell-Luker, B.. Mitchell-Luker′s Arran bus book. — Brodick (Ivy Cottage, Brodick, Isle of Arran KA27 8DD) : Kilbrannan Publishing, Aug.1982. — [200]p
ISBN 0-907939-06-6 (pbk) : £3.50 : CIP entry
B82-23846

388.3′22′09425 — England. East Midlands. Bus services & coach services: United Counties Omnibus Company Limited — *History*

Warwick, Roger M.. An illustrated history of United Counties Ominbus Company Limited / by Roger M. Warwick. — Northampton : R.M. Warwick
Pt.3: 1933 to 1937. — c1980. — 58p : ill,maps,1plan,ports ; 22cm
Includes index
ISBN 0-9505980-2-x (pbk) : Unpriced
B82-13902

Warwick, Roger M.. An illustrated history of United Counties Omnibus Company Limited / by Roger M. Warwick. — Northampton (101 Broadway East, Northampton NN3 2PP) : R.M. Warwick
Part 5: 1947 to 1952. — c1981. — 70p : ill,maps ; 22cm
Includes index
ISBN 0-9505980-4-6 (pbk) : Unpriced
B82-02318

388.3′22′094257 — Oxfordshire. Bus services, *1881-1981 — Illustrations*

Hurry along, please! : trams and buses in Oxfordshire, 1881-1981 / [text by Malcolm Graham]. — Oxford : Libraries′ Department, Oxfordshire County Council, c1981. — [16]p : all ill,1port ; 30cm
Published to accompany an exhibition of the same name. — Cover title. — Bibliography on inside cover
ISBN 0-906871-01-8 (pbk) : Unpriced
Primary classification 388.4′6′094257
B82-13702

388.3′22′094271 — Cheshire. Bus services: Crosville Motor Services, *to 1980*

Anderson, R. C. (Roy Claude). A history of Crosville motor services / R.C. Anderson. — Newton Abbot : David & Charles, c1981. — 192p : ill,2maps,1port ; 23cm
Bibliography: p187. — Includes index
ISBN 0-7153-8088-5 : £7.95 : CIP rev.
Also classified at 388.3′22′094291 B81-30370

388.3′22′094282 — South Yorkshire *(Metropolitan County).* **Bus services** — *Lists*

Hilton, Alan, *1946-*. Bus operation South Yorkshire : P.T.E. and joint operators / [compiled and published by Alan Hilton]. — [Sheffield] ([31, Warminster Crescent, Sheffield S8 39U]) : [A. Hilton], 1982. — [12]p ; 21cm. — (A Routeliner production)
£0.20 (unbound) B82-18389

388.3′22′0942845 — North Yorkshire. Tadcaster region. Road transport. Coaching, *to 1850*

Page, Ian. Tadcaster and the coaching days / by Ian Page. — Tadcaster : Tadcaster Civic Society, 1982. — 26p : ill,facsims,2maps ; 20cm. — (Occasional publications / Tadcaster Civic Society ; no.1)
Includes index
ISBN 0-9507275-1-2 (pbk) : Unpriced
B82-28135

388.3′22′094291 — North Wales. Bus services: Crosville Motor Services, *to 1980*

Anderson, R. C. (Roy Claude). A history of Crosville motor services / R.C. Anderson. — Newton Abbot : David & Charles, c1981. — 192p : ill,2maps,1port ; 23cm
Bibliography: p187. — Includes index
ISBN 0-7153-8088-5 : £7.95 : CIP rev.
Primary classification 388.3′22′094271
B81-30370

388.3′24 — International road freight transport by British registered motor vehicles — *Statistics — Serials*

International road haulage by British registered vehicles / Department of Transport. — July-Dec. 1979-. — London (Statistics Transport G Division, 2 Marsham St., SW1P 3EB) : : The Department, 1980-. — v. ; 30cm
Annual
ISSN 0262-4508 = International road haulage by British registered vehicles : £4.50
B82-04920

388.3′24044 — Great Britain. Road freight transport services. Heavy lorries. Long-distance drivers — *Case studies — For children*

Fairclough, Chris. A day with a lorry driver / Chris Fairclough. — Hove : Wayland, 1982. — 55p : ill,ports ; 24cm. — (A Day in the life)
Bibliography: p55
ISBN 0-85340-899-8 : £3.25 B82-18433

388.3′24′0681 — Road freight transport services. Costing

Lowe, David. Costing and pricing goods vehicle operations. — 3rd ed. — London : Kogan Page, Mar.1982. — [226]p
Previous ed.: 1979
ISBN 0-85038-512-1 : £11.95 : CIP entry
B82-04697

388.3′24′0681 — Road freight transport services. Financial management

Ratcliffe, Brian. Economy and efficiency in road transport operations. — London : Kogan Page, Mar.1982. — [220]p
ISBN 0-85038-535-0 : £12.00 : CIP entry
B82-04696

388.3′24′0941 — Great Britain. Road freight transport services: British Road Services, *to 1982*

Baldwin, Nick. A pictorial history of BRS : 35 years of trucking / Nick Baldwin. — [London] : Warne, [1982]. — 128p : ill(some col.),facsims,ports ; 31cm. — (An MHB book)
Ill on lining papers. — Includes index
ISBN 0-7232-2910-4 : £8.95 B82-40587

388.3′24′0941 — Great Britain. Road freight transport services. Companies — *Statistics*

Britain′s top 300 road haulage companies. — London : Jordan & Sons (Surveys), c1981. — x,17,[15]leaves ; 30cm
Includes index
ISBN 0-85938-148-x (corrected : pbk) : £45.00
B82-02694

388.3′242′094239 — Avon. Road freight transport services. Heavy lorries. Routes — *Proposals*

Lee, N. William. The control of heavy lorries in the County of Avon : (preliminary report) / N. William Lee. — [Bristol] ([P.O. Box 11, Avon House, The Haymarket, Bristol BS99 7DE]) : [County of Avon, Department of Public Relations and Publicity], 1981. — [51]p : maps (some col.) ; 30cm
Cover title
ISBN 0-86063-133-8 (pbk) : £2.00 B82-10619

388.3′4 — Great Britain. Motor vehicle hire services & motor vehicle leasing services — *Statistics — Serials*

ICC financial survey. Vehicle rental & leasing. — 1st ed.-. — London : Inter Company Comparisons, [197-]-. — v. ; 21x30cm
Annual. — Description based on: 3rd ed.
ISSN 0263-9084 = ICC financial survey. Vehicle rental & leasing : Unpriced
B82-38525

388.3′422 — Great Britain. Cars. Ownership. Forecasting. Mathematical models

Button, K. J.. Car ownership modelling and forecasting / K.J. Button, A.D. Pearman, A.S. Fowkes. — Aldershot : Gower, c1982. — xii,157p : ill,1map ; 23cm
Bibliography: p142-150. — Includes index
ISBN 0-566-00320-1 : Unpriced : CIP rev.
B81-30968

Smith, C. A.. Car ownership in the national road traffic forecasts : further research / by C.A. Smith. — London : Department of Transport, 1981. — 49p : ill ; 30cm
£2.90 (unbound) B82-40359

388.3′422′0684 — Car hire services. Project management. Teaching aids — *Case studies*

Potts, D. J.. The car hire exercise series : a teaching exercise on the financial analysis and planning of projects designed for project planners / by D.J. Potts and S. Doherty ; produced by the Teaching Materials Development Group, Project Planning Centre for Developing Countries, University of Bradford. — [Bradford] : The Centre, 1981. — 1portfolio : forms ; 34cm. — (Teaching materials series, ISSN 0262-5164 ; no.3)
ISBN 0-901945-44-7 : Unpriced B82-23563

388.3′4233′0942 — England. Bus services: Crosville Motor Services. Buses — *Lists*

Crosville Motor Services Limited. — London (52 Old Park Ridings, N21 2ES) : The P.S.V. Circle. — (Fleet history ; PC15)
Pt.3: (1953 to 1981). — [1981?]. — 74p,[6]p of plates : ill ; 30cm
Unpriced (pbk) B82-12510

388.3′4233′09421 — London. Public transport services: London Transport. Buses. Serial numbers — *Lists*

London General/London Transport body number index. — [London] ([52 Old Park Ridings, N21 2ES]) : Published jointly by the P.S.V. Circle and the Omnibus Society
Pt.2: 11310 to 12080. — [1981?]. — 24p ; 30cm. — (Publication ; LTY2)
Unpriced (unbound) B82-01517

London Transport body number index. — [London] ([52 Old Park Ridings, N21 2ES]) : Published jointly by the P.S.V. Circle and the Omnibus Society
2nd series
Pt.1: 1 to 1400. — [1981?]. — 26p ; 30cm. — (Publication ; LTY11)
Unpriced (unbound) B82-01516

388.3′4233′09423 — South-west England. Buses — *Lists*

Buses of South-East England and the Channel Islands / edited by A.M. Witton. — 3rd ed. — Manchester : A.M. Witton, 1980. — 57p : ill ; 15cm. — (Fleetbook ; no.12)
Previous ed.: 1978. — Text on inside covers
ISBN 0-86047-123-3 (pbk) : £0.80 B82-19334

388.3′4233′0942527 — Nottinghamshire. Nottingham. Bus services: Nottingham City Transport. Buses, *to 1982 — Lists*

Nottingham city transport : West Bridgford Urban District Council. — London (52, Old Park Ridings, N21 2ES) : Published jointly by the P.S.V. Circle and the Omnibus Society, 1982. — 80p,[4]p of plates : ill ; 30cm. — (Fleet history ; PE 7)
Unpriced (pbk) B82-27451

388.3′4233′094253 — Lincolnshire. Buses — *Lists*

Buses of South Yorkshire, Humberside and Lincolnshire. — 4th ed. / edited by D. Akrigg, G.R. Mills and G.W. Watts. — Manchester : A.M. Witton, 1981. — 65p : ill ; 15cm. — (Fleetbook ; no.2)
Previous ed.: published as Buses of South & East Yorkshire, 1980. — Text on inside covers
ISBN 0-86047-024-5 (pbk) : £0.80
Primary classification 388.3′4233′094282
B82-12367

388.3′4233′09426 — East Anglia. Buses — *Lists*

Buses of East Anglia / edited by G.R. Mills and G.W. Watts. — 3rd ed. — Manchester : Witton, 1982. — 57p : ill ; 15cm. — (Fleetbook ; no.10)
Previous ed.: published as Buses of eastern England. 1979. — Text on inside covers
ISBN 0-86047-103-9 (pbk) : £0.80 B82-38987

388.3′4233′094275 — Merseyside *(Metropolitan County).* **Bus services. Buses** — *Registers*

Buses of Mersey, N. Wales and Isle of Man. — 4th ed. / edited and published by A.M. Witton. — Manchester : A.M. Witton, 1981. — 57p : ill ; 15cm. — (Fleetbook ; no.5)
Previous ed.: 1979. — Text on inside covers
ISBN 0-86047-054-7 (pbk) : £0.80
Also classified at 388.3′4233′094291 ; 388.3′4233′094279
B82-05271

388.3'4233'094275 — Merseyside *(Metropolitan County).* **Public transport services: Merseyside Passenger Transport Executive. Buses —** *Registers — Serials*

Merseyside Transport fleet list. — 1st ed. (1979)-. — Southport (Hartland Ave., Southport, Merseyside PR9 9FT) : P. Gascoine, 1979-. — v. : ill ; 16cm
Annual
ISSN 0262-9593 = Merseyside Transport fleet list : £0.75 B82-14264

388.3'4233'094276 — Lancashire. Bus services. Buses — *Lists*

Buses of Lancashire and Cumbria. — 4th ed. / edited by A.M. Witton with the assistance of the Ribble Enthusiasts' Club. — Manchester : A.M. Witton, 1982. — 57p : ill ; 15cm. — (Fleetbook ; no.4)
Previous ed.: 1979
ISBN 0-86047-044-x (pbk) : £0.80
Also classified at 388.3'4233'094278
B82-29544

388.3'4233'094278 — Cumbria. Bus services. Buses — *Lists*

Buses of Lancashire and Cumbria. — 4th ed. / edited by A.M. Witton with the assistance of the Ribble Enthusiasts' Club. — Manchester : A.M. Witton, 1982. — 57p : ill ; 15cm. — (Fleetbook ; no.4)
Previous ed.: 1979
ISBN 0-86047-044-x (pbk) : £0.80
Primary classification 388.3'4233'094276
B82-29544

388.3'4233'094279 — Isle of Man. Bus services. Buses — *Registers*

Buses of Mersey, N. Wales and Isle of Man. — 4th ed. / edited and published by A.M. Witton. — Manchester : A.M. Witton, 1981. — 57p : ill ; 15cm. — (Fleetbook ; no.5)
Previous ed.: 1979. — Text on inside covers
ISBN 0-86047-054-7 (pbk) : £0.80
Primary classification 388.3'4233'094275
B82-05271

388.3'4233'094281 — West Yorkshire *(Metropolitan County).* **Bus services. Buses —** *Lists*

Buses of West Yorkshire. — 4th ed. / edited by D. Akrigg and A.M. Witton. — Manchester : A.M. Witton, 1982. — 49p : ill ; 15cm. — (Fleetbook ; no.3)
Previous ed.: 1979
ISBN 0-86047-034-2 (pbk) : £0.80 B82-29543

388.3'4233'094282 — South Yorkshire *(Metropolitan County).* **Buses —** *Lists*

Buses of South Yorkshire, Humberside and Lincolnshire. — 4th ed. / edited by D. Akrigg, G.R. Mills and G.W. Watts. — Manchester : A.M. Witton, 1981. — 65p : ill ; 15cm. — (Fleetbook ; no.2)
Previous ed.: published as Buses of South & East Yorkshire, 1980. — Text on inside covers
ISBN 0-86047-024-5 (pbk) : £0.80
Also classified at 388.3'4233'094283 ; 388.3'4233'094253 B82-12367

388.3'4233'094283 — Humberside. Buses — *Lists*

Buses of South Yorkshire, Humberside and Lincolnshire. — 4th ed. / edited by D. Akrigg, G.R. Mills and G.W. Watts. — Manchester : A.M. Witton, 1981. — 65p : ill ; 15cm. — (Fleetbook ; no.2)
Previous ed.: published as Buses of South & East Yorkshire, 1980. — Text on inside covers
ISBN 0-86047-024-5 (pbk) : £0.80
Primary classification 388.3'4233'094282
B82-12367

388.3'4233'094291 — North Wales. Bus services. Buses — *Registers*

Buses of Mersey, N. Wales and Isle of Man. — 4th ed. / edited and published by A.M. Witton. — Manchester : A.M. Witton, 1981. — 57p : ill ; 15cm. — (Fleetbook ; no.5)
Previous ed.: 1979. — Text on inside covers
ISBN 0-86047-054-7 (pbk) : £0.80
Primary classification 388.3'4233'094275
B82-05271

388.3'4233'094294 — South Wales. Buses — *Lists*

Buses of South Wales / edited by A.M. Witton. — 3rd ed. — Manchester : A.M. Witton, 1982. — 66p : ill ; 15cm. — (Fleetbook ; no.9)
Previous ed.: 1978. — Text in inside covers
ISBN 0-86047-093-8 (pbk) : £0.80 B82-22556

388.3'4233'094294 — South Wales. Independent bus services. Buses — *Lists*

Current fleets of small operators in the South Wales traffic area. — Crewe (c/o R.F.A. Neale, 11 Howard St., Sydney, Crewe CW1 1NB) : The P.S.V. Circle. — (Publication ; FGB5)
Operators H to M. — 1981. — 18p ; 30cm
Unpriced (unbound) B82-12509

388.3'44'0941 — Great Britain. Environment. Effects of lorries — *Inquiry reports*

Inquiry into Lorries, People and the Environment. Report of the Inquiry into Lorries, People and the Environment / presented to the Minister of Transport by Sir Arthur Armitage. — London : H.M.S.O., 1980. — iv,159p ; 25cm
ISBN 0-11-550536-9 (pbk) : Unpriced
B82-16632

388.3'44'0941 — Great Britain. Road freight transport services. Foreign lorries. Entry conditions

Foreign lorries in Great Britain : conditions of entry into Great Britain for vechicles used for the transport of goods by road / Department of Transport, Road Freight Division. — London (2 Marsham St, SW1P 2EB) : The Department, 1982. — 23p ; 30cm
Cover title
Unpriced (pbk) B82-36811

388.3'44'0941 — Great Britain. Road freight transport services. Heavy lorries. Policies of government, *1970-1980*

Wardroper, John. Juggernaut / John Wardroper. — London : Temple Smith, 1981. — 223p ; 23cm
Bibliography: p206-213. — Includes index
ISBN 0-85117-207-5 (cased) : Unpriced
ISBN 0-85117-208-3 (pbk) : £4.95 B82-17155

388.3'44'0941 — Great Britain. Road freight transport services. Lorries. Environmental aspects

Great Britain. *Department of Transport.* Lorries, people and the environment / Department of Transport. — London : H.M.S.O., 1981. — 11p ; 25cm. — (Cmnd. ; 8439)
ISBN 0-10-184390-9 (unbound) : £1.50
B82-11384

388.4 — LOCAL AND URBAN TRANSPORT

388.4 — Scotland. Strathclyde Region. Glasgow. Journeys by young persons

Bradley, Morris. Getting there : a survey of teenagers and young women, using cars or living without them in Glasgow / Morris Bradley and Stephen Thompson ; a report commissioned by the Scottish Consumer Council. — Glasgow : Scottish Consumer Council, 1981. — iv,68p : forms ; 30cm
ISBN 0-907067-04-2 (pbk) : £3.50 B82-06398

388.4 — Urban regions. Transport

Klaassen, Leo H.. Transport and reurbanisation / Leo H. Klaassen, Jan A. Bourdrez, Jacques Volmuller. — Aldershot : Gower, c1981. — x,214p : ill ; 24cm. — (Studies in spatial analysis)
Bibliography: p206-210. — Includes index
ISBN 0-566-00374-0 : Unpriced : CIP rev.
B81-14881

388.4'05 — Urban regions. Transport services — *Serials*

Jane's urban transport systems. — 1st ed. (1982)-. — London : Jane's Pub. Co. Ltd., 1982-. — v. : ill,maps ; 32cm
Annual
ISSN 0263-8460 = Jane's urban transport systems : £42.50 B82-32369

388.4'065'421 — London. Public transport services: London Transport

Day, John R.. A source book of London Transport / John R. Day. — London : Ward Lock, 1982. — 127p : ill ; 17x12cm
Includes index
ISBN 0-7063-6073-7 : £3.50 : CIP rev.
B82-04613

388.4'0941 — Great Brtain. Urban regions. Public transport services

The Urban transport future. — London : Construction Press, Apr.1982. — [224]p
Conference papers
ISBN 0-86095-703-9 : £19.50 : CIP entry
B82-04833

388.4'09411 — Scotland. Urban regions. Public transport services — *Proposals*

Fares please? : urban public transport - how to ease the 'mobility gap' / a report produced for the Scottish Consumer Council by the Scottish Association for Public Transport. — Glasgow : Scottish Consumer Council, [1981]. — 73p : ill ; 30cm
Cover title
ISBN 0-907067-00-x (pbk) : £3.50 B82-06399

388.4'09421 — London. Public transport services, *to 1979*

Stephens, Peter, *1930-*. London Transport Museum / [Peter Stephens, John Freeborn and Oliver Green]. — [London] ([39 Wellington St., WC2E 7BB]) : [London Transport Museum], c1980. — [32]p : ill(some col.),facsims(some col.),col.maps,plan ; 28cm
Cover title. — Text and plan on inside covers. — Bibliography: inside back cover
£0.60 (pbk) B82-35694

388.4'09427'612 — Lancashire. Skelmersdale. Transport

Lesley, Lewis. Travel in Skelmersdale : a report on the 1978 travel survey / Lewis Lesley. — Liverpool : Department of Town and Country Planning, Liverpool Polytechnic, [1982]. — 78p : ill,1map ; 30cm
ISBN 0-906442-07-9 (pbk) : Unpriced
B82-22541

388.4'0951'25 — Hong Kong. Urban regions. Transport services. Planning

Keung, John. Urban planning in Hong Kong — a political/administrative perspective / by John Keung. — Cardiff (King Edward VII Ave., Cardiff CF1 3NU) : Dept. of Town Planning, University of Wales Institute of Science and Technology, 1981. — ii,36p ; 30cm. — (Papers in planning research ; 39)
Unpriced (pbk)
Primary classification 711'.4'095125
B82-26831

388.4'0973 — United States. Urban regions. Passenger transport

Meyer, John R. (John Robert). Autos transit and cities / John R. Meyer, José A. Gómez-Ibáñez. — Cambridge, Mass. ; London : Harvard University Press, 1981. — x,360p : 1ill ; 25cm. — (A Twentieth Century Fund report)
Includes index
ISBN 0-674-05485-7 : £14.00 B82-13731

388.4'11'0941 — Great Britain. Cities. Streets. Social conditions. Effects of traffic wardens

Richman, Joel. Traffic wardens : an ethnography of street administration. — Manchester : Manchester University Press, Nov.1982. — [224]p
ISBN 0-7190-0898-0 : £19.50 : CIP entry
B82-29430

388.4'132 — Humberside. Hornsea. Horse-drawn transport services. Carr, Rose — *Biographies*

Markham, John, *1932-*. Rose Carr, (1843-1913) : the story of a remarkable Hornsea character / by John Markham. — Hornsea (Burn's Farm, 11 Newbegin, Hornsea, Humberside HU18 1AB) : North Holderness Museum of Village Life, [1982]. — 13p : ports ; 21cm
£0.75 (pbk) B82-35821

388.4'1321 — London. Taxi services

Taxi : a consumer view of the London taxi trade. — London : Consumers' Association, 1981. — 40 leaves : 1map ; 30cm
ISBN 0-85202-211-5 (spiral) : Unpriced
B82-00770

388.4'1322'0924 — London. Bus services: London Transport — *Personal observations*

Waller, Wally. The busman's story / by Wally Waller. — Bognor Regis : New Horizon, c1982. — 354p,[4]p of plates : ill ; 20cm
Includes index
ISBN 0-86116-247-1 : £6.75 B82-17487

388.4′13223′0942173 — London. Redbridge *(London Borough).* **Ilford. Trolleybus services,** *to 1959*

Thomas, L. A.. Trams and trolleybuses in Ilford / L.A. Thomson. — [Ilford] : [Ilford & District Historical Society], 1979. — 51p : ill,1coat of arms,facsims ; 22cm. — (Ilford & District Historical Society transaction ; no.2)
ISBN 0-904250-01-6 (pbk) : £1.50
Also classified at 388.4′6′0942173 B82-25198

388.4′2 — Urban regions. Light railway passenger transport services. Fares. Collection

Wyse, W. J.. Fare and ticket systems : the key to success or failure in rail transport / by W.J. Wyse. — [Dartford] ([27, Dickens Close, Hartley, Dartford, Kent DA3 8DP]) : Tramway & Light Railway Society, 1980. — 35p : ill,facsims ; 22cm. — (The Walter Gratwicke memorial lecture ; 1980)
£1.35 (pbk) B82-37735

388.4′2′094215 — London. Tower Hamlets *(London Borough).* **Railway services: London and North Eastern Railway. Blackwall branch & Millwall branch,** *to 1926*

Body, Geoffrey. The Blackwall and Millwall extension railways / by Geoffrey Body. — Weston-super-Mare : Avon-Anglia, [1982?]. — 28p : ill,maps ; 21cm. — (Avon-Anglia transport history series)
ISBN 0-905466-51-9 (pbk) : £1.60 B82-41069

388.4′2′097471 — New York *(City).* **Railway services,** *1900-1970*

Condit, Carl W.. The port of New York : a history of the rail and terminal system from the grand central electrification to the present / Carl W. Condit. — Chicago ; London : University of Chicago Press, 1981. — xii,399p : ill,maps,plans ; 25cm
Bibliography: p337-374. — Includes index
ISBN 0-226-11461-9 : £24.50 B82-17774

388.4′28′09421 — London. Underground railway services, *to 1981*

Howson, Henry F.. London′s underground / H.F. Howson. — London : Ian Allan, 1981. — 159p : ill,2maps ; 24cm
Previous ed.: 1967. — Includes index
ISBN 0-7110-1043-9 : £6.95 B82-01613

388.4′4′0942753 — Merseyside *(Metropolitan County).* **Liverpool. Railway services: Liverpool Overhead Railway**

Gahan, John W.. Seventeen stations to Dingle : the Liverpool Overhead Railway remembered / by John W. Gahan. — Birkenhead : Countryvise, c1982. — 88p : ill,facsims,1map ; 21cm
ISBN 0-907768-20-2 (pbk) : £2.95
ISBN 0-905466-54-3 (Avon-Anglia) B82-39026

388.4′6′0941443 — Scotland. Strathclyde Region. Glasgow. Tram services, *to 1960 — Illustrations*

Stewart, Ian McM.. More Glasgow by tram / Ian G. McM. Stewart. — [Glasgow] : Scottish Tramway Museum Society, 1978 (1979 [printing]). — 48p : ill ; 22cm
Facsim and text on inside covers
ISBN 0-900648-18-x (pbk) : £0.95 B82-27854

388.4′6′094167 — Belfast. Tram services: Belfast Corporation Tramways, *to 1954*

Maybin, J. M.. Belfast Corporation tramways : 1905-1954 / J.M. Maybin. — Broxbourne : Light Rail Transit Association, [1981?]. — 83p : ill,maps ; 22cm
ISBN 0-900433-83-3 (unbound) : £1.50 B82-11577

388.4′6′0942173 — London. Redbridge *(London Borough).* **Ilford. Tram services,** *to 1939*

Thomas, L. A.. Trams and trolleybuses in Ilford / L.A. Thomson. — [Ilford] : [Ilford & District Historical Society], 1979. — 51p : ill,1coat of arms,facsims ; 22cm. — (Ilford & District Historical Society transaction ; no.2)
ISBN 0-904250-01-6 (pbk) : £1.50
Primary classification 388.4′13223′0942173 B82-25198

388.4′6′094257 — Oxfordshire. Tram services, *1881-1981 — Illustrations*

Hurry along, please! : trams and buses in Oxfordshire, 1881-1981 / [text by Malcolm Graham]. — Oxford : Libraries′ Department, Oxfordshire County Council, c1981. — [16]p : all ill,1port ; 30cm
Published to accompany an exhibition of the same name. — Cover title. — Bibliography on inside cover
ISBN 0-906871-01-8 (pbk) : Unpriced
Also classified at 388.3′22′094257 B82-13702

388.4′6′0942576 — Oxfordshire. Wantage. Tram services: Wantage Tramway, *to 1945*

De Courtais, Nicholas. The Wantage tramway : 1875-1945 / by Nicholas de Courtais. — Upper Bucklebury : Wild Swan, [1982?]. — 40p : chiefly ill,maps ; 28cm
Maps on inside covers
ISBN 0-906867-06-1 (pbk) : £3-30 B82-21521

388.4′6′09426 — East Anglia. Tram services, *to 1942*

Anderson, R. C. (Roy Claude). The tramways of East Anglia. — [Networks ed.] / by R.C. Anderson and J.C. Gillham ; edited by J.H. Price. — Broxbourne : Light Rail Transit Association, [1981]. — 65p : ill,maps ; 22cm
Cover title. — Previous ed.: 1969. — Maps on inside cover
ISBN 0-900433-82-5 (pbk) : £1.25 B82-11532

388.4′74′0941 — Great Britain. Cars. Parking. Control *— Conference proceedings*

British Parking Association. *Seminar (1981 : London).* Car park control and the consumer : report of the British Parking Association Seminar held in London, November 18, 1981, and of the meetings held on March 25 and October 14, 1981. — St. Albans (17 The Croft, Chiswell Green, St Albans, Herts. AL2 3AR) : The Association, [1982]. — 41p : ill ; 30cm
£10.00 (£6.00 to members of the Association) (pbk) B82-34035

389 — MEASUREMENT AND STANDARDISATION

389′.15 — Great Britain. Weights & measures. Inspection *— Inquiry reports*

Pattern examination of weighing and measuring : report of the Joint Industry/Departmental Working Group / Chairman: E.N. Eden. — London (26 Chapter St., SW1P 4NS) : National Weights and Measures Laboratory, 1981. — iv,11p ; 30cm
At head of title: Department of Trade
Unpriced (pbk) B82-38478

389′.15 — Great Britain. Weights & measures. Inspection *— Manuals*

Manual of practical guidance for inspectors : Weights and Measures Act 1979 / Department of Trade. — Issue no.1. — London : H.M.S.O., 1980. — 144p : ill ; 30cm
ISBN 0-11-512501-9 (pbk) : £4.50 B82-19392

389′.15 — Measurement. Système International d′Unités

SI : the international system of units / translation approved by the International Bureau of Weights and Measures of its publication Le système international d′unités. — [4th ed.], editors David T. Goldman, R.J. Bell. — [Teddington] : National Physical Laboratory, 1982. — v,62p ; 21cm
Previous ed.: London : H.M.S.O for the National Physical Laboratory, 1977. — Includes index
ISBN 0-11-480050-2 (pbk) : £3.95 B82-38436

389′.15 — Random numbers *— Tables — For weights & measures inspection in Great Britain*

Supplement to manual of practical guidance for inspectors : Weights and Measures Act 1979 : random sampling numbers / Department of Trade. — London : H.M.S.O., 1980. — 90p ; 30cm
ISBN 0-11-512978-2 (pbk) : £6.75 B82-19390

390 — CUSTOMS AND FOLKLORE

390′.0943 — German customs

Russ, Jennifer M.. German festivals and customs. — London : Wolff, Oct.1982. — [166]p
ISBN 0-85496-365-0 (pbk) : £7.95 : CIP entry
Primary classification 394.2′0943 B82-25739

390′.25′097292 — Jamaica. Negro slaves. Social customs, *1770-1820*

Braithwaite, Edward. The folk culture of the slaves in Jamaica / Edward Kamau Braithwaite. — Rev. ed. — London : New Beacon, c1981. — 56p ; 22cm
Previous ed.: 1970. — Bibliography: p48-56
ISBN 0-901241-05-9 (pbk) : Unpriced B82-02807

390′.422 — Peter′s Pence, *to 1981*

Rendel, Rosemary. Peter′s pence / Rosemary Rendel. — London : Catholic Truth Society, 1982. — 15p ; 19cm
ISBN 0-85183-448-5 (unbound) : £0.35 B82-19306

391 — COSTUME AND PERSONAL APPEARANCE

391 — New Guinea. Man. Body. Decoration *— Illustrations*

Kirk, Malcolm. Man as art : New Guinea body decoration / photographs by Malcolm Kirk ; introduction by Andrew Strathern. — London : Thames and Hudson, 1981. — 143p : ill(some col.),1map ; 37cm
ISBN 0-500-54073-x : £20.00 B82-02706

391 — Nudity. Social aspects

Ableman, Paul. Anatomy of nakedness / by Paul Ableman. — London : Orbis, 1982. — 112p,[32]p of plates : ill,ports ; 25cm
Bibliography: p107. — Includes index
ISBN 0-85613-175-x (corrected) : £7.95 B82-39968

391′.009 — Clothing, *to 1980.* **Psychosocial aspects**

Lurie, Alison. The language of clothes / Alison Lurie ; with illustrations assembled by Doris Palca. — London : Heinemann, c1981. — x,272p,[8]p of plates : ill(some col.),ports(some col.) ; 25cm
Bibliography: p265-266
ISBN 0-434-43906-1 : £10.00 B82-18078

391′.009 — Clothing, *to 1981.* **Psychological aspects**

Glynn, Prudence. Skin to skin. — London : Allen & Unwin, Sept.1982. — [176]p
ISBN 0-04-391006-8 : £10.95 : CIP entry B82-19082

391′.009 — Western costume, *to 1976*

Selbie, Robert. The anatomy of costume. — London : Bell & Hyman, Mar.1982. — [137]p
Originally published: London : Owlet Books, 1977
ISBN 0-7135-2238-0 : £6.95 : CIP entry B82-03118

391′.009′04 — Fashion, *1900-1982 — Collectors′ guides*

Kennett, Frances. The collector′s book of twentieth-century fashion. — London : Granada, Feb.1983. — [256]p
ISBN 0-246-11927-6 : £12.50 : CIP entry B82-37827

391′.009′04 — Western costume, *1900-1980*

Bond, David, *19---*. The Guinness guide to 20th century fashion / David Bond. — Enfield : Guinness Superlatives, 1981. — 223p : ill(some col.),ports ; 29cm
Includes index
ISBN 0-85112-234-5 : £10.95 : CIP rev. B81-25829

391′.0094 — North-Western European costume, *1400-1500.* **Social aspects**

Scott, Margaret. Late Gothic Europe, 1400-1500 / Margaret Scott. — London : Mills & Boon, 1980. — 256p,[16]p of plates : ill(some col.),1map,ports(some col.),1geneal.table ; 29cm. — (The History of dress series)
Bibliography: p245-247. — Includes index
ISBN 0-263-06429-8 : £25.00 B82-21153

391′.009411′5 — Scottish Highland costume, *to 1900*

Dunbar, John Telfer. The costume of Scotland / John Telfer Dunbar. — London : Batsford, 1981. — 212p,[4]p of plates : ill(some col.),ports(some col.) ; 26cm
Bibliography: p207-208. — Includes index
ISBN 0-7134-2534-2 : £20.00 B82-06214

391′.009414′43 — Scotland. Strathclyde Region. Glasgow. Costume, *1730-1939*

Anderson, Douglas N.. Glasgow through the looking-glass : history of a city seen through its costume / researched and illustrated by Douglas N. Anderson. — Milngavie : Heatherbank Press, 1982. — 94p,[2]leaves of plates(1folded) : ill,1map ; 21cm
ISBN 0-905192-30-3 (pbk) : £2.95 B82-35551

391′.00942 — English costume, *1840-1914*

Gernsheim, Alison. [Fashion and reality (1840-1914)]. Victorian & Edwardian fashion : a photographic survey / by Alison Gernsheim. — New York : Dover ; London : Constable, c1981. — 104p,[128]p of plates : ill,ports ; 24cm
Originally published: London : Faber, 1963. — Bibliography: p95-100. — Includes index
ISBN 0-486-24205-6 (pbk) : £4.50 B82-34842

391′.00945 — Italian costume, *1400-1500*

Herald, Jacqueline. Renaissance dress in Italy 1400-1500. — London : Bell & Hyman, Oct.1981. — [256]p. — (History of dress ; 2)
ISBN 0-7135-1294-6 : £30.00 : CIP entry
B81-24653

391′.0097281 — Central American Indian costume: Guatemalan costume

Deuss, Krystyna. Indian costumes from Guatemala / Krystyna Deuss. — [London] ([17, Wellington Sq., SW3]) : [K. Deuss], c1981. — 72p : ill(some col.),maps ; 30cm
Bibliography: p72
ISBN 0-9507847-0-2 (pbk) : Unpriced
B82-12633

391′.00973 — American costume, *1920-1930*

Everyday fashions of the twenties : as pictured in Sears and other catalogs / edited and with text by Stella Blum. — New York : Dover ; London : Constable, 1981. — 152p : ill,facsims ; 31cm
ISBN 0-486-24134-3 (pbk) : £6.00 B82-29991

391′.04 — Working clothing, *to 1939*

Mitchell, Christobel Williams. Dressed for the job : the story of occupational costume. — Poole : Blandford, Aug.1982. — [144]p
ISBN 0-7137-1020-9 : £8.00 : CIP entry
B82-15828

391′.2 — Scotland. Strathclyde Region. Glasgow. Exhibition centres: St Enoch Exhibition Centre. Exhibits: Dresses made by Murielle *(Firm) — Catalogues*

Macfarlane, Fiona C.. Murielle : 16 December 1981-11 February 1982, St. Enoch Exhibition Centre. — [Glasgow] : Glasgow Museums and Art Galleries, c1981. — 29p,[16]p of plates : ill,ports ; 20cm
Catalogue prepared by Fiona C. Macfarlane
ISBN 0-902752-15-4 (pbk) : Unpriced
B82-12204

391′.413 — Great Britain. Clogs, *to 1978*

Dobson, Bob. Concerning clogs / Bob Dobson. — Clapham (via Lancaster) : Dalesman, 1979. — 70p : ill,facsims,2ports ; 21cm
Bibliography: p69-70
ISBN 0-85206-512-4 (pbk) : £1.25 B82-23613

391′.413′088042 — Women's shoes, *1910-1980*

Probert, Christina. Shoes in Vogue : since 1910 / Christina Probert. — London : Thames and Hudson, 1981. — 96p : ill(some col.) ; 24cm
ISBN 0-500-27222-0 (pbk) : £4.95 B82-05662

391′.413′0941 — British shoes, *1600-1980*

Swann, June. Shoes / June Swann. — London : Batsford, 1982. — 96p,[4]p of plates : ill(some col.),1facsim,ports ; 26cm. — (The Costume accessories series)
Bibliography: p87-88. — Includes index
ISBN 0-7134-0942-8 : £6.95 B82-17657

391′.42 — Corsets, *to ca 1975.* **Social aspects**

Kunzle, David. Fashion and fetishism : a social history of the corset, tight-lacing and other forms of body-sculpture in the West / David Kunzle. — Totowa : Rowan and Littlefield ; London : George Prior Associated, 1982. — xxiii,359p,[32]p of plates : ill,ports ; 25cm
Bibliography: p341-354. — Includes index
ISBN 0-8476-6276-4 : £14.95 B82-20931

391′.42 — Great Britain. Corsetry, *1856-1980*

Page, Christopher. Foundations of fashion : the Symington collection, corsetry from 1856 to the present day / by Christopher Page. — Leicester : Leicestershire Museums, c1981. — v,82p : facsims,ports ; 30cm
ISBN 0-85022-089-0 (pbk) : Unpriced
B82-16139

391′.42′0903 — Underwear, *1400-1950*

Cunnington, C. Willett. The history of underclothes / C. Willett and Phillis Cunnington. — New rev. ed. / with revisions by A.D. Mansfield and Valerie Mansfield. — London : Faber, 1981. — 185p : ill,ports ; 26cm
Previous ed.: 1951. — Bibliography: p176-177. — Includes index
ISBN 0-571-11747-3 : £11.50 : CIP rev.
B81-31089

391′.5 — Wigs, *to 1850 — Early works — Facsimiles*

Cook, Dutton. Historical notes on wigs / by Dutton Cook ; edited by J. Stevens Cox. — St Peter Port : Toucan, 1980. — [8]p : 2ill ; 26cm
Originally published in Once a week, Sept. 3, 1864
ISBN 0-85694-229-4 (pbk) : Unpriced
B82-19939

391′.5′09 — Hair styles, *to 1981 — For schools*

Huggett, Renée. Hair-styles and head-dresses / Renée Huggett. — London : Batsford Academic and Educational, 1982. — 72p : ill ; 26cm. — (History in focus)
Bibliography: p69. — Includes index
ISBN 0-7134-4067-8 : £5.95 B82-36941

391′.7 — Finger rings, *to 1980*

The King : from antiquity to the twentieth century / Anne Ward ... [et al.] ; illustration consultant Marielle Ernould Gandouet ; [drawings by Virginia Edwards, M.O. Miller]. — London : Thames and Hudson, 1981. — 214p : ill(some col.),facsims,ports(some col.) ; 29cm
Bibliography: p200-202. — Includes index
ISBN 0-500-01263-6 : £35.00 B82-04664

391′.8 — Berkshire. Newbury. Museums: Newbury District Museum. Exhibits: Wedding dresses, *1861-1981 — Catalogues*

Wedding dresses : 1861-1981. — [Newbury] : Newbury District Museum, [1981]. — [4]p ; 21cm
Published to accompany an exhibition at the Newbury District Museum, 1981
Unpriced (pbk) B82-05165

391′.8 — Mourning costume, *to 1982 — Sociological perspectives*

Taylor, Lou. Mourning dress. — London : Allen & Unwin, Nov.1982. — [368]p
ISBN 0-04-746016-4 : £15.00 : CIP entry
B82-28718

391′.8 — Staffordshire. Stoke-on-Trent. Museums: City Museum and Art Gallery *(Stoke-on-Trent).* **Exhibits: English wedding dresses,** *1865-1970 — Catalogues*

For better or for worse : a select group of wedding dresses from the City Collection 1865-1970 : City Museum & Art Gallery, Stoke-on-Trent 12th March-2nd May 1981 / exhibition and catalogue compiled by Sheila Bradbury and Liz Salmon ; photography Pam Rigby ; design Rosie Hurt. — Stoke-on-Trent ([Bethesda St., Hanley, Stoke-on-Trent, ST1 4HS]) : City Museum & Art Gallery, [1981?]. — 1portfolio : ill ; 23cm
Unpriced B82-05811

391′.8 — Women's swimming costumes, *1910-1980 — Illustrations*

Probert, Christina. Swimwear in Vogue : since 1910 / Christina Probert. — [London] : Thames and Hudson, c1981. — 96p : ill(some col.),ports ; 24cm
ISBN 0-500-27221-2 (pbk) : £4.95 B82-09641

392 — CUSTOMS OF LIFE CYCLE AND DOMESTIC LIFE

392′.0942 — Great Britain. Fertility rites, *to 1750*

Bord, Janet. Earth rites : fertility rites in pre-industrial Britain. — London : Granada, Apr.1982. — [240]p
ISBN 0-246-11431-2 : £7.95 : CIP entry
B82-04320

392′.12 — Childbirth, *to 1980 — Anthropological perspectives*

Gebbie, Donald A. M.. Reproductive anthropology : descent through woman / Donald A.M. Gebbie. — Chichester : Wiley, c1981. — xix,371p,15p of plates : ill ; 24cm
Includes bibliographies and index
ISBN 0-471-27985-4 : £19.50 : CIP rev.
B81-31204

392′.14 — Papua New Guinea. Men. Initiation rites

Rituals of manhood : male initiation in Papua New Guinea / edited by Gilbert H. Herdt ; with an introduction by Roger M. Keesing. — Berkeley ; London : University of California Press, c1982. — xxvi,365p : ill,maps ; 24cm
Includes bibliographies and index
ISBN 0-520-04448-7 : Unpriced B82-36865

392′.14 — Zambia. Northern province. Bemba women: Initiation rites *— Anthropological perspectives*

Richards, Audrey I.. Chisungu : a girl's initiation ceremony among the Bemba. — London : Tavistock, Apr.1982. — [224]p
Originally published: London : Faber, 1956
ISBN 0-422-78070-7 (pbk) : £4.95 : CIP entry
B82-04060

392′.5 — Honeymoons

Blyth, Henry. A book of honeymoons. — London : Muller, Feb.1983. — [256]p
ISBN 0-584-11043-x : £8.95 : CIP entry
B82-37653

392′.5 — Southern African marriage customs: Bridewealth

Kuper, Adam. Wives for cattle : bridewealth and marriage in Southern Africa / Adam Kuper. — London : Routledge & Kegan Paul, 1982. — xiii,202,14p : ill,maps,geneal.tables ; 23cm. — (International library of anthropology)
Bibliography: p187-197. — Includes index
ISBN 0-7100-0989-5 : £11.95 B82-24901

392′.5′0942982 — Great Britain. Young persons. Weddings *— Study regions: West Glamorgan. Swansea — Sociological perspectives*

Leonard, Diana. Sex and generation : a study of courtship and weddings. — London : Tavistock, Apr.1982. — [320]p. — (Social science paperbacks)
Originally published: 1980
ISBN 0-422-78220-3 (pbk) : £5.50 : CIP entry
Primary classification 306.7 B82-04061

393 — DEATH CUSTOMS

393 — Death customs *— Anthropological perspectives — Conference proceedings*

Research Seminar in Archaeology and Related Subjects *(1980 : University of London).* Mortality and immortality : the anthropology and archaeology of death : proceedings of a meeting of the Research Seminar in Archaeology and Related Subjects held at the Institute of Archaeology, London University, in June 1980 / edited by S.C. Humphreys and Helen King. — London : Academic Press, 1981. — x,346p : ill,1map,1port ; 24cm
Includes bibliographies and index
ISBN 0-12-361550-x : £15.80 : CIP rev.
Also classified at 393′.072 B81-36061

393′.072 — Death customs. Archaeological investigation — *Conference proceedings*

Research Seminar in Archaeology and Related Subjects *(1980 : University of London)*. Mortality and immortality : the anthropology and archaeology of death : proceedings of a meeting of the Research Seminar in Archaeology and Related Subjects held at the Institute of Archaeology, London University, in June 1980 / edited by S.C. Humphreys and Helen King. — London : Academic Press, 1981. — x,346p : ill,1map,1port ; 24cm
Includes bibliographies and index
ISBN 0-12-361550-x : £15.80 : CIP rev.
Primary classification 393 B81-36061

394 — PUBLIC AND SOCIAL CUSTOMS

394.1′2′0951 — China. Food, *to 1976* — *Anthropological perspectives*

Food in Chinese culture. — London : Yale University Press, Oct.1981. — [448]p
Originally published: 1977
ISBN 0-300-02759-1 : £6.95 : CIP entry B81-31947

394.1′3 — Martini cocktails. American drinking customs, *to 1980*

Edmunds, Lowell. The silver bullet : the martini in American civilization / Lowell Edmunds. — Westport, Conn. ; London : Greenwood, 1981. — xviii,149p : ill,facsims ; 22cm. — (Contributions in American studies ; no.52)
Bibliography: p131-141. — Includes index
ISBN 0-313-22225-8 : Unpriced B82-02612

394.1′5 — Breakfasts — *For children*

Watson, Tom. Breakfast / Tom and Jenny Watson. — Hove : Wayland, 1982. — 64p : col.ill,1col.map ; 24cm. — (What the world eats)
Includes index
ISBN 0-85340-929-3 : £3.95 B82-28020

394.1′5 — Dinners — *For children*

Watson, Tom. Evening meal / Tom and Jenny Watson. — Hove : Wayland, 1982. — 64p : col.ill,1col.map ; 24cm. — (What the world eats)
Includes index
ISBN 0-85340-931-5 : £3.95 B82-28018

394.1′5 — Japan. Tea ceremonies

Hammitzsch, Horst. Zen in the art of the tea ceremony / Horst Hammitzsch ; translated from the German by Peter Lemesurier. — Salisbury : Element, c1979. — 104p ; 23cm
Translation of: Zen in der Kunst der Tee-Zeremonie. — Bibliography: p103-104
ISBN 0-906540-02-x : £3.95 B82-05559

394.1′5 — Luncheons — *For children*

Watson, Tom. Midday meal / Tom and Jenny Watson. — Hove : Wayland, 1982. — 64p : col.ill,1col.map ; 24cm. — (What the world eats)
Includes index
ISBN 0-85340-930-7 : £3.95 B82-28019

394.2 — Festivals

Joy, Margaret. Highdays and holidays / Margaret Joy ; illustrated by Juliet Renny. — London : Faber, 1981. — 119p : ill ; 22cm
Includes index
ISBN 0-571-11771-6 : £4.50 : CIP rev. B81-28056

394.2 — Festivals — *For schools*

Purton, Rowland W.. Festivals & celebrations / Rowland Purton. — Oxford : Blackwell, 1981. — x,214p : ill ; 24cm
Bibliography: p5. — Includes index
ISBN 0-631-91570-2 : £5.95 : CIP rev. B81-30167

394.2 — United States. Bicentennial. Celebration by Great Britain

Urquhart, James. John Paul Jones : America's greatest seaman - Nithdale's greatest son 1776-1976 : a bicentennial salute and souvenir from Great Britain / written, compiled ... by James Urquhart. — Dumfries : J. Urquhart, [1982]. — 130p : ill,facsims,1geneal. table,maps,music,ports ; 25cm
Includes index
ISBN 0-9507033-4-6 (pbk) : £8.50 B82-40208

394.2′0943 — Germany. Festivals

Russ, Jennifer M.. German festivals and customs. — London : Wolff, Oct.1982. — [166]p
ISBN 0-85496-365-0 (pbk) : £7.95 : CIP entry
Also classified at 390′.0943 B82-25739

394.2′5′09729 — West Indies. Carnivals — *For children*

Menter, Ian. Carnival. — London : Hamilton, Oct.1982. — [32]p
ISBN 0-241-10833-0 : £3.50 : CIP entry B82-23451

394.2′68282 — Christmas

Daily mirror Christmas cracker : festive fun for all the family. — London : Mirror Books, 1981. — 26p : ill(some col.),ports ; 36cm. — (A Daily Mirror Christmas special)
ISBN 0-85939-291-0 (unbound) : £0.50 B82-09024

Happy Christmas from Cliff. — London : Hodder & Stoughton, 1980. — 96p : ill(some col.),ports(some col.) ; 25cm
ISBN 0-340-25835-7 (pbk) : £3.50 : CIP rev. B80-13775

Muir, Frank. A treasury of Christmas / Frank & Jamie Muir. — London : Robson, 1981, c1975. — 144p,[12]leaves : ill,facsims,ports ; 24cm
Includes index
ISBN 0-86051-154-5 : £5.95 : CIP rev. B81-27455

394.2′68282 — Christmas — *For children*

Baker, Susan. The Christmas book / [written and planned by Susan Baker]. — Rev. ed. — London : Macdonald Educational, 1981. — 48p : ill(some col.) ; 29cm
Previous ed.: 1978. — Includes index
ISBN 0-356-05914-6 : £2.95 B82-25831

Thomas, Joan Gale. My book about Christmas / Joan Gale Thomas. — Rev. and shortened ed. — Oxford : Mowbray, 1979. — 24p : col.ill ; 22cm
Cover title. — Previous ed.: 1946. — Text on inside cover
ISBN 0-264-66571-6 (pbk) : £1.25 B82-23420

394.2′68282′0924 — Cheshire. Lyme Handley. Country houses: Lyme Park. Christmas, *1906* — *Personal observations*

Sandeman, Phyllis Elinor. Treasure on Earth / Phyllis Elinor Sandeman ; illustrated by the author. — [Stockport] : Lyme Park Joint Committee, 1981. — 113p : ill,19cm
Originally published: London : Jenkins, 1952
ISBN 0-9506818-1-4 (pbk) : Unpriced B82-17410

394.2′683 — Romania. Căluș — *Anthropological perspectives*

Kligman, Gail. Căluș : symbolic transformation in Romanian ritual / Gail Kligman ; with a foreword by Mircea Eliade. — Chicago ; London : University of Chicago Press, c1981. — xvi,209p : ill ; 24cm
Bibliography: p193-206. — Includes index
ISBN 0-226-44221-7 (pbk) : £9.80 B82-09581

394.2′683 — Scotland. Borders Region. Common ridings

Common ridings and festivals : the pageantry of the horse. — [Melrose] ([Newtown St., Boswells, Melrose, TD6 0SA]) : Borders Regional Council, 1980. — [30]p : ill,col.maps ; 21cm
Cover title
£0.30 (pbk) B82-17761

394.2′683 — Scotland. Shetland. Lerwick. Festivals: Up-Helly-A′ *(Festival), to 1981*

Up-Helly-A′ : back over the years 1881-1981 / compiled by H. Jamieson and Erling J.F. Clausen. — Lerwick : Shetland Times, 1981. — 64p : ill,ports ; 22cm
Photographic collection of squads, committee members and foils. The origin of the 'Dim Riv.' The formation of the junior festival and photographs of junior jarls
ISBN 0-900662-34-4 (pbk) : Unpriced B82-02990

394′.3 — Animal disguise dancing — *Anthropological perspectives*

Lonsdale, Steven. Animals and the origins of dance / Steven Lonsdale. — [London] : Thames and Hudson, c1981. — 192p,[32]p of plates : ill ; 24cm
Bibliography: p185-187. — Includes index
ISBN 0-500-01258-x : £9.50 B82-04005

394′.4 — Tropical regions. Tribal societies. Ceremonies — *Personal observations*

Attenborough, David. Journeys to the past : travels in New Guinea, Madagascar, and the Northern Territory of Australia / David Attenborough. — Guildford : Lutterworth, 1981. — 384p : ill(some col.),maps,ports ; 25cm
Contents: abridged versions of: Zoo quest to Madagascar. Originally published: 1961 — Quest in paradise. Originally published: 1960 — Quest under Capricorn. Originally published: 1963
ISBN 0-7188-2507-1 : £9.95
Also classified at 574.909′3 B82-04534

394′.6′094267 — Essex. Fairs, *to 1981*

Walker, Wendy. Essex markets and fairs / by Wendy Walker. — [Chelmsford] : Essex Record Office, 1981. — 44p : ill,maps,facsims ; 25cm. — (Essex Record Office publication ; no.83)
Bibliography: p44
ISBN 0-900360-59-3 (pbk) : Unpriced
Primary classification 381′.18′094267 B82-12052

394′.7 — Europe. Combat sports: Tournaments. Knights, *to ca 1500* — *For children*

Morris, Neil. The Black Knight's plot. — London : Hodder & Stoughton Children's Books, Feb.1983. — [32]p. — (Story facts)
ISBN 0-340-28614-8 : £1.95 : CIP entry B82-38052

394′.7 — Europe. Combat sports: Tournaments, *to ca 1500* — *For children*

Morris, Neil. Queen of the tournament. — London : Hodder & Stoughton Children's Books, Feb.1983. — [32]p. — (Story facts)
ISBN 0-340-28612-1 : £1.95 : CIP entry B82-38050

394′.8′09415 — Ireland. Duelling, *1700-1850*

Barry, Michael, *1926-*. An affair of honour / by Michael Barry. — Fermoy : Eigse, c1981. — viii,147p : ill,ports ; 18cm
Bibliography: p137-138. — Includes index
ISBN 0-907568-04-1 (pbk) : £2.40 B82-07749

395 — ETIQUETTE

395 — Etiquette — *Manuals* — *For children*

The **New** gold medal book of things we should? do / illustrated by Colin Petty. — [London] : [Dean], c1981. — [40]p : chiefly col.ill ; 26cm
Ill on lining papers
ISBN 0-603-00256-0 : Unpriced B82-26751

395′.09182′1 — Western world. Etiquette, *1200-1977*

Elias, Norbert. The civilizing process / Norbert Elias ; translated by Edmund Jephcott. — Oxford : Blackwell, 1982
[Vol.2]: State formation and civilization. — viii,376p ; 23cm
Translation of: Über den Prozess der Zivilisation. Bd.2. — Includes index
ISBN 0-631-19680-3 : £19.50 : CIP rev.
Also classified at 320.1′09182′1 B81-10486

395′.4 — Forms of address & titles

Debrett's correct form : an inclusive guide to everything from drafting wedding invitations to addressing an archbishop / compiled and edited by Patrick Montague-Smith. — Rev. ed. — [London] : Debrett's Peerage in association with Futura, 1976 (1979 [printing]). — x,423p ; 21cm. — (A Futura book)
Previous ed.: Kingston-upon-Thames : Kelly's Directories, 1970. — Includes index
ISBN 0-7088-1500-6 (pbk) : £1.95 B82-32983

398 — FOLKLORE

398 — Folklore — *Conference proceedings*

Folklore Society. *Centenary Conference (1978 : Royal Holloway College)*. Folklore studies in the twentieth century : proceedings of the Centenary Conference of the Folklore Society / edited by Venetia J. Newall. — Woodbridge : Brewer, c1980. — xxxvi,463p : ill,maps,ports ; 26cm
Includes index
ISBN 0-85991-064-4 : £35.00 B82-02918

398′.042 — Mythology. Social aspects

Lowry, Shirley Park. Familiar mysteries : the truth in myth / Shirley Park Lowry. — New York ; Oxford : Oxford University Press, 1982. — x,339p : ill ; 22cm
Bibliography: p323-330. — Includes index
ISBN 0-19-502925-9 : £13.50 B82-33310

398′.09417′2 — Sligo *(County)* **folklore**

Yeats, W. B.. The Celtic twilight / W.B. Yeats ; with an introduction by Kathleen Raine ; illustrated by Jean Townsend. — Gerrards Cross : Smythe, 1981. — 160p : ill ; 23cm
ISBN 0-86140-069-0 (cased) : £6.75 : CIP rev.
ISBN 0-86140-070-4 (pbk) : £2.75 B81-15825

398′.0942 — English folklore — *Sociological perspectives — Conference proceedings*

British Sociological Association. *Conference (1978 : University of Sussex)*. Papers on language, culture and tradition : papers on language and folklore presented at the Annual Conference of the British Sociological Association, April 1978 [held at the University of Sussex] / edited by A.E. Green and J.D.A. Widdowson. — [Leeds] : The Institute of Dialect and Folklife Studies, School of English, University of Leeds, c1981. — viii,87p ; 21cm. — (CECTAL conference papers series, ISSN 0261-314X ; no.2)
Unpriced (pbk) B82-09894

398′.09423′7 — Cornish folklore

Cornish sayings, superstitions and remedies / compiled by Kathleen Hawke. — 3rd. ed. — Redruth : Dyllansow Truran, 1981. — 36p : ill ; 22cm
Previous ed.: 1975
ISBN 0-907566-04-9 (pbk) : Unpriced B82-11425

398′.09429′5 — Wye Valley folklore

Waters, Ivor. Folklore & dialect of the Lower Wye Valley / by Ivor Waters ; illustrations by Mercedes Waters ; map by Bryan Woodfield. — Chepstow : Moss Rose, 1982. — 81p : ill,1col.map ; 22cm
Limited ed. of 110 copies. — Bibliography: p75-76. — Includes index
ISBN 0-906134-15-3 : £8.50 B82-29839

398′.09772′99 — Indiana folklore: Calumet region folklore

Dorson, Richard M.. Land of the millrats / Richard M. Dorson. — Cambridge, Mass. ; London : Harvard University Press, 1981. — xii,251p,[12]p of plates : ill,1map,1port ; 25cm
Includes index
ISBN 0-674-50855-6 : £15.75 B82-13736

398.2 — FOLK LITERATURE

398.2 — Folk plays in English, *1400-1625*. **Special subjects: Robin Hood** — *Critical studies*

Wiles, David. The early plays of Robin Hood / David Wiles. — Cambridge : D.S. Brewer, 1981. — 97p ; 23cm
Bibliography: p94-95. — Includes index
ISBN 0-85991-082-2 : £12.00 : CIP rev. B81-30403

398.2 — Folk plays in English — *Critical studies — Serials*

Roomer : an occasional newsletter for researchers in traditional drama. — Vol.1: 1 (1980)-. — Andover (S. Roud, 22 Adelaide Rd, Andover, Hants.) : [s.n.], 1980-. — v. : facsims ; 30cm
Irregular. — Description based on: Vol.1:6 (1981)
ISSN 0262-4095 = Roomer : Unpriced B82-18525

398.2 — Tales & legends — *Anthologies — For children*

Tvrdíková, Michaela. Folk tales and legends / retold by Michaela Tvrdíková ; translated by Vera Gissing ; illustrations by Vojtěch Kubašta. — London : Cathay, 1981. — 206p : ill ; 31cm
Translated from the Czech. — Ill on lining papers
ISBN 0-86178-056-6 : £5.00 B82-01039

398.2′09423′7 — Cornish tales & legends — *Anthologies*

Bottrell, William. [Traditions and hearthside stories of West Cornwall. Selections]. Cornish ghosts and legends : compiled from William Bottrell's Traditions and hearthside stories of West Cornwall / edited by J.A. Brooks. — Norwich : Jarrold, c1981. — 144p : ill ; 21cm
ISBN 0-85306-960-3 (pbk) : Unpriced B82-03516

398.2′04922 — Aramaic folk literature. Kurdistani Jewish writers — *Anthologies*

The **Folk** literature of the Kurdistani Jews. — London : Yale University Press, July 1982. — [320]p. — (Yale Judaica series ; 23)
Translated from Hebrew and Aramaic
ISBN 0-300-02698-6 : £23.00 : CIP entry
Primary classification 398.2′04924 B82-22783

398.2′04924 — Hebrew folk literature. Kurdistani writers — *Anthologies*

The **Folk** literature of the Kurdistani Jews. — London : Yale University Press, July 1982. — [320]p. — (Yale Judaica series ; 23)
Translated from Hebrew and Aramaic
ISBN 0-300-02698-6 : £23.00 : CIP entry
Also classified at 398.2′04922 B82-22783

398.2′09411 — Scottish tales & legends — *Anthologies*

Lamont-Brown, Raymond. Mysteries and legends / Raymond Lamont-Brown ; drawings by Richard Hook. — Edinburgh : Spurbooks, c1982. — 64p : ill ; 19cm. — (Introducing Scotland)
Bibliography: p63. — Includes index
ISBN 0-7157-2083-x (pbk) : £1.25 B82-20594

Lochhead, Marion. The other country : legends and fairytales of Scotland / retold by Marion Lochhead. — London : Hamish Hamilton, 1978. — 172p : ill ; 23cm
ISBN 0-241-89773-4 : £4.25 B82-25789

Tales from Scottish lairds. — Norwich : Jarrold, [c1981]. — 140p : ill,1map ; 21cm
ISBN 0-85306-965-4 (pbk) : Unpriced B82-01365

398.2′09415 — Irish folk literature — *Anthologies*

Ó Luínse, Amhlaoibh. Seanachas / Amhlaoibh Í Luínse ; Seán Ó Cróinín a thóg síos ; Donncha Ó Cróinín a chuir in eagar. — Dublin : Comhairle Bhéaloideas Eireann, 1980. — xxxii,465p,[6]p of plates : ill,1map,1port ; 23cm. — (Scríbhinní béaloidis = Folklore studies ; 5)
Includes index
ISBN 0-906426-04-9 : Unpriced B82-20805

398.2′09415 — Irish tales & legends — *Anthologies*

Ó Catháin, Séamus. Irish life and lore / Séamas Ó Catháin. — Dublin : Mercier, c1982. — 124p ; 18cm
ISBN 0-85342-678-3 (pbk) : £2.95(Irish) B82-40405

O'Connor, Ulick. Irish tales and sagas / Ulick O'Connor ; illustrations by Pauline Bewick. — London : Granada, 1981. — 96p : col.ill ; 22cm
ISBN 0-246-11333-2 : £4.95 B82-08914

398.2′09416′3 — Fermanagh *(District)* **tales & legends** — *Anthologies*

Irish folk history : folktales from the north / [selected by] Henry Glassie ; drawings by the author. — Dublin : O'Brien Press, 1982. — x,161p : ill,maps,music ; 22cm
ISBN 0-86278-016-0 : Unpriced B82-32348

398.2′094169′3 — Donegal *(County)* **tales & legends** — *Anthologies — Irish-English parallel texts*

Fairy legends from Donegal / originally collected by Seán Ó hEochaidh ; and translated into English by Máire Mac Neill ; Irish texts edited by Séamas Ó Catháin. — Dublin (University College, Belfield, Dublin 4) : Comhairle Bhéaloideas Éireann, 1977. — 404p,vleaves of plates : ill,maps,2ports ; 23cm. — (Folklore studies ; 4)
Parallel English and Irish title pages and text; notes in English. — Maps on lining papers
Unpriced B82-14672

398.2′09429′21 — Ynys Môn tales & legends — *Anthologies — Welsh texts*

Lewis, Brenda, *1923-*. Straeon Môn / Brenda Lewis ; arluniwyd y gyfrol gan Jac Jones. — [Caernarfon] ([St. Davids Rd., Caernarfon, Gwynedd]) : Gwasg Tŷ ar y Graig, 1980. — 87p : ill,1map ; 21cm
£2.00 (pbk) B82-24400

398.2′0943 — German tales & legends — *Anthologies*

Ratcliff, Ruth. German tales and legends / Ruth Ratcliff ; illustrated by T.E. Breheny. — London : Muller, 1982. — viii,88p : ill ; 23cm
ISBN 0-584-62059-4 : £4.95 : CIP rev. B82-09301

398.2′09439 — Hungarian tales & legends — *Anthologies — For children*

Biro, Val. Hungarian folk-tales / retold from the Hungarian and illustrated by Val Biro. — Oxford : Oxford University Press, c1980. — 192p : ill ; 23cm. — (Oxford myths and legends)
ISBN 0-19-274126-8 : £4.95 B82-40114

398.2′09491′5 — Faeroese tales & legends — *Anthologies*

West, John F.. Faroese folk-tales & legends / John F. West ; illustrations by Barður Jákupsson. — Lerwick : Shetland Publishing Company, 1980. — xv,173p : ill,1map ; 22cm
Translation from the Faroese. — Bibliography: p171-173
ISBN 0-906736-01-3 : £5.95 B82-08596

398.2′0954 — Indian tales & legends — *Anthologies*

Bīdpā'ī. Kalila and Dimna / selected fables of Bidpai ; retold by Ramsay Wood ; illustrated by Margaret Kilrenny. — London : Granada, 1982, c1980. — xix,263p ; 20cm. — (A Paladin book)
ISBN 0-586-08409-6 (pbk) : £1.95 B82-35714

398.2′0956 — Sufi tales & legends — *Anthologies*

Idries Shah. Tales of the dervishes : teaching stories of the Sufi masters over the past thousand years : selected from the Sufi classics, from oral tradition, from unpublished manuscripts and schools of Sufi teaching in many countries / Idries Shah. — London : Octagon, 1977, c1982 (1982 [printing]). — 221p ; 23cm
Originally published: London : Cape, 1967
ISBN 0-900860-47-2 : Unpriced B82-21655

398.2′096 — African tales & legends — *Anthologies*

Carey, Margaret. Myths and legends of Africa / Margaret Carey ; illustrated by Ron Geary. — Feltham : Hamlyn, c1970 (1982 [printing]). — 159p : col.ill,1col.map ; 18cm. — (Hamlyn all-colour paperbacks)
Bibliography: p157. — Includes index
ISBN 0-600-00132-6 (pbk) : £1.75 B82-38338

398.2′096 — African tales & legends — *Anthologies — For children*

Fables from Africa / collected by Jan Knappert ; illustrated by Jeroo Roy. — London : Evans, 1980. — 64p : ill ; 22cm
ISBN 0-237-44985-4 : £4.75 : CIP rev. B79-36755

398.2′0979 — Navaho tales & legends — *Anthologies*

Curly, Tó Aheedlíinii. Women versus men : a conflict of Navajo emergence : the Curly Tó Aheedlíinii version / [as reported to] Berard Haile ; Navajo orthography by Irvy W. Goossen ; Karl W. Luckert, editor. — Lincoln, [Neb.] ; London : University of Nebraska Press, c1981. — viii,118p ; 24cm. — (American tribal religions. v.6)
English and Navaho text
ISBN 0-8032-2319-6 (cased) : £10.50
ISBN 0-8032-7211-1 (pbk) B82-22549

398.2′1 — Fairy tales, *ca 1650-1919* **—** *Sociological perspectives*

Zipes, Jack. Fairy tales and the art of subversion. — London : Heinemann Educational, Jan.1983. — [240]p
ISBN 0-435-82983-1 (cased) : £14.50 : CIP entry
ISBN 0-435-82982-3 (pbk) : £6.50 B82-34587

398.2′1 — Tales — *Anthologies*

Pink fairy book / collected by Andrew Lang. — Rev. ed. / edited by Brian Alderson, illustrated by Colin McNaughton. — London : Kestrel, 1982. — 331p : ill,music ; 24cm
Previous ed.: London : Longman Green, 1897
ISBN 0-7226-5703-x : £7.50 B82-40175

398.2′1 — Tales — *Anthologies — For children*

Carruth, Jane. Once upon a time storybook / retold by Jane Carruth. — London : Octopus, 1981. — 207p : col.ill ; 29cm
Translated from the Italian
ISBN 0-7064-1097-1 : £2.99 B82-03169

Manning-Sanders, Ruth. A book of heroes and heroines. — London : Methuen Children's Books, Feb.1982. — [125]p
ISBN 0-416-89310-4 : £4.95 : CIP entry
B81-35709

Nesbit, E.. The old nursery stories / E. Nesbit ; illustrated by Faith Jaques. — [Sevenoaks] : Knight Books, 1981, c1975. — 128p ; 20cm
Originally published: London : Hodder and Stoughton, 1975
ISBN 0-340-26598-1 (pbk) : £0.95 : CIP rev.
B81-26755

Sleeping Beauty & other favourite fairy tales. — London : Gollancz, Sept.1982. — [128]p
ISBN 0-575-03194-8 : £6.95 : CIP entry
B82-19560

Štovíček, Vratislav. Around the world fairy tales / retold by Vratislav ; translated by Vera Gissing ; illustrations by Zdeňka Krejčová. — London : Cathay, 1981. — 207p : ill ; 31cm
Translated from the Czech. — Ill on lining papers
ISBN 0-86178-062-0 : £5.00 B82-03188

A Time to laugh : funny stories for children / edited by Sara and Stephen Corrin ; illustrated by Gerald Rose. — [London] : Faber Fanfares, 1980, c1972. — 205p : ill ; 19cm. — (Faber fanfares)
Originally published: London : Faber, 1972
ISBN 0-571-11487-3 (pbk) : £1.25 : CIP rev.
Also classified at 823′.01′089282[J] B80-18056

398.2′1′094 — European tales — *Anthologies*

The **Trials** and tribulations of Little Red Riding Hood. — London : Heinemann Educational, Jan.1983. — [272]p
ISBN 0-435-82987-4 (cased) : £12.95 : CIP entry
ISBN 0-435-82988-2 (pbk) : £5.95 B82-34588

398.2′1′094 — European tales — *Anthologies — For children*

Robbins, Maria. Six tiny tales : six favourite tales / retold by Maria Robbins ; illustrated by Diane Dawson. — London : Pelham, [c1978]. — 1case : col.ill ; 10cm
Contents: The three billy goats gruff — The three little pigs — Goldilocks and the three bears — Mr Hedgehog and Mr Hare — The town mouse and the country mouse — The beautiful lion
ISBN 0-7207-1161-4 : £2.75 B82-12019

398.2′1′094 — North-western European tales — *Anthologies*

The **Faber** book of northern folk-tales / edited by Kevin Crossley-Holland ; illustrated by Alan Howard. — London : Faber, 1980. — 157p : ill ; 24cm
Bibliography: p155-157
ISBN 0-571-11519-5 : £5.50 : CIP rev.
B80-18666

398.2′1′09411 — Scottish tales — *Anthologies — For schools*

The **Green** man of knowledge and other Scots traditional tales. — Aberdeen : Aberdeen University Press, Oct.1981. — [128]p
ISBN 0-08-025757-7 (cased) : £9.50 : CIP entry
ISBN 0-08-025758-5 (pbk) : £5.00 B81-27360

398.2′1′094193 — Clare *(County)* **tales —** *Anthologies — Irish texts*

Ó hEalaoire, Stiofán. Leabhar Stiofáin uí Ealaoire / Séamus Ó Duilearga a bhailigh agus a chuir in eagar ; Dáithí Ó hOgain a chóirigh. — Baile Átha Cliath : Comhairle Bhéaliodeas Éireann, 1981. — xxvi,363p : ill,2ports ; 23cm
Irish text, English summary and notes
ISBN 0-906426-07-3 : Unpriced B82-21446

398.2′1′09426 — East Anglian tales — *Anthologies — For children*

Crossley-Holland, Kevin. The dead moon : and other tales from East Anglia and the Fen Country / retold by Kevin Crossley-Holland ; illustrated by Shirley Felts. — London : Deutsch, 1982. — 104p : ill ; 25cm
ISBN 0-233-97478-4 : £5.95 B82-38932

398.2′1′09429 — Welsh tales — *Anthologies — For children — Welsh texts*

Pugh, Jane. Chwedlau tylwyth teg o Gymru / Jane Pugh ; lluniau gan Alison Jenkins. — Caerdydd : Gwasg y Dref Wen, c1981. — 62p : ill ; 19cm. — (Cyfres y wiwer)
£1.70 (pbk)
B82-08970

398.2′1′0943 — German tales — *Anthologies*

Grimm, Jacob. Grimms' fairy tales. — Oxford : Oxford University Press, May 1982. — [240]p
ISBN 0-19-274529-8 : £7.95 : CIP entry
B82-10773

398.2′1′0943 — German tales — *Anthologies — Facsimiles*

Grimm, Jacob. [Kinder- und Hausmärchen. English]. Grimm's household stories / translated by Lucy Crane ; illustrated by Walter Crane. — [London] : Macmillan, [1979]. — x,269p : ill ; 25cm. — (Facsimile classics series)
Translation of: Kinder- und Hausmärchen. — Facsim. of: 1st ed. 1882
ISBN 0-333-27388-5 : £5.95 B82-13582

398.2′1′0943 — German tales — *Anthologies — For children*

Happy times book of fairytales. — London : Dean, c1981. — [20]p : col.ill ; 26cm
Ill on lining papers
ISBN 0-603-00291-9 : Unpriced B82-26821

My pop-up book of fairy tales. — London : Dean, 1982, c1973. — [8]p : col.ill ; 24cm
Cover title. — Text and ill on lining papers. — Contents: Little red riding hood — The Ugly Duckling — Hansel and Gretel
ISBN 0-603-02045-3 : Unpriced B82-26820

398.2′1′0943 — German tales — *Texts — For children*

Ash, Jutta. Rapunzel. — London : Andersen Press, Feb.1982. — [32]p
ISBN 0-86264-010-5 : £3.95 : CIP entry
B81-36965

Bechstein, Ludwig. Three fairy tales. — London : Hutchinson Junior Books, Sept.1982. — 3v
In slip case
ISBN 0-09-149310-2 : £4.50 : CIP entry
B82-20192

Grimm, Jacob. Cinderella / from Grimms' fairy tales ; pictures by Ruth Elsässer ; translated by J. Collis. — London : Steiner, c1978. — [22]p : col.ill ; 23x33cm
Translation of: Aschenputtel
ISBN 0-85440-332-9 : Unpriced B82-25000

Grimm, Jacob. Grimm's Hansel and Gretel / illustrated by Antonella Bolliger-Savelli. — Kingswood : Kaye & Ward, 1981. — [26]p : col.ill ; 24cm
Translated from the German. — Text reprinted from Grimm's fairy tales / Jacob Grimm. Oxford : Oxford University Press, 1962
ISBN 0-7182-1261-4 : £3.25 : CIP rev.
B81-04267

398.2′1′0945 — Italian tales — *Anthologies*

Italian folktales / selected and retold by Italo Calvino ; translated by George Martin. — Harmondsworth : Penguin, 1982, c1980. — xxxii,763p ; 24cm
Translation of: Fiabe italiane. — Originally published: New York : Harcourt Brace Jovanovich, 1980. — Bibliography: p759-763
ISBN 0-14-006235-1 (pbk) : £6.95 B82-34751

398.2′1′0945 — Italian tales — *Texts — For children*

De Paola, Tomie. The prince of the Dolomites. — London : Methuen, July 1981. — [40]p
ISBN 0-416-21430-4 : £3.95 : CIP entry
B81-14857

398.2′1′0947 — Russian tales — *Anthologies*

Afanas′ev, A. N.. Russian folk tales. — London : Muller, Nov.1982. — [80]p
Translated from the Russian
ISBN 0-584-62070-5 (cased) : £6.95 : CIP entry
ISBN 0-584-62071-3 (pbk) : £4.95 B82-26569

398.2′1′0947 — Russian tales — *Texts — For children*

Within-and-without-wears-his-coat-wrong-side-out : a Byelorussian folk tale / translated by Irina Zheleznova ; drawings by V. Milashevsky. — Moscow : Progress ; [London] : Central [distributor], 1975 (1982 printing). — 15p : chiefly col.ill ; 28cm
Translation of: Sin͡ia͡a svita naiznaiku sshita
ISBN 0-7147-1720-7 (pbk) : £0.55 B82-28805

398.2′1′094743 — Latvian tales — *Anthologies — Esperanto texts*

Latva fabelareto : kvar Latvaj popolaj fabeloj / tradukitaj en esperanton de Bruno Najbaro. — Gloucester : Fellowship, c1975. — 20p : ill ; 21cm
Translation of the Latvian
ISBN 0-9504146-0-3 (pbk) : Unpriced
B82-23720

398.2′1′09495 — Greek tales — *Texts — For children*

Zarambouka, Sophia. The king's apple tree. — London : Methuen Children's, Jan.1983. — [32]p. — (World folktales ; 1)
Translated from the Greek
ISBN 0-416-23250-7 : £5.50 : CIP entry
B82-34442

398.2′1′0954 — Indian tales — *Texts — For children*

Troughton, Joanna. The wizard Punchkin. — London : Blackie, Sept.1982. — [32]p
ISBN 0-216-91266-0 : £4.95 : CIP entry
B82-19002

398.2′1′0956 — Sufi tales — *Anthologies*

Idries Shah. The dermis probe / Idries Shah. — London : Octagon, 1980. — 191p ; 23cm
Originally published: London : Cape, 1970
ISBN 0-900860-83-9 : Unpriced B82-14135

Idries Shah. The magic monastery : analogical and action philosophy of the Middle East and Central Asia / Idries Shah. — London : Octagon, 1981. — 208p ; 23cm
Originally published: London : Cape, 1972
ISBN 0-900860-89-8 : £7.00 B82-17127

398.2′1′0956 — Sufi tales — *Anthologies* *continuation*

Orbeliani, Sulxan-Saba, *Prince*. A book of wisdom and lies / Sulkhan-Saba Orbeliani ; translated from the Georgian by Katharine Vivian. — London : Octagon, c1982. — xiii,174p ; 23cm
Translation of: Sibrżne sic′ruisa
ISBN 0-900860-97-9 : £7.50 B82-31189

398.2′1′095692 — Lebanese tales — *Texts*

The **Story** of Ali Baba and the forty thieves / [translated by Andrew Dalby] ; [illustrated by Elizabeth May]. — [Cambridge] ([5 Primrose Way, Linton, Cambridge CB1 6CD]) : [A. Dalby], [1981]. — [32]p : ill ; 21cm
Translation from the French. — Limited ed. of 250 copies
ISBN 0-907049-04-4 (unbound) : £0.85 B82-12968

398.2′1′0972 — Mexican Indian tales — *Anthologies* — *For children*

Hinojosa, Francisco. The old lady who ate people. — London : Methuen Children′s, Jan.1983. — [48]p
Translation of: La vieja que comia gente
ISBN 0-416-28830-8 : £5.50 : CIP entry B82-34445

398.2′1′0972 — Mexican Indian tales. Special subjects: Animals — *Anthologies* — *For children*

Kurtycz, Marcos. Tigers and opossums. — London : Methuen Children′s, Jan.1983. — [48]p
Translation of: De tigres y tlacuaches
ISBN 0-416-28850-2 : £5.50 : CIP entry B82-34446

398.2′2 — English legends. Robin Hood — *Anthologies*

The **Original** Robin Hood : a translation of the early tales / John Sheffield ; illustrated by John Clark. — Nottingham : Sheffield & Broad, 1982. — 54p : ill,1map ; 22cm
Translation of part text from: Rymes of Robyn Hood / R.B. Dobson and J. Taylor. — London : Heinemann, 1976
ISBN 0-9507457-0-7 (pbk) : £1.50 B82-21482

398.2′2 — Legends. John, *Prester* — *Anthologies*

John, *Prester*. The Hebrew Letters of Prester John / by Edward Ullendorff and C.F. Beckingham. — Oxford : Oxford University Press, 1982. — xiii,252p : facsims ; 24cm
Text in English and Hebrew. — Includes index
ISBN 0-19-713604-4 : £12.00 : CIP rev. B81-35767

398.2′2′08997 — Eskimo legends — *Texts*

Killigivuk, Asitchaq Jimmie. The shaman Aningatchaq : an Eskimo story from Tikiraq, Alaska / told by Asitchaq Jimmie Killigivuk ; translated by Tukummig Carol Omnik and Tom Lowenstein with commentaries. — London (15 Norcott Rd., London N.16) : Many Press, [1981?]. — [32]p : 1map ; 21cm
Translation from the Eskimo
Unpriced (pbk) B82-00763

398.2′2′09415 — Irish legends — *Anthologies*

[Ulster cycle]. Heroic tales from the Ulster cycle / Curriculum Development Unit. — Dublin : O′Brien Educational, 1976 (1982 [printing]). — p77-136 : ill ; 21cm
Includes one chapter in Irish. — Previously published as: The Ulster cycle
ISBN 0-86278-020-9 (pbk) : £2.30 B82-31491

398.2′2′0942353 — Devon legends: Dartmoor legends — *Anthologies*

St. Leger-Gordon, Ruth. The witchcraft and folklore of Dartmoor. — Gloucester : Sutton, July 1982. — [152]p
ISBN 0-86299-021-1 (pbk) : £3.95 : CIP entry B82-17223

398.2′2′0942383 — Somerset legends: Glastonbury legends — *Critical studies*

Ashe, Geoffrey. Avalonian quest. — London : Methuen, Oct.1982. — [288]p
ISBN 0-413-48800-4 : £7.95 : CIP entry B82-24476

398.2′2′0942383 — Somerset legends: Glastonbury Tor legends — *Critical studies*

Ditmas, E. M. R.. Glastonbury Tor : fact and legend / by E.M.R. Ditmas. — St. Peter Port, Guernsey : Toucan Press, 1981. — 21p : ill ; 19cm. — (West country folklore ; no.16)
Bibliography: p21
ISBN 0-85694-240-5 (pbk) : Unpriced B82-06456

398.2′2′0948 — Scandinavian legends — *Anthologies* — *For children*

Esping, Mikael. The Vikings : tales of gods and heroes / Mikael Esping ; illustrated by Julek Heller. — [London] : Piccolo, 1982. — 127p : ill ; 18cm
ISBN 0-330-26746-9 (pbk) : £1.00 B82-37809

398.2′2′0973 — American legends — *Critical studies*

Brunvand, Jan Harold. The vanishing hitchhiker : American urban legends and their meanings / Jan Harold Brunvand. — New York ; London : Norton, c1981. — xiv,208p ; 22cm
Includes index
ISBN 0-393-01473-8 (cased) : £10.50
ISBN 0-393-95169-3 (pbk) : Unpriced B82-37596

398.2′4529725 — North American tales & legends. Special subjects: Horses — *Anthologies*

Mister, you got yourself a horse : tales of old-time horse trading / edited, with an introduction, by Roger L. Welsch. — Lincoln, [Neb.] ; London : University of Nebraska Press, c1981. — xi,207p ; 23cm
Bibliography: p207
ISBN 0-8032-4711-7 : £10.50 B82-22953

398.2′5′09411 — Scottish tales. Special subjects: Ghosts — *Anthologies*

Campbell, Grant. Scottish hauntings / Grant Campbell ; illustrated by Jane Bottomley. — [London] : Piccolo, 1982. — 125p : ill,1map ; 19cm. — (A Piccolo original)
ISBN 0-330-26618-7 (pbk) : £1.10 B82-20430

398.2′5′094254 — Leicestershire tales & legends. Special subjects: Ghosts — *Anthologies*

Cutting, Angela. Ghost stories of Leicestershire / by Angela Cutting. — Blaby : Anderson, c1982. — 32p : ill ; 21cm
ISBN 0-907917-00-3 (pbk) : £1.10 B82-19724

398.2′6 — Tales & legends. Special subjects: Flight — *Anthologies* — *For children*

Sleigh, Barbara. Winged magic. — London : Knight, Nov.1982. — [160]p
Originally published: London : Hodder & Stoughton, 1979
ISBN 0-340-26538-8 (pbk) : £0.95 : CIP entry B82-27379

398.3/4 — FOLKLORE OF SPECIAL SUBJECTS

398′.32972′1 — Mexico. Sorcery — *Personal observations*

Castaneda, Carlos. The eagle′s gift. — London : Hodder & Stoughton, Sept.1981. — [320]p
ISBN 0-340-27086-1 : £6.95 : CIP entry B81-23933

398′.352 — English legends. Characters: Mildred, *Saint* — *Critical studies*

Rollason, D. W.. The Mildrith legend. — Leicester : Leicester University Press, Oct.1982. — [188]p. — (Studies in the early history of Britain)
ISBN 0-7185-1201-4 : £22.00 : CIP entry B82-24738

398′.352 — English legends. Characters: Robin Hood. Historicity

Holt, J. C.. Robin Hood / J.C. Holt. — London : Thames & Hudson, c1982. — 208p : ill,maps ; 24cm
Bibliography: p196-200. — Includes index
ISBN 0-500-25081-2 : £8.95 B82-27978

398′.352 — English legends. Little John — *Critical studies*

Hulbert, Martin F. H.. Let these stones live : Little John and St. Michaels and All Angels, Hathersage / by Martin F.H. Hulbert. — [Sheffield] : [M.F.H. Hulbert], [1982?]. — 20p : ill ; 21cm
ISBN 0-907602-05-3 (pbk) : Unpriced
Also classified at 942.5′13 B82-35762

398′.352 — European legends. Characters: Santa Claus. Historicity

Harrison, Shirley. Who is Father Christmas? / Shirley Harrison. — Newton Abbot : David & Charles, c1981. — 64p : ill(some col.) ; 18cm
ISBN 0-7153-8222-5 : £3.50 : CIP rev. B81-24661

398′.352 — Legends. Arthur, *King*. Historicity

Blackett, A. T.. Arthur : King of Glamorgan and Gwent / by A.T. Blackett, Alan Wilson. — Cardiff : Byrd, 1981, c1980. — 320p : ill,maps,ports,geneal.tables ; 30cm
One folded sheet attached to lining papers
ISBN 0-86285-001-0 : Unpriced
ISBN 0-86285-000-2 (presentation copies) : Unpriced B82-07857

398′.352 — Legends. Arthur, *King*. Life — *Sources of data: Western European literatures, ca 1100-ca 1500*

Morris, Rosemary. The character of King Arthur in medieval literature. — Woodbridge : Boydell, May 1982. — [192]p. — (Arthurian studies, ISSN 0261-9814 ; 4)
ISBN 0-85991-088-1 : £17.50 : CIP entry B82-08451

398′.352 — Legends. Characters: Arthur, *King*. Historical sources: Llandaff Cathedral charters

Blackett, A. T.. Arthur : and the Charters of the Kings / by A.T. Blackett, Alan Wilson. — Cardiff : Byrd, 1981, c1980. — 280p : ill,facsims,ports,geneal.tables ; 31cm
One folded sheet attached to lining papers
ISBN 0-86285-002-9 : Unpriced
ISBN 0-86285-003-7 (presentation copies) : Unpriced B82-07858

398′.352 — Legends. Heroes & heroines — *For schools*

Groves, Paul. Heroes and their journeys : in myth and legend / Paul Groves, Nigel Grimshaw. — London : Edward Arnold, 1982. — 95p : ill ; 22cm
ISBN 0-7131-0697-2 (pbk) : Unpriced : CIP rev. B82-06913

398′.355 — Irish street folklore

MacThomáis, Eamonn. Janey Mack, one shirt is black. — Dublin (20 Victoria Rd., Rathgar, Dublin 6) : O′Brien Press, Nov.1982. — [160]p
ISBN 0-905140-67-2 : £7.00 : CIP entry B82-30613

398′.3699734 — Celtic tales. Special themes: Livestock: Pigs. Occult aspects — *Critical studies*

Harte, Jeremy. White beast and sacred site / Jeremy Harte. — Cambridge (142 Pheasant Rise, Bar Hill, Cambridge CB3 8SD) : Institute of Geomantic Research, 1980. — 14p : 1ill ; 30cm. — (The Institute of Geomantic Research occasional paper ; no.17)
Bibliography: p13-14
Unpriced (unbound)
Also classified at 398′.36997358 B82-19932

398′.36997358 — Celtic tales. Special themes: Livestock: Cattle. Occult aspects — *Critical studies*

Harte, Jeremy. White beast and sacred site / Jeremy Harte. — Cambridge (142 Pheasant Rise, Bar Hill, Cambridge CB3 8SD) : Institute of Geomantic Research, 1980. — 14p : 1ill ; 30cm. — (The Institute of Geomantic Research occasional paper ; no.17)
Bibliography: p13-14
Unpriced (unbound)
Primary classification 398′.3699734 B82-19932

398′.41 — Superstitions

Planer, Felix E.. Superstition / Felix E. Planer. — London : Cassell, 1980. — 376p ; 24cm
Bibliography: p365-369. — Includes index
ISBN 0-304-30691-6 : £11.95 B82-14017

398′.42 — Agharti

Maclellan, Alec. The lost world of Agharti : the mystery of Vril power / Alec Maclellan. — London : Souvenir Press, 1982. — 231p,[16]p of plates : ill,maps,1facim,ports ; 23cm
Map on lining papers. — Bibliography: p229-231
ISBN 0-285-62521-7 : £7.95 B82-20099

398′.45 — British tales & legends. Special subjects: Fairies — *Critical studies*

Spence, Lewis. British fairy origins / by Lewis Spence. — Wellingborough : Aquarian, 1981, c1946. — ix,206p ; 22cm
Originally published: London : Watts, 1946. — Bibliography: p199-202. — Includes index
ISBN 0-85030-262-5 (pbk) : £3.95 : CIP rev. B81-20507

398′.45 — Fabulous beings — *For children*

McGowen, Tom. Hamlyn book of legendary creatures / by Tom McGowen ; illustrated by Victor G. Ambrus. — London : Hamlyn, c1982. — 62p : col.ill ; 29cm
ISBN 0-600-36681-2 : £3.99
Also classified at 398′.469 B82-19927

398′.45 — Ireland. Fairies

Logan, Patrick. The old gods : the facts about Irish fairies. — Belfast : Appletree Press, July 1981. — [160]p
ISBN 0-904651-82-7 (cased) : £6.95 : CIP entry
ISBN 0-904651-83-5 (pbk) : £3.95 B81-18069

398′.469 — Fabulous beasts — *For children*

McGowen, Tom. Hamlyn book of legendary creatures / by Tom McGowen ; illustrated by Victor G. Ambrus. — London : Hamlyn, c1982. — 62p : col.ill ; 29cm
ISBN 0-600-36681-2 : £3.99
Primary classification 398′.45 B82-19927

Mysteries / written by Christopher Fagg ... [et al.] ; illustrated by Michael Atkinson ... [et al.]. — London : Pan, 1981. — 128p : col.ill,col.maps,col.ports ; 22cm. — (A Piccolo explorer book)
Bibliography: p128. — Includes index. — Contents: Fabulous beasts — Sea mysteries — Lost cities — Missing treasure — Devils and demons — Ghosts
ISBN 0-330-26518-0 (pbk) : £1.95
Primary classification 001.9′4 B82-01584

398′.47 — Folklore. Special subjects: Ghosts

The **Folklore** of ghosts / edited by Hilda R. Ellis Davidson and W.M.S. Russell. — Cambridge : published for the Folklore Society by D.S. Brewer, c1981. — ix,271p ; 23cm. — (Mistletoe series ; v.15)
ISBN 0-85991-079-2 : £12.00 : CIP rev. B81-30472

398.8 — FOLKLORE. RHYMES, FOLK SONGS, GAMES

398′.8 — Bell rhymes in English. Shropshire bell rhymes — *Anthologies*

A **Nut** & a kernel : a collection of early Shropshire bell rhymes in the manner of 'Oranges & lemons'. — Shrewsbury (53 Belle Vue Gardens, Shrewsbury) : Ericius, 1981. — 8p : ill ; 27x12cm
Limited ed. of 150 copies
£1.50 (pbk) B82-09813

398′.8 — Children's playground rhymes in English — *Anthologies*

Inky, pinky, ponky. — London : Granada, Sept.1982. — [32]p
ISBN 0-246-11319-7 : £4.95 : CIP entry B82-18849

398′.8 — London. Street traders. Cries, *to 1884* — *Early works — Facsimiles*

Tuer, Andrew W.. Old London street cries : and the cries of to-day with heaps of quaint cuts, including hand-coloured frontispiece / by Andrew W. Tuer. — [Whitstable] : [Pryor], [c1982]. — 137p : ill(some col.),1facsim ; 14cm
Originally published: London : Field & Tuer, the Leadenhall Press, 1885. — Includes index
ISBN 0-946014-00-0 : Unpriced B82-27874

398′.8 — Nursery rhymes in English — *Anthologies*

Baa Baa Black Sheep : and other favourite nursery rhymes. — Bristol : Purnell, 1982. — [20]p : col.ill ; 21cm
ISBN 0-361-05355-x (pbk) : £0.50 B82-22336

B.B. Blacksheep and Company : a collection of favourite nusery rhymes / illustrated by Nick Butterworth. — London : Macdonald Educational, 1981. — 47p : col.ill ; 25cm
ISBN 0-356-07547-8 : Unpriced B82-00604

Bibbilibonty : more rhymes to read / [selected by June Melser]. — Leeds : E.J. Arnold, 1982, c1980. — 32p : col.ill ; 25cm. — (Story chest)
Illustrations by Robyn Belton. — Originally published: New Zealand : Shortland, 1980
ISBN 0-560-08649-0 (pbk) : Unpriced B82-31510

Favourite nursery rhymes. — London : Cathay, 1982. — 62p : col.ill ; 31cm
ISBN 0-86178-169-4 : £1.99 B82-22847

Happy times book of nursery rhymes / illustrated by Peter Adby. — London : Dean, c1981. — [20]p : col.ill ; 26cm
Ill on lining papers
ISBN 0-603-00289-7 : Unpriced B82-25973

Hillman, Priscilla. A merry-mouse book of nursery rhymes / Priscilla Hillman. — Tadworth : World's Work, 1982, c1981. — [32]p : col.ill ; 26cm. — (A World's Work children's book)
ISBN 0-437-45905-5 (pbk) : £1.95 B82-35441

Jack and Jill : and other favourite nursery rhymes. — Bristol : Purnell, 1982. — [20]p : col.ill ; 21cm
ISBN 0-361-05357-6 (pbk) : £0.50 B82-22338

Little Boy Blue : and other favourite nursery rhymes. — Bristol : Purnell, 1982. — [20]p : col.ill ; 21cm
ISBN 0-361-05356-8 (pbk) : £0.50 B82-22337

Little Miss Muffet : and other favourite nursery rhymes. — Bristol : Purnell, 1982. — [20]p : col.ill ; 21cm
ISBN 0-361-05354-1 (pbk) : £0.50 B82-22335

398′.8 — Nursery rhymes in English - *Anthologies*

My big book of nursery rhymes. — London : Ward Lock, Apr.1981. — [128]p
ISBN 0-7063-6129-6 : £3.95 : CIP entry B81-07484

398′.8 — Nursery rhymes in English — *Anthologies*

The **Nursery** rhyme book / illustrated by Ljiljana Rylands. — Cambridge : Dinosaur, c1980. — [24]p : col.ill ; 15x18cm. — (Dinosaur's Althea books)
ISBN 0-85122-226-9 (pbk) : £0.60 : CIP rev. B80-17640

Nursery rhymes / Walt Disney Productions ; illustrated by Hutchings Studio. — Bristol : Purnell, 1975 (1982 [printing]). — [28]p : col.ill ; 25cm. — (Disney colour library)
ISBN 0-361-03252-8 : Unpriced B82-25843

Nursery rhymes / [editor Janine Amos]. — Bristol : Purnell, 1982. — [26]p : col.ill ; 27cm. — (A First learning book) (My first big books)
ISBN 0-361-05381-9 : £1.99 B82-34768

Old fashioned nursery rhymes / compiled by Jennifer Mulherin ; designed by Tom Deas. — London : Granada, 1982. — 128p : ill ; 20cm. — (A Dragon book)
Includes index
ISBN 0-583-30473-7 (pbk) : £0.95 B82-28369

The **Parrot** in the garret : and other rhymes about dwellings / chosen by Lenore Blegvad ; illustrated by Erik Blegvad. — London : Julia MacRae, 1982. — [32]p : ill(some col.) ; 21cm
ISBN 0-86203-049-8 : £3.95 : CIP rev. B82-07683

To market, to market : rhymes to read / [selected by June Melser]. — Leeds : E.J. Arnold, 1982, c1980. — 16p : col.ill ; 25cm. — (Story chest)
Illustrations by Deirdre Gardiner. — Originally published: New Zealand : Shortland, 1980
ISBN 0-560-08648-2 (pbk) : Unpriced
ISBN 0-560-08719-5 (set) : Unpriced B82-31509

Tripp, Wallace. Rhymes without reason : from Mother Goose / compiled and illustrated by Wallace Tripp. — Tadworth : World's Work, 1978. — 94p : col.ill ; 29cm. — (A World's Work children's book)
ISBN 0-437-81219-7 : £3.50 B82-39243

398′.8 — Nursery rhymes in Welsh — *Anthologies*

Llyfr hwiangerddi y Dref Wen / [casgliwyd gan] John Gilbert Evans ; lluniau gan Jenny Williams. — Caerdydd : Gwasg y Dref Wen, c1981. — 128p : ill(some col.) ; 29cm
Includes index
£5.95 (pbk) B82-10640

398.8′0941 — Great Britain. Traditional games for children

Cooper, Rosaleen. Games from an Edwardian childhood. — Newton Abbot : David & Charles, Oct.1982. — [64]p
ISBN 0-7153-8317-5 : £3.95 : CIP entry B82-23011

398.9 — FOLKLORE. PROVERBS

398′.9′094 — Proverbs in European languages — *Anthologies*

Miroir de sagesse populaire européenne = Oglindă de înțelepciune populară europeană = Mirror of European popular wisdom : Românește latine, français, English, Italiano, espagñol, Português, Deutsch, norsk, Polski / sélectionnés et groupés par N.M. Goodchild, C. Michael-Titus. — London : Pamopticum, 1981. — 227p ; 21cm
ISBN 0-907256-01-5 (pbk) : Unpriced B82-09887

398′.9′21 — Proverbs in English — *Dictionaries*

The **Concise** Oxford dictionary of proverbs. — Oxford : Oxford University Press, Oct.1982. — [272]p
ISBN 0-19-866131-2 : £7.95 : CIP entry B82-23697

400 — LANGUAGE

400 — Language

Approaches to language. — Oxford : Pergamon, Jan.1983. — [166]p. — (Language & communication library ; v.4)
ISBN 0-08-028910-x : £10.50 : CIP entry B82-33611

Bolinger, Dwight. Aspects of language. — 3rd ed. / Dwight Bolinger, Donald A. Sears. — New York ; London : Harcourt Brace Jovanovich, 1981. — xvi,352p : ill ; 24cm
Previous ed.: 1975. — Includes bibliographies and index
ISBN 0-15-503872-9 (pbk) : £6.25 B82-31122

Burgess, Anthony. Language made plain / Anthony Burgess. — Rev. ed.. — [London] : Fontana, 1975 (1981 printing). — 206p : ill ; 18cm
Bibliography: p199. — Includes index
ISBN 0-00-633507-1 (pbk) : £1.75 B82-00403

Fisher, Roy. Talks for words / Roy Fisher. — Cardiff (20 Newfoundland Rd., Cardiff CF4 3LA) : Blackweir, 1980. — 29p ; 21cm
Unpriced (pbk) B82-28335

Human communication : language and its psychobiological bases / readings from Scientific American ; with introductions by William S-Y. Wang. — Oxford : Freeman, [1982]. — iv,186p : ill(some col.),facsims,maps (some col.),1plan ; 30cm
Bibliography: p181-183. — Includes index
ISBN 0-7167-1387-x (cased) : £13.30
ISBN 0-7167-1388-8 (pbk) : Unpriced B82-34391

400 — Language *continuation*

Language in use. — Milton Keynes : Open University Press. — (Educational studies : a second level course)
Block 4: Language and literature / prepared for the course team by Peter Griffith, with a contribution from John Coombes. — 1981. — 82p : ill,facsims ; 30cm. — (E263 ; block 4)
ISBN 0-335-13043-7 (pbk) : Unpriced
B82-04761

Language in use. — Milton Keynes : Open University Press. — (Educational studies : a second level course)
At head of title: The Open University
Block 5: Talk and text. — 1981. — 86p : ill ; 30cm
Includes bibliographies. — Contents: Introduction to Block 5 — Pt.1: The analysis of talk — Pt.2: Analysis of text and the reader
ISBN 0-335-13044-5 (pbk) : Unpriced
B82-04760

Language in use. — Milton Keynes : Open University Press. — (Educational studies : a second level course)
At head of title: The Open University
Resource guide / prepared by Joyce Barlow and John Greenwood for the course team. — 1981. — 32p : ill ; 30cm. — (E263)
ISBN 0-335-13046-1 (pbk) : Unpriced
B82-11345

400 — Language — *Feminist viewpoints*

Writing and sexual difference. — Brighton : Harvester Press, Dec.1982. — [320]p
ISBN 0-7108-0434-2 : £6.50 : CIP entry
B82-30079

400 — Language — *For schools*

Fitzgerald, Barry. Working with language / Barry Fitzgerald. — London : Heinemann Educational, 1982. — 58p : ill ; 24cm
Bibliography: p54-57
ISBN 0-435-10265-6 (pbk) : £1.50 B82-37617

400 — Man. Communication. Role of language — *Conference proceedings*

Perspective in communicative language teaching. — London : Academic Press, Jan.1983. — [250]p. — (Applied language studies series)
Conference papers
ISBN 0-12-387580-3 : CIP entry B82-33465

400 — Minority languages — *Conference proceedings*

International Conference on Minority Languages *(1st : 1980 : University of Glasgow)*. Minority languages today : a selection from the papers read at the First International Conference on Minority Languages held at Glasgow University from 8 to 13 September 1980 / edited by Einar Haugen, J. Derrick McClure, Derick Thomson. — Edinburgh : Edinburgh University Press, c1981. — xii,250p : ill,maps ; 24cm
Includes bibliographies and index
ISBN 0-85224-421-5 : £10.00 B82-12029

401 — Language — *Philosophical perspectives*

Bennett, Jonathan. Linguistic behaviour / Jonathan Bennett. — Cambridge : Cambridge University Press, 1976 (1979 [printing]). — ix,292p ; 22cm
Bibliography: p288-289. — Includes index
ISBN 0-521-29751-6 (pbk) : Unpriced
B82-01762

Pêcheux, Michel. Language, semantics and ideology : stating the obvious / Michel Pêcheux ; translated by Harbans Nagpal. — London : Macmillan, 1982. — xi,244p ; 23cm. — (Language, discourse, society series)
Translation of: Les Vérités de la Palice. — Bibliography: p221-230. — Includes index
ISBN 0-333-24564-4 : £20.00 B82-20953

Tugendhat, Ernst. Traditional and analytical philosophy. — Cambridge : Cambridge University Press, Aug.1982. — [440]p
Translation of: Vorlesungen zur Einführung in die sprachanalytische Philosophie
ISBN 0-521-22236-2 : £27.50 : CIP entry
B82-25493

401 — Language — *Philosophical perspectives — French texts*

Gagnepain, Jean. Du vouloir dire : traité d'épistémologie des sciences humaines. — Oxford : Pergamon. — (Language and communication library)
1: Du signe et de l'outil. — Feb.1982. — [256]p
ISBN 0-08-027079-4 : £7.30 : CIP entry
B82-11259

401 — Language. Privacy. Theories of Wittgenstein, Ludwig

Kripke, Saul A.. Wittgenstein on rules and private language. — Oxford : Blackwell, Mar.1982. — [128]p
ISBN 0-631-13077-2 : £7.95 : CIP entry
B82-03113

401 — Language. Theories

Harris, Roy, *1931-*. The language myth / Roy Harris. — London : Duckworth, 1981. — 212p ; 23cm
Bibliography: p205-208. — Includes index
ISBN 0-7156-1528-9 : £18.00 B82-00564

Spoken and written language : exploring orality and literacy / Deborah Tannen editor. — Norwood, N.J. : Ablex, c1982 ; London : Distributed by Eurospan. — xvii,267p : ill ; 24cm. — (Advances in discourse processes ; v.9)
Includes bibliographies and index
ISBN 0-89391-094-5 (cased) : Unpriced
ISBN 0-89391-099-6 (pbk) : Unpriced
B82-39725

401'.3 — International languages, *1600-1700*

Slaughter, M. M.. Universal languages and scientific taxonomy in the seventeenth century. — Cambridge : Cambridge University Press, Sept.1982. — [288]p
ISBN 0-521-24477-3 : £25.00 : CIP entry
B82-40893

401'.9 — Adults. Foreign language skills. Acquisition. Theories

Krashen, Stephen. Second language acquisition and second language learning / Stephen Krashen. — Oxford : Pergamon, 1981. — vii,151p : ill ; 21cm. — (Language teaching methodology series) (Pergamon Institute of English (Oxford))
Bibliography: p139-151
ISBN 0-08-025338-5 (pbk) : £4.95 B82-01796

401'.9 — Children. Language skills. Acquisition

Bryen, Diane Nelson. Inquiries into child language / Diane Nelson Bryen. — Boston, Mass. ; London : Allyn and Bacon, [1982?]. — x,436p : ill ; 25cm
Bibliography: p411-426. — Includes index
ISBN 0-205-07642-4 : Unpriced B82-27309

The **Child's** construction of language / edited by Werner Deutsch. — London : Academic Press, 1981. — x,393p : ill ; 24cm. — (Behavioural development)
Includes bibliographies and index
ISBN 0-12-213580-6 : £12.50 : CIP rev.
B81-34117

The **Logical** problem of language acquisition / edited by C.L. Baker and John J. McCarthy. — Cambridge, Mass. ; London : MIT, c1981. — xii,358p : ill ; 24cm. — (MIT Press series on cognitive theory and mental representation)
Bibliography: p330-344. — Includes index
ISBN 0-262-02159-5 : £19.25 B82-21016

401'.9 — Children. Language skills. Acquisition — *Conference proceedings*

Language behavior in infancy and early childhood : proceedings of a pediatric round table held at the Santa Barbara Biltmore Hotel, Santa Barbara, California, October 10-13, 1979 / editor Rachel E. Stark ; sponsored by Johnson & Johnson Baby Products Company. — New York ; Oxford : Elsevier/North-Holland, c1981. — xix,479p : ill ; 24cm
Includes bibliographies and index
ISBN 0-444-00627-3 : Unpriced B82-06112

401'.9 — Children. Language skills. Acquisition — *For teaching*

Fisher, Carol J.. Children's language and the language arts / Carol J. Fisher, C. Ann Terry. — 2nd ed. — New York ; London : McGraw-Hill, c1982. — xv,361p : ill,1map,facsims,plans ; 25cm
Previous ed.: 1977. — Includes index
ISBN 0-07-021108-6 : £14-50 B82-27573

401'.9 — Children. Language skills. Acquisition *related to* **cognitive development**

Children thinking through language / edited by Michael Beveridge. — London : Edward Arnold, 1982. — x,272p : ill ; 22cm
Includes bibliographies and index
ISBN 0-7131-6352-6 (pbk) : £7.95 : CIP rev.
Also classified at 155.4'13 B81-37563

401'.9 — Children. Language skills. Acquisition. Theories

Atkinson, Martin. Explanations in the study of child language development / Martin Atkinson. — Cambridge : Cambridge University Press, 1982. — viii,289p ; 24cm. — (Cambridge studies in linguistics, ISSN 0068-676x ; 35)
Bibliography: p265-280. — Includes index
ISBN 0-521-24302-5 (cased) : £22.50 : CIP rev.
ISBN 0-521-28593-3 (pbk) : £7.50 B82-02450

401'.9 — Children. Language skills. Development

Hastings, Phyllis. Encouraging language development. — London : Croom Helm, June 1981. — [96]p. — (Croom Helm special education series)
ISBN 0-7099-0286-7 (cased) : £8.95 : CIP entry
ISBN 0-7099-0287-5 (pbk) : £4.50 B81-12877

Lock, Andrew. The guided reinvention of language / Andrew Lock. — London : Academic Press, 1980. — xiv,205p : ill ; 24cm
Bibliography: p197-201. — Includes index
ISBN 0-12-453950-5 : £12.60 : CIP rev.
B79-36277

401'.9 — Children. Language skills. Development — *Conference proceedings*

Language and learning in home and school / edited by Alan Davies. — London : Heinemann Educational, 1982. — xi,179p : ill ; 22cm
Conference papers. — Bibliography: p164-175. — Includes index
ISBN 0-435-10192-7 (pbk) : £6.50 : CIP rev.
B81-34502

401'.9 — Children. Language skills. Development — *Manuals — For teaching*

Moyle, Donald. Children's words : a practical guide to helping children overcome difficulties in learning to read, write, speak and spell. — London : Grant McIntyre, Feb.1982. — [192]p
ISBN 0-86216-032-4 (cased) : £10.95 : CIP entry
ISBN 0-86216-033-2 (pbk) : £3.95 B81-40239

401'.9 — Children. Language skills. Tests: Sentence Comprehension Test — *Manuals*

Wheldall, Kevin. Picture booklet for Sentence comprehension test / Kevin Wheldall, Peter Mittler and Angela Hobsbaum. — [Windsor] : NFER, [1979]. — A-F,60p : all ill + score sheet
Cover title
ISBN 0-7005-0244-0 (pbk) : Unpriced
B82-35924

401'.9 — Children. Verbal deficit. Theories

Gordon, J. C. B.. Verbal deficit : a critique / J.C.B. Gordon. — London : Croom Helm, c1981. — 181p ; 23cm
Bibliography: p155-181. — Includes index
ISBN 0-85664-990-2 : £11.95 : CIP rev.
B81-13744

401'.9 — Foreign language skills. Acquisition. Psychological aspects

La Forge, Paul G.. Counselling and culture in second language acquisition. — Oxford : Pergamon, Feb.1983. — [128]p
ISBN 0-08-029477-4 (pbk) : £5.95 : CIP entry
B82-40887

401′.9 — Foreign language skills. Acquisition. Sociolinguistic aspects

Loveday, Leo. The sociolinguistics of learning and using a non-native language / Leo Loveday. — Oxford : Pergamon, 1982. — 196p : ill ; 21cm. — (Language teaching methodology series)
Bibliography: p179-196
ISBN 0-08-028668-2 (pbk) : £5.95 : CIP rev. B82-10600

401′.9 — Foreign language skills. Learning by man

Krashen, Stephen. Principles and practice in second language acquisition / Stephen D. Krashen. — Oxford : Pergamon, 1982. — ix,202p : ill ; 21cm. — (Language teaching methodology series)
Bibliography: p191-200. — Includes index
ISBN 0-08-028628-3 (pbk) : £6.25 : CIP rev. B82-10597

401′.9 — Language disordered children. Language skills. Remedial teaching

Gillham, Bill. Two words together. — London : Allen and Unwin, Jan.1983. — [64]p
ISBN 0-04-371091-3 (cased) : £10.00 : CIP entry
ISBN 0-04-371092-1 (pbk) : £4.95 B82-33594

401′.9 — Language. Psychological aspects

Steinberg, Danny D.. Psycholinguistics : language, mind and world / Danny D. Steinberg. — London : Longman, 1982. — 240p : ill ; 22cm. — (Longman linguistics library ; 28)
Bibliography: p216-231. — Includes index
ISBN 0-582-29112-7 (cased) : Unpriced : CIP rev.
ISBN 0-582-29113-5 (pbk) : £5.75 B82-01579

401′.9 — Language. Psychological aspects — *Conference proceedings*

The **Psychological** mechanisms of language : a joint symposium of the Royal Society and the British Academy / organised by H.C. Longuet-Higgins, J. Lyons and D.E. Broadbent, held on 11 and 12 March, 1981. — London : The society, 1981. — viii,209p : ill ; 31cm
'First published in Philosophical transactions of the Royal Society of London, series B, vol.295 (no.1077)'. — Pages also numbered 213-423. — Includes bibliographies
ISBN 0-85403-172-3 : £23.50 B82-06578

401′.9 — Language. Psychosocial aspects

Advances in the social psychology of language / edited by Colin Fraser and Klaus R. Scherer. — Cambridge : Cambridge University Press, 1982. — viii,264p : ill ; 24cm. — (European studies in social psychology)
Includes bibliographies and index
ISBN 0-521-23192-2 (cased) : £20.00 : CIP rev. B82-12700

401.9 — Language — *Sociological perspectives*

Attitudes towards language variation. — London : Edward Arnold, Sept.1982. — [256]p. — (Social psychology of language series)
ISBN 0-7131-6195-7 (pbk) : £7.95 : CIP entry B82-20038

401′.9 — Language. Variation. Sociolinguistic aspects

Sociolinguistic variation in speech communities. — London : Edward Arnold, Apr.1982. — [224]p
ISBN 0-7131-6355-0 (pbk) : £6.50 : CIP entry B82-04489

401′.9 — Man. Communication. Role of language. Psycholinguistic aspects

Strategies in interlanguage communication. — London : Longman, Nov.1982. — [240]p. — (Applied linguistic and language study)
ISBN 0-582-55373-3 (pbk) : £3.80 : CIP entry B82-26540

401′.9 — Man. Communication. Role of speech. Psycholinguistic aspects

Kreckel, M.. Communicative acts and shared knowledge in natural discourse / by M. Kreckel. — London : Academic Press, 1981. — xiv,316p : ill ; 24cm
Bibliography: p271-286. — Includes index
ISBN 0-12-426180-9 : £16.40 : CIP rev. B81-18128

401′.9 — Man. Speech — *Cognitive perspectives* — *Conference proceedings*

The **Cognitive** representation of speech / edited by Terry Myers, John Laver, John Anderson. — Amsterdam ; Oxford : North-Holland, c1981. — xxiii,551p : ill ; 23cm. — (Advances in psychology ; 7)
Conference papers. — Bibliography: p463-551
ISBN 0-444-86162-9 : £31.91 B82-13431

401′.9 — Mentally handicapped children. Language skills. Development — *For parents*

Sheehan, Patricia. Developmental speech problems and a guide for parents / by Patricia Sheehan. — Dublin (5 Fitzwilliam Place, Dublin 2) : National Association for the Mentally Handicapped of Ireland, [1981?]. — 9p ; 21cm
Unpriced (pbk) B82-12862

401′.9 — Mentally handicapped persons. Language skills — *Conference proceedings*

Language and the mentally handicapped, 4 : proceedings of the Conference held at Lea Castle Hospital, Wolverley, nr. Kidderminster, on Tuesday, 23rd November, 1976 / British Institute of Mental Handicap. — Kidderminster : The institute, 1979. — 42p : ill ; 21cm
Includes bibliographies
ISBN 0-906054-06-0 (pbk) : £1.25 B82-20671

401′.9 — Poor children. Language skills — *Conference proceedings*

The **Language** of children reared in poverty : implications for evaluation and intervention / edited by Lynne Feagans, Dale Clark Farran. — New York ; London : Academic Press, 1982. — xvi,286p : ill ; 24cm. — (Educational psychology)
Based on a conference held at the Frank Porter Graham Child Development Center, Chapel Hill, N.C., May 1980. — Includes bibliographies and index
ISBN 0-12-249980-8 : £16.20 B82-30110

401′.9 — Pre-school children. Language skills. Acquisition

Oksaar, Els. Language acquisition in the early years. — London : Batsford, Sept.1982. — [240]p
Translation of: Spracherwerb im Vorschulalter
ISBN 0-7134-3694-8 (pbk) : £7.50 : CIP entry B82-20045

401′.9 — Psycholinguistics

Aitchison, Jean. The articulate mammal : an introduction to psycholinguistics. — 2nd ed. — London : Hutchinson Education, Feb.1983. — [288]p
Previous ed.: 1976
ISBN 0-09-150921-1 (pbk) : £4.95 : CIP entry B82-36561

Loar, Brian. Mind and meaning / Brian Loar. — Cambridge : Cambridge University Press, 1981. — xi,268p ; 22cm. — (Cambridge studies in philosophy)
Bibliography: p261-263. — Includes index
ISBN 0-521-22959-6 : £22.00 : CIP rev.
Primary classification 401′.9 B81-37004

Speech, place, and action : studies in deixis and related topics / edited by Robert J. Jarvella and Wolfgang Klein. — Chichester : Wiley, c1982. — xii,389p : ill ; 24cm
Includes bibliographies and index
ISBN 0-471-10045-5 : £22.75 : CIP rev. B81-34475

401′.9 — Psycholinguistics — *Conference proceedings*

Mutual knowledge / edited by N.V. Smith. — London : Academic Press, c1982. — xix,272p ; 24cm
Conference papers. — Bibliography: p258-264. — Includes index
ISBN 0-12-652980-9 : £16.80 : CIP rev. B81-35909

401′.9 — Psycholinguistics — *Philosophical perspectives*

Loar, Brian. Mind and meaning / Brian Loar. — Cambridge : Cambridge University Press, 1981. — xi,268p ; 22cm. — (Cambridge studies in philosophy)
Bibliography: p261-263. — Includes index
ISBN 0-521-22959-6 : £22.00 : CIP rev.
Also classified at 401′.9 B81-37004

401′.9 — Scotland. School leavers. Language skills — *Case studies*

Gordon, Patricia. Language and the school leaver : a case study / by Patricia Gordon. — [Edinburgh] : Scottish Council for Research in Education, c1981. — 53leaves : forms ; 30cm
ISBN 0-901116-30-0 (pbk) : Unpriced B82-11855

401′.9 — Sociolinguistics

Gumperz, John J.. Discourse strategies. — Cambridge : Cambridge University Press, Sept.1982. — [228]p. — (Studies in interactional sociolinguistics)
ISBN 0-521-24691-1 (cased) : £17.50 : CIP entry
ISBN 0-521-28896-7 (pbk £5.95) B82-29358

Romaine, Suzanne. Socio-historical linguistics : its status and methodology / Suzanne Romaine. — Cambridge : Cambridge University Press, 1982. — xi,315p : ill ; 24cm. — (Cambridge studies in linguistics, ISSN 0068-6767x ; 34)
Bibliography: p290-309. — Includes index
ISBN 0-521-23750-5 : £22.00 : CIP rev. B82-07958

404′.2 — Bilingualism

Baetens Beardsmore, Hugo. Bilingualism. — Clevedon (Bank House, 8a Hill Road, Clevedon BS21 7HJ) : Tieto, Mar.1982. — [180]p
ISBN 0-905028-05-8 : £9.50 : CIP entry
ISBN 0-905028-04-x (pbk) : £4.45 B82-05776

404′.2 — Children. Bilingualism. Development

Saunders, George. Bilingual children. — Clevedon (Bank House, 8a Hill Rd., Clevedon BS21 7HH) : Multilingual Matters, Nov.1982. — [264]p. — (Multilingual matters ; 3)
ISBN 0-905028-12-0 (cased) : £13.50 : CIP entry
ISBN 0-905028-11-2 (pbk) : £5.40 B82-30322

407 — Languages. Teaching

Johnson, Keith, *1944-*. Communicative syllabus design and methodology / Keith Johnson. — Oxford : Pergamon, 1982. — x,222p : ill,forms,2maps ; 21cm. — (Language teaching methodology series)
Bibliography: p215-222
ISBN 0-08-025355-5 (pbk) : £5.95 : CIP rev. B81-28799

Surveys I : eight state-of-the-art articles on key areas in language teaching. — Cambridge : Cambridge University Press, Sept.1982. — [162]p. — (Cambridge language teaching surveys)
ISBN 0-521-24886-8 (cased) : £9.95 : CIP entry
ISBN 0-521-27046-4 (pbk) : £4.50 B82-40315

407 — Names. Learning by children

Macnamara, John, *1929-*. Names for things : a study of human learning / John Macnamara. — Cambridge, Mass. ; London : MIT, c1982. — xii,275p ; 24cm. — (A Bradford book)
Bibliography: p255-264. — Includes index
ISBN 0-262-13169-2 : £12.25 B82-37515

407′.1041 — Great Britain. Schools. Curriculum subjects: Native languages. Teaching — *National Union of Teachers viewpoints*

National Union of Teachers. Linguistic diversity and mother tongue teaching. — [London] : NUT, [1982?]. — 8p : ill ; 15x21cm. — (A National Union of Teachers policy statement)
Author: National Union of Teachers
£0.30 (pbk) B82-24876

407′.8 — England. Secondary schools. Curriculum subjects: Languages. Teaching. Use of Audio-visual aids. Research projects. Schools Council. Communication and Social Skills Project

Lorac, Carol. Communication and social skills. — Exeter : Wheaton, Apr.1981. — [206]p
ISBN 0-08-026427-1 (cased) : £8.00 : CIP entry
ISBN 0-08-026426-3 (pbk) : £4.75 B81-11946

407′.8 — Man. Language skills. Teaching aids: Games — *Manuals*

Rixon, Shelagh. How to use games in language teaching / by Shelagh Rixon. — London : Macmillan, 1981. — vi,137p : ill ; 19cm. — (Essential language teaching series)
Bibliography: p129-130. — Includes index
ISBN 0-333-27547-0 (pbk) : Unpriced B82-09824

407′.8 — Schools. Curriculum subjects: Languages. Teaching. Use of audio-visual aids: Video equipment

Video in the language classroom. — London : Allen & Unwin, Aug.1981. — [208]p. — (Practical language teaching ; no.7)
ISBN 0-04-371079-4 (pbk) : £3.50 : CIP entry B81-15880

409′.2′4 — Language. Theories of Hamann, Johann Georg

German, Terence J.. Hamann on language and religion / Terence J. German. — Oxford : Oxford University Press, 1981. — viii,187p ; 23cm. — (Oxford theological monographs)
Bibliography: p176-184. — Includes index
ISBN 0-19-826717-7 : £12.50 : CIP rev.
Also classified at 200′.92′4 B81-26752

409′.39′4 — Ancient Middle East. Languages — *Festschriften*

Societies and languages of the ancient Near East. — Warminster : Aris and Phillips, Feb.1982. — [368]p
ISBN 0-85668-205-5 (pbk) : £15.00 : CIP entry B81-35723

409′.78 — United States. Great Plains. Languages

Languages in conflict : linguistic acculturation on the Great Plains / edited by Paul Schach. — Lincoln ; London : Published by the University of Nebraska Press for the Center for Great Plains Studies University of Nebraska-Lincoln, c1980. — xi,186p : maps ; 24cm
Includes chapters translated from German and Swedish
ISBN 0-8032-2106-1 : Unpriced B82-02185

410 — LINGUISTICS

410 — Contrastive linguistics

Contrastive linguistics and the language teacher / edited by Jacek Fisiak. — Oxford : Pergamon, 1981. — x,284p : ill ; 21cm. — (Language teaching methodology series) (Pergamon Institute of English (Oxford))
Includes bibliographies and index
ISBN 0-08-027230-4 (pbk) : £4.95 : CIP rev. B81-16400

410 — Indo-European languages

Bodmer, Frederick. The loom of language : a guide to foreign languages for the home student / by Frederick Bodmer ; edited and arranged by Lancelot Hogben. — London : Merlin, 1981, c1944. — 669p : ill ; 23cm
Originally published: London : Allen & Unwin, 1943. — Includes index
ISBN 0-85036-275-x : £10.00 B82-05675

410 — Language. Change

Aitchison, Jean. Language change : progress or decay? / Jean Aitchison. — [London] : Fontana, 1981. — 266p : ill ; 20cm. — (Fontana linguistics)
Bibliography: p249-257. — Includes index
ISBN 0-00-635983-3 (pbk) : £2.95 B82-04202

410 — Linguistics

Aarsleff, Hans. From Locke to Saussure : essays on the study of language and intellectual history / Hans Aarsleff. — London : Athlone, 1982. — viii,422p ; 24cm
Includes bibliographies and index
ISBN 0-485-30001-x : £18.00 : CIP rev. B81-18038

Atkinson, Martin. Foundations of general linguistics. — London : Allen & Unwin, May 1982. — [384]p
ISBN 0-04-410003-5 (cased) : £15.00 : CIP entry
ISBN 0-04-410004-3 (pbk) : £6.95 B82-07231

Crystal, David. Linguistics / David Crystal. — Repr. with revisions. — Harmondsworth : Penguin, 1977 (1981 [printing]). — 267p : ill ; 20cm. — (Pelican books)
Bibliography: p260. — Includes index
ISBN 0-14-021332-5 (pbk) : £1.95 B82-10511

Matthews, P. H.. Do languages obey general laws? : an inaugural lecture delivered before the University of Cambridge on 17 November 1981 / P.H. Matthews. — Cambridge : Cambridge University Press, 1982. — 30p ; 19cm
Cover title
ISBN 0-521-28963-7 (pbk) : £1.95 B82-18180

SAUSSURE : course in general linguistics. — London : Duckworth, Jan.1983. — [272]p
Translation from the French
ISBN 0-7156-1670-6 (pbk) : £8.95 : CIP entry B82-32617

410 — Linguistics. Explanation

Explanation in linguistics : the logical problem of language acquisition / edited by Norbert Hornstein and David Lightfoot. — London : Longman, 1981. — 288p : ill ; 22cm. — (Longman linguistics library ; 25)
Bibliography: p272-283. — Includes index
ISBN 0-582-29114-3 (cased) : £12.00
ISBN 0-582-29115-1 (pbk) : £5.95 B82-03217

410 — Linguistics — *Festschriften*

Language, meaning and style : essays in memory of Steven Ullmann / editorial committee T.E. Hope ... [et al.]. — Leeds : Leeds University Press, c1981. — 173p : ill,1port ; 22cm
ISBN 0-9507898-0-1 : Unpriced : CIP rev. B82-01353

Linguistic controversies : essays in linguistic theory and practice in honour of F.R. Palmer / edited by David Crystal. — London : Edward Arnold, 1982. — xiv, : ill ; 24cm
Includes index
ISBN 0-7131-6349-6 : £18.50 : CIP rev. B82-04488

410 — Systemic linguistics

Readings in systemic linguistics / edited by M.A.K. Halliday and J.R. Martin ; with an introduction by M.A.K. Halliday and linking material by J.R. Martin. — London : Batsford, 1981. — 361p : ill ; 23cm
Bibliography: p347-354. — Includes index
ISBN 0-7134-3677-8 (cased) : £17.50
ISBN 0-7134-3678-6 (pbk) : Unpriced B82-01687

410′.1 — Linguistics. Functionalism. Theories of Bühler, Karl

Innis, Robert E.. Karl Bühler : semiotic foundations of language theory / Robert E. Innis. — New York ; London : Plenum, c1982. — viii,168p : ill ; 24cm. — (Topics in contemporary semiotics)
Includes index
ISBN 0-306-40791-4 : Unpriced B82-16963

410′.1 — Linguistics. Structuralism. Theories

Lepschy, Giulio C.. A survey of structural linguistics / Giulio C. Lepschy. — [New] ed. — London : Deutsch, 1982. — 206p : ill ; 22cm. — (The Language library)
Previous ed.: London : Faber and Faber, 1970. — Bibliography: p180-194. — Includes index
ISBN 0-233-97415-6 (pbk) : £4.95 B82-17731

410′.1 — Linguistics. Theories

Katz, Jerrold J.. Language and other abstract objects / Jerrold J. Katz. — Oxford : Basil Blackwell, 1981. — viii,251p : ill ; 24cm
Bibliography: p241-246. — Includes index
ISBN 0-631-12946-4 (cased) : Unpriced : CIP rev.
ISBN 0-631-12954-5 (pbk) : Unpriced B81-30171

410′.5 — Linguistics — *Serials*

Strathclyde modern language studies : occasional papers presented in the Department of Modern Languages of the University of Strathclyde. — Vol.1-. — Glasgow (Livingstone Tower, 26 Richmond St., Glasgow G1 1XH) : Department of Modern Languages, University of Strathclyde, 1981-. — v. ; 21cm
Irregular
ISSN 0261-099x = Strathclyde modern language studies : £1.00 per issue
Primary classification 809 B82-04890

410′.92′4 — Linguistics. Theories of Montague, Richard, *1930-1971*

Montague, Richard, *1930-1971*. Formal philosophy : selected papers of Richard Montague / edited and with an introduction by Richmond H. Thomason. — New Haven ; London : Yale University Press, c1974 (1979 printing). — 369p ; 22cm
Bibliography: p360-364. — Includes index
ISBN 0-300-02412-6 (pbk) : £5.55 B82-08641

410′.942 — England. Linguistics, *1780-1860*

Aarsleff, Hans. The study of language in England, 1780-1860. — London : Athlone Press, Sept.1982. — [288]p
Originally published: Princeton : Princeton University Press, 1967
ISBN 0-485-30007-9 (pbk) : £6.95 : CIP entry B82-19536

412 — Semantics

Lyons, John. Language, meaning and context / John Lyons. — [London] : Fontana, 1981. — 256p ; 20cm. — (Fontana linguistics)
Bibliography: p243-248. — Includes index
ISBN 0-00-635923-x (pbk) : £2.95 B82-04200

McCawley, James D.. Thirty million theories of grammar / James D. McCawley. — London : Croom Helm, c1982. — 223p : ill ; 23cm. — (Croom Helm linguistic series)
Bibliography: p204-217. — Includes index
ISBN 0-7099-1730-9 : £12.95 : CIP rev. B82-01212

Processes, beliefs, and questions : essays on formal semantics of natural language and natural language processing / edited by Stanley Peters and Esa Saarinen. — Dordrecht ; London : Reidel, c1982. — xxxi,231p : ill ; 23cm. — (Synthese language library ; v.16)
Includes bibliographies and index
ISBN 90-277-1314-6 : Unpriced B82-11234

412 — Semantics — *Conference proceedings*

Semantic anthropology. — London : Academic Press, Dec.1982. — [270]p. — (Association of Social Anthropologists monographs ; 22)
Conference papers
ISBN 0-12-545180-6 : CIP entry B82-32284

413 — Foreign language dictionaries, *to 1980*

Collison, Robert. A history of foreign-language dictionaries / Robert L. Collison. — London : Deutsch, 1982. — 214p,[32]p of plates : ill,facsims ; 22cm. — (The Language library)
Bibliography: p191-196. — Includes index
ISBN 0-233-97310-9 (pbk) : £12.95 B82-25772

413 — Languages — *Polyglot dictionaries*

Ray, John, *1627-1705*. Dictionariolum trilingue : editio prima 1675 / John Ray : facsimile with an introduction by William T. Stearn. — London : Ray Society, 1981. — 23,91p ; 22cm
Facsim of: 1st ed.: London : Thomae Burrel, 1675. — Bibliography: p20. — Includes index
ISBN 0-903874-16-4 : Unpriced B82-05542

413′.028′54 — Lexicography. Implications of digital computer systems — *Conference proceedings*

Lexicography in the electronic age : proceedings of a symposium held in Luxembourg, 7-9 July, 1981 / edited by J. Goetschalckx and L. Rolling. — Amsterdam ; Oxford : North-Holland, 1982. — vii,276p : ill ; 23cm
ISBN 0-444-86404-0 : £18.99 B82-39842

414 — Generative phonology

Dell, François. Generative phonology / François Dell ; translated by Catherine Cullen. — Cambridge : Cambridge University Press, 1980. — xiv,164p : ill ; 23cm
Translation of: Pt.1 of Les règles et les sons. — Bibliography: p153-161. — Includes index
ISBN 0-521-29519-x (pbk) : £3.95 B82-37897

Goldsmith, John A.. Autosegmental phonology / John A. Goldsmith. — New York ; London : Garland, 1979. — 170p : ill ; 24cm. — (Outstanding dissertations in linguistics)
Bibliography: p167-170
ISBN 0-8240-9673-8 : Unpriced B82-31071

Kenstowicz, Michael. Generative phonology : description and theory / Michael Kenstowicz, Charles Kisseberth. — New York ; London : Academic Press, c1979. — xiv,459p : ill ; 24cm
Bibliography: p441-448. — Includes index
ISBN 0-12-405160-x : £22.80 B82-07733

414 — Phonetics

Abercrombie, David. Elements of general phonetics. — Edinburgh : Edinburgh University Press, Oct.1982. — [212]p
Originally published: 1967
ISBN 0-85224-451-7 (pbk) : £5.00 : CIP entry B82-29028

Catford, John Cunnison. Fundamental problems in phonetics. — Edinburgh : Edinburgh University Press, Jan.1982. — [278]p
Originally published: 1977
ISBN 0-85224-437-1 (pbk) : £12.00 : CIP entry B81-39215

O'Connor, J. D.. Phonetics / J.D. O'Connor. — Harmondsworth : Penguin, 1973 (1982 [printing]). — 320p,[8]p of plates : ill ; 20cm. — (A Pelican book)
Bibliography: p307-314. — Includes index
ISBN 0-14-021560-3 (pbk) : £2.95 B82-20319

414'.02461 — Phonetics — *For speech disorder therapy*

Shriberg, Lawrence D.. Clinical phonetics / Lawrence D. Shriberg, Raymond D. Kent. — New York ; Chichester : Wiley, c1982. — xxvii,481p : ill,forms ; 28cm. — (Wiley series on communication disorders)
Includes bibliographies and index
ISBN 0-471-08654-1 (spiral) : £14.75 B82-26463

414'.09 — Phonetics, *to 1980* — *Festschriften*

Asher, R. E.. Towards a history of phonetics. — Edinburgh : Edinburgh University Press, Oct.1982. — [336]p
Originally published: 1981
ISBN 0-85224-450-9 (pbk) : £9.75 : CIP entry B82-29027

415 — Functional grammar

Predication and expression in functional grammar / A. Machtelt Bolkestein ... [et al.]. — London : Academic Press, 1981. — xiv,266p ; 24cm
Includes bibliographies and index
ISBN 0-12-111350-7 : £19.20 : CIP rev. B81-31333

415 — Grammar

Givón, Talmy. On understanding grammar / Talmy Givón. — New York ; London : Academic Press, 1979. — xiv,379p ; 24cm. — (Perspectives in neurolinguistics and psycholinguistics)
Bibliography: p353-365. — Includes index
ISBN 0-12-285450-0 : £17.20 B82-11651

Palmer, F. R.. Grammar / Frank Palmer. — Harmondsworth : Penguin, 1971 (1982 [printing]). — 200p : ill ; 20cm
Originally published: 1971. — Includes index
ISBN 0-14-021333-3 (pbk) : £1.95 B82-20318

415 — Grammar — *Comparative studies*

Steele, Susan. An encyclopedia of AUX : a study in cross-linguistic equivalence / Susan Steele with Adrian Akmajian ... [et al.]. — Cambridge, Mass. ; London : MIT Press, c1981. — 328p : ill ; 24cm. — (Linguistic inquiry monographs ; 5)
Bibliography: p304-312. — Includes index
ISBN 0-262-19197-0 (cased) : £21.00
ISBN 0-262-69074-8 (pbk) : Unpriced B82-13766

415 — Language. Discourse. Analysis

Stubbs, Michael. Discourse analysis : the sociolinguistic analysis of natural language. — Oxford : Basil Blackwell, Sept.1982. — [288]p. — (Language in society)
ISBN 0-631-10381-3 (cased) : £16.00 : CIP entry
ISBN 0-631-12763-1 (pbk) : £7.50 B82-20294

415 — Language. Morphology

Comrie, Bernard. Language universals and linguistic typology : syntax and morphology / Bernard Comrie. — Oxford : Blackwell, 1981. — xi,252p : 1map ; 23cm
Bibliography: p226-234. — Includes index
ISBN 0-631-12971-5 (cased) : £14.00 : CIP rev.
ISBN 0-631-12618-x (pbk) : £6.50 B81-22616

415 — Language. Quantifiers. Semantic aspects

Cushing, Steven. Quantifier meanings : a study in the dimensions of semantic competence / Steven Cushing. — Amsterdam ; Oxford : North-Holland, 1982. — xviii,388p ; 23cm. — (North-Holland linguistic series ; 48)
Bibliography: p347-360. — Includes index
ISBN 0-444-86445-8 : Unpriced B82-39970

415 — Languages. Typology

Mallinson, Graham. Language typology : cross-linguistic studies in syntax / Graham Mallinson, Barry J. Blake. — Amsterdam ; Oxford : North-Holland, c1981. — xvii,486p : ill ; 23cm. — (North-Holland linguistic studies in syntax ; 46)
Bibliography: p449-470. — Includes index
ISBN 0-444-86311-7 : £27.17 B82-07887

415 — Linguistics. Island phenomena

Grosu, Alexander. Approaches to island phenomena / Alexander Grosu. — Amsterdam ; Oxford : North-Holland, c1981. — xii,345p ; 23cm. — (North-Holland linguistics series ; 45)
Bibliography: p319-333. — Includes index
ISBN 0-444-86278-1 : £23.86 B82-06721

415 — Spoken language. Discourse. Analysis

Edmondson, Willis. Spoken discourse : a model for analysis / Willis Edmondson. — London : Longman, 1981. — 217p : ill ; 23cm. — (Longman linguistics library ; no.27)
Bibliography: p206-214. — Includes index
ISBN 0-582-29120-8 (cased) : Unpriced : CIP rev.
ISBN 0-582-29121-6 (pbk) : £5.50 B81-13793

415 — Syntax

Harris, Zellig S.. Papers on syntax / Zellig S. Harris ; edited by Henry Hiz. — Dordrecht ; London : Reidel, c1981. — vi,479p : ill ; 23cm. — (Synthese language library ; v.14)
Includes index
ISBN 90-277-1266-2 (cased) : Unpriced
ISBN 90-277-1267-0 (pbk) : Unpriced B82-06114

The **nature** of syntactic representation / edited by Pauline Jacobson and Geoffrey K. Pullum. — Dordrecht ; London : Reidel, c1982. — xix,479p : ill ; 23cm. — (Synthese language library)
Includes bibliographies and index
ISBN 90-277-1289-1 (cased) : Unpriced
ISBN 90-277-1290-5 (pbk) : Unpriced B82-34778

415 — Syntax. Transformational-generative theories

Binding and filtering / edited by Frank Heny. — London : Croom Helm, c1981. — 337p ; 23cm. — (Croom Helm linguistics series)
Includes bibliographies and index
ISBN 0-7099-0386-3 : £16.95 : CIP rev. B81-06881

Brown, E. K. (Edward Keith). Syntax : generative grammar / E.K. Brown and J.E. Miller. — London : Hutchinson, 1982. — 240p : ill ; 23cm
Bibliography: p236-238. — Includes index
ISBN 0-09-144110-2 (cased) : £15.00 : CIP rev.
ISBN 0-09-144111-0 (pbk) : £7.95 B81-22573

Radford, Andrew. Transformational syntax : a student's guide to Chomsky's extended standard theory / Andrew Radford. — Cambridge : Cambridge University Press, 1981. — ix,402p : ill ; 24cm. — (Cambridge textbooks in linguistics)
Bibliography: p397-399. — Includes index
ISBN 0-521-24274-6 (cased) : £22.50 : CIP rev.
ISBN 0-521-28574-7 (pbk) : £7.50 B81-38810

417'.2 — Dialectology

North, David. The importance of local systems in dialectology / David North. — Leeds (The School of English, The University, Leeds) : Leeds Folklore Group, 1982. — 5leaves ; 30cm. — (Leeds Folklore Group papers in folklife studies ; 2)
£0.15 1/2 (unbound) B82-30887

418 — Applied linguistics

Gray, Douglas. A marriage of mercury and philology. — Oxford : Clarendon Press, July 1982. — [18]p
ISBN 0-19-951535-2 (pbk) : £1.95 : CIP entry B82-17966

418 — Language. Standardisation

Standard languages : spoken and written / edited by W. Haas. — Manchester : Manchester University Press, c1982. — viii,192p ; 23cm. — (Mont Follick series ; v.5)
Includes bibliographies
ISBN 0-7190-0774-7 : £17.50 : CIP rev. B81-28090

418 — Language. Variety — *Serials*

CECTAL conference papers series / the Centre for English Cultural Tradition and Language, University of Sheffield. — No.1-. — [Sheffield] ([Sheffield S10 2TN]) : [The Centre], 1981-. — v. ; 21cm
Annual
ISSN 0261-314x = CECTAL conference papers series : Unpriced B82-11140

418'.0023 — Modern languages — *Career guides*

Steadman, Helen. Careers using languages / Helen Steadman. — London : Kogan Page, 1982. — 123p ; 19cm
Bibliography: p114-116
ISBN 0-85038-559-8 (cased) : Unpriced : CIP rev.
ISBN 0-85038-560-1 (pbk) : £2.50 B82-17980

418'.007 — Foreign languages. Learning

Dulay, Heidi. Language two / Heidi Dulay, Marina Burt, Stephen Krashen. — New York ; Oxford : Oxford University Press, 1982. — xv,315p : ill ; 23cm
Bibliography: p283-303. — Includes index
ISBN 0-19-502552-0 (cased) : Unpriced
ISBN 0-19-502553-9 (pbk) : £5.00 B82-40994

418'.007 — Foreign languages. Learning. Errors. Analysis

Corder, S. P.. Error analysis and interlanguage / S.P. Corder. — Oxford : Oxford University Press, 1981. — 120p : ill ; 22cm
Bibliography: p115-120
ISBN 0-19-437073-9 (pbk) : £5.00 B82-11625

418'.007 — Foreign languages. Study techniques — *Manuals*

Azzopardi, Emmanuel. Teach yourself a foreign language quickly / Emmanual Azzopardi. — London : Angus & Robertson, 1981. — 116p ; 23cm
ISBN 0-207-14351-x : £5.95 B82-10163

418'.007 — Foreign languages. Teaching

Stevick, Earl W.. Teaching and learning languages / Earl W. Stevick. — Cambridge : Cambridge University Press, 1982. — vi,215p : ill ; 24cm
Bibliography: p201-210. — Includes index
ISBN 0-521-24818-3 (cased) : £7.95 : CIP rev.
ISBN 0-521-28201-2 (pbk) : £3.95 B82-12690

418′.007 — Foreign languages. Teaching — *Conference proceedings*

Communication skills in modern languages : at school and in higher education : papers from a conference convened by CILT at the University of St Andrews, 14-16 September 1981 / editor: Helen N. Lunt. — [London] : Centre for Information on Language Teaching and Research, 1982. — viii,120p ; 21cm
Bibliography: p112-117
ISBN 0-903466-44-9 (pbk) : Unpriced
B82-38170

418′.007 — Foreign languages. Teaching. Methodology

The **Communicative** approach to language teaching / edited by C.J. Brumfit and K. Johnson. — Oxford : Oxford University Press, 1979 (1981 [printing]). — x,243p : ill,facsims ; 22cm
Bibliography: p227-238. — Includes index
ISBN 0-19-437078-x (pbk) : £5.00 B82-25895

418′.007 — Industries. Personnel. Foreign languages. Teaching. Methodology

Language incorporated : teaching foreign languages in industry / edited by Reinhold Freudenstein, Jürgen Beneke and Helmut Pönisch. — Oxford : Pergamon, 1981. — vi,202p : ill ; 21cm. — (Pergamon institute of English (Oxford) symposia)
Includes bibliographies
ISBN 0-08-024578-1 (pbk) : £6.95 : CIP rev.
B81-09995

418′.007 — Modern languages. Teaching — *Conference proceedings*

Reading : a symposium / edited by Udo O. H. Jung. — Oxford : Pergamon, 1982. — viiip,p195-301 ; 25cm. — (Language teaching methodology series)
'Published as a special issue of the journal System ... vol.9, no.3 ...'. — Includes chapters in French and German
ISBN 0-08-028614-3 (pbk) : Unpriced : CIP rev. B82-08419

418′.007′1 — Schools. Curriculum subjects: Modern languages. Syllabuses. Development

Yalden, Janice. The communicative syllabus. — Oxford : Pergamon, Jan.1983. — [160]p. — (Language teaching methodology series)
ISBN 0-08-028615-1 (pbk) : £5.95 : CIP entry
B82-33609

418′.007′1 — Schools. Curriculum subjects: Modern languages. Teaching methods

Krashen, Stephen. The natural approach. — Oxford : Pergamon, July 1982. — [128]p
ISBN 0-08-028651-8 : £5.95 : CIP entry
B82-17189

418′.007′1041 — Great Britain. Schools. Curriculum subjects: Foreign languages

Issues in language education : papers arising from the second Assembly of the National Congress on Languages in Education, 1978-80 / edited by J.M.C. Davidson. — London : Centre for Information on Language Teaching & Research, 1981. — 188p : 2ill ; 21cm. — (NCLE papers and reports ; 3)
Bibliography: p138-141
ISBN 0-903466-34-1 (pbk) : £5.00 B82-11457

418′.007′1141 — Great Britain. Higher education institutions. Curriculum subjects: Modern languages. Teaching. Resources — *Inquiry reports*

Council for National Academic Awards. *Working Party on Resources for Language Learning*. Report of the Working Party on Resources for Language Learning. — London (344 Gray's Inn Rd., WC1X 8BP) : Council for National Academic Awards, 1979. — 53p : ill,forms,1plan ; 30cm
Unpriced (pbk) B82-32776

418′.007′1141 — Great Britain. Librarians. Professional education. Curriculum subjects: Foreign languages

Foreign language studies at British library schools . — London : International and Comparative Librarianship Group of the Library Association, 1981. — 23p ; 30cm
ISBN 0-906904-01-3 (unbound) : £2.00
B82-20926

418′.007′1141 — Great Britain. Polytechnics. Curriculum subjects: Modern languages — *Conference proceedings*

Resources for modern languages in the polytechnics / Standing Conference of Heads of Modern Languages in Polytechnics and other Colleges (SCHML) ; edited by J.G. Harris. — [London] : [Centre for Information on Language Teaching and Research, for SCHML], [c1981]. — 46p ; 21cm
Conference proceedings. — Cover title
ISBN 0-903466-41-4 (pbk) : Unpriced
B82-30674

418′.007′1141 — Great Britain. Universities. Curriculum subjects: Modern languages

Reeves, Nigel. University language studies and the future of Britain / Nigel Reeves. — [Guildford] ([Guildford, Surrey GU2 5XH]) : [University of Surrey], [1976?]. — 18p ; 21cm. — (University of Surrey inaugural lecture)
Cover title
Unpriced (pbk) B82-26644

418′.007′1241 — Great Britain. Secondary schools. Curriculum subjects: Modern languages. Teaching

The **Teaching** of modern languages : a view for the 1980's : a second report on modern languages compiled for the Headmasters' Conference. — London (29 Gordon Sq., WC1H 0PS) : Headmasters' Conference, 1980. — viii,192p ; 23cm. — (HMC modern languages report ; no.2)
£3.00 (pbk) B82-10990

418.007′1241 — Great Britain. Secondary schools. Curriculum subjects: Modern languages. Teaching — *Manuals*

Handbook for modern language teachers / editor Alan W. Hornsey. — London : Methuen Educational, 1975 (1982 [printing]). — xii,449p : ill ; 22cm
At head of title: University of London Institute of Education. — Bibliography: p439-449
ISBN 0-423-51050-9 (pbk) : Unpriced : CIP rev. B82-12341

418′.007′1242 — England. Comprehensive schools. Curriculum subjects: Modern language. Teaching — *Case studies*

Modern language teaching : five case-studies in comprehensive : notes to accompany a series of five 25 minutes television programmes produced by the BBC in conjunction with the Centre for Information on Language Teaching and Research / programme notes edited by Alan Moys. — London : Centre for Information on Language Teaching and Research, 1978. — iv,44p ; 21cm
Bibliography: p41-43
ISBN 0-903466-21-x (pbk) : Unpriced
B82-11456

418′.007′15 — Foreign languages. Learning by adults. Self-assessment

Oskarsson, Mats. Approaches to self-assessment in foreign language learning / prepared for the Council of Europe by Mats Oskarsson. — Oxford : Published for and on behalf of the Council of Europe by Pergamon, 1980. — 47p : ill ; 25cm
At head of half title: Pergamon Institute of English (Oxford), Council of Europe Modern Languages Project. — Bibliography: p35-36
ISBN 0-08-024594-3 (pbk) : £1.95 : CIP rev.
B80-02720

418′.007′15 — Western Europe. Foreign languages. Courses. Adult students. Needs. Assessments

Richterich, René. Identifying the needs of adults learning a foreign language / prepared for the Council of Europe by René Richterich and Jean-Louis Chancerel. — Oxford : Published for and on behalf of the Council of Europe by Pergamon, 1980. — lx,103p : ill,forms ; 25cm
Half title page: Pergamon Institute of English (Oxford), Council of Europe Modern Languages Project. — Bibliography: p99-103
ISBN 0-08-024592-7 (pbk) : £3.95 : CIP rev.
B80-00672

418′.02 — Languages. Translation. Applications of digital computer sytems — *Conference proceedings*

Practical experience of machine translation : proceedings of a conference, London, 5-6 November 1981 / organised by Aslib and the Translators, Guild of the Institute of Linguists with the co-sponsorship of the Commission of the European Communities ; edited by Veronica Lawson. — Amsterdam ; Oxford : North-Holland, 1982. — xiv,199p : ill,facsims ; 24cm
Includes bibliographies
ISBN 0-444-86381-8 : £21.28 B82-30261

418′.02 — Languages. Translation. Semantic aspects — *Study examples: Bible*

Barnwell, Katharine G. L.. Introduction to semantics and translation : with special reference to Bible translation / [Katharine Barnwell]. — 2nd ed. — High Wycombe (Horsleys Green, High Wycombe, Bucks. HP14 3XL) : Summer Institute of Linguistics, [c1980]. — 272p : ill ; 29cm. — (Introduction to practical linguistics. English series)
Previous ed.: 1974. — Bibliography: p269-272. — Includes index
Unpriced (pbk) B82-10843

418′.02′025 — Translators & interpreters — *Directories*

Institute of Linguists. *Translators' Guild*. Index of members of the Translators' Guild. — [London] ([24a Highbury Grove, N5 2EA]) : [The Guild], 1980. — 1,ill ; 30cm
Unpriced B82-23438

419 — Deaf persons. Sign languages — *Conference proceedings*

Language in sign. — London : Croom Helm, Sept.1982. — [320]p
Conference papers
ISBN 0-7099-1528-4 : £10.95 : CIP entry
B82-19807

420 — ENGLISH LANGUAGE

420 — English language

Potter, Simeon. Our language / Simeon Potter. — Rev. ed., Repr. with rev. bibliography. — Harmondsworth : Penguin, 1976 (1982 [printing]). — 207p : ill ; 18cm. — (Pelican books)
Bibliography: p182-199. — Includes index
ISBN 0-14-020227-7 (pbk) : £1.95 B82-08525

420 — English language. Descriptive linguistics

Jackson, Howard. Analyzing English : an introduction to descriptive linguistics. — 2nd ed. — Oxford : Pergamon, Mar.1982. — [160] p. — (Language courses)
Previous ed.: 1980
ISBN 0-08-028667-4 : £6.50 : CIP entry
B82-03344

420′.1′51 — English language. Mathematical linguistics

Harris, Zellig S.. A grammar of English on mathematical principles / Zellig Harris. — New York ; Chichester : Wiley, c1982. — xvi,429p ; 24cm
Includes index
ISBN 0-471-02958-0 : £34.00 B82-36679

420′.7′1 — Schools. Curriculum subjects: English language. Teaching

Evans, Tricia. Teaching English / Tricia Evans. — London : Croom Helm, c1982. — 212p ; 23cm
Includes index
ISBN 0-7099-0901-2 : £11.95 : CIP rev.
ISBN 0-7099-0902-0 (pbk) : Unpriced
B81-30985

420′.7′1242 — England. Secondary schools & sixth form colleges. Students, 16-19 years. Curriculum. Development — *Study examples: Curriculum subjects: English language*

Adams, Anthony. Sixth sense : alternatives in education at 16-19 : English : a case study / Anthony Adams and Ted Hopkin. — Glasgow : Balckie, 1981. — ix,209p : ill ; 22cm
Bibliography: p207-209
ISBN 0-216-91074-9 (pbk) : £5.25
Also classified at 820′.7′1242 B82-05313

420′.7′1243 — West Germany. Secondary schools. Curriculum subjects: English language. Teaching methods

The **communicative** teaching of English : principles and an exercise typology / edited and translated for the English edition by Christopher N. Candlin with contributions from Christopher N. Candlin ... [et al.] ; under the auspices of the Gesellschaft zur Förderung des Englischunterrichts an Gesamtschulen e.V.. — Harlow : Longman, 1981. — 229p : ill,ports ; 22cm
Translation of: Kommunikativer Englischunterricht. — Includes bibliographies
ISBN 0-582-55064-5 (pbk) : £3.50 B82-02040

420′.7′1273 — United States. Secondary schools. Curriculum subjects: English language. Teaching

Hook, J. N.. The teaching of high school English. — 5th ed. / J.N. Hook, William H. Evans. — New York ; Chichester : Wiley, c1982. — xiii,521p ; 24cm
Previous ed.: 1972. — Includes index
ISBN 0-471-08923-0 : £15.50 B82-28034

420′.7′6 — Secondary schools. Curriculum subjects: English language. G.C.E. (O level) examinations. Techniques — *For Nigerian students*

Weir, David, *1943-*. Effective English Book 5 : teacher′s and student′s examination guide / David Weir for Michael Montgomery. — London : Evans, 1982. — 44p : ill ; 22cm
ISBN 0-237-50734-x (pbk) : Unpriced B82-37929

420′.9 — English language, *to 1937*

Jespersen, Otto. Growth and structure of the English language / Otto Jespersen. — 10th ed. / with a foreword by Randolph Quirk. — Oxford : Blackwell, 1982. — 244p ; 22cm
Previous ed.: 1938. — Includes index
ISBN 0-631-12986-3 (cased) : Unpriced : CIP rev.
ISBN 0-631-12987-1 (pbk) : Unpriced B81-37595

421 — ENGLISH LANGUAGE. WRITTEN AND SPOKEN CODES

421 — English language. Punctuation

Asibong, E. B.. Understanding punctuation. — London : Edward Arnold, July 1982. — [208]p
ISBN 0-7131-8088-9 (pbk) : £2.50 : CIP entry B82-13516

421 — English language. Punctuation — *For schools*

Payne, Philip. Punctuation. — London : Hutchinson Education, Jan.1983. — [64]p. — (Checkbooks for English)
ISBN 0-09-149281-5 (pbk) : £1.50 : CIP entry B82-33620

421′.076 — English language. Punctuation — *Questions & answers — For schools*

Smith, A. J. (Anthony John). Clear punctuation / A.J. Smith. — Slough : University Tutorial, 1981. — 80p ; 21cm
ISBN 0-7231-0822-6 (pbk) : £1.00 B82-11309

421′.1 — English language. Alphabets — *For children*

a b c : an alphabet book / editor Janine Amos ; illustrated by the County Studios. — Paulton : Purnell, 1982. — [24]p : chiefly col.ill ; 21cm. — (A First learning book)
ISBN 0-361-05372-x (pbk) : £0.50 B82-33948

Abc / illustrated by Anni Axworthy ; [editor Janine Amos]. — Bristol : Purnell, 1982. — [26]p : col.ill ; 27cm. — (A First learning book) (My first big books)
ISBN 0-361-05379-7 : £1.99 B82-34766

Adamson, Jean. Topsy and Tim′s ABC. — London : Blackie, June 1982. — [28]p
ISBN 0-216-91270-9 (cased) : £2.75 : CIP entry
ISBN 0-216-91269-5 (pbk) : £0.95 B82-09973

Allington, Richard. Letters. — Oxford : Blackwell Raintree, Nov.1982. — [32]p. — (Beginning to learn about)
ISBN 0-86256-055-1 : £2.95 : CIP entry B82-26067

Brown, Mik. Animal fun ABC : written and illustrated by Mik Brown. — London : Kingfisher, 1982. — [32]p : chiefly col.ill ; 23x25cm
ISBN 0-86272-029-x : £1.95 : CIP rev. B82-00367

Crane, Walter. An alphabet of old friends ; and, The absurd ABC / by Walter Crane. — London : Thames and Hudson, 1981. — [32]p : col.ill ; 27cm
Originally published: London : Routledge, 1874
ISBN 0-500-01260-1 : £4.95 B82-02166

. Happy times book of alphabet and numbers. — London : Dean, c1981. — [20]p : col.ill ; 26cm
Ill on lining papers
ISBN 0-603-00288-9 : Unpriced B82-25971

King, Tony. The moving alphabet book / by Tony King. — London : Heinemann, 1982. — [14]p : col.ill ; 20x21cm
Cover title. — Text on inside covers
ISBN 0-434-98018-8 (spiral) : £3.95 B82-31159

My very own abc pop-up book. — London : Dean, 1982, c1973. — [8]p : col.ill ; 24cm
Cover title
ISBN 0-603-02056-9 : Unpriced B82-25970

Sooty′s ABC. — Bristol : Purnell, 1982, c1967. — [19]p : col.ill ; 27cm. — ('Sooty' book series)
Ill on lining papers
ISBN 0-361-02749-4 : £0.99 B82-31787

Wildsmith, Brian. ABC / Brian Wildsmith. — Oxford : Oxford University Press, 1962 (1981 [printing]). — [56]p : chiefly col.ill ; 19x25cm
Ill on inside covers
ISBN 0-19-272122-4 (pbk) : £2.50 B82-11725

421′.1 — English language. Alphabets. Special subjects: Animals — *For children*

Amery, Heather. The alphabet book / Heather Amery ; illustrated by Colin King ; consultant Betty Root. — London : Usborne, 1979. — [32]p : col.ill ; 21cm. — (An Usborne first book)
ISBN 0-86020-359-x : £1.99 B82-07757

421′.1 — English language. Alphabets. Special subjects: Catholic Church — *For children*

A Child′s ABC / Catholic Truth Society. — London : Incorporated Catholic Truth Society, 1981. — [26]p ; 15cm
ISBN 0-85183-443-4 (pbk) : £0.45 B82-13712

421′.1 — English language. Alphabets. Special subjects: Christmas — *For children*

Hillman, Priscilla. A merry-mouse Christmas A.B.C. / by Priscilla Hillman. — Kingswood : World′s Work Children′s, 1981. — [30]p : col.ill ; 26cm
ISBN 0-437-45903-9 (pbk) : £1.95 B82-07753

421′.1′0222 — English language. Alphabets — *Illustrations — For children*

ABC / Walt Disney Productions. — Bristol : Purnell, 1975 (1982 [printing]). — 24p : chiefly col.ill ; 25cm. — (Disney colour library)
ISBN 0-361-03250-1 : Unpriced B82-21050

ABC colouring book. — [London] : [British Museum (Natural History)], 1980. — [12]p : chiefly ill ; 21x30cm. — (Publication / British Museum (Natural History) ; no.834)
Cover title
ISBN 0-565-00834-x (pbk) : £0.35 B82-21932

Fredman, Alan. The new gold medal book of the alphabet / illustrated by Alan Fredman. — London : Dean, 1981. — [44]p : chiefly col.ill ; 26cm
ISBN 0-603-00254-4 : Unpriced B82-26122

Svensson, Borje. Letters / [designed and illustrated by Borje Svensson] ; [paper engineering by James Diaz]. — [London] : Collins, 1982, c1981. — 1box : col.ill ; 60mmx108mmx63mm. — (A Collins block book)
1 sheet 57mmx108cm (concertina folded) attached in box containing diorama
ISBN 0-00-138380-9 : £1.25 B82-36181

421′.5 — English langauge. Phonetics — *For Spanish speaking students*

Finch, Diana F.. A course in English phonetics for Spanish speakers / Diana F. Finch, Héctor Ortiz Lira. — London : Heinemann Educational, 1982. — xiv,194p : ill ; 24cm
Bibliography: p181-184. — Includes index
ISBN 0-435-28078-3 (pbk) : Unpriced : CIP rev. B81-35887

421′.5 — English language. Phonetics

Wells, J. C.. Practical phonetics / J.C. Wells and Greta Colson. — London : Pitman, 1971 (1981 [printing]). — vii,116p : ill ; 24cm
Bibliography: p112. — Includes index
ISBN 0-273-01681-4 (pbk) : Unpriced B82-38147

421′.5′09 — English language, *to 1981.* **Phonological system**

Balmuth, Miriam. The roots of phonics : a historical introduction / by Miriam Balmuth ; foreword by Jeanne S. Chall. — New York ; London : McGraw-Hill, c1982. — xiii,251p ; 24cm
Bibliography: p225-235. — Includes index
ISBN 0-07-003490-7 : £13.50 B82-07865

421′.52 — English language. Pronunciation

Wells, J. C.. Accents of English / J.C. Wells. — Cambridge : Cambridge University Press, 1982. — 3v.(xix,673p) : ill,maps ; 23cm
Includes bibliographies and index
Unpriced : CIP rev. (v.1 : cased) : £17.50
ISBN 0-521-29719-2 (v.1 : pbk) : £5.95
ISBN 0-521-24224-x (v.2 : cased) : £15.00
ISBN 0-521-28540-2 (v.2 : pbk) : £5.50
ISBN 0-521-24225-8 (v.3 : cased) : £15.00
ISBN 0-521-28541-0 (v.3 : pbk) : £5.50 B82-01360

421′.52′019 — English language. Spelling. Psychological aspects

Frith, Uta. Cognitive processes in spelling. — London : Academic Press, Nov.1982. — [568]p
ISBN 0-12-268662-4 (pbk) : CIP entry B82-37491

422 — ENGLISH LANGUAGE. ETYMOLOGY

422′.437 — English language. Yiddish loanwords — *Dictionaries*

Rosten, Leo. Hooray for Yiddish!. — London : Hamilton, Feb.1983. — [368]p
ISBN 0-241-10944-2 (cased) : £8.95 : CIP entry
ISBN 0-241-10946-9 (pbk) : £5.95 B82-37855

423 — ENGLISH LANGUAGE. DICTIONARIES

423 — English language — *Dictionaries*

Chambers everyday paperback dictionary / edited by A.M. Macdonald and E.M. Kirkpatrick. — Rev. ed. — Edinburgh : Chambers, c1980. — xii,851p ; 20cm
Previous ed.: published as Chambers everyday paperback dictionary, 1977 ; and as Chambers everyday dictionary, 1975
ISBN 0-550-18015-x (pbk) : £2.95 B82-11411

. Chambers students′ dictionary / edited by A.M. Macdonald and E.M. Kirkpatrick. — Rev. ed. — [Edinburgh] : Chambers, c1980. — xii,851p ; 20cm
Previous ed.: 1977
ISBN 0-550-71309-3 (pbk) : Unpriced B82-32672

Collins gem English dictionary. — New ed. — London : Collins, 1981. — xii,627p ; 12cm
Previous ed.: 1963
ISBN 0-00-458326-4 : £1.40 B82-00074

423 — English language — *Dictionaries* *continuation*

The **Concise** Oxford dictionary of current English : based on the Oxford English dictionary and its supplements / first edited by H.W. Fowler and F.G. Fowler. — 7th ed. / edited by J.B. Sykes. — Oxford : Clarendon, 1982. — xxvii,1264p ; 23cm
Previous ed.: 1976
ISBN 0-19-861131-5 : £7.75 : CIP rev.
ISBN 0-19-861132-3 (Thumb index ed.) : Unpriced B82-13228

The **Nelson** contemporary English dictionary. — Walton-on-Thames : Nelson, 1981, c1977. — xiv,610p : ill ; 19cm
ISBN 0-17-443308-5 (pbk) : Unpriced B82-35138

The **New** Collins concise dictionary of the English language / managing editor, William T. McLeod ; consultant editor, Patrick Hanks. — London : Collins, 1982. — xx,1388 ; 23cm
Text on lining papers
ISBN 0-00-433091-9 : £7.50 B82-37744

The **New** Oxford illustrated dictionary / [text ... edited by J. Coulson ... et al.] ; [illustrations edited by Helen Mary Petter]. — 2nd ed. / revised by Dorothy Eagle with the assistance of Joyce Hawkins. — Sydney ; Oxford : Bay Books in association with Oxford University Press, 1978, c1976 (1981 [printing]). — 2v.(xvi,1920p) : col.ill,col.maps,ports(some col.) ; 29cm
Previous ed.: published as The Oxford illustrated dictionary, 1975
ISBN 0-19-861139-0 (cased) : £45.00 B82-09100

Oxford universal dictionary. — Oxford : Oxford University Press, July 1982. — [845]p
ISBN 0-19-861145-5 : £7.95 : CIP entry B82-14956

Purnell's family dictionary : in colour / edited by J.P. Brasier-Creagh, B.A Workman. — Bristol : Purnell, 1982. — viii,868p : col.ill,col.coats of arms,maps ; 23cm
ISBN 0-361-05425-4 : £6.95 B82-39682

A **Supplement** to the Oxford English dictionary / edited by R.W. Burchfield. — Oxford : Clarendon, 1982
Vol.3: O-Scz. — xv,1579p ; 32cm
ISBN 0-19-861124-2 : £55.00 : CIP rev. B82-14226

423 — English language — *Dictionaries — Early works*

Johnson, Samuel. [A Dictionary of the English language. Selections]. Johnson's dictionary : a modern selection / by E.L. McAdam Jr. & George Milne. — London : Macmillan, 1982, c1963. — xiv,464p ; 20cm
Originally published: London : Gollancz, 1963
ISBN 0-333-32984-8 (pbk) : £3.95 B82-14865

Johnson, Samuel, *1709-1784*. Johnson's dictionary : a modern selection. — London : Gollancz, Feb.1982. — [480]p
Originally published: 1963
ISBN 0-575-03098-4 : £8.95 : CIP entry B81-40240

423 — English language. Dictionaries: Easy English dictionary — *Questions & answers — For non-English speaking students*

Winter, Michael, *1955-*. Making the most of your easy English dictionary / Michael Winter. — London : Harrap, 1981. — 64p : ill ; 22cm
ISBN 0-245-53832-1 (pbk) : £1.00 B82-08923

423 — English language — *Dictionaries — For African students*

Longman primary dictionary / [editor-in-chief Della Summers]. — Harlow : Longman, 1982. — 336p : ill(some col.) ; 26cm
ISBN 0-582-55631-7 (cased) : £2.30
ISBN 0-582-55553-1 (pbk) : Unpriced B82-18359

423 — English language — *Dictionaries — For children*

Bevington, J. D.. Colour dictionary / Jeff Bevington ; illustrated by Peter Bailey ... [et al.]. — London : Macmillan Education, 1980. — 64p : col.ill ; 27cm
ISBN 0-333-28859-9 : Unpriced B82-38015

423 — English language - *Dictionaries - For children*

Manley, Deborah. The Kingfisher dictionary. — London (Elsley Court, 20 Great Titchfield St., W1P 7AD) : Kingfisher Books, Sept.1981. — [192]p
ISBN 0-86272-023-0 : £3.95 : CIP entry B81-20491

423 — English language — *Dictionaries — For children*

My first picture dictionary / illustrated by Peter Adby & associates. — London : Dean, c1981. — [74]p : chiefly col.ill ; 28cm
Ill on lining papers
ISBN 0-603-00250-1 : Unpriced B82-26758

Picture dictionary Aa-Zz / [illustrated by Ken McKie and Kate Lloyd-Jones]. — London : Macmillan, 1981. — 80p : col.ill ; 21cm. — (The Gay way series)
ISBN 0-333-31492-1 (pbk) : Unpriced B82-06872

Root, Betty. Starters blue dictionary / Betty Root. — London : Macdonald Educational, 1982. — 46p : ill(some col.),1col.map ; 25cm. — (Starters)
Includes index
ISBN 0-356-06939-7 : £2.95 B82-29449

Root, Betty. Starters green dictionary / Betty Root. — London : Macdonald Educational, 1982. — 61p : ill(some col.) ; 25cm. — (Starters)
Includes index
ISBN 0-356-06940-0 : £3.50 B82-29447

Root, Betty. Starters red dictionary / Betty Root. — London : Macdonald Educational, 1982. — 41p : ill(some col.) ; 25cm. — (Starters)
Includes index
ISBN 0-356-06938-9 : £2.95 B82-29448

Sansome, Rosemary. [The Oxford junior dictionary]. The Puffin Junior Dictionary / compiled by Rosemary Sansome ; illustrated by Susan Shields. — Harmondsworth : Puffin by arrangement with Oxford University Press, [1982]. — 254p : ill ; 21cm
Originally published: Oxford : Oxford University Press, 1978
ISBN 0-14-031482-2 (pbk) : £1.95 B82-40949

423 — English language — *Dictionaries — For non-English speaking students*

Collin, P. H.. Harrap's 2000 word English dictionary / P.H. Collin. — London : Harrap, 1981. — 271p ; 20cm
ISBN 0-245-53834-8 (pbk) : £1.95 B82-07476

423 — English language — *Dictionaries — For schools*

Bevington, J. D.. Macmillan illustrated dictionary / Jeff Bevington ; illustrated by KAG Design. — London : Macmillan Education, 1982. — 142p : ill ; 26cm
ISBN 0-333-30608-2 (pbk) : Unpriced B82-14796

Hawkins, Joyce M.. The Oxford senior dictionary / compiled by Joyce M. Hawkins. — Oxford : Oxford University Press, 1982. — viii,760p ; 21cm
ISBN 0-19-910222-8 : £3.75 : CIP rev.
ISBN 0-19-910221-x (non-net) : £2.50 B81-40258

423 — English language. Dictionaries: Harrap's 2000 word English dictionary — *Questions & answers*

Winter, Michael, *1955-*. Working with your 2000 word dictionary / Michael Winter. — London : Harrap, 1982. — 51p ; 20cm
Text on inside cover
ISBN 0-245-53835-6 (pbk) : £1.00 B82-25240

423 — English language. Dictionaries: Hobson, E. W.. Basic dictionary — *Questions & answers*

Hobson, E. W.. Basic dictionary exercises / compiled by E. W. Hobson. — Huddersfield : Schofield & Sims, 1980. — 56p : ill ; 21cm
'Dictionary exercises to accompany A basic dictionary'
ISBN 0-7217-0376-3 (pbk) : £0.55 B82-17398

423 — English language. Dictionaries: Oxford advanced learner's dictionary of current English & Oxford student's dictionary of current English. Use — *Questions & answers*

Underhill, Adrian. Use your dictionary : a practical book for users of Oxford advanced learner's dictionary of current English and Oxford student's dictionary of current English / Adrian Underhill. — Oxford : Oxford University Press, 1980. — 56p : ill,facsims ; 30cm
ISBN 0-19-431104-x (pbk) : £0.95 B82-05132

423 — English language. Dictionaries. Use

Kirkpatrick, E. M.. Chambers universal learners' workbook / compiled by E.M. Kirkpatrick. — Edinburgh : Chambers, c1981. — 69p ; 22cm
Published to accompany Chambers Universal Learners' Dictionary
ISBN 0-550-10637-5 (pbk) : Unpriced B82-08179

Lewis, Roger, *1944-*. Use your dictionary! / by Roger Lewis and Martin Pugmire. — [Cambridge] : National Extension College, [c1980]. — 82p ; 21cm
ISBN 0-86082-163-3 (pbk) : Unpriced B82-40819

423 — English language. Usage — *Dictionaries*

Fieldhouse, Harry. Everyman's good English guide / Harry Fieldhouse. — London : Dent, 1982. — xiii,270p ; 23cm
ISBN 0-460-04518-0 : £7.95 : CIP rev. B82-00309

Hindmarsh, Roland. Cambridge English lexicon / Roland Hindmarsh. — Cambridge : Cambridge University Press, 1980. — xiv,210p ; 21cm. — (Cambridge English language learning)
ISBN 0-521-21623-0 (pbk) : £6.50 B82-37892

McKaskill, S. G.. A dictionary of good English : a guide to current usage / S.G. McKaskill ; edited by Joan van Emden. — [Rev. ed]. — [London] : Macmillan, 1981. — 173p ; 22cm
Previous ed.: 1977
ISBN 0-333-30883-2 (pbk) : £2.95 B82-00571

423'.024054 — English language. Children's dictionaries. Use — *Questions & answers — For schools*

Ridout, Ronald. My first picture dictionary / Ronald Ridout. — Bristol : Purnell, 1982, c1980. — 125p : col.ill ; 27cm
Originally published: in six vols. 1980
ISBN 0-361-05317-7 : £2.50 B82-35133

423'.1 — English language. Entertainers' catch phrases — *Dictionaries*

Very interesting — but stupid : a book of catchphrases from the world of entertainment / compiled and introduced by Nigel Rees. — London : Unwin paperbacks, 1980. — 160p : ill,ports ; 18cm
Includes index
ISBN 0-04-827021-0 (pbk) : £1.50 : CIP rev. B80-09661

423'.1 — English language. Eponyms — *Dictionaries*

Boycott, Rosie. Batty, bloomers and boycott : a little dictionary of eponyms. — London : Hutchinson, Oct.1982. — 1v.
ISBN 0-09-149850-3 : £3.95 : CIP entry B82-28441

423'.1 — English language. Homophones — *Dictionaries*

Hagan, S. F.. Which is which : a manual of homophones / S.F. Hagan. — London : Macmillan, 1982. — vi,128p : ill ; 22cm. — (Meeds)
ISBN 0-333-27235-8 (pbk) : Unpriced B82-28531

423'.1 — English language. Idioms — *Dictionaries*

Fowler, W. S. (William Scott). Dictionary of idioms / W.S. Fowler. — New ed. — Walton-on-Thames : Nelson, 1982. — vi,224p ; 19cm
Previous ed.: 1972
ISBN 0-17-555381-5 (pbk) : £1.75 B82-28402

Wallace, Michael J.. Dictionary of English idioms / Michael J. Wallace. — Glasgow : Collins, 1981. — 222p ; 19cm
ISBN 0-00-370014-3 : £2.50 B82-05596

423'.1 — English language. Loanwords & foreign phrases — *Dictionaries*

Phythian, B. A.. A concise dictionary of foreign expressions. — London : Hodder & Stoughton, Oct.1982. — [208]p
ISBN 0-340-26294-x (cased) : £5.00 : CIP entry
ISBN 0-340-28174-x (pbk) : £2.45 B82-24812

423'.1 — English language. Rhyming words — *Dictionaries*

Walker, J.. The rhyming dictionary of the English language. — Rev. and enlarged ed.. — London : Routledge and Kegan Paul, Feb.1983. — [583]p
Originally published: 1924
ISBN 0-7100-9306-3 : £8.95 : CIP entry B82-40313

Whitfield, Jane Shaw. [The Improved rhyming dictionary]. Whitfield's university rhyming dictionary / by Jane Shaw Whitfield ; edited by Frances Stillman. — New York ; London : Barnes & Noble, 1981, c1951. — xx,283p ; 21cm
Originally published: New York : Crowell, 1951
ISBN 0-06-463538-4 (pbk) : £2.95 B82-14549

423'.1 — English language — *Thesauri*

Pocket thesaurus. — Harlow : Longman, 1982. — 435,195p ; 12cm. — (Longman top pocket series)
Includes index
ISBN 0-582-55545-0 (pbk) : £1.25 B82-29200

Roget, Peter. Roget's thesaurus of English words and phrases. — New ed. / prepared by Susan M. Lloyd. — Harlow : Longman, 1982. — xxxxxii,1247p ; 23cm
Previous ed.: / revised and modernised by Robert A. Dutch, 1962. — Includes index
ISBN 0-582-55635-x : £7.95
ISBN 0-582-55551-5 (de luxe ed) B82-25661

423'.1 — English language — *Thesauri — For children*

Wittels, Harriet. Young people's pocket thesaurus. — London : Ward Lock, Sept.1982. — [224]p
ISBN 0-7063-6183-0 : £2.95 : CIP entry B82-20014

425 — ENGLISH LANGUAGE. GRAMMAR

425 — English language. Clauses

Winter, Eugene. Towards a contextual grammar of English. — London : Allen and Unwin, Oct.1982. — [224]p
ISBN 0-04-425027-4 (cased) : £12.50 : CIP entry
ISBN 0-04-425028-2 (pbk) : £4.95 B82-23093

425 — English language. Modal verbs

Coates, Jennifer. The semantics of modal auxiliaries. — London : Croom Helm, Dec.1982. — [272]p. — (Croom Helm linguistics series)
ISBN 0-7099-0735-4 : £16.95 : CIP entry B82-35207

425 — English language. Quantifiers

Aldridge, M. V.. English quantifiers : a study of quantifying expressions in linguistic science and modern English usage / M.V. Aldridge. — [Amersham] : Avebury, 1982. — iii,272p : ill ; 22cm
Bibliography: p259-269. — Includes index
ISBN 0-86127-208-0 (pbk) : Unpriced : CIP rev. B81-30397

425 — English language. Syntax

Aarts, Flor. English syntactic structures : functions and categories in sentence analysis / Flor Aarts and Jan Aarts. — Oxford : Pergamon, 1982. — ix,189p : ill ; 25cm. — (Pergamon Institute of English (Oxford) language courses)
Includes index
ISBN 0-08-028634-8 (pbk) : £7.95 : CIP rev. B82-10598

425 — English language. Transformational-generative theories. Pseudo-cleft construction

Higgins, F. R. (Francis Roger). The pseudo-cleft construction in English / F.R. Higgins. — New York ; London : Garland, 1979. — viii,393p : ill ; 24cm. — (Outstanding dissertations in linguistics)
Bibliography: p371-393
ISBN 0-8240-9683-5 : Unpriced B82-14678

425 — English language. Verbs. Valency

Allerton, D. J.. Valency and the English verb. — London : Academic Press, Sept.1982. — 1v.
ISBN 0-12-052980-7 : CIP entry B82-19158

425 — Natural language. Parsing

Parsing natural language. — London : Academic Press, Sept.1982. — [250]p
ISBN 0-12-408280-7 : CIP entry B82-25059

427 — ENGLISH LANGUAGE. EARLY FORMS, SLANG, DIALECTS

427 — English language. Dialects

Trudgill, Peter. On dialect. — Oxford : Blackwell, Oct.1982. — [224]p
ISBN 0-631-13151-5 : £12.50 : CIP entry B82-23169

427 — English language. Dialects. Sociolinguistic aspects

Cheshire, Jenny. Variation in an English dialect. — Cambridge : Cambridge University Press, Sept.1982. — [142]p. — (Cambridge studies in linguistics, ISSN 0068-676x ; 37)
ISBN 0-521-23802-1 : £16.00 : CIP entry B82-26234

427 — English language. Foreign usage

Trudgill, Peter. International English : a guide to varieties of Standard English / Peter Trudgill and Jean Hannah. — London : Arnold, 1982. — xiii,130p : ill,1map ; 22cm
Bibliography: p117-120. — Includes index
ISBN 0-7131-6362-3 (pbk) : £3.95 : CIP rev. B81-37565

427'.02 — English language, *1066-1400*. Syntax

Warner, Anthony R.. Complementation in Middle English and the methodology of historical syntax. — London : Croom Helm, June 1982. — [256]p. — (Croom Helm linguistics series)
ISBN 0-7099-2735-5 : £12.95 : CIP entry B82-09595

427'.02 — English language, *1066-1625 — Samplers*

Partridge, A. C.. A companion to Old and Middle English. — London : Deutsch, Oct.1981. — [352]p
ISBN 0-233-97308-7 (cased) : £12.95 : CIP entry
ISBN 0-233-97410-3 (pbk) : £6.95
Also classified at 429 B81-26747

427'.23'03 — English language. Kent dialect — *Dictionaries*

Major, Alan. A new dictionary of Kent dialect / Alan Major. — [Rainham] : Meresborough, 1981. — xxvii,148p : ill ; 24cm
Bibliography: pviii
ISBN 0-905270-27-4 : £7.50 B82-36404

427'.821 — English language. Sheffield dialect

Whomersley, Derek. "Sheffieldish" : a beginner's phrase-book / by Derek Whomersley ; illustrations by Whitworth. — Sheffield : Publicity Department, Sheffield City Council, 1981. — [56]p : ill ; 20cm
ISBN 0-900660-62-7 (pbk) : Unpriced B82-40180

427'.9 — English language. Non-native usage

The Other tongue : English across cultures / edited by Braj B. Kachru. — Urbana ; London : University of Illinois Press, c1982. — xv,358p : ill ; 24cm
Includes bibliographies and index
ISBN 0-252-00896-0 : £13.15 B82-35665

427'.9'41 — English language. British usage — *For non-English speaking students*

Ford, Carol. Cultural encounters. — Oxford : Pergamon, Feb.1983. — [80]p
ISBN 0-08-029444-8 (pbk) : £1.95 : CIP entry
Primary classification 428.2'4 B82-36466

427'.9411 — English language. Scots dialect

Scotland and the Lowland tongue. — Aberdeen : Aberdeen University Press, Feb.1983. — [192]p
ISBN 0-08-028482-5 : £17.00 : CIP entry B82-36475

427'.9411'03 — English language. Scottish dialect — *Scots & English dictionaries*

Mactaggart, John. The Scottish Gallovidian encyclopedia / by John Mactaggart. — New ed. / with a note on the author by L.L. Ardern. — Strath Tay (Old Ballechin, Strath Tay, Perthshire) : Clunie Press in association with the E.A. Hornel Trust, 1981. — vi,xii,504p ; 23cm
Facsim of: edition published London : Printed for the author, 1824
ISBN 0-902965-16-6 : £15.00 B82-08322

427'.941135'03 — English language. Shetland dialect — *Dictionaries*

Miller, Stephen, *1958-*. Specimen of Shetland words from vocabulary compiled by W.A. Grant : from the Bonaparte collection in the Biblioteca Provisional de Vizcaya, Bilbao, Pais Vascos / Stephen Miller. — Leeds (c/o The School of English, The University, Leeds) : Leeds Folklore Group, 1982. — 5leaves ; 30cm. — (Leeds Folklore Group papers in folklife studies ; 3)
£0.15 1/2 (unbound) B82-30886

427'.9415 — English language. Irish dialect

Aspects of English dialects in Ireland. — [Belfast] (Queen's University of Belfast, [42, University Rd., Belfast BT7 1NJ]) : Institute of Irish Studies, 1981
Includes bibliographies
Vol.1: Papers arising from the Tape-recorded Survey of Hiberno-English Speech / edited by Michael V. Barry. — 170p : ill,maps,2facsims ; 29cm
Unpriced (pbk) B82-00633

427'.9416 — English language. Northern Irish dialect — *Phrase books*

Pepper, John. John Pepper's Ulster phrase book. — Belfast : Appletree, Oct.1982. — [64]p
ISBN 0-86281-101-5 (pbk) : £2.95 : CIP entry B82-29034

427'.9416'03 — English language. Northern Irish dialect — *Dictionaries*

Pepper, John. John Pepper's Ulster-English dictionary. — Belfast : Appletree Press, Oct.1981. — [80]p
ISBN 0-904651-88-6 (pbk) : £2.50 : CIP entry B81-30998

427'.94167 — English language. Belfast dialect. Pronunciation

Milroy, James. Belfast / James Milroy. — Belfast : Blackstaff Press, c1981. — xii,113p : ill,2maps ; 21cm. — (Regional accents of English)
Bibliography: p111-113
ISBN 0-85640-241-9 (pbk) : £5.95 : CIP rev. B81-34963

427'.9729 — English language. West Indian dialect

Sutcliffe, David. British black English / David Sutcliffe. — Oxford : Blackwell, 1982. — xiv,210p ; 23cm
Bibliography: p196-203. — Includes index
ISBN 0-631-12711-9 : £14.95 : CIP rev. B81-34293

427'.973 — English language. American usage. Comprehension — *For schools*

O'Neill, Robert. AKL : beginning / Robert O'Neill, Larry Anger and Karen Davy. — [New York] : [Longman] ; [Harlow] : [distributed by Longman]
Student's tests / Hugh Templeton, David Mills, Robert O'Neill. — 1981. — 29p : ill ; 26cm
ISBN 0-582-78341-0 (pbk) : £1.20 B82-28906

O'Neill, Robert. AKL : advanced : American kernel lessons. — New York ; Harlow : Longman. — (Longman American English)
Teacher's manual / Robert O'Neill, Penny Laporte. — 1982. — 101p : ill ; 26cm
ISBN 0-582-79763-2 (pbk) : £2.75 B82-36961

O'Neill, Robert. AKL — advanced : American kernel lessons / Robert O'Neill, Edwin T. Cornelius, Jr., Gay N. Washburn. — Harlow : Longman. — (Longman American English)
[Student's book]. — 1981. — 142p : ill ; 26cm
Includes index
ISBN 0-582-79741-1 (pbk) : Unpriced
B82-20060

O'Neill, Robert. AKL-advanced : American kernel lessons / Robert O'Neill, Edwin T. Cornelius, Jr., Guy N. Washburn. — (Longman American English)
Student's tests / Robert O'Neill, Linda Markstein. — New York : Longman Inc, 1982 ; Harlow : Distributed by Longman. — 26p ; 26cm
ISBN 0-582-79807-8 (pbk) : Unpriced
B82-37171

427'.973 — English language. American usage — *Questions & answers — For non-English speaking students*

Fassman, Paula. Gallery / Paula Fassman, Suzanne Seymour Tavares. — New York ; Oxford : Oxford University Press, 1982. — 208p : ill ; 26cm
ISBN 0-19-503132-6 (pbk) : £2.75 B82-40995

Freeman, Daniel B.. Speaking of survival / Daniel B. Freeman. — New York ; Oxford : Oxford University Press, 1982. — xii,228p : ill (some col.),1map ; 24cm
ISBN 0-19-503110-5 (pbk) : £2.75 B82-40996

Langley, Rolly. Practice tests for TOEFL : latest format / Rolly Langley. — London : Macmillan, 1981. — xvii,125p ; 26cm
ISBN 0-333-29357-6 (pbk) : Unpriced
B82-03772

427'.973 — English language. American usage, *to 1981*

Baron, Dennis E.. Grammar and good taste. — London : Yale University Press, Nov.1982. — [272]p
ISBN 0-300-02799-0 : £15.50 : CIP entry
B82-40333

427'.973 — Spoken English language. American usage — *Questions & answers — For non-English speaking students*

Bode, Sharon. Listening in & speaking out / Sharon Bode, Charles G. Whitley, Gary James. — New York ; Harlow : Longman
Advanced. — 1981. — x,99p : ill ; 26cm
ISBN 0-582-79737-3 (pbk) : £2.00 B82-02038

427'.973 — Spoken English language. Slang. Usage of American performing artists — *Dictionaries*

Wilmeth, Don B.. The language of American popular entertainment : a glossary of argot, slang, and terminology / Don B. Wilmeth. — Westport, Conn. ; London : Greenwood Press, 1981. — xxi,305p ; 25cm
Bibliography: p301-305
ISBN 0-313-22497-8 : Unpriced B82-02735

427'.973'0712 — Secondary schools. Curriculum subjects: English language. American usage. Activities — *For teaching*

Bergman, Floyd L.. The English teacher's activities handbook : an ideabook for middle and secondary schools / with text and illustrations by Floyd L. Bergman. — 2nd ed. — Boston [Mass.] ; London : Allyn and Bacon, c1982. — xviii,342p : ill,forms ; 24cm
Previous ed.: 1976. — Bibliography: p311-332. — Includes index
ISBN 0-205-07383-2 (pbk) : Unpriced
B82-06665

428 — ENGLISH LANGUAGE USAGE

428 — English language — *For schools*

Agar, Kenneth. Everyday grammar / Kenneth Agar. — London : Cassell
Bk.3. — 1980. — 64p : ill(some col.) ; 22cm
ISBN 0-304-30306-2 (pbk) : £0.95 : CIP rev.
B80-02408

Agar, Kenneth. Everyday grammar / Kenneth Agar. — London : Cassell
Bk.4. — 1980. — 80p : ill(some col.) ; 22cm
ISBN 0-304-30307-0 (pbk) : £0.95 : CIP rev.
B80-02409

Alone / edited by Francesca Greenoak. — London : Ward Lock Educational, c1978. — 128p : ill ; 21cm. — (The English project. Stage 2)
Includes index
ISBN 0-7062-3646-7 (pbk) : Unpriced
B82-19330

Brindley, D. J.. Excellence in English / D.J. Brindley ; illustrated by Ronald Oppenheim. — London : Hodder and Stoughton
Bk.5. — 1982. — viii,230p : ill,1map ; 22cm
Includes index
ISBN 0-340-24449-6 (pbk) : Unpriced : CIP rev. B81-22605

Brookes, N. F.. Andy & Anna. — Oxford : Pergamon, Apr.1982. — [128]p. — (Pergamon English course for young learners)
ISBN 0-08-025341-5 (pbk) : £2.50 : CIP entry
B82-06489

Chatfield, H. J.. Check points. — London : Bell & Hyman, Apr.1982. — [80]p
Originally published: 1980
ISBN 0-7135-1207-5 (pbk) : £1.95 : CIP entry
B82-12819

Cities / edited by Noël Hardy. — London : Ward Lock Educational, [1980]. — 128p : ill,facsims ; 21cm. — (The English project. Stage 3)
Includes index
ISBN 0-7062-3697-1 (pbk) : £1.95 B82-22195

Coles, Michael. Turning point / Michael Coles and Basil Lord. — Oxford : Oxford University Press
Workbook. — 1979. — 121p : ill ; 22cm. — (Access to English)
ISBN 0-19-453745-5 (pbk) : £1.15 B82-11636

Coles, Michael. Turning point / Michael Coles and Basil Lord. — Oxford : Oxford University Press. — (Access to English)
Workbook. — 1979 (1980 [printing]). — 121p : ill ; 22cm
ISBN 0-19-453745-5 (pbk) : Unpriced
B82-25714

Ellis, E. W.. Say, spell and write. — Cheltenham : Stanley Thornes, Sept.1982. — [48]p
ISBN 0-85950-373-9 (pbk) : £1.50 : CIP entry
B82-20199

The **English** project stage 2 teachers' handbook. — London : Ward Lock Educational, c1979. — 67p ; 22cm
ISBN 0-7062-3698-x (pbk) : £1.95 B82-19333

Faces in the crowd / edited by Myra Barrs. — London : Ward Lock Educational, [1980]. — 126p : ill ; 21cm. — (The English project. Stage 3)
Includes index
ISBN 0-7062-3645-9 (pbk) : £1.95 B82-19331

Framework English. — Walton-on-Thames : Nelson
Book 2. — 1980. — 127p : ill,facsims,ports ; 28cm
ISBN 0-17-433352-8 (pbk) : Unpriced
B82-40845

Framework English. — Walton-on-Thames : Nelson
Cover title. — Text on inside front cover
2
Teacher's bk. : with answers / Don Shiach ; [edited and designed by SGS Education]. — 1980. — 32p ; 25cm
ISBN 0-17-433357-9 (pbk) : £1.35 B82-18646

Gallon, J. P.. English : about you / J.P. & W. Gallon ; illustrations Viv Quillin. — Leeds : E.J. Arnold, c1982. — 2v. : ill,forms,maps,plans ; 23cm
ISBN 0-560-03550-0 (pbk) : Unpriced
ISBN 0-560-03551-9 (v.2) B82-31917

Grimshaw, Nigel. Read & write. — London : Cassell
Book 1. — June 1982. — [160]p
ISBN 0-304-30934-6 (pbk) : £2.75 : CIP entry
B82-09997

Grimshaw, Nigel. Read & write. — London : Cassell, Sept.1982
Book 2. — [160]p
ISBN 0-304-30935-4 (pbk) : £2.75 : CIP entry
B82-18825

Grimshaw, Nigel. Read and write. — London : Cassell
Book 3. — Jan.1983. — [144]p
ISBN 0-304-30936-2 (pbk) : £3.25 : CIP entry
B82-32850

Hapgood, Michael. English lessons. — London : Heinemann Educational, Apr.1981
1: Teachers' notes. — [32]p
ISBN 0-435-10403-9 (pbk) : £1.25 : CIP entry
B81-08928

Hapgood, Michael. English lessons two. — London : Heinemann Educational, June 1982. — [80]p
ISBN 0-435-10401-2 (pbk) : £1.95 : CIP entry
B82-16483

Jackson, David. Continuity in secondary English. — London : Methuen, Nov.1982. — [300]p
ISBN 0-416-34340-6 (cased) : £10.50 : CIP entry
ISBN 0-416-34350-3 (pbk) : £4.95 B82-23978

Jones, Barry. Basics of English. — London : Bell & Hyman, July 1981. — [64]p
ISBN 0-7135-1271-7 (pbk) : £1.95 : CIP entry
B81-16391

McNeil, Frank. Here I am / [Frank McNeil and Neil Mercer]. — London : Black, c1982. — 64p : ill(some col.) ; 20x25cm. — (The Primary language project)
Cover title. — Bibliography: p64
ISBN 0-7136-2172-9 (pbk) : £1.95 B82-25129

McNeil, Frank. Language around us / [Frank McNeil and Neil Mercer]. — London : Black, c1982. — 64p : ill(some col.),1map,1facsim ; 20x25cm. — (The Primary language project)
Cover title. — Bibliography: p64
ISBN 0-7136-2173-7 (pbk) : £1.95 B82-25127

McNeil, Frank. Talking and feeling / [Frank McNeil and Neil Mercer]. — London : Black, c1982. — 64p : ill(some col.),1col.map ; 20x25cm. — (The Primary language project)
Cover title. — Bibliography: p64
ISBN 0-7136-2174-5 (pbk) : £1.95 B82-25128

Merrick, Del. Look at language. — London : Edward Arnold, Dec.1982. — [48]p
ISBN 0-7131-0818-5 (pbk) : £1.00 : CIP entry
B82-30201

428 — English language — *For schools*
continuation

Owen, Christopher. English workshop. — London : Hodder & Stoughton Educational, May 1982
3. — [160]p
ISBN 0-340-24295-7 (pbk) : £2.50 : CIP entry B82-07430

Owen, Christopher, *1939-*. English workshop / Christopher Owen, Andrew Carter. — London : Hodder and Stoughton
2. — 1981. — 154p : ill,ports ; 25cm
ISBN 0-340-24296-5 (pbk) : £2.50 : CIP rev. B81-13567

Oxford secondary English. — Oxford : Oxford University Press
Bk.1 / John Seely and Frank Ash, Frank Green, Chris Woodhead. — 1982. — 188p : ill,1map ; 25cm
ISBN 0-19-831133-8 (pbk) : £2.50 B82-18412

Oxford secondary English. — Oxford : Oxford University Press
Book 2 / John Seely and Frank Ash, Frank Green, Chris Woodhead. — 1982. — 188p : ill,maps,plans ; 25cm
ISBN 0-19-831135-4 (pbk) : £2.50 B82-20112

Richmond, John. Investigating our language. — London : Edward Arnold, Feb.1982. — [112]p
ISBN 0-7131-0610-7 (pbk) : £2.75 : CIP entry B81-36392

Ridout, Ronald. Openings in English. — London : Hutchinson Education, Apr.1982
Coursebook 3. — [64]p
ISBN 0-09-146701-2 (pbk) : £1.95 : CIP entry B82-04117

Ridout, Ronald. Openings in English. — London : Hutchinson Educational
Spiritmaster 3. — Apr.1982. — [30]p
ISBN 0-09-146711-x (pbk) : £9.95 : CIP entry B82-03746

Rowe, Albert. Positive English / Albert Rowe. — Basingstoke : Macmillan Education, 1980
Bk.2. — 128p : ill,1map,forms ; 21cm
ISBN 0-333-27065-7 (pbk) : £1.75 : CIP rev. B80-01154

Rowe, Albert. Positive English / Albert Rowe. — Basingstoke : Macmillan Education
Bk.3. — 1980. — 159p : ill ; 21cm
ISBN 0-333-27066-5 (pbk) : £1.95 : CIP rev. B80-08179

Sam on Radio 321. — Harlow : Longman
Stage 1 of an English language course in 3 stages
[Pupil's book] / M. Iggulden, E. Melville, S. White. — 1981. — 80p : chiefly col.ill ; 24cm
Cover title
ISBN 0-582-51015-5 (pbk) : Unpriced B82-20067

Sam on Radio 321. — Harlow : Longman
Stage 1 of an English language course in 3 stages
Teacher's guide / [Eleanor Melville & Margaret Iggulden]. — 1982. — x,118p : music ; 24cm
ISBN 0-582-51013-9 (pbk) : Unpriced B82-20066

Shiach, Don. Framework : examination English / Don Shiach. — Walton-on-Thames : Nelson A. — 1982. — 192p : ill ; 25cm
ISBN 0-17-433354-4 (pbk) : Unpriced B82-26906

Taylor, Boswell. First English / Boswell Taylor. — London : Hodder and Stoughton
1 / illustrated by Terry Carter and Nicholas Ward. — 1980. — 64p : ill(some col.) ; 25cm
ISBN 0-340-23046-0 (pbk) : £1.25 : CIP rev. B80-04749

Taylor, Boswell. First English. — London : Hodder & Stoughton
4. — June 1982. — [96]p
ISBN 0-340-26226-5 (pbk) : £1.95 : CIP entry B82-10005

Woolman, Mike. Invitation to English / Mike Woolman and Ham Andrews. — Leeds : E.J. Arnold
Book 5. — 1981. — 71p : ill(some col.),maps (some col.) ; 26cm
ISBN 0-560-04110-1 (pbk) : £1.95 B82-01031

Worlds apart / edited by Peter Griffiths. — London : Ward Lock Educational, [1980]. — 128p : ill,ports ; 21cm. — (The English project. Stage 3)
Includes index
ISBN 0-7062-3758-7 (pbk) : £1.95 B82-19332

428 — English language — *For slow learning adolescents — For schools*

Ridgway, Bill. Twelve to sixteen. — London : Edward Arnold, Apr.1982
2: Your move. — [96]p
ISBN 0-7131-0648-4 (pbk) : £2.75 : CIP entry B82-04481

Ridgway, Bill. Twelve to sixteen. — London : Edward Arnold, Apr.1982
2a: Your move. — [32]p
ISBN 0-7131-0649-2 (pbk) : £1.75 : CIP entry B82-04480

Spence, Monica. Work roundabout / compiled by Monica Spence ; advised by Kathy Turton, Evelyn Bealby and the Winkfield Learning Centre. — London : Christian Education Movement, 1977. — 35p + Teachers notes ([4]p ; 22cm) : ill ; 26cm
ISBN 0-905022-22-x (unbound) : Unpriced B82-40174

428 — English language — *Games — For schools*

Granger, Colin. Play games with English / Colin Granger. — [London] : [Heinemann Educational]
Teachers' Book 2. — [1982]. — xvi,80p : ill ; 21cm
Cover title. — Includes index
ISBN 0-435-28063-5 (pbk) : £2.25
ISBN 0-435-28062-7 (Students' book) : Unpriced B81-34499

428 — English language — *Questions & answers*

English through practice. — Thirsk : Crakehill Press
Figures of speech
Pt.1 / by Alexander [i.e. Alexandar] Reid & John Lannoy. — c1981. — 48p : ill ; 21cm
ISBN 0-907105-06-8 (pbk) : Unpriced B82-03845

Griffin, John, *1935-*. English language : the pre-examination years : main book / by John Griffin and Theresa Sullivan ; illustrations by Marty Strube & Carol Foran. — Huntingdon : Cambridge Learning, [1981?]. — 143p : ill ; 24cm + Answer book(p147-222 : ill ; 24cm)
ISBN 0-905946-07-3 (pbk) : Unpriced B82-25877

Lucas, Michael. English in fact / Michael Lucas. — London : Heinemann Educational
Students' book. — 1981. — 93p : ill,maps,1facsim ; 25cm
ISBN 0-435-28420-7 (pbk) : £1.90 : CIP rev. B81-07479

Lucas, Michael. English in fact / Michael Lucas. — London : Heinemann Educational
Teachers' book. — 1981. — 63p : ill,maps ; 24cm
ISBN 0-435-28421-5 (pbk) : £2.10 : CIP rev. B81-07480

Willis, Hulon. Grammar and composition skills : generating sentences and paragraphs. — 3rd ed. / Hulon Willis, James L. Pence, Roseann Dueñas Gonzalez. — New York ; London : Holt, Rinehart and Winston, c1982. — xii,335p ; 24cm
Previous ed.: published as Grammar and composition. New York : Holt, Rinehart and Winston, 1976. — Text on lining papers. — Includes index
ISBN 0-03-059636-x (pbk) : £8.95 B82-18937

428 — English language — *Questions & answers — For children*

Arkwright, R. M.. Helping your child with home tests : for grammar and comprehensive school entrance / R.M. Arkwright. — 4th ed. — London : Harrap, 1981. — 94p : ill ; 19cm
Previous ed. published as: Home tests for grammar and comprehensive school entrance, 1970
ISBN 0-245-53786-4 (pbk) : £1.75
Primary classification 155.4'13 B82-01489

428 — English language — *Questions & answers — For Irish students*

Clarke, A. A.. Effective English. — Dublin : Educational Company of Ireland
1 / A.A. Clarke. — 1982. — iv,100p : ill ; 21cm
Unpriced (pbk) B82-25671

Lenehan, Brian. It's like this — : a first-year English course / Brian Lenehan and Patrick Murray ; [illustrations John Skelton]. — Dublin : Educational Company, 1981. — 100p : ill(some col.) ; 21cm
Unpriced (pbk) B82-02551

428 — English language — *Questions & answers — For pre-school children*

My first big talkabout book / with illustrations by Harry Wingfield, Martin Aitchison and Eric Winter. — Loughborough : Ladybird, 1978. — [58]p : chiefly ill(some col.) ; 31cm
Text and col. ill on lining papers
ISBN 0-7214-7504-3 : £1.95 B82-17509

428 — English language — *Questions & answers — For schools*

Baber, M.. 16+ English : an English coursebook for students in colleges of further education, sixth-form colleges and the 'new sixth' / M. Baber. — Cheltenham : Thornes, 1982. — x,165p : ill ; 24cm
ISBN 0-85950-325-9 (pbk) : Unpriced : CIP rev. B82-04738

Ballance, Denis. Everyday English / Denis and Helen Ballance. — London : Macmillan Education
2. — 1982. — 64p : ill ; 26cm
ISBN 0-333-30994-4 (pbk) : Unpriced B82-38810

Cooper, Alan. Revision and practice for 'O' level English. — London : Edward Arnold, Sept.1982. — [96]p
ISBN 0-7131-0810-x (pbk) : £2.25 : CIP entry B82-21982

Deadman, Ronald. Check up tests in English language / Ronald Deadman. — London : Macmillan, 1980. — 47p ; 26cm. — (Check up tests series)
ISBN 0-333-28861-0 (pbk) : £0.65 B82-15234

Fearnley, William. Choice words / William J. Fearnley. — Dublin : Gill and Macmillan, 1982. — 176p : ill
ISBN 0-7171-1146-6 (pbk) : Unpriced B82-34655

Gregory, Oliver. Oxford Junior English / Oliver Gregory. — Oxford : Oxford University Press
Teacher's book. — 2nd ed. — 1980. — 244p : 1ill ; 21cm
Previous ed.: 1978
ISBN 0-19-918138-1 (pbk) : Unpriced B82-32814

428 — English language — *Questions & answers — For schools* *continuation*

Howe, D. H.. Start with English / D.H. Howe ; [illustrations by Jonnie Ata Mak]. — Oxford : Oxford University Press
1. — 1979 (1981 [printing]). — 64p : col.ill ; 26cm
ISBN 0-19-433630-1 (pbk) : £1.15 B82-09497

Howe, D. H.. Start with English / D.H. Howe ; [illustrations by Jonnie Ata Mak]. — Oxford : Oxford University Press
2. — 1979 (1981 [printing]). — 83p : col.ill ; 26cm
ISBN 0-19-433632-8 (pbk) : £1.40 B82-09498

Howe, D. H.. Start with English / D.H. Howe ; [illustrations by Jonnie Ata Mak]. — Oxford : Oxford University Press
3. — 1979 (1981 [printing]). — 112p : col.ill ; 26cm
ISBN 0-19-433634-4 (pbk) : £1.75 B82-09499

Howe, D. H.. Start with English / D.H. Howe. — Oxford : Oxford University Press
Teacher's book 4. — 1981. — 65p ; 22cm
ISBN 0-19-433645-x (pbk) : £0.80 B82-08482

Howe, D. H.. Start with English / D.H. Howe. — Oxford : Oxford University Press
Teacher's book 5. — 1981. — 68p ; 22cm
ISBN 0-19-433646-8 (pbk) : £0.80 B82-08480

Howe, D. H.. Start with English / D.H. Howe. — Oxford : Oxford University Press
Teacher's book 6. — 1981. — 68p ; 22cm
ISBN 0-19-433647-6 (pbk) : £0.80 B82-08481

Howe, D. H.. Start with English / D.H. Howe. — Oxford : Oxford University Press
Workbook
4. — c1981. — 64p : ill ; 26cm
Cover title
ISBN 0-19-433648-4 (pbk) : £0.75 B82-03882

Hughes, D.. English : seven to twelve / D. Hughes and A. Josephs ; illustrated by T. Wanless. — Glasgow : Collins
5. — 1982. — 127p : ill(some col.) ; 23cm
ISBN 0-00-314321-x (pbk) : £2.25 B82-36494

Kitto-Jones, A.. Test your English / A. Kitto-Jones. — Glasgow : Gibson, c1982. — 47p ; 21cm
ISBN 0-7169-5515-6 (pbk) : Unpriced B82-40639

McGrath, James. Comprehensive English / James McGrath. — Edinburgh : Holmes McDougall
Bk.3. — c1981. — 94p : ill ; 25cm
ISBN 0-7157-2029-5 (pbk) : Unpriced B82-00678

McLullich, Helen H.. Wordpower / Helen H. McLullich ; [illustrated by Ray Mutimer]. — Edinburgh : Oliver & Boyd
2. — 1982. — 63p : ill(some col.),1col.map ; 25cm
Cover title
ISBN 0-05-003194-5 (pbk) : Unpriced B82-28316

Markstein, Linda. What's the story : sequential photographs for language practice / Linda Markstein, Dorien Grunbaum. — New York ; London : Longman, 1981. — 5v. : ill ; 26cm. — (Longman American English)
ISBN 0-582-79783-7 (pbk) : Unpriced
ISBN 0-582-79784-5 (students book 2) : £1.25
ISBN 0-582-79785-3 (students book 3) : £1.25
ISBN 0-85279-786-1 (students book 4) : £1.25
ISBN 0-85279-787-x (teachers book) : £1.25 B82-07454

Matthews, Alan. Themes : an integrated course for late intermediate and advanced students / Alan Matthews and Carol Read. — [Glasgow] : Collins ELT, 1982. — 189p : ill,1map ; 26cm
ISBN 0-00-370040-2 : £3.95 B82-39405

Meyer, Maricelle. Action English / Maricelle Meyer and Robert Sugg. — London : Evans
Teacher's bk.3. — 1981. — 94p : ill,music ; 25cm
ISBN 0-237-50475-8 (pbk) : Unpriced B82-06670

Milburn, Constance. Read, write and remember / Constance Milburn. — Glasgow : Blackie
Early book 1. — 1982. — 16p : ill(some col.) ; 21cm
Cover title
ISBN 0-216-91144-3 (pbk) : Unpriced B82-19596

Milburn, Constance. Read, write and remember / Constance Milburn. — Glasgow : Blackie
Early book 2. — 1982. — 16p : ill(some col.) ; 21cm
Cover title
ISBN 0-216-91145-1 (pbk) : Unpriced B82-19597

Milburn, Constance. Read, write and remember / Constance Milburn. — Glasgow : Blackie
Early book 3. — 1982. — 16p : ill(some col.) ; 21cm
Cover title
ISBN 0-216-91146-x (pbk) : Unpriced B82-19594

Milburn, Constance. Read, write and remember / Constance Milburn. — Glasgow : Blackie
Early book 4. — 1982. — 16p : ill(some col.) ; 21cm
Cover title
ISBN 0-216-91147-8 (pbk) : Unpriced B82-19595

Newby, Michael. Making language / Michael Newby ; illustrated by Paddy Mounter. — Oxford : Oxford University Press
Book 1. — 1981. — 80p : ill(some col.) ; 25cm
ISBN 0-19-831139-7 (pbk) : £1.95 B82-10928

Newby, Michael. Making language / Michael Newby ; illustrated by Paddy Mounter. — Oxford : Oxford University Press
Book 2. — c1981. — 80p : ill(some col.) ; 25cm
ISBN 0-19-831143-5 (pbk) : £1.95 B82-11254

Ridout, Ronald. Basic skills in English / Ronald Ridout. — London : Macmillan, 1980. — 2v. ; 26cm. — (A Macmillan teach and test book)
ISBN 0-333-28300-7 (pbk) : Unpriced
ISBN 0-333-29380-0 (teacher's bk) : £1.95 B82-15231

Ridout, Ronald. Positive English workbook / Ronald Ridout. — Basingstoke : Macmillan Education
3. — 1980. — 31p : ill ; 30cm
ISBN 0-333-27229-3 (unbound) : £1.95 : CIP rev. B80-02727

Ridout, Ronald. Positive English workbook / Ronald Ridout. — Basingstoke : Macmillan Education
4. — 1980. — 31p : ill ; 30cm
ISBN 0-333-27230-7 (unbound) : £0.35 : CIP rev. B80-02728

Robinson, Carole. Themes for proficiency / Carole Robinson. — Oxford : Oxford University Press, c1981. — 285p : ill ; 25cm
ISBN 0-19-432777-9 (pbk) : £3.50 B82-20439

Sadler, R. K.. Senior language / Sadler, Hayllar, Powell. — South Melbourne ; London : Macmillan, 1981. — v,280p : ill ; 26cm
ISBN 0-333-33763-8 (pbk) : Unpriced B82-35075

Seely, John. Oxford secondary English / John Seely. — Oxford : Oxford University Press
1: Teacher's book. — 1982. — xii,100p ; 25cm
Bibliography: p92
ISBN 0-19-831134-6 (pbk) : £2.75 B82-22533

Seely, John. Oxford secondary English / John Seely. — Oxford : Oxford University Press
2: Teacher's book. — 1982. — xii,84p : ill ; 25cm
Bibliography: p76
ISBN 0-19-831136-2 (pbk) : £2.75 B82-22531

Tunnicliffe, Stephen. Revise English : a complete revision course for O level and CSE / Stephen Tunnicliffe, Frances Glendenning, Denys Thompson. — Rev. ed. — London : Letts, 1981, c1979. — 221p : ill,1map,facsims ; 30cm. — (Letts study aids)
Previous ed.: 1979. — Includes index
ISBN 0-85097-367-8 (pbk) : £3.65 B82-31661

428 — English language. Usage

Becoming our own experts : the Vauxhall papers : studies of language and learning made by th Talk Workshop Group at Vauxhall Manor School, 1974-9. — London : [The Group], c1982. — vi,441p : ill ; 22cm
ISBN 0-9507910-0-8 (pbk) : Unpriced : CIP rev. B82-01735

428 — Wales. Children. Languages. Selection by bilingual mothers

Harrison, Godfrey. Bilingual mothers in Wales and the language of their children / by Godfrey Harrison, Wynford Bellin, Brec'hed Piette. — Cardiff : University of Wales Press, 1981. — 87p ; 26cm. — (Social science monographs ; no.6)
At head of title: University of Wales Board of Celtic Studies. — Bibliography: p87
ISBN 0-7083-0794-9 (pbk) : Unpriced : CIP rev. B81-30900

428'.0024553 — English language — *For geology*

Rayner, Dorothy H.. English language and usage in geology : a personal compilation / Dorothy H. Rayner. — Leeds : Leeds Geological Association, 1982. — 30p ; 25cm
Transactions of the Leeds Geological Association, special issue. — Bibliography: p29-30
ISBN 0-900483-01-6 (pbk) : £1.50 B82-28311

428'.00246238 — English language — *For sailing*

Blakey, T. N.. English for maritime studies. — Oxford : Pergamon, Nov.1982. — [192]p. — (Materials for language practice)
ISBN 0-08-028636-4 (pbk) : £4.95 : CIP entry B82-27836

428'.002465 — English language — *For business practices*

Pincott, Millie. English for business students / Millie Pincott. — 2nd ed. — London : Longman, 1982. — 142p ; 22cm
Previous ed.: 1973. — Includes index
ISBN 0-582-41261-7 (pbk) : £3.15 : CIP rev. B81-34324

Sandler, P. L.. Manage with English / P.L. Sandler, C.L. Stott. — Oxford : Oxford University Press, 1981. — 194p : ill,1map ; 25cm
Includes index
ISBN 0-19-451317-3 (pbk) : £3.00 B82-08578

Tuson, Jacqueline. Modern office English. — Cheltenham : Stanley Thornes, Aug.1982. — [192]p
ISBN 0-85950-345-3 (pbk) : £3.25 : CIP entry B82-16667

428'.02 — English language. Translation from Spanish language — *Manuals*

Translation strategies = Estrategias para traducción / by E. Brinton ... [et al.]. — London : Macmillan, 1981. — 193p ; 22cm
ISBN 0-333-32893-0 (pbk) : Unpriced
Also classified at 468'.02 B82-16153

428.1 — ENGLISH LANGUAGE USAGE. WORDS

428.1 — English language. Antonyms — *Illustrations — For children*

Woolcock, Peter. Big and small : a book of opposites / Peter Woolcock with Leonard Matthews. — London : Hodder and Stoughton, 1981. — [42]p : chiefly col.ill ; 31cm
ISBN 0-340-26647-3 : £2.50 : CIP rev. B81-23929

428.1 — English language. Pronunciation — *For non-English speaking students*

Hooke, Robert, *1929-*. A handbook of English pronunciation / Robert Hooke and Judith Rowell. — London : Edward Arnold, 1982. — xvi,248p : ill ; 23cm
English text, notes in various languages
ISBN 0-7131-8022-6 (pbk) : £3.50 : CIP rev. B81-20610

O'Connor, J. D.. Better English pronunciation / J.D. O'Connor. — 2nd ed. — Cambridge : Cambridge University Press, 1980 (1981 [printing]). — x,150p : ill ; 21cm
Previous ed.: 1967. — Bibliography: p147-148
ISBN 0-521-23152-3 (pbk) : £2.75 : CIP rev. B80-25509

Ponsonby, Mimi. How now, brown cow?. — Oxford : Pergamon, Dec.1981. — [128]p. — (English language courses)
ISBN 0-08-025354-7 (pbk) : £3.95 : CIP entry B81-31517

428.1 — English language. Pronunciation. Teaching

Baker, Ann. Introducing English pronunciation : a teacher's guide to Tree or three? and Ship or sheep? / Ann Baker. — Cambridge : Cambridge University Press, 1982. — 155p ; 23cm
ISBN 0-521-28580-1 (pbk) : £3.95 B82-36392

428.1 — English language. Sounds — *Questions & answers — For schools*

Williams, Ann, *1936-*. Sure-fire phonics / Ann Williams and Jim Rogerson ; illustrated by Oxford Illustrators Limited. — Exeter : Wheaton
Bk.1. — 1980 (1981 [printing]). — 30p : ill ; 25cm
Text and ill on inside covers
ISBN 0-08-024344-4 (pbk) : £0.75 B82-32259

Williams, Ann, *1936-*. Sure-fire phonics / Ann Williams and Jim Rogerson ; illustrated by Oxford Illustrators Limited. — Exeter : Wheaton
Bk.2. — 1980. — 30p : ill ; 25cm
ISBN 0-08-024345-2 (pbk) : £0.75 B82-32260

Williams, Ann, *1936-*. Sure-fire phonics / Ann Williams and Jim Rogerson ; illustrated by Oxford Illustrators Limited. — Exeter : Wheaton
Bk.3. — 1980. — 30p : ill ; 25cm
ISBN 0-08-024346-0 (pbk) : £0.75 B82-32261

428.1 — English language. Spelling — *Dictionaries*

Thornhill, Patrick. Spelling. — 2nd ed. — London : Teach Yourself Books, Oct.1982. — [288]p
Previous ed.: 1976
ISBN 0-340-28764-0 (pbk) : £2.45 : CIP entry B82-29647

428.1 — English language. Spelling — *For schools*

Thompson, Denys. Spelling and punctuating / Denys Thompson. — Oxford : Oxford University Press, 1981. — 79p ; 20cm
Includes index
ISBN 0-19-833162-2 (pbk) : £1.25 B82-15195

Wood, Elizabeth. Exercise your spelling. — London : Edward Arnold
Bk.1. — Dec.1981. — [50]p
ISBN 0-7131-0625-5 (pbk) : £0.50 : CIP entry B81-31538

428.1 — English language. Spelling — *Manuals*

Burt, A. M.. A guide to better spelling / A.M. Burt. — Cheltenham : Thornes, 1982. — vi,97p ; 19cm
ISBN 0-85950-343-7 (pbk) : £1.50 : CIP rev. B82-00312

428.1 — English language. Spelling — *Questions & answers — For children*

Cuff, Charles. 1st super spelling book : a basic spelling course / Charles Cuff with David Mackay ; illustrated by Chris Williamson. — Harlow : Longman, 1981. — 31p : ill ; 24cm
Cover title. — Text on inside covers
ISBN 0-582-39104-0 (pbk) : £0.70 B82-01275

Cuff, Charles. 2nd super spelling book : a basic spelling course / Charles Cuff with David Mackay ; illustrated by Chris Williamson. — Harlow : Longman, 1981. — 31p : ill ; 24cm
Cover title. — Text on inside covers
ISBN 0-582-39105-9 (pbk) : £0.70 B82-01273

Cuff, Charles. 3rd super spelling book : a basic spelling course / Charles Cuff with David Mackay ; illustrated by Chris Williamson. — Harlow : Longman, 1981. — 31p : ill ; 24cm
Cover title. — Text on inside covers
ISBN 0-582-39106-7 (pbk) : £0.70 B82-01274

Cuff, Charles. 4th super spelling book : a basic spelling course / Charles Cuff with David Mackay ; illustrated by Chris Williamson. — Harlow : Longman, 1981. — 31p : ill ; 24cm
Cover title. — Text on inside covers
ISBN 0-582-39107-5 (pbk) : £0.70 B82-01272

Cuff, Charles. 5th super spelling book : a basic spelling course / Charles Cuff with David Mackay ; illustrated by Chris Williamson. — Harlow : Longman, 1981. — 31p : ill ; 24cm
Cover title
ISBN 0-582-39108-3 (pbk) : £0.70 B82-14618

Cuff, Charles. 6th super spelling book : a basic spelling course / Charles Cuff with David Mackay ; illustrated by Chris Williamson. — Harlow : Longman, 1981. — 31p : ill ; 24cm
Cover title
ISBN 0-582-39109-1 (pbk) : £0.70 B82-14617

428.1 — English language. Spelling — *Questions & answers — For schools*

Cuff, Charles. Super spell : a basic spelling course / Charles Cuff with David Mackay ; illustrated by Chris Williamson. — Harlow : Longman, 1981. — 6v. : ill(some col.) ; 24cm
Cover title. — Text on inside covers
ISBN 0-582-19345-1 (pbk) : Unpriced
ISBN 0-582-19346-x (2) : £0.60
ISBN 0-582-19347-8 (3) : £0.60
ISBN 0-582-19348-6 (4) : £0.60
ISBN 0-582-19349-4 (5) : £0.60
ISBN 0-582-19350-8 (6) : £0.60 B82-05129

Hedley, John. Spelling practice / [John Hedley]. — Huddersfield : Schofield & Sims
2: Teacher's book : answers and additional tests. — 1980. — 24p ; 23cm
ISBN 0-7217-0384-4 (pbk) : £0.85 B82-15058

Lawley, A. H.. [How to spell and punctuate]. How to spell / by A.H. Lawley and Marian Lawley. — Slough : University Tutorial, 1962 (1982 [printing]). — vi,73p ; 18cm
ISBN 0-7231-0829-3 (pbk) : £1.05 B82-21308

Munro, Rona. Sounds for spelling / Rona Munro. — Welwyn : Nisbet
1. — 1982. — 24leaves : ill ; 28cm
Cover title. — Duplicating masters
ISBN 0-7202-1290-1 (pbk) : £7.95 B82-39899

Munro, Rona. Sounds for spelling / Rona Munro. — Welwyn : Nisbet
2. — 1982. — 24leaves : ill ; 28cm
Cover title. — Duplicating masters
ISBN 0-7202-1291-x (pbk) : £7.95 B82-39900

Sadler, Bernard R.. Spelling matters / Bernard R. Sadler. — London : Edward Arnold, 1982. — ix,150p : ill ; 22cm
ISBN 0-7131-0715-4 (pbk) : £1.95 B82-31517

White, Graham R.. Phonic spelling / Graham R. White. — Edinburgh : Oliver & Boyd
2. — 1979 (1981 [printing]). — 32p : ill(some col.) ; 25cm
ISBN 0-05-003174-0 (pbk) : £0.75 B82-02502

Wood, Elizabeth. Exercise your spelling. — London : Edward Arnold
Book 2. — Dec.1981. — [32]p
ISBN 0-7131-0626-3 (pbk) : £0.50 : CIP entry B81-31554

Wood, Elizabeth. Exercise your spelling. — London : Edward Arnold
Book 3. — Dec.1981. — [32]p
ISBN 0-7131-0627-1 (pbk) : £0.50 : CIP entry B81-31555

428.1 — English language. Vocabulary — *For non-English speaking students — For teaching*

Wallace, Michael J.. Teaching vocabulary. — London : Heinemann Educational, Aug.1982. — [144]p. — (Practical language teaching ; no.10)
ISBN 0-435-28974-8 (pbk) : £2.50 : CIP entry B82-15793

428.1 — English language. Words — *For children*

Allington, Richard. Words. — Oxford : Blackwell Raintree, Nov.1982. — [32]p. — (Beginning to learn about)
ISBN 0-86256-056-x : £2.95 : CIP entry B82-26068

428.1 — English language. Words — *For pre-school children*

East, Helen. Word book / by Helen East ; illustrated by Corinne Burrows. — London : Macdonald, 1982. — [19]p : col.ill ; 21cm. — (Macdonald 345)
ISBN 0-356-07827-2 : £1.75 B82-35130

428.1 — English language. Words — *For schools*

Foster, John, *1929-*. Words in action. — London : Macmillan Education, Jan.1983. — [64]p
ISBN 0-333-34274-7 (pbk) : £1.95 : CIP entry B82-33725

428.1 — English language. Words. Length. Analysis. Applications of statistical mathematics — *Questions & answers — For schools*

Authors anonymous / [Schools Council Project on Statistical Education]. — Slough : Published for the Schools Council by Foulsham Educational, 1981. — 16p + teachers' notes (32p ; 21cm) : ill ; 21cm. — (Statistics in your world)
ISBN 0-572-01073-7 (pbk) : Unpriced
ISBN 0-572-01100-8 (teachers' notes) : Unpriced
Also classified at 428.2 B82-13022

428.1 — English language. Words — *Lists — For children*

Matthews, Betty, *1931-*. Talk and write / Betty Matthews ; illustrated by Trevor Stubley. — Huddersfield : Schofield & Sims, c1982. — [48]p : col.ill ; 30cm
ISBN 0-7217-0429-8 (pbk) : £1.75
ISBN 0-7217-0430-1 (net ed.) : £2.35 B82-34025

428.1 — English language. Words — *Questions & answers — For Irish students*

Jennings, Barry. Work with words / Barry Jennings ; [illustrations Jon Donohoe]. — Dublin : Educational Company
1. — 1981. — 68p : ill ; 21cm
Unpriced (pbk) B82-02556

428.1 — English language. Words — *Questions & answers — For schools*

Brandling, Redvers. Using words well. — London : Edward Arnold, Feb.1983. — [64]p
ISBN 0-7131-0816-9 (pbk) : £2.00 : CIP entry B82-39441

428.1 — English language. Words. Usage — *Questions & answers*

Wenborn, Neil. Wordpower / Neil Wenborn. — London : Corgi, 1982, c1981. — 128p ; 18cm
Originally published: London : Kogan Page, 1981
ISBN 0-552-11879-6 (pbk) : £1.00 B82-18692

428.1 — Schools. Students, 7-11 years. Spelling skills. Assessment. Diagnostic Spelling Test

Vincent, Denis. Diagnostic spelling test / Denis Vincent, Jenny Claydon. — Windsor : NFER-Nelson, c1982. — 3v. : 2forms ; 30cm
ISBN 0-7005-0417-6 : Unpriced
ISBN 0-7005-0415-x (form A) : (Sold in packs of 25) £4.25
ISBN 0-7005-0416-8 (form A) : (Sold in packs of 25) £4.25 B82-25464

428.1'022'2 — English language. Words — *For children — Illustrations*

Fredman, Alan. The new gold medal book of more! words / illustrated by Alan Fredman. — London : Dean, c1981. — 43p : chiefly col.ill ; 27cm
ISBN 0-603-00255-2 : Unpriced B82-26124

Henderson, John, *19---*. Picture book one / by John Henderson & Glynis Murray. — London : Macmillan Children's, 1981. — [14]p : chiefly col.ill ; 22cm. — (Picture board books)
Cover title
ISBN 0-333-32363-7 : £0.99 B82-05972

Kikine, Seymour. First word book / compiled by Seymour Kikine ; designed and illustrated by Hurlston Design Ltd. — Loughborough : Ladybird, c1982. — 51p : chiefly col.ill ; 18cm. — (Sunbird)
ISBN 0-7214-8104-3 : Unpriced B82-37067

Little one's book of words / illustrated by Alan Fredman. — London : Dean, c1982. — [12]p : col.ill ; 21cm. — (A Dean board book)
ISBN 0-603-00313-3 (unbound) : £0.65
B82-36558

Matthews, Leonard. ABC : a book of words / Leonard Matthews and Peter Woolcock. — London : Hodder and Stoughton, 1982. — [42]p : col.ill ; 31cm
ISBN 0-340-28187-1 : £2.50 : CIP rev.
B82-10685

Scarry, Richard. Colours / Richard Scarry. — London : Collins, 1982. — [28]p : col.ill ; 9cm
Cover title. — Adaptation of: Richard Scarry's best first book ever
ISBN 0-00-138336-1 : £1.00 B82-31939

Scarry, Richard. [Lowly Worm word book]. Words / Richard Scarry. — London : Collins, 1982. — [28]p : col.ill ; 9cm
Cover title. — Originally published: New York : Random House, 1981
ISBN 0-00-138337-x : £1.00 B82-31940

428.1'076 — English language. Vocabulary — *Questions & answers — For non-English speaking students*

Bennett, S. M.. The topic dictionary : English words and idioms / S.M. Bennett and T.G. van Veen ; illustrated by Jan Sanders. — Walton-on-Thames : Nelson, c1981. — 160p : ill ; 19x25cm
Includes index
ISBN 0-17-555331-9 (pbk) : £2.95 B82-10032

Berman, Michael, *1951-*. Playing and working with words / Michael Berman. — Oxford : Pergamon, 1981. — viii,96p : facsims ; 25cm. — (Materials for language practice) (Pergamon Institute of English (Oxford))
ISBN 0-08-025352-0 (pbk) : £1.95 : CIP rev.
B81-04266

The **Words** you need / B. Rudzka ... [et al.]. — London : Macmillan, 1981. — iv,211p : ill,1map ; 25cm + Teacher's book(68p : ill ; 22cm)
Includes index
ISBN 0-333-27829-1 (pbk) : Unpriced
ISBN 0-333-28150-0 (Teacher's bk) : Unpriced
B82-10188

428.1'076 — English language. Vocabulary — *Questions & answers — For schools*

Berman, Michael, *1951-*. Key to Playing with words & Playing and working with words / by Michael Berman. — Oxford : Pergamon Press, 1981. — iii,16p ; 25cm. — (Materials for language practice)
ISBN 0-08-025353-9 (unbound) : £1.00 : CIP rev. B81-03813

Berman, Michael, *1951-*. Playing with words : exercises in increasing word power / Michael Berman. — Oxford : Pergamon Press, 1981. — vii,43p : ill ; 25cm. — (Materials for language practice)
ISBN 0-08-025351-2 (pbk) : £1.50 : CIP rev.
B81-04265

428.2 — ENGLISH LANGUAGE USAGE. GRAMMAR

428.2 — English language. Comprehension — *For slow-learning adolescents — For schools*

Hutchinson, Lynn. Which word? : graded cloze texts and comprehensive exercises / Lynn Hutchinson. — London : Hodder and Stoughton, c1981. — iv,60p ; 25cm
ISBN 0-340-27001-2 (pbk) : £0.95 : CIP rev.
B81-21584

428.2 — English language. Comprehension — *Questions & answers*

Jackson, Lionel. Message and medium : a course in critical reading / Lionel Jackson, Mary Jackson. — London : Hodder and Stoughton, 1981. — 171p ; 22cm
ISBN 0-340-26903-0 (pbk) : Unpriced : CIP rev. B81-20518

Presley, John W.. Essential reading skills / John W. Presley, William M. Dodd. — New York ; London : Holt, Rinehart and Winston, c1982. — xii,355p : forms ; 24cm
ISBN 0-03-058001-3 (pbk) : £6.85 B82-23313

428.2 — English language. Comprehension — *Questions & answers — For schools*

Cooper, John, *1928-*. More directions : reading, reference & study skills / John Cooper. — Edinburgh : Oliver & Boyd
Text on inside covers
1. — c1982. — 80p : ill,1map ; 25cm
ISBN 0-05-003498-7 (pbk) : £1.60 B82-39922

Developing comprehension / [edited by] Alan Lynskey, Margaret Stillie. — Oxford : Basil Blackwell
Blue book. — 1982. — 47p : ill ; 23cm
ISBN 0-631-91530-3 (pbk) : Unpriced
B82-35300

Developing comprehension / [edited by] Alan Lynskey, Margaret Stillie. — Oxford : Basil Blackwell
Green book. — 1982. — 47p ; 23cm
ISBN 0-631-91550-8 (pbk) : Unpriced
B82-35298

Developing comprehension / [edited by] Alan Lynskey, Margaret Stillie. — Oxford : Basil Blackwell
Orange book. — 1982. — 47p : ill ; 23cm
ISBN 0-631-91560-5 (pbk) : Unpriced
B82-35299

Developing comprehension / [edited by] Alan Lynskey, Margaret Stillie. — Oxford : Basil Blackwell
Red book. — 1982. — 47p : ill ; 23cm
ISBN 0-631-91540-0 (pbk) : Unpriced
B82-35301

Edwards, E. H.. Comprehension skills / E.H. Edwards. — South Melbourne ; London : Macmillan, 1981 (1982 [printing]). — vi,166p : ill ; 22cm
ISBN 0-333-33770-0 (pbk) : Unpriced
B82-35074

Finn, F. E. S.. In your own words : practice in summary, comprehension and composition / F.E.S. Finn. — [London] : J. Murray, c1981. — xi,84p : ill ; 22cm
ISBN 0-7195-3878-5 (pbk) : £1.10 : CIP rev.
Also classified at 808'.042'076 B81-27405

Finn, F. E. S.. In your own words : practice in summary, comprehension and composition / F.E.S. Finn. — [London] : J. Murray
[Teachers' book]. — c1981. — xi,84p : ill ; 22cm
ISBN 0-7195-3879-3 (pbk) : £1.50 : CIP rev.
Also classified at 808'.042'076 B81-27408

Gilfeather, Sandra. What's that you're reading? / Sandra Gilfeather. — London : Edward Arnold, 1982. — 32p : ill ; 25cm
ISBN 0-7131-0647-6 (pbk) : Unpriced : CIP rev. B82-01187

Jackson, Lionel. Message and medium : suggested answers / Lionel and Mary Jackson. — [London] : Hodder and Stoughton, 1982. — 44p ; 22cm
ISBN 0-340-26904-9 (unbound) : Unpriced : CIP rev. B82-05391

John, Roland. Reading comprehension passages / John Roland. — London : Collins
Answer book. — 1982. — 60p ; 21cm
£0.95 (pbk) B82-33639

Kerr, Betty. Check up tests in English comprehension / Betty Kerr. — London : Macmillan, 1980. — 48p : ill ; 26cm. — (Check up tests series)
ISBN 0-333-28863-7 (pbk) : Unpriced
B82-15235

Ní Eoghusa, Máire. Begin with words / Máire Ní Eoghusa. — Dublin : Educational Company
2. — 1982. — 43p : ill ; 30cm
Unpriced (pbk) B82-25398

Noble, James. Interpretation practice / James Noble & Alex French. — Edinburgh : Oliver & Boyd, c1982. — 63p ; 24cm
ISBN 0-05-003464-2 (pbk) : Unpriced
B82-20124

Owen, Christopher, *1939-*. English workshop / Christopher Owen, Andrew Carter. — London : Hodder and Stoughton
3. — 1980. — 185p : ill,forms ; 25cm
ISBN 0-340-24297-3 (pbk) : £2.50 : CIP rev.
B80-04750

Proud, Alan. Improve your comprehension / Alan Proud. — London : Edward Arnold, 1981. — vii,95p : ill ; 25cm
ISBN 0-7131-0584-4 (pbk) : £2.40 : CIP rev.
B81-22453

Reading with purpose. — Walton-on-Thames : Nelson
5 / [compiled by] Christopher Walker. — 1981. — 96p : ill(some col.),maps(some col.),facsims,2ports ; 25cm
ISBN 0-17-422455-9 (pbk) : £1.75 B82-02436

Ridgway, Bill. Newsmakers / Bill Ridgway ; illustrations by Brian Lythgoe. — London : Edward Arnold
1. — 1981. — 96p : ill ; 22cm
Includes index
ISBN 0-7131-0564-x (pbk) : £1.60 : CIP rev.
B81-23747

Ridgway, Bill. Newsmakers / Bill Ridgway ; illustrations by Brian Lythgoe. — London : Edward Arnold
2. — 1981. — 96p : ill ; 22cm
Includes index
ISBN 0-7131-0565-8 (pbk) : £1.60 : CIP rev.
B81-23748

Seely, John. Oxford secondary English / John Seely and Frank Ash, Frank Green, Chris Woodhead. — Oxford : Oxford University Press
Book 3. — 1982. — 188p : ill ; 25cm
ISBN 0-19-831137-0 (pbk) : £2.50
ISBN 0-19-831138-9 (Teacher's book) : Unpriced B82-20438

Tarbitt, Brian. Read and respond / Brian Tarbitt. — Edinburgh : Holmes McDougall, c1981. — 4v. : ill,1map,ports ; 22cm
ISBN 0-7157-2025-2 (pbk) : Unpriced
ISBN 0-7157-2026-0 (v.2) : £0.95
ISBN 0-7157-2027-9 (v.3) : £0.95
ISBN 0-7157-2028-7 (v.4) : £0.95 B82-24888

Taylor, Boswell. First English / Boswell Taylor. — London : Hodder and Stoughton
3 / illustrated by Margaret Chamberlain and Geraldine Spence. — 1981. — 94p : ill(some col.) ; 25cm
ISBN 0-340-26225-7 : Unpriced : CIP rev.
B81-30210

428.2 — English language. Comprehension — *Questions & answers — For schools*
continuation

Walker, Christopher, *1934-*. Reading with purpose / Christopher Walker. — Walton-on-Thames : Nelson, 1982
ISBN 0-17-422462-1 (pbk) : £1.30 B82-31689

Walker, Christopher, *1934-*. Reading with purpose / Christopher Walker. — Walton-on-Thames : Nelson
Teacher's guide. — 1981. — 28p ; 22cm
Cover title. — Text on inside covers
ISBN 0-17-422461-3 (pbk) : Unpriced
B82-29960

Williams, Eric. Secrets : introductory exercises in inferential comprehension. — London : Edward Arnold, July 1982. — [48]p
ISBN 0-7131-0696-4 (pbk) : £1.95 : CIP entry
B82-14381

Williams, Eric. What do you think? : introductory exercises in inferential comprehension. — London : Edward Arnold, July 1982. — [48]p
ISBN 0-7131-0695-6 (pbk) : £1.95 : CIP entry
B82-13013

428.2 — English language. Comprehension. Special subjects: Energy — *Questions & answers — For schools*

Scott, Roger, *1942-*. Energy / Roger Scott. — Harlow : Longman, 1981. — 28p : ill ; 24cm. — (Longman integrated comprehension and composition series. Stage 3 : non-fiction)
ISBN 0-582-55332-6 (pbk) : £0.80 B82-08913

428.2 — English language. Grammar

Burton, S. H.. Mastering English language / S.H. Burton. — [London] : Macmillan, 1982. — 172p : ill ; 23cm. — (Macmillan master series)
ISBN 0-333-31290-2 (cased) : £6.95
ISBN 0-333-31032-2 (pbk) : Unpriced
B82-17111

Herman, William. The portable English handbook : an index to grammar, usage and the research paper / William Herman. — 2nd ed. — New York ; London : Holt, Rinehart and Winston, c1982. — xiii,446p : ill,forms ; 19cm
Previous ed.: 1978. — Text on inside covers. — Includes index
ISBN 0-03-591212-x (pbk) : £6.95 B82-23308

Kolln, Martha. Understanding English grammar / Martha Kolln. — London : Macmillan, c1982. — xiii,352p ; 24cm
Includes index
ISBN 0-02-365850-9 : £6.95 B82-26290

Sparkes, Ray. Grammar without groans : an informal guide to common English usage / Ray Sparkes. — Chichester : Packard, 1981. — 48p ; 21cm
ISBN 0-906527-13-9 (pbk) : Unpriced
B82-08124

428.2 — English language. Grammar — *Questions & answers*

Herman, William. The portable English workbook / William Herman. — New York ; London : Holt, Rinehart and Winston, c1982. — ix,361p : forms ; 24cm
ISBN 0-03-059423-5 (pbk) : £6.50 B82-23307

Sullivan, Tony. Grammar / by Tony Sullivan. — Cambridge : National Extension College, 1979. — 54p ; 21cm. — (Study skills series) (National Extension College course ; no.ED20)
ISBN 0-86082-167-6 (pbk) : Unpriced
B82-40822

428.2 — English language. Grammar — *Questions & answers — For schools*

Davis, John, *19---*. Handling language / John Davis ; illustrations by Graham Humphreys and John Davis. — London : Hutchinson
Bk.2. — London : Hutchinson. — 60p : col.ill ; 24cm
ISBN 0-09-147381-0 (pbk) : Unpriced : CIP rev.
B82-04124

428.2 — English language. Sentences. Length. Analysis. Applications of statistical mathematics — *Questions & answers — For schools*

Authors anonymous / [Schools Council Project on Statistical Education]. — Slough : Published for the Schools Council by Foulsham Educational, 1981. — 16p + teachers' notes (32p ; 21cm) : ill ; 21cm. — (Statistics in your world)
ISBN 0-572-01073-7 (pbk) : Unpriced
ISBN 0-572-01100-8 (teachers' notes) : Unpriced
Primary classification 428.1 B82-13022

428.2 — English language. Vowels — *For schools*

Rogers, Jane. Vowel crowd / Jane Rogers and Jeremy Long. — London : Heinemann Educational
Bk.2. — 1980. — 46p : ill ; 21x30cm
ISBN 0-435-10764-x (pbk) : £0.75 : CIP rev.
B80-12325

Rogers, Jane. The vowel crowd / Jane Rogers and Jeremy Long. — London : Heinemann Educational
[Book 3]. — 1982. — 29p : chiefly ill ; 21x30cm
Text, ill on inside covers
ISBN 0-435-10766-6 (pbk) : £0.75 B82-22633

Rogers, Jane. The vowel crowd / Jane Rogers and Jeremy Long. — London : Heinemann Educational
Bk.3
Notes to the teacher. — 1982. — [55]p : ill ; 22cm
ISBN 0-435-10765-8 (pbk) : £2.50 B82-22276

428.24 — ENGLISH LANGUAGE. FOR FOREIGN STUDENTS

428.2'4 — English language. American usage — *For non-English speaking students*

Ford, Carol. Cultural encounters. — Oxford : Pergamon, Feb.1983. — [80]p
ISBN 0-08-029444-8 (pbk) : £1.95 : CIP entry
Also classified at 427'.9'41 B82-36466

428.2'4 — English language. Common nouns — *Questions & answers — For non-English speaking students*

Stone, Linton. Count and mass nouns / Linton Stone. — London : Harrap, 1982. — 44p ; 22cm. — (Contemporary grammar units ; 4)
ISBN 0-245-53789-9 (pbk) : £1.25 B82-32399

428.2'4 — English language. Comprehension — *Questions & answers — For Caribbean students*

Insights : an anthology of short stories / edited by Roy and Clifford Narinesingh. — Walton-on-Thames : Nelson, 1980. — vi,170p ; 22cm
ISBN 0-17-566275-4 (pbk) : £1.75 B82-16321

Narinesingh, Roy. Comprehension skills for the Caribbean / adapted by Roy Narinesingh from Once a week comprehension. — [Aylesbury] : Caribbean Universities Press
1. — 1980 (1981 [printing]). — 64p ; 21cm
ISBN 0-602-22517-5 (pbk) : Unpriced
B82-40397

Narinesingh, Roy. Comprehension skills for the Caribbean / adapted by Roy Narinesingh from Once a week comprehension. — [Aylesbury] : Caribbean Universities Press
2. — 1980 (1981 [printing]). — 64p ; 21cm
ISBN 0-602-22518-3 (pbk) : Unpriced
B82-40398

Rowe, Brian. Multiple choice questions for CXC English / Brian Rowe, Ralph Boyce. — London : Hodder and Stoughton
Basic. — 1982. — 60p ; 22cm
ISBN 0-340-27028-4 (pbk) : £1.25 : CIP rev.
B81-34649

Rowe, Brian. Multiple choice questions for CXC English / Brian Rowe, Ralph Boyce. — London : Hodder and Stoughton
General. — 1982. — 62p ; 22cm
ISBN 0-340-27029-2 (pbk) : £1.25 : CIP rev.
B81-34653

428.2'4 — English language. Comprehension — *Questions & answers — For non-English speaking students*

Dunlop, Ian, *1925 Nov.8-*. Matters of moment / by Ian Dunlop and Heinrich Schrand ; edited by G.M. Matthews. — Oxford : Pergamon, 1980. — x,84p : ill,1map,facsims,ports
Translation of: Konversationskurs Englisch. — Available as cassette
ISBN 0-08-024568-4 (pbk) : £1.95 : CIP rev.
B79-27331

Dunlop, Ian, *1925 Nov.8-*. Read and reply : comprehension and conversation / Ian Dunlop, Heinrich Schrand. — Amersham : Hulton Educational
Book 1. — 1982, c1980. — 91p : ill,1map,1plan ; 21cm
ISBN 0-7175-1008-5 (pbk) : £1.95 B82-28785

Dunlop, Ian, *1925 Nov.8-*. Read and reply : comprehension and conversation / Ian Dunlop, Heinrich Schrand. — Amersham : Hulton Educational
Book 2. — 1982, c1980. — 95p : ill,1map,1facsim ; 21cm
ISBN 0-7175-1009-3 (pbk) : £1.95 B82-28786

Dunlop, Ian, *1925 Nov.8-*. Read and reply : comprehension and conversation / Ian Dunlop, Heinrich Schrand. — Amersham : Hulton Educational
Bk.3. — 1982. — 96p : ill,facsims ; 21cm
ISBN 0-7175-1010-7 (pbk) : £1.95 B82-34834

Exploring functions. — Oxford : Oxford University Press
Teacher's ed. — 1979 (1980 [printing]). — xxi,170p : ill(some col.),2maps ; 25cm. — (Reading and thinking in English)
ISBN 0-19-451354-8 (pbk) : £3.50 B82-13816

Flowerdew, Phyllis. Reading to some purpose. — 2nd ed. — Edinburgh : Oliver & Boyd
Book 1 / Phyllis Flowerdew and Ronald Ridout. — 1981. — 32p : ill(some col.) ; 21cm
Previous ed.: 1952
ISBN 0-05-003469-3 (pbk) : £0.75 B82-14442

Flowerdew, Phyllis. Reading to some purpose. — 2nd ed. — Edinburgh : Oliver & Boyd
Book 2 / Phyllis Flowerdew and Ronald Ridout. — 1982. — 32p : ill(some col.) ; 21cm
Previous ed.: 1952
ISBN 0-05-003470-7 (pbk) : £0.75 B82-14443

Flowerdew, Phyllis. Reading to some purpose. — 2nd ed. — Edinburgh : Oliver & Boyd
Book 3 / Phyllis Flowerdew and Ronald Ridout. — 1982. — 48p : ill(some col.) ; 21cm
Previous ed.: 1953
ISBN 0-05-003471-5 (pbk) : £0.85 B82-14444

Flowerdew, Phyllis. Reading to some purpose. — 2nd ed. — Edinburgh : Oliver & Boyd
Book 4 / Phyllis Flowerdew and Ronald Ridout. — 1982. — 48p : ill(some col.) ; 21cm
Previous ed.: 1953
ISBN 0-05-003472-3 (pbk) : £0.85 B82-14445

Flowerdew, Phyllis. Reading to some purpose. — Edinburgh : Oliver & Boyd
Bk.5 / Phyllis Flowerdew and Ronald Ridout. — 2nd ed. — 1982. — 96p : ill ; 21cm
Previous ed.: 1954
ISBN 0-05-003473-1 (pbk) : £1.20 B82-21794

Flowerdew, Phyllis. Reading to some purpose. — Edinburgh : Oliver & Boyd
Bk.6 / Phyllis Flowerdew and Ronald Ridout. — 2nd ed. — 1982. — 96p : ill,maps,1plan,2forms ; 21cm
Previous ed.: 1957
ISBN 0-05-003474-x (pbk) : Unpriced
B82-20123

Flowerdew, Phyllis. Reading to some purpose. — 2nd ed. — Edinburgh : Oliver & Boyd
Bk.7 / Ronald Ridout. — 1982. — 94p : ill ; 21cm
Previous ed.: 1959
ISBN 0-05-003475-8 (pbk) : Unpriced
B82-35833

428.2'4 — English language. Comprehension — *Questions & answers — For non-English speaking students* *continuation*

Grellet, Françoise. Developing reading skills. — Cambridge : Cambridge University Press, Oct.1981. — [256]p
ISBN 0-521-28364-7 (pbk) : £5.50 : CIP entry
B81-31951

Heath, R. B. (Ray Brian). Longman English / R.B. Heath, T. McSweeney. — Harlow : Longman, 1982. — 180p : ill ; 24cm
Includes index
ISBN 0-582-22184-6 (pbk) : £2.75 B82-21784

Menné, Saxon. First certificate skills / Saxon Menné. — Oxford : Oxford University Press, 1982. — 128p : ill,maps,ports ; 20x21cm + Teachers ed.(128T : ill,maps,ports ; 20x21cm)
ISBN 0-19-453273-9 (pbk) : £2.95
ISBN 0-19-453274-7 (Teacher's ed.) : £4.00
B82-21680

Moller, Alan. Cloze in class : exercises in developing reading comprehension skills / Alan Moller and Valerie Whiteson. — Oxford : Pergamon. — (Materials for language practice)
Teacher's booklet. — 1981. — vii,32p ; 25cm
ISBN 0-08-027268-1 (pbk) : £1.00 : CIP rev.
B81-13846

Moller, Alan. Cloze in class : exercises in developing reading comprehension skills / Alan Moller and Valerie Whiteson. — Oxford : Pergamon
Workbook. — 1981. — ix,56p : ill,1map ; 25cm
ISBN 0-08-025350-4 (pbk) : Unpriced : CIP rev. B81-13454

Pint, John. Pint's passages : telephone talk and other passages. — Oxford : Pergamon. — (Materials for language practice)
Vol.2. — July 1982. — [96]p
ISBN 0-08-028621-6 (pbk) : £2.95 : CIP entry
B82-20747

Selman, Libby. Think it out / by Libby Selman. — Leeds : E.J. Arnold, c1982. — 64p : ill ; 23cm
ISBN 0-560-01039-7 (pbk) : Unpriced
B82-36785

Sim, D. D.. Reading comprehension course : selected strategies / D.D. Sim, B. Laufer-Dvorkin. — [Glasgow] : Collins ELT, 1982. — 96p : ill ; 26cm. — (Collins study skills in English)
ISBN 0-00-370005-4 (spiral) : £3.40
B82-39406

Skills for learning. — Walton-on-Thames : Nelson
Reading projects : science. — International ed. — 1981. — 220p : ill,1chart ; 25cm + Teacher's book(x,118p : ill ; 22cm)
ISBN 0-17-580094-4 (pbk) : Unpriced
ISBN 0-17-580095-2 (Teacher's bk.) : Unpriced
B82-29956

428.2'4 — English language. Comprehension. Special subjects: Electric lighting & household electric heating equipment — *Questions & answers — For non-English speaking students*

Cook, Norman, *1941-*. Electric lighting and heating / Norman Cook and Chris Ttofi. — London : Macmillan, 1980. — iv,68p : ill ; 19cm. — (Base books)
ISBN 0-333-25436-8 (pbk) : Unpriced
B82-08058

428.2'4 — English language. Comprehension. Special subjects: Medicine — *Questions & answers — For non-English speaking students*

Beitler, Lorraine. English for the medical professions / Lorraine Beitler, Barbara McDonald. — New York ; London : McGraw-Hill, c1982. — 251p : ill ; 23cm. — (Instrumental English)
ISBN 0-07-004521-6 (pbk) : £5.25 B82-24417

428.2'4 — English language. Conditional clauses — *Questions & answers — For non-English speaking students*

Robinson, Colin, *1929-*. Conditional sentences / Colin Robinson. — London : Harrap, 1982. — 48p ; 22cm. — (Contemporary grammar units ; 3)
ISBN 0-245-53788-0 (pbk) : £1.25 B82-32398

428.2'4 — English language — *For Caribbean students*

Borely, Clive. English for CXC / Clive Borely, Hazel Simmons. — Walton-on-Thames : Nelson Caribbean, 1981. — 185p : ill,1plan ; 22cm
ISBN 0-17-566301-7 (pbk) : £2.75 B82-21230

Exploring English : in the Caribbean. — London : Macmillan
Bk.1 / Ian Gordon, Desmond Clarke. — 1981. — ix,198p : ill ; 25cm
ISBN 0-333-30045-9 (pbk) : Unpriced
B82-10194

Jones, Rhodri. New English for the Caribbean. — London : Heinemann Educational
Bk.3 / by Rhodri Jones and Rosalind Wilson. — 1981. — viii,151p : ill ; 25cm
Based on New English. 3rd / Rhodri Jones. 1979. — Includes index
ISBN 0-435-10488-8 (pbk) : £2.60 B82-06292

428.2'4 — English language — *For non-English speaking pre-school children*

Schmid-Schönbein, Gisela. English for Mopsy and me / Gisela Schmid-Schönbein, Leonora Fröhlich-Ward, Heide Feder ; drawings by Elle Krings. — Oxford : Pergamon. — (English language courses)
Teacher's book 1. — 1981, c1978. — xv,112p : ill,music ; 25cm
ISBN 0-08-027226-6 (pbk) : £2.25 : CIP rev.
B81-25853

Schmid-Schönbein, Gisela. English for Mopsy and me / Gisela Schmid-Schönbein, Leonora Fröhlich-Ward, Heide Feder ; drawings by Elle Krings. — Oxford : Pergamon. — (English language courses)
Teacher's book 2. — 1981, c1978. — xv,84p ; 25cm
ISBN 0-08-027229-0 (pbk) : £2.25 : CIP rev.
B81-25850

428.2'4 — English language — *For non-English speaking students*

Abbs, Brian. Brian Abbs' and Anne Worrall's jigsaw one. — London : M. Glasgow
Activity books (single volume). — [1979] ([1980 printing]). — 80p in various pagings : col.ill ; 30cm
Cover title. — Contains activity books 1-5
ISBN 0-86158-201-2 (pbk) : Unpriced
ISBN 0-86158-213-6 (1)
ISBN 0-86158-214-4 (2)
ISBN 0-86458-215-2 (3)
ISBN 0-86158-216-0 (4)
ISBN 0-86158-217-9 (5) B82-07482

Abbs, Brian. Brian Abbs' and Anne Worrall's jigsaw one. — London : M. Glasgow
Readers (single volume). — [1979] ([1980 printing]). — 80p in various pagings : col.ill ; 30cm
Cover title. — Contains Readers 1-5
ISBN 0-86158-200-4 (pbk) : Unpriced
ISBN 0-86158-208-x (1)
ISBN 0-86158-209-8 (2)
ISBN 0-86458-210-1 (3)
ISBN 0-86158-211-x (4)
ISBN 0-86158-212-8 (5) B82-07481

Abbs, Brian. Brian Abbs' and Anne Worrall's jigsaw one. — London : M. Glasgow
Teacher's guide. — [1979] ([1981 printing]). — 80p : ill ; 30cm
ISBN 0-86158-206-3 (pbk) : Unpriced
B82-07483

Barr, Vivien. Topics and skills in English. — London : Hodder and Stoughton, Jan.1983. — [80]p
ISBN 0-340-28709-8 (pbk) : £2.25 : CIP entry
B82-37471

Brookes, N. F.. Andy and Anna. — Oxford : Pergamon, May 1982. — (Pergamon English course for young learners)
Teachers' guide. — [48]p
ISBN 0-08-025342-3 (pbk) : £1.50 : CIP entry
B82-11271

Bywater, F. V.. A proficiency course in English with key. — London : Hodder and Stoughton, Sept.1982. — [256]p
Originally published: London : University of London Press, 1969
ISBN 0-340-28628-8 (pbk) : £3.25 : CIP entry
B82-20628

Chapman, John, *19---*. Adult English / John Chapman. — Englewood Cliffs ; London : Prentice-Hall, c1978. — 3v.(ix,549p) : ill ; 28cm
ISBN 0-13-008821-8 (pbk) : Unpriced
ISBN 0-13-008839-0 (V.2) : £6.70
ISBN 0-13-008862-5 (v.3) : £6.70 B82-13450

Contemporary English / R. Rossner ... [et al.. — London : Macmillan
Pupil's book 5: Intermediate. — 1982. — iv,98p : ill,maps,forms,1port ; 25cm
ISBN 0-333-32461-7 (pbk) : Unpriced
B82-19320

Contemporary English / R. Rossner ... [et al.]. — London : Macmillan
Teacher's book for pupil book 5, intermediate. — 1982. — xi,50p ; 22cm
ISBN 0-333-32463-3 (pbk) : Unpriced
B82-23374

Cox, Geoffrey, *1944-*. O-level English for overseas candidates / by Geoffrey Cox. — London : Macmillan, 1981. — 68p ; 25cm
ISBN 0-333-32379-3 (pbk) : Unpriced
B82-18945

Gray, Joanna. Discovering English. — London : Cassell. — (Cassell's foundation English ; 2)
Teacher's book. — Dec.1981. — [72]p
ISBN 0-304-30670-3 (pbk) : £3.95 : CIP entry
B81-36988

Hartley, Bernard. Streamline English / Bernard Hartley & Peter Viney. — Oxford : Oxford University Press
Destinations : an intensive English course for intermediate students. — [Teacher's ed.]. — 1982. — 16,179p : ill(some col.),facsims,maps (some col.),ports(some col.) ; 30cm
ISBN 0-19-432242-4 (spiral) : Unpriced
B82-35996

Hartley, Bernard. Streamline English : destinations : an intensive English course for intermediate students / Bernard Hartley & Peter Viney. — Oxford : Oxford University Press
[Student's ed.]. — 1982. — [96]p : ill(some col.),facsims(some col.),1form,maps(some col.),plans ; 30cm
ISBN 0-19-432241-6 (pbk) : £2.95 B82-28188

Kernel one. — Harlow : Longman
Workbook / Muriel Higgins, Robert O'Neill. — 1982. — 58p : ill ; 25cm
ISBN 0-582-51658-7 (pbk) : £0.90 B82-21792

Kernel two. — Harlow : Longman, 1982
Teachers book / Robert O'Neill with contributions from Claire Woolford ... [et al.]. — xviii,238p : ill ; 25cm
ISBN 0-582-51640-4 (pbk) : Unpriced
B82-36490

Matreyek, Walter. Communicating in English : examples and models. — Oxford : Pergamon. — (Materials for language practice)
1: Interpersonal functions. — Jan.1983. — [128]p
ISBN 0-08-028616-x (pbk) : £2.95 : CIP entry
B82-33614

Matreyek, Walter. Communicating in English : examples and models. — Oxford : Pergamon. — (Materials for language practice)
2: Semantic dimensions. — Jan.1983. — [128]p
ISBN 0-08-028618-6 (pbk) : £2.95 : CIP entry
B82-33615

428.2′4 — English language — *For non-English speaking students* *continuation*

Matreyek, Walter. Communicating in English : examples and models. — Oxford : Pergamon. — (Materials for language practice)
3: Conversation techniques, topics and situations. — Jan.1983. — [128]p
ISBN 0-08-028617-8 (pbk) : £2.95 : CIP entry
B82-33616

O'Neill, Robert. AKL : beginning / Robert O'Neill, Larry Anger and Karen Davy. — [New York] : [Longman] ; [Harlow] : [Distributed by Longman]. — (Longman American English)
Students book. — [1981]. — 131p : ill,forms ; 26cm
Cover title. — Includes index
ISBN 0-582-79734-9 (pbk) : £2.60 B82-12360

O'Neill, Robert. AKL : beginning / Robert O'Neill, Larry Anger and Karen Davy. — [New York] : [Longman] ; [Harlow] : [distributed by Longman]
Teacher's manual. — 1981. — viii,180p : ill ; 26cm. — (Longman American English)
Includes index
ISBN 0-582-79779-9 (pbk) : £2.75 B82-22966

O'Neill, Robert. Kernel two / Robert O'Neill. — Harlow : Longman
Students' book / with listening practice contributions by Claire Woolford. — 1982. — 123p : ill,maps ; 25cm
ISBN 0-582-51642-0 (pbk) : £2.35 B82-24051

Pettigrew, Jane. Destination UK : survival skills in English / Jane Pettigrew and Shelagh Rixon. — London : Harrap
Teacher's handbook. — 1982. — xvi,64p : ill ; 22cm
ISBN 0-245-53707-4 (pbk) : £2.50 B82-27837

Robinson, Colin, *1929-*. Learn English / Colin Robinson ; illustrations John McClafferty. — London, Hamilton
Bk.3. — 1980. — xi,285p : ill ; 22cm
Includes index
ISBN 0-241-10186-7 (pbk) : £2.50 : CIP rev.
B79-34103

Romijn, Elizabeth. Live action English / by Elizabeth Romijn & Contee Seely. — 2nd ed. — Oxford : Pergamon, 1981, c1979. — xix,73p : ill ; 25cm. — (Materials for language practice) (Pergamon Institute of English (Oxford))
Originally published: s.l. : s.n., 1979
ISBN 0-08-025361-x (pbk) : £1.95 : CIP rev.
B81-05145

Schmid-Schönbein, Gisela. English for Mopsy and me. — Oxford : Pergamon. — (English language courses)
Pupils' workbook 1. — Oct.1981. — [40]p
ISBN 0-08-027227-4 (pbk) : £1.95 : CIP entry
B81-25852

Schmid-Schönbein, Gisela. English for Mopsy and me. — Oxford : Pergamon. — (English language courses)
Pupils' workbook 2. — Oct.1981. — [40]p
ISBN 0-08-027228-2 (pbk) : £1.95 : CIP entry
B81-25851

Templeton, Hugh. Kernel one / Hugh Templeton, David Mills, Robert O'Neill. — Harlow : Longman
Tests
Teacher's book. — 1982. — 9p ; 25cm
ISBN 0-582-51337-5 (pbk) : Unpriced
B82-31772

Templeton, Hugh. Kernel one tests / Hugh Templeton, David Mills, Robert O'Neill. — Harlow : Longman
Student's book. — 1982. — 28p : ill,1map ; 25cm
ISBN 0-582-51928-4 (pbk) : Unpriced
B82-37170

428.2′4 — English language — *For West Indian students*

Nelson's new West Indian readers. — Sunbury-on-Thames : Nelson
Introductory workbook 1. — 1979. — 31p : ill ; 25cm
Clive Borely
ISBN 0-17-566228-2 (unbound) : £0.35
B82-40569

Nelson's new West Indian readers. — Sunbury-on-Thames : Nelson
Introductory workbook 2. — 1979. — 31p : ill ; 25cm
Clive Borely
ISBN 0-17-566229-0 (unbound) : £0.35
B82-40570

428.2′4 — English language. Grammar — *For non-English speaking students*

Alexander, L. G.. Mainline : a functional/notional approach / L.G. Alexander. — New ed. — Harlow : Longman
Previous ed. published as: Mainline progress, 1974
Progress B
Students' book. — 1981. — 131p : ill(some col.) ; 24cm
ISBN 0-582-51540-8 (pbk) : £2.50 B82-10043

Alexander, L. G.. Mainline : a functional/notational approach. — Harlow : Longman
Progress B / L.G. Alexander
Teacher's book. — New ed. — 1981. — 126p ; 22cm
Previous ed.: published as Mainline progress. A and B. Teacher's book. 1974. — Includes index
ISBN 0-582-51541-6 (pbk) : £2.50 B82-15199

Hooper, J. S.. A quick English reference / J.S. Hooper. — Kuala Lumpur ; Oxford University Press, 1980. — vi,225p : ill ; 22cm. — (Oxford in Asia)
ISBN 0-19-581782-6 (pbk) : £2.50 B82-40788

Kernel lessons intermediate. — Harlow : Longman
Workbook / John Arnold, Frank Heyworth. — 1982. — 55p : ill ; 25cm
ISBN 0-582-51680-3 (pbk) : £0.90 B82-28176

McCarthy, Marianthy. When? Why? : teacher guide your first ESOL series / Marianthy McCarthy, Linda Barker. — New York : Macmillan ; London : Collier Macmillan, c1982. — 108p : ill ; 24cm. — (Reach out. Level 4) (Reach out. Level 5)
Includes index
ISBN 0-02-970070-1 (spiral) : Unpriced
B82-36488

Prowse, Philip. Exchanges / Philip Prowse, Judy Garton-Sprenger ; project adviser T.C. Jupp. — London : Heinemann Educational. — (Main Course English. Level 2)
Teachers' book. — 1980
Pt.A. — 92p : ill,forms,ports ; 30cm
ISBN 0-435-28464-9 (pbk) : £3.95 : CIP rev.
B80-13780

Williams, Ray, *1938-*. Panorama : an advanced course of English for study and examinations / Ray Williams. — Harlow : Longman, 1982. — 109p : ill ; 28cm + Teacher's book(46p : ill ; 24cm)
ISBN 0-582-55358-x (pbk) : £2.10
ISBN 0-582-74880-1 (Teacher's book) : £1.70
B82-39921

Woodford, Protase E.. Bridges to English / Protase E. Woodford, Doris Kernan. — New York ; London : McGraw-Hill
3. — c1981. — vii,152p : ill(some col.) ; 23cm
Includes index
ISBN 0-07-034493-0 (pbk) : £2.95 B82-16581

Woodford, Protase E.. Bridges to English / Protase E. Woodford, Doris Kernan. — New York ; London : McGraw-Hill
4. — c1981. — vii,151p : ill(some col.) ; 23cm
ISBN 0-07-034499-x (pbk) : £3.25 B82-25271

Woodford, Protase E.. Bridges to English / Protase E. Woodford, Doris Kernan. — New York ; London : McGraw-Hill
5. — c1981. — vii,152p : ill(some col.) ; 23cm
ISBN 0-07-034505-8 (pbk) : £3.25 B82-25272

Woodford, Protase E.. Bridges to English / Protase E. Woodford, Doris Kernan. — New York ; London : McGraw-Hill
6. — c1981. — vii,151p : ill(some col.) ; 23cm
ISBN 0-07-034511-2 (pbk) : £3.25 B82-25273

428.2′4 — English language. Grammar — *Questions & answers — For non-English speaking students*

Seidl, Jennifer. Grammar in practice / Jennifer Seidl. — Oxford : Oxford University Press
2. — 1982. — 135p : ill ; 22cm
Includes index
ISBN 0-19-432720-5 (pbk) : Unpriced
B82-35350

428.2′4 — English language. Idioms — *Questions & answers — For non-English speaking students*

Seidl, Jennifer. Idioms in practice / Jennifer Seidl ; illustrations by Timothy Jaques. — Oxford : Oxford University Press, 1982. — 104p : ill ; 22cm
ISBN 0-19-432769-8 (pbk) : £1.75 B82-33074

428.2′4 — English language. International usage — *Conference proceedings*

English for international communication / edited by Christopher Brumfit. — Oxford : Pergamon, 1982. — xi,98p : ill ; 25cm. — (World language English series)
Proceedings of a conference of the English-Speaking Union. — Includes bibliographies
ISBN 0-08-028613-5 (pbk) : £5.95 : CIP rev.
B82-12399

428.2′4 — English language — *Questions & answers — For Caribbean students*

Gray, Cecil, *1923-*. Language for living : a Caribbean English course for CXC / Cecil Gray, Alan Gilchrist. — [Port of Spain] : Longman Caribbean ; Harlow : Longman
Stage 4. — Rev. ed. — 1982. — x,229p : ill,1port ; 21cm
Previous ed.: 1973. — Bibliography: pviii-x
ISBN 0-582-76583-8 (pbk) : £2.15 B82-23061

Gray, Cecil, *1923-*. Language for living : a Caribbean English course for CXC / Cecil Gray, Alan Gilchrist. — [Port of Spain] : Longman Caribbean ; Harlow : Longman
Stage 5. — Rev. ed. — 1982. — ix,214p : ill,ports ; 21cm
Previous ed.: 1973. — Bibliography: pvi-ix
ISBN 0-582-76584-6 (pbk) : £2.15 B82-23060

428.2′4 — English language — *Questions & answers — For non-English speaking students*

Abbs, Brian. Studying strategies : teacher's book / Brian Abbs, Ingrid Freebairn with John Clegg, Norman Whitney. — Harlow : Longman, 1982. — xi,84p : ill ; 25cm. — (Strategies ; 4)
Includes index
ISBN 0-582-51686-2 (pbk) : £2.50 B82-24402

Abbs, Brian. Studying strategies : a core concept course for the first certificate examination / Brian Abbs, Ingrid Freebairn with John Clegg, Norman Whitney. — Harlow : Longman. — (Strategies ; 4)
[Students' book]. — 1982. — 127p : ill(some col.),maps,ports ; 26cm
Includes index
ISBN 0-582-51681-1 (pbk) : £2.75 B82-15200

Alderson, Dick. Five Cambridge first certificate texts / Dick Alderson and Vivienne Ward. — [Teacher's ed.]. — Amersham : Hulton Educational, 1981. — 159p : ill ; 24cm
£2.35 (pbk) B82-01459

Archer, Margaret. English for Cambridge Proficiency / Margaret Archer and Enid Nolan-Woods. — Walton-on-Thames : Nelson, 1980 (1981 [printing]). — 253p : ill,2maps,music,forms ; 25cm
Includes index
ISBN 0-17-555236-3 (pbk) : Unpriced
B82-23618

428.2'4 — English language — *Questions & answers — For non-English speaking students continuation*

Archer, Margaret. Working with English : a course in general and technical English / M. Archer and E. Nolan-Woods. — London : Cassell
Bk.4. — 1981. — 93p : ill,maps,forms ; 25cm + teachers book(56p : ill ; 25cm)
ISBN 0-304-30618-5 (pbk) : Unpriced : CIP rev.
ISBN 0-304-30619-3 (Teachers bk.) : Unpriced
B81-22679

Archer, Margaret. Working with English. — London : Cassell, Sept.1981
4: Teacher's book. — [80]p
ISBN 0-304-30619-3 (pbk) : £2.95 : CIP entry
B81-23955

Best, Kerry. On your marks! : revision exercises in English for lower secondary school / Kerry Best, Rodney Phillips, Clency Sooben. — Harlow : Longman, 1982. — iv,156p : ill,1facsim,maps ; 22cm
ISBN 0-582-65083-6 (pbk) : £1.30 B82-33140

Boardman, Roy. Springboard 1 : English through communication / Roy Boardman, Sirio di Giuliomaria. — Oxford : Oxford University Press, 1982. — 176p : ill(some col.) ; 27cm + Teachers book(85p ; 27cm)
ISBN 0-19-432970-4 (pbk) : Unpriced
B82-40993

Carbyn, Jessica. Proficiency use of English / Jessica Carbyn. — London : Evans, 1981. — 78p ; 22cm
ISBN 0-237-50618-1 (pbk) : Unpriced
B82-00063

Certificate of proficiency in English practice tests / University of Cambridge, Local Examinations Syndicate. — Cambridge : Cambridge University Press
[Student's book]. — 1980 (1982 [printing]). — 104p ; 25cm
ISBN 0-521-23025-x (pbk) : £1.95 B82-37900

Certificate of proficiency in English practice tests / [University of Cambridge, Local Examination Syndicate]. — Cambridge : Cambridge University Press
Teacher's book. — 1980 (1981 [printing]). — 46p : ill ; 25cm
ISBN 0-521-23007-1 (pbk) : £1.75 B82-37901

Crew, C. C.. Seek and find English / C.C. Crew. — Exeter : Wheaton, 1960 (1978 [printing]). — 2v. ; 24cm
ISBN 0-08-022869-0 (pbk) : Unpriced
ISBN 0-9802287-5-5 (teacher's ed.) : £0.90
B82-15233

Davies, Evelyn, *1931-*. Strategies for reading / Evelyn Davies and Norman Whitney. — London : Heinemann Educational. — (Reading comprehension course)
Teachers' guide. — 1982. — 94p : ill,facsims ; 22cm
Includes index
ISBN 0-435-28941-1 (pbk) : £2.50 : CIP rev.
B81-35697

Doff, Adrian. Feelings : a course in conversational English for upper-intermediate and more advanced students / Adrian Doff and Christopher Jones. — Cambridge : Cambridge University Press, 1980 (1981 [printing]). — viii,112p : ill ; 25cm + Teacher's book(135p ; 21cm)
ISBN 0-521-21847-0 (pbk) : £2.95
ISBN 0-521-21846-2 (Teacher's book)
B82-38848

Donnelly, Joan. Who? / Joan Donnelly. — New York : Macmillan ; London : Collier Macmillan. — (Reach out. Level 1)
Teacher guide. — 1982. — 85p ; 24cm
ISBN 0-02-970260-7 (spiral) : Unpriced
B82-33408

Encounters. — London : Heinemann Educational. — (Main course English. Level 1)
Workbook. — Apr.1982
Part A. — [48]p
ISBN 0-435-28447-9 (pbk) : £1.20 : CIP entry
B82-03835

Encounters. — London : Heinemann Educational. — (Main course English. Level 1)
Workbook. — Apr.1982
Part B. — [48]p
ISBN 0-435-28448-7 (pbk) : £1.20 : CIP entry
B82-03836

First certificate in English practice tests. — Cambridge : Cambridge University Press. — (Cambridge English language learning)
[Student's book]. — 1980 (1981 [printing]). — 88p : ill,1map ; 25cm
Cover title
ISBN 0-521-23009-8 (pbk) : £1.50 B82-37899

First certificate in English practice tests. — Cambridge : Cambridge University Press
Teacher's book. — 1980 (1981 [printing]). — 42p : ill ; 25cm
Cover title
ISBN 0-521-23008-x (pbk) : £1.75 B82-37898

Fowler, W. S. (William Scott). [Incentive English]. New incentive / W.S. Fowler, J. Pidcock & R. Rycroft. — Walton-on-Thames : Nelson
1
Originally published: 1979
[Students' book]. — 1982. — 91p : ill(some col.),facsims,col.ports ; 25cm
Includes index
ISBN 0-17-555372-6 (pbk) : £2.50 B82-32423

Frank, Christine. Challenge to think / Christine Frank, Mario Rinvolucri, Marge Berer. — Oxford : Oxford University Press
[Student's ed]. — 1982. — 80p : ill,facsims ; 25cm
ISBN 0-19-453250-x (pbk) : £1.95 B82-29686

Frank, Christine. Challenge to think / Christine Frank, Mario Rinvolucri, Marge Berer. — Oxford : Oxford University Press
Teacher's ed. — 1982. — 112p : ill,facsims ; 25cm
ISBN 0-19-453251-8 (pbk) : £3.00 B82-29687

Gray, Joanna. Discovering English : a new pre-intermediate course / Joanna Gray. — London : Cassell, 1982. — ix,151p : ill,facsims,forms,maps,2plans ; 25cm + Teacher's book(96p ; 25cm). — (Cassell's foundation English ; book 2)
Teacher's book by Susan Henderson and Joanna Gray. — Text on inside cover
ISBN 0-304-30669-x (pbk) : £2.75 : CIP rev.
ISBN 0-304-30670-3 (Teacher's book) : £3.95
B81-31074

Grellet, Françoise. Quartet / Françoise Grellet, Alan Maley, Wim Welsing with a contribution from Norman Coe. — Oxford : Oxford University Press
Teacher's book 1. — 1982. — 107p : ill,maps ; 25cm
ISBN 0-19-433581-x (pbk) : £3.50 B82-20441

Grellet, Françoise. Quartet / Françoise Grellet, Alan Maley, Wim Welsing with a contribution from Norman Coe. — Oxford : Oxford University Press
Students book. — 1982. — 105p : ill,maps,plans ; 25cm
ISBN 0-19-433580-1 (pbk) : £2.75 B82-20440

Kassem, Maureen J. E.. Tests in English for overseas students. — Cheltenham : Thornes, Aug.1981. — [224]p
ISBN 0-85950-464-6 (pbk) : £4.50 : CIP entry
B81-20147

Kassem, Maureen J. E.. Tests in English for overseas students. — Cheltenham : Thornes, Aug.1981
Teacher's guide. — [96]p
ISBN 0-85950-318-6 (pbk) : £1.50 : CIP entry
B81-16903

Lockwood, Jane. Let's discuss it / Jane Lockwood. — London : Macmillan, 1981. — vi,73p : ill ; 19x21cm
ISBN 0-333-32488-9 (pbk) : Unpriced
B82-12021

Maley, Alan. The mind's eye : using pictures creatively in language learning / Alan Maley, Alan Duff and Françoise Grellet. — Cambridge : Cambridge University Press, 1980. — 2v. : ill(some col.) ; 25cm. — (Cambridge English language learning)
ISBN 0-521-23332-1 (pbk) : Unpriced
ISBN 0-521-23333-x (teacher's bk) : £3.50
B82-37891

Network / John Eastwood ... [et al.]. — Oxford : Oxford University Press
3
Student's book. — 1982. — 172p : ill,ports ; 24cm
ISBN 0-19-457061-4 (pbk) : £2.75 B82-23630

Network / John Eastwood ... [et al.]. — Oxford : Oxford University Press
3
Teacher's book. — 1982. — 159p ; 25cm
ISBN 0-19-457062-2 (pbk) : £4.75 B82-23631

Palmer, Michael, *1935-*. Track / Michael Palmer and Donn Byrne. — Harlow : Longman
1. — 1982
ISBN 0-582-51347-2 (pbk) : Unpriced
B82-37167

Pettigrew, Jane. Destination UK : survival skills in English / Jane Pettigrew and Shelagh Rixon. — London : Harrap
Students bk. — 1982. — v,122p : ill,1map ; 25cm
ISBN 0-245-53635-3 (pbk) : Unpriced
B82-27116

Prowse, Philip. Exchanges / Philip Prowse, Judy Garton-Sprenger ; project adviser T.C. Jupp. — London : Heinemann Educational. — (Main course English. Level 2)
Students' book. — 1980
Pt.A. — 77p : ill(some col.),forms ; 30cm
ISBN 0-435-28469-x (pbk) : £1.95 : CIP rev.
B80-10569

Prowse, Philip. Exchanges / Philip Prowse, Judy Garton-Sprenger ; project adviser T.C. Jupp. — London : Heinemann Educational. — (Main course English. Level 2)
Teachers' book
Part B. — 1981. — 93p : ill ; 30cm
ISBN 0-435-28467-3 (pbk) : £3.95 : CIP rev.
B81-14821

Smith, Bernard, *1937-*. In your own words : integrated skills practice for EFL / Bernard Smith ; (in association with the ARELS Examinations Trust). — Sevenoaks : Hodder and Stoughton Educational, 1982. — xii,126p : ill ; 19x25cm
ISBN 0-340-25319-3 (pbk) : £2.95 : CIP rev.
B81-31161

Stone, Linton. New Cambridge First Certificate English key / Linton Stone. — London : Macmillan, 1981. — 21p ; 21cm
ISBN 0-333-32513-3 (pbk) : Unpriced
B82-01893

Werkum, Kor van. Assignments : an intermediate language practice and study skills course / Kor van Werkum, Ger van Stokkum, Robert Druce. — Glasgow : Collins, 1981. — 111p : ill,maps,facsims ; 26cm + teacher's book(30p ; 26cm) + sound cassette
ISBN 0-00-370045-3 (pbk) : £2.60
ISBN 0-00-370046-1 (teacher's book) : £0.85
ISBN 0-00-370047-x (sound cassette) : £11.00
B82-05715

What? Where?. — New York : Macmillan ; London : Collier Macmillan. — (Reach out)
Teacher guide / Talma Addes. — 1982. — xiv,110p : ill ; 24cm
ISBN 0-02-970060-4 (spiral) : Unpriced
B82-33414

428.2'4 — English language — *Questions & answers — For non-English speaking students continuation*

When?. — New York : Macmillan ; London : Collier Macmillan. — (Reach out. [Level 4])
Student book 4 / Marianthy McCarthy. — 1982. — 92p : ill(some col.) ; 24cm
ISBN 0-02-970030-2 (pbk) : Unpriced
B82-33412

Why?. — New York : Macmillan ; London : Collier Macmillan. — (Reach out. [Level 5])
Student book 5 / Linda Barker. — 1982. — 92p : ill(some col.) ; 24cm
ISBN 0-02-970040-x (pbk) : Unpriced
B82-33413

428.2'4 — English language. Sentences — *Questions & answers — For non-English speaking students*

Bander, Robert G.. Sentence making : a writing workbook in English as a second language / Robert G. Bander. — New York ; London : Holt, Rinehart and Winston, c1982. — xii,335p : facsims,forms ; 24cm
Includes index
ISBN 0-03-050631-x (pbk) : £8.95 B82-17013

428.2'4 — English language. Special subjects: Engineering — *Questions & answers — For non-English speaking students*

Rimmer, J. A.. English for foreign learners : primary technology / J.A. Rimmer and M.J. Scott. — London : Evans, c1981. — 139p : ill,plans,1form ; 19x25cm + Teacher's book (139p : ill ; 19x25cm)
ISBN 0-237-50687-4 (pbk) : Unpriced
ISBN 0-237-50688-2 (Teacher's book) : Unpriced B82-06664

428.2'4 — English language. Special subjects: Foreign trade — *For non-English speaking students*

Radice, Francis. English for international trade / Francis Radice. — London : Evans, 1981, c1982. — 112p : ill,forms ; 25cm
Includes index
ISBN 0-237-50536-3 (pbk) : Unpriced
B82-21321

428.2'4 — English language. Special subjects: Science — *For non-English speaking students*

Bates, Martin, *1935-*. General science / Martin Bates, Tony Dudley-Evans. — Harlow : Longman. — (Nucleus)
[Students' book]. — New ed. with reading texts and Arabic glossary. — 1981 (1982 [printing]). — 2v.(127,5p) : ill ; 24cm
English text, Arabic glossary. — Also published in 1 vol. without Arabic glossary. — Previous ed.: published in 1 vol. 1976
ISBN 0-582-74861-5 (pbk) : Unpriced
ISBN 0-582-74862-3 (pt.2) : Unpriced
B82-32065

Bates, Martin, *1935-*. General science / Martin Bates, Tony Dudley-Evans. — Harlow : Longman. — (Nucleus)
[Students' book]. — New ed. with reading texts. — 1982. — 135p : ill,3maps ; 24cm
Also published in 2 v. with Arabic glossary. — Previous ed.: 1976
ISBN 0-582-74860-7 (pbk) : Unpriced
B82-32067

Bates, Martin, *1935-*. General science / Martin Bates, Tony Dudley-Evans. — Harlow : Longman. — (Nucleus)
Teacher's manual / tests section by Shelley Vance. — Expanded new ed. — 1981 (1982 [printing]). — 315p : ill,3maps ; 19x25cm
Includes English/Arabic glossary. — Previous ed.: published as Teacher's notes. 1976
ISBN 0-582-74859-3 (pbk) : Unpriced
B82-32068

Bates, Martin, *1935-*. General science / Martin Bates, Tony Dudley-Evans. — Harlow : Longman. — (Nucleus)
Test book / Shelley Vance. — 1981 (1982 [printing]). — 2v. : ill ; 24cm
Text on inside covers
ISBN 0-582-74866-6 (pbk) : Unpriced
ISBN 0-582-74867-4 (pt.2) : Unpriced
B82-32066

428.2'4 — English language. Special subjects: Workshop practice — *For non-English speaking students*

Moore, C. J.. Craft in English / C.J. Moore and R.V. Allott. — London : Heinemann Educational
Craft reader. — 1982. — 71p : ill ; 30cm
ISBN 0-435-28560-2 (pbk) : £1.95 : CIP rev.
B81-30306

Moore, C. J.. Craft in English / C.J. Moore and R.V. Allott. — London : Heinemann Educational
Teachers' bk. — 1982. — 64p : ill ; 30cm
ISBN 0-435-28562-9 (pbk) : £3.25 : CIP rev.
B81-30161

428.2'4 — English language. Usage — *Questions & answers — For non-English speaking students*

Communicate 2 : English for social interaction. — Cambridge : Cambridge University Press
Teacher's book / Keith Morrow and Keith Johnson. — 1980. — 58p ; 21cm
ISBN 0-521-22741-0 (pbk) : £2.50 B82-40517

428.2'4'0245 — English language — *For science — For non-English speaking students*

Kennedy, Judith. Patterns of fact. — London : Edward Arnold, Apr.1982. — [96]p
ISBN 0-7131-8076-5 (pbk) : £2.95 : CIP entry
B82-05408

Kennedy, Judith. Patterns of fact : key. — London : Edward, Oct.1982. — [16]p
ISBN 0-7131-8092-7 (pbk) : £1.00 : CIP entry
B82-24340

Stares, Martin. Core English for general science / Martin Stares. — London : Heinemann Educational
Teachers' book. — 1980. — 69p : ill ; 24cm
ISBN 0-435-28721-4 (pbk) : £1.95 : CIP rev.
B80-11837

428.2'4'02453 — English language — *For physics — For non-English speaking students*

Blackie, David. English for basic physics / David Blackie. — Walton-on-Thames : Nelson, 1981. — 75p : ill ; 22cm
Includes index
ISBN 0-17-555319-x (pbk) : £1.70
ISBN 0-17-555320-3 (Teachers' book) : £0.75
B82-03528

428.2'4'0246 — English language — *For technology — For non-English speaking students*

Moore, C. J.. Craft in English. — London : Heinemann Educational
Language workbook. — Nov.1981. — [88]p
ISBN 0-435-28561-0 (pbk) : £1.60 : CIP entry
B81-30163

Templeton, Hugh. Basic mechanical science. — London : Heinemann Educational. — (Intermediate technical English series)
Students' book. — Nov.1982. — [80]p
ISBN 0-435-28761-3 (pbk) : £1.95 : CIP entry
B82-27503

Templeton, Hugh. Basic mechanical science. — London : Heinemann Educational. — (Intermediate technical English series)
Teachers' book. — Nov.1982. — [56]p
ISBN 0-435-28762-1 : £2.95 : CIP entry
B82-27504

428.2'4'024647 — Spoken English language — *For non-English speaking hotel personnel*

Binham, Philip. Hotel English : communicating with the international traveller / Philip Binham, Riitta Lampola, James Murray. — Oxford : Pergamon, 1982. — vii,114p : ill,for,s,1map,3plans ; 25cm. — (Materials for language practice)
ISBN 0-08-025340-7 (pbk) : £2.50 : CIP rev.
B81-12316

428'.2'402465 — English language — *For business practices — For non-English speaking students*

Guderian, Claudia. Hold on. — Oxford : Pergamon, Apr.1982. — [28]p. — (Materials for language practice)
ISBN 0-08-028638-0 (pbk) : £1.95 : CIP entry
B82-03735

428.2'4'02465 — English language — *For business practices — For non-English speaking students*

Guderian, Claudia. Hold on. — Oxford : Pergamon. — (Materials for language practice)
Teacher's manual. — Aug.1982. — [16]p
ISBN 0-08-028663-1 (pbk) : £1.00 : CIP entry
B82-17937

Pilbeam, Adrian. The economist. — London : Collins Educational, Nov.1982. — [64]p
ISBN 0-00-370329-0 (pbk) : £2.50 : CIP entry
B82-29111

428.2'4'02465 — English language — *Questions & answers — For business practices — For non-English speaking students*

Arnold, H. R.. English at work / H.R. Arnold, M.J. Fitzgerald, I.D. Maclachlan. — Amersham : Hulton Educational. — 95p : ill,forms,2maps,1plan ; 26cm
ISBN 0-7175-0989-3 (pbk) : £2.95 B82-34835

Butler, John H. Montagu. Practical business English / John H. Montagu Butler. — Amersham : Hulton, 1980. — 3v. : ill,forms ; 24cm
ISBN 0-7175-0866-8 (pbk) : Unpriced
ISBN 0-7175-0867-6 (v.2) : £1.30
ISBN 0-7175-0868-4 (v.3) : £1.50 B82-17613

Dunlop, Ian. Communication for business. — Oxford : Pergamon, Oct.1982. — [110]p. — (Materials for language practice)
ISBN 0-08-029438-3 (pbk) : £2.95 : CIP entry
B82-28437

428.2'4'05 — English language — *For non-English speaking students — Serials*

Modern English international. — No.1 (Jan. 1982)-. — Grimsby (65 Pasture St., Grimsby DN32 9AB) : Modern English International, 1982-. — v. : ill,maps,ports ; 29cm
Ten issues yearly. — Supersedes: BBC modern English
ISSN 0263-077X = Modern English international : £7.00 per year B82-15149

428.2'4'07 — Non-English speaking students. Curriculum subjects: English language. Teaching

Firkin, Margot. Home tutors kit / written by Margot Firkin in conjunction with the NEC Working Party. — London (10/12 Allington St., SW1E KEH) : Commission for Racial Equality, 1977. — 1portfolio ; 32cm
Unpriced B82-40580

Willis, Jane. Teaching English through English : a course in classroom language and techniques / Jane Willis. — Harlow : Longman, 1981. — xvi,192p : ill ; 25cm. — (Longman handbooks for language teachers)
Bibliography: p190. — Includes index
ISBN 0-582-74608-6 (pbk) : £4.20 B82-14299

428.2'4'07 — Non-English speaking students. Curriculum subjects: English language. Teaching — *Encyclopaedias*

Seaton, Brian. A handbook of English language teaching terms and practice / Brian Seaton. — London : Macmillan, 1982. — v,203p : ill ; 22cm
Bibliography: p198-202
ISBN 0-333-25448-1 (pbk) : £3.50 B82-38793

428.2'4'07 — Non-English speaking students. Curriculum subjects: English language. Teaching — *Serials*

The **EFL** gazette. — No.1 (1978)-. — London (676 Fulham Rd, S.W.6) : Gordon Publications, 1978-. — v. : ill,forms,ports ; 44cm
Monthly. — Description based on: No.31 (Apr. 1982)
ISSN 0732-5819 = EFL gazette : £4.80 per year B82-28866

428.2'4'07 — Non-English speaking students. Education. Curriculum subjects: English language

Robinson, Pauline C.. ESP : (English for specific purposes) : the present position / Pauline C. Robinson. — Oxford : Pergamon, 1980. — viii,121p : ill ; 21cm. — (Pergamon Institute of English (Oxford) position papers)
Bibliography: p93-121
ISBN 0-08-024585-4 (pbk) : £3.95 : CIP rev.
B79-30031

428.2'4'07 — Non-English speaking students. Education. Curriculum subjects: English language. Teaching — *Manuals*

Gower, Roger. Teaching practice handbook. — London : Heinemann Educational, Nov.1982. — [192]p
ISBN 0-435-28995-0 (pbk) : £4.50 : CIP entry B82-30575

Olsen, Judy E. Winn-Bell. Communication starters : techniques for the language classroom / Judy E. Winn-Bell Olsen ; edited by William R. Lee. — Oxford : Pergamon, 1982. — xii,104p : ill(some col.),maps ; 25cm. — (Language teaching techniques)
Previous ed.: 1977. — Includes index
ISBN 0-08-025360-1 (pbk) : £3.25 : CIP rev. B81-21573

The **Teaching** of English as an international language : a practical guide / Gerry Abbott ... [et al.]. — Glasgow : Collins, 1981. — 287p : ill ; 23cm
Also published in paperback: £4.95. — Includes bibliographies
ISBN 0-00-370019-4 (cased) : £8.50
ISBN 0-00-370020-8 B82-08520

428.2'4'07 — Non-English speaking students. Education. Curriculum subjects: English language. Teaching — *Serials*

World language English : the international teachers' journal of English as a world language / Pergamon Institute of English (Oxford). — Vol.1, no.1 (Oct. 1981)-. — Oxford : Pergamon, 1981-. — v. : ill ; 25cm
Quarterly
ISSN 0278-4335 = World language English : Unpriced B82-11822

428.2'4'0715 — Europe. Non-English speaking students. Adult education. Curriculum subjects: English language. European unit/credit system. Threshold level

Ek, J. A. van. Theshold level English : in a European unit/credit system for modern language learning by adults / prepared for the Council of Europe by J. Van Ek ; with appendices by L.G. Alexander. — Oxford : Published for and on behalf of the Council of Europe by Pergamon, 1980. — xi,253p ; 25cm
At head of half title: Pergamon Institute of English (Oxford), Council of Europe Modern Project. — Bibliography: p253
ISBN 0-08-024588-9 (pbk) : £2.95 : CIP rev. B80-00676

428.2'4'0715 — Europe. Non-English speaking students. Adult education. Curriculum subjects: English language. European unit/credit system. Waystage. Teaching

Ek, J. A. van. Waystage English : an intermediary objective below threshold level in a modern European Unit/credit system of modern language learning by adults / prepared for the Council of Europe by J.A. Van Ek, L.G. Alexander in association with M.A. Fitzpatrick. — Oxford : Published for and on behalf of the Council of Europe by Pergamon, 1980. — viii,101p ; 25cm
At head of half title: Pergamon Institute of English (Oxford), Council of Europe Modern Languages Project
ISBN 0-08-024590-0 (pbk) : £2.95 : CIP rev. B80-02730

428.2'4'076 — Non-English speaking students. Curriculum subjects: English language. Examinations set by University of Cambridge. First Certificate in English & Certificate of Proficiency in English. Techniques — *Manuals*

Gethin, Amorey. How to pass Cambridge First Certificate and Proficiency in English / Amorey Gethin. — Oxford : Blackwell, 1981. — 150p : 2ill ; 25cm
Includes index
ISBN 0-631-12904-9 (spiral) : £2.95 : CIP rev. B81-28069

428.2'4'078 — English language. Teaching aids: Illustrations from serials — *For teaching non-English speaking students*

McAlpin, Janet. The magazine picture library / Janet McAlpin. — London : Allen & Unwin, 1980. — 67p,24p of plates : ill,ports ; 19cm. — (Practical language teaching ; 4)
Includes index
ISBN 0-04-371061-1 (pbk) : £2.50 : CIP rev. B79-34105

428.2'4'078 — Non-English speaking students. Curriculum subjects: English language. Teaching aids: Video equipment — *For teaching*

Video in the language classroom / edited by Marion Geddes and Gill Sturtridge. — London : Heinemann Educational, 1982. — 192p : ill ; 20cm. — (Practical language teaching ; 7)
ISBN 0-435-28971-3 (pbk) : £4.50 B82-15276

428.2'4'078 — Non-English speaking students. Education. Curriculum subjects: English language. Teaching aids: Overhead projects

Jones, J. R. H.. Using the overhead projector / J.R.H. Jones. — London : Heinemann Educational, 1982. — 103p : ill ; 19cm. — (Practical language teaching ; no.8)
Bibliography: p101-103
ISBN 0-435-28972-1 (pbk) : £2.95 : CIP rev. B82-06818

428.2'4'078 — Non-English speaking students. Education. Curriculum subjects: English language. Teaching materials

Lewis, Michael. Source book for teaching English overseas. — London : Allen & Unwin, Aug.1981. — [128]p
ISBN 0-04-371086-7 (pbk) : £6.95 : CIP entry B81-15879

428.2'431 — English language. Grammar — *Questions & answers — For German speaking students*

Repair kits : a series of remedial grammar modules / [prepared by the staff of the English Language Teaching Development Unit Ltd.]. — [Bicester] ([23 Market Sq., Bicester OX6 7BR]) : ELTDU
1: Past simple and continuous, present perfect and continuous
[Workbook] 1. — c1979. — 44p : ill ; 26cm
Unpriced (pbk) B82-18645

428.2'441 — English language. Grammar - *For French students*

Culhane, Terry. English alone. — Oxford : Pergamon, June 1981. — [160]p. — (Pergamon Institute of English (Oxford) English language courses)
ISBN 0-08-025308-3 (pbk) : £15.00 : CIP entry B81-12315

428.2'451 — English language. Grammar — *For Italian students*

Edwards, Jerry. Made in England — for Italy / Jerry Edwards. — Ruislip : Bristol Language Centre
1: [illustrations by Eric Sabine]. — 2nd ed. — 1980. — 196p : ill ; 21cm
English and Italian text. — Previous ed.: 1976
ISBN 0-9505013-0-1 (pbk) : Unpriced B82-19642

428.2'4927 — English language — *For Arabic speaking students*

Allen, W. Stannard. Progressive living English for the Arab world / [W. Stannard Allen, J.M. Morgan, Alan C. McLean]. — Harlow : Longman
Pupils' book 3 / W. Stannard Allen, Alan C. McLean. — 1981. — 96p : ill(some col.) ; 24cm
Title of part: Progressive living English
ISBN 0-582-76225-1 (pbk) : £1.80 B82-16442

McLean, Alan C.. Gateway : a first English course for Arab students / Alan C. McLean. — Harlow : Longman
Language bk.2 / [illustrated by John Fraser ... et al.]. — 1981. — 75p : ill(some col.),1col.map,1col.plan ; 24cm
ISBN 0-582-76477-7 (pbk) : £1.80 B82-07459

McLean, Alan C.. Gateway : a first English course for Arab students / Alan C. McLean. — Harlow : Longman
Workbook 2A. — 1981. — 54,viiip : ill ; 24cm
Cover title
ISBN 0-582-76484-x (pbk) : £0.60 B82-22899

McLean, Alan C.. Gateway : a first English course for Arab students / Alan C. McLean. — Harlow : Longman
ISBN 0-582-76489-0 (pbk) : £0.60 B82-22900

McLean, Alan C.. Gateway : a first English course for Arab students / Alan C. McLean. — Harlow : Longman
Teacher's guide 2. — 1981. — xiv,175p : ill,forms ; 24cm
ISBN 0-582-76478-5 (pbk) : Unpriced B82-05206

428.2'496 — English language. Comprehension — *Questions & answers — For West African students*

Morakinyọ, Rosemary E.. English language tests for school certificate / R.E. Morakinyọ. — London : Macmillan, 1981. — ix,125p ; 25cm
ISBN 0-333-32611-3 (pbk) : Unpriced B82-10636

Noble, R. W.. English comprehension and summary : test exercises, for General Certificate of Education and School Certificate / R.W. Noble. — New ed, rev. and expanded. — Harlow : Longman, 1981. — 124p ; 22cm
Previous ed.: 1968. — Bibliography: p121-124
ISBN 0-582-65091-7 (pbk) : £1.50 B82-12362

428.2'496 — English language — *For Gambian students*

Hyde, Elizabeth, *1924-*. Primary English for The Gambia / Elizabeth Hyde and J.M. Stitt. — Harlow : Longman
ISBN 0-582-59191-0 (pbk) : £1.25 B82-14676

428.2'496 — English language — *For Sudanese students*

Bates, Martin, *1949-*. The NILE course for the Sudan / Martin Bates. — Harlow : Longman. — (New integrated Longman English)
Students' bk.6 / Julian Corbluth. — 1982. — 166p : ill,forms,ports ; 24cm
ISBN 0-582-76480-7 (pbk) : Unpriced B82-37169

The **Nile** course for the Sudan. — Harlow : Longman
Teachers book 6 / Julian Corbluth. — 1982. — 144p : ill ; 22cm
Includes index
ISBN 0-582-75509-3 (pbk) : Unpriced B82-31773

428.2'496 — English language — *For West African students*

Parry, Helen. Use of English course for West African students / Helen Parry. — London : Macmillan, 1979. — 277p : ill ; 22cm
ISBN 0-333-25344-2 (pbk) : Unpriced B82-09046

428.2'496 — English language — *Questions & answers — For Cameroon students*

Ndangam, Augustine. Evans Cameroon primary English / Augustine Ndangam, David Weir. — London : Evans. — 86p : ill ; 25cm
ISBN 0-237-50757-9 (pbk) : Unpriced B82-29304

Ndangam, Augustine. Evans Cameroon primary English / Augustine Ndangam, David Weir. — London : Evans
Pupil's book 5. — 1982. — 86p : ill ; 25cm
ISBN 0-237-50654-8 (pbk) : Unpriced B82-16619

428.2'496 — English language — *Questions & answers — For East African students*

Grant, Neville J. H.. English in use : an English course for secondary schools / Neville J.H. Grant, Kukubo Barasa. — Harlow : Longman
Bk.4. — 1981. — 170p : ill ; 25cm
ISBN 0-582-60177-0 (pbk) : £1.95 B82-33141

Grant, Neville J. H.. English in use / N.J.H. Grant, C.R. Wango'mbe with the advice of K. Barasa. — [Harlow] : Longman
Teacher's book for year three : with notes on reading for a purpose book 3 / by A.M. Bloor and N.J.H. Grant. — 1980. — 76p ; 22cm
ISBN 0-582-60385-4 (pbk) : £1.75 B82-21716

428.2′4963 — English language — *For Nigerian students*

Montgomery, Michael, *1940-*. New system English / Michael Montgomery with Tijjani Ismail and J.O. Bisong. — London : Evans
Student's book 1. — 1982. — 200p : ill ; 25cm
ISBN 0-237-50517-7 (pbk) : Unpriced
B82-24914

Montgomery, Michael, *1940-*. New system English / Michael Montgomery with Tijjani Ismail, J.O. Bisong. — London : Evans
Teacher's book 1. — 1982. — 156p ; 22cm
ISBN 0-237-50639-4 (pbk) : Unpriced
B82-24913

Nation-wide : a course for primary schools / by Ronald Ridout ... [et al.]. — London : Evans
6
Pupil's book / illustrated by Margaret Theakston. — 1981. — 126p : ill(some col.) ; 25cm
ISBN 0-237-50464-2 (pbk) : Unpriced
B82-04103

Nation-wide English : a course for primary schools / Ronald Ridout ... [et al.]. — London : Evans Brothers
6
Teacher's bk. — 1981. — 38p ; 22cm
ISBN 0-237-50465-0 (pbk) : Unpriced
B82-01794

428.2′4963 — English language — *Questions & answers — For Nigerian students*

Montgomery, Michael, *1940-*. New system English / Michael Montgomery with Tijjani Ismail and J.O. Bisong. — London : Evans
Student's bk.2. — 1982. — 218p : ill,1map,1form,ports ; 25cm
ISBN 0-237-50518-5 (pbk) : Unpriced
B82-27664

428.2′49928 — English language — *For Malay speaking students*

Kursus bahasa Inggeris : penerangan panduan. — London : Linguaphone Institute
[Nenmai 10]. — 1981. — 6p ; 21cm
Unpriced (pbk) B82-05976

Kursus bahasa Inggeris : buku panduan : perbendaharaan kata nota dan lampiran sinarai perkataan. — London : Linguaphone Institute
[Nenmah 11]. — 1981. — 187p : ill ; 22cm
Includes index
Unpriced B82-05977

428.3 — ENGLISH LANGUAGE. SPOKEN EXPRESSION

428.3 — Spoken English language. Comprehension — *For schools*

Aitken, Rosemary. Make up your mind / Rosemary Aitken. — London : Macmillan, 1982
Student's book. — 43p : ill,1map ; 22cm
ISBN 0-333-32198-7 (pbk) : Unpriced
B82-20924

Aitken, Rosemary. Make up your mind / Rosemary Aitken. — London : Macmillan, 1982
Teacher's book. — vi,106p : ill,1map ; 22cm
ISBN 0-333-32201-0 (pbk) : Unpriced
B82-20925

428.3 — Spoken English language — *For teaching non-English speaking students*

Christison, Mary Ann. Look who's talking. — Oxford : Pergamon, July 1982. — [128]p. — (Language teaching methodology series)
ISBN 0-08-029445-6 (pbk) : £4.25 : CIP entry
B82-17190

428.3 — Spoken English language — *Manuals — For British Broadcasting Corporation personnel*

Burchfield, Robert W.. The spoken word : a BBC guide / Robert Burchfield. — London : British Broadcasting Corporation, 1981. — 40p ; 21cm
Includes index
ISBN 0-563-17979-1 (pbk) : £1.95 B82-05718

428.3 — Spoken English language. Teaching aids: Board games

Benson, Bryan. Wordways boards. — Oxford : Pergamon. — (Materials for language practice)
Teacher's guide. — Nov.1981. — [16]p
ISBN 0-08-025362-8 (pbk) : £3.50 : CIP entry
B81-28797

428.3′4 — Spoken English language. Comprehension — *Questions & answers — For non-English speaking students*

Battaglia, John. Yoshi goes to New York. — Oxford : Pergamon, July 1982. — [64]p. — (Materials for language practice)
ISBN 0-08-028648-8 (pbk) : £1.95 : CIP entry
B82-12401

Blundell, Lesley. Task listening / Lesley Blundell and Jackie Stokes. — Cambridge : Cambridge University Press
Student's bk. — 1981. — vii,53p : ill,forms,maps ; 25cm
ISBN 0-521-23135-3 (pbk) : £1.50 B82-38585

McClintock, John. Let's listen / John McClintock and Börje Stern. — London : Heinemann Educational
Previous ed.: published as Did you get it? Malmö : Borkförlaget Corona, 1974
Students' book. — 1980
Stage 1. — 32p : ill ; 22cm
ISBN 0-435-28535-1 (pbk) : £0.55 : CIP rev.
B79-34839

McClintock, John. Let's listen / John McClintock and Börje Stern. — London : Heinemann Educational
Previous ed.: published as Did you get it? Malmö : Bokförlaget Corona, 1974
Students' book. — 1980
Stage 2. — 31p : ill,1map,forms ; 22cm
ISBN 0-435-28536-x (pbk) : £0.55 : CIP rev.
B79-34840

Mumford, Susan. Conversation pieces. — Oxford : Pergamon, Feb.1983. — (Materials for language practice)
Teacher's book. — [48]p
ISBN 0-08-029443-x (pbk) : £1.95 : CIP entry
B82-36465

Pint, John. Pint's passages. — Oxford : Pergamon, July 1982. — [96]p. — (Materials for language practice)
ISBN 0-08-028620-8 (pbk) : £2.95 : CIP entry
B82-12400

Rowlands, K. E.. Assignment in Bristol / K.E. Rowlands ; illustrated by Jolyne Knox ; photographs by L.J. Rowlands. — St. Albans : Hart-Davis Educational, c1981. — vii,87p : ill ; 22cm. — (English comprehension series)
ISBN 0-247-13024-9 (pbk) : Unpriced
B82-24518

428.3′4 — Spoken English language. Dialogues. Comprehension — *Questions & answers — For non-English speaking students*

Watcyn-Jones, Peter. Dialogues / Peter Watcyn-Jones ; with photographs, illustrations by Edward McLachlan. — Harmondsworth : Penguin, 1980. — 190p : ill ; 19x25cm. — (Penguin functional English)
ISBN 0-14-080390-4 (pbk) : £2.95 B82-25629

428.3′4 — Spoken English language. Dialogues — *For non-English speaking students*

Haycraft, Brita. It depends how you say it : dialogues in everyday social English / planned and written by Brita Haycraft in consultation with W.R. Lee ; illustrated by Madeleine Bradbury. — Oxford : Pergamon, 1982. — xii,100p : ill ; 25cm. — (Materials for language practice)
ISBN 0-08-025314-8 (pbk) : £2.50 : CIP rev.
B80-18671

428.3′4 — Spoken English language — *For non-English speaking students*

Andrews, John, *1934 Sept.8-*. Say what you mean in English / John Andrews. — Walton-on-Thames : Nelson
Bk.1
Teacher's notes / Joanna Gray. — 1980. — 55p ; 22cm
ISBN 0-17-555242-8 (pbk) : £1.25 B82-13779

Beech, Bridget. Use your English : a course in English as a second language for adults / Bridget Beech, Clarice Brierley, Marianne Moselle. — London : Hodder and Stoughton
Teacher's book. — 1981. — 64p ; 25cm
Text on inside cover. — Includes index
ISBN 0-340-25440-8 (pbk) : Unpriced : CIP rev. B80-24409

Brims, Jim. English for negotiating / by Jim Brims. — Leeds : E.J. Arnold, c1982. — 2v. : ill ; 23cm
ISBN 0-560-04169-1 (pbk) : Unpriced
ISBN 0-560-04179-9 (bk.B) B82-31916

428.3′4 — Spoken English language - *For non-English speaking students*

Cook, Vivian. English for life. — International ed. — Oxford : Pergamon, May 1981. — (Pergamon Institute of English (Oxford) English language courses)
Vol.2: Meeting people
Students' book. — [160]p
ISBN 0-08-024608-7 (pbk) : £2.95 : CIP entry
B81-08836

428.3′4 — Spoken English language — *For non-English speaking students*

Cook, Vivian. English for life. — International ed. — Oxford : Pergamon. — (English language courses)
Vol.2: Meeting people. — Mar.1982
Teacher's guide. — [48]p
ISBN 0-08-025306-7 (pbk) : £1.00 : CIP entry
B82-02620

Cook, Vivian. English for life. — International ed. — Oxford : Pergamon, Feb.1983. — (English language courses)
Vol.2: Meeting people
Workbook. — [64]p
ISBN 0-08-027236-3 (pbk) : £1.50 : CIP entry
B82-36473

Cook, Vivian. English for life. — International ed. — Oxford : Pergamon. — (English language courses)
Vol.3: Living with people. — Aug.1982
ISBN 0-08-025329-6 (pbk) : £1.50 : CIP entry
B82-15652

Cook, Vivian. English for life. — International ed. — Oxford : Pergamon. — (English language courses)
Vol.3: Living with people. — Aug.1982
Teachers' guide. — [144]p
ISBN 0-08-025330-x (pbk) : £1.50 : CIP entry
B82-15653

Cook, Vivian. People and places. — International ed. — Oxford : Pergamon, Dec.1981. — (English for life ; v.1)
Key. — [32]p
ISBN 0-08-027233-9 (pbk) : £1.00 : CIP entry
B81-36985

Cook, Vivian. People and places. — International ed. — Oxford : Pergamon, Dec.1981. — (English for life ; v.1)
Workbook. — [96]p
ISBN 0-08-027231-2 (pbk) : £2.00 : CIP entry
B81-36986

Hill, Jimmie. Flexicourse / J. Hill & M. Lewis. — Oxford : Oxford University Press
Introductory module. — 1982. — 93p : ill,1map ; 30cm
ISBN 0-19-432160-6 (pbk) : £2.25 B82-22870

Hill, Jimmie. Flexicourse / J. Hill & M. Lewis. — Oxford : Oxford University Press
Lower clubs. — 1982. — 64p : ill ; 30cm
ISBN 0-19-432163-0 (pbk) : £1.75 B82-22868

Hill, Jimmie. Flexicourse / J. Hill & M. Lewis. — Oxford : Oxford University Press
Lower diamonds. — 1982. — 64p : ill ; 30cm
ISBN 0-19-432162-2 (pbk) : £1.75 B82-22869

Hill, Jimmie. Flexicourse / J. Hill & M. Lewis. — Oxford : Oxford University Press
Lower hearts. — 1982. — 64p : ill,facsims ; 30cm
ISBN 0-19-432161-4 (pbk) : £1.75 B82-22875

428.3'4 — Spoken English language — *For non-English speaking students* *continuation*

Hill, Jimmie. Flexicourse / J. Hill & M. Lewis. — Oxford : Oxford University Press
Lower spades. — 1982. — 64p : ill,ports ; 30cm
ISBN 0-19-432164-9 (pbk) : £1.75 B82-22873

Hill, Jimmie. Flexicourse / J. Hill & M. Lewis. — Oxford : Oxford University Press
Upper clubs. — 1982. — 64p : ill ; 30cm
ISBN 0-19-432167-3 (pbk) : £1.75 B82-22871

Hill, Jimmie. Flexicourse / J. Hill & M. Lewis. — Oxford : Oxford University Press
Upper diamonds. — 1982. — 64p : ill ; 30cm
ISBN 0-19-432166-5 (pbk) : £1.75 B82-22874

Hill, Jimmie. Flexicourse / J. Hill & M. Lewis. — Oxford : Oxford University Press
Upper hearts. — 1982. — 64p : ill,facsims ; 30cm
ISBN 0-19-432165-7 (pbk) : £1.75 B82-22876

Hill, Jimmie. Flexicourse / J. Hill & M. Lewis. — Oxford : Oxford University Press
Upper spades. — 1982. — 64p : ill,facsims ; 30cm
ISBN 0-19-432168-1 (pbk) : £1.75 B82-22872

Kanelli, Sheelagh. Oral proficiency / Sheelagh Kanelli. — London : Evans Brothers, 1981. — 122p : ill ; 22cm
ISBN 0-237-50538-x (pbk) : Unpriced
B82-01795

McLean, Alan C.. Start listening / Alan C. McLean. — Harlow : Longman. — (Longman listening series. elementary level)
Workbook. — 1981. — vii,55p : ill,forms ; 25cm
ISBN 0-582-55347-4 (pbk) : Unpriced
B82-05208

Webster, Diana. Keep listening / Diana Webster. — Harlow : Longman. — (Longman listening series. pre-intermediate level)
[Study guide]. — 1981. — iv,84p : ill,maps,plans ; 25cm
ISBN 0-582-55348-2 (pbk) : Unpriced
B82-05209

428.3'4 — Spoken English language — *Questions & answers — For non-English speaking delegates*

Fitzpatrick, Anthony. English for international conferences : a language course for those working in the fields of science, economics, politics and administration / Anthony Fitzpatrick. — Oxford : Pergamon, 1982, c1979. — 63p ; 23cm. — (Materials for language practice)
Originally published: Hamburg : ILS Institut für Lernsysteme, 1979
ISBN 0-08-027277-0 (pbk) : £2.50 : CIP rev.
B81-33857

428.3'4 — Spoken English language — *Questions & answers — For non-English speaking students*

Carrier, Michael. Topics for discussion and language practice / Mike Carrier ; [illustrations Ingram Wilcox]. — Amersham : Hulton
Bk.1. — 1980. — 63p : ill ; 26cm
ISBN 0-7175-0855-2 (pbk) : £1.10 B82-16025

Carrier, Michael. Topics for discussion and language practice / [Mike Carrier] ; [illustrations Ingram Wilcox]. — Amersham : Hulton
Bk.2 / Mike Carrier and Philip Sauvain. — 1980. — 63p : ill ; 26cm
ISBN 0-7175-0856-0 (pbk) : £1.10 B82-16026

Clark, Robert, *19---*. Imaginary crimes : materials for simulation and role-playing / Robert Clark and Jo McDonough. — Oxford : Pergamon
Teacher's notes. — 1982. — 27p : ill ; 24cm. — (Materials for language practice)
ISBN 0-08-025321-0 (pbk) : £1.50 : CIP rev.
B80-23193

Hill, Jimmie. Flexicourse / J. Hill & M. Lewis. — Oxford : Oxford University Press
Teacher's book and key to exercises. — 1982. — v,57p : 1ill ; 30cm
ISBN 0-19-432159-2 (pbk) : £3.00 B82-29688

Jones, Christopher. Building strategies / Christopher Jones. — Harlow : Longman
Workbook. — 1981. — 48p : ill ; 25cm
Cover title
ISBN 0-582-51664-1 (pbk) : £0.80 B82-03299

McDowell, John, *19---*. Basic listening : authentic recordings to develop listening micro-skills through graded tasks / John McDowell and Sandra Stevens. — London : Edward Arnold, 1982
Teacher's book. — 92p : ill,facsims,maps,plans ; 25cm
ISBN 0-7131-8075-7 (pbk) : £3.75 : CIP rev.
B81-34586

McDowell, John, *1947-*. Basic listening : authentic recordings to develop listening micro-skills through graded tasks / John McDowell and Sandra Stevens. — London : Edward Arnold, 1982
[Student's book]. — 29p : ill,facsims,maps,plans ; 25cm
ISBN 0-7131-8069-2 (pbk) : £1.50 : CIP rev.
B81-34585

Morrow, Keith. Communicate 2 : English for social interaction / Keith Morrow and Keith Johnson ; with drawings by Martin Salisbury. — Cambridge : Cambridge University Press
[Student's book]. — 1980. — 155p : ill,facsims,2maps,1plan ; 25cm
ISBN 0-521-22140-4 (pbk) : £2.95 B82-37895

Murray, Heather. Murder comes to breakfast : a detective story for intermediate students of English / Heather Murray and A.M.J. Niethammer-Stott. — Oxford : Pergamon, 1981, c1980. — 32p : plans ; 21cm. — (Materials for language practice) (Pergamon Institute of English (Oxford))
ISBN 0-08-027252-5 (pbk) : £1.00 B82-01797

Peaty, David. Something to talk about / David Peaty. — Walton-on-Thames : Nelson, 1981. — 60p : ill ; 22cm + Teacher's book(37p ; 22cm)
ISBN 0-17-555369-6 (pbk) : £1.25
ISBN 0-17-555370-x (Teacher's book) : £0.95
B82-00824

428.3'4 — Spoken English language. Role-playing exercises — *For non-English speaking students*

Lamb, Michael. Factions and fictions : exercises for role-play / by Michael Lamb. — Oxford : Pergamon, 1982. — (Materials for language practice)
Students' book. — vii,35p ; 23cm
ISBN 0-08-028664-x (pbk) : £1.95 : CIP rev.
B82-03736

428.3'4 — Spoken English language. Role-playing exercises — *For non-English speaking students — For schools*

Lamb, Michael. Factions and fictions : exercises for role-play / by Michael Lamb. — Oxford : Pergamon, 1982. — x,124p ; 23cm. — (Materials for language practice / Pergamon Institute of English (Oxford))
ISBN 0-08-028612-7 (pbk) : £4.95 : CIP rev.
B81-34473

428.3'4 — Spoken English language. Role-playing exercises. Special subjects: Crimes — *For non-English speaking students — For schools*

Clark, Robert. Imaginary crimes : materials for simulation and role-playing / Robert Clark and Jo McDonough. — Oxford : Pergamon, 1982. — viii,101p : ill,maps,facsims,1plan ; 24cm. — (Language practice materials)
ISBN 0-08-025320-2 (pbk) : £2.95 : CIP rev.
B80-20554

428.3'4 — Spoken English language. Special subjects: Graphic mathematical representations — *For non-English speaking students*

Jordan, R. R.. Figures in language : describe and draw : a workbook of communicative activities / R.R. Jordan. — Glasgow : Collins, c1982. — 71p : ill,maps,plans ; 22cm. — (Collins study skills in English)
ISBN 0-00-370006-2 (pbk) : £1.40 B82-16975

428.3'4 — Spoken English language. Special subjects: Graphic representations — *For non-English speaking students*

Fletcher, Mark. Defining and verbalising / Mark Fletcher and Roger Hargreaves. — London : Evans, 1980. — 89p : ill ; 25cm. — (Evans functional units)
ISBN 0-237-50422-7 (pbk) : Unpriced
B82-41044

428.3'4 — Spoken English language. Special subjects: Great Britain. Social skills — *For non-English speaking students*

Axbey, Susan. Profiles / Susan Axbey. — Walton-on-Thames : Nelson, 1981. — 100p : ill,maps,1plan,ports ; 25cm + Teacher's book (74p : 22cm)
ISBN 0-17-555321-1 (pbk) : Unpriced
ISBN 0-17-555322-x (Teacher's book) : Unpriced B82-10159

428.3'4'024372 — Spoken English language — *For teaching non-English speaking students*

Ur, Penny. Discussions that work. — Cambridge : Cambridge University Press, Nov.1981. — [122]p. — (Cambridge handbooks for English language teachers. New series)
ISBN 0-521-28169-5 (pbk) : £2.95 : CIP entry
B81-38814

428.3'4'024642 — Spoken English language — *Questions & answers — For non-English speaking restaurant trades personnel*

Binham, Philip. Restaurant English : communicating with the international traveller / Philip Binham, Riitta Lampola, James Murray. — Oxford : Pergamon, 1982. — vii,107p : ill,facsims,1plan ; 25cm. — (Materials for language practice)
ISBN 0-08-025339-3 (pbk) : £2.50 : CIP rev.
B81-13442

428.3'4'076 — London. Westminster *(London Borough)*. **Music colleges: Trinity College** *(London)*. **Non-English speaking students. Curriculum subjects: Spoken English language. Examinations**

Maddock, Vivienne. Getting through Trinity College English / Vivienne Maddock and W.R. Lee ; with a foreword by Ernest Heberden. — Oxford : Pergamon, 1981. — ix,170p : ill ; 25cm. — (Materials for language practice)
ISBN 0-08-024574-9 (pbk) : £2.50 : CIP rev.
B81-12390

428.3'43981 — Spoken English language — *For teaching Danish speaking students*

Davidsen-Nielsen, Niels. The Danish learner / Niels Davidsen-Nielsen, Claus Færch, Peter Harder. — Tunbridge Wells : Antony Taylor, 1982. — viii,108p : ill ; 21cm. — (English language teachers' manuals ; 1)
Includes index
ISBN 0-907728-00-6 (pbk) : £3.95 B82-37348

428.3'4914 — Spoken English language — *For South Asian immigrants*

A New start : a functional course in basic spoken English / by Peter Furnborough ... [et al.]. — London : Heinemann Educational
Teacher's book. — 1980. — 187p : 2ill ; 30cm
ISBN 0-435-28045-7 (pbk) : £3.90 : CIP rev.
B79-37259

428.3'4927 — Spoken English language — *Questions & answers — For Arabic speaking students*

Adamson, Donald, *1943-*. English for a new age : a course in secondary English for Arab students / Donald Adamson. — Harlow : Longman
Students' book 2. — 1982. — 128p : ill(some col.) ; 25cm
ISBN 0-582-76159-x (pbk) : £2.50 B82-22882

428.4 — ENGLISH LANGUAGE. READING

428.4 — English language. Reading — *For non-English speaking students — For teaching*

Nuttall, Christine. Teaching reading skills in a foreign language. — London : Heinemann Educational, July 1982. — [256]p. — (Practical language teaching ; no.9)
ISBN 0-435-28973-x (pbk) : £4.95 : CIP entry
B82-12329

428.4 — Reading

Jennings, Frank G.. This is reading / Frank G. Jennings. — New York ; London : Plenum, c1982. — xiii,196p ; 22cm
Originally published: New York : Bureau of Publications, Teachers College, Columbia University, 1965
ISBN 0-306-40990-9 : Unpriced
ISBN 0-306-40992-5 (pbk) : Unpriced
B82-31526

428.4 — Schools. Students. Reading skills. Assessment. Techniques — *For teaching*

Latham, W.. Assessment procedures in the teaching of reading / W. Latham and L.S. Overall. — 3rd ed., rev. and extended. — [Sheffield] : Sheffield City Polytechnic, Language Development Centre, 1981. — 12p : 1form ; 30cm
Previous ed.: 1978. — Bibliography: p6
ISBN 0-903761-41-6 (pbk) : £0.15 B82-15261

428.4′01′9 — Reading. Learning by man. Psychological aspects

Mitchell, D. C.. The process of reading : a cognitive analysis of fluent reading and learning to read. — Chichester : Wiley, Sept.1982. — [270]p
ISBN 0-471-10199-0 : £16.00 : CIP entry
B82-22805

428.4′01′9 — Reading. Psychological aspects

Downing, John, *1922-*. Psychology of reading / John Downing, Che Kan Leong. — London : Macmillan, c1982. — ix,414p : ill ; 26cm
Bibliography: p343-392. — Includes index
ISBN 0-02-330020-5 : £12.95 B82-26288

Smith, Frank, *1928-*. Understanding reading : a psycholinguistic analysis of reading and learning to read / Frank Smith. — 3rd ed. — New York ; London : Holt, Rinehart and Winston, c1982. — xii,264p : ill ; 24cm
Previous ed.: 1978. — Bibliography: p239-258. — Includes index
ISBN 0-03-059634-3 (pbk) : £9.95 B82-25822

428.4′01′9 — Reading skills. Psycholinguistic aspects

Goodman, Kenneth S.. Language and literacy / the selected writings of Kenneth S. Goodman ; edited by Frederick V. Gollasch. — London : Routledge & Kegan Paul
Vol.2: Reading, language and the classroom teacher. — 1982. — xiv,356p : ill ; 23cm
Includes bibliographies and index
ISBN 0-7100-9005-6 : £14.95 B82-40953

428.4′01′9 — Reading skills. Psychological aspects

Henderson, Leslie. Orthography and word recognition in reading / Leslie Henderson. — London : Academic Press, 1982. — xiii,397p : ill ; 24cm
Bibliography: p361-388. — Includes indexes
ISBN 0-12-340520-3 : £27.80 : CIP rev.
B82-10421

428.4′0321 — Reading — *Encyclopaedias*

A **Dictionary** of reading and related terms. — London : Heinemann Eductional, Sept.1982. — [400]p
Originally published: Newark, Del.: International Reading Association, 1981
ISBN 0-435-10410-1 (cased) : £12.50 : CIP entry
ISBN 0-435-10411-x (pbk) : £5.95 B82-21755

428.4′07 — Children. Reading skills. Teaching — *For parents*

Meek, Margaret, *1925-*. Learning to read / Margaret Meek. — London : Bodley Head, c1982. — 254p ; 23cm
Bibliography: p228-248. — Includes index
ISBN 0-370-30154-4 : £5.95 : CIP rev.
B81-25134

428.4′07 — United States. Children. Reading skills. Teaching

Bettelheim, Bruno. On learning to read : the child′s fascination with meaning / Bruno Bettelheim & Karen Zelan. — London : Thames and Hudson, 1982, c1981. — x,306p ; 22cm
ISBN 0-500-01274-1 : £7.95 B82-18907

428.4′07′1 — Schools. Curriculum subjects: Reading. Teaching. Use of Cloze procedure tests

Rye, James. Cloze procedure and the teaching of reading. — London : Heinemann Educational, Aug.1982. — [128]p
ISBN 0-435-10781-x (pbk) : £3.50 : CIP entry
B82-18572

428.4′07′1 — Schools. Students. Reading skills. Teaching — *Manuals*

Thomas, Ellen Lamar. Improving reading in every class / Ellen Lamar Thomas, H. Alan Robinson. — Abridged 3rd ed. — Boston, [Mass.] ; London : Allyn and Bacon, c1982. — xi,337p : ill ; 24cm
Previous ed. (i.e. 3rd ed.): 1981. — Previous abridged ed.: 1978. — Includes bibliographies and index
ISBN 0-205-07730-7 (pbk) : Unpriced
B82-27108

428.4′07′1041 — Great Britain. Educational institutions. Curriculum subjects: Reading. Teaching — *Conference proceedings*

United Kingdom Reading Association. *Conference (18th : 1981 : Heriot-Watt University).* Teaching reading : the key issues : proceedings of the eighteenth annual course and conference of the United Kingdom Reading Association, Heriot-Watt University, Edinburgh, 1981 / editor Alastair Hendry. — London : Heinemann Educational, 1982. — 187p : ill ; 22cm
Includes bibliographies
ISBN 0-435-10430-6 (pbk) : £6.50 : CIP rev.
B82-14513

428.4′07′1073 — United States. Schools. Curriculum subjects: Reading. Teaching

Carnine, Douglas. Direct instruction reading / Douglas Carnine, Jerry Silbert. — Columbus ; London : Merrill, c1979. — xvi,536p : ill,2maps,facsims ; 26cm
Text on lining papers. — Bibliography: p490-507. — Includes index
ISBN 0-675-08277-3 : Unpriced B82-15055

Dillner, Martha H.. Personalizing reading instruction in middle, junior, and senior high schools : utilizing a competency-based instructional system / Martha H. Dillner, Joanne P. Olson. — 2nd ed. — New York : Macmillan ; London : Collier Macmillan, c1982. — x,598p : ill ; 26cm
Previous ed.: 1977. — Text on inside front cover. — Includes bibliographies and index
ISBN 0-02-329780-8 (pbk) : Unpriced
B82-35278

428.4′076 — English language. Reading — *Questions & answers — For non-English speaking students*

Adams, Leslie. Read it right. — Oxford : Pergamon. — (Materials for language practice)
1. — Aug.1982. — [96]p
ISBN 0-08-029435-9 (pbk) : £2.95 : CIP entry
B82-21379

Heyworth, Frank. Intermediate language skills : reading. — London : Hodder & Stoughton, June 1982. — [80]p
ISBN 0-340-25609-5 (pbk) : £2.50 : CIP entry
B82-10004

Walter, Catherine. Authentic reading. — Cambridge : Cambridge University Press
Teacher′s book and key. — Oct.1982. — [72]p
ISBN 0-521-28360-4 (pbk) : £3.25 : CIP entry
B82-40316

428.4′076 — Reading skills — *Questions & answers — For children*

Test your child′s reading. — Sevenoaks : Produced exclusively for W.H. Smith by Hodder and Stoughton, 1982. — [32]p : ill ; 25cm
ISBN 0-340-28052-2 (pbk) : £0.60 B82-27679

428.4′2′07 — Adults. Reading skills. Teaching

Jones, Edward V.. Reading instruction for the adult illiterate / Edward V. Jones. — Chicago : American Library Association ; London : distributed by Eurospan, 1981. — xi,169p : 1form ; 24cm
Bibliography: p161-166. — Includes index
ISBN 0-8389-0317-7 : £9.50 B82-21143

428.4′2′076 — English language. Reading — *Questions & answers — For slow readers*

Hoogstad, Valerie. Sounds and silents / Valerie Hoogstad. — London : Edward Arnold, 1982, c1980. — 2v. : ill(some col.),ports ; 26cm
Originally published: in one vol. Sydney : Wiley, 1975
ISBN 0-7131-0651-4 (pbk) : Unpriced
ISBN 0-7131-0652-2 (v.2) : Unpriced
B82-31545

428.4′3 — Reading skills. Development

Chapman, L. John. Reading development and cohesion. — London : Heinemann Educational, Nov.1982. — [144]p
ISBN 0-435-10161-7 (pbk) : £3.75 : CIP entry
B82-29069

428.4′3 — Reading skills. Development — *For teaching*

Thomas, Ellen Lamar. Improving reading in every class : a sourcebook for teachers / Ellen Lamar Thomas, H. Alan Robinson. — 3rd ed. — Boston [Mass.] ; London : Allyn and Bacon, c1982. — xi,431p : ill ; 25cm
Previous ed.: 1977. — Includes bibliographies and index
ISBN 0-205-07365-4 : £21.95 B82-17724

428.4′3 — Reading skills. Self-development — *Manuals*

Harri-Augstein, Sheila. Reading to learn / Sheila Harri-Augstein, Michael Smith and Laurie Thomas. — London : Methuen, 1982. — xiii,113p : ill ; 21cm
ISBN 0-416-72660-7 (pbk) : Unpriced : CIP rev.
B82-23983

428.4′3 — Speed reading — *Manuals*

Fink, Diana Darley. Speedreading : the how-to book for every busy manager, executive, and professional / Diana Darley Fink, John T. Tate, Jr, Michael D. Rose. — New York ; Chichester : Wiley, c1982. — xii,195p : ill,forms ; 25cm. — (A Self-teaching guide)
Includes index
ISBN 0-471-08407-7 (pbk) : £6.75 B82-26450

428.4′3′0712 — Secondary schools. Students. Reading skills. Development — *For teaching*

Piercey, Dorothy. Reading activities in content areas : an ideabook for middle and secondary schools / Dorothy Piercey. — 2nd ed. — Boston [Mass.] ; London : Allyn and Bacon, c1982. — xiv,284p : ill,facsims ; 24cm
Previous ed.: 1976. — Includes index
ISBN 0-205-07372-7 (pbk) : £15.50
B82-08541

428.4′3′076 — Reading skills. Development — *Questions & answers — For schools*

Cooper, John, *1928-*. Reading skills : directions 1 / John Cooper. — 2nd ed. — Edinburgh : Oliver & Boyd, 1982. — 79p : ill,2maps ; 25cm
Previous ed.: 1977
ISBN 0-05-003612-2 (pbk) : £1.45 B82-36962

Edwards, Peter, *19---*. Edwards′ reading test / Peter Edwards. — UK ed. / prepared by Ruth Nichols. — London : Heinemann Educational, 1980. — 3v. ; 25cm
Previous ed.: published as Edwards′ diagnostic reading test. Richmond, Vic. : Primary Education Publishing, 1977. — In plastic wallet
ISBN 0-435-80292-5 (pbk) : £6.50 : CIP rev.
B80-13782

428.6 — ENGLISH LANGUAGE. READING BOOKS

428.6 — English language. Reading books: Drama — *For schools*

Byrne, Donn. Three mystery plays / Donn Byrne. — Harlow : Longman, 1970 (1981 [printing]). — 52p ; 20cm. — (Longman structural readers. Stage 4. Plays)
ISBN 0-582-52700-7 (pbk) : £0.60 B82-06080

Melser, June. The dragon : a play. — Leeds : E.J. Arnold, 1982, c1981. — 16p : col.ill ; 22cm. — (Story chest. Stage 3)
Text June Melser and Joy Cowley; illustrations Deirdre Gardiner. — Originally published: New Zealand : Shortland, 1981
ISBN 0-560-08659-8 (pbk) : Unpriced
B82-21885

428.6 — English language. Reading books: Drama — *For schools* *continuation*

Methold, Ken. The music line and other short plays / Ken Methold. — Harlow : Longman, 1981. — 36p : ill ; 20cm. — (Longman structural readers. Stage 2. Plays)
ISBN 0-582-52709-0 (pbk) : £0.50 B82-13685

428.6 — English language. Reading books — *For children*

Curry, Peter. I can hear / Peter Curry. — Tadworth : World's Work, c1982. — [32]p : col.ill ; 22cm. — (A World's Work children's book)
ISBN 0-437-32946-1 : £3.50 B82-40619

Curry, Peter. I can see / Peter Curry. — Tadworth : World's Work, c1982. — [32]p : col.ill ; 22cm. — (A World's Work children's book)
ISBN 0-437-32943-7 : £3.50 B82-40620

Egan, Pamela. All this fuss about Andy / adapted by Pamela Egan ; pictures Dea de Vries. — London : CIO, c1981. — [16]p : col.ill ; 14x17cm. — (Benjamin books)
ISBN 0-7151-0397-0 (pbk) : £0.30 B82-02794

Egan, Pamela. Don and Di-next-door / adapted by Pamela Egan ; pictures Dea de Vries. — London : CIO, c1981. — [16]p : col.ill ; 14x17cm. — (Benjamin books)
ISBN 0-7151-0401-2 (pbk) : £0.30 B82-02798

Egan, Pamela. Kevin's good day / adapted by Pamela Egan ; pictures Dea de Vries. — London : CIO, c1981. — [16]p : col.ill ; 14x17cm. — (Benjamin books)
ISBN 0-7151-0400-4 (pbk) : £0.30 B82-02797

Egan, Pamela. Must Simon come too? / adapted by Pamela Egan ; pictures Dea de Vries. — London : CIO, c1981. — [16]p : ill(some col.) ; 14x17cm. — (Benjamin books)
ISBN 0-7151-0399-7 (pbk) : £0.30 B82-02793

Egan, Pamela. Sleep well, James! / adapted by Pamela Egan ; pictures Dea de Vries. — London : CIO, c1981. — [16]p : col.ill ; 14x17cm. — (Benjamin books)
ISBN 0-7151-0396-2 (pbk) : £0.30 B82-02796

Egan, Pamela. Wake up, Judy! / adapted by Pamela Egan ; pictures Dea de Vries. — London : CIO, c1981. — [16]p : ill(some col.) ; 14x17cm. — (Benjamin books)
ISBN 0-7151-0398-9 (pbk) : £0.30 B82-02795

Farmer, Derek. A rhyme in time / Derek Farmer ; pictures by Ken Astrop. — London : Longman, c1982. — 16p : col.ill ; 21cm. — (Thin King ; story 4)
Cover title. — Text on inside covers
Unpriced (pbk) B82-36107

Farmer, Derek. Runaway whale / Derek Farmer ; pictures by Ken Astrop. — Harlow : Longman, c1982. — 16p : col.ill ; 21cm. — (Thin King ; story 2)
Cover title. — Text on inside covers
Unpriced (pbk) B82-36109

Farmer, Derek. A tale of a shed / Derek Farmer ; pictures by Ken Astrop. — London : Longman, c1982. — 16p : col.ill ; 21cm. — (Thin King ; story 1)
Cover title. — Text on inside covers
Unpriced (pbk) B82-36108

Farmer, Derek. Thimbles, thistles and a thorn in the thatch / Derek Farmer ; pictures by Ken Astrop. — Harlow : Longman, c1982. — 16p : col.ill ; 21cm. — (Thin King ; story 3)
Cover title. — Text on inside covers
Unpriced (pbk) B82-36110

McMillan, Dorothy. An orange, an apple / Dorothy McMillan ; photos Terry Hobin, Trevor Hyde. — Wellington : Milburn ; London : Methuen, c1979. — [16]p : col.ill ; 11x15cm. — (PM instant reader. 1st series ; IR4)
ISBN 0-423-49470-8 (unbound) : Unpriced B82-21707

Scarry, Richard. My house / Richard Scarry. — London : Collins, 1982. — [28]p : col.ill ; 9cm
Cover title. — Adaptation of: Richard Scarry's best first book ever
ISBN 0-00-138338-8 : £1.00 B82-36784

Scarry, Richard. Things I do / Richard Scarry. — London : Collins, 1982. — [28]p : col.ill ; 9cm
Cover title. — Adaptation of: Richard Scarry's best first book ever
ISBN 0-00-138339-6 : £1.00 B82-31938

You do it too. — [Cambridge] : Brimax, 1979 (1982 printing). — [12]p : chiefly col.ill ; 16cm. — ('Tiny tots world' series) (Brimax books 2-4 years)
ISBN 0-86112-043-4 (unbound) : Unpriced B82-33949

428.6 — English language. Reading books — *For pre-school children*

Ahlberg, Allan. Bad bear / Allan Ahlberg and Eric Hill. — London : Granada, 1982. — [24]p : col.ill ; 16cm. — (Help your child to read)
ISBN 0-583-30470-2 (pbk) : £0.85 B82-39356

Ahlberg, Allan. Double ducks / Allan Ahlberg and Eric Hill. — London : Granada, 1982. — [24]p : col.ill ; 16cm. — (Help your children to read)
ISBN 0-583-30469-9 (pbk) : £0.85 B82-39353

Ahlberg, Allan. Fast frog / Allan Ahlberg and Eric Hill. — London : Granada, 1982. — [24]p : col.ill ; 16cm. — (Help your children to read)
ISBN 0-583-30467-2 (pbk) : £0.85 B82-39355

Ahlberg, Allan. Poorly pig / Allan Ahlberg and Eric Hill. — London : Granada, 1982. — [24]p : col.ill ; 16cm. — (Help your child to read)
ISBN 0-583-30471-0 (pbk) : £0.85 B82-39357

Ahlberg, Allan. Rubber rabbit / Allan Ahlberg and Eric Hill. — London : Granada, 1982. — [24]p : col.ill ; 16cm. — (Help your child to read)
ISBN 0-583-30472-9 (pbk) : £0.85 B82-39352

Ahlberg, Allan. Silly sheep / Allan Ahlberg and Eric Hill. — London : Granada, 1982. — [24]p : col.ill ; 16cm. — (Help your child to read)
ISBN 0-583-30468-0 (pbk) : £10.85 B82-39354

All by myself. — [Cambridge] : Brimax Books, 1979 (1982 printing). — [10]p : col.ill ; 16cm. — (Tiny tots world series)
Cover title
ISBN 0-86112-040-x : Unpriced B82-36915

All together. — [Cambridge] : Brimax Books, 1979 (1980 [printing]). — [10]p : col.ill ; 16cm. — (Tiny tots world series)
Cover title
ISBN 0-86112-042-6 : Unpriced B82-36918

Bathtime. — [Cambridge] : Brimax Books, 1973 (1982 printing). — [10]p : col.ill ; 16cm. — (Show baby series)
Cover title
ISBN 0-900195-29-0 : Unpriced B82-36917

Cowell, Norma C.. Read, write and colour : with Voirrey and Juan in the Isle of Man / [written and compiled by Norma C. Cowell] ; [illustrated by Mavis Kelly]. — Onchan : Shearwater
Cover title
Book 1: For infants. — 1979. — 20p : chiefly ill ; 21cm
ISBN 0-904980-36-7 (pbk) : £0.75
Also classified at 741 B82-02241

Doing. — [Cambridge] : Brimax Books, 1974 (1981 printing). — [10]p : col.ill ; 16cm. — (Show baby plus series)
Cover title
ISBN 0-900195-58-4 : Unpriced B82-36916

Gleeson, Joan. Let's go / [text Joan Gleeson] ; [illustrated by Ann Kennedy]. — Dublin : Gill and Macmillan
Stage 1
Workbook B. — 1982. — 63p : ill ; 30cm
ISBN 0-7171-1154-7 (pbk) : £0.86 B82-25247

Gleeson, Joan. Let's go! / [text by Joan Gleeson]. — Dublin : Gill and Macmillan
Stage 2
Book 2 / [illustrated by Una Guy, Della Varilly and Patricia McElroy]. — c1982. — 40p : col.ill ; 22cm
Cover title. — Text on inside covers
ISBN 0-7171-1207-1 (pbk) : £0.99 B82-39966

Hearing. — [Cambridge] : Brimax, c1974 (1981 printing). — 12p : chiefly col.ill ; 16cm. — (Show baby plus series)
ISBN 0-900195-57-6 : Unpriced B82-08608

Jungmann, Ann. My garden / stories by Ann Jungmann ; illustrated by Joanna Stubbs. — London : Purnell, 1982. — 30p : col.ill ; 22cm. — (My day storybooks)
ISBN 0-361-05376-2 : £1.25 B82-31639

Jungmann, Ann. Playing / stories by Ann Jungmann ; illustrated by Maggie Ling. — Bristol : Purnell, 1982. — 30p : col.ill ; 22cm. — (My day storybooks)
ISBN 0-361-05377-0 : £1.25 B82-31642

Kincaid, Lucy. Chicken Licken / story adapted by Lucy Kinkaid ; illustrated by Clive Spong. — Cambridge : Brimax, 1979 (1981 [printing]). — [20]p : col.ill ; 27cm. — (Now you can read)
ISBN 0-86112-001-9 : Unpriced B82-36903

Kincaid, Lucy. The gingerbread man / story adapted by Lucy Kincaid ; illustrated by Eric Rowe. — Cambridge : Brimax, 1979 (1981 [printing]). — [20]p : col.ill ; 27cm. — (Now you can read)
ISBN 0-86112-003-5 : Unpriced B82-36902

Kincaid, Lucy. Little Red Riding Hood / story adapted by Lucy Kincaid ; illustrated by Eric Rowe. — Cambridge : Brimax, [1979] ([1981 printing]). — [20]p : col.ill ; 27cm. — (Now you can read)
ISBN 0-86112-002-7 : Unpriced B82-07169

Kincaid, Lucy. The three billy-goats gruff / story adapted by Lucy Kincaid ; illustrated by Clive Spong. — Cambridge : Brimax, [1979] ([1981 printing]). — [20]p : col.ill ; 27cm. — (Now you can read)
ISBN 0-86112-000-0 : Unpriced B82-07168

Laird, Elizabeth. The big green star / Elizabeth Laird ; pictures by Leslie Smith. — [London] : Collins, c1982. — [32]p : col.ill ; 15cm. — (Let's read) (Collins colour cubs)
ISBN 0-00-123704-7 (pbk) : £0.50 B82-32185

Laird, Elizabeth. The blanket house / Elizabeth Laird ; pictures by Leslie Smith. — [London] : Collins, c1982. — [32]p : col.ill ; 15cm. — (Let's read) (Collins colour cubs)
ISBN 0-00-123702-0 (pbk) : £0.50 B82-32182

Laird, Elizabeth. The doctor's bag / Elizabeth Laird ; pictures by Leslie Smith. — [London] : Collins, c1982. — [32]p : col.ill ; 15cm. — (Let's read) (Collins colour cubs)
ISBN 0-00-123703-9 (pbk) : £0.50 B82-32183

Laird, Elizabeth. Jumper / Elizabeth Laird ; pictures by Leslie Smith. — [London] : Collins, c1982. — [32]p : col.ill ; 15cm. — (Let's read) (Collins colour cubs)
ISBN 0-00-123701-2 (pbk) : £0.50 B82-32184

Little one's book of tell the time / illustrated by Alan Fredman. — London : Dean, c1982. — [12]p : col.ill ; 21cm. — (A Dean board book)
ISBN 0-603-00311-7 (unbound) : £0.65 B82-36559

428.6 — English language. Reading books — *For pre-school children* *continuation*

Little traveller train book : fun land, zoo land, city land. — Bristol : Purnell, [1982?]. — [8]p : col.ill ; 20x30cm + 1train(plastic, col.)
ISBN 0-361-05470-x (spiral) : Unpriced B82-38733

Manley, Deborah. Going out / by Deborah Manley ; pictures by Moira Maclean. — Harlow : Longman, 1981. — [24]p : col.ill ; 16cm. — (Little me books ; 8)
ISBN 0-582-39142-3 : £1.35 B82-00500

Manley, Deborah. Me and my friend / by Deborah Manley ; pictures by Moira Maclean. — Harlow : Longman, 1981. — [24]p : col.ill ; 16cm. — (Little me books ; 5)
ISBN 0-582-39139-3 : £1.35 B82-00497

Manley, Deborah. My colours / by Deborah Manley ; pictures by Moira Maclean. — Harlow : Longman, 1981. — [24]p : col.ill ; 16cm. — (Little me books ; 6)
ISBN 0-582-39140-7 : £1.35 B82-00498

Manley, Deborah. My colours / by Deborah Manley ; pictures by Moira Maclean. — London : Scholastic, 1981. — [24]p : col.ill ; 16cm. — (Hippo books)
ISBN 0-590-70103-7 (pbk) : £0.70 B82-02272

Manley, Deborah. My house / by Deborah Manley ; pictures by Moira Maclean. — Harlow : Longman, 1981. — [24]p : col.ill ; 16cm. — (Little me books ; 7)
ISBN 0-582-39141-5 : £1.35 B82-00499

Manley, Deborah. My house / by Deborah Manley ; pictures by Moira Maclean. — London : Scholastic, 1981. — [24]p : col.ill ; 16cm. — (Hippo books)
ISBN 0-590-70102-9 (pbk) : £0.70 B82-02266

Mealtime. — [Cambridge] : Brimax, c1973 (1981 printing). — [12]p : col.ill ; 16cm. — (Show baby series)
ISBN 0-900195-28-2 : Unpriced B82-08607

Melvill, Heather. Four pigs and a bee / by Heather Melvill ; illustrated by Maureen Galvani. — Cambridge : Dinosaur, c1981. — [25]p : col.ill ; 16x19cm. — (Dinosaur's Althea books)
ISBN 0-85122-326-5 (cased) : Unpriced
ISBN 0-85122-080-0 (pbk) : Unpriced B82-34646

Morris, Neil. Anne goes to the airport / written by Neil and Ting Morris ; illustrated by Geoffrey Butcher. — London : Hodder and Stoughton, 1982. — 24p : ill(some col.) ; 18cm. — (Story word books)
ISBN 0-340-28148-0 : £1.50 : CIP rev. B82-09188

Morris, Neil. Peter goes to granny's house / written by Neil and Ting Morris ; illustrated by Geoffrey Butcher. — London : Hodder and Stoughton, 1982. — 24p : ill(some col.) ; 18cm. — (Story word books)
ISBN 0-340-28152-9 : £1.50 : CIP rev. B82-07954

Morris, Neil. Sally goes to the market / written by Neil and Ting Morris ; illustrated by Geoffrey Butcher. — London : Hodder and Stoughton, 1982. — 24p : col.ill ; 18cm. — (Story word books)
ISBN 0-340-28151-0 : £1.50 : CIP rev. B82-09190

Morris, Neil. William goes to the zoo / written by Neil and Ting Morris ; illustrated by Geoffrey Butcher. — London : Hodder and Stoughton, 1982. — 24p : ill(some col.) ; 18cm. — (Story word books)
ISBN 0-340-28149-9 : £1.50 : CIP rev. B82-09189

My little library. — [London] : Hamlyn, [1981]. — 1case : col.ill ; 17cm
ISBN 0-600-36657-x : £3.99 B82-02673

Pearce, Lisa. Going shopping / stories by Lisa Pearce ; illustrated by Pamela Storey. — Bristol : Purnell, 1982. — 30p : col.ill ; 22cm. — (My day storybooks)
ISBN 0-361-05374-6 : £1.25 B82-31641

Perkins, Diana. Going to school / stories by Diana Perkins ; illustrated by Tony Morris. — Bristol : Purnell, 1982. — 30p : col.ill ; 22cm. — (My day storybooks)
ISBN 0-361-05375-4 : £1.25 B82-31640

Playtime / illustrated by Tony Morris ; editor Janine Amos ; designer Winsome Malcolm. — Bristol : Purnell, 1982. — [24]p : col.ill ; 21cm. — (A First learning book)
ISBN 0-361-05372-x (pbk) : £0.50 B82-38471

Seeing. — [Cambridge] : Brimax, c1974 (1981 printing). — [12]p : col.ill ; 16cm. — (Show baby plus series)
Cover title
ISBN 0-900195-55-x : Unpriced B82-07165

Sharing. — [Cambridge] : Brimax, 1979 (1980 printing). — [12]p : col.ill ; 16cm. — ('Tiny tots world' series)
Cover title
ISBN 0-86112-041-8 : Unpriced B82-07166

428.6 — English language. Reading books — *For schools*

Allan, Catherine. Resource reader / Catherine Allan, George Livingstone, Jim Love. — Edinburgh : Holmes McDougall
3. — c1981. — 80p : ill(some col.),col.1map ; 21cm
ISBN 0-7157-1944-0 (pbk) : £1.95 B82-00943

Allan, Catherine. Resource reader / Catherine Allan, George Livingstone, Jim Love. — Edinburgh : Holmes McDougall
3: Teaching guide. — c1981. — 47p ; 21cm
ISBN 0-7157-1958-0 (pbk) : £1.65 B82-00944

Allan, Catherine. Resource reader / Catherine Allan, George Livingstone, Jim Love. — Edinburgh : Holmes McDougall
4. — c1981. — 96p : ill(some col.),1col.map,ports ; 21cm
ISBN 0-7157-1945-9 (pbk) : £2.25 B82-24889

Allan, Catherine. Resource reader / Catherine Allan, George Livingstone, Jim Love. — Edinburgh : Holmes McDougall
4: Teaching guide. — c1981. — 48p ; 21cm
ISBN 0-7157-1959-9 (pbk) : £2.10 B82-24890

Allan, Catherine. Resource reader / Catherine Allan, George Livingstone, Jim Love. — Edinburgh : Holmes McDougall
5: Teaching guide. — c1982. — 46p ; 21cm
ISBN 0-7157-1960-2 (pbk) : £2.10 B82-38913

Allan, Catherine. Resource reader 5 / Catherine Allan, George Livingstone, Jim Love. — Edinburgh : Homes McDougall, c1982. — 96p : ill(some col.),maps ; 21cm
ISBN 0-7157-1946-7 (pbk) : Unpriced B82-38847

Allen, Margaret Buell. "What is it?" said the dog / story by Margaret Buell Allen ; pictures by Judy Sue Goodwin. — Aylesbury : Ginn, 1978 (1981 [printing]). — 16p : col.ill ; 23cm. — (Reading 360. Magic circle books. Level 4 ; bk.3)
ISBN 0-602-24028-x (pbk) : Unpriced B82-34799

Ambler, Eric. The dark frontier / Eric Ambler ; abridged and simplified by Richard Haill ; illustrations by Scoular Anderson. — London : Collins ELT, 1982. — 109p : ill ; 18cm. — (Collins English library. Level 6) (A Collins graded reader)
ISBN 0-00-370144-1 (pbk) : £0.85 B82-37081

Anderson, Lonzo. The haganinny / by Lonzo Anderson ; illustrated by Susan Harris Andersen. — Aylesbury : Ginn, c1978 (1981 [printing]). — 31p : col.ill ; 23cm. — (Reading 360. Magic circle books. Level 9 ; bk.2)
ISBN 0-602-24073-5 (pbk) : Unpriced B82-34525

Bade, Jane. Nine on a string / written by Jane Bade ; illustrated by Dorothy Jungels. — Aylesbury : Ginn, 1978 (1981 [printing]). — 16p : col.ill ; 23cm. — (Reading 360. Magic circle books. Level 6 ; bk.1)
ISBN 0-602-24046-8 (pbk) : Unpriced B82-34925

Begley, Eve. Duck in the park, duck in the dark / by Eve Begley ; illustrated by Jon Provest. — Aylesbury : Ginn, c1978 (1981 [printing]). — 16p : chiefly col.ill ; 20x23cm. — (Reading 360. Magic circle books. Level 3 ; bk.3)
Unpriced (pbk) B82-34813

Bendick, Jeanne. The future explorers' club meets here / by Jeanne Bendick ; illustrated by Joan Paley. — Aylesbury : Ginn, 1978 (1981 [printing]). — 24p : col.ill ; 22cm. — (Reading 360. Magic circle books. Level 9 ; bk.4)
ISBN 0-602-24073-5 (pbk) : Unpriced B82-34883

Berliner, Nancy. Border kidnap / J.M. Marks ; [adapted by Nancy Berliner ; illustrated by Tomaz Mok ; simplified according to the language grading scheme especially compiled by D.H. Howe]. — Hong Kong ; Oxford : Oxford University Press, 1981. — 65p : col.ill ; 22cm. — (Oxford progressive English readers. Grade 2) (Oxford in Asia)
Adaptation of: The triangle
ISBN 0-19-581333-2 (pbk) : Unpriced B82-35347

Berry, Erick. The valiant little potter / retold by Erick Berry ; illustrated by Nahid Haghighat. — Aylesbury : Ginn, 1978 (1981 [printing]). — 32p : col.ill ; 23cm. — (Reading 360. Magic circle books. Level 9 ; bk.6)
ISBN 0-602-24073-5 (pbk) : Unpriced B82-34889

Boyce, E. R.. The magic recorder / [text by E.R. Boyce]. — London : Macmillan, 1981. — 32p : ill(some col.) ; 21cm. — (The Gay way series. The fourth violet book)
ISBN 0-333-27326-5 (pbk) : Unpriced B82-00606

Boyce, E. R.. The old key / [text by E.R. Boyce]. — London : Macmillan, 1981. — 32p : ill (some col.) ; 21cm. — (The Gay way series. The fifth violet book)
ISBN 0-333-27327-3 (pbk) : Unpriced B82-00605

Bradbury, Lynne. World Cup final in danger : featuring Naranjito / written by Lynne Bradbury ; illustrated by Graham Marlow. — Loughborough : Ladybird, 1982. — 51p : col.ill ; 18cm
Text and col. ill on lining papers
ISBN 0-7214-0743-9 : £0.50 B82-18300

Brandt, Lois. Old lion and his friends / retold by Lois Brandt ; illustrated by Marilyn Bass. — Aylesbury : Ginn, c1978 (1981 [printing]). — 15p : col.ill ; 15x18cm. — (Reading 360. Magic circle books. Level 7 ; bk.6)
ISBN 0-602-24055-7 (pbk) : Unpriced B82-34532

Bull, Norman J.. Stories from world religions. — Edinburgh : Oliver & Boyd. — (Wide range)
2: Norman J. Bull, Reginald J. Ferris. — 1982. — 128p : ill(some col.) ; 20cm
ISBN 0-05-003371-9 (pbk) : Unpriced B82-35881

Bunting, Eve. Box, fox, ox and the peacock / by Eve Bunting ; illustrated by Leslie H. Morrill. — Aylesbury : Ginn, 1978 (1981 [printing]). — 24p : col.ill ; 24cm. — (Reading 360. Magic circle books. Level 5 ; bk.4)
ISBN 0-602-24037-9 (pbk) : Unpriced B82-34806

428.6 — English language. Reading books — *For schools* *continuation*

Bunting, Eve. A gift for Lonny / written by Eve Bunting ; illustrated by Robert Quackenbush. — Aylesbury : Ginn, c1978 (1981 [printing]). — 47p : col.ill ; 23cm. — (Reading 360. Magic circle books. Level 9 ; bk.1)
ISBN 0-602-24073-5 (pbk) : Unpriced
B82-34526

Bunting, Eve. Say it fast / written by Eve Bunting ; illustrated by True Kelley. — Aylesbury : Ginn, 1978 (1981 [printing]). — 16p : col.ill ; 20cm. — (Reading 360. Magic circle books. Level 5 ; bk.2)
ISBN 0-602-24037-9 (pbk) : Unpriced
B82-34805

Bunting, Eve. The two giants / retold by Eve Bunting ; Eric von Schmidt. — Aylesbury : Ginn, c1978 (1981 [printing]). — 22p : col.ill,1col.map ; 19x23cm. — (Reading 360. Magic circle books. Level 8 ; bk.6)
ISBN 0-602-24064-6 (pbk) : Unpriced
B82-34524

Clapman, Arnold. Angel the pig / story and pictures by Arnold Clapman. — Aylesbury : Ginn, 1978 (1981 [printing]). — 32p : col.ill ; 19x23cm. — (Reading 360. Magic circle books. Level 6 ; bk.3)
ISBN 0-602-24046-8 (pbk) : Unpriced
B82-34921

Clapman, Arnold. Dancing Nadine / story and pictures by Arnold Clapman. — Aylesbury : Ginn, 1978 (1981 [printing]). — 32p : col.ill ; 19x23cm. — (Reading 360. Magic circle books. Level 7 ; bk.3)
ISBN 0-602-24055-7 (pbk) : Unpriced
B82-34929

Clymer, Theodore. At the zoo / [story by Theodore Clymer] ; [pictures by Robert Amundsen and Hillary Hayton]. — Aylesbury : Ginn, c1978 (1981 [printing]). — 24p : col.ill ; 23cm. — (Reading 360. Level 4 ; bk.1)
ISBN 0-602-23171-x (pbk) : Unpriced
B82-34219

Clymer, Theodore. A book for Kay / [story by Theodore Clymer] ; [pictures by Robert Amundsen and Hillary Hayton]. — Aylesbury : Ginn, c1978 (1981 [printing]). — 24p : col.ill ; 23cm. — (Reading 360. Level 4 ; bk.3)
ISBN 0-602-23171-x (pbk) : Unpriced
B82-34218

Clymer, Theodore. Helicopters / [story by Theodore Clymer] ; [pictures by Robert Amundsen and Hillary Hayton]. — Aylesbury : Ginn, c1978 (1981 [printing]). — 24p : col.ill ; 23cm. — (Reading 360. Level 4 ; bk.2)
ISBN 0-602-23171-x (pbk) : Unpriced
B82-34217

Clymer, Theodore. I can read / [story by Theodore Clymer] ; [pictures by Janet Folland and George Guzzi]. — 2nd ed. — Aylesbury : Ginn, 1981. — 15p : col.ill ; 23cm. — (Reading 360. Level 3 ; bk.3)
Previous ed.: 1978
ISBN 0-602-23170-1 (pbk) : Unpriced
B82-34211

Clymer, Theodore. The park / [story by Theodore Clymer] ; [pictures by Janet Folland]. — 2nd ed. — Aylesbury : Ginn, 1981. — 23p : col.ill ; 23cm. — (Reading 360. Level 3 ; bk.1)
Previous ed.: 1978
ISBN 0-602-23170-1 (pbk) : Unpriced
B82-34213

Clymer, Theodore. The tortoise / [story by Theodore Clymer] ; [pictures by Janet Folland]. — 2nd ed. — Aylesbury : Ginn, 1981. — 24p : col.ill ; 23cm. — (Reading 360. Level 3 ; bk.2)
Previous ed.: 1978
ISBN 0-602-23170-1 (pbk) : Unpriced
B82-34212

Coates, Doreen. What a surprise! / [story by Doreen Coates] ; [pictures by Jo Chesterman]. — Aylesbury : Ginn, 1981 (1982 [printing]). — 32p : col.ill ; 23cm. — (Reading 360. Level 4 ; bk.4)
Text on inside cover. — Contents: Two surprises — Mum's surprise
ISBN 0-602-23171-x (pbk) : Unpriced
ISBN 0-602-23160-4 (set) : Unpriced
B82-34203

Coates, Doreen. Where are you going? / [story by Doreen Coates] ; [pictures by Val Biro]. — Aylesbury : Ginn, c1981 (1982 [printing]). — 24p : col.ill ; 23cm. — (Reading 360. Level 3 ; bk.6)
ISBN 0-602-23170-1 (pbk) : Unpriced
B82-34215

Coates, Doreen. Where are you going? / story by Doreen Coates ; pictures by Val Biro. — Aylesbury : Ginn, c1981 (1982 [printing]). — 24p : col.ill ; 23cm. — (Reading 360. Level 3 ; bk.6)
Cover title
ISBN 0-602-23170-1 (pbk) : Unpriced
ISBN 0-602-23156-6 (set) : Unpriced
B82-35038

Conrad, Joseph. The secret sharer : and other sea stories / Joseph Conrad ; abridged and simplified by Roland John ; illustrations by Steve Parkhouse. — London : Collins ELT, 1982. — 48p : ill ; 18cm. — (Collins English library. Level 4) (A Collins graded reader)
ISBN 0-00-370145-x (pbk) : £0.75 B82-37085

Conrad, Joseph. Victory / Joseph Conrad ; abridged and simplified by Viola Huggins ; illustrations by Willie Rodger. — London : Collins ELT, 1982. — 91p : ill ; 18cm. — (Collins English library. Level 5) (A Collins graded reader)
ISBN 0-00-370125-5 (pbk) : £0.80 B82-37083

Cooper, Stella. Mike's assignment / Stella Cooper ; [photographs Bob Cathmoir]. — London : Ward Lock Educational, c1978. — 16p : ill ; 21cm. — (WLE library graded reading series 10-14. Level 1 ; 4)
ISBN 0-7062-3707-2 (pbk) : £2.00 B82-18162

Corsi, Jerome R.. The king, the dragon, and the witch / by Jerome R. Corsi ; illustrated by Sylvie Selig. — Aylesbury : Ginn, c1978 (1981 [printing]). — 30p : col.ill ; 19x20cm. — (Reading 360. Magic circle books. Level 8 ; bk.1)
ISBN 0-602-24064-6 (pbk) : Unpriced
B82-34531

Cowley, Joy. The big tease. — Leeds : E.J. Arnold, 1982. — 8p : col.ill ; 22cm. — (Story chest. Stage 7)
Text by Joy Cowley and June Melser, illustrations by Murray Grimsdale. — Originally published: New Zealand : Shortland, 1982
ISBN 0-560-08677-6 (pbk) : Unpriced
ISBN 0-560-08705-5 (set) : £3.60 B82-31472

Cowley, Joy. Captain Bumble : a play. — Leeds : E.J. Arnold, 1982. — 16p : col.ill ; 22cm. — (Story chest. Stage 5)
Text by Joy Cowley and June Melser, illustrations by Martin Bailey. — Originally published: New Zealand : Shortland, 1982
ISBN 0-560-08669-5 (pbk) : Unpriced
ISBN 0-560-08703-9 (set) : £3.60 B82-31469

Cowley, Joy. Cat on the roof. — Leeds : E.J. Arnold, 1982. — 8p : col.ill ; 22cm. — (Story chest. Stage 5)
Text by Joy Cowley and June Melser, illustrations by Annie Dickeson. — Originally published: New Zealand : Shortland, 1982
ISBN 0-560-08667-9 (pbk) : Unpriced (set) : £3.60 B82-31467

Cowley, Joy. Countdown : a play. — Leeds : E.J. Arnold, 1982. — 8p : col.ill ; 22cm. — (Story chest. Stage 7)
Text by Joy Cowley and June Melser, illustrations by David Cowe. — Originally published: New Zealand : Shortland, 1982
ISBN 0-560-08679-2 (pbk) : Unpriced
ISBN 0-560-08705-5 (set) : £3.60 B82-31473

Cowley, Joy. A day in town. — Leeds : E.J. Arnold, 1982. — 8p : col.ill ; 22cm. — (Story chest. Stage 5)
Text by Joy Cowley and June Melser, illustrations by Glenda Jones. — Originally published: New Zealand : Shortland, 1982
ISBN 0-560-08668-7 (pbk) : Unpriced
ISBN 0-560-08703-9 (set) : £3.60 B82-31468

Cowley, Joy. The ghost and the sausage. — Leeds : E.J. Arnold, 1982. — 16p : col.ill ; 22cm. — (Story chest. Stage 6)
Text by Joy Cowley and June Melser, illustrations by Deirdre Gardiner. — Originally published: New Zealand : Shortland, 1982
ISBN 0-560-08673-3 (pbk) : Unpriced
ISBN 0-560-08704-7 (set) : £3.60 B82-31506

Cowley, Joy. Grandma's stick. — Leeds : E.J. Arnold, 1982. — 8p : col.ill ; 22cm. — (Story chest. Stage 6)
Text by Joy Cowley and June Melser, illustrations by Robyn Kahukiwa. — Originally published: New Zealand : Shortland, 1982
ISBN 0-560-08671-7 (pbk) : Unpriced
ISBN 0-560-08704-7 (set) : £3.60 B82-31507

Cowley, Joy. Hatupatu and the birdwoman. — Leeds : E.J. Arnold, 1982. — 16p : col.ill ; 22cm. — (Story chest. Stage 7)
Text by Joy Cowley and June Melser, illustrations by Robyn Kahukiwa. — Originally published: New Zealand : Shortland, 1982
ISBN 0-560-08678-4 (pbk) : Unpriced
ISBN 0-560-08705-5 (set) : £3.60 B82-31470

Cowley, Joy. Little brother's haircut. — Leeds : E.J. Arnold, 1982. — 16p : col.ill ; 22cm. — (Story chest. Stage 7)
Text by Joy Cowley and June Melser, illustrations by Helen Humphries. — Originally published: New Zealand : Shortland, 1982
ISBN 0-560-08676-8 (pbk) : Unpriced
ISBN 0-560-08705-5 (set) : £3.60 B82-31471

Cowley, Joy. The pie thief : a play. — Leeds : E.J. Arnold, 1982. — 16p : col.ill ; 22cm. — (Story chest. Stage 6)
Text by Joy Cowley and June Melser, illustrations by Robyn Belton. — Originally published: New Zealand : Shortland, 1982
ISBN 0-560-08674-1 (pbk) : Unpriced
ISBN 0-560-08704-7 (set) : £3.60 B82-31508

Cowley, Joy. The sunflower that went FLOP. — Leeds : E.J. Arnold, 1982. — 16p : col.ill ; 22cm. — (Story chest. Stage 5)
Text by Joy Cowley and June Melser, illustrations by David Cowe. — Originally published: New Zealand : Shortland, 1982
ISBN 0-560-08666-0 (pbk) : Unpriced
ISBN 0-560-08703-9 (set) : £3.60 B82-31466

Cowley, Joy. Tell-tale. — Leeds : E.J. Arnold, 1982. — 8p : col.ill ; 22cm. — (Story chest. Stage 6)
Text by Joy Cowley and June Melser, illustrations by Sherry Jordan. — Originally published: New Zealand : Shortland, 1982
ISBN 0-560-08672-5 (pbk) : Unpriced
ISBN 0-560-08704-7 (set) : £3.60 B82-34652

Crume, Marion. Do you see Mouse? / story by Marion Crume ; pictures by Ray Ameijide. — Aylesbury : Ginn, c1978 (1981 [printing]). — 24p : chiefly col.ill ; 23cm. — (Reading 360. Magic circle books. Level 4 ; bk.2)
ISBN 0-602-24028-x (pbk) : Unpriced
B82-34814

Daem, Mary. The dragon with a thousand wrinkles / written by Mary Daem ; illustrated by Marc Tolon Brown. — Aylesbury : Ginn, 1978 (1981 [printing]). — 15p : col.ill ; 19x23cm. — (Reading 360. Magic circle books. Level 10 ; bk.2)
ISBN 0-602-24082-4 (pbk) : Unpriced
B82-34888

Daem, Mary. The house on the top of the hill / by Mary Daem ; illustrated by Donald Leake. — Aylesbury : Ginn, c1978 (1981 [printing]). — 22p : col.ill ; 23cm. — (Reading 360. Magic circle books. Level 8 ; bk.2)
ISBN 0-602-24064-6 (pbk) : Unpriced
B82-34530

428.6 — English language. Reading books — *For schools* *continuation*

Dailey, Jan. The Poseidon adventure / [adapted by Jan Dailey]. — Harlow : Longman, 1982. — 31p : col.ill ; 21cm. — (Longman movieworld. Stage 1. Elementary)
ISBN 0-582-53548-4 (pbk) : £0.80 B82-22109

Davidson, Alan, *1924-*. Wedding in Laos / Alan Davidson ; illustrated by Soun Vannithone. — Cambridge : Cambridge University Press, 1982. — 24p : ill(some col.),1col.map ; 22cm. — (Pole star series. How people live)
ISBN 0-521-28346-9 (pbk) : Unpriced : CIP rev. B82-11492

De Paola, Tomie. The unicorn and the moon / written and illustrated by Tomie de Paola. — Aylesbury : Ginn, 1978 (1981 [printing]). — 31p : col.ill ; 20cm. — (Reading 360. Magic circle books. Level 9 ; bk.5)
ISBN 0-602-24073-5 (pbk) : Unpriced
B82-34887

De Paola, Tomie. The wind and the sun / retold and illustrated by Tomie de Paola. — Aylesbury : Ginn, 1978 (1981 [printing]). — 23p : col.ill ; 22cm. — (Reading 360. Magic circle books. Level 6 ; bk.6)
ISBN 0-602-24046-8 (pbk) : Unpriced
B82-34922

Doyle, *Sir* Arthur Conan. Three Sherlock Holmes adventures / Sir A. Conan Doyle ; abridged and simplified by Lewis Jones ; illustrations by Willie Rodger. — London : Collins ELT, 1982. — 48p : ill ; 18cm. — (Collins English library. Level 2) (A Collins graded reader)
ISBN 0-00-370146-8 (pbk) : £0.60 B82-37082

Dueland, Joy. Beaver boy / written and illustrated by Joy Dueland. — Aylesbury : Ginn, 1978 (1981 [printing]). — 30p : col.ill ; 23cm. — (Reading 360. Magic circle books. Level 10 ; bk.4)
ISBN 0-602-24082-4 (pbk) : Unpriced
B82-34884

Dueland, Joy. The pine tree that went to sea / written by Joy Dueland ; illustrated by Louis Cary. — Aylesbury : Ginn, 1978 (1981 [printing]). — 24p : col.ill ; 23cm. — (Reading 360. Magic circle books. Level 10 ; bk.5)
ISBN 0-602-24082-4 (pbk) : Unpriced
B82-34886

Edwards, Roy, *1931-*. Good save / Roy Edwards ; [illustrations by Bob Harvey]. — London : Ward Lock Educational, c1978. — 24p : ill ; 21cm. — (WLE library graded reading series 10-14. Level 3)
ISBN 0-7062-3763-3 (pbk) : £3.00 B82-18156

The **Emperor** and the nightingale / [illustrated by Maggie Read]. — London : Macmillan, 1982. — 32p : ill(some col.) ; 21cm. — (The Gay way series. The third orange book)
Contents: The emperor and the nightingale — The ugly duckling
ISBN 0-333-31765-3 (pbk) : Unpriced
B82-16861

Farmer, Derek. BBC Radio Thin King / Derek Farmer ; pictures by Ken Astrop. — Harlow : Longman, 1982
[Unit 1]. — 4v. : col.ill ; 21cm
ISBN 0-582-30105-x (pbk) : £2.50 B82-35443

Fiddle-dee-dee / [stories selected, adapted and graded by June Melser] ; [illustrations by Philip Webb ... et al.]. — Leeds : E.J. Arnold, 1982, c1981. — 48p : col.ill ; 22cm. — (Story chest. Stage 6)
Originally published: New Zealand : Shortland, 1981
ISBN 0-560-08670-9 (pbk) : Unpriced
ISBN 0-560-08704-7 (Set) : £3.60 B82-31505

Flowerdew, Phyllis. Reading on / Phyllis Flowerdew and Sam Stewart. — 2nd ed. — Edinburgh : Oliver & Boyd
Red book 2. — 1981. — 191p : ill,maps,music,1facsim,ports,1geneal.table ; 21cm
Previous ed.: 1960
ISBN 0-05-003357-3 (pbk) : £1.75 B82-15073

Flowerdew, Phyllis. Wide range readers / Phyllis Flowerdew. — Edinburgh : Oliver & Boyd
Red book 7. — 1982. — 174p : ill(some col.) ; 20cm
ISBN 0-05-003081-7 (pbk) : Unpriced
B82-20059

Flowerdew, Phyllis. Wide range readers / Phyllis Flowerdew. — London : Oliver & Boyd
Red book 8. — 1982. — 175p : ill(some col.) ; 20cm
ISBN 0-05-003082-5 (pbk) : £1.70 B82-33451

Freschet, Berniece. The park, the park / by Berniece Freschet ; pictures by Bini Bichisecchi. — Aylesbury : Ginn, c1978 (1981 [printing]). — 16p : chiefly col.ill ; 20x23cm. — (Reading 360. Magic circle books. Level 2 ; bk.3)
ISBN 0-602-24012-3 (pbk) : Unpriced
B82-34812

Gallico, Paul. [Short stories. Selections]. Love is a gimmick and other short stories / Paul Gallico ; selected and simplified by Jan Dalley ; illustrated by Pat Ludlow. — Harlow : Longman, 1982. — 44p : ill ; 20cm. — (Longman structural readers. Stage 3. Fiction)
Text on inside covers
ISBN 0-582-52655-8 (pbk) : Unpriced
B82-38962

Gibson, Gordon. Fishing / Gordon Gibson. — Cambridge : Press Syndicate of the University of Cambridge, 1982. — 16p : ill ; 21cm. — (Openers)
Cover title
ISBN 0-521-28381-7 (pbk) : £0.95 B82-35004

Gillam, Anne-Marie. One way with words / Anne-Marie Gillam ; [illustrated by Jim Dunkley]. — Bath : Better Books
Bk.1: Tom the cat. — 1980. — [19]p : ill ; 18cm
Cover title
ISBN 0-904700-10-0 (pbk) : Unpriced
B82-34930

Gillam, Anne-Marie. One way with words / Anne-Marie Gillam ; [illustrated by Jim Dunkley]. — Bath : Better Books
Bk.2: Peg and Sam. — 1980. — [19]p : ill ; 18cm
Cover title
ISBN 0-904700-10-0 (pbk) : Unpriced
B82-34931

Gillam, Anne-Marie. One way with words / Anne-Marie Gillam ; [illustrated by Jim Dunkley]. — Bath : Better Books
Bk.3: Ned and his hen. — 1980. — [16]p : ill ; 18cm
Cover title
ISBN 0-904700-10-0 (pbk) : Unpriced
B82-34932

Gillam, Anne-Marie. One way with words / Anne-Marie Gillam ; [illustrated by Jim Dunkley]. — Bath : Better Books
Bk.4: The rat. — 1980. — [12]p : ill ; 18cm
Cover title
ISBN 0-904700-10-0 (pbk) : Unpriced
B82-34933

Gillam, Anne-Marie. One way with words / Anne-Marie Gillam ; [illustrated by Jim Dunkley]. — Bath : Better Books
Bk.5: Tom on the log. — 1980. — [12p]p : ill ; 18cm
Cover title
ISBN 0-904700-10-0 (pbk) : Unpriced
B82-34934

Gillam, Anne-Marie. One way with words / Anne-Marie Gillam ; [illustrated by Jim Dunkley]. — Bath : Better Books
Bk.6: The fog. — 1980. — [19]p : ill ; 18cm
Cover title
ISBN 0-904700-10-0 (pbk) : Unpriced
B82-34935

Gillam, Anne-Marie. One way with words / Anne-Marie Gillam ; [illustrated by Jim Dunkley]. — Bath : Better Books
Bk.7: Val and Ted. — 1980. — [12]p : ill ; 18cm
Cover title
ISBN 0-904700-10-0 (pbk) : Unpriced
B82-34936

Gillam, Anne-Marie. One way with words / Anne-Marie Gillam ; [illustrated by Jim Dunkley]. — Bath : Better Books
Bk.8: At camp. — 1980. — [20]p : ill ; 18cm
Cover title
ISBN 0-904700-10-0 (pbk) : Unpriced
B82-34937

Gillam, Anne-Marie. One way with words / Anne-Marie Gillam ; [illustrated by Jim Dunkley]. — Bath : Better Books
Bk.9: The gang at the hut. — 1980. — [23]p : ill ; 18cm
Cover title
ISBN 0-904700-10-0 (pbk) : Unpriced
B82-34938

Gillam, Anne-Marie. One way with words / Anne-Marie Gillam ; [illustrated by Jim Dunkley]. — Bath : Better Books
Bk.10: The pet shop. — 1980. — [28p]p : ill ; 18cm
Cover title
ISBN 0-904700-10-0 (pbk) : Unpriced
B82-34939

Gillam, Anne-Marie. One way with words / Anne-Marie Gillam ; [illustrated by Jim Dunkley]. — Bath : Better Books
Bk.11: Gran and the tramp. — 1980. — [36]p : ill ; 18cm
Cover title
ISBN 0-904700-10-0 (pbk) : Unpriced
B82-34941

Gillam, Anne-Marie. One way with words / Anne-Marie Gillam ; [illustrated by Jim Dunkley]. — Bath : Better Books
Bk.12: Fred and Sad Sam. — 1980. — [40]p : ill ; 18cm
Cover title
ISBN 0-904700-10-0 (pbk) : Unpriced
B82-34942

Gillam, Anne-Marie. One way with words / Anne-Marie Gillam ; [illustrated by Jim Dunkley]. — Bath : Better Books
Bk.13: Bill and the bus. — 1980. — [28]p : ill ; 18cm
Cover title
ISBN 0-904700-10-0 (pbk) : Unpriced
B82-34943

Gillam, Anne-Marie. One way with words / Anne-Marie Gillam ; [illustrated by Jim Dunkley]. — Bath : Better Books
Bk.14: Fred and the car. — 1980. — [32]p : ill ; 18cm
Cover title
ISBN 0-904700-10-0 (pbk) : Unpriced
B82-34944

Gillam, Anne-Marie. One way with words / Anne-Marie Gillam ; [illustrated by Jim Dunkley]. — Bath : Better Books
Bk.15: the start of term. — 1980. — [36]p : ill ; 18cm
Cover title
ISBN 0-904700-10-0 (pbk) : Unpriced
B82-34945

Gillam, Anne-Marie. One way with words / Anne-Marie Gillam ; [illustrated by Jim Dunkley]. — Bath : Better Books
Bk.16: Bob and the dentist. — 1980. — [40]p : ill ; 18cm
Cover title
ISBN 0-904700-10-0 (pbk) : Unpriced
B82-34946

Gillam, Anne-Marie. One way with words / Anne-Marie Gillam ; [illustrated by Jim Dunkley]. — Bath : Better Books
Bk.17: The jazz band. — 1980. — [32]p : ill ; 18cm
Cover title
ISBN 0-904700-10-0 (pbk) : Unpriced
B82-34947

428.6 — English language. Reading books — *For schools* *continuation*

Gillam, Anne-Marie. One way with words / Anne-Marie Gillam ; [illustrated by Jim Dunkley]. — Bath : Better Books
Bk.18: The skull. — 1980. — [32]p : ill ; 18cm
Cover title
ISBN 0-904700-10-0 (pbk) : Unpriced
B82-34948

Gillam, Anne-Marie. One way with words / Anne-Marie Gillam ; [illustrated by Jim Dunkley]. — Bath : Better Books
Bk.19: Dave and hope. — 1980. — [32]p : ill ; 18cm
Cover title
ISBN 0-904700-10-0 (pbk) : Unpriced
B82-34949

Gillam, Anne-Marie. One way with words / Anne-Marie Gillam ; [illustrated by Jim Dunkley]. — Bath : Better Books
Bk.20: Sunday at the barn. — 1980. — [32]p : ill ; 18cm
Cover title
ISBN 0-904700-10-0 (pbk) : Unpriced
B82-34950

Gillam, Anne-Marie. One way with words / Anne-Marie Gillam ; [illustrated by Jim Dunkley]. — Bath : Better Books
Bk.21: The pigsty. — 1980. — [32]p : ill ; 18cm
Cover title
ISBN 0-904700-10-0 (pbk) : Unpriced
B82-34951

Gooch, Pat. Come for a ride / [story by Pat Gooch and William Shepherd] ; [pictures by Jo Chesterman]. — Aylesbury : Ginn, 1980 (1981 [printing]). — 16p : col.ill ; 23cm. — (Reading 360. Level 2 ; bk.5)
Cover title. — Text on inside covers
ISBN 0-602-23169-8 (pbk) : Unpriced
ISBN 0-602-23152-3 (set) : Unpriced
B82-34200

Griffiths, Helen. Love forever / Helen Griffiths. — London : Macmillan, 1981. — 73p : ill ; 21cm. — (Range 6, Fiction)
ISBN 0-333-31472-7 (pbk) : £0.80 B82-02271

Griffiths, Joan. Amul dairy / Joan Griffiths ; illustrated by Beryl Sanders. — Cambridge : Cambridge University Press, 1982. — 24p : ill (some col.),1col.map ; 22cm. — (Pole star series. How people live)
ISBN 0-521-28345-0 (pbk) : Unpriced : CIP rev.
B82-11493

Groves, Paul. The smuggler : and other stories / Paul Groves, Nigel Grimshaw. — London : Murray, c1981. — 90p ; 22cm
ISBN 0-7195-3867-x (pbk) : £1.10 : CIP rev.
B81-21520

Hickox, Nancy. Tuloose the miserable moose / written by Nancy Hickox ; illustrated by Les Gray. — Aylesbury : Ginn, 1978 (1981 [printing]). — 16p : col.ill ; 23cm. — (Reading 360. Magic circle books. Level 7 ; bk.4)
ISBN 0-602-24055-7 (pbk) : Unpriced
B82-34927

Hill, Christopher, *1950-*. Tom Turtle / story by Christopher Hill ; pictures by Tom Hill. — Aylesbury : Ginn, 1978 (1981 [printing]). — 32p : col.ill ; 20x23cm. — (Reading 360. Magic circle books. Level 5 ; bk.1)
ISBN 0-602-24037-9 (pbk) : Unpriced
B82-34803

Hill, Susan. I'm the king of the castle : a novel / by Susan Hill ; with a specially written introduction by the author ; editorial material by Geoffrey Halson and Sarah Ray. — Harlow : Longman, 1981. — ix,222p : 1port ; 20cm. — (Longman imprint books)
I'm the king of the castle. Originally published: London : Hamilton, 1970. — Includes extracts from A change for the better and The albatross and other stories
ISBN 0-582-22173-0 (pbk) : £1.45 B82-02041

Hinckley, Helen. The opossum's table / by Helen Hinckley ; illustrated by Gail Robinson. — Aylesbury : Ginn, 1978 (1981 [printing]). — 22p : col.ill ; 20cm. — (Reading 360. Magic circle books. Level 7 ; bk.2)
ISBN 0-602-24055-7 (pbk) : Unpriced
B82-34926

Hoare, Penny. Jamaican day / Penny Hoare ; illustrated by Annabel Large. — Cambridge : Cambridge University Press, 1982. — 24p : ill (some col.),1col.map ; 22cm. — (Pole star series. How people live)
ISBN 0-521-28344-2 (pbk) : Unpriced : CIP rev.
B82-11494

Hogg, Gordon. Twists : twelve stories with questions / Gordon Hogg ; illustrations by Gavin Rowe. — London : Edward Arnold, 1981. — 76p : ill ; 22cm
ISBN 0-7131-0613-1 (pbk) : £1.50 : CIP rev.
B81-33874

Hoke, Helen. Jokes, jests and jollies / collected by Helen Hoke ; illustrated by True Kelley. — Aylesbury : Ginn, 1978 (1981 [printing]). — 31p : col.ill ; 19x23cm. — (Reading 360. Magic circle books. Level 9 ; bk.3)
ISBN 0-602-24073-5 (pbk) : Unpriced
B82-34892

Holt, Michael. Science stories / Michael Holt and Alan Ward. — Edinburgh : Oliver & Boyd, 1982. — (Wide range)
Includes index
2. — 128p : ill(some col.) ; 21cm
ISBN 0-05-003291-7 (pbk) : £1.50 B82-33453

Jensen, Margaret Mary. Inside the red and white tent / written by Margaret Mary Jensen ; illustrated by George M. Ulrich. — Aylesbury : Ginn, 1978 (1981 [printing]). — 22p : col.ill ; 20cm. — (Reading 360. Magic circle books. Level 4 ; bk.5)
ISBN 0-602-24028-x (pbk) : Unpriced
B82-34804

Johnson, Barrie. A bad break : by Barrie Johnson / illustrated by Ray Mutimer. — Huddersfield : Schofield & Sims, 1981. — 16p : ill ; 21cm. — (The Relay readers. Yellow book ; 5)
ISBN 0-7217-0408-5 (pbk) : £0.40 B82-07312

Johnson, Barrie. Bringing the house down! / by Barrie Johnson ; illustrated by Ray Mutimer. — Huddersfield : Schofield & Sims, c1982. — 16p : ill ; 21cm. — (The Relay readers. Blue book ; 5)
ISBN 0-7217-0420-4 (pbk) : £0.40 B82-19951

Johnson, Barrie. Canal junk! : by Barrie Johnson / illustrated by Ray Mutimer. — Huddersfield : Schofield & Sims, 1981. — 16p : ill ; 21cm. — (The Relay readers. Yellow book ; 6)
ISBN 0-7217-0409-3 (pbk) : £0.40 B82-07311

Johnson, Barrie. Down under / by Barrie Johnson ; illustrated by Ray Mutimer. — Huddersfield : Schofield & Sims, 1982. — 16p : ill ; 21cm. — (The Relay readers. Blue book ; 6)
ISBN 0-7217-0421-2 (pbk) : £0.40 B82-19952

Johnson, Barrie. A fighting chance! / by Barrie Johnson ; illustrated by Ray Mutimer. — Huddersfield : Schofield & Sims, c1982. — 16p : ill ; 21cm. — (The Relay readers. Green book ; 6)
ISBN 0-7217-0415-8 (pbk) : £0.40 B82-19953

Johnson, Barrie. The final score : by Barrie Johnson / illustrated by Ray Mutimer. — Huddersfield : Schofield & Sims, 1981. — 16p : ill ; 21cm. — (The Relay readers. Red book ; 6)
ISBN 0-7217-0403-4 (pbk) : £0.40 B82-07313

Johnson, Barrie. Home and away / by Barrie Johnson ; illustrated by Ray Mutimer. — Huddersfield : Schofield & Sims, c1982. — 16p : ill ; 21cm. — (The Relay readers. Green book ; 4)
ISBN 0-7217-0413-1 (pbk) : £0.40 B82-19956

Johnson, Barrie. Lost and found : by Barrie Johnson / illustrated by Ray Mutimer. — Huddersfield : Schofield & Sims, 1981. — 16p : ill ; 21cm. — (The Relay readers. Red book ; 4)
ISBN 0-7217-0401-8 (pbk) : £0.40 B82-07315

Johnson, Barrie. No contest! : by Barrie Johnson / illustrated by Ray Mutimer. — Huddersfield : Schofield & Sims, 1981. — 16p : ill ; 21cm. — (The Relay readers. Yellow book ; 4)
ISBN 0-7217-0407-7 (pbk) : £0.40 B82-07310

Johnson, Barrie. One good turn : by Barrie Johnson / illustrated by Ray Mutimer. — Huddersfield : Schofield & Sims, 1981. — 16p : ill ; 21cm. — (The Relay readers. Red book ; 5)
ISBN 0-7217-0402-6 (pbk) : £0.40 B82-07314

Johnson, Barrie. Race against the tide / by Barrie Johnson ; illustrated by Ray Mutimer. — Huddersfield : Schofield & Sims, c1982. — 16p : ill ; 21cm. — (The Relay readers. Blue book ; 4)
ISBN 0-7217-0419-0 (pbk) : £0.40 B82-19955

Johnson, Barrie. Witch hunt! : by Barrie Johnson / illustrated by Ray Mutimer. — Huddersfield : Schofield & Sims, c1982. — 16p : ill ; 21cm. — (The Relay readers. Green book ; 5)
ISBN 0-7217-0414-x (pbk) : £0.40 B82-19954

Johnson, Ryerson. Monsters that move earth / written by Ryerson Johnson ; illustrated by Willi Baum. — Aylesbury : Ginn, 1978 (1981 [printing]). — 24p : col.ill ; 19x30cm. — (Reading 360. Magic circle books. Level 6 ; bk.5)
ISBN 0-602-24046-8 (pbk) : Unpriced
B82-34920

Joyce, Carolyn. The magic donkey / by Carolyn Joyce ; illustrated by Gregorio Prestopino. — Aylesbury : Ginn, c1978 (1981 [printing]). — 16p : col.ill ; 23cm. — (Reading 360. Magic circle books. Level 8 ; bk.3)
ISBN 0-602-24064-6 (pbk) : Unpriced
B82-34529

Jungmann, Ann. Little monkey / [story by Ann Jungmann] ; [pictures by Ivan Ripley]. — Aylesbury : Ginn, 1981 (1982 [printing]). — 24p : col.ill ; 23cm. — (Reading 360. Level 4 ; bk.5)
Text on inside cover
ISBN 0-602-23171-x (pbk) : Unpriced
ISBN 0-602-23160-4 (set) : Unpriced
B82-34201

Jungmann, Ann. A picnic for tortoise / [story by Ann Jungmann] ; [pictures by Lesley Smith]. — Aylesbury : Ginn, c1981 (1982 [printing]). — 16p : col.ill ; 23cm. — (Reading 360. Level 3 ; bk.5)
ISBN 0-602-23170-1 (pbk) : Unpriced
B82-34216

Jungmann, Ann. A picnic for tortoise / [story by Ann Jungmann] ; [pictures by Lesley Smith]. — Aylesbury : Ginn, 1981 (1982 [printing]). — 16p : col.ill ; 23cm. — (Reading 360. Level 3 ; bk.5)
Cover title
ISBN 0-602-23170-1 (pbk) : Unpriced
ISBN 0-602-23156-6 (set) : Unpriced
B82-35036

Keenan-Church, Helen. Ben and Lad / [story by Helen Keenan-Church] ; [pictures by Rosie Evans]. — Aylesbury : Ginn, 1978 (1981 [printing]). — 16p : col.ill ; 23cm. — (Reading 360. Level 2 ; bk.1)
Cover title. — Text on inside covers
ISBN 0-602-23169-8 (pbk) : Unpriced
ISBN 0-602-23152-3 (set) : Unpriced
B82-34196

428.6 — English language. Reading books — *For schools* *continuation*

Keenan-Church, Helen. Ben and Sparky / [story by Helen Keenan-Church] ; [pictures by Janet Folland]. — Aylesbury : Ginn, 1980 (1981 [printing]). — 16p : col.ill ; 23cm. — (Reading 360. Level 2 ; bk.6)
Cover title. — Text on inside covers
ISBN 0-602-23169-8 (pbk) : Unpriced
ISBN 0-602-23152-3 (set) : Unpriced
B82-34197

Keenan-Church, Helen. Can we help? / [story by Helen Keenan-Church] ; [pictures by Rosie Evans]. — Aylesbury : Ginn, 1978 (1981 [printing]). — 16p : col.ill ; 23cm. — (Reading 360. Level 2 ; bk.2)
Cover title. — Text on inside covers
ISBN 0-602-23169-8 (pbk) : Unpriced
ISBN 0-602-23152-3 (set) : Unpriced
B82-34198

Keenan-Church, Helen. Horses / [story by Helen Keenan-Church] ; [pictures by Janet Folland]. — Aylesbury : Ginn, c1981 (1982 [printing]). — 24p : col.ill ; 23cm. — (Reading 360. Level 3 ; bk.4)
ISBN 0-602-23170-1 (pbk) : Unpriced
B82-34214

Keenan-Church, Helen. Horses / story by Helen Keenan-Church ; pictures by Janet Folland. — Aylesbury : Ginn, c1981 (1982 [printing]). — 24p : col.ill ; 23cm. — (Reading 360. Level 3 ; bk.4)
ISBN 0-602-23170-1 (pbk) : Unpriced
B82-35037

Keenan-Church, Helen. I can hide / [story by Helen Keenan-Church] ; [pictures by Rosie Evans]. — Aylesbury : Ginn, 1978 (1981 [printing]). — 16p : col.ill ; 23cm. — (Reading 360. Level 2 ; bk.3)
Cover title. — Text on inside covers
ISBN 0-602-23169-8 (pbk) : Unpriced
ISBN 0-602-23152-3 (set) : Unpriced
B82-34199

Kessler, Leonard. Paint me a picture, Mr. Pine / written by Leonard Kessler ; illustrated by John Kuzich. — Aylesbury : Ginn, 1978 (1981 [printing]). — 31p : col.ill ; 23cm. — (Reading 360. Magic circle books. Level 6 ; bk.2)
ISBN 0-602-24046-8 (pbk) : Unpriced
B82-34923

Kingston, Peter. Mr Noah's animals / written and illustrated by Peter Kingston. — Loughborough : Ladybird, 1981. — 51p : col.ill ; 18cm. — (Story board)
Text and ill on lining papers. — Contents: The lions — The snake
ISBN 0-7214-0680-7 : £0.50 B82-00637

Kingston, Peter. Mr. Noah's animals / written and illustrated by Peter Kingston. — Loughborough : Ladybird, 1981. — 51p : col.ill ; 18cm. — (Story board)
Text and ill on lining papers. — Contents: The Monkeys — The Foxes
ISBN 0-7214-0681-5 : £0.50 B82-00635

Kingston, Peter. Mr Noah's animals / written and illustrated by Peter Kingston. — Loughborough : Ladybird, 1982. — 51p : col.ill ; 18cm. — (Story board) (Level 5 plus)
Text and col. ill on lining papers. — Contents: The giraffes. — The polar bears
ISBN 0-7214-0724-2 : £0.50 B82-18303

Kingston, Peter. Running out of time / written and illustrated by Peter Kingston. — Loughborough : Ladybird, 1982. — 51p : col.ill ; 18cm. — (Sport Billy)
Col. ill on lining papers
ISBN 0-7214-0742-0 : £0.50 B82-18301

Kingston, Peter. The winning goal / written and illustrated by Peter Kingston. — Loughborough : Ladybird, 1982. — 51p : col.ill ; 18cm. — (Sport Billy)
Col. ill on lining papers
ISBN 0-7214-0741-2 : Unpriced B82-18302

Kingston, Peter. Zoric the spaceman / written and illustrated by Peter Kingston. — Loughborough : Ladybird, 1982. — 51p : col.ill ; 18cm. — (Story board) (Level 5 plus)
Text and col. ill on lining papers. — Contents: A new house. — Helping the birds
ISBN 0-7214-0732-3 : £0.50 B82-18299

Lane, Jerry. In the zoo / story by Jerry Lane ; pictures by Blair Drawson. — Aylesbury : Ginn, 1978 (1981 [printing]). — 24p : col.ill ; 20x23cm. — (Reading 360. Magic circle books. level 4 ; bk.4)
ISBN 0-602-24028-x (pbk) : Unpriced
B82-34800

Lane, Sheila. The monkey and the crocodile : and other stories / adapted by Sheila Lane and Marion Kemp ; illustrations by Paula Bayne. — London : Ward Lock Educational, 1982. — 32p : ill ; 24cm. — (Take part starters. Level 1)
ISBN 0-7062-4144-4 (pbk) : Unpriced
B82-32126

Lane, Sheila. The princess who wanted the moon : and other stories / adapted by Sheila Lane and Marion Kemp ; illustrations by Jane Cope. — London : Ward Lock Educational, 1982. — 32p : ill ; 24cm. — (Take part starters. Level 2)
ISBN 0-7062-4145-2 (pbk) : Unpriced
B82-32127

Lane, Sheila. The three trolls : and other stories / adapted by Sheila Lane and Marion Kemp ; illustrations by Rosie Farrell. — London : Ward Lock Educational, 1982. — 32p : ill ; 24cm. — (Take part starters. Level 3)
ISBN 0-7062-4146-0 (pbk) : Unpriced
B82-32125

Lawrence, D. H.. Sons and lovers / D.H. Lawrence ; abridged and simplified by Margery Morris ; illustrations by Dorothy Hamilton. — London : Collins ELT, 1982. — 80p : ill ; 18cm. — (Collins English library. Level 6) (A Collins graded reader)
ISBN 0-00-370120-4 (pbk) : £0.85 B82-37084

Level 9 comprehension, language and reading development : extra cards and teacher's notes. — Aylesbury : Ginn, [1980] ([1982 [printing]]). — 25pieces : ill ; 22cm. — (Reading 360. Level 9)
ISBN 0-602-23172-8 : Unpriced B82-36822

Level 10 comprehension, language and reading development : extra cards and teacher's notes. — Aylesbury : Ginn, [1980] ([1981 [printing]]). — 25pieces : col.ill ; 22cm. — (Reading 360. Level 10)
ISBN 0-602-23173-6 : Unpriced B82-36826

Lexau, Joan M.. The tail of the mouse / retold by Joan M. Lexau ; illustrated by Roberta Langman. — Aylesbury : Ginn, 1978 (1981 [printing]). — 24p : col.ill ; 23cm. — (Reading 360. Magic circle books. Level 5 ; bk.6)
ISBN 0-602-24037-9 (pbk) : Unpriced
B82-34801

Lip, Evelyn. Clever kingfisher / written and illustrated by Evelyn Lip. — Singapore : Macmillan Southeast Asia ; London : Macmillan, 1982. — 16p : col.ill ; 19x21cm. — (Picture stories for children. Blue covers)
ISBN 0-333-33102-8 (pbk) : £0.60 B82-35906

Lip, Evelyn. The frog family / written and illustrated by Evelyn Lip. — Singapore : Macmillan Southeast Asia ; London : Macmillan, 1982. — 16p : col.ill ; 19x21cm. — (Picture stories for children. Blue covers)
ISBN 0-333-33103-6 (pbk) : £0.60 B82-35909

Lip, Evelyn. The greedy sparrow / written and illustrated by Evelyn Lip. — Singapore : Macmillan Southeast Asia ; London : Macmillan, 1982. — 16p : col.ill ; 19x21cm. — (Picture stories for children. Yellow covers)
ISBN 0-333-33100-1 (pbk) : £0.60 B82-35904

Lip, Evelyn. The kind tiger / written and illustrated by Evelyn Lip. — Singapore : Macmillan Southeast Asia ; London : Macmillan, 1982. — 16p : col.ill ; 19x21cm. — (Picture stories for children. Red covers)
ISBN 0-333-33098-6 (pbk) : £0.60 B82-35905

Lip, Evelyn. The little sparrow / written and illustrated by Evelyn Lip. — Singapore : Macmillan Southeast Asia ; London : Macmillan, 1982. — 16p : col.ill ; 19x21cm. — (Picture stories for children. Red covers)
ISBN 0-333-32123-5 (pbk) : £0.60 B82-35910

Lip, Evelyn. The snail and the tortoise / written and illustrated by Evelyn Lip. — Singapore : Macmillan Southeast Asia ; London : Macmillan, 1982. — 16p : col.ill ; 19x21cm. — (Picture stories for children. Blue covers)
ISBN 0-333-32125-1 (pbk) : £0.60 B82-35903

Lip, Evelyn. The snake and the eggs / written and illustrated by Evelyn Lip. — Singapore : Macmillan Southeast Asia ; London : Macmillan, 1982. — 16p : col.ill ; 19x21cm. — (Picture stories for children. Yellow covers)
ISBN 0-333-33099-4 (pbk) : £0.60 B82-35902

Lip, Evelyn. The three monkeys / written and illustrated by Evelyn Lip. — Singapore : Macmillan Southeast Asia ; London : Macmillan, 1982. — 16p : col.ill ; 19x21cm. — (Picture stories for children. Red covers)
ISBN 0-333-32124-3 (pbk) : £0.60 B82-35908

Lip, Evelyn. The zebras and the lion / written and illustrated by Evelyn Lip. — Singapore : Macmillan Southeast Asia ; London : Macmillan, 1982. — 16p : col.ill ; 19x21cm. — (Picture stories for children. Red covers)
ISBN 0-333-33097-8 (pbk) : £0.60 B82-35907

Loxton, Margaret. Day trip / Margaret Loxton ; [illustrations by Michael Munday]. — London : Ward Lock Educational, c1978. — 23p : ill ; 21cm. — (WLE library graded reading series 10-14. Level 3)
ISBN 0-7062-3765-x (pbk) : £3.00 B82-18159

McCullagh, Sheila. The ghost train / [author Sheila McCullagh] ; [artist Ferelith Eccles Williams]. — St Albans : Hart-Davis Educational, 1982. — 16p : col.ill ; 22cm. — (One two three and away!. Red book ; 7) (Red platform readers)
Cover title
ISBN 0-247-12917-8 (pbk) : Unpriced
ISBN 0-247-13231-4 (set) : Unpriced
B82-22905

McCullagh, Sheila. The hole in the wall / [author Sheila McCullagh] ; [artist Robert Geary]. — St Albans : Hart-Davis Educational, 1982. — 16p : col.ill ; 22cm. — (One two three and away!. Red book ; 9) (Red platform readers)
Cover title
ISBN 0-247-12931-3 (pbk) : Unpriced
ISBN 0-257-13231-4 (set) : Unpriced
B82-22903

McCullagh, Sheila. The little fox / [author Sheila McCullagh] ; [artist Barry Wilkinson]. — St Albans : Hart-Davis Educational, 1982. — 16p : col.ill ; 22cm. — (One two three and away!. Red book ; 10) (Red platform readers)
Cover title
ISBN 0-247-12932-1 (pbk) : Unpriced
ISBN 0-247-12932-1 (set) : Unpriced
B82-22906

McCullagh, Sheila. Sita and the robin / [author Sheila McCullagh] ; [artist Ferelith Eccles Williams]. — St Albans : Hart-Davis Educational, 1982. — 16p : col.ill ; 22cm. — (One two three and away!. Red book ; 8) (Red platform readers)
Cover title
ISBN 0-247-12930-5 (pbk) : Unpriced
ISBN 0-247-13231-4 (set) : Unpriced
B82-22904

428.6 — English language. Reading books — *For schools continuation*

McDonald, June. Help / [story by June McDonald and Stella E. Woodroffe] ; [pictures by Bob Young]. — Aylesbury : Ginn, 1978 (1981 [printing]). — 16p : col.ill ; 23cm. — (Reading 360. Level 1 ; bk.3)
Cover title
ISBN 0-602-23168-x (pbk) : Unpriced
B82-35044

McDonald, June. Here / [story by June McDonald and Stella E. Woodroffe] ; [pictures by Jochen Kruse]. — Aylesbury : Ginn, 1978 (1981 [printing]). — 16p : col.ill ; 23cm. — (Reading 360. Level 1 ; bk.2)
Cover title
ISBN 0-602-23168-x (pbk) : Unpriced
B82-35041

McDonald, June. Look / [story by June McDonald and Stella E. Woodroffe] ; [pictures by Jack Larkin]. — Aylesbury : Ginn, 1978 (1981 [printing]). — 16p : col.ill ; 23cm. — (Reading 360. Level 1 ; bk.1)
ISBN 0-602-23168-x (pbk) : Unpriced
B82-35042

Maclean, Muriel. Mags / by Muriel Maclean ; illustrations by Ben Black. — Aylesbury : Ginn, 1978 (1981 [printing]). — 29p : ill(some col.) ; 23cm. — (Reading 360. Magic circle books. Level 10 ; bk.3)
ISBN 0-602-24082-4 (pbk) : Unpriced
B82-34891

McMillan, Dorothy. Animals at the zoo / Dorothy McMillan ; photos Terry Hobin, Trevor Hyde. — Wellington : Milburn ; London : Methuen, c1979. — [16]p : col.ill ; 11x15cm. — (PM instant readers. 1st series ; 1R23)
Unpriced (unbound) B82-18650

McMillan, Dorothy. Baby / Dorothy McMillan ; photos Ian Hulse. — Wellington : Milburn ; London : Methuen, c1979. — [16]p : col.ill ; 11x15cm. — (PM instant readers. 1st series ; 1R15)
Unpriced (unbound) B82-18656

McMillan, Dorothy. Busy / Dorothy McMillan ; photos Trevor Hyde, Leslie Haines, Jean Stanton. — Wellington : Milburn ; London : Methuen, c1979. — [16]p : col.ill ; 11x15cm. — (PM instant readers. 1st series ; 1R6)
Unpriced (unbound) B82-18655

McMillan, Dorothy. In the park / Dorothy McMillan ; photos Ian Hulse, Trevor Hyde, Jean Stanton. — Wellington : Milburn ; London : Methuen, c1979. — [16]p : col.ill ; 11x15cm. — (PM instant readers. 1st series ; 1R19)
Unpriced (unbound) B82-18654

McMillan, Dorothy. In the toy shop / Dorothy McMillan ; photos Trevor Ulyatt. — Wellington : Milburn ; London : Methuen, c1979. — [16]p : col.ill ; 11x15cm. — (PM instant readers. 1st series ; 1R8)
Unpriced (unbound) B82-18652

McMillan, Dorothy. Oh look at this / Dorothy McMillan ; photos Leslie Haines. — Wellington : Milburn ; London : Methuen, c1979. — [16]p : col.ill ; 11x15cm. — (PM instant readers. 1st series ; 1R5)
Unpriced (unbound) B82-18653

McMillan, Dorothy. Travelling / Dorothy McMillan ; photos Ian Hulse. — Wellington : Milburn ; London : Methuen, c1979. — [16]p : col.ill ; 11x15cm. — (PM instant readers. 1st series ; 1R18)
Unpriced (unbound) B82-18651

McMillan, Dorothy. Visits / Dorothy McMillan ; photos Trevor Hyde, Ann Noble, Jean Stanton. — Wellington : Milburn ; London : Methuen, c1979. — [16]p : col.ill ; 11x15cm. — (PM instant readers. 1st series ; 1R21)
Unpriced (unbound) B82-18658

McMillan, Dorothy. We like you / Dorothy McMillan ; photos Trevor Hyde, Jean Stanton. — Wellington : Milburn ; London : Methuen, c1979. — [16]p : col.ill ; 11x15cm. — (PM instant readers. 1st series ; 1R22)
Unpriced (unbound) B82-18649

McMillan, Dorothy. Where are they kept? / Dorothy McMillan ; photos Ann Noble, Trevor Hyde, Jean Stanton. — Wellington : Milburn ; London : Methuen, c1979. — [16]p : col.ill ; 11x15cm. — (PM instant readers. 1st series ; 1R20)
Unpriced (unbound) B82-18657

McPhail, David. The glerp / written and illustrated by David M. McPhail. — Aylesbury : Ginn, 1978 (1981 [printing]). — 23p : col.ill ; 23x19cm. — (Reading 360. Magic circle books. Level 6 ; bk.4)
ISBN 0-602-24046-8 (pbk) : Unpriced
B82-34924

McPhail, David. Yesterday I lost a sneaker (and found the great goob sick) / written and illustrated by David M. McPhail. — Aylesbury : Ginn, 1978 (1981 [printing]). — 24p : col.il ; 22cm. — (Reading 360. Magic circle books. Level 7 ; bk.1)
ISBN 0-602-24055-7 (pbk) : Unpriced
B82-34928

Manley, Deborah. Me and my friend / by Deborah Manley ; pictures by Moira Maclean. — London : Scholastic, 1981. — [24]p : col.ill ; 16cm
ISBN 0-590-70104-5 (pbk) : £0.70 B82-03225

Marshall, Edward. Three by the sea / by Edward Marshall ; pictures by James Marshall. — London : Bodley Head, 1982, c1981. — 48p : col.ill ; 22cm. — (Bodley beginners)
Originally published: New York : Dial Press, 1981
ISBN 0-370-30455-1 : £3.25 : CIP rev.
B81-36977

Martin, Patricia Miles. Cat / story by Patricia Miles Martin ; pictures by Jonathan Goell. — Aylesbury : Ginn, c1978 (1981 [printing]). — 15p : chiefly ill ; 23cm. — (Reading 360. Magic circle books. Level 3 ; bk.2)
ISBN 0-602-24020-4 (pbk) : Unpriced
B82-34817

Martin, Patricia Miles. Hide / story by Patricia Miles Martin ; drawings by Jon McIntosh ; photographs by Dick Rogers. — Aylesbury : Ginn, c1978 (1981 [printing]). — 24p : chiefly col.ill ; 23cm. — (Reading 360. Magic circle books. Level 2 ; bk.2)
ISBN 0-602-24012-3 (pbk) : Unpriced
B82-34818

Martin, Patricia Miles. How can you hide an elephant? / story by Patricia Miles Martin ; pictures by George M. Ulrich. — Aylesbury : Ginn, c1978 (1981 [printing]). — 24p : chiefly col.ill ; 20x23cm. — (Reading 360. Magic circle books. Level 4 ; bk.1)
ISBN 0-602-24028-x (pbk) : Unpriced
B82-34810

Marzollo, Jean. Amy goes fishing / by Jean Marzollo ; pictures by Ann Schweninger. — London : Bodley Head, 1981, c1980. — 56p : col.ill ; 22cm. — (Bodley beginners)
Originally published: New York : Dial Press, 1980
ISBN 0-370-30902-2 : £3.25 : CIP rev.
B81-27458

Maxwell, Ruth. Look with May Ling / story by Ruth Maxwell ; pictures by Kenneth Francis Dewey. — Aylesbury : Ginn, c1978 (1981 [printing]). — 16p : chiefly col.ill ; 20x23cm. — (Reading 360. Magic circle books. Level 3 ; bk.5)
ISBN 0-602-24020-4 (pbk) : Unpriced
B82-34811

Maynard, Priscilla M.. Stop! Look! / by Priscilla M. Maynard ; illustrated by Joan Paley. — Aylesbury : Ginn, c1978 (1981 [printing]). — 16p : chiefly ill(some col.) ; 20cm. — (Reading 360. Magic circle books. Level 3 ; bk.1)
ISBN 0-602-24020-4 (pbk) : Unpriced
B82-34815

Melser, June. A barrel of gold. — Leeds : E.J. Arnold, 1982, c1981. — [16]p : col.ill ; 22cm. — (Story chest. Stage 4)
Text, June Melser and Joy Cowley; illustrations Robyn Belton. — Originally published: New Zealand : Shortlands, 1981
ISBN 0-560-08661-x (pbk) : Unpriced
ISBN 0-560-08702-0 (set) : Unpriced
B82-31437

Melser, June. The bee. — Leeds : E.J. Arnold, 1982, c1981. — 8p : col.ill ; 17cm. — (Story chest. Stage 1. Ready-set-go-books. Set B)
Text, June Melser and Joy Cowley; illustrations, Christine Ross. — Originally published: New Zealand : Shortlands, 1981
ISBN 0-560-08624-5 (pbk) : Unpriced
B82-31442

Melser, June. The big toe. — Leeds : E.J. Arnold, 1982, c1980. — 16p : chiefly col.ill ; 14x17cm. — (Story chest. Stage 1. Read-together books. Small books)
Text by June Melser and Joy Cowley, illustrations by Martin Bailey. — Originally published: New Zealand : Shortland, 1980
ISBN 0-560-08609-1 (pbk) : Unpriced
ISBN 0-560-08695-4 (set) : £4.20 B82-31457

Melser, June. The birthday cake : a play. — Leeds : E.J. Arnold, 1982, c1981. — [8]p : col.ill ; 22cm. — (Story chest. Stage 2)
Text, June Melser and Joy Cowley; illustrations Philip Webb. — Originally published: New Zealand : Shortlands, 1981
ISBN 0-560-08654-7 (pbk) : Unpriced
ISBN 0-560-08700-4 (set) : Unpriced
B82-31435

Melser, June. Boo-hoo. — Leeds : E.J. Arnold, 1982, c1980. — 16p : chiefly col.ill ; 14x17cm. — (Story chest. Stage 1. Read-together books. Small books)
Text by June Melser and Joy Cowley, illustrations by Andrew Reid. — Originally published: New Zealand : Shortland, 1980
ISBN 0-560-08612-1 (pbk) : Unpriced
ISBN 0-560-08695-4 (set) : £4.20 B82-31458

Melser, June. The chocolate cake. — Leeds : E.J. Arnold, 1982, c1981. — 8p : chiefly col.ill ; 17cm. — (Story chest. Stage 1. Ready-set-go books. Set A)
Text by June Melser and Joy Cowley, illustrations by Robyn Belton. — Originally published: New Zealand : Shortland, 1981
ISBN 0-560-08619-9 (pbk) : Unpriced
ISBN 0-560-08696-2 (set) B82-31452

Melser, June. Clever Mr Brown. — Leeds : E.J. Arnold, 1982, c1981. — [16]p : col.ill ; 22cm. — (Story chest. Stage 4)
Text, June Melser and Joy Cowley; illustrations David Cowe. — Originally published: New Zealand : Shortlands, 1981
ISBN 0-560-08662-8 (pbk) : Unpriced
ISBN 0-560-08702-0 (set) : Unpriced
B82-31438

Melser, June. Come with me. — Leeds : E.J. Arnold, 1982, c1981. — 8p : chiefly col.ill ; 14x17cm. — (Story chest. Stage 1. Ready-set-go books. Set A)
Text by June Melser and Joy Cowley, illustrations by Deirdre Gardiner. — Originally published: New Zealand : Shortland, 1981
ISBN 0-560-08622-9 (pbk) : Unpriced
ISBN 0-560-08696-2 (set) B82-31455

Melser, June. Copy-cat. — Leeds : E.J. Arnold, 1982, c1981. — 8p : col.ill ; 14x17cm. — (Story chest. Stage 1. Ready-set-go books. Set B)
Text, June Melser and Joy Cowley; illustrations Murray Grimsdale. — Originally published: New Zealand : Shortlands, 1981
ISBN 0-560-08631-8 (pbk) : Unpriced
B82-31448

428.6 — English language. Reading books — *For schools continuation*

Melser, June. Flying. — Leeds : E.J. Arnold, 1982, c1981. — 8p : col.ill ; 17cm. — (Story chest. Stage 1. Ready-set-go books. Set B)
Text, June Melser and Joy Cowley; illustrations Jenni Webb. — Originally published: New Zealand : Shortlands, 1981
ISBN 0-560-08625-3 (pbk) : Unpriced
B82-31443

Melser, June. Grandpa, grandpa. — Leeds : E.J. Arnold, 1982, c1980. — 16p : col.ill ; 25cm. — (Story chest. Stage 1. Read-together books. Large books)
Text by June Melser and Joy Cowley, illustrations by David Cowe. — Originally published: New Zealand : Shortland, 1980
ISBN 0-560-08603-2 (pbk) : Unpriced
ISBN 0-560-08694-6 (set) : Unpriced
B82-31477

Melser, June. Hairy bear. — Leeds : E.J. Arnold, 1982, c1980. — 16p : col.ill ; 25cm. — (Story chest. Stage 1. Read-together books. Large books)
Text by June Melser and Joy Cowley, illustrations by Deirdre Gardiner. — Originally published: New Zealand : Shortland, 1980
ISBN 0-560-08600-8 (pbk) : Unpriced
ISBN 0-560-08694-6 (set) : Unpriced
B82-31475

Melser, June. Help me / [stories selected, adapted and graded by June Melser] ; [illustrations by Philip Webb ... [et al.]]. — Leeds : E.J. Arnold, 1982. — [48]p : col.ill ; 22cm. — (Story chest. Stage 2)
Originally published: New Zealand : Shortlands, 1980
ISBN 0-560-08650-4 (pbk) : Unpriced
ISBN 0-560-08700-4 (set) : Unpriced
B82-31431

Melser, June. The hungry giant. — Leeds : E.J. Arnold, 1982, c1980. — 16p : col.ill ; 25cm. — (Story chest. Stage 1. Read-together books. Large books)
Text by June Melser and Joy Cowley, illustrations by Jenni Webb. — Originally published: New Zealand : Shortland, 1980
ISBN 0-560-08602-4 (pbk) : Unpriced
ISBN 0-560-08694-6 (set) : Unpriced
B82-31479

Melser, June. Hungry monster. — Leeds : E.J. Arnold, 1982, c1981. — 16p : col.ill ; 22cm. — (Story chest. Stage 3)
Text June Melser and Joy Cowley; illustrations Martin Bailey. — Originally published: New Zealand : Shortland, 1981
ISBN 0-560-08656-3 (pbk) : Unpriced
B82-31888

Melser, June. I want an icecream. — Leeds : E.J. Arnold, 1982, c1981. — 8p : chiefly col.ill ; 14x17cm. — (Story chest. Stage 1. Ready-set-go books. Set A)
Text by June Melser and Joy Cowley, illustrations by Murray Grimsdale. — Originally published: New Zealand : Shortland, 1981
ISBN 0-560-08616-4 (pbk) : Unpriced
ISBN 0-560-08696-2 (set) B82-31449

Melser, June. In a dark dark wood. — Leeds : E.J. Arnold, 1982, c1980. — 16p : chiefly col.ill ; 14x17cm. — (Story chest. Stage 1. Read-together books. Small books)
Text by June Melser and Joy Cowley, illustrations by Christine Ross. — Originally published: New Zealand : Shortland, 1980
ISBN 0-560-08610-5 (pbk) : Unpriced
ISBN 0-560-08695-4 (set) : £4.20 B82-31464

Melser, June. Jack-in-the-box. — Leeds : E.J. Arnold, 1982, c1981. — 8p : col.ill ; 22cm. — (Story chest. Stage 3)
Text June Melser and Joy Cowley; illustrations Philip Webb. — Originally published: New Zealand : Shortland, 1981
ISBN 0-560-08658-x (pbk) : Unpriced
B82-31886

Melser, June. Just like me / [stories selected, adapted and graded by June Melser] ; [illustrations by Deirdre Gardiner ... [et al]. — Leeds : E.J. Arnold, 1982, c1980. — [48]p : col.ill ; 22cm. — (Story chest. Stage 4)
Originally published: New Zealand : Shortlands, 1980
ISBN 0-560-08660-1 (pbk) : Unpriced
ISBN 0-560-08702-0 (set) : Unpriced
B82-31436

Melser, June. The kick-a-lot shoes. — Leeds : E.J. Arnold, 1982. — [8]p : col.ill ; 22cm. — (Story chest. Stage 2)
Text, June Melser and Joy Cowley; illustrations Deirdre Gardiner. — Originally published: New Zealand : Shortlands, 1981
ISBN 0-560-08653-9 (pbk) : Unpriced
B82-31434

Melser, June. Lazy Mary. — Leeds : E.J. Arnold, 1982, c1980. — 16p : col.ill ; 25cm. — (Story chest. Stage 1. Read-together books. Large books)
Text by June Melser and Joy Cowley, illustrations by Judy Shanahan. — Originally published: New Zealand : Shortland, 1980
ISBN 0-560-08607-5 (pbk) : Unpriced
ISBN 0-560-08694-6 (set) : Unpriced
B82-31482

Melser, June. Let me in. — Leeds : E.J. Arnold, 1982, c1980. — 48p : col.ill ; 22cm. — (Story chest. Stage 3)
Stories selected, adapted and graded by June Melser, illustrations by David Cowe, Deirdre Gardiner, Rosemary Turner. — Originally published: New Zealand : Shortland, 1980
ISBN 0-560-08655-5 (pbk) : Unpriced
B82-31889

Melser, June. Little pig. — Leeds : E.J. Arnold, 1982, c1981. — 8p : col.ill ; 22cm. — (Story chest. Stage 1. Ready-set-go books. Set B)
Text, June Melser and Joy Cowley; illustrations Isabel Lowe. — Originally published: New Zealand : Shortlands, 1981
ISBN 0-560-08626-1 (pbk) : Unpriced
B82-31444

Melser, June. Lost. — Leeds : E.J. Arnold, 1982, c1981. — 8p : col.ill ; 17cm. — (Story chest. Stage 1. Ready-set-go books. Set B)
Text, June Melser and Joy Cowley; illustrations Philip Webb. — Originally published: New Zealand : Shortlands, 1981
ISBN 0-560-08629-6 (pbk) : Unpriced
B82-31446

Melser, June. More! more! more! / [stories selected, adapted and graded by June Melser] ; [illustrations by Liz Fuller ... et al.]. — Leeds : E.J. Arnold, 1982, c1981. — 48p : col.ill ; 22cm. — (Story chest. Stage 7)
Originally published: New Zealand : Shortland, 1981
ISBN 0-560-08675-x (pbk) : Unpriced
ISBN 0-560-08705-5 (set) : £3.60 B82-31474

Melser, June. Mrs Wishy-washy. — Leeds : E.J. Arnold, 1982, c1980. — 16p : col.ill ; 25cm. — (Story chest. Stage 1. Read-together books. Large books)
Text by June Melser and Joy Cowley, illustrations by Elizabeth Fuller. — Originally published: New Zealand : Shortland, 1980
ISBN 0-560-08604-0 (pbk) : Unpriced
ISBN 0-560-08694-6 (set) : Unpriced
B82-31476

Melser, June. My home. — Leeds : E.J. Arnold, 1982, c1981. — 8p : col.ill ; 17cm. — (Story chest. Stage 1. Ready-set-go books. Set B)
Text, June Melser and Joy Cowley; illustrations, Isabel Lowe. — Originally published: New Zealand : Shortlands, 1981
ISBN 0-560-08630-x (pbk) : Unpriced
B82-31447

Melser, June. Obadiah. — Leeds : E.J. Arnold, 1982, c1980. — 16p : chiefly col.ill ; 14x17cm. — (Story chest. Stage 1. Read-together books. Small books)
Text by June Melser and Joy Cowley, illustrations by Murray Grimsdale. — Originally published: New Zealand : Shortland, 1980
ISBN 0-560-08615-6 (pbk) : Unpriced
ISBN 0-260-08695-4 (set) : £4.20 B82-31463

Melser, June. One cold wet night. — Leeds : E.J. Arnold, 1982, c1980. — 16p : chiefly col.ill ; 14x17cm. — (Story chest. Stage 1. Read-together books. Small books)
Text by June Melser and Joy Cowley, illustrations by Deirdre Gardiner. — Originally published: New Zealand : Shortland, 1980
ISBN 0-560-08613-x (pbk) : Unpriced
ISBN 0-560-08695-4 (set) : £4.20 B82-31460

Melser, June. The pirates. — Leeds : E.J. Arnold, 1982, c1981. — [8]p : col.ill ; 22cm. — (Story chest. Stage 2)
Text, June Melser and Joy Cowley; illustrations Isabel Lowe. — Originally published: New Zealand : Shortlands, 1981
ISBN 0-560-08651-2 (pbk) : Unpriced
ISBN 0-560-08700-4 (set) : Unpriced
B82-31432

Melser, June. Plop!. — Leeds : E.J. Arnold, 1982, c1981. — 8p : col.ill ; 14x17cm. — (Story chest. Stage 1. Ready-set-go books. Set B)
Text, June Melser and Joy Cowley; illustrations Christine Ross. — Originally published: New Zealand : Shortlands, 1981
ISBN 0-560-08627-x (pbk) : Unpriced
B82-31445

Melser, June. Poor old Polly. — Leeds : E.J. Arnold, 1982, c1980. — 16p : chiefly col.ill ; 14x17cm. — (Story chest. Stage 1. Read-together books. Small books)
Text by June Melser and Joy Cowley, illustrations by Elizabeth Fuller. — Originally published: New Zealand : Shortland, 1980
ISBN 0-560-08611-3 (pbk) : Unpriced
ISBN 0-560-08695-4 (set) : £4.20 B82-31461

Melser, June. Round and round. — Leeds : E.J. Arnold, 1982, c1981. — 8p : chiefly col.ill ; 17cm. — (Story chest. Stage 1. Ready-set-go books. Set A)
Text by June Melser and Joy Cowley, illustrations by David Cowe. — Originally published: New Zealand : Shortland, 1981
ISBN 0-560-08620-2 (pbk) : Unpriced
ISBN 0-560-08696-2 (set) B82-31453

Melser, June. Sing a song. — Leeds : E.J. Arnold, 1982, c1980. — 16p : col.ill ; 25cm. — (Story chest. Stage 1. Read-together books. Large books)
Text by June Melser and Joy Cowley, illustrations by Deirdre Gardiner. — Originally published: New Zealand : Shortland, 1980
ISBN 0-560-08606-7 (pbk) : Unpriced
ISBN 0-560-08694-6 (set) : Unpriced
B82-31481

Melser, June. Smarty pants. — Leeds : E.J. Arnold, 1982, c1980. — 16p : col.ill ; 25cm. — (Story chest. Stage 1. Read-together books. Large books)
Text by June Melser and Joy Cowley, illustrations by Murray Grimsdale. — Originally published: New Zealand : Shortland, 1980
ISBN 0-560-08605-9 (pbk) : Unpriced
ISBN 0-560-08694-6 (set) : Unpriced
B82-31480

Melser, June. Splosh. — Leeds : E.J. Arnold, 1982, c1981. — 8p : chiefly col.ill ; 17cm. — (Story chest. Stage 1. Ready-set-go books. Set A)
Text by June Melser and Joy Cowley, illustrations by Philip Webb. — Originally published: New Zealand : Shortland, 1981
ISBN 0-560-08621-0 (pbk) : Unpriced
ISBN 0-560-08696-2 (set) B82-31454

428.6 — English language. Reading books — *For schools* *continuation*

Melser, June. A terrible fright : a play. — Leeds : E.J. Arnold, 1982, c1981. — 8p : col.ill ; 22cm. — (Story chest ; Stage 4)
Text, June Melser and Joy Cowley; illustrations Girvan Roberts. — Originally published: New Zealand : Shortlands, 1981
ISBN 0-560-08664-4 (pbk) : Unpriced
ISBN 0-560-08702-0 (set) : Unpriced
B82-31440

Melser, June. Three little ducks. — Leeds : E.J. Arnold, 1982, c1980. — 16p : chiefly col.ill ; 14x17cm. — (Story chest. Stage 1. Read-together books. Small books)
Text by June Melser and Joy Cowley, illustrations by David Cowe. — Originally published: New Zealand : Shortland, 1980
ISBN 0-560-08608-3 (pbk) : Unpriced
ISBN 0-560-08695-4 (set) : £4.20 B82-31459

Melser, June. To New York. — Leeds : E.J. Arnold, 1982, c1981. — 8p : chiefly col.ill ; 14x17cm. — (Story chest. Stage 1. Ready-set-go books. Set A)
Text by June Melser and Joy Cowley, illustrations by Jenni Webb. — Originally published: New Zealand : Shortland, 1981
ISBN 0-560-08618-0 (pbk) : Unpriced
ISBN 0-560-08696-2 (set) B82-31451

Melser, June. Well I never / [stories selected, adapted and graded by June Melser] ; [illustrations by Deirdre Gardiner, Robyn Belton, Christine Ross]. — Leeds : E.J. Arnold, 1982, c1980. — 48p : col.ill ; 22cm. — (Story chest. Stage 5)
Originally published: New Zealand : Shortland, 1980
ISBN 0-560-08665-2 (pbk) : Unpriced
ISBN 0-560-08703-9 (set) : £4.20 B82-31465

Melser, June. Wet grass. — Leeds : E.J. Arnold, 1982, c1981. — [8]p : col.ill ; 22cm. — (Story chest. Stage 2)
Text, June Melser and Joy Cowley; illustrations Christine Ross. — Originally published: New Zealand : Shortlands, 1981
ISBN 0-560-08652-0 (pbk) : Unpriced
ISBN 0-560-08700-4 (set) : Unpriced
B82-31433

Melser, June. Where are they going?. — Leeds : E.J. Arnold, 1982, c1981. — 8p : chiefly col.ill ; 14x17cm. — (Story chest. Stage 1. Ready-set-go books. Set A)
Text by June Melser and Joy Cowley, illustrations by Martin Bailey. — Originally published: New Zealand : Shortland, 1981
ISBN 0-560-08623-7 (pbk) : Unpriced
ISBN 0-560-08696-2 (set) B82-31456

Melser, June. Where is my spider?. — Leeds : E.J. Arnold, 1982, c1981. — [8]p : col.ill ; 22cm. — (Story chest. Stage 4)
Text, June Melser and Joy Cowley; illustrations Murray Grimsdale. — Originally published: New Zealand : Shortlands, 1981
ISBN 0-560-08663-6 (pbk) : Unpriced
ISBN 0-560-08702-0 (set) : Unpriced
B82-31439

Melser, June. Who lives here?. — Leeds : E.J. Arnold, 1982, c1981. — 8p : col.ill ; 14x17cm. — (Story chest. Stage 1. Ready-set-go books. Set B)
Text, June Melser and Joy Cowley; illustrations, David Cowe. — Originally published: New Zealand : Shortlands, 1981
ISBN 0-560-08628-8 (pbk) : Unpriced
B82-31441

Melser, June. Who's going to lick the bowl?. — Leeds : E.J. Arnold, 1982, c1981. — 8p : chiefly col.ill ; 17cm. — (Story chest. Stage 1. Ready-set-go books. Set A)
Text by June Melser and Joy Cowley, illustrations by Murray Grimsdale. — Originally published: New Zealand : Shortland, 1981
ISBN 0-560-08617-2 (pbk) : Unpriced
ISBN 0-560-08696-2 (set) B82-31450

Melser, June. Woosh!. — Leeds : E.J. Arnold, 1982, c1980. — 16p : chiefly col.ill ; 14x17cm. — (Story chest. Stage 1. Read-together books. Small books)
Text by June Melser and Joy Cowley, illustrations by Gary Hebley. — Originally published: New Zealand : Shortland, 1980
ISBN 0-560-08614-8 (pbk) : Unpriced
ISBN 0-560-08695-4 (set) : £4.20 B82-31462

Melser, June. Yes ma'am. — Leeds : E.J. Arnold, 1982, c1980. — 16p : col.ill ; 25cm. — (Story chest. Stage 1. Read-together books. Large books)
Text by June Melser and Joy Cowley, illustrations by Rosemary Turner. — Originally published: New Zealand : Shortland, 1980
ISBN 0-560-08601-6 (pbk) : Unpriced
ISBN 0-560-08694-6 (set) : Unpriced
B82-31478

Melser, June. Yum and yuk. — Leeds : E.J. Arnold, 1982, c1981. — 8p : col.ill ; 22cm. — (Story chest. Stage 3)
Text June Melser and Joy Cowley; illustrations Isabel Lowe. — Originally published: New Zealand : Shortland, 1981
ISBN 0-560-08657-1 (pbk) : Unpriced
B82-31887

Milnes, Bryan. F.I.S.H. fish / Bryan Milnes ; [illustrations by David Gibbons]. — London : Ward Lock Educational, c1978. — 24p : ill ; 21cm. — (WLE library graded reading series 10-14. Level 3)
ISBN 0-7062-3766-8 (pbk) : £3.00 B82-18157

Moon, Cliff. Once upon a time / [story adapted by Cliff Moon] ; [pictures by Caroline Sharpe]. — Aylesbury : Ginn, 1981 (1982 [printing]). — 32p : col.ill ; 23cm. — (Reading 360. Level 4 ; bk.6)
Contents: Little Red Riding Hood — Jack and the beanstalk
ISBN 0-602-23171-x (pbk) : Unpriced
ISBN 0-602-23160-4 (set) : Unpriced
B82-34202

Morpurgo, Michael. 'Do all you dare' / Michael Morpurgo ; [photographs Bob Cathmoir]. — London : Ward Lock Educational, c1978. — 16p : ill ; 21cm. — (WLE library graded reading series 10-14. Level 1 ; 1)
ISBN 0-7062-3704-8 (pbk) : £2.00 B82-18163

Morpurgo, Michael. What shall we do with it? / Michael Morpurgo ; [illustations by Priscilla Lamont]. — London : Ward Lock Educational, c1978. — 24p : ill ; 21cm. — (WLE library graded reading series 10-14. Level 2)
ISBN 0-7062-3708-0 (pbk) : £3.00 B82-18165

Mountfield, Anne. Hospital — emergency / Anne Mountfield. — London : Harrap, 1982. — 40p : ill ; 19cm. — (The Reporters series)
ISBN 0-245-53646-9 (pbk) : £0.90 B82-31574

Murphy, Frank. Stepping stones. — Dublin : Educational Company of Ireland
Cover title. — Author: F. Murphy. — Text on inside covers
Basic reader F / [illustrations by John Skelton]. — 1980. — 72p : col.ill ; 21cm
Unpriced (pbk) B82-02101

Murphy, Frank. Stepping stones. — Dublin : Educational Company of Ireland
Cover title. — Author: F. Murphy. — Text on inside covers
Extension reader F / [illustrations by John Skelton]. — 1981. — 72p : col.ill ; 21cm
Unpriced (pbk) B82-02102

Murphy, Frank. Stepping-stones. — Dublin : Educational Company of Ireland
First reader G / [illustrations by John Skelton]. — 1981. — 128p : ill(some col.) ; 21cm
Cover title. — Author: F. Murphy
Unpriced (pbk) B82-00006

Murphy, Frank. Stepping-stones. — Dublin : Educational Company of Ireland
Stage A: Workbook. — Rev. ed. / [Frank Murphy], [illustrations by Tommy McCann]. — 1981. — 64p : ill ; 30cm
Cover title. — Previous ed.: 1978
Unpriced (pbk) B82-00418

Murphy, Frank. Stepping stones. — Dublin : Education Company of Ireland
Stage F. workbook / [illustrations and cover design: Tommy McCann]. — 1982. — 111p : ill ; 21cm
Cover title. — Author: F. Murphy. — Text on inside cover
Unpriced (pbk) B82-13765

Murray, Philippa. Changes / Philippa Murray, Alison Sinclair and Susan Quilliam. — Welwyn : Nisbet, 1982. — 96p : ill(some col.),col.maps,1port ; 21cm
ISBN 0-7202-1017-8 (pbk) : £1.40 B82-33063

Murray, Philippa. Currents / Philippa Murray, Alison Sinclair and Susan Quilliam. — Welwyn : Nisbet, 1982. — 95p : ill(some col.),col.maps,1port ; 21cm
ISBN 0-7202-1018-6 (pbk) : £1.40 B82-33062

Murray, W. (William), *1912-*. Jump from the sky / by W. Murray ; with illustrations by Martin Aitchison. — Loughborough : Ladybird, c1980. — 51p : col.ill ; 18cm. — (The Ladybird key words reading scheme ; bk.9b)
Text on lining papers
ISBN 0-7214-0545-2 : £0.50 B82-35454

Perkins, Diana. Home / [story by Diana Perkins] ; [pictures by Lynne Byrnes]. — Aylesbury : Ginn, c1980 (1981 [printing]). — 16p : col.ill ; 23cm. — (Reading 360. Level 1 ; bk.4)
Cover title
ISBN 0-602-23168-x (pbk) : Unpriced
ISBN 0-602-23148-5 (set) : Unpriced
B82-35043

Perkins, Diana. Lad / [story by Diana Perkins] ; [pictures by Janet Folland]. — Aylesbury : Ginn, c1980 (1981 [printing]). — 16p : col.ill ; 13cm. — (Reading 360. Level 1 ; bk.5)
Cover title
ISBN 0-602-23168-x (pbk) : Unpriced
ISBN 0-602-23148-5 (set) : Unpriced
B82-35039

Pollock, Robert, *1930 May 11-*. Yam festival / Robert Pollock ; illustrated by Joanna Troughton. — Cambridge : Cambridge University Press, 1982. — 23p : ill(some col.),1col.map ; 22cm. — (Pole star series. How people live)
ISBN 0-521-28343-4 (pbk) : Unpriced : CIP rev. B82-11495

Randell, Beverley. After school / Beverley Randell ; photos Ann Noble, Trevor Hyde, Jean Stanton. — Wellington : Milburn ; London : Methuen, c1979. — [16]p : col.ill ; 11x15cm. — (PM instant readers. 1st series ; IR17)
Unpriced (unbound) B82-18640

Randell, Beverley. Big brother / Beverley Randell ; photos Ian Hulse. — Wellington : Milburn ; London : Methuen, c1979. — [16]p : col.ill ; 11x15cm. — (PM instant readers. 1st series ; IR14)
Unpriced (unbound) B82-18637

Randell, Beverley. Big sister / Beverley Randell ; photos Ian Hulse. — Wellington : Milburn ; London : Methuen, c1979. — [16]p : col.ill ; 11x15cm. — (PM instant readers. 1st series ; IR13)
Unpriced (unbound) B82-18634

Randell, Beverley. Father / Beverley Randell ; photos Ian Hulse. — Wellington : Milburn ; London : Methuen, c1979. — [16]p : col.ill ; 11x15cm. — (PM instant readers. 1st series ; IR12)
Unpriced (unbound) B82-18636

428.6 — English language. Reading books — *For schools* *continuation*

Randell, Beverley. Grown-ups / Beverley Randell ; photos Trevor Hyde, Jean Stanton. — Wellington : Milburn ; London : Methuen, c1979. — [16]p : col.ill ; 11x15cm. — (PM instant readers. 1st series ; IR7)
Unpriced (unbound) B82-18638

Randell, Beverley. Me / Beverley Randell ; photos Ian Hulse. — Wellington : Milburn ; London : Methuen, c1979. — [16]p : col.ill ; 11x15cm. — (PM instant readers. 1st series ; IR9)
Unpriced (unbound) B82-18633

Randell, Beverley. Mother / Beverley Randell ; photos Ian Hulse. — Wellington : Milburn ; London : Methuen, c1979. — [16]p : col.ill ; 11x15cm. — (PM instant readers. 1st series ; IR11)
Unpriced (unbound) B82-18635

Randell, Beverley. My family / Beverley Randell ; photos Ian Hulse. — Wellington : Milburn ; London : Methuen, c1979. — [16]p : col.ill ; 11x15cm. — (PM instant readers. 1st series ; IR10)
Unpriced (unbound) B82-18631

Randell, Beverley. People we know / Beverley Randell ; photos Trevor Hyde, Ian Hulse, Jean Stanton. — Wellington : Milburn ; London : Methuen, c1979. — [16]p : col.ill ; 11x15cm. — (PM instant readers. 1st series ; IR16)
Unpriced (unbound) B82-18639

Randell, Beverley. Pets / Beverley Randell ; photos Ian Hulse. — Wellington : Milburn ; London : Methuen, c1979. — [16]p : col.ill ; 11x15cm. — (PM instant readers. 1st series ; IR24)
Unpriced (unbound) B82-18632

Reid, Jessie. Link-up / [Jessie Reid, Joan Low]. — Edinburgh : Holmes McDougall
Build-up book 6a: The king who wanted to touch the moon ; The clever donkey / [illustrators Anne Roger, Sydney McK Glen, Joan Beales]. — c1982. — 24p : col.ill ; 22cm
Cover title
ISBN 0-7157-2156-9 (pbk) : £0.95 B82-35549

Reid, Jessie. Link-up / [Jessie Reid, Joan Low]. — Edinburgh : Holmes McDougall
Build-up book 6c: The lion and the mouse ; Sheba's babies / [illustrators David C. Wilson, Sydney McK Glen, Jessie Henderson]. — c1982. — 24p : col.ill ; 22cm
Cover title
ISBN 0-7157-2158-5 (pbk) : £0.95 B82-35550

Reid, Jessie. Link-up / [Jessie Reid, Joan Low]. — Edinburgh : Holmes McDougall
Build-up book 6b: The lonely scarecrow ; The baby blackbird / [illustrators Joan Beales, Anne Rodger, David C. Wilson]. — c1982. — 24p : col.ill ; 22cm
Cover title
ISBN 0-7157-2157-7 (pbk) : £0.95 B82-35548

Reid, Jessie. Link-up / [by Jessie Reid, Joan Low]. — Edinburgh : Holmes McDougall
9: Surprises. — [c1981]. — 64p : col.ill ; 22cm
Cover title
ISBN 0-7157-1935-1 (pbk) : Unpriced B82-03212

Richards, J. C.. Alice's adventures through the looking glass / by Lewis Carroll ; [retold by J.C. Richards] ; [illustrated by Kathryn Blomfield]. — Hong Kong ; Oxford : Oxford University Press, c1981. — 69p : col.ill ; 22cm. — (Oxford progressive English readers. Grade 2)
ISBN 0-19-581308-1 (pbk) : £1.10 B82-25578

Roberts, Gwyneth. Sons and lovers / D.H. Lawrence ; abridged and simplified by Gwyneth Roberts. — Harlow : Longman, 1982. — 124p ; 19cm. — (Longman simplified English series)
ISBN 0-582-52634-5 (pbk) : £0.80 B82-22108

Robson, Nancy. Where is Zip? / story by Nancy Robson ; pictures by Lynn Titleman. — Aylesbury : Ginn, c1978 (1981 [printing]). — 16p : chiefly col.ill ; 20cm. — (Reading 360. Magic circle books. Level 3 ; bk.4)
ISBN 0-602-24020-4 (pbk) : Unpriced B82-34809

Rogerson, Jim. Control to Baby One - / Jim Rogerson ; [illustrations by David Godfrey]. — London : Ward Lock Educational, c1978. — 24p : ill ; 21cm. — (WLE library graded reading series 10-14. Level 3)
ISBN 0-7062-3764-1 (pbk) : £3.00 B82-18160

Rogerson, Jim. The hunting dog / Jim Rogerson ; [photographs Bob Cathmoir]. — London : Ward Lock Educational, c1978. — 16p : ill ; 21cm. — (WLE library graded reading series 10-14. Level 1 ; 3)
ISBN 0-7062-3706-4 (pbk) : £2.00 B82-18161

Rogerson, Jim. Little girl lost / Jim Rogerson ; [photographs Bob Cathmoir]. — London : Ward Lock Educational, c1978. — 16p : ill ; 21cm. — (WLE library graded reading series 10-14. Level 1 ; 2)
ISBN 0-7062-3705-6 (pbk) : £2.00 B82-18158

Rogerson, Jim. Tiger, tiger! / Jim Rogerson ; [illustrations by Gavin Rowe]. — London : Ward Lock Educational, c1978. — 24p : ill ; 21cm. — (WLE library graded reading series 10-14. Level 2)
ISBN 0-7062-3710-2 (pbk) : £3.00 B82-18164

Russell, Solveig Paulson. Through a magic glass / written by Solveig Paulson Russell ; illustrated by Betty Fraser. — Aylesbury : Ginn, c1978 (1981 [printing]). — 16p : ill(some col.) ; 22cm. — (Reading 360. Magic circle books. Level 8 ; bk.5)
ISBN 0-602-24064-6 (pbk) : Unpriced B82-34527

Sadler, R. K.. Word skills / Sadler, Hayllar, Powell. — London : Evans
1. — 1982. — v,217p : ill,facsims ; 22cm
ISBN 0-237-29314-5 (pbk) : Unpriced B82-33806

Sadler, R. K.. Word skills / Sadler, Hayllar, Powell. — London : Evans
2. — 1982. — 235p : ill,facsims ; 22cm
ISBN 0-237-29315-3 (pbk) : Unpriced B82-33805

Sadler, R. K.. Word skills / Sadler, Hayllar, Powell. — London : Evans
3. — 1982. — 231p : ill,facsims ; 22cm
ISBN 0-237-29316-1 (pbk) : Unpriced B82-33804

Schatz, Letta. So many Henrys / by Letta Schatz ; illustrated by John Kuzich. — Aylesbury : Ginn, c1978 (1981 [printing]). — 23p : col.ill ; 19x23cm. — (Reading 360. Magic circle books. Level 8 ; bk.4)
ISBN 0-602-24064-6 (pbk) : Unpriced B82-34528

Schatz, Letta. The troubles of kings : two tales from Africa / retold by Letta Schatz ; illustrated by John Freas. — Aylesbury : Ginn, 1978 (1981 [printing]). — 48p : col.ill ; 19x23cm. — (Reading 360. Magic circle books. Level 10 ; bk.6)
ISBN 0-602-24082-4 (pbk) : Unpriced B82-34885

Sellers, Naomi. The litte elephant who liked to play / by Naomi Sellers ; illustrated by Yoko Mitsuhashi. — Aylesbury : Ginn, 1978 (1981 [printing]). — 32p : col.ill ; 23cm. — (Reading 360. Magic circle books. Level 5 ; bk.5)
ISBN 0-602-24037-9 (pbk) : Unpriced B82-39368

Shepherd, William. Ben / [story by William Shepherd] ; [pictures by Janet Folland]. — Aylesbury : Ginn, c1980 (1981 [printing]). — 16p : col.ill ; 23cm. — (Reading 360. Level 1 ; bk.6)
Cover title
ISBN 0-602-23168-x (pbk) : Unpriced
ISBN 0-602-23148-5 (set) : Unpriced B82-35040

Shepherd, William, *19---*. Can you? / [story by William Shepherd] ; [pictures by Janet Folland]. — Aylesbury : Ginn, 1980 (1981 [printing]). — 16p : col.ill ; 23cm. — (Reading 360. Level 2 ; bk.4)
Cover title. — Text on inside covers
ISBN 0-602-23169-8 (pbk) : Unpriced
ISBN 0-602-23152-3 (set) : Unpriced B82-34195

Smith, Hendy. Johnny Black, footballer / Hendy Smith ; illustrated by Ian Heard. — Exeter : Wheaton, 1981. — 16p : ill ; 22cm. — (The Johnny Black stories ; bk.1)
ISBN 0-08-024372-x (pbk) : £0.50 B82-03970

Smith, Hendy. Johnny Black, pilot / Hendy Smith ; illustrated by Ian Heard. — Exeter : Wheaton, 1981. — 16p : ill ; 22cm. — (The Johnny Black stories ; bk.4)
ISBN 0-08-024375-4 (pbk) : £0.50 B82-03975

Smith, Hendy. Johnny Black, racing driver / Hendy Smith ; illustrated by Ian Heard. — Exeter : Wheaton, 1981. — 16p : ill ; 22cm. — (The Johnny Black stories ; bk.5)
ISBN 0-08-024376-2 (pbk) : £0.50 B82-03973

Smith, Hendy. Johnny Black, show-jumper / Hendy Smith ; illustrated by Ian Heard. — Exeter : Wheaton, 1981. — 16p : ill ; 22cm. — (The Johnny Black stories ; bk.3)
ISBN 0-08-024374-6 (pbk) : £0.50 B82-03972

Smith, Hendy. Johnny Black, special agent / Hendy Smith ; illustrated by Ian Heard. — Exeter : Wheaton, 1981. — 16p : ill ; 22cm. — (The Johnny Black stories ; bk.2)
ISBN 0-08-024373-8 (pbk) : £0.50 B82-03971

Smith, Hendy. Johnny Black stops dreaming / Hendy Smith ; illustrated by Ian Heard. — Exeter : Wheaton, 1981. — 16p : ill ; 22cm. — (The Johnny Black stories ; bk.6)
ISBN 0-08-024377-0 (pbk) : £0.50 B82-03974

Smith Beattie, Sara. School on a raft / written by Sara Smith Beattie ; illustrated by Gordon Laite. — Aylesbury : Ginn, 1978 (1981 [printing]). — 45p : col.ill ; 23cm. — (Reading 360. Magic circle books. Level 10 ; bk.1)
ISBN 0-602-24082-4 (pbk) : Unpriced B82-34890

Swan, D. K.. Alice in Wonderland / Lewis Carroll ; simplified by D.K. Swan ; illustrated by Carol Tarrant. — London : Longman, 1976 (1978 [printing]). — 60p : ill ; 19cm. — (New method supplementary readers. Stage 1)
ISBN 0-582-53414-3 (pbk) : £0.40 B82-00122

Swan, D. K.. Black Beauty / Anna Sewell ; simplified by D.K. Swan. — London : Longman, 1976 (1978 [printing]). — 52p : ill ; 19cm. — (New method supplementary readers. Stage 1)
ISBN 0-582-53522-0 (pbk) : £0.40 B82-00127

Tansley, A. E.. Sound sense stories / A.E. Tansley. — Leeds : E.J. Arnold
Bk.6C: [Gorg and the Gorgans] / illustrated by Gay Galsworthy. — c1982. — 48p : ill(some col.) ; 21cm
ISBN 0-560-02789-3 (pbk) : Unpriced B82-38620

Tansley, A. E.. Sound sense stories / A.E. Tansley. — Leeds : E.J. Arnold
Bk.6A: [Stories from America and Canada] / illustrated by Malcolm S. Lea. — c1982. — 47p : ill(some col.) ; 21cm
ISBN 0-560-02769-9 (pbk) : Unpriced B82-38622

428.6 — English language. Reading books — *For schools* *continuation*

Tansley, A. E.. Sound sense stories / A.E. Tansley. — Leeds : E.J. Arnold
Bk.6B: [Tales of giants] / illustrated by Ray Mutimer. — c1982. — 48p : ill(some col.) ; 21cm
ISBN 0-560-02779-6 (pbk) : Unpriced
B82-38621

The **Touch** of gold / [illustrated by David Dowland]. — London : Macmillan, 1982. — 32p : ill(some col.) ; 21cm. — (The Gay way series. The second orange book)
Contents: The touch of gold — The inquisitive shepherd
ISBN 0-333-31764-5 (pbk) : Unpriced
B82-16862

Tyler, Deborah. Alice's adventures in Wonderland / by Lewis Carroll ; retold by Deborah Tyler. — London : Macmillan, 1982. — 46p : ill(some col.) ; 21cm. — (Ranger. Range 3, Fiction)
ISBN 0-333-31595-2 (pbk) : Unpriced
B82-34208

Tyler, Deborah. Through the looking-glass : and what Alice found there / by Lewis Carroll ; retold by Deborah Tyler. — London : Macmillan, 1982. — 440p : ill(some col.) ; 21cm. — (Ranger. Range 3, fiction)
ISBN 0-333-32835-3 (pbk) : £0.65 B82-35911

Ullstein, Sue. The secret garden / Frances Hodgson Burnett ; simplified by Sue Ullstein ; illustrated by Jane Taylor. — London : Longman, 1975 (1978 [printing]). — 92p : ill ; 19cm. — (New method supplementary readers. Stage 2)
ISBN 0-582-53417-8 (pbk) : £0.40 B82-00123

Ullstein, Sue. The wind in the willows / Kenneth Grahame ; simplified by Sue Ullstein ; illustrations from the original edition by Ernest H. Shepard. — Harlow : Longman, 1981. — 76p : ill ; 19cm
ISBN 0-582-52652-3 (pbk) : £0.75 B82-05037

Van Leeuwen, Jean. More tales of Oliver Pig / Jean van Leeuwen ; pictures by Arnold Lobel. — London : Bodley Head, 1981. — 64p : col.ill ; 22cm. — (Bodley beginners)
Originally published: New York : Dial Press, 1981
ISBN 0-370-30908-1 (pbk) : £3.25 : CIP rev.
B81-27955

Walsh, Gordon. The energy crisis / Gordon Walsh. — Harlow : Longman, 1980. — 74p : ill ; 20cm. — (Longman structural readers. Stage 4. Non-fiction)
ISBN 0-582-53834-3 (pbk) : £0.60 B82-37924

West, Michael, *1936-*. King Arthur and the knights of the Round Table / simplified by Michael West. — 2nd ed. / revised by D.K. Swan. — London : Longman, 1976 (1978 [printing]). — 60p : ill ; 19cm. — (New method supplementary readers. Stage 1)
ISBN 0-582-53415-1 (pbk) : £0.40 B82-00128

West, Michael, *1936-*. Little women / Louisa M. Alcott ; simplified by Michael West. — 2nd ed. — London : Longman, 1965 (1979 [printing]). — 121p : ill ; 19cm. — (New method supplementary readers. Stage 4)
ISBN 0-582-53489-5 (pbk) : £0.40 B82-00124

West, Michael, *1936-*. The prince and the pauper / Mark Twain ; simplified by Michael West. — 2nd ed. / revised by D.K. Swan. — London : Longman, 1976 (1979 [printing]). — 44p : ill ; 19cm. — (New method supplementary readers. Stage 2)
ISBN 0-582-53422-4 (pbk) : £0.40 B82-00126

West, Michael, *1936-*. Robinson Crusoe / Daniel Defoe ; simplified by Michael West. — New ed. / revised by D.K. Swan. — London : Longman, 1976 (1979 [printing]). — 37p : ill ; 19cm. — (New method supplementary readers. Stage 3)
ISBN 0-582-53444-5 (pbk) : £0.40 B82-00125

Wiesbauer, Marcia. The big green bean / by Marcia Wiesbauer ; illustrated by Trina Hyman. — Aylesbury : Ginn, 1978 (1981 [printing]). — 24p : col.ill ; 20cm. — (Reading 360. Magic circle books. Level 5 ; bk.3)
ISBN 0-602-24037-9 (pbk) : Unpriced
B82-34802

Wiesbauer, Marcia. Ride! Ride! Ride! / story by Marcia Wiesbauer ; pictures by Marc Tolon Brown. — Aylesbury : Ginn, c1978 (1981 [printing]). — 24p : chiefly col.ill ; 20cm. — (Reading 360. Magic circle books. Level 2 ; bk.1)
ISBN 0-602-24012-3 (pbk) : Unpriced
B82-34816

Wood, David, *1950-*. The machines / David Wood and Phyllis Edwards. — London : Edward Arnold, 1980. — 31p ; 22cm. — (Vardo ; 8)
ISBN 0-7131-0467-8 (pbk) : £0.80 : CIP rev.
B80-18530

Woodman, June. Wiff the dragon / written by June Woodman and Rita Grainge ; illustrated by Peter Kingston. — Loughborough : Ladybird, 1981. — 51p : col.ill ; 18cm. — (Story board)
Text and ill on lining papers. — Contents: To the rescue — The secret weapon
ISBN 0-7214-0695-5 : £0.50 B82-00636

Yeo, Wilma. Oliver Twister and his big little sister / by Wilma Yeo ; illustrated by Winnie Fitch. — Aylesbury : Ginn, c1978 (1981 [printing]). — 24p : ill(some col.) ; 20cm. — (Reading 360. Magic circle books. Level 7 ; bk.5)
ISBN 0-602-24055-7 (pbk) : Unpriced
B82-34523

428.6 — English language. Reading books: Gay way series — *For teaching*

The **Gay** way teacher's guide. — London : Macmillan Education, 1981. — 54p : ill ; 21cm. — (The Gay way series)
ISBN 0-333-31170-1 (pbk) : Unpriced
B82-06870

428.6 — English language. Reading books: Plays — *For schools*

Lane, Sheila. All aboard the ark / Sheila Lane and Marion Kemp. — Cambridge : Cambridge University Press, 1982. — 72p : ill,music ; 21cm. — (Playmakers)
ISBN 0-521-28634-4 (pbk) : £0.95 B82-26503

Lane, Sheila. Hans Andersen : the story teller of Odense / Sheila Lane and Marion Kemp. — Cambridge : Cambridge University Press, 1982. — 71p : ill,music ; 21cm. — (Playmakers)
ISBN 0-521-28633-6 (pbk) : £0.95 B82-26504

Lane, Sheila. The invaders' story / Sheila Lane and Marion Kemp. — Cambridge : Cambridge University Press, 1982. — 72p : ill ; 21cm. — (Playmakers)
ISBN 0-521-28637-9 (pbk) : £0.95 B82-26502

Lane, Sheila. Missions to moon base / Sheila Lane and Marion Kemp. — Cambridge : Cambridge University Press, 1982. — 72p : ill ; 21cm. — (Playmakers)
ISBN 0-521-28635-2 (pbk) : £0.95 B82-26505

428.6 — English language. Reading books: Poetry — *For pre-school children*

Halloran, Maureen. Witch in the kitchen / Maureen Halloran ; illustrated by Judith Trevelyan. — London : Methuen Educational, 1981. — [8]p : col.ill ; 30cm. — (PM readalongs. Excitements)
Unpriced (unbound) B82-36084

Randell, Beverley. The boat race / Beverly Randell ; illustrated by Judith Trevelyan. — London : Methuen Educational, 1981. — [16]p : col.ill ; 30cm. — (PM readalongs. Excitements)
Unpriced (unbound) B82-36085

Randell, Beverley. Moon shot / Beverley Randell ; illustrated by Ernest Papps. — London : Methuen Educational, 1981. — [8]p : col.ill ; 30cm. — (PM readalongs. Excitements)
Unpriced (unbound) B82-36081

Randell, Beverley. One big dinosaur / Beverley Randell ; illustrated by Lynley Dodd. — London : Methuen Educational, 1981. — [16]p : col.ill ; 30cm. — (PM readalongs. Excitements)
Unpriced (unbound) B82-36082

Randell, Beverley. Pop pop pop / adapted by Beverly Randell from a traditional rhyme ; illustrated by Lynley Dodd. — London : Methuen Educational, 1981. — [8]p : col.ill ; 30cm. — (PM readalongs. Excitements)
Unpriced (unbound) B82-36080

Randell, Beverley. Tamsy and the pirates / Beverly Randell ; illustrated by Judith Trevelyan. — London : Methuen Educational, 1981. — [16]p : col.ill ; 30cm. — (PM readalongs. Excitements)
Unpriced (unbound) B82-36083

428.6 — English language. Reading books. Special subjects: Animals. Tracks — *For children*

Branley, Franklyn M.. Big tracks, little tracks / by Franklyn M. Branley ; and illustrated by Leonard Kessler. — New ed. — London : A. & C. Black, 1979. — [37]p : ill(some col.) ; 21x22cm. — (Let's read and find out)
Previous ed.: New York : Crowell, 1960 ; London : A. & C. Black, 1967
ISBN 0-7136-2012-9 : £2.25 B82-06635

428.6 — English language. Reading books. Special subjects: California. Los Angeles. Hollywood. Cinema films. Stunting — *For schools*

Border, Rosemary. Great Hollywood stunts / by Rosemary Border ; illustrated by Malcolm Stokes. — London : Macmillan, 1982. — 32p : ill ; 14x22cm. — (Ranger. Range 2, Fact)
Text on inside covers
ISBN 0-333-28116-0 (pbk) : Unpriced
B82-17680

428.6 — English language. Reading books. Special subjects: Handicapped children

Hallworth, Grace. My mind is not in a wheelchair. — Hertford (County Hall, Hertford SG8 8EJ) : Hertfordshire Library Service, Sept.1982. — 1v.
ISBN 0-901354-21-x (pbk) : £0.50 : CIP entry
B82-31316

428.6 — English language. Reading books. Special subjects: Houses — *For children*

McMillan, Dorothy. Around the house / Dorothy McMillan ; photos Leslie Haines. — Wellington : Milburn ; London : Methuen, c1979. — [16]p : col.ill ; 11x15cm. — (PM instant reader. 1st series ; IR3)
ISBN 0-423-49470-8 (unbound) : Unpriced
B82-21705

428.6 — English language. Reading books. Special subjects: Knowledge — *For children*

Knowing. — [Cambridge] : Brimax, c1974 (1981 printing). — [10]p : col.ill ; 16cm. — (Show baby plus series)
Cover title
ISBN 0-900195-59-2 : Unpriced B82-05029

428.6 — English language. Reading books. Special subjects: Measurement — *For children*

Allington, Richard. Measuring. — Oxford : Blackwell Raintree, Nov.1982. — [32]p. — (Beginning to learn about)
ISBN 0-86256-065-9 : £2.95 : CIP entry
B82-26072

428.6 — English language. Reading books. Special subjects: Months — *For children*

Hillman, Priscilla. A merry-mouse book of months / by Priscilla Hillman. — Kingswood : World's Work Children's, 1981. — 31p : col.ill ; 26cm
ISBN 0-437-45904-7 (pbk) : £1.95 B82-07754

428.6 — English language. Reading books. Special subjects: Numeration — *For children*

Blyton, Enid. Learn to count with Noddy / by Enid Blyton. — London : Low, Marston, [c1965] ([1982 printing]). — [60]p : col.ill ; 20cm
ISBN 0-361-05363-0 : Unpriced B82-22340

428.6 — English language. Reading books. Special subjects: Oceans. Mysteries, *1700-1915 — For schools*

Garrett, Richard. Great sea mysteries / Richard Garrett ; adapted for Rangers by Carol Christian. — London : Macmillan, 1981. — 60p : ill ; 21cm. — (Range 8, Fact)
ISBN 0-333-29454-8 (pbk) : £0.80 B82-02755

428.6 — English language. Reading books. Special subjects: Pets: Dogs — *For children*

Taylor, Anne. Puppies and dogs / words by Anne Taylor. — Maidenhead : Intercontinental Book Productions, c1979. — [24]p : col.ill ; 21cm. — (My first animal library)
Originally published: Windermere, Fla. : Rourke Enterprises, 1979
ISBN 0-85047-433-7 (pbk) : £0.40 B82-16334

428.6 — English language. Reading books. Special subjects: Reading — *For children*

Allington, Richard. Reading / by Richard Allington and Kathleen Krull ; illustrated by Joel Naprstek. — Oxford : Blackwell Raintree, c1981. — 32p : col.ill ; 24cm. — (Beginning to learn about)
Originally published: Milwaukee : Raintree Childrens Books, 1980
ISBN 0-86256-041-1 : £2.50 : CIP rev.
B81-19155

428.6 — English language. Reading books. Special subjects: Science — *For schools*

Holt, Michael. Science stories / Michael Holt and Alan Ward. — Edinburgh : Oliver & Boyd. — (Wide range)
1. — 1982. — 127p : ill(some col.),maps ; 21cm
Includes index
ISBN 0-05-003290-9 (pbk) : £1.50 B82-23057

428.6 — English language. Reading books: Special subjects. Shopping — *For children*

Blyton, Enid. Learn to go shopping with Noddy / by Enid Blyton. — London : Low, Marston, [c1965] ([1982 printing]). — [60]p : col.ill ; 20cm
ISBN 0-361-05362-2 : Unpriced B82-22329

428.6 — English language. Reading books. Special subjects: Spring — *For children*

Allington, Richard. Spring / by Richard Allington and Kathleen Krull ; illustrated by Lynn Uhde. — Oxford : Blackwell Raintree, c1981. — 32p : col.ill ; 24cm. — (Beginning to learn about)
ISBN 0-86256-045-4 : £2.50 : CIP rev.
B81-30562

428.6 — English language. Reading books. Special subjects: Summer — *For children*

Allington, Richard. Summer / by Richard Allington and Kathleen Krull ; illustrated by Dennis Hockerman. — Oxford : Blackwell Raintree, c1981. — 32p : col.ill ; 24cm. — (Beginning to learn about)
ISBN 0-86256-046-2 : £2.50 : CIP rev.
B81-30563

428.6 — English language. Reading books. Special subjects: Talking — *For children*

Allington, Richard. Talking / Richard Allington and Kathleen Krull ; illustrated by Rick Thrun. — Oxford : Blackwell Raintree, c1981. — 31p : col.ill ; 24cm. — (Beginning to learn about)
Originally published: Milwaukee : Raintree Childrens Books, 1980
ISBN 0-86256-040-3 : £2.50 : CIP rev.
B81-19114

428.6 — English language. Reading books. Special subjects: Thought processes — *For children*

Allington, Richard. Thinking / by Richard Allington and Kathleen Krull ; illustrated by Tom Garcia. — Oxford : Blackwell Raintree, c1981. — 32p : col.ill ; 24cm. — (Beginning to learn about)
Originally published: Milwaukee : Raintree Childrens Books, 1980
ISBN 0-86256-042-x : £2.50 : CIP rev.
B81-19156

428.6 — English language. Reading books. Special subjects: Time — *For children*

Allington, Richard. Time. — Oxford : Blackwell Raintree, Nov.1982. — [32]p. — (Beginning to learn about)
ISBN 0-86256-059-4 : £2.95 : CIP entry
B82-26071

Blyton, Enid. Learn to tell the time with Noddy / by Enid Blyton. — London : Low, Marston, [c1965] ([1982 printing]). — [60]p : col.ill ; 20cm
ISBN 0-361-05361-4 : Unpriced B82-22339

428.6 — English language. Reading books. Special subjects: Vehicles — *For children*

McMillan, Dorothy. Traffic / Dorothy McMillan ; photos Trevor Hyde. — Wellington : Milburn ; London : Methuen, c1979. — [16]p : col.ill ; 11x15cm. — (PM instant reader. 1st series ; IR2)
ISBN 0-423-49470-8 (unbound) : Unpriced
B82-21704

428.6 — English language. Reading books. Special subjects: Vertebrates — *For children*

Blyton, Enid. Learn to read about animals with Noddy / by Enid Blyton. — London : Low, Marston, [c1965] ([1982 printing]). — [60]p : col.ill ; 20cm
ISBN 0-361-05364-9 : Unpriced B82-22330

Taylor, Anne. Animal friends / words by Anne Taylor. — Maidenhead : Intercontinental Book Productions, c1979. — [24]p : col.ill ; 21cm. — (My first animal library)
Originally published: Windermere, Fla. : Rourke Enterprises, 1979
ISBN 0-85047-435-3 (pbk) : £0.40 B82-16333

428.6 — English language. Reading books. Special subjects: Winter — *For children*

Allington, Richard. Winter / by Richard Allington and Kathleen Krull ; illustrated by John Wallner. — Oxford : Blackwell Raintree, c1981. — 32p : col.ill ; 24cm. — (Beginning to learn about)
ISBN 0-86256-044-6 : £2.50 : CIP rev.
B81-30439

428.6 — English language. Reading books. Special subjects: Writing — *For children*

Allington, Richard. Writing / by Richard Allington and Kathleen Krull ; illustrated by Yoshi Miyake. — Oxford : Blackwell Raintree, c1981. — 32p : col.ill ; 24cm. — (Beginning to learn about)
Originally published: Milwaukee : Raintree Childrens Books, 1980
ISBN 0-86256-043-8 : £2.50 : CIP rev.
B81-20616

428.6 — English language. Reding books. Special subjects: Autumn — *For children*

Allington, Richard. Autumn / by Richard Allington and Kathleen Krull ; illustrated by Bruce Bond. — Oxford : Blackwell Raintree, c1981. — 32p : col.ill ; 24cm. — (Beginning to learn about)
ISBN 0-86256-047-0 : £2.50 : CIP rev.
B81-30564

428.6 — English. Reading books. Special subjects: Agricultural industries. Farms. Livestock — *For children*

McMillan, Dorothy. Farm animals / Dorothy McMillan ; photos Terry Hobin. — Wellington : Milburn ; London : Methuen, c1979. — [16]p : col.ill ; 11x15cm. — (PM instant reader. 1st series ; IR1)
ISBN 0-423-49470-8 (unbound) : Unpriced
B82-21706

Taylor, Anne. Farm animals / words by Anne Taylor. — Maidenhead : Intercontinental Book Productions, c1979. — [24]p : col.ill ; 21cm. — (My first animal library)
Originally published: Windermere, Fla. : Rourke Enterprises, 1979
ISBN 0-85047-431-0 (pbk) : £0.40 B82-16332

428.6′2 — English language. Reading books — *For illiterate adults*

Pick and choose / Adult Literacy Support Services Fund. — Rev. [ed.]. — London (252 Western Ave., W3 6XJ) : The fund, 1979. — 1portfolio : ill,facsims,forms,1map ; 33cm
Previous ed.: 1977
£2.25 B82-40592

428.6′2 — English language. Reading books — *For severely mentally handicapped students*

Satterthwaite, Jean. Alan saves the day / [written by Jean Satterthwaite]. — Leeds ([Tongue Lane, Leeds. LS6 4QB]) : Continuing Education Unit of Meanwood Park Hospital, c1981. — 39p : ill ; 21cm
Unpriced (pbk) B82-21472

Satterthwaite, Jean. A good Saturday / [written by Jean Satterthwaite]. — Leeds ([Tongue Lane, Leeds, LS6 4QB]) : Continuing Education Unit of Meanwood Park Hospital, c1980. — 40p : ill ; 21cm
Unpriced (pbk) B82-21471

Satterthwaite, Jean. Kevin and the big problem / [written by Jean Satterthwaite]. — Leeds ([Tongue Lane, Leeds, LS6 4QB]) : Continuing Education Unit of Meanwood Park Hospital, c1980. — 40p : ill ; 21cm
Unpriced (pbk) B82-21470

Satterthwaite, Jean. Roy and the chocolate bar / [written by Jean Satterthwaite]. — Leeds (Tongue Lane, Leeds, LS6 4QB) : Continuing Education Unit of Meanwood Park Hospital, c1979. — 37p : ill ; 21cm
Unpriced (pbk) B82-21473

428.6′2 — English language. Reading books — *For slow learning adolescents*

Carew, Jan. Don′t go near the water : three stories / Jan Carew. — Harlow : Longman, 1982. — 62p : ill ; 20cm. — (Knockouts)
ISBN 0-582-25049-8 (cased) : £2.95
ISBN 0-582-21177-8 (pbk) : £0.75 B82-15555

Chilton, Irma. Flash / by Irma Chilton ; illustrations by Andy Carroll. — London : Cassell, 1981. — 63p : ill ; 19cm. — (Red lion books ; 23)
ISBN 0-304-30704-1 (pbk) : Unpriced : CIP rev.
B81-13884

Crosher, G. R.. The dogs of the marsh / by G.R. Crosher ; illustrations by Paul Blount. — London : Cassell, 1981. — 63p : ill ; 19cm. — (Red lion books ; 15)
ISBN 0-304-30628-2 (pbk) : Unpriced : CIP rev.
B81-13875

Crosher, G. R.. Journey into danger / by G.R. Crosher ; illustrations by Jim McCarthy. — London : Cassell, 1981. — 64p : ill ; 19cm. — (Red lion books ; 16)
ISBN 0-304-30629-0 (pbk) : Unpriced : CIP rev.
B81-13876

Deary, Terry. Twist of the knife : two stories / Terry Deary. — Harlow : Longman, 1981. — 136p ; 19cm. — (Knockouts)
Contents: Twist of the knife — The victim
ISBN 0-582-39098-2 (cased) : Unpriced
ISBN 0-582-20007-5 (pbk) : Unpriced
B82-03660

Edwards, Glyn. Real English : a practical guide to reading, talking and writing today / by Glyn Edwards and Frank Hayes. — Huddersfield : Scholfield & Sims
3. — 1982. — 96p : ill(some col.) ; 30cm
ISBN 0-7217-0355-0 (pbk) : £1.85 B82-17456

428.6'2 — English language. Reading books — *For slow learning adolescents* *continuation*

Escott, John. The ghost of Genny Castle / by John Escott ; illustrations by Dilys Jones. — London : Cassell, 1981. — 64p : ill ; 19cm. — (Red lion books ; 21)
ISBN 0-304-30702-5 (pbk) : Unpriced : CIP rev. B81-13881

Griffin, John, *1934-*. A person of bad character / John Griffin. — Harlow : Longman, 1981. — 153p : ill ; 19cm. — (Knockouts)
ISBN 0-582-21179-4 (pbk) : £0.80 B82-14724

Jones, Lewis, *1924-*. Japanese Red : and other short stories / Lewis Jones ; illustrated by Ivan Lapper. — Harlow : Longman, 1981. — 48p : ill ; 19cm. — (Books in easy English. Stage 1)
ISBN 0-582-52703-1 (pbk) : Unpriced B82-20117

Judge, Tony. Dave and the drug pushers / Tony Judge ; illustrations by John R. Edwards. — Amersham : Hulton Educational, 1981. — 79p : ill ; 19cm. — (Copswinger ; 6)
ISBN 0-7175-0849-8 (pbk) : £1.15 B82-05536

Judge, Tony. Dave Carter — police cadet / Tony Judge ; illustrations by John R. Edwards. — Amersham : Hulton, 1980. — 75p : ill ; 19cm. — (Copswinger ; 1)
ISBN 0-7175-0844-7 (pbk) : £1.05 B82-16089

Judge, Tony. Dave goes on the beat / Tony Judge ; illustrations by John R. Edwards. — Amersham : Hulton, 1980. — 76p : ill ; 19cm. — (Copswinger ; 2)
ISBN 0-7175-0845-5 (pbk) : £1.05 B82-16090

Judge, Tony. Dave goes under cover / Tony Judge ; illustrations by John R. Edwards. — Amersham : Hutton Educational, 1979. — 79p : ill ; 19cm. — (Copswinger ; [no.5])
ISBN 0-7175-0848-x (pbk) : Unpriced B82-00013

Judge, Tony. Dave joins the Special Patrol Group / Tony Judge ; illustrations by John R. Edwards. — Amersham : Hutton Educational, 1979. — 79p : ill ; 19cm. — (Copswinger ; [no.3])
ISBN 0-7175-0846-3 (pbk) : Unpriced B82-00014

Judge, Tony. Dave meets a challenge / Tony Judge ; illustrations by John R. Edwards. — Amersham : Hutton Educational, 1979. — 77p : ill ; 19cm. — (Copswinger ; [no.4])
ISBN 0-7175-0847-1 (pbk) : Unpriced B82-00015

Levine, Josie. Fair fight / Barry Pointon ; adapted by Josie Levine. — Abridged ed. — Harlow : Longman, 1982. — 164p ; 19cm. — (Knockouts)
Previous ed.: published as Cave / by Barry Pointon. London : Bodley Head, 1976
ISBN 0-582-20074-1 (pbk) : £0.95 B82-19019

Loxton, Margaret. Accident / Margaret Loxton. — Harlow : Longman, 1981. — 86p ; 19cm. — (Knockouts)
ISBN 0-582-21178-6 (pbk) : £0.70 B82-14723

Mays, Dennis. The knight of the road / by Dennis Mays ; illustrations by Jim McCarthy. — London : Cassell, 1981. — 46p : ill ; 19cm. — (Red lion books ; 19)
ISBN 0-304-30632-0 (pbk) : Unpriced : CIP rev. B81-13879

Melling, Frank. Project fishing / by Frank A. Melling. — London : Heinemann Educational, 1982. — 74p : ill ; 25cm
ISBN 0-435-10511-6 (pbk) : £1.95 : CIP rev. B82-14367

Melling, Frank. Project rock / by Frank A. Melling. — London : Heinemann Educational, [1982]. — 74p : ill ; 25cm
ISBN 0-435-10512-4 (pbk) : £1.95 : CIP rev. B82-19659

Pasakarnis, Ernest. The sweet secret / by Ernest Pasakarnis ; illustrations by Paul Blount. — London : Cassell, 1981. — 63p : ill ; 19cm. — (Red lion books ; 20)
ISBN 0-304-30633-9 (pbk) : Unpriced : CIP rev. B81-13880

Philbin, Kevin. The stone of Gan / by Kevin Philbin ; illustrations by Jim McCarthy. — London : Cassell, 1981. — 48p : ill ; 19cm. — (Red lion books ; 17)
ISBN 0-304-30630-4 (pbk) : Unpriced : CIP rev. B81-13877

Philbin, Kevin. A time gone by / by Kevin Philbin ; illustrations by Dilys Jones. — London : Cassell, 1981. — 63p : ill ; 19cm. — (Red lion books ; 18)
ISBN 0-304-30631-2 (pbk) : Unpriced : CIP rev. B81-13878

Rosen, Michael. Nasty! / Michael Rosen. — Harlow : Longman, 1982. — 93p : ill ; 20cm. — (Knockouts)
ISBN 0-582-25048-x (cased) : Unpriced
ISBN 0-582-20127-6 (pbk) : £0.85 B82-22522

Townson, Hazel. Walk over my grave / by Hazel Townson ; illustrations by Andy Carroll. — London : Cassell, 1981. — 48p : ill ; 19cm. — (Red lion books ; 22)
ISBN 0-304-30703-3 (pbk) : Unpriced : CIP rev. B81-13882

Townson, Hazel. Who is Sylvia? / by Hazel Townson ; illustrations by Jim McCarthy. — London : Cassell, 1981. — 48p : ill ; 19cm. — (Red lion books ; 24)
ISBN 0-304-30794-7 (pbk) : Unpriced : CIP rev. B81-13883

428.6'2 — English language. Reading books — *For slow learning children*

Chilton, Irma. The killer / by Irma Chilton ; illustrations by Sophie Kittredge. — London : Cassell, 1980. — 64p : ill ; 18cm. — (Cassell red lion books)
ISBN 0-304-30512-x (pbk) : £0.95 : CIP rev. B80-05312

Higgins, D. S.. Tales of terror / by Edgar Allan Poe ; retold by D.S. Higgins ; illustrations by Dilys Jones. — London : Cassell, 1980. — 46p : ill ; 18cm. — (Cassell red lion books)
ISBN 0-304-30513-8 (pbk) : £0.95 : CIP rev. B80-05316

McBratney, Sam. The hanging man / by Sam McBratney ; illustrations by Bruce Symons. — London : Cassell, 1980. — 32p : ill ; 18cm. — (Cassell red lion books)
ISBN 0-304-30259-7 (pbk) : £0.95 : CIP rev. B80-05317

McBratney, Sam. The man who tried to fly / by Sam McBratney ; illustrations by Bruce Symons. — London : Cassell, 1980. — 32p : ill ; 18cm. — (Cassell red lion books)
ISBN 0-304-30260-0 (pbk) : £0.95 : CIP rev. B80-05318

McBratney, Sam. The stolen Honda / by Sam McBratney ; illustrations by Bruce Symons. — London : Cassell, 1980. — 32p : ill ; 18cm. — (Cassell red lion books)
ISBN 0-304-30262-7 (pbk) : £0.95 : CIP rev. B80-05320

Machin, Noel. Jaws 2 / screenplay by Carl Gottlieb and Howard Sackler ; based on characters created by Peter Benchley ; [easy reading edition adapted by Noel Machin]. — Harlow : Longman, 1981. — 31p : col.ill ; 21cm. — (Longman movieworld. Stage 1 elementary)
ISBN 0-582-53547-6 (pbk) : £0.60 B82-09937

Machin, Noel. Roller coaster / screenplay by Richard Levinson and William Link ; story by Sanford Sheldon and Richard Levinson and William Link ; suggested by a story by Tommy Cook ; [easy reading edition adapted by Noel Machin]. — Harlow : Longman, 1981. — 31p : col.ill ; 21cm. — (Longman movieworld. Stage 1 elementary)
ISBN 0-582-52793-7 (pbk) : £0.80 B82-09936

McKenna, Terry. Tomboy / written and illustrated by Terry McKenna. — Cambridge : Dinosaur, c1982. — [48]p : ill ; 19cm
ISBN 0-85122-334-6 (cased) : Unpriced
ISBN 0-85122-320-6 (pbk) : Unpriced B82-31021

Mark, Jan. The long distance poet / by Jan Mark ; illustrated by Steve Smallman. — Cambridge : Dinosaur, c1982. — [48]p : ill ; 19cm
ISBN 0-85122-331-1 (cased) : Unpriced
ISBN 0-85122-305-2 (pbk) : Unpriced B82-31020

Philbin, Kevin. The curse of Gull House / by Kevin Philbin ; illustrations by Richard Appleby. — London : Cassell, 1980. — 47p : ill ; 18cm. — (Cassell red lion books)
ISBN 0-304-30267-8 (pbk) : £0.95 : CIP rev. B80-05322

Philbin, Kevin. Eye witness / by Kevin Philbin ; illustrations by Richard Appleby. — London : Cassell, 1980. — 45p : ill ; 18cm. — (Cassell red lion books)
ISBN 0-304-30268-6 (pbk) : £0.95 : CIP rev. B80-05323

Philbin, Kevin. No way out / by Kevin Philbin ; illustrations by Richard Appleby. — London : Cassell, 1980. — 32p : ill ; 18cm. — (Cassell red lion books)
ISBN 0-304-30269-4 (pbk) : £0.95 : CIP rev. B80-05324

Solomon, Helen. One of these days / by Helen Solomon ; illustrated by Steve Smallman. — Cambridge : Dinosaur, c1982. — [48]p : ill (some col.) ; 19cm. — (Dinosaur's strip books)
ISBN 0-85122-333-8 (cased) : £2.25
ISBN 0-85122-321-4 (pbk) : Unpriced B82-31055

Storr, Catherine. It couldn't happen to me / by Catherine Storr ; illustrated by Isabel Pearce. — Cambridge : Dinosaur, c1982. — [48]p : ill ; 19cm. — (Dinosaur's strip books)
ISBN 0-85122-332-x (cased) : Unpriced
ISBN 0-85122-319-2 (pbk) : Unpriced B82-31061

Tate, Joan. Ben and Annie / by Joan Tate ; illustrations by Malcolm Kirton. — London : Cassell, 1980. — 64p : ill ; 18cm. — (Cassell red lion books)
ISBN 0-304-30515-4 (pbk) : £0.95 : CIP rev. B80-05325

Ullstein, Sue. Star wars / based on the film Star Wars ; story by George Lucas ; [easy reading edition adapted by Sue Ullstein]. — Harlow : Longman, 1981. — 30p : col.ill ; 21cm. — (Longman movieworld. Stage 2 elementary)
ISBN 0-582-53550-6 (pbk) : £0.80 B82-09935

428.6'2 — English language. Reading books — For slow learning children — For schools

King, Clive. Snakes and snakes. — Basingstoke : Macmillan Educational, Mar.1982. — [64]p. — (Rockets)
ISBN 0-333-26091-0 (pbk) : £0.70 : CIP entry B82-01868

428.6'2 — English language. Reading books — *For slow learning children — For schools*

Marshall, James Vance. A river ran out of Eden ; [and], My boy John that went to sea. — London : Hutchinson, Jan.1983. — [112]p. — (Bulls-eye)
ISBN 0-09-149111-8 (pbk) : £0.95 : CIP entry B82-33627

428.6′2 — English language. Reading books — *For slow learning children — For schools*
continuation

Nobes, Patrick. Walkabout. — London : Hutchinson, Feb.1982. — [96]p. — (Bulls-eye)
ISBN 0-09-146891-4 (pbk) : £0.85 : CIP entry
B81-38326

Smith, Wilbur. Shout at the devil. — London : Hutchinson, Jan.1983. — [112]p. — (Bulls-eye)
ISBN 0-09-149101-0 (pbk) : £0.95 : CIP entry
B82-33626

Thornton, Rosemary. Still in trouble : stories and exercises / Rosemary Thornton ; drawings by Gavin Rowe. — London : Edward Arnold, 1980. — 103p : ill ; 22cm
ISBN 0-7131-0492-9 (pbk) : £1.60 : CIP rev.
B80-20567

428.6′2 — English language. Reading books — *For slow learning students*

Taylor, James P.. A price to pay : tales of challenge / adapted by James P. Taylor. — London : Edward Arnold, 1981. — 86p : ill ; 21cm. — (Taken from life)
ISBN 0-7131-0560-7 (pbk) : £1.75 : CIP rev.
B81-31550

428.6′2 — English language. Reading books — *For slow reading adults*

Holden, Frances. Just my luck / Frances Holden. — Manchester : Gatehouse Projet, c1981. — 14p : ill ; 21cm
ISBN 0-906253-11-x (pbk) : Unpriced
B82-10533

Wilson, Paul, *19---*. Fun at Fine Fare / Paul Wilson. — Manchester : Gatehouse Projet, c1980. — 15p : ill,ports ; 21cm
ISBN 0-906253-10-1 (pbk) : Unpriced
B82-10534

428.6′2 — English language. Reading books. Special subjects: Animals — *For slow learning students*

Taylor, James P.. How to catch a dragon : animal tales / adapted by James P. Taylor. — London : Edward Arnold, 1981. — 85p : ill ; 21cm. — (Taken from life)
ISBN 0-7131-0559-3 (pbk) : £1.75 : CIP rev.
B81-31549

428.6′4 — English language. Reading books — *For negro students*

Greenwood, Angela. Going to school / written by Angela Greenwood ; illustrated by Gay Galsworthy. — Loughborough : Ladybird, c1982. — 51p : chiefly col.ill ; 18cm. — (Sunbird)
ISBN 0-7214-8105-1 : Unpriced B82-37060

428.6′4 — English language. Reading books — *For non-English speaking students*

Ackert, Patricia. Insights and ideas : a beginning reader for students of English and a second language / Patricia Ackert. — New York ; London : Holt, Rinehart and Winston, c1982. — x,219p : ill,maps,ports ; 24cm
ISBN 0-03-058322-5 (pbk) : £7.95 B82-16910

Alderson, Jim. Walkabout / James Vance Marshall ; retold by Jim Alderson ; illustrated by Trevor Parkin. — London : Heinemann Educational, 1979. — 73p : ill ; 18cm. — (Heinemann guided readers. Intermediate level ; 20)
ISBN 0-435-27062-1 (pbk) : £0.55 B82-06480

Border, Rosemary. Dune / Frank Herbert ; adapted by Rosemary Border. — Oxford : Oxford University Press, c1980. — 144p ; 18cm
ISBN 0-19-424239-0 (pbk) : Unpriced
B82-35889

Border, Rosemary. Hard times / Charles Dickens ; adapted by Rosemary Border. — Oxford : Oxford University Press, 1979. — 96p : ill ; 18cm. — (Alpha classics)
ISBN 0-19-424182-3 (pbk) : £0.70 B82-02292

Border, Rosemary. Silas Marner / George Eliot ; adapted by Rosemary Border. — Oxford : Oxford University Press, c1979. — 92p : ill ; 18cm. — (Alpha classics)
ISBN 0-19-424183-1 (pbk) : £0.70 B82-08769

Byram, R. S.. Dialogues and situations for secondary schools. — London : Heinemann Educational, Feb.1983. — [96]p
ISBN 0-435-92066-9 (pbk) : £1.95 : CIP entry
B82-36311

Capel, Will. Stop, look and listen. — London : Hodder and Stoughton, Jan.1983. — [64]p
ISBN 0-340-27947-8 (pbk) : £2.25 : CIP entry
B82-35221

Christian, Carol. Juan′s eyes / by Carol Christian ; illustrated by James Val. — London : Macmillan, 1982. — 32p : ill(some col.) ; 14x22cm. — (Ranger. Range 1)
ISBN 0-333-28120-9 (corrected : pbk) : £0.65
B82-20998

Cowboys in Alaska / English Language Services, Inc.. — Rev. ed. — New York : Collier Macmillan International ; London : Collier Macmillan, 1981. — v,88p : ill ; 18cm. — (Collier Macmillan English readers)
Previous ed.: 1965
ISBN 0-02-970380-8 (pbk) : £0.65 B82-29941

Davey, John, *1937-*. Elephant Walk / Robert Standish ; retold by John Davey ; illustrated by Trevor Parkin. — London : Heinemann Educational, 1980. — 90p : ill ; 18cm. — (Heinemann guided readers. Intermediate level ; 25)
ISBN 0-435-27073-7 (pbk) : £0.65 : CIP rev.
B80-11841

Forbes, Duncan. The peacemakers / Duncan Forbes. — London : Heinemann Educational, 1981. — vi,58p : ill,maps,ports ; 18cm. — (Heinemann guided readers. Intermediate level ; 29)
ISBN 0-435-27077-x (pbk) : £0.70 B82-12368

Geddes, Marion. Reading links / Marion Geddes and Gill Sturtridge. — London : Heinemann Educational, c1982. — 62p : ill,maps ; 30cm
ISBN 0-435-28055-4 (pbk) : Unpriced : CIP rev. B82-09728

Hall, Tim. Wuthering Heights / Emily Bronte ; adapted by Tim Hall. — Oxford : Oxford University Press, c1980. — 91p ; 18cm. — (Alpha classic)
ISBN 0-19-424186-6 (pbk) : Unpriced
B82-34958

Homeshaw, Jane. The pathfinders / Jane Homeshaw ; illustrations by Willie Rodger. — London : Collins, 1980. — 31p : ill,maps ; 18cm. — (Collins English library. Level 1) (Collins graded readers)
ISBN 0-00-370136-0 (pbk) : £0.40 B82-40698

Huggins, Viola. Middlemarch / George Eliot ; abridged and simplified by Viola Huggins ; illustrations by Scoular Anderson. — London : Collins, 1981. — 96p : ill ; 18cm. — (Collins English library. Level 5) (A Collins graded reader)
ISBN 0-00-370130-1 (pbk) : Unpriced
B82-04514

In context : reading skills for intermediate students of English as a second language / Jean Zukowski/Faust ... [et al.]. — New York ; London : Holt, Rinehart and Winston, c1982. — xiii,246p : ill,1plan ; 24cm
Includes index
ISBN 0-03-058286-5 (pbk) : Unpriced
B82-27632

The **Island** of truth / English Language Services, Inc.. — Rev. ed. — New York : Collier Macmillan International ; London : Collier Macmillan, 1981. — iv,122p : ill ; 18cm. — (Collier Macmillan English readers)
Previous ed.: 1964
ISBN 0-02-970390-5 (pbk) : £0.65 B82-29942

Johnston, Olivia. Jaws 2 : a completely new novel / by Hank Searls ; based on a screenplay by Howard Sackler and Dorothy Tristan ; inspired by Peter Benchley′s Jaws ; abridged and simplified by Olivia Johnston. — Harlow : Longman, 1980, c1978. — 76p ; 18cm. — (Longman simplified English series)
ISBN 0-582-52527-6 (pbk) : £0.70 B82-16599

Jolly, David. Reading choices : authentic self-access reading sources for students of English / David Jolly. — [Cambridge] : Cambridge University Press, [1982]. — 1case : ill,facsims,maps,ports ; 23x32x9cm
ISBN 0-521-22933-2 : Unpriced
ISBN 0-521-28725-1 (Answer bk.) : Unpriced
ISBN 0-521-28724-3 (Teacher′s bk.) : Unpriced
B82-32684

Jones, Lewis, *1924-*. Tiger / Kailash Sankhala ; abridged and simplified by Lewis Jones ; illustrations by Susan O′Carroll. — London : Collins, 1981. — 64p : ill ; 19cm ; pbk. — (Collins English library. Level 4) (A Collins graded reader)
ISBN 0-00-370134-4 : Unpriced B82-04513

Jordan, Jane. Collins English reader : authentic and varied reading practice, with activity work, for students of English / Jane Jordan. — Glasgow : Collins, 1982. — 144p : ill,maps,facsims,1plan,ports ; 21cm
Includes index
ISBN 0-00-370021-6 (corrected : pbk) : £1.90
B82-18688

Love : a reader for students of English / [compiled by] Susan Morris. — Cambridge : Cambridge University Press, 1980. — iv,140p : ill ; 20cm
Includes index
ISBN 0-521-22641-4 (pbk) : Unpriced
B82-38818

The **Love** letter / English Language Services, Inc.. — Rev. ed. — New York : Collier Macmillan International ; London : Collier Macmillan, 1981. — iii,88p : ill ; 18cm. — (Collier Macmillan English readers)
Previous ed.: 1968
ISBN 0-02-970360-3 (pbk) : £0.65 B82-29944

McIver, Nick. Dear Jan — Love Ruth / Nick McIver ; illustrated by Chris Evans. — London : Heinemann Educational, 1982. — 29p : ill ; 18cm. — (Heinemann guided readers. beginner level ; B16)
ISBN 0-435-27078-8 (pbk) : Unpriced
B82-22523

Miller, Victor B.. Kojak : the trade-off : a novel / by Victor B. Miller ; based on the Universal Television series created by Abby Mann adapted from the episode 'The trade-off' written by Robert E. Swanson ; abridged and simplified by Michael Dean. — Harlow : Longman, 1981, c1975. — 62p ; 18cm. — (Longman simplified English series)
ISBN 0-582-53336-8 (pbk) : Unpriced
B82-30990

Mistri, A. J.. Ivanhoe / Sir Walter Scott ; simplified and abridged by A.J. Mistri ; edited by M. Choksi ; illustrations by Shaila Mohan. — London : Sangam, 1982. — 106p : ill ; 19cm. — (Sangam English supplementary readers. Grade 5)
ISBN 0-86131-283-x (pbk) : £0.55 B82-36277

Morris, Margery. Three English kings : from Shakespeare / simplified and retold by Margery Morris ; illustrations by Willie Rodger. — London : Collins, 1981. — 64p : ill ; 19cm. — (Collins English library. level 3) (A Collins graded reader)
ISBN 0-00-370128-x (pbk) : Unpriced
B82-04518

Moynahan, Brian. Airport international / Brian Moynahan ; abridged and simplified by Lewis Jones. — London : Collins ELT, 1982. — 64p : ill ; 18cm. — (Collins English library. Level 4) (A Collins graded reader)
ISBN 0-00-370138-7 (pbk) : £0.75 B82-41119

428.6'4 — English language. Reading books — *For non-English speaking students* *continuation*

Newland, Michael. Close encounters of the third kind / Steven Spielberg ; adapted by Michael Newland. — London : Macmillan, 1982. — 62p : ill ; 21cm. — (Ranger : Range 7, fiction)
ISBN 0-333-30628-7 (pbk) : Unpriced
B82-31415

The **People** speak / English Language Services, Inc.. — Rev. ed. — New York : Collier Macmillan International ; London : Collier Macmillan, 1981. — iii,57p : ill ; 18cm. — (Collier Macmillan English readers)
Previous ed.: 1965
ISBN 0-02-970350-6 (pbk) : £0.65 B82-29945

Peterson, Lennart. Hijack! and other short stories / selected and simplified by Lennart Peterson and Sheila Wylie. — Harlow : Longman, 1981. — 58p ; 18cm. — (Longman simplified English series)
ISBN 0-582-52648-5 (pbk) : £0.80 B82-15558

Pitkeathly, Naomi. Town or country? / Naomi Pitkeathly ; illustrated with photographs by Verna Evans. — St. Albans : Hart-Davis Educational, 1981. — 47p : ill ; 18cm. — (Insights into English)
ISBN 0-247-13086-9 : Unpriced B82-09829

Recollections : ten stories on five themes / edited by Alex Adkins and Mark Shackleton. — London : Edward Arnold, 1980. — 156p ; 19cm
ISBN 0-7131-8021-8 (pbk) : £1.75 : CIP rev.
B80-18672

Ridley, Con. The flight of the condor / Con Ridley. — London : Macmillan, 1981. — 78p : ill ; 21cm. — (Ranger. Range 7, fiction)
ISBN 0-333-29455-6 (pbk) : Unpriced
B82-03014

Rimmer, J. A.. Family trapped / J.A. Rimmer and M.J. Scott. — London : Evans Brothers, c1982. — 14p : ill ; 19cm
ISBN 0-237-50689-0 (pbk) : Unpriced
B82-16930

The **Silver** elephant / English Language Services, Inc.. — Rev. ed. — New York : Collier Macmillan International ; London : Collier Macmillan, 1981. — vi,72p : ill ; 18cm. — (Collier Macmillan English readers)
Previous ed.: 1965
ISBN 0-02-970370-0 (pbk) : £0.65 B82-29940

Stocks, Chris. Fixation / Jack Pullman [i.e. Pulman] ; adapted by Chris Stocks. — Adapted ed. — Oxford : Oxford University Press, 1982. — 94p ; 18cm. — (Alpha thriller)
Previous ed.: / by Jack Pulman. London : Hamilton, 1978
ISBN 0-19-424223-4 (pbk) : £0.75 B82-19996

[Stories to surprise you]. Twisted tales / English Language Services, Inc.. — New York : Collier Macmillan International ; London : Collier Macmillan, c1964 (1981 printing). — v,87p : ill ; 18cm. — (Collier Macmillan English readers)
ISBN 0-02-970400-6 (pbk) : £0.65 B82-29943

Swan, Michael, *1936-*. Kaleidoscope : teacher's book : a guide to the use of authentic written materials in class / Michael Swan. — Cambridge : Cambridge University Press, c1980. — 76p ; 21cm
ISBN 0-521-23390-9 (pbk) : £2.75 B82-39485

Taborn, Stretton. Interface / Stretton Taborn. — London : Macmillan, 1981. — 84p : ill ; 21cm. — (Ranger. Range 6, fiction)
ISBN 0-333-29456-4 (pbk) : Unpriced
B82-03137

Tarner, Margaret. Dracula / Bram Stoker ; rewritten by Margaret Tarner ; illustrated by Kay Mary Wilson. — London : Heinemann Educational, 1982. — 57p : ill,1map ; 18cm. — (Heinemann guided readers. Intermediate level)
ISBN 0-435-27086-9 (pbk) : Unpriced
B82-38611

Wagner, Rosemary. The mayor of Casterbridge / Thomas Hardy ; adapted by Rosemary Wagner. — Oxford : Oxford University Press, c1979. — 93p ; 18cm. — (Alpha classics)
ISBN 0-19-424178-5 (pbk) : Unpriced
B82-05325

Walter, Catherine. Authentic reading. — Cambridge : Cambridge University Press, Nov.1982. — [96]p
ISBN 0-521-28359-0 : £2.25 : CIP entry
B82-40325

428.6'4 — English language. Reading books for non-English speaking students: Swan, Michael, *1936-*. **Spectrum** — *For teaching*

Swan, Michael, *1936-*. Spectrum : teacher's book : a guide to the use of authentic written materials in class / Michael Swan. — Cambridge : Cambridge University Press, 1980. — 80p ; 21cm
Includes index
ISBN 0-521-23391-7 (pbk) : £2.95 B82-38837

428.6'4 — English language. Reading books. Special subjects: Advertising — *For non-English speaking students*

Malovany-Chevallier, Sheila. Advertising / Sheila Malovany-Chevallier. — London : Cassell, 1980. — 128p : ill,2forms ; 22cm
ISBN 0-304-30420-4 (pbk) : £2.65 : CIP rev.
B80-08716

428.6'4 — English language. Reading books. Special subjects: Association football — *For non-English speaking students*

Dean, Michael, *19---*. Spotlight on football / Michael Dean. — London : Cassell, 1982, c1981. — 58p : ill,1map,ports ; 19cm. — (Cassell graded readers. Level 3)
ISBN 0-304-30595-2 (pbk) : Unpriced : CIP rev. B81-23940

428.6'4 — English language. Reading books. Special subjects: Boxing. Muhammad Ali — *For non-English speaking students*

Milton, Peter. Spotlight on Muhammad Ali / Peter Milton. — London : Cassell, 1982, c1981. — 31p : ill,ports ; 19cm. — (Cassell graded readers. Level 1)
ISBN 0-304-30591-x (pbk) : Unpriced: CIP rev.
B81-25680

428.6'4 — English language. Reading books. Special subjects: British tales & legends — *For non-English speaking students*

Robinson, Philip Bedford. Spotlight on strange stories / Philip Robinson. — London : Cassell, 1982. — 62p : ill ; 19cm. — (Cassell graded readers. Level 4)
ISBN 0-304-30567-7 (pbk) : Unpriced : CIP rev. B81-25677

428.6'4 — English language. Reading books. Special subjects: Drama in English. Shakespeare, William — *For non-English speaking students*

Barnaby, David. Spotlight on Shakespeare / David Barnaby. — London : Cassell, 1982. — 63p : ill,1map,ports ; 19cm. — (Cassell graded readers. Level 4)
ISBN 0-304-30597-9 (pbk) : Unpriced : CIP rev. B81-25671

428.6'4 — English language. Reading books. Special subjects: East Sussex. Brighton. Local radio services: Radio Brighton — *For non-English speaking students*

Goodman-Stephens, Pamela. Spotlight on a radio station / Pamela and Bryan Goodman-Stephens. — London : Cassell, 1982, c1981. — 23p : ill ; 19cm. — (Cassell graded readers. Level 1)
ISBN 0-304-30592-8 (pbk) : Unpriced : CIP rev. B81-23938

428.6'4 — English language. Reading books. Special subjects: England — *For non-English speaking students*

Brookes, H. F.. Life in Britain. — London : Heinemann Educational, July 1982. — [144]p
ISBN 0-435-28041-4 (pbk) : £1.95 : CIP entry
B82-14080

428.6'4 — English language. Reading books. Special subjects: England. Political events, *1642-1660* — *For non-English speaking students*

Newhouse, Julia. Spotlight on the English Revolution / Julia Newhouse and Jan King. — London : Cassell, 1982. — vi,90p : ill,1map,1facsim,ports ; 19cm. — (Cassell graded readers. Level 6)
ISBN 0-304-30571-5 (pbk) : Unpriced : CIP rev. B81-23937

428.6'4 — English language. Reading books. Special subjects: European Economic Community — *For non-English speaking students*

Haines, Simon. Spotlight on the Common Market / Simon Haines. — London : Cassell, 1982. — viii,55p : ill,maps ; 19cm. — (Cassell graded readers. Level 3)
ISBN 0-304-30596-0 (pbk) : Unpriced : CIP rev. B81-23941

428.6'4 — English language. Reading books. Special subjects: Food: British dishes — *For non-English speaking students*

West, Christine. Spotlight on British food / Christine West. — London : Cassell, 1982, c1981. — 32p : ill ; 19cm. — (Cassell graded readers. Level 1)
ISBN 0-304-30564-2 (pbk) : Unpriced : CIP rev. B81-25678

428.6'4 — English language. Reading books. Special subjects: Food — *For non-English speaking students*

Stitt, J. M.. Knives, forks and fingers / James M. Stitt. — 2nd ed. — London : Evans, 1979. — 31p : ill ; 19cm. — (Evans graded reading. Grade 1)
Previous ed.: 1977
ISBN 0-237-50344-1 (pbk) : Unpriced
B82-21847

428.6'4 — English language. Reading books. Special subjects: General practitioners. Working life — *For non-English speaking students*

Border, Rosemary. Spotlight on a doctor's day / Rosemary Border. — London : Cassell, 1982, c1981. — 32p : ill ; 19cm. — (Cassell graded readers. Level 1)
ISBN 0-304-30562-6 (pbk) : Unpriced : CIP rev. B81-23860

428.6'4 — English language. Reading books. Special subjects: Great Britain. Churchill, Winston S. (Winston Spencer), *1874-1965* — *For non-English speaking students*

Newhouse, Julia. Spotlight on Winston Churchill / Julia Newhouse. — London : Cassell, 1982. — 92p : ill,ports ; 19cm. — (Cassell graded readers. Level 6)
ISBN 0-304-30572-3 (pbk) : Unpriced : CIP rev. B81-25653

428.6'4 — English language. Reading books. Special subjects: Great Britain. Food & drink — *For non-English speaking students*

Harris, Rosemary, *1935 May 22-*. Tastes good : food and drink in Britain today / Rosemary Harris. — London : Harrap, 1982. — 48p : ill,1map,1facsim,1port ; 22cm. — (Britain today. Intermediate)
ISBN 0-245-53657-4 (pbk) : £1.50 B82-25255

428.6'4 — English language. Reading books. Special subjects: Hoaxes — *For non-English speaking students*

Hunt, Roderick, *1939-*. [Hoaxers, tricksters and frauds]. Jokers and con-men / Rod Hunt ; glossary and exercise by Mike Samuda. — London : Edward Arnold, 1980. — 32p : ill,ports ; 19cm. — (Leaders)
Originally published: 1978
ISBN 0-7131-8018-8 (pbk) : £0.60 : CIP rev.
B80-07759

428.6'4 — English language. Reading books. Special subjects: Horror films. Monsters — *For non-English speaking students*

Samuda, Mike. Hollywood monsters / Mike Samuda ; glossary and exercises by Mike Samuda. — London : Edward Arnold, 1980. — 32p : ill ; 19cm. — (Leaders)
Originally published: 1978
ISBN 0-7131-8016-1 (pbk) : £0.60 : CIP rev.
B80-09184

428.6′4 — English language. Reading books. Special subjects: Internal combustion engines — *For non-English speaking students*

Kopf, George. The engine / George Kopf. — London : Heinemann Educational, 1981. — 32p : ill ; 19cm. — (Heinemann science and technical readers. Elementary level)
Includes index
ISBN 0-435-29005-3 (pbk) : £0.85 B82-05073

428.6′4 — English language. Reading books. Special subjects: Inventions — *For non-English speaking students*

Border, Rosemary. Spotlight on inventions / Rosemary Border. — London : Cassell, 1982, c1981. — 32p : ill ; 19cm. — (Cassell graded readers. Level 2)
ISBN 0-304-30563-4 (pbk) : Unpriced : CIP rev. B81-23861

428.6′4 — English language. Reading books. Special subjects: Money — *For non-English speaking students*

Frampton, Robin. The story of money / Robin Frampton. — London : Heinemann Educational, 1981. — 58p : ill,1map,forms ; 18cm. — (Heinemann guided readers. Upper level ; 13)
ISBN 0-435-27082-6 (pbk) : £0.75 B82-12082

428.6′4 — English language. Reading books. Special subjects: Mysteries — *For non-English speaking students*

Samuda, Mike. [Unresolved mysteries]. Truly mysterious / Mike Samuda ; glossary and exercises by Mike Samuda. — London : Edward Arnold, 1980. — 32p : ill ; 19cm. — (Leaders)
Originally published: 1978
ISBN 0-7131-8017-x (corrected : pbk) : £0.60 : CIP rev. B80-09185

428.6′4 — English language. Reading books. Special subjects: Oxford & Cambridge — *For non-English speaking students*

Tarner, Margaret. Oxford and Cambridge / Margaret Tarner. — London : Heinemann Educational, 1981. — 58p : ill,maps,1facsim,ports ; 18cm. — (Heinemann guided readers. Elementary level ; 16)
ISBN 0-435-27080-x (pbk) : £0.55 B82-01806

428.6′4 — English language. Reading books. Special subjects: Paranormal phenomena — *For non-English speaking students*

West, Christine. Spotlight on surprises of nature / Christine West. — London : Cassell, 1982. — 63p : ill ; 19cm. — (Cassell graded readers. Level 4)
ISBN 0-304-30568-5 (pbk) : Unpriced : CIP rev. B81-25674

428.6′4 — English language. Reading books. Special subjects: Pop music industries — *For non-English speaking students*

Carrier, Michael. Spotlight on the pop industry / Michael Carrier and Christine Evans. — London : Cassell, 1982. — 96p : ill,ports ; 19cm. — (Cassell graded readers. Level 5)
ISBN 0-304-30570-7 (pbk) : Unpriced : CIP rev. B81-23862

428.6′4 — English language. Reading books. Special subjects: Puzzles & optical illusions — *For non-English speaking students*

Haines, Simon. Spotlight on illusions / Simon Haines. — London : Cassell, 1982, c1981. — [32]p : ill,1map ; 19cm. — (Cassell graded readers. Level 1)
ISBN 0-304-30561-8 (pbk) : Unpriced : CIP rev. B81-23859

428.6′4 — English language. Reading books. Special subjects: Racing cars. Racing, *to 1980* — *For non-English speaking students*

Price, Roger, *1941-*. Spotlight on motor racing / Roger Price. — London : Cassell, 1982, c1981. — 63p : ill,3ports ; 19cm. — (Cassell graded readers. Level 3)
ISBN 0-304-30565-0 (pbk) : Unpriced : CIP rev. B81-25679

428.6′4 — English language. Reading books. Special subjects: Radio, *to ca 1920* — *For non-English speaking students*

Border, Rosemary. Spotlight on the beginning of radio / Rosemary Border. — London : Cassell, 1982, c1981. — 32p : ill,1facsim,3ports ; 19cm. — (Cassell graded readers. Level 2)
ISBN 0-304-30593-6 (pbk) : Unpriced : CIP rev. B81-23939

428.6′4 — English language. Reading books. Special subjects: Science — *For non-English speaking students*

Lebauer, R. Susan. Reading skills for the future. — Oxford : Pergamon, July 1982. — [128]p. — (Materials for language practice)
ISBN 0-08-028619-4 (pbk) : £3.45 : CIP entry B82-12402

428.6′4 — English language. Reading books. Special subjects: Sports — *For non-English speaking students*

McLean, Alan C.. Fair play? / Alan C. McLean. — Harlow : Longman, 1981. — 45p : ill,1map,facsims,ports ; 25cm. — (Longman structural readers. Stage 4) (LSR analysis)
ISBN 0-582-52516-0 (pbk) : £0.70 B82-15198

428.6′4 — English language. Reading books. Special subjects: Stunting — *For non-English speaking students*

Samuda, Mike. [Daredevils]. Dangermen / Mike Samuda ; glossary and exercises by Mike Samuda. — London : Edward Arnold, 1980. — 32p : ill,ports ; 19cm. — (Leaders)
Originally published: 1977
ISBN 0-7131-8015-3 (pbk) : £0.60 : CIP rev. B80-09183

428.6′4 — English language. Reading books. Special subjects: Tennis — *For non-English speaking students*

Slater, Steven. Spotlight on tennis / Steven Slater. — London : Cassell, 1982, c1981. — 32p : ill,ports ; 19cm. — (Cassell graded readers. Level 2)
ISBN 0-304-30594-4 (pbk) : Unpriced : CIP rev. B81-25654

428.6′4 — English language. Reading books. Special subjects: United States. Politics. Kennedy *(Family)* — *For non-English speaking students*

Haines, Simon. Spotlight on the Kennedys / Simon and Vicky Haines. — London : Cassell, 1982. — 62p : ill,maps,1plan,ports ; 19cm. — (Cassell graded readers. Level 3)
ISBN 0-304-30566-9 (pbk) : Unpriced : CIP rev. B81-25675

428.6′4 — English language. Reading books. Special subjects: United States. Social life — *For non-English speaking students*

Musman, Richard. Background to the USA / Richard Musman. — London : Macmillan, c1982. — 146p,[8]p of plates : ill(some col.),1map,ports ; 22cm
ISBN 0-333-29070-4 (pbk) : Unpriced B82-20928

428.6′4927 — English language. Reading books — *For Arabic speaking students*

Rimmer, J. A.. Juma and Abdulla with the policemen of Oman / J.A. Rimmer ; illustrated by John Fraser. — Harlow : Longman, 1981. — 47p : ill,maps ; 20cm. — (Longman graded structural readers for the Arab world. Stage 3. Fiction)
ISBN 0-582-76481-5 (pbk) : £0.55 B82-06160

428.6′4995 — English language. Reading books — *For Solomon Islands students*

Bickerstaff, David. Maefiti and the terrorists / Derek Bickerstaffe. — London : Evans, 1981. — 57p : ill ; 22cm. — (Wide horizon library)
ISBN 0-237-50577-0 (pbk) : Unpriced B82-04236

Bickerstaffe, Derek. Maefiti and the drug smugglers / Derek Bickerstaffe. — London : Evans Bros., 1981. — 63p : ill ; 22cm. — (Wide horizon library)
ISBN 0-237-50578-9 (pbk) : Unpriced B82-11670

Milsome, John. Yemi's big match / John Milsome. — London : Evans, 1982. — 60p : ill ; 22cm. — (Wide horizon library)
ISBN 0-237-50628-9 (pbk) : Unpriced B82-20126

429 — OLD ENGLISH LANGUAGE

429 — Old English language — *Samplers*

Partridge, A. C.. A companion to Old and Middle English. — London : Deutsch, Oct.1981. — [352]p
ISBN 0-233-97308-7 (cased) : £12.95 : CIP entry
ISBN 0-233-97410-3 (pbk) : £6.95
Primary classification 427′.02 B81-26747

429′.5 — Old English language. Grammar

Mitchell, Bruce. A guide to Old English. — 3rd ed. — Oxford : Basil Blackwell, Sept.1982. — [224]p
Previous ed.: 1968
ISBN 0-631-12798-4 (cased) : £14.00 : CIP entry
ISBN 0-631-12735-6 (pbk) : £5.50 B82-20293

Wright, Joseph. Old English grammar. — 3rd ed. — Oxford : Clarendon Press, Dec.1982. — [388]p
Previous ed.: 1914
ISBN 0-19-811942-9 (pbk) : £13.50 : CIP entry B82-29896

429′.5 — Old English language. Words. Order

Bean, Marian C.. The development of word order patterns in Old English. — London : Croom Helm, Nov.1982. — [160]p. — (Croom Helm linguistics series)
ISBN 0-7099-0681-1 : £11.95 : CIP entry B82-27933

433 — GERMAN LANGUAGE. DICTIONARIES

433′.21 — German language. Figurative usage — *German & English dictionaries*

Spalding, Keith. An historical dictionary of German figurative usage / by Keith Spalding with the assistance of Kenneth Brooke. — Oxford : Basil Blackwell
German and English text
Fasc.35: Lippc-Maul. — c1982. — p.1625-1672 ; 26cm
ISBN 0-631-04050-1 (unbound) : Unpriced B82-37228

433′.21 — German language — *German & English dictionaries*

Collins pocket German dictionary : German-English English-German / [editors: Veronika Schnorr, Ute Nicol, Peter Terrell ; assistant editor Anne Dickinson]. — London : Collins, 1982. — vi,441p ; 19cm
Text adapted from Collins gem German-English, English-German dictionary
ISBN 0-00-433202-4 : £3.50 B82-37320

Lentz, E. Ernest. A German vocabulary : the 4500 most useful words arranged in connected groups suitable for translation, conversation and composition / E. Ernest Lentz. — New ed. — London : Blackie, c1966 (1982 [printing]). — 147p ; 15cm. — (Blackie vocabularies)
Parallel German text and English translation
ISBN 0-216-91182-6 (pbk) : £0.95 B82-24497

433′.21 — German language. Idioms. Colloquial usage — *German & English dictionaries*

Anderson, Beatrix. Cassell's colloquial German : a handbook of idiomatic usage / completely revised by Beatrix Anderson and Maurice North. — Rev. ed. — London : Cassell, 1980. — 176p ; 18cm
Previous ed.: published as Beyond the dictionary in German. 1968
ISBN 0-304-07941-3 (pbk) : Unpriced B82-07744

437 — GERMAN LANGUAGE. EARLY FORMS, SLANG, DIALECTS

437′.43 — German language. Rhineland-Palatinate dialects. Sociolinguistic aspects

Reinfrank, Arno. Wisdom, wit and wine. — London : Oswald Wolff, June 1982. — [128]p
ISBN 0-85496-366-9 (pbk) : £4.00 : CIP entry B82-14935

437'.947 — Yiddish language

Geipel, John. Mame loshn : the making of Yiddish. — London : Journeyman Press, Apr.1982. — [128]p
ISBN 0-904526-72-0 (cased) : £6.95 : CIP entry
ISBN 0-904526-73-9 (pbk) : £3.25 B82-11099

438 — GERMAN LANGUAGE USAGE

438 — German language — *For schools*

Berlinka, Jane. Deutsch in Wort und Bild / Jane Berlinka ; illustrated by Marian Jermiah. — London : Edward Arnold
Book 3: A secondary German course. — 1982. — 174p : ill,maps ; 25cm
English and German text
ISBN 0-7131-0541-0 (pbk) : £4.25 : CIP rev. B81-23807

Panorama / David Shotter, Hartmut Ahrens. — London : Heinemann Educational. — (Deutscher Sprachkurs ; 4)
[Pupil's book]. — 1981. — 450p : ill ; 25cm
German text, English introduction and notes. — Includes index
ISBN 0-435-38847-9 (pbk) : Unpriced : CIP rev. B81-13476

438 — German language — *Questions & answers*

Baer, Edith R.. Signposts German / Edith Baer and Margaret Wightman. — Cambridge : Cambridge University Press, 1982. — 104p : ill ; 21cm
ISBN 0-521-28186-5 (pbk) : £2.25 B82-30686

438 — German language — *Questions & answers — For schools*

Gregory, Stan. German : in your own words / Stan Gregory. — Harlow : Longman, 1982. — xii,100p ; 20cm
German text with English preliminaries
ISBN 0-582-33077-7 (pbk) : £1.10 B82-08909

Hawkins, Terry. Look at West Germany / Terry Hawkin. — Harlow : Longman, 1981. — 32p : ill,maps ; 16x22cm. — (Longman German workbooks)
Cover title. — Ill and text on inside covers
ISBN 0-582-20070-9 (pbk) : Unpriced
Also classified at 943.087'8 B82-05153

Stroh, Franz. Lache mit Willi / Franz Stroh, Ingrid Mållberg, Barbro Börjesson. — London : Mary Glasgow, 1979. — 51p : ill ; 22cm
German text, English introduction
ISBN 0-86158-563-1 (pbk) : Unpriced B82-05980

Vorwärts. — Leeds : Published for the Nuffield Foundation by E.J. Arnold. — (Nuffield introductory German course)
Teacher's book stage 2A / prepared by the German Section, Nuffield Foreign languages Teaching Materials Project. — Rev. ed. — 1978. — 112p : music ; 23cm
Previous ed.: 1970
ISBN 0-560-48140-3 (pbk) : Unpriced B82-23607

Whitton, Kenneth S.. Zusammen : integrated language exercises for sixth form German classes / Kenneth S. Whitton, J. Marjory Whitton. — Basingstoke : Macmillan Education, 1980. — viii,111p : ill ; 22cm
Includes index
ISBN 0-333-26303-0 (pbk) : £2.25 : CIP rev. B80-05880

438 — German language — *Study examples: Signs in German — Questions & answers*

Sawers, Robin. Schildersprache : reading comprehension activities / Robin Sawers, Ursula Runde. — London : Harrap, 1981. — [59]p : ill ; 21cm
German text, introduction in English
ISBN 0-245-53376-1 (pbk) : £1.95 B82-07471

438.2'4 — German language — *For non-German speaking students*

New German self taught : the quick, practical way to reading, writing, speaking, understanding / revised by Erich W. Berger and Dorothea Berger. — New York ; Cambridge : Barnes & Noble, 1982, c1959. — xix,389p ; 21cm
Originally published: New York : Funk & Wagnalls, 1959. — Text on inside covers. — Includes index
ISBN 0-06-463615-1 (pbk) : £2.95 B82-22930

438.2'421 — German language. Comprehension — *Questions & answers*

Kilborn, Richard W.. Themen und Variationen : practice in German styles and registers / Richard W. Kilborn, Peter H. Meech. — London : Harrap
Schülerbuch. — 1980. — 112p : ill,facsims,ports ; 22cm
German text, introduction in English
ISBN 0-245-53303-6 (pbk) : £3.25 B82-17397

438.2'421 — German language. Comprehension — *Questions & answers — For schools*

Grey, Douglas. Freude am Verstehen. — London : Heinemann Educational, Dec.1982
Pupil's book. — [64]p
ISBN 0-435-38020-6 (pbk) : £2.50 : CIP entry B82-29768

Grey, Douglas. Freude am Verstehen. — London : Heinemann Educational, Dec.1982
Teacher's book. — [72]p
ISBN 0-435-38021-4 (pbk) : £3.50 : CIP entry B82-29769

Johnson, Victor, *1930-*. Aus dem Leben gegriffen / Victor Johnson and Günther Schäfer. — London : Heinemann Educational, 1980. — 57p ; 22cm
ISBN 0-435-38410-4 (pbk) : £1.40 : CIP rev. B80-10572

Shotter, David. Panorama / by David Shotter, Hartmut Ahrens. — London : Heinemann Educational. — (Deutschers Sprachkurs ; 4)
Teacher's book. — 1981. — 121p ; 22cm
ISBN 0-435-38848-7 (pbk) : Unpriced : CIP rev. B81-13477

438.2'421 — German language. Crossword puzzles — *Collections — For schools*

Barnes, Carole. German topic crosswords. — London : E. Arnold, Dec.1982. — [48]p
ISBN 0-7131-0731-6 (pbk) : £1.60 : CIP entry B82-30199

438.2'421 — German language. Grammar

Buckley, R. W.. Living German. — 4th ed. — London : Hodder & Stoughton, June 1982. — [352]p
Previous ed.: London : University of London Press, 1965
ISBN 0-340-28378-5 (pbk) : £2.95 : CIP entry B82-10473

Rogers, Paul, *1950-*. Alles klar : German grammar through cartoons : demonstration and practice to examination level / Paul Rogers ; cartoons and design by Jeremy Long. — London : Harrap, 1982. — 65p : ill ; 30cm
English and German text
ISBN 0-245-53683-3 (pbk) : Unpriced B82-27113

438'.2'421 — German language. Grammar — *For schools*

Sunday best 2. — London : Gollancz, Nov.1982. — [224]p
ISBN 0-575-03190-5 : £6.95 : CIP entry B82-26560

438.2'421 — German language. Précis. Writing — *Questions & answers — For schools*

Wild, M. R.. German passages for summary and revision / M.R. Wild. — London : Edward Arnold, 1980. — iv,68p ; 22cm
German text, English introduction and explanations
ISBN 0-7131-0450-3 (pbk) : £1.60 : CIP rev. B80-12333

438.3'421 — Spoken German language. Business German — *Phrase books*

Paton, Roderick. Business case studies, German / Roderick Paton and Bärbel Paton. — Harlow : Longman, 1981. — 124p : ill,1form ; 24cm
German text, English introduction. — Bibliography: p124
ISBN 0-582-35171-5 (pbk) : £5.50 B82-09785

438.3'421 — Spoken German language — *For schools*

Sutton, P. J.. German conversation topics / P.J. Sutton. — London : Hodder and Stoughton, 1982. — vi,88p : ill ; 24cm
German text, English introduction
ISBN 0-340-26143-9 (pbk) : £1.95 : CIP rev. B81-20603

438.3'421 — Spoken German language — *Phrase books*

Howson, Bryan. Get by in German : a quick beginners' course for holidaymakers and businesspeople / course writer and producer: Edith Bear ; study booklet: Bryan Howson ; editor: Iris Sprankling. — Lonodn : British Broadcasting Corporation, 1981. — 72p : ill,map ; 18cm
A BBC radio course first broadcast March 1977
ISBN 0-563-16372-0 (pbk) : £1.35 B82-36039

438.6'421 — German language. Reading books

Spotlight on German : life and language in Germany today / editor Paul Hartley. — London : Pan in association with Heinemann Educational Books, 1981. — 125p : ill,maps,facsims,plans ; 20cm. — (Pan language readers)
German text, English introdution
ISBN 0-330-26471-0 (pbk) : £1.75 B82-01587

438.6'421 — German language. Reading books — *For schools*

Schnurre, Wolfdietrich. Stories. — London : Bell & Hyman, June 1981. — [144]p
ISBN 0-7135-1247-4 (pbk) : £2.95 : CIP entry B81-15895

439.31 — DUTCH LANGUAGE

439.3'1321 — Dutch language — *Dutch & English dictionaries*

Renier, Fernand G.. Dutch-English and English-Dutch dictionary / by Fernand G. Renier. — London : Routledge & Kegan Paul, 1949 (1982 [printing]). — xviii,571p ; 16cm
ISBN 0-7100-9352-7 (pbk) : £3.95 B82-39702

439.3'186421 — Dutch language. Reading books

A Dutch reader / compiled by Jelly K. Williams. — Cheltenham : Thornes, 1981. — ix,102p : ill ; 24cm
ISBN 0-85950-349-6 (pbk) : £3.75 : CIP rev. B81-34207

439.5 — SCANDINAVIAN LANGUAGES

439'.65 — Old Norse language. Grammar

Valfellis, Sigrid. Old Icelandic : an introductory course / Sigrid Valfellis and James E. Cathey. — Oxford : Oxford University Press in association with the Anglo-Scandinavian Foundation, 1981. — xxiv,379p ; 23cm
Bibliography: p379
ISBN 0-19-811172-x (cased) : £15.00 : CIP rev.
ISBN 0-19-811173-8 (pbk) : Unpriced B81-23885

439.82 — NORWEGIAN LANGUAGE

439.8'282421 — Norwegian language. Grammar

Stokker, Kathleen. Norsk : Nordmenn og Norge / av Kathleen Stokker og Odd Haddal. — Madison ; London : University of Wisconsin Press, c1981. — xviii,617p : ill,maps ; 24cm
English and Norwegian text. — Includes index
ISBN 0-299-08690-9 : £12.25 B82-12774

439.8'283421 — Spoken Norwegian language. Grammar

Haugen, Einar. Spoken Norwegian / Einar Haugen, Kenneth G. Chapman. — 3rd ed. — New York ; London : Holt, Rinehart and Winston, c1982. — xiv,450p : ill,maps ; 24cm
Previous ed.: 1964
ISBN 0-03-060013-8 : £14.95 B82-25821

440 — ROMANCE LANGUAGES

440′.05 — Romance languages — *Serials*

Romance studies. — No.1 (Winter 1982)-. — Aberystwyth (Dept. of Romance Studies, Hugh Owen Building, University College of Wales, Aberystwyth (Dyfed) SY23 3DY) : B. Nelson, Dec.1982. — [120]p
ISSN 0263-9904 : £2.50 : CIP entry
B82-39256

440′.7′1241 — Great Britain. Secondary schools. Curriculum subjects: Modern languages. Teaching — *Study examples: French language*

Teaching languages in today′s schools / edited by D.G. Smith. — London : Centre for Information on Language Teaching and Research, 1981. — vii,126p : ill ; 21cm
ISBN 0-903466-35-x (pbk) : £4.50 B82-12027

441 — FRENCH LANGUAGE. WRITTEN AND SPOKEN CODES

441′.52 — French language. Pronunciation

Carduner, Sylvie. D′accord : la prononciation du français international acquisition et perfectionnement / Sylvie Carduner, M. Peter Hagiwara. — New York ; Chichester : Wiley, c1982. — xiii,304p : ill ; 24cm
English text, French exercises. — Includes index
ISBN 0-471-09729-2 : £12.50 B82-18246

442 — FRENCH LANGUAGE. ETYMOLOGY

442 — French language. Words: Défaitisme. Usage, *1917-1918*

Slater, Catherine. Defeatists and their enemies : political invective in France, 1914-1918 / Catherine Slater. — Oxford : Oxford University Press, 1981. — viii,206p : 1facsim ; 23cm. — (Oxford modern languages and literature monographs)
Bibliography: p190-198. — Includes index
ISBN 0-19-815776-2 : £12.50 : CIP rev.
B81-30565

443 — FRENCH LANGUAGE. DICTIONARIES

443′.21 — French language — *French & English dictionaries*

Cousin, Pierre-Henri. Collins pocket dictionary : French-English English-French / Pierre-Henri Cousin. — London : Collins, 1982. — v,522p ; 19cm
Text adapted from Collins French gem dictionary
ISBN 0-00-433201-6 : £3.50 B82-37318

Murray, Malcolm W.. A French vocabulary : the 3500 most useful words arranged in connected groups suitable for translation, conversation and composition / Malcolm W. Murray and E. Ernest Lentz. — New ed. / fully revised by W.B. Seacroft. — London : Blackie, 1969 ([1982] [printing]). — 128p ; 15cm. — (Blackie vocabularies)
Parallel French text and English translation
ISBN 0-216-91183-4 (pbk) : £0.95 B82-24496

445 — FRENCH LANGUAGE. GRAMMAR

445 — Romance languages. Verbs. Future tense

Fleischman, Suzanne. The future in thought and language : diachronic evidence from Romance / Suzanne Fleischman. — Cambridge : Cambridge University Press, 1982. — xii,218p : ill ; 24cm. — (Cambridge studies in linguistics, ISSN 0068-676x ; 36)
Bibliography: p194-214. — Includes index
ISBN 0-521-24389-0 : £20.00 : CIP rev.
B82-11513

447 — FRENCH LANGUAGE. EARLY FORMS, SLANG, DIALECTS

447′.01 — Old French language. Influence of Latin language, *400-1250*

Wright, Roger. Late Latin and early Romance in Spain and Carolingian France. — Liverpool (The University, P.O. Box 147, Liverpool L69 3BX) : Francis Cairns, Oct.1982. — [322]p. — (ARCA classical and medieval texts, papers and monographs, ISSN 0309-5541 ; 8)
ISBN 0-905205-12-x : £20.00 : CIP entry
Also classified at 467′.01 B82-24750

447′.942342 — French language. Guernsey dialect. Grammar

Lukis, Eric Fellowes. An outline of the Franco-Norman dialect of Guernsey / by Eric Fellowes Lukis. — Rev. ed. with augmented Guernesiès-English vocabulary. — Le camp Tréhard (Le Camp Tréhard, Guernsey) : E.F. Lukis, 1981. — 79p : 1col.map ; 15x21cm
Cover title. — previous ed.: 1978. — Includes bibliographies
ISBN 0-9507661-0-0 (pbk) : £1.80 B82-23158

448 — FRENCH LANGUAGE USAGE

448

Downes, P. J.. French for today. — London : Hodder and Stoughton
Pupil′s book A / P.J. Downes and E.A. Griffith ; drawings by F. Chalaud ; additional art-work by Jan Pickett. — c1980. — 128p : ill (some col.),music ; 25cm
French text, English instructions
ISBN 0-340-23367-2 (pbk) : £1.75 : CIP rev.
Primary classification 448 B80-06370

448 — French language — *For schools*

Buckley, Michael. Action! : graded French / Michael Buckley. — Walton-on-Thames : Nelson
Bk.3. — 1982. — 239p : ill,form,maps,1port ; 25cm
French and English text
ISBN 0-17-439038-6 (pbk) : Unpriced
B82-34643

Downes, P. J.. French for today / P.J. Downes, E.A. Griffith ; drawings by François Chalaud and Jan Pickett. — London : Hodder and Stoughton
Pupils book B. — c1981. — 128p : col.ill,maps ; 25cm
ISBN 0-340-23368-0 (pbk) : £1.95 : CIP rev.
B81-28169

Downes, P. J.. French for today / P.J. Downes, E.A. Griffith ; drawings by François Chalaud and Jan Pickett. — London : Hodder and Stoughton
Text in French and English
Workbook B1 : (unit 1-10). — 1982. — 47p : ill ; 25cm
ISBN 0-340-23365-6 (unbound) : Unpriced : CIP rev. B81-34131

En avant. — [London] : Nuffield Foundation ; Leeds : E.J. Arnold
Stage 4B. — (Nuffield introductory French course. Stage 4b)
Reader C. — New combined ed. — 1980. — 24p : ill ; 16x21cm
Previous ed.: 1971
ISBN 0-560-00627-6 (pbk) : £0.50 B82-13786

En avant. — [London] : Nuffield Foundation ; Leeds : E.J. Arnold
Stage 4B. — (Nuffield introductory French course. Stage 4b)
Reader D. — New combined ed. — 1980. — 24p : ill ; 16x21cm
Previous ed.: 1971
ISBN 0-560-00626-8 (pbk) : £0.50 B82-13787

En avant. — [London] : Nuffield Foundation ; Leeds : E.J. Arnold
Stage 4B. — (Nuffield introductory French course. Stage 4b)
Reader B. — New combined ed. — 1980. — 24p : ill ; 16x21cm
Previous ed.: 1971
ISBN 0-560-00625-x (pbk) : £0.50 B82-13785

Fyfe, James. 'O' grade French. — London : Hodder & Stoughton, July 1981
Teacher′s book. — [40]p
ISBN 0-340-26752-6 (pbk) : £1.85 : CIP entry
B81-19149

Gilbert, Mark. Le français par l′image / Mark Gilbert. — London : Hodder and Stoughton
Bk.4 / illustrations by Celia Weber. — 1981. — 128p : ill ; 25cm
ISBN 0-340-24388-0 (pbk) : £2.65 : CIP rev.
B81-04217

Gilbert, Mark. Le Français par l′image / Mark Gilbert. — [London] : Hodder and Stoughton
Teacher′s Bk.4. — c1981. — 35p ; 22cm
Text in English and French
ISBN 0-340-24389-9 (unbound) : Unpriced : CIP rev. B81-31162

Honnor, Sylvia. Tricolore / Sylvia Honnor and Heather Mascie-Taylor. — Leeds : E.J. Arnold
Stage 3
Pupil′s book. — c1982. — 200p : ill(some col.),maps(some col.) ; 25cm
French and English text
ISBN 0-560-20581-3 (pbk) : Unpriced
B82-38976

Jones, Barry, *1938-*. Découvertes : language assignments / Barry Jones. — Cambridge : Cambridge University Press
English and French text
1: [A vous de décider]. — 1981. — 32p : ill,facsims ; 16x21cm
ISBN 0-521-28077-x (pbk) : £0.55 B82-36188

Miller, Arthur J.. Bleu, blanc, rouge / Francis Grand-Clément, Sten-Gunnar Hellström, Sven G. Johansson ; adapted by Arthur J. Miller. — [Exeter] : Wheaton, 1981. — 3v. : ill ; 21cm
Adaption of: Bleu, blanc, rouge. Stockholm : Almqvist & Wiksell Läromedel AB, 1973-75
ISBN 0-08-024173-5 (pbk) : Unpriced
ISBN 0-08-024174-3 (v.2) : £2.50
ISBN 0-08-024175-1 (v.3) : £2.50 B82-00736

Moore, Sidney. D′accord / Sidney Moore, Les Antrobus, Gordon Pugh ; linguistic consultant Elisabeth Escalier des Orres. — Harlow : Longman. — (Longman audio-visual French)
Stage 1
Pupil′s book. — 1982. — 128p : ill(some col.),maps,music ; 24cm
Text in French and English. — Previous ed.: published as Longman audio-visual French. Stage A1. — Text on inside cover. — Includes index
ISBN 0-582-31044-x : Unpriced B82-31770

Moore, Sidney. D′accord / Sidney Moore, Les Antrobus, Gordon Pugh ; linguistic consultant Elisabeth Escalier des Orres. — Harlow : Longman. — (Longman audio-visual French)
Stage 1
Teacher′s book. — 1982. — 80p ; 24cm
Text in English and French. — Previous ed.: published as Longman audio-visual French. Stage A1. — Includes index
ISBN 0-582-20220-5 (pbk) : Unpriced
B82-31771

Tour de France. — London : Heinemann Educational
1
Teacher′s book / a national working party of the Scottish Central Committee on Modern Languages. — 1982. — 148p : ill ; 25cm
ISBN 0-435-37754-x (pbk) : Unpriced : CIP rev. B81-30510

Tour de France / A national working party of the Scottish Central Committee on Modern Languages. — London : Heinemann
2. — 1982. — 94p : ill ; 25cm
ISBN 0-435-37759-0 (pbk) : £1.80 : CIP rev.
B82-06031

448 — French language — *For schools continuation*

Tricolore. — Leeds : E.J. Arnold in association with the Nuffield Foundation
Stage 3
Teacher's pack. — [1982?]. — 1case : ill(some col.),maps(some col.),ports ; 38cm
Contents: Teacher's book — Pupil's book — Set of spirit duplicator masters — 6 filmstrips — 5 tapes
ISBN 0-560-20595-3 : £83.75 (with tapes) B82-38415

448 — French language — *Questions & answers — For schools*

Antrobus, Les. Bonjour L'Afrique! / Les Antrobus, Max Anyanwu, David Mills. — Harlow : Longman
Practice bk.1. — 1982. — 47p : ill,1map ; 25cm
ISBN 0-582-60462-1 (pbk) : £0.80 B82-39926

Asher, Colin. French for you / Colin Asher and David Webb. — London : Hutchinson, 1982. — 2v. : ill,maps,facsims,plans,ports ; 24cm
ISBN 0-09-146641-5 (pbk) : Unpriced : CIP rev.
ISBN 0-09-146651-2 (bk.2) B82-00269

Downes, P. J.. French for today. — London : Hodder and Stoughton
Workbook A1. — 1980
(Units 1-10) / P.J. Downes, R.M. Johnstone and E.A. Griffith ; illustrations by François Chalaud ; with additional material by Jan Pickett. — 47p : ill ; 25cm
ISBN 0-340-23363-x (unbound) : £0.65 : CIP rev. B80-04761

Downes, P. J.. French for today. — London : Hodder and Stoughton
Workbook A2. — 1980
(Units 11-20) / P.J. Downes, R.M. Johnstone, E.A. Griffith ; illustrations by François Chalaud, ; with additional material by Jan Pickett. — 48p : ill,1map ; 25cm
ISBN 0-340-23364-8 (unbound) : Unpriced : CIP rev. B80-06371

Downes, P. J.. French for today. — London : Hodder and Stoughton
Pt.A: Teacher's handbook / P.J. Downes, E.A. Griffith. — 1980. — 77p ; 25cm
English and French text
ISBN 0-340-23369-9 (pbk) : £2.95 B82-22361

Downes, P. J.. French for today / P.J. Downes, E.A. Griffith. — London : Hodder and Stoughton
Pt.B: Teacher's handbook. — 1982. — 92p : ill,2maps ; 25cm
Includes text in French
ISBN 0-340-23370-2 (pbk) : Unpriced : CIP rev. B80-02736

Downes, P. J.. French for today. — London : Hodder and Stoughton
Pupil's book A / P.J. Downes and E.A. Griffith ; drawings by F. Chalaud ; additional art-work by Jan Pickett. — c1980. — 128p : ill (some col.),music ; 25cm
French text, English instructions
ISBN 0-340-23367-2 (pbk) : £1.75 : CIP rev.
Also classified at 448 B80-06370

Downes, P. J.. French for today / P.J. Downes, E.A. Griffith ; drawings by François Chalaud and Jan Pickett. — London : Hodder and Stoughton
Workbook B2 : (Units 11-18). — 1982. — 47p : ill ; 25cm
Text in French, notes in English
ISBN 0-340-23366-4 (unbound) : Unpriced : CIP rev. B82-07943

Fenley, G. Ward. Regardez l'image! / G. Ward Fenley ; edited by Ian MacDonald. — New ed. — London : Edward Arnold, 1980. — 37p : ill ; 25cm
Previous ed.: Stokie, Ill. : National Textbook Co, 1970
ISBN 0-7131-0447-3 (pbk) : £1.35 : CIP rev. B80-03606

Le Français en faculté / Scottish Universities French Language Research Project. — London : Hodder and Stoughton, 1980
Audio Course
Student's workbook : (to be used with tapes) / prepared by John Devereux, Brian Farrington and Catherine Richardson. — 40p : 1ill ; 24cm
French and English text
ISBN 0-340-24093-8 (pbk) : £1.25 : CIP rev. B79-34120

Fyfe, James, *1925-*. 'O' grade French / James Fyfe. — London : Hodder and Stoughton, c1981
Pupil's book. — 89p : ill ; 24cm + Teacher's book(56p : 24cm)
ISBN 0-340-26288-5 (pbk) : £1.75 : CIP rev.
ISBN 0-340-26752-6 (Teacher's book) : £2.45 B81-19150

Gilogley, A. C.. French practice papers / A.C. Gilogley. — Glasgow : Blackie, 1981. — 104p ; 22cm + Teacher's guide(30p : 22cm)
French text, English preface, questions and vocabulary
ISBN 0-216-91068-4 (pbk) : £2.35
ISBN 0-216-91069-2 (Teacher's guide) : £1.50 B82-04439

Houldsworth, P. B.. Find out about France / P.B. Houldsworth. — Sevenoaks : Hodder & Stoughton, c1982. — iii,27p : 1map ; 25cm
Published to be used in conjunction with All about France
ISBN 0-340-25596-x (unbound) : Unpriced : CIP rev. B81-37590

Page, Brian. Lire / Brian Page and Alan Moys. — Cambridge : Cambridge University Press, 1982. — 72p : ill ; 21cm. — (Communication in French ; level 3)
Text on inside covers
ISBN 0-521-28624-7 (pbk) : £1.25 B82-26484

Scottish Central Committee on Modern Languages. Tour de France. — London : Heinemann Educational
2: Teacher's book. — Dec.1982. — [128]p
ISBN 0-435-37762-0 (pbk) : £5.50 : CIP entry B82-30588

Smith, Jeanne-Marie. Communiquez bien en français : practice in language skills for O level and SCE examinations / Jeanne-Marie Smith. — Amersham : Hulton Educational
Text in English and French
[Pupil's book]. — 1982. — 125p : ill ; 26cm
ISBN 0-7175-0891-9 (pbk) : £2.35 B82-21500

Smith, Jeanne-Marie. Communiquez bien en français : practice in language skills for O level and SCE examinations / Jeanne-Marie Smith. — Amersham : Hulton Educational
Text in English and French
[Teacher's book]. — 1982. — 149p : ill ; 26cm
ISBN 0-7175-0892-7 (pbk) : £2.85 B82-21501

Sprake, David. 'Communiqué' : practice for the CSE and 16+ examination / David Sprake. — Oxford : Oxford University Press, 1982. — 156p : ill ; 22cm
Includes index
ISBN 0-19-832386-7 (pbk) : £2.25 B82-18414

Tour de France / Scottish Central Committee on Modern Languages. — London : Heinemann Educational
1
Reproduction masters. — 1982. — [32]p : ill ; 30cm
ISBN 0-435-37751-5 (unbound) : £3.00 B82-15284

448 — French language - *Questions & answers - For schools*

Whitmore, P. C.. French for CSE. — 3rd ed. — London : Bell and Hyman, June 1981. — [246]p
Previous ed.: London : Bell, 1977
ISBN 0-7135-1265-2 (pbk) : £3.50 : CIP entry B81-14966

448 — French language — *Questions & answers — French texts*

Eyre, Kim. Le vif du sujet : nouveau cours monolingue de français / Kim Eyre. — Slough : University Tutorial, 1982. — 203p : ill,1map ; 21cm
French text with English preface and bibliography. — Bibliography: p203
ISBN 0-7231-0827-7 (pbk) : £2.25 B82-21309

448 — French language — *Study examples: Signs in French — Questions & answers*

Ellis, D. L.. Les mots de la rue : reading comprehension activities / D.L. Ellis, E. Shellard ; photographs by M.R. Pearce. — London : Harrap, 1981. — 64p : ill ; 21cm
French text, introduction in English
ISBN 0-245-53367-2 (pbk) : £1.95 B82-07472

448'.0024624 — French language — *For civil engineering*

Paulus, A.. Civil engineering in French : a guide to the language and practice of civil engineering in French-speaking countries / A. Paulus. — London : Telford, 1982. — 192p : ill,plans ; 22cm
Includes bibliographies
ISBN 0-7277-0138-x : £10.00 B82-36666

448'.0024642 — French language — *For catering*

Grisbrooke, John. French for catering students / John Grisbrooke. — London : Edward Arnold, 1982. — ix,144p : ill,1map ; 22cm
ISBN 0-7131-0710-3 (pbk) : £3.95 : CIP rev. B82-06914

448'.002465 — French language — *For business enterprise*

Bower, Malcolm. French for business / Malcolm Bower and Lucette Barbarin. — 2nd ed. — London : Hodder and Stoughton, 1981. — x,144p : ill,2maps ; 20cm
French text, English introduction, notes and instructions. — Previous ed.: 1977
ISBN 0-340-26920-0 (pbk) : £2.25 : CIP rev. B81-13763

Castley, Andrew. French / Andrew Castley, Tom Wight. — Harlow : Longman, 1982. — 99p ; 24cm. — (Business situations)
French exercises and dialogue, English introduction, notes and vocabulary
ISBN 0-582-35181-2 (pbk) : £3.50 B82-32639

448.1 — French language. Words — *For children — Illustrations*

Lamblin, Simone. Larousse word and picture book / text by Simone Lamblin ; illustration by Marianne Gaunt ; adaptation by Mary Ann Quinson. — London : Ward Lock, 1981. — 45p : chiefly col.ill ; 32cm
English and French text
ISBN 0-7063-6162-8 : Unpriced B82-11851

448.1'076 — French language. Vocabulary — *Questions & answers — For schools*

Wildbore, Alison M.. Comment ça se dit? / Alison M. Wildbore. — London : Arnold, 1982. — 48p : ill ; 25cm
ISBN 0-7131-0451-1 (pbk) : Unpriced : CIP rev. B81-31547

448.2 — Romance languages. Verbs — *Festschriften*

Studies in the Romance verb. — London : Croom Helm, Sept.1982. — [256]p
ISBN 0-7099-2602-2 : £12.95 : CIP entry B82-20768

448.2'4 — French language — *For non-French speaking students*

New French self taught : the quick, practical way to reading, writing, speaking, understanding / revised by Frédéric Ernst with pronunciation and phonetics by Dora Bashour. — New York ; Cambridge : Barnes & Noble, 1982, c1959. — xix,385p ; 21cm
Originally published: New York : Funk & Wagnalls, 1959. — Text on inside covers. — Includes index
ISBN 0-06-463614-3 (pbk) : £2.95 B82-22929

448.2'421 — French language. Comprehension — *Questions & answers — For schools*

Albani, Alex. En l'an 2000 / Alex Albani and Kevin Desmond. — London : Heinemann Educational, 1981. — 68p : ill ; 25cm
English and French text
ISBN 0-435-37030-8 (pbk) : £1.95 : CIP rev. B81-04254

448.2'421 — French language — *For English speaking African students*

Antrobus, Les. Bonjour l'Afrique / Les Antrobus, Max Anyanwu, David Mills. — Harlow : Longman. — (Longman French for secondary schools)
Students' book 1. — 1981. — v,128p : ill(some col.),music ; 25cm
French text, introduction in English. — Map, text on inside covers. — Includes index
ISBN 0-582-60460-5 (pbk) : Unpriced B82-20119

448.2'421 — French language — *For slow learning students — For schools*

Johnson, Christopher. D'accord. — London : Hodder & Stoughton
1: Pupils' book. — Jan.1982. — [64]p
ISBN 0-340-24951-x (pbk) : £1.35 : CIP entry B81-34146

Johnson, Christopher. D'accord. — London : Hodder and Stoughton
2: Pupils' book. — Jan.1982. — [64]p
ISBN 0-340-27709-2 (pbk) : £1.25 : CIP entry B81-34147

448.2'421 — French language. Grammar — *For schools*

Goodman-Stephens, Bryan. French language patterns / B.J. Goodman-Stephens and P.E. Goodman-Stephens. — Exeter : Wheaton, 1982. — 201p ; 21cm
Text in English and French
ISBN 0-08-025003-3 (pbk) : £2.95 B82-39565

Houldsworth, Peter. Le Français d'aujourd'hui. — New ed. — London : Hodder and Stoughton
Pt 4(B). — Sept.1982. — [208]p
Previous ed.: London : English Universities P., 1970
ISBN 0-340-28704-7 (pbk) : £3.95 : CIP entry B82-21733

Houldsworth, Peter B.. Le Français d'aujourd'hui. — New ed. — London : Hodder and Stoughton
Pt.4(B). — Sept.1982
Previous ed.: London : English Universities P., 1970
Teacher's booklet. — [64]p
ISBN 0-340-28705-5 (pbk) : £1.50 : CIP entry B82-21384

448.2'496 — French language. Grammar — *For African students — For schools*

Grandsaigne, J. de. France-Afrique. — New ed. — London : Macmillan Education
Livre de l'élève 2 / J. de Grandsaigne. — 1981. — 153p : ill ; 17x22cm
Previous ed.: 1977. — Includes index
ISBN 0-333-30573-6 (pbk) : Unpriced B82-25649

448.3'421 — Spoken French language

Marshall, S. A.. French for beginners / S.A. Marshall and D.J. Morrison. — Cambridge : National Extension College, c1968 (1978 [printing]). — 36p : ill ; 29cm. — (National Extension College correspondence texts ; course no.L2)
English and French text
ISBN 0-86082-027-0 (pbk) : Unpriced B82-40277

Neather, E.. Mastering French / E. Neather ; editorial consultant Betty Parr. — London : Macmillan, 1982. — xiii,262p : ill ; 23cm. — (Macmillan master series)
ISBN 0-333-34058-2 (cased) : Unpriced
ISBN 0-333-32347-5 (pbk) : Unpriced B82-39711

448.3'421 — Spoken French language. Comprehension — *Questions & answers*

Symonds, Pamela. A l'écoute / Pamela Symonds. — Cambridge : Cambridge University Press, 1982. — 72p : ill,maps,ports ; 22cm. — (Communication in French. Level 3)
ISBN 0-521-28601-8 (pbk) : £1.25 B82-34568

448.3'421 — Spoken French language — *Phrase books*

Harris, Julian. Basic conversational French / Julian Harris, André Lévêque. — 7th ed. — New York ; London : Holt, Rinehart and Winston, 1982. — xv,501,[12]p of plates : ill (some col.),3maps ; 24cm
Previous ed.: 1978. — Ill on lining papers. — Includes index
ISBN 0-03-060112-6 : £15.95 B82-25416

448.3'421 — Spoken French language — *Questions & answers — For schools*

McLagan, Pat. Start speaking French / Pat McLagan & Hilary Stanyer. — Glasgow : Blackie, 1981. — 48p : chiefly ill ; 22cm + Teacher's guide(29p : 22cm)
Cover title. — Text on inside cover
ISBN 0-216-91070-6 (pbk) : £2.60
ISBN 0-216-91071-4 (Teacher's guide) : £1.90 B82-04440

Moran, John F.. Guidance and practice for students in oral French at Leaving Certificate level / John Moran, Derek Johnston. — Dublin (Ballymount Road, Walkinstown, Dublin 12) : Helicon : Educational Company of Ireland [distributor], c1982. — 96p : ill ; 21cm
French text ; instructions and questions in English
Unpriced (pbk) B82-17163

Sanderson, David. Découvertes / [written and produced by the Language Materials Development Unit of the University of York] ; [authors David Sanderson, Antony Peck]. — York : Language Materials Development Unit, University of York, c1982. — 20p : ill ; 19x21cm
Text in English and French. — Cover title
ISBN 0-85600-203-8 (pbk) : Unpriced B82-24382

Simulations en français. — York : Language Materials Development Unit, University of York, c1981. — [28]p : ill ; 21cm + 34 work cards(ill ; 15x21cm)
Pamphlet and work cards in plastic bag
ISBN 0-85600-162-7 (unbound) : Unpriced B82-15415

448.6'421 — French language. Reading books

Guillot, René. Crin-blanc / René Guillot ; based on the film by Albert Lamorisse ; abridged and edited by J.R. Watson ; illustrated by Akos Szabo. — Abridged and simplified ed. — London : Harrap, 1961 (1981 [printing]). — 77p : ill ; 20cm
ISBN 0-245-53783-x (pbk) : £1.95 B82-08793

Spotlight on French : life and language in France today / editor Bryan Howson. — London : Pan in association with Heinemann Educational, 1981. — 127p : ill,facsims ; 20cm. — (Pan langauge readers)
French text, English introduction
ISBN 0-330-26469-9 (pbk) : £1.75 B82-01589

448.6'421 — French language. Reading books — *For schools*

Dufournier, Denise. Entre deux coups de téléphone / Denise Dufournier ; edited by Alison M. Wildbore ; drawings by Veronica van Vliet. — London : Arnold, 1982. — 32p : ill(some col.) ; 14x22cm
Originally published: Amsterdam : Meulenhoff, 1979
ISBN 0-7131-0659-x (pbk) : Unpriced : CIP rev. B82-11086

Dufournier, Denise. La maison du père Loriot / Denise Dufournier ; edited by Alison M. Wildbore ; drawings by Lisa Couwenbergh. — London : Edward Arnold, 1982. — 32p : ill (some col.) ; 14x22cm
Originally published: Amsterdam : Meulenhoff, 1980. — Text on inside cover
ISBN 0-7131-0660-3 (pbk) : Unpriced : CIP rev. B82-11087

Galembert, Pierre-Jean. Le collier africain / Pierre-Jean Galembert ; illustrated by Warren Linn. — London : Bell & Hyman in association with National Textbook Company, 1979, c1978. — 68p : ill ; 23cm. — (Les aventures de Pierre et de Bernard)
French text, English preface
ISBN 0-7135-1121-4 (pbk) : £1.25 B82-22454

Galembert, Pierre-Jean. Les contrebandiers / Pierre-Jean Galembert ; illustrated by Warren Linn. — London : Bell & Hyman in association with National Textbook Company, 1979, c1974. — 58p : ill ; 23cm. — (Les aventures de Pierre et de Bernard)
French text, English preface
ISBN 0-7135-1122-2 (pbk) : £1.25 B82-22453

Galembert, Pierre-Jean. Le trésor des pirates / Pierre-Jean Galembert ; illustrated by Warren Linn. — London : Bell & Hyman in association with National Textbook Company, 1979, c1974. — 56p : ill ; 23cm. — (Les aventures de Pierre et de Bernard)
ISBN 0-7135-1124-9 (pbk) : £1.25 B82-22455

Heurlin, K.. A la découverte de Paris / K. Heurlin ; adapted by Anne Constantine. — Amersham : Hulton, 1982. — 75p : ill,facsims,plans ; 21cm
ISBN 0-7175-1006-9 (pbk) : £1.75 B82-28351

MacDonald, Ian, *1947-*. Catastrophe! / Ian MacDonald ; illustrations by John Ellis. — London : Edward Arnold, 1981, c1982. — 32p : ill ; 23cm. — (Faut le croire!)
French text, English introduction
ISBN 0-7131-0545-3 (pbk) : £1.25 : CIP rev. B81-23808

Neamat, Christine. Scènes de France / Christine Neamat. — Amersham : Hulton Educational, 1982, c1979. — 48p : ill ; 18cm
French text, English foreword
ISBN 0-7175-1005-0 (pbk) : £1.00 B82-21499

Pivot, Agnes. Les aventures en mer / Agnès Pivot ; illustration by John Ellis. — London : Edward Arnold, 1981, c1982. — 32p : ill,ports ; 23cm. — (Faut le croire!)
French text, English introduction
ISBN 0-7131-0546-1 (pbk) : £1.25 : CIP rev. B81-21472

Roper, John, *1927-*. Les héros et les héroïnes de la Résistance / John Roper ; illustrations by John Ellis. — London : Edward Arnold, 1981, c1982. — 32p : ill,3ports ; 23cm. — (Faut le croire!)
French text, English introduction
ISBN 0-7131-0547-x (pbk) : £1.25 : CIP rev. B81-21488

448.6'421 — French language. Reading books. Special subjects: France. Employment — *For schools*

Chafer, Anthony. Le monde du travail / Anthony Chafer. — London : Edward Arnold, 1981. — 14p : ill ; 30cm. — (En l'etat actuel des choses)
French text, English introduction
ISBN 0-7131-0549-6 (unbound) : £1.25 : CIP rev. B81-12891

448.6'421 — French language. Reading books: Strip cartoons — *For schools*

Thorén, Nils. Le Chapeau Rouge / Nils Thorén, Staffan Wahlgren. — London : Mary Glasgow
3: La grande opération. — c1979. — 13p : col.ill ; 23cm
Cover title
ISBN 0-86158-502-x (pbk) : Unpriced B82-00614

Thorén, Nils. Le Chapeau Rouge / Nils Thorén, Staffan Wahlgren. — London : Mary Glasgow
4: La valise désirable. — c1979. — 13p : col.il ; 23cm
Cover title
ISBN 0-86158-503-8 (pbk) : Unpriced B82-00612

450 — ITALIAN, ROMANIAN, RHAETO-ROMANIC LANGUAGES

450′.7′1141 — Great Britain. Universities. Curriculum subjects: Italian language. Courses — *Statistics*

Lo **Studio** dell'italiano nelle università britanniche / a cura di Andrew Wilkin. — Londra : Istituto italiano di cultura nel Regno Unito, 1981. — 26p ; 21cm
Parallel English text and Italian translation
ISBN 0-9504663-1-x (pbk) : Unpriced B82-05180

453 — ITALIAN LANGUAGE. DICTIONARIES

453′.21 — Italian language — *Italian & English dictionaries*

Dizionario inglese italiano italiano inglese : adattamento e ristrutturazione dell' originale Advanced learner's dictionary of current English della Oxford University Press / [direttore Malcolm Skey]. — [4a ed]. — Torino : Società Editrice Internazionale ; [Oxford] : [Oxford University Press], 1981. — xxix,1894p ; 25cm
Previous ed.: 1979
ISBN 0-19-431158-9 : £19.50 B82-00001

Love, Catherine E.. Collins pocket Italian dictionary : Italian-English English-Italian / Catherine E. Love. — London : Collins, 1982. — viii,437p ; 19cm
Text adapted from Collins gem Italian-English, English-Italian dictionary
ISBN 0-00-433203-2 : Unpriced B82-37319

458 — ITALIAN LANGUAGE USAGE

458.1 — Italian language. Pronunciation — *Manuals*

Chapallaz, Marguerite. The pronunciation of Italian : a practical introduction / Marguerite Chapallaz. — London : Bell & Hyman, 1979. — xv,244p : ill ; 19cm
Bibliography: p242-244
ISBN 0-7135-1997-5 (pbk) : £4.95 B82-12039

458.2′421 — Italian language. Comprehension — *Questions & answers — For schools*

Kozma, Janice M.. Carosello : a cultural reader / Janice M. Kozma. — 2nd ed. — New York ; London : Holt, Rinehart and Winston, c1982. — viii,216p : ill,facsims ; 24cm
Text in Italian. — Previous ed.: 1978
ISBN 0-03-060066-9 (pbk) : £8.95 B82-29504

458.2′421 — Italian language. Grammar

Germano, Joseph E.. Schaum's outline of Italian grammar / by Joseph E. Germano and Conrad J. Schmitt. — New York ; London : McGraw-Hill, c1982. — 258p ; 28cm. — (Schaum's outline series)
ISBN 0-07-023031-5 (pbk) : £5.95 B82-37798

Jackson, Eugene. Italian made simple / Eugene Jackson and Joseph Lopreato ; advisory editor Gloria Ackerley. — Rep. and rev. — London : Heinemann, 1977 (1982 [printing]). — xii,340p : 1map ; 22cm. — (Made simple books)
English and Italian text. — Originally published: London W.H. Allen, 1968. — Includes index
ISBN 0-434-98536-8 (pbk) : £2.95 B82-26807

Valgimigli, Maria. Living Italian / Maria Valgimigli. — 3rd ed. / with revisions by David S. Watson. — London : Hodder and Stoughton, 1982. — 320p : ill ; 18cm
Previous ed.: 1969. — Includes index
ISBN 0-340-26030-0 (pbk) : £2.45 : CIP rev. B81-13887

458.3′421 — Spoken Italian language — *Phrase books*

New Italian self taught : the quick, practical way to reading, writing, speaking, understanding. — [New ed.] / rev. by Mario Pei. — New York ; London : Barnes & Noble, 1982. — xv,336p : ill ; 21cm
Parallel Italian text and English translation. — Previous ed.: New York : Funk & Wagnalls, 1959. — Text on inside covers. — Includes index
ISBN 0-06-463616-x (pbk) : £2.95 B82-26509

458.3′421 — Spoken Italian language — *Questions & answers*

Cremona, Joseph. Buongiorno Italia! / course writer Joseph Cremona ; language assistant Tiziana Andreis. — London : British Broadcasting Corporation, 1982. — 304p + notes for teachers(64p : ill ; 23cm) : ill(some col.),col.maps,1col.plan,ports ; 23cm
Dialogue, reading passages in Italian, introduction and notes in English
ISBN 0-563-16479-4 (pbk) : £4.95
ISBN 0-563-16539-1 (Notes for teachers) : £3.00 B82-35088

458.6′421 — Italian language. Reading books

Burney, Anna Chelotti. Tempi moderni / Anna Chelotti Burney [compiler]. — New York ; London : Holt, Rinehart and Winston, c1982. — v,197p ; 24cm
Italian text, English introduction and notes
ISBN 0-03-059557-6 (pbk) : £5.95 B82-16903

Spotlight on Italian : life and language in Italy today / editor Ottavio Negro. — London : Pan in association with Heinemann Educational, 1981. — 127p : ill,1map,facsims ; 20cm. — (Pan language readers)
Italian text, English introduction
ISBN 0-330-26472-9 (pbk) : £1.75 B82-01590

459.9 — RHAETO-ROMANIC LANGUAGES

459′.9 — Rhaeto-Romance language

Gregor, Douglas Bartlett. Romontsch : the Sursilvan Raeto-romance of Switzerland. — Cambridge : Oleander Press, Apr.1982. — [220]p. — (Oleander language and literature ; 11)
ISBN 0-900891-39-4 : £13.50 : CIP entry B82-05772

461 — SPANISH LANGUAGE. WRITTEN AND SPOKEN CODES

461′.5 — Spanish languages. Phonetics — *Spanish texts*

Barrutia, Richard. Fonética y fonología españolas / Richard Barrutia, Tracy David Terrell. — New York ; Chichester : Wiley, c1982. — xi,189p : ill,maps ; 24cm
Bibliography: p163-186. — Includes index
ISBN 0-471-08461-1 : £13.30 B82-26465

463 — SPANISH LANGUAGE. DICTIONARIES

463′.21 — Spanish language — *Spanish & English dictionaries*

Gonzalez, Mike. Collins pocket Spanish dictionary : Spanish-English English-Spanish / Mike Gonzalez. — London : Collins, 1982. — ix,436p ; 19cm
Text adapted from Collins Spanish gem dictionary
ISBN 0-00-433204-0 : £3.50 B82-37317

Lentz, E. Ernest. A Spanish vocabulary : the 3500 most useful words arranged in connected groups suitable for translation, conversation and composition / E. Ernest Lentz. — New ed. / revised by Isabel Julian. — London : Blackie, c1972 ([1982] [printing]). — 128p ; 15cm. — (Blackie vocabularies)
Parallel Spanish text, and English translation
ISBN 0-216-91181-8 (pbk) : £0.95 B82-24495

465 — SPANISH LANGUAGE. GRAMMAR

465 — Spanish language. Verbs

Connell, Tim. The Spanish verb : its forms and uses / Tim Connell and Elizabeth Van Heusden. — Cheltenham : Thornes, 1980. — 88p ; 21cm
English and Spanish text. — Includes index
ISBN 0-85950-452-2 (pbk) : £1.95 : CIP rev. B80-17644

467 — SPANISH LANGUAGE. EARLY FORMS, SLANG, DIALECTS

467′.01 — Old Spanish language. Influence of Latin language, *400-1250*

Wright, Roger. Late Latin and early Romance in Spain and Carolingian France. — Liverpool (The University, P.O. Box 147, Liverpool L69 3BX) : Francis Cairns, Oct.1982. — [322]p. — (ARCA classical and medieval texts, papers and monographs, ISSN 0309-5541 ; 8)
ISBN 0-905205-12-x : £20.00 : CIP entry
Primary classification 447′.01 B82-24750

468 — SPANISH LANGUAGE USAGE

468 — Spanish language — *Questions & answers — For schools*

Bennett, A. J.. ¡Buenos días! : an illustrated Spanish course / A.J. Bennett. — London : Hodder and Stoughton, 1981
Pt.3: Pupil's book. — 150p : ill,maps ; 22cm
ISBN 0-340-24363-5 (pbk) : Unpriced : CIP rev. B81-04223

Bennett, A. J.. ¡Buenos días! : an illustrated Spanish course / A.J. Bennett. — London : Hodder and Stoughton
Pt.3: Teacher's book. — 1981. — 47p ; 22cm
ISBN 0-340-24361-9 (unbound) : £1.65 : CIP rev. B81-28149

Carthew, Clive. Spanish in your own words / Clive Carthew, David Webb. — Harlow : Longman, 1982. — xii,100p ; 20cm
Spanish text, English introduction. — Text on inside cover
ISBN 0-582-33082-3 (pbk) : Unpriced B82-37163

Claro!. — [London] : ILEA Learning Materials Service in association with Mary Glasgow Publications
Text in English and Spanish
1. — c1980. — 12p : ill(some col.) ; 30cm
ISBN 0-86158-700-6 (unbound) : Unpriced B82-13449

Milne, Carmen B. G.. Topical Spanish / Carmen B.G. Milne. — Harlow : Longman, 1981. — 94p : ill,1map,facsims,1plan,1port ; 21cm
Spanish text with English introduction and translation passages
ISBN 0-582-35316-5 (pbk) : £2.10 B82-08908

468′.0024658 — Spanish language — *Questions & answers — For business studies*

Balfour, Sebastian. Spanish / Sebastian Balfour. — Harlow : Longman, 1982. — 124p : ill,facsims,forms ; 24cm. — (Business case studies)
Spanish text, English introduction
ISBN 0-582-35164-2 (pbk) : £3.50 B82-09106

468′.02 — Spanish language. Translation from English language — *Manuals*

Translation strategies = Estrategias para traducción / by E. Brinton ... [et al.]. — London : Macmillan, 1981. — 193p ; 22cm
ISBN 0-333-32893-0 (pbk) : Unpriced
Primary classification 428′.02 B82-16153

468.2′4 — Spanish language — *For non-Spanish speaking students*

New Spanish self taught : the guick, practical way to reading, writing, speaking, understanding / revised by Juan López-Morillas. — New York ; Cambridge : Barnes & Noble, 1982, c1959. — xix,340p ; 21cm
Originally published: New York : Funk & Wagnalls, 1959. — Text on inside covers. — Includes index
ISBN 0-06-463617-8 (pbk) : £2.95 B82-22928

Tchira, S. E.. Your invisible teacher of Spanish / by S.E. Tchira. — Cheadle ([Brook Lodge, Schools Hill, Cheadle, Cheshire]) : S.E.T. Books, 1981. — 46p : ill ; 22cm
£1.35 (pbk) B82-07745

468.2′421 — Spanish language. Comprehension — *Questions & answers*

Kattán-Ibarra, Juan. Spain after Franco : language in context / Juan Kattán-Ibarra, Tim Connell. — Cheltenham : Thornes, 1980. — 179p : ill,maps,ports ; 25cm
English and Spanish text
ISBN 0-85950-486-7 (pbk) : £4.95 : CIP rev.
B80-07336

468.2′421 — Spanish language. Comprehension — *Questions & answers — For schools*

MacDonald, Ian, *1947-*. Everyday Spanish for comprehension / Ian MacDonald, Michael Tarver. — London : Edward Arnold, 1980. — 47p : ill,1chart,forms ; 22cm
Spanish text, English questions and instructions
ISBN 0-7131-0475-9 (pbk) : £1.60 B82-18687

Zollo, M. A.. ¿Vale? ¡Si, vale! : reading and listening comprehension in Spanish / M.A. Zollo. — London : Edward Arnold, 1981. — 115p ; 22cm
Spanish text, English preface and exercises
ISBN 0-7131-0606-9 (pbk) : £2.25 : CIP rev.
B81-30604

468.2′421 — Spanish language. Grammar

Resnick, Seymour. En breve : a concise review of Spanish grammar / Seymour Resnick and William Giuliano with the collaboration of Phyllis M. Golding. — New York ; London : Holt, Rinehart and Winston, c1982. — viii,290p : ill ; 24cm
Includes index
ISBN 0-03-059356-5 (pbk) : Unpriced
B82-27631

468.2′421 — Spanish language. Grammar — *Questions & answers*

Wilden-Hart, M.. Curso practico de Espanol para mayores. — Cheltenham : Stanley Thornes, Feb.1983. — [256]p
ISBN 0-85950-385-2 (pbk) : £3.65 : CIP entry
B82-39600

468.3′421 — Spoken Spanish language

Clarke, R.. Mastering Spanish / R. Clarke ; editorial consultant Betty Parr. — London : Macmillan, 1982. — xiv,322p : ill ; 23cm. — (Macmillan master series)
ISBN 0-333-32342-4 (cased) : Unpriced
ISBN 0-333-32343-2 (pbk) : Unpriced
B82-39712

468.3′421 — Spoken Spanish language. Idioms — *Lists*

Pierson, Raymond H.. Guide to Spanish idioms : a practical guide to 2500 Spanish idioms = Guía de modismos españoles / Raymond H. Pierson. — [2nd ed.]. — Cheltenham : Thornes, 1981, c1978. — iv,174p ; 23cm
Parallel Spanish and English text. — Originally published: Skokie : National Textbook, 1978
ISBN 0-85950-334-8 (pbk) : £1.75 : CIP rev.
B81-23803

468.3′421 — Spoken Spanish language — *Phrase books*

Marles, R. J.. Richard's holiday Spanish. — Torquay : Rotographic, 1982. — 72p : ill ; 15cm. — (A Richard's pocket book)
Written by R.J. Marles. — Includes index
ISBN 0-901170-10-0 (pbk) : £1.00 B82-35767

468.6′421 — Spanish language. Reading books

Spotlight on Spanish : life and language in Spain today / editors Kenneth Hall, Derek Utley. — London : Pan in association with Heinemann Educational, 1981. — 127p : ill,maps,facsims ; 20cm. — (Pan language readers)
Spanish text, English introduction
ISBN 0-330-26470-2 (pbk) : £1.75 B82-01588

468.6′421 — Spanish language. Reading books — *For schools*

Topping, Anne. ¡ Estupendo!. — London : Edward Arnold, Apr.1982. — [64]p
ISBN 0-7131-0658-1 (pbk) : £1.50 : CIP entry
B82-04706

468.6′421 — Spanish language. Reading books. Special subjects: Spanish America, *to 1980*

Latin American history : selected texts from the beginning to modern times / edited by Salvador Ortiz-Carboneres ; with introductions by John King and Anthony McFarlane ; preface by Alistair Hennessy. — Leamington Spa : Berg, 1981. — 100p ; 22cm
ISBN 0-907582-02-8 (pbk) : £2.95 : CIP rev.
B81-24624

469 — PORTUGUESE LANGUAGE

469.83′421 — Spoken Portuguese language — *Phrase books*

Newman, Penny. Get by in Portuguese : a quick beginner's course for holidaymakers and business people / course writer: Penny Newman ; language consultant: Manuela Cook ; producer: Christopher Stone. — London : British Broadcasting Corporation, 1982. — 80p : ill,facsims,2maps ; 18cm
Text in English and Portuguese
ISBN 0-563-16508-1 (pbk) : £2.25 B82-28884

473 — LATIN LANGUAGE. DICTIONARIES

473′.21 — Latin language — *Latin & English dictionaries*

Oxford Latin dictionary. — Oxford : Clarendon
Fasc.7: Qualiterqualiter — Sopitus / edited by P.G.W. Glare. — 1980. — p1537-1792 ; 31cm
ISBN 0-19-864220-2 (pbk) : £17.50 : CIP rev.
B80-10053

Oxford Latin dictionary. — Oxford : Clarendon Press
Fasc.8: Sopor-Zythum / edited by P.G.W. Glare. — 1982. — p1793-2126 ; 31cm
ISBN 0-19-864221-0 (pbk) : £20.00 : CIP rev.
B81-36303

Woodhouse, S. C.. The Englishman's pocket Latin-English and English-Latin dictionary / by S.C. Woodhouse. — London : Routledge & Kegan Paul, 1913 (1982 [printing]). — 491p ; 16cm. — (Routledge pocket dictionaries)
Cover title: Latin dictionary
ISBN 0-7100-2325-1 (cased) : Unpriced
ISBN 0-7100-9267-9 (pbk) : £3.95 B82-26982

473′.21 — Latin language — *Latin-English dictionaries*

Oxford Latin dictionary. — Oxford : Clarendon, Nov.1982. — [2150]p
ISBN 0-19-864224-5 : £120.00 : CIP entry
B82-26870

475 — LATIN LANGUAGE. GRAMMAR

475 — Great Britain. Latin language. Grammar. Teaching, *ca 600-ca 800*

Law, Vivien. The insular Latin grammarians. — Woodbridge : Boydell Press, Dec.1981. — [128]p. — (Studies in Celtic history ; 3)
ISBN 0-85115-147-7 : £15.00 : CIP entry
B81-33878

477 — LATIN LANGUAGE. OLD, POSTCLASSICAL, VULGAR LATIN

477 — Latin language. British usage, *ca 600-ca 1200*

Latin and the vernacular languages in early medieval Britain / edited by Nicholas Brooks. — [Leicester] : Leicester University Press, 1982. — xi,170p : facsims ; 25cm. — (Studies in the early history of Britain)
Includes index
ISBN 0-7185-1209-x : £25.00 : CIP rev.
B82-09629

478 — LATIN LANGUAGE USAGE

478 — Latin language — *For schools*

Cambridge Latin course. — Cambridge : Cambridge University Press
Unit 1. — 2nd ed. — 1982. — 12v. : ill,maps ; 21 cm
Set of 12 booklets in plastic bag. — Latin and English text. — Previous ed.: 1970
ISBN 0-521-28871-1 (pbk) : £4.20 B82-35015

Cambridge Latin course. — 2nd ed. — Cambridge : Cambridge University Press for the Schools Council, 1982
Previous ed.: 1970
Unit 1
Language information. — 32p ; 21cm
Cover title
ISBN 0-521-28741-3 (pbk) : Unpriced
B82-35016

Cambridge Latin course. — 2nd ed. — Cambridge : Cambridge University Press for the Schools Council, 1982
Previous ed.: 1970
Unit 1
Teacher's handbook. — v,98p ; 21cm
Bibliography: p95-98
ISBN 0-521-28742-1 (pbk) : Unpriced
B82-35017

Cambridge Latin course. — Cambridge : Cambridge University Press
Supplementary handbook. — 1980. — vi,90p ; 22cm
Bibliography: p84-89. — List of films: p89-90
ISBN 0-521-28068-0 (pbk) : £2.25 B82-37893

478 — Latin language — *Questions & answers — For schools*

Ecce Romani : a Latin reading course / prepared by the Scottish Classics Group. — Edinburgh : Oliver & Boyd
1: Meeting the family. — 2nd ed. — 1982. — 80p : ill,2maps,plans ; 22cm + Teacher's notes (43p : 22cm)
Text in Latin and English. — Previous ed.: 1971. — Text on inside cover
ISBN 0-05-003465-0 (pbk) : £0.95
ISBN 0-05-003550-9 (Teacher's notes) : £1.50
B82-23058

Ecce Romani : a Latin reading course / prepared by the Scottish Classics Group. — Edinburgh : Oliver & Boyd
2: Rome at last. — 2nd ed. — 1982. — 89p : ill,maps ; 22cm + Teacher's notes(35p : 22cm)
Text in Latin and English. — Previous ed.: 1971. — Text on inside cover
ISBN 0-05-003466-9 (pbk) : £1.05
ISBN 0-05-003551-7 (Teacher's notes) : £1.50
B82-23059

Hillard, A. E.. Elementary Latin exercises : an introduction to North and Hillard's Latin prose composition / A.E. Hillard and C.G. Botting. — London : Duckworth, 1982. — xii,210p ; 20cm
Facsim. of ed. published: London : Rivingtons, 1910
ISBN 0-7156-1525-4 (pbk) : £4.95 : CIP rev.
B82-10873

478′.02 — Latin language. Unseens — *Collections — For schools*

Advanced Latin unseens. — [Rev. ed.] / drawn from the selection of Cook and Marchant and edited by Anthony Bowen. — Bristol : Bristol Classical Press, 1980. — iv,62p ; 21cm
Latin texts with English preliminaries. — Selections from: Passages for unseen translation selected from Latin and Greek literature / by Cook and Marchant. London : Methuen, 1898
ISBN 0-906515-54-8 (pbk) : Unpriced
B82-05340

Dale, C. M.. Latin passages for translation and comprehension / C.M. Dale. — Cambridge : Cambridge University Press, 1981. — 47p : 1map ; 22cm. — (Cambridge Latin texts)
English and Latin text
ISBN 0-521-28355-8 (pbk) : £1.05 B82-32124

478.1 — Latin language, *to 500.* **Vocabulary. Special subjects: Sex**

Adams, J. N.. The Latin sexual vocabulary. — London : Duckworth, Oct.1982. — [300]p
ISBN 0-7156-1648-x : £28.00 : CIP entry
B82-23016

478.3′421 — Latin language — *Phrase books — For schools*

Meissner, C.. Latin phrase book / C. Meissner ; translated from the sixth German edition with the addition of supplementary phrases and references by H.W. Auden. — London : Duckworth, 1981. — xiii,338p ; 20cm
Translated from the German. — Originally published: London : Macmillan, 1894. — Includes index
ISBN 0-7156-1469-x (cased) : Unpriced : CIP rev. B80-00684

481 — GREEK LANGUAGE. WRITTEN AND SPOKEN CODES

481′.5 — Greek language. Phonemes: Shwa

Lindeman, Fredrik Otto. The triple representation of Schwa in Greek and some related problems of Indo-European phonology / Fredrik Otto Lindeman. — Oslo : Universitetsforlaget, c1982 ; London : Global Book Resources [distributor]. — 75p ; 23cm. — (Instituttet for Sammenlignende kulturforskning. Serie B, ISSN 0332-6217 ; 65)
Includes index
ISBN 82-00-09533-9 : Unpriced B82-40777

481′.7 — Inscriptions in Linear B script

Hooker, J. T.. Linear B : an introduction / J.T. Hooker. — Bristol : Bristol Classical Press, 1980. — xii,204p : ill,1map ; 26cm
ISBN 0-906515-69-6 (cased) : Unpriced
ISBN 0-906515-62-0 (pbk) : Unpriced B82-05333

487 — GREEK LANGUAGE. POSTCLASSICAL GREEK

487′.4 — Biblical Greek language. Grammar

Whittaker, Molly. New testament Greek grammar / Molly Whittaker. — London : SCM
Key to exercises. — 1969 (1980 [printing]). — 42p ; 20cm
ISBN 0-334-00830-1 (pbk) : £1.50 B82-14325

Whittaker, Molly. New Testament Greek grammer : an introduction : Molly Whittaker. — Rev. ed. — London : SCM, 1980. — 192p ; 20cm
Previous ed.: 1969
ISBN 0-334-01128-0 (pbk) : £3.95 B82-10523

488 — GREEK LANGUAGE. CLASSICAL GREEK USAGE

488′.02 — English language. Translation from Greek language — *Questions & answers — For schools*

Hillard, A. E.. [Elementary Greek translation book]. Elementary Greek translation / A.E. Hillard and C.G. Botting. — London : Duckworth, 1982. — vii,209p ; 20cm
Originally published: London : Rivington, 1923
ISBN 0-7156-1654-4 (pbk) : £4.95 B82-38307

488′.02 — Greek language. Unseens — *Collections — For schools*

Advanced Greek unseens. — [Rev. ed.] / drawn from the selection of Cook and Marchant and edited by Anthony Bowen. — Bristol : Bristol Classical Press, 1980. — iv,92p ; 21cm
Greek texts with English introduction. — Selections from: Passages for unseen translation selected from Latin and Greek literature / by Cook and Marchant. London : Methuen, 1898
ISBN 0-906515-47-5 (pbk) : Unpriced B82-05341

488.6′421 — Greek language. Reading books — *For schools*

The **Intellectual** revolution : selections from Euripides, Thucydides and Plato : text and running vocabulary. — Cambridge : Cambridge University Press, 1980. — viii,159p : ill,maps ; 21cm. — (The Joint Association of Classical Teachers′ Greek course)
Classical Greek text, introduction and notes in English
ISBN 0-521-22461-6 (pbk) : £5.50 B82-37896

489.3 — MODERN GREEK LANGUAGE

489′.3152 — Modern Greek language. Pronunciation

Tofallis, Kypros. The Greek language and the one accent system / by Kypros Tofallis. — London : Greek Institute, c1982. — 13p ; 22cm
ISBN 0-905313-09-7 (pbk) : £0.90 B82-37766

489′.3321 — Modern Greek language — *Modern Greek & English dictionaries*

Hionides, Harry T.. [Collins contemporary Greek dictionary]. Collins pocket Greek dictionary : Greek-English, English-Greek / Harry T. Hionides. — London : Collins, 1982. — xiii,430p ; 19cm
Originally published: 1977
ISBN 0-00-433205-9 (pbk) : £3.50 B82-17729

Pring, J. T.. The Oxford dictionary of modern Greek : English-Greek / compiled by J.T. Pring. — Oxford : Clarendon, 1982. — x,370p ; 19cm
ISBN 0-19-864136-2 : £6.50 : CIP rev. B81-23876

Pring, J. T.. The Oxford dictionary of modern Greek : Greek-English and English-Greek / compiled by J.T. Pring. — Oxford : Clarendon, 1982. — 222,370p ; 19cm
Also published in 2 vols
ISBN 0-19-864137-0 (cased) : £9.50 : CIP rev.
ISBN 0-19-864148-6 (pbk) : £3.25 B81-23877

490 — LANGUAGES(OTHER THAN GERMANIC, ROMANCE AND GREEK)

490′.954 — South Asian languages

Zograph, G. A.. Languages of South Asia : a guide / G.A. Zograph ; translated by G.L. Campbell. — London : Routledge & Kegan Paul, 1982. — viii,231p : 2maps ; 22cm. — (Languages of Asia and Africa ; v.3)
Translation of: ÍAzyki Indii, Pakistana, Tseilona i Nepala. — Bibliography: p210-229. — Includes index
ISBN 0-7100-0914-3 (pbk) : £10.50 B82-30997

491.1 — INDO-IRANIAN LANGUAGES

491′.1′07042542 — Great Britain. Ethnic minorities. Native languages. Teaching — *Study regions: Leicestershire. Leicester — Study examples: South Asian languages*

Wilding, Jennifer. Ethnic minority languages in the classroom? : a survey of Asian parents in Leicester / Jennifer Wilding. — Leicester (58 Earl Howe St., Leicester) : Leicester Council for Community Relations, 1981. — 83,23p : forms ; 30cm
£1.50 (pbk) B82-07851

491.2/4 — INDIC LANGUAGES

491′.2 — Vedic language — *Polyglot dictionaries*

Suryakanta. A practical Vedic dictionary / Suryakanta. — Delhi ; Oxford : Oxford University Press, 1981. — xvii,750p ; 25cm
English introduction, Hindi and English text
ISBN 0-19-561298-1 : £19.00 B82-31566

491′.428 — Punjabi language — *Questions & answers — For schools*

Nagra, J. S.. O′level Panjabi / by J.S. Nagra. — Coventry (Sidney Stringer School and Community College, Cox St., Coventry CV1 5NL) : J.S. Nagra, 1981. — 100p ; 24cm
English and Panjabi text
£1.50 (pbk) B82-08245

491′.4282421 — Punjabi language. Grammar

Tolstaīā, N. I.. The Panjabi language : a descriptive grammar / N.I. Tolstaya ; translated by G.L. Campbell. — London : Routledge & Kegan Paul, 1981. — vi,78p : 1map ; 22cm. — (Languages of Asia and Africa ; v.2)
Translation of: Īazyk Pandzhabi. — Bibliography: p78
ISBN 0-7100-0939-9 (pbk) : £7.00 B82-03311

491′.4383421 — Spoken Hindi & Urdu languages. Grammar

Russel, Ralph, *1918-*. A new course in Hindustani : for learners in Britain / by Ralph Russell. — London : Extramural Division, School of Oriental and African Studies, University of London
Part 2: An outline of grammar and common usage (mainly for reference). — 1981. — 102p ; 30cm
English and Hindi/Urdu text with Englsh notes
ISBN 0-7286-0085-4 (pbk) : £2.00 : CIP rev. B81-14789

Russel, Ralph, *1918-*. A new course in Hindustani : for learners in Britain / by Ralph Russell. — London : Extramural Division, School of Oriental and African Studies, University of London
Part 3: Rapid readings. — 1981. — 180p ; 30cm
English and Hindi/Urdu text with Englsh notes
ISBN 0-7286-0086-2 (pbk) : £3.00 : CIP rev. B81-14790

491′.4383′421 — Spoken Hindi & Urdu languages. Grammar

Russell, Ralph. A new course in Hindustani for learners in Britain. — London : University of London, School of Oriental and African Studies
Pt.4: The Urdu script. — Feb.1982. — [132]p
ISBN 0-7286-0093-5 (pbk) : £2.50 : CIP entry B81-35841

491′.4383421 — Spoken Hindi language — *Phrase books*

Oldenburg, Veena Talwar. Say it in Hindi / by Veena Talwar Oldenburg. — New York : Dover Publications ; London : Constable, 1981. — xviii,238p ; 14cm. — (Dover say it series)
Text in English and Hindi. — Includes index
ISBN 0-486-23959-4 (pbk) : £2.60 B82-08959

491.5 — IRANIAN LANGUAGES

491′.59 — Kurdish language. Grammar

Akrawy, F. R.. Standard Kurdish grammar / by F.R. Akrawy. — [Aylsham] ([Balind House, 22 John of Gaunt Close, Aylsham, Norwich, NR11 6DG]) : F.R. Akrawy, 1982. — iii,200p ; 22cm
Text in English and Kurdish. — Includes index
£6.00 (pbk) B82-36382

491.6 — CELTIC LANGUAGES

491.6′2′0924 — Ireland. Irish language. Promotion. De Búrca, Uilleog — *Biographies — Irish texts*

Ó Maolmhuaidh, Proinsias. Uilleog de Búrca : athair na hathbheochana / Proinsias Ó Maolmhuaidh. — Baile Átha Cliath (29 Sráid Uí Chonaill Íocht Baile Átha Cliath 1) : Foilseacháin Náisiúnta, c1981. — 207p,[16]p of plates : ill,facsims,ports ; 20cm
Text on lining papers. — Bibliography: p199-207
£5.00 B82-20794

491.6′211 — Irish language. Alphabets — *For children*

Rosie. Piasún ar gheág / Rosie agus Paybo. — [Baile Átha Cliath] : Oifig an tSoláthair, c1981. — [48]p : col.ill ; 22cm
Unpriced B82-19588

491.6′2152 — Irish language. Pronunciation — *Irish texts*

Ó Baoill, Dónall P.. Cleachtaí foghraíochta / Dónall Ó Baoill. — Baile Átha Cliath (31 Plas Mhic Liam, Baile Atha Cliath 2) : Institiúid Teangeolaíochta, 1975 (1978 [printing]). — 72p : ill ; 25cm. — (Foilseachán / Institiúid Teangeolaíochta Éireann ; uimh.a2(G))
Unpriced (pbk) B82-40814

491.6′27 — Old Irish language. Etymology — *Old Irish & French dictionaries*

Vendryes, J.. Lexique étymologique de l′irlandais ancien / de J. Vendryes. — [Dublin] : Dublin Institute for Advanced Studies
Bibliography: p.vii-xiv
Lettre B / par les soins de E. Bachellery et P.-Y. Lambert. — c1980. — xiv,8-119p ; 25cm
ISBN 2-222-02800-0 (pbk) : £10.00 B82-08921

491.6'28 — Ireland *(Republic)*. School leavers. Written Irish language. Errors — *Irish texts*

Earráidí scríofa gaeilge. — Baile Átha Cliath (31 Plás Mhic Liam, Baile Átha Cliath 2) : Institiuid Teangeolaíochta Eireann
Cuid 3: Reamhfhocail agus conhréir : earráidí a tharla in aistí Gaeilge na hArdteikstiméireachta, 1975 / Dónall Ó Baoill. — 1981. — viii,197-319p : ill ; 30cm
£4.00 (pbk) B82-20475

491.6'28 — Irish language — *Questions & answers — For Irish students*

Nic Aogán, Úna. Muintir uí chonaill : cúrsa closamhairc don chéad bhliain / Úna Nic Aogán. — Baile Átha Cliath : Folens, c1979. — 88p : ill(some col.),1map ; 26cm
ISBN 0-86121-062-x (pbk) : Unpriced
B82-28075

Nic Aogán, Úna. Muintir uí chonaill / Úna Nic Aogán. — Bhaile Átha Cliath : Folens Leabhar saothair. — c1979. — 53p : ill ; 26cm
ISBN 0-86121-096-4 (pbk) : Unpriced
B82-28074

491.6'281 — Irish language. Spelling — *Dictionaries*

Ó hOgáin, Nollaig C.. Buntés litrithe / Nollaig C. O. hOgáin. — Baile Átha Cliath [Dublin] : Gill and Macmillan, 1982. — 33p ; 16cm
Cover title
ISBN 0-7171-1251-9 : Unpriced B82-31155

491.6'281 — Irish language. Words — *For children — Illustrations*

[The First 1000 words. *Irish*]. Buntús foclóra : leagan Gaeilge den sraithleabhar / buntéacs Heather Amery ; pictiúir Stephen Cartwright ; eagarthóir/aistritheoir Fiachra Ó Dubhthaigh. — [Dublin] : Gill and Macmillan, c1981. — 63p : chiefly col.ill ; 32cm
Translation of: The first 1000 words. — Text on lining papers
ISBN 0-7171-1194-6 : £4.30 B82-08381

491.6'282 — Irish language. Grammar — *Irish texts*

Ó Culacháin, Ciarán. Scór : forleathnú ar na cúrsaí closamhairc Bunsraith Gaeilge agus Téanam ort don Chéad Bhliain san Isarbhunscoil / Ciarán Ó Culacháin. — Baile Átha Cliath : An Comhlacht Oideachais, c1982. — 116p : ill ; 20cm
Unpriced (pbk) B82-28696

491.6'283421 — Spoken Irish language

Ó Baoill, Dónall P.. Anois is arís / le Dónall Ó Baoill agus Éamonn Ó Tuathail. — [Dublin] ([7 Merrion Sq., Dublin 2]) : RTÉ i gcomhar le Bord na Gaeilge, c1981. — 162p : ill(some col.) ; 21cm
Irish text, English introduction and notes
Unpriced (pbk) B82-25457

491.6'283'421 — Spoken Irish language — *phrase books*

Dorris, Paul. The little Irish phrasebook. — Belfast : Appletree Press, July 1982. — [72]p
ISBN 0-86281-010-8 (pbk) : £1.50 : CIP entry
B82-21761

491.6'286 — Irish language. Reading books — *For Irish speaking students*

Ní Mhaoláin, Páraicín. Lionta A / Páraicín Ní Mhaoláin, Treasa Ní Ailpín. — Baile Átha Cliath [i.e. Dublin] (Bóthar Bhaile an Aird, Baile Uailcín, Baile Átha Cliath 12) : Comhlacht Oideachais na hEireann Teoranta, c1981. — 24p : col.ill ; 21cm
Cover title. — Text on inside covers
Unpriced (pbk) B82-02100

Ní Mhaoláin, Páraicín. Lionta B / Páraicín Ní Mhaoláin, Treasa Ní Ailpín. — Baile Átha Chiath [i.e. Dublin] (Bóthar Bhaile an Aird, Baile Uailcín, Baile Átha Cliath 12) : Comhlacht Oideachais na hEireann Teoranta, c1981. — 32p : col.ill ; 21cm
Cover title. — Text on inside covers
Unpriced (pbk) B82-02099

Ní Mhaoláin, Páraicín. Lionta D / Páraicín Ní Mhaoláin, Treasa Ní Ailpín. — Baile Átha Cliath (Bóthar Bhaile an Aird, Baile, Uailcín,. Baile Átha Cliath 12) : Comhlacht Oideachais na hEireann Teoranta, c1982. — 32p : ill ; 21cm
Cover title. — Text on inside covers
Unpriced (pbk) B82-27613

491.6'38 — Scottish Gaelic language — *Questions & answers*

Gaidhlig bheo : a course leading to the Scottish Certificate of Education 'O' grade (learners) examination. — Cambridge : National Extension College in association with An Comunn Gaidhealach, 1976-1977 (1978-1980 [printing]). — 4v. : ill ; 30cm. — (National Extension College correspondence texts ; course no.L24)
English and Gaelic text
ISBN 0-902404-46-6 (pbk) : Unpriced
ISBN 0-902404-54-7 (v.1)
ISBN 0-902404-55-5 (v.2)
ISBN 0-902404-56-3 (v.3)
ISBN 0-86082-180-3 (v.4) B82-40131

491.6'382421 — Gaelic language. Grammar

Ainslie, Alan. Elementary Gaelic : twelve lessons for beginners / by Alan Ainslie. — Friockheim : A.D. Ainslie, c1981. — [30]p ; 32cm
Unpriced (unbound) B82-24214

Burns, G. N.. A welcome to Gaelic = Fàilte d'on Ghàidhlig / by G.N. Burns. — [Scotland] : Strathspey Highland Malt Whisky, 1977. — 48p : ill,music ; 21cm
Parallel English and Gaelic text. — Bibliography: p48
Unpriced (pbk) B82-24196

491.6'6'05 — Welsh language — *Serials*

Cardiff working papers in Welsh linguistics = Papurau gwaith ieithyddol Cymraeg Caerdydd. — No.1 (1981)-. — [Cardiff] ([St. Fagans, Cardiff]) : National Museum of Wales (Welsh Folk Museum), 1981-. — v. : ill,maps ; 30cm
Annual. — Text in English, introduction also in Welsh. — Joint production of: Welsh Language Research Unit, University College Cardiff, and the Department of Dialects, Welsh Folk Museum
ISSN 0263-0362 = Papurau gwaith ieithyddol Cymraeg Caerdydd : Unpriced B82-14780

491.6'682 — Welsh language. Grammar — *For Welsh speaking students*

Evans, H. Meurig. Sylfeini'r Gymraeg : gramadeg, priod-ddulliau, ymarferion, traethodau, cyfansoddi / H. Meurig Evans. — Llandysul : Gomer, 1981. — 90p ; 21cm
ISBN 0-85088-765-8 (pbk) : £1.95 B82-10275

491.6'682421 — Welsh language. Grammar

Jones, Geraint. An approach to Welsh / by Geraint Jones. — Cambridge : National Extension College
Lessons 1-10. — 1969 (1976 [printing]). — i,154p : ill ; 30cm. — (National Extension College correspondence texts ; course no.L6)
Unpriced (pbk) B82-38177

491.6'682421 — Welsh language. Idioms: Colloquialisms

Davies, Cennard. Lluniau llafar = Idioms for Welsh learners : anifeiliaid, lliwiau, rhannau'r corff / Cennard Davies. — Llandysul : Gwasg Gomer, 1980. — 151p ; 21cm
Includes definitions in English
ISBN 0-85088-782-8 (pbk) : £1.95 B82-15294

491.6'686 — Welsh language. Reading books — *For Welsh speaking persons — For children*

Gwrando a darllen 1 / [lluniau gan Wini Harbourne]. — Llandysul : Gwasg Gomer, 1982. — 62p : col.ill ; 24cm
ISBN 0-85088-966-9 (pbk) : £1.75 B82-27255

Gwrando a darllen 2 / [lluniau gan Wini Harbourne]. — Llandysul : Gwasg Gomer, 1982. — 52p : col.ill ; 24cm
ISBN 0-85088-976-6 (pbk) : £1.75 B82-27256

Seymour, Peter, *19---*. Llyfr sbonc bwyd / [testun gwreiddiol gan Peter Seymour ; lluniau gan Chuck Murphy ; cynllunwaith y papur gan Tor Lokvig ; addasiad Cymraeg gan Dilwen M. Evans. — Llandysul : Gwasg Gomer, 1981, c1980. — [12]p : col.ill ; 21cm
Cover title
ISBN 0-85088-695-3 : Unpriced B82-27254

Seymour, Peter, *19---*. Llyfr sbonc diogelwch / [testun gwreiddiol gan Peter Seymour ; lluniau gan Chuck Murphy ; cynllunwaith y papur gan Tor Lokvig ; addasiad Cymraeg gan Dilwen M. Evans. — Llandysul : Gwasg Gomer, 1981, c1980. — [12]p : col.ill ; 21cm
Cover title
ISBN 0-85088-715-1 : Unpriced B82-27253

491.6'686 — Welsh language. Reading books. Special subjects: Animals — *For Welsh speaking persons — For children*

Evans, Dilwen M.. Llyfr sbonc anifeiliaid / [testun gwreiddiol gan Larry Shapiro ; lluniau gan Chuck Murphy ; cynllunwaith y papur gan Tor Lokvig ; addasiad Cymraeg gan Dilwen M. Evans]. — Llandysul : Gwasg Gomer, 1981, c1980. — [12]p : col.ill ; 21cm
Cover title
ISBN 0-85088-725-9 : Unpriced B82-19143

491.6'686 — Welsh language. Reading books. Special subjects: Days & months — *For Welsh speaking persons — For children*

Evans, Dilwen M.. Llyfr sbonc y dyddiau / [testun gwreiddiol gan Larry Shapiro a Chuck Murphy ; lluniau gan Chuck Murphy ; cynllunwaith y papur gan Tor Lokvig ; addasiad Cymraeg gan Dilwen M. Evans]. — Llandysul : Gwasg Gomer, 1981, c1980. — [12]p : col.ill ; 21cm
Cover title
ISBN 0-85088-705-4 : Unpriced B82-19140

491.6'686 — Welsh language. Reading books. Special subjects: Sounds — *For Welsh speaking persons — For children*

Evans, Dilwen M.. Llyfr sbonc Sŵn / [testun gwreiddiol gan Larry Shapiro ; lluniau gan Chuck Murphy ; cynllunwaith y papur gan Tor Lokvig ; addasiad Cymraeg gan Dilwen M. Evans]. — Llandysul : Gwasg Gomer, 1981, c1980. — [12]p : col.ill ; 21cm
Cover title
ISBN 0-85088-735-6 : Unpriced B82-19142

491.6'686 — Welsh language. Reading books. Special subjects: Time — *For Welsh speaking persons — For children*

Evans, Dilwen M.. Llyfr sbonc amser / [testun gwreiddiol gan Larry Shapiro a Chuck Murphy ; lluniau gan Chuck Murphy ; cynllunwaith y papur gan Tor Lokvig ; addasiad Cymraeg gan Dilwen M. Evans]. — Llandysul : Gwasg Gomer, 1981, c1980. — [12]p : col.ill ; 21cm
Cover title
ISBN 0-85088-685-6 : Unpriced B82-19141

491.6'686421 — Welsh language. Reading books — *For schools*

[Airport. *Welsh*]. Maes awyr / lluniau gan Juliet Stanwell Smith. — Caerdydd : Gwasg y Dref Wen, c1981. — 28p : col.ill. — (Cychwyn. Ffeithiau. Gwyrdd ; 1)
Translation of: Airport. — Text on lining papers
£1.25 B82-33080

[Birds. *Welsh*]. Adar / lluniau gan Diana Maclean ; ymgynghorwr Berian Williams. — Caerdydd : Gwasg y Dref Wen, c1981. — 28p : col.ill ; 21cm. — (Cychwyn. Ffeithiau. Coch ; 2)
Translation of: Birds. — Text on lining papers
£1.25 B82-33078

[Cars. *Welsh*]. Ceir / lluniau gan David Mostyn. — Caerdydd : Gwasg y Dref Wen, c1981. — 28p : col.ill,1col.port ; 21cm. — (Cychwyn. Ffeithiau. Glas ; 2)
Translation of: Cars. — Text on lining papers
£1.25 B82-33079

491.6'686421 — Welsh language. Reading books — *For schools* *continuation*

Cymraeg fel Ail Iaith yn yr Ysgol Uwchradd *(Project)*. Llygaid i weld : project addysg ddwyieithog (Ysgolion uwchradd) / [Cymraeg fel Ail Iaith yn yr Ysgol Uwchradd]. — London : Schools Council, c1981. — 79p : ill,1map ; 21cm
ISBN 0-901681-58-x (pbk) : Unpriced B82-20722

Fairclough, Chris. [Let's go to Italy. Welsh]. Yr Eidal / testun a lluniau gan Chris Fairclough ; addasiad Cymraeg gan Roger Boore. — Caerdydd : Gwasg y Dref Wen, c1981. — 32p : col.ill,1col.map ; 22cm. — (Gwledydd)
Translation of: Let's go to Italy
£1.95 B82-33076

Fairclough, Chris. [Let's go to West Germany. Welsh]. Gorllewin yr Almaen / testun a lluniau gan Chris Fairclough ; addasiad Cymraeg gan Roger Boore. — Caerdydd : Gwasg y Dref Wen, c1981. — 32p : col.ill,2col.maps ; 22cm. — (Gwledydd)
Translation of: Let's go to West Germany
£1.95 B82-33077

[Going to the zoo. *Welsh*]. Mynd i'r sw / lluniau gan Suzanna Rust ; ymgynghorwr Berian Williams. — Caerdydd : Gwasg y Dref Wen, c1981. — 28p : col.ill ; 21cm. — (Cychwyn. Ffeithiau. Coch ; 1)
Translation of: Going to the zoo. — Text on lining papers
£1.25 B82-33081

[Space travel. *Welsh*]. Teithio'r gofod / lluniau gan John Cameron. — Caerdydd : Gwasg y Dref Wen, c1981. — 28p : col.ill,col.ports ; 21cm. — (Cychwyn. Ffeithiau. Glas ; 1)
Translation of: Space travel. — Text on lining papers
£1.25 B82-33082

491.6'686421 — Welsh language. Reading books. Special subjects: Animals — *For schools*

Cymraeg fel Ail Iaith yn yr Ysgol Uwchradd *(Project)*. Creaduriaid diddorol : project addysg ddwyieithog (Ysgolion uwchradd) / [Cymraeg fel Ail Iaith yn yr Ysgol Uwchradd]. — London : Schools Council, c1981. — 94p : ill ; 21cm
ISBN 0-901681-56-3 (pbk) : Unpriced B82-20719

491.6'686421 — Welsh language. Reading books. Special subjects: Heroes & heroines, *to 1980 — For schools*

Cymraeg fel Ail Iaith yn yr Ysgol Uwchradd *(Project)*. Pencampwyr : project addysg ddwyieithog (Ysgolion uwchradd) / [Cymraeg fel Ail Iaith yn yr Ysgol Uwchradd]. — London : Schools Council, c1981. — 104p : ill,1plan,ports ; 21cm
ISBN 0-901681-57-1 (pbk) : Unpriced B82-20720

491.6'686421 — Welsh language. Reading books. Special subjects: North American Indians — *For schools*

Cymraeg fel Ail Iaith yn yr Ysgol Uwchradd *(Project)*. Indiaid Gogledd America : project addysg ddwyieithog (Ysgolion uwchradd) / [Cymraeg fel Ail Iaith yn yr Ysgol Uwchradd]. — London : Schools Council, c1981. — 63p : ill,1map ; 21cm
ISBN 0-901681-55-5 (pbk) : Unpriced B82-20723

491.6'686421 — Welsh language. Reading books. Special subjects: Outer space — *For schools*

Cymraeg fel Ail Iaith yn yr Ysgol Uwchradd *(Project)*. Y Gofod : project addysg ddwyieithog (Ysgolion uwchradd) / [Cymraeg fel Ail Iaith yn yr Ysgol Uwchradd]. — London : Schools Council, c1981. — 72p : ill ; 21cm
ISBN 0-901681-54-7 (pbk) : Unpriced B82-20721

491.6'7'09 — Cornish language, *to 1600*

Fudge, Crysten. The life of Cornish / by Crysten Fudge ; illustrations by Laura Rowe. — Redruth : Truran, [1982]. — 30p : ill,1facsim,1map ; 22cm
ISBN 0-907566-25-1 (pbk) : £1.00 B82-35412

491.6'73 — Cornish language. Dictionaries. Compilation. Projects

Hawke, Andrew. The Cornish dictionary project : first progress report / Andrew Hawke. — Aberystwyth (Department of Welsh, University College of Wales, Old College, Aberystwyth, Dyfed SY23 2AY) : A. Hawke, 1982. — 28p : facsims ; 21cm
Bibliography: p22-24
Private circulation (pbk) B82-35411

491.6'782421 — Cornish language. Grammar

Smith, A. S. D.. Cornish simplified : short lessons for self-tuition pronunciation, grammar, exercises / by A.S.D. Smith (Caradar). — 2nd ed. / edited by E.G.R. Hooper (Talek). — Redruth (Trewolsta, Trewirgie Hill, Redruth, Cornwall) : Dyllansow Truran, c1972 (1981 [printing]). — 88p ; 21cm
Originally published: Exeter : Townsend, 1955
£1.50 (pbk) B82-12787

491.7 — RUSSIAN LANGUAGE

491.72'4 — Russian language. Non-Slavonic words — *Lists*

Faden, B.. Russian words of non slavonic origin : a student's handbook / compiled and edited by B. Faden. — Letchworth : Prideaux, 1981. — 73p ; 20cm. — (Russian texts for students ; no.10)
£0.90 (pbk) B82-07479

491.73'21 — Russian language — *Russian & English dictionaries*

The **Pocket** Oxford English-Russian dictionary / compiled by Nigel Rankin and Della Thompson. — Oxford : Clarendon, 1981. — xii,420p ; 14cm
ISBN 0-19-864127-3 : £4.95 : CIP rev. B80-01164

The **Pocket** Oxford Russian dictionary / Russian-English compiled by Jessie Coulson ; English-Russian compiled by Nigel Rankin and Della Thompson. — Oxford : Clarendon, 1981. — vii,420p ; 14cm
ISBN 0-19-864122-2 (pbk) : £5.95 : CIP rev. B81-23875

Wilson, Elizabeth A. M.. Conversational Russian dictionary for English speakers. — Oxford : Pergamon, Oct.1981. — [1440]p
ISBN 0-08-020554-2 : £25.00 : CIP entry B81-30203

491.782'421 — Russian language. Grammar

Jackson, Eugene. Russian made simple / Eugene Jackson and Elizabeth Bartlett Gordon ; advisory editors Geoffrey Braithwaite, and Albina Tarasova. — Rep. with revisions. — London : Heinemann, 1982. — xiii,304p ; 22cm. — (Made simple books)
English and Russian text. — Originally published: London : W.H. Allen, 1967. — Includes index
ISBN 0-434-98523-6 (cased) : Unpriced
ISBN 0-434-98524-4 (pbk) : £2.95 B82-26806

491.782'421 — Russian language. Grammar — *Questions & answers*

Meades, P. H.. An approach to Russian : a course for beginners / compiled by P.H. Meades ; based on The Penguin Russian course ; tape recording by Albina Tarasova and P.H. Meades. — Cambridge : National Extension College, 1969, (1979 [printing]). — iv,54p : ill,maps ; 30cm. — (National Extension College correspondence texts ; course no.L5)
English and Russian text
ISBN 0-86062-042-5 (pbk) : Unpriced B82-40133

Meades, P. H.. 'O' level Russian course : lessons 1-14 : designed to follow on from the NEC Approach to Russian course / compiled by P.H. Meades ; based on The Penguin Russian course ; tape recording by Albina Tarasova and P.H. Meades. — Cambridge : National Extension College, 1969, c1979 (1979 [printing]). — 111p : ill ; 30cm. — (National Extension College texts ; course no.L11)
English and Russian text
ISBN 0-86082-050-5 (pbk) : Unpriced B82-40132

Meades, P. H.. Russian : a course leading to the University of London GCE 'O' level examination : exam modules / by Peter Meades. — Cambridge : National Extension College, 1974 (1977 [printing]). — 35p : ill ; 21x30cm. — (National Extension College correspondence texts ; course no.L22)
ISBN 0-902404-40-7 (pbk) : Unpriced B82-40134

491.783'421 — Spoken Russian language — *Phrase books*

Russian phrase book. — 2nd ed. — [London] : Hodder and Stoughton, 1982. — vi,180p ; 15cm. — (Teach yourself books)
Previous ed.: 1961
ISBN 0-340-27174-4 (pbk) : £1.95 : CIP rev. B82-01096

Swinglehurst, Edmund. Russian phrase book / Edmund Swinglehurst ; Russian translation by Vera Chalidrae ; phonetic transcription by Nicholas Brown. — London : Hamlyn, 1982. — 222p ; 15cm
Includes index
ISBN 0-600-33216-0 (pbk) : £0.95 B82-34851

491.8 — SLAVIC LANGUAGES

491.8 — Slavonic languages — *Slavonic & English dictionaries*

Faden, B.. Slavonic equivalents of some English words : a list of over 400 English words and their meaning in ten Slavonic languages / compiled and edited by B. Faden. — Letchworth (P.O. Box 1, Letchworth, Herts. SG6 1DN) : Prideaux, 1982. — 79p ; 19cm
Unpriced (pbk) B82-17001

491.8'05 — Slavonic languages. Linguistics — *Serials*

Papers in Slavonic linguistics. — 1-. — [Birmingham] ([Gosta Green, Birmingham B4 7ET]) : Department of Modern Languages, University of Aston in Birmingham, 1982-. — v. ; 21cm
ISSN 0263-5798 = Papers in Slavonic linguistics : Unpriced B82-28113

491.8'283421 — Spoken Serbo-Croatian language — *Phrase books*

Serbo-Croat phrase book. — 2nd ed. — [London] : Hodder and Stoughton, 1982. — 89p ; 15cm. — (Teach yourself books)
Previous ed.: 1961
ISBN 0-340-27175-2 (pbk) : £1.45 : CIP rev. B82-01097

491.8'581 — Serials in Polish. Words. Frequency — *Lists*

Knowles, F. E.. A word-frequency dictionary of Polish journalistic texts / F.E. Knowles. — Birmingham (c/o Department of Modern Languages, University of Aston, Birmingham B4 7ET) : F.E. Knowles, c1981. — 3v. : 1ill ; 30cm
English and Polish text. — Includes index
ISBN 0-903807-91-2 (pbk) : Unpriced
ISBN 0-903807-92-0 (v.2)
ISBN 0-903807-93-9 (v.3) B82-03650

491.8'582441 — Polish language — *For French speaking students*

Cours de polonais : instructions. — London (207 Regent St., W1R 8AU) : Linguaphone Institute, 1981. — 5p ; 21cm
French text
Unpriced (pbk) B82-26360

492 — SEMITIC LANGUAGES

492 — Ancient Syrian inscriptions in Semitic languages

Gibson, John C. L.. Textbook of Syrian Semitic inscriptions / by John C.L. Gibson. — Oxford : Clarendon Press
Vol.3: Phoenician inscriptions : including inscriptions in the mixed dialect of Arslan Tash. — 1982. — xx,187p,viiip of plates : ill,1map ; 24cm
Includes index
ISBN 0-19-813199-2 : £15.00 B82-17803

492.1 — AKKADIAN LANGUAGES

492′.1 — Akkadian language — *Texts*
British Museum. Cuneiform texts from Babylonian tablets in the British Museum. — London : British Museum Publications
Pt.55. — June 1982. — [336]p
ISBN 0-7141-1106-6 : £30.00 : CIP entry
B82-10867

British Museum. Cuneiform texts from Babylonian tablets in the British Museum. — London : British Museum Publications
Pt.56. — June 1982. — [336]p
ISBN 0-7141-1107-4 : £30.00 : CIP entry
B82-10868

492′.1 — Documents in Akkadian, *B.C.605-B.C.581* — *Collections*
Weisberg, David B.. Texts from the time of Nebuchadnezzar / by David B. Weisberg ; including 21 plates by Raymond P. Dougherty. — New Haven ; London : Yale University Press, 1980. — xxvii,90p,cliv p of plates : ill ; 30cm. — (Yale oriental series. Babylonian texts ; v.17)
Bibliography: pxiii-xiv. — Includes index
ISBN 0-300-02338-3 : £18.90 : CIP rev.
B80-21776

492′.1 — Inscriptions in Akkadian — *Collections*
McEwan, Gilbert J. P.. Texts from Hellenistic Babylonia in the Ashmolean Museum / by Gilbert J.P. McEwan ; with notes on the seal impressions by the late Briggs Buchanan. — Oxford : Clarendon, 1982. — ix,115p : ill,facsims ; 32cm. — (Oxford editions of cuneiform texts ; v.9)
Text in English and Assyro-Babylonian. — Includes index
ISBN 0-19-815457-7 (pbk) : Unpriced : CIP rev.
B82-13226

492′.1 — London. Camden *(London Borough)*. **Museums: British Museum. Stock: Inscriptions in Babylonian** — *Catalogues*
British Museum. Catalogue of the Babylonian tablets in the British Museum. — London : British Museum Publications, Sept.1982
Vol.6: Tablets from Sippar 1. — [192]p
ISBN 0-7141-1109-0 : £30.00 : CIP entry
B82-21394

492.2/3 — ARAMAIC LANGUAGES

492′.3 — Syriac language. Grammar
Robinson, Theodore H.. Paradigms and exercises in Syriac grammar / by Theodore H. Robinson. — 4th ed. / revised by L.H. Brockington. — Oxford : Clarendon, 1962 (1981 [printing]). — viii,158p ; 19cm
Previous ed.: 1949. — Includes index
ISBN 0-19-815458-5 (pbk) : £5.50 : CIP rev.
B81-33826

492.4 — HEBREW LANGUAGE

492.4 — Hebrew language — *For Biblical Hebrew speaking persons*
Muraoka, T.. Modern Hebrew for biblical scholars : an annotated chrestomathy with an outline grammar and a glossary / T. Muraoka. — Sheffield : JSOT Press, 1982. — 212p ; 31cm. — (JSOT manuals, ISSN 0262-1754 ; 2)
Hebrew text, English introduction and notes. — Bibliography: p24-25
ISBN 0-905774-36-1 (cased) : Unpriced
ISBN 0-905774-37-x (pbk) : Unpriced
B82-36968

492.4′092′4 — Hebrew language. Promotion. Ben-Yehuda, Eliezer — *Conference proceedings*
Eliezer Ben-Yehuda : symposium in Oxford / edited by Eisig Silberschlag. — Oxford ([45 St. Giles, Oxford OX1 3LW]) : Oxford Centre for Postgraduate Hebrew Studies, 1981. — 68p ; 21cm
Unpriced (pbk)
B82-36430

492.4′5 — Hebrew language. Morphophonemics
Chomsky, Noam. Morphophonemics of modern Hebrew / Noam Chomsky. — New York ; London : Garland, 1979. — 74p ; 24cm. — (Outstanding dissertations in linguistics)
Bibliography: p74
ISBN 0-8240-9688-6 : Unpriced
B82-31070

492.4′7 — Biblical Hebrew language
Yahuda, Joseph. Hebrew is Greek. — Oxford (St Thomas House, Becket St., Oxford OX1 1SJ) : Becket Publications, Nov.1982. — [688]p
ISBN 0-7289-0013-0 : £60.00 : CIP entry
B82-27034

492.4′7 — Biblical Hebrew language. Verbs. Formulation. Theories, *to 1981*
McFall, Leslie. The enigma of the Hebrew verbal system. — Sheffield (24 Tapton Crescent Rd., Sheffield S10 5DA) : Almond Press, Dec.1982. — [272]p. — (Historic texts and interpretations in Biblical scholarship, ISSN 0263-1199 ; 2)
ISBN 0-907459-20-x (cased) : £17.95 : CIP entry
ISBN 0-907459-21-8 (pbk) : £8.95
B82-30723

492.7 — ARABIC LANGUAGE

492′.7 — Arabic language
Francis, T.. The Macmillan Arabic course / T. Francis, M. Frost. — London : Macmillan
English and Arabic text
Bk.1: Write to left : introduction to script and pronunciation. — 1980. — 231p : ill,2maps,facsims ; 23cm
Bibliography: p230-231
ISBN 0-333-23089-2 (pbk) : £7.95
B82-17136

492′.7′321 — Arabic language — *Arabic & English dictionaries*
The **Concise** Oxford English-Arabic dictionary of current usage. — Oxford : Oxford University Press, Jan.1982. — [544]p
ISBN 0-19-864321-7 (pbk) : £4.50 : CIP entry
B81-33997

492′.75 — Arabic language. Verbs. Passive voice
Saad, George Nehmeh. Transitivity, causation and passivization : a semantic-syntactic study of the verb in classical Arabic / George Nehmeh Saad. — London : Kegan Paul International, 1982. — xviii,121p : ill ; 25cm. — (Library of Arabic linguistics ; monograph no.4)
Includes one chapter in Arabic. — Bibliography: p105-108. — Includes index
ISBN 0-7103-0037-9 : £25.00
B82-38922

492′.77 — Spoken Arabic language. Baskinta dialect
Abu-Haidar, Farida. A study of the spoken Arabic of Baskinta / by Farida Abu-Haidar. — Leiden ; London : Published for the Royal Asiatic Society by Brill, 1979. — xv,190p : 1map ; 22cm. — (James G. Forlong Fund ; v.28)
Bibliography: p184-187. — Includes index
ISBN 90-04-05948-2 (pbk) : £13.40
B82-13911

492′.77 — Spoken Arabic language. North-eastern Arabian dialects
Ingham, Bruce. North east Arabian dialects / Bruce Ingham. — London : Kegan Paul International, 1982. — xxiii,208,[17]p : maps ; 25cm. — (Library of Arabic linguistics ; monograph ; no.3)
English text, prefaces, glossary and editor's note in English and Arabic. — Bibliography: p190-195. — Includes index
ISBN 0-7103-0018-2 : £25.00
B82-30616

492′.77 — Spoken Maltese language. Dialects. Words. Pronunciation
A **Survey** of contemporary dialectal Maltese / report on the results of field work undertaken during the years 1964-71 on behalf of the Department of Maltese and Oriental Languages in the Old University of Malta and the Department of Semitic Studies in the University of Leeds under the direction of J. Aquilina and B.S.J. Isserlin with contributions by J. Aquilina ... [et al.]. — Leeds : B.S.J. Isserlin
Vol.1: Gozo. — 1981. — xxvii,222p,[1]leaf of plates : ill,maps ; 30cm
ISBN 0-907860-00-1 (pbk) : Unpriced
B82-09819

492′.7′82 — Arabic language, *to ca 700*. **Grammar** — *Sources of data: Papyri in Arabic*
Hopkins, Simon. Studies in the grammar of early Arabic. — Oxford : Oxford University Press, Nov.1981. — [312]p. — (London oriental series ; v.37)
ISBN 0-19-713603-6 : £28.00 : CIP entry
B81-30338

492′.782421 — Arabic language. Grammar
Ayyad, A. T.. Teach yourself Arabic. — London (68a Delancy St., NW1 7RY) : Ta Ha Publishers, Dec.1981
Part 1: Rules of reading and writing. — [128]p
ISBN 0-907461-13-1 (pbk) : £2.75 : CIP entry
B81-39232

492′.783421 — Spoken Arabic language. Grammar
McLoughlin, Leslie J.. Colloquial Arabic (Levantine) / Leslie J. McLoughlin. — London : Routledge & Kegan Paul, 1982. — vi,145p ; 19cm
Bibliography: p145. — Includes index
ISBN 0-7100-0668-3 (pbk) : £5.25 : CIP rev.
B81-18152

492′.783421 — Spoken Arabic language — *Phrase books*
Peters, James. Very simple Arabic / written and illustrated by James Peters. — Tenterden : Norbury, 1980. — 75p : col.ill,1port ; 21cm
ISBN 0-904404-24-2 (pbk) : Unpriced
B82-20897

Swinglehurst, Edmund. Arabic phrase book / Edmund Swinglehurst ; Arabic translation by Zohra Inoughi ; phonetic transcription by Bruce Ingham. — London : Hamlyn, 1982. — 192p ; 15cm
Includes index
ISBN 0-600-30497-3 (pbk) : £0.95
B82-35260

492′.783421 — Spoken Arabic language. Special subjects: Koran — *For children*
Qur'an made easy. — Karachi : Islamic Seminary Pakistan ; London (284 Kilburn High Rd., NW6 2DP) : Islamic Seminary [distributor], 1980. — 130p ; 22cm
Text in English and Arabic
Unpriced (pbk)
B82-13616

492.9 — SOUTH ARABIAN LANGUAGES

492′.9 — Jibbāli language — *Jibbāli & English dictionaries*
Johnstone, T. M.. Jibbāli lexicon / by T.M. Johnstone. — Oxford : Oxford University Press, 1981. — xxxvii,328p ; 22cm
Bibliography: pxxxiii-xxxiv
ISBN 0-19-713602-8 : £26.00 : CIP rev.
B81-34414

493 — HAMITIC AND CHAD LANGUAGES

493′.1 — Ancient Egyptian hieroglyphs
Watterson, Barbara. Introducing Egyptian hieroglyphs / by Barbara Watterson. — Edinburgh : Scottish Academic Press, 1981. — vii,152p : ill ; 22cm
Includes index
ISBN 0-7073-0267-6 : £8.50
B82-02839

493′.1 — Egyptian language. Reading books
The **Story** of Sinuhe : containing complete collated hieroglyphic text with interlinear transliteration and translation, plus grammatical commentary on each facing page / by Ronald Bullock ; foreword by H.S. Smith. — 2nd ed. rev., 3rd reprint. — London : Probsthain, [1978] ([1982? reprint]). — xi,127leaves ; 30cm
Cover title. — Second edition revised by Carol Andrews. — Leaves printed on both sides
Unpriced (spiral)
B82-39033

493′.1 — Inscribed Ancient Egyptian stones: Rosetta Stone
Andrews, Carol. The Rosetta stone. — New ed. — London : British Museum Publications, Sept.1981. — [32]p
Previous ed.: 1950
ISBN 0-7141-0931-2 (pbk) : £1.25 : CIP entry
B81-28702

493′.1 — Inscriptions in Old Egyptian, *ca B.C.1350-B.C.1090* — *Collections*
Kitchen, K. A.. Ramesside inscriptions : historical and biographical / by K.A. Kitchen. — Oxford : B.H. Blackwell
Egyptian hieroglyphic text, English notes. — Cover title. — Text on inside front cover
[Vol.] 3
[Fasc.] 14. — 1980. — p417-448 ; 29cm
ISBN 0-903563-48-7 (pbk) : Unpriced
B82-20235

493'.1 — Inscriptions in Old Egyptian, *ca B.C.1350-B.C.1090 — Collections*
continuation

Kitchen, K. A.. Ramesside inscriptions : historical and biographical / by K.A. Kitchen. — Oxford : B.H. Blackwell
Egyptian hieroglyphic text, English notes. — Cover title. — Text on inside front cover
[Vol.] 3
[Fasc.] 15. — 1980. — p449-480p ; 29cm
ISBN 0-903563-49-5 (pbk) : Unpriced
B82-20236

493.1 — Late Egyptian language. Grammar

Bakir, A. M.. Notes on late Egyptian grammar. — Warminster : Aris and Phillips, Jan.1983. — [152]p
ISBN 0-85668-214-4 (pbk) : £10.00 : CIP entry
B82-33116

493'.1 — London. Camden *(London Borough)*. **Museums: British Museum. Stock: Ancient Egyptian stelae. Hieroglyphs**

Hieroglyphic texts from Egyptian stelae etc. — London : British Museum Publications, July 1982
Part 10. — [96]p
ISBN 0-7141-0926-6 : £25.30 : CIP entry
B82-14073

493.11 — Ostraca. Collections — *Catalogues*

Page, Anthea. Ancient Egyptian figured ostraca in the Petrie collection. — Warminster : Aris and Phillips, Dec.1982. — [120]p
ISBN 0-85668-216-0 (pbk) : £15.00 : CIP entry
B82-30615

493'.7282421 — Hausa language. Grammar

Smirnova, M.. The Hausa language : a descriptive grammar / M. Smirnova ; translated by G.L. Campbell. — London : Routledge & Kegan Paul, 1982. — vi,112p ; 22cm. — (Languages of Asia and Africa, ISSN 0261-0116 ; v.5)
Translation of: ÎAzyk khausa. — Bibliography: p93-112
ISBN 0-7100-9076-5 (pbk) : £6.95 B82-39665

493'.7286 — Hausa language. Reading books

Fulani, Dan. Sauna, dan sandan ciki. — London : Hodder & Stoughton Educational, Dec.1981. — [128]p
ISBN 0-340-27466-2 (pbk) : £1.50 : CIP entry
B81-31469

494.1/3 — ALTAIC LANGUAGES

494'.3 — Uzbek language — *Uzbek & English dictionaries*

Waterson, Natalie. Uzbek-English dictionary / compiled by Natalie Waterson. — Oxford : Oxford University Press, 1980. — xx,190p ; 24cm
Bibliography: pviii
ISBN 0-19-713597-8 : £18.00 : CIP rev.
B79-36781

494.4/5 — URALIC LANGUAGES

494'.5453'21 — Estonian language — *Estonian & English dictionaries*

Saagpakk, Paul F.. Eesti-Inglise sõnaraamat = Estonian-English dictionary. — London : Yale University Press, Sept.1982. — [1180]p. — (Yale linguistic series)
ISBN 0-300-02849-0 : £105.00 : CIP entry
B82-29401

495 — LANGUAGES OF EAST AND SOUTHEAST ASIA

495 — Sino-Tibetan languages. Etymology — *Dictionaries*

Luce, G. H.. A comparative word-list of Old Burmese, Chinese and Tibetan / G.H. Luce. — London : School of Oriental and African Studies, University of London, 1981. — xi,88p ; 30cm
ISBN 0-7286-0084-6 (pbk) : £3.00 : CIP rev.
B81-10506

495.1 — CHINESE LANGUAGE

495.1'11 — Chinese language. Characters

Miaoling, Lin. Everyday Chinese characters. — London : Duckworth, Apr. 1981. — [80]p
ISBN 0-7156-1552-1 (cased) : £1.50 : CIP entry
ISBN 0-7156-1553-x (pbk) : £1.50 B81-00090

495.1'152 — Chinese language. Pronunciation

Anderson, Olov Bertil. An investigation into the present state of standard Chinese pronunciation. — London : Curzon Press
Pt.1b: A character register of Chinese symbols. — Feb.1982. — [160]p
ISBN 0-7007-0157-5 (pbk) : £6.00 : CIP entry
B82-02454

495.1'5 — Classical Chinese language. Syntax

Harbsmeier, Christoph. Aspects of Classical Chinese syntax / Christoph Harbsmeier. — London : Curzon, 1981. — 303p ; 23cm. — (Scandinavian Institute of Asian Studies monograph series, ISSN 0069-1712 ; no.45)
Summary in Danish. — Bibliography: p288-292. — Includes index
ISBN 0-7007-0139-7 (pbk) : £10.00 : CIP rev.
B82-01335

495.1'7 — Chinese language. Cantonese. Classifiers — *Dictionaries*

Killingley, Siew-yue. A short glossary of Cantonese classifiers / Siew-Yue Killingley. — Newcastle upon Tyne : G. & G., 1982. — xx,54p ; 21cm
Bibliography: p53-54
ISBN 0-9507918-0-6 (pbk) : £3.35 : CIP rev.
B82-06067

495.1'7 — Chinese language. Cantonese dialect. Classifiers

Killingley, Siew-Yue. Cantonese classifiers. — Newcastle upon Tyne (9 Rectory Drive, Newcastle upon Tyne, NE3 1XT) : Grevatt & Grevatt, Feb.1983. — [160]p
ISBN 0-9507918-3-0 (pbk) : £6.00 : CIP entry
B82-39837

495.1'7 — Chinese language. Malayan Cantonese. Grammar

Killingley, Siew-Yue. The grammatical hierarchy of Malayan Cantonese / Siew-Yue Killingley. — Newcastle-upon-Tyne : Siew-Yue Killingley, 1982. — xxiv,231[i.e. 116]p ; 21x30cm
Bibliography: p215-219. — Includes index
ISBN 0-9508149-0-3 (pbk) : £6.30 : CIP rev.
B82-20792

495.1'82421 — Chinese language. Mandarin. Grammar

Li, Charles N.. Mandarin Chinese : a functional reference grammar / Charles N. Li and Sandra A. Thompson. — Berkeley ; London : University of California Press, c1981. — xviii,691p : 1map ; 24cm
Bibliography: p677-682. — Includes index
ISBN 0-520-04286-7 : £26.00 B82-13759

Modern Chinese : a second course / by the Faculty of Peking University ; with English translations of the illustrative sentences and texts by members of the Department of East Asian Languages and Civilizations, Harvard University. — New York : Dover ; London : Constable, 1981. — viii,471p ; 22cm
Text in English and Chinese
ISBN 0-486-24155-6 (pbk) : £5.25 B82-13789

495.1'83421 — Spoken Chinese language. Mandarin — *Phrase books*

Montanaro, John S.. Chinese/English phrase book for travellers / by John S. Montanaro. — New York ; Chichester : Wiley, c1981. — xvi,288p : 1map ; 16cm
Map on inside covers
ISBN 0-471-08298-8 (pbk) : £5.00 B82-05124

495.6 — JAPANESE LANGUAGE

495.6'3'21 — Japanese language — *Japanese-English dictionaries*

The **Oxford-Duden** pictorial English-Japanese dictionary. — Oxford : Oxford University Press, Jan.1983. — [848]p
ISBN 0-19-864149-4 : £15.00 : CIP entry
B82-32846

495.6'82 — Japanese language. Grammar — *Japanese texts*

Nihongo kōsu. — 8th (rev.) ed. — London : Linguaphone Institute, 1980. — 148p : ill ; 21cm
Previous ed.: 197-. — Ill on inside covers
Unpriced B82-16070

496 — AFRICAN LANGUAGES

496'.07'1 — Africa. Schools. Curriculum subjects: African languages. Teaching

Awoniyi, Timothy Adedeji. The teaching of African languages. — London : Hodder and Stoughton, Aug.1982. — [192]p
ISBN 0-340-28171-5 (pbk) : £2.95 : CIP entry
B82-18472

496.3 — NIGER-CONGO LANGUAGES

496'.39 — Mbukushu language — *Mbukushu & English dictionaries*

Wynne, R. C.. English-Mbukushu dictionary / R.C. Wynne. — [Amersham] : Avebury, 1980. — xxxiii,615p ; 31cm
ISBN 0-86127-203-x : £24.00 : CIP rev.
B79-37275

497 — NORTH AMERICAN INDIAN LANGUAGES

497'.2 — Navaho language. Questions. Transformational-generative theories

Schauber, Ellen. The syntax and semantics of questions in Navajo / Ellen Schauber. — New York ; London : Garland, 1979. — 313p : ill ; 24cm. — (Outstanding dissertations in linguistics ; 20)
Bibliography: p309-313
ISBN 0-8240-9676-2 : Unpriced B82-15185

497'.4 — Maya hieroglyphs. Decipherment

Thompson, J. Eric S.. Maya hieroglyphs without tears / J. Eric S. Thompson. — London : Published for the Trustees of the British Museum by British Museum Publications, c1972 (1980 [printing]). — 77p : ill ; 24cm
Bibliography: p75. — Includes index
ISBN 0-7141-1555-x (pbk) : £3.95 B82-16023

499.2 — AUSTRONESIAN LANGUAGES, MALAY LANGUAGES

499'.2 — Austronesian languages. Phonemes. Evolution

Dahl, Otto Christian. Early phonetic and phonemic changes in Austronesian / Otto Christian Dahl. — Oslo : Universitetsforlaget ; London : Global Book Resources [distributor], c1981. — 175p ; 23cm. — (Instituttet for sammenlignende kulturforskning. Serie B, ISSN 0332-6217 ; skrifter 63)
At head of title: Instituttet for sammenlignende kulturforskning. — Bibliography: p167-169. — Includes index
ISBN 82-00-09530-4 : £9.85 B82-11840

499'.22 — Iban language — *Iban & English dictionaries*

Richard, Anthony, *1914-*. An Iban-English dictionary / compiled by Anthony Richard. — Oxford : Clarendon Press, 1981. — xxx,417p : 1ill,1map ; 23cm
Bibliography: pxxi-xxvii
ISBN 0-19-864325-x : £25.00 B82-16130

499.221'321 — Indonesian language — *Indonesian & English dictionaries*

Schmidgall-Tellings, A. Eduard. Contemporary Indonesian-English dictionary : a supplement to the standard Indonesian dictionaries with particular concentration on new words, expressions and meanings / by A.Ed. Schmidgall-Tellings and Alan M. Stevens. — Chicago ; London : Ohio University Press, c1981. — xv,388p ; 24cm
ISBN 0-8214-0424-5 (cased) : Unpriced
ISBN 0-8214-0435-0 (pbk) : £11.25
B82-30098

499.4 — POLYNESIAN LANGUAGES

499'.4 — Maori language — *Maori & English dictionaries*

Biggs, Bruce. The complete English-Maori dictionary / Bruce Biggs. — [Auckland] : Auckland University Press ; [Oxford] : Oxford University Press, 1981. — x,227p ; 22cm
ISBN 0-19-647989-4 : £12.00 B82-05422

499'.4 — Polynesian languages

Krupa, Viktor. The Polynesian languages : a guide / Viktor Krupa ; [translated from the Russian by G.L. Campbell] ; [translation revised by Viktor Krupa]. — London : Routledge & Kegan Paul, 1982. — vii,193p ; 22cm. — (Languages of Asia and Africa, ISSN 0261-0116 ; v.4)
Translation of: Polineziiskie i͡azyki. — Bibliography: p168-193
ISBN 0-7100-9075-7 (pbk) : £8.95 B82-39666

499.9 — MINOR LANGUAGES (INCLUDING ARTIFICIAL LANGUAGES)

499'.99 — Invented languages — *Personal observations*

Hickling, Colin, *1916-*. Man ling : an essay in international communication dedicated to the 21st century, just in case there is one / by col in hik ling [sic]. — Doncaster (33 Beckett Rd., Doncaster, Yorkshire DN2 4AD) : Solonist Society, 1981. — [16]p ; 21cm
Unpriced (pbk) B82-27436

500 — SCIENCE

500 — Science

Berry, Adrian. From apes to astronauts / Adrian Berry. — [London] : Daily Telegraph, 1980. — viii,182p ; 18cm
Includes index
ISBN 0-901684-60-0 (pbk) : £1.45 B82-08784

Kapit͡sa, P. L.. Experiment, theory, practice : articles and addresses / P.L. Kapitza. — Dordrecht ; London : Reidel, c1980. — xxvi,429p : ill,1facsim,ports ; 23cm. — (Boston studies in the philosophy of science ; v.46)
Translation of: Eksperiment, teori͡a, praktika. 2 izd ispr i dop. — Bibliography: p419-424. — Includes index
ISBN 90-277-1061-9 (cased) : Unpriced
ISBN 90-277-1062-7 (pbk) : Unpriced
B82-37355

Medawar, Peter. Pluto's republic. — Oxford : Oxford University Press, Sept.1982. — [400]p
ISBN 0-19-217726-5 : £12.50 : CIP entry
B82-19181

Pyke, Magnus. Everyman's scientific facts and feats / Magnus Pyke, Patrick Moore. — London : Dent, 1981. — 310p : ill,maps,ports ; 26cm
Includes index
ISBN 0-460-04540-7 : £8.95 : CIP rev.
B81-28031

Riban, David M.. Introduction to physical science / David M. Riban. — New York ; London : McGraw-Hill, c1982. — xiii,658p : ill(some col.),col.maps,ports ; 25cm
Text on lining papers. — Includes index
ISBN 0-07-052140-9 : £15.50 B82-03303

Vergara, William C.. Science in everyday life / William C. Vergara. — London : Sphere, 1982, c1980. — 306p : ill ; 20cm
Originally published: New York : Harper & Row ; London : Souvenir, 1980. — Includes index
ISBN 0-7221-8720-3 (pbk) : £2.50
Also classified at 600 B82-24544

The **World** of science : (science for S101) : an introductory and refresher course in science for intending Open University S101 students. — Cambridge : National Extension College, 1978-1979. — 2v. : ill ; 30cm. — (National Extension College correspondence texts ; course no.S24)
Prepared by Andrew Read et al. — Vol.1 contains units 1-4, vol.2 units 5-8
ISBN 0-86082-126-9 (pbk) : Unpriced
ISBN 0-86082-124-2 (v.1) : Unpriced
ISBN 0-86082-125-0 (v.2) : Unpriced
B82-38357

500 — Science — *For Caribbean students*
Lancaster, Colin. Science step by step for the Caribbean. — [London] : Macmillan Caribbean. — (The Macmillan primary science project)
Early years
Book 3 / C. Lancaster, B.L. Young. — 1981. — 46p : ill(some col.),forms ; 24cm
ISBN 0-333-31103-5 (pbk) : Unpriced
B82-28650

500 — Science — *For children*
Allington, Richard. Science. — Oxford : Blackwell Raintree, Nov.1982. — [32]p. — (Beginning to learn about)
ISBN 0-86256-058-6 : £2.95 : CIP entry
B82-26070

Marsh, Leonard. The Guinness book for the young scientist. — Enfield (2 Cecil Court, London Rd, Enfield, Middx. EN2 6DJ) : GBR Educational, Oct.1982. — [96]p
ISBN 0-85112-631-6 (pbk) : £2.95 : CIP entry
B82-24267

Stein, Sara. The science book / Sara Stein. — London : Heinemann, 1982, c1979. — 285p : ill ; 22x24cm
Originally published: New York : Workman Publishing, 1980. — Includes index
ISBN 0-434-96460-3 : £4.95 B82-37625

500 — Science — *For Irish students*
Prior, John, *1933-*. Science : a new approach / John Prior, B.Ó Briain. — Dublin : Educational Company of Ireland
3. — 1981. — 160p : ill ; 25cm
Includes index
Unpriced (pbk) B82-00419

500 — Science — *For schools*
Basic secondary science. — London : Evans
Adaptation of: Intermediate science curriculum study
Bk.1 / writing and advisory team E.O. Aderinlewo ... [et al.]. — c1982. — vi,249p : ill (some col.) ; 28cm
ISBN 0-237-50527-4 (pbk) : Unpriced
B82-39661

Basic secondary science. — London : Evans
Teacher's bk.1 / writing and advisory team E.O. Aderinlewo ... [et al.]. — 1982. — xxii,249p : ill(some col.),ports ; 28cm
ISBN 0-237-50529-0 (pbk) : Unpriced
B82-36803

Chandrasegaran, A. L.. General science / A.L. Chandrasegaran, Leong Wing Fatt, M.P. Prabhakar. — 2nd ed. — Kuala Lumpur ; Oxford : Oxford University Press, 1980. — vi,258p : ill ; 25cm. — (Modern certificate guides)
Previous ed.: 1977?
ISBN 0-19-582800-3 (pbk) : £2.95 B82-33036

Harris, P. L.. Chemistry. — London : Murray, July 1982. — [96]p. — (Essential science series)
ISBN 0-7195-3796-7 (pbk) : £1.10 : CIP entry
B82-14525

Heasman, C. J.. Integrated science. — London : Bell & Hyman, Sept.1982. — [160]p
ISBN 0-7135-1325-x (pbk) : £3.95 : CIP entry
B82-20046

Heasman, C. J.. Integrated science. — London : Bell & Hyman, Sept.1982
Teacher's book. — [16]p
ISBN 0-7135-1355-1 (pbk) : £2.00 : CIP entry
B82-21392

Hogg, M. E.. Energy & matter, Energy & life : yellow, blue and red series : teacher's book for the complete course / M.E. Hogg. — London : Cassell, 1982. — x,96p : ill,maps ; 25cm. — (Cassell's foundation science)
Bibliography: p89-96
ISBN 0-304-30802-1 (pbk) : £4.50 B82-27075

Hogg, M. E.. Energy and matter / M.E. Hogg. — London : Cassell, 1982. — 186p : ill,1map ; 25cm. — (Cassell's foundation science. Yellow series ; part 1)
ISBN 0-304-30796-3 (pbk) : £2.95 B82-27074

Hogg, M. E.. Energy and matter / M.E. Hogg. — London : Cassell, 1982. — 192p : ill,1facsim ; 25cm. — (Cassell's foundation science. Blue series ; part 1)
Text on inside cover
ISBN 0-304-30797-1 (pbk) : £2.95 B82-27076

Jackson, Sylvia. Introducing science / Sylvia Jackson. — Glasgow : Blackie
7: Plants and animals. — 1980. — 32p : ill (some col.) ; 24cm
Cover title
ISBN 0-216-90832-9 (pbk) : £1.50 B82-12369

Jackson, Sylvia. Introducing science / Sylvia Jackson. — Glasgow : Blackie
Teacher's guide 7/8. — 1981. — 29p : ill ; 21cm
ISBN 0-216-90841-8 (pbk) : £2.00 B82-12371

Jackson, Sylvia. Introducing science / Sylvia Jackson. — Glasgow : Blackie
8: Sound. — 1980. — 32p : ill(some col.) ; 24cm
Cover title
ISBN 0-216-90833-7 (pbk) : £1.50 B82-12370

Jackson, Sylvia. Introducing science / Sylvia Jackson. — Glasgow : Blackie
9: Electricity. — 1980. — 32p : ill(some col.) ; 24cm
Cover title
ISBN 0-216-90834-5 (pbk) : £1.50 B82-34493

Jackson, Sylvia. Introducing science / Sylvia Jackson. — Glasgow : Blackie
10: Magnetism. — 1980. — 32p : ill(some col.) ; 24cm
Cover title
ISBN 0-216-90835-3 (pbk) : £1.50 B82-34494

Jackson, Sylvia. Introducing science / Sylvia Jackson. — Glasgow : Blackie
Teacher's guide 9/10. — 1982. — 30p : ill ; 21cm
ISBN 0-216-90842-6 (pbk) : £2.00 B82-34495

Kellington, Steuart. Reading about science. — London : Heinemann Educational, Sept.1982
1: Units, living things and energy. — [48]p
ISBN 0-435-57504-x (pbk) : £1.60 : CIP entry
B82-25148

Kellington, Steuart. Reading about science. — London : Heinemann Educational, Sept.1982
2: Substances, solutions, cells and seeds. — [48]p
ISBN 0-435-57505-8 (pbk) : £1.60 : CIP entry
B82-25149

Kellington, Steuart. Reading about science. — London : Heinemann Educational, Sept.1982
3: Heat, electricity and electromagnetism. — [48]p
ISBN 0-435-57506-6 (pbk) : £1.60 : CIP entry
B82-24519

Kellington, Steuart. Reading about science. — London : Heinemann Educational, Sept.1982
4: Gases, acids and the earth. — [48]p
ISBN 0-435-57507-4 (pbk) : £1.60 : CIP entry
B82-25150

Kellington, Steuart. Reading about science. — London : Heinemann Educational, Sept.1982
5: Senses, forces and transport in living things. — [48]p
ISBN 0-435-57508-2 (pbk) : £1.60 : CIP entry
B82-25151

500 — Science — *For schools continuation*

Mee, A. J.. Science 2000 / development from Science for the 70s by A.J. Mee, Patricia Boyd and David Ritchie. — London : Heinemann Educational
Bk.2. — 1981. — viii,136p : ill(some col.)
Includes index
ISBN 0-435-57567-8 (pbk) : £2.75 : CIP rev. B81-22577

Parker, Sheila. Sciencewise / Sheila Parker and Alan Ward. — Walton-on-Thames : Norton
Cover title. — Text on inside covers
Teachers' Book 4 : to accompany pupil's book 6. — 1979 (1980 [printing]). — 16p ; 22cm
ISBN 0-17-423036-2 (pbk) : Unpriced B82-37973

Science happenings. — Aylesbury : Ginn
Teachers' resource book / [Michael Holt]. — c1980. — 80p : ill ; 28cm
Bibliography: p73-75. — Includes index
ISBN 0-602-22532-9 (pbk) : Unpriced B82-35655

Smyth, Thomas N.. Intermediate Certificate science : biology, chemistry, physics / Thomas N. Smyth. — [Dublin] : Folens, c1982. — 416p : ill(some col.),1chart,facsims ; 25cm
Includes index
ISBN 0-86121-163-4 (pbk) : Unpriced B82-28189

500 — Science — *Forecasts*

Asimov, Isaac. Change!. — London : Coronet, Jan.1983. — [224]p
ISBN 0-340-28650-4 (pbk) : £1.50 : CIP entry B82-33744

Outlook for science and technology : the next five years / a report of the National Research Council. — Oxford : Published in collaboration with the National Academy of Sciences by Freeman, c1982. — xx,788p : ill ; 24cm
Includes bibliographies and index
ISBN 0-7167-1345-4 (cased) : £18.50
ISBN 0-7167-1346-2 (pbk) : £10.95
Also classified at 600 B82-23933

500 — Science. International cooperation

Knowledge and power in the global society / edited by William M. Evan. — Beverly Hills ; London : Sage, c1981. — 320p : ill ; 23cm. — (Sage focus editions ; v.30)
Includes bibliographies and index
ISBN 0-8039-1659-0 (cased) : Unpriced
ISBN 0-8039-1660-4 (pbk) : £6.50 B82-07909

500 — Science. Policies of governments

Tisdell, C. A.. Science and technology policy : priorities of governments / C.A. Tisdell. — London : Chapman and Hall, 1981. — xii,222p : ill ; 24cm
Includes index
ISBN 0-412-23320-7 : £12.00 : CIP rev.
Also classified at 600 B81-28835

500 — Science — *Quotations*

The **Harvest** of a quiet eye : a selection of scientific quotations / by Alan L. Mackay ; edited by Maurice Ebison ; with a foreword by Sir Peter Medawar. — Bristol : Institute of Physics, 1977 (1981 [printing]). — xii,192p : ill,ports ; 24cm
Includes index
ISBN 0-85498-039-3 (pbk) : Unpriced B82-38569

500 — Symmetry groups. Applications

Butler, Philip H.. Point group symmetry applications : methods and tables / Philip H. Butler. — New York ; London : Plenum, c1981. — ix,567p : ill ; 24cm
Bibliography: p553-556. — Includes index
ISBN 0-306-40523-7 : Unpriced B82-14546

500.2'0246 — Physical sciences — *Questions & answers — For technicians*

Bird, J. O.. Physical science 1 checkbook / J.O. Bird, A.J.C. May. — London : Butterworth Scientific, 1982. — viii,152p : ill ; 20cm. — (Butterworths technical and scientific checkbooks)
Includes index
ISBN 0-408-00681-1 (cased) : Unpriced : CIP rev.
ISBN 0-408-00628-5 (pbk) : Unpriced B82-10484

500.2'072041 — Physical sciences. Research in British institutions — *Directories — Serials*

Research in British universities, polytechnics and colleges. Vol.1, Physical sciences. — 1982. — Boston Spa : British Library Lending Division, RBUPC Office, July 1982. — [900]p
ISBN 0-7123-2003-2 : £34.50 : CIP entry
ISBN 0-7123-2002-4 (set) : Unpriced
ISSN 0142-2472 B82-14522

500.2'076 — Physical sciences — *Questions & answers — For schools*

Hogg, M. E.. Energy & matter / M.E. Hogg. — London : Cassell
Part 1. — 1982. — 228p : ill ; 25cm
ISBN 0-304-30798-x (pbk) : Unpriced B82-30619

500.5 — Space sciences - *Conference proceedings*

International Astronautical Congress *(31st : 1980 : Tokyo)*. Applications of space developments. — Oxford : Pergamon, July 1981. — [360]p
Conference papers
ISBN 0-08-026729-7 : £30.00 : CIP entry B81-17538

500.5 — Space sciences — *For children*

Becklake, Susan. Space discovery / Susan Becklake. — London : Macdonald, 1980. — 32p : col.ill,2col.charts ; 29cm. — (Eye openers!)
Bibliography: p30. — Includes index
ISBN 0-356-07092-1 : £2.50 B82-24547

500.5 — Space sciences — *For schools*

Thackray, James. Space science / James Thackray. — Glasgow : Blackie, 1981. — 32p : ill ; 17x25cm. — (Modular science)
ISBN 0-216-90591-5 (pbk) : £1.40 B82-02403

500.5'03'21 — Space sciences — *Encyclopaedias*

Angelo, Joseph A.. Dictionary of space technology / by Joseph A. Angelo, Jr. — London : Muller, 1982. — 380p : ill,maps,plans ; 25cm
ISBN 0-584-95011-x : £12.50 B82-30975

500.507'2 — Space sciences. Research. Use of balloons - *Conference proceedings*

Scientific ballooning - II. — Oxford : Pergamon, Apr.1981. — [274]p. — (Advances in space research ; v.1, no.11)
ISBN 0-08-028390-x : £14.50 : CIP entry B81-08934

500.5'09417 — Ireland *(Republic)*. **Space sciences** — *Conference proceedings*

Irish participation in space : proceedings of a symposium held in the Royal Irish Academy, 23 May 1980 / compiled and edited by S.M.P. McKenna-Lawlor. — Dublin : The Academy, c1982. — 72p : ill ; 21cm
Unpriced (pbk) B82-38935

501 — Philosophy of science

Horwich, Paul. Probability and evidence / Paul Horwich. — Cambridge : Cambridge University Press, 1982. — vii,146p : ill ; 23cm. — (Cambridge studies in philosophy)
Bibliography: p143-144. — Includes index
ISBN 0-521-23758-0 : £15.00 : CIP rev. B82-15934

Popper, Karl R.. Realism and the aim of science. — London : Hutchinson, Jan.1983. — [464]p
ISBN 0-09-151450-9 : £25.00 : CIP entry B82-33460

Wisdom, J. O.. Challengeability in modern science. — Amersham : Avebury, Dec.1981. — [240]p
ISBN 0-86127-106-8 : £16.00 : CIP entry B81-31635

501 — Philosophy of science — *Festschriften*

Scientific philosophy today : essays in honor of Mario Bunge / edited by Joseph Agassi and Robert S. Cohen. — Dordrecht ; London : Reidel, c1982. — x,513p : ill,1port ; 23cm. — (Boston studies in the philosophy of science ; v.67)
Includes bibliographies and index
ISBN 90-277-1262-x (cased) : Unpriced
ISBN 90-277-1263-8 (pbk) : Unpriced B82-14562

501 — Philosophy of science. Theories

Giedymin, Jerzy. Science and convention : essays on Henri Poincaré's philosophy of science and the conventionalist tradition / by Jerzy Giedymin. — Oxford : Pergamon, 1982. — xvii,229p ; 22cm. — (Foundations & philosophy of science & technology)
Bibliography: p206-216. — Includes index
ISBN 0-08-025790-9 : £12.50 : CIP rev. B81-28843

Stove, David Charles. Popper and after. — Oxford : Pergamon [May 1981]. — [192]p. — (Pergamon international library)
ISBN 0-08-026792-0 (cased) : £7.95 : CIP entry
ISBN 0-08-026791-2 (pbk) : £4.95 B81-07605

501 — Philosophy of science. Theories of Sellars, Wilfrid

Pitt, Joseph C.. Pictures, images, and conceptual change : an analysis of Wilfrid Sellars' philosophy of science / Joseph C. Pitt. — Dordrecht ; London : Reidel, c1981. — x,165p ; 23cm. — (Synthese library ; v.151)
Bibliography: p156-158. — Includes index
ISBN 90-277-1276-x (cased) : Unpriced
ISBN 90-277-1277-8 (pbk) : Unpriced B82-05343

501 — Science, *ca 1500-1980 — Philosophical perspectives*

Berman, Morris. The reenchantment of the world / Morris Berman. — Ithaca ; London : Cornell University Press, 1981. — 357p : ill ; 24cm
Includes index
ISBN 0-8014-1347-8 (cased) : Unpriced
ISBN 0-8014-9225-4 (pbk) : Unpriced B82-16162

501 — Science. Explanation — *Philosophical perspectives*

Scientific explanation : papers based on Herbert Spencer lectures given in the University of Oxford / edited by A.F. Heath. — Oxford : Clarendon, 1981. — x,123p ; 23cm. — (Herbert Spencer lecture) (Oxford science publications)
Includes index, port
ISBN 0-19-858214-5 : £7.95 : CIP rev. B81-28129

501 — Science — *Philosophical perspectives*

Brown, Harold I.. Perception, theory and commitment : the new philosophy of science / Harold I. Brown. — Chicago ; London : University of Chicago Press, 1979, c1977. — 203p ; 23cm
Originally published: Chicago : Precedent, 1977. — Bibliography: p191-200. — Includes index
ISBN 0-226-07618-0 (pbk) : Unpriced B82-21265

Dilworth, Craig. Scientific progress : a study concerning the nature of the relation between successive scientific theories / Craig Dilworth. — Dordrecht ; London : Reidel, c1981. — 155p : ill ; 23cm. — (Synthese library ; v.153)
Bibliography: p142-148. — Includes index
ISBN 90-277-1311-1 : Unpriced B82-05344

Fetzer, James H.. Scientific knowledge : causation, explanation and corroboration / James H. Fetzer. — Dordrecht ; London : Reidel, c1981. — xvi,323p ; 23cm. — (Boston studies in the philosophy of science ; v.69)
Bibliography: p297-309. — Includes index
ISBN 90-277-1335-9 (cased) : Unpriced
ISBN 90-277-1336-7 (pbk) : Unpriced B82-14561

501 — Science — *Philosophical perspectives* *continuation*

Feyerabend, Paul. Problems of empiricism / Paul K. Feyerabend. — Cambridge : Cambridge University Press, 1981. — xii,255p : ill ; 24cm. — (Philosophical papers ; v.2)
Includes index
ISBN 0-521-23964-8 : £17.50 : CIP rev.
B81-25774

Feyerabend, Paul. Realism, rationalism and scientific method / Paul K. Feyerabend. — Cambridge : Cambridge University Press, 1981. — xiv,353p : ill ; 24cm. — (Philosophical papers ; v.1)
Includes bibliographies and index
ISBN 0-521-22897-2 : £22.50 : CIP rev.
B81-25775

Munévar, Gonzalo. Radical knowledge : a philosophical inquiry into the nature and limits of science / Gonzalo Munévar ; with a foreword by Paul K. Feyerabend. — [Amersham] : Avebury, 1981. — x,125p : ill ; 24cm. — (Avebury philosophy of science series)
Includes index
ISBN 0-86127-109-2 (cased) : Unpriced : CIP rev.
ISBN 0-86127-111-9 (pbk) : Unpriced
B81-21553

Newton-Smith, W. H.. The rationality of science / W.H. Newton-Smith. — Boston, Mass. ; London : Routledge & Kegan Paul, 1981. — xii,294p ; 22cm. — (International library of philosophy)
Bibliography: p282-287. — Includes index
ISBN 0-7100-0870-8 (cased) : £9.95
ISBN 0-7100-0913-5 (pbk) : Unpriced
B82-07918

Polish essays in the philosophy of the natural sciences / edited by Władysław Krajewski. — Dordrecht ; London : Reidel, c1982. — xxviii,487p ; 23cm. — (Boston studies in the philosophy of science ; v.68)
Translated from the Polish. — Bibliography: p435-468. — Includes index
ISBN 90-277-1286-7 (cased) : Unpriced
ISBN 90-277-1287-5 (pbk) : Unpriced
B82-30370

Scientific revolutions / edited by Ian Hacking. — Oxford : Oxford University Press, 1981. — 180p : ill ; 21cm. — (Oxford readings in philosophy)
Bibliography: p169-176. — Includes index
ISBN 0-19-875051-x (pbk) : £3.50 : CIP rev.
B81-08866

Smith, Peter, *1951-*. Realism and the progress of science / Peter Smith. — Cambridge : Cambridge University Press, 1981. — 135p ; 23cm. — (Cambridge studies in philosophy)
Bibliography: p130-132. — Includes index
ISBN 0-521-23937-0 : £12.50 : CIP rev.
B81-32526

What? where? when? why? : essays on induction, space and time, explanation : inspired by the work of Wesley C. Salmon and celebrating his first visit to Australia, September-December 1978 / edited by Robert McLaughlin. — Dordrecht ; London : Reidel, c1982. — xvii,319p : ill,1port ; 23cm. — (Australasian studies in history and philosophy of science ; 1)
Bibliography: p295-302. — Includes index
ISBN 90-277-1337-5 : Unpriced B82-21456

501 — Science. Rationality — *Philosophical perspectives*

Rationality in science : studies in the foundations of science and ethics / edited by Risto Hilpinen. — Dordrecht ; London : Reidel, c1980. — vii,256p : ill ; 23cm. — (Philosophical studies series in philosophy ; v.21)
Conference papers. — Includes bibliographies and index
ISBN 90-277-1112-7 : Unpriced B82-35625

501 — Science. Relations with belief. Theories, *ca 1800-ca 1930*

Science and belief : from Darwin to Einstein. — Milton Keynes : Open University Press. — (Arts : a third level course)
At head of title: The Open University
Block 4: Modern physics and problems of knowledge / prepared for the Course Team by Paul M. Clark ... [et al.]. — 1981. — 153p : ill,ports ; 30cm. — (A381 ; block 4 (6-9))
Bibliography: p153. — Contents: Unit 6: Einstein : philosophical belief and physical theory — Unit 7: Introduction to quantum theory — Unit 8: Quantum theory ; the Bohr-Einstein debate — Unit 9: Physics and society
ISBN 0-335-11003-7 (pbk) : Unpriced
Primary classification 121′.6 B82-04649

Science and belief : from Darwin to Einstein. — Milton Keynes : Open University Press. — (Arts : a third level course)
At head of title: The Open University
Block 5: The mystery of life / prepared for the Course Team by David Goodman and Robert Olby. — 1981. — 53p : ill,ports ; 30cm. — (A381 ; block 5 (10,11))
Bibliography: p52-53. — Contents: Unit 10: The origins of life : discussions in the later nineteenth century — Unit 11: The nature of life : discovery in the twentieth century
ISBN 0-335-11004-5 (pbk) : Unpriced
Primary classification 121′.6 B82-04650

501 — Science. Theories. Applications of general systems theory — *French texts*

Laszlo, Ervin. Le systémisme. — Oxford : Pergamon, Dec.1981. — [116]p
ISBN 0-08-027051-4 (pbk) : £4.50 : CIP entry
B81-31720

501 — Scientific knowledge. Acquisition. Role of cognition

Mey, Marc de. The cognitive paradigm / Marc de Mey. — Dordrecht ; London : Reidel, 1982. — xx,314p ; 23cm. — (Sociology of the sciences)
Bibliography: p283-303. — Includes index
ISBN 90-277-1382-0 : Unpriced B82-40762

501′.4 — Science. Semantic aspects

Tondl, Ladislav. Problems of semantics : a contribution to the analysis of the language of science / Ladislav Tondl ; translated from the Czech by David Short. — Dordrecht ; London : Reidel, c1981. — xiv,403p : ill ; 23cm. — (Boston studies in the philosophy of science ; v.66)
Translation of: Problémy sémantiky. — Bibliography: p379-385. — Includes index
ISBN 90-277-0148-2 (cased) : Unpriced
ISBN 90-277-0316-7 (pbk) : Unpriced
B82-04416

501′.41 — Science. Communication. Effects of foreign languages

Large, J. A.. The foreign language barrier to scientific communication. — London : Deutsch, Oct.1982. — [240]p. — (Language library)
ISBN 0-233-97488-1 (pbk) : £8.95 : CIP entry
B82-23486

501′.8 — Science. Hypotheses. Use, *to 1980*

Laudan, Larry. Science and hypothesis : historical essays on scientific methodology / Larry Laudan. — Dordrecht ; London : Reidel, c1981. — x,258p ; 23cm. — (The University of Western Ontario series in philosophy of science ; v.19)
Includes bibliographies and index
ISBN 90-277-1315-4 (cased) : Unpriced
ISBN 90-277-1316-2 (pbk) : Unpriced
B82-09383

501′.8 — Science. Methodology — *Philosophical perspectives*

Feyerabend, Paul. Science in a free society. — London : Verso/NLB, Oct.1982. — 1v.
Originally published: 1978
ISBN 0-86091-753-3 (pbk) : £4.25 : CIP entry
B82-28598

On scientific discovery : the Erice lectures 1977 / edited by Mirko Drazen Grmek, Robert S. Cohen, Guido Cimino. — Dordrecht ; London : Reidel, c1981. — vii,333p : ill ; 24cm. — (Boston studies in the philosophy of science ; v.34)
Includes bibliographies and index
ISBN 90-277-1122-4 (cased) : Unpriced
ISBN 90-277-1123-2 (pbk) : Unpriced
B82-40795

501′.9 — Scientists. Thought processes

On scientific thinking / edited by Ryan D. Tweney, Michael E. Doherty, Clifford R. Mynatt. — New York ; Guildford : Columbia University Press, 1981. — xii,459p : ill,facsims ; 24cm
Bibliography: p419-439. — Includes index
ISBN 0-231-04814-9 (cased) : £23.50
ISBN 0-231-04815-7 (pbk) : £10.80
B82-05623

502′.07 — Science — *Humour*

Weber, Robert L.. More random walks in science. — Bristol : Institute of Physics, Oct.1982. — [209]p
ISBN 0-85498-040-7 : £10.00 : CIP entry
B82-25946

502′.12 — Science. Formulae — *For technicians*

Browning, D. R.. Science facts and formulae for TEC courses / D.R. Browning. — Harlow : Longman, 1981. — 37p : ill ; 22cm
Cover title
ISBN 0-582-41234-x (pbk) : £0.95 : CIP rev.
B81-31822

502.3′41 — Great Britain. Laboratory technicians — *Career guides*

Quinton, Anson. Working as a laboratory technician. — London : Batsford, Feb.1983. — [112]p
ISBN 0-7134-4443-6 : £5.95 : CIP entry
B82-39426

502′.3′41 — Great Britain. *Ministry of Defence.* **Scientists** — *Career guides*

Defence science 1981 : work as a scientist in the Ministry of Defence. — [London?] : [Ministry of Defence?], 1980. — 48p : ill,1map ; 30cm
Prepared by the Ministry of Defence Public Relations and the Central Office of Information
Unpriced (spiral) B82-05570

502′.4613 — Science — *For nursing*

Hinwood, Barry G.. Integrated science applied for nurses / Barry G. Hinwood. — London : Baillière Tindall, 1981. — 231p : ill ; 28cm
Originally published: North Ryde : Cassell Australia, 1981. — Bibliography: p207-209. — Includes index
ISBN 0-7020-0910-5 (pbk) : £8.50 B82-15509

502′.464 — Science — *For household management*

Rees, Ann Maree. Science of home economics and institutional management. — 3rd ed. — Oxford : Blackwell Scientific, Dec.1982. — [432]p
ISBN 0-632-01019-3 (pbk) : £10.00 : CIP entry
B82-32294

502′.4′6467 — Science — *For beauty care*

Rounce, John F.. Science for beauty therapists. — Cheltenham : Stanley Thornes, Aug.1982. — [224]p
ISBN 0-85950-331-3 (pbk) : £4.95 : CIP entry
B82-16666

502′.46467 — Science — *For hairdressing*

Lee, C. M.. Science for hairdressing students. — 3rd ed. — Oxford : Pergamon, June 1982. — [288]p. — (Pergamon international library)
Previous ed.: 1972
ISBN 0-08-027440-4 (cased) : £25.00 : CIP entry
ISBN 0-08-027439-0 (pbk) : £12.00
B82-10595

502′.8′2 — Microscopy — *Manuals*

Curry, Alan. Under the microscope / Alan Curry, Robin F. Grayson, Geoffrey R. Hosey. — Poole : Blandford, 1982. — 160p,[4]p of plates : ill(some col.) ; 23cm
Bibliography: p153-156. — Includes index
ISBN 0-7137-1030-6 : £6.95 : CIP rev.
B82-06245

502'.8'2 — Microscopy — *Manuals* *continuation*

Locquin, Marcel. Handbook of microscopy. — London : Butterworth, Oct.1982. — [360]p
ISBN 0-408-10679-4 : £50.00 : CIP entry B82-24471

502'.8'2 — Optical microscopy

Spencer, Michael, *1931-*. Fundamentals of light microscopy / Michael Spencer. — Cambridge : Cambridge University Press, 1982. — x,93p : ill,1facsim ; 24cm. — (IUPAB biophysics series ; 6)
Bibliography: p77. — Includes index
ISBN 0-521-24794-2 (cased) : £10.00
ISBN 0-521-28967-x (pbk) : £4.50 B82-38490

502'.8'205 — Microscopy — *Serials*

Advances in optical and electron microscopy. — Vol.8. — London : Academic Press, May 1982. — [300]p
ISBN 0-12-029908-9 : CIP entry
ISSN 0065-3012 B82-07261

502'.8'25 — Electron microscopy — *Conference proceedings*

Electron microscopy and analysis, 1981 : proceedings of the Institute of Physics Electron Microscopy and Analysis Group conference held at the University of Cambridge, 7-10 September 1981 (EMAG 81) / edited by M.J. Goringe. — Bristol : Institute of Physics, c1982. — xvi,563p : ill ; 24cm. — (Conference series / Institute of Physics, ISSN 0305-2346 ; no.61)
Includes bibliographies and index
ISBN 0-85498-152-7 : Unpriced : CIP rev. B81-34575

502'.8'25 — Electron microscopy. Experimental techniques

Butler, E. P.. Dynamic experiments in the electron microscope / E.P. Butler, K.F. Hale. — Amsterdam ; Oxford : North-Holland, 1981. — xv,457p : ill ; 23cm. — (Practical methods in electron microscopy ; v.9)
Includes bibliographies and index
ISBN 0-444-80285-1 (cased) : Unpriced
ISBN 0-444-80286-x (pbk) : Unpriced B82-00830

502'.8'25 — Scanning electron microscopy

Scanning electron microscopy and X-ray microanalysis : a text for biologists, materials scientists, and geologists / Joseph I. Goldstein ... [et al.]. — New York ; London : Plenum, c1981. — xiii,673p : ill ; 24cm
Bibliography: p649-664. — Includes index
ISBN 0-306-40768-x : Unpriced
Also classified at 543'.0812 B82-14544

503'.21 — Science — *Encyclopaedias*

Pocket science dictionary. — Harlow : Longman, 1982. — 329p ; 12cm. — (Longman top pocket series)
ISBN 0-582-55544-2 (pbk) : £0.75 B82-29199

503'.21 — Science, *to 1980* — *Encyclopaedias*

Dictionary of the history of science / edited by W.F. Bynum, E.J. Browne, Roy Porter. — London : Macmillan, 1981. — 494p : ill ; 25cm
Bibliography: 11p. — Includes index
ISBN 0-333-29316-9 : £17.50 B82-10638

503'.31 — Science — *German & English dictionaries*

Dorian, A. F.. Dictionary of science and technology : German-English / compiled and arranged by A.F. Dorian with the cooperation of L. Da Costa Monsanto = Handwörterbuch der Naturwissenschaft und Technik : Deutsch-Englisch / zusammengestellt durch A.F. Dorian unter Mitarbeit von L. Da Costa Monsanto. — Amsterdam ; Oxford : Elsevier Scientific, c1970 (1978 [printing]). — 879p ; 23cm
ISBN 0-444-40848-7 : £61.82
Also classified at 603'.31 B82-09152

503'.31 — Science - *German-English dictionaries*

Dorian, A. F.Dictionary of science and technology : German-English. — 2nd rev. ed. — Oxford : Elsevier Scientific, Aug.1981. — [1250]p
ISBN 0-444-41997-7 : CIP entry
Also classified at 603'.31 B81-16866

503'.41 — Science — *French & English dictionaries*

Dorian, A. F.. Dictionary of science and technology : French-English / compiled and arranged by A.F. Dorian. — Amsterdam ; Oxford : Elsevier Scientific, 1980. — 1085p ; 23cm
Added t.p. in French
ISBN 0-444-41911-x : £60.54 : CIP rev.
Also classified at 603'.41 B80-13355

505 — Science - *Serials*

Royal Institution of Great Britain. Proceedings of the Royal Institution of Great Britain. — Vol.53 (1981). — Northwood : Science Reviews, Aug.1981. — 1v.
ISBN 0-905927-71-0 (pbk) : £16.50 : CIP entry B81-19124

506'.041 — Great Britain. Science. Organisations: British Association for the Advancement of Science, *to 1981*

The **Parliament** of science. — London : Science Reviews, Aug.1981. — 1v.
ISBN 0-905927-66-4 (pbk) : £12.25 : CIP entry B81-18057

507 — Great Britain. Science teachers. Professional education — *Conference proceedings*

Science teachers for tomorrow's schools / Arthur Jennings and Richard Ingle (editors). — London : University of London Institute of Education, 1982. — 84p : ill ; 20cm. — (Bedford Way papers, ISSN 0261-0078 ; 7)
Conference papers
ISBN 0-85473-123-7 (pbk) : £2.25 B82-27689

507 — Science. Information sources

Information sources in the history of science and medicine. — London : Butterworth, Nov.1982. — [576]p. — (Butterworths guides to information sources)
ISBN 0-408-10764-2 : £18.00 : CIP entry
Primary classification 610'.7 B82-29442

507'.04 — Science. European information sources — *Directories*

European sources of scientific and technical information. — 5th ed. / editors Anthony P. Harvey and Ann Pernet. — Harlow : Hodgson, 1981. — 504p ; 24cm. — (Reference on research)
Previous ed.: published as Guide to European sources of technical information / edited by Ann Pernet. 1976. — Includes index
ISBN 0-582-90108-1 : £75.00 : CIP rev.
Also classified at 607'.4 B81-32048

507'.044 — France. Education. Curriculum subjects: Science, *1808-1914*

The **Organization** of science and technology in France 1808-1914 / edited by Robert Fox and George Weisz. — Cambridge : Cambridge University Press, 1980. — x,355p ; 24cm
Bibliography: p333-341. — Includes index
ISBN 0-521-23234-1 : £15.00 : CIP rev.
Also classified at 607'.44 B80-25534

507'.1 — Schools. Curriculum subjects: Science. Teaching

Driver, Rosalind. The pupil as scientist?. — Milton Keynes : Open University Press, Oct.1982. — [112]p
ISBN 0-335-10178-x (pbk) : £4.95 : CIP entry B82-24811

507'.1 — Schools. Curriculum subjects: Science. Teaching. Innovation

Innovation in the science curriculum : classroom knowledge and curriculum change / edited by John Olson. — London : Croom Helm, c1982. — 182p : 1ill ; 23cm. — (Croom Helm curriculum policy and research series)
Includes bibliographies and index
ISBN 0-7099-1900-x : £12.50 : CIP rev. B82-09591

507'.1141 — Great Britain. Higher education institutions. Curriculum subjects: Science. Ph.D. courses. Supervision

Research student and supervisor : a discussion document on good supervisory practice. — Swindon : SERC, 1982. — 22p ; 21cm
Cover title
Unpriced (pbk) B82-25958

507'.1241 — Great Britain. Middle schools. Curriculum subjects: Science — *Proposals*

Core intentions for science in the middle years. — [Leeds] : Leeds City Council, Dept. of Education, c1980. — [6],198p : ill ; 30cm
At head of title: The Middle Years Science Curriculum Project
ISBN 0-9508029-0-5 (spiral) : Unpriced B82-38846

507'.1241 — Great Britain. Secondary schools. Students: Girls. Curriculum subjects: Science

Girls and science : a report on an enquiry carried out in 1978 into the teaching of science to girls in coeducational comprehensive schools and an assessment of the factors influencing their choice of science subjects / Department of Education and Science. — London : H.M.S.O., 1980. — 45p ; 25cm. — (HMI series : matters for discussion ; 13)
Bibliography: p45
ISBN 0-11-270534-0 (pbk) : £3.30 B82-17177

507'.15 — England. Adult education. Curriculum subjects: Science

Advisory Council for Adult and Continuing Education. Basic science education for adults : a report on the issues affecting the provision of adult general education in the sciences and technology / ACACE. — Leicester : ACACE, [1981]. — 43p ; 21cm. — (Report / Advisory Council for Adult and Continuing Education)
ISBN 0-906436-12-5 (pbk) : £1.50 B82-39496

507'.2041 — Biology. Research in British institutions — *Directories* — *Serials*

Research in British universities, polytechnics and colleges. Vol.2, Biological sciences. — 1982. — Boston Spa : British Library Lending Division, RBUPC Office, July 1982. — [800]p
ISBN 0-7123-2004-0 (pbk) : £23.00 : CIP entry
ISBN 0-7123-2002-4 (set) : Unpriced
ISSN 0143-0734 B82-14523

507'.2041 — Great Britain. Science. Research — *Serials*

Science and Engineering Research Council. SERC bulletin / Science & Engineering Research Council. — Vol.2, no.3 (Autumn 1981)-. — Swindon : SERC, 1981-. — v. : ill ; 31cm
Three issues yearly. — Continues: Great Britain. Science Research Council. SRC bulletin
ISSN 0262-7671 = SERC bulletin : Unpriced
Also classified at 620'.0072041 B82-06773

507'.2041 — Science. Research in British Institutions — *Directories*

Research in British universities, polytechnics and colleges : Vol.2, Biological sciences. — 2nd ed. (1981). — Boston Spa (RBUPC Office, British Library Lending Division, Boston Spa, Wetherby, W.Yorks., LS23 7B9) : British Library, June 1981. — [655]p
ISBN 0-900220-88-0 (pbk) : £20.00 : CIP entry
ISSN 0143-0734
Also classified at 300'.7'2041 B81-13546

507'.208 — Latin America. Science. Research & development — *Directories*

Latin American Newsletters. Science and technology in Latin America. — London : Longman, Dec.1982. — [320]p. — (Longman guide to science and technology ; 2)
ISBN 0-582-90057-3 : £39.00 : CIP entry
Also classified at 607'.208 B82-30069

507'.24 — Research laboratories. Organisation — *Manuals*

Davy, John R.. Research : a laboratory digest / by John R. Davy. — [St. Helens] ([St. Helens, Merseyside WA10 3TT]) : Pilkington, 1981. — 58p,[1]leaf of plates : 1port ; 21cm
Unpriced (pbk) B82-02866

507'.24 — Science. Experiments — *Amateurs' manuals*

Gardner, Martin. [Science puzzlers]. Entertaining science experiments : with everyday objects / Martin Gardner ; illustrated by Anthony Ravielli. — New York : Dover ; London : Constable, 1981. — 127p : ill ; 22cm
Originally published: New York : Viking, 1960 ; London : Macmillan, 1962
ISBN 0-486-24201-3 (pbk) : £1.50 B82-18079

507'.24 — Science. Experiments — *For children*

Temple, Paul, *1951-*. How to make square eggs / Paul Temple and Ralph Levinson ; illustrated by David Mostyn. — London : Beaver, 1982. — 110p : ill ; 18cm
ISBN 0-600-20456-1 (pbk) : £0.95 B82-39074

Wicks, Keith. Science can be fun / Keith Wicks ; illustrated by Pavel Kostal. — London : Macmillan, 1982. — 32p : ill(some col.) ; 29cm. — (Help yourself books)
ISBN 0-333-30860-3 : £2.95 : CIP rev. B81-35783

507'.24 — Science. Simulations: Models — *Philosophical perspectives*

Wartofsky, Marx W.. Models : representation and the scientific understanding / Marx W. Wartofsky. — Dordrecht ; London : Reidel, c1979. — xxvi,390p : ill ; 23cm. — (Boston studies in the philosophy of science ; v.48) (Synthese library ; v.129)
Bibliography: p173-174. — Includes index
ISBN 90-277-0736-7 (cased) : Unpriced
ISBN 90-277-0947-5 (pbk) : Unpriced B82-39097

507'.6 — Science — *Questions & answers — For schools*

Brandling, Redvers. Check up tests in science / Redvers Brandling. — London : Macmillan Education, 1981. — 47p : ill ; 26cm
ISBN 0-333-31223-6 (pbk) : £1.95
ISBN 0-333-31224-4 (Teacher's book) : £0.75 B82-02581

Thomas, D. (David), *1924 Dec.14-*. Starting science / D. Thomas & W. Gibson. — Welwyn : Nisbet
Bk.3. — 1982. — 24leaves : ill ; 28cm
Cover title. — Duplicating masters
ISBN 0-7202-0812-2 (pbk) : £7.95 B82-39901

Windridge, Charles. Know science / Charles Windridge. — Huddersfield : Schofield & Sims, 1980. — 64p : ill,1map,ports ; 25cm
ISBN 0-7217-3568-1 (pbk) : £0.65 B82-13901

507'.8 — Great Britain. Schools. Curriculum subjects: Science. Teaching aids

Science resources : for primary and middle schools. — London : Published for the Schools Council by Macdonald Educational, 1982. — 80p : ill ; 22cm. — (Learning through science)
Includes bibliographies
ISBN 0-356-07816-7 (pbk) : Unpriced B82-23516

507'.8 — Schools. Curriculum subjects: Science. Teaching. Applications of microcomputer systems

Sparkes, R. A.. Microcomputers and science teaching. — London : Hutchinson Education, June 1982. — [240]p
ISBN 0-09-149021-9 (pbk) : £7.95 : CIP entry B82-12714

507'.9 — Ireland *(Republic)*. **Scientists. Awards** — *Directories*

Gillick, Mary. Fellowships and scholarships available to Irish scientists and technologists / compiled by Mary Gillick and Diarmuid Murphy. — Dublin (Shelbourne House, Shelbourne Rd., Dublin 4) : The National Board for Science and Technology, c1978. — 102p ; 21cm
Includes index
£2.00 (pbk)
Also classified at 607'.39 B82-12736

508 — Natural environment — *For children*

Humberstone, Eliot. Finding out about things outdoors / written by Eliot Humberstone ; illustrated by Louise Nevett ... [et al.]. — London : Usborne, 1981. — 32p : col.ill ; 21cm. — (Usborne explainers)
Includes index
ISBN 0-86020-464-2 (pbk) : £0.99 B82-34559

508 — Natural history — *Amateurs' manuals*

Durrell, Gerald. The amateur naturalist. — London : Hamilton, Sept.1982. — [320]p
ISBN 0-241-10841-1 : £12.50 : CIP entry B82-20164

508 — Natural history — *For schools*

Carson, Sean. BBC nature book / written by Sean Carson ; edited by Peter Ward. — London : Published at the request of the School Broadcasting Council for the United Kingdom by the British Broadcasting Corporation, 1982. — 64p : ill(some col.),maps ; 30cm
Text on inside back cover
ISBN 0-563-16520-0 (pbk) : Unpriced B82-39740

508 — Scientific expeditions by Beagle *(Ship), 1831-1836 — For children*

Law, Felicia. Darwin and the voyage of the Beagle. — London : Deutsch, Oct.1982. — [32]p
ISBN 0-233-97482-2 : £5.95 : CIP entry B82-23485

508'.074'02134 — London. Kensington and Chelsea *(London Borough)*. **Museums: British Museum (Natural History)**, *to 1980*

British Museum (Natural History). The British Museum (Natural History) / text by Peter Whitehead ; photographs by Colin Keates. — London : Published in association with the British Museum (Natural History) [by] Philip Wilson, 1981. — 128p : ill(some col.),col.facsims,1col.map,1plan,ports(some col.) ; 28cm
ISBN 0-85667-109-6 (cased) : Unpriced
ISBN 0-85667-108-8 (pbk) : £4.95 B82-33960

508'.074'02134 — London. Kensington and Chelsea *(London Borough)*. **Museums: British Museum (Natural History)** — *Visitors' guides*

British Museum (Natural History). The Natural History Museum : centenary souvenir guide 1881-1981. — [London] : British Museum (Natural History), c1981. — [32]p : col.ill,1facsim,plan,1col.port ; 30cm
Text, ill on inside covers. — Bibliography: p[3]
ISBN 0-565-00845-5 (pbk) : Unpriced B82-03310

508'.074'027 — North-west England. Natural history specimens. Collections — *Directories*

Register of natural science collections in North West England / editors E.G. Hancock and C.W. Pettitt. — Manchester : Manchester Museum on behalf of the North West Collections Research Unit, 1981. — [178]p ; 30cm
Includes index
ISBN 0-904630-04-8 (spiral) : £6.00 B82-01028

508'.092'4 — Natural history. Bonnet, Charles — *Critical studies*

Anderson, Lorin. Charles Bonnet and the order of the known / Lorin Anderson. — Dordrecht ; London : Reidel, c1982. — xv,159p ; 23cm. — (Studies in the history of modern science ; v.11)
Bibliography: p151-155. — Includes index
ISBN 90-277-1389-8 : Unpriced B82-41037

508'.092'4 — Natural history. Taylor, Fred J. — *Biographies*

Taylor, Fred J.. Reflections of a countryman. — London : Paul, Oct.1982. — [192]p
ISBN 0-09-150220-9 : £8.95 : CIP entry B82-25073

508'.092'4 — Natural history. Waterton, Charles — *Biographies*

Moore, Norman. Charles Waterton of Walton Hall 1782-1865. — Wakefield : Wakefield Historical Publications, 1981. — 5p : 2ill,2ports ; 21cm. — (W.H.P. ; 9)
Author: Norman Moore
ISBN 0-901869-11-2 (pbk) : £0.90 B82-13793

508.3 — Scientific expeditions by Beagle *(Ship), 1831-1836 — For children*

Ward, Peter, *1943-*. The adventures of Charles Darwin / Peter Ward ; illustrated by Annabel Large. — Cambridge : Cambridge University Press, 1982. — 96p : ill(some col.),1col.map ; 23cm
ISBN 0-521-24510-9 : £3.95 : CIP rev. B82-13131

508.3 — Scientific expeditions. Organisations — *Manuals*

Blashford-Snell, John. The expedition organiser's guide / by John Blashford-Snell & Richard Snailham ; written for the Scientific Exploration Society. — [London] ([135 Fleet St., E.C.4]) : [Daily Telegraph], [1982]. — 48p : ill ; 18cm. — (A Daily telegraph publication)
Bibliography: p47
£0.75 (pbk) B82-41095

508.3164 — Pacific Ocean. Scientific expeditions. Voyages by ships, *1768-1771*: **Endeavour** *(Ship)*

Craigie, Lucy Elizabeth. The voyage of the Endeavour / Lucy Elizabeth Craigie. — Bognor Regis : New Horizon, c1982. — 27p,[12]leaves of plates : ill,1map ; 21cm
ISBN 0-86116-503-9 : £3.25 B82-39723

508.41 — Great Britain. Natural environment — *Personal observations*

Jefferies, Richard. Field and hedgerow : the last essays of Richard Jefferies / collected by his widow. — Oxford : Oxford University Press, 1982. — vi,329p ; 20cm. — (Oxford paperbacks)
Originally published: London : Longman, 1889
ISBN 0-19-281355-2 (pbk) : £2.95 : CIP rev. B82-15674

508.41 — Great Britain. Natural history, *ca 1820-ca 1840*

Clare, John, *1793-1864*. The natural history prose writings of John Clare. — Oxford : Clarendon, Oct.1982. — [480]p
ISBN 0-19-818517-0 : £25.00 : CIP entry B82-23684

508.41 — Great Britain. Nature reserves — *Visitors' guides*

A nature reserves handbook : a guide to a selection of the nature reserves of the nature conservation trusts and the Royal Society for Nature Conservation / editor A.E. Smith. — Nettleham : Royal Society for Nature Conservation on behalf of its associated trusts, c1982. — 176p : ill(some col.),maps ; 21cm
Unpriced (pbk) B82-19714

508.41 — Great Britain. Seashore. Natural environment — *For schools*

Catherall, Ed. The seashore / Ed Catherall. — Hove : Wayland, 1982. — 32p : col.ill ; 23cm. — (Young scientist)
ISBN 0-85340-995-1 : £3.50 B82-34825

508.41'05 — Great Britain. Natural history — *Serials*

Dudley Natural History Society newsletter. — Jan. 1982-. — Dudley (c/o J. Coborn, Dudley Zoo, Dudley, West Midlands) : The Society, 1982-. — v. : ill ; 30cm
Monthly. — Description based on: May 1982
ISSN 0262-8422 = Dudley Natural History Society newsletter : Unpriced B82-32154

508.414'25 — Scotland. Stathclyde Region. Dumbarton. Nature trails: Overtoun Nature Trail — *Walkers' guides*

The **Overtoun** nature trail / [illustration & design by Andrew Ramsay]. — Dumbarton (c/o Civic Amenities Dept., Municipal Buildings, Dumbarton) : Dumbarton Natural History Society, [1980]. — 18p : ill,1col.map ; 21cm
Cover title. — Text, ill on inside covers
Unpriced (pbk) B82-14664

508.422'7 — Hampshire. Natural environment

Colebourn, Phil. The countryside heritage : an introduction / [written and produced in the Hampshire County Planning Department] ; [text by Phil Colebourn and Mike Hughes] ; [designed and illustrated by Paul Jones]. — [Winchester] ([The Castle, Winchester]) : [The Planning Department], [1982?]. — 22p : ill ; 30cm
£3.00 (pbk) B82-37078

508.422′74 — Hampshire. Selborne. Natural environment — *Correspondence, diaries, etc.*

White, Gilbert. [The Garden kalendar. Selections]. Gilbert White′s year : passages from ′The garden kalendar′ & ′The naturalist′s journal′ / selected by John Commander ; introduction by Richard Mabey. — Oxford : Oxford University Press, 1982. — 134p : ill ; 20cm. — (Oxford paperbacks)
Originally published: London : Scolar Press, 1979
ISBN 0-19-281354-4 (pbk) : £2.95 : CIP rev.
Also classified at 635′.09422′74 B82-10434

White, Gilbert. Journals of Gilbert White / edited by Walter Johnson. — London : Futura, 1982. — xlii,433p ; 18cm. — (Heritage)
Originally published: London : Routledge, 1931. — Includes index
ISBN 0-7088-2179-0 (pbk) : £2.50 B82-24097

508.423′31 — Dorset. Chesil Beach. Natural environment

The **Fleet** and Chesil Beach : structure and biology of a unique coastal feature : a scientific account / compiled by the Fleet Study Group ; editor M. Ladle. — [Dorchester] : [Dorset County Council], [1981]. — 74p,[18]leaves of plates : ill ; 30cm
Conference papers. — Cover title. — Bibliography: p71-74
ISBN 0-85216-288-x (pbk) : Unpriced
B82-13585

508.423′36 — Dorset. Purbeck *(District)*. *Nature reserves: Studland Heath National Nature Reserve. Nature trails: Woodland Trail — Walkers′ guides*

Nature Conservancy Council. Studland Heath National Nature Reserve : woodland trail / Nature Conservancy Council. — Taunton : Nature Conservancy Council, South West Region, c1980. — [8]p : ill ; 21cm
ISBN 0-86139-092-x (unbound) : £0.20
B82-35380

508.423′5 — Devon. Natural environment, *ca 1920 — Personal observations*

Williamson, Henry. The peregrine′s saga : and other wild tales / Henry Williamson. — London : Futura, 1982. — 151p ; 18cm. — (Heritage)
ISBN 0-7088-2201-0 (pbk) : £1.50 B82-37027

508.424 — England. Severn Estuary. Sites of special scientific interest. Effects of proposed tidal power barrages

McKirdy, A. P.. Potential effects of barrage construction and operation on sites of earth science interest : Severn tidal power / A.P. McKirdy ; report ... commissioned by the United Kingdom Atomic Energy Authority. — [Shrewsbury] : Nature Conservancy Council, 1981. — 22p : maps ; 30cm
ISBN 0-86139-150-0 (spiral) : Unpriced
B82-02087

508.425′82 — Hertfordshire. Stevenage. Nature reserves: Watery Grove Nature Reserve. Nature trails — *Visitors′ guides*

Hertfordshire & Middlesex Trust for Nature Conservation. Watery Grove : nature trail guide / Herts & Middx Trust for Nature Conservation. — [Hitchin] ([c/o Hon. Sec., Offley Place, Great Offley, Hitchin, Herts. SG5 3DS]) : [The Trust], [1981?]. — 8p : ill ; 21cm
Cover title. — Map on inside cover
£0.20 (pbk) B82-09516

508.425′85 — Hertfordshire. London Colney. Nature reserves: Broad Colney Lakes Nature Reserve — *Visitors′ guides*

Hertfordshire & Middlesex Trust for Nature Conservation. Broad Colney Lakes Nature Reserve / Herts & Middlesex Trust for Nature Conservation. — [Hitchin] ([c/o Hon. Sec., Offley Place, Great Offley, Hitchin, Herts. SG5 3DS]) : [The Trust], [1981?]. — 7p : ill,2maps ; 22cm
£0.15 (unbound) B82-09515

508.427′8′05 — Cumbria. Lake District. Natural history — *Serials*

News letter of the Cumbria Trust for Nature Conservation. — New ser. no.1 (Aug. 1981)-. — Ambleside ([Rydal Rd,] Ambleside [LA22 9AN]) : The Trust, 1981-. — v. : ill ; 30cm
Three issues yearly. — Continues: News letter (Cumbria Naturalists′ Trust)
ISSN 0263-2179 = News letter of the Cumbria Trust for Nature Conservation : £0.20 per issue
B82-19852

508.428′47 — North Yorkshire. Forge Valley. Nature reserves: Forge Valley Woods National Nature Reserve. Nuture trails — *Visitors′ guides*

Nature Conservancy Council. Forge Valley Woods National Nature Reserve / Nature Conservancy Council. — London : [The Council], c1978. — 1folded sheet([6]p) : ill (some col.) ; 22cm
ISBN 0-86139-000-8 : £0.10 B82-35382

508.428′61 — Durham *(County)*. **Upper Teesdale. Nature reserves: Upper Teesdale National Nature Reserve. Nature trails: Widdybank Fell Nature Trail** — *Walkers′ guides*

Nature Conservancy Council. Upper Teesdale National Nature Reserve : Widdybank Fell nature trail : detailed guide / Nature Conservancy Council. — Banbury : The Council, c1977. — 18p : ill(some col.),(1col.map) ; 15x21cm
ISBN 0-901204-86-2 (unbound) : £0.20
B82-35381

508.428′81 — Northumberland. Linn Burn Basin. Natural environment. Research

Bevan, J. R.. The Polytechnic experimental catchment for teaching and research : first report / [J.R. Bevan]. — Newcastle upon Tyne ([Ellison Place, Newcastle upon Tyne]) : School of Geography and Environmental Studies, Newcastle upon Tyne Polytechnic, 1981. — iv leaves,68p : ill,maps ; 30cm. — (Occasional series in geography, ISSN 0142-6370 ; no.4)
Bibliography: p62-68
Unpriced (pbk) B82-06688

508.429′25 — Gwynedd. Aber. Nature reserves: Coedydd Aber National Nature Reserve. Nature trails — *Visitors′ guides*

Nature Conservancy Council. Coedydd Aber Nature Trail : National Nature Reserve / Nature Conservancy Council/Cyngor Gwarchod Natur. — Rev. — Bangor, N. Wales : Nature Conservancy Council, North Wales Region, c1977. — [12]p : ill(some col.),1col.map ; 21cm
Previous ed.: 1975
ISBN 0-86139-081-4 (unbound) : Unpriced
B82-17445

508.491′5 — Faeroe Islands. Natural environment

The **Physical** environment of the Faeroe Islands / edited by G.K. Rutherford. — The Hague ; London : Junk, 1982. — 148p : ill(some col.),maps ; 24cm. — (Monographiae biologicae ; v.46)
Bibliography: p145-146. — Includes index
ISBN 90-619-3099-5 : Unpriced B82-24294

508.866′5 — Galápagos Islands. Natural environment

Moore, Tui De Roy. Galapagos : island lost in time / Tui De Roy Morre ; with an introduction by Peter Matthiessen. — London : Allen & Unwin, 1982, c1980. — 71p,[94]p of plates : col.ill,2maps ; 31cm
Originally published: New York : Viking, 1980. — Bibliography: p53
ISBN 0-04-918003-7 : Unpriced : CIP rev.
B82-03714

509 — SCIENCE. HISTORICAL AND GEOGRAPHICAL TREATMENT

509 — Science, *to 1700*

Webster, Charles, *1936-*. From Paracelsus to Newton : magic and the making of modern science. — Cambridge : Cambridge University Press, Jan.1983. — [116]p. — (The Eddington memorial lectures)
ISBN 0-521-24919-8 : £12.50 : CIP entry
B82-40901

509 — Science, *to 1979*

Selected studies : physics-astrophysics, mathematics, history of science : a volume dedicated to the memory of Albert Einstein / editors Thermistocles M. Rassias, George M. Rassias. — Amsterdam ; Oxford : North-Holland, 1982. — xii,392p : ill ; 23cm
Includes bibliographies
ISBN 0-444-86161-0 : £41.40
Primary classification 510 B82-28562

509′.032 — Science, *1630-1720*

Hall, A. Rupert. From Galileo to Newton / by A. Rupert Hall. — New York : Dover ; London : Constable, 1982. — 379p,[16]p of plates : ill,1facsim ; 22cm
Originally published: London : Collins, 1963. — Includes index
ISBN 0-486-24227-7 (pbk) : Unpriced
B82-34631

509′.034 — Science, *ca 1850-1930 — Conference proceedings*

Science, technology and society in the time of Alfred Nobel. — Oxford : Pergamon, Nov.1982. — [400]p
Conference papers
ISBN 0-08-027939-2 : £25.00 : CIP entry
B82-27834

509′.2′2 — Great Britain. Science. Organisations: Royal Society. Fellows. Signatures, *to 1979 — Facsimiles*

Royal Society. The signatures in the first journal-book and the charter-book of the Royal Society : being a facsimile of the signatures of the founders, patrons and fellows of the Society from the year 1660 down to the present time. — 4th ed. — London : The Society, 1980. — ix,182p : chiefly facsims,1port ; 46cm
Previous ed.: 1950. — Includes index
ISBN 0-85403-115-4 : £35.00 B82-25052

509′.2′2 — Scientists — *Biographies*

McGraw-Hill modern scientists and engineers. — [Rev. and expanded ed.]. — New York ; London : McGraw-Hill, c1980. — 3v. : ports ; 28cm
Previous ed.: published as McGraw-Hill modern men of science. 1966-1968. — In slip case. — Includes index
ISBN 0-07-045266-0 : Unpriced B82-40736

509′.2′2 — Scientists, *to 1980 — Biographies*

A **Biographical** dictionary of scientists / edited by Trevor I. Williams ; assistant editor Sonia Withers. — 3rd ed. — London : Black, 1982. — xiv,674p ; 25cm
Previous ed.: 1974. — Includes index
ISBN 0-7136-2228-8 : £15.00 : CIP rev.
B82-09606

509′.2′2 — Women scientists — *Personal observations — Collections*

Women scientists : the road to liberation / edited by Derek Richter. — London : Macmillan, 1982. — 219p ; 23cm
Includes index
ISBN 0-333-32468-4 : £10.00 B82-32339

509′.2′4 — Science. Darwin, Erasmus — *Correspondence, diaries, etc*

Darwin, Erasmus. The letters of Erasmus Darwin / edited by Desmond King-Hele. — Cambridge : Cambridge University Press, 1981. — xxxii,363p,[21]p of plates : ill,1map,facsims,ports ; 24cm
Includes index
ISBN 0-521-23706-8 : £45.00 : CIP rev.
B81-20504

509′.2′4 — Science. Theories of Descartes, René

Clarke, Desmond M.. Descartes′ philosophy of science. — Manchester : Manchester University Press, May 1982. — [389]p. — (Studies in intellectual history)
ISBN 0-7190-0868-9 : £16.50 : CIP entry
B82-07589

509′.2′4 — Science. Wren, *Sir* **Christopher** — *Biographies*

Bennett, J. A.. The mathematical science of Christopher Wren. — Cambridge : Cambridge University Press, Aug.1982. — [160]p
ISBN 0-521-24608-3 : £15.00 : CIP entry
B82-25498

509′.38 — Ancient Greece. Science, *B.C.600-A.D.199*

Science and speculation : studies in Hellenistic theory and practice. — Cambridge : Cambridge University Press, Nov.1982. — [384]p
ISBN 0-521-24689-x : £25.00 : CIP entry
B82-40327

509′.492 — Netherlands. Science, *ca 1585-ca 1695*

Struik, Dirk J.. The land of Stevin and Huygens : a sketch of science and technology in the Dutch Republic during the Golden Century / Dirk J. Struik. — Dordrecht ; London : Reidel, c1981. — xx,162p,[24]p of plates : ill,facsims,ports ; 23cm. — (Studies in the history of modern science ; v.7)
Translation of 3rd ed. of: Het land van Stevin en Huygens. — Bibliography: p147-151. — Includes index
ISBN 90-277-1236-0 (cased) : Unpriced
ISBN 90-277-1237-9 (pbk) : Unpriced
B82-00471

509′.51 — China. Science — *History*

Needham, Joseph. Science and civilisation in China. — Cambridge : Cambridge University Press
Vol.5: Chemistry and chemical technology
Pt.4: Spagyrical discovery and invention : apparatus, theories and gifts / by Joseph Needham with the collaboration of Ho Ping-Yii and Lu Gwei-Djen and a contribution by Nathan Sivin. — 1980. — xlviii,772p : ill ; 26cm
Bibliography p510-692. — Includes index
ISBN 0-521-08573-x : £48.00 : CIP rev.
Also classified at 609′.51 B80-25535

509′.51 — China. Science. Policies of government, *1949-1956*

Xu, Liangying. Science and socialist construction in China / by Xu Liangying and Fan Dainian ; edited with an introduction by Pierre M. Perrolle ; foreword to the English edition by Xu Liangying ; translated by John C.S. Hsu. — New York : Sharpe ; London : Distributed by Europan, c1982. — xxvii,225p ; 24cm. — (The China book project)
Translated from the Chinese
ISBN 0-87332-189-8 : Unpriced
Also classified at 609′.51 B82-23789

509′.51 — China. Science, *to ca 1800*

Needham, Joseph. The shorter science and civilisation in China / an abridgement of Joseph Needham's original text ; Colin A. Ronan. — Cambridge : Cambridge University Press
Vol.2. — 1981. — xii,459p : ill,charts,facsims ; 24cm
Vol.3 and a section of Vol.4, Pt.1 of the major series. — Bibliography: p389-394. — Includes index
ISBN 0-521-23582-0 : £15.00 : CIP rev.
Also classified at 609′.51 B81-31189

509′.56 — Middle East. Science

Sardar, Ziauddin. Science and technology in the Middle East. — London : Longman, Nov.1982. — [350]p. — (Longman guides to world science and technology)
ISBN 0-582-90052-2 : £38.00 : CIP entry
Also classified at 609′.56 B82-26544

509′.73 — United States. Science, *1900-1939*

Science in America : a documentary history 1900-1939 / edited, selected, and with an introduction by Nathan Reingold and Ida H. Reingold. — Chicago ; London : University of Chicago Press, 1981. — xii,490p : ill ; 24cm. — (The Chicago history of science and medicine)
Includes index
ISBN 0-226-70946-9 : £12.00 B82-19783

510 — MATHEMATICS

510 — Applied mathematics

Handbook of applicable mathematics. — Chichester : Wiley, Aug.1982
Vol.4: Analysis. — [832]p
ISBN 0-471-10141-9 : £27.50 : CIP entry
B82-15817

510 — Applied mathematics — *For schools*

Mathematics and the telegraph pole. — Cheltenham : Thornes, Sept.1982. — (Mathematics towards relevance)
Unit 1. — [56]p
ISBN 0-85950-358-5 (pbk) : £1.50 : CIP entry
B82-30704

Mathematics and the telegraph pole. — Cheltenham : Thornes, Sept.1982. — (Mathematics towards relevance)
Unit 2. — [56]p
ISBN 0-85950-359-3 (pbk) : £1.50 : CIP entry
B82-30705

Mathematics and the telegraph pole. — Cheltenham : Thornes, Sept.1982. — (Mathematics towards relevance)
Teacher's guide. — [48]p
ISBN 0-85950-363-1 (pbk) : £1.50 : CIP entry
B82-30710

510 — Great Britain. Secondary schools. Curriculum subjects: Mathematics. Problem solving — *Case studies*

Lingard, David. Mathematical investigations in the classroom / David Lingard. — Derby : Association of Teachers of Mathematics, 1980. — [57]p : ill ; 30cm
ISBN 0-900095-35-0 (spiral) : £1.35
B82-34501

510 — Mathematics

Al-Moajil, Abdullah H.. Basic mathematics : a precalculus course for science and engineering / Abdullah H. Al-Moajil and Abdelali Benharbit. — Dhahran : University of Petroleum and Minerals ; Chichester : Wiley, c1981. — xii,308p : ill ; 24cm
Includes index
ISBN 0-471-27941-2 (cased) : £14.00 : CIP rev.
ISBN 0-471-27942-0 (pbk) : Unpriced
B81-28070

Courant, Richard. What is mathematics? : an elementary approach to ideas and methods / by Richard Courant and Herbert Robbins. — Oxford : Oxford University Press, 1941, c1969 (1980 printing). — 521p : ill ; 23cm. — (A Galaxy book)
Bibliography: p511-514. — Includes index
ISBN 0-19-502517-2 (pbk) : £4.50 B82-25897

Developing mathematical thinking / [The EM235 Course Team]. — Milton Keynes : Open University Press. — (Educational studies/mathematics : a second level course)
At head of title: The Open University
Topic 2: Setting up and solving / prepared by the Course Team. — 1982. — 70p : ill ; 21x30cm. — (EM235 ; topic 2)
ISBN 0-335-13102-6 (pbk) : Unpriced
B82-31930

Developing mathematical thinking / [The EM235 Course Team]. — Milton Keynes : Open University Press. — (Educational studies/mathematics : a second level course)
At head of title: The Open University
Topic 3: Measuring. — 1982. — 75p : ill ; 21x30cm. — (EM235 ; topic 3)
Bibliography: p71
ISBN 0-335-13103-4 (pbk) : Unpriced
B82-31931

Developing mathematical thinking / [The EM235 Course Team]. — Milton Keynes : Open University Press. — (Educational studies/mathematics : a second level course)
At head of title: The Open University
Topic 4: Developing mathematical thinking / prepared by the Course Team. — 1982. — 56p : ill ; 21x30cm. — (EM235 ; topic 4)
Bibliography: p56
ISBN 0-335-13105-0 (pbk) : Unpriced
B82-31932

Developing mathematical thinking / [The EM235 Course Team]. — Milton Keynes : Open University Press. — (Educational studies/mathematics : a second level course)
At head of title: The Open University
Project guide. — 1982. — 75p : ill ; 21x30cm. — (EM235 ; PG)
ISBN 0-335-13104-2 (pbk) : Unpriced
B82-31935

Developing mathematical thinking. — [Milton Keynes] : Open University Press. — (Educational studies/mathematics : a second level course)
At head of title: The Open University
Wallet / prepared by the course team. — c1982. — 1portfolio : ill,forms ; 30cm. — (EM235 ; wallet)
Cover title
ISBN 0-335-13107-7 : Unpriced B82-21195

Devlin, Keith J.. Sets, functions and logic. — London : Chapman and Hall, Apr.1981. — [96]p
ISBN 0-412-22660-x : £6.00 : CIP entry
ISBN 0-412-22670-7 (pbk) : £2.95 B81-02370

Graham, Lynne. Maths help / by Lynne Graham. — London : British Broadcasting Corporation, 1982
Part 1. — 112p : ill ; 22cm
Published to accompany the BBC Continuing Education television series
ISBN 0-563-16487-5 (pbk) : £3.95 B82-12483

Harper, W. M.. Basic mathematics / W.M. Harper and L.W.T. Stafford. — Plymouth : Macdonald and Evans, 1981. — viii,181p : ill ; 19cm. — (The M & E handbook series)
Includes index
ISBN 0-7121-0287-6 (pbk) : £3.25 B82-01909

Hulbert, J.. Think about it. — London : Heinemann Educational, Jan.1983
Book 1. — [64]p
ISBN 0-435-50420-7 (pbk) : £0.95 : CIP entry
B82-33212

Hulbert, J.. Think about it. — London : Heinemann Educational, Jan.1983
Book 2. — [64]p
ISBN 0-435-50421-5 (pbk) : £0.95 : CIP entry
B82-33213

Hulbert, J.. Think about it. — London : Heinemann Educational, Jan.1983
Book 3. — [64]p
ISBN 0-435-50422-3 (pbk) : £0.95 : CIP entry
B82-33214

Hulbert, J.. Think about it. — London : Heinemann Educational, Jan.1983
Book 4. — [64]p
ISBN 0-435-50423-1 (pbk) : £0.95 : CIP entry
B82-33215

Hulbert, J.. Think about it. — London : Heinemann Educational, Jan.1983
Teacher's book. — 1v.
ISBN 0-435-50424-x (pbk) : £2.95 : CIP entry
B82-33216

Kudrîavtsev, V. A.. A brief course of higher mathematics / V.A. Kudryavtsev and B.P. Demidovich ; translated from the Russian by Leonid Levant. — Moscow : Mir ; [London] : Distributed by Central Books, 1981. — 693p : ill ; 23cm
Translation of: Kratkiĭ kurs vyssheĭ matematiki. — Added t.p. in Russian. — Includes index
ISBN 0-7147-1653-7 : £5.25 B82-02531

Littlewood, J. E.. Collected papers of J.E. Littlewood. — Oxford : Clarendon Press, Sept.1981
Vol.1. — [750]p
ISBN 0-19-853353-5 : £40.00 : CIP entry
B81-20530

Mason, John. Thinking mathematically. — London : Addison-Wesley, Apr.1982. — [256]p
ISBN 0-201-10238-2 (pbk) : £5.95 : CIP entry
B82-04292

Murphy, Frank. Square one : a basic maths course for adults / by Frank Murphy. — Cambridge : National Extension College, 1973 (1977 [printing]). — 3v. : ill ; 30cm. — (National Extension College correspondence texts ; course no.M10)
ISBN 0-902404-23-7 (pbk) : Unpriced
B82-38349

510 — Mathematics *continuation*

Murphy, Patrick, *1925-*. Modern mathematics made simple / Patrick Murphy. — London : Heinemann, c1982. — ix,275p : ill ; 22cm. — (Made simple books)
Includes index
ISBN 0-434-98544-9 (cased) : Unpriced
ISBN 0-434-98545-7 (pbk) : £2.95 B82-37748

Perry, Owen. Mastering mathematics / O. & J. Perry. — London : Macmillan, 1982. — xiii,386p : ill ; 23cm. — (Macmillan master series)
Includes index
ISBN 0-333-31292-9 (cased) : £8.95
ISBN 0-333-31043-8 (pbk) : Unpriced
B82-17103

Rolf, Howard L.. Mathematics / Howard L. Rolf. — Boston [Mass.] ; London : Allyn and Bacon, c1982. — 486p : ill ; 25cm
Text, ill on lining papers. — Includes index
ISBN 0-205-07627-0 : Unpriced B82-26763

Selected studies : physics-astrophysics, mathematics, history of science : a volume dedicated to the memory of Albert Einstein / editors Thermistocles M. Rassias, George M. Rassias. — Amsterdam ; Oxford : North-Holland, 1982. — xii,392p : ill ; 23cm
Includes bibliographies
ISBN 0-444-86161-0 : £41.40
Also classified at 523.01 ; 509 B82-28562

Seven years of Manifold 1968-1980 / edited by Ian Stewart, John Jaworski. — Nantwich : Shiva, c1981. — ii,94p : ill ; 24cm
ISBN 0-906812-07-0 (pbk) : Unpriced : CIP rev. B81-10008

Smithers, Graham. M23M mathematics 'A' Level : a course leading to the University of London G.C.E. 'A' Level examination in mathematics (syllabus D — subject 391) / written by Graham Smithers. — [Cambridge] : National Extension College, 1977. — 4v. : ill ; 30cm. — (National Extension College correspondence texts ; course no.M23M)
Vol.1. (1978 printing); vol.2. c1976 (1979 printing). — Vols.1 and 3 of course M23M form vols. 1 and 2 of course M23P
ISBN 0-902404-82-2 (pbk) : Unpriced
ISBN 0-902404-76-8 (v.1)
ISBN 0-902404-78-4 (v.2)
ISBN 0-902404-77-6 (v.3)
ISBN 0-902404-79-2 (v.4) B82-38174

Smithers, Graham. M23P pure mathematics 'A' Level : a course leading to the University of London G.C.E. 'A' Level examination in pure mathematics (subject 405) / written by Graham Smithers. — [Cambridge] : National Extension College, 1977. — 4v. : ill ; 30cm. — (National Extension College correspondence texts ; course no.M23P)
Vols.1 and 2 of course M23P form vols.1 and 3 of course M23M. — Vol.1 (1978 printing); vol.4. c1979. — Vol.3 has joint author Eileen Aldworth
ISBN 0-902404-83-0 (pbk) : Unpriced
ISBN 0-902404-76-8 (v.1)
ISBN 0-902404-77-6 (v.2)
ISBN 0-902404-80-6 (v.3)
ISBN 0-902404-81-4 (v.4) B82-38175

Smithers, Graham. Mathematics GCE 'O' Level / author: Graham Smithers. — Repr. with corrections. — Cambridge : National Extension College, 1980. — 3v. + Diagram supplement (27p : ill ; 30cm) : ill ; 30cm. — (National Extension College correspondence texts ; course no.M5(1))
Originally published: 1971. — Introductory course notes and worksheets (26p : ill ; 30cm) as insert. — Vol.1 contains lessons 1-8, vol.2 lessons 9-16, vol.3 lessons 17-24
ISBN 0-86082-010-6 (pbk) : Unpriced
ISBN 0-86082-006-8 (v.1) : Unpriced
ISBN 0-86082-007-6 (v.2) : Unpriced
ISBN 0-86082-008-4 (v.3) : Unpriced
B82-38358

Smithers, Graham. Modern mathematics 'O' Level / by Graham Smithers. — [Cambridge] : National Extension College, 1972 (1977 [printing]). — 3v. ; 30cm. — (National Extension College correspondence texts ; course no.M12)
ISBN 0-902404-07-5 (pbk) : Unpriced
ISBN 0-902404-13-x (v.2)
ISBN 0-902404-14-8 (v.3) B82-38176

Solomon, Charles, *1898-*. Mathematics / Charles Solomon ; illustrated by Kenneth Ody. — London : Hamlyn, 1969 (1982 printing). — 159p : col.ill ; 19cm
Includes index
ISBN 0-600-35652-3 (cased) : £2.95
ISBN 0-600-36110-1 (pbk) : £1.75 B82-37051

Sperling Abraham P.. Mathematics made simple / Abraham Sperling and Monroe Stuart ; advisory editor Patrick Murphy. — Rev. — London : Heinemann, 1981. — xi,273p : ill ; 22cm. — (Made simple books)
Originally published: London : W.H. Allen, 1977. — Includes index
ISBN 0-434-98491-4 (pbk) : £2.50 B82-20424

Studies in pure mathematics. — Milton Keynes : Open University Press. — (Mathematics : a third level course)
At head of title: The Open University
Logic
Includes indes
Units 5-8 / prepared by the [M335 Logic Option Course Team]. — 1981. — 106p ; 30cm. — (M335 ; L 5-8)
ISBN 0-335-14013-0 (pbk) : Unpriced
B82-15091

Studies in pure mathematics. — Milton Keynes : Open University Press. — (Mathematics : a third level course)
At head of title: The Open University
Metric and topological space
Units 5-8 / prepared by the Course Team. — 1982. — 117p : ill ; 30cm. — (M335 ; MT5-8)
ISBN 0-335-14017-3 (pbk) : Unpriced
B82-32215

Studies in pure mathematics. — Milton Keynes : Open University Press. — (Mathematics : a third level course)
At head of title: The Open University
Number theory
Units 5-8 / prepared by The Course Team. — 1981. — 86p : ill ; 30cm. — (M335 ; NT 5-8)
ISBN 0-335-14011-4 (pbk) : Unpriced
B82-04759

Wiener, Norbert. Collected works with commentaries / Norbert Wiener ; edited by P. Masani. — Cambridge, Mass. ; London : MIT. — (Mathematicians of our time)
Vol.3: The Hopf-Wiener integral equation, prediction and filtering, quantum mechanics and relativity, miscellaneous mathematical papers. — c1981. — xi,753p : 2ports ; 26cm
Includes articles in French and German. — Includes index
ISBN 0-262-23107-7 : £35.00 B82-37519

510 — Mathematics. Applications

Oliveira-Pinto, F.. Applicable mathematics of non-physical phenomena / F. Oliveira-Pinto and B.W. Conolly. — Chichester : Horwood, 1982. — 269p : ill ; 24cm. — (Ellis Horwood series in mathematics and its applications)
Bibliography: p264-265. — Includes index
ISBN 0-85312-366-7 (cased) : £19.50 : CIP rev.
ISBN 0-85312-413-2 (pbk) : Unpriced
ISBN 0-470-27297-x (Halsted) B81-39212

510 — Mathematics — *For African students — For schools*

Zepp, R. A.. Essential mathematics for African students. — Cheltenham : Stanley Thornes, Jan.1983
Student's edition. — [352]p
ISBN 0-85950-382-8 (pbk) : £4.65 : CIP entry
B82-33117

Zepp, R. A.. Essential mathematics for African students. — Cheltenham : Stanley Thornes, Jan.1983
Teacher's edition. — [416]p
ISBN 0-85950-391-7 (pbk) : £6.00 : CIP entry
B82-33118

510 — Mathematics — *For Caribbean students*

Singh, M. P.. Oxford mathematics for the Caribbean. — Oxford : Oxford University Press
5 / M.P. Singh, V. Bentt. — 1982. — 174p : ill ; 25cm
ISBN 0-19-914084-7 (pbk) : Unpriced
B82-39062

510 — Mathematics — *For children*

Kelsey, Edward. Mrs Witchitt works it out!. — Cambridge : Cambridge University Press, Dec.1981. — [14]p. — (Maths with a story!)
ISBN 0-521-28606-9 (pbk) : £0.65 : CIP entry
B81-34005

Snell, Gordon. Max — the Muddleville millionaire. — Cambridge : Cambridge University Press, Dec.1981. — [14]p. — (Maths with a story!)
ISBN 0-521-28607-7 (pbk) : £0.65 : CIP entry
B81-34004

Snell, Gordon. Muddleville olympics. — Cambridge : Cambridge University Press, Dec.1981. — [14]p. — (Maths with a story!)
ISBN 0-521-28609-3 (pbk) : £0.65 : CIP entry
B81-34003

Ward, Peter. Pirate gold. — Cambridge : Cambridge University Press, Dec.1981. — [14] p. — (Maths with a story!)
ISBN 0-521-28608-5 (pbk) : £0.65 : CIP entry
B81-34002

510 — Mathematics — *For computer sciences*

McKeown, G. P.. Mathematics for computing / G.P. McKeown, V.J. Rayward-Smith. — London : Macmillan, 1982. — 428p : ill ; 25cm. — (Macmillan computer science series)
Bibliography: p406. — Includes index
ISBN 0-333-29169-7 (cased) : £18.00
ISBN 0-333-29170-0 (pbk) : Unpriced
B82-38787

510 — Mathematics — *For Irish students*

O'Shea, Frank. Complete mathematics : Leaving Certificate ordinary course / Frank O'Shea. — [Tallaght] : Folens, c1982. — 544p : ill ; 25cm
ISBN 0-86121-162-6 (pbk) : Unpriced
B82-17860

510 — Mathematics — *For Nigerian students*

Okosi, C. N.. Junior secondary mathematics / C.N. Okosi, V.W. Ferris, J.N. Busbridge. — London : Evans
1
Student's book. — 1981. — 236p : ill ; 25cm
ISBN 0-237-50485-5 (pbk) : Unpriced
B82-00062

Okosi, C. N.. Junior secondary mathematics / C.N. Okosi, V.W. Ferris, J.N. Busbridge. — London : Evans
Student's book 2. — 1982. — 231p : ill ; 25cm
ISBN 0-237-50521-5 (pbk) : Unpriced
B82-24915

Okosi, C. N.. Junior secondary mathematics / C.N. Okosi, V.W. Ferris, J.N. Busbridge. — London : Evans
Tutor text 2. — 1982. — 120p : ill ; 22cm
Includes index
ISBN 0-237-50523-1 (pbk) : Unpriced
B82-24919

Okosi, C. N.. Junior secondary mathematics / C.N. Okosi, V.W. Ferris, J.N. Busbridge. — London : Evans
3
Tutor text. — 1982. — vi,117p : ill ; 22cm
ISBN 0-237-50526-6 (pbk) : Unpriced
B82-35035

510 — Mathematics — *For schools*

Bostock, L.. Further pure mathematics. — Cheltenham : Thornes, Jan.1983. — [734]p
ISBN 0-85950-103-5 (pbk) : £7.50 : CIP entry
B82-36157

510 — Mathematics — *For schools*
continuation

Bostock, L.. Mathematics — the core course for A-level / L. Bostock, S. Chandler. — Cheltenham : Thornes, 1981. — xiii,752p : ill ; 23cm
Includes index
ISBN 0-85950-306-2 (pbk) : £6.95 : CIP rev.
B81-16902

Brighouse, Alan. Peak mathematics / Alan Brighouse, David Godber, Peter Patilla. — Walton-on-Thames : Nelson
Teacher's guide 5. — c1982. — 24p ; 25cm
Cover title. — Text on inside covers
ISBN 0-17-421315-8 (pbk) : Unpriced
B82-27271

Celia, C. W.. Advanced mathematics. — Basingstoke : Macmillan Education
2 / C.W. Celia, A.T.F. Nice, K.F. Elliott. — 1982. — 411p : ill ; 24cm
Includes index
ISBN 0-333-23193-7 (pbk) : Unpriced : CIP rev.
B81-35800

Certificate mathematics / Modular Mathematics Organization. — London : Heinemann Educational
Unit M13: Variation. — 1980. — 39p : ill ; 24cm
Cover title
ISBN 0-435-50936-5 (pbk) : £0.55 : CIP rev.
B80-09195

Certificate mathematics / Modular Mathematics Organization. — London : Heinemann Educational
Units M13-M20. — 1980. — 240p : ill ; 24cm
ISBN 0-435-50935-7 (pbk) : £3.50 : CIP rev.
B80-09666

Cheah, Tat Huat. Additional mathematics / Cheah Tat Huat, Tan Beng Theam, Khor Gark Kim. — Kuala Lumpur ; Oxford : Oxford University Press, c1977 (1978 [printing]). — 236p : ill ; 26cm. — (Modern certificate guides)
ISBN 0-19-581069-4 (pbk) : £1.95 B82-33039

Graham, Duncan. Revise mathematics : a complete revision course for O level and CSE / Duncan Graham. — Rev. [ed.]. — London : Letts, 1981, c1979. — vi,205p : ill ; 30cm. — (Letts study aids)
Previous ed.: 1979. — Includes index
ISBN 0-85097-357-0 (pbk) : £3.65 B82-19113

Individualised mathematics. — Cambridge : Cambridge University Press, Mar.1982
Further matrices and transformations. — [138]p
ISBN 0-521-28675-1 (pbk) : £3.25 : CIP entry
B82-11484

Individualised mathematics. — Cambridge : Cambridge University Press
Geometry 1
Symmetry and trigonometry. — Nov.1981. — [112]p
ISBN 0-521-28377-9 (pbk) : £2.60 : CIP entry
B81-31230

Individualised mathematics. — Cambridge : Cambridge University Press, Mar.1982
Geometry 2
ISBN 0-521-28466-x (pbk) : £2.60 : CIP entry
B82-11482

Infant mathematics : a development through activity / Scottish Primary Mathematics Group. — London : Heinemann Educational
1st Stage
Teacher's book. — 1980. — 244p : ill ; 25cm
ISBN 0-435-02941-x (pbk) : £4.00 : CIP rev.
B80-20575

Infant mathematics : a development through activity / Scottish Primary Mathematics Group. — London : Heinemann Educational
2nd stage
Teacher's notes. — 1981. — 277p : ill ; 25cm + Teacher's pack
ISBN 0-435-02945-2 (pbk) : £4.95 : CIP rev.
ISBN 0-435-02946-0 (teacher's pack) : 5.75
B81-34206

Integrated mathematics scheme. — London : Bell & Hyman
Book C. — Sept.1982. — [128]p
ISBN 0-7135-1338-1 (pbk) : £4.95 : CIP entry
B82-22431

Irwin, J. R.. Essentials of pure mathematics / J.R. Irwin. — London : Edward Arnold, 1981. — viii,352p : ill ; 23cm
Includes index
ISBN 0-7131-0551-8 (pbk) : £5.95 : CIP rev.
B81-11917

Kaner, Peter. Integrated mathematics scheme. — London : Bell & Hyman, Apr.1982
Book 1A. — [192]p
ISBN 0-7135-1330-6 (pbk) : £3.95 : CIP entry
B82-07815

Kaner, Peter. Integrated mathematics scheme. — London : Bell & Hyman, Apr.1982
Book 1B. — [208]p
ISBN 0-7135-1331-4 (pbk) : £3.95 : CIP entry
B82-07816

Kaner, Peter. Integrated mathematics scheme. — London : Bell & Hyman, Sept.1982
Teachers' Book 1. — [96]p
ISBN 0-7135-1334-9 (pbk) : £3.50 : CIP entry
B82-20047

Kaner, Peter. Integrated mathematics scheme. — London : Bell & Hyman
Book A2. — Sept.1982. — [200]p
ISBN 0-7135-1332-2 (pbk) : £3.95 : CIP entry
B82-20774

Kaner, Peter. Integrated mathematics scheme. — London : Bell & Hyman
Book B2. — Sept.1982. — [216]p
ISBN 0-7135-1333-0 (pbk) : £3.95 : CIP entry
B82-20649

Kaner, Peter. Integrated mathematics scheme. — London : Bell & Hyman
ISBN 0-7135-1339-x (pbk) : £3.50 : CIP entry
B82-21391

Modern mathematics for schools / [Scottish Mathematics Group]. — Glasgow : Blackie
Extra questions to accompany mathsheets 1. — c1980. — [77]p : ill ; 30cm
ISBN 0-216-91028-5 (unbound) : £2.25
ISBN 0-550-75962-x (W. & R. Chambers)
B82-20139

Modern mathematics for schools / [Scottish Mathematics Group]. — Glasgow : Blackie
Extra questions to accompany mathsheets 1
Teachers' ed. — 1980. — [77]p : ill(some col.) ; 30cm
ISBN 0-216-91029-3 (unbound) : £2.75
ISBN 0-550-75963-8 (W. & R. Chambers)
B82-20138

Modern mathematics for schools / Scottish Mathematics Group. — Glasgow : Blackie
Mathsheets to accompany Modern mathematics for schools book 2 : Teachers' edition. — 1975, 1977 [printing]. — [142]p : ill ; 30cm
ISBN 0-216-89826-9 (unbound) : Unpriced
B82-01632

Norton, F. G. J.. Advanced mathematics / F.G.T. Norton. — London : Pan, 1982. — vi,321p : ill ; 20cm. — (Pan study aids)
Includes index
ISBN 0-330-26615-2 (pbk) : £2.95 B82-20433

Okosi, C. N.. Junior secondary mathematics / C.N. Okosi, V.W. Ferris, J.N. Busbridge. — London : Evans
1
Tutor text. — 1981. — viii,151p : ill ; 22cm
Includes index
ISBN 0-237-50486-3 (pbk) : Unpriced
B82-13396

Okosi, C. N.. Junior secondary mathematics / C.N. Okosi, V.W. Ferris, J.N. Busbridge. — London : Evans
3. — 1982
Student's book. — 215p : ill ; 25cm
ISBN 0-237-50524-x (pbk) : Unpriced
B82-27291

Perkins, Martin. Advanced maths. — London : Bell and Hyman
Book 1. — Feb.1982. — [573]p
ISBN 0-7135-1272-5 (pbk) : £5.95 : CIP entry
B81-38316

Raven, A. J.. Mathematics for everyday life / A.J. Raven and S.M. Ault. — London : Heinemann Educational
Bk.5. — 3rd ed. — 1980. — 160p : ill ; 22cm
Previous ed.: 1972. — Text on inside covers
ISBN 0-435-50774-5 (pbk) : £1.90 B82-39147

School Mathematics Project. The School Mathematics Project. — Cambridge : Cambridge University Press
New Book 3
Part 2. — Dec.1981. — [200]p
ISBN 0-521-28626-3 (pbk) : £2.95 : CIP entry
B82-01334

School Mathematics Project. The School Mathematics Project. — Cambridge : Cambridge University Press
New book 4. — Oct.1982
Part 1. — [216]p
ISBN 0-521-28945-9 (pbk) : £3.50 : CIP entry
B82-40317

Schools Mathematics Project. Individualised mathematics. — Cambridge : Cambridge University Press, June 1981
Matrix algebra and isometric transformations. — [96]p
ISBN 0-521-28265-9 (pbk) : £2.60 : CIP entry
B81-19165

Scottish Primary Mathematics Group. Topics and activities in mathematics. — London : Heinemann
Answers book. — Jan.1983. — [80]p
ISBN 0-435-02994-0 (pbk) : £3.50 : CIP entry
B82-36132

Scottish Primary Mathematics Group. Topics and activities in mathematics. — London : Heinemann
Teacher's notes. — Jan.1983. — [144]p
ISBN 0-435-02993-2 (pbk) : £5.50 : CIP entry
B82-36131

Stead, Jeffrey. Core mathematics. — Cambridge : Cambridge University Press
Book 1. — Dec.1981. — [320]p
ISBN 0-521-23232-5 (pbk) : £2.95 : CIP entry
B81-30897

Stead, Jeffrey. Core mathematics. — Cambridge : Cambridge University Press, Dec.1981
Book 2. — [304]p
ISBN 0-521-23233-3 (pbk) : £2.95 : CIP entry
B81-32599

Svennson, Leif. Hey, mathematics / [Leif Svennson, Curt Oreberg, Matts Hastad] ; general editor Jim Boucher. — [Edinburgh] : Caffrey Smith
Translated from the Swedish
Module 3
Answer book. — c1974 (1979 [printing]). — 38p ; 24cm
Cover title
ISBN 0-7024-0602-3 (pbk) : Unpriced
B82-37562

Svennson, Leif. Hey, mathematics / [Leif Svennson, Curt Oreberg, Matts Hastad] ; general editor Jim Boucher. — [Edinburgh] : Caffrey Smith
Translated from the Swedish
Module 6. — c1980
Book 1: Pineapple. — 40p : col.ill ; 23cm
Cover title
ISBN 0-7024-0130-7 (pbk) : Unpriced
B82-37561

510 — Mathematics — *For schools*
continuation

Svennson, Leif. Hey, mathematics / [Leif Svennson, Curt Oreberg, Matts Hastad] ; general editor Jim Boucher. — [Edinburgh] : Caffrey Smith
Translated from the Swedish
Module 6. — c1980
Book 2: Banana. — 40p : col.ill ; 23cm
Cover title
ISBN 0-7024-0131-5 (pbk) : Unpriced
B82-37559

Svennson, Leif. Hey, mathematics / [Leif Svennson, Curt Oreberg, Matts Hastad] ; general editor Jim Boucher. — [Edinburgh] : Caffrey Smith
Translated from the Swedish
Module 6. — c1980
Book 3: Lemon. — 48p : col.ill ; 23cm
Cover title
ISBN 0-7024-0132-3 (pbk) : Unpriced
B82-37560

Sylvester, J. E. K.. Mainstream mathematics / J.E.K. Sylvester. — Walton-on-Thames : Nelson
Bk.3: Teachers' book. — c1982. — iii,65p : ill ; 22cm
ISBN 0-17-438137-9 (pbk) : Unpriced
B82-26791

510 — Mathematics — *For slow learning students*

Rees, Ruth. Foundation numeracy. — London : E. Arnold, Sept.1982. — [112]p
ISBN 0-7131-0720-0 (pbk) : £2.50 : CIP entry
B82-18768

510 — Mathematics — *For users of pocket electronic calculators*

Bawtree, Michael. The student's calculator book : a practical guide for students and teachers in schools, colleges and universities / Michael Bawtree and Robin Bradbeer. — Bromley : Chartwell-Bratt, [1980?]. — 202p : ill ; 23cm
Includes index
ISBN 0-86238-007-3 (pbk) : Unpriced
B82-35647

Larson, Roland E.. Mathematics for everyday living / Roland E. Larson, Donald Hostetler ; exercises prepared with the assistance of David E. Heyd. — Philadelphia ; London : Saunders College Publishing, c1982. — viii,600p : ill ; 25cm
Includes index
ISBN 0-03-058954-1 : Unpriced
B82-31114

510 — Mathematics — *For West African students*

Universal primary mathematics / wadanda suka fassara A.M. Fagulu ... [et al.]. — Sabon shiri. — Ibadan ; London : Evans Brothers
Littafi na 3. — 1981. — 153p : ill(some col.) ; 23cm
Hausa text, English preliminaries. — Previous ed.: 1977
ISBN 0-237-50112-0 (pbk) : Unpriced
B82-04267

Universal primary mathematics / edited by A.M. Fagbulu ... [et al.]. — New ed. — Ibadan ; London : Evans
Previous ed.: 1976?
Bk.3 Hausa. Teachers guide. — 1982. — xiv,174p : ill(some col.) ; 28cm
ISBN 0-237-50115-5 (pbk) : Unpriced
B82-39660

Universal primary mathematics / edited by A.M. Fagbulu ... [et al.]. — New ed. — Ibadan ; London : Evans Brothers
Bk.4. — 1981. — 124p : ill(some col.) ; 23cm
Previous ed.: 1977
ISBN 0-237-50119-8 (pbk) : Unpriced
B82-04266

510 — Mathematics. Problem solving

Solving real problems with mathematics. — Cranfield (Cranfield Institute of Technology, Cranfield, Bedford MK43 0AL) : CIT Press
Vol.1. — Nov.1981. — [105]p
ISBN 0-902937-62-6 (pbk) : £4.50 : CIP entry
B81-40266

510 — Mathematics. Problem solving — *Manuals — For teaching*

Solving real problems with mathematics. — Cranfield (Cranfield Institute of Technology, Cranfield, Bedford MK43 0AL) : Cranfield Press
Vol.2. — June 1982. — [105]p
ISBN 0-902937-64-2 (pbk) : £7.50 : CIP entry
B82-17901

510 — Nonlinear mathematics

Saaty, Thomas L.. Nonlinear mathematics / Thomas L. Saaty, Joseph Bram. — New York : Dover ; London : Constable, 1981, c1964. — 381p : ill ; 22cm
Originally published: New York ; London : McGraw-Hill, 1964. — Includes index
ISBN 0-486-64233-x (pbk) : £4.90
B82-34627

510'.1 — Mathematics. Paradoxes & fallacies

Bunch, Bryan H.. Mathematical fallacies and paradoxes / Bryan H. Bunch. — New York ; London : Van Nostrand Reinhold, c1982. — xi,216p : ill ; 24cm
Bibliography: p211-212. — Includes index
ISBN 0-442-24905-5 : £14.40
B82-21851

510'.212 — Mathematics - *Tables - For schools*

Fox, R. W.. Mathematical tables and data. — 3rd ed. — London : Edward Arnold, June 1981. — [32]p
Previous ed.: 1970
ISBN 0-7131-0594-1 (pbk) : £1.25(non-net) : CIP entry
B81-14868

510'.212 — Mathematics — *Tables* — *For schools*

Three-figure tables. — [Kettering] ([Weekley Glebe Rd., Kettering, Northants. NN16 9NS]) : [Montagu School], c1981. — [16]p : ill ; 22cm
Unpriced (unbound)
B82-04189

510'.224624 — 083 Mathematics — *For civil engineering* — *For schools*

Stability of structures. — Cheltenham : Thornes, Sept.1982. — [8]p. — (Mathematics towards relevance)
ISBN 0-85950-360-7 (pbk) : £1.85 : CIP entry
B82-30711

510'.224624 — Mathematics — *For civil engineering* — *For schools*

Stability of structures. — Cheltenham : Thornes, Sept.1982. — (Mathematics towards relevance)
Teacher's guide. — [48]p
ISBN 0-85950-365-8 (pbk) : £1.85 : CIP entry
B82-30708

510'.23'41 — Great Britain. Mathematics — *Career guides*

Christie, Catherine. Careers with maths and computers / Catherine Christie. — Northampton : Hamilton House, 1981. — 32p ; 21cm. — (Careerscope ; 4)
ISBN 0-906888-22-0 (pbk) : Unpriced
B82-03065

510'.240431 — Mathematics — *For parents*

Birtwistle, Claude. Help your child with the new maths / by Claude Birtwistle. — Kingswood : Elliot Right Way, c1982. — 189p : ill ; 18cm. — (Paperfronts)
Includes index
ISBN 0-7160-0675-8 (pbk) : £0.75
B82-23914

510'.24301 — Mathematics — *For social sciences*

Anton, Howard. Mathematics with applications for the management, life, and social sciences / Howard Anton, Bernard Kolman. — 2nd ed. — New York ; London : Academic Press, 1982. — xii,851p : ill,col.maps ; 25cm
Includes index
ISBN 0-12-059561-3 : £15.20
Also classified at 510'.24574 ; 510'.24658
B82-30153

510'.2433 — Mathematics — *For economics*

Kennedy, Gavin. Mathematics for innumerate economists / Gavin Kennedy. — London : Duckworth, 1982. — vii,134p : ill ; 23cm
Bibliography: p129-131. — Includes index
ISBN 0-7156-1564-5 (cased) : Unpriced : CIP rev.
ISBN 0-7156-1609-9 (pbk) : £7.95
B81-30356

Onimode, Bade. Mathematics for economics and business. — London : Allen & Unwin, Aug.1982. — [256]p
ISBN 0-04-330326-9 : £6.95 : CIP entry
B82-15629

Pearson, J. M.. Mathematics for economists. — London : Longman, June 1982. — [240]p
ISBN 0-582-29615-3 (pbk) : £4.95 : CIP entry
B82-09446

Weber, Jean E.. Mathematical analysis : business and economic applications / Jean E. Weber. — 4th ed. — New York ; London : Harper & Row, c1982. — xii,719p : ill ; 26cm
Bibliography: p709-710. — Includes index
ISBN 0-06-046977-3 (pbk) : £9.95
B82-28709

510'.2433 — Mathematics — *For economics — for schools*

Mathematics of finance. — Cheltenham : Thornes, Sept.1982. — (Mathematics towards relevance)
Unit 1. — [1v.]
ISBN 0-85950-354-2 (pbk) : £1.50 : CIP entry
B82-30701

Mathematics of finance. — Cheltenham : Thornes, Sept.1982. — (Mathematics towards relevance)
Unit 2. — [1v.]
ISBN 0-85950-355-0 (pbk) : £1.50 : CIP entry
B82-30702

Mathematics of finance. — Cheltenham : Thornes, Sept.1982. — (Mathematics towards relevance)
Unit 3. — [1v.]
ISBN 0-85950-356-9 (pbk) : £1.50 : CIP entry
B82-30706

Mathematics of finance. — Cheltenham : Thornes, Sept.1982. — (Mathematics towards relevance)
Unit 4. — [1v.]
ISBN 0-85950-357-7 (pbk) : £1.50 : CIP entry
B82-30707

Mathematics of finance. — Cheltenham : Thornes, Sept.1982. — (Mathematics towards relevance)
Teacher's guide. — [1v.]
ISBN 0-85950-362-3 (pbk) : £1.50 : CIP entry
B82-30703

510'.24372 — Applied mathematics - *For teaching*

Evyatar, A.. Motivated mathematics. — Cambridge : Cambridge University Press, June 1981. — [280]p
ISBN 0-521-23308-9 (spiral) : £18.00 : CIP entry
B81-19117

510'.24372 — Mathematics — *For teaching*

Topics in mathematics : ideas for the secondary classroom. — London : Bell & Hyman, 1979. — 195p : ill ; 20cm
Includes index
ISBN 0-7135-1999-1 (pbk) : Unpriced
B82-04665

510'.2438 — Mathematics — *For commerce*

Pintel, Gerald. Basic business mathematics / Gerald Pintel, Jay Diamond. — 3rd ed. — Englewood Cliffs ; London : Prentice-Hall, c1982. — xi,269p : ill,facsims,forms ; 28cm
Previous ed.: 1978. — Includes index
ISBN 0-13-057380-9 (pbk) : £9.70
B82-28193

510'.245 — Mathematics — *For science*

Chirgwin, Brian H.. A course of mathematics for engineers and scientists / Brian H. Chirgwin and Charles Plumpton. — Oxford : Pergamon
Vol.2. — 2nd ed. — 1972 (1982 [printing]). — ix,533p ; 21cm
Previous ed.: 1963. — Includes index
ISBN 0-08-029145-7 (cased) : Unpriced
ISBN 0-08-015970-2
Primary classification 510'.2462
B82-28625

Walshaw, A. C.. Fundamentals of analysis in science and engineering. — Warley : Tetradon, Sept.1982. — [100]p
ISBN 0-906070-07-4 (pbk) : £4.80 : CIP entry
B82-28617

510′.2453 — Mathematics — *For physics*

Ram, Michael. Essential mathematics for college physics : a self study guide / Michael Ram. — New York ; Chichester : Wiley, c1982. — 278p : ill ; 28cm
Includes index
ISBN 0-471-86454-4 (pbk) : £6.70 B82-32703

510′.2454 — Mathematics — *For chemistry*

Masterton, William L.. Mathematical preparation for general chemistry / William L. Masterton, Emil J. Slowinski. — 2nd ed. — Philadelphia ; London : Saunders College, c1982. — vii,200p : ill ; 24cm
Previous ed.: published as Elementary mathematical preparation for general chemistry. 1974. — Includes index
ISBN 0-03-060119-3 (pbk) : £9.95 B82-25371

510′.24574 — Mathematics — *For biochemistry*

Cornish-Bowden, Athel. Basic mathematics for biochemists / Athel Cornish-Bowden. — London : Chapman and Hall, 1981. — ix,137p : ill ; 23cm
Includes index
ISBN 0-412-23000-3 (cased) : Unpriced : CIP rev.
ISBN 0-412-23010-0 (pbk) : £3.95 B81-30440

510′.24574 — Mathematics — *For biology*

Anton, Howard. Mathematics with applications for the management, life, and social sciences / Howard Anton, Bernard Kolman. — 2nd ed. — New York ; London : Academic Press, 1982. — xii,851p : ill,col.maps ; 25cm
Includes index
ISBN 0-12-059561-3 : £15.20
Primary classification 510′.24301 B82-30153

Pollard, J. H.. A handbook of numerical and statistical techniques : with examples mainly from the life sciences / J.H. Pollard. — Cambridge : Cambridge University Press, 1977 (1981 [printing]). — xvi,349p : ill ; 23cm
Bibliography: p332-335. — Includes index
ISBN 0-521-29750-8 (pbk) : £7.95 B82-08284

510′.246 — Mathematics — *For technicians*

Alldis, Blair K.. Mathematics for technicians / Blair K. Alldis. — Sydney ; London : McGraw-Hill, c1980. — 463p : ill ; 25cm
ISBN 0-07-093556-4 (pbk) : Unpriced B82-29496

Bird, J. O.. Mathematics 4 checkbook / J.O. Bird, A.J.C. May. — London : Butterworths, 1981. — viii,216p : ill ; 20cm. — (Butterworths technical and scientific checkbooks)
Includes index
ISBN 0-408-00660-9 (cased) : Unpriced : CIP rev.
ISBN 0-408-00612-9 (pbk) : Unpriced B81-23915

Bird, J. O.. Technician mathematics / J.O. Bird, A.J.C. May. — London : Longman. — (Longman technician series. Mathematics and sciences)
Level 1. — 2nd ed. — 1982. — 390p : ill ; 21cm
Previous ed.: 1977. — Includes index
ISBN 0-582-41256-0 (pbk) : £4.95 : CIP rev. B82-16467

Bird, J. O.. Technician mathematics / J.O. Bird, A.J.C. May. — London : Longman. — (Longman technician series. Mathematics and sciences)
Level 2. — 2nd ed. — 1982. — 435p : ill ; 21cm
Previous ed.: 1978. — Includes index
ISBN 0-582-41257-9 (pbk) : £4.95 : CIP rev. B82-16468

Boyce, John G.. Mathematics for technical and vocational students. — 7th ed. / John G. Boyce, Louis Margolis, Samuel Slade. — New York ; Chichester : Wiley, c1982. — xiv,561p : ill(some col.) ; 25cm
Previous ed.: published as Mathematics for technical and vocational schools. 1975. — Text on lining papers. — Includes index
ISBN 0-471-05182-9 : £14.75 B82-18066

Davies, H. G.. Mathematics II / H.G. Davies, G.A. Hicks. — London : Macmillan, 1981. — viii,177p : ill ; 21x23cm. — (Macmillan technician series)
ISBN 0-333-24072-3 (pbk) : £4.95 B82-06962

Dyball, George E.. Mathematics for technician engineers levels 4 and 5. — London : McGraw-Hill, Feb.1983. — [384]p
ISBN 0-07-084664-2 (pbk) : £7.95 : CIP entry B82-36432

Garlick, F. J.. Technical mathematics : a second level course / F.J. Garlick, J.R.M. Barnes. — London : McGraw-Hill, c1981. — x,339p : ill ; 23cm
Includes index
ISBN 0-07-084644-8 (pbk) : £4.95 : CIP rev. B81-10004

Greer, A.. Mathematics for technicians / A. Greer, G.W. Taylor. — Cheltenham : Thomas. — (Technology today series)
New level 1. — 1982. — vii,343p : ill ; 23cm
Includes index
ISBN 0-85950-352-6 (pbk) : £4.20 : CIP rev. B82-13150

Greer, A.. Mathematics for technicians Level II. — New ed. — Cheltenham : Stanley Thornes, July 1982. — [328]p
Previous ed.: 1979
ISBN 0-85950-353-4 (pbk) : £3.95 : CIP entry B82-17912

Hancox, D. J.. Mathematics for technicians 2. — London : Granada, June 1982. — [160]p
ISBN 0-246-11725-7 : £4.50 : CIP entry B82-10701

Kramer, Arthur D.. Fundamentals of technical mathematics / Arthur D. Kramer. — New York ; London : McGraw-Hill, c1982. — x,660p : ill ; 25cm
Includes index
ISBN 0-07-035427-8 : £12.25 B82-27150

Smith, Brian W.. TEC mathematics exercises Level 1. — Cheltenham : Thornes, July 1982. — [80]p
ISBN 0-85950-371-2 (pbk) : £1.50 : CIP entry B82-13151

Smithson, J. L.. Mathematics for electrical, telecommunications and science technicians : a second level course. — 2nd ed. — London : McGraw-Hill
Previous ed. published as: Mathematics for electrical and telecommunications technicians. 1969
Vol.2. — June 1982. — [320]p
ISBN 0-07-084660-x (pbk) : £4.95 : CIP entry B82-12913

Walker, Eric. Mathematics level 2. — Eastbourne : Holt-Saunders, Jan.1982. — 1v.
ISBN 0-03-910345-5 (pbk) : £1.95 : CIP entry B81-33998

Walker, Eric. Mathematics Level 3 / Eric Walker. — London : Holt, Rinehart and Winston, c1982. — xv,344p : ill ; 22cm. — (Holt technician texts)
Includes index
ISBN 0-03-910355-2 (pbk) : £4.95 : CIP rev. B82-00926

510′.246 — Mathematics — *Questions & answers* — *For technicians*

Bird, J. O.. Mathematics 3 checkbook / J.O. Bird, A.J.C. May. — London : Butterworths, 1981. — x,272p : ill ; 20cm. — (Butterworths technical and scientific checkbooks)
Includes index
ISBN 0-408-00634-x (cased) : Unpriced : CIP rev.
ISBN 0-408-00611-0 (pbk) : Unpriced B81-14852

510′.2461 — Mathematics — *For radiographic technicians*

Stefani, Stefano S.. Mathematics for techologists in radiology, nuclear medicine, and radiation therapy / Stefano S. Stefani, Lincoln B. Hubbard ; with the technical assistance of Erhard Sanders. — St. Louis, Mo. ; London : Mosby, 1979. — xii,240p : ill ; 26cm
Bibliography: p234. — Includes index
ISBN 0-8016-4762-2 (pbk) : Unpriced B82-21885

510′.2462 — Mathematics — *For engineering*

Chirgwin, Brian H.. A course of mathematics for engineers and scientists / Brian H. Chirgwin and Charles Plumpton. — Oxford : Pergamon
Vol.2. — 2nd ed. — 1972 (1982 [printing]). — ix,533p ; 21cm
Previous ed.: 1963. — Includes index
ISBN 0-08-029145-7 (cased) : Unpriced
ISBN 0-08-015970-2
Also classified at 510′.245 B82-28625

Corn, Juliana. Technical mathematics through applications / Juliana Corn, Tony Behr. — Philadelphia ; London : Saunders College Publishing, c1982. — xv,585p : ill ; 24cm
Includes index
ISBN 0-03-057721-7 : £16.95 B82-15338

Meadows, R. G.. Electrical and engineering mathematics / Richard Meadows. — London : Pitman
Vol.1. — 1980. — xiii,298p : ill ; 25cm
Includes index
ISBN 0-273-01407-2 (pbk) : £4.95 B82-13338

Wylie, C. Ray. Advanced engineering mathematics. — 5th ed. / C. Ray Wylie, Louis C. Barrett. — New York ; London : McGraw-Hill, c1982. — xiv,1103p : ill ; 25cm
Previous ed.: New York : London : McGraw-Hill, 1975. — Includes index
ISBN 0-07-072188-2 : £25.95 B82-36959

510′.2462 — Mathematics — *Questions & answers* — *For engineering*

Minorskiĭ, V. P.. Problems in higher mathematics / V.P. Minorsky ; translated from the Russian by Yuri Ermolyev. — Moscow : Mir, 1975 (1980 [printing]) ; [London] : Distributed by Central Books. — 395p : ill ; 21cm
Translation of: Sbornik zadach po vyssheĭ matematike
£4.50 B82-11408

510′.246213 — Mathematics — *For electrical engineering*

Karni, Shlomo. Mathematical methods in continuous and discrete systems / by Shlomo Karni and William J. Byatt. — New York ; London : Holt, Rinehart and Winston, c1982. — ix,312p : ill ; 21cm. — (HRW series in electrical and computer engineering)
Includes bibliographies and index
ISBN 4-8337-0089-1 (pbk) : £8.95 B82-37424

510′.246213 — Mathematics — *For electronic engineering*

Cooke, Nelson M.. Basic mathematics for electronics. — 5th ed. / Nelson M. Cooke, Herbert F.R. Adams, Peter B. Dell. — New York ; London : McGraw-Hill, c1982. — vi,698p : ill(some col.) ; 25cm
Previous ed.: 1976. — Text on lining papers. — Includes index
ISBN 0-07-012514-7 : £16.50 B82-37581

510′.24658 — Mathematics — *For business studies*

Rosenberg, R. Robert. Business mathematics / R. Robert Rosenberg, Harry Lewis, Roy W. Poe. — 9th ed. — New York ; London : McGraw-Hill, c1982. — viii,552p : ill,forms ; 24cm
Previous ed.: New York : McGraw-Hill, 1975. — Includes index
ISBN 0-07-053726-7 : £8.95 B82-00527

510′.24658 — Mathematics — *For management*

Anton, Howard. Mathematics with applications for the management, life, and social sciences / Howard Anton, Bernard Kolman. — 2nd ed. — New York ; London : Academic Press, 1982. — xii,851p : ill,col.maps ; 25cm
Includes index
ISBN 0-12-059561-3 : £15.20
Primary classification 510′.24301 B82-30153

510'.2469 — Mathematics — *For building construction*

Tabberer, Frank L.. Calculations for building craft students / Frank L. Tabberer. — London : Hutchinson, 1982. — 209p : ill,plans ; 24cm
ISBN 0-09-147201-6 (pbk) : £4.95 : CIP rev.
B82-07254

510'.2491 — Mathematics — *For geography*

Selkirk, K. E.. Pattern and place : an introduction to the mathematics of geography / K.E. Selkirk. — Cambridge : Cambridge University Press, 1982. — iv,203p : ill,maps ; 25cm
Bibliography: p195-197. — Includes index
ISBN 0-521-28208-x (pbk) : £7.50 : CIP rev.
B82-03367

510'.28 — Pocket electronic calculators — *Manuals*

Killingbeck, J. P.. The creative use of calculators / J.P. Killingbeck. — Harmondsworth : Penguin, 1981. — 220p : ill ; 18cm
Includes index
ISBN 0-14-022336-3 (pbk) : £1.95 B82-08145

510'.28'5404 — Mathematics. Applications of Sinclair ZX81 microcomputer systems

Bluston, H. S.. Mathematical & educational applications of the ZX81 microcomputer / H.S. Bluston. — [Bedford] ([24 Elm Close, Bedford MK41 8BZ]) : [H.S. Bluston], [c1982]. — 6leaves : 1ill ; 30cm
Cover title
£5.00 (pbk) B82-35525

510'.3 — Mathematics — *Polyglot dictionaries*

Eisenreich, Günther. Dictionary of mathematics : in four languages, English, German, French, Russian / compiled by Günther Eisenreich and Ralf Sube. — Amsterdam ; Oxford : Elsevier Scientific, 1982. — 2v.(1460p) ; 25cm
ISBN 0-444-99706-7 : Unpriced : CIP rev.
B81-36209

510'.3'21 — Mathematics — *Encyclopaedias* — *For schools*

Jones, Christopher. Mathematics / Christopher Jones and Peter Clamp. — London : Collins, 1982. — 251p : ill ; 12cm. — (Basic facts) (Collins revision aids)
ISBN 0-00-458889-4 (pbk) : £1.50 B82-33437

Kaner, Peter. A basic dictionary of maths. — London : Bell & Hyman, Oct.1981. — [64]p
ISBN 0-7135-1269-5 (pbk) : £1.75 : CIP entry
B81-30191

510'.7 — Education. Curriculum subjects: Mathematics. Teaching

Wells, D. G.. Three essays on the teaching of mathematics / David Wells. — Bristol : Rain Publications, 1982. — 48p : ill(some col.) ; 21cm
Cover title
ISBN 0-907944-00-0 (pbk) : Unpriced
B82-17830

510'.7'1 — Schools. Curriculum subjects: Mathematics. Learning by students. Psychological aspects

Davis, Robert B.. Learning mathematics. — London : Croom Helm, Dec.1982. — [384]p. — (Croom Helm curriculum policy and research series)
ISBN 0-7099-0225-5 : £14.95 : CIP entry
B82-30805

510'.7'1 — Schools. Curriculum subjects: Mathematics. Teaching

Rudnick, Jesse A.. A guide book for teaching general mathematics / Jesse A. Rudnick, Stephen Krulik. — Boston [Mass.] ; London : Allyn and Bacon, c1982. — viii,216p : ill,forms ; 28cm. — (A Guidebook for teaching)
ISBN 0-205-07371-9 (pbk) : Unpriced
B82-23531

Teaching mathematics. — London : Croom Helm, Aug.1982. — [256]p
ISBN 0-7099-0713-3 (cased) : £12.95 : CIP entry
ISBN 0-7099-0714-1 (pbk) : £5.95 B82-15904

510'.7'1041 — Great Britain. Schools. Curriculum subjects: Mathematics. Teaching

Dean, Peter G.. Teaching and learning mathematics. — London : Woburn Press, Jan.1982. — [280]p
ISBN 0-7130-0168-2 : £11.00 : CIP entry
B81-34570

510'.7'1042 — England. Educational institutions. Curriculum subjects: Mathematics. Teaching, *to 1981*

Howson, Geoffrey. A history of mathematics education in England. — Cambridge : Cambridge University Press, Sept.1982. — [304]p
ISBN 0-521-24206-1 : £6.95 : CIP entry
B82-26239

510'.7'1042 — England. Schools. Curriculum subjects: Mathematics. Teaching — *Inquiry reports*

Great Britain. *Committee of Inquiry into the Teaching of Mathematics in Schools.*
Mathematics counts : report of the Committee of Inquiry into the Teaching of Mathematics in Schools under the chairmanship of W.H. Cockcroft. — London : H.M.S.O., 1982. — xv,311p : ill ; 25cm
ISBN 0-11-270522-7 (pbk) : £5.75 B82-17712

510'.7'1242 — England. Secondary schools. Curriculum subjects: Mathematics. Academic achievement of students. Assessment

Mathematical development : secondary survey report no.1 / by D.D. Foxman ... [et al.]. — London : H.M.S.O., 1980. — xiii,131p : ill,forms ; 25cm
"Report on the 1978 secondary survey from the National Foundation for Educational Research in England and Wales to the Department of Education and Science, Department of Education for Northern Ireland and the Welsh Office". — At head of title: Assessment of Performance Unit. — Includes index
ISBN 0-11-270516-2 (pbk) : £6.60 B82-17173

510'.71242 — England. Secondary schools. Sixth forms. Curriculum subjects: Mathematics. N level & F level courses — *Feasibility studies*

Mathematics for sixth formers. — Nelson : Association of Teachers of Mathematics, c1978. — iv,90p : ill ; 29cm
Bibliography: p90
£1.50 (pbk) B82-34496

510'.7'1242821 — Secondary schools. Curriculum subjects: Mathematics. Academic achievement of students: Girls — *Study regions: South Yorkshire (Metropolitan County). Sheffield*

Mathematics education and girls : a report of the investigations into learning difficulties in mathematics, and attitudes to mathematics, with particular reference to girls / Sheffield City Polytechnic Department of Mathematics, Statistics and Operational Research ; sponsorship by the British Petroleum Company. — Sheffield : The Department, 1982. — iiileaves,198p : ill,forms ; 30cm
Bibliography: p193-198
ISBN 0-903761-45-9 (pbk) : Unpriced
B82-15263

510'.7'12429 — Wales. Secondary schools. Curriculum subjects: Mathematics. Academic achievement of students. Assessment

Mathematical development : secondary survey report no.1 : Wales / D.D. Foxman ... [et al.]. — Cardiff : H.M.S.O., 1980. — iii,63p : ill ; 25cm
"Report on the 1978 secondary survey from the National Foundation for Educational Research in England & Wales to the Department of Education & Science and the Welsh Office". — At head of title: Assessment of Performance Unit
ISBN 0-11-790150-4 (pbk) : £3.60 B82-17172

510'.723 — Great Britain. Adults. Mathematical skills. Surveys

Adults' mathematical ability and performance / ACACE. — Leicester : ACACE, [1982]. — 59p : ill ; 21cm. — (Report / Advisory Council for Adult and Continuing Education)
ISBN 0-906436-09-5 (pbk) : £1.50 B82-39492

Sewell, Bridgid. Use of mathematics by adults in daily life / by Bridgid Sewell. — Leicester : ACACE, [1981]. — ii,83p : ill,1form,1map ; 30cm. — (Enquiry officers report)
ISBN 0-906436-10-9 (pbk) : £2.50 B82-39497

510'.76 — Mathematics — *Questions & answers*

Higgins, Robert L.. Instructor's answer manual for Mathematics with applications for the management, life, and social sciences, 2/e / by Roberty L. Higgins. — New York ; London : Academic Press, c1982. — iv,75p : ill ; 24cm
ISBN 0-12-059563-x (pbk) : £2.40 B82-29986

Porkess, R.. Mathematics study and revision / R. Porkess. — [Glasgow] : Collins Euducational, 1982. — [64]p : ill ; 30cm. — (Collins revision aids)
ISBN 0-00-197251-0 (pbk) : £1.50
ISBN 0-00-327780-1 (non-net ed.) : Unpriced
B82-32058

510'.76 — Mathematics — *Questions & answers* — *For Caribbean students*

Greer, Alex. Multiple-choice tests in mathematics for Caribbean schools. — Cheltenham : Thornes, Feb.1982. — [96]p
ISBN 0-85950-448-4 (pbk) : £1.95 : CIP entry
B81-35722

Wardle, M. E.. Certificate maths practice for the Caribbean / Mike Wardle and Chris Weeks. — Oxford : Oxford University Press, 1981. — 283p : ill ; 24cm
ISBN 0-19-832621-1 (pbk) : £2.95 B82-00827

510'.76 — Mathematics — *Questions & answers* — *For children*

Arkwright, R. M.. Helping your child with home tests : for grammar and comprehensive school entrance / R.M. Arkwright. — 4th ed. — London : Harrap, 1981. — 94p : ill ; 19cm
Previous ed. published as: Home tests for grammar and comprehensive school entrance, 1970
ISBN 0-245-53786-4 (pbk) : £1.75
Primary classification 155.4'13 B82-01489

Griffiths, A. L.. Key maths at home / A.L. Griffiths. — Harlow : Longman, 1981, c1976
Originally published: London : Oliver & Boyd, 1976
Book 1. — 96p : ill ; 24cm
ISBN 0-582-39146-6 (pbk) : £0.99 B82-01276

Griffiths, A. L.. Key maths at home / A.L. Griffiths. — Harlow : Longman, 1981, c1976
Originally published: London : Oliver & Boyd, 1976
Book 2. — 96p : ill ; 24cm
ISBN 0-582-39145-8 (pbk) : £0.99 B82-01277

Harrison, R. S.. Helping your child with maths / R.S. Harrison. — London : Harrap, 1982. — 74p : ill ; 19cm
Includes index
ISBN 0-245-53802-x (pbk) : £1.75 B82-16972

510'.76 — Mathematics — *Questions & answers* — *For Irish students*

I can solve it! : primary maths work cards. — Dublin : Folens
Bk.5 / [by J.J. O'Neill]. — [1981?]. — 56p : ill ; 24cm
Cover title. — Text on inside cover
ISBN 0-86121-154-5 (pbk) : Unpriced
B82-00019

I can solve it. — [Dublin] : [Folens]
Book 5 and Book 6 / J.J. O'Neill. — [1981?]
Answers. — 48p ; 25cm
Cover title
ISBN 0-86121-158-8 (pbk) : Unpriced
B82-18014

Shortt, John. Revision aids in intermediate certificate mathematics : lower course / John Shortt and Jim Tully. — Dublin : Helicon, 1982. — 92p : ill ; 21cm
Unpriced (pbk) B82-27122

510′.76 — Mathematics — *Questions & answers — For Irish students* *continuation*

Shortt, John. Revision aids to Leaving Certificate mathematics (O Level) / John Shortt. — Rev. ed. — Dublin : Helicon, 1981 : Distributed by Educational Company. — 120p : ill ; 21cm
Previous ed.: 1979
Unpriced (pbk) B82-02559

Step by step maths. — Dublin : Gill and Macmillan
Answers for books 1 and 2. — 1981. — 51p ; 22cm
ISBN 0-7171-1203-9 (pbk) : Unpriced
B82-13471

510′.76 — Mathematics — *Questions & answers — For Nigerian students*

Universal primary mathematics. — New ed., [adapted by A. M. Fagbulu] ... [et al.]. — Ibadan ; London : Evans
Previous ed.: published as Kenya primary mathematics, Kenya : Jomo Kenyatta Foundation for the Kenya Institute of Education, 196-?
Book 6
Pupil′s book. — 1982. — 142p : ill(some col.) ; 23cm
ISBN 0-237-50121-x (pbk) : Unpriced
B82-24920

510′.76 — Mathematics — *Questions & answers — For schools*

Bakhda, S.. Consolidated practice mathematics / adapted by S. Bakhda and G.S. Eshiwani. — London : Ginn
Book 1. — c1980. — 80p : ill ; 22cm
ISBN 0-602-22449-7 (pbk) : Unpriced
ISBN 0-602-22450-0 (with answers) : Unpriced
B82-36820

Bakhda, S.. Consolidated practice mathematics / adapted by S. Bakhda and G.S. Eshiwani. — Aylesbury : Ginn
Book 2. — c1980. — 80p : ill ; 22cm
ISBN 0-602-22451-9 (pbk) : Unpriced
ISBN 0-602-22452-7 (with answers) : Unpriced
B82-36821

Barrett, W. G.. Essential maths revision / W.G. Barrett and R.G. Hollis. — 2nd (rev. and enl.) ed. — London : Cassell
[Pupils′ book]. — 1981. — 108p : ill ; 25cm
Previous ed.: 1980
ISBN 0-304-30888-9 (pbk) : Unpriced
B82-06901

Barrett, W. G.. Essential maths revision / W.G. Barrett and R.G. Hollis. — 2nd (rev. and enl.) ed. — London : Cassell
[Teacher′s edition]. — 1981. — 156p : ill ; 25cm
Previous ed.: 1980
ISBN 0-304-30889-7 (pbk) : Unpriced
B82-06902

Bizony, M. S.. Mathematics (Advanced level) / by M.S. Bizony. — London : Artemis, 1982. — 88p ; 22cm. — (General Certificate of Education model answers)
ISBN 0-85478-005-x (pbk) : £1.45 B82-21656

Bolt, R. L.. Mathematics to sixteen / by R.L. Bolt and C. Reynolds. — Slough : University Tutorial
Book 5 [with answers]. — 1981. — 247p : ill ; 22cm
ISBN 0-7231-0820-x (pbk) : £3.30 B82-06989

Bolt, R. L.. Mathematics to sixteen / by R.L. Bolt and C. Reynolds. — Slough : University Tutorial
Book 5 (without answers). — 1981. — 215p : ill ; 22cm
ISBN 0-7231-0821-8 (pbk) : £3.05 B82-06988

Brighouse, Alan. Peak mathematics / Alan Brighouse, David Godber, Peter Patilla. — Walton-on-Thames : Nelson
Answer bk.5. — 1982. — 55p : ill ; 22cm
Cover title
ISBN 0-17-421319-0 (pbk) : £1.25 B82-28355

Brighouse, Alan. Peak mathematics / Alan Brighouse, David Godber, Peter Patilla. — Walton-on-Thames : Nelson
5: [Pupils′ book]. — 1982. — 128p : ill(some col.),maps(some col.),plans,ports(some col.) ; 25cm
Cover title
ISBN 0-17-421310-7 (pbk) : Unpriced
B82-29464

Brighouse, Alan. Peak mathematics / Alan Brighouse, David Godber, Peter Patilla. — Walton-on-Thames : Nelson
6. — 1982. — 128p : ill(some col.) ; 25cm + Answer book(56p : ill ; 22cm. ; pbk)
Text on inside front cover
ISBN 0-17-421311-5 (pbk) : £2.25
ISBN 0-17-421320-4 (Answer book) : £1.25
B82-31026

Brighouse, Alan. Peak mathematics / Alan Brighouse, David Godber, Peter Patilla. — Walton-on-Thames : Nelson
Teacher′s guide 6. — 1982. — 24p : ill,1form ; 25cm
Cover title. — Text on inside cover
ISBN 0-17-421316-6 (pbk) : £1.95 B82-28357

Brighouse, Alan. Peak mathematics / Alan Brighouse, David Godber, Peter Patilla. — Walton-on-Thames : Nelson
Teacher′s guide 7. — 1982. — 23p : ill,1form ; 25cm
Cover title
ISBN 0-17-421341-7 (pbk) : £1.95 B82-28356

Christon, R.. Everyday maths practice / R. Christon and P. Newton. — Oxford : Oxford University Press, 1982. — 192p : ill ; 25cm
Text on inside covers
ISBN 0-19-914092-8 (pbk) : £2.50 B82-33035

Clarke, L. Harwood. Pure mathematics at advanced level / L. Harwood Clarke. — 3rd ed. / prepared by F.G.J. Norton. — London : Heinemann Educational, 1982. — xvi,477p : ill ; 22cm
Previous ed.: 1971. — Includes index
ISBN 0-435-51188-2 (pbk) : £4.95 : CIP rev.
B82-08122

Cofman, Judita. Problems for young mathematicians / by Judita Cofman. — Knebworth : Pullen, [1981]. — ii,66p : ill ; 30cm
Bibliography: p66
ISBN 0-907616-06-2 (corrected : pbk) : £3.50
B82-12865

Court, R. A.. Simple modern maths 3 / R.A. Court, A.M. Court with advice from M.B. Godsen. — Walton-on-Thames : Nelson
Pupils′ bk. — 1980. — 318p : ill(some col.) ; 24cm
ISBN 0-17-431011-0 (pbk) : Unpriced
B82-37545

Cwirko-Godycki, Jerzy. Mathematical activities from Poland / Jerzy Cwirko-Godycki. — Derby : Association of Teachers of Mathematics, [1982?]. — [38]p : ill ; 21x30cm. — (An ATM activity book)
ISBN 0-900095-27-x (spiral) : £1.50
B82-34500

De Ville, Eric. O Level and CSE mathematics. — London : Bell & Hyman, May 1982. — [109]p. — (Allman revision notes series)
Originally published: London : Mills & Boon, 1963
ISBN 0-7135-2214-3 (pbk) : £1.50 : CIP entry
B82-14055

Greer, A.. Revision practice in multiple-choice mathematics questions / A. Greer and C. Layne. — Cheltenham : Thornes, 1981. — xi,105p : ill ; 19cm. — (ST(P) revision notes series)
ISBN 0-85950-346-1 (pbk) : £1.95 : CIP rev.
B82-04818

Greer, A.. Revision practice in short-answer mathematics questions / A. Greer. — Cheltenham : Thornes, 1981. — viii,112p : ill ; 19cm. — (ST(P) revision notes series)
ISBN 0-85950-340-2 (pbk) : £1.95 : CIP rev.
B82-04817

Hawthorne, W. M.. Continuing mathematics / W.M. Hawthorne and A. Olubummo. — London : Evans
Teacher′s book 1. — 1982. — 196p : ill ; 25cm
ISBN 0-237-50643-2 (pbk) : Unpriced
B82-22059

Hawthorne, W. M.. Continuing mathematics / W.M. Hawthorne and A. Olubummo. — London : Evans
Teacher′s book 2. — 1982. — 187p : ill ; 25cm
ISBN 0-237-50642-4 (pbk) : Unpriced
B82-22058

Hawthorne, W. M.. Continuing mathematics / W.M. Hawthorne and A. Olubummo. — London : Evans
Student′s bk.2. — 1982. — 187p : ill,maps ; 25cm
ISBN 0-237-50645-9 (pbk) : Unpriced
B82-27663

Hawthorne, W. M.. Continuing mathematics / W.M. Hawthorne and A. Olubummo. — London : Evans
Teacher′s bk.2. — 1982. — 195p : ill(some col.),maps ; 25cm
ISBN 0-237-50646-7 (pbk) : Unpriced
B82-27662

Holland, Frederick J.. Question one : leaving certificate mathematics / F.J. Holland, A.D. Madden. — Dublin : Educational Company of Ireland
Higher level. — c1982. — 24p ; 21cm
Unpriced (unbound) B82-35330

Holland, Frederick J.. Question one : leaving certificate mathematics / F.J. Holland, A.D. Madden. — Dublin : Educational Company of Ireland
Ordinary level. — c1982. — 24p ; 21cm
Unpriced (unbound) B82-35329

Holt, Michael. Basic skills in mathematics / Michael Holt. — London : Macmillan, 1980. — 2v. : ill(some col.) ; 2lcm. — (A Macmillan teach and test book)
ISBN 0-333-28301-5 (pbk) : Unpriced
ISBN 0-333-29382-7 (teacher′s bk) : £1.95
B82-15232

Holt, Michael. CSE maths check-up / Michael Holt and Andrew Rothery. — London : Heinemann Educational, 1982. — vi,152p : ill ; 22cm
ISBN 0-435-50409-6 (pbk) : £2.50 : CIP rev.
B82-14514

Holt, Michael. Mathsworks / Michael Holt and Andrew Rothery. — Harlow : Longman
Bk.A. — 1982. — 96p : ill(some col.) ; 25cm
ISBN 0-582-20338-4 (pbk) : Unpriced
B82-34287

Holt, Michael. Mathsworks / Michael Holt and Andrew Rothery. — Harlow : Longman
Teachers′ bk
A. — 1982. — 16,[32]p : ill ; 28cm
ISBN 0-582-20335-x (pbk) : Unpriced
B82-34286

Judge, D. C.. Solutions to ′O′ Grade mathematics : paper 1 / D.C. Judge. — Glasgow : Gibson, c1982. — 64p : ill ; 21cm
ISBN 0-7169-3119-2 (pbk) : Unpriced
B82-19042

Kaye, Alan. Mathematics / Alan Kaye. — London : Macmillan Education, 1981. — 92p : ill ; 25cm. — (Certificate model answers)
ISBN 0-333-29123-9 (pbk) : £0.90 B82-39748

510'.76 — Mathematics — *Questions & answers — For schools* *continuation*

Lewis, G. (Gareth). Maths for life / G. Lewis. — Glasgow : Collins, 1980. — 48p : ill ; 26cm. — (A Ready for work record book)
Text on inside covers
ISBN 0-00-197014-3 (pbk) : £0.65
ISBN 0-00-322000-1 (non-net) : Unpriced
B82-39107

Morgan, J. F. (John Francis). Solutions to 'H' grade mathematics paper 1 / J.F. Morgan. — Glasgow : Gibson, 1982. — 48p : ill ; 21cm
ISBN 0-7169-6953-x (pbk) : Unpriced
B82-24398

Nolan, Melvyn. Check up tests in mathematics / Melvyn Nolan. — London : Macmillan, 1980. — 47p : ill ; 26cm. — (Check up tests series)
ISBN 0-333-28865-3 (pbk) : Unpriced
B82-16116

Nolan, Melvyn. Check up tests in mathematics / Melvyn Nolan. — London : Macmillan Education. — (Check/up)
Text on inside covers
(Teacher's book). — 1980 (1981 [printing]). — 54p : ill ; 26cm
ISBN 0-333-28866-1 (spiral) : Unpriced
B82-36189

Oliver, C.. Comprehensive mathematics practice / C. Oliver, A. Ledsham, R. Elvin. — Oxford : Oxford University Press
1. — 1981. — 82p : ill ; 25cm
ISBN 0-19-833663-2 (pbk) : Unpriced
B82-03791

Oliver, C.. Comprehensive mathematics practice / C. Oliver, A. Ledsham, R. Elvin. — Oxford : Oxford University Press
2. — 1981. — 82p : ill ; 25cm
ISBN 0-19-833664-0 (pbk) : Unpriced
B82-03790

Oliver, C.. Comprehensive mathematics practice / C. Oliver, A. Ledsham, R. Elvin. — Oxford : Oxford University Press
3. — 1981. — 82p : ill ; 25cm
ISBN 0-19-833665-9 (pbk) : Unpriced
B82-03789

Oliver, C.. Comprehensive mathematics practice / C. Oliver, A. Ledsham, R. Elvin. — Oxford : Oxford University Press
4. — 1981. — 82p : ill ; 25cm
ISBN 0-19-833666-7 (pbk) : Unpriced
B82-03788

Oliver, C.. Comprehensive mathematics practice / C. Oliver, A. Ledsham, R. Elvin. — Oxford : Oxford University Press
5. — 1981. — 90p : ill ; 25cm
ISBN 0-19-833667-5 (pbk) : £1.25 B82-10926

Oliver, C.. Comprehensive mathematics practice / C. Oliver, A. Ledsham, R. Elvin. — Oxford : Oxford University Press
6. — 1981. — 82p : ill ; 25cm
ISBN 0-19-833668-3 (pbk) : £1.25 B82-11031

Oliver, C.. Comprehensive mathematics practice / C. Oliver, A. Ledsham, R. Elvin. — Oxford : Oxford University Press
Answers. — 1981. — 77p : ill ; 25cm
ISBN 0-19-833669-1 (pbk) : £2.50 B82-08524

Plumpton, Charles. Integrated mathematics : problems and worked examples / C. Plumpton, G.M. Staley, H.M. Kenwood. — Basingstoke : Macmillan Education, 1982. — vii,119p : ill ; 24cm
ISBN 0-333-30779-8 (pbk) : £1.95 : CIP rev.
B82-07424

Plumpton, Charles. New tertiary mathematics / C. Plumpton, P.S.W. MacIlwaine. — Oxford : Pergamon. — (Pergamon international library)
Vol.1. — 1980
Pt.1: Pure mathematics : the core. — xix,401p : ill ; 26cm
Includes index
ISBN 0-08-025031-9 (cased) : £17.40 : CIP rev.
ISBN 0-08-021643-9 (pbk) : £6.90
ISBN 0-08-025030-0 (pbk : non-net) : Unpriced
ISBN 0-08-021646-3 (set) : Unpriced
B80-02740

Plumpton, Charles. New tertiary mathematics / C. Plumpton, P.S.W. MacIlwaine. — Oxford : Pergamon. — (Pergamon international library)
Vol.1. — 1980
Pt.2: Basic applied mathematics. — xiv,229p : ill ; 26cm
Includes index
ISBN 0-08-025035-1 (cased) : £17.40 : CIP rev.
ISBN 0-08-021645-5 (pbk) : £5.80
ISBN 0-08-025034-3 (pbk : non-net) : Unpriced
ISBN 0-08-021646-3 (set) : Unpriced
B80-06896

Plumpton, Charles. New tertiary mathematics / C. Plumpton, P.S.W. MacIlwaine. — Oxford : Pergamon. — (Pergamon international library)
Vol.2
Pt.1: Further pure mathematics. — 1980. — xixp,p403-804 : ill
Includes index
ISBN 0-08-025033-5 (cased) : £17.40
ISBN 0-08-021644-7 (pbk) : £5.80
ISBN 0-08-025032-7 (pbk : non-net) : Unpriced
ISBN 0-08-021646-3 (set) : Unpriced
B82-35950

Points of departure / [Tansy Hardy et al.]. — [Derby] : Association of Teachers of Mathematics, 1981
1. — [35]p : ill ; 22x30cm
ISBN 0-900095-30-x (spiral) : £1.00
B82-34502

Ridgway, Bill. Maths about town / Bill Ridgway. — London : Edward Arnold, 1982. — 47p : ill ; 25cm
ISBN 0-7131-0644-1 (pbk) : Unpriced : CIP rev.
B82-09191

Rosen, Marion. Mathscore / Marion Rosen ; illustrated by Oxford Illustrators. — Harlow : Longman, 1982. — 48p : col.ill ; 29cm
Text on inside covers
ISBN 0-582-18393-6 (pbk) : Unpriced
B82-37168

Shelton, J.. Practice in essential skills / J. Shelton and G. Lewis. — Glasgow : Collins
Calculator mathematics. — 1982. — 64p : ill,maps,plans ; 23cm
ISBN 0-00-322020-6 (pbk) : £0.95 B82-16973

Smith, Ewart. Examples in mathematics : for CSE/O/CS / Ewart Smith. — Cheltenham : Thornes
Bk.1. — 1982. — 188p : ill ; 22cm + Answers book 1(26p ; 22cm)
ISBN 0-85950-350-x (pbk) : Unpriced : CIP rev.
B82-04819

Smith, Ewart. Examples in mathematics for o/cs / Ewart Smith. — Cheltenham : Thornes
Bk.2. — 1982. — 171p : ill ; 22cm + Answer bk.(18p: ill; 22cm; pbk)
ISBN 0-85950-369-0 (pbk) : Unpriced : CIP rev.
B82-04820

Stanfield, Jan. Impact maths / Jan Stanfield, Jerzy Cwirko-Godycki ; illustrated by Anna Clarke. — London : Evans
Pupil's book 4. — 1982. — 64p : ill,maps,plans ; 25cm
ISBN 0-237-29298-x (pbk) : Unpriced
B82-30542

Striebig, R. A.. Model answers : Ordinary Level mathematics London Board syllabus B / R.A. Striebig. — London : Pandit, 1982. — 69p : ill ; 21cm
ISBN 0-9507233-3-9 (pbk) : £1.80 B82-38240

Sylvester, J. E. K.. Mainstream mathematics / J.E.K. Sylvester. — Walton-on-Thames : Nelson
Bk.3. — 1981. — 208p : ill,2facsims,maps,music,2ports ; 25cm
ISBN 0-17-438133-6 (pbk) : Unpriced
B82-29957

Universal primary mathematics. — Ibadan ; London : Evans
Book 5. — New ed, edited by A.M. Fagbulu ... [et al.]. — 1982. — 142p : ill ; 24cm
ISBN 0-237-50120-1 (pbk) : Unpriced
B82-22060

Wood, Anthony J.. Chase the numbers / Anthony J. Wood. — Oxford : Blackwell, 1982. — 2v. : ill(some col.) ; 24cm + Answers and teaching notes(24p : ill ; 25cm). — (Quicksilver maths)
ISBN 0-631-91500-1 (pbk) : Unpriced
ISBN 0-631-91920-1 (Answers and notes) : Unpriced B82-35725

Wood, Anthony J.. Criss cross / Anthony J. Wood. — Oxford : Blackwell, 1982. — 2v. : ill (some col.) ; 24cm + Answers and teaching notes(23p : ill ; 25cm). — (Quicksilver maths)
ISBN 0-631-91520-6 (pbk) : Unpriced
ISBN 0-631-91940-6 (Answers and notes) : Unpriced B82-35727

Wood, Anthony J.. Follow the shapes / Anthony J. Wood. — Oxford : Blackwell, 1982. — 3v. : ill(some col.) ; 25cm + Answers and teaching notes(21p : ill ; 25cm). — (Quicksilver maths)
ISBN 0-631-91510-9 (pbk) : Unpriced
ISBN 0-631-91930-9 (Answers and notes) : Unpriced B82-35726

510'.76 — Mathematics — *Questions & answers — For slow learning children — For schools*

Stanfield, Jan. Impact maths / Jan Stanfield, Jerzy Cwirko-Godycki ; illustrated by Anna Clarke. — London : Evans
Pupil's book 3. — 1982. — 64p : ill ; 25cm
ISBN 0-237-29295-5 (pbk) : Unpriced
B82-27290

Stanfield, Jan. Impact maths / Jan Stanfield, Jerzy Cwirko-Godycki ; illustrated by Anna Clarke. — London : Evans
Teacher's book 3. — 1982. — 32p : ill ; 25cm
ISBN 0-237-29297-1 : Unpriced B82-30510

Stanfield, Jan. Impact maths / Jan Stanfield, Jerzy Cwirko-Godycki ; illustrated by Anna Clarke. — London : Evans
Teachers book 4. — 1982. — 32p : ill,maps ; 25cm
ISBN 0-237-29300-5 (pbk) : Unpriced
B82-37930

510'.76 — Mathematics — *Questions & answers — For users of pocket electronic calculators — For schools*

Birtwistle, C. Maths with a calculator. — London : Edward Arnold, Feb.1982. — [48]p
ISBN 0-7131-0642-5 (pbk) : £1.60 : CIP entry
B81-37561

510'.76 — Mathematics — *Questions & answers — For West African students*

New general mathematics for West Africa. — New ed. / J.B. Channon ... [et al.]. — Harlow : Longman
Previous ed.: i.e. New ed. / by J.B. Channon, A. McLeish Smith, H.C. Head, 1971-78
2. — 1981. — 202p : ill ; 25cm
Includes index
ISBN 0-582-65056-9 (pbk) : £2.75 B82-09105

New general mathematics for West Africa 3. — New ed. / J.B. Channon ... [et al.]. — Harlow : Longman, 1981. — 230p : ill ; 25cm
Previous ed. i.e. New ed. / by J.B. Channon, A. McLeish Smith, H.C. Head, 1974. —
Includes index
ISBN 0-582-65057-7 (pbk) : £3.20 B82-21791

Okeke, Pius N.. Objective tests : O-Level mathematics / Pius N. Okeke, C.E. Okeke. — Harlow : Longman, 1982. — 87p : ill ; 22cm. — (Study for success)
ISBN 0-582-65079-8 (pbk) : £1.15 B82-17726

510'.9 — Mathematics. Concepts, *to 1900*

Sondheimer, Ernest. Numbers and infinity : a historical account of mathematical concepts / Ernst Sondheimer and Alan Rogerson. — Cambridge : Cambridge University Press, 1981. — x,172p : ill ; 23cm
Bibliography: p163-167. — Includes index
ISBN 0-521-24091-3 (cased) : £9.50 : CIP rev.
ISBN 0-521-28433-3 (pbk) : £3.75 B81-31282

510'.9 — Mathematics, *to 1930 — Festschriften*

Mathematical perspectives : essays on mathematics and its historical development / edited by Joseph W. Dauben. — New York ; London : Academic Press, 1981. — xv,272p : ill,1port ; 24cm
'Presented to Kurt-Reinhard Biermann on the occasion of his 60th birthday'. — Includes essays in English, French and German. — Includes index
ISBN 0-12-204050-3 : £22.60 B82-12300

510'.9 — Mathematics, *to 1965*

Bochner, Salomon. The role of mathematics in the rise of science / by Salomon Bochner. — Princeton ; Guildford : Princeton University Press, c1966 (1981 printing). — x,386p ; 21cm
Includes index
ISBN 0-691-08028-3 (cased) : £4.90 B82-06877

510'.9'04 — Mathematics, *1880-1980*

Temple, George. 100 years of mathematics / George Temple. — London : Duckworth, 1981. — xvi,316p ; 26cm
Bibliography: p283. — Includes index
ISBN 0-7156-1130-5 : £32.00 B82-00561

510'.92'2 — Mathematics — *Biographies*

Ashurst, F. Gareth. Founders of modern mathematics / F. Gareth Ashurst. — London : Muller, 1982. — 145p : ill,ports ; 21cm
Bibliography: p138-139. — Includes index
ISBN 0-584-10380-8 : £7.50 : CIP rev. B81-37578

510'.92'4 — Mathematics. Babbage, Charles — *Biographies*

Hyman, Anthony. Charles Babbage : pioneer of the computer / Anthony Hyman. — Oxford : Oxford University Press, 1982. — xv,287p,[33]p of plates : ill,facsims,plans,ports ; 24cm
List of works: p256-260. — Includes index
ISBN 0-19-858170-x : £12.50 : CIP rev. B81-34413

510'.92'4 — Mathematics. MacLaurin, Colin — *Correspondence, diaries, etc.*

MacLaurin, Colin. The collected letters of Colin MacLaurin. — Nantwich : Shiva, Jan.1982. — [420]p
ISBN 0-906812-08-9 : £15.00 : CIP entry B81-37547

510'.938 — Ancient Greek mathematics, *to 300*

Heath, *Sir* **Thomas.** A history of Greek mathematics / Sir Thomas Heath. — New York : Dover ; London : Constable, 1981. — 2v. : ill ; 21cm
Originally published: Oxford : Clarendon, 1921. — Includes index
ISBN 0-486-24073-8 (pbk) : Unpriced
ISBN 0-486-24074-6 (v.2) : £6.35 B82-09081

511 — MATHEMATICS. GENERALITIES

511 — Numerical analysis. Applications of functional analysis

Cryer, Colin W.. Numerical functional analysis. — Oxford : Clarendon Press. — (Monographs on numerical analysis)
Vol.1. — Sept.1982. — [580]p
ISBN 0-19-853410-8 : £35.00 : CIP entry B82-25510

511'.02462 — Mathematics. Numerical methods — *For engineering*

Ferziger, Joel H.. Numerical methods for engineering application / Joel H. Ferziger. — New York ; Chichester : Wiley, c1981. — xii,270p : ill ; 25cm
Bibliography: p260-261. — Includes index
ISBN 0-471-06336-3 : £16.60 B82-08619

511'.028'5425 — Mathematics. Numerical methods. Software packages: TEAPACK — *Manuals*

Johnston, R. L.. Mathematics subroutines for numerical methods / R.L. Johnston. — New York ; Chichester : Wiley, c1982. — 118p ; 28cm. — (Teapack users' manual)
ISBN 0-471-86443-9 (pbk) : Unpriced B82-38980

511'.2 — Intuitionistic mathematics

Kleene Symposium *(1978 : Madison, Wis.).* The Kleene Symposium : proceedings of the Symposium held June 18-24, 1978 at Madison, Wisconsin, U.S.A. / edited by Jon Barwise, H. Jerome Keisler and Kenneth Kunen. — Amsterdam ; Oxford : North-Holland Publishing, 1980. — xx,425p : ill,1port ; 23cm. — (Studies in logic and the foundations of mathematics ; v.101)
Includes bibliographies
ISBN 0-444-85345-6 : £24.31
Primary classification 511.3 B82-31845

511.3 — Formal languages

Salomaa, Arto. Jewels of formal language theory / Arto Salomaa. — London : Pitman, 1981. — ix,144p ; 23cm
Bibliography: p139-142. — Includes index
ISBN 0-273-08522-0 : Unpriced B82-07926

511.3 — Mathematical logic

Fisher, Alec. Formal number theory and computability : a workbook. — Oxford : Clarendon Press, June 1982. — [200]p. — (Oxford logic guides)
ISBN 0-19-853178-8 : £9.50 : CIP entry B82-12717

Rucker, Rudolf v.B. Infinity and the mind. — Brighton : Harvester, Sept.1982. — [352]p
ISBN 0-7108-0461-x : £12.95 : CIP entry B82-25938

511.3 — Mathematical logic — *Correspondence, diaries, etc.*

Boole, George. The Boole-De Morgan correspondence 1842-1864 / [edited by] G.C. Smith. — Oxford : Clarendon, 1982. — 156p : ill ; 24cm. — (Oxford science publications) (Oxford logic guides)
Bibliography: p136-151. — Includes index
ISBN 0-19-853183-4 : £17.50 : CIP rev. B82-10455

511.3 — Mathematical logic. Logic machines & diagrams

Gardner, Martin. Logic machines and diagrams. — 3rd ed. — Brighton : Harvester, Nov.1982. — [176]p
Previous ed.: New York : Dover, 1968
ISBN 0-7108-0409-1 : £4.95 : CIP entry B82-31298

511.3 — Mathematics. Proof

Solow, Daniel. How to read and do proofs : an introduction to mathematical thought process / Daniel Solow. — New York ; Chichester : Wiley, c1982. — xiv,172p : ill ; 22cm
Includes index
ISBN 0-471-86645-8 (pbk) : £5.55 B82-30694

511.3 — Mathematics. Recursive functions

Fitting, Melvin. Fundamentals of generalized recursion theory / Melvin Fitting. — Amsterdam ; Oxford : North-Holland, 1981. — xx,307p : ill ; 23cm. — (Studies in logic and the foundations of mathematics ; v.105)
Bibliography: p297-302. — Includes index
ISBN 0-444-86171-8 : £32.61 B82-07890

511.3 — Mathematics. Recursive functions — *Conference proceedings*

Kleene Symposium *(1978 : Madison, Wis.).* The Kleene Symposium : proceedings of the Symposium held June 18-24, 1978 at Madison, Wisconsin, U.S.A. / edited by Jon Barwise, H. Jerome Keisler and Kenneth Kunen. — Amsterdam ; Oxford : North-Holland Publishing, 1980. — xx,425p : ill,1port ; 23cm. — (Studies in logic and the foundations of mathematics ; v.101)
Includes bibliographies
ISBN 0-444-85345-6 : £24.31
Also classified at 511'.2 B82-31845

511'.3 — Mathematics. Recursive functions — *Conference proceedings*

Logic Colloquium '79 *(Leeds).* Recursion theory : its generalisations and applications : proceedings of Logic Colloquium '79, Leeds, August 1979 / edited by F.R. Drake and S.S. Wainer. — Cambridge : Cambridge University Press, 1980. — 319p : ill ; 22cm. — (London Mathematical Society lecture note series, ISSN 0076-0552 ; 45)
Includes index
ISBN 0-521-23543-x (pbk) : Unpriced : CIP rev. B80-25539

511'.3 — Model theory. Stability theory

Pillay, Anand. An introduction to stability theory. — Oxford : Clarendon Press, Jan.1983. — [180]p. — (Oxford logic guides)
ISBN 0-19-853186-9 : £15.00 : CIP entry B82-39294

511.3 — Propositional calculus

Segerberg, Krister. Classical propositional operators : an exercise in the foundations of logic / by Krister Segerberg. — Oxford : Clarendon, 1982. — x,151p : 1ill ; 24cm. — (Oxford logic guides ; 5)
Bibliography: p143-144. — Includes index
ISBN 0-19-853173-7 : £12.50 : CIP rev. B81-00858

511.3 — Set theory

Hamilton, A. G.. Numbers, sets and axioms : the apparatus of mathematics. — Cambridge : Cambridge University Press, Nov.1982. — [256]p
ISBN 0-521-24509-5 (cased) : £25.00 : CIP entry
ISBN 0-521-28761-8 (pbk) : £9.50 B82-40329

511.3'2 — Mathematics. Convex sets

Lay, Steven R.. Convex sets and their applications / Steven R. Lay. — New York ; Chichester : Wiley, c1982. — xvi,244p : ill ; 24cm. — (Pure and applied mathematics)
Bibliography: p234-238. — Includes index
ISBN 0-471-09584-2 : £23.00 B82-32736

511.3'2 — Multiple valued logic. Algebraization — *Conference proceedings*

Finite algebra and multiple-valued logic / edited by B. Csákány and I. Rosenberg. — Amsterdam ; Oxford : North-Holland, c1981. — 880p : ill ; 25cm. — (Colloquia mathematica Societatis János Bolyai, ISSN 0139-3383 ; 28)
Conference papers. — Includes bibliographies
ISBN 0-444-85439-8 : £61.05 B82-11225

511.3'22 — Axiomatic set theory

Kunen, Kenneth. Set theory : an introduction to independence proofs / Kenneth Kunen. — Amsterdam ; Oxford : North-Holland Publishing, 1980. — xvi,313p : 1ill ; 23cm. — (Studies in logic and the foundations of mathematics ; v.102)
Bibliography: p305-308. — Includes index
ISBN 0-444-85401-0 : £11.85 B82-31844

511.3'22 — Set theory

Dodd, A.. The core model / A. Dodd. — Cambridge : Cambridge University Press, 1982. — xxxviii,229p ; 23cm. — (London Mathematical Society lecture note series, ISSN 0076-0552 ; 61)
Bibliography: p222-226. — Includes index
ISBN 0-521-28530-5 (pbk) : £12.50 : CIP rev. B82-11508

511.3'24 — Algebra. Ordered sets — *Conference proceedings*

Ordered sets : proceedings of the NATO Advanced Study Institute held at Banff, Canada, August 28 to September 12, 1981 / edited by Ivan Rival. — Dordrecht ; London : Reidel in cooperation with NATO Scientific Affairs Division, c1982. — xviii,966p : ill ; 25cm. — (Nato advanced study institutes series. Series C, Mathematical and physical sciences ; v.83)
Bibliography: p865-966
ISBN 90-277-1396-0 : Unpriced B82-25246

511.3′3 — Mathematics. Functions

Brackx, F.. Clifford analysis. — London : Pitman, Oct.1982. — [322]p. — (Research notes in mathematics ; 76)
ISBN 0-273-08535-2 : £12.50 : CIP entry B82-25191

511′.5 — Graph theory

Cameron, Peter J.. Graphs, codes and designs / P.J. Cameron, J.H. van Lint. — Cambridge : Cambridge University Press, 1980. — vii,147p : ill ; 22cm. — (London Mathematical Society lecture note series ; 43)
Bibliography: p136-144. — Includes index
ISBN 0-521-23141-8 (pbk) : £9.25
Also classified at 519.4 B82-28967

511′.5 — Graph theory. Applications

Graphs, networks and design. — Milton Keynes : Open University Press. — (Technology/Mathematics : a third level interfaculty course)
At head of title: The Open University
[Unit 5]: Paths and cycles. — 1981. — 46p : ill ; 30cm. — (TM361 ; 5)
Bibliography: p45. — Includes index
ISBN 0-335-17059-5 (pbk) : Unpriced B82-05201

Graphs, networks and design. — Milton Keynes : Open University Press. — (Technology/mathematics : a third level interfaculty course)
At head of title: The Open University
[14]: Codes / [prepared for the course team by Elspeth Cusack]. — [1982]. — 63p : ports ; 30cm. — (TM361 ; 14)
Cover title. — Bibliography: p62. — Includes index
ISBN 0-335-17068-4 (pbk) : Unpriced B82-38950

Graphs, networks and design. — Milton Keynes : Open University Press. — (Technology/mathematics : a third level interfaculty course)
At head of title: The Open University
Conclusion. — 1981. — 54p : ill,1port ; 30cm. — (TM361 ; 16)
Cover title. — Includes index
ISBN 0-335-17070-6 (pbk) : Unpriced B82-15089

Graphs, networks and design. — Milton Keynes : Open University Press. — (Technology/mathematics : a third level interfaculty course)
At head of title: The Open University
Geometry. — 1981. — 48p : ill ; 30cm. — (TM361 ; 13)
Cover title. — Text on inside cover. — Bibliography: p48. — Includes index
ISBN 0-335-17067-6 (pbk) : Unpriced B82-15090

Graphs, networks and design. — Milton Keynes : Open University Press. — (Technology/mathematics : a third level interfaculty course)
At head of title: The Open University
Planarity and colouring. — 1981. — 31p : ill,1map,2ports ; 30cm. — (TM361 ; 12)
Cover title. — Bibliography: p50. — Includes index
ISBN 0-335-17066-8 (pbk) : Unpriced B82-15088

Temperley, H. N. V.. Graph theory and applications / H.N.V. Temperley. — Chichester : Horwood, 1981. — 130p : ill ; 24cm. — (Ellis Horwood series in mathematics and its applications)
Includes index
ISBN 0-85312-252-0 (cased) : £15.00 : CIP rev.
ISBN 0-85312-389-6 (pbk) : Unpriced
ISBN 0-470-27296-1 (Halsted) B81-30375

511′.5 — Graph theory. Applications — *Conference proceedings*

The **Theory** and applications of graphs : fourth international conference, May 6-9, 1980, Western Michigan University, Kalamazoo, Michigan / edited by G. Chartrand ... [et al.]. — New York ; Chichester : Wiley, 1981. — xvi,611p : ill ; 24cm
Includes bibliographies
ISBN 0-471-08473-5 : £22.00 B82-09879

511′.5 — Graphs. Numerical solution. Algorithms

Gondran, Michel. Graphs and algorithms. — Chichester : Wiley, Feb.1983. — [550]p. — (Wiley series in discrete mathematics)
Translation of: Graphes et algorithmes
ISBN 0-471-10374-8 : £35.00 : CIP entry B82-38706

511′.6 — Combinatorial analysis

Riordan, John. An introduction to combinatorial analysis / John Riordan. — Princeton ; Guildford : Princeton University Press, 1980, c1978. — x,244p : ill ; 25cm
Originally published: New York : Wiley, 1958. — Includes bibliographies and index
ISBN 0-691-08262-6 (cased) : £12.10
ISBN 0-691-02365-4 (pbk) : Unpriced B82-06972

511′.6 — Combinatorial analysis — *Conference proceedings*

British Combinatorial Conference *(8th : 1981 : University College, Swansea)*. Combinatorics : proceedings of the eighth British Combinatorial Conference, University College, Swansea 1981 / edited by H.N.V. Temperley. — Cambridge : Cambridge University Press, 1981. — 190p : ill ; 22cm. — (London Mathematical Society lecture note series, ISSN 0076-0552 ; 52)
Includes bibliographies
ISBN 0-521-28514-3 (pbk) : £11.95 B82-28970

511′.6 — Combinatorial optimisation. Algorithms

Papadimitriou, Christos H.. Combinatorial optimization : algorithms and complexity / Christos H. Papadimitriou, Kenneth Steiglitz. — Englewood Cliffs ; London : Prentice-Hall, c1982. — xvi,496p : ill ; 24cm
Includes index
ISBN 0-13-152462-3 : £25.50 B82-16724

511′.6 — Combinatorial optimisation — *Conference proceedings*

Applications of combinatorics. — Nantwich (4 Church La., Nantwich, Cheshire CW5 5RQ) : Shiva, Apr.1982. — [140]p. — (Shiva mathematics series ; 6)
Conference papers
ISBN 0-906812-14-3 (cased) : CIP entry
ISBN 0-906812-13-5 (pbk) : £7.50 B82-10679

Combinatorial optimization II : the proceedings of the CO79 conference held at the University of East Anglia Norwhich [i.e. Norwich], England, 9th-12th July 1979 / edited by V.J. Rayward-Smith ; [contributors] T.B. Boffey ... [et al.]. — Amsterdam ; Oxford : North-Holland, 1980. — viii,142p : ill ; 25cm. — (Mathematical programming study ; 13)
Includes bibliographies
ISBN 0-444-86040-1 (pbk) : £12.60 B82-31514

511′.66 — Dynamical systems. Nondifferentiable optimisation — *Conference proceedings*

Workshop on Numerical Techniques for Systems Engineering Problems *(1980 : Lexington, Ky.)*. Nondifferential and variational techniques in optimization : proceedings of the Workshop on Numerical Techniques for Systems Engineering Problems, part 2 / edited by D.C. Sorensen and R.J.-B. Wets. — Amsterdam ; Oxford : North-Holland, 1982. — ix,159p : ill ; 24cm. — (Mathematical programming study ; 17)
ISBN 0-444-86392-3 (pbk) : Unpriced
Also classified at 515′.64 B82-32385

511′.8 — Dynamical systems. Mathematical models

Modelling of dynamical systems / edited by H. Nicholson. — Stevenage : Peregrinus on behalf of the Institution of Electrical Engineers
Vol.1. — c1980. — x,227p : ill ; 24cm. — (IEE control engineering series ; 12)
Includes index
ISBN 0-906048-38-9 : £22.00 : CIP rev. B80-11848

511′.8 — Dynamical systems. Mathematical models. Applications of digital computer systems — *Manuals*

Cavana, R. Y.. Dysmap user manual / R.Y. Cavana and R.G. Coyle. — Bradford : System Dynamics Research Group, 1982. — 77p : ill ; 30cm
Includes index
ISBN 0-904401-06-5 (pbk) : Unpriced B82-22587

Ratnatunga, A. K.. DYSMAP user manual / A.K. Ratnatunga ; revised by R.Y. Cavana. — Bradford : System Dynamics Research Group, University of Bradford, 1980. — vii,80p : ill ; 30cm
Previous ed.: 1979. — Includes index
ISBN 0-904401-05-7 (pbk) : £2.00 B82-31761

511′.8 — Dynamical systems. Mathematical models. Applications of digital computer systems. Programming languages: DYNAMO language

Richardson, George P.. Introduction to system dynamics modeling with DYNAMO / George P. Richardson, Alexander L. Pugh III. — Cambridge, Mass. ; London : MIT Press, c1981. — xi,413p : ill ; 24cm
Bibliography: p402-405. — Includes index
ISBN 0-262-18102-9 : £17.50 B82-21010

511′.8 — Mathematical models

Dunning-Davies, J.. Mathematical methods for mathematicians, physical scientists and engineers / J. Dunning-Davies. — Chichester : Ellis Horwood, 1982. — 416p : ill ; 24cm. — (Ellis Horwood series in mathematics and its applications)
Bibliography: p412. — Includes index
ISBN 0-85312-367-5 : £19.50 : CIP rev.
ISBN 0-85312-387-x (pbk) : Unpriced B81-35876

Mathematical models and methods. — Milton Keynes : Open University Press. — (An inter-faculty second level course)
At head of title: The Open University
Unit 1: Recurrence relations / prepared for the Course Team by Mick Bromilow. — 1982. — 58p : ill ; 30cm. — (MST204 ; unit 1)
ISBN 0-335-14030-0 (pbk) : Unpriced B82-15039

Mathematical models and methods. — Milton Keynes : Open University Press. — (An inter-faculty second level course)
At head of title: The Open University
Unit 2: Differential equations I / prepared for the Course Team by Oliver Penrose and Peter Taylor. — 1981. — 50p : ill ; 30cm. — (MST204 ; unit 2)
ISBN 0-335-14031-9 (pbk) : Unpriced B82-15040

Mathematical models and methods. — Milton Keynes : Open University Press. — (An inter-faculty second level course)
At head of title: The Open University
Unit 3: Animal populations : their growth and exploitation / prepared for the course team by Bob Tunnicliffe. — 1981. — 56 : ill ; 30cm. — (MST204 ; unit 3)
ISBN 0-335-14032-7 (pbk) : Unpriced B82-17094

Mathematical models and methods. — Milton Keynes : Open University Press. — (Mathematics/Science/Technology : an inter-faculty second level course)
At head of title: The Open University
Unit 4: Newtonian mechanics in one dimension / prepared for the Course Team by John Bolton. — 1981. — 59p : ill,1port ; 30cm. — (MST204 ; 4)
ISBN 0-335-14033-5 (pbk) : Unpriced B82-15016

Mathematical models and methods. — Milton Keynes : Open University Press. — (Mathematics/Science/Technology : an inter-faculty second level course)
At head of title: The Open University
Unit 5: Complex numbers / prepared for the Course Team by Mike Thorpe. — 1981. — 59p : ill ; 30cm. — (MST204 ; 5)
ISBN 0-335-14034-3 (pbk) : Unpriced B82-15017

Mathematical models and methods. — Milton Keynes : Open University Press. — (An inter-faculty second level course)
At head of title: The Open University
Unit 6: Differential equations II / prepared for the Course Team by Bob Tunnicliffe. — 1981. — 60p : ill ; 30cm. — (MST204 ; unit 6)
ISBN 0-335-14035-1 (pbk) : Unpriced B82-15041

511′.8 — Mathematical models *continuation*

Mathematical models and methods. — Milton Keynes : Open University Press. — (Mathematics/Science/Technology : an inter-faculty second level course)
At head of title: The Open University
Unit 8: Damped and forced vibrations / prepared for the Course Team by David Broadhurst. — 1981. — 52p : ill ; 30cm. — (MST204 ; 8)
ISBN 0-335-14037-8 (pbk) : Unpriced
B82-15018

Mathematical models and methods. — Milton Keynes : Open University Press. — (Mathematics/Science/Technology : an inter-faculty second level course)
At head of title: The Open University
Unit 9: Simultaneous linear algebraic equations / prepared for the Course Team by Jen Phillips. — 1981. — 58p : ill ; 30cm. — (MST204 ; 9)
ISBN 0-335-14038-6 (pbk) : Unpriced
B82-15019

Mathematical models and methods. — Milton Keynes : Open University Press. — (Mathematics/Science/Technology : an inter-faculty second level course)
At head of title: The Open University
Unit 10: Linear programming / prepared for the Course Team by Peter Taylor an Mick Bromilow. — 1981. — 45p : ill ; 30cm. — (MST204 ; 10)
ISBN 0-335-14039-4 (pbk) : Unpriced
B82-15020

Mathematical models and methods. — Milton Keynes : Open University Press. — (Mathematics/Science/Technology : an inter-faculty second level course)
At head of title: The Open University
Unit 11: Forecasting / prepared for the Course Team by Shirley Hitchcock. — 1981. — 48p : ill ; 30cm. — (MST204 ; 11)
ISBN 0-335-14040-8 (pbk) : Unpriced
B82-15021

Mathematical models and methods. — Milton Keynes : Open University Press. — (Mathematics/science/technology : an inter-faculty second level course)
At head of title: The Open University
Unit 12: Heat transfer / prepared for the Course Team by Richard Fendrich. — 1981. — 30p : ill ; 30cm. — (MST204 ; 12)
ISBN 0-335-14041-6 (pbk) : Unpriced
B82-15022

Mathematical models and methods. — Milton Keynes : Open University Press. — (Mathematics/Science/Technology : an inter-faculty second level course)
At head of title: The Open University
Unit 14: Vector algebra / prepared for the course team by John Berry. — 1981. — 54p : ill ; 30cm. — (MST204 ; 14)
ISBN 0-335-14043-2 (pbk) : Unpriced
B82-17095

Mathematical models and methods. — Milton Keynes : Open University Press. — (Mathematics/science/technology : an inter-faculty second level course)
At head of title: The Open University
Unit 15: Newtonian mechanics in three dimensions / prepared for the Course Team by John Bolton. — 1982. — 53p : ill ; 30cm. — (MST204 ; 15)
ISBN 0-335-14044-0 (pbk) : Unpriced
B82-32009

Mathematical models and methods. — Milton Keynes : Open University Press. — (Mathematics/science/technology : an inter-faculty second level course)
At head of title: The Open University
Unit 17: Many-particle systems and Newton′s third law / prepared for the Course Team by Paul Clark and John Bolton. — 1982. — 53p : ill ; 30cm. — (MST204 ; 17)
ISBN 0-335-14046-7 (pbk) : Unpriced
B82-32008

Mathematical models and methods. — Milton Keynes : Open University Press. — (Mathematics/science/technology : an inter-faculty second level course)
At head of title: The Open University
Unit 19: Numerical methods for differential equations / prepared for the Course Team by Mick Bromilow. — 1982. — 56p : ill ; 30cm. — (MST204 ; 19)
ISBN 0-335-14048-3 (pbk) : Unpriced
B82-32004

Mathematical models and methods. — Milton Keynes : Open University Press. — (Mathematics/science/technology : an inter-faculty second level course)
At head of title: The Open University
Unit 20: Matrix algebra and determinants / prepared for the Course Team by Jen Phillips. — 1982. — 64p : ill ; 30cm. — (MST204 ; 20)
ISBN 0-335-14049-1 (pbk) : Unpriced
B82-32005

Mathematical models and methods. — Milton Keynes : Open University Press. — (Mathematics/science/technology : an inter-faculty second level course)
At head of title: The Open University
Unit 21: Eigenvalues and eigenvectors / prepared for the Course Team by Jen Phillips. — 1982. — 52p : ill ; 30cm. — (MST204 ; 21)
ISBN 0-335-14050-5 (pbk) : Unpriced
B82-32006

Mathematical models and methods. — Milton Keynes : Open University Press. — (Mathematics/science/technology : an inter-faculty second level course)
At head of title: The Open University
Unit 22: Simultaneous differential equations / prepared for the Course Team by Bob Tunnicliffe. — 1982. — 41p : ill ; 30cm. — (MST204 ; 22)
ISBN 0-335-14051-3 (pbk) : Unpriced
B82-32007

Mathematical models and methods. — Milton Keynes : Open University Press. — (Mathematics/science/technology : an inter-faculty second level course)
At head of title: The Open University
Unit 25: Functions of more than one variable / prepared for the Course Team by David Brannan. — 1982. — 51p : ill ; 30cm. — (MST204 ; 25)
ISBN 0-335-14054-8 (pbk) : Unpriced
B82-32003

Mathematical models and methods. — Milton Keynes : Open University Press. — (Mathematics/Science/Technology : an inter-faculty second level course)
At head of title: The Open University
Unit 26: Vector calculus / prepared for the course team by John Berry. — 1982. — 48p : ill,1map ; 30cm. — (MST204 ; 26)
ISBN 0-335-14055-6 (pbk) : Unpriced
B82-40144

Mathematical models and methods. — Milton Keynes : Open University Press. — (Mathematics/Science/Technology : an inter-faculty second level course)
At head of title: The Open University
Unit 27: Multiple integrals / prepared for the course team by John Berry. — 1982. — 49p : ill ; 30cm. — (MST204 ; 27)
ISBN 0-335-14056-4 (pbk) : Unpriced
B82-40145

Mathematical models and methods. — Milton Keynes : Open University Press. — (Mathematics/science/technology : an inter-faculty second level course)
At head of title: The Open University
Unit 29: Angular momentum / prepared for the course team by John Bolton and Paul Clark. — 1982. — 63p : ill ; 30cm. — (MS204 ; 29)
ISBN 0-335-14058-0 (pbk) : Unpriced
B82-38949

Mathematical models and methods. — Milton Keynes : Open University Press. — (Mathematics/science/technology : an inter-faculty second level course)
At head of title: The Open University
Unit 30: Motion under gravity prepared for the course team by David Broadhurst. — 1982. — 68p : ill ; 30cm. — (MST204 ; 30)
ISBN 0-335-14059-9 (pbk) : Unpriced
B82-38948

Mathematical models and methods. — Milton Keynes : Open University Press. — (Mathematics/Science/Technology : an inter-faculty second level course)
At head of title: The Open University
Unit 31: Fourier analysis / prepared for the course team by Richard Fendrich. — 1982. — 30p : ill ; 30cm. — (MST204 ; 31)
ISBN 0-335-14060-2 (pbk) : Unpriced
B82-40143

Mathematical models and methods. — Milton Keynes : Open University Press. — (Mathematics/science/technology : an inter-faculty second level course)
At head of title: The Open University
Unit 32: Partial differential equations / prepared for the course team by Graham Read. — 1982. — 38p : ill ; 30cm. — (MST204 ; 32)
ISBN 0-335-14061-0 (pbk) : Unpriced
B82-38947

511′.8 — Mathematical models. Applications

Burghes, D. N.. Applying mathematical modelling. — Chichester : Horwood, May 1982. — [176]p. — (Ellis Horwood series in mathematics and its applications)
ISBN 0-85312-417-5 : £15.00 : CIP entry
B82-16509

511′.8 — Mathematical models. Applications — *Case studies*

Case studies in mathematical modelling / edited by R. Bradley and R.D. Gibson and M. Cross. — London : Pentech Press, 1981. — 167p : ill ; 24cm
Conference papers
ISBN 0-7273-0311-2 : Unpriced : CIP rev.
B81-14785

Case studies in mathematical modelling / edited by D.J.G. James and J.J. McDonald. — Cheltenham : Stanley Thornes, 1981. — 214p : ill ; 23cm
ISBN 0-85950-304-6 (pbk) : £4.95 : CIP rev.
B81-16901

511′.8 — Mathematical models. Applications — *For schools*

Burkhardt, Hugh. The real world and mathematics / Hugh Burkhardt. — Glasgow : Blackie, 1981. — vi,188p : ill ; 22cm
Includes index
ISBN 0-216-91084-6 (pbk) : £5.95 B82-12182

511′.8 — Mathematical models — *For schools*

Watson, F. R.. A simple introduction to simulation / F.R. Watson. — [Keele] : University of Keele, Institute of Education, 1980. — 2v.(ii,182p) : ill ; 21cm
Cover title. — Includes index
£1.50 (pbk) B82-38115

512 — ALGEBRA

512 — Algebra

Brauer, Richard. Collected papers / Richard Brauer ; edited by Paul Fong and Warren J. Wong. — Cambridge, Mass. ; London : MIT Press, 1980. — 3v. : ports ; 27cm. — (Mathematics of our time ; 17-19)
Includes chapters in German. — Facsim. reprints. — Includes bibliographies
ISBN 0-262-02157-9 : £34.10
ISBN 0-262-02135-8 (v.1) : Unpriced
ISBN 0-262-02148-x (v.2) : Unpriced (v.3) : Unpriced
B82-38968

Carman, Robert A.. Basic algebra : a guided approach / Robert A. Carman, Marilyn J. Carman. — 2nd ed. — New York ; Chichester : Wiley, c1982. — x,575p : ill(some col.) ; 28cm
Includes index
ISBN 0-471-04174-2 (pbk) : £13.40
B82-28038

512 — Algebra *continuation*

Carnevale, Thomas. Encounters with algebra / Thomas Carnevale, Robert Shloming. — New York ; London : Harcourt Brace Jovanovich, 1981. — xiii,480p : ill(some col.) ; 28cm
Text on inside covers. — Includes index
ISBN 0-15-522593-6 (pbk) : £9.70 B82-31120

Connell, Ian. Modern algebra : a constructive introduction / Ian Connell. — London : Arnold, 1982. — x,451p : ill ; 24cm
Includes index
ISBN 0-7131-3463-1 : £16.00 B82-36009

Gulati, Bodh R.. College algebra / Bodh R. Gulati. — Boston, [Mass.] ; London : Allyn and Bacon, c1982. — xviii,514,[53]p : ill(some col.) ; 24cm
Text on lining papers. — Includes index
ISBN 0-205-07683-1 : Unpriced B82-28519

Harrison, Ian. The big red algebra book / by Ian Harrison ; and Trevor Hawkes and Bill Breckon helped him with the maths ; art by Krishna Alegeswaran ; cuteness by Eric and friends. — Warwick : 2-Manifold Publ. in association with Warwick University Mathematics Society, c1982. — 44p : ill ; 30cm
Includes index
Unpriced (pbk) B82-31428

Hungerford, Thomas W.. College algebra / Thomas W. Hungerford, Richard Mercer. — Philadelphia ; London : Saunders College, c1982. — xiv,493p : ill ; 25cm
Includes index
ISBN 0-03-059521-5 : £13.45 B82-19434

Kolman, Bernard. Algebra for college students / Bernard Kolman, Arnold Shapiro. — Rev. and expanded ed. — New York ; London : Academic Press, c1982. — xii,[537]p : ill ; 27cm
Previous ed.: 1980. — Includes index
ISBN 0-12-417875-8 : £12.00 B82-31252

McKeague, Charles P.. Intermediate algebra / Charles P. McKeague. — 2nd ed. — New York ; London : Academic Press, c1982. — 471,[87]p : ill ; 25cm
Previous ed.: 1979. — Includes index
ISBN 0-12-484770-6 : Unpriced B82-30157

Moon, Robert G.. Elementary algebra / Robert G. Moon, Robert D. Davis. — 3rd ed. — Columbus ; London : Merrill, c1980. — ix,518p : ill ; 28cm
Previous ed.: 1975. — Includes index
ISBN 0-675-08158-0 (pbk) : £10.50 B82-21000

Price, Justin J.. College algebra / Justin J. Price, Harley Flanders. — Philadelphia ; London : Saunders College Publishing, c1982. — xiii,362p : ill(some col.) ; 25cm
Text on lining papers. — Includes index
ISBN 0-03-060128-2 : £13.95 B82-19054

Stein, Edwin I.. Introductory algebra / Edwin I. Stein. — Boston, Mass. ; London : Allyn and Bacon, c1981. — 650,A1-A22p : ill(some col.) ; 24cm
Includes index
ISBN 0-205-07710-2 : £18.95 B82-00623

Thompson, J. E. (James Edgar). Algebra : for the practical worker / J.E. Thompson. — 4th ed. — New York ; London : Van Nostrand Reinhold, c1982. — xvii,277p : ill ; 21cm. — (Mathematics library for practical workers)
Previous ed.: published as Algebra for the practical man / by Max Peters and others. Princeton : Van Nostrand, 1962. — Includes index
ISBN 0-442-28273-7 (pbk) : £5.90 B82-25657

512 — Algebra — *Early works*

Jordanus, *Nemorarius.* [De numeris datis. English]. Jordanus de Nemore, De numeris datis : a critical edition and translation / by Barnabas Bernard Hughes. — Berkeley ; London : University of California Press, c1982. — xi,212p : ill,1facsim ; 25cm. — (Publications of the Center for Medieval and Renaissance Studies, UCLA ; 14)
Bibliography: p197-204. — Includes index
ISBN 0-520-04283-2 : £28.25 B82-31180

512 — Universal algebra — *Conference proceedings*

Universal algebra / edited by B. Csákány, E. Fried and E.T. Schmidt. — Amsterdam ; Oxford : North-Holland, 1982. — 804p : ill ; 25cm. — (Colloquia mathematica Societatis János Bolyai, ISSN 0139-3383 ; 29)
Conference paers. — Includes bibliographies
ISBN 0-444-85405-3 : £68.42 B82-21913

512'.00246 — Algebra — *For technicians*

Bird, J. O.. Algebra for technicians / J.O. Bird, A.J.C. May. — London : Longman, 1982. — 198p : ill ; 22cm. — (Longman technician series. Mathematics and sciences)
Includes index
ISBN 0-582-41258-7 (pbk) : £4.50 : CIP rev. B82-11303

512'.0076 — Algebra — *Questions & answers*

Drooyan, Irving. Introductory algebra : a guided worktext / Irving Drooyan, Bill Rosen. — New York ; Chichester : Wiley, c1982. — ix,410p ; 27cm
Text on inside covers. — Includes index
ISBN 0-471-06318-5 (pbk) : £12.75 B82-21538

Durbin, John R.. College algebra / John R. Durbin. — New York ; Chichester : Wiley, c1982. — lx,506p : ill ; 24cm
Text on lining papers. — Includes index
ISBN 0-471-03368-5 : £14.00 B82-26454

Kolman, Bernard. Instructor's manual for College algebra / by Bernard Kolman and Arnold Shapiro. — New York ; London : Academic Press, c1982. — 29p : ill ; 28cm
ISBN 0-12-417886-3 (pbk) : £2.40 B82-29938

McKeague, Charles P.. Instructor's resource manual for Elementary algebra, 2/e / Charles P. McKeague. — New York ; London : Academic Press, 1981. — iii,170p : ill ; 28cm
ISBN 0-12-484754-4 (pbk) : £2.40 B82-30152

McKeague, Charles P.. Instructor's resource manual for Intermediate algebra : a text/workbook / Charles P. McKeague. — New York ; London : Academic Press, 1981. — 240p : ill ; 28cm
ISBN 0-12-484761-7 (pbk) : £2.40 B82-30151

Zuckerman, Martin M.. Intermediate algebra : a straightforward approach / Martin M. Zuckerman. — 2nd ed. — New York ; Chichester : Wiley, c1982. — xvii,440,A46,I,7p : ill(some col.) ; 26cm
Previous ed.: 1976. — Text, ill on lining papers. — Includes index
ISBN 0-471-09731-4 : £14.00 B82-25865

512'.02 — Abstract algebra

Cohn, P. M.Paul Moritz. Algebra / P.M. Cohn. — Chichester : Wiley
Vol.1. — 2nd ed. — c1982. — xv,410p : ill ; 23cm
Previous ed.: 1974. — Bibliography: p400-401. — Includes index
ISBN 0-471-10169-9 (pbk) : £9.95 : CIP rev. B82-09706

512'.12 — Algebra & geometry

Ellis, A. J. (Alan John). Basic algebra and geometry for scientists and engineers / A.J. Ellis. — Chichester : Wiley, c1982. — xi,187p : ill ; 24cm
Includes index
ISBN 0-471-10174-5 (cased) : £10.95 : CIP rev.
ISBN 0-471-10175-3 (WIE ed.) : Unpriced B82-13254

512'.13 — Algebra & trigonometry

Groza, Vivian Shaw. Algebra & trigonometry / Vivian Shaw Groza, Gene Sellers. — Philadelphia ; London : Saunders College Publishing, c1982. — x,804,[90]p : ill(some col.) ; 28cm
Text on inside covers. — Includes index
ISBN 0-03-060107-x (pbk) : £13.95 B82-15345

Gulati, Bodh R.. Algebra and trigonometry : precalculus mathematics / Bodh R. Gulati, Helen Bass. — Boston, [Mass.] ; London : Allyn and Bacon, c1982. — xviii,666,[82]p : ill (some col.) ; 24cm
Text on lining papers. — Includes index
ISBN 0-205-07686-6 : Unpriced B82-28520

Hungerford, Thomas W.. Algebra & trigonometry / Thomas W. Hungerford, Richard Mercer. — Philadelphia ; London : Saunders College, c1982. — x,678p : ill(some col.) ; 25cm
Includes index
ISBN 0-03-059519-3 : £14.95 B82-16904

512'.13'076 — Algebra & trigonometry — *Questions & answers*

Kolman, Bernard. Instructor's manual for College algebra and trigonometry / by Bernard Kolman and Arnold Shapiro. — New York ; London : Academic Press, c1981. — 38p : ill ; 28cm
ISBN 0-12-417845-6 (pbk) : £2.40 B82-29981

Price, Justin J.. College algebra and trigonometry / Justin J. Price, Harley Flanders. — Philadelphia ; London : Saunders College, c1982. — xiii,496,T10,vip : ill(some col.) ; 25cm
Text on lining papers. — Includes index
ISBN 0-03-060132-0 : Unpriced B82-20605

512'.2 — Algebra. Groups. Presentation

Johnson, D. L.. Topics in the theory of group presentations / D.L. Johnson. — Cambridge : Cambridge University Press, 1980. — vii,311p : ill ; 22cm. — (London Mathematical Society lecture note series ; 42)
Includes index
ISBN 0-521-23108-6 (pbk) : £15.75 B82-28968

512'.2 — Algebra. Groups. Representations

Curtis, Charles W.. Methods of representation theory : with applications to finite groups and orders / Charles W. Curtis, Irving Reiner. — New York ; Chichester : Wiley. — (Pure and applied mathematics, ISSN 0079-8185)
Vol.1. — c1981. — xxii,819p : ill ; 24cm
Bibliography: p795-812. — Includes index
ISBN 0-471-18994-4 : £40.70 B82-06286

512'.2 — Finite groups

Tsuzuku, T.. Finite groups and finite geometries / T. Tsuzuku ; translated by A. Sevenster and T. Okuyama. — Cambridge : Cambridge University Press, 1982. — x,328p : ill ; 23cm. — (Cambridge tracts in mathematics ; v.78)
Translation of: Yugengun to yugenkika. — Includes index
ISBN 0-521-22242-7 : £22.50 : CIP rev.
Also classified at 516 B82-01329

512'.2 — Finite groups. Modular representations

Feit, Walter. The representation theory of finite groups / Walter Feit. — Amsterdam ; Oxford : North-Holland, 1982. — xiv,502p : ill ; 23cm. — (North-Holland mathematical library ; v.25)
Bibliography: p476-499. — Includes index
ISBN 0-444-86155-6 : £30.57 B82-34293

512'.2 — Finite simple groups. Classification

Gorenstein, Daniel. Finite simple groups : an introduction to their classification / Daniel Gorenstein. — New York ; London : Plenum, c1982. — x,333p ; 24cm. — (The University series in mathematics)
ISBN 0-306-40779-5 : Unpriced B82-30270

512'.2 — Locally finite groups. Sylow subgroups

Curzio, M.. Some problems of Sylow type in locally finite groups / M. Curzio. — London : Academic Press, 1979. — 69p ; 24cm. — (Institutiones mathematicae ; v.5)
At head of title: Istituto nazionale di alta matematica
Unpriced (pbk) B82-11046

512'.22 — Group theory
Representation theory. — Cambridge : Cambridge University Press, Oct.1982. — [288] p. — (London Mathematical Society lecture note series, ISSN 0076-0552 ; 69)
Translation from the Russian
ISBN 0-521-28981-5 (pbk) : £15.00 : CIP entry B82-29369

512'.22 — Group theory — *Conference proceedings*
Groups — St. Andrews 1981. — Cambridge : Cambridge University Press, Oct.1982. — [368] p. — (London Mathematical Society lecture note series, ISSN 0076-0552 ; 71)
Conference papers
ISBN 0-521-28974-2 (pbk) : £17.50 : CIP entry B82-29368

512'.22 — Group theory *expounded by* **permutations**
Glass, A. M. W.. Ordered permutation groups. — Cambridge : Cambridge University Press, Jan.1982. — [336]p. — (London Mathematical Society lecture notes series, ISSN 0076-0552 ; 55)
ISBN 0-521-24190-1 (pbk) : £12.50 : CIP entry B81-33996

512'.22'078 — Group theory. Teaching aids: Geometrical puzzles
Ewing, John, *1944-*. Puzzle it out : cubes, groups and puzzles / John Ewing, Czes Kośniowski. — Cambridge : Cambridge University Press, 1982. — 64p : ill(some col.) ; 21cm
Cover title
ISBN 0-521-28924-6 (pbk) : £2.50 B82-16194

512'.24 — Commutative algebra
Matsumura, Hideyuki. Commutative algebra / Hideyuki Matsumura. — 2nd ed. — Reading, Mass. ; London (Benjamin/Cummings), 1980. — xv,313p ; 24cm. — (Mathematics lecture note series ; 56)
Previous ed.: New York : W.A. Benjamin, 1970. — Includes index
ISBN 0-8053-7026-9 (pbk) : £12.90 B82-14748

512'.32 — Galois theory
Adamson, Iain T.. Introduction to field theory. — 2nd ed. — Cambridge : Cambridge University Press, May 1982. — [192]p
Previous ed.: Edinburgh : Oliver & Boyd, 1964
ISBN 0-521-24388-2 (cased) : £12.50 : CIP entry
ISBN 0-521-28658-1 (pbk) : £4.95 B82-11514

512'.4 — Algebra. Rings
Allenby, R. B. J. T.. Rings, fields and groups. — London : Edward Arnold, Dec.1982. — [296]p
ISBN 0-7131-3476-3 : £10.00 : CIP entry B82-30205

Kasch, F.. Modules and rings. — London : Academic Press, July 1982. — [380]p. — (London Mathematical Society monograph ; 17)
Translation of: Moduln und Ringe
ISBN 0-12-400350-8 : CIP entry
Primary classification 512'.522 B82-12442

512'.4 — Algebra. Rings. Radicals
Szász, F. A.. Radicals of rings / F.A. Szász. — Chichester : Wiley, c1981. — 287p ; 25cm
Bibliography: p215-276. — Includes index
ISBN 0-471-27583-2 : £14.75 : CIP rev. B80-00170

512'.5 — Linear algebra
Kolman, Bernard. Elementary linear algebra / Bernard Kolman. — 3rd ed. — New York : Macmillan ; London : Collier Macmillan, c1982. — xii,356p : ill ; 24cm
Previous ed.: 1977. — Text on lining papers. — Includes index
ISBN 0-02-365990-4 (cased) : £14.95
ISBN 0-02-977570-1 (pbk) : Unpriced B82-29744

Rabenstein, Albert L.. Elementary differential equations with linear algebra / Albert L. Rabenstein. — 3rd ed. — New York ; London : Academic Press, c1982. — ix,518p ; 25cm
Previous ed.: 1975. — Bibliography: p481-482. — Includes index
ISBN 0-12-573945-1 : £16.40
Primary classification 515.3'5 B82-30106

Rabenstein, Albert L.. Instructor's answer manual for Elementary differential equations with linear algebra, third edition / by Albert L. Rabenstein. — New York ; London : Academic Press, c1982. — 34p ; 23cm
ISBN 0-12-573946-x (pbk) : £2.40
Also classified at 515.3'5 B82-29937

Schneider, Dennis M.. Linear algebra : a concrete introduction / Dennis M. Schneider, Manfred Steeg, Frank H. Young. — New York : Macmillan ; London : Collier Macmillan, c1982. — xi,347p : ill ; 25cm
Includes index
ISBN 0-02-476810-3 : £15.95 B82-29743

512'.5'02433 — Linear algebra — *For economics*
Shaw, R.. Linear algebra and group representations. — London : Academic Press, Dec.1982
Vol.1: Linear algebra and introduction to group representations. — [270]p
ISBN 0-12-639201-3 : CIP entry B82-29891

Shaw, R.. Linear algebra and group representations. — London : Academic Press, Dec.1982
Vol.2: Multilinear algebra and group representations. — [300]p
ISBN 0-12-639202-1 : CIP entry B82-29892

512'.522 — Algebra. Modules
Kasch, F.. Modules and rings. — London : Academic Press, July 1982. — [380]p. — (London Mathematical Society monograph ; 17)
Translation of: Moduln und Ringe
ISBN 0-12-400350-8 : CIP entry
Also classified at 512'.4 B82-12442

512'.55 — Algebra. Rings. Left modules. Cochain complexes. Cohomology
Lubkin, Saul. Cohomology of completions / Saul Lubkin. — Amsterdam ; Oxford : North-Holland Publishing, 1980. — xxx,802p ; 24cm. — (North-Holland mathematics studies ; 42) (Notas de matemática ; 71)
Bibliography: p801-802
ISBN 0-444-86042-8 (pbk) : £29.82 B82-38412

512'.55 — Algebraic K-theory
Berrick, A. J.. An approach to algebraic K-theory / A.J. Berrick. — Boston, Mass. ; London : Pitman Advanced Publishing Program, c1982. — 108p : ill ; 25cm. — (Research notes in mathematics ; 56)
Includes index
ISBN 0-273-08529-8 (pbk) : Unpriced : CIP rev. B81-35775

Mahammed, N.. Some applications of topological K-theory / N. Mahammed, R. Piccinini, U. Suter. — Amsterdam ; Oxford : North-Holland Publishing, 1980. — ix,317p ; 24cm. — (North-Holland mathematics studies ; 45) (Notas de matemática ; 74)
Includes index
ISBN 0-444-86113-0 (pbk) : £17.10 B82-38414

512'.55 — Analytic groups. Module categories
Magid, Andy R.. Module categories of analytic groups / Andy R. Magid. — Cambridge : Cambridge University Press, 1982. — x,134p ; 23cm. — (Cambridge tracts in mathematics ; 81)
Bibliography: p132-133. — Includes index
ISBN 0-521-24200-2 : £15.00 : CIP rev. B82-14517

512'.55 — Banach algebras
Riesz and Fredholm theory in Banach algebras. — London : Pitman, July 1982. — [131]p. — (Research notes in mathematics ; 67)
ISBN 0-273-08563-8 : £7.50 : CIP entry B82-13510

512'.55 — Banach algebras. Analytic semigroups
Sinclair, Allan M.. Continuous semigroups in Banach algebras / Allan M. Sinclair. — Cambridge : Cambridge University Press, 1982. — 145p : ill ; 23cm. — (London Mathematical Society lecture note series ; 63)
Bibliography: p138-142. — Includes index
ISBN 0-521-28598-4 (pbk) : Unpriced : CIP rev. B82-12724

512'.55 — C*-algebras
Goodearl, K. R.. Notes on real and complex C*-algebras. — Nantwich (4 Church La, Nantwich, Cheshire CW5 5RQ) : Shiva, May 1982. — [180]p. — (Shiva mathematics series ; 5)
ISBN 0-906812-16-x (cased) : £12.50 : CIP entry
ISBN 0-906812-15-1 (pbk) : £7.50 B82-13273

512'.55 — Coxeter groups
Hiller, Howard. Geometry of Coxeter groups / Howard Hiller. — Boston, Mass. ; London : Pitman Advanced Publishing Program, c1982. — 213p : ill ; 25cm. — (Research notes in mathematics ; 54)
Includes index
ISBN 0-273-08517-4 (pbk) : Unpriced : CIP rev. B81-34157

512'.55 — Lie groups. Eisenstein systems
Osborne, M. Scott. The theory of Eisenstein systems / M. Scott Osborne and Garth Warner. — New York ; London : Academic Press, 1981. — xiii,385p : ill ; 24cm. — (Pure and applied mathematics ; 99)
Includes index
ISBN 0-12-529250-3 : £36.40 B82-18681

512'.55 — Mathematics. Category theory
Kelly, Gregory Maxwell. Basic concepts of enriched category theory / Gregory Maxwell Kelly. — Cambridge : Cambridge University Press, 1982. — 245p : ill ; 23cm. — (London Mathematical Society lecture note series, ISSN 0076-0522 ; 64)
Includes index
ISBN 0-521-28702-2 (pbk) : £12.50 : CIP rev. B82-03374

512'.55 — Topological groups. Uniformities
Roelcke, W.. Uniform structures on topological groups and their quotients / W. Roelcke, S. Dierolf. — New York ; London : McGraw-Hill, c1981. — ix,276p ; 25cm. — (Advanced book program)
Bibliography: p270-272. — Includes index
ISBN 0-07-053412-8 : £22.50 : CIP rev. B80-23209

512'.55 — Von Neumann algebras
Dixmier, Jacques. Von Neumann algebras / Jacques Dixmier. — Amsterdam ; Oxford : Excerpta Medica, c1981. — xxxviii,437p ; 23cm. — (North-Holland mathematical library ; v.27)
Translation of: Les algèbres d'opérateurs dans l'espace hilbertien (algèbres de Von Neumann). — Bibliography: p387-437. — Includes index
ISBN 0-444-86308-7 : £19.75 B82-08569

Strătilă, Şerban. Modular theory in operator algebras / Şerban Strătilă. — Bucureşti : Editura Academiei ; Tunbridge Wells : Abacus, 1981. — 462p ; 25cm
Translation from the Romanian. — Bibliography: p477-485. — Includes index
ISBN 0-85626-190-4 : Unpriced : CIP rev. B81-22510

512'.7 — Ancient world. Numbers. Patterns
Villiers-Stuart, Patricia. Number rhythms / by Patricia Villiers-Stuart. — London (12 Empress Place, SW6) : P. Villiers-Stuart, 1982. — 22leaves : ill ; 34cm
Unpriced (unbound) B82-22957

512'.7 — Number theory
Burn, R. P.. A pathway into number theory / R.P. Burn. — Cambridge : Cambridge University Press, 1982. — vii,257p ; 24cm
Bibliography: p244-245. — Includes index
ISBN 0-521-24118-9 (cased) : £18.00
ISBN 0-521-28534-8 (pbk) : £7.50 B82-18236

Davenport, H.. The higher arithmetic. — 5th ed. — Cambridge : Cambridge University Press, Sept.1982. — [192]p
Previous ed.: London : Hutchinson, 1970
ISBN 0-521-24422-6 (cased) : £12.00 : CIP entry
ISBN 0-521-28678-6 (pbk) : £5.00 B82-29360

512'.7 — Number theory — *Conference proceedings*
Journées arithmétiques 1980. — Cambridge : Cambridge University Press, May 1982. — [392]p. — (London Mathematical Society lecture note series, ISSN 0076-0552 ; 56)
Conference papers
ISBN 0-521-28513-5 (pbk) : £15.00 : CIP entry
B82-12689

512'.73 — Analytic number theory
Bellman, Richard. Analytic number theory : an introduction / Richard Bellman. — Reading, Mass. ; London : Benjamin/Cummings, 1980. — xvi,195p : ill ; 25cm. — (Mathematics lecture notes series ; 57)
Includes bibliographies and index
ISBN 0-8053-0360-x : £12.90 B82-31251

512'.73 — Mathematics. Continued fractions
Jones, William B.. Continued fractions : analytic theory and applications / William B. Jones and W.J. Thron ; foreword by Felix E. Browder ; introduction by Peter Henrici. — Reading, Mass. ; London : Addison-Wesley, 1980. — xxviii,428p : ill ; 25cm. — (Encyclopedia of mathematics and its applications ; v.11)
Bibliography: p404-419. — Includes index
ISBN 0-201-13510-8 : £24.80 B82-23419

512'.73 — Reciprocal equations. Asymptotic theory
De Koninck, J.-M.. Topics in arithmetical functions : asymptotic formulae for sums of reciprocals of arithmetical functions and related results / J.-M. De Koninck and A. Ivić. — Amsterdam ; Oxford : North-Holland Publishing, 1980. — xvii,262p ; 24cm. — (North-Holland mathematics studies ; 43) (Notas de matemática ; 72)
Bibliography: p251-258. — Includes index
ISBN 0-444-86049-5 (pbk) : £15.90
B82-38411

512'.74 — Algebra. Diophantine equations. Solution
Gel'fond, A. O.. Solving equations in integers / A.O. Gelfond ; translated from the Russian by O.B. Sheinin. — Moscow : Mir, 1981 ; [London] : Distributed by Central Books. — 56p ; 20cm. — (Little mathematics library)
Translation of: Reshenie uravneniĭ v t͡selykh chislakh
ISBN 0-7147-1772-x (pbk) : £0.95 B82-39306

512'.74 — Mathematics. Class field theory
Iwascwa, Ken-ichi. Local classified theory. — Oxford : Clarendon Press, July 1982. — [150] p. — (Oxford mathematical monographs)
Translation from the Japanese
ISBN 0-19-853356-x : £15.00 : CIP entry
B82-14361

512'.74 — Mathematics. Field theory
Klotz, A. H.. Macrophysics and geometry. — Cambridge : Cambridge University Press, June 1982. — [152]p
ISBN 0-521-23938-9 : £20.00 : CIP entry
B82-14506

512'.74 — P-adic numbers
Koblitz, Neal. p-adic analysis : a short course on recent work / Neal Koblitz. — Cambridge : Cambridge University Press, 1980. — 163p : ill ; 22cm. — (London Mathematical Society lecture note series, ISSN 0076-0552 ; 46)
Bibliography: p154-160. — Includes index
ISBN 0-521-28060-5 (pbk) : Unpriced : CIP rev. B80-28293

Mahler, Kurt. p-adic numbers and their functions / Kurt Mahler. — 2nd ed. — Cambridge : Cambridge University Press, 1981. — x,320p ; 23cm. — (Cambridge tracts in mathematics ; 76)
Previous ed.: published as Introduction to p-adic numbers and their functions. 1973. — Includes index
ISBN 0-521-23102-7 : £19.00 B82-31512

512.9'22 — Logarithms. Geometric representation
Markushevich, A. I.. Areas and logarithms / A.I. Markushevich ; translated from the Russian by I. Aleksanova. — Moscow : Mir ; [London] : Distributed by Central Books, 1981. — 69p : ill ; 20cm. — (Little mathematics library)
Translation of: Ploshchadi i logarifmy
ISBN 0-7147-1770-3 (pbk) : £0.95 B82-40110

512.9'25 — Magic cubes
Benson, William H.. Magic cubes : new recreations / William H. Benson and Oswald Jacoby. — New York : Dover ; London : Constable, c1981. — 142p : ill ; 22cm
ISBN 0-486-24140-8 (pbk) : £3.00 B82-26161

512.9'42 — Algebra. Linear equations. Numerical solution. Iterative methods
Hageman, Louis A.. Applied iterative methods / Louis A. Hageman, David M. Young. — New York ; London : Academic Press, 1981. — xvii,386p : ill ; 24cm. — (Computer science and applied mathematics)
Bibliography: p373-380. — Includes index
ISBN 0-12-313340-8 : £26.20 B82-10046

512.9'42 — Algebra. Nonlinear equations. Numerical solution
Rosinger, E. E.. Nonlinear equivalence, reduction of PDEs to ODEs and fast convergent numerical methods. — London : Pitman, Jan.1983. — [270]p. — (Research notes in mathematics ; 77)
ISBN 0-273-08570-0 (pbk) : £10.95 : CIP entry
B82-33715

512.9'42 — Quartic equations. Solution
Warriner, Michael. A solution of quartic equations : and others / Michael Warriner. — [Wellington] ([Trading Estate, Wellington, Somerset TA21 8ST]) : Acanthus, 1980. — 29p ; 22cm
Unpriced B82-00020

512.9'434 — Algebra. Matrices. Calculus
Graham, Alexander. Kronecker products and matrix calculus : with applications / Alexander Graham. — Chichester : Horwood, 1981. — 130p ; 24cm. — (Ellis Horwood series in mathematics and its applications)
Bibliography: p126-128. — Includes index
ISBN 0-85312-391-8 (cased) : £14.50 : CIP rev.
ISBN 0-85312-427-2 (pbk) : Unpriced
B81-31065

512.9'434 — Algebra. Matrices — *For engineering & science*
Deif, Assem S.. Advanced matrix theory for scientists and engineers / Assem S. Deif. — Tunbride Wells : Abacus, 1982. — x,241p ; 24cm
Bibliography: p234-237. — Includes index
ISBN 0-85626-327-3 (pbk) : Unpriced : CIP rev. B81-39225

512.9'434 — Algebra. Matrices. Generalised inverses
Recent applications of generalized inverses. — London : Pitman, Sept.1982. — [280]p. — (Research notes in mathematics ; 66)
ISBN 0-273-08550-6 (pbk) : £11.00 : CIP entry
B82-18873

513 — ARITHMETIC

513 — Arithmetic
Groza, Vivian Shaw. Arithmetic / Vivian Shaw Groza. — Philadelphia ; London : Saunders College Publishing, c1982. — ix,539,[18]p : ill,forms ; 28cm
Text, ill on inside covers. — Includes index
ISBN 0-03-060109-6 (pbk) : £12.95
B82-15342

Thompson, J. E. (James Edgar). Arithmetic : for the practical worker. — 4th ed. — New York ; London : Van Nostrand Reinhold, c1982. — xiv,266p : ill ; 21cm. — (Mathematics library for practical workers)
Author: J.E. Thompson. — Previous ed.: published as Arithmetic for the practical man / by Max Peters and others. Princeton : Van Nostrand, 1962. — Includes index
ISBN 0-442-28275-3 (pbk) : £5.90 B82-25654

513 — Arithmetic — *For consumers*
Pascaris, Peter A.. A guidebook for teaching consumer mathematics / Peter A. Pascaris. — Boston, [Mass.] ; London : Allyn and Bacon, 1982. — xii,322p : forms ; 28cm. — (A Guidebook for teaching)
Includes bibliographies
ISBN 0-205-07388-3 (pbk) : Unpriced
B82-27061

513 — Arithmetic. Use of fingers — *Manuals*
Pai, Hang Young. The complete book of Chisanbop : original finger calculation method : created by Sung Jin Pai and Hang Young Pai / written by Hang Young Pai ; edited by John Leonard. — New York ; London : Van Nostrand Reinhold, c1981. — vi,330p : ill ; 24cm
ISBN 0-442-27569-2 (cased) : Unpriced
ISBN 0-442-27568-4 (pbk) : £11.60
B82-08236

513 — Great Britain. Adults. Numeracy — *Statistics*
Adult numeracy study : tabulated results of a survey / conducted by Social Surveys (Gallup Poll) Ltd ; on behalf of the Advisory Council for Adult and Continuing Education in February/March 1981. — Leicester : ACACE, c1981. — 84p ; 30cm. — (Gallup report)
ISBN 0-906436-08-7 (spiral) : £6.00
B82-39325

513'.024613 — Arithmetic — *Questions & answers — For nursing*
Gatford, J. D.. Nursing calculations / J.D. Gatford. — Melbourne ; Edinburgh : Churchill Livingstone, 1982. — 100p ; 19cm
ISBN 0-443-02388-3 (pbk) : Unpriced : CIP rev. B82-12346

513'.02463 — Arithmetic — *For agriculture*
O'Loan, Arthur. Farm calculations / Arthur O'Loan. — [Blackrock] ([Frascati Rd., Blackrock, Co. Dublin]) : ACOT, c1981. — 93p : ill(some col.) ; 21x29cm
Unpriced (pbk) B82-05192

513'.076 — Arithmetic — *Questions & answers*
Brown, Ross F.. Basic arithmetic / Ross F. Brown. — Glenview ; London : Scott, Foresman, c1979. — ix,374p : ill ; 28cm
Text on inside cover
ISBN 0-673-15106-9 (pbk) : £10.50
B82-40997

513'.076 — Arithmetic — *Questions & answers — For Caribbean students*
Soon, Stephen Quan. Graded arithmetic for the Caribbean / adapted by Stephen Quan Soon. — [Eagle Hall] : Caribbean Universities Press ; Aylesbury : Ginn
Adaptation of: Two grade arithmetic / by K. Lovell and C.H.J. Smith
1. — c1980. — 96p : ill ; 21cm
ISBN 0-602-22512-4 (pbk) : Unpriced
B82-38750

Soon, Stephen Quan. Graded arithmetic for the Caribbean / adapted by Stephen Quan Soon. — [Eagel Hall] : Caribbean Univeristies Press ; Aylesbury : Ginn
Adaptation of: Two grade arithmetic / by K. Lovell and C.H.J. Smith
Answers 1 & 2. — c1980. — 64p ; 21cm
ISBN 0-602-22514-0 (pbk) : Unpriced
B82-38751

513'.076 — Arithmetic — *Questions & answers — For children*
Griffiths, A. L.. Basic 7 a day / A.L. Griffiths. — Edinburgh : Oliver & Boyd, 1981. — 77p : col.ill ; 25cm
ISBN 0-05-003435-9 (pbk) : £1.25 B82-10041

Griffiths, A. L.. Basic 7 a day / A.L. Griffiths. — Edinburgh : Oliver & Boyd
Answers. — 1981. — [12]p ; 21cm
ISBN 0-05-003441-3 (unbound) : £0.35
B82-12357

Test your child's arithmetic. — Sevenoaks : Produced exclusively for W.H. Smith by Hodder and Stoughton, 1982. — [32]p : ill (some col.) ; 25cm
ISBN 0-340-28055-7 (pbk) : £0.60 B82-27680

513'.076 — Arithmetic — *Questions & answers — For schools*
Hesse, K. A.. The four rules of number / K.A. Hesse. — Harlow : Longman
Bk.2: [Pupil's ed.]. — 1982. — 62p ; 25cm
ISBN 0-582-18438-x (pbk) : £0.72 B82-26739

513'.076 — Arithmetic — *Questions & answers — For schools* *continuation*

Hesse, K. A.. An introduction to first problems / K.A. Hesse. — Pupil's ed. — Harlow : Longman, 1982. — 30p : ill ; 25cm
ISBN 0-582-18295-6 (pbk) : Unpriced
ISBN 0-582-18296-4 (teacher's ed) B82-22881

Hesse, K. A.. An introduction to first problems / K.A. Hesse. — Harlow : Longman
Teacher's ed. — 1982. — 30p : ill ; 25cm
ISBN 0-582-18296-4 (pbk) : £0.75 B82-23062

Hollands, Roy. Foundation arithmetic / Roy Hollands. — Cambridge : Cambridge University Press, 1980. — 96p : ill ; 25cm. — (Arithmetic for living)
ISBN 0-521-23354-2 (pbk) : £1.60 B82-32119

Logan, Lindsay. Home arithmetic / Lindsay Logan. — Cambridge : Cambridge University Press, 1980. — 62p : ill ; 23cm. — (Arithmetic for living)
ISBN 0-521-29923-3 (pbk) : £1.20 B82-32118

513'.07'8 — Schools. Curriculum subjects: Arithmetic. Electronic teaching aids

Briggs, Brenda. Electronic learning aids : enquiry one / Brenda Briggs and Maurice Meredith with Hampshire teachers. — [Southampton] : University of Southampton, Department of Education, c1981. — v,98p : ill,facsims ; 30cm
Cover title
ISBN 0-85432-218-3 (spiral) : £2.50
B82-25618

513'.2 — Arithmetic. Addition — *For pre-school children*

Hurt, Roger. Addition / written by Roger and Mary Hurt ; illustrated by Peter Kingston. — Loughborough : Ladybird, c1982. — 51p : chiefly col.ill ; 18cm. — (Ladybird junior maths)
Ill on lining papers
ISBN 0-7214-0704-8 : £0.50 B82-25887

513'.2 — Arithmetic. Multiplication — *For children*

Hurt, Roger. Multiplication / written by Roger and Mary Hurt ; illustrated by Lynn N. Grundy. — Loughborough : Ladybird, 1982. — 51p : col.ill ; 18cm. — (Ladybird junior maths)
Ill on lining papers
ISBN 0-7214-0706-4 : £0.50 B82-29308

513'.2 — Arithmetic. Division — *For children*

Hurt, Roger. Division / written by Roger and Mary Hurt ; illustrated by Peter Kingston. — Loughborough : Ladybird, c1982. — 51p : col.ill ; 18cm. — (Ladybird junior maths)
Ill on lining papers
ISBN 0-7214-0707-2 : £0.50 B82-29307

513'.2 — Arithmetic. Subtraction — *For children*

Hurt, Roger. Subtraction / written by Roger and Mary Hurt ; illustrated by Peter Kingston. — Loughborough : Ladybird, c1982. — 51p : col.ill ; 18cm. — (Ladybird junior maths)
Ill on lining papers
ISBN 0-7214-0705-6 : £0.50 B82-29306

513'.2 — Numbers

Laxton, Bob. Make it count : a fresh start with numbers / Bob Laxton and Graham Rawlinson. — Cambridge : National Extension College, 1977 (1978 [printing]). — 124p : ill ; 30cm
ISBN 0-86082-101-3 (pbk) : Unpriced
B82-40278

513'.2 — Numbers — *For children*

1 2 3 : a counting book / editor Janine Amos ; illustrated by the County Studios. — Paulton : Purnell, 1982. — [24]p : chiefly col.ill ; 21cm. — (A First learning book)
ISBN 0-361-05372-x (pbk) : £0.50 B82-38472

Asimov, Isaac. How we found out about numbers / Isaac Asimov. — Harlow : Longman, 1982, c1973. — 54p : ill,1map ; 23cm. — (How we found out about series)
Originally published: New York : Walker, 1973. — Includes index
ISBN 0-582-39148-2 : £2.75 B82-33651

Brown, Mik. Animal fun 123 / written and illustrated by Mik Brown. — London : Kingfisher, 1982. — [32]p : chiefly col.ill ; 23x25cm
ISBN 0-86272-030-3 : £1.95 : CIP rev.
B82-00368

Hindley, Judy. The counting book / Judy Hindley ; illustrated by Colin King ; consultant Betty Root. — London : Usborne, 1979. — [32]p : chiefly col.ill ; 21cm. — (An Usborne first book)
ISBN 0-86020-360-3 (pbk) : £0.65 B82-13395

513'.2'0222 — Numbers — *Illustrations — For children*

Anno, Mitsumasa. [Ten little people and their new house]. Anno's counting house. — London : Bodley Head, Oct.1982. — [56]p
Originally published: Dowaya : Tokyo, 1981
ISBN 0-370-30931-6 : £4.95 : CIP entry
B82-24453

Counting / Walt Disney Productions. — Bristol : Purnell, 1976 (1982 [printing]). — [28]p : chiefly col.ill ; 25cm. — (Disney colour library)
ISBN 0-361-03493-8 : Unpriced B82-21051

Counting / illustrated by Pamela Storey ; [editor Janine Amos]. — Bristol : Purnell, 1982. — [26]p : col.ill ; 27cm. — (A First learning book) (My first big books)
ISBN 0-361-05380-0 : £1.99 B82-34767

Counting monster machines. — London : Blackie, 1980. — [24]p : col.ill ; 20cm. — (Patchwork picture books)
ISBN 0-216-90850-7 (cased) : £1.95 : CIP rev.
ISBN 0-216-90849-3 (pbk) : Unpriced
Primary classification 621.8'022'2 B80-00224

Henderson, John, *1949-*. Number book one / John Henderson & Glynis Murray. — London : Macmillan Children's, c1981. — [102]p : chiefly col.ill ; 22cm. — (Picture board books)
Cover title
ISBN 0-333-32362-9 : £0.99 B82-05971

Hutchins, Pat. 1 hunter / by Pat Hutchins. — London : Bodley Head, 1982. — [24]p : chiefly col.ill ; 26cm
ISBN 0-370-30920-0 : £3.95 : CIP rev.
B82-01152

Little one's book of numbers / illustrated by Alan Fredman. — London : Dean, c1982. — [12]p : col.ill ; 21cm. — (A Dean board book)
ISBN 0-603-00312-5 (unbound) : £0.65
B82-36557

Svensson, Borje. Numbers /. [designed and illustrated by Borje Svensson] ; [paper engineering by James Diaz]. — [London] : Collins, 1982, c1981. — 1box : col.ill ; 60mmx60mmx60mm. — (A Collins block book)
1 sheet, 57mmx108cm (concertina folded) attached in box containing diorama
ISBN 0-00-138381-7 : £1.25 B82-36184

Woolcock, Peter. One, two, three : a book of numbers / Peter Woolcock with Leonard Matthews. — London : Hodder and Stoughton, 1981. — [42]p : chiefly col.ill ; 31cm
ISBN 0-340-26646-5 : £2.50 : CIP rev.
B81-23928

Youldon, Gillian. Numbers / by Gillian Youldon. — London : Watts, 1979. — [26]p : col.ill ; 20cm. — (Picture play!)
ISBN 0-85166-756-2 (cased) : £1.99
ISBN 0-85166-900-x (pbk) : £0.99 B82-40816

513'.2'0715 — Adults. Number skills. Teaching

An **Introduction** to numeracy teaching. — London : ALBSU, 1982. — 64p : ill ; 21cm
ISBN 0-906509-19-x (pbk) : £0.60 B82-39064

513'.2'076 — Arithmetic. Decimals — *Questions & answers — For children*

Hesse, K. A.. Decimals : hundreds of sums, carefully selected and graded to give extra practice to children of all ages / K.A. Hesse. — Harlow : Longman, 1981. — 32p ; 25cm. — (Basic arithmetic practice ; 4)
ISBN 0-582-39173-3 (pbk) : £0.60 B82-01278

513'.2'076 — Arithmetic. Decimals — *Questions & answers — For schools*

Coyne, Peter. Maths quizzes : decimals / Peter Coyne. — Slough : University Tutorial, 1981. — 38p : ill ; 21cm
ISBN 0-7231-0816-1 (pbk) : £0.80 B82-06986

Heylings, M. R.. Fractions and decimals / M.R. Heylings. — Huddersfield : Schofield & Sims, 1982. — 144p : ill(some col.) ; 24cm. — (Graded examples in mathematics)
ISBN 0-7217-2323-3 (pbk) : £1.55
Primary classification 513'.26'076 B82-29675

Heylings, M. R.. Fractions and decimals answers / M.R. Heylings. — Huddersfield : Schofield & Sims, 1982. — 48p ; 24cm. — (Graded examples in mathematics)
ISBN 0-7217-2324-1 (pbk : corrected) : £0.95
Primary classification 513'.26'076 B82-35344

513'.2'076 — Arithmetic. Fundamental operations — *Questions & answers — For schools*

Hesse, K. A.. The four rules of number / K.A. Hesse. — Harlow : Longman
Bk.2: [Teacher's ed.]. — 1982. — viii,62p ; 25cm
ISBN 0-582-18439-8 (pbk) : £1.30 B82-26747

Number practice / compiled by A.J. Stables. — Huddersfield : Schofield & Sims
2. — 1981. — 37p : ill(some col.) ; 24cm + Answer book(37p : ill ; 24cm)
ISBN 0-7217-2316-0 (pbk) : £0.65
ISBN 0-7217-2320-9 (answer book) : £0.95
B82-12479

Stables, A. J.Number practice. — Huddersfield : Schofield & Sims
1 / by A.J. Stables. — 1981. — 37p : ill(some col.) ; 24cm + answer book(35p : ill ; 24cm)
ISBN 0-7217-2315-2 (pbk) : £0.95
ISBN 0-7217-2319-5 (answer book) : £0.95
B82-07001

Stables, A. J.. Number practice / compiled by A.J. Stables. — Huddersfield : Schofield & Sims
3. — 1982. — 37p : ill(some col.) ; 24cm + answer book(37p : ill ; 24cm)
ISBN 0-7217-2317-9 (pbk) : £0.65
ISBN 0-7217-2321-7 (answer book) : £0.95
B82-22322

Stables, A. J.. Number practice / compiled by A.J. Stables. — Huddersfield : Schofield & Sims
4: Answers. — 1982. — 37p : ill(some col.) ; 24cm
ISBN 0-7217-2322-5 (pbk) : Unpriced
B82-35404

513'.2'076 — Numbers — *Questions & answers — For non-English speaking students*

Elsworth, Steve. Count me in : understanding numbers in English / Steve Elsworth. — Harlow : Longman, 1982. — 48p : ill,maps ; 25cm
Text on inside back cover
ISBN 0-582-74855-0 (pbk) : Unpriced
B82-36239

513'.26'076 — Arithmetic. Fractions — *Questions & answers — For children*

Hesse, K. A.. Fractions : hundreds of sums, carefully selected and graded to give extra practice to children of all ages / K.A. Hesse. — Harlow : Longman, 1981. — 32p : ill ; 25cm. — (Basic arithmetic practice ; 3)
ISBN 0-582-39172-5 (pbk) : £0.60 B82-01279

513'.26'076 — Arithmetic. Fractions — *Questions & answers — For schools*

Coyne, Peter. Maths quizzes : fractions / Peter Coyne. — Slough : University Tutorial, 1981. — 44p : ill ; 21cm
ISBN 0-7231-0817-x (pbk) : £0.80 B82-06987

513'.26'076 — Arithmetic. Fractions — *Questions & answers — For schools* *continuation*

Heylings, M. R.. Fractions and decimals / M.R. Heylings. — Huddersfield : Schofield & Sims, 1982. — 144p : ill(some col.) ; 24cm. — (Graded examples in mathematics)
ISBN 0-7217-2323-3 (pbk) : £1.55
Also classified at 513'.2'076 B82-29675

Heylings, M. R.. Fractions and decimals answers / M.R. Heylings. — Huddersfield : Schofield & Sims, 1982. — 48p ; 24cm. — (Graded examples in mathematics)
ISBN 0-7217-2324-1 (pbk : corrected) : £0.95
Also classified at 513'.2'076 B82-35344

513'.5 — Numeration — *For children*

Adamson, Jean. Topsy and Tim's counting book. — London : Blackie, June 1982. — [24]p
ISBN 0-216-91268-7 (cased) : £2.75 : CIP entry
ISBN 0-216-91267-9 (pbk) : £0.95 B82-09972

Adamson, Jean. Topsy and Tim's counting frieze. — London : Blackie, June 1982. — [20]p
ISBN 0-216-91180-x (pbk) : £1.95 : CIP entry B82-10462

Testa, Fulvio. If you take a pencil. — London : Andersen Press, Sept.1982. — [32]p
ISBN 0-86264-032-6 : £4.50 : CIP entry B82-21560

513'.5 — Numeration — *For children — Arabic texts*

al-'**Add** wa-l-qiyās / tarğamah Fahmī 'Utmān. — London : Macmillan, 1981. — 30p : col.ill ; 18cm
Translation of: Counting and measuring. — Originally published: Amman : Royal Jordanian Scientific Society, 1979
ISBN 0-333-32337-8 : Unpriced
Primary classification 530.8 B82-13465

513'.56'05 — Numbers. Duodecimal notation — *Serials*

The **Dozenal** journal. — No.1 (Winter 1981)-. — New York : Dozenal Society of America ; Denmead (Millside, Mill Rd, Denmead, Hampshire PO7 6PA) : Dozenal Society of Great Britain, 1981-. — v. : ill,music ; 21cm
Irregular. — Merger of: The Dozenal review; and, The Duodecimal bulletin
ISSN 0260-4884 = Dozenal journal : Unpriced B82-27642

513'.93 — Business arithmetic

Boisselle, Arthur H.. Using mathematics in business / Arthur H. Boisselle, Jr., Donald M. Freeman, Lyle V. Brenna. — Reading, Mass. ; London : Addison-Wesley, c1981. — xiv,382p : ill,forms ; 28cm
Includes index
ISBN 0-201-00098-9 (pbk) : £11.20 B82-37326

Harvey, J. H.. Commercial arithmetic. — 5th ed. — Sevenoaks : Teach Yourself Books, Nov.1982. — [192]p. — (Teach Yourself series)
Previous ed.: 1977
ISBN 0-340-28269-x (pbk) : £2.25 : CIP entry B82-29070

Ochs, Robert. Introduction to business mathematics / Robert Ochs, James Gray. — Philadelphia ; London : Saunders College Publishing, c1982. — x,356p : ill ; 26cm
£12.50 (pbk) B82-13551

Smith, Karl J.. Business mathematics / Karl J. Smith. — Boston, Mass. ; London : Allyn & Bacon, c1982. — xiv,559p : ill,forms ; 28cm
Text on inside covers. — Includes index
ISBN 0-205-07622-x (pbk) : Unpriced B82-27111

Stafford, L. W. T.. Business mathematics / L.W.T. Stafford. — 2nd ed. — Plymouth : Macdonald and Evans, 1979. — xiv,384p : ill ; 18cm. — (The M & E handbook series)
Previous ed.: 1969. — Includes index
ISBN 0-7121-0282-5 (pbk) : £2.95 B82-33763

513'.93 — Business arithmetic — *For African students*

Newcomb, V. N.. Practical calculations for business studies : problems and applications for students in Africa / V.N. Newcomb. — Chichester : Wiley, c1981. — vii,156p : ill ; 24cm
Includes index
ISBN 0-471-27966-8 (cased) : £9.90 : CIP rev.
ISBN 0-471-27967-6 (pbk) : Unpriced B81-23740

513'.93 — Business arithmetic — *For schools*

Steele, D. U.. Business and commercial arithmetic / D.U. Steele. — Cambridge : Cambridge University Press, 1980. — 56p : ill ; 23cm. — (Arithmetic for living)
ISBN 0-521-29924-1 (pbk) : £1.20 B82-32121

513'.93'028 — Business arithmetic. Use of electronic calculators — *Questions & answers*

Berg, Gary A.. Using calculators for business problems / Gary A. Berg. — Chicago ; Henley-on-Thames : Science Research Associates, c1979. — 227p : ill ; 28cm
ISBN 0-574-20565-9 (pbk) : £6.85 B82-08044

513'.93'076 — Business arithmetic — *Questions & answers — For East African students*

Bishop, K. R.. Business calculations for East Africa / K.R. Bishop and Amirali Sokwala. — London : Cassell, 1981. — 106p : ill ; 22cm
ISBN 0-304-30804-8 (pbk) : Unpriced B82-03183

514 — TOPOLOGY

514'.2 — Algebraic topology

Blackett, D. W.. Elementary topology. — London : Academic Press, Sept.1982. — [250]p
Originally published: 1967
ISBN 0-12-103060-1 (pbk) : CIP entry B82-19156

514'.2 — Surface topology

Firby, P.. Surface topology. — Chichester : Ellis Horwood, June 1982. — [192]p. — (Ellis Horwood series in mathematics and its applications)
ISBN 0-85312-483-3 : £17.50 : CIP entry B82-18587

514'.223 — Topological spaces: Complex manifolds & functions of several complex variables

Field, Michael J.. Several complex variables and complex manifolds / Mike Field. — Cambridge : Cambridge University Press, 1982. — 2v. : ill ; 23cm. — (London Mathematical Society lecture note series, ISSN 0076-0552 ; 65-66)
Includes bibliographies and index
ISBN 0-521-28301-9 (pbk) : Unpriced : CIP rev.
ISBN 0-521-28888-6 (v.2) : £11.00 B82-11481

514'.223 — Topological spaces: Minimal submanifolds — *Conference proceedings*

Japan-United States Seminar on Minimal Submanifolds including Geodesics *(1977 : Tokyo)*. Minimal submanifolds and geodesics : proceedings of the Japan-United States Seminar on Minimal Submanifolds, including Geodesics Tokyo, 1977 / edited by Morio Obata. — Amsterdam ; Oxford : North-Holland Publishing, 1979, c1978. — x,292p,[1]leaf of plates : ill,ports ; 25cm
Includes bibliographies and index
ISBN 0-444-85327-8 : Unpriced B82-17880

514'.24 — Homotopy theory

Baues, Hans Joachim. Commutator calculus and groups of homotopy classes / Hans Joachim Baues. — Cambridge : Cambridge University Press, 1981. — 160p ; 22cm. — (London Mathematical Society lecture note series, ISSN 0076-0552 ; 50)
Bibliography: p156-158. — Includes index
ISBN 0-521-28424-4 (pbk) : £11.25 : CIP rev. B81-31237

Crabb, M. C.. ZZ/2 — homotopy theory / M.C. Crabb. — Cambridge : Cambridge University Press, 1980. — 128p ; 22cm. — (London Mathematical Society lecture note series, ISSN 0076-0552 ; 44)
Bibliography: p121-126. — Includes index
ISBN 0-521-28051-6 (pbk) : £7.75 : CIP rev. B80-28296

514'.3 — Low dimensional topological spaces — *Conference proceedings*

Conference on Topology in Low Dimension *(1979 : Bangor)*. Low dimensional topology : vol.1 of the proceedings of the Conference on Topology in Low Dimension, Bangor, 1979 / edited by R. Brown and T.L. Thickstun. — Cambridge : Cambridge University Press, 1982. — 245p : ill ; 23cm. — (London Mathematical Society lecture note series ; 48)
Includes bibliographies
ISBN 0-521-28146-6 (pbk) : Unpriced : CIP rev. B82-18436

514'.32 — Topological spaces. Open subsets. Chain conditions

Comfort, W. W. (William Wistar), *1933-*. Chain conditions in topology / W.W. Comfort, S. Negrepontis. — Cambridge : Cambridge University Press, 1982. — xiii,300p ; 23cm. — (Cambridge tracts in mathematics ; 79)
Bibliography: p281-294. — Includes index
ISBN 0-521-23487-5 : £22.50 : CIP rev. B82-12141

514'.7 — Differential topology

Arnol'd, V. I.. Singularity theory : selected papers / V.I. Arnold. — Cambridge : Cambridge University Press, 1981. — 266p : ill ; 22cm. — (London Mathematical Society lecture note series, ISSN 0076-0522 ; 53)
Includes bibliographies
ISBN 0-521-28511-9 (pbk) : £12.50 : CIP rev.
Primary classification 515'.2 B81-31284

514'.72 — Catastrophe theory

Sinha, D. K.Catastrophe : theory and applications / edited by D.K. Sinha. — New York ; Chichester : Wiley, c1981. — xi,158p : ill ; 23cm. — (Mathematics of mathematical sciences)
Bibliography: p132-154. — Includes index
ISBN 0-470-27303-8 : £10.95 B82-36684

514'.72 — Differential topology

Brocker, Th.. Introduction to differential topology. — Cambridge : Cambridge University Press, Sept.1982. — [160]p
Translation of: Einführung in die Differentialtopologie
ISBN 0-521-24135-9 (cased) : £13.50 : CIP entry
ISBN 0-521-28470-8 (pbk) : £5.50 B82-19539

515 — CALCULUS

515 — Calculus

Binmore, K. G.. Mathematical analysis. — 2nd ed. — Cambridge : Cambridge University Press, Oct.1982. — [376]p
Previous ed.: 1977
ISBN 0-521-24680-6 (cased) : £18.00 : CIP entry
ISBN 0-521-28882-7 (pbk) : £6.95 B82-37665

Contributions to analysis and geometry / edited by D.N. Clark, G. Pecelli, R. Sacksteder. — Baltimore ; London : Johns Hopkins University Press, c1981. — ix,357p : ill ; 24cm
Conference proceedings. — Supplement to The American journal of mathematics. — Includes bibliographies
ISBN 0-8018-2779-5 : £27.50 B82-34454

De Lillo, Nicholas J.. Advanced calculus with applications / Nicholas J. De Lillo. — New York : Macmillan ; London : Collier Macmillan, c1982. — xii,836p : ill ; 24cm
Includes index
ISBN 0-02-328220-7 (cased) : Unpriced
ISBN 0-02-977530-2 (Int. ed.) : £10.95 B82-36484

Grossman, Stanley I.. Calculus / Stanley I. Grossman. — New York ; London : Academic Press
Part 2: Multivariably calculus, linear algebra, and differential equations. — 1982. — x,721,76p : ill ; 26cm
Includes index
ISBN 0-12-304302-6 : £18.60 B82-29969

515 — Calculus *continuation*

Larson, Roland E.. Calculus : with analytic geometry / Roland E. Larson, Robert P. Hostetler ; exercises prepared with the assistance of David E. Heyd. — Lexington, Mass. : Heath ; London : Distributed by Eurospan, c1979. — xv,974p : ill(some col.) ; 24cm
Text, ill on lining papers. — Includes index
ISBN 0-669-01301-3 : Unpriced B82-25715

Maurin, Krzysztof. Analysis / Krzysztof Maurin. — Dordrecht ; London : Reidel
Translation of: Analiza
Pt.2: Integration, distributions, holomorphic functions, tensor and harmonic analysis. — c1980. — xvii,829p : ill ; 23cm
Includes index
ISBN 90-277-0865-7 : Unpriced B82-37352

Parzynski, William R.. Introduction to mathematical analysis / William R. Parzynski, Philip W. Zipse. — New York ; London : McGraw-Hill, c1982. — viii,359p : ill ; 24cm. — (International series in pure and applied mathematics)
Includes index
ISBN 0-07-048845-2 : £17.95 B82-37453

Salas, S. L.. Calculus : one and several variables : with analytic geometry / S.L. Salas, Einar Hille. — 4th ed. — New York ; Chichester : Wiley, c1982. — 2v.(xv,1038,[64]p) : ill(some col.) ; 27cm
Previous ed.: 1978. — Text on lining papers. — Includes index
ISBN 0-471-08055-1 : Unpriced
ISBN 0-471-08054-3 (pt.2) : £17.00
B82-28779

Salas, S. L.. Calculus : one and several variables : with analytic geometry / S.L. Salas, Einar Hille. — 4th ed. — New York ; Chichester : Wiley, c1982. — xvi,1038,A-93,I-5p : ill(some col.),ports ; 27cm
Previous ed.: 1978. — Text on lining papers. — Also available in two parts. — Includes index
ISBN 0-471-04660-4 : £25.00 B82-23514

Sherlock, A. J.. Calculus : pure and applied / A.J. Sherlock, E.M. Roebuck, M.G. Godfrey. — London : Edward Arnold, 1982. — x,534p : ill ; 25cm
Includes index
ISBN 0-7131-3446-1 (pbk) : Unpriced : CIP rev. B81-27937

Textbook of mathematical analysis / Leadership Project Committee (Mathematics), University of Bombay. — New Delhi : Tata McGraw-Hill ; New Delhi ; London : McGraw-Hill, 1980, (1981 [printing]). — ix,214p : ill ; 23cm
Includes index
ISBN 0-07-096393-2 (pbk) : £3.25 B82-03887

Thompson, J. E. (James Edgar). Calculus : for the practical worker / J.E. Thompson. — 4th ed. — New York ; London : Van Nostrand Reinhold, c1982. — xvi,280p : ill ; 21cm. — (Mathematics library for practical workers)
Previous ed.: published as Calculus for the practical man / by Max Peters and others. Princeton : Van Nostrand, 1962. — Includes index
ISBN 0-442-28274-5 (pbk) : £5.90 B82-25660

515 — Calculus — *Festschriften*

Mathematical analysis and applications : essays dedicated to Laurent Schwartz on the occasion of his 65th birthday / edited by Leopoldo Nachbin. — New York ; London : Academic Press
Part A. — 1981. — xviii,416p : 1port ; 24cm. — (Advances in mathematics. Supplementary studies ; V.7A)
Includes four chapters in French. — Includes bibliographies
ISBN 0-12-512801-0 : £33.80 B82-10289

Mathematical analysis and applications : essays dedicated to Laurent Schwartz on the occasion of his 65th birthday / edited by Leopoldo Nachbin. — New York ; London : Academic Press
Part B. — 1981. — xiv,417-791p : ill ; 24cm. — (Advances in mathematics. Supplementary studies ; v.78)
English and French text
ISBN 0-12-512802-9 : £32.40 B82-10061

515 — Calculus — *For users of pocket electronic calculators*

McCarty, George. Calculator calculus. — London : Spon, Dec.1982. — [276]p
Originally published: Palo Alto, Calif. : Page-Ficklin Publications, 1975
ISBN 0-419-12910-3 (pbk) : £5.95 : CIP entry
B82-29792

Rosser, J. Barkley. Pocket calculator supplement for calculus / J. Barkley Rosser, Carl de Boor. — Reading, Mass. ; London : Addison-Wesley, c1979. — ix,291p : ill ; 26cm
Includes index
ISBN 0-201-06502-9 (pbk) : Unpriced
B82-14150

515 — Location. Optimisation. Mathematical models

Optimization in locational and transport analysis / A.G. Wilson ... [et al.]. — Chichester : Wiley, c1981. — xiv,283p : ill ; 24cm
Bibliography: p263-273. — Includes index
ISBN 0-471-28005-4 : £19.80 : CIP rev.
B81-34561

515 — Mathematics. Optimisation

Gill, Philip E.. Practical optimization / Philip E. Gill, Walter Murray, Margaret H. Wright. — London : Academic Press, 1981 (1982 printing). — xvi,401p : ill ; 25cm
Bibliography: p363-387. — Includes index
ISBN 0-12-283952-8 (pbk) : £11.80 : CIP rev.
B82-12130

Ponstein, J.. Approaches to the theory of optimization / J. Ponstein. — Cambridge : Cambridge University Press, 1980. — xii,205p ; 23cm. — (Cambridge tracts in mathematics ; 77)
Bibliography: p196-201. — Includes index
ISBN 0-521-23155-8 : £16.00 : CIP rev.
B80-29571

Vincent, Thomas L.. Optimality in parametric systems / Thomas L. Vincent, Walter J. Grantham. — New York ; Chichester : Wiley, c1981. — xv,243p : ill ; 24cm
Bibliography: p236-238. — Includes index
ISBN 0-471-08307-0 : £21.45 B82-01053

515 — Mathematics. Optimisation. Applications

Fletcher, R.. Practical methods of optimization / R. Fletcher. — Chichester : Wiley
Vol.2: Constrained optimization. — c1981. — ix,224p : ill ; 24cm
Bibliography: p215-220. — Includes index
ISBN 0-471-27828-9 : £13.30 : CIP rev.
B81-34559

515 — Mathematics. Optimisation. Applications of convex functions — *Conference proceedings*

Convex analysis and optimization / J.-P. Aubin & R.B. Vinter [editors]. — Boston, Mass. ; London : Pitman Advanced Publishing Program, c1982. — 210p : ill,1ports ; 25cm. — (Research notes in mathematics ; 57)
Conference papers
ISBN 0-273-08547-6 (pbk) : Unpriced : CIP rev. B82-01863

515 — Nonlinear optimisation

Nonlinear optimization 1981 / [proceedings of the NATO Advanced Research Institute held at Cambridge in July 1981 which was sponsored by the Special Programme Panel on Systems Science of the NATO Science Committee and the Mathematical Programming Society] ; edited by M.J.D. Powell. — London : Academic Press, 1982. — xvii,559p : ill ; 24cm. — (Nato conference series. II, Systems science)
Bibliography: p493-539. — Includes index
ISBN 0-12-563860-4 : £21.20 : CIP rev.
B82-04137

515 — Optimisation

Modern applied mathematics : optimization and operations research : collection of state-of-the-art surveys based on lectures presented at the summer school 'Optimization and operations research' held at the University of Bonn, September 14-22, 1979 / edited by Bernhard Korte. — Amsterdam ; Oxford : North-Holland, 1982. — ix,693p : ill ; 23cm
Includes bibliographies
ISBN 0-444-86134-3 : Unpriced B82-33802

515 — Smooth mappings. Singularities

Gibson, C. G.. Singular points of smooth mappings / C.G. Gibson. — London : Pitman, 1979. — 239p : ill ; 25cm. — (Research notes in mathematics ; 25)
Includes index
ISBN 0-273-08410-0 (pbk) : Unpriced : CIP rev. B78-19139

Martinet, Jean. Singularities of smooth functions and maps / Jean Martinet ; translated by Carl P. Simon. — Cambridge : Cambridge University Press, 1982. — xiii,256p : ill ; 23cm. — (London Mathematical Society lecture note series, ISSN 0076-0552 ; 58) (London Mathematical Society lecture note series ; 58)
Translated from the French. — Bibliography: p249-251. — Includes index
ISBN 0-521-23398-4 (pbk) : £12.50 : CIP rev.
B82-26229

515′.0246 — Calculus — *For technicians*

Walker, Eric. Analytical mathematics level 2 / Eric Walker. — London : Holt, Rinehart and Winston, c1982. — xi,175p : ill ; 22cm. — (Holt technician texts)
Includes index
ISBN 0-03-910343-9 (pbk) : £2.95 : CIP rev.
B81-33999

515′.02462 — Calculus — *For engineering*

Kaplan, Wilfred. Advanced mathematics for engineers / Wilfred Kaplan. — Reading, Mass. ; London : Addison-Wesley, c1981. — xix,929p : ill ; 24cm. — (Addison-Wesley world student series)
Bibliography: pix-x. — Includes index
ISBN 0-201-03666-5 (pbk) : £9.50 B82-23418

515′.07 — Educational institutions. Curriculum subjects: Calculus. Teaching

Neill, Hugh. Teaching calculus / Hugh Neill and Hilary Shuard ; [illustrated by Janet M. Watson]. — Glasgow : Blackie, 1982. — 279p : ill ; 25cm
ISBN 0-216-91083-8 (pbk) : £8.95 B82-35688

515′.076 — Calculus — *Questions & answers*

Amazigo, John C.. Solutions manual for Advanced calculus, and its applications to the engineering and physical sciences / John C. Amazigo, Lester A. Rubenfeld. — New York ; Chichester : Wiley, c1981. — 140p ; 23cm
ISBN 0-471-09281-9 (pbk) : £6.85 B82-37989

Lane, Richard B.. Student′s solutions manual for Calculus, second edition chapters 1-14 and Calculus, part 1 by Stanley I. Grossman / Richard B. Lane, Carol Johnson. — New York ; London : Academic Press, c1981. — xiv,526p : ill ; 28cm
ISBN 0-12-304361-1 (pbk) : £5.80 B82-29978

515′.076 — Calculus — *Questions & answers — For schools*

[Modern mathematics for schools. Book 8-9. *Selections*]. Calculus 8 & 9 : modern mathematics for schools / Scottish Mathematics Group. — 2nd ed. — Glasgow : Blackie, 1982. — 118p : ill ; 21cm
Originally published: as calculus sections of Modern mathematics for schools. Bks. 8 & 9. 1974-75
ISBN 0-216-91271-7 (pbk) : £1.95
ISBN 0-550-75898-4 (Chambers) B82-38362

515′.15 — Calculus & analytic geometry

Shockley, James E.. Calculus : and analytic geometry / James E. Shockley. — Philadelphia ; London : Saunders College Publishing, c1982. — xii,1126,[74]p : ill(some col.],ports ; 24cm
Text on lining papers. — Includes index
ISBN 0-03-018886-5 : £23.95 B82-20711

515'.15 — Calculus & analytic geometry *continuation*

Stein, Sherman K.. Calculus and analytic geometry / Sherman K. Stein. — New York ; London : McGraw-Hill, c1982. — xvi,1026,185p : ill ; 27cm
Previous ed.: 1973. — Text on lining papers. — Includes index
ISBN 0-07-061153-x : £23.75 B82-29454

515'.2 — Mathematics. Functions. Singularities

Arnol'd, V. I.. Singularity theory : selected papers / V.I. Arnold. — Cambridge : Cambridge University Press, 1981. — 266p : ill ; 22cm. — (London Mathematical Society lecture note series, ISSN 0076-0522 ; 53)
Includes bibliographies
ISBN 0-521-28511-9 (pbk) : £12.50 : CIP rev.
Also classified at 514'.7 B81-31284

515'.223 — Calculus. Bounded analytic functions

Garnett, John B.. Bounded analytic functions / John B. Garnett. — New York ; London : Academic Press, 1981. — xvi,467p : ill ; 24cm. — (Pure and applied mathematics)
Bibliography: p444-460. — Includes index
ISBN 0-12-276150-2 : £39.00 B82-07713

515'.234 — Calculus. Asymptotic expansions

Bruijn, N. G. de. Asymptotic methods in analysis / by N.G. de Bruijn. — 3nd ed. — New York : Dover ; London : Constable, 1981. — xii,200p : ill ; 22cm
Originally published: Amsterdam : North Holland, 1970. — Includes index
ISBN 0-486-64221-6 (pbk) : £3.20 B82-29999

515'.24 — Calculus. Sequences & series. Convergence

Hall, Peter. Rates of convergence in the central limit theorem. — London : Pitman, Sept.1982. — [260]p. — (Research notes in mathematics ; 62)
ISBN 0-273-08565-4 (pbk) : £10.25 : CIP entry B82-18874

515'.2433 — Fourier analysis

Guzmán, Miguel de. Real variable methods in Fourier analysis / Miguel de Guzmán. — Amsterdam ; Oxford : North-Holland Publishing, 1980. — xiii,392p : ill ; 24cm. — (North-Holland mathematics studies ; 46) (Notas de matemática ; 75)
Bibliography: p379-387. — Includes index
ISBN 0-444-86124-6 (pbk) : £18.22 B82-38413

515'.252 — Nonlinear equations

Saaty, Thomas L.. Modern nonlinear equations / Thomas L. Saaty. — Rev. — New York : Dover ; London : Constable, 1981. — 471p ; 22cm
Previous ed.: New York : McGraw Hill, 1967. — Includes bibliographies and index
ISBN 0-486-64232-1 (pbk) : £6.35 B82-40188

515'.252 — Nonlinear equations. Numerical solution. Applications

Zangwill, Willard I.. Pathways to solutions, fixed points, and equilibria / W.I. Zangwill, G.B. Garcia. — Englewood Cliffs ; London : Prentice-Hall, c1981. — xv,479p : ill ; 24cm. — (Prentice-Hall series in computational mathematics)
Bibliography: p459-472. — Includes index
ISBN 0-13-653501-1 : £24.40 B82-16706

515.3'5 — Bifurcation theory

Vanderbauwhede, A.. Local bifurcation and symmetry. — London : Pitman, Nov.1982. — [358]p. — (Research notes in mathematics ; 75)
ISBN 0-273-08569-7 (pbk) : £12.50 : CIP entry B82-27365

515.3'5 — Differential equations

Arrowsmith, D. K.. Ordinary differential equations. — London : Chapman and Hall, Feb.1982. — [300]p. — (Chapman and Hall mathematics series)
ISBN 0-412-22600-6 (cased) : £12.00 : CIP entry
ISBN 0-412-22610-3 (pbk) : £6.00 B81-36378

Differential equations and numerical mathematics : selected papers presented to a national conference held in Novosibirsk, September 1978 / edited by G.I. Marchuk. — Oxford : Pergamon, 1982. — viii,156p : ill ; 24cm
Translation from the Russian
ISBN 0-08-026491-3 : £25.00 : CIP rev. B81-34470

Piaggio, H. T. H.. An elementary treatise on differential equations and their applications. — 2nd ed. — London : Bell & Hyman, June 1982. — [302]p
Previous ed.: 1928
ISBN 0-7135-0851-5 (pbk) : £4.50 : CIP entry B82-20772

Rabenstein, Albert L.. Elementary differential equations with linear algebra / Albert L. Rabenstein. — 3rd ed. — New York ; London : Academic Press, c1982. — ix,518p ; 25cm
Previous ed.: 1975. — Bibliography: p481-482. — Includes index
ISBN 0-12-573945-1 : £16.40
Also classified at 512'.5 B82-30106

Rabenstein, Albert L.. Instructor's answer manual for Elementary differential equations with linear algebra, third edition / by Albert L. Rabenstein. — New York ; London : Academic Press, c1982. — 34p ; 23cm
ISBN 0-12-573946-x (pbk) : £2.40
Primary classification 512'.5 B82-29937

515.3'5 — Differential equations — *Conference proceedings*

Recent advances in differential equations / edited by Robert Conti. — New York ; London : Academic Press, 1981. — xi,447p ; 24cm
Conference papers. — Includes bibliographies
ISBN 0-12-186280-1 : Unpriced B82-28665

515.3'5 — Differential equations. Qualitative methods — *Conference proceedings*

Qualitative theory of differential equations / edited by M. Farkad. — Amsterdam ; Oxford : North-Holland, 1981. — 2v(1089p) ; 25cm. — (Colloquia mathematica Societatis János Bolyai, ISSN 0139-3383 ; 30)
Conference papers
ISBN 0-444-86173-4 : £79.86 B82-23542

515.3'5 — Differential equations. Solution

Hill, J. M.. Solution of differential equations by means of one-parameter groups. — London : Pitman, Jan.1983. — [171]p
ISBN 0-273-08506-9 (pbk) : £7.00 : CIP entry B82-33714

515.3'5 — Differential equations. Solution. Green's functions

Butkovskiĭ, A. G.. Green's functions and transfer functions handbook / A.G. Butkovskiy ; translated by L.W. Longdon. — Chichester : Ellis Horwood, 1982. — 236p ; 24cm. — (Ellis Horwood series in mathematics and its applications)
Translation of: Kharakteristiki sistem s raspredelennymi parametrami. — Bibliography: p227-236. — Includes index
ISBN 0-85312-447-7 : £22.50 : CIP rev. B82-10675

Roach, G. F.. Green's functions / G.F. Roach. — 2nd ed. — Cambridge : Cambridge University Press, 1982. — xiii,325p ; 24cm
Previous ed.: Wokingham : Van Nostrand Reinhold, 1970. — Bibliography: p319-321. — Includes index
ISBN 0-521-23890-0 (cased) : Unpriced : CIP rev. B82-11499

515.3'5 — Hamilton-Jacobi equations. Solution

Lions, P. L.. Generalized solutions of Hamilton-Jacobi equations. — London : Pitman, July 1982. — [418]p. — (Research notes in mathematics ; 69)
ISBN 0-273-08556-5 (pbk) : £9.95 : CIP entry B82-16237

515.3'52 — Ordinary differential equations

Miller, Richard K.. Ordinary differential equations / Richard K. Miller, Anthony N. Michel. — New York ; London : Academic Press, 1982. — xiii,351p : ill ; 24cm
Bibliography: p342-345. — Includes index
ISBN 0-12-497280-2 : £22.80 B82-30108

Rao, M. Rama Mohana. Ordinary differential equations : theory and applications / M. Rama Mohana Rao. — London : Edward Arnold, 1981, c1980. — viii,266p : ill ; 24cm
Bibliography: p261-262. — Includes index
ISBN 0-7131-3452-6 (pbk) : £9.50 : CIP rev. B81-21500

515.3'52 — Ordinary differential equations. Singular systems

Campbell, S. L.. Singular systems of differential equations II / S.L. Campbell. — San Francisco ; London : Pitman, c1982. — 234p : ill ; 25cm. — (Research notes in mathematics ; 61)
Bibliography: p220-228. — Includes index
ISBN 0-273-08516-6 (pbk) : Unpriced : CIP rev. B82-09995

515.3'52'02854 — Ordinary differential equations. Applications of computer systems. Techniques — *Conference proceedings*

Computational techniques for ordinary differential equations : based on the proceedings of the conference on computational techniques for ordinary differential equations, held at the University of Manchester 18th-20th December, 1978 organised by The Institute of Mathematics and its Applications / edited by I. Gladwell, D.K. Sayers. — London : Academic, c1980. — viii,303p : ill ; 24cm. — (The Institute of Mathematics and its Applications conference series)
Includes bibliographies
ISBN 0-12-285780-1 : £12.60 : CIP rev. B80-03138

515.3'53 — Equations. Elliptic partial differential equations. Solution — *Conference proceedings*

Elliptic Problem Solvers Conference *(1980 : Santa Fe)*. Elliptic problem solvers / [proceedings of the Elliptic Problem Solvers Conference held in Santa Fe, New Mexico from June 30-July 2, 1980, sponsored by the Los Alomos [i.e. Alamos] Scientific Laboratory] ; edited by Martin H. Schultz. — New York ; London : Academic Press, 1981. — xiii,444p : ill ; 24cm
Includes index
ISBN 0-12-632620-7 : £18.20 B82-02070

515.3'53 — Hyperbolic differential equations. Boundary value problems. Solution

Sakamoto, Reiko. Hyperbolic boundary value problems / Reiko Sakamoto ; translated by Katsumi Miyahara. — Cambridge : Cambridge University Press, 1982. — viii,210p : ill ; 24cm
Translation from the Japanese. — Includes index
ISBN 0-521-23568-5 : £18.50 : CIP rev. B82-14372

515.3'53 — Mathematics. Boundary element methods — *For physics*

Crouch, S. L.. Boundary element methods in solid mechanics. — London : Allen and Unwin, Nov.1982. — [320]p
ISBN 0-04-620010-x : £15.00 : CIP entry B82-28717

515.3'53 — Mathematics. Boundary element methods — *Serials*

Developments in boundary element methods. — 2. — London : Applied Science, Mar.1982. — [260]p. — (The developments series)
ISBN 0-85334-112-5 : £28.00 : CIP entry B82-01413

Progress in boundary element methods. — Vol.1-. — London (Estover Rd, Plymouth, Devon) : Pentech Press, 1981-. — v. : ill ; 24cm
Annual
ISSN 0260-7018 = Progress in boundary element methods : Unpriced B82-05227

Progress in boundary element methods. — Vol.2. — London : Pentech Press, Sept.1982. — [240]p
ISBN 0-7273-1611-7 : £28.50 : CIP entry
ISSN 0260-7018 B82-20394

515.3'53 — Mathematics. Finite element methods. Applications of computer systems

Akin, J. E.. Application and implementation of finite element methods. — London : Academic Press, June 1982. — [300]p
ISBN 0-12-047650-9 : CIP entry B82-10418

515.3′53 — Mathematics. Finite element methods — *Conference proceedings*

The **Mathematics** of finite elements and applications IV—MAFELAP 1981. — London : Academic Press, July 1982. — [600]p
Conference papers
ISBN 0-12-747254-1 : CIP entry B82-12530

Numerical methods in coupled problems. — Swansea (91 West Cross La., West Cross, Swansea, W. Glamorgan) : Pineridge Press, Aug.1981. — [1000]p
Conference papers
ISBN 0-906674-13-1 : £44.00 : CIP entry B81-22584

515.3′53 — Mathematics. Finite element methods — *For engineering*

Rao, S. S.. The finite element method in engineering / by S.S. Rao. — Oxford : Pergamon, 1982. — xxvi,625p : ill ; 24cm. — (Pergamon international library)
Includes index
ISBN 0-08-025467-5 (cased) : Unpriced
ISBN 0-08-025466-7 (pbk) : £8.75 B82-14693

515.3′53 — Nonlinear partial differential equations

Integrable systems : selected papers / S.P. Novikov ... [et al.]. — Cambridge : Cambridge University Press, 1981. — 266p : ill ; 23cm. — (London Mathematical Society lecture note series ; 60)
ISBN 0-521-28527-5 (pbk) : Unpriced B82-31367

515.3′53 — Nonlinear partial differential equations. Applications — *Conference proceedings*

Nonlinear partial differential equations and their applications : Collège de France Seminar. — Boston, [Mass.] ; London : Pitman. — (Research notes in mathematics ; 60)
Vol.2 / H. Brezis & J.L. Lions (editors) ; D. Cioranescu (coordinator). — c1982. — 398p : ill ; 25cm
Includes 11 papers in French. — Includes bibliographies
ISBN 0-273-08541-7 (pbk) : Unpriced : CIP rev.
ISBN 0-273-08491-7 (v.1) B82-07420

Nonlinear partial differential equations and their applications. — London : Pitman. — (Research notes in mathematics ; 70)
Conference papers
Vol.3. — Oct.1982. — [444]p
ISBN 0-273-08568-9 : £12.50 : CIP entry B82-23483

515.3′53 — Nonlinear partial differential equations. Bäcklund transformations

Rogers, C.. Bäcklund transformations and their applications / C. Rogers and W.F. Shadwick. — New York ; London : Academic Press, 1982. — xiii,334p : ill ; 24cm. — (Mathematics in science and engineering ; v.161)
Includes index
ISBN 0-12-592850-5 : Unpriced B82-40834

515.3′53 — Partial differential equations

Farlow, Stanley J.. Partial differential equations : for scientists and engineers / Stanley J. Farlow. — [Chichester?] : Wiley, 1982. — ix,402p : ill ; 25cm
Text on lining papers. — Includes index
ISBN 0-471-08639-8 : £20.25 B82-36933

515.3′53 — Partial differential equations. Boundary value problems. Solutions. Special functions — *For physics*

Johnson, D. E.. Mathematical methods in engineering and physics / David E. Johnson, Johnny R. Johnson. — Englewood Cliffs ; London : Prentice-Hall, c1982. — x,273p : ill ; 24cm
Originally published: New York : Ronald Press, 1965. — Bibliography: p267-268. — Includes index
ISBN 0-13-561126-1 : £21.40 B82-20121

515.3′53 — Partial differential equations. Numerical solution

Lapidus, Leon. Numerical solution of partial differential equations in science and engineering / Leon Lapidus, George F. Pinder. — New York ; Chichester : Wiley, c1982. — 677p : ill ; 25cm
Includes bibliographies and index
ISBN 0-471-09866-3 : £35.00 B82-34746

515.3′53 — Partial differential equations. Numerical solution. Applications of digital computer systems

Vemuri, V.. Digital computer treatment of partial differential equations / V. Vemuri, Walter J. Karplus. — Englewood Cliffs ; London : Prentice-Hall, c1981. — xiv,449p : ill ; 25cm. — (Prentice-Hall series in computational mathematics)
Includes index
ISBN 0-13-212407-6 : £21.70 B82-07545

Vichnevetsky, Robert. Computer methods for partial differential equations / Robert Vichnevetsky. — Englewood Cliffs ; London : Prentice-Hall. — (Prentice-Hall series in computational mathematics)
Vol.1: Elliptic equations and the fininte-element method. — c1981. — x,357p : ill ; 24cm
Bibliography: p336-353. — Includes index
ISBN 0-13-165233-8 : £21.00 B82-07546

515.3′53 — Partial differential equations. Numerical solution — *Conference proceedings*

Conference on the Numerical Solutions of Partial Differential Equations *(1981 : University of Melbourne)*. Numerical solutions of partial differential equations : proceedings of the 1981 Conference on the Numerical Solutions of Partial Differential Equations held at Queen′s College, Melbourne University, Australia / edited by John Noye. — Amsterdam ; Oxford : North-Holland, 1982. — xii,647p : ill ; 23cm
Includes bibliographies
ISBN 0-444-86356-7 : Unpriced B82-21627

515.3′53 — Partial differential equations. Solution

Straughan, B.. Instability, nonexistence and weighted energy methods in fluid dynamics and related theories. — London : Pitman, Nov.1982. — [176]p. — (Research notes in mathematics ; 74)
ISBN 0-273-08564-6 (pbk) : £8.50 : CIP entry B82-27364

515.3′54 — Linear differential equations

Conti, R.. Linear differential equations and control / R. Conti. — London : Academic Press, 1976. — 174p : ill ; 24cm. — (Institutiones mathematicae ; v.1)
At head of title: Istituto nazionale di alta matematica. — Bibliography: p173-174
Unpriced (pbk) B82-00985

515.3′54′0285424 — Linear differential equations. Solution. Applications of digital computer systems. Programming languages: Fortran IV language

Smetana, Frederick O.. FORTRAN codes for classical methods in linear dynamics / Frederick O. Smetana, Andrew O. Smetana. — New York ; London : McGraw-Hill, c1982. — x,394p : ill ; 22x28cm
ISBN 0-07-058440-0 (pbk) : £7.75 B82-24553

515.3′55 — Nonlinear differential equations & boundary value problems. Numerical solution

Baker, Christopher T. H.. The numerical solution to nonlinear problems. — Oxford : Clarendon Press, Jan.1982. — [384]p
ISBN 0-19-853354-3 : £15.00 : CIP entry B81-34384

515.3′55′02466 — Nonlinear differential equations. Solution — *For chemical engineering*

Finlayson, Bruce A.. Nonlinear analysis in chemical engineering / Bruce A. Finlayson. — New York ; London : McGraw-Hill, c1980. — x,366p : ill ; 24cm. — (McGraw-Hill chemical engineering series)
Includes bibliographies and index
ISBN 0-07-020915-4 : £19.50 : CIP rev. B80-06899

515.4′2 — Ergodic theory

Parry, William. Classification problems in ergodic theory / William Parry and Selim Tuncel. — Cambridge : Cambridge University Press, 1982. — 101p : ill ; 23cm. — (London Mathematical Society lecture note series, ISSN 0076-0552 ; 67)
Includes index
ISBN 0-521-28794-4 (pbk) : £7.50 : CIP rev. B82-12688

515.4′2 — Ergodic theory — *Serials*

Ergodic theory and dynamical ststems. — Vol.1, pt.1 (Mar. 1981)-. — Cambridge : Cambridge University Press, 1981-. — v. ; 25cm
Quarterly
ISSN 0143-3857 = Ergodic theory and dynamical systems : £45.00 per year B82-09072

515.4′2 — Measure theory & integration

De Barra, G.. Measure theory and integration / G. de Barra. — Chichester : Ellis Horwood, 1981. — 239p ; 24cm. — (Ellis Horwood series in mathematics and its applications)
Includes index
ISBN 0-85312-337-3 (cased) : £21.50 : CIP rev.
ISBN 0-85312-363-2 (student ed.) : £8.50
ISBN 0-470-27232-5 (Halsted Press) : £21.50 B81-20592

515.4′3 — Calculus. Integrals

Apelblat, A.. Table of definite and indefinite integrals. — Oxford : Elsevier Scientific, Jan.1983. — [458]p. — (Physical sciences data ; v.13)
ISBN 0-444-42151-3 B82-37633

515.4′3 — Lebesque integration

Craven, B. D.. Lebesgue measure & integral / Bruce D. Craven. — Boston ; London : Pitman, c1982. — ix,221p : ill ; 25cm
Bibliography: p215-216. — Includes index
ISBN 0-273-01754-3 : Unpriced B82-37787

515.4′5 — Integral equations. Numerical solution — *Conference proceedings*

Treatment of integral equations by numerical methods. — London : Academic Press, Jan.1983. — [500]p
Conference papers
ISBN 0-12-074120-2 : CIP entry B82-37475

515′.53 — Mathematics. Subharmonic functions

Aronszajn, N.. Polyharmonic functions. — Oxford : Clarendon, Feb.1983. — [320]p. — (Oxford mathematical monographs)
ISBN 0-19-853906-1 : £25.00 : CIP entry B82-36597

515′.62 — Boundary value problems. Solution. Applications of Fourier series

Hanna, J. Ray. Fourier series and integrals of boundary value problems / J. Ray Hanna. — New York ; Chichester : Wiley, c1982. — xi,271p : ill ; 24cm. — (Pure and applied mathematics, ISSN 0079-8185)
Text on lining papers. — Includes index
ISBN 0-471-08129-9 : £23.65 B82-24062

515′.62 — Boundary value problems. Solution. Variational methods

Elliott, C. M.. Weak and variational methods for moving boundary problems / C.M. Elliott & J.R. Ockendon. — Boston, [Mass.] ; London : Pitman Advanced Publishing Program, c1982. — 213p : ill ; 25cm. — (Research notes in mathematics ; 59)
Text on inside cover. — Bibliography: p183-200. — Includes index
ISBN 0-273-08503-4 (pbk) : Unpriced : CIP rev. B82-03796

515′.624′0212 — Calculus. Numerical integration — *Tables*

Smith, H. V.. Tables for numerical integration / H.V. Smith. — London : Griffin, 1982. — v,26p ; 21cm
ISBN 0-85264-272-5 (pbk) : £1.95 B82-40638

515′.63 — Differential calculus. Vector analysis

Baxandall, P. R.. Differential vector calculus / P.R. Baxandall and H. Liebeck. — London : Longman, 1981. — viii,243p : ill ; 22cm. — (Longman mathematical texts)
Includes index
ISBN 0-582-44193-5 (pbk) : £7.95 : CIP rev. B81-14981

515′.63 — Euclidean tensor analysis

Beju, I. Euclidean tensor calculus with applications. — Tunbridge Wells : Abacus, Jan.1983. — [300]p
Translation of: Tehnici de calcul tensorial Euclidian cu aplicatii
ISBN 0-85626-330-3 : £25.00 : CIP entry B82-33114

515′.63 — Tensor analysis

Goodbody, A. M.. Cartesian tensors : with applications to mechanics, fluid mechanics and elasticity. — Chichester : Ellis Horwood, Dec.1981. — [336]p. — (The Ellis Horwood series in mathematics and its applications)
ISBN 0-85312-220-2 : £22.50 : CIP entry
B81-31379

515′.63 — Tensor analysis & vector analysis

Reddy, J. N.. Advanced engineering analysis / J.N. Reddy, M.L. Rasmussen. — New York ; Chichester : Wiley, c1982. — xiv,488p : ill ; 24cm
Includes index
ISBN 0-471-09349-1 : Unpriced B82-34519

515′.63 — Vector analysis

Krasnov, M. L.. Vector analysis / M.L. Krasnov, A.I. Kiselev, G.I. Makarenko ; translated from the Russian by George Yankovsky. — Moscow : Mir ; [London] : distributed by Central, 1981. — 190p : ill ; 20cm
Translation and revision of: Vektornyĭ analiz. — Bibliography: p187. — Includes index
ISBN 0-7147-1694-4 (pbk) : £1.25 B82-29718

515′.64 — Dynamical systems. Optimisation. Applications of variational methods — *Conference proceedings*

Workshop on Numerical Techniques for Systems Engineering Problems *(1980 : Lexington, Ky.)*. Nondifferential and variational techniques in optimization : proceedings of the Workshop on Numerical Techniques for Systems Engineering Problems, part 2 / edited by D.C. Sorensen and R.J.-B. Wets. — Amsterdam ; Oxford : North-Holland, 1982. — ix,159p : ill ; 24cm. — (Mathematical programming study ; 17)
ISBN 0-444-86392-3 (pbk) : Unpriced
Primary classification 511′.66 B82-32385

515.7 — Applied mathematics. Functional analysis

Griffel, D. H.. Applied functional analysis / D.H. Griffel. — Chichester : Ellis Horwood, 1981. — 386p : ill ; 24cm. — (Ellis Horwood series in mathematics and its applications)
Bibliography: p378-382. — Includes index
ISBN 0-85312-226-1 (cased) : £25.00 : CIP rev.
ISBN 0-85312-304-7 (student ed.) B81-20560

515.7 — Evolution equations — *Conference proceedings*

Evolution equations and their applications. — London : Pitman, Sept.1982. — [331]p. — (Research notes in mathematics ; 68)
ISBN 0-273-08567-0 : £9.50 : CIP entry
B82-18875

515.7 — Mathematics. Functional analysis

Heuser, Harro G.. Functional analysis / by Harro G. Heuser ; translated by John Horváth. — Chichester : Wiley, 1982. — xv,408p ; 24cm
Translation of: Funktionanalysis. — Bibliography: p393-400. — Includes index
ISBN 0-471-28052-6 (cased) : £25.00 : CIP rev.
ISBN 0-471-10069-2 (pbk) : Unpriced
B81-34646

Kantorovich, L. V.. Functional analysis. — 2nd ed. — Oxford : Pergamon, June 1981. — [800]p
Previous ed.: published as Functional analysis in normed spaces. 1964
ISBN 0-08-023036-9 (cased) : £45.00 : CIP entry
ISBN 0-08-026486-7 (pbk) : £15.00
B81-13534

515.7 — Mathematics. Functional analysis. Applications of convexity theory

Asimow, L.. Convexity theory and its applications in functional analysis / L. Asimow, A.J. Ellis. — London : Academic Press, 1980. — x,266p ; 24cm. — (L.M.S. monographs, ISSN 0076-0560 ; 16)
Includes index
ISBN 0-12-065340-0 : £23.20 : CIP rev.
B80-11015

515.7 — Mathematics. Functional analysis — *Conference proceedings*

Operator theory and functional analysis / I. Erdelyi (editor). — San Francisco ; London : Pitman, c1979. — 163p ; 23cm. — (Research notes in mathematics ; 38)
Conference proceedings. — Includes bibliographies
ISBN 0-273-08450-x (pbk) : Unpriced
Also classified at 515.7′24 B82-06587

515.7 — Mathematics. Functional analysis. Vector valued measures

Ziegler, H. J. W.. Vector valued Nevanlinna theory. — London : Pitman, Oct.1982. — [208] p. — (Research notes in mathematics ; 73)
ISBN 0-273-08530-1 (pbk) : £9.00 : CIP entry
B82-23482

515.7 — Mathematics. Functions. Approximation — *Conference proceedings*

Approximation and function spaces : proceedings of the international conference held in Gdańsk, August 27-31, 1979 / edited by Zbigniew Ciesielski. — Amsterdam ; Oxford : North-Holland, 1981. — xiv,897p ; 25cm
ISBN 0-444-86143-2 : £58.51 B82-13430

515.7′2 — Operational calculus

Mikusinski, Jan. Operational calculus. — 2nd ed. — Oxford : Pergamon, June 1981. — (International series in pure and applied mathematics ; v.109)
Previous ed.: 1959
Vol.1. — [320]p
ISBN 0-08-025071-8 : £12.00 : CIP entry
B81-11921

515′.723 — Integral transforms

Marichev, O. I.. Handbook of integral transforms of higher transcendental functions. — Chichester : Ellis Horwood, Oct.1982. — [336] p. — (Ellis Horwood series in mathematics and its applications)
Translation of: Metod vychisleniya integralov ot spetsial'nykh funktsii
ISBN 0-85312-528-7 : £30.00 : CIP entry
B82-31307

515.7′23 — Mathematics. Integral operators

Okikiolu, G. O.. Special integral operators / G.O. Okikiolu. — London : G.O. Okikiolu
Vol.1: Weierstrass operators and related integrals. — c1980. — 306p ; 21cm
Includes index
ISBN 0-905499-04-2 (pbk) : £6.25 : CIP rev.
B80-03140

515.7′24 — Mathematics. Operators — *Conference proceedings*

Operator theory and functional analysis / I. Erdelyi (editor). — San Francisco ; London : Pitman, c1979. — 163p ; 23cm. — (Research notes in mathematics ; 38)
Conference proceedings. — Includes bibliographies
ISBN 0-273-08450-x (pbk) : Unpriced
Primary classification 515.7 B82-06587

515.7′24 — Mathematics. Subnormal operators

Conway, John B.. Subnormal operators / John B. Conway. — Boston ; London : Pitman Advanced Publishing Program, c1981. — xvii,476p ; 25cm. — (Research notes in mathematics ; 51)
Bibliography: p455-470. — Includes index
ISBN 0-273-08520-4 : Unpriced B82-07927

515.7′242 — Mathematics. Differential operators. Spectral theory

Berthier, A. M.. Spectral theory and wave operators for the Schrödinger equation. — London : Pitamn, July 1982. — [314]p. — (Research notes in mathematics ; 71)
ISBN 0-273-08562-x (pbk) : £9.95 : CIP entry
B82-16236

515.7′242 — Mathematics. Differential operators. Spectral theory — *Conference proceedings*

Spectral theory of differential operators : proceedings of the conference held at the University of Alabama in Birmingham, Birmingham, Alabama, U.S.A. March 26-28, 1981 / edited by Ian W. Knowles and Roger T. Lewis. — Amsterdam ; Oxford : North-Holland, 1981. — xv,384p ; 24cm. — (North-Holland mathematics studies, ISSN 0304-0208 ; v.55)
Includes bibliographies
ISBN 0-444-86277-3 (pbk) : £23.91
B82-07886

515.7′3 — Locally convex spaces. Applications of differential calculus & holomorphic functions

Colombeau, Jean François. Differential calculus and holomorphy : real and complex analysis in locally convex spaces / Jean François Colombeau. — Amsterdam ; Oxford : North-Holland, 1982. — xii,455p : ill ; 24cm. — (Notas de matemática ; 84) (North-Holland mathematics series ; 64)
Bibliography: p431-452. — Includes index
ISBN 0-444-86397-4 (pbk) : £29.54
B82-39847

515.7′3 — Locally convex spaces. Functional analysis

Dineen, Seán. Complex analysis in locally convex spaces / Seán Dineen. — Amsterdam ; Oxford : North-Holland, c1981. — xiii,492p ; 24cm. — (Notas de matemática ; 83) (North-Holland mathematics studies ; 57)
Bibliography: p433-479. — Includes index
ISBN 0-444-86319-2 (pbk) : £25.26
B82-11230

515.7′3 — Orthomodular lattices

Kalmbach, G.. Orthomodular lattices. — London : Academic Press, Dec.1982. — [390]p. — (London Mathematical Society monograph series, ISSN 0076-0560)
ISBN 0-12-394580-1 : CIP entry B82-29882

515.7′32 — Banach spaces

Beauzamy, Bernard. Introduction to Banach spaces and their geometry / Bernard Beauzamy. — Amsterdam ; Oxford : North-Holland, 1982. — xi,308p : ill ; 24cm. — (North-Holland mathematical studies ; 68) (Notas de matemática ; 86)
Bibliography: p301-304. — Includes index
ISBN 0-444-86416-4 (pbk) : Unpriced
B82-39850

Notes in Banach spaces / edited by H. Elton Lacey. — Austin ; London : University of Texas Press, c1980. — 439p : ill ; 29cm
ISBN 0-292-75520-1 : £21.00 B82-13110

515.7′32 — Hp spaces

Koosis, Paul. Introduction to Hp spaces : with an appendix on Wolff's proof of the Corona Theorem / Paul Koosis. — Cambridge : Cambridge University Press, 1980. — xv,376p : ill ; 22cm. — (London Mathematical Society lecture note series ; 40)
Bibliography: p348-358. — Includes index
ISBN 0-521-23159-0 (pbk) : £10.95
B82-29920

515.7′33 — Hilbert spaces. Linear operators

Akhiezer, N. I.. Theory of linear operators in Hilbert space / N.I. Akhiezer, the late I.M. Glazman ; translated by E.R. Dawson ; English translation edited by W.N. Everitt. — Boston, [Mass.] ; London : Published in association with Scottish Academic Press by Pitman Advanced Publishing, c1981. — 2v.(xxxii, 552p) ; 24cm. — (Monographs and studies in mathematics ; 9-10)
Translation of: Teoriı͡a lineĭnykh operatorov v Gilbertovom prostranstve. 3 izd. — Includes index
ISBN 0-273-08495-x : Unpriced
ISBN 0-273-08496-8 (v.2) : £29.50 B82-40734

515.7′33 — Hilbert spaces. Operator colligations

Power, S. C.. Hankel operators on Hilbert space. — London : Pitman, July 1982. — [100]p. — (Research notes in mathematics ; 64)
ISBN 0-273-08518-2 : £7.00 : CIP entry
B82-12273

515.7′33 — Hilbert spaces. Operators

Herrero, Domingo A.. Approximation of Hilbert space operators. — London : Pitman
Vol.1. — Sept.1982. — [270]p. — (Research notes in mathematics ; 72)
ISBN 0-273-08579-4 (pbk) : £9.00 : CIP entry
B82-18876

515.7′82 — Mathematics. Generalised functions

Jones, D. S. (Douglas Samuel). The theory of generalised functions / D.S. Jones. — 2nd ed. — Cambridge : Cambridge University Press, 1982. — xiii,539p ; 23cm
Previous ed.: published as Generalised functions. London : McGraw-Hill, 1966. — Includes index
ISBN 0-521-23723-8 : £35.00 : CIP rev.
B82-03363

515.7′82 — Mathematics. Generalised functions — *For physics*

Vladimirov, V. S.. Generalized functions in mathematical physics / V.S. Vladimirov ; translated from the Russian by George Yankovsky. — Moscow : Mir, 1979 ; [London] : Distributed by Central Books. — xii,362p : ill ; 23cm
Translation of: Obobshchennye funkt͡sii v matematicheskoĭ fizike. — Bibliography: p351-356. — Includes index
£4.50 B82-11409

515.8′3 — Calculus. Functions of one real variable

Introduction to real analysis / Robert G. Bartle, Donald R. Sherbert. — New York ; Chichester : Wiley, c1982. — xii,370p : ill ; 25cm
Bibliography: p350. — Includes index
ISBN 0-471-05944-7 : £21.40 B82-28179

Van Rooij, A. C. M.. A second course on real functions / A.C.M. Van Rooij and W.H. Schikhof. — Cambridge : Cambridge University Press, 1982. — xiii,200p : ill ; 24cm
Bibliography: p196. — Includes index
ISBN 0-521-23944-3 (cased) : Unpriced : CIP rev.
ISBN 0-521-28361-2 (pbk) : Unpriced
B82-00230

515.8′4 — Calculus. Functions of several real variables

Craven, B. D.. Functions of several variables / B.D. Craven. — London : Chapman and Hall, 1981. — viii,136p : ill ; 22cm
Includes bibliographies and index
ISBN 0-412-23330-4 (cased) : £10.00 : CIP rev.
ISBN 0-412-23340-1 (pbk) : Unpriced
B81-19186

515.8′4 — Functions of several variables. Differentiation

Breckon, Bill. Differentiating functions of lots of variables : starring Derek the differentiable dinosaur : mathematics and imagination / by Bill Breckon ; art by Krishna Alageswaran ; graphics by Ian Harrison. — Warwick : Warwick University Maths Society, c1982. — 24p : ill ; 30cm
Unpriced (unbound) B82-25399

515.8′8 — Calculus. Convex functions

Fuchssteiner, Benno. Convex cones / Benno Fuchssteiner and Wolfgang Lusky. — Amsterdam ; Oxford : North-Holland, c1981. — x,429p ; 24cm. — (Notas de matemática ; (82)) (North-Holland mathematical studies, ISSN 0304-0208 ; 56)
Bibliography: p403-422. — Includes index
ISBN 0-444-86290-0 (pbk) : £23.86
B82-06720

Giles, John R.. Convex analysis with application in the differentiation of convex functions / John R. Giles. — Boston ; London : Pitman Advanced Publishing Program, c1982. — x,278p ; 25cm. — (Research notes in mathematics ; 58)
Includes index
ISBN 0-273-08537-9 (pbk) : Unpriced : CIP rev. B81-35774

515.9 — Calculus. Functions of complex variables

Complex analysis. — Milton Keynes : Open University Press. — (Mathematics : a third level course)
At head of title: The Open University
Unit 0: Real analysis review / prepared by David Brannan. — 1981. — 68p : ill ; 30cm. — (M332 ; unit 0)
ISBN 0-335-05559-1 (pbk) : Unpriced
B82-17093

515.9′02462 — Calculus. Functions of complex variables — *For engineering*

Mathews, John H.. Basic complex variables : for mathematics and engineering / John H. Mathews. — Boston [Mass.] ; London : Allyn and Bacon, c1982. — xii,319p : ill ; 24cm
Bibliography: p309-311. — Includes index
ISBN 0-205-07170-8 : £18.95 B82-08537

515.9′4 — Calculus. Functions of several complex variables

Krantz, Steven G.. Function theory of several complex variables / Steven G. Krantz. — New York ; Chichester : Wiley, c1982. — xiii,437p : ill ; 25cm. — (Pure and applied mathematics, ISSN 0079-8185)
Bibliography: p419-429. — Includes index
ISBN 0-471-09324-6 : £29.50 B82-13356

516 — GEOMETRY

516 — Finite geometry

Tsuzuku, T.. Finite groups and finite geometries / T. Tsuzuku ; translated by A. Sevenster and T. Okuyama. — Cambridge : Cambridge University Press, 1982. — x,328p : ill ; 23cm. — (Cambridge tracts in mathematics ; v.78)
Translation of: Yugengun to yugenkika. — Includes index
ISBN 0-521-22242-7 : £22.50 : CIP rev.
Primary classification 512′.2 B82-01329

516 — Geometry

Gordon, V. O.. A course in descriptive geometry / V.O. Gordon and M.A. Sementsov-Ogievskii ; edited by V.O. Gordon ; translated from the Russian by Leonid Levant. — Moscow : Mir, 1980 ; [London] : Distributed by Central Books. — 376p : ill ; 22cm
Translation of: Kurs nachertatel′noĭ geometrii. — Added t.p. in Russian. — Includes index
ISBN 0-7147-1655-3 : £3.95 B82-02699

Lawlor, Robert. Sacred geometry : philosophy and practice / Robert Lawlor. — London : Thames and Hudson, c1982. — 111p : ill(some col.),plans ; 28cm
Bibliography: p110
ISBN 0-500-81030-3 (pbk) : £3.95 B82-28187

Rees, Elmer. Supplement to Notes on geometry / Elmer Rees. — [Oxford] : Mathematical Institute, University of Oxford, 1979. — 27p : ill ; 30cm
Unpriced (pbk) B82-23718

Shuvalova, É. Z.. Geometry / E.Z. Shuvalova. — Moscow : Mir ; [London] : Distributed by Central Books, 1980. — 237p : ill ; 20cm
Translation of: Geometri͡ia. — Added t.p. in Russian. — Includes index
£2.25 (pbk) B82-39136

Thompson, J. E. (James Edgar). Geometry : for the practical worker / J.E. Thompson. — 4th ed. — New York ; London : Van Nostrand Reinhold, c1982. — xv,260p : ill ; 21cm. — (Mathematics library for practical workers)
Previous ed.: published as Geometry for the practical man / by Max Peters and others. Princeton : Van Nostrand, 1962. — Includes index
ISBN 0-442-28272-9 (pbk) : £5.90 B82-25656

516 — Shapes — *For children*

Curry, Peter. Peter Curry′s shapes. — Kingswood : World′s Work, c1981. — [32]p : col.ill ; 18x20cm. — (A World′s Work children′s book)
ISBN 0-437-32942-9 : £2.95 B82-07375

516 — Shapes — *Illustrations — For children*

Little one′s book of shapes and colours / illustrated by Alan Fredman. — London : Dean, c1982. — [12]p : col.ill ; 21cm. — (A Dean board book)
ISBN 0-603-00310-9 (unbound) : £0.65
B82-37615

Youldon, Gillian. Shapes / by Gillian Youldon. — London : Watts, 1979. — [26]p : col.ill ; 20cm. — (Picture play!)
ISBN 0-85166-755-4 (cased) : £1.99
ISBN 0-85166-901-8 (pbk) : £0.99 B82-40817

516 — Sizes — *Illustrations — For children*

Sizes / [illustrated by James Hodgson]. — London : Aladdin, [1981]. — [12]p : chiefly col.ill ; 21cm. — (All a-board story books)
Cover title
ISBN 0-85166-916-6 : £1.99 B82-04362

Youldon, Gillian. Sizes / by Gillian Youldon. — London : Watts, 1979. — [26]p : col.ill ; 20cm. — (Picture play!)
ISBN 0-85166-758-9 (cased) : £1.99
ISBN 0-85166-902-6 (pbk) : £0.99 B82-40818

516′.001′531112 — Geometry. Applications of kinematics — *For schools*

Li͡ubich, I͡U. I.. The kinematic method of geometrical problems / Yu I. Lyubich, L.A. Shor. — Moscow : Mir, 1980 ; [London] : Distributed by Central Books. — 55p : ill ; 21cm. — (Little mathematics library)
Translation of: Kinematicheskiĭ metod v geometricheskikh zadachakh
£0.75 (pbk) B82-34681

516′.0022′8 — Model geometric figures

Cundy, H. Martyn. Mathematical models / by H. Martyn Cundy and A.P. Rollett. — 3rd ed. — Norfolk : Tarquin Publications, 1981. — 286p,[1]folded leaf,4p of plates : ill ; 22cm
Previous ed.: Oxford : Clarendon Press, 1961. — Bibliography: p279-280. — Includes index
ISBN 0-906212-20-0 (pbk) : £4.50 B82-08012

516′.0022′8 — Model geometric figures. Making — *Manuals*

Jenkins, Gerald. Mathematical curiosities : a collection of interesting and curious models of a mathematical nature / Gerald Jenkins, Anne Wild. — Stradbroke : Tarquin, c1980. — 28p : ill(some col.) ; 21x30cm
Text and ill on inside covers
ISBN 0-906212-13-8 (pbk) : Unpriced
B82-20234

Jenkins, Gerald. Mathematical curiosities 3 : a collection of interesting and curious models of a mathematical nature, ready to cut out and glue together / Gerald Jenkins, Anne Wild. — Stradbroke : Tarquin, c1982. — 28p : ill(some col.) ; 21x30cm
Cover title. — Text, ill on inside covers
ISBN 0-906212-25-1 (pbk) : Unpriced
B82-40400

Martin, R. D. (Rodney David). Nets and solids / R.D. Martin. — Stradbroke : Tarquin, c1982. — 32p : ill ; 21cm
ISBN 0-906212-23-5 (pbk) : Unpriced
ISBN 0-906212-24-3 (Teacher′s guide)
B82-40401

516′.00246 — Geometry — *For technicians*

Walker, Eric. Mensuration level 2 / Eric Walker. — London : Holt, Rinehart and Winston, c1982. — ix,156p : ill ; 22cm. — (Holt technician texts)
Includes index
ISBN 0-03-910344-7 (pbk) : £2.95 : CIP rev.
B81-34000

516′.007′8 — Educational institutions. Curriculum subjects: Geometry. Teaching. Applications of digital computer systems

Abelson, Harold. Turtle geometry : the computer as a medium for exploring mathematics / Harold Abelson, Andrea A. diSessa. — Cambridge, Mass. ; London : MIT Press, c1981. — xx,477p : ill ; 24cm. — (The MIT Press series in artificial intelligence)
Includes index
ISBN 0-262-01063-1 : £14.00 B82-03916

516'.13 — Plane figures. Construction

Pritulenko, P. V.. Plane figures and sections : how to construct them given specific conditions / P.V. Pritulenko translated from the Russian by Vladimir Shokurov. — Moscow : Mir, 1980 ; [London] : Distributed by Central Books. — 162p : ill ; 23cm
Translation of: Postroenie ploskith figur i sechenii
£2.95 B82-11407

516'.15 — Curves

Vasil'ev, N. B.. Straight lines and curves / N.B. Vasilyev, V.L. Gutenmacher ; translated from the Russian by Anjan Kundu. — Moscow : Mir ; [London] : Distributed by Central Books, 1980. — 193p : ill ; 18cm
Translation of: Prīamye i krivye. — Added t.p. in Russian
£1.95 B82-39137

516'.15 — Plane curves

Markushevich, A. I.. Remarkable curves / A.I. Markushevich ; translated from the Russian by Yu. A. Zdorovov. — Moscow : Mir, 1980 ; [London] : Distributed by Central Books. — 46p : ill ; 21cm. — (Little mathematics library)
Translation of: Zamechatelnye krivye
£0.75 (pbk) B82-34682

516'.2 — Geometry. Euclid. Elements — *Critical studies*

Mueller, Ian. Philosophy of mathematics and deductive structure of Euclid's Elements / Ian Mueller. — Cambridge, Mass. ; London : MIT Press, c1981. — xv,378p : ill ; 26cm
Bibliography: p371-376. — Includes index
ISBN 0-262-13163-3 : £26.25 B82-09580

516.2'04'076 — Euclidean geometry. Problems — *Questions & answers*

Bold, Benjamin. [Famous problems of mathematics]. Famous problems of geometry : and how to solve them / Benjamin Bold. — New York : Dover ; London : Constable, 1982, c1969. — xii,112p : ill ; 22cm
Originally published: New York : Van Nostrand Reinhold, 1969
ISBN 0-486-24297-8 (pbk) : £2.25 B82-40190

516.2'4 — Trigonometry

Flanders, Harley. Trigonometry / Harley Flanders and Justin J. Price. — 2nd ed. — Philadelphia ; London : Saunders College, c1982. — xiv,345p : ill(some col.) ; 25cm. — (Flanders/Price series)
Previous ed.: 1975. — Text and ill on lining papers. — Includes index
ISBN 0-03-057802-7 : £14.50 B82-16906

Hyatt, Herman R.. Trigonometry : a calculator approach / Herman R. Hyatt, Laurence Small. — New York ; Chichester : Wiley, c1982. — ix,430p : ill(some col.) ; 25cm
Text and ill on lining papers. — Includes index
ISBN 0-471-07985-5 : £18.70 B82-32733

Thompson, J. E. (James Edgar). Trigonometry : for the practical worker / J.E. Thompson. — 4th ed. — New York ; London : Van Nostrand Reinhold, c1982. — xv,199p : ill ; 21cm. — (Mathematics library for practical workers)
Previous ed.: published as Trigonometry for the practical man / by Max Peters and others. Princeton : Van Nostrand, 1962. — Includes index
ISBN 0-442-28271-0 (pbk) : £5.95 B82-25655

516.3 — Analytic geometry

Pogorelov, A. V.. Analytical geometry / A.V. Pogorelov ; translated from the Russian by Leonid Levant. — Moscow : Mir ; [London] : Distributed by Central Books, 1980. — 240p : ill ; 20cm
Translation of: Analiticheskaīa geometriīa. — Added t.p. in Russian
£2.25 (pbk) B82-39135

Smogorzhevskiĭ, A. S.. Method of coordinates / A.S. Smogorzhevsky ; translated from the Russian by Ram S. Wadhwa. — Moscow : Mir, 1980 ; [London] : Distributed by Central Books. — 47p : ill ; 21cm. — (Little mathematics library)
Translation of: Metod koordinat
£0.75 (pbk) B82-34684

516.3'53 — Normal varieties

Greco, Silvio. Normal varieties / Silvio Greco ; notes written with the collaboration of A. di Sante. — London : Academic Press, 1978. — 72p ; 24cm. — (Institutiones mathematicae ; v.4)
At head of title: Istituto nazionale di alta matematica. — Bibliography: p71-72
Unpriced (pbk) B82-00986

516.3'6 — Differential geometry

Kock, Anders. Synthetic differential geometry / Anders Kock. — Cambridge : Cambridge University Press, 1981. — 311p : ill ; 22cm. — (London Mathematical Society lecture note series, ISSN 0076-0552 ; 51)
Bibliography: p304-309. — Includes index
ISBN 0-521-24138-3 (pbk) : £13.00 : CIP rev. B81-36241

Poor, Walter A.. Differential geometric structures / Walter A. Poor. — New York ; London : McGraw-Hill, c1981. — xiii,338p : ill ; 25cm
Bibliography: p317-323. — Includes index
ISBN 0-07-050435-0 : £30.50 B82-02281

516.3'6 — Geometric figures: Surfaces. Differential geometry

Svec, A.. Global differential geometry of surfaces / by A. Švec. — Dordrecht ; London : Reidel, c1981. — 154p ; 25cm
Bibliography: p154
ISBN 90-277-1295-6 : Unpriced B82-20801

516.3'6 — Geometric figures: Surfaces. Gaussian transformations. Cusps

Banchoff, Thomas. Cusps of Gauss mappings / Thomas Banchoff, Terence Gaffney & Clint McCrory. — Boston, [Mass.] ; London : Pitman, c1982. — 88p : ill ; 25cm. — (Research notes in mathematics ; 55)
Bibliography: p83-87. — Includes index
ISBN 0-273-08536-0 (pbk) : Unpriced B82-09955

516.3'6 — Topological spaces: Differentiable manifolds — *For physics*

Choquet-Bruhat, Yvonne. Analysis, manifolds and physics / by Yvonne Choquet-Bruhat, Cécile DeWitt-Morette with Margaret Dillard-Bleick. — Rev. ed. — Amsterdam ; Oxford : North-Holland, 1982, c1977. — xx,630p : ill ; 25cm
Previous ed.: 1977. — Bibliography: p603-609. — Includes index
ISBN 0-444-86017-7 : Unpriced B82-32388

516.3'62 — Integral geometry

Ambartzumian, R. V.. Combinatorial integral geometry. — Chichester : Wiley, Nov.1981. — [250]p. — (Wiley series in probability and mathematical statistics)
ISBN 0-471-27977-3 : £15.00 : CIP entry B81-31203

516.3'73 — Topological spaces: Riemannian manifolds. Iterated tangents

White, J. Enrico. The method of iterated tangents with applications in local Riemannian geometry / J. Enrico White. — Boston, [Mass.] ; London : Pitman Advanced Publishing Program, 1982. — xx,252p : ill ; 24cm. — (Monographs and studies in mathematics ; 13)
Bibliography: p246-247. — Includes index
ISBN 0-273-08515-8 : Unpriced : CIP rev. B82-01862

516'.4 — Affine planes. Transitive collineation groups

Kallaher, Michael J.. Affine planes with transitive collineation groups / Michael J. Kallaher. — New York ; London : Van Nostrand Reinhold, c1982. — xii,155p : ill ; 24cm
Bibliography: p149-152. — Includes index
ISBN 0-444-00620-6 : £21-74 B82-07884

516'.6 — Descriptive geometry

Descriptive geometry : metric. — 6th ed. / E.G. Paré ... [et al.]. — New York : Macmillan ; London : Collier Macmillan, c1982. — x,416p : ill ; 27cm
Previous ed.: under Eugene George Paré. 1977. — Text on lining papers. — Includes index
ISBN 0-02-390930-7 (cased) : £14.95
ISBN 0-02-977580-9 (pbk) : Unpriced B82-26199

516'.93 — Riemannian geometry

Willmore, Thomas J.. Total curvature in Riemannian geometry. — Chichester : Ellis Horwood, Oct.1982. — [160]p. — (Ellis Horwood series in mathematics and its applications)
ISBN 0-85312-267-9 : £15.00 : CIP entry B82-30310

519 — PROBABILITIES AND APPLIED MATHEMATICS

519 — Applied finite mathematics

Anton, Howard. Applied finite mathematics / Howard Anton, Bernard Kolman. — 3rd ed. — New York ; London : Academic Press, 1982. — xi,593p : ill(some col.),col.maps ; 25cm
Previous ed.: 1978. — Includes index
ISBN 0-12-059566-4 : £14-60 B82-30154

Higgins, Robert L.. Instructor's answer manual for Applied finite mathematics 3/e / by Robert L. Higgins. — New York ; London : Academic Press, c1982. — iv,48p : ill ; 24cm
ISBN 0-12-059571-0 (pbk) : £2.00 B82-29985

519.2 — Mathematics. Entropy functions

Martin, Nathaniel F. G.. Mathematical theory of entropy / Nathaniel F.G. Martin, James W. England ; foreword by James K. Brooks. — Reading, Mass. ; London : Addison-Wesley, 1981. — xxi,257p : ill ; 25cm. — (Encyclopedia of mathematics and its applications ; v.12)
Bibliography: p245-251. — Includes index
ISBN 0-201-13511-6 : £19.50 B82-37176

519.2 — Probabilities

Bauer, Heinz. Probability theory and elements of measure theory / Heinz Bauer. — 2nd English ed. / English translation by R.B. Burckel. — London : Academic, 1981. — xiii,460p ; 24cm. — (Probability and mathematical statistics)
Translation of: Wahrscheinlichkeitstheorie und Grundzuge der Masstheorie. 2 Aufl. — Previous ed.: New York ; London : Holt, Rinehart and Winston, 1972. — Bibliography: p428-433. — Includes index
ISBN 0-12-082820-0 : £38.20 : CIP rev. B81-04332

Grimmett, Geoffrey. Probability and random processes. — Oxford : Clarendon Press, May 1982. — [250]p
ISBN 0-19-853184-2 (cased) : £17.50 : CIP entry
ISBN 0-19-853185-0 (pbk) : £7.95 B82-16499

Mises, Richard von. Probability, statistics and truth / Richard von Mises. — 2nd rev. English ed. / prepared by Hilda Geiringer. — New York : Dover ; London : Constable, 1981. — vii,244p ; 22cm
Translation from the German. — Originally published: London : Allen & Unwin, 1957. — Includes index
ISBN 0-486-24214-5 (pbk) : £4.50 B82-18197

Muthu, S. K.. Probability and errors for the physical sciences / S.K. Muthu. — London : Sangam, 1982. — 568p : ill ; 25cm
Includes index
ISBN 0-86131-137-x : £8.95 B82-26741

Rowntree, Derek. Probability. — London : Edward Arnold, Sept.1982. — [160]p
ISBN 0-7131-3474-7 : £5.00 : CIP entry B82-20035

Studies in inductive logic and probability / Rudolf Carnap and Richard C. Jeffrey editors. — Berkeley ; London : University of California Press
Vol.2 / Richard C. Jeffrey, editor. — c1980. — 305p : ill ; 24cm
Includes index
ISBN 0-520-03826-6 : £12.00
Also classified at 161 B82-40424

519.2 — Probabilities & statistical mathematics

Larson, Harold J.. Introduction to probability theory and statistical inference / Harold J. Larson. — 3rd ed. — New York ; Chichester : Wiley, c1982. — xi,637p : ill ; 24cm. — (Wiley series in probability and mathematical statistics)
Previous ed.: 1974. — Includes index
ISBN 0-471-05909-9 : £21.80 B82-34742

Lee, J. D. (John David). Statistics and computer methods in BASIC / J.D. Lee and T.D. Lee. — New York ; London : Van Nostrand Reinhold, 1982. — xi,198p : ill ; 25cm
Includes index
ISBN 0-442-30474-9 (cased) : £11.50
ISBN 0-442-30474-9 (pbk) : £5.50 B82-14013

Pannonian Symposium on Mathematical Statistics *(2nd : 1981 : Bad Tatzmannsdorf).*
Probability and statistical inference / proceedings of the 2nd Pannonian Symposium on Mathematical Statistics, Bad Tatzmannsdorf, Austria, June 14-20, 1981 ; edited by Wilfried Grossmann, Georg Ch. Pflug and Wolfgang Wertz. — Dordrecht ; London : Reidel, c1982. — viii,389p : ill ; 25cm
Includes bibliographies and index
ISBN 90-277-1427-4 : Unpriced B82-37032

Trivedi, Kishor Shridharbhai. Probability and statistics with reliability queuing, and computer science applications / Kishor Shridharbhai Trivedi. — Englewood Cliffs ; London : Prentice-Hall, c1982. — x,624p : ill ; 24cm
Bibliography: p573-578. — Includes index
ISBN 0-13-711564-4 : £22.00 B82-36876

519.2 — Probabilities & statistical mathematics. Exchangeability — *Conference proceedings*

International Conference on Exchangeability in Probability and Statistics *(1981 : Rome).*
Exchangeability in probability and statistics : proceedings of the International Conference on Exchangeability in Probability and Statistics, Rome, 6th-9th April, 1981 in honour of Professor Bruno de Finetti / edited by G. Koch and F. Spizzichino. — Amsterdam ; Oxford : North-Holland, 1982. — xvii,365p : ill ; 23cm
Includes bibliographies
ISBN 0-444-86403-2 : £29.54 B82-39843

519.2 — Probabilities & statistical mathematics — *Festschriften*

Statistics and probability : essays in honor of C.R. Rao / edited by G. Kallianpur, P.R. Krishnaiah, J.K. Ghosh. — Amsterdam ; Oxford : North-Holland, 1982. — xi,722p : 1port ; 25cm
Includes bibliographies
ISBN 0-444-86130-0 : £65.82 B82-28642

519.2 — Random fields

Random fields : rigorous results in statistical mechanics and quantum field theory / edited by J. Fritz, J.L. Lebowitz and D. Szász. — Amsterdam ; Oxford : North-Holland, c1981. — 2v.(1111p) : ill ; 25cm. — (Colloquia mathematica Societatis János Bolyai, ISSN 0139-3383 ; 27)
Conference proceedings
ISBN 0-444-85441-x : Unpriced B82-21633

519.2 — Stochastic analysis

Rao, M. M.. Foundations of stochastic analysis / M.M. Rao. — New York ; London : Academic Press, 1981. — xi,295p ; 24cm. — (Probability and mathematical statistics)
Bibliography: p283-290. — Includes index
ISBN 0-12-580850-x : £26.20 B82-10055

519.2 — Stochastic differential equations

Elworthy, K. D.. Stochastic differential equations on manifolds / K.D. Elworthy. — Cambridge : Cambridge University Press, 1982. — 326p ; 23cm. — (London Mathematical Society lecture note series ; 70)
Bibliography: p308-318. — Includes index
ISBN 0-521-28767-7 (pbk) : Unpriced : CIP rev. B82-26254

519.2 — Stochastic dynamical systems. Filtering & identification — *Conference proceedings*

Stochastic systems : the mathematics of filtering and identification and applications : proceedings of the NATO Advanced Study Institute held at Les Arcs, Savoie, France, June 22 - July 5, 1980 / edited by Michiel Hazewinkel and Jan C. Willems. — Dordrecht ; London : Reidel in cooperation with NATO Scientific Affairs Division, c1981. — xi,663p : ill ; 25cm. — (NATO advanced study institutes series. Series C, Mathematical and physical sciences ; v.78)
Includes bibliographies and index
ISBN 90-277-1330-8 : Unpriced B82-06119

519.2 — Stochastic models

Neuts, Marcel F.. Matrix-geometric solutions in stochastic models : an algorithmic approach / Marcel F. Neuts. — Baltimore ; London : Johns Hopkins University Press, c1981. — xiii,332p : ill ; 24cm. — (Johns Hopkins series in the mathematical sciences ; 2)
Bibliography: p310-328. — Includes index
ISBN 0-8018-2560-1 : £22.75 B82-02225

Stoyan, Dietrich. Comparison methods for queues and other stochastic models. — Chichester : Wiley, July 1982. — [300]p. — (Wiley series in probability and mathematical statistics (applied section))
Translation and revision of: Qualitative Eigenschaften und Abschätzungen stochastischer Modelle
ISBN 0-471-10122-2 : £18.00 : CIP entry B82-13247

519.2 — Stochastic processes

Wentzell, A. D.. A course in the theory of stochastic processes / A.D. Wentzell ; translated by S. Chomet ; foreword by K.L. Chung. — New York ; London : McGraw-Hill, c1981. — x,304p : ill ; 24cm
Bibliography: p302. — Includes index
ISBN 0-07-069305-6 : £28.75 : CIP rev. B80-08724

519.2 — Stochastic processes. Probability methods

Skorokhod, A. V.. Studies in the theory of random processes / by A.V. Skorokhod. — New York : Dover ; London : Constable, 1982. — viii,199p ; 22cm
Translation of: Issledovaniīa po teorii sluchaĭnykh protsessov. — Originally published: Reading, Mass. : Addison-Wesley, 1965
ISBN 0-486-64240-2 (pbk) : £3.40 B82-34626

519.2 — Topological vector spaces. Probabilities. Distributions

Vakhania, N. N.. Probability distributions on linear spaces / N.N Vakhania. — New York ; Oxford : North-Holland, c1981. — xiv,123p ; 24cm. — (North-Holland series in probability and applied mathematics)
Translation of: Verīatnostnye raspredeleniīa v lineĭnykh prostranstvakh. — Includes index
ISBN 0-444-00577-3 : Unpriced B82-05058

519.2′01 — Probabilities. Theories — *Philosophical perspectives*

Weatherford, Roy. Philosophical foundations of probability theory / Roy Weatherford. — London : Routledge & Kegan Paul, 1982. — xi,282p ; 23cm. — (International library of philosophy)
Text on back lining papers. — Bibliography: p273-278. — Includes index
ISBN 0-7100-9002-1 : £15.00 B82-35997

519.2′02433 — Probabilities & statistical mathematics — *For economics*

Hoel, Paul G.. Basic statistics for business and economics / Paul G. Hoel and Raymond J. Jessen. — 3rd ed. — New York ; Chichester : Wiley, c1982. — x,629p : ill ; 24cm. — (Wiley series in probability and mathematical statistics)
Previous ed.: 1977. — Text on lining papers. — Bibliography: p8-9. — Includes index
ISBN 0-471-09829-9 : £17.70 B82-26451

519.2′024552 — Probabilities & statistical mathematics — *For petrology*

Le Maitre, R. W.. Numerical petrology. — Oxford : Elsevier Scientific, July 1982. — [282] p. — (Developments in petrology ; 8)
ISBN 0-444-42098-3 : CIP entry B82-20635

519.2′028′54 — Probabilities. Applications of computer systems

Probability theory and computer science. — London : Academic Press, Sept.1982. — 1v.. — (International lecture series in computer science)
ISBN 0-12-455820-8 : CIP entry B82-18830

519.2′076 — Probabilities — *Questions & answers* — *For schools*

Choice or chance / [Schools Council Project on Statistical Education]. — Slough : Published for the Schools Council by Foulsham Educational, 1981. — 20p + teachers′ notes (20p ; 21cm) : ill ; 21cm. — (Statistics in your world)
ISBN 0-572-01085-0 (pbk) : Unpriced
ISBN 0-572-01112-1 (teachers′ notes) : Unpriced B82-13023

Testing testing / [Schools Council Project on Statistical Education]. — Slough : Published for the Schools Council by Foulsham Educational, c1981. — 19p : ill ; 21cm + teachers′ notes(18p ; 21cm). — (Statistics in your world)
ISBN 0-572-01087-7 (pbk) : Unpriced
ISBN 0-572-01114-8 (teachers′ notes) : Unpriced B82-11684

519.2′33 — Markov renewal processes — *Conference proceedings*

Recent developments in Markov decision processes : based on the proceedings of an international conference on Markov decision processes / organised jointly by the Department of Decision Theory of the University of Manchester and the Institute of Mathematics and its Applications and held at the University of Manchester on July 17th to 19th, 1978 ; edited by R. Hartley, L.C. Thomas, D.J. White. — London : Academic Press, 1980. — xiv,334p : ill ; 24cm. — (The Institute of Mathematics and its Applications conference series)
ISBN 0-12-328460-0 : £15.00 : CIP rev. B80-09205

519.2′87 — Reliability theory

Goldberg, Harold. Extending the limits of reliability theory / Harold Goldberg. — New York ; Chichester : Wiley, c1981. — xii,263p : ill ; 24cm
Includes index
ISBN 0-471-07799-2 : £24.25 B82-09883

519.3 — Differential games

Basar, T.. Dynamic noncooperative game theory. — London : Academic Press, Jan.1982. — [480]p
ISBN 0-12-080220-1 : CIP entry B81-34120

519.3 — Failure time. Data. Statistical analysis

Lawless, J. F.. Statistical models and methods for lifetime data / J.F. Lawless. — New York ; Chichester : Wiley, c1982. — xi,580p ; 23cm. — (Wiley series in probability and mathematical statistics, ISSN 0271-6356)
Bibliography: p540-565. — Includes index
ISBN 0-471-08544-8 : £27.25 B82-18205

Nelson, Wayne. Applied life data analysis / Wayne Nelson. — New York ; Chichester : Wiley, c1982. — xiv,634p : ill ; 24cm. — (Wiley series in probability and mathematical statistics. Applied probability and statistics, ISSN 0271-6356)
Bibliography: p603-616. — Includes index
ISBN 0-471-09458-7 : £30.25 B82-28078

519.3 — Game theory

Colman, Andrew. Game theory and experimental games. — Oxford : Pergamon, Sept.1982. — [300]p. — (International series in experimental social psychology ; v.4)
ISBN 0-08-026070-5 (cased) : £38.00 : CIP entry
ISBN 0-08-026069-1 (pbk) : £13.90 B82-19092

519.3 — Game theory *continuation*

Dresher, Melvin. [Games of strategy]. The mathematics of games of strategy : theory and applications / by Melvin Dresher. — New York : Dover ; London : Constable, 1981. — 184p : ill ; 21cm
Originally published: Englewood Cliffs : Prentice-Hall, 1961. — Bibliography: p179-180. — Includes index
ISBN 0-486-64216-x (pbk) : £3.00 B82-29994

Venttsel', E. S.. Elements of game theory / Ye.S. Venttsel ; translated from the Russian by Vladimir Shokurov. — Moscow : Mir, 1980 ; [London] : Distributed by Central Books. — 68p : ill ; 21cm. — (Little mathematics library)
Translation of: Elementy teorii igr
£0.95 (pbk) B82-34683

519.3'024658 — Game theory — *For business studies*

Ponssard, Jean-Pierre. Competitive strategies : an advanced textbook in game theory for business students / Jean-Pierre Ponssard ; [translated by A.R.G. Heesterman]. — Amsterdam ; Oxford : North-Holland, c1981. — ix,211p : ill ; 23cm
Translation of: Logique de la negociation et théorie des jeux. — Includes bibliographies
ISBN 0-444-86230-7 : £21.69 B82-06719

519.4 — Applied mathematics. Concave functions — *Conference proceedings*

Generalized concavity in optimization and economics / [papers presented at the proceedings of the NATO Advanced Study Institute held at the University of British Columbia, Vancouver, Canada, August 4-15, 1980] ; edited by Siegfried Schaible, William T. Ziemba. — New York ; London : Academic Press, 1981. — xiv,767p : ill ; 24cm
Includes bibliographies
ISBN 0-12-621120-5 : £29.80 B82-30150

519.4 — Coding theory

Cameron, Peter J.. Graphs, codes and designs / P.J. Cameron, J.H. van Lint. — Cambridge : Cambridge University Press, 1980. — vii,147p : ill ; 22cm. — (London Mathematical Society lecture note series ; 43)
Bibliography: p136-144. — Includes index
ISBN 0-521-23141-8 (pbk) : £9.25
Primary classification 511'.5 B82-28967

519.4 — Computation by digital computer systems

McNaughton, Robert. Elementary computability, formal languages and automata / Robert McNaughton. — Englewood Cliffs ; London : Prentice-Hall, c1982. — xvi,400p : ill ; 24cm
Bibliography: p388-393. — Includes index
ISBN 0-13-253500-9 : £18.70 B82-22232

519.4 — Computer systems. Mathematics

Lipschutz, Seymour. Schaum's outline of theory and problems of essential computer mathematics / by Seymour Lipschutz. — New York ; London : McGraw-Hill, c1982. — 357p : ill ; 28cm. — (Schaum's outline series)
Includes index
ISBN 0-07-037990-4 (pbk) : Unpriced B82-29457

519.4 — Computer systems. Mathematics. Recursive functions

Péter, Rózsa. Recursive functions in computer theory / Rózsa Péter ; [translated by I. Juhász]. — Chichester : Horwood, c1981. — 179p : ill ; 24cm. — (The Ellis Horwood series in computers and their applications)
Translation of: Rekursive Funktionen in der Komputer-Theorie. — Includes index
ISBN 0-85312-164-8 : £17.50 : CIP rev. B81-08822

519.4 — Digital computer systems. Mathematics

Beckman, Frank S.. Mathematical foundations of programming / Frank S. Beckman. — Reading, Mass. ; London : Addison-Wesley, c1980 (1981 [printing]). — xviii,443p : ill,1facsim,1port ; 25cm. — (The Systems programming series)
Ill on lining papers. — Includes index
ISBN 0-201-14462-x : £18.40 B82-12651

519.4 — Error-correcting codes

Pless, Vera. Introduction to the theory of error-correcting codes / Vera Pless. — New York ; Chichester : Wiley, c1982. — xi,169p : ill ; 24cm. — (Wiley-interscience series in discrete mathematics)
Bibliography: p163-164. — Includes index
ISBN 0-471-08684-3 : £17.00 B82-13354

519.4 — Numerical analysis

Henrici, Peter. Essentials of numerical analysis : with pocket calculator demonstrations / Peter Henrici. — New York ; Chichester : Wiley, c1982. — vi,409p : ill ; 25cm
Bibliography: p399-402. — Includes index
ISBN 0-471-05904-8 : £18.85 B82-33134

Maron, Melvin J.. Numerical analysis : practical approach / Melvin J. Maron. — New York : Macmillan ; London : Collier Macmillan, c1982. — xviii,471p : ill ; 27cm
Text on lining papers. — Bibliography: p451-452. — Includes index
ISBN 0-02-475670-9 : £17.95 B82-36486

519.4 — Numerical analysis. Applications of digital computer systems

Johnston, R. L.. Numerical methods : a software approach / R.L. Johnston. — New York ; Chichester : Wiley, c1982. — ix,276p : ill ; 24cm
Bibliography: p268-269. — Includes index
ISBN 0-471-09397-1 : £18.45 B82-26479

Morris, J. Ll. Computational methods in elementary numerical analysis. — Chichester : Wiley, Mar.1982. — [450]p
ISBN 0-471-10419-1 (cased) : £19.00 : CIP entry
ISBN 0-471-10420-5 (pbk) : £10.50 B82-10658

519.4 — Numerical analysis. Applications of digital computer systems. Programming

IFIP TC2 Working Conference on the Relationship between Numerical Computation and Programming Languages *(1981 : Boulder)*. The relationship between numerical computation and programming languages : proceedings of the IFIP TC2 Working Conference on the Relationship between Numerical Computation and Programming Languages, Boulder, Colorado, USA, 3-7 August, 1981 / [organized by IFIP Working Group 2.5 (Mathematical Software) on behalf of IFIP Technical Committee 2 (Programming), International Federation for Information Processing] ; edited by John K. Reid. — Amsterdam ; Oxford : North-Holland, 1982. — x,377p : ill ; 23cm
Includes bibliographies
ISBN 0-444-86377-x : £16.38 B82-34294

519.4 — Numerical analysis — *For set theory*

Beller, A.. Coding the universe. — Cambridge : Cambridge University Press, Dec.1981. — [368]p. — (London Mathematical lecture note series, ISSN 0076-0552 ; 47)
ISBN 0-521-28040-0 : £17.50 : CIP entry B82-01354

519.4 — Numerical analysis. Use of pocket electronic calculators — *Manuals*

Henrici, Peter. Numerical analysis : demonstrations on the HP-33E / Peter Henrici, Marie Louise Henrici. — New York ; Chichester : Wiley, c1982. — 234p : ill ; 24cm
ISBN 0-471-05943-9 (pbk) : Unpriced B82-37964

519.4 — Numerical methods — *Conference proceedings*

Numerical methods / edited by P. Rózsa. — Amsterdam ; Oxford : North-Holland, 1980. — 631p : ill ; 25cm. — (Colloquia mathematica Societatis János Bolyai, ISSN 0139-3383 ; 22)
Conference papers. — Includes bibliographies
ISBN 0-444-85407-x : £38.54 B82-40937

519.4'0246 — Numerical analysis. Computation — *For technicians*

Caldwell, Jim. Computational and quantitative methods / Jim Caldwell. — Northallerton : Emjoc, 1981. — 134p : ill ; 22cm
Includes index
ISBN 0-9506994-1-1 (cased) : £10.50
ISBN 0-9506994-2-x (pbk) : £5.50 B82-22256

519.5 — Distribution free statistical methods

Maritz, J. S.. Distribution-free statistical methods / J.S. Maritz. — London : Chapman and Hall, 1981. — x,264p : ill ; 23cm
Bibliography: p259-261. — Includes index
ISBN 0-412-15940-6 : £14.00 : CIP rev. B81-18153

519.5 — Multidimensional scaling. Applications of digital computer systems. Programs

Coxon, Anthony P. M.. The user's guide to multidimensional scaling : with special reference to the MDS (X) library of computer programs / A.P.M. Coxon with the assistance of P.M. Davies. — London : Heinemann Educational, 1982. — xii,271p : ill ; 25cm
Bibliography: p254-264. — Includes index
ISBN 0-435-82251-9 (cased) : £16.50 : CIP rev.
ISBN 0-435-82252-7 (pbk) : Unpriced B82-01958

Schiffman, Susan S.. Introduction to multidimensional scaling : theory, methods, and applications / Susan S. Schiffman, M. Lance Reynolds, Forrest W. Young with contributions by J. Douglas Carroll ... [et al.] ; with a foreword by Joseph B. Kruskal. — New York ; London : Academic Press, 1981. — xvi,413p : ill ; 24cm
Includes bibliographies and index
ISBN 0-12-624350-6 : £19.60 B82-18684

519.5 — One-dimensional scaling — *For social sciences*

McIver, John P.. Unidimensional scaling / John P. McIver, Edward G. Carmines. — Beverly Hills ; London : Sage, 1981. — 96p : ill ; 22cm. — (Quantitative applications in the social sciences ; no.07-024) (Sage university papers)
Bibliography: p91-96
ISBN 0-8039-1736-8 (pbk) : £2.50 B82-17759

519.5 — Qualitative data. Statistical analysis. Applications of loglinear models — *For social sciences*

Gilbert, G. Nigel. Modelling society : an introduction to loglinear analysis for social researchers / G. Nigel Gilbert. — London : Allen & Unwin, 1981. — xii,131p : ill ; 23cm. — (Contemporary social research series ; 2)
Bibliography: p125-129. — Includes index
ISBN 0-04-312009-1 (cased) : Unpriced : CIP rev.
ISBN 0-04-312010-5 (pbk) : Unpriced B81-28787

519.5 — Statistical analysis

Cox, D. R.. Applied statistics : principles and examples / D.R. Cox, E.J. Snell. — London : Chapman and Hall, 1981. — viii,189p : ill ; 24cm
Bibliography: p181-183. — Includes index
ISBN 0-412-16560-0 (cased) : Unpriced : CIP rev.
ISBN 0-412-16570-8 (pbk) : £6.95 B81-23907

519.5 — Statistical mathematics

Barra, Jean-René. Mathematical basis of statistics / Jean-René Barra ; translation edited by Leon Herbach. — New York ; London : Academic Press, 1981. — xvi,249p ; 24cm. — (Probability and mathematical statistics)
Translation of: Notions fondamentales de statistique mathématique. — Bibliography: p243-245. — Includes index
ISBN 0-12-079240-0 : £26.20 B82-10049

Caswell, Fred. Success in statistics / Fred Caswell ; consultant editor Helen Wright. — London : Murray, 1982. — xi,344p : ill ; 22cm. — (Success studybooks)
Bibliography: p312. — Includes index
ISBN 0-7195-3902-1 (pbk) : £4.50 : CIP rev. B82-04882

Cochran, William G.. Contributions to statistics / William G. Cochran. — New York ; Chichester : Wiley, c1982. — 1v.(various pagings) : ill,1port ; 26cm
Includes chapters in French and Spanish. — Includes bibliographies
ISBN 0-471-09786-1 : £59.00 B82-27735

519.5 — Statistical mathematics
continuation

Ehrenberg, A. S. C.. A primer in data reduction : an introductory statistics textbook / A.S.C. Ehrenberg. — Chichester : Wiley, c1982. — xviii,305p : ill ; 24cm
Includes index
ISBN 0-471-10134-6 (cased) : £22.20 : CIP rev.
ISBN 0-471-10135-4 (pbk) : £6.95 B82-13250

Gilbert, Norma. Statistics / Norma Gilbert. — 2nd ed. — Philadelphia ; London : Saunders College, c1981. — xi,434p : ill ; 21cm
Previous ed.: 1976. — Text on inside cover. — Includes index
ISBN 4-8337-0040-9 (pbk) : £7.95 B82-30497

Hannagan, T. J.. Mastering statistics / T.J. Hannagan. — [London] : Macmillan, 1982. — 244p : ill ; 23cm. — (Macmillan master series)
Includes index
ISBN 0-333-31291-0 (cased) : £8.95
ISBN 0-333-30905-7 (pbk) : Unpriced B82-17110

Harper, W. M.. Statistics / W.M. Harper. — 4th ed. — Plymouth : Macdonald and Evans, 1982. — xii,387p : ill ; 19cm. — (The M & E handbook series)
Previous ed.: 1977. — Bibliography: p251. — Includes index
ISBN 0-7121-1988-4 (pbk) : £3.95 B82-39945

Kendall, *Sir* Maurice. The advanced theory of statistics. — 4th ed. — London : Griffin
Previous ed.: 1976
Vol.3: Design and analysis, and time-series. — Nov.1982. — [792]p
ISBN 0-85264-268-7 : £32.00 : CIP entry B82-30584

Sellers, Gene. Elementary statistics. — 2nd ed. / Gene R. Sellers, Stephen A. Vardeman. — Philadelphia ; London : Saunders College, c1982. — x,598p : ill ; 25cm
Previous ed.: 1977. — Text on lining papers. — Includes index
ISBN 0-03-058456-6 : £18.95 B82-25407

Walpole, Ronald E.. Introduction to statistics / Ronald E. Walpole. — 3rd ed. — New York : Macmillan ; London : Collier Macmillan, c1982. — xv,521p : ill(some col.) ; 25cm
Previous ed.: 1974. — Includes index
ISBN 0-02-424150-4 (cased) : Unpriced
ISBN 0-02-977650-3 (pbk) : £7.95 B82-29741

Wetherill, G. Barrie. Elementary statistical methods. — 3rd ed. — London : Chapman and Hall, Jan.1982. — [348]p. — (Science paperbacks)
Previous ed.: 1972
ISBN 0-412-24000-9 (pbk) : £6.95 : CIP entry B81-34403

Wonnacott, Ronald J.. Statistics : discovering its power / Ronald J. Wonnacott, Thomas H. Wonnacott. — New York ; Chichester : Wiley, c1982. — xviii,378p : ill(some col.) ; 25cm. — (Wiley series in probability and mathematical statistics)
Text on lining papers. — Bibliography: p354-356. — Includes index
ISBN 0-471-01412-5 : £13.40 B82-27726

519.5 — Statistical mathematics. Applications

Caulcutt, R.. Statistics in research and development. — London : Chapman and Hall, Nov.1982. — [250]p
ISBN 0-412-23720-2 : £15.00 : CIP entry B82-28257

519.5 — Statistical mathematics — *Conference proceedings*

International Symposium on Statistics and Related Topics *(1980 : Ottawa)*. Statistics and related topics : proceedings of the International Symposium on Statistics and Related Topics held in Ottawa, Canada, May 5-7, 1980 / edited by M. Csörgö ... [et al.]. — Amsterdam ; Oxford : North-Holland, c1981. — xiv,387p : ill ; 23cm
Includes bibliographies
ISBN 0-444-86293-5 : £26.65 B82-09910

Some recent advances in statistics / edited by J. Tiago de Oliveira and Benjamin Epstein. — London : Academic Press, 1982. — ix,248p : ill ; 24cm
Conference papers. — Includes bibliographies
ISBN 0-12-691580-6 : £24.00 : CIP rev. B82-07492

519.5′0212 — Statistical mathematics — *Tables*

Neave, Henry R.. Elementary statistics tables / Henry R. Neave. — [London] : [Allen & Unwin], [c1981]. — 45p : ill ; 30cm
Text on inside back cover
ISBN 0-04-001002-3 (pbk) : Unpriced : CIP rev. B80-19189

Statistical tables for the social, biological and physical sciences / compiled by F.C. Powell. — Cambridge : Cambridge University Press, 1982. — 96p ; 26cm
ISBN 0-521-24141-3 : £7.50 : CIP rev.
ISBN 0-521-28473-2 (pbk) : Unpriced B81-40268

White, John, *1944-*. Tables for statisticians / compiled by John White, Alan Yeats, Gordon Skipworth. — 3rd ed. — Cheltenham : Thomas, 1979, c1974. — 70p : ill ; 24cm
Previous ed.: 1977
ISBN 0-85950-012-8 (pbk) : £1.50 B82-37248

519.5′023′41 — Great Britain. Statistical mathematics — *Career guides*

Careers in statistics / [Institute of Statisticians]. — Bury St. Edmunds : The Institute, [1982?]. — [12]p : ill ; 21cm
£0.25 (pbk) B82-31964

519.5′024092 — Statistical mathematics — *For librarianship*

Simpson, Ian S.. Basic statistics for librarians. — 2nd ed. — London : Bingley, Oct.1982. — [240]p
Previous ed.: 1975
ISBN 0-85157-352-5 : £9.95 : CIP entry B82-25067

519.5′02415 — Statistical mathematics — *For psychology*

Levine, Gustav. Instructor′s manual for Introductory statistics for psychology : the logic and the methods / Gustav Levine. — New York ; London : Academic Press, c1981. — viii,92p : ill ; 28cm
ISBN 0-12-445481-x (pbk) : £2.40 B82-29939

Minium, Edward W.. Elements of statistical reasoning / Edward W. Minium, Robert B. Clarke. — New York ; Chichester : Wiley, c1982. — 400p,[85]p : ill ; 24cm
Includes index
ISBN 0-471-08041-1 : £14.00 B82-27757

519.5′0243 — Statistical mathematics — *For behavioural sciences*

Ewen, Robert B.. Workbook for Introductory statistics for the behavioral sciences, third edition / Robert B. Ewen. — New York ; London : Academic Press, c1982. — xix,235p ; 24cm
ISBN 0-12-743271-x (pbk) : £6.20 B82-29984

Lindner, William A.. Statistics : for students in the behavioral sciences / William A. Lindner. — Menlo Park ; London : Benjamin/Cummings, c1979. — xvii,438p : ill ; 25cm
Text on lining papers. — Includes index
ISBN 0-8053-6576-1 : £15.20 B82-10996

Welkowitz, Joan. Introductory statistics for the behavioral sciences / Joan Welkowitz, Robert B. Ewen, Jacob Cohen. — 3rd ed. — New York ; London : Academic Press, c1982. — xiii,369p : ill ; 25cm + Answer key(30p; 23cm)
Previous ed.: 1976. — Text on lining papers. — Includes index
ISBN 0-12-743270-1 : £12.60 B82-32789

Wynne, James D.. Learning statistics : a common-sense approach / James D. Wynne. — New York : Macmillan ; London : Collier Macmillan, c1982. — xiii,546p : ill ; 26cm
Text on lining papers. — Includes index
ISBN 0-02-430680-0 : Unpriced B82-33691

519.5′024301 — Statistical analysis — *For social sciences*

Cooper, R. A.. Data, models and statistical analysis. — Deddington : Philip Allan, Oct.1982. — [416]p
ISBN 0-86003-139-x (cased) : £18.00 : CIP entry
ISBN 0-86003-043-1 (pbk) : £8.95 B82-28592

519.5′024309 — Statistical mathematics — *For sociology*

Startup, Richard. Introducing social statistics / Richard Startup, Elwyn T. Whittaker. — London : Allen & Unwin, 1982. — x,201p : ill ; 23cm. — (Studies in sociology ; 12)
Includes index
ISBN 0-04-310012-0 (cased) : Unpriced : CIP rev.
ISBN 0-04-310013-9 (pbk) : Unpriced B81-33922

519.5′02433 — Statistical mathematics — *For economics*

Hebden, Julia. Statistics for economists / Julia Hebden. — Oxford : Philip Allan, 1981. — vi,201p : ill ; 24cm
Includes bibliographies and index
ISBN 0-86003-036-9 (cased) : £12.00 : CIP rev.
ISBN 0-86003-134-9 (pbk) : £5.95 B81-23900

519.5′02433 — Statistical mathematics — *Questions & answers — For econometrics*

Salvatore, Dominick. Schaum′s outline of theory and problems of statistics and econometrics / Dominick Salvatore. — New York ; London : McGraw-Hill, c1982. — 234p : ill ; 28cm. — (Schaum′s outline series)
Includes index
ISBN 0-07-054505-7 (pbk) : £4.50 B82-17100

519.5′0246 — Statistical mathematics — *For technicians*

Walker, Eric. Statistics level 3 / Eric Walker. — London : Holt, Rinehart and Winston, c1982. — ix,133p : ill ; 22cm. — (Holt technician texts)
Includes index
ISBN 0-03-910356-0 (pbk) : £3.95 : CIP rev. B81-40250

519.5′02461 — Statistical analysis — *For medicine*

Regier, Mary H.. Biomedical statistics with computing. — Chichester : Wiley, July 1982. — [275]p. — (Medical computing series)
ISBN 0-471-10449-3 : £16.00 : CIP entry B82-14078

519.5′02461 — Statistical mathematics — *For medicine*

Glantz, Stanton A.. Primer of biostatistics / Stanton A. Glantz. — New York ; London : McGraw-Hill, c1981. — xv,352p : ill ; 21cm
Includes index
ISBN 0-07-023370-5 (pbk) : £7.50 B82-04451

Strike, Paul W.. Medical laboratory statistics / Paul W. Strike. — Bristol : John Wright, 1981. — ix,203p : ill ; 19cm. — (Institute of Medical Laboratory Sciences monographs)
Includes bibliographies and index
ISBN 0-7236-0582-3 (pbk) : Unpriced : CIP rev. B81-20573

519.5′02462 — Statistical mathematics — *For engineering*

Guttman, Irwin. Introductory engineering statistics / Irwin Guttman, the late S.S. Wilks, J. Stuart Hunter. — 3rd ed. — New York ; Chichester : Wiley, c1982. — xi,580p : ill ; 25cm. — (Wiley series in probability and mathematical statistics)
Previous ed.: 1971. — Includes index
ISBN 0-471-07859-x : £25.00 B82-34517

Volk, William. Engineering statistics with a programmable calculator / William Volk. — New York ; London : McGraw-Hill, c1982. — iv,362p : ill ; 25cm
Includes index
ISBN 0-07-067552-x : £13.95 B82-00415

519.5′02465 — Statistical mathematics — *For business enterprise*

Freund, John E.. Elementary business statistics : the modern approach / John E. Freund, Frank J. Williams. — 4th ed. — Englewood Cliffs ; London : Prentice-Hall, c1982. — xviii,606p : ill(some col.) ; 25cm
Previous ed.: Englewood Cliffs : Prentice-Hall, 1977. — Text on lining papers. — Bibliography: p547-550. — Includes index
ISBN 0-13-253120-8 : £17.95 B82-20085

519.5′02465 — Statistical mathematics — *Questions & answers — For business enterprise*

Letchford, Stanley. Statistics workbook : for accountancy and business studies students / by Stanley Letchford. — London : Gee, 1982. — 138p ; 25cm. — (A Gee's study book)
ISBN 0-85258-220-x (pbk) : £5.75 B82-31256

519.5′024658 — Statistical mathematics — *For business studies*

Bancroft, Gordon. Maths and statistics for accounting and business studies / Gordon Bancroft and George O'Sullivan. — London : McGraw-Hill, c1981. — xi,294p : ill ; 25cm
Bibliography: p289-290. — Includes index
ISBN 0-07-084564-6 (pbk) : £7.95 : CIP rev. B81-21639

Bowen, Earl K.. Basic statistics for business and economics / Earl K. Bowen, Martin K. Starr. — New York ; London : McGraw-Hill, c1982. — xviii,730p : ill(some col.) ; 25cm. — (McGraw-Hill series in quantitative methods for management)
Ill on lining papers. — Includes index
ISBN 0-07-006725-2 : £18.95 B82-27152

Marston, Paul. Applied business statistics / Paul Marston. — London : Holt, Rinehart and Winston, c1982. — viii,374p : ill ; 22cm. — (Holt business texts)
Includes index
ISBN 0-03-910366-8 (pbk) : £4.95 : CIP rev. B82-14488

519.5′028′5404 — Statistical mathematics. Applications of microcomputer systems

Cooke, D.. Basic statistical computing / D. Cooke, A.H. Craven, G.M. Clarke. — London : Edward Arnold, 1982. — xii,156p : ill ; 25cm
Bibliography: p151. — Includes index
ISBN 0-7131-3441-0 (pbk) : £5.95 : CIP rev. B81-32047

519.5′028′542 — Statistical analysis. Applications of digital computer systems. Programs: IDA program — *Manuals*

Ling, Robert F.. [User's manual for IDA]. IDA : a user's guide to the IDA interactive data analysis and forecasting system / Robert F. Ling, Harry V. Roberts. — [Palo Alto] : Scientific Press ; New York ; London : McGraw-Hill, [1980] ([1982 printing]). — 1v.(various pagings) : ill ; 28cm. — (The SPSS series in data analysis)
Includes index
ISBN 0-07-037906-8 (pbk) : £9.50 B82-25278

519.5′028′5425 — Statistical analysis. Applications of digital computer systems. Software packages: GENSTAT — *Manuals*

Alvey, Norman. An introduction to Genstat / Norman Alvey, Nick Galwey, Peter Lane. — London : Academic Press, 1982. — vii,152p : ill ; 25cm
Bibliography: p128. — Includes index
ISBN 0-12-055550-6 (pbk) : £8.50 : CIP rev. B82-10689

519.5′028′5425 — Statistical analysis. Software packages

Francis, Ivor. Statistical software : a comparative review / Ivor Francis. — New York ; Oxford : North-Holland, 1981. — xx,542p : ill ; 24cm
Bibliography: p531. — Includes index
ISBN 0-444-00658-3 : £47.37 B82-13434

519.5′03′21 — Statistical mathematics — *Encyclopaedias*

Encyclopedia of statistical sciences / [editor-in-chief Samuel Kotz, Norman L. Johnson] ; [associate editor Campbell B. Read]. — New York ; Chichester : Wiley
Vol.1: A to Circular probable error. — 1982. — x,480p : ill ; 27cm
Includes bibliographies
ISBN 0-471-05546-8 : £55.00 B82-39344

Kendall, *Sir* Maurice G.. A dictionary of statistical terms. — 4th ed. — London : Longman, Aug.1982. — [213]p
Previous ed.: 1971
ISBN 0-582-47008-0 : £12.95 : CIP entry B82-16470

519.5′06′041 — Great Britain. Statistical mathematics. Organisations: Institute of Statisticians — *Serials*

The **professional** statistician. — Vol.1 issue 1 (Jan. 1982)-. — Bury St. Edmunds (36 Churchgate St., Bury St. Edmunds, Suffolk IP33 1RD) : Institute of Statisticians, 1982-. — v. : ports ; 25cm
Ten issues yearly. — Continues: Newsletter (Institute of Statisticians)
ISSN 0263-1563 = Professional statistician : £10.00 per year (free to members of the Institute) B82-17257

519.5′07 — Statistical mathematics - *Questions & answers*

Wetherill, G. Barrie. Solution to exercises in Intermediate statistical methods. — London : Chapman and Hall, Apr.1981. — [80]p
ISBN 0-412-23520-x (pbk) : £2.00: CIP entry B81-03688

519.5′07′1041 — Great Britain. Educational institutions. Curriculum subjects: Statistical mathematics. Projects — *For teaching*

Statistical teaching aids : a manual of laboratory experiments, classroom demonstrations, films, books and equipment. — (2nd ed.) / revision editor A.F. Bissell. — Bury St. Edmunds : Institute of Statisticians, 1977. — vi,141leaves : ill ; 30cm
Previous ed.: 1972. — Bibliography: leaf 140
Unpriced (pbk) B82-31966

519.5′07′11 — Higher education institutions. Curriculum subjects: Data. Statistical analysis. Teaching

Teaching of statistics and statistical consulting / edited by Jagdish S. Rustagi, Douglas A. Wolfe ; proceedings of a conference held at the Ohio State University, November 24-25, 1980. — New York ; London : Academic Press, 1982. — xvi,548p ; 24cm
Includes bibliographies
ISBN 0-12-604540-2 : £23.80 B82-38384

519.5′07′1242 — England. Secondary schools. Curriculum subjects: Statistical mathematics

Holmes, Peter. Statistics in schools 11-16. — London : Methuen, July 1981. — [100]p. — (Working papers / Schools Council, ISSN 0533-1668 ; 69)
ISBN 0-423-50840-7 (pbk) : £5.00 : CIP entry B81-13500

519.5′076 — Statistical mathematics. Examinations — *Syllabuses*

Institute of Statisticians. Final examinations : (stages II and III) : (units X, Y and Z) / the Institute of Statisticians. — Bury St. Edmunds : [The Institute], 1979. — 17p ; 22cm
Cover title. — "Econometrics" (1 folded sheet) as insert
Unpriced (pbk) B82-31963

Institute of Statisticians. Syllabuses for the preliminary and stage 1 examinations / the Institute of Statisticians. — Bury St. Edmunds : [The Institute], 1979. — 8p ; 22cm
Cover title
Unpriced (pbk) B82-31962

519.5′076 — Statistical mathematics — *Questions & answers — For schools*

Bolt, R. L.. Revision and practice in statistics. — London : Arnold, Nov.1982. — [64]p
ISBN 0-7131-0802-9 (pbk) : £1.75 : CIP entry B82-27944

Loveday, Robert. Everyday statistics / Robert Loveday. — Cambridge : Cambridge University Press, 1980. — 48p : ill ; 23cm. — (Arithmetic for living)
ISBN 0-521-29922-5 (pbk) : £1.20 B82-32120

519.5′2′076 — Statistical mathematics. Sampling — *Questions & answers — For schools*

Pupil poll / [Schools Council Project on Statistical Education]. — Slough : Published for the Schools Council by Foulsham Educational, c1981. — 16p : ill ; 21cm + teachers' notes(15p ; 21cm). — (Statistics in your world)
ISBN 0-572-01084-2 (pbk) : Unpriced
ISBN 0-572-01111-3 (teachers' notes) : Unpriced B82-11683

519.5′3 — Cluster analysis. Algorithms

Zupan, Jure. Clustering of large data sets. — Chichester : Wiley, June 1982. — [200]p. — (Chemometrics research studies series ; 2)
ISBN 0-471-10455-8 : £12.00 : CIP entry B82-13508

519.5′3 — Contingency tables. Statistical analysis

Fienberg, Stephen E.. The analysis of cross-classified categorical data / Stephen E. Fienberg. — 2nd ed. — Cambridge, Mass. ; London : MIT Press, c1980. — xiv,198p : ill ; 24cm
Previous ed.: 1977. — Bibliography: p177-190. — Includes index
ISBN 0-262-06071-x : £4.80 B82-22546

519.5′3 — Discriminant analysis

Hand, D. J.. Discrimination and classification / D.J. Hand. — Chichester : Wiley, c1981. — x,218p : ill ; 24cm. — (Wiley series in probability and mathematical statistics)
Bibliography: p200-209. — Includes index
ISBN 0-471-28048-8 : £15.50 : CIP rev. B81-34017

519.5′3 — Discriminant analysis. Kernel method

Hand, D. J.. Kernel discriminant analysis / D.J. Hand. — Chichester : Research Studies, c1982. — x,253p : ill ; 24cm. — (Electronic & electrical engineering studies. Pattern recognition & image processing research studies series ; 2)
Bibliography: p237-244. — Includes index
ISBN 0-471-10211-3 : £15.50 : CIP rev. B82-12905

519.5′32 — Statistical mathematics. Circular distributions — *For biology*

Batschelet, Edward. Circular statistics in biology / Edward Batschelet. — London : Academic Press, 1981. — xvi,371p : ill ; 24cm. — (Mathematics in biology)
Bibliography: p353-366. — Includes index
ISBN 0-12-081050-6 : £28.80 : CIP rev. B81-17521

519.5′32 — Statistical mathematics. Distributions — *Conference proceedings*

Statistical distributions in scientific work : proceedings of the NATO Advanced Study Institute held at the Universita degli Studi di Trieste, Trieste, Italy, July 10-August 1, 1980 / edited by Charles Taillie, Ganapati P. Patil and Bruno A. Baldesssari. — Dordrecht ; London : Reidel in cooperation with NATO Scientific Affairs Division, c1981. — 3v. : ill ; 25cm. — (NATO advanced study institutes series. Series C, Mathematical and physical sciences ; v.79)
Includes bibliographies and index
ISBN 90-277-1332-4 : Unpriced
ISBN 90-277-1333-2 (v.5)
ISBN 90-277-1334-0 (v.6) B82-06396

519.5′35 — Multivariate analysis

Gordon, A. D.. Classification. — London : Chapman and Hall, Aug.1981. — [250]p. — (Monographs on applied probability and statistics)
ISBN 0-412-22850-5 : £10.00 : CIP entry B81-18150

Johnson, Richard A.. Applied multivariate statistical analysis / Richard A. Johnson, Dean W. Wichern. — Englewood Cliffs ; London : Prentice-Hall, c1982. — xiii,594p : ill ; 25cm
Includes bibliographies and index
ISBN 0-13-041400-x : £31.15 B82-37726

519.5'35 — Multivariate analysis *continuation*

Lewi, Paul J.. Multivariate data analysis in industrial practice. — Chichester : Wiley, Aug.1982. — [250]p. — (Chemometrics research studies series ; 3)
ISBN 0-471-10466-3 (pbk) : £14.00 : CIP entry B82-15819

Muirhead, Robb J.. Aspects of multivariate statistical theory / Robb J. Muirhead. — New York ; Chichester : Wiley, c1982. — xix,673p ; 24cm. — (Wiley series in probability and mathematical statistics. Probability and mathematical statistics)
Bibliography: p650-661. — Includes index
ISBN 0-471-09442-0 : £31.00 B82-32734

Topics in applied multivariate analysis / edited by Douglas M. Hawkins. — Cambridge : Cambridge University Press, 1982. — 326p : ill ; 24cm
Includes bibliographies and index
ISBN 0-521-24368-8 : £12.50 : CIP rev. B82-01332

519.5'35 — Multivariate analysis — *Conference proceedings*

Looking at Multivariate Data *(Conference : 1980 : University of Sheffield)*. Interpreting multivariate data / [proceedings of the Conference entitled "Looking at Multivariate Data" held in the University of Sheffield, U.K. from 24-27 March 1980] ; edited by Vic Barnett. — Chichester : Wiley, c1981. — xvi,374p : ill,maps ; 24cm. — (Wiley series in probability and mathematical statistics)
Bibliography: p349-364. — Includes index
ISBN 0-471-28039-9 : £21.00 : CIP rev. B81-31826

519.5'354'0243 — Factor analysis — *For social sciences*

Measuring social judgments : the factorial survey approach / Peter H. Rossi, Steven L. Nock editors. — Beverly Hills ; London : Sage, c1982. — 255p ; 23cm
Includes bibliographies
ISBN 0-8039-1816-x : £17.00 B82-38162

519.5'36 — Linear regression analysis

Montgomery, Douglas C.. Introduction to linear regression analysis / Douglas C. Montgomery, Elizabeth A. Peck. — New York ; Chichester : Wiley, c1982. — xiii,504p ; 24cm. — (Wiley series in probability and mathematical statistics. Applied probability and statistics, ISSN 0271-6356)
Bibliography: p447-459. — Includes index
ISBN 0-471-05850-5 : Unpriced B82-23944

Toutenburg, Helge. Prior information in linear models / Helge Toutenburg. — Chichester : Wiley, c1982. — ix,215p : ill ; 24cm. — (Wiley series in probability and mathematical statistics)
Bibliography: p207-212. — Includes index
ISBN 0-471-09974-0 : £16.50 : CIP rev. B81-38305

519.5'36 — Multiple regression analysis — *For behavioural sciences*

Pedhazur, Elazar J.. Multiple regression in behavioral research : explanation and prediction. — 2nd ed. / Elazar J. Pedhazur. — New York ; London : Holt, Rinehart and Winston, c1982. — x,822p : ill ; 24cm
Previous ed.: / by Fred N. Kerlinger, Elazar J. Pedhazur. 1973. — Bibliography: p794-811. — Includes index
ISBN 0-03-041760-0 : Unpriced B82-28667

519.5'36 — Regression analysis

Cook, R. Dennis. Residuals and influence in regression. — London : Chapman and Hall, Aug.1982. — [200]p. — (Monographs on statistics and applied probability)
ISBN 0-412-24280-x : £10.00 : CIP entry B82-16638

519.5'4 — Sequential analysis. Nonparametric methods

Sen, Pranab Kumar. Sequential nonparametrics : invariance principles and statistical inference / Pranab Kumar Sen. — New York ; Chichester : Wiley, c1981. — xv,421p ; 24cm. — (Wiley series in probability and mathematical statistics)
Bibliography: p398-413. — Includes index
ISBN 0-471-06013-5 : £31.00 B82-07723

519.5'4 — Statistical inference

Barnett, Vic. Comparative statistical inference / Vic Barnett. — 2nd ed. — New York ; Chichester : Wiley, c1982. — xvi,325p : ill ; 24cm. — (Wiley series in probability and mathematical statistics. Probability and mathematical statistics)
Previous ed.: 1973. — Bibliography: p311-314. — Includes index
ISBN 0-471-10076-5 : £16.50 : CIP rev. B81-31611

519.5'4'02415 — Statistical inference — *For psychology*

Greene, Judith. Statistics for psychology experiments. — Milton Keynes : Open University Press, Aug.1982. — 1v.
ISBN 0-335-10177-1 (pbk) : CIP entry B82-25512

519.5'4'02491 — Statistical inference — *For geography*

Norcliffe, G. B.. Inferential statistics for geographers. — 2nd ed. — London : Hutchinson Education, Jan.1983. — [272]p
Previous ed.: 1977
ISBN 0-09-149811-2 (pbk) : £4.50 : CIP entry B82-33621

519.5'42 — Decision theory

Kmietowicz, Z. W.. Decision theory and incomplete knowledge / Z.W. Kmietowicz and A.D. Pearman. — Aldershot : Gower, c1981. — viii,121p : ill ; 24cm
Bibliography: p116-118. — Includes index
ISBN 0-566-00327-9 : Unpriced : CIP rev. B81-02658

White, D. J.. Optimality and efficiency. — Chichester : Wiley, Dec.1982. — [250]p
ISBN 0-471-10223-7 : £19.50 : CIP entry B82-30820

519.5'42'01 — Decision theory — *Philosophical perspectives*

Eells, Ellery. Rational decision and causality / Ellery Eells. — Cambridge : Cambridge University Press, 1982. — x,234p : ill ; 23cm. — (Cambridge studies in philosophy)
Bibliography: p225-229. — Includes index
ISBN 0-521-24213-4 : £20.00 : CIP rev. B82-15824

519.5'5 — Time series. Analysis — *Conference proceedings*

Applied time series analysis II / edited by David F. Findley. — New York ; London : Academic Press, 1981. — xii,798p : ill ; 24cm
Includes bibliographies and index
ISBN 0-12-256420-0 : £32.80 B82-29595

Time series analysis : theory and practice : proceedings of the international conference held at Valencia, Spain, June 1981 / edited by O.D. Anderson in collaboration with J.G De Gooijer and K.D.C. Stoodley. — Amsterdam ; Oxford : North-Holland, 1982. — ix,756p ; 22cm
Includes bibliographies
ISBN 0-444-86337-0 : £41.75 B82-21023

519.5'5 — Time series. Spectral analysis

Priestley, M. B.. Spectral analysis and time series. — London : Academic Press, Sept.1982. — [960]p. — (Probability and mathematical statistics)
Originally published in 2 vols., 1981
ISBN 0-12-564922-3 (pbk) : CIP entry B82-26213

519.5'5'024301 — Time series. Analysis — *For social sciences*

Gottman, John M.. Time-series analysis : a comprehensive introduction for social scientists / John M. Gottman. — Cambridge : Cambridge University Press, 1981. — xvi,400p : ill ; 24cm
Bibliography: p393-396. — Includes index
ISBN 0-521-23597-9 : £18.50 B82-15254

519.5'5'024553 — Time series. Analysis — *For hydrology — Conference proceedings*

Time series methods in hydrosciences. — Oxford : Elsevier Scientific, Aug.1982. — [614]p. — (Developments in water science ; 17)
Conference papers
ISBN 0-444-42102-5 : CIP entry B82-20636

519.7 — Mathematical programming

Kaplan, Edward L.. Mathematical programming and games / Edward L. Kaplan. — New York ; Chichester : Wiley, c1982. — xx,588p : ill ; 25cm
Bibliography: p560-574. — Includes index
ISBN 0-471-03632-3 : £27.25 B82-32735

519.7'0024658 — Mathematical programming — *For management*

Lev, Benjamin. Introduction to mathematical programming : quantitative tools for decision making / Benjamin Lev, Howard J. Weiss. — London : Edward Arnold, 1982. — xii,289p : ill ; 24cm
Includes index
ISBN 0-7131-3455-0 : £17.50 B82-31518

519.7'02491 — Mathematical programming — *For geography*

Killen, James. Mathematical programming methods for geographers and planners. — London : Croom Helm, Oct.1982. — [384]p
ISBN 0-7099-1512-8 : £14.95 : CIP entry B82-25929

519.7'03 — Dynamic programming

Denardo, Eric V.. Dynamic programming : models and applications / Eric V. Denardo. — Englewood Cliffs ; London : Prentice-Hall, c1982. — xii,227p ; 24cm
Bibliography: p210-217. — Includes index
ISBN 0-13-221507-1 : £20.20 B82-16709

519.7'03 — Optimisation. Dynamic programming

Whittle, Peter. Optimization over time : dynamic programming and stochastic control / Peter Whittle. — Chichester : Wiley. — (Wiley series in probability and mathematical statistics. Applied probability and statistics)
Vol.1. — c1982. — xi,317p : ill ; 24cm
Bibliography: p311-314. — Includes index
ISBN 0-471-10120-6 : £19.50 : CIP rev. B82-13246

519.7'2 — Linear programming

Ignizio, James P.. Linear programming in single- & multiple- objective systems / James P. Ignizio. — Englewood Cliffs ; London : Prentice-Hall, c1982. — xvii,506p : ill ; 24cm. — (Prentice-Hall international series in industrial and systems engineering)
Includes bibliographies and index
ISBN 0-13-537027-2 : £22.45 B82-16701

Vajda, S.. Linear programming. — London : Chapman and Hall, Apr.1981. — [120]p. — (Science paperbacks ; 167)
ISBN 0-412-16430-2 (pbk) : £3.95 : CIP entry B81-03686

519.7'6 — Nonlinear programming — *Conference proceedings*

Nonlinear Programming Symposium *(4th : 1980 : University of Wisconsin-Madison)*. Nonlinear programming 4 / [proceedings of the Nonlinear Programming Symposium 4 conducted by the Computer Sciences Department at the University of Wisconsin-Madison, July 14-16, 1980] ; edited by Olvi L. Mangasarian, Robert R. Meyer, Stephen M. Robinson. — New York ; London : Academic Press, 1981. — ix,549p : ill ; 24cm
Includes bibliographies and index
ISBN 0-12-468662-1 : £26.40 B82-04220

519.7′6 — Optimisation. Nonlinear programming
Algorithms for constrained minimization of smooth nonlinear functions / edited by A.G. Buckley and J.-L. Goffin ; [contributors R.M. Chamberlain ... et al.]. — Amsterdam ; Oxford : North-Holland, 1982. — vii,189p : ill ; 24cm. — (Mathematical programming study ; 16)
ISBN 0-444-86390-7 (pbk) : £12.77 B82-30262

519.7′7 — Integer programming. Applications of graph theory — *Conference proceedings*
Studies on graphs and discrete programming / P. Hansen. — Amsterdam ; Oxford : North-Holland, c1981. — viii,395p : ill ; 24cm. — (Annals of discrete mathematics ; 11) (North-Holland mathematics studies ; 59)
Conference papers. — Includes bibliographies
ISBN 0-444-86216-1 (pbk) : £41.49 B82-13433

519.8′2 — Queueing theory
Cohen, J. W.. The single server queue / J.W. Cohen. — Rev. ed. — Amsterdam ; Oxford : North-Holland, 1982. — xiv,694p ; 23cm. — (North-Holland series in applied mathematics and mechanics ; v.8)
Previous ed.: 1969. — Bibliography: p667-682. — Includes index
ISBN 0-444-85452-5 : £44.49 B82-18374

Newell, G. F.. Applications of queueing theory. — 2nd ed. — London : Chapman and Hall, Sept.1982. — [250]p. — (Monographs on statistics and applied probability)
Previous ed.: 1971
ISBN 0-412-24500-0 : £10.00 : CIP entry B82-19224

Queues and point processes. — Chichester : Wiley, Dec.1981. — [150]p. — (Wiley series in probability and mathematical statistics)
ISBN 0-471-10074-9 : £12.00 : CIP entry B81-30899

520 — ASTRONOMY

520 — Astronomy
Abell, George O.. Exploration of the universe / George O. Abell. — 4th ed. — Philadelphia ; London : Saunders College, c1982. — viii,719p,[8]p of plates : ill(some col.),charts ; 26cm
Previous ed.: 1975. — Bibliography: p659-661. — Includes index
ISBN 0-03-058502-3 : £21.95 B82-25417

Compendium in astronomy : a volume dedicated to Professor John Xanthakis on the occasion of completing twenty five years of scientific activities as fellow of the National Academy of Athens / edited by Elias G. Mariolopoulos, Pericles S. Theocaris and L.N. Mavridis. — Dordrecht ; London : Reidel, c1982. — xv,464p : ill,1port ; 25cm
Includes bibliographies and index
ISBN 90-277-1373-1 : Unpriced B82-30624

Encyclopedia of astronomy : a comprehensive survey of our solar system, galaxy and beyond / consultant editor Colin Ronan. — London : Hamlyn, c1979. — 240p : ill(some col.) ; 31cm
Ill on lining papers. — Bibliography: p234. — Includes index
ISBN 0-600-30362-4 : £7.95 B82-04365

Henbest, Nigel. The restless universe. — London : Philip, Sept.1982. — [240]p
ISBN 0-540-01069-3 : £7.95 : CIP entry B82-19542

Nicolson, Iain. Astronomy / Iain Nicolson ; illustrated by Gordon Davies. — London : Hamlyn, 1970 (1982 [printing]). — 159p : col.ill,col.charts ; 19cm
Bibliography: p156. — Includes index
ISBN 0-600-35653-1 (cased) : £2.99 B82-36014

Pananides, Nicholas A.. Introductory astronomy. — 2nd ed. / Nicholas A. Pananides, Thomas Arny. — Reading, Mass. ; London : Addison-Wesley, c1979. — xxiii,388p,[24]p of plates : ill(some col.),charts,1map,1port ; 24cm. — (Addison-Wesley series in physics)
Previous ed.: 1973. — Includes index
ISBN 0-201-05674-7 : £15.20 B82-10997

Reports on astronomy / edited by Edith A. Müller. — Dordrecht ; London : Reidel, c1979. — vii,223p : 1ill ; 26cm. — (Transactions of the International Astronomical Union ; v.27A ; pt.14)
Includes a chapter and a section in French. — At head of title: International Council of Scientific Unions International Astronomical Union. — Includes bibliographies
ISBN 90-277-1005-8 : Unpriced B82-13862

Reports on astronomy / edited by Patrick A. Wayman. — Dordrecht ; London : Reidel, c1982. — viii,669p ; 26cm. — (Translations of the International Astronomical Union ; v.18a)
At head of title: International Astronomical Union
ISBN 90-277-1423-1 : Unpriced B82-36214

Roy, A. E.. Astronomy : principles and practice / A.E. Roy, D. Clarke. — 2nd ed. — Bristol : Hilger, 1982. — xv,342p : ill ; 28cm
Previous ed.: 1977. — Includes index
ISBN 0-85274-463-3 (cased) : £9.95 : CIP rev.
ISBN 0-85274-464-1 (pbk) : £9.95 B82-11126

Zeilik, Michael. Astronomy : the evolving universe / Michael Zeilik. — 3rd ed. — New York ; London : Harper & Row, c1982. — xv,623p,[8]p of plates : ill(some col.),charts,maps,1facsim,ports ; 29cm
Previous ed.: 1979. — Charts on lining papers. — Includes bibliographies and index
ISBN 0-06-047376-2 : £18.95 B82-24032

520 — Astronomy — *Early works*
Ptolemaeus, Claudius. [Almagest. English]. Ptolemy′s Almagest. — London : Duckworth, Nov.1981. — [720]p
Translated from the Greek
ISBN 0-7156-1588-2 : £42.00 : CIP entry B81-31175

520 — Astronomy — *For schools*
Kincaid, Doug. Sky and space. — [London] : Macdonald Educational/Schools Council, [c1982]. — 48sheets : ill(some col.) ; 22x30cm + teachers′ guide(28p : ill ; 21x30cm). — (Learning through science)
Authors of this material are Doug Kincaid and Roy Richards
ISBN 0-356-07552-4 : Unpriced B82-28885

Seymour, Percy. Adventures with astronomy. — London : Murray, Feb.1983. — [80]p
ISBN 0-7195-3945-5 (cased) : £5.95 : CIP entry
ISBN 0-7195-3931-5 (pbk) : £3.25 (non-net) B82-39437

520 — Astronomy. Observation. Relationships with theories of astronomy
Revealing the universe : prediction and proof in astronomy / edited by James Cornell and Alan P. Lightman. — Cambridge, Mass. ; London : MIT Press, c1982. — xiv,246p : ill,facsims,ports ; 24cm
Includes bibliographies and index
ISBN 0-262-03080-2 : £10.85 B82-20106

520′.3′21 — Astronomy — *Encyclopaedias*
A Dictionary of astronomy / edited by Valerie Illingworth. — London : Pan in association with the Macmillan Press, 1981, c1979. — 378p : ill ; 20cm. — (Pan reference books)
Originally published: London : Macmillan, 1979
ISBN 0-330-26513-x (pbk) : £2.95 B82-04199

520′.5 — Astronomy — *Serials*
Vistas in astronomy. — Vol.24. — Oxford : Pergamon, Oct.1981. — [377]p
ISBN 0-08-028437-x : £50.00 : CIP entry B81-28123

520′.7′1041 — Great Britain. Educational institutions. Curriculum subjects: Astronomy — *Serials*
AAE news. — Vol.1, no.1 (Sept. 1981)-. — [Liverpool] ([c/o Mr J. Ravest, Liverpool Planetarium, Merseyside County Museums, William Brown St., Liverpool L3 8EN]) : Association for Astronomy Education, 1981-. — v. : ill ; 21cm
Three issues yearly
ISSN 0262-3099 = AAE news : Free to Association members B82-05222

520′.7′1141 — Great Britain. Universities. Curriculum subjects: Astronomy. Postgraduate courses — *Lists*
Postgraduate opportunities in astronomy and geophysics. — 4th ed. — London (Burlington House, Piccadilly, W1V ONL) : Royal Astronomical Society, 1979. — [60]p ; 21cm
Unpriced (pbk)
Also classified at 551′.07′1141 B82-40431

520′.7′7 — Astronomy — *Programmed instructions*
Moché, Dinah L.. Astronomy / Dinah L. Moché ; star maps by George Loui. — 2nd ed. — New York ; Chichester : Wiley, c1981. — xiii,284p,[4]leaves of plates : ill,charts,1map ; 26cm. — (A self-teaching guide)
Previous ed.: 1978. — Bibliography: p262-265. — Includes index
ISBN 0-471-09713-6 (pbk) : £5.50 B82-10185

520′.9′01 — Ancient astronomy
Archaeoastronomy in the Old World / edited by D.C. Heggie. — Cambridge : Cambridge University Press, 1982. — vii,280p : ill,plans ; 24cm
Conference papers. — Includes bibliographies and index
ISBN 0-521-24734-9 : £20.00 : CIP rev. B82-26248

520′.9′04 — Astronomy, *ca 1950-1975*
Moore, Patrick. What′s new in space? / Patrick Moore ; illustrated by Paul Doherty. — [London] : Carousel, 1982. — 112p : ill ; 20cm
Includes index
ISBN 0-552-54208-3 (pbk) : £0.95 B82-29738

520′.97 — Pre-Columbian America. Astronomy — *Conference proceedings*
Archaeoastronomy in the New World : American primitive astronomy : proceedings of an international conference held at Oxford University, September 1981 / edited by A.F. Aveni. — Cambridge : Cambridge University Press, 1982. — xi,219p : ill,maps ; 24cm
Includes bibliographies
ISBN 0-521-24731-4 : £16.00 : CIP rev. B82-25771

521 — THEORETICAL ASTRONOMY

521′.1 — Celestial mechanics. Applications of dynamics — *Conference proceedings*
Applications of modern dynamics to celestial mechanics and astrodynamics : proceedings of the NATO Advanced Study Institute held at Cortina d′Ampezzo, Italy, August 2-14, 1981 / edited by Victor Szebehely. — Dordrecht ; London : Reidel in cooperation with NATO Scientific Affairs Division, c1982. — xviii,373p : ill ; 25cm. — (NATO advanced study institutes series. Series C, Mathematical and physical sciences ; v.82)
Includes bibliographies and index
ISBN 90-277-1390-1 : Unpriced B82-25245

521′.3 — Astronomical bodies. Orbits
Roy, Archie. Orbital motion / A.E. Roy. — 2nd ed. — Bristol : Hilger, 1982. — xvi,495p : ill ; 24cm
Previous ed.: 1978. — Includes bibliographies and index
ISBN 0-85274-462-5 : £22.50 : CIP rev. B82-11127

521′.5′09 — Astronomy. Theories, *to ca 1750*
Rogers, Eric M.. Astronomy : for the inquiring mind : the growth and use of theory in science / by Eric M. Rogers. — Princeton, N.J. ; Guildford : Princeton University Press, c1982. — 163p : ill ; 28cm
Revised selections from Physics for the inquiring mind
ISBN 0-691-02370-0 (pbk) : £5.60 B82-38424

521′.5′09031 — Astronomy. Theories, *ca 1500-1679*
Koyré, Alexandre. The astronomical revolution : Copernicus, Kepler, Borelli / Alexandre Koyré ; translated by R.E.W. Maddison. — London : Methuen, 1973 (1980 [printing]). — 530p : ill ; 23cm
Translation of: La révolution astronomique. — Originally published: Paris : Hermann ; London : Methuen, 1973. — Includes index
ISBN 0-416-74410-9 : £19.50 : CIP rev. B80-08728

521′.5′0938 — Ancient Greece. Astronomy. Theories, *to ca B.C.230*
Heath, *Sir* **Thomas**. Aristarchus of Samos : the ancient Copernicus / by Sir Thomas Heath. — New York : Dover ; London : Constable, 1981. — viii,425p : ill ; 22cm
Originally published: Oxford : Clarendon, 1913. — Includes index
ISBN 0-486-24188-2 (pbk) : £5.25 B82-18195

521′.54 — Solar system. Origins
Hutchinson, R.. The search for our beginning. — Oxford : Oxford University Press, Dec.1982. — [144]p
ISBN 0-19-858505-5 : CIP entry B82-29627

521′.541 — Planets: Mercury. Perihelion. Theories, *to 1915*
Roseveare, N. T.. Mercury's perihelion : from Le Verrier to Einstein / N.T. Roseveare. — Oxford : Clarendon, 1982. — viii,208p : ill ; 24cm. — (Oxford science publications)
Bibliography: p187-201. — Includes index
ISBN 0-19-858174-2 : £20.00 : CIP rev. B82-04288

521′.542′0924 — Venus. Origins. Theories of Velikovsky, Immanuel
Forrest, Bob. Velikovsky's sources / Bob Forrest. — [Manchester] ([53 Bannerman Ave., Prestwich, Manchester M25 5DR]) : B. Forrest Pt.2. — c1981. — 81-164p ; 30cm
Unpriced (pbk) B82-02884

Forrest, Bob. Velikovsky's sources / Bob Forrest. — Manchester (53, Bannerman Ave., Prestwich, Manchester M25 5DR) : B. Forrest Part 3. — c1982. — [83]p : ill ; 30cm
Unpriced (unbound) B82-26668

Forrest, Bob. Velikovsky's sources / Bob Forrest. — Manchester (53 Bannerman Ave., Prestwich, Manchester M25 5DR) : B. Forrest Pt.4. — c1982. — p249-336 ; 30cm
Unpriced (unbound) B82-39362

522 — PRACTICAL AND SPHERICAL ASTRONOMY

522 — Astrometry
Murray, C. A.. Vectorial astrometry. — Bristol : Hilger, Dec.1982. — [340]p
ISBN 0-85274-372-6 : £24.00 : CIP entry B82-30733

522 — Astronomical bodies. Observation — *Amateurs' manuals*
Sidgwick, J. B.. Observational astronomy for amateurs / J.B. Sidgwick. — 4th ed. / prepared by James Muirden. — London : Pelham, 1982. — xix,348p : ill,1map,1form ; 23cm
Previous ed.: London : Faber, 1971. — Bibliography: p297-337. — Includes index
ISBN 0-7207-1378-1 : £14.95 : CIP rev. B81-30395

Webb Society deep-sky observer's handbook / compiled by the Webb Society. — Hillside, N.J. : Enslow ; Guildford : Lutterworth Vol.4: Galaxies / edited by Kenneth Glyn Jones written and illustrated by Edmund S. Barker ; with a foreword by Halton Arp. — 1981. — xvi,238p : ill ; 24cm
ISBN 0-7188-2527-6 (pbk) : Unpriced B82-15399

522 — Astronomy — *Amateurs' manuals*
Muirden, James. The Kingfisher astronomy handbook / James Muirden. — London, 1982. — 189p : ill(some col.) ; 20cm
Bibliography: p183. — Includes index
ISBN 0-86272-028-1 : £3.95 : CIP rev. B82-00363

Sidgwick, J. B.. Amateur astronomer's handbook / J.B. Sidgwick. — 4th ed. / prepared by James Muirden. — London : Pelham, 1979. — xxix,568p : ill,plans ; 22cm
Previous ed.: London : Faber, 1971. — Bibliography: p521-552. — Includes index
ISBN 0-7207-1164-9 : £12.50 B82-14002

522′.028′54 — Astronomy. Calculations. Use of pocket electronic calculators
Duffett-Smith, Peter. Practical astronomy with your calculator / Peter Duffett-Smith. — 2nd ed. — Cambridge : Cambridge University Press, 1981. — xvi,188p : ill,1map ; 21cm
Previous ed.: 1979. — Includes index
ISBN 0-521-24059-x (cased) : £15.00 : CIP rev.
ISBN 0-521-28411-2 (pbk) : £4.95 B81-32528

522′.1 — Astronomical observatories
Marx, Siegfried. Observatories of the world / Siegfried Marx and Werner Pfau. — Poole : Blandford, 1982. — 200p : ill(some col.),maps (some col.),ports ; 23cm
Maps on lining papers. — Bibliography: p195-197. — Includes index
ISBN 0-7137-1191-4 : £8.95 : CIP rev. B82-06249

522′.2 — Astronomical optical telescopes
Bell, Louis. The telescope / Louis Bell ; with a new introduction by Jay M. Pasachoff. — New York : Dover ; London : Constable, 1981. — xix,287p : ill,ports ; 22cm
Originally published: New York : McGraw-Hill, 1922. — Bibliography: pxii. — Includes index
ISBN 0-486-24151-3 (pbk) : £4.10 B82-09082

International Astronomical Union. *Colloquium (67th : 1981 : Zelenchukskaya)*.
Instrumentation for astronomy with large optical telescopes : proceedings of IAU colloquium no.67, held at Zelenchukskaya, U.S.S.R., 8-10 September, 1981 / edited by Colin M. Humphries. — Dordrecht ; London : Reidel, c1982. — xvii,321p : ill ; 25cm. — (Astrophysics and space science library ; v.92)
Includes bibliographies and index
ISBN 90-277-1388-x : Unpriced B82-36211

522′.2′09 — Astronomical telescopes, *to 1975*
Learner, Richard. Astronomy through the telescope / Richard Learner. — London : Evans, 1982, c1981. — 224p : ill(some col.),ports ; 32cm
Originally published: New York : Van Nostrand Reinhold, 1981. — Includes index
ISBN 0-237-45644-3 : £12.50 B82-29707

522′.294134 — Edinburgh. Radiotelescopes. Organisations: Royal Observatory, Edinburgh. *U.K. Schmidt Telescope Unit — Serials*
Royal Observatory, Edinburgh. *U.K. Schmidt Telescope Unit*. Newsletter / Science and Engineering Research Council, U.K. Schmidt Telescope Unit. — No.3 (June 1981)-. — Edinburgh (Royal Observatory, Blackford Hill, Edinburgh EH9 3HJ) : The Unit, 1981-. — v. ; 30cm
Irregular. — Continues: Royal Observatory, Edinburgh. U.K. Schmidt Telescope Unit. UKSTU newsletter
ISSN 0262-4567 = Newsletter - U.K. Schmidt Telescope Unit : Unpriced B82-04902

522′.682 — Extragalactic radio sources — *Conference proceedings*
Extragalactic radio sources / edited by David S. Heeschen and Campbell M. Wade. — Dordrecht ; London : Reidel, c1982. — xvii,490p ; 25cm. — (Symposium / International Astronomical Union ; no.97)
Symposium 'organized by IAU in cooperation with URSI held at Albuquerque, U.S.A., August 3-7, 1981'. — Includes index
ISBN 90-277-1384-7 (cased) : Unpriced
ISBN 90-277-1385-5 (pbk) : Unpriced B82-18397

522′.682 — Submillimetre radioastronomy — *Conference proceedings*
Submillimetre wave astronomy. — Cambridge : Cambridge University Press, Sept.1982. — [370]p
Conference papers
ISBN 0-521-24733-0 : £26.00 : CIP entry B82-29357

522′.682′09 — Radioastronomy, *ca 1954*
Classics in radio astronomy / selection and commentary by Woodruff Turner Sullivan. — Dordrecht ; London : Reidel, c1982. — xxiv,348p : ill,1port ; 23cm. — (Studies in the history of modern science)
Bibliography: p337-344. — Includes index
ISBN 90-277-1356-1 : Unpriced B82-36212

522′.686 — X-ray astronomy — *Conference proceedings*
Galactic X-ray sources / edited by Peter W. Sanford, Paul Laskarides, Jane Salton. — Chichester : Wiley, c1982. — xvii,450p : ill ; 24cm
Based on the Proceedings of the NATO Advanced Study Institute on Galactic X-ray Sources held in Sounion, Greece. — Includes bibliographies and index
ISBN 0-471-27963-3 : £20.00 : CIP rev. B81-03354

523 — DESCRIPTIVE ASTRONOMY

523 — Astronomical bodies
Roy, A. E.. Astronomy : structure of the universe. — 2nd ed. — Bristol : Hilger, Sept.1982. — [290]p
Previous ed.: 1977
ISBN 0-85274-465-x (cased) : £20.00 : CIP entry
ISBN 0-85274-466-8 (pbk) : £9.95 B82-20651

523 — Astronomical bodies — *Field guides*
Whitney, Charles A.. Whitney's star finder : a field guide to the heavens / Charles A. Whitney. — London : Joseph, 1982, c1981. — xxi,102p : ill,charts ; 21cm
Originally published: New York : Knopf, 1981. — Locater wheel in pocket. — Includes index
ISBN 0-7181-2129-5 (pbk) : £5.95 B82-22750

523 — Astronomical bodies — *Field guides — For children*
Henbest, Nigel. Spotter's guide to the night sky / Nigel Henbest ; illustrated by Michael Roffe ; star charts by Studio Briggs. — London : Usborne, 1979. — 64p : ill (some col.) ; 18cm. — (Spotter's guides) (Usborne pocketbooks)
Includes index
ISBN 0-86020-284-4 (pbk) : £0.75 B82-05558

523 — Astronomical bodies: Singularities
Davies, P. C. W.. The edge of infinity. — Oxford : Oxford University Press, Feb.1983. — [208]p. — (Oxford paperbacks)
Originally published: London : Dent, 1981
ISBN 0-19-286031-3 (pbk) : £2.95 : CIP entry B82-36588

523 — Black holes
Chandrasekhar, S. (Subrahmonyan). The mathematical theory of black holes. — Oxford : Clarendon Press, Dec.1982. — [750]p. — (The International series of monographs on physics)
ISBN 0-19-851291-0 : £45.00 : CIP entry B82-33329

523 — Extragalactic astronomy
Sérsic, J. L.. Extragalactic astronomy : lecture notes from Códoba / J.L. Sérsic. — Dordrecht ; London : Reidel, c1982. — xiii,245p : ill,1port ; 25cm. — (Geophysics and astrophysics monographs ; v.20)
Includes bibliographies and index
ISBN 90-277-1321-9 : Unpriced B82-32402

523 — Quasi-stellar objects
Hoyle, Fred. Quasar controversy resolved. — Cardiff : University College Cardiff Press, Oct.1981. — [80]p
ISBN 0-906449-28-6 (pbk) : £3.25 : CIP entry B81-30972

523.01 — Astrophysics
Selected studies : physics-astrophysics, mathematics, history of science : a volume dedicated to the memory of Albert Einstein / editors Thermistocles M. Rassias, George M. Rassias. — Amsterdam ; Oxford : North-Holland, 1982. — xii,392p : ill ; 23cm
Includes bibliographies
ISBN 0-444-86161-0 : £41.40
Primary classification 510 B82-28562

523.01 — Astrophysics — *Festschriften*
Investigating the universe : papers presented to Zdeněk Kopal on the occasion of his retirement, September 1981 / with a foreword by M.K.V. Bapple ; edited by F.D. Kahn. — Dordrecht ; London : Reidel, c1981. — x,458p : ill,ports ; 25cm. — (Astrophysics and space science library ; v.91)
Includes bibliographies and index
ISBN 90-277-1325-1 : Unpriced B82-02725

523′.01 — Relativistic astrophysics

Demianski, Marek. Relativistic astrophysics. — Oxford : Pergamon, Dec.1981. — [300]p. — (International series in natural philosophy ; v.110)
ISBN 0-08-025042-4 : £25.00 : CIP entry
B81-31803

523.01 — Relativistic astrophysics

Sexl, Roman. White dwarfs — black holes : an introduction to relativistic astrophysics / by Roman Sexl, Hannelore Sexl ; translated from the German by Patrick P. Weidhaas. — New York ; London : Academic Press, 1979. — ix,203p : ill ; 24cm
Translation of: Weisse Zwerge — schwarze Löcher. — Bibliography: p195-198. — Includes index
ISBN 0-12-637350-7 : £8.80 B82-12966

523.01′9 — High energy astrophysics - *Conference proceedings*

High energy astrophysics. — Oxford : Pergamon, Apr.1981. — [300]p. — (Advances in space research ; v.1, no.13)
Conference papers
ISBN 0-08-028395-0 : £17.00 : CIP entry
B81-10433

523.01′976 — High energy astrophysics

Longair, M. S.. High energy astrophysics : an informal introduction for students of physics and astronomy / M.S. Longair. — Cambridge : Cambridge University Press, 1981. — viii,412p : ill ; 24cm
Includes bibliographies and index
ISBN 0-521-23513-8 (cased) : £24.00 : CIP rev.
ISBN 0-521-28013-3 (pbk) : £8.95 B81-32533

Narlikar, Jayant. Violent phenomena in the universe / Jayant Narlikar. — Oxford : Oxford University Press, 1982. — vii, 218p,[8]p of plates : ill ; 23cm. — (OPUS)
Bibliography: p212. — Includes index
ISBN 0-19-219160-8 : £9.95 : CIP rev.
B82-00887

523.1 — ASTRONOMY. UNIVERSE

523.1 — Astronomy. Cosmology

Cosmology today / edited by John Gribbin. — London : IPC Magazines, c1982. — 64p : ill,facsims,ports ; 29cm. — (A New scientist guide)
ISBN 0-85037-518-5 (pbk) : Unpriced
B82-30525

Progress in cosmology / proceedings of the Oxford international symposium held in Christ Church, Oxford, September 14-18, 1981 ; edited by A.W. Wolfendale. — Dordrecht ; London : Reidel, c1982. — vii,360p : ill ; 25cm. — (Astrophysics and space science library ; v.99)
Includes bibliographies and index
ISBN 90-277-1441-x : Unpriced B82-40154

Sciama, D. W.. Modern cosmology. — Cambridge : Cambridge University Press, Nov.1981. — [210]p
Originally published: 1971
ISBN 0-521-28721-9 (pbk) : £5.95 : CIP entry
B81-38809

523.1 — Astronomy. Cosmology — *Conference proceedings*

Cosmologie physique = Physical cosmology : USMG NATO ASI Les Houches session XXXII 2-27 Juillet 1979 / édité par Roger Balian, Jean Audouze, David N. Schramm. — Amsterdam ; Oxford : North-Holland Publishing, 1980. — xxxiv,665p : ill,ports ; 23cm
Includes prefaces in English and French
ISBN 0-444-85433-9 : £44.73 B82-13866

523.1 — Universe

Heidmann, Jean. Extragalactic adventure : our strange universe / Jean Heidmann ; translated by Maureen Schaeffer and Ann Boesgaard ; foreword by Carl Sagan. — Cambridge : Cambridge University Press, 1982. — viii,174p : ill ; 23cm
Translation of: Au-delà de notre voie lactée — un étrange univers
ISBN 0-521-23571-5 (cased) : £12.50 : CIP rev.
ISBN 0-521-28045-1 (pbk) : £4.95 B81-40267

Henbest, Nigel. The mysterious universe / Nigel Henbest. — London : Ebury, 1981. — 184p : ill(some col.) ; 30cm
Ill on inside covers. — Includes index
ISBN 0-85223-212-8 : £8.95 B82-01307

523.1′01 — Universe. Theories, *1900-1931*

Smith, Robert W. (Robert William), *1952-*. The expanding universe : astronomy's 'great debate', 1900-1931 / Robert W. Smith. — Cambridge : Cambridge University Press, 1982. — xiv,220p : ill,ports ; 24cm
Bibliography: p202-215. — Includes index
ISBN 0-521-23212-0 : £19.00 : CIP rev.
B82-12002

523.1′01574 — Astronomy. Cosmology. Biological aspects

Hoyle, Fred. Space travellers. — Cardiff : University College Cardiff Press, May 1981. — [192]p
ISBN 0-906449-27-8 : £8.95 : CIP entry
B81-13555

523.1′09 — Astronomy. Cosmology, *to 1980*

Cronin, Vincent. The view from planet Earth : man looks at the cosmos / Vincent Cronin. — London : Collins, 1981. — 348p,[12]p of plates : ill ; 24cm
Includes index
ISBN 0-00-211397-x : £12.50 : CIP rev.
B81-25105

523.1′1 — Universe. Structure

Davies, P. C. W.. The accidental universe. — Cambridge : Cambridge University Press, Aug.1982. — [148]p
ISBN 0-521-24212-6 (cased) : £10.00 : CIP entry
ISBN 0-521-28692-1 (pbk) : £4.95 B82-21720

523.1′12 — Constellations: Orion. Interstellar space. Matter

Goudis, C.. The Orion complex : a case study of interstellar matter / by C. Goudis. — Dordrecht ; London : Reidel, 1982. — xiv,311p : ill,1chart ; 25cm. — (Astrophysics and space library ; v.90)
Bibliography: p291-306. — Includes index
ISBN 90-277-1298-0 : Unpriced B82-37034

523.1′12 — Galaxies

Ferris, Timothy. Galaxies / written and with photographs selected by Timothy Ferris ; illustrations by Sarah Landry. — [London] : Thames and Hudson, c1980. — 182p : ill(some col.) ; 34x37cm
Bibliography: p173-174. — Includes index
ISBN 0-500-01248-2 : £20.00 B82-40385

523.1′12 — Galaxies. Physical properties — *Conference proceedings*

The **Large-scale** characteristics of the galaxy : held in College Park, Maryland, U.S.A., 12-17 June, 1978 / edited by W.B. Burton. — Dordrecht ; London : Reidel, c1979. — xviii,611p : ill,ports ; 25cm. — (Symposium ; no.84)
At head of title: International Astronomical Union. — Includes bibliographies and index
ISBN 90-277-1029-5 (cased) : Unpriced
ISBN 90-277-1030-9 (pbk) : Unpriced
B82-40482

The **Structure** and evolution of normal galaxies / edited by S.M. Fall and D. Lynden-Bell. — Cambridge : Cambridge University Press, 1981. — xiii,272p : ill ; 24cm
At head of title: North Atlantic Treaty Organisation, Advanced Study Institute held at the Institute of Astronomy and Clare College, Cambridge 3-15 August 1980. — Includes bibliographies and index
ISBN 0-521-23907-9 : £15.00 : CIP rev.
B81-23749

523.1′12 — Galaxies. Physicial properties

Mihalas, Dimitri. Galactic astronomy : structure and kinematics. — 2nd ed. / Dimitri Mihalas, James Binney. — Oxford : W.H. Freeman, c1981. — xiii,597p : ill ; 24cm
Previous ed.: 1968. — Includes index
ISBN 0-7167-1280-6 : £19.50 B82-05839

523.1′12 — Interstellar molecular clouds — *Conference proceedings*

Interstellar molecules : held at Mount Tremblant, Québec, Canada, August 6-10, 1979 / edited by B.H. Andrew. — Dordrecht ; London : Reidel, c1980. — xl,704p : ill,ports ; 25cm. — (Symposium ; no.87)
At head of title: International Astronomical Union. — Includes bibliographies and index
ISBN 90-277-1160-7 (cased) : Unpriced
B82-40485

523.1′12 — Interstellar space. Matter

Spitzer, Lyman. Searching between the stars / Lyman Spitzer, Jr. — New Haven ; London : Yale University Press, c1982. — xv,179p : ill,maps ; 22cm. — (Mrs. Hepsa Ely Silliman memorial lectures)
Bibliography: p163-171. — Includes index
ISBN 0-300-02709-5 : Unpriced : CIP rev.
B82-13477

523.1′12 — Interstellar space. Molecules — *Conference proceedings*

Molecules in interstellar space : proceedings of a Royal Society discussion meeting held on 20 and 21 May 1981 / organized and edited by A. Carrington and D.A. Ramsay. — London : Royal Society, 1982, c1981. — vi,167p : ill ; 31cm
Originally published: in Philosophical Transactions of the Royal Society of London, series A, vol.303 (no.1480), pages 463-631 — title page verso. — Includes bibliographies
ISBN 0-85403-180-4 : £19.00 B82-17467

523.1′13 — Milky Way

Bok, Bart J.. The milky way / Bart J. Bok and Priscilla F. Bok. — 5th ed. — Cambridge, Mass. ; London : Harvard University Press, 1981. — viii,356p : ill ; 24cm. — (The Harvard books on astronomy)
Previous ed.: 1977. — Includes index
ISBN 0-674-57503-2 : £14.00 B82-03868

Kühn, Ludwig. The Milky Way. — Chichester : Wiley, Dec.1982. — [176]p
Translation of: Das Milchstrassensystem
ISBN 0-471-10277-6 : £14.75 : CIP entry
B82-30823

523.1′2 — Cosmogony

Atkins, P. W.. The Creation / P.W. Atkins. — Oxford : W.H. Freeman, c1981. — viii,132p : ill ; 24cm
ISBN 0-7167-1350-0 : £5.95 B82-01464

523.2 — ASTRONOMY. SOLAR SYSTEM

523.2 — Solar system

European Regional Meeting in Astronomy *(6th : 1981 : Dubrovnik)*. Sun and planetary system : proceedings of the Sixth European Regional Meeting in Astronomy, held in Dubrovnik, Yugoslavia, 19-23 October 1981 / edited by W. Fricke and G. Teleki. — Dordrecht ; London : Reidel, c1982. — xiii,538p : ill ; 25cm. — (Astrophysics and space science library ; v.96)
Includes 3 chapters in French. — Includes bibliographies and index
ISBN 90-277-1429-0 : Unpriced B82-34836

Henbest, Nigel. The mysterious universe / Nigel Henbest. — London : Marshall Cavendish, 1981. — 184p : ill(some col.),col.maps ; 30cm
Ill on lining papers. — Includes index
ISBN 0-85685-938-9 : Unpriced B82-06103

Miller, Ron. The traveller's guide to the solar system / by Ron Miller & William K. Hartmann. — London : Macmillan, 1981. — 187p : ill(some col.) ; 22x25cm
Includes index
ISBN 0-333-32694-6 : £8.95 B82-10637

The **Solar** system. — London (Burlington House, W1V 0NL) : British Astronomical Association, 1980. — 20leaves : ill(some col.) ; 23cm
Unpriced (unbound) B82-34688

523.2 — Solar system. Dynamics — *Conference proceedings*

Solar and interplanetary dynamics : held in Cambridge, Massachusetts, U.S.A., August 27-31, 1979 / edited by M. Dryer and E. Tandberg-Hanssen ; cosponsored by Scientific Committee on Solar-Terrestrial Physics and Committee for Space Research. — Dordrecht ; London : Reidel, c1980. — xix,558p : ill ; 25cm. — (Symposium ; no.91)
At head of title: International Astronomical Union. — Includes bibliographies and index
ISBN 90-277-1162-3 (cased) : Unpriced
ISBN 90-277-1163-1 (pbk) : Unpriced
B82-37359

523.2 — Solar system. Plasmas

Solar system plasmas and fields. — Oxford : Pergamon, Mar.1982. — [86]p. — (Advances in space research ; v.2, no.1)
ISBN 0-08-029125-2 (pbk) : £17.50 : CIP entry
B82-05380

523.2′0724 — Solar system. Simulation. Use of Stonehenge

Saunders, Mike, *1935-*. Solar system model / Mike Saunders. — Caterham (Caterham, Surrey) : Downs Books, 1980. — [2]leaves ; 30cm
Unpriced (unbound) B82-09261

523.2′0724 — Solar system. Simulations. Use of Silbury Hill

Saunders, Mike, *1935-*. Planets Avebury and Sanctuary, at the Silbury Planetarium / Mike Saunders. — Caterham (Caterham, Surrey) : Downs Books, 1980. — [2]leaves : 1chart ; 30cm
Unpriced (unbound) B82-09260

523.3 — ASTRONOMY. MOON

523.3 — Moon

Cadogen, Peter H.. The moon. — Cambridge : Cambridge University Press, Mar.1982. — [392]p
ISBN 0-521-23684-3 (cased) : £27.50 : CIP entry
ISBN 0-521-28152-0 (pbk) : £12.50
B82-01141

Moore, Patrick. The moon / Patrick Moore ; maps by Charles A. Cross ; foreword by Archie E. Roy. — London : Mitchell Beazley in association with the Royal Astronomical Society, c1981. — 96p : ill(some col.) ; 30cm. — (The Mitchell Beazley library of astronomical altases for amateur and professional observers)
Bibliography: p95. — Includes index
ISBN 0-85533-310-3 : £6.95 B82-03761

523.3 — Moon — *For children*

Jay, Michael, *1946-*. The moon / Michael Jay. — London : Watts, 1982. — 32p : ill(some col.) ; 22cm. — (A First look book)
Includes index
ISBN 0-85166-954-9 : £2.99 B82-23302

523.3′3 — Moon. Motion — *Conference proceedings*

International Astronomical Union. *Colloquium (63rd : 1981 : Grasse)*. High precision earth rotation and earth moon dynamics : lunar distances and related observations / proceedings of the 63rd Colloquium of the International Astronomical Union, held at Grasse, France, May 22-27, 1981 ; edited by O. Calame ; sponsored by International Astronomical Union, ICSU Committee on Space Research, International Association of Geodesy. — Dordrecht ; London : Reidel, c1982. — xix,354p : ill ; 25cm. — (Astrophysics and space science library ; v.94)
Includes bibliographies and index
ISBN 90-277-1405-3 : Unpriced
Primary classification 525′.35 B82-33821

523.4 — ASTRONOMY. PLANETS

523.4 — Solar system. Planets & satellites — *Conference proceedings*

Planetary exploration : Royal Society discussion / arranged by the British National Committee on Space Research, under the leadership of Sir Harrie Massey ... [et al.] held on 4 and 5 November 1980. — London : Royal Society, 1982, c1981. — v,167p,[6]p of plates : ill(some col.) ; 31cm
Originally published: in Philosophical Transactions of the Royal Society of London, series A, vol.303 (no.1477), pages 213-381 — title page verso. — Includes bibliographies
ISBN 0-85403-185-5 : £20.50 B82-17468

523.4 — Solar system. Planets — *Charts*

Briggs, Geoffrey. A photographic atlas of the planets. — Cambridge : Cambridge University Press, Sept.1982. — [250]p
ISBN 0-521-23976-1 : £12.50 : CIP entry
B82-25503

523.4 — Solar system. Planets — *Conference proceedings*

The **Comparative** study of the planets : proceedings of NATO Advanced Study Institute held at Vulcano (Aeoliar Islands), Italy, September 14-25, 1981 / edited by Angioletta Coradini and Marcello Fulchignoni. — Dordrecht ; London : Reidel in cooperation with NATO Scientific Affairs Division, c1982. — xi,516p : ill,1map ; 25cm. — (NATO advanced study institutes series. Series C, Mathematical and physical sciences ; v.85)
Includes index
ISBN 90-277-1406-1 : Unpriced B82-29461

523.4′2 — Venus

Hunt, Garry. The planet Venus. — London : Faber, Mar.1982. — [208]p
ISBN 0-571-09050-8 : CIP entry B82-06037

523.4′3 — Mars. Atmosphere

The **Mars** reference atmosphere. — Oxford : Pergamon, Mar.1982. — [106]p. — (Advances in space research ; v.2, no.2)
ISBN 0-08-029126-0 (pbk) : £17.50 : CIP entry
B82-05381

523.4′3 — Mars. Surface features

Carr, Michael H.. The surface of Mars / Michael H. Carr. — New Haven ; London : Yale University Press, c1981. — xi,232p : ill,maps ; 29x30cm
Bibliography: p216-226. — Includes index
ISBN 0-300-02750-8 : £31-50 : CIP rev.
B82-07098

523.4′5 — Jupiter

Hunt, Garry. Jupiter / Garry Hunt and Patrick Moore ; foreword by Archie E. Roy. — London : Mitchell Beazley in association with Royal Astronomical Society, c1981. — 96p : ill (some col.) ; 30cm. — (The Mitchell Beazley library of astronomical atlases for amateur and professional observers)
Includes index
ISBN 0-85533-309-x : £6.95 B82-03766

523.4′5 — Jupiter. Observation — *Amateurs′ manuals*

Peek, Bertrand M.. The planet Jupiter : the observer′s handbook / by Bertrand M. Peek ; with a foreword by Patrick Moore. — Rev. ed. — London : Faber, 1981. — 240p,xivp of plates : ill ; 22cm
Previous ed.: 1958. — Includes index
ISBN 0-571-18026-4 : £10.00 : CIP rev.
B81-21466

523.4′7 — Uranus — *Conference proceedings*

Uranus and the outer planets : proceedings of the IAU/RAS colloquium no.60 / edited by Garry Hunt. — Cambridge : Cambridge University Press, 1982. — ix,307p : ill ; 24cm
Includes bibliographies and index
ISBN 0-521-24573-7 : Unpriced : CIP rev.
B82-03109

523.5 — ASTRONOMY. METEORS, SOLAR WIND, ZODIACAL LIGHT

523.5′1 — Meteorites

Dodd, Robert T.. Meteorites : a petrologic-chemical synthesis / Robert T. Dodd. — Cambridge : Cambridge University Press, 1981. — xi,368p : ill ; 25cm
Bibliography: p329-358. — Includes index
ISBN 0-521-22570-1 : £35.00 B82-13984

523.5′1 — Solar system. Meteors

Mackenzie, Robert A.. Solar system debris / Robert A. Mackenzie. — Dover (26 Adrian St., Dover, Kent CR17 9AT) : British Meteor Society, c1980. — 103p : ill ; 30cm. — (Monographs in solar system astronomy ; v.1)
Unpriced (unbound) B82-11167

523.6 — ASTRONOMY. COMETS

523.6 — Comets

Brandt, John C.. Introduction to comets / John C. Brandt and Robert D. Chapman. — Cambridge : Cambridge University Press, 1981. — viii,246p : ill,facsims,1port ; 24cm
Bibliography: p229-238. — Includes index
ISBN 0-521-23906-0 : £21.00 B82-13749

Clube, Victor. The cosmic serpent : a catastrophist view of Earth history / Victor Clube and Bill Napier. — London : Faber, 1982. — 299p : ill ; 23cm
Includes index
ISBN 0-571-11816-x : £12.50 : CIP rev.
B82-06038

523.6 — Interstellar comets — *Conference proceedings*

Workshop on Interstellar Comets *(1982 : Edinburgh)*. Proceedings of the Workshop on Interstellar Comets held at Edinburgh, 13-15 April 1982. — Edinburgh (Blackford Hill, Edinburgh EH9 3HJ) : Royal Observatory, Aug.1982. — 1v.. — (Occasional reports of the Royal Observatory, Edinburgh, ISSN 0309-099x ; no.9)
ISBN 0-902553-25-9 (pbk) : CIP entry
B82-27212

523.7 — ASTRONOMY. SUN

523.7 — Sun

Nicolson, Iain. The sun / Iain Nicolson ; foreword by Archie E. Roy. — London : Mitchell Beazley published in association with the Royal Astronomical Society, 1982. — 96p : ill(some col.) ; 29cm. — (The Mitchell Beazley library of astronomical atlases for amateur and professional observers)
Bibliography: p90-91. — Includes index
ISBN 0-85533-311-1 : £6.95 B82-33659

Radio physics of the sun : held in College Park, Md, USA., August 7-10, 1979 / edited by Mukul R. Kundu and Tomas E. Gergely. — Dordrecht ; London : Reidel, c1980. — xx,475p : ill,ports ; 25cm. — (Symposium ; no.86)
At head of title: International Astronomical Union. — Includes bibliographies and index
ISBN 90-277-1120-8 (cased) : Unpriced
ISBN 0-927711-21-6 (pbk) : Unpriced
B82-39095

523.8 — ASTRONOMY. STARS

523.8 — Stars

Martin, Martha Evans. The friendly stars / Martha Evans Martin. — Rev. ed. / revised by Don Rice and Craig Foltz. — New York ; London : Van Nostrand Reinhold, 1982. — 140p : ill ; 21cm
Previous ed.: New York ; London : Harper, 1907. — Includes index
ISBN 0-442-21198-8 (pbk) : £6.75 B82-28198

523.8 — Stars. Evolution — *Conference proceedings*

International Astronomical Union. *Colloquium (69th : 1981 : Bamberg).* Binary and multiple stars as tracers of stellar evolution : proceedings of the 69th Colloquium of the International Astronomical Union held in Bamberg, F.R.G., August 31-September 3, 1981 / edited by Zdeněk Kopal and Jürgen Rahe. — Dordrecht ; London : Reidel, c1982. — xxx,503p : ill ; 25cm. — (Astrophysics and space science library ; v.98)
Includes bibliographies and index
ISBN 90-277-1436-3 : Unpriced B82-40171

523.8 — Stars. Formation — *Conference proceedings*

Regions of recent star formation : proceedings of the symposium on 'Neutral clouds near HII regions — dynamics and photochemistry', held in Penticton, British Columbia, June 24-26, 1981 / edited by R.S. Roger and P.E. Dewdney. — Dordrecht ; London : Reidel, c1982. — xvi,496p : ill ; 25cm. — (Astrophysics and space science library)
Includes bibliographies and index
ISBN 90-277-1383-9 : Unpriced B82-20800

523.8 — Stars. Physical properties

Kaplan, S. A.. The physics of stars. — Chichester : Wiley, Dec.1982. — [110]p
Translation of: 3rd ed. of Fizika zvezd
ISBN 0-471-10327-6 : £13.00 : CIP entry
B82-30824

523.8 — Symbiotic stars — *Conference proceedings*

IAU Colloquium *(70th : 1981 : Observatoire de Haute Provence).* The nature of symbiotic stars : proceedings of IAU Colloquium no. 70 held at the Observatoire de Haute Provence, 26-28 August, 1981 / edited by Michael Friedjung and Roberto Viotti. — Dordrecht ; London : Reidel, c1982. — xix,310p : ill ; 25cm. — (Astrophysics and space science library ; v.95)
Includes bibliographies and index
ISBN 90-277-1422-3 : Unpriced B82-34545

523.8 — Wolf-Rayet stars — *Conference proceedings*

Wolf-rayet stars : observations, physics, evolution / edited by C.W.H. de Loore and A.J. Willis. — Dordrecht ; London : Reidel, c1982. — xx,618p : ill,ports ; 25cm. — (Symposium / International Astronomical Union = Union Astronomique Internationale ; no.99)
Includes bibliographies and index
ISBN 90-277-1469-x (cased) : Unpriced
ISBN 90-277-1470-3 (pbk) : Unpriced
B82-40761

523.8'1 — Stars. Paths. Astrometry

Van de Kamp, Peter. Stellar paths : photographic astrometry with long-focus instruments / Peter van de Kamp ; with an introduction by Jean-Claude Pecker. — Dordrecht ; London : Reidel, c1981. — xxii,155p : ill ; 25cm. — (Astrophysics and space science library ; v.85)
Bibliography: p146-149. — Includes index
ISBN 90-277-1256-5 : Unpriced B82-07444

523.8'2 — Bright stars

Jager, Cornelis de. The brightest stars / Cornelis de Jager. — Dordrecht ; London : Reidel, c1980. — xxii,457p : ill ; 25cm. — (Geophysics and astrophysics monographs ; v.19)
Bibliography: p411-447
ISBN 90-277-1109-7 (cased) : Unpriced
ISBN 90-277-1110-0 (pbk) : Unpriced
B82-39093

523.8'41 — Binary stars

Close binary stars : observations and interpretation : held in Toronto, Canada, August 7-10, 1979 / edited by Mirek J. Plavec, Daniel M. Popper and Roger K. Ulrich. — Dordrecht ; London : Reidel, c1980. — xx,598p : ill ; 25cm. — (Symposium ; no.88)
At head of title: International Astronomical Union. — Includes bibliographies and index
ISBN 90-277-1116-x (cased) : Unpriced
ISBN 90-277-1117-8 (pbk) : Unpriced
B82-40483

523.8'41 — Binary stars. Observation — *Amateurs' manuals*

Couteau, Paul. Observing visual double stars / Paul Couteau ; translated by Alan H. Bratten. — Cambridge, Mass. ; London : MIT Press, c1981. — xvi,257p : ill,1facsim ; 21cm
Translations of: L'Observation des étoiles doubles visuelles. — Includes bibliographies and index
ISBN 0-262-03077-2 : £14.00 B82-03755

523.8'44 — Be stars — *Conference proceedings*

Be stars / edited by Mercedes Jaschek and Hans-Günter Groth. — Dordrecht ; London : Reidel, c1982. — xv,523p : ill ; 25cm. — (Symposium / International Astronomical Union ; no.98)
Includes bibliographies and index
ISBN 90-277-1366-9 (cased) : Unpriced
ISBN 90-277-1367-7 (pbk) : Unpriced
B82-13708

523.8'446 — Supernovae

Supernovae, a survey of current research : proceedings of the NATO Advanced Study Institute held at Cambridge, U.K., June 29-July 10, 1981 / edited by Martin J. Rees and Ray J. Stoneham. — Dordrecht ; London : Reidel, c1982. — xxiii,590p : ill,1port ; 25cm. — (NATO advanced study institutes series. Series C, mathematical and physical sciences, ISSN 0377-2071 ; v.90)
Includes bibliographies and index
ISBN 90-277-1442-8 : Unpriced B82-36213

523.8'5 — Star clusters — *Conference proceedings*

Star Clusters : held in Victoria, B.C., Canada, 27-30 August, 1979 / edited by James E. Hesser. — Dordrecht ; London : Reidel, c1980. — xxi,516p : ill,1 map,ports ; 25cm. — (Symposium ; no.85)
At head of title: International Astronomical Union. — Includes bibliographies and index
ISBN 90-277-1087-2 (cased) : Unpriced
ISBN 90-277-1088-0 (pbk) : Unpriced
B82-37356

523.8'7 — Hot stars. Spectra. Emission lines

Kitchin, Christopher R.. Early emission line stars / C.R. Kitchin. — Bristol : Hilger, c1982. — xi,182p : ill ; 26cm. — (Monographs on astronomical subjects, ISSN 0141-1128 ; 8)
Bibliography: p158-178. — Includes index
ISBN 0-85274-402-1 : £16.00 : CIP rev.
B82-09873

523.8'903 — Constellations — *For children*

McLeish, Kenneth. The way of the stars. — Cambridge : Cambridge University Press, Jan.1983. — [29]p
ISBN 0-521-25061-7 : £4.95 : CIP entry
B82-32431

523.8'903 — Stars — *Atlases*

Tirion, Wil. Sky atlas 2000.0 : 26 star charts, covering both hemispheres / Wil Tirion. — Deluxe ed. — Cambridge : Cambridge University Press, 1981. — 25 folded leaves : col.charts ; 41cm + 1 plastic overlay(39x26cm)
Includes index
ISBN 0-521-24467-6 (spiral) : Unpriced
B82-18392

523.8'908 — Stars — *Catalogues*

Sky catalogue 2000.0. — Cambridge : Cambridge University Press
Vol.1: Stars to magnitude 8.0 / edited by Alan Hirshfeld and Roger W. Sinnott. — 1982. — xxiv,604p : ill ; 32cm
Includes index
ISBN 0-521-24710-1 (cased) : £32.50
ISBN 0-521-28913-0 (pbk) : Unpriced
B82-26772

525 — ASTRONOMY. PLANETS. EARTH

525'.35 — Earth. Nutation. Effects of elasticity of earth's core — *Conference proceedings*

Trew, Anthony. Running wild. — London : Collins, July 1982. — [306]p
ISBN 0-00-222677-4 : £7.50 : CIP entry
B82-12428

525'.35 — Earth. Rotation — *Conference proceedings*

International Astronomical Union. *Colloquium (63rd : 1981 : Grasse).* High precision earth rotation and earth moon dynamics : lunar distances and related observations / proceedings of the 63rd Colloquium of the International Astronomical Union, held at Grasse, France, May 22-27, 1981 ; edited by O. Calame ; sponsored by International Astronomical Union, ICSU Committee on Space Research, International Association of Geodesy. — Dordrecht ; London : Reidel, c1982. — xix,354p : ill ; 25cm. — (Astrophysics and space science library ; v.94)
Includes bibliographies and index
ISBN 90-277-1405-3 : Unpriced
Also classified at 523.3'3 B82-33821

525'.35 — Earth. Rotation. Variation

Warlow, Peter. The reversing earth / Peter Warlow. — London : Dent, 1982. — x,213p,[4]p of plates : ill ; 24cm
Bibliography: p196-203. — Includes index
ISBN 0-460-04478-8 : £8.95 : CIP rev.
B81-38303

525'.6 — Tides

Melchior, Paul. The tides of the planet Earth. — 2nd ed. — Oxford : Pergamon Press, Nov.1982. — [648]p
Previous ed.: 1966
ISBN 0-08-026248-1 : £45.00 : CIP entry
B82-28723

526 — GEODESY, CARTOGRAPHY

526 — Cartography — *For children*

Green, Christopher, *1938-.* Making maps / Christopher Green ; illustrated by Paul Bryant. — London : Bodley Head, 1982. — 23p : ill (some col.),1col.map ; 22cm. — (A Young geographer)
Includes index
ISBN 0-370-30465-9 : £3.25 : CIP rev.
B82-10481

526 — North-western Europe. Thematic cartography, *to ca 1860*

Robinson, Arthur H. Early thematic mapping in the history of cartography / Arthur H. Robinson. — Chicago ; London : University of Chicago Press, 1982. — xiv,266p : ill,facsims (some col.),maps(some col.) ; 25cm
Bibliography: p241-257. — Includes index
ISBN 0-226-72285-6 : Unpriced B82-36992

526 — Thematic cartography

Cuff, David J.. Thematic maps. — London : Methuen, Oct.1982. — [192]p
ISBN 0-416-33500-4 (pbk) : £7.50 : CIP entry
B82-25079

Cuff, David J.. Thematic maps. — London : Methuen, Oct.1982
Instructor's manual. — [192]p
ISBN 0-416-34320-1 (pbk) : £2.50 : CIP entry
B82-23980

526'.028'54 — Cartography. Applications of digital computer systems

Monmonier, Mark S.. Computer-assisted cartography : principles and prospects / Mark S. Monmonier. — Englewood Cliffs ; London : Prentice-Hall, c1982. — x,214p : ill ; 25cm
Bibliography: p178-185. — Includes index
ISBN 0-13-165308-3 : Unpriced B82-28420

526'.1 — Geodesy

Theory of the earth's shape. — Oxford : Elsevier Scientific, Feb.1982. — [694]p. — (Developments in solid earth geophysics ; 13)
Translation of: Teoria figurii pămîntului
ISBN 0-444-99705-9 : £50.00 : CIP entry
ISBN 0-444-41799-0 (set) B81-36208

Vaníček, Petr. Geodesy : the concepts / Petr Vaníček, Edward J. Krakiwsky. — Amsterdam ; Oxford : North-Holland, 1982. — xv,691p : ill,maps ; 25cm
Includes bibliographies and index
ISBN 0-444-86149-1 : £58.39 B82-28564

526′.1′028542 — Geodesy. Applications of digital computer systems. Programs: Geodetic suite

Cross, P. A.. The geodetic suite / P.A. Cross. — London : North East London Polytechnic, Department of Land Surveying, 1981. — x,92p : ill ; 30cm. — (Working paper / North East London Polytechnic Department of Land Surveying, ISSN 0260-9142 ; no.4)
Bibliography: p92
ISBN 0-907382-03-7 (pbk) : Unpriced
B82-05827

526.3′6′028 — Levels

Cooper, M. A. R.. Modern theodolites and levels. — 2nd ed. — London : Granada, May 1982. — [272]p
Previous ed.: London : Lockwood, 1971
ISBN 0-246-11502-5 : £20.00 : CIP entry
Primary classification 526.9′028 B82-07406

526′.7′09989 — British Antarctic Territory. Graham Land. Gravitational fields

Renner, R. G. B.. Gravity and magnetic surveys in Graham Land / by R.G.B. Renner. — Cambridge : British Antarctic Survey, 1980. — 99p,[11]p of plates(some folded) : ill,maps(some col.) ; 31cm. — (Scientific reports / British Antarctic Survey ; no.77)
Bibliography: p95-99
ISBN 0-85665-018-8 (pbk) : Unpriced
Also classified at 538′.7′09989 B82-05874

526.8 — Maps. Design

Graphic communication and design in contemporary cartography. — Chichester : Wiley, Feb.1983. — [360]p. — (Progress in contemporary cartography ; v2)
ISBN 0-471-10316-0 : £22.50 : CIP entry
B82-38280

526.8′6′0285424 — Maps. Drawing. Applications of digital computer systems. Programs: LINPOINT program — *Manuals*

Morrison, Alastair. Linpoint : a program for drawing maps of lines and points : user manual / Alastair Morrison. — [Glasgow] : Geography Department, Glasgow University, c1981. — 75p : ill,maps ; 30cm. — (Occasional papers series ; no.6)
Unpriced (spiral) B82-21171

526.9 — SURVEYING

526.9 — British chartered surveyors. Overseas activities — *Directories*

Directory of international practices = Annuaire international = Guía internacionale / The Royal Institution of Chartered Surveyors. — 2nd ed. — [London] : [RICS], 1981. — 120p : ill ; 30cm
English text, French, Spanish and Arabic contents list and introduction. — Previous ed.: 1979
£7.00 (pbk) B82-09382

526.9 — British chartered surveyors. Overseas activities — *Practical information*

Notes for guidance for chartered surveying practices considering appointments for services outside the United Kingdom / prepared by the International Division, The Royal Institution of Chartered Surveyors. — London : Published on behalf of the Royal Institution of Chartered Surveyors by Surveyors Publications, c1981. — [8]p ; 21x10cm
ISBN 0-85406-162-2 (pbk) : £1.25 (£1.00 to members of the Institution) B82-09372

526.9 — Land. Surveying

Dent, David. Soil survey and land evaluation / David Dent and Anthony Young. — London : Allen & Unwin, 1981. — xiii,278p,4folded p of plates : ill,maps ; 24cm
Bibliography: p263-269. — Includes index
ISBN 0-04-631013-4 (cased) : Unpriced : CIP rev.
ISBN 0-04-631014-2 (pbk) : Unpriced
Primary classification 631.4′7 B81-26738

Wright, John. Ground and air survey for field scientists. — Oxford, Clarendon, May 1982. — [150]p. — (Monographs on soil and resource surveys)
ISBN 0-19-857560-2 : £14.00 : CIP entry
B82-11750

526.9 — Land. Surveying. Quantitative methods

Robinson, Carl. Quantitative methods for surveyors. — Lancaster : Construction Press, May 1981. — [224]p
ISBN 0-86095-891-4 (pbk) : CIP entry
B81-12816

526.9 — Surveying

Bouchard, Harry. Surveying. — 7th ed. / Francis H. Moffitt, the late Harry Bouchard. — New York ; London : Harper & Row, c1982. — xii,834p : ill,maps ; 25cm. — (The Harper & Row series in civil engineering)
Previous ed.: New York : Intext Educational, 1975. — Includes index
ISBN 0-06-044559-9 : £19.95 B82-16589

526.9′02462 — Surveying — *For engineering*

Shepherd, F. A.. Advanced engineering surveying : problems and solutions / F.A. Shepherd. — London : Edward Arnold, 1981. — ix,276p : ill ; 25cm
Includes index
ISBN 0-7131-3416-x (pbk) : £9.95 : CIP rev.
B79-37286

526.9′024624 — Surveying — *For construction*

Whyte, W. S.. Site surveying and levelling 2. — London : Butterworth, Oct.1981. — [160]p
ISBN 0-408-00532-7 (pbk) : £5.00 : CIP entry
B81-25310

526.9′024624 — Surveying — *Manuals* — *For civil engineering*

Kissam, Philip. Surveying for civil engineers / Philip Kissam, with contributions by Arthur J. McNair. — 2nd ed. — New York ; London : McGraw-Hill, c1981. — x,779p : ill,charts,facsims,maps,plans ; 25cm
Previous ed.: 1956. — Tables on lining papers. — Includes index
ISBN 0-07-034882-0 : £27.75 B82-33410

526.9′028 — Theodolites

Cooper, M. A. R.. Modern theodolites and levels. — 2nd ed. — London : Granada, May 1982. — [272]p
Previous ed.: London : Lockwood, 1971
ISBN 0-246-11502-5 : £20.00 : CIP entry
Also classified at 526.3′6′028 B82-07406

526.9′028′7 — Electromagnetic distance measuring instruments

Burnside, C. D.. Electromagnetic distance measurement. — 2nd ed. — London : Granada, May 1982. — [208]p
Previous ed.: London : Lockwood, 1971
ISBN 0-246-11624-2 (pbk) : £10.00 : CIP entry
B82-07407

526.9′06′01 — Commonwealth countries. Land. Surveying. Organisations: Commonwealth Association of Surveying and Land Economy

Commonwealth Association of Surveying and Land Economy. An introduction to the work of the Association and the professions it represents / Commonwealth Association of Surveying and Land Economy. — 5th ed. — [London] : The Association, 1982. — 21p ; 15x21cm
Cover title. — Previous ed.: 1977. — Text on inside cover
ISBN 0-903577-23-2 (pbk) : £1.00 B82-22898

526.9′07′11171241 — Commonwealth countries. Land surveyors. Professional education

Commonwealth Association of Surveying and Land Economy. Education for surveying and land economy / Commonwealth Association of Surveying and Land Economy. — 3rd ed. — London : The Association, 1982. — 32p ; 30cm + Appendix B(p33-38; 30cm)
Cover title. — Previous ed.: 1977. — Text on inside cover
ISBN 0-903577-24-0 (pbk) : £3.00
Also classified at 333′.007′11171241 ; 624.1′042′0711171241 B82-22897

526.9′07′1141 — Great Britain. Surveyors. Professional education — *Proposals*

Moore, Peter N. M. The general practice surveyor : pointers for education for private practice : a review of what members of the profession in small to medium-sized firms of surveyors, valuers & estate agents believe should be taught to new entrants in general practice & to those receiving post qualification training / research undertaken and report prepared by Peter N.M. Moore. — [Reading] ([Whiteknights, Reading, RG6 2AW]) : [College of Estate Management], [1981?]. — 52p : 1form ; 30cm. — (A Geoffrey Blake Benefaction report)
Unpriced (pbk) B82-01681

526.9′072041 — Land. Surveying. Research in British institutions — *Directories*

Dowman, I. J.. Directory of research and development activities in the United Kingdom in land survey and related fields / compiled and edited by I.J. Dowman. — 3rd ed. / sponsored by the Photogrammetric Society and the Royal Institution of Chartered Surveyors. — London (12 Great George St., SW1P 3AD) : Surveyors Publications, 1982. — 65p ; 21cm
Previous ed.: London : UK National Group for Communication in Surveying and Photogrammetry, 1978
£3.00 (pbk) B82-25135

526.9′09171′241 — Commonwealth countries. Land. Surveying — *Conference proceedings*

Commonwealth Association of Surveying and Land Economy. *General Assembly (4th : 1981 : Ottawa).* Commonwealth Association of Surveying and Land Economy : fourth General Assembly, Ottawa, Canada, 14-19 September 1981. — London : CASLE, [1981]. — 31p : ill,ports ; 30cm
ISBN 0-903577-25-9 (pbk) : £3.00 B82-22896

526.9′823 — Aerial photogrammetry

Sears, G. M.. First steps in photogrammetry / G.M. Sears. — [London] : North East London Polytechnic, Department of Land Surveying, 1982. — vii,158p : ill ; 30cm. — (Working paper / North East London Polytechnic. Department of Land Surveying, ISSN 0260-9142 ; no.5)
Bibliography: p158
ISBN 0-907382-04-5 (pbk) : Unpriced
B82-19911

529 — TIME

529 — Time

Shallis, Michael. On time : an investigation into scientific knowledge and human experience / Michael Shallis. — [London] : Burnett, 1982. — 208p : ill ; 25cm
Bibliography: p200-203. — Includes index
ISBN 0-09-148950-4 : £8.95 : CIP rev.
B82-09418

Whitrow, G. J.. The natural philosophy of time / G.J. Whitrow. — 2nd ed. — Oxford : Clarendon, 1980. — ix,399p : ill ; 24cm. — (Oxford science publications)
Previous ed.: London : Nelson, 1961. — Includes bibliographies and index
ISBN 0-19-858215-3 (pbk) : £7.95 : CIP rev.
B81-31193

529 — Time — *For children*

Telling the time / illustrated by Joanna Stubbs ; editor Janine Amos ; designer Winsome Malcolm. — Bristol : Purnell, 1982. — [24]p : col.ill ; 21cm. — (A First learning book)
ISBN 0-361-05372-x (pbk) : £0.50 B82-36383

529′.01 — Time. Asymmetry

Landsberg, P. T.. The enigma of time. — Bristol : Hilger, Oct.1982. — [222]p
ISBN 0-85274-545-1 : £13.00 : CIP entry
B82-24239

529′.7 — Time. Measurement. Projects — *For children*

Catherall, Ed. Clocks and time / Ed Catherall. — Hove : Wayland, 1982. — 32p : col.ill ; 24cm. — (Young scientist)
ISBN 0-85340-912-9 : £2.95 B82-18430

530 — PHYSICS

530 — Physics

Archenhold, W. F.. Physics : a course leading to the University of London G.C.E. Advanced Level examination / by W.F. Archenhold. — Cambridge : National Extension College. — (National Extension College correspondence texts ; course no.20)
Vol.1
Originally published: 1976
Units 1-10. — Repr. with amendments. — 1978, c1976. — 49p : ill ; 30cm
ISBN 0-86082-137-4 (pbk) : Unpriced
ISBN 0-902404-87-3 B82-38202

Archenhold, W. F.. Physics : a course leading to the University of London G.C.E. Advanced Level examination / by W.F. Archenhold. — Cambridge : National Extension College. — (National Extension College correspondence texts ; course no.S20)
Vol.2
Originally published: 1976
Units 11-20. — Repr. with amendments. — 1978, c1976. — 45p : ill ; 30cm
ISBN 0-86082-139-0 (pbk) : Unpriced
ISBN 0-902404-87-3 B82-38203

Archenhold, W. F.. Physics : a course leading to the University of London G.C.E. Advanced Level examination / by W.F. Archenhold. — Cambridge : National Extension College. — (National Extension College correspondence texts ; course no.S20)
Vol.3
Units 21-30. — 1977 (1978 [printing]). — iv,46p : ill ; 30cm
ISBN 0-902404-86-5 (pbk) : Unpriced
ISBN 0-902404-87-3 B82-38204

Bill, Len. Basic physical quantities. — Cheltenham : Thornes, Sept.1982. — [48]p. — (Background to technology : 1)
ISBN 0-85950-394-1 (pbk) : £2.95 : CIP entry
B82-25942

Bueche, Frederick J.. Principles of physics / F. Bueche. — 4th ed. — New York ; London : McGraw-Hill, c1982. — xx,839p,[4]p of plates : ill(some col.),ports ; 25cm
Previous ed.: 1977. — Text on lining paper. — Includes index
ISBN 0-07-008867-5 : £19.50 B82-27223

Bueche, Frederick J.. Understanding the world of physics / Frederick J. Bueche ; [editors were John J. Corrigan and James W. Bradley]. — New York ; London : McGraw-Hill, c1981. — viii,576p : ill,maps,ports ; 25cm
Text on lining paper. — Includes bibliographies and index
ISBN 0-07-008863-2 : £13.95 B82-22226

Derringh, Edward. Selected solutions for Fundamentals of physics second edition [and] second edition extended [by] David Halliday, Robert Resnick, Edward Derringh / prepared by Edward Derringh. — Chichester : Wiley, c1981. — vi,450p : ill ; 22cm
ISBN 0-471-06463-7 (pbk) : £7.45 B82-32099

Discovering physics / [S271 Course Team]. — Milton Keynes : Open University Press. — (Science : a second level course)
At head of title: The Open University
Unit 1: Surveying the Universe : an example of physical enquiry / prepared by Keith Hodgkinson for the Course Team. — 1982. — 50p,[2]p of plates : ill(some col.) ; 30cm. — (S271 ; unit 1)
Bibliography: p40
ISBN 0-335-16115-4 (pbk) : Unpriced
B82-21207

Discovering physics / [S271 Course Team]. — Milton Keynes : Open University Press. — (Science : a second level course)
At head of title: The Open University
Unit 2: Describing motion / prepared by Alan Durrant for the Course Team. — 1982. — 64p : ill ; 30cm. — (S271 ; unit 2)
ISBN 0-335-16116-2 (pbk) : Unpriced
B82-21206

Discovering physics / [S271 Course Team]. — Milton Keynes : Open University Press. — (Science : a second level course)
At head of title: The Open University
Unit 3: Dynamics — forces, energy, and motion / prepared by Raymond Mackintosh for the Course Team. — 1982. — 55p : ill,2ports ; 30cm. — (S271 ; unit 3)
ISBN 0-335-16117-0 (pbk) : Unpriced
B82-31991

Discovering physics / [S271 Course Team]. — Milton Keynes : Open University Press. — (Science : a second level course)
At head of title: The Open University
Unit 4: Equilibrium, stability and gravitation / prepared by Milo Shott for the Course Team ; [Unit 5: Mechanics revision] / [prepared by Graham Farmelo, Stuart Freake and Steve Swithenby for the Course Team]. — 1982. — 46,17p : ill ; 30cm. — (S271 ; units 4 and 5)
ISBN 0-335-16118-9 (pbk) : Unpriced
B82-31992

Discovering physics / [S271 Course Team]. — Milton Keynes : Open University Press. — (Science : a second level course)
At head of title: The Open University
Unit 6: Electrostatics / prepared by Jim Ramage, Steve Swithenby and Shelagh Ross for the Course Team. — 1982. — 51p : ill(some col.) ; 30cm. — (S271 ; unit 6)
ISBN 0-335-16119-7 (pbk) : Unpriced
B82-31993

Discovering physics / [S271 Course Team]. — Milton Keynes : Open University Press. — (Science : a second level course)
At head of title: The Open University
Unit 7: Currents and circuits / prepared by Steve Swithenby and Shelagh Ross for the Course Team ; [Unit 8: Electrodynamics] / [prepared by Bob Lambourne for the Course Team]. — 1982. — 27,61p : ill(some col.) ; 30cm. — (S271 ; units 7 and 8)
ISBN 0-335-16120-0 (pbk) : Unpriced
B82-31995

Discovering physics / [S271 Course Team]. — Milton Keynes : Open University Press. — (Science : a second level course)
At head of title: The Open University
Units 9 and 10: Vibrations and waves / prepared by Stuart Freake for the Course Team. — 1982. — 70p : ill(some col.) ; 30cm. — (S271 ; units 9 and 10)
ISBN 0-335-16121-9 (pbk) : Unpriced
B82-31994

Discovering physics / [S271 Course Team]. — Milton Keynes : Open University Press. — (Science : a second level course)
At head of title: The Open University
Unit 11: Temperature and heat : towards a microscopic explanation / prepared by Keith Hodgkinson for the Course Team. — 1982. — 63p : ill ; 30cm. — (S271 ; unit 11)
ISBN 0-335-16122-7 (pbk) : Unpriced
B82-31990

Discovering physics / [S271 Course Team]. — Milton Keynes : Open University Press. — (Science : a second level course)
At head of title: The Open University
Unit 12: Special relativity / prepared by Bob Lambourne for the Course Team. — 1982. — 60p,1folded leaf : ill(some col.),1port ; 30cm. — (S271 ; unit 12)
ISBN 0-335-16123-5 (pbk) : Unpriced
B82-34540

Discovering physics / [S271 Course Team]. — Milton Keynes : Open University Press. — (Science : a second level course)
At head of title: The Open University
Unit 13: The beginnings of modern atomic physics / prepared by Graham Farmelo for the Course Team. — 1982. — 48p : ill(some col.),ports ; 30cm. — (S271 ; unit 13)
ISBN 0-335-16124-3 (pbk) : Unpriced
B82-34541

Discovering physics / [S271 Course Team]. — Milton Keynes : Open University Press. — (Science : a second level course)
At head of title: The Open University
Unit 14: Quantum mechanics : theory / prepared by John Walters for the Course Team. [Unit 15: Quantum mechanics : applications] / [prepared by Graham Farmelo for the Course Team]. — 1982. — 72,48p : ill ; 30cm. — (S517 : units 14-15)
ISBN 0-335-16125-1 (pbk) : Unpriced
B82-40654

Discovering physics / [S271 Course Team]. — Milton Keynes : Open University Press. — (Science : a second level course)
At head of title: The Open University
Unit 16: Modern physics in dying stars / prepared by Alan Cooper for the course team. — 1982. — 61p : ill,ports ; 30cm. — (S271 : unit 16)
ISBN 0-335-16126-x (pbk) : Unpriced
B82-40652

Eisberg, Robert M.. Physics : foundations and applications / Robert M. Eisberg, Lawrence S. Lerner. — New York ; London : McGraw-Hill, c1981. — xiv,1526,C-A-15,I-15p : ill ; 26cm
'Combined volume'. — Also available as two separate volumes. — Text on lining papers. — Includes index
ISBN 0-07-019110-7 : £19.50 B82-00417

Goswami, Amit. The concepts of physics / Amit Goswami. — Lexington, Mass. : Heath ; London : distributed by Eurospan, c1979. — xxiii,584p : ill,1map ; 24cm
Includes index
ISBN 0-669-01897-x : £16.25 B82-26734

ÎAvorskiĭ, B. M.. Handbook of physics / B. Yavorsky and A. Detlaf ; translated from the Russian by Nicholas Weinstein. — 3rd ed. — Moscow : Mir ; [London] : Distributed by Central, 1980, c1975. — 1131p : ill ; 18cm
Translation and revision of: Spravochnik po fizike. 1977 ed. — Previous ed.: 1975. — Includes index
ISBN 0-7147-1691-x : £7.50 B82-29284

Isaacs, Alan. Physics / Alan Isaacs and Valerie Pitt ; illustrated by Whitecroft Designs. — Feltham : Hamlyn Paperbacks, 1982, c1972. — 159p : col.ill,2col.ports ; 19cm
Originally published: 1972. — Includes index
ISBN 0-600-35651-5 (cased) : £2.99
ISBN 0-600-36983-8 (pbk) : £1.75 B82-38105

Kitaĭgorodskiĭ, A. I.. Introduction to physics / A. Kitaigorodsky ; translated from Russian by O. Smith and L. Levant. — 2nd ed. — Moscow : Mir ; [London] : distributed by Central Books, c1981. — 589p : ill ; 25cm
Translation of: Vvedenie v fiziku. — Previous ed.: 1963. — Includes index
ISBN 0-7147-1707-x : £6.50 B82-19616

McGervey, John D.. Introduction to modern physics / John D. McGervey. — New York ; London : Academic Press
Solution manual. — [1981]. — 30p ; 22cm
ISBN 0-12-483556-2 (unbound) : Unpriced
B82-21244

Marion, Jerry B.. Physics : for science and engineering / Jerry B. Marion, William F. Hornyak. — Philadelphia ; London : Saunders College Publishing
Pt.1. — c1982. — xii,743,[18]p : ill ; 26cm. — (Saunders golden sunburst series)
Text on lining papers. — Includes index
ISBN 0-03-049486-9 : £17.95
ISBN 4-8337-0098-0 (International Edition) : £12.95 B82-20708

Marion, Jerry B.. Physics : for science and engineering / Jerry B. Marion, William F. Hornyak. — Philadelphia ; London : Saunders College Publishing. — (Saunders golden sunburst series)
Pt.2. — c1982. — xp,p745-1274 : ill ; 27cm
Text on lining papers. — Includes index
ISBN 0-03-049491-5 : Unpriced
ISBN 4-8337-0098-0 (International Edition) : £12.95 B82-27292

530 — Physics *continuation*

Radin, Shelden H.. Physics : for scientists and engineers / Shelden H. Radin, Robert T. Folk. — Englewood Cliffs ; London : Prentice-Hall, c1982. — xv,790,[22]p : ill ; 29cm
Text on lining papers. — Includes index
ISBN 0-13-674002-2 : Unpriced B82-19727

Savel'ev, I. V.. Physics : a general course / I.V. Savelyev ; translated from the Russian by G. Leib. — Moscow : Mir ; [London] : Distributed by Central Books
Translation of: Kurs obshcheĭ fiziki
Vol.3. — 1981. — 318p : ill ; 23cm
Added t.p. in Russian. — Includes index
ISBN 0-7147-1660-x : £4.50 B82-02698

Serway, Raymond A.. Physics : for scientists and engineers / Raymond A. Serway. — Philadelphia ; London : Saunders College, c1982. — 943p in various pagings : ill ; 27cm
Text on lining papers. — Includes index
ISBN 0-03-057903-1 : £22.50 B82-25408

Shive, John N.. Similarities in physics. — Bristol : Adam Hilger, May 1982. — [260]p
ISBN 0-85274-540-0 : £10.00 : CIP entry B82-07025

530 — Physics — *Conference proceedings*

Some **strangeness** in the proportion : a centennial symposium to celebrate the achievements of Albert Einstein / edited by Harry Woolf. — Reading, Mass. ; London : Addison-Wesley, 1980. — xxxi,539p : ill,ports ; 25cm
Includes index
ISBN 0-201-09924-1 : £28.70 B82-38765

530 — Physics — *For schools*

Carrick, Michael. Physics / Michael Carrick. — Walton-on-Thames : Nelson, 1982. — 204p : ill (some col.) ; 25cm
Includes index
ISBN 0-17-438236-7 (pbk) : Unpriced B82-26912

Duncan, Tom. Advanced physics. — London : J. Murray, Jan.1982. — [700]p
ISBN 0-7195-3889-0 (pbk) : £8.50 : CIP entry B81-33845

Fuller, John. Light on physics : a basic course. — Cambridge : Cambridge University Press, May 1982. — [246]p
ISBN 0-521-28207-1 (pbk) : £3.95 : CIP entry B82-11509

Gardner, David. Physics around us / David Gardner and Matthew Scott. — London : Edward Arnold, 1981. — 47p : ill ; 25cm
ISBN 0-7131-0536-4 (pbk) : £1.75 : CIP rev. B81-25697

Hobson, Art. Physics and human affairs / Art Hobson. — New York ; Chichester : Wiley, c1982. — xiii,418p : ill,ports ; 25cm
Includes bibliographies and index
ISBN 0-471-04746-5 : Unpriced B82-23946

Jones, M.. 'O' level physics : — in a nutshell / M. Jones, D.L. Jones. — Repr. with amendments. — Burton on Trent : Mercian, 1982. — 104p : ill ; 15x21cm
Originally published: 1980. — Includes index
ISBN 0-9506583-3-2 (pbk) : Unpriced B82-39563

Nelkon, M.. Advanced level physics / M. Nelkon, P. Parker. — 4th ed. — London : Heinemann Educational, 1977 (1981 [printing]). — x,1020p : ill ; 24cm
South-east Asian reprint. — Previous ed.: 1970. — Includes index
ISBN 0-435-68610-0 : £8.50 B82-08394

Nelkon, M.. Advanced level physics / M. Nelkon, P. Parker. — 5th ed. — London : Heinemann Educational, 1982. — 948p ; 23cm
Previous ed.: 1977. — Includes index
ISBN 0-435-68666-6 (pbk) : £9.50 : CIP rev. B81-35869

Nelkon, M.. Advanced physics / M. Nelkon and M.V. Detheridge. — London : Pan, 1982. — ix,358p : ill ; 20cm. — (Pan study aids)
Includes index
ISBN 0-330-26614-4 (pbk) : £2.95 B82-20432

Pople, Stephen. Explaining physics / Stephen Pople. — Oxford : Oxford University Press, 1982. — 352p : ill,ports ; 26cm
Includes index
ISBN 0-19-914085-5 (pbk) : £3.95 B82-29685

Revised Nuffield physics / general editors Eric M. Rogers, E.J. Wenham. — London : Published for the Nuffield-Chelsea Curriculum Trust by Longman
Year 5
Teacher's guide / contributors D.W. Harding, J.L. Lewis, A.W. Trotter. — Rev. ed. — 1980. — 163p : ill ; 25cm
Previous ed.: published as Physics. 1967. — Bibliography: p157. — Includes index
ISBN 0-582-04685-8 (pbk) : Unpriced B82-20241

Shepherd, Michael, *1937-*. Revise physics : a complete revision course for O level and CSE / Michael Shepherd. — Rev. [ed.]. — London : Letts, 1981, c1979. — vii,220p : ill(some col.) ; 30cm. — (Letts study aids)
Previous ed.: 1979. — Includes index
ISBN 0-85097-397-x (pbk) : £3.65 B82-19112

Warren, Peter, *1939-*. Physics alive / Peter Warren. — London : Murray, 1982. — 248p : ill(some col.) ; 28cm
Includes index
ISBN 0-7195-3782-7 (pbk) : £3.60 : CIP rev. B81-19162

Wellington, J. J.. Physics for all / J.J. Wellington. — Cheltenham : Thornes, 1982. — vi,201p : ill ; 25cm
Includes index
ISBN 0-85950-329-1 (pbk) : Unpriced : CIP rev. B82-00311

530 — Physics — *For West African students*

Ashworth, A. E.. Physics for WAEC / A.E. Ashworth. — London : Cassell. — (Cassell's 'O' level science for West Africa)
Bk.1. — 1982. — 166p : ill ; 25cm
Includes index
ISBN 0-304-30422-0 (pbk) : Unpriced B82-08929

530'.01 — Physics — *Philosophical perspectives*

Harman, P. M.. Metaphysics and natural philosophy : the problem of substance in classical physics / P.M. Harman. — Brighton : Harvester, 1982. — xvi,168p ; 23cm
Bibliography: p155-163. — Includes index
ISBN 0-7108-0451-2 : £20.00 : CIP rev. B82-27931

Jones, Roger S.. Physics as metaphor. — London : Wildwood House, June 1982. — [268]p
ISBN 0-7045-0477-4 : £7.95 : CIP entry B82-12837

Popper, Karl R.. The Open universe. — London : Hutchinson Education, June 1982. — [224]p
ISBN 0-09-146180-4 : £12.50 : CIP entry B82-10604

Powers, Jonathan. Philosophy and the new physics. — London : Methuen, Dec.1982. — [150]p
ISBN 0-416-73470-7 (cased) : £5.95 : CIP entry
ISBN 0-416-73480-4 (pbk) : £2.50 B82-29763

530'.0212 — Physics — *Tables*

Nordling, Carl. Physics handbook : elementary constants and units, tables, formulae and diagrams and mathematical formulae / Carl Nordling, Jonny Österman. — Lund : Studentlitteratur ; Bromley : Chartwell-Bratt, 1980. — 430p : ill ; 23cm
Translated from the Swedish. — Accompanied by "Chart of the nuclides". — 12th ed. (col.ill; 120x66cm). — Includes index
ISBN 0-86238-000-6 : Unpriced B82-35641

530'.0246 — Physics — *For technicians*

Bird, J. O.. Physics 1 checkbook / J.O. Bird, A.J.C. May. — London : Butterworths, 1982. — vii,120p : ill ; 20cm. — (Butterworths technical and scientific checkbooks)
Includes index
ISBN 0-408-00682-x (cased) : £7.95 : CIP rev.
ISBN 0-408-00629-3 (pbk) : Unpriced B82-10487

Bird, J. O.. Physics 2 checkbook. — London : Butterworth Scientific, Jan.1983. — [224]p. — (Butterworths technical and scientific checkbooks)
ISBN 0-408-00692-7 (cased) : £8.95 : CIP entry
ISBN 0-408-00630-7 (pbk) : £3.95 B82-34426

Deeson, Eric. Technician physics level 2. — London : Longman, Mar.1982. — [288]p. — (Longman technician series. Mathematics and sciences)
ISBN 0-582-41585-3 : £5.95 : CIP entry B82-01124

Physics for TEC Level II. — Cheltenham : Thornes, May 1982. — [224]p
ISBN 0-85950-315-1 (pbk) : £4.50 : CIP entry B82-07040

Schofield, Walter, *1931-*. Physical science for engineers / Walter Schofield. — 2nd ed. — London : McGraw-Hill, c1982. — ix,241p : ill ; 25cm
Previous ed.: 197-?. — Includes index
ISBN 0-07-084642-1 (pbk) : £5.54 : CIP rev. B81-16884

530'.028'54 — Physics. Applications of programmable electronic calculators — *Questions & answers*

Christman, J. Richard. Physics problems for programmable calculators : wave motion, optics and modern physics / J. Richard Christman. — New York ; Chichester : Wiley, c1982. — p.301-609 : ill ; 28cm
"Supplement to Physics, 3rd, and Fundamentals of physics by David Halliday and Robert Resnick"
ISBN 0-471-86062-x (pbk) : £5.00 B82-26262

530'.03'21 — Physics — *Encyclopaedias* — *For schools*

Deeson, Eric. Physics / Eric Deeson ; adviser G. Needham. — London : Collins, 1982. — xxiii,232p : ill ; 12cm. — (Basic facts) (Collins revision aids)
ISBN 0-00-458886-x (pbk) : £1.50 B82-33438

530'.07'11 — Physics teachers. Professional education

The **Education** and training of physics teachers worldwide : a survey / general editor Brian Davies. — London : Murray, 1982. — vi,260p ; 29cm
ISBN 0-7195-3922-6 (pbk) : £4.95 : CIP rev. B81-33872

530'.0724 — Physics. Experiments — *For schools*

Advanced practical physics. — London : J. Murray, Sept.1982
Student's guide. — [160]p
ISBN 0-7195-3957-9 (pbk) : £3.50 : CIP entry B82-19828

Advanced practical physics. — London : J. Murray, Sept.1982
Teacher's guide. — [32]p
ISBN 0-7195-3958-7 (pbk) : £1.95 : CIP entry B82-19827

Armitage, E.. Practical physics in SI. — 2nd ed. — London : Murray, Jan.1983. — [240]p
Previous ed.: 1972
ISBN 0-7195-4001-1 (pbk) : £3.95 : CIP entry B82-30222

Okeke, P. N.. Certificate practical physics / P.N. Okeke, B.L.N. Ndupu. — Lagos : Longman Nigeria ; Harlow : Longman, 1981. — 149p : ill ; 25cm
ISBN 0-582-60608-x (pbk) : £2.20 B82-14300

530'.0724 — Systems. Simulations. Applications of digital computer systems. Use of particle models — *Study examples: Physics. Simulations*

Hockney, Roger W.. Computer simulation using particles / Roger W. Hockney and James W. Eastwood. — New York ; London : McGraw-Hill, c1981. — xix,540p : ill ; 24cm
Bibliography: p509-523. — Includes index
ISBN 0-07-029108-x : £27.50 : CIP rev. B80-18240

530'.076 — Physics — *Questions & answers*

Deeson, Eric. Physics study and revision / E. Deeson. — [Glasgow] : Collins Educational, 1982. — [64]p : ill ; 30cm. — (Collins revision aids)
ISBN 0-00-197253-7 (pbk) : £1.50
ISBN 0-00-327781-x (non-net ed.) : Unpriced B82-32060

530'.076 — Physics — *Questions & answers — For schools*

Avery, J. H.. Objective tests in Ordinary Level physics / by J.H. Avery and A.W.K. Ingram. — Combined ed. — London : Heinemann Educational, 1980. — 97p : ill ; 22cm
Previous ed.: published in 2v. 1969-1975
ISBN 0-435-67039-5 (pbk) : £1.95 B82-35370

Bolton, W.. Multiple-choice questions for A-level physics. — London : Butterworth, Jan.1983. — [144]p. — (Study topics in physics)
ISBN 0-408-10854-1 (pbk) : £3.50 : CIP entry B82-34436

Bolton, W. (William), *1933-*. Revision and workbook : revision notes : questions with explanatory answers : questions from past examination papers / W. Bolton. — London : Butterworths, 1982. — 188p : ill ; 25cm. — (Study topics in physics)
ISBN 0-408-10829-0 (pbk) : Unpriced : CIP rev. B82-01164

Deeson, Eric. Diagnostic testing in advanced physics / Eric Deeson. — London : Hodder and Stoughton
[Complete vol.]. — 1981. — 153p : ill ; 24cm
ISBN 0-340-26281-8 (pbk) : Unpriced : CIP rev. B81-25788

Deeson, Eric. Diagnostic testing in advanced physics / Eric Deeson. — London : Hodder and Stoughton
[Test vol.]. — 1981. — 90p : ill ; 24cm
ISBN 0-340-26282-6 (pbk) : Unpriced : CIP rev. B81-25787

Harrison, D. R.. Understanding physics : a course of problems to O level / D.R. Harrison. — London : Heinemann Educational
Vol.1. — 1982. — vi,78p : ill ; 25cm
ISBN 0-435-67300-9 (pbk) : £2.50 : CIP rev. B81-33986

Harrison, D. R.. Understanding physics : a course of problems to O level / D.R. Harrison. — London : Heinemann Educational
Vol.2. — 1982. — 103p : ill ; 25cm
ISBN 0-435-67301-7 (pbk) : £2.50 : CIP rev. B81-33987

Harrison, D. R.. Understanding physics. — London : Heinemann Educational
Vol.3. — Jan.1983. — [88]p
ISBN 0-435-67302-5 (pbk) : £3.50 : CIP entry B82-34585

Hinson, Don. Physics exercises for year 5 / Don Hinson. — London : Harrap, 1982. — v,98p : ill ; 22cm
Includes index
ISBN 0-245-53556-x (pbk) : £1.95 B82-16971

Oguntonade, C. B.. Questions and answers : O level physics / C.B. Oguntonade. — Harlow : Longman, 1982. — 160p : ill ; 22cm. — (Study for success)
ISBN 0-582-60632-2 (pbk) : £1.50 B82-24401

530'.09'034 — Physics. Theories, *1800-1900*

Harman, P. M.. Energy, force, and matter : the conceptual development of nineteenth-century physics / P.M. Harman. — Cambridge : Cambridge University Press, 1982. — ix,182p : ill,facsims ; 22cm. — (Cambridge history of science)
Includes index
ISBN 0-521-24600-8 (cased) : £13.50
ISBN 0-521-28812-6 (pbk) : £5.50 B82-29931

530'.092'4 — Physics. Braun, Ferdinand — *Biographies*

Kurylo, Friedrich. Ferdinand Braun : a life of the Nobel prizewinner and inventor of the cathode-ray oscilloscope / Friedrich Kurylo and [translated by] Charles Susskind. — Rev. ed. / [revised and edited by Charles Susskind]. — Cambridge, Mass. ; London : MIT Press, c1981. — xiv,289p : ill,facsims,ports ; 24cm
Translation of: Ferdinand Braun : Leben und Wirken des Erfinders der Braunschen Röhre, Nobelpreis 1909. Verb. Aufl.. — Bibliography: p254-272 . — Includes index
ISBN 0-262-11077-6 : £21.00 B82-09574

530'.092'4 — Physics. Clerk Maxwell, James — *Biographies*

Tolstoy, Ivan. James Clerk Maxwell : a biography / Ivan Tolstoy. — Edinburgh : Canongate, 1981. — viii,184p,[8]p of plates : ill,1facsim,ports ; 23cm
Bibliography: p173-180. — Includes index
ISBN 0-86241-010-x : £9.95 B82-09055

530'.092'4 — Physics. Einstein, Albert — *Biographies*

Pais, Abraham. Subtle is the Lord — the science and life of Albert Einstein. — Oxford : Oxford University Press, Sept.1982. — [456]p
ISBN 0-19-853907-x : £15.00 : CIP entry B82-18982

530'.092'4 — Physics. Einstein, Albert — *Conference proceedings*

Jerusalem Einstein Centennial Symposium on Gauge Theories and Unification of Physical Forces *(1979)*. Albert Einstein : historical and cultural perspectives : the centennial symposium in Jerusalem / [Jerusalem Einstein Centennial Symposium, 14-23 March 1979] ; [organized by the Israel Academy of Sciences and Humanities et al.] ; edited by Gerald Holton and Yehuda Elkana. — Princeton ; Guildford : Princeton University Press, c1982. — xxxii,439p : ill ; 25cm
Includes index
ISBN 0-691-08299-5 : £24.70 B82-39034

530'.092'4 — Physics. Einstein, Albert — *Festschriften*

Einstein : the first hundred years / edited by Maurice Goldsmith, Alan Mackay and James Woudhuysen. — Oxford : Pergamon, 1980. — xiii,200p : ill,ports ; 26cm
Includes index
ISBN 0-08-025019-x : £8.95 : CIP rev. B80-06902

530'.092'4 — Physics. Einstein, Albert. Theories — *Christian viewpoints*

Paul, Iain. Science, religion and Einstein. — Belfast : Christian Journals, May 1982. — 1v.. — (Theology and scientific culture ; v.3)
ISBN 0-904302-80-6 : £9.50 : CIP entry B82-16211

530'.092'4 — Physics. Millikan, Robert Andrews — *Biographies*

Kargon, Robert H.. The rise of Robert Millikan : portrait of a life in American science / Robert H. Kargon. — Ithaca ; London : Cornell University Press, 1982. — 205p : ill,ports ; 23cm
Bibliography: p173-174. — Includes index
ISBN 0-8014-1459-8 : £17.00 B82-35761

530'.092'4 — Physics. Theories of Newton, ***Sir*** **Isaac. European criticism**

Guerlac, Henry. Newton on the Continent / Henry Guerlac. — Ithaca ; London : Cornell University Press, 1981. — 169p : ill,3ports ; 24cm
Includes index
ISBN 0-8014-1409-1 : Unpriced B82-16926

530.1 — PHYSICS. THEORIES

530.1 — Physics. Theories. Approximation — *Conference proceedings*

Structure and approximation in physical theories / [proceedings of a colloquium on structure and approximation in physical theories held at Osnabrück, FRG, in June 1980] ; edited by A. Hartkämper and H.-J. Schmidt. — New York ; London : Plenum, c1981. — viii,255p : ill ; 26cm
Includes bibliographies and index
ISBN 0-306-40882-1 : Unpriced B82-14455

530.1'1 — Physics. General theory of relativity

Buchdahl, H. A.. Seventeen simple lectures on general relativity theory / H.A. Buchdahl. — New York ; Chichester : Wiley, c1981. — xiii,174p ; 24cm
Bibliography: p165-166. — Includes index
ISBN 0-471-09684-9 : £17.75 B82-13355

530.1'1 — Physics. Relativity

Coleman, James A.. Relativity for the layman : a simplified account of the history, theory, and proofs of relativity / James A. Coleman ; illustrated by the author. — Rev. ed. — Harmondsworth : Penguin, 1969 (1981 [printing]). — 142p : ill ; 18cm
Previous ed.: 1959. — Includes index
ISBN 0-14-020442-3 (pbk) : £1.25 B82-10512

530.1'1 — Physics. Relativity. Geometrical aspects

Torretti, Roberto. Relativity and geometry. — Oxford : Pergamon, Oct.1982. — [352]p. — (Foundations and philosophy of science and technology series)
ISBN 0-08-026773-4 : £22.50 : CIP entry B82-24952

530.1'1 — Physics. Special theory of relativity

Dixon, W. G.. Special relativity. — Cambridge : Cambridge University Press, Sept.1982. — [260]p
Originally published: 1978
ISBN 0-521-27241-6 (pbk) : £9.95 : CIP entry B82-29356

Rindler, Wolfgang. Introduction to special relativity / Wolfgang Rindler. — Oxford : Clarendon, 1982. — x,185p : ill ; 23cm. — (Oxford science publications)
Includes index
ISBN 0-19-853181-8 (cased) : £15.00 : CIP rev.
ISBN 0-19-853182-6 (pbk) : £6.95 B81-36966

Winterflood, A. H.. Newton's error / A.H. Winterflood. — London (9 Grosvenor Gardens, Muswell Hill, N10 3TB) : A.H. Winterflood, 1981. — 71p : ill ; 20cm
Includes index
£3.00 (pbk) B82-08162

530.1'1 — Physics. Special theory of relativity — *Philosophical perspectives*

Pope, N. Vivian. Relativising relativity / N. Vivian Pope. — [Burton-on-Trent] : [Philosophical Enterprises], [1981]. — 10p ; 21cm
Cover title
ISBN 0-9503790-3-4 (pbk) : Unpriced B82-14995

530.1'1 — Space & time

Mehlberg, Henry. Time, causality and the quantum theory : studies in the philosophy of science / Henry Mehlberg ; edited by Robert S. Cohen ; with a preface by Adolf Grünbaum. — Dordrecht ; London : Reidel, c1980. — 2v. : ill,2ports ; 23cm. — (Boston studies in the philosophy of science ; v.19)
Bibliography: Vol.2 p262-284. — Includes index
ISBN 90-277-0721-9 : Unpriced
ISBN 90-277-1074-0 (v.1 : Pbk) : Unpriced
ISBN 90-277-1075-9 (v.2) : Unpriced
ISBN 90-277-1079-7 (v.2 : Pbk) : Unpriced
Also classified at 530.1'2 B82-39094

530.1′1′0151563 — Physics. Relativity. Tensor analysis

Lawden, D. F.. An introduction to tensor calculus, relativity and cosmology / D.F. Lawden. — 3rd ed. — Chichester : Wiley, 1982. — xiii,205p : ill ; 24cm
Previous ed.: published as An introduction to tensor calculus and relativity. London : Methuen, 1967. — Bibliography: p200. — Includes index
ISBN 0-471-10082-x : £14.75 : CIP rev.
ISBN 0-471-10096-x (pbk) : Unpriced
B82-09701

530.1′1′0924 — Physics. Relativity. Theories of Einstein, Albert

Calder, Nigel. Einstein′s universe : a guide to the theory of relativity / Nigel Calder. — Harmondsworth : Penguin, 1982, c1979. — 254p : ill,ports ; 18cm
Originally published: New York : Viking, 1979. — Includes index
ISBN 0-14-022407-6 (pbk) : £1.95 B82-26442

Miller, Arthur I.. Albert Einstein′s special theory of relativity : emergence (1905) and early interpretation (1905-1911) / Arthur I. Miller. — Reading, Mass. ; London : Addison-Wesley, 1981. — xxviii,466p : ill,facsims,ports ; 24cm
Includes index
ISBN 0-201-04680-6 : Unpriced B82-27981

530.1′2 — Physics. Non-relativistic quantum theory

Landau, L. D.. Quantum mechanics : non-relativistic theory / by L.D. Landau and E.M. Lifshitz ; translated from the Russian by J.B. Sykes and J.B. Bell. — 3rd ed. rev. & enlarged. — Oxford : Pergamon, 1977 (1981 printing). — xiv,673p : ill ; 25cm. — (Course of theoretical physics ; v.3)
Translation of: Kvantovaia mekhanika. — Includes index
ISBN 0-08-029140-6 (cased) : Unpriced
ISBN 0-08-020940-8 B82-25835

Tarasov, L. V.. [Osnovy krantovoĭ mekhaniki. English]. Basic concepts of quantum mechanics / L.V. Tarasov ; translated from the Russian by Ram S. Wadhwa. — Moscow : Mir, 1980 ; [London] : Distributed by Central Books. — 262p : ill ; 23cm
Translation of: Osnovy Krantovoĭ mekhaniki. — Includes index
£2.95 B82-11404

530.1′2 — Physics. Quantum theory

Clark, H.. A first course in quantum mechanics / H. Clark. — Rev. ed. — New York ; London : Van Nostrand Reinhold, c1982. — 368p : ill ; 22cm. — (The Modern university physics series)
Previous ed.: 1974. — Includes bibliographies and index
ISBN 0-442-30173-1 (pbk) : £4.95 B82-30761

Davies, P. C. W.. Other worlds / Paul Davies. — London : Abacus, 1982, c1980. — 207p : ill ; 20cm
Originally published: London : Dent, 1980. — Includes index
ISBN 0-349-10741-6 (pbk) : £2.50 B82-21060

Martin, J. L. (John Legat). Basic quantum mechanics / J.L. Martin. — Oxford : Clarendon, 1981. — ix,241p : ill ; 23cm. — (Oxford physics series ; 8)
Includes index
ISBN 0-19-851815-3 (cased) : £17.50 : CIP rev.
ISBN 0-19-851816-1 (pbk) : £7.95 B81-11918

530.1′2 — Physics. Quantum theory. Applications of Lagrange′s equations

Leray, Jean. Lagrangian analysis and quantum mechanics : a mathematical structure related to asymptotic expansions and the Maslov index / Jean Leray ; English translation by Carolyn Schroeder. — Cambridge, Mass. ; London : MIT Press, c1981. — xvi,271p ; 24cm
Translation from the French. — Bibliography: p269-271
ISBN 0-262-12087-9 : Unpriced B82-35064

530.1′2 — Physics. Quantum theory. Approximation

Maslov, V. P.. Semi-classical approximation in quantum mechanics / V.P. Maslov and M.V. Fedoriuk ; translated from the Russian by J. Niederle and J. Tolar. — Dordrecht ; London : Reidel, 1981. — ix,301p ; 23cm. — (Mathematical physics and applied mathematics ; v.7)
Translation of: Kvaziklassicheskoe priblizhenie dlīa uravneniĭ kvantovoĭ mekhaniki. — Bibliography: p290-294. — Includes index
ISBN 90-277-1219-0 : Unpriced B82-00487

530.1′2 — Physics. Quantum theory — *Philosophical perspectives*

Bohm, David. Wholeness and the implicate order / David Bohm. — Repr. with corrections. — London : Routledge & Kegan Paul, 1981, c1980. — xv,224p : ill ; 22cm
Includes index
ISBN 0-7100-0971-2 (pbk) : £3.95 B82-01481

Mehlberg, Henry. Time, causality and the quantum theory : studies in the philosophy of science / Henry Mehlberg ; edited by Robert S. Cohen ; with a preface by Adolf Grünbaum. — Dordrecht ; London : Reidel, c1980. — 2v. : ill,2ports ; 23cm. — (Boston studies in the philosophy of science ; v.19)
Bibliography: Vol.2 p262-284. — Includes index
ISBN 90-277-0721-9 : Unpriced
ISBN 90-277-1074-0 (v.1 : Pbk) : Unpriced
ISBN 90-277-1075-9 (v.2) : Unpriced
ISBN 90-277-1079-7 (v.2 : Pbk) : Unpriced
Primary classification 530.1′1 B82-39094

Popper, Karl R.. Quantum theory and the schism in physics. — London : Hutchinson Education, June 1982. — [256]p
ISBN 0-09-146170-7 : £15.00 : CIP entry
B82-10603

530.1′2 — Physics. Relativistic quantum theory

Berestetskiĭ, V. B.. Quantum electrodynamics / by V.B. Berestetskiĭ, E.M. Lifshitz and L.P. Pitaevskiĭ ; translated from the Russian by J.B. Sykes and J.S. Bell. — 2nd ed. — Oxford : Pergamon, 1982. — xv,652p : ill ; 26cm. — (Course of theoretical physics ; v.4)
Translation of: Kvantovaya elektrodinamika. — Previous ed.: published in 2v. as Relativistic quantum theory. 1971-1974. — Includes index
ISBN 0-08-026503-0 (cased) : Unpriced : CIP rev.
ISBN 0-08-026504-9 (pbk) : £14.75
B81-35908

530.1′2 — Quantum theory

Cassels, J. M.. Basic quantum mechanics / J.M. Cassels. — 2nd ed. — London : Macmillan, 1982. — 205p : ill ; 23cm
Previous ed.: Maidenhead : McGraw-Hill, 1970. — Includes index
ISBN 0-333-18599-4 (cased) : £25.00
ISBN 0-333-31768-8 (pbk) : Unpriced
B82-20942

Dirac, P. A. M.. The principles of quantum mechanics. — 4th ed. — Oxford : Clarendon Press, Nov.1981. — [328]p. — (The International series of monographs on physics ; 27)
Previous ed.: 1947
ISBN 0-19-852011-5 (pbk) : £7.95 : CIP entry
B81-33642

Hameka, Hendrik F.. Quantum mechanics / Hendrik F. Hameka. — New York ; London : Wiley, c1981. — xii,387p : ill ; 24cm
Includes index
ISBN 0-471-09223-1 : £24.00 B82-05126

Rae, Alastair I. M.. Quantum mechanics / Alastair I.M. Rae. — London : McGraw-Hill, c1981. — xii,237p : ill ; 23cm
Bibliography: p231-233. — Includes index
ISBN 0-07-084127-6 (pbk) : £6.25 : CIP rev.
B81-23881

Yariv, Amnon. An introduction to theory and applications of quantum mechanics / Amnon Yariv. — New York ; Chichester : Wiley, c1982. — xiii,300p : ill ; 25cm
Bibliography: p293-294. — Includes index
ISBN 0-471-06053-4 : £16.85 B82-36932

530.1′2 — Quantum theory. Applications of variational methods

Yourgrau, Wolfgang. Variational principles in dynamics and quantum theory / Wolfgang Yourgrau, Stanley Mandelstam. — 3rd ed. — New York : Dover ; London : Constable, 1979, c1968. — xiii,201p ; 21cm
Previous ed.: London : Pitman, 1960. — Bibliography: p184-186. — Includes index
ISBN 0-486-63773-5 (pbk) : £3.00
Also classified at 531′.11 B82-27464

530.1′2 — Quantum theory — *Conference proceedings*

Quantum mechanics in mathematics, chemistry, and physics / [proceedings of a special session in mathematical physics organized as a part of the 774th Meeting of the American Mathematical Society, held March 27-29, 1980, in Boulder, Colorado] ; edited by Karl E. Gustafson and William P. Reinhardt. — New York ; London : Plenum, c1981. — ix,506p : ill ; 26cm
Includes bibliographies and index
ISBN 0-306-40737-x : Unpriced B82-14708

530.1′2′09 — Quantum theory, *to 1981*

Wolf, Fred Alan. Taking the quantum leap : the new physics for nonscientists / Fred Alan Wolf. — San Francisco ; London : Harper & Row, c1981. — 262p : ill,ports ; 24cm
Bibliography: p255-257. — Includes index
ISBN 0-06-250980-2 (pbk) : Unpriced
B82-18399

530.1′24 — Wave mechanics. Schrödinger equation

Eastham, M. S. P.. Schrödinger-type operators with continuous spectra. — London : Pitman, June 1982. — [290]p. — (Research notes in mathematics ; 65)
ISBN 0-273-08526-3 (pbk) : £9.50 : CIP entry
B82-12134

530.1′3 — Statistical mechanics

Akhiezer, A. I.. Methods of statistical physics / by A.I. Akhiezer and S.V. Peletminskii ; translated by M. Schukin. — Oxford : Pergamon, 1981. — xv,450p : ill ; 24cm. — (International series in natural philosophy ; v.104)
Translation from the Russian. — Bibliography: p436-441. — Includes index
ISBN 0-08-025040-8 : £22.50 : CIP rev.
B81-28198

Bowler, M. G.. Lectures on statistical mechanics / by M.G. Bowler. — Oxford : Pergamon Press, 1982. — ix,120p ; 23cm
Bibliography: p114-116. — Includes index
ISBN 0-08-026516-2 (cased) : Unpriced : CIP rev.
ISBN 0-08-026515-4 (pbk) : £4.95 B81-34471

Rosser, W. G. V.. An introduction to statistical physics / W.G.V. Rosser. — Chichester : Ellis Horwood, 1982. — xiv,382p : ill ; 24cm. — (Ellis Horwood series in mathematics and its applications)
Includes index
ISBN 0-85312-272-5 (cased) : £17.50 : CIP rev.
ISBN 0-85312-357-8 (pbk) : Unpriced
B81-12918

Statistical mechanics and dynamics / Henry Eyring ... [et al.]. — [Rev.] 2nd ed. — New York ; Chichester : Wiley, c1982. — xiv,785p : ill ; 24cm
Previous ed.: i.e. 2nd ed. 1978. — Includes index
ISBN 0-471-37042-8 : £20.25 B82-28085

Thompson, Colin J.. Mathematical statistical mechanics / Colin J. Thompson. — Princeton, N.J. ; Guildford : Princeton University Press, 1979, c1972. — ix,278p : ill ; 25cm
Originally published: New York : Macmillan ; London : Collier-Macmillan, 1972. — Bibliography: p263-274. — Includes index
ISBN 0-691-08219-7 (cased) : Unpriced
ISBN 0-691-08220-0 (pbk) : Unpriced
B82-27059

530.1'3 — Statistical mechanics. Mathematical models

Baxter, Rodney J.. Exactly solved models in statistical mechanics / Rodney J. Baxter. — London : Academic Press, 1982. — xii,482p : ill ; 24cm
Bibliography: p474-481. — Includes index
ISBN 0-12-083180-5 : £43.60 : CIP rev. B82-04132

530.1'33 — Physics. Geometric quantization

Woodhouse, Nicholas. Geometric quantization / by Nicholas Woodhouse. — Oxford : Clarendon, 1980. — xi,314p : ill ; 24cm. — (Oxford mathematical monographs)
Includes index
ISBN 0-19-853528-7 : £27.50 B82-22534

530.1'41 — Electromagnetic fields

Becker, Richard. Electromagnetic fields and interactions / Richard Becker ; edited by Fritz Sauter. — New York : Dover ; London : Constable, 1982, c1964. — 403p : ill ; 22cm
Translation of: Theorie der Elektrizität. — Originally published: in 2 vols. New York : Blaisdell, 1964. — Includes index
ISBN 0-486-64290-9 (pbk) : £9.40 B82-40187

Florides, P. S.. The complete field of charged perfect fluid spheres and of other static spherically symmetric charged distributions / by P.S. Florides. — Dublin : Trinity College Dublin, School of Mathematics, [1982]. — 21leaves ; 30cm
Bibliography: leaf 21
Unpriced (pbk) B82-31219

Neff, Herbert P.. Basic electromagnetic fields / Herbert P. Neff Jr. — New York ; London : Harper & Row, c1981. — xxi,600p : ill ; 25cm
Includes index
ISBN 0-06-044785-0 : £15.00 B82-36845

Paul, Clayton R.. Introduction to electromagnetic fields / Clayton R. Paul, Syed A. Nasar. — New York ; London : McGraw-Hill, c1982. — xv,567p : ill ; 25cm. — (McGraw-Hill series in electrical engineering)
Text on lining papers. — Includes index
ISBN 0-07-045884-7 : £22.75 B82-16376

530.1'41 — Electromagnetic fields & waves. Theories

Skitek, G. G.. Electromagnetic concepts and applications / G.G. Skitek, S.V. Marshall. — Engelwood Cliffs ; London : Prentice-Hall, c1982. — xvii,510p : ill ; 25cm
Text on lining paper. — Bibliography: p493-494. — Includes index
ISBN 0-13-248963-5 : £20.95 B82-31819

530.1'41 — Electromagnetic waves. Interactions with plasmas

The **Dissipation** of electromagnetic waves in plasmas / edited by N.G. Basov ; translated from Russian by Donald H. McNeill. — New York ; London : Consultants Bureau, c1982. — vii,101p : ill ; 28cm. — (Proceedings (Trudy) of the P. N. Lebedev Physics Institute ; v.92)
Translation of: Dissipat͡sii͡a elektromagnitnykh voln v plazme
ISBN 0-306-10969-7 (pbk) : Unpriced B82-41107

530.1'41 — Electromagnetic waves. Scattering

Bayvel, L. P.. Electromagnetic scattering and its applications / L.P. Bayvel and A.R. Jones. — London : Applied Science, c1981. — xvi,289p : ill ; 23cm
Bibliography: p268-278. — Includes index
ISBN 0-85334-955-x : £28.00 : CIP rev. B81-17510

530.1'42 — Physics. Twistor theory

Advances in twistor theory / L.P. Hughston & R.S. Ward (editors). — San Francisco ; London : Pitman, c1979. — 335p : ill ; 25cm. — (Research notes in mathematics)
Bibliography: p324-332. — Includes index
ISBN 0-273-08448-8 (pbk) : £10.95 B82-06185

530.1'42 — Physics. Unified field theory

Rowlands, Peter. The laws of physics and fundamental particles / by Peter Rowlands. — Runcorn : Newart Visual Aids, c1979. — 36p ; 30cm
Unpriced (unbound) B82-38640

530.1'42 — Physics. Unified field theory — *Conference proceedings*

Jerusalem Einstein Centennial Symposium on Gauge Theories and Unification of Physical Forces *(1979)*. To fulfill a vision : Jerusalem Einstein Centennial Symposium on Gauge Theories and Unification of Physical Forces / [presented at the Israel Academy of Sciences and Humanities, Jerusalem, March 20-23, 1979] ; edited by Yuval Ne'eman. — Reading, Mass. ; London : Addison-Wesley, 1981. — xxxi,279p : ill ; 25cm
Includes index
ISBN 0-201-05289-x : £26.10 B82-23417

530.1'43 — Physics. Quantum field theory

Burt, Philip Barnes. Quantum mechanics and nonlinear waves / Philip Barnes Burt. — Chur ; London : Harwood, c1981. — ix,331p : ill ; 24cm. — (Physics, ISSN 0276-9025 ; v.1)
Bibliography: p309-319. — Includes index
ISBN 3-7186-0072-2 : Unpriced B82-33436

530.1'43 — Physics. Quantum field theory. Instantons & solitons

Rajaraman, R.. Solitons and instantons : an introduction to solitons and instantons in quantum field theory / R. Rajaraman. — Amsterdam ; Oxford : North-Holland, 1982. — vii,409p : ill ; 24cm
Bibliography: p394-402. — Includes index
ISBN 0-444-86229-3 : £41.49 B82-30536

530.1'43 — Physics. Relativistic quantum field theory

Birrell, N. D.. Quantum fields in curved space / N.D. Birrell and P.C.W. Davies. — Cambridge : Cambridge University Press, 1982. — ix,340p : ill ; 24cm. — (Cambridge monographs on mathematical physics)
Bibliography: p323-336. — Includes index
ISBN 0-521-23385-2 : £27.50 : CIP rev. B82-00237

530.1'44 — Physics. Many-body problem. Solution. Techniques

Umezawa, H.. Thermo field dynamics and condensed states / H. Umezawa and H. Matsumoto, M. Tachiki. — Amsterdam ; Oxford : North-Holland, 1982. — xvi,591p : ill ; 23cm
Includes index
ISBN 0-444-86361-3 : £58.02 B82-39844

530.1'5 — Indistinguishables. Mathematical models

Parker-Rhodes, A. F.. The theory of indistinguishables : a search for explanatory principles below the level of physics / A.F. Parker-Rhodes. — Dordrecht ; London : Reidel, c1981. — xiv,216p : ill ; 23cm. — (Synthese library ; v.150)
Includes index
ISBN 90-277-1214-x : Unpriced B82-09384

530.1'55 — Physics. Nonlinear analysis — *Conference proceedings*

Los Alamos Conference on Nonlinear Problems *(1st : 1981)*. Nonlinear problems : present and future : proceedings of the first Los Alamos Conference on Nonlinear Problems, Los Alamos, NM, U.S.A., March 2-6, 1981 / edited by Alan Bishop, David Campbell, Basil Nicolaenko. — Amsterdam ; Oxford : North-Holland, 1982. — xi,483p : ill ; 24cm. — (North-Holland mathematics studies ; 61)
Includes bibliographies and index
ISBN 0-444-86395-8 (pbk) : £31.65 B82-39841

NATO Advanced Study Institute on Nonlinear Phenomena in Physics and Biology *(1980 : Banff, Alta.)*. Nonlinear phenomena in physics and biology / [proceedings of a NATO Advanced Study Institute on Nonlinear Phenomena in Physics and Biology, held August 17-29, 1980, at the Banff Center, Banff, Alberta, Canada] ; edited by Richard H. Enns ... [et al.]. — New York ; London : Published in cooperation with NATO Scientific Affairs Division [by] Plenum, c1981. — x,609p : ill,1port ; 26cm. — (NATO advanced study institutes series. Series B, Physics ; v.75)
Includes bibliographies and index
ISBN 0-306-40880-5 : Unpriced
Also classified at 574'.01'515 B82-17646

530.1'5545 — Physics. Linear integral equations

Jörgens, K.. Linear integral operators / the late K. Jörgens ; translated by G.F. Roach. — Boston, [Mass.] ; London : Pitman Advanced Publishing Program, c1982. — x,379p ; 24cm. — (Surveys and reference works in mathematics ; [7])
Translation of: Lineare Integraloperatoren. — Includes index
ISBN 0-273-08523-9 : Unpriced : CIP rev. B82-03798

530.1'592 — Physics. Stochastic processes

Alberti, Peter M.. Stochasticity and partial order : doubly stochastic maps and unitary mixing / Peter M. Alberti and Armin Uhlmann. — Berlin : VEB Deutscher Verlag der Wissenschaften ; Dordrecht ; London : Reidel, c1982. — 123p ; 23cm. — (Mathematics and its applications ; v.9)
Bibliography: p116-120. — Includes index
ISBN 90-277-1350-2 : Unpriced B82-34837

Kampen, N. G. van. Stochastic processes in physics and chemistry / N.G. van Kampen. — Amsterdam ; Oxford : North-Holland, 1981. — xiv,419p : ill ; 23cm
Includes index
ISBN 0-444-86200-5 : £38.29
Also classified at 540'.1'5192 B82-13455

530.4 — PHYSICS. STATES OF MATTER

530.4 — Condensed matter — *Conference proceedings*

European Physical Society. *Condensed Matter Division. General Conference (1st : 1980 : Antwerp)*. Recent developments in condensed matter physics / [presented at the First General Conference of the European Physical Society held April 9-11, 1980, at the University of Antwerp (RUCA and UIA), Antwerp, Belgium] ; edited by J.T. Devreese ; associate editors L.F. Lemmens, V.E. van Doren, J. van Royen. — New York ; London : Plenum
Vol.2: Metals, disordered systems surfaces and interfaces. — c1981. — xvii,477p : ill ; 26cm
Includes index
ISBN 0-306-40647-0 : Unpriced B82-13996

European Physical Society. *Condensed Matter Division. General Conference (1st : 1980 : Antwerp)*. Recent developments in condensed matter physics / [contributed papers presented at the First General Conference of the Condensed Matter Division of the European Physical Society, held April 9-11, 1980, at the University of Antwerp (RUCA and UIA), Antwerp, Belgium. — New York ; London : Plenum
Vol.3: Impurities, excitons, polarons, and polaritons / edited by J.T. Devreese ... [et al.]. — c1981. — xvi,420p : ill ; 26cm
Includes index
ISBN 0-306-40648-9 : Unpriced B82-14283

European Physical Society. *Condensed Matter Division. General Conference (1st : 1980 : Antwerp)*. Recent developments in condensed matter physics / [presented at the First General Conference of the European Physical Society held April 9-11, 1980, at the University of Antwerp (RUCA and UIA), Antwerp, Belgium] ; edited by J.T Devreese ; associate editors L.F. Lemmens, V.E. van Doren, J. van Royen. — New York ; London : Plenum
Includes index
Vol.4: Low-dimensional systems, phase changes, and experimental techniques. — c1981. — xvi,448p : ill ; 26cm
ISBN 0-306-40649-7 (corrected) : Unpriced B82-16808

530.4 — Condensed matter — *Conference proceedings* *continuation*

Midwest Solid State Conference *(29th : 1981 : Argonne National Laboratory).* Novel materials and techniques in condensed matter : proceedings of the twenty-ninth Midwest Solid State Conference held 25-26 September 1981 at Argonne National Laboratory, Argonne, Illinois, U.S.A. / editors G.W. Crabtree and P. Vashishta. — New York ; Oxford : North-Holland, c1982. — xxiii,346p : ill ; 24cm
Includes index
ISBN 0-444-00694-x : Unpriced B82-33798

530.4 — Condensed matter. Mathematical models

Lovesey, S. W.. Condensed matter physics : dynamic correlations / S.W. Lovesey. — Reading, Mass. ; London : Benjamin/Cummings, 1980. — xiii,191p : ill ; 25cm. — (Frontiers in physics ; 49)
Bibliography: p185-188. — Includes index
ISBN 0-8053-6610-5 (cased) : £14.60
ISBN 0-8053-6611-3 (pbk) : Unpriced
B82-05154

530.4 — Disordered systems. Excitations — *Conference proceedings*

Excitations in disordered systems / edited by M.F. Thorpe. — New York ; London : Plenum Press published in cooperation with NATO Scientific Affairs Division, c1982. — xiv,704p : ill ; 26cm. — (NATO advanced study institutes series. Series B, Physics ; v.78)
Conference papers. — Includes bibliographies and index
ISBN 0-306-40981-x : Unpriced B82-35325

530.4 — Materials. Surfaces. Structure & physical properties — *Conference proceedings*

Sagamore Army Materials Research Conference *(26th : 1979).* Surface treatments for improved performance and properties / [proceedings of Twenty-Sixth Sagamore Army Materials Research Conference, held July 16-20, 1979, at the Sagamore Hotel, Bolton Landing, Lake George, New York] ; edited by John J. Burke and Volker Weiss. — New York ; London : Plenum, c1982. — x,224p : ill ; 26cm. — (Sagamore army materials research conference proceedings)
Includes index
Unpriced B82-25807

530.4 — Matter. Physical properties *expounded by* **physical properties of art objects**

Smith, Cyril Stanley. From art to science : seventy-two objects illustrating the nature of discovery / Cyril Stanley Smith. — Cambridge, Mass. ; London : MIT Press, c1980. — 118p : ill(some col.),1port ; 25cm
ISBN 0-262-19181-4 : Unpriced B82-35063

530.4 — States of matter

Walton, Alan J.. Three phases of matter. — 2nd ed. — Oxford : Clarendon Press, Oct.1982. — [350]p
Previous ed.: London : McGraw-Hill, 1976
ISBN 0-19-851957-5 (cased) : £17.50 : CIP entry
ISBN 0-19-851953-2 (pbk) : £7.95 B82-23694

530.4′1 — Semimetals. Structure & physical properties

Semiconductors and semimetals / edited by R.K. Willardson, Albert C. Beer. — New York ; London : Academic Press
Vol.16: Defects, (HgCd)Se, (HgCd)Te. — 1981. — ix,266p : ill ; 24cm
Includes bibliographies and index
ISBN 0-12-752116-x : £24.80
Primary classification 537.6′22 B82-13114

530.4′1 — Amorphous materials. Structure

Waseda, Yoshio. The structure of non-crystalline materials : liquids and amorphous solids / Yoshio Waseda. — New York ; London : McGraw-Hill, c1980. — xv,326p : ill ; 24cm
Bibliography: p307-315. — Includes index
ISBN 0-07-068426-x : £41.95 : CIP rev.
B80-02762

530.4′1 — Amorphous materials. Structure. Determination. Applications of diffraction

Diffraction studies on non-crystalline substances / edited by István Hargittai and W.J. Orville-Thomas. — Amsterdam ; Oxford : Elsevier Scientific, 1981. — 894p : ill ; 25cm. — (Studies in physical and theoretical chemistry ; 13)
Includes index
ISBN 0-444-99752-0 : £47.78 B82-15240

530.4′1 — Amorphous solids. Structure — *Conference proceedings*

The **Structure** of noncrystalline solids 2. — London : Taylor and Francis, Feb.1983. — [450]p
Conference papers
ISBN 0-85066-241-9 : £25.00 : CIP entry
B82-39432

530.4′1 — Gases. Adsorption by surfaces of solids

Gregg, S. J.. Adsorption, surface area and porosity / S.J. Gregg, K.S.W. Sing. — 2nd ed. — London : Academic Press, 1982. — xi,303p : ill ; 24cm
Previous ed.: 1967. — Includes index
ISBN 0-12-300956-1 : £24.00 : CIP rev.
B82-07484

530.4′1 — Solids. Defects — *Conference proceedings*

Physique des défauts = Physics of defects / édité par Roger Balian, Maurice Kléman, Jean-Paul Poirier. — Amsterdam ; Oxford : North-Holland, c1981. — xxxi,857p : ill ; 22cm
Conference papers delivered at Les Houches, session XXXV, 28 July-29 August 1980. — English text with French preface. — At head of title: USMG-NATO ASI
ISBN 0-444-86225-0 : £78.28 B82-21022

530.4′1 — Solids. Effects of radiation

Radiation effects in solids, including ion implantation : summary of the recommendations and conclusions of a review panel, 1980 / Science and Engineering Research Council Physics Committee. — [Swindon] : [The Council], [1980?]. — 12p ; 30cm
Unpriced (pbk) B82-36813

530.4′1 — Solids. Implantation of ions — *Conference proceedings*

International Conference on Modification of Surface Properties of Metals by Ion Implantation *(3rd : 1981 : Manchester).* Ion implantation in metals. — Oxford : Pergamon, June 1982. — [383]p
ISBN 0-08-027625-3 : £35.00 : CIP entry
B82-13509

530.4′1 — Solids. Phase transitions

March, N. H.. Collective effects in solids and liquids. — Bristol : Hilger, Apr.1982. — [300] p. — (Graduate student series in physics, ISSN 0261-7242)
ISBN 0-85274-528-1 (pbk) : £14.00 : CIP entry
B82-04791

530.4′1 — Solids. Phase transitions. Role of interactions between electrons & phonons

Phase transformations during irradiation. — London : Applied Science, Feb.1983. — [368]p
ISBN 0-85334-179-6 : £40.00 : CIP entry
B82-39606

530.4′1 — Solids. Structure & physical properties

Chalmers, B.. The structure and properties of solids. — London : Heyden, Apr.1982. — [150]p
ISBN 0-85501-721-x : £9.00 : CIP entry
B82-08423

530.4′1 — Solids. Surfaces. Adsorption of gases — *Conference proceedings*

Adsorption at the gas-solid and liquid-solid interface. — Oxford : Elsevier Scientific, May 1982. — [520]p. — (Studies in surface science and catalysis ; 10)
Conference papers
ISBN 0-444-42087-8 : CIP entry B82-14950

530.4′1 — Solids. Surfaces. Physical properties — *Conference proceedings*

Symposium on Physics of Solid Surfaces *(1980 : Bechyňe).* Proceedings of the Symposium on Physics of Solid Surfaces / edited by M. Láznička. — Amsterdam ; Oxford : Elsevier Scientific, 1982. — 282p : ill ; 23cm. — (Studies in surface science and catalysis ; 9)
ISBN 0-444-99716-4 (pbk) : £32.35 : CIP rev.
B81-35882

530.4′1 — Solids. Surfaces. Structure & physical properties

Electromagnetic surface modes. — Chichester : Wiley, July 1982. — [816]p
ISBN 0-471-10077-3 : £35.00 : CIP entry
B82-13242

Mikhail, Raouf Sh.. Microstructure and thermal analysis of solid surfaces. — Chichester : Wiley, Aug.1982. — [550]p
ISBN 0-471-26230-7 : £30.00 : CIP entry
B82-30604

530.4′2 — Fluids. Statistical mechanics

The **Liquid** state of matter : fluids, simple and complex / editors E.W. Montroll, J.L. Lebowitz. — Amsterdam ; Oxford : North-Holland, 1982. — vii,440p : ill ; 23cm. — (Studies in statistical mechanics ; v.8)
Includes bibliographies and index
ISBN 0-444-86334-6 : £26.54 B82-28559

530.4′2 — Liquids

Rowlinson, J. S.. Liquids and liquid mixtures. — 3rd ed. / J.S. Rowlinson, F.L. Swinton. — London : Butterworths, 1982. — viii,328p : ill ; 24cm. — (Butterworths monographs in chemistry)
Previous ed.: 1969. — Includes index
ISBN 0-408-24192-6 : Unpriced : CIP rev.
B82-09290

530.4′2 — Liquids. Two-dimensional nuclear magnetic resonance spectroscopy

Bax, Ad. Two-dimensional nuclear magnetic resonance in liquids / by Ad Bax. — Delft : Delft University Press ; Dordrecht ; London : Reidel, c1982. — 200p : ill ; 25cm
ISBN 90-277-1412-6 : Unpriced B82-26965

530.4′2′0724 — Liquids. Experiments — *For children*

Watson, Philip. Liquid magic / written by Philip Watson ; step-by-step illustrations by Elizabeth Wood ; feature illustrations by Ronald Fenton. — London : Methuen/Walker Books, 1982. — 46p : col.ill ; 28cm. — (Science club ; [1])
Includes index
ISBN 0-416-24230-8 : Unpriced : CIP rev.
B82-04847

530.4′3 — Ionised gases. Anions

Smirnov, B. M.. Negative ions / B.M. Smirnov ; translated by S. Chomet ; edited by H.S.W. Massey. — New York ; London : McGraw-Hill, c1982. — x,170p : ill ; 24cm
Translation of: Otriŧsatel′nye iony. — Includes index
ISBN 0-07-058447-8 : £41.50 : CIP rev.
B80-11020

530.4′4 — Electromagnetic fields. Interactions with plasmas

Gekker, I. R.. The interaction of strong electromagnetic fields with plasmas / I.R. Gekker ; translated from the Russian by J.B. Sykes and R.N. Franklin. — Oxford : Clarendon, 1982. — xiii,324p : ill ; 25cm. — (Oxford studies in physics)
Translation of: Élekromagnitўkh poleĭ s plazmoĭ. — Bibliography: p291-322. — Includes index
ISBN 0-19-851467-0 : £35.00 : CIP rev.
B81-20600

530.4′4 — Inertially confined plasmas. Fusion

Duderstadt, James J.. Inertial confinement fusion / James J. Duderstadt, Gregory A. Moses. — New York ; Chichester : Wiley, 1982. — x,347p : ill ; 24cm
Includes index
ISBN 0-471-09050-6 : £36.00 B82-21799

530.4′4 — Ionosphere & magnetosphere. Plasmas
Magnetospheric Substorms and Related Plasma Processes *(Conference : 1978 : Los Alamos).*
Dynamics of the magnetosphere : proceedings of the A.G.U. Chapman conference 'Magnetospheric Substorms and Related Plasma Processes', held at Los Alamos Scientific Laboratory, Los Alamos, N.M., U.S.A., October 9-13, 1978 / edited by S.-I. Akasofu. — Dordrecht ; London : Reidel, c1980. — xi,658p : ill ; 25cm. — (Astrophysics and space science library ; v.78)
Includes bibliographies and index
ISBN 90-277-1052-x : Unpriced B82-37357

530.4′4 — Ionosphere & magnetosphere. Plasmas. Research. Use of particle accelerators — *Conference proceedings*
Artificial particle beams in space plasma studies / edited by Bjørn Grandal. — New York ; London : Plenum published in co-operation with NATO Scientific Affairs Division, c1982. — xviii,704p : ill ; 26cm. — (NATO advanced study institutes series. Series B, Physics ; v.79)
Conference papers. — Includes bibliographies and index
ISBN 0-306-40985-2 : Unpriced B82-41005

530.4′4 — Plasmas. Nonlinear effects
Sitenko, A. G.. Fluctuations and non-linear wave interactions in plasmas / by A.G. Sitenko ; translated by O.D. Kocherga. — Oxford : Pergamon, 1982. — 262p ; 26cm. — (International series in natural philosophy ; v.107)
Translation from the Russian. — Bibliography: p249-255. — Includes index
ISBN 0-08-025051-3 : £25.00 : CIP rev. B81-31373

530.4′4 — Space plasmas. Waves. Instability — *Conference proceedings*
Wave instabilities in space plasmas : proceedings of a symposium organized within the XIX URSI General Assembly held in Helsinki, Finland, July 31-August 8, 1978 / edited by Peter J. Palmadesso and Konstantinos Papadopoulos ; sponsored by Commission H of URSI. — Dordrecht ; London : Reidel, c1979. — vii,309p : ill ; 25cm. — (Astrophysics and space science library ; v.74)
Includes bibliographies and index
ISBN 90-277-1028-7 : Unpriced B82-39117

530.8 — PHYSICAL UNITS, DIMENSIONS, CONSTANTS

530.8 — Dimensional analysis
Staicu, Constantin I.. Restricted and general dimensional analysis : treatment of experimental data / Constantin I. Staicu. — Tunbridge Wells : Abacus, c1982. — 303p ; 22cm
Translation of: Analiza dimensională generală. — Bibliography: p293-300. — Includes index
ISBN 0-85626-300-1 : Unpriced : CIP rev. B81-25893

530.8 — Dimensional analysis — *For geography*
Haynes, Robin M.. An introduction to dimensional analysis for geographers / by Robin Haynes. — Norwich : Geo Abstracts, c1982. — 52p : ill ; 21cm. — (Concepts and techniques in modern geography, ISSN 0306-6142 ; no.33)
Bibliography: p50-52
ISBN 0-86094-097-7 (pbk) : Unpriced B82-19777

530.8 — Measurement
Bishop, O. N.. Yardsticks of the universe / Owen Bishop. — London : Muller, 1982. — 125p : ill ; 21cm
For adolescents. — Includes index
ISBN 0-584-10381-6 : £7.50 : CIP rev. B82-11304

530.8 — Measurement — *For children — Arabic texts*
al-'Add wa-l-qiyās / tarğamah Fahmī 'Utmān. — London : Macmillan, 1981. — 30p : col.ill ; 18cm
Translation of: Counting and measuring. — Originally published: Amman : Royal Jordanian Scientific Society, 1979
ISBN 0-333-32337-8 : Unpriced
Also classified at 513′.5 B82-13465

530.8 — Measurement. Uncertainty. Recording — *Standards*
Campion, P. J.. A code of practice for the detailed statement of accuracy / P.J. Campion, J.E. Burns, A. Williams. — London : National Physical Laboratory, c1980. — vii,51p : 3ill ; 21cm
ISBN 0-9504496-6-0 (pbk) : £3.00 B82-38969

531 — MECHANICS

531 — Continuous media. Mechanics
Hunter, S. C.. Mechanics of continuous media. — 2nd ed. — Chichester : Ellis Horwood, Jan.1983. — [656]p. — (Ellis Horwood series in mathematics and its applications)
Previous ed.: 1976
ISBN 0-85312-570-8 : £30.00 : CIP entry B82-36156

531 — Continuous media. Mechanics. Partial differential equations — *Conference proceedings*
International Conference on Continuum Models of Discrete Systems *(4th : 1981 : Stockholm).*
Continuum models of discrete systems, 4 : proceedings of the Fourth International Conference on Continuum Models of Discrete Systems, Stockholm, Sweden, June 29-July 3, 1981 / edited by O. Brulin nad R.K.T. Hsieh. — Amsterdam ; Oxford : North-Holland, 1981. — xvi,517p : ill ; 23cm
Includes index
ISBN 0-444-86309-5 : £32.61 B82-07889

531 — Mechanics
Desloge, Edward A.. Classical mechanics / Edward A. Desloge. — New York ; Chichester : Wiley, c1982. — 2v.(xviii,991,I-1 to I-12p) : ill ; 25cm
Includes index
ISBN 0-471-09144-8 : Unpriced
ISBN 0-471-09145-6 (v.2) : £36.50 B82-28946

Goldstein, Herbert, *1922-*. Classical mechanics / Herbert Goldstein. — 2nd ed. — Reading, Mass. ; London : Addison-Wesley, c1980. — xiv,672p : ill ; 24cm. — (Addison-Wesley series in physics) (World student series)
Previous ed.: 1950. — Bibliography: p621-630. — Includes index
ISBN 0-201-02969-3 (pbk) : £9.95 B82-16877

Landau, L. D.. Physical bodies / L.D. Landau, A.I. Kitaigorodsky ; translated from the Russian by Martin Greendlinger. — 2nd ed. — Moscow : Mir, 1980 ; [London] : Distributed by Central Books. — 248p : ill,ports ; 18cm. — (Physics for everyone ; bk.1)
Translation of: Fizicheskie tela. — Previous English ed.: 1978
£2.25 B82-35158

Medley, D. G.. An introduction to mechanics and modelling / D.G. Medley. — London : Heinemann, 1982. — xi,340p : ill ; 24cm. — (An HEB paperback)
Includes index
ISBN 0-435-52560-3 (pbk) : £7.50 : CIP rev. B81-34500

531 — Mechanics — *For children*
Paull, John. Simple mechanics / by John and Dorothy Paull ; illustrated by Drury Lane Studios. — Loughborough : Ladybird, c1982. — 49p : col.ill ; 18cm. — (Ladybird junior science)
Text, ill on lining papers. — Includes index
ISBN 0-7214-0659-9 : £0.50 B82-12212

531 — Mechanics — *For schools*
Abbott, P.. Mechanics / P. Abbott. — Rev. ed. / revised by D.G. Kershaw. — London : Teach Yourself Books, 1971 (1981 [printing]). — 318p : ill ; 20cm. — (Teach yourself books)
Previous ed.: published as Teach yourself mechanics, 1942
ISBN 0-340-26953-7 (pbk) : £2.25 : CIP rev. B81-30906

Chapple, M.. Mechanics and heat / M. Chapple. — 2nd ed. — Plymouth : Macdonald & Evans, 1979. — xiii,318p : ill ; 18cm. — ('A' level physics ; v.1) (The M. & E. handbook series)
Previous ed.: 1974. — Includes index
ISBN 0-7121-0154-3 (pbk) : £2.25
Also classified at 536 B82-12178

531 — Solids. Mechanics — *Festschriften*
Mechanics of solids : the Rodney Hill 60th anniversary volume / edited by H.G. Hopkins and M.J. Sewell. — Oxford : Pergamon, 1982. — xxiii,693p,[1]leaf of plates : ill,1port ; 26cm
Includes bibliographies and index
ISBN 0-08-025443-8 : £39.50 : CIP rev. B81-05167

531 — Solids. Microstructure. Defects. Mechanics
Mura, Toshio. Micromechanics of defects in solids / Toshio Mura. — The Hague ; London : Nijhoff, 1982. — xii,494p : ill ; 25cm. — (Monographs and textbooks on mechanics of solids and fluids. Mechanics of elastic and inelastic solids ; 3)
Bibliography: p429-480. — Includes index
ISBN 90-247-2560-7 : Unpriced B82-34776

531′.01′51 — Mechanics. Mathematics
Sadler, A. J.. Understanding mechanics. — Oxford : Oxford University Press, Jan.1983. — [352]p
ISBN 0-19-914097-9 (pbk) : £5.00 : CIP entry B82-34104

531′.01′515 — Mechanics. Nonlinear analysis. Applications of digital computer systems
Recent advances in nonlinear computational mechanics. — Swansea (91 West Cross La., West Cross, Swansea) : Pineridge Press, Apr.1982. — [330]p
ISBN 0-906674-19-0 : CIP entry B82-12890

531′.0246 — Mechanics — *For technicians*
Bill, Len. Forces and pressures. — Cheltenham : Stanley Thornes, Sept.1982. — [120]p. — (Background to technology ; 2)
ISBN 0-85950-395-x (pbk) : £3.95 : CIP entry B82-29110

531′.02462 — Mechanics — *For engineering*
Shames, Irving H.. Engineering mechanics / Irving H. Shames. — Englewood Cliffs ; London : Prentice-Hall, c1980. — 2v.(xiv,896,xxvp) : ill ; 25cm
Previous ed.: 1966. — Ill on lining papers. — Includes index
ISBN 0-13-279141-2 : Unpriced
ISBN 0-13-279158-7 (v.2) : £18.70 B82-26455

531′.02462 — Mechanics — *For engineering — Arabic texts*
Meriam, J. L.. [Engineering mechanics. Arabic]. al-Mīkānīkā l-handasiyyah. — Niyāyurk ; Šišastar : Dār Gun Wāyilī wa-Abnā'ihi, 1982
Translation of: Engineering mechanics
al-Muğallad I: al-Istātīkā : tab'ah SI / targamah A.D. aṣ-Ṣāliḥī, A.A.M. Sāyiğ, M. Fawzī Ḥamd, [wa-] Ṣāliḥ al-'Adl. — 401p : ill (some col.) ; 24cm
ISBN 0-471-06312-6 (pbk) : £12.50 B82-23424

531.1 — DYNAMICS, STATICS, PARTICLE MECHANICS

531′.11 — Dynamics. Applications of variational methods
Yourgrau, Wolfgang. Variational principles in dynamics and quantum theory / Wolfgang Yourgrau, Stanley Mandelstam. — 3rd ed. — New York : Dover ; London : Constable, 1979, c1968. — xiii,201p ; 21cm
Previous ed.: London : Pitman, 1960. — Bibliography: p184-186. — Includes index
ISBN 0-486-63773-5 (pbk) : £3.00
Primary classification 530.1′2 B82-27464

531′.11 — Rotation
McGillivray, D.. Rotational dynamics / D. McGillivray. — Coventry : Jones-Sands, 1981. — iii,85p : ill ; 30cm. — (A Jones-Sands educational publication)
ISBN 0-9507424-1-4 (pbk) : Unpriced B82-06585

531′.11′0724 — Motion. Experiments — *For children*
Watson, Philip. Super motion / written by Philip Watson ; step-by-step illustrations by Clive Scruton ; feature illustrations by Elizabeth Falconer. — London : Methuen/Walker Books, 1982. — 46p : col.ill ; 28cm. — (Science club)
Includes index
ISBN 0-416-24260-x : Unpriced : CIP rev. B81-23775

531'.113 — Kinetic theory

Lifshits, E. M.. Physical kinetics / by E.M. Lifshitz and L.P. Pitaevskiĭ ; translated from the Russian by J.B. Sykes and R.N. Franklin. — Oxford : Pergamon, 1981. — xi,452p : ill ; 26cm. — (Course of theoretical physics ; v.10) (Pergamon international library)
Translation of: Fizicheskaya kinetika. — Includes index
ISBN 0-08-020641-7 (cased) : Unpriced : CIP rev.
ISBN 0-08-026480-8 (pbk) : £12.00
B81-31072

531'.1133 — Nonlinear dispersive waves. Asymptotic theory

Jeffrey, Alan. Asymptotic methods in nonlinear wave theory / Alan Jeffrey, Takuji Kawahara. — Boston, [Mass.] ; London : Pitman Advanced Publishing Program, 1982. — x,256p ; 24cm. — (Applicable mathematics series)
Bibliography: p237-251. — Includes index
ISBN 0-273-08509-3 : Unpriced : CIP rev.
B82-03797

531'.1133 — Nonlinear waves

Solitons and nonlinear wave equations. — London : Academic Press, July 1981. — [350]p
ISBN 0-12-219120-x : CIP entry B81-13847

531'.1133 — Random media. Waves. Multiple scattering — *Conference proceedings*

Multiple scattering and waves in random media : proceedings of the U.S. Army workshop held in Blacksburg, Virginia, 24-26 March, 1980 / edited by P.L. Chow, W.E. Kohler, G.C. Papanicolaou. — Amsterdam ; Oxford : North-Holland, c1981. — x,286p : ill ; 23cm
ISBN 0-444-86280-3 : £19.52 B82-06722

531'.1133 — Viscoelastic materials. Waves. Propagation — *Conference proceedings*

Wave propagation in viscoelastic media / F. Mainardi, editor. — Boston, [Mass.] ; London : Pitman, c1982. — 272p : ill ; 24cm. — (Research notes in mathematics ; 52)
Conference papers
ISBN 0-273-08511-5 (pbk) : Unpriced : CIP rev. B81-34156

531'.1137 — Mass transfer

Lykov, A. V.. Heat and mass transfer / A. Luikov ; translated from the Russian by T. Kortneva. — Moscow : Mir, 1980 ; [London] : Distributed by Central Books. — 623p : ill ; 23cm
Translation of: Teplomassoobmen. — Includes index
ISBN 0-7147-1742-8 : £6.95
Primary classification 536'.2 B82-39309

531'.12 — Statics

Sandori, Paul. The logic of machines and structures / Paul Sandori. — New York ; Chichester : Wiley, c1982. — xii,180p : ill,ports ; 27cm
Bibliography: p175. — Includes index
ISBN 0-471-86397-1 (cased) : £23.25
ISBN 0-471-86193-6 (pbk) : £13.50
B82-36680

531'.14 — Gravitation. Classical theories. Mathematics

Ramsey, A. S.. [An Introduction to the theory of Newtonian attraction]. Newtonian attraction / A.B. Ramsey. — Cambridge : Cambridge University Press, 1940, 1981 [printing]. — 184p : ill ; 22cm. — (Cambridge science classics)
ISBN 0-521-09193-4 (pbk) : £6.95 : CIP rev.
B81-38808

531'.14 — Gravitation. General theory of relativity

Stephani, Hans. General relativity : an introduction to the theory of the gravitational field / Hans Stephani ; edited by John Stewart ; translated by Martin Pollock and John Stewart. — Cambridge : Cambridge University Press, 1982. — xiii,298p : ill ; 24cm
Translation of: Allgemeine Relativitätstheorie. — Bibliography: p287-295. — Includes index
ISBN 0-521-24008-5 : £25.00 : CIP rev.
B82-26236

531'.14 — Gravitation. General theory of relativity — *Conference proceedings*

Marcel Grossmann Meeting on General Relativity *(2nd : 1979 : Trieste)*. Proceedings of the second Marcel Grossmann Meeting on General Relativity : organized and held at the International Centre for Theoretical Physics, Trieste 5-11 July, 1979 : held in honour of the hundredth anniversary of the birth of Albert Einstein / sponsored by International Atomic Energy Agency ... [et al.] ; edited by Remo Ruffini. — Amsterdam ; Oxford : North-Holland, 1982. — 2v.(xiv,1268p) : ill ; 25cm
Includes index
ISBN 0-444-86357-5 : Unpriced B82-32394

531'.14 — Gravitation. General theory of relativity. Research

Will, Clifford M.. Theory and experiment in gravitational physics / Clifford M. Will. — Cambridge : Cambridge University Press, 1981. — x,342p : ill,2facsims ; 24cm
Bibliography: p320-337. — Includes index
ISBN 0-521-23237-6 : £37.50 B82-15278

531'.14 — Gravity

Tsuboi, Chuji. Gravity. — London : Allen & Unwin, Oct.1982. — [256]p
ISBN 0-04-551072-5 (cased) : £20.00 : CIP entry
ISBN 0-04-551073-3 (pbk) : £9.95 B82-24703

531'.14 — Matter. Weight in air. Physical constants. Values. Definition

Conventional value of the result of weighing in air / International Organization of Legal Metrology. — Orpington : Published on behalf of the Department of Trade by the Technology Reports Centre, 1979. — 13p ; 30cm. — (International recommendation ; no.33)
French and English text. — Cover title
£2.50 (pbk) B82-20450

531.3 — SOLIDS. DYNAMICS

531'.32 — Vibration

Pippard, A. B.. The physics of vibration. — Cambridge : Cambridge University Press
Vol.2. — Jan.1983. — [208]p
ISBN 0-521-24623-7 : £20.00 : CIP entry
B82-40897

Thomson, William T.. Theory of vibration with applications. — 2nd ed. — London : Allen & Unwin, Mar.1982. — [494]p
Originally published: 1981
ISBN 0-04-620009-6 (pbk) : £5.95 : CIP entry
B82-00892

531'.32 — Vibration. Analysis — *Conference proceedings*

Applied mathematical analysis : vibration theory. — Nantwich (4 Church La., Nantwich, Cheshire, CW5 5RQ) : Shiva, Apr.1982. — [250]p. — (Shiva mathematics series ; 4)
Conference papers
ISBN 0-906812-12-7 (cased) : £12.50 : CIP entry
ISBN 0-906812-11-9 (pbk) : £8.50 B82-12807

531'.322 — Nonlinear oscillations

Hagedorn, Peter. Non-linear oscillations. — Oxford : Clarendon Press, Sept.1982. — [308]p. — (Oxford engineering science series)
Translation of: Nichtlineare Schwingungen
ISBN 0-19-856156-3 (pbk) : £9.95 : CIP entry
B82-21975

Mickens, Ronald E.. An introduction to nonlinear oscillations / Ronald E. Mickens. — Cambridge : Cambridge University Press, 1981. — xiii,224p : ill ; 24cm
Bibliography: p218-220. — Includes index
ISBN 0-521-22208-7 : £30.00 B82-03907

Starzhinskiĭ, V. M.. Applied methods in the theory of nonlinear oscillations / V.M. Starzhinskii ; translated from the Russian by V.I. Kinsin. — Moscow : Mir, 1980 ; [London] : Distributed by Central Books. — 263p : ill ; 23cm
Translation of: Prikladnye metody nelineĭnykh kolebaniĭ. — Includes index
£3.95 B82-11406

531'.3823 — Anisotropic solids. Elasticity

Lekhnitskiĭ, S. G.. Theory of elasticity of an anisotropic body / S.G. Lekhnitskii. — Moscow : Mir ; [London] : Distributed by Central Books, 1981. — 430p : ill ; 21cm
Translation of: Teoriîa uprugosti anizotropnogo tela. — Added t.p. in Russian. — Bibliography: p416-424. — Includes index
ISBN 0-7147-1657-x : £4.95 B82-02702

531'.3823 — Elastic solids. Diffraction

Achenbach, J. D.. Ray methods for waves in elastic solids with applications to scattering by cracks. — London : Pitman, Nov.1982. — [264]p. — (Monographs and studies in mathematics ; 14)
ISBN 0-273-08453-4 : £27.50 : CIP entry
B82-31293

531'.3823 — Nonlinear elasticity. Partial differential equations

Nonlinear analysis and mechanics : Heriot-Watt Symposium / R.J. Knops (editor). — San Francisco ; London : Pitman. — (Research notes in mathematics ; 39)
Vol.4. — c1979. — 212p : ill ; 25cm
Includes bibliographies
ISBN 0-273-08461-5 (pbk) : Unpriced
B82-06589

531.5 — SOLIDS. MASS, GRAVITY, BALLISTICS

531'.5 — Gravitation. Quantum theory — *Conference proceedings*

Quantum gravity 2. — Oxford : Clarendon Press, Sept.1981. — [800]p
Conference papers
ISBN 0-19-851952-4 : £35.00 : CIP entry
B81-25763

Quantum structure of space and time. — Cambridge : Cambridge University Press, Oct.1982. — [436]p
Conference papers
ISBN 0-521-24732-2 : £25.00 : CIP entry
B82-40321

531'.5 — Supergravity

Supergravity '81. — Cambridge : Cambridge University Press, Aug.1982. — [512]p
ISBN 0-521-24738-1 : £24.00 : CIP entry
B82-29350

531.6 — ENERGY

531'.6 — Energy — *For children*

Satchwell, John. Energy at work. — London (17 Hanway House, Hanway Place, W.1) : Walker Books, Apr.1981. — [48]p. — (All about earth)
ISBN 0-416-05660-1 : £3.50 : CIP entry
B81-02100

531'.6'0321 — Energy — *Encyclopaedias*

Counihan, Martin. A dictionary of energy / Martin Counihan. — London : Routledge & Kegan Paul, 1981. — x,157p : ill ; 23cm
Bibliography: p156-157
ISBN 0-7100-0847-3 : £6.95 B82-03313

531.8 — MECHANICS OF SIMPLE MACHINES

531'.8 — Great Britain. Schools. Students, 5-14 years. Curriculum subjects: Wheels — *For teaching*

Slack, Derek. Wheels / Derek Slack and John Little. — Basingstoke : Globe Education, 1982. — 60p : ill,forms ; 30cm. — (Science horizons. Level 2a)
Published for West Sussex County Council
ISBN 0-333-32162-6 (pbk) : Unpriced
B82-38807

532 — FLUIDS. MECHANICS

532 — Fluids. Mechanics

Pai, Shih-I.. Modern fluid mechanics / Shih-I. Pai. — Beijing : Science Press ; New York ; London : Distributed by Van Nostrand Reinhold, 1981. — xx,570p : ill ; 22cm
Includes bibliographies and index
ISBN 0-442-20075-7 : £31.90 B82-07867

532 — Fluids. Mechanics *continuation*

Shames, Irving H.. Mechanics of fluids / Irving H. Shames. — 2nd ed. — New York ; London : McGraw-Hill, c1982. — xxii,692,[62]p : ill ; 25cm
Previous ed.: 1962. — Text on lining papers. — Includes index
ISBN 0-07-056385-3 : £24.50 B82-37749

532'.00246 — Fluids. Mechanics — *For technicians*

Bacon, D. H.. Fluid mechanics for technicians 3/4. — London : Butterworth, Oct.1982. — [128]p
ISBN 0-408-01115-7 (pbk) : £4.95 : CIP entry B82-26702

532'.05 — Two phase systems

Handbook of multiphase systems / editor-in-chief Gad Hetsroni. — Washington ; London : Hemisphere, c1982. — 1463p in various pagings : ill ; 25cm
Includes bibliographies and index
ISBN 0-07-028460-1 : £49.50 B82-17098

532'.05'01515353 — Fluids. Dynamics. Mathematics. Finite element methods — *Serials*

Finite elements in fluids. — Vol.4. — Chichester : Wiley, Oct.1982. — [550]p. — (Wiley series in numerical methods in engineering)
ISBN 0-471-10178-8 : £32.00 : CIP entry B82-23325

532'.05'015194 — Fluids. Dynamics. Mathematics. Numerical methods — *Conference proceedings*

Numerical methods for fluid dynamics. — London : Academic Press, Dec.1982. — [450]p
Conference papers
ISBN 0-12-508360-2 : CIP entry B82-32283

532'.05'0287 — Fluids. Dynamics. Measurement. Techniques

Fluid dynamics / edited by R.J. Emrich. — New York ; London : Academic Press
Part B. — 1981. — xvi,405-877p : ill ; 24cm. — (Methods of experimental physics ; v.18)
Includes index
ISBN 0-12-475956-4 : £34.40 B82-10059

532'.051 — Fluids. Compressible flow

Anderson, John D. (John David). Modern compressible flow : with historical perspective / John D. Anderson, Jr.. — New York ; London : McGraw-Hill, c1982. — xii,466p : ill,ports ; 25cm. — (McGraw-Hill series in mechanical engineering)
Ill on lining papers. — Includes index
ISBN 0-07-001654-2 : £24.95 B82-16374

532'.051'01511 — Fluids. Flow. Mathematics. Numerical methods — *Conference proceedings*

Transonic, shock, and multidimensional flows : advances in scientific computing : proceedings of a symposium conducted by the Mathematics Research Center, the University of Wisconsin-Madison, May 13-15, 1981 / edited by Richard E. Meyer. — New York ; London : Academic Press, 1982. — ix,345p : ill ; 24cm. — (Publication no.47 of the Mathematics Research Center, the University of Wisconsin-Madison)
ISBN 0-12-493280-0 : £14.00 B82-39507

532'.051015'117 — Fluids. Flow. Mathematics. Numerical methods - *Conference proceedings*

Numerical methods in laminar and turbulent flow . — Swansea (91 West Cross Lane, West Cross, Swansea, W. Glam.) : Pineridge, June 1981. — [1200]p
Conference papers
ISBN 0-906674-15-8 : £43.00 : CIP entry B81-10512

532'.051'01515353 — Fluids. Flow. Mathematics. Finite element methods

Taylor, C.. Finite element programming in fluids. — Swansea (91 West Cross La., West Cross, Swansea, W. Glam.) : Pineridge Press, July 1981. — [240]p
ISBN 0-906674-16-6 : £11.50 : CIP entry B81-13465

532'.051028'5 — Fluids. Flow. Mathematics. Numerical methods. Applications of digital computer systems

Computational techniques in transient and turbulent fluid flow. — Swansea (91 West Cross Lane, West Cross, Swansea, West Glam.) : Pineridge, May 1981. — [350]p
ISBN 0-906674-17-4 : £19.00 : CIP entry B81-10514

532'.052 — Two-phase flow

Chisholm, D.. Two-phase flow in pipelines and heat exchangers. — London : Godwin, Nov.1982. — [336]p
ISBN 0-7114-5748-4 : £25.00 : CIP entry B82-27967

532'.0527 — Fluids. Buoyant turbulent jets & plumes

Turbulent buoyant jets and plumes / edited by Wolfgang Rodi. — Oxford : Pergamon, 1982. — viii,184p : ill ; 26cm. — (HMT ; 6)
Bibliography: p176-178. — Includes index
ISBN 0-08-026492-1 : £17.50 : CIP rev. B82-12915

532'.0527 — Fluids. Turbulence

Batchelor, G. K.. The theory of homogeneous turbulence / by G.K. Batchelor. — Cambridge : Cambridge University Press, 1953 (1982 [printing]). — xi,197p : ill ; 22cm. — (Cambridge science classics)
Bibliography: p188-195. — Includes index
ISBN 0-521-04117-1 (pbk) : £6.95 B82-30685

532'.0527 — Fluids. Turbulence — *Conference proceedings*

Transition and turbulence : proceedings of a symposium conducted by the Mathematics Research Center the University of Wisconsin - Madison, October 13-15, 1980 / edited by Richard E. Meyer. — New York ; London : Academic Press, 1981. — ix,245p : ill ; 24cm. — (Publication no.46 of the Mathematics Research Center, the University of Wisconsin-Madison)
Includes bibliographies and index
ISBN 0-12-493240-1 : £10.40 B82-02069

532'.053 — Fluids. Flow. Measurement

Developments in flow measurement / edited by R.W.W. Scott. — London : Applied Science. — (Developments series)
1. — c1982. — x,333p : ill ; 23cm
Includes index
ISBN 0-85334-976-2 : £29.00 : CIP rev. B81-31513

532'.053 — Fluids. Flow. Measurement — *Conference proceedings*

International Conference on Advances in Flow Measurement Techniques *(1981 : University of Warwick)*. Papers presented at the International Conference on Advances in Flow Measurement Techniques : held at Warwick University, Warwick, U.K., September 9-11, 1981 / sponsored and organised by BHRA Fluid Engineering ... in conjunction with CIT Fluid Engineering Unit, U.K. ; [editors H.S. Stephens, Mrs B. Jarvis]. — Cranfield : BHRA Fluid Engineering, c1981. — v,354p : ill ; 30cm
Spine title: Advances in flow measurement techniques
ISBN 0-906085-58-6 (pbk) : Unpriced : CIP rev. B81-24648

532'.053 — Fluids. Flow. Visualisation. Methods — *Conference proceedings*

International Symposium on Flow Visualization *(2nd : 1980 : Bochum)*. Flow visualization II : proceedings of the Second International Symposium on Flow Visualization, September 9-12, 1980, Bochum, West Germany / edited by Wolfgang Merzkirch. — Washington ; London : Hemisphere, c1982. — xii,803p : ill ; 29cm
Includes bibliographies and index
ISBN 0-89116-232-1 : £68-95 B82-25324

532'.0532'0287 — Fluids. Flow. Laser Doppler velocimetry

Durst, F.. Principles and practice of laser-Doppler anemometry / F. Durst, A. Melling and J.H. Whitelaw. — 2nd ed. — London : Academic Press, 1981. — ix,437p : ill ; 28cm
Previous ed.: 1976. — Bibliography: p407-425. — Includes index
ISBN 0-12-225260-8 : £24.80 : CIP rev. B81-09971

532'.0595 — Fluids. Cavitation

Hammitt, Frederick G.. Cavitation and multiphase flow phenomena / Frederick G. Hammitt. — New York ; London : McGraw-Hill, c1980. — xvii,423p : ill ; 24cm
Includes index
ISBN 0-07-025907-0 : £31.25 : CIP rev. B78-36058

532.2 — HYDROSTATICS

532'.2 — Hydrostatics

Drake, Stillman. Cause, experiment and science : a Galilean dialogue incorporating a new English translation of Galileo's 'Bodies that stay atop water, or move in it' / Stillman Drake. — Chicago ; London : University of Chicago Press, 1981. — xxix,237p : ill ; 22cm
Includes index
ISBN 0-226-16228-1 : £14.00 B82-13669

532.6 — SURFACE PHENOMENA OF LIQUIDS

532'.6 — Liquids. Bubbles. Structure & properties — *Conference proceedings*

Mechanics and physics of bubbles in liquids : proceedings IUTAM symposium, held in Pasadena, California, 15-19 June 1981 / edited by L. van Wijngaarden. — The Hague ; London : Nijhoff, 1982. — 383p : ill ; 25cm
'Reprinted from Applied scientific research, vol.38 (1982)'
ISBN 90-247-2625-5 : Unpriced B82-25212

533.1 — GASES. STATICS AND OTHER PHENOMENA

533'.13 — Gases. Diffusion

Dense gas dispersion. — Oxford : Elsevier Scientific, July 1982. — [250]p. — (Chemical engineering monographs ; 16)
ISBN 0-444-42095-9 : CIP entry B82-20634

533.2 — GASES. DYNAMICS

533'.28 — Gases. Compressible flow. Analysis. Numerical methods

Schreier, Stefan. Compressible flow / Stefan Schreier. — New York ; Chichester : Wiley, c1982. — vii,577p : ill ; 24cm
Includes index
ISBN 0-471-05691-x : £44.50 B82-13965

533.6 — AEROMECHANICS

533'.62 — Aerodynamics

Allen, John E. (John Elliston). Aerodynamics : the science of air in motion / John E. Allen. — [2nd ed.]. — New York : McGraw-Hill ; St Albans : Granada, 1982. — 205p : ill ; 25cm
Previous ed.: published as Aerodynamics, a space age survey. London : Hutchinson, 1963. — Includes index
ISBN 0-07-001074-9 : £18.95 B82-31691

Allen, John E. (John Elliston). Aerodynamics : the science of air in motion / John E. Allen. — 2nd ed. — London : Granada, 1982. — viii,205p : ill ; 25cm
Previous ed.: London : Hutchinson, 1963. — Includes index
ISBN 0-246-11300-6 : Unpriced : CIP rev. B81-33983

533'.62'02854 — Aerodynamics. Applications of computer systems — *Conference proceedings*

Numerical methods in aeronautical fluid dynamics. — London : Academic Press, June 1982. — [550]p. — (IMA conference series)
Conference papers
ISBN 0-12-592520-4 : CIP entry B82-10423

533′.6273′0287 — Subsonic wind tunnels. Air. Turbulence & laminar flow. Measurement. Applications of hot-wire anemometry

Perry, A. E. (Anthony Edward). Hot-wire anemometry / A.E. Perry. — Oxford : Clarendon, 1982. — xix,184p : ill ; 25cm. — (Oxford science publications)
Bibliography: p177-180. — Includes index
ISBN 0-19-856327-2 : £20.00 : CIP rev.
B81-36231

533.7 — KINETIC THEORY OF GASES

533′.7 — Gases. Kinetic theory

Jeans, *Sir* James. An introduction to the kinetic theory of gases. — Cambridge : Cambridge University Press, Oct.1982. — [320]p. — (Cambridge science classics)
Originally published: 1940
ISBN 0-521-09232-9 (pbk) : £8.95 : CIP entry
B82-29367

Klimontovich, Iu L.. Kinetic theory of nonideal gases and nonideal plasmas. — Oxford : Pergamon, July 1982. — [327]p. — (International series in natural philosophy ; v.105)
Translation of: Kineticheskaia teoriia neideal′nogo gaze i neideal′noĭ plazmi
ISBN 0-08-021671-4 : £17.50 : CIP entry
B82-18458

534 — SOUND AND RELATED VIBRATIONS

534 — Acoustics

Wicks, Keith. Sound and recording / [author Keith Wicks] ; [editor John Paton]. — Harlow : Longman, 1982. — 61p : ill(some col.),2ports ; 25cm. — (Understanding science)
Includes index
ISBN 0-582-39169-5 : £4.95 : CIP rev.
B82-06041

534 — Sound

Berg, Richard E.. The physics of sound / Richard E. Berg, David G. Stork. — Englewood Cliffs ; London : Prentice-Hall, c1982. — xiv,370p : ill,music ; 25cm
Includes bibliographies and index
ISBN 0-13-674283-1 : £17.20 B82-28161

Dowling, A. P.. Sound and sources of sound. — Chichester : Ellis Horwood, Nov.1982. — [258]p
ISBN 0-85312-400-0 : £22.50 : CIP entry
B82-30311

534 — Sound — *For children*

Sowry, Jo. Looking at sound / Jo Sowry. — London : Batsford Academic and Educational, 1982. — 48p : ill ; 23cm. — (Looking at science)
Bibliography: p47. — Includes index
ISBN 0-7134-3988-2 : £3.95 B82-22175

534 — Sound waves

Fundamentals of acoustics / Lawrence E. Kinsler ... [et al.]. — 3rd ed. — New York ; Chichester : Wiley, c1982. — xvi,480p : ill ; 25cm
Previous ed.: 1962. — Includes index
ISBN 0-471-02933-5 : £22.00 B82-16540

534.5′5 — Ultrasonic waves

Ultrasonics / edited by Peter D. Edmonds. — New York ; London : Academic Press, 1981. — xx,619p : ill ; 24cm. — (Methods of experimental physics ; v.19)
Includes index
ISBN 0-12-475961-0 : Unpriced B82-02573

534.5′5 — Ultrasonic waves — *Conference proceedings*

Ultrasonics International 81 *(Conference : Brighton)*. Ultrasonics International 81 : Brighton, UK 30 June-2 July 1981 : conference proceedings / conference organizer Z. Novak ; deputy conference organizer S.L. Bailey ; advisory panel E.E. Aldridge ... [et al.]. — Guildford : IPC Science and Technology Press, c1981. — xiii,473p : ill ; 24cm
Includes index
ISBN 0-86103-054-0 (pbk) : Unpriced
B82-02985

535 — LIGHT AND PARAPHOTIC PHENOMENA

535 — Light

Schmid, Alfred. A marvel of light. — London : Wildwood House, Sept.1982. — [256]p
Translation of: Traktat über das Licht
ISBN 0-7045-3066-x : £6.95 : CIP entry
B82-20010

535 — Light — *For children*

Jennings, Terry. Light and colour / Terry Jennings ; illustrated by John Barber ... [et al.]. — Oxford : Oxford University Press, 1982. — 32p : ill(chiefly col.) ; 29cm. — (The Young scientist investigates)
ISBN 0-19-918047-4 (cased) : Unpriced
ISBN 0-19-918041-5 (pbk) : £1.50
Also classified at 535.6 B82-29528

Paull, John. Light / by John and Dorothy Paull ; illustrated by David Palmer. — Loughborough : Ladybird, c1982. — 51p : col.ill ; 18cm. — (Ladybird junior science)
Text, ill on lining papers. — Includes index
ISBN 0-7214-0657-2 : £0.50 B82-12211

535 — Optics. Use of lasers

Tarasov, L. V.. Laser age in optics / L.V. Tarasov ; translated from the Russian by V. Kisin. — Moscow : Mir ; [London] : distributed by Central Books, 1981. — 206p : ill(some col.) ; 18cm
Translation of: Optika, rozhdennaia lazerom
ISBN 0-7147-1743-6 : £2.50 B82-38229

535′.0724 — Light. Experiments — *For children*

Watson, Philip. Light fantastic / written by Philip Watson ; step-by-step illustrations by Clive Scruton ; feature illustrations by Ronald Fenton. — London : Methuen/Walker Books, 1982. — 46p : col.ill ; 28cm. — (Science club ; [2])
Includes index
ISBN 0-416-24240-5 : Unpriced : CIP rev.
B82-04848

535′.1′09032 — Light. Theories, *1600-1700*

Sabra, A. I.. Theories of light : from Descartes to Newton / A.I. Sabra. — [New ed.]. — Cambridge : Cambridge University Press, 1981. — 365p : ill ; 24cm
Previous ed.: London : Oldbourne, 1967. — Bibliography: p343-355. — Includes index
ISBN 0-521-24094-8 (cased) : £20.00
ISBN 0-521-28436-8 (pbk) : £6.95 B82-21362

535′.22 — Photometry

Moon, Parry. The photic field / Parry Moon and Domina Eberle Spencer. — Cambridge, Mass. ; London : MIT, c1981. — x,257p : ill,1port ; 24cm
Includes index
ISBN 0-262-13166-8 : £17.50 B82-03756

535′.4 — Diffraction gratings

Hutley, M. C.. Diffraction gratings / M.C. Hutley. — London : Academic Press, 1982. — ix,330p : ill ; 24cm. — (Techniques of physics, ISSN 0308-5392 ; 6)
Bibliography: p319-324. — Includes index
ISBN 0-12-362980-2 : £24.00 : CIP rev.
B82-00315

535′.4 — Light. Scattering

Hulst, H. C. van de. Light scattering : by small particles / by H.C. van de Hulst. — New York : Dover ; London : Constable, 1981. — 470p : ill ; 22cm
Originally published: New York : Wiley, 1957. — Includes bibliographies and index
ISBN 0-486-64228-3 (pbk) : £5.60 B82-29992

535′.4 — Light. Scattering. Applications

Hulst, Henk C. van de. Multiple light scattering : tables, formulas and applications / H.C. van de Hulst. — New York ; London : Academic Press, 1980. — 2v.(xi,739p) : ill ; 24cm
Includes bibliographies and index
ISBN 0-12-710701-0 : Unpriced
ISBN 0-12-710702-9 (v.2) : £26.20 B82-40696

535′.4 — Volume gratings

Solymar, L.. Volume holography and volume gratings / L. Solymar and D.J. Cooke. — London : Academic Press, 1981. — x,466p : ill ; 24cm
Includes index
ISBN 0-12-654580-4 : £39.60 : CIP rev.
B81-15806

535.5′8 — Lasers. Theories

Svelto, Orazio. Principles of lasers / Orazio Svelto ; translated from Italian and edited by David C. Hanna. — 2nd ed. — New York ; London : Plenum, c1982. — xv,375p : ill ; 24cm
Previous ed.: London : Heyden, 1976. — Includes index
ISBN 0-306-40862-7 : Unpriced B82-30272

535.6 — Colour

Colour / [editor, Helen Varley]. — London : Mitchell Beazley, 1980. — 256p : col.ill ; 32cm
Bibliography: p251-254. — Includes index
ISBN 0-86134-024-8 : £9.95 B82-08378

535.6 — Colour — *For children*

Jennings, Terry. Light and colour / Terry Jennings ; illustrated by John Barber ... [et al.]. — Oxford : Oxford University Press, 1982. — 32p : ill(chiefly col.) ; 29cm. — (The Young scientist investigates)
ISBN 0-19-918047-4 (cased) : Unpriced
ISBN 0-19-918041-5 (pbk) : £1.50
Primary classification 535 B82-29528

Youngs, Betty. Pink pigs in mud. — London : Bodley Head, Oct.1982. — [32]p
ISBN 0-370-30344-x : £4.50 : CIP entry
B82-24847

535.6 — Colour — *For schools*

Richards, Roy. Colour / [authors Roy Richards, Doug Kincaid]. — [London] : Macdonald Educational, c1981. — 48pupils′ cards : col.ill ; 21x30cm + Teachers′ guide(28p : ill ; 21x30cm). — (Learning through science)
Pupils′ cards in 2 indentical sets of 24
ISBN 0-356-07550-8 : Unpriced B82-04261

535.6 — Colours — *For children*

Curry, Peter. Peter Curry′s colours. — Kingswood : World′s Work, c1981. — [32]p : col.ill ; 18x20cm. — (A World′s Work children′s book)
ISBN 0-437-32941-0 : £2.95 B82-05331

535.6′022′2 — Colours — *Illustrations* — *For children*

Colours / [illustrated by James Hodgson]. — London : Aladdin, [1981]. — [12]p : chiefly col.ill ; 21cm. — (All a-board story books)
Cover title
ISBN 0-85166-915-8 : £1.99 B82-04361

Colours / illustrated by Pat Tourret ; [editor Janine Amos]. — Bristol : Purnell, 1982. — [26]p : col.ill ; 27cm. — (My first big books) (A First learning book)
ISBN 0-361-05382-7 : £1.99 B82-34765

Colours I see. — Paulton : Purnell, 1982. — [16]p : chiefly col.ill ; 16cm. — (A First learning book)
ISBN 0-361-05370-3 (unbound) : £0.50
B82-33946

Henderson, John, *19---*. Colour book one / by John Henderson and Glynis Murray. — London : Macmillan Childrens, 1981. — [14]p : chiefly col.ill ; 22cm. — (Picture board books)
Cover title
ISBN 0-333-32364-5 : £0.99 B82-06980

Svensson, Borje. Colours / [designed and illustrated by Borje Svensson] ; [paper engineering by James Diaz. — [London] : Collins, 1982, c1981. — 1box : col.ill ; 60mmx60mmx60mm. — (A Collins block book)
1 folded sheet 57mmx108cm (concertina folded) attached in box containing diorama
ISBN 0-00-138382-5 : £1.25 B82-36182

535.6′022′2 — Colours — *Illustrations — For children* *continuation*

Wilkes, Angela. The colours book / Angela Wilkes ; illustrated by Colin King ; consultant Betty Root. — London : Usborne, 1979. — [32]p : chiefly col.ill ; 21cm. — (An Usborne first book)
ISBN 0-86020-362-x (pbk) : £0.65 B82-02240

Youldon, Gillian. Colours / by Gillian Youldon. — London : Watts, 1979. — [26]p : col.ill ; 20cm. — (Picture play!)
ISBN 0-85166-757-0 (cased) : £1.99
ISBN 0-85166-899-2 (pbk) : £0.99 B82-40815

535.8′4 — Absorption spectra. Deconvolution

Blass, William E.. Deconvolution of absorption spectra / William E. Blass, George W. Halsey. — New York ; London : Academic Press, 1981. — ix,158p : ill ; 24cm
Bibliography: p155-156. — Includes index
ISBN 0-12-104650-8 : £15.20 B82-18682

535.8′4 — Atomic absorption spectroscopy

Ebdon, L.. An introduction to atomic absorption spectroscopy. — London : Heyden, Mar.1982. — [176]p
ISBN 0-85501-714-7 (pbk) : £8.10 : CIP entry B82-02639

535.8′4 — Atomic spectroscopy — *Conference proceedings*

Colloquium Spectroscopicum Internationale *(21st : 1979 : Cambridge)*. Keynote lectures / XXI Colloquium Spectroscopicum Internationale, 8th International Conference on Atomic Spectroscopy, Cambridge, July 1-6, 1979. — London : Heyden, c1979. — x,275p : ill ; 25cm
ISBN 0-85501-487-3 : Unpriced B82-10090

535.8′4 — Fluorescence spectroscopy

Standards in fluorescence spectrometry. — London : Chapman and Hall, Nov.1981. — [160]p. — (Techniques in visible and ultraviolet spectrometry ; v.2)
ISBN 0-412-22500-x : £10.00 : CIP entry B81-30384

535.8′4 — Fluorescent spectroscopy

Modern fluorescence spectroscopy / edited by E.L. Wehry. — New York ; London : Plenum Press
3. — c1981. — xx,354p : ill ; 24cm. — (Modern analytical chemistry)
Includes index
ISBN 0-306-40690-x : Unpriced B82-01883

Modern fluorescence spectroscopy / edited by E. L. Wehry. — New York ; London : Plenum
Vol.4. — c1981. — xvi,282p : ill ; 24cm. — (Modern analytical chemistry)
Includes index
ISBN 0-306-40691-8 : Unpriced B82-01884

535.8′4 — High resolution spectroscopy

Hollas, J. Michael. High resolution spectroscopy / J. Michael Hollas. — London : Butterworth, 1982. — xv,638p : ill ; 26cm
Includes bibliographies and index
ISBN 0-408-10605-0 : £45.00 : CIP rev. B81-28819

535.8′4 — High resolution spectroscopy — *Conference proceedings*

High resolution spectroscopy. — London : Faraday Division, Royal Society of Chemistry, 1981. — 373p : ill ; 26cm. — (Faraday discussions of the Chemical Society, ISSN 0301-7249 ; no.71 (1981))
Conference papers. — Includes index
ISBN 0-85186-718-9 (pbk) : Unpriced B82-15998

535.8′4 — Inductively-coupled plasma atomic emission spectroscopy — *Conference proceedings*

Developments in atomic plasma spectrochemical analysis. — London : Heyden, Dec.1981. — [750]p
Conference papers
ISBN 0-85501-677-9 : £36.00 : CIP entry B82-00170

535.8′4 — Laser spectroscopy — *Serials*

Advances in laser spectroscopy. — Vol.1-. — London : Heyden, 1982-. — v. : ill ; 24cm
Annual
£20.00 B82-32165

535.8′42 — Near infrared spectroscopy. Spectra — *Illustrations*

The **Atlas** of near infrared spectra. — Philadelphia : Sadtler ; London : Heyden, c1981. — 1000p : all ill ; 29cm
Includes index
ISBN 0-85501-440-7 : Unpriced B82-08324

535.8′42 — Vibration spectroscopy — *Conference proceedings*

International Conference on Vibrations at Surfaces *(2nd : 1980 : Namur)*. Vibrations at surfaces / [proceedings of the second International Conference on Vibrations at Surfaces, held September 10-12, 1980, at the Facultés Notre-Dame de la Paix, Namur, Belgium] ; edited by R. Caudano, J.-M. Gilles and A.A. Lucas. — New York ; London : Plenum, c1982. — xi,585p : ill ; 26cm
Includes index
ISBN 0-306-40824-4 : Unpriced B82-23740

535.8′42 — Vibration spectroscopy — *Serials*

Vibrational spectra and structure. — Vol.11. — Oxford : Elsevier Scientific, Aug.1982. — [378]p
ISBN 0-444-42103-3 : CIP entry B82-20637

535.8′42′05 — Infrared spectroscopy — *Serials*

Advances in infrared and Raman spectroscopy. — Vol.9. — London : Heyden, May 1982. — [385]p
ISBN 0-85501-189-0 : CIP entry
Also classified at 535.8′46′05 B82-11786

535.8′46 — Light. Raman scattering

Surface enhanced Raman scattering / edited by Richard K. Chang and Thomas E. Furtak. — New York ; London : Plenum, c1982. — viii,423p : ill ; 26cm
Includes bibliographies and index
ISBN 0-306-40907-0 : Unpriced B82-28145

535.8′46 — Raman spectroscopy

Vibrational intensities in infrared and raman spectroscopy. — Oxford : Elsevier Scientific, Sept.1982. — [500]p. — (Studies in physical and theoretical chemistry ; 20)
ISBN 0-444-42115-7 : CIP entry B82-25511

535.8′46 — Raman spectroscopy — *Conference proceedings*

International Conference on Raman Spectroscopy *(8th : 1982 : Bordeaux)*. Raman spectroscopy VIII. — Chichester : Wiley, Sept.1982. — [872]p
ISBN 0-471-26241-2 : £100.00 : CIP entry B82-21092

535.8′46′05 — Raman spectroscopy — *Serials*

Advances in infrared and Raman spectroscopy. — Vol.9. — London : Heyden, May 1982. — [385]p
ISBN 0-85501-189-0 : CIP entry
Primary classification 535.8′42′05 B82-11786

535.8′9 — Optical waveguides

Adams, M. J.. An introduction to optical waveguides / M.J. Adams. — Chichester : Wiley, c1981. — xv,401p : ill ; 25cm
Bibliography: p370-396. — Includes index
ISBN 0-471-27969-2 : £21.50 : CIP rev. B81-31363

Owyang, Gilbert H.. Foundations of optical waveguides / Gilbert H. Owyang. — London : Edward Arnold, c1981. — xiv,245p : ill ; 24cm
Includes index
ISBN 0-7131-3451-8 : £25.00 B82-13571

536 — HEAT

536 — Heat — *For children*

Jennings, Terry. Heat / Terry Jennings ; illustrated by John Barber ... [et al.]. — Oxford : Oxford University Press, 1982. — 32p : ill (chiefly col.) ; 29cm. — (The Young scientist investigates)
ISBN 0-19-918048-2 (cased) : Unpriced
ISBN 0-19-918042-3 (pbk) : £1.50 B82-29526

536 — Heat — *For schools*

Chapple, M.. Mechanics and heat / M. Chapple. — 2nd ed. — Plymouth : Macdonald & Evans, 1979. — xiii,318p : ill ; 18cm. — ('A' level physics ; v.1) (The M. & E. handbook series)
Previous ed.: 1974. — Includes index
ISBN 0-7121-0154-3 (pbk) : £2.25
Primary classification 531 B82-12178

Wadsworth, Ted. Heat : an O-Level/CSE physics course for self-instruction and class learning / by Ted Wadsworth ; illustrated by Ted Wadsworth & Carol Foran. — St. Ives, Cambs. : Cambridge Learning, [1981]. — 3v. : ill ; 24cm
Includes indexes
ISBN 0-905946-10-3 (pbk) : Unpriced B82-01781

536′.2 — Heat transfer

Lykov, A. V.. Heat and mass transfer / A. Luikov ; translated from the Russian by T. Kortneva. — Moscow : Mir, 1980 ; [London] : Distributed by Central Books. — 623p : ill ; 23cm
Translation of: Teplomassoobmen. — Includes index
ISBN 0-7147-1742-8 : £6.95
Also classified at 531′.1137 B82-39309

Todd, James P.. Applied heat transfer / James P. Todd, Herbert P. Ellis. — New York ; London : Harper & Row, c1982. — x,546p : ill ; 24cm
Text on lining papers. — Includes index
ISBN 0-06-046635-9 : Unpriced B82-33817

536′.201511 — Heat transfer. Mathematics. Numerical methods - *Conference proceedings*

Numerical methods in thermal problems. — Swansea (91 West Cross La., West Cross, Swansea, W. Glam.) : Pineridge Press, June 1981. — [1400]p
Conference papers
ISBN 0-906674-12-3 : £46.00 : CIP entry B81-10424

536′.2′015194 — Heat transfer. Mathematics. Numerical methods

Hausen, Helmuth. Heat transfer in counterflow, parallel-flow and cross-flow. — London : McGraw-Hill, Dec.1981. — [576]p
Translation of: Warmeubertragung im Gegenstrom, Gleichstrom und Kreuzstrom
ISBN 0-07-027215-8 : CIP entry B81-31531

536′.25 — Two-phase flow. Heat transfer — *Conference proceedings*

Two-phase flows and heat transfer : proceedings of NATO Advanced Study Institute, August 16-27, 1976, Istanbul, Turkey / edited by S. Kakaç, F. Mayinger. — Washington ; London : Hemisphere, c1977. — 3v.(xxvii,1469p) : ill ; 25cm
Vols. 2 and 3 edited by S. Kakaç and T.N. Veziroglu. — Includes index
ISBN 0-89116-049-3 : £82.50
ISBN 0-89116-050-7 (v.2) : Unpriced
ISBN 0-89116-051-5 (v.2) : Unpriced B82-40735

536′.25′0924 — Fluids. Convection. Mathematical models — *Conference proceedings*

Polymodel 4 *(Conference : 1981 : Sunderland Polytechnic)*. Numerical modelling in diffusion convection : proceedings of Polymodel 4, the fourth annual conference of the North East Polytechnics Mathematical Modelling and Computer Simulation Group, held at Sunderland Polytechnic in May 1981 / edited by J. Caldwell and A.O. Moscardini. — London : Pentech, 1982. — 262p : ill ; 25cm
Includes bibliographies
ISBN 0-7273-1404-1 : Unpriced : CIP rev. B82-07822

536′.401 — Phase transitions — *Conference proceedings*

Cargèse Summer Institute on Phase Transitions *(1980)*. Phase transitions : Cargèse 1980 / [proceedings of the 1980 Cargèse Summer Institute on Phase Transitions, held July 16-31, 1980, in Cargèse, Corsica] ; edited by Maurice Lévy and Jean-Claude Le Guillou and Jean Zinn-Justin. — New York ; London : Plenum, c1982. — viii,462p : ill ; 25cm. — (NATO advanced study institutes series. Series B, Physics ; v.72)
Includes index
ISBN 0-306-40825-2 : Unpriced B82-28646

536'.401 — Phase transitions. Mathematics

Sinai, IA. G.. Mathematical problems in the theory of phase transitions. — Oxford : Pergamon, July 1981. — [128]p
ISBN 0-08-026469-7 : £11.00 : CIP entry
B81-14472

536'.401 — Phase transitions. Nonlinear analysis — *Conference proceedings*

Nonlinear phenomena transitions and instabilities / [proceedings of a NATO Advanced Study Institute held at Geilo, Norway, March 29-April 9, 1981] ; edited by T. Riste. — New York ; London : Plenum in co-operation with NATO Scientific Affairs Division, c1982. — xii,481p : ill ; 26cm. — (NATO advanced study institutes series. Series B, Physics ; v.77)
Includes index
ISBN 0-306-40896-1 : Unpriced B82-25805

536'.414 — Solids. High pressure physics — *Conference proceedings*

International Symposium on the Physics of Solids under High Pressure *(1981 : Bad Honnef)*. Physics of solids under high pressure : proceedings of the International Symposium on the Physics of Solids under High Pressure, Bad Honnef, Germany, August 10-14, 1981 / edited by James S. Schilling, Robert N. Shelton. — Amsterdam ; Oxford : North-Holland, c1981. — xv,419p : ill ; 27cm
Includes index
ISBN 0-444-86326-5 : £31.18 B82-11943

536'.443 — Liquids. Boiling

Stralen, Sjoerd van. Boiling phenomena : physicochemical and engineering fundamentals and applications / Sjoerd van Stralen, Robert Cole, with invited contributions. — Washington ; London : Hemisphere, c1979. — 2v.(xiii,943,18p) : ill ; 25cm. — (Series in thermal and fluids engineering)
Includes index
ISBN 0-07-079189-9 : £42.30
ISBN 0-07-067611-9 (v.1) : Unpriced
ISBN 0-07-067612-7 (v. 2) : Unpriced
B82-41015

536'.56 — Cryogenics

Arkharov, A. M.. Theory and design of cryogenic systems / A. Arkharov, I. Marfenina, and Ye. Mikulin ; translated from Russian by Boris V. Kuznetsov. — Moscow : Mir ; [London] : distributed by Central, 1981. — 430p : ill ; 23cm
Translation of: Teoriîa i raschet kriogennykh sistem. — Includes index
ISBN 0-7147-1693-6 : £5.95 B82-29288

536'.7 — Physics. Irreversible processes. Thermodynamics

Yao, Y. L.. Irreversible thermodynamics / Y.L. Yao. — Beijing : Science Press ; New York ; London : Distributed by Van Nostrand Reinhold, 1981. — xiv,343p : ill ; 22cm
Includes index
ISBN 0-442-20074-9 : £25.10 B82-07864

536'.7 — Thermodynamics

Burghardt, M. David. Engineering thermodynamics with applications / M. David Burghardt. — 2nd ed. — New York ; London : Harper & Row, c1982. — xiv,571p : ill ; 24cm. — (Harper & Row series in mechanical engineering)
Previous ed.: 1978. — Text on lining papers. — Bibliography: p501. — Includes index
ISBN 0-06-041042-6 : £15.95 B82-28715

Honig, J. M.. Thermodynamics : principles characterizing physical and chemical processes. — Oxford : Elsevier Scientific, June 1982. — [450]. — (Studies in modern thermodynamics ; 4)
ISBN 0-444-42092-4 : CIP entry B82-18455

Sonntag, Richard E.. Introduction to thermodynamics : classical and statistical / Richard E. Sonntag, Gordon J. Van Wylen. — 2nd ed. — New York ; Chichester : Wiley, c1982. — xiv,810p ; 25cm
Previous ed.: 1971. — Bibliography: p795. — Includes index
ISBN 0-471-03134-8 : Unpriced B82-40522

536'.7'02462 — Thermodynamics — *For engineering*

Rolle, Kurt C.. Introduction to thermodynamics / Kurt C. Rolle. — 2nd ed. — Columbus ; London : Merrill, c1980. — xiii,568p : ill ; 26cm
Previous ed.: 1973. — Bibliography: p555-558. — Includes index
ISBN 0-675-08268-4 : £13.50 B82-28538

537 — ELECTRICITY

537 — Continuous media. Electromechanics

Melcher James R.. Continuum electromechanics / James R. Melcher. — Cambridge, Mass. ; London : MIT, c1981. — xvi,627p : ill ; 32cm
Includes index
ISBN 0-262-13165-x : £26.25 B82-03785

537 — Electricity

Basford, Leslie. Electricity made simple. — London : Heinemann, Feb.1983. — [240]p. — (Made simple books, ISSN 0464-2902)
Originally published: London : W.H. Allen, 1976
ISBN 0-434-98492-2 (pbk) : £2.95 : CIP entry
B82-37655

Kitaĭgorodskiĭ, A. I.. Electrons / A.I. Kitaigorodsky ; translated from the Russian by Nicholas Weinstein. — Moscow : Mir ; [London] : Distributed by Central Books, 1981. — 248p : ill,ports ; 18cm. — (Physics for everyone ; book 3)
Translation of: Elektrony
ISBN 0-7147-1658-8 : £2.25 B82-02697

537 — Electricity & magnetism — *For children*

Paull, John. Magnets and electricity / by John and Dorothy Paull ; illustrated by Peter Robinson ; photographs by Tim Clark. — Loughborough : Ladybird, c1982. — 51p : col.ill ; 18cm. — (Ladybird junior science)
Text, ill on lining papers. — Includes index
ISBN 0-7214-0656-4 : £0.50 B82-12214

537 — Electricity — *For children*

Jennings, Terry. Electricity and magnetism / Terry Jennings ; illustrated by Norma Burgin ... [et al.]. — Oxford : Oxford University Press, 1982. — 32p : ill(chiefly col.) ; 29cm. — (The Young scientist investigates)
ISBN 0-19-918046-6 (cased) : Unpriced
ISBN 0-19-918040-7 (pbk) : £1.50
Also classified at 538 B82-29524

537 — Electromagnetism

Booker, H. G.. Energy in electromagnetism / H.G. Booker. — Stevenage : Peregrinus on behalf of the Institution of Electrical Engineers, c1982. — xiv,360p : ill ; 24cm. — (IEE electromagnetic waves series ; 13)
Includes index
ISBN 0-906048-59-1 : Unpriced : CIP rev.
B81-31807

537 — Electromagnetism — *For schools*

Electromagnetism / Advanced Physics Project for Independent Learning. — London : J. Murray in association with Inner London Education Authority. — (Unit EM)
Bibliography: p102
Student's guide. — c1980. — 104p : ill,1port ; 27x30cm
ISBN 0-7195-3608-1 (pbk) : £2.55 B82-34313

Electromagnetism / Advanced Physics Project for Independent Learning. — London : J. Murray in association with the Inner London Education Authority. — (Unit EM)
Teacher's guide. — 1980. — 21p : ill ; 30cm
Text on inside covers
ISBN 0-7195-3609-x (pbk) : £0.95 B82-34310

537'.09'032 — Physics, *1600-1800* — *Study examples: Electricity*

Heilbron, J. L.. Elements of early modern physics / J.L. Heilbron. — Berkeley ; London : University of California Press, c1982. — xii,301p : ill ; 25cm
Bibliography: p241-283. — Includes index
ISBN 0-520-04554-8 (cased) : £22.50
ISBN 0-520-04555-6 (pbk) : Unpriced
B82-40213

537.2 — ELECTROSTATICS

537'.24 — Dielectrics

Chełkowski, August. Dielectric physics / by August Chełkowski. — Amsterdam ; Oxford : Elsevier Scientific, 1980. — xii,396p : ill ; 25cm. — (Studies in physical and theoretical chemistry ; 9)
Translation of: Fizyka dielektryków. — Includes index
ISBN 0-444-99766-0 : £33.40 : CIP rev.
B80-07772

537'.243 — Liquid dielectrics. Rotational Brownian motion

McConnell, J.. Rotational Brownian motion and dielectric theory / James McConnell. — London : Academic Press, 1980. — xiii,300p : ill ; 24cm
Bibliography: p287-291. — Includes index
ISBN 0-12-481850-1 : £23.40 : CIP rev.
B80-18250

537.5 — ELECTRONICS

537.5 — Electronics — *For schools*

Bolton, W. (William), *1933-*. Electronic systems / W. Bolton. — London : Butterworths, 1980. — 96p : ill ; 25cm. — (Study topics in physics ; bk.8)
Bibliography: p95. — Includes index
ISBN 0-408-10659-x (pbk) : £1.60 : CIP rev.
B80-23381

537.5 — Electronics - *For schools*

Sladdin, M.. Elementary electronics. — London : Hodder & Stoughton, June 1981. — [192]p
ISBN 0-340-24643-x (pbk) : £3.95 : CIP entry
B81-09997

537.5 — Quantum electronics — *Serials*

Progress in quantum electronics. — Vol.6. — Oxford : Pergamon, Oct.1981. — [294]p
ISBN 0-08-028387-x : £31.50 : CIP entry
B81-31102

537.5'2 — Gases. Electric discharges — *Conference proceedings*

International Conference on Gas Discharges and their Applications *(7th : 1982 : Imperial College of Science and Technology)*. Seventh International Conference on Gas Discharges and their Applications, 31 August-3 September 1982 / sponsored by Central Electricity Generating Board ... [et al.] ; organised in association with the Institution of Electrical Engineers ... [et al.]. — London : Peregrinus, c1982. — 536p : ill ; 30cm
ISBN 0-906048-86-9 (pbk) : Unpriced
B82-40496

537.5'34 — Gyrotropic waveguides

Hlawiczka, Paul. Gyrotropic waveguides / Paul Hlawiczka. — London : Academic Press, 1981. — ix,100p : ill ; 24cm
Bibliography: p97. — Includes index
ISBN 0-12-349940-2 : £12.80 : CIP rev.
B81-31338

537.5'352 — Neutron capture gamma ray spectroscopy — *Conference proceedings*

International Symposium on Neutron-Capture Gamma-Ray Spectroscopy and Related Topics *(4th : 1981 : Grenoble)*. Neutron-capture gamma-ray spectroscopy and related topics 1981 : proceedings of the Fourth International Symposium on Neutron-Capture Gamma-Ray Spectroscopy and Related Topics organised by the Institut Laue-Langevin and held at the Institute des Sciences Nucléaires, Grenoble, France, 7-11 September 1981 / edited by Till von Egidy, Friedrich Gönnenwein and Bernd Maier. — Bristol : Institute of Physics, c1982. — xix,728p : ill ; 24cm. — (Conference series / Institute of Physics ; no.62)
Includes bibliographies and index
ISBN 0-85498-153-5 : Unpriced : CIP rev.
B81-39237

537.5′352 — X-ray spectroscopy — *Conference proceedings*

International Conference on X-Ray Processes and Inner-Shell Ionization *(1980 : Stirling).* Inner-shell and X-ray physics of atoms and solids / [proceedings of the International Conference on X-Ray Processes and Inner-Shell Ionization, held August 25-29, 1980, at Stirling, Scotland] ; edited by Derek J. Fabian, Hans Kleinpoppen and Lewis M. Watson. — New York ; London : Plenum, c1981. — xxv,950p : ill ; 26cm. — (Physics of atoms and molecules)
Includes index
ISBN 0-306-40819-8 : Unpriced
Primary classification 539.7′54 B82-14446

537.5′352 — X-ray spectroscopy — *Festschriften*

Advances in X-ray spectroscopy. — Oxford : Pergamon, Sept.1982. — [476]p
ISBN 0-08-025266-4 : £47.50 : CIP entry B82-20749

537.6 — ELECTRODYNAMICS AND THERMOELECTRICITY

537.6 — Electrodynamics

Novozhilov, ÎU. V.. Electrodynamics / Yu. V. Novozhilov and Yu. A. Yappa ; translated from the Russian by V.I. Kisin. — Moscow : Mir, 1981 ; [London] : Distributed by Central Books. — 352p : ill ; 23cm
Translation of: Elecktrodinamika. — Includes index
ISBN 0-7147-1764-9 : £4.95 B82-39310

537.6 — Electrodynamics. Quantum theory

Healy, W. P.. Non-relativistic quantum electrodynamics. — London : Academic Press, Oct.1982. — [250]p
ISBN 0-12-335720-9 : CIP entry B82-24940

537.6′2 — Electricity. Conduction in thin metal films

Tellier, Colette R.. Size effects in thin films. — Oxford : Elsevier Scientific, Aug.1982. — [250] p. — (Thin films science and technology ; 2)
ISBN 0-444-42106-8 : CIP entry B82-20638

537.6′2 — Electron bombardment electrical conductivity

Ehrenberg, W.. Electron bombardment induced conductivity : and its applications / by the late W. Ehrenberg and D.J. Gibbons. — London : Academic Press, 1981. — x,348p : ill ; 24cm
Bibliography: p327-339. — Includes index
ISBN 0-12-233350-0 : £39.80 : CIP rev. B81-08912

537.6′22 — Amorphous semiconductors

Amorphous semiconductor technologies & devices / editor Y. Hamakawa. — Tokyo : OHM ; Amsterdam ; London : North-Holland, 1982. — 380p,[2]p of plates : ill(some col.) ; 27cm. — (Japan annual reviews in electronics, computers & telecommunications)
£65.82 B82-33301

537.6′22 — Chromium-gallium arsenide semiconductors — *Conference proceedings*

Semi-Insulating III-V Materials *(Conference : 1980 : Nottingham).* Semi-Insulating III-V Materials : Nottingham 1980 / edited by G.J. Rees. — Orpington : Shiva, c1980. — xiii,361p : ill,ports ; 24cm
Includes index
ISBN 0-906812-05-4 : £18.00 : CIP rev. B80-21826

537.6′22 — Gallium arsenide semiconductors

GaInAsP alloy semiconductors. — Chichester : Wiley, Dec.1982. — [484]p
ISBN 0-471-10119-2 : £21.50 : CIP entry B82-30813

537.6′22 — Gallium arsenide semiconductors — *Conference proceedings*

Gallium arsenide and related compounds, 1982. — Bristol : Institute of Physics, Feb.1983. — [720]p. — (Conference series / Institute of Physics ; no.63)
Conference papers
ISBN 0-85498-156-x : £35.00 : CIP entry B82-39286

International Symposium on Gallium Arsenide and Related Compounds *(9th : 1981 : Oiso).* Gallium arsenide and related compounds, 1981 : contributed papers from the Ninth International Symposium on Gallium Arsenide and Related Compounds held at Oiso, Japan, 20-23 September 1981 / edited by T. Sugano. — 1981. — Bristol : Institute of Physics, c1982. — xvi,592p : ill,1port ; 24cm. — (Conference series / Institute of Physics ; no.63)
Includes bibliographies and index
ISBN 0-85498-154-3 : Unpriced : CIP rev. B82-01418

537.6′22 — Glassy semiconductors

Borisova, Z. U.. Glassy semiconductors / Z.U. Borisova ; translated from Russian by J. George Adashko. — New York ; London : Plenum, c1981. — ix,505p : ill ; 24cm
Translation of: Khimiia stekloobrazynkh poluprovodnikov. — Includes index
ISBN 0-306-40609-8 : Unpriced B82-17758

537.6′22 — Semiconductors

Handbook on semi-conductors / series editor T.S. Moss. — Amsterdam ; Oxford : North-Holland
Vol.1: Band theory and transport properties / volume editor William Paul. — 1982. — xvii,879p : ill ; 25cm
Includes index
ISBN 0-444-85346-4 : £73.09
ISBN 0-444-85298-0 (set) B82-38129

Handbook on semiconductors / series editor, T.S. Moss. — Amsterdam ; Oxford : North-Holland
Vol.3: Materials, properties and preparation / volume editor, Seymour P. Keller. — 1980. — xiii,925p : ill ; 25cm
Includes bibliographies and index
ISBN 0-444-85274-3 : £69.17 B82-40796

537.6′22 — Semiconductors. Defects & impurities

Jaros, M.. Deep levels in semiconductors / M. Jaros. — Bristol : Hilger, c1982. — xi,302p : ill ; 24cm
Bibliography: p282-295. — Includes index
ISBN 0-85274-516-8 : £24.00 : CIP rev. B82-04790

537.6′22 — Semiconductors. Defects — *Conference proceedings*

International Conference on Defects and Radiation Effects in Semiconductors *(11th : 1980 : Oiso).* Defects and radiation effects in semiconductors, 1980 : invited and contributed papers from the Eleventh International Conference on Defects and Radiation Effects in Semiconductors held in Oiso, Japan, 8-11 September 1980 / edited by R.R. Hasiguti. — Bristol : Institute of Physics, c1981. — xiv,571p : ill ; 25cm. — (Conference series, ISSN 0305-2346 ; no.59)
Includes bibliographies and index
ISBN 0-85498-150-0 : Unpriced : CIP rev. B81-15834

537.6′22 — Semiconductors. Energy bands

T͡Sidilkovskiĭ, I. M.. Band structure of semiconductors / by I.M. Tsidilkovski ; translated by R.S. Wadhwa. — Oxford : Pergamon, 1982. — x,406p : ill ; 24cm. — (International series on the science of the solid state ; v.19)
Translation of: Zonna͡ia struktura poluprovodnikov. — Includes index
ISBN 0-08-021657-9 : £45.00 : CIP rev. B82-12895

537.6′22 — Semiconductors. Grain boundaries — *Conference proceedings*

Grain boundaries in semiconductors : proceedings of the Materials Research Society Annual Meeting, November 1981, Boston Park Plaza Hotel, Boston, Massachusetts, USA / editors H.J. Leamy, G.E. Pike and C.H. Seager. — New York ; Oxford : North-Holland, c1982. — xi,417p : ill ; 24cm. — (Materials Research Society symposia proceedings ; v.5)
Includes index
ISBN 0-444-00697-4 : £34.81 B82-38827

537.6′22 — Semiconductors. Microstructure. Research. Applications of electron microscopy — *Conference proceedings*

Microscopy of semiconducting materials, 1981 : proceedings of the Royal Microscopical Society conference held in St. Catherine's College, Oxford, 6-10 April 1981 / edited by A.G. Cullis and D.C. Joy. — Bristol : Institute of Physics, c1981. — xi,464p : ill ; 24cm. — (Conference series / Institute of Physics, ISSN 0305-2346 ; no.60)
Includes bibliographies and index
ISBN 0-85498-151-9 : Unpriced : CIP rev. B81-28136

537.6′22 — Semiconductors. Molecular beam epitaxy

Molecular beam epitaxy / edited by Brian R. Pamplin. — Oxford : Pergamon, 1980. — c,174p : ill,ports ; 26cm
Includes index
ISBN 0-08-025050-5 : 15.75 : CIP rev. B79-35342

537.6′22 — Semiconductors. Physical properties — *Conference proceedings*

Semi-insulating III-V materials. — Nantwich : Shiva, Nov.1982. — [420]p
Conference papers
ISBN 0-906812-22-4 : £35.00 : CIP entry B82-28763

537.6′22 — Semiconductors. Quantum theory

Ridley, B. K.. Quantum processes in semiconductors / B.K. Ridley. — Oxford : Clarendon, 1982. — ix,286p : ill ; 24cm. — (Oxford science publications)
Includes bibliographies and index
ISBN 0-19-851150-7 : £28.00 : CIP rev. B81-31069

537.6′22 — Semiconductors. Structure & physical properties

Fraser, D. A.. The physics of semiconductor devices. — 3rd ed. — Oxford : Clarendon Press, Aug.1982. — [200]p. — (Oxford physics series ; 16)
Previous ed.: 1979
ISBN 0-19-851859-5 (cased) : £15.00 : CIP entry
ISBN 0-19-851860-9 (pbk) : £6.95 B82-16498

Semiconductors and semimetals / edited by R.K. Willardson, Albert C. Beer. — New York ; London : Academic Press
Vol.16: Defects, (HgCd)Se, (HgCd)Te. — 1981. — ix,266p : ill ; 24cm
Includes bibliographies and index
ISBN 0-12-752116-x : £24.80
Also classified at 530.4′1 B82-13114

537.6′23 — High temperature superconductivity

High-temperature superconductivity / edited by V.L. Ginzburg and D.A. Kirzhnits ; translated from the Russian by K.K. Agyei ; translation edited by Joseph L. Birman. — New York ; London : Consultants Bureau, c1982. — xv,364p : ill ; 24cm
Translation of: Problema vysoko-temperaturnoi sverkhprovodimosti
ISBN 0-306-10970-0 : Unpriced B82-37419

537.6′23 — Superconductors. Josephson effect

Barone, Antonio. Physics and applications of the Josephson effect / Antonio Barone, Gianfranco Paternò. — New York ; Chichester : Wiley, c1982. — xvii,529p : ill ; 24cm
Bibliography: p477-524. — Includes index
ISBN 0-471-01469-9 : £38.50 B82-37205

537.7′092′4 — Nuclear physics. Heisenberg, Werner - *Biographies*

Heisenberg, Werner. Physics and beyond. — London : Allen & Unwin, June 1981. — [264] p. — (World perspectives ; no.23)
Translation of: Der teil und das Ganze. — This translation originally published: New York : Harper & Row, 1971
ISBN 0-04-925020-5 (pbk) : £7.50 : CIP entry B81-09494

538 — MAGNETISM

538 — Magnetism — *For children*
Jennings, Terry. Electricity and magnetism / Terry Jennings ; illustrated by Norma Burgin ... [et al.]. — Oxford : Oxford University Press, 1982. — 32p : ill(chiefly col.) ; 29cm. — (The Young scientist investigates)
ISBN 0-19-918046-6 (cased) : Unpriced
ISBN 0-19-918040-7 (pbk) : £1.50
Primary classification 537 B82-29524

538′.2 — Magnets. Projects — *For children*
Catherall, Ed. Magnets / Ed Catherall. — Hove : Wayland, 1982. — 32p : col.ill ; 24cm. — (Young scientist)
ISBN 0-85340-913-7 : £2.95 B82-18429

538′.2 — Superconducting magnets. Design
Thome, Richard J.. MHD and fusion magnets : field and force design concepts / Richard J. Thome, John M. Tarrh. — New York ; Chichester : Wiley, c1982. — xvii,347p : ill ; 25cm
Includes index
ISBN 0-471-09317-3 : £30.50 B82-35310

538′.362 — Nuclear magnetic resonance
Abragam, A.. Nuclear magnetism : order and disorder / A. Abragam and M. Goldman. — Oxford : Clarendon Press, 1982. — xix,626p : ill ; 24cm. — (The International series of monographs on physics)
Bibliography: p610-616. — Includes index
ISBN 0-19-851294-5 : £45.00 : CIP rev.
B81-31071

538′.362 — Nuclear magnetic resonance spectroscopy
Triplet state ODMR spectroscopy : techniques and applications to biophysical systems / edited by Richard H. Clarke. — New York ; Chichester : Wiley, c1982. — x,566p : ill ; 24cm
Includes index
ISBN 0-471-07988-x : £43.75 B82-28944

538′.362 — Nuclear magnetic resonance spectroscopy — *Serials*
Progress in nuclear magnetic resonance spectroscopy. — Vol.14. — Oxford : Pergamon, July 1982. — [316]p
ISBN 0-08-029698-x : £56.00 : CIP entry
B82-18459

538′.362 — Pulsed nuclear magnetic resonance
Fukushima, Eiichi. Experimental pulse NMR : a nuts and bolts approach / Eiichi Fukushima, Stephen B.W. Roeder. — Reading, Mass. ; London : Addison-Wesley, 1981. — xiii,539p : ill ; 24cm
Bibliography: p513-515. — Includes index
ISBN 0-201-10403-2 : £22.80 B82-37175

538′.362′024574 — Nuclear magnetic resonance — *For biochemistry*
ESR and NMR of paramagnetic species in biological and related systems : proceedings of the NATO Advanced Study Institute held at Acquafredda di Maratea, Italy, June 3-15, 1979 / edited by Ivano Bertini and Russell S. Drago. — Dordrecht ; London : Published in cooperation with the NATO Scientific Affairs Division [by] Reidel, c1980. — xx,434p : ill ; 25cm. — (NATO advanced study institutes series. Series C, Mathematical and physical sciences ; v.52)
Includes index
ISBN 90-277-1063-5 : Unpriced B82-39112

538′.362′05 — Nuclear magnetic resonance spectroscopy — *Serials*
Nuclear magnetic resonance. — Vol.11. — London : Royal Society of Chemistry, June 1981. — [360]p. — (Specialist periodical report / Royal Society of Chemistry)
ISBN 0-85186-342-6 : CIP entry
ISSN 0305-9804 B82-12016

538′.364 — Electron spin resonance spectroscopy — *Serials*
Electron spin resonance. — Vol.7. — London : Royal Society of Chemistry, Sept.1982. — [430]p. — (Specialist periodical report / Royal Society of Chemistry)
ISBN 0-85186-811-8 : CIP entry
ISSN 0305-9578 B82-18881

538′.45 — Ferrimagnetic materials. Microwaves. Propagation
Sodha, M. S.. Microwave propagation in ferromagnetics / M.S. Sodha and N.C. Srivastava. — New York ; London : Plenum, c1981. — xxiii,403p : ill ; 24cm
Bibliography: p381-394. — Includes index
ISBN 0-306-40716-7 : Unpriced B82-14453

538.7 — GEOMAGNETISM AND RELATED PHENOMENA

538′.7′028 — Rocks. Magnetism. Techniques
Collinson, D. W.. Methods in rock magnetism and palaeomagnetism techniques and instrumentation. — London : Chapman and Hall, Dec.1982. — [500]p
ISBN 0-412-22980-3 : £30.00 : CIP entry
B82-29776

538′.7′09989 — British Antarctic Territory. Graham Land. Magnetic fields
Renner, R. G. B.. Gravity and magnetic surveys in Graham Land / by R.G.B. Renner. — Cambridge : British Antarctic Survey, 1980. — 99p,[11]p of plates(some folded) : ill,maps(some col.) ; 31cm. — (Scientific reports / British Antarctic Survey ; no.77)
Bibliography: p95-99
ISBN 0-85665-018-8 (pbk) : Unpriced
Primary classification 526′.7′09989 B82-05874

538′.767 — Schumann resonance
Bliokh, P. V.. Schumann resonances in the earth-ionosphere cavity / P.V. Bliokh, A.P. Nicholaenko, Yu. F. Fillippov. — English ed. / translated by S. Chomet ; edited by D. Llanwyn Jones. — Stevenage : Peregrinus on behalf of the Institution of Electrical Engineers, 1980. — x,166p : ill,1chart,1map ; 24cm. — (IEE electromagnetic wave series ; 8)
Translation of: Global′nye élektromagnitnye rezonansy v polosti Zemiia-ionosfera. — Includes index
ISBN 0-906048-33-8 : £20.00 : CIP rev.
B80-08737

539 — MODERN PHYSICS

539 — Atoms & molecules — *For children*
Asimov, Isaac. How we found out about atoms / Isaac Asimov. — Harlow : Longman, 1982, c1976. — 53p : ill ; 23cm. — (How we found out about series)
Originally published: New York : Walker, 1976. — Includes index
ISBN 0-582-39156-3 : £2.75 B82-33650

539 — Atoms & molecules. Structure
Kitaĭgorodskiĭ, A. I.. Order and disorder in the world of atoms / A.I. Kitaigorodsky ; translated from the Russian by Nicholas Weinstein. — Moscow : Mir ; [London] : Distributed by Central, 1980. — 164p : ill ; 20cm
Translation of: Por͡iadok i bespor͡iadok v mire atomov
ISBN 0-7147-1552-2 (pbk) : £1.95 B82-21643

Landau, L. D.. Molecules / L.D. Landau, A.I. Kitaigorodsky ; translated from the Russian by Martin Greendlinger. — 2nd ed. — Moscow : Mir, 1980 ; [London] : Distributed by Central Books. — 243p : ill ; 18cm. — (Physics for everyone ; bk.2)
Translation of: Molekuly. — Previous English ed.: 1978
£2.25 B82-35157

539 — Atoms & molecules. Structure & properties
Bransden, B. H.. Physics of atoms and molecules. — London : Longman, Aug.1981. — [640]p
ISBN 0-582-44401-2 (pbk) : £13.95 : CIP entry
B81-18161

539 — Modern physics
Anderson, Elmer E.. Introduction to modern physics / Elmer E. Anderson. — Philadelphia ; London : Saunders College Publishing, c1982. — xi,308p : ill(some col.) ; 25cm. — (Saunders golden sunburst series)
Text, ill on lining papers. — Includes index
ISBN 0-03-058512-0 : £20.50 B82-25828

Calder, Nigel. The key to the universe : a report on the new physics / Nigel Calder. — Harmondsworth : Penguin, 1982, c1977. — 199p : ill(some col.),ports ; 26cm
Originally published: London : British Broadcasting Corporation, 1977. — Includes index
ISBN 0-14-005065-5 (pbk) : £3.95 B82-18144

539′.0720421 — London. Richmond upon Thames *(London Borough)*. **Physics. Research organisations: National Physical Laboratory,** *to 1981*
Pyatt, Edward. The National Physical Laboratory : a history. — Bristol : Hilger, Dec.1982. — [1500]p
ISBN 0-85274-387-4 : £20.00 : CIP entry
B82-30734

539.1 — STRUCTURE OF MATTER

539′.1′01 — Matter. Theories
Speirs, John M. S.. A theory of matter & its application / John M.S. Speirs. — Fleet (96 Clarence Rd., Fleet, Hampshire) : KAAP Press, 1979. — 50p ; 30cm
Cover title
Unpriced (spiral) B82-25620

539′.12 — Molecules. Structure
Dmitriev, I. S.. Molecules without chemical bonds : essays on chemical topology / I.S. Dmitriev ; translated from the Russian by Yuri Atanov. — Moscow : Mir ; [London] : Central Books [distributor], 1981. — 155p : ill ; 20cm
Translation of: Molekuly bez khimicheskikh sv͡iazeĭ
ISBN 0-7147-1762-2 (pbk) : £1.95 B82-37237

539′.14 — Atoms. Structure
Newman, James A.. Atomic structures / James A. Newman. — Introductory ed. — Durham (30 St. Monica Grove, Durham) : J.A. Newman, c1981. — ii,42p : ill ; 21cm
Cover title. — Bibliography: p42
ISBN 0-9507732-0-4 (pbk) : £1.50 B82-02319

Speirs, John M. S.. The structure of the atom and Coulomb′s Law / by John M.S. Speirs. — [Fleet] ([96 Clarence Rd., Fleet, Hants.]) : [KAAP], 1981. — 37leaves : ill ; 30cm
Cover title
Unpriced (spiral) B82-10527

Speirs, John M. S.. A theory of matter and its application / John M.S. Speirs. — Fleet (96 Clarence Rd., Fleet, Hants.) : Kaap Press, 1979. — 50leaves ; 30cm
Unpriced (spiral) B82-16791

539′.14 — Atoms. Structure & spectra
Cowan, Robert D.. The theory of atomic structure and spectra / Robert D. Cowan. — Berkeley ; London : University of California Press, c1981. — xviii,731p : ill ; 26cm. — (Los Alamos series in basic and applied sciences)
Bibliography: p702-708. — Includes index
ISBN 0-520-03821-5 : £31.50 B82-13755

539.2 — RADIATION

539.2 — Radiation
Radiation / Peace Force Scotland. — Kirkcaldy (The Lantern House, Olympia Arcade, Kirkcaldy, KY1 1QF) : Peace Force Scotland, [1982]. — [4]p : ill ; 21cm. — (Fact sheet ; 4)
Bibliography: p4
Unpriced (unbound) B82-27591

539.6 — MOLECULAR PHYSICS

539′.6 — Atoms. Collisions with high energy ions — *Conference proceedings*
International Seminar on High-Energy Ion-Atom Collision Processes *(1981 : Debrecen)*.
High-energy ion-atom collisions : proceedings of the International Seminar on High-Energy Ion-Atom Collision Processes, Debrecen, Hungary 17-19 March 1981 : surveys and contributed papers / edited by D. Berényi and G. Hock. — Amsterdam ; Oxford : Elsevier Scientific, 1982. — 274p : ill ; 25cm. — (Nuclear methods monographs ; 2)
Includes bibliographies
ISBN 0-444-99703-2 : £31.58 : CIP rev.
B82-01966

539.6 — Molecules. Collisions — *Conference proceedings*

Atomic and molecular collision theory / [proceedings of a NATO advanced study institute on atomic and molecular collision theory held at Il Palazzone di Cortona, Arezzo, Italy, on September 15-26, 1980] ; edited by Franco A. Gianturco. — New York ; London : Plenum published in cooperation with NATO Scientific Affairs Division, c1982. — viii,505p : ill ; 26cm. — (NATO advanced study institutes series. Series B, Physics)
Includes bibliographies and index
ISBN 0-306-40807-4 : Unpriced
Primary classification 539.7′54 B82-31524

539′.6 — Molecules. Diffusion

Diffusion processes in environmental systems / J. Crank .. [et al.]. — London : Macmillan, 1981. — xi,160p : ill ; 25cm
Includes bibliographies and index
ISBN 0-333-30721-6 : Unpriced B82-08910

539′.6 — Molecules. Dynamics & structure — *Conference proceedings*

Bat-Sheva Seminar *(38th : Weizmann Institute of Science).* Molecular ions, molecular structure and interaction with matter : proceeding of the 38th Bat-Sheva Seminar held at the Weizmann Institute of Science, Rehovot at Ein-Bokek and at the Technion-Israel Institute of Technology, Haifa / edited by Baruch Rosner. — Bristol : Hilger in association with the American Institute of Physics, New York, c1980. — vi,290p : ill,ports ; 25cm. — (Annals of the Israel Physical Society, ISSN 0309-8710 ; v.4)
Includes index
ISBN 0-85274-441-2 : Unpriced : CIP rev.
B81-12791

539′.6 — Molecules. Interactions — *Serials*

Molecular interactions. — Vol.3. — Chichester : Wiley, June 1982. — [656]p
ISBN 0-471-10033-1 : £43.00 : CIP entry
B82-11297

539′.6 — Polyatomic molecules. Vibration spectroscopy & rotation spectroscopy. Spectra

Papoušek, D.. Molecular vibrational-rotational spectra : theory and applications of high resolution infrared, microwave and Raman spectroscopy of polyatomic molecules / by D. Papoušek, M.R. Aliev. — Amsterdam ; Oxford : Elsevier Scientific, 1982. — 323p : ill ; 25cm. — (Studies in physical and theoretical chemistry ; 17)
Includes index
ISBN 0-444-99737-7 : Unpriced : CIP rev.
B81-31832

539.7 — NUCLEAR PHYSICS

539.7 — Atoms

Crowley, J. D.. The atom and associated phenomena : physics based on one inert particle / by J.D. Crowley. — Rev. 2nd ed. — [Deal] (22 Redsull Ave., Deal, Kent) : J.D. Crawley, [1981?]. — 13leaves : ill ; 30cm
Unpriced (unbound) B82-00022

539.7 — Nuclear physics

CERN : 25 years of physics / editor M. Jacob ; with contributions by F. Combley ... [et al.]. — Amsterdam ; Oxford : North-Holland, 1981. — 560p : ill,ports ; 27cm. — (Physics reports reprint book series ; v.4)
Includes index
ISBN 0-444-86146-7 : Unpriced B82-05063

Dyson, N. A.. An introduction to nuclear physics, with applications in medicine and biology / N.A. Dyson. — Chichester : Ellis Horwood, 1981. — 244p : ill ; 24cm. — (Ellis Horwood series in medicine and biology)
Text on lining papers. — Includes bibliographies and index
ISBN 0-85312-265-2 : £19.50 : CIP rev.
ISBN 0-85312-376-4 (student edition)
ISBN 0-470-27277-5 (Halstead Press)
B81-20517

Growth points in nuclear physics. — Oxford : Pergamon
Vol.3. — Dec.1981. — [200]p
ISBN 0-08-026485-9 (cased) : £8.95 : CIP entry
ISBN 0-08-026484-0 (pbk) : £4.45 B81-31374

Klimov, A.. Nuclear physics and nuclear reactors / A. Klimov ; translated from the Russian by O. Rudnitskaya. — Moscow : Mir ; [London] : Distributed by Central, 1975 (1981 printing). — 404p : ill ; 23cm
Translation of: I͡Adernai͡a fizika i i͡adernye reaktory. — Includes index
ISBN 0-7147-1715-0 : £4.95
Also classified at 621.48′3 B82-29285

539.7 — Nuclear physics — *Conference proceedings*

International School of Mathematical Physics *(4th : 1980 : Erice, Sicily).* Rigorous atomic and molecular physics / [proceedings of the Fourth International School of Mathematical Physics, held June 1-15, 1980, in Erice, Sicily, Italy] ; edited by G. Velo and A.S. Wightman. — New York ; London : Plenum, published in cooperation with NATO Scientific Affairs Division, c1981. — viii,495p : ill ; 26cm. — (NATO advanced study institutes series. Series B, Physics ; v.74)
Includes index
ISBN 0-306-40829-5 : Unpriced B82-13927

International School of Physics 'Enrico Fermi' *(79th : 1980 : Varenna).* From nuclei to particles : proceedings of the International School of Physics 'Enrico Fermi', Course LXXIX, Varenna on Lake Como, Villa Monastero, 23rd June-5th July 1980 / edited by A. Molinari. — Amsterdam ; Oxford : North-Holland, 1981. — xii,532p : ill ; 25cm
Added t.p. in Italian. — At head of title: Italian Physical Society
ISBN 0-444-86158-0 : £53.08 B82-28641

Nuclear Physics Workshop *(1981 : Trieste).* Nuclear physics : proceedings of the Nuclear Physics Workshop, I.C.T.P., Trieste, Miramare, Italy, 5-30 October, 1981 / editor C.H. Dasso ; associate editors R.A. Broglia, A. Winther. — Amsterdam ; Oxford : North-Holland, 1982. — xi,781p : ill ; 27cm
Includes index
ISBN 0-444-86401-6 : £47.47 B82-38189

539.7′072 — Nuclear physics. Research, *1930-1980* — *Personal observations*

Mann, Wilfrid Basil. Was there a fifth man? : quintessential recollections / by Wilfrid Basil Mann. — Oxford : Pergamon, 1982. — xiv,170p,[4]p of plates : ill,ports ; 22cm
Includes index
ISBN 0-08-027445-5 : £9.50 : CIP rev.
B81-32601

539.7′072 — Nuclear physics. Research — *Correspondence, diaries, etc.*

Bohr, Niels. Niels Bohr : collected works / general editor L. Rosenfeld. — Amsterdam ; Oxford : North-Holland
Vol.2: Work on atomic physics (1912-1917) / edited by Ulrich Hoyer. — 1981. — xv,647p : ill,facsims ; 26cm
Includes index
ISBN 0-7204-1802-x : £58.39 B82-15176

539.7′072 — Nuclear physics. Research organisations — *Directories*

World nuclear directory : a guide to organizations and research activities in atomic energy. — 6th ed. / consultant editor C.W.J. Wilson. — Harlow : Francis Hodgson, c1981. — 975p ; 25cm
Previous ed.: published as Nuclear research index. 1976. — Includes index
ISBN 0-582-90010-7 : Unpriced : CIP rev.
B81-04302

539.7′072 — Nuclear physics. Research, *to ca 1980*

Keller, Alex. The infancy of atomic physics. — Oxford : Clarendon Press, Jan.1983. — [250]p
ISBN 0-19-853904-5 : £9.95 : CIP entry
B82-33487

539.7′092′2 — Nuclear physicists, *to 1955*

Jungk, Robert. Brighter than a thousand suns : a personal history of the atomic scientists / Robert Jungk ; translated by James Cleugh. — Harmondsworth : Penguin, 1960, c1958 (1982 [printing]). — 329p ; 20cm
Translation of: Heller als tausend Sonnen. — Originally published: London : Gollancz, 1958. — Bibliography: p306-307. — Includes index
ISBN 0-14-020667-1 (pbk) : £1.95 B82-37815

539.7′2 — High energy physics. Field theory & gauge theories

Aitchison, Ian J. R.. An informal introduction to gauge field theories. — Cambridge : Cambridge University Press, Nov.1982. — [168]p
ISBN 0-521-24540-0 : £12.50 : CIP entry
B82-27536

539.7′2 — High energy physics. Gauge theories

Faddeev, L. D.. Gauge fields : introduction to quantum theory / L.D. Faddeev, A.A. Slavnov ; translated from the Russian edition by D.B. Pontecorvo. — Reading, Mass. ; London : Benjamin/Cummings, 1980. — xiii,232p : ill ; 25cm. — (Frontiers in physics ; 50)
Translation of: Vvedenie v kvantovui͡u teorii͡u kali' rovochnykh polei. — Includes index
ISBN 0-8053-9016-2 : £20.80 B82-16879

Konopleva, N. P.. Gauge fields / translated from the second Russian edition and edited by N.M. Queen. — Chur ; London : Harwood Academic, c1981. — 264p : ill ; 24cm
Translation of: Kalibrovochnye poli͡a. — Includes index
ISBN 3-7186-0045-5 : Unpriced B82-24928

Leader, Elliot. An introduction to gauge theories and the 'new physics'. — Cambridge : Cambridge University Press, July 1982. — [512]p
ISBN 0-521-23375-5 (cased) : £35.00 : CIP entry
ISBN 0-521-29937-3 (pbk) : £15.00
B82-27210

Leite Lopes, J.. Gauge field theories : an introduction / by J. Leite Lopes. — Oxford : Pergamon, 1981. — xv,484p : ill ; 24cm
Bibliography: p461-477. — Includes index
ISBN 0-08-026501-4 : £17.00 : CIP rev.
B81-24600

539.7′2 — High energy physics. Gauge theories — *Conference proceedings*

Orbis Scientiae *(Conference : 1981 : University of Miami, Center for Theoretical Studies).* Gauge theories, massive neutrinos, and proton decay / [proceedings of Orbis Scientiae 1981, held by the Center for Theoretical Studies, University of Miami, Coral Gables, Florida, January 19-22, 1981] ; chairman Behram Kursunoglu, editor Arnold Perlmutter. — New York ; London : Plenum, 1981. — ix,392p : ill ; 26cm. — (Studies in natural sciences ; v.18)
Includes index
ISBN 0-306-40821-x : Unpriced
Also classified at 539.7′215 ; 539.7′212
B82-02766

539.7′2′0289 — Radiation. Safety aspects — *Conference proceedings*

Society for Radiological Protection. *International Symposium (3rd : 1982 : Inverness).* Third international symposium : radiological protection — advances in theory and practice : Inverness, Scotland 6th-11th June 1982 : proceedings. — [Didcot] : The Society for Radiological Protection, [1982?]. — 2v. : ill ; 21cm
Papers in English and French. — At head of title: Society for Radiological Protection. — Includes index
ISBN 0-9508123-0-7 (pbk) : Unpriced
B82-39642

539.7′2′05 — High energy physics — *Serials*

Surveys in high energy physics : an international journal. — Vol.1, no.1 (1979)-. — Chur ; London : Harwood Academic, 1979-. — v. ; 23cm
Quarterly. — Description based on: Vol.3, no.1 (1982)
ISSN 0142-2413 = Surveys in high energy physics : Unpriced B82-23595

539.7′21 — Bosons & fermions. Mathematical models — *Conference proceedings*

Interacting Bose-Fermi systems in nuclei / [proceedings of the second specialized seminar on interacting Bose-Fermi systems in nuclei, held June 12-19, 1980, in Erice, Sicily] ; edited by F. Iachello. — New York ; London : Plenum, c1981. — x,406p : ill ; 26cm. — (Ettore Majorana international science series. Physical sciences ; v.10)
Includes index
ISBN 0-306-40733-7 : Unpriced B82-13925

539.7'21 — Elementary particles

Kitaĭgorodskiĭ, A. I.. Photons and nuclei / A.I. Kitaigorodsky ; translated from the Russian by George Yankovsky. — Moscow : Mir ; [London] : Distributed by Central, c1981. — 235p : ill,ports ; 18cm. — (Physics for everyone ; bk.4)
Translation of: Fotony i ïadra
ISBN 0-7147-1716-9 : £2.25 B82-29277

Lee, T. D. (Tsung-Dao). Particle physics and introduction to field theory = Li zi wu li he chang lun jian yin / T.D. Lee. — Beijing : Science Press ; Chur ; London : Harwood Academic, c1981. — xvii,865p : ill ; 24cm. — (Contemporary concepts in physics, ISSN 0272-2488 ; v.1)
Includes bibliographies and index
ISBN 3-7186-0032-3 (cased) : Unpriced
ISBN 3-7186-0033-1 (pbk) : Unpriced
B82-22169

The **Nature** of matter : Wolfson College lectures 1980 / edited by J.H. Mulvey. — Oxford : Clarendon Press, 1981. — xiii,202p : ill,ports ; 25cm
Bibliography: p197-198. — Includes index
ISBN 0-19-851151-5 : £8.95 : CIP rev.
B81-15837

Progress in particle and nuclear physics. — Oxford : Pergamon
Vol.8: Quarks and the nucleus : proceedings of the International School of Nuclear Physics, Erice, 21-30 April 1981 / edited by Sir Denys Wilkinson. — 1982. — viii,446p : ill ; 26cm
Includes bibliographies and index
ISBN 0-08-029103-1 : Unpriced : CIP rev.
B81-38331

Valentin, Luc. Subatomic physics : nuclei and particles / Luc Valentin. — Paris : Hermann ; Amsterdam ; Oxford : North-Holland, c1981. — 2v.(xvi,600p) : ill ; 24cm
Translation of: Physique subatomique. — Includes index
ISBN 0-444-86117-3 : Unpriced B82-06106

539.7'21 — Elementary particles — *Conference proceedings*

International School of Subnuclear Physics *(17th : 1979 : Erice)*. Point-like structures inside and outside hadrons / [proceedings of the Seventeenth International School of Subnuclear Physics, held in Erice, Trapani, Sicily, Italy, July 31-August 11, 1979] ; edited by Antonino Zichichi. — New York ; London : Plenum, c1982. — viii,739p : ill ; 26cm. — (The Subnuclear series ; 17)
Includes index
ISBN 0-306-40568-7 : Unpriced B82-36416

International Summer Institute on Theoretical Physics *(1980 : Bad Honnef)*. Current topics in elementary particle physics / [proceedings of the International Summer Institute on Theoretical Physics held September 1-12 1980 in Bad Honnef, Germany] ; edited by K.H. Mutter and K. Schilling. — New York ; London : Plenum in cooperation with NATO Scientific Affairs Division, c1981. — viii,343p : ill ; 26cm. — (NATO advanced study institutes series. Series B, Physics ; v.70)
Includes index
ISBN 0-306-40801-5 : Unpriced B82-06142

539.7'21 — Elementary particles. Gauge theories

Aitchison, I. J. R.. Gauge theories in particle physics : a practical introduction / Ian J.R. Aitchison, Anthony J.G. Hey. — Bristol : Hilger in association with the University of Sussex Press, c1982. — xvi,341p : ill ; 24cm. — (Graduate student series in physics)
Bibliography: p329-332. — Includes index
ISBN 0-85274-534-6 (pbk) : £14.50 : CIP rev.
B81-31510

539.7'2112 — Atoms. Electrons. Energy levels — *Technical data*

Bashkin, Stanley. Atomic energy-level and Grotrian diagrams / Stanley Bashkin and John O. Stoner, Jr. — Amsterdam ; Oxford : North-Holland
Vol.3: Vanadium I-Chromium XXIV. — 1981. — xvi,549p : ill ; 30cm
Includes bibliographies
ISBN 0-444-86006-1 : £38.96 B82-01642

539.7'2112 — Electron spectroscopy - *Serials*

Electron spectroscopy. — London : Academic Press, Apr.1981
Vol.4. — [500]p
ISBN 0-12-137804-7 : CIP entry B81-06066

539.7'2112 — Electrons. Collisions — *Conference proceedings*

International Conference on the Physics of Electronic and Atomic Collisions *(12th : 1981 : Gatlinburg)*. XII International Conference on the Physics of Electronic and Atomic Collisions : abstracts of contributed papers : Gatlinburg, Tennessee, USA : July 15-21, 1978 / edited by Sheldon Datz. — Amsterdam ; Oxford : North-Holland, [1981]. — 2v.(lv,1138p) : ill ; 22cm
Includes index
ISBN 0-444-86322-2 (pbk) : Unpriced
Primary classification 539.7'54 B82-06599

539.7'212 — Protons. Decay — *Conference proceedings*

Orbis Scientiae *(Conference : 1981 : University of Miami, Center for Theoretical Studies)*. Gauge theories, massive neutrinos, and proton decay / [proceedings of Orbis Scientiae 1981, held by the Center for Theoretical Studies, University of Miami, Coral Gables, Florida, January 19-22, 1981] ; chairman Behram Kursunoglu, editor Arnold Perlmutter. — New York ; London : Plenum, 1981. — ix,392p : ill ; 26cm. — (Studies in natural sciences ; v.18)
Includes index
ISBN 0-306-40821-x : Unpriced
Primary classification 539.7'2 B82-02766

539.7'213 — Neutrons

Neutron sources. — Oxford : Pergamon, Dec.1982. — [370]p. — (Neutron physics and nuclear data in science and technology ; 2)
ISBN 0-08-029351-4 : £32.50 : CIP entry
B82-31286

539.7'213 — Neutrons — *Conference proceedings*

The **Neutron** and its applications, 1982. — Bristol : Institute of Physics, Feb.1983. — [550]p. — (Conference series / Institute of Physics, ISSN 0305-2346 ; 64)
Conference papers
ISBN 0-85498-155-1 : £30.00 : CIP entry
B82-40918

539.7'213 — Pulsed neutrons. Scattering

Windsor, C. G.. Pulsed neutron scattering / C.G. Windsor. — London : Taylor & Francis, 1981. — xi,432p : ill ; 24cm + 1sheet(ill ; 23cm)
Bibliography: px-xi. — Includes index
ISBN 0-85066-195-1 : £25.00 : CIP rev.
B81-20509

539.7'213'0212 — Neutrons. Cross sections — *Tables*

Neutron cross sections. — New York ; London : Academic Press
V.1: Neutron resonance parameters and thermal cross sections / S.F. Mughabghab, M. Divadeenam, N.E. Holden. — 1981
Pt.A: Z=1-60. — 1v. in various pagings : ill ; 24cm
ISBN 0-12-509701-8 : £38.40 B82-30019

539.7'215 — Neutrinos — *Conference proceedings*

Neutrino '80 *(Conference : Erice)*. Neutrino physics and astrophysics / [proceedings of Neutrino '80, and international conference on neutrino physics and astrophysics, held June 23-28, 1980, in Erice, Sicily] ; edited by Ettore Fiorini. — New York ; London : Plenum, c1982. — xi,421p : ill ; 26cm. — (Ettore Majorana international science series. Physical sciences ; v.12)
Includes index
Unpriced B82-22471

Orbis Scientiae *(Conference : 1981 : University of Miami, Center for Theoretical Studies)*. Gauge theories, massive neutrinos, and proton decay / [proceedings of Orbis Scientiae 1981, held by the Center for Theoretical Studies, University of Miami, Coral Gables, Florida, January 19-22, 1981] ; chairman Behram Kursunoglu, editor Arnold Perlmutter. — New York ; London : Plenum, 1981. — ix,392p : ill ; 26cm. — (Studies in natural sciences ; v.18)
Includes index
ISBN 0-306-40821-x : Unpriced
Primary classification 539.7'2 B82-02766

539.7'217 — Surfaces. Polaritons

Surface polaritons : electromagnetic waves at surfaces and interfaces / volume editors V.M. Agranovich, D.L. Mills. — Amsterdam ; Oxford : North-Holland, 1982. — xvi,717p : ill ; 25cm. — (Modern problems in condensed matter sciences ; v.1)
Includes bibliographies and index
ISBN 0-444-86165-3 : £73.88 B82-36634

539.7'222 — Accidental x-rays

Martin, E. B. M.. Adventitious X-rays. — Northwood : Science Reviews, Dec.1981. — [120]p. — (Occupational hygiene monographs, ISSN 0141-7568 ; 7)
ISBN 0-905927-90-7 (pbk) : £5.00 : CIP entry
B81-36995

539.7'222 — Grenz rays

Graham, Daniel. Grenz rays : an illustrated guide to the theory and practical application of soft X-rays / by Daniel Graham and John Thomson. — Oxford : Pergamon, 1980. — x,149p : ill,1port ; 22cm
Includes index
ISBN 0-08-025525-6 : £10.00 B82-39537

539.7'3 — Particle accelerators — *Conference proceedings*

Atomic physics : accelerators / edited by Patrick Richard. — New York ; London : Academic Press, 1980. — xxiv,641p : ill,ports ; 24cm. — (Methods of experimental physics ; v.17)
Includes index
ISBN 0-12-475959-9 : £39.20 B82-39146

539.7'3 — Particle accelerators. Targets. Preparation — *Conference proceedings*

International Nuclear Target Development Society. *World Conference (1979 : Boston, Mass.)*. Preparation of nuclear targets for particle accelerators / [proceedings of the World Conference of the International Nuclear Target Development Society, held October 1-3, 1979, in Boston, Massachusetts] ; edited by Josef Jaklovsky. — New York ; London : Plenum, c1981. — x,289p : ill ; 21cm
Includes index
ISBN 0-306-40731-0 : Unpriced B82-08344

539.7'4 — Atoms. Nuclei. Structure — *Conference proceedings*

Netherlands Physical Society International Summer School on Nuclear Structure *(1980 : Dronten)*. Nuclear structure / [proceedings of the Netherlands Physical Society 1980 International Summer School on Nuclear Structure, held August 12-23, 1980, in Dronten, The Netherlands] ; edited by K. Abrahams, K. Allaart and A.E.L. Dieperink. — New York ; London : Plenum, published in cooperation with NATO Scientific Affairs Division, c1981. — x,432p : ill ; 26cm. — (NATO advanced study institutes series. Series B, Physics ; v.67)
Includes index
ISBN 0-306-40728-0 : Unpriced B82-13926

539.7'5 — Nuclear reactions, *1896-1979*

Transmutation. — London : Heyden, Aug.1981. — [130]p. — (Nobel prize topics in chemistry)
ISBN 0-85501-685-x (cased) : £12.00 : CIP entry
ISBN 0-85501-686-8 (pbk) : 5.50 B81-22594

539.7'5 — Nuclear reactions — *Conference proceedings*

International School of Physics 'Enrico Fermi' *(81st : 1980 : Varenna)*. Theory of fundamental interactions : proceedings of the International School of Physics 'Enrico Fermi', course LXXXI, Varenna on Lake Como, Villa Monastero, 21st July-2nd August 1980 / edited by G. Costa and R.R. Gatto. — Amsterdam ; Oxford : North-Holland, 1982. — vii,299p : ill ; 25cm
At head of title: Italian Physical Society
ISBN 0-444-86156-4 : £30.72 B82-38181

539.7'523 — Atoms. Nuclei. Beta decay

Behrens, Heinrich. Electron radial wave functions and nuclear beta-decay. — Oxford : Oxford University Press, May 1982. — [600]p. — (International series of monographs in physics ; 67)
ISBN 0-19-851297-x : £55.00 : CIP entry
B82-07519

539.7'54 — Atoms. Collisions — *Conference proceedings*

Atomic and molecular collision theory / [proceedings of a NATO advanced study institute on atomic and molecular collision theory held at Il Palazzone di Cortona, Arezzo, Italy, on September 15-26, 1980] ; edited by Franco A. Gianturco. — New York ; London : Plenum published in cooperation with NATO Scientific Affairs Division, c1982. — viii,505p : ill ; 26cm. — (NATO advanced study institutes series. Series B, Physics)
Includes bibliographies and index
ISBN 0-306-40807-4 : Unpriced
Also classified at 539.6 B82-31524

International Conference on the Physics of Electronic and Atomic Collisions *(12th : 1981 : Gatlinburg)*. Physics of electronic and atomic collisions : invited papers of the XII International Conference on the Physics of Electronic and Atomic Collisions, Gatlinburg, Tennessee, 15-21 July, 1981 / edited by Sheldon Datz. — Amsterdam ; Oxford : North-Holland, 1982. — xiii,872p : ill ; 23cm
Includes index
ISBN 0-444-86323-0 : £65.26 B82-21906

International Conference on the Physics of Electronic and Atomic Collisions *(12th : 1981 : Gatlinburg)*. XII International Conference on the Physics of Electronic and Atomic Collisions : abstracts of contributed papers : Gatlinburg, Tennessee, USA : July 15-21, 1978 / edited by Sheldon Datz. — Amsterdam ; Oxford : North-Holland, [1981]. — 2v.(lv,1138p) : ill ; 22cm
Includes index
ISBN 0-444-86322-2 (pbk) : Unpriced
Also classified at 539.7'2112 B82-06599

539.7'54 — Atoms. Nuclei. Interactions

Szymánski, Zdzisław. Fast nuclear rotation. — Oxford : Oxford University Press, Sept.1982. — [200]p. — (Oxford studies in physics)
ISBN 0-19-851463-8 : £20.00 : CIP entry B82-18983

539.7'54 — Continuous spectra — *Conference proceedings*

International Symposium on Continuum Spectra of Heavy Ion Reactions *(1979 : San Antonio)*. Continuum spectra on heavy ion reactions : proceedings of the International Symposium on Continuum Spectra of Heavy Ion Reactions held in San Antonio, Texas, December 3-5, 1979 / edited by T. Tamura, J.B. Natowitz, D.H. Youngblood. — Chur ; London : Harwood Academic, c1980. — xiv,476p : ill ; 23cm. — (Nuclear science research conference series, ISSN 0250-4375 ; v.2)
Includes index
ISBN 3-7186-0028-5 (pbk) : Unpriced B82-11463

539.7'54 — Elementary particles. Weak interactions

Bailin, David. Weak interactions / David Bailin. — 2nd ed. — Bristol : Hilger in association with the University of Sussex Press, 1982, c1977. — ix,457p : ill ; 24cm. — (Graduate student series in physics)
Previous ed.: London : Chatto and Windus for Sussex University Press, 1977. — Includes index
ISBN 0-85274-539-7 (pbk) : £11.95 : CIP rev. B82-10883

539.7'54 — Heavy atoms. Nuclei. Interactions — *Technical data*

Gorbachev, V. M.. Nuclear reactions in heavy elements : a data handbook / V.M. Gorbachev, Y.S. Zamyatnin, A.A. Lbov. — Oxford : Pergamon, 1980. — 462p : ill ; 24cm
ISBN 0-08-023595-6 : £49.00 : CIP rev. B80-00177

539.7'54 — Heavy ions. Collisions

Heavy ion collisions / editor R. Bock. — Amsterdam ; Oxford : North-Holland
Vol.2. — 1980. — 471p : ill ; 25cm
Includes bibliographies and index
ISBN 0-444-85295-6 : £34.79
ISBN 0-444-85353-7 (set) : Unpriced B82-39110

539.7'54 — Heavy ions. Collisions — *Conference proceedings*

Adriatic Europhysics Study Conference on the Dynamics of Heavy-Ion Collisions *(3rd : 1981 : Hvar, Yugoslavia)*. Dynamics of heavy-ion collisions : proceedings of the 3rd Adriatic Europhysics Study Conference on the Dynamics of Heavy-Ion Collisions, Hvar, Croatia, Yugoslavia, May 25-30, 1981 / edited by Nikola Cindro, Renato A. Ricci, Walter Greiner. — Amsterdam ; Oxford : North-Holland, c1981. — xv,382p : ill ; 23cm
ISBN 0-444-86332-x : £31.91 B82-13435

539.7'54 — Heavy ions. Nuclear reactions — *Conference proceedings*

International School of Physics 'Enrico Fermi' *(77th : 1979 : Varenna)*. Nuclear structure and heavy-ion collisions : proceedings of the International School of Physics 'Enrico Fermi', course LXXVII, Varenna on Lake Como, Villa Monastero, 9th-21st July 1979 / edited by R.A. Broglia and R.A. Ricci and C.H. Dasso. — Amsterdam ; Oxford : North-Holland, 1981. — xiii,721p : ill ; 24cm
Added t.p. in Italian. — At head of title: Italian Physical Society
ISBN 0-444-85462-2 : £71.13 B82-15175

539.7'54 — High energy elementary particles. Weak interactions

Bilenky, S. M.. Introduction to the physics of electroweak interactions. — Oxford : Pergamon, Sept.1982. — [250]p
Translated from the Russian
ISBN 0-08-026502-2 : £22.70 : CIP entry B82-19094

539.7'54 — Inner-shell ionisation — *Conference proceedings*

International Conference on X-Ray Processes and Inner-Shell Ionization *(1980 : Stirling)*. Inner-shell and X-ray physics of atoms and solids / [proceedings of the International Conference on X-Ray Processes and Inner-Shell Ionization, held August 25-29, 1980, at Stirling, Scotland] ; edited by Derek J. Fabian, Hans Kleinpoppen and Lewis M. Watson. — New York ; London : Plenum, c1981. — xxv,950p : ill ; 26cm. — (Physics of atoms and molecules)
Includes index
ISBN 0-306-40819-8 : Unpriced
Also classified at 537.5'352 B82-14446

539.7'54 — Inorganic compounds. Particles. Scattering — *Conference proceedings*

Emission and scattering techniques : studies of inorganic molecules, solids, and surfaces : proceedings of the NATO Advanced Study Institute held at Alghero, Sardinia, Italy, September 14-25, 1980 / edited by Peter Day. — Dordrecht ; London : Reidel in cooperation with NATO Scientific Affairs Division, c1981. — viii,390p : ill ; 25cm. — (NATO advanced study institutes series. Series C, Mathematical and physical sciences ; v.73)
Includes index
ISBN 90-277-1317-0 : Unpriced
Primary classification 543'.0858 B82-00472

539.7'54 — Particles. Action at a distance. Relativistic theories

Brown, G. Burniston. Retarded action-at-a-distance : the change of force with motion / by G. Burniston Brown. — Luton : Cortney, 1982. — vi,145p : ill ; 23cm
Includes index
ISBN 0-904378-14-4 : £9.95 B82-32571

539.7'54'05 — Elementary particles. Interactions — *Serials*

Physics in collision. — Vol.1-. — New York ; London : Plenum, 1982-. — v. : ill ; 26cm
Annual
Unpriced B82-32355

539.7'7 — Dosimetry — *Conference proceedings*

Hospital Physicists' Association. *Meeting on Practical Radiation Protection Dosimetry (1980 : London)*. Practical radiation protection dosimetry / proceedings of the Hospital Physicists' Association Meeting on Practical Radiation Protection Dosimetry, London, 6th October, 1980 ; edited by J. Law. — [London] : [The Association], [c1981]. — 48p : ill ; 21cm. — (Conference report series / Hospital Physicists' Association ; 34)
Includes bibliographies
ISBN 0-904181-21-9 (pbk) : Unpriced B82-23222

539.7'7 — Solids. Nuclear tracks. Detection — *Conference proceedings*

Solid state nuclear track detectors : proceedings of the 11th international conference, Bristol, 7-12 September, 1981 under the joint auspices of the Parliamentary Assembly of the Council of Europe and the University of Bristol / edited by P.H. Fowler and V.M. Clapham ; editor-in-chief S.A. Durrani. — Oxford : Pergamon, 1982. — xxxiv,958p : ill ; 26cm
'Supplement no.3 to the journal Nuclear Tracks: methods, instruments and applications'. — Includes bibliographies and index
ISBN 0-08-026509-x : £87.50 : CIP rev. B81-39234

539.7'7 — Thermoluminescence dosimetry — *Conference proceedings*

Applied thermoluminescence dosimetry : lectures of a course held at the Joint Research Centre, Ispra, Italy, 12-16 November 1979 / edited by M. Oberhofer and A. Scharmann. — Bristol : Published for the Commission of the European Communities by Hilger, c1981. — xvii,414p : ill ; 24cm. — (Ispra courses)
Conference papers. — Includes bibliographies and index
ISBN 0-85274-544-3 : £35.00 : CIP rev. B81-12788

540 — CHEMISTRY(INCLUDING CRYSTALLOGRAPHY, MINERALOGY)

540 — Chemical compounds — *Conference proceedings*

International Conference on Transport in Non-stoichiometric Compounds *(1st : 1980 : Mogilany)*. Transport in non-stoichiometric compounds. — Oxford : Elsevier Scientific, Oct.1982. — 2v.([1050]p). — (Materials science monographs)
ISBN 0-444-99679-6 : £85.00 : CIP entry
ISBN 0-444-99681-8 (v.15A) : Unpriced
ISBN 0-444-99680-x (v.15B) : Unpriced B82-25902

540 — Chemistry

Brady, James E.. General chemistry : principles and structure / James E. Brady, Gerard E. Humiston. — 3rd ed. — New York ; Chichester : Wiley, c1982. — xvii,831p,[12]p of plates : ill(some col.),1port ; 27cm
Previous ed.: 1978. — Text on lining paper. — Includes index
ISBN 0-471-07806-9 : £20.70 B82-23513

Buttle, J. W.. Chemistry : a unified approach / J.W. Buttle, D.J. Daniels, P.J. Beckett. — 4th ed. — London : Butterworths, 1981. — 646p : ill,1map,facsims ; 24cm
Previous ed.: 1974. — Bibliography: p633. — Includes index
ISBN 0-408-70938-3 (pbk) : Unpriced : CIP rev. B81-19143

Chemistry 'A' Level : a course leading to the University of London examinations in 'A' Level Chemistry, syllabus B. — Cambridge : National Extension College. — (National Extension College correspondence texts ; course no.S11)
Vol.1
Units 1-10 / by Tony Mercer, W. Bland, J. Wyer. — 1974 (1977 [printing]). — iv,182p : ill ; 30cm
ISBN 0-902404-68-7 (pbk) : Unpriced
ISBN 0-902404-72-5 B82-38198

540 — Chemistry *continuation*

Chemistry 'A' Level : a course leading to the University of London examinations in A-Level Chemistry, syllabus B. — Cambridge : National Extension College. — (National Extension College correspondence texts ; course no.S11)
Vol.2
Units 11-20 / by W. Bland ... [et al.]. — 1974 (1978 [printing]). — 174p : ill ; 30cm
ISBN 0-902404-69-5 (pbk) : Unpriced
ISBN 0-902404-72-5 B82-38201

Chemistry 'A' Level : a course leading to the University of London examinations in 'A' Level Chemistry, syllabus B. — Cambridge : National Extension College. — (National Extension College correspondence texts ; course no.S11)
Vol.3
Units 21-30 / by Will Bland, Edgar Jenkins, John Wyer. — 1976 (1981 [printing]). — iv,166p : ill ; 30cm
Vol.3 lacks subtitle
ISBN 0-902404-72-5 (pbk) : Unpriced
ISBN 0-902404-72-5 B82-38200

Chemistry 'A' Level : a course leading to the University of London examinations in 'A' Level Chemistry, syllabus B. — Cambridge : National Extension College. — (National Extension College correspondence texts ; course no.S11)
Experiments handbook / by Edgar Jenkins. — c1977. — ix,158p : ill ; 30cm
Handbook lacks subtitle
ISBN 0-902404-71-7 (pbk) : Unpriced
ISBN 0-902404-72-5 B82-38199

Clark, John O. E.. Chemistry / John O.E. Clark ; illustrated by Peter Edwards. — London : Hamlyn, 1971 (1982 printing). — 159p : col.ill ; 19cm
Bibliography: p156. — Includes index
ISBN 0-600-35650-7 (cased) : £2.99
ISBN 0-600-00124-5 (pbk) : £1.75 B82-37050

Critchlow, P.. Mastering chemistry / P. Critchlow. — London : Macmillan, 1982. — xii,324p : ill ; 23cm. — (Macmillan master series)
Includes index
ISBN 0-333-31294-5 (cased) : £8.95
ISBN 0-333-30447-0 (pbk) : Unpriced
B82-17107

Holum, John R.. Fundamentals of general, organic, and biological chemistry / John R. Holum. — 2nd ed. — New York ; Chichester : Wiley, c1982. — xv,717p : ill(some col.) ; 27cm
Previous ed.: 1978. — Text on lining papers. — Includes index
ISBN 0-471-06314-2 : £19.20 B82-26495

Peters, Edward I. Introduction to chemical principles / Edward I. Peters. — 3rd ed. — Philadelphia ; London : Saunders College, c1982. — viii,654p : ill(some col.) ; 25cm. — (Saunders golden sunburst series)
Previous ed.: 1978. — Text on lining papers. — Includes index
ISBN 0-03-058432-9 : £18.95 B82-23306

Petrucci, Ralph H.. General chemistry : principles and modern applications / Ralph H. Petrucci. — New York : Macmillan ; London : Collier Macmillan, c1982. — xvii,764p : ill (some col.) ; 27cm
Previous ed.: 1977. — Includes index
ISBN 0-02-395010-2 (cased) : £16.95
ISBN 0-02-977640-6 (international ed)
B82-26389

Seager, Spencer L.. Introductory chemistry : general, organic, biological / Spencer L. Seager, Michael R. Slabaugh. — Glenview ; London : Scott, Foresman, c1979. — 684p : ill(some col.) ; 27cm
Ill on lining papers. — Includes index
ISBN 0-673-15026-7 : £18.50 B82-41000

Siebert, Eleanor Dantzler. Foundations of chemistry / Eleanor Dantzler Siebert. — New York ; London : McGraw-Hill, c1982. — xvii,661p : ill,ports ; 26cm
Text on lining papers. — Includes index
ISBN 0-07-057285-2 : £18.25 B82-27907

Ucko, David A.. Basics for chemistry / David A. Ucko. — New York ; London : Academic Press, c1982. — 636,[68]p : ill,ports ; 25cm
Ill on lining papers. — Includes index
ISBN 0-12-705960-1 : £15.20 B82-30155

540 — Chemistry — *Conference proceedings*

International Union of Pure and Applied Chemistry. *Congress (28th : 1981 : Vancouver)*.
Frontiers of chemistry : plenary and keynote lectures presented at the 28th IUPAC Congress, Vancouver, British Columbia, Canada, 16-22 August 1981 / edited by Keith J. Laidler. — Oxford : Pergamon, 1982. — x,369p : ill ; 28cm
At head of title: International Union of Pure and Applied Chemistry in conjunction with The Chemical Institute of Canada
ISBN 0-08-026220-1 : £42.50 : CIP rev.
B82-02621

540 — Chemistry — *For children*

Paull, John. Simple chemistry / written by John and Dorothy Paull ; illustrations by Peter Robinson ; photographs by Tim Clark. — Loughborough : Ladybird, c1982. — 51p : col.ill ; 18cm. — (Ladybird junior science)
Text, ill on lining papers. — Includes index
ISBN 0-7214-0660-2 : £0.50 B82-12215

540 — Chemistry — *For schools*

Ainley, D.. Chemistry in today's world. — London : Bell & Hyman, Apr.1982. — [416]p
Originally published: London : Mills and Boon, 1980
ISBN 0-7135-2182-1 (pbk) : £4.95 : CIP entry
B82-11090

Charles, David, *1931-*. Chemistry for first examinations / David Charles. — Edinburgh : Holmes McDougall, c1981. — 212p : ill(some col.) ; 28cm. — (Holmes McDougall science series)
Includes index
ISBN 0-7157-1989-0 (pbk) : Unpriced
B82-04520

Clynes, S.. A new chemistry / S. Clynes, D.J.W. Williams, J.S. Clarke. — 4th ed. — London : Hodder and Stoughton, 1981. — 372p : ill,maps,ports ; 25cm. — (The New School series)
Previous ed.: 1975. — Includes index
ISBN 0-340-27577-4 (pbk) : £3.45 B82-01227

Dempsey, Tony. Visual chemistry. — London : Edward Arnold, May 1982. — [224]p
ISBN 0-7131-0641-7 (pbk) : £3.50 : CIP entry
B82-06911

Denial, M. J.. Investigating chemistry. — 2nd ed. / M.J. Denial in conjunction with L. Davies, A.W. Locke, M.E. Reay. — London : Heinemann Educational, 1981. — xii,565p : ill ; 24cm
Previous ed.: 1973. — Includes index
ISBN 0-435-64166-2 (pbk) : £3.95 : CIP rev.
B81-13821

Gilmore, G. N.. A modern approach to comprehensive chemistry / G.N. Gilmore. — 2nd ed. — Cheltenham : Thornes, 1979 (1980 [printing]). — 387p : ill ; 25cm
Previous ed.: 1975. — Includes index
ISBN 0-85950-458-1 (pbk) : Unpriced
B82-00061

Gordon, I.. S.C.E. 'O' grade chemistry : a concise approach / I. Gordon and I. Thornton ; [illustrator Ian Fry]. — Glasgow : Collins, 1981. — 160p : ill ; 22cm
Includes index
ISBN 0-00-327746-1 (pbk) : £1.95 B82-10029

Hill, Graham, *1942-*. Chemistry in context : laboratory manual and study guide / Graham C. Hill, John S. Holman. — Walton-on-Thames : Nelson, 1982. — viii,240p : ill,1port ; 28cm
Includes index
ISBN 0-17-448059-8 (pbk) : Unpriced
B82-29553

Investigating chemistry. — London : Heinemann Educational
Notes for teachers / M.J. Denial in conjunction with L. Davies, A.N. Locke, M.E. Reay. — 1981. — 89p ; 22cm
Previous ed.: 1975
ISBN 0-435-64167-0 (pbk) : £3.75 B82-04274

Latchem, W. E.. Chemistry for you. — London : Hutchinson Education
1. — May 1982. — [160]p
ISBN 0-09-144501-9 (pbk) : £2.95 : CIP entry
B82-07967

Lewis, Michael, *1940-*. Advancing chemistry / Michael Lewis, Guy Waller. — Oxford : Oxford University Press, 1982. — 856p : ill ; 25cm
Includes index
ISBN 0-19-914083-9 : £9.50 : CIP rev.
B82-03097

McDuell, G. R.. Revise chemistry : a complete revision course for O level and CSE / Bob McDuell. — Rev. [ed.]. — London : Letts, 1981, c1979. — vii,200p : ill(some col.) ; 30cm. — (Letts study aids)
Previous ed.: 1979. — Includes index
ISBN 0-85097-387-2 (pbk) : £3.65 B82-19110

Menon, K. B.. Modern chemistry / K.B. Menon. — Kuala Lumpur ; Oxford : Oxford University Press (1979 [printing]). — vi,145p : ill ; 26cm. — (Modern certificate guides)
ISBN 0-19-581080-5 (pbk) : £1.75 B82-33037

Murray, Peter R. S.. Advanced chemistry / Peter Murray. — London : Pan, 1982. — viii,405p : ill ; 20cm. — (Pan study aids)
Includes index
ISBN 0-330-26683-7 (pbk) : £2.95 B82-20434

Slater, Bryan. A foundation course in chemistry / Bryan Slater, Jeff Thompson in conjunction with ... G. Evans, F. Lewis, J. Piper. — Basingstoke : Macmillan Education, 1982. — x,157p : ill ; 25cm
Includes index
ISBN 0-333-25515-1 (pbk) : Unpriced : CIP rev. B81-35799

540 — Chemistry — *For West African students*

Akusoba, E. U.. Certificate notes : O-level chemistry / E.U. Akusoba, G.H. Walkley. — Harlow : Longman, 1982. — 150p : ill ; 22cm. — (Study for success)
ISBN 0-582-65081-x (pbk) : £1.30 B82-22968

540'.1'12 — Alchemy

Jung, C. G.. Psychology and alchemy / C.G. Jung ; translated by R.F.C. Hull. — 2nd ed. — London : Routledge and Kegan Paul, 1968 (1980 [printing]). — xxxiv,571p : ill ; 22cm. — (The Collected works of C.G. Jung ; v.12)
Translation of: Psychologie und Alchemie. 2 revidierte Aufl. — Previous ed.: 1953. — Bibliography: p487-523. — Includes index
ISBN 0-7100-0707-8 (pbk) : £5.95 B82-13864

540'.1'51 — Chemistry. Calculations — *Questions & answers — For schools*

Ramsden, E. N.. Calculations for A-level chemistry / E.N. Ramsden. — Cheltenham : Thornes, 1982. — xiv,258p : ill ; 25cm
Includes index
ISBN 0-85950-309-7 (pbk) : Unpriced : CIP rev. B81-31813

540'.1'5192 — Chemistry. Stochastic processes

Kampen, N. G. van. Stochastic processes in physics and chemistry / N.G. van Kampen. — Amsterdam ; Oxford : North-Holland, 1981. — xiv,419p : ill ; 23cm
Includes index
ISBN 0-444-86200-5 : £38.29
Primary classification 530.1'592 B82-13455

540'.212 — Chemical elements & chemical compounds — *Technical data — For schools*

Stark, J. G.. Chemistry data book. — 3rd ed. — London : Murray, Aug.1982. — [112]p
Previous ed.: 1970
ISBN 0-7195-3951-x (pbk) : £1.60 : CIP entry
B82-15844

540'.246 — Chemistry — *For technicians*

Brockington, J.. Technician chemistry, level 1 / John Brockington, Peter Stamper. — London : Longman, 1981. — 204p : ill ; 22cm. — (Longman technician series. Mathematics and sciences)
Includes index
ISBN 0-582-41593-4 (pbk) : £3.95 : CIP rev.
B81-14942

Chivers, P. J.. Chemistry 3 checkbook / P.J. Chivers. — London : Butterworth Scientific, 1982. — viii,188p : ill ; 20cm. — (Butterworths technical and scientific checkbooks. Level 3)
Includes index
ISBN 0-408-00662-5 (cased) : Unpriced : CIP rev.
ISBN 0-408-00658-7 (pbk) : Unpriced
B82-04029

Hawkins, M. D.. Technician chemistry 1 / M.D. Hawkins. — London : Cassell, 1981. — x,278p : ill ; 22cm. — (Cassell's TEC series)
Includes index
ISBN 0-304-30730-0 (pbk) : Unpriced
B82-06900

Hawkins, M. D.. Technician chemistry 3. — London : Cassell, Sept.1982. — [288]p. — (Cassell's TEC series)
ISBN 0-304-30979-6 (pbk) : £5.95 : CIP entry
B82-29003

540'.24616 — Chemistry — *For nuclear medicine*

Billinghurst, Mervyn W.. Chemistry for nuclear medicine / Mervyn W. Billinghurst, Alan R. Fritzberg. — Chicago ; London : Year Book Medical, c1981. — xi,328p : ill ; 23cm
Includes index
ISBN 0-8151-3295-6 (pbk) : £19.75
B82-11879

540'.3'21 — Chemistry — *Encyclopaedias*

Denney, Ronald C.. Key definitions in chemistry / Ronald C. Denney. — London : Frederick Muller, 1982. — 143p : ill ; 20cm. — (A Language of its own)
ISBN 0-584-10559-2 (pbk) : £3.95 : CIP rev.
B82-04580

Hampel, Clifford A.. Glossary of chemical terms / Clifford A. Hampel and Gessner G. Hawley. — 2nd ed. — New York ; London : Van Nostrand Reinhold, c1982. — ix,306p : ill ; 24cm
Previous ed.: 1976
ISBN 0-442-23871-1 : £16.95 B82-34326

540'.3'21 — Chemistry — *Encyclopaedias* — *For schools*

Scott, W. A. H.. Chemistry / W.A.H. Scott ; adviser A. Brookes. — London : Collins, 1982. — 251p : ill ; 12cm. — (Basic facts) (Collins revision aids)
ISBN 0-00-458887-8 (pbk) : £1.50 B82-33439

540'.7 — Chemistry. Information sources

Bonchev, Danail. Information theoretic indices for characterisation of chemical structures. — Chichester : Wiley, Jan.1983. — [225]p. — (Chemometrics research studies series ; 5)
ISBN 0-471-90087-7 : £20.00 : CIP entry
B82-32427

Skolnik, Herman. The literature matrix of chemistry / Herman Skolnik. — New York ; Chichester : Wiley, c1982. — xi,297p ; 24cm
Includes index
ISBN 0-471-79545-3 : £23.50 B82-35307

Wolman, Yecheskel. Chemical information : a practical guide to utilization. — Chichester : Wiley, Feb.1983. — [250]p
ISBN 0-471-10319-5 : £11.00 : CIP entry
B82-38281

540'.76 — Chemistry — *Questions & answers*

Instructor's manual for Fundamentals of chemistry, fourth edition / Brescia ... [et al.]. — New York ; London : Academic Press, c1980. — 164p : ill ; 23cm
ISBN 0-12-132393-5 (pbk) : £0.60 B82-39143

Selvaratnam, M.. Problem solving in chemistry : M. Selvaratnam and M.J. Frazer. — London : Heinemann Educational, 1982. — ix,229p ; 22cm
Includes index
ISBN 0-435-65257-5 (pbk) : £4.95 : CIP rev.
B81-34498

Ucko, David A.. Instructor's manual for Basics for chemistry / by David A. Ucko. — New York ; London : Academic Press, 1982. — 206p : ill ; 24cm
ISBN 0-12-705962-8 (pbk) : £3.40 B82-30156

540'.76 — Chemistry — *Questions & answers* — *For schools*

Brown, Peter. Questions in 'A' level chemistry. — London : Edward Arnold, Sept.1981. — [96]p
ISBN 0-7131-0578-x (pbk) : CIP entry
B81-22485

Brown, Peter. Solutions in 'A' level chemistry. — London : Edward Arnold, Sept.1981. — [128]p
ISBN 0-7131-0579-8 (pbk) : CIP entry
B81-22513

Burdon, Margery. Solutions to 'O' grade chemistry : papers I & II / Margery Burdon. — Glasgow : Gibson, c1981. — 64p : ill ; 21cm
ISBN 0-7169-3121-4 (pbk) : Unpriced
B82-11030

Green, J. C.. Concise O-level chemistry questions / J.C. Green. — Burton upon Trent : Mercian, 1980. — 120p : ill ; 21cm
With answers. — Text on inside covers
ISBN 0-9506583-2-4 (pbk) : Unpriced
B82-32072

Holderness, A.. Worked examples and problems in Ordinary Level chemistry / by A. Holderness and John Lambert. — 3rd ed. — London : Heinemann Educational, 1982. — 74p ; 22cm
Previous ed.: 1971
ISBN 0-435-64428-9 (pbk) : £1.95 B82-39934

Moran, Michael, *1937-*. Worked examples in 'H' grade chemistry : paper 2 / Michael Moran. — Glasgow : Gibson, c1981. — 56p : ill ; 21cm. — (Prepare to pass)
ISBN 0-7169-3120-6 (pbk) : Unpriced
B82-12383

Stebbens, Derek. Objective tests in O Level chemistry. — London : Heinemann Educational, Aug.1982. — [128]p
ISBN 0-435-64844-6 (pbk) : £2.25 : CIP entry
B82-18573

Windle, Robin. Objective test questions in O-level chemistry / Robin Windle. — Cheltenham : Thornes, 1982. — v,105p : ill ; 23cm
ISBN 0-85950-341-0 (pbk) : Unpriced : CIP rev.
B82-10225

Wood, C. A.. Questions in chemistry for O and H grade / C.A. Wood. — London : Heinemann Educational, 1981. — 99p : ill ; 21cm
ISBN 0-435-64970-1 (pbk) : Unpriced : CIP rev.
B81-28166

540'.92'4 — Chemistry. Curie, Marie — *Biographies* — *For children*

Brandon, Ruth. Marie Curie. — London : Hodder and Stoughton, Sept.1981. — [128]p. — (Twentieth century people)
ISBN 0-340-25951-5 : £4.95 : CIP entry
B81-25669

540'.92'4 — Chemistry. Mendeleev, D. I. — *Biographies*

Aucken, I.. Mendeleev's guardian angel / I. Aucken. — Richmond, Surrey (28 Matthias Court, Church Rd., Richmond, Surrey TW10 6LL) : [I. Aucken], c1982. — 72p ; 23cm
£2.24 (pbk) B82-31483

541 — PHYSICAL AND THEORETICAL CHEMISTRY

541'.042 — Fluids. Chemical properties. Computation by digital computer systems

Štěrbáček, Zdeněk. Calculation of properties using corresponding-state methods / Zdeněk Štěrbáček, Bohuslav Biskup, Petr Tausk. — Amsterdam ; Oxford : Elsevier Scientific, 1979. — 308p : ill ; 25cm. — (Chemical engineering monographs ; v.5)
Translation from the Czech. — Bibliography: p295-303. — Includes index
ISBN 0-444-99807-1 : Unpriced B82-17887

541'.042'1 — Solid state materials. Reactivity — *Conference proceedings*

International Symposium on the Reactivity of Solids *(9th : 1980 : Cracow)*. Reactivity of solids. — Oxford : Elsevier Scientific, Jan.1982. — 2v. ([1500]p.). — (Materials science monographs ; 10)
ISBN 0-444-99707-5 : £100.00 : CIP entry
B81-34564

541'.0421 — Solids. Chemical properties — *Conference proceedings*

European Conference on Solid State Chemistry *(2nd : 1982 : Veldhoven)*. Solid state chemistry 1982. — Oxford : Elsevier Scientific, Jan.1983. — [852]p. — (Studies in organic chemistry ; v.3.)
ISBN 0-444-42147-5 : CIP entry B82-37632

541'.0421 — Solids. Surfaces. Chemical properties

The **Chemical** physics of solid surfaces and heterogeneous catalysis / edited by D.A. King and D.P. Woodruff. — Amsterdam ; Oxford : Elsevier Scientific
Vol.4: Fundamental studies of heterogeneous catalysis. — 1982. — 468p : ill ; 25cm
Includes index
ISBN 0-444-41987-x : £67.80
ISBN 0-444-41971-3
Also classified at 541.3'95 B82-38125

The **chemical** physics of solid surfaces and heterogenous catalysis / edited by D.A. King and D.P. Woodruff. — Amsterdam ; Oxford : Elsevier Scientific
Vol.1: Clean solid surfaces. — 1981. — 372p : ill ; 25cm
Includes index
ISBN 0-444-41924-1 : Unpriced : CIP rev.
Also classified at 541.3'95 B81-12378

541'.042'105 — Solids. Structure & chemical properties — *Serials*

Progress in solid state chemistry. — Vol.13. — Oxford : Pergamon, Sept.1982. — [377]p
ISBN 0-08-029712-9 : £56.00 : CIP entry
B82-21078

541'.0422 — Liquids. Structure & chemical properties

Murrell, J. N.. Properties of liquids and solutions / J.N. Murrell and E.A. Boucher. — Chichester : Wiley, c1982. — x,288p : ill ; 24cm
Bibliography: p280-283. — Includes index
ISBN 0-471-10201-6 (cased) : Unpriced : CIP rev.
ISBN 0-471-10202-4 (pbk) : Unpriced
B82-13255

541.2 — THEORETICAL CHEMISTRY

541.2'2 — Inorganic compounds. Electrons. Properties — *Serials*

Electronic structure and magnetism of inorganic compounds. — Vol.7. — London : Royal Society of Chemistry, June 1982. — [200]p. — (Specialist periodical report / Royal Society of Chemistry)
ISBN 0-85186-301-9 : CIP entry
ISSN 0305-9766 B82-09869

541.2'23 — Enantiomers & racemic isomers. Resolution

Jacques, Jean. Enantiomers, racemates, and resolutions / Jean Jacques, André Collet, Samuel H. Wilen. — New York ; Chichester : Wiley, c1981. — xv,447p : ill ; 24cm
Includes index
ISBN 0-471-08058-6 : £38.75 B82-04543

541.2′23 — Stereochemistry

Stereochemistry / editor Ch. Tamm. — Amsterdam ; Oxford : Elsevier Biomedical, 1982. — 342p : ill ; 25cm. — (New comprehensive biochemistry ; v.3)
Includes index
ISBN 0-444-80389-0 : £29.54 B82-38829

541.2′24 — Chemical bonding

Coulson, C. A.. The shape and structure of molecules. — 2nd ed. — Oxford : Clarendon Press, Apr.1982. — [112]p
Previous ed.: 1973
ISBN 0-19-855517-2 (cased) : £7.95 : CIP entry
ISBN 0-19-855518-0 (pbk) : £3.95 B82-12685

541.2′24 — Free radicals

Scott, P. R.. Odd-electron species : the chemistry of free radicals / P.R. Scott. — Cambridge : Cambridge University Press, 1981. — 120p : ill ; 23cm
Bibliography: p118. — Includes index
ISBN 0-521-28177-6 (pbk) : £2.50 : CIP rev. B81-31279

541.2′24 — Metal compounds containing multiple bonds

Cotton, F. Albert. Multiple bonds between metal atoms / F. Albert Cotton, Richard A. Walton. — New York ; Chichester : Wiley, 1982. — xiv,466p : ill,ports ; 24cm
Includes index
ISBN 0-471-04686-8 : £35.00 B82-26467

541.2′242 — Coordination compounds — *Conference proceedings*

International Conference on Coordination Chemistry *(20th : 1979 : Calcutta)*. Coordination chemistry, 20 : invited lectures presented at the 20th International Conference on Coordination Chemistry, Calcutta, India, 10-14 December 1979 / editor, D. Banerjea. — Oxford : Pergamon, 1980. — ix,275p : ill ; 28cm
At head of title: International Union of Pure and Applied Chemistry (Inorganic Chemistry Division) in conjunction with Indian Chemical Society (Calcutta)
ISBN 0-08-023942-0 : £34.00 : CIP rev. B80-23243

541.2′26 — Intermolecular forces — *Conference proceedings*

Jerusalem Sympsosium on Quantum Chemistry and Biochemistry *(14th : 1981)*. Intermolecular forces : proceedings of the fourteenth Jerusalem Symposium on Quantum Chemistry and Biochemistry held in Jerusalem, Israel, April 13-16, 1981 / edited by Bernard Pullman. — Dordrecht ; London : Reidel, c1981. — ix,567p : ill ; 25cm. — (The Jerusalem symposia on quantum chemistry and biochemistry ; v.14)
Includes index
ISBN 90-277-1326-x : Unpriced B82-00486

541.2′8 — Chemical reactions. Kinetics. Determination. Mass spectrometry — *Conference proceedings*

Current topics in mass spectrometry and chemical kinetics : proceedings of the symposium in honour of Professor Allan Maccoll on the occasion of his retirement from University College London in 1981 / organized and edited by J.H. Beynon and M.L. McGlashan. — London : Heyden, c1982. — xii,153p : ill ; 25cm
ISBN 0-85501-711-2 : £22.00 : CIP rev. B82-02468

541.2′8 — Chemical reactions. Rates. Determination. Nuclear magnetic resonance spectroscopy

Sandström, J.. Dynamic NMR spectroscopy / J. Sandström. — London : Academic Press, 1982. — x,226p : ill ; 24cm
Includes index
ISBN 0-12-618620-0 : £19.20 : CIP rev. B82-00335

541.2′8 — Chemistry. Fourier transform infrared spectroscopy

Fourier transform infrared spectroscopy : reactions to chemical systems / edited by J.R. Ferraro, Louis J. Basile. — New York : London : Academic Press
Vol.3. — 1982. — viii,215p : ill ; 24cm
Vol.3 has subtitle: Techniques using Fourier transform interferometry. — Includes bibliographies and index
ISBN 0-12-254103-0 : £19.20 B82-34859

541.2′8 — Chemistry. Nuclear magnetic resonance spectroscopy — *Serials*

Annual reports in NMR spectroscopy. — 13. — London : Academic Press, Feb.1983. — [440]p
ISBN 0-12-505313-4 : CIP entry
ISSN 0066-4103 B82-36573

541.2′8 — Chemistry. Quantum theory

Hanna, Melvin W.. Quantum mechanics in chemistry / Melvin W. Hanna. — 3rd ed. — Menlo Park, Calif. ; London : Benjamin/Cummings, c1981. — xv,284p : ill ; 24cm. — (Physical chemistry textbook series)
Previous ed.: 1969. — Bibliography: p273-277. — Includes index
ISBN 0-8053-3708-3 (cased) : Unpriced
ISBN 0-8053-3705-9 (pbk) : Unpriced B82-20556

Jørgensen, Poul, *1944-*. Second quantization-based methods in quantum chemistry / Poul Jørgensen, Jack Simons. — New York ; London : Academic Press, 1981. — ix,172p : ill ; 24cm
Includes bibliographies and index
ISBN 0-12-390220-7 : £19.60 B82-21242

Paul, R. (Reginald). Field theoretical methods in chemical physics / R. Paul. — Amsterdam ; Oxford : Elsevier Scientific, 1982. — vii,414p : ill ; 25cm. — (Studies in physical and theoretical chemistry ; 19)
Includes index
ISBN 0-444-42073-8 : £48.94 : CIP rev. B82-11265

Quantum theory of chemical reactions. — Dordrecht ; London : Reidel
1: Collison theory, reaction path, static indices / edited by Raymond Daudel ... [et al.]. — c1980. — vii,248p : ill ; 25cm
Includes index
ISBN 90-277-1047-3 : Unpriced B82-39694

Quantum theory of chemical reactions. — Dordrecht ; London : Reidel
2: Solvent effect, reaction mechanisms, photochemical processes / edited by Raymond Daudel ... [et al.]. — c1981. — vii,325p : ill ; 25cm
Includes index
ISBN 90-277-1182-8 : Unpriced B82-39695

541.2′8 — Chemistry. Quantum theory — *Conference proceedings*

International Symposium on Atomic, Molecular, and Solid-state Theory, Collision Phenomena, and Computational Quantum Chemistry *(1981 : Florida)*. Proceedings of the International Symposium on Atomic, Molecular, and Solid-state Theory, Collision Phenomena and Computational Quantum Chemistry : held at Flagler Beach, Florida, March 8-14, 1981 / editor in chief Per-Olov Löwdin ; editor Yngve Öhru. — New York ; Chichester : Wiley, [1982?]. — xvi,730p : ill,ports ; 23cm. — (Quantum chemistry symposium ; no.15)
At head of title International journal of quantum chemistry
ISBN 0-471-86672-5 (pbk) : Unpriced B82-39918

541.2′8 — Chemistry. Raman spectroscopy

Grasselli, Jeanette G.. Chemical applications of Raman spectroscopy / Jeanette G. Grasselli and Marcia K. Snavely, Bernard J. Bulkin. — New York ; Chichester : Wiley, c1981. — x,198p : ill ; 24cm
Includes index
ISBN 0-471-08541-3 : £22.00 B82-07790

541.2′8 — Inorganic compounds. Spectroscopy — *Serials*

Spectroscopic properties of inorganic and organometallic compounds. — Vol.14. — London : Royal Society of Chemistry, Dec.1981. — [400]p. — (Specialist periodical report / Royal Society of Chemistry)
ISBN 0-85186-123-7 : CIP entry
ISSN 0584-8555
Also classified at 547′.05 B81-32050

541.2′8 — Molecules. Electrons. Quantum theory. Calculations

The **Force** concept in chemistry / edited by B.M. Deb. — New York ; London : Van Nostrand Reinhold, c1981. — xvii,502p : ill ; 24cm
Includes bibliographies and index
ISBN 0-442-26106-3 : £29.75 B82-00752

541.2′8 — Molecules. Excited states

Dynamics of the excited state / edited by K.P. Lawley. — New York ; Chichester : Wiley, 1982. — v,667p : ill ; 24cm. — (Advances in chemical physics ; v.50)
Includes bibliographies and index
ISBN 0-471-10059-5 : £35.90 : CIP rev. B82-15811

Potential energy surfaces and dynamics calculations : for chemical reactions and molecular energy transfer / edited by Donald G. Truhlar. — New York ; London : Plenum, c1981. — xii,866p : ill ; 26cm
Includes index
ISBN 0-306-40755-8 : Unpriced B82-01478

541.2′8 — Molecules. Wave functions. Calculations

Richards, W. G.. Ab initio molecular orbital calculations for chemistry. — 2nd ed. — Oxford : Clarendon Press, Nov.1982. — [112]p
Previous ed.: 1970
ISBN 0-19-855369-2 (pbk) : £7.95 : CIP entry B82-26874

541.2′8 — Polyatomic molecules. Electrons. Quantum theory. Calculations

Mulliken, Robert S.. Polyatomic molecules : results of ab Initio calculations / Roberts S. Mulliken, Walter C. Ermler. — New York ; London : Academic Press, 1981. — xvi,431p : ill ; 24cm
Includes index
ISBN 0-12-509860-x : £32.40 B82-18356

541.3 — PHYSICAL CHEMISTRY

541.3 — Physical chemistry

Atkins, P. W.. Physical chemistry / P.W. Atkins. — 2nd ed. — Oxford : Oxford University Press, 1982. — xvii,1095p : ill ; 24cm
Previous ed.: 1978. — Text on lining papers. — Includes index
ISBN 0-19-855150-9 (cased) : £25.00
ISBN 0-19-855151-7 (pbk) : Unpriced B82-16132

Atkins, P. W.. Principles of physical chemistry / P.W. Atkins, M.J. Clugston. — London : Pitman, 1982. — x,246p : ill ; 25cm
Text on inside covers. — Bibliography: p240-242. — Includes index
ISBN 0-273-01774-8 (pbk) : £4.95 : CIP rev. B82-07419

Lesk, Arthur M.. Introduction to physical chemistry / Arthur M. Lesk. — Englewood Cliffs ; London : Prentice-Hall, c1982. — xv,746p : ill ; 25cm
Text on lining papers. — Includes index
ISBN 0-13-492710-9 : £21.70 B82-35070

Liptrot, G. F.. Modern physical chemistry. — London : Bell & Hyman, Aug.1981. — [480]p
ISBN 0-7135-2231-3 (pbk) : £6.95 : CIP entry B81-18067

Wilson, D. E.. Essential ideas in physical chemistry / D.E. Wilson. — London : Hodder and Stoughton, 1981. — 174p : ill ; 24cm
Includes index
ISBN 0-340-20830-9 (pbk) : Unpriced : CIP rev. B81-11915

541.3′014 — Physical chemistry. Measures. Units. Symbols & terminology

Manual of symbols and terminology for physicochemical quantities and units. — 1979 ed. / prepared for publication by D.H. Whiffen. — Oxford : Pergamon, 1979. — 41p ; 28cm
At head of title: International Union of Pure and Applied Chemistry. Division of Physical Chemistry. Commission on Physicochemical Symbols, Terminology and Units. — Originally published: in Pure and applied chemistry. Vol.51, no.1. — Previous ed.: London : Butterworth, 1975
ISBN 0-08-022386-9 (pbk) : £3.90 : CIP rev. B79-05688

541.3′0151 — Physical chemistry. Mathematics — *Questions & answers*

Griffiths, P. J. F.. Calculations in advanced physical chemistry. — 3rd ed. — London : Arnold, Feb.1983. — [272]p
Previous ed.: 1971
ISBN 0-7131-3483-6 (pbk) : £7.50 : CIP entry B82-39442

541.3′076 — Physical chemistry — *Questions & answers*

Atkins, P. W.. Solutions manual for physical chemistry / P.W. Atkins. — 2nd ed. — Oxford : Oxford University Press, 1982. — 457p : ill ; 23cm
Previous ed.: published as Physical chemistry. Solutions manual. 1979
ISBN 0-19-855156-8 (pbk) : £7.95 : CIP rev. B81-37524

541.3′41 — Solutions. Equilibrium constants — *Technical data — For solvent extraction*

Wisniak, Jaime. Liquid-liquid equilibrium and extraction : a literature source book / Jaime Wisniak and Abraham Tamir. — Amsterdam ; Oxford : Elsevier Scientific
Pt.A. — 1980. — xxii,1252p ; 25cm. — (Physical sciences data ; 7a)
ISBN 0-444-41909-8 : Unpriced : CIP rev. B80-12844

Wisniak, Jaime. Liquid-liquid equilibrium and extraction : a literature source book / Jaime Wisniak and Abraham Tamir. — Amsterdam ; Oxford : Elsevier Scientific. — (Physical sciences data ; 7)
Pt.B. — 1981. — xxi,1437p ; 25cm
ISBN 0-444-42023-1 : Unpriced : CIP rev. B81-28177

541.3′416 — Nonelectrolytic solutions. Classical thermodynamic properties

Van Ness, Hendrick C.. Classical thermodynamics of nonelectrolyte solutions : with applications to phase equilibria / Hendrick C. Van Ness, Michael M. Abbott. — New York ; London : McGraw-Hill, c1982. — xiv,482p : ill ; 25cm. — (McGraw-Hill chemical engineering series)
Includes bibliographies and index
ISBN 0-07-067095-1 : £30.25 B82-22165

541.3′42 — Inorganic compounds. Solubility

Broul, Miroslav. Solubility in inorganic two-component systems / Miroslav Broul, Jaroslav Nývlt and Otakar Söhnel. — Amsterdam ; Oxford : Elsevier Scientific, 1981. — 574p ; 25cm. — (Physical sciences data ; 6)
Translated from the Czech. — Includes index
ISBN 0-444-99763-6 : £35.30 : CIP rev. B80-10588

541.3′42′0212 — Chemical compounds. Solubility — *Tables*

Solubilities of inorganic and organic compounds. — Oxford : Pergamon
Translation of: Spravochnik po rastvorimosti
Vol.1: Binary systems / edited by H. Stephen and T. Stephen. — 1963 (1979 [printing])
Pt.1. — 960p ; 22cm
ISBN 0-08-009923-8 : Unpriced : CIP rev.
ISBN 0-08-023599-9 (Set) : £400.00 B79-22415

Solubilities of inorganic and organic compounds. — Oxford : Pergamon
Translation of: Spravochnik po rastvorimosti
Vol.1: Binary systems / edited by H. Stephen and T. Stephen. — 1963 (1979 [printing])
Includes index
Pt.2. — p963-1933 ; 22cm
ISBN 0-08-009924-6 : Unpriced : CIP rev.
ISBN 0-08-023599-9 (Set) : £400.00 B79-22416

Solubilities of inorganic and organic compounds. — Oxford : Pergamon
Translation of: Spravochnik po rastvorimosti
Vol.2 / edited by H. Stephen and T. Stephen. — 1964 (1979 [printing])
Pt.1: Ternary systems. — 943p ; 22cm
ISBN 0-08-009925-4 : Unpriced : CIP rev.
ISBN 0-08-023599-9 (Set) : £400.00 B79-22418

Solubilities of inorganic and organic compounds. — Oxford : Pergamon
Translation of: Spravochnik po rastvorimosti
Vol.2 / edited by H. Stephen and T. Stephen. — 1964 (1979 [printing])
Pt.2: Ternary and multicomponent systems. — p994-2053 ; 22cm
Includes index
ISBN 0-08-009926-2 : Unpriced : CIP rev.
ISBN 0-08-023599-9 (Set) : £400.00 B79-22417

Solubilities of inorganic and organic compounds. — Oxford : Pergamon
Translation of: Spravochnik po rastvorimosti
Vol.3: Ternary and multicomponent systems of inorganic substances / edited by Howard L. Silcock. — 1979. — 3v. ; 22cm
Includes index
ISBN 0-08-023570-0 : Unpriced : CIP rev.
ISBN 0-08-023599-9 (Set) : £400.00 B79-22419

541.3′423 — Non-aqueous solvents

Burger, K.. Solvation, ionic and complex formation reactions in non-aqueous solvents. — Oxford : Elsevier, Apr.1982. — [350]p. — (Studies in analytical chemistry ; 6)
ISBN 0-444-99697-4 : £35.00 : CIP entry B82-03586

541.3′45 — Colloids & surface phenomena

Surface and colloid science
Vol.12 / edited by Egon Matijević. — New York ; London : Plenum, c1982. — xi,473p : ill ; 24cm
Includes index
ISBN 0-306-40616-0 : Unpriced B82-26272

541.3′451 — Colloids. Physical properties — *Conference proceedings*

Colloidal dispersions. — London : Royal Society of Chemistry, Aug.1982. — [220]p. — (Special publication / Royal Society of Chemistry, ISSN 0260-6291 ; no.43)
Conference papers
ISBN 0-85186-865-7 (pbk) : CIP entry B82-21753

541.3′451 — Colloids. Zeta potential

Hunter, Robert J.. Zeta potential in colloid science : principles and applications / Robert J. Hunter. — London : Academic Press, 1981. — xi,386p : ill ; 24cm. — (Colloid science ; 2)
Includes bibliographies and index
ISBN 0-12-361960-2 : £35.00 : CIP rev. B81-06031

541.3′4514 — Microemulsions

Physical Chemistry of Microemulsions *(Conference : 1980 : Cambridge)*. Microemulsions : [proceedings of a conference on the Physical Chemistry of Microemulsions, organized on behalf of the Industrial Sub-Committee of the Faraday Division of the Chemical Society, and held September 15-16, 1980, in Cambridge, England] / edited by I.D. Robb. — New York ; London : Plenum, c1982. — viii,259p : ill ; 26cm
Includes index
ISBN 0-306-40834-1 : Unpriced B82-28147

541.3′453 — Adhesion

Wahe, William C.. Adhesion and the formualtion of adhesives. — 2nd ed. — London : Applied Science, July 1982. — [352]p
Previous ed.: 1976
ISBN 0-85334-134-6 : £30.00 : CIP entry
Also classified at 668′.3 B82-13138

541.3′453 — Adhesion — *Conference proceedings*

Société de chimie physique. *International Meeting (34th : 1981 : Paris)*. Microscopic aspects of adhesion and lubrication : proceedings of the 34th International Meeting of the Société de chimie physique, Paris, 14-18 September 1981 / J.M. Georges editor with the help of the Organizing Committee. — Amsterdam ; Oxford : Elsevier Scientific, 1982. — xix,812p : ill ; 25cm. — (Tribology series ; 7)
English and French text. — Includes bibliographies and index
ISBN 0-444-42071-1 : £69.15 : CIP rev.
ISBN 0-444-41677-3
Also classified at 621.8′9 B82-09294

541.3′453 — Adhesion — *Conference proceedings — Serials*

Adhesion. — 6. — London : Applied Science, Mar.1982. — [232]p
ISBN 0-85334-106-0 : £23.00 : CIP entry B82-01411

541.3′453 — Adsorption

Ościk, J.. Adsorption. — Chichester : Ellis Horwood, June 1981. — [256]p. — (Ellis Horwood series in physical chemistry)
Translation of: Adsorpcja
ISBN 0-85312-166-4 : £19.50 : CIP entry B81-10016

541.3′453 — Aqueous solutions. Solutes. Adsorption — *Conference proceedings*

Adsorption from aqueous solutions / [proceedings of a symposium on adsorption from aqueous solutions held March 24-27, 1980, as a satellite symposium to the meeting of the American Chemical Society Division of Colloid and Surface Chemistry, Houston, Texas] ; edited by P.H. Tewari. — New York ; London : Plenum, c1981. — viii,248p : ill ; 26cm
Includes index
ISBN 0-306-40747-7 : Unpriced B82-14454

Adsorption from solution. — London : Academic Press, Feb.1983. — [400]p
Conference proceedings
ISBN 0-12-530980-5 : CIP entry B82-37478

541.3′453 — Liquids. Capillarity. Mathematical models

Rowlinson, J. S.. Molecular theory of capillarity. — Oxford : Clarendon Press, June 1982. — [300]p. — (The International series of monographs on chemistry ; 8)
ISBN 0-19-855612-8 : £30.00 : CIP entry B82-10457

541.3′453′0724 — Adsorption by solids. Simulation. Applications of digital computer systems

Nicholson, D.. Computer simulation and the statistical mechanics of adsorption. — London : Academic Press, Oct.1982. — [450]p
ISBN 0-12-518060-8 : CIP entry B82-24941

541.3′5 — Photochemistry

Light, chemical change and life : a source book in photochemistry / edited by J.D. Coyle, R.R. Hill and D.R. Roberts. — Milton Keynes : Open University Press, 1982. — xi,406p,[4]p of plates : ill(some col.) ; 21cm. — (Science : a third level course)
At head of title: The Open University. — Bibliography: p402-403. — Includes index
ISBN 0-335-16100-6 (pbk) : £6.95 B82-37546

Photochemistry : light, chemical change and life / [S341 Course Team]. — Milton Keynes : Open University Press. — (Science : a third level course)
At head of title: The Open University
The course file. — 1982. — 1portolio : ill(some col.) ; 34cm. — (S341 ; [CF])
Unpriced B82-21208

541.3'5 — Photochemistry *continuation*

Rabek, J. F.. Experimental methods in photochemistry and photophysics. — Chichester : Wiley, Sept.1982. — [1200]p
ISBN 0-471-10090-0 : £75.00 : CIP entry
B82-19517

541.3'5'05 — Photochemistry - *Serials*

Photochemistry. — Vol.11. — London : Royal Society of Chemistry, Aug.1981. — [650]p. — (Specialist periodical report)
ISBN 0-85186-095-8 : CIP entry
ISSN 0556-3860 B81-15932

541.3'5'05 — Photochemistry — *Serials*

Photochemistry. — Vol.12. — London : Royal Society of Chemistry, Feb.1982. — [600]p. — (Specialist periodical report / Royal Society of Chemistry)
ISBN 0-85186-105-9 : CIP entry
ISSN 0556-3860 B81-39251

541.3'61 — Fire — *For children*

Satchwell, John. Fire. — London : Methuen/Walker, Sept.1982. — [32]p. — (The Elements ; 2)
ISBN 0-416-06480-9 : £3.50 : CIP entry
B82-19241

541.3'61 — Flames. Mathematical aspects

Buckmaster, J. D.. Theory of laminar flames / J.D. Buckmaster, G.S.S. Ludford. — Cambridge : Cambridge University Press, 1982. — xii,266p : ill ; 24cm. — (Cambridge monographs on mechanics and applied mathematics)
Bibliography: p248-260. — Includes index
ISBN 0-521-23929-x : £25.00 : CIP rev.
B82-15937

541.3'61 — Flames. Metal vapours

Metal vapours in flames / by C.Th.J. Alkemade ... [et al.]. — Oxford : Pergamon, 1982. — xxii,1029p : ill ; 24cm. — (International series in natural philosophy ; v.103)
Bibliography: p959-997. — Includes index
ISBN 0-08-018061-2 : £50.00 : CIP rev.
B82-05370

541.3'61'05 — Combustion — *Serials*

Progress in energy and combustion science. — Vol.7. — Oxford : Pergamon, Apr.1982. — [330]p
ISBN 0-08-029124-4 : £65.00 : CIP entry
B82-08429

541.3'63 — Phase transitions. Thermochemistry

Oonk, H. A. J.. Phase theory : the thermodymanics of heterogeneous equilibria / H.A.J. Oonk. — Amsterdam ; Oxford : Elsevier Scientific, 1981. — xiv,269p : ill ; 25cm. — (Studies in modern thermodynamics ; 3)
Includes index
ISBN 0-444-42019-3 : Unpriced : CIP rev.
B81-28195

541.3'69 — Chemical reactions. Thermodynamics

Eremin, E. N.. Fundamentals of chemical thermodynamics / E.N. Yeremin ; translated from the Russian by Artavaz Beknazarov. — Moscow : Mir ; [London] : distributed by Central, 1981. — 438p : ill ; 23cm
Translation of: Osnovy khimicheskoĭ termodinamiki. — Bibliography: p426-428. — Includes index
ISBN 0-7147-1774-6 : £5.95 B82-37041

Smith, E. Brian. Basic chemical thermodynamics. — 3rd ed. — Oxford : Clarendon Press, June 1982. — [160]p. — (Oxford chemistry series ; 31)
Previous ed.: 1977
ISBN 0-19-855521-0 (cased) : £7.95 : CIP entry
ISBN 0-19-855522-9 (pbk) : £3.95 B82-21954

541.3'69 — Inorganic compounds. Chemical reactions. Thermodynamics

Dasent, W. E.. Inorganic energetics : an introduction / W.E. Dasent. — 2nd ed. — Cambridge : Cambridge University Press, 1982. — xii,185p : ill ; 24cm. — (Cambridge texts in chemistry and biochemistry)
Previous ed.: Harmondsworth : Penguin, 1970. — Bibliography: p178-179. — Includes index
ISBN 0-521-24027-1 (cased) : £12.00 : CIP rev.
ISBN 0-521-28406-6 (pbk) : £4.95 B82-14515

Johnson, D. A. (David Arthur). Some thermodynamic aspects in inorganic chemistry / D.A. Johnson. — 2nd ed. — Cambridge : Cambridge University Press, 1982. — 282p : ill ; 24cm. — (Cambridge texts in chemistry and biochemistry)
Previous ed.: 1968. — Bibliography: p270-273. — Includes index
ISBN 0-521-24204-5 (cased) : £18.00 : CIP rev.
ISBN 0-521-28521-6 (pbk) : £6.95 B81-36954

541.3'7 — Electrochemistry

Comprehensive treatise of electrochemistry. — New York ; London : Plenum
Vol.4: Electrochemical materials science / edited by J. O'M. Bockris ... [et al.]. — c1981. — xxii,563p : ill ; 26cm
Includes index
ISBN 0-306-40614-4 : Unpriced B82-14003

Comprehensive treatise on electrochemistry. — New York ; London : Plenum
Vol.1: The double layer / edited by J.O'M. Bockris, Brian E. Conway, Ernest Yeager. — c1980. — xix,453p : ill ; 26cm
Includes index
ISBN 0-306-40275-0 : Unpriced B82-35365

Koryta, Jiří. Ions, electrodes, and membranes / Jiří Koryta. — Chichester : Wiley, c1982. — viii,197p : ill ; 24cm
Includes index
ISBN 0-471-10007-2 : Unpriced : CIP rev.
ISBN 0-471-10008-0 (pbk) : Unpriced
B82-02664

541.3'7 — Electrochemistry — *For industries*

Pletcher, Derek. Industrial electrochemistry. — London : Chapman and Hall, Sept.1982. — [300]p
ISBN 0-412-16500-7 : £17.50 : CIP entry
B82-19221

541.3'7 — Electrophoresis

Andrews, Andrew T.. Electrophoresis. — Oxford : Clarendon Press, Nov.1981. — [400]p
ISBN 0-19-854626-2 : £28.00 : CIP entry
B81-31070

Electrophoresis. — Oxford : Elsevier Scientific. — (Journal of chromatography library ; v.18)
Pt.B: Applications. — Sept.1982. — [350]p
ISBN 0-444-42114-9 : CIP entry B82-22804

541.3'72 — Electrochemistry. Solutions — *Technical data*

Recommended methods for purification of solvents and tests for impurities. — Oxford : Pergamon, Oct.1982. — [72]p
ISBN 0-08-022370-2 : £10.00 : CIP entry
B82-27213

541.3'72 — Ionophores. Structure

Dobler, Max. Ionophores and their structures / Max Dobler. — New York ; Chichester : Wiley, c1981. — xi,379p : ill ; 24cm
Includes index
ISBN 0-471-05270-1 : £42.50 B82-04541

541.3'72 — Solutions. Metal ions. Equilibrium constants — *Tables*

Stability constants of metal-ion complexes. — Oxford : Pergamon
Pt.A: Inorganic ligands / compiled by Erik Högfeldt. — 1982. — xiv,310p ; 28cm. — (IUPAC chemical data series ; no.21)
At head of title: International Union of Pure and Applied Chemistry (Analytical Chemistry Division, Commission on Equilibrium Data). — Includes index
ISBN 0-08-020959-9 : Unpriced : CIP rev.
B82-12707

541.3'724 — Conductive metal oxide electrodes

Electrodes of conductive metallic oxides / edited by Sergio Trasatti. — Amsterdam ; Oxford : Elsevier Scientific. — (Studies in physical and theoretical chemistry ; 11)
Pt.A. — 1980. — xvi,366p : ill ; 25cm
Includes index
ISBN 0-444-41912-8 : £36.40 : CIP rev.
B80-13798

541.3'724 — Membrane electrodes

Morf, W. E.. The principles of ion-selective electrodes and of membrane transport / W.E. Morf. — Amsterdam ; Oxford : Elsevier Scientific, 1981. — x,432p : ill ; 25cm. — (Studies in analytical chemistry ; v.2)
Includes index
ISBN 0-444-99749-0 : £30.52 : CIP rev.
B80-28330

541.3'724 — Selective ion sensitive electrodes

Ion-selective electrode reviews. — Oxford : Pergamon, Aug.1981
Vol.2. — [270]p
ISBN 0-08-028434-5 : £24.00 : CIP entry
B81-22671

541.3'724 — Selective ion sensitive electrodes — *Conference proceedings*

Ion-selective electrodes, 3 : third symposium held at Mátrafüred, Hungary, 13-15 October, 1980 / editor E. Pungor ; associate editor I. Buzás. — Amsterdam ; Oxford : Elsevier Scientific, 1981. — xi,427p : ill ; 25cm. — (Analytical chemistry symposia series ; v.8)
Includes index
ISBN 0-444-99714-8 : £45.26 : CIP rev.
B81-31619

541.3'724'0212 — Electrode potentials — *Tables*

Antelman, Marvin S.. The encyclopedia of chemical electrode potentials / Marvin S. Antelman with the assistance of Franklin J. Harris, Jr.. — New York ; London : Plenum, c1982. — xiv,288p ; 23cm
ISBN 0-306-40903-8 : Unpriced B82-28648

541.3'724'05 — Selective ion sensitive electrodes — *Serials*

Ion-selective electrode reviews. — Vol.3. — Oxford : Pergamon, June 1982. — [258]p
ISBN 0-08-029692-0 : £31.25 : CIP entry
B82-16500

541.3'8 — Radiochemistry

Choppin, Gregory R.. Nuclear chemistry : theory and applications / Gregory R. Choppin and Jan Rydberg. — Oxford : Pergamon, 1980. — viii,667p,[2] folded leaves of plates : ill,ports ; 26cm
Text on lining papers. — Includes bibliographies and index
ISBN 0-08-023826-2 (cased) : £36.00 : CIP rev.
ISBN 0-08-023823-8 (pbk) : £13.50
B79-20066

Nuclear and radiochemistry. — 3rd ed. / Gerhart Friedlander ... [et al.]. — New York ; Chichester : Wiley, c1981. — xii,684p : ill ; 24cm
Previous ed.: 1964. — Includes index
ISBN 0-471-28021-6 : £31.00
ISBN 0-471-86255-x (pbk) : Unpriced
B82-04194

541.3'8 — Radiochemistry — *Conference proceedings*

The **Study** of fast processes and transient species by electron pulse radiolysis : proceedings of the NATO Advanced Study Institute held at Capri, Italy, 7-18 September, 1981 / edited by John H. Baxendale and Fabio Busi. — Dordrecht ; London : Reidel in cooperation with NATO Scientific Affairs Division, c1982. — xvi,637p : ill ; 25cm. — (NATO advanced study institutes series. Series C, Mathematical and physical sciences ; v.86)
Includes index
ISBN 90-277-1431-2 : Unpriced B82-40166

541.3′88 — Stable isotopes — *Conference proceedings*

Stable isotopes : proceedings of the 4th International Conference, Jülich, March 23-26, 1981 / edited by H.-L. Schmidt, H. Förstel and K. Heinzinger. — Amsterdam ; Oxford : Elsevier Scientific, 1982. — xvii,775p : ill ; 25cm. — (Analytical chemistry symposia series ; v.11)
Includes index
ISBN 0-444-42076-2 : Unpriced : CIP rev. B82-12684

541.3′9 — Chemical reactions. Kinetics - *Serials*

Progress in reaction kinetics. — Vol.10. — Oxford : Pergamon, Apr.1981. — [406]p
ISBN 0-08-027155-3 : £36.00 : CIP entry B81-04201

541.3′9 — Chemical reactions. Role of electrons

Salem, Lionel. Electrons in chemical reactions : first principles / Lionel Salem. — New York ; Chichester : Wiley, c1982. — x,260p : ill ; 24cm
Includes index
ISBN 0-471-08474-3 : £27.25 B82-37202

541.3′92 — Chemical reactions. Equilibria

Martell, Arthur E.. Critical stability constants / by Arthur E. Martell and Robert M. Smith. — New York ; London : Plenum. — xvi,495p ; 28cm
Includes index
ISBN 0-306-35213-3 : Unpriced B82-35683

541.3′92 — Metal coordination compounds. Equilibria — *Technical data*

Martell, Arthur E.. Critical stability constants / by Arthur E. Martell and Robert M. Smith. — New York ; London : Plenum
Vol.5: First supplement. — c1982. — xvii,604p : ill ; 28cm
Bibliography: p479-556. — Includes index
ISBN 0-306-41005-2 : Unpriced B82-30267

541.3′93 — Homogeneous chemical reactions. Kinetics & mechanisms

Moore, John W.. Kinetics and mechanism. — 3rd ed. / John W. Moore, Ralph G. Pearson. — New York ; Chichester : Wiley, c1981. — xv,455p : ill ; 24cm
Previous ed.: Arthur A. Frost, Ralph G. Pearson. 1961. — Includes index
ISBN 0-471-03558-0 : £23.70 B82-05798

541.3′93 — Molecules. Rearrangements

Rearrangements in ground and excited states / edited by Paul de Mayo. — New York ; London : Academic Press, 1980. — 3v. : ill ; 24cm. — (Organic chemistry ; v.42)
Includes index
ISBN 0-12-481301-1 : Unpriced
ISBN 0-12-481302-x (v.2) : £42.20
ISBN 0-12-481303-8 (v.3) : £50.00 B82-41013

541.3′93 — Unsaturated compounds. Electrophilic addition reactions

De la Mare, P. B. D.. Electrophilic additions to unsaturated systems / P.B.D. de la Mare, R. Bolton. — [2nd ed.]. — Amsterdam ; Oxford : Elsevier, 1982. — xiii,377p : ill ; 27cm. — (Studies in organic chemistry ; 9)
Previous ed.: 1966. — Includes index
ISBN 0-444-42030-4 : Unpriced : CIP rev. B81-31233

541.3′94 — Chemical reactions. Kinetics & mechanisms

Butt, John B.. Reaction kinetics and reactor design / John B. Butt. — Englewood Cliffs ; London : Prentice-Hall, c1980. — xv,431p : ill ; 24cm. — (Prentice-Hall international series in the physical and chemical engineering sciences)
Includes index
ISBN 0-13-753335-7 : £21.70 B82-26462

541.3′94 — Gases. Chemical reactions. Kinetics

Collie, C. H.. Kinetic theory and entropy. — London : Longman, July 1982. — [384]p
ISBN 0-582-44368-7 : £10.95 : CIP entry B82-12992

541.3′94 — Molecules. Chemical reactions. Kinetics. Research. Applications of lasers

Bernstein, Richard B.. Chemical dynamics via molecular beam and laser techniques : the Hinshelwood lectures 1980 / Richard B. Bernstein. — Oxford : Clarendon, 1982. — viii,262p : ill,1port ; 24cm
Bibliography: p242-251. — Includes index
ISBN 0-19-855154-1 (cased) : Unpriced : CIP rev.
ISBN 0-19-855169-x (pbk) : £10.95 B82-08437

541.3′95 — Catalysis — *Conference proceedings*

International Congress on Catalysis *(7th : 1980 : Tokyo).* New horizons in catalysis : proceedings of the 7th International Congress on Catalysis, Tokyo, 30 June-4 July, 1980 / edited by T. Seiyama, K. Tanabe. — Tokyo : Kodansha ; Amsterdam ; Oxford : Elsevier Scientific, 1981. — 2v.(xxx,1537p) : ill ; 24cm. — (Studies in surface science and catalysis ; v.7)
Includes index
ISBN 0-444-99750-4 : £68.90 : CIP rev.
ISBN 0-444-99740-7 (pt.A)
ISBN 0-444-99739-3 (pt.B)
ISBN 0-444-41801-6 B81-11922

541.3′95 — Catalysis. Supported complexes

Ermakov, ÎU. I.. Catalysis by supported complexes / Yu. I. Yermakov, B.N. Kuznetsov, V.A. Zakharov. — Amsterdam ; Oxford : Elsevier Scientific, 1981. — xx,522p : ill ; 25cm. — (Studies in surface science and catalysis ; 8)
Includes bibliographies and index
ISBN 0-444-42014-2 : £41.34 : CIP rev. B81-24609

541.3′95 — Catalysts: Metals. Structure & physical properties — *Conference proceedings*

Metal-support and metal-additive effects in catalysis. — Oxford : Elsevier Scientific, Sept.1982. — [300]p. — (Studies in surface science and catalysis ; 11)
Conference papers
ISBN 0-444-42111-4 : CIP entry B82-21768

541.3′95 — Catalysts: Zeolites. Structure & physical properties

Mortier, W. J.. Compilation of extra framework sites in zeolites / W.J. Mortier. — Guildford : Butterworth on behalf of the Structure Commission of the International Zeolite Association, c1982. — 67p : ill ; 29cm
ISBN 0-86103-056-7 (pbk) : Unpriced B82-15293

541.3′95 — Catalysts: Zeolites. Structure & physical properties — *Conference proceedings*

Metal microstructure in zeolites. — Oxford : Elsevier Scientific, Sept.1982. — [284]p. — (Studies in surface science and catalysis ; 12)
Conference papers
ISBN 0-444-42112-2 : CIP entry B82-22803

541.3′95 — Enzyme catalysis — *Conference proceedings*

OHOLO Conference *(26th : 1981 : Zichron Yaacov).* Chemical approaches to understanding enzyme catalysis : biomimetic chemistry and transition-state analogs : proceedings of the 26th OHOLO Conference, Zichron Yaacov, Israel, 22-25 March 1981 / edited by B.S. Green and Y. Ashani, D. Chipman ; technical editors J. Sandler, E. Tepper. — Amsterdam ; Oxford : Elsevier Scientific, c1982. — xv,355p : ill,1port ; 25cm. — (Studies in organic chemistry ; 10)
Includes index
ISBN 0-444-42063-0 : £45.84 : CIP rev. B82-10664

541.3′95 — Heterogeneous catalysis

The **Chemical** physics of solid surfaces and heterogeneous catalysis / edited by D.A. King and D.P. Woodruff. — Amsterdam ; Oxford : Elsevier Scientific
Vol.4: Fundamental studies of heterogeneous catalysis. — 1982. — 468p : ill ; 25cm
Includes index
ISBN 0-444-41987-x : £67.80
ISBN 0-444-41971-3
Primary classification 541′.0421 B82-38125

The **chemical** physics of solid surfaces and heterogenous catalysis / edited by D.A. King and D.P. Woodruff. — Amsterdam ; Oxford : Elsevier Scientific
Vol.1: Clean solid surfaces. — 1981. — 372p : ill ; 25cm
Includes index
ISBN 0-444-41924-1 : Unpriced : CIP rev.
Primary classification 541′.0421 B81-12378

541.3′95′05 — Catalysis - *Serials*

Catalysis. — Vol.4. — London : Royal Society of Chemistry, July 1981. — [265]p. — (A Specialist periodical report)
ISBN 0-85186-554-2 : CIP entry
ISSN 0140-0568 B81-14899

541.3′95′05 — Catalysis — *Serials*

Catalysis. — 5. — London : Royal Society of Chemistry, Aug.1982. — [415]p. — (Specialist periodical report / Royal Society of Chemistry)
ISBN 0-85186-564-x : CIP entry
ISSN 0140-0568 B82-18481

542 — CHEMISTRY. LABORATORIES, APPARATUS, EQUIPMENT

542 — Chemistry. Research. Use of lasers

Applications of lasers to chemical problems / edited by Ted R. Evans. — New York ; Chichester : Wiley, c1982. — xi,291p : ill ; 24cm. — (Techniques of chemistry ; v.17)
Includes index
ISBN 0-471-04949-2 : Unpriced B82-40780

542′.4 — Distillation. Laboratory techniques

Krell, Erich. Handbook of laboratory distillation : with an introduction to pilot plant distillation / Erich Krell ; translation, exclusive of the parts retained from the 1st English edition, by Manfred Hecker. — Completely rev. 2nd ed. — Amsterdam : Elsevier Scientific, 1982. — 524p : ill ; 24cm. — (Techniques and intrumentation in analytical chemistry ; v.2)
Translation of: Handbuch der Laboratoriumsdestillation. 3rd ed. — Previous ed.: i.e. 2nd ed., 1963. — In slipcase. — Includes index
ISBN 0-444-99723-7 : £46.97 : CIP rev. B81-24630

542′.8 — Chemistry. Applications of digital computer systems — *Conference proceedings*

Data processing in chemistry : a collection of papers presented at the summer school, Rzeszów, Poland, August 26-31, 1980 / edited by Z. Hippe. — Amsterdam ; Oxford : Elsevier Scientific, 1981. — ix,286p : ill,2maps ; 25cm. — (Studies in physical and theoretical chemistry ; 16)
ISBN 0-444-99744-x : £31.98 : CIP rev. B81-03694

542′.8 — Chemistry. Calculations. Use of pocket programmable electronic calculators

Clarke, Frank H.. Calculator programming for chemistry and the life sciences / Frank H. Clarke. — New York ; London : Academic Press, 1981. — vii,226p : ill ; 24cm
Includes index
ISBN 0-12-175320-4 : £16.20 B82-30137

543 — CHEMICAL ANALYSIS

543 — Chemical analysis

Braun, Robert D.. Introduction to chemical analysis / Robert D. Braun. — New York ; London : McGraw-Hill, c1982. — xiv,462p : ill ; 25cm
Text on lining papers. — Includes index
ISBN 0-07-007280-9 : £18.25 B82-22467

Marr, Iain L.. Environmental chemical analysis. — Glasgow : International Textbook, Oct.1982. — [224]p
ISBN 0-7002-0282-x : £16.00 : CIP entry B82-25093

Pataki, L.. Basic analytical chemistry / by L. Pataki and E. Zapp ; translated by Gy Jalsovszky. — Oxford : Pergamon, 1980. — xiii,463p : ill ; 24cm. — (Pergamon series in analytical chemistry ; v.2)
Translated from the Hungarian. — Bibliography: p453-455. — Includes index
ISBN 0-08-023850-5 : £23.00 : CIP rev. B79-34160

543 — Chemical analysis *continuation*

Ramette, Richard W.. Chemical equilibrium and analysis / Richard W. Ramette. — Reading, Mass. ; London : Addison-Wesley, c1981. — xv,765p : ill ; 25cm
Text on lining papers. — Includes index
ISBN 0-201-06107-4 : Unpriced B82-20557

Skoog, Douglas A.. Fundamentals of analytical chemistry / Douglas A. Skoog, Donald M. West. — 4th ed. — Philadelphia ; London : Saunders College, c1982. — xiv,859p : ill ; 21cm. — (Saunders golden sunburst series)
Previous ed.: 1976. — Text on inside covers. — Bibliography: p825-828. — Includes index
ISBN 4-8337-0082-4 (pbk) : £9.50 B82-37427

Treatise on analytical chemistry. — New York ; Chichester : Wiley
Part 1: Theory and practice
Vol.5. — 2nd ed. / edited by Philip J. Elving ; associate editor Eli Grushka ; editor emeritus I.M. Kolthoff. — c1982. — xxix,668p : ill ; 25cm
Previous ed.: New York, London : Interscience, 1964. — Includes bibliographies and index
£48.00 B82-17807

Treatise on analytical chemistry / [edited by I.M. Kolthoff, Philip J. Elving]. — New York ; Chichester : Wiley
Pt.1: Theory and practice. — c1981
Vol.7 / edited by Philip J. Elving, associate editor Edward J. Meehan, editor Emeritus I.M. Kolthoff. — 2nd ed. — xxviii,816p : ill,ports ; 24cm
Previous ed.: 1967. — Includes bibliographies and index
ISBN 0-471-07996-0 : £48.00 B82-01808

Treatise on analytical chemistry / edited by I.M. Kolthoff and Philip J. Elving. — New York ; Chichester : Wiley
Pt.2: Analytical chemistry of inorganic and organic compounds
Vol.17: Index : vols.1-16. — c1980. — xiv,388p ; 24cm
ISBN 0-471-06481-5 : £27.00 B82-34689

Wilson and Wilson's comprehensive analytical chemistry / edited by G. Svehla. — Amsterdam ; Oxford : Elsevier Scientific
Vol.12: Thermal analysis
Pt.B: Biochemical and clinical applications of thermometric and thermal analysis / edited by Neil D. Jespersen. — 1982. — xvii,254p : ill ; 23cm
Includes index
ISBN 0-444-42062-2 : £36.25 : CIP rev.
B82-04739

Wilson and Wilson's comprehensive analytical chemistry / edited by G. Svehla. — Amsterdam ; Oxford : Elsevier Scientific
Vol.13: Analysis of complex hydrocarbon mixtures
Pt.B: Group analysis and detailed analysis / by Slavoj Hála, Mečislav Kuraš, Milan Popl. — 1981. — p383-841 : ill ; 23cm
Includes index
ISBN 0-444-99735-0 : £34.04 : CIP rev.
ISBN 0-444-99734-2 (set) : Unpriced
B81-25292

Wilson and Wilson's comprehensive analytical chemistry. — Oxford : Elsevier Scientific, May 1982
Vol.14: Ion exchangers in analytical chemistry : their properties and use in inorganic chemistry. — [550]p
ISBN 0-444-99717-2 : £40.00 : CIP entry
B82-06831

543 — Chemical analysis. Derivatization

Chemical derivatization in analytical chemistry. — New York ; London : Plenum
Vol.1: Chromatography / edited by R.W. Frei and J.F. Lawrence. — c1981. — xi,344p : ill ; 24cm
Includes index
ISBN 0-306-40608-x : Unpriced B82-01882

543 — Chemical analysis. Use of complexes

Přibil, Rudolf. Applied complexometry. — Oxford : Pergamon, Dec.1982. — [410]p. — (Pergamon series in analytical chemistry ; 5)
Translation of: Komplexometrie
ISBN 0-08-026277-5 : £37.50 : CIP entry
B82-30833

543 — Gases. Chemical analysis

Váňa, Jaroslav. Gas and liquid analyzers. — Oxford : Elsevier Scientific, Oct.1982. — [600] p. — (Wilson and Wilson's comprehensive analytical chemistry ; v.17)
Translated from the Czech
ISBN 0-444-99691-5 : £50.00 : CIP entry
B82-24018

543 — Inorganic compounds. Trace elements. Chemical analysis. Separation & preconcentration. Laboratory techniques

Minczewski, J.. Separation and preconcentration methods in inorganic trace analysis / J. Minczewski, J. Chwastowska, R. Dybczyński ; translation editor Mary R. Masson. — Chichester : Horwood, 1982. — xi,543p : ill ; 24cm. — (Ellis Horwood series in analytical chemistry)
Translation of: Analiza śladowa-metody rozdzielania i zagęszczania. — Includes index
ISBN 0-85312-165-6 : £31.50 : CIP rev.
B81-31511

543 — Trace elements. Chemical analysis

Trace analysis. — New York ; London : Academic Press
Vol.1 / edited by James F. Lawrence. — 1981. — ix,331p : ill ; 23cm
Includes bibliographies and index
ISBN 0-12-682101-1 : £26.20 B82-29972

543'.0028 — Chemical analysis. Laboratory techniques

Chalmers, R. A.. Quantitative chemical analysis. — Chichester : Ellis Horwood, July 1981. — [416]p. — (Ellis Horwood series in analytical chemistry)
ISBN 0-85312-192-3 : £25.00 : CIP entry
B81-18173

543'.0028 — Chemical analysis. Laboratory techniques — *Manuals*

Huskins, D. J.. General handbook of on-line process analysers / D.J. Huskins. — 239p : ill ; 24cm. — (Ellis Horwood series in analytical chemistry)
Includes bibliographies and index
ISBN 0-85312-329-2 : £30.00 : CIP rev.
B81-35881

543'.0028 — Chemical analysis. Laboratory techniques. Standardisation — *Conference papers*

International Symposium on Harmonization of Collaborative Analytical Studies *(1981 : Helsinki)*. Collaborative interlaboratory studies in chemical analysis : lectures presented at the International Symposium on Harmonization of Collaborative Analytical Studies, Helsinki, Finland, 20-21 August 1981 / edited by H. Egan and T.S. West. — Oxford : Pergamon, 1982. — 171p : ill ; 27cm
Includes index
ISBN 0-08-026228-7 (pbk) : Unpriced : CIP rev. B82-07989

543'.007 — Chemical analysis. Teaching

Baiulescu, G. E.. Education and teaching in analytical chemistry / G.E. Baiulescu and C. Patroescu and R.A. Chalmers. — Chichester : Ellis Horwood, 1982. — 190p : ill ; 24cm. — (Ellis Horwood series in analytical chemistry)
Includes index
ISBN 0-85312-384-5 : £15.00 : CIP rev.
B81-30492

543'.0812 — Electron probe microanalysis

Scanning electron microscopy and X-ray microanalysis : a text for biologists, materials scientists, and geologists / Joseph I. Goldstein ... [et al.]. — New York ; London : Plenum, c1981. — xiii,673p : ill ; 24cm
Bibliography: p649-664. — Includes index
ISBN 0-306-40768-x : Unpriced
Primary classification 502'.8'25 B82-14544

543'.083 — Centrifugation

Hsu, Hsien-Wen. Separations by centrifugal phenomena / Hsien-Wen Hsu ; editor Edmond S. Perry. — New York ; Chichester : Wiley, c1981. — xvi,466p : ill ; 24cm. — (Techniques of chemistry ; v.16)
Includes index
ISBN 0-471-05564-6 : £40.25 B82-12295

543'.0858 — Chemical analysis. Atomic absorption spectroscopy. Techniques

Castle, John Edward. Atomic absorption spectrometry. — Oxford : Elsevier Scientific, Sept.1982. — [400]p. — (Techniques and instrumentation in analytical chemistry ; v.5)
ISBN 0-444-42015-0 : CIP entry B82-22802

543'.0858 — Chemical analysis. Atomic spectroscopy

International Conference on Atomic Spectroscopy *(9th : 1981 : Tokyo)*. Recent advances in analytical spectroscopy : proceedings of the 9th International Conference on Atomic Spectroscopy and 22nd Colloquium Spectroscopicum Internationale, Tokyo, Japan, 4-8 September 1981 / [sponsored by] the International Union of Pure and Applied Chemistry (Analytical Chemistry Division) in conjunction with the Ministry of Education, Science and Culture of Japan ... [et al.] ; edited by Keiichiro Fuwa. — Oxford : Pergamon, 1982. — ix,325p : ill ; 28cm
ISBN 0-08-026221-x : £37.50 : CIP rev.
B82-11982

Magyar, B.. Guide-lines to planning of atomic spectrometric analysis. — Oxford : Elsevier, May 1982. — [330]p. — (Studies in analytical chemistry ; 4)
ISBN 0-444-99699-0 : £35.00 : CIP entry
B82-06832

543'.0858 — Chemical analysis. Atomic spectroscopy — *Serials*

Annual reports on analytical atomic spectroscopy. — Vol.10. — London : Royal Society of Chemistry, Nov.1981. — [350]p
ISBN 0-85186-717-0 : CIP entry
ISSN 0306-1353 B81-31186

Progress in analytical atomic spectroscopy. — Vol.3. — Oxford : Pergamon, Oct.1981. — [390]p
ISBN 0-08-029081-7 : £43.00 : CIP entry
B81-30205

Progress in analytical atomic spectroscopy. — Vol.4. — Oxford : Pergamon, Mar.1982. — [450]p
ISBN 0-08-029659-9 : £45.00 : CIP entry
B82-09187

543'.0858 — Chemical analysis. Fourier transform spectroscopy

Fourier, Hadamard, and Hilbert transforms in chemistry / edited by Alan G. Marshall. — New York ; London : Plenum, c1982. — xii,562p : ill ; 26cm
Includes index
ISBN 0-306-40904-6 : Unpriced B82-23742

543'.0858 — Chemical analysis. Matrix isolation spectroscopy — *Conference proceedings*

Matrix isolation spectroscopy : a book based on the lectures given and the discussions that took place at the NATO Advanced Study Institute held at the Université des sciences et techniques du Languedoc, Montpellier, France, July 17-31, 1980 / edited by A.J. Barnes ... [et al.]. — Dordrecht ; London : Reidel in cooperation with NATO Scientific Affairs Division, c1981. — x,605p : ill ; 25cm. — (NATO advanced study institutes series. Series C, Mathematical and physical sciences ; v.76)
Includes index
ISBN 90-277-1328-6 : Unpriced B82-03452

543'.0858 — Inorganic compounds. Chemical analysis. Emission spectroscopy — *Conference proceedings*

Emission and scattering techniques : studies of inorganic molecules, solids, and surfaces : proceedings of the NATO Advanced Study Institute held at Alghero, Sardinia, Italy, September 14-25, 1980 / edited by Peter Day. — Dordrecht ; London : Reidel in cooperation with NATO Scientific Affairs Division, c1981. — viii,390p : ill ; 25cm. — (NATO advanced study institutes series. Series C, Mathematical and physical sciences ; v.73)
Includes index
ISBN 90-277-1317-0 : Unpriced
Also classified at 539.7'54 B82-00472

543'.08584 — Chemical analysis. Nonlinear Raman spectroscopy

Chemical applications of nonlinear Raman spectroscopy / edited by Albert B. Harvey. — New York ; London : Academic Press, 1981. — xii,383p : ill ; 24cm
Includes bibliographies and index
ISBN 0-12-329050-3 : £31.80 B82-13053

543'.08586 — Chemical analysis. X-ray fluorescence spectroscopy

Tertian, R.. Principles of quantitative X-ray fluorescence analysis / R. Tertian, F. Claisse. — London : Heyden, c1982. — xviii,385p : ill ; 24cm
Includes index
ISBN 0-85501-709-0 : Unpriced : CIP rev.
B82-07115

543'.086 — Thermal analysis - *Conference proceedings*

European Symposium on Thermal Analysis *(2nd : 1981 : University of Aberdeen)*. Proceedings of the Second European Symposium on Thermal Analysis, ESTA2, University of Aberdeen, UK, 1-4 September 1981, organized by the Thermal Methods Group of the Analytical Division of the Chemical Society. — London : Heyden, Aug.1981. — [600]p
ISBN 0-85501-705-8 : £26.00 : CIP entry
B81-20526

543'.086 — Thermal analysis — *Conference proceedings*

International Conference on Thermal Analysis *(7th : 1982 : Ontario)*. Thermal analysis. — Chichester : Wiley, Oct.1982. — [1550]p
ISBN 0-471-26243-9 : £60.00 : CIP entry
ISBN 0-471-26244-7 (v.1)
ISBN 0-471-26245-5 (v.2) B82-27214

543'.0873 — Mass spectrometry

Beynon, J. H.. An introduction to mass spectrometry / by J.H. Beynon and A.G. Brenton. — Cardiff : University of Wales Press, 1982. — 57p : ill ; 21cm
Bibliography: p57
ISBN 0-7083-0810-4 (pbk) : Unpriced : CIP rev. B81-28823

Rose, M. E.. Mass spectrometry for chemists and biochemists / M.E. Rose, R.A.W. Johnstone. — Cambridge : Cambridge University Press, 1982. — xiii,307p : ill ; 24cm. — (Cambridge texts in chemistry and biochemistry)
Bibliography: p296-302. — Includes index
ISBN 0-521-23729-7 (cased) : £27.50 : CIP rev.
B82-19252

543'.0873 — Trace elements. Chemical analysis. Mass spectrometry — *Conference proceedings*

Applications of mass spectrometry to trace analysis : lectures of a course held at the Joint Research Centre, Ispra (Italy), September 29-October 3, 1980 / edited by S. Facchetti. — Amsterdam ; Oxford : Published for the Commission of the European Communities by Elsevier Scientific, 1982. — x,321p : ill,forms ; 25cm. — (Ispra courses)
Includes index
ISBN 0-444-42042-8 : £39.45 : CIP rev.
B81-37525

543'.0877 — Chemical analysis. High resolution nuclear magnetic resonance spectroscopy — *Manuals*

Brevard, C.. Handbook of high resolution multinuclear NMR / C. Brevard, P. Granger. — New York ; Chichester : Wiley, c1981. — xvii,229p : ill ; 24cm
Bibliography: p213-226. — Includes index
ISBN 0-471-06323-1 : £18.15 B82-04432

543'.089 — Chromatography — *Conference proceedings*

Chromatography, equilibria and kinetics. — London : The Faraday Division, The Royal Society of Chemistry, 1980. — 191p : ill ; 25cm. — (Faraday symposia of the Chemical Society, ISSN 0301-5696 ; no.15)
Includes index
ISBN 0-85186-728-6 (pbk) : £25.50
B82-05832

International Symposium on Chromatography in Biochemistry, Medicine and Environmental Research *(1981 : Venice)*. Chromatography in biochemistry, medicine and environmental research, 1. — Oxford : Elsevier Scientific, Feb.1983. — [600]p. — (Analytical chemistry symposia series ; v.13)
ISBN 0-444-42016-9 B82-37634

543'.0892 — Chemical analysis. Electron capture detection chromatography

Electron capture : theory and practice in chromatography / edited by A. Zlatkis, C.F. Poole. — Amsterdam ; Oxford : Elsevier Scientific, 1981. — xii,429p : ill ; 25cm. — (Journal of chromatography library ; v.20)
Includes index
ISBN 0-444-41954-3 : Unpriced B82-05060

543'.0894 — High performance liquid chromatography

Hamilton, R. J.. Introduction to high performance liquid chromatography / R.J. Hamilton and P.A. Sewell. — 2nd ed. — London : Chapman and Hall, 1982. — vii,248p : ill ; 25cm
Previous ed.: 1977. — Includes index
ISBN 0-412-23430-0 : Unpriced : CIP rev.
B82-00302

High performance liquid chromatography. — Edinburgh : Edinburgh University Press, Sept.1982. — [205]p
Originally published: 1978
ISBN 0-85224-383-9 (pbk) : £7.50 : CIP entry
B82-19834

543'.0894 — Liquid chromatography

Techniques of liquid chromatography. — Chichester : Wiley, Nov.1982. — [460]p
ISBN 0-471-26220-x : £25.00 : CIP entry
B82-29439

543'.0894 — Reversed-phase liquid chromatography

Krstulović, Ante M.. Reversed-phase high-performance liquid chromatography : theory, practice and biomedical applications / Ante M. Krstulović, Phyllis R. Brown. — New York ; Chichester : Wiley, c1982. — xi,296p : ill ; 24cm
Bibliography: p2-3. — Includes index
ISBN 0-471-05369-4 : £27.00 B82-34335

545 — QUANTITATIVE ANALYSIS

545'.33'05 — Mass spectrometry — *Serials*

Dynamic mass spectrometry. — Vol.6. — London : Heyden, Sept.1981. — [384]p
ISBN 0-85501-499-7 : £35.00 : CIP entry
B81-24607

Mass spectrometry. — Vol.6. — London : Royal Society of Chemistry, Nov.1981. — [330]p. — (Specialist periodical report / Royal Society of Chemistry)
ISBN 0-85186-308-6 : CIP entry
ISSN 0305-9987 B81-31187

546 — INORGANIC CHEMISTRY

546 — Inorganic chemistry

Moeller, Therald. Inorganic chemistry : a modern introduction / Therald Moeller. — New York ; Chichester : Wiley, 1982. — viii, : ill ; 24cm
Includes index
ISBN 0-471-61230-8 : £27.25 B82-39920

546 — Inorganic chemistry - *For schools*

Liptrot, G. F.. Modern inorganic chemistry. — 3rd ed. — London : Bell & Hyman, June 1981. — [471]p. — (Modern chemistry series)
Previous ed.: 1974
ISBN 0-7135-2183-x (pbk) : £4.95 : CIP entry
B81-15918

546 — Inorganic compounds

Chambers, C.. Inorganic chemistry / C. Chambers, A.K. Holliday. — [New ed.]. — London : Butterworths, 1982. — xi,397p : ill ; 24cm. — (Butterworths intermediate chemistry)
Previous ed.: published as Modern inorganic chemistry. 1975. — Text on inside covers. — Includes index
ISBN 0-408-10822-3 (pbk) : Unpriced : CIP rev. B82-01972

Inorganic chemistry : concepts and case studies / [S247 Course Team]. — Milton Keynes : Open University Press. — (Science : a second level course) (S247 ; Block 4)
Block 4: Molecules great and small / written by Elaine Moore in collaboration with the Course Team. — 1981. — 123p : ill(some col.) ; 30cm
At head of title: The Open University
ISBN 0-335-17023-4 (pbk) : Unpriced
B82-07729

Inorganic chemistry : concepts and case studies / [S247 Course Team]. — Milton Keynes : Open University Press. — (Science : a second level course)
At head of title: The Open University
Block 6: Spectroscopic methods in inorganic chemistry / written by Charles Harding in collaboration with the Course Team. — 1981. — 55p : ill(some col.) ; 30cm. — (S247 ; blocks 6 and 7)
ISBN 0-335-17024-2 (pbk) : Unpriced
B82-16979

Ionisation constants of inorganic acids and bases in aqueous solution. — Oxford : Pergamon, Nov.1982. — [194]p. — (IUPAC chemical data series ; 29)
ISBN 0-08-029214-3 : £25.00 : CIP entry
B82-33326

Kauffman, George B.. Inorganic chemical compounds. — London : Heyden, Apr.1981. — 1v.. — (Fundamentals of chemistry)
ISBN 0-85501-683-3 (cased) : CIP entry
ISBN 0-85501-684-1 (pbk) : Unpriced
B81-06597

Mellor, J. W.. Supplement to Mellor's Comprehensive treatise on inorganic and theoretical chemistry / prepared under the direction of an editorial board. — London : Longman
Vol.5: Boron
Part B1: Boron-hydrogen compounds. — 1981. — 616p : ill ; 24cm
Includes index
ISBN 0-582-46278-9 : £80.00 : CIP rev.
B80-07776

546'.05 — Inorganic chemistry — *Serials*

Annual reports on the progress of chemistry. Section A. Inorganic chemistry. — Vol.76 (1979)-. — London : Royal Society of Chemistry, 1980-. — v. : ill ; 23cm
Annual. — Continues in part: Annual reports on the progress of chemistry. Section A, Physical and inorganic chemistry
ISSN 0260-1818 = Annual reports on the progress of chemistry Section A. Inorganic chemistry : Unpriced B82-11803

Polyhedron : the international journal for inorganic and organometallic chemistry. — Vol.1, no.1 (1982)-. — Oxford : Pergamon, 1982-. — v. : ill ; 28cm
Monthly. — Merger of: Journal of inorganic & nuclear chemistry; and, Inorganic & nuclear chemistry letters. — Index in each December issue
ISSN 0277-5387 = Polyhedron : £243.90 per year B82-27634

546'.2 — Hydrogen. Atoms. Electron capture theory

Speirs, John M. S.. The capture of an electron by a proton / by John M.S. Speirs. — Fleet (Vernon House, 96 Clarence Rd., Fleet, Hampshire, GU13 9RS) : KAAP Press, 1982. — 5leaves ; 30cm
Cover title
Unpriced (spiral) B82-25619

546'.2248 — Water. Spectroscopy. Spectra — *Tables*

Flaud, J. -M.. Water vapour line parameters from microwave to medium infrared : an atlas of H2 O(16), H2 O(17) and H2 O(18) line positions and intensities between 0 and 4350cm-1 / by J.-M. Flaud, C. Camy-Peyret and R.A. Toth ; preface by J.N. Howard. — Oxford : Pergamon, 1981. — 259p ; 28cm. — (International tables of selected constants ; 19)
English and French text. — Added t.p. in French
ISBN 0-08-026181-7 : Unpriced : CIP rev. B81-28793

546'.24 — Acid-base balance. Theories

Finston, Harman L.. A new view of current acid-base theories / Harmon L. Finston and Allen C. Rychtman. — New York ; Chichester : Wiley, c1982. — viii,216p : ill ; 23cm. — (A Wiley-Interscience publication)
Includes index
ISBN 0-471-08472-7 : £35.00 B82-28698

546'.2642'0212 — Hydrogen. Solubility — *Tables*

Hydrogen and deuterium / volume editor Colin L. Young ; evaluators Rubin Battino, H. Lawrence Clever, Denis A. Wiesenburg ; compilers R.W. Cargill ... [et al.]. — Oxford : Pergamon, 1981. — xviii,646p : ill ; 28cm. — (Solubility data series, ISSN 0191-5622 ; v.5-6)
Includes index
ISBN 0-08-023927-7 : Unpriced : CIP rev. B81-19154

546'.3 — Diatomic metals — *Conference proceedings*

Diatomic metals and metallic clusters. — London : Faraday Division, Royal Society of Chemistry, [c1980]. — 250p,[1]leaf of plates : ill ; 26cm. — (Faraday symposia of the Royal Society of Chemistry, ISSN 0301-5696 ; no.14)
Conference papers. — Includes index
ISBN 0-85186-998-x (pbk) : Unpriced B82-37881

546'.3 — Liquid metals — *Conference proceedings*

Material behaviour and physical chemistry in liquid metal systems / edited by H.U. Borgstedt. — New York ; London : Plenum, c1982. — xiv,548p : ill ; 26cm
Conference proceedings. — Includes index
ISBN 0-306-40917-8 : Unpriced B82-38671

546'.3 — Metals. High resolution microanalysis — *Conference proceedings*

Quantitative microanalysis with high spatial resolution : proceedings of the conference, jointly sponsored by the Metals Science Committee of the Metals Society and the EMAG Group of the Institute of Physics, which was held in the Renold Building of the University of Manchester Institute of Science and Technology on 25-27 March 1981. — London : Metals Society, 1981. — ix,275p : ill(some col.) ; 31cm
Includes index
ISBN 0-904357-38-4 : Unpriced B82-16005

546'.3 — Metals. High temperature oxidation

Birks, N.. Introduction to high temperature oxidation of metals. — London : Edward Arnold, July 1982. — [208]p
ISBN 0-7131-3464-x (pbk) : £12.00 : CIP entry B82-13016

546'.4 — Actinide elements — *Conference proceedings*

Actinides — 1981 Conference *(Pacific Grove)*. Actinides in perspective : proceedings of the Actinides — 1981 Conference Pacific Grove, California, USA, 10-15 September 1981 / edited by Norman M. Edelstein. — Oxford : Pergamon, 1982. — ix,610p : ill ; 24cm
Includes bibliographies and index
ISBN 0-08-029193-7 : £37.50 : CIP rev. B82-12712

546'.4 — Rare earth elements

Busev, A. I.. Analytical chemistry of rare elements / A.I. Busev, V.G. Tiptsova, V.M. Ivanov ; translated from the Russian by Alexander Rosinkin. — Moscow : Mir ; [London] : distributed by Central, 1981. — 416p : ill ; 23cm
Translation and revision of: Rukovodstvo po analiticheskoĭ khimii redkikh ėlementov
ISBN 0-7147-1718-5 : £5.95 B82-29716

Handbook on the physics and chemistry of rare earths / editors Karl A. Gschneidner, Jr., LeRoy Eyring. — Amsterdam ; Oxford : North-Holland Publishing
Vol.4: Non-metallic compounds 2. — 1979. — xiii,602p : ill ; 25cm
Includes bibliographies and index
ISBN 0-444-85216-6 : Unpriced B82-17877

546'.431 — Uranium. Disequilibrium. Environmental aspects

Uranium series disequilibrium. — Oxford : Clarendon Press, Jan.1982. — [550]p
ISBN 0-19-854423-5 : £45.00 : CIP entry B81-34383

546'.6 — Metal hydrides — *Conference proceedings*

NATO Advanced Study Institute on Metal Hydrides *(1980 : Rhodes)*. Metal hydrides / [proceedings of a NATO Advanced Study Institute on Metal Hydrides, held June 17-27, 1980, in Rhodes, Greece] ; edited by Gust Bambakidis. — New York ; London : Plenum, published in cooperation with NATO Scientific Affairs Division, c1981. — viii,385p : ill ; 26cm. — (NATO advanced study institutes series. Series B, Physics ; v.76)
Includes index
ISBN 0-306-40891-0 : Unpriced B82-14447

546'.7 — Heterocyclic inorganic sulphur, nitrogen & phosphorus compounds

Heal, Henry G.. The inorganic heterocyclic chemistry of sulfur, nitrogen and phosphorus / Henry G. Heal. — London : Academic Press, 1980. — xv,271p ; 24cm
Includes index
ISBN 0-12-335680-6 (Corrected) : £35.80 : CIP rev. B80-20625

546'.711542'0212 — Nitrogen oxides. Solubility — *Tables*

Nitrogen and air. — Oxford : Pergamon, Oct.1982. — [618]p. — (Solubility data series ; v.10)
ISBN 0-08-023922-6 : £50.00 : CIP entry B82-25509

Oxides of nitrogen / volume editor Colin L. Young ; evaluators Rubin Battino, William Gerrard ; compilers H. Lawrence Clever ... [et al.]. — Oxford : Pergamon, 1981. — xviii,369p ; 28cm. — (Solubility data series, ISSN 0191-5622 ; v.8)
Includes index
ISBN 0-08-023924-2 : £50.00 : CIP rev. B81-31064

546'.71159 — Nitrogen. Fixation

Nitrogen fixation. — Oxford : Clarendon
Vol.1: Ecology / edited by W.J. Broughton. — 1981. — xi,306p : ill ; 24cm
Includes bibliographies and index
ISBN 0-19-854540-1 : £22.00 B82-17763

546'.7212 — Oxides

Nonstoichiometric oxides / edited by O. Toft Sørensen. — New York ; London : Academic Press, 1981. — xi,441p : ill ; 24cm. — (Materials science and technology)
Includes bibliographies and index
ISBN 0-12-655280-0 : £39.00 B82-30131

546'.7212 — Oxides. Properties — *Tables*

The **Oxide** handbook / edited by G.V. Samsonov. — 2nd ed. / translated from Russian by Robert K. Johnston. — New York ; London : IFI, c1982. — xvii,463p : ill ; 24cm
Translation of: Fiziko-khimicheskie svoĭstva okislov. — Previous ed.: 1973. — Includes index
ISBN 0-306-65177-7 : Unpriced B82-23738

546'.721542'0212 — Oxygen. Solubility — *Tables*

Oxygen and ozone / volume editor Rubin Battino ; evaluators Rubin Battino ... [et al.] ; compilers Ardis L. Cramer ... [et al.]. — Oxford : Pergamon, 1981. — xviii,519p : ill ; 28cm. — (Solubility data series ; v.7)
Includes index
ISBN 0-08-023915-3 : Unpriced : CIP rev. B81-30381

546'.7232'05 — Sulphur compounds — *Serials*

Sulfur reports. — Vol.1, no.1 (1980)-. — Chur ; London : Harwood Academic, 1980-. — v. : ill ; 25cm
Irregular. — Description based on: Vol.1, no.6 (1981)
ISSN 0196-1772 = Sulfur reports : Unpriced B82-38537

547 — ORGANIC CHEMISTRY

547 — Organic chemistry

Elvidge, J. A.. Chemistry is organic / J.A. Elvidge. — [Guildford] ([Guildford, Surrey GU2 5XH]) : [University of Surrey], [1978?]. — 29p : ill,ports ; 21cm. — (University of Surrey university lecture)
Cover title
Unpriced (pbk) B82-26655

Fernandez, Jack E.. Organic chemistry : an introduction / Jack E. Fernandez. — Englewood Cliffs ; London : Prentice-Hall, c1982. — xxii,538p : ill ; 25cm
Includes index
ISBN 0-13-640417-0 : £14.95 B82-15508

547 — Organic chemistry — *Festschriften*

R B Woodward remembered : a collection of papers in honour of Robert Burns Woodward 1917-1979 / editor-in-chief Sir Derek Barton ; editor H.H. Wasserman ... [et al.]. — Oxford : Pergamon, 1982. — xx,522p : ill ; 28cm
Includes 4 papers in French. — Bibliography: p xii-xviii
ISBN 0-08-029238-0 : Unpriced B82-39871

547 — Organic chemistry — *For schools*

Williams, Hugh J.. Introduction to organic chemistry. — Chichester : Wiley, Feb.1983. — [288]p
ISBN 0-471-10206-7 (cased) : £10.00 : CIP entry
ISBN 0-471-10207-5 (pbk) : £5.00 B82-38276

547 — Organic compounds

Applequirt, Douglas. Introduction to organic chemistry. — 3rd ed. / Douglas Applequirt, Charles H. DePuy, Kenneth L. Rinehart. — New York ; Chichester : Wiley, c1982. — xiii,384p : ill(some col.) ; 25cm
Previous ed.: / by Charles H. DePuy, Kenneth L. Rinehart, Jr. 1975. — Includes index
ISBN 0-471-05641-3 : Unpriced B82-19656

Baum, Stuart J.. Introduction to organic and biological chemistry / Stuart J. Baum. — 3rd ed. — New York : Macmillan ; London : Collier Macmillan, c1982. — xiv,560p : ill ; 26cm
Previous ed.: 1978. — Includes index
ISBN 0-02-306640-7 : £15.95 B82-19509

Comprehensive organic chemistry : the synthesis and reactions of organic compounds / chairman and deputy chairman of the editorial board Sir Derek Barton and W. David Ollis. — Oxford : Pergamon, 1979. — 6v. ; 28cm
Includes index
ISBN 0-08-021319-7 : £343.75 : CIP rev.
ISBN 0-08-021313-8 (v.1)
ISBN 0-08-021314-6 (v.2)
ISBN 0-08-021315-4 (v.3)
ISBN 0-08-021316-2 (v.4)
ISBN 0-08-021317-0 (v.5)
ISBN 0-08-022931-x (v.6) B78-33762

Norman, R.O.C.. Modern organic chemistry. — 3rd ed. — London : Bell & Hyman, June 1981. — [366]p
Previous ed.: London : Mills and Boon, 1975
ISBN 0-7135-2185-6 (pbk) : £4.75 : CIP entry B81-15912

Organic chemistry / [S246 Course Team]. — Milton Keynes : Open University Press. — (Science : a second level course)
At head of title: The Open University
Block 4: Reaction mechanisms : applications / prepared by an Open University Course Team. — 1981. — 38p : ill(some col.) ; 30cm. — (S246 ; block 4, units 10-13)
Contents: Unit 10: Aromatics — Unit 11: Carbonyl chemistry — Unit 12: Organometallic chemistry — Unit 13: Polymer chemistry
ISBN 0-335-16003-4 (pbk) : Unpriced B82-16978

547 — Organic compounds *continuation*

Organic chemistry / [S246 Course Team]. — Milton Keynes : Open University Press. — (Science : a second level course)
At head of title: The Open University
Block 5: An introduction to organic synthesis. — 1981. — 37,32,30p : ill ; 30cm. — (S246 ; units 14-16)
Contents: Unit 14: Methods of organic synthesis — Unit 15: Planning organic synthesis — Unit 16: Cholesterol
ISBN 0-335-16004-2 (pbk) : Unpriced
B82-05200

Solomons, T. W. Graham. Fundamentals of organic chemistry / T.W. Graham Solomons. — New York ; Chichester : Wiley, c1982. — 884p in various pagings : ill ; 27cm
Text on lining papers. — Bibliography: pB1-B5. — Includes index
ISBN 0-471-02980-7 : £19.95 B82-18219

Supplements to the 2nd edition (editor S. Coffey) of Rodd's chemistry of carbon compounds : a modern comprehensive treatise / edited by M. F. Ansell. — Amsterdam ; Oxford : Elsevier Scientific
Supplement to volume III Aromatic compounds. — 1981
Includes index
Part B : Benzoquinones and related compounds : derivatives of mononuclear benzenoid hydrocarbons with nuclear substituents attached through an element other than the non-metals in groups VI and VII of the periodic table. Part C : Nuclear-substituted benzenoid hydrocarbons with more than one nitrogen atom in a substituent group. — xviii,358p : ill ; 24cm
ISBN 0-444-42017-7 : £36.42 B82-00692

Supplements to the 2nd edition (editor S. Coffey) of Rodd's Chemistry of carbon compounds : a modern comprehensive treatise / edited by Martin F. Ansell. — Amsterdam ; Oxford : Elsevier-Scientific
Supplement to volume III Aromatic compounds
Pt.D: Monobenzenoid hydrocarbon derivatives with functional groups in an acyclic side chain ... Pt.E: Monobenzenoid hydrocarbon derivatives with functional groups in separate side chains ... Pt.F: Polybenzenoid hydrocarbons and their derivatives ... (Partial : Chapters 20 and 21 only in this vol.). — 1982. — xx,423p : ill ; 24cm
Includes index
ISBN 0-444-42088-6 : Unpriced B82-39977

547 — Organic salts. Thermodynamic properties & transport phenomena — *Conference proceedings*

Thermodynamic and transport properties of organic salts / prepared for publication by Paolo Franzosini and Manlio Sanesi. — Oxford : Pergamon, 1980. — x,370p : ill ; 28cm. — (IUPAC chemical data series ; no.28)
At head of title: International Union of Pure and Applied Chemistry (Physical Chemistry Division, Commission on Thermodynamics)
ISBN 0-08-022378-8 : £42.50 : CIP rev.
B80-12348

547'.00246 — Organic chemistry — *For technicians*

Brockington, John. Organic chemistry for higher education / John Brockington, Peter Stamper. — London : Longman, 1982. — 341p : ill ; 22cm
Includes index
ISBN 0-582-41230-7 (pbk) : £6.50 : CIP rev.
B82-26533

547'.0028 — Organic chemistry. Experiments — *Manuals*

Pavia, Donald L.. Introduction to organic laboratory techniques : a contemporary approach / Donald L. Pavia, Gary M. Lampman, George S. Kriz. — 2nd ed. — Philadelphia ; London : Saunders College Publishing, c1982. — xiv,676,xiiip : ill ; 27cm. — (Saunders golden sunburst series)
Previous ed.: 1976. — Text on lining papers. — Includes bibliographies and index
ISBN 0-03-058424-8 : £17.50 B82-15351

547'.0028 — Organic chemistry. Laboratory techniques

Keese, R.. Fundamentals of preparative organic chemistry / R. Keese, R.K. Müller and T.P. Toube ; illustrated by H. Brühwiler ; developed and compiled in cooperation with Hans-Ulrich Blaser ... [et al.]. — Chichester : Horwood, 1982. — 149p ; 24cm. — (Ellis Horwood series in organic chemistry)
Text on lining papers. — Includes index
ISBN 0-85312-396-9 (cased) : £15.00 : CIP rev.
ISBN 0-85312-450-7 (pbk) : Unpriced
B82-11095

Mázov, Laszlo. Methods of organic analysis. — Oxford : Elsevier Scientific, Mar.1982. — [500] p. — (Wilson and Wilson's comprehensive analytical chemistry ; v.15)
Translation and revision of: Szerves kémiai analizis
ISBN 0-444-99704-0 : £50.00 : CIP entry
B82-01967

Moore, James A.. Experimental methods in organic chemistry / James A. Moore, David L. Dalrymple, Oscar R. Rodig. — 3rd ed. — Philadelphia ; London : Saunders College Publishing, c1982. — viii,368p : ill ; 24cm. — (Saunders golden sunburst series)
Previous ed.: 1976. — Text and ill on inside cover. — Includes index
ISBN 0-03-056896-x : £16.95 B82-15357

547'.003'21 — Organic compounds — *Encyclopaedias*

Dictionary of organic compounds. — 5th ed. — London : Chapman and Hall, Sept.1982. — 7v
Previous ed.: London : Eyre & Spottiswoode, 1965
ISBN 0-412-17000-0 : £975.00 : CIP entry
B82-19222

547'.005 — Organic chemistry — *Serials*

Annual reports on the progress of chemistry. Section B, Organic chemistry. — Vol.77 (1980). — London : Royal Society of Chemistry, Oct.1981. — [410]p
ISBN 0-85186-121-0 : £40.50 : CIP entry
ISSN 0069-3030 B81-24669

547'.0076 — Organic chemistry — *Questions & answers*

Ryles, A. P.. Worked examples in essential organic chemistry / A.P. Ryles, K. Smith and R.S. Ward. — Chichester : Wiley, c1982. — ix,161p : ill ; 24cm
ISBN 0-471-27972-2 (cased) : £11.00 : CIP rev.
ISBN 0-471-27975-7 (pbk) : Unpriced
B81-19170

547'.0076 — Organic chemistry — *Questions & answers* — *For schools*

Pandit, Vijay. Advanced Level organic chemistry : (questions and answers) / Vijay Pandit. — London : V. Pandit, 1980. — 140p ; 22cm
ISBN 0-9507233-0-4 (pbk) : £2.00 B82-11036

547'.01 — 1,3-indandiones

Pharmacochemistry of 1,3-indandiones / edited by W. Th. Nauta and R.F. Rekker. — Amsterdam ; Oxford : Elsevier Scientific, 1981. — xvii,346p : ill ; 25cm. — (Pharmacochemistry library ; 3)
Includes index
ISBN 0-444-41976-4 : Unpriced : CIP rev.
B81-22640

547'.01044252 — Hydrocarbons. Thermal isomerisation

Gajewski, Joseph J.. Hydrocarbon thermal isomerizations / Joseph J. Gajewski. — New York ; London : Academic Press, 1981. — x,442p : ill ; 24cm. — (Organic chemistry ; v.44)
Includes index
ISBN 0-12-273350-9 : £29.80 B82-15469

547'.010448 — Hydrocarbons. Raman spectra — *Tables*

Sterin, K. E.. Raman spectra of hydrocarbons / by K.E. Sterin, V.T. Aleksanyan, G.N. Zhizhin. — Oxford : Pergamon, 1980. — 358p ; 24cm
Includes index
ISBN 0-08-023596-4 : £33.00 : CIP rev.
B80-00179

547'.010458 — Hydrocarbons. Effects of ionising radiation

Radiation chemistry of hydrocarbons / edited by G. Földiák. — Amsterdam ; Oxford : Elsevier Scientific, 1981. — 476p : ill ; 25cm. — (Studies in physical and theoretical chemistry ; v.14)
Includes index
ISBN 0-444-99746-6 : £41.48 B82-13444

547'.0104595 — Hydrocarbons. Conversion. Catalysis

Pines, Herman. The chemistry of catalytic hydrocarbon conversions / Herman Pines. — New York ; London : Academic Press, 1981. — xiii,305p : ill ; 24cm
Includes bibliographies and index
ISBN 0-12-557160-7 (corrected) : £23.20
B82-01624

547'.01046 — Hydrocarbons. Mixtures. Chemical analysis

Hála, Slavoj. Analysis of complex hydrocarbon mixtures / by Slavoj Hála, Mečislav Kuraš, Milan Popl. — Amsterdam ; Oxford : Elsevier Scientific
Part A: Separation methods. — 1981. — 382p : ill ; 23cm. — (Comprehensive analytical chemistry ; v.13)
Includes index
ISBN 0-444-99736-9 : £47.87 : CIP rev.
ISBN 0-444-99734-2 (set) : Unpriced
B81-25293

547'.02 — Organofluorine compounds

Preparation, properties and industrial applications of organofluorine compounds. — Chichester : Ellis Horwood, June 1982. — [304]p. — (Ellis Horwood series in chemical science)
ISBN 0-85312-276-8 : £30.00 : CIP entry
B82-18583

547'.03 — Carbon dioxide. Chemical reactions with organic compounds

Organic and bio-organic chemistry of carbon dioxide / edited by Shohei Inoue, Noboru Yamazaki. — Tokyo : Kodansha ; New York ; Chichester : Wiley, c1982. — xi,280p : ill ; 23cm
Includes index
ISBN 0-470-27309-7 : £39.00 B82-30380

547'.0350459 — Crown-ethers. Chemical reactions

Jong, F. de. Stability and reactivity of crown-ether complexes / F. de Jong, D.N. Reinhoudt. — London ; New York : Academic Press, 1981. — 163p : ill ; 24cm
Originally published: in Advances in physical organic chemistry ; vol.17. — London : Academic Press, 1980. — Bibliography: p146-155. — Includes index
ISBN 0-12-208780-1 (pbk) : Unpriced : CIP rev. B81-30303

547'.036 — Chalcones

Dhar, Durga Nath. The chemistry of chalcones and related compounds / Durga Nath Dhar ; foreword by Derek Barton. — New York ; Chichester : Wiley, c1981. — 285p : ill ; 24cm
Includes index
ISBN 0-471-08007-1 : £28.50 B82-04435

547'.04 — Organic nitrogen compounds

Supplement F : the chemistry of amino, nitroso and nitro coumpounds and their derivatives / edited by Saul Patai. — Chichester : Wiley, 1982. — 2v.(xiv,1438p) : ill ; 24cm. — (The Chemistry of functional groups)
Includes bibliographies and index
ISBN 0-471-27873-4 : £75.00 : CIP rev.
ISBN 0-471-27871-8 (v.1)
ISBN 0-471-27872-6 (v.2) B82-01170

547'.043 — Diazo compounds

Ershov, Vladimir V.. Quinonediazides. — Oxford : Elsevier, Aug.1981. — [302]p. — (Studies in organic chemistry ; v.7)
ISBN 0-444-41737-0 : CIP entry B81-25108

547'.05 — Organometallic compounds

The **Chemistry** of the metal-carbon bond. — Chichester : Wiley. — (The Chemistry of functional groups)
Vol.1. — Sept.1982. — [992]p
ISBN 0-471-10058-7 : £75.00 : CIP entry
B82-19515

547'.05 — Organometallic compounds *continuation*

Comprehensive organometallic chemistry. — Oxford : Pergamon, Sept.1982. — 9v.
ISBN 0-08-025269-9 : £1075.00 : CIP entry B82-19091

547'.05 — Organometallic compounds — *Conference proceedings*

China-Japan-United States Trilateral Seminar on Organometallic Chemistry *(1980 : Peking).* Fundamental research in organometallic chemistry : proceedings of the China-Japan-United States Trilateral Seminar on Organometallic Chemistry held at Peking, People's Republic of China, June, 1980 / edited by Minoru Tsutsui, Yoshio Ishii, Huang Yaozeng. — New York ; London : Van Nostrand Reinhold, c1982. — xxix,975p : ill,1port ; 24cm
Includes index
ISBN 0-442-27216-2 : £55.25 B82-36982

547'.05 — Organometallic compounds. Spectroscopy — *Serials*

Spectroscopic properties of inorganic and organometallic compounds. — Vol.14. — London : Royal Society of Chemistry, Dec.1981. — [400]p. — (Specialist periodical report / Royal Society of Chemistry)
ISBN 0-85186-123-7 : CIP entry
ISSN 0584-8555
Primary classification 541.2'8 B81-32050

547'.050459 — Organometallic compounds. Synthesis

Organometallic syntheses. — New York ; London : Academic Press
Bibliography: p183-186. — Includes index
Vol.2: Nontransition-metal compounds / by John J. Eisch. — 1981. — xiv,194p : ill ; 24cm
ISBN 0-12-234950-4 : £19.60 B82-04245

547'.05046 — Organometallic compounds. Carbon-13 nuclear magnetic resonance spectroscopy — *Technical data*

Mann, Brian E.. 13C nmr data for organomatellic compounds / Brian E. Mann, Brian F. Taylor. — London : Academic Press, 1981. — viii,326p : ill ; 24cm. — (Organometallic chemistry)
ISBN 0-12-469150-1 : £15.80 : CIP rev. B81-13848

547'.05'05 — Organometallic compounds — *Serials*

Organometallic chemistry. — Vol.10. — London : Royal Society of Chemistry, Mar.1982. — [480]p. — (Specialist periodical report / Royal Society of Chemistry)
ISBN 0-85186-581-x : CIP entry
ISSN 0301-0074 B82-07118

547'.0568 — Organic group IV compounds — *Serials*

Organometallic chemistry reviews. — Oxford : Elsevier Scientific, Oct.1981. — [300]p. — (Journal of Organometallic Chemistry library ; 12)
ISBN 0-444-42025-8 : CIP entry B81-27379

547'.0572'05 — Organic selenium compounds & organic tellurium compounds - *Serials*

Organic compounds of sulphur, selenium, and tellurium. — Vol.6. — London : Royal Society of Chemistry, Sept.1981. — [350]p. — (A Specialist periodical report)
ISBN 0-85186-299-3 : CIP entry
ISSN 0305-9812
Primary classification 547'.06'05 B81-20502

547'.06'05 — Organic sulphur compounds - *Serials*

Organic compounds of sulphur, selenium, and tellurium. — Vol.6. — London : Royal Society of Chemistry, Sept.1981. — [350]p. — (A Specialist periodical report)
ISBN 0-85186-299-3 : CIP entry
ISSN 0305-9812
Also classified at 547'.0572'05 B81-20502

547'.07'05 — Organic phosphorus compounds - *Serials*

Organophosphorus chemistry. — Vol.12. — London : Royal Society of Chemistry, Sept.1981. — [300]p. — (A Specialist periodical report)
ISBN 0-85186-106-7 : CIP entry
ISSN 0306-0713 B81-20565

547'.07'05 — Organic phosphorus compounds — *Serials*

Organophosphorus chemistry. — Vol.13. — London : Royal Society of Chemistry, July 1982. — [310]p. — (Specialist periodical report / Royal Society of Chemistry)
ISBN 0-85186-116-4 : CIP entry
ISSN 0306-0713 B82-14948

547'.08 — Organic silicon compounds

Silicon geochemistry and biogeochemistry. — London : Academic Press, Dec.1982. — [300]p
ISBN 0-12-065620-5 : CIP entry B82-29872

547.1'223'024372 — Organic compounds. Stereochemistry — *For teaching*

Marples, B. A.. Elementary organic stereochemistry and conformational analysis / B.A. Marples. — London : Royal Society of Chemistry, 1981. — iii,82p : ill ; 22cm. — (Royal Society of Chemistry monographs for teachers ; no.34)
Bibliography: p82
ISBN 0-85186-303-5 (pbk) : Unpriced B82-08164

547.1'224 — Organic compounds. Chemical bonding. Molecular orbital theory — *Conference proceedings*

Molecular structure and conformation. — Oxford : Elsevier Scientific, June 1982. — [346]p. — (Progress in theoretical organic chemistry ; v.3)
Conference papers
ISBN 0-444-42089-4 : CIP entry B82-15932

547.1'28 — Organic compounds. Molecules. Structure. Determination. Infrared spectroscopy

Bellamy, L. J.. The infrared spectra of complex molecules / L.J. Bellamy. — London : Chapman and Hall
Vol.2: Advances in infrared group frequencies. — 2nd ed. — 1980. — xi,299p : ill ; 24cm
Previous ed.: London : Methuen, 1968. — Includes index
ISBN 0-412-22350-3 : £15.00 : CIP rev. B80-11424

547.1'28 — Organic compounds. Molecules. Structure. Determination. Spectroscopy

Clerc, J. T.. Structural analysis of organic compounds : by combined application of spectroscopic methods / J.T. Clerc, E. Pretsch, J. Seibl. — Amsterdam ; Oxford : Elsevier Scientific, 1981. — 288p : ill ; 25cm. — (Studies in analytical chemistry ; 1)
Includes index
ISBN 0-444-99748-2 : £28.42 B82-21914

547.1'3'05 — Physical organic chemistry — *Serials*

Advances in physical organic chemistry. — Vol.18. — London : Academic Press, Mar.1982. — [300]p
ISBN 0-12-033518-2 : CIP entry
ISSN 0065-3160 B82-00292

Advances in physical organic chemistry. — Vol.19. — London : Academic Press, Dec.1982. — [480]p
ISBN 0-12-033519-0 : CIP entry
ISSN 0065-3160 B82-29870

547.1'372 — Carbanions

Comprehensive carbanion chemistry / edited by E. Buncel, T. Durst. — Amsterdam ; Oxford : Elsevier Scientific
Pt.A: Structure and reactivity. — 1980. — vii,400p : ill ; 25cm. — (Studies in organic chemistry ; 5)
Includes index
ISBN 0-444-41913-6 : £36.40 : CIP rev. B80-12349

547.1'3723 — Aqueous solutions. Organic acids. Ionisation. Equilibrium constants — *Tables*

Serjeant, E. P.. Ionisation constants of organic acids in aqueous solution / by E.P. Serjeant and Boyd Dempsey. — Oxford : Pergamon, 1979. — ix,989p ; 28cm. — (IUPAC chemical data series ; no.23)
At head of title: International Union of Pure and Applied Chemistry, Analytical Chemistry Division, Commission on Equilibrium Data
ISBN 0-08-022339-7 : £72.00 : CIP rev. B78-36066

547.1'3723 — Organic acids & bases. Ionisation. Thermodynamic properties

Perrin, D. D.. pKa prediction for organic acids and bases. — London : Chapman and Hall, Nov.1981. — [150]p
ISBN 0-412-22190-x : £10.00 : CIP entry B81-31266

547.13'88 — Isotope-labelled chemical compounds — *Conference proceedings*

International Symposium on the Synthesis and Applications of Isotopically Labeled Compounds *(1982 : Kansas City).* Synthesis and applications of isotopically labeled compounds. — Oxford : Elsevier Scientific, Jan.1983. — [508]p
ISBN 0-444-42152-1 : CIP entry B82-37631

547.1'39 — Organic compounds. Chemical reactions

Saxton, R. G.. Fundamental organic reactions / by R. G. Saxton. — Burton upon Trent : Mercian, 1980. — vi,202p : ill ; 21cm
Includes index
ISBN 0-9506583-1-6 (pbk) : Unpriced B82-31682

547.13'9 — Organic compounds. Chemical reactions. Mechanisms — *Serials*

Organic reaction mechanisms. — 1981. — Chichester : Wiley, Feb.1983. — [700]p
ISBN 0-471-10459-0 : £80.00 : CIP entry B82-38711

547.1'393 — Organic compounds. Reactivity

Klumpp, Gerhard W.. Reactivity in organic chemistry / Gerhard W. Klumpp ; translated from the German by Ludmila Birladeanu. — New York ; Chichester : Wiley, c1982. — xiii,502p : ill ; 24cm
Translation of: Reaktivität in der organischen Chemie. — Includes index
ISBN 0-471-06285-5 : £38.75 B82-34739

547.1'3'94 — Organic compounds. Chemical reactions. Linear free energy relationships. Correlation methods

Shorter, John. The correlation analysis of organic reactivity, with particular reference to multiple regression. — Chichester : Wiley, Aug.1982. — [250]p. — (Chemometrics research studies series ; 4)
ISBN 0-471-10479-5 : £15.00 : CIP entry B82-17203

547'.2 — Organic compounds. Synthesis

Mackie, Raymond K.. Guidebook to organic synthesis / Raymond K. Mackie and David M. Smith. — London : Longman, 1982. — xi,338p : ill ; 24cm
Bibliography: p326-332. — Includes index
ISBN 0-582-45592-8 (pbk) : £9.95 : CIP rev. B81-30153

547'.2 — Organic compounds. Synthesis. Electrochemical techniques

Technique of electroorganic synthesis. — New York ; Chichester : Wiley. — (Techniques of chemistry ; v.5)
Includes index
[Pt.3]: Scale-up and engineering aspects / edited by N.L. Weinberg, B.V. Tilak. — c1982. — xiv,536p : ill ; 24cm
ISBN 0-471-06359-2 : £66.00 B82-34339

547'.2 — Organic compounds. Synthesis. Reagents: Organic silicon compounds

Colvin, Ernest W.. Silicon in organic synthesis / Ernest W. Colvin. — London : Butterworths, 1981. — xi,348p : ill ; 24cm. — (Butterworths monographs in chemistry and chemical engineering)
Includes index
ISBN 0-408-10619-0 (cased) : Unpriced : CIP rev.
ISBN 0-408-10831-2 (pbk) : Unpriced B81-18175

547'.2 — Organic compounds. Synthesis. Use of organometallic compounds

Davies, Stephen G.. Organotransition metal chemistry. — Oxford : Pergamon, Nov.1982. — [428]p. — (Organic chemistry series ; v.2)
ISBN 0-08-026202-3 : £42.50 : CIP entry B82-28720

547′.2′028 — Organic compounds. Synthesis. Laboratory techniques

Warren, Stuart. Organic synthesis : the disconnection approach. — Chichester : Wiley, July 1982. — [320]p
ISBN 0-471-10160-5 (cased) : £15.00 : CIP entry
ISBN 0-471-10161-3 (pbk) : £6.00 B82-13253

547′.2′05 — Organic compounds. Synthesis — *Serials*

General and synthetic methods. — Vol.5. — London : Royal Society of Chemistry, July 1982. — [440]p. — (Specialist periodical report / Royal Society of Chemistry)
ISBN 0-85186-864-9 : CIP entry
ISSN 0141-2140 B82-13134

547′.23 — Organic compounds. Oxidation. Catalysis. Metal compounds. Mechanisms

Sheldon, Roger A.. Metal-catalyzed oxidations of organic compounds : mechanistic principles and synthetic methodology including biochemical processes / Roger A. Sheldon, Jay K. Kochi. — New York ; London : Academic Press, 1981. — xxi,424p : ill ; 24cm
Bibliography: p397. — Includes index
ISBN 0-12-639380-x : £37.00 B82-12305

547′.28 — Carbocationic polymerisation

Kennedy, Joseph P.. Carbocationic polymerization / Joseph P. Kennedy, Ernest Maréchal. — New York ; Chichester : Wiley, c1982. — xx,510p : ill ; 24cm
Includes bibliographies and index
ISBN 0-471-01787-6 : £55.50 B82-26478

547′.28 — Emulsion polymerisation

Emulsion polymerization / edited by Irja Piirma. — New York ; London : Academic Press, 1982. — xii,454p : ill ; 24cm
Includes bibliographies and index
ISBN 0-12-556420-1 : £38.40 B82-35739

Emulsion polymerization and its applications in industry / V.I. Eliseeva ... [et al.] ; translated from the Russian by Sylvia J. Teague. — New York ; London : Consultants Bureau, c1981. — xv,225p : ill ; 24cm
Translation of: Émul'sionnaīa polimerizatsiīa i ee primenenie v promyshlennosti
ISBN 0-306-10961-1 : Unpriced B82-17721

547′.28′05 — Polymerisation — *Serials*

Developments in polymerisation. — 3. — London : Applied Science, Apr.1982. — [256]p. — (The Developments series)
ISBN 0-85334-117-6 : £25.00 : CIP entry B82-04794

547.3 — Organic compounds. Chemical analysis

Lyman, Warren J.. Handbook of chemical property estimation methods : environmental behavior of organic compounds / ; Warren J. Lyman, William F. Reehl, David H. Rosenblatt. — New York ; London : McGraw-Hill, c1982. — 987p in various pagings : ill,1 form ; 25cm
Includes bibliographies and index
ISBN 0-07-039175-0 : £32.50 B82-37796

547.3′05 — Physical chemistry — *Serials*

Annual reports on the progress of chemistry. Section C, Physical chemistry. — Vol.77 (1980). — London : Royal Society of Chemistry, Sept.1981. — [230]p
ISBN 0-85186-822-3 : £36.50 : CIP entry
ISSN 0260-1826 B81-23892

547.3′0871 — Organic compounds. Chemical analysis. Use of selective ion sensitive electrodes

Ma, T. S.. Organic analysis using ion-selective electrodes / T.S. Ma and S.S.M. Hassan. — London : Academic Press. — (The Analysis of organic materials ; 14)
Vol.1: Methods. — 1982. — xiii,184p : ill ; 24cm
Includes index
ISBN 0-12-462901-6 : £19.20 : CIP rev. B82-00317

Ma, T. S.. Organic analysis using ion-selective electrodes / T.S. Ma and S.S.M. Hassan. — London : Academic Press. — (The Analysis of organic materials ; 14)
Vol.2: Applications and experimental procedures. — 1982. — xiii,284p : ill ; 24cm
Includes index
ISBN 0-12-462902-4 : £24.00 : CIP rev. B82-00318

547.3′0894 — Organic compounds. Trace elements. Chemical analysis. Liquid chromatography

Lawrence, J. F. (James Frederick). Organic trace analysis by liquid chromatography / James F. Lawrence. — New York ; London : Academic Press, 1981. — xii,288p : ill ; 24cm
Includes index
ISBN 0-12-439150-8 : £22.60 B82-12302

547.3′4 — Organic compounds. Qualitative analysis *— Laboratory manuals — For schools*

Davies, D. G.. Organic reactions at Advanced Level. — 2nd ed. — London : Bell & Hyman, Jan.1982. — [52]p
ISBN 0-7135-2197-x (pbk) : £1.50 : CIP entry B81-34291

547′.412 — Allenes

The **Chemistry** of the allenes. — London : Academic Press, Mar.1982
Vol.1: Synthesis of allenes. — [268]p
ISBN 0-12-436101-3 : CIP entry B82-03091

The **Chemistry** of the allenes. — London : Academic Press, Mar.1982
Vol.2: Reactions of allenes. — [374]p
ISBN 0-12-436102-1 : CIP entry B82-03093

The **Chemistry** of the allenes. — London : Academic Press, Mar.1982
Vol.3: Stereochemical, spectroscopic and special aspects. — [338]p
ISBN 0-12-436103-x : CIP entry B82-03092

547′.412 — Chiral olefins. Circular dichroism

Mason, Stephen F.. Molecular optical activity and the chiral discriminations. — Cambridge : Cambridge University Press, Oct.1982. — [280]p
ISBN 0-521-24702-0 : £20.00 : CIP entry B82-29370

547′.5 — Macrocyclic compounds

Hiraoka, Michio. Crown compounds. — Oxford : Elsevier Scientific, May 1982. — [290]p. — (Studies in organic chemistry ; 12)
ISBN 0-444-99692-3 : £40.00 : CIP entry B82-11276

547′.590459 — Heterocyclic compounds. Synthesis

Robinson, Brian. The Fischer indole synthesis. — Chichester : Wiley, May 1982. — [928]p
ISBN 0-471-10009-9 : £55.00 : CIP entry B82-10767

547′.59′05 — Heterocyclic compounds — *Serials*

Heterocyclic chemistry. — Vol.2. — London : Royal Society of Chemistry, Feb.1982. — [450] p. — (A Specialist periodical report)
ISBN 0-85186-813-4 : CIP entry
ISSN 0144-8773 B82-12161

Heterocyclic chemistry. — Vol.3. — London : Royal Society of Chemistry, Sept.1982. — [408]p. — (Specialist periodical report / Royal Society of Chemistry)
ISBN 0-85186-823-1 : CIP entry
ISSN 0144-8773 B82-20530

547′.592 — Coumarins

Murray, Robert D. H.. The natural coumarins : occurrence, chemistry and biochemistry / Robert D.H. Murray, Jesus Méndez and Stewart A. Brown. — Chichester : Wiley, c1982. — xi,702p : ill,ports ; 26cm
Includes index
ISBN 0-471-28057-7 : £70.00 : CIP rev. B82-04855

547′.593 — Indoles. Biosynthesis

Atta-ur-Rahman. Biosynthesis of indole alkaloids. — Oxford : Clarendon Press, June 1982. — [250]p. — (The International series of monographs on chemistry ; 7)
ISBN 0-19-855610-1 : £25.00 : CIP entry B82-10456

547′.593 — Pyrazines

Barlin, G. B.. The pyrazines / G.B. Barlin. — New York ; Chichester : Wiley, c1982. — xxi,687p : ill ; 24cm. — (The Chemistry of heterocyclic compounds ; 41)
Includes index
ISBN 0-471-38119-5 : £110.00 B82-28942

547′.596 — Quinolines

Quinolines / edited by Gurnos Jones. — Chichester : Wiley. — (The Chemistry of heterocyclic compounds ; v.32)
Pt.2. — c1982. — xi,685p : ill ; 24cm
Includes index
ISBN 0-471-28055-0 : £70.00 : CIP rev. B82-01108

547′.610457 — Aromatic hydrocarbons. Electronic properties

Pope, Martin. Electronic processes in organic crystals. — Oxford : Clarendon Press, Jan.1982. — [800]p. — (Monographs on the physics and chemistry of materials)
ISBN 0-19-851334-8 : £50.00 : CIP entry B81-34563

547.7 — Crystalline polymers — *Serials*

Developments in crystalline polymers. — 1-. — London : Applied Science, 1982-. — v. : ill ; 23cm. — (Developments series)
Irregular
ISSN 0263-6204 = Developments in crystalline polymers : £32.00 B82-28114

547.7 — Flavonoids

The **Flavonoids** : advances in research 1975-1981. — London : Chapman and Hall, Sept.1982. — [600]p
ISBN 0-412-22480-1 : £30.00 : CIP entry B82-19225

Markham, K. R.. Techniques of flavonoid identification / K.R. Markham. — London : Academic Press, 1982. — xi,113p : ill ; 24cm. — (Biological techniques series)
Bibliography: p99-103. — Includes index
ISBN 0-12-472680-1 : £9.40 : CIP rev. B82-00316

547.7 — Flavonoids — *Conference proceedings*

International Bioflavonoid Symposium *(1981 : Munich)*. Flavonoids and bioflavonoids, 1981. — Oxford : Elsevier Scientific, June 1982. — [560]p. — (Studies in organic chemistry ; 11)
ISBN 0-444-99694-x : £45.00 : CIP entry B82-09740

547.7 — Graft copolymers

Cationic graft copolymerization / editor J.P. Kennedy. — New York ; London : Wiley, c1977. — iv,193p : ill ; 23cm. — (Applied polymer symposium, ISSN 0570-4898 ; 30)
Includes index
ISBN 0-471-04426-1 (pbk) : £4.50 B82-35155

547.7 — Linear chain polymers

Extended linear chain compounds. — New York ; London : Plenum
Vol.1 / edited by Joel S. Miller. — c1982. — xvi,481p : ill ; 24cm
Includes index
ISBN 0-306-40711-6 : Unpriced B82-31529

547.7 — Linear chain polymers — *Serials*

Extended linear chain compounds. — Vol.1-. — New York ; London : Plenum Press, 1982-. — v. : ill ; 24cm
Description based on: Vol.2
Unpriced B82-26159

547.7 — Oriented polymers — *Serials*

Developments in oriented polymers. — 1. — London : Applied Science, May 1982. — [232] p. — (The Developments series)
ISBN 0-85334-124-9 : £24.00 : CIP entry B82-07027

547.7 — Polymers

Cowd, M. A.. Polymer chemistry. — London : Murray, Nov.1982. — [96]p. — (Modern chemistry background readers)
ISBN 0-7195-3961-7 (pbk) : £2.95 : CIP entry
B82-26404

Rodriguez, Ferdinand. Principles of polymer systems / Ferdinand Rodriguez. — 2nd ed. — Washington ; London : Hemisphere, c1982. — xvi,575p : ill ; 25cm
Previous ed.: 1970. — Bibliography: p507-512. — Includes index
ISBN 0-07-053382-2 : £22.50 B82-07445

Rosen, Stephen L.. Fundamental principles of polymeric materials / Stephen L. Rosen. — New York ; Chichester : Wiley, c1982. — xvi,346p : ill ; 24cm. — (SPE monographs, ISSN 0195-4288)
Previous ed.: published as Fundamental principles of polymeric materials for practicing engineers. New York : Barnes & Noble, 1971. — Bibliography: p332-333. — Includes index
ISBN 0-471-08704-1 : Unpriced B82-22636

Young, Robert J. (Robert Joseph). Introduction to polymers / Robert J. Young. — London : Chapman and Hall, 1981. — viii,331p : ill ; 24cm
Includes bibliographies and index
ISBN 0-412-22170-5 (cased) : Unpriced : CIP rev.
ISBN 0-412-22180-2 (pbk) : £7.95 B81-18159

547.7 — Polymers — *Conference proceedings*

International Symposium on Macromolecules *(27th : 1981 : Strasbourg).* Macromolecules : main lecture presented at the 27th International Symposium on Macromolecules, Strasbourg, France, 6-9 July 1981 / edited by H. Benoit and P. Rempp. — Oxford : Pergamon, 1982. — x,335p : ill ; 28cm
At head of title: International Union of Pure and Applied Chemistry (Macromolecular Division) in conjunction with Centre national de la recherche scientifique, Université Louis Pasteur de Strasbourg
ISBN 0-08-026226-0 : £37.50 : CIP rev.
B82-02622

547.7′0448 — Polymers. Vibration spectroscopy

Painter, Paul C.. The theory of vibrational spectroscopy and its application to polymeric materials / Paul C. Painter, Michael M. Coleman, Jack L. Koenig. — New York ; Chichester : Wiley, c1982. — xvii,530p : ill ; 24cm
Includes index
ISBN 0-471-09346-7 : £44.50 B82-22638

547.7′045 — Polymers. Miscibility

Olabisi, Olagoke. Polymer-polymer miscibility / Olagoke Olabisi and Lloyd M. Robeson, Montgomery T. Shaw. — New York ; London : Academic Press, 1979. — xii,370p : ill ; 24cm
Includes bibliographies and index
ISBN 0-12-525050-9 : £31.40 B82-36745

547.7′045 — Polymers. Physical properties

Hearle, J. W. S.. Polymers and their properties / J.W.S. Hearle. — Chichester : Ellis Horwood. — (Ellis Horwood series in chemical science)
Bibliography: p427-428. — Includes index
Vol.1: Fundamentals of structure and mechanics. — 1982. — 437p : ill ; 24cm
ISBN 0-85312-033-1 : £32.50 : CIP rev.
B81-32027

547.7′045453 — Solutions of polymers. Viscosity

Bohdanecký, Miloslav. Viscosity of polymer solutions / Miloslav Bohdanecký and Josef Kovář. — Amsterdam ; Oxford : Elsevier Scientific, 1982. — xii,285p : ill ; 25cm. — (Polymer science library)
Includes index
ISBN 0-444-42066-5 : £38.22 : CIP rev.
B82-09293

547.7′0455 — Polymers. Photochemistry

Developments in polymer photochemistry / edited by Norman S. Allen. — 3. — London : Applied Science Publishers. — (The Developments series)
3. — c1982. — x,353p : ill ; 24cm
Includes index
ISBN 0-85334-978-9 : £40.00 : CIP rev.
B81-27954

547.7′0456 — Polymers. Thermal analysis

Thermal characterization of polymeric materials / edited by Edith A. Turi. — New York ; London : Academic Press, 1981. — xiv,972p : ill ; 23cm
Includes bibliographies and index
ISBN 0-12-703780-2 : £64.80 B82-29974

547.7′045686 — Polymers. Low temperature properties

Perepechko, I. I.. Low-temperature properties of polymers / I. Perepechko ; translated from the Russian by A. Beknazarov. — Moscow : Mir ; Oxford : Pergamon, 1980. — ix,301p : ill ; 23cm
Translation of: Svoistva polimerov pri nizkikh temperaturakh. — Includes index
ISBN 0-08-025301-6 : £16.50 B82-28003

547.7′04572′05 — Ion-containing polymers — *Serials*

Developments in ionic polymers. — 1. — London : Applied Science, Nov.1982. — [320]p. — (The Developments series)
ISBN 0-85334-159-1 : £36.00 : CIP entry
B82-26314

547.7′046 — Polymers. Characterisation. Thermal analysis — *Conference proceedings*

Eastern Analytical Symposium *(1980 : New York City).* Thermal analysis in polymer characterization : selected papers presented at the Eastern Analytical Symposium, New York City, November 1980 / edited by Edith A. Turi. — Philadelphia ; London : Heyden, c1981. — viii,159p : ill ; 24cm
Includes index
ISBN 0-85501-626-4 : Unpriced B82-33052

547.7′046 — Vegetable fibres. Identification

Catling, Dorothy M.. Identification of vegetable fibres. — London : Chapman & Hall, Dec.1981. — [150]p
ISBN 0-412-22300-7 : £12.50 : CIP entry
B81-31729

547.7′046′028 — Polymers. Chemical analysis. Techniques

Analysis of polymer systems. — London : Applied Science, June 1982. — [312]p
ISBN 0-85334-122-2 : £28.00 : CIP entry
B82-09875

547.7′046′05 — Polymers. Chemical analysis — *Serials*

Developments in polymer characterisation. — 3. — London : Applied Science, May 1982. — [264]p. — (The Developments series)
ISBN 0-85334-119-2 : £26.00 : CIP entry
B82-07026

Developments in polymer characterisation. — 4. — London : Applied Science, Feb.1983. — [272]p. — (The Developments series)
ISBN 0-85334-180-x : £30.00 : CIP entry
B82-39602

547.7′05 — Polymers — *Serials*

Macromolecular chemistry. — Vol.2. — London : Royal Society of Chemistry, June 1982. — [420]p. — (Specialist periodical report / Royal Society of Chemistry)
ISBN 0-85186-866-5 : CIP entry
ISSN 0144-2988 B82-12845

547.7′1 — Essential oils. Carbon-13 nuclear magnetic resonance spectroscopy

Formacek, V.. Essential oils analysis by capillary gas chromatography and carbon-13 NMR spectroscopy. — Chichester : Wiley, Dec.1982. — [392]p
Originally published: London : Heyden, 1981
ISBN 0-471-26218-8 : CIP entry B82-33342

Kubeczka, K. -H.. Essential oils analysis by carbon-13 NMR spectroscopy. — London : Heyden, July 1981. — [360]p
ISBN 0-85501-704-x : CIP entry B81-20191

547.7′1′0321 — Terpenoids — *Encyclopaedias*

Glasby, John S.. Encyclopaedia of the terpenoids. — Chichester : Wiley, Dec.1981. — [1000]p
ISBN 0-471-27986-2 : £85.00 : CIP entry
B81-31364

547.7′1′05 — Terpenoids — *Serials*

Terpenoids and steroids. — Vol.11. — London : Royal Society of Chemistry, June 1982. — [270]p. — (Specialist periodicals report / Royal Society of Chemistry)
ISBN 0-85186-346-9 : CIP entry
ISSN 0300-5992
Also classified at 547.7′3′05 B82-10881

547.7′2 — Alkaloids

The Alkaloids : chemistry and physiology / founding editor R.H.F. Manske. — New York ; London : Academic Press
Vol.18 / edited by R.G.A. Rodrigo. — 1981. — xvi,411p ; 24cm
Includes index
ISBN 0-12-469518-3 : £43.00 B82-10050

547.7′2′05 — Alkaloids — *Serials*

The **alkaloids.** — Vol.11. — London : Royal Society of Chemistry, Dec.1981. — [265]p. — (Specialist periodical report / Royal Society of Chemistry)
ISBN 0-85186-347-7 : CIP entry
ISSN 0305-9707 B81-30890

547.7′3046 — Steroids. Chemical analysis

Symposium on the Analysis of Steroids *(1981 : Eger).* Advances in steroid analysis : proceedings of the Symposium on the Analysis of Steroids, Eger, Hungary, May 20-22, 1981 / edited by S. Görög. — Amsterdam ; Oxford : Elsevier Scientific, 1982. — xi,551p : ill ; 25cm. — (Analytical chemistry symposia series ; v.10)
Includes bibliographies and index
ISBN 0-444-99711-3 : £49.13 : CIP rev.
ISBN 0-444-41786-9 (set) B81-34494

547.7′3′05 — Steroids — *Serials*

Terpenoids and steroids. — Vol.11. — London : Royal Society of Chemistry, June 1982. — [270]p. — (Specialist periodicals report / Royal Society of Chemistry)
ISBN 0-85186-346-9 : CIP entry
ISSN 0300-5992
Primary classification 547.7′1′05 B82-10881

547.7′31 — Cholesterol. Autoxidation

Smith, Leland L.. Cholesterol autoxidation / Leland L. Smith. — New York ; London : Plenum, c1981. — xviii,674p : ill ; 24cm
Bibliography: p525-637. — Includes index
ISBN 0-306-40759-0 : Unpriced B82-00706

547.7′34 — Prostaglandins

Prostaglandins and thromboxanes / edited by Roger F. Newton, Stanley M. Roberts. — London : Butterworth Scientific, 1982. — xi,143p : ill ; 24cm. — (Butterworths monographs in chemistry)
Includes index
ISBN 0-408-10773-1 : Unpriced : CIP rev.
Also classified at 547.7′7 B81-37533

547.7′34 — Prostaglandins & thromboxanes. Synthesis

New synthetic routes to prostaglandins and thromboxanes. — London : Academic Press, Mar.1982. — [300]p
ISBN 0-12-589620-4 : CIP entry B82-00336

547.7′34 — Prostaglandins — *Conference proceedings*

Golden Jubilee International Congress on Essential Fatty Acids and Prostaglandins *(1980 : University of Minnesota).* Golden Jubilee International Congress on Essential Fatty Acids and Prostaglandins / editor in chief Ralph T. Holman ; guest editors Michael Crawford, James F. Mead, Anthony L. Willis. — Oxford : Pergamon, 1982. — xxiii,911p : ill ; 29cm. — (Progress in lipid research ; v.20)
Includes bibliographies and index
ISBN 0-08-028011-0 : Unpriced : CIP rev.
B81-33858

547.7′4 — Vitamin B12

B12 / edited by David Dolphin. — New York ; Chichester : Wiley, c1982. — 2v. : ill,ports ; 24cm
Includes indexes
ISBN 0-471-03655-2 : £90.00 B82-25863

547.7′5 — Amino acids, peptides & proteins — *Serials*

Amino-acids, peptides and proteins. — Vol.12. — London : Royal Society of Chemistry, Dec.1981. — [630]p. — (Specialist periodical report / Royal Society of Chemistry)
ISBN 0-85186-104-0 : CIP entry
ISSN 0306-0004 B81-32051

547.7′5 — Dopamine

Advances in dopamine research : proceedings of a satellite symposium to the 8th International Congress of Pharmacology, Okayama, Japan, July 1981 / editors M. Kohsaka ... [et al.]. — Oxford : Pergamon, 1982. — x,428p : ill ; 26cm. — (Advances in the biosciences ; v.37)
Includes bibliographies and index
ISBN 0-08-027391-2 : Unpriced : CIP rev. B82-05373

547.7′5 — Iron-sulphur proteins

Iron-sulfur proteins / edited Thomas G. Spiro. — New York ; Chichester : Wiley, c1982. — x,434p : ill ; 24cm. — (Metal ions biology, ISSN 0271-2911 ; v.4)
Includes index
ISBN 0-471-07738-0 : £62.00 B82-40415

547.7′5 — Peptides & proteins. Molecules. Amino acid sequence. Determination — *Conference proceedings*

Branched-chain amino acids. — Lancaster : MTP Press, Dec.1982. — [120]p
Conference papers
ISBN 0-85200-706-x (pbk) : £6.00 : CIP entry B82-39262

International Conference on the Chemical Synthesis and Sequencing of Peptides and Proteins *(1980 : National Institute of Health, Bethesda).* Chemical synthesis and sequencing of peptides and proteins : proceedings of the International Conference on the Chemical Synthesis and Sequencing of Peptides and Proteins held May 8-9, 1980 at the National Institute of Health, Bethesda / editors: Teh-Yung Liu ... [et al.]. — New York ; Oxford : Elsevier/North-Holland, c1981. — xxv,274p : ill,ports ; 25cm. — (Developments in biochemistry ; v.17)
Includes index
ISBN 0-444-00623-0 : £27.83
Also classified at 547.7′50459 B82-08072

547.7′5 — Proteins — *Conference proceedings*

The **Evolution** of protein structure and function : a symposium in honor of Professor Emil L. Smith / edited by David S. Sigman, Mary A.B. Brazier. — New York ; London : Academic Press, 1980. — xvii,350p : ill ; 27cm. — (UCLA forum in medical sciences ; no.21)
Includes bibliographies and index
ISBN 0-12-643150-7 : Unpriced B82-07734

547.7′5 — Proteins. Crystals. Chemical analysis

McPherson, Alexander. Preparation and analysis of protein crystals / Alexander McPherson. — New York ; Chichester : Wiley, c1982. — vii,371p : ill ; 24cm
Bibliography: p313-342. — Includes index
ISBN 0-471-08524-3 : £39.00 B82-35309

547.7′5044 — Proteins. Microstructure. Research. Applications of electron microscopy — *Serials*

Electron microscopy of proteins. — Vol.3. — London : Academic Press, 1982. — [270]p
ISBN 0-12-327603-9 : CIP entry B82-07485

547.7′50442 — Proteins. Molecules. Structure

Phillips, *Sir* **David,** *1924-.* Protein structure / D.C. Phillips and A.C.T. North. — 2nd ed.(rev.). — Burlington, N.C. : Carolina Biological Supply Co., Scientific Publications Division, c1978 ; Chichester : Distributed by Packard. — 31p : ill(some col.) ; 25cm. — (Carolina biology readers ; 34)
Previous ed.: London : Oxford University Press, 1973. — Bibliography: p31
ISBN 0-89278-234-x (unbound) : £1.35 B82-31595

547.7′50459 — Peptides & proteins. Synthesis — *Conference proceedings*

International Conference on the Chemical Synthesis and Sequencing of Peptides and Proteins *(1980 : National Institute of Health, Bethesda).* Chemical synthesis and sequencing of peptides and proteins : proceedings of the International Conference on the Chemical Synthesis and Sequencing of Peptides and Proteins held May 8-9, 1980 at the National Institute of Health, Bethesda / editors: Teh-Yung Liu ... [et al.]. — New York ; Oxford : Elsevier/North-Holland, c1981. — xxv,274p : ill,ports ; 25cm. — (Developments in biochemistry ; v.17)
Includes index
ISBN 0-444-00623-0 : £27.83
Primary classification 547.7′5 B82-08072

547.7′5046 — Proteins. Chemical analysis. Gel electrophoresis. Laboratory techniques

Gel electrophoresis of proteins : a practical approach / edited by B.D. Hames, D. Rickwood. — London : IRL, c1981. — xv,290p : ill(some col.) ; 23cm
Bibliography: p249-254. — Includes index
ISBN 0-904147-22-3 (pbk) : Unpriced : CIP rev. B81-18170

547.7′5′05 — Amino acids, peptides & proteins — *Serials*

Amino-acids, peptides, and proteins. — Vol.13. — London : Royal Society of Chemistry, Aug.1982. — [600]p. — (Specialist periodical report / Royal Society of Chemistry)
ISBN 0-85186-114-8 : CIP entry
ISSN 0306-0004 B82-19800

547′.754 — Haemoglobins

Hemoglobins / edited by Eraldo Antonini, Luigi Rossi-Bernardi, Emilia Chiancone. — New York ; London : Academic Press, 1981. — xxii,874p : ill ; 24cm. — (Methods in enzymology ; v.76)
Includes index
ISBN 0-12-181976-0 : Unpriced B82-32801

547.7′56 — Peptides

The **Peptides** : analysis, synthesis, biology. — New York ; London : Academic Press
Vol.4: Modern techniques of conformational, structural, and configurational analysis / edited by Erhard Gross, Johannes Meienhofer. — 1981. — xix,309p : ill ; 24cm
Includes bibliographies and index
ISBN 0-12-304204-6 : £34.00 B82-07558

547.7′56 — Synthetic peptides

Pettit, George R.. Synthetic peptides / George R. Pettit. — Amsterdam ; Oxford : Elsevier Scientific
Vol.6. — 1982. — viii,511p : ill ; 24cm
ISBN 0-444-42080-0 : Unpriced : CIP rev. B82-14057

547.7′58 — Allosteric enzymes. Chemical reactions. Kinetics

Kurganov, B. I.. Allosteric enzymes : kinetic behaviour. — Chichester : Wiley, Dec.1982. — [400]p
Translated from the Russian
ISBN 0-471-10195-8 : £24.00 : CIP entry B82-30817

547.7′5804594 — Enzymes. Chemical reactions. Kinetics

Engel, Paul C.. Enzyme kinetics : the steady-state approach / Paul C. Engel. — 2nd ed. — London : Chapman and Hall, 1981. — 96p : ill ; 22cm. — (Outline studies in biology)
Previous ed.: 1977. — Includes index
ISBN 0-412-23970-1 (pbk) : £2.45 : CIP rev. B81-36379

547.7′7 — Lipids — *Conference proceedings*

Current perspectives in the use of lipid emulsion. — Lancaster : MTP Press, Dec.1982. — [100]p
Conference papers
ISBN 0-85200-705-1 (pbk) : £6.00 : CIP entry B82-40917

547.7′7 — Thromboxanes

Prostaglandins and thromboxanes / edited by Roger F. Newton, Stanley M. Roberts. — London : Butterworth Scientific, 1982. — xi,143p : ill ; 24cm. — (Butterworths monographs in chemistry)
Includes index
ISBN 0-408-10773-1 : Unpriced : CIP rev.
Primary classification 547.7′34 B81-37533

547′.77046 — Lipids. Chemical analysis

Christie, William W.. Lipid analysis. — 2nd ed. — Oxford : Pergamon, July 1982. — [208]p. — (Pergamon international library)
Previous ed.: 1973
ISBN 0-08-023791-6 (cased) : £20.00 : CIP entry
ISBN 0-08-023792-4 (pbk) : £8.95 B82-12407

547.7′7′05 — Lipids — *Serials*

Progress in lipid research : an international journal. — Vol.17, no.1 (1978)-. — Oxford : Pergamon, 1978-. — v. : ill ; 28cm
Quarterly. — Continues: Progress in the chemistry of fats and other lipids. — Description based on: Vol.21, no.1 (1982)
ISSN 0163-7827 = Progress in lipid research : Unpriced B82-29047

547.7′8 — Carbohydrates

Kennedy, John F.. Bioactive carbohydrates in chemistry, biochemistry and biology. — Chichester : Ellis Horwood, June 1982. — [280]p
ISBN 0-85312-201-6 : £27.50 : CIP entry B82-18582

547.7′8 — Carbohydrates - *Serials*

Carbohydrate chemistry. — Vol.12. — London : Royal Society of Chemistry, May 1981. — [500]p. — (A Specialist periodical report)
ISBN 0-85186-940-8 : CIP entry
ISSN 0576-7172 B81-08839

547.7′8′05 — Carbohydrates — *Serials*

Carbohydrate chemistry. — Vol.13. — London : Royal Society of Chemistry, Aug.1982. — [750]p. — (Specialist periodical report / Royal Society of Chemistry)
ISBN 0-85186-112-1 : CIP entry
ISSN 0576-7172 B82-19799

547.7′82 — Cellulose

Cellulose and other natural polymer systems : biogenesis, structure, and degradation / edited by R. Malcolm Brown, Jr. — New York ; London : Plenum, c1982. — xvii,519p,4p of plates : ill(some col.) ; 26cm
Includes bibliographies and index
ISBN 0-306-40856-2 : Unpriced B82-41080

547.7′9 — Nucleic acids

Symposium on Nucleic Acids Chemistry *(10th).* 10th Symposium on Nucleic Acids Chemistry. — Eynsham : IRL Press, Nov.1982. — [400]p. — (Nucleic acids symposium series ; 11)
ISBN 0-904147-48-7 : £13.00 : CIP entry B82-33364

547.7′9′02854 — Nucleic acids. Research. Applications of digital computer systems

The **Application** of computers to research on nucleic acids. — Eynsham (P.O. Box 1, Eynsham, Oxford OX8 1JJ) : IRL Press, Jan.1982. — [450]p
ISBN 0-904147-37-1 (pbk) : £9.50 : CIP entry B82-02479

547.7′90442 — Nucleic acids. Structure

Nucleic acid biochemistry and molecular biology. — Oxford : Blackwell Scientific, Oct.1982. — [560]p
ISBN 0-632-00632-3 : £14.50 : CIP entry B82-25901

547.7′904572 — Nucleic acids. Gel electrophoresis. Laboratory techniques

Gel electrophoresis of nucleic acids. — Eynsham (1 Abbey St., Oxford OX8 1JJ) : IRL Press, Dec.1981. — [200]p
ISBN 0-904147-24-x (pbk) : £7.50 : CIP entry B81-31369

547.7'9'072 — Nucleic acids. Research — *Serials*

Nucleic acids symposium series. — No.6-. — London (1 Falconberg Court, W1V 5FG) : Information Retrieval Limited, 1979-. — v. : ill ; 23cm
Irregular. — Continues: Nucleic acids research. Special publication. — Description based on: No.8
ISSN 0261-3166 = Nucleic acids symposium series : Unpriced B82-32141

547.8'2 — Coal. Pyrolysis

Gavalas, G. R.. Coal pyrolysis. — Oxford : Elsevier Scientific, June 1982. — [300]p. — (Coal science and technology ; 4)
ISBN 0-444-42107-6 : CIP entry B82-20639

547.8'4 — Block copolymers — *Serials*

Developments in block copolymers. — 1. — London : Applied Science, Sept.1982. — [368] p. — (The Developments series)
ISBN 0-85334-145-1 : £35.00 : CIP entry B82-20829

547.8'4 — Polymers. Crystallisation

International Microsymposium on the Crystallization and Fusion of Polymers *(1976 : Université catholique de Louvain)*. Recent advances in the field of crystallization and fusion of polymers : International Microsymposium on the Crystallization and Fusion of Polymers / held under the auspices of the Société chimique belge and the Groupe français des polymères, Université catholique de Louvain, Louvain-la-Neuve, June 8-11, 1976 ; editors, J.P. Mercier, R. Legras. — New York ; London : Wiley, c1977. — 143p : ill ; 23cm. — (Polymer symposium, ISSN 0360-8905 ; no.59)
Includes index
ISBN 0-471-04425-3 (pbk) : £4.75 B82-35156

547.8'4 — Polymers. Structure, chemical & physical properties

Brydson, J. A.. Flow properties of polymer melts. — 2nd ed. — London : Godwin, May 1981. — [288]p
Previous ed.: London: Iliffe, 1970
ISBN 0-7114-5681-x : £22.00 : CIP entry B81-10443

547.8'4270455 — Synthetic polymers. Photochemistry — *Conference proceedings*

Photophysics of synthetic polymers. — Northwood : Science Reviews, May 1982. — [190]p. — (Forefronts in photochemistry)
ISBN 0-905927-95-8 (pbk) : £9.50 : CIP entry B82-12174

547.8'47272 — Synthetic rubber

Blackley, D. C.. Synthetic rubbers. — London : Applied Science, Dec.1982. — [400]p
ISBN 0-85334-152-4 : £40.00 : CIP entry B82-30717

547.8'69 — Carotenoids — *Conference proceedings*

International Symposium on Carotenoids *(6th : 1981 : Liverpool)*. Carotenoid chemistry and biochemistry : proceedings of the 6th International Symposium on Carotenoids, Liverpool, UK, 26-31 July 1981 / edited by George Britton and Trevor W. Goodwin. — Oxford : Pergamon, 1982. — vi,399p : ill ; 28cm
At head of title: International Union of Pure and Applied Chemistry, Organic Chemistry Division. — Includes index
ISBN 0-08-026224-4 : £47.50 : CIP rev. B82-12897

547.8'69 — Carotenoids. Use

Carotenoids as colorants and vitamin A precursors : technological and nutritional applications / edited by J. Christopher Bauernfeind. — New York ; London : Academic Press, 1981. — xvi,938p,[24]p of plates : ill(some col.) ; 24cm. — (Food science and technology)
Includes bibliographies and index
ISBN 0-12-082850-2 : Unpriced B82-08213

548 — CRYSTALLOGRAPHY

548 — Crystallography

Hazen, Robert M.. Comparative crystal chemistry. — Chichester : Wiley, Dec.1982. — [300]p
ISBN 0-471-10268-7 : £17.50 : CIP entry B82-30822

Steadman, R.. Crystallography / R. Steadman. — New York ; London : Van Nostrand Reinhold, c1982. — viii,120p : ill ; 24cm
ISBN 0-442-30498-6 (pbk) : £3.95 B82-28151

548'.028'54 — Crystallography. Applications of digital computer systems — *Conference proceedings*

International Summer School on Crystallographic Computing *(1981 : Ottawa)*. Computational crystallography : papers presented at the International Summer School on Crystallographic Computing held at Carleton University, Ottawa, Canada, August 7-15, 1981 / David Sayre, editor. — Oxford : Clarendon, 1982. — 539p : ill ; 24cm. — (Oxford science publications)
Includes bibliographies and index
ISBN 0-19-851954-0 : £25.00 : CIP rev. B82-06492

548'.3 — Complex solids. Crystals. Chemical bonding

Structure and bonding in crystals. — New York ; London : Academic Press
Vol.1 / edited by Michael O'Keeffe, Alexander Navrotsky. — 1981. — xviii,327p : ill ; 24cm
Includes bibliographies and index
ISBN 0-12-525101-7 : £31.80 B82-15538

548'.3 — Inorganic compounds. Crystals. Chemical bonding

Structure and bonding in crystals. — New York ; London : Academic Press
Vol.2 / edited by Michael O'Keeffe, Alexandra Navrotsky. — 1981. — xviii,357p : ill(some col.) ; 24cm
Includes bibliographies and index
ISBN 0-12-525102-5 : £33.80
Also classified at 548'.81 B82-21243

548'.5'05 — Crystals. Growth - *Serials*

Progress in crystal growth and characterization. — Vol.3. — Oxford : Pergamon, July 1981. — [394]p
ISBN 0-08-028405-1 : £51.00 : CIP entry B81-16852

548'.5'05 — Crystals. Growth — *Serials*

Progress in crystal growth and characterization. — Vol.4. — Oxford : Pergamon, May 1982. — [390]p
ISBN 0-08-029681-5 : £65.00 : CIP entry B82-11994

548'.8 — Crystals. Surfaces. Structure & physical properties

Interfacial aspects of phase transformations : proceedings of the NATO Advanced Study Institute held at Erice, Silicy [i.e. Sicily] August 29-September 9, 1981 / edited by Boyan Mutaftschiev. — Dordrecht ; London : Reidel in cooperation with NATO Scientific Affairs Division, c1982. — x,708p : ill ; 25cm. — (NATO advanced study institutes series. Series C, Mathematical and physical sciences ; v.87)
Includes index
ISBN 90-277-1440-1 : Unpriced B82-40168

548'.81 — Crystals. Defects. Theories

Kléman, M.. Points, lines and walls : in anisotropic fluids and crystalline solids. — Chichester : Wiley, Dec.1982. — [304]p
ISBN 0-471-10194-x : £23.75 : CIP entry B82-30816

548'.81 — Crystals. Structure

Krestov, G. A.. From crystal to solution / G.A. Krestov, V.A. Kobenin ; translated from the Russian by A. Rosinkin. — Moscow : Mir, 1980 ; London : Distributed by Central Books. — 140p : ill, ; 17cm
Translation of: Ot kristalla k rastvoru. — Bibliography: p137. — Includes index
£0.95 (pbk) B82-34685

Smith, Joseph V.. Geometrical and structural crystallography / Joseph V. Smith. — New York ; Chichester : Wiley, c1982. — xii,450p : ill ; 24cm. — (Smith and Wyllie intermediate geology series)
Bibliography: p419-430. — Includes index
ISBN 0-471-86168-5 : Unpriced B82-38984

548'.81 — Inorganic compounds. Crystals. Structure & physical properties

Structure and bonding in crystals. — New York ; London : Academic Press
Vol.2 / edited by Michael O'Keeffe, Alexandra Navrotsky. — 1981. — xviii,357p : ill(some col.) ; 24cm
Includes bibliographies and index
ISBN 0-12-525102-5 : £33.80
Primary classification 548'.3 B82-21243

548'.83 — X-ray diffraction

Hukins, David W. L.. X-ray diffraction by disordered and ordered systems : covering X-ray diffraction by gases, liquids and solids and indicating how the theory of diffraction by these different states of matter is related and how it can be used to solve structural problems / by David W.L. Hukins. — Oxford : Pergamon, 1981. — ix,164p : ill ; 24cm
Bibliography: p152-156. — Includes index
ISBN 0-08-023976-5 : £11.95 : CIP rev. B81-34489

Small angle x-ray scattering / edited by O. Glatter and O. Kratky. — London : Academic Press, 1982. — x,515p : ill ; 24cm
Includes bibliographies and index
ISBN 0-12-286280-5 : £43.60 : CIP rev. B82-04140

548'.842 — Crystals. Dislocations

Hirth, John Price. Theory of dislocations / John Price Hirth, Jens Lothe. — 2nd ed. — New York ; Chichester : Wiley, c1982. — xii,857p : ill ; 25cm
Previous ed.: New York : London : McGraw-Hill, 1968. — Includes bibliographies and index
ISBN 0-471-09125-1 : £57.00 B82-34748

548'.9 — Crystals. Optical properties

Gay, P.. An introduction to crystal optics. — London : Longman, Sept.1982. — [272]p
Originally published: 1967
ISBN 0-582-30112-2 (pbk) : £6.95 : CIP entry B82-20267

548'.9 — Liquid crystals

Chandrasekhar, S. (Sivaramakrishna). Liquid crystals / S. Chandrasekhar. — Cambridge : Cambridge University Press, 1977 (1980 [printing]). — x,342p : ill ; 23cm. — (Cambridge monographs on physics)
Includes index
ISBN 0-521-29841-5 (pbk) : £10.95 B82-26373

548'.9 — Nematic liquid crystals

Cognard, Jacques. Alignment of nematic liquid crystals and their mixtures / by Jacques Cognard. — London : Gordon and Breach, c1982. — 77p : ill ; 23cm. — (Molecular crystals and liquid crystals. Supplement series, ISSN 0026-8941 ; suppl.1)
Includes index
ISBN 0-677-05905-1 (pbk) : Unpriced B82-22368

549 — MINERALOGY

549 — Gemmology — *Encyclopaedias*

Read, Peter G.. Dictionary of gemmology / P.G. Read. — London : Butterworth Scientific, 1982. — vi,240p : ill ; 23cm
ISBN 0-408-00571-8 : Unpriced : CIP rev. B82-10485

549 — Minerals — *Field guides*

Tennissen, Anthony C.. Colorful mineral identifier / by Anthony C. Tennissen ; photographs by Werner Lieber. — New York : Sterling ; London : Oak Tree Press, 1971 (1981 [printing]). — 224p : ill(some col.) ; 15cm
Includes index
ISBN 0-8069-7516-4 : Unpriced B82-39883

549′.0941 — Great Britain. Mineralogy — *Serials*

Journal of the Russell Society. — Vol.1, no.1 (Mar. 1982)-. — Countesthorpe (11, Spinney Ave., Countesthorpe, Leics. LE8 3RT) : The Society, 1982-. — v. : ill ; 30cm
ISSN 0263-7839 = Journal of the Russell Society : Unpriced B82-32350

549′.1 — Gemmological equipment

Read, Peter G.. Gemmological instruments. — 2nd ed. — London : Butterworth, Feb.1983. — [224]p
Previous ed.: London : Newnes-Butterworth, 1978
ISBN 0-408-01190-4 : £12.95 : CIP entry B82-38284

549′.133 — Minerals. Chemical analysis

Johnson, Wesley M.. Rock and mineral analysis. — 2nd ed. / Wesley M. Johnson, John A. Maxwell. — New York ; Chichester : Wiley, c1981. — xi,489p : ill ; 24cm. — (Chemical analysis, ISSN 0069-2883 ; v.27)
Previous ed.: / by John A. Maxwell. New York, Chichester : Interscience, 1968. — Bibliography: p428-432. — Includes index
ISBN 0-471-02743-x : £38.85
Primary classification 552′.06 B82-05889

549′.27 — Graphite. Physical properties

Kelly, B. T.. Physics of graphite / B.T. Kelly. — London : Applied Science, c1981. — x,477p : ill ; 23cm
Includes index
ISBN 0-85334-960-6 : £48.00 : CIP rev. B81-14445

549′.6 — Rock-forming minerals

Deer, W. A.. Rock-forming minerals. — 2nd ed. — London : Longman
Vol.1A: Orthosilicates. — Feb.1982. — [928]p
Previous ed.: 1962
ISBN 0-582-46526-5 : £50.00 : CIP entry B81-36347

549′.67 — Clay. Constituents: Minerals. Chemical analysis. Techniques — *Conference proceedings*

Advanced techniques for clay mineral analysis : invited contributions from the symposium held at the 7th International Clay Conference, September 6-12, 1981, Bologna and Pavia, Italy / edited by J.J. Fripiat. — Amsterdam ; Oxford : Elsevier Scientific, 1982. — 235p : ill ; 24cm. — (Developments in sedimentology ; 34)
Includes bibliographies and index
ISBN 0-444-42002-9 : £21.25 : CIP rev. B81-20593

International Clay Conference *(7th : 1981 : Bologna and Pavia)*. International Clay Conference 1981. — Oxford : Elsevier Scientific, July 1982. — [400]p. — (Developments in sedimentology ; 35)
ISBN 0-444-42096-7 : CIP entry B82-21372

549′.68 — Zeolites

Barrer, R. M.. Hydrothermal chemistry of zeolites. — London : Academic, Oct.1982. — [380]p
ISBN 0-12-079360-1 : £7.46 : CIP entry B82-24985

550 — EARTH

550 — Earth — *For children*

Lambert, David, *1932-*. Planet earth / by David Lambert ; editor: Jacqui Bailey. — London : Kingfisher, 1982. — 89p : ill(some col.),maps (some col.) ; 19cm. — (A Kingfisher factbook)
Ill on lining papers. — Includes index
ISBN 0-86272-033-8 : £2.50 : CIP rev. B82-01404

Lye, Keith. All about our Earth / [author Keith Lye] ; [editor Linda Moore]. — London : Marshall Cavendish, 1981. — 29p : col.ill ; 30cm. — (Enigma) (An All colour fact book)
Text, ill on lining papers
ISBN 0-85685-966-4 : Unpriced B82-06076

Padget, Sheila. Planet earth / Sheila Padget. — London : Macdonald, 1980. — 32p : col.ill,1col.map ; 29cm. — (Eye openers!)
Bibliography: p30. — Includes index
ISBN 0-356-07091-3 : £2.50 B82-24548

550 — Earth sciences

The **Cambridge** encyclopedia of earth sciences / editor-in-chief David G. Smith. — Cambridge : Cambridge University Press, 1982, c1981. — 496p : ill(some col.),charts,maps,ports ; 26cm
Originally published: New York : Crown, 1981. — Includes index
ISBN 0-521-23900-1 : £19.95 : CIP rev. B81-30182

550′.28′54 — Earth sciences. Applications of computer systems — *Conference proceedings*

Geochautauqua *(8th : 1979 : Syracuse University)*. Computer applications in the earth sciences : an update of the 70s / [proceedings of the 8th Geochautauqua, held 26-27 October 1979, at Syracuse University] ; [sponsored by the Department of Geology at Syracuse University, the Division of Marine Geology and Geophysics at the University of Miami and the International Association for Mathematical Geology] ; edited by Daniel F. Merriam. — New York ; London : Plenum, c1981. — xiv,385p : ill,maps ; 26cm. — (Computer applications in the earth sciences)
Includes bibliographies and index
ISBN 0-306-40809-0 : Unpriced B82-00699

550′.3′31 — Earth sciences — *German & English dictionaries*

Dictionary of geosciences : German-English. — Oxford : Elsevier, July 1982. — [380]p
ISBN 0-444-99701-6 : £25.00 : CIP entry B82-12348

Dictionary of geosciences : English-German. — Oxford : Elsevier, Apr.1982. — [400]p
ISBN 0-444-99702-4 : £25.00 : CIP entry B82-03587

550′.720171241 — Commonwealth countries. Earth sciences. Research organisations: Commonwealth Science Council. *Earth Sciences Programme* — *Serials*

[News letter *(Commonwealth Science Council. Earth Sciences Programme)*]. News letter / Commonwealth Science Council, Earth Sciences Programme. — CSC(81)ESP/NL-1 (Oct. 1981)-. — [London] ([Marlborough House, Pall Mall, SW1Y 5HX]) : [The Programme], 1981-. — v. ; 21cm
Monthly (1981), six issues yearly (1982-). — Continues: News letter (Commonwealth Geological Liaison Office)
ISSN 0263-1636 = News letter - Commonwealth Science Council. Earth Sciences Programme (corrected) : Unpriced B82-20880

551 — GEOLOGY

551 — Geological features

Ludman, Allan. Physical geology / Allan Ludman and Nicholas K. Coch. — New York ; London : McGraw-Hill, c1982. — xx,587p,[16]p of plates : ill(some col.),maps (some col.) ; 26cm
Includes bibliographies and index
ISBN 0-07-011510-9 : £18.95 B82-16288

551 — Geological features — *For schools*

Stirrup, Martin. Geology : the science of the earth / Martin Stirrup. — Cambridge : Cambridge University Press, 1980. — 140p : ill,maps ; 25cm
Bibliography: p139. — Includes index
ISBN 0-521-22567-1 (pbk) : £3.95 : CIP rev. B80-25591

551 — Geology

Potter, A. W. R.. Geology / A.W.R. Potter and H. Robinson. — 2nd ed. — Plymouth : Macdonald and Evans, 1982. — xii,283p : ill,maps ; 19cm. — (The M & E handbook series)
Previous ed.: 1975. — Includes index
ISBN 0-7121-0742-8 (pbk) : £2.75 B82-38815

Press, Frank. Earth / Frank Press, Raymond Siever. — 3rd ed. — Oxford : Freeman, c1982. — xv,613p : ill(some col.),maps(some col.) ; 29cm
Previous ed: 1978. — Ill, map on lining papers. — Includes bibliographies and index
ISBN 0-7167-1362-4 : £18.50 B82-34392

551 — Geology — *For schools*

Atherton, M. A.. Rocks and earth history / Michael Atherton & Roger Robinson. — Sevenoaks : Hodder and Stoughton, 1981. — 80p : ill(some col.),maps ; 25cm. — (Study the earth)
Cover title. — Text on inside covers
ISBN 0-340-24187-x (pbk) : Unpriced : CIP rev. B80-12851

Atherton, M. A.. Useful materials from the earth / Michael Artherton & Roger Robinson. — Sevenoaks : Hodder and Stoughton Educational, 1982. — 80p : ill(some col.),1facsim,col.maps ; 25cm. — (Study the earth)
Cover title. — Text on inside cover
ISBN 0-340-24188-8 (pbk) : Unpriced : CIP rev. B81-34126

551 — Geology — *Quotations*

A **Geological** miscellany. — Oxford (P.O. Box 141, Oxford OX1 1TZ) : Orbital Press, Sept.1982. — [224]p
ISBN 0-946193-00-2 : £8.95 : CIP entry B82-28616

551 — Geophysical processes

Bates, Charles C.. Geophysics in the affairs of man. — Oxford : Pergamon, Oct.1982. — [512]p. — (Pergamon international library)
ISBN 0-08-024026-7 (cased) : £30.00 : CIP entry
ISBN 0-08-024025-9 (pbk) : £12.50 B82-24946

Leet, L. Don. Physical geology. — 6th ed. / L. Don Leet, Sheldon Judson, Marvin E. Kauffman. — Englewood Cliffs ; London : Prentice-Hall, c1982. — xvi,487p : ill(some col.),maps(some col.) ; 29cm
Previous ed.: 1978. — Text on lining papers. — Includes bibliographies and index
ISBN 0-13-669762-3 : £19.45 B82-31818

The **Story** of the Earth / [F.W. Dunning ... et al.]. — 2nd ed. — London : H.M.S.O., 1981. — 36p : col.ill,col.charts,col.maps ; 21x22cm
At head of title: Geological Museum, Institute of Geological Sciences. — Previous ed.: 1972. — Ill on lining papers
ISBN 0-11-884129-7 (cased) : £1.95
ISBN 0-11-884166-1 (pbk) : £0.90 B82-11203

Turcotte, Donald L.. Geodynamics : applications of continuum physics to geological problems / Donald L. Turcotte, Gerald Schubert. — New York ; Chichester : Wiley, c1982. — ix,450p : ill,maps ; 25cm
Includes bibliographies and index
ISBN 0-471-06018-6 : £20.20 B82-36951

551 — Physical geology

Robinson, Edwin Simons. Basic physical geology / Edwin Simons Robinson. — New York ; Chichester : Wiley, c1982. — vi,633p,11-120p : ill,maps ; 25cm
Maps on lining papers. — Includes bibliographies and index
ISBN 0-471-72809-8 : £19.20 B82-31115

551′.01′51 — Geophysics. Applications of inversion methods — *Conference proceedings*

International School of Applied Geophysics *(1980 : Erice)*. The solution of the inverse problem in geophysical interpretation / [proceedings of the third course of the International School of Applied Geophysics, on the solution of the inverse problem in geophysical interpretation, held March 27-April 4, 1980, in Erice, Sicily] ; edited by R. Cassinis. — New York ; London : Plenum, c1981. — ix,381p : ill,maps ; 26cm. — (Ettore Majorana international science series. Physical sciences ; v.11)
Includes bibliographies and index
ISBN 0-306-40735-3 : Unpriced B82-14282

551′.024372 — Geology — *For teaching*

Thomas, Roger D. K.. Instructor′s guide to Earth, third edition, by Frank Press and Raymond Siever / Roger D.K. Thomas. — Oxford : Freeman, c1982. — 165p ; 23cm
Includes bibliographies
ISBN 0-7167-1415-9 (pbk) : £1.00 B82-34384

551'.024624 — Geology — *For civil engineering*

Bell, F.. Fundamentals of engineering geology. — London : Butterworth, Jan.1983. — [608]p
ISBN 0-408-01169-6 : £30.00 : CIP entry
B82-34428

Carter, M.. Geotechnical engineering handbook. — London : Pentech Press, Oct.1982. — [250]p
ISBN 0-7273-0702-9 : £18.00 : CIP entry
B82-27029

Harvey, J. C.. Geology for geotechnical engineers. — Cambridge : Cambridge University Press, Oct.1982. — [129]p
ISBN 0-521-24629-6 (cased) : £12.50 : CIP entry
ISBN 0-521-28862-2 (pbk) : £5.25 B82-26245

551'.05 — Geology — *Serials*

[The Journal *(Open University. Geological Society)*]. The Journal / the Open University Geological Society. — Vol.1, no.1 (Spring 1980)-. — [Churchdown] ([c/o Mr. M. Bryan, editor, 29 Oldbury Orchard, Churchdown, Glos. GL3 2PO]) : [The Society], 1980-. — v. : ill ; 30cm
Three issues yearly. — Continues in part: Newsletter (Open University. Geological Society)
ISSN 0143-9472 = Journal - Open University Geological Society : Unpriced B82-18526

551'.05 — Geophysical processes — *Serials*

Geophysical journal : a cover-to-cover translation of Geofizicheskij zhurnal. — Vol.3, no.1 (1981)-. — New York ; London : Gordon and Breach, 1982-. — v. : ill,maps ; 23cm
Six issues yearly. — Translation of: Geofizičeskij žurnal. — Description based on: Vol.3, no.2 (1981)
ISSN 0275-9128 = Geophysical journal : £162.00 per year B82-28874

551'.07'041 — Great Britain. Geology. Sites. Documents on geological sites. Information sources

Cooper, John A.. Geological record centre handbook / by John A. Cooper with Philip W. Phillips, Kenneth W. Sedman and Michael F. Stanley. — Duxford : Museum Documentation Association, 1980. — vii,65p ; 30cm
At head of title: National Scheme for Geological Site Documentation. — Bibliography: p43-48
ISBN 0-905963-28-8 (spiral) : £1.50
B82-39100

551'.07'1141 — Great Britain. Universities. Curriculum subjects: Geophysics. Postgraduate courses — *Lists*

Postgraduate opportunities in astronomy and geophysics. — 4th ed. — London (Burlington House, Piccadilly, W1V ONL) : Royal Astronomical Society, 1979. — [60]p ; 21cm
Unpriced (pbk)
Primary classification 520'.7'1141 B82-40431

551'.0723 — Geology. Field studies — *Manuals*

Moseley, F.. Methods in field geology / F. Moseley. — Oxford : W.H. Freeman, c1981. — viii,211p : ill,maps ; 25cm
Bibliography: p205-208. — Includes index
ISBN 0-7167-1293-8 (cased) : £12.00
ISBN 0-7167-1294-6 (pbk) : £6.50 B82-05554

551'.092'4 — Geology. Sedgwick, Adam — *Biographies*

Speakman, Colin. Adam Sedgwick : geologist and dalesman, 1785-1873 : a biography in twelve themes / by Colin Speakman. — Broad Oak : Broad Oak Press, 1982. — 145p : ill,facsims,maps,ports ; 24cm
Bibliography: p139-142. — Includes index
ISBN 0-906716-01-2 (pbk) : £5.75 B82-41113

551.1 — Earth. Structure & physical properties

The Earth : structure, composition and evolution / [the S237 Course Team]. — Milton Keynes : Open University Press. — (Science : a second level course) (S237 ; Block 2)
Block 2: Earth structure : earthquakes, seismology and gravity. — 1981. — 128p : ill (some col.),maps(some col.) ; 30cm
At head of title: The Open University. — Bibliography: p118-119
ISBN 0-335-16056-5 (pbk) : Unpriced
B82-07728

The Earth : structure, composition and evolution / [the S237 Course Team]. — Milton Keynes : Open University Press. — (Science : a second level course)
At head of title: The Open University
Block 5: Surface processes : weathering to diagenesis. — 1981. — 111p : ill(some col.) ; 30cm. — (S237 ; block 5)
Bibliography: p100
ISBN 0-335-16059-x (pbk) : Unpriced
B82-15042

The Earth : structure, composition and evolution / [S237 Course Team]. — Milton Keynes : Open University Press. — (Science : a second level course)
At head of title: The Open University
Block 6: Crustal anomalies : economic deposits and pollutants. — 1982. — 104p : ill ; 30cm. — (S237 : block 6)
ISBN 0-335-16060-3 (pbk) : Unpriced
B82-40660

Lyttleton, R. A.. The earth and its mountains. — Chichester : Wiley, Oct.1982. — [220]p
ISBN 0-471-10530-9 : £15.00 : CIP entry
B82-23327

Williams, Peter J.. The surface of the earth. — London : Longman, Apr.1982. — [288]p
ISBN 0-582-30043-6 (pbk) : £5.95 : CIP entry
B82-04861

551.1'1 — Earth. Interior

Bott, Martin H. P.. The interior of the earth : its structure, constitution and evolution / Martin H.P. Bott. — 2nd ed. — London : Arnold, 1982. — ix,403p : ill,maps ; 26cm
Previous ed.: 1971. — Bibliography: p370-396. — Includes index
ISBN 0-7131-2842-9 : £25.00 : CIP rev.
B82-14504

551.1'36 — Forearc regions. Plate tectonics — *Conference proceedings*

Trench-forearc geology : sedimentation and tectonics on modern and ancient active plate margins / edited by Jeremy K. Leggett. — Oxford : Published for the Geological Society of London, by Blackwell Scientific Publications, 1982. — vii,576p,[4]leaves of plates (some folded) : ill,maps ; 26cm
Includes bibliographies
ISBN 0-632-00708-7 : £45.00 : CIP rev.
B81-30410

551.2'1 — Volcanoes — *For children*

Hancock, Gillian. The great volcanoes / Gillian Hancock ; illustrated by Laszlo Acs. — Kingswood : Kaye & Ward, 1982. — 95p : ill ; 23cm
ISBN 0-7182-2920-7 : £4.95 B82-37789

Steel, Sarah. Earthquakes and volcanoes. — London : A. & C. Black, Sept.1982. — [64]p. — (Junior reference ; 36)
ISBN 0-7136-2239-3 : £3.50 : CIP entry
Primary classification 551.2'2 B82-20359

551.2'1 — Volcanoes — *For schools*

Crystal, David. Volcanoes. — London : Edward Arnold, May 1982. — [24]p. — (Databank)
ISBN 0-7131-0632-8 (pbk) : £0.90 : CIP entry
B82-06909

551.2'1'09391 — Greece. Thera. Volcanoes. Eruptions, *ca. B.C.1450.* **Geological aspects** — *Conference proceedings*

International Scientific Congress *(2nd : 1978 : Santorini)*. Thera and the Aegean world / [editor C. Doumas]. — London : Thera and the Aegan World
2: Papers and proceedings of the Second International Scientific Congress, Santorini, Greece, August 1978. — 1980. — 427p : ill (some col.),maps(some col.) ; 29cm
"Geological maps of the Santorini Islands" (2 folded sheets) in envelope as insert. — Includes bibliographies
ISBN 0-9506133-2-0 : Unpriced
ISBN 0-9506133-3-9 (set) B82-08799

551.2'1'09953 — Papua New Guinea. Volcanoes. Eruptions, *ca 1630-ca 1670* — *Sources of data: Papua New Guinea legends*

Blong, R. J.. The time of darkness : local legends and volcanic reality in Papua New Guinea / R.J. Blong. — Seattle ; London : University of Washington Press, 1982. — xi,257p : ill,maps ; 25cm
Bibliography: p227-236. — Includes index
ISBN 0-295-95880-4 : Unpriced B82-38142

551.2'2 — Artifically generated seismic waves. Migration

Berkhout, A. J.. Seismic migration. — 2nd ed. — Oxford : Elsevier Scientific, Oct.1982. — [352] p. — (Developments in solid earth geophysics ; 14A)
Previous ed.: 1980
ISBN 0-444-42130-0 : CIP entry B82-33338

551.2'2 — Earthquakes — *For children*

Asimov, Isaac. How we found out about earthquakes / Isaac Asimov. — Harlow : Longman, 1982. — 54p : ill,maps ; 23cm. — (How we found out about series ; 4)
Includes index
ISBN 0-582-39161-x : £2.75 B82-29318

Lambert, David, *1932-*. Earthquakes / David Lambert. — London : Watts, 1982. — 32p : ill (some col.),col.maps ; 22cm. — (A First look book)
Includes index
ISBN 0-85166-956-5 : £2.99 B82-31209

Steel, Sarah. Earthquakes and volcanoes. — London : A. & C. Black, Sept.1982. — [64]p. — (Junior reference ; 36)
ISBN 0-7136-2239-3 : £3.50 : CIP entry
Also classified at 551.2'1 B82-20359

551.2'2 — Earthquakes. Identification & monitoring — *Conference proceedings*

Identification of seismic sources - earthquake or underground explosion : proceedings of the NATO Advanced Study Institute held at Voksenåsen, Oslo, Norway, September 8-18, 1980 / edited by Eystein S. Husebye and Svein Mykkeltveit. — Dordrecht ; London : D. Reidel, c1981. — xii,876p : ill,maps ; 25cm. — (NATO advanced study institutes series. Series C. Mathematical and physical sciences ; v.74)
Includes index
ISBN 90-277-1320-0 : Unpriced
Also classified at 623.4'5 B82-00485

551.2'2 — Microearthquakes. Research. Techniques

Lee, W. H. K.. Principles and applications of microearthquake networks / W.H.K. Lee and S.W. Stewart. — New York ; London : Academic Press, 1981. — xi,293p : ill,maps ; 24cm. — (Advances in geophysics ; suppl.2)
Bibliography: p231-266. — Includes index
ISBN 0-12-018862-7 : Unpriced B82-07862

551.2'2 — Seismic waves. Analysis

Kleyn, A. H.. Seismic reflection interpretation. — London : Applied Science, Dec.1982. — [272]p
ISBN 0-85334-161-3 : £30.00 : CIP entry
B82-30718

551.2'2 — Seismic waves. Analysis. Use of computer systems

Seismic signal analysis and discrimination. — Oxford : Elsevier Scientific, Nov.1982. — [200] p. — (Methods in geochemistry and geophysics ; 17)
ISBN 0-444-42136-x : CIP entry B82-36135

551.2'2'0955 — Iran. Earthquakes, *to 1979*

Ambraseys, N. N.. A history of Persian earthquakes / N.N. Ambraseys & C.P. Melville. — Cambridge : Cambridge University Press, 1982. — xvii,219p : ill,2facsims,maps ; 29cm. — (Cambridge earth science series)
Bibliography: p199-212. — Includes index
ISBN 0-521-24112-x : Unpriced : CIP rev.
B82-25496

551.3'02 — Landforms. Weathering & erosion

Trudgill, Stephen T.. Weathering and erosion. — London : Butterworth Scientific, Oct.1982. — [192]p. — (Sources and methods in geography)
ISBN 0-408-10635-2 (pbk) : £4.50 : CIP entry
B82-24470

551.3'03 — Landslides

Záruba, Quido. Landslides and their control. — 2nd completely rev. ed. — Oxford : Elsevier Scientific, Apr.1982. — [300]p. — (Developments in geotechnical engineering ; 31)
Previous ed.: 1969
ISBN 0-444-99700-8 : £25.00 : CIP entry
B82-03588

551.3'04 — Sedimentation

Leeder, M. R.. Sedimentology : process and product / M.R. Leeder. — London : Allen & Unwin, 1982. — xiv,344p : ill,maps ; 25cm
Bibliography: p320-338. — Includes index
ISBN 0-04-551053-9 (cased) : Unpriced : CIP rev.
ISBN 0-04-551054-7 (pbk) : Unpriced
B81-35919

Selley, Richard C.. Introduction to sedimentology. — 2nd ed. — London : Academic Press, Sept.1982. — [480]p
Previous ed.: 1976
ISBN 0-12-636360-9 (cased) : CIP entry
ISBN 0-12-636362-5 (pbk) B82-18734

551.3'04'028 — Sediments. Analysis. Use of electron microscopy

Smart, Peter. Electron microscopy of soils and sediments / Peter Smart and N. Keith Tovey. — Oxford : Clarendon Press. — (Oxford science publications)
Examples. — 1981. — viii,177p : ill ; 26cm
Bibliography: p170-171. — Includes index
ISBN 0-19-854515-0 : £30.00 : CIP rev.
Primary classification 631.4'1'028 B81-15841

551.3'04028 — Soils & sediments. Analysis. Use of electron microscopy

Smart, P.. Electron microscopy of soils and sediments. — Oxford : Clarendon Press, Sept.1981. — [400]p
ISBN 0-19-857574-2 : £35.00 : CIP entry
B81-21622

551.3'1 — Glaciation — *Conference proceedings*

Glacial geomorphology. — London : Allen & Unwin, Dec.1981. — [304]p. — (The 'Binghamton' symposia in geomorphology : international series ; no.5)
Conference proceedings
ISBN 0-04-551045-8 : £12.00 : CIP entry
B81-31530

551.3'14 — Glacial deposits — *Conference proceedings*

Guelph Symposium on Geomorphology *(6th : 1980)*. Research in glacial, glaciofluvial and glaciolacustrine systems : proceedings of the 6th Guelph Symposium on Geomorphology, 1980 / edited by R. Davidson-Arnott, W. Nickling, B.D. Fahey. — Norwich : Geo Abstracts in association with Geomorphology Symphosium, University of Guelph, c1982. — iv,318p : ill,maps ; 24cm
Includes bibliographies
ISBN 0-86094-083-7 (pbk) : Unpriced
B82-31974

551.3'5 — Fluvial processes

Modern and ancient fluvial systems. — Oxford : Blackwell Scientific, Dec.1982. — [584]p. — (Special publications / International Association of Sedimentologists ; 6)
ISBN 0-632-00997-7 : £35.00 : CIP entry
B82-36333

551.3'5 — Fluvial processes — *Conference proceedings*

Adjustments of the fluvial system. — London : Allen & Unwin, Aug.1982. — [351]p. — (Annual geomorphology symposia series ; 10th)
Conference papers
ISBN 0-04-551005-9 (cased) : £16.00 : CIP entry
ISBN 0-04-551060-1 (pbk) : £12.95
B82-15644

Fluvial geomorphology. — London : Allen & Unwin, Nov.1981. — [304]p. — (The 'Binghampton' symposia in geomorphology : international series ; no.4)
Conference papers
ISBN 0-04-551046-6 : £12.00 : CIP entry
B81-30215

551.3'55 — Deltas

Coleman, James M.. Deltas : processes of deposition & models for exploration / James M. Coleman. — 2nd ed. — [Champaign] : CEPCO ; Heathfield : Broad Oak [distributor], c1981. — 124p : ill,maps ; 29cm
Previous ed.: 1976. — Bibliography: p112-124
ISBN 0-8087-2942-x (cased) : Unpriced
ISBN 0-8087-2943-8 (pbk) : Unpriced
B82-28039

551.3'8 — Periglacial landforms. Mass wasting

Harris, Charles, *1947-*. Periglacial mass-wasting : a review of research / by Charles Harris. — Norwich : Geo, c1981. — vi,204p : ill,maps ; 24cm. — (British Geomorphological Research Group research monograph series ; 4)
Bibliography: p176-197. — Includes index
ISBN 0-86094-078-0 (pbk) : £8.40 B82-07322

551.4 — GEOMORPHOLOGY AND GENERAL HYDROLOGY

551.4 — Applied geomorphology

Applied geomorphology / edited by Richard G. Craig, Jesse L. Craft. — London : Allen & Unwin, 1982. — x,253p : ill,maps,1plan ; 24cm. — (The 'Binghamton' symposia. International series ; 11)
Conference proceedings. — Includes bibliographies
ISBN 0-04-551050-4 : Unpriced : CIP rev.
B82-03718

551.4 — Deserts — *For children*

Carson, James. Deserts and people / James Carson. — Hove : Wayland, 1982. — 88p : ill (some col.),1map ; 25cm. — (Nature's landscapes)
Bibliography: p85. — Includes index
ISBN 0-85340-923-4 : Unpriced B82-21935

551.4 — Deserts. Geomorphology

Cooke, R. U.. Urban geomorphology in drylands. — Oxford : Oxford University Press, June 1982. — [300]p
ISBN 0-19-823239-x : £15.00 : CIP entry
B82-12716

551.4 — Geomorphology

Clowes, Alan. Process and landform : an outline of contemporary geomorphology / Alan Clowes and Peter Comfort ; maps and diagrams drawn by Tim Smith. — Edinburgh : Oliver & Boyd, 1982. — 289p : ill,maps ; 25cm. — (Conceptual frameworks in geography)
Includes bibliographies and index
ISBN 0-05-003127-9 (pbk) : Unpriced
B82-28317

551.4 — Geomorphology — *Conference proceedings*

Pitty, Alistair F.. The nature of geomorphology. — London : Methuen, Sept.1982. — [120]p
ISBN 0-416-32110-0 (cased) : £6.00 : CIP entry
ISBN 0-416-32120-8 (pbk) : £3.50 B82-20174

Space and time in geomorphology. — London : Allen and Unwin, May 1982. — [400]p. — (The 'Binghamton' symposia in geomorphology ; no.12)
Conference papers
ISBN 0-04-551056-3 : £20.00 : CIP entry
B82-07232

551.4 — Granite landforms

Twidale, C. R.. Granite landforms. — Oxford : Elsevier Scientific, Oct.1982. — [500]p
ISBN 0-444-42116-5 : CIP entry B82-27027

551.4 — Landforms. Effects of climate

Büdel, Julius. Climatic geomorphology / by Julius Büdel ; translated by Leonore Fischer and Detlef Busche. — Princeton ; Guildford : Princeton University Press, c1982. — xix,443p : ill,maps ; 24cm
Translation of: Klima-Geomorphologie. — Map on lining paper. — Bibliography: p365-415. — Includes index
ISBN 0-691-08294-4 (cased) : £35.30
ISBN 0-691-08295-2 (pbk) : £13.10
B82-34567

551.4 — Landforms. Effects of climate — *Conference proceedings*

Land surface processes in atmospheric general circulation models. — Cambridge : Cambridge University Press, Sept.1982. — [572]p
ISBN 0-521-25222-9 : £30.00 : CIP entry
B82-29355

551.4 — Natural resources: Water. Chemical properties

Drever, James I. The geochemistry of natural waters / James I. Drever. — Englewood Cliffs ; London : Prentice-Hall, 1982. — xii,388p : ill ; 25cm
Bibliography: p363-380. — Includes index
ISBN 0-13-351403-x : £23.95 B82-28507

551.4 — Natural resources: Water. Radioisotopes

Ferronsky, V. I.. Environmental isotopes in the hydrosphere. — Oxford : Pergamon, Aug.1982. — [400]p
ISBN 0-471-10114-1 : £25.00 : CIP entry
B82-15816

551.4'028 — Geomorphology. Techniques

Dackombe, R. V.. Geomorphological field manual. — London : Allen and Unwin, Oct.1982. — [272]p
ISBN 0-04-551061-x (cased) : £16.00 : CIP entry
ISBN 0-04-551062-8 (pbk) : £7.95 B82-23094

Geomorphological techniques / edited for the British Geomorphological Research Group by Andrew Goudie with the assistance of John Lewin ... [et al.]. — London : Allen & Unwin, 1981. — xvi,395p : ill ; 26cm
Bibliography: p346-389. — Includes index
ISBN 0-04-551042-3 (cased) : Unpriced
ISBN 0-04-551043-1 (pbk) : Unpriced
B82-01222

551.4'072 — Geomorphology. Research. Methodology

Shorter technical methods. — Norwich : Published for the British Geomorphological Research Group by Geo Abstracts. — (Technical bulletin ; no.29)
Cover title. — Includes bibliographies
4 / edited by S. Trudgill and others. — c1981. — 48p : ill ; 21cm
ISBN 0-86094-095-0 (pbk) : Unpriced
B82-24692

551.4'09422 — Southern England. Landforms. Evolution

The **Shaping** of Southern England / edited by David K.C. Jones. — London : Academic Press, 1980. — xi,274p : ill,maps ; 26cm. — (Institute of British Geographers special publication, ISSN 0073-9006 ; no.11)
Includes bibliographies and index
ISBN 0-12-388950-2 : £14.60 : CIP rev.
B80-20631

551.4'1 — Continental shelf. Geological features — *Serials*

Continental shelf research : (a companion journal to Deep-sea research and Progress in oceanography). — Vol.1, no.1 (Aug. 1982)-. — Oxford : Pergamon, 1982-. — v. : ill,maps ; 25cm
Quarterly
ISSN 0278-4343 = Continental shelf research : Unpriced
B82-40067

551.4'1 — Continental shelf. Sedimentation

Sedimentary dynamics of continental shelves / edited by C.A. Nittrouer. — Amsterdam ; Oxford : Elsevier Scientific, 1981. — viii,449p : ill,maps ; 25cm. — (Developments in sedimentology ; 32)
"Reprinted from Marine geology V.42. no.1/4". — Includes bibliographies and index
ISBN 0-444-41962-4 : Unpriced : CIP rev.
B81-19139

551.4'24'09943 — Queensland. Great Barrier Reef. Landforms

Hopley, David. The geomorphology of the Great Barrier Reef : quaternary development of coral reefs / David Hopley. — New York ; Chichester : Wiley, c1982. — xiv,453p : ill,maps ; 27cm
Bibliography: p398-435. — Includes index
ISBN 0-471-04562-4 : £45.00 B82-37994

551.4′3′0941 — Great Britain. Upland regions
Marriott, Michael. Mountains and hills of Britain. — London : Collins, Oct.1982. — [176]p
ISBN 0-00-218028-6 : £8.95 : CIP entry B82-21411

551.4′32 — Mountains
Price, Larry W.. Mountains & man : a study of process and environment / Larry W. Price. — Berkeley ; London : University of California Press, c1981. — xxi,506p : ill,maps ; 26cm
Bibliography: p443-492. — Includes index
ISBN 0-520-03263-2 : £11.50 B82-02220

551.4′32 — Mountains. Formation
Miyashiro, Akiho. Orogeny. — Chichester : Wiley, Nov.1982. — [250]p. — (Texts in earth sciences)
ISBN 0-471-10376-4 (cased) : £15.00 : CIP entry
ISBN 0-471-10377-2 (pbk) : £8.00 B82-27547

551.4′32 — Mountains. Formation — *Conference proceedings*
Mountain building processes. — London : Academic Press, Nov.1982. — [350]p
Conference papers
ISBN 0-12-357980-5 : CIP entry B82-26862

551.4′36 — Hereford and Worcester. Bredon Hill. Slopes. Stability
Gerrard, J.. Mass movement forms and processes on Bredon Hill, Worcestershire / J. Gerrard and L. Morris. — Birmingham : Department of Geography, University of Birmingham, 1980. — 11p,[3] leaves of plates : ill ; 30cm. — (Working paper series / University of Birmingham. Department of Geography ; 10)
Bibliography: p11
ISBN 0-7044-0565-2 (pbk) : £0.40 B82-23552

551.4′36 — Hills. Slopes
Small, R. J.. Slopes and weathering. — Cambridge : Cambridge University Press, Oct.1982. — [ ]p. — (Cambridge topics in geography. 2nd series)
ISBN 0-521-23340-2 (cased) : £6.95 : CIP entry
ISBN 0-521-29926-8 (pbk) : £3.25 B82-23330

551.4′36 — Hills. Slopes. Geological aspects
Selby, M. J.. Hillslope materials and processes. — Oxford : Oxford University Press, Aug.1982. — [288]p
ISBN 0-19-874126-x (cased) : £18.50 : CIP entry
ISBN 0-19-874127-8 (pbk) : £9.95 B82-15684

551.4′5 — Tundra regions — *For children*
Barrett, Ian. Tundra and people / Ian Barrett. — Hove : Wayland, 1982. — 91p : ill(some col.),2maps ; 25cm. — (Nature′s landscapes)
Bibliography: p89. — Includes index
ISBN 0-85340-953-6 : Unpriced B82-21945

551.46 — Oceanography
Ross, David A.. Introduction to oceanography / David A. Ross. — 3rd ed. — Englewood Cliffs ; London : Prentice-Hall, c1982. — xvi,544p,[8]p of plates : ill(some col.),maps ; 25cm
Previous ed.: 1977. — Bibliography: p513-323. — Includes index
ISBN 0-13-491357-4 : £17.95 B82-33772

Study of the sea : the development of marine research under the auspices of the International Council for the Exploration of the Sea / edited by E.M. Thomasson. — Farnham : Fishing News, c1981. — xiv,256p : ill,charts,ports ; 26cm
Includes bibliographies and index
ISBN 0-85238-112-3 : Unpriced : CIP rev.
Also classified at 639′.22 B81-16893

Van Andel, Tjeerd. [Tales of an old ocean]. Science at sea : tales of an old ocean / Tjeerd van Andel. — Oxford : Freeman, c1981. — xii,186p : ill,maps ; 24cm
Originally published: Stanford : Stanford Alumni Association, 1977. — Bibliography: p176-178. — Includes index
ISBN 0-7167-1363-2 (cased) : £11.90
ISBN 0-7167-1364-0 (pbk) : £5.50 B82-23937

551.46 — Oceans
Gross, M. Grant. Oceanography : a view of the earth / M. Grant Gross. — 3rd ed. — Englewood Cliffs ; London : Prentice-Hall, c1982. — xii,498p : ill,maps ; 28cm
Previous ed.: 1977. — Includes bibliographies and index
ISBN 0-13-629683-1 : £20.75 B82-36881

Smith, Sandra, *1948-*. Discovering the sea / by Sandra Smith. — Harlow : Longman, 1982. — 96p : ill(some col.),maps(some col.) ; 26cm
Includes index
ISBN 0-582-25060-9 : £6.95 : CIP rev. B82-01723

551.46 — Oceans. Radiation. Measurement — *Conference proceedings*
I.U.C.R.M. Colloquium *(6th : 1978 : Patricia Bay, B.C.)*. Passive radiometry of the ocean : proceedings of the Sixth I.U.C.R.M. colloquium, Patricia Bay, B.C., Canada, June 14-21 1978 / edited by J.F.R. Gower. — Dordrecht ; London : Reidel, c1980. — 358p : ill,charts,maps ; 25cm
Includes bibliographies
Unpriced B82-37354

551.46′0028 — Oceanography. Instrumentation, *to 1900*
McConnell, Anita. No sea too deep : the history of oceanographic instruments / Anita McConnell. — Bristol : Hilger, c1982. — 162p : ill,charts,facsims,1map ; 29cm
Includes index
ISBN 0-85274-416-1 : £19.50 : CIP rev. B81-34568

551.46′0028 — Oceanography. Use of spaceborne synthetic aperture radar systems
Spaceborne synthetic aperture radar for oceanography / edited by Robert C. Beal, Pat S. DeLeoninbus, Isadore Katz. — Baltimore ; London : Johns Hopkins University Press, 1981. — 215p : ill(some col.),charts,maps ; 29cm. — (The Johns Hopkins oceanographic studies ; no.7)
Includes bibliographies
ISBN 0-8018-2668-3 : Unpriced B82-02179

551.46′0028 — Oceans. Remote sensing by artificial satellites — *Conference proceedings*
COSPAR/SCOR/IUCRM Symposium on Oceanography from Space *(1980 : Venice)*. Oceanography from space / [proceedings of the COSPAR/SCOR/IUCRM Symposium on Oceanography from Space, held May 26-30, 1980, in Venice, Italy] ; edited by J.F.R. Gower. — New York ; London : Plenum, c1981. — xix,978p : ill,maps ; 26cm. — (Marine science ; vol.13)
Includes bibliographies and index
ISBN 0-306-40808-2 : Unpriced B82-05801

Satellite microwave remote sensing. — Chichester : Ellis Horwood, Dec.1982. — [440]p. — (Ellis Horwood series on marine science)
Conference papers
ISBN 0-85312-494-9 : £40.00 : CIP entry B82-30312

551.46′003′21 — Oceans — *Encyclopaedias*
Groves, Donald G.. Ocean world encyclopedia / Donald G. Groves and Lee M. Hunt. — New York ; London : McGraw-Hill, c1980. — xv,443p : ill,maps ; 25cm
Includes index
ISBN 0-07-025010-3 : £24.95 B82-07086

551.46′005 — Oceanography - *Serials*
Oceanography and marine biology. — Vol.19. — Aberdeen : Aberdeen University Press, Sept.1981. — [655]p
ISBN 0-08-028439-6 : CIP entry
ISSN 0078-3218
Also classified at 574.92′05 B81-20511

551.46′005 — Oceanography — *Serials*
Oceanography and marine biology. — Vol.20. — Aberdeen : Aberdeen University Press, Sept.1982. — [650]p
ISBN 0-08-028460-4 : £39.00 : CIP entry
ISSN 0078-3218
Also classified at 574.92′05 B82-19099

551.4′6′005 — Oceanography — *Serials*
Progress in oceanography. — Vol.9. — Oxford : Pergamon, Oct.1981. — [258]p
ISBN 0-08-027116-2 : £38.00 : CIP entry B81-30982

551.46′005 — Oceanography — *Serials*
Progress in oceanography. — Vol.10. — Oxford : Pergamon, Feb.1982. — [236]p
ISBN 0-08-029121-x : £41.00 : CIP entry B82-03349

551.46′01 — Physical oceanography
Pickard, George L.. Descriptive physical oceanography : an introduction / by George L. Pickard and William J. Emery. — 4th enl. ed. (in SI units). — Oxford : Pergamon, 1982. — xiv,249p,[4]p of plates : ill,maps ; 24cm. — (Pergamon international library)
Previous ed.: 1979. — Bibliography: p233-241. — Includes index
ISBN 0-08-026280-5 (cased) : Unpriced : CIP rev.
ISBN 0-08-026279-1 (pbk) : Unpriced B82-10593

551.46′01 — Seawater. Chemical analysis. Electrochemical techniques
Marine electrochemistry : a practical introduction / edited by M. Whitfield and D. Jagner. — Chichester : Wiley, c1981. — xiii,529p : ill,1map ; 24cm
Includes bibliographies and index
ISBN 0-471-27976-5 : £27.50 : CIP rev. B81-28041

551.46′08 — Oceans. Bed. Geological features
Kennet, James P.. Marine geology / James P. Kennet. — Englewood Cliffs ; London : Prentice-Hall, c1982. — xv,813p : ill,maps ; 25cm
Bibliography: p752-787. — Includes index
ISBN 0-13-556936-2 : £26.20 B82-20080

The **Ocean** floor. — Chichester : Wiley, Aug.1982. — [332]p
ISBN 0-471-10091-9 : £36.00 : CIP entry B82-15815

551.46′08 — Oceans. Benthic regions. Geological features
The **Dynamic** environment of the ocean floor / edited by Kent A. Fanning, Frank T. Manheim. — Lexington, Mass. : Lexington Books : [Aldershot], Gower [distributor], 1982. — x,502p : ill,maps ; 24cm
Includes bibliographies and index
ISBN 0-669-02809-6 : £28.50 B82-24916

551.46′08 — Submarine lithosphere
The **Oceanic** lithosphere / edited by Cesare Emiliani. — New York ; Chichester : Wiley, c1981. — xii,1738p,[2]folded p of plates : ill,maps ; 27cm. — (The Sea ; v.7)
Includes bibliographies and index
ISBN 0-471-02870-3 : £110.00 B82-13992

551.46′08′0931 — North Atlantic Ocean. Bed. Geological features
Naylor, D.. Geology of offshore Ireland and West Britain. — London : Graham and Trotman, June 1982. — [224]p
ISBN 0-86010-340-4 (cased) : £25.00 : CIP entry
ISBN 0-86010-430-3 (pbk) : £12.00 B82-18590

551.46′083 — Marine sediments. Mass wasting — *Conference proceedings*
NATO Workshop on Marine Slides and Other Mass Movements *(1980 : Algarve)*. Marine slides and other mass movements / [proceedings of a NATO Workshop on Marine Slides and Other Mass Movements, held in Algarve, Portugal, December 15-21, 1980] ; edited by Svend Saxov and J.K. Nieuwenhuis. — New York ; London : Published in cooperation with NATO Scientific Affairs Division [by] Plenum, c1982. — ix,353p : ill,maps,plans ; 26cm. — (NATO conference series. IV, Marine sciences)
Includes bibliographies and index
ISBN 0-306-40888-0 : Unpriced B82-31924

551.46′083 — Oceans. Bed. Phosphorite

Baturin, G. N.. Phosphorite on the sea floor. — Oxford : Elsevier Scientific, Jan.1982. — [300] p. — (Developments in sedimentology, ISSN 0070-4571 ; 33)
Translation of: Fosfority na dne okeanov
ISBN 0-444-41990-x : CIP entry B81-34495

551.46′083 — Offshore sedimentation. Effects of tides

Offshore tidal sands. — London : Chapman and Hall, Sept.1982. — [400]p
ISBN 0-412-12970-1 : £30.00 : CIP entry B82-19220

551.46′083′336 — North Sea. Holocene strata. Marine sediments

Holocene marine sedimentation in the North Sea basin / edited by S.-D. Nio, R.T.E. Shüttenhelm and Tj.C.E. van Weering. — Oxford : Blackwell Scientific, 1981. — 515p : ill,charts,maps ; 25cm. — (Special publication of the International Association of Sedimentologists ; no.5)
Includes bibliographies
ISBN 0-632-00858-x (pbk) : £35.00 : CIP rev. B81-30979

551.46′147 — United States. Chesapeake Bay

Schubel, J. R.. The living Chesapeake / J.R. Schubel. — Baltimore ; London : Johns Hopkins University Press, c1981. — x,113p : ill,1map ; 26cm
ISBN 0-8018-2547-4 : £14.00 B82-11847

551.46′735 — Kuwait. Kuwait Bay. Sea level. Variation

Al-Asfour, Taiba A.. Changing sea-level along the north-coast of Kuwait Bay / Taiba A. Al-Asfour. — London : Kegan Paul International in association with Kuwait University, 1982. — xv,186p,[20]p of plates : ill (some col.),maps ; 24cm
Bibliography: p168-177. — Includes index
ISBN 0-7103-0010-7 : £25.00 B82-36663

551.47 — Oceans. Dynamics

International School of Physics 'Enrico Fermi' *(80th : 1980 : Varenna)*. Topics in ocean physics / edited by A.R. Osborne and by P. Malanotte Rizzoli. — Amsterdam ; Oxford : North-Holland, 1982. — xv,550p,[1]leaf of plates : ill(some col.),maps ; 25cm
"Proceedings of the International School of Physics 'Enrico Fermi', course LXXX, Varenna on Lake Como, Villa Monastero, 7th-19th July 1980". — Added t.p. in Italian. — At head of title: Italian Physical Society. — Includes index
ISBN 0-444-86160-2 : £47.67 B82-38127

551.47 — Oceans. Interactions with atmosphere. Measurement

JASIN 1978 *(Project)*. Air-sea interaction project : summary of the 1978 field experiment : (JASIN 1978) / prepared for the British National Committee for GARP by the participants. — London : Royal Society, 1979. — viii,139p : ill,maps,plans ; 30cm
ISBN 0-85403-139-1 (pbk) : Unpriced B82-25646

551.47 — Semi-enclosed seas. Hydrodynamics — *Conference proceedings*

International Liège Colloquium on Ocean Hydrodynamics *(13th : 1981)*. Hydrodynamics of semi-enclosed seas : proceedings of the 13th International Liège Colloquium on Ocean Hydrodynamics / edited by Jacques C.J. Nihoul. — Amsterdam ; Oxford : Elsevier Scientific, 1982. — xiv,555p : ill ; 25cm. — (Elsevier oceanography series ; 34)
Includes bibliographies and index
ISBN 0-444-42077-0 : £38.54
ISBN 0-444-41623-4 (set) B82-36630

551.47′01 — Oceans. Continental shelf regions. Circulation — *Conference proceedings*

Circulation and fronts in continental shelf seas : a Royal Society discussion held on 25 and 26 February 1981 / organized by J.C. Swallow ... [et al.]. — London : The Royal Society, 1981. — vii,177p,[10]p of plates : ill ; 31cm
Includes bibliographies
ISBN 0-85403-178-2 : £22.40 B82-05591

551.47′022 — Oceans. Waves. Technical data — *Conference proceedings*

Hogben, N.. Basic data requirements : a review with emphasis on wave and wind data : paper presented to a workshop on coastal engineering organized by the Engineering Committee on Oceanic Resources at the First Panamerican Conference on Oceanic Engineering in Mexico City, 20-23 October 1980 / by N. Hogben. — Feltham : National Maritime Institute, 1980. — 30p : ill,1map ; 30cm. — (SMT-M-8001) (NMI ; R92)
Cover title
Unpriced (pbk)
Also classified at 551.5′185 B82-40677

551.48 — Inland waters. Salinity — *Conference proceedings*

Land and stream salinity : an international seminar and workshop held in November 1980 in Perth, Western Australia / edited by J.W. Holmes and T. Talsma. — Amsterdam ; Oxford : Elsevier Scientific, 1981. — 392p : ill,maps ; 25cm. — (Developments in agricultural engineering ; 2)
"Reprinted from Agricultural water management V.4. no.1,2,3(1981)" — Half t.p. verso. — Includes bibliographies and index
ISBN 0-444-41999-3 : Unpriced : CIP rev.
Primary classification 631.4′16 B81-24632

551.48 — Metamorphic rocks. Interactions with fresh waters — *Study regions: Luxembourg. Haarts drainage basin*

Verstraten, J. M.. Water-rock interactions : a case study in a very low grade metamorphic shale catchment in the Ardennes, NW Luxembourg / J.M. Verstraten. — Norwich : Geo, c1980. — 243p : ill,2maps ; 24cm. — (British Geomorphological Research Group research monograph series ; 2)
Bibliography: p160-176
ISBN 0-86094-042-x (cased) : £7.40
ISBN 0-86094-043-8 (pbk) : £4.40 B82-07320

551.48 — Soil pipes

Jones, J. A. A.. The nature of soil piping : a review of research / J.A.A. Jones. — Norwich : Geo, c1981. — xiv,301p : ill,1map ; 24cm. — (British Geomorphological Research Group research monograph series ; 3)
Bibliography: p245-286. — Includes index
ISBN 0-86094-077-2 (pbk) : £12.40 B82-07321

551.48 — Surface water

Bowen, Robert. Surface water. — London : Applied Science, June 1982. — [252]p
ISBN 0-85334-128-1 : £25.00 : CIP entry B82-09878

551.48′024624 — Hydrology — *For civil engineering*

Réthátí, László. Groundwater in civil engineering. — Oxford : Elsevier Scientific, Oct.1982. — [500]p. — (Developments in geotechnical engineering ; 35)
Translation of: Talajviz a mélyépítésben
ISBN 0-444-99686-9 : £45.00 : CIP entry B82-24014

551.48′024627 — Hydrology — *For hydraulic engineering*

Linsley, Ray K.. Hydrology for engineers / Ray K. Linsley Jr., Max A. Kohler, Joseph L.H. Paulhus. — 3rd ed. — New York ; London : McGraw-Hill, c1982. — xx,508p : ill,charts,maps ; 25cm. — (McGraw-Hill series in water resources and environmental engineering)
Previous ed.: 1975. — Text on lining papers. — Includes bibliographies and index
ISBN 0-07-037956-4 : £23.95 B82-16338

551.48′028 — United States. Hydrology. Soil Conservation Service techniques

McCuen, Richard H.. A guide to hydrologic analysis using SCS methods / Richard H. McCuen. — Englewood Cliffs ; London : Prentice-Hall, c1982. — xii,145p : ill ; 29cm
ISBN 0-13-370205-7 : £17.20 B82-19725

551.48′0724 — Hydrology. Simulations. Applications of digital computer systems

Abbott, M. A.. Engineering applications of computational hydraulics. — London : Pitman Vol.2. — June 1982. — [224]p. — (Monographs and surveys in water resources engineering ; 6)
ISBN 0-273-08543-3 : £22.50 : CIP entry B82-09996

551.4′82′028 — Limnology. Experimental techniques — *Manuals*

Lind, Owen T.. Handbook of common methods in limnology / Owen T. Lind. — 2nd ed. — St. Louis ; London : Mosby, 1979. — xi,199p : ill,1form ; 21cm
Previous ed.: 1974. — Bibliography: p187-190. — Includes index
ISBN 0-8016-3019-3 (pbk) : £9.25 B82-24778

551.48′3 — Rivers — *For children*

Browne, Tom, *1950-*. Rivers and people / Tom Browne. — Hove : Wayland, 1982. — 91p : ill (some col.),maps ; 25cm. — (Nature's landscapes)
Bibliography: p89. — Includes index
ISBN 0-85340-952-8 : Unpriced B82-21934

Eden, Michael. Rivers / Michael Eden ; illustrated by Wendy Bramall. — London : Bodley Head, 1981. — 23p : col.ill ; 22cm. — (A Young geographer)
Includes index
ISBN 0-370-30388-1 : £2.95 : CIP rev. B81-30489

551.48′3 — Rivers. Geophysical processes

Richards, Keith. Rivers. — London : Methuen, Oct.1982. — [272]p
ISBN 0-416-74900-3 (cased) : £17.00 : CIP entry
ISBN 0-416-74910-0 (pbk) : £8.95 B82-23987

551.48′3′0941 — Great Britain. Rivers

British rivers. — London : Allen & Unwin, Sept.1981. — [228]p
ISBN 0-04-551047-4 : £20.00 : CIP entry B81-20483

551.48′3′0941 — Great Britain. Rivers, *to 1981*

Burton, Anthony. The changing river / Anthony Burton. — London : Gollancz, 1982. — 158p,[15]p of plates : ill,1port ; 24cm
Bibliography: p151-152. — Includes index
ISBN 0-575-02967-6 : £9.95 : CIP rev. B81-38315

551.48′9′0941 — Great Britain. Coastal regions. Flooding — *Conference proceedings*

Floods due to high winds and tides : based on the proceedings of a conference on floods due to high winds and tides arranged by the Environmental Mathematics Group of the IMA and held at the University of Bristol on January 9, 1980 / edited by D.H. Peregrine. — London : Academic Press, 1981. — viii,106p : ill,maps ; 24cm. — (The Institute of Mathematics and its Applications conference series)
Includes bibliographies
ISBN 0-12-551820-x : £9.40 : CIP rev. B81-28138

551.48′9′09421 — London. Flooding

Milne, Antony. London's drowning. — London : Thames Methuen, May 1982. — [176]p
ISBN 0-423-00390-9 : £6.50 : CIP entry B82-07662

551.49 — England. Alluvial aquifers

Monkhouse, R. A.. Alluvial aquifers in England and Wales / R.A. Monkhouse. — Reading : Central Water Planning Unit, 1978. — vi,11p ; 30cm. — (Technical note ; no.27)
Bibliography: p10
ISBN 0-904839-35-4 (spiral) : Unpriced B82-40474

551.49 — Ground water

Matthess, Georg. The properties of groundwater / Georg Matthess ; translated by John C. Harvey. — New York ; Chichester : Wiley, c1982. — xii,406p : ill,maps ; 24cm
Translation of: Die Beschaffenheit des Grundwassers. — Bibliography: p353-397. — Includes index
ISBN 0-471-08513-8 : £34.00 B82-18199

551.49 — Ground water. Flow. Mathematical models

Verruijt, A.. Theory of groundwater flow / A. Verruijt. — 2nd ed. — London : Macmillan, 1982. — vi,144p : ill ; 25cm
Previous ed.: 1970. — Bibliography: p138-141. — Includes index
ISBN 0-333-32958-9 (cased) : £18.00
ISBN 0-333-32959-7 (pbk) : Unpriced
B82-32379

Wang, Herbert F.. Introduction to groundwater modeling : finite difference and finite element methods / Herbert F. Wang, Mary P. Anderson. — Oxford : Freeman, c1982. — x,237p : ill ; 24cm. — (A series of books in geology)
Bibliography: p227-233. — Includes index
ISBN 0-7167-1303-9 : £20.70 B82-29337

551.49 — Ground water. Geochemical aspects — *Conference proceedings*

Symposium on Geochemistry of Groundwater *(1980 : Paris)*. Symposium on Geochemistry of Groundwater : 26th International Geological Congress, Paris, 1980 / edited by William Back and René Létolle. — Amsterdam ; Oxford : Elsevier Scientific, 1982. — x,369p : ill,maps ; 25cm. — (Developments in water science ; 16)
Includes two chapters in French. — "Reprinted from the Journal of hydrology, Vol.54, no.1/3 (1981)". — Includes bibliographies
ISBN 0-444-42036-3 : Unpriced : CIP rev.
B81-34008

551.49 — Ground water. Seepage

Mariño, Miguel A.. Seepage and groundwater / Miguel A. Mariño and James N. Luthin. — Amsterdam ; Oxford : Elsevier Scientific, 1982. — xv,489p : ill ; 25cm. — (Developments in water science ; 13)
Bibliography: p443-453. — Includes index
ISBN 0-444-41975-6 : Unpriced : CIP rev.
B81-18078

551.49′01′5145 — Hydrogeology. Applications of integral boundary equations

Liggett, James A.. The boundary integral equation method for porous media flow. — London : Allen & Unwin, Nov.1982. — [272]p
ISBN 0-04-620011-8 : £17.50 : CIP entry
B82-27821

551.5 — METEOROLOGY

551.5 — Atmosphere

Fotheringham, R. R.. The Earth′s atmosphere viewed from space / R.R. Fotheringham. — [Dundee] ([Dundee DD1 4HN]) : University of Dundee, c1979. — 71p : ill,1map ; 30cm
Bibliography: p69-71
Unpriced (pbk) B82-35415

551.5 — Atmosphere. Chemical composition & properties

Mészáros, E.. Atmospheric chemistry : fundamental aspects / by E. Mészáros. — Amsterdam ; Oxford : Elsevier Scientific, 1981. — 201p : ill ; 25cm. — (Studies in environmental science ; 11)
Rev. translation of: A levegőkémia alapjai. — Bibliography: p183-194. — Includes index
ISBN 0-444-99753-9 : Unpriced : CIP rev.
B80-17677

551.5 — Energy sources: Weather

Schwoegler, Bruce. Weather and energy / Bruce Schwoegler and Michael McClintock. — New York ; London : McGraw-Hill, c1981. — ix,230p : ill,charts,maps ; 24cm. — (An Energy learning systems book)
Bibliography: p225-227. — Includes index
ISBN 0-07-055746-2 : £17.50 B82-31520

551.5 — Meteorology

Barry, Roger G.. Atmosphere, weather and climate. — 4th ed. — London : Methuen, Sept.1982. — [432]p
Previous ed.: 1968
ISBN 0-416-33690-6 (cased) : £12.00 : CIP entry
ISBN 0-416-33700-7 (pbk) : £5.95 B82-20177

Dynamical meteorology. — London : Methuen, Sept.1981. — [200]p
ISBN 0-416-73830-3 (cased) : £10.00 : CIP entry
ISBN 0-416-73840-0 (pbk) : £4.95 B81-30295

Holford, Ingrid. Guinness book of weather facts and feats. — 2nd ed. — Enfield : Guinness Superlatives, Oct.1982. — [256]p
Previous ed.: 1977
ISBN 0-85112-243-4 : £8.95 : CIP entry
B82-24257

Lutgens, Frederick K.. The atmosphere : an introduction to meteorology / Frederick K. Lutgens, Edward J. Tarbuck. — 2nd ed. — Englewood Cliffs ; London : Prentice-Hall, 1982. — xvii,478p,[8]p of plates : ill(some col.),maps ; 25cm
Previous ed.: 1979. — Includes index
ISBN 0-13-050120-4 : £17.95 B82-28508

Neiburger, Morris. Understanding our atmospheric environment / Morris Neiburger, James G. Edinger, William D. Bonner. — 2nd ed. — Oxford : Freeman, c1982. — ix,453p : ill,charts,maps ; 25cm
Previous ed.: 1973. — Bibliography: p411-416. — Includes index
ISBN 0-7167-1348-9 : £13.95 B82-34390

551.5 — Meteorology — *For children*

Wright, Peter. Discovering the weather. — London : Longman, Sept.1982. — [96]p
ISBN 0-582-39103-2 : £6.95 : CIP entry
B82-20268

551.5 — Weather

Forrester, Frank H.. 1001 questions answered about the weather / by Frank H. Forrester. — New York : Dover ; London : Constable, 1981. — 419p,[14]p of plates : ill,maps,ports ; 21cm
Originally published: New York : Dodd, Mead, 1957. — Bibliography: p394-402. — Includes index
ISBN 0-486-24218-8 : £4.50 B82-29997

Miller, Albert. Meteorology. — 4th ed. / Albert Miller, Richard A. Anthes. — Columbus ; London : Merrill, c1980. — v,170p : ill,charts,maps ; 25cm. — (Merrill earth science series)
Previous ed.: 1976. — Bibliography: p162-163. — Includes index
ISBN 0-675-08181-5 (pbk) : £5.25 B82-21001

The **Weather** book / Ralph Hardy ... [et al.]. — London : Joseph, 1982. — 224p : ill(some col.),charts(some col.),maps(some col.),ports (some col.) ; 29cm
Bibliography: p223. — Includes index
ISBN 0-7181-2047-7 : £12.95 B82-26979

551.5 — Weather — *For children*

Eden, Michael. Weather / Michael Eden ; illustrated by Colin Threadgall. — London : Bodley Head, 1982. — 23p : col.ill,2charts ; 22cm. — (A Young geographer)
Includes index
ISBN 0-370-30454-3 : £3.25 : CIP rev.
B82-10479

Wilson, Francis, *19---*. Spotter′s guide to the weather / Francis Wilson and Felicity Mansfield ; illustrated by Ralph Stobart ; with additional illustrations by Peter Taylor ... [et al.] ; photography by Ken Pilsbury. — [London] : Usborne, 1979. — 64p : ill(some col.),charts ; 19cm. — (Spotter′s Guides) (Usborne pocketbooks)
Bibliography: p63. — Includes index
ISBN 0-86020-271-2 : £1.85 B82-05600

551.5 — Weather — *For schools*

Shorthouse, Michael. Weather. — London : Edward Arnold, Feb.1983. — [64]p. — (Foundation geography)
ISBN 0-7131-0668-9 (pbk) : £2.00 : CIP entry
B82-38904

551.5′0243694 — Meteorology — *For scouting*

Meteorologist / publication approved by the Scout Association, London. — 2nd ed. — Glasgow : Brown, Son & Ferguson, 1980. — 49p : ill,1map ; 19cm. — (Scout badge series ; no.2)
Previous ed.: 1967
ISBN 0-85174-385-4 (pbk) : £1.30 B82-17998

551.5′0246238 — Meteorology — *For seafaring*

Burgess, C. R.. Meteorology for seamen / by C.R. Burgess. — 4th ed. — Glasgow : Brown, Son & Ferguson, 1978 (1982 [printing]). — xi,251p,[4]folded leaves of plates : ill ; 22cm
Previous ed.: 1972. — Includes index
ISBN 0-85174-315-3 : £10.00 B82-36957

Sanderson, Ray. Meteorology at sea / Ray Sanderson. — London : Stanford Maritime, 1982. — 277p,xivp of plates : ill,charts,maps ; 24cm
Includes index
ISBN 0-540-07405-5 : £8.95 : CIP rev.
B81-34220

551.5′024624 — Weather — *Tables — For construction*

A2 : weather & solar data 1982. — London (222, Balham High Rd, SW12 9BS) : Chartered Institute of Building Services, c1982. — 95p : ill,maps ; 30cm. — (CIBS guide)
Includes index
Unpriced (pbk) B82-36401

551.5′028 — Lasers. Beams. Interactions with atmosphere

Zuev, V. E.. Laser beams in the atmosphere / V.E. Zuev ; translated from Russian by James S. Wood. — New York ; London : Consultants Bureau, c1982. — xi,504p : ill ; 24cm
Translation of: Luch lazera v atmosfere
ISBN 0-306-10967-0 : Unpriced B82-15507

551.5′028′7 — Meteorological conditions. Measurement — *Manuals*

Handbook of meteorological instruments. — 2nd ed. — London : H.M.S.O.
At head of title: Meteorological Office
Vol.1: Measurement of atmospheric pressure. — 1980. — 52p in various pagings : ill ; 30cm
Previous ed.: 1956. — Includes index
ISBN 0-11-400316-5 (pbk) : £3.80 B82-18191

Handbook of meteorological instruments. — 2nd ed. — London : H.M.S.O.
At head of title; Meteorological Office
Vol.2: Measurement of temperature. — 1981. — 81p in various pagings : ill ; 30cm
Previous ed.: 1956. — Includes index
ISBN 0-11-400324-6 (pbk) : £4.40 B82-18189

Handbook of meteorological instruments. — 2nd ed. — London : H.M.S.O
Vol.3: Measurement of humidity. — 1981. — 60p in various pagings : ill ; 30cm + 1correction sheet(1ill; 29cmx19cm)
At head of title: Meteorological Office. — Previous ed.: 1956. — Bibliography: p3-26 — 3-28. — Includes index
ISBN 0-11-400325-4 (pbk) : £3.50 B82-30492

Handbook of meteorological instruments / Meteorological Office. — 2nd ed. — London : H.M.S.O.
Vol.4: Measurement of surface wind. — 1981. — vii,38,[16]p,[10]p of plates : ill ; 30cm
Previous ed.: 1956. — Bibliography: p38. — Includes index
ISBN 0-11-400331-9 (pbk) : £4.90 B82-35633

Handbook of meteorological instruments. — 2nd ed. — London : H.M.S.O
Vol.6: Measurement of sunshine and solar and terrestrial radiation. — 1982. — 84p in various pagings : ill ; 30cm
At head of title: Meteorological Office. — Previous ed.: 1956. — Bibliography: p6-45. — Includes index
ISBN 0-11-400336-x (pbk) : £5.30 B82-30493

551.5'0999'2 — Solar system. Planets. Atmosphere — *Study examples: Venus, Mars & Jupiter*
Kondrat'ev, K. ĪĀ.. Weather and climate on planets / by K.Y. Kondratyev, G.E. Hunt. — Oxford : Pergamon, 1982. — xiii,755p : ill ; 26cm
Includes index
ISBN 0-08-026493-x : £50.00 : CIP rev. B81-30983

551.5'1 — Air — *For children*
Jennings, Terry. Air / Terry Jennings ; illustrated by John Barber ... [et al.]. — Oxford : Oxford University Press, 1982. — 32p : ill (chiefly col.) ; 29cm. — (The Young scientist investigates)
ISBN 0-19-918044-x (cased) : Unpriced
ISBN 0-19-918038-5 (pbk) : £1.50 B82-29527

Lloyd, David. Air. — London : Methuen/Walker, Sept.1982. — [32]p. — (The Elements ; 1)
ISBN 0-416-06470-1 : £3.50 : CIP entry B82-19240

Paull, John. Air / by John Paull ; illustrated by Robert Ayton. — Loughborough : Ladybird, c1982. — 51p : col.ill ; 18cm. — (Ladybird junior science)
Text, ill on lining papers. — Includes index
ISBN 0-7214-0658-0 : £0.50 B82-12213

551.5'1 — Air — *For schools*
Crystal, David. Air. — London : Edward Arnold, May 1982. — [24]p. — (Databank)
ISBN 0-7131-0633-6 (pbk) : £0.90 : CIP entry B82-06910

551.5'1'0724 — Air. Experiments — *For children*
Smith, Henry, *1946-*. Amazing air / written by Henry Smith ; step-by-step illustrations by Barbara Firth and Rosalinda Kightley ; feature illustrations by Elizabeth Falconer. — London : Methuen/Walker Books, 1982. — 46p : col.ill ; 28cm. — (Science club)
Includes index
ISBN 0-416-24250-2 : Unpriced : CIP rev. B82-19244

551.5'14 — Mesosphere - *Conference proceedings*
The **Mesosphere** and thermosphere. — Oxford : Pergamon, Apr.1981. — [238]p. — (Advances in space research ; v.1, no.12)
Conference papers
ISBN 0-08-028393-4 : £13.00 : CIP entry
Also classified at 551.5'14 B81-09972

551.5'14 — Thermosphere - *Conference proceedings*
The **Mesosphere** and thermosphere. — Oxford : Pergamon, Apr.1981. — [238]p. — (Advances in space research ; v.1, no.12)
Conference papers
ISBN 0-08-028393-4 : £13.00 : CIP entry
Primary classification 551.5'14 B81-09972

551.5'153 — Atmosphere. Dynamics
Large-scale dynamical processes in the atmosphere. — London : Academic Press, Feb.1983. — [425]p
ISBN 0-12-356680-0 : CIP entry B82-37477

551.5'17 — Atmosphere. Circulation
Atkinson, B. W.. Meso-scale atmospheric circulations / B.W. Atkinson. — London : Academic Press, 1981. — xvii,495p : ill,maps ; 24cm
Includes bibliographies and index
ISBN 0-12-065960-3 : £32.40 : CIP rev B81-08802

551.5'185 — Oceans. Winds. Technical data — *Conference proceedings*
Hogben, N.. Basic data requirements : a review with emphasis on wave and wind data : paper presented to a workshop on coastal engineering organized by the Engineering Committee on Oceanic Resources at the First Panamerican Conference on Oceanic Engineering in Mexico City, 20-23 October 1980 / by N. Hogben. — Feltham : National Maritime Institute, 1980. — 30p : ill,1map ; 30cm. — (SMT-M-8001) (NMI ; R92)
Cover title
Unpriced (pbk)
Primary classification 551.47'022 B82-40677

551.5'271 — Sun. Radiation
Solar radiation data : proceedings of the EC contractors meeting held in Brussels, 20 November 1981 / edited by W. Palz. — Dordrecht ; London : Reidel for the Commission of the European Communities, c1982. — vi,143p : ill,1map ; 24cm. — (Solar energy R & D in the European Community. Series F ; v.1)
ISBN 90-277-1387-1 : Unpriced B82-32404

551.57'1 — Atmosphere. Water vapour — *Conference proceedings*
International Workshop on Atmospheric Water Vapor *(1979 : Vail, Colo.)*. Atmospheric water vapor / [proceedings of the International Workshop on Atmospheric Water Vapor, held in Vail, Colorado, September 11-13, 1979] ; edited by Adarsh Deepak, Thomas D. Wilkerson, Lothar H. Ruhnke. — New York ; London : Academic Press, 1980. — xvi,695p : ill,maps ; 24cm
Includes index
ISBN 0-12-208440-3 : £29.80 B82-10143

551.57'2 — Natural environment. Water. Evaporation
Brutsaert, Wilfred. Evaporation into the atmosphere : theory, history, and applications / Wilfred Brutsaert. — Dordrecht ; London : Reidel, c1982. — x,299p : ill ; 25cm. — (Environmental fluid mechanics ; 1)
Bibliography: p263-291. — Includes index
Unpriced B82-18325

551.57'2'0287 — Natural environment. Water. Evaporation. Measurement — *Manuals*
Handbook of meteorological instruments. — 2nd ed. — London : H.M.S.O.
At head of title: Meteorological Office
Vol.5: Measurement of precipitation and evaporation. — 1981. — 56p in various pagings : ill ; 30cm
Previous ed.: 1956. — Includes index
ISBN 0-11-400328-9 (pbk) : £3.80 B82-18190

551.57'6'0222 — Clouds — *Illustrations*
Scorer, Richard. Clouds of the world. — 2nd rev. ed. — Newton Abbot : David & Charles, Feb.1983. — [176]p
Previous ed.: 1972
ISBN 0-7153-8442-2 : £27.50 : CIP entry B82-39455

551.57'81'0287 — Rainfall. Measurement. Use of artificial satellites
Barrett, Eric C.. The use of satellite data in rainfall monitoring / Eric C. Barrett, David W. Martin. — London : Academic Press, 1981. — xi,340p : ill,charts ; 24cm
Bibliography: p312-329. — Includes index
ISBN 0-12-079680-5 : £27.80 : CIP rev. B81-26773

551.57'81242496'0212 — West Midlands *(Metropolitan County)*. **Edgbaston. Rainfall,** *1940-1979 — Statistics*
Kings, J.. Rainfall in Birmingham 1940-1979 : a statistical analysis by weeks / J. Kings and B.D. Giles. — 2nd ed. — [Birmingham] : Department of Geography, University of Birmingham, 1982. — 87p : ill ; 30cm. — (Occasional publication ; no.14)
Previous ed.: 1981
ISBN 0-7044-0575-x (pbk) : Unpriced B82-34400

551.6 — CLIMATE AND WEATHER

551.6 — Climate. Changes
Budyko, M. I.. The earth's climate : past and future / M.I. Budyko ; translated by the author. — New York ; London : Academic Press, 1982. — x,307p : ill,maps ; 24cm. — (International geophysics series ; v.29)
Translation of Klimat v proshlom i budushchem. — Bibliography: p288-304. — Includes index
ISBN 0-12-139460-3 : Unpriced B82-40835

551.6 — Climate. Changes, *B.C.6000-0 — Conference proceedings*
Climatic change in later pre-history / A.F. Harding eidtor. — Edinburgh : Edinburgh University Press, c1982. — viii,210p : ill,maps ; 24cm
Includes bibliographies and index
ISBN 0-85224-425-8 (pbk) : £9.75 : CIP rev. B82-00182

551.6 — Climate. Changes. Theories
Hoyle, Fred. Ice. — London : New English Library, Oct.1982. — [228]p
Originally published: London : Hutchinson, 1981
ISBN 0-450-05493-4 (pbk) : £1.95 : CIP entry B82-23320

551.6 — Climate. Changes, *to 1977*
Lamb, H. H.. Climate, history and the modern world / H.H. Lamb. — London : Methuen, 1982. — xix,387p : ill,charts,maps ; 24cm
Bibliography: p377-378. — Includes index
ISBN 0-416-33430-x (cased) : Unpriced : CIP rev.
ISBN 0-416-33440-7 (pbk) : Unpriced B82-20175

551.6 — Dendroclimatology — *Conference proceedings*
Climate from tree rings / edited by M.K. Hughes ... [et al.]. — Cambridge : Cambridge University Press, 1982. — 223p : ill,maps ; 31cm
Bibliography: p199-213. — Includes index
ISBN 0-521-24291-6 : £18.50 : CIP rev. B82-12720

551.6'05 — Climate — *Serials*
Journal of climatology : a journal of the Royal Meteorological Society. — Vol.1, no.1 (Jan.-Mar. 1981)-. — Chichester : Wiley, 1981-. — v. : ill,charts,maps ; 26cm
Quarterly
ISSN 0196-1748 = Journal of climatology : £35.00 per year B82-01066

551.6'3 — Weather. Forecasting
Dunlop, S.. The Hamlyn guide to weather forecasting / S. Dunlop, F. Wilson. — London : Hamlyn, c1982. — 160p : ill(some col.),maps ; 20cm
Bibliography: p154. — Includes index
ISBN 0-600-35619-1 (cased) : £5.95
ISBN 0-600-39024-1 (pbk) : £3.95 B82-40747

551.6'3'0247971 — Weather. Forecasting — *For yachting*
Watts, Alan. Cruising weather. — London : Macmillan London, Apr.1982. — [232]p
ISBN 0-333-32217-7 : £10.95 : CIP entry B82-03801

551.6'32 — Weather. Reporting by ships. Coding — *Manuals*
Ships' code and decode book : incorporating the international meteorological codes for weather reports from and to ships and the analysis code for use of shipping / Meteorological Office. — London : H.M.S.O., c1981. — 59p,[1]folded leaf of plates : 1col.chart ; 25cm
Previous ed.: 1977. — Includes index
ISBN 0-11-400327-0 (pbk) : £1.75 B82-17769

551.6'362 — Weather. Short-range forecasting — *Conference proceedings*
Nowcasting. — London : Academic Press, Sept.1982. — [280]p
Conference papers
ISBN 0-12-137760-1 : CIP entry B82-19159

551.6914'3 — Climate & weather. Influence of mountains
Barry, Roger G.. Mountain weather and climate. — London : Methuen, Sept.1981. — [300]p
ISBN 0-416-73730-7 : £15.00 : CIP entry B81-23771

551.69173'2 — Urban regions. Climate
Landsberg, H. E.. The urban climate / Helmut E. Landsberg. — New York ; London : Academic Press, 1981. — ix,275p : ill ; 24cm. — (International geophysics series ; v.28)
Includes bibliographies and index
ISBN 0-12-435960-4 : Unpriced B82-02988

551.6941 — Great Britain. Weather
Stirling, Robin. The weather of Britain / Robin Stirling. — London : Faber, 1982. — 270p : ill,charts,maps ; 24cm
Bibliography: p253-254. — Includes index
ISBN 0-571-11695-7 : £12.50 : CIP rev. B81-30955

551.6942'012 — England. Climate. Classification — *For agricultural land use*
Bendelow, V. C.. Climatic classification of England and Wales / V.C. Bendelow and R. Hartnup. — Harpenden (Rothamsted Experimental Station, Harpenden, Herts. AL5 2JQ) : Soil Survey, 1980. — vii,27p : ill,maps ; 21cm + 4sheets(col.maps). — (Soil Survey technical monograph ; no.15)
Maps in wallet. — Bibliography: p23-27
£6.25 (pbk) B82-02927

551.7 — STRATIGRAPHY

551.7 — Historical geology
Stokes, William Lee. Essentials of earth history : an introduction to historical geology / W. Lee Stokes. — 4th ed. — Englewood Cliffs ; London : Prentice-Hall, c1982. — xiv,577p : ill,maps,ports ; 24cm
Previous ed.: 1973. — Text and ill on lining papers. — Includes bibliographies and index
ISBN 0-13-285890-8 : £19.45 B82-20075

551.7 — Phanerozoic strata
The **Mesozoic**, B. — Oxford : Elsevier Scientific, June 1982. — 1v.. — (The Phanerozoic geology of the world ; 2)
ISBN 0-444-41672-2 : CIP entry B82-09739

551.7 — Stratigraphy
Numerical dating in stratigraphy. — Chichester : Wiley, Sept.1982. — 2v.([500];[500]p)
ISBN 0-471-10085-4 : £25.00 : CIP entry B82-19516

Quantitative stratigraphic correlation. — Chichester : Wiley, Jan.1983. — [300]p. — (International geological correlations programme)
ISBN 0-471-10171-0 : £20.00 : CIP entry B82-34614

551.7 — Western English Channel. Sub-chalk strata
Evans, C. D. R.. The Zephyr (1977) wells, south-western approaches and western English Channel / C.D.R. Evans, G.K. Lott and G. Warrington (compilers) ; contributors P.J. Bigg ... [et al.]. — London : H.M.S.O., 1981. — iv,44p : ill,maps ; 30cm. — (Report / Institute of Geological Sciences ; 81/8)
4 sheets (125x27cm folded to 19x27cm) in pocket. — Bibliography: p4
ISBN 0-11-884198-x (pbk) : £7.25 B82-13529

551.7'1 — Pre-Cambrian strata. Banded iron formations
Mel'nik, ÎÛ. P.. Precambrian banded iron-formations : physicochemical conditions of formation / Y.P. Mel'nik ; translation from the Russian by Dorothy B. Vitaliano. — Amsterdam ; Oxford : Elsevier Scientific, 1982. — xii,310p : ill,maps ; 25cm. — (Developments in Precambrian geology ; 5)
Translation of: Fiziko-khimicheskie usloviîa obrazovaniîa dokembriĭskikh zhelezistykh kvartŝitov. — Bibliography: p283-306. — Includes index
ISBN 0-444-41934-9 : £36.09 : CIP rev. B81-35706

551.7'3'0956 — Middle East. Lower Palaeozoic strata
Lower Palaeozoic of the Middle East, eastern and southern Africa, and Antarctica : with essays on Lower Palaeozoic trace fossils of Africa and Lower Palaeozoic palaeoclimatology / edited by C.H. Holland. — Chichester : Wiley, c1981. — ix,331p,[27]p of plates : ill,maps ; 28cm. — (Lower Palaeozoic rocks of the world ; v.3)
Includes bibliographies and index
ISBN 0-471-27945-5 : £38.00
Also classified at 551.7'3'0967 ; 551.7'3'09989 B82-05891

551.7'3'0967 — East & Southern Africa. Lower Palaeozoic strata
Lower Palaeozoic of the Middle East, eastern and southern Africa, and Antarctica : with essays on Lower Palaeozoic trace fossils of Africa and Lower Palaeozoic palaeoclimatology / edited by C.H. Holland. — Chichester : Wiley, c1981. — ix,331p,[27]p of plates : ill,maps ; 28cm. — (Lower Palaeozoic rocks of the world ; v.3)
Includes bibliographies and index
ISBN 0-471-27945-5 : £38.00
Primary classification 551.7'3'0956 B82-05891

551.7'3'09989 — Antarctic. Lower Palaeozoic strata
Lower Palaeozoic of the Middle East, eastern and southern Africa, and Antarctica : with essays on Lower Palaeozoic trace fossils of Africa and Lower Palaeozoic palaeoclimatology / edited by C.H. Holland. — Chichester : Wiley, c1981. — ix,331p,[27]p of plates : ill,maps ; 28cm. — (Lower Palaeozoic rocks of the world ; v.3)
Includes bibliographies and index
ISBN 0-471-27945-5 : £38.00
Primary classification 551.7'3'0956 B82-05891

551.7'4'094128 — Scotland. Firth of Tay. Upper Devonian strata
Browne, M. A. E.. The Upper Devonian and Lower Carboniferous (Dinantian) of the Firth of Tay, Scotland / M.A.E. Browne. — London : H.M.S.O., 1980. — ii,13p : ill,1map ; 30cm. — (Report / Institute of Geological Sciences ; 80/9)
Bibliography: p12-13
ISBN 0-11-884186-6 (pbk) : £1.25
Also classified at 551.7'51'094128 B82-20457

551.7'5 — Carboniferous strata. Formation
Nature and origin of cretaceous carbon-rich facies . — London : Academic Press, Dec.1982. — [250]p
ISBN 0-12-624950-4 : CIP entry B82-29888

551.7'5 — Great Britain. Strata. Mobile belts. Variscan fold belt
The **Variscan** fold belt in Britain. — Bristol : Hilger, Oct.1982. — [214]p
ISBN 0-85274-383-1 : £40.00 : CIP entry B82-24238

551.7'51'094128 — Scotland. Firth of Tay. Lower Carboniferous strata
Browne, M. A. E.. The Upper Devonian and Lower Carboniferous (Dinantian) of the Firth of Tay, Scotland / M.A.E. Browne. — London : H.M.S.O., 1980. — ii,13p : ill,1map ; 30cm. — (Report / Institute of Geological Sciences ; 80/9)
Bibliography: p12-13
ISBN 0-11-884186-6 (pbk) : £1.25
Primary classification 551.7'4'094128 B82-20457

551.7'8 — Cainozoic era
Pomerol, Charles. The Cenozoic Era : tertiary and quaternary / Charles Pomerol ; translated by Derek W. Humphries and Evelyn E. Humphries ; edited by D. Curry and D.T. Donovan. — Chichester : Horwood, 1982. — 272p : ill,maps ; 25cm. — (Ellis Horwood series in geology)
Translation of: Ère cénozoique. — Bibliography: p256-262. — Includes index
ISBN 0-85312-256-3 (pbk) : £24.50 B82-25449

551.7'9 — Quaternary strata. Soils. Mechanics
. Soil mechanics in quaternary science / by M.A. Paul (editor) with contributions from M.A. Paul, E.L. Pole, T.P. Gostelow. — [London] : Quaternary Research Association, [1981]. — 121p : ill ; 21cm
Notes to accompany a course of lectures given in the Department of Civil Engineering, Heriot-Watt University, Edinburgh for members of the Quaternary Research Association, 18th-20th September, 1981. — Includes bibliographies
ISBN 0-907780-00-8 (pbk) : Unpriced B82-08297

551.7'9'05 — Quaternary strata — *Serials*
Quaternary science reviews. — Vol.1, no.1 (1982)-. — Oxford : Pergamon, 1982-. — v. : ill,maps ; 25cm
Quarterly
Unpriced B82-28857

551.7'9'094237 — West Cornwall. Quaternary strata — *For field studies*
West Cornwall field meeting, 18-21 September 1980 / Quaternary Research Association ; contributors, K. Atkinson ... [et al.] ; compiled and edited by Peter C. Sims. — [Plymouth] ([Drake Circus, Plymouth PL4 8AA]) : Published and produced by the Dept. of Geographical Sciences, Plymouth Polytechnic for the Quaternary Research Association, c1980. — 53p : ill,maps ; 21cm
Bibliography: p41-53
Unpriced (spiral) B82-34621

551.7'9'094675 — Spain. Majorca. Quarternary strata — *For field studies*
The **Quaternary** of Mallorca : field meeting guide, December, 1978 / by K. Crabtree ... [et al.]. — [Bristol] ([c/o Dept. of Geography, University of Bristol, Park St., Bristol 8]) : Quaternary Research Association, [1981?]. — v,114p : ill,maps ; 22cm
Bibliography: p103-114
Unpriced (pbk) B82-34622

551.7'9'09676 — East Africa. Quaternary era. Environmental aspects
Hamilton, A. C.. Environmental history of East Africa : a study of the Quaternary / A.C. Hamilton. — London : Academic Press, 1982. — xiv,328p : ill,maps ; 24cm
Bibliography: p294-311. — Includes index
ISBN 0-12-321880-2 : £24.00 : CIP rev. B82-04141

551.7'92'0941 — Great Britain. Ice ages
Sparks, B. W.. The Ice Age in Britain. — London : Methuen, Oct.1981. — [320]p. — (Methuen library reprints)
ISBN 0-416-32160-7 : £17.50 : CIP entry B81-25727

551.7'93'09443 — France. Champagne. Holocene strata
Beal, C. J.. Late holocene environmental change in the Champagne, France : an interim report on fieldwork 1978-1980 / C.J. Beal, P.C. Buckland and J.R.A. Greig. — Birmingham : Department of Geography, University of Birmingham, 1980. — 22p : ill,maps ; 30cm. — (Working paper series / University of Birmingham. Department of Geography ; no.6)
Bibliography: p20-22
ISBN 0-7044-0561-x (pbk) : £0.40 B82-23561

551.8 — STRUCTURAL GEOLOGY

551.8 — Geological features. Analysis. Use of geological maps
Roberts, John L.. Introduction to geological maps and structures. — Oxford : Pergamon, July 1982. — [325]p. — (Pergamon international library)
ISBN 0-08-023982-x (cased) : £20.00 : CIP entry
ISBN 0-08-020920-3 (pbk) : £8.50 B82-12408

551.8 — Geological features. Mapping — *Manuals*
Barnes, John W.. Basic geological mapping / John W. Barnes. — Milton Keynes : Open University Press, 1981. — 112p,[1]leaf of plates : ill ; 18cm. — (Geological Society of London handbook)
Ill, text on inside covers. — Bibliography: p112
ISBN 0-335-10035-x (pbk) : £4.95 : CIP rev. B81-30284

551.8 — Geological structure
Wilson, Gilbert. Introduction to small-scale geological structures / Gilbert Wilson in collaboration with J.W. Cosgrove. — London : Allen & Unwin, 1982. — 128p : ill ; 22cm
Bibliography: p113-125. — Includes index
ISBN 0-04-551051-2 (cased) : Unpriced : CIP rev.
ISBN 0-04-551052-0 (pbk) : Unpriced B81-35928

551.8 — Structural geology
Park, R. G.. Foundations of structural geology. — Glasgow : Blackie, Sept.1982. — [128]p
ISBN 0-216-91312-8 (cased) : £15.50 : CIP entry
ISBN 0-216-91311-x (pbk) : £7.75 B82-19007

551.8'961'2 — Libya. Structural geology - *Conference proceedings*
The **Geology** of Libya. — London : Academic Press, Apr.1981
Vol.1. — [461]p
ISBN 0-12-615501-1 : CIP entry B81-03680

The **Geology** of Libya. — London : Academic Press, Apr.1981
Vol.2. — [461]p
ISBN 0-12-615502-x : CIP entry B81-03681

The **Geology** of Libya. — London : Academic Press, Apr.1981
Vol.3. — [461]p
ISBN 0-12-615503-8 : CIP entry B81-03682

551.8′961′2 — Libya. Structural geology - *Conference proceedings* *continuation*

551.9 — GEOCHEMISTRY

551.9 — Cornwall. Geochemical maps

Jones, R. C.. Reconnaissance geochemical maps of parts of south Devon and Cornwall / R.C. Jones. — London : Institute of Geological Sciences, 1981. — 3leaves ; 30cm. — (Mineral reconnaissance programme report ; no.44)
Unpriced (sprial)
Primary classification 551.9 B82-15030

551.9 — Earth. High temperature fluid solutions & high pressure fluid solutions — *Conference proceedings*

Chemistry and geochemistry of solutions at high temperatures and pressures : proceedings of a Nobel Symposium / organized by the Royal Swedish Academy of Sciences and held at Bjorkborns Herrgard, Karlskoga, Sweden, 17-21 September 1979 ; editors David T. Rickard, Frans E. Wickman. — Oxford : Published for the Royal Swedish Academy of Sciences by Pergamon, c1981. — xi,562p,[1]leaf of plates : ill,1port ; 28cm. — (Physics and chemistry of the earth ; v.13 & 14)
Includes bibliographies and index
ISBN 0-08-026285-6 : Unpriced : CIP rev.
B81-31359

551.9 — Geochemistry

Henderson, Paul. Inorganic geochemistry. — Oxford : Pergamon, Mar.1982. — [372]p. — (Pergamon international library)
ISBN 0-08-020448-1 (cased) : £21.00 : CIP entry
ISBN 0-08-020447-3 (pbk) : £9.35 B82-00927

551.9 — South Devon. Geochemical maps

Jones, R. C.. Reconnaissance geochemical maps of parts of south Devon and Cornwall / R.C. Jones. — London : Institute of Geological Sciences, 1981. — 3leaves ; 30cm. — (Mineral reconnaissance programme report ; no.44)
Unpriced (sprial)
Also classified at 551.9 B82-15030

551.9′028 — Geochemistry. Laboratory techniques

Statistics and data analysis in geochemical prospecting. — Oxford : Elsevier Scientific, May 1982. — [200]p. — (Handbook of exploration geochemistry ; v.2)
ISBN 0-444-42038-x : CIP entry B82-06828

552 — PETROLOGY

552 — Rocks

Ehlers, Ernest G.. Petrology : igneous, sedimentary and metamorphic / Ernest G. Ehlers, Harvey Blatt. — Oxford : Freeman, c1982. — xvi,732p : ill,maps ; 24cm. — (A Series of books in geology)
Includes bibliographies and index
ISBN 0-7167-1279-2 : £21.95 B82-29261

552 — Rocks — *For children*

Jennings, Terry. Rocks and soil / Terry Jennings ; illustrated by Norma Burgin. — Oxford : Oxford University Press, 1982. — 32p : ill (chiefly col.) ; 29cm. — (The Young scientist investigates)
ISBN 0-19-918045-8 (cased) : Unpriced
ISBN 0-19-918039-3 (pbk) : £1.50
Also classified at 631.4 B82-29523

552′.002493 — Petrology — *For archaeology*

The **Petrology** of archaeological artefacts. — Oxford : Clarendon Press, Sept.1982. — [430]p
ISBN 0-19-854418-9 : £30.00 : CIP entry
B82-18971

552′.06 — Rocks. Chemical analysis

Johnson, Wesley M.. Rock and mineral analysis. — 2nd ed. / Wesley M. Johnson, John A. Maxwell. — New York ; Chichester : Wiley, c1981. — xi,489p : ill ; 24cm. — (Chemical analysis, ISSN 0069-2883 ; v.27)
Previous ed.: / by John A. Maxwell. New York, Chichester : Interscience, 1968. — Bibliography: p428-432. — Includes index
ISBN 0-471-02743-x : £38.85
Also classified at 549′.133 B82-05889

552.09412′95 — Scotland. Fife Region. West Wemyss. Rocks — *For teaching*

Rocks and fossils of West Wemyss. — [West Wemyss] : West Wemyss Environmental Education Centre, [1982]. — 28p,[2]leaves of plates : ill,2maps ; 21cm
Cover title. — Ill on inside cover
Unpriced (pbk)
Also classified at 560.9412′95 B82-19640

552.095 — Asia. Rocks. Metamorphism

Metamorphic complexes of Asia. — Oxford : Pergamon, Sept.1981. — [350]p
Translation of: Metamorficheskie kompleksy Azii
ISBN 0-08-022854-2 : £20.00 : CIP entry
B81-22570

552′.1 — Igneous rocks. Petrology

Hughes, Charles J.. Igneous petrology / Charles J. Hughes. — Amsterdan ; Oxford : Elsevier Scientific, 1982. — xvi,551p : ill,maps ; 25cm. — (Developments in petrology ; 7)
Bibliography: p489-519. — Includes index
ISBN 0-444-42011-8 : £14.77 : CIP rev.
B82-14050

552′.1′0222 — Igneous rocks. Textures — *Illustrations*

MacKenzie, W. S.. Atlas of igneous rocks and their textures. — London : Longman, Nov.1982. — [160]p
ISBN 0-582-30082-7 (pbk) : £9.95 : CIP entry
B82-26530

552′.1′0941 — Great Britain. Igneous rocks

Igneous rocks of the British Isles / edited by D.S. Sutherland. — Chichester : Wiley, c1982. — xv,645p : ill,maps ; 30cm
Bibliography: p583-622. — Includes index
ISBN 0-471-27810-6 : £55.00 B82-26175

552′.2 — Andesites

Andesites : orogenic andesites and related rocks / edited by R.S. Thorpe. — Chichester : Wiley, c1982. — xiii,724p : ill,maps ; 26cm
Includes bibliographies and index
ISBN 0-471-28034-8 : £59.50 : CIP rev.
B81-34647

552′.2 — Volcanic rocks: Komatiites

Komatiites. — London : Allen & Unwin, May 1982. — [544]p
ISBN 0-04-552019-4 : £35.00 : CIP entry
B82-07233

552′.23 — Tephra — *Conference proceedings*

Tephra Studies as a Tool in Quaternary Research *(Conference : 1980 : Laugarvatn and Reykjavík)*. Tephra studies : proceedings of the NATO Advanced Study Institute "Tephra Studies as a Tool in Quaternary Research", held in Laugarvatn and Reykjavik, Iceland, June 18-29, 1980 / edited by S. Self and R.S.J. Sparks. — Dordrecht ; London : Reidel in cooperation with NATO Scientific Affairs Division, c1981. — xiv,481p : ill,maps ; 25cm. — (NATO advanced study institutes series. Series C, Mathematical and physical sciences ; v.75)
Includes index
ISBN 90-277-1327-8 : Unpriced B82-03458

552′.4 — Metamorphic rocks. Petrology

Fry, Norman. The field description of metamorphic rocks. — Milton Keynes : Open University Press, Dec.1982. — [128]p. — (The Geological Society of London handbook series)
ISBN 0-335-10037-6 (pbk) : £6.95 : CIP entry
B82-29638

Turner, Francis J. (Francis John). Metamorphic petrology : mineralogical, field and tectonic aspects / Francis J. Turner. — 2nd ed. — Washington ; London : Hemisphere, c1981. — xv,524p : ill,maps ; 25cm. — (McGraw-Hill international series in the earth and planetary sciences)
Previous ed.: London : McGraw-Hill, 1968. — Bibliography: p471-499. — Includes index
ISBN 0-07-065501-4 : £25.95 B82-00412

552′.4 — Rocks. Metamorphism

Gillen, Con. Metamorphic geology : an introduction to tectonic and metamorphic processes / Con Gillen. — London : Allen & Unwin, 1982. — xii,144p : ill,maps ; 22cm
Bibliography: p136-137. — Includes index
ISBN 0-04-551057-1 (cased) : Unpriced : CIP rev.
ISBN 0-04-551058-x (pbk) : Unpriced
B82-03706

552′.4 — South Africa. Southern Cape Province. Silcretes

Summerfield, M. A.. The nature and occurrence of silcrete, Southern Cape Province, South Africa / M.A. Summerfield. — Oxford (Mansfield Rd., Oxford OX1 3TB) : School of Geography, University of Oxford, 1981. — 36p : ill,maps ; 22cm. — (Research paper / School of Geography, University of Oxford, ISSN 0305-8190 ; 28)
Unpriced (pbk) B82-05829

552′.5 — Clastic tidal sediments

Klein, George deVries. Clastic tidal facies / George deVries Klein. — Champaign : CEPCO ; Heathfield : Broad Oak [distributor], c1977. — 149p : ill,maps ; 26cm
Bibliography: p133-143. — Includes index
ISBN 0-89469-092-2 (cased) : Unpriced
ISBN 0-89469-093-0 (pbk) : Unpriced
B82-28042

552′.5 — Sedimentary basins. Formation — *Conference proceedings*

The **Evolution** of sedimentary basins : proceedings of a Royal Society discussion meeting held on 3 and 4 June 1981 / organized and edited by Sir Peter Kent ... [et al.]. — London : Royal Society, 1982. — 338p : ill,maps ; 30cm
'Overlay to figures 3-13' (1 transparent sheet) as insert. — Includes bibliographies
ISBN 0-85403-184-7 : £41.25 B82-33135

552′.5 — Sedimentary rocks

Collinson, J. D.. Sedimentary structures. — London : Allen and Unwin, Apr.1982. — [240]p
ISBN 0-04-552017-8 (cased) : £18.00 : CIP entry
ISBN 0-04-552018-6 (pbk) : £8.95 B82-03707

Tucker, Maurice E.. The field description of sedimentary rock / Maurice E. Tucker. — Milton Keynes : Open University Press, 1982. — 112p : ill ; 18cm. — (Geological Society of London handbook)
Ill on inside covers. — Bibliography: p111-112
ISBN 0-335-10036-8 (pbk) : £4.95 : CIP rev.
B81-30221

552′.5 — Sedimentary rocks. Diagenesis

Diagenesis in sediments and sedimentary rocks, 2. — Oxford : Elsevier Scientific, Jan.1983. — [550]p. — (Developments in sedimentology ; 25B)
ISBN 0-444-42013-4 : CIP entry B82-34598

552′.5 — Sedimentary rocks. Sedimentation

Allen, John R. L.. Sedimentary structures : their character and physical basis / by John R.L. Allen. — Amsterdam ; Oxford : Elsevier Scientific, 1982. — 2v. : ill ; 25cm. — (Development in sedimentology ; v.30A-v.30B)
Includes bibliographies and index
ISBN 0-444-41946-2 : Unpriced : CIP rev.
ISBN 0-444-41935-7 (v.1) : Unpriced
ISBN 0-444-41945-4 (v.2) : £55.44 B81-27380

553 — ECONOMIC GEOLOGY

553 — Energy resources. Geophysical aspects — *Conference proceedings*

Geophysical aspects of the energy problem : proceedings of the 2nd course held at the School of Geophysics Ettore Majorana International Centre for Scientific Culture, Erice, Italy, June 4-18, 1978 / edited by A. Rapolla, G.V. Keller, D.J. Moore. — Amsterdam ; Oxford : Elsevier Scientific, 1980. — xiv,325p : ill ; 25cm. — (Energy research ; v.1)
Includes bibliographies
ISBN 0-444-41845-8 : £28.36 : CIP rev.
B80-13804

553 — Mineral deposits. Geochemical aspects. Mathematical models

Conceptual models in exploration geochemistry. — Amsterdam ; Oxford : Elsevier Scientific. — (Developments in economic geology ; 13) (Association of Exploration Geochemists special publication ; no.8)
4: Australia / compiled and edited by C.R.M. Butt and R.E. Smith. — 1980. — x,275p : ill,maps ; 25cm
Bibliography: p265-275
ISBN 0-444-41902-0 : £27.83 : CIP rev.
B80-11866

553 — Minerals

O'Donoghue, Michael. Beginner's guide to minerals. — London : Newnes Technical Books, Sept.1982. — [168]p
ISBN 0-408-01119-x (pbk) : £3.95 : CIP entry
B82-19218

553 — Strategic ores. Availability — *Conference proceedings*

National Symposium on the Availability of Strategic Minerals *(1979 : London)*. Availability of strategic minerals : proceedings of the National Symposium on the Availability of Strategic Minerals, organised by the Institution of Mining and Metallurgy, in association with the Fellowship of Engineering, held in London on 20 and 21 November 1979 / edited by Michael J. Jones. — London : Institution of Mining and Metallurgy, c1980. — ix,109p : ill ; 30cm
ISBN 0-900488-48-4 (pbk) : Unpriced
B82-16009

553'.094 — Europe. Mineral deposits

Mineral deposits of Europe. — [London] : The Mineralogical Society
Vol.2: Southeast Europe / edited by F.W. Dunning, W. Mykura and D. Slater ; non-metallic minerals editor A.J.G. Notholt ; production editor A.R. Woolley. — c1982. — xi,304p : ill(some col.),maps ; 31cm
Includes bibliographies and index
ISBN 0-900488-63-8 : Unpriced B82-39903

553'.09414'95 — Scotland. Dumfries and Galloway Region. Culvennan Fell region. Mineral deposits

Mineral exploration in the area around Culvennan Fell, Kirkcowan, south-western Scotland / geophysics M.E. Parker ; geochemistry D.C. Cooper, P.J. Bide ; geology P.M. Allen. — London : Institute of Geological Sciences, 1981. — 31leaves : ill,maps ; 30cm. — (Mineral reconnaissance programme report ; no.42)
Bibliography: leaf 16
Unpriced (sprial) B82-15033

553'.09429'29 — Gwynedd. Tanygrisiau. Microgranite strata. Mineralisation. Geophysical analysis

Cornwell, J. D.. Geophysical evidence for a concealed eastern extension of the Tanygrisiau microgranite and its possible relationship to mineralisation / geophysics J.D. Cornwell, D.J. Patrick ; geology R.J. Tappin. — London : Institute of Geological Sciences, 1980. — 13leaves,1folded leaf of plates : ill ; 30cm. — (Mineral reconnaissance programme report ; no.38)
Unpriced (spiral) B82-15029

553'.1 — Ore deposits. Mineralisation — *Conference proceedings*

Metallization associated with acid magmatism / edited by A.M. Evans. — Chichester : Wiley, c1982. — ix,385p : ill,maps ; 26cm. — (Mineralization associated with acid magmatism ; v.6)
Conference papers. — Includes bibliographies
ISBN 0-471-09995-3 : £21.00 : CIP rev.
B82-04850

553'.14 — Stratabound ore deposits & stratiform ore deposits

Handbook of strata-bound and stratiform ore deposits / edited by K.H. Wolf. — Amsterdam ; Oxford : Elsevier Scientific
Part 3
Vol.10: Bibliography and ore occurrence data. — c1981. — 576p : maps ; 25cm
Includes bibliographies and index
ISBN 0-444-41825-3 : Unpriced : CIP rev.
B81-12785

553.2'4 — Coal. Geochemical aspects

Bouška, Vladimír. Geochemistry of coal / by Vladimír Bouška. — Amsterdam ; Oxford : Elsevier Scientific, 1981. — 284p : ill ; 25cm. — (Coal science and technology ; 1)
Translation of: Geochemie uhlí. 2nd ed. — Bibliography: p232-259. — Includes index
ISBN 0-444-99738-5 : Unpriced : CIP rev.
B81-30522

553.2'8 — Sandstone strata. Natural gas deposits & petroleum deposits — *For prospecting*

Klein, George deVries. Sandstone depositional models for exploration for fossil fuels / George deVries Klein. — 2nd ed. — [Champaign] : CEPCO ; Heathfield : Broad Oak [distributor], c1980. — v,149p : ill ; 29cm
Previous ed.: 1975. — Includes bibliographies and index
ISBN 0-8087-2977-2 (cased) : Unpriced
ISBN 0-8087-2978-0 (pbk) : Unpriced
B82-28041

553.2'82 — Petroleum — *For children*

Asimov, Isaac. How we found out about oil / Isaac Asimov. — Harlow : Longman, 1982, c1980. — 53p : ill,1map ; 23cm. — (How we found out about series)
Originally published: New York : Walker, 1980. — Includes index
ISBN 0-582-39157-1 : £2.75 B82-33649

553.2'82'0724 — Petroleum deposits. Reservoirs. Mathematical models

Thomas, G. W. (Gordon W). Principles of hydrocarbon reservoir simulation / G.W. Thomas. — Boston, Mass. : International Human Resources Development ; Heathfield : Broad Oak [distributor], c1982. — xiv,207p : ill ; 24cm
Includes index
ISBN 0-934634-11-4 : Unpriced B82-28046

553.2'82'09047 — Petroleum, *1969-1981*

Al-Otaiba, Mana Saeed. Essays on petroleum. — London : Croom Helm, May 1982. — [176]p
ISBN 0-7099-1921-2 : £10.00 : CIP entry
B82-15924

553.4'09423'592 — Devon. Lutton region. Metalliferous strata. Mineralisation

Metalliferous mineralisation near Lutton, Ivybridge, Devon / geology K.E. Beer, M.J. Bennett ; geochemistry T.K. Ball, R.C. Jones, K. Turton. — London : Institute of Geological Sciences, 1981. — 33leaves : ill,maps ; 30cm. — (Mineral reconnaissance programme report ; no.41)
Unpriced (spiral) B82-15034

553.4'1'0941495 — Scotland. Dumfries and Galloway Region. Loch Dee Region. Gold deposits. Mineralisation

Gold mineralisation at the southern margin of the Loch Doon granitoid complex, south-west Scotland / geochemistry and mineralisation R.C. Leake ; mineralogy H.H. Auld ; geology P. Stone ; geophysics C.E. Johnson. — London : Institute of Geological Sciences, 1981. — 41leaves : ill ; 30cm. — (Mineral reconnaissance programme report ; no.46)
Bibliography: leaf 41
Unpriced (spiral) B82-15027

553.4'3'0941495 — Scotland. Dumfries and Galloway Region. Cairngarroch Bay. Copper-bearing intrusive complexes

Copper-bearing intrusive rocks at Cairngarroch Bay, south-west Scotland / geology P.M. Allen ; geochemistry P.J. Bide, D.C. Cooper ; geophysics M.E. Parker ; mineralogy H.W. Haslam. — London : Institute of Geological Sciences, 1981. — 20leaves : ill,maps ; 30cm. — (Mineral reconnaissance programme report ; no.39)
Bibliography: leaf 20
Unpriced (sprial) B82-15032

553.4'646'0941185 — Scotland. Highland Region. Ballachulish region. Copper-molybdenum deposits. Mineralisation

Haslam, H. W.. Disseminated copper-molybdenum mineralisation near Ballachulish, Highland Region / geology and geochemistry H.W. Haslam ; geophysics G.S. Kimbell. — London : Institute of Geological Sciences, 1981. — 45leaves : ill,maps ; 30cm. — (Mineral reconnaissance programme report ; no.43)
Unpriced (spiral) B82-15028

553.4'926 — Karsts. Bauxite deposits

Bárdossy, György. Karst bauxites : bauxite deposits on carbonate rocks / by Gyŕgy Bárdossy. — Amsterdam ; Oxford : Elsevier Scientific, 1982. — 441p,[8]p of plates : ill (some col.),maps(some col.) ; 25cm. — (Developments in economic geology ; 14)
Translation of: Karsztbauxitok. — Nine folded sheets in pocket. — Bibliography: p406-424. — Includes index
ISBN 0-444-99727-x : £41.05 : CIP rev.
B81-31622

553.4'99 — Scotland. Tayside Region. Aberfeldy region. Stratabound barium-zinc ores. Mineralisation

Stratabound barium-zinc mineralisation in Dalradian schist near Aberfeldy, Scotland : final report / geology and geochemistry J.S. Coats ... [et al.] ; geophysics M.E. Parker ; mineralogy N.J. Fortey. — London : Institute of Geological Sciences, 1981. — 116p : ill,maps ; 30cm. — (Mineral reconnaissance programme report ; no.40)
Six maps (49x100cm folded to 29x16cm or smaller) in pockets
Unpriced (spiral) B82-15031

553.6'2 — Sand & gravel deposits

Chester, David K.. Predicting the quality of sand and gravel deposits in areas of fluvioglacial deposition. — Liverpool : Liverpool University Press, Oct.1982. — [77]p. — (University of Liverpool : Department of Geography research papers ; 10)
ISBN 0-85323-414-0 (pbk) : £3.00 : CIP entry
B82-36327

553.6'2'0941225 — Scotland. Grampian Region. Peterhead region. Sand & gravel deposits

McMillan, A. A.. The sand and gravel resources of the country west of Peterhead, Grampian Region : description of 1:25000 sheet NK04 and parts of NJ94 and 95, NK05, 14 and 15 / A.A. McMillan, A.M. Aitken, contributor D.L. Ross. — London : H.M.S.O., 1981. — iii,99p : ill,maps(some col.) ; 30cm. — (Mineral assessment report ; 58)
At head of title: Institute of Geological Sciences. — Map (1 folded sheet) in pocket. — Bibliography: p99
ISBN 0-11-884145-9 (pbk) : £12.00
B82-11397

553.6'2'0941469 — Scotland. Strathclyde Region. Douglas Water Valley. Sand & gravel deposits

Shaw, A. J.. The sand and gravel resources of the valley of the Douglas Water, Strathclyde : description of 1:25,000 resource sheet NS83 and parts of NS82, 92 and 93 / A.J. Shaw and E.F.P. Nickless, contributors I.B. Cameron and M.D. Issaias. — London : H.M.S.O., 1981. — iii,98p : ill,maps(some col.) ; 30cm. — (Mineral assessment report ; 63)
At head of title: Institute of Geological Sciences. — Map (1 folded sheet) in pocket. — Bibliography: p95
ISBN 0-11-884150-5 (pbk) : £11.50
B82-11398

553.6'2'0942521 — Nottinghamshire. Ranskill region. Sand & gravel deposits

Thomas, D. (David). The sand and gravel resources of the country around Ranskill and East Retford, Nottinghamshire : description of 1:25000 resource sheet SK68 and part of SK78 / D. Thomas. — London : H.M.S.O., 1981. — iii,54p : ill,maps(some col.) ; 30cm. — (Mineral assessment report ; 87)
At head of title: Institute of Geological Sciences, Natural Environment Research Council. — Map (1 folded sheet) in pocket. — Bibliography: p54
ISBN 0-11-884210-2 (pbk) : £8.50 B82-12050

553.6′2′0942538 — Lincolnshire. Stamford region. Sand & gravel deposits

Booth, S. J.. The sand and gravel resources of the country between Stamford and Peterborough : description of 1:25000 resource sheets TF00 and TF10 / S.J. Booth, contributors R.J. Wyatt and J.B.L. Wild. — London : H.M.S.O., 1981. — iii,123p : ill,maps (some col.) ; 30cm. — (Mineral assessment report ; 80)
At head of title: Institute of Geological Sciences. — Map (1 folded sheet) in pocket. — Bibliography: p.123
ISBN 0-11-884180-7 (pbk) : £14.50
Also classified at 553.6′2′0942651 B82-08388

553.6′2′0942554 — Northamptonshire. East Northamptonshire *(District)*. Sand & gravel deposits

Harrison, A. M.. The sand and gravel resources of the country south-west of Peterborough, in Cambridgeshire and east Northamptonshire : description of 1:25000 resource sheets TL09, 19 and SP98, TL08 / A.M. Harrison. — London : H.M.S.O., 1981. — 89p : ill,maps(some col.) ; 30cm. — (Mineral assessment report ; 60)
At head of title: Institute of Geological Sciences. — 2maps (2folded sheets) in pocket. — Bibliography: p89
ISBN 0-11-884147-5 (pbk) : £15.50
Primary classification 553.6′2′0942651 B82-02743

553.6′2′0942586 — Hertfordshire. Cuffley region. Sand & gravel deposits

Gozzard, J. R.. The sand and gravel resources of the country around Hatfield and Cheshunt, Hertfordshire : description of 1:25000 sheets TL20 and 30, and parts of TQ29 and 39 / J.R. Gozzard. — London : H.M.S.O., 1981. — iii,75p : ill,maps(some col.) ; 30cm. — (Mineral assessment report ; 67)
At head of title: Institute of Geological Sciences. — Folded sheet (map) in pocket. — Bibliography: p73
ISBN 0-11-884167-x (pbk) : £10.00 B82-04347

553.6′2′0942586 — Hertfordshire. Welwyn Garden City region. Sand & gravel deposits

Gozzard, J. R.. The sand and gravel resources of the country around Welwyn Garden City, Hertfordshire : description of 1:25000 resource sheet TL11 and TL21 / J.R. Gozzard. — London : H.M.S.O., 1981. — iii,83p : ill,maps (some col.) ; 30cm. — (Mineral assessment report ; 69)
At head of title: Institute of Geological Sciences. — Map (1folded sheet) in pocket. — Bibliography: p80
ISBN 0-11-884169-6 (pbk) : £10.50 B82-03641

553.6′2′0942648 — Suffolk. Nayland region. Sand & gravel deposits

Hopson, P. M.. The sand and gravel resources of the country around Nayland, Suffolk : description of 1:25000 resource sheet TL93 / P.M. Hopson. — London : H.M.S.O., 1981. — iii,179p : ill,maps(some col.) ; 30cm. — (Mineral assessment report ; 85)
At head of title: Institute of Geological Sciences, Natural Environment Research Council. — Map (1 folded sheet) in pocket. — Bibliography: p178-179
ISBN 0-11-884208-0 (pbk) : £11.25 B82-12051

553.6′2′0942651 — Cambridgeshire. Peterborough region. Sand & gravel deposits

Booth, S. J.. The sand and gravel resources of the country between Stamford and Peterborough : description of 1:25000 resource sheets TF00 and TF10 / S.J. Booth, contributors R.J. Wyatt and J.B.L. Wild. — London : H.M.S.O., 1981. — iii,123p : ill,maps (some col.) ; 30cm. — (Mineral assessment report ; 80)
At head of title: Institute of Geological Sciences. — Map (1 folded sheet) in pocket. — Bibliography: p.123
ISBN 0-11-884180-7 (pbk) : £14.50
Primary classification 553.6′2′0942538 B82-08388

Harrison, A. M.. The sand and gravel resources of the country south-west of Peterborough, in Cambridgeshire and east Northamptonshire : description of 1:25000 resource sheets TL09, 19 and SP98, TL08 / A.M. Harrison. — London : H.M.S.O., 1981. — 89p : ill,maps(some col.) ; 30cm. — (Mineral assessment report ; 60)
At head of title: Institute of Geological Sciences. — 2maps (2folded sheets) in pocket. — Bibliography: p89
ISBN 0-11-884147-5 (pbk) : £15.50
Also classified at 553.6′2′0942554 B82-02743

553.6′2′0942656 — Cambridgeshire. Wicken region. Sand & gravel deposits

Clayton, A. R.. The sand and gravel resources of the country between Ely and Cambridge, Cambridgeshire : description of 1:25000 sheets TL56 and 57 / A.R. Clayton, contributor C.E. Corser. — London : H.M.S.O., 1981. — iii,70p : ill,maps(some col.) ; 30cm. — (Mineral assessment report ; 73)
At head of title: Institute of Geological Sciences. — Map (1 folded sheet) in pocket. — Bibliography: p.70
ISBN 0-11-884173-4 (pbk) : £9.50 B82-08387

553.6′2′09426715 — Essex. Sible Hedingham region. Sand & gravel deposits

Marks, R. J.. The sand and gravel resources of the country around Sible Hedingham, Essex : description of 1:25000 resource sheet TL73 / R.J. Marks and D.W. Murray. — London : H.M.S.O., 1981. — iii,99p : ill,maps(some col.) ; 30cm. — (Mineral assessment report ; 82)
At head of title: Institute of Geological Sciences. — Map (1 folded sheet) in pocket. — Bibliography: p99
ISBN 0-11-884205-6 (pbk) : £10.75 B82-09565

553.6′2′0942842 — North Yorkshire. Kirk Hammerton region. Sand & gravel deposits

Giles, J. R. A.. The sand and gravel resources of the country around Kirk Hammerton, North Yorkshire : description of 1:25000 resource sheet SE45 / J.R.A. Giles, contributor A.H. Cooper. — London : H.M.S.O., 1981. — iii,84p : ill,maps(some col.) ; 30cm. — (Mineral assessment report ; 84)
At head of title: Institute of Geological Sciences. — Map (1 folded sheet) in pocket. — Bibliography: p84
ISBN 0-11-884207-2 (pbk) : £10.00 B82-09566

553.6′2′0942842 — North Yorkshire. Knaresborough region. Sand & gravel deposits

Dundas, D. L.. The sand and gravel resources of the country east of Harrogate, North Yorkshire : description of 1:25000 resource sheet SE35 / D. L. Dundas, contributor A.H. Cooper. — London : H.M.S.O., 1981. — 57p : ill,maps (some col.) ; 30cm(pbk). — (Mineral assessment report ; 70)
Map (1 folded sheet) in pocket. — Bibliography: p57
ISBN 0-11-884170-x : 15.50 B82-02745

553.6′2′0942881 — Northumberland. Prudhoe region. Sand & gravel deposits

Giles, J. R. A.. The sand and gravel resources of the country around Blaydon, Tyne and Wear : description of 1:25000 resource sheet NZ06, 16 / J.R.A. Giles. — London : H.M.S.O., 1981. — iii,71p : ill,maps(some col.) ; 30cm. — (Mineral assessment report ; 74)
At head of title: Institute of Geological Sciences. — Map (1 folded sheet) in pocket. — Bibliography: p71
ISBN 0-11-884174-2 (pbk) : £10.50 B82-09564

553.6′2′0942939 — Clwyd. Gresford region. Sand & gravel deposits

Dunkley, P. N.. The sand and gravel resources of the country north of Wrexham, Clwyd : description of 1:25000 resource sheet SJ35 and part of SJ25 / P.N. Dunkley ; contributors K.A.McL. Adlam, D.J. Lowe and W.J.R. Harries. — London : H.M.S.O., 1981. — 90p : ill,maps(some col.) ; 30cm. — (Mineral assessment report ; 61)
At head of title: Institute of Geological Sciences. — Map (1 folded sheet) in pocket. — Bibliography: p87
ISBN 0-11-884148-3 (pbk) : £11.75 B82-03640

553.6′32′0942449 — Hereford and Worcester. Droitwich. Keuper marls. Salt deposits

Poole, E. G.. The Keuper saliferous beds of the Droitwich area / E.G. Poole and B.J. Williams. — London : H.M.S.O., 1980. — 19p : ill,1map ; 30cm. — (Report / Institute of Geological Sciences ; 81/2)
Bibliography: p7-8
ISBN 0-11-884192-0 (pbk) : £1.50 B82-20459

553.6′68 — Sulphide ores — *Conference proceedings*

Complex Sulphide Ores Conference *(1980 : Rome)*. Complex sulphide ores : papers presented at the Complex Sulphide Ores Conference, organized by The Institution of Mining and Metallurgy in association with the Consiglio nazionale delle ricerche, Istituto per il trattamento dei minerali, and held in Rome, Italy, from 5 to 8 October, 1980 / edited by Michael J. Jones. — London : The Institution of Mining and Metallurgy, c1980. — viii,278p : ill,maps ; 30cm
English text with English, French, German and Italian summaries
ISBN 0-900488-51-4 (pbk) : Unpriced B82-15427

553.7 — Water — *For children*

Jennings, Terry. Water / Terry Jennings ; illustrated by John Barber ... [et al.]. — Oxford : Oxford University Press, 1982. — 32p : ill (chiefly col.) ; 29cm. — (The Young scientist investigates)
ISBN 0-19-918043-1 (cased) : Unpriced
ISBN 0-19-918037-7 (pbk) : £1.50 B82-29525

Leutscher, Alfred. Water. — London : Methuen/Walker, Oct.1982. — [32]p. — (The Elements ; 4)
ISBN 0-416-06460-4 : £3.50 : CIP entry B82-24483

Sowry, Jo. Looking at water / Jo Sowry. — London : Batsford Academic and Educational, 1982. — 48p : ill ; 23cm. — (Looking at science)
Bibliography: p47. — Includes index
ISBN 0-7134-4061-9 : £3.95 B82-22172

553.7′9 — National resources: Ground water. Investigation

Mandel, S.. Groundwater resources : investigation and development / S. Mandel, Z.L. Shiftan. — New York ; London : Academic Press, 1981. — ix,269p : ill,maps ; 24cm. — (Water pollution)
Includes bibliographies and index
ISBN 0-12-468040-2 : £21.20 B82-07715

553.8 — Gemstones

Webster, Robert. Gemmologists′ compendium / Robert Webster. — 6th ed. / revised by E. Allan Jobbins. — London : N.A.G. Press, 1979. — 240p,[16]p of plates : ill(some col.) ; 20cm
Previous ed.: 1970
ISBN 0-7198-0101-x : £5.95 B82-20817

553.8 — Gemstones — *Identification manuals*

Brocardo, G.. Minerals & gemstones. — Newton Abbot : David & Charles, Sept.1982. — [224]p
Translation of: Minerali a colpo d′occhio
ISBN 0-7153-8283-7 : £6.95 : CIP entry B82-20375

553.8′03′21 — Gemstones — *Encyclopaedias*

Robins, Bill. An A-Z of gems and jewellery / Bill Robins ; illustrations by Evelyn Bartlett. — Newton Abbot : David & Charles, c1982. — 96p : ill ; 23cm
Includes index
ISBN 0-7153-8279-9 : £3.95 : CIP rev. B82-01184

553.8′2 — Diamonds

Epstein, Edward Jay. The diamond invention. — London : Hutchinson, May 1982. — [224]p
ISBN 0-09-147690-9 : £7.95 : CIP entry B82-14211

Lenzen, Godehard. Diamonds and diamond grading. — London : Butterworths, July 1982. — [256]p
Translation of: Diamantenkunde
ISBN 0-408-00547-5 : £20.00 : CIP entry B82-12321

553.8′7 — Jade — *Serials*

Bulletin of the Friends of Jade. — Vol.1, no.1 (Fall 1980)-. — [Wallington] ([P.O. Box 135, Wallington, Surrey]) : Friends of Jade, 1980-. — v. ; 30cm
Two issues yearly
ISSN 0261-7080 = Bulletin of the Friends of Jade : Unpriced B82-11147

553′.92 — Pacific region. Silica deposits — *Conference proceedings*

Siliceous deposits in the Pacific region. — Oxford : Elsevier Scientific, Nov.1982. — 1v.. — (Developments in sedimentology ; 36)
Conference papers
ISBN 0-444-42129-7 : CIP entry B82-30302

554/559 — GEOLOGY OF SPECIAL LOCALITIES

554.15 — Ireland. Geological features

A **Geology** of Ireland / edited by C.H. Holland. — Edinburgh : Scottish Academic Press, 1981. — x,335p : ill,maps ; 26cm
Includes bibliographies and index
ISBN 0-7073-0269-2 : £27.50 B82-02758

554.23′41 — Jersey. Geological features — *For field studies*

Bishop, A. C.. Jersey / by A.C. Bishop and D.H. Keen. — [London] ([Geology Dept., Queen Mary College, Mile End Rd., E1 4NS]) : Geologists′ Association, c1981. — 30p : maps ; 21cm. — (Geologists′ Association guide ; no.41)
Bibliography: p30
Unpriced (pbk) B82-39628

554.25′1 — Derbyshire. Geological features

Frost, D. V.. Geology of the country north of Derby : memoir for 1:50,000 geological sheet 125 / D.V. Frost and J.G.O. Smart contributors N. Aitkenhead ... [et al.]. — London : Institute of Geological Sciences, 1979. — xiv,199p : ill(some col.),maps ; 29cm
At head of title: Geographical Survey of Great Britain. — Bibliography: p123-128. — Includes index
ISBN 0-11-884119-x : £18.00 B82-17178

554.25′11 — England. Peak District. Geological features — *For field studies*

Simpson, I. M.. The Peak District / I.M. Simpson. — London : Unwin, 1982. — 120p : ill,maps ; 20cm. — (Rocks and fossils)
Bibliography: p117. — Includes index
ISBN 0-04-554006-3 (pbk) : £3.95 : CIP rev. B82-03724

554.25′11 — England. Peak District. National parks: Peak District National Park. Geological features

Greenwood, J. A. (John Andrew). An introduction to geology in the Peak National Park / [text J.A. Greenwood]. — [Bakewell] : Peak Park Joint Planning Board, c1980. — 20p : ill,1map ; 21cm. — (A Peak National Park theme booklet)
Bibliography: p20
ISBN 0-901428-58-2 (pbk) : Unpriced B82-38437

554.25′11 — England. South Pennines. Geological features, *to 1980*

Breakell, Bill. How the South Pennines were made : 350 million years of landscape building : geology map and wallchart / [written & designed by Bill Breakell & Maria Murtagh]. — Hebden Bridge : Pennine Heritage Network, c1981. — 1sheet : ill(some col.),maps(some col.) ; 84x60cm folded to 21x15cm
ISBN 0-907613-00-4 : £1.25 B82-08815

554.27′8 — Cumbria. Lake District. Geological features — *For field studies*

The **Lake** District / The Cumberland Geological Society ; [edited by Tom Shipp]. — London : Unwin, 1982. — viii,136p : ill,maps ; 20cm. — (Rocks and fossils)
Bibliography: p122-124. — Includes index
ISBN 0-04-554007-1 (pbk) : £3.95 : CIP rev. B82-03725

554.27′84 — Cumbria. Sellafield. Nuclear reactors: British Nuclear Fuels Limited. ***Sellafield.*** **Sites. Geological features**

Holmes, D. C.. The 1977-1979 geological and hydrogeological investigations at the Windscale works, Sellafield, Cumbria / D.C. Holmes and D.H. Hall. — London : H.M.S.O., 1980. — iii,27p : ill,maps ; 30cm. — (Report / Institute of Geological Sciences ; 80/12)
Bibliography: p26
ISBN 0-11-884190-4 (pbk) : £3.50 B82-20458

554.27′86 — Cumbria. Penrith region. Geological features

Arthurton, R. S.. Geology of the country around Penrith : memoir for 1:50000 geological sheet 24 / R.S. Arthurton and A.J. Wadge, contributor J. Pattison ... [et al.]. — [London] : Institute of Geological Sciences, 1981. — 177p : ill(some col.),maps(some col.) ; 29cm
At head of title: Geological survey of Great Britain. — Includes bibliographies and index
ISBN 0-11-884142-4 : Unpriced B82-02746

554.28′81 — Northumberland. Bellingham region. Geological features

Frost, D. V.. Geology of the country around Bellingham : memoir for 1:50000 geological sheet 13 / D.V. Frost and D.W. Holliday ; contributors J. Pattison ... [et al.]. — London : Institute of Geological Sciences, 1980. — 112p : ill(some col.),maps ; 29cm
At head of title: Geological Survey of Great Britain. — Bibliography: p99-102. — Includes index
ISBN 0-11-884137-8 : Unpriced B82-40423

554.29′27 — Gwynedd. Dolgarrog region. Geological features

Dolgarrog : description of 1:25000 sheet SH76 / M.F. Howells ... [et al.]. — London : H.M.S.O., 1981. — viii,89p : ill(some col.),maps(some col.) ; 22cm. — (Classical areas of British geology)
'Institute of Geological Sciences, Natural Environment Research Council'. — Col. maps on inside covers. — Bibliography: p76-79. — Includes index
ISBN 0-11-884133-5 (pbk) : £4.00 B82-13715

554.29′6 — Dyfed. Geological features — *For field studies*

Geological excursions in Dyfed, South-West Wales / edited by M.G. Bassett. — Cardiff : Published for the Geologists′ Association, South Wales Group by the National Museum of Wales, 1982. — 327p : ill,maps ; 22cm
Includes bibliographies
ISBN 0-7200-0249-4 (pbk) : Unpriced B82-38430

555.6 — Middle East. Geological features — *Conference proceedings*

Evolution and mineralization of the Arabian-Nubian Shield : proceedings of a symposium convened by Ahmad M.S. Al-Shanti. — Oxford : Published for the Institute of Applied Geology, King Abdulaziz University by Pergamon
Vol.4. — 1980. — viii,168p : ill,maps ; 29cm. — (I.A.G. bulletin ; no.3)
English text, Arabic summaries. — Vol.2 lacks subtitle. — Vol.4 published for the Faculty of Earth Sciences, King Abdulaziz University. — Five maps on 5 folded leaves in pocket. — Includes bibliographies
ISBN 0-08-024481-5 : £15.00 : CIP rev. B80-06915

555.98 — Eastern Indonesia. Geological features — *Conference proceedings*

CCOP-IOC SEATAR Working Group Meeting *(1979 : Bandung)*. The geology and tectonics of eastern Indonesia. — Oxford : Pergamon, Sept.1981. — [356]p. — (Special publication / Geological Research and Development Centre ; no.2)
ISBN 0-08-028732-8 : £22.00 : CIP entry B81-25112

557.94 — California. Tectonic features — *Conference proceedings*

The **Geotectonic** development of California / W.G. Ernst, editor. — Englewood Cliffs ; London : Prentice-Hall, c1981. — xi,706p : ill,maps ; 25cm. — (Rubey volume ; 1)
Conference papers. — Bibliography: p615-685. — Includes index
ISBN 0-13-353938-5 : £26.95 B82-19720

559.7′11 — South Georgia. Geological features

The **Geology** of South Georgia. — Cambridge : British Antarctic Survey. — (Scientific reports / British Antarctic Survey ; no.96)
4: Barff Peninsula and Royal Bay areas / by P. Stone. — 1980. — 45p,[13]p of plates(some folded) : ill,maps(some col.) ; 31cm
Bibliography: p43-45
ISBN 0-85665-050-1 (pbk) : Unpriced B82-05875

559.8′9 — Antarctic. Geological maps

Antarctica : glaciological and geophysical folio. — Cambridge : University of Cambridge, Scott Polar Research Institute, Dec.1982. — 1v.
ISBN 0-901021-04-0 : £59.00 : CIP entry B82-40344

559.8′9 — British Antarctic Territory. Central Black Coast. Geological features

Singleton, D. G.. The geology of the central Black Coast Palmer Land / by D.G. Singleton. — Cambridge : British Antarctic Survey, 1980. — 50p,[1]folded leaf of plates : ill,2maps ; 31cm. — (Scientific reports / British Antarctic Survey ; no.102)
Bibliography: p45-47
ISBN 0-85665-082-x (pbk) : Unpriced B82-05873

559.9 — Solar system. Geological features

Glass, Billy P.. Introduction to planetary geology. — Cambridge : Cambridge University Press, Oct.1982. — [482]p
ISBN 0-521-23579-0 : £18.00 : CIP entry B82-26230

559.9′23 — Mars. Geological features

Baker, Victor R.. The channels of Mars / by Victor R. Baker. — Bristol : Hilger, 1982. — xiii,198p : ill,maps ; 29cm
Bibliography: p185-193. — Includes index
ISBN 0-85274-467-6 : £22.50 B82-28819

560 — PALAEONTOLOGY

560 — Fossil microorganisms — *Conference proceedings*

Microfossils from recent and fossil shelf seas / editors J.W. Neale and M.D. Brasier. — Chichester : Ellis Horwood for British Micropalaeontological Society, 1981. — 380p : ill,maps ; 25cm. — (British Micropalaeontological Society series)
Conference papers. — Text on lining papers. — Includes bibliographies and index
ISBN 0-85312-338-1 : £35.00 : CIP rev. B81-13852

560 — Fossils — *Field guides*

Case, Gerard R.. A pictorial guide to fossils / Gerard R. Case. — New York ; London : Van Nostrand Reinhold, c1982. — xii,514p : ill ; 29cm
Bibliography: p502-506. — Includes index
ISBN 0-442-22651-9 : £25.45 B82-34330

Prokop, Rudolf. Fossils / by Rudolf Prokop ; illustrated by Vladimír Krb ; [translated by Margot Schierlová]. — London : Hamlyn, c1981. — 224p : ill(some col.) ; 22cm. — (A Hamlyn colour guide)
Translation from the Czech. — Includes index
ISBN 0-600-35370-2 : £2.95 B82-04327

560 — Fossils — *For children*

Lawrence, J. T.. Fossils. — London : Granada, Aug.1982. — [64]p. — (Granada guide series ; 24)
ISBN 0-246-11896-2 : £1.95 : CIP entry B82-15712

560 — Micropalaeontology — *Festschriften*

Aspects of micropalaeontology. — London : Allen & Unwin, Nov.1982. — [352]p
ISBN 0-04-562003-2 : £25.00 : CIP entry B82-28996

560 — Palaeobiology

Ziegler, B.. Introduction to palaeobiology. — Chichester : Ellis Horwood, Nov.1982. — [256] p. — (Ellis Horwood series in geology)
Translation of: Einführung in die Paläobiologie
ISBN 0-85312-211-3 : £30.00 : CIP entry B82-34099

560′.1′726 — Scotland. Devonian strata. Fossil plants

Chaloner, W. G.. Plants invade the land / W.G. Chaloner and P. Macdonald. — Edinburgh : H.M.S.O. for the Royal Scottish Museum, c1980. — 16p : ill(some col.) ; 20x25cm
Cover title. — Ill on inside covers
ISBN 0-11-491698-5 (pbk) : £1.20 B82-35019

560′.74 — Museums. Stock: Fossils — *Lists*

World palaeontological collections. — London : Mansell, Oct.1982. — [480]p
ISBN 0-7201-1655-4 : £50.00 : CIP entry
ISBN 0-565-00850-1 (British Museum (Natural History)) : Unpriced B82-23026

560.92 — Fossil marine ecosystems

Boucot, Arthur J.. Principles of benthic marine paleoecology / Arthur J. Boucot with contributions on bioturbation, biodeposition, and Robert S. Carney. — New York ; London : Academic Press, 1981. — xv,463p : ill,maps ; 29cm
Bibliography: p409-445. — Includes index
ISBN 0-12-118980-5 : £38.40 B82-07559

560.941 — Great Britain. Fossils — *Collectors′ guides*

Croucher, R.. Fossils, minerals and rocks : collection and preservation / R. Croucher & A.R. Woolley. — London : British Museum (Natural History), 1982. — 60p : ill ; 22cm
Bibliography: p53. — Includes index
ISBN 0-521-24736-5 : £2.95 : CIP rev. B82-11511

560.9412′95 — Scotland. Fife Region. West Wemyss. Fossils — *For teaching*

Rocks and fossils of West Wemyss. — [West Wemyss] : West Wemyss Environmental Education Centre, [1982]. — 28p,[2]leaves of plates : ill,2maps ; 21cm
Cover title. — Ill on inside cover
Unpriced (pbk)
Primary classification 552.09412′95 B82-19640

560′.9421 — London. Palaeontology, *1850-1875*

Desmond, Adrian. Archetypes and ancestors : palaeontology in Victorian London 1850-1875. — London : Bland & Briggs, Oct.1982. — [288]p
ISBN 0-85634-121-5 : £12.95 : CIP entry B82-24114

561 — FOSSIL PLANTS

561′.13′094124 — Scotland. Grampian Region. Banchory region. Fossil pollen. Analysis

Ewan, Lorna A.. A palynological investigation of a peat deposit near Banchory : some local and regional environmental implications / by Lorna A. Ewan. — [Aberdeen] : Department of Geography, University of Aberdeen, 1981. — iv,54p : ill,maps ; 30cm. — (O′Dell memorial monograph, ISSN 0141-1454 ; no.11)
Bibliography: p48-54
Unpriced (pbk) B82-19913

561′.197 — North America. Fossil plants — *Conference proceedings*

Geobotany Conference *(1980 : Bowling Green State University)*. Geobotany II : [proceedings of the Geobotany Conference held March 1, 1980 at Bowling Green State University, Bowling Green, Ohio] / edited by Robert C. Romans. — New York ; London : Plenum, c1981. — viii,263p,2folded leaves of plates : ill,maps ; 26cm
Includes bibliographies and index
ISBN 0-306-40832-5 : Unpriced B82-14004

561′.2 — Fossil flowering plants. Evolution

Hughes, Norman F.. Palaeobiology of angiosperm origins. — Cambridge : Cambridge University Press, Nov.1981. — [242]p. — (Cambridge earth science series)
Originally published: 1976
ISBN 0-521-28726-x (pbk) : £9.95 : CIP entry B81-38811

561′.21 — Cainozoic strata. Wood. Identification — *Manuals*

Barefoot, A. C.. Identification of modern and tertiary woods / A.C. Barefoot and Frank W. Hankins ; with assistance from L.H. Daugherty. — Oxford : Clarendon Press, 1982. — vii,189p : ill ; 31cm. — (Oxford science publications)
Bibliography: p182-184. — Includes index
ISBN 0-19-854378-6 : £47.50 : CIP rev.
Also classified at 620.1′2 B79-37308

561′.93 — Great Britain. Strata. Calcareous nannofossils

A Stratigraphical index of calcareous nannofossils / editor A.R. Lord. — Chichester : Horwood, 1982. — 192p : ill,maps ; 25cm. — (British Micropalaeontological Society series)
Bibliography: p174-183. — Includes index
ISBN 0-85312-326-8 : £30.00 : CIP rev. B82-09210

562 — FOSSIL INVERTEBRATES

563′.12 — Fossil Foraminiferida

Stratigraphical atlas of fossil foraminifera / editors D.G. Jenkins and J.W. Murray. — Chichester : Ellis Horwood for the British Micropalaeontological Society, 1981. — 310p : ill,maps ; 25cm. — (British Micropalaeontological Society series)
Includes bibliographies and index
ISBN 0-85312-210-5 : £25.00 : CIP rev. B81-13851

563′.6 — Rugose corals — *Lists*

Cotton, Geoffrey. The rugose coral genera / Geoffrey Cotton. — Kidderminster : G. Cotton, 1980
Cover title. — Bibliography: p51
Supplement 3. — 51p ; 21cm
ISBN 0-905141-02-4 : £3.00 B82-24636

563′.71 — Graptolithina — *Identification manuals*

Rigby, John E.. A genus identification key for graptolites. — Witham (Fossil Hall, Boars Tye Rd, Silver End, Witham, Essex CM8 3QA) : S.A. Baldwin, Sept.1982. — [140]p
ISBN 0-9508063-0-7 : CIP entry B82-25084

564′.5′074 — Fossil cephalopoda — *Catalogues*

British Museum (Natural History). Catalogue of the type and figured specimens of fossil Cephalopoda (excluding Mesozoic Ammonoidea) in the British Museum (Natural History) / by D. Phillips. — [London] : British Museum (Natural History), c1982. — 94p ; 30cm
Bibliography: p75-87. — Includes index
ISBN 0-565-00855-2 (pbk) : Unpriced B82-39924

564′.53 — Ammonites

Lehmann, Ulrich. The ammonites : their life and their world / Ulrich Lehmann ; translated by Janine Lettau. — Cambridge : Cambridge University Press, 1981. — xi,246p : ill ; 24cm
Translation of: Ammoniten. — Includes bibliographies and index
ISBN 0-521-23627-4 : £9.95 B82-07160

564′.8′09427 — Northern England. Visean strata & Namurian strata. Gigantoproductoid Brachiopoda

Pattison, J.. The stratigraphical distribution of gigantoproductoid brachiopods in the Viséan and Namurian rocks of some areas in Northern England / J. Pattison. — London : H.M.S.O., 1981. — ii,30p : ill,1map ; 30cm. — (Report / Institute of Geological Sciences ; 81/9)
Bibliography: p17-18
ISBN 0-11-884199-8 (pbk) : £3.25 B82-04349

565′.33 — Fossil Ostracoda. Shells — *Illustrations*

A Stereo-atlas of ostracod shells / edited by R.H. Bate ... [et al.]. — Llandudno (Ty′n-y-Coed, Llanrhos, Llandudno, Gwynedd LL30 1SA) : The British Micropalaeontological Society in association with Robertson Research
Vol.8. — 1981
Pt.1. — [39]leaves : ill,1map ; 31cm
Cover title
£20.00 (spiral) B82-03330

A Stereo-atlas of ostracod shells / edited by R.H. Bate ... [et al.]. — Llandudno (Ty′n-y-Coed, Llanrhos, Llandudno, Gwynedd LL30 1SA) : British Micropalaeontological Society in association with Robertson Research International
Vol.8
Pt.2. — 1981. — [43]leaves : ill ; 31cm
Cover title. — Includes index
£30.00 (spiral) B82-12880

566 — FOSSIL VERTEBRATES

566 — Vertebrate palaeo-ecology & vertebrate taphonomy

Shipman, Pat. Life history of a fossil : an introduction to taphonomy and paleoecology / Pat Shipman. — Cambridge, Mass. ; London : Harvard University Press, 1981. — 222p : ill ; 24cm
Bibliography: p207-218. — Includes index
ISBN 0-674-53085-3 : £14.00 B82-03872

566′.0941 — Great Britain. Pleistocene vertebrates

Stuart, A. J.. Pleistocene vertebrates in the British Isles. — London : Longman, July 1982. — [304]p
ISBN 0-582-30069-x : £16.50 : CIP entry B82-12989

567.9′1 — Dinosaurs

Stout, William. The dinosaurs / illustrated by William Stout ; narrated by William Service ; edited by Byron Preiss ; introduction and scientific commentary by Peter Dodson. — New York ; London : Bantam, 1981. — [160]p : ill(some col.),1port ; 28cm. — (A Byron Preiss book)
ISBN 0-553-01335-1 (pbk) : £4.95 B82-10267

567.9′1 — Dinosaurs. Extinction. Theories

Croft, L. R.. The last dinosaurs / L.R. Croft. — Chorley : Elmwood, 1982. — 80p : ill ; 23cm
Bibliography: p77-79. — Includes index
ISBN 0-946019-00-2 (cased) : £4.95 : CIP rev.
ISBN 0-946019-01-0 (pbk) : Unpriced B82-10680

567.9′1 — Dinosaurs — *For children*

Lambert, David. Dinosaurs. — London : Kingfisher, Sept.1982. — [96]p
Originally published: London : Grisewood & Dempsey, 1978
ISBN 0-86272-039-7 : £5.95 : CIP entry B82-20185

Lambert, David, *1932-*. Dinosaur world. — London : Ward Lock, Apr.1981. — [96]p. — (Kingfisher factbook)
ISBN 0-7063-6107-5 : £2.50 : CIP entry B81-03166

Lambert, David, *1932-*. Dinosaurs / David Lambert. — London : Watts, 1982. — 32p : col.ill,col.maps ; 22cm. — (A First look book)
Includes index
ISBN 0-85166-955-7 : £2.99 B82-31208

Oliver, Rupert. Dinosaurs. — London : Hodder & Stoughton Children′s Books, Feb.1983. — [32]p
ISBN 0-340-28609-1 : £2.95 : CIP entry B82-38047

Riley, Terry, *1941-*. The amazing world of dinosaurs / written and illustrated by Terry Riley. — London : Dean, c1981. — [73]p : ill (some col.) ; 28cm
Ill on lining papers
ISBN 0-603-00252-8 : Unpriced B82-26749

567.9′1′0222 — Dinosaurs — *Illustrations* — *For children*

Althea. Dinosaur′s book of dinosaurs / by Althea ; illustrated by Ljiljana Rylands. — Cambridge : Dinosaur, c1982. — 24p : col.ill ; 16x19cm. — (Althea′s history series)
ISBN 0-85122-336-2 (cased) : Unpriced
ISBN 0-85122-335-4 (pbk) : Unpriced B82-32077

567.9′1′0222 — Dinosaurs — *Illustrations — For children* *continuation*

Barlowe, Dorothea. Dinosaurs / illustrated by Dot and Sy Barlowe. — Glasgow : Collins, c1977 (1981 [printing]). — [14]p : chiefly col.ill ; 24cm. — (A Pop-up book)
Text, ill on lining papers
ISBN 0-00-106239-5 : £3.50 B82-02853

567.9′3 — England. Ichthyosaurs. Research, *to 1980*

Howe, S. R.. Ichthyosaurs : a history of fossil 'sea-dragons' / S.R. Howe, T. Sharpe, H.S. Torrens. — Cardiff : National Museum of Wales, c1981. — 32p : ill,1map,facsims,ports ; 25cm
ISBN 0-7200-0232-x (pbk) : £0.90 B82-05303

567.9′3 — Synapsids. Evolution

Kemp, T. S.. Mammal-like reptiles and the origin of mammals / T.S. Kemp. — London : Academic Press, 1982. — xiv,363p : ill ; 24cm
Bibliography: p335-346. — Includes index
ISBN 0-12-404120-5 : £24.00 : CIP rev. B82-00319

569 — Prehistoric mammals — *For children*

Oliver, Rupert. Prehistoric animals / Rupert Oliver ; illustrated by Bernard Long. — London : Hodder and Stoughton, 1982. — 60p : col.ill ; 31cm
ISBN 0-340-27165-5 : £2.95 : CIP rev. B82-01092

569′.9′09632 — Ethiopia. Hadar. Fossil hominids

Johanson, Donald C.. Lucy : the beginnings of humankind / Donald C. Johanson and Maitland A. Edey. — London : Granada, 1981 (1982 [printing]). — 413p,[8]p of plates : 3maps,ports ; 20cm. — (A Paladin book)
Bibliography: p390-394. — Includes index
ISBN 0-586-08437-1 (pbk) : £2.95 B82-41096

572 — ETHNOLOGY

572 — Race. Biological aspects

King, James C.. The biology of race / James C. King. — [Rev. ed.]. — Berkeley ; London : University of California Press, c1981. — x,180p : ill,maps ; 23cm
Previous ed.: New York : Harcourt Brace Jovanovich, 1971. — Bibliography: p165-166. — Includes index
ISBN 0-520-04223-9 : £11.25 B82-28100

573 — PHYSICAL ANTHROPOLOGY

573 — Physical anthropology

Lasker, Gabriel Ward. Physical anthropology. — 3rd ed. / Gabriel W. Lasker, Robert N. Tyzzer. — New York ; London : Holt, Rinehart and Winston, c1982. — x,526,[8]p : ill,2maps,ports ; 24cm
Previous ed.: 1976. — Bibliography: p492-512. — Includes index
ISBN 0-03-047551-1 (pbk) : £13.95 B82-15350

Stein, Philip L.. Physical anthropology / Philip L. Stein, Bruce M. Rowe. — 3rd ed. — New York ; London : McGraw-Hill, c1982. — xii,482p : ill(some col.),col.maps ; 24cm
Previous ed.: 1978. — Includes bibliographies and index
ISBN 0-07-061151-3 (pbk) : £14.50 B82-26971

573′.028 — Biology. Use of radioactive isotopes

Ayrey, E.. The use of radioactive isotopes in life sciences. — London : Allen & Unwin, Sept.1981. — [176]p
ISBN 0-04-570011-7 (cased) : £4.95 : CIP entry
ISBN 0-04-570012-5 (pbk) : £4.95 B81-20554

573.2 — Man. Evolution

Aspects of human evolution. — London : Taylor and Francis, Apr.1981. — [230]p. — (Symposia / The Society for the Study of Human Biology, ISSN 0081-153x ; 21)
ISBN 0-85066-209-5 : £12.00 : CIP entry B81-04279

Gribbin, John. The monkey puzzle : a family tree / John Gribbin and Jeremy Cherfas. — London : Bodley Head, 1982. — 279p,[16]p of plates : ill,maps,1port ; 23cm
Includes index
ISBN 0-370-30469-1 : £8.50 : CIP rev. B82-04021

Hardy, *Sir* Alister. Darwin and the spirit of man. — London : Collins, Oct.1982. — [192]p
ISBN 0-00-215160-x : £7.95 : CIP entry B82-25534

Leakey, Richard E.. Origins : what new discoveries reveal about the emergence of our species and its possible future / Richard E. Leakey and Roger Lewin. — London : Macdonald, 1982, c1977. — 255p ; 18cm. — (A Futura book)
Originally published: London : Macdonald and Jane's, 1977. — Bibliography: p244-245. — Includes index
ISBN 0-7088-2151-0 (pbk) : £1.95 B82-16943

Wilber, Ken. Up from Eden. — London : Routledge & Kegan Paul, Feb.1983. — [355]p
ISBN 0-7100-9506-6 : £6.95 : CIP entry B82-40909

573.2 — Man. Evolution. Archaeological sources — *For children*

Asimov, Isaac. How we found out about our human roots / Isaac Asimov. — Harlow : Longman, 1982. — 53p : ill ; 23cm. — (How we found out about series ; 3)
Includes index
ISBN 0-582-39159-8 : £2.75 B82-29316

573.2 — Man. Evolution. Effects of aquatic habitats

Morgan, Elaine. The aquatic ape : a theory of human evolution / Elaine Morgan. — London : Souvenir, 1982. — 168p,8p of plates : ill,maps,1port ; 23cm
Bibliography: p160-162. — Includes index
ISBN 0-285-62509-8 : £7.95 B82-17989

573.2 — Man. Evolution — *For children*

Aiello, Leslie. Discovering the origins of mankind. — London : Longman, Feb.1983. — [96]p
ISBN 0-582-39218-7 : £6.95 : CIP entry B82-38677

573.2 — Man. Evolution. Natural selection. Aesthetic factors

Goulstone, J.. The role of aesthetic rejection and selection in human evolution / by John Goulstone. — [Bexleyheath] ([10 Haslemere Rd., Bexleyheath, Kent DA7 4NQ]) : J. Goulstone, c1981. — [16]p,[7]leaves of plates : ill ; 26cm
Unpriced (pbk) B82-06457

573.2′01 — Man. Evolution. Role of work. Theories of Engels, Friedrich

Woolfson, Charles. The labour theory of culture : a re-examination of Engels's theory of human origins / Charles Woolfson. — London : Routledge & Kegan Paul, 1982. — viii,124p ; 22cm
Bibliography: p104-116. — Includes index
ISBN 0-7100-0997-6 (pbk) : £4.95 B82-25674

573.2′1 — Man. Genetics

Novitski, Edward. Human genetics / Edward Novitski. — 2nd ed. — New York : Macmillan ; London : Collier Macmillan, c1982. — xxiii,487p : ill,maps ; 26cm
Previous ed.: 1977. — Includes bibliographies and index
ISBN 0-02-388570-x : £17.95 B82-39387

573.2′15 — Man. Population genetics

Cannings, C.. Genealogical and genetic structure / C. Cannings, E.A. Thompson. — Cambridge : Cambridge University Press, 1981. — xi,156p : ill ; 22cm. — (Cambridge studies in mathematical biology ; 3)
Bibliography: p144-151. — Includes index
ISBN 0-521-23946-x (cased) : £17.50 : CIP rev.
ISBN 0-521-28363-9 (pbk) : £6.95 B81-32527

573.2′292 — Man. Mutagenic effects of chemicals. Evaluation — *Conference proceedings*

Chemical mutagenesis, human population monitoring and genetic risk assessment : proceedings of the international symposium held 14-16 October 1980, Ottawa (Canada) / edited by K.C. Bora, G.R. Douglas and E.R. Nestmann. — Amsterdam ; Oxford : Elsevier Biomedical, 1982. — xxiv,364p : ill ; 25cm. — (Progress in mutation research ; v.3)
Includes bibliographies and index
ISBN 0-444-80352-1 : Unpriced B82-19623

573.2′292 — Man. Mutagenic effects of toxic chemicals — *Conference proceedings*

European Environmental Mutagen Society. *Meeting (10th : 1980 : Athens)*. Progress in environmental mutagenesis and carcinogenesis : proceedings of the 10th Annual Meeting of the European Environmental Mutagen Society (EEMS) Athens (Greece), 14-19 September 1980 : under the auspices of the Ministry of Culture and Science of Greece and the Greek Atomic Energy Commission / edited by A. Kappas. — Amsterdam ; Oxford : Elsevier/North-Holland Biomedical, 1981. — (Progress in mutation research ; v.2)
Includes bibliographies and index
ISBN 0-444-80334-3 : Unpriced
Also classified at 616.99′4071 B82-06110

573.2′292 — Man. Mutation. Genetic aspects — *Conference proceedings*

Population and biological aspects of human mutation / edited by Ernest B. Hook, Ian H. Porter. — New York ; London : Academic Press, 1981. — xvii,435p : ill,forms ; 24cm. — (Birth Defects Institute symposia)
Conference proceedings. — Includes index
ISBN 0-12-355440-3 : £22.80 B82-30139

573′.3 — Peking man — *Festschriften*

Homo erectus : papers in honor of Davidson Black : based on the proceedings of an international symposium in honor of Davidson Black, Cedar Glen, Ontario, October 21, 1976 / Becky A. Sigmon and Jerome S. Cybulski editors. — Toronto ; London : University of Toronto Press, c1981. — xiv,271p : ill,2maps ; 24cm. — (Symposia of the Canadian Association for Physical Anthropology ; v.1)
Bibliography: p241-264. — Includes index
ISBN 0-8020-5511-7 : £21.00 B82-13938

573′.6 — Anthropometry. Techniques

Aherne, William A.. Introduction to morphometry. — London : Edward Arnold, Sept.1982. — [176]p
ISBN 0-7131-4403-3 : £17.50 : CIP entry B82-20036

573′.6 — British men. Anthropometric features — *For clothing industries*

British male body measurements : report of a survey of men in Great Britain / carried out by Wira Clothing Services. — Leeds : Wira, 1980. — 102leaves : ill,maps,1plan ; 30cm
ISBN 0-900820-13-6 (spiral) : Unpriced B82-37306

573′.6 — Sportswomen. Anthropometric features — *Conference proceedings*

International Congress on Women and Sport *(1980 : Rome)*. The female athlete : a socio-psychological and kinanthropometric approach : selected papers of the International Congress on Women and Sport, Rome, Italy, July 4-8, 1980 / volume editors J. Borms, M. Hebbelinck and A. Venerando. — Basel ; London : Karger, c1981. — xiii,218p : ill ; 25cm. — (Medicine and sport ; v.15)
Includes bibliographies and index
ISBN 3-8055-2739-x : £36.00
Also classified at 306′.483′088042 B82-21666

573′.6′0880542 — Scotland. Newborn babies. Anthropometric features — *Statistics*

Birthweight, head circumference and length by gestational age : Scotland 1973-1979. — Edinburgh (Trinity Park House, South Trinity Road, Edinburgh EH5 3SQ) : Information Services Division, Scottish Health Service Common Services Agency, [1980?]. — [10] leaves : ill ; 30cm
Unpriced (unbound) B82-34363

574 — BIOLOGY

574 — Biology

Barrass, Robert. Modern biology made simple. — London : Heinemann, Dec.1982. — [304]p. — (Made simple books)
Originally published: London : Allen, 1979
ISBN 0-434-98538-4 (pbk) : £2.95 : CIP entry B82-31288

Thomas, Lewis. The medusa and the snail : more notes of a biology watcher / Lewis Thomas. — Harmondsworth : Penguin, 1981, c1979. — 143p ; 20cm
Originally published: New York : Viking, 1979 ; London : Allen Lane, 1980. — Includes index
ISBN 0-14-005615-7 (pbk) : £1.95 B82-07304

574 — Biology — *For schools*

Bishop, O. N.. Adventures with small plants. — London : Murray, Sept.1982. — [64]p
ISBN 0-7195-3953-6 (cased) : £4.95 : CIP entry
ISBN 0-7195-3967-6 (pbk) : £2.75 B82-19831

Life probe : a study of biology / Donald I. Galbraith ... [et al.]. — Toronto ; Chichester : Wiley, c1981. — 460p : ill(some col.) ; 25cm
Includes index
ISBN 0-471-79966-1 : £10.50 B82-26493

Roberts, M. B. V.. Biology for life / M.B.V. Roberts. — Walton-on-Thames : Nelson, 1981 (1982 [printing]). — vii,407p : ill ; 28cm
Includes index
ISBN 0-17-448083-0 (pbk) : Unpriced B82-34283

Torrance, James. 'O' Grade biology / James Torrance. — London : Edward Arnold, 1982. — 124p : ill ; 25cm
Includes index
ISBN 0-7131-0576-3 (pbk) : £3.25 : CIP rev. B81-22486

574 — Hollow trees. Organisms — *For children*

Hansen, Elvig. The hollow tree / written and illustrated by Elvig Hansen ; consultant for English edition, Anthony Wootton. — Hove : Wayland, 1982. — 63p : col.ill ; 25cm
Translation from the Danish. — Includes index
ISBN 0-85340-948-x : £4.25 B82-21940

574 — Organisms

Ambrose, E. J.. The nature and origin of the biological world. — Chichester : Horwood, May 1982. — [192]p
ISBN 0-85312-454-x : £17.50 : CIP entry B82-11114

Arms, Karen. Biology / Karen Arms, Pamela S. Camp. — 2nd ed. — Philadelphia ; London : Saunders College Publishing, 1982, c1979. — xxxii,942p : ill(some col.),col.maps,ports ; 29cm
Previous ed.: New York : London : Holt, Rinehart and Winston, 1979. — Text and ill on lining papers. — Includes bibliographies and index
ISBN 0-03-059961-x : £17.50 B82-15353

Graham, Tom M.. Biology : the essential principles / Tom M. Graham. — Philadelphia ; London : Saunders College, c1982. — xi,736p,[32]p of plates : ill(some col.),ports ; 27cm
Includes index
ISBN 0-03-057838-8 : £18.95 B82-23124

Lovelock, J. E.. Gaia : a new look at life on earth / J.E. Lovelock. — Oxford : Oxford University Press, 1979 (1982 [printing]). — xi,157p : ill,1map ; 21cm. — (Oxford paperbacks)
ISBN 0-19-286030-5 (pbk) : £2.95 B82-39669

Nelson, Gideon E.. Fundamental concepts of biology. — 4th ed. / Gideon E. Nelson, Gerald G. Robinson. — New York ; Chichester : Wiley, 1982. — ix,406p,4p of plates : ill(some col.),maps ; 26cm
Previous ed.: 1974. — Includes index
ISBN 0-471-03382-0 : £17.00 B82-13970

Noland, George B.. General biology / George B. Noland. — 10th ed. — St. Louis ; London : Mosby, c1979. — xiii,623p : ill(some col.),ports ; 25cm
Previous ed.: 1975. — Includes index
ISBN 0-8016-3673-6 : £15.00 B82-24925

Weisz, Paul B.. The science of biology. — 5th ed. / Paul B. Weisz and Richard N. Keogh. — New York ; London : McGraw-Hill, c1982. — xii,1009,[28]p : ill(some col.),maps(some col.),ports ; 24cm
Includes bibliographies and index
ISBN 0-07-069145-2 : £18.95 B82-27224

574 — Organisms — *For children*

Althea. The year around us / by Althea. — Cambridge : Dinosaur, c1982. — 72p : col.ill ; 28cm
Ill on lining papers. — Includes index
ISBN 0-85122-341-9 (cased) : £5.95
ISBN 0-85122-363-x (pbk) : Unpriced B82-32078

Nature / written by Neil Ardley ... [et al.] ; illustrated by Stephen Adams ... [et al.]. — London : Pan, 1981. — 128p : col.ill ; 22cm. — (A Piccolo explorer book)
Bibliography: p128. — Includes index. — Contents: Wild flowers — Trees — Shells — Birds — Insects — Mammals
ISBN 0-330-26575-x (pbk) : £1.95 B82-01582

Ward Lock's nature book. — London : Ward Lock, Apr.1981. — [224]p
ISBN 0-7063-6136-9 : £5.95 : CIP entry B81-02575

574 — Organisms — *For Irish students — For schools*

Duhig, Margaret. Biology : science of life / Margaret Duhig, K. Valarasan-Toomey. — Dublin : Gill and Macmillan
Workbook. — 1981. — 68p : ill ; 27cm
ISBN 0-7171-1128-8 (pbk) : Unpriced B82-00710

574 — Organisms — *For schools*

Beckett, B. S.. Biology : a modern introduction / B.S. Beckett. — 2nd ed. — Oxford : Oxford University Press, 1982. — 307p : ill ; 28cm
Previous ed.: 1976. — Includes index
ISBN 0-19-914088-x (pbk) : £3.75 B82-26511

Bunyan, P. T.. A first biology course / P.T. Bunyan. — Cheltenham : Thornes, 1982. — x,229p : ill ; 22cm
Includes index
ISBN 0-85950-339-9 (pbk) : Unpriced : CIP rev. B82-04816

Clegg, Colin. Advanced biology / Colin Clegg. — London : Pan, 1982. — xx,332p : ill ; 20cm. — (Pan study aids)
Includes index
ISBN 0-330-26616-0 (pbk) : £2.95 B82-20435

Ford-Robertson, Julian. Revise biology : a complete revision course for O level and CSE / Julian Ford-Robertson. — Rev. [ed.]. — London : Letts, 1981. — ix,224p : ill(some col.),1map ; 30cm. — (Letts study aids)
Previous ed.: 1979. — Includes index
ISBN 0-85097-377-5 (pbk) : £3.65 B82-19111

Price, Richard. Beginning biology. — Cambridge : Cambridge University Press, Nov.1982. — [198]p
ISBN 0-521-28209-8 (pbk) : £3.50 : CIP entry B82-40326

Reid, Donald. Biology for the individual / Donald Reid, Philip Booth. — London : Heinemann Educational
Teacher's guide to Books 1-7. — 1982. — 124p : ill,1facsim ; 25cm
ISBN 0-435-59765-5 (pbk) : £6.50 : CIP rev. B81-34395

Roberts, M. B. V.. Biology : a functional approach / M.B.V. Roberts. — 3rd ed.. — Walton-on-Thames : Nelson, 1982. — xv,655p : ill,maps,ports ; 28cm
Previous ed.: 1976. — Bibliography: p637-646. — Includes index
ISBN 0-17-448015-6 (pbk) : Unpriced B82-30360

Simpkins, J.. Biology of the cell, mammal and flowering plant. — London : Bell & Hyman, Apr.1982. — [454]p
Originally published: London : Mills & Boon, 1980
ISBN 0-7135-2204-6 (pbk) : £7.95 : CIP entry B82-11093

Smallman, Clare. Biology for you. — London : Hutchinson, Apr.1981
2. — [176]p
ISBN 0-09-141131-9 (pbk) : £2.25 : CIP entry B81-00884

Smith, Barry A.. Life & living / by Barry A. Smith. — 2nd ed. / revised by John T.C. Sellick. — Thirsk : Crakehill, 1982. — 78p : ill ; 30cm
Previous ed.: Helperby : Cundall Manor : 1979. — Includes index
ISBN 0-907105-07-6 (pbk) : Unpriced B82-13208

Understanding biology. — London : Bell & Hyman, Apr.1982. — [304]p
Originally published: London : Mills & Boon, 1976
ISBN 0-7135-2198-8 (pbk) : £4.60 : CIP entry B82-11091

574 — Organisms — *For schools — Irish texts*

De Buitléar, ÉamonAn saol beo. — Baile Átha Cliath : An Gúm
3 / údar Éamon de Buitléar ; líníocht dhaite Freddy Eldnar ; dearadh Henry Sharpe. — c1982. — 52p : ill(some col.) ; 18x25cm
Translation of: Out and about
Unpriced (pbk) B82-40288

574 — Organisms — *For students in tropical regions*

Soper, R.. Biology / R. Soper and S. Tryell Smith. — [London] : Macmillan, [1981]. — 93p : ill ; 28cm. — (Certificate revision series)
Includes index
ISBN 0-333-31061-6 (pbk) : Unpriced B82-25552

574 — Organisms — *For West African students*

Mackean, D. G.. Introduction to biology / D.G. Mackean. — 2nd West African ed. — London : Heinemann Educational (Nigeria) in association with John Murray, 1982. — 256p : ill ; 30cm
Previous ed.: 1977. — Bibliography: p240. — Includes index
ISBN 0-7195-3887-4 (pbk) : £3.95 : CIP rev.
ISBN 978-12-9087-0 (Heinemann Educational (Nigeria)) B81-28007

574 — Plants. Leaves. Organisms — *For children*

Hansen, Elvig. Life on a leaf / written and illustrated by Elvig Hansen ; consultant for English edition, Ralph Whitlock. — Hove : Wayland, 1982. — 64p : ill(some col.) ; 25cm
Translation from the Danish. — Includes index
ISBN 0-85340-950-1 : £4.25 B82-21944

574'.00724 — Biology. Mathematical models

Jeffers, J. N. R.. Modelling. — London : Chapman and Hall, Nov.1982. — [80]p. — (Outline studies in ecology)
ISBN 0-412-24360-1 (pbk) : £2.75 : CIP entry B82-28259

574'.01 — Biology - *Philosophical perspectives*

Against biological determinism. — London : Allison & Busby, Sept.1981. — [192]p
ISBN 0-85031-423-2 (cased) : £9.95 : CIP entry
ISBN 0-85031-424-0 (pbk) : £4.95 B81-20129

574'.01 — Biology — *Philosophical perspectives*

Towards a liberatory biology. — London : Allison and Busby, Sept.1981. — [192]p
ISBN 0-85031-425-9 (pbk) : £9.95 : CIP entry
ISBN 0-85031-426-7 (pbk) : £4.95 B81-25111

574'.01 — Biology. Theories

Mercer, E. H.. The foundations of biological theory / E.H. Mercer. — New York ; Chichester : Wiley, c1981. — vi,232p : ill ; 24cm
Includes bibliographies and index
ISBN 0-471-08797-1 : £25.90 B82-03751

574'.01 — Biology. Theories — *French texts*

Duchesneau, François. La physiologie des lumières : empirisme, modèles et théories / par François Duchesneau. — Hague ; London : Nijhoff, 1982. — xxi,611p ; 25cm. — (Archives internationales d'histoire des idées = International archives of the history of ideas ; 95)
Bibliography: p583-601. — Includes index
ISBN 90-247-2500-3 : Unpriced B82-20798

574'.01 — Biology. Theories, *to 1980*

Mayr, Ernst. The growth of biological thought : diversity, evolution and inheritance / Ernst Mayr. — Cambridge, Mass. ; London : Belknap Press, 1982. — ix,974p ; 24cm
Bibliography: p893-955. — Includes index
ISBN 0-674-36445-7 : £21.00 B82-38450

574'.012 — Europe. Taxonomy. Research

Taxonomy in Europe : final report of the European Science Research Councils' ad hoc Group on Biological Recordings, Systematics and Taxonomy / edited by V.H. Heywood and R.B. Clark. — Amsterdam ; Oxford : North-Holland for the European Science Foundation, 1982. — vi,170p ; 24cm. — (ESRC review ; no.17)
Text on inside covers. — Bibliography: p168-169
ISBN 0-444-86363-x (pbk) : £6.46 B82-36632

574'.012 — Numerical taxonomy

Dunn, G.. An introduction to mathematical taxonomy / G. Dunn & B.S. Everitt. — Cambridge : Cambridge University Press, 1982. — ix,152p : ill ; 23cm. — (Cambridge studies in mathematical biology ; 5)
Bibliography: p138-144. — Includes index
ISBN 0-521-23979-6 (cased) : £15.00 : CIP rev.
ISBN 0-521-28388-4 (pbk) : Unpriced
B82-06863

574'.012 — Organisms. Taxonomy. Evolutionary aspects

Margulis, Lynn. Five kingdoms : an illustrated guide to the phyla of life on earth / Lynn Margulis, Karlene V. Schwartz. — Oxford : Freeman, c1982. — xiv,338p : ill(some col.),ports ; 23cm
Includes bibliographies and index
ISBN 0-7167-1212-1 (cased) : £17.30
ISBN 0-7167-1213-x (pbk) : Unpriced
B82-29340

Wiley, E. O.. Phylogenetics : the theory and practice of phylogenetic systematics / E.O. Wiley. — New York ; Chichester : Wiley, c1981. — xv,439p : ill,maps,port ; 24cm
Bibliography: p401-419. — Includes index
ISBN 0-471-05975-7 : £27.75 B82-00117

574'.012 — Taxonomy, *to 1980* — *Conference proceedings*

History in the service of systematics : papers from the conference to celebrate the centenary of the British Museum (Natural History) 13-16 April, 1981 / [organized by the Society for the Bibliography of Natural History and the Systematics Association] ; edited by Alwyne Wheeler & James H. Price. — London : The society, 1981. — v,164p ; 25cm. — (Society for the Bibliography of Natural History special publication ; 1)
Includes bibliographies
ISBN 0-901843-05-9 (pbk) : Unpriced
B82-17425

574'.01'515 — Biology. Nonlinear analysis — *Conference proceedings*

NATO Advanced Study Institute on Nonlinear Phenomena in Physics and Biology *(1980 : Banff, Alta.)*. Nonlinear phenomena in physics and biology / [proceedings of a NATO Advanced Study Institute on Nonlinear Phenomena in Physics and Biology, held August 17-29, 1980, at the Banff Center, Banff, Alberta, Canada] ; edited by Richard H. Enns ... [et al.]. — New York ; London : Published in cooperation with NATO Scientific Affairs Division [by] Plenum, c1981. — x,609p : ill,1port ; 26cm. — (NATO advanced study institutes series. Series B, Physics ; v.75)
Includes bibliographies and index
ISBN 0-306-40880-5 : Unpriced
Primary classification 530.1'55 B82-17646

574'.01'51535 — Biology. Differential equations
Jones, D. S. (Douglas Samuel). Differential equations and mathematical biology. — London : Allen & Unwin, Sept.1982. — [320]p
ISBN 0-04-515001-x : £15.00 : CIP entry
B82-19083

574'.01'516 — Organisms. Geometrical aspects
Edwards, Lawrence. The field of form : research concerning the outer world of living forms and the inner world of geometrical imagination / Lawrence Edwards. — Edinburgh : Floris, 1982. — 223p : ill ; 22cm
Includes index
ISBN 0-903540-50-9 (pbk) : £8.50 : CIP rev.
B82-10858

574'.022'2 — Organisms — *Illustrations* — *For children*
Colouring book. — [London] : [British Museum (Natural History)], c1981. — [12]p : ill ; 21x30cm
Cover title. — Text on inside covers
ISBN 0-565-00846-3 (pbk) : Unpriced
B82-05545

574'.022'2 — Organisms. Illustrations. Techniques — *Manuals*
Wood, Phyllis. Scientific illustration : a guide to biological, zoological, and medical rendering techniques, design, printing, and display / Phyllis Wood. — New York ; London : Van Nostrand Reinhold, c1979 (1982 [printing]). — 148p,[4]p of plates : ill(some col.) ; 28cm
Bibliography: p146. — Includes index
ISBN 0-442-29307-0 (pbk) : £8.45 B82-36641

574'.024372 — Biology — *For teaching*
Biology in the '80s : a lecture series for teachers in upper school. — [Lancaster] : University of Lancaster
Vol.1: Plant physiology / edited by W.J. Davies and P.G. Ayres. — 1982. — 167p,[4]p of plates : ill ; 21cm
Includes index
ISBN 0-901699-88-8 (pbk) : Unpriced
B82-37349

574'.028 — Biology. Experiments. Laboratory techniques — *For teaching*
Abramoff, Peter. Instructor's handbook for Laboratory outlines in biology — III / Peter Abramoff, Robert G. Thomson. — Oxford : Freeman, c1982. — vii,104p : ill ; 28cm
Includes bibliographies
ISBN 0-7167-1404-3 (unbound) : £1.00
B82-34386

574'.028 — Biology — *Laboratory manuals*
Higher biology laboratory manual. — London : Edward Arnold, Sept.1982. — [64]p
ISBN 0-7131-0640-9 (pbk) : £2.95 : CIP entry
B82-21981

574'.028 — Biology. Nuclear magnetic resonance spectroscopy
Gadian, David G.. Nuclear magnetic resonance and its applications to living systems. — Oxford : Clarendon, Nov.1981. — [250]p
ISBN 0-19-854627-0 : £15.00 : CIP entry
B81-30527

574'.028 — Biology. Nuclear magnetic resonance spectroscopy — *Serials*
Magnetic resonance in biology. — Vol.1-. — New York ; Chichester : Wiley, 1980-. — v. : ill ; 24cm
£17.50 B82-19864

574'.028 — Biology. Statistics. Visual presentation — *Manuals*

Charts & graphs : guidelines for the visual presentation of statistical data in the life sciences / editor Doig Simmonds ; contributors Gillian Bragg ... [et al.] ; illustrations Gillian Bragg. — Lancaster : MTP published in association with the Institute of Medical and Biological Illustration, 1980. — xii,93p : ill (some col.),2ports ; 23cm
ISBN 0-85200-293-9 (pbk) : Unpriced : CIP rev.
Also classified at 610'.28 B79-30071

574'.028 — Organisms. Nuclear magnetic resonance spectroscopy

Mansfield, P.. NMR imaging in biomedicine : supplement 2, Advances in magnetic resonance / P. Mansfield, P.G. Morris. — New York ; London : Academic, 1982. — ix,354p : ill ; 24cm
Includes index
ISBN 0-12-025562-6 : £32.80 B82-38080

574'.028'542 — Biology. Data. Statistical analysis. Applications of ditital computer systems. Programs: BMDP programs

BMDP statistical software 1981 / W.J. Dixon, chief editor ; [edited by] M.B. Brown ... [et al.]. — Berkeley ; London : University of California Press, 1981. — x,725p : ill ; 28cm
Text on inside covers. — Bibliography: p714-719. — Includes index
ISBN 0-520-04408-8 (pbk) : £12.25
B82-25277

574'.028'5424 — Biology. Statistical methods. Applications of digital computer systems. Programming languages: Basic language

Lee, J. D. (John David). Statistics and numerical methods in BASIC for biologists / J.D. Lee and T.D. Lee. — New York ; London : Van Nostrand Reinhold, c1982. — xi,267p : ill ; 26cm
Bibliography: p255-256. — Includes index
ISBN 0-442-30476-5 (cased) : £13.50
ISBN 0-442-30481-1 (pbk) : £6.95 B82-37523

574'.028'7 — Biology. Measurement

Woodward, F. I.. Principles and measurements in environmental biology. — London : Butterworths, Feb.1983. — [350]p
ISBN 0-408-10637-9 : £35.00 : CIP entry
B82-38289

574'.03'21 — Biology — *Encyclopaedias*

Dictionary of biology / editor Elizabeth Tootill. — Maidenhead : Intercontinental Book Productions in conjunction with Seymour Press, 1980. — 282p : ill ; 18cm. — (Key facts)
ISBN 0-85047-935-5 (pbk) : £2.25 B82-36095

574'.03'21 — Biology — *Encyclopaedias* — *For schools*

McCahill, T.. Biology / T.A. McCahill ; adviser K. Davison. — London : Collins, [1982]. — xxxv,213p : ill ; 12cm. — (Basic facts) (Collins revision aids)
ISBN 0-00-458888-6 (pbk) : Unpriced
B82-33440

574'.03'9171 — Biology — *Russian & English dictionaries*

English-Russian biological dictionary / edited by O.I. Chibisova and L.A. Koziar. — 4th ed. — Oxford : Pergamon, 1980. — 732p ; 23cm
Previous ed.: 1978
ISBN 0-08-023163-2 : £55.00 : CIP rev.
B78-10925

574'.05 — Biology — *Serials*

Soviet scientific reviews. Section D, Biology reviews. — Vol.1 (1980)-. — Chur ; London (37 Chancery La., WC2A 1EL) : Harwood Academic, 1980-. — v. : ill ; 22cm
Annual
ISSN 0143-0424 = Soviet scientific reviews. Section D. Biology reviews : £20.74
B82-19869

574'.05 — Organisms — *Serials*

Young naturalist's news / British Naturalists' Association. — No.1 (Spring 1981)-. — Burnley (c/o R. Freethy, 15 Lower Manor La., Burnley) : The Association, 1981-. — v. : ill,ports ; 23cm
ISSN 0263-7650 = Young naturalist's news : £2.00 per year B82-32173

574'.07 — Biology. Information sources

Guide to sources for agricultural and biological research / edited by J. Richard Blanchard and Lois Farrell ; sponsored by the United States National Agricultural Library United States Department of Agriculture, Beltsville, Maryland. — Berkeley, [Calif.] ; London : University of California Press, c1981. — xi,735p ; 29cm
Includes index
ISBN 0-520-03226-8 : Unpriced
Primary classification 630'.7 B82-28301

574'.07'1141235 — Scotland. Grampian Region. Aberdeen. Universities: University of Aberdeen. *Institute of South-East Asian Biology, to 1979*

University of Aberdeen. *Institute of South-East Asian Biology.* The Institute of South-East Asian Biology : the first ten years 1969-1979. — Aberdeen : University of Aberdeen, 1980. — ii,12p ; 30cm
Includes bibliographies
Unpriced (unbound) B82-18390

574'.07'12411 — Scotland. Secondary schools. Curriculum subjects: Biology. Teaching

Burchill, Jane. From school to university : the biological sciences. — Aberdeen : Aberdeen University Press, June 1982. — [84]p
ISBN 0-08-028472-8 (pbk) : £4.00 : CIP entry B82-16224

574'.072 — Biometrics

Sokal, Robert R.. Biometry : the principles and practice of statistics in biological research / Robert R. Sokal and F. James Rohlf. — 2nd ed.. — Oxford : W.H. Freeman, c1981. — xviii,859p : ill ; 24cm
Previous ed.: 1969. — Text on lining papers. — Bibliography: p826-837. — Includes index
ISBN 0-7167-1254-7 : £19.50 B82-05840

574'.072 — Biometrics — *Tables*

Rohlf, F. James. Statistical tables / F. James Rohlf, Robert R. Sokal. — 2nd ed. — Oxford : W.H. Freeman, c1981. — xiii,219p : ill ; 24cm
Previous ed.: 1969
ISBN 0-7167-1257-1 (cased) : £15.20
ISBN 0-7167-1258-x (pbk) : £6.95 B82-05842

574'.072041 — Biology. Research projects supported by Science and Engineering Research Council. *Biological Sciences Committee*

Science and Engineering Research Council. Current grants in the life sciences : 1 June 1981. — [Swindon] : SERC, 1981. — ii leaves,209p ; 30cm
Unpriced (pbk) B82-35085

574'.072041 — Biology. Research. Role of Great Britain. *Science and Engineering Research Council. Biological Sciences Committee*

Achievements in biology : the role of the Science and Engineering Research Council / [prepared by Members of the SERC Biological Sciences Committee]. — Swindon : The Council, 1982. — v,37p : ill ; 25cm
ISBN 0-901660-46-9 (pbk) : Unpriced B82-20109

574'.07'24 — Biology. Experiments

Abramoff, Peter. Laboratory outlines in biology — III / Peter Abramoff, Robert G. Thomson. — [3rd ed.]. — Oxford : Freeman, c1982. — ix,479p : ill,forms ; 28cm
Previous ed.: 1972. — Includes bibliographies
ISBN 0-7167-1323-3 (pbk) : £8.95 B82-35102

574'.0724 — Biology. Experiments — *For schools*

Mackean, D. G.. Class experiments in biology. — London : J. Murray, July 1982
Students' book. — [88]p
ISBN 0-7195-3852-1 (pbk) : £1.40 : CIP entry B82-13074

Mackean, D. G.. Class experiments in biology. — London : J. Murray, July 1982
Teachers' book. — [96]p
ISBN 0-7195-3853-x (pbk) : £2.80 : CIP entry B82-13075

574'.0724 — Biology. Mathematical models — *Conference proceedings*

Biomathematics in 1980 : papers presented at a workshop on Biomathematics: current status and future perspectives, Salerno, April 1980 / edited by Luigi Ricciardi and Alwyn Scott. — Amsterdam ; Oxford : North Holland, 1982. — xiv,297p : ill ; 24cm. — (North-Holland mathematical studies ; 58)
Includes index
ISBN 0-444-86355-9 (pbk) : Unpriced B82-25699

574'.0724 — Organisms. Cells. Culture — *Serials*

Advances in cell culture. — Vol.1 (1981)-. — New York ; London : Academic Press, 1981-. — v. : ill,port ; 24cm
ISSN 0275-6358 = Advances in cell culture : Unpriced B82-07643

574'.076 — Biology — *Questions & answers — For Irish students — For schools*

Clegg, C. J.. Test your biology. — London : Murray
Teachers' answer book. — Dec.1982. — [96]p
ISBN 0-7195-3920-x (pbk) : £2.25 : CIP entry B82-30221

574'.076 — Biology — *Questions & answers — For schools*

Clarke, Sheila. Solutions to 'O' grade biology : paper 2 / Sheila Clarke. — Glasgow : Gibson, c1981. — 64p : ill ; 21cm. — (Prepare to pass)
ISBN 0-7169-3122-2 (pbk) : Unpriced B82-12384

Clegg, C. J.. Test your biology. — London : Murray, Jan.1982. — [128]p
ISBN 0-7195-3863-7 (pbk) : £1.80 : CIP entry B81-33850

Interpretation tests in biology / writing team: James Torrance ... [et al.] ; team co-ordinator: James Torrance. — London : Edward Arnold, 1981. — v,48p : ill ; 23cm + answers(13p ; 22cm)
ISBN 0-7131-0550-x (pbk) : £5.95 : CIP rev. B81-21489

Usher, George, *1930-*. Objective tests in certificate biology / George Usher. — Estover : Macdonald & Evans, 1981. — x,140p : ill ; 19cm
ISBN 0-7121-1518-8 (pbk) : £2.25 B82-08510

574'.076 — Organisms — *Questions & answers*

McCahill, T.. Biology study and revision / T.A. McCahill. — [Glasgow] : Collins Educational, [1982]. — [63]p : ill ; 30cm. — (Collins revision aids)
Cover title
ISBN 0-00-197250-2 (pbk) : £1.50
ISBN 0-00-327749-6 (non-net ed.) : Unpriced B82-32059

574'.092'2 — Great Britain. Biology — *Biographies*

Some famous biologists. — London : Royal Society, c1982. — [16]p : ports(some col.) ; 25cm
ISBN 0-85403-187-1 (unbound) : Unpriced B82-35345

574'.092'4 — Great Britain. Biology. Hickin, Norman E. — *Biographies*

Hickin, Norman E.. [Forest refreshed]. Wyre forest refreshed : the autobiographical notes of a biologist / Norman E. Hickin. — Kidderminster : Kenneth Tomkinson, 1981, c1965. — 184p : ill ; 23cm
Originally published: London : Hutchinson, 1965. — Bibliography: p172-173. — Includes index
Unpriced (pbk) B82-16029

574'.092'4 — United States. Natural history. Coues, Elliott — *Biographies*

Cutright, Paul Russell. Elliott Coues : naturalist and frontier historian / Paul Russell Cutright and Michael J. Brodhead. — Urbana ; London : University of Illinois Press, c1981. — xv,509p,[10]p of plates : ill,2maps,ports ; 24cm
Bibliography: p439-480. — Includes index
ISBN 0-252-00802-2 : £19.95 B82-05713

574.1 — ORGANISMS. PHYSIOLOGY

574.1 — Organisms. Physiology

Biology : form and function. — Milton Keynes : Open University Press. — (Science : a second level course) (S202 ; Units 16-18)
Animal physiology 1 / prepared by the S202 Course Team. — 1981. — ix,63,25,34p : ill (some col.) ; 30cm
At head of title: The Open University. — Includes bibliographies. — Contents: Unit 16: Communication : Nerves and hormones — Unit 17: Blood sugar regulation — Unit 18: Control mechanisms in reproduction
ISBN 0-335-16036-0 (pbk) : Unpriced B82-07732

Biology : form and function. — Milton Keynes : Open University Press. — (Science : a second level course) (S202 ; Units 22 & 23)
Animal physiology III / prepared by the S202 Course Team. — 1981. — 64p : ill(some col.) ; 30cm
At head of title: The Open University. — Bibliography: p64. — Contents: Units 22 and 23 : Osmoregulation and excretion
ISBN 0-335-16038-7 (pbk) : Unpriced B82-07730

Biology : form and function. — Milton Keynes : Open University Press. — (Science : a second level course)
Development II / prepared by the S202 Course Team. — 1981. — 60,15p : ill(some col.) ; 30cm. — (S202 ; Units 14 & 15)
At head of title: The Open University. — Includes bibliographies. — Contents: Unit 14: Pattern specification and morphogenesis — Unit 15: Chicken or egg?
ISBN 0-335-16035-2 (pbk) : Unpriced B82-07731

Biology : form and function. — Milton Keynes : Open University Press. — (Science : a second level course)
At head of title: The Open University
Explaining biological form and function / prepared by the S202 Course Team. — 1981. — 32p : ill,ports ; 30cm. — (S202 ; EBFF)
Bibliography: p31-32
ISBN 0-335-16043-3 (pbk) : Unpriced B82-21204

Biology form and function / prepared by the S202 Course Team. — Milton Keynes : Open University Press. — (Science : a second level course)
At head of title: The Open University
Plant physiology II. — 1981. — 57p : ill ; 30cm. — (S202 ; units 29-31)
Bibliography: p56. — Contents: Unit 29: Plant cells : growth and differentiation — Units 30 and 31: Morphogenesis in flowering plants
ISBN 0-335-16041-7 (pbk) : Unpriced B82-15043

574.1'33 — Organisms. Metabolism. Monitoring. Non-invasive techniques — *Conference proceedings*

Noninvasive probes of tissue metabolism / Jack S. Cohen, editor. — New York ; Chichester : Wiley, c1982. — xiv,270p : ill ; 24cm
Includes bibliographies and index
ISBN 0-471-08893-5 : £36.50 B82-18223

574.1'66 — Sex. Evolution

Bell, Graham, *1949-*. The masterpiece of nature : the evolution and genetics of sexuality / Graham Bell. — London : Croom Helm, c1982. — 635p : ill,maps ; 24cm
Bibliography: p514-593. — Includes index
ISBN 0-85664-753-5 : £25.00 : CIP rev. B81-22541

574.16'6'05 — Sexual reproduction — *Serials*
Oxford reviews of reproductive biology. — Vol.4 (1982). — Oxford : Clarendon Press, July 1982. — [300]p
ISBN 0-19-857537-8 : £30.00 : CIP entry B82-12552

574.1'7 — Organisms. Tissues. Differentiation. Laboratory techniques: In vitro methods — *Conference proceedings*
British Society for Cell Biology. *Symposium (4th : 1980 : University of Edinburgh)*. Differentiation in vitro / the forth symposium of the British Society for Cell Biology ; edited by M.M. Yeoman, D.E.S. Truman. — Cambridge : Cambridge University Press, 1982. — ix,286p : ill ; 24cm
Includes bibliographies and index
ISBN 0-521-23926-5 : £30.00 : CIP rev.
Also classified at 574.87'612'028 B81-39254

574.1'8 — Organisms. Behaviour. Neurophysiological aspects
Symposium on the Neural Basis of Behavior *(1979 : Alfred I. du Pont Institute)*. The neural basis of behavior / [based on the symposium on the Neural Basis of Behavior, June 7-8, 1979, Alfred I. du Pont Institute, Wilmington, Delaware] ; edited by Alexander L. Beckman. — Lancaster : MTP, c1982. — 337p : ill ; 24cm
Includes bibliographies and index
ISBN 0-85200-588-1 : £29.95 B82-17277

574.1'8 — Organisms. Virus receptors
Virus receptors. — London : Chapman and Hall. — (Receptors and recognition. Series B ; v.7)
Pt.1: Bacterial viruses / edited by L.L. Randall and L. Philipson. — 1980. — xii,147p : ill ; 25cm
Includes bibliographies and index
ISBN 0-412-15660-1 : £15.00 : CIP rev. B80-18285

574.1'88 — Organisms. Receptors. Regulation
Receptor regulation / edited by R.J. Lefkowitz. — London : Chapman and Hall, 1981. — viii,253p : ill ; 24cm. — (Receptors and recognition. Series B ; v.13)
Includes bibliographies and index
ISBN 0-412-15930-9 : £25.00 : CIP rev. B81-31749

574.1'882 — Organisms. Biological rhythms
Applin, D. G.. Biological periodicities : a new interpretation / D.G. Applin and J.L. Cloudsley-Thompson. — Shildon : Meadowfield, c1982. — 52p : ill ; 20cm. — (Patterns of progress. Zoology series ; 17)
Bibliography: p46-49. — Includes index
ISBN 0-904095-35-5 (pbk) : £2.80 B82-28226

Biological timekeeping / edited by John Brady. — Cambridge : Cambridge University Press, 1982. — xvii,197p : ill ; 24cm. — (Society for Experimental Biology seminar series ; 14)
Includes bibliographies and index
ISBN 0-521-23307-0 (cased) : £22.50 : CIP rev.
ISBN 0-521-29899-7 (pbk) : Unpriced B82-12699

The **Rhythms** of life / consultant editors Edward S. Ayensu and Philip Whitfield. — London : Marshall, 1982. — 199p : ill(some col.) ; 31cm
Includes index
ISBN 0-9507901-0-9 : £14.95 B82-23397

574.19 — Biology. Quantum theory
Davydov, A. S.. Biology & quantum mechanics / by A.S. Davydov ; translated by D. Oliver. — Oxford : Pergamon, 1982. — ix,229p : ill ; 24cm. — (International series in natural philosophy ; v.109)
Translation from the Russian. — Includes index
ISBN 0-08-026392-5 : £22.50 : CIP rev. B81-31360

Muller, Margaret. The sacred enigma : a personal conception of the brain-mind relationship based on the quantum theory / Margaret Muller. — Edgware (51 Lodge Close, Canons Drive, Edgware, Middx) : M. Muller, c1981. — 166leaves ; 30cm
Bibliography: leaves 163-166
Unpriced B82-02529

574.19'1 — Biophysics
Chandler, E. C.. The holosystem : a theory relating biosystems to astrosystems / E.C. Chandler. — Chichester : E.C. Chandler, 1982. — 88p : ill ; 25cm
ISBN 0-9508120-0-5 (pbk) : Unpriced B82-39533

Hallet, F. R.. Physics for the biological sciences : a topical approach to biophysical concepts / F.R. Hallet, R.H. Stinson, P.A. Speight in association with W.G. Graham. — Toronto ; London : Methuen, c1982. — xi,255p : ill ; 24cm
Bibliography: p242-243. — Includes index
ISBN 0-458-95280-x (pbk) : Unpriced
ISBN 0-412-24750-x (Chapman and Hall) B82-38380

574.19'1 — Water. Biophysics — *Conference proceedings*
Biophysics of water. — Chichester : Wiley, Dec.1982. — [424]p
ISBN 0-471-10229-6 : £27.00 : CIP entry B82-30821

574.19'1'05 — Biophysics - *Serials*
Progress in biophysics and molecular biology. — 36. — Oxford : Pergamon, June 1981. — [146]p
ISBN 0-08-028394-2 : £29.50 : CIP entry B81-16854

574.1'91'05 — Biophysics — *Serials*
Progress in biophysics and molecular biology. — 37. — Oxford : Pergamon, Feb.1982. — [242]p
ISBN 0-08-029120-1 : £31.20 : CIP entry B82-03348

Progress in biophysics and molecular biology. — 38. — Oxford : Pergamon, May 1982. — [222]p
ISBN 0-08-029683-1 : £38.75 : CIP entry B82-11993

574.19'1'072 — Biophysics. Research. Applications of synchrotron radiation
Uses of synchrotron radiation in biology. — London : Academic Press, July 1982. — [390]p
ISBN 0-12-674850-0 : CIP entry B82-12528

574.19'12 — Biological materials. Mechanical properties
Vincent, J. F. V.. Structural biomaterials / Julian F.V. Vincent. — London : Macmillan, 1982. — vii,206p : ill ; 25cm
Bibliography: p196-197. — Includes index
ISBN 0-333-26125-9 (cased) : Unpriced
ISBN 0-333-26126-7 (pbk) : Unpriced B82-16151

574.19'12 — Organisms. Mechanics
Mechanical design in organisms / S.A. Wainwright ... [et al.]. — Princeton ; Guildford : Princeton University Press, c1982. — xii,423p : ill ; 24cm
Originally published: London : Edward Arnold, 1976. — Bibliography: p369-374. — Includes index
ISBN 0-691-08306-1 (cased) : Unpriced
ISBN 0-691-08308-8 (pbk) : £8.85 B82-36960

574.19'121 — Bioenergetics
Of oxygen, fuels, and living matter. — Chichester : Wiley. — (Evolving life sciences series)
Part 1 / edited by G. Semenza. — 1981. — xi,349p : ill,ports ; 26cm
Includes index
ISBN 0-471-27923-4 : £29.50 B82-11343

Of oxygen, fuels and living matter / edited by G. Semenza. — Chichester : Wiley. — (Evolving life sciences series ; v.1)
Pt.2. — c1982. — xi,508p : ill,ports ; 27cm
Includes bibliographies and index
ISBN 0-471-27924-2 : £27.50 B82-28781

574.19'121 — Bioenergetics — *Conference proceedings*
Energy and effort. — London : Taylor & Francis, Sept.1982. — [250]p. — (Symposia of the Society for the Study of Human Biology, ISSN 0081-153X ; 22)
Conference papers
ISBN 0-85066-224-9 : £15.00 : CIP entry B82-24357

574.19'121 — Organisms. Energy conversion
Fox, Ronald F.. Biological energy transduction : the uroboros / Ronald F. Fox. — New York ; Chichester : Wiley, c1982. — vii,279p : ill ; 24cm
Includes index
ISBN 0-471-09026-3 : Unpriced B82-19655

574.19'121'01 — Bioenergetics. Chemiosmotic theory
Nicholls, David G.. Bioenergetics : an introduction to the chemiosmotic theory / David G. Nicholls. — London : Academic Press, 1982. — xi,190p : ill ; 24cm
Ill on lining papers. — Bibliography: p179-183. — Includes index
ISBN 0-12-518120-5 (cased) : £13.40 : CIP rev.
ISBN 0-12-518122-1 (pbk) : £5.50 B81-36062

574.19'125 — Bioluminescence
Bioluminescence : current perspectives / Kenneth H. Nealson, editor. — [Champaign] : CEPCO ; Heathfield : Broad Oak [distributor], c1981. — 165p : ill ; 24cm
Includes bibliographies and index
ISBN 0-8087-2971-3 (pbk) : Unpriced B82-28048

574.19'15 — Organisms. Effects of radiation
Coggle, J. E.. Biological effects of radiation. — 2nd ed. — London : Taylor and Francis, Feb.1983. — [250]p
Previous ed.: London : Wykeham, 1971
ISBN 0-85066-238-9 : £12.50 : CIP entry B82-39431

574.19'15'072 — Radiobiology. Research
Cell Biology and Disorders Board. *Cell Board Subcommittee*. Radiobiology : report of the Cell Board Subcommittee. — London : Medical Research Council, 1981. — 67p : ill ; 30cm
Bibliography: p53-58
Unpriced (pbk) B82-05434

574.19'153 — Light. Scattering in biological materials — *Conference proceedings*
Scattering techniques applied to supramolecular and nonequilibrium systems / [proceedings of a NATO Advanced Study Institute on scattering techniques applied to supramolecular and nonequilibrium systems, held August 3-12, 1980, at Wellesley College, Wellesley, Mass.] ; edited by Sow-Hsin Chen, Benjamin Chu and Ralph Nossal. — New York ; London : Plenum ... in co-operation with NATO Scientific Affairs Division, c1981. — xiv,928p : ill ; 26cm. — (NATO advanced study institutes series. Series B, Physics ; v.73)
Includes bibliographies and index
ISBN 0-306-40828-7 : Unpriced B82-14703

574.19'153 — Photobiology
Truscott, T. G.. Flash photolysis and pulse radiolysis in biology and medicine. — Oxford : Pergamon, Jan.1983. — [272]p
ISBN 0-08-024949-3 : £25.00 : CIP entry B82-33324

574.19'153 — Photobiology — *Conference proceedings*
Trends in photobiology / [proceedings of the Eighth International Congress on Photobiology and of the Colloque international du CNRS on Les effets biologiques et la bioconversion du rayonnement solaire held July 20-25, 1980, in Strasbourg, France] ; edited by C. Hélène ... [et al.]. — New York ; London : Plenum, c1982. — xiii,673p : ill ; 26cm
Includes index
ISBN 0-306-40644-6 : Unpriced B82-22012

574.19'2 — Biochemistry
Berlow, Peter P.. Introduction to the chemistry of life / Peter P. Berlow, Donald J. Burton, Joseph I. Routh. — Philadelphia ; London : Saunders College, c1982. — xvi,757,A1-A87,xviip : ill(some col.),ports ; 25cm. — (Saunders golden sunburst series)
Text on lining papers. — Includes index
ISBN 0-03-058516-3 : £20.50 B82-25369

574.19'2 — Biochemistry *continuation*

Campbell, Peter N.. Biochemistry illustrated : being an illustrated summary of the subject for medical and other students of biochemistry / Peter N. Campbell, Anthony D. Smith ; illustrator Sue Harris. — Edinburgh : Churchill Livingstone, 1982. — xv,225p : ill ; 25cm
Includes index
ISBN 0-443-02176-7 (pbk) : £7.50 : CIP rev. B81-14946

Comprehensive biochemistry / edited by Marcel Florkin and Elmer H. Stotz. — Amsterdam ; Oxford : Elsevier Scientific
Vol.19B: Protein metabolism
Pt.2 / [edited by] Albert Neuberger, Laurens L.M. van Deenen. — 1982. — xxii,593p : ill ; 23cm
Bibliography: p566-573. — Includes index
ISBN 0-444-80346-7 : £37.47
ISBN 0-444-80151-0 (set) B82-36624

Science and scientists : essays by biochemists, biologists and chemists / edited by M. Kageyama ... [et al.]. — Tokyo : Japan Scientific Societies Press ; Dordrecht ; London : Reidel, c1981. — xv,454p : ill(some col.),ports ; 27cm
Includes index
ISBN 90-277-1357-x : Unpriced B82-17268

Wood, E. J.. Introducing biochemistry. — London : J. Murray, June 1982. — [144]p
ISBN 0-7195-3897-1 (pbk) : £3.50 : CIP entry B82-09832

574.19'2 — Biochemistry — *Festschriften*

Experiences in biochemical perception / edited by L. Nicholas Ornston, Stephen G. Sligar. — New York ; London : Academic Press, 1982. — xx,381p : ill,1port ; 24cm
In honour of I.C. Gunsalus. — Includes bibliographies and index
ISBN 0-12-528420-9 : £31.20 B82-39505

574.19'2 — Biological materials — *Conference proceedings*

World Biomaterials Congress *(1st : 1980 : Baden)*. Biomaterials 1980 : proceedings of the first World Biomaterials Congress held in Baden, Vienna, Austria, in April 1980, in conjunction with the 12th International Biomaterials Symposium and the 6th Annual Meeting of the Society for Biomaterials, U.S.A. / edited by George D. Winter, Donald F. Gibbons, Hanns Plenk Jr. — Chichester : Wiley, c1982. — xxii,829p : ill ; 24cm. — (Advances in biomaterials ; v.3) (A Wiley-interscience publication)
Includes index
ISBN 0-471-10126-5 : £29.75 : CIP rev. B81-34477

574.19'2 — Biologically active compounds

Advances in natural products chemistry : extraction and isolation of biologically active compounds / edited by Sinsaku Natori, Nobuo Ikekawa and Makoto Suzuki. — Tokyo : Kodansha ; New York ; Chichester : Wiley, c1981. — xii,599p : ill ; 24cm
Includes index
ISBN 0-470-27245-7 : £66.00 B82-18227

574.1'92 — Organisms. Effects of pesticides. Biochemical aspects — *Serials*

Progress in pesticide biochemistry. — Vol.2. — Chichester : Wiley, July 1982. — [260]p
ISBN 0-471-10118-4 : £20.00 : CIP entry B82-13245

574.19'2'02461 — Biochemistry — *For medicine*

O'Sullivan, D. G.. Pocket examiner in biochemistry. — London : Pitman, Jan.1983. — [208]p
ISBN 0-272-79644-1 (pbk) : £4.95 : CIP entry B82-33713

574.19'2'028 — Biochemistry. Laboratory techniques

Data for biochemical research / edited by R.M.C. Dawson ... [et al.]. — 2nd ed. — Oxford : Clarendon Press, 1969 (1982 [printing]). — xii,654p : ill ; 24cm. — (Oxford science publications)
Includes index
ISBN 0-19-855334-x : £25.00 B82-20448

Laboratory techniques in biochemistry and molecular biology / edited by T.S. Work, E. Work. — Amsterdam ; Oxford : Elsevier/North Holland Biomedical
[Vol.1]
[Pt.3]: Immunochemical techniques for the identification and estimation of macromolecules / J. Clausen. — 2nd fully rev. ed. — 1981. — xiv,387p : ill ; 21cm
Previous ed.: 1969. — Bibliography: p338-362. — Includes index
ISBN 0-444-80245-2 (cased) : £36.56
ISBN 0-444-80244-4 (pbk) : Unpriced
ISBN 0-7204-4200-1 B82-11938

574.19'2'028 — Biochemistry. Magnetic resonance spectroscopy

Biological magnetic resonance. — New York ; London : Plenum
Vol.3 / edited by Lawrence J. Berliner and Jacques Reuben. — c1981. — xx,268p : ill ; 24cm
Includes bibliographies and index
ISBN 0-306-40612-8 : Unpriced B82-00704

574.19'2'05 — Biochemistry — *Serials*

Essays in biochemistry. — Vol.17. — London : Academic Press, Nov.1981. — 1v.
ISBN 0-12-158117-9 : CIP entry
ISSN 0071-1365 B81-28139

Life chemistry reports. — Vol.1, no.1 (1982)-. — Chur ; London (c/o STBS Ltd., P.O. Box 197, WC2N 4DE) : Harwood Academic, 1982-. — v. : ill ; 23cm
Irregular
Unpriced B82-38511

574.19'2'076 — Biochemistry — *Questions & answers*

Biochemistry: pre-test self-assessment and review. — 2nd ed. / edited by Ian D.K. Halkerston. — New York ; London : McGraw-Hill, c1980. — vii,176p : ill ; 22cm. — (Pre-test series)
Previous ed.: / edited by J.M. Kirkwood, 1976. — Bibliography: p175-176
ISBN 0-07-050963-8 (pbk) : £6.95 B82-25266

574.19'2'0924 — Biochemistry. Krebs, *Sir* Hans — *Biographies*

Krebs, *Sir* Hans. Reminiscences and reflections / Hans Krebs in collaboration with Anne Martin. — Oxford : Clarendon Press, 1981. — vii,298p,[8]p of plates : ill,facsims,ports ; 23cm
Bibliography: p263-289. — Includes index
ISBN 0-19-854702-1 : £12.50 : CIP rev. B81-21606

574.19'214 — Animals. Inorganic compounds. Crystals. Growth

Inorganic biological crystal growth. — Oxford : Pergamon, Oct.1981. — [280]p. — (Progress in crystal growth and characterization)
ISBN 0-08-028420-5 : £26.00 : CIP entry B81-30176

574.19'214 — Nitrogen cycle — *Conference proceedings*

The **Nitrogen** cycle : a Royal Society discussion held on 17 and 18 June 1981 / organized by W.D.P. Stewart, and T. Rosswall. — London : The Society, 1982. — ix,274p : ill,maps ; 31cm
Pages also numbered 303-576. — Includes bibliographies
ISBN 0-85403-183-9 : £29.80 B82-20959

574.19'214 — Organisms. Iron

The **Biological** chemistry of iron : a look at the metabolism of iron and its subsequent uses in living organisms : proceedings of the NATO Advanced Study Institute held at Edmonton, Alberta, Canada, August 23-September 4, 1981 / edited by H. Brian Dunford ... [et al.]. — Dordrecht ; London : Reidel in cooperation with NATO Scientific Affairs Division, c1982. — xii,517p : ill ; 25cm. — (NATO advanced study institutes series. Series C, Mathematical and physical sciences ; v.89)
Includes index
ISBN 90-277-1444-4 : Unpriced B82-40167

574.19'214 — Organisms. Oxygen — *Conference proceedings*

Oxygen and oxy-radicals in chemistry and biology / edited by M.A.J. Rodgers, E.L. Powers. — New York ; London : Academic Press, 1981. — xxx,808p : ill,1map ; 24cm
Conference papers. — Includes index
ISBN 0-12-592050-4 : £41.00 B82-15534

574.19'214 — Organisms. Oxygen — *For children — Arabic texts*

al-**Uksiğin** wa-l-hayāt / tarğamah Nā'ilah ar-Riğal. — London : Macmillan, 1981. — 30p : col.ill ; 18cm
Translation of: Oxygen keeps you alive
ISBN 0-333-32334-3 : Unpriced B82-13474

574.19'214 — Organisms. Strontium

Handbook of stable strontium / edited by Stanley C. Skoryna. — New York ; London : Plenum, c1981. — xv,644p : ill ; 24cm
Includes index
ISBN 0-306-40417-6 : Unpriced B82-02732

574.19'214'05 — Inorganic compounds. Biochemistry — *Serials*

Inorganic biochemistry. — Vol.3. — London : Royal Society of Chemistry, May 1982. — [400]p. — (Specialist periodical report / Royal Society of Chemistry)
ISBN 0-85186-565-8 : CIP entry
ISSN 0142-9698 B82-07022

574.19'218 — Organisms. Flavins — *Conference proceedings*

International Symposium on Flavins and Flavoproteins *(7th : 1981 : Ann Arbor)*. Flavins and flavoproteins : proceedings of the Seventh International Symposium on Flavins and Flavoproteins : Ann Arbor, Michigan, June 21-26, 1981 / editors Vincent Massey, Charles H. Williams. — New York ; Oxford : Elsevier/North Holland, c1982. — xxvii,890p : ill ; 25cm. — (Developments in biochemistry ; v.21)
Includes index
ISBN 0-444-00672-9 : Unpriced B82-32393

574.19'24 — Biopolymers. Pyrolysis mass spectroscopy

Mewzelaar, Henk L. C.. Pyrolysis mass spectrometry of recent and fossil biomaterials : compendium and atlas. — Oxford : Elsevier Scientific, June 1982. — [300]p. — (Techniques and instrumentation in analytical chemistry ; v.3)
ISBN 0-444-42099-1 : CIP entry B82-21366

574.19'24 — Organisms. Cyanides — *Conference proceedings*

Cyanide in biology / edited by B. Vennesland ... [et al.]. — London : Academic Press, 1981. — xiii,548p : ill ; 24cm
Conference papers. — Includes bibliographies and index
ISBN 0-12-716980-6 : £22.00 : CIP rev. B81-14871

574.19'24 — Organisms. Sulphates. Metabolism — *Conference proceedings*

Sulfate metabolism and sulfate conjugation. — London : Taylor & Francis, Aug.1982. — [321]p
Conference proceedings
ISBN 0-85066-233-8 : £18.00 : CIP entry B82-15852

574.19'2431 — Organisms. Cholesterol. Biochemistry

Gibbons, G. F.. Biochemistry of cholesterol / G.F. Gibbons, K.A. Mitropoulos and N.B. Myant. — Amsterdam ; Oxford : Elsevier Biomedical, 1982. — xvii,369p : ill ; 25cm
Includes bibliographies and index
ISBN 0-444-80348-3 : Unpriced B82-34484

574.19'245 — Organisms. Copper proteins

Copper proteins / edited by Thomas G. Spiro. — New York ; Chichester : Wiley, c1981. — ix,363p : ill ; 24cm. — (Metal ions in biology, ISSN 0271-2911 ; v.3)
Includes index
ISBN 0-471-04400-8 : £40.50 B82-13357

574.19'245 — Organisms. Glycoproteins

Hughes, R. C.. Glycoproteins. — London : Chapman and Hall, Feb.1983. — [80]p. — (Outline studies in biology)
ISBN 0-412-24150-1 (pbk) : £2.75 : CIP entry
B82-38293

574.19'245 — Organisms. Metallothionein — *Conference proceedings*

Biological roles of metallothionein : proceedings of a USA-Japan Workshop held at the University of Cincinnati, Cincinnati, Ohio, March 22-27, 1981 / editor E.C. Foulkes. — New York ; Oxford : Elsevier/North-Holland, c1982. — xiii,327p : ill ; 24cm. — (Developments in toxicology and environmental science ; v.9)
Includes bibliographies and index
ISBN 0-444-00653-2 : £32.26 B82-11941

574.19'245 — Organisms. Proteins. Biochemistry

Structural and contractile proteins. — New York ; London : Academic Press. — (Methods in enzymology ; v.82)
Part A: Extracellular matrix / edited by Leon W. Cunningham, Dixie W. Frederiksen. — 1982. — xxiii,913p : ill ; 24cm
Includes index
ISBN 0-12-181982-5 : Unpriced B82-33520

574.19'245 — Organisms. Proteins. Interactions with lipids

Lipid-protein interactions / edited by Patricia C. Jost and O. Hayes Griffith. — New York ; Chichester : Wiley
Includes bibliographies and index
Vol.2. — c1982. — xi,307p : ill ; 24cm
ISBN 0-471-06456-4 : £54.50
Also classified at 574.19'247 B82-34337

574.19'245 — Organisms. Proteins. Interactions with nucleic acids — *Conference proceedings*

Mobility and function in proteins and nucleic acids. — London : Pitman, Dec.1982. — [320]p. — (Ciba Foundation symposium ; 93)
Conference papers
ISBN 0-272-79657-3 : £22.50 : CIP entry
Primary classification 574.87'328 B82-29636

574.19'245 — Organisms. Proteins. Microstructure. Electron microscopy

Electron microscopy of proteins / edited by James R. Harris. — London : Academic Press
Vol.1. — 1981. — x,352p : ill ; 24cm
Includes bibliographies and index
ISBN 0-12-327601-2 : £35.00 : CIP rev.
B81-25847

Electron microscopy of proteins / edited by James R. Harris. — London : Academic Press
Vol.2. — 1982. — x,315p : ill ; 24cm
Bibliography: p303-305. — Includes index
ISBN 0-12-327602-0 : £30.00 : CIP rev.
B81-36063

574.19'245 — Organisms. Proteins. Structure — *Conference proceedings*

Molecular approaches to gene expression and protein structure / edited by M.A.Q. Siddiqui, Manuel Krauskopf, Herbert Weissbach. — New York ; London : Academic Press, 1981. — xiii,371p : ill ; 24cm
Conference papers. — Includes index
ISBN 0-12-641820-9 : £18.00
Primary classification 574.87'322 B82-04219

574.19'247 — Organisms. Lipids

Progress in lipid research. — Vol.18. — Oxford : Pergamon, Aug.1981. — [243]p
ISBN 0-08-027129-4 : £32.00 : CIP entry
B81-23789

574.19'247 — Organisms. Lipids. Interactions with proteins

Lipid-protein interactions / edited by Patricia C. Jost and O. Hayes Griffith. — New York ; Chichester : Wiley
Includes bibliographies and index
Vol.2. — c1982. — xi,307p : ill ; 24cm
ISBN 0-471-06456-4 : £54.50
Primary classification 574.19'245 B82-34337

574.19'247046'028 — Organisms. Lipids. Chemical analysis. Laboratory techniques

Lipids / edited by John M. Lowenstein. — New York ; London : Academic Press
Pt.D. — 1981. — xxvi,842p : ill ; 24cm. — (Methods in enzymology ; v.72)
Includes index
ISBN 0-12-181972-8 : £43.00 B82-15468

574.19'24'705 — Organisms. Lipids — *Serials*

Progress in lipid research. — Vol.19. — Oxford : Pergamon, Dec.1981. — [230]p
ISBN 0-08-021000-7 : £38.00 : CIP entry
B81-34221

574.19'25 — Biology. Enzymology

Price, Nicholas C.. Fundamentals of enzymology / by Nicholas C. Price and Lewis Stevens. — Oxford : Oxford University Press, 1982. — xvi,454p : ill ; 24cm. — (Oxford science publications)
Includes index
ISBN 0-19-857175-5 (cased) : £25.00 : CIP rev.
ISBN 0-19-857176-3 (pbk) : £12.50
B82-01110

Royer, G. P.. Fundamentals of enzymology : rate enhancement, specificity, control and applications / G.P. Royer. — New York ; Chichester : Wiley, c1982. — xii,232p : ill ; 24cm
Includes index
ISBN 0-471-04675-2 : Unpriced B82-23947

574.19'25 — Enzymes. Inhibitors — *Lists*

Jain, Mahendra Kumar. Handbook of enzyme inhibitors (1965-1977) / Mahendra Kumar Jain. — New York ; Chichester : Wiley, c1982. — ix,447p : ill ; 29cm
ISBN 0-471-86727-6 : £73.50 B82-37996

574.19'25 — Organisms. Enzymes

The **Enzymes** / edited by Paul D. Boyer. — 3rd ed. — New York ; London : Academic Press
Previous ed.: 1959-1963. — Includes index
Vol.14: Nucleic acids. Pt.A. — 1981. — xviii,655p : ill ; 24cm
ISBN 0-12-122714-6 : £49.60 B82-36385

The **Enzymes** / edited by Paul D. Boyer. — 3rd ed. — New York ; London : Academic Press
Previous ed.: 1959-1963. — Includes index
Vol.15: Nucleic acids. Pt.B. — 1982. — xiii,659p : ill ; 24cm
ISBN 0-12-122715-4 : Unpriced B82-36386

Hammes, Gordon G.. Enzyme catalysis and regulation / Gordon G. Hammes. — New York ; London : Academic, 1982. — x,263p : ill ; 24cm. — (Molecular biology)
Includes index
ISBN 0-12-321960-4 (cased) : Unpriced
ISBN 0-12-321962-0 (pbk) : Unpriced
B82-38079

574.19'25 — Organisms. Enzymes. Biochemistry. Immunochemical techniques

Immunochemical techniques. — New York ; London : Academic Press. — (Methods in enzymology ; v.74)
Part C / edited by John J. Langone, Helen Van Vunakis. — 1981. — xxiv,729p : ill ; 24cm
Includes index
ISBN 0-12-181974-4 : Unpriced B82-33518

Immunochemical techniques / edited by John J. Langone, Helen Van Vunakis. — New York ; London : Academic Press
Pt.B. — New York ; London : Academic Press. — xxii,739p : ill ; 24cm
ISBN 0-12-181973-6 : Unpriced B82-07863

574.19'25 — Organisms. Isoenzymes

Moss, D. W.. Isoenzymes / D.W. Moss. — London : Chapman and Hall, 1982. — ix,204p : ill ; 25cm
Bibliography: p185-198. — Includes index
ISBN 0-412-22200-0 : Unpriced : CIP rev.
B82-12328

574.19'256 — Organisms. Proteinases

Proteolytic enzymes. — New York ; London : Academic Press. — (Methods in enzymology ; v.80)
Part C / edited by Laszlo Lorand. — 1981. — xxvii,919p : ill ; 24cm
Includes index
ISBN 0-12-181980-9 : Unpriced B82-33519

574.19'256 — Organisms. Proteinases - *Conference proceedings*

Proteinases and their inhibitors. — Oxford : Pergamon, June 1981. — [500]p
Conference papers
ISBN 0-08-027377-7 : £33.00 : CIP entry
B81-09490

574.19'258 — Biochemistry. Oxidation & reduction — *Conference proceedings*

International Symposium on Oxidases and Related Redox Systems *(3rd : 1979 : State University of New York)*. Oxidases and related redox systems. — Oxford : Pergamon, Oct.1981. — 2v.[(1250p.)]. — (Advances in the biosciences ; v.33 and 34)
ISBN 0-08-024421-1 : £125.00 : CIP entry
B81-28187

574.19'258 — Organisms. Cytochrome oxidases

Wikström, Mårten. Cytochrome oxidase : a synthesis / Mårten Wikström, Klaas Krab and Matti Saraste. — London : Academic Press, 1981. — xi,198p : ill ; 24cm
Bibliography: p174-189. — Includes index
ISBN 0-12-752020-1 : £14.60 : CIP rev.
B81-31352

574.19'258 — Organisms. Superoxides & superoxide dismutases — *Conference proceedings*

Biological and clinical aspects of superoxide and superoxide dismutase : proceedings of the Federation of European Biochemical Societies symposium no.62 / editors W.H. Bannister, J.V. Bannister ; organizing committee J.V. Bannister ... [et al.]. — New York ; Oxford : Elsevier/North-Holland, c1980. — ix,434p : ill ; 25cm. — (Developments in biochemistry ; v.11B)
Includes index
ISBN 0-444-00443-2 : Unpriced B82-34317

Chemical and biochemical aspects of superoxide and superoxide dismutase : proceedings of the Federation of European Biochemical Societies symposium no.62 / editors J.V. Bannister, H.A.O. Hill ; organizing committee, J.V. Bannister ... [et al.]. — New York ; Oxford : Elsevier/North-Holland, c1980. — ix,414p : ill ; 25cm. — (Developments in biochemistry ; v.11A)
Includes index
ISBN 0-444-00442-4 : Unpriced B82-34316

574.19'282 — Organisms. Chemical compounds. Molecules. Stereochemistry — *Conference proceedings*

Steric effects in biomolecules. — Oxford : Elsevier Scientific, June 1982. — [400]p. — (Studies in physical and theoretical chemistry ; 18)
Conference papers
ISBN 0-444-99693-1 : £50.00 : CIP entry
B82-21769

574.1'9285 — Biochemistry. Affinity chromatography — *Conference proceedings*

Affinity chromatography and related techniques : theoretical aspects/industrial and biomedical applications : proceedings of the 4th international Symposium, Veldhoven, The Netherlands, June 22-26, 1981 / edited by T.C.J. Gribnau, J. Visser and R.J.F. Nivard. — Amsterdam ; Oxford : Elsevier Scientific, 1982. — xviii,584p : ill ; 25cm. — (Analytical chemistry symposia series ; v.9)
Includes index
ISBN 0-444-42031-2 (corrected) : £41.05 : CIP rev.
B81-33644

574.19'285 — Biochemistry. Chemical analysis. Laboratory techniques

Evaluation of analytical methods in biological systems. — Oxford : Elsevier Scientific
Pt. A: Analysis of biogenic amines. — Sept.1982. — [300]p. — (Techniques and instrumentation in analytical chemistry ; v.4)
ISBN 0-444-42110-6 : CIP entry B82-21767

574.19′285 — Biochemistry. Mass spectrometry — *Conference proceedings*

Chemical Society Symposium on Advances in Mass Spectrometry Soft Ionization Methods *(1980 : London).* Soft ionization biological mass spectrometry : proceedings of the Chemical Society Symposium on Advances in Mass Spectrometry Soft Ionization Methods, London, July 1980 / edited by H.R. Morris. — London : Heyden, c1981. — xii,156p : ill,1map ; 24cm
Includes index
ISBN 0-85501-706-6 : Unpriced : CIP rev.
B81-36990

International Symposium on Mass Spectrometry in Biochemistry, Medicine and Environmental Research *(7th : 1980 : Milan).* Recent developments in mass spectrometry in biochemistry, medicine and environmental research, 7 : proceedings of the 7th International Symposium on Mass Spectrometry in Biochemistry, Medicine and Environmental Research, Milan, 16-18 June, 1980 / edited by Alberto Frigerio. — Amsterdam ; Oxford : Elsevier Scientific, 1981. — ix,360p : ill ; 25cm. — (Analytical chemistry symposia series ; v.7)
Includes index
ISBN 0-444-42029-0 : £36.96 : CIP rev.
B81-30197

574.19′29 — Biologically active compounds. Synthesis — *Conference proceedings*

International Kyoto Conference on New Aspects of Organic Chemistry *(1st : 1980).* New synthetic methodology and biologically active substances : proceedings of the 1st International Kyoto Conference on New Aspects of Organic Chemistry / edited by Zen-ichi Yoshida. — Tokyo : Kodansho ; Amsterdam ; Oxford : Elsevier Scientific, 1981. — x,281p : ill ; 26cm. — (Studies in organic chemistry ; 6)
Includes index
ISBN 0-444-99742-3 : Unpriced B82-01653

574.19′29 — Natural products. Biosynthesis

Thomas, Robert, *1927-.* The chemistry of life / Robert Thomas. — [Guildford] ([Guildford, Surrey GU2 5XH]) : [University of Surrey], [1978?]. — 34p : ill,1port ; 21cm. — (University of Surrey inaugural lecture)
Cover title
Unpriced (pbk) B82-26653

574.19′29 — Natural products. Biosynthesis. Mechanisms

Torssell, Kurt. Natural product chemistry. — Chichester : Wiley, Feb.1983. — [432]p
ISBN 0-471-10378-0 (cased) : £23.00 : CIP entry
ISBN 0-471-10379-9 (pbk) : £9.50 B82-38707

574.19′29 — Secondary metabolites. Biosynthesis

Herbert, R. B. (Raymond Breckon). The biosynthesis of secondary metabolites / R.B. Herbert. — London : Chapman and Hall, 1981. — ix,178p : ill ; 22cm
Includes index
ISBN 0-412-16370-5 (cased) : £14.00 : CIP rev.
ISBN 0-412-16380-2 (pbk) : Unpriced
B81-14855

574.19′296 — Organisms. Eukaryotic cells. Proteins. Biosynthesis — *Conference proceedings*

Protein biosyntheses in eukaryotes / [proceedings of a NATO advanced study institute on protein biosynthesis in eukaryotes, held in Maratea, Italy, September 7-17, 1980] ; edited by R. Pérez-Bercoff. — New York ; London : Plenum published in cooperation with NATO Scientific Affairs Division, c1982. — xviii,501p : ill ; 26cm. — (NATO advanced study institute series. Series A, Life sciences)
Includes bibliographies and index
ISBN 0-306-40893-7 : Unpriced B82-31530

574.19′296 — Proteins. Biosynthesis

Jackson, R. J.. Protein biosynthesis / R.J. Jackson. — Burlington, N.C. : Carolina Biological Supply Co., Scientific Publications Division, c1978 ; Chichester : Distributed by Packard. — 32p : ill(some col.) ; 25cm. — (Carolina biology readers ; 86)
Bibliography: p32
ISBN 0-89278-286-2 (unbound) : £1.35
B82-31601

574.2 — ORGANISMS. DISEASES

574.2′34 — Organisms. Virus diseases. Diagnosis

Comparative diagnosis of viral diseases / edited by Edouard Kurstak and Christine Kurstak. — New York ; London : Academic Press
Vol.3: Vertebrate animal and related viruses
Part A: DNA viruses. — 1981. — xvi,429p : ill,1map,1facsim ; 24cm
Includes bibliographies and index
ISBN 0-12-429703-x : £35.80 B82-18354

Comparative diagnosis of viral diseases. — New York ; London : Academic Press
Vol.4: Vertebrate animal and related viruses. Pt.B—RNA viruses / edited by Edouard Kurstak, Christine Kurstak. — 1981. — xxii,694p : ill ; 24cm
Includes bibliographies and index
ISBN 0-12-429704-8 : £52.20 B82-12303

574.2′9 — Immunochemistry

Antibody as a tool : the applications of immunochemistry. — Chichester : Wiley, Aug.1982. — [624]p
ISBN 0-471-10084-6 : £26.00 : CIP entry
B82-15814

Johnstone, Alan. Immunochemistry in practice / Alan Johnstone, Robin Thorpe. — Oxford : Blackwell Scientific, 1982. — xii,298p : ill ; 24cm
Bibliography: p289-292. — Includes index
ISBN 0-632-00836-9 (pbk) : £9.80 : CIP rev.
B82-07127

574.2′9 — Immunocytochemistry

Immunocytochemistry. — Bristol : J. Wright, Jan.1983. — [400]p
ISBN 0-7236-0669-2 : £25.00 : CIP entry
B82-35206

Techniques in immunocytochemistry. — London : Academic Press
Vol.1 / edited by Gillian R. Bullock and Peter Petrusz. — 1982. — xii,306p,[3]p of plates : ill (some col.) ; 24cm
Includes bibliographies and index
ISBN 0-12-140401-3 : £24.00 : CIP rev.
B82-06221

574.2′9 — Immunogenetics — *Conference proceedings*

Frontiers in immunogenetics : proceedings of a symposium in honor of Professor Ray D. Owen with contributions from former students and colleagues held at the California Institute of Technology, Pasadena, California, June 2 and 3, 1980 / editor William H. Hildemann. — New York ; Oxford : Elsevier/North Holland, c1981. — 268p : ill,ports ; 24cm
Includes bibliographies and index
ISBN 0-444-00624-9 : Unpriced B82-00804

Mid-West Autumn Immunology Conference *(8th : 1979 : Detroit).* Immunoglobulin genes and B cell differentiation : proceedings of the 8th annual Mid-West Autumn Immunology Conference, Detroit, Michigan, U.S.A., November 4-6, 1979 / editors Jack R. Battisto and Katherine L. Knight. — New York ; Oxford : Elsevier/North-Holland, c1980. — xi,212p : ill ; 25cm. — (Developments in immunology ; v.12)
Includes index
ISBN 0-444-00580-3 : £18.97 B82-38488

574.2′9 — Immunology

Cooper, Edwin L.. General immunology / by Edwin L. Cooper. — Oxford : Pergamon, 1982. — xii,343p : ill ; 25cm. — (Pergamon international library)
Bibliography: p325-330. — Includes index
ISBN 0-08-026368-2 (cased) : Unpriced : CIP rev.
ISBN 0-08-026369-0 (pbk) : £12.00
B81-20617

Kirkwood, Eve M.. An introduction to practical immunology. — Chichester : Wiley, June 1982. — [200]p. — (A Wiley medical publiction)
ISBN 0-471-10529-5 (pbk) : £7.50 : CIP entry
B82-22773

574.3 — ORGANISMS. DEVELOPMENT

574.3 — Organisms. Development

McFarland, David. Functional ontogeny. — London : Pitman, Sept.1982. — [204]p. — (Research notes in animal behaviour ; v.1)
ISBN 0-273-08545-x (pbk) : £9.00 : CIP entry
B82-21081

Saunders, John W.. Developmental biology : patterns, problems, principles / John W. Saunders, Jr. — New York : Macmillan ; London : Collier Macmillan, c1982. — xii,559p : ill ; 25cm
Includes bibliographies and index
ISBN 0-02-406370-3 : £16.95 B82-29749

574.3 — Organisms. Development. Genetic aspects

Stewart, Alistair D.. The genetic basis of development / Alistair D. Stewart and David M. Hunt. — Glasgow : Blackie, 1982. — ix,221p : ill ; 22cm. — (Tertiary level biology)
Bibliography: p200-214. — Includes index
ISBN 0-216-91161-3 (cased) : £18.95 : CIP rev.
ISBN 0-216-91160-5 (pbk) : £8.95 B81-27429

574.3 — Organisms. Patterns. Development — *Conference proceedings*

Theories of biological pattern formation : a Royal Society discussion held on 25 and 26 March 1981 / organized by S. Brenner, J.D. Murray and L. Wolpert. — London : Royal Society, 1981. — 191p,[4]p of plates : ill ; 31cm
Includes bibliographies
ISBN 0-85403-176-6 : £23.00 B82-05592

574.3′0724 — Organisms. Patterns. Development. Mathematical models

Meinhardt, Hans. Models of biological pattern formation. — London : Academic Press, Oct.1982. — [275]p
ISBN 0-12-488620-5 : CIP entry B82-24944

574.3′2 — Organisms. Gametes. Genetic aspects — *Conference proceedings*

Genetic control of gamete production and function. — London : Academic Press, July 1982. — [300]p. — (Serono clinical colloquia on reproduction ; 3)
ISBN 0-12-790947-8 : CIP entry B82-14225

574.5 — ECOLOGY

574.5 — Ecology

Conceptual issues in ecology / edited by Esa Saarinen. — Dordrecht ; London : Reidel, c1982. — vii,374p ; 23cm. — (A Pallas paperback ; 23)
Includes bibliographies and index
ISBN 90-277-1391-x (pbk) : Unpriced
B82-34544

Handbook of contemporary developments in world ecology / edited by Edward J. Kormondy and J. Frank McCormick. — Westport ; London : Greenwood Press, 1981. — xxviii,776p : ill ; 25cm
Includes bibliographies and index
ISBN 0-313-21381-x : Unpriced B82-18018

574.5 — Ecology. Biochemical aspects

Harborne, J. B.. Introduction to ecological biochemistry / J.B. Harborne. — 2nd ed. — London : Academic Press, 1982. — xvi,278p : ill ; 24cm
Previous ed.: 1977. — Includes bibliographies and index
ISBN 0-12-324680-6 (cased) : £12.30 : CIP rev.
ISBN 0-12-324682-2 (pbk) : Unpriced
B81-36066

574.5 — Ecology. Biochemical aspects — *Serials*

Chemistry in ecology. — Vol.1, no.1 (1982)-. — New York ; London : Gordon and Breach, 1982-. — v. : ill ; 23cm
Quarterly
ISSN 0275-7540 = Chemistry in ecology : Unpriced B82-25475

574.5 — Ecosystems
Tivy, Joy. Biogeography : a study of plants in the ecosphere / Joy Tivy. — 2nd ed. — London : Longman, 1982. — xvii,459p : ill,maps ; 22cm
Previous ed.: Edinburgh : Oliver and Boyd, 1971. — Includes bibliographies and index
ISBN 0-582-30009-6 (pbk) : £6.95 : CIP rev. B81-28110

574.5 — Environment. Chemical constituents
Fergusson, J. E.. Inorganic chemistry and the earth. — Oxford : Pergamon, Nov.1982. — [400]p. — (Pergamon series on environmental science) (Pergamon international library)
ISBN 0-08-023995-1 (cased) : £20.00 : CIP entry
ISBN 0-08-023994-3 (pbk) : £9.95 B82-29852

574.5 — Environment. Chemical constituents — *Serials*
Environmental chemistry. — Vol.2. — London : Royal Society of Chemistry, Mar.1982. — [280]p. — (Specialist periodical report / Royal Society of Chemistry)
ISBN 0-85186-765-0 : CIP entry
ISSN 0305-7712 B82-03378

574.5'03'21 — Ecology — *Encyclopaedias*
Lincoln, R. J.. A dictionary of ecology. — Cambridge : Cambridge University Press, Oct.1982. — [305]p
ISBN 0-521-23957-5 : £25.00 : CIP entry B82-29381

574.5'05 — Ecology — *Serials*
Advances in ecological research. — Vol.12. — London : Academic Press, Mar.1982. — [250]p
ISBN 0-12-013912-x : CIP entry B82-00326

574.5'072 — Ecology. Research. Use of radioisotopes
Schultz, Vincent. Radioecological techniques / Vincent Schultz and F. Ward Whicker. — New York ; London : Plenum, c1982. — xi,298p : ill ; 24cm
Bibliography: p261-292. — Includes index
ISBN 0-306-40797-3 : Unpriced B82-25808

574.5'0724 — Ecology. Mathematical models
Application of ecological modelling in environmental management. — Oxford : Elsevier Scientific
Part A. — Jan.1983. — [800]p. — (Developments in environmental modelling ; v.4A)
ISBN 0-444-42155-6 B82-37630

574.5'076 — Ecology — *Questions & answers*
Brewer, Richard. Laboratory and field manual of ecology / Richard Brewer, Margaret T. McCann. — Philadelphia ; London : Saunders College, c1982. — ix,269p : ill,forms ; 28cm
Text, index on covers. — Includes bibliographies and index
ISBN 0-03-057879-5 (pbk) : Unpriced B82-33168

574.5'0912 — Mediterranean climatic regions. Ecosystems
Money, D. C.. Mediterranean environments / D.C. Money. — London : Evans, 1982. — 48p : ill,maps ; 21cm. — (Environmental systems)
Bibliography: p45
ISBN 0-237-29271-8 (pbk) : Unpriced B82-18293

574.5'0912 — Mediterranean climatic regions. Ecosystems — *Conference proceedings*
International Symposium on Photosynthesis, Primary Production and Biomass Utilization in Mediterranean-type Ecosystems *(1980 : Kassandra)*. Components of productivity of Mediterranean-climate regions : basic and applied aspects : proceedings of the International Symposium on Photosynthesis, Primary Production and Biomass Utilization in Mediterranean-type Ecosystems, held in Kassandra, Greece, September 13-15, 1980 / edited by N.S. Margaris and H.A. Mooney. — The Hague ; London : Junk, 1981. — viii,279p : ill ; 27cm. — (Tasks for vegetation science ; 4)
Includes bibliographies
ISBN 90-619-3944-5 : Unpriced
ISBN 90-619-3897-x (set) : Unpriced B82-05350

574.5'0995 — New Guinea. Organisms. Ecology
Biogeography and ecology of New Guinea / edited by J.L. Gressitt. — The Hague ; London : Junk, 1982. — 2v.(983p) : ill,maps ; 25cm. — (Monographiae biologicae ; v.42)
Includes bibliographies and index
ISBN 90-619-3094-4 : Unpriced
Also classified at 574.995 B82-11236

574.5'2 — Earth. Carbon cycle. Mathematical models — *Conference proceedings*
Carbon cycle modelling / edited by Bert Bolin. — Chichester : Published on behalf of the Scientific Committee on Problems of the Environment (SCOPE) of the International Council of Scientific Unions (ICSU) by Wiley, c1981. — xiv,390p : ill ; 24cm. — (SCOPE ; 16)
Conference papers. — Includes bibliographies and index
ISBN 0-471-10051-x : £18.95 : CIP rev. B81-20564

574.5'222 — Ecosystems. Effects of stress — *Conference proceedings*
Stress effects on natural ecosystems / edited by Gary W. Barrett and Rutger Rosenberg. — Chichester : Wiley, c1981. — xviii,305p : ill ; 24cm. — (Environmental monographs and symposia)
Conference papers. — Includes bibliographies and index
ISBN 0-471-27834-3 : £19.50 : CIP rev. B81-02106

574.5'222 — Hydroelectric power industries. Ecological aspects
Langford, T. E.. Electricity generation and the ecology of natural waters. — Liverpool : Liverpool University Press, Oct.1982. — [376]p
ISBN 0-85323-334-9 (pbk) : £18.50 : CIP entry B82-24265

574.5'222 — North America. Ecosystems. Effects of fires
Wright, Henry A.. Fire ecology : United States and southern Canada / Henry A. Wright and Arthur W. Bailey. — New York ; Chichester : Wiley, c1982. — xxi,501p : ill ; 24cm
Includes bibliographies and index
ISBN 0-471-09033-6 : £33.25 B82-28943

574.5'222 — Organisms. Effects of climatic changes
Ford, Michael J. (Michael John). The changing climate : responses of the natural fauna and flora / Michael J. Ford. — London : Allen and Unwin, 1982. — 190p : ill,maps ; 24cm
Bibliography: p155-174. — Includes index
ISBN 0-04-574017-8 : Unpriced : CIP rev. B82-00895

574.5'222'091813 — Northern hemisphere. Ecosystems. Effects of fires — *Conference proceedings*
The **Role** of fire in northern circumpolar ecosystems. — Chichester : Wiley, Feb.1983. — [350]p. — (SCOPE ; 18)
Conference papers
ISBN 0-471-10222-9 : £24.00 : CIP entry B82-38278

574.5'222'09424 — England. Severn Estuary. Ecosystems. Effects of proposed tidal power barrages
Mitchell, R.. The natural environment : Severn tidal power / R. Mitchell & P.K. Probert ; report ... commissioned by the United Kingdom Atomic Energy Authority ... — [Shrewsbury] : Nature Conservancy Council, 1981. — 27p : ill,maps ; 30cm
Bibliography: p26-27
ISBN 0-86139-148-9 (pbk) : Unpriced B82-02084

574.5'223 — Ecosystems. Effects of extinction of organisms
Ehrlich, Paul R.. Extinction : the causes and consequences of the disappearance of species / Paul and Anne Ehrlich. — London : Gollancz, 1982, c1981. — xiv,305p ; 24cm
Includes index
ISBN 0-575-03114-x : £9.95 : CIP rev. B82-04610

574.5'223 — Ecosystems. Influence of man — *For schools*
Tivy, Joy. Human impact on the ecosystem / Joy Tivy, Greg O'Hare ; maps and diagrams drawn by Ann Rooke and Andy Skinner. — Edinburgh : Oliver & Boyd, c1981. — 243p,[4]p of plates : ill,maps(some col.) ; 24cm. — (Conceptual frameworks in geography)
Bibliography: p227-235. — Includes index
ISBN 0-05-003424-3 (cased) : Unpriced : CIP rev.
ISBN 0-05-003203-8 (pbk) : £4.95 B81-25786

574.5'223 — Environment. Role of microorganisms
Burdick, Eric. Invisible life. — London : Macmillan, Sept.1981. — [192]p
ISBN 0-333-29142-5 : £6.95 : CIP entry B81-23943

574.5'24 — Organisms. Competition. Ecological aspects
Pontin, A. J.. Competition and coexistence of species / A.J. Pontin. — Boston, Mass. ; London : Pitman Advanced Publishing Program, c1982. — vii,102p : ill ; 24cm
Includes bibliographies and index
ISBN 0-273-08489-5 : Unpriced : CIP rev. B81-35777

Tilman, David. Resource competition and community structure / David Tilman. — Princeton ; Guildford : Princeton University Press, c1982. — xi,296p ; 23cm
Bibliography: p273-290. — Includes index
ISBN 0-691-08301-0 (cased) : £19.40
ISBN 0-691-08302-9 (pbk) : Unpriced B82-40618

574.5'247 — Ecological commnunities — *Festschriften*
Ecology and evolution of communities / Martin L. Cody and Jared M. Diamond, editors. — Cambridge, Mass. ; London : Belknap Press of Harvard University Press, c1975 (1979 printing). — xii,545p : ill,maps,1port ; 23cm
Conference papers. — Includes bibliographies and index
ISBN 0-674-22446-9 (pbk) : £8.75 B82-26460

574.5'247'01519535 — Ecological communities. Data. Multivariate analysis
Gauch, Hugh G.. Multivariate analysis in community ecology / Hugh G. Gauch, Jr. — Cambridge : Cambridge University Press, 1982. — x,298p : ill ; 24cm. — (Cambridge studies in ecology)
Bibliography: p248-294. — Includes index
ISBN 0-521-23820-x (cased) : £20.00
ISBN 0-521-28240-3 (pbk) : £7.95 B82-24435

574.5'248'0724 — Organisms. Population. Dynamics. Mathematical models
Hoppensteadt, Frank C.. Mathematical methods of population biology / Frank C. Hoppensteadt. — Cambridge : Cambridge University Press, 1982. — viii,149p : ill ; 23cm. — (Cambridge studies in mathematical biology ; 4)
Bibliography: p141-143. — Includes index
ISBN 0-521-23846-3 (cased) : £15.00
ISBN 0-521-28256-x (pbk) : £6.50 B82-20994

Nisbet, R. M.. Modelling fluctuating populations / R.M. Nisbet and W.S.C. Gurney. — Chichester : Wiley, 1982. — xiii,379p : ill ; 23cm
Bibliography: p361-370. — Includes index
ISBN 0-471-28058-5 : £19.50 : CIP rev. B81-34412

574.5'248'0724 — Organisms. Population. Dynamics. Mathematical models: Differential equations
Differential equations and applications in ecology, epidemics, and population problems / edited by Stavros N. Busenberg, Kenneth L. Cooke. — New York ; London : Academic Press, 1981. — xv,359p : ill ; 24cm
Conference papers. — Includes index
ISBN 0-12-148360-6 : £22.80 B82-21253

574.5'249 — Parasites — *Conference proceedings*

International Congress of Parasitology *(5th : 1982 : Toronto)*. Parasites : their world and ours : proceedings of the Fifth International Congress of Parasitology held in Toronto, Canada, on 7-14 August 1982 / under the auspices of the World Federation of Parasitologists ; editors D.F. Mettrick and S.S. Desser. — Amsterdam ; Oxford : Elsevier Biomedical, 1982. — xiii,465p : ill ; 25cm
Includes index
ISBN 0-444-80433-1 : £31.65 B82-38194

574.5'249 — Parasitology

Modern parasitology. — Oxford : Blackwell Scientific, Aug.1982. — [352]p
ISBN 0-632-00612-9 (pbk) : £13.50 : CIP entry B82-17936

Trends and perspectives in parasitology / edited by D.W.T. Crompton and B.A. Newton. — Cambridge : Cambridge University Press
2. — c1982. — viii,91p : ill,1map ; 27cm
Includes bibliographies
ISBN 0-521-24830-2 (cased) : £8.50 : CIP rev.
ISBN 0-521-28989-0 (pbk) : £3.95
ISSN 0260-6763 B82-11510

574.5'263 — Aquatic ecosystems

Angel, Heather. The family water naturalist / Heather Angel & Pat Wolseley ; photography by Heather Angel. — London : Joseph, 1982. — 192p : ill(some col.),maps(some col.) ; 30cm
Bibliography: p188. — Includes index
ISBN 0-7181-1912-6 : £9.95 B82-29701

574.52'63 — Aquatic ecosystems. Effects of toxic materials — *Conference proceedings*

Ecotoxicology and the aquatic environment. — Oxford : Pergamon, Dec.1981. — [100]p. — (Water science and technology)
Conference papers
ISBN 0-08-029092-2 : £17.50 : CIP entry B81-32040

574.5'2632 — Freshwater ecosystems

Cole, Gerald A.. Textbook of limnology / Gerald A. Cole. — 2nd ed. — St Louis ; London : Mosby, 1979. — xvi,426p : ill ; 27cm
Previous ed.: 1975. — Bibliography: p378-402. — Includes index
ISBN 0-8016-1016-8 : £17.25 B82-38657

574.5'2632 — Swamp ecosystems

Mires. — Oxford : Elsevier Scientific. — (Ecosystems of the world ; v.4)
A: Analytical studies. — July 1982. — [450]p
ISBN 0-444-42003-7 : CIP entry
ISBN 0-444-42005-3 (set) B82-12349

574.5'2632'0967 — Africa. Tropical regions. Freshwater ecosystems

Beadle, L. C.. The inland waters of tropical Africa : an introduction to tropical limnology / L.C. Beadle. — 2nd ed. — London : Longman, 1981. — x,475p : ill,maps ; 25cm
English text, French foreword. — Previous ed.: 1974. — Bibliography: p417-462. — Includes index
ISBN 0-582-46341-6 : £22.50 : CIP rev. B81-30154

574.5'26322'094897 — Finland. Lake ecosystems — *Conference proceedings*

Lakes and water management : proceedings of the 30 years jubilee symposium of the Finnish Limnological Society, held in Helsinki, Finland, 22-23 September 1980 / edited by V. Ilmavirta, R.I. Jones and P.-E. Persson. — The Hague ; London : Junk, 1982. — ix,222p : ill,maps ; 27cm. — (Developments in hydrobiology ; 7)
"Reprinted from Hydrobiologia, Vol.86, no.1/2 (1982)". — Includes bibliographies
ISBN 90-619-3758-2 : Unpriced
Primary classification 333.91 B82-19407

574.5'26323 — Streams. Ecology

Perspectives in running water ecology / edited by Maurice A. Lock and D. Dudley Williams. — New York ; London : Plenum, c1981. — x,430p : ill,maps ; 26cm
Includes bibliographies and index
ISBN 0-306-40898-8 : Unpriced B82-17647

574.5'26325 — Marshland ecosystems

Wilson, Ron. The marshland world. — Poole : Blandford Press, Sept.1982. — [160]p
ISBN 0-7137-1199-x : £9.95 : CIP entry B82-21097

574.5'26325'09424 — England. Severn Estuary. Wetlands. Drainage. Effects of proposed tidal power barrages. Ecological aspects

Probert, P. K.. Potential effects of altered drainage patterns on freshwater wetlands : Severn tidal power / P.K. Probert ; report ... commissioned by the United Kingdom Atomic Energy Authority .. : ill. — [Shrewsbury] : Nature Conservancy Council, 1981. — 18p : maps ; 30cm
Bibliography: p15
ISBN 0-86139-149-7 (spiral) : Unpriced B82-02086

574.5'26325'0975 — South-eastern United States. Bottomland hardwood forests. Wetlands. Ecology — *Conference proceedings*

Wetlands of bottomland hardwood forests : proceedings of a workshop on bottomland hardwood forest wetlands of the southeastern United States held at Lake Lanier, Georgia June 1-5, 1980 / edited by J.R. Clark and J. Benforado. — Amsterdam ; Oxford : Elsevier Scientific, 1981. — xviii,401p : ill,maps ; 25cm. — (Developments in agricultural and managed-forest ecology ; 11)
Includes bibliographies and index
ISBN 0-444-42020-7 : £40.00 : CIP rev. B81-28179

574.5'2636 — Coastal ecosystems

Mann, K. H.. Ecology of coastal waters : a systems approach / by K.H. Mann. — Oxford : Blackwell Scientific, 1982. — x,322p : ill ; 25cm. — (Studies in ecology ; v.8)
Bibliography: p285-312. — Includes index
ISBN 0-632-00669-2 (cased) : £25.00 : CIP rev.
ISBN 0-632-00953-5 (pbk) : £10.00 B81-38291

574.5'2636 — Marine ecosystems

Barnes, R. S. K.. An introduction to marine ecology. — Oxford : Blackwell Scientific, Dec.1982. — [240]p
ISBN 0-632-00892-x (pbk) : £9.50 : CIP entry B82-30047

Estuaries and enclosed seas. — Oxford : Elsevier Scientific, Dec.1981. — [350]p. — (Ecosystems of the world ; v.26)
ISBN 0-444-41921-7 : CIP entry
Primary classification 574.5'26365 B81-31621

Marine ecology : a comprehensive, integrated treatise on life in oceans and coastal waters / editor Otto Kinne. — Chichester : Wiley
Vol.5: Ocean management
Pt.1. — 1982. — xix,642p : ill ; 26cm
Includes bibliographies and index
ISBN 0-471-27997-8 : Unpriced : CIP rev. B81-35922

574.5'2636 — Marine ecosystems. Effects of pollution of oceans by petroleum

The **Effects** of oil pollution : some research needs : a memorandum / prepared by the Marine Pollution Subcommittee of the British National Committee on Oceanic Research. — London : Royal Society, 1980. — 103p ; 21cm
Includes bibliographies
ISBN 0-85403-156-1 (pbk) : £2.25 B82-37923

574.5'2636 — Marine ecosystems. Effects of pollution of oceans by petroleum — *Conference proceedings*

The **Long-term** effects of oil pollution on marine populations, communities and ecosystems : proceedings of a Royal Society discussion meeting held on 28 and 29 October 1981 / organized by H.A. Cole and R.B. Clark ; edited by R.B. Clark. — London : Royal Society, 1982. — viii,259p : ill,maps ; 31cm
Originally published in Philosophical Transactions of the Royal Society of London. Series B, Vol.297 (no.1087) p183-443. — Includes bibliographies
ISBN 0-85403-188-x : £32.00 B82-35343

574.5'2636 — Marine organisms. Ecology

Levinton, Jeffrey S.. Marine ecology / Jeffrey S. Levinton. — Englewood Cliffs ; London : Prentice-Hall, c1982. — xv,526p : ill,maps ; 25cm
Bibliography: p461-508. — Includes index
ISBN 0-13-556852-8 : £26.95 B82-28156

574.5'2636'072041 — Marine ecosystems. Research organisations: Institute for Marine Environmental Research — *Serials*

Institute for Marine Environmental Research. IMER / Institute for Marine Environmental Research. — 1980-. — Plymouth (Prospect Place, The Hoe, Plymouth PL1 3DH) : The Institute, 1980-. — v. : ill ; 24cm
Irregular. — Continues: Institute for Marine Environmental Research. Report
ISSN 0263-4082 = IMER : Unpriced B82-19867

574.5'26365 — Estuary ecosystems

Estuaries and enclosed seas. — Oxford : Elsevier Scientific, Dec.1981. — [350]p. — (Ecosystems of the world ; v.26)
ISBN 0-444-41921-7 : CIP entry
Also classified at 574.5'2636 B81-31621

574.5'2638 — Rocky seashore. Ecology

Brehaut, Roger N.. Ecology of rocky shores / Roger N. Brehaut. — London : Edward Arnold, 1982. — 58p : ill ; 22cm. — (The Institute of Biology studies in biology, ISSN 0537-9024 ; no.139)
Bibliography: p54-55. — Includes index
ISBN 0-7131-2839-9 (pbk) : £2.25 : CIP rev. B81-30996

574.5'2638'0941 — Great Britain. Seashore ecosystems — *For schools*

Jenkins, Morton. Seashore studies. — London : Allen & Unwin, Jan.1983. — [104]p. — (Practical ecology)
ISBN 0-04-574019-4 : £3.50 : CIP entry B82-33599

574.5'2638'09415 — Ireland. Seashore ecosystems — *For schools*

O'Keefe, Ciaran. School projects in coastal ecology / Ciaran O'Keeffe. — Dublin : An Foras Forbartha, [1982]. — v,65p : ill ; 21cm
Bibliography: p63-65
ISBN 0-906120-58-6 (pbk) : £2.00(Irish) B82-40396

574.5'264 — Europe. Wall ecosystems

Darlington, Arnold. Ecology of walls / Arnold Darlington. — London : Heinemann Educational, 1981. — 138p : ill ; 24cm
Bibliography: p132. — Includes index
ISBN 0-435-60222-5 (cased) : £10.50 : CIP rev.
ISBN 0-435-60223-3 (pbk) : £4.95 B81-22635

574.5'2642 — Far East. Tropical rain forest ecosystems

Whitmore, T. C.. Tropical rain forests of the Far East. — Oxford : Clarendon Press, Nov.1982. — [296]p
Originally published: 1975
ISBN 0-19-442391-3 (pbk) : £5.95 : CIP entry B82-26215

574.5'2642 — Forest ecosystems — *For children*

Morris, Neil. Secret of the forest. — London : Hodder & Stoughton Children's Books, Feb.1983. — [32]p. — (Story facts)
ISBN 0-340-28611-3 : £1.95 : CIP entry B82-38049

574.5'2642 — Forests

The **International** book of the forest. — London : Mitchell Beazley, c1981. — 224p : ill(some col.),maps(some col.),ports (some col.) ; 30cm
Includes index
ISBN 0-85533-345-6 : £14.95 B82-02190

574.5'2642 — Forests. Biomass — *Statistics*

World forest biomass and primary production data / compiled by M.G.R. Cannell. — London : Academic Press, 1982. — viii,391p ; 26cm
Includes index
ISBN 0-12-158780-0 : £27.00 : CIP rev. B82-10419

574.5'2642 — Jungle ecosystems — *For children*
Morgan, Gillian C.. Jungles and people / Gillian Morgan. — Hove : Wayland, 1982. — 88p : ill (some col.),1col.map ; 25cm. — (Nature's landscapes)
Bibliography: p85. — Includes index
ISBN 0-85340-924-2 : £4.95 B82-33433

574.5'2642 — Woodland ecosystems
Packham, John R.. Ecology of woodland processes. — London : Edward Arnold, June 1982. — [240]p. — (Contemporary biology)
ISBN 0-7131-2834-8 (pbk) : £8.00 : CIP entry B82-09603

574.5'2642'0913 — Tropical rain forest ecosystems
Tropical rain forest ecosystems. — Oxford : Elsevier Scientific, Apr.1982. — 1v.. — (Ecosystems of the world ; v.14A)
ISBN 0-444-41986-1 : CIP entry B82-03590

574.5'2642'0913 — Tropical rain forest ecosystems — *For children*
Eden, Michael. Rain-forests / Michael Eden ; illustrated by Colin Threadgall. — London : Bodley Head, 1981. — 23p : col.ill,1col.map ; 22cm. — (A Young geographer)
Includes index
ISBN 0-370-30369-5 : £3.95 : CIP rev. B81-25769

574.5'2642'0913 — Tropical regions. Forests. Assessment — *Conference proceedings*
Conference on Forest Land Assessment and Management for Sustainable Uses *(1979 : Honolulu)*. Assessing tropical forest lands : their suitability for sustainable uses : (proceedings of the Conference on Forest Land Assessment and Management for Sustainable Uses, June 19-28, 1979, Honolulu, Hawaii) / Richard A. Carpenter, editor. — Dublin : Tycooly International, 1981. — 337p : ill,maps ; 25cm. — (Natural resources and the environment series ; v.3)
Includes bibliographies
ISBN 0-907567-02-9 (cased) : Unpriced
ISBN 0-907567-07-x (pbk) : Unpriced B82-29728

574.5'2642'0951 — China. Forests
The **Forestry** mission to China 1979. — Edinburgh : Forestry Commission, [1980]. — 94p : ill,2maps ; 21cm
Includes bibliographies
ISBN 0-85538-085-3 (pbk) : £1.50 B82-15519

574.5'2643 — Cornfield ecosystems — *For children*
Hansen, Elvig. In the cornfield / written and illustrated by Elvig Hansen ; consultant for English edition, Anthony Wootton. — Hove : Wayland, 1982. — 63p : col.ill ; 25cm
Translation from the Danish. — Includes index
ISBN 0-85340-947-1 : £4.25 B82-21939

574.5'2643 — Grassland ecosystems — *For children*
Horton, Catherine. Grasslands and people / Catherine Horton. — Hove : Wayland, 1982. — 90p : ill(some col.),1facsim,1col.map ; 25cm. — (Nature's landscapes)
Bibliography: p88. — Includes index
ISBN 0-85340-925-0 : £4.95 B82-33434

574.5'2643 — Great Britain. Hedgerows
Streeter, David. Discovering hedgerows / David Streeter, Rosamond Richardson. — London : British Broadcasting Corporation, 1982. — 160p : ill(some col.) ; 26cm
Bibliography: p153-154. — Includes index
ISBN 0-563-16452-2 (cased) : £10.50
ISBN 0-563-16528-6 (pbk) : £5.95 B82-24408

574.5'2643'0912 — Temperate regions. Grassland ecosystems
Money, D. C.. Temperate grasslands / D.C. Money. — London : Evans, 1982. — 48p : ill,maps ; 21cm. — (Environmental systems)
Bibliography: p46
ISBN 0-237-29270-x (pbk) : Unpriced B82-06667

574.5'2643'0913 — Tropical regions. Savanna ecosystems
Tropical savannas. — Oxford : Elsevier Scientific, Dec.1982. — [400]p. — (Ecosystems of the world ; 13)
ISBN 0-444-42035-5 : CIP entry B82-29807

574.5'265 — Arid region ecosystems
Money, D. C.. Arid lands / D.C. Money. — London : Evans, 1982. — 48p : ill,maps ; 21cm. — (Environmental systems)
Bibliography: p45
ISBN 0-237-29269-6 (pbk) : Unpriced B82-18287

574.5'2652 — Desert ecosystems
Louw, Gideon. Ecology of desert organisms / Gideon Louw and Mary Seely. — London : Longman, 1982. — 194p,4p of plates : ill(some col.),maps ; 24cm
Bibliography: p174-183. — Includes index
ISBN 0-582-44393-8 (pbk) : £8.50 : CIP rev. B82-06510

574.5'2652'0912 — Temperate regions. Desert ecosystems
Temperate deserts and semi-deserts. — Oxford : Elsevier Scientific, Nov.1981. — [250]p. — (Ecosystems of the world ; 5)
ISBN 0-444-41931-4 : CIP entry B81-31195

574.5'267'099435 — Island ecosystems — *Study regions: Queensland. Great Barrier Reef. One-Tree Island*
Heatwole, Harold. A coral island : the story of One Tree Island and its reef / Harold Heatwole ; based in part on manuscripts contributed by W.G. Allaway ... [et al.]. — Sydney ; London : Collins, 1981. — 200p,[16]p of plates : ill(some col.),2maps ; 23cm
Bibliography: p181-190. — Includes index
ISBN 0-00-216442-6 : £9.50 B82-09959

574.5'268 — Urban regions. Ecology — *Conference proceedings*
European Ecological Symposium *(2nd : 1980 : Berlin)*. Urban ecology : the second European Ecological Symposium, Berlin, 8-12 September 1980 / edited by R. Bornkamm, J.A. Lee and M.R.D. Seaward ; sponsoring societies the British Ecological Society ... [et al.]. — Oxford : Blackwell Scientific, 1982. — xiv,370p : ill,maps ; 25cm
Includes bibliographies and index
ISBN 0-632-00943-8 : £27.50 : CIP rev. B82-07128

574.5'3 — Estuaries. Organisms. Feeding behaviour — *Conference proceedings*
Feeding and survival strategies of estuarine organisms / edited by N.V. Jones and W.J. Wolff. — New York ; London : Plenum, c1981. — xi,304p : ill,maps ; 26cm. — (Marine science ; v.15)
Conference proceedings
ISBN 0-306-40813-9 : Unpriced B82-01885

574.5'3 — Food webs. Analysis. Mathematical models
Pimm, Stuart L.. Food webs. — London : Chapman & Hall, Sept.1982. — [300]p. — (Population and community biology)
ISBN 0-412-23100-x (cased) : £20.00 : CIP entry
ISBN 0-412-23110-7 (pbk) : £10.00 B82-19226

574.5'3 — Organisms. Feeding & nutrition. Evolutionary aspects
Physiological ecology : an evolutionary approach to resource use / edited by Colin R. Townsend and Peter Calow. — Oxford : Blackwell Scientific, 1981. — xi,393p : ill ; 25cm
Bibliography: p346-382. — Includes index
ISBN 0-632-00555-6 (cased) : £21.00 : CIP rev.
ISBN 0-632-00617-x (pbk) : £11.80 B81-20590

574.5'42 — Biometeorology
Tromp, S. W.. Biometeorology : the impact of the weather and climate on human and their environment (animals and plants) / S.W. Tromp. — London : Heyden, c1980. — xiv,346p : ill,maps ; 25cm. — (Heyden international topics in science)
Includes index
ISBN 0-85501-453-9 : Unpriced B82-08353

574.54'2 — Cold. Adaptation of organisms — *Conference proceedings*
International Symposium for Survival in the Cold *(1980 : Prague)*. Survival in the cold : hibernation and other adaptations : proceedings of the International Symposium for Survival in the Cold held in Prague, Czechoslovakia, July 2-5, 1980 / editors: X.J. Musacchia, L. Jansky. — New York ; Oxford : Elsevier/North Holland, c1981. — xiii,225p : ill ; 24cm
Includes bibliographies and index
ISBN 0-444-00635-4 : Unpriced B82-00805

574.5'43 — Great Britain. Organisms. Winter life — *For schools*
Bishop, O. N.. Winter biology / Owen Bishop. — Cambridge : Cambridge University Press, 1981. — 58p : ill ; 25cm
Bibliography: p58
ISBN 0-521-28176-8 (pbk) : £1.95 : CIP rev. B81-30481

574.5'43 — Seasons — *For children*
Ichikawa, Satomi. A child's book of seasons / Satomi Ichikawa. — London : Heinemann, 1975 (1982 [printing]). — 32p : col.ill ; 24x25cm
ISBN 0-434-94360-6 : £3.95 B82-27554

574.5'43'0924 — Leicestershire. Leicester. Gardens. Organisms. Seasonal variation — *Personal observations*
Owen, Jennifer. Garden life. — London : Chatto & Windus, Jan.1983. — [224]p
ISBN 0-7011-2610-8 : £8.50 : CIP entry B82-32521

574.8 — ORGANISMS. HISTOLOGY AND CYTOLOGY

574.8'028 — Organisms. Cells & tissues. Microprobe analysis — *Conference proceedings*
Conference on Techniques and Applications of Microprobe Analysis of Cells and Tissues *(1980 : Seattle)*. Microprobe analysis of biological systems / [proceedings of the Conference on Techniques and Applications of Microprobe Analysis of Cells and Tissues held in Seattle, Washington, 30 July-1 August 1980] ; edited by Thomas E. Hutchinson, Andrew P. Somlyo. — New York ; London : Academic Press, 1981. — xiii,427p : ill,ports ; 24cm
Includes bibliographies and index
ISBN 0-12-362880-6 : £23.80 B82-18680

574.8'2 — Plants. Tissues
Juniper, B. E.. Plant surfaces. — London : Edward Arnold, Dec.1982. — [128]p
ISBN 0-7131-2856-9 (pbk) : £4.95 : CIP entry B82-30203

574.8'212 — Histochemistry
Histochemistry : the widening horizons of its applications in the biomedical sciences / edited by Peter J. Stoward and Julia M. Polak. — Chichester : Wiley, c1981. — xx,293p,8p of plates : ill(some col.) ; 24cm
Includes bibliographies and index
ISBN 0-471-10010-2 : £25.00 : CIP rev. B81-30519

Horobin, Richard W.. Histochemistry : an explanatory outline of histochemistry and biophysical staining / Richard W. Horobin. — Stuttgart : Fischer ; London : Butterworths, c1982. — xi,310p : ill ; 25cm
Bibliography: p260-283. — Includes index
ISBN 0-407-00248-0 : Unpriced B82-34365

574.87 — Animals. Extracellular matrices. Cells. Structure & properties
Cell biology of extracellular matrix / edited by Elizabeth D. Hay. — New York ; London : Plenum, c1981. — xv,417p,[1]leaf of plates : ill ; 26cm
Includes bibliographies and index
ISBN 0-306-40785-x : Unpriced B82-21842

574.87 — Organisms. Cells
Bonney, Brian H.. Cell biology, level II / Brian H. Bonney. — Plymouth : Macdonald and Evans, 1982. — xv,331p,[47]p of plates : ill ; 22cm. — (The M. & E. TECbook series)
Includes index
ISBN 0-7121-0389-9 (pbk : corrected) : £4.95 B82-32788

574.87 — Organisms. Cells *continuation*

Cell biology : a comprehensive treatise / edited by David M. Prescott, Lester Goldstein. — New York ; London : Academic Press
Vol.4: Gene expression : translation and the behavior of proteins. — c1980. — xiv,496p : ill ; 24cm
Includes bibliographies and index
ISBN 0-12-289504-5 : £27.80 B82-35617

574.87'0246 — Organisms. Cells — *For technicians*

Thorpe, N. A.. Cell biology for technicians, level 2. — London : Longman, Apr.1982. — [288]p. — (Longman technician series. Mathematics & science)
ISBN 0-582-41580-2 (pbk) : £4.50 : CIP entry B82-07108

574.87'028 — Organisms. Cells. Electron microscopy. Laboratory techniques

Toner, Peter G.. Cell structure. — 3rd ed. — Edinburgh : Churchill Livingstone, Mar.1982. — [404]p
Previous ed.: 1971
ISBN 0-443-02324-7 (pbk) : £15.00 : CIP entry B82-01964

574.87'2 — Organisms. Cells. Structure

Cytoskeletal elements and plasma membrane organization / edited by George Poste and Garth L. Nicolson. — Amsterdam ; Oxford : North-Holland, 1981. — xx,349p : ill ; 25cm. — (Cell surface reviews ; v.7)
Includes bibliographies and index
ISBN 0-444-80335-1 : £49.79
ISBN 0-444-80201-0 B82-30263

Hillman, H.. The living cell : a re-examination of its fine structure / H. Hillman and P. Sartory. — Chichester : Packard, 1980. — 112p : ill ; 22cm
Bibliography: p88-97. — Includes index
ISBN 0-906527-02-3 (cased) : Unpriced
ISBN 0-906527-01-5 (pbk) : Unpriced B82-08133

574.87'32 — Chromosomes

Jones, R. N.. B. chromosomes. — London : Academic Press, Aug.1982. — [280]p
ISBN 0-12-390060-3 : CIP entry B82-15667

574.87'32 — Organisms. Cells. Nuclei

The **Cell** nucleus / edited by Harris Busch. — New York ; London : Academic Press
Vol.9: Nuclear particles
Pt.B. — 1981. — xxi,372p : ill ; 24cm
Includes index
ISBN 0-12-147609-x : £32.80 B82-15463

574.87'32 — Organisms. Cells. Nucleolus

Jordan, E. G.. The nucleolus / E.G. Jordan. — 2nd ed.(rev.). — Burlington, N.C. : Carolina Biological Supply Co., Scientific Publications Division, c1978 ; Chichester : Distributed by Packard. — 16p : ill(some col.) ; 25cm. — (Carolina biology readers ; 16)
Previous ed.: London : Oxford University Press, 1971. — Bibliography: p16
ISBN 0-89278-216-1 (unbound) : £0.80 B82-31594

574.87'32 — Organisms. Cells. Nucleolus — *Conference proceedings*

The **Nucleolus** / edited by E.G. Jordan and C.A. Cullis. — Cambridge : Cambridge University Press, 1982. — ix,218p : ill ; 24cm. — (Society for Experimental Biology seminar series ; 15)
Conference proceedings. — Includes bibliographies and index
ISBN 0-521-23734-3 : £25.00 : CIP rev.
ISBN 0-521-28189-x (pbk) : £9.95 B82-19253

574.87'32 — Organisms. Chromatin

Bradbury, E. Morton. DNA, chromatin and chromosomes. — Oxford : Blackwell Scientific Publications, June 1981. — [224]p
ISBN 0-632-00554-8 (pbk) : £8.50 : CIP entry B81-09497

574.87'322 — Chromosomes — *Conference proceedings*

Genome evolution. — London : Academic Press, Feb.1982. — [300]p. — (The Systematics Association special volume, ISSN 0309-2593 ; no.20)
Conference papers
ISBN 0-12-221380-7 (cased) : CIP entry
ISBN 0-12-221382-3 (pbk) : Unpriced B82-00157

574.87'322 — Chromosomes. HMG proteins

The **HMG** chromosomal proteins / edited by E.W. Johns. — London : Academic Press, 1982. — x,251p : ill ; 24cm
Includes bibliographies and index
ISBN 0-12-386050-4 : £19.20 : CIP rev. B82-04142

574.87'322 — Gene expression — *Conference proceedings*

Molecular approaches to gene expression and protein structure / edited by M.A.Q. Siddiqui, Manuel Krauskopf, Herbert Weissbach. — New York ; London : Academic Press, 1981. — xiii,371p : ill ; 24cm
Conference papers. — Includes index
ISBN 0-12-641820-9 : £18.00
Also classified at 574.19'245 B82-04219

574.87'322 — Genetic information. Translation. Role of metal ions

Metal ions in genetic information transfer / editors Gunther L. Eichhorn, Luigi G. Marzilli with the assistance of Patricia A. Marzilli. — New York ; Oxford : Elsevier/North-Holland, c1981. — xviii,340p,[4]p of plates : ill(some col.),1port ; 25cm. — (Advances in inorganic biochemistry ; 3)
Includes index
ISBN 0-444-00637-0 : Unpriced B82-05061

574.87'3223 — Sister chromatids. Exchanges

Sister chromatid exchange / edited by Sheldon Wolff. — New York ; Chichester : Wiley, c1982. — viii,306p : ill ; 24cm
Includes bibliographies and index
ISBN 0-471-05987-0 : £51.50 B82-25456

574.87'3224 — Genetics. Biochemical aspects

Physiological genetics / edited by John G. Scandalios. — New York ; London : Academic Press, 1979. — xii,280p : ill ; 24cm. — (Physiological ecology)
Includes index
ISBN 0-12-620980-4 : £19.60 B82-24161

574.87'328 — Molecular genetics — *Conference proceedings*

Miami Winter Symposium *(1981)*. Cellular responses to molecular modulators : proceedings of the Miami Winter Symposium, January 1981 / sponsored by the Department of Biochemistry, University of Miami School of Medicine, Miami, Florida ... and by the Papanicolaou Cancer Research Institute, Miami, Florida ... ; edited by Lee W. Mozes ... [et al.]. — New York ; London : Academic Press, 1981. — xxii,558p : ill ; 24cm. — (Miami winter symposia ; v.18)
Includes index
ISBN 0-12-509380-2 : £29.80 B82-13113

574.87'328 — Organisms. Nucleic acids. Biochemistry

The **Biochemistry** of the nucleic acids. — 9th ed / R.L.P. Adams ... [et al.]. — London : Chapman and Hall, 1981. — xiv,517p : ill ; 25cm
Previous ed.: published as Davidson's The biochemistry of the nucleic acids / by James Norman Davidson. 1976. — Includes index
ISBN 0-412-22680-4 (cased) : Unpriced : CIP rev.
ISBN 0-412-22690-1 (pbk) : £8.50 B81-15916

574.87'328 — Organisms. Nucleic acids. Interactions with proteins — *Conference proceedings*

Mobility and function in proteins and nucleic acids. — London : Pitman, Dec.1982. — [320]p. — (Ciba Foundation symposium ; 93)
Conference papers
ISBN 0-272-79657-3 : £22.50 : CIP entry
Also classified at 574.19'245 B82-29636

574.87'328 — Organisms. Nucleic acids. Sequences

Nucleic acid sequences handbook. — Eastbourne : Praeger
Vol.1. — Nov.1981. — [320]p
ISBN 0-03-060626-8 : £8.00 : CIP entry B81-31231

Nucleic acid sequences handbook. — Eastbourne : Praeger
Vol.2. — Nov.1981. — [320]p
ISBN 0-03-060627-6 : £8.00 : CIP entry B81-31232

574.87'3282 — Organisms. Cells. Genes. DNA. Transcription to RNA

Travers, A. A.. Transcription of DNA / A.A. Travers. — 2nd ed.(rev.). — Burlington, N.C. : Carolina Biological Supply Co., Scientific Publications Division, c1978 ; Chichester : Distributed by Packard. — 16p : col.ill ; 25cm. — (Carolina biology readers ; 75)
Previous ed.: London : Oxford University Press, 1974. — Bibliography: p16
ISBN 0-89278-275-7 (unbound) : £0.80 B82-31598

574.87'3282 — Organisms. DNA. Repair. Mechanisms

Chromosome damage and repair / [proceedings of a NATO Advanced Study Institute and an EMBO Lecture course on Chromosome Damage and Repair held at Godøysund Fjord Hotel, near Bergen, on May 27-June 5, 1980] ; edited by Erling Seeberg and Kjell Kleppe. — New York ; London : Plenum published in cooperation with NATO Scientific Affairs Division, c1981. — xiv,623p : ill ; 26cm. — (NATO advanced study institutes series. Series A, Life sciences ; v.40)
Includes index
ISBN 0-306-40886-4 : Unpriced B82-26797

574.87'3282 — Organisms. DNA. Replication & recombination

Whitehouse, Harold L. K.. Genetic recombination : understanding the mechanisms. — Chichester : Wiley, Nov.1982. — [350]p
ISBN 0-471-10205-9 : £25.00 : CIP entry B82-27545

574.87'3282 — Organisms. DNA. Replication & recombination — *Conference proceedings*

ICN-UCLA Symposia on Structure and DNA-Protein Interactions of Replication Origins *(1981 : Salt Lake City)*. The initiation of DNA replication / [proceedings of the 1981 ICN-UCLA Symposia on Stru[c]ture and DNA-Protein Interactions of Replication Origins held in Salt Lake City, Utah, on March 8-13, 1981] ; edited by Dan S. Ray. — New York ; London : Academic Press, 1981. — xx,628p : ill ; 24cm. — (ICN-UCLA symposia on molecular and cellular biology ; v.22)
Includes bibliographies and index
ISBN 0-12-583580-9 : Unpriced B82-28669

574.87'3282 — Organisms. Eukaryotic cells. DNA. Mutagenesis & repair — *Conference proceedings*

DND repair, chromosome alterations and chromatin structure : proceedings of an international meeting held at Noordwijkerhout, The Netherlands, 23-24 April 1981 / edited by A.T. Natarajan, G. Obe and H. Altmann. — Amsterdam ; Oxford : Elsevier Biomedical, 1982. — xv,390p : ill ; 25cm. — (Progress in mutation research ; v.4)
Includes bibliographies and index
ISBN 0-444-80367-x : £44.78 B82-30031

574.87'3282 — Organisms. Recombinant DNA — *Conference proceedings*

Cleveland Symposium on Macromolecules *(3rd : 1981)*. Recombinant DNA : proceedings of the Third Cleveland Symposium on Macromolecules, Cleveland, Ohio, 22-26 June 1981 / edited by A.G. Walton. — Amsterdam ; Oxford : Elsevier Scientific, 1981. — vii,310p : ill ; 25cm
Includes index
ISBN 0-444-42039-8 : Unpriced : CIP rev. B81-33862

574.87'3282 — Organisms. Recombinant DNA. Molecules. Cloning. Research, *to 1980*

The DNA story : a documentary history of gene cloning / [compiled by] James D. Watson, John Tooze. — Oxford : W.H. Freeman, c1981. — xii,605p,[8]p of plates : ill(some col.),facsims,ports ; 29cm
Bibliography: p589-594. — Includes index
ISBN 0-7167-1292-x : £13.95 B82-10625

574.87'3283 — Organisms. Development & reproduction. Role of RNA — *Conference proceedings*

The Role of RNA in development and reproduction : proceedings of the second international symposium, April 25-30, 1980 / edited by M.C. Niu, H.H. Chuang. — Beijing : Science Press ; New York ; London : Van Nostrand Reinhold [distributor], 1981. — xiii,932p : ill,ports ; 24cm
Includes index
ISBN 0-442-20090-0 : £51.00 B82-08238

574.87'33 — Organisms. Cells. Chloroplasts

Prebble, J. N.. Mitochondria chloroplasts and bacterial membranes / J.N. Prebble. — London : Longman, 1981. — xiv,378p : ill ; 25cm
Bibliography: p354-364. — Includes index
ISBN 0-582-44133-1 : £12.00
Primary classification 574.87'342 B82-09107

574.87'34 — Flagella

Prokaryotic and eukaryotic flagella. — Cambridge : Cambridge University Press published for the Society for Experimental Biology, 1982. — viii,632p : ill ; 24cm. — (Symposia of the Society for Experimental Biology ; no.35)
Conference proceedings. — Includes bibliographies and index
ISBN 0-521-24228-2 : £40.00 : CIP rev. B82-11516

574.87'34 — Organisms. Centrioles

Wheatley, D. N.. The centriole : a central enigma of cell biology / D.N. Wheatley. — Amsterdam ; Oxford : Elsevier Biomedical, 1982. — xiii,232p : ill ; 25cm
Bibliography: p205-224. — Includes index
ISBN 0-444-80359-9 : Unpriced B82-21628

574.87'34 — Organisms. Liposomes — *Conference proceedings*

Liposomes : from physical structure to therapeutic applications / editor C.G. Knight. — Amsterdam ; Oxford : Elsevier/North-Holland Biomedical, 1981. — xix,497p : ill ; 25cm. — (Research monographs in cell and tissue physiology ; v.7)
Includes bibliographies and index
ISBN 0-444-80320-3 : £55.43 B82-09909

Liposomes, drugs and immunocompetent cell functions / [Proceedings of a conference held 1-3 September 1980 in Grignon, France] ; edited by Claude Nicolau and Alain Paraf. — London : Academic Press, 1981. — xiv,194p : ill ; 24cm
Includes bibliographies and index
ISBN 0-12-518660-6 : £14.00 : CIP rev. B81-14885

574.87'342 — Organisms. Cells. Mitochondria

Prebble, J. N.. Mitochondria chloroplasts and bacterial membranes / J.N. Prebble. — London : Longman, 1981. — xiv,378p : ill ; 25cm
Bibliography: p354-364. — Includes index
ISBN 0-582-44133-1 : £12.00
Also classified at 574.87'33 B82-09107

Tzagoloff, Alexander. Mitochondria / Alexandra Tzagoloff. — New York ; London : Plenum, c1982. — xiv,342p ; 27cm. — (Cellular organelles)
Includes bibliographies and index
ISBN 0-306-40799-x (cased) : Unpriced
ISBN 0-306-40778-7 (pbk) : Unpriced B82-30266

574.87'342 — Organisms. Cells. Mitochondria. Biosynthesis

Chappell, J. B.. The energetics of mitochondria. — 2nd ed.(rev.) / J.B. Chappell. — Burlington, N.C. : Carolina Biological Supply Co., Scientific Publications Division, c1979 ; Chichester : Distributed by Packard. — 32p : ill(some col.) ; 25cm. — (Carolina biology readers ; 19)
Previous ed.: Published as Mitochondria. London : Oxford University Press, 1972. — Bibliography: p32
ISBN 0-89278-219-6 (unbound) : £1.35 B82-31591

574.87'342 — Organisms. Cells. Mitochondria. Inhibitors

Inhibitors of mitochondrial functions / section editors Maria Erecińska and David F. Wilson. — Oxford : Pergamon, 1981. — x,334p ; 28cm. — (International encyclopedia of pharmacology and therapeutics ; section 107)
Includes bibliographies and index
ISBN 0-08-027380-7 : £36.00 : CIP rev. B81-22565

574.87'342 — Organisms. Cells. Mitochondria. Ions & elections. Transport — *Conference proceedings*

International Symposium on Vectorial Reactions in Electron and Ion Transport in Mitochondria and Bacteria *(1981 : Selva di Fasano).* Vectorial reactions in electron and ion transport in mitochondria and bacteria : proceedings of the International Symposium on Vectorial Reactions in Electron and Ion Transport in Mitochondria and Bacteria held in Selva di Fasano (Italy), May 19-22, 1981 / editors F. Palmieri ... [et al.]. — Amsterdam ; Oxford : Elsevier-North-Holland Biomedical, 1981. — xi,429p : ill ; 25cm. — (Developments in bioenergetics and biomembranes ; v.5)
Includes index
ISBN 0-444-80372-6 : £34.63
Also classified at 589.9'0875 B82-01639

574.87'5 — Organisms. Cells. Membranes

Biological membranes. — London : Academic Press, 1982
Vol.4 / edited by Dennis Chapman. — xv,526p : ill ; 24cm
Includes bibliographies and index
ISBN 0-12-168545-4 : £36.20 : CIP rev. B82-00329

Membrane research : classic origins and current concepts / edited by A.L. Muggleton-Harris. — New York ; London : Academic Press, 1981. — xxiv,428p : ill,1port ; 24cm. — (International review of cytology. Supplement ; 12)
Includes bibliographies and index
ISBN 0-12-364373-2 : Unpriced B82-02571

574.87'5 — Organisms. Cells. Membranes — *Conference proceedings*

Membrane recycling. — London : Pitman, Oct.1982. — [320]p. — (Ciba Foundation symposium ; 92)
Conference papers
ISBN 0-272-79656-5 : £22.50 : CIP entry B82-23478

Totts Gap Colloquium on the Relation of Cell Membranes to Membrane-Bound Enzymes *(1980)* . Composition and function of cell membranes : application to the pathophysiology of muscle diseases / [an edited transcript of the Totts Gap Colloquium on the Relation of Cell Membranes to Membrane-Bound Enzymes held May 19-21, 1980 and sponsored by the Muscular Dystrophy Association] ; edited by Stewart Wolf and Allen K. Murray.. — New York ; London : Plenum, c1981. — xi,287p : ill ; 26cm. — (Advances in experimental medicine and biology ; v.140)
Bibliography: p261-282. — Includes index
ISBN 0-306-40883-x : Unpriced B82-13532

574.87'5 — Organisms. Cells. Membranes. Transport phenomena

Membranes and transport / edited by Anthony N. Martonosi. — New York ; London : Plenum
Vol.1. — c1982. — xxxiv,688p : ill ; 26cm
Includes bibliographies and index
Unpriced B82-41103

574.87'5 — Organisms. Cells. Plasma membranes

Lucy, J. A.. The plasma membrane / J.A. Lucy. — 2nd ed.(rev.). — Burlington, N.C. : Carolina Biological Supply Co., Scientific Publications Division, c1978 ; Chichester : Distributed by Packard. — 16p : ill(some col.) ; 25cm. — (Carolina biology readers ; 81)
Previous ed.: London : Oxford University Press, 1975. — Bibliography: p16
ISBN 0-89278-281-1 (unbound) : £0.80 B82-31599

574.87'5 — Organisms. Membranes. Biochemistry

Sim, E.. Membrane biochemistry. — London : Chapman and Hall, Nov.1982. — [80]p. — (Outline studies in biology)
ISBN 0-412-23810-1 (pbk) : £2.75 : CIP entry B82-28258

574.87'5 — Organisms. Membranes. Effects of low temperature — *Conference proceedings*

Effects of Low Temperatures on Biological Membranes *(Conference : Royal Free Hospital, London : 1980).* Effects of low temperatures on biological membranes / [based on a meeting 'Effects of Low Temperatures on Biological Membranes' held 25 September 1980 at the Royal Free Hospital, London, UK] ; edited by G.J. Morris, A. Clarke. — London : Academic Press, 1981. — xxii,432p : ill ; 24cm
Bibliography: p379-417. — Includes index
ISBN 0-12-507650-9 : £22.00 : CIP rev. B81-27369

574.87'5 — Organisms. Membranes. Interactions

Membranes, molecules, toxins, and cells / edited by Konrad Bloch, Liana Bolis, Daniel C. Tosteson. — Boston [Mass.] ; Bristol : John Wright, c1981. — xv,315p : ill ; 25cm
Includes index
ISBN 0-88416-309-1 : Unpriced B82-06971

574.87'5 — Organisms. Membranes. Physiology

Houslay, Miles D.. Dynamics of biological membranes. — Chichester : Wiley, Aug.1982. — [400]p
ISBN 0-471-10080-3 (cased) : £20.00 : CIP entry
ISBN 0-471-10095-1 (pbk) : £9.00 B82-15813

574.87'5 — Organisms. Receptors. Biochemical aspects

Towards understanding receptors / edited by John W. Lamble ; foreword by G. Alan Robinson. — Amsterdam ; Oxford : Elsevier/North-Holland, 1981. — xiv,232p : ill,2ports ; 24cm. — (Current reviews in biomedicine ; 1)
Includes index
ISBN 0-444-80339-4 (pbk) : £7.00 B82-39930

574.87'5'0712411 — Scotland. Secondary schools. Curriculum subjects: Biology. Concepts: Organisms. Cells. Membranes. Osmosis. Diagnostic tests

Arnold, Brian. Concept development and diagnostic testing : osmosis in 'O' grade biology / Brian Arnold, Mary Simpson. — [Aberdeen] : Aberdeen College of Education, 1982. — vi,86,[41]p : ill ; 30cm
Bibliography: p84-86
Unpriced (unbound) B82-37947

Arnold, Brian. Diagnostic testing for pupil difficulties in osmosis / B. Arnold, M. Simpson. — [Aberdeen] : Aberdeen College of Education, 1981. — 27leaves : ill ; 30cm
Unpriced (unbound) B82-37948

574.87'6 — Organisms. Cells. Analysis

Cell analysis / edited by Nicholas Catsimpoolas. — New York ; London : Plenum
Vol.1. — c1982. — xiii,336p : ill ; 24cm
Includes bibliographies and index
ISBN 0-306-40864-3 : Unpriced B82-40413

574.87'6 — Organisms. Cells. Interactions

Cellular interactions / [edited by] J.T. Dingle and J.L. Gordon. — Amsterdam ; Oxford : Elsevier/North-Holland, 1981. — xiii,295p : ill,2ports ; 25cm. — (Research monographs in cell and tissue physiology ; v.6)
Conference papers. — Includes bibliographies and index
ISBN 0-444-80330-0 : £40.78 B82-06718

574.87'6041 — Organisms. Cells. Electrical activity

Cellular pacemakers / edited by David O. Carpenter. — New York ; Chichester : Wiley
Vol.2: Function in normal and disease states. — c1982. — xii,371p : ill ; 24cm
Includes bibliographies and index
ISBN 0-471-09608-3 : £33.25 B82-26464

574.87'6041 — Organisms. Cells. Kinetics. Mathematical models — *Conference proceedings*

Biomathematics and cell kinetics : proceedings of a workshop held at Asilomar, California, 4-6 March, 1981 / edited by Manuel Rotenberg. — Amsterdam ; Oxford : Elsevier-North-Holland Biomedical, 1981. — xiv,423p : ill ; 25cm. — (Developments in cell biology ; v.8)
Includes index
ISBN 0-444-80371-8 : £33.12 B82-01636

574.87'6042 — Organisms. Cells. Biochemistry

Cohen, Annabelle. Handbook of cellular chemistry / Annabelle Cohen. — 2nd ed. — St. Louis ; London : C.V. Mosby, 1979. — xiv,226p : ill ; 25cm
Previous ed.: 1975. — Bibliography: p209-210. — Includes index
ISBN 0-8016-1006-0 (pbk) : £8.75 B82-33560

574.87'6042 — Organisms. Excitable cells. Ions. Measurement. Use of selective ion sensitive microelectrodes — *Conference proceedings*

Ion-selective microelectrodes and their use in excitable tissues / edited by Eva Syková, Pavel Hník and Ladislav Vyklický. — New York ; London : Plenum, c1981. — xi,369p : ill ; 26cm
Conference proceedings. — Includes bibliographies and index
ISBN 0-306-40723-x : Unpriced B82-01886

574.87'61 — Organisms. Cells. Energy metabolism

Reich, J. G.. Energy metabolism of the cell : a theoretical treatise / by J.G. Reich and E.E. Sel'kov. — London : Academic Press, 1981. — vii,345p : ill ; 23cm
Bibliography: p321-338. — Includes index
ISBN 0-12-585920-1 : £36.00 : CIP rev. B81-18127

574.87'61 — Organisms. Cells. Growth

Wheatley, Denys N.. Cell growth and division. — London : Edward Arnold, Nov.1982. — [64]p. — (Studies in biology ; no.148)
ISBN 0-7131-2859-3 (pbk) : £2.25 : CIP entry B82-33209

574.87'61 — Organisms. Cells. Growth — *Conference proceedings*

Cell growth / [proceedings of a Nato advanced study institute on cell growth, held October 18-31, 1980, in Erice, Sicily] ; edited by Claudio Nicolini. — New York ; London : Plenum published in cooperation with NATO Scientific Affairs Division, c1982. — xvi,821p : ill ; 26cm. — (Nato advanced study institute series. Series A, Life sciences ; v.38)
Includes index
ISBN 0-306-40815-5 : Unpriced B82-22892

574.87'61 — Organisms. Cells. Metabolism. In vitro regulation

The **Growth** requirements of vertebrate cells in vitro / edited by Charity Waymouth, Richard G. Ham, Paul J. Chapple. — Cambridge : Cambridge University Press, 1981. — xi,542p : ill ; 29cm
ISBN 0-521-23019-5 : £35.00 B82-15280

574.87'61 — Organisms. Cells. Metabolism. Regulation

NATO Advanced Study Institute on Control of the Growth and Function of Differentiated Cells by Intracellular Signals *(1980 : Nivelles).* Cell regulation by intracellular signals / [proceedings of a NATO Advanced Study Institute on Control of the Growth and Function of Differentiated Cells by Intracellular Signals, held July 14-23, 1980 in Nivelles, Belgium] ; edited by Stéphane Swillens and Jacques E. Dumont. — New York ; London : Plenum in cooperation with NATO Scientific Affairs Division, c1982. — ix,334p : ill ; 26cm. — (NATO advanced study institute series. Series A, Life Sciences ; v.44)
Includes bibliographies and index
ISBN 0-306-40980-1 : Unpriced B82-38668

574.87'61 — Organisms. Cells. Metabolism. Regulation. Role of calcium

Rasmussen, Howard. Calcium and cAMP as synarchic messengers / Howard Rasmussen. — New York ; Chichester : Wiley, c1981. — xiv,370p : ill ; 25cm
Bibliography: p319-361. — Includes index
ISBN 0-471-08396-8 : £29.25 B82-09885

Thomas, M. V.. Techniques in calcium research. — London : Academic Press, Sept.1982. — [250]p. — (Biological techniques series)
ISBN 0-12-688680-6 : CIP entry B82-18735

574.87'61 — Organisms. Cells. Metabolism. Regulation. Role of hormones — *Conference proceedings*

INSERM European Symposium on Hormones and Cell Regulation *(6th : 1981 : Bischoffsheim).* Hormones and cell regulation : proceedings of the sixth INSERM European Symposium on Hormones and Cell Regulation, held at Le Bischenberg, Bischoffsheim (France), 5-8 October, 1981 / sponsored by Institut national de la santé et de la recherche médicale ; edited by J.E. Dumont, J. Nunez and G. Schultz. — Amsterdam ; Oxford : Elsevier Biomedical, 1982. — xii,319p : ill ; 25cm. — (European symposium ; v.6)
Includes index
ISBN 0-444-80419-6 : £33.19
ISBN 0-7204-0657-9 (set) B82-36626

574.87'61 — Organisms. Stem cells

Stem cells. — Edinburgh : Churchill Livingstone, Dec.1982. — [320]p
ISBN 0-443-02451-0 : £20.00 : CIP entry B82-29803

574.87'612 — Organisms. Cells. Differentiation

Bownes, Mary. Differentiation in cells. — London : Chapman and Hall, Sept.1981. — [80]p. — (Outline studies in biology)
ISBN 0-412-22830-0 (pbk) : £2.45 : CIP entry B81-25776

574.87'612 — Organisms. Cells. Differentiation. Regulation

Regulation of growth in neoplasia / editor G.V. Sherbet. — Basel ; London : Karger, 1981. — vii,201p : ill ; 25cm
Includes bibliographies and index
ISBN 3-8055-2305-x : £34.80
Primary classification 616.99'407 B82-07726

Unilever Jubilee Symposium *(1980 : Vlaardingen)* . Cellular controls in differentiation / [based on the Unilever Jubilee Symposium held in Vlaardingen, Holland during December 1980] ; Clive W. Lloyd, David A. Rees. — London : Academic Press, 1981. — x,324p : ill ; 24cm
Includes bibliographies
ISBN 0-12-453580-1 : £12.40 : CIP rev. B81-19209

574.87'612 — Organisms. Cells. Differentiation. Role of gene expression

Gurdon, J. B.. Gene expression during cell differentiation / J.B. Gurdon. — 2nd ed.(rev.). — Burlington, N.C. : Carolina Biological Supply Co., Scientific Publications Division, c1978 ; Chichester : Distributed by Packard. — 32p : ill(some col.). — (Carolina biology readers ; 25)
Previous ed.: London : Oxford University Press, 1973. — Bibliography: p32
ISBN 0-89278-225-0 (unbound) : £1.35 B82-31596

574.87'612'028 — Organisms. Cells. Differentiation. Laboratory techniques: In vitro methods — *Conference proceedings*

British Society for Cell Biology. *Symposium (4th : 1980 : University of Edinburgh).* Differentiation in vitro / the forth symposium of the British Society for Cell Biology ; edited by M.M. Yeoman, D.E.S. Truman. — Cambridge : Cambridge University Press, 1982. — ix,286p : ill ; 24cm
Includes bibliographies and index
ISBN 0-521-23926-5 : £30.00 : CIP rev.
Primary classification 574.1'7 B81-39254

574.87'62 — Organisms. Cells. Cycles

The **Cell** cycle / edited by P.C.L. John. — Cambridge : Cambridge University Press, 1981. — vii,276p : ill ; 24cm. — (Seminar series / Society for Experimental Biology ; 10)
Includes bibliographies and index
ISBN 0-521-23912-5 (cased) : £20.00 : CIP rev.
ISBN 0-521-28342-6 (pbk) : £8.95 B81-34016

574.87'62 — Organisms. Cells. Division. Temporal regulation

Lloyd, David, *1940-*. The cell division cycle : temporal organization and control of cellular growth and reproduction / David Lloyd, Robert K. Poole, Steven W. Edwards. — London : Academic Press, 1982. — xi,523p : ill ; 24cm
Bibliography: p443-503. — Includes index
ISBN 0-12-453760-x : £38.60 : CIP rev. B81-35914

574.87'62 — Organisms. Eukaryotic cells. Reproduction

Mitosis/cytokinesis / edited by Arthur M. Zimmerman, Arthur Forer. — New York ; London : Academic Press, 1981. — xvi,479p : ill ; 24cm. — (Cell biology)
Includes bibliographies and index
ISBN 0-12-781240-7 : £36.40 B82-34644

Prescott, David M.. The reproduction of the eukaryotic cells / David M. Prescott. — Burlington, N.C. : Carolina Biological Supply Co., Scientific Publications Division, c1978 ; Chichester : Distributed by Packard. — 16p : ill(some col.) ; 25cm. — (Carolina biology readers ; 96)
Bibliography: p16
ISBN 0-89278-296-x (unbound) : £0.80 B82-31603

574.87'64 — Organisms. Cells. Chemotaxis

Biology of the chemotactic respone / edited by J.M. Lackie and P.C. Wilkinson. — Cambridge : Cambridge University Press, 1981. — xiii,177p : ill ; 24cm. — (Society for Experimental Biology seminar series ; 12) (Seminar series / Society for Experimental Biology ; 12)
Includes bibliographies and index
ISBN 0-521-23305-4 : £20.00 : CIP rev.
ISBN 0-521-29897-0 (pbk) B81-37002

574.87'64 — Organisms. Cells. Contraction & secretion. Role of calcium

Rubin, Ronald P.. Calcium and cellular secretion / Ronald P. Rubin. — New York ; London : Plenum, c1982. — xi,276p : ill ; 24cm
Bibliography: p219-264. — Includes index
ISBN 0-306-40978-x : Unpriced B82-36622

574.87'64 — Organisms. Cells. Motility — *Festschriften*

Cell behaviour : a tribute to Michael Abercrombie / edited by Ruth Bellairs, Adam Curtis, Graham Dunn. — Cambridge : Cambridge University Press, 1982. — viii,615p : ill ; 24cm
Includes bibliographies and index
ISBN 0-521-24107-3 : £45.00 : CIP rev. B82-00233

574.87'64 — Organisms. Cells. Motility — *Serials*

Cell and muscle motility. — Vol.1-. — New York ; London ([88 Middlesex St., E1 7EX]) : Plenum, 1981-. — v. : ill ; 26cm
Unpriced
Also classified at 591.1'852 B82-07633

574.87'65 — Organisms. Cells. Ageing

Aging and cell structure. — New York ; London : Plenum
Vol.1 / edited by John E. Johnson Jr. — c1981. — xvi,385p : ill ; 26cm
Includes bibliographies and index
ISBN 0-306-40695-0 : Unpriced B82-20991

574.87'65 — Organisms. Cells. Death

Cell death in biology and pathology / edited by I.D. Bowen and R.A. Lockshin. — London : Chapman and Hall, 1981. — xvii,493p : ill ; 24cm
Includes bibliographies and index
ISBN 0-412-16010-2 : £30.00 B82-17597

574.8′8 — Molecular biology — *Conference proceedings*

Structural molecular biology : methods and applications / [proceedings of a NATO Advanced study institute and FEBS Advanced Course No. 78 on current methods in structural molecular biology, held May 3-16, 1981, in Maratea, Italy] edited by David B. Davies, Wolfram Saenger and Steven S. Danyluk. — New York ; London : Plenum in cooperation with Nato Scientific Affairs Division, c1982. — x,530p : ill ; 26cm. — (NATO advanced study institutes series. Series A, Life sciences ; v.45)
Includes index
ISBN 0-306-40982-8 : Unpriced B82-36414

574.8′8′015193 — Molecular biology *expounded by* **game theory**

Eigen, Manfred. Laws of the game : how the principles of nature govern chance / by Manfred Eigen and Ruthild Winkler ; translated by Robert and Rita Kember. — London : Allen Lane, 1982, c1981. — xiv,347p : ill(some col.),music ; 22cm
Translation of: Das Spiel. — Originally published: New York : Knopf, distributed by Random House, 1980. — Includes index
ISBN 0-7139-1484-x : £14.95 B82-19052

574.8′8′0222 — Organisms. Molecules. Structure — *Illustrations*

Atlas of molecular structures in biology / edited by D.C. Phillips and F.M. Richards. — Oxford : Clarendon Press
2: Haemoglobin and myoglobin / by G. Fermi and M.F. Perutz. — 1981. — vi,104p : ill(some col.) ; 32cm + 1 stereoscopic viewer
Stereoscopic viewer in pocket. — Bibliography: p103-104
ISBN 0-19-854706-4 (spiral) : £20.00 : CIP rev. B80-39389

574.8′8′028 — Molecular biology. Laboratory techniques

Techniques in molecular biology. — London : Croom Helm, Feb.1983. — [304]p
ISBN 0-7099-2747-9 (cased) : £17.95 : CIP entry
ISBN 0-7099-2755-x (pbk) : £8.95 B82-38898

574.8′8′028 — Molecular biology. Nuclear magnetic resonance spectroscopy

Jardetzky, Oleg. NMR in molecular biology / Oleg Jardetzky, G.C.K. Roberts. — New York : London : Academic Press, 1981. — xiii,681p : ill ; 24cm. — (Molecular biology)
Bibliography: p591-635. — Includes index
ISBN 0-12-380580-5 : £39.00 B82-34858

574.8′8′05 — Molecular biology — *Serials*

The **EMBO** journal. — Vol.1, no.1 (1982)-. — Eynsham (P.O. Box 1, Eynsham, Oxford OX8 1JJ) : IRL Press for the European Molecular Biology Organization, 1982-. — v. : ill ; 28cm
Monthly
ISSN 0261-4189 = EMBO journal : £155.00 per year (£40.00 to individuals and members of EMBO) B82-20874

Molecular aspects of medicine. — Vol.3. — Oxford : Pergamon, Dec.1981. — [562]p
ISBN 0-08-028871-5 : £47.00 : CIP entry B81-32039

Molecular aspects of medicine. — Vol.4. — Oxford : Pergamon, Sept.1982. — [457]p
ISBN 0-08-030007-3 : £75.00 : CIP entry B82-21079

574.9 — BIOLOGY. GEOGRAPHICAL TREATMENT

574.9 — Biogeography

Furley, Peter A.. Geography of the biosphere. — London : Butterworths, Aug.1982. — [384]p
ISBN 0-408-70801-8 : £35.00 : CIP entry B82-15783

574.9 — Naturalised organisms. Geographical aspects

Jarvis, P. J.. The biogeography and ecology of introduced species / P.J. Jarvis. — Birmingham : Department of Geography, University of Birmingham, 1980. — 40p : ill,maps ; 30cm. — (Working paper series / University of Birmingham. Department of Geography ; 1)
Bibliography: p33-40
ISBN 0-7044-0556-3 (pbk) : £0.60 B82-23558

574.9 — Organisms. Distribution. Geographical aspects

Rapoport, Eduardo H.. Areography : geographical strategies of species / by Eduardo H. Rapoport ; translated by Barbara Drausal. — Oxford : Published on behalf of the Fundación Bariloche by Pergamon, 1982. — 269p : ill,maps ; 22cm. — (The Fundación Bariloche series)
Translation of: Areografía. — Bibliography: p242-255. — Includes index
ISBN 0-08-028914-2 : £14.75 : CIP rev. B81-35947

574.9 — Organisms. Distribution. Geographical aspects — *For schools*

Simmons, I. G.. Biogeographical processes / I.G. Simmons. — London : Allen & Unwin, 1982. — vi,97p : ill(some col.),maps(some col.) ; 25cm. — (Processes in physical geography ; 5)
Bibliography: p92. — Includes index
ISBN 0-04-574016-x (pbk) : Unpriced : CIP rev. B81-33912

574.909′3 — Tropical regions. Organisms. Diversification — *Conference proceedings*

Association for Tropical Biology. *International Symposium (5th : 1979 : Caracas)*. Biological diversification in the tropics : proceedings of the Fifth International Symposium of the Association for Tropical Biology, held at Macuto Beach, Caracas, Venezuela, February 8-13, 1979 / edited by Ghillean T. Prance. — New York ; Guildford : Columbia University Press, 1982. — xvi,714p : ill,maps ; 27cm
Includes bibliographies and index
ISBN 0-231-04876-9 : £44.50 B82-36926

574.909′3 — Tropical regions. Organisms — *For West African students*

Maxwell-Ojo, Bola. Modern tropical biology : teacher′s book / Bola Maxwell-Ojo. — London : Evans, 1982. — 108p ; 22cm
To accompany ′Introduction to modern tropical biology′. — Bibliography: p104-108
ISBN 0-237-50548-7 (pbk) : Unpriced B82-18292

Maxwell-Ojo, Bola. Modern tropical biology / Bola Maxwell-Ojo. — London : Evans
Student′s book. — 1982. — 295p : ill(some col.),1col.map,ports ; 28cm
Includes index
ISBN 0-237-50509-6 (pbk) : Unpriced B82-24912

574.909′3 — Tropical regions. Organisms — *Personal observations*

Attenborough, David. Journeys to the past : travels in New Guinea, Madagascar, and the Northern Territory of Australia / David Attenborough. — Guildford : Lutterworth, 1981. — 384p : ill(some col.),maps,ports ; 25cm
Contents: abridged versions of: Zoo quest to Madagascar. Originally published: 1961 — Quest in paradise. Originally published: 1960 — Quest under Capricorn. Originally published: 1963
ISBN 0-7188-2507-1 : £9.95
Primary classification 394′.4 B82-04534

574.909′45 — Tundra regions. Organisms — *For children*

Arctic lands / consultant editor Henry Pluckrose ; illustrated by Maurice Wilson. — London : Hamilton, 1982. — 28p : col.ill ; 20cm. — (Small world)
Includes index
ISBN 0-241-10724-5 : £2.75 B82-23157

574.909′52 — Jungles. Organisms — *For children*

Jungles / consultant editor Henry Pluckrose ; illustrated by Richard Orr. — London : Hamilton, 1982. — 28p : col.ill ; 20cm. — (Small world)
Includes index
ISBN 0-241-10726-1 : £2.75 B82-23163

574.909′73′2 — Urban regions. Organisms

Jenkins, Alan C.. Wildlife in the city. — Exeter : Webb & Bower, June 1982. — [160]p
ISBN 0-906671-56-6 : £8.95 : CIP entry B82-10896

574.909′822 — Mediterranean region. Organisms

Harris, Tegwyn. The natural history of the Mediterranean / Tegwyn Harris ; foreword by Oleg Polunin ; illustrated by Franklin Coombs ... [et al.]. — London : Pelham, 1982. — 224p : col.ill,col.maps ; 21cm
Bibliography: p212-213. — Includes index
ISBN 0-7207-1391-9 : £7.95 B82-27044

574.92 — Marine biology

Nybakken, James W.. Marine biology : an ecological approach / James W. Nybakken. — Cambridge, [Mass.] ; London : Harper & Row, c1982. — xvii,446p[8]p of plates : ill(some col.) ; 25cm
Bibliography: p423-432. — Includes index
ISBN 0-06-044849-0 : Unpriced B82-34019

574.92 — Marine biology. Experimental techniques

Experimental biology at sea. — London : Academic Press, Feb.1983. — [440]p
ISBN 0-12-464160-1 : CIP entry B82-36577

574.92 — Marine plankton

Raymont, John E. G.. Plankton and productivity in the oceans. — 2nd ed. — Oxford : Pergamon
Previous ed.: 1963
Vol.2: Zooplankton. — Dec.1982. — [700]p
ISBN 0-08-024404-1 (cased) : £40.00 : CIP entry
ISBN 0-08-024403-3 (pbk) : £23.00 B82-29867

574.92′05 — Marine biology — *Serials*

Advances in marine biology. — Vol.19. — London : Academic Press, Mar.1982. — [310]p
ISBN 0-12-026119-7 : CIP entry
ISSN 0065-2881 B82-00321

Advances in marine biology. — Vol.20. — London : Academic Press, Sept.1982. — [430]p
ISBN 0-12-026120-0 : CIP entry
ISSN 0065-2881 B82-19155

574.92′05 — Marine biology - *Serials*

Oceanography and marine biology. — Vol.19. — Aberdeen : Aberdeen University Press, Sept.1981. — [655]p
ISBN 0-08-028439-6 : CIP entry
ISSN 0078-3218
Primary classification 551.46′005 B81-20511

574.92′05 — Marine biology — *Serials*

Oceanography and marine biology. — Vol.20. — Aberdeen : Aberdeen University Press, Sept.1982. — [650]p
ISBN 0-08-028460-4 : £39.00 : CIP entry
ISSN 0078-3218
Primary classification 551.46′005 B82-19099

574.92′072 — Marine biology. Research. Policies of Natural Environment Research Council

Natural Environment Research Council. Policy and support for research in marine life sciences / The Natural Environment Research Council. — Swindon : The Council, c1981. — 11p ; 30cm
Cover title
Unpriced (pbk) B82-05049

Natural Environment Research Council. Policy and support for research in marine life sciences / The Natural Environment Research Council. — Swindon (Polaris House, North Star Ave., Swindon SN2 1EU) : The Council, c1981. — 11p ; 30cm
Cover title
Unpriced (pbk) B82-30491

574.92'134 — Gulf of Bothnia. Coastal waters. Organisms

Coastal research in the Gulf of Bothnia / edited by Karl Müller. — Hague ; London : Dr. W. Junk, 1982. — xiv,462p : ill,maps ; 25cm. — (Monographiae biologicae ; v.45)
Includes bibliographies and index
ISBN 90-619-3098-7 : Unpriced B82-30372

574.92'9 — Freshwater organisms

Sterry, Paul. Pond watching. — London : Severn House, Sept.1982. — [160]p. — (Severn House naturalist's library)
ISBN 0-7278-2025-7 : £8.95 : CIP entry B82-20397

574.92'9'41 — Great Britain. Ponds & streams. Freshwater organisms

Russell, Ian, *1949-*. Ponds and streams / Ian Russell. — Newton Abbot : David & Charles, c1982. — 52p : ill(some col.) ; 21cm. — (Wildlife)
ISBN 0-7153-8162-8 (pbk) : £1.95 : CIP rev. B82-01178

574.92'9'41 — Great Britain. Rivers & canals. Organisms

Hopkins, Anthony J.. Wildlife of rivers and canals. — Ashbourne : Moorland, Aug.1982. — [192]p
ISBN 0-86190-061-8 : £7.95 : CIP entry B82-22789

574.92'9'41 — Great Britain. Rivers. Organisms — *For children*

Luff, Vanessa. The river / Vanessa Luff. — London : Black, 1981. — [32]p : ill(some col.) ; 22cm
ISBN 0-7136-2198-2 : £3.95 B82-02594

574.94 — Europe. Coastal waters. Marine organisms

De Haas, Werner. The illustrated guide to marine life / Werner de Haas and Fredy Knorr ; translated by Heather J. Fisher ; edited and adapted by Roderick C. Fisher ; introduction by A.E. Brafield ; illustrated by Fredy Knorr and Roderick C. Fisher. — Expanded ed. — London : Starke, 1982. — viii,356p,[6]p of plates : ill(some col.) ; 21cm
Translation of: Was lebt im Meer?. — Previous ed.: 1979. — Bibliography: p332-334. — Includes index
ISBN 0-287-00056-7 : £8.95 B82-27284

574.941 — Great Britain. Coastal waters. Marine organisms — *Field guides*

Quigley, Michael. An introductory field guide : to the more common animals and plants of rocky shores / by Michael Quigley and Robin Crump. — Rev. 2nd ed. — Northampton : Nene College, 1982. — 39p : ill ; 23cm
Cover title. — Previous ed.: 1981. — Text on inside cover. — Bibliography: p35-36
ISBN 0-9508096-0-8 (spiral) : Unpriced B82-35089

574.941 — Great Britain. Gardens & parks. Organisms

Russell, Ian, *1949-*. Garden and park / Ian Russell. — Newton Abbot : David & Charles, c1982. — 51p : ill(some col.) ; 21cm. — (Wildlife)
ISBN 0-7153-8186-5 (pbk) : £1.95 : CIP rev. B82-01177

574.941 — Great Britain. Hedgerows & roadsides. Organisms

Major, Alan. Hedgerow and wayside / Alan Major. — Newton Abbot : David & Charles, c1982. — 51p : ill(some col.) ; 21cm. — (Wildlife)
ISBN 0-7153-8185-7 (pbk) : £1.95 : CIP rev. B82-01180

574.941 — Great Britain. Organisms — *For children*

Wilson, Ron. The nature detective's notebook / Ron Wilson ; illustrated by Susan Edwards. — [Sevenoaks] : Knight Books, 1979. — 156p : ill ; 18cm
Bibliography: p153-154
ISBN 0-340-24248-5 (pbk) : £0.65 : CIP rev. B79-10283

574.941 — Great Britain. Ponds. Organisms — *Field guides — For children*

Swallow, Su. Pond life / Su Swallow ; illustrated by Trevor Boyer ... [et al.] ; designed by Sally Burrough and Niki Overy ; edited by Sue Jacquemier and Jim Roberts. — London : Usborne, c1979. — 32p : col.ill ; 16cm. — (Younger spotter's guides)
ISBN 0-86020-329-8 : £0.75 B82-05555

574.941 — Great Britain. Ponds. Organisms — *For schools*

Hutchinson, Ken. Pond life / Ken Hutchinson. — London : Macmillan Education, 1981. — 31p : ill(some col.) ; 26cm. — (Living science)
ISBN 0-333-29251-0 (pbk) : £0.95 B82-07004

574.941 — Great Britain. Rural coastal regions. Organisms — *Walkers' guides*

Coastal walks. — London : Hamlyn, c1982. — 124p : ill(some col.),ports(some col.) ; 28cm. — (Discovering the countryside with David Bellamy)
Bibliography: p122. — Includes index
ISBN 0-600-35588-8 : £3.99 B82-21662

574.941 — Great Britain. Rural regions. Organisms — *Field guides*

Morris, Pat. The Hamlyn guide to the countryside of Britain and Northern Europe / editor Pat Morris. — London : Hamlyn, c1982. — 320p : col.ill ; 20cm
Includes index
ISBN 0-600-35607-8 (cased) : £5.95
ISBN 0-600-35606-x (pbk) : £3.95 B82-34850

574.941 — Great Britain. Seashore. Organisms

Russell, Ian, *1949-*. The seashore / Ian Russell. — Newton Abbot : David & Charles, c1982. — 52p : ill(some col.) ; 21cm. — (Wildlife)
ISBN 0-7153-8161-x (pbk) : £1.95 : CIP rev. B82-01179

574.941 — Great Britain. Seashore. Organisms — *For children*

Gilman, David. Life on the seashore / David Gilman. — London : Macdonald, 1981. — 45p : col.ill ; 29cm. — (Nature in focus)
Bibliography: p43-44. — Includes index
ISBN 0-356-07123-5 : £3.95 B82-00116

574.941 — Great Britain. Upland regions. Organisms — *For children*

Anderson, Penny. The wildlife of mountains & moorlands / Penny Anderson. — London : Macdonald, c1982. — 45p : ill(some col.) ; 29cm. — (Nature in focus)
Col. ill on lining papers. — Bibliography: p43-44. — Includes index
ISBN 0-356-07124-3 : £3.95 B82-38343

574.941 — Great Britain. Woodlands. Organisms — *Walkers' guides*

Woodland walks. — London : Hamlyn, c1982. — 125p : ill(some col.),ports(some col.) ; 28cm. — (Discovering the countryside with David Bellamy)
Bibliography: p123. — Includes index
ISBN 0-600-35587-x : £3.99 B82-21661

574.9411 — Scotland. Organisms, *ca 1845-1852 — Personal observations*

St. John, Charles. A Scottish naturalist : the sketches and notes of Charles St. John 1809-1856. — London : Deutsch, 1982. — 192p,[32]p of plates : ill(some col.) ; 26cm
Edited by Antony Atha
ISBN 0-233-97390-7 : £10.95 B82-23925

574.9411 — Scotland. Organisms — *Field guides*

Fry, Gareth. Nature guide to Scotland / Gareth Fry. — London : Usborne, 1981. — 127p : ill (some col.),maps(some col.) ; 20cm. — (Usborne regional guides)
Bibliography: p122. — Includes index
ISBN 0-86020-406-5 (cased) : £3.99
ISBN 0-86020-405-7 (pbk) : £2.50 B82-39044

574.9412'35 — Scotland. Grampian Region. Aberdeen. Organisms

Marren, Peter. A natural history of Aberdeen / by Peter Marren. — Finzean : Callander, 1982. — 184p : ill,maps,2ports ; 23cm
Map on a folded leaf attached to inside cover. — Bibliography: p171-174. — Includes index
ISBN 0-907184-03-0 (cased) : £7.25
ISBN 0-907184-04-9 (pbk) : Unpriced B82-21587

574.9412'95 — Scotland. Fife Region. West Wemyss. Seashore. Organisms — *For teaching*

Marine study. — [West Wemyss] : West Wemyss Environmental Education Centre, [1982]. — 40p,[2]leaves of plates : ill,1map ; 21cm
Cover title. — Text on inside cover
Unpriced (pbk) B82-19638

574.9422'3 — Kent. Organisms — *Personal observations*

Crompton, John. A fox under my bed / John Crompton ; illustrated by Benjamin Edwards. — Basingstoke : Macmillan, 1980, c1979. — 111p : ill ; 18cm. — (Topliners)
ISBN 0-333-27447-4 (pbk) : £0.70 : CIP rev.
Also classified at 574.9422'8 B80-12863

574.9422'5 — East Sussex. Organisms

Wildlife in East Sussex : some places to see and enjoy natural history. — Lewes : East Sussex County Council County Planning Department, 1980. — 28p : ill,1col.map ; 21cm. — (Publication ; no.P/229)
Bibliography: p28
ISBN 0-900348-99-2 (pbk) : Unpriced B82-11412

574.9422'74 — Hampshire. Selborne. Natural environment — *Early works*

White, Gilbert. The illustrated natural history of Selborne / Gilbert White. — Redesigned and illustrated ed. with additional material / compiled by Ronald Davidson-Houston ; introduction by June E. Chatfield. — Exeter : Published in collaboration with the Gilbert White Museum [by] Webb & Bower, 1981. — 256p : col.ill,1col.map ; 26cm
Previous ed.: published as The natural history of Selborne. London : White & Son, 1789. — Ill on lining papers. — Includes index
ISBN 0-906671-47-7 : £12.50 : CIP rev. B81-30485

574.9422'75 — Hampshire. New Forest. Organisms

Hawkins, Desmond. Wild life in the New Forest / by Desmond Hawkins ; with photographs by Eric Ashby ; based on the BBC TV film. — Bournemouth : Newsome, [1982]. — 32p : ill ; 17cm
Bibliography: p32
ISBN 0-906742-02-1 (pbk) : Unpriced B82-32812

574.9422'8 — Isle of Wight. Organisms — *Personal observations*

Crompton, John. A fox under my bed / John Crompton ; illustrated by Benjamin Edwards. — Basingstoke : Macmillan, 1980, c1979. — 111p : ill ; 18cm. — (Topliners)
ISBN 0-333-27447-4 (pbk) : £0.70 : CIP rev.
Primary classification 574.9422'3 B80-12863

574.9423 — South-west England. Organisms

Mercer, Ian, *1933-*. Nature guide to the West Country : Somerset, Dorset, Devon & Cornwall / Ian Mercer. — London : Usborne, 1981. — 127p : ill(some col.),maps(some col.) ; 19cm. — (Usborne regional guides)
Includes index
ISBN 0-86020-397-2 (pbk) : £2.50 B82-34472

574.9423'592 — Devon. Dart Estuary. Animals

Soper, Tony. Wildlife of the Dart Estuary. — Dartmouth (12 Fairfax Place, Dartmouth, Devon TQ6 9AE) : Harbour Books, Apr.1982. — [64]p
ISBN 0-907906-00-1 (pbk) : £1.50 : CIP entry B82-05794

574.9424′41 — Hereford and Worcester. Wyre Forest. Organisms — *Personal observations*

Fletcher, Simon. A Wyre Forest diary / Simon Fletcher ; illustrated by Margaret Layton. — Kidderminster : Kenneth Tomkinson, 1981. — 178p : ill,1map ; 21cm
Includes index
ISBN 0-907083-06-4 (pbk) : Unpriced
B82-13950

574.9425′45 — Leicestershire. Rutland Water region. Organisms, *1971-1976*

Before Rutland Water : report of a survey of the wildlife of the site before and during the construction of the reservoir, 1971-76 / Rutland Natural History Society. — [Leicester] : Leicestershire Museums, Art Galleries and Records Service, 1981. — 66p,[14]p of plates (2fold) : ill,2maps ; 30cm
ISBN 0-85022-098-x (spiral) : £2.50
B82-24567

574.9425′46 — North-east Leicestershire. Coal fields. Organisms

North-east Leicestershire coalfield : report of a biological survey 1978 / edited by I.M. Evans. — Leicester : Leicestershire Museums, Art Galleries & Records Service, 1979. — 269p : ill,maps ; 30cm. — (Leicestershire Museums publication ; 16)
Text on inside cover. — Includes bibliographies
ISBN 0-85022-056-4 (spiral) : Unpriced
B82-11047

574.9426 — East Anglia. Organisms — *Field guides*

Evans, Ros. Nature guide to East Anglia & Lincolnshire / Ros Evans. — London : Usborne, 1981. — 127p : ill(some col.),maps (some col.) ; 20cm. — (Usborne regional guides)
Bibliography: p123. — Includes index
ISBN 0-86020-400-6 (cased) : £3.99
ISBN 0-86020-399-9 (pbk) : £2.50 B82-39043

574.9427′51 — Merseyside *(Metropolitan County).* **Hilbre Islands. Organisms**

Hilbre : the Cheshire island : its history and natural history / edited by J.D. Craggs. — Liverpool : Liverpool University Press, 1982. — xix,306p : ill,charts,maps ; 26cm
Includes bibliographies and index
ISBN 0-85323-314-4 : £20.00 : CIP rev.
B81-33788

574.9427′8 — Cumbria. Organisms — *Field guides*

Waller, Cliff. Nature guide to the Lake District, Cumbria & North Lancashire / Cliff Waller. — London : Usborne, 1981. — 125p : ill(some col.),maps(some col.) ; 20cm. — (Usborne regional guides)
Bibliography: p120. — Includes index
ISBN 0-86020-404-9 : £3.99 B82-39042

574.9429 — Wales. Organisms — *Field guides*

Chatfield, June E.. Nature guide to Wales / June E. Chatfield. — London : Usborne, c1981. — 127p : ill(some col.),maps(some col.) ; 20cm. — (Usborne regional guides)
Bibliography: p123. — Includes index
ISBN 0-86020-402-2 (cased) : £3.99
ISBN 0-86020-401-4 (pbk) : £2.50 B82-39045

574.9598 — Malay Archipelago. Organisms. Distribution. Implications of Wallace′s line

Wallace′s line and plate tectonics / edited by T.C. Whitmore. — Oxford : Clarendon Press, 1981. — x,90p : ill,maps ; 25cm. — (Oxford monographs on biogeography) (Oxford science publications)
Maps on lining papers. — Bibliography: p81-88. — Includes index
ISBN 0-19-854545-2 : £15.00 : CIP rev.
B81-21605

574.9719′5 — Northwest Territories. Ellesmere Island. Princess Marie Bay. Biological expeditions: Joint Services Expedition to Princess Marie Bay, Ellesmere Island *(1980)*

Joint Services Expedition to Princess Marie Bay, Ellesmere Island *(1980).* The report of the Joint Services Expedition to Princess Marie Bay, Ellesmere Island 1980. — Weymouth (30 Gallwey Rd, Weymouth, Dorset DT4 9AH) : [The Expedition], [1982?]. — 405p in various pagings : ill,1facsim,maps(some col.),ports ; 30cm
Cover title. — Two maps on sheet 58x46cm folded to 25x15cm in pocket attached to back cover
Unpriced (spiral) B82-40590

574.98 — Andes. Organisms — *Personal observations*

Andrews, Michael, *1938-.* The flight of the condor : a wildlife exploration of the Andes / Michael Alford Andrews. — London : Collins, 1982. — 158p,[88]p of plates : ill(some col.),maps ; 26cm
Bibliography: p149. — Includes index
ISBN 0-00-219545-3 : £12.95
ISBN 0-563-17991-0 (British Broadcasting Corporation) B82-12945

574.99312′2 — New Zealand. Lake Taupo region. Organisms — *Personal observations*

Gillett, Alex. The Taupo fishing diary. — London : Hodder & Stoughton, Aug.1982. — [160]p
ISBN 0-340-26951-0 : £14.95 : CIP entry
B82-15721

574.994 — Australia. Organisms

Morcombe, Michael. The nature of Australia / Michael Morcombe. — Adelaide ; London : Rugby, 1980, c1972. — 110p : col.ill,maps ; 29cm
Originally published: Gadesville : Golden Press ; London : Muller, 1972. — Maps on lining papers
ISBN 0-7270-1373-4 : £8.25 B82-13056

574.995 — New Guinea. Organisms. Distribution

Biogeography and ecology of New Guinea / edited by J.L. Gressitt. — The Hague ; London : Junk, 1982. — 2v.(983p) : ill,maps ; 25cm. — (Monographiae biologicae ; v.42)
Includes bibliographies and index
ISBN 90-619-3094-4 : Unpriced
Primary classification 574.5′0995 B82-11236

574.999 — Extraterrestrial life

Life in the universe / John Billingham, editor. — Cambridge, Mass. ; London : MIT, 1981. — xix,461p : ill ; 27cm
Conference papers. — Includes bibliographies and index
ISBN 0-262-02155-2 : £14.00 B82-29483

574.999 — Extraterrestrial life. Theories, *to 1800*

Dick, Steven J.. Plurality of worlds : the origins of the extraterrestrial life debate from Democritus to Kant / Steven J. Dick. — Cambridge : Cambridge University Press, 1982. — x,246p : ill,facsims ; 24cm
Bibliography: p222-235. — Includes index
ISBN 0-521-24308-4 : £19.00 B82-26773

575 — EVOLUTION AND GENETICS

575 — Evolution

Day, William, *1928-.* Genesis on planet Earth : the search for life′s beginning / William Day. — Nantwich : Shiva, 1981, c1979. — xii,408p : ill ; 24cm
Originally published: East Lansing : House of Talos, 1979. — Bibliography: p393-394. — Includes index
ISBN 0-906812-09-7 : Unpriced : CIP rev.
B81-28182

Evolution / [S364 Course Team]. — Milton Keynes : Open University Press. — (Science : a third level course)
Unit 5: The evolution of fish and amphibians ; Unit 6: The evolution of reptiles, birds and mammals / prepared by an Open University Course Team. — 1981. — 45,49p : ill ; 30cm. — (S364 ; Units 5 and 6)
At head of title: The Open University. — Includes bibliographies
ISBN 0-335-16087-5 (pbk) : Unpriced
B82-04679

Evolution / [S364 Course Team]. — Milton Keynes : Open University Press. — (Science : a third level course)
Unit 7: The evolution of land plants ; Unit 8: Patterns of evolution ; Unit 9: Physical influences on evolution / prepared by an Open University Course Team. — 1981. — 67,52,35p : ill(some col.),maps(some col.) ; 30cm. — (S364 ; Units 7,8 and 9)
At head of title: The Open University. — Includes bibliographies
ISBN 0-335-16088-3 (pbk) : Unpriced
B82-04678

Evolution / [S364 Course Team]. — Milton Keynes : Open University Press. — (Science : a third level course)
At head of title: The Open University
Unit 14: The Evolution of behaviour ; Unit 15: Human evolution / prepared by an Open University Course Team. — 1981. — 52p : ill ; 30cm. — (S364 ; unit 14 and 15)
Bibliography: p49
ISBN 0-335-16091-3 (pbk) : Unpriced
B82-15035

575 — Organisms. Evolution

Evolution now : a century after Darwin / edited by John Maynard Smith. — London : Nature in association with Macmillan, 1982. — 239p : ill ; 23cm
ISBN 0-333-33595-3 (cased) : £12.00
ISBN 0-333-33603-8 (pbk) : Unpriced
B82-38804

Goldschmidt, Richard. The material basis of evolution / Richard Goldschmidt ; with an introduction by Stephen Jay Gould. — New Haven ; London : Yale University Press, c1982. — xlii,436p : ill,maps ; 22cm. — (Silliman milestones in science)
Facsim of ed. published: 1940. — Bibliography: p401-423. — Includes index
ISBN 0-300-02822-9 (cased) : Unpriced : CIP rev.
ISBN 0-300-02823-7 (pbk) : Unpriced
B82-13485

Medawar, P. B.. The uniqueness of the individual / by P.B. Medawar. — 2nd rev. ed. — New York : Dover Publications ; London : Constable, 1981. — xxv,162p ; 21cm
Previous ed.: London : Methuen, 1957. — Includes index
ISBN 0-486-24042-8 (pbk) : £3.00 B82-26162

Russell, Peter. The awakening earth. — London : Routledge and Kegan Paul, Oct.1982. — [256]p
ISBN 0-7100-9318-7 (pbk) : £4.95 : CIP entry
B82-23206

Stanley, Steven M.. The new evolutionary timetable : fossils, genes and the origin of the species / Steven M. Stanley. — New York : Basic Books ; London : Harper & Row, c1981. — xvi,222p : ill ; 24cm
Includes index
ISBN 0-06-337022-0 : £9.50 B82-08949

575 — Organisms. Evolution *expounded by* **organisms,** *1978* — *For children*

Attenborough, David. Discovering life on earth : a natural history / David Attenborough. — Rev. ed. — London : Collins, 1981. — 224p : col.ill ; 26cm
Previous ed.: published as Life on earth, 1979. — Includes index
ISBN 0-00-195147-5 (cased) : £6.95
ISBN 0-00-195148-3 (pbk) : Unpriced
B82-07393

575 — Organisms. Evolution. Molecular biolgoy

Ninio, Jacques. Molecular approaches to evolution / Jacques Ninio ; translated by Robert Lang. — London : Pitman, 1982. — v,133p : ill ; 24cm
Translation of: Approches moleculaires de l′évolution. — Bibliography: p123-133
ISBN 0-273-08521-2 (pbk) : Unpriced : CIP rev.
B81-34158

575 — Organisms. Evolution. Physiological aspects

Cordon, Faustino. The origin, nature and evolution of protoplasmic individuals and their associations. — Oxford : Pergamon, Apr.1982. — [650]p
ISBN 0-08-027990-2 : £44.50 : CIP entry B82-06490

575′.001′5193 — Evolution. Game theory

Smith, John Maynard. Evolution and the theory of games. — Cambridge : Cambridge University Press, Oct.1982. — 1v.
ISBN 0-521-24673-3 (cased) : £18.00 : CIP entry
ISBN 0-521-28884-3 (pbk) : £6.50 B82-40322

575′.0092′4 — Evolution. Darwin, Charles — *Biographies*

Brent, Peter. Charles Darwin : a man of enlarged curiosity / Peter Brent. — London : Heinemann, 1981. — 536p,[12]p of plates : ill,1coat of arms,ports ; 25cm
Maps on lining papers. — Bibliography: p525-528. — Includes index
ISBN 0-434-08595-2 : £12.50 B82-03897

575′.0092′4 — Evolution. Wallace, Alfred Russel — *Biographies*

Clements, Harry. Alfred Russel Wallace : biologist and social reformer. — London : Wildwood House, June 1982. — [220]p
ISBN 0-7045-3064-3 : £7.95 : CIP entry B82-09585

575′.0092′4 — Organisms. Evolution. Darwin, Charles — *Biographies*

Charles Darwin : a commemoration 1882-1982 / edited by R.J. Berry. — London : Published for the Linnean Society of London [by] Academic Press, c1982. — 135p : 1ill,3geneal.tables,music ; 26cm
'Reprinted from the Biological journal of the Linnean Society, vol.17, no.1, 1982'. — Includes bibliographies and index
ISBN 0-12-093180-x (pbk) : £6.60 B82-32790

575′.0092′4 — Organisms. Evolution. Darwin, Charles — *Biographies — Welsh texts*

Hughes, R. Elwyn. Darwin / R. Elwyn Hughes. — [Denbigh] ([Chapel St., Denbigh, Clwyd]) : Gwasg Gee, 1981. — 126p : ill ; 19cm. — (Y Meddwl modern)
Bibliography: p125-126
£1.50 (pbk) B82-12200

575.01 — Organisms. Evolution. Theories

Calow, Peter. Evolutionary principles. — Glasgow : Blackie, Jan.1983. — [120]p. — (Tertiary level biology)
ISBN 0-216-91396-9 (cased) : £15.50 : CIP entry
ISBN 0-216-91395-0 (pbk) : £7.50 B82-33495

Taylor, Gordon Rattray. The great evolution mystery. — London : Secker & Warburg, Feb.1983. — [288]p
ISBN 0-436-51633-0 : £10.50 : CIP entry B82-40890

575.01′6 — Evolution. Theories, *ca 1850-1981.* Genetic factors

Berry, R. J.. Genes in ecology and evolution. — London : Edward Arnold, July 1982. — [64]p. — (The Institute of Biology's studies in biology ; no.144)
ISBN 0-7131-2849-6 (pbk) : £2.25 : CIP entry B82-13015

575.01′6 — Organisms. Evolution. Theories, *1859-1900*

Bratchell, D. F.. The impact of Darwinism : texts and commentary illustrating nineteenth century religious, scientific and literary attitudes / D.F. Bratchell. — Amersham : Avebury, 1981. — 140p ; 22cm
Includes bibliographies
ISBN 0-86127-204-8 (pbk) : Unpriced : CIP rev. B80-21879

575.01′62 — Evolution. Natural selection. Theories of Darwin, Charles. Formulation, *1838-1859*

Gale, Barry. Evolution without evidence. — Brighton : Harvester, Sept.1982. — [256]p
ISBN 0-7108-0442-3 : £18.95 : CIP entry B82-20024

Ospovat, Dov. The development of Darwin's theory : natural history, natural theology, and natural selection, 1838-1859 / Dov Ospovat. — Cambridge : Cambridge University Press, 1981. — xii,301p : ill,1facsim,ports ; 24cm
Bibliography: p278-290. — Includes index
ISBN 0-521-23818-8 : £20.00 B82-02677

575.01′62 — Organisms. Evolution. Darwin, Charles. On the origin of species by means of natural selection — *Concordances*

A Concordance to Darwin's Origin of species, first edition / edited by Paul H. Barrett, Donald J. Weinshank, and Timothy T. Gottleber. — Ithaca ; London : Cornell University Press, 1981. — xv,834p ; 25cm
ISBN 0-8014-1319-2 : Unpriced B82-16980

575.01′62 — Organisms. Evolution. Natural selection — *Early works*

Darwin, Charles. [On the origin of species]. The origin of species by means of natural selection, or, The preservation of favoured races in the struggle for life / Charles Darwin ; edited with an introduction by J.W. Burrow. — Harmondsworth : Penguin, 1968 (1982 [printing]). — 476p : 1ill ; 19cm. — (Penguin English Library)
Originally published: London : John Murray, 1859. — Bibliography: p461-462
ISBN 0-14-043205-1 (pbk) : £2.25 B82-37816

575.01′62 — Organisms. Evolution. Theories of Darwin, Charles

George, Wilma. Darwin / Wilma George. — [London] : Fontana, 1982. — 160p ; 18cm. — (Fontana modern masters)
Bibliography: p159-160
ISBN 0-00-636502-7 (pbk) : £1.75 B82-22563

Hitching, Francis. The neck of the giraffe, or, Where Darwin went wrong / Francis Hitching. — London : Pan, 1982. — 288p : ill,ports ; 20cm
Bibliography: p272-279. — Includes index
ISBN 0-330-26643-8 (pbk) : £2.50 B82-23289

Howard, Jonathan, *19---*. Darwin / Jonathan Howard. — Oxford : Oxford University Press, 1982. — viii,101p ; 19cm. — (Past masters)
Bibliography: p97-98. — Includes index
ISBN 0-19-287557-4 (cased) : Unpriced : CIP rev.
ISBN 0-19-287556-6 (pbk) : £1.25 B82-00883

575.1 — Evolution. Genetic factors

Cairns-Smith, A. G.. Genetic takeover and the mineral origins of life. — Cambridge : Cambridge University Press, Aug.1982. — [479]p
ISBN 0-521-23312-7 : £15.00 : CIP entry B82-25495

575.1 — Evolution. Genetic factors — *Conference proceedings*

Problems of phylogenetic reconstruction. — London : Academic Press, Mar.1982. — [450] p. — (The Systematics Association special volume, ISSN 0309-2593 ; no.21)
Conference papers
ISBN 0-12-391250-4 : CIP entry B82-01707

575.1 — Genetic engineering

Cherfas, Jeremy. Man made life. — Oxford : Blackwell, July 1982. — [256]p
ISBN 0-631-13026-8 (cased) : £12.50 : CIP entry
ISBN 0-631-13027-6 (pbk) : £4.50 B82-14519

Genetic technology : a new frontier / Office of Technology Assessment. — Boulder : Westview ; London : Croom Helm, 1982. — xvii,331p : ill ; 23cm
Bibliography: p265-266
ISBN 0-7099-1913-1 : £13.95 B82-26931

Old, R. W.. Principles of gene manipulation : an introduction to genetic engineering / R.W. Old, S.B. Primrose. — 2nd ed. — Oxford : Blackwell Scientific, 1981. — x,214p : ill ; 24cm. — (Studies in microbiology ; v.2)
Previous ed.: 1980. — Bibliography: p195-210. — Includes index
ISBN 0-632-00856-3 (pbk) : £6.50 : CIP rev. B81-31082

575.1 — Genetic engineering — *Conference proceedings*

From genetic experimentation to biotechnology — the critical transition / edited by William J. Whelan and Sandra Black. — Chichester : Wiley, c1982. — xx,266p : ill ; 24cm
An international symposium sponsored by the Consiglio Nazionale delle Ricerche, Rome and the Committee on Genetic Experimentation. — 'Proceedings of a symposium From genetic experimentation to biotechnology — the critical transition held at Consiglio Nazionale delle Ricerche ... Rome, Italy, 20-23 September 1981' — preliminaries. — Includes bibliographies and index
ISBN 0-471-10148-6 : £17.50 : CIP rev. B81-37596

575.1 — Genetics

Genetics : readings from Scientific American / with introductions by Cedric I. Davern. — Oxford : W.H. Freeman, 1981. — 331p : ill (some col.),ports ; 30cm
Bibliography: p315-323. — Includes index
ISBN 0-7167-1200-8 (cased) : £13.40
ISBN 0-7167-1201-6 (pbk) : £6.20 B82-01463

ICN-UCLA Symposia on Developmental Biology Using Purified Genes *(1981 : Keystone).*
Developmental biology using purified genes / [proceedings of the 1981 ICN-UCLA Symposia on Developmental Biology Using Purified Genes held in Keystone, Colorado, on March 15-20, 1981] ; edited by Donald D. Brown. — New York ; London : Academic Press, 1981. — xxi,702p : ill ; 24cm. — (ICN-UCLA symposia on molecular and cellular biology ; v.23)
Includes index
ISBN 0-12-137420-3 : Unpriced B82-28668

575.1 — Organisms. Evolution. Genetic factors

Dobzhansky, Theodosius. Genetics and the origin of species / by Theodosius Dobzhansky ; with an introduction by Stephen Jay Gould. — New York ; Guildford : Columbia University Press, 1937, c1982 (1982 [printing]). — xli,364p : ill,maps ; 23cm. — (Columbia classics in evolution series)
Includes bibliographies and index
ISBN 0-231-05475-0 (pbk) : £9.30 B82-39008

575.1′028 — Biometrical genetics

Mather, *Sir* Kenneth. Biometrical genetics : the study of continuous variation / Sir Kenneth Mather, John L. Jinks. — 3rd ed. — London : Chapman and Hall, 1982. — xiv,396p : ill ; 25cm
Previous ed.: 1971. — Bibliography: p377-387. — Includes index
ISBN 0-412-22890-4 : Unpriced : CIP rev. B82-12327

575.1′05 — Genetic engineering — *Serials*

Genetic engineering. — Vol.2. — London : Academic Press, Oct.1981. — [180]p
ISBN 0-12-270302-2 : CIP entry B81-27368

575.1′092′4 — Genetics. Muller, H. J. — *Biographies*

Carlson, Elof Axel. Genes, radiation, and society : the life and work of H.J. Muller / Elof Axel Carlson. — Ithaca ; London : Cornell University Press, 1981. — xiv,457p : ill,ports ; 24cm
Includes index
ISBN 0-8014-1304-4 : Unpriced B82-16927

575.1′2 — Organisms. Evolution. Role of genes

Dawkins, Richard. The extended phenotype : the gene as the unit of selection / Richard Dawkins. — Oxford : Freeman, c1982. — viii,307p ; 24cm
Bibliography: p265-281. — Includes index
ISBN 0-7167-1358-6 : £9.95 B82-11649

575.1′5 — Population genetics

Falconer, D.S.. Introduction to quantitative genetics / D.S. Falconer. — 2nd ed. — London : Longman, 1981. — viii,340p : ill ; 24cm
Previous ed.: Edinburgh : Oliver & Boyd, 1960. — Bibliography: p321-334. — Includes index
ISBN 0-582-44195-1 (pbk) : £9.95 : CIP rev. B81-15941

575.1'5 — Population genetics. Ecological aspects

Merrell, David J.. Ecological genetics / David J. Merrell. — London : Longman, 1981. — xii,500p : ill ; 24cm
Originally published: Minneapolis : University of Minnesota Press, 1981. — Bibliography: p453-491. — Includes index
ISBN 0-582-46349-1 : £15.00 : CIP rev. B81-30280

575.2'2 — Environment. Effects of man. Adaptation of organisms. Genetic aspects

Genetic consequences of man made change : edited by J.A. Bishop, L.M. Cook. — London : Academic Press, 1981. — xiv,409p : ill,maps ; 24cm
Bibliography: p343-400. — Includes index
ISBN 0-12-101620-x : £23.60 : CIP rev. B81-17522

575.2'92 — Chemical mutagenesis

Chemical mutagens : principles and methods for their detection. — New York ; London : Plenum Press
'Sponsored by the Environmental Mutagen Society'. — Includes index
edited by Frederick J. de Serres and Alexander Hollaender. — c1982. — xxvi,497p : ill ; 24cm
ISBN 0-306-40771-x : Unpriced B82-21158

575.2'92 — Laboratory organisms. Mutagenic effects of chemicals — *Conference proceedings*

Workshop on Comparative Chemical Mutagenesis *(1977 : Raleigh)*. Comparative chemical mutagenesis / [proceedings of the Workshop on Comparative Chemical Mutagenesis, sponsored by NIEHS and held October 30-November 4, 1977, at the Crabtree Valley Mall, Raleigh, North Carolina] ; edited by Frederick J. de Serres and Michael D. Shelby. — New York ; London : Plenum, c1981. — viii,1117p,[4]p of plates : ill(some col.) ; 26cm. — (Environmental science research ; v.24)
Includes index
ISBN 0-306-40930-5 : Unpriced B82-26277

576 — MICROORGANISMS

576 — Methylotrophs. Biochemistry

Anthony, C.. The biochemistry of methylotrophs / C. Anthony. — London : Academic Press, 1982. — xv,431p : ill ; 24cm
Bibliography: p351-378. — Includes index
ISBN 0-12-058820-x : £24.00 : CIP rev. B82-07262

576 — Microbiology

The **Microbial** perspective / Eugene W. Nester ... [et al.] ; assisted by Martha T. Nester ; illustrations by Iris J. Nichols. — Philadelphia ; London : Saunders College, c1982. — vi,730p,[16]p of plates : ill(some col.),1map ; 25cm
Text on lining covers. — Includes bibliographies and index
ISBN 0-03-047041-2 : £21.95 B82-23311

New dimensions in microbiology : mixed substrates, mixed cultures and microbial communities : proceedings of a Royal Society discussion meeting held on 11 and 12 November 1981 / organized and edited by J.R. Quayle and A.T. Bull. — London : The Society, 1982. — viii,193p,1 leaf of plates : ill ; 31cm
Originally published: in Philosphical transactions of the Royal Society of London, series B, vol. 297 (no. 1088), p445-639. — Pages also numbered 447-639. — Includes bibliographies
ISBN 0-85403-189-8 : £25.20 B82-33755

576 — Microorganisms

Pîatkin, K. D.. Microbiology : with virology and immunology / K.D. Pyatkin, Yu. S. Krivoshein ; translated from the Russian by L. Aksenova and V. Lisovskaya. — 2nd enl. and rev. ed. — Moscow : Mir ; [London] : distributed by Central, 1980. — 560p,[16]p of plates : ill(some col.),ports ; 23cm
Translation of: Mikrobiologiîa. — Previous ed.: 1967. — Includes index
ISBN 0-7147-1719-3 : £6.50 B82-29715

576 — Microorganisms — *For schools*

Williams, J. I.. Micro-organisms. — 2nd ed. — London : Bell & Hyman, Jan.1982. — [176]p
Previous ed.: London : Mills and Boon, 1976
ISBN 0-7135-1321-7 (pbk) : £3.75 : CIP entry B81-38841

576'.03 — Microbiology - *Encyclopedias*

Singleton, Paul. Dictionary of microbiology. — Chichester : Wiley, June 1981. — [496]p
Originally published: 1978
ISBN 0-471-28036-4 (pbk) : £4.95 : CIP entry B81-09978

576'.0724 — Higher education institutions. Curriculum subjects: Microbiology. Laboratory techniques — *For teaching*

Source book of experiments for the teaching of microbiology / edited by S.B. Primrose, A.C. Wardlaw. — London : Academic Press, 1982. — xvii,766p : ill ; 26cm. — (Special publications of the Society for General Microbiology)
ISBN 0-12-565680-7 : £28.20 : CIP rev. B82-07487

576'.11 — Microorganisms. Physiology — *Serials*

Advances in microbial physiology. — Vol.22. — London : Academic Press, Sept.1981. — [250]p
ISBN 0-12-027722-0 : CIP entry
ISSN 0065-2911 B81-21610

576'.11'05 — Microorganisms. Physiology — *Serials*

Advances in microbial physiology. — Vol.23. — London : Academic Press, Mar.1982. — [260]p
ISBN 0-12-027723-9 : CIP entry
ISSN 0065-2911 B82-00320

576'.11924 — Microorganisms. Carbon. Metabolism

Dawes, Edwin A.. The biochemist in a microbial wonderland / Edwin A. Dawes. — [St Andrews] : University of St Andrews, 1982. — 64p : ill ; 21cm. — (The American Medical Alumni lectures ; 1980-81)
'Delivered on 3rd, 5th, 6th and 7th November 1980 in the Department of Biochemistry'
Unpriced (pbk) B82-31430

576'.15 — Microorganisms. Ecological communities. Research. Laboratory techniques

Experimental microbial geology / edited by Richard G. Burns and J. Howard Slater. — Oxford : Blackwell Scientific, 1982. — x,683p : ill ; 26cm
Includes bibliographies and index
ISBN 0-632-00765-6 : £55.00 : CIP rev. B82-12835

576'.15 — Microorganisms. Ecology

Atlas, Ronald M.. Microbial ecology : fundamentals and applications / Ronald M. Atlas, Richard Bartha. — Reading, Mass. ; London : Addison-Wesley, c1981. — xi,560p : ill ; 24cm. — (Addison-Wesley series in the life sciences)
Includes bibliographies and index
ISBN 0-201-00051-2 : Unpriced B82-27983

Grant, W. D.. Environmental microbiology / W.D. Grant, P.E. Long. — Glasgow : Blackie, 1981. — viii,215p : ill ; 22cm. — (Tertiary level biology)
Includes bibliographies and index
ISBN 0-216-91153-2 (cased) : £17.50 : CIP rev.
ISBN 0-216-91152-4 (pbk) : £8.50 B81-22491

576'.15 — Microorganisms. Habitats: Man. Mouth

Oral microbiology : with basic microbiology and immunology / edited by William A. Nolte. — 4th ed. — St. Louis ; London : Mosby, 1982. — xi,795p : ill ; 28cm
Previous ed.: 1977. — Includes bibliographies and index
ISBN 0-8016-3697-3 : £26.25
Also classified at 616.3'101 B82-31868

576'.16 — Applied microbiology

Essays in applied microbiology / edited by J.R. Norris and M.H. Richmond. — Chichester : Wiley, c1981. — 360p in various pagings : ill ; 24cm
Includes bibliographies and index
ISBN 0-471-27998-6 : £19.50 : CIP rev. B81-34562

576'.16 — Microorganisms. Exploitation — *Conference proceedings*

Overproduction of microbial products. — London : Academic Press, Aug.1982. — [800]p
Conference papers
ISBN 0-12-426920-6 : CIP entry B82-15669

576'.163 — Food. Contaminants: Microorganisms

Developments in food microbiology. — 1. — London : Applied Science Publishers. — (The Developments series)
1 / edited by R. Davies. — c1982. — x,219p : ill ; 25cm
Includes index
ISBN 0-85334-999-1 : £24.00 : CIP rev. B81-35855

576'.163 — Food. Contaminants: Psychrophilic microorganisms — *Conference proceedings*

International Symposium on Food Microbiology *(11th : 1980 : Aalborg)*. Psychrotrophic microorganisms in spoilage and pathogenicity / [based on the proceedings of the XIth International Symposium on Food Microbiology organised by the Committee on Food Microbiology and Hygiene of the International Union of Microbiological Societies held at Aalborg, Denmark on 6-11 July, 1980] ; edited by T.A. Roberts ... [et al.]. — London : Academic Press, 1981. — xix, 502p : ill ; 24cm
Includes bibliographies and index
ISBN 0-12-589720-0 : £24.00 : CIP rev. B81-35910

576'.163'028 — Food. Contaminants: Microorganisms. Identification. Laboratory techniques

Isolation and identification methods for food poisoning organisms. — London : Academic Press, Aug.1982. — [460]p. — (The Society for Applied Bacteriology technical series ; no.17)
ISBN 0-12-189950-0 : CIP entry B82-15663

576'.192 — Marine sediments. Microorganisms

Sediment microbiology / edited by D.B. Nedwell and C.M. Brown. — London : Published for the Society for General Microbiology by Academic Press, 1982. — viii,234p : ill ; 24cm. — (Special publications of the Society for General Microbiology ; 7)
Includes bibliographies and index
ISBN 0-12-515380-5 : £14.20 : CIP rev. B82-04136

576'.64 — Negative strand viruses. Replication — *Conference proceedings*

International Symposium on Negative Strand Viruses *(4th : 1980 : Saint Thomas)*. The replication of negative strand viruses : proceedings of the 4th International Symposium on Negative Strand Viruses held October 26-November 1, 1980 at Frenchman's Reef, Saint Thomas, U.S. Virgin Islands / editors, David H.L. Bishop and Richard W. Compans. — New York ; Oxford : Elsevier/North-Holland, c1981. — xxii,990p : ill ; 25cm
Includes index
ISBN 0-444-00606-0 : Unpriced B82-01662

576'.64 — Viruses

Comprehensive virology / edited by Heinz Fraenkel-Conrat and Robert R. Wagner. — New York ; London : Plenum
16: Virus-host interactions : viral invasion, persistence, and disease. — c1980. — 372p : ill ; 26cm
Includes bibliographies and index
ISBN 0-306-40488-5 : Unpriced B82-37148

576'.6483 — Plants. Pathogens: Viruses

Matthews, R. E. F.. Plant virology / R.E.F. Matthews. — 2nd ed. — New York ; London : Academic Press, c1981. — xvii,897p : ill ; 24cm
Previous ed.: 1970. — Bibliography: p735-857. — Includes index
ISBN 0-12-480560-4 : £39.40 B82-21298

576'.6483 — Plants. Pathogens: Viruses. Antigens. Serology & immunology

Van Regenmortel, M. H. V.. Serology and immunochemistry of plant viruses / M.H.V. Van Regenmortel. — New York : London : Academic Press, 1982. — xiv,302p : ill ; 24cm
Bibliography: p206-267. — Includes index
ISBN 0-12-714180-4 : £29.20 B82-34861

576′.6484 — Oncogenic viruses
Gross, Ludwik. Oncogenic viruses. — 3rd ed. — Oxford : Pergamon, Jan.1983. — [1200]p
Previous ed.: 1970
ISBN 0-08-026830-7 : £60.00 : CIP entry
B82-35197

577 — BIOLOGY. PROPERTIES OF LIFE

577 — Life. Origin
Crick, Francis. Life itself : its origin and nature / Francis Crick. — London : Macdonald, 1982, c1981. — 192p : ill ; 22cm
Originally published: New York : Simon & Schuster, 1981. — Bibliography: p177-178. — Includes index
ISBN 0-356-07736-5 (corrected) : £7.95
B82-08627

Gribbin, John. Genesis : the origins of man and the universe. — Oxford : Oxford University Press, Sept.1982. — [378]p
Originally published: London : Dent, 1981
ISBN 0-19-283035-x (pbk) : £3.95 : CIP entry
B82-18988

Hublin, Jean-Jacques. Origins of man. — London : Hart-Davis Educational, May 1982. — [64]p. — (Signposts series)
Translation of: Les origines de l'homme
ISBN 0-247-13039-7 : £3.50 : CIP entry
B82-07413

577 — Life. Origin — *For children*
Bantock, Cuillin. The story of life. — London : Walker, Sept.1982. — [48]p. — (Life sciences)
ISBN 0-906785-01-4 : £4.50 : CIP entry
B82-21576

578 — BIOLOGY. MICROSCOPY

578′.45 — Biology. Electron probe microanalysis
X-ray microanalysis in biology / edited by M.A. Hayat. — London : Macmillan, 1981, c1980. — viii,488p : ill ; 24cm
Originally published: Baltimore : University Park Press, 1980. — Includes bibliographies and index
ISBN 0-333-32355-6 : Unpriced B82-06632

579 — BIOLOGICAL SPECIMENS. COLLECTION AND PRESERVATION

579 — Insects. Collecting
Smithers, Courtenay. Handbook of insect collecting : collection, preparation, preservation and storage / Courtenay Smithers. — Newton Abbot : David & Charles, 1982, c1981. — 120p : ill ; 26cm
Bibliography: p118. — Includes index
ISBN 0-7153-8278-0 : £6.95 : CIP rev.
B82-01183

579 — Marine molluscs. Collecting — *Manuals*
Smith, Shelagh M.. How to collect marine mollusca (including so-called rare species) / by Shelagh M. Smith. — Luton ([c/o Mrs. E.B. Rands, 51 Wychwood Ave, Luton, LU2 7HT]) : Conchological Society of Great Britain and Ireland, 1981. — 24p ; 30cm. — (Papers for students / Conchological Society of Great Britain and Ireland, ISSN 0141-4593 ; no.18)
Bibliography: p18
Unpriced (unbound) B82-11946

579′.1 — Vertebrates. Skull. Collecting — *Amateurs′ manuals*
Steel, Richard. Skulls! / Richard Steel ; illustrated by Gerry Gaston. — [London] : Piccolo in association with Heinemann, 1982, c1980. — 86p : ill ; 20cm
Originally published: London : Heinemann, 1980. — Includes index
ISBN 0-330-26655-1 (pbk) : £1.00 B82-23288

580 — BOTANICAL SCIENCES

580′.74′44 — Europe. Botanical gardens, *ca 1500-ca 1800*
Prest, John. The Garden of Eden : the botanic garden and the re-creation of Paradise / John Prest. — New Haven ; London : Yale University Press, 1981. — 122p : ill(some col.),2maps,plans ; 27cm
Bibliography: p114-119. — Includes index
ISBN 0-300-02726-5 : Unpriced B82-15439

580′.74′442134 — London. Kensington and Chelsea *(London Borough).* **Botanical gardens: Chelsea Physic Garden,** *to 1979*
Chelsea Physic Garden. The Chelsea Physic Garden. — Rev. ed. — [London] ([66 Royal Hospital Rd., SW3 4HS]) : [Chelsea Physic Garden], 1980. — 30p : ill,1plan ; 25cm
Previous ed.: 195-?
£0.75 (pbk) B82-06405

580′.74′442195 — London. Richmond upon Thames *(London Borough).* **Botanical gardens: Royal Botanic Gardens** *(Kew), to 1977*
Royal Botanic Gardens Kew : gardens for science & pleasure / edited by F. Nigel Hepper. — London : H.M.S.O., 1982. — 194p : ill(some col.),1facsim,2col.maps,ports ; 29cm
Bibliography: p188. — Includes index
ISBN 0-11-241181-9 : £9.95 B82-32959

580′.74′49451 — Australia. Victoria. Melbourne. Botanical gardens: Royal Botanic Gardens *(Melbourne), to 1970*
Pescott, R. T. M.. The Royal Botanic Gardens, Melbourne : a history from 1845 to 1970 / R.T.M. Pescott. — Melbourne ; Oxford : Oxford University Press, 1982. — xii,212p : ill (some col.),maps(some col.),ports ; 25x27cm
Bibliography: p209. — Includes index
ISBN 0-19-554256-8 : £23.00 B82-31497

581 — BOTANY

581 — Plants
Botany : an introduction to plant biology / T. Elliot Weier ... [et al.]. — 6th ed. — New York ; Chichester : Wiley, c1982. — xii,720p : ill(some col.),maps ; 29cm
Previous ed.: 1974. — Includes index
ISBN 0-471-01561-x : £20.65 B82-18217

The **Encyclopedia** of the plant kingdom / [botanical editor, Anthony Huxley]. — London : Corgi, 1981, c1977. — 240p : ill(some col.) ; 30cm
Originally published: Feltham : Hamlyn, 1977. — Bibliography: p240. — Includes index
ISBN 0-552-98204-0 (pbk) : £5.95 B82-08151

Höhn, Reinhardt. Curiosities of the plant kingdom / Reinhardt Höhn in collaboration with Johannes Petermann ; [translated from the German by Herbert Liebscher]. — London : Cassell, 1980. — 212p : ill(some col.),maps (some col.) ; 28cm
Bibliography: p211-212. — Includes index
ISBN 0-304-30463-8 : £8.95 B82-13475

Miller, Ruth N.. Plant types / Ruth N. Miller. — London : Hutchinson
1: Algae, fungi and lichens. — 1982. — 120p : ill ; 24cm
ISBN 0-09-144481-0 (pbk) : Unpriced : CIP rev. B82-03744

581 — Plants — *For children*
Hepper, F. Nigel. Know about plants. — London : Ark, [1981?]. — [16]p : col.ill ; 21cm. — (Know about nature series)
Cover title. — Author: Nigel Hepper
ISBN 0-86201-055-1 (pbk) : £0.50 B82-05605

Lambert, Mark, *1946-*. Plant life / by Mark Lambert ; editor Jacqui Bailey. — London : Pan, 1982. — 91p : ill(some col.) ; 18cm. — (A Piccolo factbook)
Includes index
ISBN 0-330-26620-9 (pbk) : £1.35 B82-20156

Lambert, Mark, *1946-*. Plant life / by Mark Lambert ; editor Jacqui Bailey. — London : Kingfisher, 1982. — 91p : ill(some col.),col.maps ; 19cm. — (A Kingfisher factbook)
Includes index
ISBN 0-86272-032-x : £2.50 : CIP rev.
B82-01403

581 — Plants — *For schools*
Fenton, E.. Systematic botany for 'A' level / E. Fenton. — Staines (5, Wendover Rd, Staines, Middx.) : E. Fenton, c1982. — [12]p : ill ; 29cm
Cover title
Unpriced (pbk) B82-28844

581 — Plants — *Identification manuals*
Perry, Frances. Tropical and subtropical plants. — London : Ward Lock, Mar.1982. — [136]p
ISBN 0-7063-6137-7 (cased) : £4.50 : CIP entry
ISBN 0-7063-5964-x (pbk) : £2.95 B82-03114

581 — Plants mentioned in Bible
Zohary, Michael. Plants of the Bible. — Cambridge : Cambridge University Press, Nov.1982. — [224]p
ISBN 0-521-24926-0 : £9.50 : CIP entry
B82-29388

581 — Plants, *to 1980*
The **Green** planet : the story of plant life on earth. — Cambridge : Cambridge University Press, Sept.1982. — [288]p
ISBN 0-521-24610-5 : £13.50 : CIP entry
B82-19540

581 — Scented plants
Verey, Rosemary. The scented garden / Rosemary Verey. — London : Joseph, 1981. — 167p : ill(some col.) ; 27cm
Bibliography: p167. — Includes index
ISBN 0-7181-2050-7 : £10.95 B82-02312

581′.012 — Plants. Taxonomy
Jeffrey, Charles. An introduction to plant taxonomy / C. Jeffrey. — 2nd ed. — Cambridge : Cambridge University Press, 1982. — vii,153p : ill ; 23cm
Previous ed.: London : Churchill, 1968. — Bibliography: p140-148. — Includes index
ISBN 0-521-24542-7 (cased) : £12.50 : CIP rev.
ISBN 0-521-28775-8 (pbk) : Unpriced
B82-25492

581′.022′2 — Plants, *to 1980 — Illustrations*
Rix, Martyn. The art of the botanist / Martyn Rix. — Guildford : Lutterworth, c1981. — 224p : ill(some col.) ; 34cm
Bibliography: p220. — Includes index
ISBN 0-7188-2482-2 : £30.00 B82-04430

581′.028 — Botany. Laboratory techniques — *Manuals*
Balbach, Margaret. A laboratory manual for general botany / Margaret Balbach, Lawrence C. Bliss. — 6th ed. / prepared with the assistance of Harold E. Balbach. — Philadelphia ; London : Saunders College, c1982. — vii,350p : ill ; 27cm
Previous ed.: New York ; London : Holt, Rinehart and Winston, 1977. — Includes index
ISBN 0-03-058514-7 (pbk) : £10.95
B82-33814

581′.03 — Botany — *Polyglot dictionaries*
Macura, P.. Elsevier′s dictionary of botany / compiled by P. Macura. — Amsterdam ; Oxford : Elsevier Scientific
2: General terms : in English, French, German and Russian. — c1982. — 743p ; 23cm
Includes index
ISBN 0-444-41977-2 : £55.08 : CIP rev.
B81-31197

581′.05 — Botany — *Serials*
Advances in botanical research. — Vol.9. — London : Academic Press, Feb.1982. — [280]p
ISBN 0-12-005909-6 : CIP entry
ISSN 0065-2296 B81-36037

581′.072 — Botany. Applications of nuclear technology
Vose, Peter B.. Introduction to nuclear techniques in agronomy and plant biology / by Peter B. Vose. — Oxford : Pergamon, 1980. — xiii,391p : ill ; 25cm. — (Pergamon international library of science, technology, engineering and social studies)
Includes bibliographies and index
ISBN 0-08-024924-8 (cased) : Unpriced : CIP rev.
ISBN 0-08-024923-x (pbk) : £11.95
Primary classification 630′.72 B79-34938

581'.0724 — Plants. Tissues. In vitro culture. Laboratory techniques

Dodds, John H.. Experiments in plant tissue culture / John H. Dodds and Lorin W. Roberts ; foreword by J. Heslop-Harrison. — Cambridge : Cambridge University Press, 1982. — xiii,178p : ill ; 24cm
Includes bibliographies and index
ISBN 0-521-23477-8 (cased) : £15.00
ISBN 0-521-29965-9 (pbk) : £5.95 B82-24221

581'.09 — Botany, *to ca 1980*

Morton, A. G.. History of botanical science : an account of the development of botany from ancient times to the present day / A.G. Morton. — London : Academic Press, 1981. — xii,474p : ill,ports ; 24cm
Includes index
ISBN 0-12-508380-7 (cased) : £18.80 : CIP rev.
ISBN 0-12-508382-3 (pbk) : Unpriced
B81-27376

581'.09'033 — Botany, *1700-1800*

Delaporte, François. Nature's second kingdom : explorations of vegetality in the eighteenth century / François Delaporte ; translated by Arthur Goldhammer. — Cambridge, Mass. ; London : MIT, c1982. — xii,266p : ill ; 21cm
Translation of: Le second règne de la nature. — Bibliography: p233-252. — Includes index
ISBN 0-262-04066-2 : £14.00 B82-35670

581.1 — PLANTS. PHYSIOLOGY

581.1'0428 — Plants. Roots — *Conference proceedings*

Structure and function of plant roots : proceedings of the 2nd International Symposium, held in Bratislava, Czechoslovakia, September 1-5, 1980 / edited by R. Brouwer ... [et al.]. — The Hague ; London : Nijhoff, 1981. — xix,415p : ill ; 25cm. — (Developments in plant and soil sciences ; v.4)
Includes bibliographies and index
ISBN 90-247-2510-0 : Unpriced B82-14564

581.1'0724 — Plants. Physiology. Mathematical models — *Conference proceedings*

Crop Science Model Builders' Group. *Meeting (10th : 1980 : Glasshouse Crops Research Institute).* Mathematics and plant physiology : [proceedings of the tenth annual meeting of the Crop Science Model Builders' Group of the Agricultural Research Council, held at the Glasshouse Crops Research Institute, 27-28 March 1980] / edited by D.A. Rose and D.A. Charles-Edwards. — London : Academic, 1981. — xviii,320p : ill ; 24cm. — (Experimental botany)
Includes bibliographies and index
ISBN 0-12-596880-9 : £28.60 : CIP rev.
B81-12356

581.1'16 — Vascular plants. Phloem

Wooding, F. B. P.. Phloem / F.B.P. Wooding. — 2nd ed.(rev.). — Burlington, N.C. : Carolina Biological Supply Co., Scientific Publications Division, c1978 ; Chichester : Distributed by Packard. — 16p : ill(some col.) ; 25cm. — (Carolina biology readers ; 15)
Previous ed.: London : Oxford University Press, 1971. — Bibliography: p16
ISBN 0-89278-215-3 (unbound) : £0.80
B82-31593

581.1'33 — Plants. Metabolism

Phytochemical Society of North America. *Meeting (21st : 1981 : Cornell University).* Cellular and subcellular localization in plant metabolism / [proceedings of the Twenty-first Annual Meeting of the Phytochemical Society of North America held August 10-14, 1981 at Cornell University, Ithaca, New York] ; edited by Leroy L. Creasy and Ceza Hrazdina. — New York ; London : Plenum, c1982. — ix,277p : ill ; 24cm. — (Recent advances in phytochemistry ; v.16)
Includes index
ISBN 0-306-41023-0 : Unpriced B82-38662

581.1'33 — Plants. Metabolism. Effects of drought

The **Physiology** and biochemistry of drought resistance in plants / edited by L.G. Paleg and D. Aspinall. — Sydney ; London : Academic Press, 1981. — xv,492p : ill ; 24cm
Bibliography: p411-466. — Includes index
ISBN 0-12-544380-3 : £46.20 B82-32782

581.1'33 — Plants. Symbiotic microorganisms. Nitrogen. Fixation. Genetic engineering — *Conference proceedings*

Genetic engineering of symbiotic nitrogen fixation and conservation of fixed nitrogen / [proceedings of a symposium of enhancing biological production of ammonia from atmospheric nitrogen and soil nitrate, held June 29-July 3, 1980, at Granlibakken, Lake Tahoe, California, co-sponsored by NSF, Grant PFR 77-07301, and the College of Agricultural and Environmental Sciences, University of California, Davis] ; edited by J.M. Lyons ... [et al.]. — New York ; London : Plenum, c1981. — xiv,698p : ill,ports ; 26cm. — (Basic life sciences ; v.17)
Includes bibliographies and index
ISBN 0-306-40730-2 : Unpriced B82-13922

581.1'3342 — Plants. Growth. Effects of photosynthesis. Measurement

Techniques in bioproductivity and photosynthesis / edited by J. Coombs and D.O. Hall ; sponsored by the United Nations Environment Programme. — Oxford : Pergamon, 1982. — xix,171p : ill,1map ; 25cm. — (Pergamon international library)
Includes bibliographies and index
ISBN 0-08-027382-3 (cased) : Unpriced : CIP rev.
ISBN 0-08-027383-1 (pbk) : £7.50 B81-09489

581.1'3342 — Plants. Photophosphorylation. Electron transfer

Electron transport and photophosphorylation / edited by J. Barber. — Amsterdam ; Oxford : Elsevier Biomedical, 1982. — xi,287p : ill,1port ; 25cm. — (Topics in photosynthesis ; v.4)
Includes bibliographies and index
ISBN 0-444-80375-0 : Unpriced B82-21632

581.1'3342 — Plants. Photosynthesis

Edwards, G.. C3, C4 : mechanisms, cellular and environmental regulation of photosynthesis. — Oxford : Blackwell Scientific, Dec.1982. — [550]p
ISBN 0-632-00757-5 (cased) : £32.00 : CIP entry
ISBN 0-632-00767-2 (pbk) : £18.00
B82-30045

Hall, D. O.. Photosynthesis / D.O. Hall, K.K. Rao. — 3rd ed. — London : Edward Arnold, 1981. — 84p : ill ; 22cm. — (The Institute of Biology's studies in biology, ISSN 0537-9024 ; no.37)
Previous ed.: 1977. — Bibliography: p80-82. — Includes index
ISBN 0-7131-2827-5 (pbk) : £2.75 : CIP rev.
B81-30608

581.1'3342 — Plants. Photosynthesis. Energy transfer — *Conference proceedings*

Harry Steenbock Symposium *(11th : 1981 : University of Wisconsin-Madison).* Energy coupling in photosynthesis : proceedings of the Eleventh Harry Steenbock Symposium held 6-8 July, 1981 at the University of Wisconsin-Madison, Wisconsin, U.S.A. / editors Bruce R. Selman and Susanne Selman-Reimer. — New York ; Oxford : Elsevier/North-Holland, c1981. — xv,374p : ill ; 25cm. — (Developments in biochemistry, ISSN 0165-1714 ; v.20)
Includes index
ISBN 0-444-00675-3 : £31.58 B82-11227

581.1'3342'0724 — Plants. Photosynthesis. Research. Mathematical models

Charles-Edwards, D. A.. The mathematics of photosynthesis and productivity / D.A. Charles-Edwards. — London : Academic Press, 1981. — x,127p : ill ; 24cm. — (Experimental botany ; v.17)
Includes bibliographies and index
ISBN 0-12-170580-3 : £10.40 : CIP rev.
B81-13461

581.1'335 — Plants. Nutrition. Minerals — *Conference proceedings*

Metals and micronutrients. — London : Academic Press, Dec.1982. — [350]p. — (Annual proceedings of the Phytochemical Society of Europe, ISSN 0309-9393 ; no.21)
Conference papers
ISBN 0-12-589580-1 : CIP entry B82-29887

581.1'3356 — Plants. Copper — *Conference proceedings*

Copper in soils and plants : proceedings of the Golden Jubilee International Symposium on 'Copper in Soils and Plants' held at Murdoch University, Perth, Western Australia on May 7-9, 1981 under the sponsorship of the Australian Academy of Technological Sciences / edited by J.F. Loneragan, A.D. Robson, R.D. Graham. — Sydney ; London : Academic Press, 1981. — xv,380p : ill ; 24cm
Includes bibliographies and index
ISBN 0-12-455520-9 : £16.00
Primary classification 631.4'16 B82-07560

581.19'12 — Plants. Transport phenomena

Moorby, Jeffrey. Transport systems in plants / Jeffrey Moorby. — London : Longman, 1981. — 169p : ill ; 22cm. — (Integrated themes in biology)
Bibliography: p161-162. — Includes index
ISBN 0-582-44379-2 (pbk) : £6.95 B82-01700

581.19'153 — Plants. Effects of daylight — *Conference proceedings*

British Photobiology Society. *International Symposium (1st : 1981 : Leicester).* Plants and the daylight spectrum / [proceedings of the First International Symposium of the British Photobiology Society, Leicester, 5-8 January 1981] ; edited by H. Smith. — London : Academic Press, 1981. — xix,508p : ill,3maps ; 24cm
Includes bibliographies
ISBN 0-12-650980-8 : £22.00 : CIP rev.
B81-31347

581.19'2 — Plants. Biochemistry

The **Biochemistry** of plants : comprehensive treatise / [P.J. Stumpf and E.E. Conn, editor-in-chief]. — New York ; London : Academic Press
Vol.1: The plant cell / N.E. Tolbert, editor. — 1980. — xvi,705p : ill ; 25cm
Includes bibliographies and index
ISBN 0-12-675401-2 : £36.40 B82-39139

The **Biochemistry** of plants : a comprehensive treatise / [P.K. Stumpf and E.E. Conn, editors-in-chief]. — New York ; London : Academic Press
Vol.2: Metabolism and respiration / David D. Davies, editor. — 1980. — xvi,687p : ill ; 25cm
Includes bibliographies and index
ISBN 0-12-675402-0 : £34.60 B82-39140

The **Biochemistry** of plants : a comprehensive treatise. — New York ; London : Academic Press
Vol 3: Carbohydrates structure and function / Jack Preiss, editor. — 1980. — xvi,644p : ill ; 25cm
Includes bibliographies and index
ISBN 0-12-675403-9 : £46.00 B82-21280

The **Biochemistry** of plants : a comprehensive treatise / [P.K. Stumpf and E.E. Conn, editors-in-chief]. — New York ; London : Academic Press
Vol.5: Amino acids and derivatives / B.J. Miflin, editor. — 1980. — xvi,670p : ill ; 25cm
Includes bibliographies and index
ISBN 0-12-675405-5 : £36.40 B82-39141

The **Biochemistry** of plants / [P.K. Stumpf and E.E. Conn, editors-in-chief]. — New York ; London : Academic Press
Vol.7: Secondary plant products / E.E. Conn, editor. — 1981. — xx,798p : ill ; 25cm
Includes bibliographies and index
ISBN 0-12-675407-1 : £56.20 B82-21296

Goodwin, T. W.. Introduction to plant biochemistry. — 2nd ed. — Oxford : Pergamon, Apr.1982. — [400]p. — (Pergamon international library)
Previous ed.: 1972
ISBN 0-08-024922-1 (cased) : £35.00 : CIP entry
ISBN 0-08-024921-3 (pbk) : £14.00
B82-03729

581.19'24 — Isoprenoid compounds. Biosynthesis

Biosynthesis of isoprenoid compounds / edited by John W. Porter and Sandra L. Spurgeon. — New York ; Chichester : Wiley
Includes index
Vol.1. — c1981. — xiii,558p : ill ; 24cm
ISBN 0-471-04807-0 : £44.00 B82-08720

581.2 — PLANTS. DISEASES

581.2 — Plants. Diseases

Plant disease : an advanced treatise. — New York ; London : Academic Press
Vol.5: How plants defend themselves / edited by James G. Horsfall, Ellis B. Cowling. — 1980. — xxii,534p : ill ; 24cm
Includes bibliographies and index
ISBN 0-12-356405-0 : £27.80 B82-35368

581.2 — Plants. Pathology

Manners, J. G.. Principles of plant pathology / J.G. Manners. — Cambridge : Cambridge University Press, 1982. — viii,264p : ill ; 24cm
Bibliography: p229-251. — Includes index
ISBN 0-521-24301-7 (cased) : £22.50 : CIP rev.
ISBN 0-521-28592-5 (pbk) : £8.95 B82-11497

581.2'1 — Plants. Physiology. Effects of diseases — *Conference proceedings*

Effects of disease on the physiology of the growing plant / edited by P.G. Ayres. — Cambridge : Cambridge University Press, 1981. — viii,228p : ill ; 24cm. — (Seminar series / Society for Experimental Biology ; 11)
Conference papers. — Includes bibliographies and index
ISBN 0-521-23306-2 (cased) : £20.00 : CIP rev.
ISBN 0-521-29898-9 (pbk) : £8.95 B81-34013

581.2'3 — Plants. Pathogens: Microorganisms

Dickinson, C. H.. Plant pathology and plant pathogens / C.H. Dickinson, J.A. Lucas. — 2nd ed. — Oxford : Blackwell Scientific, 1982. — viii,229p : ill ; 24cm. — (Basic microbiology ; 6)
Previous ed.: 1977. — Includes bibliographies and index
ISBN 0-632-00918-7 (pbk) : £7.80 : CIP rev. B82-12932

581.2'3 — Plants. Pathogens: Microorganisms — *Conference proceedings*

Bacteria and plants / edited by Muriel E. Rhodes-Roberts and F.A. Skinner. — London : Academic Press, c1982. — xiii,264p : ill ; 24cm. — (The Society for Applied Bacteriology symposium series ; 10)
Includes bibliographies and index
ISBN 0-12-587080-9 : £14.20 : CIP rev. B82-00337

581.2'3 — Plants. Pathogens: Microorganisms. Toxins

Toxins in plant disease / edited by R.D. Durbin. — New York ; London : Academic Press, 1981. — xii,515p : ill ; 24cm. — (Physiological ecology)
Includes bibliographies and index
ISBN 0-12-225050-8 : £34.40 B82-21247

581.2'322 — Plants. Mycoplasma diseases

Plant and insect mycoplasma techniques / edited by M.J. Daniels and P.G. Markham. — London : Croom Helm, c1982. — 369p : ill ; 23cm
Includes bibliographies and index
ISBN 0-7099-0272-7 : £12.50 : CIP rev.
Also classified at 595.7'02322 B81-24656

581.2'326 — Phytoalexins

Phytoalexins / general editors John A. Bailey and John W. Mansfield. — Glasgow : Blackie, 1982. — x,334p : ill ; 24cm
Includes bibliographies and index
ISBN 0-216-91162-1 : £28.00 : CIP rev. B81-31459

581.2'34 — Plants. Virus diseases

Bos, L.. Introduction to plant virology. — London : Longman, Feb.1983. — [132]p
ISBN 0-582-44680-5 (pbk) : £6.95 : CIP entry B82-38679

581.2'4 — Plants. Toxic effects of heavy metals

Effect of heavy metal pollution on plants / edited by N.W. Lepp. — London : Applied Science, c1981. — 2v. : ill,1map ; 23cm. — (Pollution monitoring series)
Includes bibliographies and index
ISBN 0-85334-959-2 : Unpriced : CIP rev.
ISBN 0-85334-923-1 (v.2) : £21.00 B81-14811

581.3 — PLANTS. DEVELOPMENT

581.3 — Plants. Development. Molecular biology

The **Molecular** biology of plant development. — Oxford : Blackwell Scientific, June 1982. — [600]p. — (Botanical monographs ; v.18)
ISBN 0-632-00727-3 : £35.00 : CIP entry B82-14218

581.3'1 — Plants. Abscission

Addicott, Frederick T.. Abscission / Frederick T. Addicott. — Berkeley ; London : University of California Press, c1982. — xviii,369p : ill ; 25cm
Bibliography: p315-354. — Includes index
ISBN 0-520-04288-3 : £29.75 B82-34977

581.3'1 — Plants. Growth. Analysis. Quantitative methods

Hunt, Roderick, *1945-*. Plant growth curves : the functional approach to plant growth analysis / Roderick Hunt. — London : Edward Arnold, 1982. — vii,248p : ill ; 23cm
Bibliography: p194-228. — Includes index
ISBN 0-7131-2844-5 (pbk) : £8.75 : CIP rev. B82-11988

581.3'1 — Plants. Growth. Effects of soil properties

Davidescu, David. Evaluation of fertility by plant and soil analysis / David Davidescu, Velicica Davidescu. — Bucuresti : Editura Academiei ; Tunbridge Wells : Abacus, c1982. — 560p : ill ; 25cm
Translation of: Testarea stării de fertilitate prin plantă şi sol. — Bibliography: p518-544. — Includes index
ISBN 0-85626-123-8 : Unpriced : CIP rev. B81-40261

581.3'1 — Plants. Growth hormones — *Conference proceedings*

Plant growth substances 1982. — London : Academic Press, Dec.1982. — [650]p
Conference papers
ISBN 0-12-735380-1 : CIP entry B82-29894

581.3'1 — Plants. Growth. Regulation

Wareing, P. F.. Growth and differentiation in plants / P.F. Wareing and I.D.J. Phillips. — 3rd ed. — Oxford : Pergamon Press, 1981. — xi,343p : ill ; 25cm. — (Pergamon international library)
Previous ed.: published as The control of growth and differentiation in plants. 1978. — Includes bibliographies and index
ISBN 0-08-026350-x (cased) : Unpriced B82-02317

581.3'1 — Plants. Growth. Regulation — *Conference proceedings*

'Aspects and prospects of plant growth regulators' : proceedings of a symposium organised jointly by the Dutch Committee for Plant Growth Regulators and the British Plant Growth Regulator Group held at the International Agricultural Centre, Wageningen, the Netherlands on 3-7th November, 1980 / edited by B. Jeffcoat. — Wantage : British Plant Growth Regulator Group, 1981. — x,249p : ill ; 21cm. — (Mongraph / British Plant Growth Regulator Group ; no.6)
ISBN 0-906673-04-6 (pbk) : £5.00 B82-02025

581.3'1 — Plants. Leaves. Growth

Dale, John E.. The growth of leaves / John E. Dale. — London : Edward Arnold, 1982. — 60p : ill ; 22cm. — (The Institute of Biology's studies in biology, ISSN 0537-9024 ; no.137)
Bibliography: p58-59. — Includes index
ISBN 0-7131-2836-4 (pbk) : £2.25 : CIP rev. B81-31631

581.3'8 — Plants. Evolution — *Early works*

Church, A. H.. Revolutionary botany : 'thalassiophyta' and other essays of A.H. Church / edited by D.J. Mabberley with a recollection by E.J.H. Corner. — Oxford : Clarendon, 1981. — xii,256p,27plates : ill ; 24cm. — (Oxford Science publications)
ISBN 0-19-854548-7 : £21.00
Also classified at 581.9425'7 B82-02983

581.3'8 — Plants. Speciation

Grant, Verne. Plant speciation / Verne Grant. — 2nd ed. — New York ; Guildford : Columbia University Press, 1981. — xii,563p : ill,maps ; 24cm
Previous ed.: 1977. — Bibliography: p489-540. — Includes index
ISBN 0-231-05112-3 (cased) : £28.00
ISBN 0-231-05113-1 (pbk) : £10.50 B82-17718

581.4 — PLANTS. ANATOMY

581.4 — Plants. Anatomy

Fahn, A.. Plant anatomy. — 3rd ed. — Oxford : Pergamon, Feb.1982. — [400]p. — (Pergamon international library)
Previous ed.: 1974
ISBN 0-08-028030-7 (cased) : £27.00 : CIP entry
ISBN 0-08-028029-3 (pbk) : £12.50 B81-35943

581.4'028 — Plants. Anatomy. Laboratory techniques

O'Brien, T. P. (Terry P.). The study of plant structure : principles and selected methods / T.P. O'Brien, M.E. McCully. — Melbourne : Termarcarphi ; Oxford : Distributed by Blackwell, c1981. — 357p in various pagings : ill(some col.) ; 31cm
Includes bibliographies
ISBN 0-9594174-0-0 : Unpriced B82-28986

581.4'6 — Plants. Spores

Zoosporic plant pathogens. — London : Academic Press, Feb.1983. — [370]p
ISBN 0-12-139180-9 : CIP entry B82-36576

581.4'7 — Plants. Cuticles — *Conference proceedings*

The **Plant** cuticle : papers presented at an international symposium organized by the Linnean Society of London, held at Burlington House, London, 8-11 September 1980 / editors D.F. Cutler, K.L. Alvin and C.E. Price. — London : Published for the Linnean Society of London [by] Academic Press, c1982. — x,461p : ill,maps ; 27cm. — (Linnean Society symposium series ; no.10)
Includes bibliographies and index
ISBN 0-12-199920-3 : Unpriced : CIP rev. B81-32049

581.5 — PLANTS. ECOLOGY

581.5 — Plants. Ecology

Etherington, John R.. Environment and plant ecology. — 2nd ed. — London : Wiley, July 1982. — [400]p
Previous ed.: 1975
ISBN 0-471-10136-2 (cased) : £19.50 : CIP entry
ISBN 0-471-10146-x (pbk) : £8.00 B82-13251

Grace, John. Plant-atmosphere relationships. — London : Chapman and Hall, Feb.1983. — [80] p. — (Outline studies in ecology)
ISBN 0-412-23180-8 (pbk) : £2.75 : CIP entry B82-38292

Silvertown, Jonathan W.. Introduction to plant population ecology. — London : Longman, July 1982. — [198]p
ISBN 0-582-44265-6 (pbk) : £7.95 : CIP entry B82-16469

581.5'0973 — United States. Plants. Ecology, *1895-1955*

Tobey, Ronald C.. Saving the prairies : the life cycle of the founding school of American plant ecology 1895-1955 / Ronald C. Tobey. — Berkeley ; London : University of California Press, c1981. — x,315p : ill ; 24cm
Bibliography: p285-298. — Includes index
ISBN 0-520-04352-9 : £17.50 B82-28103

581.5′222 — Plants. Effects of atmosphere pollutants

Effects of gaseous air pollution in agriculture and horticulture / [edited by] M.H. Unsworth, D.P. Ormrod. — London : Butterworth Scientific, 1982. — xiv,532p : ill,maps ; 25cm
Conference proceedings. — Includes bibliographies and index
ISBN 0-408-10705-7 : Unpriced : CIP rev. B82-00223

581.5′247 — Plants. Ecological communities — *Conference proceedings — Festschriften*

The **Plant** community as a working mechanism. — Oxford : Blackwell Scientific, Mar.1982. — [128]p. — (A Special publication of the British Ecological Society ; 1)
Conference papers
ISBN 0-632-00839-3 (pbk) : £3.50 : CIP entry B82-06235

581.5′247 — Plants. Ecological communities. Ordination

Ordination of plant communities / edited by Robert H. Whittaker. — The Hague ; London : Junk, 1982. — 388p : ill ; 24cm
Includes bibliographies and index
ISBN 90-619-3565-2 (pbk) : Unpriced B82-38747

581.5′247′09411 — Scotland. Plants. Ecological communities — *Technical data*

Birse, E. L.. Plant communities of Scotland : revised and additional tables : a preliminary phytocoenonia / by E.L. Birse. — Aberdeen (Craigiebuckler, Aberdeen, AB9 2QJ) : Macaulay Institute for Soil Research, c1980. — 235p : ill(some col.) ; 28cm. — (Bulletin / Soil Survey of Scotland ; no.4)
Bibliography: p230-231
ISBN 0-7084-0228-3 (pbk) : Unpriced B82-25107

581.5′26323′0941 — Great Britain. Rivers. Plants. Ecology

Haslam, S. M.. Vegetation in British rivers / S.M. Haslam. — London : Nature Conservancy Council, Chief Scientist′s Team, c1982. — 2v. : maps ; 30cm
Includes index
ISBN 0-86139-203-5 (spiral) : Unpriced B82-39978

581.5′264 — England. Upland regions. Vegetation. Change. Ecological aspects

Ecology of vegetation change in upland landscapes / D.F. Ball ... [et al.]. — Bangor (Bangor Research Station, Penrhos Rd., Bangor, Gwynedd LL57 2LQ) : Institute of Terrestrial Ecology, 1981. — 2v. : ill,maps ; 30cm. — (Bangor occasional paper, ISSN 0260-6925 ; v.2, 3)
Cover title. — Includes bibliographies
Unpriced (pbk) B82-16082

581.5′2642 — Woodlands. Vegetation. Dynamics — *Conference proceedings*

Vegetation dynamics in grasslands, heathlands and Mediterranean ligneous formations : symposium of the Working Groups for Succession research on permanent plots, and data-processing in phytosociology of the International Society for Vegetation Science, held at Montpellier, France, September 1980 / edited by P. Poissonet ... [et al.]. — Hague ; London : Junk, 1981. — x,286p : ill,maps ; 27cm. — (Advances in vegetation science ; 4)
Reprinted from Vegetatio, vols. 46-47, 1981. — Includes bibliographies
ISBN 90-619-3636-5 : Unpriced
Also classified at 581.5′2643 B82-19362

581.5′2642′098133 — Brazil. Areia region. Mata de Pau Ferro. Vegetation

Mayo, S. J.. Mata de Pau Ferro : a pilot study of the Brejo Forest of Paraíba, Brazil / S.J. Mayo & V.P.B. Fevereiro. — Kew : Royal Botanic Gardens (Bentham-Moxon Trust) in association with the Winston Churchill Memorial Trust, Great Britain, 1982. — 29p : ill,maps ; 30cm
'Travelling Fellowship to Northeast Brazil 1980-1981. Second report to the Winston Churchill Memorial Trust.'. — Summary in Portuguese. — Bibliography: p29
Unpriced (spiral) B82-26632

581.5′2643 — Grassland & heathland. Vegetation. Dynamics — *Conference proceedings*

Vegetation dynamics in grasslands, heathlands and Mediterranean ligneous formations : symposium of the Working Groups for Succession research on permanent plots, and data-processing in phytosociology of the International Society for Vegetation Science, held at Montpellier, France, September 1980 / edited by P. Poissonet ... [et al.]. — Hague ; London : Junk, 1981. — x,286p : ill,maps ; 27cm. — (Advances in vegetation science ; 4)
Reprinted from Vegetatio, vols. 46-47, 1981. — Includes bibliographies
ISBN 90-619-3636-5 : Unpriced
Primary classification 581.5′2642 B82-19362

581.5′265 — Halophytes. Ecology

Contributions to the ecology of halophytes / edited by David N. Sen and Kishan S. Rajpurohit. — Hague ; London : Junk, 1982. — viii,272p : ill,maps ; 27cm. — (Tasks for vegetation science ; 2)
Includes bibliographies and index
ISBN 90-619-3942-9 : Unpriced B82-23507

581.5′7 — Plants. Defence mechanisms — *Conference proceedings*

Active defense mechanisms in plants / [proceedings of a NATO advanced study institute on active defense mechanisms in plants, held April 21-May 3, 1980, in Cape Sounion, Greece] ; edited by R.K.S. Wood. — New York ; London : Plenum published in cooperation with NATO Scientific Affairs Division, c1982. — x,381p : ill ; 26cm. — (NATO advanced study institutes series. Series A, Life sciences ; v.37)
Includes bibliographies and index
ISBN 0-306-40814-7 : Unpriced B82-22891

581.6 — ECONOMIC BOTANY

581.6′1 — Plants useful to man

Langenheim, Jean H.. Botany : plant biology and its relation to human affairs / Jean H. Langenheim, Kenneth V. Thimann. — New York ; Chichester : Wiley, c1982. — xi,624p : ill(some col.),maps(some col.) ; 25cm
Text on lining papers. — Bibliography: p573-579. — Includes index
ISBN 0-471-85880-3 : £17.90 B82-28083

581.6′1′0321 — Plants useful to man — *Encyclopaedias*

Popular encyclopedia of plants / chief editor Vernon H. Heywood ; associate editor Stuart R. Chant. — Cambridge : Cambridge University Press, 1982. — 368p : col.ill ; 29cm
Bibliography: p368. — Includes index
ISBN 0-521-24611-3 : £15.00 : CIP rev. B82-03616

581.6′1′0941 — Great Britain. Plants useful to man. Use by agricultural communities, ***1600-1800***

Palliser, Susan. Plants and their uses in the agricultural community : some examples / Susan Palliser. — Leeds (The School of English, The University, Leeds) : Leeds Folklore Group, 1982. — 13leaves ; 30cm. — (Leeds Folklore Group papers in folk life studies ; 1)
£0.28 (unbound) B82-30881

581.6′3′094 — Europe. Herbs — *Field guides*

Sloover, Jacques de. Wild herbs : a field guide : aromatic, medicinal, culinary / Jacques de Sloover & Martine Goossens ; English translation by Lucia Wildt. — Newton Abbot : David & Charles, [1981]. — 213p : chiefly ill (some col.),col.maps ; 22cm + key to symbols (1sheet : ill ; 21cm)
Translation of: Guide des herbes sauvages. — Ill on lining papers. — Bibliography: p203-205. — Includes index
ISBN 0-7153-8221-7 : £6.95 : CIP rev. B81-21509

581.6′34 — Medicinal plants

Hamilton, Edward. The Flora Homoeopathica. — London : Homoeopathic Trust, Aug.1981. — [626]p
Facsim. of: 1st ed. London : Bailliere, 1852
ISBN 0-9507629-0-3 : £40.00 : CIP entry B81-24627

581.6′52 — Weeds

Biology and ecology of weeds / edited by W. Holzner and M. Numata. — Hague ; London : Junk, 1982. — ix,461p : ill ; 27cm. — (Geobotany ; 2)
Includes bibliographies and index
ISBN 90-619-3682-9 : Unpriced B82-30377

581.6′52′094 — Western Europe. Weeds — *Polyglot dictionaries*

Elsevier′s dictionary of weeds of Western Europe : their common names and importance in Latin, Danish, German, English, Spanish, Finnish, French, Icelandic, Italian, Dutch, Norwegian, Portuguese and Swedish / compiled by Gareth Williams. — Amsterdam ; Oxford : Elsevier Scientific, 1982. — 320p ; 24cm
ISBN 0-444-41978-0 (pbk) : £37.15 : CIP rev. B81-31196

581.8 — PLANTS. HISTOLOGY AND CYTOLOGY

581.87′33 — Plants. Cells. Chloroplasts

Tribe, Michael A.. Chloroplasts and mitochondria / Michael Tribe, Peter Whittaker. — 2nd ed. — London : Edward Arnold, 1982. — 83p : ill ; 22cm. — (The Institute of Biology′s studies in biology, ISSN 0537-9024 ; no.31)
Previous ed.: 1972. — Bibliography: p83. — Includes index
ISBN 0-7131-2828-3 (pbk) : £2.75 : CIP rev.
Also classified at 581.87′342 B81-30607

581.87′33 — Plants. Cells. Chloroplasts. Biochemistry

Halliwell, Barry. Chloroplast metabolism : the structure and function of chloroplasts in green leaf cells / Barry Halliwell. — Oxford : Clarendon, 1981. — xi,257p : ill ; 24cm
Includes bibliographies and index
ISBN 0-19-854549-5 : £20.00 : CIP rev. B81-30337

581.87′33 — Plants. Cells. Chloroplasts. Evolution — *Conference proceedings*

On the origins of chloroplasts / edited by Jerome A. Schiff with the assistance of Harvard Lyman. — New York ; Oxford : Elsevier/North-Holland, c1982. — xxvi,336p : ill,1port ; 24cm
Conference papers. — Includes bibliographies and index
ISBN 0-444-00669-9 : £42.10 B82-21907

581.87′34 — Plants. Cells. Cytoplasm

The **Cytoskeleton** in plant growth and development. — London : Academic Press, Nov.1982. — [450]p
ISBN 0-12-453780-4 : CIP entry B82-26863

581.87′342 — Plants. Cells. Mitochondria

Tribe, Michael A.. Chloroplasts and mitochondria / Michael Tribe, Peter Whittaker. — 2nd ed. — London : Edward Arnold, 1982. — 83p : ill ; 22cm. — (The Institute of Biology′s studies in biology, ISSN 0537-9024 ; no.31)
Previous ed.: 1972. — Bibliography: p83. — Includes index
ISBN 0-7131-2828-3 (pbk) : £2.75 : CIP rev.
Primary classification 581.87′33 B81-30607

581.87′5 — Plants. Cells. Membranes

Isolation of membranes and organelles from plant cells. — London : Academic Press, Feb.1983. — 1v.
ISBN 0-12-318820-2 : CIP entry B82-36575

581.87′5 — Plants. Cells. Membranes — *Conference proceedings*

International Workshop on Plasmalemma and Tonoplast of Plant Cells ***(1981 : Strasbourg)***.
Plasmalemma and tonoplast : their functions in the plant cell : proceedings of the International Workshop on Plasmalemma and Tonoplast of Plant Cells held in Strasbourg, France, September 8-11, 1981 / editors D. Marmé, E. Marrè and R. Hertel. — Amsterdam ; Oxford : Elsevier Biomedical, 1982. — x,446p : ill ; 25cm. — (Developments in plant biology ; v.7)
Includes index
ISBN 0-444-80409-9 : £37.89 B82-21909

581.87'61 — Plants. Cells. Metabolism

Hall, J. L.. Plant cell structures and metabolism. — 2nd ed. — London : Longman, Mar.1982. — [560]p
Previous ed.: 1974
ISBN 0-582-44408-x (pbk) : £10.95 : CIP entry
B82-00213

581.9 — BOTANY. GEOGRAPHICAL TREATMENT

581.9 — Plants. Distribution. Geographical aspects. Mathematical models

Box, Elgene Owen. Macroclimate and plant forms : an introduction to predictive modeling in phytogeography / Elgene Owen Box. — The Hague ; London : Junk, 1981. — xiii,258p : ill,maps ; 27cm. — (Tasks for vegetation science ; 1)
Bibliography: p243-258
ISBN 90-619-3941-0 : Unpriced B82-04397

581.909'3 — Tropical regions. Plants useful to bees — *Lists*

International Bee Research Association. Planting for bees in developing countries. — Gerrards Cross : International Bee Research Association, Apr.1982. — [10]p. — (Source materials for apiculture ; no.3)
ISBN 0-86098-113-4 (pbk) : £1.00 : CIP entry
B82-17217

581.92 — Marine plants

Dawes, Clinton J.. Marine botany / Clinton J. Dawes. — New York ; Chichester : Wiley, c1981. — x,628p : ill,maps ; 24cm
Includes bibliographies and index
ISBN 0-471-07844-1 : £33.50 B82-13990

Dring, Matthew J.. The biology of marine plants. — London : E. Arnold, Nov.1982. — [256]p. — (Contemporary biology)
ISBN 0-7131-2860-7 : £9.95 : CIP entry
B82-27948

581.94 — Europe. Plants — *Field guides*

Spotter's guide to wild plants : trees, flowers, fungi, seaweeds, ferns, grasses, mosses, lichens and liverworts / [edited by Sue Jacquemier and Patricia Monahan]. — London : Usborne, 1981. — 191p : ill(some col.) ; 20cm
Includes index
ISBN 0-86020-507-x : £3.99 B82-39038

581.94'0216 — Europe. Plants — *Lists*

Moore, D. M.. Flora Europaea check-list and chromosome index / D.M. Moore. — Cambridge : Cambridge University Press, 1982. — x,423p ; 24cm
Bibliography: p366-408. — Includes index
ISBN 0-521-23759-9 : £30.00 B82-36886

581.941 — Great Britain. Chalk regions. Plants — *Field guides*

A **Brief** guide to plants of our chalk downs. — Hitchin ([c/o Hon. Sec., Offley Place, Great Offley, Hitchin, Herts. SG5 3DS]) : Hertfordshire & Middlesex Trust for Nature Conservation, [1981?], c1978. — 21p : ill ; 15x21cm
Text on inside cover. — Produced by P.E. Taylor
£0.30 (pbk) B82-09513

581.941 — Great Britain. Plants — *Field guides*

Nicholson, B. E.. Plants of the British Isles / Barbara Nicholson ; introduced and described by Frank Brightman. — London : Collins in association with the British Museum (Natural History), 1982. — 76p : ill(some col.) ; 27cm
Ill on lining papers. — Includes index
ISBN 0-00-410416-1 : £7.95 B82-16969

581.9412'95 — Scotland. Fife Region. West Wemyss. Plants. Observation — *For schools*

The **Flora** of West Wemyss. — [West Wemyss] : West Wemyss Environmental Education Centre, [1982]. — 30p,[2]leaves of plates : ill,1map ; 22cm
Cover title. — Bibliography: p30
Unpriced (pbk) B82-19482

581.9423'8 — Somerset. Plants — *Lists*

Roe, R. G. B.. The flora of Somerset / R.G.B. Roe. — Taunton : Somerset Archaeological and Natural History Society, 1981. — xv,345p,[20]p of plates : ill(some col.) ; 19cm
Bibliography: p313-315. — Includes index
ISBN 0-902152-12-2 (pbk) : Unpriced
B82-08278

581.9425'7 — Oxfordshire. Plants

Church, A. H.. Revolutionary botany : 'thalassiophyta' and other essays of A.H. Church / edited by D.J. Mabberley with a recollection by E.J.H. Corner. — Oxford : Clarendon, 1981. — xii,256p,27plates : ill ; 24cm. — (Oxford Science publications)
ISBN 0-19-854548-7 : £21.00
Primary classification 581.3'8 B82-02983

581.9425'97 — Buckinghamshire. Chalfont St Giles. Parks: Newland Park. Plants

The **Natural** history of Newland Park. — [Aylesbury] : [Buckinghamshire County Council]
1: Introduction and preliminary survey / by C.J. Smith. — [1981]. — 17p : ill,maps,plans ; 21cm
Bibliography: p16-17
ISBN 0-86059-245-6 (pbk) : Unpriced
B82-14418

581.9561 — Turkey. Plants

The **Flora** of Turkey and the East Aegean islands . — Edinburgh : Edinburgh University Press
Vol.7. — Sept.1982. — [968]p
ISBN 0-85224-396-0 : £60.00 : CIP entry
B82-20208

581.959 — ASEAN countries. Plants

Flora malesiana. — The Hague ; London : [Published by] Nijhoff under the auspices of Lembaga Biologi Nasional (Botanic Gardens of Indonesia), Bogor, Indonesia and the Rijksherbarium, Leyden, Holland. — (Systematic revisions)
Ser.1: Spermatophyta flowering plants. — 1982
General editor: C.G.G.J. van Steenis
Vol.9
Pt.2: Dipterocarpaceae. — p237-552 : ill,maps ; 24cm
Cover title. — Text on inside covers. — Includes index
ISBN 90-247-2696-4 (pbk) : Unpriced
B82-40149

581.9595 — Malaysia. Plants

Flora malesiana ... / prepared on an international co-operative basis under the supervision of several directors of botanic gardens, keepers of herbaria and various prominent botanists ; general editors C.G.G.J. van Steenis & R.E. Holttum. — Hague ; London : Published under the auspices of Lembaga Biologi Nasional, Botanic Gardens of Indonesia, Bogor, Java and of the Rijksherbarium, Leyden, Netherlands by Nijhoff. — (Taxonomical revisions)
Subtitle: being an illustrated systematic account of the Malesian flora — including keys for determination — diagnostic descriptions — references to the literature — synonymy — and distribution — and notes on the ecology of its wild and commonly cultivated plants. — At head of title: Indonesian Institute of Sciences
Ser.2: Pteridophyta
Vol.1
Pt. 5: Thelypteridaceae. — 1982. — 20,p331-599 : ill ; 24cm
Maps on inside covers. — Includes index
ISBN 90-247-2652-2 (pbk) : Unpriced
B82-26968

Flora malesiana ... / prepared on an international co-operative basis under the supervision of several directors of botanic gardens, keepers of herbaria and various prominent botanists ; general editors C.G.G.J. van Steenis & R.E. Holttum. — Hague ; London : Published under the auspices of Lembaga Biologi Nasional, Botanic Gardens of Indonesia, Bogor, Java and of the Rijksherbarium, Leyden, Netherlands by Nijhoff. — (Taxonomical revisions)
Subtitle: being an illustrated systematic account of the Malesian flora — including keys for determination — diagnostic descriptions — references to the literature synonymy — and distribution and notes on the ecology of its wild and commonly cultivated plants. — At head of title: Indonesian Institute of Sciences
Ser.2: Pteridophyta
Vol.1. — c1982. — 20,xxiii,599p : ill ; 25cm
Includes index
ISBN 90-247-2653-0 : Unpriced B82-26967

581.969'9 — South Africa. Prince Edward Islands. Plants

Gremmen, N. J. M.. The vegetation of the subantarctic islands, Marion and Prince Edward / N.J.M. Gremmen. — The Hague ; London : Junk, 1982. — x,149p : ill,maps ; 27cm. — (Geobotany ; 3)
Bibliography: p129-135. — Includes index
ISBN 90-619-3683-7 : Unpriced B82-17265

581.974 — United States. Middle Atlantic states. Coastal regions. Plants — *Field guides*

Silberhorn, Gene M.. Common plants of the mid-Atantic coast : a field guide / Gene M. Silberhorn ; illustrations by Mary Warinner. — Baltimore ; London : Johns Hopkins University Press, c1982. — xiii,255p : ill,1map ; 24cm
Bibliography: p249-252. — Includes index
ISBN 0-8018-2319-6 (cased) : Unpriced
ISBN 0-8018-2725-6 (pbk) : Unpriced
B82-36872

581.9946'022'2 — Tasmania. Plants — *Illustrations*

Stones, Margaret. The endemic flora of Tasmania / painted by Margaret Stones ; botanical and ecological text by Winifred Curtis. — London : Ariel
Pt.6. — c 1978. — p391-478,[36]leaves of plates : chiefly col.ill,2col.maps ; 41cm
Maps on lining papers. — Includes index
Unpriced B82-40386

582 — SPERMATOPHYTES

582'.0014 — Seed plants. Terminology — *Lists*

Index Kewensis : plantarum phanerogamarum. — Oxonii : E Prelo Clarendoniano
Supplementum sextum decimum: Nomina et synonyma omnium familiarum et graduum inframiliarum ab initio anni MDCCCCLXXI ad finem anni MDCCCCLXXV nonnulla etiam antea edita complectens / ductu et consilio Patricii Brenan confecerunt herbarii horti regii botanici Kewensis curatores. — 1981. — 309p ; 22cm
ISBN 0-19-854531-2 : £60.00 : CIP rev.
B81-13872

582'.0333 — Seeds. Germination

Mayer, A. M.. The germination of seeds / by A.M. Mayer and A. Poljakoff-Mayber. — 3rd ed. — Oxford : Pergamon, 1982. — ix,211p : ill ; 26cm
Previous ed.: 1975. — Includes bibliographies and index
ISBN 0-08-028854-5 (cased) : Unpriced : CIP rev.
ISBN 0-08-028853-7 (pbk) : £9.50 B82-00284

582'.0463 — Flowering plants. Flowers

Wilson, Ron. Wild flowers / Ron Wilson. — London : Albany, 1979. — 93p : col.ill ; 29cm
Includes index
Unpriced B82-36217

582'.0463 — Pollen — *Identification manuals — For bee-keeping*

Sawyer, R. W.. Pollen identification for beekeepers. — Cardiff : University College Cardiff Press, Oct.1981. — [112]p
ISBN 0-906449-29-4 (pbk) : £5.95 : CIP entry
B81-30174

582.13 — Flowering plants

Ewart, Neil. The lore of flowers. — Poole : Blandford, Sept.1982. — 1v.
ISBN 0-7137-1176-0 : £10.95 : CIP entry B82-30212

582.13 — Flowering plants — *For children*

Clarke, Lea. Wild flowers. — London : Granada, Apr.1982. — [64]p. — (Granada guide series ; 14)
ISBN 0-246-11721-4 : £1.95 : CIP entry B82-05387

Cox, Rosamund Kidman. Flowers / Rosamund Kidman Cox and Barbara Cork ; [illustrated by Wendy Bramall ... et al.]. — London : Usborne, 1980. — 24p : ill(some col.) ; 21cm. — (Usborne first nature)
Text on inside covers. — Includes index
ISBN 0-86020-479-0 (pbk) : £0.90 B82-39721

582.13 — Meadows & marshes. Flowering plants

Větvička, Václav. Wildflowers of meadows and marshes / by Václav Větvička ; illustrated by Zdenka Krejčová ; [translated by Olga Kuthanová]. — London : Hamlyn, c1981. — 224p : ill(some col.) ; 22cm. — (A Hamlyn colour guide)
Translation from the Czech. — Includes index
ISBN 0-600-35586-1 : £2.95 B82-04326

582.13′04234 — Flowering plants. Virus diseases

Stevens, W. A.. Virology of flowering plants. — Glasgow : Blackie, Jan.1983. — [176]p. — (Tertiary level biology)
ISBN 0-216-91357-8 (cased) : £16.00 : CIP entry
ISBN 0-216-91356-x (pbk) : £8.00 B82-33494

582.13′0452 — North-western Europe. Flowering plants. Habitats

Wild flowers : their habitats in Britain and northern Europe / edited by Geoffrey Halliday and Andrew Malloch. — London : Peter Lowe, c1981. — 180p : chiefly ill,1col.map ; 28cm
Includes index
ISBN 0-85654-618-6 : £6.95 : CIP rev. B81-13834

582.13′04524 — Flowering plants. Interactions with insects — *For children*

Flowers and insects. — Poole : Blandford, 1982, c1981. — 30p : col.ill ; 25cm. — (Finding out about (Blandford))
Translation of the Japanese
ISBN 0-7137-1152-3 : £2.95 : CIP rev.
Also classified at 595.7052′4 B81-04355

582.13′0913 — Tropical regions. Flowering plants — *Field guides*

Flowering plants in the landscape / Mildred E. Mathias, editor ; foreword by Sir George Taylor. — Berkeley ; London : University of California Press, c1982. — xiii,240p : ill(some col.) ; 24cm
Bibliography: p237-240. — Includes index
ISBN 0-520-04350-2 : £12.75 B82-40216

582.13′0914′3 — Mountainous regions. Flowering plants — Field guides

Stefenelli. Mountain flowers. — Newton Abbot : David & Charles, Oct.1982. — [208]p
Translation of: I fiori della montagna
ISBN 0-7153-8339-6 : £6.95 : CIP entry B82-23012

582.13′094 — Europe. Flowering plants — *Field guides*

Schauer, Thomas. A field guide to the wild flowers of Britain and Europe / Thomas Schauer ; illustrated by Claus Caspari ; translated and adapted by Richard Pankhurst. — London : Collins, 1982. — 464p : ill(some col.) ; 20cm
Includes index
ISBN 0-00-219256-x (cased) : £7.95
ISBN 0-00-219257-8 (pbk) : Unpriced B82-22886

Tebbs, B. M.. Usborne guide to wild flowers of Britain & Europe / Barry Tebbs. — London : Usborne, 1981. — 128p : ill(some col.) ; 20cm
Bibliography: p124. — Includes index
ISBN 0-86020-497-9 : £3.99 B82-39039

Tomanová, Eliška. The Hamlyn book of wild flowers / by Eliška Tomanová ; [translated by Olga Kuthanová] ; [illustrations by Eduard Demartini and Věra Ničová]. — London : Hamlyn, c1981. — 304p : ill(some col.),maps (some col.) ; 30cm
Translated from the Czech. — Bibliography: p38. — Includes index
ISBN 0-600-35582-9 : £4.95 B82-19314

582.13′094 — Europe. Flowering plants — *Field guides — For children*

Bonar, Ann. Wild flowers / Ann Bonar ; illustrated by Cynthia Pow. — London : Hamlyn, 1982. — 128p : ill(some col.) ; 18cm. — (Hamlyn junior pocket books)
Includes index
ISBN 0-600-36451-8 : £1.99 B82-23624

582.13′094 — North-western Europe. Flowering plants

Blackmore, Stephen. Illustrated guide to wild flowers / Stephen Blackmore. — London : Kingfisher, 1982. — 197p : ill(some col.),col.maps ; 27cm
Bibliography: p193. — Includes index
ISBN 0-86272-007-9 : £7.95 : CIP rev. B82-00364

582.13′094 — North-western Europe. Flowering plants — *Field guides*

Blamey, Marjorie. Wild flowers : the wild flowers of Britain and Northern Europe / Marjorie Blamey, Richard Fitter, Alastair Fitter ; with a foreword by Geoffrey Grigson. — London : Collins, c1977 (1981 [printing]). — xv,82p,126p of plates : ill(some col.),1map ; 29cm
Based on: Wild flowers of Britain and Northern Europe / text by Richard Fitter, Alastair Fitter ; illustrated by Marjorie Blamey. 1974. — Includes index
ISBN 0-00-219757-x (cased) : Unpriced
ISBN 0-00-636457-8 (pbk(Fontana)) : Unpriced B82-03967

582.13′0941 — Great Britain. Flowering plants

Cameron, Elizabeth. A floral ABC. — Exeter : Webb & Bower, Nov.1982. — [64]p
ISBN 0-906671-28-0 (pbk) : £4.95 : CIP entry B82-32321

Mabey, Richard. The flowering of Britain / Richard Mabey and Tony Evans. — London : Arrow, 1982, c1980. — 173p : col.ill ; 23cm
Originally published: London : Hutchinson, 1980. — Bibliography: p163-167. — Includes index
ISBN 0-09-928060-4 (pbk) : Unpriced B82-22764

582.13′0941 — Great Britain. Flowering plants — *Field guides*

Field guide to the wild flowers of Britain / [edited and designed by the Reader′s Digest Association]. — Repr. with amendments. — London : Reader′s Digest Association, 1981. — 447p : col.ill ; 16x21cm. — (Reader′s Digest nature lover′s library)
Includes index
Unpriced B82-10283

Field guide to the wild flowers of Britain. — Repr. with amendments. — London : Reader′s Digest Association, 1981 (1982 [printing]). — 447p : col.ill ; 16x20cm. — (Reader′s Digest nature lover′s library)
Includes index
Unpriced B82-33548

Martin, W. Keble. The new concise British flora / W. Keble Martin ; with nomenclature edited and revised by Douglas H. Kent ; and foreword by The Duke of Edinburgh. — [New ed.]. — London : Ebury, 1982. — 247p : chiefly ill(some col.) ; 29cm
Previous ed: published as Concise British flora in colour. 1974. — Bibliography: p216. — Includes index
ISBN 0-7181-2126-0 : £12.50 B82-26977

Press, J. R.. Field guide to the wild flowers of Britain / [edited and designed by the Reader′s Digest Association] ; [principal consultants and authors, J.R. Press, D.A. Sutton, B.M. Tebbs] ; [additional writers, Ruth Cleary ... et al.] ; [artists, Leonora Box ... et al.]. — London : Reader′s Digest Association, c1981. — 447p : col.ill ; 16x21cm. — (Reader′s digest nature lover′s library)
Includes index
Unpriced B82-37890

582.13′0941 — Great Britain. Flowering plants — *Illustrations*

Martin, W. Keble. The concise British flora in colour / W. Keble Martin ; with nomenclature edited and revised by Douglas H. Kent ; and foreword by H.R.H. The Prince Philip, Duke of Edinburgh. — London : Sphere in association with Ebury Press and Michael Joseph, 1978. — 254p : chiefly ill(some col.) ; 26cm
4th ed. Previous ed.: 1976. — Includes index
ISBN 0-7221-0503-7 (pbk) : £4.50 B82-00577

Ross-Craig, Stella. Drawings of British plants : being illustrations of the species of flowering plants growing naturally in the British Isles / by Stella Ross-Craig. — London : Bell & Hyman, 1979. — 8v. : chiefly ill ; 25cm
Originally published in 32 pts. London : Bell, 1948-1974. — Includes index
ISBN 0-7135-1110-9 : Unpriced B82-09756

582.13′0941 — Great Britain. Woodlands. Flowering plants

Tanner, Heather. Woodland plants / Heather & Robin Tanner. — London : Robin Garton, 1981. — 215p : ill ; 29cm
Limited ed. of 950 numbered copies. — Bibliography: p209-212. — Includes index
ISBN 0-906030-15-3 : Unpriced B82-08635

582.13′09411′82 — Scotland. Highland Region. Skye & Raasay. Flowering plants — *Lists*

The **Botanist** in Skye : check-list of the plants of the islands of Skye and Raasay as known to the end of 1979 / compiled by C.W. Murray with contributions from H.J.B. Birks and R.M. Murray. — [London] : Botanical Society of the British Isles, 1980. — vi,62p,[1]leaf of plates : col.ill,maps ; 20cm
Previous ed.: Portree : Portree High School, 1974. — Bibliography: p62. — Includes index
Unpriced (pbk)
Also classified at 587′.31′0941182 B82-29205

582.13′09429′21 — Gwynedd. Ynys Môn. Flowering plants — *Lists*

Roberts, R. H.. The flowering plants and ferns of Anglesey / by R.H. Roberts. — Cardiff : Amgueddfa Genedlaethol Cymru, 1982. — xv,88p ; 21cm
Bibliography: p79. — Includes index
ISBN 0-7200-0241-9 (pbk) : £3.50
Also classified at 587′.31′0942921 B82-30548

582.13′095496 — Nepal. Flowering plants

Hara, H.. An enumeration of the flowering plants of Nepal / H. Hara and L.H.J. Williams with the collaboration of ... [others]. — London : British Museum (Natural History)
Vol.3 / H. Hara, A.O. Chater and L.H.J. Williams with the assistance of S.Y. Sutton and with the collaboration of specialists. — 1982. — 226p : 1map ; 28cm. — (Publication ; no.854)
"A Joint Project of the British Museum (Natural History) and the University of Tokyo" — t.p.. — Includes index
ISBN 0-565-00854-4 (pbk) : Unpriced : CIP rev. B82-14499

582.13′09676′2 — Kenya. Flowering plants

Blundell, *Sir* **Michael.** The wild flowers of Kenya / Michael Blundell ; with additional photographs by Tim Campbell, Peter Davey & Nigel Pavitt. — London : Collins, 1982. — 160p,48p of plates : ill(some col.),maps(some col.) ; 23cm
Maps on lining papers. — Bibliography: p138. — Includes index
ISBN 0-00-219317-5 : £8.95 B82-27665

582.13′09687 — South Africa. Cape Peninsula. Flowering plants

Jackson, W. P. U.. Wild flowers of the fairest Cape / by W.P.U. Jackson. — Aylesbury : Timmins, 1980. — 126p : ill(some col.),maps ; 30cm
Maps on lining papers. — Bibliography: p126. — Includes index
ISBN 0-86978-194-4 : £15.00 B82-13055

582.1′4 — Succulents

Succulent scene one. — Burgess Hill (11 Wingle Tye Rd., Burgess Hill, West Sussex RH15 9HR) : Southern Reprographics, Oct.1981. — [80]p
ISBN 0-907678-00-9 (pbk) : £2.95 : CIP entry B81-30904

582.1′4 — Succulents — *Field guides*

Scott, S. H.. The observer′s book of cacti : and other succulents / S.H. Scott. — 2nd ed., completely rev., reset and reill. / revised by J.W.P. Mullard. — London : Warne, 1981. — 185p : ill(some col.) ; 15cm
Previous ed.: 1975. — Bibliography: p177. — Includes index
ISBN 0-7232-1607-x : £1.95 B82-38817

582.1′504116 — Wood. Xylem. Development

Xylem cell development / edited by J.R. Barnett. — Tunbridge Wells : Castle House, c1981. — viii,307p : ill ; 25cm
Includes bibliographies and index
ISBN 0-7194-0050-3 : £29.50 B82-14460

582.16 — Great Britain. Deciduous trees. Leaves — *For children*

Althea. Leaves from trees / by Althea ; illustrated by Barbara McGirr. — Over : Dinosaur, c1981. — 24p : col.ill ; 16x19cm. — (Althea′s nature series)
ISBN 0-85122-281-1 (cased) : £2.25
ISBN 0-85122-265-x (pbk) : £0.70 B82-08268

582.16 — Trees

Edlin, Herbert L.. The illustrated encyclopedia of trees, timbers and forests of the world / Herbert Edlin, Maurice Nimmo et al. ; consultants A. Bourdo Jr, Hugh Fraser ; illustrated by Ian Garrard, Olivia Beasley and David Nockels. — London : Corgi, 1981, c1978. — 256p : col.ill ; 30cm
Originally published: London : Salamander, 1978. — Includes index
ISBN 0-552-98205-9 (pbk) : £5.95 B82-08152

582.16 — Trees — *Field guides*

The **Macdonald** encyclopedia of trees / English translation by Hugh Young. — London : Macdonald, 1982, c1977. — 299p : ill(some col.) ; 19cm
Translation of the Italian. — Includes index
ISBN 0-356-08574-0 (pbk) : £4.95 B82-16360

Procter, Ray. Trees of the world / Ray Procter ; illustrated by Karel Tholé and Ross Wardle. — London : Hamlyn, 1972 (1982 [printing]). — 159p : col.ill ; 19cm
Bibliography: p159. — Includes index
ISBN 0-600-35656-6 (cased) : £2.99
ISBN 0-600-10070-7 (pbk) : £1.75 B82-36011

582.16 — Trees — *For children*

Briquebec, John. Trees. — London : Granada, Apr.1982. — [64]p. — (Granada guide series ; 13)
ISBN 0-246-11720-6 : £1.95 : CIP entry B82-06498

Thomson, Ruth. Trees / Ruth Thomson ; [illustrated by Bob Brampton ... et al.]. — London : Usborne, 1980. — 24p : ill(some col.) ; 21cm. — (Usborne first nature)
Text on inside covers. — Includes index
ISBN 0-86020-473-1 (pbk) : £0.90 B82-39720

582.16 — Trees — *For schools*

Catherall, Ed. Trees / Ed Catherall. — Hove : Wayland, 1982. — 32p : col.ill ; 23cm. — (Young scientist)
ISBN 0-85340-991-9 : £3.50 B82-34826

582.16′0014 — Great Britain. Naturalised trees. Names — *Lists*

Jarvis, P. J.. Botanical nomenclature of trees and shrubs introduced into Great Britain by 1813 : a provisional index of polynomial and binomial synonyms / P.K. Jarvis. — Birmingham : Department of Geography, University of Birmingham, 1980. — 69p ; 30cm. — (Working paper series / University of Birmingham. Department of Geography ; 8)
Bibliography: p4-5
ISBN 0-7044-0563-6 (pbk) : £2.00
Also classified at 582.1′7′014 B82-23557

582.16′02322 — Trees. Mycoplasma diseases — *Conference proceedings*

Mycoplasma diseases of trees and shrubs / edited by Karl Maramorosch, S.P. Raychaudhuri. — New York ; London : Academic Press, 1981. — xii,362p : ill ; 24cm
Conference papers. — Includes bibliographies and index
ISBN 0-12-470220-1 : £19.60
Also classified at 582.1′7042322 B82-29598

582.16′031 — Dendrochronology

Baillie, M. G. L.. Tree-ring dating and archaeology / M.G.L. Baillie. — London : Croom Helm, c1982. — 274p : ill ; 23cm
Bibliography: p265-270. — Includes index
ISBN 0-7099-0613-7 : £16.95 : CIP rev. B81-16873

582.16094 — Europe. Trees — *Field guides*

Barrett, Mary, *1949-*. Usborne guide to trees of Britain & Europe / Mary Barrett. — London : Usborne, 1981. — 128p : ill(some col.) ; 20cm
Bibliography: p126. — Includes index
ISBN 0-86020-498-7 (pbk) : £2.50 B82-39040

582.160941 — Great Britain. Trees — *Field guides*

Field guide to the trees and shrubs of Britain / [edited and designed by the Reader′s Digest Association]. — Repr. with amendments. — London : Reader′s Digest Association, 1981. — 303p : col.ill,1col.map ; 16x21cm. — (Reader′s Digest nature lover′s library)
Includes index
Unpriced
Also classified at 582.1′7′0941 B82-10285

Field guide to the trees and shrubs of Britain. — Repr. with amendments. — London : Reader′s Digest Association, 1981 (1982 [printing]). — 303p : col.ill ; 16x20cm. — (Reader′s Digest nature lover′s library)
Includes index
Unpriced
Also classified at 582.1′7′0941 B82-33547

582.16′0941 — Great Britain. Trees — *Field guides*

Harris, Esmond. Field guide to the trees and shrubs of Britain / [edited and designed by the Reader′s Digest Association] ; [consultants and authors, Esmond Harris, Jeanette Harris] ; [artists, Dick Bonson ... et al.]. — London : Reader′s Digest Association, c1981. — 303p : col.ill,1col.map ; 16x20cm. — (Reader′s digest nature lover′s library)
Includes index
Unpriced
Also classified at 582.1′7′0941 B82-37889

582.160941 — Great Britain. Trees — *Field guides*

Mitchell, Alan, *1922-*. The trees of Britain and northern Europe / text by Alan Mitchell ; illustrated by John Wilkinson. — London : Collins, 1982. — 288p : ill(some col.) ; 20cm
Includes index
ISBN 0-00-219037-0 (cased) : £6.95
ISBN 0-00-219035-4 (pbk) : Unpriced B82-17730

582.160941 — Great Britain. Trees, *to 1980*

Wilkinson, Gerald. A history of Britain′s trees / Gerald Wilkinson. — London : Hutchinson, 1981. — 176p : ill(some col.),maps,ports ; 26cm
Bibliography: p6. — Includes index
ISBN 0-09-146000-x : £9.95 : CIP rev. B81-26793

582.1609428′8 — Northumberland. National parks: Northumberland National Park. Broad-leaved woodlands — *Statistics*

A **Classification** and evaluation of broadleaved woodlands in the Northumberland National Park. — Hexham : Northumberland National Park and Countryside Committee, 1981. — 90p : ill,maps ; 30cm. — (Occasional paper / Northumberland National Park and Countryside Committee ; no.2)
Unpriced (spiral) B82-11948

582.1′7′014 — Great Brtain. Naturalised shrubs. Names — *Lists*

Jarvis, P. J.. Botanical nomenclature of trees and shrubs introduced into Great Britain by 1813 : a provisional index of polynomial and binomial synonyms / P.K. Jarvis. — Birmingham : Department of Geography, University of Birmingham, 1980. — 69p ; 30cm. — (Working paper series / University of Birmingham. Department of Geography ; 8)
Bibliography: p4-5
ISBN 0-7044-0563-6 (pbk) : £2.00
Primary classification 582.16′0014 B82-23557

582.1′7042322 — Shrubs. Mycoplasma diseases — *Conference proceedings*

Mycoplasma diseases of trees and shrubs / edited by Karl Maramorosch, S.P. Raychaudhuri. — New York ; London : Academic Press, 1981. — xii,362p : ill ; 24cm
Conference papers. — Includes bibliographies and index
ISBN 0-12-470220-1 : £19.60
Primary classification 582.16′02322 B82-29598

582.1′7′0941 — Great Britain. Shrubs — *Field guides*

Field guide to the trees and shrubs of Britain / [edited and designed by the Reader′s Digest Association]. — Repr. with amendments. — London : Reader′s Digest Association, 1981. — 303p : col.ill,1col.map ; 16x21cm. — (Reader′s Digest nature lover′s library)
Includes index
Unpriced
Primary classification 582.160941 B82-10285

Field guide to the trees and shrubs of Britain. — Repr. with amendments. — London : Reader′s Digest Association, 1981 (1982 [printing]). — 303p : col.ill ; 16x20cm. — (Reader′s Digest nature lover′s library)
Includes index
Unpriced
Primary classification 582.160941 B82-33547

Harris, Esmond. Field guide to the trees and shrubs of Britain / [edited and designed by the Reader′s Digest Association] ; [consultants and authors, Esmond Harris, Jeanette Harris] ; [artists, Dick Bonson ... et al.]. — London : Reader′s Digest Association, c1981. — 303p : col.ill,1col.map ; 16x20cm. — (Reader′s digest nature lover′s library)
Includes index
Unpriced
Primary classification 582.16′0941 B82-37889

583 — DICOTYLEDONS

583′.044 — Dicotyledons. Anatomy

Metcalfe, C. R.. Anatomy of the dicotyledons. — 2nd ed. — Oxford : Clarendon Press
Previous ed.: 1950
Vol.2. — Oct.1982. — [330]p
ISBN 0-19-854559-2 : £40.00 : CIP entry B82-23106

583′.32 — Leguminosae

Allen, O. N.. The leguminosae : a source book of characteristics, uses and nodulation / O.N. Allen & Ethel K. Allen. — London : Macmillan, 1981. — lxiv,812p : ill ; 24cm
Bibliography: p731-798. — Includes index
ISBN 0-333-32221-5 : £35.00 B82-06698

583′.32041′0428 — Legumes. Root nodules

Bergersen, F. J.. Root nodules of legumes : structure and functions / F.J. Bergersen. — Chichester : Research Studies, c1982. — x,164p : ill ; 24cm. — (Botanical research studies ; 1)
Bibliography: p129-159. — Includes index
ISBN 0-471-10456-6 : £13.25 : CIP rev. B82-13511

583′.55 — Dandelions — *For children*

Ingves, Gunilla. The dandelion. — London : Black, Jan.1983. — [28]p. — (First nature books)
Translation of: Har du sett på : Maskrosen
ISBN 0-7136-2289-x : £1.95 : CIP entry
B82-32604

583′.55′09824 — Argentina. North-western Argentina. Compositae — *Field guides*

Giberti, G. C.. Medicinal Mutisieae (Compositae) of North-western Argentina : a contribution to their identification / by G.C. Giberti. — [Kew] : [Jodrell Laboratory, Royal Botanic Gardens], [1981]. — 44p : ill ; 30cm. — (Notes from the Jodrell Laboratory ; 9)
Bibliography: p43-44
Unpriced (pbk) B82-07776

583′.672 — Cyclamen — *Conference proceedings*

Cyclamen 1980 : proceedings of the second conference of the Cyclamen Society held at Wye College, University of London, Ashford, Kent, 4-5 October 1980 / editor R.H. Bailey. — Ilford (c/o Dr M. Summers, 7 Montreal Rd., Ilford, Essex) : The Society, 1981. — 27p ; 21cm. — (Conference report / the Cyclamen Society, ISSN 0143-3571)
Includes bibliographies
Unpriced (pbk) B82-25684

583′.72 — Asclepiadaceae — *Serials*

[Asklepios *(International Asclepiad Society)*]. Askepios. — 23 (Aug. 1981)-. — [S.l.] (c/o L. Delderfield, 136 Chanctonbury Rd., Burgess Hill, Sussex) : The Society, 1981-. — v. : ill (some col.) ; 30cm
Quarterly. — Continues: Asclepiadaceae
ISSN 0260-9533 = Asklepios (International Asclepiad Society) : £4.00 per year
B82-12449

584 — MONOCOTYLEDONS

584 — Monocotyledons

Dahlgren, Rolf M. T.. The monocotyledons : a comparative study / by Rolf M.T. Dahlgren and H. Trevor Clifford in cooperation with U. Hamann ... [et al.]. — London : Academic Press, 1982. — xiv,378p : ill ; 29cm. — (Botanical systematics ; v.2)
One card ′Abbreviations′ as insert. — Bibliography: p346-356. — Includes index
ISBN 0-12-200680-1 : £48.00 : CIP rev.
B81-28142

584′.044 — Monocotyledons. Anatomy

Anatomy of the monocotyledons / edited by C.R. Metcalfe. — Oxford : Clarendon Press, c1982. — (Oxford science publications)
Bibliography: p484-509. — Includes index
7: Helobiae (Alismatidae) : (including the seagrasses) / P.B. Tomlinson; with the assistance of Priscilla Fawcett ... [et al.]. — xiv,559p : ill ; 25cm
ISBN 0-19-854502-9 : £50.00 : CIP rev.
B81-31738

584′.15′096 — Africa. Orchids

Stewart, J.. Orchids of Africa : a select review / text by J. Stewart ; illustrations by E.F. Hennessy. — London : Macmillan, 1981. — ix,159p : ill(some col.) ; 36cm
Ill on lining papers. — Bibliography: p155-157. — Includes index
ISBN 0-333-32536-2 : £27.50 B82-01941

584′.24 — Irises

Mathew, Brian. The iris / Brian Mathew. — London : Batsford, 1981. — xvii,202p,[32]p of plates : ill(some col.) ; 24cm
Bibliography: p191-192. — Includes index
ISBN 0-7134-3390-6 : £17.50 B82-06208

585 — GYMNOSPERMS

585′.2 — Redwood trees

Hewes, Jeremy Joan. Redwoods : the world′s largest trees / Jeremy Joan Hewes. — London : Hamlyn, 1981. — 192p : ill(some col.),maps (some col.),ports ; 32cm
Bibliography: p187-189. — Includes index
ISBN 0-600-35581-0 : £7.95 B82-04358

586 — CRYPTOGAMS

586 — Cryptogams

Esser, Karl. Cryptogams : cyanobacteria, algae, fungi, lichens : textbooks and practical guide / Karl Esser ; photographs Dieter Graw ... [et al.] ; drawings Hans-Jürgen Rathke ; English translation of the revised text by Michael G. Hackston and John Webster. — Cambridge : Cambridge University Press, 1982. — xi,610p : ill ; 24cm
Translation of: Kryptogamen. — Bibliography: p580-590. — Includes index
ISBN 0-521-23621-5 : £37.90 : CIP rev.
B82-12696

587 — PTERIDOPHYTES

587′.31′0941182 — Scotland. Highland Region. Skye & Raasay. Ferns — *Lists*

The **Botanist** in Skye : check-list of the plants of the islands of Skye and Raasay as known to the end of 1979 / compiled by C.W. Murray with contributions from H.J.B. Birks and R.M. Murray. — [London] : Botanical Society of the British Isles, 1980. — vi,62p,[1]leaf of plates : col.ill,maps ; 20cm
Previous ed.: Portree : Portree High School, 1974. — Bibliography: p62. — Includes index
Unpriced (pbk)
Primary classification 582.13′09411′82
B82-29205

587′.31′0942921 — Gwynedd. Ynys Môn. Ferns — *Lists*

Roberts, R. H.. The flowering plants and ferns of Anglesey / by R.H. Roberts. — Cardiff : Amgueddfa Genedlaethol Cymru, 1982. — xv,88p ; 21cm
Bibliography: p79. — Includes index
ISBN 0-7200-0241-9 (pbk) : £3.50
Primary classification 582.13′09429′21
B82-30548

588 — BRYOPHYTES

588′.045 — Bryophytes. Ecology

Bryophyte ecology / edited by A.J.E. Smith. — London : Chapman and Hall, 1982. — x,511p : ill,maps ; 24cm
Includes bibliographies and index
ISBN 0-412-22340-6 : Unpriced : CIP rev.
B82-19223

588′.0941 — Great Britain. Bryophytes. Distribution — *Lists*

Corley, M. F. V.. Distribution of bryophytes in the British Isles : a census catalogue of their occurrence in vice-counties / prepared by M.F.V. Corley and M.O. Hill. — Cardiff : British Bryological Society, 1981. — 160p : maps ; 22cm
Bibliography: p140-141. — Includes index
ISBN 0-9507639-0-x (pbk) : Unpriced
B82-12026

588′.2′0941 — Great Britain. Mosses — *Field guides*

Watson, E. V.. British mosses and liverworts : an introductory work, with full descriptions and figures of over 200 species, and keys for the identification of all except the very rare species / written and illustrated by E. Vernon Watson ; with a foreword by Paul Richards. — 3rd ed. — Cambridge : Cambridge University Press, 1981. — xviii,519p : ill ; 23cm
Previous ed.: 1968. — Bibliography: p15-17. — Includes index
ISBN 0-521-24004-2 (cased) : £25.00 : CIP rev.
ISBN 0-521-28536-4 (pbk) : £12.95
Also classified at 588′.33′0941 B81-34014

588′.3′097 — North America. Hornworts & liverworts

Schuster, Rudolf M.. The Hepaticae and Anthocerotae of North America : east of the hundredth meridian / Rudolf M. Schuster. — New York ; Guildford : Columbia University Press
Vol.4. — 1980. — xviii,1334p : ill ; 26cm
Includes index
ISBN 0-231-04608-1 : £41.50 B82-39138

588′.33′0941 — Great Britain. Liverworts — *Field guides*

Watson, E. V.. British mosses and liverworts : an introductory work, with full descriptions and keys for the figures of over 200 species, and keys for the identification of all except the very rare species / written and illustrated by E. Vernon Watson ; with a foreword by Paul Richards. — 3rd ed. — Cambridge : Cambridge University Press, 1981. — xviii,519p : ill ; 23cm
Previous ed.: 1968. — Bibliography: p15-17. — Includes index
ISBN 0-521-24004-2 (cased) : £25.00 : CIP rev.
ISBN 0-521-28536-4 (pbk) : £12.95
Primary classification 588′.2′0941 B81-34014

589 — THALLOPHYTES

589′.04133 — Plants. Nitrogen. Fixation

Nitrogen fixation. — Oxford : Oxford University Press
Vol.2: Rhizobium. — Feb.1982. — [400]p
ISBN 0-19-854552-5 : £28.00 : CIP entry
B81-36230

Nitrogen fixation. — Oxford : Clarendon Press
Vol.3: Legumes. — Oct.1982. — [400]p
ISBN 0-19-854555-x : £35.00 : CIP entry
B82-23696

589.2 — Fungi — *For children*

Schliemann, Eva Raupp. Fungi round the year / written and illustrated by Eva Raupp Schliemann. — London : Black, c1982. — 37p : col.ill ; 25x26cm
Translation of: Die Pilz-Uhr. — Ill on lining papers
ISBN 0-7136-2217-2 : £3.95 : CIP rev.
B82-07577

589.2′041 — Fungi. Physiology

Griffin, David H.. Fungal physiology / David H. Griffin. — New York ; Chichester : Wiley, c1981. — xii,383p : ill ; 25cm
Includes bibliographies and index
ISBN 0-471-05748-7 : £24.25 B82-09880

589.2′0446 — Fungi. Spores — *Conference proceedings*

International Fungal Spore Symposium *(3rd : 1980 : Gwatt).* The fungal spore : morphogenetic controls / [proceedings of the Third International Fungal Spore Symposium (3IFSS) held 18-22 August 1980 at Gwatt near Thun, Switzerland] ; edited by G. Turian and H.R. Hohl. — London : Academic Press, 1981. — xiii,670p : ill ; 24cm
Includes bibliographies and index
ISBN 0-12-703660-6 : £27.80 : CIP rev.
B80-29668

589.2′045′24 — Mycorrhizas

Harley, J. L.. Mycorrhizal symbiosis. — London : Academic Press, Feb.1983. — [500]p
ISBN 0-12-325560-0 : CIP entry B82-36579

589.2′045249 — Plants. Parasites: Fungi

Deverall, Brian J.. Fungal parasitism / Brian J. Deverall. — 2nd ed. — London : Edward Arnold, 1981. — 66p : ill,1map ; 22cm. — (The Institute of Biology′s studies in biology, ISSN 0537-9024 ; no.17)
Previous ed.: 1968. — Bibliography: p64. — Includes index
ISBN 0-7131-2832-1 (pbk) : £2.40 : CIP rev.
B81-30610

589.2′0464 — Industrial mycology

Smith, George, *1895-.* Smith′s introduction to industrial mycology. — 7th ed. / A.H.S. Onions, D. Allsopp, H.O.W. Eggins. — London : Edward Arnold, 1981. — viii,398p : ill ; 24cm
Previous ed.: published as An introduction to industrial mycology. 1969. — Includes bibliographies and index
ISBN 0-7131-2811-9 : £37.50 : CIP rev.
B81-30605

589.2′048732 — Fungi. Cells. Nuclei — *Conference proceedings*

The **Fungal** nucleus : symposium of the British Mycological Society held at Queen Elizabeth College, London, April 1980 / edited by K. Gull & S.G. Oliver. — Cambridge : Cambridge University Press, 1981. — x,358p : ill ; 24cm. — ([British Mycological Society symposium series] ; [5])
Includes bibliographies and index
ISBN 0-521-23492-1 : £32.50 : CIP rev.
B81-36244

589.2′2 — Basidiomycetes — *Conference proceedings*

Decomposer basidiomycetes. — Cambridge : Cambridge University Press, Aug.1982. — [358]p. — (British Mycological Society symposia)
Conference papers
ISBN 0-521-24634-2 : £37.50 : CIP entry
B82-20761

589.2′2′0941 — Great Britain. Basidiomycetes — *Field guides*

Wakefield, Elsie M.. Common British fungi : a guide to the more common larger Basidiomycetes of the British Isles / by Elsie M. Wakefield and R.W.G. Dennis. — 2nd ed. / by R.W.G. Dennis. — Hindhead : Saiga, c1981. — viii,212p,111p of plates : ill(some col.) ; 26cm. — (Know the countryside series)
Previous ed.: London : Gawthorn, 1950. — Includes index
ISBN 0-904558-94-0 : £38.00 B82-10709

589.2′2′0973 — United States. Basidiomycetes — *Field guides*

Courtenay, Booth. A field guide to mushrooms and their relatives / Booth Courtenay, Harold H. Burdsall, jr. — New York ; London : Van Nostrand Reinhold, c1982. — 144p : ill(some col.) ; cm
Includes index
ISBN 0-442-23117-2 (cased) : £16.10
Also classified at 589.2′3′0973 B82-36540

589.2′22 — Mushrooms — *For children*

Ingves, Gunilla. The mushroom. — London : Black, Jan.1983. — [28]p. — (First nature books)
Translation of: Har du sett på : Svampen
ISBN 0-7136-2288-1 : £1.95 : CIP entry
B82-32603

589.2′22′094 — Europe. Agaricales — *Field guides*

Nonis, U.. Mushrooms & toadstools : a colour field guide / U. Nonis ; English translation by Lucia Wildt. — Newton Abbot : David & Charles, 1982. — 229p : ill(some col.) ; 22cm
Translated from the Italian. — 'Key to symbols used' (1sheet) as inset. — Includes index
ISBN 0-7153-8282-9 : £6.95 : CIP rev.
B82-15838

Pegler, David. The Mitchell Beazley pocket guide to mushrooms and toadstools / David N. Pegler. — London : Mitchell Beazley, 1981. — 168p : ill(some col.) ; 20cm
Includes index
ISBN 0-85533-347-2 : £3.95 B82-08306

589.2′22′0941 — Great Britain. Agaricales — *Field guides*

Wilkinson, John, *1934-*. Mushrooms & toadstools / John Wilkinson, Stefan Buczacki. — London : Collins, 1982. — 240p : col.ill ; 12cm. — (Collins gem guides)
Includes index
ISBN 0-00-458812-6 (pbk) : £1.75 B82-29302

589.2′25 — Rust fungi

The **Rust** fungi. — London : Academic Press, July 1982. — [290]p
ISBN 0-12-633520-6 : CIP entry B82-12445

589.2′3 — Penicillium. Taxonomy

Pitt, John I.. The genus Penicillium : and its teleomorphic states : Eupenicillium and Talaromyces / John I. Pitt. — London : Academic Press, 1979. — vi,634p : ill ; 24cm
Bibliography: p604-612. — Includes index
ISBN 0-12-557750-8 : £44.00 : CIP rev.
B79-35858

Ramirez, Carlos. Manual and atlas of the penicillia / Carlos Ramirez ; with the technical assistance in scanning electron micrography of Angel T. Martinez. — Amsterdam ; Oxford : Elsevier Biomedical, 1982. — xv,874p : ill(some col.) ; 25cm
Bibliography: p631-640. — Includes index
ISBN 0-444-80369-6 : £74.47 B82-30538

589.2′3′0973 — United States. Ascomycetes — *Field guides*

Courtenay, Booth. A field guide to mushrooms and their relatives / Booth Courtenay, Harold H. Burdsall, jr. — New York ; London : Van Nostrand Reinhold, c1982. — 144p : ill(some col.) ; cm
Includes index
ISBN 0-442-23117-2 (cased) : £16.10
Primary classification 589.2′2′0973 B82-36540

589.2′33 — Yeasts

Berry, David R.. Biology of yeast / David R. Berry. — London : Edward Arnold, 1982. — 59p : ill ; 22cm. — (The Institute of Biology's studies in biology, ISSN 0537-9024 ; no.140)
Bibliography: p59. — Includes index
ISBN 0-7131-2838-0 (pbk) : £2.50 : CIP rev.
B81-30995

589.2′33 — Yeasts — *For children*

Struwe, Sten. The micro-life of yeast / written by Sten Struwe ; translated by E. Meyland-Smith ; edited by Su Swallow. — Harlow : Longman, 1981. — 31p : col.ill,1col.map ; 23cm. — (A First look at microbiology)
Translated from the Danish
ISBN 0-582-39131-8 : £2.50 B82-21052

589.2′4 — Hyphomycetes. Taxonomy

Subramanian, C. V.. Hyphomycetes. — London : Academic Press, Oct.1982. — [450]p
ISBN 0-12-675620-1 : CIP entry B82-24942

589.2′5 — Fungi: Moulds

Malloch, David, *1940-*. Moulds : their isolation, cultivation and identification / David Malloch. — Toronto ; London : University of Toronto Press, c1981. — vii,97p : ill ; 28cm
Bibliography: p91-94. — Includes index
ISBN 0-8020-2418-1 (sprial) : £9.75
B82-13700

589.2′9 — Physarum & Didymium

Cell biology of physarum and didymium / edited by Henry C. Aldrich, John W. Daniel. — New York ; London : Academic. — (Cell biology)
Vol.1: Organisms, nucleus and cell cycle. — 1982. — xii,444p : ill ; 24cm
Includes bibliographies and index
ISBN 0-12-049601-1 : £36.40 B82-38076

589.2′9 — Physarum polycephalum. Development

Sauer, Helmut. Developmental biology of Physarum. — Cambridge : Cambridge University Press, Sept.1982. — [249]p. — (Developmental and cell biology series ; 11)
ISBN 0-521-22703-8 : £32.00 : CIP entry
B82-26226

589.29′424′9 — England. West Midlands. Birds. Distribution

The **Birds** of the West Midlands / Graham R. Harrison, editor ... [et al.]. — Studley : West Midland Bird Club, 1982. — 494p : ill,maps ; 25cm
Bibliography: p479-486. — Includes index
ISBN 0-9507881-0-4 : £15.00 B82-30116

589.3 — Algae

Daly, W. Marshall. Algal biology. — Oxford : Blackwell Scientific, July 1982. — [176]p. — (Basic microbiology ; v.9)
ISBN 0-632-00608-0 : £8.50 : CIP entry
B82-14520

589.3′05 — Algae — *Serials*

Progress in phycological research. — Vol.1-. — Amsterdam ; Oxford : Elsevier Biomedical Press, 1982-. — v. : ill ; 25cm
£49.13 B82-32354

589.3′5 — Algae. Ecology

Round, F. E.. The ecology of algae / F.E. Round. — Cambridge : Cambridge University Press, 1981. — 653p : ill,maps ; 26cm
Bibliography: p574-627. — Includes index
ISBN 0-521-22583-3 : £60.00 B82-08357

589.3′92 — Seaweeds

The **Biology** of seaweeds / edited by Christopher S. Lobban and Michael J. Wynne. — Oxford : Blackwell Scientific, 1981. — xi,786p : ill ; 25cm. — (Botanical monographs ; v.17)
Includes bibliographies and index
ISBN 0-632-00672-2 : £45.00 : CIP rev.
B81-22644

589.4′6 — Blue-green algae

The **Biology** of cyanobacteria. — 2nd ed. — Oxford : Blackwell Scientific, July 1982. — [704]p. — (Botanical monographs ; v.9)
Previous ed. published as: The biology of blue-green algae. 1973
ISBN 0-632-00695-1 : £35.00 : CIP entry
B82-17921

589.4′7 — North America. Desmids

A **Synopsis** of North American desmids. — Lincoln [Neb.] ; London : University of Nebraska Press
Pt.2: Desmidiaceae : Placodermae / G.W. Prescott ... [et al.]
Bibliography: p681-702. — Includes index
Section 3. — c1981. — 720p : ill ; 28cm
ISBN 0-8032-3660-3 : Unpriced B82-02046

589.4′8104875 — Diatoms. Frustules. Structure

Barber, Horace G.. A guide to the morphology of the diatom frustule : with a key to the British freshwater genera / by Horace G. Barber and Elizabeth Y. Haworth. — Ambleside : Freshwater Biological Association, 1981. — 112p : ill ; 21cm. — (Scientific publication / Freshwater Biological Association, ISSN 0367-1887 ; no.44)
Bibliography: p110-112
ISBN 0-900386-42-8 (pbk) : Unpriced
B82-01643

589.9 — Bacteria

Singleton, Paul, *1937-*. Introduction to bacteria : for students in the biological sciences / Paul Singleton, Diana Sainsbury. — Chichester : Wiley, c1981. — vii,167p : ill ; 24cm
Includes index
ISBN 0-471-10034-x (cased) : £11.00 : CIP rev.
ISBN 0-471-10035-8 (pbk) : Unpriced
B81-33885

589.9′00216 — Bacteria — *Lists*

Supplement to Index Bergeyana / Norman E. Gibbons, Kathleen B. Pattee and John G. Holt, co-editors. — Baltimore ; London : Williams & Wilkins, c1981. — vii,442p ; 24cm
Bibliography: p313-442
ISBN 0-683-04106-1 : Unpriced B82-02562

589.9′019214 — Bacteria. Denitrification

Payne, W. J.. Denitrification / W.J. Payne. — New York ; Chichester : Wiley, c1981. — xiv,214p : ill ; 24cm
Bibliography: p185-208. — Includes index
ISBN 0-471-04764-3 : £25.90 B82-05818

589.9′0192482 — Bacteria. Amphiphiles — *Conference proceedings*

Conference on Chemistry and Biological Activities of Bacterial Surface Amphiphiles *(1981 : New Orleans)*. Chemistry and biological activities of bacterial surface amphiphiles / [proceedings of the Conference on Chemistry and Biological Activities of Bacterial Surface Amphiphiles, held in New Orleans, Louisiana, January 12, 1981] ; edited by Gerald D. Shockman, Anthony J. Wicken. — New York ; London : Academic Press, 1981. — xiv,390p : ill ; 24cm
Includes index
ISBN 0-12-640380-5 : £27.60 B82-30114

589.9′046 — Bacteria. Spores

Russell, A. D.. The destruction of bacterial spores / A.D. Russell. — London : Academic Press, 1982. — ix,333p : ill ; 24cm
Includes bibliographies and index
ISBN 0-12-604060-5 : £19.20 : CIP rev.
B82-04131

589.9'08732 — Bacteria. Transfection & transformation — *Conference proceedings*

European Meeting on Bacterial Transformation and Transfection *(4th : 1978 : York).*
Transformation - 1978 : proceedings of the Fourth European Meeting on Bacterial Transformation and Transfection, York, England, August 29th-September 1st 1978 / editors S.W. Glover and L.O. Butler. — Oxford : Cotswold Press, 1979. — 466p : ill ; 26cm
Includes index
ISBN 0-906649-01-3 : Unpriced B82-19404

European Meeting on Bacterial Transformation and Transfection *(5th : 1980 : Florence).*
Transformation - 1980 : proceedings of the Fifth European Meeting on Bacterial Transformation and Transfection, Florence, Italy, 2-5 September 1980 / editors M. Polsinelli and G. Mazza. — Oxford : Cotswold Press, 1981. — xiii,453p : ill ; 25cm
Includes index
ISBN 0-906649-02-1 : Unpriced B82-19408

589.9'08734 — Plasmids

Day, M. J.. Plasmids. — London : Edward Arnold, July 1982. — [56]p. — (The Institute of Biology's studies in biology, ISSN 0537-9024 ; no.142)
ISBN 0-7131-2846-1 (pbk) : £2.25 : CIP entry B82-16229

Hardy, Kimber. Bacterial plasmids / Kimber Hardy. — Walton-on-Thames : Nelson, 1981. — 104p : ill ; 22cm. — (Aspects of microbiology ; 4)
Includes bibliographies and index
ISBN 0-17-771104-3 (pbk) : £2.95 B82-02433

589.9'08734 — Plasmids — *Conference proceedings*

International Plasmid Conference on Molecular Biology, Pathogenicity and Ecology of Bacterial Plasmids *(1981 : Santo Domingo).* Molecular biology, pathogenicity, and ecology of bacterial plasmids / [proceedings of the International Plasmid Conference on Molecular Biology, Pathogenicity, and Ecology of Bacterial Plasmids, held January 5-9, 1981, in Santo Domingo, Dominican Republic] ; edited by Stuart B. Levy, Royston C. Clowes and Ellen L. Koenig. — New York ; London : Plenum, c1981. — xii,708p : ill ; 26cm
Includes index
ISBN 0-306-40753-1 : Unpriced B82-00672

589.9'0875 — Bacteria. Ions & elections. Transport — *Conference proceedings*

International Symposium on Vectorial Reactions in Electron and Ion Transport in Mitochondria and Bacteria *(1981 : Selva di Fasano).* Vectorial reactions in electron and ion transport in mitochondria and bacteria : proceedings of the International Symposium on Vectorial Reactions in Electron and Ion Transport in Mitochondria and Bacteria held in Selva di Fasano (Italy), May 19-22, 1981 / editors F. Palmieri ... [et al.]. — Amsterdam ; Oxford : Elsevier-North-Holland Biomedical, 1981. — xi,429p : ill ; 25cm. — (Developments in bioenergetics and biomembranes ; v.5)
Includes index
ISBN 0-444-80372-6 : £34.63
Primary classification 574.87'342 B82-01639

589.9'2 — Mycobacteria

The **Biology** of the mycobacteria / edited by Colin Ratledge and John Stanford. — London : Academic Press
Vol.1: Physiology, identification and classification. — 1982. — viii,544p : ill ; 24cm
Includes bibliographies and index
ISBN 0-12-582301-0 : £41.20 : CIP rev. B82-00328

Chadwick, Maureen V.. Mycobacteria / Maureen V. Chadwick. — Bristol : John Wright, 1981. — 114p ; 19cm. — (Institute of Medical Laboratory Sciences monographs)
Bibliography: p107-109. — Includes index
ISBN 0-7236-0595-5 (pbk) : Unpriced : CIP rev. B81-21588

589.9'5 — Escherichia coli. Genes. Molecular biology

Glass, Robert E.. Gene function : E. coli and its heritable elements / Robert E. Glass. — London : Croom Helm, c1982. — 487p : ill ; 24cm
Includes bibliographies and index
ISBN 0-7099-0081-3 (cased) : £19.95 : CIP rev.
ISBN 0-7099-0081-3 (pbk) : Unpriced B81-24658

589.9'5 — Rhizobium

Biology of the Rhizobiaceae / edited by Kenneth L. Giles, Alan G. Atherly. — New York ; London : Academic Press, 1981. — xv,336p : ill ; 24cm. — (International review of cytology. Supplement ; 13)
Includes bibliographies and index
ISBN 0-12-364374-0 : Unpriced B82-29988

589.9'504133 — Microorganisms. Nitrogen. Fixation

Postgate, J. R.. The fundamentals of nitrogen fixation. — Cambridge : Cambridge University Press, Dec.1982. — [254]p
ISBN 0-521-24169-3 (cased) : £20.00 : CIP entry
ISBN 0-521-28494-5 (pbk) : £7.95 B82-40892

590 — ZOOLOGICAL SCIENCES

590'.74'4 — Zoos — *For children*

Lenga, Rosalind. Let's go to the zoo / Rosalind Lenga ; general editor Henry Pluckrose ; photography by Mike Dyer. — London : Watts, c1978 (1982 [printing]). — 32p : col.ill ; 22cm. — (Let's go series)
ISBN 0-85166-714-7 : £2.99 B82-26838

Standring, Gillian. The zoo book / Gillian Standring. — London : Macdonald, 1982. — 61p : col.ill,1col.map ; 29cm
Includes index
ISBN 0-356-05972-3 : £4.50 B82-19115

590'.74'40222 — Zoos. Animals — *Illustrations — for children*

Campbell, Rod. Dear zoo. — London : Abelard-Schuman, Sept.1982. — [24]p
ISBN 0-200-72779-6 : £2.95 : CIP entry B82-18962

591 — ZOOLOGY

591 — Animals

Black, David, *1944-*. Animal wonders of the world / David Black. — London : Orbis, 1981. — 208p : ill(some col.),maps(some col.) ; 30cm
Bibliography: p204-206. — Includes index
ISBN 0-85613-391-4 : £12.95 B82-08553

Blow, Catherine. World of colour animal encyclopedia / Catherine Blow. — London : Octopus, 1980. — 348p : col.ill ; 25cm
Ill on lining papers. — Includes index
ISBN 0-7064-1356-3 : £5.95 B82-01008

Bradshaw, Jeremy. Giants / Jeremy Bradshaw ; introduction by Keith Shackleton. — London : ITV Books in association with Anglia Television, 1982. — 47p : ill(some col.) ; 26cm. — (Animals in action)
Text on lining papers. — Includes index
ISBN 0-900727-07-1 : £2.50 B82-30166

Burton, Robert, *1941-*. The family library of wild animals / Robert Burton. — London : Octopus, 1982, c1981. — 80p : ill(chiefly col.) ; 33cm
Ill on lining papers. — Includes index
ISBN 0-7064-1461-6 : £2.95 B82-30162

Hickman, Cleveland P. (Cleveland Pendleton), *1895-*. Biology of animals / Cleveland P. Hickman Jr., Larry S. Roberts, Frances M. Hickman ; original artwork by William C. Ober. — 3rd ed. — St. Louis ; London : Mosby, 1982. — viii,646p : ill(some col.),2maps ; 29cm
Previous ed.: 1978. — Ill on lining papers. — Includes bibliographies and index
ISBN 0-8016-2167-4 : £17.75 B82-31869

Wood, Gerald L.. The Guinness book of animal facts and feats / Gerald L. Wood. — 3rd ed. — Enfield : Guinness Superlatives, c1982. — 252p : ill(some col.),ports(some col.) ; 24cm
Previous ed.: 1976. — Text on lining papers. — Bibliography: p224-239. — Includes index
ISBN 0-85112-235-3 : £8.95 : CIP rev. B82-08426

591 — Animals — *For children*

I am an owl / [English text Yvonne Hooker]. — London : Methuen, 1981, c1978. — [24]p : col.ill ; 22x25cm
These illustrations originally published with an Italian text
ISBN 0-416-21830-x (spiral) : £3.25 B82-15604

Kilpatrick, Cathy. Animals / Cathy Kilpatrick. — London : Hamlyn, 1982. — 128p : ill(some col.) ; 18cm. — (Hamlyn junior pocket books)
Includes index
ISBN 0-600-30499-x : £1.99 B82-23622

Lambert, David, *1932-*. Animal wonders. — London : Ward Lock, Apr.1981. — [96]p. — (Kingfisher factbook)
ISBN 0-7063-6106-7 : £2.50 : CIP entry B81-03165

Roffey, Maureen. Home sweet home. — London : Bodley Head, Sept.1982. — [32]p
ISBN 0-370-30481-0 : £4.50 : CIP entry B82-18750

591 — Nocturnal animals

Burton, Robert, *1941-*. Nature's night life / Robert Burton. — Poole : Blandford, 1982. — 160p : ill(some col.) ; 26cm
Includes index
ISBN 0-7137-1111-6 : £8.95 : CIP rev. B82-00297

591 — Zoology

Hickman, Cleveland P. (Cleveland Pendleton), *1895-*. Integrated principles of zoology / Cleveland P. Hickman, Cleveland P. Hickman, Jr., Frances M. Hickman ; in association with Larry S. Roberts ; with 1205 illustrations, including original drawings by William C. Ober. — 6th ed. — St. Louis ; London : Mosby, 1979. — xvii,1086p : ill ; 27cm
Previous ed.: 1974. — Ill on lining papers. — Includes bibliographies and index
ISBN 0-8016-2172-0 : £19.50 B82-28892

591'.012 — Animals. Taxonomy

Goto, H. E.. Animal taxonomy. — London : Edward Arnold, Aug.1982. — [64]p. — (The Institute of Biology's studies in biology ; no.143)
ISBN 0-7131-2847-x (pbk) : £2.25 : CIP entry B82-15917

591'.012 — Animals. Taxonomy. Evolutionary aspects

Mayr, Ernst. Systematics and the origin of species / by Ernst Mayr ; with an introduction by Niles Eldredge. — New York ; Guildford : Columbia University Press, c1982. — xxxvii,334p : ill,maps ; 23cm. — (Columbia classics in evolution series)
Originally published: 1942. — Includes bibliographies and index
ISBN 0-231-05449-1 (pbk) : £10.40 B82-39007

591'.01'515 — Zoology. Mathematics. Optimisation

Alexander, R. McNeill. Optima for animals / R. McNeill Alexander. — London : Arnold, 1982. — vii,112p : ill ; 23cm
Bibliography: p107-109. — Includes index
ISBN 0-7131-2843-7 (pbk) : £5.25 : CIP rev. B82-13014

591'.022'2 — Animals — *Illustrations — For children*

Herbert, Helen. Animals in famous pictures : colouring book / by Helen Herbert. — Cambridge : Dinosaur, c1982. — [22]p : ill ; 21x30cm
ISBN 0-85122-317-6 (pbk) : £0.80 B82-32080

591'.022'2 — Animals — *Illustrations — For children* *continuation*

Svensson, Borje. Animals / [designed and illustrated by Borje Svensson] ; [paper engineering by James Diaz]. — [London] : Collins, 1982, c1981. — 1box : col.ill ; 60mmx60mmx60mm. — (A Collins block book)
1 sheet 57mmx108cm (concertina folded) attached in box containing diorama
ISBN 0-00-138383-3 : £1.25 B82-36183

591'.07'1041 — Great Britain. Schools. Students, 5-14 years. Curriculum subjects: Animals — *For teaching*

Thorpe, Peter. Looking at animals / Peter Thorpe. — Basingstoke : Globe Education, 1982. — 48p : ill,forms ; 30cm. — (Science horizons. Level 2a)
Published for West Sussex County Council. — Bibliography: p13
ISBN 0-333-28535-2 (pbk) : Unpriced B82-38805

591'.092'4 — Tropical regions. Zoological expeditions — *Personal observations*

Attenborough, David. The Zoo quest expeditions : travels in Guyana, Indonesia & Paraguay / David Attenborough. — Abridged combined ed. — Harmondsworth : Penguin, 1982, c1980. — 355p,[16]p of plates : ill ; 18cm
Originally published: Guildford : Lutterworth, 1980. — Contents: Zoo quest to Guiana. Previous ed.: Guildford : Lutterworth, 1956 — Zoo quest for a dragon. Previous ed.: Guildford : Lutterworth, 1957 — Zoo quest in Paraguay. Previous ed.: Guildford : Lutterworth, 1959
ISBN 0-14-005765-x (pbk) : £1.95 B82-22487

591'.092'4 — Zoology. Durrell, Gerald — *Biographies*

Durrell, Gerald. My family and other animals. — London : Granada, Sept.1982. — [256]p
Originally published: London : Hart-Davis, 1956
ISBN 0-246-63690-4 : £6.95 : CIP entry B82-18865

591'.092'4 — Zoology. Jacobs, George — *Biographies*

Jacobs, George. Memoirs of a coarse zoo keeper. — London : Muller, July 1982. — [272]p
ISBN 0-584-11025-1 : £7.95 : CIP entry B82-17205

591.1 — ANIMALS. PHYSIOLOGY

591.1 — Animals. Physiology — *Conference proceedings*

International Conference on Comparative Physiology *(5th : 1980 : Sandbjerg)*. A companion to animal physiology / [papers from the Fifth International Conference on Comparative Physiology held at Sandbjerg, Denmark, July 22-26, 1980] ; editors C. Richard Taylor, Kjell Johansen, Liana Bolis. — Cambridge : Cambridge University Press, 1982. — xv,365p : ill ; 24cm. — (Comparative physiology perspectives)
Includes bibliographies and index
ISBN 0-521-24437-4 (cased) : £20.00
ISBN 0-521-28685-9 (pbk) : £7.95 B82-36431

591.1 — Small animals. Physiology. Projects — *For children*

Bishop, O. N.. Adventures with small animals. — London : J. Murray, Oct.1982. — [64]p
ISBN 0-7195-3944-7 (cased) : £4.95 : CIP entry
ISBN 0-7195-3930-7 (pbk) : £2.75 B82-23019

591.1'13 — Animals. Blood. White cells

Leukocyte function / edited by Martin J. Cline. — New York ; Edinburgh : Churchill Livingstone, 1981. — ix,149p : ill ; 24cm. — (Methods in hematology ; v.3)
Includes index
£15.00 B82-17808

591.1'13 — Animals. Blood. White cells. Chemotropism

Wilkinson, Peter C.. Chemotaxis and inflammation. — 2nd ed. — Edinburgh : Churchill Livingstone, Apr.1982. — [280]p
Previous ed.: 1974
ISBN 0-443-02085-x : £17.00 : CIP entry B82-03579

591.1'16 — Animals. Peripheral arteries. Chemoreceptors. Physiology - *Conference proceedings*

Arterial chemoreceptors. — Leicester : Leicester University Press, Apr.1981. — [554]p
Conference papers
ISBN 0-7185-1205-7 : £20.00 : CIP entry B81-05129

591.1'3 — Animals. Nutrition

Human nutrition and animal feeding / volume editor Geoffrey H. Bourne. — Basel ; London : Karger, 1981. — xii,290p : ill ; 25cm. — (World review of nutrition and dietetics ; v.37)
Includes bibliographies and index
ISBN 3-8055-2143-x : £74.00
Primary classification 613.2 B82-06281

591.1'32 — Animals. Pancreas. Islets

The **Islets** of Langerhans : biochemistry, physiology and pathology / edited by S.J. Cooperstein, Dudley Watkins. — New York ; London : Academic Press, 1981. — xxi,497p : ill ; 24cm
Includes bibliographies and index
ISBN 0-12-187820-1 : £40.00 B82-30113

591.1'32 — Animals. Teeth — *For children*

LeSieg, Theo.. The tooth book / by Theo. LeSieg ; illustrated by Roy McKie. — Glasgow : Collins, 1982, c1981. — [40]p : chiefly col.ill ; 24cm. — (A Beginning beginner book)
Originally published: New York : Beginner Books, 1981
ISBN 0-00-171227-6 (cased) : £2.95
ISBN 0-00-171285-3 (pbk) : Unpriced B82-25284

591.1'33 — Animals. Nutrition. Trace elements. Deficiency — *Conference proceedings*

Trace element deficiency : metabolic and physiological consequences / a Royal Society discussion organized by L. Fowden, G.A. Garton and C.F. Mills, held on 28 and 29 January 1981. — London : Royal Society, 1981. — v,213p,[2]leaves of plates : ill ; 31cm
Originally published: in Philosophical transactions of the Royal Society of London, series B, vol.294(no.1071). — Includes bibliographies
ISBN 0-85403-171-5 : £24.25 B82-00661

591.1'4 — Animals. Endocrine system — *Serials*

Oxford reviews of reproductive biology. — Vol.3 (1981). — Oxford : Clarendon Press, Sept.1981. — [325]p
ISBN 0-19-857536-x : £30.00 : CIP entry
Primary classification 591.1'6 B81-21621

591.1'4 — Animals. Reticuloendothelial system

The **Reticuloendothelial** system : a comprehensive treatise. — New York ; London : Plenum
Vol.2: Biochemistry and metabolism / edited by Anthony J. Sbarra and Robert R. Strauss. — c1980. — xxiv,432p : ill ; 26cm
Includes bibliographies and index
ISBN 0-306-40292-0 : Unpriced B82-40421

591.1'42 — Animals. Endocrine system. Regulation. Effects of olfactory perception — *Conference proceedings*

Olfaction and endocrine regulation. — Eynsham (1 Abbey St., Eynsham, Oxford OX8 1JJ) : IRL Press, Jan.1982. — [350]p
Conference papers
ISBN 0-904147-35-5 (pbk) : £12.00 : CIP entry B81-37540

591.1'5 — Animals. Genes

Hutt, Frederick B.. Animal genetics / Frederick B. Hutt, Benjamin A. Rasmusen. — 2nd ed. — New York ; Chichester : Wiley, c1982. — x,582p : ill ; 24cm
Previous ed.: New York : Ronald Press Co, 1964. — Includes bibliographies and index
ISBN 0-471-08497-2 : £21.90 B82-34516

591.1'6 — Animals. Reproductive system — *Serials*

Oxford reviews of reproductive biology. — Vol.3 (1981). — Oxford : Clarendon Press, Sept.1981. — [325]p
ISBN 0-19-857536-x : £30.00 : CIP entry
Also classified at 591.1'4 B81-21621

591.1'8 — Animals. Control systems — *Conference proceedings*

European Society for Comparative Physiology and Biochemistry. *Congress (3rd : 1981 : Noordwijkerhout)*. Exogenous and endogenous influences on metabolic and neural control of respiration, feeding, activity and energy supply in muscles, ion- and osmoregulation, reproduction perception and orientation / editors A.D.F. Addink, N. Spronk. — Oxford : Pergamon, 1982. — 2v. : ill ; 26cm
"Proceedings of the third Congress of the European Society for Cooperative Physiology and Biochemistry, August 31-September 3, 1981, Noordwijkerhout, Netherlands". — Includes index
ISBN 0-08-027986-4 : Unpriced : CIP rev.
ISBN 0-08-028845-6 (v.2) : £25.00 B82-10596

591.1'82 — Animals. Neurotransmitter receptors

Neurotransmitter receptors. — London : Chapman and Hall
Pt.1: Amino acids, peptides and benzodiazepines / edited by S.J. Enna and H.I. Yamamura. — 1980. — xi,212p : ill ; 24cm. — (Receptors and recognition. Series B ; v.9)
Includes bibliographies and index
ISBN 0-412-16250-4 : £15.00 : CIP rev. B80-25619

591.1'82 — Animals. Senses — *For children*

Sully, Nina. Looking at the senses / Nina Sully. — London : Batsford Academic and Educational, 1982. — 48p : ill ; 23cm. — (Looking at science)
Bibliography: p47. — Includes index
ISBN 0-7134-4059-7 : £3.95 B82-22174

591.1'823 — Animals. Eyes. Retinas — *Serials*

Progress in retinal research. — Vol.1. — Oxford : Pergamon, Oct.1982. — [245]p
ISBN 0-08-028901-0 : £36.00 : CIP entry B82-24957

591.1'826 — Animals. Olfactory perception & gustatory perception. Biochemistry

Perception of behavioral chemicals / edited by Dale Melvin Norris. — Amsterdam ; Oxford : Elsevier/North-Holland Biomedical, 1981. — x,,328p : ill ; 25cm
Includes bibliographies and index
ISBN 0-444-80347-5 : £43.22 B82-18375

591.1'852 — Animals. Collagen. Genetic aspects

Collagen in health and disease. — Edinburgh : Churchill Livingstone, Oct.1982. — [480]p
ISBN 0-443-02142-2 : £45.00 : CIP entry B82-24019

591.1'852 — Animals. Locomotion

Alexander, R. McNeill. Animal mechanics. — 2nd ed. — Oxford : Blackwell Scientific, Nov.1982. — [320]p
Previous ed.: London : Sidgwick and Jackson, 1968
ISBN 0-632-00956-x : £15.00 : CIP entry B82-29438

591.1'852 — Animals. Movement

Alexander, R. McNeill. Locomotion of animals / R. McNeill Alexander. — Glasgow : Blackie, 1982. — vii,163p : ill ; 21cm. — (Tertiary level biology)
Bibliography: p154-158. — Includes index
ISBN 0-216-91159-1 (cased) : £15.95 : CIP rev.
ISBN 0-216-91158-3 (pbk) : £7.95 B81-36035

The **Ecology** of animal movement. — Oxford : Oxford University Press, Jan.1983. — [350]p
ISBN 0-19-857575-0 : £25.00 : CIP entry B82-33484

591.1'852 — Animals. Muscles. Contraction

Squire, John. The structural basis of muscular contraction / John Squire. — New York ; London : Plenum, c1981. — xvii,698p : ill ; 24cm
Bibliography: p685-687. — Includes index
ISBN 0-306-40582-2 : Unpriced B82-05800

591.1'852 — Animals. Muscles. Motility — *Serials*

Cell and muscle motility. — Vol.1-. — New York ; London ([88 Middlesex St., E1 7EX]) : Plenum, 1981-. — v. : ill ; 26cm
Unpriced
Primary classification 574.87'64 B82-07633

591.1′852 — Animals. Voluntary muscles. Sarcoplasmic reticulum. Calcium. Transport phenomena

Meis, Leopoldo de. The sarcoplasmic reticulum : transport and energy transduction / Leopoldo de Meis. — New York ; Chichester : Wiley, c1981. — xv,163p : ill ; 24cm. — (Transport in the life sciences, ISSN 0271-6208 ; v.2)
Bibliography: p145-153. — Includes index
ISBN 0-471-05025-3 : £29.25 B82-05817

591.1′852 — Lincolnshire. Lincoln. Flaxengate. Animals. Bones, *ca 870-1500*. Archaeological investigation

O'Connor, Terry. Animal bones from Flaxengate, Lincoln, c.870-1500. — London : Council for British Archaeology, Mar.1982. — [52]p. — (The Archaeology of Lincoln ; v.18-1)
ISBN 0-906780-13-6 (pbk) : £5.00 : CIP entry
B82-10663

591.1′852 — South Africa. Animals. Bones. Archaeological investigation

Brain, C. K.. The hunters or the hunted? : an introduction to African cave taphonomy / C.K. Brain. — Chicago ; London : University of Chicago Press, c1981. — x,365p : ill,maps,ports ; 31cm
Bibliography: p347-361. — Includes index
ISBN 0-226-07089-1 : £24.50 B82-13699

591.1′858 — Animals. Skin. Sensory nerves. Conduction

Sinclair, David, *1915-*. Mechanisms of cutaneous sensation / David Sinclair. — 2nd ed. — Oxford : Oxford University Press, 1981. — xi,363p : ill ; 23cm. — (Oxford medical publications)
Previous ed.: published as 'Cutaneous sensation', 1967. — Includes index
ISBN 0-19-261174-7 : £20.00 : CIP rev.
B81-28854

591.1′858 — Dermatoglyphics

Loesch, Danuta Z.. Quantitative dermatoglyphics. — Oxford : Oxford University Press, July 1982. — [450]p. — (Oxford monographs on medical genetics ; 10)
ISBN 0-19-261305-7 : £30.00 : CIP entry
B82-12537

591.1′88 — Animals. Brain. Electrical stimulation. Techniques

Electrical stimulation research techniques / edited by Michael M. Patterson, Raymond P. Kesner ; with a foreword by Richard F. Thompson. — New York ; London : Academic Press, 1981. — xv,370p : ill ; 24cm. — (Methods in physiological psychology ; v.3)
Includes bibliographies and index
ISBN 0-12-547440-7 : £25.80 B82-07552

591.1′88 — Animals. Nerve fibres. Electrochemistry

Tasaki, Ichiji. Physiology and electrochemistry of nerve fibers / Ichiji Tasaki. — New York ; London : Academic Press, 1982. — xiv,348p : ill ; 24cm. — (Biophysics and bioengineering series ; 3)
Includes bibliographies and index
ISBN 0-12-683780-5 : £23.80 B82-34855

591.1′88 — Animals. Nerves. Growth

Liu, H. Mei. Biology and pathology of nerve growth / H. Mei Liu. — New York ; London : Academic Press, c1981. — xi,308p : ill ; 24cm
Bibliography: p270-302. — Includes index
ISBN 0-12-452960-7 : £23.20 B82-29693

591.1′88 — Animals. Nervous system

Biology, brain and behaviour : summer school, introduction and guide. — [Milton Keynes] : Open University Press, c1981. — 4p ; 30cm. — (SD286 ; SSIG)
At head of title: The Open University
Unpriced (pbk)
Also classified at 591.51 B82-15052

Biology, brain and behaviour / [SD286 Course Team]. — Milton Keynes : Open University Press
At head of title: The Open University
Module B1: Neuronal structure and function ; Module B2: Nauronal systems / prepared by a Course Team from the Faculties of Science and Social Sciences. — 1981. — 50,22p : ill(some col.) ; 30cm. — (SD286 ; block B)
ISBN 0-335-16065-4 (pbk) : Unpriced
Also classified at 591.51 B82-04958

Biology, brain and behaviour / [SD286 Course Team]. — Milton Keynes : Open University Press
At head of title: The Open University
Module C1: Plasticity and specificity in the nervous systems. — 1981. — 35p : ill(some col.) ; 30cm. — (SD286 ; block C)
Cover title. — Bibliography: p34
ISBN 0-335-16068-9 (pbk) : Unpriced
Also classified at 591.51 B82-04955

Biology, brain and behaviour / [SD286 Course Team]. — Milton Keynes : Open University Press
At head of title: The Open University
Module C2: Learning, memory and the brain. — 1981. — 23p : ill ; 30cm. — (SD286 ; block C)
Cover title. — Bibliography: p23
ISBN 0-335-16069-7 (pbk) : Unpriced
Also classified at 591.51 B82-04954

Biology, brain and behaviour / [the SD286 Course Team]. — Milton Keynes : Open University Press
At head of title: The Open University
Module C3: The hippocampus. — 1981. — 30p : ill(some col.) ; 30cm. — (SD286 ; block C)
ISBN 0-335-16070-0 (pbk) : Unpriced
Also classified at 591.51 B82-15044

Biology, brain and behaviour / [the SD286 Course Team]. — Milton Keynes : Open University Press
At head of title: The Open University. — Bibliography: p42
Module C4: Motivation. — 1981. — 43p : ill (some col.) ; 30cm. — (SD286 ; block C)
ISBN 0-335-16071-9 (pbk) : Unpriced
Also classified at 591.51 B82-15045

Biology, brain and behaviour / [the SD286 Course Team]. — Milton Keynes : Open University Press
At head of title: The Open University
Module C5: Chemical pathways in the brain. — 1981. — 23p : ill(some col.) ; 30cm. — (SD286 ; block C)
ISBN 0-335-16072-7 (pbk) : Unpriced
Also classified at 591.51 B82-15046

Biology, brain and behaviour / [the SD286 Course Team]. — Milton Keynes : Open University Press
At head of title: The Open University
Module C6: Pain. — 1981. — 30p : ill(some col.) ; 30cm. — (SD286 ; block C)
Bibliography: p28
ISBN 0-335-16073-5 (pbk) : Unpriced
Also classified at 591.51 B82-15047

Biology, brain and behaviour / [the SD286 Course Team]. — Milton Keynes : Open University Press
At head of title: The Open University
Module C8: Aggression. — 1981. — 35p : ill (some col.) ; 30cm. — (SD286 ; block C)
Bibliography: p34
ISBN 0-335-16075-1 (pbk) : Unpriced
Also classified at 591.51 B82-15048

Biology, brain and behaviour / [SD286 Course Team]. — Milton Keynes : Open University Press
At head of title: The Open University
Module C9: Hormones and sexual behaviour. — 1981. — 27p : ill(some col.) ; 30cm. — (SD286 ; block C)
ISBN 0-335-16076-x (pbk) : Unpriced
Also classified at 591.51 B82-04957

Biology, brain and behaviour / [SD286 Course Team]. — Milton Keynes : Open University Press
At head of title: The Open University
Module C10: Mother-infant relationships. — 1981. — 24p : ill(some col.) ; 30cm. — (SD286 ; block C)
Cover title
ISBN 0-335-16077-8 (pbk) : Unpriced
Also classified at 591.51 B82-04956

591.1′88 — Animals. Nervous system. Genetic aspects

Hall, Jeffrey C.. Genetic neurobiology / Jeffrey C. Hall, Ralph J. Greenspan, and William A. Harris ; ... based in part on ideas developed at a Neurosciences Research Program Work Session chaired by Seymour Benzer, Richard L. Sidman, and Jeffrey C. Hall. — Cambridge, Mass. ; London : MIT Press, c1982. — 284p : ill ; 24cm
Bibliography: p212-268. — Includes index
ISBN 0-262-08111-3 : £21.00 B82-35397

591.1′88 — Animals. Neurons. Development

Neuronal development / edited by Nicholas C. Spitzer. — New York ; London : Plenum, c1982. — xxiii,424p : ill ; 24cm. — (Current topics in neurobiology)
Includes index
ISBN 0-306-40956-9 : Unpriced B82-38670

591.1′88 — Animals. Neurons. Interactions with glia cells — *Conference proceedings*

Glial-neurone interactions. — Cambridge : Cambridge University Press, Jan.1982. — [244] p. — (The Journal of Experimental Biology, ISSN 0022-0949 ; v.95)
Conference papers
ISBN 0-521-24556-7 : £22.00 : CIP entry
B82-03365

591.1′88 — Animals. Neurosecretion

International Symposium on Neurosecretion *(8th : 1980 : Friday Harbour, Wash.).* Neurosecretion : molecules, cells, systems / [proceedings of the Eighth International Symposium on Neurosecretion, held September 4-10, 1980, in Friday Harbour, Washington] ; edited by Donald S. Farner and Karl Lederis. — New York ; London : Plenum, c1981. — xxv,531p : ill ; 24cm
Includes bibliographies and index
ISBN 0-306-40760-4 : Unpriced B82-31925

591.1′88 — Neurobiology

Mill, Peter J.. Comparative neurobiology. — London : Edward Arnold, Dec.1981. — [224]p. — (Contemporary biology)
ISBN 0-7131-2810-0 : £8.95 : CIP entry
B81-31556

591.1′88 — Neurobiology — *Festschriften*

Studies in developmental neurobiology : essays in honor of Viktor Hamburger / edited by W. Maxwell Cowan. — New York ; Oxford : Oxford University Press, 1981. — xv,454p : ill,1port ; 25cm
Includes bibliographies and index
ISBN 0-19-502927-5 : £30.00 B82-16080

591.1′88 — Neurobiology. Laboratory techniques

Methods in neurobiology / edited by Robert Lahue. — New York ; London : Plenum
Includes bibliographies and index
Vol.2. — c1981. — xvi,665p : ill ; 26cm
ISBN 0-306-40518-0 : Unpriced B82-03029

591.1′88′02854044 — Neurobiology. Applications of digital computer systems

Bureš, Jan. Practical guide to computer applications in neurosciences. — Chichester : Wiley, Dec.1982. — [350]p
ISBN 0-471-10012-9 : CIP entry B82-30811

591.1′88′05 — Neurobiology — *Serials*

Progress in neurobiology. — Vol.15. — Oxford : Pergamon, Nov.1981. — [350]p
ISBN 0-08-029084-1 : £43.00 : CIP entry
B81-31078

Progress in neurobiology. — Vol.16. — Oxford : Pergamon, Feb.1982. — [320]p
ISBN 0-08-029105-8 : £45.00 : CIP entry
B82-01313

Progress in neurobiology. — Vol.17. — Oxford : Pergamon, July 1982. — [290]p
ISBN 0-08-029697-1 : £115.00 : CIP entry
B82-20748

591.19′121 — Animals. Bioenergetics

Brafield, Alan E.. Animal energetics / Alan E. Brafield, Michael J. Llewellyn. — Glasgow : Blackie, 1982. — viii,168p : ill ; 21cm. — (Tertiary level biology)
Bibliography: p158-162. — Includes index
ISBN 0-216-91255-5 (cased) : £16.95 : CIP rev.
ISBN 0-216-91254-7 (pbk) : £7.95 B82-04301

591.19′2 — Animals. Proteins, trace minerals & vitamins. Interactions — *Serials*

Vitamin/trace mineral/protein interactions. — Vol.1-. — Westmount, Québec : Eden Press ; Edinburgh : Churchill Livingstone, 1979-. — v. ; 22cm. — (Annual research reviews)
Annual. — Description based on: Vol.3
ISSN 0708-5923 = Vitamin, trace mineral, protein interactions : Unpriced B82-18712

591.19′218 — Animals. Pigments

Vevers, Gwynne. The colours of animals. — London : Edward Arnold, Sept.1982. — [80]p. — (The Institute of Biology's studies in biology, ISSN 0537-9024 ; no.146)
ISBN 0-7131-2858-5 (pbk) : £2.25 : CIP entry B82-25915

591.19′2454 — Animals. Cells. Lipoproteins

Lipid-protein interactions / edited by Patricia C. Jost and O. Hayes Griffith. — New York ; Chichester : Wiley, c1982
Vol. 1. — x,338p : ill ; 24cm
Includes index
ISBN 0-471-06457-2 : £58.50 B82-32710

591.19′25 — Animals. Co-enzyme Q — *Conference proceedings*

Biomedical and clinical aspects of coenzyme Q. — Amsterdam ; Oxford : Elsevier/North-Holland Biomedical Press
Vol.3: Proceedings of the Third International Symposium on Coenzyme Q, held in Austin, Texas, U.S.A., January 18-21 1981 / editors K. Folkers and Y. Yamamura. — 1981. — xv,414p : ill ; 25cm
Includes index
ISBN 0-444-80319-x : Unpriced B82-05986

591.19′27 — Animals. Steroid hormone receptors

Mechanisms of steroid action / edited by G.P. Lewis and M. Ginsburg. — London : Macmillan, 1981. — ix,179p : ill ; 25cm
Conference papers. — At head of title: Biological Council the Co-ordinating Committee for Symposia on Drug Action. — Includes bibliographies and index
ISBN 0-333-32455-2 : £3.50 B82-20937

591.2 — ANIMALS. DISEASES

591.2′1113 — Animals. Blood. Leukemia — *Conference proceedings*

International Symposium for Comparative Research on Leukemia and Related Diseases *(10th : 1981 : University of California)*. Advances in comparative leukemia research 1981 : proceedings of the Xth International Symposium for Comparative Research on Leukemia and Related Diseases, held at the University of California, Los Angeles, USA, August 31-September 4, 1981 / edited David S. Yohn, James R. Blakeslee. — New York ; Oxford : Elsevier Biomedical, c1982. — xliii,649p : ill ; 25cm
Includes index
ISBN 0-444-00720-2 : £53.19 B82-30535

591.2′188 — Animals. Nervous system. Diseases. Genetic aspects

Neurogenetics : genetic approaches to the nervous system / Xandra O. Breakefield, editor-in-chief. — New York ; Oxford : Elsevier, c1979. — xvii,377p : ill ; 24cm
Includes bibliographies and index
ISBN 0-444-00295-2 : Unpriced B82-15242

591.2′3 — Animals. Pathogens: Microorganisms

Linton, Alan H.. Microbes, men and animals : the natural history of microbial interactions / Alan H. Linton with contributions by Mary P. English ... [et. al.]. — Chichester : Wiley, c1982. — xvi,342p : ill,maps ; 24cm
Includes bibliographies and index
ISBN 0-471-10083-8 : £19.50 : CIP rev. B82-09702

591.2′3′05 — Animals. Parasitic diseases — *Serials*

Advances in parasitology. — Vol.19. — London : Academic Press, Oct.1981. — [360]p
ISBN 0-12-031719-2 : CIP entry
ISSN 0065-308x B81-28141

Advances in parasitology. — Vol.20. — London : Academic Press, Apr.1982. — [520]p
ISBN 0-12-031720-6 : CIP entry B82-04130

Advances in parasitology. — Vol.21. — London : Academic Press, Sept.1982. — [310]p
ISBN 0-12-031721-4 : CIP entry
ISSN 0065-308x B82-19157

591.2′34 — Animals. Pathogens: Viruses. Persistence — *Conference proceedings*

Society for General Microbiology. *Symposium (33rd : 1982 : University of Cambridge)*. Virus persistence : thirty-third symposium of the Society for General Microbiology held at the University of Cambridge, March 1982 / edited by B.W.J. Mahy, A.C. Minson and G.K. Darby. — Cambridge : Cambridge University Press for the Society for General Microbiology, 1982. — x,300p : ill ; 24cm
Includes bibliographies and index
ISBN 0-521-24454-4 : Unpriced : CIP rev. B82-14484

591.3 — ANIMALS. DEVELOPMENT

591.3 — Animals. Development

Davenport, Richard, *1930-*. An outline of animal development / Richard Davenport. — Reading, Mass. ; London : Addison-Wesley, c1979. — xvii,412p : ill ; 24cm. — (Addison-Wesley series in life sciences)
Includes index
ISBN 0-201-01814-4 : £12.95 B82-16072

591.3′33 — Animals. Embryos. In vitro culture

Fertilization and embryonic development in vitro / edited by Luigi Mastroianni, Jr. and John D. Biggers. — New York ; London : Plenum, c1981. — xi,371p : ill ; 24cm
Includes bibliographies and index
ISBN 0-306-40783-3 : Unpriced
Primary classification 591.3′33 B82-13923

591.3′1 — Animals. Growth. Role of nutrition

Physiology of growth and nutrition / volume editor M. Rechcigl, Jr. — Basel ; London : Karger, c1981. — xii,341p : ill ; 25cm. — (Comparative animal nutrition ; v.4)
Includes bibliographies and index
ISBN 3-8055-1199-x : £79.20 B82-11588

591.3′3 — Embryos

Le Douarin, Nicole M.. The neural crest. — Cambridge : Cambridge University Press, Dec.1982. — [259]p. — (Developmental and cell biology series ; 12)
ISBN 0-521-24770-5 : £37.50 : CIP entry B82-26249

591.3′3 — Embryos. Development

Cohen, Jack, *1933-*. Living embryos. — 3rd ed. / by Jack Cohen and Brendan Massey. — Oxford : Pergamon, 1982. — xii,173p,xivp of plates : ill ; 21cm
Previous ed.: 1967. — Bibliography: p162. — Includes index
ISBN 0-08-025926-x (cased) : Unpriced
ISBN 0-08-025925-1 (pbk) : £3.95 B82-39021

Growth and the development of pattern. — Cambridge : Cambridge University Press, Feb.1982. — [324]p. — (Journal of embryology and experimental morphology. Supplement, ISSN 0022-0752 ; v.65)
Conference papers
ISBN 0-521-24557-5 : £21.00 : CIP entry B82-07960

591.3′3′0222 — Embryos — *Illustrations*

Mathews, Willis W.. Atlas of descriptive embryology / Willis W. Mathews. — 3rd ed. — New York : Macmillan ; London : Collier Macmillan, c1982. — x,230p : chiefly ill ; 28cm
Previous ed.: 1976
ISBN 0-02-377130-5 (pbk) : £5.95 B82-39384

591.3′33 — Animals. Ova. In vitro fertilisation

Fertilization and embryonic development in vitro / edited by Luigi Mastroianni, Jr. and John D. Biggers. — New York ; London : Plenum, c1981. — xi,371p : ill ; 24cm
Includes bibliographies and index
ISBN 0-306-40783-3 : Unpriced
Also classified at 591.3′33 B82-13923

591.3′34 — Animals. Complete metamorphosis

Metamorphosis : a problem in developmental biology. — 2nd ed. / edited by Lawrence I. Gilbert and Earl Frieden. — New York ; London : Plenum, c1981. — xx,578p : ill ; 26cm
Previous ed.: New York : Appleton-Century-Crofts, 1968. — Includes bibliographies and index
ISBN 0-306-40692-6 : Unpriced B82-14277

591.3′8 — Animals. Evolution. Ecological aspects

Colombo, Federica. Animal evolution / Federica Colombo ; adapted by Isabelle Rabourdin ; translated by R.D. Martin, and A.-E. Martin. — London : Burke, 1981. — 92p : col.ill,maps,1port ; 28cm. — (Animal behaviour)
Translation of: Les animaux et leur environnement. — Includes index
ISBN 0-222-00822-9 : £4.95 : CIP rev. B81-30301

591.3′8 — Animals. Evolution — *For children*

Sortwell, Andrew. Animals of the past / Andrew Sortwell. — London : Macdonald, 1980. — 32p : col.ill ; 29cm. — (Eye openers!)
Bibliography: p30. — Includes index
ISBN 0-356-07090-5 : £2.50 B82-24549

591.3′8 — Animals. Evolution — *Forecasts*

Dixon, Dougal. After man : a zoology of the future / by Dougal Dixon ; introduction by Desmond Morris. — London : Granada, 1981. — 124p : ill(some col.),maps ; 29cm
Bibliography: p124. — Includes index
ISBN 0-246-11577-7 : £8.95 B82-09235

591.5 — ANIMALS. ECOLOGY

591.5 — Animals. Ecology

Wildlife population ecology / edited by James S. Wakeley. — University Park ; London : Pennsylvania State University Press, c1982. — x,385p : ill,maps ; 27cm
Includes bibliographies
ISBN 0-271-00303-0 (cased) : Unpriced
ISBN 0-271-00304-9 (pbk) : Unpriced B82-38144

591.5 — Environment. Adaptation of animals — *For children*

Jenkins, Alan Charles. Secrets of nature. — London : Hodder and Stoughton, Apr.1981. — [128]p
ISBN 0-340-26526-4 (pbk) : £1.25 : CIP entry B81-02563

591.51 — Animal sociobiology

Baldwin, John D.. Beyond sociobiology / John D. Baldwin and Janice I. Baldwin. — New York ; Oxford : Elsevier, c1982. — x,325p : ill ; 24cm
Bibliography: p263-297. — Includes index
ISBN 0-444-99086-0 : Unpriced B82-18373

591.51 — Animals. Behaviour

Barnard, C. J.. Animal behaviour. — London : Croom Helm, June 1982. — [384]p
ISBN 0-7099-0636-6 (cased) : £14.95 : CIP entry
ISBN 0-7099-0673-0 (pbk) : £7.95 B82-09586

Barnett, S. A.. Modern ethology : the science of animal behavior / S.A. Barnett. — New York ; Oxford University Press, 1981. — xi,705p : ill ; 24cm
Bibliography: p637-679. — Includes index
ISBN 0-19-502780-9 : £12.95 B82-01005

Biology, brain and behaviour : summer school, introduction and guide. — [Milton Keynes] : Open University Press, c1981. — 4p ; 30cm. — (SD286 ; SSIG)
At head of title: The Open University
Unpriced (pbk)
Primary classification 591.1′88 B82-15052

591.51 — Animals. Behaviour *continuation*

Biology, brain and behaviour / [SD286 Course Team]. — Milton Keynes : Open University Press
At head of title: The Open University
Module B1: Neuronal structure and function ; Module B2: Neuronal systems / prepared by a Course Team from the Faculties of Science and Social Sciences. — 1981. — 50,22p : ill(some col.) ; 30cm. — (SD286 ; block B)
ISBN 0-335-16065-4 (pbk) : Unpriced
Primary classification 591.1'88 B82-04958

Biology, brain and behaviour / [SD286 Course Team]. — Milton Keynes : Open University Press
At head of title: The Open University
Module C1: Plasticity and specificity in the nervous systems. — 1981. — 35p : ill(some col.) ; 30cm. — (SD286 ; block C)
Cover title. — Bibliography: p34
ISBN 0-335-16068-9 (pbk) : Unpriced
Primary classification 591.1'88 B82-04955

Biology, brain and behaviour / [SD286 Course Team]. — Milton Keynes : Open University Press
At head of title: The Open University
Module C2: Learning, memory and the brain. — 1981. — 23p : ill ; 30cm. — (SD286 ; block C)
Cover title. — Bibliography: p23
ISBN 0-335-16069-7 (pbk) : Unpriced
Primary classification 591.1'88 B82-04954

Biology, brain and behaviour / [the SD286 Course Team]. — Milton Keynes : Open University Press
At head of title: The Open University
Module C3: The hippocampus. — 1981. — 30p : ill(some col.) ; 30cm. — (SD286 ; block C)
ISBN 0-335-16070-0 (pbk) : Unpriced
Primary classification 591.1'88 B82-15044

Biology, brain and behaviour / [the SD286 Course Team]. — Milton Keynes : Open University Press
At head of title: The Open University. — Bibliography: p42
Module C4: Motivation. — 1981. — 43p : ill (some col.) ; 30cm. — (SD286 ; block C)
ISBN 0-335-16071-9 (pbk) : Unpriced
Primary classification 591.1'88 B82-15045

Biology, brain and behaviour / [the SD286 Course Team]. — Milton Keynes : Open University Press
At head of title: The Open University
Module C5: Chemical pathways in the brain. — 1981. — 23p : ill(some col.) ; 30cm. — (SD286 ; block C)
ISBN 0-335-16072-7 (pbk) : Unpriced
Primary classification 591.1'88 B82-15046

Biology, brain and behaviour / [the SD286 Course Team]. — Milton Keynes : Open University Press
At head of title: The Open University
Module C6: Pain. — 1981. — 30p : ill(some col.) ; 30cm. — (SD286 ; block C)
Bibliography: p28
ISBN 0-335-16073-5 (pbk) : Unpriced
Primary classification 591.1'88 B82-15047

Biology, brain and behaviour / [the SD286 Course Team]. — Milton Keynes : Open University Press
At head of title: The Open University
Module C8: Aggression. — 1981. — 35p : ill (some col.) ; 30cm. — (SD286 ; block C)
Bibliography: p34
ISBN 0-335-16075-1 (pbk) : Unpriced
Primary classification 591.1'88 B82-15048

Biology, brain and behaviour / [SD286 Course Team]. — Milton Keynes : Open University Press
At head of title: The Open University
Module C9: Hormones and sexual behaviour. — 1981. — 27p : ill(some col.) ; 30cm. — (SD286 ; block C)
ISBN 0-335-16076-x (pbk) : Unpriced
Primary classification 591.1'88 B82-04957

Biology, brain and behaviour / [SD286 Course Team]. — Milton Keynes : Open University Press
At head of title: The Open University
Module C10: Mother-infant relationships. — 1981. — 24p : ill(some col.) ; 30cm. — (SD286 ; block C)
Cover title
ISBN 0-335-16077-8 (pbk) : Unpriced
Primary classification 591.1'88 B82-04956

Broom, Donald M.. Biology of behaviour : mechanisms, functions and applications / Donald M. Broom ; with animal drawings by Robert Gillmor. — Cambridge : Cambridge University Press, 1981. — ix,320p : ill ; 24cm
Bibliography: p263-304. — Includes index
ISBN 0-521-23316-x (cased) : £20.00 : CIP rev.
ISBN 0-521-29906-3 (pbk) : £7.95 B81-33622

The **Oxford** companion to animal behaviour. — Oxford : Oxford University Press, June 1981. — [600]p
ISBN 0-19-866120-7 : £15.00 : CIP entry B81-11942

591.51 — Animals. Behaviour. Development

Behavioral development / the Bielefeld Interdisciplinary Project ; edited by Klaus Immelmann ... [et al.]. — Cambridge : Cambridge University Press, 1981. — xiv,754p : ill ; 25cm
Includes bibliographies and index
ISBN 0-521-24058-1 (cased) : £35.00
ISBN 0-521-28410-4 (pbk) : £12.50 B82-13985

591.51 — Animals. Behaviour. Development — *Conference proceedings*

The **Development** of behaviour : comparative and evolutionary aspects / [edited by] Gordon M. Burghardt, Marc Bekoff. — New York ; London : Garland STPM, c1978. — xiii,429p : ill ; 24cm
Conference papers. — Includes bibliographies and index
ISBN 0-8240-7015-1 : Unpriced B82-02772

591.51 — Animals. Behaviour. Neurobiological aspects

Guthrie, D. M.. Neuroethology : an introduction / D.M. Guthrie. — Oxford : Blackwell Scientific, 1980. — viii,221p : ill ; 24cm
Includes bibliographies and index
ISBN 0-632-00303-0 (pbk) : £8.75 : CIP rev. B80-02447

591.51 — Animals. Grooming

Vevers, Gwynne. Animal cleaners. — London : Bodley Head, July 1982. — [24]p. — (Bodley Head young naturalists)
ISBN 0-370-30460-8 : £2.95 : CIP entry B82-12317

591.51 — Animals. Play

Fagen, Robert. Animal play behavior / Robert Fagen. — New York ; Oxford : Oxford University Press, 1981. — xvii,684p : ill ; 24cm
Bibliography: p562-652. — Includes index
ISBN 0-19-502760-4 (cased) : £21.00 B82-05633

591.51 — Animals. Social behaviour

Animal societies and evolution : readings from Scientific American / with an introduction by Howard Topoff. — Oxford : W.H. Freeman, c1981. — viii,106p : ill(some col.),2maps ; 30cm
Bibliography: p101-102. — Includes index
ISBN 0-7167-1333-0 (cased) : £11.95 (pbk) : £5.50 B82-16150

Colombo, Federica. Animal society / Federica Colombo ; adapted by Paul-Henri Plantain ; translated by R.D. Martin, and A.-E. Martin. — London : Burke, 1981. — 91p : col.ill ; 28cm. — (Animal behaviour)
Translation of: Les animaux en société. — Includes index
ISBN 0-222-00823-7 : £4.95 : CIP rev. B81-30188

591.51 — Animals. Social behaviour — *For children*

Vevers, Gwynne. Animals that live in groups / Gwynne Vevers ; illustrated by Colin Threadgall. — London : Bodley Head, 1981. — 23p : col.ill ; 22cm. — (A Bodley Head young naturalist)
Includes index
ISBN 0-370-30400-4 : £2.95 B82-02492

591.51 — Ethology

Hinde, Robert A.. Ethology : its nature and relations with other sciences / Robert A. Hinde. — [Glasgow] : Fontana, 1982. — 320p : ill ; 18cm. — (Fontana masterguides)
Bibliography: p283-312. — Includes index
ISBN 0-00-636237-0 (pbk) : £2.95 B82-18954

Hinde, Robert A.. Ethology : its nature and relations with other sciences / Robert A. Hinde. — New York ; Oxford : Oxford University Press, 1982. — 320p : ill ; 22cm
Bibliography: p283-312. — Includes index
ISBN 0-19-520370-4 : £9.50 B82-27096

591.51 — Livestock. Self perception — *Conference proceedings*

Self awareness in domesticated animals : proceedings of a workshop held at Keble College, Oxford, 7th and 8th July 1980 / edited by D.G.M. Wood-Gush, M. Dawkins, R. Ewbank. — Potters Bar : Universities Federation for Animal Welfare, c1981. — 55p ; 21cm
Includes bibliographies
ISBN 0-900767-26-x (pbk) : £5.60 B82-28305

591.51 — Zoos. Animals. Behaviour. Projects

Markowitz, Hal. Behavioral enrichment in the zoo / Hal Markowitz. — New York ; London : Van Nostrand Reinhold, c1982. — ix,210p : ill ; 24cm
Bibliography: p200-203. — Includes index
ISBN 0-442-25125-4 : £20.40 B82-34329

591.51'01 — Animal sociobiology — *Philosophical perspectives*

Clark, Stephen R. L.. The nature of the beast : are animals moral?. — Oxford : Oxford University Press, Sept.1982. — [160]p
ISBN 0-19-219130-6 : £7.95 : CIP entry B82-19182

591.51'0724 — Animals. Behaviour. Mathematical models

McFarland, David. Quantitative ethology : the state space approach / David McFarland and Alasdair Houston. — Boston, Mass. ; London : Pitman Advanced Publishing Program, c1981. — viii,204p : ill ; 24cm. — (Pitman series in neurobiology and behaviour)
Bibliography: p187-201. — Includes index
ISBN 0-273-08417-8 : Unpriced : CIP rev. B81-28781

591.52'48 — Animals. Population

Moss, Robert. Animal population dynamics. — London : Chapman and Hall, Nov.1982. — [80]p. — (Outline studies in ecology)
ISBN 0-412-22240-x (pbk) : £2.75 : CIP entry B82-28256

591.52'48 — Animals. Population. Growth & regulation

Slobodkin, Lawrence B.. Growth and regulation of animal populations / Lawrence B. Slobodkin. — 2nd enl. ed. — New York : Dover ; London : Constable, 1980. — xii,234p : ill ; 21cm
Previous ed.: New York : Holt, Rinehart & Winston, 1961. — Bibliography: p185-198. — Includes index
ISBN 0-486-63958-4 (pbk) B82-40546

591.52'48'072 — Animals. Population. Research. Statistical methods

Seber, G. A. F.. The estimation of animal abundance : and related parameters / G.A.F. Seber. — 2nd ed. — London : Griffin, 1982. — xvii,654p : ill ; 25cm
Previous ed.: 1973. — Bibliography: p588-643. — Includes index
ISBN 0-85264-262-8 : £26.50 : CIP rev. B82-03380

591.52′482 — Animals. Symbiosis — *For children*
Vevers, Gwynne. Animal partners. — London : Bodley Head, July 1982. — [24]p. — (Bodley Head young naturalists)
ISBN 0-370-30461-6 : £2.95 : CIP entry B82-12319

591.52′5 — Animals. Migration — *Conference proceedings*
Animal migration / edited by D.J. Aidley. — Cambridge : Cambridge University Press, 1981. — 264p : ill,maps ; 23cm. — (Seminar series / Society for Experimental Biology ; 13)
Includes bibliographies and index
ISBN 0-521-23274-0 (cased) : £20.00 : CIP rev.
ISBN 0-521-29888-1 (pbk) : £9.95 B82-01355

591.52′5 — Animals. Migration. Evolutionary aspects
Baker, R. Robin. Migration. — London : Hodder & Stoughton, Jan.1982. — [208]p
ISBN 0-340-26079-3 (pbk) : £4.95 : CIP entry B81-34149

591.52′5 — Animals. Migration — *For children*
Vevers, Gwynne. Animals that travel / Gwynne Vevers ; illustrated by Matthew Hillier. — London : Bodley Head, 1981. — 23p : col.ill,1col.map ; 22cm. — (A Bodley Head young naturalist)
Includes index
ISBN 0-370-30399-7 : £2.95 : CIP rev. B81-14940

591.52′64 — Great Britain. Small gardens. Animals. Ecology
Garden wildlife : the living world of your garden / introduction by Derek Jones ; illustrated by Phil Weare. — London : Ebury, 1981. — 152p : ill(some col.) ; 30cm
Ill on lining papers. — Includes index
ISBN 0-85223-213-6 : £7.95 B82-06101

591.52′6404 — Soils. Animals. Effects of manure & fertilisers
Marshall, V. G.. Effects of manures and fertilizers on soil fauna : a review / V.G. Marshall. — Slough : Commonwealth Agricultural Bureaux, 1977. — 79p ; 25cm. — (Special Publication / Commonwealth Bureau of Soils ; no.3)
Bibliography: p47-76
ISBN 0-85198-384-7 (pbk) : Unpriced B82-13878

591.53 — Animals. Foraging behaviour — *Conference proceedings*
Foraging behavior : ecological, ethological, and psychological approaches / edited by Alan C. Kamil and Theodore D. Sargent. — New York ; London : Garland STPM, c1981. — xvii,534p : ill ; 24cm. — (Garland series in ethology)
Conference papers. — Bibliography: p475-514. — Includes index
ISBN 0-8240-7068-2 : Unpriced B82-26823

591.57′2 — Animals. Camouflage
Foy, Sally. The grand design : shape and colour in the animal kingdom. — London : Dent, Sept.1982. — [240]p
ISBN 0-460-04571-7 : £12.50 : CIP entry B82-19701

Penny, Malcolm. Camouflage / Malcolm Penny ; introduction by Keith Shackleton. — London : ITV Books in association with Anglia Television, 1982. — 47p : ill(some col.) ; 26cm. — (Animals in action)
Text on lining papers. — Includes index
ISBN 0-900727-09-8 : £2.50 B82-30163

591.59 — Animals. Communication
Bioacoustics. — London : Academic Press, Dec.1982. — [550]p
ISBN 0-12-446550-1 : CIP entry B82-29883

591.6 — ECONOMIC ZOOLOGY

591.6 — Animals. Relationships with man
Brett, Caroline. Animals and people / Caroline Brett ; introduction by Keith Shackleton. — London : ITV Books in association with Anglia Television, 1982. — 47p : ill(some col.) ; 26cm. — (Animals in action)
Text on lining papers. — Includes index
ISBN 0-900727-08-x : £2.50 B82-30165

Hall, Rebecca. Animals are equal : an exploration of animal consciousness / Rebecca Hall. — London : Wildwood House, 1980 (1981 [printing]). — viii,256p : 1ill ; 22cm
Includes index
ISBN 0-7045-0438-3 (pbk) : Unpriced
Also classified at 304.2 B82-37452

591.6′5 — Animals dangerous to man
Banks, Martin, *19---*. Dangerous animals / Martin Banks ; introduction by Keith Shackleton. — London : ITV Books in association with Anglia Television, 1982. — 47p : ill(some col.),1map ; 26cm. — (Animals in action)
Text on lining papers. — Includes index
ISBN 0-900727-06-3 : £2.50 B82-30164

591.6′9′0994 — Australia. Venomous animals
Sutherland, Struan K.. Venomous creatures of Australia : a field guide with notes on First Aid / Struan K. Sutherland. — Melbourne ; Oxford : Oxford University Press, 1981. — 128p : ill(some col.),maps ; 21cm
Bibliography: p126. — Includes index
ISBN 0-19-554317-3 (cased) : Unpriced
ISBN 0-19-554318-1 (pbk) : Unpriced B82-37363

591.8 — ANIMALS. HISTOLOGY AND CYTOLOGY

591.87 — Mononuclear phagocytes — *Conference proceedings*
Mononuclear phagocytes : functional aspects / edited by Ralph Van Furth. — The Hague ; London : Nijhoff, 1980. — 2v. ; xviii,1938p : ill ; 25cm
Conference papers. — Includes bibliographies and index
ISBN 90-247-2211-x : Unpriced
ISBN 90-247-2293-4 (pt.1) : Unpriced
ISBN 90-247-2294-2 (pt.2) : Unpriced B82-40697

591.87 — Mononuclear phagocytes. Research. Laboratory techniques
Methods for studying mononuclear phagocytes / edited by Dolph O. Adams, Paul J. Edelson, Hillel S. Koren. — New York : London : Academic Press, 1981. — xxiv, 1023p : ill ; 24cm
Includes index
ISBN 0-12-044220-5 : £39.40 B82-34860

591.87′5 — Animals. Cells. Membranes. Calcium. Transport phenomena
Membrane transport of calcium / edited by Ernesto Carafoli. — London : Academic Press, 1982. — xi,266p : ill ; 24cm
Includes bibliographies and index
ISBN 0-12-159320-7 : £21.00 : CIP rev. B81-34118

U.S.-Japan International Symposium on Gated Calcium Transport *(1981 : Hawaii)*. The mechanism of gated calcium transport across biological membranes / [based on the U.S.-Japan International Symposium on Gated Calcium Transport, sponsored by the National Science Foundation and Japan Society for the Promotion of Science, held in Hawaii, August 14-18 1981] ; edited by S. Tsuyoshi Ohnishi, Makoto Endo. — New York ; London : Academic Press, 1981. — xvii,324p : ill ; 24cm
Includes index
ISBN 0-12-524980-2 : £19.60 B82-39506

591.87′6 — Animals. Cells. Control systems. Mechanisms — *Conference proceedings*
Physiology : The Next Decade *(Conference : 1981 : Cornell University)*. Functional regulation at the cellular and molecular levels : proceedings of the symposium, Physiology : The Next Decade : Functional Regulation at the Cellular and Molecular Levels, held 21-24 July 1981 at Cornell University, Ithaca, New York, USA / editor Robert A. Corradino. — New York ; Oxford : Elsevier/North-Holland, c1982. — viii,325p : ill ; 24cm
Includes bibliographies and index
ISBN 0-444-00676-1 : Unpriced B82-39849

591.87′6 — Animals. Cells. Interactions
British Society for Cell Biology. *Symposium (5th)*. The functional integration of cells in animal tissues / the fifth symposium of the British Society for Cell Biology ; edited by John D. Pitts and Malcolm E. Finbow. — Cambridge : Cambridge University Press, 1982. — viii,360p : ill ; 24cm
Includes bibliographies and index
ISBN 0-521-24199-5 : £35.00 : CIP rev. B82-12693

591.87′6 — Animals. Excitable cells. Physiology — *Festschriften*
The **Biophysical** approach to excitable systems : a volume in honor of Kenneth S. Cole on his 80th birthday / edited by William J. Adelman, Jr. and David E. Goldman. — New York ; London : Plenum, c1981. — xi,258p : ill,1port ; 24cm
Includes bibliographies and index
ISBN 0-306-40784-1 : Unpriced B82-13924

591.87′6 — Animals. Neurons. Surfaces
The **Cell** surface and neuronal function / edited by Carl W. Cotman, George Poste and Garth L. Nicolson. — Amsterdam ; Oxford : North-Holland Publishing, 1980. — xxiv,546p : ill ; 25cm. — (Cell surface reviews ; v.6)
Includes bibliographies and index
ISBN 0-444-80202-9 : Unpriced B82-40727

591.87′65 — Animals. Cells. Ultrastructure. Pathology
Ghadially, Feroze N.. Ultrastructural pathology of the cell and matrix : a text and atlas of physiological and pathological alterations in the fine structure of cellular and extracellular components / Feroze N. Ghadially. — 2nd ed. — London : Butterworths, 1982. — xx,971p : ill ; 26cm
Previous ed.: published as Ultrastructural pathology of the cell. 1975. — Includes bibliographies and index
ISBN 0-407-00166-2 : Unpriced : CIP rev. B81-33636

591.9 — ZOOLOGY. GEOGRAPHICAL TREATMENT

591.909′1 — Polar regions. Animals — *For children*
Colombo, Federica. Animals of the Polar regions. — London : Burke, Aug.1982. — [80]p. — (Animals and their environment)
ISBN 0-222-00853-9 : £3.95 : CIP entry B82-17967

591.909′43 — Mountainous regions. Animals — *For children*
Colombo, Federica. Animals of the mountains and forests. — London : Burke, Aug.1982. — [80]p. — (Animals and their environment)
ISBN 0-222-00855-5 : £3.95 : CIP entry
Also classified at 591.909′52 B82-17969

591.909′45 — Prairies. Animals — *For children*
Colombo, Federica. Animals of the prairie and savannah. — London : Burke, Aug.1982. — [80]p. — (Animals and their environment)
ISBN 0-222-00854-7 : £3.95 : CIP entry B82-17968

591.909′46 — Seashore. Animals — *For children*
Roux, Charles. Animals of the seashore / written by Charles Roux ; edited by Michael Chinery ; illustrated by Carl Brenders ; translated by Anne-Marie Moore. — London : Kingfisher, 1981. — 44p : ill(some col.) ; 29cm. — (Nature′s hidden world)
Translation of: Les bords de la mer
ISBN 0-86272-025-7 : £3.50 : CIP rev. B82-07693

591.909′46 — Tidal marshes. Animals
Daiber, Franklin C.. Animals of the tidal marsh / Franklin C. Daiber. — New York ; London : Van Nostrand Reinhold, c1982. — x,422p : ill ; 24cm
Bibliography: p377-406. — Includes index
ISBN 0-442-24854-7 : £16.95 B82-09815

591.909′52 — Forests. Animals — *For children*

Colombo, Federica. Animals of the mountains and forests. — London : Burke, Aug.1982. — [80]p. — (Animals and their environment)
ISBN 0-222-00855-5 : £3.95 : CIP entry
Primary classification 591.909′43 B82-17969

591.909′52 — Tropical rain forests. Animals — *For children*

Colombo, Federica. Animals of the tropical forest. — London : Burke, Aug.1982. — [80]p. — (Animals and their environment)
ISBN 0-222-00858-x : £3.95 : CIP entry
B82-17972

591.909′54 — Deserts. Animals — *For children*

Colombo, Federica. Animals of the desert. — London : Burke, Aug.1982. — [80]p. — (Animals and their environment)
ISBN 0-222-00857-1 : £3.95 : CIP entry
B82-17971

591.92 — Marine animals & freshwater animals — *For children*

Colombo, Federica. Animals of the seas and inland waters. — London : Burke, Aug.1982. — [80]p. — (Animals and their environment)
ISBN 0-222-00856-3 : £3.95 : CIP entry
B82-17970

591.941 — Great Britain. Ponds. Animals — *For children*

Clay, Pat. Pond life / Pat and Helen Clay. — London : Black, 1982. — 25p : ill(some col.) ; 22cm. — (Nature in close-up)
Includes index
ISBN 0-7136-2212-1 : £3.50 : CIP rev.
B82-06955

591.9412′95 — Scotland. Fife Region. West Wemyss. Animals — *For teaching*

Mammals and mini beasts of West Wemyss. — [West Wemyss] : West Wemyss Environmental Education Centre, [1982]. — 22p,[2]leaves of plates : ill,1map ; 22cm
Cover title. — Text on inside covers. — Bibliography: p22
Unpriced (pbk) B82-19639

591.9669′5 — Nigeria. Game reserves: Yonkari Game Reserve. Animals

Jia, Alhaji Jibirin. A guide to the Yankari Game Reserve / Alhaji Jibirin Jia, Philip Marshall, Humphrey Crick. — Zaria ; Sevenoaks : Hudahuda in association with Hodder and Stoughton, 1982. — [31]p : col.ill ; 15x17cm
Map and text on inside covers
ISBN 0-340-28270-3 (pbk) : Unpriced : CIP rev. B82-03817

591.9688 — Namibia. Wildlife reserves: National parks: Etosha National Park. Animals — *Personal observations*

Reardon, Mitch. Life & death on an African plain / Mitch & Margot Reardon. — London : Hamlyn, 1981. — 160p : col.ill ; 29cm
ISBN 0-600-35591-8 : £7.95 B82-00688

591.97 — North America. Animals

Felix, Jiří. Animals of the Americas / Jiří Felix ; illustrated by Květoslau Hísek ... [et al.] ; [translated by Dana Hábová]. — London : Hamlyn, c1982. — 301p : col.ill,col.maps ; 28cm
Translated from the Czech. — Maps on lining papers. — Includes index
ISBN 0-600-36643-x : £4.95
Also classified at 591.98 B82-19311

591.98 — South America. Animals

Felix, Jiří. Animals of the Americas / Jiří Felix ; illustrated by Květoslau Hísek ... [et al.] ; [translated by Dana Hábová]. — London : Hamlyn, c1982. — 301p : col.ill,col.maps ; 28cm
Translated from the Czech. — Maps on lining papers. — Includes index
ISBN 0-600-36643-x : £4.95
Primary classification 591.97 B82-19311

591.998 — Arctic. Animals — *For children*

Cuisin, Michel. The frozen north / written by Michel Cuisin ; edited by Michael Chinery ; translated by Alison Carter ; illustrated by John Barber. — London : Kingfisher, 1981. — 44p : ill(some col.),1col.map ; 29cm. — (Nature′s hidden world)
Translation of: Le grand Nord
ISBN 0-86272-024-9 : £3.50 : CIP rev.
B82-07692

592 — INVERTEBRATES

592 — Invertebrates

Barth, Robert H.. The invertebrate world / Robert H. Barth, Robert E. Broshears. — Philadelphia ; London : Saunders College, c1982. — ix,646p : ill ; 26cm
Includes bibliographies and index
ISBN 4-8337-0106-5 (pbk) : £10.95
B82-37426

592 — Invertebrates — *For children*

Kilpatrick, Cathy. Creepy crawlies : insects and other tiny animals / Cathy Kilpatrick. — London : Usborne, 1982. — 24p : col.ill ; 21cm. — (Usborne first nature)
Text on inside covers. — Includes index
ISBN 0-86020-630-0 (pbk) : £1.00 B82-35841

592′.032 — Invertebrates. Primordial germ cells

Nieuwkoop, Pieter D.. Primordial germ cells in the invertebrates : from epigenesis to preformation / Pieter D. Nieuwkoop, Lien A. Sutasurya. — Cambridge : Cambridge University Press, 1981. — xii,258p : ill ; 24cm. — (Developmental and cell biology series)
Bibliography: p189-231. — Includes index
ISBN 0-521-22189-7 : £30.00 : CIP rev.
B81-33618

592′.0526365 — Estuaries. Marine invertebrates. Effects of pollution

Pollution ecology of estuarine invertebrates / edited by C.W. Hart, Jr. and Samuel L.H. Fuller. — New York ; London : Academic Press, 1979. — xiii,406p : ill ; 24cm. — (Water pollution)
Bibliography: p390-396. — Includes index
ISBN 0-12-328440-6 : £27.20 B82-24158

592.092′9 — Freshwater invertebrates

Jones, Clive, *1939-*. Freshwater invertebrates / the author Clive Jones. — Coventry : Jones-Sands, 1982. — 91p : ill ; 22cm. — (A Jones-Sands educational publication)
Bibliography: p91
ISBN 0-9507424-3-0 (pbk) : Unpriced
B82-22043

592.092′9 — Still waters. Invertebrates

Price, Taff. Taff Price′s stillwater flies : a modern account of natural history, flydressing and fishing technique. — London : Benn
Book 3. — 1981. — p193-260,[4]p of plates : ill(some col.) ; 25cm
ISBN 0-510-22543-8 (pbk) : £5.95
Primary classification 799.1′755 B82-05909

593.1′041′88 — Protozoa. Nervous system

Electrical conduction and behaviour in 'simple' invertebrates. — Oxford : Clarendon Press, Jan.1982. — [400]p
ISBN 0-19-857171-2 : £30.00 : CIP entry
B81-34554

593.1′045249 — Animals. Parasites: Protozoa

Baker, John R. (John Robin). The biology of parasitic protozoa / John R. Baker. — London : Edward Arnold, 1982. — 60p : ill ; 22cm. — (The Institute of Biology′s studies in biology, ISSN 0537-9024 ; no.138)
Bibliography: p56-58. — Includes index
ISBN 0-7131-2837-2 (pbk) : £2.25 B82-23651

593.1′2′024553 — Foraminiferida — *For geology*

Haynes, John Roland. Foraminifera / John R. Haynes. — London : Macmillan, 1981. — x,433p,[32]p of plates : ill,maps,ports ; 26cm
Bibliography: p349-389. — Includes index
ISBN 0-333-28681-2 : Unpriced B82-10165

593.1′72′09169 — Freshwater ciliates — *Field guides*

British and other freshwater ciliated protozoa. — Cambridge : Cambridge University Press for the Linnean Society of London and The Estuarine and Brackish-water Sciences Association. — (Synopses of the British fauna. A new series ; no.22)
Part 1: Ciliophora : kinetofragminophora, keys and notes for indentification of the free-living genera / Colin R. Curds. — 1982. — v,387p : ill ; 23cm
Bibliography: p371-384. —Includes index
ISBN 0-521-24257-6 (cased) : £27.50 : CIP rev.
ISBN 0-521-28558-5 (pbk) : £11.95
B82-14490

593.1′8 — Great Britain. Coastal waters. Marine Dinoflagellata

Dodge, John D.. Marine dinoflagellates of the British Isles / John D. Dodge with the assistance of Barbara Hart-Jones. — London : Her Majesty′s Stationery Office, 1982. — 303p : ill ; 25cm
Bibliography: p273-288. — Includes index
ISBN 0-11-241196-7 (pbk) : £19.50
B82-25965

593.1′9 — Carnivores. Parasites: Coccidia

Levine, Norman D.. The coccidian parasites (Protozoa, Apicomplexa) of carnivores / Norman D. Levine and Virginia Ivens. — Urbana ; London : University of Illinois Press, c1981. — 248p : ill ; 23cm. — (Illinois biological monographs ; 51)
Bibliography: p169-204. — Includes index
ISBN 0-252-00856-1 (pbk) : £11.20
B82-08801

593.1′9 — Coccidia

The **Biology** of the coccidia / edited by Peter L. Long. — London : Edward Arnold, 1982. — x,502p : ill ; 29cm
Includes bibliographies and index
ISBN 0-7131-2845-3 : £45.00 B82-31546

593′.5 — Cnidaria — *For children*

Coldrey, Jennifer. Jellyfish and other sea jellies / by Jennifer Coldrey ; photographs by Peter Parks. — London : Deutsch, 1981. — 32p : col.ill ; 20x25cm. — (Nature′s way)
ISBN 0-233-97379-6 : £2.95 : CIP rev.
B81-26744

594 — Great Britain. Freshwater molluscs & land molluscs

The **Illustrated** guide to molluscs / Horst Janus translated, edited and adapted ; illustrated by Walter Sölner and Cynthia O′Brien. — Expanded ed. — London : Starke, 1982. — vii,179p,[4]p of plates : ill ; 21cm
Translation of: Unsere Schnecken und Muscheln. — Previous ed.: 1965. — Bibliography: p168-170. — Includes index
ISBN 0-287-00055-9 : £7.45 B82-27286

594′.0074 — Molluscs — *Catalogues*

National Museum of Wales. *Department of Zoology*. The Melvill-Tomlin collection. — Cardiff : National Museum of Wales. — (Handlists of the molluscan collections in the Department of Zoology, National Museum of Wales. Series 1)
Pts.8 and 9: Carditacea and crassatellacea / compiled by P. Graham Oliver. — [1982]. — 49p in various paging ; 30cm
Cover title. — Includes bibliographies and index
Unpriced (spiral) B82-28498

National Museum of Wales. *Department of Zoology*. The Melvill-Tomlin collection. — Cardiff : National Museum of Wales. — (Handlists of the molluscan collections in the Department of Zoology, National Museum of Wales. Series 1)
Pt.10: Conacea (Conidae) / compiled by Alison Trew. — [1982]. — 28,xip ; 30cm
Cover title. — Bibliography: pxi
Private circulation (spiral) B82-32640

594′.0074′0292987 — Cardiff. Museums: National Museum of Wales. *Department of Zoology*. Stock: Molluscs. Collections: Melvill-Tomlin Collection — *Catalogues*

National Museum of Wales. *Department of Zoology*. The Melvill-Tomlin collection. — Cardiff : National Museum of Wales
Pt.1: Arcacea / compiled by P. Graham Oliver. — [1981?]. — 10,vii,vi,iip ; 30cm. — (Handlists of the molluscan collections in the Department of Zoology, National Museum of Wales. Series 1)
Cover title. — Includes bibliographies and index
Unpriced (spiral) B82-05474

National Museum of Wales. *Department of Zoology*. The Melvill-Tomlin collection. — Cardiff : National Museum of Wales
Pt.2: Tonnacea including Colubrariinae / compiled by Alison Trew and P. Graham Oliver. — [1981?]. — 19,xiii,ivp ; 30cm. — (Handlists of the molluscan collections in the Department of Zoology, National Museum of Wales. Series 1)
Cover title. — Includes bibliographies and index
Unpriced (spiral) B82-05475

National Museum of Wales. *Department of Zoology*. The Melvill-Tomlin collection. — Cardiff : National Museum of Wales
Pts.3, 4 and 5: Pholadomyacea, Pandoracea and Poromyacea / compiled by P. Graham Oliver. — [1981?]. — 24p in various pagings ; 30cm. — (Handlists of the molluscan collections in the Department of Zoology, National Museum of Wales. Series 1)
Cover title. — Includes bibliographies and index
Unpriced (spiral) B82-05476

National Museum of Wales. *Department of Zoology*. The Melvill-Tomlin collection. — Cardiff : National Museum of Wales
Pt.6: Muricacea / compiled by Alison Trew and P. Graham Oliver. — [1981?]. — 1v.(various pagings) ; 30cm. — (Handlists of the molluscan collections in the Department of Zoology, National Museum of Wales. Series 1)
Cover title. — Bibliography: 3p. — Includes index
Private circulation (spiral) B82-05477

National Museum of Wales. *Department of Zoology*. The Melvill-Tomlin collection. — Cardiff : National Museum of Wales. — (Handlists of the molluscan collections in the Department of Zoology, National Museum. Series 1)
Cover title. — Bibliography: pi-v. — Includes index
Pt.7: Strombacea / compiled by Aileen F. Blake and P. Graham Oliver. — 1981. — 9,v,vp ; 30cm
Unpriced (spiral) B82-11602

594′.0471 — Marine molluscs. Shells — *Collectors′ guides*

Dance, S. Peter. Seashells / S. Peter Dance. — Feltham : Hamlyn, 1971 (1982 [printing]). — 159p : col.ill,col.maps ; 19cm
Bibliography: p156. — Includes index
ISBN 0-600-35655-8 (cased) : £2.99
ISBN 0-600-37908-6 (pbk) : £1.75 B82-38108

594′.0471 — Molluscs. Shells — *Field guides*

The **Macdonald** encyclopedia of shells. — London : Macdonald, 1982, c1980. — 512p : ill (some col.),maps ; 19cm
Includes index
ISBN 0-356-08575-9 (pbk) : £4.95 B82-15097

594′.0471′075 — Land molluscs. Shells. Collecting — *Serials*

[Helix *(Nottingham)*]. Helix / Land Shell Studies Group. — Vol.1, no.1 (Spring 1981)-. — Nottingham (c/o R. Morrell, 43 Eugene Gardens, Nottingham NG2 3LF) : The Group, 1981-. — v. : ill,ports ; 21cm
Quarterly
ISSN 0263-0788 = Helix (Nottingham) : Free to Group members B82-15148

594′.0471′095353 — Oman. Marine molluscs. Shells — *Field guides*

Bosch, Donald. Seashells of Oman. — London : Longman, July 1981. — [208]p
ISBN 0-582-78309-7 : £14.70 : CIP entry B81-14948

594′.0471′09536 — Persian Gulf countries. Marine molluscs. Shells — *Field guides*

Smythe, Kathleen R.. Seashells of the Arabian Gulf / Kathleen R. Smythe. — London : Allen & Unwin, 1982. — 123p,20p of plates : ill (some col.),2maps ; 21cm. — (The Natural history of the Arabian Gulf)
Map on lining papers. — Bibliography: p117. — Includes index
ISBN 0-04-594001-0 : Unpriced : CIP rev. B82-10581

594′.061 — Molluscs of economic importance

Boyle, P. R.. Molluscs and man / P.R. Boyle. — London : Edward Arnold, 1981. — 59p : ill,maps ; 22cm. — (The Institute of Biology′s studies in biology, ISSN 0537-9024 ; no.134)
Bibliography: p58-59. — Includes index
ISBN 0-7131-2824-0 (pbk) : £2.25 : CIP rev. B81-30606

594.0953′8 — Saudi Arabia. Marine molluscs

Sharabati, Doreen. Saudi Arabian seashells : selected Red Sea and Arabian Gulf molluscs / Doreen Sharabati. — [London] : VNU Books International, 1981. — 119p : ill(some col.),1col.map ; 29cm
Bibliography: p109-111. — Includes index
ISBN 0-9507641-0-8 : Unpriced : CIP rev. B81-25743

594′.3 — Snails — *For children*

Ingves, Gunilla. The garden snail. — London : Black, Jan.1983. — [28]p. — (First nature books)
Translation of: Har du sett på : Vinbergssnäckan
ISBN 0-7136-2287-3 : £1.95 : CIP entry B82-32602

594′.38′0941 — Great Britain. Land slugs — *Field guides*

Ellis, A. E.. Key to British slugs / by A.E. Ellis. — New ed. / amended and updated by A. Norris. — [Luton] ([c/o Mrs E.B. Rands, 51 Wychwood Ave, Luton LU2 7HT]) : [Conchological Society of Great Britain and Ireland], 1979. — 12leaves,[3]leaves of plates : ill ; 26cm. — (Papers for students / The Conchological Society of Great Britain and Ireland, ISSN 0141-4593 ; no.12)
Previous ed.: 1969. — Bibliography: p11-12
Unpriced (unbound) B82-17709

Eversham, Brian. Slugs : an impetus to their study / Brian Eversham and Noel Jackson. — Durham : N. Jackson, 1980. — [12]leaves : ill ; 30cm
ISBN 0-9507324-0-0 (unbound) : Unpriced B82-37303

595.1′2045249 — Amphibians. Parasites: Flatworms. Taxonomy

Prudhoe, Stephen. Platyhelminth parasites of the amphibia / Stephen Prudhoe & Rodney A. Bray. — London : British Museum (Natural History), 1982. — 217p : ill ; 26cm. — (Publication ; no.853)
Four microfiche in pocket. — Bibliography on microfiche
ISBN 0-565-00853-6 : Unpriced : CIP rev.
ISBN 0-19-858509-8 (Oxford University Press) B82-10778

595.1′23 — Turbellaria — *Conference proceedings*

The **Biology** of the turbellaria : proceedings of the Third International Symposium held in Diepenbeek, Belgium / edited by Ernest R. Schockaert and Ian R. Ball. — The Hague ; London : Junk, 1981. — xiii,300p : ill,maps,ports ; 27cm. — (Developments in hydrobiology ; 6)
"Reprinted from Hydrobiologia, vol.84 (1981)". — Includes bibliographies and index
ISBN 90-619-3757-4 : Unpriced B82-04418

595.1′23′0941 — Great Britain. Turbellaria

Ball, Ian R.. British planarians : Platyhelminthes: Tricladida : keys and notes for the identification of the species / Ian R. Ball, T.B. Reynoldson ; illustrated by Julian Mulock and Maria Tran Thi Vinh-Hao. — Cambridge : Published for the Linnean Society of London and The Estuarine and Brackish-water Sciences Association by Cambridge University Press, 1981. — vi,141p : ill,1map ; 23cm. — (Synopses of the British fauna. New series ; 19)
Bibliography: p126-137. — Includes index
ISBN 0-521-23875-7 (cased) : £16.00 : CIP rev.
ISBN 0-521-28272-1 (pbk) : £6.95 B81-38812

595.1′24′0941 — Great Britain. Nemertea

Gibson, Ray. British nemerteans. — Cambridge : Cambridge University Press, Sept.1982. — [212]p. — (Synopses of the British fauna. New series ; no.23)
ISBN 0-521-24619-9 (cased) : £18.00 : CIP entry
ISBN 0-521-28837-1 (pbk) : £7.95 B82-26244

595.1′4604873 — Oligochaeta. Cells. Ultrastructure

Jamieson, B. G. M.. The ultrastructure of the Oligochaeta / Barrie G.M. Jamieson. — London : Academic Press, 1981. — xvi,462p : ill ; 25cm
Bibliography: p395-437. — Includes index
ISBN 0-12-380180-x : £68.00 : CIP rev. B81-26772

595.1′46′0916 — Aquatic Oligochaeta

Brinkhurst, Ralph O.. British and other marine and estuarine oligochaetes : keys and notes for the identification of the species / R.O. Brinkhurst. — Cambridge : Cambridge University Press for The Linnean Society of London and The Estuarine and Brackish-water Sciences Association, 1982. — 127p : ill ; 23cm. — (Synopses of the British fauna. New series ; no.21)
Bibliography: p116-123. — Includes index
ISBN 0-521-24258-4 (cased) : £15.50 : CIP rev.
ISBN 0-521-28559-3 (pbk) : £6.50 B82-14532

595.1′47′09411 — Scotland. Coastal waters. Polychaeta — *Field guides*

Tebble, Norman. Polychaetes from Scottish waters : a guide to identification / Norman Tebble and Susan Chambers. — Edinburgh : Royal Scottish Museum. — (Royal Scottish Museum studies)
Part 1: Family Polynoidae. — 1982. — 73p : ill ; 26cm
Bibliography: p71-72. — Includes index
ISBN 0-900733-26-8 (corrected : pbk) : Unpriced B82-37262

595.1′82 — Roundworms

Nematodes as biological models / edited by Bert M. Zuckerman. — New York ; London : Academic Press, 1980. — 2v. : ill ; 24cm
Includes bibliographies and index
ISBN 0-12-782401-4 : Unpriced
ISBN 0-12-782402-2 (v.2) : £19.60 B82-39697

595.1′82′012 — Roundworms. Taxonomy — *Conference proceedings*

Concepts in nematode systematics. — London : Academic Press, Dec.1982. — 1v.. — (The Systematics Association special volume, ISSN 0309-2593 ; no.22)
Conference papers
ISBN 0-12-672680-9 : CIP entry B82-29899

595.1′82045249 — Plants. Parasites: Roundworms

Plant parasitic nematodes. — New York ; London : Academic Press
Vol.3 / edited by Bert M. Zuckerman, Richard A. Rohde. — 1981. — xix,508p : ill ; 24cm
Includes bibliographies and index
ISBN 0-12-782203-8 : £43.00 B82-18357

595′.2 — Man. Vectors: Arthropoda

Furman, Deane P.. Manual of medical entomology / Deane P. Furman and E. Paul Catts. — 4th ed. — Cambridge : Cambridge University Press, c1982. — vii,207p : ill ; 28cm
Previous ed.: 1980. — Includes bibliographies
ISBN 0-521-29920-9 (pbk) : £7.95 B82-31815

595'.2 — Man. Vectors: Arthropoda
continuation

Grundy, John Hull. John Hull Grundy's arthropods of medical importance / edited by Nicholas R.H. Burgess. — Chilbolton : Noble Books, c1981. — 223p : ill ; 22cm
Includes index
ISBN 0-902068-11-3 : Unpriced B82-13330

595'.2041852 — Arthropoda. Locomotion — *Conference proceedings*

Locomotion and energetics in arthropods / [proceedings of a symposium on Locomotion and Exercise of Arthropods, held December 27-28, 1980, as part of the 1980 Seattle meeting of the American Society of Zoologists, held at the University of Washington, Seattle, Washington ; edited by Clyde F. Herreid II and Charles R. Fourtner. — New York ; London : Plenum, c1981. — viii,546p : ill ; 26cm
Includes bibliographies and index
ISBN 0-306-40830-9 : Unpriced B82-05802

595'.2041858 — Arthropoda. Epidermis. Cuticles

Neville, Charles. The biology of arthropod cuticle / Charles Neville. — Burlington, N.C. : Carolina Biological Supply Co., Scientific Publications Division, c1978 ; Chichester : Distributed by Packard. — 16p : ill(some col.) ; 25cm. — (Carolina biology readers ; 103)
Bibliography: p16
ISBN 0-89278-303-6 (unbound) : £0.80 B82-31605

595'.20457 — Arthropoda. Defence mechanisms: Organic compounds

Blum, Murray S.. Chemical defenses of arthropods / Murray S. Blum. — New York ; London : Academic Press, 1981. — xii,562p : ill ; 24cm
Bibliography: p513-538. — Includes index
ISBN 0-12-108380-2 : £36.40 B82-21252

595.3'3 — Ostracoda

Fossil and recent ostracods / editors R.H. Bate, E. Robinson and L.M. Sheppard. — Chichester : Ellis Horwood for the British Micropalaeontological Society, c1982. — 492p : ill,maps,1port ; 25cm. — (British Micropalaeontological Society series)
Includes bibliographies and index
ISBN 0-85312-324-1 : £38.50 : CIP rev. B82-01338

595.4'2'041 — Ticks

Physiology of ticks. — Oxford : Pergamon, Feb.1982. — [450]p. — (Current themes in tropical science ; v.1)
ISBN 0-08-024937-x : £62.50 : CIP entry B81-35907

595.4'4 — Spiders — *For children*

Lane, Margaret. The spider. — London : Methuen/Walker, Oct.1982. — [32]p
ISBN 0-416-06360-8 : £3.50 : CIP entry B82-24482

595'.44'012 — Spiders. Taxonomy

Brignoli, Paolo M.. Catalogue of the Araneae described between 1940 and 1980. — Manchester : Manchester University Press, June 1982. — [500]p
ISBN 0-7190-0856-5 : £40.00 : CIP entry B82-09630

595.4'40459 — Spiders. Communication

Spider communication : mechanisms and ecological significance / edited by Peter N. Witt and Jerome S. Rovner. — Princeton ; Guildford : Princeton University Press, c1982. — ix,440p : ill ; 25cm
Conference papers. — Bibliography: p393-432. — Includes index
ISBN 0-691-08291-x : £21.10 B82-24310

595.4'4'0941 — Great Britain. Spiders — *For schools*

Hutchinson, Ken. Spiders / Ken Hutchinson. — London : Macmillan Education, 1981. — 31p : ill(some col.) ; 26cm. — (Living science)
ISBN 0-333-29248-0 (pbk) : £0.95 B82-07002

595.7 — Entomology

Ross, Herbert H.. A textbook of entomology. — 4th ed. / Herbert H. Ross, Charles A. Ross, June R.P. Ross. — New York ; Chichester : Wiley, c1982. — viii,666,30p : ill,maps,ports ; 25cm
Previous ed.: 1965. — Includes bibliographies and index
ISBN 0-471-73694-5 : £20.25 B82-36950

595.7 — Insects

Chapman, R. F.. The insects. — 3rd ed. — London : Hodder & Stoughton, May 1982. — [976]p
Previous ed.: 1971
ISBN 0-340-26453-5 (pbk) : £19.50 : CIP entry B82-12702

595.7 — Insects — *For children*

Sully, Nina. Looking at insects / Nina Sully. — London : Batsford Academic and Educational, 1982. — 48p : ill ; 23cm. — (Looking at science)
Bibliography: p47. — Includes index
ISBN 0-7134-3990-4 : £3.95 : CIP rev. B81-33837

595.7'01'05 — Insects. Physiology — *Serials*

Advances in insect physiology. — Vol.16. — London : Academic Press, June 1982. — [420]p
ISBN 0-12-024216-8 : CIP entry
ISSN 0065-2806 B82-10417

595.7'013 — Insects. Feeding behaviour

Hodkinson, I. D.. Insect herbivory. — London : Chapman and Hall, Dec.1982. — [80]p. — (Outline studies in ecology)
ISBN 0-412-23870-5 (pbk) : £2.75 : CIP entry B82-29777

595.7'014 — Insects. Pheromones

Birch, M. C.. Insect pheromones. — London : E. Arnold, Nov.1982. — [64]p. — (The Institute of Biology's studies in biology, ISSN 0537-9024 ; 147)
ISBN 0-7131-2852-6 (pbk) : £2.50 : CIP entry B82-27949

595.7'0188 — Insects. Nervous system. Effects of drugs — *Conference proceedings*

Neuropharmacology of insects. — London : Pitman, 1982. — x,330p ; 24cm. — (Ciba Foundation symposium ; 88)
Includes bibliographies and index
ISBN 0-272-79652-2 : Unpriced : CIP rev. B82-05390

595.7'01882 — Insects. Circadian rhythms

Saunders, D. S.. Insect clocks / by D.S. Saunders. — 2nd ed. — Oxford : Pergamon, 1982. — xvii,409p : ill ; 26cm. — (Pergamon international library)
Previous ed.: 1976. — Bibliography: p365-402. — Includes index
ISBN 0-08-028848-0 (cased) : Unpriced : CIP rev.
ISBN 0-08-028847-2 (pbk) : £24.00 B82-00283

595.7'01927 — Insects. Juvenile hormones — *Conference proceedings*

International Congress on Juvenile Hormone Biochemistry — Action, Agonism and Antagonism *(3rd : 1981 : Brighton).* Juvenile hormone biochemistry : action, agonism and antagonism : proceedings of the Third International Congress on Juvenile Hormone Biochemistry — Action, Agonism and Antagonism, held in Brighton, United Kingdom, July 7-10, 1981 / G.E. Pratt and G.T. Brooks editors. — Amsterdam ; Oxford : Elsevier/North-Holland Biomedical, 1981. — x,455p : ill ; 25cm. — (Developments in endocrinology ; v.15)
Includes index
ISBN 0-444-80390-4 : £36.81 B82-13443

595.7'02322 — Insects. Mycoplasma diseases

Plant and insect mycoplasma techniques / edited by M.J. Daniels and P.G. Markham. — London : Croom Helm, c1982. — 369p : ill ; 23cm
Includes bibliographies and index
ISBN 0-7099-0272-7 : £12.50 : CIP rev.
Primary classification 581.2'322 B81-24656

595.7052'4 — Insects. Interactions with flowering plants — *For children*

Flowers and insects. — Poole : Blandford, 1982, c1981. — 30p : col.ill ; 25cm. — (Finding out about (Blandford))
Translation of the Japanese
ISBN 0-7137-1152-3 : £2.95 : CIP rev.
Primary classification 582.13'04524 B81-04355

595.7'05249 — Parasites: Insects

Marshall, A. G.. The ecology of ectoparasitic insects. — London : Academic Press, Dec.1981. — [550]p
ISBN 0-12-474080-4 : CIP entry B81-33870

595.7'052623 — Tropical regions. Insects. Population

Young, Allen M.. Population biology of tropical insects / Allen M. Young. — New York ; London : Plenum, c1982. — xiii,511p : ill ; 24cm
Includes index
ISBN 0-306-40843-0 : Unpriced B82-36384

595.70941 — Great Britain. Insects — *Field guides*

The **Oxford** book of insects / illustrations by Joyce Bee, Derek Whiteley, and Peter Parks ; text by John Burton with I.H.H. Yarrow ... [et al.]. — Pocket ed. — Oxford : Oxford University Press, 1981. — viii,201p : col.ill ; 15cm
Bibliography: p201. — Includes index
ISBN 0-19-217725-7 (pbk) : £2.50 : CIP rev. B81-16856

595.70966 — West Africa. Insects

Boorman, John, *19---.* West African insects / John Boorman. — Harlow : Longman, 1981. — viii,88p : ill(some col.) ; 20cm. — (West African nature handbooks)
Bibliography: p82-83. — Includes index
ISBN 0-582-60626-8 (pbk) : £1.90 B82-20968

595.70981'1 — South America. Amazon River Basin. Tropical rain forests. Insects

Penny, Norman D.. Insects of an Amazon forest / Norman D. Penny, Jorge R. Arias ; illustrations by Artêmio Coelho da Silva, Alberto Coelho da Silva. — New York ; Guildford : Columbia University Press, 1982. — xvii,269p : ill ; 24cm
Bibliography: p253-261. — Includes index
ISBN 0-231-05266-9 : £26.35 B82-19582

595.7'22 — American cockroaches

The **American** cockroach / edited by William J. Bell and K.G. Adiyodi. — London : Chapman and Hall, 1982, c1981. — xvi,529p : ill ; 24cm
Bibliography: p445-521. — Includes index
ISBN 0-412-16140-0 : £35.00 : CIP rev. B81-31750

595.7'22 — Cockroaches

Cornwell, P. B.. The cockroach / P.B. Cornwell. — (The Rentokil library)
Vol.2: Insecticides and cockroach control : an account of the insecticides, formulations and equipment used for cockroach control, together with details of safety, resistance and test procedures. — London : Associated Business Programmes. — 1976. — 557p : ill,facsims,1plan ; 24cm
Bibliography: p499-536. — Includes index
ISBN 0-85227-102-6 : Unpriced B82-29677

595.7'26 — Grasshoppers — *For children*

Ingves, Gunilla. The grasshopper. — London : Black, Jan.1983. — [28]p. — (First nature books)
Translation of: Har du sett på : Gräshoppan
ISBN 0-7136-2286-5 : £1.95 : CIP entry B82-32601

595.7'26 — North America. Grasshoppers

Otte, Daniel. The North American grasshoppers / Daniel Otte. — Cambridge, Mass. ; London : Harvard University Press
Vol.1: Acrididae : gomphocerinae and acridinae. — 1981. — ix,275p,16p of plates : ill (some col.),maps ; 25cm
Bibliography: p255-267. — Includes index
ISBN 0-674-62660-5 : £31.50 B82-17780

595.7'45 — Caddis flies — *Conference proceedings*

International Symposium on Trichoptera *(3rd : 1980 : Perugia).* Proceedings of the Third International Symposium on Trichoptera, Perugia, July 28-August 2, 1980 / edited by G.P. Moretti. — The Hague ; London : Junk, 1981. — xxi,472p : ill,maps ; 25cm. — (Series entomologica ; v.20)
Includes bibliographies and index
ISBN 90-619-3130-4 : Unpriced
ISBN 90-619-3190-9 (set) : Unpriced
B82-05349

595.7'52 — Great Britain. Typhlocybinae

Le Quesne, W. J.. Cicadellidae (Typhlocybinae) with a check list of the British Auchenorhyncha (Hemiptera, Homoptera) / by W.J. Le Quesne and K.R. Payne. — London : Royal Entomological Society of London, 1981. — 95p : ill ; 23cm. — (Handbooks for the identification of British insects ; v.II, pt.2(c))
Includes index
Unpriced (pbk) B82-18702

595.76'9 — Ladybirds — *For children*

Ingves, Gunilla. The ladybird. — London : Black, Jan.1983. — [28]p. — (First nature books)
Translation of: Har du sett på : Nyckelpigan
ISBN 0-7136-2284-9 : £1.95 : CIP entry
B82-32599

Wootton, Anthony, *1935-*. Life of the ladybird / photographs and text by Andreas and Heiderose Fischer-Nagel ; adapted by Anthony Wootton. — London : Dent, 1981. — 40p : col.ill ; 24cm
Translation and adaptation of: Marienkäfer
ISBN 0-460-06085-6 : £3.95 : CIP rev.
B81-22632

595.77 — Flies — *For children*

Ingves, Gunilla. The fly. — London : Black, Jan.1983. — [28]p. — (First nature books)
Translation of: Har du sett på : Flugan
ISBN 0-7136-2285-7 : £1.95 : CIP entry
B82-32600

595.77'1 — Chironomidae — *Connference proceedings*

International Symposium on Chironomidae *(7th : 1979 : Dublin).* Chironomidae : ecology, systematics, cytology and physiology : proceedings of the 7th International Symposium on Chironomidae, Dublin, August 1979 / editor D.A. Murray. — Oxford : Pergamon, 1980. — xix,354p : ill ; 26cm
Includes bibliographies and index
ISBN 0-08-025889-1 : £33.00 : CIP rev.
B80-00190

595.77'1 — European stratiomyidae

Rozkošný, Rudolf. A biosystematic study of the European Stratiomyidae (Diptera) / Rudolf Rozkošný. — Hague ; London : Junk. — (Series entomologica ; v.21)
Vol.1: Introduction, beridinae, sarginae and stratiomyinae. — c1982. — viii,401p : ill,maps ; 25cm
Includes index
ISBN 90-619-3132-0 : Unpriced B82-34542

595.77'1 — Great Britain. Orthocladiinae. Larvae — *Field guides*

Cranston, P. S.. A key to the larvae of the British Orthocladiinae (Chironomidae) / by P.S. Cranston. — [Ambleside] : Freshwater Biological Association, 1982. — 152p : ill ; 21cm. — (Scientific publication / Freshwater Biological Association, ISSN 0367-1887 ; no.45)
Bibliography: p144-149. — Includes index
ISBN 0-900386-43-6 (pbk) : Unpriced
B82-25337

595.77'4 — Drosophila. Development

A **Handbook** of Drosophila development / edited by Robert Ransom. — Amsterdam ; Oxford : Elsevier Biomedical, 1982. — xviii,289p : ill ; 25cm
Includes bibliographies and index
ISBN 0-444-80366-1 : Unpriced B82-21625

595.77'4 — Drosophila. Genetics

Dobzhansky, Theodosius. Dobzhansky's Genetics of natural populations I-XLIII / edited by R.C. Lewontin ... [et al.]. — New York ; Guildford : Columbia University Press, 1981. — xiv,942p,[16]p of plates : ill,maps,ports ; 24cm
Papers by Dobzhansky and colleagues originally published between 1937 and 1975. — Bibliography: p897-929. — Includes index
ISBN 0-231-05132-8 : £29.85 B82-19503

The **Genetics** and biology of Drosophila. — London : Academic Press
Vol.2d / edited by M. Ashburner and T.R.F. Wright. — 1980. — xi,702,lviiip : ill ; 24cm
Includes bibliographies and index
ISBN 0-12-064943-8 : £54.00 : CIP rev.
B79-34189

The **Genetics** and biology of Drosophila. — London : Academic Press
Vol.3a / edited by M. Ashburner, H.L. Carson and J.N. Thompson, Jr. — 1981. — xvi,429,Ilxxp : ill,maps ; 24cm
Includes index
ISBN 0-12-064945-4 : Unpriced : CIP rev.
B81-08914

The **Genetics** and biology of Drosophila. — London : Academic Press
Vol.36. — May 1982. — [500]p
ISBN 0-12-064946-2 : CIP entry B82-07263

595.77'5'07402134 — London. Kensington and Chelsea *(London Borough).* **Museums: British Museum (Natural History). Stock: Fleas** — *Catalogues*

British Museum (Natural History). An illustrated catalogue of the Rothschild collection of fleas (siphonaptera) in the British Museum (Natural History) : with keys and short descriptions for the identification of families, genera, species and subspecies of the order. — London : Trustees of the British Museum (Natural History)
Vol.6: Pygiopsyllidae / by D.K. Mardon. — 1981. — 298p : ill ; 29cm
Bibliography: 294-296. — Includes index
ISBN 0-565-00820-x : Unpriced : CIP rev.
B81-07939

595.78 — Butterflies & moths — *For children*

Cox, Rosamund Kidman. Butterflies and moths / Rosamund Kidman Cox and Barbara Cork ; [illustrated by Joyce Bee ... et al.]. — London : Usborne, 1980. — 24p : ill(some col.) ; 21cm. — (Usborne first nature)
Text on inside covers. — Includes index
ISBN 0-86020-477-4 (pbk) : £0.90 B82-39719

595.78 — Butterflies & moths — *For schools*

Hutchinson, Ken. Butterflies and moths / Ken Hutchinson. — London : Macmillan Education, 1981. — 31p : ill(some col.) ; 26cm. — (Living science)
Text on inside cover
ISBN 0-333-29249-9 (pbk) : £0.95 B82-06958

595.78'094 — Europe. Butterflies & moths — *Illustrations*

Carter, David. Butterflies and moths in Britain and Europe / by David Carter ; designed by Roger Phillips. — London : Heinemann published in association with the British Museum (Natural History), 1982. — 192p : col.ill ; 30cm
Includes index
ISBN 0-434-10965-7 : £12.50 B82-30649

595.78'0941 — Great Britain. Butterflies & moths — *Illustrations*

Wilkes, Benjamin. Benjamin Wilkes the British Aurelian / with an essay by R.S. Wilkinson. — Faringdon, Oxon. : Classey, 1982. — Portfolio : chiefly ill ; 35cm. — (Classica entomologica ; no.3)
Twelve new designs of English butterflies originally published: B. Wilkes, 1742. — Limited ed. of 745 copies. — Includes Facsim reprints of Twelve new designs of English butterflies and of Directions for making a collection
ISBN 0-86096-011-0 : Unpriced B82-30565

595.78'09422'5 — East & West Sussex. Butterflies & moths, *ca 1830-1980*

Pratt, Colin, *19---*. A history of the butterflies and moths of Sussex : being a history and modern-day survey of the macro-lepidoptera of East and West Sussex / by Colin Pratt. — [Brighton] : Borough of Brighton, Booth Museum of Natural History, c1981. — 356p,8p of plates : ill(some col.,maps ; 22cm
Bibliography: p17-23. — Includes index
ISBN 0-9502372-7-2 : Unpriced B82-01903

595.78'09424'62 — Staffordshire. Keele. Universities: University of Keele. Woodlands. Butterflies & moths

Emley, David W.. The butterflies and moths of Keele University / David W. Emley. — [Keele] : Keele University Library, 1982. — 41p : ill,1map ; 21cm. — (Occasional publication ; no.18)
Bibliography: p2
Unpriced (pbk) B82-25009

595.78'1 — Kenya. Nairobi. Warehouses. Ephestia cautella. Fertilisation. Effects of synthetic female sex pheromones

Haines, C. P.. The effects of synthetic female sex pheromones on fertilization in a warehouse population of Ephestia cautella (Walker) (Lepidoptera, Phycitidae) / C.P. Haines and J.S. Read. — London : Tropical Products Institute, 1977. — iv,10p : ill ; 30cm
English text, English, French and Spanish summaries. — At head of title: Tropical Products Institute. — Bibliography: p10
£0.50 (pbk) B82-07462

595.78'1'012 — Moths. Genera. Names

The **Generic** names of moths of the world / edited by I.W.B. Nye. — London : Trustees of the British Museum (Natural History)
Vol.2: Noctuoidea (part) : Arctiidae, Cocytiidae, Ctenuchidae, Dilobidae, Dioptidae, Lymantriidae, Notodontidae, Strepsimanidae, Thaumetopoeidae, Thyretidae / by Allan Watson, D.S. Fletcher and I.W.B. Nye. — 1980. — xiv,228p,[1]leaf of plate : ill ; 31cm
Includes index
ISBN 0-565-00811-0 : £22.50 : CIP rev.
B80-19773

The **Generic** names of moths of the world / edited by I.W.B. Nye. — London : British Museum (Natural History)
Vol.4: Bombycoidea, Castnioidea, Cossoidea, Mimallonoidea, Sesioidea, Sphingoidea, Zygaenoidea / by D.S. Fletcher and I.W.B. Nye. — 1982. — xiv,192p,[1]p of plates : ill ; 31cm
Includes index
ISBN 0-565-00848-x : Unpriced : CIP rev.
B82-06867

595.78'9 — Butterflies

Smart, Paul. The illustrated encyclopedia of the butterfly world / Paul Smart. — London : Salamander Books ; [London] : New English Library [distributor], 1975 (1981 [printing]). — 275p : ill(some col.),1map,ports ; 30cm
Ill on lining papers. — Includes index
ISBN 0-86101-101-5 : £6.95 B82-08014

595.78'9 — European white admirals — *For children*

Sheehan, Angela. The butterfly / by Angela Sheehan ; illustrated by Maurice Pledger. — London : New Caxton Library Service, c1976. — [26]p : col.ill ; 23cm. — (Eye-view library)
Originally published: London : Angus and Robertson, 1976. — Ill on lining papers
Unpriced B82-13223

595.78'9 — Great Britain. Meadow browns. Life cycle. Research

Dowdeswell, W. H.. The life of the meadow brown / W.H. Dowdeswell. — London : Heinemann, 1981. — viii,165p : ill,maps ; 22cm
Includes index
ISBN 0-435-60224-1 (pbk) : £5.95 : CIP rev.
B81-30258

595.78'9 — Large cabbage butterflies

Feltwell, John. Large white butterfly : the biology, biochemistry and physiology of Pieris brassicae (linnaeus) / John Feltwell. — The Hague ; London : Junk, c1982. — xxvi,535p : ill ; 25cm. — (Series entomologica ; v.18)
Includes bibliographies and index
ISBN 90-619-3128-2 : Unpriced B82-08862

595.78′9′094 — Europe. Butterflies — *Field guides*

Carter, David. Butterflies and moths in Britain and Europe / by David Carter ; designed by Roger Phillips. — London : Pan in association with Heinemann and the British Museum (National History), 1982. — 192p : chiefly col.ill ; 30cm
Includes index
ISBN 0-330-26642-x (pbk) : £6.95 B82-23292

Higgins, Lionel G.. A field guide to the butterflies of Britain and Europe / Lionel G. Higgins and Norman D. Riley ; over 800 illustrations in colour by Brian Hargreaves. — 4th ed. rev. and reset. — London : Collins, 1980, c1970. — 384p : ill(chiefly col.),maps ; 20cm. — (Collins guides)
Previous ed.: 1975. — Col. ill on lining papers. — Bibliography: p372-373. — Includes index
ISBN 0-00-219241-1 : £7.95 B82-38770

Whalley, Paul Ernest Sutton. The Mitchell Beazley guide to butterflies / Paul Whalley. — London : Mitchell Beazley, c1981. — 168p : col.ill,1col.map ; 20cm
Includes index
ISBN 0-85533-348-0 : £3.95 B82-08305

595.78′9′094 — Europe. Butterflies — *Lists*

Cribb, Peter W.. A Label list of butterflies : (Rhopalocera) : North, Western & Southern Europe / compiled by Peter W. Cribb. — Feltham (355 Hounslow Rd, Hanworth, Feltham, Middx.) : Amateur Entomologists' Society, 1981. — 20p ; 21cm. — (Pamphlet ; 11)
Cover title
Unpriced (pbk) B82-40861

595.78′9′094 — North-western Europe. Butterflies

Dal, Björn. The butterflies of Northern Europe / Björn Dal ; edited by Michael Morris ; translated by Roger Littleboy. — London : Croom Helm, c1982. — 127p : col.ill,col.maps ; 21cm
Translated from the Swedish. — Bibliography: p123. — Includes index
ISBN 0-7099-0810-5 : £5.95 : CIP rev. B81-34315

595.78′9′0941 — Great Britain. Butterflies

Brooks, Margaret. A complete guide to British butterflies : their entire life histories described and illustrated in colour from photographs taken in their natural surroundings / Margaret Brooks and Charles Knight. — London : Cape, 1982. — viii,159p : ill(some col.) ; 26cm
Includes index
ISBN 0-224-01958-9 : £10.95 : CIP rev. B82-01171

595.78′9′094244 — Hereford and Worcester. Worcestershire. Butterflies — *Field guides*

Green, Jack. A practical guide to the butterflies of Worcestershire. — Birmingham (The Lodge, Beacon Lane, Rednal, Birmingham B45 9XN) : Worcester Nature Conservation Trust, June 1982. — [40]p
ISBN 0-9508008-0-5 (pbk) : £2.80 : CIP entry B82-12003

595.78′9′0942962 — Dyfed. Presali *(District)* **& South Pembrokeshire** *(District)*. **Butterflies**

Kruys, Ivan. Butterflies of Pembrokeshire / Ivan Kruys. — Newport, Dyfed : Published by Greencroft for the Pembrokeshire Coast National Park Authority, 1981. — 32p : ill ; 21cm. — (Pembrokeshire Coast National Park Subject guide, ISSN 0143-5507)
Text on inside covers. — Bibliography: on inside cover
ISBN 0-905559-47-9 (pbk) : Unpriced B82-02847

595.78′9′096 — Africa. Butterflies — *Field guides*

D'Abrera, Bernard. Butterflies of the afrotropical region : based on Synonymic catalogue of the butterflies of the Ethiopian region by R.H. Carcasson / Bernard D'Abrera. — East Melbourne : Lansdowne ; Farringdon : Classey [distributor], 1980. — xx,593p : chiefly col.ill,maps(some col.) ; 35cm. — ([Butterflies of the world] ; [v.2])
Bibliography: p577-582. — Includes index
ISBN 0-7018-1029-7 : £57.50 B82-38642

595.78′9′098 — South America. Tropical regions. Butterflies

D'Abrera, Bernard. Butterflies of the neotropical region / Bernard D'Abrera. — East Melbourne ; Farringdon : Lansdowne Editions in association with E.W. Classey, 1981. — ([Butterflies of the world] ; [v.3])
Bibliography: p167-168. — Includes index
Part 1: Papilionidae & pieridae. — xiv,172p : col.ill,maps ; 35cm
ISBN 0-7018-1033-5 : Unpriced B82-39692

595.79 — Social insects

Social insects / edited by Henry R. Hermann. — New York ; London : Academic Press
In 4 vols
Vol.2. — 1981. — xiii,491p : ill ; 24cm
Includes bibliographies and index
ISBN 0-12-342202-7 : £36.40 B82-21246

595.79 — Social insects — *Conference proceedings*

Biosystematics of social insects / edited by P.E. Howse, J.-L. Clement. — London : Published for the Systematics Association by Academic Press, 1981. — 346p : ill,maps ; 24cm. — (The Systematics Association special volume ; no.19)
Proceedings of an international symposium held in Paris. — English text with French summaries. — Includes bibliographies and index
ISBN 0-12-357180-4 : Unpriced : CIP rev. B81-18129

595.79′6 — Ants — *For children*

Ants. — Poole : Blandford, 1982, c1981. — 29p : col.ill ; 25cm. — (Finding out about (Blandford))
Translation of the Japanese
ISBN 0-7137-1153-1 : £2.95 : CIP rev. B81-04330

595.79′6′0941 — Great Britain. Ants — *For schools*

Hutchinson, Ken. Ants / Ken Hutchinson. — London : Macmillan Education, 1981. — 31p : ill(some col.) ; 26cm. — (Living science)
ISBN 0-333-29250-2 (pbk) : £0.95 B82-07003

595.79′8 — Wasps — *For children*

Clay, Pat. Wasps / Pat and Helen Clay. — London : A. & C. Black, 1981. — 25p : col.ill ; 22cm. — (Nature in close-up ; 14)
Includes index
ISBN 0-7136-2153-2 : £3.50 : CIP rev. B81-22530

595.79′9 — Bees

Free, John B.. Bees and mankind. — London : Allen & Unwin, Oct.1982. — [176]p
ISBN 0-04-638001-9 (pbk) : £9.50 : CIP entry B82-23096

595.79′9 — Bees — *Early works*

Corney, Richard. Some observations experimental touching bees. — Gerrards Cross : International Bee Research Association, June 1982. — [10]p. — (Texts of early bee books ; no.2)
Text of original 1670 manuscript
ISBN 0-86098-098-7 : £6.00 : CIP entry B82-16218

Remnant, Richard. A discourse or historie of bees. — Gerrards Cross : International Bee Research Association, June 1982. — [34]p. — (Texts of early bee books ; no.6)
Originally published: London : Printed by Robert Young for Thomas Slater, 1637
ISBN 0-86098-121-5 : £12.00 : CIP entry B82-16217

595.79′9 — Bumblebees — *For children*

Sheehan, Angela. The bumblebee / by Angela Sheehan ; illustrated by Maurice Pledger. — London : New Caxton Library Service, c1976. — [26]p : col.ill ; 23cm. — (Eye-view library)
Originally published: London : Angus and Robertson, 1976. — Ill on lining papers
Unpriced B82-13221

595.79′9 — Honey-bees. Life cycle — *For children*

Fischer-Nagel, Andreas. Life of the honeybee / photographs and text by Andreas and Heiderose Fischer-Nagel ; translated by Noel Simon. — London : Dent, 1982. — 40p : col.ill ; 24cm
Translation of: Im Bienenstock
ISBN 0-460-06099-6 : £4.50 : CIP rev. B82-06849

596 — VERTEBRATES

596 — Extinct vertebrates

Day, David, *1947-*. The doomsday book of animals : a unique natural history of three hundred vanished species / by David Day ; foreword by the Duke of Edinburgh ; illustrated by Tim Bramfitt ... [et al.]. — London : Ebury Press, 1981. — 288p : ill(some col.),1col.map ; 32cm
Bibliography: p282-284. — Includes index
ISBN 0-85223-183-0 : £14.95 B82-31490

596 — Extinct vertebrates — *For chidren*

Rice, Shawn. As dead as a dodo / portraits of extinct animals by Shawn Rice ; text by Paul Rice and Peter Mayle. — London : Methuen, 1981. — [32]p : col.ill ; 28cm
ISBN 0-416-21420-7 : £4.95 : CIP rev. B81-25840

596 — Vertebrates

Orr, Robert T.. Vertebrate biology / Robert T. Orr. — 5th ed. — Philadelphia ; London : Saunders College, c1982. — viii,568p : ill,maps ; 25cm
Previous ed.: 1976. — Includes bibliographies and index
ISBN 0-03-057959-7 : Unpriced B82-20601

596 — Vertebrates — *Stories, anecdotes*

Ingledew, B.. True stories about animals and birds / B. Ingledew ; illustrated by ABE. — Ilfracombe : Stockwell, 1981. — 30p : ill ; 19cm
ISBN 0-7223-1531-7 (pbk) : £0.82 B82-06269

596′.0022′2 — Vertebrates — *Illustrations* — *For children*

Adby, Peter. Happy times book of zoo fun / illustrated and written by Peter Adby. — London : Dean, c1981. — [20]p : col.ill ; 26cm
Ill on lining papers
ISBN 0-603-00290-0 : Unpriced B82-28848

596′.0074 — Zoos. Vertebrates — *For children*

Taylor, Anne. Zoo animals / words by Anne Taylor. — Maidenhead : Intercontinental Book Productions, c1979. — [24]p : col.ill ; 21cm. — (My first animal library)
Originally published: Windermere, Fl. : Rourke Enterprises, 1979
ISBN 0-85047-430-2 (pbk) : £0.40 B82-18924

596′.01′028 — Vertebrates. Physiology. Telemetry — *Conference proceedings*

Telemetric studies of vertebrates : (the proceedings of a symposium held at the Zoological Society of London on 21 and 22 November 1980) / edited by C.L. Cheeseman and R.B. Mitson. — London : Published for Zoological Society of London by Academic Press, 1982. — xix,368p : ill,maps ; 24cm. — (Symposia of the Zoological Society of London, ISSN 0084-5612 ; no.49)
Includes bibliographies and index
ISBN 0-12-613349-2 : Unpriced : CIP rev. B82-04145

596′.0116 — Vertebrates. Heart. Creatine kinase — *Conference proceedings*

Heart creatine kinase : the integration of isozymes for energy distribution / edited by William E. Jacobus and Joanne S. Ingwall. — Baltimore ; London : Williams & Wilkins, c1980. — xiv,198p : ill ; 26cm
Conference papers. — Includes bibliographies and index
ISBN 0-683-04353-6 : Unpriced B82-25292

596'.0132 — Vertebrates. Liver. Cytochrome P-450

Hepatic cytochrome p-450 monooxygenase system / section editors John B. Schenkman and David Kupfer. — Oxford : Pergamon, 1982. — xvi,841p : ill ; 27cm. — (International encyclopedia of pharmacology and therapeutics ; section 108)
Includes bibliographies and index
ISBN 0-08-027381-5 : £79.50 : CIP rev.
B81-21559

596'.014 — Vertebrates. Pineal gland — *Conference proceedings*

International Congress of Endocrinology. *Satellite Symposium (1980 : Melbourne).* Pineal function : proceedings of the Satellite Symposium, Sixth International Congress of Endocrinology, Melbourne, Australia, February 1980 / edited by Colin D. Matthews and R.F. Seamark. — Amsterdam ; Oxford : Elsevier/North-Holland Biomedical, 1981. — xvii,271p : ill ; 25cm
Includes bibliographies and index
ISBN 0-444-80313-0 : Unpriced B82-05985

596'.0142 — Vertebrates. Adrenal cortex. Physiology

General, comparative and clinical endocrinology of the adrenal cortex / edited by I. Chester Jones and I.W. Henderson. — London : Academic Press
Vol.3. — 1980. — xiv,627p : ill ; 24cm
Includes bibliographies and index
ISBN 0-12-171503-5 : £55.00 : CIP rev.
B80-20667

596'.0142 — Vertebrates. Pineal gland — *Conference proceedings*

European Pineal Study Group. *Colloquium (2nd : 1981 : Giessen).* The pineal organ : photobiology-biochronometry-endocrinology : proceedings of the Second Colloquium of the European Pineal Study Group (EPSG) at the Department of Anatomy and Cytobiology, Justus Liebig University, Giessen, Federal Republic of Germany, July 1-4, 1981 / editors A. Oksche and P. Pévet. — Amsterdam ; Oxford : Elsevier/North-Holland Biomedical, 1981. — xiii,366p : ill ; 25cm. — (Developments in endocrinology ; v.14)
Includes index
ISBN 0-444-80387-4 : £29.79 B82-13445

596'.016 — Vertebrates. Reproduction — *Early works*

Harvey, William, *1578-1657.* Disputations touching the generation of animals / by William Harvey ; translated with introduction and notes by Gweneth Whitteridge. — Oxford : Blackwell Scientific, 1981. — lxvi,502p,4p of plates : ill(some col.) ; 23cm
Translation of: De generatione animalium. — Bibliography: plxv-lxvi. — Includes index
ISBN 0-632-00492-4 : £25.00 : CIP rev.
B78-16230

596'.0182 — Vertebrates. Sensory perception. Development

Development of perception : psychobiological perspectives / edited by Richard N. Aslin, Jeffrey R. Alberts, Michael R. Peterson. — New York ; London : Academic Press. — (Behavioral biology)
Vol.2: The visual system. — 1981. — xvii,387p : ill ; 24cm
Includes bibliographies and index
ISBN 0-12-065302-8 : £21.00 B82-04244

596'.01823 — Vertebrates. Colour vision

Jacobs, Gerald H.. Comparative color vision / Gerald H. Jacobs. — New York ; London : Academic Press, 1981. — viii,209p : ill ; 24cm. — (Academic Press series in cognition and perception)
Bibliography: p183-197. — Includes index
ISBN 0-12-378520-0 : £16.00 B82-30147

596'.01823 — Vertebrates. Eyes. Physiology

Analysis of visual behavior / edited by David J. Ingle, Melvyn A. Goodale, Richard J.W. Mansfield. — Cambridge, Mass. ; London : MIT Press, c1982. — x,834p : ill ; 26cm
Includes bibliographies and index
ISBN 0-262-09022-8 : Unpriced B82-35065

Weale, R. A.. The vertebrate eye / R.A. Weale. — 2nd ed.(rev.). — Burlington, N.C. : Carolina Biological Supply Co., Scientific Publications Division, c1978 ; Chichester : Distributed by Packard. — 16p : ill(some col.) ; 25cm. — (Carolina biology readers ; 71)
Previous ed.: London : Oxford University Press, 1974. — Bibliography: p16
ISBN 0-89278-271-4 (unbound) : £0.80
B82-31597

596'.01826 — Vertebrates. Olfactory perception & gustatory perception. Biochemistry

Biochemistry of taste and olfaction / edited by Robert H. Cagan, Morley R. Kare. — New York ; London : Academic Press, 1981. — xxiv,539p : ill ; 24cm. — (The Nutrition Foundation)
Text on lining papers. — Includes bibliographies and index
ISBN 0-12-154450-8 : £25.60 B82-02153

596'.01852 — Vertebrates. Locomotion — *Conference proceedings*

Vertebrate locomotion : the proceedings of a symposium held at the Zoological Society of London on 27 and 28 March 1980 / edited by M.H. Day. — London : Published for the Zoological Society of London by Academic Press, 1981. — xvii,471p : ill,1facsim ; 24cm. — (Symposia of the Zoological Society of London, ISSN 0084-5612 ; no.48)
Includes bibliographies and index
ISBN 0-12-613348-4 : £37.20 : CIP rev.
B81-28140

596'.01852 — Vertebrates. Muscles. Nerves. Physiology

Keynes, R. D.. Nerve and muscle / R.D. Keynes and D.J. Aidley. — Cambridge : Cambridge University Press, 1981. — vi,163p : ill ; 23cm. — (Cambridge texts in the physiological sciences ; 2)
Bibliography: p157-160. — Includes index
ISBN 0-521-23945-1 (cased) : £15.00 : CIP rev.
ISBN 0-521-28362-0 (pbk) : £4.95
Also classified at 612'.74 B81-31190

596'.01858 — Vertebrates. Skin — *Conference proceedings*

The **Skin** of vertebrates : papers presented at a symposium / organized by the Linnean Society of London and the British Association of Dermatologists, held at Queen Elizabeth College, University of London, 25-27 September 1978 ; editors, R.I.C. Spearman and P.A. Riley. — London : Published for the Linnean Society of London by Academic Press, c1980. — xiii,321p,[70]p of plates : ill(some col.) ; 27cm. — (Linnean Society symposium series ; no.9)
Includes bibliographies and index
ISBN 0-12-656950-9 : £42.00 : CIP rev.
B80-09685

596'.0188 — Vertebrates. Brain — *Comparative studies*

Macphail, E. M.. Brain and intelligence in vertebrates / E.M. Macphail. — Oxford : Clarendon Press, 1982. — viii,423p : ill ; 25cm. — (Oxford science publications)
Bibliography: p344-385. — Includes index
ISBN 0-19-854550-9 (cased) : £20.00 : CIP rev.
ISBN 0-19-854551-7 (pbk) : Unpriced
B81-30528

596'.0188 — Vertebrates. Cholinergic nervous system — *Conference proceedings*

Cholinergic mechanisms : phylogenetic aspects, central and peripheral synapses, and clinical significance / edited by Giancarlo Pepeu and Herbert Ladinsky. — New York ; London : Plenum, c1981. — xx,989p : ill ; 26cm. — (Advances in behavioral biology ; v.25)
Conference papers. — Includes bibliographies and index
ISBN 0-306-40810-4 : Unpriced B82-08345

596'.0188 — Vertebrates. Nervous system

Nathan, Peter, *1914-.* The nervous system / Peter Nathan. — 2nd ed. — Oxford : Oxford University Press, 1982. — xv,398p,[8]p of plates : ill ; 23cm
Previous ed.: Harmondsworth : Penguin, 1969. — Includes index
ISBN 0-19-261344-8 : £12.50 : CIP rev.
B81-18125

596'.0188 — Vertebrates. Nervous system. Development — *Conference proceedings*

Development in the nervous system : the fifth symposium of the British Society for Developmental Biology / edited by D.R. Garrod & J.D. Feldman. — Cambridge : Cambridge University Press, 1981. — x,403p : ill ; 24cm
Includes bibliographies and index
ISBN 0-521-23493-x : £40.00 : CIP rev.
B81-31276

596'.0188 — Vertebrates. Nervous system. Evolution

Sarnat, Harvey B.. Evolution of the nervous system / Harvey B. Sarnat, Martin G. Netsky. — 2nd ed. — New York ; Oxford : Oxford University Press, 1981. — xiv,504p : ill ; 24cm
Previous ed.: 1974. — Bibliography: p413-490. — Includes index
ISBN 0-19-502775-2 (cased) : Unpriced
ISBN 0-19-502776-0 (pbk) : £9.95 B82-18952

596'.019245 — Vertebrates. Gamma-aminobutyric acid — *Conference proceedings*

Problems in GABA research : from brain to bacteria : proceedings of an international symposium on recent advances in GABA study — GABA in neural and non-neural tissues, Hakone, Japan, July 15-18, 1981 / editors Yasuhiro Okada, Eugene Roberts. — Amsterdam ; Oxford : Excerpta Medica, 1982. — xx,443p : ill ; 25cm. — (International congress series ; no.565)
Includes bibliographies and index
ISBN 90-219-0510-8 : £55.08
ISBN 0-444-90236-8 (Elsevier) : Unpriced
B82-18376

596'.019258 — Vertebrates. Monoamine oxidases — *Conference proceedings*

Monoamine oxidase : basic and clinical frontiers : proceedings of a symposium held in Hakone, Japan, July 25-27, 1981 / editors K. Kamijo, E. Usdin, T. Nagatsu. — Amsterdam ; Oxford : Excerpta Medica, 1982. — xi,378p : ill ; 25cm. — (International congress series ; no.564)
Includes bibliographies and index
ISBN 90-219-0509-4 : £45.55
ISBN 0-444-90235-x (Elsevier) : Unpriced
B82-18377

596'.02 — Vertebrates. Decomposition — *For children*

Hansen, Gerth. When animals die / written and illustrated by Gerth Hansen ; consultant for English edition, Ralph Whitlock. — Hove : Wayland, 1982. — 63p : ill(some col.),1port ; 25cm
Translation from the Danish. — Includes index
ISBN 0-85340-949-8 : £4.25 B82-21941

596'.0234 — Vertebrates. Pathogens: Coronaviruses — *Conference proceedings*

Biochemistry and biology of coronaviruses / [proceedings of an international symposium held in October 1980 at the Institute of Virology and Immunobiology of the University of Würzburg, FRG] ; edited by V. ter Meulen, S. Siddell, and H. Wege. — New York ; London : Plenum, c1981. — x,438p : ill ; 26cm. — (Advances in experimental medicine and biology ; v.142)
Includes bibliographies and index
ISBN 0-306-40806-6 : Unpriced B82-22011

596'.0234 — Vertebrates. Pathogens: Herpesviruses

International Symposium on Herpesvirus *(1981 : Tokushima City).* Herpesvirus : clinical, pharmacological and basic aspects : proceedings of the International Symposium on Herpesvirus held in Tokushima City, Japan, July 27-30, 1981 / editors Hiroshi Shiota, Yung-Chi Cheng, William H. Prusoff. — Amsterdam ; Oxford : Excerpta Medica, 1982. — xv,459p : ill ; 25cm. — (International congress series ; no.571)
Includes index
ISBN 90-219-0519-1 : Unpriced B82-34481

596'.0234 — Vertebrates. Pathogens: Herpesviruses. DNA

Herpesvirus DNA : recent studies on the organization of viral genomes, MRNA transcription, DNA replication, defective DNA, and viral DNA sequences in transformed cells and bacterial plasmids / edited by Yechiel Becker. — The Hague ; London : Nijhoff, 1981. — xiv,466p : ill ; 25cm. — (Developments in molecular virology ; v.1)
Includes bibliographies and index
ISBN 90-247-2512-7 : Unpriced B82-04420

596'.029 — Vertebrates. Histocompatibility gene complex

Current trends in histocompatibility / edited by Ralph A. Reisfeld and Soldano Ferrone. — New York ; London : Plenum, c1981. — 2v. : ill ; 24cm
Includes bibliographies and index
ISBN 0-306-40480-x : Unpriced
ISBN 0-306-40481-8 (v.2) : Unpriced
B82-00697

596'.03 — Vertebrates. Development. Variation. Psychophysiological aspects

Developmental plasticity : behavioral and biological aspects of variations in development / edited by Eugene S. Gollin. — New York ; London : Academic Press, 1981. — xi,282p : ill ; 24cm. — (Developmental psychology series)
Includes bibliographies and index
ISBN 0-12-289620-3 : £16.60 B82-02208

596'.038 — Vertebrates. Evolution — *Conference proceedings*

The **Terrestrial** environment and the origin of land vertebrates : [proceedings of an international symposium held at the University of Newcastle upon Tyne] / edited by A.L. Panchen. — London : Published for the Systematics Association by Academic Press, 1980. — xii,633p : ill,maps ; 24cm. — (The Systematics Association special volume, ISSN 0309-2593 ; no.15)
Includes bibliographies and index
ISBN 0-12-544780-9 : £38.00 : CIP rev.
B80-18303

596'.04 — Vertebrates. Anatomy

King, G. M.. Colour atlas of vertebrate anatomy. — London (Middlesex House, 34 Cleveland St., W1P 5FB) : Bolsover Press, Sept.1982. — [136]p
ISBN 0-9507676-0-3 : £9.80 : CIP entry
ISBN 0-632-01007-x (Blackwell Scientific)
B82-24353

596'.048 — Vertebrates. Telencephalon. Anatomy

Comparative correlative neuroanatomy of the vertebrate telencephalon / edited by Elizabeth C. Crosby, H.N. Schnitzlein. — New York : Macmillan ; London : Baillière Tindall, c1982. — xiii,830p : ill ; 29cm
Includes bibliographies and index
ISBN 0-02-325690-7 : Unpriced B82-40791

596'.05 — Vertebrates. Species identity

Species identity and attachment : a phylogenetic evaluation / edited by M. Aaron Roy. — New York ; London : Garland STPM, c1980. — xiii,414p : ill ; 24cm. — (Garland series in ethology)
Includes bibliographies and index
ISBN 0-8240-7052-6 : Unpriced B82-10718

596'.0564 — Vertebrates. Habitations — *For children*

Althea. Animals at home / by Althea ; illustrated by Maureen Galvani. — Over : Dinosaur, c1981. — 24p : col.ill ; 16x19cm. — (Althea's nature series)
ISBN 0-85122-282-x (cased) : £2.25
ISBN 0-85122-266-8 (pbk) : £0.70 B82-08275

596'.059 — Vertebrates. Sounds — *For children*

Althea. Can you moo? / by Althea ; illustrated by Ljiljana Rylands. — Over : Dinosaur, c1981. — [24]p : col.ill ; 16x19cm. — (Dinosaur's Althea books)
ISBN 0-85122-299-4 (cased) : £2.25
ISBN 0-85122-298-6 (pbk) : £0.70 B82-08269

596'.08'028 — Vertebrates. Cells & tissues. Microstructure. Scanning electron microscopy — *Conference proceedings*

International Symposium on SEM in Cell Biology and Medicine *(1980 : Kyoto)*. Scanning electron microscopy in cell biology and medicine : proceedings of the International Symposium on SEM in Cell Biology and Medicine, Kyoto, 11-15 May, 1980 / edited by Keiichi Tanaka, Tsuneo Fujita. — Amsterdam ; Oxford : Excerpta Medica, 1981. — xxv,499p : ill ; 27cm. — (International congress series ; 545)
Includes bibliographies and index
ISBN 90-219-0477-2 : Unpriced
ISBN 0-444-90191-4 (Elsevier North-Holland)
B82-00798

596.092 — Large marine vertebrates — *For children*

Oliver, Rupert. Monsters of the seas / Rupert Oliver ; illustrated by Bernard Long. — London : Hodder and Stoughton, 1982. — 59p : col.ill ; 31cm
Ill on lining papers
ISBN 0-340-27139-6 : £2.95 : CIP rev.
B82-01091

596.0994 — Australia. Vertebrates — *Encyclopaedias*

Morcombe, Michael. An illustrated encyclopaedia of Australian wildlife / Michael Morcombe. — Adelaide ; London : Rigby, 1980, c1974. — 125p : ill(some col.) ; 30cm
Originally published: Melbourne ; London : Macmillan, 1974. — Bibliography: p125. — Includes index
ISBN 0-7270-1354-8 : £8.95 B82-13057

596.0998'9'0222 — Antarctic. Vertebrates — *Illustrations*

Hosking, Eric. Antarctic wildlife. — London : Croom Helm, June 1982. — [160]p
ISBN 0-7099-1215-3 : £10.95 : CIP entry
B82-09587

596'.2'0941 — Great Britain. Coastal waters. Tunicates

Fraser, J. H.. British pelagic tunicates : keys and notes for the identification of the species / J.H. Fraser. — Cambridge : Published for the Linnean Society of London and Estuarine and Brackish-water Sciences Association by Cambridge University Press, 1981. — vi,57p : ill ; 22cm. — (Synopses of the British fauna. New series : no.20)
Bibliography: p53-55. — Includes index
ISBN 0-521-28367-1 (pbk) : £4.95 : CIP rev.
B82-14375

597 — Fish

Moyle, Peter B.. Fishes : an introduction to ichthyology / Peter B. Moyle, Joseph J. Cech, Jr. — Englewood Cliffs ; London : Prentice-Hall, c1982. — xiv,593p : ill,1map ; 24cm
Bibliography: p539-581. — Includes index
ISBN 0-13-319723-9 : Unpriced B82-28416

597 — Fish — *For children*

Cansdale, George. Know about fish. — London : Ark, [1981?]. — [16]p : col.ill ; 21cm. — (Know about nature series)
Cover title. — Author: George Cansdale
ISBN 0-86201-058-6 (pbk) : £0.50 B82-05601

Wheeler, Alwyne. Fishes / Alwyne Wheeler. — London : Usborne, 1982. — 24p : ill(some col.) ; 21cm. — (Usborne first nature)
Text on inside covers. — Includes index
ISBN 0-86020-626-2 (pbk) : £1.00 B82-35839

597 — Fish — *For schools*

Bone, Q.. Biology of fishes. — Glasgow : Blackie, Aug.1982. — [267]p. — (Tertiary level biology)
ISBN 0-216-91017-x (pbk) : £11.95 : CIP entry
B82-16244

597'.01826 — Fish. Chemoreception

Chemoreception in fishes / edited by Toshiaki J. Hara. — Amsterdam ; Oxford : Elsevier Scientific, 1982. — x,433p : ill ; 24cm. — (Developments in aquaculture and fisheries science ; 8)
Includes bibliographies and index
ISBN 0-444-42040-1 : £45.65 : CIP rev.
B81-34479

597'.0192 — Fish. Biochemistry

Love, R. Malcolm. The chemical biology of fishes / R. Malcolm Love. — London : Academic Press
Vol.2: Advances 1968-1977 : with a supplementary key to the chemical literature. — 1980. — xviii,943p : ill ; 24cm
Bibliography: p753-928. — Includes index
ISBN 0-12-455852-6 : £50.00 : CIP rev.
B79-20944

597'.02 — Fish. Deaths due to water pollution. Investigation — *Manuals*

Boelens, R. G.. A guide to the investigation of fish kills / R.G. Boelens, C.M. O'Sullivan. — Dublin : Institute for Industrial Research and Standards, [1982]. — [24]p : ill,2forms ; 18cm
ISBN 0-900450-67-3 (pbk) : £0.75 B82-37928

597'.023 — Fish. Pathogens: Microorganisms — *Conference proceedings*

Microbial diseases of fish. — London : Academic Press, Sept.1982. — [340]p. — (Special publications of the Society for General Microbiology ; 9)
Conference papers
ISBN 0-12-589660-3 : CIP entry B82-19167

597'.0334 — Marine fish. Larvae

Marine fish larvae : morphology, ecology, and relation to fisheries / Reuben Lasker, editor. — [Seattle?] : Washington Sea Grant Program ; Seattle ; London : University of Washington Press [distributor], [1982]. — 131p : ill,2maps ; 23cm
Includes bibliographies
ISBN 0-295-95883-9 (pbk) : Unpriced
B82-37325

597'.051 — Fish. Stress

Stress and fish / edited by A.D. Pickering. — London : Academic Press, 1981. — xiv,367p : ill ; 24cm
Includes bibliographies and index
ISBN 0-12-554550-9 : £24.60 : CIP rev.
B81-27351

597'.052632 — Europe. Freshwater fish. Effects of water quality. Criteria

Water quality criteria for freshwater fish / [edited by] J.S. Alabaster ; assisted by R. Lloyd. — 2nd ed. — London : Published by arrangement with the Food and Agriculture Organization of the United Nations by Butterworth Scientific, 1982. — xix,361p : ill ; 25cm
Previous ed.: 1980. — Includes bibliographies and index
ISBN 0-408-10849-5 : Unpriced : CIP rev.
B82-10496

597'.053 — Fish. Feeding behaviour — *For angling*

Walker, Richard, *1918-*. Catching fish : knowing their feeding habits / Richard Walker. — Newton Abbot : David & Charles, c1981. — 158p ; 22cm
ISBN 0-7153-8198-9 : £6.50 : CIP rev.
B81-28175

597.092'35 — Caribbean Sea. Coral reefs. Fish

Took, Ian F.. Fishes of the Caribbean Reefs, the Bahamas and Bermuda / Ian F. Took. — London : Macmillan Caribbean, 1979, c1978. — 92p : col.ill,1map ; 22cm
Includes index
ISBN 0-333-25874-6 (pbk) : Unpriced
B82-25852

597.092'733 — Red Sea. Coral reefs. Marine fish — *Field guides*

Randall, John E.. Red Sea reef fishes. — London (34 Stansfield Road, SW9 9RZ) : IMMEL, Oct.1982. — [128]p
ISBN 0-907151-04-3 : £14.95 : CIP entry
B82-24610

597.092'733 — Red Sea. Coral reefs. Marine fish — *Field guides — For recreational underwater diving*

Randall, John E.. The diver's guide to Red Sea reef fishes. — London (34 Stansfield Rd., SW9 9RZ) : IMMEL, Oct.1982. — [96]p
ISBN 0-907151-05-1 : £9.95 : CIP entry
B82-24611

597.092′94 — Europe. Freshwater fish — *Identification manuals*
Wheeler, Alwynne. Freshwater fishes. — London : Kingfisher Books, Sept.1982. — [128]p. — (Kingfisher guides ; 18)
ISBN 0-86272-036-2 : £2.95 : CIP entry B82-21562

597.092′941 — Great Britain. Freshwater fish. Contamination by pesticides
Hider, R. C.. Chlorinated hydrocarbon pesticides and polychlorinated biphenyls in freshwater fishes in the United Kingdom, 1980-1981 / R.C. Hider, C.F. Mason, M.E. Bakaj. — London : Vincent Wildlife Trust, 1982. — 19p : 1map ; 21cm
Bibliography: p17-19
ISBN 0-946081-00-x (pbk) : Unpriced B82-32836

597′.2 — Agnatha: Cyclostomata
Biology of lampreys. — London : Academic Press
Vol.4a. — Feb.1983. — [300]p
ISBN 0-12-324804-3 : CIP entry B82-36572

Biology of lampreys. — London : Academic Press
Vol.46. — Feb.1983. — [300]p
ISBN 0-12-324824-8 : CIP entry B82-37660

597′.2 — Lampreys
The **Biology** of lampreys / edited by M.W. Hardisty and I.C. Potter. — London : Academic Press, 1981
Vol.3. — xiv,469p : ill ; 24cm
Includes bibliographies and index
ISBN 0-12-324803-5 : £43.60 : CIP rev. B81-36064

597′.31 — Sharks — *For children*
Riley, Terry, *1941-*. Sharks : and other hunters of the deep / written and illustrated by Terry Riley. — London : Dean, c1982. — [26]p : ill (some col.) ; 28cm
Ill on lining papers
ISBN 0-603-00263-3 : £1.25 B82-29535

597′.53 — Sticklebacks — *For children*
Lane, Margaret, *1907-*. The stickleback / by Margaret Lane ; illustrations by John Butler. — London : Methuen/Walker, 1981. — [28]p : col.ill ; 24cm. — (Animal lives)
ISBN 0-416-05830-2 : £3.50 : CIP rev. B81-30461

597′.55 — North America. Salmon & trout — *For angling*
Willers, W. B.. Trout biology : an angler′s guide / W.B. Willers. — Madison ; London : University of Wisconsin Press, 1981. — xvi,206p : ill(some col.) ; 24cm
Bibliography: p195-198. — Includes index
ISBN 0-299-08720-4 : £12.85 B82-19648

597′.58 — East Africa. Rift Valley. Lakes. Cichlidae
Axelrod, Glen S.. Rift lake cichlids / by Glen S. Axelrod. — Neptune, N.J. ; Reigate : T.F.H., c1979. — 93p : ill(some col.) ; 21cm
Ill on lining papers. — Bibliography: p93
ISBN 0-87666-514-8 : Unpriced B82-08310

597′.58 — Freshwater angel fish
Axelrod, Herbert R.. Freshwater angelfishes / by Herbert R. Axelrod and Warren E. Burgess. — Neptune, N.J. ; Reigate : T.F.H., c1979. — 93p : ill(some col.),ports ; 21cm
Ill on lining papers
ISBN 0-87666-516-4 : Unpriced B82-08311

597.8′7 — Great Britain. Natterjack toads
Beebee, Trevor J. C.. The natterjack toad. — Oxford : Oxford University Press, Sept.1982. — [200]p
ISBN 0-19-217709-5 : £9.95 : CIP entry B82-19180

597.8′9 — Common frogs — *For children*
Sheehan, Angela. The frog / by Angela Sheehan ; illustrated by Bernard Robinson. — London : New Caxton Library Service, c1976. — [26]p : col.ill ; 23cm. — (Eye-view library)
Originally published: London : Angus and Robertson, 1976. — Ill on lining papers
Unpriced B82-13218

597.8′9 — Frogs — *For children*
Lane, Margaret, *1907-*. The frog / by Margaret Lane ; illustrations by Grahame Corbett. — London : Methuen/Walker, 1981. — [28]p : col.ill ; 24cm. — (Animal lives)
ISBN 0-416-05780-2 : £3.50 : CIP rev. B81-25864

Snow, Keith. I am a frog / Keith Snow ; [illustrated by] Ferelith Eccles Williams. — Kingswood : World′s Work, c1982. — [32]p : chiefly col.ill ; 17cm
ISBN 0-437-76109-6 : £3.20 B82-30440

597.9 — Reptiles
Biology of the reptilia. — Vol.13. — London : Academic Press, Sept.1982. — [350]p
ISBN 0-12-274613-9 : CIP entry B82-19817

Biology of the reptilia. — London : Academic Press
Vol.12. — Sept.1982. — [570]p
ISBN 0-12-274612-0 : CIP entry B82-19160

Spellerberg, Ian F.. Biology of reptiles : an ecological approach / Ian F. Spellerberg. — Glasgow : Blackie, 1982. — viii,158p : ill,maps ; 21cm. — (Tertiary level biology)
Bibliography: p145-154. — Includes index
ISBN 0-216-91257-1 (cased) : £17.95 : CIP rev.
ISBN 0-216-91256-3 : £8.95 B82-07529

597.9′042 — Reptiles. Diseases
Diseases of the Reptilia / edited by John E. Cooper and Oliphant F. Jackson. — London : Academic Press, 1981. — 2v.(xi,584,xxxiip) : ill ; 24cm
Includes bibliographies and index
ISBN 0-12-187901-1 : Unpriced : CIP rev.
ISBN 0-12-187902-x (v.2) : £19.00 B81-15804

597.9′0994 — Australia. Reptiles
Cogger, Harold G.. Australian reptiles in colour / Harold Cogger. — Sydney ; London : A.H. & A.W. Reed, 1967 (1978 [printing]). — 112p : col.ill ; 18x19cm
Includes index
ISBN 0-589-50060-0 : £4.90 B82-02059

597.92 — Hampshire. Selborne. Tortoises — *Personal observations — Correspondence, diaries, etc. — Early works*
White, Gilbert1720-1793. The portrait of a tortoise : extracted from the journals & letters of Gilbert White / with an introduction and notes by Sylvia Townsend Warner. — London : Virago, 1981. — 63p : ill,ports ; 19cm
Originally published: London : Chatto & Windus, 1946. — Ill on lining papers. — Bibliography: p6
ISBN 0-86068-218-8 : £3.50 : CIP rev. B81-22480

597.96 — Rattlesnakes
Klauber, Laurence M.. Rattlesnakes : their habits, life histories and influence on mankind / Laurence M. Klauber ; abridged by Karen Harvey McClung. — Berkeley ; London : University of California Press for the Zoological Society of San Diego, c1981. — xxii,350p,[16]p of plates ; 24cm
Bibliography: p337-339. — Includes index
ISBN 0-520-04038-4 : £14.00 B82-28099

598 — Birds
Welty, Joel Carl. The life of birds / Joel Carl Welty. — 3rd ed. — Philadelphia ; London : Saunders College Publishing, c1982. — xiv,754p : ill,maps(some col.) ; 25cm
Previous ed.: 1975. — Maps on lining papers. — Bibliography: p652-716. — Includes index
ISBN 0-03-057917-1 : £19.95 B82-25829

598 — Birds — *Early works — Facsimiles*
Michelet, Jules. The bird / by Jules Michelet ; with 210 illustrations by Giacomelli. — London : Wildwood House, 1981. — 350p : ill ; 22cm. — (A Wildwood rediscovery)
Translation of: L′oiseau. — Facsim of: ed. published London : Nelson, 1872. — Includes index
ISBN 0-7045-0444-8 (pbk) : £4.50 : CIP rev. B81-23796

598 — Birds — *For children*
Cox, Rosamund Kidman. Birds / Rosamund Kidman Cox and Barbara Cork ; [illustrated by Roy Hutchison ... et al.]. — London : Usborne, 1980. — 24p : ill(some col.) ; 21cm. — (Usborne first nature)
Text on inside covers. — Includes index
ISBN 0-86020-475-8 (pbk) : £0.90 B82-39718

Elcome, David. Bird life / David Elcome. — London : Macdonald, 1980. — 32p : col.ill ; 29cm. — (Eye openers!)
Bibliography: p30. — Includes index
ISBN 0-356-07089-1 : £2.50 B82-24546

Rankin, W. T. C.. Know about birds. — London : Ark, [1981?]. — [16]p : col.ill ; 21cm. — (Know about nature series)
Cover title. — Author: W.T.C. Rankin
ISBN 0-86201-057-8 (pbk) : £0.50 B82-05603

598′.0216 — Birds — *Lists*
Clements, James. Birds of the world : a checklist / James Clements. — [3rd ed.]. — London : Croom Helm, 1981. — xxxviii,526p : 1col.map ; 25cm
Previous ed.: 1978. — Map on lining papers. — Bibliography: p527-531. — Includes index
ISBN 0-7099-0724-9 : £11.95 B82-25792

598′.022′2 — Birds — *Illustrations*
Ching, Raymond. Studies & sketches of a bird painter / paintings, drawings and text by Raymond Ching ; with additional text by Errol Fuller. — Melbourne ; London : Lansdowne ; [London] : [Collins] [[distributor]], 1981. — 260p : ill(some col.) ; 42cm
In slip case. — Bibliography: p256. — Includes index
ISBN 0-7018-1042-4 : £75.00 B82-15397

598′.022′2 — Birds — *Illustrations — For children*
Read, Derek. The life of birds / [written by Derek Read]. — London : Proteus, 1981. — [32]p : ill(some col.) ; 28cm. — (Pictorial learning books)
ISBN 0-906071-85-2 (pbk) : £1.25 B82-22021

598′.07′23441 — Great Britain. Birds. Observation — *Manuals*
Bird study. — [West Wemyss] : West Wemyss Environmental Education Centre, [1982]. — 33p : ill,forms ; 21cm
Cover title
Unpriced (pbk) B82-19484

Whitlock, Ralph. Bird watch in an English village / by Ralph Whitlock. — Evershot : Gavin Press, 1982. — xiii,194p,[8]p of plates : ill ; 23cm
ISBN 0-905868-09-9 : £7.95 : CIP rev. B82-17228

598′.07′23441 — Great Britain. Birds. Observation — *Serials*
Birdwatcher′s yearbook. — 1982. — Buckingham (Rostheme, Hall Close, Maids Moreton, Buckingham MK18 1RH) : Buckingham Press, Oct.1981. — [320]p
ISBN 0-9506478-2-9 (pbk) : £5.95 : CIP entry
ISSN 0144-364x B81-31950

598′.07′2344114 — Scotland. Western Isles. Benbecula, North Uist & South Uist. Birds. Observation
A **Guide** to birds and birdwatching on the Uists. — Benbecula (Royal Artillery Range Hebrides, Benbecula, Scotland PA88 5LN) : Royal Artillery Range Hebrides Natural History Society, 1981. — 20p ; 30cm
Unpriced (unbound) B82-27776

598′.07′23441295 — Scotland. Fife Region. West Wemyss. Birds. Observation — *Manuals*
Bird study in West Wemyss. — [West Wemyss] : West Wemyss Environmental Education Centre, [1982]. — 38p : ill ; 22cm
Cover title
Unpriced (pbk) B82-19481

598'.074'02371 — Cornwall. Padstow. Zoological bird gardens: Tropical Bird & Butterfly Gardens — *Visitors' guides*

Tropical Bird & Butterfly Gardens. Tropical Bird & Butterfly Gardens, Padstow. — Padstow (Fentonluna Lane, Padstow, Cornwall) : [Jack Brown], [1980?]. — [19]p : ill(some col.),1col.plan ; 21cm
Unpriced (unbound) B82-37287

598'.09'033 — Ornithology, *1760-1850*

Farber, Paul Lawrence. The emergence of ornithology as a scientific discipline : 1760-1850 / Paul Lawrence Farber. — Dordrecht ; London : Reidel, c1982. — xxi,191p : ports ; 23cm. — (Studies in the history of modern science ; v.12)
Includes index
ISBN 90-277-1410-x : Unpriced B82-40151

598.2'07234'0321 — Birds. Observations — *Encyclopaedias*

Weaver, Peter, *1944-*. The birdwatcher's dictionary / by Peter Weaver ; with drawings by Michael Hodgson. — Calton : Poyser, 1981. — 155p : ill,maps ; 23cm
ISBN 0-85661-028-3 : £5.00 B82-08224

598.2'074'02561 — Bedfordshire. Stagsden. Zoological bird gardens: Stagsden Bird Gardens — *Visitors' guides*

Rayment, Rod. Stagsden Bird Gardens / [by Rod Rayment]. — Derby : English Life, c1982. — 8p : ill(some col.),1map,1plan ; 22cm
Cover title. — Map, ill on inside covers
ISBN 0-85101-191-8 (pbk) : £0.30 B82-28024

598.2'1 — Birds. Physiology

Freethy, Ron. How birds work. — Poole : Blandford Press, Oct.1982. — [176]p
ISBN 0-7137-1156-6 : £9.95 : CIP entry B82-22994

598.2'18 — Birds. Navigation

Gerrard, Edward. Instinctive navigation of birds / Edward Gerrard. — Skye : Scottish Research Group, 1981. — v,182p : ill,maps ; 21cm
Bibliography: p176-181. — Includes index. — Incorporating: Bird navigation, the controversy
ISBN 0-907629-01-6 (pbk) : £4.50 B82-08360

598.2'1858 — Birds. Feathers — *For schools*

About feathers. — [Stirling] : Scottish Panel of Advisers in Outdoor Education, [c1979]. — 24p : ill ; 21cm. — (About ; 1)
ISBN 0-86223-000-4 (pbk) : Unpriced B82-20674

598.25 — Birds. Adaptation

Andrews, John, *1939-*. Adaptable birds. — London : Dent, Oct.1982. — [48]p
ISBN 0-460-06061-9 : £3.50 : CIP entry B82-24371

598.251 — Birds. Behaviour

Sparks, John. Bird behaviour / John Sparks ; illustrated by David Andrews. — London : Hamlyn, 1969 (1982 [printing]). — 159p : col.ill,1col.map ; 19cm
Bibliography: p156. — Includes index
ISBN 0-600-35654-x (cased) : £2.99 (pbk) : £1.75 B82-36012

598.252'0941 — Great Britain. Birds. Habitats

Fuller, R. J.. Bird habitats in Britain / by R.J. Fuller ; drawings by Donald Watson. — Calton : Poyser, 1982. — 320p,32p of plates : ill,maps ; 24cm
Bibliography: p239-252. — Includes index
ISBN 0-85661-031-3 : £13.00 B82-39564

598.252'5 — Birds. Migration — *For children*

Gill, Peter, *1924-*. Migrating birds / by Peter Gill ; illustrated by the author. — Cambridge : Dinosaur, c1982. — 24p : col.ill ; 16x19cm
ISBN 0-85122-338-9 (cased) : Unpriced
ISBN 0-85122-337-0 (pbk) : Unpriced B82-32079

598.2'525 — Great Britain. Summer migrant birds. Arrival & departure. Dates

Riddiford, Nick. Seasonal movements of summer migrants / Nick Riddiford, Peter Findley. — Tring (Beech Grove, Tring, Herts.) : British Trust for Ornithology, 1981. — 84p : ill ; 21cm. — (BTO guide ; 18)
Bibliography: p84
Unpriced (pbk) B82-17459

598.2'525'096 — Africa. Birds. Migration

Curry-Lindahl, Kai. Bird migration in Africa : movements between six continents / Kai Curry-Lindahl. — London : Academic Press, 1981. — 2v.(xxiii,695p,[16]p of plates) : ill,maps ; 24cm
Bibliography: p619-652. — Includes index
ISBN 0-12-200101-x : Unpriced
ISBN 0-12-200102-8 (v.2) : £20.60 B82-12626

598.256'094 — Europe. Birds. Breeding behaviour

Pforr, Manfred. The breeding birds of Europe : a photographic handbook / Manfred Pforr and Alfred Limbrunner ; translated by Richard Stoneman ; edited by Iain Robertson. — London : Croom Helm
Translated from the German
2: Sandgrouse to crows. — 1982. — 394p : ill (some col.),col.maps ; 20x22cm
Bibliography: p394. — Includes index
ISBN 0-7099-2020-2 : £17.95 : CIP rev. B82-06948

Pforr, Manfred. The breeding birds of Europe 1 : a photographic handbook : divers to auks / Manfred Pforr and Alfred Limbrunner ; translated by Richard Stoneman ; edited by Iain Robertson. — London : Croom Helm, c1981. — 327p : col.ill,col.maps ; 21x23cm
Translation from the German. — Includes index
ISBN 0-7099-2013-x : £14.95 B82-07146

598.29'13 — Tropical regions. Birds

Roots, Clive. Tropical birds / Clive Roots ; illustrated by John Rignal. — [Feltham] : Hamlyn Paperbacks, 1982, c1971. — 159p : col.ill,col.maps ; 18cm
Originally published: 1971. — Bibliography: p156. — Includes index
ISBN 0-600-38606-6 (pbk) : £1.75 B82-36015

598.291'822 — Mediterranean region. Birds

Handbook of the birds of Europe, the Middle East and North Africa : the birds of the Western Palearctic. — Oxford : Oxford University Press
Vol.3: Waders to gulls. — Feb.1983. — [850]p
ISBN 0-19-857506-8 : £45.00 : CIP entry
Primary classification 598.294 B82-37867

598.29'182'2 — Mediterranean region. Birds — *Field guides*

Jonsson, Lars. Birds of the Mediterranean and Alps. — London : Croom Helm, Aug.1982. — [128]p
Translation from the Swedish
ISBN 0-7099-1413-x : £5.95 : CIP entry
Also classified at 598.29494'7 B82-15907

598.294 — Europe. Birds

Handbook of the birds of Europe, the Middle East and North Africa : the birds of the Western Palearctic. — Oxford : Oxford University Press
Vol.3: Waders to gulls. — Feb.1983. — [850]p
ISBN 0-19-857506-8 : £45.00 : CIP entry
Also classified at 598.291'822 B82-37867

598.294 — Europe. Birds — *Field guides*

Hammond, Nicholas. Birds of Britain and Europe / Nicholas Hammond and Michael Everett ; designed by Roger Phillips. — London : Pan, 1980. — 256p : chiefly col.ill,col.maps ; 29cm
Includes index
ISBN 0-330-26023-5 (pbk) : £6.50 B82-25838

Hume, Rob. Usborne guide to birds of Britain & Europe / Rob Hume. — London : Usborne, 1981. — 128p : ill(some col.) ; 20cm
Includes index
ISBN 0-86020-495-2 : £3.99 B82-39041

598.294 — Europe. Freshwater regions. Birds

Ogilvie, M. A.. Birdwatching : on inland fresh waters / M.A. Ogilvie ; with drawings by Carol Ogilvie. — London : Severn House, c1981. — 160p : ill(some col.),2maps ; 22cm. — (Severn House naturalists' library)
Bibliography: p156-157. — Includes index
ISBN 0-7278-2004-4 : £8.95 : CIP rev. B82-00378

598.2941 — Great Britain. Birds

Flegg, Jim. Bird of the week / Jim Flegg ; illustrated by Robert Gillmor. — London : British Broadcasting Corporation, 1981. — 111p : ill ; 21cm
ISBN 0-563-17950-3 (pbk) : £3.25 B82-08371

Gooders, John. Collins British birds / John Gooders ; paintings by Terence Lambert and by Norman Arlott. — London : Collins, 1982. — 384p : ill(some col.),col.maps ; 27cm
Bibliography: p378-379. — Includes index
ISBN 0-00-219121-0 : £12.95 B82-23524

Soper, Tony. Birdwatch / Tony Soper ; illustrations by Robert Gillmor. — Exeter : Webb & Bower, 1982. — 208p : ill(some col.),1col.map ; 26cm
Includes index
ISBN 0-906671-55-8 : £9.95 : CIP rev. B82-07701

598.2941 — Great Britain. Birds, *1969-1979*

Wallace, Ian, *1933-*. Birdwatching in the seventies / Ian Wallace. — London : Macmillan, 1981. — viii,183p : ill,maps ; 23cm
Bibliography: p169. — Includes index
ISBN 0-333-30026-2 : £7.95 : CIP rev. B81-23944

598.2941 — Great Britain. Birds — *Field guides*

Dougall, Robert. British birds / by Robert Dougall ; photographs by Natural History Photographic Agency and Aquila ; illustrations by Hilary Jarvis. — Loughborough : Ladybird, c1982. — 151p : col.ill ; 25cm
Cover title: The Ladybird book of British birds. — Includes index
ISBN 0-7214-7519-1 : £3.95 B82-39057

Field guide to the birds of Britain / [edited and designed by the Reader's Digest Association]. — Repr. with amendments. — London : Reader's Digest Association, 1981. — 319p : col.ill,col.maps ; 16x21cm. — (Reader's Digest nature lover's library)
Includes index
Unpriced B82-10284

Field guide to the birds of Britain / [edited and designed by the Reader's Digest Association] ; [consultants and authors, Philip J.K. Burton ... et al.] ; [artists, Stephen Adams ... et al.]. — London : Reader's Digest Association, c1981. — 319p : col.ill,col.maps ; 15x21cm. — (Reader's digest nature lover's library)
Includes index
Unpriced B82-37888

Field guide to the birds of Britain. — Repr. with amendments. — London : Reader's Digest Association, c1981 (1982 [printing]). — 319p : col.ill,maps(some col.) ; 16x21cm. — (Reader's Digest nature lover's library)
Includes index
Unpriced B82-33546

Kilbracken, John Godley, *Baron*. The easy way to bird recognition / John Kilbracken. — London : Kingfisher, 1982. — v,[130]p : ill (some col.) ; 20cm
Includes index
ISBN 0-86272-027-3 : £3.50 : CIP rev. B82-00366

598.2941 — Great Britain. Birds — *Illustrations*

Rickman, Philip. A selection of bird paintings and sketches / written and illustrated by Philip Rickman ; foreword by HRH The Duke of Edinburgh. — [Holt] ([Romndway, High St., Holt, Norfolk]) : Curpotten for Fine Sporting Interests, 1979. — [138]p : ill(some col.) ; 42cm
Limited ed. of 500 copies. — In slip case
Unpriced B82-14187

598.2941 — Great Britain. Birds — *Illustrations continuation*

Tunnicliffe, C. F.. Sketches of bird life / C.F. Tunnicliffe ; introduction and commentary by Robert Gillmor. — London : Gollancz, 1981. — [144p] : ill(some col.) ; 25cm
Includes index
ISBN 0-575-03036-4 : £10.95 B82-05795

598.2941 — Great Britain. Coastal regions. Marine birds. Distribution, *1978-1980*

Jones, P. Hope. Seabird movement at coastal sites around Great Britain and Ireland 1978-80 / P. Hope Jones and M.L. Tasker. — Aberdeen : The Nature Conservancy Council, 1982. — iii,76p : maps ; 30cm
Prepared for the Seabird Group
ISBN 0-86139-155-1 (spiral) : Unpriced B82-23758

598.2941 — Great Britain. Estuaries. Birds

Prater, A. J.. Estuary birds : of Britain and Ireland / by A.J. Prater ; illustrated by John Busby. — Calton : Poyser, 1981. — 440p,[16]p of plates : ill,maps ; 24cm
Bibliography: p426-433. — Includes index
ISBN 0-85661-029-1 : £14.00 B82-08225

598.2941 — Great Britain. Gardens. Birds

The **Garden** bird book. — London : Macmillan, Sept.1982. — [224]p
ISBN 0-333-33151-6 : £7.95 : CIP entry B82-18828

Mockler, Mike. Birds : in the garden. — Poole : Blandford, 1982. — 160p : col.ill ; 26cm
Bibliography: p157. — Includes index
ISBN 0-7137-1129-9 : £8.95 : CIP rev. B82-04499

598.2'941 — Great Britain. Gardens. Birds — *For children*

Cooke, Jean. Garden birds. — London : Granada, Apr.1982. — [64]p. — (Granada guide series ; 16)
ISBN 0-246-11723-0 : £1.95 : CIP entry B82-05389

598.2941 — Great Britain. Gardens. Birds — *For children*

Snow, Keith. A garden of birds / written by Keith Snow ; illustrated by Norman Arlott. — Tadworth : World's Work, c1981. — 32p : ill (some col.) ; 22cm
ISBN 0-437-76107-x : £3.95 B82-13553

598.2941 — Great Britain. Marine birds — *For children*

Richards, Alan. Sea birds / Alan Richards. — London : Black, 1982. — 25p : col.ill ; 22cm. — (Nature in close-up)
Includes index
ISBN 0-7136-2213-x : £3.50 : CIP rev. B82-06956

598.2941'022'2 — Great Britain. Birds — *Illustrations — For children*

Grimes, Brian. British wild birds. — London : Hodder & Stoughton Children's Books, Sept.1982. — [96]p
ISBN 0-340-27970-2 : £9.95 : CIP entry B82-18811

598.29422'3 — Kent. Birds

The **Birds** of Kent : a review of their status and distribution / edited by D.W. Taylor, D.L. Davenport and J.J.M. Flegg. — Meopham : Kent Ornithological Society, 1981. — vii,438p : ill(1col.),maps ; 24cm
Bibliography: p426-427. — Includes index
ISBN 0-9507418-0-9 : £13.95 B82-15096

598.29423'1 — Wiltshire. Birds

The **Birds** of Wiltshire / edited for The Wiltshire Ornithological Society by John Buxton. — Trowbridge : Wiltshire Library & Museum Service, 1981. — xiii,194p,32p of plates : ill,maps,1facsim ; 20cm
Bibliography: p191-192. — Includes index
ISBN 0-86080-080-6 (pbk) : £5.50 B82-10821

598.29424'1 — Gloucestershire. Birds

Swaine, Christopher M.. Birds of Gloucestershire. — Gloucester : Alan Sutton, Aug.1982. — [240]p
ISBN 0-86299-012-2 : £7.95 : CIP entry B82-19268

598.29424'63 — Staffordshire. Westport Lake. Birds

Emley, David W.. The birds of Westport lake / D.W. Emley & W.J. Low. — Stoke-on-Trent : City Museum & Art Gallery, [1982?]. — 47p : ill,3maps ; 21cm. — (Staffordshire biological recording scheme ; no.9)
ISBN 0-905080-14-9 (pbk) : Unpriced B82-33687

598.29425'9'05 — Buckinghamshire. Birds — *Serials*

Buckinghamshire bird report. — 1980. — Grendon Underwood (c/o C. Fisher, Fairings, High St., Grendon Underwood, Aylesbury, Bucks. HP18 0SL) : Buckinghamshire Bird Club, Feb.1982. — [32]p
ISBN 0-907823-00-9 (pbk) : £2.00 : CIP entry
ISSN 0262-0561 B81-38824

598.294259'05 — Buckinghamshire. Birds — *Serials*

Buckinghamshire bird report. — 1981. — Grendon Underwood (c/o Mr C. Fisher, Fairings, High St., Grendon Underwood, Aylesbury, Bucks. HP18 0SC) : Buckinghamshire Bird Club, Sept.1982. — [36]p
ISBN 0-907823-01-7 (pbk) : £2.00 : CIP entry
ISSN 0262-0561 B82-25744

598.29426'54 — Cambridgeshire. Huntingdon *(District).* **Natural resources: Water. Reservoirs: Grafham Water. Birds**

Cooke, Arnold. The birds of Grafham Water 2 : 1976-1980. — Ely : EARO, c1981. — 21p : ill,1map ; 21cm
ISBN 0-904463-79-6 (pbk) : £1.00 B82-30532

598.29427'1'05 — Cheshire. Birds — *Serials*

[Bird report *(Cheshire Ornithological Association)*]. Bird report / Cheshire Ornithological Association. — 1978-. — [Heald Green] ([c/o A. W. Martin, 6 Avon Rd, Heald Green, Cheshire SK8 3LS]) : The Association, [197-]-. — v. : ill,maps ; 21cm
Annual. — Continues: Cheshire bird report. — Description based on: 1980 issue
ISSN 0262-7655 = Bird report - Cheshire Ornithological Association : £1.40 B82-06788

598.2946'75 — Spain. Balearic Islands. Birds

Bannerman, David A.. The birds of the Balearics. — London : Croom Helm, Jan.1983. — [450]p
ISBN 0-7099-0679-x : £25.00 : CIP entry B82-32552

598.29484'5 — Norway. Varanger Peninsula. Birds

Vaughan, Richard, *1927-*. Arctic summer : birds in North Norway / Richard Vaughan. — Shrewsbury : A. Nelson, 1979. — 152p,[4]p of plates : ill(some col.),maps ; 24cm
Bibliography: p152
ISBN 0-904614-01-8 : £7.50 B82-39403

598.29494'7 — Europe. Alps. Birds — *Field guides*

Jonsson, Lars. Birds of the Mediterranean and Alps. — London : Croom Helm, Aug.1982. — [128]p
Translation from the Swedish
ISBN 0-7099-1413-x : £5.95 : CIP entry
Primary classification 598.29'182'2 B82-15907

598.2953'6 — Arabia. Gulf States. Birds — *Field guides*

Jennings, Michael C.. Birds of the Arabian Gulf / Michael C. Jennings. — London : Allen & Unwin, 1981. — 167p,12p of plates : ill(some col.) ; 21cm. — (The Natural history of the Arabian Gulf)
Maps on lining papers. — Bibliography: p99-101. — Includes index
ISBN 0-04-598009-8 : Unpriced : CIP rev. B81-20482

598.2954 — South Asia. Birds — *Field guides*

Ali, Sálim. Handbook of the birds of India and Pakistan : together with those of Bangladesh, Nepal, Bhutan and Sri Lanka / Sálim Ali and S. Dillon Ripley ; sponsored by the Bombay Natural History Society. — 2nd ed. — Delhi ; London : Oxford University Press
Vol.1: Diver to hawks; synopsis nos. 1-224, colour plates 1-18, monochrome plates M1-M4. — 1978 (1981 [printing]). — lviii,384p,[24] leaves of plates : ill(some col.),maps(some col.) ; 25cm
Previous ed.: 1968. — Text on lining papers. — Bibliography: p371-373. — Includes index
ISBN 0-19-561115-2 : £15.00 B82-29511

598.296 — Africa. Birds

Brown, Leslie, *1917-1980*. The birds of Africa. — London : Academic Press, July 1982
Vol.1. — [600]p
ISBN 0-12-137301-0 : CIP entry B82-17193

598.2966 — West & Central Africa. Birds — *Field guides*

Mackworth-Praed, C. W.. Birds of West Central and Western Africa / C.W. Mackworth-Praed and C.H.B. Grant. — London : Longman
Vol.1. — 1970 (1981 [printing]). — xxxii,671p,[45]p of plates : ill(some col.),maps ; 23cm. — (African handbook of birds. Series 3)
Includes index
ISBN 0-582-46086-7 : £30.00 : CIP rev. B81-28774

Mackworth-Praed, C. W.. Birds of West Central and Western Africa / C.W. Mackworth-Praed and C.H.B. Grant. — London : Longman
Vol.2. — 1973 (1981 [printing]). — x,818p,[47]p of plates : ill(some col.),maps ; 23cm. — (African handbook of birds. Series 3)
Includes index
ISBN 0-582-46087-5 : £30.00 : CIP rev. B81-28775

598.2966'51 — Gambia. Birds — *Lists*

Gore, M. E. J.. Birds of the Gambia : an annotated check-list / by M.E.J. Gore. — London : British Ornithologists Union, 1981. — 130p,[8]p of plates : ill,maps ; 25cm. — (B.O.U. check-list ; no.3)
Bibliography: p116-118. — Includes index
ISBN 0-907446-02-7 : Unpriced B82-37983

598.29669 — Nigeria. Birds

Elgood, J. H.. The birds of Nigeria : an annotated check-list / by J.H. Elgood. — London : British Ornithologists Union, 1982. — 246p : ill ; 25cm. — (B.O.U. check list ; no.4)
Bibliography: p237-242. — Includes index
ISBN 0-907446-03-5 (pbk) : Unpriced B82-30885

598.29678'1 — Tanzania. Zanzibar & Pemba. Birds — *Lists*

Pakenham, R. H. W.. The birds of Zanzibar and Pemba : an annotated check-list / R.H.W. Pakenham. — London (c/o Zoological Society, Regent's Park, NW1 4RY) : British Ornithologist's Union, 1979. — 134p : maps ; 25cm. — (B.O.U. check-list ; no.2)
Bibliography: p108-113. — Includes index
Unpriced (pbk) B82-39372

598.2968 — Southern Africa. Birds — *Field guides*

Birds of Southern Africa. — Johannesburg : Macmillan South Africa ; London : Macmillan
Includes index
1: Kruger National Park : a comprehensive checklist. — c1980 (1981 [printing]). — xii,242p : ill(some col.),col.maps ; 20cm
ISBN 0-86954-103-x : Unpriced B82-28428

Mackworth-Praed, C. W.. Birds of the southern third of Africa / C.W. Mackworth-Praed and C.H.B. Grant. — London : Longman
Vol.1. — 1962 (1981 [printing]). — xxvi,688p,[49]p of plates : ill(some col.),maps ; 23cm. — (African handbook of birds. Series 2)
Includes index
ISBN 0-582-46084-0 : £30.00 : CIP rev. B81-28111

598.2968 — Southern Africa. Birds — *Field guides continuation*

Mackworth-Praed, C. W.. Birds of the southern third of Africa / C.W. Mackworth-Praed and C.H.B. Grant. — London : Longman
Vol.2. — 1963 (1981 [printing]). — x,747p,[47]p of plates : ill(some col.),maps ; 23cm. — (African handbook of birds. Series 2)
Includes index
ISBN 0-582-46085-9 : £30.00 : CIP rev. B81-28004

598.297 — North America. Birds

Peterson, Roger Tory. Audubon's Birds of America / by Roger Tory Peterson & Virginia Marie Peterson. — London : Heinemann, 1981. — [169]p,435p of plates : ill(some col.),1 col.map ; 39cm
At head of title: The Audubon Society Baby Elephant Folio. — Includes index
ISBN 0-434-58701-x : £65.00 B82-11558

598.29729 — West Indies. Birds

Bond, James, *1900-*. Birds of the West Indies / James Bond ; with colour illustrations by Don R. Eckelberry and Arthur B. Singer ; and line drawings by Earl L. Poole. — 4th ed. — London : Collins, 1979. — 256p,[16]p of plates : ill(some col.),1map ; 20cm
Previous ed.: 1974. — Maps on lining papers. — Includes index
ISBN 0-00-219190-3 : Unpriced B82-25681

598.2994 — Australia. Birds

Serventy, Vincent. Australian birds / Vincent and Carol Serventy. — Adelaide ; London : Rigby, 1981. — 80p : col.ill ; 31cm
ISBN 0-7270-1500-1 : Unpriced B82-40539

598′.33 — Birds: Waders

Hosking, Eric. Eric Hosking's waders. — London : Pelham, Feb.1983. — [160]p
ISBN 0-7207-1430-3 : £12.95 : CIP entry B82-39430

Soothill, Eric. Wading birds of the world. — Poole : Blandford Press, Mar.1982. — [320]p
ISBN 0-7137-0913-8 : £10.95 : CIP entry B82-07831

598′.33 — Great Britain. Coastal regions. Birds

Bennett, Linda. The Guinness book of sea and shore birds / Linda Bennett and Michael Everett ; line drawings by Pamela Dowson. — Enfield : Guinness Superlatives, 1982. — 160p : ill(some col.),maps(some col.) ; 21cm. — (British natural heritage)
Includes index
ISBN 0-85112-307-4 : £4.50 : CIP rev. B82-01447

598′.33 — Northern hemisphere. Wetlands. Birds: Waders — *Field guides*

Prater, A. J.. Guide to the identification and ageing of Holarctic waders / Tony Prater and John Marchant and Juhani Vuorinen. — Tring : British Trust for Ornithology, 1977. — 168p,[17]p of plates : ill(some col.),1map ; 21cm. — (British Trust for Ornithology field guide ; 17)
Bibliography: p164-168
Unpriced (pbk) B82-36687

598′.33 — Shorebirds

Johnsgard, Paul A.. The plovers, sandpipers, and snipes of the world / Paul A. Johnsgard. — Lincoln [Neb.] ; London : University of Nebraska Press, 1981. — xvi,493p,[64]p of plates : ill(some col.),maps ; 29cm
Ill on lining papers. — Bibliography: p473-487. — Includes index
ISBN 0-8032-2553-9 : £31.50 B82-13112

598′.338 — Gulls — *Field guides*

Grant, P. J. (Peter James). Gulls : a guide to indentification / by P.J. Grant ; illustrated by the author. — Calton : Poyser, 1982. — 280p : ill,maps ; 24cm
Bibliography: p149
ISBN 0-85661-030-5 : £12.00 B82-37385

598′.34 — Herons — *For schools*

About the heron. — Stirling : Scottish Panel of Advisers in Outdoor Education in conjunction with B.P. Educational Service, c1979. — 24p : ill,2maps ; 21cm. — (About ; 6)
Bibliography: p24
ISBN 0-86223-006-3 (pbk) : Unpriced B82-20675

598.4′1 — Austria. Alm River region. Greylag geese. Social behaviour — *Personal observations*

Lorenz, Konrad. The year of the greylag goose / Konrad Lorenz ; photographs by Sybille and Klaus Kalas ; translated by Robert Martin. — London : Eyre Methuen, 1979 (1981 [printing]). — 199p : col.ill ; 28cm
Translation of: Das Jahr der Graugans
ISBN 0-413-49130-7 (pbk) : £3.95 B82-17547

598.4′1 — Ducks — *For children*

Althea. Ducks and drakes / by Althea ; illustrated by Joe Blossom. — Cambridge : Dinosaur in co-operation with The Wildfowl Trust, 1982. — 24p : col.ill ; 16x19cm
ISBN 0-85122-343-5 (cased) : £2.25
ISBN 0-85122-342-7 (pbk) : Unpriced B82-32076

The **Duck** / translated by Erica and Arthur Propper ; illustrated by Peter Barrett. — London : Macdonald Educational, 1979. — 19p : col.ill,1col.map ; 24cm. — (Animal world)
Translated from the French
ISBN 0-356-06533-2 : £1.25 B82-40685

598.4′1 — Europe. Wildfowl

Ogilvie. Wildfowl of Britain and Europe. — Oxford : Oxford University Press, Oct.1982. — [96]p
ISBN 0-19-217723-0 : £6.95 : CIP entry B82-23660

598.4′1 — Greenland. White-fronted geese

Greenland White-fronted Goose Study. Report of the 1979 Greenland White-fronted Goose Study expedition to Eqalungmiut Nunât, West Greenland. — Aberystwyth (Dept. of Zoology, University College of Wales, Aberystwyth) : The Study, Aug.1981. — [200]p
ISBN 0-9507667-0-4 (pbk) : £5.00 : CIP entry B81-24642

598.4′1 — Mallards — *For children*

Sheehan, Angela. The duck / by Angela Sheehan ; illustrated by Maurice Pledger and Bernard Robinson. — London : New Caxton Library Service, c1979. — [26]p : col.ill ; 23cm. — (Eye-view library)
Ill on lining papers
Unpriced B82-13216

598.4′1 — Shelducks. Social behaviour

Patterson, I. J.. The shelduck — a study in behavioural ecology. — Cambridge : Cambridge University Press, Sept.1982. — [277]p
ISBN 0-521-24646-6 : £27.50 : CIP entry B82-26246

598.4′1042 — Wildfowl. Diseases

Wobeser, Gary A.. Diseases of wild waterfowl / Gary A. Wobeser. — New York ; London : Plenum, c1981. — xii,300p : ill ; 24cm
Bibliography: p248-286. — Includes index
ISBN 0-306-40764-7 : Unpriced B82-19053

598.4′2 — Petrels

Lockley, R. M.. Flight of the storm petrel. — Newton Abbot : David & Charles, Jan.1983. — [192]p
ISBN 0-7153-8219-5 : £7.50 : CIP entry B82-32607

598.4′41 — Adélie penguins — *Stories, anecdotes — For children*

Bonners, Susan. A penguin year / written and illustrated by Susan Bonners. — London : Gollancz, 1981. — [46]p : col.ill ; 20x25cm
ISBN 0-575-03025-9 : £4.95 B82-07752

598′.617 — Chickens: Hens — *For children*

Ingves, Gunilla. Hens. — London : A. & C. Black, Sept.1982. — [32]p. — (Farm animals)
Translation of: Hons
ISBN 0-7136-2237-7 : £3.50 : CIP entry B82-20357

598′.617 — Peafowl

Bergmann, Josef. The peafowl of the world / Josef Bergmann. — Hindhead : Saiga, 1980. — ix,99p : ill(some col.) ; 30cm
Bibliography: p99. — Includes index
ISBN 0-904558-51-7 : £12.00 B82-12632

598′.617 — Pheasants — *Illustrations*

Elliot, Daniel Giraud. The birds of Daniel Giraud Elliot : a selection of pheasants and peacocks / painted by Joseph Wolf ... ; edited and introduced by Adrian Thorpe. — London : Ariel Press, c1979. — [36]p,xii leaves of plates : col.ill,1facsim ; 57cm
Selections from Monographs of the phasianidae originally published : New York : The Author, 1872. — Limited ed. of 1000 numbered copies of which 500 are reserved for North American distribution
ISBN 0-900074-33-7 : Unpriced B82-20254

598′.71 — Parrots — *For children — Welsh texts*

Hope, Ffransis. Y parot / [testun gan Ffransis Hope ; ymgynghorwr Berian Williams ; lluniau gan The Tjong Khing]. — Caerdydd : Gwasg y Dref Wen, c1981. — 16p : ill(some col.) ; 22cm. — (Cyfres y seren)
Translated and adapted from the Dutch. — Cover title. — Text on inside covers
£0.85 (pbk) B82-10535

598′.74 — Europe. Cuckoos

Wyllie, Ian. The cuckoo / Ian Wyllie. — London : Batsford, 1981. — 176p,[16]p of plates : ill (some col.),maps ; 24cm
Bibliography: p160-169. — Includes index
ISBN 0-7134-0266-0 : £8.95 B82-03563

598.8′11 — Cotingas

Snow, David. The cotingas. — London : British Museum (Natural History), June 1982. — [202]p
ISBN 0-565-00833-1 : £30.00 : CIP entry
ISBN 0-19-858511-x (Oxford University Press) B82-11527

598.8′13 — Swallows

Tate, Peter, *1926-*. Swallows / Peter Tate ; illustrations by Alan Harris. — London : Witherby, 1981. — 96p,2leaves of plates : ill (some col.) ; 23cm
Bibliography: p87-89. — Includes index
ISBN 0-85493-140-6 : £5.95 B82-01937

598.8′32 — Dippers — *For schools*

About the dipper. — Stirling : Scottish Panel of Advisers in Outdoor Education in conjunction with Educational Service, c1979. — 20p : ill,2maps ; 21cm. — (About ; 2)
Cover title. — Bibliography: p20
ISBN 0-86223-001-2 (pbk) : Unpriced B82-20676

598.8′42 — Song thrushes — *For children*

Sheehan, Angela. The song thrush / by Angela Sheehan ; illustrated by George Thompson. — London : New Caxton Library Service, c1976. — [26]p : col.ill ; 23cm. — (Eye-view library)
Ill on lining papers
Unpriced B82-13214

598.8′73 — Weaver finches

Goodwin, Derek. Estrildid finches of the world / Derek Goodwin ; colour plates by Martin Woodcock. — London : British Nuseum (Natural History), 1982. — 328p,[8]p of plates : ill(some col.),maps ; 29cm
Includes bibliographies and index
ISBN 0-565-00832-3 : £25.00 : CIP rev.
ISBN 0-19-858506-3 (Oxford University Press) B82-14359

598.8′83 — House sparrows & tree sparrows — *For children*

Sparrows. — Poole : Blandford, 1982, c1981. — 31p : col.ill ; 25cm. — (Finding out about (Blandford))
Translation of the Japanese
ISBN 0-7137-1151-5 : £2.95 : CIP rev. B81-04327

598.8'92 — Kingfishers
Boag, David. The kingfisher / David Boag. — Poole : Blandford Press, 1982. — viii,120p : ill (some col.) ; 25cm
Bibliography: p117. — Includes index
ISBN 0-7137-1170-1 : £8.95 : CIP rev. B82-09608

598'.91 — Vultures — *For children*
Cloudsley-Thompson, J. L.. Vultures / John Cloudsley-Thompson. — Hove : Wayland, 1981. — 60p : col.ill ; 23cm. — (Animals of the world)
Includes index
ISBN 0-85340-851-3 : £3.95 B82-16519

598'.91042 — Birds of prey. Diseases — *Conference proceedings*
International Symposium on Diseases of Birds of Prey *(1980 : London)*. Recent advances in the study of raptor diseases : proceedings of the International Symposium on Diseases of Birds of Prey, 1st-3rd. July 1980, London / edited by J.E. Cooper and A.G. Greenwood. — Keighley : Chiron, 1981. — x,178p : ill ; 31cm
Limited ed. of 100 numbered and signed copies. — Includes bibliographies and index
ISBN 0-9507716-0-0 : Unpriced B82-07942

598'.916 — Eagles — *For children*
Riley, Terry, *1941-*. Eagles : and other hunters of the sky / written and illustrated by Terry Riley. — London : Dean, c1982. — [26]p : ill (some col.) ; 28cm
Ill on lining papers
ISBN 0-603-00266-8 : £1.25 B82-29538

598'.918 — Falcons
Cade, Tom J.. The falcons of the world / by Tom J. Cade ; with paintings by R. David Rigby. — London : Collins, 1982. — 188p : ill (some col.) ; 32cm
Bibliography: 3p. — Includes index
ISBN 0-00-219251-9 : £15.00 B82-18384

598'.97 — Barn owls — *For schools*
About the barn owl. — Stirling : Scottish Panel of Advisers in Outdoor Education in conjunction with B.P. Educational Service, c1979. — 28p : ill ; 21cm. — (About ; 7)
Cover title. — Bibliography: p28
ISBN 0-86223-007-1 (pbk) : Unpriced B82-20677

598'.97 — Owls
Hosking, Eric. Eric Hosking's owls / Eric Hosking with Jim Flegg ; foreword by Ian Prestt. — London : Pelham, 1982. — 169p : ill (some col.) ; 29cm
Ill on lining papers. — Includes index
ISBN 0-7207-1390-0 : £12.95 : CIP rev. B82-04965

599 — MAMMALS

599 — Mammals
Delany, M. J.. Mammal ecology. — Glasgow : Blackie, Sept.1982. — [160]p. — (Tertiary level biology)
ISBN 0-216-91310-1 (cased) : £15.00 : CIP entry
ISBN 0-216-91309-8 (pbk) : £7.95 B82-19006

Eisenberg, John F.. The mammalian radiations : an analysis of trends in evolution, adaptation, and behaviour / John F. Eisenberg. — London : Athlone Press, 1981. — xx,610p : ill,maps ; 27cm
Includes index
ISBN 0-485-30008-7 : £32.00 : CIP rev. B81-30558

599 — Mammals — *For children*
Cansdale, George. Know about mammals. — London : Ark, [1981?]. — [16]p : col.ill ; 21cm. — (Know about nature series)
Cover title. — Author: George Cansdale
ISBN 0-86201-056-x (pbk) : £0.50 B82-05604

Cork, Barbara. Wild animals : land and sea mammals / Barbara Cork. — London : Usborne, 1982. — 24p : col.ill ; 21cm. — (Usborne first nature)
Text on inside covers. — Includes index
ISBN 0-86020-628-9 (pbk) : £1.00 B82-35840

Riley, Terry, *1941-*. The wonderful world of wild animals / cover illustration and text by Terry Riley. — London : Dean, c1981. — [73]p : col.ill,maps ; 27cm
Ill on lining papers
ISBN 0-603-00251-x : Unpriced B82-26757

599.01 — Mammals. Physiology
Allen, Phyllis A.. Mammalian physiology Level II / Phyllis A. Allen. — Plymouth : Macdonald and Evans, 1981. — viii,144p : ill ; 22cm. — (The M. & E. TECbook series)
Includes index
ISBN 0-7121-1283-9 (pbk) : £3.95 B82-09752

599.01'13 — Mammals. Blood. Angiotensin. Role of renin — *Conference proceedings*
Heterogeneity of renin and renin-substrate : proceedings of a satellite to the Seventh Scientific Meeting of the International Society of Hypertension, New Orleans, Louisiana, USA, May 14 and 15, 1980 / editor Mohinder P. Sambhi. — New York ; Oxford : Elsevier/North-Holland, c1981. — xxii,425p : ill ; 24cm
Includes bibliographies and index
ISBN 0-444-00618-4 : £37.33 B82-06717

599.01'1 — Mammals. Microcirculatory system — *Conference proceedings*
European Conference on Microcirculation *(9th : 1976 : Antwerp)*. Recent advances in basic microcirculatory research / 9th European Conference on Microcirculation, Antwerp, July 5-9, 1976 (Part I) ; editor D.H. Lewis. — Basel ; London : Karger, 1977. — xxv,572p : ill ; 25cm. — (Bibliotheca anatomica ; no.15)
Includes bibliographies and index
ISBN 3-8055-2757-8 : £63.00 B82-15408

European Conference on Microcirculation *(9th : 1976 : Antwerp)*. Recent advances in clinical microcirculatory research / 9th European Conference on Microcirculation, Antwerp, July 5-9, 1976 (Part II) ; editor D.H. Lewis. — Basel ; London : Karger, 1977. — xxv,553p : ill ; 25cm. — (Bibliotheca anatomica ; no.16)
Includes bibliographies and index
ISBN 3-8055-2758-6 : £63.00 B82-15409

599.01'1 — Mammals. Microcirculatory system. Regulation by ions
Ionic regulation of the microcirculation / volume editor B.M. Altura. — Basel ; London : Karger, c1982. — viii,173p : ill ; 25cm. — (Advances in microcirculation ; v.11)
Includes index
ISBN 3-8055-3429-9 : Unpriced B82-40348

599.01'13 — Mammals. Blood. White cells. Immunity — *Conference proceedings*
International Leucocyte Conference *(14th : 1981 : Heidelberg)*. Mechanisms of lymphocyte activation : proceedings of the 14th International Leucocyte Conference held in Heidelberg, FRG, 7-11 June, 1981 / editors Klaus Resch and Holger Kirchner. — Amsterdam ; Oxford : Elsevier/North-Holland Biomedical, 1981. — xxii,713p : ill ; 25cm
Includes index
ISBN 0-444-80376-9 : £50.76 B82-06716

599.01'13 — Megakaryocytes — *Conference proceedings*
Symposium on Megakaryocytes In Vitro *(1980 : Atlanta)*. Megakaryocyte biology and precursors : in vitro cloning and cellular properties : proceedings of the Symposium on Megakaryocytes in Vitro held at the Centers for Disease Control, Public Health Service, U.S. Department of Health and Human Services, Atlanta, Georgia, U.S.A., May 1-2, 1980 / editors Bruce Lee Evalt, Richard F. Levine, Neil T. Williams. — New York ; Oxford : Elsevier/North-Holand, c1981. — xiv,349p : ill ; 24cm
Includes bibliographies and index
ISBN 0-444-00585-4 : £37.15 B82-15172

599.01'16 — Mammals. Heart beat
Cardiac rate and rhythm : physiological morphological and developmental aspects / edited by Lennart N. Bouman and Habo J. Jongsma. — Hague ; London : Nijhoff, 1982. — xiv,682p : ill ; 25cm. — (Developments in cardiovascular medicine ; v.17)
Includes bibliographies and index
ISBN 90-247-2626-3 : Unpriced B82-30374

599.01'32 — Mammals. Appetite. Effects of drugs
Drugs and appetite / edited by T. Silverstone. — London : Academic Press, 1982. — xi,187p : ill ; 24cm
Includes bibliographies and index
ISBN 0-12-643780-7 : £14.20 : CIP rev. B82-00332

599.01'33 — Mammals. Metabolic compartmentation
Metabolic compartmentation. — London : Academic Press, Apr.1982. — [560]p
ISBN 0-12-642750-x : CIP entry B82-11269

599.01'3305 — Mammals. Xenobiotics. Metabolism - *Serials*
Foreign compound metabolism in mammals. — Vol.6. — London : Royal Society of Chemistry, Aug.1981. — [480]p. — (A Specialist periodical report)
ISBN 0-85186-058-3 : CIP entry
ISSN 0300-3493 B81-18083

599.01'42 — Mammals. Neuroendocrine system. Physiology
Advances in neuroendocrine physiology / volume editors K.B. Ruf, G. Tolis. — Basel ; London : Karger, c1982. — 140p : ill ; 25cm. — (Frontiers of hormone research ; v.10)
ISBN 3-8055-2949-x : £28.50 B82-21669

599'.0142 — Mammals. Neuroendocrine system. Physiology
Bennett, Geoffrey W.. Mammalian neuroendocrinology. — London : Croom Helm, Jan.1983. — [320]p
ISBN 0-7099-0638-2 (cased) : £15.95 : CIP entry
ISBN 0-7099-0674-9 (pbk) : £8.95 B82-40912

599.01'49 — Mammals. Detoxication — *Conference proceedings*
Symposium on Renal Ammonia Metabolism *(1981 : Athens)*. Renal ammonia metabolism : symposium on Renal Ammonia Metabolism, Athens, June 1981 / volume editors R.L. Tannen ... [et al.]. — Basel : S. Karger, c1982. — 153p : ill ; 23cm. — (Contributions to nephrology ; 31)
Includes bibliographies
ISBN 3-8055-3481-7 (pbk) : £26.95 B82-40289

599.01'49 — Mammals. Detoxication. Role of enzymes
Detoxication and drug metabolism : conjugation and related systems / edited by William B. Jakoby. — New York ; London : Academic Press, c1981. — xxii,476p : ill ; 24cm. — (Methods in enzymology ; v.77)
Includes index
ISBN 0-12-181977-9 : Unpriced B82-29575

Enzymatic basis of detoxication / edited by William B. Jakoby. — New York ; London : Academic Press, 1980. — (Biochemical pharmacology and toxicology)
Vol.1. — xv,415p : ill ; 24cm
Includes index
ISBN 0-12-380001-3 : £24.20 B82-06537

599.01'49 — Mammals. Kidneys. Biochemistry — *Conference proceedings*
International Symposium on the Biochemistry of Kidney Functions *(6th : 1981 : Bischoffsheim)*. Biochemistry of kidney functions : proceedings of the 6th International Symposium on the Biochemistry of Kidney Functions held at Le Bischenberg, Bischoffsheim (France), 7-10 December, 1981 / sponsored by the Institut national de la santé et de la recherche médicale and supported by the Centre national de la recherche scientifique and the Fondation Hugot ; editor François Morel. — Amsterdam ; Oxford : Elsevier Biomedical, 1982. — xvii,462p : ill ; 25cm. — (INSERM symposium ; no.21)
Includes index
ISBN 0-444-80417-x : £40.08 B82-27159

599.01′49 — Mammals. Urine. Concentration. Regulation by renal medulla

Jamison, Rex L.. Urinary concentrating mechanism : structure and function / Rex L. Jamison, Wilhelm Kriz. — New York ; Oxford : Oxford University Press, 1982. — viii,340p : ill ; 24cm
Bibliography: p295-332. — Includes index
ISBN 0-19-502801-5 : £25.00 B82-27297

599.01′49 — Mammals. Water-electrolyte balance. Regulation by kidneys

Moffat, D. B.. The control of water balance by the kidney / D.B. Moffat. — 2nd ed.(rev.). — Burlington, N.C. : Carolina Biological Supply Co., Scientific Publications Division, c1978 ; Chichester : Distributed by Packard. — 16p : ill(some col.) ; 25cm. — (Carolina biology readers ; 14)
Previous ed.: London : Oxford University Press, 1971. — Bibliography: p16
ISBN 0-89278-214-5 (unbound) : £0.80 B82-31592

599.01′6 — Mammals. Contraception. Use of gossypol

Neville, Peter, *1958-*. Gossypol : a literature review of gossypol as an oral contraceptive and an assessment of its potential in the control of feral cats and dogs / by Peter Neville. — Potters Bar : Universities Federation for Animal Welfare, c1982. — 11p ; 26cm. — (A UFAW technical publication)
Cover title. — Bibliography: p10-11
Unpriced (pbk) B82-24877

599.01′6 — Mammals. Relaxin — *Conference proceedings*

Midwest Conference on Endocrinology and Metabolism *(15th : 1979 : University of Missouri)*. Relaxin / [proceedings of the Fifteenth Midwest Conference on Endocrinology and Metabolism, held October 11-12, 1979, at the University of Missouri, Columbia, Missouri, and sponsored by: National Science Foundation ... et el.] ; edited by Ralph R. Anderson. — New York ; London : Plenum, c1982. — xiii,359p : ill ; 26cm. — (Advances in experimental medicine and biology ; v.143)
Includes bibliographies and index
ISBN 0-306-40901-1 : Unpriced B82-25810

Workshop on the Chemistry and Biology of Relaxin *(1980 : University of Hawaii)*. Relaxin : proceedings of a Workshop on the Chemistry and Biology of Relaxin held at the East-West Center, the University of Hawaii, Honolulu, Hawaii, June 10-14, 1980 / editors G.D. Bryant-Greenwood, H.D. Niall, F.C. Greenwood. — New York ; Oxford : Elsevier/North-Holland, c1981. — xiv,401p : ill ; 24cm
Includes index
ISBN 0-444-00643-5 : Unpriced B82-19312

599.01′6 — Mammals. Reproduction

Reproduction in mammals. — Cambridge : Cambridge University Press
Book 1: Germ cells and fertilization / edited by C.R. Austin, R.V. Short ; drawings by John R. Fuller. — 2nd ed. — 1982. — ix,177p : ill ; 26cm
Previous ed.: 1972. — Includes bibliographies and index
ISBN 0-521-24628-8 (cased) : £15.00 : CIP rev.
ISBN 0-521-28861-4 (pbk) : £5.95 B82-15877

Reproduction in mammals. — 2nd ed. — Cambridge : Cambridge University Press
Previous ed.: 1972
Book 2: Embryonic and fetal development. — Oct.1982. — [190]p
ISBN 0-521-24786-1 (cased) : £16.00 : CIP entry
ISBN 0-521-28962-9 (pbk) : £6.95 B82-40320

Reproduction in mammals / edited by C.R. Austin and R.V. Short ; illustrations by John R. Fuller. — Cambridge : Cambridge University Press
Bk.8: Human sexuality. — 1980. — xiii : ill,1port ; 23cm
Includes bibliographies and index
ISBN 0-521-22361-x (cased) : £12.00 : CIP rev.
ISBN 0-521-29461-4 (pbk) : £3.95 B80-25651

599.01′6 — Mammals. Reproduction. Immunological aspects

Hogarth, Peter J.. Immunological aspects of mammalian reproduction / Peter J. Hogarth. — Glasgow : Blackie, 1982. — viii,196p : ill ; 24cm
Bibliography: p169-185. — Includes index
ISBN 0-216-91247-4 (cased) : Unpriced : CIP rev.
ISBN 0-216-91248-2 (pbk) : Unpriced B82-01710

599.01′6 — Mammals. Reproductive system. Development — *Conference proceedings*

Workshop on the Development and Function of the Reproductive Organs *(5th : 1981 : Copenhagen)*. Development and function of reproductive organs : proceedings of the Vth Workshop on the Development and Function of the Reproductive Organs, Copenhagen, July 6-9 1981 / editors Anne Grete Byskov and Hannah Peters. — Amsterdam ; Oxford : Excerpta Medica, 1981. — xiii,366p : ill,ports ; 25cm. — (International congress series ; no.559)
Includes index
ISBN 90-219-0504-3 : £29.79 B82-13452

599.01′82 — Mammals. Sensory perception. Role of brain — *Conference proceedings*

Brain mechanisms of sensation : the third Taniguchi symposium of brain sciences / edited by Yasuji Katsuki, Ralph Norgren, Masayasu Sato ; [sponsor the Taniguchi Foundation]. — New York ; Chichester : Wiley, c1981. — xi,329p,2p of plates : ill(some col.) ; 27cm
Includes index
ISBN 0-471-08148-5 : £24.00 B82-00119

599.01′823 — Mammals. Eyes. Movements — *Conference proceedings*

International Conference on Oculomotor Research *(1980 : Schloss Reisensburg, Ulm)*. Progress in oculomotor research : proceedings of the International Conference on Oculomotor Research held July 28-31, 1980 at Schloss Reisensburg near Ulm, West Germany / editors Albert F. Fuchs and Wolfgang Becker. — New York ; Oxford : Elsevier/North-Holland, c1981. — xxi,685p : ill,ports ; 25cm. — (Developments in neuroscience ; v.12)
Bibliography: p601-673. — Includes index
ISBN 0-444-00589-7 : Unpriced B82-06600

599.01′825 — Mammals. Echolocation

Purves, P. E.. Echolocation in whales and dolphins. — London : Academic Press, Feb.1983. — [275]p
ISBN 0-12-567960-2 : CIP entry B82-36582

599.01′825′05 — Mammals. Hearing — *Serials*

Hearing research and theory. — Vol.1-. — New York ; London : Academic Press, 1981-. — v. : ill ; 24cm
ISSN 0730-1480 = Hearing research and theory : £19.20 B82-07625

599.01′88 — Mammals. Brain. Microcirculatory system — *Conference proceedings*

Microcirculation : current physiologic, medical, and surgical concepts / edited by Richard M. Effros, Holger Schmid-Schönbein, Jørn Ditzel. — New York ; London : Academic Press, 1981. — xv,317p ; 24cm
Conference proceedings. — Includes bibliographies and index
ISBN 0-12-232560-5 : £29.80 B82-07556

599.01′88 — Mammals. Brain. Physiology — *Conference proceedings*

International School of Medical Sciences *(11th : 1980 : Erice)*. Investigation of brain function / edited by A.W. Wilkinson. — New York ; London : Plenum, c1981. — viii,262p : ill ; 26cm. — (Ettore Majorana international science series. Life sciences ; v.7)
′Proceedings of the 11th course of the International School of Medical Sciences, held May 3-11, 1980 at the Ettore Majorana Center for Scientific Culture, Erice, Sicily, Italy′ — title page verso. — Includes bibliographies and index
ISBN 0-306-40811-2 : Unpriced B82-02149

599.01′88 — Mammals. Central nervous system. Neurotransmitters: Peptides — *Conference proceedings*

OHOLO Biological Conference on Neuroactive Compounds and their Cell Receptors *(24th : 1979 : Zichron Ya′acov)*. Endogenous peptides and centrally acting drugs : 24th Annual OHOLO Biological Conference on Neuroactive Compounds and their Cell Receptors, Zichron Ya′acov, April 1-4, 1979 / volume editors, A. Levy ... [et al.] ; technical editor, S.R. Smith. — Basel ; London : Karger, c1980. — xiv,159p : ill ; 25cm. — (Progress in biochemical pharmacology ; v.16)
Includes index
ISBN 3-8055-0831-x : £21.50 B82-38649

Pfizer International Symposium *(11th : 1981 : Edinburgh)*. Neuropeptides : basic and clinical aspects : proceedings of the eleventh Pfizer International Symposium, September 1981 / edited by George Fink, Lawrence J. Whalley ; foreword by John Gillingham. — Edinburgh : Churchill Livingstone, 1982. — 286p : ill ; 24cm
Includes index
ISBN 0-443-02537-1 : Unpriced : CIP rev. B82-07665

599.01′88 — Mammals. Nervous system. Biochemistry — *Conference proceedings*

Substance P in the nervous system. — London : Pitman, Sept.1982. — [336]p. — (Ciba Foundation symposium ; 91)
Conference papers
ISBN 0-272-79655-7 : £25.00 : CIP entry B82-18869

599.01′88 — Mammals. Nervous system — *Conference proceedings*

Nerve cells, transmitters and behaviour : proceedings of a study week at the Pontifical Academy of Sciences, October 9-14, 1978 / edited by Rita Levi-Montalcini. — Amsterdam ; Oxford : Elsevier/North-Holland Biomedical, 1980. — xvi,679p : ill,ports ; 25cm. — (Pontificiae Academiae Scientiarum scripta varia ; 45)
Includes bibliographies
ISBN 0-444-80243-6 : £43.85 B82-31843

599.01′88 — Mammals. Nervous system. Molecules

Molecular approaches to neurobiology / edited by Ian R. Brown. — New York ; London : Academic Press, 1982. — xi,419p : ill ; 24cm. — (Cell biology)
Includes bibliographies and index
ISBN 0-12-137020-8 : £32.80 B82-34853

599.01′88 — Mammals. Nervous system. Proteins

Nervous-system-specific proteins / edited by Elisabeth Bock. — Oxford : Published for the Scandinavian Society for Immunology by Blackwell Scientific, c1982. — ix,356p : ill ; 26cm. — (Scandinavian journal of immunology. Supplement no.9, ISSN 0301-6323 ; v.15)
Includes bibliographies
ISBN 0-632-00937-3 : £35.00 : CIP rev. B82-02666

599.01′88 — Mammals. Neurons

Jones, D. Gareth. Neurons and synapses / D.G. Jones. — London : Edward Arnold, 1981. — 60p : ill ; 22cm. — (The Institute of Biology′s studies in biology, ISSN 0537-9024 ; no.135)
Bibliography: p57. — Includes index
ISBN 0-7131-2825-9 (pbk) : £2.25 : CIP rev. B81-30609

599′.0188 — Mammals. Paraneurons — *Conference proceedings*

International Symposium on Paraneurons *(1979 : Shikotsuko)*. Paraneurons, their features and function : proceedings of the International Symposium on Paraneurons, Shikotsuko, Hokkaido, Japan July 24-27, 1979 / edited by Tomio Kanno. — Amsterdam ; Oxford : Excerpta Medica, 1981. — vi,193p : ill ; 27cm. — (International congress series ; no.552)
Includes bibliographies and index
ISBN 90-219-0479-9 : Unpriced B82-10629

599.01′88 — Mammals. Presynaptic receptors

Presynaptic receptors. — Chichester : Ellis Horwood, May 1982. — [192]p
ISBN 0-85312-407-8 : £21.00 : CIP entry B82-11113

599.01′882 — Mammals. Circadian rhythms

Moore-Ede, Martin C.. The clocks that time us : physiology of the circadian timing system / Martin C. Moore-Ede, Frank M. Sulzman, and Charles A. Fuller. — Cambridge, Mass. ; London : Harvard University Press, 1982. — xii,448p : ill ; 25cm
Bibliography: p384-439. — Includes index
ISBN 0-674-13580-6 : £17.50 B82-34320

599.01′924 — Herbivores. Food: Plants. Secondary metabolites. Interactions with herbivores

Herbivores : their interaction with secondary plant metabolites / edited by Gerald A. Rosenthal, Daniel H. Jawzen. — New York ; London : Academic Press, 1979. — xiii,718p : ill ; 24cm
Includes bibliographies and index
ISBN 0-12-597180-x : £41.40 B82-04335

599.01′924 — Mammals. Taurine — *Conference proceedings*

Taurine in nutrition and neurology / [proceedings of a symposium on taurine, questions and answers, held November 17-19, 1980, at the Universidad Nacional Autónoma de México, Mexico] ; edited by Ryan J. Huxtable and Herminia Pasantes-Morales. — New York ; London : Plenum, c1982. — xiii,551p : ill ; 26cm. — (Advances in experimental medicine and biology ; v.139)
Includes bibliographies and index
ISBN 0-306-40839-2 : Unpriced B82-21032

599.01′9245 — Mammals. Adrenergic nervous system. Catecholamines. Release. Mechanisms — *Conference proceedings*

Synthesis, storage & secretion of adrenal catecholamines. — Oxford : Pergamon, Mar.1982. — [302]p. — (Advances in the biosciences ; v.36)
Conference papers
ISBN 0-08-028012-9 : £25.00 : CIP entry B82-05377

599.01′9245 — Mammals. Interferons

Interferons / edited by Sidney Pestka. — New York ; London : Academic Press. — xxxiv,677p : ill ; 24cm. — (Methods in enzymology ; v.79)
ISBN 0-12-181979-5 : Unpriced B82-39502

Interferons / edited by Sidney Pestka. — New York ; London : Academic Press. — (Methods in enzymology ; v.78)
Includes index
Pt.A. — 1981. — xxx,632p : ill ; 24cm
ISBN 0-12-181978-7 : Unpriced B82-32807

599.01′9245 — Mammals. Phsyiology. Effects of glutamic acids

The **Biological** effects of glutamic acid and its derivatives / edited by V.A. Najjar. — The Hague ; London : Nijhoff, c1981. — 405p : ill ; 27cm. — (Developments in molecular and cellular biochemistry ; 1)
'Reprinted from Molecular and cellular biochemistry, vols. 38 and 39, 1981'
ISBN 90-619-3841-4 : Unpriced B82-17295

599.01′92456 — Mammals. Endorphins

The **Role** of endorphins in neuropsychiatry / volume editor H.M. Emrich. — Basel ; London : Karger, c1981. — vi,290p : ill ; 24cm. — (Modern problems of pharmacopsychiatry ; v.17)
Includes bibliographies and index
ISBN 3-8055-2918-x : £38.60 B82-18198

599.01′92456 — Mammals. Polypeptides. Immunological aspects

Immunologically active peptides / edited by V.A. Najjar. — The Hague ; London : Nijhoff, c1981. — 136p : ill ; 27cm. — (Developments in molecular and cellular biochemistry ; 2)
'Reprinted from Molecular and cellular biochemistry, vol.41, 1981'. — Includes index
ISBN 90-619-3842-2 : Unpriced B82-17294

599.01′925 — Mammals. Monoamine enzymes — *Conference proceedings*

Function and regulation of monoamine enzymes : basic and clinical aspects : proceedings of a conference held at Airlie House, March 6-8, 1981 / edited by Earl Usdin, Norman Weiner, Moussa B.H. Youdim. — London : Macmillan, 1981. — xxiii,961p : ill ; 25cm
Includes index
ISBN 0-333-32746-2 : £50.00 B82-14873

599.01′9256 — Mammals. Proteinases. Properties — *Lists*

McDonald, J. K.. Mammalian proteases : a glossary and bibliography. — London : Academic Press, July 1982
Vol.2. — [300]p
ISBN 0-12-079502-7 : CIP entry
Also classified at 016.59901′9256 B82-12437

599.01′927 — Mammals. Hormones: Peptides & proteins

Hormonal proteins and peptides / edited by Choh Hao Li. — New York ; London : Academic Press
Vol.10: β-Endorphin. — 1981. — xvii,359p : ill ; 24cm
Includes bibliographies and index
ISBN 0-12-447210-9 : £29.40 B82-21297

599.01′927′05 — Mammals. Hormones — *Serials*

Progress in hormone biochemistry and pharmacology. — Vol.1-. — Westmount, Quebec : Eden Press ; Lancaster : MTP Press, 1980-. — v. ; 21cm
Issued every two years
£15.95 B82-18541

599.02 — Mammals. Cancer. Cells. Organelles

Cancer-cell organelles / edited by E. Reid, G.M.W. Cook and D.J. Morré. — Chichester : Ellis Horwood, 1982. — 415p : ill ; 24cm. — (Methodological surveys. Sub-series (B) Biochemistry)
Includes index
ISBN 0-85312-344-6 : £27.50 : CIP rev. B81-21548

599.02 — Mammals. Cancer. Pathogens: Oncogenic viruses

T-W-Fiennes, Richard N.. Infectious cancers of animals and man. — London : Academic Press, Sept.1982. — [180]p
ISBN 0-12-256040-x : CIP entry B82-20750

599.02′149 — Mammals. Kidneys. Cortex. Necrosis. Role of hormones

László, F. A.. Renal cortical necrosis : experimental induction by hormones / F.A. László ; translated by M. Kertai. — Basel ; London : Karger, c1981. — viii,215p : ill ; 23cm. — (Contributions to nephrology ; v.28)
Translation from the Hungarian. — Bibliography: p183-203. — Includes index
ISBN 3-8055-2109-x (pbk) : £20.00 B82-01055

599.02′1823 — Mammals. Eyes. Diseases. Physiological aspects — *Conference proceedings*

Pathophysiology of the visual system : proceedings of a workshop held at the Scuola Normale Superiore, Pisa, Italy on December 12-15, 1980 / sponsored by the Commission of the European Communities, as advised by the Committee on Medical and Public Health Research ; editor L. Maffei. — The Hague ; London : Junk for the Commission of the European Communities, 1981. — viii,278p : ill ; 24cm. — (Documenta ophthalmologica. Proceedings series, ISSN 0303-6405 ; v.30)
Includes bibliographies
ISBN 90-619-3726-4 : Unpriced B82-00473

599.02′322 — Mammals. Pathogens: Haemophilus, pasteurella & actinobacillus — *Conference proceedings*

Haemophilus, pasteurella and actinobacillus / edited by M. Kilian, W. Frederiksen, E.L. Biberstein. — London : Academic Press, 1981. — xiv,294p : ill ; 24cm
Based on the Proceedings of an International Symposium held in Copenhagen, Denmark, 20-23 August, 1980. — Includes index
ISBN 0-12-406780-8 : £14.20 : CIP rev. B81-20591

599.02′9 — Mammals. Major histocompatibility system. Immunogenetic aspects

The **Role** of the major histocompatibility complex in immunobiology / edited by Martin E. Dorf. — Chichester : Wiley, c1981. — ix,406p : ill ; 26cm
Includes index
ISBN 0-471-10124-9 : £27.00 : CIP rev. B81-32021

599.02′92 — Mammals. Major histocompatibility system. Antigens

Histocompatibility antigens : structure and function / edited by P. Parham and J. Strominger. — London : Chapman and Hall, 1982. — xi,246p : ill ; 24cm. — (Receptors and recognition. Series B ; v.14)
Includes bibliographies and index
ISBN 0-412-22410-0 : Unpriced : CIP rev. B82-25078

599.02′93 — Mammals. Immunoglobulin idiotypes — *Conference proceedings*

Immunoglobulin idiotypes / edited by Charles Janeway, Eli E. Sercarz, Hans Wigzell. — New York ; London : Academic Press, 1981. — xli,902p : ill ; 24cm. — (ICN-UCLA symposia on molecular and cellular biology ; v.xx, 1981)
Conference papers. — Includes index
ISBN 0-12-380380-2 : £35.80 B82-21251

599.02′93 — Mammals. Monoclonal immunoglobulins

Monoclonal antibodies and T-cell hybridomas : perspectives, and technical advances / editors Günter J. Hämmerling, Ulrich Hämmerling, and John F. Kearney. — Amsterdam ; Oxford : Elsevier/North-Holland Biomedical, 1981. — xxxii,587p : ill ; 25cm. — (Research monographs in immunology ; v.3)
ISBN 0-444-80351-3 : £49.79 B82-13439

599.02′95 — Mammals. Immune reactions — *Festschriften*

The **Immune** system : festschrift in honor of Niels Kaj Jerne on the occasion of his 70th birthday / edited by Charles M. Steinberg and Ivan Lefkovits with the assistance of Catherine di Lorenzo. — Basel ; London : Karger, 1981. — 2v. : ill(some col.),ports ; 25cm
Includes bibliographies and index
ISBN 3-8055-3407-8 : Unpriced
ISBN 3-8055-3408-6 (v.2) : £80.40 B82-07721

599.02′95 — Mammals. Immune reactions. Regulation by central nervous system

Psychoneuroimmunology / edited by Robert Ader ; with a foreword by Robert A. Good. — New York ; London : Academic Press, 1981. — xxiii,661p : ill ; 24cm. — (Behavioral medicine)
Includes bibliographies and index
ISBN 0-12-043780-5 : £39.00 B82-07718

599.02′95 — Mammals. Immune reactions. Role of phagocytes — *Conference proceedings*

European Conference on Phagocytic Leucocytes *(2nd : 1980 : Trieste)*. Biochemistry and function of phagocytes / [proceedings of the Second European Conference on Phagocytic Leucocytes, held in Trieste, Italy, September 15-18, 1980] ; edited by F. Rossi and P. Patriarca. — New York ; London : Plenum, c1982. — xvi,699p : ill ; 26cm. — (Advances in experimental medicine and biology ; v.141)
Includes index
ISBN 0-306-40887-2 : Unpriced B82-30346

599.03 — Mammals. Development. Effects of toxic chemicals

Developmental toxicology / edited by Keith Snell. — London : Croom Helm, c1982. — 350p : ill ; 23cm
Includes bibliographies and index
ISBN 0-7099-2306-6 : £22.50 : CIP rev. B81-28059

599.03′2 — Mammals. Oogenesis & ovulation — *Conference proceedings*

Reinier de Graaf Symposium *(4th : 1981 : Nijmegen)*. Follicular maturation and ovulation : proceedings of the IVth Reinier de Graaf Symposium, Nijmegen, August 20-22, 1982 / editors R. Rolland ... [et al.]. — Amsterdam ; Oxford : Excerpta Medica, 1982. — xii,432p : ill(some col.) ; 25cm. — (International congress series ; 560)
Includes index
ISBN 90-219-0505-1 : £41.58 B82-23539

599.03′2 — Mammals. Spermatogenesis. Effects of lonidamine

Lonidamine : a new pharmacological approach to the study and control of spermatogenesis and tumors / editors B. Silvestrini and A. Caputo. — Basel ; London : Karger, [1981]. — 120p : ill ; 26cm
Supplement to : Chemotherapy
ISBN 3-8055-3438-8 (pbk) : Unpriced B82-06294

599.03′33 — Mammals. Ova. Delayed implantation — *Conference proceedings*

Embryonic diapause in mammals : proceedings of a symposium held at Thredbo, New South Wales, Australia, February 1980 / edited by A.P.F. Flint, Marilyn B. Renfree and Barbara J. Weir. — Cambridge : Journal of Reproduction & Fertility ; Colchester : Biochemical Society Book Depot [distributor], 1981. — v,260p,[22]p of plates : ill,ports ; 26cm. — (Journal of reproduction & fertility, ISSN 0449-3087 ; supplement no.29)
Includes bibliographies and index
ISBN 0-906545-05-6 : Unpriced B82-08386

599.03′33 — Mammals. Ova. In vitro fertilisation — *Conference proceedings*

In vitro fertilization and embryo transfer / editors E.S.E. Hafez, K. Semm. — Lancaster : MTP, c1982. — xiii,393p : ill ; 25cm
Conference papers. — Includes bibliographies and index
ISBN 0-85200-438-9 : £29.95 : CIP rev. B81-38819

599.03′34 — Mammals. Foetuses. Development — *Conference proceedings*

The **Fetus** and independent life. — London : Pitman, 1981. — ix,372p : ill ; 24cm. — (Ciba Foundation symposium ; 86)
Conference papers. — Includes bibliographies and index
ISBN 0-272-79650-6 : Unpriced : CIP rev. B81-31461

599.03′34 — Mammals. Placenta — *Conference proceedings*

Placenta : receptors, pathology and toxicology / edited by R.K. Miller and H.A. Thiede. — London : Saunders, 1981. — xiii,374p : ill ; 25cm
Proceedings of the 8th Trophoblast Conference. — Includes bibliographies and index
ISBN 0-7216-6353-2 : £24.75 : CIP rev. B81-26693

599.04 — Mammals. Anatomy

Progress in anatomy. — Cambridge : Cambridge University Press
Vol.2. — June 1982. — [232]p
ISBN 0-521-24420-x : £30.00 : CIP entry B82-25097

599.04′3 — Mammals. Teeth. Anatomy. Development — *For dentistry*

Dental anatomy and embryology / edited by J.W. Osborn. — Oxford : Blackwell Scientific, 1981. — xiii,447p : ill ; 26cm. — (A Companion to dental studies ; v.1. Bk.2)
Includes bibliographies and index
ISBN 0-632-00799-0 : £12.00 : CIP rev. B81-24649

599.05′096 — Africa. Large mammals. Ecology

Eltringham, S. K.. The ecology and conservation of large African mammals / S.K. Eltringham. — London : Macmillan, 1979. — x,286p,[8]p of plates : ill,2maps ; 24cm
Bibliography: p247-266. — Includes index
ISBN 0-333-23580-0 : £15.00 : CIP rev. B79-25187

599.052′48 — Large mammals. Population. Dynamics — *Conference proceedings*

Dynamics of large mammal populations / [edited by] Charles W. Fowler, Tim D. Smith. — New York ; Chichester : Wiley, c1981. — xviii,477p : ill ; 24cm
Conference papers. — Includes bibliographies and index
ISBN 0-471-05160-8 : £31.50 B82-13359

599.08′24′028 — Mammals. Histology. Laboratory techniques

Ratcliffe, N. A.. Practical illustrated histology / N.A. Ratcliffe ; illustrations by P.J. Llewellyn. — London : Macmillan, 1982. — vii,228p : ill ; 27cm
Bibliography: p219. — Includes index
ISBN 0-333-32653-9 (cased) : Unpriced
ISBN 0-333-25635-2 (pbk) : Unpriced B82-39710

599.08′24′076 — Mammals. Tissues — *Questions & answers*

Wheater, Paul R.. Self-assessment in histology : questions and quiz micrographs / Paul R. Wheater, H. George Burkitt. — Edinburgh : Churchill Livingstone, 1981, c1982. — 198p : col.ill ; 22cm
ISBN 0-443-02109-0 (pbk) : £3.95 : CIP rev. B81-14984

599.08′76 — Mammals. Cells. Endogenous pacemakers

Cellular pacemakers. — New York ; Chichester : Wiley
Vol.1: Mechanisms of pacemaker generation / edited by David O. Carpenter. — c1982. — xii,332p : ill ; 24cm
Includes bibliographies and index
ISBN 0-471-06509-9 : £33.30 B82-21798

599.08′764 — Mammals. Cells. Secretion. Regulation — *Conference proceedings*

The **Control** of secretion : a Royal Society discussion : held on 28 and 29 May 1981 / organized by R.A. Gregory, O.H. Petersen and Sir Arnold Burgen. — London : The society, 1982, c1981. — 193p,[24]p of plates : ill ; 31cm
Originally published: as Philosophical transactions of the Royal Society of London, series B, vol.296 (no.1080), p1-193. — Includes bibliographies
ISBN 0-85403-179-0 : £27.30 B82-15373

599.08′765 — Mammals. Cells. Carcinogenic effects of chemicals. Short term tests. Evaluation — *Conference proceedings*

Evaluation of short-term tests for carcinogens : report of the international collaborative program / edited by Frederick J. de Serres and John Ashby. — New York ; Oxford : Elsevier/North-Holland, c1981. — xiii,827p : ill ; 28cm
Includes bibliographies and index
ISBN 0-444-00570-6 : Unpriced B82-01665

599.094 — Europe. Mammals — *For children*

Bishop, Iain. Mammals of Britain and Europe / Iain Bishop ; illustrated by Bernard Robinson. — London : Kingfisher, 1982. — 123p : ill (some col.),col.maps ; 20cm. — (A Kingfisher guide)
Includes index
ISBN 0-86272-026-5 : £2.95 : CIP rev. B82-00365

Deedes, Paul. Wild animals. — London : Granada, Apr.1982. — [64]p. — (Granada guide series ; 15)
ISBN 0-246-11722-2 : £1.95 : CIP entry B82-05388

599.0941 — Great Britain. Mammals

Burton, John A.. The Guinness book of mammals / John A. Burton ; line drawings by Jean Vaughan. — Enfield : Guinness Superlatives, 1982. — 160p : ill(some col.),maps(some col.) ; 21cm. — (Britain's natural heritage)
Includes index
ISBN 0-85112-305-8 : £4.50 : CIP rev. B82-01446

Kinns, Geoffrey. British wild animals : wild mammals of the British Isles / photographs by Geoffrey Kinns ; devised and written by Brian Grimes. — London : Hodder and Stoughton, c1981. — 125p : col.ill ; 30cm
Ill on lining papers. — Bibliography: p121. — Includes index
ISBN 0-340-26888-3 : £7.95 : CIP rev. B81-28849

599.09411 — Scotland. Mammals

Stephen, David, *1910-*. Wildlife / David Stephen ; drawings by Richard Hook. — Edinburgh : Spurbooks, c1982. — 64p : ill ; 19cm. — (Introducing Scotland)
Bibliography: p63. — Includes index
ISBN 0-7157-2085-6 (pbk) : £1.25 B82-20592

599′.0967 — East Africa. Mammals

Kingdon, Jonathan. East African mammals : an atlas of evolution in Africa / Jonathan Kingdon. — London : Academic Press
Vol.3
Pt.C: Bovids. — 1982. — 393p,[1]p of plates : ill(some col.),maps ; 29cm
ISBN 0-12-408344-7 : £49.90 : CIP rev. B81-39219

Kingdon, Jonathan. East African mammals : an atlas of evolution in Africa / Jonathan Kingdon. — London : Academic Press
Vol.3
Bibliography: p643-704. — Includes index
Pt.D: Bovids. — 1982. — 395-746p : ill,maps ; 29cm
ISBN 0-12-408345-5 : £49.90 : CIP rev. B81-39220

599.09712 — Western Canada. Mammals

Savage, Arthur. Wild mammals of Northwest America / Arthur and Candace Savage. — Baltimore ; London : Johns Hopkins University Press, c1981. — 209p : col.ill,col.maps ; 29cm
Bibliography: p177-200. — Includes index
ISBN 0-8018-2627-6 : £19.50 B82-22607

599.0973 — United States. National parks. Mammals

Van Gelder, Richard G.. Mammals of the national parks / Richard G. Van Gelder. — Baltimore ; London : Johns Hopkins University Press, c1982. — xvi,310p,[8]p of plates : ill (some col.),maps ; 23cm
Bibliography: p307-308. — Includes index
ISBN 0-8018-2688-8 (cased) : Unpriced
ISBN 0-8018-2689-6 (pbk) : Unpriced B82-40383

599.2 — Kangaroos — *For children* — *Welsh texts*

Hope, Ffransis. Y cangarŵ / [testun gan Ffransis Hope ; ymgynghorwr Berian Williams ; lluniau gan C. Teeuwisse]. — Caerdydd : Gwasg y Dref Wen, c1981. — 16p : ill(some col.) ; 22cm. — (Cyfres y seren)
Translated and adapted from the Dutch. — Cover title. — Text on inside covers
£0.85 (pbk) B82-10537

599.2′04132 — Marsupials. Digestive system. Physiology

Hume, Ian D.. Digestive physiology and nutrition of marsupials / Ian D. Hume. — Cambridge : Cambridge University Press, 1982. — ix,256p : ill,1map ; 24cm. — (Monographs on marsupial biology)
Bibliography: p231-252. — Includes index
ISBN 0-521-23892-7 : £25.00 : CIP rev. B82-19254

599.32′2 — Rabbits & hares — *For children*

Snow, Keith. I am a rabbit / Keith Snow ; [illustrated by] Ferelith Eccles Williams. — Kingswood : World's Work, c1982. — [32]p : chiefly col.ill ; 17cm
ISBN 0-437-76108-8 : £3.20 B82-30439

599.32′2 — Rabbits — *For children*

Feder, Jan. The life of a rabbit / Jan Feder ; illustrated by Tilman Michalski ; translated by Anthea Bell. — London : Hutchinson, 1982. — 32p : col.ill ; 25cm. — (Animal lives)
ISBN 0-09-145020-9 : £2.95 : CIP rev. B81-12323

599.32′32 — Beavers — *For children*

Clarkson, Ewan. Beavers / Ewan Clarkson. — Hove : Wayland, 1981. — 60p : col.ill ; 23cm. — (Animals of the world)
Ill on lining papers. — Includes index
ISBN 0-85340-853-x : £3.95 B82-16518

Lane, Margaret, *1907-*. The beaver / by Margaret Lane ; illustrations by David Nockels. — London : Methuen/Walker, 1981. — 28p : col.ill ; 23cm. — (Animal lives)
ISBN 0-416-05800-0 : £3.50 : CIP rev. B81-30455

599.32′32 — Red squirrels — *For children*

Sheehan, Angela. The squirrel / by Angela Sheehan ; illustrated by Maurice Pledger. — London : New Caxton Library Service, c1976. — [26]p : col.ill ; 23cm. — (Eye-view library)
Originally published: London : Angus and Robertson, 1976. — Ill on lining papers
Unpriced B82-13222

Wildsmith, Brian. Squirrels / [Brian Wildsmith]. — Oxford : Oxford University Press, 1974 (1979 [printing]). — [32]p : chiefly col.ill ; 29cm
ISBN 0-19-272105-4 (pbk) : £1.25 B82-08864

599.32′32 — Squirrels — *For children*

Lane, Margaret, *1907-*. The squirrel / by Margaret Lane ; illustrations by Kenneth Lilly. — London : Methuen/Walker, 1981. — [28]p : col.ill ; 24cm
ISBN 0-416-05820-5 : £3.50 : CIP rev. B81-25865

599.32′33 — Gerbils. Behaviour

Thiessen, Del. The gerbil in behavioral investigations : mechanisms of territoriality and olfactory communication / by Del Thiessen and Pauline Yahr. — Austin ; London : University of Texas Press, c1977. — xxi,224p : ill ; 27cm. — (The Dan Danciger publication series)
Bibliography: p203-221. — Includes index
ISBN 0-292-72709-7 : £18.30 B82-35393

599.32′33 — Great Britain. Harvest mice — *For children*

Coldrey, Jennifer. Harvest mouse / by Jennifer Coldrey ; photographs by George Bernard, Sean Morris and David Thompson. — London : Deutsch, 1981. — 30p : col.ill ; 20x25cm. — (Nature's way)
ISBN 0-233-97378-8 : £2.95 : CIP rev. B81-26745

599.32′33 — Hamsters — *For children*

Feder, Jan. The life of a hamster / Jan Feder ; illustrated by Tilman Michalski ; translated by Anthea Bell. — London : Hutchinson, 1982. — 32p : col.ill ; 25cm. — (Animal lives)
ISBN 0-09-145430-1 : £2.95 : CIP rev. B81-25667

599.32′33 — Mammals. Germ cells & somatic cells. Development. Mechanisms — *Study examples: Mice*

McLaren, Anne. Germ cells and soma : a new look at an old problem / Anne McLaren. — New Haven ; London : Yale University Press, c1981. — 119p : ill ; 22cm. — (Yale University Mrs. Hepsa Ely Silliman memorial lectures)
Bibliography: p97-113. — Includes index
ISBN 0-300-02694-3 : Unpriced : CIP rev. B81-22683

599.32′33 — Rats

Hart, Martin. Rats / Martin Hart ; translated by Arnold Pomerans. — London : Allison & Busby, 1982. — 172p,[24]p of plates : ill ; 23cm
Translated from the Dutch. — Bibliography: p167. — Includes index
ISBN 0-85031-297-3 : £8.95 : CIP rev. B80-09230

599.32′33 — Rats. Brain. Ventricles. Anatomy

Mitro, A.. Morphology of the rat brain ventricles, ependyma, and periventricular structures / A. Mitro and M. Palkovits. — Basel ; London : Karger, 1981. — 109p : ill(some col.) ; 29cm. — (Bibliotheca anatomica ; no.21)
Bibliography: p101-107. — Includes index
ISBN 3-8055-2546-x (pbk) : £31.00 B82-15410

599.32′33 — Wood mice — *For children*

Sheehan, Angela. The mouse / by Angela Sheehan ; illustrated by Maurice Pledger. — London : New Caxton Library Service, c1976. — [26]p : col.ill ; 23cm. — (Eye-view library)
Originally published: London : Angus and Robertson, 1976. — Ill on lining papers
Unpriced B82-13219

599.3′3 — Europe. Hedgehogs — *For children*

Sheehan, Angela. The hedgehog / by Angela Sheehan ; illustrated by Maurice Pledger. — London : New Caxton Library Service, c1976. — [26]p : col.ill ; 23cm. — (Eye-view library)
Originally published: London : Angus and Robertson, 1976. — Ill on lining papers
Unpriced B82-13220

599.3′3 — Hedgehogs — *For schools*

About the hedgehog. — Stirling : Scottish Panel of Advisers in Outdoor Education in conjunction with BP Educational Service, c1979. — 28p : ill,2maps ; 21cm. — (About ; 5)
Cover title. — Bibliography: p28
ISBN 0-86223-003-9 (pbk) : Unpriced B82-20678

599.5 — Dolphins & whales

Watson, Lyall. Sea guide to whales of the world / Lyall Watson ; illustrated by Tom Ritchie. — London : Hutchinson, 1981. — 302p : col.ill,col.maps ; 25cm
Ill on lining papers. — Bibliography: p287-297. — Includes index
ISBN 0-09-146600-8 : £12.95 : CIP rev. B81-24611

599.5 — Ireland. Coastal waters. Whales

Fairley, James. Irish whales and whaling / James Fairley. — Belfast : Blackstaff, c1981. — 218p : ill,maps,ports ; 22cm
Bibliography: p205-212. — Includes index
ISBN 0-85640-232-x : £8.95 : CIP rev.
Also classified at 639′.28′09415 B80-21929

599.5 — Marine mammals

Handbook of marine mammals / edited by Sam H. Ridgway and Richard J. Harrison. — London : Academic Press
Vol.2: Seals. — 1981. — xv,359p : ill,maps ; 24cm
Includes bibliographies and index
ISBN 0-12-588502-4 : £20.20 : CIP rev. B81-05120

599.5 — Whales

Ellis, Richard, *1938-*. The book of whales / written and illustrated by Richard Ellis. — London : Hale, 1981 [i.e. 1982], c1980. — xvii,202p,[24]p of plates : ill(some col.),1map ; 32cm
Ill on lining papers. — Bibliography: p161-194. — Includes index
ISBN 0-7091-9761-6 : £14.95 B82-27139

599.5 — Whales — *For children*

Simon, Noel. Whales / Noel Simon ; illustrated by Terry Riley. — London : Dent, 1981. — 46p : ill(some col.) ; 22cm. — (Animal families)
Text and ill on lining papers
ISBN 0-460-06957-8 : £3.25 : CIP rev. B81-28057

599.5′0451 — Cetacea. Behaviour

Gaskin, D. E.. The ecology of whales and dolphins. — London : Heinemann Educational, Sept.1982. — [480]p
ISBN 0-435-62286-2 : £19.50 : CIP entry B82-19675

599.5′3 — Dolphins

Doak, Wade. Dolphin dolphin. — London : Hodder and Stoughton, Mar.1982. — [250]p
ISBN 0-340-27225-2 : £12.95 : CIP entry B82-03103

599.5′3 — Dolphins — *Personal observations*

Dobbs, Horace E.. Save the dolphins / Horace E. Dobbs ; foreword by HRH the Duke of Edinburgh. — London : Souvenir, 1981. — 128p,[8]p of plates : ill(some col.),ports ; 23cm
ISBN 0-285-62437-7 : £7.95 B82-05024

599.5′3 — Southern hemisphere. Sperm whales. Food: Cephalopoda

Clarke, Malcolm R.. Cephalopoda in the diet of sperm whales of the Southern Hemisphere and their bearing on sperm whale biology / by Malcolm R. Clarke. — [Godalming] : Institute of Oceanographic Sciences, c1979. — iv,324p,[1]leaf of plates : ill ; 31cm. — (Discovery reports ; v.37)
Bibliography: p319-324
Unpriced (pbk) B82-13213

599.6′1 — Elephants

Eltringham, S. K.. Elephants / S.K. Eltringham. — Poole : Blandford, 1982. — x,262p,[8]p of plates : ill(some col.),maps ; 23cm. — (Blandford mammal series)
Bibliography: p248-255. — Includes index
ISBN 0-7137-1041-1 : £10.95 : CIP rev. B82-04498

599.6′1′0222 — Elephants — *Illustrations* — *For children*

Hewett, Joan. The mouse and the elephant / text by Joan Hewett ; photographs by Richard Hewett. — London : Angus & Robertson, 1981, c1977. — [28]p : chiefly ill ; 24cm
Originally published: Boston, Mass. : Little Brown, 1977. — Ill on lining papers
ISBN 0-207-14816-3 : £2.95 B82-10164

599.72′8 — Rhinoceroses

Martin, Esmond Bradley. Run, rhino, run. — London : Chatto & Windus, Sept.1982. — [128]p
ISBN 0-7011-2632-9 : £9.95 : CIP entry B82-20301

599.72′8 — Rhinoceroses — *For children*

Simon, Noel. Rhinos. — London : Dent, Oct.1981. — [32]p. — (Animal families)
ISBN 0-460-06065-1 : £3.50 : CIP entry B81-30452

599.73′4 — Hippopotamuses — *For children* — *Welsh texts*

Hope, Ffransis. Yr hipopotamws / [testun gan Ffransis Hope ; ymgynghorwr Berian Williams ; lluniau gan Jan van Wijngaarden]. — Caerdydd : Gwasg y Dref Wen, c1981. — 16p : ill(some col.) ; 22cm. — (Cyfres y seren)
Translated and adapted from the Dutch. — Cover title. — Text on inside covers
£0.85 (pbk) B82-10536

599.73′57 — Giraffes — *For children*

Simon, Noel. Giraffes. — London : Dent, Oct.1981. — [32]p. — (Animal families)
ISBN 0-460-06066-x : £3.50 : CIP entry B81-30453

599.73′57 — Great Britain. Deer — *Field guides*

Page, F. J. Taylor. Field guide to British deer. — 3rd ed. — Oxford : Blackwell Scientific, July 1982. — [96]p
Previous ed. : 1971
ISBN 0-632-00978-0 (pbk) : £3.95 : CIP entry B82-17960

599.73′57 — Scotland. Highland Region. Rhum. Red deer. Behaviour

Clutton-Brock, T. H.. Red deer. — Edinburgh : Edinburgh University Press, Sept.1982. — [400]p
ISBN 0-85224-446-0 (cased) : £18.00 : CIP entry
ISBN 0-85224-447-9 (pbk) : £9.00 B82-18776

599.73′58 — American bison. Taxonomy. Evolutionary aspects

McDonald, Jerry N.. North American bison : their classification and evolution / Jerry N. McDonald. — Berkeley ; London : University of California Press, c1981. — 316p,[16]p of plates : ill,maps ; 26cm
Bibliography: p286-309. — Includes index
ISBN 0-520-04002-3 : £24.50 B82-06995

599.73′58 — Antelopes — *For children*

Wootton, Anthony, *1935-*. Antelopes / Anthony Wootton. — Hove : Wayland, 1981. — 60p : col.ill ; 23cm. — (Animals of the world)
Ill on lining papers. — Includes index
ISBN 0-85340-850-5 : £3.95 B82-16517

599.7′3′58 — Uganda. Waterbucks. Territoriality

Spinage, C. A.. A territorial antelope : the Uganda waterbuck / C.A. Spinage. — London : Academic Press, 1982. — xvi,334p : ill,maps ; 24cm
Bibliography: p314-325. — Includes index
ISBN 0-12-657720-x : £24.00 : CIP rev. B82-00331

599.73'58 — Yaks — *For children*

Whitlock, Ralph. Llamas and yaks / Ralph Whitlock. — Hove : Wayland, 1981. — 60p : col.ill ; 23cm. — (Animals of the world)
Ill on lining papers. — Includes index
ISBN 0-85340-852-1 : £3.95
Also classified at 599.73'6 B82-16520

599.73'6 — Camels. Diseases

Singh, R. P.. Diseases of camels / by R.P. Singh, M.S. Vashishta, Chander Kala. — Hyderabad, India : Seven Seas ; Luton : Apex Books Concern [distributor], 1980. — x,47p ; 17cm
£1.40 (pbk) B82-33170

599.73'6 — Llamas — *For children*

Whitlock, Ralph. Llamas and yaks / Ralph Whitlock. — Hove : Wayland, 1981. — 60p : col.ill ; 23cm. — (Animals of the world)
Ill on lining papers. — Includes index
ISBN 0-85340-852-1 : £3.95
Primary classification 599.73'58 B82-16520

599.74 — Carnivores — *For children*

Riley, Terry, *1941-*. Lions : and other hunters of the plain / written and illustrated by Terry Riley. — London : Dean, c1982. — [26]p : ill (some col.) ; 28cm
Ill on lining papers
ISBN 0-603-00264-1 : £1.25 B82-29536

599.74'428 — Cats. Anatomy *compared with* **human anatomy**

Walker, Warren F.. A study of the cat : with reference to human beings / Warren F. Walker, Jr. — 4th ed. — Philadelphia ; London : Saunders College, c1982. — xi,244p : ill(some col.) ; 24cm
Previous ed.: 1977. — Bibliography: p236-238. — Includes index
ISBN 0-03-057914-7 (pbk) : Unpriced
Also classified at 611 B82-20598

599.74'428 — Feral cats. Social behaviour

Allaby, Michael. The curious cat / Michael Allaby and Peter Crawford. — London : Joseph, 1982. — 159p : ill,ports ; 25cm
Map on lining papers. — Includes index
ISBN 0-7181-2065-5 : £8.95 B82-14881

599.74'428 — Great Britain. Pumas

Francis, Di. Cat country. — Newton Abbot : David & Charles, Jan.1983. — [168]p
ISBN 0-7153-8425-2 : £4.95 : CIP entry
B82-32613

599.74'428 — India *(Republic)*. **Dudhwa. Wildlife reserves: Tiger Haven. Tigers** — *Personal observations*

Singh, Arjan. Tara : a tigress / Arjan Singh ; edited by John Moorehead. — London : Quartet, 1981. — xii,99p,[24]p of plates : ill (some col.),maps,ports(some col.) ; 29cm
Bibliography: p99
ISBN 0-7043-2282-x : £9.95 : CIP rev.
B81-16869

599.74'428 — India *(Republic)*. **Leopards** — *Personal observations*

Singh, Arjan. Prince of cats. — London : Cape, Oct.1982. — [208]p
ISBN 0-224-02034-x : £8.50 : CIP entry
B82-25161

599.74'428 — Kenya. Wildlife reserves: Maasai Mara Reserve. Lions — *Personal observations*

Jackman, Brian. The Marsh lions. — London : Hamilton, Sept.1982. — [224]p
ISBN 0-241-10827-6 : £12.50 : CIP entry
B82-18834

599.74'428 — Mammals. Physiology — *Study examples: Cats*

Donnelly, Patricia J.. Laboratory manual for anatomy and physiology : with cat dissections / Patricia J. Donnelly, George A. Wistreich. — New York ; London : Harper & Row, c1982. — xvii,636p : ill(some col.),forms ; 28cm
Includes index
ISBN 0-06-046644-8 (spiral) : Unpriced
B82-33815

599.74'428 — Tanzania. Wildlife reserves: National parks: Serengeti National Park. Lions — *Personal observations*

Hanby, Jeannette. Lions share. — London : Collins, June 1982. — [224]p
ISBN 0-00-216455-8 : £9.95 : CIP entry
B82-12710

599.74'442 — Foxes — *For children*

Lane, Margaret, *1907-*. The fox. — London : Methuen/Walker Books, Sept.1982. — [32]p. — (Animal lives ; 5)
ISBN 0-416-06350-0 : £3.50 : CIP entry
B82-19235

599.74'442 — Foxes — *Personal observations — For children*

Hill, Pat. Foxes in the family / Pat Hill ; photographs by Richard Smallwood. — London : Dent, 1981. — [46]p : ill,ports ; 22cm
Text and ill on lining papers
ISBN 0-460-06972-1 : £3.50 B82-02764

599.74'442 — Red foxes — *For children*

Sheehan, Angela. The fox / by Angela Sheehan ; illustrated by Bernard Robinson. — London : New Caxton Library Service, c1976. — [26]p : col.ill ; 23cm. — (Eye-view library)
Originally published: London : Angus and Robertson, 1976. — Ill on lining papers
Unpriced B82-13217

599.74'442 — Wolves — *For children*

Simon, Noel. Wolves / Noel Simon ; illustrated by Terry Riley. — London : Dent, 1981. — 45p : ill(some col.) ; 22cm. — (Animal families)
Ill on lining papers
ISBN 0-460-06975-6 : £3.25 : CIP rev.
B81-30451

599.74'443 — Giant pandas

Belson, Jenny. The giant panda book / Jenny Belson and James Gilheany ; foreword by Sir Peter Scott. — London : Collins, 1981. — 77p : ill,1map,1port ; 32cm
ISBN 0-00-216392-6 (pbk) : £4.95 : CIP rev.
B81-36991

Morris, Ramona. The giant panda. — Revised ed. — London : Kegan Page, Aug.1981. — [192]p
Previous ed. published as: Men and pandas. London : Hutchinson, 1966
ISBN 0-85038-489-3 : £7.95 : CIP entry
B81-20462

599.74'443 — Giant pandas — *For children*

Bonners, Susan. Panda / written and illustrated by Susan Bonners. — London : Scholastic, 1981, c1978. — [46]p : ill ; 19x23cm. — (A Hippo book)
Originally published: New York : Delacorte, 1978 ; London : Gollancz, 1979
ISBN 0-590-72054-6 (pbk) : £0.85 B82-15576

Pandas. — Poole : Blandford, 1982, c1981. — 30p : col.ill ; 25cm. — (Finding out about (Blandford))
Translation of the Japanese
ISBN 0-7137-1150-7 : £2.95 : CIP rev.
B81-04325

599.74'446 — Bears — *For children*

Riley, Terry, *1941-*. Bears : and other hunters of the north / written and illustrated by Terry Riley. — London : Dean, c1982. — [26]p : ill (some col.) ; 28cm
Ill on lining papers
ISBN 0-603-00265-x : £1.25 B82-29537

599.74'446 — Polar bears — *For children — Welsh texts*

Hope, Ffransis. Yr arth wen / [testun gan Ffransis Hope ; ymgynghorwr Berian Williams ; lluniau gan Kees de Kiefte]. — Caerdydd : Gwasg y Dref Wen, c1981. — 16p : ill(some col.) ; 22cm. — (Cyfres y seren)
Translated and adapted from the Dutch. — Cover title. — Text on inside covers
£0.85 (pbk) B82-10538

599.74'447 — Badgers

Briefly on badgers / produced by the Gwent Badger Group ; foreword by Eric Ashby. — [Newport] : [Gwent Badger Group], [1982?]. — 36p : ill ; 22cm
Bibliography: p35-36
ISBN 0-9506774-0-x (pbk) : Unpriced
B82-36024

599.74'447 — Common otters — *For children*

Sheehan, Angela. The otter / by Angela Sheehan ; illustrated by Bernard Robinson. — London : New Caxton Library Service, c1979. — [26]p : col.ill ; 23cm. — (Eye-view library)
Ill on lining papers
Unpriced B82-13215

599.74'447 — Great Britain. Common otters

Laidler, Liz. Otters in Britain / Liz Laidler. — Newton Abbot : David & Charles, c1982. — 200p : ill(some col.),maps ; 22cm
Bibliography: p191-196
ISBN 0-7153-8069-9 : £7.95 : CIP rev.
B81-36395

Weir, Vincent. The otter / by Vincent Weir for the Otter Haven Project of the Fauna Preservation Society and the Vincent Wildlife Trust. — London (21 Bury St., London EC3A 5AU) : Vincent Wildlife Trust, 1978. — 7p : ill ; 20cm
Unpriced (pbk) B82-24299

599.74'447 — Ireland *(Republic)*. **Common otters. Distribution**, *1980-1981*

Chapman, P. J. (Peter John), *1950-*. Otter survey of Ireland = Suirbhé dobharchú na h-Éireann 1980-81 / P.J. and L.L. Chapman. — London (Baltic Exchange Buildings, 21 Bury St., EC3A 5AU) : Vincent Wildlife Trust, 1982. — 40p : ill,1facsim,col.maps ; 30cm
Bibliography: p34-35
Unpriced (pbk) B82-35400

599.74'447 — Otters — *For children*

Simon, Noel. Otters / Noel Simon ; illustrated by Terry Riley. — London : Dent, 1981. — 45p : ill(some col.) ; 22cm. — (Animal families)
Ill on lining papers
ISBN 0-460-06974-8 : £3.25 : CIP rev.
B81-30454

599.74'447 — Otters — *Stories, anecdotes*

Williamson, Henry. Tarka the otter. — London : Bodley Head, June 1982. — [256]p
Originally published: London : Putnam, 1927
ISBN 0-370-30919-7 : £4.95 : CIP entry
B82-10482

599.74'447 — Scotland. Common otters. Distribution, *1977-1979*

Green, Jim. Otter survey of Scotland 1977-79 / Jim & Rosemary Green. — London (Baltic Exchange Buildings, 21 Bury St., EC3A 5AU) : Vincent Wildlife Trust, 1980. — 46p : ill (some col.),1form,col.maps ; 30cm
Bibliography: p39
Unpriced (pbk) B82-35399

599.74'447 — South America. Otters

Laidlet, Keith. The river wolf. — London : Allen and Unwin, Feb.1983. — [176]p
ISBN 0-04-599008-5 : £8.95 : CIP entry
B82-36447

599.74'8 — Northumberland. Farne Islands. Grey seals

Grey seals at the Farne Islands and the Isle of May 1979 and 1980 / editor Grace Hickling. — Newcastle upon Tyne (The Hancock Museum, Newcastle upon Tyne. NE2 4PT) : The Natural History Society of Northumbria, 1981. — 16p : 1map ; 25cm. — (Transactions of the Natural History Society of Northumbria, ISSN 0144-221x ; v.47)
Bibliography: p16
£0.80 (pbk)
Also classified at 599.74'8 B82-19916

599.74'8 — Scotland. Fife Region. Isle of May. Grey seals

Grey seals at the Farne Islands and the Isle of May 1979 and 1980 / editor Grace Hickling. — Newcastle upon Tyne (The Hancock Museum, Newcastle upon Tyne. NE2 4PT) : The Natural History Society of Northumbria, 1981. — 16p : 1map ; 25cm. — (Transactions of the Natural History Society of Northumbria, ISSN 0144-221x ; v.47)
Bibliography: p16
£0.80 (pbk)
Primary classification 599.74'8 B82-19916

599.74'8 — Weddell seals

Kooyman, Gerald L.. Weddell seal : consummate diver / Gerald L. Kooyman. — Cambridge : Cambridge University Press, 1981. — viii,135p : ill ; 24cm
Bibliography: p127-131. — Includes index
ISBN 0-521-23657-6 : £18.00 B82-09019

599.8'04132 — Primates. Teeth

Swindler, Daris R.. The teeth of primates / Daris R. Swindler. — Burlington, N.C. : Carolina Biological Supply Co., Scientific Publications Division, c1978 ; Chichester : Distributed by Packard. — 16p : ill(some col.) ; 25cm. — (Carolina biology readers ; 97)
Bibliography: p16
ISBN 0-89278-297-8 (unbound) : £0.80 B82-31604

599.8'04188 — Primates. Brain. Evolution — *Conference proceedings*

Primate brain evolution : methods and concepts / [based on the proceedings of a satellite symposium of the International Primatological Society Meeting, held July 4-5, 1980, in Turin, Italy, and of a symposium at the annual meeting of the American Association of Physical Anthropologists, held April 19, 1980, in Niagara Falls, New York] ; edited by Este Armstrong and Dean Falk. — New York ; London : Plenum, c1982. — xiii,332p : ill ; 26cm
Includes bibliographies and index
ISBN 0-306-40914-3 : Unpriced B82-22010

599.8'04333 — Primates. Foetuses. Endocrine system. Physiology — *Conference proceedings*

Fetal endocrinology / Miles J. Novy, John A. Resko. — New York ; London : Academic Press, 1981. — xv,423p : ill ; 24cm. — (ORPRC symposia on primate reproductive biology ; 1)
Includes bibliographies and index
ISBN 0-12-522601-2 : £23.80 B82-30017

599.8'04524 — Primates. Social organisation — *Conference proceedings*

Primate ecology and human origins : ecological influences on social organization / edited by Irwin S. Bernstein, Euclid O. Smith. — New York ; London : Garland STPM, c1979. — xviii,362p : ill,maps ; 24cm. — (Garland series in ethology)
Conference proceedings. — Includes bibliographies and index
ISBN 0-8240-7080-1 : Unpriced B82-21236

599.8'1 — Lemurs

Tattersall, Ian. The primates of Madagascar / Ian Tattersall. — New York ; Guildford : Columbia University Press, 1982. — xiv,382p : ill,maps ; 24cm
Bibliography: p341-365. — Includes index
ISBN 0-231-04704-5 : £28.80 B82-28063

599.8'2 — South America. Monkeys. Reproduction

Reproduction in new world primates. — Lancaster : MTP Press, June 1982. — [220]p
ISBN 0-85200-407-9 : £25.00 : CIP entry B82-21955

599.88'2 — Indonesia. Siberut. Beelow gibbons. Social behaviour — *Personal observations*

Whitten, Tony. The gibbons of Siberut / Tony Whitten ; foreword by Sir Peter Scott. — London : Dent, 1982. — xii,207p,[8]p of plates : ill(some col.) ; 24cm
Includes index
ISBN 0-460-04476-1 : £9.50 : CIP rev. B81-36199

599.88'4'096 — Africa. Great apes — *Conference proceedings*

The **Great** apes of Africa : proceedings of a symposium held at the Centre International de Récherche Medicale de Franceville, Gabon, West Africa, December 1979 / edited by R.V. Short and Barbara J. Weir. — Cambridge : Journal of Reproduction & Fertility ; Colchester : Biochemical Society Book Depot [distributor], 1980. — 173p,[18]p of plates : ill (some col.),1map,1plan,1port ; 26cm. — (Journal of reproduction & fertility, ISSN 0449-3087 ; supplement no.28)
Includes bibliographies
ISBN 0-906545-04-8 : Unpriced B82-10175

599.88'440451 — Netherlands. Arnhem. Zoos: Burgers Dierenpark *(Arnhem)*. **Chimpanzees. Social behaviour**

Waal, Frans de. Chimpanzee politics : power and sex among apes / Frans de Waal ; with photographs and drawings by the author. — London : Cape, 1982. — 223p : ill ; 24cm
Ill on lining papers. — Bibliography: p214-218. — Includes index
ISBN 0-224-01874-4 : £8.95 : CIP rev. B82-25157

599.88'460451 — Gorillas. Behaviour

Maple, Terry L.. Gorilla behavior / Terry L. Maple, Michael P. Haff. — New York ; London : Van Nostrand Reinhold, c1982. — ix,290p : ill ; 24cm. — (Van Nostrand Reinhold primate behavior and development series)
Bibliography: p271-282. — Includes index
ISBN 0-442-25152-1 : £27.20 B82-14304

599.9 — Man. Biology

Practical human biology / [edited by] J.S. Weiner and J.A. Lourie. — London : Academic Press, 1981. — xv,439p : ill ; 24cm
Includes bibliographies and index
ISBN 0-12-741960-8 : £16.00 : CIP rev. B81-13484

599.9 — Man. Biology — *For children*

Howard, Joanna. Me and you / Joanna Howard. — London : Macdonald Educational, 1982. — 30p : ill(some col.) ; 29cm. — (My first encyclopedia ; 1)
Includes index
ISBN 0-356-07817-5 : £2.95 B82-35811

600 — TECHNOLOGY

600 — Technological development — *Forecasts*

Clarke, Arthur C.. Profiles of the future. — New rev. ed. — London : Gollancz, Nov.1982. — [256]p
Previous ed.: 1973
ISBN 0-575-03210-3 : £7.95 : CIP entry B82-26563

600 — Technological innovation

Brave new world?. — Oxford : Pergamon, Dec.1982. — [188]p
ISBN 0-08-025847-6 : £7.95 : CIP entry B82-37509

Marsh, Ken. The way the new technology works. — London (76 Old Compton St., W1V 5PA) : Century, Nov.1982. — [224]p
ISBN 0-7126-0013-2 (cased) : £8.95 : CIP entry
ISBN 0-7126-0046-9 (pbk) : £6.95 B82-27036

600 — Technology

Vergara, William C.. Science in everyday life / William C. Vergara. — London : Sphere, 1982, c1980. — 306p : ill ; 20cm
Originally published: New York : Harper & Row ; London : Souvenir, 1980. — Includes index
ISBN 0-7221-8720-3 (pbk) : £2.50
Primary classification 500 B82-24544

600 — Technology — *Forecasts*

Outlook for science and technology : the next five years / a report of the National Research Council. — Oxford : Published in collaboration with the National Academy of Sciences by Freeman, c1982. — xx,788p : ill ; 24cm
Includes bibliographies and index
ISBN 0-7167-1345-4 (cased) : £18.50
ISBN 0-7167-1346-2 (pbk) : £10.95
Primary classification 500 B82-23933

600 — Technology — *Forecasts — For children*

Gatland, Kenneth. The Usborne book of the future : a trip in time to the year 2000 and beyond / Kenneth Gatland & David Jefferis. — London : Usborne, 1979. — 97p : ill(some col.),col.maps ; 29cm
Includes index
ISBN 0-86020-290-9 : £4.25 B82-17750

600 — Technology. Policies of governments

Tisdell, C. A.. Science and technology policy : priorities of governments / C.A. Tisdell. — London : Chapman and Hall, 1981. — xii,222p : ill ; 24cm
Includes index
ISBN 0-412-23320-7 : £12.00 : CIP rev.
Primary classification 500 B81-28835

600.2'42 — Books on medicine. Illustrations, *to 1982*

Thornton, John L.. Medical book illustration. — Cambridge : Oleander, Dec.1982. — [160]p. — (Oleander medical books series ; v.2)
ISBN 0-906672-07-4 : £15.00 : CIP entry B82-30745

601 — Technology — *Philosophical perspectives*

Feibleman, James K.. Technology and reality / James K. Feibleman. — The Hague ; London : Nijhoff, 1982. — xii,210p ; 25cm
Includes index
ISBN 90-247-2519-4 : Unpriced B82-40859

Thakur, Shivesh Chandra. Philosophy and the choice of a technology / S.C. Thakur. — [Guildford] ([Guildford, Surrey GU2 5XH]) : [University of Surrey], [1976?]. — 11p ; 21cm. — (University of Surrey inaugural lecture)
Cover title
Unpriced (pbk) B82-26649

601 — Technology — *Philosophical perspectives — Serials*

Research in philosophy & technology : official annual publication of the Society for Philosophy & Technology. — Vol.1 (1978)-. — Greenwich, Conn. : JAI Press ; London (3 Henrietta St., WC2E 8LU) : Distributed by JAICON Press, 1978-. — v. ; 24cm
Description based on: Vol.2 (1979)
ISSN 0161-7249 = Research in philosophy & technology : £28.90 B82-02350

601'.48 — Technology — *Abbreviations*

Pugh, Eric. Pugh's dictionary of acronyms and abbreviations : abbreviations in management, technology and information science / compiled by Eric Pugh. — London : Bingley, 1981. — 344p ; 30cm
ISBN 0-85157-292-8 : Unpriced : CIP rev. B81-13758

602'.18 — British goods. Standards — *Inquiry reports*

Great Britain. *Department of Trade*. Standards, quality and international competitiveness / Department of Trade. — London : H.M.S.O., 1982. — 22p ; 25cm. — (Cmnd. ; 8621)
ISBN 0-10-186210-5 (unbound) : £2.55 B82-38224

602'.2'2 — Great Britain. Architecture. Organisations: Architectural Association. Exhibits: European technical drawings — *Catalogues*

The **Engineers** / [... designed by Ron Herron and Tony Meadows]. — London : Architectural Association, c1982. — 48p : ill,facsims ; 18cm
Published to accompany an exhibition of books, prints and drawings at the Architectural Association, London, 1982
ISBN 0-904503-16-x (pbk) : Unpriced B82-27434

602'.3'41 — Great Britain. Technology — *Career guides*

Technicians in industry / [prepared jointly by COIC and the Central Office of Information]. — [London] : [Manpower Services Commission], [1982]. — 9v. : col.ill ; 30cm. — (Close-up)
ISBN 0-86110-196-0 : Unpriced
ISBN 0-86110-197-9 (CU83)
ISBN 0-86110-198-7 (CU84)
ISBN 0-86110-199-5 (CU85)
ISBN 0-86110-201-0 (CU86)
ISBN 0-86110-202-9 (CU87)
ISBN 0-86110-203-7 (CU88)
ISBN 0-86110-204-5 (CU89)
ISBN 0-86110-206-1 (CU90) B82-40365

602'.75 — Great Britain. Companies. Trade names — *Encyclopaedias*

Room, Adrian. Dictionary of trade name origins / Adrian Room. — London : Routledge & Kegan Paul, 1982. — 217p ; 24cm
Bibliography: p208-211
ISBN 0-7100-0839-2 : £7.95 B82-24528

603'.21 — Technology — *Encyclopaedias — For children*

Vincent, Hugh. A basic dictionary of technical terms. — London : Bell and Hyman, June 1981. — [48]p
ISBN 0-7135-1270-9 (pbk) : £1.60 : CIP entry B81-10478

603'.31 — Technology — *German & English dictionaries*

Dorian, A. F.. Dictionary of science and technology : German-English / compiled and arranged by A.F. Dorian with the cooperation of L. Da Costa Monsanto = Handwörterbuch der Naturwissenschaft und Technik : Deutsch-Englisch / zusammengestellt durch A.F. Dorian unter Mitarbeit von L. Da Costa Monsanto. — Amsterdam ; Oxford : Elsevier Scientific, c1970 (1978 [printing]). — 879p ; 23cm
ISBN 0-444-40848-7 : £61.82
Primary classification 503'.31 B82-09152

603'.31 — Technology - *German-English dictionaries*

Dorian, A. F.Dictionary of science and technology : German-English. — 2nd rev. ed. — Oxford : Elsevier Scientific, Aug.1981. — [1250]p
ISBN 0-444-41997-7 : CIP entry
Primary classification 503'.31 B81-16866

603'.41 — Technology — *French & English dictionaries*

Dorian, A. F. Dictionary of science and technology : French-English / compiled and arranged by A.F. Dorian. — Amsterdam ; Oxford : Elsevier Scientific, 1980. — 1085p ; 23cm
Added t.p. in French
ISBN 0-444-41911-x : £60.54 : CIP rev.
Primary classification 503'.41 B80-13355

604.2 — Engineering. Design. Technical drawings

Graphics in engineering design. — New York ; Chichester : Wiley
Series A. — c1980
Workbook 1: A general treatment of engineering graphics ... / A.S. Levens, F.H. Schneider, L.C. Walter. — 130leaves : ill ; 28cm
Ill, text on inside covers
ISBN 0-471-03133-x (pbk) : £5.00 B82-38645

Graphics in engineering design. — New York ; Chichester : Wiley
Series A. — c1980
Workbook 2: An emphasis on fundamental principles and applications of orthogonal projection with graphical solutions and computations / A.S. Levens, F.H. Schneider. — 125leaves : ill ; 28cm
Ill, text on inside covers
ISBN 0-471-03214-x (pbk) : £5.00 B82-38646

Graphics in engineering design. — New York ; Chichester : Wiley
Series A. — c1980
Workbook 3: An emphasis on engineering graphics in the design process : problems and project suggestions / A.S. Levens, W.S. Chalk. — 132p : ill ; 28cm
Ill, text on inside covers
ISBN 0-471-03215-8 (pbk) : £5.00 B82-38647

Jeary, L. N.. Engineering drawing I checkbook / L.N. Jeary. — London : Butterworth Scientific, 1982. — vi,154p : ill ; 20cm. — (Butterworths technical and scientific checkbooks)
Includes index
ISBN 0-408-00667-6 (cased) : £7.95 : CIP rev.
ISBN 0-408-00647-1 (pbk) : £3.95 B81-34113

604'.2 — Technical drawings

Collier, P.. Engineering drawing : second level / P. Collier & R. Wilson. — London : Hutchinson, 1982. — 238p : ill,plans ; 24cm. — (Hutchinson TEC texts)
Includes index
ISBN 0-09-146611-3 (pbk) : £6.95 : CIP rev. B81-22581

604.2'076 — Engineering. Design. Technical drawings — *Questions & answers*

Bland, Stuart. Graded exercises in technical drawing / Stuart Bland. — [Harlow] : Longman, [1982]. — iv,188p : ill ; 21x28cm
ISBN 0-582-65095-x (pbk) : £2.90 B82-36963

604.2'4 — Technical drawings. Draftsmanship

Engineering and industrial graphics handbook / George E. Rowbotham, editor in chief. — New York ; London : McGraw-Hill, c1982. — 1v.(various pagings) : ill ; 29cm
Includes index
ISBN 0-07-054080-2 : £37.95 B82-25220

Holmes, Clive. Beginner's guide to technical illustration / Clive Holmes. — London : Newnes Technical, 1982. — 166p : ill,plans ; 20cm
Includes index
ISBN 0-408-00582-3 (pbk) : Unpriced : CIP rev. B81-34161

604.2'4 — Technical drawings. Draftsmanship — *For civil engineering*

Jude, D. V.. Civil engineering drawing. — 2nd ed. — London : Granada, Nov.1982. — [176]p
Previous ed.: London : McGraw-Hill, 1971
ISBN 0-246-11752-4 (pbk) : £9.95 : CIP entry B82-27360

604.2'4 — Technical drawings. Draftsmanship — *For Irish students*

Goodison, P.. Technical drawing for leaving certificate : plane and solid geometry & building / P. Goodison and M. Ward. — Tallaght : Folens, c1981. — 269p : ill ; 30cm
ISBN 0-86121-148-0 (pbk) : Unpriced B82-01027

604.2'4 — Technical drawings. Draftsmanship — *For schools*

Barnett, P. J.. Technical drawing / P. Barnett. — London : Letts, 1982. — 222p : ill ; 19cm. — (GCE O-level passbooks)
Includes index
ISBN 0-85097-433-x (pbk) : £1.75 B82-31588

Cuthbert, B. G.. Graphical communication : a three-book course intended for students preparing for examination in graphical communication and technical drawing at the age of sixteen plus / authors B.G. Cuthbert, M.R. Pattenden. — Glasgow : Collins Educational
[Bk.1]. — c1982. — 96p : ill(some col.),maps,plans ; 30cm
ISBN 0-00-322050-8 (pbk) : £2.95 B82-26728

604.2'4 — Technical drawings. Draftsmanship — *For technicians*

Jeary, L. N.. Engineering drawing 2 checkbook. — London : Butterworths, Sept.1982. — [160]p
ISBN 0-408-00683-8 (cased) : £6.95 : CIP entry
ISBN 0-408-00648-x (pbk) : £3.50 B82-19216

Maguire, Dennis E.. Progressive engineering drawing for TEC students. — London : Hodder and Stoughton, July 1982. — [192]p
ISBN 0-340-26196-x (pbk) : £4.95 : CIP entry B82-12252

Yarwood, A.. Engineering drawing / A. Yarwood. — London : Cassell, 1982. — 176p : ill ; 25cm. — (Cassell's technical craft series)
Includes index
ISBN 0-304-30950-8 (pbk) : £4.95 B82-33761

604.2'4'076 — Technical drawings. Draftsmanship — *Questions & answers — For schools*

Donaldson, Stanley S.. Test papers in technical drawing. — 2nd ed. — Freeland : Technical Press, July 1981. — [104]p
Previous ed.: 1972
ISBN 0-291-39488-4 (pbk) : £3.95 : CIP entry B81-22575

Examination questions in technical graphics / [compiled by] B. Halliwell and S. Waterhouse ; drawings by Barry & Tim Davies. — Huddersfield : Schofield & Sims, 1982. — 96p : ill ; 24x30cm
ISBN 0-7217-4009-x (spiral) : £2.25 B82-40259

Green, J. N.. Technical drawing for GCE & CSE. — 3rd metric ed. — London : Bell & Hyman, Apr.1982. — [264]p
Originally published: London : Mills & Boon, 1974
ISBN 0-7135-2047-7 (pbk) : £3.50 : CIP entry B82-11089

604.2'5 — Blueprints. Interpretation — *Manuals*

Weaver, Rip. Blueprint reading basics / Rip Weaver. — Houston ; London : Gulf, c1982. — vii,295p : ill,plans ; 28cm
Includes index
ISBN 0-87201-075-9 (pbk) : Unpriced B82-39739

604.6 — Great Britain. Drinks containers. Re-use & recycling — *Proposals*

Study of returnable and non-returnable containers / Waste Management Advisory Council Packaging and Containers Working Party. — London : H.M.S.O., 1981. — 135p : ill ; 30cm
ISBN 0-11-512939-1 (pbk) : £6.50 B82-00431

604.6 — Waste materials. Recycling — *Manuals — For teaching*

Silverman, Eleanor. Trash into treasure : recycling ideas for library/media centers / by Eleanor Silverman. — Metuchen ; London : Scarecrow, 1982. — ix,138p : ill ; 28cm
Includes index
ISBN 0-8108-1489-7 (pbk) : £10.00 B82-17480

604.6'01'576 — Waste materials. Microorganisms — *For children*

Jansen, Mogens. Micro-life in rubbish / written by Morgens [i.e. Mogens] Jansen ; translated by E. Meyland-Smith ; edited by Su Swallow. — Harlow : Longman, 1981. — 31cm : ill (some col.) ; 23cm. — (A First look at microbiology)
Translated from the Danish
ISBN 0-582-39130-x : £2.50 B82-21055

605 — Alternative technology — *Serials*

Natta newsletter. — 1 (Sept.-Oct. 1979)-. — Milton Keynes (c/o Alternative Technology Group, Faculty of Technology, Open University, Walton Hall, Milton Keynes, Bucks.) : Natta, 1979-. — v. : ill ; 30cm
Six issues yearly. — Description based on : 10 (Mar.-Apr. 1981)
ISSN 0262-7221 = Natta newsletter : Unpriced B82-10349

607 — Technology. Information sources

Buchanan, H. J.. Information technology. — London : British Library, Science Reference Library, Oct.1982. — [15]p. — (Guide (British Library Science Reference Library), ISSN 0306-4298)
ISBN 0-7132-0707-8 (pbk) : CIP entry B82-33210

607 — Technology. Information sources. Directories. Feasibility studies

Parsons, R. B.. Report on the feasibility study and pilot project for a directory of sources of technical digests / R.B. Parsons. — London : British Library, 1982. — 155p in various pagings : ill ; 30cm. — (BL R & D report ; no.5691)
Unpriced (pbk) B82-16790

607'.01724 — Commonwealth developing countries. Technical education

Commonwealth Fund for Technical Co-operation. Commonwealth skills for Commonwealth needs / Commonwealth Fund for Technical Co-operation. — London (Marlborough House, SW1Y 5HX) : Commonwealth Secretariat, 1979. — 24p : ill(some col.),ports ; 25cm
Cover title
Unpriced (pbk) B82-40433

607'.068'8 — United States. Clothing. Retailing — *Manuals*

Segal, Marvin E.. From rags to riches : success in apparel retailing / Marvin E. Segal. — New York ; Chichester : Wiley, c1982. — xi,228p : ill ; 21cm. — (The Wiley small business series)
Includes index
ISBN 0-471-09156-1 (pbk) : Unpriced B82-39915

607'.12 — Secondary schools. Curriculum subjects: Crafts, design & technology. Projects — *For teaching*

Hodder, W. R.. Projects for design and technology in wood, metal and plastics / W.R. Hodder and S.L. Molesworth. — London : Murray, 1982. — 92p : ill ; 30cm
ISBN 0-7195-3952-8 (spiral) : Unpriced : CIP rev. B82-06048

607'.1241 — Great Britain. Secondary schools. Technical education

Harrison, Geoffrey. The British technic / by Geoffrey Harrison. — Sheffield : The Education Department, Stanley Tools, c1981. — 13p : 1ill ; 30cm. — (The Stanley lecture ; [4])
"At the Royal Society of Arts, London on Wednesday, 21st October 1981"
Unpriced (pbk) B82-29560

607'.208 — Latin America. Technology. Research — *Directories*

Latin American Newsletters. Science and technology in Latin America. — London : Longman, Dec.1982. — [320]p. — (Longman guide to science and technology ; 2)
ISBN 0-582-90057-3 : £39.00 : CIP entry
Primary classification 507'.208 B82-30069

607'.2'41 — Technology. Research in British institutions — *Directories*

Industrial research in the United Kingdom : a reference guide to organizations and establishments. — 9th ed. / Consultant editor Trevor I. Williams. — Harlow : Hodgson, 1980. — 872p ; 24cm. — (Reference on research)
Previous ed.: 1976. — Includes index
ISBN 0-582-90008-5 : £60.00 : CIP rev. B80-18748

607'.2'427 — Research & development by industries in Northern England

Buswell, R. J.. A survey of industrial research and development in the Northern Region / R.J. Buswell, M. Vallely. — [Newcastle upon Tyne] ([Department of Humanities, Ellison Place, Newcastle upon Tyne]) : [Division of Geography, Newcastle upon Tyne Polytechnic], [1979]. — i,62p ; 30cm. — (Occasional series in geography, ISSN 0142-6370 ; no.1)
Cover title. — Bibliography: p61-62
Unpriced (pbk) B82-06687

607'.34'7471 — New York *(City)*. Exhibitions: New York World's Fair *(1939-1940)*

Dawn of a new day : the New York World's Fair, 1939/40 / Helen A. Harrison, guest curator ; essays by Joseph P. Cusker ... [et al.]. — New York : Queens Museum ; New York ; London : New York University Press, c1980. — xi,123p : ill(some col.),1plan,ports ; 25cm
Published to accompany an exhibition held at the Queens Museum, New York, 1980
ISBN 0-8147-3407-3 (cased) : £22.30
ISBN 0-8147-3408-1 (pbk) : £11.10 B82-36625

607'.39 — Ireland *(Republic)*. Technologists. Awards — *Directories*

Gillick, Mary. Fellowships and scholarships available to Irish scientists and technologists / compiled by Mary Gillick and Diarmuid Murphy. — Dublin (Shelbourne House, Shelbourne Rd., Dublin 4) : The National Board for Science and Technology, c1978. — 102p ; 21cm
Includes index
£2.00 (pbk)
Primary classification 507'.9 B82-12736

607'.4 — Technology. European information sources — *Directories*

European sources of scientific and technical information. — 5th ed. / editors Anthony P. Harvey and Ann Pernet. — Harlow : Hodgson, 1981. — 504p ; 24cm. — (Reference on research)
Previous ed.: published as Guide to European sources of technical information / edited by Ann Pernet. 1976. — Includes index
ISBN 0-582-90108-1 : £75.00 : CIP rev.
Primary classification 507'.04 B81-32048

607'.41 — Great Britain. Technical education. Distance study

Open learning for technicians : report of an investigation carried out by Guildford Educational Services Ltd for the Council for Educational Technology, The Technician Education Council and The Manpower Services Commission / edited by John Twining. — Cheltenham : Thornes, 1982. — xii,259p : maps ; 22cm. — (S.T. (P) Handbooks for further education)
ISBN 0-85950-380-1 (pbk) : £7.50 : CIP rev. B82-08116

607'.42 — England. Secondary schools. Curriculum subjects: Crafts, design & technology

Technology in schools : developments in craft, design and technology departments / Department of Education and Science. — London : H.M.S.O., 1982. — 32p : ill ; 30cm
ISBN 0-11-270555-3 (pbk) : £2.25 B82-32956

607'.44 — France. Education. Curriculum subjects: Technology, *1808-1914*

The **Organization** of science and technology in France 1808-1914 / edited by Robert Fox and George Weisz. — Cambridge : Cambridge University Press, 1980. — x,355p ; 24cm
Bibliography: p333-341. — Includes index
ISBN 0-521-23234-1 : £15.00 : CIP rev.
Primary classification 507'.044 B80-25534

608 — Patent system

Grubb, Philip W.. Patents for chemists / by Philip W. Grubb. — Oxford : Clarendon, c1982. — x,273p : ill,facsims ; 24cm. — (Oxford science publications)
Includes index
ISBN 0-19-855153-3 : £20.00 : CIP rev. B82-04287

609 — TECHNOLOGY. HISTORICAL AND GEOGRAPHICAL TREATMENT

609 — Inventions, *to 1981* — *Encyclopaedias*

The **Inventions** that changed the world : an illustrated guide to man's practical genius through the ages / [consultant editor Gordon Rattray Taylor]. — London (25, Berkeley Square, W1X 6AB) : Reader's Digest Association, c1982. — 368p : ill(some col.),facsims,(some col.),ports ; 28cm
Includes index
£10.95 B82-23782

609 — Inventions, *to 1981* — *Illustrations* — *For children*

Burgess, Jan. Everyday inventions / Jan Burgess. — London : Macdonald, 1982. — 32p : col.ill ; 29cm. — (Eye openers!)
Includes index
ISBN 0-356-07095-6 : £2.95 B82-23732

609 — Technology — *History* — *Serials*

History of technology. — 6th annual volume (1981). — London : Mansell, Dec.1981. — [192]p
ISBN 0-7201-1634-1 : £18.00 : CIP entry B81-31535

609'.04 — Technology, *ca 1900-ca 1950*

Williams, Trevor I.. A short history of twentieth-century technology c.1900-c.1950. — Oxford : Clarendon Press, May 1982. — [352]p
ISBN 0-19-858159-9 : £12.50 : CIP entry B82-07520

609'.047 — Appropriate technology, *1965-1979*

McRobie, George. Small is possible / George McRobie. — London : Abacus, c1982, c1981. — xv,331p ; 20cm
Originally published: London : Cape, 1981. — Bibliography: p316-318. — Includes index
ISBN 0-349-12307-1 (pbk) : £3.25 B82-39056

609'.3611 — Scotland. Technology, *to 125* — *Conference proceedings*

Scottish Archaeological Forum *(11th : 1979 : University of Glasgow)*. Early technology in North Britain : Scottish Archaeological Forum 11 / edited by James Kenworthy. — Edinburgh : Edinburgh University Press, c1981. — 85p : ill,maps ; 24cm
Conference papers. — Includes bibliographies
ISBN 0-85224-398-7 (pbk) : Unpriced B82-02882

609'.41 — Great Britain. Industrial archaeology, *1900-1980*

Hudson, Kenneth. The archaeology of the consumer society. — London : Heinemann, Apr.1981. — [144]p
ISBN 0-435-32959-6 : £12.50 : CIP entry B81-03690

609'.41 — Great Britain. Technological innovation. Role of universities

Bailey, J. E.. University education for technological purposes / J.E. Bailey. — [Guildford] ([Guildford, Surrey GU2 5XH]) : [University of Surrey], [1976?]. — 24p : ill ; 21cm. — (University of Surrey inaugural lecture)
Cover title
Unpriced (pbk) B82-26642

609'.424'56 — Shropshire. Ironbridge Gorge region. Industrial antiquities

Teachers handbook / Ironbridge Gorge Museum. — Ironbridge : Ironbridge Gorge Museum Trust, 1981. — 36p : ill,facsims,maps,ports ; 30cm
Bibliography: p32-36
ISBN 0-903971-10-0 (pbk) : Unpriced B82-35603

609'.425'32 — Lincolnshire. Louth. Industrial antiquities — *Walkers' guides*

Louth industrial trail / [researched, written and produced by the Local History Group based at Louth Teachers' Centre]. — [Lincoln] : Lincolnshire Library Service, 1981. — 24p : ill,maps,plans ; 21cm
Cover title. — Originally published: Louth : Louth Teachers' Centre, 1977. — Text, map on inside covers
ISBN 0-86111-103-6 (pbk) : Unpriced B82-17261

609'.426'1 — Norfolk. Industrial antiquities — *Visitors' guides*

Alderton, David. Industrial archaeology in and around Norfolk / by David Alderton. — Telford ([The Wharfage, Ironbridge, Telford, Shropshire TF8 7AW]) : [Association for Industrial Archaeology in conjunction with the Norfolk Industrial Archaeological Society], [1981?]. — 23p : ill,maps ; 21cm
Bibliography: p3
Unpriced (unbound) B82-02705

609'.427 — North-west England. Industrial antiquities — *Gazetteers*

Ashmore, Owen. The industrial archaeology of North-West England / Owen Ashmore. — Manchester : Manchester University Press, c1982. — 241p : ill,maps,plans ; 24cm
Bibliography: p231-235. — Includes index
ISBN 0-7190-0820-4 : £9.50 : CIP rev. B81-22509

609′.428′19 — West Yorkshire *(Metropolitan County)*. **Leeds. Bank. Industrial antiquities** — *Walkers′ guides*

Leeds. — London : Published for the Yorkshire Archaeological Society, Industrial History Section by SELIA, 1981. — (Walks in industrial Yorkshire series)
1: The Bank / by Janet Douglas and Ken Powell. — 16p : ill,1map ; 22cm
ISBN 0-907370-00-4 (pbk) : Unpriced
B82-24431

609′.429′95 — Gwent. Blaenau Gwent *(District)*. **Industrial antiquities** — *Walkers′ guides*

Van Laun, John. The Clydach Gorge : industrial archaeology trails in a north Gwent valley / [devised, researched by John van Laun] ; [drawings by Michael Blackmore]. — 2nd ed. — [Brecon] : Produced by Brecon Beacons National Park Committee in co-operation with Gwent County Council, 1980. — 24p : ill,2col.maps
Cover title. — Previous ed.: 1980. — Text and illustrations on inside folded cover
ISBN 0-905293-05-3 (pbk) : £0.60 B82-31036

609′.51 — China. Technology — *History*

Needham, Joseph. Science and civilisation in China. — Cambridge : Cambridge University Press
Vol.5: Chemistry and chemical technology
Pt.4: Spagyrical discovery and invention : apparatus, theories and gifts / by Joseph Needham with the collaboration of Ho Ping-Yii and Lu Gwei-Djen and a contribution by Nathan Sivin. — 1980. — xlviii,772p : ill ; 26cm
Bibliography p510-692. — Includes index
ISBN 0-521-08573-x : £48.00 : CIP rev.
Primary classification 509′.51 B80-25535

609′.51 — China. Technology. Policies of government, *1949-1956*

Xu, Liangying. Science and socialist construction in China / by Xu Liangying and Fan Dainian ; edited with an introduction by Pierre M. Perrolle ; foreword to the English edition by Xu Liangying ; translated by John C.S. Hsu. — New York : Sharpe ; London : Distributed by Eurospan, c1982. — xxvii,225p ; 24cm. — (The China book project)
Translated from the Chinese
ISBN 0-87332-189-8 : Unpriced
Primary classification 509′.51 B82-23789

609′.51 — China. Technology, *to ca 1800*

Needham, Joseph. The shorter science and civilisation in China / an abridgement of Joseph Needham′s original text ; Colin A. Ronan. — Cambridge : Cambridge University Press
Vol.2. — 1981. — xii,459p : ill,charts,facsims ; 24cm
Vol.3 and a section of Vol.4, Pt.1 of the major series. — Bibliography: p389-394. — Includes index
ISBN 0-521-23582-0 : £15.00 : CIP rev.
Primary classification 509′.51 B81-31189

609′.56 — Middle East. Technology

Sardar, Ziauddin. Science and technology in the Middle East. — London : Longman, Nov.1982. — [350]p. — (Longman guides to world science and technology)
ISBN 0-582-90052-2 : £38.00 : CIP entry
Primary classification 509′.56 B82-26544

609′.6 — Africa. Technology — *Conference proceedings*

Technology & information : how can Africans help Africa? : conference report / by Africa Technology Discussion Group. — London (c/o Africa Educational Trust, Africa Centre, 38 King St., WC2E 8JS) : Africa Technology Discussion Group, c1982. — 43p ; 30cm
Cover title
£1.00 (pbk)
B82-23046

609′.99 — Outer space. Colonisation — *Forecasts*

Calder, Nigel. Spaceships of the mind / Nigel Calder. — Harmondsworth : Penguin, 1979, c1978. — 144p : ill(some col.) ; 26cm
Originally published: New York : Viking Press ; London : British Broadcasting Corporation, 1978. — Includes index
ISBN 0-14-005231-3 (pbk) : £3.95 B82-08026

610 — MEDICINE

610 — Medicine

Burton, J. L.. Essential medicine / J.L. Burton. — Edinburgh : Churchill Livingstone, 1981. — 157p : ill ; 25cm
'A version of this book was published in 1976 under the title "Aids to medicine for nurses"'. — Includes bibliographies and index
ISBN 0-443-02438-3 (pbk) : Unpriced : CIP rev. B81-18079

Companion to the life sciences / edited by Stacey B. Day. — New York ; London : Van Nostrand Reinhold
Vol.3: Life stress. — c1982. — xviii,409p : ill,1port ; 24cm
Includes bibliographies and index
ISBN 0-442-26294-9 : £28.90 B82-30959

610 — Medicine — *For general practice*

Practice : a handbook of primary care. — London : Kluwer, Nov.1982. — [938]p
ISBN 0-903393-59-x : £25.00 : CIP entry
B82-36296

610 — Medicine — *For medical assistants*

Bodanza, Mary F.. Clinical and laboratory procedures in the physician′s office / Mary F. Bodanza. — New York ; Chichester : Wiley, c1982. — x,313p : ill,forms ; 24cm
Bibliography: p297-298. — Includes index
ISBN 0-471-06497-1 : £13.50
Primary classification 610.69′53 B82-15405

610 — Medicine. Influence of technology — *Conference proceedings*

The **Technological** imperative in medicine / [proceedings of a Totts Gap colloquium held June 15-17, 1980 at Totts Gap Medical Research Laboratories, Bangor, Pennsylvania] ; edited by Stewart Wolf and Beatrice Bishop Berle. — New York ; London : Plenum, c1981. — ix,150p : ill ; 24cm
Bibliography: p143-145. — Includes index
ISBN 0-306-40889-9 : Unpriced B82-14452

610 — Medicine — *Welsh texts*

Edwards, Huw. Y pryfyn yn yr afal / Huw Edwards. — [Denbigh] ([Chapel St., Denbigh, Clwyd]) : Gwasg Gee, c1981. — 139p,17p of plates : ill,facsims ; 22cm
Includes bibliographies
£3.50 (pbk) B82-12198

610′.9′034 — Medicine, *1840-1940*

Biology, medicine and society 1840-1940 / edited by Charles Webster. — Cambridge : Cambridge University Press, 1981. — ix,344p : 1ill ; 23cm. — (Past and present publications)
Includes index
ISBN 0-521-23770-x : £22.50 : CIP rev.
Primary classification 306′.45 B81-30183

610′.1 — Medicine — *Philosophical perspectives*

Culver, Charles M.. Philosophy in medicine : conceptual and ethical issues in medicine and psychiatry / Charles M. Culver, Bernard Gert. — New York ; Oxford : Oxford University Press, 1982. — xi,201p : 1ill ; 22cm
Includes bibliographies and index
ISBN 0-19-502979-8 (cased) : £15.50
ISBN 0-19-502908-1 (pbk) : Unpriced
B82-37012

610′.14 — Medicine. Terminology

Progress in medical terminology / editor A. Manuila. — Basel ; London : Karger, c1981. — xi,116p ; 23cm
ISBN 3-8055-2112-x (pbk) : £23.00
B82-06293

Spatola, Anthony L.. Mastering medical language / Anthony L. Spatola. — Englewood Cliffs ; London : Prentice-Hall, c1982. — xiii,496p : ill ; 24cm
Includes index
ISBN 0-13-560151-7 (pbk) : £12.70
B82-16844

Young, Clara Gene. Learning medical terminology : step by step. — 4th ed. / Clara Gene Young, Miriam G. Austrin. — St. Louis ; London : Mosby, 1979. — xvi,351p : ill,forms ; 25cm
Previous ed.: 1975. — Bibliography: p322. — Includes index
ISBN 0-8016-5654-0 : Unpriced B82-19321

610′.1′5195 — Medicine. Statistical mathematics — *Conference proceedings*

European Symposium on Medical Statistics *(1980 : Rome)*. Perspectives in medical statistics : proceedings of the European Symposium on Medical Statistics, Rome, 1980 / edited by J.F. Bithell, R. Coppi. — London : Academic Press, 1981. — xviii,330p : ill ; 24cm
Includes bibliographies and index
ISBN 0-12-102520-9 : £22.00 : CIP rev.
B81-36059

610′.1′53 — Medicine. Physics

Brown, B. H.. Medical physics and physiological measurement / B.H. Brown & R.H. Smallwood. — Oxford : Blackwell Scientific, 1981. — viii,558p : ill ; 24cm
Bibliography: p546-548. — Includes index
ISBN 0-632-00704-4 : £14.00 : CIP rev.
B81-30473

Jensen, J. Trygve. Physics for the health professions / J. Trygve Jensen. — 3rd ed. — New York ; Chichester : Wiley, c1982. — xi,329p : ill ; 24cm
Previous ed.: Philadelphia : Lippincott, c1976. — Bibliography: p315-319. — Includes index
ISBN 0-471-08696-7 (pbk) : £9.75 B82-28947

610′.1′53 — Medicine. Physics — *Conference proceedings*

International School of Physics ′Enrico Fermi′ *(76th : 1979 : Varenna)*. Medical physics : proceedings of the International School of Physics ′Enrico Fermi′, course LXXVI, Varenna on Lake Como, Villa Monastero, 25th June-7th July 1979. — Amsterdam ; Oxford : North-Holland, 1981. — xvii,521p : ill ; 25cm
At head of title: Italian Physical Society
ISBN 0-444-85457-6 : £47.37 B82-13813

610′.1′535014 — Medicine. Applications of ultraviolet radiation

Diffey, B. L.. Ultraviolet radiation in medicine / B.L. Diffey. — Bristol : Hilger in collaboration with the Hospital Physicists′ Association, c1982. — ix,163p : ill ; 22cm. — (Medical physics handbooks, ISSN 0143-0203 ; 11)
Bibliography: p154-157. — Includes index
ISBN 0-85274-535-4 : £13.95 : CIP rev.
B82-04792

610′.1′535014 — Medicine. Applications of ultraviolet radiation — *Conference proceedings*

Hospital Physicists′ Association. *Conference on Ultraviolet Radiation and its Medical Applications*. Ultraviolet radiation and its medical applications : proceedings of the Hospital Physicists′ Association Conference on Ultraviolet Radiation and its Medical Applications / the Hospital Physicists′ Association. — [London] : The Association, c1978. — 46p ; 22cm. — (Conference report series ; 28)
Includes bibliographies
ISBN 0-904181-10-3 (pbk) : Unpriced
B82-14178

610′.1′9 — Medicine. Psychological aspects — *Conference proceedings*

International Conference on Psychology and Medicine *(1979 : Swansea)*. Research in psychology and medicine / edited by D.J. Oborne, M.M. Gruneberg, J.R. Eiser. — London : Academic Press
Vol.2: Social aspects, attitudes, communications, care and training / [based on the proceedings of the International Conference on Psychology and Medicine held under the auspices of the Welsh Branch of the British Psychological Society in Swansea from June 23-27 1979]. — 1979. — xv,488p : ill ; 24cm
Includes bibliographies and index
ISBN 0-12-523702-2 : £10.80 : CIP rev.
B79-34195

610′.207 — Medicine — *Humour*

Gordon, Richard, *1921-*. Bedside manners : a patient′s guide to doctors and hospitals / Richard Gordon. — London : Weidenfeld and Nicolson, c1982. — viii,172p : ill ; 22cm
ISBN 0-297-78104-9 : £6.50 B82-26753

610′.22′2 — Medicine. Illustrations. Rymsdyk, Jan van — *Critical studies*

Thornton, John L.. Jan van Rymsdyk : medical artist of the eighteenth century / by John L. Thornton. — Cambridge : Oleander, 1982. — ix,111p : ill,3facsims,2ports ; 22cm
Bibliography: p94-99. — Includes index
ISBN 0-906672-02-3 : £9.95 : CIP rev. B81-31519

610′.246171 — Medicine — *Questions & answers — For surgeons*

Primary FRCS revision book : multiple choice questions / edited by Mary L. Forsling, Peter H. Abrahams, Timothy J. Chambers. — Hemel Hempstead : Pastest Service, 1982. — viii,151p ; 22cm
ISBN 0-906896-07-x (pbk) : Unpriced : CIP rev. B82-04729

610′.28 — Bioengineering. Applications of biochemistry

Applied biochemistry and bioengineering / edited by Lemuel B. Wingard, Jr, Ephraim Katchalski-Katzir, Leon Goldstein. — New York ; London : Academic Press
Vol.2: Analytical applications of immobilized enzymes and cells. — c1981. — xiv,314p : ill ; 24cm
Includes bibliographies and index
ISBN 0-12-041103-2 : £28.20 B82-29603

610′.28 — Bioengineering — *Conference proceedings*

Biotechnology. — London : City of London Polytechnic, July 1982. — [33]p
Conference papers
ISBN 0-904264-65-3 : £3.50 : CIP entry B82-23838

Control aspects of prosthetics and orthotics. — Oxford : Pergamon, Jan.1983. — [238]p
Conference papers
ISBN 0-08-029350-6 : £30.00 : CIP entry B82-35199

610′.28 — Bioengineering — *Serials*

University College, London. *Bioengineering Centre.* Report / Department of Mechanical Engineering, Bioengineering Centre, University College London. — 1981-. — London ([Roehampton La., SW15 5PR]) : The Centre, [1981]-. — v. : ill ; 30cm
Annual. — Spine title: Bioengineering Centre report. — Continues: Great Britain. Biomechanical Research and Development Unit. Report
ISSN 0262-8619 = Report - Department of Mechanical Engineering, Bioengineering Centre, University College London : Unpriced B82-10113

610′.28 — Medical technology

Comprehensive review for medical technologists / edited by Alice M. Semrad. — 2nd ed. — St. Louis, Mo. ; London : Mosby, 1979. — xviii,222p : ill ; 22cm. — (Mosby′s comprehensive review series)
Previous ed.: 1975. — Bibliography: p209-210. — Includes index
ISBN 0-8016-4487-9 (pbk) : Unpriced B82-21893

610′.28 — Medicine. Biological materials — *Conference proceedings*

European Conference on Biomaterials *(2nd : Gothenburg : 1981)*. Clinical applications of biomaterials. — Chichester : Wiley, May 1982. — [350]p. — (Advances in biomaterials ; v.4)
ISBN 0-471-10403-5 : £16.00 : CIP entry B82-07987

610′.28 — Medicine. Laboratory techniques — *Manuals*

Basic medical laboratory technology / editor, Clive J.C. Kirk ; authors, R. Nigel Peel ... [et al.]. — 2nd ed. — London : Pitman, 1982. — xi,366p : ill ; 26cm
Previous ed.: Tunbridge Wells : Pitman Medical, 1975. — Includes bibliographies and index
ISBN 0-272-79630-1 : Unpriced : CIP rev. B81-34159

Gradwohl, R. B. H.. Gradwohl′s Clinical laboratory methods and diagnosis. — 8th ed. / edited by Alex C. Sonnenwirth, Leonard Jarett. — St. Louis ; London : Mosby, 1980. — 2v.(xxi,2339,201p) : ill(some col.),forms ; 28cm
Previous ed.: 1970. — Includes index
ISBN 0-8016-4741-x : £85.00 B82-39698

610′.28 — Medicine. Laboratory techniques. Reference values

Reference values in laboratory medicine : the current state of the art / [based on a NORDKEM workshop, Hanaholmen (Hanasaari), Espoo, Finland, 4-6 May 1980] ; edited by R. Gräsbeck, T. Alström ; discussions edited by H.E. Solberg. — Chichester : Wiley, c1981. — xiv,413p : ill ; 24cm
Includes bibliographies and index
ISBN 0-471-28025-9 : £18.75 : CIP rev. B81-34662

610′.28 — Medicine. Statistics. Visual presentation — *Manuals*

Charts & graphs : guidelines for the visual presentation of statistical data in the life sciences / editor Doig Simmonds ; contributors Gillian Bragg ... [et al.] ; illustrations Gillian Bragg. — Lancaster : MTP published in association with the Institute of Medical and Biological Illustration, 1980. — xii,93p : ill (some col.),2ports ; 23cm
ISBN 0-85200-293-9 (pbk) : Unpriced : CIP rev.
Primary classification 574′.028 B79-30071

610′.28 — Medicine. Techniques

Eknoyan, Garabed. Medical procedures manual / Garabed Eknoyan ; illustrations by Barry Baker. — Chicago ; London : Year Book Medical, c1981. — xii,230p : ill ; 22cm
Includes bibliographies
ISBN 0-8151-3053-8 (pbk) : £10.75 B82-18072

610′.28 — Medicine. Use of lasers — *Serials*

Lasers in medicine. — Vol.1-. — Chichester : Wiley, 1980-. — v. : ill ; 25cm
£39.50 B82-11802

610′.28 — Medicine. Use of ultrasonic waves

Morley, Patricia. Normal ultrasonic sectional anatomy. — Edinburgh : Churchill Livingstone, June 1982. — [240]p
ISBN 0-443-01690-9 : £24.00 : CIP entry B82-09712

610′.28′54 — Medicine. Applications of digital computer systems

Covvey, H. Dominic. Computers in the practice of medicine. — Reading [Mass.] ; London : Addison-Wesley. — (Addison-Wesley series computers in the practice of medicine)
Vol.1: Introduction to computing concepts / H. Dominic Covvey, Neil Harding McAlister. — c1980. — xv,266p : ill ; 24cm
Bibliography: p233-240. — Includes index
ISBN 0-201-01251-0 : £13.00 B82-08714

Kember, N. F.. An introduction to computer applications in medicine / N.F. Kember. — London : Edward Arnold, 1982. — ix,163p : ill ; 23cm
Bibliography: p149-154. — Includes index
ISBN 0-7131-4414-9 (pbk) : £7.25 : CIP rev. B82-01192

610′.28′54 — United States. Medicine. Applications of digital computer systems

Computers for medical office and patient management / edited by Stacey B. Day and Jan F. Brandejs. — New York ; London : Van Nostrand Reinhold, c1982. — ix,201p : ill,maps,1plan ; 24cm
Includes bibliographies and index
ISBN 0-442-21316-6 : £16.95 B82-23713

610′.3′21 — English language. Eponyms. Special subjects: Medicine — *Dictionaries*

Lourie, J. A.. Medical eponyms : who was Coudé?. — London : Pitman, Aug.1982. — [224]p
ISBN 0-272-79643-3 (pbk) : £4.95 : CIP entry B82-15713

610′.3′21 — Medicine — *Encyclopaedias*

Concise medical dictionary. — London : Corgi, 1982. — 695p : ill ; 20cm
Originally published: Oxford : Oxford University Press, 1980
ISBN 0-552-11934-2 (pbk) : £4.95 B82-21597

Dorland, William Alexander Newman. Dorland′s pocket medical dictionary. — 23rd ed. — Philadelphia ; London : Saunders, c1982. — xxi,754p ; 19cm. — (Saunders dictionaries and vocabulary aids)
Abridged from Dorland′s illustrated medical dictionary. — Previous ed.: 1977
ISBN 0-7216-3167-3 : £8.95
ISBN 0-7216-3166-5 (indexed copy) : £10.95 B82-31897

Playfair, A. S.. Purnell′s A-Z of family health : a guide to coping with illness and accident in the home / A.S. Playfair. — Bristol : Purnell, 1982. — 221p : ill(some col.) ; 20cm. — (A Charles Herridge book)
ISBN 0-361-05086-0 (cased) : £5.99
ISBN 0-361-05087-9 (pbk) : Unpriced B82-32753

Pocket medical dictionary / [checked and approved] in association with the Royal Society of Medicine. — Harlow : Longman, 1982. — 278p ; 12cm. — (Longman top pocket series)
ISBN 0-582-55546-9 (pbk) : £0.90 B82-29201

Stedman′s medical dictionary : illustrated. — 24th ed. — Baltimore ; London : Williams & Wilkins, c1982. — xlvii,1678p,24p of plates : ill (some col.),1port ; 26cm
Previous ed.: 1976
ISBN 0-683-07915-8 : Unpriced B82-19368

610′.3′9162 — Medicine — *Irish & English dictionaries*

Fiseolaíocht agus sláinteachas = Physiology and hygiene. — Baile Átha Cliath [Dublin] : Oifig an tSoláthair, c1981. — v,74p ; 24cm
At head of title: An Roinn Oideachais
Unpriced (pbk) B82-30527

610′.5 — Medicine — *For Middle Eastern countries — Serials*

Medical forum. — No.1 (1981)-. — Oxford (52 New Inn Hall St., Oxford OX1 2BS) : Medical Education Services, 1981-. — v. : ill ; 28cm
Quarterly
ISSN 0261-3646 = Medical forum : Unpriced B82-11813

610′.5 — Medicine - *Serials*

Advanced medicine. — 17. — Tunbridge Wells : Pitman Medical, July 1981. — [330]p
ISBN 0-272-79633-6 (pbk) : £16.50 : CIP entry
ISSN 0308-3888 B81-14784

610′.5 — Medicine — *Serials*

Advanced medicine. — 18. — London : Pitman, Aug.1982. — [496]p
ISBN 0-272-79686-7 : £17.00 : CIP entry
ISSN 0308-3888 B82-21378

The **Medical** annual. — 100th year. — Bristol : Wright, July 1982. — [416]p
ISBN 0-7236-0655-2 : £15.50 : CIP entry B82-17916

610′.6 — Medicine. Organisations — *Directories*

Directory of international and national medical societies. — Oxford : Pergamon, Sept.1981. — [350]p
ISBN 0-08-027991-0 : £29.00 : CIP entry B81-21585

610′.6′042 — Great Britain. General practitioners. Organisations: Royal College of General Practitioners, *to 1979*

The **Royal** College of General Practitioners. — Lancaster : MTP Press, Dec.1982. — [270]p
ISBN 0-85200-495-8 : £15.00 : CIP entry
B82-31306

610′.6′0421 — England. Physicians. Organisations: Royal College of Physicians of London — *Directories — Serials*

Munk′s roll. — Vol.6 (1966-1975). — Oxford : IRL Press, July 1982. — [550]p
ISBN 0-904147-38-x : £15.00 : CIP entry
B82-17986

610.69 — Great Britain. Medicine — *Career guides*

Careers in medicine. — Edinburgh : Scottish Council for Postgraduate Medical Education, 1982. — 80p ; 21cm
Text on inside covers
ISBN 0-905830-05-9 (pbk) : Unpriced
B82-27476

Humphries, Judith. Careers in medicine, dentistry and mental health / Judith Humphries. — London : Kogan Page, 1981. — 112p : ill ; 19cm
Bibliography: p112
ISBN 0-85038-514-8 (cased) : Unpriced : CIP rev.
ISBN 0-85038-515-6 (pbk) : £2.50 B81-34216

The **IHG** directory. — London : Kogan Page, Feb.1983. — [500]p
ISBN 0-85038-608-x : £25.00 : CIP entry
B82-39279

610.69′5 — Great Britain. *Medical Advisory Service.* **Local medical officers. Duties —** *Manuals*

Local medical officers′ guidebook. — [London] : Medical Advisory Service, Civil Service Department, 1981. — 22p ; 30cm
Includes index
Unpriced (spiral) B82-00558

610.69′5′0924 — Labrador. Christian medical missions. Grenfell, ***Sir*** **Wilfred —** *Biographies — For children*

Wilfred Grenfell : doctor in the frozen North. — London : Marshall, Morgan & Scott, Feb.1982. — [96]p. — (Heroes of the cross)
ISBN 0-551-00944-6 (pbk) : £0.95 : CIP entry
B82-07805

610.69′52′02541 — Great Britain. Medical profession — *Directories*

The **Medical** directory. — 138th annual issue (1982). — Edinburgh : Churchill Livingstone, Aug.1982. — 2v. ([3648]p.)
ISBN 0-582-90350-5 : £47.50 : CIP entry
ISSN 0305-3342 B82-17973

610.69′53 — Medical assistants. Duties — *Manuals*

Bodanza, Mary F.. Clinical and laboratory procedures in the physician′s office / Mary F. Bodanza. — New York ; Chichester : Wiley, c1982. — x,313p : ill,forms ; 24cm
Bibliography: p297-298. — Includes index
ISBN 0-471-06497-1 : £13.50
Also classified at 610 B82-15405

610.69′6 — Doctors. Communication with patients — *For general practice*

Bendix, Torben. The anxious patient : the therapeutic dialogue in clinical practice / Torben Bendix ; edited by H. J. Wright ; translated by Mogens Schou assisted by David M. Shaw and Douglas Henderson. — Edinburgh : Churchill Livingstone, 1982. — x,70p ; 22cm
Translation of: Din Nervøse Patient
ISBN 0-443-02295-x (pbk) : Unpriced : CIP rev. B82-09718

610.69′6 — Doctors. Interpersonal relationships with patients — *Conference proceedings*

Doctors, patients, and society : power and authority in medical care / edited by Martin S. Staum and Donald E. Larsen ; essays by David J. Roy ... [et al.]. — Waterloo, Ont. : Wilfred Laurier University Press for the Calgary Institute for the Humanities ; Gerrards Cross : distributed by Smythe, c1981. — xii,285p ; 23cm
Conference papers
ISBN 0-88920-111-0 (pbk) : £6.75 B82-33133

610.69′6 — Great Britain. Medical specialists. Professional conduct — *Manuals*

Osmond, A. H.. The complete medical consultant / by A.H. Osmond ; irreverently illustrated by A.B. Richard. — London : H.K. Lewis, 1982. — 114p : ill ; 23cm
ISBN 0-7186-0453-9 : £7.00 B82-27384

610′.7 — Medicine. Information sources

Information sources in the history of science and medicine. — London : Butterworth, Nov.1982. — [576]p. — (Butterworths guides to information sources)
ISBN 0-408-10764-2 : £18.00 : CIP entry
Also classified at 507 B82-29442

610′.7′11 — Medical schools. Curriculum subjects: Medicine. Teaching — *Manuals*

The **Medical** teacher / edited by Kenneth R. Cox, Christine E. Ewan. — Edinburgh : Churchill Livingstone, 1982. — xii,248p : ill ; 25cm
Includes index
ISBN 0-443-02446-4 (pbk) : £10.00 : CIP rev.
B81-34506

610′.7′1141 — Great Britain. Doctors. Professional education — *Inquiry reports*

Great Britain. *Parliament. House of Commons. Social Services Committee.* Fourth report from the Social Services Committee, session 1980-81 : medical education : with special reference to the number of doctors and the career structure in hospitals : together with the proceedings of the committee, the minutes of evidence and appendices. — London : H.M.S.O., [1981]
Vol.1: Report. — cxxxiip : ill,1map ; 25cm. — ([HC] ; 31-I)
ISBN 0-10-008961-5 (pbk) : £6.35 B82-03339

Great Britain. *Parliament. House of Commons. Social Services Committee.* Fourth report from the Social Services Committee, session 1980-81 : medical education : with special reference to the number of doctors and the career structure in hospitals : together with the proceedings of the committee, the minutes of evidence and appendices. — London : H.M.S.O., [1981]
Vol.2: Evidence : 26 November 1980-18 February 1981. — xv,513p ; 25cm. — ([HC] ; 31-II)
ISBN 0-10-008971-2 (pbk) : £13.85
B82-03340

Great Britain. *Parliament. House of Commons. Social Services Committee.* Fourth report from the Social Services Committee, session 1980-81 : medical education : with special reference to the number of doctors and the career structure in hospitals : together with the proceedings of the committee, the minutes of evidence and appendices. — London : H.M.S.O., [1981]
Vol.3: Evidence : 2 March-6 May 1981. — xvp,p514-1047 : ill ; 25cm. — ([HC] ; 31-III)
ISBN 0-10-008981-x (pbk) : £14.35
B82-03341

Great Britain. *Parliament. House of Commons. Social Services Committee.* Fourth report from the Social Services Committee, session 1980-81 : medical education : with special reference to the number of doctors and the career structure in hospitals : together with the proceedings of the committee, the minutes of evidence and appendices. — London : H.M.S.O., [1981]
Vol.4: Appendices. — xvp,1048-1181 : ill ; 25cm. — ([HC] ; 31-IV)
ISBN 0-10-009001-x (pbk) : £7.00 B82-03342

610′.7′1141 — Great Britain. Doctors. Professional education — *Proposals*

General Medical Council. *Education Committee.* Recommendations on basic medical education : issued in pursuance of section 15 of the Medical Act 1978 / General Medical Council, Education Committee. — [London] : [The Committee], 1980. — 29p ; 22cm
Cover title
Unpriced B82-15994

610′.7′1141 — Great Britain. General practitioners. Professional education. Vocational training

Gray, D. J. Pereira. Training for general practice / D.J. Pereira Gray. — Plymouth : Macdonald and Evans, 1982. — xii,324p : ill,forms ; 22cm
Bibliography: p229-241. — Includes index
ISBN 0-7121-2004-1 : Unpriced B82-16245

610′.7′1141 — Great Britain. General practitioners. Professional education. Vocational training — *Inquiry reports*

National Trainee Conference *(4th : 1980 : Exeter)*. Fourth National Trainee Conference : report, recommendations and questionnaire Exeter, 1980 / editors Clare Ronalds ... [et al.]. — London : Royal College of General Practitioners, 1981. — vii,84p : ill ; 28cm. — (Occasional paper / Royal College of General Practitioners)
Includes bibliographies
ISBN 0-85084-083-x (pbk) : Unpriced
B82-03485

610′.7′1141 — Great Britain. Medical personnel. Professional education. Curriculum subjects: National health services. Cooperation with welfare services — *Conference proceedings*

Symposium on Interprofessional Learning *(1979 : University of Nottingham).* Education for co-operation in health and social work : papers from the Symposium on Interprofessional Learning, University of Nottingham, July 1979 / [organized by] Central Council for Education and Training in Social Work ... [et al.] ; edited by Hugh England. — London : Journal of the Royal College of General Practitioners, [1980]. — 31p : ill ; 29cm. — (Occasional paper ; 14)
Bibliography: p31
ISBN 0-85084-075-9 (pbk) : £3.00
Primary classification 361′.007′1141
B82-40678

610′.7′114134 — Edinburgh. Universities. Medical schools: Edinburgh Medical School, *to 1900 — For schools*

Lobban, R. D.. Edinburgh and the medical revolution / R.D. Lobban. — Cambridge : Cambridge University Press, 1980. — 48p : ill,maps,ports ; 21x22cm. — (Cambridge introduction to the history of mankind. Topic book)
ISBN 0-521-22028-9 (pbk) : £1.95 B82-38819

610′.7′1142 — England. Doctors. Part-time postgraduate professional education — *Practical information*

Part-time in medicine. — London (7, Marylebone Rd, NW1 5HH) : Council for Postgraduate Medical Education, 1981. — 48p ; 21cm
Cover title
£2.00 (pbk) B82-08392

610′.7′1142 — England. General practitioners. In-service training — *Case studies*

Freeling, Paul. In-service training : a study of the Nuffield courses of the Royal College of General Practitioners / Paul Freeling, Susie Barry. — Windsor : NFER/Nelson, 1982. — xii,219p ; 22cm
Bibliography: p212-219
ISBN 0-85633-239-9 (pbk) : £8.95 B82-25347

610′.7′1142819 — West Yorkshire *(Metropolitan County).* **Leeds. Universities. Medical schools: Leeds School of Medicine,** *to 1981*

Anning, S. T.. A history of the Leeds School of Medicine : one and a half centuries, 1831-1981 / S.T. Anning and W.K.J. Walls. — [Leeds] : Leeds University Press, c1982. — xiv,170p : ill,facsims,maps,plans,ports ; 22cm
Includes index
ISBN 0-85316-131-3 : Unpriced B82-38333

610′.72 — Medicine. Research. Use of control groups

The **Case-control** study : consensus and controversy / edited by Michel A. Ibrahim ; co-ordinating associate editor Walter O. Spitzer. — Oxford : Pergamon, 1979. — viii,148p : ill,2ports ; 28cm
Conference papers. — Published as a special issue of Journal of chronic diseases. Vol.32, no. 1/2. — Bibliography: p145-148. — Includes index
ISBN 0-08-024907-8 : £13.00 : CIP rev. B79-23273

610′.7204 — Europe. Medicine. Research

Collaboration in medical research in Europe / [edited by David Evered, Maeve O'Connor]. — [London] : Ciba Foundation, 1981. — viii,153p ; 23cm. — (A Ciba Foundation study group)
Conference papers. — Includes bibliographies
ISBN 0-272-79634-4 (pbk) : Unpriced : CIP rev. B81-28121

610′.72041 — Great Britain. Medicine. Research — ***Directories***

Wiley medical research directory. — Chichester : Wiley, Feb.1983. — [650]p. — (A Wiley medical publication)
ISBN 0-471-10335-7 : £50.00 : CIP entry B82-38703

610′.72073 — United States. Medicine. Research & innovation

Biomedical innovation / edited by Edward B. Roberts. — Cambridge, Mass. ; London : MIT Press, c1981. — xvi,395p : ill ; 24cm. — (MIT Press series in health and public policy ; 3)
Includes bibliographies and index
ISBN 0-262-18103-7 : £19.25 B82-21009

610′.72073 — United States. Medicine. Research, ***1905-1945***

Harvey, A. McGehee. Science at the bedside : clinical research in American medicine, 1905-1945 / A. McGehee Harvey. — Baltimore ; London : Johns Hopkins University Press, c1981. — xix,554p : 1port ; 24cm
Includes index
ISBN 0-8018-2562-8 : £12.25 B82-06990

610′.7207526 — Medicine. Research by Johns Hopkins Medical Institutions, ***1889-ca 1960***

Harvey, A. McGehee. Research and discovery in medicine : contributions from Johns Hopkins / A. McGehee Harvey. — Baltimore ; London : Johns Hopkins University Press, c1981. — xiii,322p : ill,ports ; 29cm
Includes bibliographies
ISBN 0-8018-2723-x : £17.50 B82-17791

610.73 — Hospitals. Patients. Care. Participation of patients

Mutual goal setting in patient care / CURN Project ; principal investigator Jo Anne Horsley ; project director Joyce Crane ; the protocol manuscript for this book was prepared by Karen B. Haller, Margaret A. Reynolds. — New York ; London : Grune & Stratton, c1982. — xvii,95p : ill ; 23cm. — (Using research to improve nursing practice)
Bibliography: p91-92. — Includes index
ISBN 0-8089-1436-7 (spiral) : £9.60 B82-32778

610.73 — Medicine. Nursing

Baillière's pocket book of ward information. — 13th ed. / Douglas Middleton. — London : Baillière Tindal, 1980. — 205p : ill ; 14cm
Previous ed.: 1971. — Includes index
ISBN 0-7020-0819-2 (pbk) : £1.10 : CIP rev. B80-24485

Bower, Fay Louise. The process of planning nursing care : nursing practice models / Fay Louise Bower. — 3rd ed. — St. Louis ; London : Mosby, 1982. — xii,207p : ill ; 23cm
Previous ed.: 1977. — Bibliography: p196-199. — Includes index
ISBN 0-8016-0721-3 (pbk) : £7.25 B82-31871

Brunt, Marguerita. Physiology of nursing. — London : Harper and Row, May 1982. — [256]p
ISBN 0-06-318227-0 (pbk) : £6.50 : CIP entry B82-07985

Chapple, Mary. Fundamentals of nursing / Mary Chapple, Annette Drew. — London : McGraw-Hill, c1981. — 246p : ill ; 24cm. — (McGraw-Hill nursing studies series)
Bibliography: p234-235. — Includes index
ISBN 0-07-084237-x (pbk) : £4.50 B82-14990

Coakley, Davis. Nursing and the doctor. — London : Pitman, May 1982. — [208]p
ISBN 0-272-79649-2 : £9.95 : CIP entry B82-07416

Dison, Norma. Clinical nursing techniques / Norma Dison. — 4th ed. — St. Louis ; London : C.V. Mosby, 1979. — xiv,491p : ill ; 24cm
Previous ed.: 1975. — Includes bibliographies and index
ISBN 0-8016-1308-6 (pbk) : £12.00 B82-33562

Handbook of nursing procedures / edited by Mary E. Scholes, Jane L. Wilson, Sheila Macrae. — Oxford : Blackwell Scientific, 1982. — viii,371p : col.ill ; 19cm
Includes index
ISBN 0-632-00687-0 (pbk) : £4.80 : CIP rev. B81-34783

Hegyvary, Sue Thomas. The change to primary nursing : a cross-cultural view of professional nursing practice / Sue Thomas Hegyvary. — St. Louis, Mo. ; London : Mosby, 1982. — xiii,190p : ill ; 23cm
Includes index
ISBN 0-8016-2127-5 (pbk) : £8.50 B82-34464

McFarlane of Llandaff, Jean Kennedy McFarlane, ***Baroness***. A guide to the practice of nursing using the nursing process. — London : Year Book Medical Publishers, July 1982. — [120]p
ISBN 0-8016-3278-1 (pbk) : £4.50 : CIP entry B82-16490

Medical-surgical nursing : concepts and clinical practice : with 731 illustrations Barbara C. Long, Nancy Fugate Woods. — St. Louis ; London : Mosby, 1979. — xiv,1634p : ill ; 29cm
Includes bibliographies and index
ISBN 0-8016-3932-8 : £25.50 B82-24892

Narrow, Barbara W.. Fundamentals of nursing practice / Barbara W. Narrow, Kay Brown Buschle. — New York ; Chichester : Wiley, c1982. — xxvi,676p : ill ; 29cm. — (A Wiley medical publication)
Ill on lining papers. — Includes bibliographies and index
ISBN 0-471-05950-1 : Unpriced B82-19898

The **Nursing** process : a scientific approach to nursing care / [compiled by] Ann Marriner. — 2nd ed. — St. Louis ; London : Mosby, 1979. — x,276p : ill,1form ; 25cm
Previous ed.: 1975. — Includes bibliographies and index
ISBN 0-8016-3122-x (pbk) : £8.75 B82-24781

Nursing process : application of theories, frameworks, and models / edited by Janet W. Griffith, Paula J. Christensen. — St. Louis, Mo. ; London : Mosby, 1982. — xii,301p : ill,2ports ; 28cm
Includes bibliographies and index
ISBN 0-8016-1984-x (pbk) : £7.75 B82-34463

Nursing science in nursing practice / [edited by] James P. Smith. — London : Butterworths, 1981. — vii,272p : ill ; 22cm
Includes bibliographies and index
ISBN 0-407-00202-2 (pbk) : Unpriced B82-00554

Roper, Nancy. Principles of nursing / Nancy Roper. — 3rd ed. — Edinburgh : Churchill Livingstone, 1982. — viii,388p : ill ; 21cm. — (Churchill Livingstone nursing texts)
Previous ed.: 1973. — Includes bibliographies and index
ISBN 0-443-02343-3 (pbk) : £4.25 : CIP rev. B81-34001

Spencer, May. Introduction to nursing / May Spencer, Katherine M. Tait. — 5th ed. — Oxford : Blackwell Scientific, 1981. — x,528p : ill ; 24cm
Previous ed.: 1976. — Includes bibliographies and index
ISBN 0-632-00705-2 (pbk) : £7.50 : CIP rev. B81-30999

610.73 — Medicine. Nursing — ***Early works***

Nightingale, Florence. Notes on nursing : what it is and what it is not / Florence Nightingale. — Edinburgh : Churchill Livingstone, 1980. — 2v. ; 23cm
Originally published: London : Harrison, 1859. — In slip case. — Includes: Notes on nursing : the science and the art / by Muriel Skeet
ISBN 0-443-02130-9 : £7.95 : CIP rev. B80-10618

610.73 — Medicine. Nursing — ***Manuals***

Brunner, Lillian. Lippincott manual of medical-surgical nursing. — London : Harper and Row, June 1982
Vol.1. — [512]p
ISBN 0-06-318207-6 : £5.95 : CIP entry B82-11282

Brunner, Lillian. Lippincott manual of medical-surgical nursing. — London : Harper and Row, June 1982
Vol.2. — [512]p
ISBN 0-06-318208-4 : £5.95 : CIP entry B82-11283

Brunner, Lillian. Lippincott manual of medical-surgical nursing. — London : Harper and Row, June 1982
Vol.3. — [512]p
ISBN 0-06-318209-2 : £5.95 : CIP entry B82-11284

Medical-surgical nursing. — 6th ed., International student ed. / Kathleen Newton Shafer ... [et al] ; British version prepared by Janet Spruce. — St. Louis, Mo. ; London : Mosby, 1979, c1975. — xvi,1031p : ill ; 26cm
Previous ed.: 1971. — Includes bibliographies and index
ISBN 0-8016-4511-5 (pbk) : Unpriced B82-21883

610.73 — Medicine. Nursing. Problem oriented systems — ***Manuals***

Vaughan-Wrobel, Beth C.. The problem-oriented system in nursing : a workbook / Beth C. Vaughan-Wrobel, Betty S. Henderson. — 2nd ed. — St. Louis, Mo. ; London : Mosby, 1982. — xii,194p : ill,forms ; 24cm
Previous ed.: 1976. — Includes bibliographies and index
ISBN 0-8016-5222-7 (pbk) : £8.50 B82-31862

610.73 — Medicine. Practical nursing

Becker, Betty Glore. Vocational and personal adjustment in practical nursing / Betty Glore Becker, Dolores T. Fendler. — 4th ed. / with a chapter on ethical and legal aspects by Laura Reilly and James Abrams. — St. Louis ; London : Mosby, 1982. — ix,180p : ill ; 23cm
Previous ed.: 1978. — Includes bibliographies and index
ISBN 0-8016-0566-0 (pbk) : £7.50
Also classified at 302′.024613 B82-31870

Mosby's review of practical nursing. — 8th ed. / Mary Elizabeth Faircloth ... [et al.]. — St. Louis ; London : Mosby, 1982. — 352,[29]p : ill,forms ; 24cm
Previous ed.: 1978. — Includes bibliographies and index
ISBN 0-8016-3538-1 (pbk) : £9.25 B82-31882

610.73 — Patients. Lifting & carrying — ***Manuals***

The **Handling** of patients : a guide for nurse managers / by Paul Lloyd ... [et al.] ; and the design and illustrations by Don Charlesworth. — Teddington : Back Pain Association in conjunction with the Royal College of Nursing, 1981. — 46p : ill(some col.) ; 30cm
Bibliography: p44
ISBN 0-9507726-0-7 (spiral) B82-11957

610.73 — Patients. Lifting & carrying — *Manuals continuation*

Hollis, Margaret. Safer lifting for patient care / Margaret Hollis ; with a foreword by P.R. Davis. — Oxford : Blackwell Scientific, 1981. — xiii,138p : ill ; 19cm
Bibliography: p133-134. — Includes index
ISBN 0-632-00825-3 (pbk) : £4.80 : CIP rev. B81-32024

610.73'09756 — United States. General practice. Nursing — *Study regions: North Carolina*

Yedidia, Michael J.. Delivering primary health care : nurse practitioners at work / Michael J. Yedidia. — Boston, Mass. : Auburn House ; London : distributed by Eurospan, c1981. — xviii,152p ; 24cm
Includes index
ISBN 0-86569-075-8 : £14.95 B82-08670

610.73'01'9 — Medicine. Nursing. Psychological aspects

Jasmin, Sylvia. Behavioral concepts and the nursing process / Sylvia Jasmin, Louise N. Trygstad. — St. Louis ; London : Mosby, 1979. — ix,193p : ill ; 23cm
Includes index
ISBN 0-8016-2435-5 (pbk) : £8.00 B82-28168

610.73'05 — Medicine. Nursing — *Serials*

Recent advances in nursing. — 3. — Edinburgh : Churchill Livingstone, Feb.1982. — [256]p
ISBN 0-443-01935-5 : £7.00 : CIP entry
ISSN 0144-6592 B81-35717

Recent advances in nursing. — 5. — Edinburgh : Churchill Livingstone, Nov.1982. — [220]p
ISBN 0-443-02367-0 (pbk) : £6.95 : CIP entry
ISSN 0144-6592 B82-27539

610.73'068 — United States. Medicine. Nursing. Management

Contemporary nursing management : issues and practice / edited by Ann Marriner. — St. Louis ; London : Mosby, 1982. — xi,403p : ill,forms ; 24cm
Includes bibliographies and index
ISBN 0-8016-3168-8 (pbk) : £9.25 B82-31880

610.73'06'9 — England. Medicine. Nursing. Attitudes of ward sisters

Redfern, Sally J.. Hospital sisters. — London (Henrietta Place, W1M 0AB) : Royal College of Nursing, July 1981. — [123]p
ISBN 0-902606-65-4 : £4.00 : CIP entry B81-20644

610.73'06'9 — Medicine. Nursing. Change. Role of nurses

The **Nurse** as a change agent / edited by Jeanette Lancaster, Wade Lancaster. — St. Louis ; London : Mosby, 1982. — xv,476p : ill ; 24cm. — (Concepts for advanced nursing practice)
Includes bibliographies and index
ISBN 0-8016-2832-6 (pbk) : £9.75 B82-22834

610.73'06'99 — Hospitals. Nurses. Nonverbal communication with patients

Blondis, Marion Nesbitt. Nonverbal communication with patients : back to the human touch / Marion Nesbitt Blondis, Barbara E. Jackson. — 2nd ed. — New York ; Chichester : Wiley, c1982. — xvii,260p ; 22cm
Previous ed.: 1977. — Bibliography: p249-251. — Includes index
ISBN 0-471-08217-1 (pbk) : £8.75 B82-25864

610.73'06'99 — Hospitals. Ward sisters. Interpersonal relationships with student nurses

Ogier, Margaret E.. An ideal sister? : a study of the leadership style and verbal interactions of ward sisters with nurse learners in general hospitals. — London : Royal College of Nursing, Jan.1982. — [82]p
ISBN 0-902606-68-9 (pbk) : £3.25 : CIP entry B82-00175

610.73'06'99 — Medicine. Nursing. Communication

Bradley, Jean C.. Communication in the nursing context / Jean C. Bradley, Mark A. Edinberg. — New York : Appleton-Century-Crofts ; London : Prentice-Hall, c1982. — xiii,353p : ill ; 23cm
Includes bibliographies and index
ISBN 0-8385-1180-5 (pbk) : Unpriced B82-34726

Ceccio, Joseph F.. Effective communication in nursing : theory and practice / Joseph F. Ceccio, Cathy M. Ceccio. — New York ; Chichester : Wiley, c1982. — xi,315p : ill,forms ; 24cm
Includes bibliographies and index
ISBN 0-471-07911-1 (pbk) : £10.25 B82-25866

610.73'06'99 — United States. Medicine. Nursing. Leadership

Moloney, Margaret M.. Leadership in nursing : theory, strategies and action / Margaret M. Moloney. — St. Louis ; London : Mosby, 1979. — xiv,221p : ill ; 24cm
Includes bibliographies and index
ISBN 0-8016-3471-7 (pbk) : £9.50 B82-24780

610.73'07'11 — Nurses. Professional education

Nursing education. — Edinburgh : Churchill Livingstone, Aug.1982. — [224]p. — (Recent advances in nursing, ISSN 0144-6592 ; 4)
ISBN 0-443-02496-0 (pbk) : £6.50 : CIP entry B82-15800

610.73'07'11 — Nurses. Professional education. Curriculum. Planning

Torres, Gertrude. Curriculum process in nursing : a guide to curriculum development / Gertrude Torres, Marjorie Stanton. — Englewood Cliffs ; London : Prentice-Hall, c1982. — x,198p ; 24cm
Bibliography: p179-191. — Includes index
ISBN 0-13-196261-2 : £12.70 B82-20079

610.73'07'1141 — Great Britain. Hospitals. Ward sisters. Professional education

The **Ward** sister : her role and preparation. — London : Baillière Tindall, Sept.1982. — [192]p
ISBN 0-7020-0950-4 (pbk) : £6.75 : CIP entry B82-20009

610.73'07'1142 — England. Nurses. Professional education. Joint Board of Clinical Nursing Studies approved courses. Students. Assessment

Joint Board of Clinical Nursing Studies. Assessment strategy : guidance for staff involved in Joint Board courses. — London (178-202 Great Portland St, W1N 5TB) : The Joint Board of Clinical Nursing Studies, 1982. — 16p : 1ill ; 21cm. — (Occasional publication ; 4)
Cover title. — Bibliography: p16
Unpriced (pbk) B82-38207

610.73'071'142 — Great Britain. Hospitals. Wards. Student nurses. Professional education. Role of head nurses

Orton, Helen D.. Ward learning climate. — London : Royal College of Nursing, Nov.1981. — [95]p
ISBN 0-902606-67-0 (pbk) : £4.00 : CIP entry B81-34958

610.73'072 — Medicine. Nursing. Research

Research — a base for the future? : proceedings. — [Edinburgh] : University of Edinburgh, Nursing Studies Research Unit, c1982. — ix,590p : ill ; 21cm
Includes bibliographies
ISBN 0-9507824-0-8 (pbk) : Unpriced B82-37430

610.73'072 — Medicine. Nursing. Research. Methodology

Treece, Eleanor Walters. Elements of research in nursing / Eleanor Walters Treece, James William Treece, Jr. — 3rd ed. — St. Louis, Mo. ; London : Mosby, 1982. — vii,424p : ill,forms ; 24cm
Previous ed.: 1977. — Includes bibliographies and index
ISBN 0-8016-5109-3 (pbk) : £11.25 B82-34468

610.73'076 — Medicine. Nursing — *Questions & answers*

Copcutt, Lynn. SRN 2 : case histories and objective test questions for student nurses. — Hemel Hempstead : PasTest Service, Dec.1982. — [112]p
ISBN 0-906896-09-6 : £3.75 : CIP entry B82-36151

Hull, E. J.. Do-it-yourself revision for nurses / E.J. Hull and B.J. Isaacs. — 2nd ed. — London : Baillière Tindall, 1982. — 4v. : ill ; 20cm
Previous ed.: in 6 vols. 1970. — Includes bibliographies
ISBN 0-7020-0911-3 (pbk) : Unpriced : CIP rev.
ISBN 0-7020-0912-1 (pbk) : £2.50
ISBN 0-7020-0913-x (pbk) : £2.50
ISBN 0-7020-0914-8 (pbk) : £2.50 B81-37567

Mosby's assess test : for evaluation of basic professional nursing knowledge / [editor Dolores F. Saxton] ; [associate editors Phyllis K. Pelikan, Patricia M. Nugent, Selma R. Needleman] ; [statistical consultant William H. Ward] ; [consultant Patricia Ryan]. — St. Louis, Mo. ; London : Mosby, 1982. — vii,86p : 1facsim,forms ; 28cm
ISBN 0-8016-4326-0 (pbk) : £16.50 B82-34466

Multiple choice questions. — London : Baillière Tindall. — (Nurses' aids series)
Psychology for nurses / Annie Altschul. Pharmacology for nurses / Rosemary E. Bailey. — 1980. — xiii,74p : ill ; 18cm
ISBN 0-7020-0723-4 (pbk) : £1.50 : CIP rev. B79-37324

Riddle, Janet T. E.. Objective tests for nurses / compiled and edited by Janet T.E. Riddle. — Edinburgh : Churchill Livingstone
Bk.3: The circulatory system and the respiratory system / with contributions from Joan Dinner, May Lee, Rosa M. Sacharin ; foreword by Margaret W. Thomson. — 1981. — 102p : ill ; 25cm
ISBN 0-443-01741-7 (pbk) : £2.75 : CIP rev. B81-21570

Riddle, Janet T. E.. Objective tests for nurses / compiled and edited by Janet T.E. Riddle. — Edinburgh : Churchill Livingstone
Bk.4: The digestive system and the urinary system / with contributions from May Lee ... [et al.] ; foreword by Margaret W. Thomson. — 1982. — [9],115p : ill ; 25cm
Bibliography: 6th prelim. page
ISBN 0-443-01742-5 (pbk) : £2.95 : CIP rev. B82-09713

Riddle, Janet T. E.. Objective tests for nurses. — Edinburgh : Churchill Livingstone
Book 5: The nervous system and the special senses. — Feb.1983. — [128]p
ISBN 0-443-01743-3 (pbk) : £2.95 : CIP entry B82-38273

610.73'092'4 — Great Britain. Medicine. Nursing — *Personal observations*

Prentis, Evelyn. A nurse in parts / Evelyn Prentis. — Large print ed. — Bath : Chivers, 1982, c1980. — 297p ; 23cm. — (A new Portway large print book)
Originally published: London : Hutchinson, 1980
ISBN 0-85119-177-0 : Unpriced : CIP rev. B82-14528

Prentis, Evelyn. A nurse near by. — Large print ed. — Bath : Chivers, Feb.1983. — [320]p. — (A New Portway large print book)
Originally published: London : Hutchinson, 1981
ISBN 0-85119-207-6 : £6.90 : CIP entry B82-39463

Strathern, Nadine. Sisters / Nadine Strathern & Moira Harvey. — Bognor Regis : New Horizon, c1982. — 184p ; 21cm
ISBN 0-86116-628-0 : £5.75 B82-22239

610.73'092'4 — Medicine. Nursing. Nightingale, Florence — *Biographies*

Boyd, Nancy. Josephine Butler, Octavia Hill, Florence Nightingale : three Victorian women who changed their world / Nancy Boyd. — London : Macmillan, 1982. — xviii,276p ; 23cm
Bibliography: p263-270. — Includes index
ISBN 0-333-30057-2 : £15.00
Also classified at 362'.92'4 ; 333.7'2'0924 B82-28832

610.73'092'4 — Medicine. Nursing. Nightingale, Florence — *Biographies* *continuation*

Smith, F. B.. Florence Nightingale : reputation and power / F.B. Smith. — London : Croom Helm, c1982. — 216p ; 23cm
Bibliography: p205-211. — Includes index
ISBN 0-7099-2314-7 : £12.95 : CIP rev. B81-33890

610.73'092'4 — Medicine. Nursing. Prentis, Evelyn — *Biographies*

Prentis, Evelyn. A nurse near by / Evelyn Prentis ; with decorations by Douglas Hall. — London : Arrow, 1982, c1981. — 198p : ill ; 18cm
Originally published: London : Hutchinson, 1981
ISBN 0-09-928860-5 (pbk) : £1.50 B82-35588

Prentis, Evelyn. A turn for the nurse / Evelyn Prentis ; with decorations by Douglas Hall. — London : Hutchinson, 1982. — 197p ; 23cm
ISBN 0-09-147600-3 : £6.95 : CIP rev. B82-10607

610.73'092'6 — Medicine. Nursing — *Case studies*

Saxton, Dolores F.. Planning and implementing nursing intervention : stress and adaptation applied to patient care / Dolores F. Saxton, A. Hyland. — 2nd ed. — St. Louis, Mo. ; London : Mosby, 1979. — xi,195p : ill ; 24cm
Previous ed.: 1975. — Bibliography: p181-190. — Includes index
ISBN 0-8016-4337-6 (pbk) : Unpriced B82-21890

610.73'0941 — Great Britain. Medicine. Nursing

Armstrong-Esther, C. A.. Nursing : in sickness or in health / C.A. Armstrong-Esther. — [Guildford] ([Guildford, Surrey GU2 5XH]) : [University of Surrey], [1980?]. — 30p : ill ; 21cm. — (University of Surrey inaugural lecture)
Cover title. — Bibliography: p29
Unpriced (pbk) B82-26648

610.73'0942 — England. Medicine. Nursing, *1881-1914*

Maggs, Christopher J.. The origins of general nursing. — London : Croom Helm, Nov.1982. — [176]p
ISBN 0-7099-1734-1 : £11.95 : CIP entry B82-27937

610.73'0973 — United States. Hospitals. Patients: Adults. Nursing

Current practice in nursing care of the adult : issues and concepts / [editors] Maureen Shawn Kennedy, Gail Molnar Pfeifer. — St. Louis ; London : Mosby, 1979. — (Mosby current practice and perspectives in nursing series ; v.1)
Includes bibliographies
Vol.1. — xiii,314p : ill,forms ; 25cm
ISBN 0-8016-2646-3 (cased) : £9.50
ISBN 0-8016-2635-8 (pbk) : £6.75 B82-24776

610.73'0973 — United States. Medicine. Nursing. Efficiency

Marram, Gwen D.. Primary nursing : a model for individualised care / Gwen Marram, Margaret W. Barrett, Em Olivia Bevis. — 2nd ed. — St. Louis ; London : Mosby, 1979. — xiii,216p : ill,forms ; 23cm
Previous ed.: 1974. — Includes bibliographies and index
ISBN 0-8016-3125-4 (pbk) : £9.00 B82-24777

610.73'0973 — United States. Medicine. Nursing. Small groups

Loomis, Maxine E.. Group process for nurses / Maxine E. Loomis. — St. Louis ; London : Mosby, 1979. — x,170p : ill ; 23cm
Includes index
ISBN 0-8016-3037-1 (pbk) : £8.75 B82-24775

610.73'099 — Australasia. Medicine. Nursing

Issues in Australasian nursing / edited by Enid Jenkins, Billee King, Genevieve Gray ; foreword by June F. Cochrane. — Melbourne ; Edinburgh : Churchill Livingstone, 1982. — xii,202p : ill,forms ; 22cm
Includes bibliographies and index
ISBN 0-443-02275-5 (pbk) : Unpriced : CIP rev. B82-06838

610.73'43'0924 — France. Strasbourg. Medicine. District nursing, *1954-ca 1975 — Personal observations*

Holfert, Elisabeth. Vignettes from life / Elisabeth Holfert. — Bognor Regis : New Horizon, c1982. — 81p ; 21cm
Translated from the French
ISBN 0-86116-872-0 : £3.50 B82-23285

610.73'43'0941 — Great Britain. Medicine. District nursing

A **New** approach to district nursing / edited by Monica E. Baly. — London : Heinemann Medical, 1981. — xi,362p : ill ; 22cm
Includes bibliographies and index
ISBN 0-433-01162-9 (pbk) : £9.95 B82-03470

610.73'43'0941 — Great Britain. Medicine. District nursing — *Serials*

Journal of district nursing. — Vol.1 no.1 (July 1982)-. — Sutton (282 High St., Sutton, Surrey SM1 1PQ) : PTM Publishers, 1982-. — v. : ill (some col.),ports ; 30cm
Monthly. — Continues: Journal of community nursing
ISSN 0263-4465 = Journal of district nursing : £9.00 per year B82-32179

610.73'43'0942 — England. Medicine. District nursing — *Inquiry reports*

Dunnell, Karen. Nurses working in the community : a survey carried out on behalf of the Department of Health and Social Security in England and Wales in 1980 / Karen Dunnell, Joy Dobbs. — London : H.M.S.O., 1982. — ix,94p : ill ; 30cm
At head of title: Office of Population, Censuses and Surveys, Social Survey Division
ISBN 0-11-690909-9 (pbk) : £11.80 B82-34047

610.73'43'0973 — United States. Medicine. District nursing

Fromer, Margot Joan. Community health care and the nursing process / Margot Joan Fromer. — St. Louis ; London : Mosby, 1979. — xiii,467p : ill,forms ; 27cm
Includes bibliographies and index
ISBN 0-8016-1707-3 : £16.25 B82-33157

610.73'46 — Industrial health. Nursing. Counselling

Williams, M. Margaret Durrant. Counselling in occupational health nursing. — London (Henrietta Place, W1M 0AB) : Royal College of Nursing, Sept.1981. — [102]p
ISBN 0-902606-66-2 : £4.00 : CIP entry B81-28809

610.73'46'0711 — Industrial nurses. Professional education

Silverstone, Rosalie. The role and educational needs of occupational health nurses. — London : Royal College of Nursing, Sept.1982. — [114]p
ISBN 0-902606-71-9 (pbk) : £3.50 : CIP entry B82-29151

610.73'61 — Critically ill patients. Nursing — *Manuals*

Methods in critical care : the AACN manual / by the American Association of Critical-Care Nurses ; editor-in-chief Sally Millar ; editors Leslie K. Sampson, Maurita Soukup, Sylvan Lee Weinberg. — Philadelphia ; London : Saunders, 1980. — xxi,484p : ill,forms ; 27cm
Includes bibliographies and index
ISBN 0-7216-1006-4 : £7.95 B82-31260

610.73'61 — Medicine. Emergency treatment. Nursing

Essential accident and emergency care / F. Wilson ... [et al.]. — Lancaster : MTP, 1981. — x,308p : ill ; 22cm
Includes index
ISBN 0-85200-307-2 (pbk) : Unpriced : CIP rev. B81-19208

610.73'61 — Terminally ill patients. Nursing

Hector, Winifred. Nursing care for the dying patient and the family / Winifred Hector and Sarah Whitfield. — London : Heinemann Medical, 1982. — viii,142p ; 22cm
Bibliography: p137-138. — Includes index
ISBN 0-433-14219-7 (pbk) : Unpriced B82-25351

610.73'61 — Terminally ill persons. Nursing

Charles-Edwards, Alison. The nursing care of the dying patient. — Beaconsfield : Beaconsfield Publishers, Jan.1983. — [276]p
ISBN 0-906584-08-6 (pbk) : £6.95 : CIP entry B82-33246

610.73'62 — Children. Nursing

Aspects of sick children's nursing : a learning package. — [London] : General Nursing Council for England and Wales, c1981. — 1v.(loose-leaf) : ill,forms ; 32cm + 160 slides (col.) ; 5x5cm + 3 sound cassettes
Includes bibliographies
ISBN 0-907474-00-4 : Unpriced B82-22179

King, Heather. Applied paediatric nursing / Heather King, T.J. David. — London : Pitman, 1982. — vii,248p : ill ; 23cm
Includes index
ISBN 0-272-79675-1 (pbk) : Unpriced : CIP rev. B82-12270

Whaley, Lucille F.. Essentials of pediatric nursing / Lucille F. Whaley, Donna L. Wong. — St. Louis ; London : Mosby, 1982. — x,942p : ill ; 29cm
Includes bibliographies and index
ISBN 0-8016-5422-x : £19.75 B82-22970

610.73'62 — Children. Nursing — *Manuals*

Weller, Barbara F.. The Lippincott manual of paediatric nursing / adapted for the UK by Barbara F. Weller. — London : Harper & Row, c1981. — 688p : ill ; 21cm. — (Lippincott nursing series)
Adapted from: The Lippincott manual of nursing practice / by Lillian Sholtis Brunner, Doris Smith Suddarth. 2nd ed.. — Includes bibliographies and index
ISBN 0-06-318183-5 (pbk) : Unpriced : CIP rev. B81-30202

Whaley, Lucille F.. Nursing care of infants and children / Lucille F. Whaley, Donna L. Wong. — St. Louis ; London : Mosby, 1979. — xvi,1718p : ill ; 29cm
Includes bibliographies and index
ISBN 0-8016-5417-3 : Unpriced B82-19327

610.73'62 — Newborn babies. Intensive care. Nursing — *Manuals*

Halliday, Henry L.. Handbook of neonatal intensive care / Henry L. Halliday, Garth McClure, Mark Reid. — London : Baillière Tindall, 1981. — 307p : ill ; 19cm
Bibliography: p289-292. — Includes index
ISBN 0-7020-0884-2 (pbk) : £7.50 : CIP rev. B81-25834

610.73'62'0222 — Children. Nursing — *Illustrations — For children*

Swayne, Dick. I am a nurse. — London : Dent, Sept.1982. — [32]p
ISBN 0-460-06087-2 : £3.50 : CIP entry B82-19703

610.73'65 — Old persons. Nursing

Care of the aging / edited by Laurel Archer Copp ; foreword by Thelma J. Wells. — Edinburgh : Churchill Livingstone, 1981. — 238p ; 22cm. — (Recent advances in nursing, ISSN 0144-6592 ; 2)
Bibliography: p209-231. — Includes index
ISBN 0-443-02187-2 (pbk) : Unpriced : CIP rev. B81-25299

Gerontology and geriatric nursing / Sir W. Ferguson Anderson ... [et al.] ; foreword by Doreen Norton. — London : Hodder and Stoughton, 1982. — viii,215p,[2]p of plates : ill (some col.),1form ; 22cm. — (Modern nursing series)
Bibliography: p205-207. — Includes index
ISBN 0-340-26252-4 (pbk) : £3.95 B82-36427

610.73'677 — Medicine. Orthopaedics. Nursing

Powell, Mary. Orthopaedic nursing and rehabilitation / Mary Powell ; foreword by Robert B. Duthie. — 8th ed. — Edinburgh : Churchill Livingstone, 1982. — 629p : 1port ; 25cm
Previous ed.: 1976. — Bibliography: p603-615. — Includes index
ISBN 0-443-01994-0 (pbk) : Unpriced B82-25663

610.73′677 — Medicine. Surgery. Nursing

Dixon, Eileen. Theatre technique. — 5th ed. — London : Baillière Tindall, July 1982. — [272] p. — (Nurses′ aids series)
Previous ed.: / Marjorie Houghton. 1967
ISBN 0-7020-0866-4 : £3.95 : CIP entry
B82-12996

Moroney, James. Surgery for nurses / the late James Moroney. — 15th ed. — Edinburgh : Churchill Livingstone, 1982. — 609p : ill,1port ; 25cm
Previous ed.: 1978. — Includes bibliographies and index
ISBN 0-443-02241-0 (pbk) : £9.50 : CIP rev.
B82-24334

610.73′677 — Medicine. Surgery. Operations. Nursing — *Manuals*

Graves, F. T.. Seeing theatre nursing / F.T. Graves and Dorothy Graves ; contributor D.W. Eyre-Walker ; advisors in theatre nursing O.J. Downes, Pauline Pearsall. — London : Heinemann Medical, 1981. — 247p : ill,plans ; 19x27cm
Bibliography: p239-240. — Includes index
ISBN 0-433-12570-5 (pbk) : £12.50
B82-08326

610.73′678 — Great Britain. Midwifery. Organisations: Royal College of Midwives, *to 1981*

Cowell, Betty. Behind the blue door / the history of the Royal College of Midwives, 1881-1981 ; Betty Cowell and David Wainwright. — London : Baillière Tindall, 1981. — 111p : ill,1coat of arms,1facsim,ports ; 22cm
Includes index
ISBN 0-7020-0881-8 (pbk) : £2.50 B82-02599

610.73′678 — Gynaecology & obstetrics. Nursing

Bailey, Rosemary E.. Obstetric and gynaecological nursing. — 3rd ed. — London : Tindall, Nov.1982. — [384]p. — (Nurses′ aids series)
Previous ed.: 1975
ISBN 0-7020-0934-2 (pbk) : £3.50 : CIP entry
B82-28742

610.73′68 — Mentally disordered patients. Nursing

Dreyer, Sharon. Guide to nursing management of psychiatric patients / Sharon Dreyer, David Bailey, Will Doucet. — 2nd ed. — St. Louis ; London : C.V. Mosby, 1979. — xvi,247p ; 27cm
Previous ed.: 1975. — Includes bibliographies
ISBN 0-8016-0832-5 (pbk) : £9.75 B82-33563

Maddison, David. Psychiatric nursing / the late David Maddison, Kevin J. Kellehear ; with additional chapters by Peter Eisen ... [et al.] ; with additional material by Bruce S. Singh ; illustrated by Bernard Hesling. — 5th ed. — Edinburgh : Churchill Livingstone, 1982. — 570p : ill ; 22cm
Previous ed.: 1975. — Bibliography: p552-557. — Includes index
ISBN 0-443-02547-9 (pbk) : £9.75 : CIP rev.
B82-24347

Mereness, Dorothy A.. Mereness′ Essentials of psychiatric nursing. — 11th ed. / Cecelia Monat Taylor. — St. Louis ; London : Mosby, 1982. — xvii,699p : ill ; 25cm
Previous ed.: published as Essentials of psychiatric nursing. 1978. — Includes bibliographies and index
ISBN 0-8016-4890-4 : Unpriced B82-34552

Saxton, Dolores F.. Care of patients with emotional problems / Dolores F. Saxton, Phyllis W. Haring. — 3rd ed. — St. Louis, Mo. ; London : Mosby, 1979. — viii,132p : ill ; 23cm
Previous ed.: 1975. — Bibliography: p113-117. — Includes index
ISBN 0-8016-4341-4 (pbk) : Unpriced
B82-21888

Stuart, Gail Wiscarz. Principles and practice of psychiatric nursing / Gail Wiscarz Stuart, Sandra J. Sundeen. — St. Louis, Mo. ; London : Mosby, 1979. — xix,636p : ill ; 25cm
Includes bibliographies and index
ISBN 0-8016-4821-1 : Unpriced B82-21884

610.73′68 — Psychiatric nursing — *Manuals*

Darcy, P. T.. Theory and practice of psychiatric care. — London : Hodder & Stoughton, Nov.1981. — [224]p
ISBN 0-340-26564-7 (pbk) : £4.95 : CIP entry
B81-30133

610.73′68′071141 — Great Britain. Psychiatric nurses. Professional education. Attitudes of student nurses

Powell, Dennis. Learning to relate?. — London : Royal College of Nursing, Aug.1982. — [96]p
ISBN 0-902606-69-7 : £3.50 : CIP entry
B82-25053

610.73′68′076 — Mentally disordered patients. Nursing — *Questions & answers*

Mereness, Dorothy A.. Mereness′ Essentials of psychiatric nursing. — St. Louis ; London : Mosby
Previous ed.: published as Essentials of psychiatric nursing. 1978
Learning and activity guide / Carol Ruth Lofstedt ; with a foreword by Cecelia Monat Taylor. — 1982. — xiv,237p : ill ; 24cm
ISBN 0-8016-4892-0 (pbk) : £7.00 B82-22833

610.73′692 — Respiratory patients. Nurisng

Respiratory nursing : the science and the art / edited by Gayle A. Traver. — New York ; Chichester : Wiley, c1982. — xiv,474p : ill ; 24cm
Includes bibliographies and index
ISBN 0-471-04539-x : £14.75 B82-26477

610′.74′02134 — London. Kensington and Chelsea *(London Borough).* **Museums: Wellcome Museum of the History of Medicine** — *Visitors′ guides*

Wellcome Museum of the History of Medicine. The Wellcome Museum of the History of Medicine : a part of the Science Museum. — London : Science Museum, c1981. — [32]p : col.ill,2plans(some col.) ; 28cm
ISBN 0-901805-17-3 (pbk) : Unpriced
B82-14863

610′.76 — Educational institutions. Curriculum subjects: Medicine. Academic achievement of students. Assessment. Multiple-choice tests

Anderson, John, *1921-*. The multiple choice question in medicine / John Anderson. — 2nd ed. — London : Pitman, 1982. — xii,216p ; 22cm
Previous ed.: Tunbridge Wells : Pitman Medical, 1976. — Bibliography: p85-88. — Includes index
ISBN 0-272-79642-5 (pbk) : Unpriced : CIP rev.
B82-01864

610′.76 — Medicine — *Questions & answers*

Medical specialities : review and assessment / [edited by] Richard M. Stillman, Eli A. Friedman. — New York : Appleton-Century-Crofts ; London : Prentice-Hall, c1982. — viii,288p : ill ; 23cm
Includes bibliographies
ISBN 0-8385-6267-1 (pbk) : £13.15
B82-29233

610′.76 — Medicine — *Questions & answers — For general practice*

Bell, P.. Multiple choice questions in medicine : for the MRCP examination (Part 1) / P. Bell ; with a foreword by J. Vallance-Owen. — Bristol : Wright, 1981. — xi,164p ; 22cm
ISBN 0-7236-0630-7 (pbk) : Unpriced : CIP rev.
B81-27422

610′.76 — Medicine — *Questions & answers — For physicians*

Mills, K. R.. MRCP Part 1 review book : multiple choice questions / K.R. Mills, A.E. Champion, Vasantha Machado. — Hemel Hempstead : Pastest, 1980. — 153p ; 22cm
ISBN 0-906896-00-2 (pbk) : £4.95 : CIP rev.
B79-35361

610′.76 — Medicine — *Questions & answers — For schools*

Jordan, Chris. Medieval medicine / Chris Jordan and Tim Wood. — London : Edward Arnold, 1982. — 14p : ill,2facsims ; 30cm. — (History action pack)
Role playing exercise instructions (4 sheets) as inserts
ISBN 0-7131-0703-0 (unbound) : Unpriced : CIP rev.
B82-06242

610′.880816 — Developing countries. Physically handicapped persons. Medical aspects

A Cry for health. — Somerset (16, Bath St., Frome, Somerset BA11 1DN) : Third World Group, Nov.1982. — [96]p
ISBN 0-946279-00-4 (pbk) : £2.50 : CIP entry
ISBN 0-907320-04-x (A.H.R.T.A.G.)
B82-32867

610′.9 — Medicine, *to 1975*

Ackerknecht, Erwin H.. A short history of medicine / Erwin H. Ackerknecht. — Rev. ed. — Baltimore ; London : Johns Hopkins University Press, 1982. — xx,277p : ill,ports ; 23cm
Previous ed.: New York : Ronald Press, 1968. — Bibliography: p245-263. — Includes index
ISBN 0-8018-2726-4 (pbk) : Unpriced
B82-36866

A Celebration of medical history : the fiftieth anniversary of The Johns Hopkins Institute of the History of Medicine and The Welch Medical Library / edited by Lloyd G. Stevenson. — Baltimore ; London : Johns Hopkins University Press, c1982. — vi,228p,1leaf of plates : ports(1col.) ; 24cm. — (The Henry E. Sigerist supplements to the Bulletin of the history of medicine. New series ; no.6)
ISBN 0-8018-2733-7 : Unpriced B82-36867

610′.9′034 — Medicine, *1800-1900*

Williams, Guy R.. The age of miracles : medicine and surgery in the nineteenth century / Guy Williams. — London : Constable, 1981. — 234p : ill,ports ; 23cm
Includes index
ISBN 0-09-462360-0 : £7.95 B82-08697

610′.92′2 — England. Physicians. Organisations: Royal College of Physicians of London. Registrars, *to 1960 — Biographies*

Whitfield, George, *1909-*. The first thirty seven registrars of the college / George Whitfield. — [Birmingham] : [University of Birmingham], [1981]. — 193p : ports ; 22cm
At head of title: The Royal College of Physicians. — Includes bibliographies and index
ISBN 0-7044-0585-7 : Unpriced B82-08492

610′.92′4 — Great Britain. Medicine. Pole, K.F.M. — *Biographies*

Pole, K. F. M.. Two halves of a life / K.F.M. Pole. — Rainham : Meresborough, 1982. — 158p : ill,ports ; 22cm
ISBN 0-905270-50-9 : £5.95 B82-36405

610′.92′4 — Hawaii. Molokai. Catholic medical missions. Damien, *Father — Biographies*

O′Brien, Felicity. Father Damien / Felicity O′Brien. — London : Catholic Truth Society, 1982. — 14p ; 19cm
ISBN 0-85183-459-0 (pbk) : £0.40 B82-21898

610′.92′4 — Medicine. Galen — *Conference proceedings*

Galen : problems and prospects / [a collection of papers submitted at the 1979 Cambridge conference] ; edited by Vivian Nutton. — [London] ([183 Euston Rd, NW1 2BP]) : The Wellcome Institute for the History of Medicine, [c1981]. — iii,281p ; 21cm
Unpriced (pbk) B82-28080

610′.92′4 — Somerset. Rural regions. Medicine — *Personal observations*

Clifford, Robert. Look out, doctor!. — London : Pelham, Feb.1983. — [176]p
ISBN 0-7207-1423-0 : £7.95 : CIP entry
B82-39429

Clifford, Robert. Oh dear, doctor! / Robert Clifford ; illustrated by Nick Baker. — London : Sphere, 1982, c1981. — 191p : ill ; 18cm
Originally published: London : Pelham, 1981
ISBN 0-7221-2379-5 (pbk) : £1.25 B82-21273

610′.941 — Great Britain. Medicine — *Practical information — For patients*

Coleman, Vernon. The good medicine guide / Vernon Coleman. — [London] : Thames and Hudson, c1982. — 352p ; 21cm
Bibliography: p338-340. — Includes index
ISBN 0-500-01270-9 : £6.50 B82-17158

610'.941 — Great Britain. Medicine. Statistics

Statistics in practice : articles published in the British Medical Journal. — London : British Medical Association, c1982. — 100p : ill ; 30cm
Includes index. — Contents: Statistics in question / Sheila M. Gore — Statistics and ethics in medical research / Douglas G. Altman
ISBN 0-7279-0085-4 (pbk) : Unpriced
B82-18887

610'.951'5 — Tibetan medicine

Finckh, Elisabeth. Foundations of Tibetan medicine. — London : Watkins
Vol.2. — Mar.1982. — [120]p
ISBN 0-7224-0192-2 (cased) : CIP entry
ISBN 0-7224-0193-0 (pbk) : Unpriced
B82-03377

611 — MAN. ANATOMY

611 — Man. Anatomy

Beck, Ernest W.. Mosby's atlas of functional human anatomy / Ernest W. Beck with Maureen Groër ; edited by Harry Monsen. — St. Louis, Mo. ; London : Mosby, 1982. — xvi,310p : ill(some col.) ; 28cm
Includes index
ISBN 0-8016-0554-7 (pbk) : £7.50 B82-34469

Gray, Henry. Gray's anatomy. — 36th ed. / edited by Peter L. Williams & Roger Warwick ; associate editors, Mary Dyson & Lawrence H. Bannister with the assistance of Richard E.M. Moore ... [et al.]. — Edinburgh : Churchill Livingstone, 1980. — xvii,1578p : ill(some col.),ports ; 31cm
Previous ed.: Harlow : Longman, 1973. — Bibliography: p1467-1530. — Includes index
ISBN 0-443-01505-8 : £32.00 B82-38648

Green, J.H.. An introduction to human anatomy / J.H. Green, P.H.S. Silver. — Oxford : Oxford University Press, 1981. — x,424p : ill ; 26cm. — (Oxford medical publications)
Includes index
ISBN 0-19-261196-8 (pbk) : £12.50
B82-00002

Murphy, T. R.. Practical human anatomy : laboratory handbook and pictorial guide / T.R. Murphy. — London : Lloyd-Luke
Section 3: Head and neck. — 1982. — 154p : ill ; 19cm
Includes index
ISBN 0-85324-160-0 (pbk) : £3.00 B82-14415

Murphy, T. R.. Practical human anatomy : laboratory handbook and pictorial guide / T.R. Murphy. — London : Lloyd-Luke
Section 5: Lower limb. — 1982. — 154p : ill ; 19cm
Includes index
ISBN 0-85324-162-7 (pbk) : £3.00 B82-29255

Murphy, T.R.. Practical human anatomy : laboratory handbook and pictorial guide / T.R. Murphy. — London : Lloyd-Luke
Section 4: Upper limb. — 1982. — 154p : ill ; 19cm
Includes index
ISBN 0-85324-161-9 (pbk) : £3.00 B82-23241

Practical human anatomy : laboratory handbook and pictorial guide. — London : Lloyd-Luke
Section 2: Abdomen / T.R. Murphy. — 1981. — 154p : ill ; 19cm
Includes index
ISBN 0-85324-159-7 (pbk) : £3.00 B82-06875

611 — Man. Anatomy *compared with* **anatomy of cats**

Walker, Warren F.. A study of the cat : with reference to human beings / Warren F. Walker, Jr. — 4th ed. — Philadelphia ; London : Saunders College, c1982. — xi,244p : ill(some col.) ; 24cm
Previous ed.: 1977. — Bibliography: p236-238. — Includes index
ISBN 0-03-057914-7 (pbk) : Unpriced
Primary classification 599.74'428 B82-20598

611'.0022'2 — Man. Anatomy — *Illustrations*

Kiss, Ferenc. Atlas of human anatomy / by Ferenc Kiss, János Szentágothai. — 3rd English ed. / in collaboration with G.N.C. Crawford. — The Hague ; London : Nijhoff, 1980. — 3v. : all ill(some col.) ; 30cm
Translation of: Az ember anatómiájának atlasza. — Previous ed.: Oxford : Pergamon, 1964. — Includes index
ISBN 90-247-2264-0 : Unpriced
ISBN 90-247-2265-0 (v.1) : Unpriced
ISBN 90-247-2266-7 (v.2) : Unpriced
ISBN 90-247-2267-5 (v.3) : Unpriced
B82-31513

Matt, Margaret. Human anatomy coloring book / Margaret Matt ; text by Joe Ziemian ; scientific adviser, Donald Wernsing. — New York : Dover ; London : Constable, 1982. — 43p : chiefly ill(some col.) ; 28cm. — (Dover coloring book)
Ill on inside covers
ISBN 0-486-24138-6 (pbk) : £2.30 B82-37388

611'.0024616 — Man. Anatomy — *For radiography*

Frik, W.. Roentgenologic anatomy : an introduction / W. Frik, U. Goering ; translated by L.G. Rigler, P. Spiegler. — Chicago ; London : Year Book Medical, 1980. — vi,138p : ill ; 19cm
Translation of: Röntgenanatomie. 2 Aufl.. — Bibliography: p134. — Includes index
ISBN 0-8151-3292-1 (pbk) : £6.75 B82-31765

Johnson, W. H.. Johnson and Kennedy radiographic skeletal anatomy. — 2nd ed. — Edinburgh : Churchill Livingstone, Oct.1982. — [288]p
Previous ed.: London : Livingstone, 1961
ISBN 0-443-01627-5 : £14.00 : CIP entry
B82-24720

611'.0028 — Man. Dissection — *Manuals*

Zuckerman, Solly Zuckerman, *Baron*. A new system of anatomy : a dissector's guide and atlas / Lord Zuckerman. — 2nd ed. / revised in collaboration with Deryk Darlington, F. Peter Lisowski. — Oxford : Oxford University Press, 1981. — 1v.(various pagings) : ill ; 29cm. — (Oxford medical publications)
Previous ed.: 1961. — Includes index
ISBN 0-19-263137-3 : £30.00 : CIP rev.
B80-04806

611'.0076 — Man. Anatomy — *Questions & answers*

Joseph, J.. Multiple choice questions in anatomy. — 2nd ed / J. Joseph. — London : Baillière Tindall, 1982. — 139p : ill ; 22cm
Previous ed.: 1972
ISBN 0-7020-0920-2 (pbk) : £4.25 : CIP rev.
B82-04623

611'.018 — Man. Cells & tissues. Microstructure

Johnson, Kurt E.. Histology : microscopic anatomy and embryology / Kurt E. Johnson. — New York ; Chichester : Wiley, c1982. — xii,415p : ill ; 26cm
Includes index
ISBN 0-471-08092-6 (pbk : corrected) : £12.95
B82-31112

611'.018 — Man. Cells & tissues. Structure

Krause, William J.. Concise text of histology / William J. Krause, J. Harry Cutts. — Baltimore ; London : Williams & Wilkins, c1981. — xi,429p : ill ; 26cm
Includes index
ISBN 0-683-04784-1 (pbk) : Unpriced
B82-02564

Rogers, A. W.. Cells and tissues. — London : Academic Press, Feb.1983. — [296]p
ISBN 0-12-593120-4 : CIP entry B82-40310

611'.018'0222 — Man. Cells & tissues. Microstructure — *Illustrations*

Kühnel, Wolfgang. Pocket atlas of cytology and microscopic anatomy / by Wolfgang Kühnel ; translated by H.M. Beier. — 2nd rev. ed. — Chicago ; London : Year Book Medical Publishers, 1981. — 303p : ill(some col.) ; 19cm. — (Thieme flexibook)
Translation of: Taschenatlas der Zytologie und mikroskopischen Anatomie. 5th ed. — Previous ed.: published as Atlas of histology / Ernst von Herrath. New York ; London : Hafner, 1966. — Includes index
ISBN 0-8151-5208-6 (pbk) : £12.25
B82-16349

611'.018'0222 — Man. Tissues. Diseases — *Illustrations*

Curran, R. C.. Colour atlas of histopathology / by R.C. Curran ; foreword by Sir Roy Cameron. — London : Harvey Miller, 1972 (1981 [printing]). — 94p : chiefly col.ill ; 32cm
Previous ed.: London : Baillière, Tindall & Cassell, 1966. — Includes index
ISBN 0-905203-98-4 : £19.00
ISBN 0-19-921002-0 (Oxford University Press)
B82-20350

611'.018'0724 — Man. Tissues. Culture — *Conference proceedings*

Tissue culture in medical research (II) : proceedings of the second international symposium, Cardiff, Wales, U.K., 1-3 April 1980 / editors R.J. Richards and K.T. Rajan. — Oxford : Pergamon, 1980. — xiii,257p : ill,ports ; 26cm
Includes bibliographies and index
ISBN 0-08-025924-3 : £20.00 : CIP rev.
B80-17710

611'.0181 — Man. Brain stem. Cells. Anatomy

Olszewski, Jerzy. Cytoarchitecture of the human brain stem / by Jerzy Olszewski and Donald Baxter. — 2nd ed. — Basel ; London : Karger, 1982. — 199p : ill ; 33cm
Previous ed.: Philadelphia : Lippincott, 1954. — Bibliography: p199
ISBN 3-8055-2210-x : £80.90 B82-21530

611'.0185 — Man. Lymphoid tissue. Histopathology. Laboratory techniques

Reynolds, G. J.. Lymphoid tissue : a histological approach. — Bristol : Wright, Oct.1982. — [130]p. — (Institute of Medical Laboratory Sciences monographs)
ISBN 0-7236-0645-5 (pbk) : £5.00 : CIP entry
B82-24272

611.2 — MAN. ANATOMY. RESPIRATORY SYSTEM

611'.24'072 — Man. Lungs. Anatomy. Research, *150-1980*

Meban, C.. The breath of life : an inaugural lecture delivered before the Queen's University of Belfast on 10 March 1981 / C. Meban. — [Belfast] : Queens University of Belfast, c1981. — 20p : ill,1facsim,2ports ; 21cm. — (New lecture series ; no.126)
ISBN 0-85389-196-6 (pbk) : £0.40 B82-11692

611.3 — MAN. ANATOMY. DIGESTIVE SYSTEM

611'.31 — Man. Mouth. Anatomy

Brand, Richard W.. Anatomy of orofacial structures / Richard W. Brand, Donald E. Isselhard. — 2nd ed. — St Louis ; London : Mosby, 1982. — ix,405p : ill ; 26cm
Previous ed.: St Louis : Mosby ; London : distributed by Kimpton, 1977. — Includes bibliographies and index
ISBN 0-8016-0857-0 (pbk) : £15.00
Also classified at 611'.91 B82-35105

611'.314 — Man. Teeth. Anatomy

Scott, James Henderson. Introduction to dental anatomy / the late James Henderson Scott and Norman Barrington Bray Symons. — 9th ed. — Edinburgh : Churchill Livingstone, 1982. — 417p : ill ; 22cm
Previous ed.: 1977. — Includes index
ISBN 0-443-02561-4 (pbk) : £12.00
B82-38388

611′.314 — Man. Teeth. Identification

Van Beck, G. C.. Dental morphology. — 2nd ed. — Bristol : J. Wright, Jan.1983. — [144]p
Previous ed.: 1975 / by G.C. Downer
ISBN 0-7236-0666-8 (pbk) : £5.50 : CIP entry
B82-40305

611′.34 — Man. Intestines. Anatomy

Structure of the gut / edited by J.M. Polak ... [et al.]. — Ware : Glaxo Group Research, 1982. — iv,488p : ill ; 26cm. — (Basic science in gastroenterology)
Includes bibliographies and index
ISBN 0-9500593-2-3 (cased) : Unpriced
ISBN 0-9500593-3-1 (pbk) : Unpriced
B82-36743

611.4 — MAN. ANATOMY. LYMPHATIC AND GLANDULAR SYSTEMS

611′.47 — Man. Intermediate pituitary gland. Intermediate lobe peptides - *Conference proceedings*

. Peptides of the pars intermedia. — London : Pitman Medical, May 1981. — [320]p. — (Ciba Foundation symposium ; 81)
Conference papers
ISBN 0-272-79617-4 : £19.50 : CIP entry
B81-04375

611.6 — MAN. ANATOMY. UROGENITAL SYSTEM

611′.6 — Man. Urinary tract. Anatomy

Gosling, John A.. Functional anatomy of the urinary tract. — London (34 Cleveland St., WIP 5FB) : Gower Medical, Sept.1982. — [160]p
ISBN 0-906923-03-4 : £37.50 : CIP entry
B82-22442

611.8 — MAN. ANATOMY. NERVOUS SYSTEM

611′.8 — Man. Central nervous system. Anatomy

Miller, Richard A. (Richard Avery). Atlas of the central nervous system in man / Richard A. Miller, Ethel Burack. — 3rd ed. — Baltimore ; London : Williams & Wilkins, c1982. — ix,81 [i.e. 162]p : ill ; 29cm
Previous ed.: 1977. — Text, ill on lining papers. — Includes index
ISBN 0-683-05933-5 : Unpriced B82-18002

611′.8 — Man. Nervous system. Anatomy

Angevine, Jay B.. Principles of neuroanatomy / Jay B. Angevine Jr, Carl W. Cotman. — New York ; Oxford : Oxford University Press, 1981. — xviii,393p : ill ; 24cm
Bibliography: p376-378. — Includes index
ISBN 0-19-502885-6 (cased) : Unpriced
ISBN 0-19-502886-4 (pbk) : £8.95 B82-16133

611′.81 — Man. Brain. Anatomy

Nolte, John. The human brain : an introduction to its functional anatomy / John Nolte. — St. Louis ; London : Mosby, 1981. — ix,322p : ill ; 28cm
Includes bibliographies and index
ISBN 0-8016-3702-3 (pbk) : £14.00
B82-04111

611′.81′028 — Man. Brain. Microdissection. Laboratory techniques

Brain microdissection techniques. — Chichester : Wiley, Feb.1983. — [160]p. — (IBRO handbook series : methods in neurosciences ; v.2)
ISBN 0-471-10523-6 (cased) : £16.00 : CIP entry
ISBN 0-471-90019-2 (pbk) : £8.00 B82-38712

611.9 — MAN. REGIONAL ANATOMY

611′.9 — Man. Back & limbs. Anatomy

Hollinshead, W. Henry. The back and limbs / W. Henry Hollinshead. — 3rd ed. — Philadelphia, [Pa.] ; London : Harper & Row, c1982. — viii,878p : ill ; 27cm. — (Anatomy for surgeons ; .3)
Previous ed.: 1969. — Includes bibliographies and index
ISBN 0-06-141266-x : £56.00 B82-31190

611′.9′0222 — Man. Regional anatomy — *Illustrations*

Jamieson, Edward Bald. Jamieson's Illustrations of regional anatomy. — Edinburgh : Churchill Livingstone
Section 2: Head and neck. — 10th ed. / [revised by] Robert Walmsley and T.R. Murphy. — 1982. — vii,73p : chiefly ill(some col.) ; 21cm
Previous ed.: 1972. — Includes index
ISBN 0-443-02266-6 (spiral) : Unpriced : CIP rev. B81-30486

611′.9′076 — Man. Regional anatomy — *Questions & answers*

Abrahams, Peter H., *1947 Aug.5-*. Pocket examiner in regional and clinical anatomy / Peter H. Abrahams, Matthew J. Thatcher. — London : Pitman, 1981. — ix,274p ; 21x10cm
ISBN 0-272-79621-2 (pbk) : Unpriced : CIP rev. B81-23856

611′.91 — Man. Head & neck. Anatomy

Brand, Richard W.. Anatomy of orofacial structures / Richard W. Brand, Donald E. Isselhard. — 2nd ed. — St Louis ; London : Mosby, 1982. — ix,405p : ill ; 26cm
Previous ed.: St Louis : Mosby ; London : distributed by Kimpton, 1977. — Includes bibliographies and index
ISBN 0-8016-0857-0 (pbk) : £15.00
Primary classification 611′.31 B82-35105

Hiatt, James L.. Textbook of head and neck anatomy / James L. Hiatt, Leslie P. Gartner ; illustrated by Jerry L. Gadd. — New York ; Appleton-Century-Crofts ; London : Prentice-Hall International, c1982. — xiv,350p : ill ; 27cm
Bibliography: p331-332. — Includes index
ISBN 0-8385-8876-x : £21.70 B82-23646

611′.91′0222 — Man. Head & neck. Anatomy — *Illustrations — For computerised tomography*

Palacios, Enrique. Multiplanar anatomy of the head and neck for computed tomography / Enrique Palacios, Michael Fine, Victor M. Haughton. — New York ; Chichester : Wiley, c1980. — xv,206p : chiefly ill(some col.) ; 29cm
Bibliography: p199. — Includes index
ISBN 0-471-05820-3 : £70.00 B82-11555

612 — MAN. PHYSIOLOGY

612 — Man. Body — *For schools*

Foster, John. You and your body. — London : Edward Arnold, Feb.1983. — [48]p. — (Lifescan)
ISBN 0-7131-0694-8 (pbk) : £1.75 : CIP entry
B82-38906

612 — Man. Physiology

Despopoulos, Agamemnon. Color atlas of physiology / Agamemnon Despopoulos, Stefan Silbernagl ; 145 color plates by Wolf-Rüdiger Gay and Barbara Gay. — Chicago ; London : Year Book Medical, 1981. — 328p : ill(some col.) ; 19cm. — (Thieme flexibook)
Translation of: Taschenatlas der Physiologie. — Includes index
ISBN 0-8151-2434-1 (pbk) : £7.75 B82-11877

Essential sciences for clinicians / editor in chief V.R. Tindall ; editors M.E. Dodson, A.H. Gowenlock ; coordinators D. Charlesworth, J.E. MacIver. — Oxford : Blackwell Scientific, 1981. — ix,518p : ill ; 25cm
Includes bibliographies and index
ISBN 0-632-00733-8 : £18.50 : CIP rev.
B81-22689

Guyton, Arthur C.. Human physiology and mechanisms of disease / Arthur C. Guyton. — 3rd ed. — Philadelphia ; London : Saunders, 1982. — x,709p : ill(some col.) ; 28cm
Previous ed.: published as Basic human physiology. 1977. — Includes bibliographies and index
ISBN 0-7216-4384-1 : £17.95 B82-16909

Human biology : an exhibition of ourselves. — 2nd ed. — London : British Museum (Natural History), c1981. — 120p : ill(some col.) ; 22cm
Previous ed.: 1977. — Includes index
ISBN 0-521-23832-3 (cased) : £12.00 : CIP rev.
ISBN 0-521-28247-0 (pbk) : £3.95 B81-34418

Scratcherd, T.. Aids to physiology / T. Scratcherd. — Edinburgh : Churchill Livingstone, 1981. — 310p ; 22cm
Includes index
ISBN 0-443-01959-2 (pbk) : £5.95 : CIP rev.
B81-31841

Winter, H. Frank. Review of human physiology / H. Frank Winter, Melvin L. Shourd. — Philadelphia ; London : Saunders, 1982. — xiv,563p : ill ; 26cm
'A companion to Guyton's Textbook of medical physiology and Human physiology and mechanisms of disease'
ISBN 0-7216-9469-1 (pbk) : Unpriced
B82-30690

Wright, Samson. Samson Wright's applied physiology. — 13th ed. — Oxford : Oxford University Press, Oct.1982. — [650]p. — (Oxford medical publications)
Previous ed.: 1971
ISBN 0-19-263211-6 (cased) : £30.00 : CIP entry
ISBN 0-19-263210-8 (pbk) : £15.00
B82-26696

612 — Man. Physiology — *For children*

Taylor, Ron, *1927-*. How the body works / [author Ron Taylor] ; [editor Linda Moore]. — London : Marshall Cavendish, 1981. — 29p : col.ill ; 30cm. — (Enigma) (An All colour fact book)
Text, ill on inside covers
ISBN 0-85685-971-0 : Unpriced B82-06075

Taylor, Ron, *1927-*. Human body. — London : Granada, Apr.1982. — [64]p. — (Granada guide series ; 10)
ISBN 0-246-11638-2 : £1.95 : CIP entry
B82-06496

612 — Man. Physiology — *For schools*

Freeman, Joan. Human biology and hygiene / Joan Freeman ; illustrated by R.A. Neave. — 2nd ed. — Exeter : Wheaton, 1981, c1968. — viii,273p,[2]leaves of plates : ill(some col.) ; 22cm
Previous ed.: Oxford : Pergamon, 1968. — Includes index
ISBN 0-08-025602-3 (pbk) : £2.95 B82-02397

Mackean, D. G.. Study guides in human physiology. — London : Murray
Series C. — June 1982. — [52]p
ISBN 0-7195-3780-0 (unbound) : £11.00 : CIP entry B82-11777

Mackean, D. G.. Study guides in human physiology. — London : Murray
Series A, B, C (complete). — June 1982. — [208]p
ISBN 0-7195-3959-5 (unbound) : £35.00 : CIP entry B82-11778

Mackean, D. G.. Study guides in human physiology. — London : Murray
Series A. — June 1982. — [86]p
ISBN 0-7195-3778-9 (unbound) : £14.00 : CIP entry B82-11775

Mackean, D. G.. Study guides in human physiology. — London : Murray
Series B. — June 1982. — [78]p
ISBN 0-7195-3779-7 (unbound) : £14.00 : CIP entry B82-11776

Minett, P. M.. A concise human biology and hygiene. — 2nd revised ed. — London : Bell & Hyman, Apr.1982. — [160]p
Originally published: London : Mills & Boon, 1979
ISBN 0-7135-2200-3 (pbk) : £3.95 : CIP entry
B82-11092

Richards, Roy. Ourselves / [authors Roy Richards, Doug Kincaid]. — [London] : Macdonald Educational, c1981. — 48pupils' cards : col.ill ; 21x30cm + Teachers' guide(28p : ill ; 21x30cm). — (Learning through science)
Pupils' cards in 2 identical sets of 24
ISBN 0-356-07549-4 : Unpriced B82-04262

612 — Man. Physiology — *For schools continuation*

Robson, M. D.. Human biology today : a course for first examinations / M.D. Robson, A.G. Morgan. — Basingstoke : Macmillan Education, 1982. — 176p : ill,3maps ; 30cm
Bibliography: p169. — Includes index
ISBN 0-333-27879-8 (corrected : pbk) : Unpriced : CIP rev. B81-35798

Suppiah, Rajoo. Human and social biology / Rajoo Suppiah. — Kuala Lumpur ; Oxford : Oxford University Press, c1979 (1981 [printing]). — vi,258p : ill ; 26cm. — (Modern certificate guides) (Oxford in Asia)
ISBN 0-19-581081-3 (pbk) : £2.95 B82-33040

612′.001 — Man. Physiology. Theories

Maturana, Humberto R.. Autopoiesis and cognition : the realization of the living / Humberto R. Maturana and Francisco J. Varela ; with a preface to Autopoiesis by Sir Stafford Beer. — Dordrecht ; London : Reidel, c1980. — xxx,141p : 1ill ; 25cm. — (Boston studies in the philosophy of science ; v.42)
Bibliography: p139-140. — Includes index
ISBN 90-277-1015-5 (cased) : Unpriced
ISBN 90-277-1016-3 (pbk) : Unpriced
Primary classification 153.4 B82-37353

612′.0024613 — Man. Physiology — *For nursing*

Taverner, Deryck. Taverner's physiology. — 4th ed. — London : Hodder & Stoughton, Jan.1982. — [256]p
Previous ed.: published as: Physiology for nursing. London : English Universities Press, 1972
ISBN 0-340-23763-5 (pbk) : £3.95 : CIP entry B81-34121

612′.0028′7 — Man. Physiology. Telemetry — *Serials*

Biotelemetry and patient monitoring : official organ of the International Society on Biotelemetry. — Vol.5 (1978)-. — Basel ; London : Karger ; Chichester : Wiley [distributor], 1978-. — v. : ill ; 26cm
Quarterly. — Continues: Biotelemetry. — Description based on: Vol.8, no.1-2 (1981)
ISSN 0378-309x = Biotelemetry and patient monitoring : £19.80 per issue B82-03402

612′.00724 — Man. Physiology. Mathematical models. Applications of microcomputer systems — *For teaching*

Randall, James E.. Microcomputers and physiological simulation / James E. Randall ; foreword by Arthur C. Guyton. — Reading, Mass. ; London : Addison-Wesley, 1980. — xv,235p : ill ; 24cm
Includes index
ISBN 0-201-06128-7 (pbk) : £9.60 B82-08626

612′.0076 — Man. Physiology — *Questions & answers*

Forsling, Mary L.. Pocket examiner in physiology / Mary L. Forsling. — London : Pitman, 1981. — x,170p ; 21x10cm
ISBN 0-272-79635-2 (pbk) : Unpriced : CIP rev. B81-23858

Jenkins, Morton. Human biology questions for assessment at 16+. — Cambridge : Cambridge University Press, Aug.1982. — [88]p
ISBN 0-521-28504-6 (pbk) : £1.95 : CIP entry B82-26251

Nicpon-Marieb, Elaine. Human anatomy and physiology : laboratory manual / Elaine Nicpon-Marieb. — Cat ed. — Menlo Park, Calif. ; London : Benjamin/Cummings, c1981. — viii,384,RS216p : ill,forms ; 28cm
Includes index
ISBN 0-8053-6723-3 (spiral) : £12.00 B82-39902

612′.0076 — Man. Physiology — *Questions & answers* — *For schools*

Rowlinson, Pat. Human biology : an activity approach / Pat Rowlinson and Morton Jenkins. — Cambridge : Cambridge University Press, 1982. — iv,284p : ill ; 28cm
Includes index
ISBN 0-521-28200-4 (pbk) : £4.95 : CIP rev. B82-14495

612′.009′04 — Medicine. Physiology, *1934-1976*

The **Pursuit** of nature : informal essays on the history of physiology / A.L. Hodgkin ... [et al.]. — Cambridge : Cambridge University Press, 1977 (1979 [printing]). — 180p : ill ; 23cm
These essays were written as part of the celebrations of the Centenary of the Physiological Society in 1976. — Includes bibliographies and index
ISBN 0-521-29617-x (pbk) : £3.95 B82-01770

612′.014 — Man. Circadian rhythms

Minors, D. S.. Circadian rhythms and the human / D.S. Minors, J.M. Waterhouse ; with a foreword by R.T.W.L. Conroy. — Bristol : John Wright, 1981. — xv,332p : ill,1plan ; 25cm
Includes bibliographies and index
ISBN 0-7236-0592-0 : Unpriced : CIP rev. B81-23849

612′.014 — Man. Tissues. Effects of radiation. Medical aspects

Cytotoxic insult to tissues : effects on cell lineages. — Edinburgh : Churchill Livingstone, Oct.1982. — [708]p
ISBN 0-443-02418-9 : £20.00 : CIP entry B82-24021

612′.01426 — Man. Body heat. Conservation

Total warmth : the complete guide to winter well-being / Geri Harrington ... [et al.]. — New York : Collier Books ; London : Collier Macmillan, 1981. — xiv,210p : ill ; 28cm
Includes index
ISBN 0-02-548460-5 (cased) : Unpriced
ISBN 0-02-080070-3 (pbk) : Unpriced
Primary classification 697 B82-28916

612′.01445 — Man. Effects of mechanical vibration — *Conference proceedings*

International CISM-IFToMM-WHO Symposium *(1979 : Udine)*. Man under vibration : suffering and protection : proceedings of the International CISM-IFToMM-WHO Symposium, Udine, Italy, April 3-6, 1979 / edited by G. Bianchi, K.V. Frolov, A. Olędzki. — Amsterdam ; Oxford : Elsevier Scientific, 1981. — xiv,437p : ill ; 25cm. — (Studies in environmental science ; 13)
English text, notes, references and summaries in French, German and Russian
ISBN 0-444-99743-1 : £37.31 : CIP rev. B81-03825

612′.01448 — Medicine. Dosimetry

Isodose atlas : for use in radiotherapy / edited by Gy. Németh, H. Kuttig ; [English translation by K. Takácsi-Nagy]. — The Hague ; London : Nijhoff, 1981. — 269p : ill ; 25cm. — (Series in radiology ; v.5)
Translation from the Hungarian. — Bibliography: p263-268. — Includes index
ISBN 90-247-2476-7 : Unpriced B82-07453

612′.01448 — Medicine. Dosimetry — *Conference proceedings*

Symposium on Advances in Radiation Protection Dosimetry in Medicine *(1979 : Erice)*. Advances in radiation protection and dosimetry in medicine : [proceedings of the Symposium on Advances in Radiation Protection Dosimetry in Medicine held in Italy, September 16-25, 1979] / edited by Ralph H. Thomas and Victor Perez-Mendez. — New York ; London : Plenum, c1980. — lx,658p : ill ; 26cm. — (Ettore Majorana international science series. life sciences ; v.2)
Includes bibliographies and index
ISBN 0-306-40468-0 : Unpriced B82-40681

612′.015 — Man. Biochemistry

McMurray, W. C.. A synopsis of human biochemistry : with medical applications / W.C. McMurray. — Philadelphia ; London : Harper & Row, c1982. — xi,319p : ill ; 23cm
Includes bibliographies and index
ISBN 0-06-141642-8 (pbk) : Unpriced B82-33819

Orton, James M.. Human biochemistry / James M. Orten, Otto W. Neuhaus. — 10th ed. — St. Louis ; London : Mosby, 1982. — ix,984p : ill ; 28cm
Previous ed.: 1975. — Includes bibliographies and index
ISBN 0-8016-3730-9 : £23.25 B82-31906

Textbook of biochemistry : with clinical correlations / edited by Thomas M. Devlin. — New York ; Chichester : Wiley, c1982. — xxxvi,1265p : ill ; 24cm
Includes bibliographies and index
ISBN 0-471-05039-3 : £26.50 B82-25396

612′.015 — Man. Organic acids

Chalmers, R. A.. Organic acids in man. — London : Chapman and Hall, Jan.1982. — [400]p
ISBN 0-412-14890-0 : £27.50 : CIP entry B81-34402

612′.015 — Medicine. Biochemistry — *Conference proceedings*

Medicinal Chemistry Symposium *(1st : 1981 : Cambridge)*. Chemical regulation of biological mechanisms. — London : Royal Society of Chemistry, May 1982. — [340]p. — (Special publication / Royal Society of Chemistry, ISSN 0260-6291 ; no.42)
ISBN 0-85186-855-x (pbk) : CIP entry B82-07677

612′.015′05 — Medicine. Biochemistry - *Serials*

Recent advances in clinical biochemistry. — No.2. — Edinburgh : Churchill Livingstone, Aug.1981. — [302]p
ISBN 0-443-02005-1 : £20.00 : CIP entry
ISSN 0143-6767 B81-16411

612′.015′0973 — United States. Medicine. Biochemistry, *to 1980*

Kohler, Robert E.. From medical chemistry to biochemistry : the making of biomedical discipline / Robert E. Kohler. — Cambridge : Cambridge University Press, 1982. — ix,399p : ill ; 24cm. — (Cambridge monographs on the history of medicine)
Includes index
ISBN 0-521-24312-2 : £22.50 B82-34880

612′.0151 — Man. Phenolsulphotransferase

Phenolsulfotransferase in mental health research / edited by Merton Sandler, Earl Usdin. — London : Macmillan, 1981. — xii,225p : ill ; 24cm
Includes bibliographies and index
ISBN 0-333-32016-6 : £22.00 B82-10635

612′.01513 — Man. Leukotrienes — *Serials*

Prostaglandins, leukotrienes and medicine. — Vol.8, no.1 (Jan. 1982)-. — Edinburgh : Churchill Livingstone, 1982-. — v. : ill ; 25cm
Monthly. — Continues: Prostaglandins and medicine
ISSN 0262-1746 = Prostaglandins leukotrienes and medicine : £80.00 per year
Primary classification 612′.405 B82-18544

612′.01522 — Man. Acid-base balance, electrolyte balance & fluid balance

Willatts, Sheila M.. Lecture notes on fluid and electrolyte balance / Sheila M. Willatts. — Oxford : Blackwell Scientific, 1982. — ix,308p : ill ; 22cm. — (Lecture notes)
Bibliography: p296-297. — Includes index
ISBN 0-632-00862-8 (pbk) : Unpriced : CIP rev. B82-01555

612′.01522 — Man. Body fluids. Electrolytes — *Programmed instructions* — *For nursing*

Kee, Joyce LeFever. Fluids and electrolytes with clinical applications : a programmed approach / Joyce LeFever Kee. — 3rd ed. — New York ; Chichester : Wiley, c1982. — xvii,526p : ill ; 24cm
Previous ed.: 1978. — Bibliography: p517-520. — Includes index
ISBN 0-471-08989-3 (pbk) : £13.20 B82-34745

612′.01524 — Man. Effects of lead — *Conference proceedings*

International Symposium on Low Level Lead Exposure and its Effects on Human Beings *(1982 : London)*. Lead versus health. — Chichester : Wiley, Nov.1982. — [250]p
ISBN 0-471-90028-1 : £16.00 : CIP entry B82-28741

612′.0157 — Man. Histamine — *Conference proceedings*

International Histamine Symposium *(1981 : Okayama)*. Advances in histamine research : proceedings of the International Histamine Symposium held at Okayama, Japan, 26-27 July 1981 / editors B. Uvnas, K. Tasaka. — Oxford : Pergamon, 1982. — vii,261p : ill ; 26cm. — (Advances in the biosciences ; v.33)
Includes bibliographies and index
ISBN 0-08-028006-4 : Unpriced : CIP rev. B82-02625

612′.0157 — Man. Histamine receptors

Pharmacology of histamine receptors / edited by C.R. Ganellin, M.E. Parsons ; with a foreword by Sir William Paton. — Bristol : John Wright, 1982. — xvii,521p : ill ; 24cm
Includes bibliographies and index
ISBN 0-7236-0589-0 : Unpriced : CIP rev. B82-04969

612′.022 — Man. Circadian rhythms. Effects of drugs — *Conference proceedings*

International Congress of Pharmacology *(8th : 1981 : Japan)*. Toward chronopharmacology. — Oxford : Pergamon, Jan.1983. — [456]p. — (Advances in the biosciences ; v.41)
ISBN 0-08-027977-5 : £40.00 : CIP entry B82-33607

612′.04 — Man. Physiology. Effects of underwater diving

The **Physiology** and medicine of diving and compressed air work. — 3rd ed. — London : Baillière Tindall, Sept.1982. — [608]p
Previous ed.: 1975
ISBN 0-7020-0821-4 : £35.00 : CIP entry
Primary classification 616.98′022 B82-20003

612′.042 — Man. Work. Physiological aspects

Stegemann, Jürgen. Exercise physiology : physiologic bases of work and sport / by Jürgen Stegemann ; translated and edited by James S. Skinner. — Chicago ; London : Year Book Medical, 1981. — xi,345p : ill ; 19cm. — (Thieme flexibook)
Translation of: Leistungsphysiologie. — Includes index
ISBN 0-8151-8171-x (pbk) : £9.75
Also classified at 612′.044 B82-07475

612′.044 — Man. Exercise capacity. Effects of lung diseases — *Conference proceedings*

Muscular exercise in chronic lung disease = L′Exercice musculaire dans les maladies pulmonaires chroniques / editors M. Gimenez, C. Saunier. — Oxford : Pergamon, 1980. — 436p : ill ; 25cm. — (Entretiens de physio-pathologie respiratoire, Nancy. 11e série)
Conference papers. — Text in English and French
ISBN 0-08-024930-2 : £20.00 : CIP rev. B79-25738

612′.044 — Man. Exercise. Physiological aspects — *Conference proceedings*

International Course on Physiological Chemistry of Exercise and Training *(1st : 1979 : Fiuggi Terme)*. Physiological chemistry of exercise and training : First International Course on Physiological Chemistry of Exercise and Training, Fiuggi Terme, October 1-4, 1979 / volume editors P.E. di Prampero and J. Poortmans. — Basel ; London : Karger, c1981. — viii,219p : ill ; 25cm. — (Medicine and sport ; v.13)
Includes bibliographies and index
ISBN 3-8055-2028-x : £26.00 B82-01060

612′.044 — Man. Exercise. Physiological aspects — *For physical education*

Wilmore, Jack H.. Training for sport and activity : the physiological basis of the conditioning process / Jack H. Wilmore. — 2nd ed. — Boston, Mass. ; London : Allyn and Bacon, c1982. — ix,294p : ill ; 25cm
Previous ed.: published as Athletic training and physical fitness, 1977. — Includes bibliographies and index
ISBN 0-205-07761-7 : Unpriced B82-27114

612′.044 — Sports & games. Physiological aspects

Stegemann, Jürgen. Exercise physiology : physiologic bases of work and sport / by Jürgen Stegemann ; translated and edited by James S. Skinner. — Chicago ; London : Year Book Medical, 1981. — xi,345p : ill ; 19cm. — (Thieme flexibook)
Translation of: Leistungsphysiologie. — Includes index
ISBN 0-8151-8171-x (pbk) : £9.75
Primary classification 612′.042 B82-07475

612.1 — MAN. PHYSIOLOGY. CARDIOVASCULAR SYSTEM

612′.1 — Man. Blood. Circulation — *For children*

Ward, Brian. The heart and blood / Brian R. Ward. — London : Watts, 1982. — 48p : col.ill ; 26cm. — (The Human body)
Includes index
ISBN 0-85166-945-x : £3.99 B82-23819

612′.1 — Man. Cardiovascular system

Cardiovascular system dynamics : models and measurements / [proceedings of a symposium on Cardiovascular System Dynamics: Models and Measurements, a Satellite symposium to the 28th International Congress of Physiological Sciences, held July 10-12, 1980, in Graz, Austria] ; edited by Thomas Kenner, Rudi Busse and Helmut Hinghofer-Szalkay. — New York ; London : Plenum, c1982. — xviii,668p : ill ; 26cm
Includes bibliographies and index
ISBN 0-306-40727-2 : Unpriced B82-26278

612′.1 — Man. Cardiovascular system. Prostaglandins — *Conference proceedings*

International Symposium on Prostaglandins and Thromboxanes in the Cardiovascular System *(3rd : 1980 : Halle)*. Prostaglandins and thromboxanes. — Oxford : Pergamon, May 1981. — [500]p
ISBN 0-08-027369-6 : £33.00 : CIP entry B81-09986

612′.1′0924 — Man. Blood. Circulation. Harvey, William, *1578-1657* — *Biographies*

Rose, Kenneth, *19---*. William Harvey / by Kenneth Rose. — [London] : Gilbey Jubilee Collection, 1978. — 32p ; 22cm
ISBN 0-9506160-0-1 (pbk) : Unpriced B82-13547

612′.11 — Man. Blood. Cells — *Illustrations*

Hayhoe, F. G. J.. A colour atlas of haematological cytology / F.G.J. Hayhoe, R.J. Flemans. — 2nd ed. — London : Wolfe Medical, 1982. — 240p : chiefly col.ill ; 27cm
Previous ed.: published as An Atlas of haematological cytology, 1969. — Includes index
ISBN 0-7234-0778-9 : Unpriced B82-19919

612′.11 — Medicine. Haemodilution — *Conference proceedings*

International Symposium on Hemodilution *(3rd : 1980 : Pontresina)*. Hemodilution and flow improvement : 3rd International Symposium on Hemodilution, Pontresina, December 7-10, 1980 / volume editors H. Schmid-Schönbein, K. Messmer and H. Rieger. — Basel ; London : Karger, 1981. — vii,356p : ill ; 24cm. — (Bibliotheca haematologica ; no.47)
Includes index
ISBN 3-8055-2899-x (pbk) : £54.80 B82-24061

612′.11′05 — Man. Blood — *Serials*

Biotest bulletin. — No.1-no.6 ; Vol.1, no.1-. — Birmingham (171 Alcester Rd., Moseley, Birmingham B13 8JR) : Biotest, 1976-. — v. ; 25cm
Two issues yearly. — Description based on: Vol.1, no.1
ISSN 0261-1597 = Biotest bulletin : Unpriced B82-07644

612′.11′0722 — Man. Blood. Research, *to 1981*

Rapson, Helen. Circulation of the blood — a history. — London : Muller, June 1982. — [144]p
ISBN 0-584-11013-8 : £7.95 : CIP entry B82-12725

612′.111 — Man. Blood. Red cells. Membranes

Red cell membranes. — London : Academic Press, Aug.1982. — [390]p. — (Biological techniques)
ISBN 0-12-237140-2 : CIP entry B82-15665

612′.1111 — Man. Blood. Haemoglobins. Allosterism

Imai, Kiyohiro. Allosteric effects in haemoglobin / Kiyohiro Imai. — Cambridge : Cambridge University Press, 1982. — xvi,275p : ill,ports ; 24cm
Bibliography: p251-265. — Includes index
ISBN 0-521-22575-2 : £30.00 : CIP rev. B82-07957

612′.112 — Man. Blood. White cells

White blood cells : morphology and rheology as related to function / proceedings, with commentary, of the Symposium held at London, England October 3-4, 1981 ; edited by U. Bagge, G.V.R. Born, P. Gaehtgens. — The Hague ; London : Nijhoff, 1982. — xi,169p ; 25cm. — (Microcirculation reviews ; 1)
ISBN 90-247-2681-6 : Unpriced B82-37030

612′.115 — Man. Fibrinolysis

Marsh, Neville. Fibrinolysis / Neville Marsh. — Chichester : Wiley, c1981. — xv,254p : ill ; 24cm
Includes bibliographies and index
ISBN 0-471-28029-1 : £16.50 : CIP rev. B81-20126

612′.117 — Man. Blood. Platelets

Laboratory evaluation of platelets for transfusion / editors Joseph Fratantoni, John Milton Mishler, IV. — Basel ; London : Karger, [1981]. — vi,124p : ill ; 26cm
Supplement to: Vox sanguinis
Unpriced (pbk) B82-06295

612′.117 — Man. Blood. Platelets. Interactions with blood vessel walls — *Conference proceedings*

Interactions between platelets and vessel walls / a Royal Society discussion organized by G.V.R. Born and J.R. Vane, held on 20 and 21 November 1980. — London : Royal Society, 1981. — viii,412p,[3]leaves of plates : ill ; 31cm
Originally published: in Philosophical transactions of the Royal Society of London, series B, vol.294(no.1072). — Includes bibliographies
ISBN 0-85403-164-2 : £23.00 B82-00662

612′.1181 — Man. Blood. Flow

Blood flow. — London : Academic Press, Dec.1982. — [340]p
ISBN 0-12-683880-1 : CIP entry B82-35214

612′.1181 — Man. Blood. Flow. Measurement

Blood flow measurement in man. — Tunbridge Wells : Castle House Publications, Nov.1982. — [208]p
ISBN 0-7194-0078-3 : £19.50 : CIP entry B82-29021

612′.118223 — Man. Blood. Lymphocytes. Regulation. Role of immunoglobulin idiotypes

Bona, Constantin. Idiotypes and lymphocytes / Constantin A. Bona. — New York ; London : Academic Press, 1981. — xii,211p : ill ; 24cm. — (Immunology)
Bibliography: p193-204. — Includes index
ISBN 0-12-112950-0 : £18.60 B82-21241

612′.118223 — Man. Monoclonal immunoglobins

Monoclonal antibodies in clinical medicine / edited by Andrew J. McMichael and John W. Fabre. — London : Academic Press, 1982. — xii,663p : ill ; 24cm
Includes bibliographies and index
ISBN 0-12-485580-6 : £34.00 : CIP rev. B82-12444

612′.11825 — Man. Blood groups. Compatibility. Testing — *Manuals*

Lockyer, W. John. Essentials of ABO-Rh grouping and compatibility testing : theoretical aspects and practical application / W. John Lockyer ; with a foreword by H.H. Gunson. — Bristol : J. Wright, 1982. — xi,140p : ill,1form ; 22cm
Includes index
ISBN 0-7236-0635-8 (pbk) : Unpriced : CIP rev. B82-04972

612'.11825 — Man. Blood groups. Distribution — *Statistics*

Tills, D.. The distribution of the human blood groups and other polymorphisms. Supplement 1. — Oxford : Oxford University Press, Feb.1982. — [300]p. — (Oxford monographs on medical genetics)
ISBN 0-19-261129-1 : £30.00 : CIP entry
B81-35773

612'.12 — Man. Blood. Biochemistry

Blood biochemistry. — London : Croom Helm, Sept.1982. — [160]p. — (Croom Helm biology in medicine series)
ISBN 0-7099-0003-1 (cased) : £11.95 : CIP entry
ISBN 0-7099-0004-x (pbk) : £5.75 B82-20642

612'.12 — Man. Blood. Gases. Analysis

Adams, A. P.. Principles and practice of blood-gas analysis. — 2nd ed. — Edinburgh : Churchill Livingstone, May 1982. — [104]p
Previous ed.: 1979
ISBN 0-443-02521-5 (pbk) : £10.00 : CIP entry
B82-06842

612'.12 — Man. Blood plasma. Proteins. Chemical analysis, *to 1980*

Rosenfeld, Louis. Origins of clinical chemistry : the evolution of protein analysis / Louis Rosenfeld. — New York : London : Academic Press, 1982. — xviii,366p : ill,ports ; 24cm
Bibliography: p332-355. — Includes index
ISBN 0-12-597580-5 : £25.20 B82-34862

612'.13 — Man. Blood vessels. Smooth muscles

Vascular smooth muscle : metabolic, ionic and contractile mechanisms / edited by M.F. Crass III, C.D. Barnes. — New York ; London : Academic Press, 1982. — xii,205p : ill ; 24cm. — (Research topics in physiology ; 4)
Includes bibliographies and index
ISBN 0-12-195220-7 : £21.20 B82-35740

612'.13 — Man. Cardiovascular system. Blood. Circulation

Berger, Edward C.. The physiology of adequate perfusion / Edward C. Berger ; with 48 illustrations by Bruce D. Bentzen ; with technical assistance by Thomas A. Koelz. — St Louis ; London : Mosby, 1979. — xiv,183p : ill ; 24cm
Bibliography: p158-160. — Includes index
ISBN 0-8016-0618-7 : £16.25 B82-38658

Oka, Syoten. Cardiovascular hemorheology / Syoten Oka. — Cambridge : Cambridge University Press, 1981. — xii,208p : ill ; 22cm
Bibliography: p193-205. — Includes index
ISBN 0-521-23650-9 : £20.00 : CIP rev.
B81-33620

612'.13 — Man. Microcirculatory system

Wiedeman, Mary Purcell. An introduction to microcirculation / Mary Purcell Wiedeman, Ronald F. Tuma, Harvey Norman Mayrovitz. — New York ; London : Academic Press, 1981. — xi,226p : ill,2ports ; 24cm. — (Biophysics and bioengineering series ; v.2)
Includes bibliographies and index
ISBN 0-12-749350-6 : £19.80 B82-12304

612'.13 — Man. Microcirculatory system — *Conference proceedings*

Tokyo International Symposium on Microcirculation *(1981).* Basic aspects of microcirculation : proceedings of the Tokyo International Symposium on Microcirculation, July 26, 1981 / editors Masaharu Tsuchiya, Makishige Asano, Masaya Oda. — Amsterdam ; Oxford : Excerpta Medica, 1982. — xv,376p : ill ; 25cm. — (International congress series ; no.578)
Includes bibliographies and index
ISBN 90-219-0578-7 : £42.19 B82-38830

612'.133 — Man. Arteries

O'Rourke, Michael F.. Arterial function in health and disease / Michael F. O'Rourke. — Edinburgh : Churchill Livingstone, 1982. — 276p : ill ; 25cm
Includes bibliographies and index
ISBN 0-443-02179-1 : £22.00 : CIP rev.
B82-03580

612'.17 — Man. Heart. Cells. Physiology — *Conference proceedings*

Cellular biology of the heart. — London : Academic Press, July 1982. — [180]p
Conference papers
ISBN 0-12-506960-x (pbk) : CIP entry
B82-14509

612'.178 — Man. Heart. Atria. Receptors

Linden, R. J.. Atrial receptors / R.J. Linden and C.T. Kappagoda. — Cambridge : Cambridge University Press, 1982. — xiv,363p : ill ; 23cm. — (Monographs of the Physiological Society ; no.39)
Bibliography: p323-357. — Includes index
ISBN 0-521-24188-x : £37.50 : CIP rev.
B82-14501

612.2 — MAN. PHYSIOLOGY. RESPIRATORY SYSTEM

612'.2 — Man. Respiration — *Early works — Facsimiles*

Saumarez, Richard. On the function of respiration : in health and in disease : and more especially in cholera, typhus &c. : also on the formation of atmospheric air / by Richard Saumarez. — St. Peter Port : Toucan, 1982. — 36p ; 22cm
Facsim of: 1832 ed
ISBN 0-85694-256-1 (pbk) : Unpriced
B82-10030

612'.2 — Man. Respiratory system. Physiology

Levitzky, Michael G.. Pulmonary physiology / Michael G. Levitzky. — New York ; London : McGraw-Hill, 1982. — xiv,271p : ill ; 24cm
Bibliography: p238-245. — Includes index
ISBN 0-07-037431-7 (pbk) : £7.75 B82-25270

Slonim, N. Balfour. Respiratory physiology. — 4th ed. / N. Balfour Slonim, Lyle H. Hamilton. — St. Louis ; London : Mosby, 1981. — x,301p : ill ; 24cm
Previous ed.: 1976. — Bibliography: p274-275. — Includes index
ISBN 0-8016-4668-5 (pbk) : £14.25
B82-08263

612'.21 — Man. Breathing. Physiology — *For children*

Ward, Brian. The lungs and breathing / Brian R. Ward. — London : Watts, 1982. — 48p : col.ill ; 25cm. — (The Human body)
Includes index
ISBN 0-85166-946-8 : £3.99 B82-23818

612'.22 — Man. Respiration. Gas exchange

Pulmonary gas exchange / edited by John B. West. — New York ; London : Academic Press, 1980. — 2v. : ill ; 24cm
Includes bibliographies and index
ISBN 0-12-744501-3 : Unpriced
ISBN 0-12-744502-1 (v.2) : £22.20 B82-39145

612.3 — MAN. PHYSIOLOGY. DIGESTIVE SYSTEM

612'.3 — Man. Digestive system. Physiology

Davenport, Horace W.. Physiology of the digestive tract : an introductory text / Horace W. Davenport. — 5th ed. — Chicago ; London : Year Book Medical, 1982. — vii,245p : ill ; 25cm. — (Physiology textbook series)
Previous ed.: 1977. — Includes bibliographies and index
ISBN 0-8151-2330-2 (cased) : Unpriced
ISBN 0-8151-2329-9 (pbk) : Unpriced
B82-36092

Sanford, Paul A.. Digestive system physiology / Paul A. Sanford. — London : Arnold, 1982. — x,150p ; 23cm. — (Physiological principles in medicine)
Includes bibliographies and index
ISBN 0-7131-4380-0 (pbk) : £5.25 : CIP rev.
B81-30593

612'.3 — Man. Nutrition. Medical aspects

Bender, Arnold E.. Nutrition for medical students / Arnold E. Bender and David A. Bender. — Chichester : Wiley, c1982. — vii,380p : ill ; 24cm
Includes bibliographies and index
ISBN 0-471-28041-0 : £16.00 : CIP rev.
B81-36234

Enteral and parental nutrition : a clinical handbook. — Oxford : Blackwell Scientific, May 1982. — [192]p
ISBN 0-632-00732-x (pbk) : £6.00 : CIP entry
B82-16213

Nutrition and medical practice / editor, Lewis A. Barness with Yank D. Coble, Donald I. Macdonald, George Christakis. — Lancaster : MTP, 1981. — xvii,408p : ill ; 24cm
Includes index
ISBN 0-85200-601-2 : Unpriced B82-29342

612'.3 — Man. Nutrition. Medical aspects - *Conference proceedings - Serials*

Recent advances in clinical nutrition. — 1st (9-11 July 1980). — London (80 Bondway, SW8 2JF) : John Libbey, Apr.1981. — [312]p
Conference papers
ISBN 0-86196-009-2 : £18.00 : CIP entry
ISSN 0260-8170 B81-07459

612'.3 — Man. Nutrition. Medical aspects — *Serials*

Human nutrition. Clinical nutrition. — Vol.36C, no.1 (1982)-. — London : John Libbey, 1982-. — v. : ill ; 25cm
Six issues yearly. — Continues in part: Journal of human nutrition
ISSN 0263-8290 = Human nutrition. Clinical nutrition (corrected) : £37.00 per year
B82-32366

612'.3 — Man. Nutrition. Physiology

Physiology and social nutrition and nutritional education / volume editor Geoffrey H. Bourne. — Basel ; London : Karger, c1981. — ix,229p : ill ; 25cm. — (World review of nutrition and dietetics ; v.38)
Includes index
ISBN 3-8055-3048-x : £47.25
Also classified at 613.2'07'11 B82-21668

612'.3'05 — Man. Digestive system — *Serials — For general practice*

GI for the GP. — Vol.1, no.1 (Nov. 1978)-. — Welwyn Garden City (Welwyn Garden City, Herts.) : Smith Kline & French Laboratories Ltd, 1978-. — v. : col.ill ; 24cm
Six issues yearly
ISSN 0262-9194 = GI for the GP : Only available to general practitioners B82-15166

612'.3'0880542 — Babies. Nutrition. Physiology

Workshop on Metabolic-Endocrine Responses to Food Intake in Infancy *(1981 : Bern).* Metabolic-endocrine responses to food intake in infancy / Workshop on Metabolic-Endocrine Responses to Food Intake in Infancy, Bern, September 24, 1981 ; volume editor G. Zoppi. — Basel ; London : Karger, c1982. — vii,115p : ill ; 24cm. — (Monographs in paediatrics ; v.16)
Includes bibliographies and index
ISBN 3-8055-3477-9 (pbk) : £18.85
B82-30383

612'.31 — Man. Periodontium

The **Periodontal** ligament in health and disease. — Oxford : Pergamon, Feb.1982. — [464]p
ISBN 0-08-024412-2 (cased) : £38.00 : CIP entry
ISBN 0-08-024411-4 (pbk) : £19.00
B81-35905

612'.311 — Man. Teeth. Calcium phosphates

Driessens, F. C. M.. Mineral aspects of dentistry / F.C.M. Driessens. — Basel ; London : Karger, c1982. — xiii,215p : ill ; 25cm. — (Monographs in oral science ; v.10)
Bibliography: p178-212. — Includes index
ISBN 3-8055-3469-8 : £41.00 B82-40292

612'.33 — Man. Intestines. Adaptation — *Conference proceedings*

International Conference on Intestinal Adaptation *(2nd : 1981 : Titisee).* Mechanisms of intestinal adaptation : proceedings of the Second International Conference on Intestinal Adaptation (Falk Symposium 30) held at Titisee, West Germany, May 24-26, 1981 / edited by J.W.L. Robinson, R.H., Dowling, E.-O. Riecken. — Lancaster : MTP. Press, c1982. — 646p : ill ; 25cm. — (Falk symposium ; 30)
Includes index
ISBN 0-85200-442-7 : Unpriced : CIP rev.
B81-38818

612'.34 — Man. Insulin receptors — *Conference proceedings*

Current views on insulin receptors / edited by D. Andreani ... [et al.]. — London : Academic Press, 1981. — xi,625p : ill ; 24cm. — (Proceedings of the Serono symposia ; v.41)
Conference papers. — Includes bibliographies and index
ISBN 0-12-058620-7 : £34.80 : CIP rev.
B81-34116

612'.35 — Man. Liver

Sherlock, Sheila. The human liver / Sheila Sherlock. — Burlington, N.C. : Carolina Biological Supply Co., Scientific Publications Division, c1978 ; Chichester : Distributed by Packard. — 16p : ill(some col.) ; 25cm. — (Carolina biology readers ; 83)
Bibliography: p16
ISBN 0-89278-283-8 (unbound) : £0.80
B82-31600

612'.35 — Man. Liver. Metabolism. Regulation — *Festschriften*

Short-term regulation of liver metabolism / editors Louis Hue and Gerald Van de Werve. — Amsterdam ; Oxford : Elsevier/North-Holland Biomedical, 1981. — xxv,464p : ill ; 25cm
Essays in honour of Douglas Hems. — Includes bibliographies and index
ISBN 0-444-80333-5 : £54.74 B82-11226

612'.391 — Man. Thirst. Psychophysiological aspects

Rolls, Barbara J.. Thirst / Barbara J. Rolls and Edmund T. Rolls. — Cambridge : Cambridge University Press, 1982. — xiii,194p : ill ; 23cm. — (Problems in the behavioural sciences)
Bibliography: p171-190. — Includes index
ISBN 0-521-22918-9 (cased) : £15.00 : CIP rev.
ISBN 0-521-29718-4 (pbk) : £5.50 B82-03362

612'.392 — Man. Minerals. Metabolism

Eastham, R. D.. A guide to water electrolyte and acid-base metabolism. — Bristol : J. Wright, Jan.1983. — [244]p
ISBN 0-7236-0662-5 (pbk) : £8.50 : CIP entry
B82-37466

612'.3924 — Man. Calcium & phosphates. Transport — *Conference proceedings*

Calcium and phosphate transport across biomembranes / [based on an international workshop on calcium and phosphate transport across biomembranes held in Vienna, Austria, March 2-4, 1981] ; edited by Felix Bronner, Meinrad Peterlik. — New York ; London : Academic Press, 1981. — xxi,300p : ill ; 24cm
Includes bibliographies and index
ISBN 0-12-135280-3 : £18.60 B82-29602

612.3924 — Man. Nitrogen. Metabolism — *Conference proceedings*

Nitrogen metabolism in man / international symposium organised by the Rank Prize Funds and held at Kingston, Jamaica on 21-25 November, 1980 ; edited by J.C. Waterlow and J.M.L. Stephen. — London : Applied Science Publishers, c1981. — xvi,558p : ill ; 23cm
Includes bibliographies and index
ISBN 0-85334-991-6 : Unpriced : CIP rev.
B81-31515

612'.3924 — Man. Trace elements

Rose, J.. Trace elements in health. — London : Butterworth, Nov.1982. — [256]p
ISBN 0-407-00255-3 : £18.00 : CIP entry
B82-28277

612'.397 — Man. Lipids. Metabolism

Brisson, Germain J.. Lipids in human nutrition : an appraisal of some dietary concepts / Germain J. Brisson. — Lancaster : MTP, 1982, c1981. — xiv,175p : ill ; 21cm
Originally published: Englewood, N.J. : J.K. Burgess, 1981. — Includes index
ISBN 0-85200-600-4 : Unpriced B82-13381

612'.399 — Man. Vitamin C

Basu, T. K.. Vitamin C in health and disease / T.K. Basu, C.J. Schorah. — London : Croom Helm, c1982. — 152p : ill ; 23cm
Bibliography: p128-147. — Includes index
ISBN 0-7099-0445-2 : £11.95 : CIP rev.
B81-34307

Mervyn, Leonard. Vitamin C : enemy of the common cold / by Leonard Mervyn. — Wellingborough : Thorsons, 1981. — 94p ; 18cm
Includes index
ISBN 0-7225-0717-8 (pbk) : £0.95 : CIP rev.
B81-30279

Nobile, Silvia. Vitamin C : the mysterious redox-system a trigger of life? / Silvia Nobile and Joan Mary Woodhill. — Lancaster : MTP, c1981. — 185p : ill ; 24cm
Bibliography: p145-159. — Includes index
ISBN 0-85200-419-2 : Unpriced : CIP rev.
B81-18177

612'.399 — Man. Vitamin C — *Conference proceedings*

Vitamin C : (ascorbic acid) / [an international symposium organised and sponsored by Roche Products Limited at the University of Warwick, Coventry, on the 9th and 10th of April 1981] ; edited by J.N. Counsell and D.H. Hornig. — London : Applied Science Publishers, c1981. — xii,383p : ill ; 24cm
Includes index
ISBN 0-85334-109-5 : £32.00 : CIP rev.
B81-33876

612.4 — MAN. PHYSIOLOGY. LYMPHATIC, EXOCRINE, ENDOCRINE SYSTEMS

612'.4 — Man. Cells. Secretory granules

The **Secretory** granule / edited by A.M. Poisner and J.M. Trifaró. — Amsterdam ; Oxford : Elsevier Biomedical, 1982. — xviii,415p : ill ; 25cm. — (The Secretory process ; v.1)
Includes bibliographies and index
ISBN 0-444-80383-1 : £56.14 B82-38179

612'.4 — Man. Endocrine system

Fregly, Melvin J.. Human endocrinology : an interactive text / Melvin J. Fregly, William G. Luttge. — New York ; Oxford : Elsevier Biomedical, c1982. — viii,365p : ill ; 26cm
Includes bibliographies and index
ISBN 0-444-00662-1 (pbk) : £14.83
B82-38130

Hardy, Richard N.. Endocrine physiology / Richard N. Hardy. — London : Edward Arnold, 1981. — xiv,174p : ill ; 23cm. — (Physiological principles in medicine)
Bibliography: pxiv. — Includes index
ISBN 0-7131-4378-9 (pbk) : £4.95 : CIP rev.
B81-14856

612'.4'0088042 — Pregnant women. Endocrine system — *Conference proceedings*

Symposium on Gynecologic Endocrinology *(5th : 1980 : University of Tennessee)*. Endocrinology of pregnancy : based on the proceedings of the Fifth Annual Symposium on Gynecologic Endocrinology held March 3-5, 1980 at the University of Tennessee, Memphis, Tennessee / editor James R. Givens ; associate editor Garland D. Anderson. — Chicago ; London : Year Book Medical, c1981. — x,393p : ill ; 24cm
Includes index
ISBN 0-8151-3529-7 : £43.50 B82-18073

612'.405 — Man. Development. Role of hormones

Hormones in development and aging / edited by Antonia Vernadakis, Paola S. Timiras. — Lancaster : MTP, c1982. — 686p : ill ; 26cm
Includes bibliographies and index
ISBN 0-85200-578-4 (corrected) : Unpriced
B82-29676

612'.405 — Man. Hormone receptors

Hormone receptors / volume editor L.D. Kohn. — Chichester : Wiley, c1982. — xi,392p : ill ; 24cm. — (Horizons in biochemistry and biophysics, ISSN 0096-2708 ; v.6)
Includes bibliographies and index
ISBN 0-471-10049-8 : £28.50 : CIP rev.
B82-03603

612'.405 — Man. Prostaglandins

Prostaglandins / edited by James B. Lee. — New York ; Oxford : Elsevier, c1982. — xvi,377p : ill ; 24cm. — (Current endocrinology)
Includes bibliographies and index
ISBN 0-444-00645-1 : £27.70 B82-23544

612'.405 — Man. Prostaglandins — *Serials*

Prostaglandins, leukotrienes and medicine. — Vol.8, no.1 (Jan. 1982)-. — Edinburgh : Churchill Livingstone, 1982-. — v. : ill ; 25cm
Monthly. — Continues: Prostaglandins and medicine
ISSN 0262-1746 = Prostaglandins leukotrienes and medicine : £80.00 per year
Also classified at 612'.01513 B82-18544

612'.43 — Man. Thymus — *Conference proceedings*

The **Thymus** gland / edited by Marion D. Kendall. — London : Academic Press, 1981. — xii,218p : ill ; 24cm. — (The Anatomical Society of Great Britain and Ireland Symposium ; no.1)
Includes bibliographies and index
ISBN 0-12-404180-9 : £13.80 : CIP rev.
B81-30213

Thymus, thymic hormones and T lymphocytes / edited by F. Aiuti and H. Wigzell. — London : Academic Press, 1980. — ix,445p : ill ; 24cm. — (Proceedings of the Serono symposia, ISSN 0308-5503 ; v.38)
Conference papers. — Includes bibliographies and index
ISBN 0-12-046450-0 : £25.00 B82-12365

612'.46 — Man. Sodium. Excretion. Regulation. Role of hormones — *Conference proceedings*

Regulation of Renal Sodium Excretion by Hormones *(Conference : 1980 : Bratislava)*. Hormonal regulation of sodium excretion : proceedings of the Satellite Symposium of the 28th I.U.P.S. Congress. Regulation of Renal Sodium Excretion by Hormones held in Bratislava, Czechoslovakia, 8-12 July 1980 / Branislav Lichardus, Robert W. Schrier and Jozef Ponec editors. — Amsterdam ; Oxford : Elsevier/North-Holland Biomedical, c1980. — xiv,410p : ill ; 25cm. — (Developments in endocrinology ; v.10)
Includes index
ISBN 0-444-80289-4 : £25.71 B82-34315

612'.463 — Man. Kidneys

Gower, P. E.. Nephrology. — Oxford : Blackwell Scientific, Oct.1982. — [272]p. — (Pocket consultants)
ISBN 0-86286-025-3 (pbk) : £6.95 : CIP entry
B82-29412

O'Connor, W. J.. Normal renal function : the excretion of water, urea and electrolytes derived from food and drink / W.J. O'Connor. — London : Croom Helm, c1982. — viii,433p : ill ; 23cm
Bibliography: p387-420. — Includes index
ISBN 0-7099-1917-4 : £15.95 : CIP rev.
B82-09592

612'.463 — Man. Kidneys. Physiology

Catto, Graeme R. D.. Clinical aspects of renal physiology / Graeme R.D. Catto, John A.R. Smith ; with a foreword by John Richmond. — London : Baillière Tindall, 1981. — 147p,viiip of plates : ill ; 24cm
Includes bibliographies and index
ISBN 0-7020-0893-1 (pbk) : £7.75 : CIP rev.
B81-30166

Hawker, Ross Wilson. Notebook of medical physiology : renal and body fluids : a revision text for candidates preparing for examinations in basic medical sciences ; includes multiple choice questions / Ross Wilson Hawker. — Edinburgh : Churchill Livingstone, 1982. — 190p : ill ; 22cm
Includes bibliographies and index
ISBN 0-443-02502-9 (pbk) : £4.95 : CIP rev.
B82-06841

Lote, Christopher J.. Principles of renal physiology / Christopher J. Lote. — London : Croom Helm, c1982. — 179p : ill ; 23cm
Includes bibliographies and index
ISBN 0-7099-0078-3 (cased) : £12.95 : CIP rev.
ISBN 0-7099-0079-1 (pbk) : Unpriced
B81-34305

612'.492 — Man. Posterior pituitary gland. Hormones: Peptides — *Conference proceedings*

Pituitary hormones and related peptides / edited by M. Motta, M. Zanisi and F. Piva. — London : Academic Press, 1982. — xv,406p : ill ; 24cm. — (Proceedings of the Serono symposia, ISSN 0308-5503 ; v.49)
Includes bibliographies and index
ISBN 0-12-509160-5 : Unpriced : CIP rev.
B82-10777

612.6 — MAN. PHYSIOLOGY. REPRODUCTIVE SYSTEM AND DEVELOPMENT

612'.6 — Man. Development. Medical aspects

Human growth and development throughout life : a nursing perspective / edited by Patty Maynard Hill, Patricia Humphrey. — New York ; Chichester : Wiley, c1982. — xiv,496p : ill ; 25cm
Includes bibliographies and index
ISBN 0-471-05814-9 : £14.75 B82-28033

612.6 — Man. Fertility. Regulation. Immunological aspects

Jones, Warren R.. Immunological fertility regulation. — Oxford : Blackwell Scientific, Feb.1983. — [282]p
ISBN 0-86793-008-x : £29.50 : CIP entry
B82-39835

612'.6 — Man. Reproduction

Basic reproductive medicine / edited by David Hamilton and Frederick Naftolin. — Cambridge, Mass. ; London : MIT
Vol.1: Basis and development of reproduction. — c1981. — xii,174p : ill ; 24cm
Includes bibliographies and index
ISBN 0-262-08089-3 : £15.75 B82-21017

Basic reproductive medicine / edited by David Hamilton and Frederick Naftolin. — Cambridge, Mass. ; London : MIT
Vol.2: Reproductive function in men. — c1982. — xvi,350p : ill ; 24cm
Includes bibliographies and index
ISBN 0-262-08102-4 (cased) : £17.50
ISBN 0-262-58046-2 (pbk) : Unpriced
B82-37520

Stirrat, Gordon M.. Aids to reproductive biology. — Edinburgh : Churchill Livingstone, Oct.1982. — [160]p
ISBN 0-443-02233-x : £3.95 : CIP entry
B82-24020

612'.6 — Man. Reproduction — *Conference proceedings*

Atlas of human reproduction. — Lancaster : MTP, Oct.1982. — [250]p
Conference papers
ISBN 0-85200-485-0 : £29.95 : CIP entry
B82-23876

Human reproduction : proceedings of III World Congress, Berlin, March 22-26, 1981 / editors K. Semm, K. Mettler. — Amsterdam ; Oxford : Excerpta Medica, 1981. — xv,585p : ill ; 25cm. — (International congress series ; no.551)
Includes bibliographies and index
ISBN 90-219-0493-4 : £39.50 B82-08564

612'.6 — Man. Reproduction *expounded by* **reproduction of primates**

Non-human primate models for study of human reproduction : satellite symposium to the 7th Congress of the International Primatological Society on relevance of researches on non-human primates to the understanding of human reproduction, Bangalore, January 8-12, 1979 / editor T.C. Anand Kumar. — Basel ; London : Karger, c1980. — vi,232p : ill ; 23cm
Includes bibliographies
ISBN 3-8055-0540-x (pbk) : £28.30
B82-11587

612'.6 — Man. Sex

Godow, Annette G.. Human sexuality / Annette G. Godow. — St. Louis, Mo. ; London : Mosby, 1982. — xvi,669p : ill,ports ; 24cm
Bibliography: p622-630. — Includes index
ISBN 0-8016-1861-4 (pbk) : £12.75
B82-22841

612.6 — Man. Sexual intercourse

Havil, Anthony. The technique of sex. — 6th ed. — Wellingborough : Thorsons, Jan.1983. — [128]p
Previous ed.: 1975
ISBN 0-7225-0799-2 (pbk) : £3.50 : CIP entry
B82-32628

612'.6 — Man. Sexuality

Carrera, Michael. Sex : the facts, the acts and your feelings / Michael Carrera. — London : Mitchell Beazley, c1981. — 448p : ill ; 27cm
Bibliography: p435-436. — Includes index
ISBN 0-85533-346-4 : £9.95 B82-02150

Hyde, Janet Shibley. Understanding human sexuality / Janet Shibley Hyde. — 2nd ed. — New York ; London : McGraw-Hill, c1982. — xxv,623p : ill(some col.),ports ; 24cm
Previous ed.: 1979. — Bibliography: p590-609. — Includes index
ISBN 0-07-031567-1 : £14.50 B82-24906

The **Little** blue book. — 5th ed. — Oxford (c/o Sally Hirsh, 43 Woodstock Rd., Oxford OX2 6HE) : WOLS, c1978. — 56p : ill,1map ; 21cm
Cover title. — Previous ed.: 1977
£0.50 (pbk) B82-38651

Masters, William H.. Human sexual response / William H. Masters, Virginia E. Johnson. — Toronto ; London : Bantam, 1980, c1966. — xiii,363p : ill ; 18cm
Originally published: Boston, Mass. : Little, Brown, 1966. — Bibliography: p313-333. — Includes index
ISBN 0-553-13761-1 (pbk) : £1.95 B82-35025

Woods, Nancy Fugate. Human sexuality in health and illness / Nancy Fugate Woods. — 2nd ed. — St. Louis ; London : Mosby, 1979. — xii,400p : ill ; 23cm
Previous ed.: 1975. — Includes bibliographies and index
ISBN 0-8016-5619-2 (pbk) : Unpriced
B82-19325

612.6'0024613 — Man. Sexuality — *For nursing*

Human sexualilty in nursing process / edited by Elizabeth M. Lion. — New York ; Chichester : Wiley, c1982. — xiv,496p : ill ; 24cm
Includes bibliographies and index
ISBN 0-471-03869-5 (pbk) : £11.75
B82-28087

612'.6'0097292 — Jamaica. Man. Sex

Brody, Eugene B.. Sex, contraception, and motherhood in Jamaica / Eugene B. Brody. — Cambridge, Mass. ; London : Harvard University Press, 1981. — 278p : ill ; 24cm. — (A Commonwealth Fund book)
Bibliography: p263-272. — Includes index
ISBN 0-674-80277-2 : £14.00 B82-13734

612'.61 — Men. Reproductive system

Silber, Sherman J.. The male. — London : Granada, May 1982. — [192]p
Originally published: New York : Scribners, 1981
ISBN 0-246-11776-1 : £5.95 : CIP entry
B82-07409

612'.61 — Men. Sex

Llewellyn-Jones, Derek. Every man. — Oxford : Oxford University Press, Sept.1982. — [312]p. — (Oxford paperbacks)
Originally published: 1981
ISBN 0-19-286026-7 (pbk) : £2.50 : CIP entry
B82-18993

612'.62 — Man. Conception

Edwards, R. G.. Conception in the human female / Robert G. Edwards. — London : Academic Press, 1980. — xvi,1087p : ill(some col.) ; 26cm
Includes index
ISBN 0-12-232450-1 : £48.50 : CIP rev.
B80-13833

612'.62 — Women. Gonadotrophins — *Conference proceedings*

The **Gonadotrophins** : basic science and clinical aspects in females / edited by C. Flamigni, J.R. Givens. — London : Academic Press, 1982. — xvii,492p : ill ; 24cm. — (Proceedings of the Serono symposia, ISSN 0308-5503 ; v.42)
Includes bibliographies and index
ISBN 0-12-258550-x : Unpriced : CIP rev.
B81-38310

612'.64 — Man. Embryos & foetuses. Development

Moore, Keith L.. The developing human : clinically orientated embryology / Keith L. Moore ; illustrated primarily by Glen Reid. — 3rd ed. — Philadelphia ; London : Saunders, 1982. — xii,479p : ill(some col.) ; 27cm
Previous ed.: 1977. — Ill on lining papers. — Includes bibliographies and index
ISBN 0-7216-6472-5 : £16.95 B82-36825

612'.64'076 — Man. Embryos & foetuses. Development — *Questions & answers*

Moore, Keith L.. Study guide and review manual of human embryology / Keith L. Moore. — 2nd ed. — Philadelphia ; London : Saunders, c1982. — xi,286p : ill ; 26cm
Previous ed.: 1976
ISBN 0-7216-6476-8 (pbk) : Unpriced
B82-38910

612'.647 — Man. Placenta. Proteins. Immunological aspects

Immunology of human placental proteins. — Eastbourne : Saunders, Apr.1982. — [160]p
ISBN 0-03-062117-8 : £15.00 : CIP entry
B82-11503

612'.647'00724 — Man. Foetuses. Physiology. Research. Use of laboratory animals: Mammals

Animal models in fetal medicine / edited by P.W. Nathanielsz. — Amsterdam ; Oxford : Elsevier/North-Holland Biomedical. — (Monographs in fetal physiology ; v.2)
1. — 1980. — xv,368p : ill ; 25cm
Includes index
ISBN 0-444-80153-7 : £34.75 B82-40733

612'.65 — Children. Growth

Nelms, Bobbie Crew. Growth and development : a primary health care approach / Bobbie Crew Nelms, Ruth G. Mullins. — Englewood Cliffs ; London : Prentice-Hall, c1982. — xii,803p : ill,forms ; 24cm
Bibliography: p782-787. — Includes index
ISBN 0-13-365528-8 : £24.70 B82-24086

612'.65 — Children. Growth. Assessment

Brook, Charles G. D.. Growth assessment in childhood and adolescence. — Oxford : Blackwell Scientific, July 1982. — [176]p
ISBN 0-632-00955-1 (pbk) : £8.00 : CIP entry
B82-20762

612'.65 — Children. Growth. Control

Control of growth / edited by J.M. Tanner. — London : Published for the British Council by Churchill Livingstone, c1981. — 208-304p : ill,1form ; 28cm
Cover title. — Reprint of September 1981 issue of British medical bulletin (Vol.37, No.3). — Includes bibliographies and index
ISBN 0-443-02526-6 (pbk) : Unpriced
B82-05239

612'.65 — Children. Growth *related to* **physical fitness**

Shephard, Roy J.. Physical activity and growth / Roy J. Shephard. — Chicago ; London : Year Book Medical, c1982. — xi,340p : ill ; 23cm
Bibliography: p250-315. — Includes index
ISBN 0-8151-7643-0 : £26.50
Primary classification 613.7'042 B82-22923

612'.65 — Children. Physical development

Scientific foundations of paediatrics / edited by John A. Davis and John Dobbing. — 2nd ed. — London : Heinemann Medical, 1981. — xv,1095p : ill ; 29cm
Previous ed.: 1974. — Includes bibliographies and index
ISBN 0-433-07191-5 : £75.00 B82-04010

612'.65 — Young persons. Growth. Assessment. Parent-specific adjustments

Himes, J. H.. Parent-specific adjustments for assessment of recumbent length and stature / J.H. Himes, A.F. Roche and D. Thissen. — Basel ; London : Karger, 1981. — vi,88p : ill ; 24cm. — (Monographs in paediatrics ; v.13)
Bibliography: p81-88
ISBN 3-8055-2594-x (pbk) : £19.80
B82-07725

612'.65'0222 — Children. Growth — *Illustrations*

Tanner, J. M.. Atlas of children's growth : normal variation and growth disorders / J.M. Tanner and R.H. Whitehouse. — London : Academic Press, 1982. — 206p : ill ; 36x40cm
Bibliography: p196
ISBN 0-12-683340-0 : Unpriced : CIP rev.
B81-18126

612'.654 — Children, to 4 years. Physical development. Screening

Illingworth, Ronald S.. Basic developmental screening : 0-4 years / Ronald S. Illingworth. — 3rd ed. — Oxford : Blackwell Scientific, 1982. — 62p : ill ; 19cm
Previous ed.: 1977. — Bibliography: p62. — Includes index
ISBN 0-632-00945-4 (pbk) : £2.80 : CIP rev.
B82-10862

612'.661 — Man. Puberty — *For children*

Mayle, Peter. What's happening to me? : the answer to some of the world's most embarrassing questions / written by Peter Mayle ; illustrated by Arthur Robins. — London : Macmillan, 1978, c1975. — [51]p : ill (some col.) ; 26cm
Originally published: Secaucus, N.J. : Lyle Stuart, 1975
ISBN 0-333-24179-7 (pbk) : £1.95 : CIP rev.
B78-08308

612'.664 — Women. Breasts

Stanway, Penny. The breast : Penny and Andrew Stanway / illustrated by Giovanni Casselli. — London : Granada, 1982. — 250p : ill ; 20cm. — (A Mayflower book)
Includes index
ISBN 0-583-13464-5 (pbk) : £1.95 B82-16156

612'.665 — Women. Menopause

Women's change of life. — 6th ed. — Wellingborough : Science of Life Books, Jan.1983. — [80]p
Previous ed.: 1969
ISBN 0-909911-98-3 (pbk) : £0.95 : CIP entry
B82-36167

612'.665 — Women. Menopause — *Conference proceedings*

International Congress on the Menopause *(3rd : 1981 : Ostend)*. The controversial climacteric : the workshop moderators' reports presented at the Third International Congress on the Menopause, held in Ostend, Belgium, in June 1981, under the auspices of the International Menopause Society / edited by P.A. van Keep, W.H. Utian and A. Vermeulen ; ... assisted by Pamela Freebody. — Lancaster : MTP, c1982. — xvi,182p : ill ; 24cm
Includes bibliographies and index
ISBN 0-85200-410-9 : Unpriced : CIP rev.
B82-06523

The **Menopause** : clinical, endocrinological and pathophysiological aspects / edited by P. Fioretti ... [et al.]. — London : Academic Press, 1982. — xxii,584p : ill ; 24cm. — (Proceedings of the Serono symposia ; v.39)
Includes bibliographies
ISBN 0-12-256080-9 : £36.20 : CIP rev.
B82-03090

612'.67 — Adults. Ageing

Aging / [James G. March, editor in chief]. — New York ; London : Academic Press
Social change / edited by Sara B. Kiesler, James N. Morgan, Valerie Kincade Oppenheimer. — c1981. — xxiv,631p : ill ; 24cm
Conference papers. — Includes bibliographies and index
ISBN 0-12-040002-2 (cased) : £32.80
ISBN 0-12-040022-7 (pbk) : £16.20
B82-27136

Evans, Peter, *1940-*. Getting on : caring for the elderly / Peter Evans. — London : Granada, 1982. — viii,136p ; 21cm
Bibliography: p130-131. — Includes index
ISBN 0-246-11136-4 : £4.95 : CIP rev.
B82-01151

612'.67 — Gerontology

Lectures in gerontology. — London : Academic Press, May 1982
Vol.1a. — [280]p
ISBN 0-12-721601-4 : CIP entry B82-07494

Lectures in gerontology. — London : Academic Press, May 1982
Vol.1b. — [280]p
ISBN 0-12-721641-3 : CIP entry B82-07493

612'.67 — Man. Ageing

Aging : a challenge to science and society. — Oxford : Published on behalf of l'Institut de la vie and the World Health Organization Regional Office for Europe by Oxford University Press. — (Oxford medical publications)
Vol.2. — 1981. — xvi,403p : ill ; 24cm
Includes bibliographies and index. — Contents: Part I: Medicine / edited by A.J.J. Gilmore, A. Svanborg, M. Marois — Part II: Social issues and social policy / edited by Walter M. Beattie, Jr, Jerzy Piotrowski, M. Marois
ISBN 0-19-261255-7 : £30.00 : CIP rev.
B80-18752

Aging. — Oxford : Oxford University Press. — (Oxford medical publications)
Conference papers
Vol.3: Behavioural sciences and conclusions. — Dec.1981. — [350]p
ISBN 0-19-261256-5 : £30.00 : CIP entry
B81-31353

Aging / [James G. March, editor in chief]. — New York ; London : Academic Press
In 3 vols
Biology and behavior / edited by James L. McGaugh, Sara B. Kiesler. — c1981. — xx,407p : ill ; 24cm
Conference papers. — Includes bibliographies and index
ISBN 0-12-040001-4 (cased) : Unpriced
ISBN 0-12-040021-9 (pbk) : £9.60 B82-21240

Fries, James F.. Vitality and aging : implications of the rectangular curve / James F. Fries, Lawrence M. Crapo. — Oxford : W.H. Freeman, c1981. — xii,172p : ill ; 24cm
Bibliography: p153-165. — Includes index
ISBN 0-7167-1308-x : £10.95
ISBN 0-7167-1309-8 (pbk) : £4.95 B82-05843

Neuhaus, Ruby Hart. Successful aging / Ruby Hart Neuhaus, Robert Henry Neuhaus. — New York ; Chichester : Wiley, c1982. — xviii,285p ; 24cm
Bibliography: p250-274. — Includes index
ISBN 0-471-08448-4 : £12.50
Also classified at 305.2'6'0973 B82-26472

612.7 — MAN. PHYSIOLOGY. MOTOR AND INTEGUMENTARY SYSTEMS

612'.74 — Man. Muscles. Fatigue

Human muscle fatigue. — London : Pitman Medical, May 1981. — [362]p. — (Ciba Foundation symposium ; 82)
ISBN 0-272-79618-2 : £19.50 : CIP entry
B81-07472

612'.74 — Man. Muscles. Physiology

Keynes, R. D.. Nerve and muscle / R.D. Keynes and D.J. Aidley. — Cambridge : Cambridge University Press, 1981. — vi,163p : ill ; 23cm. — (Cambridge texts in the physiological sciences ; 2)
Bibliography: p157-160. — Includes index
ISBN 0-521-23945-1 (cased) : £15.00 : CIP rev.
ISBN 0-521-28362-0 (pbk) : £4.95
Primary classification 596'.01852 B81-31190

612'.741 — Man. Muscles. Contraction

Bagshaw, C. R.. Muscle contraction. — London : Chapman and Hall, Sept.1982. — [80]p. — (Outline studies in biology)
ISBN 0-412-13450-0 (pbk) : £2.75 : CIP entry
B82-22801

612'.744 — Man. Muscles. ATP

Chappell, J. B.. ATP / J.B. Chappell. — Burlington, N.C. : Carolina Biological Supply Co., Scientific Publications Division, c1977 ; Chichester : Distributed by Packard. — 32p : ill ; 25cm. — (Carolina biology readers ; 50)
Bibliography: p32
ISBN 0-89278-250-1 (unbound) : £1.35
B82-31590

612'.744'0321 — Man. Voluntary muscles. Chemical constituents — *Encyclopaedias*

Walter, W. G.. Skeletal muscle pharmacology : glossary of muscle constituents and chemical research tools, with reference to muscle physiology and neuromuscular disorders : an alphabetical list of these substances and their synonyms and a bibliography of the literature on skeletal muscles from which the data are derived / compiled by W.G. Walter. — Amsterdam ; Oxford : North-Holland, 1981. — ix,473p ; 25cm
Includes index
ISBN 90-219-3064-1 : £51.06
ISBN 0-444-90226-0 (Elsevier North-Holland)
Primary classification 616.7'4061'0321
B82-13432

612'.75 — Man. Face. Bones. Growth

Goose, Denys H.. Human dentofacial growth / by Denys H. Goose and John Appleton. — Oxford : Pergamon, 1982. — ix,228p : ill ; 24cm
Includes bibliographies and index
ISBN 0-08-026394-1 (cased) : Unpriced : CIP rev.
ISBN 0-08-026393-3 (pbk) : £8.95 B82-03733

612'.75 — Man. Joints. Physiology

Kapandji, I. A.. The physiology of the joints. — 2nd ed. — Edinburgh : Churchill Livingstone
Translation of: Physiologie articulaire
Vol.1: Upper limb. — Dec.1981. — [208]p
Previous ed. of this translation: London : Livingstone, 1970
ISBN 0-443-02504-5 (pbk) : £6.50 : CIP entry
B81-31833

612'.75 — Man. Mineral connective tissues — *Conference proceedings*

International Conference on the Chemistry and Biology of Mineralized Connective Tissues *(1st : 1981 : Northwestern University Dental School)*. The chemistry and biology of mineralized connective tissues : proceedings of the First International Conference on the Chemistry and Biology of Mineralized Connective Tissues held 3-7 May 1981 at the Northwestern University Dental School, Chicago, Illinois, U.S.A. / editor Arthur Veis. — New York ; Oxford : Elsevier/North Holland, c1981. — xxiv,680p : ill ; 25cm. — (Developments in biochemistry ; v.22)
Includes index
ISBN 0-444-00678-8 : £53.76 B82-11942

612'.75 — Man. Skeletal system. Mechanics - *Conference proceedings*

Mechanical factors and the skeleton. — London (80 Bondway, SW8 1SF) : John Libbey, Apr.1981. — [224]p
Conference papers
ISBN 0-86196-006-8 : £14.00 : CIP entry
B81-07458

612'.75 — Man. Synovial joints — *Conference proceedings*

International Symposium on Articular Synovium *(1981 : Bruges)*. Articular synovium : anatomy, physiology, pathology, pharmacology, and therapy : International Symposium on Articular Synovium, Bruges, October 15-17, 1981 / editor P. Franchimont. — Basel ; London : Karger, c1982. — vi,183p : ill ; 23cm
Includes bibliographies
ISBN 3-8055-3461-2 (pbk) : £31.70
B82-40293

612'.76 — Biomechanics

Anthropometry and biomechanics : theory and application / [proceedings of a NATO symposium on anthropometry and biomechanics: theory and application, held July 7-11, 1980, at Queens' College, Cambridge, England] ; edited by Ronald Easterby, K.H.E. Kroemer and Don B. Chaffin. — New York ; London : Published in cooperation with NATO Scientific Affairs Division [by] Plenum, c1982. — x,327p : ill ; 26cm. — (NATO conference series. 111, Human factors)
Includes bibliographies and index
ISBN 0-306-40745-0 : Unpriced
Primary classification 620.8'2 B82-33765

612'.76 — Gymnastics. Techniques. Biomechanics

Smith, Tony. Gymnastics. — London : Hodder and Stoughton, Nov.1982. — [192]p
ISBN 0-340-28164-2 (cased) : £8.50 : CIP entry
ISBN 0-340-28165-0 (pbk) : £4.50 B82-27348

612'.76 — Kinesiology

Cooper, John M. (John Miller). Kinesiology. — 5th ed. / John M. Cooper, Marlene Adrian, Ruth B. Glassow. — St. Louis ; London : Mosby, 1982. — ix,452p : ill ; 25cm
Previous ed.: 1976. — Includes bibliographies and index
ISBN 0-8016-1040-0 : £13.50 B82-16567

612'.76 — Man. Exercise. Bioenergetics & biomechanics

Human body dynamics : impact, occupational, and athletic aspects / edited by Dhanjoo N. Ghista. — Oxford : Clarendon, 1982. — xii,549p : ill ; 24cm. — (Oxford medical engineering series)
Includes index
ISBN 0-19-857548-3 : £40.00 : CIP rev. B81-34415

612'.76 — Man. Movement

Luttgens, Kathryn. Kinesiology : scientific basis of human motion / Kathryn Luttgens, Katharine F. Wells. — 7th ed. — Philadelphia ; London : Saunders College Publishing, c1982. — xv,656p : ill ; 25cm
Previous ed.: / by Katherine F. Wells, Kathryn Luttgens. 1977. — Includes index
ISBN 0-03-058358-6 : £16.95 B82-25827

Movement. — [London] : British Museum (Natural History), 1980. — 18p : ill(some col.) ; 21cm. — (Publication / British Museum (Natural History) ; no.829)
Bibliography: p18
ISBN 0-565-00829-3 (unbound) : £0.30 B82-37882

612'.76 — Man. Movement. Mechanics

Watkins, James. An introduction to the mechanics of human movement. — Lancaster : MTP Press, Dec.1982. — [150]p
ISBN 0-85200-492-3 : £9.00 : CIP entry B82-37503

612'.76 — Man. Movement. Mechanics — *For physical education*

Hay, James G.. The anatomical and mechanical bases of human motion / James G. Hay, J. Gavin Reid. — Englewood Cliffs ; London : Prentice-Hall, c1982. — xv,443p : ill,1map ; 25cm
Includes bibliographies and index
ISBN 0-13-035139-3 : £14.95 B82-20083

612'.76'01515353 — Biomechanics. Mathematics. Finite element methods

Finite elements in biomechanics / edited by R.H. Gallagher ... [et al.]. — Chichester : Wiley, c1982. — xiv,404p : ill ; 24cm. — (Wiley series in numerical methods in engineerng)
Conference papers. — Includes bibliographies and index
ISBN 0-471-09996-1 : Unpriced : CIP rev. B82-02663

612'.76'024616 — Man. Movement. Mechanics — *For physiotherapy*

Galley, P. M.. Human movement : an introductory text for physiotherapy students / P.M. Galley, A.L. Forster. — Edinburgh : Churchill Livingstone, 1982. — 212p ; 25cm
Includes bibliographies and index
ISBN 0-443-02068-x (pbk) : £6.95 : CIP rev. B82-09714

612'.76'05 — Biomechanics — *Serials*

Perspectives in biomechanics. — Vol.1-. — Chur ; London (61 Grays Inn Rd, WC1X 8TL) : Harwood Academic Publishers, 1980-. — v. ; 24cm
ISSN 0272-6327 = Perspectives in biomechanics : Unpriced B82-01065

612'.76'071141 — Great Britain. Higher education institutions. Curriculum subjects: Man. Movement — *Conference proceedings*

Human Movement Studies Conference *(1979 : University of Nottingham Conference Centre).* Human Movement Studies Conference 28-29 September 1979 University of Nottingham Conference Centre, Sutton Bonington : the conference report. — London (344 Gray's Inn Rd, WC1X 8BP) : Council for National Academic Awards, 1980. — 80p : ill ; 30cm
At head of title: Council for National Academic Awards, Calouste Gulbenkian Foundation. — Includes index
Unpriced (pbk) B82-31762

612'.78 — Man. Speech. Physiology

Speech motor control : proceedings of an international symposium on speech motor control, held at the Wenner-Gren Center, Stockholm, May 11 and 12, 1981 / editors Sten Grillner ... [et al.]. — Oxford : Pergamon, 1982. — xiii,281p : ill ; 26cm. — (Wenner-Gren Center international symposium series ; v.36)
Includes bibliographies and index
ISBN 0-08-028892-8 : £30.00 : CIP rev. B82-07246

612'.79 — Man. Skin

Some fundamental approaches in skin research / volume editor J.W.H. Mali. — Basel ; London : Karger, c1981. — vi,149p : ill ; 23cm. — (Current problems in dermatology ; v.9)
Includes bibliographies
ISBN 3-8055-3080-3 (pbk) : £26.00 B82-01059

612'.79'05 — Man. Skin. Physiology — *Serials*

The Physiology and pathophysiology of the skin. — Vol.7. — London : Academic Press, Aug.1982. — [330]p
ISBN 0-12-380607-0 : CIP entry B82-15666

612'.791 — Man. Skin. Biophysics — *Conference proceedings*

Bioengineering and the skin / based on the proceedings of the European Society for Dermatological Research Symposium, held at the Welsh National School of Medicine, Cardiff, 19-21 July 1979 ; edited by R. Marks, P.A. Payne. — Lancaster : MTP, c1981. — xv,327p : ill ; 24cm
Includes index
ISBN 0-85200-314-5 : Unpriced B82-06368

612'.7921 — Man. Mucus — *Conference proceedings*

International Symposium on Mucus in Health and Disease *(2nd : 1981 : University of Manchester).* Mucus in health and disease - II / [proceedings of the Second International Symposium on Mucus in Health and Disease, held September 1-4, 1981, at Manchester University, Manchester, England] ; edited by Eric N. Chantler, James B. Elder and Max Elstein. — New York ; London : Plenum, c1982. — xv,441p : ill ; 26cm. — (Advances in experimental medicine and biology ; v.144)
Includes bibliographies and index
ISBN 0-306-40906-2 : Unpriced B82-31052

612.8 — MAN. PHYSIOLOGY. NERVOUS SYSTEM

612'.8 — Man. Neuroendocrine system

Neuroendocrine perspectives / edited by Eugenio E. Müller and Robert M. MacLeod. — Amsterdam ; Oxford : Elsevier Biomedical
Vol.1. — 1982. — xx,405p : ill ; 25cm
Includes bibliographies and index
ISBN 0-444-80365-3 : £45.44 B82-28638

612'.8 — Neurophysiology

Feldberg, W. S.. Fifty years on : looking back on some developments in neurohumoral physiology / W.S. Feldberg. — Liverpool : Liverpool University Press, 1982. — xiii,106p : ill ; 22cm. — (The Sherrington lectures ; 16)
Bibliography: p81-93. — Includes index
ISBN 0-85323-364-0 : £6.25 : CIP rev. B81-30630

Mann, Michael D.. The nervous system and behavior / Michael D. Mann. — Philadelphia ; London : Harper & Row, c1981. — x,386p : ill ; 26cm
Includes bibliographies and index
ISBN 0-06-141576-6 (pbk) : £13.95 B82-11964

Stein, J. F.. An introduction to neurophysiology. — Oxford : Blackwell Scientific, Aug.1982. — [384]p
ISBN 0-632-00582-3 (pbk) : £12.00 : CIP entry B82-18474

612'.8 — Senses

The Senses / edited by H.B. Barlow and J.D. Mollon. — Cambridge : Cambridge University Press, 1982. — xii,490p : ill ; 23cm. — (Cambridge texts in the physiological sciences ; 3)
Includes bibliographies and index
ISBN 0-521-24474-9 (cased) : £30.00 : CIP rev.
ISBN 0-521-28714-6 (pbk) : £12.50 B82-25999

612'.8042 — Man. Cerebrospinal fluid. Hormones: Peptides — *Conference proceedings*

International Symposium on Cerebrospinal Fluid and Peptide Hormones *(1st : 1980 : Valdivia).* Cerebrospinal fluid (CSF) and peptide hormones : 1st International Symposium on Cerebrospinal Fluid and Peptide Hormones, Valdivia, November 24-25, 1980 / volume editors E.M. Rodriguez, Tj. B. van Wimersma Greidanus. — Basle ; London : Karger, c1982. — viii,220p : ill ; 25cm. — (Frontiers of hormone research ; v.9)
Includes bibliographies and index
ISBN 3-8055-2823-x : Unpriced B82-19568

612'.8042 — Man. Cerebrospinal fluid — *Serials*

Neurobiology of cerebrospinal fluid. — 1-. — New York ; London : Plenum Press, 1980-. — v. : ill ; 27cm
Unpriced B82-11805

612'.8042 — Man. Nervous system. Biochemistry

Eadie, M. J.. Biochemical neurology. — Lancaster : MTP Press, Nov.1982. — [280]p
ISBN 0-85200-494-x : £20.00 : CIP entry B82-30611

612'.8042 — Medicine. Neurochemistry

Handbook of neurochemistry / edited by Abel Lajtha. — 2nd ed. — New York ; London : Plenum
Previous ed.: 1969-1972
Vol.1: Chemical and cellular architecture. — c1982. — xix,496p : ill ; 26cm
Includes index
ISBN 0-306-40861-9 : Unpriced B82-31406

612'.8042 — Medicine. Neurochemistry — *Conference proceedings*

International Society for Neurochemistry. *Meeting (8th : 1981 : Nottingham).* Abstracts / 8th Meeting of the International Society for Neurochemistry, September 7-11, 1981, Nottingham. — [Great Britain] : [s.n.], [1981]. — v,466p
Includes index
Unpriced B82-31922

612'.8042 — Medicine. Neurochemistry — *Festschriften*

Chemisms of the brain : proceedings of a symposium held in London, September 1980, in honour of Professor Henry McIlwain / edited by Richard Rodright, Herman S. Bachelard and William L. Stahl. — Edinburgh : Churchill Livingstone, 1981. — 334p : ill,1port ; 24cm
Includes bibliographies and index
ISBN 0-443-02409-x : £25.00 : CIP rev. B81-22597

612′.8′05 — Neurophysiology — *Serials*
Developmental neuroscience. — Vol.1, no.1 (1978)-. — Basel ; London : Karger, 1978-. — v. : ill(some col.) ; 26cm
Six issues yearly. — Description based on: Vol.5, no.1 (1982)
ISSN 0378-5866 = Developmental neuroscience : Unpriced B82-36721

612′.8′076 — Man. Senses — *Questions & answers — For schools*
Moran, Jane. Explore your senses. — London : E. Arnold, Nov.1982. — [48]p
ISBN 0-7131-0693-x (pbk) : £1.50 : CIP entry B82-27950

612′.8′0880542 — Babies. Nervous system. Development
Davis, John A. (John Allen). The human nature of very young infants / John A. Davis. — [Exeter] : University of Exeter, 1981. — 14p ; 21cm. — (Greenwood lecture 1981)
Bibliography: p13-14
ISBN 0-85989-123-2 (pbk) : £0.60 B82-06271

612′.8′09 — Neurophysiology, *to 1830*
Neuburger, Max. The historical development of experimental brain and spinal cord physiology before Flourens / Max Neuburger ; translated and edited, with additional material, by Edwin Clarke. — Baltimore, Md. ; London : Johns Hopkins University Press, c1981. — xxv,391p : 1port ; 24cm
Translation of: Die historische Entwicklung der experimentellen Gehirn- und Rückenmarksphysiologie vor Flourens. — Bibliography: p375-376. — Includes index
ISBN 0-8018-2380-3 : Unpriced B82-28092

612′.81 — Man. Nervous system. Synapses. Tracing. Use of horseradish peroxidases
Tracing neural connections with horseradish peroxidase / edited by M-Marsel Mesulam. — Chichester : Wiley, c1982. — xvi,251p : ill ; 24cm. — (IBRO handbook series. Methods in the neurosciences)
Includes bibliographies and index
ISBN 0-471-10028-5 (cased) : £22.00 : CIP rev.
ISBN 0-471-10029-3 (pbk) : Unpriced B81-34510

612′.813 — Man. Nervous system. Biophysics
Vasilescu, V.. Introduction to neurobiophysics. — Tunbridge Wells : Abacus Press, Dec.1981. — [267]p
Translation of: Introducere in neurobiofizica
ISBN 0-85626-302-8 : £22.50 : CIP entry B81-31651

612′.82 — Man. Brain
Gilling, Dick. The human brain / Dick Gilling and Robin Brightwell. — London : Orbis by arrangement with British Broadcasting Corporation, 1982. — 191p : ill(some col.),1facsim,ports ; 26cm
Bibliography: p188-191. — Includes index
ISBN 0-85613-424-4 : £8.95 B82-27551

Parkins, E. J.. Brain/mind : a description in terms of the representation and processing of information and homeostatic control / E.J. Parkins. — Blackburn (Haydn House, 166 Shear Brow, Blackburn, Lancashire BB1 8DZ) : E.J. Parkins, 1982. — 76p : ill ; 22cm
£1.00 B82-31038

612′.82 — Man. Brain. Development
Brain and behavioural development : interdisciplinary perspectives on structure and function / edited by John W.T. Dickerson and Harry McGurk. — [Guildford] : Surrey University Press, 1982. — ix,266p : ill ; 24cm
Includes bibliographies and index
ISBN 0-903384-27-2 : £27.50 : CIP rev. B81-30372

612′.82 — Man. Brain. Neurophysiological aspects
Grossberg, Stephen. Studies of mind and brain : neural principles of learning, perception, development, cognition, and motor control / Stephen Grossberg. — Dordrecht ; London : Reidel, c1982. — xvii,662p : ill ; 23cm. — (Boston studies in the philosophy of science ; 70)
Includes bibliographies and index
ISBN 90-277-1359-6 : Unpriced B82-37028

612′.82 — Man. Brain. Neurophysiological aspects — *Festschriften — Conference proceedings*
Psychiatry and the biology of the human brain : a symposium dedicated to Seymour S. Kety / [proceedings of the October 12-13, 1979 conference on Psychiatry and the Biology of the Human Brain, Pierce Hall, the McLean Hospital, Belmont, Massachussetts] ; editor Steven Matthysse. — New York ; Oxford : Elsevier/North-Holland, c1981. — vii,310p : ill ; 24cm
Includes bibliographies and index
ISBN 0-444-00649-4 : £26.52 B82-07885

612′.82 — Man. Brain *related to* **mind**
Kuhlenbeck, Hartwig. The human brain and its universe / Hartwig Kuhlenbeck ; edited by Joachim Gerlach. — 2nd rev. and enl. ed. — Basel ; London : Karger
Vol.1: The world of natural sciences and its phenomenology. — c1982. — xiii,281p : ill ; 24cm
Previous ed.: published in 1 vol. as Brain and consciousness. 1957. — Bibliography: p265-276. — Includes index
ISBN 3-8055-1817-x : £48.00
Primary classification 128′.2 B82-28702

Kuhlenbeck, Hartwig. The human brain and its universe / Hartwig Kuhlenbeck ; edited by Joachim Gerlach. — 2nd rev. and enl. ed. — Basel ; London : Karger
Vol.2: The brain and its mind. — c1982. — xiii,374p : ill ; 24cm
Previous ed.: published in 1 vol. as Brain and consciousness. 1957. — Bibliography: p347-368. — Includes index
ISBN 3-8055-2403-x : £67.25
Primary classification 128′.2 B82-28703

612′.82 — Man. Central nervous system. Nerve tracts. Tracing. Experimental techniques
Neuroanatomical tract-tracing methods / edited by Lennart Heimer and Martine J. Robards. — New York ; London : Plenum, c1981. — xxiii,567p,[5]leaves of plates : ill(some col.) ; 26cm
Includes bibliographies and index
ISBN 0-306-40593-8 : Unpriced B82-17861

612′.82 — Man. Central nervous system. Neurotransmitters — *Conference proceedings*
Neurotransmitter vesicles. — London : Academic Press, Apr.1982. — [400]p
ISBN 0-12-413680-x : CIP entry B82-04135

Nobel Conference *(2nd : 1980 : Stockholm)*. Chemical neurotransmission : 75 years / [based on proceedings of the Second Nobel Conference held at the Wenner-Gren Centre, Stockholm, 7-9 December 1980] ; edited by Lennart Stjärne ... [et al.]. — London : Academic Press, 1981. — xxiii,562p : ill,1port ; 24cm
Includes bibliographies and index
ISBN 0-12-671480-0 : £43.40 : CIP rev. B81-34410

612′.82 — Man. Central nervous system. Neurotransmitters: Peptides — *Conference proceedings*
Current status of centrally acting peptides. — Oxford : Pergamon, June 1982. — [288]p. — (Advances in the biosciences ; v.38)
Conference papers
ISBN 0-08-028008-0 : £25.00 : CIP entry B82-11998

Neuroendocrinology of vasopressin, and opiomelanocortins corticoliberin. — London : Academic Press, Sept.1982. — [300]p
ISBN 0-12-072440-5 : CIP entry B82-22800

612′.82′0724 — Man. Brain. Experiments
Fisher, Richard B.. Brain games / Richard B. Fisher. — [London] : Fontana, 1981. — 249p : ill ; 18cm
Bibliography: p238-239. — Includes index
ISBN 0-00-636095-5 (pbk) : £2.75 B82-04196

612′.821 — Man. Performance. Role of sleep
Biological rhythms, sleep and performance / edited by Wilse B. Webb. — Chichester : Wiley, c1982. — xv,279p : ill ; 24cm. — (Wiley series on studies in human performance)
Includes bibliographies and index
ISBN 0-471-10047-1 : £15.50 : CIP rev. B82-03602

612′.821 — Man. Sleep
Oswald, Ian. Get a better night's sleep. — London : Dunitz, Feb.1983. — [128]p. — (Positive health guide)
ISBN 0-906348-40-4 (cased) : £7.95 : CIP entry
ISBN 0-906348-39-0 (pbk) : £2.95 B82-39833

612′.821 — Man. Sleep — *Anthroposophical viewpoints*
McAllen, Audrey E.. Sleep : an unobserved element in education / Audrey E. McAllen. — [Gloucester] ([Chessel, 4 Campden Rd, Tuffley, Gloucester GL4 0HX]) : [A.E. McAllen], 1981. — 67p,[8]p of plates : ill(some col.) ; 21cm
Bibliography: p66-67
Unpriced (pbk) B82-13546

612′.821 — Man. Sleep — *Conference proceedings*
European Congress on Sleep Research *(5th : 1980 : Amsterdam)*. Sleep 1980 : circadian rhythms, dreams, noise and sleep, neurophysiology, therapy : fifth European Congress on Sleep Research, Amsterdam, September 2-5, 1980 / editor W.P. Koella. — Basel ; London : Karger, c1981. — xi,464p : ill ; 25cm
Includes bibliographies and index
ISBN 3-8055-2045-x : £74.50 B82-05125

612′.821 — Man. Sleep. Effects of shiftwork — *Conference proceedings*
Biological rhythms, sleep and shift work / edited by Laverne C. Johnson ... [et al.]. — Lancaster : MTP Press, c1981. — 618p : ill ; 26cm. — (Advances in sleep research ; v.7)
"Proceedings of a conference on Variations in Work-Sleep Schedules : Effects on Health and Performance ... held in San Diego, California, September 19-23, 1979" — t.p. verso. — Includes bibliographies and index
ISBN 0-85200-581-4 : £38.75 B82-01783

612′.822 — Children. Brain. Evoked electric potentials — *Conference proceedings*
International Conference on Clinical Application of Cerebral Evoked Potentials in Pediatric Neurology *(1982 : Milan)*. Clinical application of cerebral evoked potentials in pediatric medicine : proceedings of the International Conference on Clinical Application of Cerebral Evoked Potentials in Pediatric Neurology, Milan, Italy, January 14-16, 1982 / editors G.A. Chiarenza, D. Papakostopoulos. — Amsterdam ; Oxford : Excerpta Medica, 1982. — xvii,415p : ill ; 25cm. — (International congress series ; no.595)
Includes index
ISBN 0-444-90278-3 : £31.57 B82-38135

612′.822 — Man. Brain. Auditory evoked & visual evoked electric potentials. Laboratory techniques
Evoked potentials in clinical testing. — Edinburgh : Churchill Livingstone, Oct.1981. — [250]p. — (Clinical neurology and neurosurgery monographs ; v.3)
ISBN 0-443-01791-3 : £15.00 : CIP entry B81-30629

612′.822 — Man. Brain. Event-related electric potentials. Psychophysiological aspects
Howard, R. C. (Richard Charles). Event-related brain potentials in personality and psychopathology : a Pavlovian approach / R.C. Howard, G.W. Fenton and P.B.C. Fenwick. — Chichester : Research Studies, c1982. — xvii,112p : ill ; 24cm. — (Psychophysiology research studies series)
Bibliography: p97-109. — Includes index
ISBN 0-471-10454-x : £12.75 : CIP rev. B82-11300

612′.822 — Man. Brain. Evoked electric potentials — *Conference proceedings*
Current clinical neurophysiology : update on EEG and evoked potentials / [from the Fifteenth Annual Course in Clinical Electroencephalography sponsored by the American Electroencephalographic Society] ; editor C.E. Henry. — New York ; Oxford : Elsevier/North-Holland, c1980. — x,577p : ill,forms ; 24cm
Includes bibliographies and index
ISBN 0-444-00639-7 : £37.65
Primary classification 616.8′047547 B82-13451

612'.822 — Man. Central nervous system. Serotonin. Role — *Conference proceedings*
Biology of serotonergic transmission / edited by Neville N. Osborne. — Chichester : Wiley, c1982. — xiii,522p : ill ; 24cm
Includes bibliographies and index
ISBN 0-471-10032-3 : £30.00 : CIP rev.
B82-04851

Serotonin : current aspects of neurochemistry and function / [proceedings of an International Society for Neurochemistry Symposium on Serotonin: Current Aspects of Neurochemistry and Function, held September 11-16, 1979, in Athens, Greece] ; edited by Bernard Haber ... [et al.]. — New York ; London : Plenum, c1981. — xvi,824p : ill ; 26cm. — (Advances in experimental medicine and biology ; v.133)
Includes bibliographies and index
ISBN 0-306-40579-2 : Unpriced B82-00701

612'.822 — Man. Learning & memory. Role of peptides
Endogenous peptides and learning and memory processes / edited by Joe L. Martinez, Jr ... [et al.]. — New York ; London : Academic Press, 1981. — xx,587p : ill ; 24cm. — (Behavioral biology)
Includes bibliographies and index
ISBN 0-12-474980-1 : £32.80 B82-16317

612'.825 — Man. Amygdala — *Conference proceedings*
International Symposium on the Amygdaloid Complex *(1981 : Senlis, France)*. The amygdaloid complex : proceedings of the International Symposium on the Amygdaloid Complex held in the Château de Fillerval, Senlis (France), 1-4 September, 1981 / sponsored by the Institut national de la santé et de la recherche médicale and the Centre national de la recherche scientifique ; editor Yehezkel Ben-Ari. — Amsterdam ; Oxford : Elsevier/North-Holland Biomedical, 1981. — xviii,516p : ill ; 25cm. — (INSERM symposium ; no.20)
Includes index
ISBN 0-444-80397-1 : £44.89 B82-13438

612'.825 — Man. Brain. Right hemisphere. Psychophysiological aspects
Wilson, Colin, *1931-*. Frankenstein's castle : the double brain : door to wisdom / Colin Wilson. — Sevenoaks : Ashgrove, 1980. — 128p ; 22cm
ISBN 0-906798-11-6 : £4.95 B82-17580

612'.826 — Man. Brain. Neostriatum — *Conference proceedings*
The Neostriatum : proceedings of a workshop sponsored by the European Brain and Behaviour Society, Denmark, 17-19 April 1978 / editors, Ivan Divac and R. Gunilla E. Öberg. — Oxford : Pergamon, 1979. — vi,325p : ill ; 25cm
Includes index
ISBN 0-08-023174-8 : £21.00 : CIP rev.
B79-19256

612'.84 — Man. Colour vision. Theories, *1800-1860*
Sherman, Paul D.. Colour vision in the nineteenth century : the Young-Helmholtz-Maxwell theory / Paul D. Sherman ; foreword by W.D. Wright. — Bristol : Adam Hilger, c1981. — xiii,233p,4p of col.plates : ill(some col.),ports ; 24cm
Bibliography: p223-229. — Includes index
ISBN 0-85274-376-9 : £35.00 : CIP rev.
B81-18081

612'.84 — Man. Sight — *For children*
Catherall, Ed. Sight / Ed Catherall. — Hove : Wayland, 1981. — 32p : col.ill ; 24cm. — (Young scientist)
ISBN 0-85340-866-1 : £2.95 B82-06543

Ward, Brian. The eye and seeing / Brian R. Ward. — London : Watts, 1981. — 48p : ill (some col.) ; 26cm. — (The Human body)
Includes index
ISBN 0-85166-929-8 : £3.99 B82-04742

612'.84 — Man. Sight — *For children — Arabic texts*
al-**'Ayn** wa-l-ibsār. — London : Macmillan, 1981. — 30p : col.ill ; 18cm
Translation of: The eye and vision. — Originally published: Amman : Royal Jordanian Scientific Society, 1978
ISBN 0-333-32338-6 : Unpriced B82-13464

612'.84 — Man. Sight — *For schools*
Kincaid, Doug. Eyes and looking / Doug Kincaid and Peter Coles. — Exeter : Wheaton, c1981. — 24p : ill(some col.) ; 22cm. — (Read and do)
ISBN 0-08-027885-x : £1.95 B82-01671

612'.84 — Man. Sight. Neurophysiological aspects
Divided visual field studies of cerebral organisation / edited by J. Graham Beaumont. — London : Academic Press, 1982. — xiii,305p : ill ; 24cm
Bibliography: p253-297. — Includes index
ISBN 0-12-084080-4 : £18.00 : CIP rev.
B82-00323

612'.84 — Man. Visual perception. Physiological aspects
Dolezal, Hubert. Living in a world transformed : perceptual and performatory adaptation to visual distortion / Hubert Dolezal. — New York ; London : Academic Press, c1982. — xvi,388p : ill ; 24cm. — (Academic Press series in cognition and perception)
Bibliography: p349-367. — Includes index
ISBN 0-12-219950-2 : £24.60 B82-29691

612'.84'02854 — Man. Binocular vision. Analysis. Applications of digital computer systems
Grimson, William Eric Leifur. From images to surfaces : a computational study of the human early visual system / William Eric Leifur Grimson. — Cambridge, Mass. ; London : MIT, c1981. — 274p : ill ; 24cm. — (The MIT Press series in artificial intelligence)
Bibliography: p247-267. — Includes index
ISBN 0-262-07083-9 : £17.50 B82-21014

612'.84'088054 — Children. Sight. Development
Gardiner, P. A.. The development of vision / P.A. Gardiner. — Lancaster : MTP, c1982. — 141p,[2]p of plates : ill(some col.) ; 23cm. — (Studies in developmental paediatrics ; v.3)
Includes index
ISBN 0-85200-303-x : £11.95 : CIP rev.
B81-22681

612'.85 — Man. Hearing — *For children*
Catherall, Ed. Hearing / Ed Catherall. — Hove : Wayland, 1981. — 32p : col.ill ; 24cm. — (Young scientist)
ISBN 0-85340-867-x : £2.95 B82-06544

Ward, Brian. The ear and hearing / Brian R. Ward. — London : Watts, 1981. — 40p : col.ill ; 26cm. — (The Human body)
Includes index
ISBN 0-85166-930-1 : £3.99 B82-04741

612'.85 — Man. Hearing — *For schools*
Kincaid, Doug. Ears and hearing / Doug Kincaid and Peter Coles. — Exeter : Wheaton, c1981. — 24p : ill(some col.) ; 22 cm. — (Read and do)
ISBN 0-08-027883-3 : £1.95 B82-01673

612'.85 — Man. Hearing. Physiology
Katsuki, Yasuji. Receptive mechanisms of sound in the ear / Yasuji Katsuki. — Cambridge : Cambridge University Press, c1982. — viii,155p : ill ; 24cm
Bibliography: p136-150. — Includes index
ISBN 0-521-24346-7 : £20.00 : CIP rev.
B82-11515

Pickles, James O.. An introduction to the physiology of hearing / James O. Pickles. — London : Academic Press, c1982. — ix,341p : ill ; 24cm
Bibliography: p303-327. — Includes index
ISBN 0-12-554750-1 (cased) : £16.00 : CIP rev.
ISBN 0-12-554752-8 (pbk) : Unpriced
B82-04144

612'.86 — Man. Chemoreception. Structure-activity relationships — *Conference proceedings*
European Chemoreception Research Organization. *Minisymposium (5th : 1981 : Jerusalem)*. The determination of behaviour by chemical stimuli : proceedings of the Vth European Chemoreception Research Organization Minisymposium. — Eynsham (P.O. Box 1, Eynsham, Oxford, OX8 1JJ) : IRL Press, Feb.1982. — [350]p
ISBN 0-904147-33-9 (pbk) : £12.00 : CIP entry
B82-00177

612'.86 — Man. Nose. Physiology
The Nose : upper airway physiology and the atmospheric environment / edited by Donald F. Proctor and Ib Andersen. — Amsterdam ; Oxford : Elsevier Biomedical, 1982. — xviii,509p : ill,1facsim ; 25cm
Includes bibliographies and index
ISBN 0-444-80377-7 : £66.38 B82-36628

612'.86 — Man. Senses: Smell — *For schools*
Kincaid, Doug. Taste and smell / Doug Kincaid and Peter Coles. — Exeter : Wheaton, c1981. — 24p : ill(some col.) ; 22cm. — (Read and do)
ISBN 0-08-027884-1 : £1.95
Also classified at 612'.87 B82-01670

612'.86 — Man. Smell — *For children*
Catherall, Ed. Taste and smell / Ed Catherall. — Hove : Wayland, 1982. — 32p : col.ill ; 23cm. — (Young scientist)
ISBN 0-85340-869-6 : £2.95
Also classified at 612'.87 B82-16421

612'.87 — Man. Senses: Taste — *For schools*
Kincaid, Doug. Taste and smell / Doug Kincaid and Peter Coles. — Exeter : Wheaton, c1981. — 24p : ill(some col.) ; 22cm. — (Read and do)
ISBN 0-08-027884-1 : £1.95
Primary classification 612'.86 B82-01670

612'.87 — Man. Taste — *For children*
Catherall, Ed. Taste and smell / Ed Catherall. — Hove : Wayland, 1982. — 32p : col.ill ; 23cm. — (Young scientist)
ISBN 0-85340-869-6 : £2.95
Primary classification 612'.86 B82-16421

612'.88 — Man. Senses: Touch — *For schools*
Kincaid, Doug. Touch and feel / Doug Kincaid and Peter Coles. — Exeter : Wheaton, c1981. — 24p : ill(some col.) ; 22cm. — (Read and do)
ISBN 0-08-027882-5 : £1.95 B82-01672

612'.88 — Man. Touch — *For children*
Catherall, Ed. Touch / Ed Catherall. — Hove : Wayland, 1982. — 32p : col.ill ; 23cm. — (Young scientist)
ISBN 0-85340-868-8 : £2.95 B82-16422

612'.89 — Man. Adrenergic receptors
Adrenoceptors and catecholamine action / edited by George Kunos. — New York ; Chichester : Wiley. — (Neurotransmitter receptors ; v.1)
Part A. — c1981. — vii,343p : ill ; 24cm
Includes index
ISBN 0-471-05725-8 : £37.00 B82-05122

612'.89 — Man. Autonomic nervous system. Development — *Conference proceedings*
Development of the autonomic nervous system. — London : Pitman Medical, 1981. — x,389p : ill ; 24cm. — (Ciba Foundation symposium ; 83)
Conference papers. — Includes bibliographies and index
ISBN 0-272-79619-0 : £22.50 : CIP rev.
B81-09464

612.9 — MAN. REGIONAL PHYSIOLOGY

612'.92 — Man. Oral region — *For dentistry*
Oral biology / [edited by] Gerald I. Roth, Robert Calmes. — St. Louis ; London : Mosby, 1981. — xii,482p : ill ; 24cm
Includes bibliographies and index
ISBN 0-8016-4182-9 (pbk) : £18.75
B82-08264

612'.92 — Man. Oral region. Physiology — *Conference proceedings*
The Environment of the teeth : symposium in honour of G.N. Jenkins, Newcastle upon Tyne, September 1980 / volume editor D.B. Ferguson. — Basel ; London : Karger, c1981. — x,173p : ill ; 25cm. — (Frontiers of oral physiology ; v.3)
Includes index
ISBN 3-8055-2577-x : £28.50 B82-21667

613 — England. Population. Health. Inequalities. Influence of social class

Black, *Sir* **Douglas**. Inequalities in health / by Sir Douglas Black. — [Birmingham] : University of Birmingham, 1981. — 10p ; 21cm. — (Christie Gordon lecture)
Bibliography: p10
ISBN 0-7044-0581-4 (pbk) : Unpriced
B82-13694

Inequalities in health : the Black report / Sir Douglas Black ... [et al.] ; edited and with an introduction by Peter Townsend and Nick Davidson. — Harmondsworth : Penguin, 1982, c1980. — 240p : ill ; 20cm. — (Pelican books)
Bibliography: p222-233. — Includes index
ISBN 0-14-022420-3 (pbk) : £2.50 B82-37609

613 — Families. Health

Everyday guide to family health. — London : Faber, Sept.1982. — [640]p
ISBN 0-571-11933-6 (pbk) : £5.95 : CIP entry
B82-19550

The **Family** good health guide : common sense on common health problems / by John Fry ... [et al.]. — Lancaster : MTP, c1982. — vii,292p : ill ; 24cm
Includes index
ISBN 0-85200-308-0 : Unpriced : CIP rev.
B81-27424

613 — Great Britain. Man. Health. Holism. Organisations — *Directories*

New life directory / production team Bill Anderton ... [et al.]. — Forest of Dean : Soluna, c1982. — [52]p : ill,1map ; 22cm. — (A Soluna publication)
Text on inside covers
ISBN 0-907522-01-7 (pbk) : £1.20 B82-26787

613 — Great Britain. Sedentary occupations. Personnel. Health

Melhuish, Andrew. Work and health / Andrew Melhuish. — Extensively rev. ed. — Harmondsworth : Penguin, 1982, c1978. — 208p : ill ; 20cm. — (A Penguin handbook)
Previous ed.: published as Executive health. London : Business Books, 1978. —
Bibliography: p202-203. — Includes index
ISBN 0-14-046450-6 (pbk) : £2.50 B82-40772

613 — Man. Health

Pearse, Innes H.. The case for action : a survey of everyday life under modern industrial conditions, with special reference to the question of health / by Innes H. Pearse and G. Scott Williamson ; with prefaces by the late Lord Moynihan and A.D. Lindsay. — 4th ed. — [Edinburgh] : Scottish Academic Press, c1982. — xv,162p : 3plans ; 19cm
Previous ed.: London : Faber, 1938. —
Includes index
ISBN 0-7073-0318-4 (pbk) : Unpriced
B82-30668

Turner, Clair E.. Turner's personal and community health. — 15th ed. / revised by Stewart M. Brooks and Natalie A. Brooks. — St. Louis ; London : Mosby, 1979. — xiv,403p : ill ; 25cm
Previous ed.: 1971. — Includes bibliographies and index
ISBN 0-8016-5536-6 : Unpriced B82-19322

Weston, Trevor. Live to be 100 / Trevor Weston. — London : W.H. Allen, 1982. — 224p ; 23cm
Includes index
ISBN 0-491-02897-0 : £8.95 B82-34876

613 — Man. Health — *For West African students*

Kurien, A. V.. Objective tests in health science for WAEC O level. — London : Hodder & Stoughton, July 1982. — [128]p
ISBN 0-340-27595-2 (pbk) : £2.75 : CIP entry
B82-14084

613 — Man. Health. Holism

Health for the whole person : the complete guide to holistic medicine / edited by Arthur C. Hastings, James Fadiman and James S. Gordon. — Toronto ; London : Bantam, 1981. — xix,569p : ill ; 18cm
Originally published: Boulder : Westview, 1980. — Includes bibliographies and index
ISBN 0-553-20322-3 (pbk) : £2.50 B82-18408

Mind, body and spirit : the journey toward health and wholeness / edited by Peter Albright & Bets Parker Albright. — U.K. ed. — Findhorn : Thule Press, 1981. — 324p : ill ; 21cm
Previous ed.: published as Body, mind and spirit. Brattleboro, Vt. : Stephen Greene Press, 1980. — Bibliography: p312-320. — Includes index
ISBN 0-906191-63-7 (pbk) : £3.95 B82-03998

613 — Man. Health. Holism — *Manuals*

Shames, Richard. The gift of health : a holistic approach to higher-quality, lower-cost health care / Richard Shames and Karilee Halo Shames. — Toronto ; London : Bantam, 1982. — xii,162p ; 18cm
ISBN 0-553-20052-6 (pbk) : £1.50 B82-36737

613 — Man. Health. Improvement — *Manuals*

Brannin, Marilyn. Your body in mind : the key to health and happiness through body sense therapy / by Marilyn Brannin. — London : Souvenir, 1982. — 174p : ill ; 24cm
ISBN 0-285-62498-9 : £7.95 B82-11685

The **Good** health guide / the Open University in association with the Health Education Council and the Scottish Health Education Unit. — London : Pan, 1982, c1980. — 256p : ill(some col.) ; 28cm
Originally published: London : Harper & Row, 1980. — Includes bibliographies and index
ISBN 0-330-26629-2 (pbk) : £5.95 B82-11644

613 — Man. Health. Self-care

The **Beecham** manual of family medicine. — Lancaster : MTP Press, Aug.1982. — [230]p
ISBN 0-85200-456-7 : £10.00 : CIP entry
B82-21969

613 — Man. Health. Self-care — *Manuals*

The **Health** care manual. — Lancaster : MTP Press, Apr.1982. — [304]p
ISBN 0-85200-445-1 (pbk) : £2.50 : CIP entry
B82-12814

The **Healthy** body : a maintenance manual / the Diagram Group. — London : Muller, 1982, c1981. — 191p : ill ; 28cm
Originally published: New York : New American Library, 1981. — Includes index
ISBN 0-584-11031-6 (pbk) : £4.95 : CIP rev.
B82-12687

The **Macmillan** guide to family health / editor-in-chief Tony Smith. — London : Macmillan, 1982. — 832p : ill(some col.) ; 25cm
Includes index
ISBN 0-333-27870-4 : £14.95 : CIP rev.
B82-00306

Marley, William P.. Health and physical fitness : taking charge of your health / William P. Marley. — Philadelphia, [Pa.] ; London : Saunders College, c1982. — ix,412p : ill ; 24cm
Includes index
ISBN 0-03-058363-2 (pbk) : Unpriced
B82-28296

Parker, Derek. Do it yourself health / Derek and Julia Parker. — London : Thames and Hudson, c1982. — 143p : ill,forms ; 24cm
Bibliography: p136-138. — Includes index
ISBN 0-500-01275-x : £6.50 B82-28656

613 — Man. Mental health — *Serials*

Research in community and mental health : an annual compilation of research. — Vol.1 (1979)-. — Greenwich, Conn. : JAI Press ; London (3 Henrietta St., WC2E 8LU) : Distributed by JAICON Press, 1979-. — v. ; 24cm
ISSN 0192-0812 = Research in community and mental health : £26.20 B82-03432

613′.0243694 — Man. Health — *For Brownie Guides*

The **Brownie** painting book : keeping healthy / illustrated by Barbara Walker. — London : Girl Guides Association, [1981?]. — [20]p : ill ; 22cm
£0.45 (pbk) B82-15092

613′.04244 — Women. Health

Fogel, Catherine Ingram. Health care of women : a nursing perspective / Catherine Ingram Fogel, Nancy Fugate Woods. — St. Louis, Mo. ; London : Mosby, 1981. — x,643p,[2]p of plates : ill(some col.) ; 28cm
Includes bibliographies and index
ISBN 0-8016-1605-0 (pbk) : £19.75
B82-34462

613′.04244 — Women. Health — *For women*

Stoppard, Miriam. Everywoman's lifeguide / Miriam Stoppard. — London : Macdonald, 1982. — 448p : ill(some col.),ports ; 25cm
Includes index
ISBN 0-356-08588-0 : £9.95 B82-26520

613′.0432 — Children. Health

Pringle, Sheila M.. Promoting the health of children : a guide for caretakers and health care professionals / Sheila M. Pringle, Brenda E. Ramsey. — St. Louis ; London : Mosby, 1982. — xi,275p : ill ; 28cm
Bibliography: p258-265. — Includes index
ISBN 0-8016-4048-2 (pbk) : £9.00 B82-16560

613′.0432 — Preventive paediatrics — *German texts*

Präventive Aspekte in der Pädiatrie / Herausgeber des Bandes G. Stalder und C.P. Fliegel. — Basel ; London : Karger, c1981. — 179p : ill ; 23cm. — (Pädiatrische Fortbildungskurse für die Praxis = Cours de perfectionnement en pédiatrie pour le praticien ; Bd.52)
Includes 2 articles in French. — Includes bibliographies
ISBN 3-8055-1980-x (pbk) : £23.65
B82-01058

613′.0432 — Scotland. Children. Health. Attitudes of working class mothers

Blaxter, Mildred. Mothers and daughters : a three-generational study of health attitudes and behaviour / Mildred Blaxter and Elizabeth Paterson with the assistance of Sheila Murray. — London : Heinemann Educational, 1982. — viii,211p ; 23cm. — (Studies in deprivation and disadvantage ; 5)
Includes index
ISBN 0-435-82055-9 : £14.50 : CIP rev.
B82-04062

613′.0432′0240431 — Children. Health — *For parents*

McPherson, Ann. Mum — I feel funny!. — London : Chatto & Windus, Sept.1982. — [32]p
ISBN 0-7011-2631-0 : £3.50 : CIP entry
B82-20300

613′.0432′024613 — Children. Health — *For nursing*

Child and family : concepts of nursing practice / Marjorie J. Smith ... [et al.]. — New York ; London : McGraw-Hill, c1982. — xxxii,1246p : ill,forms ; 26cm
Includes index
ISBN 0-07-048720-0 : £22.95 B82-33698

613′.0432′0941 — Great Britain. Preventive paediatrics — *Conference proceedings*

Study day report (International Year of the Child) : the preventive aspects of child health : 28 November 1979, Scottish Health Service Centre / [editor Gerald H. France]. — Edinburgh (Crewe Rd South, Edinburgh EH4 2LF) : The Centre, [1980]. — 28p : 1ill,1form,ports ; 30cm
Unpriced (pbk) B82-35006

613′.05 — Man. Health — *Serials*

[**You** *(London)*]. You. — [1 (Spring 1982)?]-. — London (67 Upper Berkeley St., W1H 7DH) : You, [198-]-. — v. ; 30cm
Quarterly. — Description based on: 1 (Spring 1982)
ISSN 0263-7545 = You (London) : £40.00 per year B82-32136

613'.05 — Man. Health — *Serials*
continuation

[Your health *(London)*]. Your health. — Issue 1 (Nov. 1981)-. — London (24 Grays Inn Rd., WC1X 8HR) : Your Health Ltd., 1981-. — v. : ill ; 27cm
Monthly
ISSN 0262-9232 = Your health (London) : £0.80 per issue B82-11825

613'.07 — Health education

Participation in health. — London : Croom Helm, Jan.1983. — [200]p
ISBN 0-7099-1754-6 : £11.95 : CIP entry B82-35209

613'.07 — Health education. Role of mass media — *Conference proceedings*

Health education and the media : proceedings of an international conference organized jointly by the Scottish Health Education Group, Edinburgh, and the Advertising Research Unit, Department of Marketing, University of Strathclyde, Edinburgh, 24-27 March 1981 / editors D.S. Leathar, G.B. Hastings, J.K. Davies. — Oxford : Pergamon, 1981. — xxiii,602p : ill,2facsims ; 24cm
ISBN 0-08-027982-1 : £40.00 : CIP rev. B81-30204

613'.07 — Patients. Health education — *For nursing*

Patient teaching. — Edinburgh : Churchill Livingstone, Feb.1983. — [200]p. — (Recent advances in nursing, ISSN 0144-6592 ; 6)
ISBN 0-443-02499-5 (pbk) : £6.95 : CIP entry B82-38275

613'.07'041 — Great Britain. Health education officers. Recruitment & training

Great Britain. *National Staff Committee for Administrative and Clerical Staff.* The recruitment, training and development of health education officers / a report by the National Staff Committee for Administrative and Clerical Staff. — [Great Britain] : The Committee, 1981. — iii,28p ; 30cm
Cover title. — At head of title: National Health Service
Unpriced (pbk) B82-40281

613'.07'0429 — Wales. Health education

Joint Working Group on Health Education in Wales. Report of the Joint Working Group on Health Education in Wales. — [Cardiff] : [H.M.S.O.], 1981. — 19,3leaves ; 30cm
Cover title
Unpriced (spiral) B82-23764

613'.07'1041 — Great Britain. Schools. Curriculum subjects: Health education

A Guide to school health education / compiled by Jeff Lee & Hugh Graham. — London (78 New Oxford St, WC1A 1AH) : Health Education Council, 1982. — 65p : ill ; 30cm
Unpriced (spiral) B82-39055

613'.07'1273 — United States. Secondary schools. Health education. Teaching methods

Willgoose, Carl E.. Health teaching in secondary schools / Carl E. Willgoose. — 3rd ed. — Philadelphia ; London : Saunders College, c1982. — v,426p : ill ; 25cm
Previous ed.: 1977. — Includes bibliographies and index
ISBN 0-03-058493-0 : £19.50 B82-25406

613'.0943'46 — West Germany. Heidelberg. Man. Health

Arab, L.. Nutrition and health : a survey of young men and women in Heidelberg / L. Arab, B. Schellenberg and G. Schlierf with the assistance of M. Blum ... [et al.]. — Basel ; London : Karger, c1981. — xi,244p : ill ; 26cm
Translation of: Ernährung und Gesundheit. — First supplement to Annals of nutrition and metabolism 1982. — Includes index
ISBN 3-8055-3465-5 (pbk) : £13.35 B82-40290

613.1 — HYGIENE. ENVIRONMENTAL FACTORS

613'.122'0941 — Great Britain. Spas, *to 1980*

Denbigh, Kathleen. A hundred British spas : a pictorial history : with 42 maps and 81 illustrations based on old prints and photographs, drawn by the author / Kathleen Denbigh. — London : Spa, c1981. — xxi,287p : ill,maps ; 22cm
Bibliography: p281-282. — Includes index
ISBN 0-9507574-0-3 : £6.00 B82-00576

613'.122'0942978 — Mid Glamorgan. Taff's Well. Spas: Ffynnon Taf, *to ca 1980*

Brown, Roger Lee. Taffs Well & Ffynnon Taf / by Roger Lee Brown. — [Taffs Well] ([The Vicarage, Merthyr Rd, Tongwynlais, Cardiff CF4 7LF]) : R.L. Brown, c1981. — 25p,[7]p of plates : ill,2maps ; 21cm
Unpriced (pbk) B82-35595

613'.192 — Physical fitness. Breathing. Exercises

Nakamura, Takashi. Oriental breathing therapy / Takashi Nakamura. — Tokyo : Japan Publications ; Hemel Hempstead : International Book Distributors, 1981. — 160p : ill ; 26cm
Includes index
ISBN 0-87040-478-4 (pbk) : £8.10 B82-14458

613'.192 — Pranayama

Lysebeth, André van. Pranayama : the yoga of breathing / André Van Lysebeth. — London : Unwin Paperbacks, 1979. — viii,230p : ill ; 20cm. — (Mandala books)
ISBN 0-04-149050-9 (pbk) : £2.95 : CIP rev. B79-01179

613'.194 — Europe. Naturist beaches — *Directories — Serials*

Free-sun. Europe. — 1982-. — Hastings (16 Viewbank, Hastings, Sussex, TN35 5HB) : Free-Sun Publications, 1982-. — v. : ill(some col.),ports ; 21cm
Annual. — Continues: Free-sun (Europe's beaches)
ISSN 0262-589x = Free-sun. Europe : £6.00 B82-31709

613.2 — HYGIENE. DIETETICS

613.2 — Babies & pregnant women. Health. Effects of diet

Davis, Adelle. Let's have healthy children. — New expanded and rev. ed. — London : Unwin Paperbacks, Oct.1981. — [400]p
Previous ed.: 1974
ISBN 0-04-612032-7 (pbk) : £1.95 : CIP entry B81-30883

613.2 — Man. Health. Effects of diet

Bircher-Benner, M.. The prevention of incurable disease. — Cambridge : James Clarke, Feb.1982. — [128]p
Translated from the German. — Originally published: 1959
ISBN 0-227-67571-1 (pbk) : £2.95 : CIP entry B82-07102

British Nutrition Foundation. Preventive nutrition and society / [Proceedings of the British Nutrition Foundation Second Annual Conference held at the Royal Society, July 1-2, 1980] ; edited by M.R. Turner. — London : Academic Press, 1981. — xii,228p : ill,facsims ; 24cm
Includes bibliographies and index
ISBN 0-12-704450-7 : £16.40 : CIP rev.
Also classified at 613.2'07'041 B81-28783

Implementation of dietary guidelines. — London : British Nutrition Foundation, June 1982. — [56]p. — (BNF monograph series ; 1)
ISBN 0-907667-01-5 (pbk) : £2.95 : CIP entry B82-17900

Nutrition in disease and development / volume editor Geoffrey H. Bourne. — Basel ; London : Karger, 1982. — ix,194p : ill ; 25cm. — (World review of nutrition and dietetics ; v.39)
Includes bibliographies and index
ISBN 3-8055-3459-0 : £46.40 B82-32047

613.2 — Man. Health. Effects of diet — *Serials*

[Nutrition and health *(Berkhamsted)*]. Nutrition and health. — Vol.1, no.1 (1982)-. — Berkhamsted (P.O. Box 97, Berkhamsted, Herts. HP4 2PX) : AB Academic Publishers, 1982-. — v. : ill ; 25cm
Quarterly
ISSN 0260-1060 = Nutrition and health (Berkhamsted) : £25.00 per year B82-30480

613.2 — Man. Nutrition

Controversies in nutrition / edited by Leon Ellenbogen. — New York ; Edinburgh : Churchill Livingstone, 1981. — xi,176p : ill ; 24cm. — (Contemporary issues in clinical nutrition ; v.2)
Includes index
ISBN 0-443-08127-1 : £13.00 B82-16434

Davis, Adelle. Let's stay healthy : a guide to lifelong nutrition / Adelle Davis ; edited and expanded by Ann Gildroy ; foreword by Leonard Lustgarten. — London : Allen & Unwin, 1982, c1981. — xxi,391p : ill ; 23cm
Originally published: New York : Harcourt Brace Jovanovich, 1981. — Bibliography: p354-356. — Includes index
ISBN 0-04-641041-4 : Unpriced : CIP rev. B82-01535

Deutsch, Ronald M.. Realities of nutrition / Ronald M. Deutsch. — Palo Alto : Bull, 1976 ; London. — xiii,405p : ill ; 25cm. — (Berkeley series in nutrition)
Includes index
ISBN 0-915950-07-3 : £10.50 B82-34996

Guthrie, Helen Andrews. Introductory nutrition / Helen Andrews Guthrie. — 4th ed. — St. Louis ; London : Mosby, 1979. — vii,693p : ill ; 27cm
Previous ed.: 1975. — Includes index
ISBN 0-8016-2001-5 : £17.50 B82-28893

Hildreth, E. M.. Elementary science of food. — 2nd ed. — London : Bell & Hyman, Aug.1981. — [306]p
Previous ed.: London : Allman, 1952
ISBN 0-7135-2059-0 (pbk) : £4.25 : CIP entry B81-20650

Human nutrition : current issues and controversies / edited by A. Neuberger, T.H. Jukes. — Lancaster : MTP, 1982. — x,249p : ill ; 25cm
Includes index
ISBN 0-85200-393-5 : £16.95 : CIP rev. B82-01563

Human nutrition and animal feeding / volume editor Geoffrey H. Bourne. — Basel ; London : Karger, 1981. — xii,290p : ill ; 25cm. — (World review of nutrition and dietetics ; v.37)
Includes bibliographies and index
ISBN 3-8055-2143-x : £74.00
Also classified at 591.1'3 B82-06281

Lesser, Michael. Nutrition and vitamin therapy / Michael Lesser. — Toronto ; London : Bantam, 1981. — 239p : ill ; 18cm
Originally published: New York : Grove Press, 1980. — Includes index
ISBN 0-553-14437-5 (pbk) : £1.25
Also classified at 615.8'54 B82-14450

Robinson, Corinne H.. Normal and therapeutic nutrition. — 16th ed. / Corinne H. Robinson, Marilyn R. Lawler. — New York : Macmillan ; London : Collier Macmillan, 1982. — x,849p : ill ; 25cm
Previous ed.: 1977. — Tables on lining papers. — Includes bibliographies and index
ISBN 0-02-402370-1 : Unpriced
Also classified at 615.8'54 B82-40793

Weiner, Michael A.. The way of the skeptical nutritionist : a strategy for designing your own nutritional profile / Michael A. Weiner. — New York : Macmillan ; London : Collier Macmillan, c1981. — 253p ; 25cm
Bibliography: p238-241. — Includes index
ISBN 0-02-625620-7 : £7.95 B82-26204

613.2 — Man. Nutrition *continuation*
Williams, Sue Rodwell. Essentials of nutrition and diet therapy / Sue Rodwell Williams. — 3rd ed. — St. Louis ; London : Mosby, 1982. — x,390p : ill ; 24cm
Previous ed.: 1978. — Includes bibliographies and index
ISBN 0-8016-5575-7 (pbk) : Unpriced
B82-31879

613.2 — Man. Nutrition — *Conference proceedings*
Advances in human clinical nutrition / edited by Joseph J. Vitale, Selwyn A. Broitman. — The Hague ; London : Nijhoff, 1982. — ix,217p : ill ; 25cm
Conference papers. — Includes index
ISBN 90-247-2485-6 : Unpriced B82-14565

Clinical nutrition ′81. — Edinburgh : Churchill Livingstone, Sept.1982. — [304]p
Conference papers
ISBN 0-443-02700-5 (pbk) : £18.00 : CIP entry
B82-26223

613.2 — Man. Nutrition - *For adolescents*
Creese, Angela[Guide to nutrition]. The young homemaker guide to nutrition. — London : Bell & Hyman, Aug.1981. — [96]p. — (The Young homemaker series)
Originally published as: Guide to nutrition. London : Mills & Boon, 1969
ISBN 0-7135-2065-5 (pbk) : CIP entry
B81-16362

613.2 — Man. Nutrition. Health aspects
Atkins, Robert C.. Dr Atkins′ nutrition breakthrough : how to treat your medical condition without drugs / Robert C. Atkins. — Toronto ; London : Bantam, 1982, c1981. — viii,377p ; 18cm
Originally published: New York : Morrow, 1981. — Includes index
ISBN 0-553-20279-0 (pbk) : £1.50 B82-29739

613′.2 — Man. Nutrition. Health aspects
Nutritional problems in modern society. — London (80 Broadway, Vauxhall, SW8 1SF) : Libbey, Apr.1981. — [160]p
ISBN 0-86196-007-6 : £9.50 : CIP entry
B81-04273

613.2 — Man. Nutrition. Health aspects
Taylor, T. Geoffrey. Nutrition and health. — London : Edward Arnold, May 1982. — [64]p. — (The Institute of Biology′s studies in biology, ISSN 0537-9024 ; no.141)
ISBN 0-7131-2840-2 (pbk) : £2.25 : CIP entry
B82-06919

613.2 — Man. Nutrition. Health aspects — *Conference proceedings*
Advances in clinical nutrition. — Lancaster : MTP Press, Dec.1982. — [400]p
Conference papers
ISBN 0-85200-496-6 : £24.95 : CIP entry
B82-34103

British Nutrition Foundation. *Conference (3rd : 1981 : London)*. Nutrition and health : a perspective : the status of research on diet-related diseases : proceedings of the British Nutrition Foundation third annual conference held at the Royal College of Physicians, London, 23 and 24 June 1981 / edited by Michael R. Turner. — Lancaster : MTP press, c1982. — ix,261p : ill,1map ; 25cm
Includes bibliographies and index
ISBN 0-85200-441-9 : Unpriced : CIP rev.
B82-04734

613.2 — Man. Nutrition — *Practical information*
Bender, Arnold E.. Pocket encyclopedia of calories and nutrition / Arnold E. Bender with Tony Nash. — London : Mitchell Beazley, c1979 (1982 [printing]). — 128p ; 20cm
ISBN 0-85533-150-x : £3.95 B82-33579

613.2′03′21 — Man. Nutrition — *Encyclopaedias*
Bender, Arnold E.. Dictionary of nutrition and food technology. — 5th ed. — London : Butterworths, Nov.1982. — [320]p
Previous ed.: London : Newnes-Butterworths, 1975
ISBN 0-408-10855-x : £15.00 : CIP entry
Also classified at 664′.00321 B82-28273

613.2′05 — Man. Nutrition — *Serials*
Human nutrition. Applied nutrition. — Vol.36A, no.1 (Feb. 1982)-. — London : John Libbey, 1982-. — v. : ill ; 25cm
Six issues yearly. — Continues in part: Journal of human nutrition
ISSN 0263-8495 = Human nutrition. Applied nutrition (corrected) : £37.00 per year
B82-32365

613.2′07′041 — Great Britain. Health education. Curriculum subjects: Man. Nutrition
British Nutrition Foundation. Preventive nutrition and society / [Proceedings of the British Nutrition Foundation Second Annual Conference held at the Royal Society, July 1-2, 1980] ; edited by M.R. Turner. — London : Academic Press, 1981. — xii,228p : ill,facsims ; 24cm
Includes bibliographies and index
ISBN 0-12-704450-7 : £16.40 : CIP rev.
Primary classification 613.2 B81-28783

Lennon, Dorothy. Community dietetics / Dorothy Lennon, Paul Fieldhouse. — London : Forbes, 1979. — 127p : ill,1map ; 22cm
Bibliography: p119-120
ISBN 0-901762-30-x (pbk) : Unpriced
B82-06879

613.2′07′11 — Medical personnel. Professional education. Curriculum subjects: Man. Nutrition
Physiology and social nutrition and nutritional education / volume editor Geoffrey H. Bourne. — Basel ; London : Karger, c1981. — ix,229p : ill ; 25cm. — (World review of nutrition and dietetics ; v.38)
Includes index
ISBN 3-8055-3048-x : £47.25
Primary classification 612′.3 B82-21668

613.2′072 — Man. Nutrition. Research — *Conference proceedings*
Human nutrition research : invited papers presented at a symposium held May 6-9, 1979 at the Beltsville Agricultural Research Center (BARC), Beltsville, Maryland 20705 / Gary R. Beecher, editor ; organized by the BARC Symposium IV Committee ; sponsored by The Beltsville Agricultural Research Center ... — Totowa : Allenheld, Osmun ; London : Granada, 1981. — xiv,303p : ill ; 25cm. — (Beltsville symposia in agricultural research ; 4)
Includes bibliographies and index
ISBN 0-246-11456-8 : Unpriced B82-24200

613.2′076 — Man. Nutrition — *Questions & answers*
Shannon, Barbara. Student supplement for Realities of nutrition / Barbara Shannon. — Palo Alto : Bull ; London : distributed by Eurospan, c1977. — [206]p : ill,forms ; 28cm
ISBN 0-915950-13-8 (pbk) : Unpriced
B82-41102

613.2′088042 — Pregnant women. Health. Effects of diet
Davis, Adelle. Let′s have healthy children / Adelle Davis. — 3rd ed., new, expanded and rev. ed. / updated by Marshall Mandell. — London : Unwin Paperbacks, 1981. — xiii,386p : ill ; 18cm
Previous ed.: 1974. — Includes index
ISBN 0-04-612030-0 (pbk) : £1.95 : CIP rev.
Primary classification 613.2′0880542
B79-12940

613.2′088054 — Children. Nutrition
Cameron, Margaret. Manual on feeding infants and young children. — 3rd ed. — Oxford : Oxford University Press, Jan.1983. — [240]p. — (Oxford medical publications)
Previous ed.: S.l. : Protein Advisory Group, 1976
ISBN 0-19-261403-7 (pbk) : £3.00 : CIP entry
B82-33480

613.2′088054 — Children. Nutrition. Health aspects
Textbook of paediatric nutrition / edited by Donald S. McLaren, David Burman ; foreword by Reginald Lightwood. — 2nd ed. — Edinburgh : Churchill Livingstone, 1982. — x,464p : ill ; 25cm
Previous ed.: 1976. — Includes bibliographies and index
ISBN 0-443-02285-2 (pbk) : £16.00 : CIP rev.
B81-25300

613.2′0880542 — Babies. Diet
Mac Keith, Ronald. MacKeith′s infant feeding and feeding difficulties. — 6th ed. / Christopher B.S. Wood, John A. Walker-Smith. — Edinburgh : Churchill Livingstone, 1981. — viii,334p : ill ; 22cm
Previous ed.: published as Infant feeding and feeding difficulties. 1977. — Includes bibliographies and index
ISBN 0-443-01945-2 (pbk) : £8.00 : CIP rev.
B81-00122

613.2′0880542 — Babies. Health. Effects of diet
Davis, Adelle. Let′s have healthy children / Adelle Davis. — 3rd ed., new, expanded and rev. ed. / updated by Marshall Mandell. — London : Unwin Paperbacks, 1981. — xiii,386p : ill ; 18cm
Previous ed.: 1974. — Includes index
ISBN 0-04-612030-0 (pbk) : £1.95 : CIP rev.
Also classified at 613.2′088042 B79-12940

613.2′088055 — Adolescents. Nutrition. Health aspects
Adolescent nutrition / edited by Myron Winick. — New York ; Chichester : Wiley, c1982. — viii,188p : ill ; 24cm. — (Current concepts in nutrition, ISSN 0090-0443 ; v.11)
Includes index
ISBN 0-471-86543-5 : £31.25 B82-32707

613.2′0880565 — Great Britain. Old persons. Nutrition
Davies, Louise. Three score years — and then? : a study of the nutrition and wellbeing of elderly people at home / Louise Davies. — London : Heinemann Medical, 1981. — vii,228p : ill ; 22cm
Bibliography: p178-182. — Includes index
ISBN 0-433-07193-1 (pbk) : Unpriced
B82-08640

613.2′088796 — Athletes. Nutrition
Morella, Joseph J.. Nutrition and the athlete / Joseph J. Morella and Richard J. Turchetti ; foreword by James F. Fixx. — Rev. ed. — New York ; London : Van Nostrand Reinhold, 1982. — 272p ; 22cm
Previous ed.: New York : Mason/Charter, 1976. — Includes index
ISBN 0-442-26369-4 (cased) : Unpriced
ISBN 0-442-26368-6 (pbk) : £6.75 B82-17628

613.2′0941 — Great Britain. Man. Nutrition
Dickerson, John W. T.. Nutrition in an age of technology / J.W.T. Dickerson. — [Guildford] ([Guildford, Surrey GU2 5XH]) : [University of Surrey], [1979?]. — 17p ; 21cm. — (University of Surrey inaugural lecture)
Cover title. — Bibliography: p16-17
Unpriced (pbk) B82-26645

613.2′5 — Physical fitness. Slimming
Burton, Penny. Slimmer′s mirror : a his ′n′ hers guide to fitness and health : diets, exercise, slimming tips / by Penny Burton. — London : Mirror Books for Mirror Group Newspapers, c1982. — 26p : ill(some col.),ports ; 26cm. — (A Daily mirror slimmers club special)
ISBN 0-85939-304-6 (unbound) : £0.50
B82-25248

Slimming : the complete guide / by the experts of Slimming magazine ; [editors: Sybil Greatbatch and Vera Segal] ; [writer: Gaynor Hagan] ; introduction by Audrey Eyton. — London : Collins, 1982. — 224p : ill(some col.),ports (some col.) ; 29cm
Includes index
ISBN 0-00-411675-5 (cased) : £9.95
ISBN 0-00-411813-8 (pbk) : Unpriced
B82-39412

613.2′5 — Physical fitness. Slimming. Diet
Eyton, Audrey. The F-plan / Audrey Eyton. — Harmondsworth : Penguin, 1982. — 204p ; 19cm
ISBN 0-14-006422-2 (pbk) : £1.50 B82-33152

Katahn, Martin. The 200 calorie solution. — London : Arlington, Oct.1982. — [280]p
ISBN 0-85140-595-9 : £5.95 : CIP entry
B82-25066

613.2'5 — Physical fitness. Slimming. Diet *continuation*

Kennedy, Lynn. The Daily Express guide to successful slimming / Lynn Kennedy. — [London] : Star, 1982, c1981. — 125p ; 18cm
ISBN 0-352-31102-9 (pbk) : £1.50 B82-20315

Mazel, Judy. The Beverly Hills diet / Judy Mazel with Susan Shultz. — London : Sidgwick & Jackson, 1982, c1981. — xxv,262p ; 23cm
Originally published: New York : Macmillan, 1981. — Includes index
ISBN 0-283-98845-2 : £4.95 B82-20214

Pinkus, Susan. Slimming diets. — Havant : Mason, Aug.1981. — [32]p
Originally published: 1973
ISBN 0-85937-102-6 (pbk) : £0.20 : CIP entry B81-18049

Pritikin, Nathan. The Pritikin permanent weight-loss manual / by Nathan Pritikin ; illustrated by Joann T. Rounds. — Toronto ; London : Bantam, 1982, c1981. — xiii,396p : ill ; 18cm
Originally published: New York : Grosset & Dunlap, c1981. — Includes index
ISBN 0-553-17778-8 (pbk) : £1.50 B82-36739

Spira, Michael. The no-diet book : a guide to permanent weight control / Michael Spira. — [London] : Fontana, 1982. — 156p ; 18cm
Includes index
ISBN 0-00-636491-8 (pbk) : £1.50 B82-28904

Trimmer, Eric. The complete book of slimming & diets / Eric Trimmer. — Loughton : Piatkus, 1981. — 160p : ill(some col.) ; 25cm
Includes index
ISBN 0-86188-081-1 (cased) : Unpriced : CIP rev.
ISBN 0-86188-116-8 (pbk) : £4.95 B81-21523

613.2'5'088042 — Women. Physical fitness. Slimming

Voak, Sally Ann. The SHE book of slimming / Sally Ann Voak. — London : Arthur Barker, c1982. — 112p : ill ; 23cm
Includes index
ISBN 0-213-16802-2 (cased) : £5.95
ISBN 0-213-16807-3 (pbk) : £3.95 B82-09921

613.2'6 — Man. Chang ming diet

Soo, Chee. The Tao of long life. — Wellingborough : Aquarian Press, Aug.1982. — [176]p
Originally published: London : Gordon & Cremonesi, 1979
ISBN 0-85030-320-6 (pbk) : £3.50 : CIP entry B82-16653

613.2'6 — Man. Health. Effects of sugar

Brekhman, I. I.. Brown or white : the sugar controversy. — Oxford : Pergamon, Nov.1982. — [100]p
Translation from the Russian
ISBN 0-08-026837-4 : £12.50 : CIP entry B82-31282

613.2'6 — Man. Health. Improvement. Use of natural food

Meredith, Bronwen. Vogue natural health and beauty / Bronwen Meredith. — Harmondsworth : Penguin, 1981, c1979. — 300p,[16]p of plates : ill(some col.),facsims ; 25cm
Originally published: London : Allen Lane, 1979. — Includes index
ISBN 0-14-005040-x (pbk) : £4.95
Also classified at 646.7'2 B82-07285

Wheatley, Michael. A way of living. — London : Allen & Unwin, Nov.1982. — [384]p
Originally published: London : Corgi, 1977
ISBN 0-04-613048-9 (pbk) : £3.95 : CIP entry B82-27820

613.2'62 — Vegetarianism

Bargen, Richard. The vegetarian's self-defense manual / by Richard Bargen. — Wheaton ; London : Theosophical Publishing House, c1979. — vii,160p : ill ; 21cm. — (A Quest book)
Bibliography: p137-160
ISBN 0-8356-0530-2 (pbk) : Unpriced B82-31195

613.2'62'088054 — Children, to 12 years: Vegetarians. Nutrition

Elliot, Rose. Rose Elliot's vegetarian baby book. — Altrincham : Vegetarian Society, June 1982. — [48]p
ISBN 0-900774-22-3 (pbk) : £1.95 : CIP entry B82-14965

613.2'8 — Fish oil. Fatty acids. Nutritional aspects. Analysis — *Conference proceedings*

Nutritional evaluation of long-chain fatty acids in fish oil. — London : Academic Press, Aug.1982. — [340]p
Conference papers
ISBN 0-12-078920-5 : CIP entry B82-16637

613.2'8 — Man. Diet. Role of fibre — *Conference proceedings*

Dietary fiber in health and disease / edited by George V. Vahouny and David Kritchevsky. — New York ; London : Plenum, c1982. — xiv,330p : ill ; 24cm. — (GWUMC Department of Biochemistry annual spring symposia)
Includes bibliographies and index
ISBN 0-306-40926-7 : Unpriced B82-40412

Dietary fibre. — London : Applied Science, Feb.1983. — [280]p
Conference papers
ISBN 0-85334-178-8 : £36.00 : CIP entry B82-39605

613.2'8 — Man. Health. Effects of vitamins

Gildroy, Ann. Vitamins and your health / by Ann Gildroy ; illustrated by Clive Sandall. — London : Allen & Unwin, 1982. — 132p : ill ; 23cm
Bibliography: p125-127. — Includes index
ISBN 0-04-641039-2 : Unpriced : CIP rev. B81-33909

Mindell, Earl. The vitamin bible. — London : Arlington Books, Aug.1982. — [208]p
ISBN 0-85140-583-5 (pbk) : £4.95 : CIP entry B82-15874

Vitamins / [edited by Eileen Lloyd]. — Aylesbury : Rodale, 1982. — 48p ; 18cm. — (Prevention health guides)
ISBN 0-87857-431-x (pbk) : Unpriced B82-36760

Vitamins in medicine. — London : Heinemann Medical
Vol.2. — 4th ed / [edited by] Brian M. Barker, David A. Bender. — 1982. — 350p : ill ; 24cm
Previous ed.: / Franklin Bicknell, Frederick Prescott. 1953. — Includes bibliographies and index
ISBN 0-433-02806-8 : Unpriced B82-32098

613.2'8 — Man. Nutrients: Trace elements & vitamins

Pfeiffer, Carl C.. [Dr. Pfeiffer's total nutrition]. Total nutrition / Carl C. Pfeiffer and Jane Banks. — London : Granada, 1982, c1980. — 161p ; 21cm
Originally published: New York : Simon and Schuster, 1980. — Includes index
ISBN 0-246-11686-2 : £4.95 : CIP rev.
Also classified at 641.5'637 B81-35797

613.2'8 — Man. Nutrients: Vitamins

Colgan, Michael. Your personal vitamin profile. — London : Blond & Briggs, Feb.1983. — [304]p
ISBN 0-85634-140-1 : £6.95 : CIP entry B82-37649

613.2'8 — Man. Nutrition. Role of selenium

Lewis, Alan, *19---*. Selenium : the facts about this essential mineral / by Alan Lewis. — Wellingborough : Thorsons, 1982. — 96p ; 18cm
Includes index
ISBN 0-7225-0734-8 (pbk) : £0.95 : CIP rev. B82-09216

613.4 — HYGIENE. CARE OF PERSON

613'.482 — Great Britain. Children. Footwear. Health aspects — *Inquiry reports*

Bad fit, bad feet : children's footwear and health. — London : National Consumer Council, 1981. — 16p : ill ; 30cm + 1 poster(ill ; 30x42cm folded to 30x21cm)
ISBN 0-905653-35-1 (pbk) : Unpriced B82-08170

613.5/6 — HYGIENE. ARTIFICIAL ENVIRONMENTS

613.6'2 — Industrial health — *Serials*

Recent advances in occupational health. — No.1. — Edinburgh : Churchill Livingstone, Oct.1981. — [259]p
ISBN 0-443-02300-x : £16.00 : CIP entry
ISSN 0261-1449 B81-25301

613.6'2 — Personnel. Health. Effects of shiftwork & night work — *Conference proceedings*

International Symposium on Night and Shift Work *(5th : 1980 : Rouen)*. Night and shift work. — Oxford : Pergamon, June 1981. — [516]p. — (Advances in the biosciences ; v.30)
ISBN 0-08-025516-7 : £33.00 : CIP entry B81-13510

613.6'6 — Self-defence — *Manuals*

Hoare, Syd. Self defence. — London : Hodder & Stoughton, July 1982. — [192]p. — (Teach yourself books)
ISBN 0-340-26834-4 (pbk) : £2.25 : CIP entry B82-12263

613.6'6'088042 — Self-defence by women — *Manuals*

Barthol, Robert G.. Protect yourself : a self-defense guide for women from prevention to counter-attack / Robert G. Barthol. — Englewood Cliffs ; London : Prentice-Hall, c1979. — xii,222p : ill ; 25cm. — (A Spectrum book)
Includes index
ISBN 0-13-731430-2 (cased) : £10.45
ISBN 0-13-731422-1 (pbk) : Unpriced B82-06994

Butler, Pat. Self-defence for women. — London : New English Library, Nov.1982. — [96]p
ISBN 0-450-05530-2 (pbk) : £1.25 : CIP entry B82-27516

613.6'8 — Travel. Health aspects — *Practical information*

Birch, C. Allan. How to survive your holiday : the traveller's guide to health / C. Allan Birch. — London : Wigmore House, 1982. — 130p ; 23cm
Includes index
ISBN 0-907070-04-3 (cased) : £8.95 : CIP rev.
ISBN 0-907070-05-1 (pbk) : £3.95 B82-12175

Dick, George. Health on holiday : and other travels / by George Dick. — London : British Medical Association, [1982]. — 31p : 1map ; 19cm. — (A Family doctor booklet)
£0.50 (unbound) B82-19049

613.6'9 — Survival. Techniques — *Manuals* — *For children*

Hildreth, Brian. How to survive / written by Brian Hildreth ; illustrated by Conrad Bailey. — Harmondsworth : Puffin, 1976 (1982 [printing]). — 192p : ill ; 19cm
Includes index
ISBN 0-14-030856-3 (pbk) : £0.95 B82-20316

613.7 — PHYSICAL FITNESS

613.7 — Physical fitness — *Manuals*

Body workshop / [editor Brenda Marshall]. — London : Marshall Cavendish, c1979. — 19p : ill(some col.) ; 28cm. — (Your body)
Includes index
ISBN 0-85685-350-x (pbk) : £0.99 B82-37309

Cooper, Henry, *1934-*. Get fit for life / Henry Cooper. — London : Sphere, 1982. — x,150p : ill ; 18cm
ISBN 0-7221-2498-8 (pbk) : £1.25 B82-11193

Dowson, Jeff. Fit for living / Jeff Dowson. — London : Independent Television Books, 1981. — 112p : ill ; 20cm
ISBN 0-900727-92-6 (pbk) : Unpriced B82-09489

The **Health** & fitness handbook : a family guide / edited by Miriam Polunin. — [London] : Windward, c1981. — 256p : ill ; 26cm
Bibliography: p249-250. — Includes index
ISBN 0-7112-0208-7 : £9.95 B82-01586

Newton-Dunn, Esme. The bodywork book. — London : Collins, Oct.1982. — [128]p
ISBN 0-00-218007-3 : £3.95 : CIP entry B82-23077

Percival, Jan. The complete guide to total fitness / Jan Percival, Lloyd Percival, Joe Taylor. — Wakefield : EP, 1982, c1977. — 224p : ill ; 24cm
Originally published: Scarborough, Ont. : Prentice-Hall, 1977. — Includes index
ISBN 0-7158-0804-4 (pbk) : £3.95 B82-34875

613.7 — Physical fitness. Wushu — *Manuals*

Wushu! : the Chinese way to family health and fitness / [editor Jane Garton ; art editor Ingrid Mason ; editorial assistant Maxine Stait ; illustrators Russell Barnett, Nick Ward, the Mitchell Beazley Studio] ; introduction by Dame Margot Fonteyn. — London : Mitchell Beazley, 1981. — 144p : ill(some col.) ; 26cm
ISBN 0-85533-315-4 (pbk) : £3.50 B82-30496

613.7'042 — Children. Physical fitness — *For schools*

Carre, F. Alex. Fitness for life / F. Alex Carre, Charles B. Corbin, Ruth Lindsey. — Toronto : Gage ; [Basingstoke] : Macmillan Education [[distributor]], c1980. — 192p : ill,forms ; 28cm. — (Physical education concepts)
Bibliography: p192
ISBN 0-333-32961-9 (pbk) : Unpriced
ISBN 0-333-32960-0 (Teachers ed.) : Unpriced B82-28390

613.7'042 — Children. Physical fitness *related to* growth

Shephard, Roy J.. Physical activity and growth / Roy J. Shephard. — Chicago ; London : Year Book Medical, c1982. — xi,340p : ill ; 23cm
Bibliography: p250-315. — Includes index
ISBN 0-8151-7643-0 : £26.50
Also classified at 612'.65 B82-22923

613.7'045 — Women. Physical fitness — *Manuals*

Fonda, Jane. Jane Fonda's workout book / by Jane Fonda ; photographs by Steve Schapiro. — London : Allen Lane, 1982, c1981. — 252p : ill,ports ; 29cm
Originally published: New York : Simon & Schuster, 1981
ISBN 0-7139-1437-8 : £7.95 B82-19047

613.7'046 — Acu-yoga — *Manuals*

Gach, Michael Reed. Acu-yoga : self help techniques to relieve tension / Michael Reed Gach with Carolyn Marco. — Tokyo : Japan Publications ; Hemel Hempstead : International Book Distributors, 1981. — 247p : ill ; 26cm
Bibliography: p239-241. — Includes index
ISBN 0-87040-489-x (pbk) : £7.75 B82-14459

613.7'046 — Physical fitness. Hatha-yoga

Hoare, Sophy. Tackle yoga / Sophy Hoare. — London : Stanley Paul, 1982. — 119p : ill ; 24cm
ISBN 0-09-145410-7 (cased) : £6.50 : CIP rev.
ISBN 0-09-145411-5 (pbk) : £3.95 B81-13440

613.7'046 — Physical fitness. Hatha-yoga — *Manuals*

Patel, Shivabhai. Yogasana self teacher : (pictorial book teaching asanas for healthy life) / author Shivabhai Patel ; foreword by Swami Chidanand. — Chaklashi (Shiv Yoga Niketan) ; London (143 Upton La., E7 8PJ) : S. Patel, 1980. — 178p,[2]leaves of plates : ill,ports ; 22cm
Includes index
£3.00 B82-01894

Volin, Michael. Challenging the years : Yoga wisdom and modern knowledge for healthier and longer life / Michael Volin. — London : Sphere
Originally published: in 1v. London : Pelham, 1979
Vol.2. — 1981, c1979. — 119p,[8]p of plates : ill ; 18cm
ISBN 0-7221-8744-0 (pbk) : £1.25 B82-02171

613.7'046'0880816 — Handicapped persons. Physical fitness. Hatha-yoga — *Manuals*

Brosnan, Barbara. Yoga for handicapped people / Barbara Brosnan. — London : Souvenir, 1982. — 208p,[24]p of plates : ill ; 22cm. — (Human horizons series) (A Condor book)
Bibliography: p198. — Includes index
ISBN 0-285-64947-7 (cased) : £6.95
ISBN 0-285-64952-3 (pbk) : £4.95 B82-23042

613.7'07'1 — Schools. Curriculum subjects: Physical education. Curriculum. Design

Annarino, Anthony A.. Curriculum theory and design in physical education. — 2nd ed. / Anthony A. Annarino, Charles C. Cowell, Helen W. Hazelton. — St Louis ; London : Mosby, 1980. — xvi,420p : forms ; 25cm
Previous ed.: published as Curriculum designs in physical education / Charles C. Cowell, Helen W. Hazelton. New York : Prentice-Hall ; London : Bailey & Swinfen, 1955. — Bibliography: p388-414. — Includes index
ISBN 0-8016-0297-1 : £11.25 B82-14972

613.7'07'1041 — Great Britain. Schools. Curriculum subjects: Physical education. Safety measures

British Association of Advisers and Lecturers in Physical Education. Safety in physical education / compiled and published by the British Association of Advisers and Lecturers in Physical Education. — Chester (c/o Public Relations Officer, 7 Edinburgh Way, Queen's Park, Chester) : The Association, 1979 (1980 [printing]). — 111p ; 24cm
Unpriced (pbk) B82-31663

613.7'1 — Lawn tennis players. Physical fitness — *Manuals*

Bolliger, A.. Get fit for tennis / A. Bolliger. — London : Pelham, 1982. — 189p : ill,ports ; 23cm
Translation of: Top fit im Tennis. — Bibliography: p180-183. — Includes index
ISBN 0-7207-1350-1 : £7.95 : CIP rev. B81-17505

613.7'1 — Physical fitness. Exercises

Burke, Edmund J.. Fit to exercise / Edmund J. Burke, John H.L. Humphreys ; foreword by Ron Hill. — London : Pelham, 1982. — 175p : ill ; 23cm
Bibliography: p163-170. — Includes index
ISBN 0-7207-1224-6 : £7.95 : CIP rev. B81-27932

Gaines, Charles. Staying hard : the only exercise book you will ever need / written by Charles Gaines ; photographs by George Butler ; designed by Martin Stephen Moskof. — London : Macmillan, 1981, c1980. — 191p : ill ; 29cm
Originally published: New York : Kenan, 1980
ISBN 0-333-31996-6 (cased) : £6.95
ISBN 0-333-31927-3 (pbk) : Unpriced B82-36372

Getchell, Bud. Being fit : a personal guide / Bud Getchell with Wayne Anderson. — New York ; Chichester : Wiley, c1982. — viii,312p : ill ; 23cm
Includes index
ISBN 0-471-86353-x (pbk) : Unpriced B82-37975

Prudden, Suzy. Suzy Prudden's I can exercise anywhere book. — Loughton : Piatkus, Oct.1982. — [160]p
Originally published: New York : Workman, 1981
ISBN 0-86188-217-2 (cased) : £6.95 : CIP entry
ISBN 0-86188-220-2 (pbk) : £3.95 B82-24579

613.7'1 — Physical fitness. Sports

Handbook for the young athlete / Bob Gaillard ... [et al.]. — Palo Alto : Bull Publishing ; London : distributed by Eurospan, c1978. — 201p : ill ; 22cm
ISBN 0-915950-18-9 (pbk) : Unpriced B82-36620

613.7'1 — Physical fitness. Stretching exercises — *Manuals*

Balaskas, Arthur. Soft exercise. — London : Unwin Paperbacks, Nov.1982. — [144]p
ISBN 0-04-613047-0 (pbk) : £4.95 : CIP entry B82-28998

613.7'1'0880544 — Children, 4-10 years. Physical fitness. Coordination. Exercises — *For teaching*

Learmouth, John. Small apparatus in practice / by John Learmouth. — Huddersfield : Schofield & Sims, 1982. — 109p : ill ; 21cm
ISBN 0-7217-4516-4 (pbk) : £2.45 B82-13353

613.7'1'0880565 — Old persons. Physical fitness. Exercises

Gibbs, Russell. Exercises for the elderly. — London : Jill Norman, July 1981. — [152]p
ISBN 0-906908-52-3 (cased) : £6.95 : CIP entry
ISBN 0-906908-53-1 (pbk) : £3.50 B81-13504

Movement for the over-sixties / East Midland Keep Fit Association. — [Nottingham] ([12 Dark La., Aslockton, Nottingham NG13 9AA]) : East Midland Keep Fit Association in association with the Sports Council, East Midland Region, [1982?]. — 22p ; 21cm
Bibliography: p20
Unpriced (pbk) B82-39913

613.7'1'0880816 — Handicapped persons. Physical fitness. Exercises

Hollis, Katy. Progress to improved movement : for handicapped children and adults with poor posture / Katy Hollis ; illustrations David Baird. — New ed. — Kidderminster : British Institute of Mental Handicap, 1980. — v,26p : ill ; 21cm
Previous ed.: 1977. — Bibliography: pv
ISBN 0-906054-17-6 (pbk) : £1.65 B82-36512

613.7'9 — Man. Relaxation — *Manuals*

Eagle, Robert. Taking the strain / Robert Eagle. — London : British Broadcasting Corporation, 1982, c1981. — 96p : ill,ports ; 21cm
Bibliography: p94
ISBN 0-563-16499-9 (pbk) : £2.75 B82-27856

Hewitt, James. Relaxation East and West : a manual of poised living / James Hewitt. — London : Rider, 1982. — 213p ; 22cm
Bibliography: p204-207. — Includes index
ISBN 0-09-146281-9 (pbk) : £4.95 : CIP rev. B82-10605

613.8 — ADDICTIONS AND HEALTH

613.8 — Drug taking

Duncan, David, *1947-*. Drugs and the whole person / David Duncan, Robert Gold. — New York ; Chichester : Wiley, c1982. — xii,260p : ill,2facsims ; 24cm
Bibliography: p242-253. — Includes index
ISBN 0-471-04120-3 (pbk) : £8.95 B82-28141

613.8'1 — Alcoholic drinks. Consumption. Health aspects — *For adolescents*

Foster, Fiona. All about drinking / Fiona Foster, Alexander McCall Smith ; illustrated by Iain McIntosh. — Edinburgh : Macdonald, c1981. — 46p : ill ; 24cm
ISBN 0-904265-52-8 : £2.95 B82-36096

613.8'5 — Cigarette smoking. Health aspects

. Smoking and arterial disease. — Tunbridge Wells : Pitman Medical, Apr.1981. — [336]p
ISBN 0-272-79604-2 (pbk) : £20.00 : CIP entry B81-06073

613.8′5 — Cigarette smoking. Health aspects *continuation*

Williams, Howard, *1919-*. Facts about smoking for young and old / Howard Williams. — London (Tavistock House North, Tavistock Sq., WC1H 9JE) : Chest, Heart and Stroke Association, [1981?]. — 7p ; 22cm
Unpriced (unbound) B82-08056

613.8′5 — Cigarette smoking. Stopping — *Manuals*

Ogle, Jane. The stop-smoking diet book. — Loughton : Piatkus, July 1982. — [160]p
ISBN 0-86188-198-2 : £5.95 : CIP entry B82-12927

613.8′5 — Developing countries. Cigarette smoking. Health aspects

Nath, Uma Ram. Smoking : Third World alert. — Oxford : Oxford University Press, Nov.1982. — [200]p. — (Oxford medical publications)
ISBN 0-19-261402-9 (cased) : £5.95 : CIP entry
ISBN 0-19-261325-1 (pbk) : £1.00 B82-26893

613.8′5 — Man. Health. Effects of tobacco smoking. Psychosocial aspects

Eysenck, H. J.. The causes and effects of smoking / H.J. Eysenck with contributions by L.J. Eaves. — London : Temple Smith, 1980. — 397p : ill ; 23cm
Bibliography: p358-383. — Includes index
ISBN 0-85117-186-9 : £16.50 B82-21339

613.8′5 — Tobacco smoking

Ashton, Heather. Smoking : psychology and pharmacology. — London : Tavistock, Feb.1982. — [250]p
ISBN 0-422-77700-5 : £10.00 : CIP entry B81-35728

613.8′5 — Tobacco smoking. Health aspects

Shephard, Roy J.. The risks of passive smoking / Roy J. Shephard. — London : Croom Helm, c1982. — 195p : ill ; 23cm
Bibliography: p160-191. — Includes index
ISBN 0-7099-2334-1 : £12.95 : CIP rev. B82-04470

613.8′5′024055 — Cigarette smoking. Health aspects — *For adolescents*

Williams, Howard, *1919-*. To smoke or not to smoke / Howard Williams. — London (Tavistock House North, Tavistock Sq., WC1H 9JE) : Chest, Heart and Stroke Association, c1981. — 11p ; 18cm
Unpriced (unbound) B82-08055

613.9 — BIRTH CONTROL AND SEX HYGIENE

613.9′4 — Man. Artificial insemination — *Conference proceedings*

Instrumental insemination / edited by E.S.E. Hafez and K. Semm. — The Hague ; London : Nijhoff, 1982. — x,231p ; 28cm. — (Clinics in andrology ; 8)
Includes bibliographies and index
ISBN 90-247-2530-5 : Unpriced B82-34546

International Symposium on Artificial Insemination and Semen Preservation *(1979 : Paris)*. Human artificial insemination and semen preservation / [proceedings of the International Symposium on Artificial Insemination and Semen Preservation held in Paris, France April 9-11, 1979] ; edited by Georges David and Wendel S. Price. — New York ; London : Plenum, c1980. — xvi,639p : ill,maps,1facsim,2ports ; 26cm
Includes bibliographies and index
ISBN 0-306-40547-4 : Unpriced
Also classified at 613.9′4 B82-11043

613.9′4 — Man. Contraception. Political aspects

Djerassi, Carl. The politics of contraception : the present and the future / Carl Djerassi. — Oxford : W.H. Freeman, 1981. — xxi,282p : ill,facsims,1port ; 25cm
Originally published: Stanford, Calif. : Stanford Alumni Association, 1979. — Includes index
ISBN 0-7167-1341-1 (cased) : £14.80
ISBN 0-7167-1341-1 (pbk) : £6.95 B82-16157

613.9′4 — Man. Semen. Preservation — *Conference proceedings*

International Symposium on Artificial Insemination and Semen Preservation *(1979 : Paris)*. Human artificial insemination and semen preservation / [proceedings of the International Symposium on Artificial Insemination and Semen Preservation held in Paris, France April 9-11, 1979] ; edited by Georges David and Wendel S. Price. — New York ; London : Plenum, c1980. — xvi,639p : ill,maps,1facsim,2ports ; 26cm
Includes bibliographies and index
ISBN 0-306-40547-4 : Unpriced
Primary classification 613.9′4 B82-11043

613.9′4 — Men. Contraception

Progress towards a male contraceptive. — Chichester : Wiley, Dec.1982. — [272]p. — (Current topics in reproductive endocrinology ; v.2) (A Wiley medical publication)
ISBN 0-471-10417-5 : £19.00 : CIP entry B82-30827

613.9′42 — Women. Sterilisation

Female sterilization. — London : International Planned Parenthood Federation, Jan.1982. — [44]p. — (IPPF medical publications)
ISBN 0-86089-045-7 (pbk) : £1.50 : CIP entry B82-03127

Saidi, M. H.. Female sterilization : a handbook for women / M.H. Saidi & Carla M. Zainie. — New York ; London : Garland STPM, 1979. — xiii,119p : ill ; 24cm
Bibliography: p110-113. — Includes index
ISBN 0-8240-7136-0 : Unpriced B82-31072

613.9′42 — Women. Tubal sterilisation

Brown, Herbert P.. Female sterilization : an overview with emphasis on the vaginal route and the organization of a sterilization program / Herbert P. Brown, Stephan N. Schanzer. — Boston, Mass. ; Bristol : John Wright, 1982. — ix,111p : ill,forms ; 23cm
Includes index
ISBN 0-88416-356-3 : Unpriced B82-16119

613.9′432 — Oral contraceptives — *Conference proceedings*

Benefits and risks of hormonal contraception : has the attitude changed? / edited by A.A. Haspels and R. Rolland. — Lancaster : M.T.P. Press, c1982. — xvi,192p : ill ; 23cm
Conference proceedings. — Includes index
ISBN 0-85200-457-5 : £13.95 : CIP rev. B82-19276

Non-steroidal regulators in reproductive biology & medicine. — Oxford : Pergamon, Mar.1982. — [266]p. — (Advances in the biosciences ; v.34)
Conference papers
ISBN 0-08-027976-7 : £55.00 : CIP entry B82-02623

613.9′434 — Man. Contraception. Billings method

Billings, Evelyn. The Billings method : controlling fertility without drugs or devices / Evelyn Billings and Ann Westmore. — London : Allen Lane, 1981, c1980. — 254p : ill(some col.) ; 23cm
Originally published: Carlton, Vic. : Anne O'Donovan, 1980. — Includes index
ISBN 0-7139-1454-8 : £5.95 B82-06618

613.9′435 — Intrauterine devices — *Conference proceedings*

IUD technology / editors E.S.E. Hafez, A.J.M. Audebert. — Lancaster : MTP, c1982. — 201p : ill ; 24cm. — (Progress in contraceptive delivery systems ; v.4)
Conference papers. — Includes bibliographies and index
ISBN 0-85200-356-0 : £18.50 : CIP rev. B81-30634

613.9′435 — Intrauterine devices — *Illustrations*

Thomsen, Russel J.. An atlas of intrauterine contraception / Russel J. Thomsen. — London : Hemisphere, c1982. — ix,169p : ill ; 24cm
Includes bibliographies and index
ISBN 0-89116-246-1 : £52.50
ISBN 0-07-060238-8 (McGraw-Hill) B82-37794

613.9′5′07073 — United States. Sex education

Sex education in the eighties : the challenge of healthy sexual evolution / edited by Lorna Brown. — New York ; London : Plenum, c1981. — xiv,264p ; 26cm. — (Perspectives in sexuality)
Includes bibliographies and index
ISBN 0-306-40762-0 : Unpriced B82-13921

613.9′6 — Man. Sexual intercourse — *Manuals*

Castleman, Michael. How to last longer : and other sexual solutions / Michael Castleman. — London : Souvenir, 1980. — 267p : ill ; 24cm
Originally published: New York : Simon and Schuster, 1980. — Bibliography: p252-255. — Includes index
ISBN 0-285-62514-4 : £7.95 B82-22178

Feigel, Marcel. How to have sex in public without being noticed. — London : Muller, Feb.1983. — [96]p
ISBN 0-584-11062-6 (pbk) : £1.95 : CIP entry B82-37482

613.9′6′088042 — Women. Sex relations — *Manuals — For women*

Kassorla, Irene. Nice girls do — : and now you can too! / Irene Kassorla. — London : Granada, 1981, c1980. — 239p : ill ; 18cm. — (A Mayflower book)
Originally published: Los Angeles : Stratford Press, 1980. — Bibliography: P237-239
ISBN 0-583-13557-9 : £5.95 B82-24534

613.9′6′08808166 — Spinal cord injury victims. Rehabilitation. Sexual aspects

Human sexuality and rehabilitation medicine / sexual functioning following spinal cord injury ; edited by Ami Sha'ked. — Baltimore ; London : Williams & Wilkins, c1981. — xix,210p : ill ; 24cm. — (Rehabilitation medicine library)
Includes bibliographies and index
ISBN 0-683-07749-x : Unpriced B82-02569

614 — PUBLIC HEALTH

614 — Public health

Public health and preventive medicine / Maxcy, Rosenau. — 11th ed. / editor, John M. Last ; editor emeritus, Philip E. Sartwell ; associate editors, James Chin, Irving J. Selikoff. — New York : Appleton-Century-Crofts ; London : Prentice-Hall, c1980. — xxv,1926p : ill,maps ; 26cm
Previous ed.: Published as Preventive medicine and public health. New York : Appleton-Century-Crofts, 1974. — Includes bibliographies and index
ISBN 0-8385-6186-1 : £41.95 B82-40724

614′.0941′443 — Scotland. Strathclyde Region. Glasgow. Public health & hygiene, *1830-1900* — *Sociological perspectives*

Health care as social history. — Aberdeen : Aberdeen University Press, Mar.1982. — [380]p
ISBN 0-08-028444-2 : £20.00 : CIP entry B82-00289

614.1 — FORENSIC MEDICINE

614′.1 — Forensic medicine

Gordon, I.. Forensic medicine. — 2nd ed. — Edinburgh : Churchill Livingstone, Aug.1982. — [400]p
Previous ed.: 1975
ISBN 0-443-02393-x : £16.00 : CIP entry B82-15798

614′.1 — Great Britain. Mentally disordered persons. Legal aspects

Trick, K. L. K.. Forensic psychiatry : an introductory text / K.L.K. Trick, T.G. Tennent. — London : Pitman, 1981. — viii,207p ; 23cm
Includes bibliographies and index
ISBN 0-272-79637-9 : Unpriced : CIP rev. B81-30344

614'.1'0924 — Great Britain. Forensic medicine, *1912-1953 — Personal observations*
Smith, *Sir* **Sydney,** *d. 1969*. Mostly murder / Sir Sydney Smith ; with a foreword by Keith Simpson. — London : Harrap, 1959 (1982 [printing]). — 318p,[23]p of plates : ill,ports ; 23cm
Includes index
£8.50 B82-25332

614.4 — PUBLIC HEALTH. INCIDENCE, DISTRIBUTION AND CONTROL OF DISEASE

614.4 — Man. Communicable diseases. Epidemiology
The **Population** dynamics of infectious diseases. — London : Chapman and Hall, Sept.1982. — [300]p
ISBN 0-412-21610-8 : £15.00 : CIP entry B82-19227

614.4 — Man. Diseases. Epidemiology
Epidemiology of diseases / edited by D.L. Miller, R.D.T. Farmer ; foreword by Sir Richard Doll. — Oxford : Blackwell Scientific, 1982. — xiii,492p : ill,maps ; 24cm
Includes index
ISBN 0-632-00686-2 : £28.50 : CIP rev. B82-01554

614.4 — Man. Diseases. Epidemiology — *Festschriften*
Donald Darnley Reid 1914-1977 : a memorial volume from colleagues and friends. — London : London School of Hygiene and Tropical Medicine, 1979. — 88p : ill,1port ; 26cm
Spine title: D.D. Reid memorial volume. — Originally published: in the Journal of epidemiology and community health, v.32, 1978. — Bibliography: p3-6
ISBN 0-902657-06-2 : £6.50 B82-08323

614.4 — Man. Diseases. Epidemiology. Genetic aspects
Morton, Newton E.. Outline of genetic epidemiology / Newton E. Morton. — Basel ; London : Karger, c1982. — vii,252p : ill ; 23cm
Includes bibliographies and index
ISBN 3-8055-2269-x (pbk) : Unpriced B82-40350

614.4 — Scotland. Man. Foodborne diseases. Epidemiology — *Serials*
Surveillance programme for foodborne infections and intoxications, Scotland. — Rept. no.1 (1980)-. — Glasgow (Ruchill Hospital, Glasgow G20 9NB) : Communicable Diseases Scotland Unit ; Edinburgh : Information Services Division, Scottish Health Service Common Services Agency, 1981-. — v. ; 30cm
Annual
ISSN 0263-8754 = Surveillance programme for foodborne infections and intoxications, Scotland : Unpriced B82-36696

614.4'072 — Man. Diseases. Epidemiology. Use of control groups
Schlesselman, James J.. Case control studies : design, conduct, analysis / James J. Schlesselman, with contributions by Paul D. Stolley. — New York ; Oxford : Oxford University Press, 1982. — xv,354p : ill ; 24cm. — (Monographs in epidemiology and biostatistics)
Bibliography: p325-343. — Includes index
ISBN 0-19-502933-x : £18.00 B82-25201

614.4'2 — Man. Diseases. Epidemiology. Geographical aspects - *Conference proceedings*
International Geographical Congress *(24th : 1980 : Tokyo)*. The geography of health. — Oxford : Pergamon, July 1981. — [270]p
ISBN 0-08-027434-x : £8.50 : CIP entry B81-16851

614.4'22724 — Developing countries. Man. Diseases. Epidemiology
Barker, D. J. P.. Practical epidemiology / D.J.P. Barker with chapters by F.J. Bennett. — 3rd ed. — Edinburgh : Churchill Livingstone, 1982. — viii,159p : ill,1map,2forms ; 22cm. — (Medicine in the tropics series)
Previous ed.: 1976. — Bibliography: p155. — Includes index
ISBN 0-443-02303-4 (pbk) : £4.25 B82-11850

614.4'322 — Man. Vectors: Blood-sucking flies
Muirhead-Thomson, R. C.. Behaviour patterns of blood-sucking flies / E.[i.e. R.]C. Muirhead-Thomson. — Oxford : Pergamon, 1982. — vii,224p : ill ; 24cm
Bibliography: p207-221. — Includes index
ISBN 0-08-025497-7 : £25.00 : CIP rev. B82-00303

614.4'323 — Man. Vectors: Mosquitoes. Genetic control — *Conference proceedings*
Cytogenetics and genetics of vectors : proceedings of a symposium of the XVIth International Congress of Entomology / editors R. Pal, J.B. Kitzmiller, T. Kanda. — Tokyo : Kodansha ; Amsterdam ; Oxford : Elsevier Biomedical, c1981. — x,265p : ill ; 27cm
Includes bibliographies and index
ISBN 0-444-80382-3 : £29.72 B82-28555

614.4'323'072 — Man. Malaria. Vectors: Mosquitoes. Research. Methodology
Bailey, Norman T. J.. The biomathematics of malaria. — London : Charles Griffin, June 1982. — [216]p
ISBN 0-85264-266-0 : £12.00 : CIP entry B82-11128

614.4'4 — Great Britain. Hospitals. Patients. Nosocomial infections: Creutzfeldt-Jakob disease. Control
Advisory Group on the Management of Patients with Spongiform Encephalopathy (Creutzfeldt-Jakob Disease (CJD)). Advisory Group on the Management of Patients with Spongiform Encephalopathy (Creutzfeldt-Jakob Disease (CJD)) : report to the Chief Medical Officers of the Department of Health and Social Security, the Scottish Home and Health Department and the Welsh Office. — London : H.M.S.O., 1981. — 5p ; 25cm
ISBN 0-11-320778-6 (unbound) : £1.00 B82-17684

614.4'4 — Hospitals. Patients. Nosocomial infections. Control
Ayliffe, G. A. J.. Hospital-acquired infection : principles and prevention / G.A.J. Ayliffe, B.J. Collins and Lynda J. Taylor ; with a foreword by E.J.L. Lowbury. — Bristol : J. Wright, 1982. — x,147p : ill ; 22cm
Bibliography: p140-142. — Includes index
ISBN 0-7236-0608-0 (pbk) : Unpriced : CIP rev. B82-09308

Control of hospital infection : a practical handbook / edited by E.J.L. Lowbury ... [et al.]. — 2nd ed. — London : Chapman and Hall, 1981. — xiv,325p ; 24cm
Previous ed.: / Working Party on Control of Hospital Infection. 1975. — Bibliography: p316. — Includes index
ISBN 0-412-16300-4 : £16.50 : CIP rev. B81-30462

614.4'8 — Swimming pools. Disinfectants: Sodium hypochlorite & calcium hypochlorite. Effectiveness
Swimming pool disinfection systems using sodium hypochlorite and calcium hypochlorite : a survey of the efficacy of disinfection / Department of the Environment, National Water Council, Standing Technical Advisory Committee on Water Quality, Sub-Committee on the Treatment of Water of Swimming Pools. — London : H.M.S.O., 1981. — 44p : ill ; 21cm
ISBN 0-11-751550-7 (pbk) : £3.30 B82-39645

614.5'18 — United States. Man. Swine flu. Epidemics. Public health measures, *1976.* **Political aspects**
Silverstein, Arthur M.. Pure politics and impure science : the swine flu affair / Arthur M. Silverstein. — Baltimore ; London : Johns Hopkins University Press, c1981. — xv,176p : ill,maps,facsims ; 24cm
Bibliography: p171-172. — Includes index
ISBN 0-8018-2632-2 : Unpriced B82-22603

614.5'21 — Man. Smallpox. Vaccination. Jenner, Edward — *Biographies*
Saunders, Paul. Edward Jenner : the Cheltenham years, 1795-1823 : being a chronicle of the vaccination campaign / by Paul Saunders ; preface by William Le Fanu. — Hanover [N.H.] ; London : University Press of New England, 1982. — xviii,469p,[12]p of plates : ill,facsims,ports ; 24cm
Includes index
ISBN 0-87451-215-8 : Unpriced B82-36990

614.5'21 — Man. Smallpox. Vaccination. Role of Jesty, Benjamin
Wallace, E. Marjorie. The first vaccinator : Benjamin Jesty of Yetminster and Worth Matravers and his family / by E. Marjorie Wallace ; with an additional illustration by Joan Begbie. — [Swanage] ([Lobster Cottage, Worth Matravers, Swanage, Dorset BH19 3LQ]) : [E.M. Wallace], [1981]. — 20p : ill,1facsim,2ports ; 22cm
Cover title
Unpriced (pbk) B82-05813

614.5'43 — Children. Whooping cough. Vaccination. Adverse reactions — *Inquiry reports*
Whooping cough : reports from the Committee on Safety of Medicines and The Joint Committee on Vaccination and Immunisation. — London : H.M.S.O., 1981. — xiii,184p : ill,facsims,forms ; 25cm
At head of title: Department of Health and Social Security
ISBN 0-11-320764-6 (pbk) : £6.90 B82-00698

614.5'7 — Man. Virus diseases. Epidemiology & control measures
Viral infections of humans : epidemiology and control / edited by Alfred S. Evans. — 2nd ed., completely rev. and expanded. — New York ; London : Plenum Medical, c1982. — xxxvii,720p : ill,maps ; 26cm
Previous ed.: London : Wiley, 1976. — Includes bibliographies and index
ISBN 0-306-40676-4 : Unpriced B82-41006

614.5'732'0094 — Western Europe. Man. Black Death. Epidemics, *ca 1340-ca 1350*
Ziegler, Philip. The Black Death / Philip Ziegler. — Harmondsworth : Penguin, 1970 (1982 [printing]). — 331p ; 20cm
Originally published: London : Collins, 1969. — Bibliography: p311-321. — Includes index
ISBN 0-14-006076-6 (pbk) : £2.50 B82-40776

614.5'732'0094 — Western Europe. Man. Black Death. Epidemics, *ca 1340-ca 1350 — Questions & answers — For schools*
Jordan, Chris. The Black Death / Chris Jordan and Tim Wood. — London : Edward Arnold, 1982. — ill,maps ; 30cm. — (History action pack)
Role playing exercise instructions (5 sheets) as inserts
ISBN 0-7131-0704-9 (unbound) : Unpriced : CIP rev. B82-05406

614.5'9241 — Man. Legionnaires' diseases. Epidemics, *to 1980*
Thomas, Gordon. Trauma : the search for the cause of legionnaires' disease / by Gordon Thomas and Max Morgan-Witts. — London : Hamilton, 1981. — xv,445p,[8]p of plates : ill,ports ; 23cm
Bibliography: p435-436. — Includes index
ISBN 0-241-10366-5 : £8.95 : CIP rev. B81-25705

614.5'996 — Water supply. Fluoridation. Public health aspects
Dillon, Charles. The fluoridation forgery / by Charles Dillon. — Fort William (c/o Bank of Scotland, 62 High Street, Fort William, Inverness-shire) : C. Dillon, [1982]. — 20p : ill ; 21cm
Unpriced (unbound) B82-27462

614.5'997 — Man. Eyes. Trachoma. Public health measures
Dawson, C. R.. Guide to trachoma control : in programmes for the prevention of blindness / C.R. Dawson, B.R. Jones, M.L. Tarizzo. — Geneva : World Health Organisation ; [London] : [H.M.S.O.] [distributor], 1981. — 56p,4p of plates : ill(some col.) ; 24cm
Bibliography: p55-56
ISBN 92-415-4157-1 (pbk) : £2.70 B82-05102

614.5'999 — Man. Cancer. Epidemiology

Doll, Richard. The causes of cancer : quantitative estimates of avoidable risks of cancer in the United States today / Richard Doll and Richard Peto. — Oxford : Oxford University Press, 1981. — p1197-1312 : ill ; 24cm. — (Oxford medical publications)
Originally published: in the Journal of the National Cancer Institute. v.66. June 1981. — Bibliography: p1260-1265. — Includes index
ISBN 0-19-261359-6 (pbk) : £4.95 B82-16081

614.6 — PUBLIC HEALTH. DISPOSAL OF THE DEAD

614'.6'0941 — Great Britain. Funeral directors. Duties — *Manuals*

Manual of funeral directing / National Association of Funeral Directors. — London (57 Doughty St., WC1N 2NE) : The Association, 1981. — 1v.(loose-leaf) : ill,forms ; 31cm
Includes index
Unpriced B82-09743

615 — PHARMACOLOGY AND THERAPEUTICS

615 — Pharmacology & therapeutics — *Conference proceedings*

International Congress of Pharmacology *(8th : 1981 : Tokyo)*. Advances in pharmacology and therapeutics II : proceeding of the 8th International Congress of Pharmacology, Tokyo 1981 / editors H. Yoshida, Y. Hayihara, S. Ebashi. — Oxford : Pergamon, 1982. — 6v : ill ; 24cm
Includes bibliographies and indices
ISBN 0-08-027975-9 : £182.00 : CIP rev. B81-39244

615'.05 — Pharmacology & therapeutics — *Serials*

Recent advances in clinical therapeutics. — Vol.1-. — New York ; London : Academic Press, 1981-. — v. : ill ; 25cm
Annual
£19.60 B82-11151

615.1 — DRUGS

615'.1 — Drugs

Taylor, J. B. (John B.). Introductory medicinal chemistry / J.B. Taylor and P.D. Kennewell. — Chichester : Ellis Horwood, 1981. — 202p : ill ; 24cm. — (Ellis Horwood series in chemical science)
Bibliography: p189-191. — Includes index
ISBN 0-85312-207-5 (cased) : £20.00 : CIP rev.
ISBN 0-85312-311-x (pbk) : Unpriced B81-20516

Turner, Paul, *1933-*. Clinical pharmacology / Paul Turner, Alan Richens. — 4th ed. — Edinburgh : Churchill Livingstone, 1982. — 270p : ill ; 22cm. — (Churchill Livingstone medical text)
Previous ed.: 1978. — Includes index
ISBN 0-443-02531-2 (pbk) : £4.50 B82-12056

615'.1 — Drugs — *Conference proceedings*

International Symposium on Medicinal Chemistry *(6th : 1978 : Brighton)*. Medicinal chemistry VI : proceedings of the 6th International Symposium on Medicinal Chemistry, Brighton, U.K., September 4-7, 1978 / editor M.A. Simkins. — Oxford : Cotswold, 1979. — 477p : ill ; 26cm
ISBN 0-906649-00-5 : Unpriced B82-19360

615'.1 — Pharmacology

Bentley, P. J.. Elements of pharmacology : a primer on drug action / P.J. Bentley. — Cambridge : Cambridge University Press, 1981. — ix,154p : ill ; 24cm
Bibliography: p140-144. — Includes index
ISBN 0-521-23617-7 (cased) : £15.00
ISBN 0-521-28074-5 (pbk) : £4.95 B82-00663

Reid, John L.. Lecture notes on clinical pharmacology. — Oxford : Blackwell Scientific, July 1982. — [160]p
ISBN 0-632-00896-2 (pbk) : £4.00 : CIP entry B82-14521

615'.1'014 — Drugs. Names — *Lists* — *Serials*

British approved names / British Pharmacopoeia Commission. — 1981-. — London : H.M.S.O., 1981-. — v. ; 21cm
Issued every four years. — Continues: Approved names. — Supplement: British approved names. Supplement
ISSN 0262-3773 = British approved names : £6.95 B82-03436

615'.1'024613 — Drugs — *For nursing*

Hahn, Anne Burgess. Pharmacology in nursing / Anne Burgess Hahn, Robert L. Barkin, Sandy Jeanne Klarman Oestreich. — 15th ed. — St Louis ; London : Mosby, 1982. — x,1078p : ill ; 29cm
Previous ed.: 1979. — Text, ill on lining papers. — Includes bibliographies and index
ISBN 0-8016-0633-0 : £21.00 B82-33958

615'.1'024613 — Pharmacology — *For nursing*

Connechan, James. Pharmacology for nurses. — 5th ed. — London : Baillière Tindall, Sept.1982. — [256]p. — (Nurses' aids series)
Previous ed.: 1975
ISBN 0-7020-0868-0 (pbk) : £3.95 : CIP entry B82-20004

Drugs in nursing practice. — Edinburgh : Churchill Livingstone, Sept.1982. — [544]p
ISBN 0-443-02172-4 (pbk) : £7.50 : CIP entry B82-19682

615'.1'024617 — Pharmacology — *For anaesthesia*

Calvey, T. N.. Principles and practice of pharmacology for anaesthetists. — Oxford : Blackwell Scientific, Sept.1982. — [336]p
ISBN 0-632-00868-7 : £16.50 : CIP entry B82-20763

615'.1'0246176 — Pharmacology — *For dentistry*

Cawson, R. A.. Clinical pharmacology in dentistry / R.A. Cawson R.G. Spector. — 3rd ed. — Edinburgh : Churchill Livingstone, 1982. — 352p : ill ; 22cm. — (Churchill Livingston dental series)
Originally published: 1978. — Includes index
ISBN 0-443-02576-2 (pbk) : £6.95 : CIP rev. B82-24346

Pennington, George W.. Dental pharmacology. — 4th ed. / George W. Pennington, T.N. Calvey, T.C.A. O'Neil. — Oxford : Blackwell Scientific, 1980. — ix,236p : ill ; 22cm
Previous ed.: 1977. — Includes bibliographies and index
ISBN 0-632-00539-4 (pbk) : £8.75 : CIP rev. B80-11899

615'.1'05 — Drugs — *Serials*

Advances in pharmaceutical sciences. — Vol.5. — London : Academic Press, Dec.1981. — [220]p
ISBN 0-12-032305-2 : CIP entry B81-31330

615'.1'0688 — Pharmaceutical products. Marketing. Regulation — *Proposals*

An **International** code of pharmaceutical marketing practice : a discussion document. — London (c/o C. Medawar, Social Audit Ltd, 9 Poland St., W1V 3DG) : Health Action International, [1981]. — 10,ivp ; 21cm
Unpriced (pbk) B82-03775

615'.1'0688 — United States. Pharmaceutical industries. Unbranded products. Marketing

James, Barrie G.. The marketing of generic drugs : a guide to counter-strategies for the technology intensive pharmaceutical companies / by Barrie G. James. — London : Associated Business Press, 1981. — xi,211p : ill ; 23cm
Bibliography: p196-202. — Includes index
ISBN 0-85227-268-5 : Unpriced B82-20159

615'.1'07 — Prescription drugs. Information sources — *Directories*

Coni, Nicholas. Aids to prescribing. — Oxford : Blackwell Scientific, Oct.1982. — [144]p
ISBN 0-632-00599-8 (pbk) : £5.50 : CIP entry B82-29404

615'.1'072 — Pharmacology. Research. Methodology — *Conference proceedings*

IUPAC-IUPHAR Symposium *(2nd : 1981 : Noordwijkerhout)*. Strategy in drug research : proceedings of the Second IUPAC-IUPHAR Symposium held in Noordwijkerhout (The Netherlands), August 25-28, 1981 / edited by J.A. Keverling Buisman. — Amsterdam : Oxford : Elsevier Scientific, 1982. — viii,420p : ill ; 25cm. — (Pharmacochemistry library ; v.4)
Conference papers
ISBN 0-444-42053-3 : £34.44 : CIP rev. B81-38828

615'.1'072 — Pharmacology. Research. Use of radioisotopes

Radionuclide imaging in drug research / edited by Clive George Wilson and John G. Hardy with M. Frier and S.S. Davis. — London : Croom Helm, c1982. — 330p : ill ; 22cm
Includes bibliographies and index
ISBN 0-7099-2716-9 : £19.95 : CIP rev. B81-31098

615'.1'076 — Pharmacology — *Questions & answers*

Bleehan, Tirza. Pocket examiner in pharmacology. — London : Pitman, Feb.1983. — [272]p
ISBN 0-272-79645-x (pbk) : £4.95 : CIP entry B82-37818

D'Mello, A.. Multiple choice questions in pharmacology. — London : Edward Arnold, Nov.1982. — [64]p
ISBN 0-7131-4418-1 (pbk) : £3.00 : CIP entry B82-26047

Laurence, D. R.. MCQs on clinical pharmacology. — Edinburgh : Churchill Livingstone, Dec.1982. — [200]p
ISBN 0-443-02786-2 (pbk) : £3.95 : CIP entry B82-29805

615'.1'0941 — Great Britain. Non-prescription drugs — *For self-treatment*

Li Wan Po, Alain. Non-prescription drugs. — Oxford : Blackwell Scientific, Aug.1982. — [480]p
ISBN 0-632-00857-1 (pbk) : £18.00 : CIP entry B82-17206

615'.19 — Drugs. Quality control

Progress in the quality control of medicines / P.B. Deasy and R.F. Timoney editors. — Amsterdam ; Oxford : Elsevier Biomedical, 1981. — x,297p : ill ; 25cm
Includes index
ISBN 0-444-80344-0 : Unpriced B82-17461

615'.19 — Pharmaceutics

Progress in pharmaceutical research / edited by K.R.H. Wooldridge. — Oxford : Published for the Society of Chemical Industry by Blackwell Scientific Publications, c1982. — vii,186p : ill ; 24cm. — (Critical reports on applied chemistry ; v.4)
Includes index
ISBN 0-632-00787-7 (pbk) : Unpriced : CIP rev. B81-30470

615'.19 — Pharmacology. Use of electrocardiography of rats — *Conference proceedings*

The **Rat** electrocardiogram in pharmacology and toxicology : proceedings of an international workshop held in Hannover, Federal Republic of Germany, July 1980 : (an official satellite symposium of the second International Congress on Toxicology, Brussels, Belgium, July 1980) / editors R. Budden, D.K. Detweiler, G. Zbinden. — Oxford : Pergamon, 1981. — xi,272p : ill ; 23cm
Bibliography: p265-272
ISBN 0-08-026867-6 : £30.00 : CIP rev.
Also classified at 615.9'07 B81-14430

615'.19015 — Drugs. Chemical analysis. Use of membrane electrodes

Coşofreţ, Vasile V.. Membrane electrodes in drug-substances analysis / by Vasile V. Cosofret ; translation editor J.D.R. Thomas. — Oxford : Pergamon, 1982. — xvi,362p : ill ; 24cm
Translated from the Romanian. — Includes index
ISBN 0-08-026264-3 : £29.50 : CIP rev. B81-34218

615'.19015 — Man. Body fluids. Drugs. Chemical analysis

Smith, Robert V.. Textbook of biopharmaceutic analysis : a description of methods for the determination of drugs in biologic fluids / Robert V. Smith, James T. Stewart. — Philadelphia : Lea & Febiger ; London : Kimpton, 1981. — xii,308p : ill ; 27cm
Includes index
ISBN 0-8121-0770-5 : Unpriced B82-37558

615.191 — Drugs. Development

Chronicles of drug discovery / edited by Jasjit S. Bindra, Daniel Lednicer. — New York ; Chichester : Wiley
Vol.1. — c1982. — xiii,283p : ill ; 24cm
Includes index
ISBN 0-471-06516-1 : £24.00 B82-16537

615.3 — ORGANIC DRUGS

615'.3142 — Cimetidine — *Conference proceedings*

Cimetidine in the 80s / edited by J.H. Baron. — Edinburgh : Churchill Livingstone, 1981. — xiii,285p : ill ; 24cm
Includes bibliographies and index
ISBN 0-443-02540-1 : £16.00 : CIP rev.
B81-38820

615'.32 — Medicine. Natural remedies: Aromatic plant essential oils

Valnet, Jean. The practice of aromatherapy / Jean Valnet ; translated from the French by Robin Campbell and Libby Houston ; edited by Robert B. Tisserand. — Saffron Walden : Daniel, 1982. — 279p ; 23cm
Translation of: Aromathérapie. — Bibliography: p277-279. — Includes index
ISBN 0-85207-141-8 (corrected) : £11.25
B82-20730

615'.32 — Medicine. Natural remedies: Raw juices

Charmine, Susan E.. The complete raw juice therapy. — Wellingborough : Thorsons, Oct.1981. — [128]p
Originally published: 1977
ISBN 0-7225-0732-1 (pbk) : £1.00 : CIP entry
B81-28181

615'.32 — Medicine. Plant remedies

Barnard, Julian, *1947-*. A guide to the Bach flower remedies / by Julian Barnard. — Saffron Walden (1 Church Path, Saffron Walden, Essex CB10 1JP) : C.W. Daniel Co., 1979. — 36p ; 21cm
Bibliography: p36
£0.75 (pbk) B82-31854

615'.32'096 — Africa. Drugs obtained from plants

Sofowora, Abayomi. Medicinal plants and traditional medicine in Africa. — Chichester : Wiley, Feb.1983. — [250]p
ISBN 0-471-10367-5 : £11.00 : CIP entry
B82-38705

615'.321 — Herbal drugs — *British pharmacopoeias*

British herbal pharmacopoeia / produced by the ... Scientific Committee [British Herbal Medicine Association]. — Keighley (Lane House, Cowling, Keighley, W. Yorkshire BD22 0LX) : The Association
Pt.1 : 1976. — 1976 (1980 [printing]). — vii,248p ; 23cm
Originally published: in 3v. 1971-1974. — Includes index
Unpriced B82-35623

615'.321 — Medicine. Herbal remedies

Duff, Gail. The countryside cook book : recipes & remedies / Gail Duff ; illustrated by Linda Garland ; with line illustrations by Roger Garland. — Dorchester : Prism, 1982. — 191p : ill(some col.) ; 26cm
Bibliography: p187. — Includes index
ISBN 0-907061-21-4 : £8.95
Primary classification 641.6 B82-21266

Griggs, Barbara. Barbara Griggs' home herbal. — London : Norman & Hobhouse, Oct.1982. — [192]p
ISBN 0-906908-91-4 (pbk) : £1.95 : CIP entry
B82-24609

Griggs, Barbara. Green pharmacy : a history of herbal medicine. — London : Jill Norman & Hobhouse, Oct.1981. — [384]p
ISBN 0-906908-64-7 : £7.95 : CIP entry
B81-27418

Griggs, Barbara. Green pharmacy : a history of herbal medicine. — London : Jill Norman & Hobhouse, July 1982. — [384]p
Originally published: 1981
ISBN 0-906908-84-1 (pbk) : £4.50 : CIP entry
B82-13274

Williams, Ann, *1938-*. Country cures / by Ann Williams. — Clapham, N. Yorkshire : Dalesman, 1981. — 64p : ill ; 21cm
Bibliography: p62. — Includes index
ISBN 0-85206-651-1 (pbk) : £1.50 B82-03633

615'.321 — Medicine. Herbal remedies — *Manuals*

De Baïracli-Levy, Juliette. The illustrated herbal handbook / Juliette de Baïracli Levy ; illustrated by Heather Wood. — 2nd, rev. ed. — London : Faber, 1982. — 224p : ill ; 20cm
Previous ed.: 1974. — Includes index
ISBN 0-571-11894-1 (pbk) : £3.50 : CIP rev.
B82-10783

615'.321 — Tanzania. Medicine. Herbal remedies

Harjula, Raimo. Mirau and his practice : a study of the ethnomedicinal repertoire of a Tanzanian herbalist / Raimo Harjula. — London : Tri-Med, 1980. — xvi,223p : ill,2maps,ports ; 22cm
Bibliography: p221-223
ISBN 0-905402-07-3 (pbk) : Unpriced
B82-25458

615'.323'687 — Medicine. Herbal remedies: Ginseng

Fulder, Stephen. An end to ageing?. — Wellingborough : Thorsons, Feb.1983. — [128]p
ISBN 0-7225-0769-0 (pbk) : CIP entry
B82-39469

615'.324324 — Medicine. Herbal remedies: Garlic

Binding, G. J.. About garlic. — 2nd ed. — Wellingborough : Thorsons, Feb.1982. — [64]p
Previous ed.: 1970
ISBN 0-7225-0754-2 (pbk) : £0.75 : CIP entry
B82-00188

615'.329 — Antibiotics. Action

Pharmacokinetics II / volume editor H. Schönfeld. — Basel ; London : S. Karger, c1982. — xi,224p : ill ; 25cm. — (Antibiotics and chemotherapy ; v.31)
Includes bibliographies
ISBN 3-8055-2448-x : Unpriced B82-19710

615'.329 — Beta-lactam antibiotics

Greenwood, David. Antibiotics of the beta-lactam groups. — Chichester : Wiley, July 1982. — [85]p. — (Antimicrobial chemotherapy research studies series ; 2)
ISBN 0-471-10473-6 : £14.00 : CIP entry
B82-14232

615'.329 — Medicine. Drug therapy. Antibiotics

Emmerson, A. M.. The microbiology and treatment of life-threatening infections. — Chichester : Wiley, Oct.1982. — [175]p. — (Antimicrobial chemotherapy research studies series ; 3)
ISBN 0-471-90049-4 : £17.00 : CIP entry
B82-25094

Sanderson, P. J.. Antibiotics for surgical infections. — Chichester : Wiley, Feb.1983. — [260]p. — (Antimicrobial chemotherapy research studies series ; 4)
ISBN 0-471-90109-1 : £16.00 : CIP entry
B82-38716

615'.329 — Medicine. Drug therapy. Netilmicin — *Conference proceedings*

Netilmicin. — London : Academic Press, Aug.1982. — [100]p. — (International congress and symposia series / Royal Society of Medicine, ISSN 0142-2367 ; no.50)
Conference papers
ISBN 0-12-793533-9 : CIP entry B82-21963

615'.329'05 — Antibiotics. Chemical properties — *Serials*

Topics in antibiotic chemistry. — Vol.6. — Chichester : Ellis Horwood, June 1982. — [288]p
ISBN 0-85312-457-4 : £30.00 : CIP entry
B82-17952

615'.32995 — Augmentin — *Conference proceedings*

Augmentin : clavulanate-potentiated amoxycillin : proceedings of the Second Symposium, 17 July, 1981 / editors D.A. Leigh, O.P.W. Robinson. — Amsterdam ; Oxford : Excerpta Medica, 1982. — vii,245p : ill ; 25cm. — (International congress series ; no.590)
Includes index
ISBN 90-219-0590-6 : £32.21 B82-27158

615'.36 — Medicine. Drug therapy. Drugs obtained from oysters

Lewis, Alan, *19---*. The Japanese oyster : amazing healing properties from the sea / by Alan Lewis. — Wellingborough : Thorsons, 1981. — 62p ; 18cm
Includes index
ISBN 0-7225-0721-6 (pbk) : £0.75 : CIP rev.
B81-28183

615'.36 — Medicine. Drug therapy. Steroid hormones. Quantitative analysis

Görög, S.. Quantitative analysis of steroids. — Oxford : Elsevier Scientific, May 1982. — [300] p. — (Studies in analytical chemistry ; 5)
ISBN 0-444-99698-2 : £35.00 : CIP entry
B82-06829

615'.364 — Medicine. Drug therapy. Adrenocorticotrophic hormones

Pharmacology of adrenal cortical hormones / contributors J.D. Baxter ... [et al.] ; [section editor, Gordon N. Gill]. — Oxford : Pergamon, 1979. — xi,243p : ill ; 28cm. — (International encyclopedia of pharmacology and therapeutics ; section 100)
'Published as a supplement to the review journal, Pharmacology & therapeutics'. — Includes bibliographies and index
ISBN 0-08-019619-5 : Unpriced : CIP rev.
B78-12807

615'.364 — Medicine. Drug therapy. Corticosteroids

Clinical Symposium *(6th : 1981 : Tallahassee)*. Progress in research and clinical applications of corticosteroids : proceedings of the Sixth Annual Clinical Symposium, February 20-22, 1981, Tallahassee, Florida, USA / edited by Henry J. Lee and Thomas J. Fitzgerald. — Philadelphia ; London : Heyden, c1982. — x,302p : ill ; 24cm
Conference papers. — Includes bibliographies and index
ISBN 0-85501-722-8 : Unpriced : CIP rev.
B82-05746

615'.366 — Anti-androgens

Androgens and anti-androgen therapy. — Chichester : Wiley, Aug.1982. — [250]p. — (Current topics in reproductive endocrinology v.1) (A Wiley medical publication)
ISBN 0-471-10154-0 : £15.00 : CIP entry
B82-15818

615'.366 — Medicine. Drug therapy. Oestrogens

Chaudhury, Ranjit RoyPharmacology of estrogens / section editor Ranjit Roy Chaudhury. — Oxford : Pergamon, 1981. — viii,165p : ill ; 28cm. — (International encyclopedia of pharmacology and therapeutics ; Section 106)
'Published as Supplement no.4 1981 to the review journal Pharmacology & therapeutics'. — Includes bibliographies and index
ISBN 0-08-026869-2 : Unpriced : CIP rev.
B81-16398

615'.37 — Medicine. Drug therapy. Antivirals — *Conference proceedings*

Antiviral chemotherapy : design of inhibitors of viral functions / edited by K.K. Gauri. — New York ; London : Academic Press, 1981. — xv,366p : ill ; 24cm
Conference papers. — Includes index
ISBN 0-12-277720-4 : £19.20 B82-10053

615'.39 — Critically ill patients. Fluid therapy

Fluid and blood component therapy in the critically ill and injured / edited by Suellyn Ellerbe. — New York ; Edinburgh : Churchill Livingstone, 1981. — 122p : ill ; 24cm. — (Contemporary issues in critical care nursing ; v.1)
Includes index
ISBN 0-443-08129-8 : £11.50 B82-16436

615'.39 — Medicine. Immunohaemotherapy. Immunoglobulins — *Conference proceedings*

Immunohemotherapy : a guide to immunoglobulin prophylaxis and therapy / [proceedings of a workshop on immunological and pathological aspects of immunoglobulin prophylaxis and therapy held in Interlaken, Switzerland, 24-26 August, 1981] ; edited by U.E. Nydegger. — London : Academic Press, 1981. — xiii,475p : ill ; 24cm
Includes index
ISBN 0-12-523280-2 : £18.00 : CIP rev. B81-34010

615.4 — PHARMACY

615'.4 — Pharmacy — *Conference proceedings*

European Symposium on Clinical Pharmacy *(10th : 1981 : Stresa)*. Progress in clinical pharmacy IV : proceedings of the tenth European Symposium on Clinical Pharmacy held in Stresa, Italy, 14-17 October, 1981 / editors G. Ostino, N. Martini and E. van der Kleijn. — Amsterdam ; Oxford : Elsevier Biomedical, 1982. — ix,273p : ill ; 25cm
Includes index
ISBN 0-444-80437-4 : £29.54 B82-38826

International Congress of Pharmaceutical Sciences of F.I.P. *(41st : 1981 : Vienna)*. Topics in pharmaceutical sciences : proceedings of the 41st International Congress of Pharmaceutical Sciences of F.I.P., held in Vienna, Austria, September 7-11, 1981 / editors D.D. Breimer, P. Speiser. — Amsterdam ; Oxford : Elsevier/North-Holland Biomedical, 1981. — xiii,535p : ill ; 25cm
Includes index
ISBN 0-444-80403-x : £31.85 B82-15241

615'.4'01513 — Drugs. Dosage. Arithmetical calculations — *For nursing*

Pirie, Susan. Mathematics in the ward : drug dosage calculations. — Cheltenham : Stanley Thornes, Dec.1982. — [40]p
ISBN 0-85950-367-4 (pbk) : £1.00 : CIP entry B82-32313

615'.4'01513 — Drugs. Dosage. Arithmetical calculations — *Questions & answers — For nursing*

Saxton, Dolores F.. Programmed instruction in arithmetic, dosages, and solutions / Dolores F. Saxton, Norma H. Ercolano, John F. Walter. — 5th ed. — St. Louis, Mo. ; London : Mosby, 1982. — viii,84p : 1ill ; 24cm
Previous ed.: 1977. — Template in pocket
ISBN 0-8016-4327-9 (spiral) : £6.50 B82-31858

615'.4'02341 — Great Britain. Pharmacy — *Career guides*

Tomski, Werner. Careers in pharmacy. — London : Kogan Page, Nov.1982. — [100]p
ISBN 0-85038-594-6 (cased) : £6.95 : CIP entry
ISBN 0-85038-595-4 (pbk) : £2.50 B82-26418

615'.4'05 — Pharmacy — *Serials*

The **Year** book of clinical pharmacy. — 1981-. — Chicago ; London : Year Book Medical Publishers, 1981-. — v. : ill,maps ; 24cm
ISSN 0271-7956 : Unpriced B82-06166

615'.4'068 — Pharmacies. Management

Tharp, C. Patrick. Pharmacy management : for students and practitioners / C. Patrick Tharp, Pedro J. Lecca. — 2nd ed. — St. Louis, Mo. ; London : Mosby, 1979. — xiv,226p : ill ; 26cm
Previous ed.: 1974. — Includes bibliographies and index
ISBN 0-8016-4898-x : Unpriced B82-21891

615'.4'0941 — Great Britain. Rural regions. Pharmacy — *Serials*

The **Rural** pharmacist : the journal of the Rural Pharmacists Association. — Issue 1 (Sept. 1981)-. — Plymouth (Chelfam House, 1 Saltburn Rd, St. Budeaux, Plymouth, Devon) : The Association, 1981-. — v. : ports ; 21cm
ISSN 0263-1393 = Rural pharmacist : Unpriced B82-17241

615'.4'0973 — United States. Pharmacy

Smith, Mickey C.. Pharmacy, drugs and medical care / Mickey C. Smith, David A. Knapp. — 3rd ed. — Baltimore ; London : William & Wilkins, c1981. — xvii,330p : ill ; 23cm
Previous ed.: 1976. — Includes index
ISBN 0-683-07761-9 (pbk) : Unpriced B82-02561

615.5 — MEDICINE. THERAPY

615.5 — Alternative medicine

Drury, Nevill. The healing power : a handbook of alternative medicine and natural health / Nevill Drury with contributions by John Newton & Merren Parker. — London : Muller, 1981. — 231p : ill(some col.),ports(some col.) ; 29cm
Bibliography: p224-227. — Includes index
ISBN 0-584-97078-1 : £7.95 : CIP rev.
ISBN 0-584-97106-0 (pbk) : £5.95 B81-28107

Eagle, Robert. A guide to alternative medicine / Robert Eagle. — London : British Broadcasting Corporation, 1980 (1981 [printing]). — 96p : ill,2ports ; 21cm
Published in conjunction with the BBC Radio series Alternative medicine, six programmes starting on 26 September 1980
ISBN 0-563-16454-9 (pbk) : £2.70 B82-08868

Easthope, Gary. Healers' work. — London : Wildwood House, May 1982. — [220]p
ISBN 0-7045-3057-0 : £7.95 : CIP entry B82-09208

615.5 — Great Britain. Alternative medicine

Fulder, Stephen. The status of complementary medicine in the United Kingdom / Stephen Fulder, Robin Monro. — London (7 Regency Terrace, Elm Place, SW7 3QW) : Threshold Foundation, c1981. — 50p : ill ; 90cm
Unpriced (pbk) B82-21221

615.5'028 — Medical therapeutic equipment

Therapeutic medical devices : application and design / edited by Albert M. Cook, John G. Webster. — Englewood Cliffs ; London : Prentice-Hall, c1982. — xiii,588p : ill ; 25cm
Includes bibliographies
ISBN 0-13-914796-9 : £28.50 B82-16850

615.5'05 — Medicine. Therapy — *Serials*

[Current therapy *(International edition)***]**. Current therapy. — International ed. — 1980-1981-. — Philadelphia ; London : W.B. Saunders, 1980-. — v. : ill,forms ; 27cm
Issued every two years. — Paperback edition of the annual publication: Current therapy
£10.95 B82-19882

615.5'092'6 — Oxfordshire. Oxford. Patients. Therapy, *1650-1652 — Case studies — Early works*

Willis, Thomas. Willis's Oxford casebook (1650-52) / introduced and edited by Kenneth Dewhurst. — Oxford : Sandford, c1981. — xi,199p,[9]leaves of plates : ill(some col.),2maps,1coat of arms,facsims,1port,2geneal.tables ; 22cm
Limited ed. of 750 copies. — Includes index
ISBN 0-9501528-5-4 : £12.00 B82-16878

615.5'32 — Medicine. Homeopathy

George, R. L.. Homoeopathy : the first step to a 'return to nature' / by R.L. George and M.J.F. Whitaker. — [Bearstead] ([6 Cavendish Way, Bearstead, Kent]) : [R.L. George and M.J.F. Whitaker], c1981. — 89p : ill ; 21cm
Bibliography: p89. — Includes index
Unpriced (pbk) B82-09751

Scott, Keith. Homoeopathy. — Wellingborough : Thorsons, Oct.1982. — [128]p
ISBN 0-7225-0780-1 (cased) : £6.95 : CIP entry
ISBN 0-7225-0779-8 (pbk) : £3.95 B82-24244

Shepherd, Dorothy. Two lectures / Dorothy Shepherd. — Holsworthy : Unity Teaching and Healing Trust, c1981. — 32p : 1port ; 22cm
Contents: The new art and science of medicine — The philosophy of homoeopathy
ISBN 0-907707-01-7 (pbk) : Unpriced B82-01528

615.5'32 — Medicine. Homeopathy. Remedies

Borland, Douglas. Homoeopathy in practice / Douglas Borland ; edited for publication by Kathleen Priestman. — Beaconsfield : Beaconsfield Publishers, 1982. — xii,173p ; 22cm
Includes index
ISBN 0-906584-06-x (pbk) : £4.95 : CIP rev. B81-30619

Panos, Maesimund B.. Homeopathic medicine at home / Maesimund B. Panos and Jane Heimlich ; with a foreword by Robert Mendelsohn. — [London] : Corgi, 1982, c1980. — 304p ; 20cm
Originally published: Los Angeles : Tarcher, 1980. — Bibliography: p291-300. — Includes index
ISBN 0-552-11954-7 (pbk) : £2.95 B82-29733

Smith, Trevor, *1934-*. Homoeopathic medicine : a doctor's guide to remedies for common ailments / by Trevor Smith. — Wellingborough : Thorsons, 1982. — 256p ; 22cm
Includes index
ISBN 0-7225-0775-5 (cased) : £4.95 : CIP rev.
ISBN 0-7225-0735-6 (pbk) : Unpriced B82-13080

615.5'32 — Medicine. Homeopathy. Remedies — *Encyclopaedias*

Coats, Peter, *1905-*. The homœopathic aide-memoire / Peter Coats. — Saffron Waldon : Health Science Press, c1980. — 96p ; 19cm
ISBN 0-85032-165-4 : £3.95 B82-00089

615.5'32'05 — Medicine. Homeopathy — *Serials*

Homeopathy and health. — Vol.2, no.3 (Spring 1982)-. — Newcastle upon Tyne (21 Leazes Park Rd, Newcastle upon Tyne, Tyne and Wear NE1 4PF) : National Foundation for Homeopathic Medicine, 1982-. — v. : ill,ports ; 21cm
Quarterly. — Continues: Homoeopathic , alternative
ISSN 0263-8282 = Homeopathy and health : £3.00 per year B82-32144

[The Homœopath *(Society of Homœopaths)***]**. The Homœopath : the journal of the Society of Homœopaths. — Vol.1, no.1 (Autumn 1980)-. — Brentwood (101 Sebastian Av., Shenfield, Brentwood, Essex CM15 8PP) : The Society, 1980-. — v. ; 21cm
Quarterly. — Description based on: Vol.2, no.2 (Winter 1981)
ISSN 0263-3256 = Homœopath (Society of Homœopaths) : £1.50 per year B82-31714

615.5'32'0924 — Medicine. Homeopathy. Hahnemann, Samuel — *Biographies*

Cook, T. M. (Trevor Morgan). Samuel Hahnemann : the founder of homoeopathic medicine / by Trevor M. Cook. — Wellingborough : Thorsons, 1981. — 192p : ill,ports,1geneal.table ; 23cm
Bibliography: p189-190. — Includes index
ISBN 0-7225-0689-9 (cased) : £7.95 : CIP rev.
ISBN 0-7225-0740-2 (pbk) : Unpriced B81-30488

615.5'33 — Medicine. Cranial osteopathy

Brookes, Denis. Lectures on cranial osteopathy : a manual for practitioners and students / by Denis Brookes. — Wellingborough : Thorsons, 1981. — 144p : ill ; 26cm
Includes index
ISBN 0-7225-0698-8 : £12.50 : CIP rev. B81-24666

615.5'33 — Medicine. Osteopathy

Chaitow, Leon. Osteopathy. — Wellingborough : Thorsons, Oct.1982. — [128]p
ISBN 0-7225-0782-8 (cased) : £6.95 : CIP entry
ISBN 0-7225-0745-3 (pbk) : £3.95 B82-24246

615.5′33 — Medicine. Osteopathy
continuation

Osteopathy : an explanation. — Eastbourne (12 College Rd, Eastbourne, East Sussex BN21 4HZ) : Society of Osteopaths, [1982]. — 1sheet : 1col.ill ; 21x40cm folded to 21x10cm
Unpriced B82-15221

Scofield, Arthur G.. Chiropractice. — Wellingborough : Thorsons, June 1981. — [224]p
ISBN 0-7225-0702-x (pbk) : £3.95 : CIP entry B81-12909

615.5′33 — Medicine. Osteopathy — *Early works*

Ashmore, Edythe F.. Osteopathic mechanics : a text book / by Edythe F. Ashmore. — London : Tamor Pierston, 1981. — 237p : ill ; 23cm
Facsim. of: 1st ed. Kirksville, Mo. : Journal Printing Co., 1915. — Includes index. — Limited ed. of 650 copies
Unpriced B82-24897

Page, Leon E.. Osteopathic fundamentals / by Leon E. Page. — London : Tamor Pierston, 1981. — 182p : ill,1port ; 25cm
Facsim. of 1st ed. Kirksville, Mo. : Journal Printing Co., 1927. — Limited ed. of 500 copies
ISBN 0-907457-03-7 : Unpriced B82-20667

615.5′34′094 — Europe. Medicine. Chiropractic — *Serials*

European journal of chiropractic. — Vol.30, no.1 (Mar. 1982)-. — London : Grant McIntyre for the European Chiropractors′ Union, 1982-. — v. : ill,ports ; 25cm
Quarterly. — Continues: Bulletin (European Chiropractors′ Union). — Description based on: Vol.30, no.2 (June 1982)
ISSN 0263-9114 = European journal of chiropractic (corrected) : Unpriced B82-32373

615.5′35 — Medicine. Natural remedies. Making — *Manuals*

Lotions and potions. — London : WI Books, June 1982. — [32]p
Originally published: 1955
ISBN 0-900556-63-3 (unbound) : £0.95 : CIP entry
Also classified at 668′.5 B82-19269

615.5′42 — Children. Therapy

Pediatric therapy / editor Harry C. Shirkey. — 6th ed. / associate editors, Heinz F. Eichenwald ... [et al.]. — St. Louis ; London : Mosby, 1980. — xxvi,1321p : ill,forms ; 28cm
Previous ed.: 1975. — Text on lining papers. — Includes bibliographies and index
ISBN 0-8016-4596-4 : £45.50 B82-40387

615.5′8 — Children. Drug therapy

Catzel, Pincus. The paediatric prescriber. — 5th ed. / Pincus Catzel, Richard Olver ; Foreword to the first edition by Sir Wilfrid Sheldon. — Oxford : Blackwell Scientific, c1981. — xiii,432p : ill ; 18cm
Previous ed.: 1974. — Includes index
ISBN 0-632-00586-6 (pbk) : £6.80 : CIP rev. B81-09985

615.5′8 — Hospitals. Patients. Drug therapy — *For pharmacists*

Clinical pharmacy and hospital drug management . — London : Chapman and Hall, Nov.1981. — [300]p
ISBN 0-412-22760-6 : £15.00 : CIP entry B81-30355

615.5′8 — Medicine. Drug therapy

Drug therapeutics : concepts for physicians. — 1982 ed. / Kenneth L. Melmon, editor-in-chief. — New York ; Oxford : Elsevier, c1982. — xii,225p : ill ; 24cm. — (Drug therapeutics, ISSN 0163-1705)
Includes index
ISBN 0-444-00647-8 : £15.96 B82-34285

Lewis, Peter J.. Essential clinical pharmacology / Peter Lewis. — Lancaster : MTP, 1981. — vii,180p : ill ; 22cm
Includes index
ISBN 0-85200-372-2 (pbk) : Unpriced : CIP rev. B81-21546

Melville, Arabella. Cured to death. — London : Secker and Warburg, Oct.1982. — [256]p
ISBN 0-436-27686-0 : £8.50 : CIP entry B82-26222

615.5′8 — Medicine. Drug therapy — *For patients*

Lewis, R. J. R.. Is your medicine really necessary? / by R.J.R. Lewis. — London : British Medical Association, [1982?]. — 30p ; 19cm. — (A Family doctor booklet)
Unpriced (unbound) B82-14296

615.5′8 — Medicine. Long-term drug therapy

Long-term prescribing : drug management of chronic disease and other problems / edited by Eric Wilkes. — London : Faber, 1982. — 269p : ill ; 26cm
Includes bibliographies and index
ISBN 0-571-11898-4 (cased) : £15.00 : CIP rev. B82-14238

615.5′8′024613 — Drug therapy - *For district nursing*

Anderson, David J.. Drugs and the community nurse. — London (Henrietta Place, W1M 0AB) : Royal College of Nursing, May 1981. — [180]p
ISBN 0-902606-64-6 (pbk) : £4.00 : CIP entry B81-09980

615.5′8′0880565 — Old persons. Drug therapy

Drug therapy for the elderly / edited by Kenneth A. Conrad, Rubin Bressler. — St. Louis ; London : Mosby, 1982. — x,371p : ill ; 24cm
Includes bibliographies and index
ISBN 0-8016-0782-5 (pbk) : £16.00 B82-08262

Drug treatment in the elderly. — Chichester : Wiley, Oct.1982. — [220]p. — (Disease management in the elderly ; v.1) (A Wiley medical publication)
ISBN 0-471-10216-4 : £12.50 : CIP entry B82-24728

Influence of old age on the effect of drugs : satellite symposium to the XII International Congress of Gerontology, Bremen, July 10-11, 1981 / editor M. Bergener ; co-editor H.P. von Hahn. — Basel ; London : Karger, [1982]. — 136p : ill ; 26cm
Suppl.1 to Gerontology v.28, 1982. — Includes index
Unpriced (pbk) B82-40352

615.6 — DRUG THERAPY. MEDICATION

615′.6 — Drugs. Controlled release

Drug delivery systems : characteristics and biomedical applications / edited by R.L. Juliano. — New York ; Oxford : Oxford University Press, 1980. — 320p : ill ; 24cm
Includes bibliographies and index
ISBN 0-19-502700-0 : £16.00 B82-22745

615′.63 — Intravenous drugs

Trissel, Lawrence A.. Handbook on injectable drugs / by Lawrence A. Trissel. — 2nd ed. — Amsterdam ; Oxford : Elsevier-North-Holland Biomedical, 1980. — xxxi,613p ; 24cm
"American Society of Hospital Pharmacists". — Previous ed.: Washington, D.C. : American Society of Hospital Pharmacists, 1977. — Includes index
ISBN 0-444-80361-0 (cased) : £35.71
ISBN 0-444-80362-9 (pbk) : Unpriced B82-01638

615′.63 — Man. Intravenous therapy. Dextran — *Conference proceedings — German texts*

Infusionstherapie mit Dextranen : ein aktueller Überblick : Symposium in Krens, 10 Mai 1980 / Bandherausgeber K. Steinbereithner und W.F. List. — Basel ; London : Karger, c1981. — 111p : ill ; 23cm. — (Beiträge zu Infusionstherapie und klinische Ernährung ; Bd.8)
Includes bibliographies
ISBN 3-8055-2840-x (pbk) : £6.65 B82-01056

615′.63 — Medicine. Intravenous therapy. Nitroglycerin — *Conference proceedings*

International Symposium on the Clinical Use of Tridil, Intravenous Nitroglycerin *(Guys Hospital : 1981)*. The International Symposium on the Clinical Use of Tridil, Intravenous Nitroglycerin. — Oxford (52 New Inn Hall St., Oxford OX1 2BS) : Medicine Publishing Foundation, Mar.1982. — [80]p. — (The Medicine Publishing Foundation Symposium series, ISSN 0260-0242 ; 4)
ISBN 0-906817-18-8 (pbk) : £3.50 : CIP entry B82-08118

615′.63 — Medicine. Intravenous therapy. Research — *For nursing*

Intravenous cannula change / CURN project ; principal investigator Jo Anne Horsley ; director Joyce Crane ; the protocol manuscript ... prepared by Karen B. Haller. — New York ; London : Grune & Stratton, c1981. — xvii,137p : ill,forms ; 23cm. — (Using research to improve nursing practice)
Bibliography: p127-128. — Includes index
ISBN 0-8089-1389-1 (spiral) : Unpriced B82-10558

615′.63 — Medicine. Parenteral feeding — *Conference proceedings*

Advances in Clinical Nutrition *(2nd : 1982 : Bermuda)*. Home parenteral nutrition. — Lancaster : MTP Press, Dec.1982. — [96]p
ISBN 0-85200-499-0 : £6.00 : CIP entry B82-37502

615′.65 — Man. Blood. Plasmapheresis — *Conference proceedings*

Arbeitsgemeinschaft Internistische Onkologie. *Symposium (1980 : Göttingen)*. Plasmapheresis in immunology and oncology / Symposium of Arbeitsgemeinschaft Internistische Onkologie (AIO) der Deutschen Krebsgesellschaft, Göttingen, December 5-6, 1980 ; volume editors, J.-H. Beyer ... [et al.]. — Basel ; London : Karger, c1982. — viii,266p : ill ; 23cm. — (Beiträge zur Onkologie = Contributions to oncology)
Includes bibliographies
ISBN 3-8055-3467-1 (pbk) : £20.30 B82-30379

615′.65 — Man. Blood. Transfusion

Clinical practice of blood transfusion / edited by Lawrence D. Petz and Scott N. Swisher. — New York ; Edinburgh : Churchill Livingstone, 1981. — xxi,856p : ill,facsims,2ports ; 26cm
Includes index
ISBN 0-443-08067-4 : £45.00 B82-14437

Mollison, P. Loudon. Blood transfusion in clinical medicine. — 7th ed. — Oxford : Blackwell Scientific, Feb.1983. — [1010]p
Previous ed.: 1979
ISBN 0-632-01037-1 : £32.50 : CIP entry B82-40906

615′.65 — Man. Haemoperfusion — *Conference proceedings*

International Meeting on Hemoperfusion *(1981 : Bologna)*. Hemoperfusion / International Meeting on Hemoperfusion, Bologna, March 16, 1981 ; volume editors V. Bonomini and T.M.S. Chang. — Basel ; London : Karger, 1982. — 148p : ill ; 23cm. — (Contributions to nephrology ; 29)
Includes index
ISBN 3-8055-3421-3 (pbk) : £25.80 B82-32046

615.7 — PHARMACODYNAMICS

615′.7 — Antimicrobials. Biochemistry

Franklin, T. J.. Biochemistry of antimicrobial action. — 3rd ed. — London : Chapman and Hall, Apr.1981. — [256]p
Previous ed.: 1975
ISBN 0-412-22440-2 (cased) : £15.00 : CIP entry
ISBN 0-412-22450-x (pbk) : £6.95 B81-00126

Principles and practice of disinfection, preservation and sterilisation / edited by A.D. Russell, W.B. Hugo, G.A.J. Ayliffe. — Oxford : Blackwell Scientific, 1982. — x,653p : ill ; 26cm
Includes bibliographies and index
ISBN 0-632-00547-5 : £32.00 : CIP rev. B81-32023

615'.7 — Clinical trials. Methodology

Friedman, Lawrence M.. Fundamentals of clinical trials / Lawrence M. Friedman, Curt D. Furberg, David L. DeMets. — Boston [Mass.] : PSG ; Bristol : John Wright, 1981. — ix,225p : ill ; 25cm
Includes index
ISBN 0-88416-296-6 : Unpriced B82-08361

Schwartz, Daniel. Clinical trials / Daniel Schwartz, Robert Flamant, Joseph Lellouch ; translated by M.J.R. Healy. — London : Academic Press, 1980. — xiii,281p : ill ; 23cm
Translation of: L'essai thérapeutique chez l'homme. — Bibliography: p277. — Includes index
ISBN 0-12-632440-9 (pbk) : £15.00 : CIP rev. B80-18326

Whitehead, John. The design and analysis of sequential clinical trials. — Chichester : Ellis Horwood, Dec.1982. — [312]p. — (Ellis Horwood series mathematics and its applications)
ISBN 0-85312-404-3 : £25.00 : CIP entry B82-35189

615'.7 — Drugs. Action

Basic pharmacology in medicine / Joseph R. DiPalma, editor. — 2nd ed. — New York ; London : McGraw-Hill, c1982. — x,517p : ill ; 25cm
Previous ed.: 1976. — Includes bibliographies and index
ISBN 0-07-017011-8 : £17.50 B82-25217

Julien, Robert M.. A primer of drug action / Robert M. Julien. — 3rd ed. — Oxford : W.H. Freeman, c1981. — xiii,306p : ill ; 24cm. — (A Series of books in psychology)
Previous ed.: 1978. — Bibliography: p292-297. — Includes index
ISBN 0-7167-1287-3 : £12.30
ISBN 0-7167-1288-1 (pbk) : £5.95 B82-05841

615'.7 — Drugs. Action. Molecular biology

Topics in molecular pharmacology / edited by Arnold S.V. Burgen and Gordon C.K. Roberts. — Amsterdam ; Oxford : Elsevier/North-Holland Biomedical
Vol.1. — 1981. — 249p : ill ; 25cm
Includes bibliographies and index
ISBN 0-444-80354-8 : Unpriced B82-34485

615'.7 — Man. Behaviour. Effects of drugs — *Conference proceedings*

OHOLO Conference *(27th : 1982 : Zichron Ya'acov)*. Behavioral models and the analysis of drug action. — Oxford : Elsevier Scientific, Oct.1982. — [500]p
ISBN 0-444-42125-4 : CIP entry B82-28453

615'.7 — Man. Drugs. Adverse reactions

Textbook of adverse drug reactions / edited by D.M. Davies. — 2nd ed. — Oxford : Oxford University Press, 1981. — 693p : ill ; 26cm
Previous ed.: 1977. — Includes bibliographies and index
ISBN 0-19-261270-0 : £28.00 B82-26799

615'.7 — Man. Drugs. Adverse reactions. Evaluation

Workshop on Standardizing Methods of Assessing Causality of Adverse Drug Reactions *(1981 : Morges)*. Assessing causes of adverse drug reactions : with special reference to standardized methods / editor Jan Venulet ; coeditors Garry-Claude Berneker, Antonio G. Ciucci ; [based on the Workshop on Standardizing Methods of Assessing Causality of Adverse Drug Reactions, held 14-18 June 1981 in Morges, Switzerland and sponsored by Ciba-Geigy Medical Department, Basle, Switzerland]. — London : Academic Press, 1982. — xvi,233p,[1]leaf of plates : ill(some col.) ; 24cm
Includes bibliographies
ISBN 0-12-717350-1 : Unpriced : CIP rev. B82-14061

615'.7 — Man. Drugs. Adverse reactions — *Serials*

Adverse drug reactions and acute poisoning reviews. — Vol.1, no.1 (Spring 1982)-. — Oxford : Oxford University Press, 1982-. — v. : ill ; 24cm
Quarterly
ISSN 0260-647X = Adverse drug reactions and acute poisoning reviews : £27.00 per year B82-38501

615'.7 — Man. Drugs. First-pass metabolism

Presystemic drug elimination / edited by Charles F. George and David G. Shand ; guest editor Andrew G. Renwick. — London : Butterworth Scientific, 1982. — 213p : ill ; 24cm. — (Clinical pharmacology and therapeutics, ISSN 0260-0099 ; 1) (Butterworths international medical reviews)
Includes bibliographies and index
ISBN 0-407-02322-4 : £15.00 : CIP rev. B82-01544

615'.7 — Man. Effects of drugs

Gossop, Michael. Living with drugs / Michael Gossop. — London : Temple Smith, 1982. — 233p ; 22cm
Bibliography: p224-230. — Includes index
ISBN 0-85117-224-5 (pbk) : £3.95 : CIP rev. B82-07825

615'.7 — Man. Intravenous drugs. Adverse reactions — *Conference proceedings*

Infusions and infections?. — Oxford (36 Pembroke St., Oxford OX1 1BL) : Medicine Publishing Foundation, Aug.1982. — [48]p. — (The Medicine Publishing Foundation series)
Conference proceedings
ISBN 0-906817-30-7 (pbk) : £3.50 : CIP entry B82-24336

615'.7 — Medicine. Drug therapy. Antibacterials. Testing. Laboratory techniques

Bryant, M. C.. Laboratory control of antibacterial chemotherapy / M.C. Bryant. — Bristol : Wright, 1981. — ix,140p : ill ; 19cm. — (Institute of Medical Laboratory Sciences monographs)
Bibliography: p134-136. — Includes index
ISBN 0-7236-0594-7 (pbk) : Unpriced : CIP rev. B81-32026

615'.7 — Multicentre clinical trials

Multicentre trials / volume editors N. Sartorius and H. Helmchen. — Basel ; London : Karger, 1981. — viii,114p : ill ; 25cm. — (Modern problems of pharmacopsychiatry ; v.16)
Includes bibliographies and index
ISBN 3-8055-2806-x : £25.25 B82-13385

615'.7 — Nitroimidazoles — *Conference proceedings*

Nitroimidazoles : chemistry, pharmacology, and clinical applications / [proceedings of an international conference on nitroimidazoles: chemistry, pharmacology, and clinical application, held August 27-30, 1980, in Cesenatico, Italy] ; edited by A. Breccia, B. Cavalleri, G.E. Adams. — New York ; London : Plenum in cooperation with NATO Scientific Affairs Division, c1982. — xii,211p : ill ; 26cm. — (NATO Advanced Study Institutes series. Series A, Life sciences)
Includes index
ISBN 0-306-40916-x : Unpriced B82-33764

615'.7 — Non-steroid anti-inflammatory drugs — *Conference proceedings*

Are all non-steroidal anti-inflammatory drugs the same? : a workshop held at Kildwick Hall, West Yorkshire, 14 March 1981 / chaired by George Nuki. — Oxford : Medicine Publishing Foundation, 1981. — 12p : col.ill ; 20cm. — (Medicine forum, ISSN 0260-9312 ; 1)
Bibliography: p12
ISBN 0-906817-11-0 (pbk) : £2.50 : CIP rev. B81-12902

615'.7 — Xenobiotics. Biodegradation — *Conference proceedings*

FEMS Symposium *(12th : 1980 : Zürich)*. Microbial degradation of xenobiotics and recalcitrant compounds : FEMS Symposium no.12 / edited by T. Leisinger ... [et al.]. — London : Academic Press for the Swiss Academy of Sciences and the Swiss Society of Microbiology on behalf of the Federation of European Microbiological Societies, 1981. — xiv,415p : ill ; 24cm
Includes bibliographies and index
ISBN 0-12-442920-3 : £32.00 : CIP rev. B81-31341

615'.7 — Xenobiotics — *Conference proceedings*

International Symposium on Biological Reactive Intermediates *(2nd : 1980 : University of Surrey)*. Biological reactive intermediates II : chemical mechanisms and biological effects / [proceedings of the Second International Symposium on Biological Reactive Intermediates, held at the University of Surrey, July 14-17, 1980] ; edited by Robert Snyder ... [et al.] ; associate editors Beatrice N. Engelsberg, George F. Kay, Stephen L. Longacre. — New York ; London : Plenum, c1982. — 2v.(xx,1476p) : ill ; 26cm. — (Advances in experimental and biology ; v.136)
Includes bibliographies and index
ISBN 0-306-40802-3 : Unpriced B82-31408

615'.7'024613 — Drugs. Action — *For nursing*

Clark, Julia B.. Pharmacological basis of nursing practice / Julia B. Clark, Sherry F. Queener, Virginia Burke Karb. — St. Louis ; London : Mosby, 1982. — x,692p,1p of plate : ill(some col.) ; 29cm
Includes bibliographies and index
ISBN 0-8016-4061-x : £17.75 B82-31905

615'.7'0246176 — Drugs. Action — *For dental hygiene*

Requa, Barbara S.. Applied pharmacology for the dental hygienist / Barbara S. Requa, Sam V. Holroyd. — St. Louis ; London : Mosby, 1982. — xvii,348p : ill,forms ; 24cm
Includes index
ISBN 0-8016-2239-5 (pbk) : £12.25 B82-16563

615'.7042 — Man. Diseases caused by drugs

Iatrogenic diseases. — 2nd ed., update 1981. — Oxford : Oxford University Press, June 1981. — [200]p. — (Oxford medical publications)
Second ed. originally published: 1978
ISBN 0-19-261263-8 : £15.00 : CIP entry B81-12870

Iatrogenic diseases. — 2nd ed., update 1982. — Oxford : Oxford University Press, Oct.1982. — [250]p. — (Oxford medical publications)
ISBN 0-19-261356-1 : £17.50 : CIP entry B82-23665

615'.7045 — Drugs. Interactions

Stockley, Ivan H.. Drug interactions : a source book of adverse interactions, their mechanisms, clinical importance and management / Ivan H. Stockley. — Oxford : Blackwell Scientific, 1981. — x,495p : ill ; 25cm
Includes index
ISBN 0-632-00843-1 (pbk) : £15.00 : CIP rev. B81-28016

615'.7045'024617 — Drugs. Interactions — *For anaesthesia*

Smith, N. Ty. Drug interactions in anesthesia / N. Ty Smith, Ronald D. Miller, Aldo N. Corbascio. — Philadelphia, Pa. : Lea & Febiger ; London : Kimpton, 1981. — xiv,351p : ill ; 27cm
Includes index
ISBN 0-8121-0683-0 : Unpriced B82-26966

615'.705 — Man. Drugs. Metabolism — *Serials*

Progress in drug metabolism. — Vol.6. — Chichester : Wiley, Nov.1981. — [320]p
ISBN 0-471-28023-2 : £20.50 : CIP entry B81-30523

615'.71 — Anti-hypertensive drugs

Anti-hypertensive drugs / section editor A. Doyle. — Oxford : Pergamon, 1982. — xiii,241p : ill ; 27cm. — (International encyclopedia of pharmacology and therapeutics ; section 109)
Includes bibliographies and index
ISBN 0-08-028849-9 : £27.50 : CIP rev.
B81-35945

615'.71 — Man. Beta adrenergic receptors. Blocking agents — *Conference proceedings*

Advances in beta-blocker therapy II : proceedings of the 2nd international symposium Venice, October 16-17, 1981, / editor A. Zanchetti. — Amsterdam ; Oxford : Excerpta Medica, 1982. — vii,312p : ill ; 25cm. — (International congress series ; no.593)
Includes index
ISBN 90-219-0593-0 : Unpriced
ISBN 0-444-90276-7 (Elsevier/North-Holland)
B82-32390

615'.71 — Man. Cardiovascular system. Drug therapy

Cardiac pharmacology / edited by R. Douglas Wilkerson. — New York ; London : Academic Press, 1981. — xv,447p : ill ; 24cm. — (Physiologic and pharmacologic bases of drug therapy ; 2)
Includes bibliographies and index
ISBN 0-12-752050-3 : £39.40 B82-30149

Recent developments in cardiovascular drugs / edited by John Coltart, David E. Jewitt. — Edinburgh : Churchill Livingstone, 1982. — 355p : ill ; 25cm
Includes bibliographies and index
ISBN 0-443-02629-7 : £24.00 : CIP rev.
B82-14368

615'.71 — Man. Cardiovascular systems. Drug therapy. Urokinase

Urokinase : basic and clinical aspects / edited by P.M. Mannucci and A. D'Angelo. — London : Academic Press, 1982. — ix,265p : ill ; 24cm. — (Proceedings of the Serono symposia ; v.48)
Includes bibliographies and index
ISBN 0-12-469280-x : Unpriced : CIP rev.
B81-33981

615'.71 — Medicine. Drug therapy. Nadolol — *Conference proceedings*

The **Haemodynamics** of nadolol. — London : Academic Press, Sept.1982. — [100]p. — (Royal Society of Medicine series. International congress and symposium series, ISSN 0142-2367 ; 51)
Conference papers
ISBN 0-12-792048-x : CIP entry B82-25525

615'.71 — Nifedipine — *Conference proceedings*

International Adalat Symposium *(4th : 1979 : Paris)*. 4th International Adalat Symposium : new therapy of ischemic heart disease : proceedings of the Symposium held at Paris, October 19-20, 1979 / edited by Paul Puech and Rolf Krebs. — Amsterdam ; Oxford : Excerpta Medica, 1980. — xi,298p : ill ; 25cm. — (International congress series ; no.516)
Includes index
ISBN 90-219-9440-2 : £23.71 B82-32256

615'.718 — Man. Blood. Drug therapy. Hydroxyethyl starch

Mishler, John Milton. Pharmacology of hydroxyethyl starch : use in therapy and blood banking / John Milton Mishler IV. — Oxford : Oxford University Press, 1982. — xii,207p : ill ; 23cm. — (Oxford medical publications)
Bibliography: p171-207. — Includes index
ISBN 0-19-261239-5 : £20.00 : CIP rev.
B82-12535

615'.72 — Man. Respiratory system. Drug therapy

Cole, R. B.. Drug treatment of respiratory disease / R.B. Cole. — New York ; Edinburgh : Churchill Livingstone, 1981. — viii,334p : ill ; 24cm. — (Monographs in clinical pharmacology ; v.5)
Includes bibliographies and index
ISBN 0-443-08012-7 : £19.00 B82-09786

615'.76 — Men. Urogenital system. Drug therapy

Pharmacology of the urinary tract and the male reproductive system / [edited by] Alex E. Finkbeiner, Galen L. Barbour, Nabil K. Bissada. — New York : Appleton-Century-Crofts ; London : Prentice-Hall, c1982. — x,356p : ill ; 24cm
Includes index
ISBN 0-8385-7841-1 : £18.70
Also classified at 615'.761 B82-20070

615'.761 — Man. Urinary tract. Drug therapy

Pharmacology of the urinary tract and the male reproductive system / [edited by] Alex E. Finkbeiner, Galen L. Barbour, Nabil K. Bissada. — New York : Appleton-Century-Crofts ; London : Prentice-Hall, c1982. — x,356p : ill ; 24cm
Includes index
ISBN 0-8385-7841-1 : £18.70
Primary classification 615'.76 B82-20070

615'.766 — Aphrodisiacs — *Encyclopaedias*

The **Biodisiac** book. — London (3 Clifford St., W1) : Biodisiac Institute, Oct.1981. — [64]p
ISBN 0-85140-548-7 : £3.95 : CIP entry
B81-28161

615'.766 — Drugs: Sex hormones. Use — *Conference proceedings*

Symposium on Gynecologic Endocrinology *(4th : 1979 : University of Tennessee)*. Clinical use of sex steroids : based on the proceedings of the Fourth Annual Symposium on Gynecologic Endocrinology held May 7-9, 1979 at the University of Tennessee, Memphis, Tennessee / editor James R. Givens ; associate editors Richard N. Andersen, Brian M. Cohen, Anne Colston Wentz. — Chicago ; London : Year Book Medical, c1980. — xiv,376p : ill,1port ; 24cm
Includes index
ISBN 0-8151-3528-9 : Unpriced B82-38428

615'.766 — Man. Placenta. Effects of drugs

Placenta : the largest human biopsy : based on papers from meetings at Harvard Medical School and the National Institute of Health, November 1980; the Istituto Superiore di Sanità, Rome and SCIP Research Unit, Bedford College, University of London, November 1981 / editors Rebecca Beaconsfield, George Birdwood. — Oxford : Pergamon, 1982. — xii,160p : ill ; 24cm
ISBN 0-08-028028-5 : Unpriced : CIP rev.
B82-09185

615'.77 — Man. Muscles. Relaxants — *For anaesthesia*

Feldman, Stanley A.. Muscle relaxants : Stanley A. Feldman with a contribution by M.A. Skivington. — 2nd ed. — Philadelphia ; London : Saunders, 1979. — 240p : ill ; 25cm. — (Major problems in anesthesia ; v.1)
Previous ed.: 1973. — Includes bibliographies and index
ISBN 0-7216-3592-x : £15.00 B82-01387

615'.78 — Anti-depressant drugs

Non-tricyclic and non-monoamine oxidase inhibitors / volume editor H.E. Lehmann. — Basel ; London : Karger, c1982. — viii,212p : ill ; 25cm. — (Modern problems of pharmacopsychiatry ; v.18)
ISBN 3-8055-3428-0 : Unpriced B82-40354

615'.78 — Anti-depressant drugs — *Conference proceedings*

Trazodone clinical workshop. — London : Medicine Publishing Foundation, Sept.1982. — [40]p
Conference papers
ISBN 0-906817-33-1 : £2.50 : CIP entry
B82-25919

615'.78 — Antipsychotic drugs & anti-depressant drugs

Clinical pharmacology in psychiatry : neuroleptic and antidepressant research / edited by Earl Usdin ... [et al.]. — London : Macmillian, 1981. — xviii,409p : ill ; 25cm
Includes bibliographies and index
ISBN 0-333-31088-8 : £40.00 B82-10827

615'.78 — Man. Behaviour. Effects of drugs

Leavitt, Fred. Drugs and behavior / Fred Leavitt. — 2nd ed. — New York ; Chichester : Wiley, c1982. — vii,515p : ill ; 25cm
Previous ed.: Philadelphia ; London : Saunders, 1974. — Includes bibliographies and index
ISBN 0-471-08226-0 : £29.75 B82-30695

615'.78 — Man. Nervous system. Effects of aminopyridines — *Conference proceedings*

Aminopyridines & similarly acting drugs. — Oxford : Pergamon, Mar.1982. — [352]p
Conference papers
ISBN 0-08-028000-5 : £32.50 : CIP entry
B82-05376

615'.78 — Neuropharmacology

Green, A. Richard. Pharmacology and biochemistry of psychiatric disorders / A. Richard Green and David W. Costain. — Chichester : Wiley, c1981. — xiv,217p ; 24cm
Bibliography: p191-203. — Includes index
ISBN 0-471-09998-8 (cased) : £14.00 : CIP rev.
ISBN 0-471-10000-5 (pbk) : Unpriced
Primary classification 616.89'18 B81-28044

615'.78 — Neuropsychopharmacology — *Conference proceedings*

Collegium Internationale Neuro-Psychopharmacologicum. *Congress (12th : 1980 : Göteborg)*. Recent advances in neuro-psychopharmacology. — Oxford : Pergamon, Apr.1981. — [422]p
ISBN 0-08-026382-8 : £33.00 : CIP entry
B81-00917

615'.78 — Old persons. Psychopharmacology — *Conference proceedings*

Psychopharmacology of old age. — Oxford : Oxford University Press, Aug.1982. — [200]p. — (British Association for Psychopharmacology monograph ; 3) (Oxford medical publications)
Conference papers
ISBN 0-19-261373-1 : £17.50 : CIP entry
B82-14358

615'.78 — Psychotropic drugs — *For physicians*

Ban, Thomas A.. Psychopharmacology for everyday practice / Thomas A. Ban, Marc H. Hollender. — Basel ; London : Karger, 1981. — viii,194p ; 24cm
Includes bibliographies
ISBN 3-8055-2241-x : £11.25 B82-06284

615'.78'0287 — Man. Nervous system. Effects of drugs. Measurement

Central nervous system / edited by M.H. Lader & A. Richens. — London : Macmillan, 1981. — 164p : ill ; 26cm. — (Methods in clinical pharmacology ; [3])
Originally published: in British journal of clinical pharmacology, vol.10, 1980 and vol.11, 1981. — Includes bibliographies
ISBN 0-333-31726-2 : £20.00 B82-14870

615'.78'05 — Psychopharmacology — *Serials*

Advances in human psychopharmacology. — Vol.1 (1980)-. — Greenwich, Conn. : JAI Press ; London (3 Henrietta St., WC2E 8LU) : Distributed by JAICON Press, 1980-. — v. ; 24cm
ISSN 0272-068x = Advances in human psychopharmacology : £26.20 B82-02373

Theory in psychopharmacology. — Vol.1-. — London : Academic Press, 1981-. — v. : ill ; 24cm
£19.20 B82-14789

615'.781 — Anaesthetics — *Conference proceedings*

Developments in drugs used in anaesthesia / edited by J. Spierdijk ... [et al.]. — The Hague ; London : Leiden University Press, 1981. — xi,244p : ill ; 25cm. — (Boerhaave series for postgraduate medical education ; v.23)
Conference papers. — Includes index
ISBN 90-602-1492-7 : Unpriced B82-18400

615'.782 — Hypnotics — *Conference proceedings*

Hypnotics in clinical practice. — Oxford : Medicine Publishing Foundation, Sept.1982. — [80]p pbk. — (The Medicine Publishing Foundation symposium series, ISSN 0260-0242 ; 7)
Conference papers
ISBN 0-906817-32-3 : £3.50 : CIP entry
B82-25753

615'.782 — Hypnotics — *Questions & answers*

Hypnotics in clinical practice. — Oxford (36 Pembroke St., Oxford OX1 1BL) : Medicine Publishing Foundation, Sept.1982. — [16]p. — (Medicine forum, ISSN 0260-9312 ; 4)
ISBN 0-906817-31-5 (pbk) : £2.50 : CIP entry
B82-29040

615'.782 — Man. Effects of opioids — *Conference proceedings*

International Narcotic Research Conference *(1981 : Kyoto)*. Advances in endogenous and exogenous opioids : proceedings of the International Narcotic Research Conference (satellite symposium of the 8th International Congress of Pharmacology) held in Kyoto, Japan on July 26-30, 1981 / edited by Hiroshi Takagi and Eric J. Simon. — Tokyo : Kodansha ; Amsterdam ; Oxford : Elsevier Biomedical, 1981. — xxvi,493p : ill ; 27cm
Includes index
ISBN 0-444-80402-1 : £45.22 B82-28563

615'.7827 — Man. Effects of cannabis

Expert Group on the Effects of Cannabis Use. Report of the Expert Group on the Effects of Cannabis Use / Advisory Council on the Misuse of Drugs. — London : Home Office, 1982. — v,62p ; 30cm
ISBN 0-86252-031-2 (pbk) : £3.10 B82-31976

Russell, George K.. Marihuana today : a compilation of medical findings for the layman / by George K. Russell. — Rev. ed. — New York : Myrin Institute for Adult Education, 1978 ; Oxford : Distributed by Pergamon. — 75p : 1ill ; 23cm
Previous ed.: 1976
ISBN 0-08-025509-4 (pbk) : Unpriced : CIP rev. B79-31780

615'.7828 — Man. Physiology. Effects of alcohol

Alcohol and disease / edited by Sheila Sherlock. — London : published for the British Council by Churchill Livingstone, c1982. — 116p, 4p of plates : ill ; 28cm
Reprinted from British medical bulletin v.38, no.1. — Includes bibliographies and index
ISBN 0-443-02532-0 (pbk) : £9.50 B82-16441

615'.783 — Medicine. Drug therapy. Buprenorphine — *Conference proceedings*

A New route to pain relief? : a workshop held at the Barber-Surgeons' Hall, London / chaired by J.W. Lloyd. — Oxford : Medicine Publishing Foundation, 1982. — 16p : col.ill ; 21cm. — (Medicine forum, ISSN 0260-9312 ; 2)
Conference papers. — Bibliography: p16
ISBN 0-906817-16-1 (pbk) : £2.50 : CIP rev.
B81-32046

615'.788 — Psychotropic drugs

DuQuesne, J. T.. A handbook of psychoactive medicines. — London : Quartet, Nov.1981. — [512]p
ISBN 0-7043-2270-6 (pbk) : £6.95 : CIP entry
B81-30353

615.8 — PHYSICAL AND OTHER THERAPIES

615.8 — Non-medical healing

Coddington, Mary. In search of the healing energy / Mary Coddington ; foreword by William Gutman. — Wellingborough : Excalibur, 1981, c1976. — 191p ; 22cm
Originally published: New York : Destiny, 1976. — Bibliography: p181-186. — Includes index
ISBN 0-85454-078-4 (pbk) : £3.50 : CIP rev.
B81-15926

615.8'043 — Hospitals. Patients. Resuscitation

Wilson, Frank, *1927-*. Basic resuscitation and primary care / F. Wilson and W.G. Park. — Lancaster : MTP, c1980. — x,339p : ill ; 22cm
Bibliography: p333. — Includes index
ISBN 0-85200-316-1 : £9.95 : CIP rev.
B80-17720

615.8'2 — Medicine. Physiotherapy

Arnould-Taylor, W. E.. The principles and practice of physical therapy / by W.E. Arnould-Taylor. — 2nd ed. — Cheltenham : Thornes, 1982, c1977. — 189p : ill ; 23cm
Previous ed.: 1977. — Includes index
ISBN 0-85950-351-8 (pbk) : £4.95 : CIP rev.
B82-06528

615.8'2 — Medicine. Physiotherapy diagnosis

Coates, Heather. The patient assessment. — Edinburgh : Churchill Livingstone, Oct.1982. — [160]p
ISBN 0-443-02421-9 (pbk) : £3.25 : CIP entry
B82-24359

615.8'20153 — Physiotherapy. Applications of physics — *Conference proceedings*

Joint Meeting on Physics in Physiotherapy *(1980 : Birmingham)*. Physics in physiotherapy : proceedings of the Hospital Physicists' Association and Chartered Society of Physiotherapy Joint Meeting on Physics in Physiotherapy, Birmingham, 2nd May 1980 / edited by M.F. Docker. — London : Hospital Physicists' Association, c1982. — 42p ; 21cm. — (Conference report series ; 35)
Includes bibliographies
ISBN 0-904181-23-5 (pbk) : Unpriced
B82-32803

615.8'205 — Medicine. Physiotherapy — *Serials*

Abstracts quarterly, physiotherapy : journal of the Irish Board of the Chartered Society of Physiotherapy. — Vol.1, no.1 (Spring 1980)-. — Dublin (P.O. Box 1119, James's St., Dublin 8) : The Board, 1980-. — v. : ill,ports ; 30cm
Description based on: Vol.1, no.3 (Autumn 1980)
Unpriced B82-09061

615.8'2068 — Great Britain. Medicine. Physiotherapy. Private practice. Management — *Manuals*

Starting in private practice / the Organisation of Chartered Physiotherapists in Private Practice. — London (14 Bedford Row, WC1R 4ED) : Chartered Society of Physiotherapy, [1982?]. — 24p : ill ; 21cm
Cover title
Unpriced (pbk) B82-30560

615.8'22 — Man. Shiatzu. Use of pressure points of ears — *Manuals*

Chan, Pedro. Ear acupressure : the ancient Chinese art of healing and treating pain with finger pressure / by Pedro Chan. — Wellingborough : Thorsons, 1981, c1977. — 110p : ill ; 22cm
Originally published: Monterey Park, Calif. : Chan's Corporation, 1977
ISBN 0-7225-0727-5 (pbk) : £2.95 : CIP rev.
B81-30587

615.8'22 — Man. Spine. Manipulation

Barrington, B.. Backache and manipulation / by B. Barrington. — [Grouville] (["Pied De Cotil", La Rigondaine, Grouville, Jersey]) : [Lisfinny], [1981]. — 44p : ill,1port ; 22cm
Cover title. — Includes one chapter by E.F. Rabey
£1.50 (pbk) B82-18914

Bourdillon, J. F.. Spinal manipulation / J.F. Bourdillon. — 3rd ed. — London : Heinemann Medical, 1982. — ix,230p : ill ; 22cm
Previous ed.: 1973. — Includes index
ISBN 0-433-03632-x (pbk) : Unpriced
B82-25816

615.8'22 — Man. Therapy. Use of foot massage

Bayly, Doreen E.. Reflexology today. — 2nd ed. — Wellingborough : Thorsons, Sept.1982. — [64]p
Previous ed.: 1978
ISBN 0-7225-0705-4 (pbk) : £3.50 : CIP entry
B82-20209

615.8'22 — Medicine. Self-treatment. Use of Shiatzu — *Manuals*

Bahr, Frank. The acupressure health book / Frank Bahr ; translated from the German by Philip Dale in association with First Edition. — London : Unwin, 1982. — 160p : ill ; 25cm
Translation of: Akupressur
ISBN 0-04-613044-6 (pbk) : £5.50 : CIP rev.
B82-07234

615.8'36 — Critically ill patients. Intensive care. Respiratory therapy

Respiratory monitoring in intensive care. — Edinburgh : Churchill Livingstone, Jan.1982. — [176]p. — (Clinics in critical care)
ISBN 0-443-02062-0 : £14.00 : CIP entry
B82-06034

615.8'36 — Man. Lungs. Artificial ventilation

Clinical use of mechanical ventilation / edited by Christen C. Rattenborg, Enrique Via-Reque. — Chicago ; London : Year Book Medical, c1981. — xx,363p : ill ; 23cm
Includes index
ISBN 0-8151-7072-6 (pbk) : £14.75
B82-02994

Martz, Kathren V.. Management of the patient-ventilator system : a team approach / Kathren V. Martz, Jerry Joiner, Rodger M. Shepherd. — St. Louis ; London : Mosby, 1979. — xv,254p : ill,forms ; 28cm
Includes index
ISBN 0-8016-3139-4 (pbk) : £11.75
B82-24773

615.8'36 — Respiratory therapy equipment — *Questions & answers*

Shoup, Cynthia A.. Laboratory exercises in respiratory therapy / Cynthia A. Shoup, Ronald N. McHenry. — St. Louis, Mo. ; London : Mosby, 1979. — xi,251p : ill,forms ; 28cm
Includes bibliographies
ISBN 0-8016-4593-x (pbk) : Unpriced
B82-21887

615.8'36'077 — Medicine. Respiratory therapy — *Programmed instructions*

Kelsey, Neal. Respiratory therapy review : a workbook and study guide / Neal Kelsey. — 2nd ed. — St. Louis, Mo. ; London : Mosby, 1982. — x,402p : ill,forms ; 28cm
Previous ed.: 1979. — Bibliography: p401
ISBN 0-8016-2638-2 (pbk) : £17.00
B82-22840

615.8'42 — Medicine. Radiotherapy

Hendee, William R.. Radiation therapy physics / William R. Hendee. — Chicago ; London : Year Book Medical, c1981. — x,195p : ill ; 23cm
Includes index
ISBN 0-8151-4234-x (pbk) : £19.75
B82-11878

Interventional radiology / editor Benjamin Felson. — New York ; London : Grune & Stratton, c1981. — v,152p : ill ; 29cm. — (A Seminars in roentgenology reprint)
Includes index
ISBN 0-8089-1414-6 : £19.60 B82-04243

Interventional radiology / edited by Robert A. Wilkins, Manuel Viamonte Jr. — Oxford : Blackwell Scientific, 1982. — xiv,480p : ill ; 25cm
Includes bibliographies and index
ISBN 0-632-00769-9 : Unpriced : CIP rev.
B82-12143

615.8'4202854 — Medicine. Radiotherapy. Applications of digital computer systems

Wood, Raymond G.. Computers in radiotherapy planning / Raymond G. Wood. — Chichester : Research Studies Press, c1981. — ix,171p,[1] leaf of plates : ill(some col.) ; 24cm. — (Medical computing series ; 5)
Includes index
ISBN 0-471-09994-5 : £19.00 : CIP rev.
B81-18123

615.8'45 — Medicine. Electrotherapy

Clayton, E. Bellis. Clayton's electrotherapy : theory & practice. — 8th ed. / [by] Angela Forster, Nigel Palastanga. — London : Baillière Tindall, c1981. — vi,233p : ill ; 22cm
Previous ed.: published as Clayton's electrotherapy and actinotherapy. 1975. — Bibliography: p227. — Includes index
ISBN 0-7020-0902-4 (pbk) : £7.75 : CIP rev.
B81-35929

Electrotherapy / edited by Steven L. Wolf. — New York ; Edinburgh : Churchill Livingstone, 1981. — ix,204p : ill ; 25cm. — (Clinics in physical therapy ; v.2)
Includes index
ISBN 0-443-08146-8 : £11.50 B82-11711

Fraser, Morris. E.C.T. : a clinical guide. — Chichester : Wiley, Sept.1982. — [150]p. — (A Wiley medical publication)
ISBN 0-471-10416-7 : £12.00 : CIP entry
B82-19529

615.8'51 — Medicine. Applications of biofeedback training

Gaarder, Kenneth R.. Clinical biofeedback : a procedural manual for behavioral medicine. — 2nd ed. / Kenneth R. Gaarder, Penelope S. Montgomery with the contribution of Charles G. Burgar. — Baltimore ; London : Williams & Wilkins, c1981. — xxii,261p : ill,forms ; 23cm
Previous ed.: 1977. — Bibliography: p227-232. — Includes index
ISBN 0-683-03401-4 (pbk) : Unpriced
B82-13534

615.8'51 — Mental healing

Shattock, E. H.. A manual of self-healing / by E.H. Shattock ; illustrations by Belinda Shattock and Karin Chu. — Wellingborough : Turnstone, 1982. — 96p : ill ; 22cm
Includes index
ISBN 0-85500-169-0 (pbk) : £2.95 : CIP rev.
B82-04801

615.8'512'088054 — Children. Hypnotherapy

Gardner, G. Gail. Hypnosis and hypnotherapy with children / G. Gail Gardner, Karen Olness. — New York ; London : Grune & Stratton, c1981. — xvii,397p : ill ; 24cm
Includes bibliographies and index
ISBN 0-8089-1413-8 : £19.60 B82-21292

615.8'5152 — Medicine. Occupational therapy — *Manuals*

Pedretti, Lorraine Williams. Occupational therapy : practice skills for physical dysfunction / Lorraine Williams Pedretti. — St. Louis ; London : Mosby, 1981. — viii,339p : ill,forms ; 28cm
Includes bibliographies and index
ISBN 0-8016-3772-4 (pbk) : £17.75
B82-08265

the **Practice** of occupational therapy : an introduction to the treatment of physical dysfunction / edited by Ann Turner ; foreword by Katherine Inganells. — Edinburgh : Churchill Livingstone, 1981. — viii,498p : ill,forms ; 25cm
Includes bibliographies and index
ISBN 0-443-01878-2 (pbk) : £16.50
B82-01271

615.8'5153 — Medicine. Recreational therapy

Austin, David R.. Therapeutic recreation processes and techniques / David R. Austin. — New York ; Chichester : Wiley, c1982. — xi,241p : ill ; 24cm
Includes bibliographies and index
ISBN 0-471-08666-5 : £14.00 B82-34740

615.8'52 — Christianity. Spiritual healing

Beard, Rebecca. Everyman's mission : the development of the Christ-self / Rebecca Beard. — Evesham : James, 1952, c1969 (1979 [printing]). — xviii,184p ; 19cm
ISBN 0-85305-217-4 (pbk) : £2.50 B82-11250

Bennett, George, *b.1912.* The heart of healing : a handbook on healing / by George Bennett. — Evesham : James, 1971 (1979 [printing]). — 125p ; 20cm
ISBN 0-85305-218-2 (pbk) : £2.00 B82-11249

Portsmouth, William. Healing prayer : with daily prayers for a month / by William Portsmouth. — 7th ed. — Evesham : James, 1980, c1954. — 156p ; 19cm
Originally published: 1974
ISBN 0-85305-230-1 (pbk) : £2.50 B82-17142

Wright, Gordon, *1916-*. Our quest for healing / by Gordon Wright. — [Cheltenham] ([PO Box 38, Cheltenham, Glos.]) : [Grenehurst Press], c1981. — 168p : 1ill ; 20cm
Unpriced (pbk) B82-08589

615.8'52 — Man. Therapy. Metamorphic technique

Saint-Pierre, Gaston. The metamorphic technique : the principles and practice / Gaston Saint-Pierre and Barbara D'Arcy Thompson. — London (26 Chalcot Sq, NW1 8YA) : Metamorphic Association, c1981. — 19p : ill ; 21cm
Cover title
£1.25 (pbk) B82-02778

Saint-Pierre, Gaston. The metamorphic technique : the principles and practice / Gaston Saint-Pierre. — London (Chalcot Sq, NW1 8YA) : Metamorphic Association, [1981]. — [8]p : ill ; 22cm + Information leaflet(4p ; 22cm)
Abridged version of: The metamorphic technique / Gaston Saint Pierre and Barbara D'Arcy Thompson. — Cover title
£0.75 (pbk) B82-02779

615.8'52 — Spiritual healing. Communication — *Texts*

Lascelles, *Dr. (Spirit).* The magic of angels / [based on the teachings of Dr. Lascelles received through his medium the late Mr. C.A. Simpson] ; edited and revised by Stanley King. — Addington Park (Addington Park, Maidstone, Kent, ME19 5BL) : Seekers Trust, c1979. — 178p ; 19cm
Unpriced (pbk) B82-27714

615.8'52 — Spiritual healing — *Poems*

Heaton, John W.. The minstrel / John W. Heaton. — Bognor Regis : New Horizon, c1979. — 65p : music ; 21cm
ISBN 0-86116-137-8 : £2.95 B82-07934

615.8'52 — Spiritual healing. White Eagle methods

White Eagle *(Spirit).* Heal thyself / White Eagle. — Liss : White Eagle Publishing Trust, 1962 (1976 [printing]). — 61p ; 20cm
ISBN 0-85487-015-6 : £0.75 B82-02842

615.8'52'0924 — Christianity. Spiritual healing. Edwards, Harry, *1893-1976* **— *Biographies***

Branch, Ramus. Harry Edwards : the story of the greatest healer since the time of Christ / by Ramus Branch. — [Guildford] : [Healer], c1982. — 299p,[64]p of plates : ill,ports ; 23cm
Includes index
£5.00 B82-26924

615.8'52'0924 — Christianity. Spiritual healing — *Personal observations*

McAll, Kenneth. Healing the family tree. — London : Sheldon Press, Nov.1982. — [176]p
ISBN 0-85969-364-3 (pbk) : £2.95 : CIP entry
B82-26330

615.8'52'0924 — Spiritual healing. Pilgrim, Tom — *Biographies*

Pilgrim, Tom. Tom Pilgrim : autobiography of a spiritualist healer / Tom Pilgrim with Nadia Fowler. — London : Sphere, 1982. — 150p ; 18cm
ISBN 0-7221-6868-3 (pbk) : £1.50 B82-39059

615.8'53 — Medicine. Hydrotherapy. Exercises

Duffield's exercise in water. — 3rd ed. — London : Baillière Tindall, Feb.1983. — [160]p
Previous ed.: 1976
ISBN 0-7020-0925-3 (pbk) : £8.50 : CIP entry
B82-38871

615.8'54 — Clinical dietetics

Mason, Marion. The dynamics of clinical dietetics / Marion Mason, Burness G. Wenberg, P. Kay Welsch. — 2nd ed. — New York ; Chichester : Wiley, c1982. — xv,354p : ill ; 24cm
Previous ed.: 1977. — Ill on lining papers. — Includes bibliographies and index
ISBN 0-471-06088-7 : £14.00 B82-25453

615.8'54 — Critically ill patients. Nutrition — *Serials*

Clinical nutrition : official journal of the European Society of Parenteral and Enteral Nutrition. — Vol.1, no.1 (Mar. 1982)-. — Edinburgh : Churchill Livingstone, 1982-. — v. : ill ; 25cm
Quarterly
ISSN 0261-5614 = Clinical nutrition : £40.00 per year B82-33875

615.8'54 — Medicine. Therapy. Cider vinegar

Scott, Cyril. Cider vinegar. — 8th ed. — Wellingborough : Athlene Publishing, Feb.1982. — [48]p
Previous ed.: 1973
ISBN 0-7225-0755-0 (pbk) : £0.60 : CIP entry
B82-00189

615.8'54 — Medicine. Therapy. Diet

The **Cantamac** dietary system : a dietary regime designed to eliminate gluten, refined sugar and saturated fat from the diet : with recipes and food guide. — 2nd ed. — London : Cantassium Co., 1978. — 19p ; 19cm
Previous ed.: 197-?
ISBN 0-906185-07-6 (unbound) : Unpriced
B82-37150

Lesser, Michael. Nutrition and vitamin therapy / Michael Lesser. — Toronto ; London : Bantam, 1981. — 239p : ill ; 18cm
Originally published: New York : Grove Press, 1980. — Includes index
ISBN 0-553-14437-5 (pbk) : £1.25
Primary classification 613.2 B82-14450

Robinson, Corinne H.. Normal and therapeutic nutrition. — 16th ed. / Corinne H. Robinson, Marilyn R. Lawler. — New York : Macmillan ; London : Collier Macmillan, 1982. — x,849p : ill ; 25cm
Previous ed.: 1977. — Tables on lining papers. — Includes bibliographies and index
ISBN 0-02-402370-1 : Unpriced
Primary classification 613.2 B82-40793

615.8'54 — Medicine. Therapy. Honey — *Early works*

Hill, John, *1716?-1775.* The virtues of honey / John Hill. — 2nd ed. — London : International Bee Research Association, c1981. — 24leaves ; 30cm
Transcript of: 2nd ed. published: London : s.n., 1759
ISBN 0-86098-099-5 (pbk) : Unpriced : CIP rev. B81-21601

615.8'54 — Medicine. Therapy. Role of nutrition

Nutrition in clinical care / [edited by] Rosanne Beatrice Howard, Nancie Harvey Herbold. — 2nd ed. — New York ; London : McGraw-Hill, c1982. — xv,776p : ill(some col.) ; 25cm
Previous ed.: 1978. — Ill on lining papers. — Includes index
ISBN 0-07-030514-5 : £16.95 B82-37795

615.8'9 — Man. Therapy. Use of karma

Williston, Glenn. Soul search : spiritual growth through a knowledge of past lifetimes. — Wellingborough : Turnstone Press, June 1982. — [224]p
ISBN 0-85500-161-5 (pbk) : £4.95 : CIP entry
B82-10217

615.8'92 — Acupuncture

Lewith, G. T.. Acupuncture : its place in Western medical science / by G.T. Lewith. — Wellingborough : Thorsons, 1982. — 127p : ill ; 22cm. — (Alternative therapies)
Bibliography: p123. — Includes index
ISBN 0-7225-0760-7 (cased) : Unpriced : CIP rev.
ISBN 0-7225-0693-7 (pbk) : £3.95 B82-04968

615.8'92 — Acupuncture *continuation*

Low, Royston H.. The secondary vessels of acupuncture. — Wellingborough : Thorsons, Feb.1983. — [192]p
ISBN 0-7225-0736-4 : £15.00 : CIP entry
B82-39468

Macdonald, Alexander, *1941-*. Acupuncture : from an ancient art to modern medicine / by Alexander Macdonald. — London : Allen & Unwin, 1982. — xiv,184p,7p of plates : ill ; 23cm. — (The Medicine today series)
Includes index
ISBN 0-04-616023-x : Unpriced : CIP rev.
B82-10582

615.8'92 — Acupuncture. Points — *Illustrations*

Cooperative Group of Shandong Medical College and Shandong College of Traditional Chinese Medicine. Anatomical atlas of Chinese acupuncture points. — Oxford : Pergamon, Oct.1982. — [265]p
ISBN 0-08-029784-6 : £16.00 : CIP entry
B82-29112

615.8'92 — Moxibustion — *Manuals*

Newman Turner, R.. The principles and practice of moxibustion : a guide to the therapeutic application of heat to acupuncture points / by Roger Newman Turner and Royston H. Low ; illustrations by Giles Newman Turner. — Wellingborough : Thorsons, 1981. — 95p : ill,1map ; 23cm
Includes index
ISBN 0-7225-0675-9 : £5.95 : CIP rev.
B81-21514

615.8'99 — Brazil. Iguape region. Primitive medicine

Souza Queiroz, Marcos de. 'Hot and cold' : a fundamental system of classification to the traditional medicine in Iguape / Marcos de Souza Queiroz. — Manchester : Department of Sociology, University of Manchester, [1982?]. — 40p ; 30cm. — (Occasional paper ; no.8)
Bibliography: p39-40
ISBN 0-946180-07-5 (pbk) : £1.00 B82-40645

615.9 — TOXICOLOGY

615.9 — Formaldehyde. Toxic effects

Fielder, R. J.. Formaldehyde / compiled by R.J. Fielder in consultation with G.S. Sorrie ... [et al.]. — London : H.M.S.O., 1981. — 18p ; 30cm. — (Toxicity review ; 2)
At head of title: Health and Safety Executive
ISBN 0-11-883452-5 (pbk) : £2.20 B82-11663

615.9 — Man. Health. Toxic effects of environmental pollutants — *Conference proceedings*

Genotoxic effects of airborne agents / edited by Raymond R. Tice, Daniel L. Costa and Karen M. Schaich. — New York ; London : Plenum Press, c1982. — xiii,658p : ill ; 26cm. — (Environmental science research ; v.25)
Conference papers. — Includes index
ISBN 0-306-40983-6 : Unpriced B82-35327

615.9 — Man. Liver. Toxic effects of drugs

Drug reactions and the liver. — Tunbridge Wells : Pitman Medical, May 1981. — [376]p
ISBN 0-272-79620-4 (pbk) : £25.00 : CIP entry
B81-08843

615.9 — Man. Organs. Toxic effects of chemicals — *Conference proceedings*

Symposium on Chemical Indices and Mechanisms of Organ-Directed Toxicity *(1981 : Barcelona)*. Organ-directed toxicity : chemical indices and mechanisms : proceedings of the Symposium on Chemical Indices and Mechanisms of Organ-Directed Toxicity, Barcelona, Spain, 4-7 March 1981 / edited by Stanley S. Brown and Donald S. Davies. — Oxford : Pergamon, 1981. — xii,341p : ill ; 28cm
At head of title: International Union of Pure and Applied Chemistry (Clinical Chemistry Division) ... [et al.]. — Includes index
ISBN 0-08-026197-3 : 37.50 : CIP rev.
B81-28178

615.9 — Medicine. Toxicology

Tu, Anthony T. Survey of contemporary toxicology. — New York ; Chichester : Wiley
Vol.2 / edited by Anthony T. Tu. — c1982. — xi,248p : ill ; 24cm
Includes index
ISBN 0-471-06352-5 : £37.00 B82-21801

615.9'005 — Medicine. Toxicology — *Serials*

Human toxicology : an international journal. — Vol.1, no.1 (1981)-. — Basingstoke : Macmillan, 1981-. — v. : ill ; 25cm
Quarterly
ISSN 0144-5952 = Human toxicology : £40.00 per year B82-11819

615.9'007'073 — United States. Toxicology. Information sources

Wexler, Philip. Information resources in toxicology / Philip Wexler. — New York ; Oxford : Elsevier/North-Holland, c1982. — xiv,333p ; 24cm
Includes index
ISBN 0-444-00616-8 : £22.34 B82-13436

615.9'0072 — Toxicology. Research. Quality control

Scientific considerations in monitoring and evaluating toxicological research / edited by Edward J. Gralla. — Washington [D.C.] ; London : Hemisphere, c1981. — xv,221p : ill ; 24cm. — (A CIIT series)
Includes index
ISBN 0-89116-209-7 : £22.25 B82-02521

615.9'00941 — Great Britain. Man. Poisons

McCaughey, Helen. Is it poisonous? : a home guide to poisoning prevention and first aid with quick-reference poisons index / Helen McCaughey. — U.K. ed. / revised and adapted by Deanna Wilson. — London : Angus and Robertson, 1980 c1979. — 185p : ill
Previous ed.: 1976. — Includes index
ISBN 0-207-95867-x (pbk) : £2.95 B82-03044

615.9'01'574192 — Medicine. Toxicology. Biochemical aspects

Timbrell, John A.. Principles of biochemical toxicology / John A. Timbrell. — London : Taylor & Francis, 1982. — x,249p : ill ; 24cm
Includes bibliographies and index
ISBN 0-85066-221-4 : £13.50 : CIP rev.
B82-09845

615.9'07 — Drugs. Toxic effects. Testing

Testing for toxicity / edited by J.W. Gorrod. — London : Taylor & Francis, 1981. — xiv,381p : ill ; 24cm
Includes bibliographies and index
ISBN 0-85066-218-4 : £18.00 : CIP rev.
B81-21587

615.9'07 — Medicine. Toxicology. Use of electrocardiagrams of rats — *Conference proceedings*

The **Rat** electrocardiogram in pharmacology and toxicology : proceedings of an international workshop held in Hannover, Federal Republic of Germany, July 1980 : (an official satellite symposium of the second International Congress on Toxicology, Brussels, Belgium, July 1980) / editors R. Budden, D.K. Detweiler, G. Zbinden. — Oxford : Pergamon, 1981. — xi,272p : ill ; 23cm
Bibliography: p265-272
ISBN 0-08-026867-6 : £30.00 : CIP rev.
Primary classification 615'.19 B81-14430

615.9'08 — Man. Acute poisoning. Therapy

Proudfoot, A. T.. Diagnosis and management of acute poisoning / Alexander T. Proudfoot. — Oxford : Blackwell Scientific, 1982. — viii,237p ; 22cm
Includes bibliographies and index
ISBN 0-632-00584-x (pbk) : £7.50 : CIP rev.
B81-22618

615.9'08 — Man. Poisoning. Emergency treatment — *Manuals*

Toxicologic emergencies : a comprehensive handbook in problem solving. — 2nd ed. / edited by Lewis R. Goldfrank ; associate editors Neal E. Flomenbaum, Neal A. Lewin, Richard S. Weisman. — New York : Appleton-Century-Crofts ; London : Prentice-Hall, c1982. — xv,432p : ill ; 25cm
Previous ed.: 1978. — Includes bibliographies and index
ISBN 0-8385-8965-0 : £25.90 B82-28191

615.9'1 — Man. Toxic effects of diesel engines. Exhaust gases

Diesel Emissions Symposium *(1981 : Raleigh, N.C.)*. Toxicological effects of emissions from diesel engines : proceedings of the Environmental Protection Agency 1981 Diesel Emissions Symposium held in Raleigh, North Carolina, U.S.A., October 5-7, 1981 / editor Joellen Lewtas. — New York ; Oxford : Elsevier Biomedical, c1982. — xi,380p : ill ; 25cm. — (Developments in toxicology and environmental science ; v.10)
Includes index
ISBN 0-444-00687-7 : £36.17 B82-30259

615.9'25'3 — Man. Toxic effects of heavy metals. Analysis

Martin, M. H.. Biological monitoring of heavy metal pollution : land and air. — London : Applied Science, Aug.1982. — [480]p. — (Pollution monitoring series)
ISBN 0-85334-136-2 : £45.00 : CIP entry
B82-16659

615.9'2539224 — Man. Toxic effects of asbestos

Peters, George A.. Sourcebook on asbestos diseases : medical, legal, and engineering aspects / George A. Peters, Barbara J. Peters. — New York ; London : Garland STPM, c1980. — 454p in various pagings ; 24cm. — (Garland safety management series)
Bibliography: (177p). — Includes index
ISBN 0-8240-7175-1 : Unpriced B82-26824

615.9'51 — Styrene. Toxic effects

Fielder, R. J.. Styrene / compiled by R.J. Fielder, R. Lowing in consultation with G.S. Sorrie ... [et al.]. — London : H.M.S.O., 1981. — 42p : 1ill ; 30cm. — (Toxicity review ; 1)
At head of title: Health and Safety Executive
ISBN 0-11-883451-7 (pbk) : £3.00 B82-11665

615.9'511 — Industrial chemicals: Benzene. Toxic effects

Great Britain. *Health and Safety Executive*. Review of the toxicology of benzene. — London : H.M.S.O., Apr.1982. — [50]p
ISBN 0-11-883627-7 (pbk) : £3.00 : CIP entry
B82-10667

615.9'511 — Polychlorinated dibenzodioxins. Toxic effects. Environmental aspects — *Conference proceedings*

Chlorinated dioxins and related compounds : impact on the environment : proceedings of a workshop held at the Istituto Superiore di Sanità, Rome, Italy, 22-24 October 1980 / editors O. Hutzinger ... [et al.]. — Oxford : Pergamon, 1982. — xii,658p : ill,maps ; 24cm. — (Pergamon series on environmental science ; v.5)
Includes bibliographies and index
ISBN 0-08-026256-2 : £37.50 : CIP rev.
B81-32043

615.9'516 — Carbon disulphide. Toxic effects

Fielder, R. J.. Carbon disulphide / compiled by R.J. Fielder and R.O. Shillaker in consultation with G.S. Sorrie ... [et al.]. — London : H.M.S.O., 1981. — 42p ; 30cm. — (Toxicity review ; 3)
At head of title: Health and Safety Executive
ISBN 0-11-883453-3 (pbk) : £3.00 B82-11664

615.9'5292 — Fungi. Metabolites: Toxins — *Technical data*

Cole, Richard J.. Handbook of toxic fungal metabolites / Richard J. Cole, Richard H. Cox. — New York ; London : Academic Press, 1981. — xviii,937p : ill ; 25cm
Includes bibliographies and index
ISBN 0-12-179760-0 : £52.20 B82-10147

615.9'5292 — Fungi. Metabolites: Toxins — *Technical data* *continuation*

Turner, W. B.. Fungal metabolites II. — London : Academic Press, Sept.1982. — [500]p
ISBN 0-12-704551-1 : CIP entry B82-19169

615.9'54 — Man. Food poisoning

Foulger, Richard. The food poisoning handbook : a guide to food hygiene for everyone who produces or prepares food and drink / Richard Fouler, Edward Routledge ; illustrations by Fred Pipes. — Bromley : Chartwell-Bratt, c1981. — 104p : ill ; 23cm
ISBN 0-86238-019-7 (pbk) : Unpriced B82-40505

615.9'54 — Man. Toxic effects of food

Adverse effects of foods / edited by E.F. Patrice Jelliffe and Derrick B. Jelliffe. — New York ; London : Plenum, c1982. — xv,614p : ill,maps ; 26cm
Includes bibliographies and index
ISBN 0-306-40870-8 : Unpriced B82-36623

616 — MAN. DISEASES

616 — Ambulatory patients. Treatment. Decision making. Applications of digital computer systems

McDonald, Clement J.. Action-oriented decisions in ambulatory medicine / Clement J. McDonald. — Chicago ; London : Year Book Medical, c1981. — xix,374p : ill,1form ; 26cm
Includes index
ISBN 0-8151-5809-2 : Unpriced B82-38426

616 — Diseases caused by pathogens from outer space

Hoyle, Fred. Diseases from space / Fred Hoyle and N.C. Wickramasinghe. — London : Sphere, 1981, c1979. — xii,241p : ill,maps ; 18cm
Originally published: London : Dent, 1979. — Bibliography: p235-238. — Includes index
ISBN 0-7221-4754-6 (pbk) : £1.50 B82-02174

616 — Internal medicine

Harrison, T. R.. Harrison's principles of internal medicine. — Update 2 with CME Examination, editors Kurt J. Isselbacher ... [et al.]. — New York ; London : McGraw-Hill, c1982. — xi,238,20p : ill ; 29cm
Previous ed.: 1981
ISBN 0-07-032132-9 : £22.50 B82-14034

Harrison's principles of internal medicine : with CME examination. — 9th ed. / editors Kurt J. Isselbacher ... [et al.], Update 1. — New York ; London : McGraw-Hill, c1981. — x,263,21p : ill,1facsim ; 29cm. — (Update ; 1)
Previous ed.: 1977. — Includes bibliographies
ISBN 0-07-032131-0 : £29.50 B82-35772

Internal medicine : review and assessment / [edited by] Eli A. Friedman, Richard M. Stillman. — New York : Appleton-Century-Crofts ; London : Prentice-Hall, c1982. — xi,420p : ill ; 23cm
Includes bibliographies
ISBN 0-8385-4040-6 (pbk) : Unpriced B82-35118

616 — Man. Acute diseases. Recovery. Psychological factors

Wilson-Barrett, Jenifer. Recovery from illness. — Chichester : Wiley, Sept.1982. — [150]p. — (Wiley series in development and nursing research ; v.1)
ISBN 0-471-10408-6 : £12.00 : CIP entry B82-19528

616 — Man. Diseases

Dickinson, Ken. Doctor / Ken Dickinson. — London : ITV
Book 2. — 1981. — 107p : ill ; 20cm
ISBN 0-900727-88-8 (pbk) : £1.50 B82-05300

Disorders of neurohumoural transmission. — London : Academic Press, Dec.1982. — [420]p
ISBN 0-12-195980-5 : CIP entry B82-29877

Fry, John, *1922-*. Common diseases. — 3rd ed. — Lancaster : MTP Press, Oct.1982. — [450]p
Previous ed.: 1979
ISBN 0-85200-454-0 : £10.95 : CIP entry B82-31305

Houston, J. C.. A short textbook of medicine. — 7th ed. / J.C. Houston, C.L. Joiner, J.R. Trounce. — London : Hodder and Stoughton, 1982. — 772p : ill ; 22cm. — (University medical texts)
Previous ed. / by J.C. Houston. 1979. — Includes bibliographies and index
ISBN 0-340-26758-5 (pbk) : £7.95 : CIP rev. B81-24629

Lambert, Harold P.. Infectious diseases illustrated : an integrated text and colour atlas. — London : Gower Medical, Apr.1982. — [314]p
ISBN 0-906923-02-6 : £40.00 : CIP entry B82-05786

Medical resident's manual. — 4th ed. / Stephen M. Ayres ... [et al.]. — New York : Appleton-Century-Crofts ; London : Prentice-Hall, c1982. — xxiii,644p : ill ; 18cm
Previous ed.: / by William J. Grace, Richard J. Kennedy, Frank B. Flood. 1971. — Includes bibliographies and index
ISBN 0-8385-6253-1 (pbk) : £11.95 B82-23155

Rubenstein, David. Multiple choice questions on lecture notes on clinical medicine. — 2nd ed. — Oxford : Blackwell Scientific, Sept.1982. — [80]p
Previous ed.: 1976
ISBN 0-632-00976-4 (pbk) : £2.25 : CIP entry B82-23851

616 — Man. Diseases & injuries

Weston, Trevor. Don't panic : a basic guide to handling illness and medical emergencies in the family / Trevor Weston. — London : W.H. Allen, 1981. — 240p : ill ; 23cm
Includes index
ISBN 0-491-02765-6 : £5.95 B82-00110

616 — Man. Diseases — *For general practice*

Common problems in primary care / [edited by] Lynne Lesak Gorline, Cheryl Cummings Stegbauer. — St. Louis ; London : Mosby, 1982. — xii,286p : ill ; 24cm
Includes bibliographies and index
ISBN 0-8016-1931-9 (pbk) : £11.25 B82-08267

616 — Man. Diseases — *For radiography*

Bloomfield, John A.. Pathology for radiographers : and allied health professionals / John A. Bloomfield. — Chicago ; London : Year Book Medical, c1982. — xiv,167p : ill ; 17cm
Includes index
ISBN 0-8151-0946-6 (pbk) : Unpriced B82-31748

616 — Man. Diseases. Geographical aspects

Biocultural aspects of disease / edited by Henry Rothschild ; coordinating editor Charles F. Chapman. — New York ; London : Academic Press, c1981. — xix,653p : ill,maps ; 24cm
Includes bibliographies and index
ISBN 0-12-598720-x : £43.00 B82-29697

616 — Medicine. Diagnosis & therapy — *Conference proceedings*

Problems of the medically ill : new agents and approaches to diagnosis and therapy : the fifty-fourth Hahnemann symposium on medical practice for the 1980s / edited by David A. Major ... [et al.]. — New York ; London : Grune & Stratton, c1981. — xiii,255p : ill ; 27cm
Includes index
ISBN 0-8089-1388-3 : £29.40 B82-21293

616'.001'9 — Man. Diseases. Psychological aspects

Clinical psychology and medicine : a behavioural perspective / edited by Chris J. Main ; associate editor William R. Lindsay. — New York ; London : Plenum, c1982. — xi,372p : ill ; 26cm
Includes bibliographies and index
ISBN 0-306-40900-3 : Unpriced B82-22890

616'.001'9 — Medicine. Diagnosis & therapy. Decision making

Normal values in medicine. — Oxford : Medicine Publishing Foundation, Oct.1982. — [40]p
ISBN 0-906817-36-6 (pbk) : £2.50 : CIP entry B82-29414

616'.001'9 — Medicine. Diagnosis & therapy. Decision making — *Questions & answers*

Beck, Paul. Case exercises in clinical reasoning / Paul Beck with contributions by Richard L. Byyny, Kirk S. Adams. — Chicago ; London : Year Book Medical, c1981. — xiii,320p : ill ; 25cm
Includes index
ISBN 0-8151-0597-5 : £18.00 B82-16613

616'.001'9 — Medicine. Diagnosis & therapy. Decision making, *to 1981*

King, Lester S.. Medical thinking : a historical preface / Lester S. King. — Princeton, N.J. ; Guildford : Princeton University Press, c1982. — vii,336p ; 24cm
Includes index
ISBN 0-691-08297-9 : £13.80 B82-24505

616'.0022'2 — Man. Diseases. Illustrations: Transparencies. Interpretation — *Manuals*

Parfrey, P. S.. Slide interpretation. — Oxford : Oxford University Press. — (Oxford medical publications)
Vol.2: Clinical signs in postgraduate medicine. — Jan.1983. — [150]p
ISBN 0-19-261397-9 (pbk) : £9.50 : CIP entry B82-33479

616'.0024613 — Man. Acute diseases — *For nursing*

Concepts common to acute illness : identification and management / edited by Laura K. Hart, Jean L. Reese, Margery O. Fearing. — St. Louis, Mo. ; London : Mosby, 1981. — ix,371p : ill ; 25cm
Includes index
ISBN 0-8016-2117-8 : £14.25 B82-22844

616'.0024613 — Man. Diseases — *For nursing*

Billings, Diane McGovern. Medical-surgical nursing : common health problems of adults and children across the life span / Diane McGovern Billings, Lillian Gatlin Stokes. — St. Louis ; London : Mosby, 1982. — x,1440p : ill ; 29cm
Includes bibliographies and index
ISBN 0-8016-0736-1 : £24.75 B82-31867

Fream, William C.. Notes on medical nursing / William C. Fream. — 3rd ed. — Edinburgh : Churchill Livingstone, 1982. — 207p : ill ; 19cm
Previous ed.: 1977. — Includes index
ISBN 0-443-02422-7 (pbk) : Unpriced : CIP rev. B82-24331

616'.0024617 — Man. Diseases — *For anaesthesia*

Medicine for anaesthetists / edited by M.D. Vickers ; foreword by William W. Mushin. — 2nd ed. — Oxford : Blackwell Scientific, 1982. — xii,647p : ill,2ports ; 25cm
Previous ed.: 1977. — Includes bibliographies and index
ISBN 0-632-00737-0 : £32.50 : CIP rev. B81-16934

To make the patient ready for anesthesia : medical care of the surgical patient / edited by Leroy D. Vandam. — Menlo Park ; London : Addison-Wesley, c1980. — xix,245p : ill ; 24cm. — (The Addison-Wesley clinical practice series)
Includes bibliographies and index
ISBN 0-201-07999-2 : Unpriced B82-27980

616'.00246171 — Man. Diseases — *Illustrations — For surgery*

Guthrie, W.. A colour atlas of surgical pathology / W. Guthrie, R. Fawkes. — London : Wolfe Medical, 1982. — 229p : ill(some col.) ; 27cm. — (Wolfe Medical atlases)
Includes index
ISBN 0-7234-0759-2 : Unpriced B82-21880

616'.00246176 — Man. Diseases & injuries — *For dentistry*

Kennedy, A. C.. Essentials of medicine and surgery for dental students. — 4th ed. — Edinburgh : Churchill Livingstone, June 1982. — [288]p
Previous ed.: 1977
ISBN 0-443-02534-7 (pbk) : £8.50 : CIP entry B82-09719

616'.00246176 — Man. Diseases - *For dentistry*

Human disease for dental students. — London : Pitman Medical, Apr.1981. — [368]p
ISBN 0-272-79608-5 (pbk) : £9.95 : CIP entry B81-03685

616'.00246176 — Man. Diseases — *For dentistry*

Scully, Crispian. Medical problems in dentistry / Crispian Scully, Roderick A. Cawson ; with a foreword by D.K. Mason. — Bristol : Wright, 1982. — ix,514p : ill ; 24cm
Includes index
ISBN 0-7236-0607-2 (pbk) : Unpriced : CIP rev. B82-10875

Tullman, Michael J.. Systemic disease in dental treatment / Michael J. Tullman, Spencer W. Redding. — New York ; Appleton-Century-Crofts ; London : Prentice-Hall, c1982. — xiv,512p : ill,1form ; 25cm
Includes bibliographies and index
ISBN 0-8385-8793-3 : £21.70 B82-23314

616'.003'21 — Man. Diseases — *Encyclopaedias*

Collins family medical handbook. — London : Collins, 1981. — viii,436p : ill ; 19cm
ISBN 0-00-434322-0 : £3.95 B82-00722

616'.005 — Man. Diseases — *Serials* — *For general practice*

Second opinion. — 1980-. — Guildford (LMS House, Riverway Estate, Portsmouth Rd., Guildford, Surrey) : Baskerville Publishers, 1980-. — v. : col.ill ; 28cm
Two issues yearly. — Description based on: Pt.1 (1982)
ISSN 0262-9895 = Second opinion : Unpriced B82-32137

616'.0076 — Man. Diseases — *Questions & answers*

Joshi, Pankaj. Multiple choice questions for the MRCP. — London : Butterworth Scientific, Sept.1982. — [248]p
ISBN 0-407-00247-2 : £5.95 : CIP entry B82-19211

MRCP part 2 revision book. — Hemel Hempstead (P.O. Box 81, Hemel Hempstead, Herts.) : PasTest Service, May 1982. — [160]p
ISBN 0-906896-08-8 (pbk) : £9.50 : CIP entry B82-11109

616'.0076 — Man. Diseases — *Questions & answers* — *Serials* — *For general practice*

CHECK : programme of self assessment / the Royal Australian College of General Practitioners. — Unit 1 (Apr. 1980)-. — Jolimont, Vic. : The College ; London : Update Publications, 1980-. — v. : ill ; 30cm
Description based on: Unit 9 (Dec. 1980)
Unpriced B82-19888

616'.008996073 — United States. Negroes. Diseases. Racial factors

Kiple, Kenneth F.. Another dimension to the black diaspora : dirt, disease, and racism / Kenneth F. Kiple, Virginia Himmelsteib King. — Cambridge : Cambridge University Press, 1981. — xix,295p : 1map ; 24cm
Includes index
ISBN 0-521-23664-9 : £20.00 B82-13983

616'.01 — Man. Drugs. Resistance of pathogens: Microorganisms

Bryan, L. E.. Bacterial resistance and susceptibility in chemotherapeutic agents / L.E. Bryan. — Cambridge : Cambridge University Press, 1982. — viii,234p : ill ; 23cm
Includes bibliographies and index
ISBN 0-521-23039-x (cased) : £17.50 : CIP rev.
ISBN 0-521-29785-0 (pbk) : £7.95 B82-12138

616'.01 — Man. Pathogens: Microorganisms

Shanson, D. C.. Microbiology in clinical practice / D.C. Shanson. — Bristol : J. Wright, 1982. — xxiii,574p : ill ; 24cm
Includes bibliographies and index
ISBN 0-7236-0577-7 (pbk) : Unpriced : CIP rev. B82-05411

616'.01 — Medicine. Microbiology

Collee, J. G.. Applied medical microbiology / J.G. Collee. — 2nd ed. — Oxford : Blackwell Scientific, 1981. — vii,150p ; 24cm. — (Basic microbiology ; v.3)
Previous ed.: 1976. — Bibliography: p140-142. — Includes index
ISBN 0-632-00853-9 (pbk) : £5.50 : CIP rev. B81-19218

Cooke, E. M.. Clinical microbiology for medical students. — Chichester : Wiley, Feb.1983. — [200]p
ISBN 0-471-90074-5 : £5.50 : CIP entry B82-38714

A Short textbook of medical microbiology. — 5th ed. — London : Hodder and Stoughton, Dec.1982. — [416]p. — (University medical texts)
Previous ed.: 1978
ISBN 0-340-32388-4 (pbk) : £5.95 : CIP entry B82-29657

616'.01 — Medicine. Microbiology — *For children*

Struwe, Sten. Micro-life in medicine / written by Sten Struwe ; translated by E. Meyland-Smith ; edited by Su Swallow. — Harlow : Longman, 1981. — 31p : ill(some col.),2ports ; 23cm. — (A First look at microbiology)
Translated from the Danish
ISBN 0-582-39144-x : £2.50 B82-21056

616'.01'024613 — Medicine. Microbiology — *For nursing*

Parker, Margaret J.. Microbiology for nurses. — 6th ed. / Margaret J. Parker, Vivien A. Stucke ; foreword by the late R.E.M. Thompson. — London : Baillière Tindall, 1982. — xi,260p : ill,ports ; 19cm. — (Nurses' aids series)
Previous ed.: 1978. — Bibliography: p247-250. — Includes index
ISBN 0-7020-0924-5 (pbk) : £3.25 : CIP rev. B82-06939

616'.01'024613 — Medicine. Microbiology — *For tropical nursing*

Akinsanya, Justus A.. Microbiolgogy, health and hygiene / Justus A. Akinsanya with a special contribution by Malcolm J.W. Hughes. — London : Macmillan, 1980. — 112p : ill,2maps,1form,ports ; 25cm. — (Macmillan tropical nursing and health science series)
Bibliography: p102. — Includes index
ISBN 0-333-27580-2 (pbk) : Unpriced : CIP rev. B80-24506

616'.01'0246176 — Medicine. Microbiology — *For dentistry*

Melville, T. H.. Microbiology for dental students. — 3rd ed. / T.H. Melville, C. Russell. — London : Heinemann Medical, 1981. — xi,394p,[11]p of plates : ill(some col.) ; 22cm
Previous ed.: 1975. — Bibliography: p380. — Includes index
ISBN 0-433-21151-2 (pbk) : £12.50 B82-10972

616'.01'028 — Medicine. Microbiology. Laboratory techniques

Bailey, W. Robert. Bailey and Scott's Diagnostic microbiology. — 6th ed. / Sydney M. Finegold, William J. Martin. — St. Louis, Mo. ; London : Mosby, 1982. — xiii,705p,[39]p of plates : ill(some col.) ; 25cm
Previous ed.: 1978. — Includes bibliographies and index
ISBN 0-8016-1577-1 : £19.75 B82-34461

616.01'05 — Medicine. Microbiology — *Serials*

Medical microbiology. — Vol.1. — London : Academic Press, Sept.1982. — [400]p
ISBN 0-12-228001-6 : CIP entry B82-19161

616'.014 — Man. Pathogens: Bacteria

Notes on medical bacteriology / edited by J. Douglas Sleigh, Morag C. Timbury ; foreword by Sir James W. Howie. — Edinburgh : Churchill Livingstone, 1981. — 354p : ill,1port ; 22cm. — (Churchill Livingstone medical text)
Includes index
ISBN 0-443-02264-x (pbk) : Unpriced : CIP rev. B81-22639

616'.014 — Man. Pathogens: Bacteria. Resistance to antibiotics

The **Control** of antibiotic-resistant bacteria. — London : Academic Press, Sept.1982. — [300] p. — (The Beecham colloquia)
Conference papers
ISBN 0-12-674750-4 : CIP entry B82-19168

616'.014'2 — Man. Staphylococci - *Conference proceedings*

The **Staphylococci**. — Aberdeen : Aberdeen University Press, Apr.1981. — [152]p
Conference papers
ISBN 0-08-025749-6 : CIP entry B81-04351

616'.0145 — Man. Diseases caused by streptococci — *Conference proceedings*

International Symposium on Streptococci and Streptococcal Diseases *(8th : 1981 : Lund)*. Basic concepts of streptococci and streptococcal diseases. — Chertsey : Reedbooks, July 1982. — [320]p
ISBN 0-906544-05-x : £32.00 : CIP entry B82-16233

616'.0145 — Man. Pathogens: Pseudomonas aeruginosa

A **Comprehensive** guide to the therapeutic use of cefsulodin. — Basel ; London : Karger, c1980. — 94p : ill ; 23cm. — (Pharmanual ; 1)
ISBN 3-8055-1042-x (pbk) : £6.50 B82-39119

616'.015'0222 — Man. Pathogens: Fungi — *Illustrations*

Frey, Dorothea. A colour atlas of pathogenic fungi / Dorothea Frey, Ronald Jowett Oldfield, Ronald C. Bridger. — London : Wolfe Medical, 1979. — 168p : col.ill ; 27cm
Bibliography: p154-164. — Includes index
ISBN 0-7234-0744-4 : Unpriced B82-06100

616'.0194 — Man. Pathogens: Cytomegaloviruses

Ho, Monto. Cytomegalovirus : biology and infection / Monto Ho. — New York ; London : Plenum, c1982. — xvii,309p : ill ; 24cm. — (Current topics in infectious disease)
Bibliography: p245-279. — Includes index
ISBN 0-306-40844-9 : Unpriced B82-38664

616'.0194 — Man. Pathogens: Herpesviruses — *Conference proceedings*

International Conference on Human Herpesviruses *(1980 : Emory University)*. The human herpesviruses : an interdisciplinary perspective / [proceedings of the International Conference on Human Herpesviruses, Emory University, Atlanta, Georgia, March 17-21, 1980] ; edited by André J. Nahmias, Walter R. Dowdle, Raymond F. Schinazi. — New York ; Oxford : Elsevier, c1981. — xxi,721p : ill ; 28cm
Includes index
ISBN 0-444-00553-6 : Unpriced B82-00803

616'.0194 — Medicine. Virology

Fraenkel-Conrat, Heinz. Virology / Heinz Fraenkel-Conrat, Paul C. Kimball. — Englewood Cliffs ; London : Prentice-Hall, c1982. — x,406p : ill ; 25cm
Includes bibliographies and index
ISBN 0-13-942144-0 : £24.70 B82-29235

Hsiung, G. D.. Diagnostic virology. — 3rd ed. — London : Yale University Press, Nov.1982. — [296]p
Previous ed.: 1973
ISBN 0-300-02888-1 : £19.50 : CIP entry B82-40332

Sommerville, R. G.. Clinical virology. — Oxford : Blackwell Scientific, Jan.1983. — [192]p
Originally published: London : Grant McIntyre, 1982
ISBN 0-86286-009-1 (pbk) : £7.50 : CIP entry B82-36160

616'.0194 — Tropical medicine. Virology

Metselaar, D.. Practical virology : for medical students and practitioners in tropical countries / D. Metselaar, D.I.H. Simpson with contributions from E.T.W. Bowen ... [et al.]. — Oxford : Oxford University Press, 1982. — ix,496p : ill ; 24cm. — (Oxford medical publications)
Includes bibliographies and index
ISBN 0-19-261317-0 (pbk) : £6.50 : CIP rev. B81-35771

616'.025 — Medicine. Emergency treatment
Rund, Douglas A.. Essentials of emergency medicine / Douglas A. Rund. — New York : Appleton-Century-Crofts ; London : Prentice-Hall, c1982. — x,453p : ill ; 23cm
Includes index
ISBN 0-8385-2243-2 (pbk) : £14.65 B82-21691

616'.025 — Medicine. Emergency treatment — *Conference proceedings*
International Congress of Emergency Surgery *(5th : 1981 : Brighton)*. Care of the acutely ill and injured. — Chichester : Wiley, Apr.1982. — [350]p. — (A Wiley medical publication)
ISBN 0-471-10238-5 : £17.50 : CIP entry B82-07125

616'.025 — Medicine. Emergency treatment — *For general practice*
Emergencies in the home : articles published in the British medical journal. — London : British Medical Association, c1982. — 112p ; 22cm
Includes index
ISBN 0-7279-0088-9 (pbk) : Unpriced B82-36538

Moulds, A. J.. Emergencies in general practice. — Lancaster : MTP Press, Nov.1982. — [210]p
ISBN 0-85200-475-3 : £10.00 : CIP entry B82-29026

616'.025 — Medicine. Emergency treatment — *For hospital doctors*
Modern emergency department practice. — London : Edward Arnold, Feb.1983. — [416]p
ISBN 0-7131-4423-8 : £45.00 : CIP entry B82-38905

616'.025 — Medicine. Emergency treatment — *Manuals*
Flint, Thomas. Flint's Emergency treatment and management. — 6th ed. / Harvey D. Cain. — Philadelphia ; London : Saunders, 1980. — xvii,846p : ill,forms ; 21cm
Previous ed.: published as Emergency treatment and management. 1975. — Text on lining papers. — Includes index
ISBN 0-7216-2312-3 : £11.50 B82-35023

Smith, Bradley F.. The emergency book / Bradley Smith and Gus Stevens. — Revised and adapted ed. — Harmondsworth : Penguin, 1982. — 138p : ill ; 21cm. — (Penguin handbooks)
Previous ed.: New York : Simon & Schuster, 1978
ISBN 0-14-046448-4 (pbk) : £2.50 B82-35261

616'.025'05 — Medicine. Emergency treatment — *Serials*
The **Year** book of emergency medicine. — 1981-. — Chicago ; London : Year Book Medical Publishers, 1981-. — v. : ill,plans ; 24cm
ISSN 0271-7964 : £29.00 B82-06167

616.02'52 — Expeditions. First aid — *Manuals*
Sheen, Brian. Expedition first aid and emergency treatments : including tropical supplement / by Brian Sheen. — 2nd rev. ed. — Par (92 Par Green, Par, Cornwall PL24 2AG) : B. Sheen, c1982. — i,23p ; 21cm
Bibliography: p22
£0.75 (pbk) B82-22510

616.02'52 — First aid
Basic emergency care of the sick and injured / [edited by] Guy S. Parcel. — 2nd ed. — St. Louis, Mo. ; London : Mosby, 1982. — xix,293p : ill ; 24cm
Previous ed.: published as First aid in emergency care. 1977. — Includes bibliographies and index
ISBN 0-8016-3754-6 (pbk) : £8.50 B82-34465

616.02'52 — First aid — *For industries*
Great Britain. *Health and Safety Commission*. Health and Safety (First-Aid) Regulations 1981. — London : Health & Safety Executive, Aug.1981. — [20]p
ISBN 0-11-883447-9 (pbk) : CIP entry B81-25132

Great Britain. *Health and Safety Executive*. First aid at work. — London : Health and Safety Executive, Aug.1981. — [50]p. — (Health & safety series booklet ; HS(R)11)
ISBN 0-11-883446-0 (pbk) : CIP entry B81-24608

616.02'52 — First aid — *Manuals*
Accident action : the essential family guide to home safety and first aid. — London : Macmillan, c1978. — 117p : ill ; 27cm
Text on lining papers. — Includes index
ISBN 0-333-25266-7 : £3.95 : CIP rev.
Also classified at 643'.028'9 B78-27385

Judd, Richard L.. The first responder : 'the critical first minutes!' / Richard L. Judd, Dwight D. Ponsell ; with a foreword by Norman E. McSain, Jr. — St. Louis ; London : Mosby, 1982. — xv,281p : ill ; 24cm
Bibliography: p257-258. — Includes index
ISBN 0-8016-2599-8 (pbk) : £7.75 B82-31875

Nisbet, Margaret. Book of first aid and safety / Margaret Nisbet. — Poole : Blandford, [1981]. — 95p : ill(some col.),1port ; 15cm. — ('How to')
Includes index
ISBN 0-7137-1054-3 (pbk) : £1.95 B82-20225

St. John Ambulance. The first aid manual. — London (9 Henrietta St., WC2E 8PS) : Dorling Kindersley, Sept.1982. — [224]p
Replaces 3rd ed. London : St John Ambulance, 1972
ISBN 0-86318-000-0 (cased) : £5.95 : CIP entry
ISBN 0-86318-001-0 (pbk) : £3.95 B82-21563

616.02'52 — First aid — *Manuals — For children*
Roy, Ian, *1938-*. First steps in first aid / by Ian Roy ; with illustrations by Drury Lane Studios. — Loughborough : Ladybird, c1981. — 51p : col.ill ; 18cm. — (Series 819)
Text, ill on lining papers. — Includes index
ISBN 0-7214-0686-6 : £0.50 B82-06288

Winch, Brenda. First aid / Brenda Winch ; illustrated by Paul Wrigley. — London : Macmillan, 1982. — 32p : ill(some col.) ; 28cm. — (Help yourself books)
ISBN 0-333-30861-1 : £2.95 : CIP rev. B81-35781

616.02'52 — Man. Wounds. Bandaging — *Manuals*
Bickerton, J.. Bandaging / J. Bickerton, J. Small. — London : Heinemann Medical, 1982. — 88p : ill ; 20cm
ISBN 0-433-02831-9 (pbk) : £2.95 B82-23398

616.02'52'024372 — First aid — *Manuals — For playgroup leaders*
Mayers, Pat. Accident prevention and first aid / Pat Mayers. — Rev. and rewritten. — [London] : [Pre-school Playgroups Association], [1981, c1970]. — 24p : ill ; 21cm. — (PPA publication)
Cover title. — Previous ed.: 1970?
ISBN 0-901755-35-4 (pbk) : £0.50 B82-37594

616.02'52'024649 — First aid - *Manuals - For housewives*
Creese, Angela. Safety for your family. — 2nd ed. — London : Bell & Hyman, Aug.1981. — [281]p
Previous ed.: London : Mills & Boon, 1968
ISBN 0-7135-2070-1 (pbk) : CIP entry
Primary classification 643'.028'9 B81-16361

616'.028 — Critically ill patients. Intensive care — *Manuals*
Handbook of intensive care. — Bristol : J. Wright, Jan.1983. — [592]p
ISBN 0-7236-0597-1 : £35.00 : CIP entry B82-33352

616'.028 — Medicine. Intensive care
Burrell, Lenette Owens. Critical care. — 4th ed. / Lenette Owens Burrell, Zeb L. Burrell, Jr. ; drawings by Weona Wright. — St. Louis ; London : Mosby, 1982. — xiii,622p : ill,1form ; 25cm
Previous ed.: 1977. — Text on lining papers. — Bibliography: p585-589. — Includes index
ISBN 0-8016-0906-2 : £14.25 B82-08261

Intensive care / edited by Eric Sherwood Jones. — Lancaster : MTP, c1982. — xi,464p : ill ; 25cm
Includes index
ISBN 0-85200-340-4 : Unpriced : CIP rev. B81-33647

616'.028 — Medicine. Intensive care. Instrumentation
Hill, D. W.. Intensive care instrumentation. — 2nd ed. — London : Academic Press, July 1982. — [430]p. — (Medical physics series)
Previous ed.: 1976
ISBN 0-12-791981-3 : CIP entry
ISBN 0-8089-1474-x (U.S.) B82-12532

616'.042 — Man. Diseases. Genetic factors — *Forecasts*
Harsanyi, Zolt. Genetic prophecy. — London : Granada, May 1982. — [250]p
ISBN 0-246-11760-5 : £7.95 : CIP entry B82-07408

616'.042'0246181 — Man. Genetic disorders — *For gynaecology & obstetrics*
Genetics in obstetrics and gynecology / Joe Leigh Simpson ... [et al.]. — New York ; London : Grune & Stratton, c1982. — vii,322p : ill ; 26cm
Bibliography: p267-303. — Includes index
ISBN 0-8089-1421-9 : £19.60 B82-39088

616'.043 — Great Britain. Man. Prader-Willi syndrome. Organisations: Prader-Willi Syndrome Association — *Serials*
[Newsletter *(Prader-Willi Syndrome Association)***]**. Newsletter / Prader-Willi Syndrome Association. — No.1 (Dec. 1981)-. — Abbots Langley (30 Follett Drive, Abbots Langley, Herts. WD5 0LP) : The Association, 1981-. — v. ; 30cm
ISSN 0263-449X = Newsletter - Prader-Willi Syndrome Association : Free to Association members only B82-24757

616'.043 — Man. Congenital abnormalities
Cardiovascular, respiratory, gastrointestinal and genitourinary malformations / edited by T.V.N. Persaud and M.P. Persaud. — Lancaster : MTP, 1982. — ix,232p : ill ; 24cm. — (Advances in the study of birth defects ; vol.6)
Includes index
ISBN 0-85200-397-8 : £21.95 : CIP rev. B81-22580

Genetic disorders, syndromology and prenatal diagnosis / edited by T.V.N. Persaud. — Lancaster : MTP, 1982. — ix,256p : ill ; 24cm. — (Advances in the study of birth defects ; vol.5)
Includes index
ISBN 0-85200-396-x : £21.95 : CIP rev. B81-22682

616'.043 — Medicine. Teratology
Handbook of teratology / edited by James G. Wilson and F. Clarke Fraser. — New York ; London : Plenum
2: Mechanisms and pathogenesis. — c1977. — xi,491p : ill ; 26cm
Includes bibliographies and index
ISBN 0-306-36242-2 : Unpriced B82-40425

616'.047 — Immunocompromised patients. Infection
Clinical approach to infection in the compromised host / edited by Robert H. Rubin and Lowell S. Young ; with a foreword by Martin J. Cline. — New York ; London : Plenum Medical, c1981. — xxii,653p : ill ; 26cm
Includes index
ISBN 0-306-40679-9 : Unpriced B82-20990

International Symposium on Infections in the Immunocompromised Host *(2nd : 1982 : Stirling)*. Second International Symposium on Infections in the Immunocompromised Host. — London : Academic Press, Feb.1983. — [250]p
Conference papers
ISBN 0-12-228020-2 : CIP entry B82-37476

616'.047 — Man. Fevers. Therapy — *Early works*
al-Isrā'īlī, Isḥāq ibn Sulaymān. Kitāb al-ḥummayāt / li-Isḥāq ibn Sulaymān al-Isrā'īlī = On fevers / Isaac Judaeus. — [Cambridge] : Published for the Cambridge Middle East Centre by Pembroke Arabic Texts. — (Arabic technical and scientific texts ; v.8)
al-Maqāla al-thālitha : fī al-sill = The third discourse : on consumption : together with an appendix containing a facsimile of the Latin version of this discourse (Venice, 1576) / edited and translated with introduction and notes by J.D. Latham and H.D. Isaacs. — 1981, c1980. — xxv,113,[92]p ; 20cm
Arabic text with English and Latin translations. — Bibliography: p110-112
ISBN 0-906308-09-7 (pbk) : Unpriced
B82-15289

616'.047 — Pyrogens
Whittet, T. D.. Pyrogens in the modern setting / by T.D. Whittet. — Harpenden (8 Lyndhurst Drive, Harpenden, AL5 5QN) : T.D. Whittet, [1980?]. — 17p : ill,3ports ; 28cm. — (The 1980 Todd lecture)
Bibliography: p13-17
£0.50 (spiral) B82-12485

616'.0472 — Man. Head. Headaches
Headaches and migraine / [edited by Eileen Lloyd]. — Aylesbury : Rodale, 1982. — 47p : ill ; 18cm. — (Prevention health guides)
ISBN 0-87857-430-1 (pbk) : Unpriced
B82-36762

Lance, James W.. Mechanism and management of headache. — 4th ed. — London : Butterworths, Dec.1982. — [300]p
Previous ed.: 1978
ISBN 0-407-26458-2 : £15.00 : CIP entry
B82-29783

Wilkinson, Marcia. Migraine & headaches : understanding, controlling and avoiding the pain / Marcia Wilkinson. — London : Dunitz, 1982. — 108p : ill(some col.) ; 23cm. — (Positive health guide)
Includes index
ISBN 0-906348-17-x (cased) : Unpriced : CIP rev.
ISBN 0-906348-18-8 (pbk £2.50)
Primary classification 616.8'57 B81-16918

616'.0472 — Man. Pain. Mental healing
Janov, Arthur. Prisoners of pain : unlocking the power of the mind to end suffering / Arthur Janov. — [London] : Abacus, 1982, c1980. — x,276p : ill ; 20cm
Originally published: Garden City, N.Y. : Anchor, 1980. — Includes index
ISBN 0-349-11844-2 (pbk) : £3.50 B82-24541

616'.0472 — Man. Pain. Relief
Persistent pain. — London : Academic Press, June 1981
Vol.3. — [220]p
ISBN 0-12-792573-2 : CIP entry B81-12330

616'.0472 — Man. Pain. Relief — *Conference proceedings*
Contemporary topics in pain management. — London : Academic Press, Sept.1982. — [100] p. — (Royal Society of Medicine series. International congress and symposium series, ISSN 0142-2367 ; no.52)
Conference proceedings
ISBN 0-12-790579-0 (pbk) : CIP entry
B82-25908

616'.0473 — Man. Cells. Diseases. Inflammatory reactions
Cellular functions in immunity and inflammation / editors-in-chief Joost J. Oppenheim, David L. Rosenstreich, Michael Potter. — London : Edward Arnold, c1981. — xvii,479p : ill ; 27cm
Includes bibliographies and index
ISBN 0-7131-4396-7 : £29.50
Primary classification 616.07'95 B82-05066

616.07 — Man. Cells. Diseases
Dixon, K. C.. Cellular defects in disease. — Oxford : Blackwell Scientific, July 1981. — [464]p
ISBN 0-632-00734-6 : £16.50 : CIP entry
B81-15919

616.07 — Man. Diseases. Biochemical aspects
Biochemical aspects of human diseases. — Oxford : Blackwell Scientific, July 1982. — [704]p
ISBN 0-632-00012-0 : £32.00 : CIP entry
B82-17922

616.07 — Man. Diseases. Physiological aspects
Cawson, R. A.. Pathologic mechanisms and human disease / Roderick A. Cawson, Alexander W. McCracken, Peter B. Marcus. — St Louis ; London : Mosby, 1982. — xi,594p : ill ; 28cm
Includes bibliographies and index
ISBN 0-8016-0939-9 (pbk) : £15.25
B82-33956

Groër, Maureen E.. Basic pathophysiology : a conceptual approach / Maureen E. Groër, Maureen E. Shekleton, with a contribution by Kenneth J. Kant. — St. Louis ; London : Mosby, 1979. — x,524p : ill ; 26cm
Includes bibliographies and index
ISBN 0-8016-1983-1 (pbk) : £16.50
B82-28166

Pathophysiology : clinical concepts of disease processes / [edited by] Sylvia Anderson Price, Lorraine McCarty Wilson. — 2nd ed. — New York ; London : McGraw-Hill, c1982. — xv,973p : ill(some col.) ; 29cm
Previous ed.: 1978. — Ill on lining paper. — Includes bibliographies and index
ISBN 0-07-050863-1 : £21.25 B82-15978

616.07 — Man. Palaeopathology
Živanoirć, Srboljub. Ancient diseases. — London : Methuen, Apr.1982. — [220]p
Translated from the Serbo-Croatian
ISBN 0-416-31140-7 : £13.00 : CIP entry
B82-04049

616.07 — Medicine. Pathology
Anderson, W. A. D.. Synopsis of pathology / W.A.D. Anderson, Thomas M. Scotti. — 10th ed. — St Louis ; London : Mosby, 1980. — ix, 804p : ill ; 24cm
Previous ed.: 1976. — Includes bibliographies and index
ISBN 0-8016-0231-9 (pbk) : £14.75
B82-40699

Outlines of pathology / edited by Herbert Braunstein. — St. Louis ; London : Mosby, 1982. — xi,605p : ill ; 22cm
Includes index
ISBN 0-8016-0869-4 (spiral) : £15.25
B82-22916

Reese, A. J. M.. The principles of pathology / A.J.M. Reese. — 2nd ed. — Bristol : Wright, 1981. — xi,267p : ill ; 22cm
Previous ed.: 1974. — Bibliography: p238-239. — Includes index
ISBN 0-7236-0603-x (pbk) : Unpriced : CIP rev. B81-24638

Thomson, A. D.. Lecture notes on pathology. — 3rd ed. — Oxford : Blackwell Scientific, Jan.1983. — [800]p
ISBN 0-632-00032-5 (pbk) : £18.00 : CIP entry
B82-40907

616.07 — Medicine. Pathology — *Conference proceedings*
World Congress of the World Association of Societies of Pathology (Anatomic and Clinical) *(11th : 1981 : Jerusalem)*. Advances in pathology anatomic and clinical. — Oxford : Pergamon, Sept.1982
Vol.1: Microbiology, biochemistry, immunology, hematology. — [542]p
ISBN 0-08-028878-2 : £60.00 : CIP entry
B82-20206

World Congress of the World Association of Societies of Pathology (Anatomic and Clinical) *(11th : 1981 : Jerusalem)*. Advances in pathology anatomic and clinical. — Oxford : Pergamon, Sept.1982
Vol.2: Anatomic pathology, cytopathology, forensic pathology and toxicology. — [606]p
ISBN 0-08-028879-0 : £67.50 : CIP entry
B82-20207

616.07'024613 — Medicine. Pathology — *For nursing*
Jackson, Sheila. Pathology and patient care. — Oxford : Blackwell Scientific, Sept.1982. — [128]p
ISBN 0-632-00875-x (pbk) : £4.50 : CIP entry
B82-23852

616.07'05 — Medicine. Pathology — *Serials*
Clinical laboratory annual. — Vol.1 (1982)-. — New York : Appleton-Century-Crofts ; London : Prentice-Hall International [distributor], 1982-. — v. : ill(some col.) ; 25cm
Unpriced B82-23587

616.07'076 — Medicine. Pathology — *Questions & answers*
Lennox, Bernard. MCQ tutor for students of pathology / Bernard Lennox. — London : Heinemann Medical, 1981. — viii,156p : 1ill ; 22cm. — (Second series)
ISBN 0-433-19152-x (pbk) : Unpriced
B82-23733

Smiddy, F. G.. Multiple choice questions in general pathology / F.G. Smiddy, J.L. Turk. — London : Pitman, 1981. — xi,352p ; 21x10cm
ISBN 0-272-79631-x (pbk) : Unpriced : CIP rev. B81-23857

616.07'1 — Developing countries. Man. Diseases *related to* **sanitation**
Sanitation and disease. — Chichester : Wiley, Feb.1983. — [500]p. — (World Bank studies in water supply and sanitation)
ISBN 0-471-90094-x : £20.00 : CIP entry
B82-38715

616.07'1 — Man. Diseases. Aetiology. Parapsychological aspects
Reyner, J. H.. Psionic medicine : the study and treatment of the causative factors in illness / J.H. Reyner in collaboration with George Laurence and Carl Upton. — 2nd ed. — London : Routledge & Kegan Paul, 1982. — 151p ; 22cm
Previous ed.: 1974. — Bibliography: p147-148. — Includes index
ISBN 0-7100-9088-9 (pbk) : £3.95 B82-25672

616.07'1 — Man. Diseases. Environmental factors — *Conference proceedings*
Society for Environmental Therapy. *Inaugural Conference (1981 : Oxford)*. Disease and the environment : proceedings of the Inaugural Conference of the Society for Environmental Therapy, held in Oxford, 21-23 March 1981 / edited by A.R. Rees, H.J. Purcell. — Chichester : Wiley, c1982. — xii,206p : ill ; 24cm
Includes bibliographies and index
ISBN 0-471-10203-2 : £13.50 : CIP rev.
B82-01546

616.07'1 — Man. Diseases. Role of mast cells — *Conference proceedings*
The **Mast** cell : its role in health and disease : based on an international symposium, held in Davos, Switzerland, April 23-26, 1979 / with an introduction by J. Pepys ; sponsored by Fisons Limited, Pharmaceutical Division ; compiled and edited by the publishers of the journal 'Medicine'. — Oxford : Medical Education, c1979. — 32p : ill(some col.),ports ; 30cm. — (A 'Medicine' digest)
ISBN 0-906817-02-1 (unbound) : Unpriced
B82-23719

616.07'1'0941 — Great Britain. Man. Diseases. Aetiology
National health and social sickness — what are the real causes of illness? How can we be healthy / [prepared by the Sheffield Branch of the Socialist Health Association]. — London : Socialist Health Association, [1982]. — 24p : ill ; 21cm. — (A charter for health publication)
Cover title
£0.50 (pbk) B82-37449

616.07'5 — Medical laboratories. Management. Supervision — *Manuals*
Textbook of clinical laboratory supervision / edited by Kathleen Becan-McBride. — New York : Appleton-Century-Crofts ; London : Prentice-Hall, c1982. — xii,340 : ill ; 25cm
Includes bibliographies and index
ISBN 0-8385-8871-9 : £16.50 B82-21693

616.07'5 — Medicine. Diagnosis

Beck, Eric R.. Tutorials in differential diagnosis. — London : Pitman, Mar.1982. — [256]p
ISBN 0-272-79638-7 (pbk) : £7.50 : CIP entry
B82-01861

Bouchier, Ian A. D.. Clinical skills. — 2nd ed. — Eastbourne : Holt-Saunders, Jan.1982. — [735]p
Previous ed.: London : Saunders, 1976
ISBN 0-7216-1893-6 : £9.50 : CIP entry
B81-34656

Howells, John G.. Integral clinical investigation : an aspect of pananthropic medicine / John G. Howells. — London : Macmillan, 1982. — xvi,258p : ill ; 25cm
Bibliography: p251-253. — Includes index
ISBN 0-333-29446-7 (cased) : £20.00
ISBN 0-333-29447-5 (pbk) : Unpriced
B82-39152

New diagnostic techniques : the fifty-fifth Hahnemann Symposium / editors Howard A. Miller, Steven K. Teplick, Lawrence R. Goodman ; consulting editor Eugene L. Coodley. — New York ; London : Grune & Stratton, c1982. — xii,259p : ill ; 27cm
Includes index
ISBN 0-8089-1416-2 : £24.80 B82-27130

616.07'5 — Medicine. Diagnosis. Decision making

Kraytman, Maurice. Guide to clinical reasoning / Maurice Kraytman. — New York ; London : McGraw-Hill, c1981. — xii,561p ; 21cm
Includes bibliographies and index
ISBN 0-07-035451-0 (pbk) : £9.25 B82-05550

616.07'5 — Medicine. Diagnosis — *Manuals*

Ford, Michael J.. Practical procedures in clinical medicine / Michael J. Ford, John F. Munro ; foreword by John Macleod. — Edinburgh : Churchill Livingstone, 1980. — x,116p : ill ; 23cm
Includes index
ISBN 0-443-02120-1 (pbk) : £4.25 : CIP rev.
B80-13849

616.07'5 — Medicine. Differential diagnosis

Gunn, Alexander D. G.. Differential diagnosis : a guide to symptoms and signs of common diseases and disorders, presented in systematic form / Alexander D.G. Gunn. — Lancaster : MTP, 1981. — 311p : ill ; 24cm
Includes index
ISBN 0-85200-399-4 : Unpriced : CIP rev.
B81-21598

616.07'5 — Medicine. Immunodiagnosis

Principles of immunological diagnosis in medicine / [edited by] F. Milgrom, C.J. Abeyounis, K. Kano. — Philadelphia : Lea & Febiger ; London : Kimpton, 1981. — xvi,520p : ill ; 27cm
Includes bibliographies and index
ISBN 0-8121-0720-9 : Unpriced B82-37557

616.07'5'024613 — Medicine. Diagnosis — *For nursing*

Gordon, Marjory. Nursing diagnosis : process and application / Marjory Gordon. — New York ; London : McGraw-Hill, c1982. — xii,387p : ill ; 25cm
Ill on lining paper. — Bibliography: p364-378. — Includes index
ISBN 0-07-023815-4 : £12.95 B82-27229

Pagana, Kathleen Deska. Diagnostic testing & nursing implications : a case study approach / Kathleen Deska Pagana, Timothy James Pagana. — St. Louis ; London : Mosby, 1982. — xii,347p : ill ; 24cm
Includes bibliographies and index
ISBN 0-8016-3746-5 (pbk) : £8.50 B82-31881

616.07'5'028 — Medicine. Diagnosis. Laboratory techniques

Notes on clinical method. — 2nd ed. / edited by David Tunbridge. — Manchester : Manchester University Press, 1982. — 160p : ill ; 19cm
Previous ed.: / University of Manchester, Medical School. 1971
ISBN 0-7190-0851-4 (pbk) : £4.95 : CIP rev.
B81-33828

616.07'5'076 — Medicine. Diagnosis. Data interpretation — *Questions & answers*

Gabriel, Roger. Medical data interpretation for MRCP. — 2nd ed. — London : Butterworths, Nov.1981. — [216]p
Previous ed.: 1978
ISBN 0-407-00217-0 (pbk) : £3.95 : CIP entry
B81-30549

616'.07'54 — Man. Diagnosis. Applications of radiesthesia

Mermet, *Abbé*. Principles & practice of radiesthesia. — Dulverton : Watkins, Nov.1981. — [232]p
Translation of: Comment j'opère
ISBN 0-7224-0140-x (pbk) : £4.00 : CIP entry
B81-30371

616.07'54 — Man. Diagnosis. Physical examination

DeGowin, Elmer L.. Bedside diagnostic examination / Elmer L. DeGowin, Richard L. DeGowin. — 4th ed. / illustrations by Elmer L. DeGowin. — New York : Macmillan ; London : Baillière Tindall, c1981. — xiii,1039p : ill ; 19cm
Previous ed.: 1976. — Bibliography: p956-961. — Includes index
ISBN 0-02-328030-1 : £14.00 B82-10161

Physical diagnosis : the history and examination of the patient. — 6th ed. / [edited by] John A. Prior, Jack S. Silberstein, John M. Stang. — St. Louis ; London : Mosby, 1981. — xiv,525p : ill ; 24cm
Previous ed.: 1977. — Includes bibliographies and index
ISBN 0-8016-4054-7 : £23.50 B82-04112

Thompson, Richard, *19---*. An introduction to physical signs / Richard Thompson. — Oxford : Blackwell Scientific, 1980. — viii,231p : ill ; 22cm
Bibliography: pviii. — Includes index
ISBN 0-632-00054-6 (pbk) : £7.50 : CIP rev.
B80-20722

616.07'54 — Man. Diagnosis. Physical examination. Techniques

Lodewick, L.. The physical examination : an atlas for general practice. — Lancaster : MTP Press, Mar.1982. — [280]p
Translation of: 2nd ed of Het lichamelijk onderzoek
ISBN 0-85200-395-1 : £20.00 : CIP entry
B82-09183

616.07'54 — Medicine. Diagnosis. Imaging

Imaging for medicine. — New York ; London : Plenum
Vol.1: Nuclear medicine, ultrasonics, and thermography / edited by Sol Nudelman, Dennis D. Patton. — c1980. — xiv,498p : ill ; 24cm
Includes bibliographies and index
ISBN 0-306-40384-6 : Unpriced B82-35618

Scientific basis of medical imaging / edited by P.N.T. Wells. — Edinburgh : Churchill Livingstone, 1982. — 284p : ill ; 26cm
Includes index
ISBN 0-443-01986-x : £22.00 : CIP rev.
B81-31348

Sutton, David, *1917-*. Radiology and imaging for medical students / David Sutton. — 4th ed. — Edinburgh : Churchill Livingstone, 1982. — vii,221p : ill ; 22cm
Previous ed.: published as Radiology for medical students. 1977. — Includes index
ISBN 0-443-02669-6 (pbk) : £8.95 : CIP rev.
B82-24329

616.07'54 — Medicine. Diagnosis. Imaging — *Conference proceedings*

Physical aspects of medical imaging : proceedings of a meeting held at the University of Manchester, 25th-27th June, 1980 [organised by] the Hospital Physicists Association / edited by B.M. Moores, R.P. Parker, B.R. Pullan. — Chichester : Wiley, c1981. — xi,342p : ill ; 24cm
Includes bibliographies and index
ISBN 0-471-10039-0 : £14.50 : CIP rev.
B81-16880

616.07'54 — Medicine. Diagnosis. Imaging — *Questions & answers*

Finlay, David. Multiple choice questions in imaging sciences. — London : Baillière Tindall, Dec.1982. — [150]p
ISBN 0-7020-0954-7 (unbound) : £5.00 : CIP entry B82-30041

616.07'54 — Medicine. Diagnosis. Infrared thermography

Woodrough, R. E.. Medical infra-red thermography : principles and practice / R.E. Woodrough. — Cambridge : Cambridge University Press, 1982. — xi,251p : ill(some col.) ; 24cm. — (Techniques of measurement in medicine ; 7)
Includes index
ISBN 0-521-23879-x (cased) : £25.00 : CIP rev.
ISBN 0-521-28277-2 (pbk) : £9.95 B81-38815

616.07'54 — Medicine. Iridodiagnosis

Hall, Dorothy. Iridology : personality and health analysis through the iris / Dorothy Hall ; [illustrations by Richard Gregory]. — [London] : Angus & Robertson, 1980. — 241p : ill(some col.) ; 22cm
Originally published: West Melbourne, Vic. : Nelson, 1980. — Ill on lining papers. — Includes index
ISBN 0-207-95965-x (cased) : £7.95
ISBN 0-207-95971-4 (pbk) : £4.50 B82-08397

616.07'54'024613 — Man. Diagnosis. Physical examination — *For nursing*

Nurses handbook of investigations. — London : Harper & Row, Sept.1982. — [224]p
ISBN 0-06-318235-1 (pbk) : £4.95 : CIP entry
B82-18731

616.07'543 — Critically ill patients. Diagnosis. Ultrasonography

Ultrasound in emergency medicine / edited by Kenneth J.W. Taylor and Gregory N. Viscomi. — New York ; Edinburgh : Churchill Livingstone, 1981. — xi,208p : ill ; 25cm. — (Clinics in diagnostic ultrasound ; v.7)
Includes index
ISBN 0-443-08156-5 : £12.95 B82-01697

616.07'543 — Man. Diagnosis. Doppler ultrasonography

Atkinson, P.. Doppler ultrasound and its use in clinical measurement. — London : Academic Press, Mar.1982. — [300]p. — (Medical physics series ; v.5)
ISBN 0-12-066260-4 : CIP entry B82-00330

616.07'543 — Man. Diagnosis. Ultrasonography — *Case studies*

Case studies in diagnostic ultrasound / edited by Harris J. Finberg. — New York ; Edinburgh : Churchill Livingstone, 1981. — x,260p : ill ; 25cm. — (Clinics in diagnostic ultrasound ; v.9)
Includes bibliographies
ISBN 0-443-08172-7 : £15.00 B82-21057

616.07'543 — Man. Diagnosis. Ultrasonography — *Conference proceedings*

European Congress on Ultrasonics in Medicine *(4th : 1981 : Dubrovnik-Cavtat)*. Recent advances in ultrasound diagnosis 3 : proceedings of the 4th European Congress on Ultrasonics in Medicine, Dubrovnik, May 17-24, 1981 / editors A. Kurjak, A. Kratochwil. — Amsterdam ; Oxford : Excerpta Medica, 1981. — xiv,541p : ill ; 24cm. — (International congress series ; no.553)
Includes bibliographies and index
ISBN 90-219-0495-0 : £33.91 B82-08563

616.07'543 — Man. Diagnosis. Ultrasonography — *Manuals*

Meire, Hylton B.. Basic clinical ultrasound / by Hylton B. Meire and Pat Farrant. — London : British Institute of Radiology, c1982. — 170p : ill ; 19cm. — (BIR teaching series, ISSN 0262-8341 ; no.4)
Includes index
ISBN 0-905749-10-3 (pbk) : Unpriced
B82-39624

616.07'543 — Man. Diagnosis. Use of ultrasonic waves - *Conference proceedings*

Investigative ultrasonology. — Tunbridge Wells : Pitman Medical, June 1981
Conference papers
2: Clinical advances. — [340]p
ISBN 0-272-79576-3 : £18.00 : CIP entry
B81-13559

616.07'543'0926 — Man. Diagnosis. Ultrasonography — *Case studies — Serials*

Cases in diagnostic ultrasound. — Vol.1-. — New York ; Chichester : Wiley, 1980-. — v. : ill ; 29cm
Annual
£13.50 B82-19889

616.07'545 — Man. Diagnosis. Fibre-optic endoscopy — *Conference proceedings*

Hospital Physicists' Association. *Conference on Fibre Optics and Endoscopy (1979 : London).* Fibre optics and endoscopy : proceedings of the Hospital Physicists' Association Conference on Fibre Optics and Endoscopy, London, 8th November 1979 / the Hospital Physicists' Association. — [London] : The Association, c1980. — 54p ; 22cm. — (Conference report series ; 31)
Includes bibliographies
ISBN 0-904181-16-2 (pbk) : Unpriced
B82-14180

616.07'56 — Man. Diagnosis. Use of electrophoresis of cells — *Conference proceedings*

Workshop on Cell Electrophoresis *(2nd : 1981 : Bristol).* Cell electrophoresis in cancer and other clinical research : proceedings of the 2nd Workshop on Cell Electrophoresis, comparison of techniques for assessment of cell surface phenomena, Bristol, United Kingdom, May 26-29, 1981 / editors A.W. Preece and P. Ann Light. — Amsterdam ; Oxford : Elsevier/North-Holland Biomedical, 1981. — ix,314p : ill ; 25cm. — (Developments in cancer research ; v.6)
Includes index
ISBN 0-444-80374-2 : Unpriced B82-05984

616.07'56 — Medicine. Diagnosis. Applications of amino oxidase

Gorkin, V. Z.. Amine oxidases in clinical research. — Oxford : Pergamon, Jan.1983. — [300]p
Translation from the Russian
ISBN 0-08-025523-x : £40.00 : CIP entry
B82-33604

616.07'56 — Medicine. Diagnosis. Chemical analysis

Baron, D. N.. A short textbook of chemical pathology / D.N. Baron. — 4th ed. — London : Hodder and Stoughton, 1982. — xi,292p : ill ; 22cm. — (University medical texts)
Previous ed.: London : English Universities Press, 1972. — Includes bibliographies and index
ISBN 0-340-26522-1 (pbk) : £5.25 : CIP rev.
B81-14914

Clinical biochemistry : contemporary theories and techniques / edited by Herbert E. Spiegel. — New York ; London : Academic Press
Vol.1. — 1981. — xiii,232p : ill ; 24cm
Includes bibliographies and index
ISBN 0-12-657101-5 : £19.60 B82-30134

Natelson, Samuel. Principles of applied clinical chemistry : chemical background and medical applications / Samuel Natelson and Ethan A. Natelson
Vol.3: Plasma proteins in nutrition and transport. — New York ; London : Plenum, c1980. — xvi,554p : ill ; 24cm
Includes bibliographies and index
ISBN 0-306-40276-9 : Unpriced B82-39678

616.07'56 — Medicine. Diagnosis. Microanalysis — *Manuals*

Wootton, I. D. P.. Microanalysis in medical biochemistry. — 6th ed. — Edinburgh : Churchill Livingstone, Sept.1982. — [320]p
Previous ed.: 1974
ISBN 0-443-02661-0 (pbk) : £8.00 : CIP entry
B82-19681

616.07'56 — Medicine. Diagnosis. Use of enzymes

Adolph, L.. Enzyme diagnosis in diseases of the heart, liver and pancreas / L. Adolph and R. Lorenz. — Basel ; London : Karger, c1982. — 123p : ill(some col.) ; 22cm
Translation of: Enzymdiagnostik bei Herz-, Leber- und Pankreaserkrankungen. — Bibliography: p114. — Includes index
ISBN 3-8055-3079-x (pbk) : £9.85 B82-28700

616.07'56 — Medicine. Immunoassay — *Conference proceedings*

Immunoassays for clinical chemistry. — Edinburgh : Churchill Livingstone, Nov.1982. — [800]p
Conference papers
ISBN 0-443-02704-8 : £25.00 : CIP entry
B82-30612

International Conference on Radioimmunoassay *(3rd : 1981 : Gardone Riviera).* Monoclonal antibodies and developments in immunoassay : proceedings of the 3rd International Conference on Radioimmunoassay 1981, held in Gardone Riviera, Italy, May 6-9, 1981 / editors Alberto Albertini and Roger Ekins. — Amsterdam ; Oxford : Elsevier/North-Holland Biomedical, 1981. — ix,402p : ill ; 25cm. — (Symposia of the Giovanni Lorenzini Foundation ; v.11)
Includes index
ISBN 0-444-80373-4 : Unpriced B82-05062

616.07'56 — Medicine. Immunoassay. Quality control

Jeffcoate, S. L.. Efficiency and effectiveness in the endocrine laboratory / S.L. Jeffcoate. — London : Academic Press, 1981. — vi,223p : ill ; 24cm
Includes bibliographies and index
ISBN 0-12-382160-6 : £19.20 : CIP rev.
B81-13444

616.07'56 — Medicine. Radioimmunoassay

Radioimmunoassay design and quality control. — Oxford : Pergamon, Oct.1982. — [145]p
ISBN 0-08-027095-6 : £10.00 : CIP entry
ISBN 0-08-026405-0 (set) : £250.00
B82-31284

Radioimmunoassay of antibody : and its clinical applications / David Parratt ... [et al.]. — Chichester : Wiley, c1982. — xvii,156p : ill ; 24cm
Includes bibliographies and index
ISBN 0-471-10061-7 : £15.00 : CIP rev.
B82-01105

616.07'56'076 — Medicine. Diagnosis. Chemical analysis — *Questions & answers*

Whitby, L. G.. Multiple choice questions on clinical chemistry / L.G. Whitby, A.F. Smith. — London : Blackwell Scientific, 1981. — xi,91p ; 19cm
Bibliography: p91
ISBN 0-632-00694-3 (pbk) : £2.80 : CIP rev.
B81-08801

616.07'561 — Man. Blood. Testing. Laboratory techniques. Quality control

Quality control / edited by I. Cavill. — Edinburgh : Churchill Livingstone, 1982. — viii,191p : ill,forms ; 24cm. — (Methods in hematology ; v.4)
Includes index
ISBN 0-443-02229-1 : £14.00 : CIP rev.
B81-36212

616.07'561 — Medicine. Diagnosis. Haematology

Brown, Barbara A. (Barbara Ann). Hematology : principles and procedures / Barbara A. Brown. — 3rd ed. — Philadelphia, Pa. : Lea & Febiger ; London : Kimpton, 1980. — x,358p,6leaves of plates : ill(some col.) ; 27cm
Previous ed.: 1976. — Bibliography: p339-343. — Includes index
ISBN 0-8121-0707-1 : Unpriced B82-26970

616.07'561 — Medicine. Diagnosis. Use of determination of blood viscosity — *Conference proceedings*

Blood viscosity in heart disease and cancer : based in part on the proceedings of a conference held under the auspices of the University of Sydney in the Stephen Roberts Lecture Theatre, The University of Sydney, Australia, 29th May 1978 and updated through April 1981 / edited by Leopold Dintenfass and Geoffrey V.F. Seaman. — Oxford : Pergamon, 1981. — xi,174p : ill ; 26cm
Includes index
ISBN 0-08-024954-x : £18.00 : CIP rev.
B81-31518

616.07'566 — Man. Urine. Analysis. Methods

Focus on urine analysis. — Oxford : Medicine Publishing Foundation, Jan.1983. — [36]p
ISBN 0-906817-39-0 (pbk) : £5.00 : CIP entry
B82-32848

616.07'57 — Forensic medicine. Radiography

Evans, Kenneth T.. Forensic radiology / K.T. Evans, B. Knight with contributions from D.K. Whittaker. — Oxford : Blackwell Scientific, 1981. — viii,212p : ill ; 25cm
Bibliography: p196-207. — Includes index
ISBN 0-632-00587-4 : £15.00 : CIP rev.
B81-21595

616.07'57 — Man. Diagnosis. Radiography

Hoxter, Erwin A.. Practical radiography. — London : Heyden, Apr.1982. — [200]p
Translation of: Röntgenaufnahmetechnik
ISBN 0-85501-292-7 (pbk) : CIP entry
B82-14200

Innovations in diagnostic radiology / edited by Alexander R. Margulis, Charles A. Gooding. — New York ; London : Academic Press, 1981. — xiii,507p : ill ; 29cm
ISBN 0-12-788491-2 : £64.80 B82-21254

Interventional radiologic techniques : computed tomography and ultrasonography / edited by Albert A. Moss, Henry I. Goldberg, David Norman. — New York ; London : Academic Press, 1981. — x,370p : ill ; 29cm
ISBN 0-12-788526-9 : £56.20 B82-21250

616.07'57 — Medicine. Applications of ionising radiation

Kouris, Kypros. Imaging with ionizing radiations. — Glasgow : Surrey University Press, July 1982. — [216]p. — (Progress in medical and environmental physics ; v.1)
ISBN 0-903384-30-2 : £27.50 : CIP entry
B82-13169

616.07'57 — Medicine. Emergency treatment. Diagnosis. Radiography

Harris, John H.. The radiology of emergency medicine / John H. Harris, William H. Harris. — 2nd ed. — Baltimore ; London : Williams & Wilkins, c1981. — xvi,699p : ill ; 29cm
Previous ed.: 1975. — Includes index
ISBN 0-683-03883-4 : Unpriced B82-13536

616.07'57 — Medicine. Emergency treatment. Radiology

Radiology of the emergency patient : an atlas approach / edited by Edward I. Greenbaum ; section on osseous trauma co-edited by Deborah M. Forrester ; section on trauma to the skull and spine co-edited by Henry F.W. Pribram. — New York ; Chichester : Wiley, c1982. — xviii,831p : ill ; 27cm
ISBN 0-471-08562-6 : £56.00 B82-39916

616.07'57 — Medicine. Radiology

Chapman, Stephen. A guide to radiological procedures / Stephen Chapman and Richard Nakielny with contributions from W.D. Jeans ; foreword by Sir Howard Middlemiss. — London : Ballière Tindall, 1981. — 250p : ill ; 20cm
Includes bibliographies and index
ISBN 0-7020-0885-0 (pbk) : £6.50 : CIP rev.
B81-25835

616.07'57 — Medicine. Radiology *continuation*

Hendee, William R.. Medical radiation physics : roentgenology, nuclear medicine & ultrasound / William R. Hendee. — 2nd ed. — Chicago ; London : Year Book Medical, c1979. — xv,517p : ill ; 24cm
Previous ed.: 1970. — Includes index
ISBN 0-8151-4240-4 : £32.58 B82-04566

616.07'57 — Medicine. Radiology — *Conference proceedings*

International Symposium on Interventional Radiology *(2nd : 1981 : Venice-Lido).*
Intervention radiology 2 : proceedings of the Second International Symposium on Interventional Radiology, Venice-Lido, Italy, September 27-October 1, 1981 / editors L. Oliva, J.A. Veiga-Pires. — Amsterdam ; Oxford : Excerpta Medica, 1982. — xiii,390p : ill ; 25cm. — (International congress series ; no.575)
Includes index
ISBN 90-219-0523-x : Unpriced B82-34482

616.07'57'024613 — Man. Diagnosis. Radiography — *For nursing*

Gunn, Christine. Guidelines on patient care in radiography. — Edinburgh : Churchill Livingstone, July 1982. — [160]p
ISBN 0-443-02545-2 (pbk) : £2.95 : CIP entry B82-12347

616.07'57'02854 — Medicine. Diagnosis. Radiography. Applications of digital computer systems — *Serials*

Computerized radiology : the international journal of radiological diagnosis using CT, NMR, PET, digital fluoroscopy, computer imaging : the official journal of the Computerized Tomography Society. — Vol.6, no.1 (Jan./Feb. 1982)-. — New York ; Oxford : Pergamon, 1982-. — v. : ill ; 28cm
Six issues yearly. — Continues: Computerized tomography
ISSN 0730-4862 = Computerized radiology : Unpriced B82-26137

616.07'57'0321 — Man. Diagnosis. Radiography — *Encyclopaedias*

Goldman, Myer. A radiographic index / Myer Goldman, David Cope. — 7th ed. — Bristol : John Wright, 1982. — x,99p ; 17cm
Previous ed.: 1978
ISBN 0-7236-0660-9 (pbk) : Unpriced : CIP rev. B82-17917

616.07'57'05 — Medicine. Radiology — *Serials*

Current radiology. — Vol.1-. — New York ; Chichester : Wiley, 1978-. — v. : ill ; 26cm
Annual. — Description based on: Vol.3
ISSN 0161-7818 = Current radiology : £40.70 B82-11153

Progress in medical radiation physics. — Vol.1-. — New York ; London : Plenum Press, 1982-. — v. : ill ; 24cm
Unpriced B82-26158

616.07'57'076 — Man. Diagnosis. Radiography — *Questions & answers*

Carter, P. H.. Objective tests in diagnostic radiography / P.H. Carter. — Edinburgh : Churchill Livingstone, 1982. — 80p ; 25cm
ISBN 0-443-02408-1 (pbk) : £2.25 : CIP rev. B81-36211

616.07'572 — Man. Diagnosis. Computerised tomography

Husband, Janet E.. Computed tomography of the body : a radiological and clinical approach / Janet E. Husband and Ian Kelsey Fry. — London : Macmillan, 1981. — x,222p : ill ; 26cm
Includes bibliographies and index
ISBN 0-333-25584-4 (cased) : Unpriced
ISBN 0-333-25585-2 (pbk) : Unpriced B82-23054

616.07'572 — Man. Diagnosis. Emission tomography. Applications of computer systems

Computed emission tomography. — Oxford : Oxford University Press, July 1982. — [500]p. — (Oxford medical publications)
ISBN 0-19-261347-2 : £30.00 : CIP entry B82-13231

616.07'572 — Man. Diagnosis. Radiography. Use of x-rays

Parfrey, P. S.. X-ray interpretation for the MRCP. — Edinburgh : Churchill Livingstone, Jan.1983. — [240]p
ISBN 0-443-02594-0 : £6.50 : CIP entry B82-37673

Simon, George. Clinical radiology. — 4th ed. — London : Butterworth Scientific, Feb.1983. — [288]p
Previous ed. published as: X-ray diagnosis for clinical students. 1975
ISBN 0-407-00224-3 : £22.50 : CIP entry B82-38283

616.07'572 — Man. Diagnosis. Radiography. Use of x-rays. Techniques

Eastman, Terry R.. Radiographic fundamentals and technique guide / Terry R. Eastman. — St. Louis ; London : C.V. Mosby, 1979. — ix,175p : ill ; 23cm
Includes index
ISBN 0-8016-1493-7 (pbk) : £10.50 B82-33559

616.07'572 — Man. Diagnosis. Tomography. Applications of digital computer systems

Computed tomography, ultrasound and x-ray : an integrated approach / edited by Albert A. Moss, Henry I. Goldberg. — New York ; London : Academic Press, c1980. — xi,564p : ill ; 29cm
ISBN 0-89352-055-1 : £50.80 B82-31852

616.07'575 — Man. Diagnosis. Radiography. Use of radioisotope scanning. Techniques

Principles of radionuclide emission imaging. — Oxford : Pergamon, Oct.1982. — [307]p
ISBN 0-08-027093-x : £12.50 : CIP entry
ISBN 0-08-026405-0 (set) : £250.00 B82-31283

616.07'575 — Man. Diagnosis. Radiography. Use of radioisotopes

Horton, P. W.. Radionuclide techniques in clinical investigation / P.W. Horton. — Bristol : Hilger in collaboration with the Hospital Physicists' Association, c1982. — xiv,170p : ill ; 22cm. — (Medical physics handbooks ; 12)
Bibliography: p164. — Includes index
ISBN 0-85274-503-6 : £13.95 : CIP rev. B82-09874

Radionuclide section scanning. — London : Chapman & Hall, Dec.1981. — [200]p
ISBN 0-412-23200-6 : £25.00 : CIP entry B81-31730

616.07'575 — Nuclear medicine

Clinical nuclear medicine. — London : Chapman & Hall, Oct.1982. — [650]p
ISBN 0-412-22040-7 : £35.00 : CIP entry B82-24473

Early, Paul J.. Textbook of nuclear medicine technology / Paul J. Early, Muhammad Abdel Razzak, D. Bruce Sodee. — 3rd ed. — St. Louis ; London : C.V. Mosby, 1979. — ix,691p : ill,forms ; 25cm
Previous ed.: 1975. — Ill on lining papers. — Includes bibliographies and index
ISBN 0-8016-1488-0 : £27.75 B82-33564

616.07'575 — Nuclear medicine — *Conference proceedings*

World Congress of Nuclear Medicine and Biology *(3rd : 1982 : Paris).* Nuclear medicine & biology advances. — Oxford : Pergamon, Oct.1982. — [3850]p
ISBN 0-08-026405-0 : £250.00 : CIP entry B82-33325

616.07'58 — Medicine. Diagnosis. Electron microscopy

Electron microscopy in human medicine / edited by Jan Vincents Johannessen. — New York ; London : McGraw-Hill
Vol.3: Infectious agents. — c1980. — 397p : ill ; 29cm
Includes bibliographies and index
ISBN 0-07-032503-0 : £49.95 : CIP rev. B80-06943

Electron microscopy in human medicine / edited by Jan Vincents Johannessen. — New York ; London : McGraw-Hill
Vol.4: Soft tissues, bones and joints. — c1981. — xxi,325p : ill ; 29cm
Includes index
ISBN 0-07-032504-9 : £49.95 : CIP rev. B81-09969

Electron microscopy in human medicine / edited by Jan Vincents Johannessen. — New York ; London : McGraw-Hill
Vol.5: Cardiovascular system, lymphoreticular and hematopoietic system. — c1980. — xix,501p : ill ; 29cm
Includes bibliographies and index
ISBN 0-07-032505-7 : £48.50 : CIP rev. B80-12373

Electron microscopy in human medicine / edited by Jan Vincents Johannessen. — New York ; London : McGraw-Hill
Vol.10: Endocrine organs. — c1981. — xx,215p : ill ; 29cm
Includes bibliographies and index
ISBN 0-07-032509-x : £29.50 : CIP rev. B80-18760

Electron microscopy in human medicine. — London : McGraw-Hill
Vol.11b: Special techniques and applications. — Sept.1982. — [256]p
ISBN 0-07-032524-3 : CIP entry B82-19087

616.07'582 — Medicine. Diagnosis. Use of cell markers

Cell markers / volume editor G. Jasmin. — Basel ; London : Karger, c1981. — xi,293p : ill ; 25cm. — (Methods and achievements in experimental pathology ; v.10)
Includes bibliographies and index
ISBN 3-8055-1736-x : £53.00 B82-09886

616.07'583 — Medicine. Diagnosis. Histology

Theory and practice of histological techniques / editors John D. Bancroft, Alan Stevens ; foreword by I.M.P. Dawson. — 2nd ed. — Edinburgh : Churchill Livingstone, 1982. — xiv,662p : ill ; 26cm
Previous ed.: 1977. — Includes bibliographies and index
ISBN 0-443-02006-x : £32.00 : CIP rev. B82-03577

616.07'583 — Medicine. Diagnosis. Needle biopsy

Percutaneous needle biopsy / edited by Jesus Zornoza. — Baltimore ; London : Williams & Wilkins, c1981. — xvi,207p : ill ; 26cm
Includes bibliographies and index
ISBN 0-683-09400-9 : Unpriced B82-26958

616.07'59 — Medicine. Post-mortem examination

Helpern, Milton. Autopsy / by Milton Helpern with Bernard Knight ; with a foreword by Keith Simpson. — London : W.H. Allen, 1982, c1977. — xii,273p,[4]p of plates : ill,ports ; 18cm. — (A Star book)
Originally published: New York : St. Martin's Press, 1977. — Includes index
ISBN 0-352-31188-6 (pbk) : £1.75 B82-39014

616.07'9 — Immunopathology — *Conference proceedings*

Advances in immunopathology / William O. Weigle, editor. — London : Edward Arnold, c1981. — xiv,352p : ill ; 24cm
Conference papers. — Includes index
ISBN 0-7131-4395-9 : £39.50 B82-22967

616.07'9 — Man. Diseases. Immunological aspects

Immunology of human infection. — New York ; London : Plenum Medical
Pt.1: Bacteria, mycoplasmae, chlamydiae and fungi / edited by André J. Nahmias and Richard J. O'Reilly. — c1981. — xxvii,651p : ill ; 27cm. — (Comprehensive immunology ; 8)
Includes bibliographies and index
ISBN 0-306-40257-2 : Unpriced B82-05266

616.07'9 — Man. Diseases. Immunological aspects *continuation*

Immunology of human infection. — New York ; London : Plenum medical, c1982
Pt.2: Viruses and parasites : immunodiagnosis and prevention of infectious diseases / edited by André J. Nahmias and Rihcard J. O'Reilly. — xxvii,601p : ill ; 26cm. — (Comprehensive immunology ; 9)
Includes bibliographies and index
ISBN 0-306-40258-0 : Unpriced B82-22018

616.07'9 — Man. Diseases. Immunological aspects — *Conference proceedings*

Immunological aspects of leprosy, tuberculosis and leishmaniasis : proceedings of a meeting held in Addis Ababa, Ethiopia, 27-30 October 1980 / editor David P. Humber ; conference committee Ayele Belehu ... [et al.]. — Amsterdam ; Oxford : Excerpta Medica, 1981. — xiii,312p : ill ; 25cm. — (International congress series ; no.574)
Includes index
ISBN 90-219-0522-1 : Unpriced
Also classified at 616.9'364079 ; 616.9'95079 ; 616.9'98079 B82-13454

616.07'9 — Man. Interferons — *Conference proceedings*

International Expert Meeting of the Deutsche Stiftung für Krebsforschung *(3rd : 1981 : Bonn).* Interferon : properties, mode of action, production, clinical application : proceedings of the 3rd International Expert Meeting of the Deutsche Stiftung für Krebsforschung, Bonn, March 13-16, 1981 / volume editors K. Munk and H. Kirchner. — Basel ; London : Karger, c1982. — ix,233p : ill ; 23cm. — (Beiträge zur Onkologie = Contributions to oncology ; v.11)
ISBN 3-8055-3482-5 (pbk) : £16.50
B82-40296

616.07'9 — Man. Interferons — *Serials*

Interferon. — Vol.3 (1981). — London : Academic Press, Dec.1981. — [150]p
ISBN 0-12-302252-5 : CIP entry B81-31001

Interferon. — Vol.4 (1982). — London : Academic Press, Dec.1982. — [220]p
ISBN 0-12-302253-3 : CIP entry B82-29880

616.07'9 — Man. Plasma. Complement

Recent trends in allergen and complement research / volume editor Paul Kallós ; contributors S. Ahlstedt ... [et al.]. — Basel ; London : Karger, c1982. — xiv,234p : ill ; 25cm. — (Progress in allergy ; v.30)
ISBN 3-8055-2580-x : £38.50
Primary classification 616.97 B82-24058

616.07'9 — Medicine. Immunology

Clinical aspects of immunology. — 4th ed. / edited by P.J. Lachmann, D.K. Peters. — Oxford : Blackwell Scientific, 1982. — 2v.(xvi,1751p) : ill ; 26cm
Previous ed.: / edited by P.G.H. Gell, R.P.A. Coombs, P.J. Lachmann. 1975. — In a slip-case. — Includes bibliographies and index
ISBN 0-632-00702-8 : £90.00 : CIP rev.
B81-34637

Playfair, J. H. L. Immunology at a glance / J.H.L. Playfair. — 2nd ed. — Oxford : Blackwell Scientific, 1982. — 35p : ill ; 28cm
Previous ed.: 1979. — Bibliography: 1p. — Includes index
ISBN 0-632-00805-9 (pbk) : Unpriced : CIP rev. B81-31646

Richter, Maxwell Asher. Clinical immunology : a physician's guide / Maxwell Asher Richter. — 2nd ed. — Baltimore ; London : Williams & Wilkins, c1982. — xviii,328p : ill ; 21cm
Previous ed.: published as A physician's guide to the theory and practice of clinical immunology. Ottawa : University of Ottawa Press, 1980. — Bibliography: p316-320. — Includes index
ISBN 0-683-07255-2 (pbk) : Unpriced
B82-16582

616.07'9'05 — Medicine. Immunology — *Serials*

Human lymphocyte differentiation. — Vol.1, no.1 (Jan.-Mar. 1981)-. — Eastbourne : W.B. Saunders, 1981-. — v. : ill ; 25cm
Quarterly
ISSN 0144-3909 = Human lymphocyte differentiation : £30.00 per year B82-09684

Recent advances in clinical immunology. — No.3. — Edinburgh : Churchill Livingstone, Feb.1983. — [337]p
ISBN 0-443-02641-6 (pbk) : £18.00 : CIP entry
ISSN 0140-6957 B82-36318

616.07'92 — Man. Histocompatibility gene complex. Human leucocyte antigen system

HLA antigens in clinical medicine and biology / edited by Soldano Ferrone, Emilio S. Curtoni, Sergio Gorini. — New York ; London : Garland STPM, c1979. — xii,256p : ill ; 24cm
Includes bibliographies and index
ISBN 0-8240-7051-8 : Unpriced B82-24163

616.07'95 — Man. Immune reactions

Cellular functions in immunity and inflammation / editors-in-chief Joost J. Oppenheim, David L. Rosenstreich, Michael Potter. — London : Edward Arnold, c1981. — xvii,479p : ill ; 27cm
Includes bibliographies and index
ISBN 0-7131-4396-7 : £29.50
Also classified at 616'.0473 B82-05066

616.07'95 — Man. Immune reactions. Microbiological aspects — *Conference proceedings*

Immunomodulation by microbial products and related synthetic compounds : proceedings of an international symposium, Osaka, July 27-29, 1981 / chief editors Yuichi Yamamura, Shozo Kotani ; advisory editors Ichiro Azuma, Akihide Koda, Tetsuo Shiba. — Amsterdam ; Oxford : Excerpta Medica, 1982. — xvi,562p : ill ; 25cm. — (International congress series ; no.563)
Includes index
ISBN 90-219-0563-9 : £53.53 B82-36633

Microbial perturbation of host defences / editors Francis O'Grady, Harry Smith. — London : Academic Press, 1981. — xii,254p : ill ; 24cm. — ([The Beecham colloquia] ; 3)
Includes bibliographies and index
ISBN 0-12-524750-8 : £14.80 : CIP rev.
B81-23873

616.079'5 — Man. Immune reactions. Role of antibodies

Chandra, Ranjit Kumar. Immunodeficiency disorders. — Edinburgh : Churchill Livingstone, Jan.1983. — [400]p
ISBN 0-443-02101-5 : £25.00 : CIP entry
B82-34594

616.07'95 — Man. Immune reactions. Role of antibodies — *Conference proceedings*

Receptors, antibodies and disease. — London : Pitman, Aug.1982. — [320]p. — (Ciba Foundation symposium ; 90)
Conference papers
ISBN 0-272-79654-9 : £22.50 : CIP entry
B82-15714

616.07'95 — Man. Immune reactions. Role of cytotoxic cells — *Conference proceedings*

International Workshop on Mechanisms in Cell-Mediated Cytotoxicity *(1st : 1981 : Carry-le-Rouet).* Mechanisms of cell-mediated cytotoxicity / [proceedings of the First International Workshop on Mechanisms in Cell-Mediated Cytotoxicity, held September 14-16, 1981, in Carry-le-Rouet, France] ; edited by William R. Clarke and Pierre Golstein. — New York ; London : Plenum, c1982. — xiii,597p : ill ; 26cm. — (Advances in experimental medicine and biology)
Includes index
ISBN 0-306-41012-5 : Unpriced B82-36412

616.07'95'0724 — Man. Immune reactions. Research. Use of laboratory animals

Animal models of immunological processes / edited by John B. Hay. — London : Academic Press, 1982. — xi,295p : ill ; 24cm
Includes bibliographies and index
ISBN 0-12-333520-5 : £21.20 : CIP rev.
B81-33869

616.08 — Man. Diseases. Psychophysiological aspects

Phenomenology and treatment of psychophysiological disorders / edited by William E. Fann ... [et al.]. — Lancaster : MTP, c1982. — 297p : ill ; 24cm
Includes index
ISBN 0-85200-589-x : £22.75 B82-17278

616.08 — Man. Diseases. Psychosomatic aspects

Neurological evaluation of the psychogenic patient / editors, W. Lynn Smith, Michael H. Hitchcock, Lavar G. Best. — New York ; London : SP Medical & Scientific, c1982. — 134p : ill ; 24cm
Includes bibliographies and index
£10.25 (corrected) B82-32900

616.08 — Man. Psychosomatic diseases

Biological and psychological basis of psychosomatic diseases. — Oxford : Pergamon, Dec.1982. — [304]p. — (Advances in the biosciences)
ISBN 0-08-029774-9 : £12.50 : CIP entry
B82-30596

Foundations of psychosomatics / edited by Margaret J. Christie and Peter G. Mellett. — Chichester : Wiley, c1981. — xi,428p : ill ; 24cm
Includes bibliographies and index
ISBN 0-471-27855-6 : £17.50 : CIP rev.
B81-27951

Medicine and psychiatry. — London : Pitman, Jan.1983. — [512]p
ISBN 0-272-79668-9 : £35.00 : CIP entry
B82-33717

The **Psychosomatic** approach to illness / editor Robert L. Gallon. — New York ; Oxford : Elsevier Biomedical, c1982. — xv,308p : ill,forms ; 24cm
Includes bibliographies and index
ISBN 0-444-00656-7 : Unpriced B82-34483

616'.09 — Man. Diseases — *Case studies*

Perlroth, Mark G. Fifty diseases, fifty diagnoses / Mark G. Perlroth, Douglas J. Weiland. — Chicago ; London : Year Book Medical, c1981. — x,336p : 1ill ; 23cm
Includes bibliographies and index
ISBN 0-8151-6661-3 (pbk) : £14.00
B82-18071

Spalton, David J. 100 case histories for the MRCP. — 2nd ed. — Edinburgh : Churchill Livingstone, Aug.1982. — [208]p
Previous ed.: 1976
ISBN 0-443-02140-6 (pbk) : £4.95 : CIP entry
B82-24335

616.1 — MAN. DISEASES OF CARDIOVASCULAR SYSTEM

616.1 — Man. Cardiovascular system. Diseases

The **Heart,** arteries and veins / editor-in-chief J. Willis Hurst ; editors R. Bruce Logue ... [et al.]. — 5th ed. — New York ; London : McGraw-Hill, c1982. — xxvii,1953,60p,8p of plates : ill(some col.),forms ; 29cm
Previous ed.: 1978. — Also available in 2v. set. — Includes index
ISBN 0-07-031481-0 : £52.50
ISBN 0-07-079033-7 (set) : Unpriced
ISBN 0-07-031483-7 (v.1) : Unpriced
ISBN 0-07-031484-5 (v.2) : Unpriced
B82-17164

Hurst, the heart : pretest self assessment and review / edited by J. Willis Hurst and and John W. Hurst, Jr. — 2nd ed. — New York ; London : McGraw-Hill Health Professions Division, c1982. — xiii,224p ; 28cm + CME examination(ix,21p : 1ill ; 28cm)
To be used in conjunction with The Heart, arteries and veins. 5th ed.. — Previous ed.: c1978. — CME answer sheet and mailing envelope as inserts. — Bibliography: p209-210. — Includes index
ISBN 0-07-050993-x (pbk) : Unpriced
ISBN 0-07-050992-1 (CME examination) : Unpriced B82-34048

616.1 — Man. Cardiovascular system. Diseases — *Conference proceedings*

Topics in cardiovascular medicine / [condensed proceedings of a symposium organized by CIBA and held on September 14th 1979, at the Hôpital Necker, Paris] ; edited by R.W. Elsdon-Dew, G.F.B. Birdwood and C.A.S. Wink. — London : Royal Society of Medicine, 1980. — ix,46p : ill ; 25cm. — (Royal Society of Medicine. International congress and symposium series, ISSN 0142-2367 ; no.34)
Includes bibliographies
ISBN 0-12-791156-1 (pbk) : £4.80 : CIP rev. B80-18762

616.1′0024613 — Man. Cardiovascular system. Diseases — *Questions & answers — For nursing*

The **Patient** with a cardiovascular disorder. — London : Harper & Row, Oct.1982. — [96]p. — (Patient related multiple choice questions)
ISBN 0-06-318232-7 (pbk) : £2.25 : CIP entry B82-28432

616.1′0024616 — Man. Cardiovascular system — *For physiotherapy*

Cash′s textbook of chest, heart and vascular disorders for physiotherapists. — 3rd ed. — London : Faber, Jan.1983. — [488]p
Previous ed.: 1979
ISBN 0-571-18078-7 (pbk) : CIP entry
Also classified at 616.2′0024616 B82-32452

616.1′005 — Man. Cardiovascular system. Diseases — *Serials*

Cardiovascular review. — 1979-. — New York ; London : Academic Press, 1979-. — v. : ill ; 24cm
Irregular. — Description based on: 1982 issue
ISSN 0271-4779 = Cardiovascular review : Unpriced B82-29057

616.1′0072 — Man. Cardiovascular system. Diseases. Research

Success in heart research. — London (57 Gloucester Place, W1H 4DH) : British Heart Foundation, 1980. — 11p ; 18cm. — (Heart research series ; no.2)
(unbound) B82-19761

616.1′05 — Man. Cardiovascular system. Diseases. Prevention. Drug therapy — *Study examples: Men, 45-59 years — Study regions: Lithuania. Kaunas*

The **Kaunas** Rotterdam intervention study : behavioural and operational components on health intervention programmes / editors I.S. Glasunov ... [et al.]. — Amsterdam ; Oxford : Elsevier/North-Holland Biomedical, 1981. — 330p in various pagings : ill ; 25cm
Bibliography: pD1-D12
ISBN 0-444-80386-6 (pbk) : £27.23
Also classified at 616.1′05 B82-13440

616.1′05 — Man. Cardiovascular system. Diseases. Prevention. Drug therapy — *Study examples: Men 45-59 years — Study regions: Netherlands. Rotterdam*

The **Kaunas** Rotterdam intervention study : behavioural and operational components on health intervention programmes / editors I.S. Glasunov ... [et al.]. — Amsterdam ; Oxford : Elsevier/North-Holland Biomedical, 1981. — 330p in various pagings : ill ; 25cm
Bibliography: pD1-D12
ISBN 0-444-80386-6 (pbk) : £27.23
Primary classification 616.1′05 B82-13440

616.1′06 — Man. Cardiovascular system. Behaviour therapy

Surwit, Richard S.. Behavioral approaches to cardiovascular disease / Richard S. Surwit, Redford B. Williams, David Shapiro. — New York ; London : Academic Press, 1982. — xiv,233p : ill ; 24cm. — (Behavioral medicine)
Includes bibliographies and index
ISBN 0-12-677480-3 : £16.20 B82-30012

616.1′07 — Man. Cardiovascular system. Cells. Membranes. Effects of diseases. Physiological aspects — *Conference proceedings*
Argenteuil Symposium *(5th : 1980 : Waterloo)*. Cell membrane in function and dysfunction of vascular tissue : proceedings of the Fifth Argenteuil Symposium held under the auspices of the Fondation cardiologique Princesse Liliane in Waterloo, Belgium, 30 June and 1 July 1980 / editors T. Godfraind, P. Meyer. — Amsterdam ; Oxford : Elsevier-North-Holland Biomedical, 1981. — xxi,270p : ill,1port ; 25cm
Includes index
ISBN 0-444-80316-5 : £37.88 B82-01640

616.1′071 — Man. Cardiovascular system. Diseases. Role of diet
Holmes, David, *1927-*. Save yourself and your family from heart attack. — Emsworth (1 Western Parade, Emsworth, Hants. PO10 7HS) : D. Holmes ; Chichester : Wiley, distributor Aug.1982. — [56]p
ISBN 0-471-90041-9 : £2.50 : CIP entry B82-25100

616.1′07543 — Man. Cardiovascular system. Diagnosis. Ultrasonography — *Conference proceedings*
Cardiovascular diagnosis by ultrasound : transesophageal, computerized, contrast, doppler echocardiography / edited by Peter Hanrath, Walter Bleifeld and Jacques Souquet. — The Hague ; London : Nijhoff, 1982. — xiii,320p : ill ; 25cm. — (Developments in cardiovascular medicine ; v.22)
Conference papers
ISBN 90-247-2692-1 : Unpriced B82-40147

616.1′07575 — Man. Cardiovascular system. Diagnosis. Radiography. Use of radioisotope scanning
Ennis, Joseph T.. Vascular radionuclide imaging : a clinical atlas. — London : Heyden, May 1982. — [232]p
ISBN 0-85602-084-2 B82-10693

Ennis, Joseph T.. Vascular radionuclide imaging. — Chichester : Wiley, Jan.1983. — [256]p
ISBN 0-471-25670-6 : £39.00 : CIP entry B82-32425

616.1′07575 — Man. Cardiovascular system. Diagnosis. Use of radioisotopes
Clinical nuclear cardiology / edited by Daniel S. Berman, Dean T. Mason. — New York ; London : Grune & Stratton, c1981. — xiii,494p : ill ; 27cm. — (Clinical cardiology monographs)
Includes index
ISBN 0-8089-1356-5 : £32.40 B82-04218

616.1′1 — Man. Heart. Endocardium. Bacterial endocarditis — *Conference proceedings*
The **Nature** and prevention of bacterial endocarditis : proceedings of a symposium held at the Charing Cross Hospital, London, UK, 16 November 1981 / edited by R.A. Cawson. — Oxford : Medicine Publishing Foundation, 1982. — 41p ; 24cm. — (The Medicine Publishing Foundation symposium series, ISSN 0260-0242 ; 3)
ISBN 0-906817-19-6 (pbk) : Unpriced : CIP rev. B82-06063

616.1′1 — Man. Heart. Endocardium. Bacterial endocarditis. Therapy — *Conference proceedings*
Treatment of infective endocarditis / edited by Alan L. Bisno. — New York ; London : Grune & Stratton, c1981. — xvii,340p : ill,1port ; 24cm
Conference papers. — Includes index
ISBN 0-8089-1450-2 : £22.80 B82-18677

616.1′1 — Man. Heart. Pericardium
Shabetai, Ralph. The pericardium / Ralph Shabetai. — New York ; London : Grune & Stratton, c1981. — xii,432p : ill,facsims,ports ; 27cm. — (Clinical cardiology monographs)
Includes index
ISBN 0-8089-1402-2 : £29.40 B82-29983

616.1′2 — Cardiology
Julian, Desmond G.. Cardiology. — 4th ed. — London : Baillière Tindall, Oct.1982. — [350]p. — (Concise medical textbooks)
Previous ed.: 1978
ISBN 0-7020-0953-9 (pbk) : £7.50 : CIP entry B82-23209

616.1′2 — Man. Heart. Conduction disorders — *Conference proceedings*

Alboni, Paolo. Intraventricular conduction disturbances / by Paolo Alboni. — The Hague ; London : Nijhoff, 1981. — xii,397p : ill ; 25cm. — (Developments in cardiovascular medicine ; v.12)
Includes index
ISBN 90-247-2483-x : Unpriced B82-03454

616.1′2 — Man. Heart. Conduction disorders. Diagnosis

Davies, M. J.. The conduction system of the heart. — London : Butterworth, Sept.1982. — [340]p
ISBN 0-407-00133-6 : £35.00 : CIP entry B82-19212

616.1′2 — Man. Heart. Diseases

The **Heart** / editor J. Willis Hurst. — New York ; London : McGraw-Hill, c1981. — xi,290p : ill ; 27cm. — (Update ; 5)
Includes index
ISBN 0-07-031495-0 : £21.95 B82-02326

The **Heart** and its problems : a layman′s guide. — London (102 Gloucester Place, W1H 4DH) : British Heart Foundation, c1980 (1982 [printing]). — 16p : ill(some col.) ; 18cm. — (Heart research series ; no.11)
Cover title
Unpriced (pbk) B82-40599

Hunter, Alastair. The heart : what it does; how it can go wrong; how to keep it healthy / by Alastair Hunter. — Kingswood : Elliot Right Way, c1982. — 159p : ill ; 18cm. — (Paperfronts)
Includes index
ISBN 0-7160-0676-6 (pbk) : £0.75 B82-23918

Oram, Samuel. Clinical heart disease / Samuel Oram. — 2nd ed. — London : Heinemann Medical, 1981. — viii,853p : ill ; 26cm
Previous ed.: 1971. — Includes bibliographies and index
ISBN 0-433-24201-9 : Unpriced B82-08638

Textbook of clinical cardiology / [edited by] Emanuel Goldberger. — St. Louis ; London : Mosby, 1982. — xvi,1069p : ill ; 25cm
Includes bibliographies and index
ISBN 0-8016-1864-9 : £59.00 B82-16568

Wharton, Christopher F. P.. Problems in cardiology / Christopher F.P. Wharton. — Lancaster : MTP, 1981. — 158p : ill ; 24cm. — (Problems in practice series)
Includes index
ISBN 0-85200-277-7 : £7.95 B82-02827

616.1′2 — Man. Heart. Diseases — *For patients*

Ross, Donald N.. Surgery and your heart. — Beaconsfield : Beaconsfield Publishers, Apr.1982. — [80]p
ISBN 0-906584-07-8 (pbk) : £3.50 : CIP entry B82-05782

616.1′2 — Man. Heart. Diseases — *Polish texts*

Dzikowski, Włodzimierz. Jak dbać o swoje serce / Włodzimierz Dzikowski. — Londyn : Polska Fundacja Kulturalna, 1981. — 174p ; 22cm
Includes index
Unpriced (pbk) B82-05881

616.1′2 — Man. Heart. Ventricles. Septum. Congenital abnormalities

The **Ventricular** septum of the heart / edited by Arnold C.G. Wenink, Arentje Oppenheimer-Dekker, André J. Moulaert. — The Hague ; London : Leiden University Press, 1981. — xii,238p : ill ; 25cm. — (Boerhaave series for postgraduate medical education ; v.21)
Includes index
ISBN 90-602-1486-2 : Unpriced B82-12046

616.1′2′0024613 — Man. Heart. Diseases — *For nursing*

Comprehensive cardiac care : a text for nurses, physicians and other health practitioners / Kathleen G. Andreoli ... [et al.]. — 4th ed. — St Louis ; London : Mosby, 1979. — viii,398p : ill ; 26cm
Previous ed.: 1975. — Includes bibliographies and index
ISBN 0-8016-0256-4 (pbk) : £12.00 B82-38660

616.1′2′0024613 — Medicine. Cardiology — *For nursing*

Thompson, David R.. Cardiac nursing / David R. Thompson ; with a foreword by Pat Ashworth. — London : Baillière Tindall, 1982. — viii,286p : ill ; 20cm. — (Nurses' aids series. Special interest text)
Includes bibliographies and index
ISBN 0-7020-0900-8 (pbk) : £7.50 : CIP rev. B82-06937

616.1′2′005 — Medicine. Cardiology — *Serials*

Cardiology. — 1. — London : Butterworth Scientific, June 1982. — [320]p. — (Butterworths international medical reviews)
ISBN 0-407-02266-x : £15.00 : CIP entry
ISSN 0260-0064 B82-11294

616.1′2′00904 — Medicine. Cardiology, *1895-1980* — *Conference proceedings*

History and perspectives of cardiology : catheterization, angiography, surgery and concepts of circular control / edited by H.A. Snellen, A.J. Dunning and A.C. Arntzenius. — The Hague ; London : Leiden University Press, c1981. — xii,204p : ill,facsims,ports ; 25cm
Conference papers. — Includes bibliographies
ISBN 90-602-1480-3 : Unpriced B82-00475

616.1′2025 — Man. Heart. Emergency treatment

Goldberger, Emanuel. Treatment of cardiac emergencies / Emanuel Goldberger ; Chapter 13 ... by Myron W. Wheat, Jr. — 3rd ed. — St. Louis ; London : Mosby, 1982. — ix,416p : ill ; 24cm
Previous ed.: 1977. — Includes bibliographies and index
ISBN 0-8016-1857-6 (pbk) : £21.50 B82-31873

616.1′2028 — Man. Heart. Diseases. Intensive care

Intensive care of the heart and lungs : a text for nurses and other staff / J.-M. Neutze ... [et al.] ; foreword by Sir Brian Barratt-Boyes. — 3rd ed. — Oxford : Blackwell Scientific, 1982. — xi,324p : ill ; 22cm
Previous ed.: 1978. — Bibliography: p311-312. — Includes index
ISBN 0-632-00925-x (pbk) : £7.50 : CIP rev.
Also classified at 616.2′00428 B82-00190

616.1′2043 — Man. Heart. Congenital abnormalities. Diagnosis. Echocardiography

Gussenhoven, Elma J.. Congenital heart disease. — Edinburgh : Churchill Livingstone, Dec.1982. — [304]p. — (Modern pediatric cardiology)
ISBN 0-443-02262-3 : £35.00 : CIP entry B82-29800

616.1′2043 — Man. Heart. Congenital diseases. Pathology

Becker, Anton E.. Pathology of congenital heart disease / Anton E. Becker, Robert H. Anderson. — London : Butterworths, 1981. — xii,498p : ill ; 25cm. — (Postgraduate pathology series)
Includes bibliographies and index
ISBN 0-407-00137-9 : Unpriced : CIP rev. B81-23918

616.1′205 — Man. Heart. Diseases. Prevention

Heart disease and your lifestyle / [edited by Eileen Lloyd]. — Aylesbury : Rodale, 1982. — 46p ; 18cm. — (Prevention health guides)
ISBN 0-87857-406-9 (pbk) : Unpriced B82-36763

616.1′20624 — Heart disease victims. Rehabilitation. Physical activities

Cardiac rehabilitation / edited by Louis R. Amundsen. — New York ; Edinburgh : Churchill Livingstone, 1981. — xii,170p : ill,forms ; 25cm. — (Clinics in physical therapy ; v.1)
Includes index
ISBN 0-443-08147-6 : £11.50 B82-11849

616.1′207 — Man. Heart. Pathology

Olsen, E. G. J.. The pathology of the heart / E.G.J. Olsen. — 2nd ed. — London : Macmillan, 1980. — xii,402p : ill ; 26cm
Previous ed.: New York : Intercontinental Medical, 1973. — Includes bibliographies and index
ISBN 0-333-24265-3 : £35.00 : CIP rev. B80-08779

616.1′2071 — Man. Heart. Diseases. Role of diet — *Conference proceedings*

American College of Nutrition. *Meeting (19th : 1978 : Bloomington, Minn.).* Nutrition and heart disease / [proceedings of the 19th annual meeting of the American College of Nutrition] ; edited by Herbert K. Naito. — Lancaster : M.T.P. Press, c1982. — 356p : ill,1form ; 24cm. — (Monographs of the American College of Nutrition ; v.5)
Includes bibliographies and index
ISBN 0-85200-583-0 : £23.50 B82-39878

616.1′2075 — Man. Heart. Diagnosis

Winwood, R. S.. Essentials of clinical diagnosis in cardiology / Robert S. Winwood. — London : Edward Arnold, 1981. — ix,269p : ill ; 23cm
Bibliography: p258-259. — Includes index
ISBN 0-7131-4388-6 (pbk) : £11.00 : CIP rev. B81-12858

616.1′20754 — Man. Heart. Ambulatory monitoring — *Conference proceedings*

ISAM-GENT-1981. — London : Academic Press, Apr.1982. — [700]p
Conference papers
ISBN 0-12-672360-5 : CIP entry B82-08428

616.1′20754 — Man. Heart. Diagnosis. Catheterisation

A Manual of practical central venous catheterization and parenteral nutrition. — Bristol : J. Wright, Jan.1983. — [288]p
ISBN 0-7236-0549-1 : £15.00 : CIP entry B82-32629

616.1′20754 — Man. Heart. Diagnosis. Exercise testing — *Conference proceedings*

Prognostic values of exercise testing and drug effects on the exercise ECG : proceedings of the symposium of the Working Group on Exercise Physiology, Physiopathology and Electrocardiography, Conference of the European Society of Cardiology, Vienna, April 2-4, 1981 / editors F. Kaindl and M. Niederberger. — Basel ; London : Karger, 1981. — v,214p : ill ; 26cm
Cardiology, v.68, Supplement 2, 1981. — Includes bibliographies and index
ISBN 3-8055-3437-x (pbk) : Unpriced B82-19498

616.1′20754 — Man. Heart. Diagnosis. Non-invasive techniques

Benchimol, Alberto. Non-invasive diagnostic techniques in cardiology / Alberto Benchimol. — 2nd ed. — Baltimore ; London : Williams & Wilkins, c1981. — xxi,547p : ill ; 23cm
Previous ed.: 1977. — Includes bibliographies and index
ISBN 0-683-00523-5 : Unpriced B82-08063

616.1′207543 — Man. Heart. Diagnosis. Echocardiography

Cardiac ultrasound workbook : M-mode and two-dimensional echocardiography / [edited by] James V. Talano. — New York ; London : Grune & Stratton, c1982. — ix,243p : ill ; 29cm
Bibliography: p208-219. — Includes index
ISBN 0-8089-1437-5 : £13.00 B82-39092

Diagnostic echocardiography / edited by Joseph W. Linhart, Claude R. Joyner. — St. Louis, Mo. ; London : Mosby, 1982. — xi,373p : ill ; 29cm
Includes index
ISBN 0-8016-3042-8 : £39.00 B82-22842

616.1′207543 — Man. Heart. Diagnosis. Echocardiography — *Serials*

Echocardiography. — 1-. — Edinburgh : Churchill Livingstone, 1982-. — v. : ill ; 24cm
ISSN 0263-5453 = Echocardiography : £22.00 B82-27661

616.1′207543′05 — Man. Heart. Diagnosis. Echocardiography — *Serials*

Echocardiography. — 1. — Edinburgh : Churchill Livingstone, May 1982. — [328]p
Conference papers
ISBN 0-443-02492-8 : £22.00 : CIP entry B82-24323

616.1′207547 — Man. Heart. Cardiac output. Measurement. Electrical impedance techniques

Mohapatra, Surya. Non-invasive cardiovascular monitoring by electrical impedance technique. — London : Pitman Medical, July 1981. — [304]p
ISBN 0-272-79612-3 : £26.00 : CIP entry B81-13903

616.1′207547 — Man. Heart. Diagnosis. Electrocardiography

Schamroth, Leo. An introduction to electrocardiography / by Leo Schamroth. — 6th ed. — Oxford : Blackwell Scientific, 1982. — xiv,317p : ill ; 24cm
Previous ed.: 1976. — Includes bibliographies and index
ISBN 0-632-00973-x (pbk) : £7.80 : CIP rev. B82-12145

616.1′207547 — Man. Heart. Diagnosis. Electrocardiography — *Conference proceedings*

International Congress on Electrocardiology *(7th : 1980 : Lisbon).* New frontiers of electrocardiology : proceedings of the 7th international congress on electrocardiology, Lisbon, June 1980 / edited by F. de Padua and P.W. Macfarlane. — Chichester : Research Studies Press, c1981. — xix,538p,[2]p of plates : ill(some col.) ; 24cm
Includes index
ISBN 0-471-10041-2 : £27.50 : CIP rev. B81-18058

Models and measurements of the cardiac electric field / [proceedings of the Satellite Symposium at the twenty-eighth International Congress of Physiological Sciences on the Cardiac Electric Field, its Measurement and Modeling, held July 8-11, 1980 in Dresden, German Democratic Republic] ; edited by E. Schubert. — New York ; London : Plenum, c1982. — x,232p : ill ; 26cm
Includes bibliographies and index
ISBN 0-306-41011-7 : Unpriced B82-38661

616.1′207572 — Man. Heart. Diagnosis. Radiography. Use of x-rays

Daves, Marvin L.. Cardiac roentgenology : shadows of the heart / Marvin L. Daves. — Chicago ; London : Year Book Medical, c1981. — xiv,594p : ill ; 24cm
Includes index
ISBN 0-8151-2323-x : £55.75 B82-18070

616.1′22 — Man. Heart. Angina pectoris

What is angina? : explanation and advice for the patient who has been told he has angina. — Rev. & repr. — London : British Heart Foundation, 1981. — 9p ; 18cm. — (Heart research series ; no.4)
Previous ed.: 197-?
Unpriced (unbound) B82-11394

616.1′23 — Man. Heart. Coronary arteries. Diseases

The Coronary artery / edited by Stanley Kalsner. — London : Croom Helm, c1982. — 775p : ill ; 25cm
Includes bibliographies and index
ISBN 0-7099-1503-9 : £45.00 B82-37775

616.1'23 — Man. Heart. Coronary diseases

Coronary artery disease today : diagnosis, surgery and prognosis : proceedings of an international symposium, held in Utrecht, 25-27 May, 1981 / editors A.V.G. Bruschke, G. van Herpen, F.E.E. Vermeulen. — Amsterdam ; Oxford : Excerpta Medica, 1982. — xi,455p : ill ; 25cm. — (International congress series ; no.557)
Includes index
ISBN 90-219-0503-5 : £48.73
ISBN 0-444-90229-5 (Elsevier) : Unpriced
B82-18378

Shillingford, J. P.. Coronary heart disease : the facts / J.P. Shillingford. — Oxford : Oxford University Press, 1981 (1982 [printing]). — 99p,[2]p of plates : ill ; 20cm. — (Oxford paperbacks)
Includes index
ISBN 0-19-286028-3 (pbk) : £2.50 : CIP rev.
B82-15677

616.1'23 — Man. Heart. Coronary diseases. Effects of diet — *Conference proceedings*

Diet and coronary heart disease : report of a conference at the Zoological Society, London May 1980 / chairman: Malcolm Carruthers. — Tunbridge Wells (2 Nevill St., Tunbridge Wells, Kent) : Butter Information Council, [1981]. — 51p ; 21cm
Unpriced (pbk) B82-11039

616.1'2305 — Man. Heart. Coronary diseases. Prevention

Prevention and health : avoiding heart attacks. — London : H.M.S.O., 1981. — 69p : ill,1 map ; 21cm
At head of title: Department of Health and Social Security. — Bibliography: p68-69
ISBN 0-11-320771-9 (pbk) : £1.50 B82-08167

616.1'2305 — Man, Heart. Coronary diseases. Prevention. Role of diet & exercise

Passwater, Richard. Supernutrition for healthy hearts. — Wellingborough : Thorsons, June 1981. — [416]p
ISBN 0-7225-0690-2 (pbk) : £4.50 : CIP entry
B81-09481

616.1'2306 — Man. Heart. Coronary diseases. Therapy

[The Heart patient]. Handbook of cardiac care / K.P. Ball ... [et al.]. — Lancaster : MTP, c1981. — vii,232p : ill ; 23cm
Originally published: London : Update, 1981. — Includes index
ISBN 0-85200-460-5 : £11.95 : CIP rev.
B82-17959

616.1'23061 — Man. Heart. Coronary diseases. Drug therapy — *Practical information*

Modern heart medicines. — London (57 Gloucester Place, W1H 4DH) : British Heart Foundation, c1980. — 9p ; 18cm. — (Heart research series ; no.6)
Unpriced (unbound) B82-19763

616.1'23071 — Man. Heart. Coronary diseases. Effects of diet

Yellowlees, Walter. The experience of a general practitioner : Stirling Conference, May 1980 / Walter Yellowlees. — [Scotland] : [W. Yellowlees], 1980. — 5p ; 21cm
Cover title
Unpriced B82-35024

616.1'23071 — Man. Heart. Coronary diseases. Effects of tobacco smoking

Smoking and your heart. — London (102 Gloucester Place, W1H 4DH) : British Heart Foundation, c1980 (1982 [printing]). — 8p ; 18cm. — (Heart research series ; no.10)
Unpriced (unbound) B82-33001

616.1'23071 — Man. Heart. Coronary diseases. Role of diet

Diet and your heart. — London (57 Gloucester Place, W1H 4DH) : British Heart Foundation, 1980 (1981 printing). — 10p : ill ; 18cm. — (Heart research series ; no.7)
Unpriced (unbound) B82-19762

616.1'232 — Man. Heart. Arteries. Atherosclerosis *related to* **hyperlipoproteinaemia** — *Conference proceedings*

International Symposium on Lipoproteins and Coronary Atherosclerosis *(1981 : Lugano)*. Lipoproteins and coronary atherosclerosis : proceedings of the International Symposium on Lipoproteins and Coronary Atherosclerosis held in Lugano, Switzerland, October 1-3, 1981 / editors: G. Noseda ... [et al.]. — Amsterdam ; Oxford : Elsevier Biomedical, 1982. — xi,450p : ill ; 25cm. — (Symposia of the Giovanni Lorenzini foundation ; v.13)
Includes index
ISBN 0-444-80408-0 : Unpriced
Also classified at 616.3'99 B82-25698

616.1'237 — Man. Heart. Muscles. Infarction — *Conference proceedings*

Myocardial ischaemia and protection. — Edinburgh : Churchill Livingston, Jan.1983. — [320]p
Conference papers
ISBN 0-443-02896-6 : £29.00 : CIP entry
B82-36317

616.1'237 — Man. Heart. Muscles. Infarction. Measurement & treatment

Myocardial infarction : measurement and intervention / edited by Galen S. Wagner. — The Hague ; London : Nijhoff, 1982. — xiii,551p : ill ; 25cm. — (Developments in cardiovascular medicine ; v.14)
Includes index
ISBN 90-247-2513-5 : Unpriced B82-29462

616.1'237'0019 — Heart muscle infarction patients. Psychological problems — *Conference proceedings*

Meeting on Psychological Problems before and after Myocardial Infarction *(1981 : Mas d'Artigny)*. Psychological problems before and after myocardial infarction : Meeting on Psychological Infarction, Mas d'Artigny, June 10-13, 1981 / volume editor H. Denolin. — Basel ; London : Karger, c1982. — vi,155p : ill ; 25cm. — (Advances in cardiology ; v.29)
ISBN 3-8055-3424-8 : £28.50 B82-21670

616.1'24 — Man. Heart. Myocardium. Diseases

Myocardial infarction. — Edinburgh : Churchill Livingstone, Apr.1982. — [320]p. — (International seminars in cardiovascular medicine)
ISBN 0-443-02056-6 : £16.00 : CIP entry
B82-03578

616.1'25 — Man. Heart. Valves. Diseases

Davies, M. J.. Pathology of cardiac valves / M.J. Davies. — London : Butterworths, 1980. — 180p : ill ; 24cm. — (Postgraduate pathology series)
Includes bibliographies and index
ISBN 0-407-00179-4 : £17.50 : CIP rev.
B80-36109

616.1'28 — Man. Heart. Arrhythmia

Harris, Celia C.. A primer of cardiac arrhythmias : a self-instructional programm / Celia C. Harris. — St. Louis ; London : Mosby, 1979. — xi,112p : ill ; 26cm
Template in pocket. — Bibliography: p112
ISBN 0-8016-2070-8 (spiral) : £8.00
B82-28171

616.1'28061 — Man. Heart. Arrhythmia. Drug therapy — *Conference proceedings*

Prognosis and pharmacotherapy of life : threatening arrhythmias / [proceedings of an international symposium sponsored by the Janssen Research Foundation and by the University of Mainz at the Hilton Hotel Mainz, on 12th and 13th December, 1980] ; edited by E. Jähnchen, Th. Meinertz and G. Towse. — London : Royal Society of Medicine, 1981. — xiv,216p : ill ; 25cm. — (Royal Society of Medicine. International symposium series, ISSN 0142-2367 ; no.49)
Includes bibliographies
ISBN 0-12-792161-0 (pbk) : Unpriced
B82-11403

Prognosis and pharmacotherapy of life-threatening arrhythmias. — London : Academic Press, Nov.1981. — [250]p. — (International congress and symposium series / Royal Society of Medicine ; no.49)
Conference papers
ISBN 0-12-794635-7 (pbk) : CIP entry
B81-30340

616.1'2807 — Man. Heart. Arrhythmia. Electrophysiology — *Conference proceedings*

Cardiac electrophysiology today. — London : Academic Press, Dec.1982. — [580]p
Conference papers
ISBN 0-12-478150-0 : CIP entry B82-29886

616.1'29025 — Man. Heart. Heart failure. Emergency treatment

Huszar, Robert J.. Emergency cardiac care / Robert J. Huszar. — 2nd ed. — Bowie ; London : Brady, c1982. — 442p : ill(some col.) ; 28cm
Previous ed.: 1974. — Includes index
ISBN 0-87619-863-9 (pbk) : Unpriced
B82-28422

616.1'3 — Man. Blood vessels. Diseases

Vascular diseases : current controversies / [edited by] Philip N. Sawyer, Richard M. Stillman. — New York : Appleton-Century-Crofts ; London : Prentice-Hall, c1981. — xiii,251p : ill ; 24cm
Includes bibliographies and index
ISBN 0-8385-9372-0 : £18.40 B82-07549

Vascular diseases : a concise guide to diagnosis, management, pathogenesis, and prevention / edited by Sandor A. Friedman. — Boston, Mass. ; Bristol : John Wright, 1982. — xii,576p : ill ; 24cm
Includes bibliographies and index
ISBN 0-7236-7000-5 : Unpriced B82-34896

616.1'3 — Man. Blood vessels. Lesions

Variceal bleeding. — Tunbridge Wells : Pitman, Sept.1982. — 1v.
Conference papers
ISBN 0-272-79683-2 (pbk) : £25.00 : CIP entry
B82-29115

616.1'3 — Man. Ischaemia — *Conference proceedings*

Symposium on Induced Skeletal Muscle Ischemia in Man *(1980 : Linköping)*. Induced skeletal muscle ischemia in man : Symposium on Induced Skeletal Muscle Ischemia in Man, Linköping, November 6-7, 1980 / editor D.H. Lewis. — Basel ; London : Karger, c1982. — iv,180p : ill ; 22cm
Includes bibliographies and index
ISBN 3-8055-3427-2 (pbk) : £33.50
B82-28704

616.1'3 — Man. Ischaemia. Physiological aspects

Pathophysiology of shock, anoxia, and ischemia / editors R. Adams Cowley, Benjamin F. Trump. — Baltimore ; London : Williams & Wilkins, c1982. — xvi,710p : ill ; 29cm
Includes bibliographies and index
ISBN 0-683-02149-4 : Unpriced
Also classified at 616.1'5 ; 617'.21 B82-19367

616.1'3025 — Man. Blood vessels. Emergency treatment

Vascular emergencies / [edited by] Henry Haimovici. — New York : Appleton-Century-Crofts ; London : Prentice-Hall, c1982. — xvi,634p : ill ; 27cm
Includes index
ISBN 0-8385-9361-5 : £43.90 B82-28192

616.1'307 — Man. Microcirculatory system. Pathology

Raynaud features, acrocyanosis, cryoimmunoproteins / volume editor E. Davis. — Basel ; London : Karger, c1982. — viii,114p : ill ; 25cm. — (Advances in microcirculation ; v.10)
Includes index
ISBN 3-8055-2790-x : Unpriced B82-40349

616.1'3071 — Man. Vascular diseases. Role of hormones

Hormones and vascular disease. — Tunbridge Wells : Pitman Medical, June 1981. — [360]p
ISBN 0-272-79622-0 : £20.00 : CIP entry
B81-13558

616.1'3075 — Man. Blood vessels. Diagnosis

Investigation of vascular disorders / edited by Andrew N. Nicolaides and James S.T. Yao. — New York ; Edinburgh : Churchill Livingstone, 1981. — 635p : ill ; 26cm
Includes bibliographies and index
ISBN 0-443-08020-8 : £60.00 B82-08748

616.1'30754 — Man. Blood vessels. Diagnosis. Non-invasive techniques

Noninvasive diagnostic techniques in vascular disease / edited by Eugene F. Bernstein ; associate editors Robert W. Barnes ... [et al.]. — 2nd ed. — St. Louis ; London : Mosby, 1982. — xiii,626p,[4]p of plates : ill(some col.) ; 28cm
Previous ed.: 1978. — Includes bibliographies and index
ISBN 0-8016-0807-4 : £54.75 B82-22922

616.1'307572 — Man. Blood vessels. Diagnosis. Angiography

Pioneers in angiography : the Portuguese School of angiography / edited by J.A. Veiga-Pires and Ronald G. Grainger. — Lancaster : MTP, c1982. — 131p : ill,1facsim,1port ; 22cm
Translation and revision of 2nd Portuguese ed. of: Escola Portuguese de Angiografia. — Bibliography: p101-127. — Includes index
ISBN 0-85200-448-6 : £9.95 B82-13380

616.1'307572 — Man. Blood vessels. Diagnosis. Digital subtraction angiography

Digital subtraction arteriography : an application of computerized fluoroscopy / [edited by] Charles A. Mistretta ... [et al.]. — Chicago ; London : Yearbook Medical, c1982. — xi,164p : ill ; 26cm
Conference proceedings. — Includes index
ISBN 0-8151-5915-3 : £26.00 B82-22921

616.1'31 — Man. Arms. Blood vessels. Diagnosis. Angiography

Janevski, Blagoja K.. Angiography of the upper extremity / Blagoja K. Janevski. — The Hague ; London : Nijhoff, 1982. — xiv,226p : ill ; 28cm. — (Series in radiology ; 7)
Includes bibliographies and index
ISBN 90-247-2684-0 : Unpriced
ISBN 90-247-2427-9 (series) B82-40763

616.1'32 — Man. Blood. Hypertension

Hypertension / edited by Barry M. Brenner and Jay H. Stein. — New York ; Edinburgh : Churchill Livingstone, 1981. — viii,383p : ill ; 24cm. — (Contemporary issues in nephrology ; v.8)
Includes bibliographies and index
ISBN 0-443-08145-x : £25.00 B82-14438

Is it blood pressure?. — London (102 Gloucester Place, W1H 4DH) : British Heart Foundation, c1980 (1982 [printing]). — 14p ; 18cm. — (Heart research series ; no.8)
Cover title
Unpriced (pbk) B82-40600

616.1'32 — Man. Blood. Hypertension — *Conference proceedings*

Hypertension in primary care : an international symposium held at Reykjavik, Iceland, April 1978 / convenor, John Coope. — London : Journal of the Royal College of General Practitioners, 1980. — vi,38p : ill,4forms ; 28cm. — (Occasional paper ; 12)
Includes bibliographies
ISBN 0-85084-072-4 (pbk) : £3.00 B82-34314

International Symposium on Hypertension *(3rd : 1979 : Mexico City)*. Hypertension / Third International Symposium on Hypertension [Mexico City, February 12 to 14, 1979] ; edited by Herman Villarreal. — New York ; Chichester : Wiley, c1981. — xv,320p : ill ; 26cm. — (Perspectives in nephrology and hypertension, ISSN 0092-2900)
Includes index
ISBN 0-471-07900-6 : £25.90 B82-07722

616.1'32 — Man. Blood. Hypertension. Role of endocrine system — *Conference proceedings*

Endocrinology of hypertension. — London : Academic Press, Dec.1982. — [400]p. — (Proceedings of the Serono symposia, ISSN 0308-5503 ; no.53)
ISBN 0-12-469980-4 : CIP entry B82-29885

616.1'3205 — Man. Blood. Hypertension. Prevention & control

O'Brien, Eoin. High blood pressure : what it means for you and how to control it / Eoin O'Brien and Kevin O'Malley ; foreword by Walter Somerville. — London : Dunitz, 1982. — 108p : ill(some col.) ; 23cm. — (Positive health guide)
Includes index
ISBN 0-906348-23-4 (cased) : Unpriced : CIP rev.
ISBN 0-906348-24-2 (pbk) : £2.50 B81-37585

616.1'320654 — Man. Blood. Hypertension. Therapy. Diet

High blood pressure / prepared and produced by the Editorial Committee of Science of Life Books. — 11th ed., rev. and reset. — Melbourne : Science of Life Books ; Wellingborough : Thorsons [distributor], 1982. — 96p : ill ; 18cm. — (Science of life series)
Previous ed.: 197-?. — Includes index
ISBN 0-909911-96-7 (pbk) : Unpriced : CIP rev. B82-13176

616.1'35 — Man. Blood vessels. Thrombosis

Pitney, W. R.. Venous and arterial thrombosis : evaluation, prevention and management / W.R. Pitney with contributions by D.J. Allison, J.P. Lavender and J. Ludbrook. — Edinburgh : Chruchill Livingstone, 1981. — viii,231p : ill ; 24cm
Includes bibliographies and index
ISBN 0-443-01973-8 (pbk) : Unpriced : CIP rev. B81-30379

Thrombosis and atherosclerosis / edited by Nils U. Bang ... [et al.]. — Chicago ; London : Year Book Medical, c1982. — xviii,466p : ill ; 24cm
"A Publication from the Division of Continuing Medical Education, Indiana University School of Medicine". — Includes index
ISBN 0-8151-0413-8 : £47.00
Also classified at 616.1'36 B82-18068

616.1'36 — Man. Arteries. Atherosclerosis

Thrombosis and atherosclerosis / edited by Nils U. Bang ... [et al.]. — Chicago ; London : Year Book Medical, c1982. — xviii,466p : ill ; 24cm
"A Publication from the Division of Continuing Medical Education, Indiana University School of Medicine". — Includes index
ISBN 0-8151-0413-8 : £47.00
Primary classification 616.1'35 B82-18068

Woolf, Neville. Pathology of atherosclerosis / Neville Woolf. — London : Butterworth Scientific, 1982. — xv,322p : ill ; 25cm. — (Postgraduate pathology series)
Includes bibliographies and index
ISBN 0-407-00125-5 : Unpriced : CIP rev. B82-04025

616.1'36 — Man. Arteries. Atherosclerosis — *Conference proceedings*

International Meeting on Atherosclerosis *(4th : 1981 : Bologna)*. Atherosclerosis : clinical evaluation and therapy. — Lancaster : MTP Press, May 1982. — [250]p
ISBN 0-85200-449-4 : £29.95 : CIP entry B82-16206

616.1'3605 — Man. Arteries. Atherosclerosis. Prevention

Aegerter, Ernest. Save your heart / Ernest Aegerter. — New York ; London : Van Nostrand Reinhold, c1981. — 182p : ill ; 24cm
Includes index
ISBN 0-442-23112-1 : £11.00 B82-07875

616.1'360654 — Man. Arteries. Atherosclerosis. Diet therapy — *Conference proceedings*

Soy protein in the prevention of atherosclerosis. — Lancaster : MTP Press, Sept.1982. — [120]p
Conference papers
ISBN 0-85200-450-8 : £11.95 : CIP entry B82-29137

616.1'36071 — Man. Arteries. Atherosclerosis. Role of hormones

Stout, Robert W.. Hormones and atherosclerosis. — Lancaster : MTP Press, July 1982. — [300]p
ISBN 0-85200-417-6 : £15.95 : CIP entry B82-21957

616.1'40754 — Man. Veins. Catheterisation. Techniques

Rosen, Michael. Handbook of percutaneous central venous catheterisation / Michael Rosen, Ian P. Latto, W. Shang Ng. — London : Saunders, 1981. — ix,134p : ill ; 26cm
Includes index
ISBN 0-7216-7697-9 : £6.95 B82-00829

616.1'40757 — Man. Legs & pelvis. Veins. Diagnosis. Phlebography

Lea Thomas, M.. Phlebography of the lower limb / M. Lea Thomas ; foreword by Michael Hume. — Edinburgh : Churchill Livingstone, 1982. — viii,220p : ill ; 24cm
Includes bibliographies and index
ISBN 0-443-01841-3 : £21.00 : CIP rev. B81-35718

616.1'40757 — Man. Legs. Veins. Diagnosis. Phlebography — *Illustrations*

Chermet, Jacques. Atlas of phlebography of the lower limbs : including the iliac veins / Jacques Chermet. — The Hague ; London : Nijhoff, 1982. — 294p : chiefly ill ; 27cm. — (Series in radiology ; 6)
ISBN 90-247-2525-9 : Unpriced B82-27293

616.1'43 — Man. Veins. Varicose veins

Ellis, Harold. Varicose veins. — London : Martin Dunitz, Sept.1982. — [112]p. — (Positive health guide)
ISBN 0-906348-37-4 (cased) : £6.95 : CIP entry
ISBN 0-906348-36-6 (pbk) : £2.50 B82-21572

616.1'45 — Man. Veins. Thromboembolism

Hirsh, Jack. Venous thromboembolism / Jack Hirsh, Edward Genton, Russell Hull. — New York ; London : Grune & Stratton, c1981. — vii,335p : ill ; 27cm
Includes bibliographies and index
ISBN 0-8089-1408-1 : £19.60 B82-29980

616.1'5 — Man. Blood. Anoxia. Physiological aspects

Pathophysiology of shock, anoxia, and ischemia / editors R. Adams Cowley, Benjamin F. Trump. — Baltimore ; London : Williams & Wilkins, c1982. — xvi,710p : ill ; 29cm
Includes bibliographies and index
ISBN 0-683-02149-4 : Unpriced
Primary classification 616.1'3 B82-19367

616.1'5 — Man. Blood. Diseases

Blood and its disorders. — 2nd ed. — Oxford : Blackwell Scientific, Apr.1982. — 2v.([1530]p)
Previous ed.: 1974
ISBN 0-632-00833-4 : £90.00 : CIP entry B82-11263

Child, J. A.. Aids to clinical haematology / J.A. Child. — Edinburgh : Churchill Livingstone, 1982. — viii,134p : ill ; 22cm
Bibliography: p130. — Includes index
ISBN 0-443-01984-3 (pbk) : £3.95 : CIP rev. B81-31362

Hematology / edited by William G. Figueroa. — New York ; Chichester : Wiley, c1981. — xiii,414p : ill ; 25cm
'CME post-test' (9p) as insert. — Includes bibliographies and index
ISBN 0-471-09515-x : £25.90 B82-07793

616.1'5 — Medicine. Haematology

Miale, John B.. Laboratory medicine hematology / John B. Miale. — 6th ed. — St Louis ; London : Mosby, 1982. — 1084p,64p of plates : ill(some col.) ; 29cm
Previous ed: 1977. — Bibliography: p939-1042. — Includes index
ISBN 0-8016-3422-9 : £39.50 B82-33957

Richards, John D. M.. A synopsis of haematology. — Bristol : J. Wright, Jan.1983. — [312]p. — (Synopsis series)
ISBN 0-7236-0650-1 (pbk) : £15.00 : CIP entry B82-35204

616.1′5 — Medicine. Haematology
continuation

Topical reviews in haematology. — Bristol : John Wright
Vol.2 / edited by S. Roath. — 1982. — ix,222p ; 23cm
Includes index
ISBN 0-7236-0615-3 : Unpriced : CIP rev.
B82-08119

616.1′506 — Man. Blood. Monitoring — *Conference proceedings*

International Conference on Monitoring of Blood Gases, Blood Ion Concentrations and Respiratory Gas Exchange in View of Its Application during Extracorporeal Perfurion *(1980 : Nijmegen).*
Monitoring of vital parameters during extracorporeal circulation : International Conference on Monitoring of Blood Gases, Blood Ion Concentrations and Respiratory Gas Exchange in View of Its Application during Extracorporeal Perfusion, Nijmegen, March 9-12, 1980 / editor H.P. Kimmich. — Basel ; London : Karger, 1981. — ix,332p : ill ; 25cm
Includes index
ISBN 3-8055-2059-x : Unpriced B82-19652

616.1′52 — Man. Blood. Haemoglobins. Abnormalities — *Conference proceedings*

Comprehensive Sickle Cell Center Symposium on the Molecular Basis of Mutant Hemoglobin Dysfunction *(1979 : University of Chicago).* The molecular basis of mutant hemoglobin dysfunction / [proceedings of the Comprehensive Sickle Cell Center Symposium on the Molecular Basis of Mutant Hemoglobin Dysfunction at the University of Chicago, Chicago, Illinois, U.S.A., October 7-10, 1979] ; editor Paul B. Sigler. — New York ; Amsterdam : Elsevier/North Holland, c1981. — xii,338p : ill ; 24cm. — (The University of Chicago Sickle Cell Center Hemoglobin Symposia ; v.1)
Includes index
ISBN 0-444-00631-1 : £31.85 B82-15190

616.1′52042 — Man. Blood. Thalassaemia. Diagnosis

The **Thalassaemias**. — Edinburgh : Churchill Livingstone, Jan.1983. — [146]p. — (Methods in hematology ; v.6)
ISBN 0-443-02565-7 : £12.00 : CIP entry
B82-34597

616.1′52061 — Man. Blood. Iron-loading anaemia. Drug therapy. Iron chelating agents — *Conference proceedings*

Symposium on the Development of Iron Chelators for Clinical Use *(2nd : 1980 : San Francisco).* Development of iron chelators for clinical use : proceedings of the Second Symposium on the Development of Iron Chelators for Clinical Use held August 23-24, 1980 in San Francisco, California / editors Arthur E. Martell, W. French Anderson, David G. Badman. — New York ; Oxford : Elsevier/North-Holland, c1981. — xviii,311p : ill ; 24cm
Includes index
ISBN 0-444-00650-8 : £30.53 B82-11229

616.1′527 — Man. Blood. Sickle cell disease

Sickle-cell disease : a handbook for the general clinician / edited by A.F. Fleming ; foreword by H. Lehmann. — Edinburgh : Churchill Livingstone, 1982. — xviii,145p : ill ; 22cm. — (Medicine in the tropics series)
Includes bibliographies and index
ISBN 0-443-02037-x (pbk) : £4.95 : CIP rev.
B81-35720

616.1′527 — Man. Blood. Sickle cell disease — *Conference proceedings*

Comprehensive Sickle Cell Center Symposium on the Comparative Clinical Aspects of Sickle Cell Disease *(2nd : 1980 : University of Chicago).* Comparative clinical aspects of sickle cell disease : proceedings of the Second Annual Comprehensive Sickle Cell Center Symposium on the Comparative Clinical Aspects of Sickle Cell Disease at the University of Chicago, Chicago, Illinois, U.S.A., 21-22 October 1980 / editor Walter Fried. — New York ; Oxford : Elsevier/North Holland, 1982. — xi,191p : ill,maps ; 24cm. — (The University of Chicago Sickle Cell Center Hemoglobin Symposia ; v.2)
Includes bibliographies and index
ISBN 0-444-00673-7 : £25.48 B82-28645

616.1′57 — Man. Blood. Haemostatic disorders

Ingram, G. I. C.. Bleeding disorders : investigation and management. — 2nd ed. / G.I.C. Ingram, M. Brozović, N.G.P. Slater with a chapter on dermatological purpura by D.H. McGibbon. — Oxford : Blackwell Scientific, 1982. — xiii,413p : ill ; 24cm
Previous ed.: 1965. — Bibliography: p338-390. — Includes index
ISBN 0-632-00867-9 : £27.50 : CIP rev.
B82-04618

616.1′57 — Man. Haemophilia — *Conference proceedings*

Unresolved problems in haemophilia : proceedings of an international symposium held at the Royal College of Physicians and Surgeons, Glasgow, September 1980 / edited by Charles D. Forbes and Gordon D.O. Lowe. — Lancaster : MTP, 1982. — x,245p : ill ; 24cm
Includes index
ISBN 0-85200-388-9 (pbk) : £11.95 : CIP rev.
B81-36998

616.1′57′0028 — Man. Blood. Coagulation disorders. Laboratory techniques

The **Hemophilias** / edited by Arthur L. Bloom. — Edinburgh : Churchill Livingstone, 1982. — vii,201p : ill ; 25cm. — (Methods in hematology ; v.5)
Includes index
ISBN 0-443-02439-1 : Unpriced : CIP rev.
B82-15799

616.1′572 — Haemophiliacs. Joints. Radiology

Forrai, Jenő. Radiology of haemophilic arthropathies / Jenő Forrai ; technical assistance Éva Sümeghy. — 2nd rev., enl. ed. — The Hague ; London : Nijhoff, 1979. — 144p : ill ; 25cm
Translated from the Hungarian. — Previous ed.: 1976
ISBN 90-247-2130-x : Unpriced B82-35373

616.2 — MAN. DISEASES OF RESPIRATORY SYSTEM

616.2 — Man. Respiratory system. Diseases

Clinical investigation of respiratory disease / edited by T.J.H. Clark. — London : Chapman and Hall, 1981. — xiv,526p : ill ; 24cm
Includes bibliographies and index
ISBN 0-412-15780-2 : £22.50 : CIP rev.
B81-31748

Sproule, Brian J.. Fundamentals of respiratory disease / Brian J. Sproule, Patricia Lynne-Davies, E. Garner King. — New York ; Edinburgh : Churchill Livingstone, 1981. — 211p : ill ; 23cm
Includes bibliographies and index
ISBN 0-443-08139-5 (pbk) : £11.00
B82-03224

616.2 — Man. Respiratory system. Diseases — *Conference proceedings*

International Conference on Bronchial Hyperreactivity *(1982 : The Hague).* International conference on bronchial hyperreactivity held at the Hague. — Oxford : Medicine Publishing Foundation, Sept.1982. — [80]p
ISBN 0-906817-37-4 (pbk) : £3.50 : CIP entry
B82-29400

616.2′0022′2 — Man. Respiratory system. Diseases — *Illustrations*

James, D. Geraint. A colour atlas of respiratory diseases / D. Geraint James, Peter R. Studdy. — London : Wolfe Medical Publications, 1981. — 272p : ill(some col.) ; 27cm
Includes index
ISBN 0-7234-0762-2 : £45.00 B82-07710

616.2′0024613 — Man. Respiratory system. Diseases — *Questions & answers — For nursing*

The **Patient** with a respiratory disorder. — London : Harper & Row, Oct.1982. — [96]p. — (Patient related multiple choice questions)
ISBN 0-06-318231-9 (pbk) : £2.25 : CIP entry
B82-28433

616.2′0024616 — Man. Respiratory system — *For physiotherapy*

Cash′s textbook of chest, heart and vascular disorders for physiotherapists. — 3rd ed. — London : Faber, Jan.1983. — [488]p
Previous ed.: 1979
ISBN 0-571-18078-7 (pbk) : CIP entry
Primary classification 616.1′0024616
B82-32452

616.2′00425 — Man. Respiratory system. Acute respiratory failure. Emergency treatment

Respiratory emergencies. — 2nd ed. / edited by Kenneth M. Moser, Roger G. Spragg. — St. Louis ; London : Mosby, 1982. — xi,316p : ill ; 24cm
Previous ed.: 1977. — Includes bibliographies and index
ISBN 0-8016-4584-0 (pbk) : Unpriced
B82-31883

616.2′00428 — Man. Respiratory system. Diseases. Intensive care

Intensive care of the heart and lungs : a text for nurses and other staff / J.-M. Neutze ... [et al.] ; foreword by Sir Brian Barratt-Boyes. — 3rd ed. — Oxford : Blackwell Scientific, 1982. — xi,324p : ill ; 22cm
Previous ed.: 1978. — Bibliography: p311-312. — Includes index
ISBN 0-632-00925-x (pbk) : £7.50 : CIP rev.
Primary classification 616.1′2028 B82-00190

616.2′0046 — Man. Respiratory system. Therapy

Current topics in the management of respiratory diseases. — New York : Edinburgh : Churchill Livingstone
Vol.1 / by the staff of the Pulmonary Section, Boston University School of Medicine ; edited by Jerome S. Brody and Gordon L. Snider. — 1981. — ix,182p : ill ; 24cm
Includes index
ISBN 0-443-08104-2 (pbk) : £10.50
B82-09103

616.2′0046 — Man. Respiratory system. Therapy — *For house physicians*

Marini, John J.. Respiratory medicine and intensive care for the house officer / John J. Marini. — Baltimore ; London : Williams & Wilkins, c1981. — ix,273p : ill ; 20cm
Includes index
ISBN 0-683-05551-8 (corrected pbk) : Unpriced
B82-10177

616.2′0046′077 — Man. Respiratory system. Therapy — *Programmed instructions*

Hirnle, Robert W.. Clinical simulations in respiratory care / Robert W. Hirnle, Constance J. Hirnle. — New York ; Chichester : Wiley, c1982. — 329p : ill ; 24cm
Bibliography: p327-329
ISBN 0-471-08265-1 (spiral) : £11.75
B82-18061

616.2′00471 — Man. Respiratory system. Pathogens: Atmospheric particles — *Conference proceedings*

Inhaled particles V. — Oxford : Pergamon, Sept.1982. — [900]p
Conference papers
ISBN 0-08-026838-2 : £75.00 : CIP entry
B82-19095

616.2′02061 — Man. Hay fever. Drug therapy

Widdicombe, J. G.. The current role of Rynacrom in the management of allergic rhinitis. — Oxford (36 Pembroke St., Oxford OX1 1BL) : Medicine Publishing Foundation, July 1982. — [24]p
ISBN 0-906817-27-7 (pbk) : £2.00 : CIP entry
B82-19286

616.2′030194 — Man. Influenza. Pathogens: Viruses — *Conference proceedings*

Working Group on Epidemiological Models of Influenza and their Practical Application *(1981 : Hemingford Grey).* Influenza models. — Lancaster : MTP, May 1982. — [275]p
ISBN 0-85200-459-1 : £14.95 : CIP entry
B82-17942

616.2'030194 — Man. Influenza. Pathogens: Viruses. Genes. Variation — *Conference proceedings*

ICN-UCLA Symposia on Genetic Variation among Influenza Viruses *(1981 : Salt Lake City).* Genetic variation among influenza viruses / [proceedings of the 1981 ICN-UCLA Symposia on Genetic Variation among Influenza Viruses held in Salt Lake City, Utah, on March 8-13, 1981] ; edited by Debi P. Nayak. — New York ; London : Academic Press, 1981. — xxi,672p : ill ; 24cm. — (ICN-UCLA symposia on molecular and cellular biology ; v.21)
Includes bibliographies and index
ISBN 0-12-515080-6 : Unpriced B82-28670

616.2'107572 — Man. Ears. Diagnosis. Radiography

Phelps, Peter D.. Radiology of the ear. — Oxford : Blackwell Scientific, Dec.1982. — [168]p
ISBN 0-632-01083-5 : £30.00 : CIP entry B82-40908

616.2'2 — Otolaryngology

Maran, A. G. D.. Otolaryngology. — Lancaster : MTP Press, Feb.1983. — [200]p. — (New medicine ; 4)
ISBN 0-85200-402-8 : £9.95 : CIP entry B82-39597

616.2'307545 — Man. Bronchi. Diagnosis. Bronchoscopy

Stradling, Peter. Diagnostic bronchoscopy / Peter Stradling. — 4th ed. — Edinburgh : Churchill Livingstone, 1981. — xii,159p : ill (some col.) ; 26cm
Previous ed.: 1976. — Includes index
ISBN 0-443-02277-1 : £30.00 : CIP rev. B81-13762

616.2'34061 — Man. Bronchi. Bronchitis. Herbal remedies

Gosling, Nalda. Herbs for bronchial troubles / by Nalda Gosling ; drawings by A.R. Gosling. — Wellingborough : Thorsons, 1981. — 64p : ill ; 18cm. — (Everybody's home herbal)
ISBN 0-7225-0714-3 (pbk) : £0.75 : CIP rev. B81-32053

616.2'38 — Man. Bronchi. Asthma

Lane, Donald J.. Asthma : the facts / by Donald J. Lane ; with a chapter based on personal experience by Anthony Storr. — Oxford : Oxford University Press, 1979 (1981 [printing]). — 163p : ill ; 21cm
Includes index
ISBN 0-19-286021-6 (pbk) : £2.95 B82-15411

616.2'38 — Man. Bronchi. Asthma — *Conference proceedings*

Interasma Congress *(10th : 1981 : Paris).* Interasma : Xe Congrès d'Interasma, Paris, 28 septembre-2 octobre 1981 : résumés : Xth Interasma Congress, Paris, September 28-October 2, 1981 : abstracts. — Basel ; London : Karger, 1981. — 144p ; 26cm
Supplement 1 to v.42 of Respiration. — Includes abstracts in French and and Spanish. — Includes index
ISBN 3-8055-3425-6 (pbk) : £13.90 B82-06283

616.2'38 — Man. Bronchi. Asthma — *For asthmatics*

Hilton, Sean. Understanding asthma / Sean Hilton. — London (Tavistock House North, Tavistock Sq., WC1H 9JE) : Chest, Heart and Stroke Association, c1981. — 27p : ill ; 18cm
£0.40 (unbound) B82-08057

616.2'38061 — Man. Bronchi. Asthma. Drug therapy — *Conference proceedings*

Bronchial hyperreactivity. — London : Academic Press, Oct.1982. — [250]p
Conference papers
ISBN 0-12-506450-0 : CIP entry B82-29403

616.2'38061 — Man. Bronchi. Asthma. Drug therapy. Intal — *Conference proceedings*

The **Current** role of INTAL in the management of asthma : proceedings of a workshop, Ruthin Castle, Clwyd, 28th & 29th April 1981 / sponsored by Fisons Limited, Pharmaceutical Division ; produced by Medical Education Services. — Oxford : Medicine Publishing Foundation, 1981. — 36p : ill(some col.) ; 30cm
Cover title
ISBN 0-906817-14-5 (pbk) : Unpriced B82-13328

616.2'4 — Lung disease victims. Physical fitness — *Manuals*

Better living and breathing : a manual for patients. — 2nd ed. / Kenneth M. Moser ... [et al.] ; with 129 illustrations by Steve Pileggi. — St Louis ; London : Mosby, 1980. — xi,94p : ill ; 23cm
Previous ed.: 1975. — Includes index
ISBN 0-8016-3565-9 (pbk) : £3.75 B82-31035

616.2'4 — Man. Lungs. Diseases

International School of Thoracic Medicine *(5th : 1981 : Erice).* Cellular biology of the lung / [proceedings of the fifth course of the International School of Thoracic Medicine held March 1-6, 1981 in Erice, Italy] ; edited by G. Cumming and G. Bonsignore. — New York ; London : Plenum, c1982. — viii,488p : ill ; 26cm. — (Ettore Majorana international science series. Life sciences ; v.10)
Includes bibliographies and index
ISBN 0-306-40910-0 : Unpriced B82-38672

Pulmonary disease / edited by Paul A. Selecky. — New York ; Chichester : Wiley, c1982. — xii,345p : ill ; 25cm. — (Internal medicine today)
Includes bibliographies and index
ISBN 0-471-09554-0 : £31.00 B82-36682

Pulmonary disease in the adult / edited by Douglas R. Gracey. — Chicago ; London : Year Book Medical, c1981. — xvi,410p : ill ; 24cm
Includes index
ISBN 0-8151-3850-4 : £29.50 B82-04270

Synopsis of clinical pulmonary disease. — 3rd ed. / edited by Roger S. Mitchell, Thomas L. Petty. — St. Louis, Mo. ; London : Mosby, 1982. — xii,352p : ill ; 24cm
Previous ed.: 1978. — Bibliography: p336-337. — Includes index
ISBN 0-8016-3474-1 (pbk) : £12.75 B82-31857

Tisi, Gennaro M.. Pulmonary physiology in clinical medicine / Gennaro M. Tisi. — Baltimore ; London : Williams & Wilkins, c1980. — ix,282p : ill ; 26cm
Includes index
ISBN 0-683-08250-7 : Unpriced B82-03546

Whitcomb, Michael E.. The lung : normal and diseased / Michael E. Whitcomb. — St. Louis ; London : Mosby, 1982. — viii,360p : ill ; 24cm
Includes index
ISBN 0-8016-5421-1 (pbk) : Unpriced B82-31884

616.2'4 — Man. Lungs. Diseases — *Conference proceedings*

Pulmonary and circulatory abnormalities. — London : Academic Press, Jan.1983. — [60]p. — (International congress and symposium series / Royal Society of Medicine, ISSN 0142-2367 ; 56)
Conference papers
ISBN 0-12-793534-7 (pbk) : CIP entry B82-36321

616.2'4 — Man. Lungs. Industrial diseases

Parkes, W. Raymond. Occupational lung disorders / W. Raymond Parkes ; with a foreword by Margaret Turner- Warwick. — 2nd ed. — London : Butterworths, 1982. — xv,529p : ill ; 29cm
Previous ed.: 1974. — Includes bibliographies and index
ISBN 0-407-33731-8 : Unpriced B82-16616

616.2'407 — Man. Lungs. Pathology

Dunnill, M. S.. Pulmonary pathology / M.S. Dunnill. — Edinburgh : Churchill Livingstone, 1982. — 496p : ill ; 26cm
Includes bibliographies and index
ISBN 0-443-01996-7 : £30.00 : CIP rev. B82-24326

Gibbs, A. R.. Atlas of pulmonary pathology / by A.R. Gibbs and R.M.E. Seal with a chapter by J.G. Leopold. — Lancaster : MTP, c1982. — 135p : ill(some col.) ; 31cm. — (Current histopathology ; v.3)
Includes index
ISBN 0-85200-331-5 : £27.95 : CIP rev. B81-38817

616.2'4071 — Man. Lungs. Effects of shock

Schells, Günther. Shock : acute progressive lung failure / Günther Schnells ; preface by Thomas M. Glenn. — Oxford : Medicine Publishing Foundation, 1982. — 54p : ill(some col.) ; 20x21cm
ISBN 0-906817-10-2 (pbk) : £14.95 : CIP rev. B81-30632

616.2'4075 — Man. Lungs. Diagnosis. Tests

Assessment of pulmonary function / [edited by] Alfred P. Fishman. — New York ; London : McGraw-Hill, c1980. — xii,307p,1leaf of plates : ill(some col.) ; 29cm
Based on chapters of Pulmonary diseases and disorders / by Alfred P. Fishman. — Includes bibliographies and index
ISBN 0-07-021117-5 : £12.50 B82-07361

Ruppel, Gregg. Manual of pulmonary function testing / Gregg Ruppel. — 2nd ed. — St. Louis, Mo. ; London : Mosby, 1979. — ix,162p : ill,forms ; 22cm
Previous ed.: 1975. — Includes bibliographies and index
ISBN 0-8016-4209-4 (pbk) : Unpriced B82-21889

616.2'407572 — Man. Lungs. Diagnosis. Radiography. Use of x-rays

Freundlich, Irwin M.. Pulmonary masses, cysts, and cavities : a radiologic approach / Irwin M. Freundlich. — Chicago ; London : Year Book Medical, c1981. — ix,223p : ill ; 26cm
Bibliography: p134-137. — Includes index
ISBN 0-8151-3330-8 : £26.00 B82-16614

616.2'44 — Man. Farmer's lung

Mouldy hay is dangerous. — [Blackrock] ([Frascati Rd., Blackrock, Co. Dublin]) : [ACOT], 1980. — [4]p : ill(some col.) ; 21cm
Unpriced (unbound) B82-05189

616.2'44 — Man. Lungs. Byssinosis

Honeybourne, D.. Byssinosis : causative agent and clinical aspects. — Manchester : Shirley Institute, July 1982. — [180]p. — (Shirley Institute publications, ISSN 0306-5154 ; S43)
ISBN 0-903669-40-4 : £45.00 : CIP entry B82-24327

616.3 — MAN. DISEASES OF DIGESTIVE SYSTEM

616.3 — Man. Alimentary canal. Sphincters. Diseases

Alimentary sphincters and their disorders / edited by Paul A. Thomas and Charles V. Mann. — London : Macmillan, 1981. — x,236p : ill ; 24cm
Includes index
ISBN 0-333-24099-5 : £35.00 B82-14871

616.3 — Man. Digestive system. Diseases

Bouchier, Ian A. D.. Gastroenterology / Ian A.D. Bouchier. — 3rd ed. — London : Baillière Tindall, c1982. — 389p : ill ; 22cm. — (Concise medical textbooks)
Previous ed.: 1977. — Includes bibliographies and index
ISBN 0-7020-0921-0 (pbk) : £8.00 : CIP rev. B82-09463

616.3 — Man. Digestive system. Diseases *continuation*

Dworken, Harvey J.. Gastroenterology : pathophysiology and clinical applications / Harvey J. Dworken. — Boston, [Mass.] ; London : Butterworths, c1982. — xviii,660p : ill ; 24cm
Includes bibliographies and index
Unpriced B82-24900

Gastroenterology. — 3rd ed. — Edinburgh : Churchill Livingstone, Mar.1983. — [320]p
Previous ed.: 1977
ISBN 0-443-02342-5 (pbk) : £6.95 : CIP entry B82-38274

Hobsley, Michael. Disorders of the digestive system / Michael Hobsley. — London : Edward Arnold, 1982. — x,178p : ill ; 23cm. — (Physiological principles in medicine)
Bibliography: p161-162. — Includes index
ISBN 0-7131-4381-9 (pbk) : £5.25 : CIP rev. B81-30594

Langman, M. J. S.. A concise textbook of gastroenterology / M.J.S. Langman. — 2d ed. — Edinburgh : Churchill Livingstone, 1982. — 249p : ill ; 22cm. — (Churchill Livingstone medical texts)
Previous ed.: 1973. — Includes bibliographies and index
ISBN 0-443-02055-8 (pbk) : £4.95 B82-24050

Practical gastroenterology / edited by Ronald L. Koretz. — New York ; Chichester : Wiley, c1982. — xviii,395p : ill ; 22cm + 1pamphlet (20p; 21cm). — (Family practice today)
With pamphlet of test questions. — Includes bibliographies and index
ISBN 0-471-09513-3 : £22.00 B82-15404

Shearman, David J. C.. Diseases of the gastrointestinal tract and liver / David J.C. Shearman, Niall D.C. Finlayson. — Edinburgh : Churchill Livingstone, 1982. — viii,974p : ill ; 26cm
Includes bibliographies and index
ISBN 0-443-01498-1 : £32.00 : CIP rev.
Also classified at 616.3'62 B82-06033

616.3 — Medicine. Gastroenterology. Applications of glucagon — *Conference proceedings*

Glucagon in gastroenterology and hepatology. — Lancaster : MTP Press, Apr.1982. — [175]p
Conference papers
ISBN 0-85200-447-8 : £20.00 : CIP entry B82-14391

616.3'07543 — Man. Digestive system. Diagnosis. Ultrasonography

Weill, Francis S.. Ultrasonography of digestive diseases / Francis S. Weill. — 2nd ed. — St. Louis, Mo. ; London : Mosby, 1982. — xiv,537p : ill ; 28cm
Previous ed.: 1978. — Includes bibliographies and index
ISBN 0-8016-5376-2 : £54.75 B82-34470

616.3'07'543 — Man. Digestive system. Ultrasonography

Cosgrove, David O.. Ultrasound imaging : liver, spleen, pancreas. — Chichester : Wiley, July 1982. — [350]p. — (A Wiley medical publication)
ISBN 0-471-10068-4 : £35.00 : CIP entry B82-13241

616.3'0757 — Man. Digestive system. Diagnosis. Radiography

Alimentary tract roentgenology / edited by Alexander R. Margulis and H. Joachim Burhenne
Vol.3. — St. Louis ; London : Mosby, 1979. — xii,689p : ill(some col.) ; 29cm
Vol.3 has title: Alimentary tract radiology: abdominal imaging. — Includes bibliographies and index
ISBN 0-8016-3134-3 : £72.00 B82-37428

Bartram, Clive I.. Clinical radiology in gastroenterology / Clive I. Bartram, Parveen Kumar. — Oxford : Blackwell Scientific, 1981. — vi,245p : ill ; 23cm
Includes bibliographies and index
ISBN 0-632-00213-1 : £16.00 : CIP rev. B81-13455

616.3'101 — Man. Mouth. Diseases. Microbiological aspects

Oral microbiology : with basic microbiology and immunology / edited by William A. Nolte. — 4th ed. — St. Louis ; London : Mosby, 1982. — xi,795p : ill ; 28cm
Previous ed.: 1977. — Includes bibliographies and index
ISBN 0-8016-3697-3 : £26.25
Primary classification 576'.15 B82-31868

616.3'101'0246176 — Man. Mouth. Diseases. Microbiological aspects — *For dentistry*

Dental microbiology / [edited by] Jerry R. McGhee, Suzanne M. Michalek, Gail H. Cassell. — Cambridge, [Mass] ; London : Harper & Row, c1982. — xix,914p,[3]leaves of plates : ill(some col.),1port ; 27cm
Includes bibliographies and index
ISBN 0-06-141590-1 : Unpriced B82-34015

Microbiology in clinical dentistry / [volume editor] Frank J. Orland. — Boston, Mass. ; Bristol : John Wright, 1982. — xii,270p : ill ; 25cm. — (Postgraduate dental handbook series ; v.13)
Includes index
ISBN 0-88416-171-4 : Unpriced B82-16122

616.3'1079 — Man. Mouth. Diseases. Immunological aspects — *For dentistry*

Dolby, A. E.. Introduction to oral immunology / A.E. Dolby, D.M. Walker, N. Matthews. — London : Edward Arnold, 1981. — viii,102p : ill ; 23cm
Includes bibliographies and index
ISBN 0-7131-4404-1 (pbk) : £5.95 : CIP rev. B81-31633

616.3'2 — Man. Oesophagus. Diseases — *Conference proceedings*

Medical and surgical problems of the esophagus / edited by S. Stipa, R.H.R. Belsey, A. Moraldi. — London : Academic Press, 1981. — xv,407p : ill ; 24cm. — (Proceedings of the Serono symposia, ISSN 0308-5503 ; v.43)
Conference proceedings. — Includes bibliographies
ISBN 0-12-671450-9 : £25.00 : CIP rev. B81-16846

616.3'3 — Man. Gastrointestinal tract. Diseases. Nutritional aspects

Nutrition in gastrointestinal disease / edited by Robert C. Kurtz. — New York ; Edinburgh : Churchill Livingstone, 1981. — xiii,146p : ill ; 24cm. — (Contemporary issues in clinical nutrition ; v.1)
Includes index
ISBN 0-443-08128-x : £13.00 B82-16435

616.3'3 — Man. Gastrointestinal tract. Mucous membranes. Cells. Diseases

Basic mechanisms of gastrointestinal mucosal cell injury and protection / edited by John W. Harmon. — Baltimore ; London : Williams & Wilkins, c1981. — xvi,415p : ill ; 24cm
Includes index
ISBN 0-683-03892-3 : Unpriced B82-15514

616.3'3 — Man. Stomach. Diseases

The **Stomach** / volume editor Leo van der Reis. — Basel ; London : Karger, c1980. — x,186p : ill,1map ; 25cm. — (Frontiers of gastrointestinal research ; v.6)
Includes bibliographies and index
ISBN 3-8055-3071-4 : £24.20 B82-34691

616.3'3 — Medicine. Gastroenterology

Lancaster-Smith, M.. Problems in gastroenterology. — Lancaster : MTP Press, June 1982. — [200]p. — (Problems in practice series)
ISBN 0-85200-261-0 : £7.95 : CIP entry B82-16220

616.3'3'0024613 — Man. Gastrointestinal tract. Diseases — *For nursing*

Aspects of gastroenterology for nurses / edited by Mary Sykes. — London : Pitman Medical, 1981. — x,241p : ill ; 24cm
Includes bibliographies and index
ISBN 0-272-79607-7 : Unpriced : CIP rev. B81-25778

616.3'3'005 — Medicine. Gastroenterology — *Serials*

Current gastroenterology. — Vol.1-. — New York ; Chichester : Wiley, 1980-. — v. : ill ; 26cm
Annual. — Continues in part: Current gastroenterology and hepatology. — Description based on: Vol.2
ISSN 0198-8085 = Current gastroenterology : £44.50 B82-26160

Topics in gastroenterology. — 9. — Oxford : Blackwell Scientific, Dec.1981. — [336]p
ISBN 0-632-00898-9 (pbk) : £18.00 : CIP entry B81-40260

616.3'306 — Man. Gastrointestinal tract. Therapy — *Conference proceedings*

International Congress on Stomach Diseases *(13th : 1981 : Antwerp)*. Stomach diseases : proceedings of the 13th International Congress on Stomach Diseases, Antwerp, May 1-2, 1981 / editors Y.M.F. Van Maercke, E.M.J. Van Moer, P.A.R. Pelckmans. — Amsterdam ; Oxford : Excerpta Medica, 1981. — xiii,434p : ill ; 25cm. — (International congress series ; no.555)
Includes bibliographies and index
ISBN 90-219-0500-0 : £32.32 B82-08561

616.3'3061 — Man. Gastrointestinal tract. Drug therapy. Ranitidine — *Conference proceedings*

The **Clinical** use of ranitidine. — Oxford (52 New Inn Hall St., Oxford OX1 2BS) : Medicine Publishing Foundation, July 1982. — [300]p. — (The Medicine Publishing Foundation symposium series, ISSN 0260-0242 ; 5)
ISBN 0-906817-22-6 (pbk) : £7.00 : CIP entry B82-16234

616.3'30654 — Man. Gastrointestinal tract. Therapy. Diet

Floch, Martin H.. Nutrition and diet therapy in gastrointestinal disease / Martin H. Floch. — New York ; London : Plenum Medical, c1981. — xxii,480p : ill ; 26cm. — (Topics in gastroenterology)
Includes index
ISBN 0-306-40508-3 : Unpriced B82-00529

616.3'3071 — Man. Stomach. Effects of stress

Coleman, Vernon. Stress and your stomach. — London : Sheldon Press, Jan.1983. — [96]p. — (Overcoming common problems)
ISBN 0-85969-375-9 (pbk) : £2.50 : CIP entry B82-33122

616.3'3075 — Man. Gastrointestinal tract. Diagnosis

Bouchier, Ian A. D.. Clinical investigation of gastrointestinal function. — 2nd ed. / Malcolm C. Bateson and Ian A.D. Bouchier. — Oxford : Blackwell Scientific, 1981. — xii,232p : ill ; 22cm
Previous ed.: 1969. — Includes bibliographies and index
ISBN 0-632-00742-7 (pbk) : £7.50 : CIP rev. B81-13456

616.3'30754 — Man. Digestive system. Endoscopy

Cotton, Peter B.. Practical gastrointestinal endoscopy. — 2nd ed. — Oxford : Blackwell Scientific, Sept.1982. — [182]p
Previous ed.: 1980
ISBN 0-632-01004-5 : £14.00 : CIP entry B82-29007

616.3'4 — Man. Intestines. Coeliac diseases. Therapy. Diet

Greer, Rita. Diets to help coeliacs and wheat sensitivity / by Rita Greer. — Wellingborough : Thorsons, 1982. — 47p ; 18cm
ISBN 0-7225-0756-9 (pbk) : £0.60 : CIP rev. B82-07603

616.3'4 — Man. Large intestine. Diseases

Colorectal diseases : an introduction for surgeons and physicians / edited by James P.S. Thomson, R.J. Nicholls and Christopher B. Williams ; with illustrations by Geoffrey Lyth ; foreword contributed by Malcolm C. Veidenheimer. — London : Heinemann Medical, 1981. — xv,381p : ill ; 26cm
Includes bibliographies and index
ISBN 0-433-32310-8 : £20.00 B82-11952

616.3'4 — Man. Small intestine. Diseases

Small intestine. — London : Butterworth, Oct.1982. — [360]p. — (Gastroenterology ; 2) (Butterworths international medical reviews, ISSN 0260-0110)
ISBN 0-407-02288-0 : £15.00 : CIP entry
B82-24460

616.3'4014 — Man. Intestines. Pathogens: Campylobacters — *Conference proceedings*

International Workshop on Campylobacter Infections *(1981 : University of Reading).* Campylobacter : epidemiology, pathogenesis and biochemistry / proceedings of an International Workshop on Campylobacter Infections held at University of Reading 24-26th March 1981 under the auspices of the Public Health Laboratory Service ; edited by D.G. Newell. — Lancaster : MTP, c1982. — xviii,308p : ill ; 25cm
ISBN 0-85200-455-9 : £27.50 : CIP rev.
B82-03123

616.3'4071 — Man. Colon. Diseases. Role of diet

Falk Symposium *(32nd : 1981 : Titisee).* Colon and nutrition : proceedings of the 32nd Falk Symposium held during Intestinal Week, Titisee, May 29-31, 1981 / edited by H. Kasper, H. Goebell. — Lancaster : MTP, c1982. — xiv,310p : ill ; 24cm. — (Falk symposium ; 32)
Includes index
ISBN 0-85200-444-3 : Unpriced : CIP rev.
B82-03379

616.3'407'56 — Man. Intestines. Peptides. Radioimmunoassay

Radioimmunoassay of gut regulatory peptides. — Eastbourne : Saunders, June 1982. — [256]p
ISBN 0-7216-1750-6 : £9.50 : CIP entry
B82-12838

616.3'427 — Man. Diarrhoeal diseases

How should we manage acute diarrhoea? : a workshop held at Eastbourne, Sussex, 18 March 1982 / chaired by John Badenoch ; summarized by William Jackson. — Oxford : MEDICINE Publishing Foundation, 1982. — 24p : ill,1port ; 22cm. — (Medicine forum, ISSN 0260-9312)
Ill on inside front cover
ISBN 0-906817-29-3 (pbk) : £4.00 : CIP rev.
B82-19287

616.3'42806 — Man. Constipation. Therapy

Fuller, Richard R.. Constipation control : an exercise program to achieve regularity / Richard R. Fuller. — Smithtown : Exposition Press ; [Witham] ([5 Berwell Way, Witham, Essex]) : [R. Fuller] [[distributor]], c1981. — vii,43p ; 21cm
ISBN 0-682-49690-1 : Unpriced B82-17159

616.3'428061 — Man. Constipation. Herbal remedies

Gosling, Nalda. Herbs for constipation and other bowel disorders. — Wellingborough : Thorsons, Aug.1982. — [64]p
ISBN 0-7225-0715-1 (pbk) : £0.95 : CIP entry
B82-16652

616.3'43 — Man. Gastrointestinal tract. Peptic ulcers — *Conference proceedings*

Aspects of peptic ulceration / edited by J. Eric Murphy. — Northampton : Cambridge Medical, c1978. — 74p : ill ; 25cm
Conference papers. — Includes bibliographies
ISBN 0-904052-01-x (pbk) : Unpriced
B82-14404

616.3'43061 — Ranitidine — *Conference proceedings*

The Clinical use of ranitidine : 8-9 October 1981 Barbican Conference Centre, London : a Glaxo international symposium / [sponsored by Glaxo Operations UK Limited]. — Oxford : Medical Education Services, 1982. — ii,30p : col.ill ; 28cm. — (A Medicine International review)
ISBN 0-906817-20-x (unbound) : Unpriced
B82-22958

616.3'44 — Colitis victims & Crohn's disease victims. Diet

The **Role** of diet / National Association for Colitis and Crohn's Disease. — St Albans : N.A.C.C., 1981. — 12p : ill ; 21cm
Cover title
ISBN 0-9507436-0-7 (pbk) : Unpriced
B82-15202

616.3'44 — Man. Intestines. Inflammatory diseases — *Conference proceedings*

Inflammatory bowel disease : experience and controversy : a teaching seminar on inflammatory bowel disease / sponsored by Lenox Hill Hospital (New York) and the American College of Gastroenterology ; edited by Burton I. Korelitz. — The Hague ; London : Martinus Nijhoff, 1982. — ix,237p : ill ; 24cm
Includes bibliographies and index
ISBN 90-247-2489-9 : Unpriced B82-18401

616.3'44 — Man. Intestines. Pathogens: Entamoeba histolytica

Martínez-Palomo, Adolfo. The biology of Enatamoeba histolytica / Adolfo Martínez-Palomo. — Chichester : Research Studies, c1982. — xii,161p : ill ; 24cm. — (Tropical medicine research studies series ; 2)
Bibliography: p123-154. — Includes index
ISBN 0-471-10404-3 : £17.00 : CIP rev.
B82-07988

616.3'5 — Man. Anus & rectum. Diseases

MacLeod, James H.. A method of proctology / James H. MacLeod. — Hagerstown ; London : Harper & Row, c1979. — x,194p : ill ; 26cm
Includes bibliographies and index
ISBN 0-06-141571-5 : Unpriced B82-02597

616.3'5 — Man. Haemorrhoids

The **Haemorrhoid** syndrome / edited by H.D. Kaufman. — Tunbridge Wells : Abacus, 1981. — x,156p : ill ; 24cm
Includes index
ISBN 0-85626-306-0 : Unpriced : CIP rev.
B81-13741

616.3'62 — Man. Liver. Diseases

Basic and clinical hepatology / edited by P.M. Motta and L.J.A. DiDio. — The Hague ; London : Nijhoff, 1982. — xii,236p : ill(some col.) ; 28cm. — (Developments in gastroenterology ; v.2)
Includes index
ISBN 90-247-2404-x : Unpriced B82-12045

Shearman, David J. C.. Diseases of the gastrointestinal tract and liver / David J.C. Shearman, Niall D.C. Finlayson. — Edinburgh : Churchill Livingstone, 1982. — viii,974p : ill ; 26cm
Includes bibliographies and index
ISBN 0-443-01498-1 : £32.00 : CIP rev.
Primary classification 616.3 B82-06033

616.3'62'005 — Man. Liver. Diseases — *Serials*

Current hepatology. — Vol.1-. — New York ; Chichester : Wiley, 1980-. — v. : ill ; 26cm
Annual. — Description based on: Vol.2
ISSN 0198-8093 = Current hepatology : £40.75 B82-24768

[The Liver *(Amsterdam)*]. The Liver : a series of critical surveys of the international literature. — Annual 1 (1981)-. — Amsterdam ; Oxford : Excerpta Medica, 1981-. — v. : ill ; 25cm
Annual
Unpriced B82-30478

616.3'62061 — Man. Liver. Drug therapy. (+)-cyanidanol-3 — *Conference proceedings*

International Workshop on (+)-Cyanidanol-3 in Diseases of the Liver *(1981 : Crans-Montana).* International Workshop on (+)-Cyanidanol-3 in Diseases of the Liver / editor Harold O. Conn ; administrative editor Clive Wood. — London : Published jointly by the Royal Society of Medicine, Academic Press, 1981. — xv,267p : ill,ports ; 24cm. — (Royal Society of Medicine series. International congress and symposium series, ISSN 0142-2367 ; no.47)
At head of title: Royal Society of Medicine. — Bibliography: p263-267
ISBN 0-12-790898-6 (pbk) : Unpriced : CIP rev.
B81-25110

616.3'6207 — Man. Liver. Pathology

Patrick, R. S.. Colour atlas of liver pathology. — London : Harvey Miller, Oct.1982. — [192]p. — (Oxford colour atlases of pathology)
ISBN 0-19-921033-0 : £45.00 : CIP entry
B82-25530

Wight, Derek G. D.. Atlas of liver pathology. — Lancaster : MTP, Apr.1982. — [200]p. — (Current histopathology series ; 4)
ISBN 0-85200-205-x : £30.00 : CIP entry
B82-11783

616.3'6207575 — Man. Liver. Diagnosis. Cholescintigraphy

Cholescintigraphy / edited by P.H. Cox. — The Hague ; London : Nijhoff, 1981. — xi,219p : ill ; 25cm. — (Developments in nuclear medicine ; v.1)
Includes index
ISBN 90-247-2524-0 : Unpriced B82-03864

616.3'623 — Man. Liver. Viral hepatitis

Non-A, non-B hepatitis / edited by R.J. Gerety. — New York ; London : Academic Press, 1981. — xv,301p : ill ; 24cm
Includes bibliographies and index
ISBN 0-12-280680-8 : £30.20 B82-29596

616.3'6230194 — Man. Hepatitis. Pathogens: Viruses

Zuckerman, Arie J.. Hepatitis viruses of man / Arie J. Zuckerman and Colin R. Howard. — London : Academic Press, 1979. — vi,269p : ill ; 24cm. — (Experimental virology)
Bibliography: p227-260. — Includes index
ISBN 0-12-782150-3 : £18.60 : CIP rev.
B79-27489

616.3'7 — Man. Pancreas. Cystic fibrosis — *Conference proceedings*

European Working Group for Cystic Fibrosis. *Conference (10th : 1981 : Bern).* Current problems and new trends in cystic fibrosis : 10th meeting of the European Working Group for Cystic Fibrosis, Bern, September 22-23, 1981 / volume editors M. Schöni and R. Kraemer. — Basel ; London : Karger, c1981. — ix,215p : ill ; 24cm. — (Monographs in paediatrics ; v.14)
ISBN 3-8055-3417-5 (pbk) : £44.70
B82-05123

616.3'7 — Man. Pancreas. Diseases

Pancreatic disease in clinical practice / edited by C.J. Mitchell, J. Kelleher. — London : Pitman, 1981. — xv,432p : ill ; 23cm
Conference papers. — Includes index
ISBN 0-272-79605-0 : Unpriced : CIP rev.
B81-34153

616.3'9 — Industrialised countries. Man. Deficiency diseases — *Conference proceedings*

Group of European Nutritionists. *Symposium (17th : 1979 : Santiago de Compostela).* Nutritional deficiencies in industrialized countries : 17th Symposium of the Group of European Nutritionists, Santiago de Compostela, October 7-9, 1979 / volume editors J.C. Somogyi and G. Varela. — Basel ; London : Karger, 1981. — 172p : ill ; 24cm. — (Bibliotheca nutritio et dieta ; no.30)
Includes a chapter in French. — Includes bibliographies
£38.50 (pbk) B82-05930

616.3'9 — Man. Metabolic disorders

Current endocrine concepts. — Eastbourne : Praeger, Apr.1982. — [224]p. — (Endocrinology and metabolism series ; 2)
ISBN 0-03-062119-4 : £15.00 : CIP entry
Primary classification 616.4 B82-11504

616.3'9 — Man. Metabolic disorders. Therapy

Tweedle, D. E. F.. Metabolic care. — Edinburgh : Churchill Livingstone, Dec.1982. — [320]p
ISBN 0-443-01867-7 (pbk) : £10.00 : CIP entry
B82-29798

616.3'9'00724 — Man. Metabolic disorders. Models

Quantitative approaches to metabolism : the role of tracers and models in clinical medicine. — Chichester : Wiley, Oct.1982. — [416]p
ISBN 0-471-10172-9 : £23.00 : CIP entry
B82-24727

616.3'9042 — Man. Genetic metabolic disorders — *Conference proceedings*

Inborn errors of metabolism in humans. — Lancaster : MTP, May 1982. — [300]p. — (Symposia of the Society for the Study of Inborn Errors of Metabolism ; 18)
ISBN 0-85200-412-5 : £24.95 : CIP entry B82-17943

616.3'9042 — Man. Genetic metabolic disorders. Role of transport phenomena in cell membranes — *Conference proceedings*

Society for the Study of Inborn Errors of Metabolism. *Symposium (17th : 1979 : Leeds).* Transport and inherited disease : monograph based upon proceedings of the seventeenth Symposium of the Society for the Study of Inborn Errors of Metabolism / edited by N.R. Belton and C. Toothill. — Lancaster : MTP, c1981. — xiv,380p : ill ; 24cm
Includes index
ISBN 0-85200-391-9 : Unpriced B82-06370

616.3'9042 — Man. Genetic metabolic disorders. Therapy — *Conference proceedings*

Clinical Research Centre. *Symposium (2nd : 1981 : Harrow).* Advances in the treatment of inborn errors of metabolism : proceedings of the 2nd Clinical Research Centre Symposium held in September 1981 / edited by M.d'A. Crawford, Dorothy A. Gibbs, R.W.E. Watts. — Chichester ; New York : Wiley, c1982. — xvii,365p : ill ; 24cm
Includes bibliographies and index
ISBN 0-471-10123-0 : £17.50 : CIP rev. B82-03607

616.3'9061 — Man. Metabolic disorders. Drug therapy. Acarbose — *Conference proceedings*

International Symposium on Acarbose *(1st : 1981 : Montreux).* First International Symposium on Acarbose : effects on carbohydrate and fat metabolism, Montreux, October 8-10, 1981 : proceedings / editor W. Creutzfeldt. — Amsterdam ; Oxford : Excerpta Medica, 1982. — xiii,573p : ill ; 25cm. — (International congress series ; no.594)
Includes index
ISBN 90-219-9540-9 : £40.80 B82-38823

616.3'90792 — Man. Metabolic disorders. Role of human leucocyte antigen system

HLA in endocrine and metabolic disorders / contributors Lester Baker ... [et al.] ; edited by Nadir R. Farid. — New York ; London : Academic Press, 1981. — xiii,357p : ill ; 24cm
Includes bibliographies and index
ISBN 0-12-247780-4 : £25.80
Primary classification 616.4'0792 B82-16318

616.3'98 — Man. Obesity

Serial changes in subcutaneous fat thicknesses of children and adults / A.F. Roche ... [et al.]. — Basel ; London : Karger, c1982. — 110p : ill ; 23cm. — (Monographs in paediatrics ; v.17)
Bibliography: p101-108. — Includes index
ISBN 3-8055-3496-5 (pbk) : £21.95 B82-40295

616.3'98'0019 — Man. Obesity. Psychological aspects

Psychological aspects of obesity : a handbook / Benjamin B. Wolman editor ; Stephen DeBerry editorial associate. — New York ; London : Van Nostrand Reinhold, c1982. — ix,318p : ill ; 24cm
Includes bibliographies and index
ISBN 0-442-22609-8 : £20.85 B82-14012

616.3'99 — Man. Blood. Hyperlipoproteinaemia *related to* **atherosclerosis of heart** — *Conference proceedins*

International Symposium on Lipoproteins and Coronary Atherosclerosis *(1981 : Lugano).* Lipoproteins and coronary atherosclerosis : proceedings of the International Symposium on Lipoproteins and Coronary Atherosclerosis held in Lugano, Switzerland, October 1-3, 1981 / editors: G. Noseda ... [et al.]. — Amsterdam ; Oxford : Elsevier Biomedical, 1982. — xi,450p : ill ; 25cm. — (Symposia of the Giovanni Lorenzini foundation ; v.13)
Includes index
ISBN 0-444-80408-0 : Unpriced
Primary classification 616.1'232 B82-25698

616.3'99 — Man. Calcium metabolic disorders

Calcium disorders / edited by David Heath and Stephen J. Marx. — London : Butterworth Scientific, 1982. — 286p : ill ; 24cm. — (Clinical endocrinology, ISSN 0260-0072 ; 2) (Butterworths international medical reviews)
Includes bibliographies and index
ISBN 0-407-02273-2 : Unpriced : CIP rev. B82-10668

616.3'99 — Man. Metabolic acidosis — *Conference proceedings*

Metabolic acidosis. — London : Pitman, 1982. — x,393p : ill ; 24cm. — (Ciba Foundation symposium ; 87)
Conference papers. — Editors: Ruth Porter and Geralyn Lawrenson. — Includes bibliographies and index
ISBN 0-272-79651-4 : Unpriced : CIP rev. B81-35780

616.3'99 — Man. Mineral metabolic disorders

Disorders of mineral metaboliam. — New York ; London : Academic Press
Vol.3: Pathophysiology of calcium phosphorus, and magnesium / edited by Felix Bronner, Jack W. Coburn. — 1981. — xiv,522p,[2]p of plates : ill(some col.) ; 23cm
Bibliography: p482-506. — Includes index
ISBN 0-12-135303-6 : £47.00 B82-29973

Disorders of mineral metabolism. — New York ; London : Academic Press
Vol.1: Trace minerals : edited by Felix Bronner, Jack W. Coburn. — 1981. — xvi,499p : ill ; 24cm
Includes bibliographies and index
ISBN 0-12-135301-x : £39.00 B82-15539

616.3'998 — Man. Intestines. Lactose. Malabsorption

Lactose digestion : clinical and nutritional implications / David M. Paige, Theodore M. Bayless editors. — Baltimore ; London : Johns Hopkins University Press, c1981. — xix,280p : ill ; 24cm
Includes bibliographies and index
ISBN 0-8018-2647-0 : £15.75 B82-06982

616.3'998042 — Man. Genetic carbohydrate metabolic disorders

Stock, Michael. Obesity and leanness. — London (80 Bondway, SW8 1SF) : John Libbey, May 1982. — [104]p
ISBN 0-86196-014-9 : £10.00 : CIP entry B82-12894

616.4 — MAN. DISEASES OF BLOOD-FORMING, LYMPHATIC, ENDOCRINE SYSTEMS

616.4 — Man. Endocrine system. Diseases

Current endocrine concepts. — Eastbourne : Praeger, Apr.1982. — [224]p. — (Endocrinology and metabolism series ; 2)
ISBN 0-03-062119-4 : £15.00 : CIP entry
Also classified at 616.3'9 B82-11504

Fletcher, Ronald F.. Lecture notes on endocrinology / Ronald F. Fletcher. — 3rd ed. — Oxford : Blackwell Scientific, 1982. — vi,229p : ill ; 22cm
Previous ed.: 1978. — Includes index
ISBN 0-632-00842-3 (pbk) : £6.50 : CIP rev. B82-05400

Fundamentals of clinical endocrinology. — 3rd ed. / Reginald Hall ... [et al.]. — Tunbridge Wells : Pitman Medical, 1980. — vii,788p : ill ; 24cm
Previous ed.: 1974. — Includes bibliographies and index
ISBN 0-272-79559-3 : £28.00 : CIP rev. B80-07801

Toft, Anthony D.. Diagnosis and management of endocrine diseases / Anthony D. Toft, Ian W. Campbell, John Seth. — Oxford : Blackwell Scientific, 1981. — viii,404p : ill ; 22cm
Includes index
ISBN 0-632-00553-x (pbk) : £12.50 : CIP rev. B81-16933

616.4 — Man. Endocrine system. Effects of alcoholism — *Conference proceedings*

Conference on Alcoholism *(4th : 1980 : El Paso).* Endocrinological aspects of alcoholism : 4th Annual Conference on Alcoholism, El Paso, Tex., Feb.22-23, 1980 : volume editors F.S. Messiha and G.S. Tyner. — Basel ; London : Karger, c1981. — ix,232p : ill ; 25cm. — (Progress in biochemical pharmacology ; v.18)
Includes bibliographies and index
ISBN 3-8055-2689-x : £49.30 B82-11586

616.4 — Man. Endocrine system. Effects of liver diseases — *Conference proceedings*

The Endocrines and the liver. — London : Academic Press, Sept.1982. — [500]p. — (Proceedings of the Serono symposia, ISSN 0308-5503 ; 51)
ISBN 0-12-436580-9 : CIP entry B82-18733

616.4 — Medicine. Endocrinology

Daggett, P. R.. Clinical endocrinology / Peter Daggett. — London : Edward Arnold, 1981. — xi,180p : ill ; 23cm. — (Physiological principles in medicine)
Includes bibliographies and index
ISBN 0-7131-4379-7 (pbk) : Unpriced B82-05879

Endocrinology. — Lancaster : MTP Press, Mar.1982. — [250]p. — (New medicine)
ISBN 0-85200-401-x : £9.95 : CIP entry B82-01428

Essentials of endocrinology / edited by J.L.H. O'Riordan, P.G. Malan, R.P. Gould. — Oxford : Blackwell Scientific, 1982. — x,230p : ill ; 24cm
Includes bibliographies and index
ISBN 0-632-00643-9 (pbk) : £7.50 : CIP rev. B82-11990

Lee, Julius. Essential endocrinology. — 2nd ed. — Oxford : Oxford University Press, Oct.1982. — [240]p. — (Oxford medical publications)
Previous ed.: 1978
ISBN 0-19-261290-5 (pbk) : £6.95 : CIP entry B82-23664

616.4 — Medicine. Endocrinology — *Conference proceedings*

International Congress of Endocrinology *(6th : 1980 : Melbourne).* Endocrinology 1980 : proceedings of the VI International Congress of Endocrinology, Melbourne, Australia, February 10-16, 1980 / edited by I.A. Cumming, J.W. Funder, F.A.O. Mendelsohn. — Amsterdam ; Oxford : Elsevier/North-Holland Biomedical, 1980. — xii,736p : ill ; 26cm
Includes index
ISBN 0-444-80267-3 : £22.57 B82-31853

616.4 — Medicine. Endocrinology. Quality control — *Conference proceedings*

Tenovus Workshop *(8th : 1979). Cardiff.* Quality control in clinical endocrinology : proceedings of the Eighth Tenovus Workshop : Cardiff May 1979 / edited by D.W. Wilson, S.J. Gaskell, K.W. Kemp. — Cardiff : Alpha Omega, c1981. — 275p : ill ; 22cm
ISBN 0-900663-09-x : Unpriced B82-20334

616.4 — Medicine. Endocrinology, *to 1981*

Medvei, Victor Cornelius. A history of endocrinology / Victor Cornelius Medvei. — Lancaster : MTP, c1982. — xviii,913p : ill,ports ; 24cm
Includes index
ISBN 0-85200-245-9 : Unpriced : CIP rev. B81-33793

616.4'0022'2 — Man. Endocrine system. Diseases — *Illustrations*

Hall, Reginald. A colour atlas of endocrinology / Reginald Hall, David Evered, Raymond Greene. — London : Wolfe Medical, 1979. — 176p : col.ill ; 27cm
Includes index
ISBN 0-7234-0411-9 : Unpriced B82-05989

616.4′079 — Man. Endocrine system. Diseases. Immunological aspects — *Conference proceedings*

Autoimmune aspects of endocrine disorders / edited by A. Pinchera ... [et al.]. — London : Academic Press, 1980. — xi,434p : ill ; 24cm. — (Proceedings of the Serono symposia, ISSN 0308-5503 ; v.33)
Conference papers. — Includes bibliographies and index
ISBN 0-12-556750-2 : £25.00 : CIP rev. B80-10092

616.4′0792 — Man. Endocrine system. Diseases. Role of human leucocyte antigen system

HLA in endocrine and metabolic disorders / contributors Lester Baker ... [et al.] ; edited by Nadir R. Farid. — New York ; London : Academic Press, 1981. — xiii,357p : ill ; 24cm
Includes bibliographies and index
ISBN 0-12-247780-4 : £25.80
Also classified at 616.3′90792 B82-16318

616.4′10758 — Man. Bone marrow. Diagnosis. Biopsy

Bone marrow biopsy / edited by John R. Krause ; with four contributors. — New York ; Edinburgh : Churchill Livingstone, 1981. — x,232p,ivp of plates : ill(some col.) ; 25cm
Includes bibliographies and index
ISBN 0-443-08110-7 : £22.00 B82-18334

616.4′2 — Man. Lymphatic system. Diseases

Kinmonth, J. B.. The lymphatics : surgery, lymphography and diseases of the chyle and lymph systems / J.B. Kinmonth. — [2nd ed.]. — London : Edward Arnold, 1982. — xii,428p,3leaves of plates : ill(some col.),1ports ; 26cm
Previous ed.: 1972. — Includes bibliographies and index
ISBN 0-7131-4410-6 : £67.50 : CIP rev. B82-04485

616.4′2 — Man. Non-Hodgkin′s lymphomas. Diagnosis

Lymphomas other than Hodgkin′s disease / the British Lymphoma Pathology Group ; edited by A.E. Stuart, A.G. Stansfeld, I. Lauder. — Oxford : Oxford University Press, 1981. — viii,69p : ill ; 26cm. — (Oxford medical publications)
ISBN 0-19-261296-4 : £12.50 : CIP rev. B81-02358

616.4′2′00222 — Man. Lymph nodes. Diseases — *Illustrations*

Henry, Kristin. A colour atlas of thymus and lymph node histopathology : with ultrastructure / Kristin Henry, Geoffrey Farrer-Brown. — London : Wolfe, 1981. — 328p : ill(some col.) ; 27cm
Bibliography: p321. — Includes index
ISBN 0-7234-0743-6 : Unpriced
Also classified at 616.4′3′00222 B82-05690

616.4′3′00222 — Man. Thymus. Diseases — *Illustrations*

Henry, Kristin. A colour atlas of thymus and lymph node histopathology : with ultrastructure / Kristin Henry, Geoffrey Farrer-Brown. — London : Wolfe, 1981. — 328p : ill(some col.) ; 27cm
Bibliography: p321. — Includes index
ISBN 0-7234-0743-6 : Unpriced
Primary classification 616.4′2′00222 B82-05690

616.4′4 — Man. Thyroid. Diseases

The Thyroid : physiology and treatment of disease / section editors Jerome M. Hershman and George A. Bray. — Oxford : Pergamon, 1979. — xii,634p : ill ; 28cm. — (International encyclopedia of pharmacology and therapeutics ; section 101)
Includes bibliographies and index
ISBN 0-08-017685-2 : £53.00 : CIP rev. B78-33819

616.4′407 — Man. Thyroid. Diseases

Bayliss, R. I. S.. Thyroid disease. — Oxford : Oxford University Press, Aug.1982. — [150]p. — (Oxford medical publications)
ISBN 0-19-261350-2 : £5.95 : CIP entry B82-14357

616.4′4′0754 — Man. Thyroid. Diagnosis. Radioimmunoassay

Thyroid diseases. — Oxford : Pergamon, Oct.1982. — [227]p
ISBN 0-08-027094-8 : £12.50 : CIP entry
ISBN 0-08-026405-0 (set) : £250.00 B82-31285

616.4′40756 — Man. Thyroid. Diagnosis. Radioimmunoassay — *Conference proceedings*

Free T4. — Oxford : Medicine Publishing Foundation, Oct.1982. — [48]p
Conference papers
ISBN 0-906817-38-2 (pbk) : £3.50 : CIP entry B82-29156

616.4′44 — Man. Thyroid. Hypothyroidism

International Congress of Therapeutics *(15th : 1979 : Brussels)*. Recent progress in diagnosis and treatment of hypothyroid conditions : proceedings of the XVth International Congress of Therapeutics, Brussels, September 5-9 1979. — Amsterdam ; Oxford : Excerpta Medica Theme 1 / P.A. Bastenie, M. Bonnyns, L. Vanhaelst. — 1980. — viii,157p : ill ; 25cm. — (International congress series ; no.529)
Includes index
ISBN 90-219-0448-9 : Unpriced B82-40732

616.4′62 — Man. Diabetes

Davidson, Mayer B.. Diabetes mellitus : diagnosis and treatment / Mayer B. Davidson. — New York ; Chichester : Wiley, c1981. — vii,480p : ill,forms ; 24cm
Includes bibliographies and index
ISBN 0-471-09543-5 : £12.50 B82-01052

Diabetes : reach for health and freedom / edited by Dorothea F. Sims ; prepared under the auspices of the Vermont Affiliate American Diabetes Association 1976-1979 ; contributors Margaret Calahan .. [et al.] ; illustrations by Meri Bourgard. — St. Louis ; London : Mosby, 1980. — xii,128p : ill,forms ; 26cm
Includes bibliographies and index
ISBN 0-8016-4657-x (spiral) : £4.75 B82-35045

Handbook of diabetes mellitus / edited by Michael Brownlee ; foreword by George F. Cahill, Jr. — Chichester : Wiley, c1981
Originally published: New York : Garland, 1981
Vol.1: Etiology/hormone physiology. — xi,366p : ill ; 24cm. — (A Wiley medical publication)
Includes index
ISBN 0-471-10017-x : £30.00 : CIP rev. B81-18090

Handbook of diabetes mellitus / edited by Michael Brownlee ; foreword by George F. Cahill, Jr. — Chichester : Wiley, c1981
Originally published: New York : Garland, 1981
Vol.2: Islet cell function/insulin action. — xi,255p : ill ; 24cm. — (A Wiley medical publication)
Includes index
ISBN 0-471-10016-1 : £17.00 : CIP rev. B81-18163

Handbook of diabetes mellitus / edited by Michael Brownlee ; foreword by George F. Cahill, Jr. — Chichester : Wiley, c1981
Originally published: New York : Garland, 1981
Vol.3: Intermediary metabolism and its regulation. — xi,317p : ill ; 24cm. — (A Wiley medical publication)
Includes index
ISBN 0-471-10015-3 : £23.00 : CIP rev. B81-25821

Handbook of diabetes mellitus / edited by Michael Brownlee ; foreword by George F. Cahill, Jr. — Chichester : Wiley, c1981
Originally published: New York : Garland, 1981
Vol.4: Biochemical pathology. — xiii,297p : ill ; 24cm. — (A Wiley medical publication)
Includes index
ISBN 0-471-10018-8 : £20.00 : CIP rev. B81-25822

Handbook of diabetes mellitus / edited by Michael Brownlee ; foreword by George F. Cahill, Jr. — Chichester : Wiley, c1981
Originally published: New York : Garland, 1981
Vol.5: Current and future therapies. — xiii,427p : ill ; 24cm. — (A Wiley medical publication)
Includes index
ISBN 0-471-10019-6 : £27.00 : CIP rev. B81-25823

616.4′62 — Man. Diabetes. Complications

Complications of diabetes / edited by Harry Keen and John Jarrett. — 2nd ed. — London : Arnold, 1982. — ix,331p : ill ; 26cm
Previous ed.: 1975. — Bibliography: p287-325. — Includes index
ISBN 0-7131-4409-2 : £25.00 : CIP rev. B82-01191

Diabetes and its late complications. — London : Libbey, Jan.1983. — [184]p
ISBN 0-86196-025-4 : £14.95 : CIP entry B82-33358

616.4′62 — Man. Diabetes. Complications: Foot diseases

Faris, Irwin. The management of the diabetic foot. — Edinburgh : Churchill Livingstone, Dec.1982. — [160]p
ISBN 0-443-02315-8 (pbk) : £10.00 : CIP entry B82-29801

616.4′62 — Man. Diabetes — *Conference proceedings*

The Genetics of diabetes mellitus. — London : Academic Press, July 1982. — [350]p. — (Proceedings of the Serono symposia, ISSN 0308-5503 ; no.47)
Conference papers
ISBN 0-12-417280-6 : CIP entry B82-12443

616.4′62 — Man. Diabetes — *For diabetics*

Anderson, James W.. Diabetes : a practical new guide to healthy living / James W. Anderson ; foreword by Harry Keen. — London : Dunitz, 1981. — 157p : ill(some col.) ; 23cm. — (Positive health guide)
Includes index
ISBN 0-906348-21-8 (cased) : Unpriced : CIP rev.
ISBN 0-906348-22-6 (pbk) : £2.50 B81-16919

Tattersall, Robert, *1943-*. Diabetes : a practical guide for patients on insulin / Robert Tattersall. — Edinburgh : Churchill Livingstone, 1981. — 89p : ill ; 19cm. — (Churchill Livingstone patient handbook ; 9)
ISBN 0-443-02318-2 (pbk) : £1.25 : CIP rev. B81-14982

616.4′62 — Man. Diabetes. Nutritional aspects - *Conference proceedings*

Nutrition and diabetes. — London (80 Bondway, SW8 1SF) : John Libbey, June 1981. — [160]p
Conference papers
ISBN 0-86196-008-4 : £9.00 : CIP entry B81-12882

616.4′6206 — Man. Diabetes. Therapy

Management of diabetes mellitus / edited by Rubin Bressler, David G. Johnson. — Boston, Mass. ; Bristol : John Wright, 1982. — viii,314p : ill ; 25cm
Includes index
ISBN 0-88416-259-1 : Unpriced B82-16123

616.4′62071 — Man. Diabetes. Environmental factors & genetic factors — *Conference proceedings*

Symposium on Diabetes Mellitus in Asia and Oceania *(3rd : 1981 : Honolulu)*. Genetic environmental interaction in diabetes mellitus : proceedings of the Third Symposium on Diabetes Mellitus in Asia and Oceania, Honolulu, February 6-7, 1981 / editors John S. Melish, J. Hanna, S. Baba. — Amsterdam ; Oxford : Excerpta Medica, 1982. — xv,437p : ill,maps ; 25cm. — (International congress series ; no.549)
Includes bibliographies and index
ISBN 90-219-0484-5 : £35.86 B82-27160

616.4'66 — Man. Hypoglycaemia

Marks, V.. Hypoglycaemia / Vincent Marks, F. Clifford Rose. — 2nd ed. / with contributions by James B. Brierley, Herman Bachelard. — Oxford : Blackwell Scientific, 1981. — iv,521p,[1]folded leaf : ill ; 25cm
Previous ed.: 1964. — Includes index
ISBN 0-632-00673-0 : £30.00 : CIP rev. B81-14968

616.4'7 — Man. Pituitary gland. Diseases

The **Pituitary** / edited by Colin Beardwell and Gary L. Robertson. — London : Butterworths, 1981. — 337p : ill ; 24cm. — (Clinical endocrinology, ISSN 0260-0072 ; 1) (Butterworths international medical reviews)
Includes index
ISBN 0-407-02272-4 : Unpriced : CIP rev. B81-16921

616.5 — MAN. DISEASES OF INTEGUMENTARY SYSTEM

616.5 — Man. Skin. Diseases

Dermatology : current concepts and practice. — 3rd ed. / edited by Patrick Hall-Smith, R.J. Cairns. — London : Butterworths, 1981. — xii,408p,[42]p of plates : ill(some col.) ; 24cm
Previous ed.: St. Albans : Crosby Lockwood Staples, 1973. — Includes index
ISBN 0-407-00208-1 (pbk) : Unpriced : CIP rev. B81-16920

Fry, Lionel. Illustrated encyclopaedia of dermatology / Lionel Fry, Fenella T. Wojnarowska, Parvin Shahrad. — Lancaster : MTP, 1981. — vii,567p : ill ; 24cm
Includes index
ISBN 0-85200-309-9 : Unpriced B82-06369

Progress in diseases of the skin. — New York ; London : Grune & Stratton
Vol.1 / edited by Raúl Fleischmajer. — c1981. — xii,280p : ill ; 27cm
Includes index
ISBN 0-8089-1412-x : £26.20 B82-21294

Solomons, Bethel. Lecture notes on dermatology. — 5th ed. — Oxford : Blackwell Scientific, Feb.1983. — [296]p
Previous ed.: 1977
ISBN 0-632-01065-7 (pbk) : £8.50 : CIP entry B82-38865

616.5 — Man. Skin. Effects of psoralens

Psoralens in cosmetics and dermatology. — Oxford : Pergamon, Nov.1981. — [350]p
Conference papers
ISBN 0-08-027057-3 : £25.00 : CIP entry B81-35026

616.5 — Medicine. Dermatology

MacKie, Rona M.. Clinical dermatology : an illustrated textbook / Rona M. MacKie. — Oxford : Oxford University Press, 1981. — ix,301p : ill(some col.) ; 22cm. — (Oxford medical publications)
Bibliography: p289-292. — Includes index
ISBN 0-19-261271-9 (pbk) : £8.95 : CIP rev. B81-13501

616.5 — Medicine. Dermatology — *For developing countries*

Canizares, Orlando. A manual of dermatology for developing countries. — Oxford : Oxford University Press, Feb.1982. — [350]p. — (Oxford medical publications)
ISBN 0-19-261366-9 (cased) : £15.00 : CIP entry
ISBN 0-19-261185-2 (pbk) : £5.00 B81-35770

616.5'0194 — Man. Skin. Virus diseases

Robinson, T. W. E.. Virus diseases of the skin. — Edinburgh : Churchill Livingstone, Feb.1983. — [272]p
ISBN 0-443-01428-0 : £10.00 : CIP entry B82-38272

616.5'06 — Man. Skin. Therapy

Office dermatology / [edited by] Henry J. Roenigk, Jr. — Baltimore ; London : Williams & Wilkins, c1981. — xviii,363p : ill(some col.) ; 26cm
Includes index
ISBN 0-683-07316-8 : Unpriced B82-02565

616.5'061 — Man. Skin. Combined drug therapy & ultraviolet radiotherapy

Weber, Gerhard. Photochemotherapy : information for doctors and patients / Gerhard Weber ; translated by Gerhard Behr. — Chicago ; London : Year Book Medical, 1980. — vi,106p : ill(some col.) ; 19cm
Translation of: Photochemotherapie. — Includes index
ISBN 0-8151-9155-3 (pbk) : £8.75 B82-31764

616.5'079 — Man. Skin. Diseases. Immunological aspects

Cormane, Rudi H.. Immunology and skin diseases / Rudi H. Cormane, Syed Shafi Asghar. — London : Edward Arnold, 1981. — viii,230p : ill ; 24cm. — (Current topics in immunology, ISSN 0305-8204 ; 15)
Includes bibliographies and index
ISBN 0-7131-4346-0 : £18.00 B82-00526

616.5'26 — Man. Psoriasis — *For psoriasis sufferers*

Marks, Ronald. Psoriasis : a guide to one of the commonest skin diseases / Ronald Marks. — London : Dunitz, 1981. — 107p : ill(some col.) ; 23cm. — (Positive health guide)
Includes index
ISBN 0-906348-19-6 (cased) : Unpriced : CIP rev.
ISBN 0-906348-20-x (pbk) : £2.50 B81-16917

616.5'26 — Man. Skin. Psoriasis — *Conference proceedings*

Psoriasis : proceedings of the third international symposium, Stanford University 1981 / edited by Eugene M. Farber ... [et al.]. — New York ; London : Grune & Stratton, c1982. — xxxvii,530p : ill ; 27cm
Includes bibliographies and index
ISBN 0-8089-1472-3 : £23.20 B82-35738

616.5'260654 — Man. Skin. Psoriasis. Therapy. Diet

Clements, Harry, *1928-*. Diets to help psoriasis / by Harry Clements. — Wellingborough : Thorsons, 1981. — 48p ; 18cm
ISBN 0-7225-0708-9 (pbk) : £0.60 : CIP rev. B81-21515

616.5'44 — Man. Skin. Warts

Bunney, Mary H.. Viral warts. — Oxford : Oxford University Press, Dec.1981. — [92]p. — (Oxford medical publications)
ISBN 0-19-261335-9 : £8.50 : CIP entry B81-31354

616.5'45 — Man. Legs. Ulcers. Therapy

Ryan, Terence J.. The management of leg ulcers. — Oxford : Oxford University Press, Jan.1983. — [100]p. — (Oxford medical publications)
ISBN 0-19-261338-3 (pbk) : £5.95 : CIP entry B82-33478

616.5'46 — Man. Hair & scalp. Diseases

Rook, Arthur. Diseases of the hair and scalp / Arthur Rook, Rodney Dawber. — Oxford : Blackwell Scientific, 1982. — ix,571p : ill ; 24cm
Includes bibliographies and index
ISBN 0-632-00822-9 : £35.00 : CIP rev. B81-37544

616.5'47 — Man. Nails. Diseases

The **Nail** / edited by Maurice Pierre in collaboration with G. Achten ... [et al.]. — Edinburgh : Churchill Livingstone, 1981. — 118p : ill ; 29cm. — (GEM monograph series ; [5])
Includes bibliographies and index
ISBN 0-443-02102-3 : £22.00 : CIP rev. B81-15843

616.5'5 — Man. Albinism — *Serials*

[Newsletter *(Albino Fellowship)***]**. Newsletter / Albino Fellowship. — [No.2] (Apr. 1980)-. — Ayr (c/o Jim Wiseman, 15 Goukscroft Park, Ayr, Ayrshire KA7 4DS) : The Fellowships, 1980-. — v. ; 30cm
Four issues yearly. — Series title did not appear on B.M.J. article reprint which was later designated No.1. — Description based on: No.7 (Nov. 1981)
ISSN 0263-1652 = Newsletter - Albino Fellowship : Unpriced B82-36726

616.6 — MAN. DISEASES OF UROGENITAL SYSTEM

616.6 — Man. Urinary tract. Diagnosis & therapy

Brown, R. B.. Clinical urology illustrated / R.B. Brown ; with foreword by Willard E. Goodwin. — Lancaster : MTP, c1982. — xi,401p : ill ; 29cm
Includes bibliographies and index
ISBN 0-85200-595-4 : £29.95 B82-13382

616.6 — Man. Urinary tract. Diseases

Jones, J. Michael Boulton. Diagnosis and management of renal and urinary diseases. — Oxford : Blackwell Scientific, Mar.1982. — [176]p
ISBN 0-632-00677-3 (pbk) : £8.50 : CIP entry
Primary classification 616.6'1 B82-05399

Maskell, Rosalind. Urinary tract infection / Rosalind Maskell. — London : Edward Arnold, 1982. — viii,144p,ill ; 24cm. — (Current topics in infection)
Bibliography: p126-139. — Includes index
ISBN 0-7131-4416-5 : £15.50 : CIP rev. B82-20037

Stamey, Thomas A.. Pathogenesis and treatment of urinary tract infections / Thomas A. Stamey. — Baltimore ; London : Williams & Wilkins, c1980. — ix,612p : ill(some col.) ; 26cm
Includes index
ISBN 0-683-07909-3 : Unpriced B82-03547

616.6 — Man. Urogenital system. Diseases

Blandy, John P.. Lecture notes on urology / John Blandy. — 3rd ed. — Oxford : Blackwell Scientific, 1982. — viii,384p : ill ; 24cm
Previous ed.: 1977. — Includes index
ISBN 0-632-00688-9 (pbk) : £9.80 : CIP rev. B81-34634

Brooks, David, *19---*. Renal medicine and urology / David Brooks, Netar Mallick. — Edinburgh : Churchill Livingstone, 1982. — 294p : ill,forms ; 22cm. — (Library of general practice ; 4)
Includes bibliographies and index
ISBN 0-443-01718-2 (pbk) : £8.50 : CIP rev. B81-31842

Newsam, J. E.. Urology and renal medicine / J.E. Newsam, J.J.B. Petrie. — 3rd ed. — Edinburgh : Churchill Livingstone, 1981. — 277p : ill ; 22cm. — (Churchill Livingstone medical text)
Previous ed.: 1975. — Includes bibliographies and index
ISBN 0-443-02391-3 (pbk) : Unpriced : CIP rev. B81-07417

616.6 — Medicine. Urology

Scott, Roy. Urology illustrated / Roy Scott, R. Fletcher Deane, Robin Callander. — 2nd ed. — Edinburgh : Churchill Livingstone, 1982. — 487p : ill ; 25cm
Previous ed.: 1981. — Includes index
ISBN 0-443-02376-x (pbk) : £10.00 B82-25662

616.6'061 — Man. Urinary tract. Drug therapy. Phenoxybenzamine — *Conference proceedings*

Phenoxybenzamine in disorders of micturition : proceedings of a symposium held at the Cavendish Conference Centre, London, November 1981 / edited by W. Keith Yeates. — Welwyn Garden City : Smith Kline & French, 1982. — vii,103p : ill,1form ; 24cm
Includes bibliographies
ISBN 0-9503292-2-3 (pbk) : Unpriced B82-31681

616.6'071 — Man. Reproductive system. Effects of toxic chemicals

Sullivan, F. M.. Reproductive hazards of industrial chemicals. — London : Academic Press, Aug.1982. — [620]p
ISBN 0-12-676250-3 : CIP entry B82-17194

616.6'0754 — Man. Urinary tract. Catheterisation — *For nursing*

Clean intermittent catheterization / CURN Project ; principal investigator : Jo Anne Horsley ; ... director : Joyce Crane ; ... manuscript ... prepared by Margaret A. Reynolds. — New York ; London : Grune & Stratton, c1982. — xvii,102p : ill ; 23cm. — (Using research to improve nursing practice)
Bibliography: p95-96. — Includes index
ISBN 0-8089-1463-4 (spiral) : £9.40
B82-39087

Closed urinary drainage systems / CURN Project ; principal investigator Jo Anne Horsley ; director Joyce Crane ; the protocol manuscript ... prepared by Karen B. Haller, Janet D. Bingle. — New York ; London : Grune & Stratton, c1981. — xvii,107p : ill,1form ; 23cm. — (Using research to improve nursing practice)
Bibliography: p97-98. — Includes index
ISBN 0-8089-1390-5 (spiral) : £6.40
B82-18350

616.6'1 — Man. Kidneys. Diseases

Asscher, A. W.. Nephrology illustrated : an integrated text and colour atlas / A. William Asscher, David B. Moffat, Eric Sanders ; foreword by Barry M. Brenner. — Oxford : Pergamon Medical, c1982. — 252p in various pagings : ill(some col.),1col.map ; 32cm
Includes index
ISBN 0-08-028851-0 : £48.00 B82-23413

Jones, J. Michael Boulton. Diagnosis and management of renal and urinary diseases. — Oxford : Blackwell Scientific, Mar.1982. — [176]p
ISBN 0-632-00677-3 (pbk) : £8.50 : CIP entry
Also classified at 616.6 B82-05399

Nephrology / edited by Jay H. Stein. — New York ; London : Grune & Stratton, c1980. — xxiii,458p : ill ; 29cm. — (The Science and practice of clinical medicine ; v.7)
Includes bibliographies and index
ISBN 0-8089-1246-1 : £22.50 B82-35682

Rose, Burton David. Patho-physiology of renal disease / Burton David Rose. — New York ; London : McGraw-Hill, c1981. — xii,745p : ill ; 25cm
Illustrations for pp.354-355 as insert. — Includes index
ISBN 0-07-053616-3 (cased) : Unpriced
ISBN 0-07-053615-5 (pbk) : £11.95
B82-27153

616.6'1 — Man. Kidneys. Toxic effects of chemicals — *Conference proceedings*

International Symposium on Nephrotoxicity *(1981 : University of Surrey)*. Nephrotoxicity. — Chichester : Wiley, Oct.1982. — [500]p. — (Monographs in applied toxicology ; 1)
ISBN 0-471-26212-9 : £30.00 : CIP entry
B82-25193

616.6'1'0024613 — Man. Kidneys. Diseases — *For nursing*

Development of the clinical nephrology practitioner : a focus on independent learning / by the staff of the Division of Nursing Services, University of Washington Hospital, Seattle, Washington ; edited by Elaine Larson, Lisa Lindbloom, Karen Braschel Davis. — St. Louis, Mo. ; London : Mosby, 1982. — xiii,328p : ill,forms ; 28cm
Includes bibliographies and index
ISBN 0-8016-2868-7 (spiral) : £17.75
B82-31866

616.6'1'005 — Man. Kidneys. Diseases — *Serials*

Current nephrology. — Vol.1-. — New York ; Chichester : Wiley, 1977-. — v. : ill ; 26cm
Annual. — Description based on: Vol.5
ISSN 0148-4265 = Current nephrology : Unpriced B82-38512

Recent advances in renal medicine. — No.2. — Edinburgh : Churchill Livingstone, Aug.1982. — [270]p
ISBN 0-443-02278-x (pbk) : £15.00 : CIP entry
ISSN 0309-2429 B82-15797

616.6'107 — Man. Kidneys. Diseases. Physiological aspects

Harrington, Avery R.. Renal pathophysiology / Avery R. Harrington, Stephen W. Zimmerman. — New York ; Chichester : Wiley, c1982. — xi,258p : ill ; 24cm. — (Wiley pathophysiology series)
Includes bibliographies and index
ISBN 0-471-07815-8 (pbk) : £12.95
B82-13620

Leaf, Alexander. Renal pathophysiology / Alexander Leaf, Ramzi S. Cotran. — 2nd ed. — New York ; Oxford : Oxford University Press, 1980. — xiii,410p : ill ; 23cm
Previous ed.: 1976. — Includes index
ISBN 0-19-502688-8 (cased) : Unpriced
ISBN 0-19-502689-6 (pbk) : £7.95 B82-22748

616.6'107 — Man. Kidneys. Pathology

Risdon, R. A.. Atlas of renal pathology / by R.A. Risdon and D.R. Turner. — Lancaster : MTP, c1980. — 90p : ill(some col.) ; 31cm. — (Current histopathology ; v.2)
Includes index
ISBN 0-85200-204-1 : £17.50 : CIP rev.
B80-29770

616.6'10757 — Man. Kidneys. Diagnosis. Radiography

Radionuclides in nephrology / edited by A.M. Joekes ... [et al.]. — London : Academic, 1982. — xxii,354p : ill ; 24cm
Conference proceedings. — Includes index
ISBN 0-12-792186-9 : £19.20 B82-38074

616.6'10757 — Man. Kidneys. Diagnosis. Radiography — *Conference proceedings*

Radionuclides in nephrology. — London : Academic Press, May 1982. — [300]p
Conference papers
ISBN 0-12-385480-6 : CIP entry B82-08435

616.6'1079 — Man. Kidneys. Diseases. Immunological aspects — *Conference proceedings*

International Nephrourological Course *(3rd : 1980 : Erice)*. Advances in nephrourology / [proceedings of the Third International Nephrourological Course, held May 12-18, 1980, in Erice, Sicily] ; edited by Michele Pavone-Macaluso and Philip H. Smith ; associate editors Antonio Vercellone, Rosario Maiorca, Ugo Rotolo. — New York ; London : Plenum, c1981. — x,481p : ill ; 26cm. — (Ettore Majorana international science series. Life sciences ; v.9)
Includes bibliographies and index
ISBN 0-306-40836-8 : Unpriced B82-14701

616.6'14 — Man. Kidneys. Acute renal failure — *Conference proceedings*

Acute renal failure. — London : John Libbey, June 1982. — [320]p
Conference proceedings
ISBN 0-86196-013-0 : £24.00 : CIP entry
B82-17951

616.6'14 — Man. Kidneys. Chronic renal failure

Chronic renal failure / edited by Barry M. Brenner and Jay H. Stein. — New York ; Edinburgh : Churchill Livingstone, 1981. — viii,337p : ill ; 24cm. — (Contemporary issues in nephrology ; v.7)
Includes bibliographies and index
ISBN 0-443-08141-7 : £24.00 B82-16438

616.6'1406 — Man. Kidneys. Acute renal failure. Therapy

The **Treatment** of renal failure / edited by J.E. Castro. — Lancaster : MTP, c1982. — vii,392p : ill ; 25cm
Includes index
ISBN 0-85200-336-6 : £17.95 : CIP rev.
B81-21544

616.6'1406 — Man. Kidneys. Acute renal failure. Therapy — *Conference proceedings*

Renal failure — who cares?. — Lancaster : MTP Press, Nov.1982. — [260]p
Conference papers
ISBN 0-85200-476-1 : £19.50 : CIP entry
B82-37488

616.6'1406 — Man. Kidneys. Chronic renal failure. Therapy — *For patients*

Gabriel, Roger. A patient's guide to dialysis and transplantation. — 2nd ed. — Lancaster : M.T.P. Press, Aug.1982. — [128]p
Previous ed.: 1980
ISBN 0-85200-486-9 (pbk) : £5.00 : CIP entry
B82-25763

616.6'1406'0973 — United States. Man. Kidneys. Chronic renal failure. Therapy — *For welfare work*

Fortner-Frazier, Carrie L.. Social work and dialysis : the medical and psychosocial aspects of kidney disease / Carrie L. Fortner-Frazier. — Berkeley ; London : University of California Press, c1981. — xvi,228p : ill ; 24cm
Bibliography: p203-219. — Includes index
ISBN 0-520-03674-3 : £11.50 B82-13754

616.6'22 — Man. Urinary tract. Calculi

Urinary stones : clinical and laboratory aspects / G. Alan Rose with contributions from J.E.A. Wickham ... [et al.]. — Lancaster : MTP, c1982. — x,272p : ill ; 24cm
Includes index
ISBN 0-85200-342-0 : £16.95 : CIP rev.
B81-28023

616.6'23 — Man. Bladder. Cystitis

Fisk, Peter. Pocket guide to cystitis / by Peter Fisk. — London : Arlington, 1982. — 96p ; 13cm
ISBN 0-85140-563-0 (pbk) : £0.95 B82-21284

616.6'3 — Man. Incontinence

McLaughlin, Eve. Incontinence explained / Eve McLaughlin. — Hornchurch : Ian Henry, 1981. — 137p : ill ; 21cm
Includes index
ISBN 0-86025-850-5 : £4.95 B82-05578

616.6'50143 — Man. Reproductive system. Diseases caused by Chlamydia trachomatis

Oriel, J. D.. Genital infection by Chalamydia trachomatis / J.D Oriel, G.L. Ridgway. — London : Edward Arnold, 1982. — viii,144p : ill ; 24cm. — (Current topics in infection, ISSN 0260-1664 ; 2)
Bibliography: p117-135. — Includes index
ISBN 0-7131-4376-2 : £13.50 : CIP rev.
B82-01190

616.6'5061 — Man. Reproductive system. Drug therapy. Hormones

International Study Group for Steroid Hormones. *Meeting (10th : 1981 : Rome)*. Hormonal factors in fertility, infertility and contraception : proceedings of the X Meeting of the International Study Group for Steroid Hormones, Rome, December 2-4, 1981 / editors H.J. van der Molen ... [et al.]. — Amsterdam ; Oxford : Excerpta Medica, 1982. — vi,317p : ill ; 25cm. — (International congress series ; no.580)
Includes bibliographies and index
ISBN 90-219-0580-9 : £39.61 B82-36629

616.6'50654 — Men. Prostate gland. Therapy. Diet

Prostate problems / [edited by Eileen Lloyd]. — Aylesbury : Rodale, 1982. — 46p : 1ill ; 18cm. — (Prevention health guides)
ISBN 0-87857-405-0 (pbk) : Unpriced
B82-36761

616.6'5079 — Man. Reproduction. Immunological aspects — *Conference proceedings*

Immunological factors in human reproduction / edited by Sidney Shulman, Franco Dondero, Maria Nicotra. — London : Academic Press, 1982. — xiii,254p ; 24cm. — (Proceedings of the Serono symposia, ISSN 0308-5503 ; v.45)
Includes bibliographies and index
ISBN 0-12-640780-0 : Unpriced : CIP rev.
B82-00333

616.6'906 — Man. Sexual disorders. Therapy

Krohne, Eric C.. Sex therapy handbook : a clinical manual for the diagnosis and treatment of sexual disorders / Eric C. Krohne. — Lancaster : MTP Press, c1982. — 100p : ill ; 26cm
Bibliography: p91-97. — Includes index
ISBN 0-85200-593-8 : Unpriced B82-33528

616.6′906 — Man. Sexual disorders. Therapy *continuation*

Masters, William H.. Human sexual inadequacy / William H. Masters, Virginia E. Johnson. — Toronto ; London : Bantam, 1980, c1970. — x,463p : ill ; 18cm
Originally published: Boston, Mass. : Little, Brown, 1970. — Bibliography: p385-447. — Includes index
ISBN 0-553-13739-5 (pbk) : £1.95 B82-35026

Offit, Avodah K.. Night thoughts : reflections of a sex therapist / [by Avodah K. Offit]. — London : Weidenfeld and Nicolson, 1982, c1981. — 256p ; 23cm
Includes index
ISBN 0-297-78043-3 : £6.95 B82-13971

Sex problems in practice. — London : British Medical Association, c1982. — viii,81p : ill ; 22cm
Includes index
ISBN 0-7279-0087-0 (pbk) : Unpriced B82-34791

Stephan, Peter. Sexual rejuvenation / Peter Stephan and Dick Richards. — London : Frederick Muller, 1982. — 163p ; 22cm
Includes index
ISBN 0-584-10494-4 (pbk) : £3.95 : CIP rev. B82-04579

616.6′92 — Man. Infertility

Thompson, William, *1937-*. Denied a child : an inaugural lecture delivered before the Queen′s University of Belfast on 6 January 1981 / William Thompson. — [Belfast] : Queen′s University of Belfast, c1982. — 20p,[8]p of plates : ill,ports ; 21cm. — (New lecture series ; no.129)
Bibliography: p19-20
ISBN 0-85389-206-7 (pbk) : £0.40 B82-31364

616.6′92 — Men. Infertility. Role of epididymis

International Colloquium on Epididymis and Fertility *(1980 : Strasbourg)*. Epididymis and fertility : biology and pathology : International Colloquium on Epididymis and Fertility, Strasbourg, October 24-25, 1980 / volume editors C. Bollack, A. Clavert. — Basel ; London : Karger, 1981. — vii,173p : ill ; 25cm. — (Progress in reproductive biology ; v.8)
Includes bibliographies
ISBN 3-8055-2157-x : £35.70 B82-03752

616.6′9206 — Man. Infertility. Therapy — *For infertile couples*

Stanway, Andrew. Why us? : a common-sense guide for the childless / Andrew Stanway. — London : Granada, 1980. — 221p : ill ; 20cm. — (A Mayflower book)
Includes index
ISBN 0-583-13179-4 (pbk) : £1.95 B82-24513

616.7 — MAN. DISEASES OF MUSCULOSKELETAL SYSTEM

616.7 — Man. Motor disorders

Disorders of the motor unit / edited by Donald L. Schotland. — New York ; Chichester : Wiley, c1982. — xvii,954p : ill ; 27cm
Includes index
ISBN 0-471-09507-9 : £55.50 B82-26494

Jayson, Malcolm I. V.. Locomotor disability in general practice. — Oxford : Oxford University Press, Feb.1983. — [350]p. — (Oxford general practice series ; 5)
ISBN 0-19-261331-6 (pbk) : £9.95 : CIP entry B82-37479

616.7′1 — Man. Bones. Osteoporosis — *Conference proceedings*

Osteoporosis. — London : Academic Press, Dec.1982. — [300]p. — (International congress and symposium series / Royal Society of Medicine, ISSN 0142-2367 ; 55)
Conference papers
ISBN 0-12-791054-9 : CIP entry B82-36320

Osteoporosis. — Chichester : Wiley, June 1982. — [360]p. — (A Wiley medical publication)
Conference papers
ISBN 0-471-10156-7 : £25.00 : CIP entry B82-09705

616.7′1 — Man. Jaws & teeth. Diseases. Diagnosis. Use of X-rays

Browne, R. M.. A radiological atlas of diseases of the teeth and jaws. — London : Heyden, May 1982. — [232]p
ISBN 0-85602-094-x : £25.00 : CIP entry B82-10692

616.7′1042 — Man. Bones. Osteogenesis imperfecta

Smith, Roger. The brittle bone syndrome. — London : Butterworth Scientific, Jan.1983. — [272]p
ISBN 0-407-00211-1 : £20.00 : CIP entry B82-34424

616.7′1075 — Man. Bones. Diagnosis — *Conference proceedings*

European Symposium on Calcified Tissue Research *(16th : 1981 : Belgium)*. Non-invasive bone measurements. — Oxford (P.O. Box 1, Eynsham, Oxford OX8 1JJ) : IRL Press, Oct.1982. — [300]p
ISBN 0-904147-47-9 (pbk) : £12.00 : CIP entry B82-32887

616.7′107572 — Man. Bones. Diagnosis. Radiography. Use of x-rays

Edeiken, Jack. Roentgen diagnosis of diseases of bone / Jack Edeiken. — 3rd ed. — Baltimore ; London : Williams & Wilkins, c1981. — 2v.(1557,xlviip,1folded leaf of plates) : ill ; 26cm. — (Golden′s diagnostic radiology ; section 6)
Previous ed.: 1973. — Includes bibliographies and index
ISBN 0-683-02744-1 : Unpriced B82-02595

616.7′12 — Man. Joints. Osteoarthritis. Therapy — *Conference proceedings*

International Symposium on New Trends in Osteoarthritis *(1981 : Monte Carlo)*. New trends in osteoarthritis / International Symposium on New Trends in Osteoarthritis, Monte Carlo, October 9 1981 ; volume editors E.C. Huskisson, G. Katona. — Basel ; London : Karger, 1982. — 198p ; 25cm. — (Rheumatology ; 7)
ISBN 3-8055-3487-6 (pbk) : £23.20 B82-32045

616.7′2 — Man. Arthritis & rheumatic diseases

Fox, William W.. Arthritis : is your suffering really necessary?. — London : Sheldon, Sept.1982. — [128]p
Originally published: London : Hale, 1981
ISBN 0-85969-372-4 (pbk) : £1.50 : CIP entry B82-20849

Golding, Douglas N.. Problems in arthritis and rheumatism / Douglas N. Golding. — Lancaster : MTP, 1981. — 160p : ill ; 24cm. — (Problems in practice series)
Includes index
ISBN 0-85200-394-3 : Unpriced : CIP rev. B81-21604

Scott, J. T.. Arthritis and rheumatism : the facts / by J.T. Scott ; with an introduction by Dorothy Eden. — Oxford : Oxford University Press, 1980 (1981 [printing]). — xi,123p : ill ; 21cm. — (Oxford medical publications)
Includes index
ISBN 0-19-286022-4 (pbk) : £2.95 B82-15412

616.7′2 — Man. Joints. Diseases

Dieppe, P. A.. Crystals and joint disease. — London : Chapman and Hall, Oct.1982. — [250]p
ISBN 0-412-22150-0 : £15.00 : CIP entry B82-24474

616.7′205 — Man. Arthritis & rheumatic diseases. Prevention. Self-help

Arthritis and rheumatism / [edited by Eileen Lloyd]. — Aylesbury : Rodale, 1982. — 46p ; 18cm. — (Prevention health guides)
ISBN 0-87857-408-5 (pbk) : Unpriced B82-36765

616.7′206 — Man. Joints. Arthritis & rheumatic diseases. Therapy — *Conference proceedings*

International Seminar on Treatment of Rheumatic Diseases *(2nd : 1980 : Herzliya)*. Progress in rheumatology : Second International Seminar on Treatment of Rheumatic Diseases / edited by Israel Machtey. — Boston, Mass. ; Bristol : Wright, 1982. — xxiii,211p : ill ; 24cm
Includes index
ISBN 0-7236-7007-2 : Unpriced : CIP rev. B81-35843

616.7′2062 — Man. Joints. Arthritis & rheumatic diseases. Physiotherapy

Hyde, Sylvia A.. Physiotherapy in rheumatology / Sylvia A. Hyde with contributions by O.M. Scott, R.E. Jarvis, R.A. Harrison. — Oxford : Blackwell Scientific, 1980. — x,194p : ill ; 22cm
Includes index
ISBN 0-632-00373-1 (pbk) : £8.80 : CIP rev. B80-19784

616.7′2065 — Man. Joints. Arthritis & rheumatic diseases. Naturopathy

Quick, Clifford. Why endure rheumatism and arthritis? / Clifford Quick ; foreword by Douglas Latto. — London : Unwin, 1982. — xiii,188p : ill ; 20cm
Originally published: London : Allen & Unwin, 1980. — Bibliography: p182-183. — Includes index
ISBN 0-04-616022-1 (pbk) : £2.50 : CIP rev. B81-33911

616.7′2068 — Man. Joints. Arthritis & rheumatic diseases. Self-treatment

Pemble, Edna. [Home therapy for your arthritis]. Self help for your arthritis. — London : Sheldon, Jan.1983. — [80]p. — (Overcoming common problems)
Originally published: Sydney : Reed, 1981
ISBN 0-85969-367-8 (pbk) : £1.95 : CIP entry B82-33120

616.7′2206 — Man. Joints. Arthritis. Therapy

Freeman, Julian. Arthritis : the treatments / Julian Freeman. — London : Orbis, 1982, c1981. — xiv,160p : ill ; 23cm
Originally published: Chicago : Contemporary Books, 1979. — Includes index
ISBN 0-85613-408-2 (pbk) : £3.50 B82-24027

Hunton, Mollie. Treatment for your arthritis : a guide to the treatment of arthritis orthodox and alternative / Mollie Hunton. — Stourbridge : Mark & Moody, 1982. — 42p : ill ; 21cm
Bibliography: p42. — Includes index
ISBN 0-9506439-2-0 (pbk) : Unpriced B82-24634

616.7′220654 — Man. Arthritis. Therapy. Diet — *Recipes*

Andrews, Judy. Food for arthritics : based on Dr Dong′s diet / Judy and Jim Andrews. — London : Faber, 1982. — 187p ; 21cm
Bibliography: p181-182. — Includes index
ISBN 0-571-11876-3 (cased) : £6.95 : CIP rev.
ISBN 0-571-11911-5 (pbk) : Unpriced B82-09433

616.7′2207 — Man. Joints. Osteoarthritis. Biomechanical aspects

Osteoarthromechanics / editor Dhanjoo N. Ghista. — Washington ; London : Hemisphere, c1982. — x,485p : ill ; 25cm
Includes index
ISBN 0-07-023168-0 : £37.75 B82-07446

616.7′23 — Man. Rheumatic diseases

Bluestone, Rodney. Practical rheumatology diagnosis and management / Rodney Bluestone. — Menlo Park ; London : Addison-Wesley, c1980. — xvi,239p : ill ; 24cm. — (The Addison-Wesley clinical practice series)
Includes index
ISBN 0-201-00094-6 : Unpriced B82-27979

616.7′23 — Man. Rheumatic diseases *continuation*

Clinical rheumatology / edited by John H. Talbott. — New York ; Oxford : Elsevier, c1978. — xii,198p : ill ; 24cm. — (Fundamental and clinical aspects of internal medicine)
Includes bibliographies and index
ISBN 0-444-00270-7 (cased) : Unpriced
ISBN 0-444-00251-0 (pbk) : Unpriced B82-21626

Currey, H. L. F.. Essentials of rheumatology. — London : Pitman, Jan.1983. — [152]p
ISBN 0-272-79677-8 (pbk) : £4.25 : CIP entry B82-33716

Golding, Douglas N.. A synopsis of rheumatic diseases / Douglas N. Golding. — 4th ed. — Bristol : John Wright, 1982. — viii,306p : ill ; 19cm
Previous ed. : 1978. — Includes index
ISBN 0-7236-0627-7 (pbk) : Unpriced : CIP rev. B82-01558

Hall, Hamilton. Rheumatology. — Lancaster : MTP Press, Mar.1982. — [175]p. — (New medicine)
ISBN 0-85200-400-1 : £9.95 : CIP entry B82-01429

Rogers, Michael, *1947-*. Rheumatology in general practice / Michael Rogers, Norman Williams. — Edinburgh : Churchill Livingstone, 1981. — 266p : ill ; 21cm. — (Library of general practice ; 3)
Includes bibliographies and index
ISBN 0-443-01720-4 (pbk) : £7.50 : CIP rev. B81-16412

Scientific basis of rheumatology. — Edinburgh : Churchill Livingstone, June 1982. — [320]p
ISBN 0-443-02155-4 : £25.00 : CIP entry B82-09715

616.7′23 — Man. Rheumatic diseases. Complications: Kidney diseases

The **Kidney** and rheumatic disease / edited by Paul A. Bacon and Nortin M. Hadler. — London : Butterworth Scientific, 1982. — 396p : ill ; 24cm. — (Butterworths international medical reviews. Rheumatology, ISSN 0260-017x ; 1)
Includes bibliographies and index
ISBN 0-407-02352-6 : Unpriced : CIP rev.
ISSN 0260-017x B82-10683

616.7′23′005 — Rheumatology — *Serials*

Rheumatology in practice. — Vol.1, no.1 (Oct. 1981)-. — London (1 Bedford St., WC2E 9HD) : Medical News Group, 1981-. — v. : ill,ports ; 27cm
Six issues yearly
ISSN 0262-5512 = Rheumatology in practice : £15.00 per year B82-18520

Topical reviews in rheumatic disorders. — Vol.2. — Bristol : Wright, Sept.1982. — [256]p
ISBN 0-7236-0642-0 : £18.00 : CIP entry B82-20393

616.7′23061 — Man. Rheumatic diseases. Drug therapy

Anti-rheumatic drugs. — Eastbourne : Praeger, Feb.1983. — [704]p
ISBN 0-03-062353-7 : £30.00 : CIP entry B82-37473

Bird, H. A.. Applied drug therapy of the rheumatic diseases / H.A. Bird, V. Wright. — Bristol : John Wright, 1982. — xiii,309p : ill ; 24cm
Includes index
ISBN 0-7236-0658-7 (pbk) : Unpriced : CIP rev. B82-17213

616.7′23061 — Man. Rheumatic diseases. Drug therapy. Benoxaprofen

Benoxaprofen : symptomatic or suppressive relief? : a workshop held at University College, Oxford, 18 December 1981 / chaired by I.A. Jaffe. — Oxford : MEDICINE Publishing Foundation, 1982. — 16p : ill ; 22cm
ISBN 0-906817-26-9 (pbk) : £2.50 : CIP rev. B82-14197

616.7′23061 — Man. Rheumatic diseases. Drug therapy. Diflunisal — *Conference proceedings*

Dolobid : a review of current studies : collected summaries of papers read at a meeting held in London on 23 November 1978, sponsored by Thomas Morson Pharmaceuticals, division of Merck, Sharp & Dohme Limited / editor V. Wright. — Tunbridge Wells (33 Vale Rd, Tunbridge Wells, Kent TN1 1BP) : MCS Consultants, c1979. — 31p : ill ; 25cm
Includes bibliographies
Unpriced (pbk) B82-15387

616.7′23061 — Man. Rheumatic diseases. Drug therapy. Fenclofenac — *Conference proceedings*

International Congress of Rheumatology *(15th : 1981 : Paris)*. Fenclofenac : a step beyond symptomatic relief : papers presented at the XV International Congress of Rheumatology, Paris, France on 22 June 1981 / foreword by B.M. Ansell. — Oxford : Medicine Publishing Foundation, 1981. — 24p : ill ; 21cm
Includes bibliographies
ISBN 0-906817-15-3 (pbk) : Unpriced B82-09754

616.7′2307572 — Man. Rheumatic diseases. Radiography. Use of x-rays

Dequeker, J.. An atlas of radiology of rheumatic disorders / J. Dequeker ; English version by D.H. Bosman. — London : Wolfe, 1982. — 176p : ill ; 27cm. — (Wolfe medical atlases)
Includes index
ISBN 0-7234-0773-8 : Unpriced B82-16159

616.7′23079 — Man. Rheumatic diseases. Immunological aspects

Immunological aspects of rheumatology / edited by W. Carson Dick. — Lancaster : MTP, 1981. — ix,262p : ill ; 25cm
Includes index
ISBN 0-85200-164-9 : £19.95 : CIP rev. B81-18176

616.7′2309 — Man. Rheumatic diseases - *Case studies*

Golding, Douglas N.. Tutorials in clinical rheumatology. — Tunbridge Wells : Pitman Medical, May 1981. — [128]p
ISBN 0-272-79611-5 : £6.95 : CIP entry B81-06035

616.7′3 — Man. Back. Backache

Evans, David P.. Backache : its evolution and conservative treatment / David P. Evans. — Lancaster : MTP, 1982. — viii,244p : ill ; 25cm
Bibliography: p229-235. — Includes index
ISBN 0-85200-430-3 : £11.95 : CIP rev. B81-28130

Management of low back pain / edited by Harold Carron, Robert E. McLaughlin. — Boston [Mass.] ; Bristol : John Wright, 1982. — xii,246p : ill ; 24cm
Includes index
ISBN 0-7236-7001-3 : Unpriced B82-30123

Porter, R. W.. Understanding back pain. — Edinburgh : Churchill Livingstone, Feb.1983. — [128]p. — (Churchill Livingstone patient handbook ; 13)
ISBN 0-443-02711-0 (pbk) : £1.95 : CIP entry B82-36319

616.7′3043 — Man. Spine. Spina bifida occulta

James, C. C. Michael. Spina bifida occulta : orthopaedic, radiological and neurosurgical aspects / C.C. Michael James, L.P. Lassman. — London : Academic Press, 1981. — x,230p : ill ; 24cm
Includes bibliographies and index
ISBN 0-12-792162-1 : £20.00 : CIP rev. B81-15805

616.7′306 — Man. Back. Backache. Therapy

Marshall, Leon. Your bad back / Leon Marshall. — Hornchurch : Henry, 1982, c1978. — 92p : ill ; 21cm
Originally published: South Melbourne : Sun Books, 1978. — Includes index
ISBN 0-86025-857-2 : £4.95 B82-28068

616.7′30622 — Man. Back. Backache. Relief. Use of Shiatzu — *Manuals*

Kurland, Howard. Quick backache relief without drugs / Howard Kurland. — London : Orbis, 1982, c1981. — 144p : ill ; 22cm
Originally published: New York : Morrow, 1981. — Includes index
ISBN 0-85613-407-4 : £4.95 B82-24031

616.7′307572 — Man. Spine. Diagnosis. Radiography. Use of x-rays

Gehweiler, John A.. The radiology of vertebral trauma / John A. Gehweiler, Jr., Raymond L. Osborne, Jr., R. Frederick Becker. — Philadelphia ; London : Saunders, 1980. — xiii,460p : ill ; 27cm. — (Saunders monographs in clinical radiology ; v.16)
Includes index
ISBN 0-7216-4065-6 : £22.25 B82-34690

616.7′4 — Man. Movement disorders

Movement disorders / edited by C. David Marsden and Stanley Fahn. — London : Butterworth Scientific, 1982, c1981. — 379p : ill ; 24cm. — (Butterworths international medical reviews. Neurology, ISSN 0260-0137 ; 2)
Includes bibliographies and index
ISBN 0-407-02295-3 : Unpriced : CIP rev. B81-36373

616.7′4 — Man. Muscles. Diseases — *Conference proceedings*

Foundation for Life Sciences *(Symposium) (2nd : 1981 : Sydney)*. New approaches to nerve and muscle disorders : basic and applied contributions : proceedings of the Second Symposium of the Foundation for Life Sciences, Sydney, February 3-6 1981 / editors Antony D. Kidman, John K. Tomkins, Roderick A. Westerman. — Amsterdam ; Oxford : Excerpta Medica, 1981. — 418p : ill ; 25cm. — (International congress series ; no.546)
Includes bibliographies and index
ISBN 90-219-0492-6 : £32.47
ISBN 0-444-90213-9 (Elsevier North-Holland)
Also classified at 616.8 B82-01641

616.7′4 — Man. Voluntary muscles. Diseases

Skeletal muscle pathology. — Edinburgh : Churchill Livingstone, Dec.1982. — [688]p
ISBN 0-443-02028-0 : £40.00 : CIP entry B82-29799

616.7′4061′0321 — Man. Voluntary muscles. Drug therapy. Drugs — *Encyclopaedias*

Walter, W. G.. Skeletal muscle pharmacology : glossary of muscle constituents and chemical research tools, with reference to muscle physiology and neuromuscular disorders : an alphabetical list of these substances and their synonyms and a bibliography of the literature on skeletal muscles from which the data are derived / compiled by W.G. Walter. — Amsterdam ; Oxford : North-Holland, 1981. — ix,473p ; 25cm
Includes index
ISBN 90-219-3064-1 : £51.06
ISBN 0-444-90226-0 (Elsevier North-Holland)
Also classified at 612′.744′0321 B82-13432

616.7′407547 — Man. Muscles. Electromyography

Practical electromyography / edited by Ernest W. Johnson. — Baltimore ; London : Williams & Wilkins, c1980. — xviii,457p : ill,forms ; 24cm. — (Rehabilitation medicine library)
Includes index
ISBN 0-683-04464-8 : Unpriced B82-03545

616.7′44 — Man. Myasthenia gravis

Myasthenia gravis. — London : Chapman and Hall, Jan.1983. — [560]p
ISBN 0-412-16310-1 : £30.00 : CIP entry B82-34441

616.7′48′00924 — Man. Muscular dystrophy — *Personal observations*

Smith, Christine, *1944 Oct.19-*. Clouds got in my way / Christine Smith. — London : Eyre & Spottiswoode, 1981. — 240p ; 22cm
ISBN 0-413-80240-x : £7.50 : CIP rev. B81-25288

616.8 — MAN. DISEASES OF NERVOUS SYSTEM, PSYCHIATRIC DISORDERS

616.8 — Brain damaged persons. Recovery — *Conference proceedings*

Functional recovery from brain damage / edited by M.W. van Hof and G. Mohn. — Amsterdam ; Oxford : Elsevier/North-Holland Biomedical, 1981. — ix,449p : ill,1port ; 25cm. — (Developments in neuroscience ; v.13)
Conference papers. — Includes bibliographies and index
ISBN 0-444-80394-7 : £37.45
Also classified at 636.089'68 B82-13437

616.8 — Lesbians. Stress

Brooks, Virginia R.. Minority stress and lesbian women / Virginia R. Brooks. — Lexington, Mass. : Lexington Books ; Aldershot : Gower [distributor], 1982, c1981. — xv,219p : ill ; 24cm
Includes bibliographies and index
ISBN 0-669-03953-5 : £15.00 B82-08996

616.8 — Man. Brain. Brain damage. Therapy. Neuropsychological aspects

Powell, Graham E.. Brain function therapy / Graham E. Powell. — Aldershot : Gower, c1981. — xiv,310p : ill ; 23cm
Bibliography: p276-297. — Includes index
ISBN 0-566-00315-5 : Unpriced : CIP rev.
B81-12913

616.8 — Man. Brain. Brain failure. Resuscitation

Brain failure and resuscitation / edited by Ake Grenvik, Peter Safar. — New York ; Edinburgh : Churchill Livingstone, 1981. — x,268p : ill ; 25cm. — (Clinics in critical care medicine)
Includes bibliographies and index
ISBN 0-443-08143-3 : £25.00 B82-09101

616.8 — Man. Brain. Metabolic disorders

Brain. — Lancaster : MTP Press, Nov.1982. — [138]p
ISBN 0-85200-484-2 : £17.95 : CIP entry
B82-32307

616.8 — Man. Nervous system. Diseases

Matthews, W. B.. Diseases of the nervous system. — 4th ed. — Oxford : Blackwell Scientific, Aug.1982. — [328]p
Previous ed.: 1979
ISBN 0-632-00832-6 (pbk) : £9.80 : CIP entry
B82-18578

Neurology for the non-neurologist / edited by William J. Weiner and Christopher G. Goetz. — Philadelphia ; London : Harper & Row, 1981. — xv,426p : ill ; 24cm
Includes bibliographies and index
ISBN 0-06-142654-7 (pbk) : Unpriced
B82-08785

Spillane, John D.. An atlas of clinical neurology. — 3rd ed. — Oxford : Oxford University Press, Mar.1982. — [550]p. — (Oxford medical publications)
Previous ed.: 1975
ISBN 0-19-261286-7 : £40.00 : CIP entry
B82-00890

Walton, *Sir* **John,** *1922-*. Essentials of neurology. — 5th ed. — London : Pitman, Aug.1982. — [496]p
Previous ed.: 1975
ISBN 0-272-79673-5 (pbk) : £10.95 : CIP entry
B82-25527

616.8 — Man. Nervous system. Diseases — *Conference proceedings*

Foundation for Life Sciences *(Symposium) (2nd : 1981 : Sydney)*. New approaches to nerve and muscle disorders : basic and applied contributions : proceedings of the Second Symposium of the Foundation for Life Sciences, Sydney, February 3-6 1981 / editors Antony D. Kidman, John K. Tomkins, Roderick A. Westerman. — Amsterdam ; Oxford : Excerpta Medica, 1981. — 418p : ill ; 25cm. — (International congress series ; no.546)
Includes bibliographies and index
ISBN 90-219-0492-6 : £32.47
ISBN 0-444-90213-9 (Elsevier North-Holland)
Primary classification 616.7'4 B82-01641

World Congress of Neurology *(12th : 1981 : Kyoto)*. Neurology : proceedings of the 12th World Congress of Neurology, Kyoto, Japan, September 20-25, 1981 / editors Shibanosuke Katsuki, Tadao Tsubaki, Yasuo Toyokura. — Amsterdam ; Oxford : Excerpta Medica, 1982. — ix,449p : ill ; 25cm. — (International congress series ; no.568)
Includes bibliographies and index
ISBN 90-219-0511-6 : £55.08
ISBN 0-444-90237-6 (Elsevier Science)
B82-38195

616.8 — Man. Nervous system. Diseases — *For physiotherapy*

Cash's textbook of neurology for physiotherapists. — 3rd ed. / edited by Patricia A. Downie. — London : Faber, 1982. — 464p : ill ; 22cm
Previous ed.: published as Neurology for physiotherapists / edited by Joan Cash. 1977. — Includes bibliographies and index
ISBN 0-571-18038-8 (pbk) : £6.25 : CIP rev.
B82-08081

616.8 — Man. Nervous system. Diseases — *For psychiatry*

Lechtenberg, Richard. The psychiatrist's guide to diseases of the nervous system / Richard Lechtenberg. — New York ; Chichester : Wiley, c1982. — xvii,478p : ill ; 25cm
Includes index
ISBN 0-471-08727-0 : £27.25 B82-35304

616.8 — Man. Nervous system. Effects of cancer

Henson, R. A.. Cancer and the nervous system. — Oxford : Blackwell Scientific, Mar.1982. — [640]p
ISBN 0-632-00845-8 : £40.00 : CIP entry
B82-08417

616.8 — Man. Nervous system. Metabolic disorders

Metabolic disorders of the nervous system / edited by F. Clifford Rose. — London : Pitman, 1981. — 524p : ill ; 24cm. — (Progress in neurology series, ISSN 0260-0013)
Includes index
ISBN 0-272-79624-7 : Unpriced : CIP rev.
B81-31367

616.8 — Man. Nervous system. Parasitic diseases

Brown, W. Jann. Neuropathology of parasitic infections / W. Jann Brown, Marietta Voge. — Oxford : Oxford University Press, 1982. — 240p : ill ; 25cm. — (Oxford medical publications)
Includes bibliographies and index
ISBN 0-19-261246-8 : Unpriced : CIP rev.
B81-34377

616.8 — Man. Spatial ability. Disorders

De Renzi, Ennio. Disorders of space exploration and cognition / Ennio De Renzi. — Chichester : Wiley, c1982. — xv,268p : ill ; 24cm
Includes bibliographies and index
ISBN 0-471-28024-0 : £16.95 : CIP rev.
B81-38338

616.8 — Man. Stress

Dobson, C. B.. Stress. — Lancaster : MTP, May 1982. — [370]p
ISBN 0-85200-381-1 : £15.00 : CIP entry
B82-17944

Dyce, James M.. Stress. — Suffolk (47 Water St., Lavenham, Suffolk CO10 9RN) : Stress Publications, Dec.1982. — [176]p
ISBN 0-9508277-0-3 : £12.50 : CIP entry
B82-40928

Living with stress / [edited by Edith Rudinger]. — London : Consumers' Association, c1982. — 138p ; 21cm. — (A Consumer publication)
Includes index
ISBN 0-85202-208-5 (pbk) : Unpriced
ISBN 0-340-27486-7 (Hodder & Stoughton)
B82-25651

Poteliakhoff, Alex. Real health : the ill effects of stress and their prevention / Alex Poteliakhoff and Malcolm Carruthers. — London : Davis-Poynter, 1981, c1980. — x,229p : ill ; 23cm
Includes index
ISBN 0-7067-0246-8 : £9.95 B82-05131

Spielberger, Charles D.. Understanding stress and anxiety / Charles Spielberger. — London : Harper & Row, c1979. — 128p : ill(some col.) ; 23cm. — (The life cycle series)
Bibliography: p122. — Includes index
ISBN 0-06-318138-x (cased) : Unpriced
ISBN 0-06-318139-8 (pbk) : £2.50 B82-00935

616.8 — Man. Stress. Behaviour therapy

Beech, H. R.. A behavioural approach to the management of stress : a practical guide to techniques / H.R. Beech, L.E. Burns, B.F. Sheffield. — Chichester : Wiley, c1982. — viii,132p ; 24cm. — (Wiley series on studies in occupational stress)
Bibliography: p126-129. — Includes index
ISBN 0-471-10054-4 : Unpriced : CIP rev.
B82-01104

616.8 — Man. Stress. Self-treatment

Shaffer, Martin. Life after stress / Martin Shaffer. — New York ; London : Plenum, c1982. — xv,273p,[8]p of plates : ill ; 22cm
Bibliography: p257-266. — Includes index
ISBN 0-306-40869-4 : Unpriced B82-20896

616.8 — Man. Stress. Therapy

Bennet, Glin. Beyond endurance. — London : Secker & Warburg, Jan.1983. — [304]p
ISBN 0-436-04010-7 : £12.50 : CIP entry
B82-34590

Hambly, Kenneth. Overcoming tension. — London : Sheldon Press, Jan.1983. — [96]p. — (Overcoming common problems)
ISBN 0-85969-373-2 (pbk) : £2.50 : CIP entry
B82-33121

616.8 — Man. Stress. Therapy. Alternative methods

Treatment of stress by alternative medicine / [edited] by R.P. Saxena. — [Laindon] : [International Society for the Prevention of Stress], [c1981]. — v,269p : ill ; 27cm
Includes bibliographies and index
ISBN 0-906482-07-0 : Unpriced B82-01024

616.8 — Medicine. Neurology

Atrens, Dale M.. The neurosciences and behaviour : an introduction / Dale M. Atrens, Ian S. Curthoys. — 2nd ed. — Sydney ; London : Academic Press, c1982. — x,214p : ill ; 24cm
Previous ed.: Marrickville, N.S.W. : Science Press, 1978. — Bibliography: p199-206. — Includes index
ISBN 0-12-066850-5 (pbk) : £5.50 B82-40160

Davidson, D. L. W.. Neurological therapeutics. — London : Pitman Medical, Apr.1981. — [264]p
ISBN 0-272-79616-6 : £15.00 : CIP entry
B81-08827

Principles of neural science / edited by Eric R. Kandel and James H. Schwartz ; art rendered by B. Andrew Mudryk. — London : Edward Arnold, c1981. — xxxi,731p : ill,facsims ; 28cm
Includes bibliographies and index
ISBN 0-7131-4405-x (cased) : Unpriced
ISBN 0-7131-4406-8 (pbk) : £22.50
B82-05065

Suchenwirth, Richard. Pocket book of clinical neurology / by Richard Suchenwirth ; with 86 figures including 69 diagrams by Dieter Freiherr Von Andrian ; translated and adapted by E.H. Burrows and E. Peter Bosch. — Chicago ; London : Year Book Medical, c1979. — 214p : ill(some col.) ; 20cm
Translation of: Taschenbuch der klinischen Neurologie. 2 Aufl.. — Bibliography: p207. — Includes index
ISBN 0-8151-8600-2 (pbk) : £13.00
B82-17991

616.8 — Medicine. Neurology — *Conference proceedings*

World Congress of Neurology *(12th : 1981 : Kyoto).* 12th World Congress of Neurology : Kyoto, Japan, September 20-25, 1981 : abstracts of papers presented / under the auspices of The Japanese Society of Neurology, World Federation of Neurology ; with the co-operation of Ministry of Education ... [et al.]. — Amsterdam ; Oxford : Excerpta Medica, 1981. — xi,418p ; 24cm. — (International congress series ; no.548)
Includes index
ISBN 90-219-1247-3 (pbk) : Unpriced
B82-04429

616.8 — Medicine. Neurology — *For psychiatry*

Kellam, A. M. P.. Brain sciences in psychiatry. — London : Butterworth
Study guide. — Oct.1982. — [64]p
ISBN 0-407-00260-x (pbk) : £3.95 : CIP entry
B82-31292

Shaw, David M.. Brain sciences in psychiatry. — London : Butterworth Scientific, June 1982. — [368]p
ISBN 0-407-00236-7 (cased) : £25.00 : CIP entry
ISBN 0-407-00237-5 (pbk) : £15.00
B82-11757

616.8 — Medicine. Neurology — *Serials*

Recent advances in clinical neurology. — 3. — Edinburgh : Churchill Livingstone, Oct.1981. — [272]p
ISBN 0-443-02121-x : £14.00 : CIP entry
ISSN 0307-7403 B81-25298

616.8 — Medicine. Neuropsychology

Beaumont, J. Graham. Introduction to neuropsychology. — London : Grant McIntyre, Aug.1982. — [320]p
ISBN 0-86286-017-2 (cased) : £14.95 : CIP entry
ISBN 0-86286-018-0 (pbk) : £6.95 B82-17984

616.8 — Women. Stress

Morse, Donald Roy. Women under stress / Donald Roy Morse, M. Lawrence Furst. — New York ; London : Van Nostrand Reinhold, c1982. — x,473p : ill ; 24cm
Includes index
ISBN 0-442-26648-0 : £17.00 B82-13186

616.8′024613 — Man. Nervous system. Diseases — *For nursing*

Carini, Esta. Carini and Owens Neurological and neurosurgical nursing / Barbara Lang Conway-Rutkowski. — 8th ed. — St Louis ; London : Mosby, 1982. — x,803p,[1]leaf of plates : ill(some col.) ; 25cm
Previous ed: 1978. — Includes bibliographies and index
ISBN 0-8016-1035-4 : £16.75 B82-33955

616.8′0442 — Man. Nervous system. Diseases. Genetic aspects

Baraitser, Michael. The genetics of neurological disorders. — Oxford : Oxford University Press, June 1982. — [350]p. — (Oxford medical publications) (Oxford monographs on medical genetics)
ISBN 0-19-261155-0 : £35.00 : CIP entry
B82-10431

616.8′0442 — Man. Nervous system. Genetic disorders

Neurogenetic directory / edited by Ntinos C. Myrianthopoulos. — Amsterdam ; Oxford : North-Holland. — (Handbook of clinical neurology ; 43)
Part 2. — c1982. — xvii,636p : ill ; 27cm
Includes bibliographies and index
ISBN 0-7204-0675-7 : Unpriced
ISBN 0-7204-7200-8 (set) B82-35354

616.8′0442 — Man. Nervous system. Genetic disorders — *Conference proceedings*

International Congress of Neurogenetics and Neuro-ophthalmology *(6th : 1981 : Zürich).* Neurogenetics and neuro-opthalmology : proceedings of the 6th International Congress of Neurogenetics and Neuro-ophthalomology held in Zürich, Switzerland on 9-12 June, 1981 / editors A. Huber and D. Klein. — Amsterdam ; Oxford : Elsevier/North-Holland Biomedical, 1981. — xvi,432p : ill ; 25cm. — (Developments in neurology ; v.5)
Includes index
ISBN 0-444-80378-5 : £36.46 B82-09912

616.8′0443 — Newborn babies. Central nervous system. Congenital abnormalities. Detection — *Polyglot texts*

Nevin, Norman C.. The recognition of malformations of the central nervous system at birth. — Edinburgh : Churchill Livingstone, Dec.1982. — [48]p
Text in English, French and German
ISBN 0-443-02635-1 (pbk) : £5.00 : CIP entry
B82-29804

616.8′046 — Man. Nervous system. Diseases. Therapy

Fowler, T.. Guide for house physicians in the neurological unit / T. Fowler. — London : Heinemann Medical, 1982. — 150p,16p of plates : ill ; 18cm
Bibliography: p138. — Includes index
ISBN 0-433-10688-3 (pbk) : £5.25 B82-23402

Therapy for neurological disorders / edited by Wigbert C. Weiderholt. — New York ; Chichester : Wiley, c1982. — xi,437p ; 27cm
Includes index
ISBN 0-471-09508-7 : Unpriced B82-34522

616.8′04′6 — Man. Nervous system. Diseases. Therapy — *Conference proceedings*

Treatment of neoplastic lesions of the nervous system. — Oxford : Pergamon, Oct.1982. — [178]p
Conference papers
ISBN 0-08-027989-9 : £25.00 : CIP entry
B82-24956

616.8′047 — Medicine. Neuropathology

Leech, Richard W.. Neuropathology : a summary for students / Richard W. Leech, Robert M. Shuman ; illustrations by G. David Brown. — Philadelphia ; London : Harper & Row, c1982. — xi,257p : ill ; 24cm
Includes index
ISBN 0-06-141526-x (pbk) : Unpriced
B82-35120

The **Molecular** basis of neuropathology / edited by A.N. Davison and R.H.S. Thompson. — London : Edward Arnold, 1981. — x,693p,[1] leaf of plates : ill(some col.) ; 26cm
Includes bibliographies and index
ISBN 0-7131-4374-6 : £65.00 : CIP rev.
B81-30313

616.8′047 — Medicine. Neuropathology — *Serials*

Recent advances in neuropathology. — No.2. — Edinburgh : Churchill Livingstone, July 1982. — [285]p
ISBN 0-443-02427-8 (pbk) : £20.00 : CIP entry
ISSN 0144-0535 B82-24325

616.8′0475 — Man. Nervous system. Diagnosis

Denny-Brown, D.. Handbook of neurological examination and case recording. — 3rd ed. / D. Denny-Brown, D.M. Dawson, H.R. Tyler. — Cambridge, Mass. ; London : Harvard University Press, 1982. — viii,87p : ill ; 18cm
Previous ed.: 1957
ISBN 0-674-37101-1 (spiral) : £4.90
B82-33394

616.8′0475 — Man. Nervous system. Diagnosis — *Case studies*

Tyrer, John H.. Exercises in neurological diagnosis : with brief notes on treatment, multiple choice questions and answers. — 3rd ed. / John H. Tyrer, John M. Sutherland, Mervyn J. Eadie. — Edinburgh : Churchill Livingstone, 1981. — 337p : ill ; 22cm
Previous ed.: 1975. — Includes index
ISBN 0-443-01785-9 (pbk) : £9.50 : CIP rev.
B81-25767

616.8′047547 — Man. Brain. Electroencephalography

Clinical electroencephalography. — 4th ed. / L.G. Kiloh ... [et al.]. — London : Butterworths, 1981. — xii,292p : ill ; 29cm
Previous ed.: 1972. — Includes bibliographies and index
ISBN 0-407-00160-3 : Unpriced : CIP rev.
B81-14887

Nunez, Paul L.. Electric fields of the brain / Paul L. Nunez : the neurophysics of EEC with contributions by Ron D. Katznelson. — New York ; Oxford : Oxford University Press, 1981. — xix,484p : ill ; 24cm
Includes index
ISBN 0-19-502796-5 : £27.50 B82-39521

616.8′047547 — Man. Brain. Electroencephalography — *Conference proceedings*

Current clinical neurophysiology : update on EEG and evoked potentials / [from the Fifteenth Annual Course in Clinical Electroencephalography sponsored by the American Electroencephalographic Society] ; editor C.E. Henry. — New York ; Oxford : Elsevier/North-Holland, c1980. — x,577p : ill,forms ; 24cm
Includes bibliographies and index
ISBN 0-444-00639-7 : £37.65
Also classified at 612′.822 B82-13451

616.8′047547 — Man. Brain. Electroencephalography — *Manuals*

Binnie, C. D.. A manual of electroencephalographic technology / C.D. Binnie, A.J. Rowan and Th. Gutter. — Cambridge : Cambridge University Press, 1982. — x,363p : ill ; 24cm. — (Techniques of measurement in medicine ; 6)
Bibliography: p340-353. — Includes index
ISBN 0-521-23847-1 (cased) : £30.00 : CIP rev.
ISBN 0-521-28257-8 (pbk) : £11.95
B82-00191

Spehlmann, R.. EEG primer / R. Spehlmann. — Amsterdam ; Oxford : Elsevier/North-Holland Biomedical, 1981. — xiii,473p : ill ; 17x25cm
Includes bibliographies and index
ISBN 0-444-80260-6 (cased) : £30.43
ISBN 0-444-80299-1 (pbk) : Unpriced
B82-31856

616.8′047547 — Man. Brain. Electroencephalography. Techniques

Cooper, R.. EEG technology / R. Cooper, J.W. Osselton, J.C. Shaw. — 3rd ed. — London : Butterworths, 1980. — xx,344p : ill ; 25cm
Previous ed.: 1974. — Includes bibliographies and index
ISBN 0-407-16002-7 : £14.00 : CIP rev.
B80-12907

616.8′04757 — Man. Nervous systems. Diagnosis. Radiography

Burrows, Edmund H.. Neuroradiology / Edmund H. Burrows and Norman E. Leeds. — New York ; Edinburgh : Churchill Livingstone, 1981. — 2v(529,14,E1-E352p) : ill ; 29cm
Includes bibliographies and index
ISBN 0-443-08016-x : £95.00 B82-01698

616.8′04757′0222 — Man. Central nervous system. Diagnosis. Radiography — *Illustrations*

Taveras, Juan M.. Normal neuroradiology : and atlas of the skull, sinuses and facial bones / Juan M. Taveras, Francesco Morello. — Chicago ; London : Year Book Medical, c1979. — ix,752p : chiefly ill ; 24x31cm
Includes bibliographies and index
ISBN 0-8151-8732-7 : £147.50
Also classified at 617′.5140757′0222
B82-04568

616.8′047575 — Medicine. Neurology. Applications of nuclear medicine

Neuronuclear medicine / volume editors O. Juge and A.Donath. — Basel ; London : Karger, c1981. — vi,176p,1leaf of plates : ill(some col.) ; 25cm. — (Progress in nuclear medicine ; v.7)
Includes index
ISBN 3-8055-2319-x : £49.30 B82-11585

616.8'04759 — Man. Nervous system. Post-mortem examination

Adams, J. Hume. Atlas of post-mortem techniques in neuropathology. — Cambridge : Cambridge University Press, July 1982. — [153]p
ISBN 0-521-24121-9 : £12.50 : CIP entry B82-25490

616.8'0479 — Man. Nervous system. Immunology

Neuroimmunology / edited by Jeremy Brockes. — New York ; London, Plenum, c1982. — xv,256p : ill ; 24cm. — (Current topics in neurobiology)
Includes bibliographies and index
ISBN 0-306-40955-0 : Unpriced B82-34995

616.8'07 — Patients. Health education. Special subjects: Man. Nervous system. Diseases — *For nursing*

Neurologic care : a guide for patient education / Margie J. van Meter, editor. — New York : Appleton-Century-Crofts ; London : Prentice-Hall, c1982. — ix,198p : ill ; 24cm. — (Appleton patient education series)
Includes bibliographies and index
ISBN 0-8385-6706-1 (pbk) : £10.45 B82-23151

616.8'092'4 — Neuropsychiatry. Theories of Möbius, Paul

Schiller, Francis. A möbius strip : fin-de-siècle neuropsychiatry and Paul Möbius / Francis Schiller. — Berkeley ; London : University of California Press, 1982. — 134p ; 23cm
Includes index
ISBN 0-520-04467-3 : £12.00 B82-31092

616.8'1 — Man. Brain. Arteries. Diseases

Vascular disease of the central nervous system. — 2nd ed. — Edinburgh : Churchill Livingstone, Dec.1982. — [320]p
Previous ed. published as: Cerebral arterial disease. 1976
ISBN 0-443-02415-4 : £24.00 : CIP entry B82-29802

616.8'1 — Man. Brain. Blood vessels. Diseases — *Conference proceedings*

Cerebrovascular diseases : new trends in surgical and medical aspects : a satellite of the VIIth International Congress of Neurological Surgery held in Gardone Riviera, Italy, July 2-4, 1981 / editors Henry J.M. Barnett ... [et al.]. — Amsterdam ; Oxford : Elsevier/North Holland Biomedical, 1981. — vii,405p : ill ; 25cm. — (Symposia of the Giovanni Lorenzini Foundation ; v.12)
Includes index
ISBN 0-444-80381-5 : £36.56 B82-11937

616.8'1 — Man. Brain. Diseases & injuries. Role of blood flow

Cerebral blood flow : basic knowledge and clinical implications / editor J.M. Minderhoud. — Amsterdam ; Oxford : Excerpta Medica, 1981. — x,313p : ill ; 25cm. — (The Jonxis lectures ; v.7)
Includes bibliographies and index
ISBN 90-219-6007-9 : £18.34 B82-09906

616.8'1 — Man. Brain. Strokes. Physiotherapy

Johnstone, Margaret. Restoration of motor function in the stroke patient. — 2nd ed. — Edinburgh : Churchill Livingstone, Nov.1982. — [208]p
Previous ed.: 1978
ISBN 0-443-02604-1 (pbk) : £5.95 : CIP entry B82-27543

616.8'107543 — Man. Brain. Blood vessels. Diagnosis. Doppler ultrasonography

Doppler ultrasound in the diagnosis of cerebrovascular disease / edited by Robert S. Reneman and Arnold P.G. Hoeks. — Chichester : Research Studies, c1982. — xvii,294p : ill ; 24cm. — (Ultrasound in biomedicine research series ; 5)
Includes bibliographies and index
ISBN 0-471-10165-6 : £19.50 : CIP rev. B82-03610

616.8'3 — Man. Ataxia-telangiectasia. Genetic aspects

Bridges, B. A.. Ataxia-telangiectasia : a cellular and molecular link between cancer, neuropathology, and immune deficiency / edited by B.A. Bridges, D.G. Harnden. — Chichester : Wiley, c1982. — xix,402p : ill ; 24cm
Includes bibliographies and index
ISBN 0-471-10055-2 : £19.75 : CIP rev. B82-09696

616.8'3 — Man. Tardive dyskinesia

Tardive dyskinesia and related involuntary movement disorders, : the long-term effects of antipsychotic drugs / edited by Joseph DeVeaugh-Geiss. — Boston, Mass. ; Bristol : John Wright, 1982. — viii,214p : ill ; 24cm
Includes bibliographies and index
ISBN 0-7236-7006-4 : Unpriced : CIP rev. B81-35844

616.8'33 — Man. Parkinson's disease

Stern, Gerald. Parkinson's disease : the facts / Gerald Stern and Andrew Lees. — Oxford : Oxford University Press, 1982. — ix,74p,[4]p of plates : ill ; 23cm. — (Oxford medical publication)
Includes index
ISBN 0-19-261293-x : £5.95 : CIP rev. B81-35772

616.8'34 — Man. Multiple sclerosis

Multiple sclerosis. — London : Chapman and Hall, Nov.1982. — [500]p
ISBN 0-412-14190-6 : £30.35 : CIP entry B82-28254

616.8'340654 — Man. Multiple sclerosis. Therapy. Diet

Greer, Rita. Diets to help multiple sclerosis / by Rita Greer. — Wellingborough : Thorsons, 1982. — 47p ; 18cm
ISBN 0-7225-0744-5 (pbk) : £0.60 : CIP rev. B82-07601

616.8'36061 — Man. Muscles. Cerebral origin spasticity. Drug therapy. Baclofen — *Conference proceedings*

Baclofen : spasticity and cerebral pathology / edited by A.M. Jukes. — Northampton : Cambridge Medical, c1978. — 115p : ill ; 25cm
Conference papers. — Includes bibliographies
ISBN 0-904052-02-8 (pbk) : Unpriced B82-17376

616.8'41 — Man. Dizziness

Evaluation and clinical management of dizziness and vertigo / edited by Albert J. Finestone. — Boston, Mass. ; Bristol : John Wright, 1982. — vi,218p : ill ; 24cm
Includes index
ISBN 0-7236-7003-x : Unpriced : CIP rev. B81-34779

616.8'41 — Man. Vertigo. Diagnosis & therapy

Cinnarizine and the vertiginous syndrome / edited by G. Towse. — London : Royal Society of Medicine, 1980. — vii,56p : ill ; 25cm. — (Royal Society of Medicine series. International congress and symposium series, ISSN 0142-2367 ; no.33)
Includes bibliographies
ISBN 0-12-794645-4 (pbk) : Unpriced : CIP rev. B80-18338

616.8'49 — Women. Stress enuresis

Urinary incontinence / edited by Edward J. McGuire. — New York ; London : Grune & Stratton, c1981. — x,167p : ill ; 24cm
Includes index
ISBN 0-8089-1352-2 : £20.80 B82-04338

616.85'2 — Man. Anorexia nervosa

Crisp, A. H.. Anorexia nervosa : let me be / A.H. Crisp. — Repr. with corrections. — London : Academic Press, 1982, c1980. — vii,200p : ill ; 23cm
Originally published: 1980. — Bibliography: p192-196. — Includes index
ISBN 0-12-790941-9 (pbk) : Unpriced B82-37755

616.8'52 — Man. Anorexia nervosa. Therapy

Lambley, Peter. How to survive anorexia. — London : Muller, Jan.1983. — [192]p
ISBN 0-584-11012-x : £7.95 : CIP entry B82-32509

616.85'2 — Man. Neuroses

Chadwick, David. (Not) the last word on emotional illness / David Chadwick. — [Radcliffe on Trent] ([39, Cliff Way, Radcliffe on Trent, Notts. NG12 1AQ]) : D. Chadwick, [1981?]. — 32p ; 22cm
Unpriced (unbound) B82-04233

Lowen, Alexander. Fear of life / Alexander Lowen. — New York : Collier Books ; London : Collier Macmillan, c1981, c1980. — 274p ; 18cm
Originally published: New York : Macmillan ; London : Collier Macmillan, 1980
ISBN 0-02-077330-7 (pbk) : £2.25 B82-26206

Snaith, Philip. Clinical neurosis / Philip Snaith. — Oxford : Oxford University Press, 1981. — viii,233p ; 22cm. — (Oxford medical publications)
Includes bibliographies and index
ISBN 0-19-261251-4 (pbk) : Unpriced B82-38476

616.8'5206 — Man. Neuroses. Group therapy

Bovill, Diana. Tutorial therapy : teaching neurotics to treat themselves / by Diana Bovill. — Lancaster : MTP Press, c1982. — 221p : ill ; 23cm
Bibliography: p206. — Includes index
ISBN 0-85200-451-6 : Unpriced : CIP rev. B82-02463

616.85'2071 — Man. Neuroses. Effects of social environment

Henderson, Scott. Neurosis and the social environment / Scott Henderson with D.G. Byrne and Paul Duncan-Jones. — Sydney ; London : Academic Press, c1981. — xiv,279p : ill ; 24cm. — (Personality and psychopathology)
Bibliography: p253-264. — Includes index
ISBN 0-12-340580-7 : £21.60 B82-32780

616.85'21 — Man. Hallucinations. Psychotherapy — *Case studies*

Schatzman, Morton. The story of Ruth / Morton Schatzman. — Harmondsworth : Penguin, 1982, c1980. — 286p ; 19cm
Originally published: New York : Putnam ; London : Duckworth, 1980
ISBN 0-14-005344-1 (pbk) : £1.95 B82-35581

616.85'21 — Man. Post-traumatic neuroses

Trimble, Michael R.. Post-traumatic neurosis : from railway spine to the whiplash / Michael R. Trimble. — Chichester : Wiley, c1981. — 156p : ill,facsims, ports ; 23cm
Includes bibliographies and index
ISBN 0-471-09975-9 : £13.60 : CIP rev. B81-30520

616.85'22307 — Man. Neuroses: Anxiety. Physiological aspects

Gray, Jeffrey A.. The neuropsychology of anxiety : an enquiry into the functions of the septo-hippocampal system / Jeffrey A. Gray. — Oxford : Clarendon Press, 1982. — 548p : ill ; 24cm. — (Oxford psychology series)
Bibliography: p463-525. — Includes index
ISBN 0-19-852109-x : £27.50 : CIP rev. B81-26762

616.85'225 — Man. Agoraphobia

Mathews, Andrew M.. Agoraphobia : nature and treatment / Andrew M. Mathews, Michael G. Gelder, Derek W. Johnston. — London : Tavistock, 1981. — xiii,233p : ill ; 24cm
Bibliography: p214-223. — Includes index
ISBN 0-422-78060-x : £15.00 : CIP rev. B81-28061

616.85'225 — Man. Agoraphobia — *Personal observations*

Vose, Ruth Hurst. Agoraphobia / Ruth Hurst Vose. — London : Faber, 1981. — 204p ; 21cm
Bibliography: p189-191. — Includes index
ISBN 0-571-11752-x (cased) : £7.95 : CIP rev.
ISBN 0-571-11753-8 (pbk) : Unpriced B81-23758

616.85'22506 — Man. Phobias. Therapy
Phobia : psychological and pharmacological treatment / edited by Matig Mavissakalian and David H. Barlow. — New York ; London : Guilford, c1981. — vii,256p : ill ; 24cm
Includes bibliographies and index
ISBN 0-89862-602-1 : £15.25 B82-05622

616.85'227 — Man. Neuroses: Obsession. Behaviour therapy
Behavior in excess : an examination of the volitional disorders / edited by S. Joseph Mulé. — New York : Free Press ; London : Collier Macmillan, c1981. — xv,396p : ill ; 25cm
Includes index
ISBN 0-02-922220-6 : £17.50 B82-20405

616.85'24 — Man. Hysteria
Hysteria / edited by Alec Roy. — Chichester : Wiley, c1982. — xiii,316p : ill ; 24cm
Includes bibliographies and index
ISBN 0-471-28033-x : £18.00 : CIP rev. B82-04854

616.85'27 — Man. Depression
Stanway, Andrew. Overcoming depression / Andrew Stanway. — Feltham : Hamlyn, 1981. — 240p ; 18cm
Includes index
ISBN 0-600-20332-8 (pbk) : £1.50 B82-30957

616.85'27 — Man. Depression — *Conference proceedings*
Recent advances in depression. — Oxford : Pergamon Press, Dec.1982. — [152]p
Conference papers
ISBN 0-08-027954-6 : £9.00 : CIP entry B82-32277

616.85'27 — Man. Depression. Psychopharmacological aspects — *Conference proceedings*
Symposium on Depressive Illness *(1980 : Amsterdam)*. Depressive illness : biological and psychopharmacological issues : Symposium on Depressive Illness, Amsterdam, September 11-12, 1980 / volume editors J. Mendlewicz, A. Coppen and H.M. van Praag. — Basel ; London : Karger, 1981. — vi,241p : ill ; 23cm. — (Advances in biological psychiatry ; 7)
Includes bibliographies and index
ISBN 3-8055-2482-x (pbk) : Unpriced B82-19654

616.85'27 — Man. Depression. Psychosocial aspects
Fredén, Lars. Psychosocial aspects of depression : no way out? / Lars Fredén. — Chichester : Wiley, c1982. — xii,202p : ill ; 24cm
Bibliography: p194-198. — Includes index
ISBN 0-471-10023-4 : £14.50 : CIP rev. B81-34509

616.85'27 — Man. Depression. Therapy
Horwood, Janet. Comfort. — London : Allen and Unwin, Apr.1982. — [144]p
ISBN 0-04-613046-2 (pbk) : £1.95 : CIP entry B82-03705

616.85'2706 — Man. Depression. Psychotherapy
Short-term psychotherapies for depression : behavioral, interpersonal, cognitive, and psychodynamic approaches / edited by A. John Rush. — Chichester : Wiley, 1982. — xii,339p : ill,forms ; 24cm
Originally published: New York : Guilford Press, 1982. — Includes bibliographies and index
ISBN 0-471-10210-5 : £16.60 B82-28180

616.85'27061 — Man. Depression. Drug therapy
Ban, Thomas A.. Psychopharmacology of depression : a guide for drug treatment / Thomas A. Ban. — Basel ; London : Karger, 1981. — 127p : ill ; 20cm
Bibliography: p83-120. — Includes index
ISBN 3-8055-1154-x (pbk) : £10.20 B82-13383

616.85'27061 — Man. Depression. Drug therapy — *Conference proceedings*
Depressive illness — far horizons / edited by J.N.M. McIntyre. — Northampton : Cambridge Medical, c1982. — 93p : ill ; 25cm
Conference papers. — Includes bibliographies
ISBN 0-904052-10-9 (pbk) : Unpriced B82-30916

New vistas in depression. — Oxford : Pergamon, Sept.1982. — [339]p. — (Advances in the biosciences ; v.40)
Conference papers
ISBN 0-08-027388-2 : £30.00 : CIP entry B82-19096

616.8'53 — Man. Epilepsy
For the young adult with epilepsy / [British Epilepsy Association]. — Wokingham ([Crowthorne House, Bigshotte, New Wokingham Rd., Wokingham, Berks. RG11 3AY]) : British Epilepsy Association, [1982?]. — 7p ; 21cm. — (Action for epilepsy)
Unpriced (unbound) B82-37563

A Textbook of epilepsy / edited by John Laidlaw, Alan Richens ; foreword by Denis Williams ; introduction by Maurice Parsonage. — 2nd ed. — Edinburgh : Churchill Livingstone, 1982. — xxv,549p : ill ; 26cm
Previous ed.: 1976. — Includes index
ISBN 0-443-02039-6 : Unpriced : CIP rev. B82-07123

616.8'53 — Man. Epilepsy — *Conference proceedings*
European Regional Conference on Epilepsy *(2nd : 1978 : Warsaw)*. Epilepsy : a clinical and experimental research : proceedings of the Second European Regional Conference on Epilepsy, Warsaw, October 5-7, 1978 / volume editor Jerzy Majkowski. — Basel ; London : Karger, 1980. — xiii,306p : ill ; 23cm. — (Monographs in neural sciences ; v.5)
Includes bibliographies and index
ISBN 3-8055-0635-x (pbk) : £30.00 B82-13384

616.8'53 — Man. Epilepsy. Psychiatric aspects
Epilepsy and psychiatry / edited by E.H. Reynolds, M.R. Trimble. — Edinburgh : Churchill Livingstone, 1981. — xiv,379p : ill,1port ; 25cm
Includes bibliographies and index
ISBN 0-443-02311-5 : £22.00 : CIP rev. B81-31834

616.8'53 — Man. Temporal lobe epilepsy *related to* **psychoses** — *Conference proceedings*
Temporal lobe epilepsy, mania, and schizophrenia and the limbic system : symposium presented during the 3rd World Congress of Biological Psychiatry, Stockholm, June 28-July 3, 1981 / volume editors W.P. Koella and M.R. Trimble. — Basel ; London : Karger, c1982. — ix,165p : ill ; 23cm. — (Advances in biological psychiatry ; v.8)
Includes bibliographies and index
ISBN 3-8055-3494-9 (pbk) : Unpriced
Also classified at 616.89 B82-40294

616.8'53061 — Man. Epilepsy. Drug therapy. Anticonvulsants
Psychopharmacology of anticonvulsants / edited by Merton Sandler. — Oxford : Oxford University Press, 1982. — xii,163p : ill ; 24cm. — (A British Association for Psychopharmacology monograph ; no.2) (Oxford medical publications)
Includes bibliographies and index
ISBN 0-19-261341-3 : £15.00 : CIP rev. B82-07501

616.85'5 — Man. Language disorders — *Conference proceedings*
Seminar on Language Disability *(2nd : 1982 : Dublin)*. Language disability — congenital and acquired : proceedings of the Second Seminar on Language Disability held in Trinity College, Dublin, Ireland on 16th and 17th April, 1982 / sponsored by UNESCO ; edited by Marie de Montfort Supple. — Dublin : Boole, 1982. — ix,70p ; 24cm
Includes bibliographies
ISBN 0-906783-10-0 (pbk) : Unpriced B82-40254

616.85'5 — Speech disordered persons. Vocal communication systems: Talking brooch
Turley, Raymond V.. Understanding the structure of scientific and technical literature. — London : Library Association, Feb.1983. — [176]p
ISBN 0-85365-516-2 (pbk) : £8.00 : CIP entry B82-37651

616.85'5'0072 — Man. Communication disorders. Research. Methodology
Shearer, William M.. Research procedures in speech, language, and hearing / William M. Shearer. — Baltimore ; London : Williams & Wilkins, c1982. — x,262p : ill ; 23cm
Bibliography: p253-256. — Includes index
ISBN 0-683-07724-4 (pbk) : Unpriced B82-16583

616.85'506 — Man. Speech therapy. Role of assessment of language skills
Müller, David J. Language assessment for remediation / David J. Müller, Siân M. Munro and Christopher Code. — London : Croom Helm, 1981. — 169p : ill,forms ; 23cm
Bibliography: p151-161. — Includes index
ISBN 0-7099-1706-6 (cased) : £11.95 : CIP rev.
ISBN 0-7099-1707-4 (pbk) : Unpriced B81-16850

616.85'5075 — Man. Language disorders & speech disorders. Diagnosis
Crystal, David. Profiling linguistic disability. — London : Edward Arnold, July 1982. — [256]p
ISBN 0-7131-6354-2 : £7.50 : CIP entry B82-13061

616.85'5075 — Man. Speech disorders. Assessment. Applications of phonology
Grunwell, Pamela. Clinical phonology / Pamela Grunwell. — London : Croom Helm, c1982. — 224p ; 23cm
Bibliography: p216-219. — Includes index
ISBN 0-7099-1108-4 (cased) : £12.95 : CIP rev.
ISBN 0-7099-1109-2 (pbk) : £7.95 B81-25713

616.85'5075 — Man. Speech disorders. Diagnosis
Speech evaluation in medicine / edited by John K. Darby, Jr. — New York ; London : Grune & Stratton, c1981. — xv,456p : ill ; 24cm
Includes bibliographies and index
ISBN 0-8089-1359-x : Unpriced B82-10559

616.85'52 — Man. Aphasia
Acquired aphasia / edited by Martha Taylor Sarno. — New York ; London : Academic Press, c1981. — xvi,537p : ill ; 24cm
Includes bibliographies and index
ISBN 0-12-619320-7 : £19.60 B82-16316

616.85'53 — Man. Dyslexia
Miles, T. R.. Dyslexia. — London : Granada, Jan.1983. — [256]p
ISBN 0-246-11345-6 (pbk) : £9.95 : CIP entry B82-36128

616.85'53 — Man. Dyslexia — *Conference proceedings*
Dyslexia : neuronal, cognitive and linguistic aspects : proceedings of an international symposium held at the Wenner-Gren Center, Stockholm, June 3-4, 1980 / edited by Yngve Zotterman ; organizing committee Curt von Euler ... [et al.]. — Oxford : Pergamon, 1982. — xix,153p : ill ; 25cm. — (Wenner-Gren Center international symposium series ; v.35)
Includes bibliographies
ISBN 0-08-026863-3 : £20.00 : CIP rev. B81-34472

616.85'53 — Man. Reading disorders
Reading disabilities : the interaction of reading, language, and neuropsychological deficits / Donald G. Doehring ... [et al.]. — New York ; London : Academic Press, 1981. — xiii,280p : ill ; 24cm. — (Perspectives in neurolinguistics, neuropsychology, and psycholinguistics)
Bibliography: p255-270. — Includes index
ISBN 0-12-219180-3 : £18.00 B82-15541

616.85'54 — Man. Stuttering
Conture, Edward G.. Stuttering / Edward G. Conture. — Englewood Cliffs ; London : Prentice-Hall, c1982. — xiv,186p : ill ; 24cm. — (Remediation of communication disorders series)
Bibliography: p172-179. — Includes index
ISBN 0-13-858977-1 : £14.20 B82-16857

Van Riper, Charles. The nature of stuttering / Charles Van Riper. — 2nd ed. — Englewood Cliffs ; London : Prentice-Hall, c1982. — ix,468p : ill,1facsim ; 24cm
Previous ed.: 1971. — Includes bibliographies and index
ISBN 0-13-610709-5 : £16.45 B82-28163

616.85′54075 — Man. Stuttering. Diagnosis

Preus, Alf. Identifying subgroups of stutterers / Alf Preus. — Oslo : Universitetsforlaget ; London : Global [distributor], c1981. — 230p : ill ; 24cm. — (Norwegian studies in education ; no.7)
Bibliography: p214-220. — Includes index
ISBN 82-00-05801-8 (pbk) : £13.35 B82-15527

616.8′57 — Man. Migraine

Wilkinson, Marcia. Migraine & headaches : understanding, controlling and avoiding the pain / Marcia Wilkinson. — London : Dunitz, 1982. — 108p : ill(some col.) ; 23cm. — (Positive health guide)
Includes index
ISBN 0-906348-17-x (cased) : Unpriced : CIP rev.
ISBN 0-906348-18-8 (pbk £2.50)
Also classified at 616′.0472 B81-16918

616.8′57 — Man. Migraine — *Conference proceedings*

Treatment of migraine : pharmacological & biofeedback considerations / edited by Roy J. Mathew ; technical editors Lore Feldman, Karen Hanson Stuyck ; [proceedings of symposium, November 30-December 1, 1979, sponsored by the Texas Research Institute of Mental Sciences, Houston]. — Lancaster : MTP, c1981. — 171p : ill ; 24cm
Includes index
ISBN 0-85200-591-1 : £16.25 B82-09890

616.8′57′005 — Man. Migraine — *Serials*

Progress in migraine research. — 1-. — London : Pitman, 1981-. — v. : ill ; 24cm. — (Progress in neurology series, ISSN 0260-0013)
ISSN 0262-6330 = Progress in migraine research : Unpriced B82-06794

616.8′57069 — Man. Migraine. Therapy. Applications of dentistry

Migraine : the dental involvement. — Carlisle : Country, c1982. — [14]p : ill ; 22cm
Cover title. — Bibliography: p[14]
ISBN 0-907903-00-2 (pbk) : £1.25 B82-19051

616.8′5707 — Man. Migraine. Neurophysiological aspects

Cerebral hypoxia in the pathogenesis of migraine. — London : Pitman, May 1982. — [224]p. — (Progress in neurology series, ISSN 0260-0013 ; 8)
ISBN 0-272-79669-7 : £20.00 : CIP entry B82-12903

616.8′57071 — Man. Migraine. Role of diet

Wentworth, Josie A.. The migraine guide & cookbook / Josie A. Wentworth ; with an introduction by Katharina Dalton. — London : Corgi, 1982, c1981. — 220p : ill ; 18cm
Originally published: London : Sidgwick & Jackson, 1981. — Bibliography: p210-212. — Includes index
ISBN 0-552-11897-4 (pbk) : £1.50
Primary classification 641.5′631 B82-18418

616.85′8 — Man. Personality disorders

Personality disorders : diagnosis and management / [edited by] John R. Lion. — 2nd ed. (revised for DSM III) / with 33 contributors. — Baltimore ; London : Williams & Wilkins, c1981. — xiv,592p ; 24cm
Previous ed.: 1974. — Includes bibliographies and index
ISBN 0-683-05044-3 : Unpriced B82-02592

616.85′83 — Man. Sex reversal. Ashley, April — *Biographies*

Fallowell, Duncan. April Ashley′s odyssey / Duncan Fallowell & April Ashley. — London : Cape, 1982. — viii,287p,[16]p of plates : ports ; 23cm
Includes index
ISBN 0-224-01849-3 : £8.50 : CIP rev. B82-10771

616.85′88 — Man. Mental handicaps

Spencer, Douglas A.. Information handouts on mental handicap and associated topics / Douglas A. Spencer. — Leeds : Meanwood Park Hospital Tutorial Service, 1982. — 140leaves ; 31cm
ISBN 0-946031-01-0 (unbound) : Unpriced B82-24042

616.85′88065153 — Mentally handicapped persons. Educational rhythmics — *Manuals*

Moule, Shirley. Educational rhythmics in practice : starting a programme with the mentally handicapped / Shirley Moule, Leslie F. Williams, John Holland. — Kidderminster : British Institute of Mental Handicap, 1979. — 24p : ill ; 21cm
Accompanied by 4 cassettes
ISBN 0-906054-14-1 (pbk) : £7.50 : (including 4 cassettes) B82-35265

616.85′88065153 — Mentally handicapped persons. Therapy. Use of puppetry

Astell-Burt, Caroline. Puppetry for mentally handicapped people / Caroline Astell-Burt. — London : Souvenir, 1981. — 198p,[16]p of plates : ill ; 22cm. — (Human horizons series) (A Condor book)
Bibliography: p194. — Includes index
ISBN 0-285-64932-9 (cased) : £6.95
ISBN 0-285-64933-7 (pbk) : £4.95 B82-05518

616.85′88072 — Man. Mental retardation. Syndromes

Lemeshow, Seymour. The handbook of clinical types in mental retardation / Seymour Lemeshow. — Boston [Mass.] ; London : Allyn and Bacon, c1982. — xiii,143p : ill ; 28cm
Bibliography: p138-143
ISBN 0-205-07641-6 (spiral) : £15.95 B82-23393

616.85′89′0019 — Adults. Brain. Minimal brain dysfunction. Psychological aspects — *Conference proceedings*

Adult MBD Conference *(1978 : Scottsdale)*. Psychiatric aspects of minimal brain dysfunction in adults / [Adult MBD Conference, March 3-4, 1978 Scottsdale, Arizona] ; edited by Leopold Bellak. — New York ; London : Grune & Stratton, c1979. — xi,208p : ill ; 24cm
Includes index
ISBN 0-8089-1192-9 : £14.20 B82-11652

616.86 — Addiction

The **Dependence** phenomenon. — Lancaster : MTP Press, Sept.1982. — [250]p
ISBN 0-85200-414-1 : £19.95 : CIP entry B82-22435

616.86′1 — Alcoholism. Medical aspects — *Conference proceedings*

Currents in alcoholism / edited by Marc Galanter. — New York ; London : Grune & Stratton
Vol.8: Recent advances in research and treatment / managing editor Jeanette Mason ; associate editors Henri Begleiter ... [et al.]. — c1981. — xii,527p : ill ; 24cm
Includes index
ISBN 0-8089-1458-8 : £32.20
Also classified at 362.2′92 B82-27137

616.86′1 — Alcoholism. Psychiatric aspects

Alcoholism and clinical psychiatry / edited by Joel Solomon. — New York ; London : Plenum Medical, c1982. — 238p : ill ; 24cm
Includes index
ISBN 0-306-40794-9 : Unpriced B82-23741

616.86′1′0024613 — Alcoholism. Medical aspects — *For nursing*

Rix, Keith J. B.. Alcohol problems : a guide for nurses and other health professionals. — Bristol : Wright, Jan.1983. — [208]p
ISBN 0-7236-0654-4 (pbk) : £6.00 : CIP entry B82-35205

616.86′106 — Alcoholism. Dynamic psychotherapy — *Conference proceedings*

Dynamic approaches to the understanding and treatment of alcoholism / by Margaret H. Bean ... [et al.] ; edited by Margaret H. Bean and Norman E. Zinberg. — New York : Free Press ; London : Collier Macmillan, c1981. — x,214p ; 25cm
Conference papers. — Bibliography: p189-206. — Includes index
ISBN 0-02-902110-3 : £10.95 B82-18902

616.86′106 — Alcoholism. Therapy

Edwards, Griffith. The treatment of drinking problems : a guide for the helping professions / Griffith Edwards. — London : Grant McIntyre Medical & Scientific, 1982. — vii,334p ; 24cm
Includes bibliographies and index
ISBN 0-86286-019-9 (cased) : £14.95 : CIP rev.
ISBN 0-86286-020-2 (pbk) : £6.95 B82-20765

616.86′106′025411 — Scotland. Alcoholism. Therapy. Organisations — *Directories*

Advice and help on alcoholism : some useful addresses / [compiled in association with the Scottish Council on Alcoholism]. — [Edinburgh] ([c/o 49 York Place, Edinburgh EH1 3JD]) : Scottish Health Education Group, [1980?]. — [15]p ; 21cm
Unpriced (unbound) B82-40545

616.86′1071 — Alcoholism. Influence of heredity & environmental factors

Goodwin, Donald W.. Is alcoholism hereditary? / Donald Goodwin. — Oxford : Oxford University Press, 1978 c1976. — ix,171p : 1ill ; 21cm. — (A Galaxy book)
Originally published: New York : Oxford University Press, 1976. — Includes index
ISBN 0-19-502432-x (pbk) : £2.95 B82-25894

616.8′8 — Man. Autonomic nervous system. Diseases

Autonomic failure. — Oxford : Oxford University Press, Nov.1982. — [500]p. — (Oxford medical publications)
ISBN 0-19-261339-1 : £35.00 : CIP entry B82-26891

616.89 — Man. Behavioural disorders

Behavioral medicine : assessment and treatment strategies / edited by Daniel M. Doleys, R.L. Meredith and Anthony R. Ciminero. — New York ; London : Plenum, c1982. — xix,628p : ill ; 26cm
Includes bibliographies and index
ISBN 0-306-40841-4 : Unpriced B82-31525

MacSweeney, David. The crazy ape : sanity, madness, your brain and you / David MacSweeney. — London : Peter Owen, 1982. — 244p : ill ; 23cm
Bibliography: p234-238. — Includes index
ISBN 0-7206-0565-2 : £10.95 B82-34471

Meyer, Robert G.. Case studies in abnormal behavior / Robert G. Meyer, Yvonne Hardaway Osborne. — Boston ; London : Allyn and Bacon, 1982. — viii,292p ; 24cm
Includes bibliographies and index
ISBN 0-205-07744-7 (pbk) : Unpriced B82-31403

616.89 — Man. Cognitive disorders

The **Pathology** and psychology of cognition. — London : Methuen, Oct.1982. — [256]p. — (Psychology in progress)
ISBN 0-416-30810-4 (cased) : £10.50 : CIP entry
ISBN 0-416-30820-1 (pbk) : £4.95 B82-24491

616.89 — Man. Mental disorders

Gallatin, Judith. Abnormal psychology : concepts, issues, trends / Judith Gallatin. — New York : Macmillan ; London : Collier Macmillan, c1982. — xxix,750,G-49,R-67,I-45p : ill,2facsims,ports ; 24cm
Text on lining papers. — Bibliography: pR-1—R-67. — Includes index
ISBN 0-02-475510-9 : Unpriced B82-33416

Korkina, M. V.. Psychiatric ward practice : a handbook for medical students / M. Korkina, M. Tsivilko, E. Kossova ; translated from the Russian by Elena Koltsova. — Moscow : Mir ; [London] : distributed by Central Books, 1981. — 167p ; 20cm
Translation of: Praktikum po psikhiatrii. — Includes index
ISBN 0-7147-1766-5 (pbk) : £2.95 B82-38236

616.89 — Man. Mental disorders
continuation

Mental disorder or madness? : alternative theories / [edited by] Erica M. Bates, Paul R. Wilson. — [St Lucia] : University of Queensland Press ; Hemel Hempstead : Distributed by Prentice-Hall, c1979. — vi,257p ; 23cm
Includes index
ISBN 0-7022-1388-8 (cased) : £14.25
ISBN 0-7022-1389-6 (pbk) : Unpriced
B82-07152

Treatment and management in adult psychiatry. — London : Baillière Tindall, Sept.1982. — [250]p
ISBN 0-7020-0927-x : £20.00 : CIP entry
B82-20007

White, John. The masks of melancholy. — Leicester : Inter-Varsity Press, Sept.1982. — [256]p
ISBN 0-85110-442-8 (pbk) : £2.65 : CIP entry
B82-19843

616.89 — Man. Mental disorders. Biological factors *— Conference proceedings*

World Congress of Biological Psychiatry *(3rd : 1981 : Stocholm)*. Biological psychiatry 1981 : proceedings of the IIIrd World Congress of Biological Psychiatry held from June 28th to July 3rd, 1981 in Stockholm, Sweden / editors C. Perris, G. Struwe and B. Jansson. — Amsterdam ; London : Elsevier/North-Holland Biomedical, 1981. — xxx,1327p : ill ; 25cm. — (Developments in psychiatry ; v.5)
Includes index
ISBN 0-444-80404-8 : £90.24 B82-15239

616.89 — Man. Nervous breakdowns

Lake, Tony. How to cope with your nerves / Tony Lake. — London : Sheldon, 1982. — 99p ; 20cm. — (Overcoming common problems)
Includes index
ISBN 0-85969-338-4 (pbk) : £2.50 B82-20143

616.89 — Man. Psychoses

Saul, Leon J.. The psychotic personality / by Leon J. Saul and Silas L. Warner. — New York ; London : Van Nostrand Reinhold, c1982. — xiv,306p ; 24cm
Includes index
ISBN 0-442-27764-4 : £16.10 B82-38589

616.89 — Man. Psychoses *related to* **temporal lobe epilepsy** *— Conference proceedings*

Temporal lobe epilepsy, mania, and schizophrenia and the limbic system : symposium presented during the 3rd World Congress of Biological Psychiatry, Stockholm, June 28-July 3, 1981 / volume editors W.P. Koella and M.R. Trimble. — Basel ; London : Karger, c1982. — ix,165p : ill ; 23cm. — (Advances in biological psychiatry ; v.8)
Includes bibliographies and index
ISBN 3-8055-3494-9 (pbk) : Unpriced
Primary classification 616.8'53 B82-40294

616.89 — Medicine. Psychiatry

Bird, Jonathan. Examination notes on psychiatry / Jonathan Bird, Glynn Harrison ; with a foreword by G.F.M. Russell. — Bristol : John Wright, 1982. — x,278p ; 22cm
Includes bibliographies and index
ISBN 0-7236-0593-9 (pbk) : Unpriced : CIP rev.
B82-02658

Davison, Gerald C.. Abnormal psychology : an experimental clinical approach / Gerald C. Davison, John M. Neale. — 3rd ed. — New York ; Chichester : Wiley, c1982. — xxiii,823p : ill(some col.),facsims,forms,ports ; 27cm
Previous ed.: 1978. — Text on lining papers. — Bibliography: p723-764. — Includes index
ISBN 0-471-06159-x : £15.95 B82-21444

Handbook of psychiatry. — Cambridge : Cambridge University Press, Sept.1982
Vol.1: General psychopathology. — [277]p
ISBN 0-521-23649-5 (cased) : £27.50 : CIP entry
ISBN 0-521-28137-7 (pbk) : £9.95 B82-26231

Handbook of psychiatry. — Cambridge : Cambridge University Press, Aug.1982
Vol.3: Psychoses of uncertain aetiology. — [306]p
ISBN 0-521-24101-4 (cased) : £27.50 : CIP entry
ISBN 0-521-28438-4 (pbk) : £9.95 B82-22795

Hughes, Jennifer. An outline of modern psychiatry / Jennifer Hughes. — Chichester : Wiley, c1981. — viii,211p ; 23cm. — (A Wiley medical publication)
Includes bibliographies and index
ISBN 0-471-10073-0 (cased) : £9.75 : CIP rev.
ISBN 0-471-10024-2 (pbk) : Unpriced
B81-33884

Kaplan, Harold I.. Modern synopsis of Comprehensive textbook of psychiatry, III. — 3rd ed. / Harold I. Kaplan, Benjamin J. Sadock. — Baltimore ; London : William & Wilkins, c1981. — xviii,1034,xxp : ill,ports ; 26cm
Previous ed.: / Alfred M. Freedman, Harold I. Kaplan, Benjamin J. Sadock. 1976. — Includes bibliographies and index
ISBN 0-683-04512-1 (pbk) : Unpriced
B82-02560

Laing, R. D.. The voice of experience / R.D. Laing. — London : Allen Lane, 1982. — 179p ; 23cm
Bibliography: p172-179
ISBN 0-7139-1330-4 : £7.50 B82-23571

Price, John Harding. A synopsis of psychiatry. — Bristol : J. Wright, May 1982. — [496]p. — (Synopsis series)
ISBN 0-7236-0611-0 (pbk) : £11.50 : CIP entry
B82-07606

Psychiatrists on psychiatry. — Cambridge : Cambridge University Press, Nov.1982. — [205]p
ISBN 0-521-24480-3 (cased) : £17.50 : CIP entry
ISBN 0-521-28863-0 (pbk) : £7.95 B82-29392

Readings in psychiatry and neurology. — Oxford : Medicine Publishing Foundation, Nov.1982. — [96]p
ISBN 0-906817-35-8 (pbk) : £5.00 : CIP entry
B82-32322

Rees, Linford. A short textbook of psychiatry. — 3rd ed. — London : Hodder and Stoughton, Nov.1982. — [352]p. — (University medical texts)
Previous ed.: 1976
ISBN 0-340-28706-3 (pbk) : £5.65 : CIP entry
B82-27343

Slaby, Andrew Edmund. Clinical psychiatric medicine / Andrew E. Slaby, Laurence R. Tancredi, Julian Lieb. — Philadelphia ; London : Harper & Row, c1981. — xxi,742p ; 25cm
Includes bibliography and index
ISBN 0-06-141542-1 : Unpriced B82-06588

Strayhorn, Joseph M.. Foundations of clinical psychiatry / Joseph M. Strayhorn, Jr. — Chicago ; London : Year Book Medical, c1982. — xviii,590p : ill,forms ; 23cm
Includes bibliographies and index
ISBN 0-8151-8503-0 (pbk) : £26.50
B82-22843

Szasz, Thomas. Ideology and insanity. — London : Boyars, Sept.1982. — [270]p
Originally published: 1973
ISBN 0-7145-1054-8 (pbk) : £5.95 : CIP entry
B82-20368

616.89 — Medicine. Psychiatry *— For general practice — Conference proceedings*

Psychiatry and general practice. — London : Academic Press, July 1982. — [200]p
Conference papers
ISBN 0-12-174720-4 : CIP entry B82-21373

616.89 — Medicine. Psychiatry *— Phenomenological viewpoints*

Phenomenology and psychiatry / edited by A.J.J. De Koning, F.A. Jenner. — London : Academic Press, 1982. — xvii,277p : ill ; 24cm
Includes bibliographies and index
ISBN 0-12-791022-0 : £19.20 : CIP rev.
ISBN 0-8089-1432-4 (Grune & Stratton)
B82-04147

616.89 — Mentally handicapped persons. Mental illness. Diagnosis & therapy

Reid, Andrew H.. The psychiatry of mental handicap / Andrew H. Reid ; with a foreword by Sir Ivor Batchelor. — Oxford : Blackwell Scientific, 1982. — viii,145p : ill ; 19cm
Bibliography: p124-139. — Includes index
ISBN 0-632-00929-2 (pbk) : £6.00 : CIP rev.
B81-39218

616.89'001 — Medicine. Psychiatry. Theories. Political aspects

Sedgwick, Peter. Psycho politics / Peter Sedgwick. — London : Pluto, 1982. — 292p ; 19cm. — (The politics of health)
Includes index
ISBN 0-86104-352-9 (pbk) : £4.95 B82-20684

616.89'0014 — Psychiatry. Terminology

Malik, S. M. A.. A synopsis of the cosmophobia theory / by S.M.A. Malik. — Worcester Park : Roseneath Scientific, c1981. — 30p ; 21cm
Includes index
ISBN 0-903306-14-x (pbk) : £4.50 B82-08343

616.89'002436 — Man. Mental disorders *— For welfare workers*

Kahn, Jack. The cry for help : and the professional response. — Oxford : Pergamon, June 1982. — [130]p. — (Social work series)
ISBN 0-08-027438-2 (cased) : £10.00 : CIP entry
ISBN 0-08-027437-4 (pbk) : £5.25 B82-10594

616.89'0024613 — Man. Mental disorders *— For nursing*

Dally, Peter. Psychology and psychiatry / Peter Dally. — 5th ed. — London : Hodder and Stoughton, 1982. — 285p : ill ; 22cm. — (Modern nursing series)
Previous ed.: Psychology and psychiatry for nurses, 1975. — Bibliography: p280-281. — Includes index
ISBN 0-340-27126-4 (pbk) : £4.75 : CIP rev.
B81-28804

Koshy, Koshy Tharayil. Revision notes on psychiatry / Koshy Tharayil Koshy ; foreword by M.S. Perinpanayagan. — 2nd ed. — London : Hodder and Stoughton, 1982. — x,241p ; 22cm. — (Modern nursing series)
Previous ed.: 1977. — Bibliography: p239-241
ISBN 0-340-27049-7 (pbk) : £3.65 : CIP rev.
B81-31443

Trick, K. L. K.. Understanding mental illness and its nursing. — 3rd ed. — London : Pitman, Oct.1982. — [336]p
Previous ed.: 1976
ISBN 0-272-79678-6 (pbk) : £8.50 : CIP entry
B82-23480

616.89'005 — Medicine. Psychiatry *— Serials*

Psychiatry in practice. — Vol.1 no.1 (Sept. 1981)-. — Londnon (1 Bedford St., WC2E 9HD) : Medical News Group, 1981-. — v. : ill(some col.),ports ; 28cm
Issued every two months (1981-1982), monthly (Mar. 1982-)
ISSN 0262-5377 = Psychiatry in practice : Unpriced
B82-17253

Recent advances in clinical psychiatry. — 4. — Edinburgh : Churchill Livingstone, Sept.1982. — [311]p
ISBN 0-443-02570-3 (pbk) : £15.00 : CIP entry
ISSN 0144-1086 B82-24356

616.89'0072 — Medicine. Psychiatry. Research. Methodology

Methods of biobehavioral research / edited by E.A. Serafetinides. — New York ; London : Grune & Stratton, c1979. — xii,218p : ill ; 24cm. — (Seminars in psychiatry)
Includes index
ISBN 0-8089-1173-2 : £17.20 B82-07735

616.89′0072 — Medicine. Psychiatry. Research. Methodology. Study examples: Community surveys

What is a case?. — London : Grant McIntyre, May 1981. — [352]p
ISBN 0-86216-050-2 : £20.00 : CIP entry
B81-07916

616.89′0076 — Medicine. Psychiatry — *Questions & answers*

Bird, Dorcas. Psychiatry revision : aids for postgraduate trainees / Dorcas Bird, Jonathan Bird, Glynn Harrison ; foreword by H.G. Morgan. — Edinburgh : Churchill Livingstone, 1982. — 352p ; 22cm
Includes bibliographies and index
ISBN 0-443-02290-9 (pbk) : £6.00 : CIP rev.
B82-01963

Glew, Geoffrey. Multiple choice questions in psychiatry / Geoffrey Glew. — 2nd ed. — London : Butterworths, 1981. — xii,134p ; 22cm
Previous ed.: 1978. — Bibliography: pxi-xii
ISBN 0-407-00225-1 : £4.25 : CIP rev.
B81-30491

Psychiatry : pretest self-assessment and review. — 2nd ed. / edited by J. Craig Nelson, David Greenfeld. — New York ; London : McGraw-Hill, c1982. — ix,209p : ill ; 22cm. — (Pretest series)
Previous ed.: Wallingford, Con. : PreTest Service, 1977. — Bibliography: p203-209
ISBN 0-07-050974-3 (pbk) : £7.75 B82-14994

616.89′0088042 — Women. Mental disorders. Role of childbirth

Motherhood and mental illness. — London : Academic Press, July 1982. — [250]p
ISBN 0-12-790666-5 : CIP entry B82-12531

616.89′0092′4 — United States. Psychiatry. Sullivan, Harry Stack — *Biographies*

Perry, Helen Swick. Psychiatrist of America : the life of Harry Stack Sullivan / Helen Swick Perry. — Cambridge, Mass. ; London : Belknap Press of Harvard University Press, 1982. — 462p,[16]p of plates : ill,1map,ports ; 24cm
Includes index
ISBN 0-674-72076-8 : £14.00 B82-35398

616.89′00941 — Great Britain. Man. Mental disorders. Diagnosis & therapy by general practitioners

Psychiatric illness in general practice / Michael Shepherd ... [et al.]. — 2nd ed. / with new material for this ed. by Michael Shepherd and Anthony Clare. — Oxford : Oxford University Press, 1981. — xii,238p : ill,forms ; 23cm. — (Oxford medical publications)
Previous ed.: 1966. — Bibliography: p224-234. — Includes index
ISBN 0-19-261243-3 : £15.00 : CIP rev.
B81-28853

616.89′022 — Adolescents. Psychiatry

Evans, J.. Adolescent and pre-adolescent psychiatry. — London : Academic Press, Oct.1982. — [520]p
ISBN 0-12-791168-5 : CIP entry
Also classified at 618.92′89 B82-24943

Steinberg, Derek. The clinical psychiatry of adolescence. — Chichester : Wiley, June 1982. — [350]p. — (Wiley series on studies in child psychiatry)
ISBN 0-471-10314-4 : £20.00 : CIP entry
B82-22774

616.89′023 — United States. Psychiatrists. Communication — *Case studies*

Interfaces : a communications case book for mental health decision makers / by the Committee on Mental Health Services, Group for the Advancement of Psychiatry. — San Francisco ; London : Jossey-Bass, 1981. — 167p ; 24cm
Includes index
ISBN 0-87589-510-7 : £8.95 B82-21509

616.89′025 — Man. Mental disorders. Emergency treatment — *Manuals*

Fauman, Beverly J.. Emergency psychiatry for the house officer / Beverly J. Fauman, Michael A. Fauman. — Baltimore ; London : Williams & Wilkins, c1981. — xii,170p ; 20cm
Includes bibliographies and index
ISBN 0-683-03046-9 (pbk) : Unpriced
B82-03909

616.89′07 — Man. Mental disorders. Biochemical aspects — *Conference proceedings*

Biological markers in psychiatry and neurology : proceedings of a conference held at the Ochsner Clinic, New Orleans on May 8-10, 1981 / edited by Earl Usdin and Israel Hanin. — Oxford : Pergamon, 1982. — xvi,548p : ill ; 24cm
Includes bibliographies and index
ISBN 0-08-027987-2 : £37.50 : CIP rev.
B81-38332

616.89′07 — Medicine. Psychopathology

Coles, E. M.. Clinical psychopathologyan introduction / E.M. Coles. — London : Routledge & Kegan Paul, 1982. — xxii,502p : ill ; 23cm. — (Introductions to modern psychology)
Bibliography: p391-471. — Includes index
ISBN 0-7100-0864-3 (cased) : £15.00
ISBN 0-7100-0867-8 (pbk) : £8.95 B82-23817

616.89′07 — Medicine. Psychopathology. Applications of electroencephalography — *Conference proceedings*

International Symposium on Clinical Neurophysiological Aspects of Psychopathological Conditions *(2nd : 1980 : Capri)*.
Electroneurophysiology and psychopathology : 2nd International Symposium on Clinical Neurophysiological Aspects of Psychopathological Conditions, Capri, September 23-26, 1980 / volume editors C. Perris, D. Kemali and L. Vacca. — Basel ; London : Karger, 1981. — vi,200p : ill ; 23cm. — (Advances in biological psychiatry ; v.6)
Includes bibliographies and index
ISBN 3-8055-2420-x (pbk) : £18.50
B82-06282

616.89′07′077 — Medicine. Psychopathology — *Programmed instructions*

Basic psychopathology : a programmed text / edited by C.W. Johnson, J.R. Snibbe and L.A. Evans. — 2nd ed. — Lancaster : MTP Press, c1981. — ix,350p : ill,forms ; 23cm
Previous ed.: New York : Spectrum ; London : Distributed by Wiley, 1975. — Includes bibliographies
ISBN 0-85200-548-2 (pbk) : £9.75 B82-01780

616.89′071 — Man. Mental disorders. Role of neuroendocrine system

Handbook of psychiatry and endocrinology / edited by Pierre J.V. Beumont and Graham D. Burrows. — Amsterdam ; Oxford : Elsevier Biomedical, 1982. — xxviii,448p : ill ; 24cm
Includes bibliographies and index
ISBN 0-444-80355-6 : £53.44 B82-21021

616.89′071 — Man. Mental disorders. Role of stress

Psychological stress and psychopathology / edited by Richard W.J. Neufeld ; foreword by Hans Selye. — New York ; London : McGraw-Hill, c1982. — v,360p : ill ; 25cm
Includes bibliographies and index
ISBN 0-07-046309-3 : £20.50 B82-23890

616.89′075 — Adults. Behavioural disorders. Diagnosis

Behavioral assessment of adult disorders / edited by David H. Barlow. — New York ; London : Guilford, c1981. — xii,500p : ill ; 24cm
Includes bibliographies and index
ISBN 0-89862-140-2 : £18.95 B82-05618

616.89′075 — Great Britain. Ethnic minorities. Mental disorders. Diagnosis. Cultural aspects

Rack, Philip. Race, culture, and mental disorder. — London : Tavistock, Dec.1982. — [280]p
ISBN 0-422-78160-6 (cased) : £12.00 : CIP entry
ISBN 0-422-78170-3 (pbk) : £5.95 B82-29795

616.89′075 — Man. Mental disorders. Diagnosis

Diagnosis and drug treatment of psychiatric disorders : adults and children. — 2nd ed. / Donald F. Klein ... [et al.]. — Baltimore ; London : Williams & Wilkins, c1980 (1981 [printing]). — xxxii,849p : ill ; 24cm
Previous ed.: / by Donald F. Klein and John Davis, 1969. — Text on lining papers. — Includes bibliographies and index
ISBN 0-683-04653-5 : Unpriced
Primary classification 616.89′18 B82-03549

Leff, J. P.. Psychiatric examination in clinical practice / J.P. Leff, A.D. Isaacs. — 2nd ed. — Oxford : Blackwell Scientific, c1981. — 140p : ill ; 22cm
Previous ed.: 1978. — Includes bibliographies and index
ISBN 0-632-00818-0 (pbk) : £6.50 : CIP rev.
B81-27381

616.89′075 — Medicine. Psychiatry. Diagnosis

Kellerman, Henry. Handbook of psychodiagnostic testing : personality analysis and report writing / Henry Kellerman, Anthony Burry. — New York ; London : Grune & Stratton, c1981. — xv,222p ; 24cm
Bibliography: p212-215. — Includes index
ISBN 0-8089-1403-0 : £16.20
Also classified at 808′.066616021 B82-18351

616.89′0751 — Medicine. Psychiatry. Interviewing — *Manuals*

Leon, Robert L.. Psychiatric interviewing : a primer / Robert L. Leon. — New York ; Oxford : Elsevier/North-Holand, c1982. — xii,180p ; 22cm
Includes bibliographies and index
ISBN 0-444-00646-x (pbk) : £11.68
B82-15178

616.89′09 — Medicine. Psychiatry — *Case studies*

Neale, John M.. Case studies in abnormal psychology / John M. Neale, Thomas F. Oltmanns, Gerald C. Davison. — New York ; Chichester : Wiley, c1982. — xi,316p ; 23cm
Bibliography: p297-316
ISBN 0-471-08088-8 (pbk) : £7.35 B82-21534

616.89′1 — Man. Mental disorders. Therapy. Role of consolation

Horton, Paul C.. Solace : the missing dimension in psychiatry / Paul C. Horton. — Chicago ; London : University of Chicago Press, c1981. — vii,176p ; 23cm
Bibliography: p163-170. — Includes index
ISBN 0-226-35386-9 : £9.00 B82-09669

616.89′122 — Man. Mental disorders. Electroconvulsive therapy

Electroconvulsive therapy : biological foundations and clinical applications / edited by Richard Abrams, Walter B. Essman. — Lancaster : M.T.P. Press, c1982. — xiv,270p : ill ; 24cm
Includes bibliographies and index
ISBN 0-85200-571-7 : £30.25 B82-39879

616.89′13 — Man. Mental disorders. Therapy. Physical methods

Dally, Peter. An introduction to physical methods of treatment in psychiatry. — 6th ed / Peter Dally, Joseph Connolly. — Edinburgh : Churchill Livingstone, 1981. — 165p ; 22cm
Previous ed.: 1972. — Includes bibliographies and index
ISBN 0-443-02019-1 (pbk) : Unpriced : CIP rev.
B81-03147

616.89′14 — Medicine. Brief psychotherapy

Forms of brief therapy / edited by Simon H. Budman ; foreword by Mardi J. Horowitz. — New York ; London : Guilford, c1981. — xiv,482p : ill 24cm
Includes bibliographies and index
ISBN 0-89862-608-0 : £18.95 B82-05620

616.89′14 — Medicine. Client-centred psychotherapy

Boy, Angelo V.. Client-centered counseling : a renewal / Angelo V. Boy and Gerald J. Pine. — Boston, Mass. ; London : Allyn and Bacon, c1982. — viii,277p ; 25cm
Includes bibliographies and index
ISBN 0-205-07639-4 : £19.95 B82-11465

616.89'14 — Medicine. Cognitive therapy — *Case studies*

New directions in cognitive therapy : a casebook / edited by Gary Emery, Steven D. Hollon, Richard C. Bedrosian. — New York ; London : Guilford, c1981. — xv,294p : ill ; 24cm
Includes bibliographies and index
ISBN 0-89862-606-4 : £15.25 B82-05621

616.89'14 — Medicine. Psychotherapy

Bloch, Sidney, *1941-*. What is psychotherapy?. — Oxford : Oxford University Press, Jan.1983. — [160]p
ISBN 0-19-219154-3 : £9.95 : CIP entry B82-10430

Cohen, Abraham I.. Confrontation analysis : theory and pactice / Abraham I. Cohen. — New York ; London : Grune & Stratton, c1982. — xviii,512p ; 24cm
Bibliography: p501-512. — Includes index
ISBN 0-8089-1417-0 : £19.80 B82-27129

Lazarus, Arnold A.. The practice of multimodal therapy : systematic, comprehensive, and effective psychotherapy / Arnold A. Lazarus. — New York ; London : McGraw-Hill, c1981. — x, 272p : ill ; 24cm
Bibliography: p245-255. — Includes index
ISBN 0-07-036813-9 : £13.50 B82-02330

Resistance : psychodynamic and behavioral approaches / edited by Paul L. Wachtel. — New York ; London : Plenum, c1982. — xx,267p ; 24cm
Includes bibliographies and index
ISBN 0-306-40769-8 : Unpriced B82-28146

Ryle, Anthony. Psychotherapy : a cognitive integration of theory and practice / Anthony Ryle. — London : Academic Press, 1982. — vii,196p : ill ; 24cm
Bibliography: p177-182. — Includes index
ISBN 0-12-793710-2 : £11.80 : CIP rev. B82-07495

616.89'14 — Medicine. Psychotherapy. Crisis intervention

Aguilera, Donna C.. Crisis intervention : theory and methodology. — 4th ed. / Donna C. Aguilera, Janice M. Messick. — St. Louis ; London : Mosby, 1982. — xiii,194p : ill ; 24cm
Previous ed.: 1978. — Includes bibliographies and index
ISBN 0-8016-0087-1 (pbk) : £9.25 B82-08258

616.89'14 — Medicine. Psychotherapy. Long-term effectiveness

Maximizing treatment gains : transfer enhancement in psychotherapy / edited by Arnold P. Goldstein, Frederick H. Kanfer. — New York ; London : Academic Press, c1979. — xii,487p : ill ; 24cm
Includes bibliographies and index
ISBN 0-12-288050-1 : £23.80 B82-02207

616.89'14 — Medicine. Psychotherapy — *Manuals*

Haldane, J. D.. Models for psychotherapy. — Aberdeen : Aberdeen University Press, Oct.1982. — [96]p
ISBN 0-08-028446-9 (pbk) : £5.00 : CIP entry B82-25096

616.89'14 — Medicine. Psychotherapy. Role of influence of psychotherapists

Pentony, Patrick. Models of influence in psychotherapy / Patrick Pentony. — New York : Free Press ; London : Collier Macmillan, c1981. — xiv,210p ; 25cm
Bibliography: p200-204. — Includes index
ISBN 0-02-924950-3 : £11.95 B82-20406

616.89'14 — Psychotherapy. Counselling

Brammer, Lawrence M.. Therapeutic psychology : fundamentals of counseling and psychotherapy / Lawrence M. Brammer, Everett L. Shostrom. — 4th ed. — Englewood Cliffs ; London : Prentice-Hall, c1982. — xii,466p : ill ; 25cm
Previous ed.: 1977. — Bibliography: p438-452. — Includes index
ISBN 0-13-914614-8 : Unpriced B82-28421

616.89'14 — United States. Medicine. Brief psychotherapy — *Case studies*

Mann, James, *1913-*. A casebook in time-limited psychotherapy / James Mann, Robert Goldman. — New York ; London : McGraw-Hill, c1982. — xi,179p ; 24cm
Includes index
ISBN 0-07-039905-0 : £13.95 B82-03529

616.89'14'0973 — United States. Psychotherapy

The **Newer** therapies : a sourcebook / edited by Lawrence Edwin Abt, Irving R. Stuart. — New York ; London : Van Nostrand Reinhold, c1982. — viii,402p : ill ; 24cm
Includes bibliographies and index
ISBN 0-442-27942-6 : £16.10 B82-35485

616.89'142 — Man. Nervous system. Diseases. Behaviour therapy

Lubar, Joel F.. Behavioral approaches to neurology / Joel F. Lubar, William M. Deering. — New York ; London : Academic Press, 1981. — xii,209p : ill ; 24cm. — (Behavioral medicine)
Includes bibliographies and index
ISBN 0-12-458020-3 : £14.60 B82-07555

616.89'142 — Medicine. Behaviour therapy

Applied techniques in behavioral medicine / edited by Charles J. Golden ... [et al.]. — New York ; London : Grune & Stratton, c1981. — x,454p : ill ; 24cm
Includes bibliographies and index
ISBN 0-8089-1404-9 : £19.60 B82-21291

Barker, Philip J.. Behaviour therapy nursing. — London : Croom Helm, Aug.1982. — [256]p
ISBN 0-7099-0637-4 : £7.95 : CIP entry B82-30335

Future perspectives in behavior therapy / edited by Larry Michelson, Michel Hersen and Samuel M. Turner. — New York ; London : Plenum, c1981. — xvi,350p : ill ; 24cm. — (Applied clinical psychology)
Includes bibliographies and index
ISBN 0-306-40680-2 : Unpriced B82-02733

Schwartz, Arthur. The behavior therapies : theories and applications / Arthur Schwartz. — New York : Free Press ; London : Collier Macmillan, c1982. — ix,326p ; 22cm. — (Treatment approaches in the human services)
Bibliography: p281-309. — Includes index
ISBN 0-02-928150-4 : £12.95 B82-30027

616.89'142 — Medicine. Behaviour therapy — *Conference proceedings*

Learning theory approaches to psychiatry / edited by John C. Boulougouris. — Chichester : Wiley, c1982. — xxi,262p : ill ; 24cm
Conference papers. — Includes bibliographies and index
ISBN 0-471-28042-9 : £24.00 : CIP rev. B81-36233

616.89'142 — Medicine. Behavioural psychotherapy

The **Comprehensive** handbook of behavioral medicine / edited by James M. Ferguson and C. Barr Taylor. — Lancaster : MTP
Vol.1: Systems intervention. — c1980. — xxiii,303p : ill ; 24cm
Includes index
ISBN 0-85200-540-7 : £15.95 B82-35620

The **Comprehensive** handbook of behavioral medicine / edited by James M. Ferguson and C. Barr Taylor. — Lancaster : MTP
Vol.3: Extended applications & issues. — c1980. — vi,343p : ill,1form ; 24cm
Includes index
ISBN 0-85200-542-3 : £15.95 B82-35619

Pinkerton, Susan S.. Behavioral medicine : clinical applications / Susan S. Pinkerton, Howard Hughes, W.W. Wenrich. — New York ; Chichester : Wiley, c1982. — xiv,376p : ill,forms ; 25cm. — (Wiley series on personality processes)
Includes bibliographies and index
ISBN 0-471-05619-7 : £21.50 B82-12296

Strong, Stanley R.. Change through interaction : social psychological processes of counseling and psychotherapy / Stanley R. Strong, Charles D. Claiborn. — New York ; Chichester : Wiley, c1982. — xiv,259p : ill ; 24cm. — (Wiley series of personality processes, ISSN 0195-4008)
Bibliography: p221-246. — Includes index
ISBN 0-471-05902-1 : £18.45 B82-26265

616.89'142 — Mentally handicapped persons. Behaviour therapy — *For nursing*

Bailey, Roy D.. Therapeutic nursing for the mentally handicapped / Roy D. Bailey. — Oxford : Oxford University Press, 1982. — 143p : ill ; 22cm. — (Oxford medical publications)
Bibliography: p142-143. — Includes index
ISBN 0-19-261314-6 (pbk) : £6.95 : CIP rev. B81-30531

616.89'142'05 — Medicine. Behaviour therapy — *Serials*

Advances in behaviour research and therapy. — Vol.3. — Oxford : Pergamon, Apr.1982. — [205]p
ISBN 0-08-029671-8 : £53.00 : CIP entry B82-08430

616.89'142'06041 — Medicine. Behaviour therapy. Organisations: British Association for Behavioural Psychotherapy — *Serials*

Newsletter of the British Association for Behavioural Psychotherapy. — Issue no.1 (1981)-. — [Bangor] ([c/o Ms J. Hutchings, Abbey Rd Clinic, Abbey Rd, Bangor, Gwynedd]) : The Association, 1981-. — v. ; 21cm
Quarterly. — Description based on: Issue no.3 (July 1981)
ISSN 0262-3110 = Newsletter of the British Association for Behavioural Psychotherapy : Unpriced B82-04900

616.89'143 — Medicine. Gestalt psychotherapy

Gestalt therapy primer / edited by F. Douglas Stephenson. — 2nd ed. — New York ; London : Aronson ; London, c1978. — xviii,214p ; 24cm
Previous ed.: Springfield, Ill. : Thomas, 1975. — Includes bibliographies and index
ISBN 0-87668-358-8 : Unpriced B82-23965

616.89'15 — Medicine. Psychotherapy. Use of social networks

Rueveni, Uri. Networking families in crisis : intervention strategies with families and social networks / Uri Rueveni. — New York ; London : Human Sciences, c1979 ; London : Distributed by Eurospan. — 162p ; 22cm
Bibliography: p155-158. — Includes index
ISBN 0-87705-374-x : £17.50 B82-21462

616.89'152 — Medicine. Group therapy

International Congress of Group Psychotherapy *(7th : 1980 : Copenhagen)*. The individual and the group boundaries and interrelations / [proceedings of the VII International Congress of Group Psychotherapy, held August 3-8, 1980 at the University of Copenhagen, Copenhagen, Denmark] ; edited by Malcolm Pines and Lise Rafaelsen. — New York ; London : Plenum, c1982. — 2v. : ill ; 26cm
Includes bibliographies and index
ISBN 0-306-40837-6 : Unpriced
ISBN 0-306-40838-4 (v.2) : Unpriced B82-38673

616.89'1523'05 — Medicine. Drama therapy — *Serials*

Dramatherapy : [the journal of the British Association of Dramatherapy]. — Vol.1, no.1 (Summer 1977)-. — [St. Albans] ([7 Hatfield Rd, St Albans, Herts.]) : [The Association], 1977-. — v. ; 21cm
Quarterly. — Subtitle, Vol.1, no.1 (Summer 1977)-v.1, no.2 (Autumn 1977): Journal of the Association for Dramatherapists
ISSN 0263-0672 = Dramatherapy : £8.00 per year (Free to Association members) B82-15155

616.89'156 — Married couples. Psychotherapy

Handbook of marital therapy : a positive approach to helping troubled relationships / Robert P. Liberman ... [et. al.]. — New York ; London : Plenum, c1980. — xv,262p : ill ; 24cm + 1client's workbook(42p : forms ; 22cm). — (Applied clinical psychology)
Bibliography: p239-257. — Includes index
ISBN 0-306-40235-1 : Unpriced B82-32257

616.89'156 — Medicine. Couples therapy

Wile, Daniel B.. Couples therapy : a nontraditional approach / Daniel B. Wile. — New York ; Chichester : Wiley, c1981. — xviii,229p ; 24cm
Bibliography: p213-219. — Includes index
ISBN 0-471-07811-5 : £17.50 B82-04540

616.89'156 — Medicine. Family therapy

Developments in family therapy : theories and applications since 1948 / [edited by] Sue Walrond-Skinner. — London : Routledge & Kegan Paul, 1981. — ix,373p ; 24cm
Includes bibliographies and index
ISBN 0-7100-0812-0 (pbk) : £8.95 : CIP rev. B81-17540

Family therapy. — London : Academic Press, June 1982
Vol.1. — [350]p
ISBN 0-12-790545-6 : CIP entry B82-12715

Psychotherapy with families : an analytic approach / Sally Box ... [et al.]. — London : Routledge & Kegan Paul, 1981. — xii,179p ; 24cm
Bibliography: p173-176. — Includes index
ISBN 0-7100-0854-6 (pbk) : £5.50 : CIP rev. B81-30599

616.89'156 — Medicine. Family therapy — *Conference proceedings*

Family therapy supervision : recent developments in practice / edited by Rosemary Whiffen and John Byng-Hall. — London : Academic, 1982. — xiv,271p : ill ; 24cm
Includes bibliographies and index
ISBN 0-12-794815-5 : £14.20 : CIP rev. B82-04146

616.89'156'024613 — Medicine. Family therapy — *For nursing*

Family therapy : a nursing perspective / Imelda W. Clements, Diane M. Buchanan [editors]. — New York ; Chichester : Wiley, c1982. — xxi,356p ; 24cm. — (A Wiley medical publication)
Includes bibliographies and index
ISBN 0-471-08146-9 (pbk) : Unpriced B82-26497

616.89'156'05 — Medicine. Family therapy — *Serials*

Advances in family intervention, assessment and theory : a research annual. — Vol.1 (1980)-. — Greenwich, Conn. : JAI Press ; London (3 Henrietta St., WC2E 8LU) : Distributed by JAICON Press, 1980-. — v. ; 24cm
ISSN 0270-9228 = Advances in family intervention, assessment and theory : £22.85 B82-02374

616.89'156'0973 — United States. Psychiatric hospitals. Patients. Family therapy

The **Psychiatric** hospital and the family / edited by Henry T. Harbin. — Lancaster : M.T.P. Press, c1982. — 341p ; 24cm
Includes index
ISBN 0-85200-597-0 : £26.75 B82-39877

616.89'162 — Man. Mental disorders. Hypnotherapy

Phillips, Arthur, *19---*. Transformational psychotherapy : an approach to creative hypnotic communication / Arthur Phillips. — New York ; Oxford : Elsevier, c1981. — xi,145p : ill ; 22cm
Includes index
ISBN 0-444-00652-4 : Unpriced B82-05022

616.89'1652 — Man. Mental disorders. Occupational therapy

Handbook of occupational therapy in psychiatry / edited by Anna King & Katriona O'Keeffe. — Blackrock, Co. Dublin : Grove Publications, [1980]. — 160p : ill,forms ; 21cm
Cover title. — Includes bibliographies
Unpriced (pbk) B82-40481

616.89'17 — Medicine. Psychoanalysis. Dynamic psychotherapy — *Conference proceedings*

Curative factors in dynamic psychotherapy / edited by Samuel Slipp. — New York ; London : McGraw-Hill, c1982. — xii,397p ; 24cm
Conference papers. — Includes bibliographies and index
ISBN 0-07-058190-8 : £17.50 B82-14026

616.89'17 — Medicine. Psychoanalysis. Free association

Kris, Anton O.. Free association : method and process / Anton O. Kris. — New Haven ; London : Yale University Press, c1982. — xiv,113p ; 22cm
Bibliography: p107-110. — Includes index
ISBN 0-300-02733-8 : Unpriced : CIP rev. B82-07978

616.89'17 — Medicine. Psychoanalysis. Group therapy

Kutter, Peter. Basic aspects of psychoanalytic group therapy / Peter Kutter ; translated by Angela Molnos. — London : Routledge & Kegan Paul, 1982. — xii,124p : 2ill ; 22cm. — (The International library of group psychotherapy and group process)
Translation of: Elemente der Gruppentherapie. — Includes index
ISBN 0-7100-9244-x (pbk) : £5.95 B82-38565

616.89'17'0924 — Medicine. Psychoanalysis. Freudian system — *Interviews*

Obholzer, Karim. The wolf-man sixty years later. — London : Routledge & K. Paul, Nov.1982. — [256]p
Translation of: Gespräche mit dem Wolfsmann
ISBN 0-7100-9354-3 : £10.00 : CIP entry B82-27973

616.89'18 — Man. Mental disorders. Drug therapy

Diagnosis and drug treatment of psychiatric disorders : adults and children. — 2nd ed. / Donald F. Klein ... [et al.]. — Baltimore ; London : Williams & Wilkins, c1980 (1981 [printing]). — xxxii,849p : ill ; 24cm
Previous ed.: / by Donald F. Klein and John Davis, 1969. — Text on lining papers. — Includes bibliographies and index
ISBN 0-683-04653-5 : Unpriced
Also classified at 616.89'075 B82-03549

Green, A. Richard. Pharmacology and biochemistry of psychiatric disorders / A. Richard Green and David W. Costain. — Chichester : Wiley, c1981. — xiv,217p ; 24cm
Bibliography: p191-203. — Includes index
ISBN 0-471-09998-8 (cased) : £14.00 : CIP rev.
ISBN 0-471-10000-5 (pbk) : Unpriced
Also classified at 615'.78 B81-28044

Kalinowsky, Lothar B.. Biological treatments in psychiatry / Lothar B. Kalinowsky, Hanns Hippius, Helmfried E. Klein. — New York ; London : Grune & Stratton, c1982. — xv,424p : ill ; 27cm
Bibliography: p326-408. — Includes index
ISBN 0-8089-1423-5 : £32.80 B82-39089

Silverstone, Trevor. Drug treatment in psychiatry / Trevor Silverstone, Paul Turner. — London : Routledge & Kegan Paul, 1982. — vii,287p : ill ; 22cm. — (Social and psychological aspects of medical practice)
Previous ed.: 1978. — Includes bibliographies and index
ISBN 0-7100-9050-1 (pbk) : £7.95 B82-37014

616.89'18 — Man. Mental disorders. Drug therapy — *Conference proceedings*

Abstracts of the 12th CINP Congress : Göteborg, Sweden, 22-26 June 1980. — Oxford : Pergamon, 1980. — 380p ; 26cm
Includes index
ISBN 0-08-026383-6 : £26.70 : CIP rev. B80-21977

616.89'18 — Man. Mental disorders. Drug therapy. Lithium compounds — *Conference proceedings*

Basic mechanisms in the action of lithium : proceedings of a symposium held at Schloss Ringberg, Bavaria, F.R.G., October 4-6, 1981 / editors H.M. Emrich, J.B. Aldenhoff and H.D. Lux. — Amsterdam ; Oxford : Excerpta Medica, 1982. — xiv,265p : ill,ports ; 25cm. — (International congress series ; no.572)
Includes bibliographies and index
ISBN 90-219-0520-5 : £37.08
ISBN 0-444-90249-x (Elsevier Science) B82-38196

616.89'18 — Man. Mental disorders. Drug therapy. Psychotropic drugs

Drugs in psychiatric practice. — London : Butterworth Scientific, Oct.1982. — [480]p
ISBN 0-407-00212-x : £25.00 : CIP entry B82-25077

616.89'18 — Man. Mental disorders. Drug therapy. Psychotropic drugs. Epidemiological aspects — *Conference proceedings*

International Seminar on Epidemiological Impact of Psychotropic Drugs *(1981 : Milan)*.
Epidemiological impact of psychotropic drugs : proceedings of the International Seminar on Epidemiological Impact of Psychotropic Drugs held in Milan, Italy 24-26, 1981 / editors G. Tognoni, C. Bellantuono, M. Lader. — Amsterdam ; Oxford : Elsevier/North-Holland Biomedical. — ix,395p : ill ; 25cm. — (Clinical pharmacology and drug epidemiology ; v.3)
Includes index
ISBN 0-444-80388-2 : £33.33 B82-11940

616.89'5 — Man. Affective disorders

Handbook of affective disorders / edited by E.S. Paykel. — Edinburgh : Churchill Livingstone, 1982. — viii,457p : ill ; 25cm
Includes bibliographies and index
ISBN 0-443-02036-1 : £25.00 : CIP rev. B81-16410

616.89'5'0924 — Man. Psychoses: Manic depression — *Personal observations*

Endler, Norman S.. Holiday of darkness : a psychologist's personal journey out of his depression / Norman S. Endler. — New York ; Wiley, c1982. — xvii,169p : 1ill ; 22cm
ISBN 0-471-86250-9 : £11.00 B82-26468

616.89'82 — Man. Schizophrenia

Smith, Andrew Croyden. Schizophrenia and madness. — London : Allen & Unwin, Oct.1982. — [176]p
ISBN 0-04-157008-1 (cased) : £11.95 : CIP entry
ISBN 0-04-157009-x (pbk) : £4.95 B82-23085

Tsuang, Ming T.. Schizophrenia : the facts / by Ming T. Tsuang. — Oxford : Oxford University Press, 1982. — xi,95p,2p of plates : ill ; 23cm. — (Oxford medical publications)
Bibliography: p91-92. — Includes index
ISBN 0-19-261336-7 : £5.95 : CIP rev. B82-07500

616.89'82 — Man. Schizophrenia — *Conference proceedings*

Biological aspects of schizophrenia and addiction / edited by Gwynneth Hemmings. — Chichester : Wiley, c1982. — xv,277p : ill ; 24cm
Includes bibliographies and index
ISBN 0-471-10117-6 : £18.50 : CIP rev. B82-09704

616.89'82 — Man. Schizophrenia — *Conference proceedings* — *Festschriften*

Psychobiology of schizophrenia. — Oxford : Pergamon, June 1982. — [342]p. — (Advances in the biosciences ; v.39)
Conference papers
ISBN 0-08-028007-2 : £30.00 : CIP entry B82-14953

616.89'82 — Schizophrenics. Attention. Neurobiological aspecats

Oades, Robert D.. Attention and schizophrenia : neurobiological bases / Robert D. Oades. — Boston ; London : Pitman Advanced Publishing Program, c1982. — 343p : ill ; 25cm
Bibliography: p257-328. — Includes index
ISBN 0-273-08490-9 : Unpriced : CIP rev. B81-34155

616.9 — MAN. GENERAL DISEASES

616.9 — Man. Communicable diseases

Ball, A. P.. Notes on infectious diseases / edited by A.P. Ball ; foreword by A.B. Christie. — Edinburgh : Churchill Livingstone, 1982. — xii,263p ; 22cm
Includes index
ISBN 0-443-02424-3 (pbk) : £4.50 : CIP rev. B81-31623

Christie, A. B.. Infectious diseases : epidemiology and clinical practice / A.B. Christie. — 3rd ed. — Edinburgh : Churchill Livingstone, 1980. — xv,1033p ; 26cm
Previous ed.: 1974. — Includes index
ISBN 0-443-02263-1 : £37.50 B82-36979

Emond, R. T. D.. Infection / R.T.D. Emond, J.M. Bradley & N.S. Galbraith. — London : Grant McIntyre Medical & Scientific, 1982. — 288p ; 19cm. — (Pocket consultant)
Cover title. — Text on inside covers. — Includes index
ISBN 0-86286-008-3 (pbk) : £5.95 : CIP rev. B81-34652

Infectious diseases / edited by Jay P. Sanford, James P. Luby. — New York ; London : Grune & Stratton, c1981. — xxi,426p : ill,1map ; 29cm. — (The Science and practice of clinical medicine ; v.8)
Includes bibliographies and index
ISBN 0-8089-1322-0 : £26.20 B82-18675

The **Management** of infectious diseases in clinical practice / Phillip K. Peterson ... [et al.]. — New York ; London : Academic Press, 1982. — xiii,441p ; 24cm
Includes bibliographies
ISBN 0-12-788610-9 : £15.20 B82-29599

Mims, Cedric A.. The pathogenesis of infectious disease / Cedric A. Mims. — 2nd ed. — London : Academic Press, 1982. — ix,297p : ill ; 24cm
Previous ed.: 1976. — Includes index
ISBN 0-12-498254-9 (cased) : £11.80 : CIP rev.
ISBN 0-12-498455-x (pbk) : Unpriced B82-11270

616.9'024613 — Man. Communicable diseases — *For nursing*

Blackwell, C. Caroline. Principles of infection and immunity in patient care / C. Caroline Blackwell, D.M. Weir. — Edinburgh : Churchill Livingstone, 1981. — 178p : ill ; 22cm. — (Churchill Livingstone nursing texts)
Bibliography: p171. — Includes index
ISBN 0-443-01906-1 (pbk) : £3.95 : CIP rev. B81-14466

616.9'0461 — Man. Communicable diseases. Drug therapy. Antibiotics

Conte, John E.. Manual of antibiotics and infectious diseases / John E. Conte, Jr., Steven L. Barriere. — 4th ed. — Philadelphia : Lea & Febiger ; London : Kimpton, 1981. — xiv,233p : ill ; 22cm
Previous ed.: 197-?. — Includes bibliographies
ISBN 0-8121-0768-3 (spiral) : Unpriced B82-36741

616.9'0461 — Man. Communicable diseases. Drug therapy — *For general practice*

Kolff, Cornelius A.. Handbook for infectious disease management / Cornelius A. Kolff, Ramón C. Sánchez. — Menlo Park, Calif. ; London : Addison-Wesley, c1979. — vii,280p : ill ; 23cm
Bibliography: p267-268. — Includes index
ISBN 0-201-03892-7 (pbk) : £32.40 B82-14598

616.9'0461 — Man. Diseases caused by microorganisms. Drug therapy — *Conference proceedings*

International Workshop on Combined Antimicrobial Therapy *(1978 : Rome)*. Combined antimicrobial therapy : proceedings of the International Workshop on Combined Antimicrobial Therapy held in Rome, April 21-22, 1978 in collaboration with Università di Roma, Facoltà di Scienze, 2a Cattedra di Microbiologia / edited by W. Brumfitt, L. Curcio, L. Silvestri. — The Hague ; London : Nijhoff, 1979. — xvi,323p : ill ; 25cm. — (New perspectives in clinical microbiology ; 3)
Includes index
ISBN 90-247-2280-2 : Unpriced B82-35409

616.9'047 — Man. Communicable diseases. Physiological aspects

Infection : the physiologic and metabolic responses of the host / edited by M.C. Powanda and P.G. Canonico. — Amsterdam ; Oxford : Elsevier North-Holland Biomedical, 1981. — xii,435p : ill ; 25cm
Includes bibliographies and index
ISBN 0-444-80336-x : Unpriced B82-25695

616.9'05 — Man. Communicable diseases — *Serials*

Recent advances in infection. — No.2. — Edinburgh : Churchill Livingstone, Apr.1982. — [232]p
ISBN 0-443-02410-3 (pbk) : £15.00 : CIP entry
ISSN 0144-1078 B82-03584

616.9'2 — Man. Anaerobic diseases. Drug therapy. Metronidazole

Metronidazole in the prevention and treatment of anaerobic infections : experience from the Luton & Dunstable Hospital 1973-1979. — Old Woking : Published by Gresham on behalf of May & Baker Ltd., 1980. — vii,141p : ill ; 21cm
Includes bibliographies
ISBN 0-905418-82-4 (pbk) : £5.00 B82-00767

616.9'2 — Man. Chlamydial diseases

International Symposium on Human Chlamydial Infections *(5th : 1982 : Lund)*. Chlamydial infections : proceedings of the 5th International Symposium on Human Chlamydial Infections, held in Lund (Sweden) on 15-19 June, 1982 / editors P.-A. Mårdh ... [et al.]. — Amsterdam ; Oxford : Elsevier Biomedical, 1982. — xiv,454p : ill ; 25cm. — (Fernström Foundation series ; v.2)
Includes index
ISBN 0-444-80431-5 : Unpriced B82-33800

616.9'2 — Man. Mycobacterial diseases

Grange, John M.. Mycobacterial diseases / John M. Grange. — London : Edward Arnold, 1980. — ix,115p : ill ; 24cm. — (Current topics in infection ; 1)
Bibliography: p101-110. — Includes index
ISBN 0-7131-4367-3 : £9.75 : CIP rev. B80-23347

616.92'000240431 — Children. Diseases — *Encyclopaedias — For parents*

Stanway, Andrew. Pears encyclopaedia of child health / Andrew Stanway, Penny Stanway ; advisory editor Aidan Macfarlane. — London : Sphere, 1981, c1979. — v,234p : ill ; 24cm
Originally published: London : Pelham, 1979
ISBN 0-7221-8101-9 (pbk) : £4.95 B82-07081

616.9'22 — Man. Rickettsial diseases — *Conference proceedings*

Conference on Rickettsiae and Rickettsial Diseases *(1980 : Hamilton, Mont.)*. Rickettsiae and rickettsial diseases : based on the Conference on Rickettsiae and Rickettsial Diseases held at the Rocky Mountain Laboratories, Hamilton, Montana, September 3-5, 1980 / edited by Willy Burgdorfer, Robert L. Anacker. — New York ; London : Academic Press, 1981. — xxii,650p : ill ; 23cm
Includes index
ISBN 0-12-143150-9 : £31.40 B82-29971

616.9'25 — Man. Virus diseases — *Conference proceedings*

International Symposium on Medical Virology *(1981 : Anaheim)*. Medical virology : proceedings of the 1981 International Symposium on Medical Virology, held on October 8-10, 1981, in Anaheim, California, U.S.A. / editors Luis M. de la Maza and Ellena M. Peterson. — New York ; Oxford : Elsevier Biomedical, c1982. — x,407p : ill ; 24cm
Includes bibliographies and index
ISBN 0-444-00709-1 : Unpriced B82-34486

616.9'25079 — Man. Virus diseases. Immunological aspects

McLean, Donald M.. Immunological investigation of human virus disease. — Edinburgh : Churchill Livingstone, Nov.1982. — [150]p. — (Practical methods in clinical immunology series ; v.15)
ISBN 0-443-02536-3 : £16.00 : CIP entry B82-27541

616.9'25079 — Man. Virus diseases. Immunological aspects — *Conference proceedings*

Munich Symposium on Microbiology *(6th : 1981)*. Biological products for viral diseases / [proceedings of the 6th Munich Symposium on Microbiology, held on 3-4 June 1981, and organized by the WHO Collaborating Centre for Collection and Evaluation of Data on Comparative Virology] ; edited by Peter A. Bachmann. — London : Taylor & Francis, 1981. — viii,260p : ill ; 23cm. — (Munich symposia on microbiology)
Includes index
ISBN 0-85066-226-5 (pbk) : £12.50 : CIP rev. B81-32006

616.92'80471 — Children. Brain. Development. Effects of malnutrition

Winick, Myron. Early nutrition and brain development / Myron Winick. — Burlington, N.C. : Carolina Biological Supply Co., Scientific Publications Division, c1978 ; Chichester : Distributed by Packard. — 15p : ill(some col.) ; 25cm. — (Carolina biology readers ; 93)
Bibliography: p15
ISBN 0-89278-293-5 (unbound) : £0.80 B82-31602

616.9'315 — Man. Botulism — *Conference proceedings*

Biomedical aspects of botulism / [the proceedings of an international conference on the biomedical aspects of botulism, convened at Fort Detrick, Frederick, Maryland, on March 16-18, 1981, sponsored by the U.S. Army Medical Research Institute of [i.e. for] Infectious Diseases] ; edited by George E. Lewis, Jr ; assistant editor Phebe Summers Angel. — New York ; London : Academic Press, 1981. — xv,366p : ill,maps ; 24cm
Includes index
ISBN 0-12-447180-3 : £19.20 B82-29696

616.9'318 — Man. Tetanus

Tetanus : important new concepts / edited by R. Veronesi. — Amsterdam ; Oxford : Excerpta-Medica, 1981. — xiii,284p : ill ; 25cm. — (Symposia Fondation Merieux ; 5)
Includes bibliographies and index
ISBN 90-219-0485-3 : Unpriced B82-01650

616.9'36 — Man. Toxoplasmosis. Diagnosis. Laboratory techniques

Fleck, D. G.. The laboratory diagnosis of toxoplasmosis / D.G. Fleck, W. Kwantes. — London : H.M.S.O., 1980. — iii,20p : ill ; 25cm. — (Public Health Laboratory Service monograph series ; 13)
Bibliography: p18-20
ISBN 0-11-887104-8 (pbk) : £2.00 B82-40725

616.9'362 — Man. Malaria

Malaria / edited by S. Cohen. — London : Churchill Livingstone, c1982. — p115-218,4p of plates : ill ; 28cm
Originally published: in British Medical Bulletin, vol.38, no.2, 1982. — Includes bibliographies and index
ISBN 0-443-02577-0 (pbk) : Unpriced B82-34308

616.9'363 — Man. Trypanosomiasis — *Conference proceedings*

Trypanosomiasis Seminar *(21st : 1981 : London)*. Perspectives in trypanosomiasis research. — Chichester : Wiley, Aug.1982. — [250]p. — (Tropical medicine research studies series ; 3)
ISBN 0-471-10478-7 : £15.00 : CIP entry B82-15822

616.9'364079 — Man. Leishmaniasis. Immunological aspects — *Conference proceedings*

Immunological aspects of leprosy, tuberculosis and leishmaniasis : proceedings of a meeting held in Addis Ababa, Ethiopia, 27-30 October 1980 / editor David P. Humber ; conference committee Ayele Belehu ... [et al.]. — Amsterdam ; Oxford : Excerpta Medica, 1981. — xiii,312p : ill ; 25cm. — (International congress series ; no.574)
Includes index
ISBN 90-219-0522-1 : Unpriced
Primary classification 616.07'9 B82-13454

616.95'1 — Man. Sexually transmitted diseases

Catterall, Duncan. Sexually transmitted diseases and V.D. / by Duncan Catterall. — [London] : British Medical Association, [1982]. — 30p : ill ; 19cm. — (A Family doctor booklet)
£0.50 (unbound) B82-32746

Corsaro, Maria. Sexually transmitted diseases : a commonsense guide / Maria Corsaro and Carole Korzeniowsky ; introduction by Joseph Sonnabend. — London : Sphere, 1981, c1980. — 118p : ill ; 18cm
Originally published: New York : St. Martin's Press, 1980. — Includes index
ISBN 0-7221-2559-3 (pbk) : £1.35 B82-07074

616.95'1 — Man. Venereal diseases

Thin, R. Nicol. Lecture notes on sexually transmitted diseases / R. Nicol Thin. — Oxford : Blackwell Scientific, 1982. — vii,264p : ill,2maps ; 22cm. — (Lecture notes series)
Includes index
ISBN 0-632-00834-2 (pbk) : £7.25 : CIP rev. B82-01221

Willcox, R. R.. Venereological medicine / R.R. Willcox and J.R. Willcox. — London : Grant McIntyre, 1982. — 351p : ill ; 19cm. — (Pocket consultant)
Cover title. — Includes index
ISBN 0-86286-001-6 (pbk) : £9.95 : CIP rev. B81-14459

616.95'105 — Man. Sexuality transmitted diseases. Contacts. Tracing

Handbook on contact tracing in sexually transmitted diseases / [written by Isobel Hunter ... et al.]. — London (78 New Oxford St., WC1 1AH) : Health Education Council, 1980. — 1v.(loose-leaf) : ill,forms ; 31cm
Forms and booklets, including Sexually transmitted diseases clinics 1980 (iii,523p), in pocket
£5.00 B82-32199

616.9'6 — Man. Parasitic diseases

Blecka, Lawrence J.. Concise medical parasitology / Lawrence J. Blecka. — Menlo Park, Calif. ; London : Addison-Wesley, c1980. — xii,291p : ill ; 24cm
Includes bibliographies and index
ISBN 0-201-00756-8 (pbk) : £14.40 B82-12653

Desowitz, Robert S.. New Guinea tapeworms and Jewish grandmothers : tales of parasites and people / Robert S. Desowitz. — New York ; London : Norton, c1981. — 224p ; 22cm
Bibliography: p206-217. — Includes index
ISBN 0-393-01474-6 : £9.25 B82-33704

Knight, Richard. Parasitic disease in man / Richard Knight. — Edinburgh : Churchill Livingstone, 1982. — viii,244p : ill ; 25cm. — (Churchill Livingstone medical texts)
Includes bibliographies and index
ISBN 0-443-01952-5 (pbk) : £8.50 : CIP rev. B81-31840

616.9'6'00222 — Man. Parasitic diseases — *Illustrations*

A **Colour** atlas of clinical parasitology / edited by Tomio Yamaguchi ; contributors Seiichi Inatomi ... [et al.]. — London : Wolfe Medical, 1981. — x,293p : ill(some col.) ; 31cm. — (Wolfe medical atlases)
Translation from the Japanese. — Includes index
ISBN 0-7234-0768-1 : £35.00 B82-02984

616.9'6079 — Man. Parasitic zoonoses. Immunological aspects

Immunology of parasitic infections. — 2nd ed. — Oxford : Blackwell Scientific, Sept.1982. — [864]p
Previous ed.: 1976
ISBN 0-632-00852-0 : £48.00 : CIP entry B82-18767

616.9'62061 — Man. Helminthic diseases. Drug therapy: Albendazole — *Conference proceedings*

Albendazole in helminthiasis. — London : Academic Press, Feb.1983. — [60]p. — (International congress and symposium series / Royal Society of Medicine, ISSN 0142-2367 ; 57)
Conference papers
ISBN 0-12-791264-9 (pbk) : CIP entry B82-36323

616.9'69 — Immunocompromised patients. Mycoses. Treatment

Fungal infection in the compromised patient / edited by D.W. Warnock and M.D. Richardson. — Chichester : Wiley, c1982. — xi,260p : ill ; 24cm
Includes bibliographies and index
ISBN 0-471-10204-0 : £16.75 : CIP rev. B82-09707

616.9'69'0028 — Medicine. Mycology. Laboratory techniques — *Manuals*

McGinnis, Michael R.. Laboratory handbook of medical mycology / Michael R. McGinnis. — New York ; London : Academic Press, 1980. — xiii,661p : ill ; 24cm
Bibliography: p627-643. — Includes index
ISBN 0-12-482850-7 : £36.40 B82-36746

616.97 — Man. Allergens

Recent trends in allergen and complement research / volume editor Paul Kallós ; contributors S. Ahlstedt ... [et al.]. — Basel ; London : Karger, c1982. — xiv,234p : ill ; 25cm. — (Progress in allergy ; v.30)
ISBN 3-8055-2580-x : £38.50
Also classified at 616.07'9 B82-24058

616.97 — Man. Allergies

Current perspectives in allergy. — Edinburgh : Churchill Livingstone, Jan.1983. — [200]p. — (Contemporary issues in clinical immunology and allergy ; 1)
ISBN 0-443-02503-7 (pbk) : £9.50 : CIP entry B82-34596

Eaton, Keith. Allergy therapeutics / Keith Eaton, Anne Adams, Janet Duberley. — London : Baillière Tindall, 1982. — 126p : ill,1form ; 20cm
Bibliography: p119. — Includes index
ISBN 0-7020-0933-4 (pbk) : £5.50 : CIP rev. B82-13000

Randolph, Theron G.. [An Alternative approach to allergies]. Allergies : your hidden enemy : how the new science of clinical ecology is unravelling the causes of mental and physical illness / by Theron G. Randolph and Ralph W. Moss ; foreword by Richard Mackarness. — Wellingborough : Turnstone, 1981, c1980. — xiii,268p ; 22cm
Originally published: New York : Lippincott and Crowell, 1980. — Bibliography: p243-244. — Includes index
ISBN 0-85500-151-8 (pbk) : £3.50 : CIP rev. B81-28124

Rapp, Doris J.. Allergies & your family / Doris J. Rapp. — New York : Sterling ; London : Oak Tree, c1980. — 352p : ill ; 23cm
Includes index
ISBN 0-7061-2735-8 (cased) : £7.95
ISBN 0-8069-8878-9 (pbk) : £3.95 B82-21874

Speer, Frederic. Handbook of clinical allergy : a practical guide to patient management / Frederic Speer ; contributing authors Jeremy E. Baptist, Terry R. Denison, Cynthia L. Romito. — Boston, Mass. ; Bristol : John Wright, 1982. — xi,258p,[2]p of plates : ill(some col.) ; 25cm
Includes index
ISBN 0-7236-7014-5 : Unpriced B82-34899

616.97 — Man. Allergies — *Conference proceedings*

The **Clinical** aspects of allergic diseases. — Oxford : Medicine Publishing Foundation, Sept.1982. — [40]p
Conference papers
ISBN 0-906817-34-x : £5.00 : CIP entry B82-25754

616.97 — Man. Allergies — *For patients*

Bright, Michael. Living with your allergy / Michael Bright. — London : Granada, 1982. — 130p ; 21cm
Includes index
ISBN 0-246-11114-3 : Unpriced : CIP rev. B82-01168

616.97'06 — Man. Allergies. Therapy

Lieberman, Phil L.. Management of the allergic patient : a text for the primary care physician / Phil L. Lieberman, Lloyd V. Crawford. — New York : Appleton-Century-Crofts ; London : Prentice-Hall, c1982. — x,385p,[2]p of plates : ill(some col.) ; 24cm
Includes bibliographies and index
ISBN 0-8385-6115-2 : £25.15 B82-20063

616.97'079 — Man. Allergies. Immunological aspects — *Conference proceedings*

Collegium Internationale Allergologicum. *Symposium (13th : 1980 : Konstanz)*. Cellular interactions in allergy : 13th symposium of the Collegium Internationale Allergologicum, Konstanz, July 27-31, 1980 / editors Flemming Kristensen, Alain L. de Weck, Peter Dukor. — Basel ; London : Karger, 1981. — vi,298p : ill ; 26cm
Supplement: International archives of allergy and applied immunology. — Includes index
ISBN 3-8055-3439-6 (pbk) : Unpriced B82-34289

International Congress of Allergology *(10th : 1979 : Jerusalem)*. Advances in allergology and clinical immunology : proceedings of the 10th International Congress of Allergology, Jerusalem, November 1979 / editors A. Oehling ... [et al.] ; co-editors J.M. Cortada Macias ... [et al.]. — Oxford : Pergamon, 1980. — xix,795p ; 26cm
Includes bibliographies and index
ISBN 0-08-025519-1 : £55.00 : CIP rev. B80-05400

616.97'5 — Man. Allergens: Food

Clinical reactions to food. — Chichester : Wiley, Feb.1983. — [250]p
ISBN 0-471-10436-1 : £18.00 : CIP entry B82-38709

616.97'5 — Man. Drugs. Cell-mediated pseudo-allergic reactions

Cell mediated reactions miscellaneous topics / editors P. Dukor ... [et al.]. — Basel ; London : Karger, 1982. — vii,160p ; 24cm. — (PAR, pseudo-allergic reactions ; v.3)
Includes bibliographies and index
ISBN 3-8055-0960-x : Unpriced B82-25555

616.97'5 — Man. Drugs. Pseudo-allergic reactions — *Serials*

PAR : pseudo-allergic reactions : involvement of drugs ad chemicals. — Vol.1-. — Basel ; London : Karger, 1980-. — v. : ill ; 25cm
£34.25 B82-11809

616.97'5075 — Man. Food allergies. Diagnosis. Use of diet

Help yourself to less pain. — Gt. Yarmouth ('Heronbay', Riverside, Martham, Gt. Yarmouth, Norfolk) : Help, [1982?]. — 4leaves ; 22cm
Unpriced (unbound) B82-34709

616.97'5075 — Man. Food allergies. Diagnosis. Use of diet *continuation*

McEwen, L. M.. It's something you ate : a patient's guide to elimination diets / L.M. McEwen, J.E. Morgan. — Oxford : Medical Education Services, 1981, c1979. — [28]p : ill (some col.) ; 21cm
Text and ill on inside covers
Unpriced (pbk) B82-22956

616.9'78061 — Man. Autoimmune diseases. Immunotherapy — *Conference proceedings*

Immunodynamics Conference *(3rd : 1980 : Cleveland Clinic)*. Immunoregulation and autoimmunity : proceedings of the third Immunodynamics Conference, the Cleveland Clinic, Cleveland, Ohio, USA, May 12-13, 1980 / editors Randall S. Krakauer and Martha K. Cathcart. — New York ; Oxford : Elsevier/North-Holland, c1980. — xiv,257p : ill ; 25cm. — (Developments in immunology ; v.13)
Includes index
ISBN 0-444-00579-x : £22.33 B82-34318

616.9'8021 — Aerospace medicine

Aviation medicine / editor-in-chief Sir Geoffrey Dhenin ; editorial board T.C.D. Whiteside ... [et al.]. — London : Tri-Med
[2]: Health and clinical aspects. — 1978. — xviii,333p,[1]leaf of plates : ill ; 23cm
Includes index
ISBN 0-905402-05-7 : £12.00 B82-05560

616.9'80213 — Aviation medicine — *For pilots*

Hansen, W. Bryce. Fit to fly : an aeromedicine handbook for pilots / W. Bryce Hansen. — 2nd ed. — New York ; London : Van Nostrand Reinhold, 1982, c1980. — ix,132p : ill ; 22cm
Previous ed.: published as Flying is safe — are you?. 1969. — Includes index
ISBN 0-442-23608-5 : £9.30 B82-36539

Read, Keith E. E.. Aeromedicine for aviators / Keith E.E. Read ; foreword by Rex. A. Smith. — Shrewsbury : Airlife, 1976, c1971 (1981 [printing]). — xiv,80p : ill ; 19cm
Originally published: London : Pitman, 1971. — Includes index
ISBN 0-9504543-1-1 : Unpriced B82-21434

616.98'022 — Underwater diving. Medical aspects

The **Physiology** and medicine of diving and compressed air work. — 3rd ed. — London : Baillière Tindall, Sept.1982. — [608]p
Previous ed.: 1975
ISBN 0-7020-0821-4 : £35.00 : CIP entry
Also classified at 612'.04 B82-20003

616.9'803 — Industrial medicine

Current approaches to occupational health / edited by A. Ward Gardner. — Bristol : J. Wright, 1982
Vol.1 published as: Current approaches to occupational medicine. — Includes index
2. — xviii,396p : ill ; 23cm
ISBN 0-7236-0618-8 : Unpriced : CIP rev. B82-05413

616.9'88 — Man. Hypothermia - *Conference proceedings*

International 'Action for Disaster' Conference *(3rd : 1979 : Aberdeen)*. Hypothermia - ashore and afloat. — Aberdeen : Aberdeen University Press, May 1981. — [216]p
Conference papers
ISBN 0-08-025750-x : £18.00 : CIP entry B81-14824

616.9'88'3 — Tropical medicine

Nwokolo, Chukwuedu. An introduction to clinical medicine / Chukwuedu Nwokolo ; with a chapter on introductory dermatology by James Eger. — Edinburgh : Churchill Livingstone, 1982. — 243p : ill ; 22cm. — (Medicine in the tropics series)
Includes index
ISBN 0-443-02127-9 (pbk) : £4.95 : CIP rev. B81-35719

616.9'88'3 — Tropical medicine. Immunology

Greenwood, B. M.. Immunology of medicine in the tropics / B.M. Greenwood, H.C. Whittle. — London : Edward Arnold, 1981. — xiv,306p : ill ; 24cm. — (Current topics in immunology, ISSN 0305-8204 ; [14])
Includes bibliographies and index
ISBN 0-7131-4368-1 : £18.50 : CIP rev. B81-03169

616.9'88'3 — Tropical regions. Man. Diseases

Manson, *Sir* Patrick. Manson's tropical diseases. — 18th ed. / [revised by] P.E.C. Manson-Bahr, F.I.C. Apted. — London : Baillière Tindall, 1982. — xiv,843p,4p of plates : ill(some col.),maps ; 27cm
Previous ed.: 1972. — Includes bibliographies and index
ISBN 0-7020-0830-3 : £30.00 : CIP rev. B81-20618

616.9'88'30222 — Tropical regions. Man. Diseases — *Illustrations*

Peters, Wallace, *1924-*. A colour atlas of tropical medicine and parasitology / Wallace Peters, Herbert M. Gilles. — 2nd ed. — London : Wolfe Medical, 1981. — 400p : ill(some col.),maps ; 20cm
Previous ed.: 1977. — Bibliography: p385. — Includes index
ISBN 0-7234-0772-x : £22.00 B82-02993

616.9'88'30922 — Tropical medicine. Cantlie, *Sir* James & Cantlie, *Lady* Mabel — *Biographies*

Stewart, Jean Cantlie. The quality of mercy : the lives of Sir James and Lady Cantlie. — London : Allen & Unwin, Nov.1982. — [288]p
ISBN 0-04-920066-6 : £9.95 : CIP entry B82-28719

616.9'91 — Man. Rheumatic fever

Taranta, Angelo. Rheumatic fever : a guide to its recognition, prevention and cure with special reference to developing countries / Angelo Taranta and Milton Markowitz. — Boston, Mass. ; Lancaster : MTP, c1981. — 96p : ill ; 22cm
Bibliography: p92-93. — Includes index
ISBN 0-85200-431-1 : £9.95 B82-12783

616.99'2'005 — Oncology — *Serials*

European journal of cancer & clinical oncology. — Vol.17, no.7 (July 1981)-. — Oxford : Pergamon, 1981-. — v. : ill ; 30cm
Monthly. — Continues: European journal of cancer. — Description based on: Vol.18, no.3 (Mar. 1982)
Unpriced B82-26136

Topical reviews in radiotherapy and oncology. — Vol.2. — Bristol : J. Wright, Apr.1982. — [240]p
ISBN 0-7236-0616-1 : £14.50 : CIP entry
Primary classification 616.99'40642'05 B82-04970

616.99'2075 — Man. Tumour markers — *Conference proceedings*

German Foundation for Cancer Research. *International Expert Meeting (2nd : 1979 : Bonn)*. Critical evaluation of tumor markers : proceedings of the 2nd International Expert Meeting of the German Foundation for Cancer Research, Bonn, May 11-14, 1979 / volume editors S. von Kleist, H. Breuer. — Basel ; London : Karger, c1981. — viii,120p : ill ; 23cm. — (Beiträge zur Onkologie = Contributions to oncology ; v.7)
Includes bibliographies
ISBN 3-8055-2353-x (pbk) : £10.65 B82-01057

616.99'20758 — Man. Tumours. Diagnosis. Electron microscopy

Ultrastructural appearance of tumours : a diagnostic atlas / Douglas W. Henderson, John M. Papadimitriou ; foreword by Richard L. Kempson ; and with the technical assistance of Peter J. Leppard and Terry A. Robertson. — Edinburgh : Churchill Livingstone, 1982. — xiii,409p : chiefly ill ; 29cm
Bibliography: p341-404. — Includes index
ISBN 0-443-02435-9 : £38.00 : CIP rev. B81-35923

616.99'221 — Man. Nose & paranasal sinuses. Tumours

Friedmann, Imrich. Pathology of granulomas and neoplasms of the nose and paranasal sinuses / Imrich Friedmann, Denis A. Osborn. — Edinburgh : Churchill Livingstone, 1982. — 306p : ill ; 25cm
Includes bibliographies and index
ISBN 0-443-01410-8 : £30.00 : CIP rev. B81-31629

616.99'247 — Man. Pituitary gland. Tumours. Transsphenoidal surgery

Management of pituitary adenomas and related lesions : with emphasis on transsphenoidal microsurgery / editors Edward R. Laws ... [et al.] ; illustrated by William B. Westwood. — New York : Appleton-Century-Crofts ; London : Prentice-Hall, c1982. — xi,376p : ill ; 25cm
Includes bibliographies and index
ISBN 0-8385-6122-5 : £39.40 B82-32052

616.99'263 — Man. Testes. Non-seminomal tumours — *Conference proceedings* — *German texts*

Arbeitsgemeinschaft Internistische Onkologie. *Symposium (1981 : Bad Neuenahr)*. Nicht-seminomatöse Hodentumoren : Symposium der Arbeitsgemeinschaft Internistische Onkologie (AIO) der Deutschen Krebsgesellschaft, Bad Neuenahr, 6.-7. Februar 1981 / bandherausgeber H.J. Illiger ... [et al.]. — Basel ; London : Karger, c1982. — viii,296p : ill ; 23cm. — (Beiträge zur Onkologie = Contributions to oncology ; v.8)
ISBN 3-8055-3065-x (pbk) : £17.40 B82-24060

616.99'263 — Men. Prostate gland. Tumours. Endocrine therapy

The **Endocrinology** of prostate tumours. — Lancaster : MTP, Oct.1982. — [310]p
ISBN 0-85200-416-8 : £19.95 : CIP entry B82-29023

616.99'281 — Man. Brain. Tumours. Therapy — *Conference proceedings*

International Symposium on Neuro-Oncology *(1979 : Noordwijkerhout)*. Neuro-oncology : clinical and experimental aspects : proceedings of the International Symposium on Neuro-Oncology, Noordwijkerhout, The Netherlands, October 25-27, 1979 / edited by B.W. Ongerboer de Visser, D.A. Bosch, W.M.H. van Woerkom-Eykenboom. — The Hague ; London : Nijhoff, 1980. — ix,261p : ill ; 25cm. — (Developments in oncology ; v.3)
ISBN 90-247-2421-x : Unpriced B82-39113

616.99'284 — Man. Eyes. Tumours

Tumors of the ocular adnexa and orbit / edited by Albert Hornblass. — St. Louis ; London : Mosby, 1979. — xii,336p : ill ; 27cm
Includes bibliographies and index
ISBN 0-8016-2246-8 : £47.00 B82-28169

616.99'4 — Man. Cancer

Cancer : a comprehensive treatise. — New York ; London : Plenum
1: Etiology : chemical and physical carcinogenesis / Frederick F. Becker. — 2nd ed. — c1982. — xxii,714p : ill ; 26cm
Previous ed.: 1975. — Includes bibliographies and index
ISBN 0-306-40701-9 : Unpriced B82-22017

Creasey, William A.. Cancer : introduction / William A. Creasey. — New York ; Oxford : Oxford University Press, 1981. — xiii,271p : ill ; 23cm
Includes index
ISBN 0-19-502951-8 (cased) : Unpriced
ISBN 0-19-502952-6 (pbk) : £10.00 B82-18339

Currie, Graham. Cancer. — London : Edward Arnold, Oct.1982. — [128]p
ISBN 0-7131-4400-9 (pbk) : £10.00 : CIP entry B82-22982

Methods in cancer research. — New York ; London : Academic Press
Vol.19: Tumor markers / edited by Harris Busch and Lynn C. Yeoman. — 1982. — xxii,423p : ill ; 24cm
Includes bibliographies and index
ISBN 0-12-147679-0 : Unpriced B82-33521

616.99'4 — Man. Cancer *continuation*

Oncology / edited by Jerome B. Block. — New York ; Chichester : Wiley, c1982. — xii,350p : ill ; 25cm + CME post-test(17p ; 21cm). — (Internal medicine today)
Includes bibliographies and index
ISBN 0-471-09511-7 : £27.75 B82-18218

Oppenheimer, Steven B.. Cancer : a biological and clinical introduction / Steven B. Oppenheimer. — Boston, Mass. ; London : Allyn and Bacon, c1982. — viii,279p : ill ; 25cm
Includes bibliographies and index
ISBN 0-205-07652-1 : Unpriced B82-27310

Richards, Dick, *19---*. The topic of cancer : when the killing has to stop / by Dick Richards. — Oxford : Pergamon, 1982. — vii,147p ; 24cm
Bibliography: p147
ISBN 0-08-025937-5 : £4.95 : CIP rev.
B81-34469

Ruddon, Raymond W.. Cancer biology / Raymond W. Ruddon. — New York ; Oxford : Oxford University Press, 1981. — viii,344p : ill,maps ; 24cm
Includes index
ISBN 0-19-502942-9 (cased) : Unpriced
ISBN 0-19-502943-7 (pbk) : £10.00
B82-39524

616.99'4 — Man. Cancer — *Conference proceedings*

Free radicals, lipid peroxidation and cancer / edited by D.C.H. McBrien and T.F. Slater. — London : Academic Press, 1982. — xii,447p,[3]p of plates : ill ; 24cm. — (NFCR cancer symposia ; no.1)
Conference papers. — Includes bibliographies and index
ISBN 0-12-481780-7 : £24.00 B82-29989

Free radicals, lipid peroxidation and cancer. — London : Academic Press, Feb.1982. — [450]p
Conference papers
ISBN 0-12-649180-1 : CIP entry B81-40234

International Cancer Congress *(12th : 1978 : Buenos Aires)*. Advances in medical oncology, research and education : proceedings of the 12th International Cancer Congress, Buenos Aires, 1978 / [general editors A. Canonico ... et al.]. — Oxford : Pergamon, 1979. — 12v. : ill ; 26cm
Includes 4 chapters in Spanish. — Includes bibliographies and index
ISBN 0-08-023777-0 : £368.00 B82-35751

616.99'4 — Man. Cancer. Diagnosis & treatment

Williams, Chris. All about cancer. — Chichester : Wiley, Feb.1983. — [386]p. — (A Wiley medical publication)
ISBN 0-471-90037-0 (pbk) : £5.00 : CIP entry
B82-37480

616.99'4 — Man. Cancer. Metastasis

Tumor invasion and metastasis / edited by L.A. Liotta and I.R. Hart. — The Hague ; London : Nijhoff, 1982. — 534p : ill ; 25cm. — (Developments in oncology ; 7)
Includes index
ISBN 90-247-2611-5 : Unpriced B82-40766

616.99'4 — Man. Kaposi's sarcoma — *Conference proceedings*

Kaposi's Sarcoma Symposium *(2nd : 1980 : Kampala)*. Kaposi's sarcoma : 2nd Kaposi's Sarcoma Symposium, Kampala, January 8-11, 1980 / volume editors C.L.M. Olweny, M.S.R. Hutt, R. Owor. — Basel ; London : Karger, c1981. — 101p : ill ; 25cm. — (Antibiotics and chemotherapy ; v.29)
Includes bibliographies and index
ISBN 3-8055-2076-x : £26.70 B82-06297

616.99'4 — Man. Malignant tumours

Sherbet, G. V.. The biology of tumour malignancy / G.V. Sherbet. — London : Academic Press, 1982. — xii,255p : ill ; 24cm
Includes index
ISBN 0-12-639880-1 : £19.20 : CIP rev.
B82-07489

616.99'4'0024372 — Man. Cancer — *For teaching*

Cancer information for schools / issued by Tenovus Cancer Information Centre, Cardiff in conjunction with South Glamorgan Health Authority (Teaching), County of South Glamorgan Education Department. — Cardiff : Alpha Omega, 1981. — 52p : ill(some col.) ; 30cm
ISBN 0-900663-11-1 (pbk) : Unpriced
B82-18893

616.99'4'005 — Man. Cancer — *Serials*

Cancer surveys : advances & prospects in clinical, epidemiological and laboratory oncology. — Vol.1, no.1 (Spring 1982)-. — Oxford : Oxford University Press for Imperial Cancer Research Fund, 1982-. — v. : ill,ports ; 24cm
Quarterly
ISSN 0261-2429 = Cancer surveys : £36.00 per year B82-38502

616.99'4'005 — Man. Malignant tumours — *Serials*

Recent advances in clinical oncology. — No.1. — Edinburgh : Churchill Livingstone, Nov.1981. — [358]p
ISBN 0-443-02230-5 (pbk) : £19.50 : CIP entry
ISSN 0261-7013 B81-30896

616.99'4'007 — Patients. Health education. Special subjects: Man. Cancer — *For nursing*

Cancer care : a guide for patient education / edited by Marilee Ivers Donovan. — New York : Appleton-Century Crofts ; London : Prentice-Hall, c1981. — xii,306p : ill,forms ; 24cm. — (Appleton patient education series)
Includes bibliographies and index
ISBN 0-8385-1028-0 : £10.90 B82-07787

616.99'405 — Man. Cancer. Prevention

Cancer risk and your diet / [edited by Eileen Lloyd]. — Aylesbury : Rodale, 1982. — 47p ; 18cm. — (Prevention health guides)
ISBN 0-87857-407-7 (pbk) : Unpriced
B82-36764

The **Prevention** of cancer / edited by Michael Alderson. — London : Edward Arnold, 1982. — viii,296p : ill ; 24cm. — (The Management of malignant disease series ; 4)
Includes bibliographies and index
ISBN 0-7131-4401-7 : £18.00 : CIP rev.
B82-13018

616.99'4059 — Man. Cancer. Surgery

Alfonso, Antonio E.. The practice of cancer surgery / Antonio E. Alfonso, Bernard Gardner ; illustrated by Lynn B. McDowell. — New York : Appleton-Century-Crofts ; London : Prentice-Hall, c1982. — xv,477p : ill ; 24cm
Includes bibliographies and index
ISBN 0-8385-7861-6 : £31.90 B82-20061

616.99'406 — Cancer patients. Psychotherapy

Psychotherapeutic treatment of cancer patients / edited by Jane G. Goldberg. — New York : Free Press ; London : Collier Macmillan, c1981. — xxvi,364p ; 25cm
Includes bibliographies and index
ISBN 0-02-911960-x : £17.95 B82-18004

616.99'406 — Man. Cancer. Cells. Growth. Long-term regulation

Prolonged arrest of cancer. — Chichester : Wiley, Oct.1982. — [448]p. — (New horizons in oncology ; v.1) (A Wiley medical publication)
ISBN 0-471-10221-0 : £24.75 : CIP entry
B82-24729

616.99'406 — Man. Cancer. Therapy

Brohn, Penny. Working your way back to health / Penny Brohn. — Bristol (7 Downfield Rd., Clifton, Bristol BS8 2TG) : Cancer Help Centre, [1980]. — 12p ; 21cm. — (C.H. ; 3)
Unpriced (pbk) B82-34040

Cancer Help Centre. Cancer Help Centre. — Bristol (7 Downfield Rd., Clifton, Bristol BS8 2TG) : [The Centre], [1980]. — [4]p ; 21cm. — (C.H. ; 1)
Unpriced (unbound) B82-34045

Coffee enemas and retention enemas. — Bristol (7 Downfield Rd., Clifton, Bristol BS8 2TG) : Cancer Help Centre, [1980]. — 5p ; 21cm. — (C.H. ; 6 & 7)
Unpriced (unbound) B82-34044

Controversies in oncology / edited by Peter H. Wiernik. — New York ; Chichester : Wiley, c1982. — xvii,415p : ill ; 27cm. — (A Wiley medical publication)
Includes index
ISBN 0-471-05925-0 : £28.70 B82-13293

Daily programme. — Bristol (7 Downfield Rd., Clifton, Bristol BS8 2TG) : Cancer Help Centre, [1980]. — [3]p ; 21cm. — (C.H. ; 5)
Unpriced (unbound) B82-34043

The **Diet** / compiled by Ute Brookman. — Bristol (7 Downfield Rd., Clifton, Bristol BS8 2TG) : Cancer Help Centre, [1982]. — 22p ; 21cm. — (C.H. ; 9)
Unpriced (unbound) B82-34039

Forbes, Alec. Cancer and its non-toxic treatment / by Alec Forbes. — Bristol (7 Downfield Rd., Clifton, Bristol BS8 2TG) : Cancer Help Centre, [1980]. — 18p ; 21cm. — (C.H. ; 2)
Bibliography: p16
Unpriced (unbound) B82-34038

Forbes, Alec. Non-toxic metabolic cancer therapy / by Alec Forbes. — Bristol (7 Downfield Rd., Clifton, Bristol BS8 2TG) : Cancer Help Centre, [1980]. — 9p ; 21cm. — (C.H. ; 4)
Unpriced (unbound) B82-34041

Holmes, David, *1927-*. New hope and improved treatments for cancer patients. — Chichester : Wiley, May 1982. — [80]p
ISBN 0-471-90039-7 (pbk) : £3.00 : CIP entry
B82-22394

How, Ludi. Relaxation and meditation / by Ludi How and Michael Brookman. — Bristol (7 Downfield Rd., Clifton, Bristol BS8 2TG) : Cancer Help Centre, [1982]. — 4p ; 21cm. — (C.H. ; 10)
Bibliography: p4
Unpriced (pbk) B82-34046

Practitioner's guide to amygatrile injections. — Bristol (7 Downfield Rd., Clifton, Bristol BS8 2TG) : Cancer Help Centre, [1980]. — [3]p ; 21cm. — (C.H. ; 8)
Unpriced (unbound) B82-34042

Principles of cancer treatment / [edited by] Stephen K. Carter, Eli Glatstein, Robert B. Livingston. — New York ; London : McGraw-Hill, c1982. — xix,951p : ill ; 29cm
Includes bibliographies and index
ISBN 0-07-010183-3 : £59.25 B82-03304

616.99'4061 — Man. Cancer. Adjuvant therapy — *Conference proceedings*

International Conference on the Adjuvant Therapy of Cancer *(3rd : 1981 : Tucson)*. Adjuvant therapy of cancer III / [proceedings of the Third International Conference on the Adjuvant Therapy of Cancer, Tucson, Arizona March 18-21, 1981] ; edited by Sydney E. Salmon, Stephen. E. Jones. — New York ; London : Grune & Stratton, c1981. — xiv,603p : ill ; 24cm
Includes bibliographies and index
ISBN 0-8089-1407-3 : £19.60 B82-04246

616.99'4061 — Man. Cancer. Drug therapy

Cancer and chemotherapy / edited by Stanley T. Crooke, Archie W. Prestayko ; editorial assistant, Nancy Alder. — New York (London) : Academic Press
Vol.1: Introduction to neoplasia and antineoplastic chemotherapy. — 1980. — xv,373p : ill ; 24cm
Includes bibliographies and index
ISBN 0-12-197801-x : £22.50 B82-35616

616.99'4061 — Man. Cancer. Drug therapy. Bestatin

Small molecular immunomodifiers of microbial origin. — Oxford : Pergamon, Aug.1981. — [300]p
Originally published: Baltimore : University Park Press, 1980
ISBN 0-08-027993-7 : £21.00 : CIP entry
B81-15929

616.99'4061 — Man. Cancer. Drug therapy. Cisplatin — *Conference proceedings — German text*

CISPLATIN : Derzeitiger Stand und neue Entwicklungen in der Chemotherapie maligner Neoplasien : Symposium am 16. November 1979, Frankfurt a.M. / Bandherausgeber, S. Seeber ... [et al.]. — Basel ; London : Karger, 1980. — 176p : ill ; 23cm. — (Beiträge zur Onkologie ; Bd.3)
Includes 4 papers in English
ISBN 3-8055-1364-x (pbk) : £10.50
B82-40728

616.99'4061 — Man. Cancer. Drug therapy — *Conference proceedings — German texts*

Neue Erfahrungen mit Oxazaphosphorinen unter besonderer Berücksichtigung des Uroprotektors Uromitevan : Gemeinsames Symposium der Arbeitsgemeinschaft für internistische Onkologie (AIO) der Deutschen Krebsgesellschaft und der ASTA-Werke AG, Bielefeld, am 29. Februar 1980 in Düsseldorf / Bandherausgeber, H. Burkert und G.A. Nagel. — Basel ; London : Karger, 1980. — ix,124p : ill ; 23cm. — (Beiträge zur Onkologie ; Bd.5)
Includes 1 paper in English
ISBN 3-8055-1381-x (pbk) : £10.50
B82-40731

616.99'4061 — Man. Cancer. Drug therapy. Doxorubicin — *Conference proceedings — German texts*

Adriamycin-Symposium : Ergebnisse und Aspekte : Gemeinsames symposium der Arbeitsgemeinschaft Internistische Onkologie (AIO) der Deutschen Krebsgesellschaft und der Farmitalia Carlo Erba, Freiburg i. Br. / Bandherausgeber D. Füllenbach, G.A. Nagel, S. Seeber. — Basel ; London : Karger, 1981. — viii,461p,vp of plates : ill(some col.) ; 23cm. — (Beiträge zur Onkologie = Contributions to oncology ; bd.9)
Includes bibliographies and index
ISBN 3-8055-2966-x (pbk) : £30.25
B82-13618

616.99'4061 — Man. Cancer. Drug therapy. Drugs. Testing — *Conference proceedings*

Design of models for testing cancer therapeutic agents : third in a series of technology assessment workshops sponsored by Litton Bionetics, Inc. / edited by Isaiah J. Fidler and Richrd J. White. — New York ; London : Van Nostrand Reinhold, c1982. — x,278p : ill ; 24cm. — (Litton Bionetics workshop series ; 3)
Includes index
ISBN 0-442-23897-5 : £23.40 B82-13189

616.99'4061 — Man. Cancer. Drug therapy. Nucleosides — *Conference proceedings*

Nucleosides and cancer treatment : rational approaches to antimetabolite selectivity and modulation : proceedings of a symposium held at the Ludwig Institute for Cancer Research (Sydney Branch) in October 1980 / edited by M.H.N. Tattersall, R.M. Fox. — Sydney ; London : Academic Press, 1981. — xix,442p : ill ; 24cm. — (Ludwig symposia ; 2)
Includes index
ISBN 0-12-683820-8 : £24.80 B82-10144

616.99'4061 — Women. Cancer. Drug therapy

Barker, Graham H.. Chemotherapy of gynaecological malignancies. — Tunbridge Wells : Castle House Publications, Jan.1983. — [144]p
ISBN 0-7194-0082-1 : £18.00 : CIP entry
B82-37467

616.99'40642 — Man. Cancer. Radiotherapy

Cancer topics and radiotherapy / edited by C.A.F. Joslin. — London : Pitman, 1982. — x,253p : ill ; 23cm
Includes bibliographies and index
ISBN 0-272-79662-x (pbk) : Unpriced : CIP rev. B82-07417

616.99'40642'05 — Man. Cancer. Radiotherapy — *Serials*

Topical reviews in radiotherapy and oncology. — Vol.2. — Bristol : J. Wright, Apr.1982. — [240]p
ISBN 0-7236-0616-1 : £14.50 : CIP entry
Also classified at 616.99'2'005 B82-04970

616.99'4069 — Man. Cancer. Therapy. Use of bacteria — *Conference proceedings*

Bacteria and cancer. — London : Academic Press, Jan.1983. — [550]p
Conference papers
ISBN 0-12-383820-7 : CIP entry B82-33464

616.99'407 — Man. Cancer. Cells. Growth. Regulation

Regulation of growth in neoplasia / editor G.V. Sherbet. — Basel ; London : Karger, 1981. — vii,201p : ill ; 25cm
Includes bibliographies and index
ISBN 3-8055-2305-x : £34.80
Also classified at 574.87'612 B82-07726

616.99'407 — Man. Malignant tumours. Cells. Growth. Kinetics

Ėmanuėl', N. M.. Kinetics of experimental tumour processes / by N.M. Ėmanuel. — Oxford : Pergamon, 1982. — xi,336p : ill ; 24cm
Translation of: Kinetika eksperimental'nykh opukholevykh protšessov. — Bibliography: p291-326. — Includes index
ISBN 0-08-024909-4 : Unpriced : CIP rev.
B81-35906

616.99'4071 — Man. Cancer. Pathogens: Chemicals — *Conference proceedings*

European Environmental Mutagen Society. *Meeting (10th : 1980 : Athens).* Progress in environmental mutagenesis and carcinogenesis : proceedings of the 10th Annual Meeting of the European Environmental Mutagen Society (EEMS) Athens (Greece), 14-19 September 1980 : under the auspices of the Ministry of Culture and Science of Greece and the Greek Atomic Energy Commission / edited by A. Kappas. — Amsterdam ; Oxford : Elsevier/North-Holland Biomedical, 1981. — (Progress in mutation research ; v.2)
Includes bibliographies and index
ISBN 0-444-80334-3 : Unpriced
Primary classification 573.2'292 B82-06110

616.99'4071 — Man. Cancer. Pathogens: Polycyclic aromatic hydrocarbons

Polycyclic hydrocarbons and cancer / edited by Harry V. Gelboin, Paul O.P. Ts'o. — New York ; London : Academic Press
Vol.3. — 1981. — xvi,351p : ill ; 24cm
Includes index
ISBN 0-12-279203-3 : £32.80 B82-30135

616.9'94071 — Man. Carcinogenic effects of benzidine based dyes

Wilson, Gordon, *1946-*. Cancer at work : dyes / by Gordon Wilson and advisers of the Cancer Prevention Society. — Glasgow (102 Inveroran Drive, Bearsden, Glasgow G61 2AT) : The Society, 1980. — 12p ; 22cm
Cover title
£0.35 (pbk) B82-31855

616.99'4071 — Man. Carcinogenic effects of chemicals. Research. Use of laboratory animals

Holmberg, Bo. Estimation and evaluation of carcinogenic activity : guidelines and viewpoints / Bo Holmberg, Jorma Rantanen, Erik Arrhenius ; [translation, Frances Van Stant]. — Lund : Studentlitteratur ; Bromley : Chartwell-Bratt, 1981, c1979. — 160p : ill ; 23cm
Bibliography: p118-152
ISBN 0-86238-015-4 (pbk) : Unpriced
B82-35644

616.99'4071 — Man. Carcinogenic effects of wood dust

The **Carcinogenicity** and mutagenicity of wood dust. — Southampton (c/o South Academic Block, Southampton General Hospital, Southampton SO9 4XY) : MRC Environmental Epidemiology Unit, 1982. — viii,43p : ill ; 30cm. — (Scientific report / MRC Environmental Epidemiology Unit ; no.1)
Unpriced (pbk) B82-31233

616.99'4071 — Personnel. Cancer. Pathogens: Industrial chemicals. Control — *Conference proceedings*

Identification and control of chemical carcinogens in the workplace : June 30 and July 1, 1981, London. — [London] : Scientific and Technical Studies, c1981. — iv,111p : 1ill ; 30cm
Conference proceedings. — Includes bibliographies
ISBN 0-9505774-7-2 (pbk) : £35.00
B82-11460

616.99'4075 — Man. Cancer. Diagnosis

Cancer diagnosis : new concepts and techniques / editors Richard J. Steckel, A. Robert Kagan. — New York ; London : Grune & Stratton, c1982. — xi,340p : ill ; 29cm
Includes index
ISBN 0-8089-1451-0 : £22.80 B82-39091

616.99'407582 — Man. Cancer. Diagnosis. Use of cell markers

Markers of diagnosis and monitoring of human cancer / edited by M.I. Colnaghi, G.L. Buraggi and M. Ghione. — London : Academic Press, 1982. — xii,280p : ill ; 24cm. — (Proceedings of the Serono symposia ; v.46)
Conference papers. — Includes bibliographies and index
ISBN 0-12-181520-x : £21.60 : CIP rev.
B81-34012

616.99'4079 — Man. Cancer. Immunological aspects — *Conference proceedings*

International Conference on Fundamental Mechanisms in Human Cancer Immunology *(1st : 1980 : Galveston).* Fundamental mechanisms in human cancer immunology : proceedings of the First International Conference on Fundamental Mechanisms in Human Cancer Immunology, Galveston, Texas, U.S.A., October 27-29, 1980 / editor J. Palmer Saunders ; associate editors Jerry C. Daniels, Bernard Serrou, Claude Rosenfeld ; associate editor Constance B. Denney. — New York ; Oxford : Elsevier/North-Holland, c1981. — xii,533p : ill ; 25cm. — (Developments in cancer research ; v.5)
Includes bibliographies and index
ISBN 0-444-00648-6 : £44.78 B82-09905

International Symposium on Current Concepts in Human Immunology and Cancer Immunomodulation *(1982 : Montpellier).* Current concepts in human immunology and cancer immunomodulation : proceedings of the International Symposium on Current Concepts in Human Immunology and Cancer Immunomodulation held in Montpellier, France, 18-20 January, 1982 / editors B. Serrou ... [et al.]. — Amsterdam ; Oxford : Elsevier Biomedical, 1982. — xi,664p : ill ; 25cm. — (Developments in immunology, ISSN 0163-5921 ; v.17)
Includes bibliographies and index
ISBN 0-444-80426-9 : Unpriced B82-33796

616.99'4079 — Man. Cancer. Immunology

The **Handbook** of cancer immunology / edited by Harold Waters. — New York ; London : Garland STPM
Vol.2: Cellular escape from immune destruction. — c1978. — viii,276p : ill ; 24cm
Includes index
ISBN 0-8240-7001-1 : Unpriced B82-39116

616.99'4079 — Man. Cancer. Immunology. Psychosomatic aspects — *Conference proceedings*

Biological mediators of behavior and disease : neoplasia : proceedings of a symposium on behavioral biology and cancer, held May 15, 1981 at the National Institutes of Health, Bethesda, Maryland, USA / editor Sandra M. Levy. — New York ; Oxford : Elsevier Biomedical, c1982. — xvi,260p : ill ; 24cm
Includes bibliographies and index
ISBN 0-444-00708-3 : £26.77 B82-36631

616.99'4079 — Man. Cancer. Immunotherapy

Immunological approaches to cancer therapeutics / edited by Enrico Mihich. — New York ; Chichester : Wiley, c1982. — x,587p : ill ; 24cm
Includes index
ISBN 0-471-06049-6 : £49.50 B82-38985

616.99'4079 — Man. Cancer. Suppressor cells

Suppressor cells in human cancer / edited by B. Serrou and C. Rosenfeld. — Amsterdam ; Oxford : Elsevier/North-Holland Biomedical, 1981. — xiii,215p : ill ; 25cm. — (Human cancer immunology ; v.2)
Includes bibliographies and index
ISBN 0-444-80306-8 : £32.28 B82-00693

616.99'419 — Man. Blood. Granulocytic leukaemia

Chronic granulocytic leukaemia. — Eastbourne : Praeger, Nov.1981. — [264]p
ISBN 0-03-060053-7 : £14.50 : CIP entry B81-30901

616.99'419 — Man. Blood. Leukaemia

Adult leukemias. — Hague ; London : Nijhoff 1 / edited by Clara D. Bloomfield. — 1982. — xii,415p : ill ; 25cm. — (Cancer treatment and research ; 5)
Includes bibliographies and index
ISBN 90-247-2478-3 : Unpriced B82-30376

616.99'422059 — Man. Larynx. Cancer. Surgery

Silver, Carl E.. Surgery for cancer of the larynx : and related structures / Carl E. Silver ; illustrated by Hugh Thomas. — New York ; Edinburgh : Churchill Livingstone, 1981. — xii,250p : ill(some col.) ; 29cm
Includes bibliographies and index
ISBN 0-443-08064-x : £42.00 B82-16440

616.99'424 — Man. Lungs. Cancer — *Conference proceedings*

European Symposium on Lung Cancer *(1st : 1980 : Chalkidiki).* Lung cancer : etiology, epidemiology, prevention, early diagnosis, treatment : proceedings of the 1st European Symposium on Lung Cancer, Chalkidiki, September 7-13, 1980 / editor Gregory Pontifex. — Amsterdam ; London : Excerpta Medica, 1982. — xiv,381p : ill ; 25cm. — (International congress series ; no.558)
Includes bibliographies and index
ISBN 90-219-0499-3 : £41.13 B82-27157

Lung cancer 1980 : postgraduate course : II World Congress [i.e. Conference] on Lung Cancer, Copenhagen, Denmark June 9-13, 1980 / editors Heine H. Hansen and Mikael Rørth. — Amsterdam ; Oxford : Excerpta Medica, 1980. — 152p : ill(some col.) ; 23cm. — (International congress series ; no.525)
ISBN 90-219-0447-0 : £15.91 B82-31846

616.99'431'00222 — Man. Mouth. Cancer — *Illustrations*

Burkhardt, Arne. A colour atlas of oral cancers : the diagnosis and classification of leukoplakias, precancerous conditions and carcinomas / Arne Burkhardt, Reinhard Maerker ; translated from the German by R.E.K. Meuss. — London : Wolfe Medical, 1981. — 186p : chiefly ill(some col.) ; 27cm. — (Wolfe medical atlases)
Translated from the German. — Bibliography: p184. — Includes index
ISBN 0-7234-0769-x : Unpriced B82-02247

616.99'433 — Man. Gastrointestinal tract. Cancer

Gastrointestinal cancer / edited by Jerome J. Decosse and Paul Sherlock. — The Hague ; London : Nijhoff. — (Cancer treatment and research ; v.3)
1. — 1981. — xii,452p : ill ; 25cm
Includes index
ISBN 90-247-2461-9 : Unpriced B82-05455

616.99'433 — Man. Gastrointestinal tract. Cancer — *Conference proceedings*

BSG. SK & F International Workshop *(2nd : 1981 : Chepstow).* Early gastric cancer : proceedings of the second BSG SK & F International Workshop / organised by the Education and Science Committee of the British Society of Gastroenterology, Chepstow, 20th-22nd September 1981 ; edited by P.B. Cotton. — [Welwyn Garden City] : Smith Kline & French Laboratories, c1982. — 83p : ill ; 24cm
Includes bibliographies
Unpriced (pbk) B82-31041

616.99'43306 — Man. Gastrointestinal tract. Cancer. Therapy — *Conference proceedings*

Progress and perspectives in the treatment of gastrointestinal tumors : proceedings of a symposium sponsored by the European Organization for Research and [i.e. on] Treatment of Cancer (E.O.R.T.C.), Gastro-intestinal Tumors Cooperative Group, Brussels, May 22-23, 1980 / editor A. Gerard. — Oxford : Pergamon, 1981. — vii,120p : ill ; 21cm
"Published as Supplement No.2 (1981) to the European journal of cancer and clinical oncology" — title page verso
ISBN 0-08-027979-1 : £15.00 : CIP rev. B81-26784

616.99'4347 — Man. Colon. Cancer. Pathogenesis — *Conference proceedings*

Falk Symposium *(31st : 1981 : Titisee).* Colonic carcinogenesis : proceedings of the 31st Falk Symposium held during Intestinal Week, Titisee, May 27-29, 1981 / edited by Ronald A. Malt, Robin C.N. Williamson. — Lancaster : MTP, c1982. — xv,406p : ill ; 25cm. — (Falk symposium ; 31)
Includes index
ISBN 0-85200-443-5 : £26.50 : CIP rev. B81-36974

616.99'436 — Man. Liver. Cancer

Carcinoma of the liver, biliary tract and pancreas. — London : Edward Arnold, Jan.1983. — [160]p. — (The Management of malignant disease series, ISSN 0144-8692 ; 5)
ISBN 0-7131-4333-9 : £15.00 : CIP entry B82-32592

616.99'446 — Man. Malignant lymphomas

Lymphomas 1 : including Hodgkin's disease / edited by John M. Bennett. — The Hague ; London : Nijhoff, c1981. — xii,450p : ill ; 25cm. — (Cancer treatment and research ; v.4)
Includes index
ISBN 90-247-2479-1 : Unpriced
ISBN 90-247-2426-0 (set) : Unpriced B82-05348

Malignant lymphomas : etiology, immunology, pathology, treatment / edited by Saul A. Rosenberg, Henry S. Kaplan. — New York ; London : Academic Press, 1982. — xxxii,682p : ill ; 24cm. — (Bristol-Myers cancer symposia ; 3)
Conference papers. — Includes index
ISBN 0-12-597120-6 : £31.40 B82-39508

616.99'449 — Women. Breasts. Cancer

Diagnosis and treatment of breast cancer : international clinical forum / edited by Edward F. Lewison, Albert C. W. Montague. — Baltimore ; London : Williams & Wilkins, c1981. — xxi,322p : ill,1facsim,1port ; 26cm
Conference papers. — Includes bibliographies and index
ISBN 0-683-04954-2 : Unpriced B82-07783

Faulder, Carolyn. Breast cancer : a guide to early detection and treatment / Carolyn Faulder. — New rev. ed. — London : Virago, 1982. — 166p ; 20cm
Previous ed.: London : Pan, 1979. — Bibliography: p156-160. — Includes index
ISBN 0-86068-287-0 (pbk) : £2.95 : CIP rev. B82-07116

Systemic control of breast cancer / edited by Basil A. Stoll. — London : Heinemann Medical, 1981. — xii,364p : ill ; 22cm. — (New aspects of breast cancer ; v.4)
Includes bibliographies and index
ISBN 0-433-31738-8 (pbk) : £12.50 B82-04113

616.99'449 — Women. Breasts. Cancer. Effects of hormones

Endocrine relationships in breast cancer / edited by Basil A. Stoll. — London : Heinemann Medical, 1932. — xii,349p : ill ; 22cm. — (New aspects of breast cancer ; v.5)
Includes bibliographies and index
ISBN 0-433-31737-x (pbk) : £12.50 B82-14550

616.99'4'49 — Women. Breasts. Cancer. Psychological aspects

Gyllenskōbl, Karin. Breast cancer : the psychological effects of the disease and its treatment. — London : Methuen, Mar.1982. — [300]p
Translation of: Visst blir man radd
ISBN 0-422-76820-0 (cased) : £12.00 : CIP entry
ISBN 0-422-76830-8 (pbk) : £5.50 B82-01163

616.99'449059 — Women. Breasts. Cancer. Surgery — *German texts*

Österreichische Chirurgentagung *(1. : 1978 : Salzburg).* Chirurgische Therapie des Mammakarzinoms / 1. Österreichische Chirurgentagung, September 1978, Salzburg ; Bandherausgeber, F. Judmaier. — Basel ; London : Karger, 1980. — 60p : ill,1map ; 23cm. — (Beiträge zur Onkologie ; Bd.2)
ISBN 3-8055-1350-x (pbk) : £7.50 B82-40730

616.99'44906 — Women. Breasts. Cancer. Cancer therapy. Clinical trials — *Serials*

[**News bulletin** *(Co-ordinating Committee on Cancer Research. Breast Cancer Trials Co-ordinating Subcommittee)*]. News bulletin / Breast Cancer Trials Co-ordinating Subcommittee. — No.1 (Sept. 1980)-. — Edinburgh (55 George Sq., Edinburgh EH8 9JV) : The Subcommittee, 1980-. — v. ; 30cm
ISSN 0263-7510 = News bulletin - Breast Cancer Trials Co-ordinating Subcommittee : Unpriced B82-31729

616.99'44906 — Women. Breasts. Cancer. Therapy

Cope, Oliver. The breast : a health guide for women of all ages / Oliver Cope. — Rev. ed. — London : Proteus, 1979. — 219p : ill ; 23cm
Previous ed.: Boston, Mass.: Mifflin, 1977. — Includes index
ISBN 0-906071-30-5 : £5.95 B82-03319

616.99'449061 — Women. Breasts. Cancer. Drug therapy. Aminoglutethimide

Aminoglutethimide : an alternative therapy for breast cancer. — London : Academic Press, Dec.1982. — [60]p. — (Royal Society of Medicine. International congress & symposia series, ISSN 0142-2367 ; v.53)
Conference papers
ISBN 0-12-791157-x (pbk) : CIP entry B82-32285

A Comprehensive guide to the therapeutic use of amino-glutethimide / editors Richard J. Santen, I. Craig Henderson. — 2nd rev. ed. — Basel ; London : Karger, c1982. — 160p,[3]p of plates : ill(some col.) ; 23cm. — (Pharmanual ; 2)
Previous ed.: 1981. — Includes bibliographies
ISBN 3-8055-3452-3 (pbk) : £13.70 B82-11591

616.99'449061 — Women. Breasts. Cancer. Drug therapy. Use of non-steroidal oestrogen antagonists

Non-steroidal antioestrogens : molecular pharmacology and antitumor activity / edited by Robert L. Sutherland and V. Craig Jordan. — Sydney ; London : Academic Press, 1981. — xxii,496p : ill ; 24cm
ISBN 0-12-677880-9 : £45.00 B82-32779

616.99'46 — Man. Urogenital system. Cancer

Genitourinary tumours : fundamental principles and surgical techniques / edited by Douglas E. Johnson, Michel A. Boileau. — New York ; London : Grune & Stratton, c1982. — xvii,554p : ill ; 26cm
Includes index
ISBN 0-8089-1471-5 : £52.60 B82-39090

616.99'462 — Man. Bladder. Cancer — *Conference proceedings*

Clinical bladder cancer / [proceedings of an international symposium on bladder cancer and a selection of urological papers presented at the Antwerp Medical days, held September 19-20, in Antwerp, Belgium] ; edited by L. Denis, P.H. Smith and M. Pavone-Macaluso. — New York ; London : Plenum, c1982. — xi,202p : ill ; 26cm
Includes bibliographies and index
ISBN 0-306-40835-x : Unpriced B82-18615

616.99'463 — Men. Testes. Cancer

The **Management** of testicular tumours / edited by Michael Peckham. — London : Edward Arnold, c1981. — 288p,[2]p of plates : ill(some col.) ; 24cm. — (The Management of malignant disease series, ISSN 0144-8692 ; 3)
Includes bibliographies and index
ISBN 0-7131-4326-6 : £17.50 : CIP rev.
B81-30579

616.99'463 — Men. Testes. Germ cells. Cancer — *Conference proceedings*

Germ cell tumours / edited by C.K. Anderson, W.G. Jones, A. Milford Ward. — London : Taylor & Francis, 1981. — xxi,427p : ill ; 24cm
Conference papers. — Includes bibliographies and index
ISBN 0-85066-223-0 : £18.00 : CIP rev.
B81-30257

616.99'465 — Women. Reproductive system. Cancer

Gynecologic oncology : fundamental principles and clinical practice / edited by Malcolm Coppleson ; foreword by Howard Ulfelder. — Edinburgh : Churchill Livingstone, 1981. — 2v.(xv,1059p) : ill ; 29cm
Includes bibliographies and index
ISBN 0-443-01977-0 : Unpriced : CIP rev.
B81-15847

Modern concepts of gynecologic oncology / edited by John R. van Nagell, Jr., Hugh R.K. Barber. — Boston, Mass. ; Bristol : John Wright, 1982. — xvi,686p : ill ; 24cm
Includes bibliographies and index
ISBN 0-88416-268-0 : Unpriced B82-34898

616.99'46506 — Women. Reproductive system. Cancer. Therapy. Sequelae

Management of complications in gynecologic oncology / edited by Gregorio Delgado, Julian P. Smith. — New York ; Chichester : Wiley, c1982. — xiv,287p : ill ; 27cm
Includes index
ISBN 0-471-05993-5 : £29.75 B82-32708

616.99'46506 — Women. Reproductive system. Cancer. Therapy. Sequelae — *German texts*

Probleme der Krebsnachsorge : Prognose, Begutachtung und Rehabilitation bei gynäkologischen Karzinomen / Bandherausgeber, A. Pfleiderer und W. Eissenhauer ; mit Beiträgen von M. Beck ... [et al.]. — Basel ; London : Karger, c1980. — 140p : ill ; 23cm. — (Beiträge zur Onkologie ; Bd.4)
Conference papers. — Includes bibliographies
ISBN 3-8055-1378-x (pbk) : £12.00
B82-40729

616.99'466 — Women. Uterus. Cervix. Cancer

Carcinoma of the cervix : biology and diagnosis / edited by E.S.E. Hafez and J.P. Smith. — The Hague ; London : Nijhoff, c1982. — xiii,258p : ill ; 28cm. — (Developments in obstetrics and gynecology ; v.6)
Bibliography: p242-251. — Includes index
ISBN 90-247-2574-7 : Unpriced B82-39569

616.99'466 — Women. Uterus. Cervix. Cancer — *Questions & answers*

Brown, G. Stephen. Cancer of the cervix / G. Stephen Brown, Philip J. DiSaia. — New York ; Oxford : Pergamon, c1981. — xvi,239,[56]p : ill ; 28cm. — (Oncologic, mutlidisciplinary decisions in oncology ; v.14)
Bibliography: p231-236. — Includes index
ISBN 0-08-027465-x (pbk) : Unpriced
B82-05256

616.99'466'0076 — Women. Uterus. Malignant tumours — *Questions & answers*

Glassburn, John R.. Malignant tumours of the uterine corpus and trophoblastic disease / John R. Glassburn, Thomas V. Sedlacek, Luther W. Bradly. — New York ; Oxford : Pergamon, 1982. — 292p in various pagings : ill ; 28cm. — (Oncologic, multidisciplinary decisions in oncology, ISSN 0272-5495 ; v.15)
Includes bibliographies and index
ISBN 0-08-027466-8 (pbk) : Unpriced
B82-31687

616.99'4'67 — Women. Vulva. Cancer

Way, Stanley. Malignant disease of the vulva / Stanley Way assisted by David Guthrie, Peter Philips. — Edinburgh : Churchill Livingstone, 1982. — 83p : ill,ports ; 24cm
Includes index
ISBN 0-443-02366-2 : £9.95 : CIP rev.
B82-06840

616.99'477 — Man. Skin. Cancer

Cancer-associated genodermatoses / edited by Henry T. Lynch and Ramon M. Fusaro. — New York ; London : Van Nostrand Reinhold, c1982. — vii,559p : ill ; 24cm
Includes index
ISBN 0-442-22471-0 : £27.20 B82-38590

616.99'477 — Man. Skin. Malignant tumours

Malignant skin tumours. — Edinburgh : Churchill Livingstone, June 1982. — [288]p
ISBN 0-443-02268-2 : £28.00 : CIP entry
B82-09717

616.99'48 — Man. Central nervous system. Cancer — *Conference papers*

CNS complications of malignant disease / edited by J.M.A. Whitehouse and H.E.M. Kay. — London : Macmillan, 1979. — xv,419p : ill ; 24cm
Conference papers. — Includes bibliographies and index
ISBN 0-333-25642-5 : Unpriced : CIP rev.
B79-30689

616.9'95079 — Man. Tuberculosis. Immunological aspects — *Conference proceedings*

Immunological aspects of leprosy, tuberculosis and leishmaniasis : proceedings of a meeting held in Addis Ababa, Ethiopia, 27-30 October 1980 / editor David P. Humber ; conference committee Ayele Belehu ... [et al.]. — Amsterdam ; Oxford : Excerpta Medica, 1981. — xiii,312p : ill ; 25cm. — (International congress series ; no.574)
Includes index
ISBN 90-219-0522-1 : Unpriced
Primary classification 616.07'9 B82-13454

616.9'9524'009411 — Scotland. Man. Lungs. Pulmonary tuberculosis

Forbes, G. I.. Working Party on Tuberculosis report / by G.I. Forbes, V.K. Howie, J. Urquhart. — Edinburgh (Trinity Park House, South Trinity Rd., Edinburgh EH5 3SQ) : Information Services Division, Scottish Health Service, Common Services Agency
At head of title: Scottish Pulmonary Tuberculosis Survey (SMR14)
No.1: Information on notifications recorded between July and December 1977. — 1978. — 37leaves : ill,1form ; 30cm
Unpriced (spiral) B82-34154

Forbes, G. I.. Working Party on Tuberculosis report / by G.I. Forbes, V.K. Howie, J. Urquhart. — Edinburgh (Trinity Park House, South Trinity Rd., Edinburgh EH5 3SQ) : Information Services Division, Scottish Health Service, Common Services Agency
At head of title: Scottish Pulmonary Tuberculosis Survey (SMR14)
No.2 (Supplement): Randomised health board data. — 1980. — 15leaves ; 30cm
Unpriced (unbound) B82-34158

Forbes, G. I.. Working Party on Tuberculosis report / by G.I. Forbes, V.K. Howie, J. Urquhart. — Edinburgh (Trinity Park House, South Trinity Rd., Edinburgh EH5 3SQ) : Information Services Division, Scottish Health Service, Common Services Agency
At head of title: Scottish Pulmonary Tuberculosis Survey (SMR14)
No.3: Information on notifications recorded January to December 1978. — 1980. — 27leaves ; 30cm
Unpriced (pbk) B82-34155

Forbes, G. I.. Working Party on Tuberculosis report / by G.I. Forbes, V.K. Howie, J. Urquhart. — Edinburgh (Trinity Park House, South Trinity Rd., Edinburgh EH5 3SQ) : Information Services Division, Scottish Health Service, Common Services Agency
At head of title: Scottish Pulmonary Tuberculosis Survey (SMR14)
No.4: Clinical data on notifications recorded between January and December 1978. — 1980. — 40leaves ; 30cm
Cover title
Unpriced (spiral) B82-34156

Forbes, G. I.. Working Party on Tuberculosis report / by G.I. Forbes, V.K. Howie, J. Urquhart. — Edinburgh (Trinity Park House, South Trinity Rd., Edinburgh EH5 3SQ) : Information Services Division, Scottish Health Service, Common Services Agency
At head of title: Scottish Pulmonary Tuberculosis Survey (SMR14)
No.5 and 6: Information and clinical data on notifications recorded between January and December 1979. — 1981. — 61p ; 30cm
Unpriced (spiral) B82-34157

616.9'98079 — Man. Leprosy. Immunological aspects — *Conference proceedings*

Immunological aspects of leprosy, tuberculosis and leishmaniasis : proceedings of a meeting held in Addis Ababa, Ethiopia, 27-30 October 1980 / editor David P. Humber ; conference committee Ayele Belehu ... [et al.]. — Amsterdam ; Oxford : Excerpta Medica, 1981. — xiii,312p : ill ; 25cm. — (International congress series ; no.574)
Includes index
ISBN 90-219-0522-1 : Unpriced
Primary classification 616.07'9 B82-13454

617 — MEDICINE. SURGERY

617 — Man. Surgery

Essential surgical practice. — Bristol : Wright, July 1982. — [1280]p
ISBN 0-7236-0622-6 : £35.00 : CIP entry
B82-16230

617 — Medicine. Surgery

Bailey, Hamilton. Bailey & Love's short practice of surgery. — 18th ed. / revised by A.J. Harding Rain and H. David Ritchie. — London : H.K. Lewis, 1981. — ix,1370p : ill (some col.) ; 26cm
Previous ed.: 1977. — Includes index
ISBN 0-7186-0450-4 : £23.00 B82-10707

Current surgical practice. — London : Edward Arnold, 1981
Includes index
Vol.3 / edited on behalf of the Royal College of Surgeons of England by John Hadfield and Michael Hobsley ; with a foreword by Sir Alan Parks. — xiv,313p : ill ; 24cm
ISBN 0-7131-4397-5 (pbk) : £14.95 : CIP rev.
ISSN 0141-3368 B81-31632

Davis, Loyal. Davis-Christopher textbook of modern surgical practice : the biological basis of modern surgical practice. — 12th ed., edited by David C. Sabiston, Jr. — Philadelphia ; London : Saunders, 1981. — 2v. : ill ; 28cm
Previous ed.: 1977. — Includes bibliographies and index
ISBN 0-7216-7878-5 : £35.00
ISBN 0-7216-7876-9 (v.1)
ISBN 0-7216-7877-7 (v.2)
ISBN 0-7216-7850-5 (single vol.) B82-03343

Frontiers in general surgery / edited by D.W. Jirsch. — Lancaster : MTP, c1982. — x,390p : ill ; 24cm
Includes index
ISBN 0-85200-249-1 : £22.50 : CIP rev.
B81-21603

Gray, F. J.. Principles of surgery : an illustrated text for health professionals / F.J Gray ; foreword by Maurice Ewing. — Melbourne ; Edinburgh : Churchill Livingstone, 1981. — 97p : ill ; 25cm
Includes index
ISBN 0-443-02166-x (pbk) : £3.25 : CIP rev.
B81-30380

617 — Medicine. Surgery *continuation*

Guide for house surgeons in the surgical unit / G.J. Fraenkel ... [et al.]. — 7th ed. — London : Heinemann Medical, 1982. — viii,215p : ill ; 18cm
Previous ed.: 1978. — Includes index
ISBN 0-433-10803-7 (pbk) : Unpriced
B82-37586

Scientific foundations of surgery. — 3rd ed. / edited by James Kyle and James D. Hardy. — London : Heinemann Medical, 1981. — xiv,712p : ill ; 29cm
Previous ed.: edited by Charles Wells, James Kyle and J. Englebert Dunphy. 1974. — Includes bibliographies and index
ISBN 0-433-18901-0 : £48.00 B82-00717

Smiddy, F. G.. Tutorials in surgery / F.G. Smiddy. — Tunbridge Wells : Pitman Medical
3: Operative surgery. — 1982. — ix,246p ; 22cm
ISBN 0-272-79661-1 (pbk) : Unpriced : CIP rev. B82-03100

Taylor, Selwyn. A short textbook of surgery / Selwyn Taylor, Leonard Cotton. — 5th ed. — London : Hodder Stoughton, 1982. — viii,631p : ill ; 22cm
Previous ed.: 1977. — Includes bibliographies and index
ISBN 0-340-27140-x (pbk) : £7.95 : CIP rev.
B81-28763

Thomas, J. M. (John Meirion). Aids to postgraduate surgery / J. Meirion Thomas, John S. Belstead. — 2nd ed. — Edinburgh : Churchill Livingstone, 1982. — 232p ; 22cm
Previous ed.: 1976. — Includes bibliographies and index
ISBN 0-443-02514-2 (pbk) : £4.25 : CIP rev.
ISBN 0-443-02639-4 (pbk) : £1.50 B81-34513

617 — Medicine. Surgery — *Conference proceedings*

Access surgery. — Lancaster : MTP Press, Dec.1982. — [400]p
ISBN 0-85200-453-2 : £29.95 : CIP entry
B82-37504

617'.0024613 — Medicine. Surgery — *For nursing*

Nash, D. F. Ellison. The principles and practice of surgery for nurses. — 7th ed. / D.F. Ellison Nash assisted by Cynthia M. Gilling, Mary Gillman. — London : Edward Arnold, 1980. — x,791p : ill(some col.),forms,1plans ; 25cm
Previous ed.: 1976. — Includes index
ISBN 0-7131-4366-5 (pbk) : £18.50 : CIP rev.
B80-23349

617'.005 — Medicine. Surgery — *Serials*

Recent advances in surgery. — No.11. — Edinburgh : Churchill Livingstone, Nov.1982. — [240]p
ISBN 0-443-02546-0 (pbk) : £10.00 : CIP entry
ISSN 0143-8395 B82-27542

Surgical review. — London : Pitman, May 1982. — [328]p
ISBN 0-272-79665-4 : £17.00 : CIP entry
ISSN 0144-882x B82-12902

617'.0076 — Medicine. Surgery — *Questions & answers*

Pickleman, Jack. Problems in general surgery / Jack Pickleman. — New York ; London : Plenum Medical, 1982. — xvii,363p : ill ; 24cm. — (Reviewing surgical topics)
Includes index
ISBN 0-306-40765-5 : Unpriced B82-30349

617'.01 — Hospitals. Patients. Infection during surgery. Control

Infection and the surgical patient. — Edinburgh : Churchill Livingstone, Nov.1982. — [200]p. — (Clinical surgery international ; v.4)
ISBN 0-443-02517-7 : £15.00 : CIP entry
B82-27540

617'.01 — Man. Infection during surgery — *Conference proceedings*

Infection in surgery : basic and clinical aspects / edited by J. McK. Watts ... [et al.] ; foreword by David Tonkin. — Edinburgh : Churchill Livingstone, 1980. — 404p : ill,1facsim ; 24cm
Conference papers. — Includes bibliographies and index
ISBN 0-443-02246-1 : £26.00 : CIP rev.
B80-31688

617'.01 — Postoperative patients. Diseases

Surgical infectious diseases / edited by Richard L. Simmons, Richard J. Howard with Angela I. Henriksen. — New York : Appleton-Century-Crofts ; London : Prentice-Hall, c1982. — xv,1172p : ill ; 29cm
Includes index
ISBN 0-8385-8729-1 : £101.25 B82-23153

617'.05 — Medicine. Surgery. Use of carbon dioxide lasers

Microscopic and endoscopic surgery with the CO2 laser / Albert H. Andrews, Jr editor ; Thomas G. Polanyi, associate editor. — Boston, Mass. ; Bristol : John Wright, 1982. — xv,370p : ill ; 24cm
Includes index
ISBN 0-7236-7009-9 : Unpriced B82-34895

617'.07 — Medicine. Surgery. Pathology

Myers, K. A.. Principles of pathology in surgery / K.A. Myers, R.D. Marshall, J. Freidin ; foreword by Lord Smith ; illustrated by J. Freidin. — Oxford : Blackwell Scientific, 1980. — xii,453p : ill ; 23cm
Includes index
ISBN 0-632-00413-4 (pbk) : £12.00 : CIP rev.
B80-06446

617'.079 — Medicine. Surgery. Immunology

Trauma, stress and immunity in anaesthesia and surgery / [edited by] John Watkins, Matti Salo. — London : Butterworth Scientific, 1982. — viii,378p,[1]leaf of plates : ill(some col.) ; 24cm
Includes bibliographies and index
ISBN 0-407-00207-3 : Unpriced : CIP rev.
B82-04024

617'.092'4 — Medicine. Surgery. Hunter, John, *1728-1793* — *Biographies*

Quist, George. John Hunter 1728-1793 / George Quist. — London : Heinemann Medical, 1981. — xvi,216p : ill,1coat of arms,facsims,1port,1geneal.table ; 23cm
Bibliography: p201-202. — Includes index
ISBN 0-433-27095-0 : £8.50 B82-18080

617'.092'4 — Medicine. Surgery. Keynes, *Sir* Geoffrey — *Biographies*

Keynes, *Sir* Geoffrey. The gates of memory / Geoffrey Keynes Kt. — Oxford : Clarendon, 1981. — xi,428p : ill,ports ; 23cm
Includes index
ISBN 0-19-812657-3 : £12.50 B82-05172

617.1 — MAN. WOUNDS AND INJURIES

617'.1 — Man. Injuries caused by accidents. Surgery

Topical reviews in accident surgery. — Bristol : John Wright
Vol.2 / edited by N. Tubbs and P.S. London. — 1982. — ix,258p : ill ; 23cm
Includes bibliographies and index
ISBN 0-7236-0614-5 : Unpriced : CIP rev.
B81-35846

617'.1 — Man. War injuries. Surgery

Field surgery pocket book. — New ed. / edited by Norman G. Kirby, Guy Blackburn. — London : H.M.S.O., 1981. — xvii,305p : ill ; 20cm
At head of title: Ministry of Defence. — Previous ed.: 1962. — Includes index
ISBN 0-11-772360-6 : £7.95 B82-05027

617'.1'0088054 — Battered children. Injuries

O'Doherty, Neil. The battered child : recognition in primary care / Neil O'Doherty. — London : Baillière Tindall, 1982. — 57p : ill(some col.) ; 26cm
Bibliography: p53. — Includes index
ISBN 0-7020-0734-x : Unpriced : CIP rev.
B81-13463

617'.1026 — Man. Injuries. Emergency treatment

Huckstep, R. L.. A simple guide to trauma / R.L. Huckstep ; illustrations by W. Serumaga and Franca Rubiu. — 3rd ed. — Edinburgh : Churchill Livingstone, 1982. — xii,397p : ill ; 20cm
Previous ed.: 1978. — Bibliography: p386-387. — Includes index
ISBN 0-443-02495-2 (pbk) : £4.95 : CIP rev.
B81-34512

617'.1027 — Association footballers. Injuries

Gray, Muir. Football injuries. — London : Edward Arnold, Oct.1982. — [128]p
Originally published: Oxford : Offox Press, 1980
ISBN 0-7131-0848-7 (pbk) : £3.95 : CIP entry
B82-30572

617'.1027 — Man. Injuries caused by combat sports

McLatchie, Greg. Injuries in combat sports. — Oxford (59 Lakeside, Oxford OX2 8JQ) : Offox Press, Oct.1982. — [192]p
ISBN 0-9506989-2-x : £5.95 : CIP entry
B82-28619

617'.1027 — Rackets & squash rackets. Medical aspects

Scott, Robert S.. The physician and sportsmedicine guide to racquetball and squash / Robert S. Scott ; foreword by Bob Mathias. — New York ; London : McGraw-Hill, c1980. — x,97p : ill ; 21cm. — (The physician and sportsmedicine series)
Bibliography: p89-90. — Includes index
ISBN 0-07-055586-9 : £6.50 B82-25216

617'.1027 — Recreations: Hang gliding. Medical aspects

Hadley, Dunstan. Air medical notes for hang-glider pilots / Dunstan Hadley. — [Shrewsbury] : Airlife, c1981. — 92p : ill ; 23cm
Bibliography: p89-90. — Includes index
ISBN 0-906393-13-2 : £5.95 B82-08511

617'.1027 — Rugby football. Injuries

Dunnill, Tony. Rugby injuries. — London : Edward Arnold, Oct.1982. — [224]p
Originally published: Oxford : Offox Press, 1982
ISBN 0-7131-0847-9 (pbk) : £4.95 : CIP entry
B82-30573

617'.1027 — Sports & games. Injuries

Muckle, David Sutherland. Injuries in sport : a guide for the accident department and general practice / David Sutherland Muckle. — 2nd ed. — Bristol : John Wright, 1982. — vii,159p : ill ; 23cm
Previous ed.: 1978. — Bibliography: p151-155. — Includes index
ISBN 0-7236-0620-x : Unpriced : CIP rev.
B81-34660

Relevant topics in athletic training / edited by Kent Scriber, Edmund J. Burke. — Ithaca, N.Y. : Mouvement Publications, c1978 ; Gayton (19 Oaksway, Gayton, Wirral L60 3SP) : M.E. Brodie [[distributor]]. — 140p : ill ; 28cm
ISBN 0-932392-02-4 (pbk) : Unpriced
B82-07711

617'.1027 — Sports & games. Medical aspects

Apple, David F.. Medicine for sport / by David F. Apple Jr and John D. Cantwell. — Chicago ; London : Year Book Medical Publishers, c1979. — xiii,241p : ill,ports ; 22cm
Includes bibliographies and index
ISBN 0-8151-1422-2 : £19.00 B82-09966

Davies, Bruce. Science and sporting performance. — Oxford : Clarendon Press, July 1982. — [250]p
ISBN 0-19-857594-7 : £16.00 : CIP entry
B82-17965

617'.1027 — Sports. Performance. Medical aspects — *Conference proceedings*

Coaching support services : Sunday November 30th 1980 / presented by the Sports Council (Southern Region) in conjunction with the Association of Chartered Physiotherapists in Sports Medicine ; conference main sponsor Niagara Therapy (U.K.) Ltd. — Reading (Watlington House, Watlington St., Reading RG1 4RJ) : Sports Council (Southern Region), [1981?]. — 17leaves ; 31cm. — (Conference report)
Unpriced (pbk) B82-15125

617'.1106 — Man. Burns. Therapy

Clinical burn therapy : a management and prevention guide / edited by Robert P. Hummel. — Boston [Mass.] ; Bristol : John Wright, 1982. — ix,567p : ill ; 24cm
Includes index
ISBN 0-88416-284-2 : Unpriced B82-30124

MacMillan, Bruce G.. The surgical and medical support of burn patients / Bruce G. MacMillan. — Boston, Mass. ; Bristol : J. Wright, 1982. — xxi,180p : ill,forms,col.plans ; 22cm
Text, plans on inside covers. — Bibliography: p117-120
ISBN 0-7236-7004-8 (pbk) : Unpriced B82-32588

617'.1107 — Man. Burns. Physiological aspects

Davies, J. W. L.. Physiological responses to burning injury. — London : Academic Press, Aug.1982. — [700]p
ISBN 0-12-206080-6 : CIP entry B82-15664

617.1'23707547 — Man. Heart. Muscles. Infarction. Diagnosis. Electrocardiograms. Interpretation

Goldberger, Ary Louis. Myocardial infarction : electrocardiographic differential diagnosis / Ary Louis Goldberger ; foreword by Lawrence S. Cohen. — 2nd ed. — St. Louis ; London : Mosby, 1979. — xvi,277p : ill ; 26cm
Previous ed.: 1975. — Bibliography: p247-268. — Includes index
ISBN 0-8016-1860-6 : £27.50 B82-28172

617'.1406 — Man. Wounds. Therapy

Finley, John M.. Practical wound management : a manual of dressings / John M. Finley ; illustrations by Barbara Siede. — Chicago ; London : Year Book Medical, c1981. — x,216p : ill ; 26cm
Includes index
ISBN 0-8151-3225-5 (spiral) : Unpriced B82-38433

617'.15 — Man. Bones. Fractures

Browne, Patrick S. H.. Basic facts of fractures. — Oxford : Blackwell Scientific, Dec.1982. — [200]p
ISBN 0-632-00854-7 (pbk) : £7.50 : CIP entry B82-30046

617'.15 — Man. Bones. Fractures. External fixation

Concepts in external fixation / [edited by] David Seligson, Malcolm Pope. — New York ; London : Grune & Stratton, c1982. — xii,321p : ill,ports ; 27cm
Includes index
ISBN 0-8089-1453-7 : £32.80 B82-29982

617'.15 — Man. Bones. Fractures. Therapy

McRae, Ronald. Practical fracture treatment / Ronald McRae ; with original drawings and illustrations by the author. — Edinburgh : Churchill Livingstone, 1981. — vi,316p : ill ; 25cm
Includes index
ISBN 0-443-01694-1 (pbk) : £8.95 : CIP rev. B81-16349

McRae, Ronald. Practical fracture treatment / Ronald McRae. — Edinburgh : Churchill Livingstone, 1981 (1982 [printing]). — vi,316p : ill ; 25cm
Includes index
ISBN 0-443-02697-1 (pbk) : £4.50 B82-21053

617'.15 — Man. Bones. Fractures. Therapy — *Early works*

Bennett, George Matthews. The art of the bone-setter : a testimony and a vindication / with notes and illustrations by George Matthews Bennett. — London : Tamor Pierston, 1981. — xii,144p,viiileaves of plates : ill,1port ; 19cm
Facsim. of 1st ed. London : Murby, 1884. — Limited ed. of 650 copies
ISBN 0-907457-02-9 : Unpriced B82-20668

Moulton, Thomas. The compleat bone-setter. — Isleworth : Tamor Pierston, 1981. — [48]p ; 14cm
Facsim of: parts of 1st ed. London : Printed by J.C. for Martha Harison, 1656
ISBN 0-907457-04-5 (pbk) : Unpriced B82-20666

617'.156 — Man. Maxillofacial region. Bones. Fractures — *For dentistry*

Killey, H. C.. Killey's fractures of the middle third of the facial skeleton. — 4th ed. / Peter Banks. — Bristol : Wright, 1981. — vii,96p : ill ; 22cm. — (A Dental practitioner handbook ; no.3)
Previous ed. published as: Fractures of the middle third of the facial skeleton. 1977. — Bibliography: p83-91. — Includes index
ISBN 0-7236-0625-0 (pbk) : Unpriced : CIP rev. B81-24660

617'.21 — Man. Shock. Physiological aspects

Pathophysiology of shock, anoxia, and ischemia / editors R. Adams Cowley, Benjamin F. Trump. — Baltimore ; London : Williams & Wilkins, c1982. — xvi,710p : ill ; 29cm
Includes bibliographies and index
ISBN 0-683-02149-4 : Unpriced
Primary classification 616.1'3 B82-19367

617'.21 — Man. Trauma

Trauma / edited by David C. Carter and Hiram C. Polk, Jr. — London : Butterworths, 1981. — 327p : ill ; 24cm. — (Butterworths international medical reviews. Surgery, ISSN 0260-0188 ; 1)
Includes index
ISBN 0-407-02316-x : Unpriced : CIP rev. B81-19125

Trauma and after. — London : Pitman Medical, July 1981. — [128]p. — (Ciba Foundation occasional volume)
ISBN 0-272-79623-9 : £4.95 : CIP entry B81-13427

617.3 — MEDICINE. ORTHOPAEDICS

617'.3 — Medicine. Orthopaedics

Apley, A. Graham. Apley's system of orthopaedics and fractures. — 6th ed. / A. Graham Apley, Louis Solomon. — London : Butterworth Scientific, 1982. — x,497p : ill (some col.) ; 26cm
Previous ed.: published as System of orthopaedics and fractures. 1977. — Includes bibliographies and index
ISBN 0-407-40655-7 : Unpriced : CIP rev. B82-00920

Corrigan, Brian. Practical orthopaedic medicine. — London : Butterworth Scientific, Oct.1982. — [540]p
ISBN 0-407-00238-3 : £35.00 : CIP entry B82-25926

Cotta, Horst. Orthopaedics : a brief textbook / Horst Cotta with contributions by Peter Hinz and Wolfhart Puhl ; translated by Gottfried Stiasny. — Chicago ; London : Year Book Medical, 1980. — ix,418p : ill ; 19cm
Translation of: Orthopädie. — Bibliography: p403. — Includes index
ISBN 0-8151-1864-3 (pbk) : £8.75 B82-31766

Cyriax, James. Textbook of orthopaedic medicine. — London : Baillière Tindall
Vol.1: Diagnosis of soft-tissue lesions. — 8th ed. — Aug.1982. — [600]p
Previous ed.: 1978
ISBN 0-7020-0935-0 : £21.00 : CIP entry B82-15901

Mercer, *Sir* Walter. Mercer's orthopaedic surgery. — 8th ed. — London : Arnold, Oct.1982. — [1200]p
Previous ed.: 1973
ISBN 0-7131-4417-3 : £75.00 : CIP entry B82-22987

617'.3 — Physically handicapped persons. Orthopaedic rehabilitation

Orthopedic rehabilitation / edited by Vernon L. Nickel. — New York ; Edinburgh : Churchill Livingstone, 1982. — xxi,594p : ill ; 27cm
Includes bibliographies and index
ISBN 0-443-08060-7 : £45.00 B82-39671

617'.3'0014 — Medicine. Orthopaedics. Terminology

Blauvelt, Carolyn Taliaferro. A manual of orthopaedic terminology / Carolyn Taliaferro Blauvelt, Fred R.T. Nelson. — 2nd ed. — St. Louis ; London : Mosby, 1981. — xiii,257p : ill ; 24cm
Previous ed.: 1977. — Bibliography: p206. — Includes index
ISBN 0-8016-0752-3 (pbk) : £17.75 B82-34869

617'.3'0024613 — Medicine. Orthopaedics — *For nursing*

Norton, Thomas H.. Orthopaedic surgery / Thomas H. Norton, Judith M. Tait. — 2nd ed. — London : Heinemann Medical, 1979. — 172p : ill(some col.) ; 19cm. — (Modern practical nursing series ; 8)
Previous ed.: 1971. — Includes index
ISBN 0-433-23340-0 (pbk) : Unpriced B82-18916

617'.3'0028 — Medicine. Orthopaedics. Applications of engineering

Orthopaedic mechanics : procedures and devices / edited by D.N. Ghista, R. Roaf. — London : Academic Press
Vol.2. — 1981. — xii,308p : ill ; 24cm
Includes index
ISBN 0-12-281602-1 : £34.60 : CIP rev. B81-06065

Orthopaedic mechanics : procedures and devices / edited by Dhanjoo N. Ghista, Robert Roaf. — London : Academic Press
Vol.3. — 1981. — xi,207p : ill ; 24cm
Includes bibliographies and index
ISBN 0-12-281603-x : £27.80 : CIP rev. B81-06064

617'.3'0088054 — Children. Orthopaedics

Ferguson, Albert B.. Orthopaedic surgery in infancy and childhood / Albert B. Ferguson, Jr. — 5th ed. — Baltimore ; London : Williams & Wilkins, c1981. — xxiv,935p : ill ; 26cm
Previous ed.: 1975. — Includes bibliographies and index
ISBN 0-683-03167-8 : Unpriced B82-08064

Orthopaedic management in childhood. — Oxford : Blackwell Scientific, July 1982. — [512]p
ISBN 0-632-00879-2 : £32.50 : CIP entry B82-12994

617'.307'072042574 — Oxfordshire. Oxford. Orthopaedic appliances. Bioengineering. Research organisations: Oxford Orthopaedic Engineering Centre — *Serials*

Oxford Orthopaedic Engineering Centre. Annual report of the Oxford Orthopaedic Engineering Centre. — (Jan. 1975)-. — .1 Oxford ([Headington, Oxford OX3 7LD]) : Oxford Orthopaedic Engineering Centre, University of Oxford, 1975-. — v. : ill ; 30cm
Report year irregular. — Description based on: 4 (Dec. 1977)
ISSN 0263-2535 = Annual report of the Oxford Orthopaedic Engineering Centre : Unpriced B82-22652

617'.371 — Man. Head. Congenital abnormalities

Central nervous system and craniofacial malformations. — Lancaster : MTP Press, Sept.1982. — [190]p. — (Advances in the study of birth defects ; v.7)
ISBN 0-85200-398-6 : £18.50 : CIP entry B82-20531

617′.375 — Man. Lumbar spine. Disorders — *Conference proceedings*

Symposium on the lumbar spine, Rancho Mirage, California, November, 1979 / American Academy of Orthopaedic Surgeons ; edited by Frederic W. Brown. — St. Louis ; London : Mosby, 1981. — xi,271p : ill,forms ; 26cm
Includes bibliographies and index
ISBN 0-8016-0080-4 : £37.75 B82-08332

617′.375 — Man. Lumbar spine. Disorders — *German texts*

Basler Fortbildungskurs für Rheumatologie *(6th : 1980 : Basel).* Die Lumboischialgie : Diagnose, Differentialdiagnose, Therapie : 6. Basler Fortbildungskurs für Rheumatologie, Basel, 7.-8. März 1980 / W. Müller, F.J. Wagenhäuser. — Basel ; London : Karger, 1981. — 255p : ill ; 22cm. — (Fortbildungskurse für Rheumatologie ; 6)
German text. — Includes bibliographies
ISBN 3-8055-2207-x (pbk) : Unpriced B82-25554

617′.375 — Man. Spine. Disorders

Grieve, Gregory P.. Common vertebral joint problems / Gregory P. Grieve ; foreword by Philip H. Newman. — Edinburgh : Churchill Livingstone, 1981. — xiv,576p : ill ; 29cm
Bibliography: p535-557. — Includes index
ISBN 0-443-02106-6 : Unpriced : CIP rev. B81-16409

617′.375 — Man. Spine. Surgery — *Manuals*

Manual of spinal surgery / D.H.R. Jenkins ... [et al.]. — London : Butterworths, 1981. — vii,106p : ill ; 26cm
Bibliography: p101-103. — Includes index
ISBN 0-407-00159-x : £15.00 : CIP rev. B81-21625

617′.376043 — Man. Hips. Congenital dislocations. Therapy

Congenital dislocation of the hip / edited by Mihran O. Tachdjian. — New York ; Edinburgh : Churchill Livingstone, 1982. — xvi,798p : ill ; 27cm
Bibliography: p745-775. — Includes index
ISBN 0-443-08069-0 : £52.00 B82-39672

617.4 — MEDICINE. SURGICAL OPERATIONS BY SYSTEM

617′.41 — Man. Cardiovascular system. Surgery

Jamieson, Crawford. Surgical management of vascular disease / Crawford Jamieson. — London : Heinemann Medical, 1982. — 394p : ill ; 23cm
Bibliography: p382-383. — Includes index
ISBN 0-433-17120-0 : Unpriced B82-37583

617′.41 — Man. Cardiovascular system. Surgery. Artificial circulation

Techniques in extracorporeal circulation / edited by Marian I. Ionescu. — 2nd ed. — London : Butterworths, 1981. — xxix,721p : ill ; 25cm
Previous ed.: 1976. — Includes bibliographies and index
ISBN 0-407-00173-5 : Unpriced : CIP rev. B81-07930

617′.41 — Man. Cardiovascular system. Surgery — *Conference proceedings*

International Vascular Symposium *(1981 : London).* International Vascular Symposium : Royal Festival Hall complex 14-17 September 1981. — London : Macmillan, 1981. — [310]p in various pagings : maps,plans,1ports
Text on inside front cover. — Includes index
ISBN 0-333-32607-5 (pbk) : Unpriced B82-09123

617′.412 — Man. Heart. Aortocoronary bypass surgery

Stack, Madonna C.. Coronary artery bypass surgery / Madonna C. Stack. — New York : Appleton-Century-Crofts ; London : Prentice-Hall, c1980. — viii,68p : ill ; 23cm. — (Continuing education in cardiovascular nursing. Series 2, Surgical aspects of cardiovascular disease-nursing intervention ; Unit 5)
Includes bibliographies
ISBN 0-8385-1208-9 (pbk) : £4.50 B82-40801

617′.412 — Man. Heart. Surgery

Heart surgery for adults. — London (102 Gloucester Place, W1H 4DH) : British Heart Foundation, c1981 (1982 [printing]). — 12p : ill ; 18cm. — (Heart research series ; no.12)
Cover title
Unpriced (pbk) B82-40604

Monro, James L.. A colour atlas of cardiac surgery : acquired heart disease / James L. Monro, Gerald Shore. — London : Wolfe Medical, 1982. — 165p : col.ill ; 32cm. — (Wolfe medical atlases)
Includes index
ISBN 0-7234-0771-1 : Unpriced B82-39774

617′.412 — Man. Heart. Vascular grafts

Vineberg, Arthur M.. Myocardial revascularization by arterial/ventricular implants / Arthur M. Vineberg with contributions by Lorene Freeman ... [et al.]. — Boston ; Bristol : John Wright, 1982. — xxi,468p : ill(some col.) ; 24cm
Includes index
ISBN 0-88416-191-9 : Unpriced B82-24798

617′.4120592 — Man. Heart. Transplantation

Shinn, Julie A.. Cardiac transplantation and the artificial heart / Julie A. Shinn. — New York : Appleton-Century-Crofts ; London : Prentice-Hall, c1980. — 70p : ill ; 23cm. — (Continuing education in cardiovascular nursing. Series 2, Surgical aspects of cardiovascular disease-nursing intervention ; Unit 7)
Includes bibliographies
ISBN 0-8385-1045-0 (pbk) : £4.50 B82-40800

617′.4120592′0924 — Man. Heart. Transplantation — *Personal observations*

Barlow, Andrew. Beat on / Andrew Barlow. — London : Golden Eagle, 1982. — 205p,[16]p of plates : ill,ports ; 23cm
ISBN 0-901482-29-3 : £7.95 B82-16586

617′.4120645 — Man. Heart. Cardiac pacemakers

Pacemakers. — London (57 Gloucester Place, W1H 4DH) : British Heart Foundation, [1980?] (1981 [printing]). — 4p ; 18cm. — (Heart research series ; no.9)
Unpriced (unbound) B82-40601

617′.412′0924 — Man. Heart. Surgery — *Personal observations*

Waxberg, Joseph D.. Bypass : a doctor's recovery from open heart surgery / by Joseph D. Waxberg. — New York : Appleton-Century-Crofts ; London : Prentice-Hall, c1981. — vii,165p ; 24cm
ISBN 0-8385-0935-5 : £8.20 B82-16840

617′.413 — Man. Arteries. Surgery

Femoro-distal bypass. — Tunbridge Wells : Pitman Medical, June 1981. — [296]p
ISBN 0-272-79632-8 : £20.00 : CIP entry B81-13781

617′.413 — Man. Arteries. Surgery. Techniques

Bell, P. R. F.. Operative arterial surgery / P.R.F. Bell, W. Barrie. — Bristol : Wright, 1981. — xiii,185p : ill ; 26cm
ISBN 0-7236-0610-2 : Unpriced : CIP rev. B81-24639

617′.413 — Man. Blood vessels. Surgery

Critical problems in vascular surgery / edited by Frank J. Veith. — New York : Appleton-Century-Crofts ; London : Prentice-Hall, c1982. — xvi,472p : ill,facsims,ports ; 24cm
Conference papers. — Includes index
ISBN 0-8385-1245-3 : £31-90 B82-28190

Kester, Ralph C.. A practice of vascular surgery / Ralph C. Kester and Stephen H. Leveson. — London : Pitman, 1981. — xi,372p : ill ; 24cm
Includes bibliographies and index
ISBN 0-272-79640-9 : Unpriced : CIP rev. B81-34154

617′.413 — Man. Peripheral arteries. Surgery

Peripheral arterial diseases. — London : Academic Press, Apr.1982. — [450]p. — (Proceedings of the Serono symposia, ISSN 0308-5503 ; no.44)
ISBN 0-12-671460-6 : CIP entry B82-11505

617′.414′05 — Man. Veins. Surgery — *Serials*

Topical reviews in vascular surgery. — Vol.1. — Bristol : John Wright, Oct.1982. — [240]p
ISBN 0-7236-0575-0 : £18.50 : CIP entry B82-24271

617′.44 — Man. Bone marrow. Transplantation — *Conference proceedings*

Bone marrow transplantation in Europe. — Amsterdam ; Oxford : Excerpta Medica. — (Symposia Fondation Merieux ; 6)
Vol.2: Proceedings of the Fifth European Symposium on Bone Marrow Transplantation, Courchevel, Savoie, France, March 16-18, 1980 / editors Jean-Louis Touraine, Eliane Gluckman, Claude Griscelli ; assistant editors René Triau, Ferry Zwaan. — 1981. — xi,309p : ill ; 25cm
Includes index
ISBN 90-219-0486-1 : Unpriced B82-06111

617′.44 — Man. Endocrine system. Surgery

Endocrine surgery. — London : Butterworth, Dec.1982. — [320]p. — (Butterworths international medical reviews. Surgery, ISSN 0260-0188)
ISBN 0-407-02317-8 : £15.00 : CIP entry B82-29782

617′.460757 — Postoperative patients: Children. Urinary tract. Diagnosis. Radiography

Lebowitz, Robert L.. Postoperative pediatric uroradiology / Robert L. Lebowitz. — New York : Appleton-Century-Crofts ; London : Prentice-Hall, c1981. — x,207p : ill ; 29cm
Includes bibliographies and index
ISBN 0-8385-7859-4 : £23.90 B82-23152

617′.461059 — Man. Kidneys. Peritoneal dialysis — *Conference proceedings*

International Symposium on Peritoneal Dialysis *(2nd : 1981 : Berlin).* Advances in peritoneal dialysis : proceedings of the Second International Symposium on Peritoneal Dialysis Berlin (-West), June 16-19, 1981 editors / G.M. Gahl, M. Kessel, K.D. Nolph. — Amsterdam ; Oxford : Excerpta Medica, 1981. — xx,508p : ill ; 25cm. — (International congress series ; no.567)
Includes index
ISBN 90-219-9537-9 : £38.71 B82-11936

617′.461059′05 — Man. Kidneys. Haemodialysis & transplantation — *Conference proceedings — Serials*

Proceedings of the European Dialysis and Transplant Association. — Vol.18. — London : Pitman, Dec.1981. — [816]p
ISBN 0-272-79666-2 (pbk) : £35.00 : CIP entry
ISSN 0308-9401 B81-33871

617′.473044 — Athletes. Muscles. Injuries

Krejci, Vladimir. Muscle and tendon injuries in athletes : diagnosis, treatment, muscle training, rehabilitation / Vladimir Krejci and Peter Koch ; translated by David Le Vay. — Chicago ; London : Year Book Medical, 1979, c1976. — vi,96p : ill ; 20cm. — (Thieme Flexibooks)
Translation of: Muskelverletzungen und Tendopathien der Sportler. — Bibliography: p92-94. — Includes index
ISBN 0-8151-5195-0 (pbk) : £5.25
Also classified at 617′.474044 B82-00728

617′.474044 — Athletes. Tendons. Injuries

Krejci, Vladimir. Muscle and tendon injuries in athletes : diagnosis, treatment, muscle training, rehabilitation / Vladimir Krejci and Peter Koch ; translated by David Le Vay. — Chicago ; London : Year Book Medical, 1979, c1976. — vi,96p : ill ; 20cm. — (Thieme Flexibooks)
Translation of: Muskelverletzungen und Tendopathien der Sportler. — Bibliography: p92-94. — Includes index
ISBN 0-8151-5195-0 (pbk) : £5.25
Primary classification 617′.473044 B82-00728

617′.477 — Man. Skin. Surgery

Stegman, Samuel J.. Basics of dermatologic surgery / Samuel J. Stegman, Theodore A. Tromovitch, Richard G. Glogau. — Chicago ; London : Year Book Medical, c1982. — xi,134p : ill ; 26cm
Bibliography: p126-127. — Includes index
ISBN 0-8151-8168-x (spiral) : £22.50 B82-18069

617'.48 — Man. Central nervous system. Surgery

World Society for Stereotactic and Functional Neurosurgery. *Meeting (8th : 1981 : Zurich)*. Proceedings of the Eighth Meeting of the World Society and the Fifth Meeting of the European Society for Stereotactic and Functional Neurosurgery : Zurich, July 9-11, 1981 / editors Ph.L. Gildenberg, J. Siegfried, J. Gybels ; associate editor Patricia O. Franklin. — Basel ; London : Karger, 1982. — x,554p : ill(some col.) ; 25cm. — (Advances in stereoencephalotomy ; v.9)
Includes bibliographies and index
ISBN 3-8055-3501-5 (pbk) : £45.00
B82-30700

617'.48 — Man. Nervous system. Surgery

Pásztor, Emil. Concise neurosurgery for practitioners and students / by Emil Pásztor ; [English text revised by L. Bakay]. — Basel ; London : Karger, c1980. — 291p : ill ; 25cm
Translated from the Hungarian. — Includes bibliographies and index
ISBN 3-8055-1431-x : £24.70 B82-11405

Topical reviews in neurosurgery. — Bristol : John Wright. — (Topical reviews series)
Vol.1 / edited by J.M. Rice Edwards. — 1982. — ix,192p : ill ; 23cm
Includes index
ISBN 0-7236-0576-9 : Unpriced : CIP rev.
B81-37599

617'.48'008054 — Children. Nervous system. Surgery

Concepts in pediatric neurosurgery II / American Society for Pediatric Neurosurgery. — Basel, London : Karger, c1982. — x,219p : ill ; 25cm
Includes bibliographies and index
ISBN 3-8055-3454-x : £52.80 B82-40291

617'.48'0088054 — Children. Nervous system. Surgery — *Serials*

Concepts in pediatric neurosurgery / American Society for Pediatric Neurosurgery. — 1-. — Basel ; London : Karger, 1981-. — v. : ill ; 25cm
Unpriced B82-31706

617'.4807 — Man. Nervous system. Surgery. Pathology

Burger, Peter C.. Surgical pathology of the nervous system and its coverings / Peter C. Burger, F. Stephen Vogel. — 2nd ed. — New York ; Chichester : Wiley, c1982. — xiii,739p : ill ; 26cm
Previous ed.: 1976. — Includes index
ISBN 0-471-05876-9 : £50.54 B82-34750

617'.481 — Medicine. Psychosurgery

O'Callaghan, Mark A. J.. Psychosurgery. — Lancaster : MTP Press, June 1982. — [320]p
ISBN 0-85200-458-3 : £20.00 : CIP entry
B82-21953

617'.481 — United States. Man. Brain. Lobotomy, *to 1980*

Shutts, David. Lobotomy : resort to the knife / David Shutts. — New York ; London : Van Nostrand Reinhold, c1982. — xxi,284p : ill,ports ; 24cm
Bibliography: p261-267. — Includes index
ISBN 0-442-20252-0 : £14.40 B82-23712

617'.48101 — Man. Brain. Injuries. Sequelae

Levin, Harvey S.. Neurobehavioral consequences of closed head injury / Harvey S. Levin, Arthur L. Benton, Robert G. Grossman. — New York ; Oxford : Oxford University Press, 1982. — xiii,279p : ill ; 24cm
Bibliography: p231-253. — Includes index
ISBN 0-19-503008-7 : £20.00 B82-38568

617'.4820645 — Man. Spinal cord. Electrical stimulation — *Conference proceedings*

International Meeting on Spinal Cord Stimulation *(3rd : 1980 : Houston)*. Proceedings of the Third International Meeting on Spinal Cord Stimulation : Houston, Tex., May, 1980 / editor Philip L. Gildenberg. — Basel ; London : Karger, [1981]. — 715p,[1]leaf of plates : ill (some col.) ; 26cm
Includes bibliographies
Unpriced (pbk) B82-06296

617.5 — REGIONAL MEDICINE AND SURGERY

617'.51 — Man. Ears, nose & throat. Diseases

DeWeese, David D.. Textbook of otolaryngology / David D. DeWeese, William H. Saunders. — 6th ed. — St. Louis, Mo. ; London : Mosby, 1982. — ix,495p : ill ; 28cm
Previous ed.: 1977. — Includes bibliographies and index
ISBN 0-8016-1273-x : £24.25 B82-31865

Hall, I. Simson. Diseases of the nose, throat and ear : a handbook for students and practitioners / I. Simson Hall, Bernard H. Colman. — 12th ed. — Edinburgh : Churchill Livingstone, 1981. — 407p : ill ; 22cm
Previous ed.: 1975. — Includes index
ISBN 0-443-02355-7 (pbk) : Unpriced
B82-16552

Turner, Arthur Logan. Logan Turner's diseases of the nose, throat and ear. — 9th ed. / edited by J.F. Birrell. — Bristol : John Wright, 1982. — xiii,445p : ill ; 22cm
Previous ed.: 1977. — Includes index
ISBN 0-7236-0617-x (pbk) : Unpriced : CIP rev. B82-00361

617'.51 — Man. Ears, nose & throat. Diseases. Role of allergies

Otolaryngologic allergy / Hueston C. King, editor. — Miami : Symposia Specialists ; New York ; Oxford : Distributed by Elsevier/North-Holland, c1981. — x,507p : ill ; 24cm
Includes index
ISBN 0-444-00592-7 : £34.75 B82-09911

617'.51 — Otorhinolaryngology

Browning, G. G.. Updated ENT. — London : Butterworth Scientific, June 1982. — [144]p
ISBN 0-407-00249-9 : £3.95 : CIP entry
B82-11758

617'.51 — Otorhinolaryngology — *Conference proceedings*

World Congress of Otorhinolaryngology *(12th : 1981 : Budapest)*. Borderline problems in otorhinolaryngology : proceedings of the XIIth World Congress of Otorhinolaryngology, Budapest, Hungary 21-27 June 1981 / edited by L. Surján, Gy. Bodó. — Amsterdam ; Oxford : Excerpta Medica, 1982. — xxvii,723p : ill ; 25cm
Includes bibliographies and index
ISBN 90-219-0582-5 : Unpriced B82-33803

617'.51'0024613 — Man. Ears, eyes, nose & throat. Diseases — *For nursing*

Nursing care in eye, ear, nose, and throat disorders. — 4th ed. / William H. Saunders ... [et al.]. — St. Louis, Mo. ; London : Mosby, 1979. — viii,520p : ill ; 26cm
Previous ed.: 1974. — Includes bibliographies and index
ISBN 0-8016-2113-5 : Unpriced B82-21881

617'.51044 — Man. Head. Injuries

Bagchi, Asoke K.. An introduction to head injuries / Asoke K. Bagchi. — Calcutta ; Oxford : Oxford University Press, 1980. — viii,111p,[19]p of plates : ill,1port ; 22cm
Bibliography: p101. — Includes index
ISBN 0-19-561151-9 : £6.95 B82-05418

617'.51044 — Man. Head. Injuries — *Conference proceedings*

Head Injuries — a Preventable Epidemic *(Conference : 1979 : Sydney)*. Head injuries : an integrated approach / [proceedings of a national symposium Head Injuries — a Preventable Epidemic, Sydney, Australia, 1979] ; [held under the auspices of the Australian Neurological Foundation] ; edited by T.A.R. Dinning and T.J. Connelley. — Brisbane ; Chichester : Wiley, 1981. — xiv,266p : ill,1form ; 22cm
Includes index
ISBN 0-471-33379-4 (pbk) : £6.75 B82-13987

617'.51044 — Man. Head. Injuries. Sequelae — *Study regions: Tyne and Wear (Metropolitan County). Newcastle upon Tyne*

Cartlidge, N. E. F.. Head injury / N.E.F. Cartlidge, D.A. Shaw with a contribution by R.M. Kalbag. — London : Saunders, 1981. — ix,203p : ill ; 25cm. — (Major problems in neurology ; 10)
Includes bibliographies and index
ISBN 0-7216-2443-x : £13.50 : CIP rev.
B81-30391

617'.510592 — Man. Head & neck. Plastic surgery — *Conference proceedings*

Plastic and reconstructive surgery of the head and neck : the third international symposium / edited by Leslie Bernstein. — New York ; London : Grune & Stratton, c1981. — 2v. : ill ; 29cm
Includes index
ISBN 0-8089-1372-7 : Unpriced
ISBN 0-8089-1373-5 (v.2) B82-10555

617'.510592 — Man. Head. Plastic surgery

Atlas of craniomaxillofacial surgery / Ian T. Jackson ... [et al.] ; William Winn and Scott Barrows, illustrators. — St Louis ; London : Mosby, 1982. — xv,752p : ill ; 29cm
Includes bibliographies and index
ISBN 0-8016-4295-7 : £93.75 B82-22918

617'.514 — Man. Hydrocephalus. Surgery: Shunting — *Conference proceedings*

Symposium on Shunts and Problems in Shunts *(1980 : Marseille)*. Shunts and problems in shunts / Symposium on Shunts and Problems in Shunts, Marseille, June 24-25, 1980 ; volume editor M. Choux. — Basel ; London : Karger, c1982. — x,228p : ill ; 25cm. — (Monographs in neural sciences ; v.8)
Includes bibliographies
ISBN 3-8055-2465-x : £33.35 B82-30382

617'.5140757 — Man. Skull. Diagnosis. Radiography

Rakosi, Thomas. An atlas and manual of cephalometric radiography / Thomas Rakosi ; translated by R.E.K. Meuss. — London : Wolfe, c1982. — 228p : ill ; 27cm. — (Wolfe medical atlases)
Translation of: Atlas und Anleitung zur Praktischen Fernöntgenanalyse. — Includes index
ISBN 0-7234-0767-3 : Unpriced B82-16158

617'.5140757'0222 — Man. Skull. Diagnosis. Radiography — *Illustrations*

Taveras, Juan M.. Normal neuroradiology : and atlas of the skull, sinuses and facial bones / Juan M. Taveras, Francesco Morello. — Chicago ; London : Year Book Medical, c1979. — ix,752p : chiefly ill ; 24x31cm
Includes bibliographies and index
ISBN 0-8151-8732-7 : £147.50
Primary classification 616.8'04757'0222
B82-04568

617'.52044 — Man. Face. Injuries. Surgery

Facial trauma and concomitant problems : evaluation and treatment / edited by William B. Irby. — 2nd ed. — St. Louis ; London : Mosby, 1979. — ix,340p : ill
Previous ed.: 1974. — Includes bibliographies and index
ISBN 0-8016-2349-9 : £39.00 B82-28170

617'.52059 — Man. Maxillofacial region. Surgery

Textbook of oral and maxillofacial surgery / edited by Gustav O. Kruger ; art editor B. John Melloni. — 5th ed. — St. Louis ; London : Mosby, 1979. — xvii,743p : ill,forms ; 26cm
Previous ed.: published as Text book of oral surgery. 1974. — Includes index
ISBN 0-8016-2792-3 : Unpriced B82-34998

617'.52059'088054 — Children. Maxillofacial region. Surgery

Sanders, Bruce, *1943-*. Pediatric oral and maxillofacial surgery / Bruce Sanders ; original artwork by Irene Petravicius. — St. Louis, Mo. ; London : Mosby, 1979. — xii,606p : ill ; 27cm
Includes bibliographies and index
ISBN 0-8016-4308-2 : Unpriced B82-21882

617'.520592 — Man. Maxillofacial region. Prosthesis

Maxillofacial rehabilitation : prosthodontic and surgical considerations / [edited by] John Beumer III, Thomas A. Curtis, David N. Firtell. — St. Louis ; London : Mosby, 1979. — xiv,549p : ill ; 27cm
Includes bibliographies and index
ISBN 0-8016-0676-4 : Unpriced B82-34997

617'.522059 — Man. Oral region. Surgery

Moore, J. R.. Principles of oral surgery / J.R. Moore, G.V. Gillbe. — 3rd ed. — Manchester : Manchester University Press, c1981. — 256p : ill ; 21cm
Previous ed.: 1976. — Includes bibliographies and index
ISBN 0-7190-0801-8 (pbk) : £7.95 : CIP rev. B81-33880

617'.52207 — Man. Oral region. Virus diseases. Pathology — *Conference proceedings*

International Symposium on Viruses and Oral Diseases *(1980 : National Institutes of Health)*.
Viral infections in oral medicine : proceedings of the International Symposium on Viruses and Oral Diseases held 22-23 September 1980 at the National Institutes of Health, Bethesda, Maryland, U.S.A. / editors John J. Hooks and George W. Jordan. — New York ; Oxford : Elsevier/North-Holland, c1982. — xiv,327p : ill ; 24cm
Includes bibliographies and index
ISBN 0-444-00674-5 : £27.72 B82-24662

617'.532 — Scotland. Hospitals. In-patients. Adenoids & tonsils. Adenotonsillectomy — *Statistics*

Adeno-tonsillectomy : a study of Scottish hospitals in-patient data. — Edinburgh (Trinity Park House, South Trinity Rd, Edinburgh EH5 3SQ) : Information Services Division, Scottish Health Service Common Services Agency, [1982?]. — 15[i.e.13]leaves : ill ; 30cm. — (Scripps reviews ; no.1) (Occasional papers)
Unpriced (unbound) B82-40983

617'.533059 — Laryngectomy

Laryngectomy. — London : Croom Helm, Nov.1982. — [336]p
ISBN 0-7099-0907-1 : £16.95 : CIP entry B82-28749

617'.533059 — Man. Larynx. Surgery

Tucker, Harvey M.. Surgery for phonatory disorders / Harvey M. Tucker ; illustrated by James T. Suchy. — New York ; Edinburgh : Churchill Livingstone, 1981. — viii,130p : ill ; 26cm. — (Monographs in clinical otolaryngology ; v.3)
Includes bibliographies and index
ISBN 0-443-08058-5 : £19.50 B82-18616

617'.54 — Man. Thorax. Diseases — *Conference proceedings*

Oesophageal and other thoracic problems : sixth Coventry conference : edited by W.G. Williams and R.E. Smith / with a foreword by Bryan P. Moore. — Bristol : John Wright, 1982. — xi,184p : ill ; 22cm
Includes bibliographies and index
ISBN 0-7236-0640-4 (pbk) : Unpriced : CIP rev. B81-40264

617'.54 — Man. Thorax. Surgery

Holden, M. P.. A practice of cardiothoracic surgery / M.P. Holden ; with a foreword by M.I. Ionescu. — Bristol : Wright, 1982. — xvi,432p : ill ; 24cm
Includes bibliographies and index
ISBN 0-7236-0626-9 : Unpriced : CIP rev. B82-10876

617'.54 — Man. Thorax. Surgery. - *Conference proceedings*

The **Present** state of thoracic surgery. — Tunbridge Wells : Pitman Medical, Apr.1981. — [232]p
Conference papers
ISBN 0-272-79592-5 (pbk) : £15.00 : CIP entry B81-07614

617'.54'006041 — Great Britain. Man. Thorax. Diseases. Organisations: British Thoracic Association, *to 1978*

British Thoracic Association. The British Thoracic Association : (the first fifty years). — London (30 Britten St., Brompton [SW3 6NN]) : The Association, 1978. — 110p,[12]p of plates : ports ; 21cm
Text on inside cover. — Includes index
£4.50 (pbk) B82-17862

617'.54059'024613 — Man. Thorax. Surgery — *For nursing*

Moghissi, K.. Thoracic surgery for nurses. — London : Kimpton Medical, Sept.1982. — [312]p
ISBN 0-85313-811-7 (pbk) : £12.50 : CIP entry B82-20825

617'.54062 — Hospitals. Intensive care units. Patients. Thorax. Physiotherapy

Chest physiotherapy in the intensive care unit / Colin F. Mackenzie editor ; [contributors] Nancy Ciesla, P. Cristina Imle, Nancy Klemic. — Baltimore ; London : Williams & Wilkins, c1981. — x,260p : ill ; 26cm
Includes bibliographies and index
ISBN 0-683-05328-0 (pbk) : Unpriced B82-15513

617'.540757 — Man. Thorax. Diagnosis. Radiography

Chest imaging : an integrated approach / Richard A. Mintzer, editor. — Baltimore ; London : Williams & Wilkins, c1981. — xv,177p : ill ; 26cm
Includes index
ISBN 0-683-06051-1 : Unpriced B82-13535

617'.55 — Man. Abdomen. Communicable diseases

Wilson, Samuel E.. Intra-abdominal infection / Samuel Eric Wilson, Sydney M. Finegold, Russell A. Williams. — New York ; London : McGraw-Hill, c1982. — xvi,495p : ill(some col.) ; 24cm
Ill on lining papers. — Includes index
ISBN 0-07-070815-0 : £33.95 B82-16381

617'.55059'0222 — Women. Pelvic region. Surgery — *Illustrations*

Wheeless, Clifford R.. Atlas of pelvic surgery / Clifford R. Wheeless, Jr. ; John Parker, medical illustrator. — Philadephia, Pa. : Lea & Febiger ; London : Kimpton, 1981. — xi,399p : ill ; 32cm
ISBN 0-8121-0727-6 : Unpriced B82-26972

617'.55075 — Man. Abdomen. Acute abdomen. Diagnosis

Shepherd, John A.. Management of the acute abdomen. — Oxford : Oxford University Press, July 1982. — [275]p. — (Oxford medical publications)
ISBN 0-19-261322-7 : £15.00 : CIP entry B82-10432

617'.550757 — Man. Abdomen. Diagnosis. Radiography

Abdominal radiology / James J. McCort, editor ... [et al.]. — Baltimore ; London : Williams & Wilkins, c1981. — x,344p : ill ; 26cm
Includes bibliographies and index
ISBN 0-683-05751-0 : Unpriced B82-18000

Interventional radiology of the abdomen / [edited by] Joseph T. Ferrucci, Jack Wittenberg. — Baltimore ; London : Williams & Wilkins, c1981. — xviii,243p : ill ; 26cm
Includes index
ISBN 0-683-03174-0 : Unpriced B82-02567

617'.553 — Man. Gastrointestinal tract. Surgical stomata

Stoma care. — Beaconsfield (20 Chiltern Hills Rd., Beaconsfield, Bucks. HP9 1PL) : Beaconsfield, July 1981. — 1v.
ISBN 0-906584-04-3 : £9.50 : CIP entry
Also classified at 617'.919 B81-13874

617'.5530592 — Man. Gastrointestinal tract. Surgical stomata

Principles of ostomy care / edited by Debra C. Broadwell, Bettie S. Jackson. — St. Louis ; London : Mosby, 1982. — xv,815p,[13]p of plates : ill(some col.),forms ; 29cm
Includes bibliographies and index
ISBN 0-8016-2378-2 : £27.50 B82-22971

617'.554 — Man. Digestive system. Fistulae

Alexander-Williams, John. Intestinal fistulas / John Alexander-Williams, Miles Irving ; with a foreword by Jonathan E. Rhoads. — Bristol : John Wright, 1982. — x,230p : ill ; 23cm
Includes index
ISBN 0-7236-0555-6 : Unpriced : CIP rev. B82-00360

617'.554 — Man. Intestines. Obstruction. Surgery

Ellis, Harold, *1926-*. Intestinal obstruction / Harold Ellis with contributions by: Duncan Forrest, Joseph Gleeson, Joan F. Zilva. — New York : Appleton-Century-Crofts ; London : Prentice-Hall, c1982. — xi,367p : ill ; 26cm
Includes bibliographies and index
ISBN 0-8385-4310-3 : £36.40 B82-22220

617'.556 — Man. Gall bladder. Cholecystectomy

Cholecystectomy. — London : Royal Society of Medicine for Allied Medical Group, c1982. — 17p : col.ill ; 26cm. — (Operative surgery. General surgery ; v.1 no.1)
Text on inside cover
ISBN 0-905958-05-5 (pbk) : Unpriced B82-33002

617'.556059 — Man. Biliary tract. Surgery

The **Biliary** tract. — Edinburgh : Churchill Livingstone, Nov.1982. — [260]p. — (Clinical surgery international ; v.5)
ISBN 0-443-02322-0 : £15.00 : CIP entry B82-27538

617'.559065 — Man. Stomach. Hiatus hernia. Naturopathy

Lay, Joan. Self-help for hiatus hernia / Joan Lay. — Wellingborough : Thorsons, 1982. — 63p : ill ; 18cm. — (Self-help series)
ISBN 0-7225-0713-5 (pbk) : Unpriced : CIP rev. B82-00383

617'.572 — Man. Shoulders. Disorders

Kessel, Lipmann. Clinical disorders of the shoulder / Lipmann Kessel. — Edinburgh : Churchill Livingstone, 1982. — 182p : ill,1port ; 26cm
Includes index
ISBN 0-443-01904-5 : £20.00 : CIP rev. B81-20506

617'.574 — Man. Elbows. Diseases

The **Elbow** : edited by Thomas G. Wadsworth / foreword by S. Benjamin Fowler. — Edinburgh : Churchill Livingstone, 1982. — 354p : ill ; 26cm
Includes bibliographies and index
ISBN 0-443-01931-2 : £28.00 : CIP rev. B79-31800

617'.574044 — Industries. Personnel. Arms. Vibration induced injuries. Prevention. Standards

Griffin, M. J.. Vibration injuries of the hand and arm : their occurrence and the evolution of standards and limits / M.J. Griffin. — London : H.M.S.O., 1980. — 36p : ill ; 30cm. — (Research paper)
At head of title: Health & Safety Executive. — Bibliography: p34-36
ISBN 0-11-883271-9 (pbk) : £1.50 B82-11051

617'.575044 — Man. Hands. Injuries. Therapy

Flatt, Adrian E.. The care of minor hand injuries / Adrian E. Flatt ; with forewords by Robert E. Rakel and Sir Reginald Watson-Jones. — 4th ed. — St. Louis ; London : Mosby, 1979. — xi,327p : ill ; 26cm
Previous ed.: 1972. — Bibliography: p319-322. — Includes index
ISBN 0-8016-1581-x : £37.50 B82-33158

617'.575059 — Man. Hands. Surgery

Hand surgery / [edited by] J. Edward Flynn. — 3rd ed. — Baltimore ; London : Williams & Wilkins, c1982. — xxi,983p : ill ; 26cm
Previous ed.: 1975. — Includes bibliographies and index
ISBN 0-683-03268-2 : Unpriced B82-19366

Operative hand surgery / edited by David P. Green. — New York ; Edinburgh : Churchill Livingstone, 1982. — 2v.(xx,1754,44p) : ill ; 27cm
Includes index
ISBN 0-443-08090-9 : Unpriced B82-38977

617′.575059 — Man. Hands. Surgery *continuation*

Usolt︠s︡eva, E. V.. Surgery of diseases and injuries of the hand / E.V. Usoltseva, K.I. Mashkara ; translated from the Russian by V.V. Shiffer and V.P. Pavlov. — St. Louis ; London : Mosby, 1979. — viii,338p : ill(some col.) ; 25cm
Translation of: Khirurgiya zabolevanii i povrezhdenii kisti. — Bibliography: p313-317. — Includes index
ISBN 0-8016-5198-0 : £31.25 B82-04572

617′.575075 — Man. Hands. Diagnosis — *For surgery*

American Society for Surgery of the Hand. The hand. — 2nd ed. — Edinburgh : Churchill Livingstone, Aug.1982. — [128]p
Previous ed.: 1978
ISBN 0-443-02310-7 (pbk) : £2.95 : CIP entry B82-24333

617′.58044 — Man. Limbs. Injuries. Emergency treatment

Simon, Robert R.. Orthopedics in emergency medicine : the extremities / Robert R. Simon, Steven J. Koenigsknecht ; with illustrations by Susan Gilbert and William G. Jacobson. — New York : Appleton-Century-Crofts ; London : Prentice-Hall, c1982. — xi,449p : ill ; 29cm
Includes index
ISBN 0-8385-7531-5 : Unpriced B82-32048

617′.58059 — Man. Limbs. Amputation

Amputation surgery and rehabilitation : the Toronto experience / edited by John P. Kostuik ; co-editor for children Robert Gillespie. — New York ; Edinburgh : Churchill Livingstone, 1981. — xv,448p : ill,music,forms ; 26cm
Includes bibliographies and index
ISBN 0-443-08024-0 : £32.00
Also classified at 362.4′38 B82-16548

617′.581 — Children. Hips. Diseases

Chung, Stanley M. K.. Hip disorders in infants and children / Stanley M.K. Chung. — Philadelphia : Lea & Febiger ; London : Kimpton, c1981. — x,396p : ill ; 27cm
Includes bibliographies and index
ISBN 0-8121-0706-3 : Unpriced B82-37460

617′.58207572 — Man. Knees. Diagnosis. Arthrography

Stoker, Dennis J.. Knee arthrography / Dennis J. Stoker. — London : Chapman and Hall, 1980. — xii,167p : ill ; 26cm
Includes bibliographies and index
ISBN 0-412-21860-7 : £12.00 : CIP rev. B80-24526

617′.584 — Man. Legs. Arteries. Reconstructive surgery

Extra-anatomic and secondary arterial reconstruction. — Tunbridge Wells : Pitman, Oct.1982. — 1v.
ISBN 0-272-79685-9 : £23.00 : CIP entry B82-29116

617′.584044 — Man. Legs. Trauma — *Conference proceedings*

Symposium on trauma to the leg and its sequelae, Monterey, California, April, 1979 / American Academy of Orthopaedic Surgeons ; edited by Tillman M. Moore. — St. Louis ; London : Mosby, 1981. — xiv,388p : ill ; 26cm
Includes bibliographies and index
ISBN 0-8016-0081-2 : £43.25 B82-08333

617′.585 — Man. Feet. Clubfoot

Turco, Vincent J.. Clubfoot : Vincent J. Turco. — New York ; Edinburgh : Churchill Livingstone, 1981. — xiii,193p : ill ; 25cm. — (Current problems in orthopaedics)
Includes bibliographies and index
ISBN 0-443-08033-x : Unpriced B82-05238

617′.585 — Man. Feet. Diseases

The **Foot** and its disorders. — 2nd ed. — Oxford : Blackwell Scientific, Oct.1982. — [480]p
Previous ed.: 1976
ISBN 0-632-00863-6 : £30.00 : CIP entry B82-23176

617′.585061 — Chiropody. Homeopathic techniques. Use of medicinal plants

Khan, M. Taufiq. Homœopathic medicinal plants used in chiropody / by M. Taufiq Khan. — London : Institute of Molecular Medicine, 1982. — 40p : ill ; 21cm
ISBN 0-906956-07-2 (pbk) : £1.50 B82-27437

617.6 — DENTISTRY

617.6 — Dentistry

A **Companion** to dental studies. — Oxford : Blackwell Scientific
Vol.1. — Mar.1982
Bk.1: Anatomy, biochemistry and physiology. — [800]p
ISBN 0-632-00797-4 : £20.00 : CIP entry B82-07126

617.6′001′9 — Dentistry. Psychological aspects

Ingersoll, Barbara D.. Behavioral aspects in dentistry / Barbara D. Ingersoll. — New York : Appleton-Century-Crofts ; London : Prentice-Hall, c1982. — xiii : ill ; 23cm
Includes index
ISBN 0-8385-0631-3 (pbk) : £12.60 B82-21692

617.6′0023′41 — Great Britain. Dentistry — *Career guides*

Caring for teeth / [written, designed and produced by SGS Education ; photographs by André Gordon ; illustrations by John Plumb ; careers adviser Brian Heap]. — Walton on Thames : Nelson, 1981. — 15p : ill,ports ; 28cm. — (Career profiles ; 24)
ISBN 0-17-438364-9 (unbound) : Unpriced B82-14311

617.6′003′21 — Dentistry — *Encyclopaedias*

Boucher's clinical dental terminology : a glossary of accepted terms in all disciplines of dentistry. — 3rd ed. / editor Thomas J. Zwemer ; associate editors Thomas R. Dirksen ... [et al.]. — St. Louis, Mo. ; London : Mosby, 1982. — xx,378p : ill,1port ; 25cm
Previous ed.: published as Current clinical dental terminology / compiled and edited 1974 by Carl O. Boucher
ISBN 0-8016-0712-4 : £20.75 B82-31864

617.6′007′1141 — Great Britain. Dentists. Professional education — *Inquiry reports*

Dental education : the report of a Committee of Inquiry appointed by the Nuffield Foundation. — London : The Foundation, 1980. — viii,115p ; 21cm
Includes index
ISBN 0-904956-20-2 (pbk) : £4.50 B82-13319

617.6′0076 — Dentistry — *Questions & answers*

Review of dentistry : questions and answers. — 7th ed. / editor, Maynard K. Hine, coeditor Ralph W. Phillips. — St. Louis ; London : Mosby, 1979. — x,763p ; 26cm
Previous ed.: 1975. — Includes index
ISBN 0-8016-2197-6 (pbk) : £18.50 B82-28165

617.6′0076 — Dentistry — *Questions & answers* — *For dental assistants*

Sapp, Jacqueline Walker. Comprehensive review of dental assisting / Jacqueline Walker Sapp. — New York ; Chichester : Wiley, c1981. — x,228p : ill ; 24cm. — (Wiley exam review)
ISBN 0-471-05728-2 (pbk) : £9.60 B82-04190

617.6′00941 — Great Britain. Dentistry, *to 1951*

Menzies Campbell, J.. Dentistry then and now / by J. Menzies Campbell. — Rev. and enl. 3rd ed. — [Glasgow] ([c/o Dr. M.W. Menzies Campbell, 70 Great George St., Glasgow G12 8RU]) : Privately printed, 1981, c1963. — xvi,394p,[1]leaf of plates : 1port ; 21cm
Previous ed.: i.e. 2nd ed. 1963. — Limited ed. of 1000 numbered copies. — Includes bibliographies and index
Unpriced B82-01928

617.6′01′07 — London. Hillingdon *(London Borough)*. **Children, to 5 years. Mothers. Dental health education**

Dental health education of mothers with young children in the Borough of Hillingdon / undertaken on behalf of the General Dental Council by Gerald B. Winter ... [et al.]. — [London] ([37 Wimpole St., W1M 8DQ]) : The Council, 1981. — xi,129p : ill,forms ; 21cm
Bibliography: p98-101
£2.00 (pbk) B82-14408

617.6′01′0880542 — England. Children, to 5 years. Dental health — *Inquiry reports*

Dental health in infancy : a report of a seminar organised by the Health Education Council / compiled and edited by Jennifer M. King. — [London] : Health Education Council, [1981?]. — 17p ; 30cm
Cover title
Unpriced (spiral) B82-02925

617.6′059 — Dentistry. Surgery

Howard, William W.. Atlas of operative dentistry. — 3rd ed. / William W. Howard, Richard C. Moller. — St. Louis ; London : Mosby, 1981. — xvii,292p : ill ; 28cm
Previous ed.: 1973. — Includes index
ISBN 0-8016-2282-4 (pbk) : £17.75 B82-30682

Operative dentistry / H. William Gilmore ... [et al.]. — 4th ed. — St. Louis ; London : Mosby, 1982. — ix,379p : ill ; 28cm
Previous ed.: 1977. — Includes bibliographies and index
ISBN 0-8016-1823-1 : £26.25 B82-31874

Principles and practice of operative dentistry / [Gerald T. Charbeneau ... et al.] ; [with contributions by M. Ash ... et al.]. — 2nd ed. — Philadelphia, Pa. : Lea & Febiger ; London : Kimpton, 1981. — x,474p : ill ; 27cm
Previous ed.: 1975. — Includes index
ISBN 0-8121-0775-6 : Unpriced B82-26969

617.6′059 — Dentistry. Surgery — *Manuals*

Pickard, H. M.. A manual of operative dentistry. — 5th ed. — Oxford : Oxford University Press, May 1982. — [200]p. — (Oxford medical publications)
Previous ed.: 1976
ISBN 0-19-261327-8 (pbk) : £7.50 : CIP entry B82-12705

617.6′059 — Man. Teeth. Transplantation

International Symposium on Oral Immunogenetics and Tissue Transplantation *(1981 : University of California, Los Angeles)*. Oral immunogenetics and tissue transplantation : proceedings of the International Symposium on Oral Immunogenetics and Tissue Transplantation held at the University of California, in the Center for the Health Sciences, Los Angeles, California, March 12th and 13th, 1981 / editors George R. Riviere, William H. Hildemann. — New York ; Oxford : Elsevier/North Holland, c1982. — xiii,326p : ill,ports ; 25cm. — (Developments in immunology, ISSN 0163-5921 ; v.16)
Includes bibliographies and index
ISBN 0-444-00659-1 : £33.12 B82-28644

617.6′0757 — Dentistry. Diagnosis. Radiography

Bhaskar, S. N.. Radiographic interpretation for the dentist / S.N. Bhaskar. — 3rd ed. — St Louis ; London : Mosby, 1979. — viii,295p : ill ; 27cm
Previous ed.: 1975. — Includes bibliographies and index
ISBN 0-8016-0690-x : £27.50 B82-38659

617.6′07′57 — Dentistry. Diagnosis. Radiography

Mason, Rita A.. A guide to dental radiography. — 2nd ed. — Bristol : Wright, Oct.1981. — [176]p. — (A Dental practitioner handbook ; no.27)
Previous ed.: 1977
ISBN 0-7236-0623-4 (pbk) : £7.75 : CIP entry B81-28185

617.6′0757 — Man. Teeth. Diagnosis. Radiography

Browne, R. M.. A radiological atlas of diseases of the teeth and jaws. — Chichester : Wiley, Feb.1983. — [232]p
ISBN 0-471-25616-1 : £25.00 : CIP entry B82-38713

617.6'0757 — Man. Teeth. Diagnosis. Radiography *continuation*

Wuehrmann, Arthur H.. Dental radiology / Arthur H. Wuehrmann, Lincoln R. Manson-Hing. — 5th ed. — St. Louis ; London : Mosby, 1981. — xiii,508p : ill,1plan ; 26cm
Previous ed.: 1977. — Bibliography: p472-483. — Includes index
ISBN 0-8016-5643-5 : £29.75 B82-30683

617.6'3 — Man. Mouth. Pain — *For dentistry*

Mumford, J. M.. Orofacial pain. — 3rd ed. — Edinburgh : Churchill Livingstone, Aug.1982. — [408]p
Previous ed. published as: Toothache and orofacial pain. 1976
ISBN 0-443-02631-9 (pbk) : £16.00 : CIP entry B82-24345

617.6'3 — Man. Teeth. Diseases

European Symposium on the Borderland between Caries and Periodontal Disease *(2nd : 1980 : Geneva).* The borderland between caries and periodontal disease II / [proceedings of the 2nd European Symposium on the Borderland between Caries and Periodontal Disease held in Geneva, Switzerland, between 28-29 February 1980] ; edited by T. Lehner and G. Cimasoni. — London : Academic Press, 1980. — x,288p : ill ; 24cm
Includes bibliographies and index
ISBN 0-12-792506-6 : £18.20 : CIP rev. B80-23351

617.6'3206 — Man. Periodontal diseases. Therapy

Astley Hope, Humphrey D.. Diseases, drugs and the dentist. — Chichester : Wiley, Jan.1983. — [160]p
ISBN 0-471-90016-8 : £7.45 : CIP entry B82-32426

617.6'342 — Dentistry. Endodontics

Harty, F. J.. Endodontics in clinical practice / F.J. Harty. — 2nd ed. — Bristol : John Wright, 1982. — xiv,280p : ill ; 22cm. — (A Dental practitioner handbook ; no.24)
Previous ed.: 1976. — Includes bibliographies and index
ISBN 0-7236-0643-9 (pbk) : Unpriced : CIP rev. B82-12839

Weine, Franklin S.. Endodontic therapy / Franklin S. Weine. — 3rd ed. — St. Louis ; London : Mosby, 1982. — ix,692p : ill,1form ; 28cm
Previous ed.: 1976. — Includes bibliographies and index
ISBN 0-8016-5380-0 : £31.75 B82-31907

617.6'342'00222 — Dentistry. Endodontics — *Illustrations*

Besner, Edward. Practical endodontics : a clinical guide / Edward Besner, Peter D. Ferrigno ; illustrations by Jane Kobukata Gordon. — Baltimore ; London : Williams & Wilkins, c1981. — xi,164p : ill ; 29cm
Includes index
ISBN 0-683-00607-x : Unpriced B82-07785

617.6'342059 — Dentistry. Endodontics. Surgery

Endodontic surgery / edited by Donald E. Arens, William Ray Adams, Rolando A. DeCastro ; with 12 contributors. — Philadelphia ; London : Harper & Row, c1981. — xvii,238p : ill ; 26cm
Includes bibliographies and index
ISBN 0-06-140267-2 : Unpriced B82-08629

617.6'43 — Children. Cleft lip & cleft palate. Orthodontics

Robertson, Norman. Oral orthopaedics and orthodontics for cleft lip and palate. — London : Pitman, Feb.1983. — [144]p
ISBN 0-272-79681-6 : £25.00 : CIP entry B82-37819

617.6'43 — Dentistry. Orthodontics

Foster, T. D.. A textbook of orthodontics. — 2nd ed. — Oxford : Blackwell Scientific, Sept.1982. — [368]p
Previous ed.: 1975
ISBN 0-632-00837-7 (pbk) : £15.00 : CIP entry B82-22807

Mills, J. R. E.. Principles and practice of orthodontics. — Edinburgh : Churchill Livingstone, Apr.1982. — [320]p
ISBN 0-443-02533-9 : £20.00 : CIP entry B82-04849

Walther, D. P.. Walther's orthodontic notes. — 4th ed. — Bristol : J. Wright, Feb.1983. — [224]p
Previous ed.: 1976
ISBN 0-7236-0670-6 (pbk) : £6.00 : CIP entry B82-39277

617.6'43 — Man. Teeth. Occlusion

Advances in occlusion / [edited by] Harry C. Lundeen, Charles H. Gibbs. — Boston, Mass. ; Bristol : J. Wright, 1982. — xi,232p : ill ; 26cm. — (Postgraduate dental handbook series ; v.14)
Includes index
ISBN 0-88416-168-4 : Unpriced B82-32589

Cross, Martin D.. Occlusion in restorative dentistry. — Edinburgh : Churchill Livingstone, July 1982. — [256]p
ISBN 0-443-01702-6 (pbk) : £10.00 : CIP entry B82-12344

617.6'43'0028 — Man. Begg orthodontic appliances

Fletcher, G. G. T.. The Begg appliance and technique / by G.G.T. Fletcher. — Bristol : Wright, 1981. — ix,169p : ill ; 26cm
Bibliography: p164-165. — Includes index
ISBN 0-7236-0570-x : Unpriced : CIP rev. B81-24667

617.6'43'0028 — Man. Edgewise orthodontic appliances

Thurow, Raymond C.. Edgewise orthodontics / Raymond C. Thurow. — 4th ed. — St. Louis ; London : Mosby, 1982. — vii,351p : ill ; 26cm
Previous ed.: 1972. — Includes index
ISBN 0-8016-4947-1 : £32.25 B82-16564

617.6'43075 — Dentistry. Orthodontics. Diagnosis

Houston, W. J. B.. Orthodontic diagnosis / W.J.B. Houston. — 3rd ed. — Bristol : John Wright, 1982. — vii,123p : ill ; 22cm. — (A Dental practitioner handbook ; no.4)
Previous ed.: 1975. — Includes bibliographies and index
ISBN 0-7236-0637-4 (pbk) : Unpriced : CIP rev. B81-35845

617.6'4307544 — Man. Malocclusion. Gnathosonic diagnosis

Watt, David M.. Gnathosonic diagnosis and occlusal dynamics / David M. Watt. — Eastbourne : Praeger, 1981. — viii,218p : ill ; 24cm + 1sound cassette. — (Praeger special studies)
Bibliography: p199-205. — Includes index
ISBN 0-03-059624-6 : £18.50 : CIP rev. B81-14823

617.6'45 — Children. Dentistry

Holloway, P. J.. Child dental health : a practical introduction / P.J. Holloway, J.N. Swallow. — 3rd ed. — Bristol : John Wright, 1982. — vii,225p : ill ; 22cm
Previous ed.: 1975. — Includes bibliographies and index
ISBN 0-7236-0629-3 (pbk) : Unpriced : CIP rev. B82-04971

Pediatric dentistry : scientific foundations and clinical practice / edited by Ray E. Stewart ... [et al.]. — St. Louis ; London : Mosby, 1982. — xvi,1027p : ill,forms ; 29cm
Includes bibliographies and index
ISBN 0-8016-4804-1 : £59.50 B82-08337

617.6'45 — Children. Dentistry — *Manuals*

Andlaw, R. J.. A manual of paedodontics / R.J. Andlaw, W.P. Rock ; with illustrations by G.C. Downer. — Edinburgh : Churchill Livingstone, 1982. — 209p : ill ; 25cm
Includes bibliographies and index
ISBN 0-443-01752-2 (pbk) : £9.75 : CIP rev. B81-31361

Barber, Thomas K.. Pediatric dentistry / Thomas K. Barber, Larry S. Luke. — Boston ; London : John Wright, 1982. — xiv,434p : ill ; 24cm. — (Postgraduate dental handbook series ; v.17)
Includes index
ISBN 0-88416-167-6 : Unpriced B82-34673

617.6'7 — Man. Teeth. Cavities — *Conference proceedings*

Methodological aspects related to the study of surface and colloid phenomena in the oral cavity. — Eynsham (PO Box 1, Eynsham, Oxford OX8 1JJ) : IRL Press, Feb.1982. — [260]p
Conference papers
ISBN 0-904147-36-3 (pbk) : £12.00 : CIP entry B82-03132

617.6'7052 — Man. Teeth. Caries. Prevention

Dillon, Charles. Prevention of dental caries by subtraction / by Charles Dillon. — [Scotland] : C. Dillon, 1981. — [8]p : ill ; 21cm
£5.00 (unbound) B82-27461

617.6'7052 — Man. Teeth. Caries. Prevention. Use of fluorides

Murray, John J.. Fluorides in caries prevention. — 2nd ed. — Bristol : Wright, Oct.1982. — [272]p. — (A Dental practitioner handbook)
Previous ed.: 1976
ISBN 0-7236-0644-7 (pbk) : £8.50 : CIP entry B82-24339

617.6'75 — Man. Teeth. Cavities. Resin based fillings

Deubert, L. W.. Tooth coloured filling materials in clinical practice / L.W. Deubert and C.B.G. Jenkins. — 2nd ed. — Bristol : John Wright, 1982. — ix,146p : ill ; 22cm. — (A Dental practitioner handbook ; no.16)
Previous ed.: 1972. — Bibliography: p132-139. — Includes index
ISBN 0-7236-0628-5 (pbk) : Unpriced : CIP rev. B81-37548

617.6'92 — Man. Removable partial dentures. Design

Walter, J. D.. Removable partial denture design / J.D. Walter. — London : British Dental Association, 1980. — 81p : ill ; 19cm
Reprinted from British dental journal. — Bibliography: p80-81
ISBN 0-904588-04-1 (pbk) : £2.00 B82-34687

617.6'92 — Man. Removable partial dentures. Precision attachments

Baker, James L.. Theory and practice of precision attachment removable partial dentures / James L. Baker, Richard J. Goodkind. — St. Louis ; London : Mosby, 1981. — xi,282p : ill,forms ; 28cm
Includes bibliographies and index
ISBN 0-8016-0427-3 : £36.00 B82-08336

617.6'95 — Dental materials

Reisbick, M. H.. Dental materials in clinical dentistry / M.H. Reisbick. — Boston [Mass.] ; Bristol : John Wright, 1982. — xii,372p : ill ; 24cm. — (Postgraduate dental handbook series ; v.11)
Includes index
ISBN 0-88416-166-8 : Unpriced B82-30125

617.7 — OPHTHALMOLOGY

617.7 — Man. Eyes. Diseases

Principles and practice of ophthalmology / edited by Gholam A. Peyman, Donald R. Sanders and Morton F. Goldberg. — Philadelphia ; London : Saunders, c1980. — 2v.(xix,2512,xlivp,xvip of plates) : ill(some col.) ; 27cm
Includes index
ISBN 0-7216-7228-0 : Unpriced
ISBN 0-7216-7211-6 (v.1) : £47.00
ISBN 0-7216-7212-4 (v.2) : £47.00
ISBN 0-7216-7213-2 (v.3) : £48.50 B82-40797

617.7 — Man. Eyes. Diseases — *Conference proceedings*

Functional basis of ocular motility disorders. — Oxford : Pergamon, July 1982. — [624]p. — (Wenner-Gren Center international symposium series ; v.37)
Conference proceedings
ISBN 0-08-029772-2 : £50.00 : CIP entry B82-14223

617.7 — Man. Eyes. Diseases — *Conference proceedings* *continuation*

New directions in ophthalmic research / edited by Marvin L. Sears. — New Haven ; London : Yale University Press, c1981. — x,358p : ill ; 25cm
ISBN 0-300-02749-4 : Unpriced : CIP rev. B81-31941

Ophthalmology / editor N.M.J. Schweitzer. — Amsterdam ; Oxford : Excerpta Medica, 1982. — x,221p : ill ; 25cm. — (The Jonxis lectures ; v.8)
Includes index
ISBN 90-219-6008-7 : Unpriced B82-34480

617.7 — Man. Eyes. Metabolic disorders

Metabolic disorders, methods of examination / volume editor W. Straub. — Basel ; London : Karger, c1981. — 217p,[3]p of plates : ill(some col.) ; 25cm. — (Developments in ophthalmology ; v.4)
Text in English and German. — Includes bibliographies
ISBN 3-8055-2014-x : £44.25 B82-01225

617.7 — Man. Sight disorders — *Conference proceedings*

Clinical applications of visual psychophysics : proceedings of a symposium sponsored by the Committee on Vision of the National Research Council in conjunction with the Second Study Group on Human Vision / edited by Luis M. Proenza, Jay M. Enoch, Arthur Jampolsky. — Cambridge : Cambridge University Press, 1981. — x,304p : ill ; 24cm
Bibliography: 281-299. — Includes index
ISBN 0-521-24056-5 : £21.00 B82-07387

617.7 — Ophthalmology

Bankes, James L. Kennerley. Clinical ophthalmology. — Edinburgh : Churchill Livingstone, Feb.1982. — [132]p
ISBN 0-443-02157-0 : £10.00 : CIP entry B81-35716

Glasspool, Michael. Problems in ophthalmology / Michael Glasspool. — Lancaster : M.T.P. Press, 1982. — 141p : ill(some col.) ; 24cm. — (Problems in practice series)
Includes index
ISBN 0-85200-322-6 : £7.95 : CIP rev. B82-09182

Glasspool, Michael G.. Ophthalmology. — Lancaster : MTP Press, Sept.1981. — [128]p
ISBN 0-85200-434-6 : £14.95 : CIP entry B81-28266

Hollwich, Fritz. Ophthalmology : a short textbook / Fritz Hollwich ; translated by Gerhard W. Cibis. — Chicago ; London : Year Book Medical, 1979. — xvii,336p : ill(some col.) ; 19cm
Translation of: Augenheil Kunde. 9 Aufl.. — Bibliography: p314. — Includes index
ISBN 0-8151-4642-6 (pbk) : £10.75 B82-34654

Parr, John. Introduction to ophthalmology / John Parr. — 2nd ed. — Oxford : Oxford University Press, 1982. — 216p : ill(some col.) ; 25cm. — (Oxford medical publications)
Previous ed.: 1978. — Includes index
ISBN 0-19-261363-4 (pbk) : £8.95 B82-33810

Ruben, Montague. Revision clinical optics / Montague Ruben and E. Geoffrey Woodward ; drawings by Terry Tarrant. — London : Macmillan, 1982. — 197p : ill ; 25cm
ISBN 0-333-26107-0 (cased) : £12.95
ISBN 0-333-30705-4 (pbk) : Unpriced B82-38778

Trevor-Roper, Patrick D.. Ophthalmology. — London : Grant McIntyre [May 1981]. — [120] p. — (Pocket consultants)
ISBN 0-86216-031-6 (pbk) : £4.95 : CIP rev. : CIP entry B81-07917

617.7′003′21 — Ophthalmology — *Encyclopaedias*

Stein, Harold A.. Manual of ophthalmic terminology / Harold A. Stein, Bernard J. Slatt, Penny Cook. — St. Louis ; London : Mosby, 1982. — xii,269p : ill ; 24cm
Bibliography: p236-237. — Includes index
ISBN 0-8016-4769-x (pbk) : Unpriced B82-31878

617.7′005 — Ophthalmology — *Serials*

Recent advances in ophthalmology. — No.6. — Edinburgh : Churchill Livingstone, Dec.1982. — [118]p
ISBN 0-443-01660-7 (pbk) : £9.50 : CIP entry
ISSN 0309-2437 B82-29797

617.7′061 — Man. Eyes. Drug therapy

Ellis, Philip P.. Ocular therapeutics and pharmacology. — 6th ed. / [by] Philip P. Ellis. — St. Louis ; London : Mosby, 1981. — x,320p ; 26cm
Previous ed.: 1977. — Includes bibliographies and index
£22.25 B82-06099

617.7′061 — Man. Eyes. Drug therapy: Opticrom — *Conference proceedings*

The **Current** role of opticrom in the management of allergic conjunctivitis. — Oxford : Medical Publishing Foundation, Oct.1982. — [24]p
Conference papers
ISBN 0-906817-28-5 (pbk) : £2.60 : CIP entry B82-37486

617.7′068 — Man. Sight disorders. Self-treatment

Markert, Christopher. Seeing well again without your glasses / Christopher Markert. — Saffron Walden : C.W. Daniel, c1981. — 123p : ill ; 23cm
Bibliography: p213
ISBN 0-85207-151-5 : £6.00 B82-05520

617.7′096 — Africa. Man. Eyes. Diseases

Evans, Stanley C.. Prevention of blindness in Nigeria and other African states / by Stanley C. Evans. — Oulton : Teecoll, 1981. — x,235p : ill ; 22cm
Bibliography: p231-235
ISBN 0-7109-0008-2 : Unpriced B82-36937

617.7′1 — Man. Eyes. Diseases. Immunological aspects

Allansmith, Mathea R.. The eye and immunology / Mathea R. Allansmith. — St. Louis ; London : Mosby, 1982. — xii,209p : ill ; 24cm
Includes bibliographies and index
ISBN 0-8016-0117-7 (pbk) : £27.50 B82-22919

617.7′1 — Man. Eyes. Effects of tobacco smoking & consumption of alcoholic drinks

Evans, Stanley C.. The effect of alcohol and tobacco on eye health : the health of your eyes depends on what you eat and drink / by Stanley C. Evans. — Oulton : Teecoll, 1981. — vi,48p : ill ; 22cm
ISBN 0-7109-0006-6 : Unpriced B82-36940

617.7′1 — Man. Eyes. Microsurgery

International Microsurgery Group. *Meeting (1980 : Mallorca).* Microsurgery of the anterior and posterior segments of the eye : meeting of the International Microsurgical Group, Mallorca, 1980 / volume editor M.J. Roper-Hall. — Basel ; London : Karger, c1981. — vi,134p : ill ; 24cm. — (Developments in ophthalmology ; v.5)
Includes bibliographies
ISBN 3-8055-2711-x : £26.00 B82-28701

617.7′1 — Man. Eyes. Pathology

Yanoff, Myron. Ocular pathology : a text and atlas / Myron Yanoff, Ben S. Fine. — 2nd ed. — Cambridge, [Mass.] ; London : Harper & Row, c1982. — xviii,916p,[4]leaves of plates : ill(some col.) ; 26cm
Previous ed.: 1975. — Bibliography: p885-888. — Includes index
ISBN 0-06-142781-0 : Unpriced B82-34016

617.7′1 — Man. Eyes. Surgery

Girard, Louis J.. Ultrasonic fragmentation for intraocular surgery / Louis J. Girard. — St. Louis ; London : Mosby, 1979. — xvii,285p,2leaves of plates : ill(some col.) ; 29cm. — (Advanced techniques in ophthalmic microsurgery ; v.1)
Twenty stereograph reels (view-master) and lorgnette in pocket. — Bibliography: p268-271. — Includes index
ISBN 0-8016-1837-1 : £75.00 B82-28167

617.7′1 — Ophthalmology. Plastic surgery. Techniques

Smith, Byron C.. Practical techniques in ophthalmic plastic surgery / Byron C. Smith, Frank A. Nesi ; with 307 illustrations in 69 plates by Virginia Hoyt Cantarella. — St. Louis ; London : Mosby, 1981. — viii,227p : ill ; 28cm
Includes index
ISBN 0-8016-4662-6 : £36.00 B82-08331

617.7′12 — Man. Blindness

Dobree, John H.. Blindness and visual handicap : the facts / John H. Dobree and Eric Boulter. — Oxford : Oxford University Press, 1982. — 241p,[12]p of plates : ill ; 23cm. — (Oxford medical publications)
Bibliography: p227-228. — Includes index
ISBN 0-19-261328-6 : £6.95 : CIP rev.
Also classified at 362.4′18′0941 B82-11748

617.7′15 — Man. Eyes. Diagnosis

Diagnostic techniques and clinical questions / volume editor W. Straub. — Basel ; London : Karger, c1982. — 137p : ill ; 25cm. — (Developments in ophthalmology ; v.6)
Includes 1 chapter in German
ISBN 3-8055-3431-0 : Unpriced B82-40353

617.7′154 — Man. Eyes. Diagnosis. Physical examination

Ball, Geoffrey V.. Symptoms in eye examination. — London : Butterworths, Nov.1982. — [192]p
ISBN 0-407-00205-7 (pbk) : £19.50 : CIP entry B82-28275

617.7′1543 — Man. Eyes. Diagnosis. Ultrasonography — *Conference proceedings*

SIDUO Congress *(8th : 1980? : Nijmegen).* Ultrasonography in ophthalmology : proceedings of the 8th SIDUO Congress / edited by J.M. Thijssen and A.M. Verbeek. — The Hague ; London : Junk, 1981. — xiv,538p : ill ; 24cm. — (Documenta ophthalmologica. Proceedings series ; v.29)
Includes bibliographies
ISBN 90-619-3724-8 : Unpriced B82-11238

617.7′1545 — Man. Eyes. Diagnosis. Perimetry

Anderson, Douglas R.. Testing the field of vision / Douglas R. Anderson ; illustrated by Leona M. Allison. — St. Louis ; London : Mosby, 1982. — xi,301p : ill(some col.) ; 29cm
Bibliography: p289-292. — Includes index
ISBN 0-8016-0207-6 : £29.25 B82-16559

Bedwell, C. H.. Visual fields : a basis for efficient investigation / C.H. Bedwell. — London : Butterworth Scientific, 1982. — xii,219p : ill ; 25cm
Bibliography: p208-212. — Includes index
ISBN 0-407-00215-4 : Unpriced : CIP rev. B82-06738

617.7′19 — Man. Eyes. Corneas. Diseases

Grayson, Merrill. Diseases of the cornea / Merrill Grayson. — St. Louis ; London : Mosby, 1979. — x,552p : ill(some col.) ; 26cm
Includes bibliographies and index
ISBN 0-8016-1964-5 : £62.75 B82-04574

617.7′2 — Man. Eyes. Choroids. Dystrophy

Bloome, Michael A.. Manual of retinal and choroidal dystrophies / Michael A. Bloome, Charles A. Garcia. — New York : Appleton-Century-Crofts ; London : Prentice-Hall, c1982. — vii,129p : ill ; 23cm
Bibliography: p107-119. — Includes index
ISBN 0-8385-6126-8 (pbk) : £12.40
Primary classification 617.7′3 B82-20102

617.7′3 — Man. Eyes. Retinas. Diseases — *Conference proceedings*

Problems of normal and genetically abnormal retinas. — London : Academic Press, Nov.1982. — [375]p
ISBN 0-12-176180-0 : CIP entry B82-26865

617.7′3 — Man. Eyes. Retinas. Dystrophy

Bloome, Michael A.. Manual of retinal and choroidal dystrophies / Michael A. Bloome, Charles A. Garcia. — New York : Appleton-Century-Crofts ; London : Prentice-Hall, c1982. — vii,129p : ill ; 23cm
Bibliography: p107-119. — Includes index
ISBN 0-8385-6126-8 (pbk) : £12.40
Also classified at 617.7′2 B82-20102

617.7′3 — Man. Eyes. Retinas. Photocoagulation. Use of argon lasers

Constable, Ian J.. Laser : its clinical uses in eye diseases : with 143 illustrations, 115 in colour / by Ian J. Constable, Arthur Lin Siew Ming. — Edinburgh : Churchill Livingstone, 1981. — 123p : ill(some col.) ; 28cm
Includes index
ISBN 0-443-02538-x : Unpriced B82-05240

617.7′3 — Man. Eyes. Retinas. Retinitis pigmentosa

Marshall, G. H.. Retinitis pigmentosa / G.H. Marshall. — [Coventry] ([Exhall Grange School, Wheelwright Lane, Coventry]) : [G.H. Marshall], [1981?]. — 6p : ill ; 22cm
Cover title. — Text and ill on inside cover
Unpriced (pbk) B82-03787

617.7′307547 — Man. Eyes. Retinas. Electroretinography

ISCEV Symposium *(9th : 1981 : Horgen-Zurich)*. Techniques in clinical electrophysiology of vision / proceedings of the 19th I.S.C.E.V. Symposium Horgen-Zurich, June 1-5, 1981 ; edited by G. Niemeyer and Ch. Huber. — The Hague ; London : Junk, 1982. — xii,523p : ill ; 24cm. — (Documenta ophthalmologica. proceedings series ; v.31)
Includes bibliographies and index
ISBN 90-619-3727-2 : Unpriced B82-37033

617.7′4 — Man. Eyes. Fundus oculi. Diseases

Michaelson, Isaac C.. Textbook of the fundus of the eye. — 3rd ed. / by Isaac C. Michaelson with the assistance of David Benezra. — Edinburgh : Churchill Livingstone, 1980. — xxxi,910p : ill(some col.) ; 26cm
Previous ed.: / by Arthur J. Ballantyne and Isaac C. Michaelson. 1970. — Includes bibliographies and index
ISBN 0-443-01782-4 : £65.00 : CIP rev. B79-34916

617.7′41 — Man. Eyes. Glaucoma

Leydhecker, Wolfgang. All about glaucoma : questions and answers for people with glaucoma / by Wolfgang Leydhecker and Ronald Pitts Crick ; translations from the German by Alan Pitts Crick. — London : Faber, 1981. — 76p : ill ; 21cm
Adapted and rewritten in English from: Alles über grünen Star. — Includes index
ISBN 0-571-11764-3 (pbk) : £4.95 : CIP rev.
ISBN 0-571-11765-1 (pbk) : Unpriced B81-24657

617.7′42 — Man. Eyes. Cataracts. Surgery — *Conference proceedings*

Cataract Surgical Congress *(7th : 1980 : Houston)*. Current concepts in cataract surgery : selected proceedings of the Seventh Biennial Cataract Surgical Congress / editors Jared M. Emery, Adrienne C. Jacobson. — New York : Appleton-Century-Crofts ; London : Prentice-Hall, c1982. — xiv,338p : ill ; 27cm
Includes index
ISBN 0-8385-1405-7 : £44.05 B82-23156

617.7′46059 — Man. Eyes. Vitreous bodies. Microsurgery

Charles, Steve. Vitreous microsurgery / Steve Charles ; illustrated by Arthur Goodman ; edited by Walter S. Schachat. — Baltimore ; London : Williams & Wilkins, c1981. — xiii,191p : ill ; 26cm. — (Handbooks in ophthalmology)
Bibliography: p183. — Includes index
ISBN 0-683-01550-8 B82-15511

617.7′5 — Man. Eyes. Functional disorders. Optics

Obstfeld, Henri. Optics in vision. — 2nd ed. — London : Butterworths, Aug.1982. — [432]p
Previous ed.: 1978
ISBN 0-407-00240-5 : £19.50 : CIP entry B82-18571

617.7′5′0287 — Man. Sight. Testing. Instrumentation

Henson, David B.. Optometric instrumentation. — London : Butterworth, Feb.1983. — [250]p
ISBN 0-407-00241-3 : £20.00 : CIP entry B82-38287

617.7′52 — Ophthalmic lenses

Jalie, M.. Practical ophthalmic lenses. — 2nd ed. — London : Butterworths, Feb.1983. — [384]p
Previous ed.: 1974
ISBN 0-407-50006-5 : £17.50 : CIP entry B82-38288

617.7′52 — Ophthalmic lenses — *Technical data*

Rubin, Leroy. Optometry handbook / by Leroy Rubin. — 2nd ed. — Boston [Mass.] ; London : Butterworths, c1981. — 374p : ill ; 25cm
Previous ed.: 1975. — Includes index
ISBN 0-409-95180-3 : Unpriced B82-09156

617.7′52′02341 — Great Britain. Opticians — *Career guides*

Caring for eyes. — Walton on Thames : Nelson, 1981. — 15p : ill,ports ; 28cm. — (Career profiles ; 30) (An SGS production)
ISBN 0-17-438368-1 (unbound) : Unpriced B82-29530

617.7′523 — Contact lenses

Contact lenses : a textbook for practitioner and student / edited by Janet Stone and Anthony J. Phillips. — 2nd ed. — London : Butterworths
Previous ed.: London : Barrie and Jenkins, 1972
Vol.1: Background, pre-fitting care and basic hard lens techniques. — 1980. — xiv,375,I17p,[16]p of plates : ill ; 26cm
Includes bibliographies and index
ISBN 0-407-93270-4 : £29.50 : CIP rev. B80-13860

Lowther, Gerald E.. Contact lenses : procedures and techniques / Gerald E. Lowther. — Boston, [Mass.] ; London : Butterworths, c1982. — 413p : ill,1form ; 24cm
Includes index
ISBN 0-409-95012-2 : Unpriced B82-28565

Ruben, Montague. A colour atlas of contact lenses (& prosthetics) / Montague Ruben. — London : Wolfe Medical, 1982. — 151p : ill (some col.) ; 27cm
Includes index
ISBN 0-7234-0774-6 : Unpriced B82-35832

617.7′523 — Contact lenses. Fitting — *Manuals*

Jenkin, Lawrence. Theory and practice of contact lens fitting / by Lawrence Jenkin, R. Tyler-Jones. — London : Association of Dispensing Opticians. — 149p : ill ; 25cm
Originally published: London : Hatton, 1964. — Bibliography: p145-146. — Includes index
ISBN 0-900099-14-3 (pbk) : Unpriced B82-36098

617.7′523′0212 — Contact lenses. Curvature — *Tables*

Musset, Anthony. Contact lens design tables : tables for the determination of surface radii of curvature of hard contact lenses to give a required axial edge lift / Anthony Musset, Janet Stone. — London : Butterworths, 1981. — xiii,154p ; 28cm
ISBN 0-407-00219-7 (pbk) : Unpriced : CIP rev. B81-20588

617.7′55 — Man. Eyes. Hypermetropia

Marshall, G. H.. Hypermetropia / by G.H. Marshall. — [Coventry] ([Exhall Grange School, Wheelwright Lane, Coventry]) : [G.H. Marshall], [1981?]. — 4p : ill ; 21cm
Cover title
Unpriced (pbk) B82-03786

617.7′55 — Man. Eyes. Myopia — *Conference proceedings*

International Conference on Myopia *(3rd : 1980 : Copenhagen)*. Third International Conference on Myopia : Copenhagen, August, 24-27, 1980 / edited by H.C. Fledelius, P.H. Alsbirk and E. Goldschmidt. — The Hague ; London : Junk, 1981. — 253p : ill ; 24cm. — (Documenta ophthalmologica. Proceedings series ; v.25)
Includes bibliographies
ISBN 90-619-3725-6 : Unpriced B82-00488

617.7′62 — Man. Eyes. Strabismus — *Conference proceedings*

Strabismus Symposium *(1981 : Amsterdam)*. Strabismus Symposium, Amsterdam, September 3-4 1981 / edited by A.Th.M. van Balen and W.A. Houtman. — The Hague ; London : Junk, 1982. — vii,284p : ill ; 24cm. — (Documenta ophthalmologica. Proceedings series ; v.32)
Includes four chapters in French, German and Spanish. — Includes bibliographies and index
ISBN 90-619-3728-0 : Unpriced B82-40150

617.7′6207547 — Man. Eyes. Nystagmus. Diagnosis. Electronystagmography — *Manuals*

Barber, Hugh O.. Manual of electronystagmography / Hugh O. Barber, Charles W. Stockwell. — 2nd ed. — St. Louis ; London : Mosby, 1980. — ix,230p : ill,1plan ; 26cm
Previous ed.: 1976. — Includes index
ISBN 0-8016-0449-4 : £26.00 B82-31759

617.7′6207572 — Man. Eyes. Nerves. Diagnosis. Tomography. Applications of digital computer systems

Moseley, I. F.. Computerized tomography in neuro-ophthalmology / I.F. Moseley, M.D. Sanders. — London : Chapman and Hall, 1982. — x,302p : ill,1port ; 26cm
Includes bibliographies and index
ISBN 0-412-21840-2 : Unpriced : CIP rev. B81-23908

617.7′7 — Man. Eyes. Xerophthalmia

Sommer, Alfred. Nutritional blindness : xerophthalmia and keratomalacia / Alfred Sommer. — New York ; Oxford : Oxford University Press, 1982. — xiii,282p,[8]p of plates : ill(some col.) ; 24cm
Includes index
ISBN 0-19-502977-1 : £20.00 B82-38566

617.7′71059 — Man. Eyes. Eyelids. Surgery

Collin, J. R. O.. A manual of systematic eyelid surgery. — Edinburgh : Churchill Livingstone, Oct.1982. — [160]p
ISBN 0-443-02475-8 : £12.00 : CIP entry B82-24022

617.8 — OTOLOGY AND AUDIOLOGY

617.8 — Audiology

Audiology for the physician / edited by Robert W. Keith. — Baltimore ; London : Williams & Wilkins, c1980. — xviii,327p : ill,forms ; 26cm
Includes bibliographies and index
ISBN 0-683-04551-2 : Unpriced B82-03550

617.8 — Man. Hearing disorders

Hearing science and hearing disorders. — London : Academic Press, Dec.1982. — [300]p
ISBN 0-12-460440-4 : CIP entry B82-29884

617.8 — Man. Hearing disorders — *For audiology*

Audiology and audiological medicine. — Oxford : Oxford University Press, Aug.1981. — 2v. [(800p.)]. — (Oxford medical publications)
ISBN 0-19-261154-2 : £50.00 : CIP entry B81-18080

617.8 — Man. Sudden deafness. Aetiology — *Conference proceedings*

Sudden loss of cochlear and vestibular function / volume editors M. Hoke and M.E. Wigand. — Basel ; London : Karger, 1981. — viii,197p : ill ; 25cm. — (Advances in oto-rhino-laryngology ; v.27)
Includes bibliographies
ISBN 3-8055-2630-x : £47.00 B82-13386

617.8 — Man. Tinnitus — *Conference proceedings*

Tinnitus. — London : Pitman, 1981. — viii,325p : ill ; 24cm. — (Ciba Foundation symposium ; 85)
Includes bibliographies and index
ISBN 0-272-79639-5 : Unpriced : CIP rev.
B81-25761

617.8 — Medicine. Otology

Otology. — London : Butterworths, Dec.1982. — [264]p. — (Butterworths international medical reviews, ISSN 0260-0102 ; 1)
ISBN 0-407-02318-6 : £20.00 : CIP entry
B82-31291

617.8′0022′2 — Man. Ears. Diseases — *Illustrations*

Chole, Richard A.. A colour atlas of ear disease / Richard A. Chole. — London : Wolfe Medical, 1982. — 75p : chiefly ill(some col.) ; 27cm. — (Wolfe medical atlases)
Includes index
ISBN 0-7234-0776-2 : Unpriced B82-24628

617.8′006′01 — Audiology. Organisations: International Association of Physicians in Audiology — *Serials*

[Bulletin *(International Association of Physicians in Audiology)*]. Bulletin / IAPA. — No.1 (Oct. 1981)-. — London (c/o D. Stephens, 309 Grays Inn Rd, WC1 8DA) : International Association of Physicians in Audiology, 1981-. — v. : ill,maps ; 21cm
Irregular
ISSN 0262-6853 = IAPA bulletin : Unpriced
B82-07628

617.8′042 — Man. Ears. Diseases. Genetic aspects

Beighton, Peter. Genetics and otology. — Edinburgh : Churchill Livingstone, July 1982. — [256]p. — (Genetics in medicine and surgery)
ISBN 0-443-02284-4 : £18.00 : CIP entry
B82-12345

617.8′052 — Great Britain. Industries. Personnel. Hearing disorders. Prevention

Some aspects of noise and hearing loss : notes on the problem of noise at work and report of the HSE Working Group on Machinery Noise / Health and Safety Commission. — London : H.M.S.O., 1981. — 66p : ill ; 30cm
"Background to the HSC consultative document on the protection of hearing at work" — cover. — Bibliography: p62-66
ISBN 0-11-883432-0 (pbk) : £3.50
Also classified at 620.2′3 B82-00429

617.8′052 — Great Britain. Industries. Personnel. Hearing disorders. Prevention. Standards — *Proposals*

Protection of hearing at work : content of proposed Regulations and draft Approved Code of Practice and Guidance Note / Health and Safety Commission. — London : H.M.S.O., 1981. — 52p : ill ; 30cm. — (Consultative document / Health and Safety Commission)
ISBN 0-11-883431-2 (pbk) : £3.00 B82-00430

617.8′82 — Man. Ears. Vestibular system. Diseases — *Conference proceedings*

Symposium on Vestibular Neurotology *(1980 : Montreal)*. Vestibular neurotology / Symposium on Vestibular Neurotology, Montreal, September 9-12, 1980 ; volume editors P. Molina-Negro, R.A. Bertrand. — Basel ; London : Karger, c1982. — vii,148p : ill ; 25cm. — (Advances in oto-rhino-laryngology ; v.28)
Includes index
ISBN 3-8055-3490-6 : Unpriced B82-40347

617.8′86 — Man. Sensorineural deafness — *Conference proceedings*

Sensorineural hearing loss, vertigo and tinnitus / edited by Michael M. Paparella, William L. Meyerhoff. — Baltimore ; London : Williams & Wilkins, c1981. — xiii,181p : ill ; 26cm. — (Ear clinics international ; v.1)
Conference papers. — Includes bibliographies and index
ISBN 0-683-06750-8 : Unpriced B82-15512

617.8′9 — Electric response audiometry

Beagley, H. A.. Manual of audiometric techniques. — Oxford : Oxford University Press, Nov.1982. — [96]p. — (Oxford medical publications)
ISBN 0-19-261372-3 : £4.95 : CIP entry
B82-26892

617.8′9′0287 — Man. Hearing. Testing — *For children*

Althea. Having a hearing test / by Althea ; illustrated by Maureen Galvani. — Over : Dinosaur, c1981. — 24p : col.ill ; 16x19cm. — (Dinosaur's Althea books)
ISBN 0-85122-279-x (cased) : £2.25
ISBN 0-85122-263-3 (pbk) : £0.70 B82-08273

617.9 — MEDICINE. SURGICAL TECHNIQUES AND SPECIALITIES

617′.9 — Medicine. Surgery. Techniques

General surgery therapy / Oliver H. Beahrs, editor Robert W. Beart Jr, associate editor. — New York ; Chichester : Wiley, 1981. — xiii,[519]p : ill ; 29cm
Includes indexes
ISBN 0-471-09548-6 : £48.00 B82-10044

617′.91 — Medicine. Surgery. Operations

Rob, Charles. Rob & Smith's operative surgery. — London : Butterworth Scientific
General principles, breast and extracranial endocrines. — 4th ed. — Sept.1982. — [456]p
Previous ed.: 1977
ISBN 0-407-00650-8 : £55.00 : CIP entry
B82-25056

617′.9101 — Hospitals. Patients. Infection during surgery. Drug therapy. Antibiotics

Surgical infections : selective antibiotic therapy / editors Robert E. Condon, Sherwood L. Gorbach with the assistance of Don deKoven. — Baltimore ; London : Williams & Wilkins, c1981. — xiv,180p : ill ; 26cm
Includes index
ISBN 0-683-02031-5 : Unpriced B82-19326

617′.917 — Hospitals. Operating theatres — *Manuals*

Grubb, Reba Douglas. Operating room guidelines : an illustrated manual / Reba Douglass [i.e. Douglas] Grubb, Geraldine Ondov, major contributor Lorraine Bagley. — St. Louis ; London : Mosby, 1979. — xiii,317p : ill,forms ; 28cm
Bibliography: p307-308. — Includes index
ISBN 0-8016-1985-8 (spiral) : £14.25
B82-28173

Mather, S. James. Basic concepts for operating room and critical care personnel. — Bristol : Wright, Oct.1982. — [288]p. — (Emergency care series)
ISBN 0-7236-0667-6 (pbk) : £7.50 : CIP entry
B82-26051

617′.919 — Critically ill patients. Surgery. Intensive, preoperative & postoperative care

Critical care for surgical patients / edited by John M. Beal. — New York : Macmillan ; London : Baillière Tindall, c1982. — xiii,606p : ill ; 27cm
Includes bibliographies and index
ISBN 0-02-307410-8 : £32.00 B82-17150

617′.919 — Man. Surgery. Postoperative care

Stoma care. — Beaconsfield (20 Chiltern Hills Rd., Beaconsfield, Bucks. HP9 1PL) : Beaconsfield, July 1981. — 1v.
ISBN 0-906584-04-3 : £9.50 : CIP entry
Primary classification 617′.553 B81-13874

617′.919 — Surgical patients. Nutrition

Nutrition and the surgical patient / edited by Graham L. Hill. — Edinburgh : Churchill Livingstone, 1981. — xii,323p : ill ; 24cm. — (Clinical surgery international ; v.2)
Includes bibliographies and index
ISBN 0-443-02249-6 : £12.00 : CIP rev.
B81-30427

Surgical nutrition / edited by Michael F. Yarborough, P. William Curreri. — New York ; Edinburgh : Churchill Livingstone, 1981. — ix,156p : ill ; 25cm. — (Contemporary issues in clinical nutrition ; v.3)
Includes index
ISBN 0-443-08160-3 : £13.00 B82-16551

617′.919 — Tropical regions. Surgical patients. Care — *For nursing*

Wosornu, Lade. Principles of surgical care in the Tropics. — London : Pitman, Sept.1982. — [256]p
ISBN 0-272-79672-7 (pbk) : £4.95 : CIP entry
B82-18870

617′.95 — Man. Organs & tissues. Preservation — *Conference proceedings*

Organ preservation : basic and applied aspects : a symposium of the Transplantation Society / edited by D.E. Pegg, I.A. Jacobsen and N.A. Halasz. — Lancaster : M.T.P. Press, c1982. — xxi,.433p : ill ; 25cm
Includes index
ISBN 0-85200-418-4 : £24.95 : CIP rev.
B82-08104

617′.95 — Man. Organs & tissues. Transplantation

Tissue transplantation / edited by Peter J. Morris. — Edinburgh : Churchill Livingstone, 1982. — ix,257p : ill,ports ; 25cm. — (Clinical surgery international ; v.3)
Includes bibliographies and index
ISBN 0-443-02460-x : £12.00 : CIP rev.
B81-36210

617′.95 — Man. Organs & tissues. Transplantation. Immunology. Monitoring — *Conference proceedings*

International Symposium on Immunologic Monitoring of the Transplant Patient *(2nd : 1980 : Noordwijkerhout)*. Second International Symposium on Immunologic Monitoring of the Transplant Patient / edited by Bernard Cohen, Jon J. van Rood, Calvin R. Stiller. — New York ; London : Grune & Stratton, c1981. — xi,194p : ill ; 27cm
Originally published: as Transplantation proceedings, vol.XIII no.3, September 1981. — Includes index
ISBN 0-8089-1459-6 : £29.40 B82-27135

617′.95 — Man. Organs. Transplantation

Organ transplants. — Bristol : Wright, Feb.1982. — [630]p
ISBN 0-7236-7008-0 : £27.75 : CIP entry
B81-35842

617′.95 — Medicine. Cosmetic surgery

Devine, Elizabeth. Appearances : a complete guide to cosmetic surgery / Elizabeth Devine. — Loughton : Piatkus, 1982. — 225p ; 22cm
ISBN 0-86188-178-8 : £6.95 : CIP rev.
B82-05762

617′.95 — Medicine. Plastic surgery. Techniques

Fundamentals of plastic and reconstructive surgery / edited by Wallace H.J. Chang. — Baltimore ; London : Williams & Wilkins, c1980. — xvi,392p : ill ; 26cm
Includes bibliographies and index
ISBN 0-683-01515-x : Unpriced B82-03548

McKinney, Peter. Handbook of plastic surgery / Peter McKinney, Bruce Langdon Cunningham. — Baltimore ; London : Williams & Wilkins, c1981. — xv,252p : ill ; 26cm
Bibliography: p252. — Includes index
ISBN 0-683-05865-7 (pbk) : Unpriced
B82-02563

617′.95 — Medicine. Reconstructive surgery

Reconstructive procedures in surgery / edited by P. Gilroy Bevan. — Oxford : Blackwell Scientific, 1982. — xiii,454p : ill ; 25cm
Includes bibliographies and index
ISBN 0-632-00602-1 : Unpriced : CIP rev.
B81-33864

617'.95 — Medicine. Surgically implantable materials. Mechanical properties — *Conference proceedings*

Mechanical properties of biomaterials : proceedings of a conference / organized by the Biomaterials Group of the Biological Engineering Society in conjunction with the British Ceramics Society and the European Society for Biomaterials held at Keele University, September 1978 ; edited by G.W. Hastings and D.F. Williams. — Chichester : Wiley, 1980. — xxiii,566p : ill ; 24cm. — (Advances in biomaterials ; V.2)
Includes bibliographies and index
ISBN 0-471-27761-4 : £48.50 : CIP rev.
B80-31706

617'.95'0088041 — Men. Cosmetic surgery

Male aesthetic surgery / edited by Eugene H. Courtiss. — St. Louis ; London : Mosby, 1982. — xiv,426p : ill ; 28cm
Includes bibliographies and index
ISBN 0-8016-1115-6 : £29.75 B82-16562

617'.95'009 — Medicine. Plastic surgery, *to 1981*

Wallace, Antony F.. The progress of plastic surgery : an introductory history / Antony F. Wallace. — Oxford : Meeuws, 1982. — xii,184p : ill ; 22cm
Includes bibliographies and index
ISBN 0-902672-51-7 (cased) : Unpriced : CIP rev.
ISBN 0-902672-52-5 (pbk) : Unpriced
B82-16208

617'.95'088054 — Children. Plastic surgery — *Conference proceedings*

Symposium on pediatric plastic surgery. — St. Louis ; London : Mosby
Vol.21 / editors Desmond A. Kernahan, Hugh G. Thomson ; associate editor Bruce S. Bauer. — 1982. — x,453p : ill ; 29cm
'Proceedings of the Symposium of the Plastic Surgery Educational Foundation of the American Society of Plastic and Reconstructive Surgeons Inc., held in Chicago, Illinois, October 19-21. — Includes index
ISBN 0-8016-2691-9 : £63.75 B82-22969

617'.96 — Medicine. Anaesthesia

Anesthesia / edited by Ronald D. Miller. — New York ; Edinburgh : Churchill Livingstone, 1981. — 2v.(xxii,1535,32p) : ill ; 26cm
Includes index
ISBN 0-443-08082-8 : £65.00 B82-08749

Clarke, Richard S. J.. The compleat anaesthetist / Richard S.J. Clarke. — Belfast : Queen's University of Belfast, c1981. — 16p : ill ; 21cm. — (New lecture series / Queen's University of Belfast)
ISBN 0-85389-210-5 (pbk) : £0.40 B82-35098

Lee, J. Alfred. A synopsis of anaesthesia. — 6th ed. / R.S. Atkinson, G.B. Rushman, J. Alfred Lee. — Bristol : Wright, c1982. — x,962p ; 19cm
Includes index
ISBN 0-7236-0621-8 (pbk) : Unpriced : CIP rev. B82-07607

Lunn, John N.. Lecture notes on anaesthetics. — 2nd ed. — Oxford : Blackwell Scientific, Oct.1982. — [192]p
Previous ed.: 1979
ISBN 0-632-00983-7 (pbk) : £5.50 : CIP entry
B82-25092

Scientific foundations of anaesthesia / edited by Cyril Scurr and Stanley Feldman. — 3d ed. — London : Heinemann Medical, 1982. — xv,643p : ill ; 29cm
Previous ed.: 1974. — Includes bibliographies and index
ISBN 0-433-31862-7 : £39.95 B82-21299

617'.96'05 — Anaesthesia — *Serials*

Anaesthesia. — Review 1. — Edinburgh : Churchill Livingstone, Mar.1982. — [208]p
ISBN 0-443-02370-0 (pbk) : £10.00 : CIP entry
B82-01965

617'.96'05 — Medicine. Anaesthesia & analgesia — *Serials*

Recent advances in anaesthesia and analgesia. — No.14. — Edinburgh : Churchill Livingstone, June 1982. — [192]p
ISBN 0-443-02571-1 (pbk) : £10.00 : CIP entry
ISSN 0309-2305 B82-09720

617'.96'05 — Medicine. Anaesthesia — *Serials*

[Anaesthesia *(Edinburgh)***]**. Anaesthesia. — Review 1-. — Edinburgh : Churchill Livingstone, 1982-. — v. : ill ; 24cm
Cover title: Anaesthesia review
ISSN 0263-1512 = Anaesthesia (Edinburgh) : £9.95 B82-19856

617'.96'088054 — Children. Anaesthesia

Pediatric anesthesia : current practice. — New York ; London : Academic Press
Vol.1 / edited by M. Ramez Salem. — 1981. — ix,158p : ill ; 24cm
Includes bibliographies and index
ISBN 0-12-615201-2 : £18.20 B82-28066

Some aspects of paediatric anaesthesia / edited by D.J. Steward. — Amsterdam ; Oxford : Excerpta Medica, 1982. — 377p : ill ; 25cm. — (Monographs in anaesthesiology ; v.10)
Includes bibliographies and index
ISBN 0-444-80327-0 : Unpriced B82-17464

617'.96'09 — Medicine. Anaesthesia, *to 1975*

Smith, W. D. A.. Under the influence : a history of nitrous oxide and oxygen anaesthesia / W.D.A. Smith. — London : Macmillan, 1982. — xxviii,188p : ill,ports ; 26cm
Includes bibliographies and index
ISBN 0-333-31681-9 : Unpriced B82-35275

617'.96'09 — Medicine. Anaesthesia, *to ca 1950*

Sykes, W. Stanley. Essays on the first hundred years of anæsthesia / by W. Stanley Sykes. — Edinburgh : Churchill Livingstone
Vol.1. — 1982. — 171p,[40]p of plates : ill,facsims,ports ; 23cm
Originally published: 1960. — Includes index
ISBN 0-443-02823-0 : Unpriced : CIP rev.
B82-18574

Sykes, W. Stanley. Essays on the first hundred years of anæsthesia / W. Stanley Sykes. — Edinburgh : Churchill Livingston
Vol.2. — Edinburgh : Churchill Livingston. — viii,187p of plates : ill,facsims,ports ; 23cm
ISBN 0-443-02824-9 : £14.00 : CIP rev.
B82-20759

Sykes, W. Stanley. Essays on the first hundred years of anaesthesia / by W. Stanley Sykes. — Edinburgh : Churchill Livingstone
Vol.3 / edited by Richard H. Ellis ; foreword by C. Langton Hewer. — 1982. — xviii,272p : ill,facsims,ports ; 23cm
Includes index
ISBN 0-443-02658-0 : £16.00 : CIP rev.
B82-24344

617'.9673 — Orthopaedics. Anaesthesia. Techniques

Anaesthesia and related subjects in orthopaedic surgery / edited by David W. Barron. — Oxford : Blackwell Scientific, 1982. — x,201p : ill ; 23cm
Includes bibliographies and indexes
ISBN 0-632-00675-7 : £12.00 : CIP rev.
B82-07836

617'.96741 — Man. Cardiovascular system. Anaesthesia

Cardiovascular anesthesia and postoperative care / edited by Sait Tarhan. — Chicago ; London : Year Book Medical, c1982. — xvii,515p : ill ; 26cm
Includes bibliographies and index
ISBN 0-8151-8702-5 : £57.50 B82-28202

617'.967412 — Man. Heart. Anaesthesia

Chung, David C.. Anaesthesia in patients with ischaemic heart disease / David C. Chung. — London : Edward Arnold, 1982. — xii,178p : ill ; 24cm. — (Current topics in anaesthesia ; 6)
Includes bibliographies and index
ISBN 0-7131-4407-6 : £14.00 : CIP rev.
B82-06920

617'.96751 — Man. Ears, eyes, nose & throat. Anaesthesia

Snow, John C.. Anesthesia in otolaryngology and ophthalmology / John C. Snow. — 2nd ed / with a foreword by Martin L. North. — New York : Appleton-Century-Crofts ; London : Prentice-Hall International, c1982. — xv,278p : ill ; 25cm
Previous ed.: Springfield, Ill. : Charles C. Thomas, 1971. — Bibliography: p259. — Includes index
ISBN 0-8385-0096-x : £19.90 B82-23643

617'.96754 — Man. Thorax. Anaethesia

Gothard, J. W. W.. Anaesthesia for thoracic surgery / J.W.W. Gothard, M.A. Branthwaite ; foreword by I.C.W. English. — Oxford : Blackwell Scientific, 1982. — vii,199p : ill ; 24cm
Includes bibliographies and index
ISBN 0-632-00578-5 : £12.50 : CIP rev.
B81-36969

617'.9676 — Dentistry. Anaesthesia & analgesia

Kaufman, L.. General anaesthesia, local analgesia and sedation in dentistry / L. Kaufman, J.H. Sowray, J.P. Rood. — Oxford : Blackwell Scientific, 1982. — vi,170p : ill ; 22cm
Includes index
ISBN 0-632-00847-4 (pbk) : £9.50 : CIP rev.
B81-30902

617'.9676 — Dentistry. Local anaesthesia — *Programmed instructions*

Matthews, R. W.. Dental local analgesia. — Bristol : J. Wright, Oct.1982. — [80]p
ISBN 0-7236-0664-1 (pbk) : £4.95 : CIP entry
B82-28575

617'.9682 — Childbirth. Labour. Analgesia — *For midwifery*

Moir, Donald D.. Pain relief in labour : a handbook for midwives / Donald D. Moir. — 4th ed. — Edinburgh : Churchill Livingstone, 1982. — 158p : ill ; 19cm
Previous ed.: 1978. — Includes index
ISBN 0-443-02395-6 (pbk) : £2.95 B82-38468

617'.9682 — Childbirth. Labour. Epidural analgesia

Waldron, B. A.. Management of epidural analgesia in child birth. — Edinburgh : Churchill Livingstone, Sept.1982. — [64]p
ISBN 0-443-02299-2 (pbk) : £1.95 : CIP entry
B82-19683

617'.9682 — Obstetrics. Anaesthesia & analgesia

Crawford, J. Selwyn. Obstetric analgesia and anaesthesia / J. Selwyn Crawford. — Edinburgh : Churchill Livingstone, 1982. — viii,154p : 2ill ; 22cm. — (Current reviews in obstetrics and gynaecology ; 1)
Includes bibliographies and index
ISBN 0-443-02289-5 (pbk) : £6.00 : CIP rev.
B82-03582

617'.98 — Children. Surgery

Holder, Thomas M.. Pediatric surgery / Thomas M. Holder and Keith W. Ashcraft. — Philadephia ; London : Saunders, 1980. — xxv,1166p : ill ; 27cm
Includes bibliographies and index
ISBN 0-7216-4737-5 : £39.00 B82-36980

617'.9801 — Children. Surgery. Complications

Complications of pediatric surgery / edited by Pieter A. De Vries, Stephen R. Shapiro. — New York ; Chichester : Wiley, c1982. — xvii,581p : ill ; 26cm
Includes index
ISBN 0-471-04887-9 : £42.50 B82-38983

617'.98075 — Children. Surgery. Diagnosis — *For general practice*

Filston, Howard C.. Surgical problems in children : recognition and referral / Howard C. Filston ; with foreword by Samuel L. Katz. — St. Louis ; London : Mosby, 1982. — xvii,596p : ill,forms ; 28cm
Includes bibliographies and index
ISBN 0-8016-1574-7 : £39.50 B82-08334

618 — GYNAECOLOGY AND OBSTETRICS

618 — Gynaecology & obstetrics

Integrated obstetrics and gynaecology for postgraduates / edited by Sir John Dewhurst. — 3rd ed. — Oxford : Blackwell Scientific, 1981. — xiii,810p : ill ; 26cm
Previous ed.: 1976. — Includes bibliographies and index
ISBN 0-632-00684-6 : £47.50 : CIP rev. B81-30328

Llewellyn-Jones, Derek. Everywoman : a gynaecological guide for life. — 3rd ed. — London : Faber, Sept.1982. — [400]p
Previous ed.: 1978
ISBN 0-571-18061-2 (cased) : £8.50 : CIP entry
ISBN 0-571-18062-0 (pbk) : £2.50 B82-25173

Llewellyn-Jones, Derek. Fundamentals of obstetrics and gynaecology / Derek Llewellyn-Jones. — 3rd ed. — London : Faber and Faber, c1982. — 2v. : ill(some col.),1map ; 26cm
Previous ed.: v.1, 1977 ; v.2, 1978. — Includes bibliographies and index
Unpriced (cased)
ISBN 0-571-18040-x (v.1 : pbk) : Unpriced
ISBN 0-571-18041-8 (v.2 : cased) : £11.50
ISBN 0-571-18042-6 (v.2 : pbk) : Unpriced B82-00373

Obstetrics and gynecology. — 4th ed. / editor David N. Danforth ; associate editors William J. Dignam, Charles H. Hendricks, John van S. Maeck. — Philadelphia ; London : Harper & Row, c1982. — xxv,1316p : ill ; 27cm
Previous ed.: 1977. — Includes bibliographies and index
ISBN 0-06-140696-1 : Unpriced B82-27781

Willocks, James. Essentials of obstetrics and gynaecology / James Willocks. — 2nd ed. — Edinburgh : Churchill Livingstone, 1982. — viii,250p ; 22cm. — (Churchill Livingstone medical text)
Previous ed.: published as Essential obstetrics and gynaecology. 1978. — Bibliography: p245-246. — Includes index
ISBN 0-443-02364-6 (pbk) : £5.95 : CIP rev. B82-24332

Willson, J. Robert. Obstetrics and gynecology. — 6th ed. / J. Robert Willson, Elsie Reid Carrington. — St. Louis ; London : Mosby, 1979. — viii,667p : ill ; 26cm
Previous ed.: / by J. Robert Willson, Clayton T. Beecham, Elsie Reid Carrington. 1975. — Includes bibliographies and index
ISBN 0-8016-5595-1 : £25.50 B82-04573

618 — Gynaecology & obstetrics — *Conference proceedings*

World Congress of Gynecology and Obstetrics *(9th : 1979 : Tokyo)*. Gynecology and obstetrics : proceedings of the IX World Congress of Gynecology and Obstetrics, Tokyo, October 25-31, 1979 / editors, Shoichi Sakamoto, Shimpei Tojo, Tetsuya Nakayama. — Amsterdam ; Oxford : Excerpta Medica, 1980. — xxviii,1343p : ill ; 25cm. — (International congress series ; no.512)
Includes bibliographies and index
ISBN 90-219-0440-3 : £91.09 B82-39109

618 — Gynaecology & obstetrics. Drug therapy

Ledward, R. S.. Drug treatment in obstetrics. — London : Chapman and Hall, Nov.1982. — [280]p
ISBN 0-412-24770-4 (cased) : £12.00 : CIP entry
ISBN 0-412-15020-4 (pbk) : £7.50 B82-28734

618 — Gynaecology & obstetrics. Drug therapy. Antibiotics

Antibiotics in obstetrics and gynecology / edited by William J. Ledger. — The Hague ; London : Nijhoff, 1982. — viii,255p : ill ; 25cm. — (Developments in perinatal medicine ; 2)
Includes bibliographies and index
ISBN 90-247-2529-1 : Unpriced B82-28045

618 — Gynaecology & obstetrics. Emergency treatment — *Manuals*

Emergencies in obstetrics and gynecology / edited by Arnold W. Cohen. — New York ; Edinburgh : Churchill Livingstone, 1981. — viii,150p : ill ; 24cm. — (Clinics in emergency medicine ; v.1)
Includes bibliographies and index
ISBN 0-443-08130-1 : Unpriced B82-09104

618 — Gynaecology & obstetrics — *For general practice*

Women's problems in general practice. — Oxford : Oxford University Press, Jan.1983. — [275]p. — (Oxford medical publications) (Oxford general practice series ; 4)
ISBN 0-19-261345-6 (pbk) : £9.95 : CIP entry B82-36127

618 — Women. Medical aspects

The **Woman** patient : medical and psychological interfaces / edited by Carol C. Nadelson and Malkah T. Notman. — New York ; London : Plenum. — (Women in context)
Vol.2: Concepts of feminity and the life cycle. — c1982. — x,206p ; 24cm
Vol.2 lacks subtitle. — Includes index
ISBN 0-306-40846-5 : Unpriced B82-37758

618'.05 — Gynaecology & obstetrics - *Serials*

Progress in obstetrics and gynaecology. — Vol.1. — Edinburgh : Churchill Livingstone, May 1981. — [324]p
ISBN 0-443-02178-3 (pbk) : £12.00 : CIP entry B81-07583

618'.05 — Gynaecology & obstetrics — *Serials*

Progress in obstetrics and gynaecology. — Vol.2. — Edinburgh : Churchill Livingstone, Apr.1982. — [256]p
ISBN 0-443-02396-4 (pbk) : £14.00 : CIP entry B82-03583

Recent advances in obstetrics and gynaecology. — 14. — Edinburgh : Churchill Livingstone, June 1982. — [324]p
ISBN 0-443-02209-7 (pbk) : £17.00 : CIP entry
ISSN 0143-6848 B82-09716

618'.07'1141 — Great Britain. General practitioners. Professional education. Curriculum subjects: Gynaecology & obstetrics — *Inquiry reports*

Report on training for obstetrics and gynaecology for general practitioners / by a joint working party of the RCOG and RCGP. — London : Royal College of Obstetricians and Gynaecologists, 1981. — 26p : 1ill ; 21cm
At head of title: Royal College of Obstetricians and Gynaecologists, Royal College of General Practitioners
ISBN 0-902331-21-3 (pbk) : Unpriced B82-16595

618'.09 — Gynaecology & obstetrics — *Records of achievement*

Records and curiosities in obstetrics and gynaecology / compiled by I.L.C. Fergusson, R.W. Taylor, J.M. Watson ; with a foreword by Sir John Dewhurst. — London : Baillière Tindall, 1982. — x,115p ; 23cm
ISBN 0-7020-0896-6 : Unpriced : CIP rev. B81-30165

618'.0942 — England. Gynaecology & obstetrics, *1540-1740*

Eccles, Audrey. Obstetrics and gynaecology in Tudor and Stuart England / Audrey Eccles. — London : Croom Helm, c1982. — 145p,[8]p of plates : ill ; 23cm
Includes index
ISBN 0-7099-0909-8 : £10.95 : CIP rev. B82-06239

618.1 — GYNAECOLOGY

618.1 — Gynaecology

Gynecology. — 3rd ed. / Georgeanna Seegar Jones, Howard W. Jones ; condensed from Novak's Textbook of Gynecology, 10th ed.. — Baltimore ; London : Williams & Wilkins, c1982. — x,507p : ill ; 26cm
Previous ed.: 1975. — Includes bibliographies and index
ISBN 0-683-04467-2 (pbk) : Unpriced B82-19365

Novak, Edmund R.. Novak's textbook of gynecology. — 10th ed. / Howard W. Jones Jr, Georgeanna Seegar Jones. — Baltimore ; London : Williams & Wilkins, c1981. — xvi,871p : ill(some col.) ; 26cm
Previous ed.: 1975. — Includes bibliographies and index
ISBN 0-683-06588-2 : Unpriced B82-25241

Read, Michael D.. Guidelines to gynaecology / Michael D. Read, Stuart Mellor. — Oxford : Blackwell Scientific, 1982. — ix,124p : ill ; 22cm
Includes index
ISBN 0-632-00932-2 (pbk) : £6.50 : CIP rev. B82-12821

618.1 — Women. Reproductive system. Diseases

Barnes, Josephine. Lecture notes on gynaecology. — 5th ed. — Oxford : Blackwell Scientific, Dec.1982. — [240]p
Previous ed.: 1980
ISBN 0-632-00954-3 (pbk) : £6.80 : CIP entry B82-30048

Gynecologic disorders : differential diagnosis and therapy / edited by Carl J. Pauerstein. — New York ; London : Grune & Stratton, c1982. — xii,400p : ill ; 27cm
Includes index
ISBN 0-8089-1419-7 : £19.00 B82-29979

Office gynecology / [edited by] Robert H. Glass. — 2nd ed. — Baltimore ; London : Williams & Wilkins, c1981. — xii,360p : ill ; 26cm
Previous ed.: 1976. — Includes index
ISBN 0-683-03548-7 : Unpriced B82-15510

618.1 — Women. Reproductive system. Disorders

Fox, H.. Pathology for gynaecologists. — London : E. Arnold, Nov.1982. — [256]p
ISBN 0-7131-4402-5 : £25.00 : CIP entry B82-27947

618.1 — Women. Reproductive system. Disorders — *For women*

Welburn, Vivienne. Below the belt : a guide to gynaecological problems / Vivienne Welburn. — London : W.H. Allen, 1982. — 143p : ill ; 18cm. — (A Star book)
Bibliography: p142-143
ISBN 0-352-30685-8 (pbk) : £1.95 B82-33971

618.1'07 — Women. Reproductive system. Pathology

Fox, Harold. Atlas of gynaecological pathology. — Lancaster : MTP, Dec.1982. — [170]p. — (Current histopathology ; v.5)
ISBN 0-85200-333-1 : £24.50 : CIP entry B82-39261

618.1'2 — Women. Fallopian tubes. Infertility. Diagnosis & treatment

Tubal infertility. — Oxford : Blackwell Scientific, Aug.1982. — [168]p
ISBN 0-632-00785-0 : £12.00 : CIP entry B82-17935

618.1'4'00222 — Women. Uterus. Cervix. Lesions — *Illustrations — For colposcopy*

Kolstad, Per. Atlas of colposcopy. — 3rd rev. ed. — London : Churchill Livingstone, Dec.1982. — [168]p
Previous ed.: Oslo; London : Universitetsforlaget, 1977
ISBN 0-443-02778-1 : £30.00 : CIP entry B82-29806

618.1'72 — Women. Menstrual problems

Birke, Lynda. Why suffer? : periods and their problems. — 2nd ed. — London : Virago, Jan.1982. — [80]p
Previous ed.: 1979
ISBN 0-86068-284-6 (pbk) : £1.95 : CIP entry B81-33761

618.1'72 — Women. Menstruation. Dysmenorrhea — *Conference proceedings*

Dysmenorrhea / M. Yusoff Dawood, editor. — Baltimore ; London : Williams & Wilkins, c1981. — xiv,288p : ill(some col.) ; 24cm
Includes index
ISBN 0-683-02364-0 : Unpriced B82-15416

618.1′78059 — Man. In vitro conception

Human conception in vitro / proceedings of the first Bourn Hall meeting ; edited by R.G. Edwards and Jean M. Purdy. — London : Academic Press, 1982. — xvi,435p : ill ; 24cm
Includes bibliographies and index
ISBN 0-12-232740-3 : £20.00 : CIP rev. B82-12440

618.1′78′059 — Women. Infertility. Microsurgery

Principles of microsurgical techniques in infertility / edited by J. Victor Reyniak and Niels H. Lauersen. — New York ; London : Plenum Medical, c1982. — xv,294p : ill ; 26cm
Includes index
ISBN 0-306-40781-7 : Unpriced B82-25806

618.1′7807543 — Women. Infertility. Diagnosis. Ultrasonography — *Conference proceedings*

Symposium on the Role of Ultrasound in the Management of Infertility *(1st : 1981 : Liverpool)*. Ultrasound and infertility : the proceedings of the first Symposium on the Role of Ultrasound in the Management of Infertility, Walton Hospital, Liverpool, England, 16th April 1981 / edited by A.D. Christie. — Bromley : Chartwell-Bratt, c1981. — vii,179p : ill ; 23cm
ISBN 0-86238-017-0 (pbk) : Unpriced B82-35645

618.1′9 — Women. Breasts. Diseases — *Conference proceedings*

Society for the Study of Breast Disease. *meeting (4th : 1980 : Philadelphia)*. Breast disease : diagnosis and treatment / [from the Annual Meeting of the Society for the Study of Breast Disease, Philadelphia, Pa.] ; editors, Gordon F. Schwartz, Douglas Marchant. — Miami : Symposia Specialists ; New York ; Oxford : Distributed by Elsevier, c1981. — xii,340p : ill ; 24cm
Includes index
ISBN 0-444-00593-5 : Unpriced B82-25701

618.1′9′00222 — Women. Breasts. Diseases — *Illustrations*

Nathan, Ted. An atlas of normal and abnormal mammograms / Ted Nathan. — Oxford : Oxford University Press, 1982. — xxi,118p : ill (some col.) ; 29cm. — (Oxford medical publications)
Bibliography: p117-118
ISBN 0-19-261346-4 : £30.00 : CIP rev. B81-32044

618.1′9075 — Women. Breasts. Diseases. Diagnosis

Diagnosis of breast disease. — London : Chapman and Hall, Nov.1982. — [350]p
ISBN 0-412-22130-6 : £25.30 : CIP entry B82-28255

618.2 — OBSTETRICS

618.2 — Obstetrics

Huang, C. L.-H.. Companion to obstetrics. — Lancaster : MTP Press, Jan.1982. — [260]p
ISBN 0-85200-379-x : £8.95 : CIP entry B81-34579

Obstetrics / by ten teachers. — 13th ed. / under the direction of Stanley G. Clayton ; edited by Stanley G. Clayton, T.L.T. Lewis, G. Pinker. — London : Edward Arnold, 1980 (1982 [printing]). — x,541p : ill ; 22cm
Includes index
ISBN 0-7131-4415-7 (pbk) : £9.75 B82-23496

Practical manual of obstetric care : a pocket reference for those who treat the pregnant patient / edited by Frederick P. Zuspan, Edward J. Quilligan. — St. Louis ; London : Mosby, 1982. — xiii,414p : ill ; 22cm
Includes index
ISBN 0-8016-4064-4 (spiral) : £8.75 B82-22917

Stirrat, G. M.. Obstetrics. — London (39 Great Russell St., WC1B 3PH) : Grant McIntyre, Apr.1981. — [250]p. — (Pocket consultants)
ISBN 0-86216-011-1 (pbk) : £5.95 : CIP entry B81-08858

618.2 — Obstetrics — *For midwifery*

Mayes, Mary. Mayes′ midwifery : a textbook for midwives / Betty R. Sweet. — 10th ed. — London : Baillière Tindall, 1982. — viii,630p ; 24cm
Previous ed.: 1976. — Bibliography: p611-614. — Includes index
ISBN 0-7020-0919-9 (pbk) : £9.50 : CIP rev. B82-12999

618.2 — Perinatal medicine

Perinatal medicine. — London : Butterworth, Dec.1982. — [320]p. — (Butterworths international medical reviews. Pediatrics, ISSN 0260-0161 ; 2)
ISBN 0-407-02309-7 : £15.00 : CIP entry B82-29781

618.2 — Woman. Pregnancy — *For pregnant women*

A **Guide** for the expectant mother. — London : National Dairy Council, 1980. — 15p : col.ill ; 21cm
ISBN 0-902748-23-8 (unbound) : Unpriced B82-21708

618.2 — Women. Pregnancy & childbirth

Kitzinger, Sheila. Birth over thirty / Sheila Kitzinger ; illustrations by Jo Nesbitt. — London : Sheldon, 1982. — viii,151p : ill ; 21cm. — (Overcoming common problems)
Includes index
ISBN 0-85969-368-6 (cased) : Unpriced
ISBN 0-85969-365-1 (pbk) : £2.50 B82-35104

Macy, Christopher. Pregnancy and birth : pleasures and problems / Christopher Macy and Frank Falkner. — London ; New York : Harper & Row, c1979. — 128p : ill(some col.) ; 24cm. — (The Life cycle series)
Bibliography: p125. — Includes index
ISBN 0-06-318101-0 (cased) : Unpriced
ISBN 0-06-318102-9 (pbk) : Unpriced B82-17586

Wiggins, Jayne DeClue. Childbearing : physiology, experiences, needs / Jayne DeClue Wiggins. — St. Louis ; London : Mosby, 1979. — x,178p : ill ; 24cm
Bibliography: p164-166. — Includes index
ISBN 0-8016-5543-9 (pbk) : Unpriced B82-19309

618.2 — Women. Pregnancy & childbirth — *For children*

Alex, Marlee. Our new baby / Marlee and Benny Alex ; photographs by Benny Alex, Jørgen Vium Olesen. — Tring : Lion, 1982, c1981. — 43 : col.ill ; 32cm
ISBN 0-85648-433-4 : £2.95 B82-23751

Jessel, Camilla. The joy of birth. — London : Methuen Children′s Books, May 1982. — [64]p
ISBN 0-416-89970-6 : £4.95 : CIP entry B82-09291

Nilsson, Lennart. How you began : a story in pictures / by Lennart Nilsson. — Harmondsworth : Kestrel, 1975 (1982 [printing]). — 31p : ill(some col.) ; 25cm
Translation of: Så blev du till
ISBN 0-7226-5776-3 : £4.50 B82-31079

618.2 — Women. Pregnancy, childbirth & parenthood — *For families with children*

Weiss, Joan Solomon. Your second child / Joan Solomon Weiss. — London : Sphere, 1982, c1981. — xxiii,260p ; 18cm
Originally published: New York : Summit, 1981. — Includes index
ISBN 0-7221-9016-6 (pbk) : £1.95 B82-39060

618.2 — Women. Pregnancy — *Correspondence, diaries, etc*

Gunn, Alexander. Questions and answers on pregnancy / Alexander Gunn. — London : Illustrated Publications, 1980. — 174p ; 18cm. — (A Mother & baby publication)
ISBN 0-85242-696-8 (pbk) : £1.95 B82-05261

618.2′00240431 — Women. Pregnancy & childbirth — *For fathers*

Parsons, Betty, *1915-*. The expectant father : a practical guide to pregnancy for the anxious man / by Betty Parsons ; illustrated by Mel Calman. — Rev. ed. — Sunbury : Quartermaine House, 1981. — 93p : ill ; 22cm
Previous ed.: [Great Britain?] : Yeatman, 1975
ISBN 0-905898-12-5 (pbk) : Unpriced B82-34353

618.2′00240431 — Women. Pregnancy & childbirth — *For mothers*

Chamberlain, Geoffrey. Pregnancy questions answered / Geoffrey Chamberlain. — Edinburgh : Churchill Livingstone, 1982. — 147p : ill ; 19cm. — (Churchill Livingstone patient handbook ; 11)
ISBN 0-443-02177-5 (pbk) : £1.75 : CIP rev. B82-01962

You and your baby / executive editor Evelyn Brown ; drawings Richard Brooks, Pat McNeil, Alan Morgan ; authors David Brown ... [et al.]. — London (Tavistock) : British Medical Association
1: Pregnancy and birth. — c1982. — 96p : ill (some col.) ; 20cm
Unpriced (pbk) B82-34641

618.2′00240431 — Women. Pregnancy & childbirth — *Manuals — For mothers*

Pregnancy : what you need to know. — London : Health Education Council, [1981?]. — [12]p : col.ill ; 21cm
Unpriced (unbound) B82-02494

618.2′005 — Women. Pregnancy & childbirth — *Serials*

Maternity action : the bulletin of the Maternity Alliance. — No.1 (Sept. 1981)-. — London (309 Kentish Town Rd, NW5 2TJ) : The Alliance, 1981-. — v. : ill ; 30cm
Six issues yearly. — Description based on: No.4 (Mar./Apr. [1982])
ISSN 0263-922X = Maternity action : £3.00 per year (free to members of the Alliance) B82-38515

New generation. — Vol.1, no.1 (Mar. 1982)-. — London (9 Queensborough Terrace, W2 3TB) : National Childbirth Trust, 1982-. — v. : ill ; 29cm
Quarterly
ISSN 0263-5429 = New generation : £6.00 per year B82-27652

618.2′0088055 — United States. Adolescent girls. Pregnancy

Pregnancy in adolescence : needs, problems, and management / edited by Irving R. Stuart and Carl F. Wells. — New York ; London : Van Nostrand Reinhold, 1982. — xxvi,441p ; 24cm
Includes bibliographies and index
ISBN 0-442-21225-9 : £22.55 B82-24921

618.2′00913 — Tropical regions. Obstetrics — *For midwifery*

Ojo, O. A.. A textbook for midwives in the tropics / O.A. Ojo and Enang Bassey Briggs. — 2nd ed. — London : Arnold, 1982. — xii,468p : ill ; 22cm
Previous ed.: 1976. — Includes index
ISBN 0-7131-4413-0 (pbk) : £6.50 : CIP rev. B81-36393

618.2′00941 — Great Britain. Women. Pregnancy & childbirth

The **British** way of birth / compiled by Catherine Boyd and Lea Sellers ; foreword by Gordon Bourne ; introduction by Esther Rantzen. — London : Pan in association with the Spastics Society′s ′Save a Baby′ campaign, 1982. — xvii,238p : ill ; 18cm
ISBN 0-330-26687-x (pbk) : £1.50 B82-20445

Elbourne, Diana. Is the baby all right? : current trends in British perinatal health / Diana Elbourne. — London : Junction, c1981. — ix,206p : ill,maps ; 23cm
Bibliography: p184-200. — Includes index
ISBN 0-86245-012-8 (cased) : £12.50
ISBN 0-86245-013-6 (pbk) : £5.95 B82-33160

618.2′025 — Obstetrics. Emergency treatment — *Manuals*

Cavanagh, Denis. Obstetric emergencies. — 3rd ed. / Denis Cavanagh ... [et al.]. — Philadelphia ; London : Harper & Row, c1982. — xiii,479p : ill ; 24cm
Previous ed.: 1978. — Includes bibliographies and index
ISBN 0-06-140627-9 (pbk) : £17.50
B82-26275

618.2′2 — Obstetrics. Diagnosis. Ultrasonography

Obstetric ultrasound : applications and principles / edited by W.S. Van Bergen. — Menlo Park, Calif. ; London : Addison-Wesley, c1980. — 157p : ill ; 24cm
Includes bibliographies and index
ISBN 0-201-08001-x : Unpriced B82-20550

618.2′4 — Antenatal medicine. Diagnosis — *Conference proceedings*

The **Future** of prenatal diagnosis. — Edinburgh : Churchill Livingstone, Sept.1982. — [240]p
Conference papers
ISBN 0-443-02603-3 : £15.00 : CIP entry
B82-19684

618.2′4 — Childbirth. Preparation. Exercises — *Manuals*

Heardman, Helen. Relaxation and exercise for childbirth / the late Helen Heardman. — 5th ed. / revised and re-edited by Maria Ebner ; foreword by Josephine Barnes. — Edinburgh : Churchill Livingstone, 1982. — 35p : ill ; 19cm. — (Churchill Livingstone patient handbook ; 12)
Previous ed.: 1975
ISBN 0-443-02194-5 (pbk) : Unpriced : CIP rev. B82-27209

618.2′4 — Natural childbirth. Preparation. Exercises — *Manuals*

Bing, Elisabeth. Six practical lessons for an easier childbirth / by Elisabeth Bing. — 2nd rev. ed. / photographs by Norman McGath ; drawings by Howard S. Friedman and Vivien Cohen. — Toronto ; London : Bantam. — 162p : ill ; 21cm
Previous ed.: 1977
ISBN 0-553-01371-8 (pbk) : £2.95 B82-38958

618.2′5 — Man. Multiple birth

Linney, Judi. Multiple births. — Chichester : Wiley, June 1983. — [100]p. — (Topics in community health)
ISBN 0-471-25849-0 : £8.00 : CIP entry
B82-33341

618.3 — Pregnant women. Interactions with foetuses. Immunological aspects

Cauchi, Maurice N.. Obstetric and perinatal immunology / Maurice N. Cauchi. — London : Edward Arnold, 1981. — 148p : ill ; 24cm. — (Current topics in immunology, ISSN 0305-8204 ; 16)
Bibliography: p115-140. — Includes index
ISBN 0-7131-4384-3 : Unpriced : CIP rev.
B81-27930

618.3′042 — Pregnant women. Genetic disorders

Genetic diseases in pregnancy : maternal effects and fetal outcome / edited by Joseph D. Schulman, Joe Leigh Simpson. — New York ; London : Academic Press, 1981. — xvi,492p : ill ; 24cm
Includes bibliographies and index
ISBN 0-12-630940-x : £32.40 B82-07716

618.3′2 — Man. Embryos. Congenital abnormalities. Role of malnutrition of mothers

Wynn, Margaret. The prevention of handicap of early pregnancy origin : some evidence for the value of good health before conception / by Margaret Wynn and Arthur Wynn. — London (27 Walpole St., SW3) : Foundation for Education and Research in Childbearing, 1981. — 68p : ill ; 30cm
Bibliography: p62-68
Unpriced (pbk) B82-14621

618.3′2 — Man. Foetuses & newborn babies. Patholgy

Fetal and neonatal pathology : perspectives for the general pathologist. — Eastbourne : Praeger, Feb.1982. — [272]p
ISBN 0-03-061714-6 : £15.00 : CIP entry
B81-39235

618.3′2 — Perinatal medicine

Perinatal medicine : clinical and biochemical aspects. — Washington, [D.C.] ; London : Hemisphere
Vol.2 / edited by Manohar Rathi and Sudhir Kumar. — c1982. — xii,237p : ill ; 24cm
Includes index
ISBN 0-89116-181-3 : £29.95
ISBN 0-07-051208-6 (McGraw-Hill)
B82-33703

Topics in perinatal medicine 2 / edited by Brian Wharton. — London : Pitman, c1982. — x,177p : ill ; 24cm
ISBN 0-272-79663-8 : Unpriced : CIP rev.
B82-07979

618.3′2 — Perinatal medicine — *Conference proceedings*

Eugenics Society. *Symposium (17th : 1980 : London)*. Changing patterns of child-bearing and child rearing : proceedings of the Seventeenth Annual Symposium of the Eugenics Society, London 1980 / edited by R. Chester, Peter Diggory, Margaret B. Sutherland. — London : Academic Press, 1981. — x,180p : ill ; 24cm
Includes bibliographies and index
ISBN 0-12-171660-0 : £10.80 : CIP rev.
Also classified at 362.7 B81-35915

618.3′2′0024613 — Perinatal medicine — *For nursing*

Protocols for perinatal nursing practice / [edited by] Rosanne Harrigan Perez. — St. Louis ; London : Mosby, 1981. — xv,536p : ill,forms ; 25cm
Includes bibliographies and index
ISBN 0-8016-3805-4 : £15.50 B82-08335

618.3′2043 — Man. Foetuses. Congenital abnormalities. Diagnosis

Brock, David J. H.. Early diagnosis of fetal defects. — Edinburgh : Churchill Livingstone, Jan.1983. — [148]p. — (Current reviews in obstetrics and gynaecology)
ISBN 0-443-02302-6 (pbk) : £6.00 : CIP entry
B82-34595

618.3′207543 — Man. Foetuses. Diagnosis. Ultrasonography — *Conference proceedings*

International Meeting on the Secret Prenatal Life *(1981 : Verona)*. Fetal ultrasonography : the secret prenatal life / [proceedings of the International Meeting on the Secret Prenatal Life, Verona, 10-11 April 1981] ; [editors] Franco Borruto, Manfred Hansmann, Juri W. Wladimiroff. — Chichester : Wiley, c1982. — 162p : ill(some col.) ; 25cm
Includes index
ISBN 0-471-10162-1 : £11.50 : CIP rev.
B82-06836

618.3′207545 — Man. Foetuses. Foetoscopy

Fetoscopy / edited by I. Rocker and K.M. Laurence. — Amsterdam ; Oxford : Elsevier/North-Holland Biomedical, 1981. — xii,335p : ill ; 25cm
Includes bibliographies and index
ISBN 0-444-80337-8 : £43.50 B82-09913

618.3′261 — Pregnant women. Blood. Hypertension. Drug therapy. Labetalol — *Conference proceedings*

The **Investigation** of labetalol in the management of hypertension in pregnancy : proceedings of a symposium at the Royal College of Physicians, London, 2nd December, 1981 / editors A. Riley, E.M. Symonds. — Amsterdam ; Oxford : Excerpta Medica, 1982. — viii,166p : ill ; 25cm
Includes index
ISBN 0-444-90272-4 : £26.54 B82-28557

618.3′268 — Man. Foetuses. Brain. Developmental disorders — *Conference proceedings*

Fetal brain disorders - recent approaches to the problem of mental deficiency / edited by Basil S. Hetzel and Richard M. Smith. — Amsterdam ; Oxford : Elsevier/North-Holland Biomedical, 1981. — xiii,489p : ill,maps ; 25cm
Conference papers. — Includes bibliographies and index
ISBN 0-444-80321-1 : Unpriced B82-00835

618.3′268′005 — Man. Foetuses & newborn babies. Nervous system. Diseases — *Serials*

Progress in perinatal neurology. — Vol.1-. — Baltimore, Md. ; London : Williams & Wilkins, 1981-. — v. : ill ; 24cm
Unpriced B82-06774

618.3′92 — Women. Miscarriages

Pizer, Hank. Coping with a miscarriage. — London : Jill Norman, July 1981. — [192]p
Originally published: New York : Dial, 1980
ISBN 0-906908-54-x (cased) : £6.50 : CIP entry
ISBN 0-906908-55-8 (pbk) : £3.50 B81-13503

618.4 — Childbirth — *Correspondence, diaries, etc*

Gunn, Alexander. Questions and answers on labour and birth / Alexander Gunn. — London : Illustrated Publications, 1980. — 160p ; 18cm. — (A Mother & baby publication)
ISBN 0-85242-697-6 (pbk) : £1.95 B82-05262

618.4 — Childbirth. Home confinement

Inch, Sally. Birthrights. — London : Hutchinson, Sept.1982. — 1v.
ISBN 0-09-146031-x (pbk) : £5.95 : CIP entry
B82-22413

618.4 — Developing countries. Rural regions. Childbirth. Emergency treatment — *Algorithms*

Essex, B. J.. Management of obstetric emergencies in a health centre : a handbook for midwives / B. Essex ; [illustrations A. Barrett]. — Edinburgh : Churchill Livingstone, 1981. — 77p : ill ; 30cm
Originally published: Geneva : World Health Organisation, 1978
ISBN 0-582-77700-3 (pbk) : £1.95 B82-11533

618.4′028′7 — Childbirth. Labour. Monitoring. Use of medical electronic equipment

Cibils, Luis A.. Electronic fetal-maternal monitoring : antepartum, intrapartum / Luis A. Cibils. — Boston [Mass.] ; Bristol : John Wright, c1981. — x,495p : ill ; 27cm
Includes bibliographies and index
ISBN 0-88416-192-7 : Unpriced B82-08858

618.8 — Africa. Women. Circumcision & infibulation

Abdalla, Raqiya Haji Dualeh. Sisters in affliction. — London : Zed Press, Oct.1982. — [128]p
ISBN 0-86232-093-3 (cased) : £11.95 : CIP entry
ISBN 0-86232-094-1 (pbk) : £5.50 B82-29410

618.8 — Obstetrics. Surgery

Douglas, R. Gordon. Operative obstetrics / Douglas-Stromme. — 4th ed. / Edward J. Quilligan, Frederick Zuspan, contributions by William J. Ledger, Barry S. Schifrin, Feizal Waffarn. — New York : Appleton-Century-Crofts ; London : Prentice-Hall, c1982. — x,967p : ill ; 27cm
Previous ed.: 1976. — Includes bibliographies and index
ISBN 0-8385-1752-8 : £51.40 B82-23316

Kerr, J. M. Munro. Munro Kerr's Operative obstetrics. — 10th ed. / P.R. Myerscough. — London : Baillière Tindall, 1982. — 508p : ill ; 26cm
Previous ed.: 1977. — Includes index
ISBN 0-7020-0904-0 : £25.00 : CIP rev.
B82-06938

618.8 — Sudan. Women. Circumcision & infibulation

Dareer, Asma El. Woman, why do you weep?. — London : Zed Press, Nov.1982. — [144]p
ISBN 0-86232-098-4 (cased) : £10.95 : CIP entry
ISBN 0-86232-099-2 (pbk) : £4.95 B82-29419

618.8′5 — Women. Perineum. Episiotomy

Episiotomy : physical and emotional aspects / edited by Sheila Kitzinger. — London (9 Queensborough Terr., W2 3TB) : National Childbirth Trust, 1981. — 56p : ill ; 22cm
Cover title
ISBN 0-9502256-1-4 (pbk) : £1.50 B82-11027

618.8′5 — Women. Perineum. Episiotomy *continuation*

Kitzinger, Sheila. Some women′s experiences of episiotomy / Sheila Kitzinger with Rhiannon Walters. — London (9 Queensborough Terr., W2 3TB) : National Childbirth Trust, 1981. — 20p ; 22cm
Cover title
£0.60 (pbk) B82-11028

618.8′6′0240431 — Childbirth. Caesarean section — *For parents*

Caesarian birth : a handbook for parents. — Cambridge ([7, Green St., Willingham, Cambs.]) : Caesarian Support Group of Cambridge, c1982. — 52p : ill ; 22cm
Cover title. — Text, ill on inside covers. — Bibliography: p51-52
£1.25 (pbk) B82-38855

618.8′6′024613 — Childbirth. Caesarean section — *For nursing*

The **Cesarean** experience : theoretical and clinical perspectives for nurses / edited by Carole Fitzgerald Kehoe. — New York : Appleton-Century-Crofts ; London : Prentice-Hall, c1981. — xvi,319p : ill ; 24cm
Includes bibliographies and index
ISBN 0-8385-1107-4 : £12.70 B82-07548

618.8′8 — Second-trimester abortion. Medical aspects

Second-trimester abortion : perspectives after a decade of experience / edited by Gary S. Berger, Wiliam E. Brenner, Louis G. Keith ; forewords by Irvin M. Cushner and Jeffrey E. Grossman. — The Hague ; London : Nijhoff, 1981. — xxii,340p : ill ; 25cm
Includes index
Unpriced (corrected : pbk) B82-06415

618.92 — PAEDIATRICS

618.92 — Children. Chronic diseases — *German texts*

Das **Chronisch** kranke Kind / Herausgeber des Bandes S. Fink. — Basel ; London : Karger, c1982. — 87p : ill ; 22cm. — (Pädiatrische Fortbildungskurse für die Praxis ; v.54)
Includes bibliographies
ISBN 3-8055-3422-1 (pbk) : £11.50 B82-28699

618.92 — Children. Developmental disorders. Assessment — *Behaviourist perspectives*

Behavioral assessment of childhood disorders / edited by Eric J. Mash and Leif G. Terdal ; foreword by Gerald R. Patterson. — Chichester : Wiley, 1981. — xv,749p : ill,forms ; 24cm
Includes bibliographies and index
ISBN 0-471-10042-0 : £21.00 B82-05128

618.92 — Children. Diseases

Valman, H. B.. ABC of 1 of 7 / H.B. Valman with contributions from S.K. Goolamali ... [et al.]. — London : British Medical Association, c1982. — 108p : ill ; 30cm
Includes index
ISBN 0-7279-0086-2 (pbk) : Unpriced B82-34792

618.92 — Children. Diseases — *For general practice*

Child care in general practice. — 2nd ed. — Edinburgh : Churchill Livingstone, July 1982. — [336]p
Previous ed.: 1977
ISBN 0-443-02591-6 (pbk) : £10.00 : CIP entry B82-24328

618.92 — Children. Medical aspects

Davis, Alan G.. Children in clinics. — London : Tavistock, Nov.1982. — [240]p
ISBN 0-422-77370-0 : £12.50 : CIP entry B82-27507

618.92 — Paediatrics

Barnes, N. D.. Paediatrics / N.D. Barnes and N.R.C. Roberton. — London : Update, 1981. — ix,130p : ill(some col.) ; 29cm
Includes bibliographies and index
ISBN 0-906141-15-x : Unpriced B82-19598

Habel, Alex. Aids to paediatrics / Alex Habel. — Edinburgh : Churchill Livingstone, 1982. — 136p : ill ; 22cm
Includes index
ISBN 0-443-02205-4 (pbk) : £3.95 : CIP rev. B81-31624

Hood, John, *1935-*. Problems in paediatrics / John Hood. — Lancaster : MTP Press, c1982. — 178p ; 24cm. — (Problems in practice series)
Includes index
ISBN 0-85200-263-7 : Unpriced : CIP rev. B82-12805

Meadow, Roy. Lecture notes on paediatrics / S.R. Meadow, R.W. Smithells. — 4th ed. — Oxford : Blackwell Scientific, 1981. — x,323p : ill ; 19cm
Previous ed.: 1978. — Bibliography: p312. — Includes index
ISBN 0-632-00824-5 (pbk) : £6.00 : CIP rev. B81-21596

A **Paediatric** vade-mecum. — 10th ed. / edited by Jack Insley and Ben Wood. — London : Lloyd-Luke, 1982. — xiv,282p : ill ; 18cm
Previous ed.: 1977. — Includes index
ISBN 0-85324-158-9 (pbk) : £7.00 B82-40632

618.92 — Paediatrics — *For general practice*

Modell, Michael. Paediatric problems in general practice. — Oxford : Oxford University Press, July 1982. — [230]p. — (Oxford general practice series ; no.1) (Oxford medical publications)
ISBN 0-19-261264-6 (pbk) : £9.95 : CIP entry B82-12536

618.92 — Paediatrics — *For house physicians*

The **Harriet** Lane handbook : a manual for pediatric house officers / the Harriet Lane Service, Children′s Medical and Surgical Center, Johns Hopkins Hospital. — 9th ed., editors Jeffrey A. Biller, Andrew M. Yeager. — Chicago ; London : Year Book Medical, c1981. — x,328p : ill ; 17cm
Previous ed.: 1978. — Includes index
ISBN 0-8151-4922-0 (pbk) : £9.50 B82-02992

618.92 — Paediatrics — *Manuals*

Nutbeam, Helen M.. A handbook for examinations in paediatrics. — Oxford : Blackwell Scientific, July 1981. — [144]p
ISBN 0-632-00703-6 : £4.80 : CIP entry B81-22690

Paediatric handbook / edited by D.C. Geddis. — London : Heinemann Medical, 1982. — 159p,[1]folded leaf of plates : ill ; 19cm
Includes index
ISBN 0-433-11530-0 (pbk) : Unpriced B82-27322

618.92 — Physically handicapped children. Medical aspects — *For teaching*

Physically handicapped children : a medical atlas for teachers / edited by Eugene E. Bleck, Donald A. Nagel. — 2nd ed. — New York ; London : Grune & Stratton, c1982. — xxii,530p : ill,forms ; 29cm
Previous ed.: 1975. — Includes index
ISBN 0-8089-1391-3 : £22.80 B82-27134

618.92 — Pre-school children. Developmental disorders — *Conference proceedings*

Developmental disabilities : theory assessment and intervention / edited by Michael Lewis, Lawrence T. Taft. — Lancaster : M.T.P. Press, c1982. — xiv,439p : ill ; 24cm
Conference papers. — Includes bibliographies and index
ISBN 0-85200-616-0 : £23.50 B82-39875

618.92 — United States. Children. Abuse & neglect by adults. Medical aspects

Child abuse and neglect : a medical reference / edited by Norman S. Ellerstein. — New York ; Chichester : Wiley, c1981. — xiv,355p : ill ; 26cm
Includes index
ISBN 0-471-05877-7 : £21.00 B82-05820

618.92′00012 — Children. Diseases — *Classification schedules*

British Paediatric Association. British Paediatric Association classification of diseases : successor to the Cardiff Diagnostic Classification : a paediatric supplement compatible with the ninth revision of the WHO international classification of diseases, 1977. — London : The Association, 1979. — 2v. ; 22cm
Includes index
ISBN 0-9500491-1-5 (spiral) : Unpriced B82-03060

618.92′0001′9 — Children. Chronic diseases. Psychosocial aspects — *Conference proceedings*

Psychosocial family interventions in chronic pediatric illness / [proceedings of a symposium on family dynamics, family therapy and pediatric medical illness, held December 12-13, 1980 at Downstate Medical Center, Brooklyn, New York] ; edited by Adolph E. Christ and Kalman Flomenhaft. — New York ; London : Plenum Press, c1982. — xi,211p : ill ; 26cm. — (The Downstate series of research in psychiatry and psychology ; v.4)
Includes bibliographies and index
ISBN 0-306-41013-3 : Unpriced B82-36894

618.92′0001′9 — Children. Diseases. Psychological aspects

Handbook for the practice of pediatric psychology / edited by June M. Tuma. — New York ; Chichester : Wiley, c1982. — xv,356p : ill,1form ; 24cm. — (Wiley series on personality processes, ISSN 0195-4008)
Includes bibliographies and index
ISBN 0-471-06284-7 : £23.00 B82-24059

618.92′00024613 — Paediatrics - *For nursing*

Speirs, A. L.. Paediatrics for nurses. — London : Pitman Medical, Apr.1981. — [256]p ; pbk
ISBN 0-272-79613-1 : £5.95 : CIP entry B81-04343

618.92′0005 — Chldren. Diseases. Psychosocial aspects — *Serials*

Advances in behavioral pediatrics : a research annual. — Vol.1 (1980)-. — Greenwich, Conn. : JAI Press ; London (3 Henrietta St., WC2E 8LU) : Distributed by JAICON Press, 1980-. — v. ; 24cm
ISSN 0198-7089 = Advances in behavioral pediatrics : £22.85 B82-03431

618.92′0005 — Paediatrics — *Serials*

Advances in international maternal and child health. — Vol.2. — Oxford : Oxford University Press, July 1982. — [250]p. — (Oxford medical publications)
ISBN 0-19-261370-7 : £17.50 : CIP entry B82-12538

Topics in paediatrics. — 3. — London : Pitman, May 1982. — [176]p
ISBN 0-272-79664-6 (pbk) : £14.50 : CIP entry
ISSN 0144-8668 B82-12901

618.92′00076 — Paediatrics — *Questions & answers*

Hoekelman, principles of pediatrics : patient management problems : PreTest self-assessment and review / edited by Robert A. Hoekelman. — New York ; London : McGraw-Hill, c1982. — xiii,364p : ill ; 28cm. — (PreTest series)
Includes bibliographies
ISBN 0-07-051653-7 (pbk) : £21.00 B82-03263

Johnston, Derek I.. Essential paediatric MCQs / Derek I. Johnston, David Hull. — Edinburgh : Churchill Livingstone, 1982. — 130p ; 22cm
ISBN 0-443-02235-6 (pbk) : £3.95 : CIP rev. B81-34638

Uttley, W. S.. MCQs in paediatrics / W.S. Uttley ; with a foreword by John O. Forfar. — Edinburgh : Churchill Livingstone, 1982. — xii,168p ; 22cm
ISBN 0-443-02185-6 (pbk) : £3.95 : CIP rev. B81-21567

618.92'0009172'4 — Developing countries. Children. Diseases

Ebrahim, G. J.. Paediatric practice in developing countries / G.J. Ebrahim. — London : Macmillan, 1981. — vii,321p : ill,maps ; 26cm. — (Macmillan tropical community health manuals)
Includes bibliographies and index
ISBN 0-333-27559-4 (cased) : £25.00
ISBN 0-333-27560-8 (pbk) : Unpriced
B82-02580

618.92'0025 — Children. Emergency treatment

Bacon, Christopher, *1935-*. Paediatric emergencies : a houseman's pocketbook / Christopher Bacon. — London : Heinemann Medical, 1982. — x,190p : ill ; 19cm
Includes index
ISBN 0-433-01051-7 (pbk) : Unpriced
B82-37351

Lissauer, Tom. Paediatric emergencies : a practical guide to acute paediatrics / Tom Lissauer. — Lancaster : Published, in association with Update Publications, by MTP, c1982. — viii,328p : ill ; 23cm
Includes bibliographies and index
ISBN 0-85200-436-2 : Unpriced : CIP rev.
B82-09181

618.92'0025 — Great Britain. Hospitals. Casualty departments. Patients: Children. Emergency treatment — *Manuals*

Illingworth, Cynthia M.. The diagnosis and primary care of accidents and emergencies in children. — 2nd ed. — Oxford : Blackwell Scientific, July 1982. — [176]p
Previous ed.: 1978
ISBN 0-632-00946-2 (pbk) : £6.80 : CIP entry
B82-16243

618.92'0043'0240431 — Newborn babies. Congenital abnormalities — *For parents*

Zachary, R. B.. Disabled from birth : what parents should know / by R.B. Zachary. — London : Catholic Truth Society, 1982. — 14p ; 19cm
ISBN 0-85183-470-1 (pbk) : £0.35 B82-29840

618.92'0072 — Children. Diseases. Symptoms

Illingworth, Ronald S.. Common symptoms of disease in children / R.S. Illingworth. — 7th ed. — Oxford : Blackwell Scientific, 1982. — xiii,367p : ill ; 23cm
Also available in Spanish, Greek and Italian. — Previous ed.: 1979. — Bibliography: p354-355. — Includes index
ISBN 0-632-00814-8 : £9.50 : CIP rev.
B81-39226

618.92'0075 — Children. Diagnosis. Problem solving

Fulginiti, Vincent A.. Pediatric clinical problem solving / Vincent A. Fulginiti. — Baltimore ; London : Williams & Wilkins, c1981. — viii,182p ; 26cm
Bibliography: p181-182
ISBN 0-683-03383-2 (pbk) : Unpriced
B82-02566

618.92'007543 — Children. Diagnosis. Ultrasonography

Canty, Timothy G.. Ultrasonography of pediatric surgical disorders / Timothy G. Canty, George R. Leopold, Deborah A. Wolf. — New York ; London : Grune & Stratton, c1982. — xiv,268p : ill ; 29cm
Includes bibliographies and index
ISBN 0-8089-1395-6 : £32.80 B82-27131

Ultrasound in pediatrics / edited by Jack O. Haller and Arnold Shkolnik. — New York ; Edinburgh : Churchill Livingstone, 1981. — xi,306p : ill ; 25cm. — (Clinics in diagnostic ultrasound ; v.8)
Includes index
ISBN 0-443-08155-7 : Unpriced B82-09102

618.92'0079 — Children. Immunology

Paediatric immunology. — Oxford : Blackwell Scientific, Feb.1983. — [496]p
ISBN 0-632-00724-9 : £32.00 : CIP entry
B82-38864

618.92'01 — Newborn babies. Diseases

Craig, W. S.. Craig's care of the newly born infant. — 7th ed. / A.J. Keay and D.M. Morgan in collaboration with Norah J. Stephen. — Edinburgh : Churchill Livingstone, 1982. — viii,528p : ill,1form,1map,1port ; 22cm
Previous ed.: 1978. — Includes bibliographies and index
ISBN 0-443-02344-1 (pbk) : £11.50
B82-37226

Kelnar, C. J. H.. The sick newborn baby / C.J.H. Kelnar, David Harvey ; with a foreword by Margaret E. Adams. — London : Baillière Tindall, 1981. — xi,351p : ill ; 22cm
Includes bibliographies and index
ISBN 0-7020-0728-5 (pbk) : £8.50 : CIP rev.
B81-23813

Vulliamy, David G.. The newborn child. — 5th ed. — Edinburgh : Churchill Livingstone, Aug.1982. — [256]p
Previous ed.: 1977
ISBN 0-443-02482-0 (pbk) : £6.00 : CIP entry
B82-24330

618.92'01 — Newborn babies. Intensive care

Roberton, N. R. C.. A manual of neonatal intensive care / N.R.C. Roberton ; with a chapter on cardiological problems by Douglas Pickering. — London : Edward Arnold, 1981. — x,278p : ill ; 20cm
Includes bibliographies and index
ISBN 0-7131-4372-x (pbk) : £9.95 : CIP rev.
B81-00131

618.92'01 — Newborn babies. Medical aspects

Daniels, Victor G.. Companion to neonatal medicine / Victor G. Daniels, Christopher L.-H. Huang. — Lancaster : MTP Press, c1982. — 240p : ill ; 23cm
Bibliography: p221-222. — Includes index
ISBN 0-85200-380-3 : Unpriced : CIP rev.
B82-12815

618.92'01 — Newborn babies. Resusitation

Neonatal resuscitation : a practical guide / edited by David J. Roberts. — New York ; London : Academic Press, 1981. — xv,172p : ill ; 25cm
Includes bibliographies and index
ISBN 0-12-788701-6 : £13.00 B82-10052

618.92'01'012 — Newborn babies. Diseases — *Classification schedules*

British Paediatric Association. British Paediatric Association classification of diseases : successor to the Cardiff Diagnostic Classification : a perinatal supplement compatible with the ninth revision of the WHO International Classification of Diseases, 1977 : perinatal supplement : codes designed for use in the classification of perinatal disorders. — London : The Association, 1979. — 168p ; 22cm
Includes index
ISBN 0-9500491-2-3 (spiral) : Unpriced
B82-03061

618.92'09751407543 — Babies. Cranium. Diagnosis. Ultrasonography

Babcock, Diane S.. Cranial ultrasonography of infants / Diane S. Babcock and Bokyung K. Han. — Baltimore ; London : Williams & Wilkins, c1981. — xvii,246p : chiefly ill ; 26cm
Includes index
ISBN 0-683-00300-3 : Unpriced B82-18001

618.92'0975507543 — Children. Pelvic region. Diagnosis. Ultrasonography

Kangarloo, Hooshang. Ultrasound of the pediatric abdomen and pelvis : a correlative imaging appproach / Hooshang Kangarloo, W. Fred Sample. — Chicago ; London : Year Book Medical, c1980. — xvi,375p : ill ; 24cm
Includes bibliographies and index
ISBN 0-8151-4972-7 : £33.73 B82-40703

618.92'0977 — Children. Eyes. Diseases - *Conference proceedings*

International Society for Paediatric Ophthalmology. *Meeting (2nd : 1979 : Verona)*. Paediatric ophthalmology. — Chichester : Wiley, Aug.1981. — [600]p. — (A Wiley medical publication)
Conference papers
ISBN 0-471-10040-4 : £40.00 : CIP entry
B81-16868

618.92'0978 — Children. Hearing disorders

Yeates, Sybil. The development of hearing : its progress and problems / Sybil Yeates. — Lancaster : MTP, 1980. — 237p : ill ; 23cm. — (Studies in developmental paediatrics ; v.2)
Includes index
ISBN 0-85200-301-3 : £7.95 B82-40799

618.92'12 — Children. Heart. Diseases

Jordan, S. C.. Heart disease in paediatrics / S.C. Jordan and Olive Scott. — 2nd ed. — London : Butterworths, 1981. — viii,374p : ill ; 23cm. — (Postgraduate paediatrics series)
Previous ed.: 1973. — Includes bibliographies and index
ISBN 0-407-19941-1 : Unpriced : CIP rev.
B81-09508

618.92'12 — Children. Heart. Diseases — *Conference proceedings*

Paediatric cardiology. — Edinburgh : Churchill Livingstone
Vol.3 / edited by Anton E. Becker ... [et al.] ; foreword by Dirk Durrer. — 1981. — 485p : ill ; 24cm
Includes bibliographies and index
ISBN 0-443-02015-9 : £26.00 B82-03218

Paediatric cardiology. — Edinburgh : Churchill Livingstone
Proceedings of the World Congress of Paediatric Cardiology, London, 1980
Vol.4 / edited by M.J. Godman ; foreword by Fergus J. Macartney and Jane Somerville. — 1981. — 788p : ill ; forms ; 25cm
Includes bibliographies and index
ISBN 0-443-02139-2 : £38.00 : CIP rev.
B81-30895

618.92'12043'0240431 — Children. Heart. Congenital diseases — *Practical information — For parents*

Congenital heart disease. — London (57 Gloucester Place, W1H 4DH) : British Heart Foundation, 1980. — 12p ; 18cm. — (Heart research series ; no.5)
Unpriced (unbound) B82-19760

Congenital heart disease : advice to the parents of children born with heart disease. — Rev. and repr. — London (102 Gloucester Place, W1H 4DH) : British Heart Foundation, 1982. — 10p ; 18cm. — (Heart research series ; no.5)
Previous ed.: 1980
Unpriced (unbound) B82-40603

618.92'1205 — United States. Children. Heart. Diseases. Prevention. Role of cholesterol control

Berwick, Donald M.. Cholesterol, children, and heart disease : an analysis of alternatives / Donald M. Berwick, Shan Cretin, Emmett B. Keeler. — New York ; Oxford : Oxford University Press, 1980. — xiii,399p : ill ; 24cm
Bibliography: p366-392. — Includes index
ISBN 0-19-502669-1 : £18.00 B82-17273

618.92'15 — Children. Blood. Diseases

Ekert, Henry. Clinical paediatric haematology and oncology. — Oxford : Blackwell Scientific, Mar.1982. — [248]p
ISBN 0-632-00777-x : £20.00 : CIP entry
B82-14041

Hematology and oncology / edited by Michael Willoughby and Stuart E. Siegel. — London : Butterworth Scientific, 1982. — 306p : ill,1map ; 24cm. — (Butterworths international medical reviews. Pediatrics, ISSN 0260-0161 ; 1)
Includes bibliographies and index
ISBN 0-407-02308-9 : Unpriced : CIP rev.
Also classified at 618.92'994 B82-08078

618.92'15 — Children. Blood. Diseases — *Illustrations*

Colour atlas of paediatric haematology. — Oxford : Oxford University Press, Aug.1982. — [150]p
ISBN 0-19-261227-1 : £30.00 : CIP entry
B82-22798

618.92′2 — Children. Respiratory system. Diseases

Pediatric respiratory disease / edited by Jacques Gerbeaux, Jacques Couvreur, Guy Tournier ; translated by Edward H. Cooper. — 2nd ed. — New York ; Chichester : Wiley, c1982. — x,939p : ill ; 27cm
Translation of: Pathologie respiratoire de l'enfant. 2 éd. — Includes index
ISBN 0-471-03456-8 : £70.00 B82-21441

Phelan, P. D.. Respiratory illness in children. — 2nd ed. — Oxford : Blackwell Scientific, Sept.1982. — [512]p
Previous ed.: 1975
ISBN 0-632-01006-1 : £32.00 : CIP entry B82-28479

618.92′2 — Children. Respiratory system. Diseases — *Conference proceedings*

European Paediatric Respiratory Society. *Meeting (2nd : 1980 : Baden/Vienna)*. Paediatric respiratory disease : 2nd annual meeting of the European Paediatric Respiratory Society, Baden/Vienna, October 9-12, 1980 / volume editors M.H. Götz and O.B. Stur. — Basel ; London : S. Karger, c1981. — vii,306p : ill ; 25cm. — (Progress in respiration research, ISSN 0079-6751 ; v.17)
Includes bibliographies and index
ISBN 3-8055-2658-x : Unpriced B82-19715

618.92′2 — Children. Respiratory system. Respiratory failure

Respiratory failure in the child / edited by George A. Gregory. — New York ; Edinburgh : Churchill Livingstone, 1981. — xi,205p : ill ; 24cm. — (Clinics in critical care medicine ; 3)
Includes bibliographies and index
ISBN 0-443-08112-3 : £21.00 B82-16439

618.92′2′00222 — Children. Upper respiratory system. Diseases — *Illustrations*

Benjamin, Bruce. Atlas of paediatric endoscopy : upper respiratory tract and oesophagus / Bruce Benjamin. — Oxford : Oxford University Press, 1981. — 133p : ill(some col.) ; 25cm. — (Oxford medical publications)
ISBN 0-19-261179-8 : £30.00 : CIP rev.
Also classified at 618.92′32′00222 B79-21789

618.92′20046′077 — Newborn babies. Respiratory system. Therapy — *Programmed instructions*

Hirnle, Robert W.. Clinical simulations in neonatal respiratory therapy / Robert W. Hirnle ; consultant Edmund Egan. — New York ; Chichester : Wiley, c1982. — 316p ; 24cm
Bibliography: p315-316
ISBN 0-471-08266-x (spiral) : £11.75 B82-18062

618.92′32′00222 — Children. Oesophagus. Diseases — *Illustrations*

Benjamin, Bruce. Atlas of paediatric endoscopy : upper respiratory tract and oesophagus / Bruce Benjamin. — Oxford : Oxford University Press, 1981. — 133p : ill(some col.) ; 25cm. — (Oxford medical publications)
ISBN 0-19-261179-8 : £30.00 : CIP rev.
Primary classification 618.92′2′00222 B79-21789

618.92′3427 — Children. Diarrhoeal diseases — *Conference proceedings*

Acute enteric infections in children. New prospects for treatment and prevention : proceedings of the Third Nobel Conference, sponsored by the Marcus Wallenberg Foundation for International Cooperation in Science and the World Health Organization / edited by Tord Holme ... [et al.]. — Amsterdam ; London : Elsevier/North-Holland Biomedical, 1981. — xxi,549p : ill ; 25cm
Includes index
ISBN 0-444-80328-9 : £62.42 B82-15243

618.92′3623′00724 — Children. Liver. Viral hepatitis. Research. Applications of mathematical models

Mathematical methods in clinical practice / editors in chief, G.I. Marchuk and N.I. Nisevich. — Oxford : Pergamon, 1980. — viii,105p : ill ; 26cm
Translation of: Matematicheskie metody v klinicheskoĭ praktike. — Includes index
ISBN 0-08-025493-4 : £25.00 : CIP rev. B80-27101

618.92′39 — Children. Metabolic disorders & nutritional disorders

Krieger, Ingeborg. Pediatric disorders of feeding, nutrition and metabolism / Ingeborg Krieger. — New York ; Chichester : Wiley, c1982. — ix,409p : ill ; 25cm
Includes index
ISBN 0-471-08730-0 : £23.00 B82-34336

618.92′4 — Children. Endocrine system. Diseases

Clinical paediatric endocrinology / edited by Charles G.D. Brook. — Oxford : Blackwell Scientific, 1981. — ix,684p : ill ; 26cm
Includes bibliographies and index
ISBN 0-632-00698-6 : £48.00 : CIP rev. B81-08799

A **Practical** approach to pediatric endocrinology / George E. Bacon ... [et al.]. — 2nd ed. — Chicago ; London : Year Book Medical, c1982. — xi,275p : ill ; 24cm
Previous ed.: 1975. — Includes index
ISBN 0-8151-0404-9 : £38.25 B82-36091

618.92′5 — Children. Skin. Diseases

Verbov, Julian. Colour atlas of paediatric dermatology. — Lancaster : MTP Press, Oct.1982. — [160]p
ISBN 0-85200-474-5 : £26.95 : CIP entry B82-29024

618.92′6 — Children. Urinary tract. Diseases

Pediatric urology. — 2nd ed. / edited by D. Innes Williams, J.H. Johnston. — London : Butterworths, 1982. — x,581p : ill ; 25cm
Previous ed.: 1968. — Includes bibliographies and index
ISBN 0-407-35152-3 : £45.00 : CIP rev. B81-34665

618.92′61 — Children. Kidneys. Diseases — *Conference proceedings*

International Pediatric Nephrology Symposium *(5th : 1980 : Philadelphia)*. Pediatric nephrology : proceedings of the Fifth International Pediatric Nephrology Symposium, held in Philadelphia, PA, October 6-10, 1980 / edited by Alan B. Gruskin and Michael E. Norman. — The Hague ; London : Nijhoff, 1981. — xii,530p : ill ; 25cm. — (Developments in nephrology ; v.3)
ISBN 90-247-2514-3 : Unpriced B82-03461

Symposium on Pediatric Nephrology. *(3rd : 1979 : San Juan)*. Recent advances in pediatric nephrology : 3rd Symposium on Pediatric Nephrology, San Juan, December 4-7, 1979 / volume editors J.F. Pascual, Ph.L. Calcagno. — Basel ; London : Karger, c1981. — 97p : ill ; 23cm. — (Contributions to nephrology ; v.27)
Includes bibliographies and index
ISBN 3-8055-1851-x (pbk) : £19.50 B82-06298

618.92′63 — Children. Enuresis. Prevention — *Manuals — For parents*

Marshall, Margaret. Mike. — London : Bodley Head, Jan.1983. — [32]p
ISBN 0-370-30934-0 : £3.95 : CIP entry B82-34423

618.92′63 — Children. Incontinence

Morgan, Roger, *1949-*. Childhood incontinence : a guide to problems of wetting and soiling for parents and professionals / Roger Morgan ; illustrations by Bill Brennan. — London : Published for the Disabled Living Foundation by Heinemann Medical, 1981. — xi,[96]p : ill,forms ; 21cm
Bibliography: p96
ISBN 0-433-22220-4 (pbk) : Unpriced B82-17179

618.92′72 — Children. Arthrogryposis

Arthrogryposis / [text and photographs by members of Chailey Heritage staff]. — North Chailey (North Chailey, Lewes, Sussex) : Chailey Heritage, [1982?]. — 17p : ill ; 21cm. — (Chailey Heritage information for independence ; 2)
£0.30 (unbound) B82-36551

618.92′72 — Children. Hips. Joints. Perthes′ disease

Catterall, Anthony. Legg-Calvé-Perthes′ disease / Anthony Catterall ; foreword by G.C. Lloyd-Roberts. — Edinburgh : Churchill Livingstone, 1982. — xii,115p : ill,ports ; 26cm. — (Current problems in orthopaedics)
Includes bibliographies and index
ISBN 0-443-01942-8 : £16.00 : CIP rev. B82-01960

618.92′74 — Children. Motor delay. Therapy

Levitt, Sophie. Treatment of cerebral palsy and motor delay / Sophie Levitt ; with a foreword by Mary D. Sheridan. — 2nd ed. — Oxford : Blackwell Scientific, c1982. — xiii,267p : ill ; 24cm
Previous ed.: 1977. — Includes index
ISBN 0-632-00916-0 (pbk) : £11.75 : CIP rev.
Primary classification 618.92′83606 B82-12144

618.92′8 — Children. Brain. Intracranial pressure

International Society for Paediatric Neurosurgery. *Meeting (9th : 1981 : Budapest)*. ICP in infancy and childhood / 9th Meeting of the International Society for Paediatric Neurosurgery, Budapest, July 20-22, 1981 ; volume editor E. Paraicz. — Basel ; London : Karger, c1982. — vii,146p : ill ; 24cm. — (Monographs in paediatrics ; v.15)
ISBN 3-8055-3475-2 (pbk) : Unpriced B82-40351

618.92′8 — Children. Nervous system. Diseases

Hosking, Gwilym. An introduction to paediatric neurology / Gwilym Hosking. — London : Faber, 1982. — 252p : ill ; 21cm
Includes bibliographies and index
ISBN 0-571-11848-8 (cased) : £11.50 : CIP rev.
ISBN 0-571-11849-6 (pbk) : Unpriced B82-06946

The **Practice** of pediatric neurology / [edited by] Kenneth F. Swaiman, Francis S. Wright with the collaboration of 46 contributors. — 2nd ed. — St Louis ; London : Mosby, 1982. — 2v. : ill(some col.) ; 29cm
Previous ed: 1975. — Includes bibliographies and index
ISBN 0-8016-4829-7 : £125.00 B82-33954

Vasella, F.. Neuropädiatrie II / F. Vasella. — Basel ; London : Karger, c1982. — 189p : ill ; 23cm. — (Pädiatrische Fortbildungskurse für die Praxis)
Chapters in German, French and English. — Includes bibliographies
ISBN 3-8055-3434-5 (pbk) : Unpriced B82-35976

618.92′8 — Great Britain. Children. Stress

Wolff, Sula. Children under stress / Sula Wolff. — 2nd ed. — Harmondsworth : Penguin, 1981. — 267p ; 20cm
Previous ed.: i.e. rev. ed. 1973. — Bibliography: p245-256. — Includes index
ISBN 0-14-021548-4 (pbk) : £1.95 B82-01392

618.92′80442 — Children. Nervous system. Genetic metabolic disorders

Adams, Raymond D.. Neurology of hereditary metabolic diseases of children / Raymond D. Adams, Gilles Lyon. — Washington ; London : Hemisphere, c1982. — xiv,442p : ill ; 24cm
Includes index
ISBN 0-07-000318-1 : £37.95 B82-28056

618.92′804754 — Newborn babies. Nervous system. Diagnosis. Physical examination — *Manuals*

Dubowitz, Lilly M. S.. The neurological assessment of the preterm and full-term newborn infant / Lilly Dubowitz and Victor Dubowitz. — [London] : Spastics International Medical Publications, 1981. — viii,103p : ill,facsims ; 25cm. — (Clinics in developmental medicine ; no.79)
Bibliography: p102-103
ISBN 0-433-07903-7 : Unpriced B82-04275

618.92′836 — Children. Cerebral palsy — *Polyglot texts*
Zerebrale Bewegungsstörungen : Aktuelle Fragen der Klinik und Forschung : Jubiläumstagung 25 Jahre Schweizerische Zentren für zerebrale Bewegungsstörungen, Bern, 15. und 16. September 1980 / Herausgeber des Bandes E. Köng. — Basel ; London : Karger, 1982. — 197p : ill ; 22cm. — (Pädiatrische Fortbildungskurse für die Praxis ; 53)
English, German and French text. — Includes bibliographies
ISBN 3-8055-3413-2 (pbk) : Unpriced B82-25553

618.92′836 — Children. Hemiplegic cerebral palsy. Therapy. Serial splints
Jones, Margaret, *1936-*. Serial splitting in hemiplegic cerebral palsy / Margaret Jones. — Menston : The Association of Paediatric Chartered Physiotherapists, [1982?]. — 40p : ill ; 21cm
ISBN 0-906815-06-1 (pbk) : Unpriced B82-38973

618.92′83606 — Children. Cerebral palsy. Therapy
Levitt, Sophie. Treatment of cerebral palsy and motor delay / Sophie Levitt ; with a foreword by Mary D. Sheridan. — 2nd ed. — Oxford : Blackwell Scientific, c1982. — xiii,267p : ill ; 24cm
Previous ed.: 1977. — Includes index
ISBN 0-632-00916-0 (pbk) : £11.75 : CIP rev.
Also classified at 618.92′74 B82-12144

618.92′853′0024372 — England. Children. Epilepsy — *For teaching*
Epilepsy : a guide for teachers / [British Epilepsy Association]. — Wokingham ([Crowthorne House, Bigshotte, New Wokingham Rd., Wokingham, Berks. RG11 3AY]) : British Epilepsy Association, [1982?]. — 4p ; 22cm. — (Action for epilepsy)
Cover title
Unpriced (pbk) B82-37564

618.92′855 — Children. Language disorders
Aram, Dorothy M.. Child language disorders / Dorothy M. Aram, James E. Nation. — St. Louis ; London : Mosby, 1982. — xii,302p : ill ; 25cm
Bibliography: p257-279. — Includes index
ISBN 0-8016-0288-2 : £12.75 B82-25709

Carrow-Woolfolk, Elizabeth. An integrative approach to language disorders in children / Elizabeth Carrow-Woolfolk, Joan I. Lynch. — New York ; London : Grune & Stratton, c1982. — xi,494p : ill ; 27cm
Bibliography: p451-484. — Includes index
ISBN 0-8089-1406-5 : £19.60 B82-27132

Wood, Mary Lovey. Language disorders in school age children / Mary Lovey Wood. — Englewood Cliffs ; London : Prentice-Hall, c1982. — xiii,156p ; 24cm. — (Remediation of communication disorders series)
Bibliography: p140-150. — Includes index
ISBN 0-13-522946-4 : £14.20 B82-33768

618.92′855 — Children. Speech disorders — *For children*
Althea. I can't talk like you / by Althea ; illustrated by Isabel Pearce. — Cambridge : Dinosaur, c1982. — [24]p : col.ill ; 16x19cm
ISBN 0-85122-345-1 (cased) : Unpriced
ISBN 0-85122-344-3 (pbk) : Unpriced B82-31817

618.92′85506 — Pre-school children. Language disorders. Therapy. Intervention programmes
Cole, Patricia R.. Language disorders in preschool children / Patricia R. Cole. — Englewood Cliffs ; London : Prentice-Hall, c1982. — xiv,178p : ill ; 24cm
Bibliography: p165-174. — Includes index
ISBN 0-13-522862-x : £14.20 B82-29486

618.92′85506 — United States. Schools. Students. Speech disorders. Therapy
Taylor, Joyce S.. Speech-language pathology : services in the schools / Joyce S. Taylor. — New York ; London : Grune & Stratton, c1981. — xiii,205p : ill,plans,forms ; 24cm
Includes bibliographies and index
ISBN 0-8089-1385-9 : Unpriced B82-10557

618.92′8553 — Children. Reading disorders
Brown, Don A.. Reading diagnosis and remediation / Don A. Brown. — Englewood Cliffs ; London : Prentice-Hall, c1982. — xi,385p : ill,forms ; 25cm
Includes index
ISBN 0-13-754952-0 : £15.70 B82-35168

618.92′858 — Children. Emotional problems. Treatment
Emotional disorders in children and adolescents : medical and psychological approaches to treatment / edited by G. Pirooz Sholevar with Ronald M. Benson and Barton J. Blinder. — Lancaster : MTP, c1980. — 710p ; 27cm. — (Child behavior and development)
Includes bibliographies and index
ISBN 0-85200-545-8 : £35.00 B82-31261

618.92′8588′071 — Children. Mental handicaps. Causes & prevention
Some facts on cause and prevention of mental handicap / prepared and published by the National Association for the Mentally Handicapped of Ireland. — Dublin (5 Fitzwilliam Place, Dublin 2) : The Association, 1976. — 8p : ill ; 22cm
Unpriced (pbk) B82-17863

618.92′8588075 — Children. Mental handicaps. Assessment — *Conference proceedings*
Assessing the handicaps and needs of mentally retarded children / edited by Brian Cooper. — London : Academic, 1981. — xii,269p : ill ; 24cm
Conference papers. — Includes bibliographies and index
ISBN 0-12-188020-6 : £11.80 : CIP rev. B81-11930

618.92′8589 — Children. Hyperactivity
Ross, Dorothea M.. Hyperactivity : current issues, research and theory / Dorothea M. Ross, Sheila A. Ross. — 2nd ed. — New York ; Chichester : Wiley, c1982. — xiii,491p : ill ; 25cm. — (Wiley series on personality processes, ISSN 0195-4008)
Previous ed.: 1976. — Text on lining papers. — Bibliography: p405-464. — Includes index
ISBN 0-471-06331-2 : Unpriced B82-38322

618.92′8589 — Children. Hyperactivity. Diagnosis & therapy
Barkley, Russell A.. Hyperactive children : a handbook for diagnosis and treatment / Russell A. Barkley ; foreword by Dennis P. Cantwell. — Chichester : Wiley, 1982, c1981. — xvii,458p : ill,forms ; 24cm
Includes bibliographies and index
ISBN 0-471-10147-8 : £19.50 B82-12298

618.92′858906 — Children. Hyperactivity. Behaviour therapy
Strategic intervention for hyperactive children / edited by Martin Gittelman ; with a foreword by Joseph Wolpe. — Armonk, N.Y. : Sharpe ; London : distributed by Eurospan, c1981. — vii,215p : ill ; 24cm
Includes bibliographies
ISBN 0-87332-202-9 : £15.00 B82-17301

618.92′89 — Children. Behavioural disorders
Erickson, Marilyn T.. Child psychopathology : behavior disorders and developmental disabilities / Marilyn T. Erickson. — 2nd ed. — Englewood Cliffs ; London : Prentice-Hall, c1982. — xii,354p : ill ; 25cm
Previous ed.: 1978. — Bibliography: p313-341. — Includes index
ISBN 0-13-131094-1 : £16.45 B82-20081

Weiner, Irving B.. Child and adolescent psychopathology / Irving B. Weiner. — New York ; Chichester : Wiley, c1982. — x,529p : ill,ports ; 25cm
Includes bibliographies and index
ISBN 0-471-04709-0 : £15.95 B82-34521

618.92′89 — Children. Behavioural disorders — *For medicine*
Behavioral pediatrics : research and practice / edited by Dennis C. Russo, James W. Varni. — New York ; London : Plenum, c1982. — xiv,417p : ill ; 24cm
Includes bibliographies and index
ISBN 0-306-40961-5 : Unpriced B82-38665

Block, Robert W.. Handbook of behavioral pediatrics / Robert W. Block, Francis C. Rash. — Chicago ; London : Year Book Medical, c1981. — xiii,231p ; 16cm
Includes bibliographies and index
ISBN 0-8151-0835-4 (pbk) : £10.75 B82-18076

618.92′89 — Children. Psychiatry
Evans, J.. Adolescent and pre-adolescent psychiatry. — London : Academic Press, Oct.1982. — [520]p
ISBN 0-12-791168-5 : CIP entry
Primary classification 616.89′022 B82-24943

Steinberg, Derek. Using child psychiatry : the functions and operations of a specialty / Derek Steinberg ; illustrated by Vanessa Pancheri. — [London] : Teach Yourself, 1981. — x,204p : ill ; 18cm. — (Care and welfare)
Bibliography: p191-200. — Includes index
ISBN 0-340-26835-2 (pbk) : £1.95 : CIP rev. B81-28077

618.92′89′0024362 — Children. Psychiatry — *For welfare workers*
Lask, Judith. Child psychiatry and social work / Judith Lask & Bryan Lask. — London : Tavistock, 1981. — xiv,209p ; 22cm. — (Tavistock library of social work practice)
Bibliography: p181-199. — Includes index
ISBN 0-422-77080-9 (cased) : Unpriced : CIP rev.
ISBN 0-422-77090-6 (pbk) : £4.50 B81-21556

618.92′89′007 — Children. Psychiatry. Information sources
Tite, Catherine. A guide to media resources on child psychiatry. — London (Calcutta House, Old Castle St., E1 7NT) : LLRS Publications, Dec.1982. — [33]p
ISBN 0-904264-68-8 (pbk) : £1.00 : CIP entry B82-37494

618.92′8907 — Children. Psychopathology
Achenbach, Thomas M.. Developmental psychopathology / Thomas M. Achenbach. — 2nd ed. — New York ; Chichester : Wiley, c1982. — xiv,770p : ill ; 24cm
Previous ed.: 1974. — Bibliography: p657-730. — Includes index
ISBN 0-471-05536-0 : Unpriced B82-37960

Lavigne, John V.. Pediatric psychology : an introduction for pediatricians and psychologists / ; John V. Lavigne, William J. Burns. — New York ; London : Grune & Stratton, c1981. — xi,375p ; 26cm
Includes index
ISBN 0-8089-1365-4 : £22.80 B82-18676

618.92′89075 — Children. Psychiatry. Interviewing — *Manuals*
Greenspan, Stanley I.. The clinical interview of the child / Stanley I. Greenspan with the collaboration of Nancy Thorndike Greenspan. — New York ; London : McGraw-Hill, c1981. — 203p ; 24cm
Bibliography: p193-194. — Includes index
ISBN 0-07-024340-9 : £13.50 B82-04450

618.92′8914 — Children of divorced parents. Psychotherapy
Children of separation and divorce : management and treatment / edited by Irving R. Stuart, and Lawrence Edwin Abt. — New York ; London : Van Nostrand Reinhold, c1981. — xv,365p ; 24cm
Includes bibliographies and index
ISBN 0-442-24431-2 B82-00852

618.92′89′14 — Maladjusted children. Psychotherapy
Methods in social and educational caring. — Aldershot : Gower, Mar.1982. — [152]p
ISBN 0-566-00386-4 : £12.00 : CIP entry B82-00196

618.92′89142 — Children. Behaviour therapy
Ollendick, Thomas H.. Clinical behavior therapy with children / Thomas H. Ollendick and Jerome A. Cerny. — New York ; London : Plenum, c1981. — xii,351p : ill ; 24cm. — (Applied clinical psychology)
Bibliography: p304-347. — Includes index
ISBN 0-306-40774-4 : Unpriced B82-14278

618.92'89'17 — Children. Psychoanalysis

Sandler, Joseph. The technique of child psychoanalysis : discussions with Anna Freud / by Joseph Sandler, Hansi Kennedy and Robert L. Tyson. — London : Hogarth, 1980. — 277p ; 23cm. — (The International psycho-analytical library ; no.110)
Includes index
ISBN 0-7012-0512-1 : £12.50 : CIP rev.
B80-19793

618.92'89'170926 — Children. Psychoanalysis — *Case studies — Serials*

The **Psychoanalytic** study of the child. — Vol.36. — London : Yale University Press, Jan.1982. — [554]p
ISBN 0-300-02762-1 : £24.50 : CIP entry
B82-02446

618.92'8'982 — Children. Autism

Tinebergen, N.. Autistic children. — London : Allen and Unwin, Jan.1983. — [320]p
ISBN 0-04-157010-3 : £19.50 : CIP entry
B82-33593

618.92'9 — Children. Communicable diseases

Illingworth, Ronald S.. Infections — and immunisation of your child / Ronald S. Illingworth. — Edinburgh : Churchill Livingstone, 1981. — 73p ; 19cm. — (Churchill Livingstone patent handbook ; 6)
ISBN 0-443-02238-0 (pbk) : £1.20 : CIP rev.
B81-19159

618.92'9883'05 — Tropical regions. Children. Diseases — *Serials*

Annals of tropical paediatrics. — Vol.1, no.1 (Mar. 1981)-. — London : Academic Press for Liverpool School of Tropical Medicine, 1981-. — v. : ill ; 25cm
Quarterly. — Description based on: Vol.1, no.2 (June 1981)
ISSN 0272-4936 = Annals of tropical paediatrics (corrected) : £35.00 per year
B82-07629

618.92'994 — Children. Cancer

Hematology and oncology / edited by Michael Willoughby and Stuart E. Siegel. — London : Butterworth Scientific, 1982. — 306p : ill,1map ; 24cm. — (Butterworths international medical reviews. Pediatrics, ISSN 0260-0161 ; 1)
Includes bibliographies and index
ISBN 0-407-02308-9 : Unpriced : CIP rev.
Primary classification 618.92'15 B82-08078

618.92'994 — Children. Cancer — *Conference proceedings*

San Francisco Cancer Symposium *(16th : 1981)*. Childhood cancer : triumph over tragedy : 16th annual San Francisco Cancer Symposium, San Francisco, Calif. March 13-14, 1981 / editor Jerome M. Vaeth. — Basel ; London : Karger, 1982. — vi,191p : ill ; 24cm. — (Frontiers of radiation therapy and oncology ; v.16)
Includes bibliographies
ISBN 3-8055-3020-x : £42.00 B82-28705

618.92'994 — Children. Malignant tumours

International Society of Pediatric Oncology. *Meeting (13th : 1981 : Marseilles)*. Pediatric oncology : proceedings of the XIIIth Meeting of the International Society of Pediatric Oncology, Marseilles, September 15-19, 1981 / editors C. Raybaud ... [et al.]. — Amsterdam ; Oxford : Excerpta Medica, 1982. — xiv,407p : ill ; 25cm. — (International congress series ; no.570)
Includes bibliographies and index
ISBN 90-219-0518-3 : Unpriced
ISBN 0-444-90247-3 (Elsevier/North-Holland)
B82-32391

618.92'994'0019 — Children. Cancer. Psychosocial aspects — *Conference proceedings*

Living with childhood cancer / edited by John J. Spinetta, Patricia Deasy-Spinetta in consultation with Shirley L. Brandt. — St. Louis ; London : Mosby, 1981. — xvii,279p : ill ; 24cm
Conference papers. — Includes bibliographies and index
ISBN 0-8016-4764-9 (pbk) : £12.75
B82-08266

618.92'995 — Children. Tuberculosis

Miller, F. J. W.. Tuberculosis in children : evolution, epidemiology, treatment, prevention / F.J.W. Miller. — Edinburgh : Churchill Livingstone, 1982. — xvii,294p : ill,1map ; 22cm. — (Medicine in the tropics series)
Bibliography: p263-277. — Includes index
ISBN 0-443-01574-0 (pbk) : £8.00 : CIP rev.
B81-22688

618.97 — GERIATRICS

618.97 — Geriatrics

Adams, George F.. Essentials of geriatric medicine / George F. Adams. — 2nd ed. — Oxford : Oxford University Press, 1981. — xiv,146p ; 24cm. — (Oxford medical publications)
Previous ed.: 1977. — Bibliography: p133-137. — Includes index
ISBN 0-19-261352-9 (pbk) : £4.95 : CIP rev.
B81-21638

Hodgkinson, H. M.. An outline of geriatrics. — London : Academic Press, Apr.1981. — [160]p. — (Monographs for students of medicine)
Previous ed.: 1975
ISBN 0-12-351460-6 (pbk) : £4.80 : CIP entry
B81-06625

618.97 — Geriatrics — *For general practice*

Wilcock, G. K.. Geriatric problems in general practice. — Oxford : Oxford University Press, July 1982. — [325]p. — (Oxford medical publications) (Oxford general practice series ; 2)
ISBN 0-19-261313-8 (pbk) : £9.95 : CIP entry
B82-16501

618.97 — Man. Diseases. Effects of ageing

Dilman, V. M.. The law of deviation of homeostasis and diseases of aging / Vladimir M. Dilman ; edited by Herman T. Blumenthal. — Boston, [Mass.] ; Bristol : John Wright, c1981. — xiii,380p : ill ; 25cm
Bibliography: p331-372. — Includes index
ISBN 0-88416-250-8 : Unpriced B82-16121

618.97 — Old persons. Medical aspects

Brocklehurst, J. C.. Geriatric medicine for students / J.C. Brocklehurst, T. Hanley. — 2nd ed. — Edinburgh : Churchill Livingstone, 1981. — 236p : ill ; 22cm. — (Churchill Livingstone medical texts)
Previous ed.: 1976. — Includes bibliographies and index
ISBN 0-443-02491-x (pbk) : £4.95 : CIP rev.
B81-28049

618.97 — Old persons. Medical care

Medical care for the elderly / editor, Ian Smith. — Lancaster : MTP, 1982. — 269p : ill ; 24cm
Includes bibliographies and index
ISBN 0-85200-582-2 : £23.25 B82-29343

618.97'005 — Geriatrics - *Serials*

Advanced geriatric medicine. — 1. — London : Pitman Medical, Sept.1981. — [176]p
ISBN 0-272-79629-8 : £10.00 : CIP entry
B81-20569

618.97'005 — Geriatrics — *Serials*

Advanced geriatric medicine. — 1-. — London : Pitman, 1981-. — v. : ill,forms ; 24cm
Annual
ISSN 0261-2763 = Advanced geriatric medicine : Unpriced B82-07631

Advanced geriatric medicine. — 2. — London : Pitman, June 1982. — 1v.
ISBN 0-272-79670-0 (pbk) : £12.50 : CIP entry
ISSN 0261-2763 B82-14959

Recent advances in geriatric medicine. — No.2. — Edinburgh : Churchill Livingstone, Jan.1982. — [280]p
ISBN 0-443-02320-4 (pbk) : £14.00 : CIP entry
ISSN 0144-0519 B81-34505

618.97'061 — Old persons. Drug therapy

Judge, T. G.. Drug treatment of the elderly patient. — 2nd ed. — London : Pitman, Oct.1982. — [144]p
Previous ed.: 1978
ISBN 0-272-79676-x : £5.95 : CIP entry
B82-23479

618.97'68 — Old persons. Nervous system. Diseases

Neurological disorders in the elderly / edited by F.I. Caird ; with a foreword by John A. Simpson. — Bristol : John Wright, 1982. — xi,250p : ill ; 23cm
Includes index
ISBN 0-7236-0632-3 : Unpriced : CIP rev.
B82-02659

618.97'68527 — Old persons. Depression

Blazer, Dan G.. Depression in late life / Dan G. Blazer II. — St. Louis ; London : Mosby, 1982. — xiv,304p : ill ; 25cm
Includes bibliographies and index
ISBN 0-8016-0820-1 : £18.25 B82-16566

618.97'689 — Geriatrics. Psychiatry

The **Psychiatry** of late life. — Oxford : Blackwell Scientific, Sept.1982. — [304]p
ISBN 0-632-00962-4 : £15.50 : CIP entry
B82-20764

618.97'689 — Old persons. Mental disorders

Butler, Robert N.. Aging & mental health : positive psychosocial and biomedical approaches / Robert N. Butler, Myrna I. Lewis. — 3rd ed. — St. Louis ; London : Mosby, 1982. — xxii,483p : ill,forms,ports ; 24cm
Previous ed.: 1977. — Includes bibliographies and index
ISBN 0-8016-0924-0 (pbk) : £12.00
B82-16561

Pitt, Brice. Psychogeriatrics : an introduction to the psychiatry of old age / Brice Pitt ; foreword by W. Ferguson Anderson. — 2nd ed. — Edinburgh : Churchill Livingstone, 1982. — viii,224p ; 22cm
Previous ed.: 1974. — Bibliography: p214-215. — Includes index
ISBN 0-443-01598-8 (pbk) : Unpriced : CIP rev. B82-09711

618.97'689 — United States. Old persons. Mental disorders. Assessment & therapy — *For welfare work*

Zarit, Steven H.. Aging and mental disorders : psychological approaches to assessment and treatment / Steven H. Zarit with a chapter by Robert M. Tager. — New York : Free Press ; London : Collier Macmillan, c1980. — x,454p : ill ; 25cm
Bibliography: p409-444. — Includes index
ISBN 0-02-935850-7 : £12.95 B82-18899

618.97'68983 — Old persons. Senile dementia

Reisberg, Barry. Brain failure : an introduction to current concepts of senility / Barry Reisberg. — New York : Free Press ; London : Collier Macmillan, c1981. — xvi,198p : ill ; 25cm
Bibliography: p184-189. — Includes index
ISBN 0-02-926260-7 : £12.95 B82-18010

618.97'68983 — Old persons. Senile dementia. Epidemiology

The **Epidemiology** of dementia / edited by James A. Mortimer and Leonard M. Schuman. — New York ; Oxford : Oxford University Press, 1981. — xii,187p : ill ; 24cm. — (Monographs in epidemiology and biostatistics)
Includes bibliographies and index
ISBN 0-19-502906-2 : £16.00 B82-18948

618.97'6898306 — Senile dementia victims. Psychotherapy. Reality orientation therapy

Holden, Una P.. Reality orientation : psychological approaches to the confused elderly / Una P. Holden, Robert T. Woods. — Edinburgh : Churchill Livingstone, 1982. — vii,283p : ill ; 22cm
Bibliography: p263-273. — Includes index
ISBN 0-443-02276-3 (pbk) : Unpriced : CIP rev. B82-06839

618.97'7585 — Old persons. Feet. Diseases

Clinical podogeriatrics / Arthur E. Helfand, editor. — Baltimore ; London : Williams & Wilkins, c1981. — xxi,285p : ill,2forms ; 26cm
Bibliography: p208-213. — Includes index
ISBN 0-683-03951-2 : Unpriced B82-07784

619 — EXPERIMENTAL MEDICINE

619 — Man. Strokes. Models: Strokes in laboratory animals — *Conference proceedings*

Stroke : animal models. — Oxford : Pergamon, Dec.1982. — [200]p. — (Advances in the biosciences)
Conference papers
ISBN 0-08-029799-4 : £25.00 : CIP entry
B82-30594

619 — Medicine. Research. Use of laboratory animals

Methods of animal experimentation / edited by William I. Gay. — New York ; London : Academic Press
Vol.6. — 1981. — xiv,365p : ill ; 24cm
Includes index
ISBN 0-12-278006-x : £31.40 B82-37235

619'.93 — Medicine. Research. Laboratory animals: Nude mice

The **Nude** mouse in experimental and clinical research / edited by Jørgen Fogh, Beppino C. Giovanella. — New York ; London : Academic Press
Vol.2. — 1982. — xx,587p : ill ; 24cm
Includes index
ISBN 0-12-261862-9 : £38.40 B82-37793

619'.93 — Medicine. Research. Use of laboratory animals: Mice

The **Mouse** in biomedical research. — New York ; London : Academic Press. — (American College of Laboratory Animal Medicine series)
Vol.1: History, genetics, and wild mice / edited by Henry L. Foster, J. David Small, James G. Fox. — 1981. — xiii,306p : ill,1map,ports ; 29cm
Includes bibliographies and index
ISBN 0-12-262501-3 : £35.80 B82-11401

620 — ENGINEERING

620 — Consulting engineering

Stanley, C. Maxwell. The consulting engineer / C. Maxwell Stanley. — 2nd ed. — New York ; Chichester : Wiley, c1982. — viii,303p : ill ; 24cm
Previous ed.: 1961. — Bibliography: p295-296. — Includes index
ISBN 0-471-08920-6 : £19.60 B82-13387

620 — Engineering

Bird, J. O.. Engineering science 2 checkbook. — London : Butterworths, Nov.1982. — [192]p. — (Butterworths technical and scientific checkbooks)
ISBN 0-408-00691-9 (cased) : £8.95 : CIP entry
ISBN 0-408-00627-7 (pbk) : £3.95 B82-28276

Blotter, P. Thomas. Introduction to engineering / P. Thomas Blotter. — New York ; Chichester : Wiley, c1981. — xii,289p : ill ; 24cm
Text on lining papers. — Includes index
ISBN 0-471-04935-2 : £13.40 B82-03901

Duderstadt, James J.. Principles of engineering / James J. Duderstadt, Glenn F. Knoll, George S. Springer. — New York ; Chichester : Wiley, c1982. — xiii,558p : ill(some col.) ; 25cm
Includes index
ISBN 0-471-08445-x : £18.70 B82-30698

Laithwaite, E. R.. Engineer through the looking-glass / Eric Laithwaite. — London : British Broadcasting Corporation, 1980. — 114p : ill ; 26cm
Includes index
ISBN 0-563-12979-4 : £8.25 B82-40471

620 — Engineering. Decision making

Decision models for industrial systems engineers and managers. — Oxford : Pergamon, June 1981. — [476]p
ISBN 0-08-027612-1 : £29.00 : CIP entry
B81-17535

620 — Engineering science — *For technicians*

McDonagh, I.. Engineering science for technicians / I. McDonagh and G. Waterworth ; illustrated by R.P. Phillips. — London : Edward Arnold
Previous ed.: 1977. — Includes index
Vol.1. — 2nd ed. — 1982. — vii,248p : ill ; 22cm
ISBN 0-7131-3465-8 (pbk) : £4.25 : CIP rev.
B82-01189

Page, M. G.. Technician engineering science II. — London : Hodder and Stoughton, Aug.1982. — [192]p
ISBN 0-340-22365-0 (pbk) : £3.95 : CIP entry
B82-21377

Redford, G. D.. Science for mechanical engineers for TEC Level II. — Cheltenham : Thornes, May 1982. — [264]p
ISBN 0-85950-313-5 (pbk) : £4.50 : CIP entry
B82-07038

Titherington, D.. Engineering science / D. Titherington, J.G. Rimmer. — London : McGraw-Hill
Vol.2: A third level course. — c1982. — ix,184p : ill ; 22cm. — (Technical education series)
Includes index
ISBN 0-07-084646-4 (pbk) : £4.25 : CIP rev.
B81-39249

620 — Harbours. Equipment — *For children*

Hudson, Kenneth. Waterside furniture / Kenneth Hudson. — London : Bodley Head, 1982. — 48p : ill ; 25cm
Includes index
ISBN 0-370-30393-8 : £3.95 : CIP rev.
Primary classification 942 B82-03837

620 — Sensor systems — *Serials*

Sensor review : international quarterly. — Vol.1, no.1 (Jan. 1981)-. — Bedford (35 High St., Kempston, Bedford MK42 7BT) : IFS, 1981-. — v. : ill,facsims ; 30cm
ISSN 0260-2288 = Sensor review : £34.00 per year
B82-04887

620'.001'51 — Engineering. Mathematics

The **Application** of mathematics in industry / edited by Robert S. Anderssen and Frank R. de Hoog. — The Hague ; London : Nijhoff, 1982. — xiv,202p : ill,1plan ; 25cm
Conference papers. — Includes bibliographies and index
ISBN 90-247-2590-9 : Unpriced B82-21454

620'.001'51 — Engineering. Mathematics — *For technicians*

Bird, J. O.. Engineering mathematics and science 3 checkbook / J.O. Bird, A.J.C. May, D.S. Ayling. — London : Butterworths, 1982. — viii,166p : ill ; 20cm. — (Butterworths technical and scientific checkbooks)
Includes index
ISBN 0-408-00670-6 (cased) : Unpriced : CIP rev.
ISBN 0-408-00625-0 (pbk) : Unpriced
B81-34114

620'.001'515353 — Engineering. Mathematics. Boundary element methods

Banerjee, P. K.. Boundary element methods in engineering science / P.K. Banerjee and R. Butterfield. — London : McGraw-Hill, c1981. — xiv,452p : ill ; 23cm
Includes index
ISBN 0-07-084120-9 (pbk) : £14.95
B82-03527

Mukherjee, Subrata. Boundary element methods in creep and fracture. — London : Applied Science, Nov.1982. — [200]p
ISBN 0-85334-163-x : £26.00 : CIP entry
B82-26316

620'.001'515353 — Engineering. Mathematics. Finite element methods

Bathe, Klaus-Jürgen. Finite element procedures in engineering analysis / Klaus-Jürgen Bathe. — Englewood Cliffs ; London : Prentice-Hall, c1982. — xiii,735p : ill ; 24cm. — (Prentice-Hall civil engineering and engineering mechanics series)
ISBN 0-13-317305-4 : £28.50 B82-27560

620'.00228 — Engineering models. Making — *Manuals*

Cain, Tubal. Model engineers handbook / Tubal Cain. — Watford : Model & Allied, c1981. — 170p : ill ; 21cm
Includes index
ISBN 0-85242-715-8 (pbk) : £4.95 B82-31834

620'.00228 — Engineering. Models. Use

David, F. W.. Experimental modelling in engineering / F.W. David and H. Nolle. — London : Butterworths, 1982. — 185p : ill ; 24cm
Includes index
ISBN 0-408-01139-4 : Unpriced : CIP rev.
B81-25306

620'.00228 — Radio controlled models — *Manuals*

Warring, R. H. Radio control for modellers / by R.H. Warring. — Guildford : Lutterworth, 1981. — 132p : ill,plans ; 23cm. — (Practical handbook series)
Includes index
ISBN 0-7188-2519-5 : £6.95 B82-05796

620'.00228 — Radio controlled models. Radio controls

Newell, Paul. Radio control : a handbook of theory and practice / by Paul Newell. — Guildford ([P.O. Box 81], Guildford, Surrey, GU1 3RL) : RM Books, 1981. — 181p,[1]p of plates : ill,1port ; 21cm
Unpriced (pbk) B82-05517

620'.0023 — Engineering as a profession

Kemper, John Dustin. Engineers and their profession / John Dustin Kemper. — 3rd ed. — New York ; London : Holt, Rinehart and Winston, c1982. — xv,310p : ill ; 24cm
Previous ed.: published as The engineer and his profession, 1975. — Includes index
ISBN 0-03-059042-6 (pbk) : £11.95
B82-15360

620'.0023'41 — Great Britain. Engineering — *Career guides* — *For graduates*

The **DOG** guide to engineering / [editor Iris Rosier]. — [London] : [VNU Business Publications], [1981?]. — 60p : ill ; 25cm
Cover title
ISBN 0-86271-018-9 (corrected : pbk) : Unpriced B82-05186

620'.0028 — Industrial equipment — *For Middle Eastern countries* — *Serials*

MEIP : Middle East industrial products. — Vol.1, no.1 (Nov. 1981)-. — Sutton : IPC Middle East Pub. Co., 1981-. — v. : ill ; 30cm
Eleven issues yearly
ISSN 0144-512X = MEIP. Middle East industrial products : £30.00 per year
B82-15150

620'.0028 — Industrial equipment — *Serials*

Industrial products. — Specimen issue (Oct. 1979) ; Oct. 1979-. — Stanford-le-Hope (One Grover Walk, Corringham Town Centre, Stanford-le-Hope, Essex SS17 7LU) : Patey Doyle, 1979-. — v. : ill ; 31cm
Monthly. — Specimen issue and first issue of main sequence both designated October 1979. — Description based on: Sept. 1981 issue
ISSN 0263-1490 = Industrial products : Unpriced B82-18730

Local authority plant & vehicles : the specialist plant, vehicles and equipment journal. — Vol.1, no.1 (June 1982)-. — Watford (32 Vale Rd, Bushey, Watford, Herts.) : Hamerville for Shannon Business Press, 1982-. — v. : ill (some col.),ports ; 29cm
Monthly
ISSN 0263-9246 = Local authority plant & vehicles : Unpriced B82-38518

620'.0028'54 — Great Britain. Engineering. Applications of digital computer systems — *Serials*

Engineering computers : hardware, software and commonsense. — Vol.1, no.1 (Mar. 1982)-. — [Beckenham] ([1 Copers Cope Rd, Beckenham, Kent BR3 1NB) : [Innopress], 1982-. — v. : ill(some col.) ; 29cm
Six issues yearly
ISSN 0263-4759 = Engineering computers : Unpriced B82-27641

620'.0028'5404 — Engineering. Applications of microcomputer systems — *Conference proceedings*

Desk top computing for engineers : seminar sponsored by the Engineering Manufacturing Industries Division of the Institution of Mechanical Engineers and the Institution of Production Engineers. — London : Published by Mechanical Engineering Publications Limited for the Institution of Mechanical Engineers, 1982. — 58p : ill ; 30cm
ISBN 0-85298-503-7 (pbk) : Unpriced
B82-29482

620'.0028'9 — Great Britain. Engineering plants. Hazards — *Conference proceedings*

Conway, Arthur. Engineering hazards : assessment, frequency and control / [a report prepared by Arthur Conway from papers delivered at a conference in 1980 organised by the Scientific and Technical Studies Division of Oyez International Business Communications Ltd.]. — [London] : Oyez, [1981]. — 95leaves : ill ; 30cm
ISBN 0-85120-568-2 (spiral) : Unpriced
B82-00036

620'.0042 — Engineering. Systems analysis. Bond graphs

Blundell, A. J.. Bond graphs for modelling engineering systems. — Chichester : Ellis Horwood, Oct.1982. — [160]p
ISBN 0-85312-510-4 : £16.50 : CIP entry
B82-32310

620'.00425 — Engineering. Design

Brooks, M. D.. Engineering design for TEC Level III / M.D. Brooks and D. Oldham. — Cheltenham : Thornes, 1981. — xii,228p : ill ; 25cm. — (ST(P) technology today series)
Bibliography: p223-224. — Includes index
ISBN 0-85950-303-8 (pbk) : £4.25 : CIP rev.
B81-16900

Hubka, Vladimir. Principles of engineering design / Vladimir Hubka ; translated and edited by W.E. Eder. — London : Butterworth Scientific, 1982. — 118p : ill ; 24cm
Translation of: Allgemeines Vorgehensmodell des Konstruierens. — Bibliography: p90-94. — Includes index
ISBN 0-408-01105-x : Unpriced : CIP rev.
B81-12892

Jeary, L. N.. Engineering design 2 checkbook. — London : Butterworth Scientific, Jan.1983. — [144]p. — (Butterworths technical and scientific checkbooks)
ISBN 0-408-00694-3 (cased) : £7.95 : CIP entry
ISBN 0-408-00653-6 (pbk) : £3.95 B82-34427

Oldham, D. (Derek). Engineering drawing for TEC level II. — Cheltenham : Thornes, Sept.1982. — [336]p
ISBN 0-85950-387-9 (pbk) : £4.95 : CIP entry
B82-25760

Sherwin, Keith. Engineering design for performance. — Chichester : Ellis Horwood, July 1982. — [144]p. — (Ellis Horwood series in civil and mechanical engineering)
ISBN 0-85312-471-x : £16.50 : CIP entry
B82-20654

620'.00425 — Engineering. Design. Implications of quality assurance — *Conference proceedings*

Quality assistance in design : joint IMechE-IChemE symposium, University of Manchester Institute of Science and Technology, 23 February 1982 / [symposium sponsored by the North Western Branch of the Institution of Mechanical Engineers and the Institution of Chemical Engineers]. — London : Mechanical Engineering Publications, 1982. — 51p : ill,2facsims ; 30cm
ISBN 0-85298-502-9 (pbk) : Unpriced
B82-25793

620'.00425 — Industrial plants & industrial equipment. Design. Safety aspects

Designing for safety : package / produced by the Food, Drink and Tobacco Industry Training Board. — Gloucester (Barton House, Barton St., Gloucester GL1 1QQ) : The Board, [1982?]. — 1v(loose-leaf) : ill(some col.) ; 32cm
Forty colour slides in envelope as insert
£50.00 B82-23752

620'.00425'02854 — Developing countries. Engineering. Design. Applications of digital computer systems — *Conference proceedings*

IFIP WG5.2 Working Conference on CAD/CAM as a Basis for the Development of Technology in Developing Nations *(1981 : Sao Paulo)*. CAD/CAM as a basis for the development of technology in developing nations : proceedings of the IFIP WG5.2 Working Conference on CAD/CAM as a Basis for the Development of Technology in Developing Nations, Sao Paulo, Brazil, October 21-23, 1981 / [sponsored by IFIP Working Group 5.2, Computer-Aided Design, International Federation for Information Processing and SUCESU Society of Computer and Subsidiary Equipment Users] ; edited by José L. Encarnaçao, Oswaldo F.F. Torres and Ernest A. Warman. — Amsterdam ; Oxford : North-Holland, c1981. — xii,437p : ill,maps ; 23cm
Includes index
ISBN 0-444-86320-6 : £38.14
Also classified at 338.4'567'091724 B82-18326

620'.00425'02854 — Engineering. Design. Applications of computer systems

Besant, Colin B.. Computer-aided design and manufacture. — 2nd ed. — Chichester : Ellis Horwood, Nov.1982. — [228]p. — (Ellis Horwood series in engineering science)
Previous ed.: 1980
ISBN 0-85312-452-3 : £21.00 : CIP entry
B82-32863

620'.00425'02854 — Engineering. Design. Applications of computer systems — *Conference proceedings*

CAD 82 *(Conference : Brighton)*. CAD 82 : 5th international conference and exhibition on computers in design engineering : Brighton Metropole Sussex UK 30 March-1 April 1982 / edited by Alan Pipes. — Guildford : Butterworths, c1982. — xii,709p,[2]p of plates : ill(some col.) ; 24cm
Includes index
ISBN 0-86103-058-3 (pbk) : Unpriced
B82-27115

620'.00425'02854 — Engineering. Design. Applications of interactive computer systems — *Conference proceedings*

IFIP WG5.2-5.3 Working Conference on Man-Machine Communication in CAD/CAM *(1980 : Tokyo)*. Man-machine communication in CAD/CAM : proceedings of the IFIP WG5.2-5.3 working conference held in Tokyo, Japan, 2-4 October 1980 / [IFIP WG5.2-5.3 Working Conference on Man-Machine Communication in CAD/CAM ... ; organized by Working Group 5.2 and 5.3 IFIP Technical Committee 5, Computer Applications in Technology, International Federation for Information Processing] ; edited by Toshio Sata and Ernest Warman. — Amsterdam ; Oxford : North-Holland, c1981. — ix,274p : ill ; 23cm
ISBN 0-444-86224-2 : Unpriced B82-06109

620'.00425'0285404 — Engineering. Design. Applications of microcomputer systems

Roberts, Steven K.. Industrial design with microcomputers / Steven K. Roberts. — Englewood Cliffs ; London : Prentice-Hall, c1982. — xviii,382p : ill ; 25cm
Includes index
ISBN 0-13-459461-4 : £21.70 B82-36879

620'.00425'071 — Educational institutons. Curriculum subjects: Engineering. Design — *Conference proceedings*

Education of tomorrow's engineering designers : conference sponsored by the Cambridge Engineering Department, the Design Council and the Qualifications, Education and Training Division of the Institution of Mechanical Engineers, 15-16 September 1981, Robinson College, Cambridge. — London : Published by Mechanical Engineering Publications for the Institution of Mechanical Engineers, 1981. — 112p : ill ; 30cm. — (I Mech E conference publications ; 1981-6)
ISBN 0-85298-482-0 (pbk) : Unpriced : CIP rev. B81-28172

620'.00425'072 — Engineering. Design. Research — *Conference proceedings*

Engineering research and design — bridging the gap : papers originally prepared for a conference sponsored by the Engineering Sciences Division of the Institution of Mechanical Engineers and the Joint British Committee for Stress Analysis. — London : Published by Mechanical Engineering Publications for the Institution of Mechanical Engineers, 1981. — 78p : ill ; 30cm. — (I Mech E conference publications ; 1981-7)
ISBN 0-85298-475-8 (pbk) : Unpriced : CIP rev. B81-27820

620'.0044 — Automatic testing equipment

Davis, Brendan P.. The economics of automatic testing. — London : McGraw-Hill, Sept.1982. — [324]p
ISBN 0-07-084584-0 : £19.95 : CIP entry
B82-21976

620'.0044 — Engineering equipment. Automatic testing — *Conference proceedings*

Automatic Testing 80 *(Conference : Palais des Congrès)*. Automatic Testing 80 : conference proceedings, Palais des Congrès, Paris, France, 23, 24, 25 September, 1980. — [Buckingham] : [Network], [c1980]. — 3v. : ill ; 30cm
Text in English and French. — Cover title
ISBN 0-904999-78-5 (pbk) : Unpriced
ISBN 0-904999-79-3 (session 2) : £15.00
ISBN 0-904999-80-7 (session 3) : £15.00
B82-38452

Automatic Testing '81 & Test Instrumentation *(Conference : Brighton)*. Automatic Testing 81 & Test Instrumentation. — Buckingham : Network, c1981. — 6v. : ill ; 30cm
Includes bibliographies
ISBN 0-904999-88-2 (pbk) : Unpriced
ISBN 0-904999-89-0 (v.2) : £20.00
ISBN 0-904999-90-4 (v.3) : £20.00
ISBN 0-904999-91-2 (v.4) : £20.00
ISBN 0-904999-92-0 (v.6) : £20.00
ISBN 0-904999-93-9 (v.7) : £20.00 B82-15189

620'.0044 — Engineering. Measurement

Collett, C. V.. Engineering measurements. — 2nd ed. — London : Pitman, Feb.1983. — [406]p
Previous ed.: 1974
ISBN 0-273-01758-6 (pbk) : £9.75 : CIP entry
B82-37820

Handbook of measurement science / edited by P.H. Sydenham. — Chichester : Wiley
Vol.1: Theoretical fundamentals. — c1982. — xxiv,654p : ill ; 24cm
Includes bibliographies and index
ISBN 0-471-10037-4 : £29.00 : CIP rev.
B82-11298

620'.0044 — Engineering. Measurement & control — *For technicians*

Adams, L. F.. Engineering Instrumentation and Control IV / L.F. Adams. — London : Hodder and Stoughton, 1981. — xii,256p : ill ; 22cm. — (The Higher technician series)
Bibliography: p240. — Includes index
ISBN 0-340-26147-1 (pbk) : £5.95 CIP : rev.
B81-13489

620'.0044 — Engineering. Measurement — *For technicians*

Haslam, J. A.. Engineering instrumentation and control / J.A. Haslam, G.R. Summers, D. Williams. — London : Edward Arnold, 1981. — ix,310p : ill ; 22cm
Bibliography: p303. — Includes index
ISBN 0-7131-3431-3 (pbk) : £6.50 : CIP rev.
Also classified at 629.8 B81-27979

620'.0044 — Engineering. Measuring instruments

Huskins, D. J.. Quality measuring instruments in on-line process analysis. — Chichester : Ellis Horwood, June 1982. — [256]p. — (Ellis Horwood series in analytical chemistry)
ISBN 0-85312-320-9 : £30.00 : CIP entry
B82-18584

Ramsay, D. C.. Engineering instrumentation and control / D.C. Ramsay. — Cheltenham : Stanley Thornes, 1981. — 262p : ill ; 24cm. — (ST(P) Technology today)
Includes index
ISBN 0-85950-439-5 (pbk) : £4.75
Also classified at 629.8 B82-01263

620'.0044 — Engineering. Measuring instruments *continuation*

Sutton, H. B.. Engineering instrumentation and control 4 checkbook / H.B. Sutton. — London : Butterworth Scientific, 1982. — viii,191p : ill ; 20cm. — (Butterworths technical and scientific checkbooks)
Includes index
ISBN 0-408-00680-3 (cased) : £8.95 : CIP rev.
ISBN 0-408-00617-x (pbk)
Also classified at 629.8 B82-10483

620'.0044 — Instrumentation systems. Applications of microprocessors — *Conference proceedings*

Application of Microprocessors in Devices for Instrumentation and Automatic Control *(Conference : 1980 : London)*. Application of micoprocessors in devices for instrumentation and automatic control : [collected papers from a symposium, 'Application of Micoprocessors in Devices for Instrumentation and Automatic Control', in London, 18-20 November 1980] / [The Institute of Measurement and Control ... organised the symposium]. — [London] : [The Institute], c1980. — 404p : ill ; 30cm
Unpriced (pbk)
Also classified at 629.8'95 B82-09380

620'.0044 — Instrumentation systems. Intrinsic safety

Garside, Robin. Intrinsically safe instrumentation : a guide to the protection technique of intrinsic safety, its application and uses / [Robin Garside]. — Feltham : Safety Technology, 1982. — vii,209p : ill ; 21cm
ISBN 0-9508188-0-1 (pbk) : Unpriced
B82-40162

620'.0044 — Measuring instruments

Instrument science and technology. — Bristol : Hilger
Includes bibliographies and index
Vol.1 / edited by Barry E. Jones. — c1982. — x,144p : ill ; 28cm
ISBN 0-85274-438-2 (pbk) : £6.95 : CIP rev.
B81-34775

620'.00452 — Engineering equipment. Reliability

Billinton, R.. Reliability evaluation of engineering systems. — London : Pitman, Jan.1983. — [360]p
ISBN 0-273-08484-4 : £16.50 : CIP entry
B82-33719

620'.00452 — Engineering equipment. Reliability — *Conference proceedings*

Third national reliability conference : 29 April-1 May 1981 Birmingham : Reliability '81 : proceedings. — Warrington (Wigshaw La, Culcheth, Warrington WA3 NNE) : National Centre of Systems Reliability
[Vol.1]. — [1982?]. — 1v.(various pagings) : ill ; 30cm
Unpriced (pbk) B82-40759

620'.00452 — Reliability engineering

Jensen, Finn. Burn-in : an engineering approach to the design and analysis of burn-in procedures. — Chichester : Wiley, Nov.1982. — [180]p
ISBN 0-471-10215-6 : £15.00 : CIP entry
B82-27546

620'.00452'01 — Reliability engineering. Bayesian theories

Martz, Harry F.. Bayesian reliability analysis / Harry F. Martz and Ray A. Waller. — New York ; Chichester : Wiley, c1982. — xix,745p : ill ; 24cm. — (Wiley series in probability and statistics)
Includes bibliographies and index
ISBN 0-471-86425-0 : £35.00 B82-37201

620'.0046 — Engineering equipment. Planned maintenance

Systematic fault diagnosis : principles and documentation / prepared by EEUA as their handbook no.37. — [London] : Godwin in association with the Engineering Equipment Users Association, c1982. — 127,xxxvp,[2] folded p of plates : ill,forms ; 25cm. — (EEUA handbook ; no.37)
Bibliography: p125. — Contains Guide to user needs for technical documentation (engineering), EEUA handbook no.36
ISBN 0-7114-5739-5 : Unpriced : CIP rev.
B81-40237

620'.0046 — Industrial plants. Maintenance & repair — *Conference proceedings*

8th national maintenance engineering conference : 12-14 May 1981, Café Royal, London, W1 : conference papers / organised by Conference Communication. — [Farnham] ([Monks Hill, Tilford, Farnham, Surrey GU10 2AJ]) : [Conference Communication], [1982?]. — 1v.(various pagings) : ill ; 30cm
Cover title
Unpriced (spiral) B82-40006

PEMEC 77 *(Conference : National Exhibition Centre)*. PEMEC 77 : International Plant Engineering & Maintenance Exhibition + Conference : 31 October-4 November 1977 National Exhibition Centre, Birmingham, England : conference papers. — [Farnham, Surrey] ([Monks Hill, Tilford, Farnham, Surrey, GU10 2AJ]) : [Conference Communications], [c1977]. — 474p in various pagings : ill,forms,1port ; 30cm
Cover title
Unpriced (spiral) B82-11700

PEMEC 78 *(Conference : National Exhibition Centre)*. PEMEC 78 : International Plant Engineering & Maintenance Exhibition + Conference : 4-8 December 1978, National Exhibition Centre, Birmingham : conference papers. — [Farnham, Surrey] ([Monks Hill, Tilford, Farnham, Surrey, GU10 2AJ]) : [Conference Communications], [1978]. — 488p in various pagings : ill,forms ; 30cm
Cover title. — Includes bibliographies
Unpriced (spiral) B82-11701

620'.005 — Engineering — *Serials*

Soviet engineering research / PERA. — Vol.1, no.1 (1981)-. — Melton Mowbray (Melton Mowbray, Leicestershire) : Production Engineering Research Association of Great Britain under contract to the British Library, Lending Division, 1981-. — v. : ill ; 30cm
Monthly. — Merger of: Russian engineering journal ; and, Machines & tooling (Melton Mowbray). — Combined selective translation of: Vestnik mashinostroeniia ; and, Stanki i instrument
ISSN 0144-6622 = Soviet engineering research : £125.00 per year B82-11838

620'.0068 — United States. Consulting engineering. Private practice. Management — *Manuals*

Tomczak, Steven P.. Successful consulting for engineers and data processing professionals / Steven P. Tomczak. — New York ; Chichester : Wiley, c1982. — xiii,337p : forms ; 29cm
Includes index
ISBN 0-471-86135-9 : £31.00 B82-37995

620'.0068'1 — Engineering. Parametric costing. Techniques

Gallagher, Paul F.. Parametric estimating for executives and estimators / Paul F. Gallagher. — New York ; London : Van Nostrand Reinhold, c1982. — ix,308p : ill ; 24cm
Includes index
ISBN 0-442-23997-1 : £16.95 B82-07876

620'.0068'1 — United States. Engineering industries. Financial management

Grant, Eugene L.. Principles of engineering economy / Eugene L. Grant, W. Grant Ireson, Richard S. Leavenworth. — 7th ed. — New York ; Chichester : Wiley, c1982. — x,687p : ill ; 24cm
Previous ed.: New York : Ronald Press Co., 1976. — Bibliography: p662-668. — Includes index
ISBN 0-471-06436-x : £16.00 B82-23512

620'.0068'4 — Engineering industries. Management. Group decision making

Group planning and problem-solving methods in engineering management / edited by Shirley A. Olsen. — New York ; Chichester : Wiley, c1982. — xii,455p : ill,forms ; 24cm. — (Construction management and engineering, ISSN 0193-9750)
Includes index
ISBN 0-471-08311-9 : £38.50 B82-37204

620'.0068'5 — United States. Engineering. Research & development. Management

Gibson, John E.. Managing research and development / John E. Gibson. — New York ; Chichester : Wiley, c1981. — xv,367p : ill ; 24cm
Includes index
ISBN 0-471-08799-8 : £26.00 B82-11632

Glasser, Alan. Research and development management / Alan Glasser. — Englewood Cliffs, N.J. ; London : Prentice-Hall, c1982. — xi,320p : ill ; 25cm
Includes index
ISBN 0-13-774091-3 : Unpriced B82-28342

620'.007'1141 — Great Britain. Engineers. Lifelong professional education

Cannell, R. L.. The updating of professional engineers / R.L. Cannell. — Loughborough : Loughborough University of Technology, Centre for Extension Studies, 1982. — 60p ; 30cm
ISBN 0-905078-05-5 (pbk) : Unpriced
B82-39911

620'.007'1141 — Great Britain. Engineers. Professional education — *Inquiry reports*

Berthoud, Richard. The education, training and careers of professional engineers / by Richard Berthoud and David J. Smith ; prepared for the Committee of Inquiry into the Engineering Profession by the Policy Studies Institute. — London : H.M.S.O., 1980. — xii,121p : ill,forms ; 30cm
At head of title: Department of Industry. — Includes index
ISBN 0-11-512927-8 (pbk) : £5.00 B82-20454

620'.007'1143 — West Germany. Engineers. Professional education

Hutton, Stanley. German engineers : the anatomy of a profession / Stanley Hutton and Peter Lawrence. — Oxford : Clarendon, 1981. — x,151p ; 23cm
Bibliography: p144-148. — Includes index
ISBN 0-19-827245-6 : £15.00 : CIP rev.
B82-01086

620'.007'1144361 — France. Paris. Engineering colleges: École centrale des arts et manufactures, *to 1848*

Weiss, John Hubbel. The making of technological man : the social origins of French engineering education / John Hubbel Weiss. — Cambridge, Mass. ; London : MIT, c1982. — xviii,377p : ill,1port ; 24cm
Bibliography: p313-364. — Includes index
ISBN 0-262-23112-3 : £21.00 B82-35671

620'.0072041 — Great Britain. Engineering. Research — *Serials*

Science and Engineering Research Council. SERC bulletin / Science & Engineering Research Council. — Vol.2, no.3 (Autumn 1981)-. — Swindon : SERC, 1981-. — v. : ill ; 31cm
Three issues yearly. — Continues: Great Britain. Science Research Council. SRC bulletin
ISSN 0262-7671 = SERC bulletin : Unpriced
Primary classification 507'.2041 B82-06773

620'.0072042582 — Engineering. Research organisations: Warren Spring Laboratory

Directory of specialist services and facilities to industry / Warren Spring. — Stevenage (Gunnels Wood Rd, Stevenage, Herts. SG1 2BX) : Warren Spring Laboratory, [1979]. — [44]p : ill(some col.) ; 30cm
Cover title. — Text, ill on inside covers
Unpriced (pbk) B82-36817

620'.0072042582 — Engineering. Research organisations: Warren Spring Laboratory — *Serials*

Warren Spring Laboratory. Warren Spring Laboratory / Department of Industry. — 1981-. — Stevenage (Gunnels Wood Rd, Stevenage, Herts. SG1 2BX) : The Laboratory, 1982-. — v. : ill,maps ; 30cm
Annual. — Continues: Warren Spring Laboratory. Annual report
ISSN 0263-3086 = Warren Spring Laboratory (1982) : Unpriced B82-22698

620'.0092'4 — Great Britain. Engineering. Weslake, Harry — *Biographies*
Clew, Jeff. Lucky all my life : the biography of Harry Weslake / Jeff Clew. — Yeovil : Haynes, 1979. — 176p : ill,facsims,ports ; 24cm. — (A Foulis motoring book)
Includes index
ISBN 0-85429-254-3 : Unpriced B82-07390

620'.00973 — United States. Consulting engineering — *Manuals*
Consulting engineering practice manual / edited by Stanley Cohen ; sponsored by American Consulting Engineers Council. — New York ; London : McGraw-Hill, c1982. — ix,195p : ill,forms ; 24cm
Includes index
ISBN 0-07-001352-7 : £19.50 B82-15976

620.1 — ENGINEERING MECHANICS AND MATERIALS

620.1 — Applied mechanics
Edmunds, H. G.. Mechanical foundations of engineering science / H.G. Edmunds. — Chichester : Ellis Horwood, 1981. — 429p : ill ; 24cm. — (Ellis Horwood series in engineering science)
Text on lining papers. — Includes index
ISBN 0-85312-281-4 (cased) : £17.50
ISBN 0-85312-354-3 (students ed) B82-03898

McLean, W. G.. Schaum's outline of theory and problems of engineering mechanics : statics and dynamics. — 3rd (SI metric) ed. / by W.G. McLean and E.W. Nelson ; adapted for SI Units by A.H. Bassim. — New York ; London : McGraw-Hill, c1980. — 408p : ill ; 28cm. — (Schaum's outline series)
Previous ed.: i.e. 3rd ed. 1978. — Includes index
ISBN 0-07-084354-6 (pbk) : £4.95 : CIP rev. B80-07402

Smith, Charles E.. Applied mechanics / Charles E. Smith. — New York ; Chichester : Wiley Statics. — 2nd ed. — c1982. — xiv,316p : ill ; 24cm
Previous ed.: 1976. — Ill on lining papers. — Includes index
ISBN 0-471-02965-3 : £15.50 B82-37261

Titherington, D.. Applied mechanics : mechanical science III / D. Titherington and J.G. Rimmer. — 2nd ed. — London : McGraw-Hill, c1982. — ix,177p : ill ; 22cm
Previous ed.: 1970. — Includes index
ISBN 0-07-084659-6 (pbk) : £4.25 : CIP rev. B82-10590

620.1 — Applied mechanics — *For technicians*
Ayling, D. S.. Mechanical science 3 checkbook / D.S. Ayling. — London : Butterworths, 1981. — vi,93p : ill ; 19cm. — (Butterworths technical and scientific checkbooks. Level 3)
Includes index
ISBN 0-408-00665-x (pbk) : Unpriced : CIP rev.
ISBN 0-408-00649-8 (pbk) : Unpriced B81-30517

McDonagh, Ian. Mechanical science for technicians. — London : Edward Arnold Vol.2. — Aug.1982. — [192]p
ISBN 0-7131-3445-3 (pbk) : £4.75 : CIP entry B82-15918

620.101'51'7 — Applied mechanics. Mathematics. Numerical methods
Naylor, D. J.. Finite elements in geotechnical engineering. — Swansea (91 West Cross Lane, West Cross, Swansea, W. Glam.) : Pineridge, Apr.1981. — [220]p
ISBN 0-906674-11-5 : £12.00 : CIP entry B81-10461

620.1'06 — Fluid power — *Conference proceedings*
International Fluid Power Symposium *(6th : 1981 : St John's College, Cambridge)*. Papers presented at the sixth International Fluid Power Symposium : held at St John's College Cambridge, England, April 8-10, 1981 / symposium sponsored and organised by BHRA Fluid Engineering. — Cranfield : BHRA Fluid Engineering, c1981. — vi,430p : ill ; 30cm
ISBN 0-906085-53-5 (pbk) : Unpriced : CIP rev. B81-04352

620.1'064'01511 — Fluids. Applied dynamics. Mathematics. Numerical methods — *Conference proceedings*
Conference on Numerical Methods in Applied Fluid Dynamics *(1978 : University of Reading)*. Numerical methods in applied fluid dynamics : based on the proceedings of the Conference on Numerical Methods in Applied Fluid Dynamics held at the University of Reading from 4-6 January 1978 / organised by the Institute of Mathematics and its Applications ; edited by B. Hunt. — London : Academic Press, 1980. — xviii,651p : ill ; 24cm. — (The Institute of Mathematics and its Applications conference series)
ISBN 0-12-362150-x : £26.80 : CIP rev. B80-20615

620.1'1 — Materials
Engineering materials : an introduction. — Milton Keynes : Open University Press. — (Technology : a second level course)
At head of title: The Open University
Unit 1: Materials and models ; Unit 2: Putting materials to work. — 1982. — 89p : ill(some col.) ; 30cm. — (T252 : units 1 and 2)
ISBN 0-335-17100-1 (pbk) : Unpriced B82-21205

Engineering materials : an introduction. — Milton Keynes : Open University Press. — (Technology : a second level course)
At head of title: The Open University
Unit 3: From liquid to solid ; Unit 4: Crystal or glass ; 5: Solids under stress. — 1982. — 114p : ill(some col.) ; 30cm. — (T252 ; units 3, 4 and 5)
ISBN 0-335-17101-x (pbk) : Unpriced B82-32014

Engineering materials : an introduction. — Milton Keynes : Open University Press. — (Technology : a second level course)
At head of title: The Open University
Unit 6: Composite materials. — 1982. — 39p : ill(some col.) ; 30cm. — (T252 ; unit 6)
ISBN 0-335-17102-8 (pbk) : Unpriced B82-32015

Engineering materials : an introduction. — Milton Keynes : Open University Press. — (Technology : a second level course)
At head of title: The Open University
Unit 7: Phase diagrams ; Unit 8: Phase diagrams and heat treatment. — 1982. — 72p : ill(some col.) ; 30cm. — (T252 ; units 7 and 8)
ISBN 0-335-17103-6 (pbk) : Unpriced B82-32013

Engineering materials : an introduction. — Milton Keynes : Open University Press. — (Technology : a second level course)
At head of title: The Open University
Unit 9: Steels — how to treat them. — 1982. — 35p : ill(some col.) ; 30cm. — (T252 ; unit 9)
ISBN 0-335-17104-4 (pbk) : Unpriced B82-34537

Engineering materials : an introduction. — Milton Keynes : Open University Press. — (Technology : a second level course)
At head of title: The Open University
Unit 10: Hacksaw blades — a case study. — 1982. — 33,[17]p : ill,facsims ; 30cm. — (T252 ; unit 10)
ISBN 0-335-17105-2 (pbk) : Unpriced B82-34538

Engineering materials : an introduction. — Milton Keynes : Open University Press. — (Technology : a second level course)
At head of title: The Open University
Unit 77: Bike frames — a case study. — 1982. — 39p : ill,1port ; 30cm. — (T252 ; unit 11)
ISBN 0-335-17106-0 (pbk) : Unpriced B82-40139

Gourd, L. M.. An introduction to engineering materials / L.M. Gourd. — London : Edward Arnold, 1982. — ix,166p : ill ; 22cm
Includes index
ISBN 0-7131-3444-5 (pbk) : £4.25 : CIP rev. B82-04484

Indo-U.S. Workshop on the Preparation and Characterization of Materials *(1981 : Bangalore)*. Preparation and characterization of materials / [the proceedings of the Indo-U.S. Workshop on the Preperation and Characterization of Materials held February 19-23, 1981, Indian Institute of Science, Bangalore, India] ; edited by J.M. Honig, C.N.R. Rao. — New York ; London : Academic Press, 1981. — xii,609p : ill,24 ; 24cm
Includes index
ISBN 0-12-355040-8 : £28.20 B82-32793

620.1'1 — Materials — *For schools*
Kincaid, Doug. Materials. — [London] : Macdonald Educational/Schools Council, [c1982]. — 48sheets : ill(some col.) ; 22x30cm + teachers' guide(28p : ill ; 21x30cm). — (Learning through science)
Authors of this material are Doug Kincaid and Roy Richards
ISBN 0-356-07551-6 : Unpriced B82-28886

620.1'1 — Materials science
Chanda, Manas. Science of engineering materials / Manas Chanda. — London : Macmillan, 1981, c1979. — 3v. : ill ; 22cm
Originally published: New Delhi : Macmillan, 1979. — Includes bibliographies and index
ISBN 0-333-31815-3 (pbk) : Unpriced
ISBN 0-333-31816-1 (v.2) : Unpriced
ISBN 0-333-31818-8 (v.3) : Unpriced B82-06868

620.1'1 — Materials science — *For schools*
Materials technology / John McShea ... [et al.]. — Edinburgh : Oliver & Boyd in association with the National Centre for School Technology, 1981. — 92p : ill ; 24cm. — (Schools Council modular courses in technology)
ISBN 0-05-003395-6 (pbk) : £2.50 B82-11467

Materials technology / John McShea ... [et al.]. — Edinburgh : Oliver & Boyd in association with the National Centre for School Technology, 1981. — (Schools Council modular courses in technology)
Teacher's guide / David Byrne ... [et al.]. — 44p : ill ; 24cm
Bibliography: p39-40. — List of films: p41
ISBN 0-05-003396-4 (pbk) : £2.50 B82-11468

Materials technology / John McShea ... [et al.]. — Edinburgh : Oliver & Boyd in association with the National Centre for School Technology, 1981. — (Schools Council modular courses in technology)
Workbook. — 19p : ill ; 27cm
ISBN 0-05-003397-2 (unbound) : £2.40 for set of 5 copies B82-11469

620.1'1 — Materials science — *For technicians*
Bolton, W. (William), *1933-*. Materials technology for technicians 2 / W. Bolton. — Sevenoaks : Butterworths, 1981. — 74p : ill ; 25cm. — (Butterworths technician series)
ISBN 0-408-01117-3 (pbk) : Unpriced : CIP rev. B81-30516

Bolton, W. (William), *1933-*. Materials technology for technicians 3 / W. Bolton. — Sevenoaks : Butterworths, 1981. — 93p : ill ; 25cm. — (Butterworths technician series)
ISBN 0-408-01116-5 (pbk) : Unpriced : CIP rev. B81-36951

620.1'1 — Strong solid materials
Gordon, J. E. (James Edward). The new science of strong materials, or, Why you don't fall through the floor / J.E. Gordon. — 2nd ed. — London : Pitman, 1979, c1976. — 287p,[16]p of plates : ill ; 23cm
Originally published: Harmondsworth : Penguin, 1976. — Bibliography: p280-281. — Includes index
ISBN 0-273-01457-9 : Unpriced B82-06591

620.1'1'0287 — Materials. Testing

Davis, Harmer E.. The testing of engineering materials / Harmer E. Davis, George Earl Troxell, George F.W. Hauck. — 4th ed. — New York ; London : McGraw-Hill, c1982. — xvi,478p : ill ; 25cm
Previous ed.: published as The testing and inspection of engineering materials. 1964. — Text on lining papers. — Bibliography: p448-453. — Includes index
ISBN 0-07-015656-5 : £22.95 B82-25323

620.1'1'05 — Materials science — *Serials*

Journal of materials science letters. — Vol.1, no.1 (Jan. 1982)-. — London : Chapman and Hall, 1982-. — v. : ill ; 25cm
Monthly. — Description based on: Vol.1, no.2 (Feb. 1982)
ISSN 0261-8028 = Journal of materials science letters : Unpriced B82-19859

Progress in materials science. — Vol.25. — Oxford : Pergamon, Dec.1981. — [420]p
ISBN 0-08-029096-5 : £48.00 : CIP entry B81-33853

Progress in materials science. — Vol.26. — Oxford : Pergamon, Mar.1982. — [405]p
ISBN 0-08-029122-8 : £60.00 : CIP entry B82-03350

620.1'12 — Materials. Defects — *Conference proceedings*

International Symposium on Defects and Fracture *(1st : 1980 : Tuczno)*. Defects and fracture : proceedings of First International Symposium on Defects and Fracture, held at Tuczno, Poland, October 13-17, 1980 / edited by G.C. Sih, H. Zorski. — The Hague ; London : Nijhoff, c1982. — xiv,276 : ill,ports ; 25cm
ISBN 90-247-2589-5 : Unpriced
Primary classification 620.1'123 B82-17293

620.1'12 — Materials. Mechanics

Beer, Ferdinand P.. Mechanics of materials / Ferdinand P. Beer, E. Russell Johnston, Jr. — New York ; London : McGraw-Hill, c1981. — xv,616p : ill(some col.) ; 25cm
Text, ill on lining papers. — Includes index
ISBN 0-07-004284-5 : £18.95 B82-00414

Olsen, Gerner A.. Elements of mechanics of materials / Gerner A. Olsen. — 4th ed. — Englewood Cliffs ; London : Prentice-Hall, c1982. — xx,636p : ill ; 24cm
Previous ed.: 1974. — Text on lining papers. — Includes index
ISBN 0-13-267013-5 : £20.20 B82-20065

620.1'12 — Materials. Processing. Applications of electron beams & lasers — *Conference proceedings*

Materials Research Society. *Meeting (1981 : Boston, Mass.)*. Laser and electron-beam interactions with solids : proceedings of the Materials Research Society Annual Meeting, November 1981, Boston Park Plaza Hotel, Boston, Massachusetts, U.S.A. / editors B.R. Appleton and G.K. Celler ; [sponsored by the Division of Materials Sciences, U.S. Department of Energy under contract W-7405-eng-26 with Union Carbide Corporation]. — Amsterdam ; Oxford : North-Holland, c1982. — xvii,812p : ill ; 24cm. — (Materials Research Society symposia proceedings ; v.4)
Includes index
ISBN 0-444-00693-1 : £52.97 B82-38191

620.1'12 — Materials. Strength — *For schools*

Neathery, Raymond F.. Applied strength of materials / Raymond F. Neathery. — New York ; Chichester : Wiley, 1982. — xii,419p : ill ; 25cm
Includes index
ISBN 0-471-07991-x : £16.25 B82-21803

620.1'12 — Materials. Structure & physical properties

Lewis, Gladius. Properties of engineering materials : theory, worked examples and problems / Gladius Lewis. — London : Macmillan, 1981. — vii,161p : ill ; 24cm
Bibliography: p158-159
ISBN 0-333-30741-0 (pbk) : £4.95 B82-00572

Treatise on materials science and technology. — New York ; London : Academic Press
Vol.20: Ultrarapid quenching of liquid alloys / edited by Herbert Herman. — 1981. — xiv,448p : ill ; 24cm
Includes bibliographies and index
ISBN 0-12-341820-8 : £44.40 B82-28065

Treatise on materials science and technology. — New York ; London : Academic Press
Vol.21: Electronic structure and properties / edited by Frank Y. Fradin. — 1981. — xii,448p : ill ; 24cm
Includes bibliographies and index
ISBN 0-12-341821-6 : £33.80 B82-10058

620.1'12 — Materials. Surfaces. Roughness

Rough surfaces / edited by T.R. Thomas. — London : Longman, 1982. — xix,261p : ill ; 26cm
Bibliography: p241-252. — Includes index
ISBN 0-582-46816-7 : £25.00 : CIP rev. B81-25877

620.1'12 — Outer space. Materials. Processing

Materials Research Society. *Meeting (1981 : Boston, Mass.)*. Materials processing in the reduced gravity environment of space : proceedings of the Materials Research Society Annual Meeting, November 1981, Boston Park Plaza Hotel, Boston, Massachusetts, U.S.A. / editor Guy E. Rindone. — New York ; Oxford : North-Holland, c1982. — xiii,676p : ill ; 24cm. — (Materials Research Society symposia proceedings ; v.9)
Includes index
ISBN 0-444-00691-5 : Unpriced B82-33794

620.1'12 — Particulate materials. Mechanics

Feda, Jaroslav. Mechanics of particulate materials : the principles / by Jaroslav Feda. — Amsterdam ; Oxford : Elsevier Scientific, 1982. — 446p : ill ; 25cm. — (Developments in geotechnical engineering ; v.30)
Translation of: Základy mechaniky partikulárních látek. — Bibliography: p399-432. — Includes index
ISBN 0-444-99713-x : Unpriced : CIP rev. B82-03589

620.1'12'028 — European Community countries. Materials testing equipment: Reactors — *Technical data*

Handbook of materials testing reactors and associated hot laboratories in the European Community : nuclear science and technology / edited by Peter von der Hardt and Heinz Röttger. — Rev ed. — Dordrecht ; London : Reidel, 1981. — vii,151p : ill,plans ; 24cm
At head of title: Commission of the European Communities. — Previous ed.: 1975
ISBN 90-277-1347-2 : Unpriced B82-00474

620.1'1217 — High temperature materials — *Conference proceedings*

Analysis of high temperature materials. — London : Applied Science, Feb.1983. — [272]p
ISBN 0-85334-172-9 : £30.00 : CIP entry B82-39603

620.1'1217 — High temperature materials. Joints. Physical properties — *Conference proceedings*

Behaviour of joints in high temperature materials. — London : Applied Science, Jan.1983. — [280]p
Conference papers
ISBN 0-85334-187-7 : £20.00 : CIP entry B82-24098

620.1'122 — Biodeterioration — *Conference proceedings*

International Biodeterioration Symposium *(5th : 1981 : Aberdeen)*. Biodeterioration 5. — Chichester : Wiley, Feb.1983. — [736]p
ISBN 0-471-10296-2 : £35.00 : CIP entry B82-38279

620.1'1223 — Biodegradation

Microbial biodeterioration / edited by A.H. Rose. — London : Academic Press, 1981. — xiv,516p : ill ; 24cm. — (Economic microbiology ; v.6)
Includes bibliographies and index
ISBN 0-12-596556-7 : Unpriced : CIP rev. B81-31346

620.1'1223 — Corrosion

Shreir, L. L.. Electrochemical principles of corrosion : a guide for engineers / L.L. Shreir. — [London] (National Corrosion Service, National Physical Laboratory, Teddington, Middx TW11 0LW) : Department of Industry, 1982. — 66p : ill ; 30cm
Bibliography: p66
Unpriced (pbk) B82-40360

620.1'1223 — Corrosion. Causes & control

Corrosion : aqueous processes and passive films. — London : Academic Press, Dec.1982. — [450]p. — (Treatise on materials science and technology ; v.23)
ISBN 0-12-633670-9 : CIP entry B82-29889

620.1'123 — Materials. Deformation. Mechanics

Frost, H. J.. Deformation-mechanism maps. — Oxford : Pergamon, Oct.1982. — [250]p
ISBN 0-08-029338-7 (cased) : £30.00 : CIP entry
ISBN 0-08-029337-9 (pbk) : £15.00 B82-24959

620.1'123 — Materials. Elasticity & plasticity. Analysis. Applications of variational methods

Washizu, Kyuichiro. Variational methods in elasticity and plasticity. — 3rd ed. — Oxford : Pergamon, Feb.1982. — [540]p
Previous ed.: 1974
ISBN 0-08-026723-8 : £42.00 : CIP entry B81-35952

620.1'123 — Materials. Elasticity & plasticity. Mathematical models

Chen, Wai-Fah. Constitutive equations for engineering materials / Wai-Fah Chen and Atef F. Saleeb. — New York ; Chichester : Wiley
Vol.1: Elasticity and modeling. — c1982. — xii,580p : ill ; 24cm
Includes bibliographies and index
ISBN 0-471-09149-9 : £51.75 B82-30699

620.1'123 — Materials. Fatigue & fracture — *Conference proceedings*

International Symposium on Defects and Fracture *(1st : 1980 : Tuczno)*. Defects and fracture : proceedings of First International Symposium on Defects and Fracture, held at Tuczno, Poland, October 13-17, 1980 / edited by G.C. Sih, H. Zorski. — The Hague ; London : Nijhoff, c1982. — xiv,276 : ill,ports ; 25cm
ISBN 90-247-2589-5 : Unpriced
Also classified at 620.1'12 B82-17293

620.1'123 — Materials. Fatigue & fracture. Mechanics — *Conference proceedins*

Fracture mechanics of ductile and tough materials and its applications to energy related structures : proceedings of the USA-Japan joint seminar held at Hyama, Japan, November 12-16, 1979 / H.W. Liu ... [et al.] (editors). — The Hague ; London : Nijhoff, c1981. — xix,314p : ill,ports ; 25cm
ISBN 90-247-2536-4 : Unpriced B82-17292

620.1'123 — Materials. Fracture

Recent advances in creep and fracture of engineering materials and structures. — Swansea (91 West Cross La., West Cross, Swansea) : Pineridge Press, May 1982. — [400]p
ISBN 0-906674-18-2 : £28.00 : CIP entry B82-09220

620.1'123 — Materials. High temperature fatigue

Fatigue at high temperature. — London : Applied Science, Dec.1982. — [400]p
ISBN 0-85334-167-2 : £45.00 : CIP entry B82-30720

620.1'123 — Stress analysis

Heyman, Jacques. Elements of stress analysis / Jacques Heyman. — Cambridge : Cambridge University Press, 1982. — viii,106p : ill ; 24cm
Bibliography: p106. — Includes index
ISBN 0-521-24523-0 : £15.00 : CIP rev. B82-11496

620.1′123′028 — Strain gauges

Strain gauge technology / edited by A.L. Window and G.S. Holister. — London : Applied Science : c1982. — x,356p : ill ; 23cm
Includes index
ISBN 0-85334-118-4 : £38.00 : CIP rev.
B82-04795

620.1′123′028542 — Stress analysis. Applications of digital computer systems. Programming languages: BASIC language

Iremonger, M. J.. BASIC stress analysis. — London : Butterworth, June 1982. — [150]p
ISBN 0-408-01113-0 (pbk) : £6.50 : CIP entry
B82-11523

620.1′1233 — Materials. Creep — *Conference proceedings*

International conference on engineering aspects of creep : conference sponsored by the Institution of Mechanical Engineers ... [et al.], University of Sheffield, 15-19 September 1980. — London : Published by Mechanical Engineering Publications for the Institution of Mechanical Engineers. — (I Mech E conference publications ; 1980-5)
Vol.3. — 1981. — 76p : ill ; 30cm
ISBN 0-85298-486-3 (pbk) : Unpriced
ISBN 0-85298-454-5 (set) B82-02693

620.1′1233 — Materials. Creep. Stress analysis

Boyle, J. T.. Stress analysis for creep. — London : Butterworth, Jan.1983. — [192]p
ISBN 0-408-01172-6 : £18.00 : CIP entry
B82-34429

620.1′1233 — Materials. High temperature creep — *Conference proceedings*

Creep and fracture of engineering materials and structures. — Swansea (91 West Cross Lane, West Cross, Swansea, West Glamorgan) : Pineridge Press, Apr.1981. — [800]p
ISBN 0-906674-10-7 : £38.00 : CIP entry
Also classified at 620.1′126 B81-02674

620.1′1233 — Metals. Plastic deformation

Johnson, W.. Plane strain slip line fields for metal deformation processes. — Oxford : Pergamon, Sept.1981. — [270]p
ISBN 0-08-025452-7 : £16.50 : CIP entry
B81-21530

620.1′125 — Materials. Effects of impact

Impact dynamics / Jonas A. Zukas ... [et al.]. — New York ; Chichester : Wiley, c1982. — xi,452p : ill ; 24cm
Includes bibliographies and index
ISBN 0-471-08677-0 : £35.00 B82-18933

620.1′126 — Energy engineering equipment. Solid materials. Fracture. Mechanics — *Conference proceedings*

Canadian Fracture Conference *(5th : 1981 : Winnipeg)*. Fracture problems and solutions in the energy industry : proceedings of the Fifth Canadian Fracture Conference Winnipeg, Canada, 3-4 September 1981 / edited by Leonard A. Simpson. — Oxford : Pergamon, 1982. — x,252p : ill ; 24cm
Includes bibliographies and index
ISBN 0-08-028671-2 : £25.00 : CIP rev.
B82-02626

620.1′126 — Materials. Fracture. Mechanics

Broek, David. Elementary engineering fracture mechanics / David Broek. — 3rd rev. ed. — The Hague ; London : Nijhoff, 1982. — xiv,469p : ill ; 23cm
Previous ed.: Alphen Aan Den Rijn : Sijthoff & Noordhoff, 1978. — Includes index
ISBN 90-247-2580-1 (cased) : Unpriced
ISBN 90-247-2656-5 (pbk) : Unpriced
B82-40856

620.1′126 — Materials. Fracture. Mechanics. Analysis. Experimental technique

Experimental evaluation of stress concentration and intensity factors : useful methods and solutions to experimentalist in fracture machanics / edited by G.C. Sih. — The Hague ; London : Nijhoff, 1981. — lvi,354p : ill(some col.) ; 24cm. — (Mechanics of fracture ; 7)
Includes index
ISBN 90-247-2558-5 : Unpriced B82-09386

620.1′126 — Materials. Fracture. Mechanics — *Conference proceedings*

International Symposium on Absorbed Specific Energy and/or Strain Energy Density Criterion *(1980 : Budapest)*. Proceedings of an international Symposium on Absorbed Specific Energy and/or Strain Energy Density Criterion : in memory of the late Professor László Gillemot : held at the Hungarian Academy of Sciences, Budapest, Hungary, September 17-19, 1980 / editors G.C. Sih, E. Czoboly, F. Gillemot. — The Hague ; London : Nijhoff, 1982. — xxiv,409p : ill,ports ; 25cm
Includes index
ISBN 90-247-2598-4 : Unpriced B82-29468

620.1′126 — Materials. Fracture. Role of cavities

Cavities and cracks in creep and fatigue / edited by John Gittus. — London : Applied Science, c1981. — x,296p : ill ; 23cm
Includes index
ISBN 0-85334-965-7 : £28.00 : CIP rev.
B81-20546

620.1′126 — Materials. High temperature fracture — *Conference proceedings*

Creep and fracture of engineering materials and structures. — Swansea (91 West Cross Lane, West Cross, Swansea, West Glamorgan) : Pineridge Press, Apr.1981. — [800]p
ISBN 0-906674-10-7 : £38.00 : CIP entry
Primary classification 620.1′1233 B81-02674

620.1′126 — Solid materials. Fracture — *Conference proceedings*

International Conference on Fracture *(5th : 1981 : Cannes)*. Advances in fracture research. — Oxford : Pergamon, Oct.1981. — [3000]p. — (International series on the strength and fracture of materials and structures)
ISBN 0-08-025428-4 : £200.00 : CIP entry
B81-27988

620.1′127 — Materials. Structure. Determination. Applications of diffraction

Schultz, Jerold M.. Diffraction for materials scientists / Jerold M. Schultz. — Englewood Cliffs ; London : Prentice-Hall, c1982. — xii,287p : ill ; 24cm. — (Prentice-Hall international series in the physical and chemical engineering sciences)
Includes bibliographies and index
ISBN 0-13-211920-x : £26.20 B82-16722

620.1′127 — Non-destructive testing — *Serials*

Research techniques in non-destructive testing. — Vol.6. — London : Academic Press, Dec.1982. — [340]p
ISBN 0-12-639056-8 : CIP entry B82-29890

620.1′127′05 — Non-destructive testing — *Serials*

Research techniques in nondestructive testing. — Vol.5. — London : Academic Press, Feb.1982. — [400
ISBN 0-12-639055-x : CIP entry
ISSN 0277-7045 B81-35911

620.1′1272 — Non-destructive testing. Applications of radiography

Halmshaw, R.. Industrial radiology : theory and practice / R. Halmshaw. — London : Applied Science, 1982. — xii,329p : ill ; 23cm
Includes index
ISBN 0-85334-105-2 : £32.00 B82-32903

620.1′1274 — Materials. Testing. Use of ultrasonic waves

Ultrasonic testing : non-conventional testing techniques / edited by J. Szilard. — New York ; Chichester : Wiley, c1982. — xii,648p : ill ; 24cm
Includes index
ISBN 0-471-27938-2 : £37.50 : CIP rev.
B81-22548

620.1′1296 — Nonmetallic materials. Low temperature properties & low temperature applications — *Conference proceedings*

ICMC Symposium on Nonmetallic Materials and Composites at Low Temperatures *(2nd : 1980 : Geneva)*. Nonmetallic materials and composites at low temperatures 2 / [proceedings of the Second ICMC Symposium on Nonmetallic Materials and Composites at Low Temperatures, held August 4-5, 1980 in Geneva, Switzerland] ; edited by Günther Hartwig and David Evans. — New York ; London : Plenum, c1982. — xi,399p : ill ; 26cm. — (Cryogenic materials series)
Includes index
ISBN 0-306-40894-5 : Unpriced B82-38669

620.1′1297 — Materials. Dielectric properties — *Conference proceedings*

Dielectrics Society. *Meeting (1982 : Pembroke College, Cambridge)*. Dielectric properties of molecular liquids and biological systems : the Dielectrics Society 1982 meeting, 30 March-1 April 1982, Pembroke College, Cambridge. — [Salford] ([c/o Dr. C.W. Smith, Electrical Engineering Dept., University of Salford, Salford M5 4WT]) : [Dielectrics Society], [1982]. — [56]p : ill ; 30cm
Cover title
Unpriced (spiral) B82-41016

620.1′18 — Composite materials

Handbook of composites / edited by George Lubin ; sponsored by the Society of Plastics Engineers. — New York ; London : Van Nostrand Reinhold, c1982. — x,786p : ill ; 26cm
Includes index
ISBN 0-442-24897-0 : £59.10 B82-36983

620.1′18 — Composite materials — *Conference proceedings*

Composite materials : mechanics, mechanical properties and fabrication : Japan-US conference Tokyo, Japan 1981 / editors Kozo Kawata, Takashi Akasaka. — Barking : Applied Science Publishers for Japan Society for Composite Materials, Tokyo, 1982, c1981. — xi,562p : ill ; 23cm
Includes index
ISBN 0-85334-144-3 : £34.00 : CIP rev.
B82-06526

620.1′18′05 — Composite materials - *Serials*

Developments in composite materials. — London : Applied Science, July 1981. — (Developments series)
2: Stress analysis. — [200]p
ISBN 0-85334-966-5 : £16.00 : CIP entry
B81-13748

620.1′186 — Composite materials. Fracture. Fractures

Sih, G. C.. Cracks in composite materials : a compilation of stress solutions for composite systems with cracks / G.C. Sih and E.P. Chen. — The Hague ; London : Nijhoff, 1981. — lxxxi,538p : ill ; 24cm. — (Mechanics of fracture ; 6)
Includes index
ISBN 90-247-2559-3 : Unpriced B82-09387

620.1′1892 — Composite materials. Dynamic properties

Hull, Derek. An introduction to composite materials / Derek Hull. — Cambridge : Cambridge University Press, 1981. — x, 246p : ill ; 22cm. — (Cambridge solid state science series)
Includes bibliographies and index
ISBN 0-521-23991-5 (cased) : £22.50 : CIP rev.
ISBN 0-521-28392-2 (pbk) : £7.95 B81-33621

620.1′2 — Wood

Crane, Alfred. Trees, timber and woodworking / Alfred Crane. — Bognor Regis : New Horizon, c1980. — 147p : ill ; 21cm
ISBN 0-86116-112-2 : £4.25 B82-07936

620.1′2 — Wood. Identification — *Manuals*

Barefoot, A. C.. Identification of modern and tertiary woods / A.C. Barefoot and Frank W. Hankins ; with assistance from L.H. Daugherty. — Oxford : Clarendon Press, 1982. — vii,189p : ill ; 31cm. — (Oxford science publications)
Bibliography: p182-184. — Includes index
ISBN 0-19-854378-6 : £47.50 : CIP rev.
Primary classification 561′.21 B79-37308

620.1'2 — Wood. Structure — *Conference proceedings*

New perspectives in wood anatomy : published on the occasion of the 50th anniversary of the International Association of Wood Anatomists / edited by P. Baas. — The Hague ; London : Nijhoff, 1982. — vi,252p : ill,ports ; 25cm. — (Forestry sciences)
Includes bibliographies and index
ISBN 90-247-2526-7 : Unpriced B82-34839

620.1'292 — Wood & wood-based composite materials. Mechanical properties

Bodig, Jozsef. Mechanics of wood and wood composites / Jozsef Bodig, Benjamin A. Jayne. — New York ; London : Van Nostrand Reinhold, c1982. — xxi,712p : ill ; 24cm
Includes index
ISBN 0-442-00822-8 : £36.15 B82-40851

620.1'292 — Wood-based composite materials. Adhesion — *Conference proceedings*

Adhesion in cellulosic and wood-based composites / [proceedings of a conference on adhesion in cellulosic and wood-based composites sponsored by the NATO Science Committee (Materials Science Panel) and held May 12-15, 1980, at Queen's University, Kingston, Ontario, Canada] ; edited by John F. Oliver. — New York ; London : Plenum in cooperation with Nato Scientific Affairs Division, c1981. — vi,261p : ill ; 26cm. — (NATO conference series. VI, Materials science ; v.3)
Includes bibliographies and index
ISBN 0-306-40812-0 : Unpriced
Also classified at 620.1'97 B82-14543

620.1'36 — Materials: Concrete. Properties

Neville, A. M.. Properties of concrete / A.M. Neville. — 3rd ed. — London : Pitman, 1981. — xii,779p : ill ; 24cm. — (A Pitman international text)
Previous ed.: 1973. — Includes index
ISBN 0-273-01641-5 (cased) : Unpriced
ISBN 0-273-01642-3 (pbk) : Unpriced B82-00060

620.1'36 — Materials: Concrete. Quality control

Quality assurance / prepared by the Technical Committee. — [Doncaster] ([Torridge, Bagsby Rd., Owston Ferry, Doncaster, S. Yorks.]) : Institute of Concrete Technology, 1980. — [11]p ; 30cm. — (Information review ; IR1)
Unpriced (unbound) B82-37567

620.1'3616 — Cryogenic concrete — *Conference proceedings*

Cryogenic concrete. — London : Construction Press, Oct.1982. — [335]p
Conference proceedings
ISBN 0-86095-705-5 : £25.00 : CIP entry B82-24617

620.1'363 — Concrete. Stresses & strains

Concrete strength and strains / Constantin Avram ... [et al.]. — Amsterdam ; Oxford : Elsevier Scientific, 1981. — 557p : ill ; 25cm. — (Developments in civil engineering ; 3)
Translation of: Rezistenţele şi deformaţüle betonului. 1971. — Includes bibliographies and index
ISBN 0-444-99733-4 : Unpriced : CIP rev. B81-25291

620.1'3633 — Concrete. Creep & contraction — *Conference proceedings*

Fundamental research on creep and shrinkage of concrete / edited by F.H. Wittmann. — The Hague ; London : Nijhoff, c1982. — x,528p : ill ; 25cm
Conference papers. — Includes index
ISBN 90-247-2549-6 : Unpriced B82-21451

620.1'367 — Concrete. Non-destructive testing

Bungey, J. H.. The testing of concrete in structures / J.H. Bungey. — Glasgow : Surrey University Press, 1982. — x,207p : ill ; 24cm
Includes index
ISBN 0-903384-29-9 : Unpriced : CIP rev. B82-11792

620.1'623 — Metals. Corrosion

Corrosion processes. — London : Applied Science, Sept.1982. — [320]p
ISBN 0-85334-147-8 : £28.00 : CIP entry B82-20831

620.1'623 — Metals. Corrosion inhibitors

Rozenfel'd, I. L.. Corrosion inhibitors / I.L. Rosenfeld ; translated for Keterpress Enterprises by Ron and Hilary Hardin. — New York ; London : McGraw-Hill, c1981. — xi,327p : ill ; 24cm
Translation of: Ingibitory korrozii. — Includes index
ISBN 0-07-054170-1 : £29.95 : CIP rev. B81-12880

620.1'623 — Metals. Corrosion. Prevention

Practical aspects of corrosion inhibition / proceedings of a symposium sponsored by the Society of Chemical Industry Materials Preservation Group and held at the National Physical Laboratory, Teddington, Middlesex, England on 28 February 1979. — London : Society of Chemical Industry, 1980. — viii,71p : ill ; 30cm
ISBN 0-901001-64-3 (pbk) : Unpriced B82-31369

620.1'623 — Metals. Corrosion resistance. Testing

Institute of Metal Finishing. *Working Party on Corrosion Testing in Metal Finishing.* Corrosion testing for metal finishing. — London : Butterworths, Nov.1982. — [128]p
ISBN 0-408-01194-7 : £10.00 : CIP entry B82-28274

620.1'6'3 — Metals. Strength

Strength of metals and alloys. — Oxford : Pergamon, Dec.1982. — 3v.. — (International series on the strength and fracture of materials and structures)
Conference proceedings
ISBN 0-08-029325-5 : £110.00 : CIP entry B82-29869

620.1'633 — Metals. Creep — *Conference proceedings*

International Conference on Engineering Aspects of Creep *(1980 : University of Sheffield).* International Conference on Engineering Aspects of Creep : University of Sheffield, 15-19 September 1980 / conference sponsored by the Institution of Mechanical Engineers ... [et al.]. — London : Mechanical Engineering Publications for the Institution. — (I Mech E conference publications ; 1980-5)
Vol.1. — 1980. — 296p : ill ; 30cm
ISBN 0-85298-455-3 (pbk) : Unpriced
ISBN 0-85298-454-5 (set) : £140.00 B82-40931

International Conference on Engineering Aspects of Creep *(1980 : University of Sheffield).* International Conference on Engineering Aspects of Creep : University of Sheffield, 15-19 September 1980 / conference sponsored by the Institution of Mechanical Engineers ... [et al.]. — London : Mechanical Engineering Publications for the Institution. — (I Mech E conference publications ; 1980-5)
Vol.2. — 1980. — 262p : ill ; 30cm
ISBN 0-85298-454-5 (pbk) : Unpriced B82-40932

620.1'66 — Metals. Fracture — *Conference proceedings*

National Conference on Fracture *(1st : 1979 : Johannesburg).* Engineering applications of fracture analysis : proceedings of the First National Conference on Fracture held in Johannesburg, South Africa, 7-9 November 1979 / edited by G.G. Garrett and D.L. Marriott. — Oxford : Pergamon, 1980. — 429p : ill ; 26cm. — (International series on the strength and fracture of materials and structures)
Includes bibliographies and index
ISBN 0-08-025437-3 : £25.00 : CIP rev. B80-18784

620.1'66 — Metals. Fracture. Fractures. Crack opening displacement. Measurement

Harrison, J. D. (John David). COD testing and analysis : the present state of the art / J. D. Harrison. — Cambridge : Welding Institute, 1981. — 30p : ill ; 30cm
ISBN 0-85300-144-8 (pbk) : £5.40 B82-08610

620.1'66 — Metals. Fracture. Fractures. Crack opening displacement. Measurement. Data. Correlation with Charpy test data — *Technical data*

Dolby, R. E.. COD and Charpy V test data correlation : ferritic steel weld metals / R.E. Dolby. — Cambridge : Welding Institute, 1981. — 15p : ill ; 30cm
ISBN 0-85300-143-x (pbk) : £5.40 B82-08609

620.1'8935233 — Zircaloy-2. Anisotropic creep & irradiation creep

Lucas, Glenn E.. Effects of anisotropy and irradiation on the creep behaviour of zircaloy-2 / Glenn E. Lucas. — New York ; London : Garland, 1979. — 375p : ill ; 21cm. — (Outstanding dissertations on energy)
ISBN 0-8240-3987-4 : Unpriced B82-10715

620.1'9 — Non-ductile materials. Design

Creyke, W. E. C.. Design with non-ductile materials. — London : Applied Science, Sept.1982. — [300]p
ISBN 0-85334-149-4 : £35.00 : CIP entry B82-20833

620.1'92 — Materials: Polymers. Blends

Matthews, George. Polymer mixing technology. — London : Applied Science, July 1982. — [292]p
ISBN 0-85334-133-8 : £27.00 : CIP entry B82-13137

620.1'92 — Materials: Polymers. Mechanical properties — *Conference proceedings*

International Conference on Deformation, Yield and Fracture of Polymers *(5th : 1982 : Cambridge).* Fifth International Conference on Deformation, Yield and Fracture of Polymers : Churchill College, Cambridge 29 March to 1 April 1982 / [organized by The Plastics and Rubber Institute]. — London (11 Hobart Place SW1N 0HL) : The Institute, [1982?]. — 1v (various pagings) : ill ; 21cm
Text on inside cover
£15.00 (pbk) B82-20157

620.1'92 — Polymer cellular materials — *Serials*

Cellular polymers : an international journal. — Vol.1, no.1 (1982)-. — London : Applied Science, 1982-. — v. : ill ; 24cm
Quarterly. — Continues: European journal of cellular plastics
ISSN 0262-4893 = Cellular polymers : £35.00 per year B82-40049

620.1'92 — Polymer composite materials & polymer blends

Sheldon, R. P.. Composite polymeric materials. — London : Applied Science, July 1982. — [248]p
ISBN 0-85334-129-x : £24.00 : CIP entry B82-13135

620.1'920426 — Materials: Polymers. Fracture

Kuksenko, V. S.. Fracture micromechanics of polymer materials / V.S. Kuksenko and V.P. Tamuzs. — The Hague ; London : Nijhoff, 1981. — xvi,311p : ill ; 25cm. — (Series on fatigue and fracture)
Translation of: Mikromekhanika razrusheniĭa polimernykh materialov. — Includes index
ISBN 90-247-2557-7 : Unpriced B82-07451

620.1'9204297 — Conductive polymers — *Conference proceedings*

Conductive polymers / [Proceedings of a symposium on conductive polymers sponsored by the American Chemical Society Division of Organic Coatings and Plastics Chemistry, held August 26-27, 1980, at the Second Chemical Congress of the North American Continent in Las Vegas, Nevada] ; edited by Raymond B. Seymour. — New York ; London : Plenum, c1981. — ix,237p : ill ; 26cm. — (Polymer science and technology ; v.15)
Includes index
ISBN 0-306-40805-8 : Unpriced B82-00531

620.1'923 — Materials: Thermoplastics

Mascia, L.. Thermoplastics. — London : Applied Science, Sept.1982. — [480]p
ISBN 0-85334-146-x : £42.00 : CIP entry B82-20830

620.1′923 — Plastics cellular materials. Mechanical properties

Mechanics of cellular plastics / edited by N.C. Hilyard. — London : Appiled Science, c1982. — x,401p : ill ; 23cm
Includes index
ISBN 0-85334-982-7 : £32.00 : CIP rev. B81-25719

620.1′92323 — Materials: Corrosion resistant plastics

Seymour, Raymond B.. Plastics vs. corrosives / Raymond B. Seymour. — New York ; Chichester : Wiley, c1982. — xii,285p : ill ; 24cm. — (SPE monographs, ISSN 0195-4288)
Includes bibliographies and index
ISBN 0-471-08182-5 : £37.00 B82-35306

620.1′97 — Collulosic composite materials. Adhesion — *Conference proceedings*

Adhesion in cellulosic and wood-based composites / [proceedings of a conference on adhesion in cellulosic and wood-based composites sponsored by the NATO Science Committee (Materials Science Panel) and held May 12-15, 1980, at Queen′s University, Kingston, Ontario, Canada] ; edited by John F. Oliver. — New York ; London : Plenum in cooperation with Nato Scientific Affairs Division, c1981. — vi,261p : ill ; 26cm. — (NATO conference series. VI, Materials science ; v.3)
Includes bibliographies and index
ISBN 0-306-40812-0 : Unpriced
Primary classification 620.1′292 B82-14543

620.2 — ENGINEERING. SOUND AND RELATED VIBRATIONS

620.2′3 — Great Britain. Factories. Machinery. Noise. Control measures

Some aspects of noise and hearing loss : notes on the problem of noise at work and report of the HSE Working Group on Machinery Noise / Health and Safety Commission. — London : H.M.S.O., 1981. — 66p : ill ; 30cm
"Background to the HSC consultative document on the protection of hearing at work" — cover. — Bibliography: p62-66
ISBN 0-11-883432-0 (pbk) : £3.50
Primary classification 617.8′052 B82-00429

620.2′3 — Industries. Noise. Control measures

Fader, Bruce. Industrial noise control / Bruce Fader. — New York ; Chichester : Wiley, c1981. — vii,251p : ill ; 24cm
Includes index
ISBN 0-471-06007-0 : £21.85 B82-04542

620.2′3 — Noise

Noise and vibration. — Chichester : Ellis Horwood, Sept.1982. — [800]p
ISBN 0-85312-502-3 : £40.00 : CIP entry B82-25086

620.2′3 — Noise. Control measures

Lord, Harold W.. Noise control for engineers / Harold W. Lord, William S. Gatley, Harold A. Evensen. — New York ; London : McGraw-Hill, c1980. — xi,435p : ill ; 24cm
Includes index
ISBN 0-07-038738-9 : £20.75 B82-25267

620.2′3 — Urban regions. Noise. Measurement. Noise ratings

Schultz, Theodore John. Community noise rating. — 2nd ed. — London : Applied Science, Aug.1982. — [330]p
Previous ed.: 1972
ISBN 0-85334-137-0 : £32.00 : CIP entry B82-16660

620.2′3′071141 — Great Britain. Higher education institutions. Curriculum subjects: Noise. Teaching — *Conference proceedings*

British Conference on the Teaching of Vibration and Noise *(4th : 1982 : Sheffield City Polytechnic)*. Proceedings of the Fourth British Conference on the Teaching of Vibration and Noise : held at Sheffield City Polytechnic 6th-8th July, 1982 / edited by J.L. Wearing ... [et al.]. — Sheffield : Sheffield City Polytechnic Industrial Development and Liaison Services, 1982. — 289p : ill ; 30cm
ISBN 0-903761-57-2 : Unpriced
Also classified at 620.3′07′1141 B82-37981

620.2′8 — Ultrasonic waves. Use

Puškár, Anton. The use of high-intensity ultrasonics. — Oxford : Elsevier Scientific, Oct.1982. — [300]p. — (Materials science monographs ; 13)
Translation of: Fyzikálne metalurgické a technologické aspekty využitia intenzívneho ultrazvuku
ISBN 0-444-99690-7 : £45.00 : CIP entry B82-24017

620.3 — ENGINEERING. MECHANICAL VIBRATION

620.3′07′1141 — Great Britain. Higher education institutions. Curriculum subjects: Engineering aspects of mechanical vibration. Teaching — *Conference proceedings*

British Conference on the Teaching of Vibration and Noise *(4th : 1982 : Sheffield City Polytechnic)*. Proceedings of the Fourth British Conference on the Teaching of Vibration and Noise : held at Sheffield City Polytechnic 6th-8th July, 1982 / edited by J.L. Wearing ... [et al.]. — Sheffield : Sheffield City Polytechnic Industrial Development and Liaison Services, 1982. — 289p : ill ; 30cm
ISBN 0-903761-57-2 : Unpriced
Primary classification 620.2′3′071141 B82-37981

620.3′7 — Low-frequency mechanical ground-borne vibration. Absorption. Use of natural rubber. Engineering aspects

Rose, I. G.. Vibration isolation with natural rubber / I.G. Rose. — [Brickendonbury] : Malaysian Rubber Producers′ Research Association, [1982?]. — ii,10p : ill,1port ; 30cm. — (NR background, ISSN 0144-7734 ; 5)
Cover title
Unpriced (pbk) B82-38738

620.4 — ENGINEERING TECHNOLOGIES

620′.4162 — Concrete marine structures

Sea operations / [FIP Commission on Concrete Sea Structures]. — Slough : Fédération Internationale de la Précontrainte, 1982. — 19p ; 30cm. — (State of art report / Fédération Internationale de la Précontrainte)
Cover title
ISBN 0-907862-15-2 (pbk) : Unpriced B82-37102

620′.4162 — Ocean engineering. Applications of electronics — *Conference proceedings*

Electronics for ocean technology : Birmingham 8-10 September 1981. — London : Institution of Electronic and Radio Engineers, 1981. — 348p : ill,maps ; 30cm. — (Proceedings / Institution of Electronic and Radio Engineers ; no.51)
ISBN 0-903748-46-0 (pbk) : Unpriced B82-05106

620′.4162 — Offshore engineering — *Conference proceedings*

International Symposium on Offshore Engineering *(3rd : 1981 : Federal University of Rio de Janeiro)*. Offshore engineering : proceedings of the 3rd International Symposium on Offshore Engineering held at COPPE, Federal University of Rio de Janeiro, Brazil, September 1981 / sponsored by PETROBRAS (The Brazilian State Oil Company), CPNq [i.e. CNPq] (The Brazilian Council for Scientific and Technological Development) ; edited by F.L.L.B. Carneiro, A.J. Ferrante and R.C. Batista. — London : Pentech Press, 1982. — 584p : ill,maps ; 24cm
Includes one contribution in French
ISBN 0-7273-1503-x : Unpriced : CIP rev. B82-13500

620′.4162′072041 — Great Britain. Ocean engineering. Research organisations: National Maritime Institute. Facilities for testing hydrodynamics of marine structures

Hydrodynamic experiment facilities for ships and marine structures / [prepared by the Department of Industry and the Central Office of Information]. — [Feltham] ([Faggs Rd., Feltham, Middx., TW14 0LQ]) : National Maritime Institute, [1981]. — 24p : ill ; 21x30cm
Cover title
Unpriced (pbk)
Primary classification 620′.4162′072041 B82-00627

620′.4162′072041 — Great Britain. Ocean engineering. Research organisations: National Maritime Institute. Facilities for testing hydrodynamics of ships

Hydrodynamic experiment facilities for ships and marine structures / [prepared by the Department of Industry and the Central Office of Information]. — [Feltham] ([Faggs Rd., Feltham, Middx., TW14 0LQ]) : National Maritime Institute, [1981]. — 24p : ill ; 21x30cm
Cover title
Unpriced (pbk)
Also classified at 620′.4162′072041 B82-00627

620′.4162′072041 — Great Britain. Ocean engineering. Research organisations: National Maritime Institute — *Serials*

NMI news / National Maritime Institute. — [No.1] (Nov. 1980)-. — Feltham (Feltham, Middx. TW14 0LQ) : The Institute, 1980-. — v. : ill,maps, ports ; 30cm
Irregular
ISSN 0260-4817 = NMI news : Unpriced B82-06177

620′.43 — Fine particles. Size & shape. Determination

Kaye, Brian H.. Direct characterization of fineparticles / Brian H. Kaye. — New York ; Chichester : Wiley, c1981. — xviii,398p : ill ; 24cm. — (Chemical analysis ; v.61)
Includes index
ISBN 0-471-46150-4 : £44.40 B82-04544

620′.43 — Fine particles. Size & shape. Determination. Techniques

Testing and characterization of powders and fine particles / edited by J.K. Beddow and T.P. Meloy. — London : Heyden, c1980. — xxiii,195p : ill ; 24cm
Includes index
ISBN 0-85501-460-1 : Unpriced B82-10087

620′.43 — Particles. Size. Measurement — *Conference proceedings*

Particle Size Analysis Conference *(4th : 1981 : Loughborough University of Technology)*. Particle size analysis. — London : Heyden, July 1982. — [400]p
ISBN 0-85501-719-8 : CIP entry B82-14937

620′.43 — Powders. Adhesion

Zimon, A. D.. Adhesion of dust and powder / Anatolii D. Zimon ; translated from Russian by Robert K. Johnson. — 2nd ed. — New York ; London : Consultants Bureau, c1982. — xi,438p : ill ; 24cm
Translation of: Adgeziia pyli i poroshkov
ISBN 0-306-10962-x : Unpriced B82-25804

620.7 — SYSTEMS ENGINEERING

620.7 — Systems engineering

Gheorghe, Adrian. Applied systems engineering. — Chichester : Wiley, July 1982. — [288]p
Translation and revision of: Ingineria sistemelor
ISBN 0-471-09997-x : £12.50 : CIP entry B82-14370

620.7′068 — Systems engineering. Management - *Conference proceedings*

Industrial systems engineering and management in developing countries. — Oxford : Pergamon, June 1981. — [928]p
Conference papers
ISBN 0-08-027611-3 : £56.00 : CIP entry B81-18073

620.8 — ENVIRONMENT ENGINEERING

620.8 — Environment engineering
Salvato, Joseph A.. Environmental engineering and sanitation / Joseph A. Salvato. — 3rd ed. — New York ; Chichester : Wiley, c1982. — xxiv,1163p : ill,forms,plans ; 25cm. — (Environmental science and technology, ISSN 0194-0287)
Previous ed.: 1972. — Includes bibliographies and index
ISBN 0-471-04942-5 : £40.50 B82-28780

620.8 — Environment engineering — *Conference proceedings*
Environmental systems planning, design and control : proceedings of the IFAC symposium, Kyoto, Japan, 1-5 August 1977 / edited by Y. Sawaragi and H. Akashi. — Oxford : Published for the International Federation of Automatic Control by Pergamon, 1978. — 2v.(xv,927p) : ill,maps ; 31cm
Includes index
ISBN 0-08-022016-9 : £72.00 : CIP rev. B78-21256

620.8′2 — Ergonomics
Bailey, Robert W.. Human performance engineering : a guide for system designers / Robert W. Bailey. — Englewood Cliffs ; London : Prentice-Hall, c1982. — xxiii,656p : ill ; 25cm
Bibliography: p610-633. — Includes index
ISBN 0-13-445320-4 : £27.00 B82-33767

McCormick, Ernest J.. Human factors in engineering and design / Ernest J. McCormick, Mark S. Sanders. — 5th ed. — New York ; London : McGraw-Hill, c1982. — viii,615p : ill ; 25cm
Previous ed.: 1976. — Bibliography: p599-601. — Includes index
ISBN 0-07-044902-3 : £23.75 B82-22170

Oborne, D. J.. Ergonomics at work / David J. Oborne. — Chichester : Wiley, c1982. — ix,321p : ill ; 24cm
Bibliography: p291-309. — Includes index
ISBN 0-471-10030-7 : £12.50 : CIP rev. B81-35730

620.8′2 — Ergonomics. Anthropometry
Anthropometry and biomechanics : theory and application / [proceedings of a NATO symposium on anthropometry and biomechanics: theory and application, held July 7-11, 1980, at Queens′ College, Cambridge, England] ; edited by Ronald Easterby, K.H.E. Kroemer and Don B. Chaffin. — New York ; London : Published in cooperation with NATO Scientific Affairs Division [by] Plenum, c1982. — x,327p : ill ; 26cm. — (NATO conference series. 111, Human factors)
Includes bibliographies and index
ISBN 0-306-40745-0 : Unpriced
Also classified at 612′.76 B82-33765

620.8′2 — Ergonomics — *Conference proceedings*
Manned systems design : methods, equipment, and applications / edited by J. Moraal and K.-F. Kraiss. — New York ; London : Plenum in cooperation with NATO Scientific Affairs Division, c1981. — ix,487p : ill ; 26cm. — (NATO conference series. III, Human factors ; v.17)
Conference papers. — Includes bibliographies and index
ISBN 0-306-40804-x : Unpriced B82-01482

621 — MECHANICAL ENGINEERING

621 — Applied physics
Harris, Norman C.. Introductory applied physics / Norman C. Harris, Edwin M. Hemmerling. — 4th ed. — New York ; London : McGraw-Hill, c1980. — xiii,785p : ill ; 25cm
Previous ed.: 1972. — Includes index
ISBN 0-07-026816-9 : £15.75 B82-14028

621 — Mechanical engineering — *For technicians*
Smith, Ken, *1924-*. Mechanical and engineering principles / Ken Smith. — London : Pitman
Vol.2: Fluid mechanics, thermodynamics and instrumentation. — 1982. — x,182p : ill ; 25cm
Includes index
ISBN 0-273-01674-1 (pbk) : Unpriced B82-15306

Timings, R. L.. Manufacturing technology 2 checkbook. — London : Butterworth Scientific, Dec.1982. — [192]p. — (Butterworths technical and scientific checkbooks)
ISBN 0-408-00684-6 (cased) : £7.95 : CIP entry
ISBN 0-408-00618-8 (pbk) : £3.95 B82-29788

621.042 — Energy sources
Harder, Edwin L.. Fundamentals of energy production / Edwin L. Harder. — New York ; Chichester : John Wiley & Sons, 1982. — xvi,368p : ill,maps,plans ; 29cm. — (Alternate energy)
Includes index
ISBN 0-471-08356-9 : Unpriced B82-34699

Hodgson, Peter. Our nuclear future?. — Belfast : Christian Journals, Oct.1982. — [148]p
ISBN 0-904302-81-4 : £7.50 : CIP entry B82-29413

621.042 — Energy sources: Household waste materials
Secondary materials in domestic refuse as energy sources : a report / prepared for the Environment and Consumer Protection Service of the Commission of the European Communities by Europool. — London : Graham & Trotman for the Commission, 1977. — 72p ; 30cm
ISBN 0-86010-064-2 (pbk) : £7.50 B82-34138

621.042 — Energy. Storage
Jensen, J.. Energy storage. — London : Butterworth, July 1982. — [101]p
Originally published: 1980
ISBN 0-408-01225-0 (pbk) : £7.50 : CIP entry B82-11759

621.042 — Energy. Storage — *Conference proceedings*
International Conference on Energy Storage *(1981 : Brighton)*. Papers presented at the International Conference on Energy Storage held at the Bedford Hotel, Brighton, U.K. April 29-May 1, 1981 / sponsored and organised by BHRA Fluid Engineering, Cranfield, Bedford MK43 0AJ, U.K. in conjunction with the Energy Technology Support Unit of the UK Department of Energy and the Science Research Council. — Bedford : BHRA Fluid Engineering
Vol.1. — c1981. — v,386p : ill,maps ; 30cm
ISBN 0-906085-50-0 (pbk) : Unpriced : CIP rev.
ISBN 0-906085-42-x (set) : Unpriced B81-08880

International Conference on Energy Storage *(1981 : Brighton)*. Papers presented at the International Conference on Energy Storage held at the Bedford Hotel, Brighton, U.K. April 29-May 1, 1981 / ... in conjunction with the Energy Technology Support Unit of the UK Department of Energy and the Science Research Council. — Bedford : BHRA Fluid Engineering
Vol.2. — c1981. — p387-551 : ill ; 30cm
Includes index
ISBN 0-906085-61-6 (pbk) : Unpriced
ISBN 0-906085-42-x (set) : Unpriced B82-37600

621.042 — Engineering systems. Energy efficiency. Calculation. Applications of thermodynamics
Moran, Michael J.. Availability analysis : a guide to efficient energy use / Michael J. Moran. — Englewood Cliffs ; London : Prentice-Hall, c1982. — xi,260p : ill ; 24cm
Includes bibliographies and index
ISBN 0-13-054874-x : £22.45 B82-20062

621.042 — Great Britain. Energy. Conservation. Demonstration projects: Energy Conservation Demonstration Projects Scheme
Currie, W. M.. The Energy Conservation Demonstration Projects Scheme : what it is all about / W.M. Currie. — Harwell (Building 156, AERE, Harwell, Didcot, Oxon. OX11 0RA) : Energy Technology Support Unit, 1981. — 31p : ill ; 30cm
Unpriced (spiral) B82-38372

Project profile. — Harwell (Building 156, AERE, Harwell, Didcot, Oxon. OX11 0RA) : Energy Technology Support Unit, 1981. — 1portfolio : ill(some col.) ; 31cm
Energy Conservation Demonstration Projects Scheme
Unpriced B82-38373

621.042′01′54 — Energy engineering. Chemical aspects — *Conference proceedings*
Energy and chemistry : the proceedings of a symposium organised by the Industrial Division of the Royal Society of Chemistry as part of the Annual Chemical Congress, 1981, University of Surrey, Guildford, April 7th-9th, 1981 / edited by R. Thompson. — London : Royal Society of Chemistry, c1981. — viii,359p : ill,maps ; 21cm. — (Special publication / Royal Society of Chemistry, ISSN 0260-6291 ; no.41)
ISBN 0-85186-845-2 (pbk) : Unpriced : CIP rev. B81-38853

621.042′028 — Small scale energy engineering equipment — *Buyers′ guides*
Fraenkel, Peter. The power guide : a catalogue of small scale power equipment / compiled by Peter Fraenkel. — London : Intermediate Technolgy, c1979. — 240p : ill ; 30cm
Includes index
ISBN 0-903031-59-0 (pbk) : £7.50 B82-07853

621.042′03 — Energy engineering — *Polyglot dictionaries*
Energy terminology : a multi-lingual glossary. — Oxford : Pergamon, Apr.1982. — [275]p
ISBN 0-08-029314-x (cased) : £50.00 : CIP entry
ISBN 0-08-029315-8 (pbk) : £17.50 B82-05383

621.042′03′21 — Energy engineering — *Encyclopaedias*
Gilpin, Alan. Dictionary of energy technology / Alan Gilpin in collaboration with Alan Williams. — London : Butterworth Scientific, 1982. — 392p : ill ; 23cm
Bibliography: p387-392
ISBN 0-408-01108-4 : Unpriced : CIP rev. B81-31732

621.042′072 — Energy sources. Research organisations — *Directories*
World energy directory : a guide to organizations and research activities in non-atomic energy / consultant editors J.A. Bauly and C.B. Bauly. — [Harlow] : Hodgson, c1981. — 567p ; 24cm. — (Reference on research)
Includes index
ISBN 0-582-90011-5 : £70.00 : CIP rev. B81-15936

621.1 — STEAM ENGINEERING

621.1′09 — Steam engines, *to ca 1965*
Briggs, Asa. The power of steam : an illustrated history of the world′s steam age / Asa Briggs. — London : Joseph, 1982. — 208p : ill(some col.),facsims,ports ; 26cm
Ill on lining papers. — Includes index
ISBN 0-7181-2076-0 : £10.50 B82-11324

Watkins, George. Steam power. — Newton Abbot : David & Charles, Nov.1982. — [32]p
Originally published: 1967
ISBN 0-7153-8436-8 (pbk) : £1.50 : CIP entry B82-26049

621.1′092′2 — Steam engineering. Boulton, Matthew & Watt, James, *1736-1819* — *Correspondence, diaries, etc.*
Boulton, Matthew. The selected papers of Boulton & Watt / edited by Jennifer Tann. — London : Diploma
Vol.1: The engine partnership. — 1981. — xv,425p,[14]p of plates : ill,facsims ; 24cm
Bibliography: p407-414. — Includes index
ISBN 0-86015-070-4 : Unpriced B82-20110

621.1′092′4 — Steam engineering. Watt, James — *Biographies*
Nahum, Andrew. James Watt and the power of steam / Andrew Nahum. — Hove : Wayland, 1981. — 71p : ill,1facsim,ports ; 24cm. — (Pioneers of science and discovery)
Bibliography: p68. — Includes index
ISBN 0-85340-826-2 : £3.95 B82-00863

621.1′6′0228 — Model stationary steam engines. Construction — *Manuals*

Cain, Tubal. Building simple model steam engines / Tubal Cain. — [Watford] : Model & Allied, [1980]. — 107p : ill ; 21cm
ISBN 0-85242-717-4 (pbk) : £3.95 B82-31833

621.1′8 — Boilers

Elonka, Stephen Michael. Standard boiler room questions & answers. — 3rd ed. / Stephen Michael Elonka, Alex Higgins. — New York ; London : McGraw-Hill, c1982. — x,434p : ill,forms ; 22cm
Previous ed.: published as Boiler room questions and answers / Alex Higgins, Stephen Michael Elonka. 1976. — Includes bibliographies and index
ISBN 0-07-019301-0 : £22.95 B82-15972

621.1′8 — Boilers. Operation — *Manuals*

Spring, Harry M.. Boiler operator′s guide : boiler construction, operation, inspection, maintenance, and repair, with typical boiler questions and answers for plant, operating and maintenance engineers. — 2nd ed. / Harry M. Spring, Jr, Anthony Lawrence Kohan. — New York ; London : McGraw-Hill, c1981. — x,469p : ill ; 24cm
Previous ed.: 1940. — Bibliography: p458. — Includes index
ISBN 0-07-060511-4 : £16.50 B82-02328

621.1′8 — Shell boilers. Water. Treatment

The **Treatment** of water for shell boilers : a short guide / compiled by the Technical Committee of the Association of Shell Boilermakers. — 3rd ed. — [Manchester] ([12 Booth St., Manchester M60 2ED]) : The Association, 1979. — 29p : ill ; 30cm
Cover title. — Previous ed.: 1976. — Bibliography: p26. — Includes index
£3.00 (pbk) B82-12801

621.1′8 — Steam boilers — *Conference proceedings*

Steam boiler plant technology : convention sponsored by the Power Industries Division of the Institution of Mechanical Engineers, 7 October, Institution Headquarters, London. — London : Published by Mechanical Engineering Publications for the Institution of Mechanical Engineers, 1981. — 70p : ill ; 30cm. — (I Mech E conference publications ; 1981-9)
ISBN 0-85298-483-9 (pbk) : Unpriced B82-02690

621.1′97 — Steam condensers — *Conference proceedings*

Modern Developments in Marine Condensers *(Conference : 1980 : Naval Postgraduate School, Monterey)*. Power condenser heat transfer technology : computer modeling, design, fouling / [proceedings of the workshop titled ′Modern Developments in Marine Condensers′ held at the Naval Postgraduate School, Monterey, California, March 26-28, 1980, and sponsored by the Naval Sea Systems Command and the Office of Naval Research] ; edited by P.J. Marto and R.H. Nunn. — Washington ; London : Hemisphere, c1981. — x,490p : ill ; 25cm
Includes index
ISBN 0-07-040662-6 : £34.75 B82-04444

621.2 — HYDRAULIC POWER

621.2 — Hydraulic power engineering

Animated lecturing aids for hydraulic equipment / Sperry Vickers. — [Portsmouth] ([Grove Rd, Cosham, Portsmouth PO6 1PZ]) : [Sperry Vickers], [1980?]. — 1v.(loose-leaf) : ill(some col.) ; 34cm
Text in English, French, German and Spanish. — Cover title
Unpriced B82-34686

621.2′0422 — Water power — *For children*

Payne, Sherry Neuwirth. Wind and water energy. — Oxford : Blackwell Raintree, Nov.1982. — [42]p. — (A Look inside)
ISBN 0-86256-067-5 : £3.25 : CIP entry
Also classified at 621.4′5 B82-26073

621.2′52 — Developing countries. Solar energy water pumps — *Conference proceedins*

Solar energy for developing countries : refrigeration & water pumping : conference proceedings / conference organised by the UK section of the International Solar Energy Society (UK-ISES) at the Geological Society, Burlington House, Piccadilly, London, W1, UK on Wednesday, January 27, 1982 ; edited by Bernard McNelis. — London : UK-ISES, 1982. — 109p : ill ; 21cm. — (Conference / International Solar Energy Society. UK Section, ISSN 0306-7874 ; C28)
ISBN 0-904963-29-2 (pbk) : Unpriced
Primary classification 621.5′7 B82-17796

621.2′6 — Hydraulic equipment

Hydraulic handbook. — 6th ed. — Morden : Trade & Technical Press, [1975]. — xii,787p : ill ; 23cm
Previous ed.: 1972. — Includes index
ISBN 0-85461-061-8 : £34.00 B82-32252

621.3 — ELECTRICAL, ELECTRONIC, ELECTROMAGNETIC ENGINEERING

621.3 — Electrical engineering

Basic electricity : a series of basic training manuals developed for the United States Navy / by ... Van Valkenburgh, Nooger & Neville, Inc. ; adapted to British and Commonwealth usage. — Oxford : Technical Press. — (A Common core book)
Previous ed.: 1975
Part 3. — 3rd British ed. / rev. and enlarged under the technical supervision of J.M. Chapman. — c1981. — vi,138p : ill ; 25cm
Includes index
ISBN 0-291-39632-1 (pbk) : Unpriced : CIP rev. B81-14781

Basic electricity. — Oxford : Technical
Pt.4. — 3rd ed. — May 1982. — [144]p
Previous ed.: 1975
ISBN 0-291-39633-x (pbk) : £3.95 : CIP entry B82-12704

Elgerd, Olle I.. Electric energy systems theory : an introduction / Olle I. Elgerd. — 2nd ed. — New York ; London : McGraw-Hill, c1982. — xviii,533p : ill ; 25cm. — (McGraw-Hill series in elctrical engineering. Power and energy)
Previous ed.: 1971. — Includes index
ISBN 0-07-019230-8 : £24.50 B82-23891

Lewis, Rhys. Electrical and electronic principles 2. — London : Granada, May 1982. — [192]p
ISBN 0-246-11575-0 (pbk) : £4.95 : CIP entry B82-12132

Neidle, Michael. Electrical installation technology. — 3rd ed. — London : Butterworths, June 1982. — [400]p
Previous ed.: London : Newnes-Butterworths, 1975
ISBN 0-408-01146-7 (pbk) : £6.00 : CIP entry B82-10491

Penketh, J. R.. Light current applications 3 checkbook. — London : Butterworth Scientific, Nov.1982. — [128]p. — (Butterworth technical and scientific checkbooks)
ISBN 0-408-00689-7 (cased) : £7.95 : CIP entry
ISBN 0-408-00687-0 (pbk) : £3.95 B82-28272

Tyler, D. W.. Electrical and electronic applications 2 checkbook / D.W. Tyler. — London : Butterworths, 1982. — viii,216p : ill ; 20cm. — (Butterworths technical and scientific checkbooks)
Includes index
ISBN 0-408-00661-7 (cased) : £8.95 : CIP rev.
ISBN 0-408-00661-7 (pbk) : Unpriced B81-25286

Venikov, V. A.. Introduction to energy technology : electric power-engineering / V.A. Venikov, E.V. Putyatin ; edited by V.A. Venikov ; translated from Russian by B. Nikolayev. — Moscow : Mir ; [London] : Distributed by Central Books, 1981. — 304p : ill ; 23cm
Translation of: Vvedenie v speťsial′nost′. — Added t.p. in Russian. — Includes index
ISBN 0-7147-1659-6 : £3.95 B82-02530

621.3 — Electrical engineering — *For technicians*

Bird, J. O.. Electrical science 3 checkbook / J.O. Bird, A.J.C. May, J.R. Penketh. — London : Butterworths, 1981. — viii,128p : ill ; 20cm. — (Butterworths technical and scientific checkbooks)
Includes index
ISBN 0-408-00657-9 (cased) : £6.95 : CIP rev.
ISBN 0-408-00626-9 (pbk) : £3.50 B81-32030

Knight, S. A.. Electrical and electronic principles 4/5 / S.A. Knight. — [London] : Butterworth, 1982. — 197p : ill ; 25cm. — (Butterworths technician series)
ISBN 0-408-01109-2 (pbk) : £7.95 : CIP rev. B82-04034

Meadows, R. G.. Technician electrical and electronic principles 3 / R.G. Meadows. — London : Cassell, 1981. — xiii,287p : ill ; 22cm. — (Cassell′s TEC series)
Includes index
ISBN 0-304-30296-1 (pbk) : Unpriced B82-03187

Morris, Noel M.. Electrical and electronic applications / Noel M. Morris. — London : Pitman, 1982. — xii,252p : ill ; 25cm
Includes index
ISBN 0-273-01330-0 (pbk) : Unpriced B82-15307

Pratley, John B.. Study notes for technicians. — London : McGraw-Hill
Electrical and electronic principles / John B. Pratley
Vol.1. — c1982. — 72p : ill ; 25cm
ISBN 0-07-084661-8 (pbk) : £3.25 : CIP rev. B82-12914

Pratley, John B.. Study notes for technicians. — London : McGraw-Hill
Electrical and electronic principles / John B. Pratley
Vol.2. — c1982. — 141p : ill ; 25cm
ISBN 0-07-084662-6 (pbk) : £3.25 : CIP rev. B82-17188

Roots, K.. Heavy current applications level 4. — London : Longman, Sept.1982. — [272]p. — (Longman technician series. Electrical and electronic engineering)
ISBN 0-582-41219-6 (pbk) : £6.95 : CIP entry B82-22427

Waterworth, G.. Electrical principles for technicians / G. Waterworth ; illustrated by R.P. Phillips. — London : Edward Arnold
Vol.2. — 1982. — iv,252p : ill ; 22cm
Includes index
ISBN 0-7131-3443-7 (pbk) : £5.50 : CIP rev. B82-01188

621.3 — Great Britain. Electrical engineering. Daywork. Standard prime costs

Definition of prime cost of day work carried out under an electrical contract. — 2nd ed. — London : Royal Institution of Chartered Surveyors, 1971 (1981 [printing]). — 9p ; 21cm
Text on inside cover
£0.70(£0.60 to members of RICA) (pbk) B82-25801

621.3 — Static electricity. Control measures

Horváth, T.. Static elimination / T. Horváth and I. Berta. — Chichester : Research Studies Press, c1982. — x,118p : ill ; 24cm. — (Electronic & electrical engineering research studies. Electrostatics and electrostatic applications series ; 1)
Bibliography: p107-115. — Includes index
ISBN 0-471-10405-1 : £10.50 : CIP rev. B82-09218

621.3′076 — Electrical engineering — *Questions & answers* — *For technicians*

Dagger, A.. Multiple choice questions in electrical principles : for TEC Levels I, II and III / A. Dagger. — Plymouth : Macdonald & Evans, 1981. — xiii,88p : ill ; 22cm. — (The M & E TEC book series)
Bibliography: p86. — Includes index
ISBN 0-7121-1274-x (pbk) : £2.95 B82-07282

621.3′09 — Electrical engineering, *to 1900*
Davis, Henry B. O.. Electrical and electronic technologies : a chronology of events and inventors to 1900 / by Henry B.O. Davis. — Metuchen ; London : Scarecrow, 1981. — vii,213p ; 23cm
Bibliography: p176-181. — Includes index
ISBN 0-8108-1464-1 : £12.80 B82-08576

621.3′092′4 — Electrical engineering. Edison, Thomas A. — *Biographies — For children*
Ross, Josephine. Thomas Edison / Josephine Ross ; illustrated by Peter Gregory. — London : Hamilton, 1982. — 63p : ill,ports ; 22cm. — (Profiles (Hamilton))
ISBN 0-241-10713-x : £3.25 B82-20816

621.31 — Electricity supply. Generation & transmission
Generation and transmission of electricity. — Dorchester : Planning Department, Dorset County Council, 1981. — 16p ; 21cm. — (Nuclear power stations ; information paper no.2)
Cover title. — Text on inside cover
ISBN 0-85216-297-9 (pbk) : Unpriced
B82-12740

621.31 — Electricity supply systems. Analysis
Stevenson, William D.. Elements of power system analysis / William D. Stevenson, Jr.. — 4th ed. — New York ; London : McGraw-Hill, c1982. — xii,436p : ill ; 25cm. — (McGraw-Hill series in electrical engineering)
Previous ed.: 1975. — Includes index
ISBN 0-07-061278-1 : £24.50
ISBN 0-07-061279-x (Solutions manual)
B82-28057

621.31′042 — Electric equipment
Faber, Rodney B.. Applied electricity and electronics for technology / Rodney B. Faber. — 2nd ed. — New York ; Chichester : Wiley, c1982. — xi,477p : ill,facsims ; 24cm. — (Electronic technology series, ISSN 0422-910x)
Previous ed.: 1978. — Includes bibliographies and index
ISBN 0-471-05792-4 : £16.25 B82-18936

Mottershead, Allen. Introduction to electricity and electronics : conventional current version / Allen Mottershead. — New York ; Chichester : Wiley, c1982. — xix,674p : ill ; 27cm
Includes index
ISBN 0-471-05751-7 : £15.35 B82-25452

Mottershead, Allen. Introduction to electricity and electronics : electron-flow version / Allen Mottershead. — New York ; Chichester : Wiley, c1982. — xix,674p : ill(some col.) ; 27cm
Includes index
ISBN 0-471-09851-5 : £15.35 B82-28037

621.31′042 — Electric equipment — *For schools*
Buban, Peter. Understanding electricity and electronics / Peter Buban and Marshall L. Schmitt. — 4th ed. — New York ; London : McGraw-Hill, c1982. — viii,472p : ill(some col.),1forms ; 24cm. — (McGraw-Hill publications in industrial education)
Previous ed.: 1975. — Includes index
ISBN 0-07-008678-8 : £12.00 B82-02523

621.31′042 — Electric equipment. Installation
Neidle, Michael. Electrical installation theory and practice. — London : McGraw-Hill, Feb.1983. — [192]p
ISBN 0-07-084668-5 (pbk) : £5.25 : CIP entry
B82-36308

621.31′042 — Electric equipment — *Questions & answers*
Hickman, Ian. Electronics. — 2nd ed. — London : Newnes Technical Books, Mar.1982. — [128] p. — (Questions & answers)
Previous ed.: 1966
ISBN 0-408-00578-5 (pbk) : £1.95 : CIP entry
B82-00910

621.31′042 — Electric machinery
Morgan, A. T.. General theory of electrical machines / A.T. Morgan. — London : Heyden, c1979. — xvi,448p : ill ; 24cm
Includes index
ISBN 0-85501-461-x (pbk) : Unpriced
B82-05369

Slemon, G. R.. Electric machines / G.R. Slemon, A. Straughen. — Reading, Mass. ; London : Addison-Wesley, 1980. — xv,575p : ill ; 24cm
Text on lining papers. — Includes index
ISBN 0-201-07730-2 : £9.95 B82-05156

621.31′042′05 — Electric industrial equipment — *Serials*
GEC journal for industry. — Vol.1, no.1 (Oct. 1977)-. — Rugby (Mill Rd, Rugby, Warwicks. CV21 1BD) : GEC Large Machines Ltd., 1977-. — v. : ill,ports ; 30cm
Three issues yearly. — Description based on: Vol.5, no.2 (June 1981)
ISSN 0262-8236 = GEC journal for industry : Unpriced B82-09064

621.31′042′0973 — United States. Electrical equipment. Standards — *For British exporters*
Electrical equipment for the United States of America : requirements and approval procedures applicable to domestic, commercial and industrial equipment. — Hemel Hempstead : Technical Help to Exporters, 1980. — viii,74p ; 30cm. — (Technical guide)
ISBN 0-905877-96-9 (pbk) : Unpriced
B82-39120

621.31′0941 — Great Britain. Electricity. Generation & use, *to 1981*
Bowers, Brian. A history of electric light and power / Brian Bowers. — London : Peregrinus in association with the Science Museum, c1982. — vii,278p : ill,facsims ; 24cm. — (History of technology series ; 3)
Includes index
ISBN 0-906048-68-0 (cased) : Unpriced : CIP rev.
ISBN 0-906048-71-0 (pbk) : Unpriced
B82-04730

621.31′2 — Electricity supply. Generation. Risks
Cohen, A. V.. Comparative risks of electricity production systems : a critical survey of the literature / A.V. Cohen and D.K. Pritchard. — London : H.M.S.O., 1980. — 31p ; 30cm. — (Research paper ; 11)
At head of title: Health & Safety Executive
ISBN 0-11-883274-3 (pbk) : £2.00 : CIP rev.
B80-13868

621.31′2132 — Great Britain. Electricity supply. Generation. Use of coal
England, Glyn. Electricity from coal / by Glyn England ; based on a talk to the Coal Industry Society in London on 2 November 1981. — London : Central Electricity Generating Board, 1981. — [8]p : 1port ; 21cm
Cover title. — At head of title: Central Electricity Generating Board. — Text, port on inside covers
Unpriced (pbk) B82-09572

621.31′2134 — Electricity supply. Generation by water power — *Amateurs′ manuals*
McGuigan, Dermot. Small scale water power / Dermot McGuigan. — Dorchester : Prism, 1978 (1979 [printing]). — 113p : ill ; 23cm
Bibliography: p111-113
ISBN 0-904727-33-5 (cased) : £5.95
ISBN 0-904727-32-7 B82-12526

621.31′2134 — Oceans. Wave power. Conversion
McCormick, Michael E.. Ocean wave energy conversion / Michael E. McCormick. — New York ; Chichester : Wiley, 1981. — xxiv,233p : ill ; 24cm. — (Alternate energy)
Bibliography: p196-201. — Includes index
ISBN 0-471-08543-x : £29.50 B82-03903

621.31′2134 — Tidal power & wave power — *Conference proceedings*
International Symposium on Wave & Tidal Energy *(2nd : 1981 : Cambridge)*. Papers presented at the Second International Symposium on Wave & Tidal Energy held at Cambridge England September 23-25, 1981 / ... sponsored and organised by BHRA Fluid Engineering ; [editors H.S. Stephens, C.A. Stapleton]. — Bedford : BHRA Fluid Engineering, [1981?]. — viii,440p : ill,maps ; 30cm
ISBN 0-906085-43-8 (pbk) : Unpriced : CIP rev. B81-27970

621.31′2134 — Wave power
Shaw, R.. Wave energy. — Chichester : Ellis Horwood, July 1982. — [160]p. — (Ellis Horwood series in energy and fuel science)
ISBN 0-85312-382-9 : £14.00 : CIP entry
B82-20653

621.31′2136 — Electricity supply. Generation. Wind turbine generators
Le Gouriérès, Désiré. Wind power plants. — Oxford : Pergamon, Oct.1982. — [300]p
ISBN 0-08-029967-9 (cased) : £25.00 : CIP entry
ISBN 0-08-029966-0 (pbk) : £12.50
B82-32844

621.31′24 — Direct power generation
Angrist, Stanley W.. Solutions manual to accompany Direct energy conversion, fourth ed. / Stanley W. Angrist. — Boston, [Mass.] ; London : Allyn and Bacon, c1982. — 128p : ill ; 22cm
ISBN 0-205-07759-5 (unbound) : Unpriced
B82-27105

621.31′24 — Direct power generation — *Conference proceedings*
Power sources : research and development in non-mechanical electrical power sources. — London : Academic Press
8: Proceedings of the 12th International Power Sources Symposium held at Brighton, September 1980 / sponsored by the Joint Services Electrical Power Sources Committee ; edited by J. Thompson. — 1981. — xi,630p : ill,1port ; 24cm
Includes bibliographies
ISBN 0-12-689155-9 : £62.40 : CIP rev.
B81-31350

621.31′242 — Lithium batteries
Lithium batteries. — London : Academic Press, Jan.1983. — [510]p
ISBN 0-12-271180-7 : CIP entry B82-33461

621.31′242 — Small batteries
Crompton, T. R.. Small batteries / T.R. Crompton. — London : Macmillan
Vol.1: Secondary cells. — 1982. — vi,226p : ill ; 26cm
Includes index
ISBN 0-333-26418-5 : Unpriced B82-14737

621.31′244 — Cadmium sulphide-cadmium telluride heterojunction solar cells
Mitchell, Kim Warner. Evaluation of the CdS-CdTe heterojunction solar cell / Kim Warner Mitchell. — New York ; London : Garland, 1979. — xv,136p : ill ; 24cm. — (Outstanding dissertations on energy)
ISBN 0-8240-3991-2 : Unpriced B82-10720

621.31′244 — Solar cells
Fonash, Stephen J.. Solar cell device physics / Stephen J. Fonash. — New York ; London : Academic Press, 1981. — xix,332p : ill ; 24cm. — (Energy science and engineering)
Includes index
ISBN 0-12-261980-3 : £23.20 B82-30015

Green, Martin A.. Solar cells : operating principles, technology, and system applications / Martin A. Green. — Englewood Cliffs ; London : Prentice-Hall, c1982. — xiv,274p : ill ; 24cm. — (Prentice-Hall series in solid state physical electronics)
Bibliography: p269. — Includes index
ISBN 0-13-822270-3 : £20.95 B82-16856

621.31′244 — Solar energy. Conversion — *Conference proceedings*
Nato Advanced Study Institute on Photovoltaic and Photoelectrochemical Solar Energy Conversion *(1980 : Ghent)*. Photovoltaic and photoelectrochemical solar energy conversion / [proceedings of a NATO Advanced Study Institute on Photovoltaic and Photoelectrochemical Solar Energy Conversion held August 25-September 5, 1980, at Gent, Belgium] ; edited by F. Cardon, W.P. Gomes and W. Dekeyser. — New York ; London : Plenum, published in cooperation with NATO Scientific Affairs Division, c1981. — xiii,422p : ill ; 26cm. — (NATO advanced study institutes series. Series B, Physics ; v.69)
Includes index
ISBN 0-306-40800-7 : Unpriced B82-13928

621.31'244 — Solar energy. Conversion. Use of hydrogen
Photogeneration of hydrogen. — London : Academic Press, Dec.1982. — [250]p
ISBN 0-12-326380-8 : CIP entry B82-33202

621.31'244 — Solar energy. Photochemical conversion & storage — *Conference proceedings*
International Conference on Photochemical Conversion and Storage of Solar Energy *(3rd : 1980 : Boulder).* Photochemical conversion and storage of solar energy / [proceedings of the third International Conference on Photochemical Conversion and Storage of Solar Energy held in Boulder, Colorado on August 3-8, 1980] ; [sponsored by the Solar Energy Research Institute, Golden Colorado and the Division of Chemical Sciences, Office of Basic Energy Sciences, U.S. Department of Energy, Washington, D.C.] ; edited by John S. Connolly. — New York ; London : Academic Press, 1981. — xi,444p : ill ; 24cm
Includes index
ISBN 0-12-185880-4 : £26.20 B82-21281

621.31'25 — Nuclear power stations. Fast breeder reactors — *Conference proceedings*
European symposium on fast breeder reactors : May 11 & 12 1981 : conference transcript / edited by Catherine O'Keeffe. — [London] : Scientific & Technical Studies, [1981]. — iv,182p : ill ; 30cm
ISBN 0-9505774-6-4 (pbk) : £35.00 B82-05672

621.31'25 — Suffolk. Sizewell. Proposed nuclear power stations. Safety measures
Sizewell B : a review by HM Nuclear Installations Inspectorate of the pre-construction safety report / Health and Safety Executive. — London : H.M.S.O., 1982. — vi,88p ; 30cm
ISBN 0-11-883652-8 (pbk) : £5.50 B82-38345

621.31'25'0941 — Great Britain. Nuclear power stations
Nuclear power stations and their operation. — [Dorchester] : Planning Department, Dorset County Council, 1981. — 12p : ill ; 21cm. — (Nuclear power stations ; information paper no.5)
Cover title
ISBN 0-85216-300-2 (pbk) : Unpriced B82-12742

621.31'25'094233 — Dorset. Proposed nuclear power stations
Investigation of possible sites for a power station in the South West by the Central Electricity Generating Board : joint report by a working party of Dorset county and district officers. — [Dorchester] ([County Hall, Dorchester DT1 1XJ]) : [Dorset County Council], [1981]. — 42p,11leaves of plates : ill,maps ; 30cm
ISBN 0-85216-303-7 (unbound) : Unpriced B82-12860

621.31'37 — Semiconductor power rectifiers
Wells, R. (Robert). Solid state power rectifiers : an applied technology / R. Wells. — London : Granada, 1982. — 186p : ill ; 24cm
Includes index
ISBN 0-246-11751-6 : Unpriced : CIP rev. B82-10798

621.31'7 — Electric equipment. Circuit-breakers
Power circuit breakers. — Rev. ed. — Stevenage : Peregrinus, Feb.1982. — [608]p. — (IEE power engineering ; 1)
Previous ed.: 1975
ISBN 0-906048-70-2 (pbk) : £32.00 : CIP entry B82-06060

621.31'7 — Electric equipment. Fuses
Wright, A.. Electric fuses. — Stevenage : Peregrinus, May 1982. — [208]p. — (Power engineering ; 2)
ISBN 0-906048-78-8 : £17.00 : CIP entry B82-12911

621.319 — Electricity transmission systems. Protective equipment
Power system protection. — 2nd ed. — Stevenage : Peregrinus
Previous ed.: London : Macdonald & Co., 1969
Vol.3: Application. — Nov.1981. — [496]p
ISBN 0-906048-54-0 : £22.00 : CIP entry B81-30289

621.319'1 — Electric equipment. Effects of disturbances in electricity supply systems — *Conference proceedings*
Third international conference on sources and effects of power system disturbances, 5-7 May 1982 / organised by the Power Division of the Institution of Electrical Engineers in association with the Institute of Electrical and Electronic Engineers Inc (United Kingdom and Republic of Ireland Section), the Institute of Mathematics and its Applications, the Institute of Physics, venue the Institution of Electrical Engineers, Savoy Place, London WC2. — London : Institution of Electrical Engineers, c1982. — xii,301p : ill ; 30cm. — (Conference publication, ISSN 0537-9989 ; no.210)
Cover title: Sources and effects of power system disturbances
ISBN 0-85296-257-6 (pbk) : Unpriced B82-32820

621.319'1 — Electricity transmission systems. Stability. Analysis. Lyapunov functions
Pai, M. A.. Power system stability : analysis by the direct method of Lyapunov / M.A. Pai. — Amsterdam ; Oxford : Excerpta Medica, 1981. — xiii,251p : ill ; 23cm. — (North-Holland systems and control series ; v.3)
ISBN 0-444-86310-9 : £17.95 B82-08562

621.319'1 — High voltage electricity transmission systems. Stability. Analysis. Z-transform analysis
Humpage, W. Derek. Z-transform electromagnetic transient analysis in high-voltage networks. — Stevenage : Peregrinus, Mar.1982. — [224]p. — (Power engineering ; 3)
ISBN 0-906048-79-6 : £24.00 : CIP entry B82-17229

621.319'13 — Electric equipment. Alternating current circuits. Responses. Determination. Pole zero diagrams
Maddock, R. J.. Poles and zeros : in electrical and control engineering / R.J. Maddock. — London : Holt, Rinehart and Winston, c1982. — viii,216p : ill ; 25cm
Includes index
ISBN 0-03-910346-3 (pbk) : £4.95 : CIP rev. B82-01532

621.319'2 — Electric equipment. Circuits
Durney, Carl H.. Electric circuits : theory and engineering applications / Carl H. Durney, L. Dale Harris, Charles L. Alley. — New York ; London : Holt, Rinehart and Winston, c1982. — xiv,481p : ill ; 25cm. — (HRW series in electrical and computer engineering)
Includes index
ISBN 0-03-057951-1 : Unpriced B82-23126

Hubert, Charles I.. Electric circuits AC/DC : an intergrated approach / Charles I. Hubert. — New York ; London : McGraw-Hill, c1982. — xx,776p : ill ; 25cm. — (McGraw-Hill series in electrical engineering. Electronics and electronic circuits)
Includes index
ISBN 0-07-030845-4 : £20.50 B82-22026

Nelkon, M.. Electrical principles / M. Nelkon and H.I. Humphreys. — 4th ed. — London : Heinemann Educational, 1981. — viii,189p : ill ; 22cm
Previous ed.: published as part of Electronics and radio. 1976. — Includes index
ISBN 0-435-68330-6 (pbk) : £3.95 B82-08396

621.319'2 — Electric equipment. Circuits. Analysis
Alvarez, E. Charles. Polyphase systems with computer solutions : supplement to Fundamental circuit analysis / by E. Charles Alvarez, John W. Tontsch. — Chicago ; Henley-on-Thames : Science Research Associates, c1979. — 44p : ill ; 28cm
ISBN 0-574-21530-1 (pbk) : Unpriced B82-40120

O'Malley, John. Schaum's outline of theory and problems of basic circuit analysis / by John O'Malley. — New York ; London : McGraw-Hill, c1982. — 339p : ill ; 28cm. — (Schaum's outline series)
Includes index
ISBN 0-07-047820-1 (pbk) : £4.95 B82-02505

621.319'2 — Electric equipment. Linear circuits
Van Valkenburg, M. E.. Linear circuits / M.E. van Valkenburg, B.K. Kinariwala. — Englewood Cliffs ; London : Prentice-Hall, c1982. — xiii,427p : ill ; 25cm
Includes index
ISBN 0-13-536722-0 : £20.95 B82-29232

621.319'2 — Electricity transmission equipment
Kurtz, Edwin B.. The lineman's and cableman's handbook. — 6th ed. / Edwin B. Kurtz (deceased), Thomas M. Shoemaker. — New York ; London : McGraw-Hill, c1981. — 1v.(various pagings) : ill,1map,plans ; 23cm
Previous ed.: 1976. — Includes index
ISBN 0-07-035678-5 : £33.50 B82-02519

621.319'2'01 — Electric equipment. Circuits. Theories — *Conference proceedings*
European Conference on Circuit Theory and Design *(1981 : The Hague).* Circuit theory and design : proceedings of the 1981 European Conference on Circuit Theory and Design, The Hague, The Netherlands 25-28 August, 1981 / edited by R. Boite and P. Dewilde. — Delft : Delft University Press ; Oxford : North-Holland, 1981. — xxi,1090p : ill ; 21cm
ISBN 0-444-86307-9 (corrected) : £50.53 B82-11232

621.319'24 — Buildings. Electric equipment
Porges, F.. The design of electrical services for buildings / F. Porges. — 2nd ed. — London : Spon, 1982. — x,309p : ill,1map ; 25cm
Previous ed.: 1975. — Bibliography: p299. — Includes index
ISBN 0-419-12360-1 (cased) : Unpriced : CIP rev.
ISBN 0-419-12370-9 (pbk) : Unpriced B82-06764

621.319'24 — Buildings. Electric equipment. Installation
Essential electricity — a user's guide. — 10th ed. — London : Hodder and Stoughton, Nov.1982. — [320]p
Previous ed. published as: The E.A.W. electrical handbook. London : English Universities Press, 1971
ISBN 0-340-27211-2 (pbk) : £6.95 : CIP entry B82-27344

Scaddam, Brian. Modern electrical installation for craft students. — 2nd ed. — London : Butterworth
Previous ed.: Guildford : IPC Science & Technology Press, 1979
Vol.1. — Aug.1982. — [184]p
ISBN 0-408-01245-5 (pbk) : £5.50 : CIP entry B82-21961

Scaddan, Brian. Modern electrical installation for craft students. — 2nd ed. — London : Butterworths
Previous ed.: Guildford : IPC & Technology Press, 1979
Vol.2. — Aug.1982. — [160]p
ISBN 0-408-01246-3 (pbk) : £5.50 : CIP entry B82-22412

Scaddan, Brian. Modern electrical installation for craft students. — London : Butterworth
Vol.3. — 2nd ed. — Jan.1983. — [166]p
Previous ed.: Guildford : IPC Science & Technology Press, 1979
ISBN 0-408-01247-1 (pbk) : £5.50 : CIP entry B82-34434

621.319'24 — Buildings. Electric equipment. Installation — *Manuals*
Electrical installations handbook / editor Günter G. Seip. — Berlin : Siemens AG ; London : Heyden, c1979. — 2v(xix,1184p) : ill(some col.) ; 22cm
Translation of: Elektrische Installationstechnik. — Includes index
ISBN 0-85501-260-9 : £58.00 B82-23627

621.319'24 — Buildings. Electric wiring systems
Guillou, F.. Beginner's guide to electric wiring / F. Guillou, C. Gray. — 3rd ed. — London : Newnes Technical, 1982. — 156p : ill ; 19cm
Previous ed.: 1975. — Includes index
ISBN 0-408-01130-0 (pbk) : £3.95 : CIP rev. B82-04036

621.319'24 — Buildings. Electric wiring systems *continuation*

Neidle, Michael. Electrical installation : questions and answers / Michael Neidle. — London : Pitman, 1982. — 109p : ill,2forms ; 22cm
Previous ed.: 1975. — Includes index
ISBN 0-273-01723-3 (pbk) : Unpriced B82-30618

621.319'24 — Buildings. Electric wiring systems. Installation

Steward, W. E.. Modern wiring practice. — 9th ed. / W.E. Steward and J. Watkins. — [London] : Newnes Technical Books, c1982. — 297p : ill ; 22cm
Previous ed.: 1976. — Includes index
ISBN 0-408-00518-1 (pbk) : Unpriced : CIP rev. B81-34128

621.319'24 — Buildings. Electrical equipment. Installation. Regulations: Institution of Electrical Engineers. Regulations for electrical installations — *Critical studies*

Jenkins, B. D.. Commentary on the 15th edition of the IEE wiring regulations / B.D. Jenkins ; with the co-operation and support of the Electrical Contractors' Association ... [et al.]. — Stevenage : Peregrinus on behalf of the Institution of Electrical Engineers, 1981. — xvi,211p : ill ; 22cm
Includes index
ISBN 0-906048-51-6 (pbk) : Unpriced B82-31044

Whitfield, J. F.. A guide to the 15th edition of the IEE wiring regulations / J.F. Whitfield. — Stevenage : Peregrinus on behalf of the Institution of Electrical Engineers, 1981. — ix,163p : ill ; 21cm
Includes index
ISBN 0-906048-50-8 (pbk) : Unpriced B82-31045

621.319'24 — Buildings. Interiors. Electric wiring systems

Turner, W.. Electric wiring. — 2nd ed. / revised by W. Turner. — London : Newnes Technical, 1982. — 137p : ill ; 17cm. — (Questions & answers)
Previous ed.: published as Questions and answers on electrical wiring / by Henry A. Miller. London : Newnes-Butterworths, 1974. — Includes index
ISBN 0-408-01141-6 (pbk) : £1.95 : CIP rev. B82-01968

621.319'24 — Great Britain. Buildings. Electric equipment. Installation

Hall, F.. Electrical services in buildings for architects, builders and surveyors. — London : Construction Press, Feb.1983. — 1v.
ISBN 0-86095-036-0 : £9.95 : CIP entry B82-39829

621.319'24 — Great Britain. Buildings. Electric wiring systems. Installation — *Questions & answers*

Lewis, M. L.. Multiple choice questions in electrical installation work / M.L. Lewis. — 2nd ed. — London : Hutchinson, 1981. — 63p : ill ; 25cm
Previous ed.: 1977
ISBN 0-09-146401-3 (pbk) : £3.50 : CIP rev. B81-20562

621.319'24 — United States. Buildings. Electric wiring systems. Installation

Richter, H. P.. Practical electrical wiring : residential, farm, and industrial. — 12th ed. / H.P. Richter, W. Creighton Schwan. — New York ; London : McGraw-Hill, c1981. — ix,662p : ill,plans ; 22cm
'Based on the 1981 National Electrical Code'. — Previous ed.: 1978. — Bibliography: p603. — Includes index
ISBN 0-07-052389-4 : £18.50 B82-04449

621.319'24 — United States. Commercial buildings. Electric wiring systems — *Manuals*

Mullin, Ray C.. Electrical wiring commercial : code, theory, plans, specifications, installation methods / Ray C. Mullin, Robert L. Smith. — [Rev. ed.] / based on 1981 National Electrical Code, fourth ed. — New York ; London : Van Nostrand Reinhold, c1981. — vii,230p : ill ; 29cm
Previous ed.: Albany, N.Y. : Delmar Publishers, 1977. — Seven folded sheets in pocket. — Includes index
ISBN 0-442-26592-1 : £11.00 B82-23708

621.319'34 — Electric cables

Electric cables handbook. — London : Granada, Aug.1982. — [896]p
ISBN 0-246-11467-3 : £45.00 : CIP entry B82-15706

621.319'34 — Underground electric cables

King, S. Y.. Underground power cables / S.Y. King, N.A. Halfter. — London : Longman, 1982. — 411p : ill ; 23cm
Includes index
ISBN 0-582-46344-0 : £30.00 : CIP rev. B82-00214

621.319'37 — Electric equipment. Insulation — *Conference proceedings*

BEAMA International Electrical Insulation Conference *(4th : 1982 : Brighton)*. Fourth BEAMA International Electrical Insulation Conference : Brighton, May 10-13, 1982 / organised jointly by BEAMA, ERA, EEIA. — London (8 Leicester St., WC2H 7BN) : British Electrical and Allied Manufacturers' Association, [1982]. — 319p : ill ; 30cm
£40.00 (pbk) B82-35529

621.32'2 — Great Britain. Industrial buildings. Electric lighting

Lyons, Stanley L.. Handbook of industrial lighting / Stanley L. Lyons. — London : Butterworths, 1981. — x,213p : ill ; 25cm
Includes index
ISBN 0-408-00525-4 : £15.00 : CIP rev. B81-27984

621.32'2 — Lighting

Developments in lighting. — London : Applied Science Publishers. — (The Developments series)
2: Industrial / edited by D.C. Pritchard. — c1982. — x,235p : ill ; 24cm
Includes index
ISBN 0-85334-985-1 : Unpriced : CIP rev. B81-31514

Meshkov, V. V.. Fundamentals of illumination engineering / V.V. Meshkov ; translated from the Russian by V.M. Matskovsky. — Moscow : Mir ; [London] : distributed by Central, 1981. — 371p : ill ; 21cm
Translation of: Osnovy svetotekhniki. — Includes index
ISBN 0-7147-1773-8 : £4.95 B82-37040

621.32'254'024658 — Industrial buildings. Lighting — *For management*

Lyons, Stanley L.. Management guide to modern industrial lighting. — 2nd ed. — London : Butterworth, Feb.1983. — [176]p
Previous ed.: Barking : Applied Science, 1972
ISBN 0-408-01147-5 : £10.00 : CIP entry B82-38286

621.32'28 — Residences. Lighting — *Manuals*

Lyons, Stanley L.. Domestic lighting / Stanley L. Lyons. — London : Newnes Technical, 1981. — 90p : ill,plans ; 17cm. — (Questions & answers)
Includes index
ISBN 0-408-00554-8 (pbk) : Unpriced : CIP rev. B81-34129

621.32'4 — West Yorkshire *(Metropolitan County)*. **Leeds. Gas street lights. Preservation**

Hickmott, S. J. B.. The surviving gas lights of central Leeds / S.J.B. Hickmott, P.G. Hopkinson. — Batley (4 Broomsdale Rd., Soothill, Batley) : D. Wright, [1982?]. — 12p : ill,1map ; 30x11cm
£0.30 (unbound) B82-39069

621.34 — Electromagnetic suspension & electromagnetic leviation

Jayawant, B. V.. Electromagnetic levitation and suspension techniques / B.V. Jayawant. — London : Edward Arnold, 1981. — vi,140p : ill ; 24cm
Includes index
ISBN 0-7131-3428-3 (pbk) : £11.50 B82-02395

621.36 — Electro-optical equipment

Wilson, J.. Optoelectronics. — London : Prentice-Hall, Jan.1983. — [400]p
ISBN 0-13-638395-5 (cased) : £24.95 : CIP entry
ISBN 0-13-638353-x (pbk) : £11.95 B82-33470

621.36 — Electro-optical equipment — *Conference proceedings*

Electro-Optics Laser International 82 UK *(Brighton)*. Electro-Optics/Laser International 82 UK. — London : Butterworth, Sept.1982. — [416]p
Conference proceedings
ISBN 0-408-01235-8 : £27.00 : CIP entry B82-25910

621.36'05 — Electro-optical equipment — *Serials*

Electro optics newsletter. — Vol.1, no.1 (Sept. 1981)-. — London (28 Craven St., WC2N 5PD) : Milton Pub., 1981-. — v. ; 30cm
Monthly
ISSN 0261-5657 = Electro optics newsletter : £90.00 per year B82-09070

621.36'6 — Free-electron lasers

Free-electron generators of coherent radiation : based on lectures of the Office of Naval Research sponsored workshop, August 13-17, 1979, Telluride, Colorado / edited by Stephen F. Jacobs ... [et al.]. — Reading, Mass. ; London : Addison-Wesley, 1980. — xix,813p : ill ; 24cm. — (Physics of quantum electronics ; v.7)
Includes index
ISBN 0-201-05687-9 : £26.10 B82-12657

621.36'6 — High energy lasers — *Conference proceedings*

International School of Physics 'Enrico Fermi' *(74th : 1978 : Varenna)*. Developments in high-power lasers and their applications : proceedings of the International School of Physics 'Enrico Fermi', course LXXIV, Varenna on Lake Como, Villa Monastero, 10-22nd July 1978 / edited by C. Pellegrini. — Amsterdam ; Oxford : North-Holland, 1981. — ix,477p : ill ; 24cm
Added t.p. in Italian. — At head of title: Italian Physical Society
ISBN 0-444-85459-2 : £40.34 B82-15177

621.36'6 — Lasers

Burroughs, William, *1942-*. Lasers / [author William Burroughs] ; [editors Mark Lambert, John Paton]. — Harlow : Longman, 1982. — 61p : ill ; 25cm. — (Understanding science)
Includes index
ISBN 0-582-39167-9 : £4.95 : CIP rev. B82-06040

Thyagarajan, K.. Lasers : theory and applications / K. Thyagarajan and A.K. Ghatak. — New York ; London : Plenum, c1981. — xii,431p : ill ; 24cm. — (Optical physics and engineering)
Bibliography: p425-428. — Includes index
ISBN 0-306-40598-9 : Unpriced B82-13997

621.36'6 — Lasers — *For children*

Johnson, James, *1943-*. Lasers / by James Johnson ; illustrated by Jay Blair and Mark Mille. — Oxford : Blackwell Raintree, c1981. — 48p : col.ill ; 24cm. — (A Look inside)
Includes index
ISBN 0-86256-031-4 : £2.95 B82-08585

621.36′6 — Mode-locked lasers. Ultra-short pulses — *Conference proceedings*

Ultra-short laser pulses : a Royal Society discussion / organized by D.J. Bradley, Sir George Porter and M.H. Key, held on 23 and 24 May 1979. — London : The Society, 1980. — viii,204p : ill ; 31cm
Originally published: in Philosophical transactions of the Royal Society of London. Series A, Vol.298, no.1439. — Includes bibliographies
ISBN 0-85403-147-2 : £19.50 B82-31847

621.36′61 — Semiconductor lasers

Demokan, M. S.. Mode-locking in solid-state and semi-conductor lasers. — Chichester : Wiley, Sept.1982. — [250]p. — (Lasers and fibre optics research studies series)
ISBN 0-471-10498-1 : £20.00 : CIP entry B82-19532

621.36′73 — Microfocal radiography

Ely, R. V.. Microfocal radiography / R.V. Ely. — London : Academic Press, 1980. — xi,295p : ill ; 24cm
Includes bibliographies and index
ISBN 0-12-238140-8 : £28.80 : CIP rev. B80-11054

621.36′73 — Neutron radiography

Neutron radiography handbook : nuclear science and technology / edited by P. von der Hardt and H. Röttger. — Dordrecht ; London : Reidel, c1981. — x,170p : ill ; 24cm
At head of title: Commission of the European Communities
ISBN 90-277-1378-2 : Unpriced B82-11235

621.36′73 — Radiographic photography

Barrett, Harrison H.. Radiological imaging : the theory of image formation, detection and processing / Harrison H. Barrett, William Swindell. — New York ; London : Academic Press
Vol.1. — 1981. — xxiii,358,xxip : ill ; 24cm
Bibliography: p349-358. — Includes index
ISBN 0-12-079601-5 : £36.40 B82-30145

Barrett, Harrison H.. Radiological imaging : the theory of image formation, detection, and processing / Harrison H. Barrett, William Swindell. — New York ; London : Academic Press
Vol.2. — 1981. — xxip,p359-693 : ill ; 24cm
Bibliography: p663-672. — Includes index
ISBN 0-12-079602-3 : £36.40 B82-30146

Chesney, D. Noreen. Radiographic imaging / D. Noreen Chesney and Muriel O. Chesney. — 4th ed. — Oxford : Blackwell Scientific, 1981. — 530p : ill ; 24cm
Previous ed.: published as Radiographic photography. 1971. — Includes index
ISBN 0-632-00562-9 : £16.50 : CIP rev. B81-31645

621.36′78 — Remote sensing. Optical techniques

Slater, Philip N.. Remote sensing : optics and optical systems / Philip N. Slater. — Reading, Mass. ; London : Addison-Wesley, 1980. — xvi,575p,[2]p of plates : ill(some col.) ; 25cm. — (Remote sensing)
Includes bibliographies and index
ISBN 0-201-07250-5 : £22.80 B82-14751

621.36′78 — Remote sensing systems — *For environmental studies*

Barrett, E. C.. Introduction to environmental remote sensing. — 2nd ed. — London : Chapman and Hall, Aug.1982. — [850]p
Previous ed.: 1976
ISBN 0-412-23080-1 (cased) : £24.00 : CIP entry
ISBN 0-412-23090-9 (pbk) : £12.00 B82-15785

621.36′78′05 — Remote sensing — *Serials*

Soviet journal of remote sensing : a cover-to-cover translation of Issledovanie zemli iz kosmosa. — No.1 (1981)-. — Chur ; London : Harwood Academic, 1981-. — v. : ill ; 23cm
Six issues yearly. — Description based on: No.3 (1981)
ISSN 0275-911X = Soviet journal of remote sensing : Unpriced B82-32135

621.36′92 — Fibre-optic equipment

Lacy, Edward A.. Fiber optics / Edward A. Lacy. — Englewood Cliffs ; London : Prentice-Hall, c1982. — xiv,222p : ill ; 24cm
Bibliography: 212-213. — Includes index
ISBN 0-13-314278-7 : £16.95 B82-21697

621.36′92 — Fibre optics

Kao, Charles K.. Optical fiber systems : technology, design, and applications / Charles K. Kao. — New York ; London : McGraw-Hill, c1982. — xi,204p : ill ; 24cm
Bibliography: p197. — Includes index
ISBN 0-07-033277-0 : £17.95 B82-27570

Okoshi, Takanori. Optical fibers / Takanori Okoshi. — New York ; London : Academic, 1982. — xii,299p : ill ; 24cm
Translation of: Hikari faiba no kiso. — Includes index
ISBN 0-12-525260-9 : £25.00 B82-38082

Williams, D. G. (David Gordon). Fibre optics / D.S. & S.G. Williams. — Liverpool (53 Marlborough Rd., Liverpool L13 8EA) : Quantum Jump, 1982. — 43p : ill ; 20cm
Unpriced (pbk) B82-32835

621.36′92 — Fibre optics — *Conference proceedings*

Fibre optics : London, 1-2 March 1982. — [London] : [Institution of Electronic and Radio Engineers], [1982]. — 200p : ill ; 30cm. — (Proceedings / Institution of Electronic and Radio Engineers ; no.53)
Conference papers
ISBN 0-903748-48-7 (pbk) : Unpriced B82-22366

New frontiers in fibre optics : international conference at Mount Royal Hotel, London, 20th & 21st March 1980. — [London] ([2 Serjeants' Inn, Fleet St., E.C.4]) : [Engineers' Digest], [1981?]. — 119p in various foliations : ill ; 30cm. — (Engineers' Digest technical conferences)
Unpriced (spiral) B82-08005

Optical Fibre Electronics and Communications : 23 March 1982 London : conference transcript. — [Great Britain] : Scientific and Technical Studies, c1982. — iii,71p : ill ; 30cm
ISBN 0-907822-04-5 (pbk) : Unpriced : CIP rev. B82-19293

Suematsu, Yasuharu. Introduction to optical fiber communications / Yasuharu Suematsu, Ken-ichi Iga ; translated by H. Matsumura ; text edited and revised by W.A. Gambling. — New York ; Chichester : Wiley, c1982. — xviii,208p : ill ; 24cm. — (Wiley series in pure and applied optics)
Translation of: Hikari faiba tsūshin nyūmon. — Ill on lining papers. — Includes index
ISBN 0-471-09143-x : £23.25 B82-39919

621.36′92′0287 — Fibre optics. Measurement

Marcuse, Dietrich. Principles of optical fiber measurements / Dietrich Marcuse. — New York ; London : Academic Press, 1981. — ix,360p : ill ; 24cm
Includes index
ISBN 0-12-470980-x : £26.20 B82-02063

621.36′92′05 — Fibre-optic equipment — *Serials*

Optical devices & fibers. — 198?-. — Tokyo : OHM ; Amsterdam ; Oxford : North-Holland, [198-]-. — v. : ill(some col.),ports ; 27cm. — (Japan annual reviews in electronics, computers & telecommunications)
Description based on: 1982 issue
£65.96 B82-28859

621.36′93 — Integrated optics — *Conference proceedings*

European Conference on Integrated Optics *(1st : 1981 : London)*. First European Conference on Integrated Optics, 14-15 September 1981 / organised by the Electronics Division of the Institution of Electrical Engineers in association with the Institute of Mathematics and its Applications [and the] Institute of Physics, with the support of the Convention of National Societies of Electrical Engineers of Western Europe (EUREL), venue the Institution of Electrical Engineers, Savoy Place, London WC2, UK. — [London] : [Institution of Electrical Engineers], c1981. — viii,112p : ill ; 30cm. — (Conference publication, ISSN 0537-9989 ; no.201)
ISBN 0-85296-246-0 (pbk) : Unpriced B82-00819

621.37 — Electricity. Measurement

Anastasiou, Stavros. Electrical measurements : S.I. units / by Stavros Anastasiou. — London : [A.S. Anastasiou], 1982. — 176p : ill ; 24cm
Bibliograhy: p173. — Includes index
ISBN 0-9507241-1-4 (pbk) : Unpriced B82-37284

621.37′068′5 — Great Britain. Electric measuring instruments industries. New products. Management

Johne, F. A.. The organisation of product innovation in high technology manufacturing firms : some preliminary results / by F.A. Johne. — London : [City University Business School], c1982. — ii,21leaves ; 30cm. — (Working paper series / City University Business School, ISSN 0140-1041 ; no.35)
Bibliography: leaf 21
Unpriced (pbk) B82-21197

621.37′9 — Measuring instruments: Transducers — *Conference proceedings*

Sensor ′82 *(Conference : Halle)*. Sensor ′82 : Transducer-Technik u. Temperaturmessung = Transducer-technology and temperature measurement : Konferenzunterlagen = conference proceedings. — [Wunstorf] ; [Buckingham] : [Network], [c1982]. — 3v. : ill ; 30cm
Includes papers in German and in English. — Cover title
ISBN 0-904999-94-7 (pbk) : Unpriced
ISBN 0-904999-95-5 (v.2) : £30.00
ISBN 0-904999-96-3 (v.3) : £30.00 B82-15188

621.38 — ELECTRONIC AND COMMUNICATIONS ENGINEERING

621.38 — Communication systems — *Conference proceedings*

Conference on communications equipment and systems, 20-22 April 1982 / organised by the Electronics Division of the Institution of Electrical Engineers in association with the British Computer Society ... [et al.] with the support of the Convention of National Societies of Electrical Engineers of Western Europe (EUREL), venue Birmingham Metropole Hotel, U.K.. — [London] : [Institution of Electrical Engineers], [c1982]. — xi,328p : ill ; 30cm. — (Conference publication, ISSN 0537-9989 ; no.209)
Cover title: Communications 82. Spine title: Communications equipment and systems
ISBN 0-85296-258-4 (pbk) : Unpriced B82-32819

621.38 — Communication systems. Control devices

Morris, D. J.. Communication for command & control systems. — Oxford : Pergamon, July 1982. — [470]p. — (International series on systems and control ; v.5) (Pergamon international library)
ISBN 0-08-027597-4 (cased) : £35.00 : CIP entry
ISBN 0-08-027596-6 (pbk) : £9.95 B82-12416

621.38 — Telecommunication systems

Pierce, John R.. Signals : the telephone and beyond / John R. Pierce. — Oxford : Freeman, c1981. — viii,181p : ill(some col.),ports ; 25cm
Includes index
ISBN 0-7167-1311-x (cased) : £11.80
ISBN 0-7167-1336-5 (pbk) : £5.50 B82-11650

621.38 — Telecommunication systems *continuation*

Temes, Lloyd. Schaum's outline of theory and problems of electronic communication / by Lloyd Temes. — New York ; London : McGraw-Hill, c1979. — 138p : ill ; 28cm. — (Schaum's outline series)
Includes index
ISBN 0-07-063495-5 (pbk) : £4.50 B82-03531

Tischler, Morris. Experiments in telecommunications / Morris Tischler. — New York ; London : McGraw-Hill, c1981. — 186p : ill ; 28cm. — (Linear integrated circuit applications)
Bibliography: p186
ISBN 0-07-064782-8 (pbk) : £6.50 B82-03532

621.38 — Telecommunication systems. Technological innovation — *Conference proceedings*

Innovations in telecommunications / edited by Jamal T. Manassah ; sponsored by KFAS Kuwait Foundation for the Advancement of Sciences. — New York : London : Academic Press. — (International symposia of the Kuwait Foundation)
Pt.A. — 1982. — xi,562p : ill ; 25cm
Conference papers. — Includes bibliographies
ISBN 0-12-467401-1 (cased) : £39.40
ISBN 0-12-467421-6 (pbk) : Unpriced
B82-34857

621.38'024092 — Telecommunication systems — *For librarianship*

Telecommunications and libraries : a primer for librarians and information managers / Donald W. King ... [et al.]. — White Plains, N.Y. : Knowledge Industry ; London : Eurospan [distributor], c1981. — iii,184p : ill ; 29cm. — (Professional librarian series)
Bibliography: p165-177. — Includes index
ISBN 0-914236-88-1 (cased) : Unpriced
ISBN 0-914236-51-2 (pbk) : Unpriced
B82-08808

621.38'028 — Telecommunication equipment. Transmission equipment — *For technicians*

Freeman, Roger L.. Telecommunication transmission handbook / Roger L. Freeman. — 2nd ed. — New York ; Chichester : Wiley, c1981. — xxvii,706p : ill,maps ; 24cm
Previous ed.: 1975. — Includes index
ISBN 0-471-08029-2 : £36.75 B82-13986

621.38'028'3 — Adaptive-array sensor systems

Hudson, J. E.. Adaptive array principles / J.E. Hudson. — Stevenage : Peregrinus on behalf of the Institution of Electrical Engineers, c1981. — xiv,253p : ill ; 24cm. — (IEE electromagnetic waves series ; 11)
Bibliography: p229-234p. — Includes index
ISBN 0-906048-55-9 : Unpriced : CIP rev.
B81-20521

621.38'028'3 — Antennas. Design — *Manuals*

The **Handbook** of antenna design. — Stevenage : Peregrinus
Vol.1. — May 1982. — [688]p. — (Electromagnetic waves ; 14)
ISBN 0-906048-82-6 : £35.00 : CIP entry
B82-12912

621.38'028'3 — Antennas. Projects — *Amateurs' manuals*

Penfold, R. A. Aerial projects / by R.A. Penfold. — London : Babani, 1982. — 84p : ill ; 18cm
ISBN 0-85934-080-5 (pbk) : £1.95 : CIP rev.
B82-13148

621.38'028'3 — Telecommunication equipment. Antennas

Balanis, Constantine A.. Antenna theory : analysis and design / Constantine A. Balanis. — Cambridge, [Mass.] ; London : Harper & Row, c1982. — xvii,790p : ill ; 25cm. — (The Harper & Row series in electrical engineering)
Includes index
ISBN 0-06-040458-2 : Unpriced B82-34020

621.38'028'3 — Wire antennas. Synthesis

Popovic, B. D.. Analysis and synthesis of wire-antennas. — Chichester : Wiley, Aug.1982. — [200]p. — (Research studies on antennas series ; 2)
ISBN 0-471-90008-7 : £13.50 : CIP entry
B82-24343

621.380'412 — Speech. Representation by digital signals

Witten, I. H.. Principles of computer speech. — London : Academic Press, Nov.1982. — [330] p. — (Computer and people)
ISBN 0-12-760760-9 : CIP entry B82-26864

621.38'0413 — Digital communication systems

Roden, Martin S.. Digital and data communication systems / Martin S. Roden. — Englewood Cliffs ; London : Prentice-Hall, c1982. — xiv,363p : ill ; 24cm
Includes index
ISBN 0-13-212142-5 : £22.45 B82-29234

621.38'0413 — Digital communication systems. Signals. Detection. Mathematical models. Parameters. Estimation

Lucantoni, D. M.. An algorithmic analysis of a communications model with retransmission of flawed messages. — London : Pitman, Jan.1983. — [180]p. — (Research notes in mathematics ; 81)
ISBN 0-273-08571-9 (pbk) : £8.95 : CIP entry
B82-35217

621.38'0413 — Digital integrated communication systems

Inose, Hiroshi. An introduction to digital integrated communications systems / Hiroshi Inose. — Repr. with revisions. — Stevenage : Peregrinus on behalf of the Institution of Electrical Engineers and University of Tokyo Press, 1981, c1979. — xiv,342p : ill ; 22cm
Originally published: 1979. — Includes index
ISBN 0-906048-61-3 (pbk) : Unpriced
B82-03646

621.38'0413 — Electronic communication systems

Clayton, *Sir* **Robert,** *1915-*. To calculate, communicate, command and remember / by Sir Robert Clayton. — London (2 Little Smith St., Westminster, SW1P 3DL) : Fellowship of Engineering, c1981. — 36p : ill ; 22cm. — (The Christopher Hinton lecture)
Lecture given 29th September 1981. — Cover title
Unpriced (pbk) B82-35556

621.38'0413 — Telecommunication systems. Pulse code modulation systems

Owen, Frank F. E.. PCM and digital transmission systems / Frank F.E Owen. — New York ; London : McGraw-Hill, c1982. — xi,295p : ill ; 27cm. — (Texas Instruments electronics series)
Bibliography: p283-288. — Includes index
ISBN 0-07-047954-2 : £22.50 B82-22236

621.38'0414 — Digital image processing

Multicomputers and image processing : algorithms and programs / edited by Kendall Preston, Jr, Leonard Uhr. — New York ; London : Academic Press, 1982. — xx,470p : ill ; 24cm. — (Notes and reports in computer science and applied mathematics ; 3)
Includes bibliographies and index
ISBN 0-12-564480-9 : £22.60 B82-38383

621.38'0414 — Digital image processing — *Conference proceedings*

Digital image processing : proceedings of the NATO Advanced Study Institute held at Bonas, France, June 23-July 4, 1980 / edited by J.C. Simon and R.M. Haralick. — Dordrecht ; London : Reidel in cooperation with NATO Scientific Affairs Division, c1981. — vii,596p : ill ; 25cm. — (NATO advanced study institutes series. Series C, Mathematical and physical sciences ; v.77)
Includes bibliographies and index
ISBN 90-277-1329-4 : Unpriced B82-06118

621.38'0414 — Electronic alphanumeric display systems

Weston, G. F.. Alphanumeric displays. — London : Granada, Sept.1982. — [208]p
ISBN 0-246-11702-8 : £16.50 : CIP entry
B82-18737

621.38'0414 — Electronic display systems

Sherr, Sol. Video and digital electronic displays : a user's guide / Sol Sherr. — New York ; Chichester : Wiley, c1982. — ix,252p : ill ; 24cm
Includes index
ISBN 0-471-09037-9 : £23.00 B82-36681

621.38'0414 — Electronic visual displays

Robot vision. — Kempston : IFS Publications, Nov.1982. — [350]p
ISBN 0-903608-32-4 : £28.00 : CIP entry
B82-33362

621.38'0414 — Electronic visual displays — *Conference proceedings*

Electronic Displays '81 *(Conference : Kensington Exhibition Centre)*. Electronic Displays '81 : conference proceedings : Kensington Exhibition Centre, London, UK 23, 24, 25 September 1981. — Buckingham : Network, c1981
Cover title
Session 1: Display device technology. — 97leaves : ill ; 30cm
ISBN 0-904999-85-8 (pbk) : £20.00
B82-03506

Electronic Displays '81 *(Conference : Kensington Exhibition Centre)*. Electronic Displays '81 : conference proceedings : Kensington Exhibition Centre, London, UK 23, 24, 25 September 1981. — Buckingham : Network, c1981
Cover title
Session 2: Teletext display systems. — 76leaves : ill ; 30cm
ISBN 0-904999-86-6 (pbk) : £20.00
B82-03507

Electronic Displays '81 *(Conference : Kensington Exhibition Centre)*. Electronic Displays '81 : conference proceedings : Kensington Exhibition Centre, London, UK 23, 24, 25 September 1981. — Buckingham : Network, c1981
Cover title
Session 3: Display applications. — 96leaves : ill ; 30cm
ISBN 0-904999-87-4 (pbk) : £20.00
B82-03508

621.38'0414 — Image processing — *Conference proceedings*

Scandinavian Conference on Image Analysis *(1st : 1980 : Linköping)*. Proceedings of the First Scandinavian Conference on Image Analysis / arranged by SSAB, Svenska Sällskapet för Automatiserad Bildanalys ; sponsored by International Association for Pattern Recognition ; Roger Cederberg (secr.). — Lund : Studentlitteratur ; Bromley : Chartwell-Bratt, 1980. — 388p : ill ; 22cm
Includes bibliographies
ISBN 0-86238-001-4 (pbk) : Unpriced
B82-36836

621.38'0414 — Image processing. Mathematical techniques

Serra, J.. Image analysis and mathematical morphology / by J. Serra. — London : Academic Press, 1982. — xviii,610p : ill ; 24cm
Bibliography: p590-601. — Includes index
ISBN 0-12-637240-3 : £48.40 : CIP rev.
B82-00334

621.38'0414 — Image processing. Stochastic models — *Conference proceedings*

Image modeling / edited by Azriel Rosenfeld. — New York ; London : Academic Press, 1981. — xiii,445p : ill ; 24cm
Conference papers
ISBN 0-12-597320-9 : £18.60 B82-10047

621.38'0414 — Optical communication systems

Clarricoats, P. J. B.. Progress in optical communication. — Stevenage : Peregrinus, Sept.1982. — [xiii,328]p. — (IEE reprint ; 4)
ISBN 0-906048-84-2 (pbk) : £21.00 : CIP entry
B82-32889

621.38'0414 — Optical communication systems — *Conference proceedings*

European Conference on Optical Communication *(7th : 1981 : Copenhagen)*. 7th European Conference on Optical Communication, Copenhagen, Bella Center, September 8-11, 1981 : conference proceedings / organised by Electromagnetics Institute. — Stevenage : published on behalf of the Electromagnetics Institute, Technical University of Denmark by Peregrinus, 1981. — 459p in various pagings : ill ; 30cm + 1pamphlet(44p : ill ; 30cm)
Unpriced (pbk) B82-05988

621.38'0414 — Telecommunication systems. Applications of fibre optics

Fundamentals of optical fiber communications / edited by Michael K. Barnoski. — 2nd ed. — New York ; London : Academic Press, 1981. — xi,351p : ill ; 24cm
Previous ed.: 1976
ISBN 0-12-079151-x : £19.60 B82-15537

621.38'0422 — Digital communication systems. Use of artificial satellites

Digital communications by satellite : modulation, multiple access and coding / Vijay K. Bhargava ... [et al.]. — New York ; Chichester : Wiley, c1981. — xxi,569p : ill ; 25cm
Includes index
ISBN 0-471-08316-x : £33.00 B82-16014

621.38'0422 — Maritime communications satellites — *Serials*

Ocean voice : the journal of the International Maritime Satellite Organization. — Vol.1, no.1 (Oct. 1981)-. — London (Market Towers, 1 Nine Elms La., SW8 5NQ) : INMARSAT, 1981-. — v. : ill(some col.),col.maps,ports ; 30cm
Quarterly
ISSN 0261-6777 = Ocean voice : Unpriced
B82-04891

621.38'043 — Digital signals. Processing systems using very large scale integrated circuits. Design

Bowen, B. A.. VLSI systems design for digital signal processing / B.A. Bowen and W.R. Brown. — Englewood Cliffs ; London : Prentice Hall
Vol 1: Signal processing and signal processors. — c1982. — xvii,304p : ill ; 25cm
Bibliography: p292-300. — Includes index
ISBN 0-13-942706-6 : £22.45 B82-35163

621.38'043 — Discrete time systems. Signals. Processing

Jong, M. T.. Methods of discrete signal and system analysis / M.T. Jong. — New York ; London : McGraw-Hill, c1982. — xii,452p : ill ; 25cm. — (McGraw-Hill series in electrical engineering)
Includes bibliographies and index
ISBN 0-07-033025-5 : £24.50
ISBN 0-07-033026-3 (solutions manual) : Unpriced B82-15977

621.38'043 — Telecommunication systems. Digital signals. Processing

Digital signal processing. — Stevenage : Peregrinus, Sept.1982. — [500]p. — (IEE control engineering series ; 22)
ISBN 0-906048-91-5 (pbk) : CIP entry
B82-29155

621.38'043 — Telecommunication systems. Signals

Connor, F. R.. Signals. — 2nd ed. — London : Edward Arnold, Jan.1982. — [196]p. — (Introductory topics in electronics and telecommunications)
Previous ed.: 1972
ISBN 0-7131-3458-5 (pbk) : £3.95 : CIP entry
B81-35888

621.38'043 — Telecommunication systems. Signals. Modulation

Connor, F. R.. Modulation. — 2nd ed. — London : Edward Arnold, Jan.1982. — [196]p
Previous ed.: 1973
ISBN 0-7131-3457-7 (pbk) : £3.95 : CIP entry
B81-33904

621.38'043 — Telecommunication systems. Signals. Transmission

Tugal, Dogan A.. Data transmission : analysis, design, applications / Dogan A. Tugal, Osman Tugal. — New York ; London : McGraw-Hill, c1982. — xiii,393p : ill ; 24cm
Includes bibliographies and index
ISBN 0-07-065427-1 : £18.50 B82-15974

621.38'043'02854044 — Telecommunication systems. Signals. Processing. Applications of microcomputer systems

Yuen, C. K.. Microprocessor systems and their application to signal processing. — London : Academic Press, Sept.1982. — [360]p. — (Microelectronics and signal processing)
ISBN 0-12-774950-0 : CIP entry B82-19170

621.38'0432 — Telecommunication systems: Spread spectrum systems

Holmes, Jack K.. Coherent spread spectrum systems / Jack K. Holmes. — New York ; Chichester : Wiley, c1982. — xii,624p : ill ; 24cm
Includes index
ISBN 0-471-03301-4 : £46.25 B82-26471

621.38'0433 — Digital signals. Processing. Applications of spectral analysis

Chen, C. H.. Nonlinear maximum entropy spectral analysis methods for signal recognition. — Chichester : Wiley, Sept.1982. — [170]p. — (Pattern recognition and image processing research studies series)
ISBN 0-471-10497-3 : £17.00 : CIP entry
B82-19531

621.38'0941 — Great Britain. Telecommunication engineering — *Serials*

British telecommunications engineering : the journal of the Institution of British Telecommunications Engineers. — Vol.1, pt.1 (Apr. 1982)-. — London (2 Gresham St., EC2V 7AG) : British Telecommunications Engineering Journal, 1982-. — v. : ill,maps ; 30cm
Quarterly. — Continues: Post Office electrical engineers' journal. — Supplement: Supplement to British telecommunications engineering
ISSN 0262-401X = British telecommunications engineering : £5.20 per year B82-28125

Supplement to British telecommunications engineering. — Vol.1, pt.1 (Apr. 1982)-. — London (2 Gresham St., EC2V 7AG) : British Telecommunications Engineering, 1982-. — v. : ill ; 29cm
Quarterly. — Continues: Supplement to the Post Office electrical engineers' journal. — Supplement to: British telecommunications engineering
ISSN 0262-4028 = Supplement to British telecommunications engineering : Unpriced
B82-28126

621.38'0941 — Great Britain. Telecommunication systems, *to 1981*

Bleazard, G. B.. Telecommunications in transition. — Manchester : NCC Publications, Mar.1982. — [100]p. — (Communications in the '80s)
ISBN 0-85012-378-x (pbk) : £6.50 : CIP entry
B82-11083

621.381 — ELECTRONIC ENGINEERING

621.381 — Analogue electronic equipment — *For technicians*

Green, D. C.. Electronics IV : a textbook covering the analogue (linear) content of the Level IV syllabus of the Technician Education Council / D.C. Green. — London : Pitman, 1981. — ix,278p : ill ; 25cm
Includes index
ISBN 0-273-01504-4 (pbk) : Unpriced
B82-01666

621.381 — Electronic equipment

Bishop, O. N.. Beginner's guide to electronics. — 4th ed. / Owen Bishop. — Sevenoaks : Newnes Technical, c1982. — 240p : ill ; 19cm
Previous ed.: / by Terence L. Squires and Michael Deason. 1974. — Includes index
ISBN 0-408-00413-4 (pbk) : £3.60 : CIP rev.
B81-23921

Bohlman, K. J.. Core studies (electronic devices) / K.J. Bohlman. — London : N. Price, c1980. — 100p : ill ; 22cm. — (Electronics servicing 224 course for radio, television and electronics mechanics ; v.2)
Includes index
ISBN 0-85380-145-2 (pbk) : £2.25 B82-39142

Boyce, Jefferson C.. Modern electronics : a survey of the new technology / Jefferson C. Boyce. — New York ; London : McGraw-Hill, c1982. — viii,232p : ill ; 28cm
Bibliography: p229. — Includes index
ISBN 0-07-006915-8 (pbk) : £7.45 B82-17016

Electronics engineers' handbook. — 2nd ed. / Donald G. Fink, editor in chief ; Donald Christiansen, associate editor. — New York ; London : McGraw-Hill, c1982. — 2-251p in various pagings : ill,2maps ; 25cm
Previous ed.: 1976. — Includes bibliographies and index
ISBN 0-07-020981-2 : £49.95 B82-15987

Ibrahim, K. F.. Basic electronic systems : full coverage of C & G 224 part 1 / K.F. Ibrahim. — 2nd ed. — London : Pitman, c1979 (1982 [printing]). — 132p : ill ; 21cm
Previous ed.: published as Principles and systems for radio & TV mechanics. 1976. — Includes index
ISBN 0-273-01421-8 (pbk) : Unpriced
B82-33656

Jacobowitz, Henry. Electronics made simple / Henry Jacobwitz ; advisory editor Leslie Basford. — London : Heinemann, 1967 (1982 [printing]). — xi,307p : ill ; 22cm. — (Made simple books)
Includes index
ISBN 0-434-98559-7 (pbk) : £2.95 B82-32244

Kaufman, Milton. Schaum's outline of theory and problems of electronics technology / Milton Kaufman and J.A. Wilson ; consulting editor, Peter Brooks. — New York ; London : McGraw-Hill, c1982. — 373p : ill ; 28cm. — (Schaum's outline series)
Includes index
ISBN 0-07-070690-5 (pbk) : £5.95 B82-16286

Nelkon, M.. Electronics and radio principles / M. Nelkon and H.I. Humphreys. — 4th ed. — London : Heinemann Educational, 1981. — viii,155p : ill ; 22cm
Previous ed.: published as part of Electronics and radio. 1976. — Includes index
ISBN 0-435-68331-4 (pbk) : £3.95 B82-08395

Olsen, G. H.. Electronics. — 2nd ed. — London : Butterworths, July 1982. — [358]p
Previous ed.: 1968
ISBN 0-408-01193-9 (cased) : £17.50 : CIP entry
ISBN 0-408-00491-6 (pbk) : £9.95 B82-12325

Sprott, Julien C.. Introduction to modern electronics / Julien C. Sprott. — New York ; Chichester : Wiley, c1981. — xii,349p : ill ; 24cm
Bibliography: p303-305. — Includes index
ISBN 0-471-05840-8 : £15.95 B82-00120

Uffenbeck, John E.. Introduction to electronics : devices and circuits / John E. Uffenbeck. — Englewood Cliffs ; London : Prentice-Hall, c1982. — xii,401p : ill ; 24cm
Includes index
ISBN 0-13-481507-6 : £16.45 B82-23230

Wilson, F. A.. Elements of electronics / by F.A. Wilson. — London : Babani
Bk.4: Microprocessing systems and circuits. — 1980. — 231p : ill ; 18cm
Includes index
ISBN 0-900162-97-x (pbk) : £2.95 : CIP rev.
B80-17758

621.381 — Electronic equipment — *For schools*

Electronics / Paul Fay ... [et al.]. — London : Oliver & Boyd in association with the National Centre for School Technology, 1980. — 142p : ill ; 24cm + teacher's guide(47p : ill ; 24cm). — (Schools Council modular courses in technology)
ISBN 0-05-003383-2 (pbk) : Unpriced
ISBN 0-05-003384-0 (teacher's guide)
B82-17625

Electronics / Schools Council Modular Courses in Technology. — Edinburgh : Oliver & Boyd in association with the National Centre for School Technology
Workbook. — 1980. — 31p : ill ; 27cm
ISBN 0-05-003385-9 (unbound) : £2.40
B82-21523

621.381 — Electronic equipment — *For technicians*

Cooper, A. L.. Electronics for TEC Level II / A.L. Cooper, T.R. Ball. — Cheltenham : Thornes, 1981. — 262p : ill ; 25cm. — (ST(P) technology today series)
Includes index
ISBN 0-85950-300-3 (pbk) : £5.25 : CIP rev.
B81-16899

Knight, S. A.. Electronics 2 checkbook / S.A. Knight. — London : Butterworths, 1981. — 112p : ill ; 20cm. — (Butterworths technical and scientific checkbooks)
Includes index
ISBN 0-408-00639-0 (cased) : Unpriced : CIP rev.
ISBN 0-408-00615-3 (pbk) : Unpriced
B81-16924

Smith, A. V.. Electronics for technicians level 3. — London : Granada Publishing, May 1982. — [120]p
ISBN 0-246-11488-6 (pbk) : £5.00 : CIP entry
B82-07982

621.381 — Electronic equipment. Manufacture

Villanucci, Robert S.. Electronic shop fabrication : a basic course / Robert S. Villanucci, Alexander W. Avtgis, William F. Megow. — Englewood Cliffs ; London : Prentice-Hall, c1982. — xvii,220p : ill ; 25cm
Bibliography: p214. — Includes index
ISBN 0-13-251959-3 : £13.45 B82-24089

621.381 — Electronic equipment. Projects — *Amateurs' manuals*

Bishop, Owen. Electronic science projects. — London : Babani, Nov.1982. — [144]p. — (BP ; 104)
ISBN 0-85934-079-1 (pbk) : £2.25 : CIP entry
B82-26328

621.381 — Electronic equipment. Projects. Faults. Detection — *Amateurs' manuals*

Penfold, R. A.. How to get your electronic projects working. — London : Babani, Oct.1982. — [96]p. — (BP ; 110)
ISBN 0-85934-085-6 (pbk) : £1.95 : CIP entry
B82-25738

621.381 — Electronic instruments

Malmstadt, Howard V.. Electronics and instrumentation for scientists / Howard V. Malmstadt, Christie G. Enke, Stanley R. Crouch. — Reading, Mass. ; London : Benjamin/Cummings, c1981. — xii,543p : ill ; 24cm
Ill, text on lining paper. — Includes index
ISBN 0-8053-6917-1 : £16.95 B82-37166

621.381'0245 — Electronic equipment — *For science*

Brown, Paul B.. Electronics for the modern scientist / Paul B. Brown, Gunter N. Franz, Howard Moraff. — New York ; Oxford : Elsevier, c1982. — x,496p : ill ; 26cm
Includes bibliographies and index
ISBN 0-444-00660-5 : £18.56 B82-34299

621.381'02461 — Electronic equipment — *For medical laboratory technicians*

Schmidt, L. M.. Labtronics : electronics for laboratory scientists / L.M. Schmidt. — St. Louis, Mo. ; London : Mosby, 1979. — xii,171p : ill ; 26cm
Bibliography: p168. — Includes index
ISBN 0-8016-4342-2 (pbk) : Unpriced
B82-21886

621.381'028 — Electronic devices. Materials

Jowett, C. E.. Materials and processes in electronics / C.E. Jowett. — London : Hutchinson, 1982. — 329p : ill ; 24cm
Includes index
ISBN 0-09-145100-0 : £20.00 : CIP rev.
B81-20174

621.381'028'8 — Electronic equipment. Servicing — *For technicians*

Sinclair, Ian R.. Electronics for the service engineer : a textbook for the City and Guilds of London Institute course no.224 and for the Technician Education Council Level II course in electronics / by Ian R. Sinclair. — Oxford : Technical Press
Vol.1. — c1980. — vi,170p : ill ; 25cm
Includes index
ISBN 0-291-39638-0 (pbk) : £4.95 : CIP rev.
B80-18790

621.381'042 — Electronic equipment. Design — *Serials*

Electronic product design. — Apr. 1980-. — Bromley (93 High St., Bromley, Kent BR1 1JW) : Techpress Pub. Co., 1980-. — v. : ill ; 29cm
Monthly. — Description based on: Jan. 1982 issue
ISSN 0263-1474 = Electronic product design : £15.00 per year B82-18492

621.381'042 — Electronic equipment. Reliability & maintainability

Smith, David J.. Reliability and maintainability in perspective : technical aspects / David J. Smith. — London : Macmillan, 1981. — viii,243p : ill ; 25cm
Bibliography: p236-237. — Includes index
ISBN 0-333-31048-9 (cased) : Unpriced
ISBN 0-333-31049-7 (pbk) : Unpriced
B82-10190

621.381'042 — Electronic equipment. Reliability - *Manuals*

Electronic reliability data. — Hitchin (Station House, Nightingale Rd, Hitchin, Herts.) : INSPEC, June 1981. — [300]p
ISBN 0-85296-240-1 : £125.00 : CIP entry
B81-16352

621.381'042 — Electronic systems. Design — *Conference proceedings*

European Conference on Electronic Design Automation *(1981 : Brighton)*. European Conference on Electronic Design Automation : 1-4 September 1981 / organised by the Electronics and Management and Design Divisions of the Institution of Electrical Engineers, in association with the British Computer Society (BCS) .. [et al.], venue University of Sussex, Brighton, United Kingdom. — London : Institution of Electrical Engineers, c1981. — vi,290p : ill ; 30cm. — (Conference publication, ISSN 0537-9989 ; no.200)
ISBN 0-85296-243-6 (pbk) : Unpriced
B82-00820

621.381'046 — Electronic equipment. Packaging. Design — *Manuals*

Matisoff, Bernard S.. Handbook of electronics packaging design and engineering / Bernard S. Matisoff. — New York ; London : Van Nostrand Reinhold, c1982. — viii,471p : ill,forms ; 24cm
Includes index
ISBN 0-442-20171-0 : £27.65 B82-34325

621.381'05 — Electronic equipment — *Serials*

Radio & electronics world. — Vol.1, issue 1 (Oct. 1981)-. — Brentwood (117a High St., Brentwood, Essex CM14 4SG) : Broadercasting Ltd. ; London (16 Trinity Gardens, SW9 8DX) : Distributed by SM Distribution Ltd., 1981-. — v. : ill,maps ; 29cm
Monthly
ISSN 0262-2572 = Radio & electronics world : £9.00 per year B82-06180

621.381'068'5 — Electronics industries. Technological development. Management

Vedin, Bengt-Arne. Corporated culture for innovation : conditions for growth in electronics / Bengt-Arne Vedin. — Lund : Studentlitteratur ; Bromley : Chartwell-Bratt, 1980. — 80p : ill ; 23cm
ISBN 0-86238-003-0 (pbk) : Unpriced
B82-36839

621.381'076 — Electronic equipment — *Questions & answers* — *For technicians*

Electronics servicing 224 course. — London : Price
Vol.3: Core studies (electronic circuits) / K.J. Bohlman. — 1982. — 149p : ill ; 22cm
Includes index
ISBN 0-85380-150-9 (pbk) : £3.50 B82-29755

Knight, S. A.. Electronics 3 checkbook / S.A. Knight. — London : Butterworths, 1982. — vi,105p : ill ; 20cm. — (Butterworths technical and scientific checkbooks)
Includes index
ISBN 0-408-00669-2 (cased) : Unpriced : CIP rev.
ISBN 0-408-00623-4 (pbk) : Unpriced
B81-31425

621.381'09 — Electronic engineering, *to 1980*

Pugh, A.. Electronic vision / A. Pugh. — [Hull] : University of Hull, 1981. — 17p ; 20cm
ISBN 0-85958-435-6 (pbk) : £0.75 B82-16522

621.381'1 — Electronic control systems

Fröhr, Friedrich. Introduction to electronic control engineering / Friedrich Fröhr and Fritz Orttenburger. — Berlin : Siemens ; London : Heyden, c1982. — 338p : ill ; 21cm
Translation of: Einführung in die elektronische Regelungstechnik. — Bibliography: p331-333. — Includes index
ISBN 0-85501-290-0 : £18.00 : CIP rev.
ISBN 3-8009-1340-2 (Siemens AG)
B81-34776

621.381'3 — Microwave equipment. Semiconductor devices

Advanced solid state technology for radar / edited by J. Clarke. — [Sevenoaks] ([Temple House, 34-36 High St., Sevenoaks, Kent TN13 1JG]) : Microwave Exhibitions & Publishers, c1982. — 571p : ill ; 30cm. — (MEPL reprint series)
Unpriced (pbk) B82-35000

White, Joseph F.. Microwave semiconductor engineering / Joseph F. White. — New York ; London : Van Nostrand Reinhold, c1982. — xvii,558p : ill ; 24cm. — (Van Nostrand Reinhold electrical/computer science and engineering series)
Includes index
ISBN 0-442-29144-2 : £24.25 B82-14008

621.381'32 — Microwave equipment. Digital circuits & strip transmission lines. Design. Applications of digital computer systems

Edwards, T. C.. Foundations for microstrip circuit design / T.C. Edwards. — Chichester : Wiley, c1981. — xiv,265p : ill ; 24cm
Includes index
ISBN 0-471-27944-7 : £12.75 B82-02487

621.381'323 — Electronic equipment. Microwave oscillators. Design

Vendelin, George D.. Design of amplifiers and oscillators by the S-parameter method / George D. Vendelin. — New York ; Chichester : Wiley, c1982. — xii,190p : ill ; 24cm
Includes bibliographies and index
ISBN 0-471-09226-6 : Unpriced
Primary classification 621.381'325 B82-23948

621.381'325 — Electronic equipment. Microwave amplifiers. Design

Vendelin, George D.. Design of amplifiers and oscillators by the S-parameter method / George D. Vendelin. — New York ; Chichester : Wiley, c1982. — xii,190p : ill ; 24cm
Includes bibliographies and index
ISBN 0-471-09226-6 : Unpriced
Also classified at 621.381'323 B82-23948

621.381'33 — Microwave equipment. Field effect transistors

Pengelly, Raymond S.. Microwave field-effect transistors — theory, design and applications / Raymond S. Pengelly. — Chichester : Research Studies, c1982. — xvii,470p : ill ; 24cm. — (Electronic & electrical engineering research studies. Electronic devices and systems research studies series)
Includes bibliographies and index
ISBN 0-471-10208-3 : £15.50 : CIP rev.
B82-03611

621.381'33 — Microwave equipment: Flat dipole antennas

Dubost, G.. Flat radiating dipoles and applications to arrays / G. Dubost. — Chichester : Research Studies Press, c1981. — xiv,103p : ill ; 24cm. — (Electronic & electrical engineering research studies. Research studies on antennas series ; 1)
Bibliography: p97-100. — Includes index
ISBN 0-471-10050-1 : £12.90 : CIP rev.
B81-19206

621.381'33 — Microwave equipment: Microstrip antennas. Design

James, J. R.. Microstrip antenna : theory and design / J.R. James, P.S. Hall, C. Wood. — Stevenage : Peregrinus on behalf of the Institution of Electrical Engineers, c1981. — x,290p : ill ; 24cm. — (IEE control engineering series ; 12)
Includes bibliographies and index
ISBN 0-906048-57-5 : Unpriced : CIP rev.
B81-20495

621.3815 — Digital electronic equipment

Davio, M.. Digital systems. — Chichester : Wiley, Jan.1983. — [500]p
ISBN 0-471-10413-2 (cased) : £19.95 : CIP entry
ISBN 0-471-10414-0 (pbk) : £11.50
B82-34618

Duncan, Tom. Adventures with digital electronics / Tom Duncan. — London : Murray, 1982. — 64p : ill(some col.) ; 25cm
ISBN 0-7195-3943-9 (cased) : £4.50 : CIP rev.
ISBN 0-7195-3875-0 (pbk) : £2.75 B82-09833

Gothmann, William H.. Digital electronics : an introduction to theory and practice / William H. Gothmann. — 2nd ed. — Englewood Cliffs ; London : Prentice-Hall, c1982. — xiv,383p : ill ; 24cm
Previous ed.: 1977. — Includes index
ISBN 0-13-212084-4 (pbk) : £9.95 B82-36877

Heap, Nick. Introductory digital electronics. — Milton Keynes : Open University Press, Jan.1983. — [224]p
ISBN 0-335-10184-4 (pbk) : £7.95 : CIP entry
B82-33330

Warring, R. H.. Understanding digital electronics / by R.H. Warring. — Guildford : Lutterworth Press, 1982. — 156p : ill ; 23cm
Includes index
ISBN 0-7188-2521-7 : £6.95 B82-39471

621.3815 — Digital electronic equipment. Experiments

Pasahow, Edward J.. Learning digital electronics through experiments / Edward J. Pasahow. — New York ; London : Gregg Division, McGraw-Hill, c1981. — vii,215p : ill ; 23cm. — (Electro skills series)
Includes index
ISBN 0-07-048722-7 (pbk) : £8.50 B82-07448

621.3815 — Digital electronic equipment — *For technicians*

Sinclair, I. R.. Digital techniques level 2. — Eastbourne : Holt, Rinehart & Winston, Sept.1982. — [96]p
ISBN 0-03-910379-x (pbk) : £2.95 : CIP entry
B82-20614

621.3815 — Discrete electronic components

Mazda, F. F.. Discrete electronic components / F.F. Mazda. — Cambridge : Cambridge University Press, 1981. — vii,177p : ill ; 26cm
Bibliography: p165. — Includes index
ISBN 0-521-23470-0 : £18.00 : CIP rev.
B81-30898

621.3815'1 — Electronic equipment. Ferroelectric transducers

Herbert, J. M.. Ferroelectric transducers and sensors / J.M. Herbert. — New York ; London : Gordon and Breach, c1982. — xxv,437p : ill ; 24cm. — (Electrocomponent science monographs ; v.3)
Includes index
ISBN 0-677-05910-8 : Unpriced B82-31148

621.3815'2 — Applied solid state physics

Applied solid state science : advances in materials and device research / editor Raymond Wolfe. — New York ; London : Academic Press
Supplement 1: Magnetic domain walls in bubble materials / A.P Malozemoff and J.C. Slonczewski. — c1979. — vii,326p : ill ; 24cm
Includes index
ISBN 0-12-002951-0 : £31.80 B82-21279

621.3815'2 — Metal oxide semiconductor devices

McCarthy, Oliver J.. MOS device and circuit design / Oliver J. McCarthy. — Chichester : Wiley, c1982. — xiv,261p : ill ; 24cm
Includes index
ISBN 0-471-10026-9 : £19.50 : CIP rev.
B81-36237

MOS devices. — Edinburgh : Edinburgh University Press, Sept.1982. — [216]p
ISBN 0-85224-415-0 (pbk) : £12.00 : CIP entry
B82-24358

Nicollian, E. H.. MOS (metal oxide semiconductor) physics and technology / E.H. Nicollian, J.R. Brews. — New York ; Chichester : Wiley, c1982. — xv,906p : ill ; 24cm
Includes index
ISBN 0-471-08500-6 : £51.75 B82-28777

621.3815'2 — Power semiconductor devices

Penketh, J. R.. Electronic power control for technicians / J.R. Penketh. — Sevenoaks : Butterworth, 1982. — 71p : ill ; 25cm. — (Butterworths technician series)
ISBN 0-408-01154-8 (pbk) : Unpriced : CIP rev. B82-24466

621.3815'2 — Semiconductor devices

Brown, M. A. (Michael Alan). A gentle introduction to semiconductor devices / by M.A. Brown. — [Loughborough] : [M.A. Brown], [1981?]. — 23p : ill ; 30cm
ISBN 0-904641-11-2 (pbk) : Unpriced
B82-09095

Close, K. J.. An introduction to semiconductor electronics. — 2nd ed. — London : Heinemann Educational, Jan.1982. — [224]p
Previous ed.: 1971
ISBN 0-435-68082-x (pbk) : £4.50 : CIP entry
B82-00161

Frederiksen, Thomas M.. Intuitive IC electronics : a sophisticated primer for engineers and technicians / Thomas M. Frederiksen. — New York ; London : McGraw-Hill, c1982. — xxi, 183p : ill ; 24cm
Bibliography: p173-174. — Includes index
ISBN 0-07-021923-0 : £14.25 B82-16285

Sze, S. M.. Physics of semiconductor devices / S.M. Sze. — 2nd ed. — New York ; Chichester : Wiley, c1981. — xii,868p : ill ; 24cm
Previous ed.: 1969. — Includes index
ISBN 0-471-05661-8 : 28.00 B82-06285

621.3815'2 — Semiconductor devices. Degradation

Reliability and degradation : semiconductor devices and circuits / edited by M.J. Howes, D.V. Morgan. — Chichester : Wiley, c1981. — xii,444p : ill ; 24cm. — (The Wiley series in solid state devices and circuits)
Includes index
ISBN 0-471-28028-3 : £22.00 : CIP rev.
B81-33800

621.3815'2 — Semiconductor devices. Silicon. Doping

Impurity doping processes in silicon / edited by F.F.Y. Wang. — Amsterdam ; Oxford : North-Holland, c1981. — 643p : ill ; 23cm. — (Materials processing — theory and practices ; v.2)
Includes index
ISBN 0-444-86095-9 : Unpriced B82-05059

621.3815'2 — Semiconductor devices. Silicon. Neutron-transmutation doping — *Conference proceedings*

International Conference on Neutron Transmutation Doping of Silicon *(3rd : 1980 : Copenhagen)*. Neutron-transmutation-doped silicon / [proceedings of the Third International Conference on Neutron Transmutation Doping of Silicon, held August 27-29, 1980 in Copenhagen, Denmark] ; edited by Jens Guldberg. — New York ; London : Plenum, c1981. — x,505p : ill ; 26cm
Includes index
ISBN 0-306-40738-8 : Unpriced B82-14705

621.3815'2'015194 — Semiconductor devices. Design. Applications of numerical analysis

An **Introduction** to the numerical analysis of semiconductor devices and integrated circuits : lecture notes of a short course held at Trinity College, Dublin from 15th to 16th June, 1981 in association with the NASECODE II Conference / edited by J.J.H. Miller. — Dublin : Boole, 1981. — viii,75p : ill ; 24cm
ISBN 0-906783-04-6 (pbk) : Unpriced
Also classified at 621.381'73'015194
B82-02199

Kurata, Mamoru. Numerical analysis for semiconductor devices / Mamoru Kurata. — Lexington, Mass. : Lexington ; [Aldershot] : Gower [distributor], c1982. — xviii,269p : ill ; 24cm
Includes index
ISBN 0-669-04043-6 : £22.50 B82-31790

621.3815'2'015194 — Semiconductor devices. Design. Applications of numerical analysis — *Conference proceedings*

NASECODE II *(Conference : 1981 : Trinity College, Dublin)*. Numerical analysis of semiconductor devices and integrated circuits : proceedings of the NASECODE II Conference held at Trinity College, Dublin, from 17th to 19th June, 1981 / edited by B.T. Browne, J.J.H. Miller. — Dublin : Boole, 1981. — xii,288p : ill ; 25cm
ISBN 0-906783-03-8 : Unpriced
Also classified at 621.381'73'015194
B82-02198

621.3815'2'0212 — Semiconductor devices — *Technical data*

Michael, Adrian. International diode equivalents guide. — London : Babani, Aug.1982. — [96]p. — (BP ; 108)
ISBN 0-85934-083-x (pbk) : £1.95 : CIP entry
B82-16665

621.3815'2'05 — Semiconductor devices — *Serials*

Semiconductor technologies. — 1982-. — Tokyo : OHM ; Amsterdam ; Oxford : North-Holland, 1981-. — v. : ill ; 27cm. — (Japan annual reviews in electronics, computers & telecommunications)
£65.40
B82-26147

621.3815'2'0904 — Semiconductor devices, *to 1980*

Braun, Ernest. Revolution in miniature : the history and impact of semiconductor electronics. — 2nd rev. ed. — Cambridge : Cambridge University Press, Sept.1982. — [243]p
Previous ed.: 1978
ISBN 0-521-24701-2 (cased) : £15.00 : CIP entry
ISBN 0-521-28903-3 (pbk) : £5.95 B82-28456

621.3815'28'0288 — Transistor equipment. Servicing — *Manuals*

King, Gordon J.. Servicing radio, hi-fi and TV equipment / Gordon J. King. — 3rd ed. — London : Newnes Technical Books, 1982. — 205p : ill ; 22cm
Previous ed.: published as Rapid servicing of transistor equipment. London : Newnes-Butterworths, 1973. — Includes index
ISBN 0-408-01132-7 (pbk) : Unpriced : CIP rev.
B81-31267

621.3815'3 — Digital circuits

Markus, John. Digital circuits ready-reference / John Markus. — New York ; London : McGraw-Hill, c1982. — xvii,162p : ill,1port ; 28cm
Includes index
ISBN 0-07-040457-7 (pbk) : £9.50 B82-37907

621.3815′3 — Digital circuits. Design. Applications of mathematical logic

Bird, J. O.. Digital techniques 2 checkbook / J.O. Bird, A.J.C. May. — London : Butterworths, 1982. — viii,55p : ill ; 19cm
Includes index
ISBN 0-408-00674-9 (pbk) : £2.50 : CIP rev. B81-34408

621.3815′3 — Digital circuits. Logic design

Holdsworth, B.. Digital logic design / B. Holdsworth. — London : Butterworths, 1982. — xiii,338p : ill ; 22cm
Bibliography: p331-332. — Includes index
ISBN 0-408-00404-5 (cased) : £17.95
ISBN 0-408-00566-1 (pbk) : £9.95 B82-08857

621.3815′3 — Electronic equipment. Circuits

Belove, Charles. A first circuits course for engineering technology / Charles Belove. — New York ; London : Holt, Rinehart and Winston, c1982. — x,742p : ill ; 21cm
Includes index
ISBN 4-8337-0086-7 (pbk) : £8.50 B82-37425

Boylestad, Robert. Electronic devices and circuit theory / Robert Boylestad, Louis Nashelsky. — 3rd ed. — London : Prentice-Hall, c1982. — xvi,752p : ill ; 24cm
Previous ed.: 1978. — Includes index
ISBN 0-13-250373-5 (pbk) : £9.95 B82-16700

Dennis, W. H.. Electronic components and systems / W.H. Dennis. — London : Butterworth Scientific, 1982. — xiii,258p : ill ; 23cm
Bibliography: p254. — Includes index
ISBN 0-408-01111-4 : Unpriced : CIP rev. B81-34420

Grob, Bernard. Electronic circuits and applications / Bernard Grob. — New York ; London : McGraw-Hill, c1982. — x,468p : ill ; 25cm
Bibliography: p433. — Includes index
ISBN 0-07-024931-8 : £15.95 B82-15979

Lenk, John D.. Handbook of practical electronic circuits / John D. Lenk. — Englewood Cliffs ; London : Prentice-Hall, c1982. — xii,334p : ill ; 24cm
Includes index
ISBN 0-13-380741-x : £16.48 B82-20120

621.3815′3 — Electronic equipment. Circuits. Design

Bonebreak, Robert L.. Practical techniques of electronic circuit design / Robert L. Bonebreak. — New York ; Chichester : Wiley, c1982. — xv,306p : ill ; 24cm
Includes index
ISBN 0-471-09612-1 : Unpriced B82-19657

621.3815′3 — Electronic equipment. Circuits. Electrical noise

Connor, F. R.. Noise. — 2nd ed. — London : Edward Arnold, June 1982. — [220]p
Previous ed.: 1973
ISBN 0-7131-3459-3 (pbk) : £3.95 : CIP entry B82-12156

621.3815′3 — Electronic equipment. Circuits. Projects — *Amateurs′ manuals*

Penfold, R. A.. 30 solderless breadboard projects. — London : Babani, Oct.1982. — [128]p. — (BP ; 107)
ISBN 0-85934-082-1 (pbk) : £1.95 : CIP entry B82-24121

Penfold, R. A.. Mini-matrix board projects / by R.A. Penfold. — London : Babani, 1982. — 102p : ill ; 18cm
ISBN 0-85934-074-0 (pbk) : £1.95 : CIP rev. B82-08450

Penfold, R. A.. Popular electronic circuits / by R.A. Penfold. — London : Babani
Bk.1. — 1980. — 149p : ill ; 18cm
ISBN 0-85934-055-4 (pbk) : £1.95 : CIP rev. B80-22054

Penfold, R. A.. Popular electronic circuits / by R.A. Penfold. — London : Babani. — (BP ; 98)
Bk.2. — 1982. — 146p : ill ; 18cm
ISBN 0-85934-073-2 (pbk) : £2.25 : CIP rev. B82-04814

621.3815′3 — Electronic equipment. Circuits using solar cells. Projects — *Amateurs′ manuals*

Bishop, O. N.. Electronic projects using solar cells / by Owen Bishop. — London : Babani, 1981. — 110p : ill ; 18cm. — (Bernard Babani ; BP82)
ISBN 0-85934-057-0 (pbk) : £1.95 : CIP rev. B81-22542

621.3815′3 — Telecommunication systems. Circuits

Markus, John. Communications circuits ready-reference / John Markus. — New York ; London : McGraw-Hill, c1982. — xvii,216p : ill,1port ; 28cm
Includes index
ISBN 0-07-040460-7 (pbk) : £9.50 B82-37908

621.3815′3′0212 — Electronic equipment. Circuits — *Technical data*

Markus, John. Electronics projects ready-reference / John Markus. — New York ; London : McGraw-Hill, c1982. — xvii,181p : ill,1port ; 28cm
Includes index
ISBN 0-07-040459-3 (pbk) : £9.50 B82-37904

Markus, John. Popular circuits ready-reference / John Markus. — New York ; London : McGraw-Hill, c1982. — xvii,216p : ill,1port ; 28cm
Includes index
ISBN 0-07-040458-5 (pbk) : £9.50 B82-37905

Markus, John. Special circuits ready reference / John Markus. — New York ; London : McGraw-Hill, c1982. — xvii,234p : ill,1port ; 28cm
Includes index
ISBN 0-07-040461-5 (pbk) : £9.50 B82-37906

621.3815′30422 — Transistor circuits

Amos, S. W.. Principles of transistor circuits : introduction to the design of amplifiers, receivers and digital circuits / S.W. Amos. — 6th ed. — London : Butterworths, 1981. — 331p : ill ; 23cm
Previous ed.: Newnes-Butterworth, 1975. — Includes index
ISBN 0-408-01106-8 (cased) : Unpriced : CIP rev.
ISBN 0-408-00599-8 (pbk) : Unpriced B81-25287

621.3815′324 — Active filters. Design

Huelsman, Lawrence P.. Introduction to the theory and design of active filters / L.P. Huelsman, P.E. Allen. — New York ; London : McGraw-Hill, c1980. — xv,429p : ill ; 25cm
Includes index
ISBN 0-07-030854-3 : £23.95 B82-07359

Van Valkenburg, M. E.. Analog filter design / M.E. Van Valkenburg. — New York ; London : Holt, Rinehart and Winston, c1982. — xi,608p : ill ; 25cm. — (HRW series in electrical and computer engineering)
Bibliography: p601-604. — Includes index
ISBN 0-03-059246-1 : £24.95
ISBN 4-8337-0091-3 (International edition) : £9.50 B82-25402

621.3815′324 — Electric filters. Design

Ghausi, Mohammed S.. Modern filter design : active RC and switched capacitor / M.S. Ghausi, K.R. Laker. — Englewood Cliffs ; London : Prentice-Hall, c1981. — xiii,546p : ill ; 24cm. — (Prentice-Hall series in electrical and computer engineering)
Includes index
ISBN 0-13-594663-8 : £27.00 B82-07547

621.3815′33 — Electronic equipment. Quartz crystal oscillators

Bottom, Virgil E.. Introduction to quartz crystal unit design / by Virgil E. Bottom. — New York ; London : Van Nostrand Reinhold, c1982. — xvii,265p : ill ; 24cm. — (Van Nostrand Reinhold electrical-computer science and engineering series)
Bibliography: p259-260. — Includes index
ISBN 0-442-26201-9 : £22.55 B82-23709

621.3815′34 — Electronic equipment. Pulse circuits

Pettit, F. R.. Post-digital electronics / F.R. Pettit. — Chichester : Horwood, 1982. — 176p : ill ; 24cm. — (The Ellis Horwood series in computers and their applications)
Includes index
ISBN 0-85312-421-3 : Unpriced : CIP rev. B82-06254

621.3815′35 — Electronic equipment. Broadband feedback circuits

Maclean, D. J. H.. Broadband feedback amplifiers / D.J.H. Maclean. — Chichester : Research Studies, c1982. — xxviii,295p : ill ; 24cm. — (Electronic & electric engineering research studies. Electronic circuits and systems series ; 1)
Includes index
ISBN 0-471-10214-8 : £14.75 : CIP rev. B82-07124

621.3815′35 — Electronic equipment. Negative feedback amplifiers. Design

Nordholt, Ernst H.. Design of high-performance negative feedback amplifiers. — Oxford : Elsevier Scientific, Dec.1982. — [234]p. — (Studies in electrical and electronic engineering ; v.7)
ISBN 0-444-42140-8 : CIP entry B82-35229

621.3815′35 — Electronic equipment. Operational amplifiers

Clayton, G. B.. Operational amplifier experimental manual. — London : Butterworth, Jan.1983. — [112]p
ISBN 0-408-01240-4 (cased) : £12.00 : CIP entry
ISBN 0-408-01239-0 (pbk) : £5.95 B82-34433

Faulkenberry, Luces M.. An introduction to operational amplifiers : with linear IC applications / Luces M. Faulkenberry. — 2nd ed. — New York ; Chichester : Wiley, c1982. — xiv,530p : ill ; 24cm. — (Electronic technology series)
Previous ed.: 1977. — Includes index
ISBN 0-471-05790-8 : £17.00 B82-28945

Shepherd, I. E.. Operational amplifiers / I.E. Shepherd. — London : Longman, 1981. — xiii,318p : ill ; 23cm
Includes index
ISBN 0-582-46089-1 : £25.00 : CIP rev. B81-30466

621.3815′35 — Electronic equipment. Operational amplifiers. Projects

Parr, E. A.. How to use OP amps / by E.A. Parr. — London : Babani, 1982. — 154p : ill ; 18cm
ISBN 0-85934-063-5 (pbk) : £2.25 : CIP rev. B81-27967

621.3815′363 — Frequency synthesisers. Design

Robins, W. R.. Phase noise in signal sources. — Stevenage : Peregrinus, Apr.1982. — [336]p. — (Telecommunications ; 9)
ISBN 0-906048-76-1 : £28.00 : CIP entry B82-11974

621.3815′37 — Logic circuits

Boyce, Jefferson C.. Digital logic : operation and analysis / Jefferson C. Boyce. — 2nd ed. — Englewood Cliffs ; London : Prentice-Hall, c1982. — xiii,492p : ill ; 24cm
Previous ed.: published as Digital logic and switching circuits. 1975. — Bibliography: p485-486. — Includes index
ISBN 0-13-214619-3 : £18.70 B82-33775

621.3815'48 — Cathode ray oscilloscopes
Lenk, John D.. Handbook of oscilloscopes : theory and application / John D. Lenk. — Revised and enlarged [ed.]. — Englewood Cliffs, N.J. ; London : Prentice-Hall, c1982. — xii,340p : ill ; 24cm
Previous ed.: 1968. — Includes index
ISBN 0-13-380576-x : Unpriced B82-28348

621.3815'48 — Electronic equipment. Testing — *Manuals*
Lenk, John D.. Handbook of electronic test procedures / John D. Lenk. — Englewood Cliffs ; London : Prentice-Hall, c1982. — xiv,300p : ill ; 24cm
Includes index
ISBN 0-13-377457-0 : £14.95 B82-23234

621.3815'48 — Electronic measuring instruments
Norton, Harry N.. Sensor and analyser handbook / Harry N. Norton. — Englewood Cliffs, N.J. ; London : Prentice-Hall, c1982. — xiii,562p : ill ; 25cm
Includes bibliographies and index
ISBN 0-13-806760-0 : Unpriced B82-28346

Prensky, Sol D.. Electronic instrumentation. — 3rd ed. / Sol D. Prensky, Richard L. Castellucis. — Englewood Cliffs ; London : Prentice-Hall, c1982. — xiii,465p : ill ; 25cm
Previous ed.: 1971. — Bibliography: p444-445. — Includes index
ISBN 0-13-251611-x : £18.70 B82-21675

621.3815'48 — Electronic testing equipment
Electronic test equipment : operation and applications / edited by A.M. Rudkin. — London : Granada, 1981. — 316p : ill ; 24cm
Includes index
ISBN 0-246-11478-9 : Unpriced : CIP rev. B81-30392

621.3815'48 — Electronic timers. Construction — *Amateurs' manuals*
Rayer, F. G.. Electronic timer projects / by F.G. Rayer. — London : Babani, 1981. — 88p : ill ; 18cm. — (BP ; 93)
ISBN 0-85934-068-6 (pbk) : £1.95 : CIP rev. B81-30406

621.381'7'071041 — Great Britain. Educational institutions. Curriculum subjects: Microelectronic devices
Morton, Pamela. The microelectronic revolution : can the education system be made to cope? : presented to the House of Commons Computer Forum March 21st 1979 / Pamela Morton. — [London] ([c/o Thames Polytechnic, School of Mathematics, Statistics and Computing, Wellington St., SE18 6PF]) : P. Morton, 1979. — 15,[12]leaves : ill ; 30cm
Unpriced (spiral) B82-23715

621.381'71 — Microelectronic devices
Eurocon '80 *(Conference : Stuttgart)*. From electronics to microelectronics : Fourth European Conference on Elecrotechnics — EUROCON '80, Stuttgart, Germany, March 24-80 [i.e.28], 1980 / EUREL + IEEE + VDE ; edited by W.A. Kaiser and W.E. Proebster. — Amsterdam ; Oxford : North-Holland Publishing, 1980. — xxii,792p : ill,ports ; 31cm
Includes a paper in French and introduction and 3 papers in German. — Includes index
ISBN 0-444-85481-9 : £30.27 B82-32204

Microelectronic systems Level 1. — London : Hutchinson Education, May 1982. — [208]p
ISBN 0-09-147191-5 (pbk) : £4.95 : CIP entry B82-07253

Microelectronics : the new technology / [prepared by the Department of Industry and the Central Office of Information]. — Repr. with amendments. — [London] : Department of Industry, 1981. — 24p : ill(some col.) ; 30cm
Cover title. — Originally published: 1978. — Ill on inside covers
Unpriced (pbk) B82-40099

Microelectronics and microcomputer applications. — Manchester : Manchester University Press, Nov.1982. — [256]p
ISBN 0-7190-0905-7 : £12.50 : CIP entry
Also classified at 621.3819'5835 B82-36329

Woolons, D. J.. Microelectronic systems Level 3. — London : Hutchinson Education, May 1982. — [272]p
ISBN 0-09-147801-4 (pbk) : £5.95 : CIP entry B82-07249

621.381'71 — Microelectronic devices. Design & manufacture
Brodie, Ivor. The physics of microfabrication / Ivor Brodie and Julius J. Muray. — New York ; London : Plenum, c1982. — xix,503p : ill ; 24cm
Includes index
ISBN 0-306-40863-5 : Unpriced B82-33760

621.381'71 — Microelectronic devices — *For business firms*
Microelectronics — the options. — London ([Room 524, Dean Bradley House, 52 Horseferry Rd., SW1]) : MAP, Department of Industry, c1979. — 16p : col.ill ; 30cm
Cover title. — Ill on inside covers
Unpriced (pbk) B82-38328

621.381'71 — Microelectronic devices — *For technicians*
Curtis, G. H.. An introduction to microprocessor systems. — Cheltenham : Stanley Thornes, May 1982. — [296]p
ISBN 0-85950-316-x (pbk) : £4.50 : CIP entry B82-07842

Microelectronic systems Level III. — London : Hutchinson Education, June 1982. — [224]p
ISBN 0-09-148901-6 (pbk) : £5.50 : CIP entry B82-12713

621.381'71'024631 — Microelectronic devices — *For farming*
Cox, S. W. R.. Microelectronics in agriculture and horticulture. — London : Granada, July 1982. — [240]p
ISBN 0-246-11717-6 : £9.95 : CIP entry B82-12230

621.381'73 — Digital electronic equipment using integrated circuits. Experiments
Levine, Morris E.. Digital theory and experimentation using integrated circuits / Morris E. Levine. — Rev. and enl. — Englewood Cliffs ; London : Prentice-Hall, c1982. — xiii,241p : ill ; 28cm
Previous ed.: 1974. — Bibliography: p237-238
ISBN 0-13-212688-5 (pbk) : £11.95 B82-35167

621.381'73 — Digital integrated circuits
Taub, Herbert. Digital circuits and microprocessors / Herbert Taub. — New York ; London : McGraw-Hill, c1982. — xvii,541p : ill ; 25cm. — (McGraw-Hill series in electrical engineering)
Includes index
ISBN 0-07-062945-5 : £21.95 B82-25880

621.381'73 — Digital integrated circuits. Design
Kampel, Ian. Practical design of digital circuits. — London : Newnes Technical Books, Jan.1983. — [352]p
ISBN 0-408-01183-1 (pbk) : £5.00 : CIP entry B82-34437

621.381'73 — Electronic equipment. Integrated circuits
Sedra, Adel S.. Microelectronic circuits / Adel S. Sedra, Kenneth C. Smith. — New York ; London : Holt, Rinehart and Winston, c1982. — xiii,927p : ill ; 25cm. — (HRW series in electrical and computer engineering)
Includes index
ISBN 0-03-056729-7 : £25.00
ISBN 4-8337-0090-5 (International Edition) : £8.50 B82-29503

Till, William C.. Integrated circuits : materials, devices, and fabrication / William C. Till, James T. Luxon. — Englewood Cliffs ; London : Prentice-Hall, c1982. — xiii,462p : ill ; 24cm
Includes index
ISBN 0-13-469031-1 : £24.70 B82-16702

621.381'73 — Electronic equipment. Integrated circuits. Analysis & design
Chirlian, Paul M.. Analysis and design of integrated electronics circuits / Paul M. Chirlian. — London : Harper & Row, c1982. — 2v.(xvii,1029p) : ill ; 21cm
Includes bibliographies and index
ISBN 0-06-318213-0 (pbk) : Unpriced : CIP rev.
ISBN 0-06-318215-7 (Vol.2)
ISBN 0-06-318214-8 (Vol.3) B81-35878

621.381'73 — Electronic equipment: Integrated circuits. Design & construction
Elliott, David J.. Integrated circuit fabrication technology / by David J. Elliott. — New York ; London : McGraw-Hill, c1982. — xvii,405p : ill ; 24cm
Bibliography: p391-396. — Includes index
ISBN 0-07-019238-3 : £20.95 B82-23889

621.381'73 — Electronic equipment. Integrated circuits. Projects — *Amateurs' manuals*
Rayer, F. G.. IC projects for beginners / by F.G. Rayer. — London : Babani, 1982. — 96p : ill ; 18cm
ISBN 0-85934-072-4 (pbk) : £1.95 : CIP rev. B81-38317

621.381'73 — Electronic equipment. Large scale integrated circuits
Large scale integration : devices, circuits and systems / edited by M.J. Hawes, D.V. Morgan. — Chichester : Wiley, c1981. — xii,346p : ill ; 24cm. — (The Wiley series in solid state devices and circuits)
Includes index
ISBN 0-471-27988-9 : £17.50 : CIP rev. B81-31073

VLSI electronics microstructure science. — New York ; London : Academic Press
Vol.1 / edited by Norman G. Einspruch. — 1981. — xvi,340p : ill ; 24cm
Includes index
ISBN 0-12-234101-5 : £31.20c B82-04336

621.381'73 — Electronic equipment. Large scale integrated circuits — *Conference proceedings*
VLSI81. — London : Academic Press, Aug.1981. — [350]p
Conference papers
ISBN 0-12-683420-2 : CIP entry B81-20478

621.381'73 — Electronic equipment. Large scale metal oxide semiconductor integrated circuits
Mavor, John. Introduction to MOS LSI design. — London : Addison-Wesley, Oct.1982. — [288]p. — (Microelectronics systems design series)
ISBN 0-201-14402-6 (pbk) : £12.95 : CIP entry B82-23702

621.381'73 — Electronic equipment. Very high speed digital integrated circuits
Barna, Arpad. VHSIC : very high speed integrated circuits : technologies and tradeoffs / Arpad Barna. — New York ; Chichester : Wiley, c1981. — xi,114p : ill ; 24cm
Includes index
ISBN 0-471-09463-3 : £12.95 B82-03902

621.381'73 — Electronic equipment. Very large scale integrated circuits
VLSI electronics microstructure science / edited by Norman G. Einspruch. — New York ; London : Academic Press. — xvi,333p : ill ; 24cm
ISBN 0-12-234102-3 : £31.20 B82-07557

VLSI electronics microstructure science / edited by Norman G. Einspruch. — New York ; London : Academic Press
Vol.3. — 1982. — xiv,453p : ill ; 24cm
Includes index
ISBN 0-12-234103-1 : £37.00 B82-38381

621.381'73 — Large scale integrated circuits. Design. Applications of integrated circuits
Comer, David J.. Electronic design : with integrated circuits / David J. Comer. — Reading, Mass. ; London : Addison-Wesley, c1981. — xi,353p : ill ; 24cm. — (Addison-Wesley series in electrical engineering)
Includes index
ISBN 0-201-03931-1 : £8.25 B82-37178

621.381'73'015194 — Electronic equipment. Integrated circuits. Design. Applications of numerical analysis

An **Introduction** to the numerical analysis of semiconductor devices and integrated circuits : lecture notes of a short course held at Trinity College, Dublin from 15th to 16th June, 1981 in association with the NASECODE II Conference / edited by J.J.H. Miller. — Dublin : Boole, 1981. — viii,75p : ill ; 24cm
ISBN 0-906783-04-6 (pbk) : Unpriced
Primary classification 621.3815'2'015194
B82-02199

621.381'73'015194 — Electronic equipment. Integrated circuits. Design. Applications of numerical analysis — *Conference proceedings*

NASECODE II *(Conference : 1981 : Trinity College, Dublin).* Numerical analysis of semiconductor devices and integrated circuits : proceedings of the NASECODE II Conference held at Trinity College, Dublin, from 17th to 19th June, 1981 / edited by B.T. Browne, J.J.H. Miller. — Dublin : Boole, 1981. — xii,288p : ill ; 25cm
ISBN 0-906783-03-8 : Unpriced
Primary classification 621.3815'2'015194
B82-02198

621.381'73'05 — Electronic equipment. Integrated circuits — *Serials*

Integrated circuits international : incorporating Microcomputer news international. — Vol.6, no.5 (July 1982)-. — Oxford (256 Banbury Rd, Oxford OX2 7DH) : Elsevier International Bulletins, 1982-. — v. : ill ; 30cm
Monthly. — Also entitled: IC international. — Continues: MNI Microcomputer news international
ISSN 0263-6522 = Integrated circuits international : £95.00 per year B82-40070

621.381'735 — Electronic equipment: Integrated circuits. Operational amplifiers

Johnson, D. E.. Operational amplifier circuits : design and application / David E. Johnson and V. Jayakumar. — Englewood Cliffs ; London : Prentice-Hall, c1982. — x,285p : ill ; 24cm
Includes index
ISBN 0-13-637447-6 : £17.95 B82-23649

621.381'735 — Electronic equipment: Integrated circuits. Operational amplifiers. Projects — *Amateurs' manuals*

Penfold, R. A.. Modern OP amp projects. — London : Babani, Nov.1982. — [96]p. — (BP ; 106)
ISBN 0-85934-081-3 (pbk) : £1.95 : CIP entry
B82-26329

621.381'735 — Electronic equipment: Linear integrated circuits. Operational amplifiers

Coughlin, Robert F.. Operational amplifiers and linear integrated circuits / Robert F. Coughlin, Frederick F. Driscoll. — 2nd ed. — Englewood Cliffs ; London : Prentice-Hall, c1982. — xxiii,376p : ill ; 24cm
Previous ed.: 1977. — Includes bibliographies and index
ISBN 0-13-637785-8 : £16.45 B82-16720

621.381'74 — Electronic equipment. Printed circuits. Construction — *Amateurs' manuals*

Penfold, R. A.. Multi-circuit board projects. — London : Babani, July 1982. — [96]p
ISBN 0-85934-078-3 (pbk) : £1.95 : CIP entry
B82-13147

621.3819'5'0922 — Computers — *Biographies*

Ashurst, F. Gareth. Pioneers of computing. — London : Muller, Feb.1983. — [224]p
ISBN 0-584-10382-4 : £7.95 : CIP entry
B82-38859

621.3819'58 — Microcomputers & microprocessors

Morris, Noel M.. Microprocessor and microcomputer technology / Noel M. Morris. — London : Macmillan, 1981. — xii,225p : ill ; 25cm. — (Macmillan basis books in electronics)
Bibliography: p250. — Includes index
ISBN 0-333-32005-0 (cased) : Unpriced
ISBN 0-333-29268-5 (pbk) : Unpriced
B82-08911

621.3819'58 — Microcomputers & microprocessors — *For technicians*

Microprocessor principles Level 1V. — London : Hutchinson Education, June 1982. — [192]p
ISBN 0-09-148921-0 (pbk) : £4.95 : CIP entry
B82-11292

Pasahow, Edward J.. Microprocessors and microcomputers : for electronics technicians / Edward J. Pasahow. — New York ; London : Gregg Division, McGraw-Hill, c1981. — viii,264p : ill ; 28cm
Includes index
ISBN 0-07-048713-8 (pbk) : £8.35 B82-03889

Vears, R. E.. Microelectronic systems 2 checkbook. — London : Butterworths Scientific, Oct.1982. — [192]p. — (Butterworths technical and scientific checkbooks)
ISBN 0-408-00678-1 (cased) : £7.95 : CIP entry
ISBN 0-408-00659-5 (pbk) : £4.95 B82-24462

621.3819'58 — Small digital computers. Interfaces — *Amateurs' manuals*

Bishop, O. N.. Interfacing to microprocessors and microcomputers / Owen Bishop. — [London] : Newnes Technical, 1982. — 147p : ill ; 22cm. — (Newnes microcomputer books)
Includes index
ISBN 0-408-01129-7 (pbk) : Unpriced : CIP rev. B82-10489

621.3819'580212 — Microcomputers & microprocessors — *Technical data*

Money, S. A.. Microprocessor data book. — London : Granada, Nov.1982. — [272]p
ISBN 0-246-11531-9 (pbk) : £16.00 : CIP entry
B82-27359

621.3819'582 — Small digital computers. Design

Townsend, R.. Digital computer structure and design / R. Townsend. — 2nd ed. — London : Butterworth Scientific, 1982. — 252p : ill ; 23cm
Previous ed.: 1975. — Includes index
ISBN 0-408-01158-0 (cased) : Unpriced : CIP rev.
ISBN 0-408-01155-6 (pbk) : Unpriced
B82-17197

621.3819'583 — Digital computers. Hardware. Design

Mano, M. Morris. Computer system architecture / M. Morris Mano. — 2nd ed. — Englewood Cliffs ; London : Prentice-Hall, c1982. — xii,531p : ill ; 25cm
Previous ed.: 1976. — Includes index
ISBN 0-13-166611-8 : £22.40 B82-37732

621.3819'583 — Digital computers. Hardware. Design. Applications of digital computer systems. Description languages

IFIP TC-10 International Conference on Computer Hardware Description Languages and Their Applications *(5th : 1981 : Kaiserlautern).* Computer hardware description languages and their applications : proceedings of the IFIP TC-10 Fifth International Conference on Computer Hardware Description Languages and Their Applications, Kaiserlautern, F.R.G., 7-9 September, 1981 / edited by M. Breuer, R. Hartenstein. — Amsterdam ; Oxford : North-Holland, c1981. — xii,349p : ill ; 23cm
Includes bibliographies and index
ISBN 0-444-86279-x : £17.93 B82-38183

621.3819'5833 — Digital computers. Semiconductor storage devices

Triebel, Walter A.. Handbook of semiconductor and bubble memories / Walter A. Triebel, Alfred E. Chu. — Englewood Cliffs ; London : Prentice-Hall, c1982. — xii,401p : ill ; 25cm
Bibliography: p378-380. — Includes index
ISBN 0-13-381251-0 : £18.70
Also classified at 621.3819'5833 B82-16985

621.3819'5833 — Digital computers. Storage devices. Bubble domain materials

Triebel, Walter A.. Handbook of semiconductor and bubble memories / Walter A. Triebel, Alfred E. Chu. — Englewood Cliffs ; London : Prentice-Hall, c1982. — xii,401p : ill ; 25cm
Bibliography: p378-380. — Includes index
ISBN 0-13-381251-0 : £18.70
Primary classification 621.3819'5833
B82-16985

621.3819'58'35 — Digital computers. Circuits

VLSI architecture. — Hemel Hempstead : Prentice-Hall, Feb.1983. — [480]p
ISBN 0-13-942672-8 : £21.95 : CIP entry
B82-39270

621.3819'5835 — Digital computers. Logic circuits

Scott, John R.. Basic computer logic / John R. Scott. — Lexington, Mass. : Lexington Books ; [Aldershot] : Gower [distributor], 1981. — xviii,233p : ill ; 24cm. — (Lexington Books series in computer science)
Bibliography: p223. — Includes index
ISBN 0-669-03706-0 : £12.50 B82-00398

621.3819'5835 — Great Britain. Industrial training. Curriculum subjects: Microprocessors. Applications. Management aspects

A **Guide** to training in the application of microprocessors / prepared by the National Computing Centre on behalf of the Department of Industry. — [London] ([Ashdown House, Victoria St., SW1E 6RB]) : The Department, 1981. — 7p ; 30cm
Cover title. — At head of title: Microprocessor Applications Project
Unpriced (pbk) B82-38477

621.3819'58'35 — Industrial equipment. Microprocessors. Software. Design

Foulger, R. J.. Programming embedded microprocessors. — Manchester : NCC Publications, Feb.1982. — [230]p
ISBN 0-85012-344-5 (pbk) : £15.00 : CIP entry
B81-37594

621.3819'5835 — Microcomputers. Circuits. Construction. Projects — *Study examples: Motorola 6800 — Amateurs' manuals*

Clements, Alan. Building your own microcomputer. — London : Prentice-Hall, Feb.1982. — [600]p
ISBN 0-13-086223-1 : £17.95 : CIP entry
B81-35790

621.3819'5835 — Microprocessor systems. Design & development

Microprocessor development and development systems. — London : Granada, July 1982. — [224]p
ISBN 0-246-11490-8 : £17.50 : CIP entry
B82-12228

621.3819'5835 — Microprocessors

Cahill, S. J.. Digital and microprocessor engineering / S.J. Cahill. — Chichester : Ellis Horwood, 1982. — 513p : ill ; 24cm. — (Ellis Horwood series in electrical and electronic engineering)
Includes index
ISBN 0-85312-351-9 : £35.00 : CIP rev.
ISBN 0-85312-412-4 (student ed.) : Unpriced
B81-35877

Microelectronics and microcomputer applications. — Manchester : Manchester University Press, Nov.1982. — [256]p
ISBN 0-7190-0905-7 : £12.50 : CIP entry
Primary classification 621.381'71 B82-36329

Nichols, K. G.. Theory and practice of microprocessors / K. G. Nichols and E.J. Zaluska. — New York ; Crane Russak ; London : Edward Arnold, c1982. — xiii,297p : ill ; 24cm. — (Computer systems engineering series)
Includes index
ISBN 0-7131-3442-9 (cased) : Unpriced
ISBN 0-7131-3454-2 (pbk) : £9.50
ISBN 0-8448-1384-2 (U.S. (cased))
ISBN 0-8448-1410-5 (U.S. (pbk)) B82-26727

Parr, E. A.. Beginner's guide to microprocessors / E.A. Parr. — London : Newnes Technical Books, 1982. — 218p : ill ; 19cm
Includes index
ISBN 0-408-00579-3 (pbk) : £3.95 : CIP rev.
B82-04027

Sinclair, Ian R.. Introducing microprocessors / Ian R. Sinclair. — London : Keith Dickson, 1981. — 121p : ill ; 22cm
Includes index
ISBN 0-907266-01-0 (pbk) : £4.50 B82-02887

621.3819′5835 — Microprocessors *continuation*

Zaks, Rodnay. From chips to systems : an introduction to microprocessers / Rodnay Zaks. — [Berkeley, Calif.] : Sybex ; Birmingham : Computer Bookshop [[distributor]], 1981. — xvi,552p : ill ; 23cm
Includes index
ISBN 0-89588-063-6 (pbk) : Unpriced B82-27628

621.3819′5835 — Microprocessors. Applications

Chips in the 1980s : the application of microeletronic technology in products for consumer and business markets. — London : Economist Intelligence Unit, 1979. — 57p : ill ; 30cm. — (EIU special report ; no.67)
Bibliography: p57
Unpriced (pbk) B82-07782

Information technology : the age of electronic information / Department of Industry. — London : The Department, c1982. — 16p : ill (some col.),1col.map ; 22x30cm. — (It)
Cover title. — Ill on inside covers
Unpriced (pbk) B82-40102

Lund, Robert T.. Microprocessor applications : cases of observations : a report / prepared for the Department of Industry by the Massachusetts Institute of Technology ; by Robert T. Lund, Marvin A. Sirbu Jr, James M. Utterback, with Michael J. Brand ... [et al.]. — London : H.M.S.O., 1980. — ix,166p : ill ; 22cm
ISBN 0-11-512500-0 (pbk) : £5.00 B82-31511

621.3819′5835 — Microprocessors — *Conference proceedings*

EUROMICRO Symposium on Microprocessing and Microprogramming *(7th : 1981 : Paris).*
Implementing functions : microprocessors and firmware : seventh EUROMICRO Symposium on Microprocessing and Microprogramming, Paris, September 8-10, 1981 / edited by Lutz Richter ... [et al.] ; [sponsored by CNRS ... et al.]. — Amsterdam ; Oxford : North-Holland, c1981. — xiv,499p : ill ; 27cm
Includes index
ISBN 0-444-86282-x : £37.08 B82-38188

621.3819′5835 — Microprocessors. Design

Klingman, Edwin E.. Microprocessor systems design / Edwin E. Klingman. — Englewood Cliffs ; London : Prentice-Hall
Vol.2: Microcoding, array logic, and architectural design. — c1982. — xiv,349p : ill ; 25cm
Includes index
ISBN 0-13-581231-3 : £20.65 B82-34459

621.3819′5835 — Microprocessors. Design & applications

Microprocessor applications handbook / David F. Stout, editor-in-chief. — New York ; London : McGraw-Hill, c1982. — 477p in various pagings : ill ; 24cm
Includes index
ISBN 0-07-061798-8 : £29.95 B82-16377

621.3819′5835 — Microprocessors — *Encyclopaedias*

Chandor, Anthony. The Penguin dictionary of microprocessors / Anthony Chandor. — London : Allen Lane, 1981. — 183p ; 24cm
Originally published: Harmondsworth : Penguin, 1981
ISBN 0-7139-1445-9 : £6.95 B82-07923

621.3819′5835 — Microprocessors. Experiments

Hall, Douglas V.. Experiments in microprocessors and digital systems / Douglas V. Hall, Marybelle B. Hall. — New York ; London : McGraw-Hill, c1981. — ix,150p : ill ; 28cm
ISBN 0-07-025576-8 (pbk) : £5.75
Primary classification 001.64′0724 B82-00533

621.3819′5835 — Microprocessors — *For technicians*

Microprocessor appreciation. — London : Hutchinson Education
3. — May 1982. — [120]p
ISBN 0-09-146821-3 (pbk) : £4.95 : CIP entry B82-07252

Microprocessor-based systems Level 5. — London : Hutchinson Education, May 1982. — [336]p
ISBN 0-09-147361-6 (pbk) : £7.50 : CIP entry B82-07255

Sinclair, Ian R.. Microelectronic systems : level 2 / Ian Sinclair. — London : Holt, Rinehart and Winston, c1982. — v,182p : ill ; 22cm
Includes index
ISBN 0-03-910373-0 (pbk) : Unpriced : CIP rev. B82-07986

Sinclair, Ian R.. Microelectronic systmes : level 1 / Ian Sinclair. — London : Holt, Rinehart and Winston, c1982. — viii,93p : ill ; 22cm. — (Holt technician texts)
Includes index
ISBN 0-03-910313-7 (pbk) : £2.50 : CIP rev. B81-35899

621.3819′5835 — Microprocessors. Testing — *Conference proceedings*

Microtest : the testing, maintenance and reliability of microprocessor-based equipment : 2nd-5th April 1979, University of Sussex, Brighton : a symposium / organised by the Society of Electronic and Radio Technicians in association with the Microprocessor Application Group of the Institution of Electrical Engineers and the Institution of Electronic and Radio Engineers. — [London] ([8 Charing Cross Rd., WC2H 0HP]) : The Society, c1979. — 188p : ill ; 30cm
Text on inside covers
£10.00 (£8.00 to members of SERT) (pbk) B82-41137

621.3819′5835′0287 — Digital computers. Circuits. Testing

Bennetts, R. G.. Introduction to digital board testing / R.G. Bennetts. — New York : Crane Russak ; London : Edward Arnold, c1982. — xvi,304p : ill ; 24cm. — ([Computer systems engineering series])
Text on lining papers. — Includes index
ISBN 0-7131-3450-x : £22.50 B82-24376

621.3819′596 — Digital-to-analogue converters & analogue-to-digital converters

Clayton, G. B.. Data converters / G.B. Clayton. — London : Macmillan, 1982. — ix,242p : ill ; 25cm
Includes index
ISBN 0-333-29494-7 (cased) : £18.00
ISBN 0-333-29495-5 (pbk) : Unpriced B82-21623

Loriferne, Bernard. Analog-digital and digital-analog conversion. — London : Heyden, May 1982. — [190]p
Translation of: La conversion analogique-numérique, numérique-analogique
ISBN 0-85501-497-0 : £13.00 : CIP entry B82-14936

621.3819′598 — Image processing by digital computer systems

Ballard, Dana H.. Computer vision / Dana H. Ballard, Christopher M. Brown. — Englewood Cliffs ; London : Prentice-Hall, c1982. — xx,523p,[4]p of plates : ill(some col.) ; 25cm
Includes bibliographies and index
ISBN 0-13-165316-4 : £31.95 B82-38576

Languages and architectures for image processing / edited by M.J.B. Duff and S. Levialdi. — London : Academic Press, 1981. — xi,327p : ill ; 24cm
Includes bibliographies and index
ISBN 0-12-223320-4 : £16.40 : CIP rev. B81-14873

621.3819′598 — Speech. Recognition by computers — *Conference proceedings*

Automatic speech analysis and recognition / proceedings of the NATO Advanced Study Institute held at Bonas, France, June 29-July 10, 1981 ; edited by Jean-Paul Haton. — Dordrecht ; London : Reidel in cooperation with NATO Scientific Affairs Division, c1982. — xii,371p : ill ; 25cm. — (NATO advanced study institutes series. Series C, Mathematical and physical sciences ; v.88)
Includes bibliographies and index
ISBN 90-277-1443-6 : Unpriced B82-40153

621.382 — TELEGRAPHY

621.382′0941 — Great Britain. Telecommunication systems. Cables

Information Technology Advisory Panel. Report on cable systems. — London : H.M.S.O., 1982. — 54p ; 20cm
At head of title: Cabinet Office. Information Technology Advisory Panel
ISBN 0-11-630821-4 (pbk) : £3.60 B82-29712

621.384 — RADIO AND RADAR

621.3841 — Radio engineering

Gonorovskiĭ, I. S.. Radio circuits and signals / I.S. Gonorovsky ; translated from the Russian by N. Utkin. — Moscow : Mir ; [London] : Distributed by Central Books, 1981. — 639p : ill ; 23cm
Translation of: Radiotekhnicheskie t͡sepi i signaly. — Added t.p. in Russian. — Bibliography: p629-631. — Includes index
ISBN 0-7147-1656-1 : £5.25 B82-02696

621.3841 — Radio equipment. Electromagnetic compatibility

Electromagnetic compatibility in radio engineering / edited by Wilhelm Rotkiewicz. — Amsterdam ; Oxford : Elsevier Scientific, 1982. — ix,312p : ill,maps ; 25cm. — (Studies in electrical and electronic engineering ; 6)
Rev. translation of: Kompatybilność elektromagnetyczna w radiotechnice. — Text on folded sheet in pocket. — Includes index
ISBN 0-444-99722-9 : £30.05 : CIP rev.
ISBN 0-444-41713-3 B81-31613

621.3841 — Radio equipment — *For technicians*

Danielson, G. L.. Radio systems for technicians 3 / G.L. Danielson, R.S. Walker. — [Sevenoaks] : Butterworths, 1982. — 117p : ill ; 25cm. — (Butterworths TEC technician series)
ISBN 0-408-00588-2 (pbk) : Unpriced : CIP rev. B81-36376

621.3841′092′4 — Ecuador. Christian radio services. Engineering. Cockerham, Robert — *Biographies*

Roberts, Geoff. Mightier than the waves : the Cockerhams′ story / Geoff Roberts ; line drawings by Anne Cockerham. — [Shipley] ([c/o Ms. D. Scott, 51 Nab Wood Crescent, Shipley, W. Yorkshire]) : [A. Cockerham and G. Roberts], 1981. — 48p : ill,1map,ports ; 15x21cm
£0.95 (pbk) B82-20158

621.3841′0941 — Great Britain. Commercial broadcasting services: Independent Broadcasting Authority. Radio equipment

Broadcasting technology for the 1980s / [technical editor Pat Hawker]. — [London] ([70 Brompton Rd, SW3 1EY]) : Independent Broadcasting Authority, 1980. — 11p : ill(some col.),1port ; 30cm
Unpriced (unbound)
Primary classification 621.388′00941 B82-35012

621.3841′1 — Radio waves. Diffractin by aperture antennas

Jull, E. V.. Aperture antennas and diffraction theory / E.V. Jull. — Stevenage : Peregrinus on behalf of the Institution of Electrical Engineers, c1981. — x,173p : ill ; 24cm. — (IEE electromagnetic waves series ; 10)
Bibliography: p147-152. — Includes index
ISBN 0-906048-52-4 : Unpriced : CIP rev. B81-13899

621.3841′1 — Radio waves. Underground propagation

Delogne, P.. Leaky feeders and subsurface radio communication / P. Delogne. — Stevenage : Peregrinus on behalf of the Institution of Electrical Engineers, c1982. — 283p : ill ; 24cm. — (IEE electromagnetic waves series ; 14)
Bibliography: p263-270. — Includes index
ISBN 0-906048-77-x : Unpriced : CIP rev. B82-11973

621.3841'3 — Amateur radio equipment. Construction — *Manuals*

Helfrick, Albert D.. Amateur radio equipment fundamentals / Albert D. Helfrick. — Englewood Cliffs ; London : Prentice-Hall, c1982. — xii,284p : ill ; 24cm
Includes index
ISBN 0-13-023655-1 : £14.20 B82-19947

621.3841'35 — 2m waveband frequency modulation radio equipment: Receivers. Antennas — *Amateurs' manuals*

Judd, F. C.. Two-metre antenna handbook / F.C. Judd. — London : Newnes Technical, 1980. — 157p : ill ; 19cm
Bibliography: p154. — Includes index
ISBN 0-408-00402-9 (pbk) : Unpriced : CIP rev. B79-27522

621.3841'35 — Amateur high frequency radio equipment. Antennas

Moxon, L. A.. HF antennas for all locations / L.A. Moxon. — London : Radio Society of Great Britain, 1982. — 260p : ill ; 26cm
Includes index
ISBN 0-900612-57-6 : Unpriced B82-23726

621.3841'366 — Radio equipment: Crystal receivers. Projects — *Amateurs' manuals*

Wilson, F. A.. Electronics simplified : crystal set construction / by F.A. Wilson. — London : Babani, 1982. — 72p : ill ; 18cm
ISBN 0-85934-067-8 (pbk) : £1.75 : CIP rev. B81-27413

621.3841'366 — Shortwave radio equipment: Receivers — *Amateurs' manuals*

Penfold, R. A.. An introduction to radio Dxing / by R.A. Penfold. — London : Babani, 1981. — 96p : ill ; 18cm. — (Bernard Babani ; BP91)
ISBN 0-85934-066-x (pbk) : £1.95 : CIP rev. B81-22539

621.3841'5 — Radio frequency equipment. Design

Hayward, W. H.. Introduction to radio frequency design / W.H. Hayward. — Englewood Cliffs ; London : Prentice-Hall, c1982. — xi,383p : ill ; 25cm
Includes index
ISBN 0-13-494021-0 : £20.95 B82-28158

621.3841'51 — Amateur radio equipment

Benbow, G. L.. Radio amateurs' examination manual. — 9th ed. / G.L. Benbow. — London : Radio Society of Great Britain, 1981. — 132p : ill ; 25cm
Previous ed.: 1979. — Includes index
ISBN 0-900612-55-x (pbk) : Unpriced B82-05523

Shrader, Robert L.. Amateur radio : theory and practice / written and illustrated by Robert L. Shrader. — New York ; London : McGraw-Hill, c1982. — xi,340p : ill,1form ; 24cm
Includes index
ISBN 0-07-057146-5 (pbk) : £11.50 B82-29274

621.3841'51 — Amateur radio equipment — *Buyers' guides*

Rayer, F. G.. Beginner's guide to amateur radio. — London : Newnes, Oct.1982. — [240]p
ISBN 0-408-01126-2 (pbk) : £3.95 : CIP entry B82-30338

621.3841'51 — Shortwave radio links

Braun, Gerhard. Planning and design of shortwave links. — London : Heyden, July 1982. — [550]p
Translation of: Planung und Berechnung von Kurzwellenverbindungen
ISBN 0-85501-521-7 (pbk) : CIP entry B82-14393

Wiesner, Lothar. Telegraph and data transmision over shortwave radio links. — 2nd ed. — London : Heyden, Apr.1981. — [200]p
Translation of: Fernschreib- und Datenübertragung über Kurzwelle. — Previous ed.: 1977
ISBN 0-85501-291-9 (pbk) : CIP entry B81-07464

621.3841'6'025 — Radio stations — *Directories*

The World's radio broadcasting stations : and European FM/TV / [edited by] C.J. Both. — Sevenoaks : Newnes Technical, 1981. — ix,214p ; 22cm
ISBN 0-408-01156-4 (pbk) : Unpriced B82-00963

621.3841'6'094 — Europe. Radio stations — *Lists*

Wilcox, George. Dial search : the listener's check list of European radio stations / [compiled by George Wilcox]. — 2nd ed. — Eastbourne (9 Thurrock Close, Eastbourne, East Sussex BN20 9NF) : G. Wilcox, 1981. — 15p ; 21cm
Cover title. — Previous ed.: 1974
£0.80 (pbk) B82-09096

621.3841'6'0941 — Great Britain. Radio broadcasting. Technical aspects

Latest developments in sound broadcasting / technical editor John Lovell. — London : I.B.A., 1981. — 72p : ill,2col.maps,ports ; 23cm. — (IBA technical review, ISSN 0308-423x ; 14)
English text, French, German and Italian résumés
(pbk) B82-02575

621.3841'65 — Mobile microwave radio systems

Lee, William C. Y.. Mobile communications engineering / William C.Y. Lee. — New York ; London : McGraw-Hill, c1982. — xi,464p : ill ; 24cm
Includes index
ISBN 0-07-037039-7 : Unpriced B82-35771

621.3841'66 — Amateur radio stations. Operation — *Manuals*

Amateur radio operating manual / editor R.J. Eckersley ; contributors P.J. Aitchison ... [et al.]. — 2nd ed. — London : Radio Society of Great Britain, 1982. — 203p : ill,maps,forms ; 25cm
Previous ed.: 1979. — Includes index
ISBN 0-900612-56-8 (pbk) : Unpriced B82-18082

621.3841'66'0285404 — Amateur radio communication. Applications of microcomputer systems

Anderson, Phil. Computers and the radio amateur / Phil Anderson. — Englewood Cliffs ; London : Prentice-Hall, c1982. — xii,208p : ill ; 24cm
Includes index
ISBN 0-13-166306-2 : £14.20 B82-20073

621.3841'66'0941 — Great Britain. Amateur radio communication — *Rules*

How to become a radio amateur / with the compliments of the Secretary of State for the Home Department. — [London] : [Home Office], [198-?]. — 40p ; 30cm
Cover title
Unpriced (pbk) B82-35483

621.3841'7 — Broadcasting. Radio frequency wavebands. Allocation — *Proposals*

World Administrative Radio Conference for Mobile Telecommunications *(1983 : Geneva)*. Provisional proposals of the United Kingdom for the World Administrative Radio Conference for Mobile Telecommunications : 1983. — [London] ([Queen Anne's Gate, SW1H 9AT]) : Home Office Radio Regulatory Dept., 1981. — 117p : 1ill ; 30cm
Unpriced (pbk) B82-40593

621.3841'85 — Radio equipment: Receivers using integrated circuits. Construction — *Amateurs' manuals — For children*

Davey, Gilbert. Fun with silicon chips in modern radio / Gilbert Davey ; edited by Jack Cox. — London : Kaye & Ward, 1981. — 64p : ill ; 23cm
ISBN 0-7182-1325-4 : £4.25 B82-00745

621.3841'87 — Radio equipment: Valve receivers. Servicing — *Amateurs' manuals*

Miller, Chas. E.. Practical handbook of valve radio repair. — London : Newnes Technical Books, Mar.1982. — [144]p
ISBN 0-408-00593-9 : £5.00 : CIP entry B82-00911

621.3845'4 — Citizens' Band radio equipment. Accessories. Construction — *Amateurs' manuals*

Penfold, R. A.. CB projects / by R.A. Penfold. — London : Babani, 1981. — 83p : ill ; 18cm. — (BP ; 96)
ISBN 0-85934-071-6 (pbk) : £1.95 : CIP rev. B81-30885

621.3845'4'0941 — Great Britain. Citizens' Band radio

Ainslie, Alan C.. The UK CB handbook / Alan C. Ainslie. — London : Newnes Technical, 1982. — 150p : ill ; 22cm
Includes index
ISBN 0-408-01177-7 (pbk) : Unpriced : CIP rev. B81-34576

Big Hal's CB handbook. — London (124 Cornwall Rd., S.E.1) : Grant Jarvis, Sept.1981. — [80]p
ISBN 0-907741-00-2 (pbk) : £0.95 : CIP entry B81-27880

Nichols, Richard. The complete CB radio / Richard Nichols ; illustrated by Ian Sowerby. — London : W.H. Allen, 1981. — 220p : ill,1map ; 20cm. — (A star book)
ISBN 0-352-31014-6 (pbk) : £2.50 B82-07896

621.3845'4'0941 — Great Britain. Citizens' Band radio communication

Chippindale, Peter. The British CB book / Peter Chippindale ; illustrated by Steve Bell. — London : Kona, c1981. — 225p : ill,facsims,ports ; 22cm
ISBN 0-907684-00-9 (pbk) : £2.95 B82-31247

Christos, George. CB for the serious user : the practical handbook for citizens' band radio / by George Christos ; foreword by John Spencer. — Amersham : Woodside Books, 1981. — 144p : ill ; 18cm
ISBN 0-9507884-0-6 (pbk) : £2.99 : CIP rev. B81-38296

Judd, F. C.. CB radio. — London : Newnes Technical Books, Nov.1982. — [120]p. — (Questions and answers)
ISBN 0-408-01216-1 (pbk) : £1.95 : CIP entry B82-28248

Nichols, Richard. The complete CB radio / Richard Nichols ; illustrated by Ian Sowerby. — London : W.H. Allen, 1982, c1981. — 220p : ill ; 20cm
ISBN 0-491-02787-7 : £5.95 B82-13372

Open channel : a system of personal short range radio communications in the United Kingdom : a discussion document. — London (Waterloo Bridge House, Waterloo Rd, SE1 8UA) : Radio Regulatory Department, Home Office, [1980?]. — 14p ; 21cm
Unpriced (pbk) B82-35366

621.3848'5 — Radar systems

Ewell, George W.. Radar transmitters / George W. Ewell. — New York ; London : McGraw-Hill, c1981. — xiv,338p : ill ; 24cm
Includes bibliographies and index
ISBN 0-07-019843-8 : £17.50 B82-02522

621.385 — TELEPHONY

621.385 — Business facsimile transmission equipment

Cawkell, A. E.. An investigation of commercially available facsimile systems. — London : British Library Research and Development Department, Sept.1982. — [54]p. — (British Library research and development reports, ISSN 0308-2385 ; no.5719)
ISBN 0-7123-3013-5 (spiral) : CIP entry B82-28751

621.385 — Business facsimile transmission equipment — *Buyers' guides*

Welch, W. J.. Facsimile equipment : a practical evaluation guide. — Manchester : NCC Publications, Jan.1982. — [105]p. — (Office technology in the '80s ; 2)
ISBN 0-85012-358-5 (pbk) : £4.00 : CIP entry B82-03120

621.385 — Private telephone exchanges — *For management*

Scott, P. R. D.. Choosing a PABX. — Manchester : NCC Publications, Oct.1982. — [50]p
ISBN 0-85012-364-x : £6.50 : CIP entry B82-24739

621.385 — Telephone systems. Digital signals

Bellamy, John, *1941-*. Digital telephony / John Bellamy. — New York ; Chichester : Wiley, c1982. — xviii,526p : ill ; 25cm
Bibliography: p519-521. — Includes index
ISBN 0-471-08089-6 : £33.00 B82-18221

621.388 — TELEVISION

621.388 — Teletex systems

Price, S. G.. Preparing for Teletex. — Manchester : NCC Publications, Apr.1982. — [100]p. — (Office technology in the ′80s ; 4)
ISBN 0-85012-372-0 (pbk) : £6.50 : CIP entry B82-16198

621.388 — Television

Colour & mono television for City & Guilds and Tec courses. — London : Price
Vol.1: Television reception : principles and circuits / K.J. Bohlman. — c1980. — 168p,[2] folded leaves of plates : ill(some col.) ; 22cm
Includes index
ISBN 0-85380-135-5 (pbk) : £5.00 B82-30176

White, Gordon, *1935-*. Video techniques / Gordon White. — London : Newnes Technical, 1982. — 299p : ill ; 23cm
Includes index
ISBN 0-408-00506-8 : £10.95 : CIP rev. B81-31735

621.388 — Video equipment

Matthewson, David K.. Beginner′s guide to video / David K. Matthewson. — London : Newnes Technical, 1982. — 192p : ill ; 19cm
Includes index
ISBN 0-408-00577-7 (pbk) : Unpriced : CIP rev. B81-31366

621.388 — Video equipment — *Amateurs′ manuals*

Money, S. A.. Video equipment. — Sevenoaks : Newnes, Sept.1981. — [112]p. — (Questions and answers)
ISBN 0-408-00553-x (pbk) : £1.95 : CIP entry B81-23922

621.388 — Video equipment — *Buyers′ guides*

Smith, Tim. The complete video guide / Tim Smith. — London : Virgin, 1981. — 207p : ill ; 18cm
ISBN 0-907080-26-x (pbk) : £1.95 B82-28511

621.388 — Video equipment — *Buyers′ guides — Serials*

Video for leisure. — Vol.1, no.1 (Oct. 1981)-. — London (40 Long Acre, WC2E 9JT) : Spotlight Publications, 1981-. — v. : ill,ports ; 30cm
Monthly
ISSN 0262-2122 = Video for leisure : Unpriced B82-03428

621.388 — Videotex systems

Firth, R. J.. Viewdata systems : a practical evaluation guide / R.J. Firth. — Manchester : NCC Publications, 1982. — 86p,[ie 114]p : ill ; 22cm. — (Office technology in the ′80s)
Bibliography: p81
ISBN 0-85012-370-4 (pbk) : Unpriced : CIP rev. B82-12818

Managing office automation : videotex : public and private systems. — Farnham Common : Urwick Nexos, [1982]. — ii,45p : ill ; 30cm. — (Urwick Nexos report series ; 7)
ISBN 0-907535-08-9 (pbk) : Unpriced B82-19779

Yeates, Robin. A librarian′s introduction to private viewdata systems / by Robin Yeates. — London : LASER, 1982. — 51leaves ; 30cm
British Library project no.SI/G/518. — Cover title
ISBN 0-903764-14-8 (pbk) : £5.00 B82-35768

621.388′00941 — Great Britain. Commercial broadcasting services: Independent Broadcasting Authority. Television equipment

Broadcasting technology for the 1980s / [technical editor Pat Hawker]. — [London] ([70 Brompton Rd, SW3 1EY]) : Independent Broadcasting Authority, 1980. — 11p : ill(some col.),1port ; 30cm
Unpriced (unbound)
Also classified at 621.3841′0941 B82-35012

621.388′00973 — United States. Television

Sklar, Robert. Prime-time America : life on and behind the television screen / Robert Sklar. — Oxford : Oxford University Press, 1980 (1982 [printing]). — xi,200p ; 21cm
ISBN 0-19-503046-x (pbk) : £3.50 B82-37367

621.388′04 — Colour television — *Manuals*

Cole, H. A. (Horace Albert). Basic colour television. — Oxford : Technical Press. — (Common core series)
Pt.1. — July 1982. — [128]p
ISBN 0-291-39641-0 (pbk) : £3.95 : CIP entry B82-16497

621.388′33 — Video discs

Barrett, R.. Optical video disc technology and applications. — London : British Library, Research and Development Dept., Aug.1982. — [50]p. — (Library and information research reports, ISSN 0263-1709 ; 7)
ISBN 0-7123-3010-0 (pbk) : £9.00 : CIP entry B82-28568

Sigel, Efrem. Video discs : the technology, the applications and the future / by Efrem Sigel, Mark Schubin, Paul F. Merrill with Kenneth S. Christie, John Rusche and Alan Horder. — White Plains, N.Y. : Knowledge Industry ; London : Eurospan [distributor], c1980. — iii,183p : ill,forms ; 24cm. — (Video bookshelf)
Includes index
ISBN 0-914236-56-3 : Unpriced B82-08804

621.388′87 — Television equipment: Portable receivers. Servicing — *Manuals*

Monoportables vol.1 / from information by R. Laverick ... [et al.]. — Larkhall : T.V. Technic, 1982. — 134p ; 25cm. — (T.V. repairs made easy)
Cover title
Unpriced (pbk) B82-41079

621.388′87 — Television equipment: Receivers. Servicing — *Manuals*

Goldberg, Joel. Fundamentals of television servicing / Joel Goldberg. — Englewood Cliffs ; London : Prentice-Hall, c1982. — ix,276p : ill ; 25cm
Includes index
ISBN 0-13-344598-4 : £14.20 B82-35159

Television engineers′ pocket book. — 7th ed. — London : Newnes Technical Books, May 1982. — [400]p
Previous ed.: / edited by P.J. McGoldrick. London : Newnes-Butterworths, 1973
ISBN 0-408-00444-4 (pbk) : £7.00 : CIP entry B82-06739

621.388′872 — Monochrome television equipment: Portable receivers. Servicing — *Manuals*

Wilding, George. Servicing monochrome portable television. — London : Newnes, Oct.1982. — [160]p
ISBN 0-408-01143-2 (pbk) : £6.50 : CIP entry B82-24465

621.389 — PUBLIC ADDRESS SYSTEMS, SOUND RECORDING, ETC

621.389′2 — Public address systems

Capel, Vivian. Public address handbook / Vivian Capel. — 2nd ed. — London : Keith Dickson Publishing, 1981. — 238p : ill ; 23cm
Previous ed.: London : Fountain Press, 1971. — Includes index
ISBN 0-907266-02-9 : £7.95 B82-08634

621.389′2′06041 — Great Britain. Public address systems. Organisations: Association of Sound & Communications Engineers — *Directories*

Association of Sound & Communications Engineers. Directory / [Association of Sound and Communications Engineers]. — Stoke Poges (4 Snitterfield Farm, Grays Park Rd., Stoke Poges, SL2 4HX) : The association, [1982?]. — 92p : ill(some col.) ; 21cm
Unpriced (pbk) B82-41135

621.389′3 — High-fidelity sound recording & reproduction equipment

Borwick, John. The Gramophone guide to hi-fi / John Borwick. — Newton Abbot : David & Charles, c1982. — 256p : ill,ports ; 24cm
Bibliography: p240. — List of sound discs: p234-240. — Includes index
ISBN 0-7153-8231-4 : £12.50 : CIP rev. B82-15839

621.389′3 — High-fidelity sound recording & reproduction equipment — *Buyers′ guides*

The **Which?** guide to hi-fi. — London : Consumers′ Association and Hodder & Stoughton, c1981. — 130p : ill ; 20cm
Includes index
ISBN 0-340-26629-5 (pbk) : £5.95 B82-02589

621.389′3 — High-fidelity sound recording & reproduction equipment — *Serials*

Hi-fi annual and test. — ′78-. — [Teddington] ([38 Hampton Rd, Teddington, Middx TW11 0JE]) : Haymarket Publishing, [1977]-. — v. : ill ; 29cm
Continues: Hi-fi annual and guide
ISSN 0262-446x = Hi-fi annual and test : £1.25 B82-03401

621.389′3 — Sound recording & reproduction equipment

Alkin, Glyn. Sound recording and reproduction / Glyn Alkin. — London : Focal, 1981. — 224p : ill ; 23cm
Bibliography: p215
ISBN 0-240-51070-4 : Unpriced B82-06376

621.389′32 — Tape-slide presentations. Making — *For careers guidance*

Charles, Tony. Slide-tape presentations in careers work / by Tony Charles. — Stourbridge : Institute of Careers Officers, [1981?]. — [4]p : ill ; 31cm. — (Occasional paper / Institute of Careers Officers ; no.2)
ISBN 0-903076-20-9 (unbound) : £0.75 B82-00762

621.389′32 — Tape-slide presentations. Making — *Manuals*

Sunier, John. Slide/sound and filmstrip production / John Sunier. — London : Focal, 1981. — 160p : ill ; 23cm
Bibliography: p154-157
ISBN 0-240-51074-7 : Unpriced B82-00760

621.389′32 — Videorecording. Techniques — *Manuals*

Dean, Richard. Home video. — London : Newnes Technical Books, Apr.1982. — [160]p
ISBN 0-408-01166-1 (pbk) : £3.50 : CIP entry B82-04040

621.39 — ELECTRICAL ENGINEERING. SPECIAL BRANCHES

621.39 — Superconducting magnetic systems

Wilson, Martin N.. Superconducting magnets. — Oxford : Clarendon Press, Dec.1982. — [400]p. — (Monographs on cryogenics)
ISBN 0-19-854805-2 : £30.00 : CIP entry B82-32286

621.39 — Superconductors. Applications

NATO Advanced Study Institute on the Science and Technology of Superconducting Materials *(Sintra : 1980)*. Superconductor materials science : metallurgy, fabrication, and applications / [proceedings of a NATO Advanced Study Institute on the Science and Technology of Superconducting Materials, held in August 20-30, 1980, in Sintra, Portugal]. — New York ; London : Plenum, c1981. — xxix,969p : ill ; 26cm. — (NATO advanced study institutes series. Series B, Physics ; v.68)
Conference papers. — Includes index
ISBN 0-306-40750-7 : Unpriced B82-08342

621.4 — HEAT ENGINEERING AND PRIME MOVERS

621.4 — Alternative energy sources

Flood, Mike. Solar prospects. — London : Wildwood House, Aug.1982. — [208]p
ISBN 0-7045-0473-1 (pbk) : £5.95 : CIP entry B82-18475

621.4 — Alternative energy sources — *Conference proceedings*

Alternative energy sources : an international compendium / edited by T. Nejat Veziroğlu. — Washington [D.C.] ; London : Hemisphere, c1978. — 11v.(xxi,5170p) : ill,charts,maps,plans ; 25cm
Conference papers. — Includes bibliographies and index
ISBN 0-89116-129-5 : £295.75
ISBN 0-07-079200-3 (McGraw-Hill) : £295.75 B82-02416

Alternative energy sources / edited by Jamal T. Manassah. — New York ; London : Academic Press. — (International symposium of the Kuwait Foundation)
Pt.A. — 1981. — xi,.517p : ill,maps ; 25cm
Conference papers. — 'Sponsored by KFAS Kuwait Foundation for the Advancement of Science'
ISBN 0-12-467101-2 (cased) : £32.80
ISBN 0-12-467121-7 (pbk) : Unpriced B82-10149

621.4 — Great Britain. Stationary engines, ***to 1950***

Edgington, David W.. Old stationary engines / David W. Edgington. — Aylesbury : Shire, 1980. — 32p : ill ; 21cm. — (Shire album ; 49)
Ill, text on inside covers
ISBN 0-85263-500-1 (pbk) : £0.75 B82-40935

621.4 — Stirling engines

Reader, Graham T.. Stirling engines. — London : Spon, Nov.1982. — [450]p
ISBN 0-419-12400-4 : £15.00 : CIP entry B82-28250

621.4 — Stirling engines — *Conference proceedings*

Stirling engines — progress towards reality / conference sponsored by The Power Industries Division of The Institution of Mechanical Engineers with the patronage of Fédération Internationale des Sociétés d'Ingenieurs des Techniques de l'Automobile (FISITA), 25-26 March 1982, University of Reading. — London : Published by Mechanical Engineering Publications Limited for The Institution of Mechanical Engineers, 1982. — 176p : ill ; 30cm. — (I Mech E conference publications ; 1982-2)
ISBN 0-85298-489-8 (pbk) : Unpriced B82-22280

621.4'002'46238 — Engines — *For marine engineering*

Morton, Thomas D.. Reed's motor engineering knowledge for marine engineers / by Thomas D. Morton. — 2nd ed. — Sunderland : Reed, 1978. — 212p : ill ; 22cm. — (Reed's marine engineering series)
Previous ed.: 1975. — Includes index
ISBN 0-900335-52-1 : £6.00 B82-08533

621.402 — Great Britain. Waste heat. Recovery — *Conference proceedings*

Energy Management & Waste Heat Reovery Conference *(1980 : London)*. Energy Management & Waste Heat Recovery Conference : 25 and 26 March 1980 : Waldorf Hotel, London WC2 / [sponsored by the Institution of Plant Engineers] ; [organised by Conference Communication]. — [London?] ([138 Buckingham Palace Rd., SW1W 9SG?]) : [Institution of Plant Engineers?], [1980?]. — 132p in various pagings : ill ; 30cm
Unpriced (spiral)
Primary classification 333.79'0941 B82-09410

621.402 — Heat engineering

The **Efficient** use of energy. — 2nd ed. — London : Butterworth, May 1982. — [616]p
Previous ed.: Guildford : IPC Science and Technology Press, 1975
ISBN 0-408-01250-1 : £35.00 : CIP entry B82-11760

621.402 — Heat. Storage

Thermal energy storage : lectures of a course held at the Joint Research Centre, Ispra, Italy, June 1-5, 1981 / edited by G. Beghi. — Dordrecht ; London : Reidel, c1982. — 505p : ill ; 24cm. — (Ispra courses on energy systems and technology)
Includes index
ISBN 90-277-1428-2 : Unpriced B82-37035

621.402'1 — Fluids. Thermodynamics. Engineering aspects

Thermofluid mechanics and energy / [Thermofluid Mechanics and Energy Course Team]. — Milton Keynes : Open University Press. — (Technology : a second level course)
At head of title: The Open University
3: The second law of thermodynamics ; 4: Available energy, entropy and experiments / prepared by the Course Team. — 1982. — 85p : ill ; 30cm. — (T233 ; 3 and 4)
ISBN 0-335-17076-5 (pbk) : Unpriced B82-32010

Thermofluid mechanics and energy / [Thermofluid Mechanics and Energy Course Team]. — Milton Keynes : Open University Press. — (Technology : a second level course)
At head of title: The Open University
5: Modelling fluids ; 6: Similarity analysis and dimensionless groups / prepared by the Course Team. — 1982. — 102p : ill(some col.) ; 30cm. — (T233 ; 5 and 6)
ISBN 0-335-17077-3 (pbk) : Unpriced B82-32011

Thermofluid mechanics and energy / [Thermofluid Mechanics and Energy Course Team]. — Milton Keynes : Open University Press. — (Technology : a second level course)
At head of title: The Open University
7/8: The first and second laws of thermodynamics for flow processes / prepared by the Course Team. — 1982. — 75p : ill ; 30cm. — (T233 ; 7/8)
ISBN 0-335-17078-1 (pbk) : Unpriced B82-32012

Thermofluid mechanics and energy / [The Thermofluid Mechanics and Energy Course Team]. — Milton Keynes : Open University Press. — (Technology : a second level course)
At head of title: The Open University
9/10: Fluid mechanics : energy and momentum / prepared by the Course Team. — 1982. — 67p : ill(some col.) ; 30cm. — (T233 ; 9/10)
ISBN 0-335-17079-x (pbk) : Unpriced B82-39132

Thermofluid mechanics and energy / [The Thermofluid Mechanics and Energy Course Team]. — Milton Keynes : Open University Press
At head of title: The Open University
13/14: Heat transfer analysis / prepared by the Course Team. — 1982. — 72p : ill(some col.) ; 30cm. — (T233 ; 13-14)
ISBN 0-335-17075-7 (pbk) : Unpriced B82-40659

621.402'1 — Heat engineering. Thermodynamics

Cravalho, Ernest G.. Engineering thermodynamics / Ernest G. Cravalho, Joseph L. Smith. — Boston, Mass. ; London : Pitman, c1981. — xi,548p : ill ; 24cm
At head of title: Massachusetts Institute of Technology. — Includes index
ISBN 0-273-01604-0 (pbk) : Unpriced B82-03565

621.402'1 — Heat engineering. Thermodynamics — *For technicians*

Bacon, D. H.. Thermodynamics for technicians 3/4 / D.H. Bacon and R.C. Stephens. — Sevenoaks : Butterworths Scientific, 1982. — 95p : ill ; 24cm. — (Butterworths TEC technician series)
ISBN 0-408-01114-9 (pbk) : Unpriced : CIP rev. B82-04035

621.402'2'028 — Heat transfer equipment — *Conference proceedings*

The **Selection** and use of heat transfer equipment : Manchester 1st October 1981 / edited Adin L. Clarke. — [Manchester] : Institution of Chemical Engineers, North Western Branch, [c1982]. — 50p in various pagings : ill ; 30cm. — (Symposium papers 1981 ; no.4)
ISBN 0-906636-11-6 (pbk) : £6.00 (£5.00 to members of the Branch) B82-34399

621.402'3 — Combustion engineering

Energy and combustion science : selected papers from Progress in energy and combustion science / edited by N.A. Chigier. — Student ed.1. — Oxford : Pergamon, 1979. — vii,325p : ill ; 28cm. — (Pergamon international library)
ISBN 0-08-024781-4 (cased) : £15.75 : CIP rev.
ISBN 0-08-024780-6 (pbk) : £6.25 B79-27398

621.402'3 — Combustion engineering: Swirl flows

Gupta, A. K.. Swirl flows. — Tunbridge Wells : Abacus Press, Sept.1982. — [300]p. — (Energy and engineering science series)
ISBN 0-85626-175-0 : £20.00 : CIP entry B82-20844

621.402'3 — Fuels. Fluidised combustion — *Conference proceedings*

Fluidised combustion : systems and applications : an international conference held in London, UK, 3-5 November 1980 / The Institute of Energy in association with American Society of Mechanical Engineers ... [et al.]. — London : The Institute. — (Institute of Energy symposium series ; no.4)
Vol.3. — c1980. — 498p in various pagings : ill ; 30cm
ISBN 0-902597-20-5 (pbk) : Unpriced B82-02196

621.402'3 — Furnaces. Combustion. Mathematical models

Khalil, Essam Eldin. Modelling of furnace and combustor flows. — Tunbridge Wells : Abacus Press, Jan.1982. — [300]p. — (Energy and engineering science series)
ISBN 0-85626-303-6 : £17.50 : CIP entry B81-33776

621.402'5 — Heat exchangers — *Conference proceedings*

Heat exchangers : thermal-hydraulic fundamentals and design : Advanced Study Institute book / edited by S. Kakaç, A.E. Bergles, F. Mayinger. — Washington ; London : Hemisphere, c1981. — xi,1131p : ill ; 25cm
Conference proceedings. — Includes index
ISBN 0-07-033284-3 : £45.75 B82-17096

Practical applications of heat transfer / sponsored by the Process Industries Division of the Institution of Mechanical Engineers, 31st March 1982, Institution Headquarters, 1 Birdcage Walk, Westminster, London. — London : Mechanical Engineering Publications for the Institution of Mechanical Engineers, 1982. — 80p : ill ; 30cm. — (I Mech E conference publications ; 1982-4)
Conference papers
ISBN 0-85298-490-1 : Unpriced B82-25797

621.402'5 — Heat exchangers — *Serials*

Developments in heat exchanger technology. — 1-. — London : Applied Science, 1980-. — v. : ill ; 23cm. — (Developments series)
Irregular
ISSN 0263-371x = Developments in heat exchanger technology : £26.00 B82-18539

621.402'5 — Heat pipes

Dunn, P.. Heat pipes. — 3rd ed. — Oxford : Pergamon, Nov.1982. — [320]p. — (Pergamon international library)
Previous ed.: 1978
ISBN 0-08-029356-5 (cased) : £25.00 : CIP entry
ISBN 0-08-029355-7 (pbk) : £9.50 B82-28722

Ivanovskiĭ, M. N.. The physical principles of heat pipes / by M.N. Ivanovskii, V.P. Sorokin, and I.V. Yagodkin ; translated by R. Berman ; translation edited by G. Rice. — Oxford : Clarendon, 1982. — x,262p : ill ; 24cm. — (Oxford studies in physics)
Translation of the Russian. — Includes index
ISBN 0-19-851466-2 : Unpriced : CIP rev. B81-22610

621.402′5 — Heat pipes — *Conference proceedings*

International Heat Pipe Conference *(4th : 1981 : London)*. Advances in heat pipe technology : proceedings of the IVth International Heat Pipe Conference, 7-10 September 1981, London, U.K. / edited by D.A. Reay. — Oxford : Pergamon, 1982. — xi,818p : ill ; 26cm
Includes index
ISBN 0-08-027284-3 : £42.00 : CIP rev. B81-31357

621.402′5 — Heat pumps

Cube, Hans Ludwig von. Heat pump technology / Hans Ludwig von Cube and Fritz Steimle ; translated by Ilse M. Heinrich. — English ed. / edited by E.G.A. Goodall. — London : Butterworths, 1981. — xi,379p : ill ; 24cm
Translation of: Wärmepumpen-grundlagen und praxis. — Bibliography: p373. — Includes index
ISBN 0-408-00497-5 : Unpriced B82-02201

McMullan, J. T.. Heat pumps / J.T. McMullan and R. Morgan ; consultant editor N.H. Lipman. — Bristol : Hilger, c1981. — viii,156p : ill ; 24cm
Bibliography: p147-152. — Includes index
ISBN 0-85274-419-6 : £15.00 : CIP rev. B81-20547

Sumner, John A.. An introduction to heat pumps / John A. Sumner. — 2nd ed. — Dorchester : Prism, 1980. — 64p : ill ; 22cm
Previous ed.: 1976
ISBN 0-907061-00-1 (pbk) : £1.95 B82-21416

621.402′5 — Heat pumps — *Technical data* — *For design*

Holland, F. A.. Thermodynamic design for heat pump systems : a comprehensive data base and design manual / by F.A. Holland, F.A. Watson and S. Devotta. — Oxford : Pergamon, 1982. — vii,347p : ill ; 31cm
Includes index
ISBN 0-08-028727-1 : £75.00 : CIP rev. B82-04740

621.402′5 — Industries. Applications of heat pumps

Papers presented at the international symposium on industrial application of heat pumps. — Cranfield : BHRA Fluid Engineering, Mar.1982. — [320]p
ISBN 0-906085-65-9 (pbk) : £35.00 : CIP entry B82-09211

621.402′5 — Small drop forging slot furnaces. Self-recuperative burners

Oglesby, R. H.. Condensed report on the evaluation of self-recuperative burners for use in small drop forging slot furnaces : main report prepared for the Department of Energy / by R.H. Oglesby. — [Harwell] ([Building 156, AERE Harwell, Oxon. OX11 0RA]) : [Energy Technology Support Unit], 1981. — 11p,[4]leaves of plates : ill ; 30cm
Energy Conservation Demonstration Projects Scheme
Unpriced (spiral) B82-38368

621.43 — INTERNAL COMBUSTION ENGINES

621.43 — Internal combustion engines

Nunney, M. J.. Engine technology 2. — London : Butterworth, Dec.1982. — [160]p
ISBN 0-408-00516-5 (pbk) : £3.95 : CIP entry B82-29785

621.43 — Internal combustion engines. Alternative fuels

Goodger, Eric M.. Alternative fuels for transport. — Cranfield (Cranfield Institute of Technology, Cranfield, Beds., MK43 OAL) : Cranfield Press, Apr.1982. — [36]p. — (Alternative fuel technology series ; v.1)
ISBN 0-902937-63-4 (pbk) : £7.00 : CIP entry B82-17888

621.43 — Internal combustion engines. Gases. Flow

Benson, Rowland S.. The thermodynamics and gas dynamics of internal combustion engines. — Oxford : Clarendon Press
Vol.1. — Jan.1982. — [500]p
ISBN 0-19-856210-1 : £40.00 : CIP entry B81-34382

621.43 — Internal combustion engines. Noise. Control measures

Noise control in internal combustion engines / edited by Donald E. Baxa. — New York ; London : Wiley, c1982. — xi,511p : ill ; 24cm
Includes bibliographies and index
ISBN 0-471-05870-x : £42.50 B82-32725

621.43 — Internal combustion engines. Turbocharging

Allard, Alan. Turbocharging and supercharging. — Cambridge : Stephens, Mar.1982. — [192]p
ISBN 0-85059-494-4 : £10.95 : CIP entry B82-01422

621.43 — Internal combustion engines. Turbocharging — *Conference proceedings*

Turbocharging and Turbochargers *(Conference : 1982 : London)*. Turbocharging and turbochargers 1982 / sponsored by the Power Industries Division and the Automobile Division of the Institution of Mechanical Engineers under the patronage of Fédération Internationale des Sociétés d'Ingénieurs des Techniques de l'Automobile (FISISTA). — London : Published by Mechanical Engineering Publications Limited for the Institution of Mechanical Engineers, 1982. — 237p : ill ; 30cm. — (I Mech E conference publications ; 1982-3)
ISBN 0-85298-491-x (pbk) : Unpriced B82-29480

621.43′3′028 — Gas turbines. Materials

The **Development** of gas turbine materials / edited by G.W.Meetham. — London : Applied Science, c1981. — xi,306p : ill ; 23cm
Includes index
ISBN 0-85334-952-5 : £20.00 : CIP rev. B81-10501

621.43′6 — Diesel engines

Seale, J. N.. Diesel engines / J.N. Seale. — 2nd ed. / revised by John Hartley. — Sevenoaks : Newnes Technical, 1980. — 113p : ill ; 17cm. — (Questions and answers)
Previous ed.: published as Questions and answers on diesel engines. London : Newnes, 1964. — Includes index
ISBN 0-408-00474-6 (pbk) : £1.75 : CIP rev. B80-12921

621.43′68 — Diesel engines. Maintenance & repair — *Manuals*

Dagel, John F.. Diesel engine repair / John F. Dagel. — New York ; Chichester : Wiley, c1982. — xv,586p : ill ; 28cm
Includes index
ISBN 0-471-03542-4 : £14.70 B82-13626

621.44 — GEOTHERMAL ENGINEERING

621.44 — Energy sources: Geothermal energy — *Conference proceedings*

International Conference on Geothermal Energy *(1982 : Florence)*. Papers presented at the International Conference on Geothermal Energy : Florence, Italy May 1982 / organised and sponsored by BHRA Fluid Engineering England in conjunction with Ente nazionale per l'energia elettrica (ENEL) Italy. — Bedford : BHRA Fluid Engineering, c1982. — 2v : maps,plans ; 30cm
ISBN 0-906085-68-3 (pbk) : Unpriced
ISBN 0-906085-69-1 (v.1)
ISBN 0-906085-70-5 (v.2) B82-37599

621.44 — Great Britain. Energy sources: Geothermal energy

Investigation of the geothermal potential of the UK. — London : Institute of Geological Sciences, 1982
The production test and resource assessment of the Marchwood geothermal borehole / by M. Price and D.J. Allen with contributions by J.A. Barker, W.G. Burgess and W.M. Edmunds. — 34p,[12]p of plates : ill ; 30cm
Unpriced (spiral) B82-36814

621.45 — WIND POWER

621.4′5 — Wind engineering

Melaragno, Michele. Wind in architectural and environmental design / Michele Melaragno. — New York ; London : Van Nostrand Reinhold, c1982. — xvii,684p : ill,maps,plans ; 27cm
Bibliography: p589-677. — Includes index
ISBN 0-442-25130-0 : £31.05 B82-13193

621.4′5 — Wind power

Wind energy for the eighties : a review by members of the British Wind Energy Association / British Wind Energy Association ; [editors N.H. Lipman, P.J. Musgrove, G.W-W.Pontin]. — Stevenage : Peregrinus, c1982. — xv,372p : ill,maps ; 24cm
Includes bibliographies and index
ISBN 0-906048-73-7 : Unpriced : CIP rev. B82-07132

621.4′5 — Wind power equipment

Warne, D. F.. Wind power equipment. — London : Spon, Nov.1982. — [300]p
ISBN 0-419-11410-6 : £25.00 : CIP entry B82-28251

621.4′5 — Wind power — *For children*

Payne, Sherry Neuwirth. Wind and water energy. — Oxford : Blackwell Raintree, Nov.1982. — [42]p. — (A Look inside)
ISBN 0-86256-067-5 : £3.25 : CIP entry
Primary classification 621.2′0422 B82-26073

621.4′5 — Wind power systems — *Conference proceedings*

BWEA Wind Energy Conference *(3rd : 1981 : Cranfield)*. Proceedings of the Third BWEA Wind Energy Conference : held at Cranfield April 1981 / organised by British Wind Energy Association. — Bedford : BHRA Fluid Engineering, c1981. — iv,219p : ill,maps ; 30cm
Includes bibliographies
ISBN 0-906085-56-x (pbk) : Unpriced : CIP rev. B81-22587

BWEA Wind Energy Workshop *(1st : 1979)*. Proceedings of the First BWEA Wind Energy Workshop April 1979 / [organized by BWEA in co-operation the IEE and RAeS]. — London : Multi-Science, c1979. — 233p : ill ; 30cm
Unpriced (pbk) B82-07854

International Colloquium on Wind Energy *(1981 : Brighton)*. Proceedings of the International Colloquium on Wind Energy : held at Brighton, UK, August 1981 / edited by L.F. Jesch ; organised by the British Wind Energy Association in conjunction with the International Solar Energy Society's solar world forum congress and exhibition. — Cranfield : BHRA Fluid Engineering, c1981. — 263p : ill,charts,maps ; 30cm
ISBN 0-906085-59-4 (pbk) : Unpriced B82-15128

621.4′5′072073 — United States. Wind power. Research, *1934-1980*

Putnam, Palmer Cosslett. Putnam's Power from the wind. — 2nd ed. / Gerald W. Koeppl. — New York ; London : Van Nostrand Reinhold, c1982. — xviii,470p : ill,maps ; 24cm
Previous ed.: published as Power from the wind. 1974. — Bibliography: p445-456. — Includes index
ISBN 0-442-23299-3 : £23.40 B82-14309

621.46 — ELECTRIC MOTORS, ION MOTORS, PLASMA MOTORS

621.46′2 — Direct current electric motors. Control devices: Phase-locked loops

Geiger, Dana F.. Phaselock loops for DC motor speed control / Dana F. Geiger. — New York ; Chichester : Wiley, c1981. — ix,206p : ill ; 24cm
Bibliography: p201. — Includes index
ISBN 0-471-08548-0 : £18.45 B82-04545

621.46'2 — Electric motors — *Conference proceedings*
International Conference on Small and Special Electrical Machines *(2nd : 1981 : Institution of Electrical Engineers, London)*. Second International Conference on Small and Special Electrical Machines : 22-24 September 1981 / organised by the Power Division of the Institution of Electrical Engineers in association with the Institute of Electrical and Electronics Engineers Inc (Industry Applications Society) ... [et al.]. — London : Institution of Electrical Engineers, c1981. — vii,181p : ill ; 30cm. — (IEE conference publication ; no.202)
ISBN 0-85296-245-2 (pbk) : Unpriced
B82-03986

621.46'2 — Stepping motors
Acarnley, P. P.. Stepping motors. — Stevenage : Peregrinus, Apr.1982. — [160]p. — (IEE control engineering series ; no.20)
ISBN 0-906048-75-3 : £20.00 : CIP entry
B82-11975

Acarnley, P. P.. Stepping motors : a guide to modern theory and practice / P.P. Acarnley. — Stevenage : Peregrinus on behalf of the Institution of Electrical Engineers, c1982. — viii,150p : ill ; 24cm. — (IEE control engineering series ; v.19)
Bibliography: p46-148. — Includes index
ISBN 0-906048-83-4 : Unpriced B82-30906

621.46'2'076 — Electric motors — *Questions & answers*
Hindmarsh, John. Worked examples in electrical machines and drives / John Hindmarsh. — Oxford : Pergamon, 1982. — xvi,283p : ill ; 22cm. — (Applied electricity and electronics) (Pergamon international library)
Bibliography: p283
ISBN 0-08-026131-0 (cased) : Unpriced : CIP rev.
ISBN 0-08-026130-2 (pbk) : £6.50 B81-16396

621.47 — SOLAR ENERGY ENGINEERING

621.47 — Solar energy
Garg, H. P.. Treatise on solar energy. — Chichester : Wiley
Vol.1: Fundamentals of solar energy. — Dec.1982. — [580]p
ISBN 0-471-10180-x : £23.30 : CIP entry
B82-30815

Jesch, Leslie F. Solar energy today / Leslie F. Jesch ; prepared for the UK Section of the International Solar Energy Society. — London : UK-ISES, c1981. — 223p : ill,plans ; 21cm
Includes bibliographies and index
ISBN 0-904963-27-6 (pbk) : £10.00
B82-01688

Wieder, Sol. An introduction to solar energy for scientists and engineers / Sol Wieder. — New York ; Chichester : Wiley, c1982. — xii,301p : ill ; 24cm
Includes bibliographies and index
ISBN 0-471-06048-8 : £19.45 B82-28706

621.47 — Solar energy. Applications
McVeigh, J. C.. Sun power. — 2nd ed. — Oxford : Pergamon, Jan.1983. — [240]p. — (Pergamon international library)
Previous ed.: 1977
ISBN 0-08-026148-5 (cased) : £20.00 : CIP entry
ISBN 0-08-026147-7 (pbk) : £6.75 B82-33605

621.47 — Solar energy — *Conference proceedings*
International Solar Energy Society. *Conference (1981 : Brighton)*. Solar world forum. — Oxford : Pergamon, Mar.1982. — 4v.
ISBN 0-08-026730-0 : £225.00 : CIP entry
B82-05371

621.47 — Solar energy — *For children*
Kaplan, Sheila. Solar energy. — Oxford : Blackwell Raintree, Nov.1982. — [42]p. — (A Look inside)
ISBN 0-86256-068-3 : £3.25 : CIP entry
B82-26076

Spetgang, Tilly. The children's solar energy book : even grown-ups can understand / by Tilly Spetgang and Malcolm Wells. — New York : Sterling ; Poole : Distributed by Blandford Press, c1982. — 156p : ill ; 28cm
Includes index
ISBN 0-8069-3118-3 (cased) : Unpriced
ISBN 0-8069-3119-1 (Library) : Unpriced
ISBN 0-8069-7584-9 (pbk) : £3.95 B82-39690

621.47 — Solar energy — *For engineering*
Howell, John R.. Solar-thermal energy systems : analysis and design / John R. Howell, Richard B. Bannerot, Gary C. Vliet. — New York ; London : McGraw-Hill, c1982. — x,406p : ill,maps ; 25cm
Includes index
ISBN 0-07-030603-6 : £22.50 B82-36846

621.48 — NUCLEAR ENGINEERING

621.48 — Nuclear power
Atom club / Peace Force Scotland. — Kirkcaldy (The Lantern House, Olympia Arcade, Kirkcaldy, KY1 1QF) : Peace Force Scotland, [1982]. — [4]p : ill ; 21cm. — (Fact sheet ; 12)
Bibliography: p4
Unpriced (unbound) B82-27599

Atom link / Peace Force Scotland. — Kirkcaldy (The Lantern House, Olympia Arcade, Kirkcaldy, KY1 1QF) : Peace Force Scotland, [1982]. — [4]p : ill ; 21cm. — (Fact sheet ; 11)
Bibliography: p4
Unpriced (unbound) B82-27598

Nuclear power technology. — Oxford : Clarendon Press
Vol.1: Reactor technology. — Dec.1982. — [500]p
ISBN 0-19-851948-6 : £35.00 : CIP entry
B82-29626

Nuclear power technology. — Oxford : Clarendon Press
Vol.2: Fuel cycle. — Dec.1982. — 1v.
ISBN 0-19-851958-3 : CIP entry B82-30602

Nuclear power technology. — Oxford : Clarendon Press
Vol.3: Nuclear radiation. — Dec.1982. — 1v.
ISBN 0-19-851959-1 : CIP entry B82-30603

621.48 — Nuclear power — *Conference proceedings*
Uranium Institute. *International Symposium (6th : 1981 : London)*. Uranium and nuclear energy 1981 : proceedings of the sixth International Symposium held by the Uranium Institute, London, 2-4 September, 1981. — Sevenoaks : Butterworth Scientific in cooperation with the Uranium Institute, 1982. — xvi,400p : ill,forms,maps ; 25cm
Includes bibliographies
ISBN 0-408-22151-8 : Unpriced : CIP rev.
B82-01327

Uranium Institute. *International Symposium (7th : 1982 : London)*. Uranium and nuclear energy : 1982. — Sevenoaks : Butterworths, Jan.1983. — [304]p
ISBN 0-408-22160-7 : £32.00 : CIP entry
B82-37470

621.48 — Nuclear power — *For children*
Asimov, Isaac. How we found out about nuclear power / Isaac Asimov. — Harlow : Longman, 1982. — 53p : ill ; 23cm. — (How we found out about series ; 2)
Includes index
ISBN 0-582-39150-4 : £2.75 B82-29314

Cable, Charles. Nuclear energy. — Oxford : Blackwell Raintree, Nov.1982. — [42]p. — (A Look inside)
ISBN 0-86256-066-7 : £3.25 : CIP entry
B82-26075

621.48 — Nuclear power — *For schools*
Lacey, Colin. The nuclear question : an issue to debate / [written by Colin Lacey] ; [illustrated by Pauline Jay]. — Brighton : Tressell, 1981. — 27p : ill,maps,1port ; 24cm
Cover title. — Text on inside cover. — Bibliography: p27
ISBN 0-907586-02-3 (pbk) : Unpriced
B82-14290

621.48 — Nuclear power — *Students Against Nuclear Energy viewpoints*
Anti Nuclear now — or never : a comprehensive guide to nuclear power / produced by Students Against Nuclear Energy. — London (9, Poland St., W.1.) : S.A.N.E., [1982?]. — 35p : ill,2maps,facsims,1plan,1port ; 30cm
Bibliography: p35
£0.50 (unbound) B82-22040

621.48'05 — Nuclear power — *Serials*
Progress in nuclear energy. — Vol.7. — Oxford : Pergamon, Nov.1981. — [234]p
ISBN 0-08-029090-6 : £40.00 : CIP entry
B81-32015

Progress in nuclear energy. — Vol.8. — Oxford : Pergamon, May 1982. — [330]p
ISBN 0-08-029684-x : £60.00 : CIP entry
B82-11992

621.48'06'041 — Great Britain. Nuclear power. Organisations: British Nuclear Forum — *Directories*
British Nuclear Forum. Directory of BNF : British Nuclear Forum members. — London (1 St. Alban's St., SW1Y 4SL) : BNF, 1981. — 25p : ill,1map,ports ; 30cm
Cover title
Unpriced (pbk) B82-24855

621.48'072041 — Great Britain. Nuclear power. Research organisations: Atomic Energy Research Establishment
Atomic Energy Research Establishment. Harwell : research laboratory of the United Kingdom Atomic Energy Authority. — Harwell : AERE, c1980. — 52p : ill(some col.),1col.map ; 30cm
Text and map on inside covers
ISBN 0-7058-0573-5 (pbk) : £3.00 B82-17091

621.48'091724 — Developing countries. Nuclear power
Poneman, Daniel. Nuclear power in the developing world. — London : Allen & Unwin, Nov.1982. — [272]p
ISBN 0-04-338100-6 : £14.95 : CIP entry
B82-27808

621.48'0941 — Great Britain. Nuclear power
Tombs, *Sir* **Francis**. Nuclear energy : past, present and future : Institution of Nuclear Engineers anniversary lecture, Nov. 1980 / by Sir Francis Tombs. — London (30 Millbank SW1P 4RD) : Electricity Council, Public Relations Department, [1980]. — 15p ; 30cm
Cover title
Unpriced (pbk) B82-31849

621.48'0941 — Great Britain. Nuclear power — *British Nuclear Forum viewpoints*
The **Need** for nuclear power / British Nuclear Forum. — London (1 St. Alban's St., SW1Y 4SL) : BNF, 1977. — [13]p ; 21cm
Unpriced (unbound) B82-24856

621.48'0941 — Great Britain. Nuclear power — *For schools*
Nuclear energy questions : a critical look at nuclear energy and the alternatives for today and tomorrow. — Edinburgh (2A Ainslie Place, Edinburgh 3) : Information Service on Energy, [1982?]. — 1portfolio : ill,maps ; 23cm
ISBN 0-907357-06-7 : £4.95
ISBN 0-907357-04-0 (Alternatives now)
ISBN 0-907357-05-9 (Future energy choices)
ISBN 0-907357-02-4 (Reactors and radiation)
ISBN 0-907357-01-6 (Uranium mining)
ISBN 0-907357-03-2 (Nuclear waste)
B82-26651

621.48'0954 — India *(Republic)*. **Nuclear power**
Hart, David. Nuclear power in India. — London : Allen & Unwin, Jan.1983. — [192]p
ISBN 0-04-338101-4 : £12.00 : CIP entry
B82-33598

621.48'1 — Light water reactors. Structural components — *Conference proceedings*
Structural integrity of light water reactor components. — London : Applied Science, Oct.1982. — [352]p
Conference papers
ISBN 0-85334-157-5 : £40.00 : CIP entry
B82-24260

621.48′1 — Suffolk. Sizewell. Proposed nuclear power stations. Environmental aspects — *Conference proceedings*

Seminar on the Sizewell 'B' power station proposal : held at the Wolsey Theatre, Ipswich on 10th June, 1981 : report of proceedings / Suffolk County Council. — Ipswich : The Council, 1981. — 78p in various pagings ; 30cm
ISBN 0-86055-085-0 (pbk) : Unpriced
Primary classification 363.1′79 B82-01258

621.48′3 — Nuclear reactors

Klimov, A.. Nuclear physics and nuclear reactors / A. Klimov ; translated from the Russian by O. Rudnitskaya. — Moscow : Mir ; [London] : Distributed by Central, 1975 (1981 printing). — 404p : ill ; 23cm
Translation of: IAdernaia fizika i iadernye reaktory. — Includes index
ISBN 0-7147-1715-0 : £4.95
Primary classification 539.7 B82-29285

Stamm′ler, R. J. J.. Methods of steady state reactor physics in nuclear design. — London : Academic Press, Dec.1982. — [600]p
ISBN 0-12-663320-7 : CIP entry B82-29893

621.48′3 — Nuclear reactors. Noise — *Conference proceedings*

Specialists Meeting on Reactor Noise *(3rd : 1981 : Tokyo).* Reactor noise — SMORN III. — Oxford : Pergamon, Mar.1982. — [725]p. — (Progress in nuclear energy ; v.9)
ISBN 0-08-027619-9 : £70.00 : CIP entry
B82-07991

621.48′3′0720177 — Organisation for Economic Co-operation and Development countries. Nuclear reactors. Research projects: Organisation for Economic Co-operation and Development. *Dragon Project, to 1981*

Shaw, E. N.. High temperature and cold comfort from nuclear politics. — Oxford : Pergamon, Sept.1982. — [300]p
ISBN 0-08-029324-7 : £12.50 : CIP entry
B82-19097

621.48′32 — Nuclear reactors. Prestressed concrete pressure vessels & prestressed concrete containments. Inspection

An **International** survey of in-service inspection experience with prestressed concrete pressure vessels and containments for nuclear reactors / [FIP Commission on Concrete Pressure and Storage Vessels]. — Slough : Fédération Internationale de la Précontrainte, 1982. — 47p : ill ; 30cm. — (Technical report / Fédération Internationale de la Précontrainte)
Cover title. — Bibliography: p38-42
ISBN 0-907862-06-3 (pbk) : Unpriced
B82-37105

621.48′323 — Nuclear reactors. Ionising radiation. Shields. Design. Applications of digital computer systems

Wood, James, *1929-.* Computational methods in reactor shielding / by James Wood. — Oxford : Pergamon, 1982. — vii,441p : ill,1plan ; 24cm. — (Pergamon international library)
Includes bibliographies and index
ISBN 0-08-028685-2 (cased) : Unpriced : CIP rev.
ISBN 0-08-028686-0 (pbk) : £9.50 B81-33856

621.48′33 — Nuclear reactors. Structural components. Mechanical properties — *Conference proceedings*

International Conference on Structural Mechanics in Reactor Technology *(6th : 1981 : Paris).* Transactions of the 6th International Conference on Structural Mechanics in Reactor Technology : Palais des Congrès, Paris, France, 17-21 August 1981 / conference organization by International Association for Structural Mechanics in Reactor Technology, Commission of the European Communities, Brussels, SFEN — Société française d'énergie nucléaire, Paris. — Amsterdam ; Oxford : North-Holland for The Commission of the European Communities, c1981. — 13v. : ill,ports ; 24cm
English text with French and German introductions. — Includes index
ISBN 0-444-86268-4 (pbk) : Unpriced
B82-04422

621.48′335 — Fast reactors. Fuel cycles — *Conference proceedings*

Fast reactor fuel cycles : proceedings of an international conference organized by the British Nuclear Energy Society and co-sponsored by the Royal Society of Chemistry and the Institution of Metallurgists : London, 9-12 November 1981. — London : British Nuclear Energy Society, 1982. — 406p : ill ; 30cm
ISBN 0-7277-0157-6 (pbk) : £40.00
B82-38002

621.48′335 — Fast reactors. Use of plutonium

Marshall, W.. The use of plutonium : the fifth Chancellor′s lecture / W. Marshall. — [Salford] ([Salford, Lancs. M5 4WT]) : University of Salford, [1980?]. — [44]p : ill ; 21cm
Unpriced (pbk) B82-19964

621.48′335 — Nuclear reactors. Fuel elements

Frost, Brian R. T.. Nuclear fuel elements : design, fabrication and performance / by Brian R.T. Frost. — Oxford : Pergamon, 1982. — viii,275 : ill ; 23cm. — (Pergamon international library of science, technology, engineering and social sciences) ([International series in nuclear energy])
Bibliography: p269. — Includes index
ISBN 0-08-020412-0 (cased) : Unpriced : CIP rev.
ISBN 0-08-020411-2 (pbk) : £8.75 B82-12406

621.48′335 — Nuclear reactors. Fuels. Management

Silvennoinen, P.. Nuclear fuel cycle optimization. — Oxford : Pergamon, Nov.1982. — [138]p
ISBN 0-08-027310-6 : £12.50 : CIP entry
B82-26697

621.48′34 — Great Britain. Pressurised water reactors — *Conference proceedings*

Pressurised water reactor in the United Kingdom / sponsored by the Power Industries Division of the Institution of Mechanical Engineers 11 May 1982, Institution Headquarters, 1 Birdcage Walk, Westminster London. — London : Published by Mechanical Engineering Publications Limited for the Institution of Mechanical Engineers, 1982. — 74p : ill ; 30cm. — (I Mech E conference publications ; 1982-5)
ISBN 0-85298-492-8 (pbk) : Unpriced
B82-29481

621.48′34 — Scotland. Highland Region. Dounreay. Fast reactors. Siting — *Proposals*

The **Case** for Dounreay. — [Inverness] : [Highland Regional Council], 1979. — 1folded sheet([6]p) : 2maps ; 30cm
Unpriced B82-07349

621.48′34 — West Germany. Nuclear power stations. Fast breeder reactors. Policies of government, *1955-1980*

Keck, Otto. Policymaking in a nuclear program : the case of the West German fast breeder reactor / Otto Keck. — Lexington, Mass. : Lexington Books ; [Aldershot] : Gower [distributor], 1981. — xxvii,274p : ill ; 24cm
Includes index
ISBN 0-669-03519-x : £16.50 B82-00844

621.48′35 — Cumbria. Sellafield. Nuclear reactors: British Nuclear Fuels Limited *Windscale and Calder Works.* **Safety measures**

Great Britain. *Health and Safety Executive.* Windscale : management of safety. — London : Health & Safety Executive, Apr.1981. — [40]p
ISBN 0-7176-0076-9 (pbk) : CIP entry
B81-10515

621.48′35 — Great Britain. Advanced gas-cooled nuclear reactors. Safety aspects

The **Safety** of the AGR / edited by G.C. Dale ; written and compiled by J.M. Bowerman. — London : Central Electricity Generating Board ; Glasgow : South of Scotland Electricity Board, 1982. — 111p : ill(some col.) ; 28x30cm + 1sheet(col.ill ; 54x89cm folded to 27x18cm)
Diagram of Heysham 2 / Torness (1 folded sheet) as insert. — Bibliography: p103. — Includes index
ISBN 0-902543-64-4 (pbk) : £10.00
B82-17336

621.48′35 — Great Britain. Pressurised water reactors. Safety measures

Nuclear safety : a report by the Health and Safety Executive to the Secretary of State for Energy on a review of the generic safety issues of pressurised water reactors / Health and Safety Executive. — London : H.M.S.O., 1979 (1982 [printing]). — v,52p : ill ; 30cm
ISBN 0-11-883653-6 (pbk) : £4.50 B82-38342

621.48′35 — Liquid metal fast breeder reactors. Decay heat. Removal by natural convection systems — *Conference proceedings*

Decay heat removal and natural convection in fast breeder reactors / edited by Ashok K. Agrawal and James G. Guppy. — Washington [D.C.] ; London : Hemisphere Publishing ; Auckland ; London : Distributed by McGraw-Hill, c1981. — xvi,423p : ill ; 25cm
Conference papers. — Includes index
ISBN 0-89116-196-1 : £45.95 B82-16331

621.48′35 — Nuclear reactors. Heat transfer. Safety aspects

Heat transfer in nuclear reactor safety / edited by S. George Bankoff and N.H. Afgan. — Washington ; London : Hemisphere ; Auckland ; London : Distributed by McGraw-Hill, c1982. — xii,964p : ill ; 25cm. — (Proceedings of the International Centre for Heat and Mass Transfer, ISSN 0272-880x ; 13)
Conference papers. — Includes index
ISBN 0-07-003601-2 : £66.50 B82-28058

Nuclear reactor safety heat transfer / edited by Owen C. Jones, Jr. — Washington ; London : Hemisphere, 1981. — xix,959p : ill ; 25cm. — (Proceedings of the International Centre for Heat and Mass Transfer, ISSN 0272-880x ; 12)
Includes index
ISBN 0-89116-224-0 : £123.50 B82-23041

621.48′35 — Nuclear reactors. Steel pressure vessels. Fracture toughness. Non-destructive testing — *Conference proceedings*

Advances in non-destructive examination for structural integrity. — London : Applied Science, Oct.1982. — [420]p
Conference papers
ISBN 0-85334-158-3 : £48.00 : CIP entry
B82-24105

621.48′37 — Radioactive materials. Handling — *Serials*

Active systems. — Bull. no.1 (May 1978)-. — Harwell (Engineering Publications, Building 401.4, AERE, Harwell, Oxon. OX11 ORA) : Active Systems Centre, 1978-. — v. : ill,ports ; 30cm
Irregular. — Description based on: Bull. no.7 (Apr. 1981)
ISSN 0260-1346 = Active systems : Unpriced
B82-28121

621.48′38 — Cumbria. Sellafield. Nuclear reactors: British Nuclear Fuels Limited. *Windscale and Calder Works.* **Thermal oxide reprocessing plants. Economic aspects**

Jones, Peter, *1956-.* The economics of nuclear fuel reprocessing : a case study of the Windscale Thorp plant / by Peter Jones, David Pearce. — Aberdeen : University of Aberdeen, Department of Political Economy, [1980]. — 53,lxp : ill ; 30cm. — (Discussion paper, ISSN 0143-4543 ; 80-09)
Bibliography: p51-53
Unpriced (pbk) B82-40680

621.48′38 — Fast reactors. Spent fuels. Reprocessing — *Conference proceedings*

Fast reactor fuel reprocessing : proceedings of a symposium sponsored by the Society of Chemical Industry and held at UKAEA Dounreay Nuclear Power Development Establishment, 15-18 May 1979. — London : SCI, 1980. — 217p : ill ; 30cm
Includes index
ISBN 0-901001-62-7 (pbk) : Unpriced
B82-31246

621.48′38 — Nuclear waste materials. Disposal

Lindblom, Ulf. Nuclear waste disposal. — Oxford : Pergamon, June 1981. — [80]p
ISBN 0-08-027608-3 (cased) : £7.50 : CIP entry
ISBN 0-08-027595-8 (pbk) : £3.95 B81-16853

621.48′38 — Radioactive waste materials. Disposal

Dlouhý, Zdeněk. Disposal of radioactive wastes / Zdeněk Dlouhý ; contributors František Cejnar ... [et al.]. — Amsterdam ; Oxford : Elsevier Scientific, 1982. — 264p : ill ; 24cm
Translated from the Czech. — Includes index
ISBN 0-444-99724-5 : £29.22 : CIP rev. B81-31615

Nuclear waste disposal / British Nuclear Forum. — London (1 St. Alban's St., SW1Y 4SL) : BNF, [1978?]. — [10]p : 4ill ; 21cm
Unpriced (unbound) B82-24861

Saunders, P. A. H.. The management of radioactive wastes / P.A.H. Saunders. — London (11 Charles II St., SW1Y 4QP) : Information Services Branch, United Kingdom Atomic Energy Authority, 1982. — 32p : col.ill ; 20x21cm
Unpriced (pbk) B82-35629

621.48′38 — Radioactive waste materials. Disposal — *Conference proceedings*

Radioactive waste management in perspective : September 26th, 1980 London : conference transcript / edited by N.G. Coles and Suzanne Mayhew. — [London] : Scientific & Technical Studies, [1982?]. — 170p : ill,maps ; 30cm
Includes bibliographies
ISBN 0-9505774-3-x (pbk) : Unpriced B82-40455

621.48′38 — Radioactive waste materials. Disposal — *Serials*

Radioactive waste management : an international journal. — Vol.1, no.1 (1980)-v.2, no.4 (June 1982). — Chur ; London : Harwood Academic, 1980-1982. — 2v. : ill ; 23cm
Quarterly. — Continued by: Radioactive waste management and the nuclear fuel cycle. — Description based on: Vol.2, no.3 (1982)
ISSN 0142-2405 = Radioactive waste management : Unpriced B82-36691

621.48′38 — Radioactive waste materials. Disposal within rock. Geological aspects — *Conference proceedings*

Predictive geology : with emphasis on nuclear-waste disposal : proceedings of papers presented at sessions sponsored by the International Association for Mathematical Geology at the 26th International Geological Congress in Paris, July 1980 / edited by Ghislain de Marsily and Daniel F. Merriam. — Oxford : Pergamon, 1982. — xv,,206p : ill,maps ; 24cm. — (Computers and geology ; v.4)
Includes bibliographies and index
ISBN 0-08-026246-5 : £17.50 : CIP rev. B81-32042

621.48′4 — Fusion reactions. Plasmas — *Conference proceedings*

Physics of plasmas close to thermonuclear conditions : proceedings of the Course held in Varenna, Italy 27 August-8 September 1979 / edited by B. Coppi ... [et al.]. — Oxford : Published for the Commission of the European Communities by Pergamon, 1981. — 2v.(xii,871p) : ill,ports ; 25cm
At head of title: International School of Plasma Physics. — Includes bibliographies and index
ISBN 0-08-024475-0 (pbk) : £31.00 : CIP rev. B81-17528

621.48′4 — Fusion reactors

Fusion. — New York ; London : Academic Press
Vol.1: Magnetic confinement
Part B / edited by Edward Teller. — 1981. — xi,529p : ill ; 24cm
Includes index
ISBN 0-12-685241-3 : £39.00 B82-21282

621.48′4 — Toroidal magnetic confinement devices. Plasmas. Heating — *Conference proceedings*

Joint Grenoble-Varenna International Symposium *(2nd : 1980 : Como)*. Heating in toroidal plasmas II : proceedings of the 2nd Joint Grenoble-Varenna International Symposium, Como, Italy, 3-12 September 1980 / edited by E. Canobbio ... [et al.]. — Oxford : Published for the Commission of the European Communities by Pergamon, 1982, c1981. — 2v.(xii,1210p,[1]leaf of plates) : ill,1map ; 30cm
English text, introduction in English and Italian. — At head of title: International School of Plasma Physics, Varenna, Italy and Association Euratom-Commissariat à l'énergie atomique (CEA), France. — Includes index
ISBN 0-08-029347-6 : £75.00 : CIP rev. B82-12129

Joint Varenna-Grenoble International Symposium *(3rd : 1982 : Grenoble)*. Heating in toroidal plasmas III. — Oxford : Pergamon, Nov.1982. — [3v.(1200p)]
ISBN 0-08-029984-9 : £75.00 : CIP entry B82-35196

621.48′4′07204 — Europe. Nuclear fusion technology. Research organisations: Joint European Torus, *1965-1980*

Willson, Denis. A European experiment : the launching of the JET project / Denis Willson ; foreword by Sir Monty Finniston. — Bristol : Hilger, c1981. — xiv,181p : ill,2maps,facsims,ports ; 23cm
Includes index
ISBN 0-85274-543-5 (cased) : £10.50 : CIP rev.
ISBN 0-85274-549-4 (pbk) : £6.95 B81-27377

621.5 — PNEUMATIC, VACUUM, LOW TEMPERATURE TECHNOLOGY

621.5 — Icehouses, *to 1981*

Ellis, Monica. Ice and icehouses through the ages : with a gazetteer for Hampshire / Monica Ellis. — [Southampton] : Southampton University Industrial Archaeology Group, [1982]. — v,86p : ill,facsims,2maps,plans ; 30cm
Bibliography: p84-85
ISBN 0-905280-04-0 (pbk) : Unpriced B82-38594

621.5′1 — Compressed air equipment. Energy. Conservation — *Manuals*

Compressed air and energy use. — London (Thames House South, Millbank SW1P 4QJ) : Department of Energy, [1980]. — 10p : ill ; 21cm. — (Fuel efficiency booklet ; 4)
Cover title
Unpriced (pbk) B82-31838

621.5′5 — Vacuum technology

Roth, A.. Vacuum technology / A. Roth. — 2nd rev. ed. — Amsterdam ; Oxford : North-Holland, 1982. — xiv,531p : ill ; 23cm
Previous ed.: 1976. — Bibliography: p464-517. — Includes index
ISBN 0-444-86027-4 : Unpriced B82-33797

621.5′6 — Refrigeration

Gosney, W. B.. Principles of refrigeration / W.B. Gosney. — Cambridge : Cambridge University Press, 1982. — xiii,666p : ill ; 24cm
Bibliography: p635-643. — Includes index
ISBN 0-521-23671-1 : £47.50 : CIP rev. B82-00229

621.5′7 — Developing countries. Solar energy refrigeration equipment — *Conference proceedings*

Solar energy for developing countries : refrigeration & water pumping : conference proceedings / conference organised by the UK section of the International Solar Energy Society (UK-ISES) at the Geological Society, Burlington House, Piccadilly, London, W1, UK on Wednesday, January 27, 1982 ; edited by Bernard McNelis. — London : UK-ISES, 1982. — 109p : ill ; 21cm. — (Conference / International Solar Energy Society. UK Section, ISSN 0306-7874 ; C28)
ISBN 0-904963-29-2 (pbk) : Unpriced
Also classified at 621.2′52 B82-17796

621.5′7 — Refrigeration equipment — *Manuals*

Reed, G. H. (George Henry), *1915-*. Refrigeration : a practical manual for mechanics / by G.H. Reed. — 2nd ed. — London : Applied Science, 1981. — xi,232p : ill ; 23cm
Previous ed.: 1972. — Includes index
ISBN 0-85334-964-9 : £11.00 : CIP rev. B81-13735

621.5′9 — Cryogenic liquids. Prestressed concrete storage tanks

Cryogenic behaviour of materials for prestressed concrete / [FIP Commission on Prestressing Steels and Systems]. — Slough : Fédération Internationale de la Précontrainte, 1982. — 84p : ill ; 30cm. — (State of art report / Fédération Internationale de la Précontrainte)
Cover title
ISBN 0-907862-04-7 (pbk) : Unpriced B82-37103

621.6 — ENGINEERING. FANS, BLOWERS, PUMPS

621.6 — Pumps — *Conference proceedings*

British Pump Manufacturers' Association. *Technical Conference (7th : 1981 : University of York)*. Pumps — the developing needs : papers presented at the seventh Technical Conference of the British Pump Manufacturers' Association : conference held at University of York, 31st March-2nd April 1981. — Cranfield : BHRA Fluid Engineering, 1981. — vi,314p : ill,1map ; 30cm
ISBN 0-906085-52-7 (corrected : pbk) : Unpriced : CIP rev. B81-04336

621.6 — Pumps. Design

Pump design course : four-day course 19-22 October 1981. — Glasgow : Conference Section, National Engineering Laboratory, [1981]. — [262]p,[93]p of plates : ill ; 30cm
Cover title
Unpriced (spiral) B82-25302

621.6′03 — Pumps — *Polyglot dictionaries*

Europump terminology : Pumpenanwendung : pump applications : utilization des pompes : impiego delle pompe : utilización de la bombas / [editor, Europump]. — [2nd ed.]. — Morden : Trade & Technical, 1978. — xix,427,A46p : ill,1port ; 31cm
Previous ed.: 1968. — Includes index
ISBN 0-85461-071-5 : £48.00 B82-40930

621.6′05 — Pumps — *Serials*

World pumps : an international technical review of pumps and their applications : une revue technique internationale des pompes et de leurs applications : internationale technische Zeitschrift für Pumpen und ihre Anwendungen / Europump. — No.1 (1982)-. — Morden : Trade & Technical Press, 1982-. — v. : ill ; 30cm
Monthly. — Text in English, summaries in French and German. — Continues: Pumps & their applications
ISSN 0262-1762 = World pumps : £30.00 per year B82-18729

621.6′1 — Ventilation equipment: Fans — *Conference proceedings*

International Conference on Fan Design and Applications *(1982 : Guildford)*. Papers presented at the International Conference on Fan Design & Applications. — Cranfield : BHRA Fluid Engineering, Sept.1982. — [450]p
ISBN 0-906085-72-1 (pbk) : £33.00 : CIP entry B82-25751

621.6′5 — Great Britain. Beam engines, *1712-1975*

Crowley, T. E.. Beam engines / T.E. Crowley. — 3rd ed. — Princes Risborough : Shire, 1982. — 32p : ill ; 21cm. — (Shire album ; 15)
Previous ed.: 1978. — Bibliography: p32
ISBN 0-85263-595-8 (pbk) : £0.95 B82-31138

621.8 — MACHINERY, FASTENINGS, ETC

621.8 — Large machinery — *For children*

Berry, Roland. Mechanical giants / Roland Berry. — London : Hamilton, 1982. — [30]p : col.ill ; 20x25cm
ISBN 0-241-10765-2 : £3.95 : CIP rev. B82-04311

621.8 — Mechanical power transmission equipment

Kolstee, Hans M.. Motion and power / Hans M. Kolstee. — Englewood Cliffs ; London : Prentice-Hall, c1982. — xii,240p : ill,plans ; 24cm
Includes index
ISBN 0-13-602953-1 : £14.95 B82-16991

621.8 — Mechanisms — *For schools*

Mechanisms / Omry Bailey ... [et al.]. — Edinburgh : Oliver & Boyd in association with the National Centre for School Technology, 1981. — 174p : ill ; 24cm + Teacher's book (56p : ill : 24cm). — (Schools Council modular courses in technology)
ISBN 0-05-003386-7 (pbk) : £3.50
ISBN 0-02-003387-5 (Teacher's book) : £2.50 B82-05834

Mechanisms. — Edinburgh : Oliver & Boyd in association with the National Centre for School Technology
Workbook. — 1981. — 51p : ill ; 27cm
ISBN 0-05-003388-3 (unbound) : £3.75 for set of 5 copies B82-03300

621.8′022′1 — Machinery. Technical drawings. Draftsmanship

Yankee, Herbert W.. Machine drafting and related technology / Herbert W. Yankee. — 2nd ed. — New York ; London : Gregg Division, McGraw-Hill, c1981. — viii,584p : ill ; 25cm
Previous ed.: 1966. — Bibliography: p575-577. — Includes index
ISBN 0-07-072252-8 : £11.75 B82-05114

621.8′022′2 — Machinery — *Illustrations — For children*

Counting monster machines. — London : Blackie, 1980. — [24]p : col.ill ; 20cm. — (Patchwork picture books)
ISBN 0-216-90850-7 (cased) : £1.95 : CIP rev.
ISBN 0-216-90849-3 (pbk) : Unpriced
Also classified at 513′.2′0222 B80-00224

621.8′11 — Machinery. Mechanics

Hannah, J.. Mechanics of machines : elementary theory and examples. — 4th ed. — London : Edward Arnold, Dec.1982. — [272]p
Previous ed.: 1970
ISBN 0-7131-3471-2 (pbk) : £6.50 : CIP entry B82-30204

Paul, Burton. Kinematics and dynamics of planar machinery / Burton Paul. — Englewood Cliffs ; London : Prentice-Hall, c1979. — xvii,670p : ill ; 25cm
Bibliography: p640-653. — Includes index
ISBN 0-13-516062-6 : £26.20 B82-07154

621.8′11 — Mechanisms. Kinematics

Martin, George H.. Kinematics and dynamics of machines / George H. Martin. — 2nd ed. — New York ; London : McGraw-Hill, c1982. — xiii,492p : ill ; 25cm. — (McGraw-Hill series in mechanical engineering)
Previous ed.: 1969. — Text on lining papers. — Includes index
ISBN 0-07-040657-x : £24.25 B82-21127

621.8′11 — Rotating machinery. Vibration — *Conference proceedings*

Vibrations in rotating machinery (1980) : second international conference / conference sponsored by the Institution of Mechanical Engineers ... [et al.], Churchill College, Cambridge 1-4 September 1980. — London : Mechanical Engineering Publications for the Institution of Mechanical Engineers, 1980. — 461p : ill ; 30cm. — (I Mech E conference publications ; 1980-4)
ISBN 0-85298-453-7 (pbk) : £40.00 B82-40692

621.8′11 — Turbomachinery. Heat transfer & fluid flow

Morris, W. David. Heat transfer and fluid flow in rotating coolant channels / W. David Morris. — Chichester : Research Studies, c1981. — xv,228p : ill ; 24cm. — (Mechanical engineering research studies ; 2)
Bibliography: p223-226. — Includes index
ISBN 0-471-10121-4 : £13.00 : CIP rev. B81-34476

621.8′15 — Machinery. Design

Molian, S.. Mechanism design : an introductory text / S. Molian. — Cambridge : Cambridge University Press, 1982. — ix,158p : ill ; 24cm
Bibliography: p155. — Includes index
ISBN 0-521-23193-0 (cased) : £15.00 : CIP rev.
ISBN 0-521-29863-6 (pbk) : £5.95 B82-12001

621.8′16 — Machinery. Monitoring — *Conference proceedings*

National Conference on Condition Monitoring *(3rd : 1981 : Royal Garden Hotel, Kensington)*. 3rd National Conference on Condition Monitoring : 18th & 19th February 1981, Royal Garden Hotel, Kensington : conference papers / organised by Conference Communication. — [Farnham] (Monks Hill, Tilford, Farnham, Surrey GU10 2AJ]) : [Conference Communication], [1981?]. — 166p in various pagings : ill ; 30cm
Unpriced (spiral) B82-22543

621.8′22 — Ball bearings. Lubrication

Hamrock, Bernard J.. Ball bearing lubrication : the elastohydrodynamics of elliptical contacts / Bernard J. Hamrock, Duncan Dowson. — New York ; Chichester : Wiley, c1981. — xxv,386p : ill ; 24cm
Bibliography: p362-371. — Includes index
ISBN 0-471-03553-x : £36.95 B82-07724

621.8′22 — Gas bearings — *Conference proceedings*

International Gas Bearing Symposium *(8th : 1981 : Leicester Polytechnic)*. Papers presented at the 8th International Gas Bearing Symposium 1981 at Leicester Polytechnic / organised by Leicester Polytechnic in conjunction with BHRA Fluid Engineering. — Bedford : BHRA Fluid Engineering, c1981. — vi,322p : ill ; 30cm
ISBN 0-906085-54-3 (pbk) : Unpriced : CIP rev. B81-07936

621.8′22 — Plain bearings

Welsh, R. J.. Plain bearing design handbook. — London : Butterworth, Jan.1983. — [200]p
ISBN 0-408-01186-6 : £10.00 : CIP entry B82-34430

621.8′24′0212 — Engineering components: Mechanical springs — *Technical data — For design*

Brown, A. A. D.. Mechanical springs / A.A.D. Brown on behalf of the Spring Research and Manufacturers' Association. — [Oxford] : Published for the Design Council, the British Standards Institution, and the Council of Engineering Institutions by Oxford University Press, c1981. — 44p : ill ; 30cm. — (Engineering design guides ; 42)
Bibliography: p44
ISBN 0-19-859181-0 (pbk) : £5.95 : CIP rev. B81-05122

621.8′4 — Fluid transport systems. Valves. Design

Lyons, Jerry L.. Lyons' valve designer's handbook / Jerry L. Lyons. — New York ; London : Van Nostrand, 1982. — xiii,882p : ill ; 28cm
Bibliography: p843-848. — Includes index
ISBN 0-442-24963-2 : £53.15 B82-16327

621.8′4 — Valves. Selection

Zappe, R. W.. Valve selection handbook / R.W. Zappe. — Houston, Texas ; London : Gulf Publishing, c1981. — xiii,278p : ill ; 24cm
Bibliography: p268-272. — Includes index
ISBN 0-87201-892-x : £29.25 B82-29488

621.8′6 — Bulk materials. Materials handling & transport — *Conference proceedings*

Bulk Handling and Transport Conference *(2nd : 1979 : Amsterdam)*. Bulk handling and transport. — Worcester Park, Surrey (54 Cheam Common Rd., Worcester Park, Surrey KT4 8RJ) : CS Publications, c1979
Vol.2 / proceedings of the 2nd Bulk Handling and Transport Conference organised by CS Publications and held in Amsterdam, June 1979... — [241]p : ill,1map,ports ; 30cm
Unpriced (spiral) B82-22895

621.8′6 — Construction. Sites. Materials handling equipment

Illingworth, J. R.. Site handling equipment / J.R. Illingworth. — London : Telford, 1982. — 67p : ill ; 15x21cm. — (ICE works construction guides)
ISBN 0-7277-0141-x (pbk) : £2.50 B82-37808

621.8′6 — Container handling equipment — *Technical data*

The **Handling** of ISO containers in low throughput situations : an ICHCA survey / Technical Advisory Sub-Committee ; edited by M. Green. — London : International Cargo Handling Co-ordination Association, c1982. — iv,42p : ill,plans ; 30cm
ISBN 0-906297-27-3 (pbk) : £25.00 (free to members of the Association) B82-28330

621.8′6 — Materials handling equipment

Aleksandrov, M. P.. Materials handling equipment / M.P. Alexandrov ; translated from the Russian by O.K. Sapunov. — Moscow : Mir, 1981 ; [London] : Distributed by Central Books. — 549p : ill ; 23cm
Translation of: Pod″emno-transportnye mashiny. — Bibliography: p542-543. — Includes index
ISBN 0-7147-1745-2 : £6.50 B82-39311

621.8′6′0289 — Mobile mechanical handling equipment. Safety measures

Great Britain. *Health and Safety Executive*. Safety in working with power-operated mobile work platforms. — London : H.M.S.O., Apr.1982. — [20]p. — (HS(G) ; 19)
ISBN 0-11-883628-5 (pbk) : CIP entry B82-08075

621.8′6′05 — Materials handling. Logistics — *Serials*

Logistics today. — Vol.1, no.1 (Jan. 1982)-. — Bedford (Cranfield Institute of Technology, Cranfield, Bedford MK43 0AL) : National Materials Handling Centre, 1982-. — v. : ill,ports ; 30cm
ISSN 0262-4354 = Logistics today : Unpriced B82-15770

621.8′63 — Great Britain. Industries. Fork-lift trucks. Safety measures

Safety in working with lift trucks. — London : H.M.S.O., 1979. — 33p : ill ; 21cm. — (HS(G) series ; 6)
At head of title: Health and Safety Executive
ISBN 0-11-883284-0 (pbk) : £1.00 : CIP rev. B79-23311

621.8′63′07 — Great Britain. Fork-lift trucks. Driving. Training courses — *Directories*

Sources of information on training facilities for fork lift truck drivers. — Gloucester (Barton House, Barton St., Gloucester GL1 1QQ) : The Food, Drink and Tobacco Industry Training Board, [1982]. — 16leaves ; 30cm
Bibliography: leaf 16
Unpriced (pbk) B82-26490

621.8′672 — Industries. Piping systems

Kentish, D. N. W.. Industrial pipework / D.N.W. Kentish. — London : McGraw-Hill, c1982. — x,327p : ill ; 31cm
Bibliography: p314-315. — Includes index
ISBN 0-07-084557-3 : Unpriced : CIP rev B81-27345

621.8′672 — Pipelines. Design

Pipeline and energy plant piping : design and technology. — Toronto ; Oxford : Pergamon, c1980. — ix,374p : ill ; 26cm
Proceedings of a conference organised by the Welding Institute of Canada. — Includes bibliographies and index
ISBN 0-08-025368-7 : £22.50 B82-28002

621.8′672 — Pipelines. Protection — *Conference proceedings*

International Conference on the Internal & External Protection of Pipes *(4th : 1981 : Leeuwenhort Congres Centre)*. Papers presented at the Fourth International Conference on the Internal & External Protection of Pipes : held Noordwijkerhout, Netherlands, September 15-17, 1981 / conference sponsored and organised by BHRA Fluid Engineering. — Cranfield : BHRA Fluid Engineering, [1981]. — v,328p : ill ; 30cm
ISBN 0-906085-60-8 (pbk) : Unpriced
B82-15533

International Conference on the Internal and External Protection of Pipes *(3rd : 1979 : Imperial College of Science and Technology)*. Proceedings of the 3rd International Conference on the Internal and External Protection of Pipes : London, England, September 5th-7th, 1979 / organised by BHRA Fluid Engineering. — Cranfield : BHRA Fluid Engineering, c1980. — 2v. : ill ; 30cm
Includes index
ISBN 0-906085-18-7 (pbk) : Unpriced : CIP rev.
ISBN 0-906085-19-5 (v.1) : Unpriced
ISBN 0-906085-20-9 (v.2) : Unpriced
B79-27529

621.8′672′0212 — Piping systems — *Technical data*

Kentish, D. N. W.. Pipework design data / D.N.W. Kentish. — London : McGraw-Hill, c1982. — viii,239p : ill ; 31cm
Includes index
ISBN 0-07-084558-1 : £30.00 : CIP rev.
B81-27346

621.8′73 — Lifting equipment: Cranes — *For children*

Dixon, Annabelle. Cranes / Annabelle Dixon ; illusrated by John Shackell. — London : Black, c1982. — 32p : ill ; 23cm. — (Science explorers)
Includes index
ISBN 0-7136-2161-3 : £2.95 : CIP rev.
B81-33849

621.8′82 — Fastenings: Nuts. Manufacture

McBain, N. S.. Choice of technique in bolt and nut manufacture / N.S. McBain and S.J. Uhlig. — Edinburgh : Scottish Academic Press, 1982. — 154p : ill ; 26cm. — (David Livingstone Institute series on choice of technique in developing countries ; v.5)
Bibliography: p145-146. — Includes index
ISBN 0-7073-0302-8 (cased) : Unpriced
ISBN 0-7073-0310-9 (pbk) : Unpriced
B82-36395

621.8′9 — Cams & gears. Effectiveness of lubricants. Evaluation - *Conference proceedings*

Performance and testing of gear oils and transmission fluids. — London : Heyden, June 1981. — [451]p
Conference papers
ISBN 0-85501-326-5 : £40.00 : CIP entry
B81-14417

621.8′9 — Cutting oils

Project to survey and evaluate metal cutting fluids and machine lubricants for use in automated small batch production (ASP) systems / Production Engineering Research Association of Great Britain and Machine Tool Industry Research Association. — [East Kilbride] : [Department of Industry, National Engineering Laboratory], [1982]. — 3v. : ill ; 30cm
Cover title: Survey & evaluation of metal cutting fluids & machine lubricants
Unpriced (pbk) B82-38759

621.8′9 — Friction & wear

Kragel′skiĭ, I. V.. Friction and wear. — Oxford : Pergamon, May 1981. — [450]p
Translation of: Osnovy raschetov na trenie i iznos
ISBN 0-08-025461-6 : £31.00 : CIP entry
B81-05169

621.8′9 — Lubrication

Billett, Michael. Industrial lubrication : a practical handbook for lubrication and production engineers / Michael Billett. — Oxford : Pergamon, 1979. — viii,136p : ill ; 26cm
Bibliography: p132. — Includes index
ISBN 0-08-024232-4 : £10.50 : CIP rev.
B79-16025

Lansdown, A. R.. Lubrication : a practical guide to lubricant selection / A.R. Lansdown. — Oxford : Pergamon, 1982. — xiv,252p,[1]leaf of plates : ill,1facsim ; 24cm. — (The Pergamon materials engineering practice series)
Bibliography: p243. — Includes index
ISBN 0-08-026728-9 (cased) : Unpriced : CIP rev.
ISBN 0-08-026727-0 (pbk) : £5.95 B81-35934

621.8′9 — Lubrication — *Conference proceedings*

Société de chimie physique. *International Meeting (34th : 1981 : Paris)*. Microscopic aspects of adhesion and lubrication : proceedings of the 34th International Meeting of the Société de chimie physique, Paris, 14-18 September 1981 / J.M. Georges editor with the help of the Organizing Committee. — Amsterdam ; Oxford : Elsevier Scientific, 1982. — xix,812p : ill ; 25cm. — (Tribology series ; 7)
English and French text. — Includes bibliographies and index
ISBN 0-444-42071-1 : £69.15 : CIP rev.
ISBN 0-444-41677-3
Primary classification 541.3′453 B82-09294

621.8′9 — Materials. Erosion — *Conference proceedings*

International Conference on Erosion by Liquid and Solid Impact *(5th : 1979 : Newnham College)*. Proceedings of the Fifth International Conference on Erosion by Liquid and Solid Impact : Newnham College, Cambridge, UK, 3-6 September 1979. — Cambridge : Cavendish Laboratory, University of Cambridge, [1979?]. — 1v.(various pagings) : ill,ports ; 20cm
Unpriced (spiral) B82-00092

621.8′9 — Materials: Polymers. Friction & wear

Bartenev, G. M.. Friction and wear of polymers / G.M. Bartenev, V.V. Lavrentev ; translated by D.B. Payne ; edited by Lieng-Huang Lee and K.C. Ludema. — Amsterdam ; Oxford : Elsevier Scientific, 1981. — xvii,320p : ill ; 25cm. — (Tribology series ; 6)
Includes index
ISBN 0-444-42000-2 : £29.62 : CIP rev.
B81-18074

Friction and wear in polymer-based materials / by V.A. Bely ... [et al.] ; translated by P. Granville-Jackson. — Oxford : Pergamon, 1982. — ix,415p : ill ; 24cm
Translation of: Trenie i iznos materialov na osnove polimerov. — Includes bibliographies and index
ISBN 0-08-025444-6 : £40.00 : CIP rev.
B81-07600

621.8′9 — Thin film lubricants

Iliuc, Ivan. Tribology of thin layers / Ivan Iliuc. — Bucureşti : Editura Academiei Republicii Socialiste România ; Amsterdam ; Oxford : Elsevier Scientific, 1980. — ix,225p : ill ; 25cm. — (Tribology series ; 4)
Translation of: Tribologia straturilor subtiri. — Bibliography: p215-222. — Includes index
ISBN 0-444-99768-7 : £24.31 : CIP rev.
B80-07824

621.8′9 — Tribology — *Conference proceedings*

International Tribology Congress *(3rd : 1981 : Warsaw)*. 3rd International Tribology Congress Eurotrib 81 21-24 September 1981, Warsaw, Poland. — Oxford : Elsevier Scientific, Dec.1982. — 8v.([2778]p)
ISBN 0-444-99655-9 : £250 : CIP entry
B82-36332

Leeds-Lyon Symposium on Tribology *(8th : 1981 : Lyon)*. The running in process in tribology : proceedings of the 8th Leeds-Lyon Symposium on Tribology held in the Institut National des Sciences Appliquées de Lyon, France 8-11 September 1981 / edited by D. Dowson ... [et al.]. — Guildford : Butterworths for the Institute of Tribology, Leeds University and The Institut National des Sciences Appliquées de Lyon, c1982. — vii,254p : ill ; 31cm
Includes index
ISBN 0-408-01226-9 : Unpriced B82-37680

Tribology — key to the efficient engine / conference sponsored by the Tribology Group and the Automobile Division of the Institution of Mechanical Engineers, 19 January 1982, Institution Headquarters, 1 Birdcage Walk, Westminster, London. — London : Published by Mechanical Engineering Publications for the Institution of Mechanical Engineers, 1982. — 85p : ill ; 30cm. — (I Mech E conference publications ; 1982-1)
ISBN 0-85298-488-x (pbk) : Unpriced
B82-23229

621.8′9 — Tribology - *Manuals*

Friction, wear and lubrication. — Oxford : Pergamon, Sept.1981. — 3v.
Translation of: Trenie, iznashivanie i smazka
ISBN 0-08-027591-5 : £60.00 : CIP entry
B81-20115

621.8′9′072041 — Tribology. Research in British higher education institutions

Stanton, Chris. Research in tribology and bearings / prepared for the Science Research Council by Chris Stanton and Harry Challis. — [Swindon] : [The Council], 1980. — 52p : ill ; 20x21cm
ISBN 0-901660-39-6 (pbk) : Unpriced
B82-11011

621.9 — WORKSHOP TOOLS

621.9 — Mechanical engineering. Tools

Martin, S. J.. Principles of engineering production. — 2nd ed. — London : Hodder & Stoughton, Aug.1982. — [480]p
Previous ed.: London : English University Press, 1964
ISBN 0-340-28173-1 (pbk) : £8.95 : CIP entry
B82-20626

621.9 — Woodworking tools — *Manuals*

Hill, Jack, *1933-*. Wood working tools and how to use them : based on the classic work by Alfred P. Morgan / Jack Hill. — Rev. ed. — Newton Abbot : David & Charles, 1982. — 191p : ill ; 23cm
Previous ed.: published as Tools and how to use them for woodworking. New York : Crown, 1948. — Includes index
ISBN 0-7153-8058-3 : £8.50 : CIP rev.
B82-09617

621.9′003 — Tools — *Polyglot dictionaries*

Clason, W. E.. Elsevier′s dictionary of tools and ironware. — Oxford : Elsevier Scientific, May 1982. — 1v.
ISBN 0-444-42085-1 : CIP entry B82-14949

621.9′02 — Machine tools

Weck, Manfred. Machine tools. — London : Heyden
Vol.1: Types of machine, forms of construction and applications. — Sept.1982. — 1v.
Translation of: Werkzeugmaschinen. Bd.1. Maschinenarten, Bauformen und Anwendungsbereiche
ISBN 0-85501-731-7 (pbk) : CIP entry
B82-21754

621.9′02 — Machine tools. Design — *Conference proceedings*

International Machine Tool Design and Research Conference *(22nd : 1981 : Manchester)*. Proceedings of the Twenty-Second International Machine Tool Design and Research Conference : held in Manchester 16th-18th September 1981 / edited by B.J. Davies. — Manchester : Department of Mechanical Engineering, University of Manchester Institute of Science and Technology in association with Macmillan, 1982. — xiv,579p : ill ; 31cm
ISBN 0-333-32767-5 : £52.00 B82-33837

621.9′023′02854 — Machine tools. Numerical control. Applications of digital computer systems — *Conference proceedings*

Numerical engineering : the key to success : international technical conference 30th March-31st March 1981. — [London] ([c/o the Secretary, 66 Little Ealing La., W5 4XX]) : British Numerical Control Society in conjunction with the Institution of Production Engineers, [1981]. — 4v. : ill,ports ; 30cm
Cover title
Unpriced (pbk) B82-38840

621.9′08′0901 — Prehistoric stone tools — *Serials*

Lithics : the newsletter of the Lithic Studies Society. — No.1 (1980)-. — [Cheltenham] ([c/o Mr A. Saville, Art Gallery and Museum, Clarence St., Cheltenham, Gloucestershire GL50 3NX]) : The Society, 1980-. — v. : ill ; 21cm
Annual. — Description based on: No.2 (Dec. 1981)
ISSN 0262-7817 = Lithics : £1.00 (Free to Society members only) B82-19848

621.9′08′09361 — Great Britain. Prehistoric flint tools

Pierpoint, Stephen. Prehistoric flintwork in Britain / by Stephen Pierpoint. — [Highworth] : [VORDA], [c1981]. — 50p : ill,1map ; 30cm. — (VORDA research series ; 3) (VORDA archaeological and historical publications)
Bibliography: p45-50
ISBN 0-907246-02-8 (pbk) : Unpriced B82-25046

621.9′2 — Grinding wheels

Crawshaw, Margaret. Abrasive wheels. — London : Health and Safety Executive, May 1981. — [15]p
ISBN 0-7176-0075-0 (pbk) : £1.00 : CIP entry B81-12374

621.9′2′0289 — Great Britain. Portable grinding machines. Safety measures

Great Britain. *Health and Safety Executive*. Portable grinding machines. — London : Health and Safety Executive, Oct.1981. — [40] p. — (HS(G)18)
ISBN 0-11-883444-4 (pbk) : CIP entry B81-24631

621.9′3 — Australian aboriginal stone hatchets

Dickson, F. P.. Australian stone hatchets : a study in design and dynamics / F.P. Dickson. — Sydney ; London : Academic Press, 1981. — viii,240p : ill ; 24cm. — (Studies in archaeological sciences)
Bibliography: p221-227. — Includes index
ISBN 0-12-215220-4 : £22.60 B82-32781

621.9′3 — Cutting machines: Guillotines. Safety measures

Guillotines and shears. — London : Health & Safety Executive, July 1981. — [36]p. — (HS (G))
ISBN 0-11-883434-7 (pbk) : CIP entry B81-13835

621.9′3 — Cutting tools. Materials — *Conference proceedings*

Towards improved performance of tool materials : proceedings of the international conference sponsored and organized jointly by the National Physical Laboratory and the Metals Society and held at the National Physical Laboratory, Teddington, Middlesex on 28 and 29 April 1981. — London : Metals Society, 1982. — x,252p : ill ; 31cm
ISBN 0-904357-39-2 : Unpriced
Also classified at 621.9′84 B82-25874

621.9′3 — Jet cutting — *Conference proceedings*

International Symposium on Jet Cutting Technology *(6th : 1982 : University of Surrey)*. Papers presented at the Sixth International Symposium on Jet Cutting Technology held at the University of Surrey, U.K., 6-8 April 1982 / conference sponsored and organised by BHRA Fluid Engineering. — Bedford : BHRA Fluid Engineering, c1982. — vi,524p : ill ; 30cm
ISBN 0-906085-67-5 (pbk) : Unpriced : CIP rev. B82-14485

621.9′52′0289 — Workshop equipment: Drilling machines. Safety measures

Drilling machines : guarding of spindles and attachments / Health and Safety Executive. — London : H.M.S.O., c1974 (1980 [printing]). — 31p : ill ; 21cm. — (Health and safety at work ; 20)
Cover title
ISBN 0-11-883363-4 (pbk) : £1.25 B82-35801

621.9′84 — Moulds & dies. Manufacture

Challis, Harry. Dies & moulds : research on the problems involved in manufacture / prepared for the Science and Engineering Research Council by Harry Challis and Chris Stanton in collaboration with Peter Gough. — Swindon : The Council, 1982. — 36p : ill ; 30cm
ISBN 0-901660-47-7 (pbk) : Unpriced B82-23770

621.9′84 — Press tools. Materials — *Conference proceedings*

Towards improved performance of tool materials : proceedings of the international conference sponsored and organized jointly by the National Physical Laboratory and the Metals Society and held at the National Physical Laboratory, Teddington, Middlesex on 28 and 29 April 1981. — London : Metals Society, 1982. — x,252p : ill ; 31cm
ISBN 0-904357-39-2 : Unpriced
Primary classification 621.9′3 B82-25874

622 — MINING

622 — Cut and fill mining. Applications of rock mechanics

Application of rock mechanics to cut and fill mining : proceedings of the Conference on the Application of Rock Mechanics to Cut and Fill Mining, organized by the departments of Rock Mechanics and Soil Mechanics, University of Luleå, The Swedish Rock Mechanics Research Foundation and The Institution of Mining and Metallurgy, held at the University of Luleå, Sweden, from 1 to 3 June, 1980 / editors Ove Stephansson and Michael J. Jones. — London : The Institution of Mining and Metallurgy, 1981. — x,376p : ill,maps ; 30cm
Includes index
ISBN 0-900488-60-3 (pbk) : Unpriced B82-15428

622′.028 — Mining machinery, *to 1981*

Stack, Barbara. Handbook of mining and tunnelling machinery / Barbara Stack. — Chichester : Wiley, c1982. — xxix,742p : ill ; 28cm
Text on lining papers. — Includes index
ISBN 0-471-27937-4 : £38.00
Also classified at 624.1′93′028 B82-18222

622′.074′02513 — Derbyshire. Matlock Bath. Museums: Peak District Mining Museum — *Visitors′ guides*

Willies, L. M.. Peak District Mining Museum / [text by Lynn Willies]. — Derby : Derbyshire Countryside, c1980. — 12p : ill(some col.) ; 24cm
Cover title. — Ill on inside covers
ISBN 0-85100-071-1 (pbk) : £0.40 B82-14969

622′.0942 — England. Disused mines — *Visitors guides*

Naylor, Peter. Discovering lost mines / Peter Naylor. — Princes Risborough : Shire, 1981. — 63p : ill,maps ; 18cm
Bibliography: p60. — Includes index
ISBN 0-85263-544-3 (pbk) : £1.25 B82-31005

622′.1 — Minerals. Prospecting — *Manuals — Early works — Facsimiles*

Plattes, Gabriel. A discovery of subterraneall treasure, viz. Of all manner of mines and mineralls, from the gold to the coale ; with plaine directions and rules for the finding of them in all kingdomes and countries ... — Ilkley : Reprinted for the Institution of Mining and Metallurgy London by the Scolar Press, 1980. — 60p ; 19cm
Author: Gabriel Plattes. — Facsim of: ed. published London : I. Okes for Jasper Emery, 1639
Unpriced B82-15996

622′.1′0942371 — Cornwall. Bodmin region. Mineral deposits. Exploration

Mineral investigations near Bodmin, Cornwall. — London : Institute of Geological Sciences. — (Mineral reconnaissance programme report ; no.45)
Pt.2: New uranium, tin and copper occurrences in the Tremayne area of St. Columb Major / geochemistry B.C. Tandy ; geology B.R. Mountford ; mineralogy I.R. Basham ; data treatment R.C. Jones ; edited by U.McL. Michie. — 1981. — 37leaves : ill,maps ; 30cm
Bibliography: leaf 30
Unpriced (spiral) B82-15026

622′.1′094897 — Finland. Glaciated regions. Mineral deposits. Prospecting

Excursion guide : IMM prospecting in glaciated terrain, August 1977 Finland. — [London] : Institution of Mining and Metallurgy, [1977?]. — 49leaves : ill,maps ; 30cm
Unpriced (unbound) B82-16007

622′.13 — Mineral deposits. Chemical analysis. Laboratory techniques

Fletcher, W. K.. Analytical methods in geochemical prospecting / by W.K. Fletcher. — Amsterdam ; Oxford : Elsevier Scientific, 1981. — xiii,255p : ill ; 25cm. — (Handbook of exploration geochemistry ; v.1)
Bibliography: p217-240. — Includes index
ISBN 0-444-41930-6 : £27.56 B82-00690

622′.13 — Mineral deposits. Estimation. Applications of nonparametric statistical mathematics

Henley, Stephen. Nonparametric geostatistics / Stephen Henley. — London : Applied Science, c1981. — xiv,145p : ill ; 23cm
Bibliography: p137-140. — Includes index
ISBN 0-85334-977-0 : £12.00 : CIP rev. B81-20160

622′.13 — Mineral deposits. Prospecting. Applications of geochemistry

Govett, G. J. S.. Rock geochemistry in mineral exploration. — Oxford : Elsevier Scientific, Jan.1982. — [355]p. — (Handbook of exploration geochemistry ; v.3)
ISBN 0-444-42021-5 : CIP entry B81-34491

622′.13 — Mineral deposits. Prospecting. Applications of geochemistry — *Conference proceedings*

Geochemical exploration 1980 / edited by A.W. Rose and H. Gundlach. — Amsterdam ; Oxford : Elsevier Scientific, 1981. — x,698p : ill,maps ; 25cm. — (Developments in economic geology ; 15) (Association of Exploration Geochemists special publication ; no.9)
Includes bibliographies
ISBN 0-444-42012-6 : Unpriced : CIP rev. B81-28197

622′.13 — Particulate mineral deposits. Sampling

Gy, Pierre M.. Sampling of particulate materials : theory and practice / Pierre M. Gy. — 2nd rev. ed. — Amsterdam ; Oxford : Elsevier Scientific, 1982. — xvii,431p : ill ; 25cm. — (Developments in geomathematics ; 4)
Previous ed.: 1979. — Bibliography: p425-426. — Includes index
ISBN 0-444-42079-7 : Unpriced B82-25702

622′.15 — Mineral deposits. Prospecting. Applications of geophysics

Beck, A. E.. Physical principles of exploration methods : an introductory text for geology and geophysics students / A.E. Beck. — London : Macmillan, 1981. — xii,234p : ill ; 25cm. — (Geomac)
Includes bibliographies and index
ISBN 0-333-26393-6 (cased) : £14.00
ISBN 0-333-26394-4 (pbk) : Unpriced B82-02579

Developments in geophysical exploration methods . — 3. — London : Applied Science, June 1982. — [296]p. — (The Developments series)
ISBN 0-85334-126-5 : £28.00 : CIP entry B82-11125

Developments in geophysical exploration methods . — 4. — London : Applied Science, Jan.1983. — [200]p. — (The Developments series)
ISBN 0-85334-174-5 : £26.00 : CIP entry B82-33111

622'.15 — Mineral deposits. Prospecting. Applications of plate tectonics

Mitchell, A. H. G.. Mineral deposits and global tectonic settings / A.H.G. Mitchell, M.S. Garson. — London : Academic Press, 1981. — xvii,405p : ill,maps ; 24cm. — (Academic Press geology series)
Bibliography: p340-375. — Includes index
ISBN 0-12-499050-9 : £23.60 : CIP rev.
B81-31344

622'.153 — Mineral deposits. Prospecting. Applications of electromagnetic fields — *Tables*

Verma, Rajni K.. Electromagnetic sounding interpretation data over three-layer earth / Rajni K. Verma. — New York ; London : IFI/Plenum, c1982. — 2v. : ill ; 29cm. — (IFI Data base library)
ISBN 0-306-65204-8 : Unpriced B82-39489

622'.1828 — Natural gas deposits & petroleum deposits. Prospecting. Applications of organic geochemistry

Waples, Douglas. Organic geochemistry for exploration geologists / Douglas Waples. — [Champaign] : CEPCO ; Heathfield : Broad Oak [distributor], c1981. — viii,151p : ill ; 29cm
Bibliography: p138-142. — Includes index
ISBN 0-8087-2961-6 (cased) : Unpriced
ISBN 0-8087-2980-2 (pbk) : Unpriced
B82-28040

622'.1828 — Offshore natural gas & petroleum deposits. Prospecting — *Conference proceedings*

New technologies for exploration and exploitation of oil and gas resources / [organization of the conference ... by Commission of the European Communities, Directorate-General Energy, Brussels, and Directorate-General Scientific and Technical Information and Information Management, Luxembourg]. — London : Graham & Trotman, 1979. — 2v.(1359p) : ill ; 24cm
ISBN 0-86010-158-4 (pbk) : Unpriced
ISBN 0-86010-159-2 (v.2) : £20.00
Also classified at 622'.338 B82-41012

622'.18282 — Carbonate sediments. Petroleum deposits. Prospecting

Exploration for carbonate petroleum reservoirs / Elf-Aquitaine, Centres de Recherches de Boussens et de Pau ; [translated, revised and updated by] Anne Reeckmann, Gerald M. Friedman. — New York ; Chichester : Wiley, c1982. — xiv,213p,1folded leaf : ill,maps ; 26cm
Translation of: Essai de caractérisation sédimentologique des dépôts carbonatés, pt.2. — Bibliography: p207-210. — Includes index
ISBN 0-471-08603-7 : £31.00 B82-32053

622'.18282 — Petroleum. Prospecting. Applications of geophysics

Dohr, Gerhard. Applied geophysics : introduction to geophysical prospecting / by Gerhard Dohr ; [translated by A. Franc de Ferriere and R.A. Dawe]. — 2., completely rev. ed. — New York : Halsted ; Chichester : Wiley, c1981. — viii,231p : ill ; 23cm. — (Geology of petroleum, ISSN 0720-8863 ; v.1)
Translation from the German. — Previous ed.: 1975. — Bibliography: p220-222. — Includes index
ISBN 0-471-09984-8 (pbk) : £9.90 B82-12048

622'.1841'0924 — Australia. Victoria. Gold. Prospecting, *1852-1856* — *Personal observations*

Korzelinski, Seweryn. Memoirs of gold-digging in Australia / Seweryn Korzelinski ; translated and edited by Stanley Robe ; foreword and notes by Lloyd Robson. — St. Lucia : University of Queensland Press ; Hemel Hempstead : Distributed by Prentice-Hall, c1979. — xiv,160p : ill ; 22cm
Translation of: Opis podróży do Australii i pobytu tamże od 1852 do 1856 roku. — Bibliography: p156-157. — Includes index
ISBN 0-7022-1346-2 : £8.40 B82-20104

622'.184932 — Uranium. Prospecting. Applications of geochemistry

Boyle, R. W.. Geochemical prospecting for thorium and uranium deposits. — Oxford : Elsevier Scientific, May 1982. — [550]p. — (Developments in economic geology ; v.7)
ISBN 0-444-42070-3 : CIP entry B82-10698

622'.2 — Mines. Strata. Deformation

Symposium on Strata Mechanics *(1982 : Newcastle upon Tyne)*. Strata mechanics : proceedings of the Symposium on Strata Mechanics held in Newcastle upon Tyne, 5-7 April 1982 / edited by I.W. Farmer. — Amsterdam ; Oxford : Elsevier Scientific, 1982, c1981. — 289p : ill ; 30cm. — (Developments in geotechnical engineering ; v.32)
Includes index
ISBN 0-444-42086-x : £42.19 B82-38192

622'.334'02341 — Great Britain. Coal. Mining — *Career guides*

Birtles, W.. Working at a coal mine / W. Birtles ; photography by Chris Fairclough. — Hove : Wayland, 1982. — 94p : ill,ports ; 25cm. — (People at work)
Includes index
ISBN 0-85340-976-5 : £4.95 B82-33428

White, C. J. (Cyril John). So you want to be a coal miner / by C.J. White. — Melksham : Venton, [1982]. — 154p,20p of plates : ill ; 21cm. — (White horse library)
Bibliography: p153. — Includes index
ISBN 0-85993-003-3 : Unpriced B82-36374

622'.334'028 — Great Britain. Coal mines. Hand picks — *Standards*

Hand picks for use underground. — London (Hobart House, Grosvenor Place SW1 7AE) : National Coal Board, [1980]. — 21p : ill ; 21cm. — (NCB specification ; no.650/1980)
£1.40 (unbound) B82-31837

622'.334'028 — Great Britain. Coal mines. Storage equipment: Staple shaft bunkers. Design & construction

Design and construction of staple shaft bunkers : National Coal Board Mining Department working party report 1981. — [London] : National Coal Board, c1981. — 68p : ill ; 30cm
Unpriced (pbk) B82-25012

622'.334'068 — Coal mines. Management — *Manuals*

Britton, Scott G.. Practical coal mine management / Scott G. Britton. — New York ; Chichester : Wiley, c1981. — 233p : ill,forms ; 24cm
Bibliography: p229-230. — Includes index
ISBN 0-471-09035-2 : £22.00 B82-08620

622'.334'0941 — Great Brtain. Coal mines. Coal miners — *For children*

Aston, Phillippa. A day with a miner / Phillippa Aston & Chris Fairclough. — Hove : Wayland, 1981. — 55p : ill ; 23cm. — (A day in the life)
Bibliography: p55
ISBN 0-85340-900-5 : £3.25 B82-16513

622'.334'0941295 — Scotland. Fife Region. West Wemyss. Coal. Mining, *to 1980* — *For schools*

Coal mining in West Wemyss. — [West Wemyss] : West Wemyss Environmental Education Centre, [1982]. — 32p : ill,maps ; 22cm
Cover title
Unpriced (pbk) B82-19483

622'.338 — Offshore natural gas & petroleum deposits. Extraction — *Conference proceedings*

New technologies for exploration and exploitation of oil and gas resources / [organization of the conference ... by Commission of the European Communities, Directorate-General Energy, Brussels, and Directorate-General Scientific and Technical Information and Information Management, Luxembourg]. — London : Graham & Trotman, 1979. — 2v.(1359p) : ill ; 24cm
ISBN 0-86010-158-4 (pbk) : Unpriced
ISBN 0-86010-159-2 (v.2) : £20.00
Primary classification 622'.1828 B82-41012

622'.3382 — Oil fields. Flooding. Calculations. Applications of pocket programmable electronic calculators. Programming — *Manuals*

Garb, Forrest A.. Waterflood calculations for hand-held computers / Forrest A. Garb. — Houston ; London : Gulf, c1982. — vii,94p : forms ; 28cm
ISBN 0-87201-895-4 (spiral) : Unpriced
B82-40393

622'.3382 — Petroleum deposits. Enhanced recovery — *Conference proceedings*

European Symposium on Enhanced Oil Recovery *(3rd : 1981 : Bournemouth)*. Enhanced oil recovery : proceedings of the third European Symposium on Enhanced Oil Recovery, held in Bournemouth, U.K., September 21-23, 1981 / edited by F. John Fayers. — Amsterdam ; Oxford : Elsevier Scientific, 1981. — ix,596p : ill ; 25cm. — (Developments in petroleum science ; 13)
Includes index
ISBN 0-444-42033-9 : £37.04 B82-05119

622'.3382 — Petroleum deposits. Extraction. Chemical flooding — *Conference proceedings*

Surface phenomena in enhanced oil recovery / [proceedings of a symposium on Surface Phenomena in Enhanced Oil Recovery, organized as part of the Third International Conference on Surface and Colloid Science, and held August 20-25, 1979, in Stockholm, Sweden ; edited by Dinesh O. Shah. — New York ; London : Plenum, c1981. — xii,874p : ill ; 26cm
Includes index
ISBN 0-306-40757-4 : Unpriced B82-05443

622'.3382 — Petroleum deposits. Fractured reservoirs. Engineering aspects

Golf-Racht, T. D. van. Fundamentals of fractured reservoir engineering / by T.D. van Golf-Racht. — Amsterdam ; Oxford : Elsevier Scientific, 1982. — 710p : ill ; 25cm. — (Developments in petroleum science ; 12)
Includes index
ISBN 0-444-42046-0 : £42.55 : CIP rev.
ISBN 0-444-41625-0 B81-37526

622'.3382 — Petroleum deposits. Reservoirs. Exploitation. Engineering aspects

Dake, L. P.. Fundamentals of reservoir engineering. — Oxford : Elsevier, Mar.1982. — [350]p. — (Developments in petroleum science, ISSN 0376-7361 ; 8)
Originally published: 1978
ISBN 0-444-41830-x (pbk) : CIP entry
B82-05395

622'.3382 — Petroleum. Production

Skinner, D. R.. Introduction to petroleum production / D.R. Skinner. — Houston ; London : Gulf Publishing
Vol.1: Reservoir engineering, drilling, well completions. — c1981. — vii,190p : ill ; 24cm
Includes index
ISBN 0-87201-767-2 : £15.50 B82-02242

622'.3382'01576 — Petroleum deposits. Enhanced recovery. Use of microorganisms

Moses, V.. Bacteria and the enhancement of oil recovery / V. Moses and D.G. Springham. — London : Applied Science Publishers, c1982. — xi,178p ; 23cm
Includes bibliographies and index
ISBN 0-85334-995-9 : Unpriced : CIP rev.
B81-33785

622'.3382'024553 — Petroleum reservoir engineering — *For economic geology*

Hocott, Claude R.. Basic reservoir engineering for geologists / by Claude R. Hocott ; sponsored by Geological Society of London, Petroleum Exploration Society of Great Britain. — London ([Burlington House, Piccadilly, W1V 0JU]) : [Geological Society of London], 1978. — 24p : ill ; 30cm. — (AAPG lecture series) (Geological Society miscellaneous paper ; no.8)
Cover title. — Bibliography: p24
Unpriced (pbk) B82-35933

622'.3382'028 — Petroleum drilling equipment — *Technical data*

Lynch, Philip F.. A primer in drilling & production equipment / Philip F. Lynch. — Houston ; London : Gulf
Vol.2: Rig equipment. — c1981. — vi,134p : ill ; 28cm
Includes index
ISBN 0-87201-199-2 (pbk) : Unpriced
B82-29170

622'.3382'028 — Petroleum drilling equipment — *Technical data* *continuation*

Lynch, Philip F.. A primer in drilling & production equipment / Philip F. Lynch
Vol.3: Downhole operations. — Houston ; London : Gulf. — c1981. — viii,120p : ill ; 28cm
Includes index
ISBN 0-87201-201-8 (pbk) : Unpriced
B82-12785

622'.33'820289 — Offshore petroleum industries. Safety measures: Automatic control systems — *Conference proceedings*

Automation for safety in shipping and offshore petroleum operations : proceedings of the IFIP/IFAC symposium, Trondheim, Norway, June 16-18, 1980 / edited by A.B. Aune and J. Vlietstra. — Amsterdam ; Oxford : North-Holland, 1980. — x,475p : ill ; 31cm. — (Computer applications in shipping and shipbuilding ; v.8)
Includes index
ISBN 0-444-85498-3 : £42.25
Also classified at 623.88'8 B82-31516

622'.3382'07 — Great Britain. Petroleum industries. Clerical personnel. In-service training — *Manuals*

The **Training** of office staff / Petroleum Industry Training Board. — Aylesbury (Kingfisher House, Walton St., Aylesbury, Bucks. HP21 2TQ) : The Board, c1982. — ii,43p ; 22x30cm
Unpriced (spiral) B82-38441

622'.3382'09162 — Oceans. Bed. Petroleum deposits. Extraction. Tension leg platforms

Bluston, H. S.. The tension leg platform / by H.S. Bluston. — [Bedford] : [Energy Consultancy], [1981]. — 7,14leaves,[2]leaves of plates : 2ill ; 30cm
Unpriced (pbk) B82-03331

622'.3385'0287 — Natural gas deposits. Wells. Testing

Donohue, David A. T.. Gaswell testing : theory, practice & regulation / David A.T. Donohue, Turgay Ertekin with the assistance of Howard B. Bradley. — Boston, Mass. : International Human Resources Development ; Heathfield : Broad Oak [distributor], c1982. — lx,214p : ill,forms ; 24cm
Includes index
ISBN 0-934634-10-6 (cased) : Unpriced
ISBN 0-934634-12-2 (pbk) : Unpriced
B82-28043

622'.34'094294 — South Wales. Nonferrous metals mines, *to 1980*

Foster-Smith, J. R.. The non ferrous mines of the South Wales area : by J.R. Foster-Smith. — Sheffield : Northern Mine Research Society, 1981. — 54p : ill,maps ; 30cm. — (British mining, ISSN 0308-2199 ; no.18) (A Monograph of the Northern Mine Research Society)
Bibliography: p49. — Includes index
ISBN 0-901450-15-4 (pbk) : Unpriced
B82-01506

622'.34'094687 — Spain. Huelva *(Province)*. Metals mines. Industrial antiquities. Excavation of remains

Rothenberg, Beno. Studies in ancient mining and metallurgy in south-west Spain : explorations and excavations in the Province of Huelva / by Beno Rothenberg and Antonio Blanco-Freijeiro ; with contributions by H.G. Bachmann ... [et al.]. — London : IAMS, c1981. — 320p : ill,maps ; 29cm. — (Metal in history ; 1)
Includes index
ISBN 0-906183-01-4 : £18.00 : CIP rev.
B81-38836

622'.343'0901 — Copper. Prehistoric mining

Scientific studies in early mining and extractive metallurgy / edited by P.T. Craddock. — London : British Museum, 1980. — 173p : ill,maps,plans ; 30cm. — (Occasional paper, ISSN 0142-4815, ISSN no.20)
Conference papers. — Includes bibliographies
ISBN 0-86159-019-8 (pbk) : Unpriced
Primary classification 669'.3'0901 B82-36198

622'.3453'0942376 — Cornwall. Illogan. Tin mines: South Crofty Mine, *to 1980*

Buckley, J. A.. A history of South Crofty mine / by J.A. Buckley. — Redruth : Dyllansow Truran, [1980?]. — 224p,[32]p of plates : ill,maps,1facsims,plans,ports ; 23cm
Bibliography: p212-213. — Includes index
ISBN 0-907566-17-0 : £7.95 B82-20793

622'.353 — Surrey. Merstham. Firestone mines. Industrial antiquities

Tadd, Malcolm. Merstham's football field mine / a survey directed by Chris Bayley ; notes by Malcolm Tadd. — South Nutfield (65 Trindles Rd., South Nutfield, Surrey RH1 4JL) : Unit Two Cave Research and Exploration, 1981. — [4]leaves ; 30cm + 1plan(85x32cm folded to 32x22cm)
Unpriced (unbound) B82-28331

622'.3672'0922 — New Zealand. South Island. Asbestos. Mining. Chaffey, Annie & Chaffey, Henry — *Biographies*

Henderson, Jim. The exiles of Asbestos Cottage / Jim Henderson. — Auckland ; London : Hodder and Stoughton, 1981. — 248p,[12]p of plates : ill(some col.),maps,1plan,ports(some col.) ; 22cm
Ill on lining papers
ISBN 0-340-26503-5 : £8.50 : CIP rev.
B82-01144

622'.42 — Mines. Air conditioning & ventilation

Mine ventilation and air conditioning / [principle author] Howard L. Hartman. — 2nd ed. / co-editors Jan M. Mutmansky, Y.J. Wang. — New York ; Chichester : Wiley, 1982. — xviii,791p : ill ; 24cm
Previous ed.: 19--?. — Includes index
ISBN 0-471-05690-1 : £37.00 B82-38986

622'.48 — Coal mines. Flexible multicore galvanised steel armoured electric cables — *Standards*

Flexible multicore screened auxiliary cables with galvanised steel pliable armouring. — London (Secetariat, Quality Control Branch, Mining Department, The Lodge, South Parade, Doncaster DN1 2DX) : National Coal Board, [1980]. — 13p : ill ; 21cm. — (NCB specification ; no.653/1980)
£0.80 (unbound) B82-40726

622'.5 — Great Britain. Mines. Drainage. Steam pumping engines — *Early works — Facsimiles*

Savery, Thomas. The miners friend, or, An engine to raise water by fire described and of the manner of fixing it in mines : with an account of the several other uses it is applicable unto and an answer to the objections made against it / by Tho. Savery. — Edinburgh : Antiquarian Facsimiles, 1979. — A4leaves,84p,[1] folded leaf of plates : ill ; 18cm
Facsim. of: ed. originally published: London : S. Crouch, 1702. — Limited ed. of 300 numbered copies. — In slip case
ISBN 0-9506732-0-x : £29.50 B82-01901

622'.67 — Mines. Electric winding equipment

Chatterjee, P. K.. Winding engine calculations for the mining engineer. — 2nd ed. — London : Spon, Feb.1982. — [192]p
Previous ed.: / by Alexander Bernard Price. London : General Electric Co., 1955
ISBN 0-419-12650-3 : £15.00 : CIP entry
B81-35729

622'.73 — Minerals. Grinding

Beke, Béla. The process of fine grinding / Béla Beke. — The Hague ; London : Nijhoff, 1981. — 150p : ill ; 25cm. — (Developments in mineral science and engineering ; v.1)
Translation from the Hungarian. —
Bibliography: p141-146. — Includes index
ISBN 90-247-2462-7 : Unpriced B82-02728

622'.752 — Ores. Froth flotation

Leja, Jan. Surface chemistry of froth flotation / Jan Leja. — New York ; London : Plenum, c1982. — xxi,758p : ill ; 24cm
Includes bibliographies and index
ISBN 0-306-40588-1 : Unpriced B82-33004

622'.8 — European Community countries. Coal mines. Air. Pollutants: Methane. Control measures — *Conference proceedings*

Methane, climate, ventilation in the coalmines of the European communities, Luxembourg, 4 to 6 November 1980 : information symposium / [organization of the information symposium by the Commission of the European Communities Directorate-General Energy and Directorate-General for Information Market and Innovation]. — English language ed. — Redhill : Colliery Guardian
Vol.1. — c1980. — v,533p : ill ; 24cm
Also available in French and German. — At head of title: Commission of the European Communities
ISBN 0-86108-080-7 (pbk) : Unpriced
B82-39133

622'.8 — Great Britain. Coal mines. Accidents — *Inquiry reports*

The **Explosion** at Cardowan colliery, Stepps, Strathclyde Region 27 January 1982 / a report by HM Inspectorate of Mines and Quarries. — [London] : H.M.S.O., 1982. — vi,9p,[2]folded leaves of plates : col.plans ; 30cm
ISBN 0-11-883644-7 (pbk) : £2.50 B82-39982

622'.8 — Great Britain. Coal mines. Electrical equipment. Safety measures

The **Explosive** atmospheres directives. — London : H.M.S.O., Feb.1982. — [28]p. — (HS(R))
ISBN 0-11-883620-x (pbk) : CIP entry
B82-02440

622'.8 — Great Britain. Disused coal mines. Shafts. Safety measures

The **Treatment** of disused mine shafts and adits / Mining Department, National Coal Board. — London (Hobart House, Grosvenor Place, SW1X 7AE) : The Department, 1982. — 88p : ill ; 21cm
Bibliography: p86. — Includes index
Unpriced (pbk) B82-30838

622'.8 — Great Britain. Offshore natural gas & petroleum industries. Safety measures

Offshore safety, emergency techniques and environmental protection. — [London] ([192 Sloane St, SW1X 9QX]) : United Kingdom Offshore Operators Association, [1980?]. — [40]p : ill ; 30cm
Cover title
Unpriced (pbk) B82-26588

622'.8 — Petroleum deposits. Extraction. Accidents: Blowouts. Prevention & control

Managing technological accidents : two blowouts in the North Sea : incorporating the proceedings of an IIASA Workshop on Blowout Management, April 1978 / David W. Fischer, editor. — Oxford : Pergamon, 1982. — xii,234p : ill,maps ; 26cm. — (IIASA proceedings series ; v.16)
Bibliography: p90-91. — Includes index
ISBN 0-08-029346-8 : £25.00 : CIP rev.
B82-12706

623 — MILITARY ENGINEERING

623 — Great Britain. Military equipment. Packaging

Design requirements for service packaging / Ministry of Defence. — 3rd ed. — London : H.M.S.O., 1980. — 176p : ill,forms ; 30cm. — (Defence guide ; DG-11)
Previous ed.: 1976
ISBN 0-11-772427-0 (pbk) : £12.50
B82-18619

623 — Leather military equipment, *to 1945*

Waterer, John W.. Leather and the warrior : an account of the importance of leather to the fighting man from the time of the ancient Greeks to World War II / John W. Waterer ; edited by Lysbeth Merrifield ; consultant editor, Claude Blair. — Northampton : The Museum of Leathercraft, 1981. — xix,180p : ill (some col.) ; 29cm
Bibliography: p178. — Includes index
ISBN 0-9504182-1-8 : Unpriced : CIP rev.
B81-34727

623 — Military forces. Combat support equipment — *Serials*

Jane's military vehicles and ground support equipment. — 2nd ed. (1981)-. — London : Jane's Pub. Co., 1980-. — v. : ill ; 32cm
Continues: Jane's combat support equipment
ISSN 0263-2594 = Jane's military vehicles and ground support equipment : £40.00 B82-18531

623'.0218 — Military equipment. Standards — *Serials*

Standards in defence news. — Serial 1-. — [London] ([First Ave. House, High Holborn, WC1V 6HE]) : [Directorate of Standardization, Ministry of Defence], 1976-. — v. ; 30cm
Issued every eight weeks
ISSN 0263-8266 = Standards in defence news : Unpriced B82-32143

623'.05 — Military equipment — *For Latin American military forces — Spanish texts — Serials*

Égida : revista iberoamericana para la defensa. — Vol.1, no.1 (jul.-set. 1981)-. — Londres (267 Kensal Rd., W10) : D-ALS International Ltd., 1981-. — v. : ill ; 29cm
Quarterly
ISSN 0262-7086 = Égida : Unpriced B82-06791

623'.05 — Military equipment — *Serials*

IDE&A : international defence exhibitions and advertising. — Vol.1, no.1-. — Colchester (1 East Stockwell St., Colchester CO1 1SR) : Vineyard Press, [1982]-. — v. : ill(some col.),maps,ports ; 30cm
Quarterly
ISSN 0263-6646 = IDE&A. International defence exhibitions and advertising : £25.00 per year B82-28878

623'.09182'1 — North Atlantic Treaty Organization military forces. Military equipment. Standardisation

Cornell, Alexander H.. International collaboration in weapons and equipment development and production by the NATO allies : ten years later — and beyond / Alexander H. Cornell. — The Hague ; London : Nijhoff, 1981. — xii,233p ; 24cm. — (Atlantic series ; no.11)
Bibliography: p197-222. — Includes index
ISBN 90-247-2564-x : Unpriced B82-07450

Hartley, Keith. NATO arms co-operation. — London : Allen & Unwin, Dec.1982. — [240]p
ISBN 0-04-341022-7 : £18.50 : CIP entry B82-32276

623'.094 — Europe. Military equipment, *700-1500*

Funcken, Liliane. The age of chivalry / Liliane and Fred Funcken. — London : Ward Lock. — (Arms and uniforms)
Pt.1: The 8th to the 15th century : helmets and mail, tournaments and heraldic bearings, bows and crossbows. — 1980. — 102p : ill(some col.) ; 25cm
Includes index
ISBN 0-7063-5808-2 : £6.95 : CIP rev.
Primary classification 355.1'4'094 B80-04120

Funcken, Liliane. The age of chivalry / Liliane and Fred Funcken. — London : Ward Lock. — (Arms and uniforms)
Translation of: Le costume, l'armure et les armes au temps de la chevalerie
Pt.3: The Renaissance : arms, horses and tournaments ; helmets and armour ; tactics and artillery. — 1982. — 104p : col.ill,col.ports ; 25cm
Ill on lining papers. — Includes index
ISBN 0-7063-5937-2 : £7.95 : CIP rev.
Primary classification 355.1'4'094 B81-37566

623'.0941 — Great Britain. Military equipment

Perrett, Bryan. Weapons of the Falklands conflict. — Poole : Blandford Press, Nov.1982. — [192]p
ISBN 0-7137-1315-1 : £5.95 : CIP entry
Also classified at 623'.0982 ; 997.11 B82-32861

623'.0947 — Union of Soviet Socialist Republics. *Armiia*. Army equipment — *Technical data*

An **Illustrated** guide to weapons of the modern Soviet ground forces / edited by Ray Bonds. — London : Salamander, c1981. — 158p : ill (some col.),1map ; 23cm
Ill on lining papers
ISBN 0-86101-115-5 : £3.95 B82-07995

623'.0982 — Argentina. Military equipment

Perrett, Bryan. Weapons of the Falklands conflict. — Poole : Blandford Press, Nov.1982. — [192]p
ISBN 0-7137-1315-1 : £5.95 : CIP entry
Primary classification 623'.0941 B82-32861

623'.1'09 — Fortifications, *to 1975*

Hogg, Ian V.. The history of fortification / Ian Hogg. — London : Orbis, c1981. — 256p : ill (some col.),maps,plans,ports ; 30cm
Plan on lining papers. — Bibliography: p252. — Includes index
ISBN 0-85613-028-1 : £12.50 B82-08550

623'.1'09411 — Scotland. Fortifications, *1100-1800*

Scottish weapons and fortifications 1100-1800 / edited by David H. Caldwell. — Edinburgh : John Donald, 1981. — xvii,452p : ill,maps,plans,ports ; 25cm
Bibliography: pvii-x. — Includes index
ISBN 0-85976-047-2 : £18.00
Primary classification 623.4'41'09411 B82-08869

623.1'09422'78 — Hampshire. Gosport. Fortifications, *1400-1800*

Williams, G. H. (Godfrey Hamilton). The western defences of Portsmouth Harbour 1400-1800. — Portsmouth : Portsmouth City Council, 1979. — 74p : ill,maps,2facsims,plans,ports ; 25cm. — (The Portsmouth papers ; no.30)
Cover title. — Written by G.H. Williams. — Includes index
ISBN 0-901559-37-7 (pbk) : £1.80 B82-11414

623'.12'093611 — Scotland. Ancient Roman fortifications

Breeze, David J.. The Northern frontiers of Roman Britain / David J. Breeze. — London : Batsford Academic and Educational, 1982. — 188p,[8]p of plates : ill,maps,plans ; 24cm
Bibliography: p171-180. — Includes index
ISBN 0-7134-0345-4 : £9.95
Also classified at 623'.12'093627 B82-17658

623'.12'093627 — Northern England. Ancient Roman fortifications

Breeze, David J.. The Northern frontiers of Roman Britain / David J. Breeze. — London : Batsford Academic and Educational, 1982. — 188p,[8]p of plates : ill,maps,plans ; 24cm
Bibliography: p171-180. — Includes index
ISBN 0-7134-0345-4 : £9.95
Primary classification 623'.12'093611 B82-17658

623'.19422395 — Kent. Romney Marsh. Martello towers, *to 1980*

Glendinning, I. H.. The hammers of Invicta : being a history of the martello towers round Romney Marsh / by I.H. Glendinning. — Hythe (Beacon Hill, School Rd., Hythe, Kent) : I.H. Glendinning, c1981. — 68p : ill,charts,maps,plans ; 21cm
Bibliography: p68
Unpriced (pbk) B82-32038

623'.38 — Residences. Nuclear shelters. Construction — *Manuals*

Domestic nuclear shelters : technical guidance / [prepared by the Home Office and the Central Office of Information]. — 2nd ed. — London : H.M.S.O., 1982. — ii,128p : ill,plans ; 30cm
Cover title. — Previous ed.: 1981
ISBN 0-11-340777-7 (pbk) : £5.95 B82-17324

623.4 — Military equipment: Weapons

Beckett, Brian. Weapons of tomorrow / Brian Beckett. — London : Orbis, 1982. — 160p,[16]p of plates : ill ; 23cm
Includes index
ISBN 0-85613-347-7 : £7.95 B82-39070

Koenig, William J.. Weapons of World War 3 / William J. Koenig. — London : Hamlyn, 1981. — 192p : ill(some col.) ; 29cm. — (A Bison book)
Includes index
ISBN 0-600-34219-0 : £6.95 B82-00735

623.4 — Weapon systems

Lee, R. G.. Introduction to battlefield weapons systems and technology / R.G. Lee. — Oxford : Brassey's, 1981. — xiv,198p : ill ; 26cm
Includes index
ISBN 0-08-027043-3 (cased) : Unpriced : CIP rev.
ISBN 0-08-027044-1 (pbk) : £6.50 B81-20477

623.4'028'5404 — Weapon systems. Applications of microcomputer systems

Ward, J. W. D.. Military data processing & microcomputers. — Oxford : Pergamon, Sept.1982. — [225]p. — (Battlefield weapons systems & technology ; v.9)
ISBN 0-08-028338-1 (cased) : £13.00 : CIP entry
ISBN 0-08-028339-x (pbk) : £6.50 B82-21077

623.4'09 — Military equipment: Weapons & armour, *to ca 1945 — Illustrations*

Weapons & armor : a pictorial archive of woodcuts & engravings / edited by Harold H. Hart. — New York : Dover ; London : Constable, 1982, c1978. — 191p : chiefly ill,ports ; 31cm. — (Dover pictorial archive series)
Originally published under the general editorship of Harold H. Hart ; compiled by Robert Sietsema. — New York : Hart, 1978. — Bibliography: p187. — Includes index
ISBN 0-486-24242-0 (pbk) : £5.25 B82-36249

623.4'094 — Europe. Military equipment: Weapons & body armour, *800-1980*

Wilkinson-Latham, Robert. Phaidon guide to antique weapons and armour / Robert Wilkinson-Latham ; illustrated by Malcolm McGregor, Peter Sarson and Tony Bryan. — Oxford : Phaidon, 1981. — 256p : ill(some col.) ; 23cm
Bibliography: p252. — Includes index
ISBN 0-7148-2173-x : £9.95 : CIP rev. B82-22999

623.4'1 — Artillery

Ryan, J. W.. Guns, mortars & rockets / J.W. Ryan. — Oxford : Brassey's, 1982. — xiii,227p : ill,forms ; 26cm. — (Battlefield weapons systems & technology ; v.2)
Bibliography: p219-220. — Includes index
ISBN 0-08-028324-1 (cased) : Unpriced : CIP rev.
ISBN 0-08-028325-x (pbk) : £6.50 B82-12418

623.4'1'0212 — Artillery — *Technical data*

Brassey's artillery of the world : guns, howitzers, mortars, guided weapons, rockets and ancillary equipment in service with the regular and reserve forces of all nations / editor and chief consultant Shelford Bidwell ; co-authors, compilers and consultants Brian Blunt ... [et al.]. — 2nd ed. fully rev. and updated, co-ordinating editor John Buchanan-Brown. — Oxford : Brassey's, 1981. — 246p : ill ; 32cm
Previous ed.: 1977. — Includes index
ISBN 0-08-027035-2 : £22.50 : CIP rev. B81-16399

623.4'1'094 — Napoleonic Wars. Military forces. Artillery

Wise, Terence. Artillery equipments of the Napoleonic Wars / text by Terence Wise ; colour plates by Richard Hook. — London : Osprey, 1979 (1980 [printing]). — 40p,A-Hp of plates : ill(some col.) ; 25cm. — (Men-at-arms series ; 96)
English text, English, French and German captions to plates
ISBN 0-85045-336-4 (pbk) : Unpriced B82-10733

623.4'2'0228 — Scale model cannon. Construction — *Manuals*

Stewart, Richard. Scale model cannon. — London : Murray, June 1982. — [64]p
ISBN 0-7195-3888-2 : £4.95 : CIP entry B82-14502

623.4'4 — Military equipment: Firearms

Marchant Smith, C. J.. Small arms & cannons / C.J. Marchant Smith and P.R. Haslam. — Oxford : Brassey's, 1982. — xvi,202p : ill,forms ; 26cm. — (Battlefield weapons systems & technology ; v.5)
Bibliography: p197. — Includes index
ISBN 0-08-028330-6 (cased) : Unpriced : CIP rev.
ISBN 0-08-028331-4 (pbk) : £6.50 B82-12419

623.4'41 — European swords, *1050-1850*

North, Anthony. An introduction to European swords / Anthony North. — London : H.M.S.O., 1982. — 48p : ill(some col.),1port ; 26cm
At head of cover title: Victoria & Albert Museum. — Bibliography: p47-48
ISBN 0-11-290378-9 : £3.50 B82-14858

623.4'41'09411 — Scotland. Military equipment: Weapons & armour, *1100-1800*

Scottish weapons and fortifications 1100-1800 / edited by David H. Caldwell. — Edinburgh : John Donald, 1981. — xvii,452p : ill,maps,plans,ports ; 25cm
Bibliography: pvii-x. — Includes index
ISBN 0-85976-047-2 : £18.00
Also classified at 623'.1'09411 B82-08869

623.4'425 — Essex. Epping Forest *(District)*. Military equipment industries: Firearms industries. Factories. Pattern rooms: Enfield Pattern Room. Stock: British rifles, *1695-1958 — Catalogues*

British rifles : a catalogue of the Enfield Pattern Room. — London : H.M.S.O., 1981. — vii,79p : ill ; 30cm
At head of title: Ministry of Defence
ISBN 0-11-771930-7 (pbk) : £5.75 B82-08168

623.4'43 — Military equipment: Pistols & revolvers, *to 1945*

Ezell, Edward C.. Handguns of the world. — London : Arms & Armour Press, Nov.1981. — [768]p
ISBN 0-85368-504-5 : £18.50 : CIP entry B81-30426

623.4'5 — Military equipment: Ammunition

Goad, K. J. W.. Ammunition : (including grenades and mines) / K.J.W. Goad and D.H.J. Halsey. — Oxford : Brassey's, 1982. — xix,289p : ill ; 26cm. — (Battlefield weapons systems & technology ; v.3)
Includes index
ISBN 0-08-028326-8 (cased) : Unpriced : CIP rev.
ISBN 0-08-028327-6 (pbk) : £8.75 B82-03730

623.4'5 — Underground nuclear explosions. Identification & monitoring — *Conference proceedings*

Identification of seismic sources - earthquake or underground explosion : proceedings of the NATO Advanced Study Institute held at Voksenåsen, Oslo, Norway, September 8-18, 1980 / edited by Eystein S. Husebye and Svein Mykkeltveit. — Dordrecht ; London : D. Reidel, c1981. — xii,876p : ill,maps ; 25cm. — (NATO advanced study institutes series. Series C. Mathematical and physical sciences ; v.74)
Includes index
ISBN 90-277-1320-0 : Unpriced
Primary classification 551.2'2 B82-00485

623.4'5119 — Nuclear weapons. Development. International political aspects, *to 1982*

Jacobsen, C. G.. The nuclear era. — Nottingham : Spokesman, Nov.1982. — [200]p
ISBN 0-85124-346-0 (cased) : £14.50 : CIP entry
ISBN 0-85124-347-9 (pbk) : £4.50 B82-32303

623.4'5119'072042646 — Suffolk. Orford. Nuclear weapons. Research organisations: A.W.R.E. Orfordness, *to 1971*

Kinsey, Gordon. Orfordness - secret site : a history of the establishment 1915-1980 / by Gordon Kinsey ; foreword by Arnold Fredric Wilkins ; Mr Wilkins also provided the chapters on the early development of radar at Orfordness. — Lavenham : Terence Dalton, 1981. — xi,180p : ill,maps,ports ; 24cm
Maps on lining papers. — Includes index
ISBN 0-86138-006-1 : £8.95 B82-09922

623.4'51954 — Cruise missiles

Sorrels, Charles A.. Cruise missiles. — London : Croom Helm, Nov.1982. — [384]p
ISBN 0-7099-2359-7 : £14.95 : CIP entry B82-27939

623.74'6 — Military aeroplanes. Design — *Conference proceedings*

Design for military aircraft operability : Thursday 7th February 1980 / The Royal Aeronautical Society. — London (4 Hamilton Place, W1V 3BQ) : The Society, [1980?]. — 1v.(various pagings) : ill ; 30cm
Conference papers
Unpriced (pbk) B82-07063

623.74'6 — Military aircraft

Green, William, *1927-*. Observer's directory of military aircraft / William Green, Gordon Swanborough. — London : Warne, c1982. — 256p : ill ; 25cm
Includes index
ISBN 0-7232-2796-9 : £9.95 B82-35424

World encyclopedia of military aircraft / edited by Enzo Angelucci ; [written by Paolo Matricardi ; translated from the Italian by S.M. Harris]. — London : Jane's, 1981. — 546p : ill (some col.),plans(some col.) ; 32cm
Translation of: Atlante enciclopedico degli aerei militari del mondo dal 1914 a oggi. — Bibliography: p520-522. — Includes index
ISBN 0-7106-0148-4 : £40.00 B82-00024

623.74'6'0212 — Military aircraft — *Technical data*

Munson, Kenneth. The Blandford book of warplanes / by Kenneth Munson ; illustrated by John W. Wood and associates. — Poole : Blandford, 1981. — vi,122p : ill(some col.) ; 26cm
Includes index
ISBN 0-7137-1106-x : £5.95 B82-04398

Swanborough, Gordon. Military aircraft of the world. — [New ed.] / Gordon Swanborough. — London : Ian Allan, 1981. — 224p : ill ; 23cm
Previous ed.: i.e.4th ed. / by John W.R. Taylor and Gordon Swanborough. 1979. — Includes index
ISBN 0-7110-1139-7 : £6.95 B82-07366

623.74'6044'0943 — Germany. *Luftwaffe*. Military jet aeroplanes, *to 1945 — Technical data*

Masters, David. German jet genesis / David Masters. — London : Jane's, 1982. — 142p : ill ; 29cm
Bibliography: p142
ISBN 0-7106-0186-7 : £8.95 B82-27875

623.74'6047 — Harrier aeroplanes

Gunston, Bill. Harrier / Bill Gunston. — London : Ian Allan, 1981. — 112p : ill(some col.) ; 24cm. — (Modern combat aircraft ; 13)
ISBN 0-7110-1071-4 : £6.95 B82-07363

623.74'6047 — Military helicopters — *Technical data*

Polmar, Norman. Military helicopters of the world : military rotary-wing aircraft since 1917 / by Norman Polmar and Floyd D. Kennedy, Jr. — London : Arms and Armour, c1981. — x,370p : ill ; 26cm
Ill on lining papers. — Includes index
ISBN 0-85368-238-0 : £14.50 B82-08160

623.74'6047 — Military helicopters, *to 1981 — Technical data*

Gunston, Bill. An illustrated guide to military helicopters / Bill Gunston. — London : Salamander, c1981. — 159p : ill(some col.) ; 23cm
Ill on lining papers
ISBN 0-86101-110-4 : £3.95 B82-07994

623.74'6'09 — Military aircraft, *to 1980 — For children*

Kershaw, Andrew. Guide to combat aircraft / Andrew Kershaw ; illustrated by Ron Jobson and Jim Dugdale ; edited by Bill Bruce. — London : Pan, 1980. — 24p : col.ill ; 22cm. — (A Piccolo explorer book)
Bibliography: p24. — Includes index
ISBN 0-330-26160-6 (pbk) : £0.75 B82-13178

623.74'6'0904 — Military aeroplanes, *1918-1939 — Technical data*

Taylor, Michael J. H.. Warplanes : of the world 1918-1939 / Michael J.H. Taylor. — London : Ian Allan, 1981. — 192p : ill ; 23cm
Includes index
ISBN 0-7110-1078-1 : £6.95 B82-01611

623.74'6'091717 — Warsaw Pact air forces. Military aircraft — *Illustrations*

Gething, M. J.. Warsaw Pact air power in the 1980s. — London : Arms & Armour Press, Sept.1982. — [68]p. — (Warbirds illustrated ; 8)
ISBN 0-85368-546-0 (pbk) : £3.95 : CIP entry B82-20837

623.74'6'091821 — North Atlantic Treaty Organization air forces. Military aircraft — *Illustrations*

Gething, M. J.. NATO air power in the 1980s. — London : Arms & Armour Press, Sept.1982. — [68]p. — (Warbirds illustrated ; 7)
ISBN 0-85368-545-2 (pbk) : £3.95 : CIP entry B82-20836

623.74'6'0941 — Great Britain. Military aircraft, *1914-1980*

Bowyer, Chaz. The encyclopedia of British military aircraft. — London : Arms and Armour Press, Apr.1982. — [224]p
ISBN 0-85368-517-7 : £10.95 : CIP entry B82-04796

623.74'6'0941 — Great Britain. *Royal Air Force*. Aeroplanes, *to 1980*

Turner, Michael, *1934-*. Royal Air Force : the aircraft in service since 1918 / paintings by Michael Turner ; main text by Chaz Bowyer ; foreword by Raymond Baxter. — London : Hamlyn, c1981. — 208p : ill(some col.) ; 29cm
Bibliography: p205. — Includes index
ISBN 0-600-34933-0 : £8.95 B82-00072

Turner, Michael, *1934-*. Royal Air Force : the aircraft in service since 1918 / paintings by Michael Turner ; main text by Chaz Bowyer ; foreword by Raymond Baxter. — London : Hamlyn, c1981 (1982 [printing]). — 208p : ill (some col.) ; 29cm
Bibliography: p205. — Includes index
ISBN 0-600-34933-0 : £8.95 B82-27140

623.74'6'0941 — Great Britain. *Royal Flying Corps*. Aircraft, *1912-1918*

Bruce, J. M.. The aeroplanes of the Royal Flying Corps (Military Wing). — London : Putnam, May 1982. — [600]p
ISBN 0-370-30084-x : £25.00 : CIP entry B82-06733

623.74'6'0941 — Great Britain. *Royal Navy*. Aircraft, *to 1981*

Ellis, Paul, *1946-*. Aircraft of the Royal Navy / Paul Ellis. — London : Jane's, 1982. — 176p : ill ; 27cm
Includes index
ISBN 0-7106-0135-2 : £8.95 B82-22936

623.74'6'0943 — German military forces. Military aircraft, *to 1980 — Encyclopedias*

Philpott, Bryan. The encyclopedia of German military aircraft / Bryan Philpott. — London : Arms and Armour, 1980. — 192p : ill(some col.) ; 29cm. — (A Bison book)
Bibliography: p192. — Includes index
ISBN 0-85368-427-8 : £10.95 : CIP rev. B81-23820

623.74'6'0973 — American military forces. Military aircraft, *1939-1945 — Encyclopaedias*

Munson, Kenneth. American aircraft of World War 2 in colour / Kenneth Munson ; design and art editor John W. Wood. — Poole : Blandford, 1982. — 160p : ill(some col.),1map ; 26cm
Bibliography: p158. — Includes index
ISBN 0-7137-0944-8 : £9.95 : CIP rev. B81-00949

623.74'6'0973 — United States. *Air Force*. Military aircraft, *1970-1979 — Illustrations*
Peacock, Lindsay T.. U.S. Air Force in the 1970s. — London : Arms and Armour Press, Jan.1982. — [68]p. — (Warbirds illustrated series ; 3)
ISBN 0-85368-438-3 : £3.50 : CIP entry
B81-33782

623.74'6'0973 — United States. *Air Force*. Military aircraft, *ca 1950-1980*
Nalty, Bernard C.. An illustrated guide to the air war over Vietnam : aircraft of the Southeast Asia conflict / Bernard C. Nalty, George M. Watson, Jacob Neufeld. — London : Salamander, c1981. — 159p : ill(some col.) ; 23cm
Ill on lining papers
ISBN 0-86101-080-9 : £3.95 B82-07996

623.74'6'0973 — United States. *Navy*. Military aircraft, *1970-1979 — Illustrations*
Peacock, Lindsay T.. U.S. Navy combat aircraft in the 1970s. — London : Arms and Armour Press, Jan.1982. — [68]p. — (Warbirds illustrated series ; 4)
ISBN 0-85368-458-8 : £3.50 : CIP entry
B81-33781

623.74'63 — Avro Lancaster aeroplanes, *to ca 1970*
Franklin, Neville. Lancaster : their history and how to model them / Neville Franklin and Gerald Scarborough. — Cambridge : Stephens, 1979. — 96p : ill ; 26cm. — (Classic aircraft ; no.6)
Ill on lining papers. — Bibliography: p96
Unpriced (corrected) B82-17092

Sweetman, Bill. Avro Lancaster / text by Bill Sweetman ; illustrations by Rikyu Watanabe. — London : Jane's, 1982. — 56p,8folded : ill (some col.) ; 33cm. — (Jane's aircraft spectaculars)
ISBN 0-7106-0132-8 : £6.95 B82-40635

623.74'63 — Boeing B-17 aeroplanes
Lloyd, Alwyn T.. B-17 Flying Fortress : in detail & scale / Alwyn T. Lloyd, Terry D. Moore. — Fallbrook, Ca. : Aero ; London : Arms and Armour. — (Detail & scale series)
Pt.1: Production versions. — c1981. — 72p : ill (some col.) ; 28cm
Text on inside cover. — Bibliography: p72
ISBN 0-85368-500-2 (pbk) : Unpriced : CIP rev. B81-25735

623.74'63 — Boeing B17 aeroplanes, *to 1979*
Scutts, Jerry. B-17 Flying Fortress / Jerry Scutts. — Cambridge : Stephens, 1982. — 120p : ill ; 25cm. — (Classic aircraft)
Ill on lining papers
ISBN 0-85059-464-2 : £7.95 : CIP rev.
B82-01420

623.74'63 — British Aerospace Harrier aeroplanes, *to 1980*
Mason, Francis K.. Harrier / Francis K. Mason. — Cambridge : Stephens, 1981. — 185p : ill ; 25cm
Bibliography: p179-180. — Includes index
ISBN 0-85059-501-0 : £9.95 : CIP rev.
B81-27992

623.74'63 — DeHavilland Mosquito aeroplanes, *to 1963*
Sweetman, Bill. Mosquito / text by Bill Sweetman ; illustrated by Rikyu Watanabe. — London : Jane's, 1981. — 52p : ill(some col.),plans ; 34cm. — (Jane's aircraft spectaculars)
ISBN 0-7106-0131-x : £5.95 B82-07910

623.74'63 — Dive bombers, *to 1959*
Smith, Peter C. (Peter Charles), *1920-*. Dive bomber!. — Ashbourne : Moorland, Sept.1982. — [192]p
ISBN 0-86190-062-6 : £7.95 : CIP entry
B82-22818

623.74'63 — McDonnell Douglas F-18 Hornet aeroplanes, *to 1981*
Linn, Don. F-18 in detail and scale. — London : Arms and Armour, Sept.1982. — [64]p
ISBN 0-85368-524-x (pbk) : £3.95 : CIP entry
B82-25918

623.74'64 — British Aerospace AV-8B Harrier II aeroplanes
Harrier : V/STOL report : January 1982. — [Great Britain] : [S.n.], [1982] (Camberley : Staffmace). — [16]p : ill(some col.),ports ; 30cm
Unpriced (pbk) B82-23270

623.74'64 — Falcon F-16 aeroplanes
Kinzey, Bert. F-16 A & B Fighting Falcon : in detail and scale / Bert Kinzey. — Fallbrook : Aero ; London : Arms and Armour, 1982. — 72p : ill(some col.),plans ; 28cm. — (Detail & scale series)
Bibliography: p72
ISBN 0-85368-552-5 (pbk) : Unpriced : CIP rev. B82-11112

623.74'64 — General Dynamics F-111 aeroplanes, *to 1981*
Kinzey, Bert. F-111, Aardvark. — London : Arms and Armour, July 1982. — [96]p
ISBN 0-85368-512-6 (pbk) : £3.95 : CIP entry
B82-17216

623.74'64 — McDonnell Douglas F-15 Eagle aeroplanes, *to 1980*
Ethell, Jeffrey. F-15 Eagle / Jeff Ethell. — London : Ian Allan, 1981. — 128p : ill(some col.) ; 24cm. — (Modern combat aircraft ; 12)
ISBN 0-7110-1073-0 : £7.95 B82-11218

623.74'64 — McDonnell Douglas Phantom II aeroplanes, *to 1980*
Kinsey, Bert. F-4 Phantom II (USAF) in detail and scale. — London : Arms and Armour Press. — (Detail and scale series ; 1)
Part 1. — Oct.1981. — [72]p
ISBN 0-85368-501-0 (pbk) : £3.95 : CIP entry
B81-25736

Kinzey, Bert. F-4 Phantom II in detail & scale. — London : Arms and Armour
Pt.2. — Sept.1982. — [64]p
ISBN 0-85368-525-8 (pbk) : £3.94 : CIP entry
B82-25917

623.74'64 — Mitsubishi Zero aeroplanes, *to 1945*
Horikoshi, Jiro. Eagles of Mitsubishi : the story of Zero fighter / by Jiro Horikoshi ; translated by Shojiro Shindo and Harold N. Wantiez. — London : Orbis, 1982, c1981. — xi,160p,[8]p of plates : ill,1port ; 24cm
Translated from the Japanese. — Includes index
ISBN 0-85613-397-3 : £10.00 B82-16571

623.74'64 — Northrop F-5E & F Tiger II aeroplanes, *to 1981*
Kinzey, Bert. F-5E & F Tiger II. — London : Arms and Armour, Aug.1982. — [96]p
ISBN 0-85368-553-3 (pbk) : £3.95 : CIP entry
B82-21970

623.74'64 — Supermarine Spitfire aeroplanes, *to 1968*
Eastman, Gary. The Spitfire / by Gary Eastman. — [Ivybridge] ([29 Fore St., Ivybridge, South Devon]) : [G. Eastman], [1981]. — 16p : ill ; 21cm
Unpriced (pbk) B82-11076

Price, Alfred. The Spitfire story / Alfred Price ; foreword by Jeffrey Quill. — London : Jane's, 1982. — 256p,[6]p of plates : ill(some col.),1map,ports ; 29cm
Bibliography: p252. — Includes index
ISBN 0-7106-0188-3 : £15.00 B82-29487

623.74'64'09044 — Axis air forces. Fighter aeroplanes, *1939-1945*
Gunston, Bill. An illustrated guide to German, Italian and Japanese fighters of World War II : major fighters and attack aircraft of the Axis powers / Bill Gunston. — London : Salamander, c1980. — 159p : ill(some col.) ; 23cm
Col. ill on lining papers
ISBN 0-86101-064-7 : £2.95 B82-17716

623.74'64'09045 — Fighter aeroplanes, *1950-1960*
Gunston, Bill. Fighters of the fifties / Bill Gunston. — Cambridge : Stephens, 1981. — 248p : ill ; 25cm
ISBN 0-85059-463-4 : £10.95 : CIP rev.
B81-20128

623.74'7 — Austin K5 army land vehicles — *Technical data*
Conniford, Mike. Austin K5 / by Mike Conniford. — Reading : Inkpen Art, c1982. — 9p : ill ; 15x21cm. — (Military vehicle series ; MV2)
Cover title. — Text on inside cover
ISBN 0-907403-12-3 (pbk) : Unpriced
B82-14998

623.74'7 — Bedford & Vauxhall military vehicles, *to 1981*
Vanderveen, Bart H.. Kaleidoscope of Bedford and Vauxhall military vehicles / by Bart Vanderveen. — [London] : Warne, 1982. — 96p : ill,2ports ; 31cm
Ill on lining papers. — Includes index
ISBN 0-7232-2875-2 : £6.95 B82-30621

623.74'7 — Germany. *Wehrmacht*. Military half-tracked vehicles: SdKfz 251, *to 1945*
Culver, Bruce. The SdKfz 251 half track. — London : Osprey, Jan.1983. — [40]p. — (Vanguard ; 32)
ISBN 0-85045-429-8 (pbk) : £3.50 : CIP entry
B82-32636

623.74'7 — Military vehicles: A.E.C. Matador lorries
Conniford, Mike. A.E.C. matador / researched by Mike Conniford. — Reading : Inkpen Art, c1980. — 17p : ill ; 30cm. — (Military vehicle pamphlet ; no.4)
Cover title
ISBN 0-907403-03-4 (pbk) : £1.00 B82-36196

623.74'7 — Military vehicles: Austin K6 lorries
Conniford, Mike. Austin K6 / researched by Mike Conniford. — Reading : Inkpen Art, 1980. — 17p : ill ; 30cm. — (Military vehicle pamphlet ; no.3)
Cover title
ISBN 0-907403-02-6 (pbk) : £1.00 B82-36193

623.74'7 — Military vehicles: Bedford OY lorries
Conniford, Mike. Bedford OY / researched by Mike Conniford. — Reading : Inkpen Art, 1979. — 17p : ill ; 30cm. — (Military vehicle pamphlet ; no.1)
Cover title
ISBN 0-907403-00-x (pbk) : £1.00 B82-36194

623.74'7 — Military vehicles: Leyland Retriever lorries
Conniford, Mike. Leyland retriever / researched by Mike Conniford. — Reading : Inkpen Art, c1979. — 17p : ill ; 30cm. — (Military vehicle pamphlet ; no.2)
Cover title
ISBN 0-907403-01-8 (pbk) : £1.00 B82-36195

623.74'7 — United States. *Army*. Military half-tracked vehicles, *to 1945*
Zaloga, Steven J.. US half tracks of World War II. — London : Osprey, Jan.1983. — [40]p. — (Vanguard ; 31)
ISBN 0-85045-481-6 (pbk) : £3.50 : CIP entry
B82-32637

623.74'7'09 — Military wheeled vehicles, *to 1980 — Technical data*
Vanderveen, Bart H.. A source book of military support vehicles / compiled for the Olyslager Organisation by Bart H. Vanderveen. — London : Ward Lock, 1980. — 128p : ill ; 12x17cm
Includes index
ISBN 0-7063-6051-6 : £2.95 B82-06539

623.74'72 — Humber four-wheel-drive light military vehicles
Conniford, Mike. Humber F.W.D.. — Reading : Inkpen Art Productions, c1982. — 9p : ill ; 21cm. — (Military vehicle series ; MV4)
Author: Mike Conniford
ISBN 0-907403-16-6 (pbk) : Unpriced
B82-26617

623.74'72'09044 — Military land support vehicles, *1939-1945*
Church, John. Military vehicles of World War 2 / John Church. — Poole : Blandford, 1982. — 160p : ill(some col.) ; 26cm
Includes index
ISBN 0-7137-1044-6 : £8.95 : CIP rev.
B82-04863

623.74′722′09 — Jeep military vehicles, ***to 1980***

Clayton, Michael, *1924-*. Jeep. — Newton Abbot : David & Charles, c1982. — 125p : ill,3ports ; 24cm
Includes index
ISBN 0-7153-8066-4 : £9.95 : CIP rev.
B82-21101

Jeudy, Jean-Gabriel. The Jeep / Jean-Gabriel Jeudy, Marc Tararine ; translated by Gordon Wilkins. — [London] : Warne, c1981. — 272p : ill(some col.),ports ; 23x25cm. — (Warne's transport library)
Translation of: La Jeep un défi au temps
ISBN 0-7232-2872-8 : £12.95 B82-05171

623.74′75 — Vietnamese wars. Armoured combat vehicles, ***1945-1975***

Dunstan, Simon. Vietnam tracks : armour in battle 1945-75. — London : Osprey, Oct.1982. — [192]p
ISBN 0-85045-472-7 : £9.95 : CIP entry
B82-24254

623.74′75′0212 — Armoured combat vehicles — ***Technical data***

Foss, Christopher F.. Armoured fighting vehicles of the world / Christopher F. Foss. — [New ed.]. — London : Ian Allan, 1982. — 208p : ill ; 23cm
Previous ed. ie 3rd ed.: 1977. — Includes index
ISBN 0-7110-1105-2 : £7.95 B82-26953

Messenger, Charles. The observer's book of tanks : and other armoured vehicles / Charles Messenger ; with silhouettes by Michael Badrocke. — London : Warne, 1981. — 192p : ill ; 15cm
Includes index
ISBN 0-7232-1602-9 : £1.95 B82-38816

A **Source** book of armoured fighting vehicles / compiled for the Olyslager Organisation by Bart H. Vanderveen. — London : Ward Lock, 1981. — 128p : chiefly ill ; 12x17cm. — (Source books)
Originally published: 1973. — Includes index
ISBN 0-7063-6096-6 : Unpriced B82-11461

623.74′75′0973 — United States. ***Army.*** **Armoured combat vehicles**

Zaloga, Steven J.. Modern American armour. — London : Arms and Armour Press, Jan.1982. — [88]p
ISBN 0-85368-248-8 : £6.95 : CIP entry
B81-33780

623.74′752 — Armoured combat vehicles: Leopard tanks

Barker, A. J.. Leopard / A.J. Barker. — London : Ian Allan, 1981. — 112p : ill ; 25cm
Bibliography: p111-112
ISBN 0-7110-1036-6 : £6.95 B82-01617

623.74′752 — Armoured combat vehicles: M48 tanks, ***to 1980***

Tillotson, Geoffrey, *1948-*. M48 / Geoffrey Tillotson. — London : Ian Allan, 1981. — 112p : ill,plans ; 24cm. — (Modern combat vehicles ; 4)
ISBN 0-7110-1107-9 : £6.95 B82-11219

623.74′752′0941 — Great Britain. ***Army.*** **Armoured combat vehicles: Tanks,** ***1939-1945***

Chamberlain, Peter. The British and American tanks of World War II : the complete illustrated history of British, American and Commonwealth tanks, gun motor carriages and special purpose vehicles, 1939-1945 / by Peter Chamberlain and Chris Ellis. — London : Arms and Armour, 1969 (1981 [printing]). — 222p : ill ; 29cm
Unpriced (cased)
ISBN 0-85368-033-7
Also classified at 623.74′752′0973 B82-01621

623.74′752′0947 — Union of Soviet Socialist Republics. ***Armiia.*** **Armoured combat vehicles: Heavy tanks,** ***1935-1967***

Zaloga, Steven J.. Soviet heavy tanks / text by Steven J. Zaloga and James Grandsen ; colour plates by Steven J. Zaloga. — London : Osprey, 1981. — 40p,A-Hp of plates : ill(some col.),1plan,2ports ; 25cm. — (Vanguard series ; 24)
English text, English, French and German captions to plates
ISBN 0-85045-422-0 (pbk) : Unpriced
B82-10738

623.74′752′0973 — United States. ***Army.*** **Armoured combat vehicles: Tanks,** ***1939-1945***

Chamberlain, Peter. The British and American tanks of World War II : the complete illustrated history of British, American and Commonwealth tanks, gun motor carriages and special purpose vehicles, 1939-1945 / by Peter Chamberlain and Chris Ellis. — London : Arms and Armour, 1969 (1981 [printing]). — 222p : ill ; 29cm
Unpriced (cased)
ISBN 0-85368-033-7
Primary classification 623.74′752′0941
B82-01621

623.74′9 — Military artificial satellites

Outer space — a new dimension of the arms race / edited by Bhupendra Jasani ; Stockholm International Peace Research Institute. — London : Taylor & Francis, 1982. — xviii,423p : ill,maps ; 24cm
Conference papers. — Includes index
ISBN 0-85066-231-1 : £18.50 : CIP rev.
B82-11985

623.8 — SHIPS, SHIPBUILDING AND SEAMANSHIP

623.8′009469 — Portuguese vernacular boats

Filgueiras, Octavio Lixa. The decline of Portuguese regional boats / by Octavio Lixa Filgueiras ; edited by Eric McKee. — London : Trustees of the National Maritime Museum, 1980. — iv,39p : ill,1map ; 30cm. — (Maritime monographs and reports, ISSN 0307-8590 ; no.47)
Translated from the Portuguese. —
Bibliography: p38-39
ISBN 0-905555-40-6 (pbk) : Unpriced
B82-11050

623.8′1 — Boats. Design

Kemmish, R. E. W. Yacht and boat design / R.E.W. Kemmish. — Sevenoaks : Newnes Technical, 1980. — 100p : ill ; 17cm. — (Questions & answers)
Bibliography: p97. — Includes index
ISBN 0-408-00460-6 (pbk) : £1.75 : CIP rev.
B80-12926

623.8′2 — Indonesia. Praus

Hawkins, Clifford W.. Praus of Indonesia / Clifford W. Hawkins. — London : Nautical Books, 1982. — 134p : ill(some col.),1map ; 31cm
Bibliography: p133. — Includes index
ISBN 0-333-31810-2 : £22.00 B82-35081

623.8′2 — Ships. Construction

Kemp, John F. (John Frederick). Ship construction sketches and notes / Kemp & Young. — 3rd ed. — London : Stanford Maritime, 1971, c1976 (1981 [printing]). — 135p : ill,plans ; 21cm
Previous ed.: 1967. — Includes index
ISBN 0-540-00360-3 (pbk) : £2.95 B82-05043

623.8′2′00321 — Ships — ***Encyclopaedias***

Blackburn, Graham. The illustrated dictionary of nautical terms / Graham Blackburn. — Newton Abbot : David & Charles, 1982. — 349p : ill ; 24cm
Originally published: New York : Overlook Press, 1981
ISBN 0-7153-8296-9 : £9.95 : CIP rev.
B81-38302

623.8′2′007 — Great Britain. Shipbuilding industries. Glass fibre reinforced plastics laminators. Industrial training — ***Proposals***

Shipbuilding Industry Training Board. Recommendations for the training of G.R.P. laminators / Shipbuilding Industry Training Board. — [South Harrow] ([Raeburn House, Northolt Rd., South Harrow, Middx]) : [The Board], [1980]. — 21p : forms ; 21cm. — (Training policy statement / Shipbuilding Industry Training Board ; no.9)
Cover title
£2.25 (pbk) B82-36190

623.8′2′0071041 — Great Britain. Schools. Students, 5-14 years. Curriculum subjects: Ships — ***For teaching***

Bryant, John, *1945-*. Shipshape / John Bryant. — Basingstoke : Globe Education, 1982. — 53p : ill,forms ; 30cm. — (Science horizons. Level 2b)
Published for West Sussex County Council. —
Bibliography: p13
ISBN 0-333-32153-7 (pbk) : Unpriced
B82-38806

623.8′2′009 — Ships, ***to 1980***

The Ship. — London : H.M.S.O.
1: Rafts, boats and ships : from prehistoric times to the medieval era / Sean McGrail. — 1981. — 88p : ill,2maps ; 21cm
At head of title: National Maritime Museum. — Maps on lining papers. — Bibliography: p83-86. — Includes index
ISBN 0-11-290312-6 : £2.95 B82-02761

The Ship. — London : H.M.S.O.
3: Tiller and whipstaff : the development of the sailing ship 1400-1700 / Alan McGowan. — 1981. — 59p : ill,2maps ; 21cm
At head of title: National Maritime Museum. — Maps on lining papers. — Bibliography: p58. — Includes index
ISBN 0-11-290313-4 : £2.95 B82-02762

The Ship. — London : H.M.S.O.
10: The revolution in merchant shipping 1950-1980 / Ewan Corlett. — 1981. — 60p : ill,1map,1plan ; 21cm
At head of title: National Maritime Museum. — Ill on lining papers. — Includes index
ISBN 0-11-290320-7 : £2.95 B82-02763

623.8′2′00941 — Great Britain. Preserved ships

Burton, Anthony. The past afloat / Anthony Burton ; photography by Clive Coote. — London : Deutsch, 1982. — 191p : ill(some col.),2ports ; 26cm
Accompanies a series broadcast on BBC2, Spring 1982. — Bibliography: p185. — Includes index
ISBN 0-233-97433-4 : £12.95
ISBN 0-563-16480-8 (BBC) B82-20810

623.8′2′00941 — Great Britain. Preserved ships — ***Serials***

Maritime Trust. *Friends of the Maritime Trust.* Newsletter / Friends of the Maritime Trust. — No.1 (Spring 1981)-. — London (16 Ebury St., SW1W OLH) : Maritime Trust, 1981-. — v. : ill,maps,ports ; 22cm
Quarterly
ISSN 0263-1350 = Newsletter - Friends of the Maritime Trust : Unpriced B82-17238

623.8′2′0094107402 — England. Art galleries. Exhibits: Items associated with British ships, ***to 1982 — Catalogues***

The **Voyage** of life : ship imagery in art, literature and life. — Nottingham (Department of Fine Art, Portland Building, University Park, Nottingham) : Nottingham University Art Gallery, 1982. — [36]p : ill ; 19x23cm
Catalogue of an exhibition in celebration of Maritime England Year. — Text on inside cover
Unpriced (pbk) B82-25682

623.8′201 — Model ships. Construction

Mansir, Richard. A guide to ship modelling. — London : Arms & Armour Press, Sept.1981. — [320]p
ISBN 0-85368-505-3 : £18.50 : CIP entry
B81-28206

623.8′201 — Model ships. Construction — *Manuals*
Veenstra, André. Handbook of ship modelling / André Veenstra. — Watford : Model & Allied Publications, 1981. — 242p : ill ; 21cm
Translated from the Dutch
ISBN 0-85242-714-x (pbk) : £5.95 B82-19148

Wilson, Robert A. (Robert Allan). The art of modelling merchant ships / by Robert A. Wilson. — [Preston] ([16 Padway, Penwortham, Preston, Lancs. PR1 9EL]) : [R.A. Wilson], [1982]. — 63p : ill,plans ; 21cm
Ill on inside covers. — Bibliography: p62-63
Unpriced (pbk) B82-31160

623.8′201 — Radio controlled model boats. Construction — *Manuals*
Warring, R. H.. Radio controlled model boats / R.H. Warring. — Watford : Model & Allied Publications, 1981. — 124p : ill ; 21cm
£4.25 (pbk) B82-22218

623.8′202 — Small boats. Construction — *Amateurs′ manuals*
Nicolson, Ian. Build your own boat : building and fitting out for sail and power / Ian Nicolson. — London : Allen & Unwin, 1982. — 198p : ill ; 26cm
Bibliography: p193-194. — Includes index
ISBN 0-04-623014-9 : Unpriced : CIP rev. B81-33910

623.8′202 — Small boats. Hulls. Fitting out — *Amateurs′ manuals*
Everett, David. Home boat-completion : a guide for amateurs to fitting out GRP, ferro-cement, and steel hulls / David Everett. — London : Hale, 1982. — 236p : ill ; 23cm
Includes index
ISBN 0-7091-9480-3 : £9.50 B82-27046

623.8′203′05 — Sailing vessels — *Serials*
Traditional sail review. — Issue 1 (Summer 1981)-. — Maldon (28 Spital Rd, Maldon, Essex CM9 6EB) : Anglian Yacht Services, 1981-. — v. : ill ; 30cm
Quarterly. — Description based on: Issue 2 (Autumn 1981)
ISSN 0263-1431 = Traditional sail review : £7.00 per year B82-18505

623.8′205 — Submersibles. Surveying — *Manuals*
Survey of submersible craft : instructions for the guidance of surveyors / Deparment of Trade. — London ([Ashdown House, Victoria St., SW1E 6RB]) : The Department, 1982. — 91p ; 30cm
£15.00 (pbk) B82-38480

623.8′207 — Glass fibre reinforced plastics boats. Construction — *Amateurs′ manuals*
Flett, John. Building small boats, surf craft and canoes in fibreglass : (materials, equipment, plugs and moulds, trouble shooting, repairs) / John Flett, Jeff Toghill. — London : Stanford Maritime, 1981. — 103p : ill ; 24x17cm
Includes index
ISBN 0-540-07196-x (pbk) : £3.95 B82-05042

623.8′22 — Prahus
Horridge, G. Adrian. The prahu : traditional sailing boat of Indonesia / Adrian Horridge ; with drawings by Chris Snoek. — Kuala Lumpur ; Oxford : Oxford University Press, 1981. — xv,106p,24,Qp of plates : ill(some col.),maps ; 26cm
Maps on lining papers. — Bibliography: p100-101. — Includes index
ISBN 0-19-580499-6 : £22.50 B82-41065

623.8′22 — Wind surfers. Design & construction
Fichtner, Hans. Sailboards custom-made. — London : Stanford Maritime, July 1982. — [128]p
Translation of: Surfboard custom-made
ISBN 0-540-07411-x (pbk) : £6.95 : CIP entry B82-14235

623.8′223 — Yachts: Spray *(Ship)*
Slack, Kenneth E.. In the wake of the Spray / Kenneth E. Slack. — Havant : Mason, 1982, c1966. — xii,274p,[12]p of plates : ill ; 24cm
Originally published: New Brunswick : Rutgers University Press, 1966. — Includes index
ISBN 0-85937-274-x : £9.95 : CIP rev. B81-30282

623.8′224 — South-east England. Sailing barges, *1949-1979 — Personal observations*
Bennett, A. S.. Us bargemen / A.S. Bennett. — Rainham : Meresborough, 1980. — 199p : ill,maps,ports ; 22cm
Maps on lining papers. — Includes index
ISBN 0-905270-20-7 : £6.95 B82-36406

623.8′224′0941 — Great Britain. Merchant sailing ships. Design & constuction, *1775-1815*
MacGregor, David R.. Merchant sailing ships, 1775-1815 : their design and construction / by David R. MacGregor ; drawings and diagrams by the author or from contemporary sources ; additional drawings by P.A. Roberts, T.W. Ward and others. — Watford : Model and Allied Publications, 1980. — viii,218p : ill,facsims ; 25cm
Includes index
ISBN 0-85242-663-1 : £12.50 B82-05904

623.8′231 — Motorboats
Hewitt, Dick. Motor boat and yachting manual. — 19th ed. / Dick Hewitt. — London : Stanford Maritime, 1982. — 336p : ill ; 24cm
Previous ed.: / edited by Tom Cox. 1973. — Includes index
ISBN 0-540-07400-4 : £9.95 : CIP rev. B81-35032

623.8′231 — Small motor cruisers
Gibbs, Tony. The coastal cruiser : a complete guide to the design, selection, purchase, and outfitting of auxiliary sailboats under 30 feet — with a portfolio of successful designs / by Tony Gibbs. — New York ; London : Norton, c1981. — xiii,326p : ill,plans ; 24cm
Bibliography. — Includes index
ISBN 0-393-03267-1 : £17.25 B82-35680

623.8′2314 — Steam launches: Turbinia *(Ship), 1894-1981*
Osler, Adrian. Turbinia. — [Newcastle Upon Tyne] : Tyne and Wear County Council, Museums, [1981?]. — [8]p : ill ; 21cm
Cover title. — Author: Adrian Osler
Unpriced (pbk) B82-05598

623.8′232 — Steamships: Charlotte Dundas *(Ship)*
Bowman, A. Ian. Symington and the Charlotte Dundas / A. Ian Bowman. — [Falkirk] : Falkirk District Council, Dept. of Libraries and Museums, [1981]. — 28p,[16]p of plates : ill,1facsim,3ports ; 21cm. — (Famous residents series) (Falkirk museums publication)
Bibliography: p27
Unpriced (pbk) B82-36924

623.8′234′0916336 — England. Solent. Ferry services. Passenger steamships, *to 1900*
O′Brien, F. T.. Early Solent steamers : a history of local steam navigation / F.T. O′Brien. — 2nd ed. — Glasgow : Brown, Son & Ferguson, 1981. — 254p : ill,facsims,maps,ports ; 22cm
Previous ed.: Newton Abbot : David & Charles, 1973. — Facsims on lining papers. — Includes index
ISBN 0-85174-417-6 : £12.00 B82-27124

623.8′24 — Merchant ships. Construction
Merchant ships : construction, maintenance and operational problems / sponsored by the Society of Consulting Marine Engineers and Ship Surveyors ; organised by Lloyd′s of London Press Ltd. — [London] : [Lloyds of London Press], [1982?]. — 1v.(various pagings) ; 31cm. — (Europort ′81 conferences)
ISBN 0-907432-16-6 : Unpriced B82-31128

623.8′24′0212 — Merchant ships — *Technical data — Serials*
Jane′s merchant ships. — 1982-. — London : Jane′s, 1982-. — v. : ill ; 33cm
ISSN 0263-7030 = Jane′s merchant ships : £45.00 B82-31724

623.8′243′09931 — New Zealand. Passenger ships, *1876-1980*
Plowman, Peter. Passenger ships : of Australia & New Zealand / Peter Plowman. — Greenwich : Conway Maritime
Vol.1: 1876-1912. — 1981. — 224p : ill(some col.) ; 22x28cm
Col.ill on lining papers. — Includes index
ISBN 0-85177-246-3 : £12.50
Primary classification 623.8′243′0994 B82-19944

623.8′243′0994 — Australia. Passenger ships, *1876-1980*
Plowman, Peter. Passenger ships : of Australia & New Zealand / Peter Plowman. — Greenwich : Conway Maritime
Vol.1: 1876-1912. — 1981. — 224p : ill(some col.) ; 22x28cm
Col.ill on lining papers. — Includes index
ISBN 0-85177-246-3 : £12.50
Also classified at 623.8′243′09931 B82-19944

623.8′2432 — Scotland. Strathclyde Region. Firth of Clyde. Passenger paddle steamers, *1850-1968*
Paterson, Alan J. S.. Classic Scottish paddle steamers / Alan J.S. Paterson. — Newton Abbot : David & Charles, c1982. — 207p : ill,2ports ; 23cm
Bibliography: p201-202. — Includes index
ISBN 0-7153-8335-3 : £7.95 : CIP rev. B82-13071

623.8′2432 — Ships: Steam liners
Brinnin, John Malcolm. Beau voyage : life aboard the last great ships / John Malcolm Brinnin ; conceived, compiled and designed by Michel Mohrt and Guy Feinstein ; 331 illustrations. — London : Thames and Hudson, 1982, c1981. — 271p : chiefly ill,1facsim,ports ; 33cm
Originally published: New York : St. Martin′s Press, 1981. — Illustrations originally published as Pacquebots. — Ill on lining papers. — Includes index
ISBN 0-500-01272-5 : £28.00 B82-20419

623.8′245 — Cardiff. Shipping services: D. L. Street Ltd.. Ships: Redbrook *(Ship), 1960-1965*
Heaton, P. M.. The ′Redbrook′, a deep-sea tramp : an account of the management and operation of a South Wales owned vessel in the 1960s / by P.M. Heaton. — Risca : Starling Press, 1981. — 80p,[16]p of plates : ill,forms,1port ; 22cm
Form on lining papers
ISBN 0-9507714-0-6 : £5.00 B82-01930

623.8′245 — Cargo ships. Inspection — *Standards*
International Maritime Organization. Guidelines on mandatory annual surveys, unscheduled inspections of all cargo ships as well as intermediate surveys on tankers of ten years of age and over, under the protocol of 1978 relating to the International Convention for the Safety of Life at Sea, 1974 : (resolution A.413 (XI) as amended by resolution A.465 (XII)). — London : International Maritime Organization, 1982. — 17p : forms ; 25cm
Cover title: Guidelines on surveys under the 1978 SOLAS protocol
ISBN 92-8011-135-3 (pbk) : Unpriced B82-38370

623.8′245 — England. Narrow boats, *to ca 1960 — Illustrations*
Ware, Michael E.. Narrow boats at work / Michael E. Ware. — Ashborne : Moorland, c1980. — 212p : ill,ports ; 26cm
Includes index
ISBN 0-86190-006-5 : £7.95 : CIP rev. B80-24383

623.8′245 — Great Britain. Cargo ships: Steam coasters. Operation, *1920-1940 — Personal observations — Collections*
Spargo, Owen G.. Old time steam coasting / Owen G. Spargo & Thomas H. Thomason ; illustrated by C.V. Waine. — Albrighton : Waine Research, 1982. — 135p : ill(some col.),1facsim,maps(some col.),plans,ports ; 31cm
Includes index
ISBN 0-905184-05-x : £10.95 B82-31752

623.8′245 — Western Scotland. Cargo ships: Steam coasters, *to 1970*
Burrows, George W.. Puffer ahoy! / by George W. Burrows. — Glasgow : Brown, Son & Ferguson, 1981. — xiii,119p : ill(some col.),ports ; 25cm
ISBN 0-85174-419-2 : £14.00 B82-32412

623.8′25 — Warships — *Identification manuals*
Lyon, Hugh. Fighting ships. — London (Elsley Court, 20 Great Titchfield St., W1P 7AD) : Kingfisher, Oct.1981. — [128]p. — (Kingfisher guides)
ISBN 0-86272-006-0 : £2.50 : CIP entry B81-27448

623.8′25′09 — Warships, *to 1980 — For children*

Kershaw, Andrew. Guide to fighting ships / Andrew Kershaw ; illustrated by Cliff and Wendy Meadway ; edited by Bill Bruce. — London : Pan, 1980. — 24p : col.ill,1col.map ; 22cm. — (A Piccolo explorer book)
Bibliography: p24. — Includes index
ISBN 0-330-26159-2 (pbk) : £0.75 B82-13179

623.8′25′0947 — Union of Soviet Socialist Republics. *Voenno-morskoĭ flot.* **Warships** — *Technical data*

Moore, John E.. Warships of the Soviet Navy / John E. Moore. — London : Jane′s, 1981. — 192p : ill,1port ; 27cm
Includes index
ISBN 0-7106-0103-4 : £8.95 B82-07915

623.8′25′0973 — Confederate States of America. *Navy.* **Warships**

Williams, K. J.. Ghost ships of the Mersey : a brief history of Confederate cruisers with Mersey connections / by K.J. Williams. — Birkenhead : Countryvise, [1982?]. — 38p : ill,facsims,ports ; 22cm
Bibliography: p33
ISBN 0-907768-10-5 (pbk) : Unpriced B82-38923

623.8′251 — Naval weapon systems — *Technical data*

Richardson, Doug. Naval armament / Doug Richardson. — London : Jane′s, 1981. — 144p : ill ; 27cm
Includes index
ISBN 0-7106-0127-1 : £8.95 B82-06192

623.8′252′09 — Battleships, *to 1945*

Simkins, Peter. Battleship : the development and decline of the dreadnought / by Peter Simkins. — [London] ([Lambeth Rd, SE1 6HZ]) : Imperial War Museum, 1979. — 80p : ill,ports ; 20x21cm
Cover title. — Text on inside cover. — Bibliography: p76-77
Unpriced (pbk) B82-03981

623.8′252′09 — Battleships, *to 1967*

Preston, Antony. Battleships / Antony Preston. — London : Hamlyn, 1981. — 192p : ill(some col.),col.maps,ports ; 31cm. — (A Bison book)
Includes index
ISBN 0-600-34942-x : £6.95 B82-02721

623.8′252′0941 — Great Britain. *Royal Navy.* **Battle cruisers: Hood** *(Ship) — Illustrations*

Roberts, John, *1945-*. The battlecruiser Hood / by John Roberts. — Greenwich : Conway Maritime, 1982. — 127p : ill,plans ; 25cm. — (Anatomy of the ship)
ISBN 0-85177-250-1 : £8.50 B82-19943

623.8′252′0941 — Great Britain. Royal Navy. Battleships, *1914-1918 — Illustrations*

Burt, R. A.. Battleships of the Grand Fleet. — London : Arms & Armour Press, Dec.1982. — 1v.
ISBN 0-85368-550-9 : £8.95 : CIP entry B82-30716

623.8′252′0943 — Germany. *Kriegsmarine.* **Capital ships,** *1939-1945 — Illustrations*

German capital ships : a selection of German wartime photographs from the Bundesarchiv, Koblenz / [compiled by] Paul Beaver. — Cambridge : Stephens, 1980. — 95p : chiefly ill,1map,ports ; 24cm. — (World War 2 photo album ; no.14)
ISBN 0-85059-396-4 (pbk) : £3.50 : CIP rev. B80-02478

623.8′254′0941 — Great Britain. *Royal Navy.* **Destroyer,** *1893-1981*

Cocker, Maurice. Destroyers of the Royal Navy 1893-1981 / Maurice Cocker. — London : Ian Allan, 1981. — 136p : ill ; 25cm
Ill on lining papers. — Bibliography: p128. — Includes index
ISBN 0-7110-1075-7 : £8.95 B82-01610

623.8′255′0941 — Great Britain. *Royal Navy.* **Aircraft carriers,** *to 1981*

Beaver, Paul. The British aircraft carrier / Paul Beaver. — Cambridge : Stephens, 1982. — 224p : ill,ports ; 24cm
Includes index
ISBN 0-85059-493-6 : £9.95 : CIP rev. B82-01421

623.8′255′0973 — United States. *Navy.* **Escort aircraft carriers,** *to 1970*

Terzibaschitsch, Stefan. Escort carriers and aviation support ships of the US Navy / Stefan Terzibaschitsch. — Greenwich, London : Conway Maritime, 1981. — 208p : ill ; 31cm
Translation of: Flugzeugträger der US Navy. Bd.2. Geleitflugzeugträger. — Bibliography: p192. — Includes index
ISBN 0-85177-242-0 : £15.00 B82-02602

623.8′255′0994 — Australia. *Royal Australian Navy.* **Aircraft carriers: Melbourne** *(Ship), 1955-1981*

Hall, Timothy. HMAS Melbourne. — London : Allen and Unwin, Jan.1983. — [224]p
ISBN 0-86861-284-7 : £10.00 : CIP entry B82-33240

623.8′257′09 — Submarines, *to 1981 — For children*

Compton-Hall, Richard. Submarines / Richard Compton-Hall. — Hove : Wayland, 1982. — 64p : ill(some col.),ports(some col.) ; 24cm. — (Transport and society)
Bibliography: p62. — Includes index
ISBN 0-85340-956-0 : £4.25 B82-28027

623.8′257′0973 — United States. *Navy.* **Submarines,** *to 1980*

Polmar, Norman. The American submarine / Norman Polmar. — Cambridge : Stephens, 1981. — xi,172p : ill,ports ; 26cm
Originally published: Annapolis : Nautical and Aviation Publishing Company of America, 1981. — Includes index
ISBN 0-85059-567-3 : £9.95 B82-12022

623.8′28 — Fishing boats. Stability

Hind, J. Anthony. Stability and trim of fishing vessels : and other small ships / J. Anthony Hind. — 2nd ed. — Farnham : Fishing News Books, 1982. — 132p : ill ; 23cm
Previous ed.: 1967. — Includes index
ISBN 0-85238-121-2 : £7.50 : CIP rev. B82-00183

623.8′28 — Great Britain. Lifeboats, *to 1981*

Kipling, Ray. A source book of lifeboats / Ray Kipling. — London : Ward Lock, 1982. — 127p : ill,1map ; 12x17cm. — (Source books)
Includes index
ISBN 0-7063-6158-x : £3.50 : CIP rev. B82-02632

623.8′29 — Great Britain. Rowing & sailing lifeboats, *to 1957*

Kipling, Ray. Rescue by sail and oar : the story of lifeboats before the days of engine power / by Ray Kipling. — Sulhamstead : Tops′l, 1982. — 64p : chiefly ill,plans ; 25cm
″Published in co-operation with the R.N.L.I.″. — Ill on cover
ISBN 0-906397-08-1 (pbk) : £2.50 B82-31919

623.8′3 — Great Britain. Dockyards. Lifting equipment: Electric overhead mobile cranes. Operators. Industrial training — *Proposals*

Shipbuilding Industry Training Board. Guide to the training of the drivers of cab-operated electric overhead travelling cranes / Shipbuilding Industry Training Board. — South Harrow (Raebarn House, Northolt Rd., South Harrow, Middx.) : The Board, 1981. — 6p : 1form ; 30cm. — (Information paper ; no.6)
£1.00 (pbk) B82-02417

623.8′3 — Great Britain. Dockyards. Personnel: Production managers & supervisors. Industrial training — *Proposals*

Shipbuilding Industry Training Board. The training of shipbuilding and shiprepair production managers and head foremen on first appointment / Shipbuilding Industry Training Board. — South Harrow (Raebarn House, Northolt Rd., South Harrow Middx.) : The Board, 1981. — 9p ; 30cm. — (Information paper ; no.7)
£1.20 (pbk) B82-02421

623.8′3 — Great Britain. *Royal Navy.* **Dockyards,** *to 1981*

MacDougall, Philip. Royal dockyards. — Newton Abbot : David & Charles, Oct.1982. — [216]p
ISBN 0-7153-8148-2 : £11.50 : CIP entry B82-23008

623.8′3 — Ships. Design

Clayton, B. R.. Mechanics of marine vehicles. — London : Spon, May 1982. — [600]p
ISBN 0-419-12110-2 (cased) : £20.00 : CIP entry
ISBN 0-419-12660-0 (pbk) : £10.00 B82-06763

623.8′5 — Ships. Automatic control systems — *Conference proceedings*

Ship operation automation, III : proceedings of the 3rd IFIP/IFAC Symposium, Tokyo, Japan, November 26-29, 1979 / edited by J. Vlietstra. — Amsterdam ; Oxford : North-Holland, 1980. — x,335p : ill ; 31cm. — (Computer applications in shipping and shipbuilding ; v.7)
Includes index
ISBN 0-444-86033-9 : £29.41 B82-31515

623.8′501 — Ships. Auxiliary machinery

Marine auxiliary machinery. — 6th ed. — London : Butterworths, Oct.1982. — [502]p
Previous ed.: 1975
ISBN 0-408-01123-8 : £20.00 : CIP entry B82-24463

623.8′501 — Ships. Machinery. Commissioning & sea trials

Norris, A.. Commissioning and sea trials of machinery in ships / by A. Norris. — London : Published for the Institute of Marine Engineers by Marine Management (Holdings), c1976 (1981 [printing]). — 94p : ill ; 21cm. — (Marine engineering practice ; v.2, pt.12)
ISBN 0-900976-60-8 (pbk) : Unpriced B82-23803

623.8′503 — Ships. Storage batteries

Bagshaw, Norman E.. Batteries on ships. — Chichester : Wiley, Sept.1982. — [200]p. — (Battery applications book series)
ISBN 0-471-90021-4 : £14.00 : CIP entry B82-20641

623.8′504 — Boats. Electronic equipment. Projects — *Amateurs′ manuals*

Penfold, R. A.. Electronic projects for cars and boats / by R.A. Penfold. — London : Babani, 1981. — 85p : ill ; 18cm. — (Bernard Babani ; BP94)
ISBN 0-85934-069-4 (pbk) : £1.95 : CIP rev.
Primary classification 629.2′7 B81-30192

623.8′504 — Ships. Electronic equipment — *Conference proceedings*

Conference on Operation of Ships in Rough Weather *(1980 : Institute of Marine Engineers)*. Conference on Operation of Ships in Rough Weather : the use of onboard instrumentation : Thursday, 21 February, 1980. — London : Institute of Marine Engineers, c1980. — 56p : ill ; 30cm. — (Transactions (C) / Institute of Marine Engineers ; paper C52-C57)
Cover title
ISBN 0-900976-88-8 (pbk) : Unpriced B82-38644

623.8′54 — Ships: Oil tankers. Washing systems

International Maritime Organization. Crude oil washing systems. — Rev. ed. — London : International Maritime Organization, 1982. — 95p : ill,plans ; 30cm
Previous ed.: 197-?
ISBN 92-8011-133-7 (pbk) : Unpriced B82-38369

623.8′56 — British ships. Lights & signalling equipment. Surveying — *Manuals*

Survey of lights and signalling equipment : instructions for the guidance of surveyors. — 2nd ed. — London : H.M.S.O., 1982. — vi,56p : ill ; 29cm
At head of title: Department of Trade. — Previous ed.: 1977. — Includes index
ISBN 0-11-513494-8 (pbk) : £4.20 B82-29711

623.8′6′0294 — Sailing equipment — *Buyers′ guides*

Under sail : equipment for the serious sailor / edited by Tony Meisel ; illustrated by Peter Milne. — [London] : Nautical Books, 1982. — 192p : ill(some col.) ; 28cm. — (A Quarto book)
Includes index
ISBN 0-333-32883-3 : £11.95 B82-32929

623.8′62 — Yachts. Self steering gears. Construction — *Amateurs′ manuals*

Belcher, Bill, *1912-*. Yacht wind-vane steering : how to plan and make your own / Bill Belcher ; foreword by H.G. Hasler. — Newton Abbot : David & Charles, c1982. — 128p : ill ; 26cm
Bibliography: p128
ISBN 0-7153-8176-8 : £8.95 : CIP rev. B81-30576

623.8′7 — Marine engineering

Taylor, D. A.. Introduction to marine engineering. — London : Butterworth, Dec.1982. — [208]p
ISBN 0-408-00586-6 (cased) : £15.00 : CIP entry
ISBN 0-408-00585-8 (pbk) : £8.50 B82-29786

623.8′7234 — Boats. Engines. Conversion from car engines

Warren, Nigel. Marine conversions. — 2nd ed. — London : Granada, Oct.1982. — [192]p
Previous ed.: London : Coles, 1972
ISBN 0-229-11678-7 : £7.95 : CIP entry B82-25922

623.8′72368 — Ships. Diesel engines. Maintenance & repair

Thompson, Chris. The care and repair of small marine diesels. — London : Granada, May 1982. — [120]p
ISBN 0-229-11635-3 : £7.50 : CIP entry B82-10687

623.8′74 — Ships. Fuels. Conservation

Fuel economy in shipping : a Seatrade study. — [Colchester] ([Fairfax House, Colchester CO1 1RJ]) : [Seatrade], [1981]. — 68p : ill(some col.),1map ; 30cm
Cover title
Unpriced (pbk) B82-17264

623.88 — Seamanship — *Stories, anecdotes*

The **Bunkside** companion / [edited by] Robin Knox-Johnston with Ian Dear. — London : Stanley Paul, 1981. — 254p : ill,2maps ; 23cm
ISBN 0-09-146250-9 : £6.95 : CIP rev. B81-26802

623.88′023′41 — Great Britain. Occupations involving the sea — *Career guides*

Watts, Alan S.. Careers at sea. — London : Kogan Page, Oct.1982. — [100]p
ISBN 0-85038-596-2 (cased) : £6.95 : CIP entry
ISBN 0-85038-597-0 (pbk) : £2.50 B82-24742

623.88′03′21 — Seamanship — *Encyclopaedias*

Layton, C. W. T.. Dictionary of nautical words and terms : 8,000 definitions in navigation ... / by C.W.T. Layton. — Rev. 2nd ed. / revised by Peter Clissold. — Glasgow : Brown, Son & Ferguson, c1982. — 393p ; 22cm
Previous ed.: (i.e. rev. ed.) 1973
ISBN 0-85174-422-2 (cased) : £14.00
ISBN 0-85174-296-3 (pbk) : Unpriced B82-30126

623.88′22 — Small sailing boats. Sailing. Seamanship — *Manuals*

Seaway code : a guide for small boat users / HM Coastguard. — Rev. ed. — [London] : HMSO, 1981. — 43p : col.ill,1col.map ; 19cm
Previous ed.: i.e. 2nd ed. London : Department of Trade, 1980. — Bibliography: p40
ISBN 0-11-513491-3 (unbound) : £0.75 B82-30643

Taylor, L. G.. Boat work / by L.G. Taylor. — Glasgow : Brown, Son & Ferguson, 1981. — viii,107p : ill,charts ; 19cm
Includes index
ISBN 0-85174-398-6 : £7.00 B82-00725

623.88′223 — Deep sea yachts. Seamanship

Hiscock, Eric C.. Cruising under sail : incorporating Voyaging under sail / by Eric Hiscock ; with 253 photographs by the author and 102 diagrams. — 3rd ed. — Oxford : Oxford University Press, 1981. — xxiii,551p,64p of plates : ill(some col.),charts (some col.) plans ; 23cm
Previous ed.: 1965. — Ill on lining papers. — Includes index
ISBN 0-19-217599-8 : £12.50 B82-01790

623.88′223 — Sailing boats. Downwind sailing — *Manuals*

Oakeley, John. This is down wind sailing / John Oakeley. — London : Nautical Books, 1981. — 141p : col.ill ; 21cm
ISBN 0-333-32214-2 : £8.95 B82-10630

623.88′223 — Sailing boats. Spinnakers. Handling — *Manuals*

King, R. Bunty. Spinnaker / R. ′Bunty′ King. — vi,185p : ill(some col.) ; 26cm
Bibliography: p182. — Includes index
ISBN 0-229-11605-1 : £8.95 B82-09522

623.88′223 — Seamanship — *For yachting* — *Manuals*

Fairhall, David. Pass your yachtmaster′s / David Fairhall and Mike Peyton. — London : Macmillan, 1982. — xiv,88p,8p of plates : ill (some col.),charts ; 22cm
ISBN 0-333-31957-5 : £5.95 : CIP rev. B81-34142

623.88′223 — Seamanship — *For yachting* — *Practical information* — *Serials*

[The Yachtman′s pocket almanac *(London)*]. The Yachtman′s Pocket almanac. — 1980-. — London : Mitchell Beazley, 1979-. — v. : ill (some col.) ; 20cm
Annual. — Spine title: Mitchell Beazley yachtsman′s pocket almanac. — Description based on: 1982
ISSN 0262-7264 = Yachtman′s pocket almanac (London) : £3.95 B82-11138

623.88′8 — Shipping. Safety measures

Marine personnel safety manual. — [Luton] ([41 Adelaide St., Luton LU1 5DB, Beds.]) : [Lorne & Maclean Marine Publishers], [c1977]. — 58p : ill ; 30cm
At head of title: Polytech International
Unpriced (spiral) B82-38654

623.88′8 — Shipping. Safety measures — *Conference proceedings*

International Marine Safety Symposium *(1980)*. International Marine Safety Symposium 1980 : the human factor aboard ship : ship handling in the 1980′s / sponsored by Safety at Sea. — [London?] : [Safety at Sea] ; [Birmingham] ([Queen′s Way House, Birmingham B4 6BS]) : [Fuel & Metallurgical Journals] [[distributor]], [1980?]. — 170p : ill ; 30cm
Cover title
Unpriced (spiral) B82-35046

International Marine Safety Symposium *(1981)*. International marine safety symposium 1981 : the price of safety / sponsored by Safety at sea. — [London] ([Queensway House, Queensway, Redhill, Surrey]) : [Safety at sea], [1982?]. — 167leaves in various foliations : ill,charts ; 30cm
Cover title
Unpriced (spiral) B82-09527

623.88′8 — Ships. Safety measures

Rutherford, D.. Ship safety personnel. — London : Griffin, Aug.1982. — [128]p
ISBN 0-85264-269-5 : £8.00 : CIP entry B82-23844

623.88′8 — Ships. Safety measures: Automatic control systems — *Conferenc proceedings*

Automation for safety in shipping and offshore petroleum operations : proceedings of the IFIP/IFAC symposium, Trondheim, Norway, June 16-18, 1980 / edited by A.B. Aune and J. Vlietstra. — Amsterdam ; Oxford : North-Holland, 1980. — x,475p : ill ; 31cm. — (Computer applications in shipping and shipbuilding ; v.8)
Includes index
ISBN 0-444-85498-3 : £42.25
Primary classification 622′.33′820289 B82-31516

623.88′81 — Freight transport. Shipping. Ships. Cargoes. Stowage

Kemp, John F. (John Frederick). Notes on cargo work / Kemp & Young. — New ed. — London : Stanford Maritime, 1980. — 112p : ill(some col.) ; 21cm
Previous ed.: i.e. 3rd ed. 1971. — Includes index
ISBN 0-540-07332-6 (pbk) : Unpriced B82-05044

623.88′81 — Ships. Cargo handling

Taylor, L. G.. Cargo work : the care, handling and carriage of cargoes including the management of marine cargo transportation / by L.G. Taylor in association with L.D. Conway. — 10th ed. — Glasgow : Brown, Son & Ferguson, 1981. — xiv,401p,[1]folded leaf of plates : ill(some col.),1map,plans,forms ; 22cm
Previous ed.: 1978. — Ten forms and three plans on folded sheets in pocket. — Includes index
ISBN 0-85174-408-7 : £16.00 B82-12290

623.88′82 — Knots — *Manuals*

Fry, Eric C.. The Shell combined book of knots and ropework : (practical and decorative) / Eric C. Fry ; photographs by Peter Wilson. — Newton Abbot : David & Charles, c1981. — [174]p : ill ; 26cm
Originally published: in 2 bks. as The Shell book of knots and ropework, 1977 and The Shell book of practical and decorative ropework, 1978. — Includes index
ISBN 0-7153-8197-0 : £7.50 : CIP rev.
Also classified at 746.42 B81-22507

623.88′82 — Knots - *Manuals*

Russell, John. Knots. — London : Ward Lock, May 1981. — [96]p. — (Concorde)
ISBN 0-7063-6010-9 (pbk) : £2.95 : CIP entry B81-07469

623.88′82 — Sailing ships. Rigging. Wire ropes. Splicing — *Manuals*

Popple, Leonard. Marline-spike seamanship : the art of handling, splicing and knotting wire / by Leonard Popple. — Glasgow : Brown, Son & Ferguson, 1949 (1981 [printing]). — x,82p : ill ; 21cm
ISBN 0-85174-138-x : £4.00 B82-17999

623.88′82 — Seamanship. Ropework

Maclean, William P.. Modern marlinspike seamanship : knots, splices, cordage terminals and rigging / William P. Maclean. — Newton Abbot : David & Charles, c1982. — 224p : ill ; 26cm
Originally published: Indianapolis : Bobbs-Merrill, c1979. — Includes index
ISBN 0-7153-8328-0 : £8.95 : CIP rev. B82-13070

623.88′84 — Great Britain. Coastal waters. Ships carrying dangerous cargoes. Collisions & stranding. Prevention. Great Britain. *Parliament. House of Commons. Industry and Trade Committee.* **Second report ... session 1980-81** — *Critical studies*

Great Britain. Second special report from the Industry and Trade Committee, session 1980-81 : follow-up to the second report by the former Expenditure Committee on measures to prevent collisions and strandings of noxious cargo carriers in waters around the United Kingdom : observations by the government on the third report of the committee in session 1979-80. — London : H.M.S.O., 1980. — ivp ; 25cm. — ([HC] ; 72)
ISBN 0-10-207281-7 (unbound) : £0.70 B82-10331

623.88'84 — Ships. Collisions. Prevention. Regulations: International Regulations for Preventing Collisions at Sea 1972 — *Commentaries*
Cockcroft, A. N.. A guide to the collision avoidance rules. — 3rd ed. — London : Stanford Maritime, Sept.1982. — [240]p
Previous ed.: 1976
ISBN 0-540-07278-8 : £6.95 : CIP entry
B82-21385

623.89 — Distances between ports — *Tables*
Caney, R. W.. Reed's marine distance tables / compiled for the publishers by R.W. Caney and J.E. Reynolds. — 5th ed. — London : Reed, 1981. — 202p,[1]folded leaf of plate : 1col.map ; 21cm
Previous ed.: 1978. — Includes index
ISBN 0-900335-71-8 (pbk) : £7.50 B82-05902

623.89 — Seamanship. Celestial navigation — *Questions & answers — For yachting*
Watkins, G. G.. Exercises in astro-navigation / Gordon Watkins. — London : Stanford Maritime, 1981. — 174p : ill,facsims ; 24cm
ISBN 0-540-07190-0 (pbk) : £3.95 : CIP rev.
B81-25724

623.89 — Seamanship. Navigation — *Manuals*
Dahl, Norman. Yacht navigator's handbook. — London : Ward Lock, Mar.1982. — [192]p
ISBN 0-7063-5920-8 : £9.95 : CIP entry
B82-00218

623.89 — Shipping. Navigational aids: Charts — *Manuals*
Moore, D. A.. Marine chartwork / D.A. Moore. — 2nd ed. — London : Stanford Maritime, 1981. — 109p : ill ; 24cm
Previous ed. published as: Marine chartwork and navaids, 1967
ISBN 0-540-07269-9 (pbk) : £2.95 : CIP rev.
B81-30181

623.89'0247971 — Seamanship. Navigation — *For yachting*
Derrick, David. Navigation for offshore and ocean sailors / David Derrick. — Newton Abbot : David & Charles, c1981. — 144p : ill,charts,maps,forms ; 26cm
Includes index
ISBN 0-7153-8086-9 : £8.50 : CIP rev.
B81-30389

Navigation : an RYA manual. — Newton Abbot : Royal Yachting Association in association with David & Charles, c1981. — 157p,[8]p of plates : ill(some col.),charts,maps ; 26cm
ISBN 0-7153-8246-2 (cased) : £6.95 : CIP rev.
ISBN 0-7153-8258-6 (pbk) : Unpriced
B81-21536

Quarrie, Stuart. Race navigation. — London : Stanford Maritime, Aug.1982. — [152]p
ISBN 0-540-07408-x : £5.95 : CIP entry
B82-21090

623.89'0247971 — Seamanship. Navigation — *Questions & answers — For yachting*
Anderson, Bill. Navigation exercises for yachtsmen / Bill Anderson ; produced in conjunction with the Royal Yachting Association. — 2nd ed. — London : Stanford Maritime, 1981. — 75p : ill,charts, maps ; 22cm
Previous ed.: 1974. — Chart in pocket
ISBN 0-540-07275-3 (pbk) : £3.50 : CIP rev.
B81-25725

623.89'028'54 — Seamanship. Navigation. Use of pocket electronic calculators
Keys, Gerald. Practical navigation by calculator. — London : Stanford Maritime, June 1982. — [176]p
ISBN 0-540-07410-1 (pbk) : £5.95 : CIP entry
B82-14940

623.89'09'24 — Seamanship. Navigation. Taylor, Janet, *1804-1870 — Biographies*
Alger, K. R.. Mrs. Janet Taylor "authoress and instructress in navigation and nautical astronomy" (1804-1870). — London (Calcutta House, Old Castle St., E1 7NT) : LLRS Publications, Dec.1982. — [25]p. — (Fawcett Library papers ; no.6)
ISBN 0-904264-69-6 (pbk) : £2.00 : CIP entry
B82-39266

623.89'2 — Ships. Navigation instruments, *ca 1400-1900*
Randier, Jean. Marine navigation instruments / Jean Randier ; translated from the French by John E. Powell. — London : Murray, 1980. — 219p : ill(some col.),maps,facsims ; 29cm
Translation of: L'Instrument de marine. — Bibliography: p216-217. — Includes index
ISBN 0-7195-3733-9 : £17.50 : CIP rev.
B80-04247

623.89'22 — Yachts. Pilotage — *Manuals*
Howard-Williams, Jeremy. Practical pilotage / Jeremy Howard-Williams. — 2nd ed. — London : Granada, 1982, c1981. — 96p : ill (some col.),col.charts ; 21cm
Previous ed.: 1977. — Includes index
ISBN 0-229-11657-4 : £5.95 B82-09233

623.89'29'163336 — Western English Channel. Harbours — *Pilots' guides — For yachting*
Coles, K. Adlard. Channel harbours and anchorages. — 6th ed. — London : Macmillan, Oct.1982. — [208]p
Previous ed.: Lymington : Nautical Publishing Co., 1977
ISBN 0-333-32526-5 : £12.00 : CIP entry
B82-24804

623.89'2916336 — Western English Channel. Harbours — *Pilots' guides — For yachting*
Coles, K. Adlard. The Shell pilot to the south coast harbours / K. Adlard Coles. — New and rev. ed. / by J.O. Coote, with plans by James Petter. — London : Faber, 1982. — 233p : ill,charts(some col.) ; 17x22cm
Previous ed.: i.e. 5th ed. Lymington : Nautical Publishing, 1977. — Ill on lining papers
ISBN 0-571-18060-4 : £10.00 : CIP rev.
B82-09436

623.89'294 — Western Europe. Harbours — *Pilots' guides — For cruising*
The **Cruising** Association handbook. — Rev. ed. / revised by the Council of the Cruising Association. — London : Cruising Association, 1971 (1978 [printing]). — xiv,490p : ill(some col.),charts ; 26cm
Previous ed.: 1961. — Ill on lining papers. — Includes index
ISBN 0-9503742-0-2 : Unpriced B82-35061

623.89'29441'0247971 — North-western France. Coastal waters — *Pilots' guides — For yachting*
Jefferson, David. Brittany and Channel Islands cruising guide. — 2nd ed. — London : Stanford Maritime, Aug.1982. — [208]p
Previous ed.: 1981
ISBN 0-540-07416-0 : £10.95 : CIP entry
B82-21091

623.89'29495'0247971 — Greece. Coastal waters — *Pilots' guides — For yachting*
Heikell, Rod. Greek waters pilot : a yachtsman's guide to the coasts and islands of Greece / Rod Heikell. — St. Ives, Cambs. : Imray, Laurie, Norie & Wilson, 1982. — vii,348p : ill,col.charts,maps(some col.) ; 31cm
Bibliography: p336-337. — Includes index
ISBN 0-85288-074-x : £17.50 B82-17630

623.89'3 — Great Britain. Merchant ships. Electronic navigation equipment. Simulators — *Standards*
Great Britain. *Department of Trade*. Specification for a marine navigational equipments simulator (1980) / Department of Trade. — London : The Department, 1980. — 15p ; 30cm
Replaces Specification for a marine radar simulator. 1971
Unpriced (pbk) B82-40103

623.89'33 — Ships. Automatic radar plotting aids. Use — *Manuals*
Bole, A. G.. Automatic radar plotting aids manual : a mariner's guide to the use of ARPA / A.G. Bole, K.D. Jones. — London : Heinemann, 1981. — x,131p : ill ; 25cm
Includes index
ISBN 0-434-90160-1 : £10.00 B82-23218

623.89'33 — Warships. Radar equipment
Friedman, Norman, *1946-*. Naval radar / Norman Friedman ; drawings by John Roberts. — Greenwich : Conway Maritime, 1981. — 240p : ill ; 29cm
Bibliography: p234-235. — Includes index
ISBN 0-85177-238-2 : £18.00 B82-07912

623.89'38'0212 — Echo sounding — *Tables*
Carter, D. J. T.. Echo-sounding correction tables. — 3rd ed. / by D.J.T. Carter. — Taunton : Hydrographic Department, Ministry of Defence, 1980. — 150p : charts ; 31cm. — (NP139)
Previous ed.: published as Tables of the velocity of sound in pure water and sea water for use in echo-sounding and sound-ranging / D.J. Matthews. 1939. — Bibliography: p150
Unpriced B82-40694

623.89'4 — Seamanship. Signalling — *Manuals*
Gibbs-Smith, C. H.. How to remember the international signal flags and the morse code / by Charles H. Gibbs-Smith. — Glasgow : Brown, Son & Ferguson, [198-?]. — 1folded sheet : ill(some col.) ; 21x54cm.folded to 21x11
ISBN 0-85174-402-8 : £0.80 B82-36089

623.89'4 — Ships. Signals — *Standards*
International code of signals 1969 / Department of Trade. — London : H.M.S.O., c1969 (1982). — xv,149p : ill(some col.) ; 30cm
Includes index
ISBN 0-11-513492-1 (pbk) : £6.60 B82-31239

Moore, D. A.. International light, shape and sound signals / by D.A. Moore. — London : Stanford Maritime, c1976 (1981 [printing]). — 143p : ill(some col.) ; 26cm
ISBN 0-540-07271-0 : £5.95 B82-10744

Moore, D. A.. International light, shape and sound signals. — 2nd ed. — London : Stanford Maritime, Dec.1982. — [141]p
Previous ed.: 1976
ISBN 0-540-07279-6 : £5.95 : CIP entry
B82-34091

624 — CIVIL ENGINEERING

624 — Ancient Rome. Towns. Construction, *B.C.300-A.D.150 — For children*
Macaulay, David. City : a story of Roman planning and construction / David Macaulay. — London : Collins, 1975, c1974 (1982 [printing]). — 112p : ill,plans ; 31cm
Originally published: Boston, Mass. : Houghton Mifflin, 1974
ISBN 0-00-192143-6 (pbk) : £3.50
Primary classification 711'.4'0937 B82-15441

624 — Civil engineering
Christian, John, *19---*. Management, machines and methods in civil engineering / John Christian. — New York ; Chichester : Wiley, 1981. — xix,360p : ill ; 24cm. — (Construction management and engineering)
Bibliography: p353. — Includes index
ISBN 0-471-06334-7 : £27.35 B82-03900

Fletcher, B. G.. Civil engineering technology 3 / B.G. Fletcher, S.A. Lavan ; additional material by D.C. Wallis ; illustrations prepared by Peter R. Bowyer. — [London] : TEC, 1980. — 88p : ill,forms ; 25cm
ISBN 0-408-00426-6 (pbk) : £4.95 : CIP rev.
B80-00769

624 — Civil engineering. Contracts: International Federation of Consulting Engineers. Conditions of contract (international) for works of civil engineering construction — *Critical studies*
Sawyer, John G.. The FIDIC conditions : digest of contractual relationships and responsibilities / John G. Sawyer and C.A. Gillott. — London : Telford, c1981. — 110p ; 30cm
Includes index
ISBN 0-7277-0127-4 (pbk) : £8.50 B82-02214

624 — Civil engineering. Environmental aspects
Planning and the civil engineer : proceedings of a joint conference of the American Society of Civil Engineers, the Canadian Society for Civil Engineering and the Institution of Civil Engineers held in Torquay 20-25 September 1981. — London : Telford, 1982. — 150p : ill,maps ; 31cm
Includes index
ISBN 0-7277-0152-5 : £15.00 B82-36221

624 — Civil engineering — *For schools*

Kincaid, Doug. Roads, bridges and tunnels / Doug Kincaid, Peter S. Coles ; designed and illustrated by John Hill. — [Amersham] : Hulton, 1979. — 64p : ill(some col.),1col.map ; 25cm. — (Science in a topic)
Text, ill on covers. — Bibliography on inside back cover
ISBN 0-7175-0852-8 (pbk) : Unpriced
B82-37153

624 — Civil engineering. Measurement. Standards: Institution of Civil Engineers. Civil engineering standard method of measurement. Use — *Manuals*

McCaffrey, R. G.. The civil engineering standard method of measurement in practice. — London : Granada, Jan.1983. — [256]p
ISBN 0-246-11928-4 (pbk) : £12.00 : CIP entry
B82-33712

Reynolds, Gerald. Measurement of civil engineering work / G.J. Reynolds. — London : Granada, 1980. — xii,132p : ill,forms ; 32cm
Includes index
ISBN 0-246-11375-8 (cased) : Unpriced : CIP rev.
ISBN 0-246-11376-6 (pbk) : £5.95 B80-12400

624 — Civil engineering. Quantity surveying

Hughes, Geoffrey Arthur. Civil engineering quantities. — Hornby : Construction Press, July 1981. — [220]p
ISBN 0-86095-878-7 : £12.50 : CIP entry
B81-14440

624 — Construction

Fullerton, R. L.. Construction technology, level two / R.L. Fullerton. — Oxford : Technical Press, 1982. — 2v.(x,272p) : ill,plans ; 30cm
Bibliography: p262. — Includes index
ISBN 0-291-39653-4 (pbk) : Unpriced : CIP rev.
ISBN 0-291-39654-2 (v.2) : £4.95 B81-32028

624 — Construction. Environmental aspects

Fabrick, Martin N.. Environmental planning for design and construction / Martin N. Fabrick, Joseph J. O'Rourke. — New York ; Chichester : Wiley, c1982. — xv,304p : ill,maps ; 24cm. — (Construction management and engineering, ISSN 0193-9750)
Bibliography: p243-244. — Includes index
ISBN 0-471-05848-3 : Unpriced B82-38319

624 — Construction. Estimating. Measurement

Gardner, M.. Measurement, level 2 / M. Gardner ; illustrated by the author. — London : Longman, 1981. — vii,209p : ill,forms ; 24cm. — (Longman technician series. Construction and civil engineering)
Bibliography: p207. — Includes index
ISBN 0-582-41584-5 (pbk) : £5.95 : CIP rev.
B81-30292

Jones, T. F.. Building measurement 3 checkbook. — London : Butterworth Scientific, Dec.1982. — [144]p. — (Butterworths technical and scientific checkbooks)
ISBN 0-408-00693-5 (cased) : £6.95 : CIP entry
ISBN 0-408-00652-8 (pbk) : £3.95 B82-29789

624 — Construction. Sites. Investigation

Robb, Andrew D.. Site investigation / Andrew D. Robb. — London : Telford, 1982. — 27p : ill ; 15x22cm. — (ICE works construction guides)
ISBN 0-7277-0142-8 (pbk) : £2.00 B82-37807

624 — Construction. Sites. Levelling & surveying

Clayton, C. R. I.. Site investigation. — London : Granada, May 1982. — [400]p
ISBN 0-246-11641-2 : £25.00 : CIP entry
B82-09285

Rawlinson, H.. Site surveying and levelling, level 2 / H. Rawlinson. — London : Longman, 1982. — 165p : ill,1map,plans ; 22cm. — (Longman technician series. Construction and civil engineering)
Includes index
ISBN 0-582-41597-7 (pbk) : £4.95 B82-04938

624 — Construction. Sites. Management — *Manuals*

Forster, G.. Construction site studies : production, administration and personnel / G. Forster. — London : Longman, 1981. — 264p : ill,forms,1map,plans ; 25cm. — (Longman technician series. Construction and civil engineering)
Includes index
ISBN 0-582-41567-5 (pbk) : £9.95 : CIP rev.
B81-30293

624 — Construction. Sites. Safety measures

Laney, J. C.. Site safety. — London : Longman, Nov.1982. — [192]p. — (Site practice series)
ISBN 0-582-40601-3 (pbk) : £4.95 : CIP entry
B82-26532

624 — Construction. Sites. Surveying. Use of lasers. Safety measures — *Proposals*

A **Guide** to the safe use of lasers in surveying and construction. — London : Royal Institution of Chartered Surveyors, [1980?]. — 1v.(loose-leaf) : ill(some col.) ; 32cm
£7.50 B82-35952

624 — Great Britain. Civil engineering. Contracts — *Manuals*

Marsh, P. D. V.. Contracting for engineering and construction projects / P.D.V. Marsh. — 2nd ed. — Aldershot : Gower in association with the Institute of Purchasing and Supply, 1981. — viii,257p : ill ; 23cm
Previous ed.: 1969. — Includes index
ISBN 0-566-02232-x : Unpriced : CIP rev.
Also classified at 692'.8'0941 B81-14815

624 — Great Britain. Construction equipment. Hire. Contracts. Standard conditions — *Texts*

Powell-Smith, Vincent. Contractors guide to the model conditions for the hiring of plant / by Vincent Powell-Smith. — Sutton, Surrey : IPC Building and Contract Journals, c1981. — 32p : 1form ; 30cm
ISBN 0-617-00251-7 (pbk) : £3.95 B82-21435

624 — Ireland *(Republic)*. **Construction industries. Overseas work**

Jennings, R. (Robert), *1947-*. A study of foreign work of the Irish construction industry / R. Jennings. — Dublin : An Foras Forbartha, 1981. — 48p ; 30cm
ISBN 0-906120-52-7 (spiral) : £3.00
B82-15379

624 — Large structures — *For children*

Lewis, Alun, *19---*. Super structures / author Alun Lewis. — London : Marshall Cavendish Children's Books, 1979. — 59p : col.ill ; 30cm. — (Woodpecker books)
Text and ill on lining papers. — Includes index
ISBN 0-85685-689-4 : Unpriced B82-11166

624 — Structures

Gordon, J. E. (James Edward). Structures, or, Why things don't fall down / J.E. Gordon. — London : Pitman, 1979, c1978. — 395p,24p of plates : ill ; 23cm
Originally published: Harmondsworth : Penguin, 1978. — Bibliography: p388-390. — Includes index
ISBN 0-273-01458-7 : Unpriced B82-06590

624 — Structures. Failure — *Case studies*

LePatner, Barry B.. Structural and foundation failures : a casebook for architects, engineers, and lawyers / by Barry B. LePatner & Sidney M. Johnson. — New York ; London : McGraw-Hill, c1982. — x,249p : ill ; 24cm
Includes index
ISBN 0-07-032584-7 : £18.95 B82-34919

624 — United States. Construction industries. Contracting. Financial management — *Manuals*

Financial management for contractors / The Fails Management Institute ; edited by Ira Jerome Jackson III and Marita H. Gilliam. — New York ; London : McGraw-Hill, c1981. — xi,236p : ill,forms ; 24cm
Includes bibliographies and index
ISBN 0-07-019887-x : £18.50 B82-14671

624'.01'5515 — Civil engineering. Applications of meteorology

Engineering meteorology. — Oxford : Elsevier Scientific, Apr.1982. — [750]p. — (Studies in wind engineering and industrial aerodynamics ; 1)
ISBN 0-444-41972-1 : CIP entry B82-14951

624'.022'1 — Civil engineering. Design. Technical drawings. Draftsmanship

Thomas, M. V.. A guide to the preparation of civil engineering drawings / M.V. Thomas. — London : Macmillan, 1982. — 180p : ill,maps,plans ; 27cm
Includes index
ISBN 0-333-28081-4 (cased) : Unpriced
ISBN 0-333-32699-7 (pbk) : Unpriced
B82-19296

624'.022'2 — Structures of historical importance — *Illustrations — For children*

Bahree, Patricia. Building wonders of the world / Patricia Bahree. — London : Macdonald, 1982. — 32p : col.ill ; 29cm. — (Eye openers!)
Includes index
ISBN 0-356-07096-4 : £2.95 B82-23731

624'.023'41 — Great Britain. Construction industries — *Career guides*

Construction / [prepared jointly by COIC and the Central Office of Information]. — [London] : [Manpower Services Commission], [1982?]. — 12v. : col.ill ; 30cm. — (Close-up)
Unpriced B82-40364

624'.028 — Construction equipment

Harris, Frank, *1944-*. Construction plant. — London : Granada, Sept.1982. — [272]p
ISBN 0-246-11240-9 (pbk) : £9.95 : CIP entry
B82-18847

624.028'54 — Civil engineering. Applications of digital computer systems

Cope, R. J.. Computer methods for civil engineers / R.J. Cope, F. Sawko, R.G. Tickell. — London : McGraw-Hill, c1982. — xiv,361p : ill ; 23cm. — (University series in civil engineering)
Includes index
ISBN 0-07-084129-2 (pbk) : £9.95 : CIP rev.
B82-06021

624'.03'21 — Construction — *Encyclopaedias*

Definitions of construction terms 1981 / [compiled by CIT Agency of the Polytechnic of the South Bank]. — [Rev. ed.]. — London (90 Shaftesbury Ave., W.1) : Infodoc Services, [1981]. — 937p ; 30cm
Cover title. — Previous ed.: 1977
£95.00 (pbk) B82-06120

Stein, J. Stewart. Construction glossary : an encyclopedic reference and manual / J. Stewart Stein. — New York ; Chichester : Wiley, c1980. — xvii,1013p ; 27cm. — (Wiley series of practical construction guides)
Includes index
ISBN 0-471-04947-6 : £51.40 B82-08719

624'.03'21 — Geotechnics — *Encyclopaedias*

Somerville, S. H.. Dictionary of geotechnics. — London : Butterworth, Oct.1982. — [325]p
ISBN 0-408-00437-1 : £15.00 : CIP entry
B82-24461

624'.068 — Construction industries. Management

Maher, Richard Patrick. Introduction to construction operations / Richard Patrick Maher. — New York ; Chichester : Wiley, c1982. — xi,402p : ill,forms ; 26cm
Includes index
ISBN 0-471-86136-7 : £25.50 B82-37991

Thomsen, Charles B.. CM : developing, marketing, and delivering construction management services / Charles B. Thomsen. — New York ; London : Mc-Graw-Hill, c1982. — x,209p : ill,forms ; 24cm
Includes index
ISBN 0-07-064490-x : £18.95 B82-16293

624'.068 — Construction. Sites. Management
Davies, W. H. (William Henry), *1935-.*
Construction site production 4 checkbook / W.H. Davies. — London : Butterworth Scientific, 1982. — viii,189p : ill ; 20cm. — (Butterworths technical and scientific checkbooks. Level 4)
Includes index
ISBN 0-408-00675-7 (cased) : Unpriced : CIP rev.
ISBN 0-408-00656-0 (pbk) : Unpriced
B82-04032

Murphy, Roy W.. Site engineering. — London : Construction Press, Nov.1982. — [224]p. — (Site practice series)
ISBN 0-582-40606-4 (pbk) : £6.00 : CIP entry
B82-26572

The **Practice** of site management / compiled and edited by P.A. Harlow. — Ascot : Institute of Building
[Vol.1]. — 2nd ed. — [1980]. — 170p : ill,1map,1plan ; 30cm
Previous ed.: published in 1v. 1976. — Includes index
ISBN 0-906600-18-9 (pbk) : £5.25 : CIP rev.
B80-02833

624'.068 — Great Britain. Construction industries. Organisation structure — *For technicians*
Ward, Peter A.. Organisation and procedures in the construction industry / Peter A. Ward. — Plymouth : Macdonald and Evans, 1979. — viii,212p : ill,plans,forms ; 22cm. — (The M & E TECbook series)
Includes index
ISBN 0-7121-1530-7 (pbk) : £4.25 B82-12177

624'.068'1 — Construction industries. Applications of value engineering
Zimmerman, Larry W.. Value engineering : a practical approach for owners, designers and contractors / Larry W. Zimmerman, Glen D. Hart. — New York ; London : Van Nostrand Reinhold, 1982. — xii,279p : ill,forms ; 26cm
Bibliography: p275-276. — Includes index
ISBN 0-442-29587-1 : £20.85 B82-24923

624'.068'1 — Construction industries. Financial management
Mott, Charles H.. Accounting and financial management for construction / Charles H. Mott. — New York ; Chichester : Wiley, c1981. — xiv,214p ; 24cm. — (Construction management and engineering)
Includes bibliographies and index
ISBN 0-471-07959-6 : £17.00 B82-07792

624'.068'1 — Great Britain. Construction industries. Financial management
Construction projects : their financial policy and control / edited by R.A. Burgess. — London : Construction, 1982. — 135p : 1map ; 30cm
Conference papers. — Includes index
ISBN 0-86095-876-0 : £16.50 : CIP rev.
B81-36371

624'.068'1 — United States. Construction industries. Costing
Neil, James M.. Construction cost estimating for project control / James M. Neil. — Englewood Cliffs ; London : Prentice-Hall, c1982. — xiv,331p : ill ; 24cm
Includes index
ISBN 0-13-168757-3 : £18.70 B82-16852

624'.068'4 — Construction industries. Critical path analysis
Antill, James M.. Critical path methods in construction practice / James M. Antill, Ronald W. Woodhead. — 3rd ed. — New York ; Chichester : Wiley, c1982. — xii,425p : ill ; 24cm
Previous ed.: 1970. — Includes index
ISBN 0-471-86612-1 : £29.00 B82-34338

624'.068'4 — Construction industries. Project management
Fisk, Edward R.. Construction project administration / Edmund R. Fisk. — 2nd ed. — New York ; Chichester : Wiley, c1982. — xiii,434p : ill ; 24cm
Previous ed.: 1978. — Includes bibliographies and index
ISBN 0-471-09186-3 : £18.45 B82-30693

624'.068'4 — Construction industries. Risks. Management. Decision making
Lifson, Melvin W.. Decision and risk analysis for construction management / Melvin W. Lifson, Edward F. Shaifer, Jr. — New York ; Chichester : Wiley, c1982. — xi,222p : ill ; 24cm. — (Construction management and engineering, ISSN 0193-9750)
Includes bibliographies and index
ISBN 0-471-03167-4 : £24.00 B82-32705

624'.068'8 — Great Britain. Construction industries. International marketing
Cox, Victor L.. International construction : marketing, planning and execution. — London : Construction Press, Dec.1982. — [192]p
ISBN 0-582-30510-1 : £15.00 : CIP entry
B82-30062

624'.07'11 — Civil engineers. Professional education — *Conference proceedings*
Future needs in civil engineering education : proceedings of the conference on civil engineering education and training organized by the Institution of Civil Engineers and held at the University of Birmingham on 15-16 September 1981. — London : Telford, 1982. — 135p : ill ; 31cm
ISBN 0-7277-0153-3 : £15.00 B82-36218

624'.07'1141 — Great Britain. Civil engineers. In-service training. Courses — *Directories — Serials*
Guide to in-career training courses for civil engineers. — 1 Sept. 1981-. — London (Great George St., SW1P 3AA) : The Institution of Civil Engineers, 1981-. — v. ; 21cm
Three issues yearly
ISSN 0261-5207 = Guide to in-career training courses for civil engineers : £10.00 per year
B82-09688

624'.072041 — Great Britain. Civil engineering. Research & development — *Proposals*
Long-term research and development requirements in civil engineering : a report commissioned by the Science and Engineering Research Council and the Departments of Environment and Transport and prepared by a Civil Engineering Task Force set up by the sponsors. — [London] ([6 Storey's Gate, SW1P 3AU]) : [CIRIA], 1981. — ii,73p ; 30cm
Unpriced (spiral) B82-00950

624'.092'4 — Civil engineering. Vignoles, Charles Blacker — *Biographies*
Vignoles, Keith H.. Charles Blacker Vignoles : romantic engineer / K.H. Vignoles. — Cambridge : Cambridge University Press, 1982. — xii,187p : ill,1facsim,geneal.table,maps,ports ; 26cm
Bibliography: p179-181. — Includes index
ISBN 0-521-23930-3 : £18.00 : CIP rev.
B82-12006

624'.092'4 — Great Britain. Civil engineering. Smeaton, John
John Smeaton, FRS / edited by A.W. Skempton. — London : Telford, 1981. — 291p : ill,maps,facsims,1port ; 24cm
Includes index
ISBN 0-7277-0088-x : £12.50 B82-15394

624'.0937 — Ancient Rome. Civil engineering — *For schools*
Hamey, L. A.. The Roman engineers / L.A. and J.A. Hamey. — Cambridge : Cambridge University Press, 1981. — 48p : ill,facsims, maps ; 21x22cm. — (Cambridge introduction to the history of mankind. Topic book)
ISBN 0-521-22511-6 (pbk) : £1.80 B82-38377

624'.0941 — Great Britain. Construction — *Technical data*
Builder's reference book. — 11th ed. / edited by Leslie Black. — London : Northwood, 1980. — 432p : ill ; 22cm. — (A Building trades journal book)
Previous ed.: 1974
ISBN 0-7198-2810-4 : Unpriced B82-39023

624'.09423'93 — Avon. Bristol. Structures. Design & construction. Role of Brunel, Isambard Kingdom, *1828-1848*
Buchanan, R. A.. Brunel's Bristol / R.A. Buchanan and M. Williams. — Bristol : Redcliffe published for Bristol & West Building Society, 1982. — 96p : ill,1facsim,1map,plans,ports ; 24cm
Bibliography: p96
ISBN 0-905459-39-3 (cased) : Unpriced
ISBN 0-905459-45-8 (pbk) : £3.95 B82-33661

624.1 — STRUCTURAL ENGINEERING

624.1 — Structural engineering
Lauer, Kenneth R.. Structural engineering for architects / Kenneth R. Lauer. — New York ; London : McGraw-Hill, c1981. — xviii,540p : ill,2maps ; 25cm
Includes index
ISBN 0-07-036622-5 : £18.50 B82-22171

624.1'0212 — Structural engineering — *Technical data*
Morgan, W.. Students structural handbook. — 3rd ed. — London : Butterworth, Sept.1982. — [112]p
Previous ed.: 1973
ISBN 0-408-01151-3 (pbk) : £4.95 : CIP entry
B82-21974

624.1'042 — Great Britain. Quantity surveying. Billing. Applications of digital computer systems
Enviro BQ system. — Croydon : Directorate of Quantity Surveying Services
Part 4: Instructions for computer working. — c1980. — 1v.(loose-leaf) : forms ; 32cm
Unpriced B82-33401

624.1'042'0711171241 — Commonwealth countries. Quantity surveyors. Professional education
Commonwealth Association of Surveying and Land Economy. Education for surveying and land economy / Commonwealth Association of Surveying and Land Economy. — 3rd ed. — London : The Association, 1982. — 32p ; 30cm + Appendix B(p33-38; 30cm)
Cover title. — Previous ed.: 1977. — Text on inside cover
ISBN 0-903577-24-0 (pbk) : £3.00
Primary classification 526.9'07'11171241
B82-22897

624.1'042'076 — Structural engineering. Quantity surveying — *Questions & answers*
Wilcox, Chris. Measurement of construction work / Chris Wilcox and John A. Snape. — London : G. Godwin
Vol.1. — 2nd ed. — 1980. — 163p : ill,plans ; 31cm
Previous ed.: published as Worked examples in measurement of construction work. 1972
ISBN 0-7114-5510-4 : £7.50: CIP rev.
B79-37356

624.1'042'0941 — Great Britain. Quantity surveying
Ashworth, A.. Advanced quantity surveying. — London : Butterworth, Dec.1982. — [192]p
ISBN 0-408-01192-0 (pbk) : £9.95 : CIP entry
B82-29780

Hughes, G. A.. The anatomy of quantity surveying / G.A. Hughes. — 2nd ed. — Lancaster : Construction Press, 1981. — 229p : ill,forms ; 31cm
Previous ed.: 1978. — Includes index
ISBN 0-86095-896-5 : £13.50 B82-15192

624.1'076 — Structural engineering — *Questions & answers*
Handa, Inder Jit. Handbook of worked examples in structural engineering / Inder Jit Handa. — Englewood Cliffs ; London : Prentice-Hall, c1982. — xi,452p : ill ; 29cm
Bibliography: p449. — Includes index
ISBN 0-13-382903-0 : £29.95 B82-23395

624.1'09411 — Scotland. Structural engineering, *1931-1981 — Conference proceedings*
Structural engineering in Scotland : a review of developments 1931-1981 / prepared for the Golden Jubilee Symposium of the Scottish Branch of the Institution of Structural Engineers. — London : Pentech Press, 1981. — 143p : ill ; 24cm
ISBN 0-7273-1902-7 : Unpriced : CIP rev.
B81-28088

624.1'5 — Structures. Foundations. Design

Bowles, Joseph E.. Foundation analysis and design / Joseph E. Bowles. — 3rd ed. — New York ; London : McGraw-Hill, c1982. — xiv,816p : ill,1facsim,2maps ; 25cm
Previous ed.: 1977. — Text on lining papers. — Bibliography: p788-806. — Includes index
ISBN 0-07-006770-8 : £24.75 B82-34510

624.1'51 — Civil engineering. Geotechnical aspects

Joyce, Michael D.. Site investigation practice. — London : Spon, July 1982. — [300]p
ISBN 0-419-12260-5 : £15.00 : CIP entry
B82-12338

624.1'51 — Engineering geology

Roberts, A.. Applied geotechnology : a text for students and engineers on rock excavation and related topics / by A. Roberts. — Oxford : Pergamon, 1981. — xvi,344p : ill ; 25cm. — (Pergamon international library)
Includes index
ISBN 0-08-024015-1 (cased) : Unpriced
ISBN 0-08-024014-3 (pbk) : £10.50
B82-02409

624.1'513 — Rocks & soils. Mechanics — *For technicians*

Williams, A. G.. Geotechnics : level IV / A.G. Williams. — New York ; London : Van Nostrand, 1982. — xvii,365p : ill ; 23cm. — (Higher technical education courses)
Includes index
ISBN 0-442-30349-1 (cased) : Unpriced
ISBN 0-442-30350-5 (pbk) : £8.50 B82-16324

624.1'5132 — Avon. Bristol. Avon Gorge. Rock faces. Stabilisation

Avon Gorge gallery / Avon County Council, Planning, Highways & Transport Committee. — Bristol (P.O. Box 11, Avon House, The Haymarket, Bristol BS99 7DE) : Avon County Public Relations and Publicity Dept., [1981]. — 16p : ill(some col.),col.map ; 15c21cm
Text, ill on inside covers
ISBN 0-86063-122-2 (pbk) : Unpriced
B82-01931

624.1'5136 — Soils. Artificial freezing — *Conference proceedings*

International Symposium on Ground Freezing *(2nd : 1980 : Trondheim)*. Ground freezing 1980 : selected papers of the Second International Symposium on Ground Freezing, held in Trondheim, June 24-26, 1980 / edited by P.E. Frivik ... [et al.]. — Amsterdam ; Oxford : Elsevier Scientific, 1982. — viii,411p : ill ; 25cm. — (Developments in geotechnical engineering ; v.28)
Reprinted from the journal, Engineering geology v.18, nos.1-4. — Includes bibliographies
ISBN 0-444-42010-x : £42.37 : CIP rev.
B81-38297

624'.1'5136 — Soils. Dynamics

Prakash, Shamsher. Soil dynamics / Shamsher Prakash. — New York ; London : McGraw-Hill, c1981. — xiv,426p : ill ; 25cm
Includes bibliographies and index
ISBN 0-07-050658-2 : £18.75 B82-17167

624.1'5136 — Soils. Dynamics

Soil mechanics : transient and cyclic loads : constitutive relations and numerical treatment / edited by G.N. Pande, O.C. Zienkiewicz. — Chichester : Wiley, 1982. — xii,627p : ill ; 24cm. — (Wiley series in numerical methods in engineering)
Includes index
ISBN 0-471-10046-3 : £34.50 : CIP rev.
B82-06835

624.1'5136 — Soils. Geotechnical properties — *For civil engineering*

Cernica, John N.. Geotechnical engineering / John N. Cernica. — New York ; London : Holt, Rinehart and Winston, c1982. — xviii,488p : ill ; 25cm
Text on lining papers. — Includes index
ISBN 0-03-059182-1 : Unpriced
ISBN 4-8337-0087-5 (International Edition) : £9.50 B82-20604

Spangler, Merlin G.. Soil engineering / Merlin G. Spangler, Richard L. Handy. — 4th ed. — New York ; London : Harper & Row, c1982. — xxvi,819p : ill,maps ; 25cm. — (The Harper & Row series in civil engineering)
Previous ed.: New York : Intext Educational, 1973. — Includes index
ISBN 0-7002-2533-1 : Unpriced B82-37278

624.1'5136 — Soils. Mechanics

Smith, G. N.. Elements of soil mechanics for civil and mining engineers. — 5th ed. — London : Granada, June 1982. — [512]p
Previous ed.: London : Crosby Lockwood Staples, 1978
ISBN 0-246-11765-6 (pbk) : £8.95 : CIP entry
B82-09988

624.1'5136 — Soils. Subsidence. Geotechnical aspects

Simons, N. E.. Slips, settlements and sinkholes / N.E. Simons. — [Guildford] ([Guildford, Surrey GU2 5XH]) : [University of Surrey], [1977?]. — 52p : ill ; 21cm. — (University of Surrey inaugural lecture)
Cover title. — Bibliography: p50-52
Unpriced (pbk) B82-26652

624.1'5136 — Structures. Foundations. Clay soils. Geotechnical properties

Soft clay engineering / edited by Edward William Brand and Rolf Peter Brenner. — Amsterdam ; Oxford : Elsevier Scientific, 1981. — 779p : ill,maps,ports ; 25cm. — (Developments in geotechnical engineering ; 20)
Includes bibliographies and index
ISBN 0-444-41784-2 : Unpriced B82-35555

624.1'5136 — Structures. Foundations. Design & construction. Applications of soil mechanics

Sowers, George F.. Introductory soil mechanics and foundations : geotechnical engineering. — 4th ed. / [by] George F. Sowers. — New York : Macmillan ; London : Collier Macmillan, c1979. — xvii,621p : ill,plans ; 24cm
Previous ed.: 1970. — Includes bibliographies and index
ISBN 0-02-979510-9 (pbk) : Unpriced
B82-05139

624.1'5136'01515353 — Soils. Mechanics. Mathematics. Finite element methods. Applications of digital computer systems

Smith, I. M.. Programming the finite element method : with application to geomechanics / I.M. Smith. — Chichester : Wiley, c1982. — ix,351p : ill ; 24cm
Includes bibliographies and index
ISBN 0-471-28003-8 (cased) : £20.00 : CIP rev.
ISBN 0-471-10098-6 (pbk) : Unpriced
B81-34580

624.1'5136'0287 — Soils. Testing. Laboratory techniques — *For civil engineering*

Head, K. H.. Manual of soil laboratory testing / K.H. Head. — London : Pentech
Vol.2: Permeability, shear strength and compressibility tests. — 1982. — p335-749 : ill,forms ; 26cm
Errata appearing in Vol.1 on p.749. — Includes bibliographies and index
ISBN 0-7273-1305-3 : Unpriced : CIP rev.
B81-23824

Vickers, Brian. Laboratory work in soil mechanics. — 2nd ed. — London : Granada, Jan.1983. — [192]p
Previous ed.: London : Crosby-Lockwood Staples, 1978
ISBN 0-246-11819-9 (pbk) : £7.95 : CIP entry
B82-33710

624.1'51363 — Rock slopes & soil slopes. Stabilisation. Techniques

Gray, Donald H.. Biotechnical slope protection and erosion control / Donald H. Gray, Andrew T. Leiser. — New York ; London : Van Nostrand Reinhold, c1982. — xiv,271p : ill,maps ; 29cm
Bibliography: p259-263. — Includes index
ISBN 0-442-21222-4 : £22.55 B82-36640

624.1'52 — Civil engineering. Excavation

Church, Horace K.. Excavation handbook / Horace K. Church. — New York ; London : McGraw-Hill, c1981. — xvi,[963]p : ill,maps,forms ; 24cm
Bibliography: 2p. — Includes index
ISBN 0-07-010840-4 : £34.50 B82-14027

624.1'54 — Structures. Foundations. Piles

Piles and foundations / edited by F.E. Young. — London : Telford, 1981. — 329p : ill ; 23cm
Includes index
ISBN 0-7277-0118-5 : Unpriced B82-15395

624.1'6 — Rock slopes. Design

Hoek, Evert. Rock slope engineering / Evert Hoek and John Bray. — Rev. 3rd ed. — London : The Institution of Mining and Metallurgy, 1981. — 358p : ill ; 28cm
Previous ed.: 1977. — Includes index
ISBN 0-900488-57-3 (pbk) : Unpriced
B82-15429

624.1'6 — Structures. Diaphragm walls. Construction — *Manuals*

Hajnal, I.. Construction of diaphragm walls. — Chichester : Wiley, July 1982. — [400]p
Translation of: Résfalak építése
ISBN 0-471-10002-1 : £20.00 : CIP entry
B82-14371

624.1'7 — Structures. Theories

Charlton, T. M.. A history of theory of structures in the nineteenth century / T.M. Charlton. — Cambridge : Cambridge University Press, 1982. — viii,194p : ill ; 24cm
Bibliography: p175-186. — Includes index
ISBN 0-521-23419-0 : £22.00 : CIP rev.
B82-25830

624.1'71 — Buildings. Steel frames. Design. Applications of plasticity theory

Horne, M. R.. Plastic design of low-rise frames. — London : Granada, May 1981. — [232]p
ISBN 0-246-11199-2 : £25.00 : CIP entry
B81-04248

624.1'71 — Civil engineering. Structural analysis

Vine, G. B.. Structural analysis / G.B. Vine. — London : Longman, 1982. — ix,251p : ill ; 22cm. — (Longman technician series. Construction and civil engineering)
Includes index
ISBN 0-582-41618-3 (pbk) : £4.95 : CIP rev.
B82-01128

624.1'71 — Structural components. Statics & strength

Harris, Charles O.. Statics and strength of materials / Charles O. Harris. — New York ; Chichester : Wiley, c1982. — xi,552p : ill ; 25cm
Includes index
ISBN 0-471-08293-7 : £14.70 B82-28948

624.1'71 — Structures. Analysis

Hsieh, Yuan-Yu. Elementary theory of structures / Yuan-Yu Hsieh. — 2nd ed. — Englewood Cliffs ; London : Prentice-Hall, c1982. — xi,416p : ill ; 24cm. — (Prentice-Hall international series in dynamics)
Previous ed.: 1970. — Includes index
ISBN 0-13-261545-2 : £19.45 B82-23642

624.1'71 — Structures. Analysis. Applications of virtual work

Davies, Glyn A. O.. Virtual work in structural analysis / Glyn A.O. Davies. — Chichester : Wiley, c1982. — xvi,325p : ill ; 24cm
Includes index
ISBN 0-471-10112-5 (cased) : Unpriced : CIP rev.
ISBN 0-471-10113-3 (pbk) : Unpriced
B82-13244

624.1'71 — Structures. Dynamics

Szuladzinski, Gregory. Dynamics of structures and machinery : problems and solutions / Gregory Szuladzinski. — New York ; Chichester : Wiley, c1982. — xi,297p : ill ; 29cm
ISBN 0-471-09027-1 : £34.00 B82-28030

624.1'71 — Structures. Dynamics. Mathematical models. Applications of digital computer systems

Craig, Roy R.. Structural dynamics : an introduction to computer methods / Roy R. Craig, Jr. — New York ; Chichester : Wiley, c1981. — xv,527p : ill ; 24cm
Includes index
ISBN 0-471-04499-7 : £20.45 B82-02490

624.1'71 — Structures. Mechanics & analysis — *For technicians*

Jenkins, W. M.. Structural mechanics and analysis : level IV/V / W.M. Jenkins. — New York ; London : Van Nostrand, 1982. — xiii,417p : ill ; 23cm. — (Higher technical education courses)
Includes index
ISBN 0-442-30360-2 (cased) : Unpriced
ISBN 0-442-30361-0 (pbk) : Unpriced B82-16323

624.1'71 — Structures. Reliability — *Conference proceedings*

ICOSSAR '81 *(Conference : Norwegian Institute of Technology)*. Structural safety and reliability : proceedings of ICOSSAR '81, the 3rd International Conference on Structural Safety and Reliability, the Norwegian Institute of Technology, Trondheim, Norway, June 23-25, 1981 / edited by T. Moan and M. Shinozuka. — Amsterdam ; Oxford : Elsevier Scientific, 1981. — 820p : ill ; 25cm. — (Developments in civil engineering ; 4)
ISBN 0-444-41994-2 : Unpriced : CIP rev. B81-15818

624.1'71 — Structures. Safety. Assessment. Probabilistic methods

Hart, Gary C.. Uncertainty analysis, loads, and safety in structural engineering / Gary C. Hart. — Englewood Cliffs ; London : Prentice-Hall, c1982. — x,224p : ill,maps ; 25cm. — (Prentice-Hall civil engineering and engineering mechanics series)
Includes bibliographies and index
ISBN 0-13-935619-3 : £19.45 B82-35391

624.1'71 — Structures. Stability

Axially compressed structures. — London : Applied Science, Sept.1982. — [300]p
ISBN 0-85334-139-7 : £33.00 : CIP entry B82-20828

624.1'71 — Structures. Vibration induced by fluid flow — *Conference proceedings*

International Conference on Flow Induced Vibrations in Fluid Engineering *(1982 : Reading)*. Papers presented at the International Conference on Flow Induced Vibrations in Fluid Engineering, Reading, England, September 1982. — Cranfield : BHRA Fluid Engineering, Sept.1982. — [400]p
ISBN 0-906085-73-x (pbk) : £33.00 : CIP entry B82-28610

624.1'71 — Three-dimensional structures. Analysis

Tuma, Jan J.. Schaum's outline of theory and problems of space structural analysis / by Jan J. Tuma and M.N. Reddy. — New York ; London : McGraw-Hill, c1982. — 217p : ill ; 28cm. — (Schaum's outline series)
Bibliography: p212. — Includes index
ISBN 0-07-065432-8 (pbk) : £5.95 B82-02500

624.1'71'015129434 — Structures. Analysis. Applications of matrices

Bhatt, P.. Problems in structural analysis by matrix methods / P. Bhatt. — Harlow : Construction Press, 1981. — 465p : ill ; 24cm
ISBN 0-86095-881-7 (pbk) : £9.95 : CIP rev. B81-06589

624.1'71'02854 — Structures. Analysis. Applications of digital computer systems

Ross, C. T. F.. Computer analysis of skeletal structures / C.T.F. Ross and T. Johns. — London : Spon, 1981. — viii,96p : ill ; 24cm
Bibliography: p95. — Includes index
ISBN 0-419-11970-1 : £11.00 : CIP rev. B81-31268

624.1'71'0285424 — Structures. Mechanics. Applications of microcomputer programs written in Basic language

Ross, C. T. F.. Computational methods in structural and continuum mechanics / C.T.F. Ross. — Chichester : Ellis Horwood, 1982. — 176p : ill ; 24cm. — (Ellis Horwood series in engineering science)
Includes index
ISBN 0-85312-432-9 : £15.00 : CIP rev.
ISBN 0-85312-442-6 (student ed.) : Unpriced B82-00187

624.1'75 — Structures. Wind loads — *Conference proceedings*

Wind engineering in the eighties : proceedings of the CIRIA conference held on 12/13 November 1980. — London : Construction Industry Research and Information Association, c1981. — 454p in various pagings : ill ; 30cm
ISBN 0-86017-170-1 (pbk) : £30.00 (£20.00 to members) B82-11191

624.1'76 — Structures. Fatigue & fracture

Developments in fracture mechanics. — London : Applied Science Publishers, Sept.1981. — (The Developments series)
2. — [328]p
ISBN 0-85334-973-8 : £25.00 : CIP entry B81-20162

Osgood, Carl C.. Fatigue design / by Carl C. Osgood. — 2nd ed. — Oxford : Pergamon, 1982. — ix,606p : ill ; 24cm. — (International series on the strength and fracture of materials and structures) (Pergamon international library)
Previous ed.: New York ; Chichester : Wiley-Interscience, 1970. — Bibliography: p593-596. — Includes index
ISBN 0-08-026167-1 (cased) : Unpriced : CIP rev.
ISBN 0-08-026166-3 (pbk) : £9.95 B82-00285

624.1'76 — Structures. Fatigue. Testing — *Conference proceedings*

Structural fatigue testing and analysis / two day conference, 16-17 March 1982. — Glasgow (East Kilbride, Glasgow G75 0QU) : Conference Section, National Engineering Laboratory, 1982. — [128]p : ill ; 30cm
Cover title
Unpriced (spiral) B82-26638

624.1'762 — Concrete earthquake resistant structures. Design

Englekirk, Robert E.. Earthquake design of concrete masonry buildings / Robert E. Englekirk, Gary C. Hart and the Concrete Masonry Association of California and Nevada. — Englewood Cliffs ; London : Prentice-Hall
Vol.1: Response spectra analysis and general earthquake modeling considerations. — c1982. — ix,144p : ill ; 24cm
Includes index
ISBN 0-13-223065-8 : £19.45 B82-29228

624.1'762'05 — Earthquake engineering — *Serials*

International journal of soil dynamics and earthquake engineering. — Vol.1, no.1 (Jan. 1982)-. — Southampton (125 High St., Southampton) : CML Publications, 1982-. — v. : ill ; 30cm
Quarterly. — Spine title: Soil dynamics and earthquake engineering
ISSN 0261-7277 = International journal of soil dynamics and earthquake engineering : £49.00 per year B82-28127

624.1'77 — Thin-walled structures — *Serials*

Developments in thin-walled structures. — 1. — London : Applied Science, June 1982. — [276] p. — (The Developments series)
ISBN 0-85334-123-0 : £28.00 : CIP entry B82-09877

624.1'771 — Structural components. Design

Engel, Heinrich. Structure systems / Heinrich Engel ; preface by Ralph Rapson ; conclusion by Hannskarl Bandel. — New York ; London : Van Nostrand Reinhold, 1981, c1967. — 256p : ill ; 30cm
Originally published: London : Iliffe, 1968. — Bibliography: p253. — Includes index
ISBN 0-442-28664-3 (pbk) : £14.40 B82-09794

624.1'771 — Structural engineering. Design. Use of dynamic models — *Conference proceedings*

Dynamic modelling of structures. — London : Construction Press, Aug.1982. — [357]p
Conference papers
ISBN 0-86095-706-3 : £25.00 : CIP entry B82-16492

624.1'771 — Structures. Design

Cowan, Henry J.. Structural systems / Henry J. Cowan, Forrest Wilson. — New York ; London : Van Nostrand Reinhold, c1981. — 256p : ill,plans ; 22x28cm
Bibliography: p241-242. — Includes index
ISBN 0-442-21714-5 (cased) : £21.20
ISBN 0-442-21713-7 (pbk) : £14.00 B82-09765

624.1'771 — Structures. Design — *For technicians*

Smyrell, A. G.. Design of structural elements. — London : Longman. — (Longman technician series. Construction and civil engineering)
Vol.1. — Jan.1983. — [288]p
ISBN 0-582-41229-3 (pbk) : £6.95 : CIP entry B82-32467

624.1'771 — Structures. Design. Optimisation — *Conference proceedings*

Foundations of structural optimization. — Chichester : Wiley, Oct.1982. — [576]p. — (Wiley series in numerical methods in engineering)
Conference papers
ISBN 0-471-10200-8 : £26.00 : CIP entry B82-23326

624.1'771'02854 — Structures. Design. Applications of computer systems

Iyengar, N. G. R.. Programming methods in structural design / N.G.R. Iyengar and S.K. Gupta in collaboration with N.C. Nigam. — London : Edward Arnold, 1981, c1980. — xii,248p : ill ; 24cm
Includes index
ISBN 0-7131-3453-4 (pbk) : £9.50 : CIP rev. B81-33873

624.1'773 — Space structures. Double-layer grids

Analysis, design and construction of double-layer grids / edited by Z.S. Makowski. — London : Applied Science, c1981. — x,414p : ill ; 28cm
Includes index
ISBN 0-85334-910-x : £40.00 : CIP rev. B81-12787

624.1'774 — Structures. Anchorages

Schnabel, Harry. Tiebacks in foundation engineering and construction / Harry Schnabel, Jr. — New York ; London : McGraw-Hill, c1982. — vi,170p : ill ; 24cm
Bibliography: p161-164. — Includes index
ISBN 0-07-055516-8 : £21.50 B82-16292

624.1'774 — Structures. Anchorages in rocks

Hobst, Leoš. Anchoring in rock and soil. — 2nd completely rev. ed. — Oxford : Elsevier Scientific, Nov.1982. — [450]p. — (Developments in geotechnical engineering ; 33)
Translation of: Kotvení do hornin. — Previous ed.: 1977
ISBN 0-444-99689-3 : £45.00 : CIP entry B82-27549

624.1'775 — Structures. Arches. Dynamics

Heyman, Jacques. The masonry arch. — Chichester : Horwood, July 1982. — [104]p. — (Ellis Horwood series in civil engineering)
ISBN 0-85312-500-7 : £15.00 : CIP entry B82-20655

624.1'7762 — Structures. Thin shells. Theories

Dikmen, M.. Theory of thin elastic shells / M. Dikmen. — Boston, [Mass.] ; London : Pitman, c1982. — xii,364p : ill ; 24cm. — (Surveys and reference works in mathematics ; 8)
Bibliography: p341-361. — Includes index
ISBN 0-273-08431-3 : £32.50 : CIP rev. B82-12272

Møllmann, H.. Introduction to the theory of thin shells / H. Møllmann. — Chichester : Wiley, c1981. — ix,181p : ill ; 24cm
Bibliography: p175-177. — Includes index
ISBN 0-471-28056-9 : £14.75 : CIP rev. B81-36245

624.1′7765 — Structures. Plates. Mechanics

Lowe, P. G.. Basic principles of plate theory / P.G. Lowe. — London : Surrey University Press, 1982. — ix,180p : ill ; 23cm
Includes index
ISBN 0-903384-26-4 (cased) : £18.95 : CIP rev.
ISBN 0-903384-25-6 (pbk) : £8.95 B81-33757

624.1′7765′0724 — Structures. Plates. Vibration. Mathematical models

Gorman, Daniel J.. Free vibration analysis of rectangular plates / D.J. Gorman. — New York ; Oxford : Elsevier, c1982. — xii,324p : ill ; 24cm
Includes index
ISBN 0-444-00601-x : Unpriced B82-05981

624.1′8 — Structures. Composite materials — *Conference proceedings*

International Conference on Composite Structures *(1st : 1981 : Paisley College of Technolgy)*. Composite structures / [proceedings of the 1st International Conference on Composite Structures, held at Paisley College of Technology, Scotland, from 16 to 18 September 1981, organised in association with the Institution of Mechanical Engineers and the National Engineering Laboratory] ; edited by I.H. Marshall. — London : Applied Science, c1981. — xvi,722p : ill ; 23cm
Includes index
ISBN 0-85334-988-6 : £65.00 : CIP rev.
B81-19205

624.1′821 — Steel structural components. Corrosion. Protection — *Manuals*

Steelwork corrosion protection guide. — London : British Constructional Steelwork Association, Nov.1982. — [8]p. — (Brown book ; 10/82)
ISBN 0-85073-012-0 : £1.00 : CIP entry
B82-36153

624.1′821 — Steel structural components: Fastenings — *Technical data*

Boston, R. M.. Structural fasteners : and their application / by R.M. Boston and J.W. Pask. — London (1 Vincent Sq, SW1P 2PJ) : British Constructional Steelwork Association, 1978. — 59p : ill(some col.) ; 30cm
Unpriced (pbk) B82-09480

624.1′821 — Steel structural components. Metric sizes — *Standards* **—** *For draftsmanship*

Metric practice for structural steelwork : an aid to design, drawing office and workshop personnel / [British Constructional Steelwork Association Metrication Task Group]. — 3rd ed. — London (1, Vincent Sq., SW1P 2JP) : British Constructional Steelwork Association, [1981?]. — 195p : ill ; 30cm
Bibliography: p.156-157
Unpriced (pbk) B82-09479

624.1′821 — Steel structural components — *Technical data*

Bates, William. Structural steelwork : design of components : conforming with the requirements of BS449: Part 2 : 1969 / by William Bates. — London (1 Vincent Sq, SW1P 2PJ) : British Constructional Steelwork Association, [1981?]. — 101p : ill ; 30cm
Bibliography: p101
Unpriced (pbk) B82-09478

International structural steelwork handbook. — London : British Constructional Steelwork Association, Jan.1983. — [56]p. — (Brown book ; 6/82)
ISBN 0-85073-011-2 (pbk) : £9.00 : CIP entry
B82-35223

Structural steel sections : to BS4 : Part 1: 1980, BS4848 : Part 4: 1972, BS4848 : Part 2: 1975 : a check list of designers. — 3rd ed. — Croydon : Constrado, c1981. — 11p : ill ; 30cm
Previous ed.: 197-
Unpriced (unbound) B82-17746

624.1′821 — Steel structures. Design

Lambert, F. W.. Structural steelwork / F.W. Lambert. — 3rd ed. — London : Godwin, 1982. — xi,141p : ill ; 22cm. — (Godwin study guides)
Previous ed.: London : Macdonald and Evans, 1977. — Includes index
ISBN 0-7114-5712-3 (pbk) : £4.95 : CIP rev.
B81-16378

MacGinley, T. J.. Steel structures : practical design studies / T.J. MacGinley. — London : Spon, 1981. — xxiii,319p : ill ; 24cm
Includes bibliographies and index
ISBN 0-419-12560-4 (cased) : Unpriced : CIP rev.
ISBN 0-419-11710-5 (pbk) : £7.95 B81-31269

624.1′821 — Structural components: Steel sections — *Tables*

British sections : a guide to replacement by continental sections : incorporating dimensions and properties of continental steel specifications. — 3rd ed. — London (92-96 Vauxhall Bridge Rd, SW1V 2RL) : British Constructional Steelwork Association, 1980. — 32p : ill ; 30cm
Previous ed.: 1978
Unpriced (pbk) B82-09477

624.1′821 — Structures. Steel composite materials. Joints — *Conference proceedings*

Joints in structural steelwork. — London : Pentech Press
Conference papers
Vol.2: Discussion. — Jan.1983. — [248]p
ISBN 0-7273-1002-x (pbk) : £15.00 : CIP entry
B82-40304

624.1′821 — Structures. Stressed steel diaphragm walls. Design — *Manuals*

Davies, J. M.. Manual of stressed skin diaphragm design. — London : Granada, July 1982. — [464]p
ISBN 0-246-11484-3 : £30.00 : CIP entry
B82-14510

624.1′821′07204 — Steel structures. Research in European institutions — *Directories*

Research and development in steel construction / European Convention for Constructional Steelwork ... ; prepared by the Technical General Secretariat of the ECCS. — London : Construction Press, 1981. — vii,163p ; 24cm
ISBN 0-86095-871-x (pbk) : £9.95 : CIP rev.
B82-00951

624.1′83 — Construction materials: Prestressed & reinforced masonry — *Conference proceedings*

Reinforced and prestressed masonry. — London : Thomas Telford, Nov.1982. — [166]p
Conference papers
ISBN 0-7277-0161-4 : £10.00 : CIP entry
B82-29428

624.18′3 — Masonry structural components. Design — *Manuals*

Structural masonry designers′ manual. — London : Granada, July 1982. — [512]p
ISBN 0-246-11208-5 : £30.00 : CIP entry
B82-12574

624.1′833 — Construction materials: Fibre reinforced cement — *Conference proceedings*

Fibre reinforced cement & concrete : Rilem symposium 1975 / edited by Adam Neville in association with D.J. Hannant ... [et al.]. — Lancaster : Construction Press
Vol.2. — 1976. — p463-450p : ill ; 31cm
Includes index
ISBN 0-904406-27-x : £9.50
Also classified at 624.1′8341 B82-08473

624.1′833 — Construction materials: Glass fibre reinforced cement

Fordyce, M. W.. GRC and buildings. — London : Butterworth, Dec.1982. — [224]p
ISBN 0-408-00395-2 : £9.00 : CIP entry
B82-29784

624.1′834 — Concrete. Aggregates. Mixes. Design. Applications of digital computer systems

Lewis, P. A.. Mixing aggregates to achieve a grading curve : theory, method and tutorial advantages / by P.A. Lewis. — Birmingham : Department of Transportation and Environmental Planning, University of Birmingham, 1982. — 37p ; 30cm. — (Departmental publication ; no.59)
Cover title
ISBN 0-7044-0616-0 (pbk) : Unpriced
B82-27445

624.1′834 — Concrete. Formwork

Hurst, Michael P.. Formwork. — London : Construction Press, Dec.1982. — [240]p
ISBN 0-582-41108-4 : £24.00 : CIP entry
B82-30063

624.1′834 — Concrete. Mixes

Lydon, F. D.. Concrete mix design. — 2nd ed. — London : Applied Science, Nov.1982. — [200]p
Previous ed.: 1972
ISBN 0-85334-162-1 : £23.00 : CIP entry
B82-26315

624.1′834 — Concrete. Mixes. Design

Design mix manual for concrete construction / Leslie D. "Doc" Long ... [et al.]. — New York ; London : McGraw-Hill, c1982. — xiv,391p : facsims,forms ; 29cm. — (An Engineering news-record book)
Bibliography: p387. — Includes index
ISBN 0-07-038683-8 : £35.50 B82-31564

624.1′834 — Concrete structures. Creep & shrinkage. Analysis. Applications of digital computer systems

Creep and shrinkage in concrete structures. — Chichester : Wiley, Jan.1983. — [350]p. — (Wiley series in numerical methods in engineering)
ISBN 0-471-10409-4 : £23.50 : CIP entry
B82-34617

624.1′834 — Construction materials: Concrete

Special concretes / [FIP Commission on Lightweight Concrete]. — Slough : Fédération Internationale de la Précontrainte, 1982. — 68p : ill ; 30cm. — (State of art report / Fédération Internationale de la Précontrainte)
Cover title
ISBN 0-907862-18-7 (pbk) : Unpriced
B82-37100

624.1′834 — Construction materials: Concrete. Defects. Control measures

Monks, William. The control of blemishes in concrete / William Monks. — Slough : Cement and Concrete Association, 1981. — 20p : ill ; 30cm. — (Appearance matters, ISSN 0144-0977 ; 3)
Bibliography: p18-19
ISBN 0-7210-1247-7 (pbk) : Unpriced
B82-11342

624.1′834 — Construction materials: Concrete — *For technicians*

Troy, J. F.. Concrete : materials technology / J.F. Troy. — London : Telford, 1982. — 27p : ill ; 15x21cm. — (ICE works construction guides)
Bibliography: p27
ISBN 0-7277-0139-8 (pbk) : £2.00 B82-18033

624.1′834 — Construction materials: Concrete. Internal ice. Effects

Turner, F. H.. The interaction of hardened concrete and internal ice at very low temperatures / by F.H. Turner. — [Doncaster] ([Torridge, Bagsby Rd., Owston Ferry, Doncaster, S. Yorks.]) : Institute of Concrete Technology, 1980. — 4p : ill ; 30cm. — (Technical note ; TN1)
Unpriced (unbound) B82-37566

624.1′834′0682 — Construction. Sites. Construction materials: Concrete. Use. Management aspects

Concrete on site : a checklist / [prepared by the Concrete Society Working Party functioning in conjunction with the Royal Military College of Science, Shrivenham]. — London : Concrete Society, 1980. — 40p : ill ; 22cm
ISBN 0-7210-1201-9 (pbk) : Unpriced
B82-35022

624.1′8341 — Construction materials: Fibre reinforced concrete — *Conference proceedings*
Fibre reinforced cement & concrete : Rilem symposium 1975 / edited by Adam Neville in association with D.J. Hannant ... [et al.]. — Lancaster : Construction Press
Vol.2. — 1976. — p463-450p : ill ; 31cm
Includes index
ISBN 0-904406-27-x : £9.50
Primary classification 624.1′833 B82-08473

624.1′8341 — Construction materials: Steel reinforced concrete. Reinforcing materials: Steel. Corrosion — *Conference proceedings*
Corrosion of steel reinforcements in concrete construction : proceedings of a symposium sponsored by the Society of Chemical Industry Materials Preservation Group, in conjunction with the Road and Building Materials Group, and held at the Society′s premises, 14 Belgrave Square, London SW1X 8PS, England, on 15 February 1978. — London : Society of Chemistry Industry, 1979. — 143p : ill ; 30cm
ISBN 0-901001-56-2 (pbk) : Unpriced
B82-31245

624.1′8341 — Reinforced & prestressed concrete structures. Design
CEB/FIP manual on bending and compression : design of sections under axial action effects at the ultimate limit state / prepared by Comité Euro-International du Béton (CEB) in co-operation with Fédération Internationale de la Précontrainte (FIP) ; editorial team E. Grasser ... [et al.]. — London : Construction Press, 1982. — xii,111p : ill,1port ; 31cm
Spine title: Bending and compression
ISBN 0-86095-701-2 : £15.00 : CIP rev.
B82-13166

624.1′8341 — Reinforced concrete. Bonding
International Conference on Bond in Concrete *(1982 : Paisley College of Technology)*. Bond in concrete / [proceedings of the International Conference on Bond in Concrete, held at Paisley College of Technology, Scotland, from 14 to 16 June 1982, organised in association with the Concrete Society (Scotland), the Institution of Structural Engineers and the American Concrete Institute] ; edited by P. Bartos. — London : Applied Science, c1982. — x,466p : ill ; 23cm
ISBN 0-85334-156-7 : £39.00 : CIP rev.
B82-12848

624.1′8341 — Reinforced concrete structural components. Design
Clements, R. W.. Design of reinforced concrete elements : (in accordance with CP 110 : 1972) / R.W. Clements. — 2nd ed. — London : Godwin, 1981. — xv,174p : ill ; 22cm. — (Godwin study guides)
Previous ed.: 1977. — Includes index
ISBN 0-7114-5646-1 (pbk) : £4.95 B82-30447

624.1′8341 — Reinforced concrete structures. Design
Leet, Kenneth. Reinforced concrete design / Kenneth Leet. — New York ; London : McGraw-Hill, c1982. — xi,544p : ill ; 25cm
Includes index
ISBN 0-07-037024-9 : £22.95 B82-37743

624.1′8341 — Reinforced concrete structures. Plasticity. Analysis
Chen, Wai-Fah. Plasticity in reinforced concrete / W.F. Chen. — New York ; London : McGraw-Hill, c1982. — xv,474p : ill ; 24cm
Includes bibliographies and index
ISBN 0-07-010687-8 : £28.95 B82-16284

624.1′83412 — Construction materials: Post-tensioned prestressed concrete
Wilby, C. B.. Post-tensioned prestressed concrete / C.B. Wilby. — London : Applied Science, c1981. — xviii,265p : ill ; 24cm
Includes index
ISBN 0-85334-944-4 : £22.00 B82-00568

624.1′83412 — Prestressed concrete structural components. Design
Naaman, Antoine E.. Prestressed concrete analysis and design : fundamentals / Antoine E. Naaman. — New York ; London : McGraw-Hill, c1982. — xxii,670p : ill,1chart ; 25cm
Includes index
ISBN 0-07-045761-1 : £24.75 B82-35770

624.1′83462 — Structures. Thin reinforced concrete shells. Analysis & design
Billington, David P.. Thin shell concrete structures / David P. Billington. — 2nd ed. — New York ; London : McGraw-Hill, c1982. — xviii,373p : ill ; 25cm
Previous ed.: 1965. — Includes index
ISBN 0-07-005279-4 : £30.50 B82-15975

624.1′84 — Adverse environments. Structural engineering materials: Timber — *Conference proceedings*
Structural use of wood in adverse environments / edited by Robert W. Meyer, Robert M. Kellogg ; [for the] Society of Wood Science and Technology. — New York ; London : Van Nostrand Reinhold, c1982. — xi,510p : ill ; 27cm
Conference proceedings. — Includes bibliographies and index
ISBN 0-442-28744-5 : £36.15 B82-30965

624.1′84 — Construction materials: Plywood
Plywood : its manufacture and uses / TRADA. — New ed. — High Wycombe : Timber Research and Development Association, 1981. — 58p : ill ; 30cm
Previous ed.: 1972. — Bibliography: p57-58
ISBN 0-901348-54-6 (pbk) : Unpriced
B82-14185

624.1′84 — Construction materials: Timber. Pests
Timber pests and their control. — 2nd ed. — High Wycombe : Timber Research and Development Association, 1981. — 59p : ill ; 30cm
Previous ed.: 1964. — Bibliography: p56-59
ISBN 0-901348-57-0 (pbk) : Unpriced
B82-14183

624.1′84 — Temporary structures. Construction materials: Timber
Timber in excavations / Timber in Temporary Works. — High Wycombe : Timber Research and Development Association, 1981. — 76p : ill ; 30cm
ISBN 0-901348-58-9 (pbk) : Unpriced
B82-14177

624.1′84 — Timber structural components. Design — *Manuals*
Structural timber design and technology. — London : Construction Press, Feb.1982. — [240]p
ISBN 0-86095-889-2 : £19.95 : CIP entry
B81-36348

624.1′84 — Timber structural components. Finger joints — *Conference proceedings*
Production, marketing and use of finger-jointed sawnwood : proceedings of an international seminar organized by the Timber Committee of the United Nations Economic Commission for Europe, held at Hamar, Norway, at the invitation of the Government of Norway, 15 to 19 September 1980 / edited by C.F.L. Prins. — The Hague ; London : Martinus Nijhof for the United Nations, 1982. — ix,282p : ill ; 25cm. — (Forestry sciences)
ISBN 90-247-2569-0 : Unpriced B82-18402

624.1′84 — Timber structures. Metal plate joints. Moment-rotation relationships
Morris, E. N.. The moment-rotation relationship for joints with metal plate connectors / E.N. Morris. — Glasgow : Information Services (Publications), Department of Architecture & Building Science, University of Strathclyde, 1978. — 14leaves : 3ill ; 30cm. — (Occasional paper / University of Strathclyde Department of Architecture & Building Science ; 78/5)
Bibliography: leaves 13-14
Unpriced (spiral) B82-22371

624.1′8923 — Plastics structural components
Benjamin, B. S.. Structural design with plastics / by B.S. Benjamin. — 2nd ed., rev. and enl. — New York ; London : Van Nostrand Reinhold, c1982. — xi,387p : ill ; 24cm
Previous ed.: 1969. — Includes index
ISBN 0-442-20167-2 : £27.20 B82-08234

624.1′8923 — Structural engineering materials: Plastics — *Conference proceedings*
Plastics in material and structural engineering : proceedings of the ICP-RILEM-IBK International Symposium, Prague, June 23-25 1981 / edited by Richard A. Bares in association with K. Gamski, L. Hollaway, H.J. Saechtling. — Amsterdam ; Oxford : Elsevier Scientific, c1982. — vii,954p : ill ; 25cm. — (Developments in civil engineering ; 5)
Includes index
ISBN 0-444-99710-5 : £82.09 : CIP rev.
B81-34493

624.1′9 — Underground structures. Construction
Hoek, Evert. Underground excavations in rock / E. Hoek, E.T. Brown. — London : The Institution of Mining and Metallurgy, 1980. — 527p : ill ; 29cm
Includes index
ISBN 0-900488-54-9 (cased) : Unpriced
ISBN 0-900488-55-7 (pbk) : Unpriced
B82-15430

624.1′93 — Tunnels & tunnelling
Megan, T. M.. Tunnelling. — London : Telford, Dec.1982. — [44]p. — (ICE works construction guides)
ISBN 0-7277-0160-6 (pbk) : £2.00 : CIP entry
B82-32297

Megaw, T. M.. Tunnels : planning, design, construction / T.M. Megaw and J.V. Bartlett. — Chichester : Ellis Horwood. — (Ellis Horwood series in engineering science)
Vol.2. — 1982. — 321p : ill,maps ; 24cm
Text on lining papers. — Bibliography: p276-315. — Includes index
ISBN 0-85312-361-6 : Unpriced : CIP rev.
ISBN 0-470-27209-0 (Halstead) B81-08939

Tunnel engineering handbook / edited by John O. Bickel, T.R. Kuesel. — New York ; London : Van Nostrand Reinhold, c1982. — vii,670p : ill ; 27cm
Includes index
ISBN 0-442-28127-7 (pbk) : £44.65
B82-30961

624.1′93 — Tunnels. Waterproofing
Tunnel waterproofing. — London : Construction Industry Research and Information Association, 1979 (1981 [printing]). — 55p : ill ; 30cm. — (CIRIA report, ISSN 0305-408x ; 81)
Bibliography: p42-43
ISBN 0-86017-125-6 (pbk) : £20.00 (£5.00 to members of CIRIA) B82-00818

624.1′93 — Vehicle tunnels. Aerodynamics & ventilation — *Conference proceedings*
International Symposium on the Aerodynamics & Ventilation of Vehicle Tunnels *(4th : 1982 : York)*. Papers presented at the Fourth International Symposium on the Aerodynamics & Ventilation of Vehicle Tunnels held at York, England March 23-25, 1982 / conference sponsored and organised by BHRA Fluid Engineering. — Bedford : BHRA Fluid Engineering, [1982]. — viii,504p : ill ; 30cm
ISBN 0-906085-63-2 (pbk) : Unpriced
B82-31359

624.1′93′028 — Tunnelling machinery, *to 1981*
Stack, Barbara. Handbook of mining and tunnelling machinery / Barbara Stack. — Chichester : Wiley, c1982. — xxix,742p : ill ; 28cm
Text on lining papers. — Includes index
ISBN 0-471-27937-4 : £38.00
Primary classification 622′.028 B82-18222

624.1′93′094 — Europe. Tunnels. Construction — *Conference proceedings*
Eurotunnel ′80 *(Conference : Basle)*. Eurotunnel ′80 : papers presented at the Eurotunnel ′80 conference, organized by The Institution of Mining and Metallurgy, held in Basle, Switzerland, from 16 to 19 September, 1980 / edited by Michael J. Jones. — London : The Institution of Mining and Metallurgy, c1980. — vii,156p : ill ; 30cm
English text with English, French and German summaries
ISBN 0-900488-50-6 (pbk) : Unpriced
B82-15424

624.2 — BRIDGES

624′.2 — England. Thames River. River crossings

Phillips, Geoffrey, *1921-*. Thames crossings : bridges, tunnels and ferries / Geoffrey Phillips. — Newton Abbot : David & Charles, c1981. — 268p : ill,2maps ; 24cm
Bibliography: p260-262. — Includes index
ISBN 0-7153-8202-0 : £14.95 : CIP rev. B81-30591

624′.2 — Great Britain. Road bridges. Effects of heavy lorries

EEC vehicles : lorries and the environment : report on study into the effects of heavy vehicles on bridges. — London : Department of Transport, 1980. — 73p : ill ; 30cm
£3.20 (spiral) B82-13343

624′.2 — Prestressed concrete bridges. Design & construction

Podolny, Walter. Construction and design of prestressed concrete segmental bridges / Walter Podolny, Jr., Jean M. Muller. — New York ; Chichester : Wiley, c1982. — xi,561p : ill ; 29cm
Includes index
ISBN 0-471-05658-8 : £48.00 B82-37997

624′.2′09413 — South-east Scotland. Bridges, ***to 1973***

Paxton, Roland. A heritage of bridges between Edinburgh, Kelso and Berwick / by Roland Paxton and Ted Ruddock. — Edinburgh (c/o D. Haldane, Department of Civil Engineering, Heriot-Watt University, Riccarton, Currie EH14 4AS) : Institution of Civil Engineers, Edinburgh and East of Scotland Association, [1980]. — [36]p : ill,2maps ; 22cm
Text and ill on inside covers
£1.50 (pbk) B82-16037

624′.25 — Bridges. Aerodynamics — ***Conference proceedings***

Bridge aerodynamics : proceedings of a conference held at the Institution of Civil Engineers, London, 25-26 March 1981. — London : Telford for the Institution, 1981. — 123p : ill ; 30cm
ISBN 0-7277-0135-5 : £14.00 B82-15390

624′.25 — Concrete bridges. Design — ***Manuals***

Clark, L. A.. Concrete bridge design to BS 5400. — London : Construction Press, Aug.1982. — [256]p
ISBN 0-86095-893-0 : £30.00 : CIP entry B82-16681

624′.37 — Steel & concrete composite plate girder bridges. Steel structural components — ***Technical data***

Knowles, P. R.. Simply supported composite plate girder highway bridge / P.R. Knowles. — Croydon : Constrado, c1976. — 27p : ill ; 30cm. — (Design of structural steelwork)
Cover title. — Bibliography: p27
Unpriced (pbk) B82-17739

624′.4′0941 — Great Britain. Steel box girder bridges. Design. Standards: British Standards Institution. Steel, concrete and composite bridges — ***Conference proceedings***

Code of practice for the design of steel bridges : symposium on BS5400 pt.3 Draft for public comment : Wednesday, 29 January 1980 Bloomsbury Centre Hotel, London W.C.1. — London (11 Upper Belgrave St., SW1X 8BH) : Institution of Structural Engineers, 1980. — 44p : ill ; 30cm
£8.00 (£5.00 to members of the Institution) (pbk) B82-34144

624′.6′099441 — New South Wales. Sydney. Arch bridges: Sydney Harbour Bridge, ***to 1981***

Spearritt, Peter. Sydney Harbour Bridge. — London : Allen and Unwin, Mar.1982. — [120]p
ISBN 0-86861-331-2 (cased) : £10.95 : CIP entry
ISBN 0-86861-339-8 (pbk) : £5.50 B82-11487

624′.67′0942812 — West Yorkshire ***(Metropolitan County).*** **Brighouse. Iron bridges: Kirklees Iron Bridge**

Nortcliffe, David. A preliminary report on the Kirklees Iron Bridge of 1769 and its builder / by David Nortcliffe. — [Leeds] ([Claremont, Clarendon Rd., Leeds LS2 9NZ]) : [Yorkshire Archaeological Society], 1979. — 3leaves,[1]leaf of plates : 1ill,1facsim ; 30cm
At head of title: Yorkshire Archaeological Society, Industrial History Section
Unpriced (unbound) B82-23421

625 — RAILWAY ENGINEERING AND ROAD CONSTRUCTION

625′.092′2 — Central Southern England. Railway construction contractors & railway engineers, ***1840-1914 — Lists***

Popplewell, Lawrence. A gazetteer of the railway contractors and engineers of Central Southern England 1840-1914. — Ferndown (30 Trent Way, Heatherlands Estate, Tricketts Cross, Ferndown, Dorset) : Melledgen Press, Oct.1982. — [44]p
ISBN 0-906637-02-3 (pbk) : £2.25 : CIP entry B82-31320

625.1 — RAILWAY ENGINEERING

625.1 — Railway engineering

Hay, William W.. Railroad engineering / William W. Hay. — 2nd ed. — New York ; Chichester : Wiley, c1982. — xvi,758p : ill ; 24cm
Previous ed.: 1953. — Includes index
ISBN 0-471-36400-2 : £37.00 B82-39917

625.1 — Tyne and Wear ***(Metropolitan County).*** **Coal industries. Industrial railway services: Bowes Railway. Industrial antiquities —** ***Visitors' guides***

Tyne & Wear Industrial Monuments Trust. Tyne & Wear Industrial Monuments Trust : a visitors brochure / Colin E. Mountford. — [Newcastle-upon-Tyne] : [The Trust], [c1980]. — 28p : ill,maps,1plan,1port ; 22cm
ISBN 0-906283-08-6 (pbk) : Unpriced B82-38652

625.1′00941 — Great Britain. Railway services. Lines — ***Technical data***

Oakley, Michael. Diesel enthusiasts pocket guide : including electrics / Michael Oakley. — Truro : Barton
[5]: L.M. Region north west. — [1981?]. — [48]p : ill,1map ; 19cm
Text on inside covers
ISBN 0-85153-406-6 (pbk) : £0.75 B82-10910

Oakley, Michael. Diesel enthusiasts pocket guide : including electrics / Michael Oakley. — Truro : Barton
[6]: Wales and Borders. — [1981?]. — [48]p : ill,maps ; 19cm
Text on inside covers
ISBN 0-85153-407-4 (pbk) : £0.75 B82-10913

Oakley, Michael. Diesel enthusiasts pocket guide : including electrics / Michael Oakley. — Truro : Barton
[7]: Thames-Cotswolds. — [1981?]. — [48]p : 1map ; 19cm
Text on inside covers
ISBN 0-85153-408-2 (pbk) : £0.75 B82-10914

Oakley, Michael. Diesel enthusiasts pocket guide : including electrics / Michael Oakley. — Truro : Barton
[8]: Wessex and West Country. — [1981?]. — [48]p : ill,maps ; 19cm
Text on inside covers
ISBN 0-85153-409-0 (pbk) : £0.75 B82-10915

Oakley, Michael. Diesel enthusiasts pocket guide : including electrics / Michael Oakley. — Truro : Barton
[9]: South and South East. — [1981]. — [48]p : ill,maps ; 19cm
Text on inside covers
ISBN 0-85153-410-4 (pbk) : £0.75 B82-10911

Oakley, Michael. Diesel enthusiasts pocket guide : including electrics / Michael Oakley. — Truro : Barton
[10]: Scottish Region. — [1981?]. — [48]p : ill,maps ; 19cm
Text on inside covers
ISBN 0-85153-411-2 (pbk) : £0.75 B82-10912

625.1′009423′5 — Devon. Railways. Industrial antiquities

Hall, Jean, *1925-*. Railway landmarks in Devon / Jean Hall. — Newton Abbot : David & Charles, c1982. — 48p : ill,1map ; 21cm
Bibliography: p47-48. — Includes index
ISBN 0-7153-8363-9 (pbk) : £1.95 : CIP rev. B82-10872

625.1′00957′5 — Russia ***(RSFSR).*** **Eastern Siberia. Railway services: BAM. Construction —** ***For children***

Raksha, Irina. An unusual journey / Irina Raksha ; designed by Edward Zaryansky ; translated from the Russian by Jan Butler. — Moscow : Progress, c1980 ; [London] : Distributed by Central Books. — 38[i.e.66]p : ill(some col.) ; 29cm
Translation from the Russian. — Ill on lining papers
ISBN 0-7147-1663-4 : £2.25 B82-03865

625.1′63 — Great Britain. Level crossings. Safety measures — ***Standards***

Railway construction and operation requirements : level crossings / Department of Transport. — London : H.M.S.O., 1981. — iv,55p,[1]folded leaf : ill ; 25cm
ISBN 0-11-550540-7 (pbk) : £3.50 B82-13830

625.1′65′0924 — England. Railway services: British Rail. ***London Midland Region.*** **Signalling systems,** ***ca 1950-1965 — Personal observations***

Burke, M.. Signalman / M. Burke. — Truro : Barton, [1982?]. — 112p : ill,2maps ; 22cm
ISBN 0-85153-423-6 (pbk) : £3.50 B82-35712

625.1′65′0941 — Great Britain. Railways. Signalling systems. Engineering aspects

Railway signalling : a treatise on the recent practice of British Railways / prepared under the direction of a committee of the Institution of Railway Signal Engineers, under the general editorship of O.S. Nock. — London : A. & C. Black, 1980. — viii,312p : ill ; 20x26cm
Includes index
ISBN 0-7136-2067-6 : £15.00 : CIP rev. B80-06467

625.1′9 — Miniature railways & model railways

Andress, Michael. PSL model railway guide. — Cambridge : Stephens
7: Modern railways. — Oct.1982. — [64]p
ISBN 0-85059-452-9 (pbk) : £2.95 : CIP entry B82-26054

Andress, Michael. PSL model railway guide. — Cambridge : Stephens
8: Narrow-gauge railways. — Oct.1982. — [64]p
ISBN 0-85059-453-7 (pbk) : £2.95 : CIP entry B82-26055

Williams, Guy R.. The world of model trains / Guy R. Williams. — London : Deutsch in association with Rainbird, 1970 (1980 [printing]). — 256p : ill(some col.) ; 26cm
Ill on lining papers. — Bibliography: p245. — Includes index
ISBN 0-233-96227-1 : £8.95 B82-03963

625.1′9 — Model railway equipment. Electronic equipment. Projects — ***Amateurs' manuals***

Penfold, R. A.. Model railway projects / by R.A. Penfold. — London : Babani, c1981. — 96p : ill ; 18cm. — (Bernard Babani ; BP95)
ISBN 0-85934-070-8 (pbk) : £1.95 : CIP rev. B81-30404

625.1′9 — Model railways

Andress, Michael. PSL model railway guide / Michael Andress. — Cambridge : Stephens, 1981. — 64,64p : ill ; 25cm
Originally published: in 2 vols. 1979
ISBN 0-85059-587-8 : £4.95 B82-12035

625.1′9 — Model railways *continuation*
Andress, Michael. PSL model railway guide / Michael Andress. — Cambridge : Stephens, 1982. — 62,63p : ill ; 25cm
Originally published: in 2 vols. 1980
ISBN 0-85059-588-6 : Unpriced B82-22261

Corkill, W. A.. Beginner′s guide to railway modelling. — Newton Abbot : David & Charles, Oct.1982. — [64]p
ISBN 0-7153-8127-x (pbk) : £3.95 : CIP entry B82-23007

625.1′9 — Model railways. Construction
Leigh, Chris. Model railway constructor special. — Shepperton : Ian Allan
2: Scenery. — 1982. — 48p : ill ; 29cm
ISBN 0-7110-1190-7 (pbk) : £1.75 B82-26190

Simmons, Norman. How to go railway modelling. — 4th ed. — London : Cambridge : Stephens, Sept.1981. — [216]p
Previous ed.: 1980
ISBN 0-85059-557-6 : £8.95 : CIP entry B81-21590

625.1′9 — Model railways. Construction — *Manuals*
Leigh, Chris. Model railway constructor special / Chris Leigh. — London : Ian Allan
3: Baseboards and trackwork. — 1982. — 48p : chiefly ill ; 29cm
ISBN 0-7110-1195-8 (pbk) : £1.95 B82-34787

625.1′9 — Model steam locomotives: Evening Star. Construction — *Manuals*
Evans, Martin. Evening Star / by Martin Evans and L.B.S.C.. — [Watford] : Model & Allied, 1980. — 224p : ill ; 24cm
Includes index
ISBN 0-85242-634-8 (pbk) : £5.95 B82-10313

625.1′9 — 'N' & 'Z' gauge model railways. Construction — *Manuals*
Kelly, Robert. Micro-model railways. — Newton Abbot : David and Charles, Nov.1982. — [96]p
ISBN 0-7153-8326-4 (pbk) : £5.95 : CIP entry B82-26398

625.1′9 — ′O′ gauge model railway equipment — *Lists*
Trade directory / Gauge ′O′ Guild. — 2nd ed. / compiled by Keith Paling, Phil Williams, assisted by John Chamney ... [et al.]. — Slough (7 Sawmill Cottages, Black Park Rd., Slough) : Gauge ′O′ Guild, 1981. — 144p ; 20cm
Previous ed.: 1973
£3.00 (pbk) B82-03570

625.1′9 — 'O' gauge model railways. Signals. Construction — *Manuals*
Signal construction : with prototype notes / edited by Martin Bloxsom and Dennis McCann. — Gillingham, Dorset (40 Shreen Way, Gillingham, Dorset) : Gauge O Guild, [1980]. — 66p : ill ; 21cm. — (Gauge 'O' Guild handbook ; no.5)
£1.25 (unbound) B82-35800

625.1′9 — United States. ′S′ gauge model railway equipment — *Buyers′ guides*
Greenberg′s price guide American flyer S Gauge / Paul G. Yorkis ... [et al.]. — Sykesville, Md. : Greenberg ; Wokingham : Distributed by Van Nostrand Reinhold, 1980. — 175p : ill(some col.),1facsim,1form,ports ; 29cm
ISBN 0-442-21209-7 : Unpriced B82-21713

625.1′9′028 — Model railways. Electronic equipment. Circuits. Construction — *Manuals*
Amos, Roger. Practical electronics for railway modellers. — Cambridge : Patrick Stephens, Sept.1982. — [120]p
ISBN 0-85059-555-x : £7.95 : CIP entry B82-20490

625.1′9′05 — Model railways. Construction — *Serials*
Scale trains. — Vol.1, no.1 (Apr. 1982)-. — Leicester (P.O. Box 80, Smith Dorrien Rd, Leicester LE5 4BS) : Blackfriars Press, 1982-. — v. : ill ; 30cm
Monthly
ISSN 0262-8406 = Scale trains : £9.75 per year B82-20891

625.1′9′05 — Model railways — *Serials*
Model trains. — Vol.1, no.1 (Jan. 1980)-. — Old Woking : Gresham Books for Airfix Products, 1980-. — v. : ill,plans ; 30cm
Monthly
ISSN 0263-1369 = Model trains : £7.25 per year B82-17258

PSL′s practical guide to railway modelling. — No.1. — Cambridge : Stephens, Sept.1981. — [96]p
ISBN 0-85059-548-7 : £3.95 : CIP entry B81-20510

625.2′0941 — Great Britain. Railway services: British Rail. Rolling stock — *History*
British rail fleet survey / Brian Haresnape. — London : Ian Allan
2: Western Region diesel-hydraulics. — 1982. — 79p : ill ; 28cm
ISBN 0-7110-1122-2 (pbk) : £2.95 B82-14760

British Rail fleet survey / Brian Haresnape. — London : Ian Allan
3: Production diesel-electrics, types 4 and 5. — 1982. — 79p : chiefly ill ; 29cm
ISBN 0-7110-1189-3 (pbk) : £2.95 B82-34786

625.2′0941 — Great Britain. Railway services: London, Midland and Scottish Railway. Rolling stock, *to ca 1940* — *Illustrations*
Twells, H. N.. L.M.S. miscellany : a pictorial record of the Company′s activities in the public eye and behind the scenes / [compiled] by H.N. Twells. — Oxford : Oxford Publishing, c1982. — [128]p : chiefly ill,facsims,1map,ports ; 28cm
Map on lining papers
ISBN 0-86093-172-2 : £7.95 B82-35851

625.2′09411 — Scotland. Railway passenger transport services. Disused routes. Trains, *to 1977* — *Illustrations*
The Last trains. — Edinburgh : Moorfoot
3: South-West Scotland / edited by W.S. Sellar & J.L. Stevenson. — c1981. — [24]p : ill,ports ; 21cm
ISBN 0-906606-03-9 (pbk) : Unpriced B82-06404

625.2′09415 — Ireland. Rolling stock — *Technical data*
Doyle, Oliver. Locomotives and rolling stock of Coras Iompair Eireann and Northern Ireland Railways / by Oliver Doyle and Stephen Hirsch. — 2nd ed. — Malahide : Signal, 1981. — 96p : ill ; 16cm
Previous ed.: 1979. — Ill on inside covers
ISBN 0-906591-00-7 (pbk) : £1.95 B82-26926

625.2′0942 — England. Railway services: Great Western Railway. Rolling stock. Preservation, *to 1980*
Hollingsworth, J. B.. Great Western adventure / Brian Hollingsworth. — Newton Abbot : David & Charles, c1981. — 174p,[16]p of plates : ill ; 23cm
Includes index
ISBN 0-7153-8108-3 : £5.95 : CIP rev. B81-28052

625.2′09421 — London. Railway services: London Passenger Transport Board. Rolling stock, *to 1948* — *Illustrations*
L.P.T.B. rolling stock 1933-1948 / [compiled by Brian Hardy]. — Truro : Barton, [1981]. — 71p : chiefly ill ; 23cm
ISBN 0-85153-436-8 : £5.95 B82-12385

625.2′3′0942 — England. Railway services: Great Western Railway. Rolling stock: Coaches — *Illustrations*
Great Western coaches appendix / [compiled] by J.H. Russell. — Oxford : Oxford Publishing
Vol.1: Standard passenger stock. — c1980. — viii,208p : chiefly ill,plans ; 31cm
Includes index
ISBN 0-86093-084-x : £11.90 B82-10066

625.2′4 — Great Britain. Rolling stock: Petroleum tankers, *to 1979*
Tourret, R.. Petroleum tail tank wagons of Britain / by R. Tourret. — Abingdon : Tourret Publishing, c1980. — x,140p : ill,1map ; 31cm
Includes index
ISBN 0-905878-02-7 : £8.85 B82-17311

625.2′4′0941 — Great Britain. Gloucester Railway Carriage & Wagon Company privately owned goods wagons — *Illustrations*
Private owner wagons : from The Gloucester Railway Carriage and Wagon Company Ltd / compiled by Keith Montague. — Oxford : Oxford Publishing, c1981. — x,182p : ill,plans ; 28cm
ISBN 0-86093-124-2 : £9.90 B82-10070

625.2′4′0941 — Great Britain. Railway services: London, Midland and Scottish Railway. Freight rolling stock. Engineering aspects — *Illustrations — For modelling*
Essery, R. J.. An illustrated history of Midland wagons / by R.J. Essery. — Oxford : Oxford Publishing
Vol.2. — c1980. — 169p : ill,1coat of arms,facsims,plans ; 28cm
ISBN 0-86093-041-6 : £7.95 B82-40794

An **Illustrated** history of L.M.S. wagons / [compiled] by R.J. Essery. — Oxford : Oxford Publishing, c1981
Vol.1. — viii,179p : chiefly ill,plans ; 28cm
Includes index
ISBN 0-86093-127-7 : £9.90 B82-31353

625.2′4′0942 — England. Railway services: British Rail. *Western Region*. Freight rolling stock, *1909-1964* — *Illustrations*
Freight wagons and loads in service on the Great Western Railway and British Rail, Western Region / [compiled] by J.H. Russell. — Oxford : Oxford Publishing, c1981. — ca.250p : chiefly ill ; 31cm
Includes index
ISBN 0-86093-155-2 : £11.90 B82-23038

625.2′6 — Great Britain. Railway services: British Rail. Locomotives. Engines — *Technical data*
BR traction. — Solihull (PO Box 77, Solihull, B91 3LX) : Confederal, c1982. — [62]p : ill ; 11x21cm
Cover title. — Text on inside cover
Unpriced (pbk) B82-21337

625.2′6 — West Germany. Industrial railway services. Locomotives — *Technical data*
Existing industrial locomotives of West Germany = Ein Verzeichnis der gegenwärtigen Werkslokomotiven in der Deutschen Bundesrepublik. — London : Industrial Railway Society. — (Industrial Railway Society pocket book ; GE 1)
English and German text. — Includes index
Book 1 = Teil 1: Hessen/Rheinland-Pfalz/Saar / compiled by Brian Rumary ; German translations by M. Murray and A. Christopher. — c1981. — 72p[16]p of plates : ill,maps ; 22cm
ISBN 0-901096-39-3 (pbk) : Unpriced B82-00965

625.2′6′0941 — Great Britain. Locomotives designed by Robinson, J. G., *to ca 1950*
Haresnape, Brian. Robinson locomotives : a pictorial history / by Brian Haresnape and Peter Rowledge. — London : Ian Allan, 1982. — 128p : ill ; 24cm
Ill on lining papers. — Bibliography: p128
ISBN 0-7110-1151-6 : £6.95 B82-30641

625.2′6′0941 — Great Britain. Locomotives manufactured by Hudswell Clarke & Company, *to 1971* — *Technical data*
Hardy, Clive. Hudswell Clarke & Company Ltd : locomotive works list / Clive Hardy. — Birmingham : Aleksandr, 1982, c1981. — 368p : ill,1facsim ; 22cm
ISBN 0-906829-06-2 : Unpriced B82-38019

625.2′6′0941 — Great Britain. Locomotives manufactured by Manning, Wardle & Company, *to 1926* — *Technical data*
Mabbott, F. W.. Manning Wardle & Company Ltd : locomotive works list / F.W. Mabbott. — Birmingham : Aleksandr, 1982, c1981. — 288p : ill ; 22cm
ISBN 0-906829-08-9 : Unpriced B82-38018

625.2′6′0941 — Great Britain. Railway services: British Rail. Locomotive depots. Locomotives — *Illustrations*

Diesels and electrics on shed / [compiled] by Rex Kennedy. — Oxford : Oxford Publishing
Vol.4: Scottish region. — c1982. — [112p] : chiefly ill,1map ; 29cm
ISBN 0-86093-043-2 : £5.95 B82-23039

625.2′6′0941 — Great Britain. Railway services: British Rail. Rolling stock. Locomotives & multiple units — *Lists*

British Railways spotters companion / compiled by the National Railway Enthusiasts Association. — Oxford : Oxford Publishing, c1979. — 79p : ill ; 18cm
Text on inside cover
ISBN 0-86093-097-1 (pbk) : £0.50 B82-40567

625.2′6′0942 — England. Railway services: British Rail. *Western Region.* **Locomotives & multiple units,** *1957-1981*

Body, Geoffrey. Western motive power / written and compiled by Geoffrey Body. — Weston-super-Mare : Avon-Anglia in association with British Rail (Western), c1982. — 32p : ill ; 21cm. — (Western at work ; no.2)
ISBN 0-905466-40-3 (pbk) : Unpriced B82-35816

625.2′6′0947 — Soviet Union. Locomotives, *1928-1952*

Westwood, J. N.. Soviet locomotive technology during industrialization, 1928-1952 / J.N. Westwood. — London : Macmillan in association with the Centre for Russian and East European Studies University of Birmingham, 1982. — x,240p,[16]p of plates : ill,2facsims,ports ; 23cm. — (Studies in Soviet history and society)
Bibliography: p232-233. — Includes index
ISBN 0-333-27516-0 : £20.00 B82-28680

625.2′61 — Great Britain. Steam locomotives. Boilers. Accidents: Explosions, *to 1962*

Hewison, C. H.. Locomotive boiler explosions. — Newton Abbot : David & Charles, Feb.1983. — [144]p
ISBN 0-7153-8305-1 : £6.50 : CIP entry B82-39443

625.2′61 — Great Britain. Steam locomotives. Preservation

Ransom, P. J. G.. Your book of steam railway preservation. — London : Faber, Oct.1982. — 1v.
ISBN 0-571-11931-x : £5.25 : CIP entry B82-28470

625.2′61′0222 — Steam locomotives — *Illustrations*

Garratt, Colin. Railway photographer / Colin Garratt. — London : New English Library, 1982. — 168p : col.ill ; 24cm
ISBN 0-450-04861-6 : £9.95 B82-21943

625.2′61′05 — Railway services. Steam locomotives — *Serials*

Steam world. — No.1 (Apr. 1981)-. — Sutton (Surrey House, Throwley Way, Sutton, Surrey SM1 4QQ) : IPC Specialist & Professional Press, 1981-. — v. : ill(some col.),ports ; 30cm
Monthly. — Description based on: No.6 (Sept. 1981)
ISSN 0263-0877 = Steam world : £15.00 per year B82-18512

625.2′61′06041 — Great Britain. Preserved steam locomotives. Organisations — *Lists* **—** *Serials*

Guide to steam trains in the British Isles. — 1977-. — Sheringham (Sheringham Station, Norfolk) : Association of Railway Preservation Societies, 1977-. — v. ; 43x19cm folded to 9x19cm
Annual. — Description based on: 1981 issue
ISSN 0262-3943 = Guide to steam trains in the British Isles : Unpriced B82-13411

625.2′61′09 — Garratt articulated steam locomotives, *to 1980*

Durrant, A. E.. Garratt locomotives of the world / A.E. Durrant. — Rev. and enl. ed. — Newton Abbot : David & Charles, 1981. — 207p : ill(some col.) ; 31cm
Previous ed.: published as The Garratt locomotive. 1969. — Bibliography: p201-202. — Includes index
ISBN 0-7153-7641-1 : £10.95 : CIP rev. B81-17492

625.2′61′09 — Steam locomotives, *to 1980*

Garratt, Colin. Colin Garratt's world of steam. — [London] : Octopus, [1981]. — 157p : chiefly col.ill ; 30cm
Includes index
ISBN 0-7064-1506-x : £6.95 B82-16303

625.2′61′0924 — Great Britain. Railway services. Steam locomotives. Firing, *1930-1950* **—** *Personal observations*

Bushell, George. LMS locoman : Wellingborough footplate memories / George Bushell. — Truro : Barton, [1982?]. — 112p : ill ; 22cm
ISBN 0-85153-424-4 (pbk) : £3.50 B82-35704

Bushell, George. LMS locoman : Willesden footplate memories / George Bushell. — Truro : Barton, [1982?]. — 112p : ill ; 22cm
ISBN 0-85153-425-2 (pbk) : £3.50 B82-35705

625.2′61′0924 — Great Britain. Steam locomotives designed by Gresley, *Sir* **Nigel**

Haresnape, Brian. Gresley locomotives : a pictorial history / by Brian Haresnape. — London : Ian Allan, 1981. — 176p : ill,plans ; 24cm
Ill on lining papers. — Bibliography: p176
ISBN 0-7110-0892-2 : £7.95 B82-11213

625.2′61′0924 — Southern England. Railway services: British Rail. *Southern Region.* **Steam locomotives. Firing,** *1946-1955* **—** *Personal observations*

Jackman, Michael. Engineman S.R. / Michael Jackman. — Truro : Barton, [1982?]. — 112p : ill ; 22cm
ISBN 0-85153-439-2 (pbk) : £3.50 B82-35706

625.2′61′0924 — Southern England. Railway services: British Rail. *Southern Region.* **Steam locomotives. Firing,** *1946-1965* **—** *Personal observations*

Hollands, George. Southern locoman / George Hollands. — Truro : Barton, [1982?]. — 110p : ill ; 22cm
ISBN 0-85153-422-8 (pbk) : £3.50 B82-35710

625.2′61′0941 — Great Britain. Gresley Pacific type steam locomotives

Nock, O. S.. The Gresley Pacifics / O.S. Nock. — New omnibus ed. combining parts 1 and 2. — Newton Abbot : David & Charles, 1982. — 284p : ill,plans,ports ; 26cm
Previous ed.: published in 2 vols. Pt.1, 1973 ; Pt.2, 1975. — Bibliography: p279. — Includes index
ISBN 0-7153-8388-4 : Unpriced : CIP rev. B82-15842

625.2′61′0941 — Great Britain. Preserved steam locomotives

Garratt, Colin. Preserved steam locomotives of Britain. — Poole : Blandford Press, Oct.1982. — [160]p. — (Colour series)
ISBN 0-7137-0917-0 : £6.95 : CIP entry B82-25090

625.2′61′0941 — Great Britain. Preserved steam locomotives — *Serials*

Steam. — ′82. — London : Allen and Unwin, Feb.1982. — [250]p
ISBN 0-04-385091-x (pbk) : £4.95 : CIP entry B81-39243

625.2′61′0941 — Great Britain. Railway services: British Rail. Main lines. Privately preserved steam locomotives

Main line steam : Steam Locomotive Operators Association handbook. — London : Ian Allan, 1982. — 58p : ill,1map ; 24cm
ISBN 0-7110-1235-0 (pbk) : £2.95 B82-26191

625.2′61′0941 — Great Britain. Railway services: British Rail. Standard classes steam locomotives, *1951-1967.* **Engineering aspects**

Allen, Geoffrey Freeman. The Riddles standard types in traffic / G. Freeman Allen. — London : Allen & Unwin, 1982. — 111p : ill ; 23cm. — (Steam past)
Includes index
ISBN 0-04-385092-8 : Unpriced : CIP rev. B82-10580

Beattie, Ian. B.R. standard locomotives : to scale / Ian Beattie. — Truro : Barton, c1981. — 59p : ill,plans ; 22x30cm
ISBN 0-85153-390-6 : £5.95 B82-11001

625.2′61′0941 — Great Britain. Railway services: British Rail. Standard classes steam locomotives, *1951-* **—** *Illustrations*

BR standard steam in close-up / edited by Tony Fairclough and Alan Wills. — Truro : Barton
Vol.2. — [1980]. — 95p : chiefly ill ; 23cm
ISBN 0-85153-356-6 : £5.95 B82-14970

625.2′61′0941 — Great Britain. Railway services: British Rail. Steam locomotives, *1970-1980* **—** *Illustrations*

Siviter, Roger. Steam specials : British Rail's return to steam / Roger Siviter ; with special feature by Bernard Staite. — Newton Abbot : David & Charles, c1981. — 89p : chiefly ill,maps ; 25cm
ISBN 0-7153-8126-1 : £5.95 : CIP rev. B81-21511

625.2′61′0941 — Great Britain. Railway services: British Rail. Steam locomotives, *1971-1981*

Nixon, L. A.. A decade of BR steam running : 1971-1981 / L.A. Nixon. — London : Ian Allan, 1981. — 95p : ill,1map ; 24cm
ISBN 0-7110-1177-x (pbk) : £3.50 B82-11212

625.2′61′0941 — Great Britain. Railway services: British Rail. Steam locomotives. Firing & driving, *1950-1965*

Forsythe, H. G.. Men of steam : a portrait of life on the footplate / H.G. Forsythe. — St Day : Atlantic, 1982. — [48]p : ill,ports ; 20cm
ISBN 0-906899-04-4 (pbk) : £1.95 B82-37532

625.2′61′0941 — Great Britain. Railway services: London and North Eastern Railway. 4-6-2 steam locomotives, *1922-1965* **—** *Illustrations*

Whiteley, J. S.. Power of the A1s, A2s and A3s / by J.J. Whiteley and G.W. Morrison. — Oxford : Oxford Railway Publishing, c1982. — [128p] : ill ; 28cm. — (Power series)
Text on lining papers
ISBN 0-86093-133-1 : £6.95 B82-23037

625.2′61′0941 — Great Britain. Railway services: London and North Eastern Railway. Steam locomotives, *1924-1967.* **Engineering aspects**

Beattie, Ian. L.N.E.R. locomotives : to scale / Ian Beattie. — Truro : Barton, c1981. — 61p : ill,plans ; 22x30cm
ISBN 0-85153-398-1 : £5.95 B82-11004

625.2′61′0941 — Great Britain. Railway services: London, Midland and Scottish Railway. Steam locomotives, *1923-1967.* **Engineering aspects**

Beattie, Ian. L.M.S.R. locomotives : to scale / Ian Beattie. — Truro : Barton, c1981. — 61p : ill,plans ; 22x30cm
ISBN 0-85153-399-x : £5.95 B82-11002

625.2′61′0941 — Great Britain. Railway services: London, Midland and Scottish Railway. Steam locomotives — *History*

Essery, R. J.. An illustrated history of LMS locomotives / by Bob Essery and David Jenkinson. — Oxford : Oxford Publishing
Vol.1: General review and locomotive liveries. — c1981. — vii,236p : ill(some col.) ; 28cm
Bibliography: p233. — Includes index
ISBN 0-86093-087-4 : £15.00 B82-10067

625.2′61′0941 — Great Britain. Railway services. West Coast main line. 4-6-0 steam locomotives, *1900-1945*

Atkins, C. P.. West coast 4-6-0s at work / C.P. Atkins. — London : Ian Allan, 1981. — 128p : ill,plans ; 30cm
Ill on lining papers. — Bibliography: p126. — Includes index
ISBN 0-7110-1159-1 : £7.95 B82-11221

625.2′61′0941 — Great Britain. Steam locomotives, *1830-1870*
Whitcombe, H. M.. After Rocket : the forgotten years 1830-1870 / H.M. Whitcombe ; paintings by the author ; foreword by J.A. Coiley. — Waddesdon : Kylin, 1981. — 64p : col.ill ; 22x31cm
ISBN 0-907128-02-5 : £16.50 B82-13801

625.2′61′0941 — Great Britain. Steam locomotives, *ca 1955- — Illustrations*
Trails of steam. — Oxford : Oxford Publishing
Vol.7: Trails along the Welsh border / [compiled] by Colin Walker. — c1980. — [64]p : chiefly ill ; 22x26cm
ISBN 0-86093-006-8 : £4.95 B82-17592

625.2′61′0941 — Great Britain. Steam locomotives manufactured by E. B. Wilson & Co., *to 1857 — Technical data*
Hardy, Clive. E.B. Wilson & Co. : locomotive works list / Clive Hardy. — Birmingham : Aleksandr, 1982, c1981. — 96p : ill ; 22cm
ISBN 0-906829-11-9 : Unpriced B82-38017

625.2′61′0941 — Great Britain. Steam locomotives, *to 1967 — Illustrations*
Vaughan, J. A. M.. Sunset of British steam / John Vaughan. — Oxford : Oxford Publishing, [1981?]. — [130]p : chiefly ill ; 28cm
ISBN 0-86093-163-3 : £6.95 B82-31352

625.2′61′09415 — Ireland. Steam locomotives, *1920-1939*
Nock, O. S.. Irish steam : a twenty year survey 1920-1939 / O.S. Nock. — Newton Abbot : David & Charles, c1982. — 207p : ill,1map ; 23cm
Includes index
ISBN 0-7153-7961-5 : £6.95 : CIP rev. B82-13105

625.2′61′0942 — England. Preserved steam locomotives, *1974-1979 — Illustrations*
Trevena, Nigel. Steam exposure : photography on Britain′s preserved railways / Nigel Trevena. — Penryn : Atlantic, 1979. — [88]p : ill ; 21x30cm
ISBN 0-906899-00-1 (pbk) : £3.95 B82-37528

625.2′61′0942 — England. Railway services: Great Western Railway. Steam locomotives, *1903-1967.* **Engineering aspects**
Beattie, Ian. G.W.R. locomotives : to scale / Ian Beattie. — Truro : Barton, c1981. — 60p : ill,plans ; 22x30cm
ISBN 0-85153-400-7 : £5.95 B82-11003

625.2′61′0942 — England. Railway services: London and North Eastern Railway. Steam locomotives, *1898-1965 — Illustrations*
North Eastern main line steam / compiled by ′61648′. — Truro : Barton, [1981?]. — 95p : chiefly ill ; 23cm
ISBN 0-85153-434-1 : £5.95 B82-11008

625.2′61′0942 — England. Railway services: London, Midland and Scottish Railway. Midland lines. Steam locomotives, *1930-1940*
Whitehead, Alan, *1913-*. The Midland in the 1930s / Alan Whitehead. — London : Ian Allan, 1982. — 112p : ill,facsims,1map ; 25cm
Map on lining paper. — Bibliography: p5
ISBN 0-7110-1202-4 : £6.50 B82-40629

625.2′61′0942132 — London. Westminster *(London Borough).* **Railways. Stations: Paddington Station. Steam locomotives,** *to 1981 — Illustrations*
Paddington steam / [compiled by] Keith Montague. — Norwich : Becknell, 1982. — 32p : chiefly ill ; 24cm
ISBN 0-907087-18-3 (pbk) : £2.50 B82-26195

625.2′61′09422 — Southern England. Railway services: British Rail. *Southern Region.* **King Arthur Class steam locomotives,** *1951-1957*
The **Standard** Arthurs : the named standard class fives of the Southern Region of British Railways / compiled by P.W. Gibbs ; with personal reminiscences by Peter W. Smith. — [Harpenden] : 73082 Camelot Locomotive Society, c1981. — 30p : ill ; 21cm
ISBN 0-9507761-0-6 (pbk) : Unpriced B82-11933

625.2′61′09422 — Southern England. Railway services: Southern Railway Company. Schools class steam locomotives, *to 1967*
Winkworth, D. W.. The Schools 4-4-0s. — London : Allen & Unwin, Nov.1982. — [112]p
ISBN 0-04-385095-2 : £6.95 : CIP entry B82-27817

625.2′61′09422 — Southern England. Railway services: Southern Railway Company. Steam locomotives, *1924-1967.* **Engineering aspects**
Beattie, Ian. Southern locomotives : to scale / Ian Beattie. — Truro : Barton, c1981. — 63p : ill,plans ; 22x30cm
ISBN 0-85153-389-2 : £5.95 B82-11000

625.2′61′09422 — Southern England. Railway services: Southern Railway. Steam locomotives, *to 1975 — Illustrations*
Southern steam miscellany / [compiled by] Tony Fairclough and Alan Wills. — Truro : Barton. — (Southern steam series)
Ill on lining papers
[1]. — [1982?]. — 95p : chiefly ill ; 23cm
ISBN 0-85153-384-1 : £6.95 B82-35713

625.2′61′09423 — South-west England. Railway services: British Rail. Somerset & Dorset Joint line. Steam locomotives, *1950-1959 — Illustrations*
Peters, Ivo. The Somerset and Dorset in the ′fifties / by Ivo Peters. — Oxford : Oxford Publishing Co.
Pt.1: 1950-1954. — c1980. — [110]p : chiefly ill,ports ; 28cm
ISBN 0-86093-101-3 : £5.95 B82-34692

625.2′61′094246 — Northern Staffordshire. Railway services: North Staffordshire Railway. Steam locomotives *— Illustrations*
Rush, R. W.. North Staffordshire railway locomotives and rolling stock / R.W. Rush. — [Trowbridge] : Oakwood, 1981. — 72p : ill ; 24cm
ISBN 0-85361-275-7 (pbk) : Unpriced B82-01823

625.2′61′0942483 — Warwickshire. Nuneaton region. Railway services: British Rail. *London Midland Region.* **Steam locomotives,** *1951-1966 — Illustrations*
Steam around Nuneaton : a pictorial reminiscence of the final 15 years of steam operations / [compiled by] Keith Robey, Raymond J. Green. — Leicester : K. Robey and R.J. Green in association with Midland Counties Publications, 1981. — 96p : chiefly ill,1map ; 22cm
Ill on lining papers
ISBN 0-904597-36-9 : £6.95 B82-10838

625.2′61′09426 — Eastern England. Railway services: British Rail. *Eastern Region.* **Kettering-Cambridge line. Steam locomotives,** *to 1958 — Illustrations*
Sawford, E. H.. Cambridge-Kettering line steam / E.H. Sawford. — Norwich : Becknell, 1981. — 32p : chiefly ill,1map ; 24cm
ISBN 0-907087-06-x (pbk) : £2.50 B82-11900

625.2′61′0942612 — Northern Norfolk. Railway services: British Rail. *Eastern Region.* **Steam locomotives,** *to 1968 — Illustrations*
Steam around North Norfolk / [compiled by] C.G. Beckett. — Norwich : Becknell, 1981. — 32p : chiefly ill,1map ; 24cm
ISBN 0-907087-03-5 (pbk) : £1.95 B82-11904

625.2′61′0942615 — Norfolk. Norwich region. Railway services: British Rail. *Eastern Region.* **Steam locomotives,** *to 1968 — Illustrations*
Steam around Norwich / [compiled by] Richard Adderson. — Norwich : Becknell, 1981. — 32p : chiefly ill,1map ; 24cm
ISBN 0-907087-02-7 (pbk) : £2.50 B82-11903

625.2′61′0942651 — Cambridgeshire. Peterborough region. Steam locomotives, *1957-1963 — Illustrations*
Fincham, A. V.. Before the diesels came! : a nostalgic look at the last days of steam around Peterborough / edited [and photographs] by A.V. Fincham. — Peterborough (717 Lincoln Road, Peterborough PE1 3HD) : The Model Shop, [1976?]. — 66p : of ill ; 15x21cm
Cover title
£0.90 (pbk) B82-26640

Fincham, A. V.. Steam near the Nene : further memories from the last days of steam / edited [and photographs] by A.V. Fincham. — Peterborough (717 Lincoln Road, Peterborough PE1 3HD) : The Model Shop, [1978]. — 66p : of ill(some col.) ; 15x21cm
Cover title
£0.99 (pbk) B82-26639

625.2′61′0942651 — Cambridgeshire. Peterborough region. Steam locomotives, *ca 1950-1964 — Illustrations*
Sawford, E. H.. Steam around Peterborough / [E.H. Sawford]. — Norwich : Becknell, 1982. — 32p : chiefly ill,1map ; 24cm
ISBN 0-907087-16-7 (pbk) : £2.50 B82-26192

625.2′61′0942714 — Cheshire. Chester region. Steam locomotives, *1957-1965 — Illustrations*
Wainwright, S. D.. Steam in West Cheshire : and the North Wales border / S.D. Wainwright. — London : Ian Allan, 1981. — 95p : ill ; 25cm
ISBN 0-7110-1141-9 : £4.95 B82-01616

625.2′61′094294 — South Wales. Steam locomotives, *to 1965 — Illustrations*
Hale, Michael. Steam in South Wales / by Michael Hale. — Oxford : Oxford Publishing
Vol.2: North and West of Swansea. — c1981. — [84]p : chiefly ill,maps ; 28cm
ISBN 0-86093-152-8 : £6.95 B82-10071

625.2′63′0941 — Great Britain. Railway services: British Rail. Class 76 & Class 77 electric locomotives, *to 1980 — Illustrations*
Profile of the class 76s & 77s / [compiled by] David Maxey. — Oxford : Oxford Publishing, c1981. — [78]p : chiefly ill,1map ; 28cm. — (Profile series)
ISBN 0-86093-156-0 : £5.95 B82-16357

625.2′63′0941 — Great Britain. Railway services: British Rail. Rolling stock: Electric multiple units *— Technical data*
Marsden, C. J.. EMUs / Colin J. Marsden. — London : Ian Allan, 1982. — 144p : ill ; 19cm. — (Motive power recognition ; 2)
ISBN 0-7110-1165-6 (pbk) : £1.95 B82-14464

625.2′63′0941 — Great Britain. Rolling stock: Electric multiple units *— Illustrations*
British electric trains in camera / [compiled by] John Glover. — London : Ian Allan, 1982. — 127p : chiefly ill ; 24cm
ISBN 0-7110-1163-x : £5.95 B82-26954

625.2′63′0942 — England. Railway services: British Rail. *London Midland Region.* **Class 87 electric locomotives** *— Illustrations*
The **87′s** : British Rail London Midland Region 500 HP 25kv electrics. — Temple Cloud : Rail Photoprints, c1981. — [40]p : chiefly ill ; 15x22cm. — (Named diesel and electric locomotives of British Rail ; Part 2)
Cover title. — Ill on inside covers
ISBN 0-906883-02-4 (pbk) : £1.25 B82-05108

625.2′66′0924 — Great Britain. Railway services: British Rail. Diesel locomotives. Driving, *1960-1970 — Personal observations*
Jacks, L. C.. Diesels : a driver′s reminiscences / L.C. Jacks. — Truro : Barton, c1982. — 112p : ill ; 22cm
ISBN 0-85153-437-6 (pbk) : £3.50 B82-35707

625.2′66′0941 — Great Britain. Preserved diesel locomotives *— Illustrations*
Nicholson, Pete. Diesel locomotives in preservation. — Cheltenham : Pete Nicholson Railway Publishing
Author Pete Nicholson
No.2: Former British Rail and L.M.S.R. locomotives. — c1980. — [24]p : ill ; 22cm. — (Rail-heritage illustrated)
ISBN 0-907036-01-5 (pbk) : £1.25 B82-39328

625.2′66′0941 — Great Britain. Railway freight transport services: British Rail. Diesel locomotives, *1965-1979 — Illustrations*
BR freight services in focus / [compiled by] Barry J. Nicolle. — London : Ian Allan, 1982. — 111p : chiefly ill ; 24cm
ISBN 0-7110-1169-9 : £5.95 B82-30640

625.2′66′0941 — Great Britain. Railway services: British Rail. Diesel locomotives — *Illustrations*

Postcard album : for the OPC collectors series of postcards 65-128. — Oxford : Oxford Publishing, [1980?]. — [32]p : all ill ; 25cm
Cover title
ISBN 0-86093-095-5 (pbk) : £0.75 B82-40571

625.2′66′0941 — Great Britain. Railway services: British Rail. *London Midland Region.* **Diesel locomotives,** *to 1980* — *Illustrations*

Diesels : on the London Midland / [compiled by] John Vaughan. — London : Ian Allan, 1981. — 112p : ill(some col.) ; 25cm
Ill on lining papers
ISBN 0-7110-1146-x : £5.95 B82-01614

625.2′66′0941 — Great Britain. Railway services: British Rail. Rolling stock: Diesel multiple units — *Identification manuals*

DMUs / [compiled by] Colin J. Marsden. — London : Ian Allan, 1982. — 128p : ill ; 19cm. — (Motive power recognition ; 3)
ISBN 0-7110-1201-6 (pbk) : £2.50 B82-38014

625′.2′66′0942 — England. Railway services: British Rail. *Western Region.* **Diesel locomotives,** *to 1981* — *Illustrations*

Diesels on the Western / [compiled by] John Vaughan. — London : Ian Allan, 1982. — 108p : ill ; 25cm
ISBN 0-7110-1200-8 : £5.95 B82-38009

625.2′66′09425 — South-east England. Railway services: British Rail. *Eastern Region.* **Great Northern lines. Diesel locomotives,** *1969-1980* — *Illustrations*

Dobson, Peter, *19---*. Diesels out of Kings Cross / Peter Dobson. — London : Ian Allan, 1981. — 96p : chiefly ill ; 24cm
ISBN 0-7110-1142-7 : £4.95 B82-07367

625.2′66′09426 — Eastern England. Railway services: British Rail. *Eastern Region.* **Diesel multiple units,** *1952-1981* — *Illustrations*

Diesel multiple units : Eastern England / [compiled by] S.E. Smithson. — Norwich : Becknell, 1981. — 32p : chiefly ill ; 24cm
ISBN 0-907087-08-6 (pbk) : £2.50 B82-11906

625.2′66′0942712 — Cheshire. Crewe region. Railway services: British Rail. *London Midland Region.* **Diesel locomotives,** *1974-1979* — *Illustrations*

Nicolle, B.. Diesels under the wires around Crewe / Barry Nicolle. — Gloucester : Peter Watts, c1979. — [48]p : ill,1map ; 19x22cm. — (A Railway pictorial book)
ISBN 0-906025-21-4 (pbk) : £1.80 B82-05491

625.2′662′0941 — Great Britain. Railway services: British Rail. Class 20 diesel-electric locomotives, *to 1968*

Oakley, Michael. BR Class 20 diesels / Michael Oakley. — Truro : Barton, c1981. — [32]p : ill,maps ; 22cm
ISBN 0-85153-419-8 (pbk) : £0.95 B82-10905

625.2′662′0941 — Great Britain. Railway services: British Rail. Class 24 & Class 25 diesel-electric locomotives, *to 1980* — *Illustrations*

Profile of the class 24s & 25s / [compiled by] C.J. Marsden. — Oxford : Oxford Publishing, c1981. — [80]p : chiefly ill,plans ; 28cm. — (Profile series)
ISBN 0-86093-135-8 : £5.95 B82-10068

625.2′662′0941 — Great Britain. Railway services: British Rail. Class 26 & Class 27 diesel-electric locomotives, *to 1980*

Oakley, Michael. BR Class 26/27 diesels / by Michael Oakley. — Truro : Barton, c1981. — [32]p : ill,1map ; 22cm
ISBN 0-85153-418-x (pbk) : £0.95 B82-10906

625.2′662′0941 — Great Britain. Railway services: British Rail. Class 31 diesel-electric locomotives, *to 1978*

Oakley, Michael. BR Class 31 diesels / by Michael Oakley. — Truro : Barton, c1981. — [32]p : ill,1map ; 22cm
ISBN 0-85153-417-1 (pbk) : £0.95 B82-10908

625.2′662′0941 — Great Britain. Railway services: British Rail. Class 33 diesel-electric locomotives, *to 1980* — *Illustrations*

The **Power** of the 33S / [compiled] by Brian Morrison and John Vaughan. — Oxford : Oxford Publishing, c1982. — [128]p : chiefly ill,2ports ; 28cm
Ill on lining paper
ISBN 0-86093-157-9 : £6.95 B82-35849

625.2′662′0941 — Great Britain. Railway services: British Rail. Class 40 diesel-electric locomotives, *to 1980* — *Ilustrations*

Whiteley, J. S.. Profile of the class 40s / J.S. Whiteley and G.W. Morrison. — Oxford : Oxford Publishing, c1981. — [78]p : chiefly ill ; 28cm. — (Profile series)
ISBN 0-86093-144-7 : £5.95 B82-16359

625.2′662′0941 — Great Britain. Railway services: British Rail. Class 50 diesel-electric locomotives — *Illustrations*

The **50s** : English Electric 2700 HP diesel electrics. — [Bristol] : [Rail Photoprints], [c1981]. — [52]p : chiefly ill ; 15x21cm. — (Named diesel and electric locomotives of British Rail ; pt.3)
Cover title. — Ill on inside covers
ISBN 0-906883-03-2 (pbk) : £1.45 B82-31775

625.2′662′0941 — Great Britain. Railway services: British Rail. Class 50 diesel-electric locomotives, *to 1979* — *Illustrations*

Chalcraft, John. Book of the fifties : British Rail Class 50′s / John Chalcraft and Graham Scott-Lowe. — Gloucester : Peter Watts, 1979. — [32]p : chiefly ill ; 22cm. — (Motive power review)
ISBN 0-906025-10-9 (pbk) : £1.35 B82-07707

625.2′662′0941 — Great Britain. Railway services: British Rail. Deltic class diesel-electric locomotives, *to 1980*

Guppy, Antony. BR Class 55 diesels : the Deltics / by Antony Guppy ; edited with additional material by Michael Oakley. — Truro : Barton, c1981. — [40]p : ill,1map ; 22cm
ISBN 0-85153-416-3 (pbk) : £0.95 B82-10907

625.2′662′0941 — Great Britain. Railway services: British Rail. Deltic class diesel-electric locomotives, *to 1980* — *Illustrations*

The **Deltics** : British Rail Class 55′s. — [Temple Cloud] : Rail Photoprints, c1980. — [24]p ; 15x21cm. — (Named diesel and electric locomotives of British Rail ; Part 1)
Ill on inside covers
ISBN 0-906883-01-6 (pbk) : £1.00 B82-05101

Heavyside, G. T.. Tribute to the Deltics / Tom Heavyside. — Newton Abbot : David & Charles, c1982. — 48p : ill ; 25cm
ISBN 0-7153-8281-0 : £4.95 : CIP rev. B82-07579

625.2′662′0941 — Great Britain. Railway services: British Rail. Deltic Class diesel-electric locomotives, *to 1981*

Webb, Brian, *1934-1981?*. The Deltic locomotives of British Rail / Brian Webb. — Newton Abbot : David & Charles, c1982. — 96p : ill ; 25cm
Includes index
ISBN 0-7153-8110-5 : £6.95 : CIP rev. B81-33822

625.2′662′0941 — Great Britain. Railway services: British Rail. Deltic class diesel-electric locomotives, *to 1981* — *Illustrations*

Rose, Peter J.. Deltic twilight / Peter J. Rose. — Sheffield : Pennine, 1982. — 64p : chiefly ill (some col.) ; 25x21cm
ISBN 0-946055-00-9 (pbk) : £3.95 B82-41108

625.2′662′0941 — Greater Manchester *(Metropolitan County).* **Railway services: British Rail.** *London Midland Region.* **Class 40 diesel-electric locomotives** — *Illustrations*

Class 40′s in and around Manchester. — [Temple Cloud] : Rail Photoprints, c1979. — [32]p : chiefly ill ; 15x21cm
Ill on inside covers
ISBN 0-906883-00-8 (pbk) : £1.00 B82-05107

625.2′664′0941 — Great Britain. Railway services: British Rail. Class 14 diesel hydraulic locomotives, *to 1980*

Hembry, P. J.. Class 14 : the Cinderellas of the diesel-hydraulic era / written by P.J. Hembry. — 2nd ed. / edited with additional information by Michael Oakley. — Sutton Coldfield : Diesel & Electric Group, c1982. — 15p : ill,1map ; 30cm
Previous ed.: 1980. — Text and ill on inside covers
ISBN 0-906375-09-6 (pbk) : £0.95 B82-40252

625′.42 — London. Underground railway services: London Transport Railways. COP surface electric multiple units, *to 1981*

Connor, Piers. The ′COP′ stock story / by Piers Connor. — London (1 Marchwood Cres., Ealing, London W5) : London Underground Railway Society, [1981]. — 60p : ill,1plan ; 21cm
£1.95 (pbk) B82-00984

625′.42′09421 — London. Underground railway services: Waterloo & City Railway. Construction

Pennick, Nigel. Waterloo and City Railway / Nigel Pennick. — Cambridge (142 Pheasant Rise, Bar Hill, Cambridge CB3 8SD) : Electric Traction, 1981. — 16p : ill,1map,facsims,1plan ; 21cm
Unpriced (pbk) B82-07939

625′.66 — London. Tram services. Trailers, *1905-1930*

Willsher, M. J. D.. The L.C.C. trailers / by M.J.D. Willsher. — Broxbourne : Light Rail Transit Association, [1982?]. — 59p : ill,facsims,1map ; 22cm
Text and map on inside covers
ISBN 0-900433-84-1 (pbk) : £0.95 B82-28818

625′.66 — Trolleybuses, *to 1980*

Green, Oliver. By trolleybus / [written by Oliver Green]. — [London] ([39 Wellington St., WC2E 7BB]) : London Transport Museum, c1981. — [4]p : ill ; 30cm
Bibliography: p.[4]
£0.10 (spiral) B82-35692

625′.66′0228 — Model trams. Construction — *Manuals*

Voice, David. How to go tram and tramway modelling. — Cambridge : Patrick Stephens, Aug.1982. — [150]p
ISBN 0-85059-564-9 : £8.95 : CIP entry B82-16654

625′.66′07402516 — Derbyshire. Crich. Museums: National Tramway Museum — *Visitors′ guides*

The **National** Tramway Museum. — [Matlock] ([Museum premises, Crich, Matlock, Derbyshire DE4 5DP]) : [The Museum], c1981. — [32]p : ill(some col.),col.coats of arms,1col.map ; 25cm
Unpriced (unbound) B82-26298

625′.66′0941 — Great Britain. Electric trains, *1879-1979*

Bond, A. Winstan. The British tram : history′s orphan / by A. Winstan Bond. — [Dunstable] : Tramway & Light Railway Society with the co-operation of the Tramway Museum Society, c1980. — 75p : ill,maps,facsims ; 22cm. — (The Walter Gratwicke memorial lecture ; 1979)
Unpriced (pbk) B82-00788

625′.66′0941 — Great Britain. Trams & trolleybuses, *1950-1960* — *Illustrations*

Thompson, Julian. Trolley buses and trams of the 1950s / Julian Thompson. — London : Ian Allan, 1982. — 112p : chiefly ill ; 25cm
Bibliography: p7
ISBN 0-7110-1181-8 : £5.95 B82-34782

625′.66′09421 — London. Trams, *ca 1930-1940*

Sitters, Ken. Living with London′s trams in the thirties : a passenger looks back / by Ken Sitters. — [London] ([39 Wellington St., WC2E 7BB]) : London Transport Museum, c1982. — 1folded sheet([6]p) : ill ; 30cm
£0.30 B82-35695

625′.66′094214 — North Inner London. Tram services. Trams, *to 1952* — *Illustrations*

Trams in inner North London : a pictorial souvenir / [compiled by] D.W. Willoughby, E.R. Oakley. — Hartley : D.W. Willoughby and E.R. Oakley, 1980. — 44p : ill,1map ; 22cm
′Tram map′ (1folded leaf of plates) as insert
ISBN 0-903479-14-1 (pbk) : £0.95 B82-00406

625′.66′094215 — East London. Tram services. Trams, *to 1940* — *Illustrations*

Trams in East London : a pictorial souvenir / [compiled by] D.W. Willoughby, E.R. Oakley. — Hartley : D.W. Willoughby and E.R. Oakley, [c1981]. — 44p : ill,1map ; 22cm
′Tram map′ (1folded leaf of plates) as insert
ISBN 0-903479-12-5 (pbk) : £0.95 B82-00405

625′.66′094217 — North Outer London. Tram services. Trams, *to 1939* — *Illustrations*

Trams in outer North London : a pictorial souvenir / [compiled by] D.W. Willoughby, E.R. Oakley, D.W.K. Jones. — Hartley : D.W. Willoughby, E.R. Oakley and D.W.K. Jones, 1981. — 44p : ill,1map ; 22cm
′Tram map′ (1folded leaf of plates) as insert
ISBN 0-903479-16-8 (pbk) : £0.95 B82-00404

625′.66′0942819 — West Yorkshire *(Metropolitan County)*. Leeds. Trams, *to 1959* — *Illustrations*

Leeds City tramways : a pictorial souvenir / [compiled by] Robert F. Mack. — Rev. ed. — Sheffield : Turntable, 1979. — 40p : all ill ; 22cm
Previous ed.: 1972
ISBN 0-902844-50-4 (pbk) : £1.00 B82-17394

625.7 — ROAD CONSTRUCTION

625.7 — Farms. Roads. Construction materials: Ready-mixed concrete. Use — *Manuals*

Barnes, Maurice M.. Laying roads with ready-mixed concrete / Maurice M. Barnes. — 7th ed. — Slough : Cement and Concrete Association, 1980. — 15p : ill,1map ; 30cm. — (Farm construction) (Cement and Concrete Association publication ; 47.506)
Previous ed.: 1979. — Text, map on inside covers
ISBN 0-7210-1209-4 (pbk) : Unpriced B82-35005

625.7 — Roads. Engineering aspects

Oglesby, Clarkson H.. Highway engineering. — 4th ed / Clarkson H. Oglesby, R. Gary Hicks. — New York ; Chichester : Wiley, c1982. — xiii,844p,[1]folded sheet : ill ; 24cm
Previous ed.: 1975. — Includes index
ISBN 0-471-02936-x : £21.00 B82-21537

625.7′09172′4 — Developing countries. Roads. Construction & maintenance — *Conference proceedings*

Institution of Civil Engineers. Highway investment in developing countries. — London : Telford, Dec.1982. — [199]p
Conference papers
ISBN 0-7277-0163-0 : £23.00 : CIP entry B82-33353

625.7′25 — Ireland *(Republic)*. Road junctions. Geometric aspects. Design. Standards — *Proposals*

Devlin, J.. Geometric design guidelines : (intersections at grade) / J. Devlin, P. McGuinness. — Dublin (St. Martin′s House, Waterloo Rd., Dublin 4) : An Foras Forbartha, 1981. — 72p : ill ; 30cm. — (RT ; 181)
£5.00 (spiral) B82-15383

625.7′25′09417 — Ireland *(Republic)*. Roads. Design. Aesthetic aspects — *Manuals*

Hyde, N. (Niall). Guidelines on road design aesthetics / N. Hyde. — Dublin : An Foras Forbartha, 1981. — 56p : ill ; 30cm. — (RT ; 182)
ISBN 0-906120-42-x (spiral) : £5.00 B82-15377

625.7′6′0942393 — Avon. Bristol. Streets. Maintenance, *1317-1806*
Ralph, Elizabeth. The streets of Bristol / by Elizabeth Ralph. — Bristol (74 Bell Barn Rd., Stoke Bishop, Bristol [BS9 2DG]) : Bristol Branch of the Historical Association, 1981. — 19p,[4]p of plates : ill ; 22cm. — (Local history pamphlets / Bristol Branch of the Historical Association ; 49)
Cover title
£0.60 (pbk) B82-00038

625.7′94 — England. Bridleways & footpaths. Waymarking
Waymarking. — London : Ramblers′ Association, 1979. — 1folded sheet([8]p) : 2ill ; 21cm. — (Guidance note ; 2)
ISBN 0-900613-38-6 (corrected) : £0.10 B82-39680

625.7′94 — Road traffic control systems — *Conference proceedings*
International Conference on Road Traffic Signalling *(1982 : Institution of Electrical Engineers)*. International Conference on Road Traffic Signalling : 30 March-1 April 1982 / organised by the Computing and Control Division of the Institution of Electrical Engineers in association with the Association pour le Development des Techniques de Transport d′Environnement et de Circulation (ATEC) ; venue The Institution of Electrical Engineers, London, U.K.. — London : Institution of Electrical Engineers, c1982. — viii,202p : ill,1map ; 30cm. — (IEE conference publication ; no.207)
ISBN 0-85296-259-2 (pbk) : Unpriced B82-27687

625.7′94 — Signal-controlled road traffic control systems. Applications of digital computer systems. Programs: SIGSET program
Allsop, Richard E.. Computer program SIGSET for calculating delay-minimising traffic signal timings : description and manual for users / Richard E. Allsop. — [London] : University College London, Transport Studies Group, 1981. — 32p : ill ; 30cm. — (Research report, ISSN 0142-6052)
Unpriced (spiral) B82-05046

625.7′94 — Urban regions. Automatic road traffic control systems
Strobel, Horst. Computer controlled urban transportation / Horst Strobel. — Chichester : Wiley, c1982. — xv,500p : ill ; 24cm. — (International series on applied systems analysis ; 10)
Includes bibliographies and index
ISBN 0-471-10036-6 : Unpriced : CIP rev. B82-09695

625.8′2 — Northern England. Limestone pavements. Conservation
The **Conservation** of limestone pavements / Nature Conservancy Council. — Windermere : Nature Conservancy Council, North West Region, c1980. — [8]p : ill,1col.map ; 21cm
ISBN 0-86139-093-8 (unbound) : £0.20 B82-17440

625.8′4 — Agricultural industries. Farms. Concrete pavements. Construction — *Manuals*
Barnes, Maurice M.. Farm construction: laying concrete / Maurice M. Barnes. — Slough : Cement and Concrete Association, 1982. — [8]p : col.ill ; 10x15cm. — (Pocket guide ; 1)
Cover title
ISBN 0-7210-1268-x (spiral) : Unpriced B82-40243

625.8′5 — Ireland *(Republic)*. Roads. Surface dressings: Cut-back bitumen. Viscosity grades. Selection — *Standards*
Jamieson, I. L.. The selection of the appropriate grade of cutback bitumen for surface dressing / I.L. Jamieson. — Dublin (St. Martins House, Waterloo Road, Dublin 4) : National Institute for Physical Planning and Construction Research, 1981. — 24p : ill ; 30cm
Unpriced (unbound) B82-13803

627 — HYDRAULIC ENGINEERING

627 — Hydraulic engineering — *Manuals*
Featherstone, R. E.. Civil engineering hydraulics. — London : Granada, July 1982. — [384]p
ISBN 0-246-11483-5 (pbk) : £10.00 : CIP entry B82-12227

627′.003 — Hydraulic engineering — *Polyglot dictionaries*
Troskolanski, Adam Tadeusz. Dictionary of hydraulic machinery. — Oxford : Elsevier Scientific, Dec.1981. — [800]p
ISBN 0-444-99728-8 : £70.00 : CIP entry B81-31616

627′.0228 — Hydraulic engineering scale models. Design & construction
Kramer, A. E.. Hydraulic scale model design / by A.E. Kramer. — [Birmingham] : [A.E. Kramer], [1979]. — 96p,3leaves of plates : ill ; 21cm
ISBN 0-9506623-0-5 (pbk) : £3.00 B82-11205

627′.0228 — Hydraulic engineering. Use of models
Hydraulic Modelling Applied to Maritime Engineering Problems *(Conference : 1981 : London)*. Hydraulic modelling in maritime engineering : proceedings of the conference organized by the Institution of Civil Engineers, held in London on 13-14 October 1981. — London : Telford, 1982. — 146p : ill,maps,plans ; 31cm
'Conference entitled Hydraulic modelling applied to maritime engineering problems'. — Includes index
ISBN 0-7277-0154-1 : £16.00 B82-40227

627′.028 — Hydraulic engineering. Use of rubber & plastics — *Conference proceedings*
Use of Plastics and Rubber in Water and Effluents *(Conference : 1982 : London)*. International conference The Use of Plastics and Rubber in Water and Effluents : 15-17 February 1982 : at the Royal Lancaster Hotel, London / sponsored by Institute of Water Pollution control ... [et al.]. — London (11 Hobart Place SW1N 0HL) : The Plastics and Rubber Institute, [1982?]. — 1v. : ill ; 21cm
£16.00 (pbk)
Also classified at 628′.028 B82-20153

627′.028′54 — Hydraulic engineering. Applications of digital computer systems
Brebbia, C. A.. Computational hydraulics. — London : Butterworths Scientific, Aug.1982. — [288]p
ISBN 0-408-01153-x : £19.00 : CIP entry B82-15780

Koutitas, C. G.. Elements of computational hydraulics. — London : Pentech Press, Sept.1982. — [144]p
ISBN 0-7273-0503-4 : £11.50 : CIP entry B82-20396

627′.072041 — Great Britain. Hydraulic engineering. Research organisations: Hydraulics Research Station. Transfer of equipment from Great Britain. *Department of the Environment* — *Proposals*
Great Britain. *Treasury*. Treasury minute dated 22nd March 1982 relative to the transfer, free of charge, of consumable stores and vehicles to Hydraulics Research Station Limited. — London : H.M.S.O., [1982?]. — [2]p ; 25cm. — (Cmnd. ; 8528)
ISBN 0-10-185280-0 (unbound) : £0.30 B82-26759

627′.0724 — Hydraulic engineering. Mathematical models — *Conference proceedings*
International Conference on the Hydraulic Modelling of Civil Engineering Structures *(1982 : Coventry)*. Papers presented at the International Conference on the Hydraulic Modelling of Civil Engineering Structures, Coventry, England, September 1982. — Cranfield : BHRA Fluid Engineering, Sept.1982. — [500]p
ISBN 0-906085-75-6 (pbk) : £38.00 : CIP entry B82-28611

627′.0724 — Hydraulic engineering. Mathematical models — *Festschriften*
Engineering applications of computational hydraulics. — Boston ; London : Pitman Advanced Pub.
Vol.1: Homage to Alexandre Preissmann / edited by M.B. Abbott and J.A. Cunge ; contributors M.B. Abbott ... [et al.]. — c1982. — ix,262p : ill,maps ; 24cm
Includes bibliographies
ISBN 0-273-08512-3 : Unpriced : CIP rev. B81-35776

627'.1 — Inland waterways. Design & construction — *Conference proceedings*

International Navigation Congress *(25th : 1981 : Edinburgh)*. Inland & maritime waterways & ports : design, construction, operation : proceedings of the technical sessions, XXV International Navigation Congress, Edinburgh, 10-16th May 1981 = Voies navigables et ports interieurs et maritimes : conception, construction, exploitation : compte rendu des sessions techniques, XXV Congrès internationale de navigation. — [Oxford] : [Published for the Permanent International Association of Navigation Congresses by Pergamon], [1982]. — xi,270p : ill ; 30cm
English and French text. — Includes index
ISBN 0-08-026732-7 : £20.00 : CIP rev.
ISBN 0-08-026750-5 (set) : Unpriced
Also classified at 627'.2 B82-39337

627'.1'094252 — Nottinghamshire. Inland waterways. Industrial antiquities

The **Navigable** waterways of Nottinghamshire : a survey in industrial archaeology / University of Nottingham, Delegacy for Extra-Mural Studies, Department of Adult Education, Workers' Educational Association, East Midlands District. — [Church Broughton] ([Forge House, Sutton Heath, Church Broughton, Derbyshire]) : [Published by Ian G.T. Duncan for the Department of Adult Education, University of Nottingham], 1981. — 77p : ill,2maps,2plans ; 30cm
Cover title
£2.00 (pbk) B82-06190

627'.12 — Gravel-bed rivers. Flow. Regulation. Engineering aspects — *Conference proceedings*

Gravel-bed rivers. — Chichester : Wiley, Nov.1982. — [750]p
Conference papers
ISBN 0-471-10139-7 : £36.00 : CIP entry
B82-27544

627'.13'094271 — England. Canals: Cheshire Canal Ring. Industrial antiquities — *Illustrations*

A **Tour** along part of the Cheshire canal ring, covering the Ashton, Peak Forest and Macclesfield canals : an industrial archaeological survey / Department of Adult Education, University of Nottingham and the Workers Educational Association, Nottingham Branch. — [Church Broughton] ([Forge House, Sutton Heath, Church Broughton, Derbyshire]) : [Published on behalf of the Department of Adult Education, University of Nottingham by Ian G.I. Duncan], 1981. — 49p : ill ; 22x30cm
£2.00 (pbk) B82-06189

627'.132 — Canals & rivers. Embankments. Design & construction

Peter, Pavol. Canal and river levées / by Pavol Peter. — Amsterdam ; Oxford : Elsevier Scientific, 1982. — 540p : ill ; 25cm. — (Developments in geotechnical engineering ; 29)
Translation of: Kanálové a ochranné hrádze. — Bibliography: p515-526. — Includes index
ISBN 0-444-99726-1 : Unpriced : CIP rev.
Primary classification 627'.8 B81-31618

627'.136'060422 — Southern England. Canals. Restoration. Organisations: Kennet and Avon Canal Trust, *to 1981*

The **Kennet** and Avon Canal and its Trust / photographs and text by Trust members. — [Devizes] ([Membership Office, The Wharf, Couch La., Devizes SN10 1EB]) : Kennet & Avon Canal Trust, [1981?]. — 30p : ill,1map ; 22cm
Ill on inside covers
£0.45 (pbk) B82-17372

627'.2 — Ports. Design & construction — *Conference proceedings*

International Navigation Congress *(25th : 1981 : Edinburgh)*. Inland & maritime waterways & ports : design, construction, operation : proceedings of the technical sessions, XXV International Navigation Congress, Edinburgh, 10-16th May 1981 = Voies navigables et ports interieurs et maritimes : conception, construction, exploitation : compte rendu des sessions techniques, XXV Congrès internationale de navigation. — [Oxford] : [Published for the Permanent International Association of Navigation Congresses by Pergamon], [1982]. — xi,270p : ill ; 30cm
English and French text. — Includes index
ISBN 0-08-026732-7 : £20.00 : CIP rev.
ISBN 0-08-026750-5 (set) : Unpriced
Primary classification 627'.1 B82-39337

627'.5 — Marshes. Reclamation — *Conference proceedings*

The **Evolution** of marshland landscapes : papers presented to a conference on marshland landscapes held in Oxford in December 1979. — Oxford : Oxford University Department for External Studies, 1981. — vi,177p : ill,maps,plans ; 30cm
Includes bibliographies
ISBN 0-903736-12-8 : Unpriced B82-00579

627'.54'09427 — North-west England. Land. Drainage

First report of survey of land drainage functions : Water Act 1973 section 24 (5). — Warrington (Dawson House, Great Sankey, Warrington WA5 3LW) : North West Water, Rivers Division, 1980. — 303p in various pagings : maps ; 30cm + Maps and overlays(2v. looseleaf : 47cm)
Cover title
£5.00 (spiral) B82-38455

627'.54'09931 — New Zealand. Wetlands. Drainage

Bowler, Dermot G.. The drainage of wet soils / Dermot G. Bowler. — Auckland ; London : Hodder and Stoughton, 1980. — 259p : ill,plans ; 21cm
Bibliography: p249-256. — Includes index
ISBN 0-340-25690-7 : Unpriced B82-24501

627'.56 — Aquifers. Ground water. Recharging

Huisman, L.. Artificial groundwater recharge. — London : Pitman, Jan.1983. — [336]p
ISBN 0-273-08544-1 : £12.50 : CIP entry
B82-33721

627'.58'094223 — Coasts. Protection — *Study regions: Kent*

Thorn, Roland Berkeley. Sea defence and coast protection works : a guide to design. — 3rd ed. / Roland Berkeley Thorn, Andrew G. Roberts. — London : Telford, 1981. — 216p : ill ; 23cm
Previous ed.: published as Sea defence works. London : Butterworths, 1971. — Includes index
ISBN 0-7277-0085-5 : £13.00 B82-15396

627'.72 — Underwater diving

The **Professional** divers handbook. — London (19 Roland Way, London SW7 3RF) : Submex, Nov.1982. — [328]p
ISBN 0-9508242-0-8 : £27.00 : CIP entry
B82-32873

627'.72 — Underwater engineering. Diving — *Manuals*

Haux, Gerhard F. K.. Subsea manned engineering / Gerhard F.K. Haux ; with contributions by Jörg Haas and Anthony Lovell Smith ; English translation by Eberhard Kern and Anthony Lovell Smith. — London : Baillière Tindall, 1982. — x,538p : ill ; 26cm
Bibliography: p527-528. — Includes index
ISBN 0-7020-0749-8 : £35.00 : CIP rev.
B81-16936

627'.72'06042358 — Devon. Plymouth. Underwater diving. Organisations: Fort Bovisand Underwater Centre. Courses

Fort Bovisand Underwater Centre. Inshore air diving training / Fort Bovisand Underwater Centre. — Plymouth : The Centre, 1981. — 5p : ill ; 30cm
Unpriced (unbound) B82-08950

627'.72'07041185 — Scotland. Highland Region. Fort William. Underwater diving. Training centres: Underwater Training Centre. Finance — *Inquiry reports*

Great Britain. *Parliament. House of Commons. Committee of Public Accounts*. Thirty-fifth report from the Committee of Public Accounts : together with the proceedings of the committee : session 1979-80 : Manpower Services Commission : the Underwater Training Centre, Fort William. — London : H.M.S.O., [1980]. — 21p ; 25cm. — ([HC] ; 847)
ISBN 0-10-028479-5 (unbound) : £2.40
B82-11187

627'.8 — Dams. Design & construction

Peter, Pavol. Canal and river levées / by Pavol Peter. — Amsterdam ; Oxford : Elsevier Scientific, 1982. — 540p : ill ; 25cm. — (Developments in geotechnical engineering ; 29)
Translation of: Kanálové a ochranné hrádze. — Bibliography: p515-526. — Includes index
ISBN 0-444-99726-1 : Unpriced : CIP rev.
Also classified at 627'.132 B81-31618

627'.8 — Earthquake resistant dams. Design & construction — *Conference proceedings*

Dams and earthquake : proceedings of a conference held at the Institution of Civil Engineers, London, on 1-2 October 1980. — London : Telford for the Institution, 1981. — 313p : ill ; 31cm
ISBN 0-7277-0123-1 : £26.00 B82-15391

627'.8 — England. Severn Estuary. Proposed tidal power barrages. Environmental aspects

An **Environmental** appraisal of tidal power stations : with particular reference to the Severn barrage / T.L. Shaw (editor). — Belmont, Calif. : Fearon Pitman ; London : Pitman, c1980. — 220p : ill,maps ; 25cm. — (Current reports in civil and environmental engineering ; 1) (Pitman advanced publishing program)
Includes bibliographies
ISBN 0-273-08463-1 (pbk) : Unpriced
B82-21719

627'.8 — England. Severn Estuary. Tidal power barrages — *Conference proceedings*

Severn barrage : proceedings of a symposium organized by the Institution of Civil Engineers, held in London on 8-9 October 1981. — London : Telford, 1982. — 240p : ill,maps ; 31cm
ISBN 0-7277-0156-8 : £22.00 B82-36220

627'.86'0941656 — Down *(District)*. **Natural resources: Water. Reservoirs: Silent Valley Reservoir. Construction,** *1923-1933*

Carson, W. H.. The dam builders : the story of the men who built the Silent Valley reservoir / W.H. Carson. — Newcastle, Co. Down : Mourne Observer Press, 1981. — xv,102p : ill,1 map,1facsim,ports ; 25cm
£5.50 B82-18403

627'.98 — North Sea. Offshore natural gas & petroleum industries offshore structures. Personnel. Working life — *For children*

Milton, Barry. Oil-rig worker. — London : A. & C. Black, Sept.1982. — [32]p. — (Beans)
ISBN 0-7136-2242-3 : £2.95 : CIP entry
B82-20361

627'.98 — Offshore drilling rigs. Moorings — *Conference proceedings*

Offshore moorings. — London : Telford, Nov.1982. — [144]p
Conference papers
ISBN 0-7277-0158-4 : £16.00 : CIP entry
B82-29107

627'.98 — Offshore petroleum industries. Offshore structure. Design & construction

Graff, W. J.. Introduction to offshore structures : design, fabrication, installation / W.J. Graff. — Houston ; London : Golf Publishing, c1981. — xi,375p : ill ; 24cm
Includes index
ISBN 0-87201-694-3 : £26.75 B82-02248

627'.98 — Offshore structures. Design

Gaythwaite, John. The marine environment and structural design / John Gaythwaite. — New York ; London : Van Nostrand Reinhold, c1981. — xvi,313p : ill ; 24cm
Bibliography: p307. — Includes index
ISBN 0-442-24834-2 : £19.15 B82-00855

627′.98 — Offshore structures. Design & construction — *Conference proceedings*

International Symposium on Integrity of Offshore Structures *(2nd : 1981 : Glasgow).* Integrity of offshore structures / [papers presented at the second International Symposium on Integrity of Offshore Structures, 1-3 July 1981, held at the University, Glasgow, Scotland] ; [organised by the University, Glasgow, and the Institution of Engineers and Shipbuilders in Scotland] ; edited by D. Faulkner, M.J. Cowling and P.A. Frieze. — London : Applied Science Publishers, c1981. — viii,662p : ill ; 24cm
ISBN 0-85334-989-4 : £40.00 : CIP rev.
B81-25721

627′.98 — Offshore structures: Industrial islands — *Conference proceedings*

Industrial islands : international conference sponsored by the Institution of Mechanical Engineers with the Council of Engineering Institutions — Council of Science and Technology Institutes Interdisciplinary Technical Committee, 17-19 November 1981, Institution Headquarters 1 Birdcage Walk, Westminster, London. — London : Published by Mechanical Engineering Publications for the Institution of Mechanical Engineers, c1981. — 188p : ill,maps,plans ; 30cm. — (I Mech E conference publications ; 1981-12)
ISBN 0-85298-478-2 (pbk) : Unpriced
B82-12090

627′.98 — Offshore structures. Permament anchorages

Permanent anchorages for offshore structures / [FIP Commission on Concrete Sea Structures]. — Slough : Fédération Internationale de la Précontrainte, 1982. — 56p : ill ; 30cm. — (State of art report / Fédération Internationale de la Précontrainte)
Cover title
ISBN 0-907862-10-1 (pbk) : Unpriced
B82-37101

627′.98 — Offshore structures. Steel shells. Buckling

Buckling of shells in offshore structures / edited by J.E. Harding, P.J. Dowling and N. Agelidis. — London : Granada, 1982. — 581p : ill ; 24cm
Includes bibliographies and index
ISBN 0-246-11754-0 : Unpriced B82-24514

627′.98 — Offshore structures. Steel structural components. Fatigue. Measurement & analysis. Research projects: UK Offshore Steels Research Project — *Conference proceedings*

Fatigue in offshore structural steels : implications of the Department of Energy's research programme : proceedings of a conference organized by the Institution of Civil Engineers, held in London on 24-25 February 1981. — London : Telford for the Institution, 1981. — 130p : ill ; 31cm
ISBN 0-7277-0108-8 : £14.00 B82-15388

628 — SANITARY ENGINEERING

628 — Sanitary engineering

Payne, Rolf. Drainage and sanitation. — London : Longman, Nov.1982. — [208]p
ISBN 0-582-41241-2 : £12.50 : CIP entry
B82-27960

628 — Sanitary engineering. Hydraulic engineering

Bartlett, Ronald E.. Hydraulics for public health engineers. — London : Applied Science, Sept.1982. — [180]p
ISBN 0-85334-148-6 : £29.00 : CIP entry
B82-20832

628′.028 — Sanitary engineering. Use of rubber & plastics — *Conference proceedings*

Use of Plastics and Rubber in Water and Effluents *(Conference : 1982 : London).* International conference The Use of Plastics and Rubber in Water and Effluents : 15-17 February 1982 : at the Royal Lancaster Hotel, London / sponsored by Institute of Water Pollution control ... [et al.]. — London (11 Hobart Place SW1N 0HL) : The Plastics and Rubber Institute, [1982?]. — 1v. : ill ; 21cm
£16.00 (pbk)
Primary classification 627′.028 B82-20153

628.1 — WATER SUPPLY

628.1 — Great Britain. Water supply. Losses — *Conference proceedings*

Symposium on an Understanding of Water Losses *(1981 : London).* Symposium on an Understanding of Water Losses : proceedings of symposium held in London, England 1st and 2nd December 1981. — London (31 High Holborn WC1V 6AX) : Institution of Water Engineers and Scientists, [1982?]. — 209p in various pagings : ill ; 21cm
Unpriced (pbk) B82-41143

628.1 — Waste water — *Festschriften*

Water science and technology. — Oxford : Pergamon, Dec.1981. — [500]p
ISBN 0-08-029095-7 (pbk) : £25.00 : CIP entry
B81-33855

628.1′02463 — Water supply engineering — *For agriculture*

Waterhouse, James. Water engineering for agriculture / James Waterhouse. — London : Batsford Academic and Educational, 1982. — 395p : ill,1map ; 23cm
Includes bibliographies and index
ISBN 0-7134-1409-x : £17.95 : CIP rev.
B81-30358

628.1′028 — Water supply equipment & waste water treatment equipment — *Serials*

Aquatechnic international : products and services for the water and wastewater industries. — Aug./Sept. 1981-. — Chislehurst (75 Lower Camden, Chislehurst, Kent BR7 5JD) : Marlborough Pub., 1981-. — v. : ill ; 42cm
Ten issues yearly
ISSN 0261-5355 = Aquatechnic international : £20.00 per year B82-06777

628.1′091724 — Developing countries. Water supply & waste water — *Conference proceedins*

WEDC Conference *(7th : 1981 : Loughborough).* Water, people and waste in developing countries : 7th WEDC Conference, 23-25 September 1981 : proceedings / edited by Susan Ball and John Pickford. — Loughborough : WEDC Group, Department of Civil Engineering, University of Technology Loughborough, 1982. — 112p : ill,maps ; 30cm. — (Water and waste engineering for developing countries)
ISBN 0-906055-12-1 (pbk) : £15.00
B82-25955

628.1′0945′85 — Malta. Water supply

Oglethorpe, Miles. Maltese development issues / Miles Oglethorpe. — [Glasgow] : University of Glasgow, Department of Geography, 1982. — i,150p : ill,maps ; 30cm. — (Occasional papers / Geography Department Glasgow University ; no.8)
Unpriced (spiral)
Primary classification 338.4′7914585
B82-27873

628.1′12 — England. Regulated rivers. Water. Losses

River regulation losses in English and Wales. — Reading : Central Water Planning Unit, c1979. — viii,92p : ill,maps ; 30cm
Bibliography: p91
ISBN 0-904839-43-5 (pbk) : Unpriced
B82-31848

628.1′14′0942262 — West Sussex. Chichester *(District).* **Water supply. Wells** — *Lists*

Hargreaves, Rosemary. Records of wells in the Chichester area : inventory for 1:50 000 geological sheet 317 / Rosemary Hargreaves and Judith Parker, contributor, geological classification of well records, M.R. Henson. — London : H.M.S.O., 1980. — 82p : maps ; 30cm. — (Metric well inventory)
At head of title: Institute of Geological Sciences
ISBN 0-11-884165-3 (pbk) : £5.00 B82-20451

628.1′5 — Water pipelines. Design

Stephenson, David. Pipeline design for water engineers / David Stephenson. — 2nd ed. — Amsterdam ; Oxford : Elsevier Scientific, 1981. — xi,234p : ill ; 25cm. — (Developments in water science ; 15)
Previous ed.: 1976. — Includes index
ISBN 0-444-41991-8 : £22.64 : CIP rev.
B81-13839

628.1′61 — Ponds. Water. Quality control — *For fish farming*

Boyd, Claude E.. Water quality management for pond fish culture / Claude E. Boyd. — Amsterdam ; Oxford : Elsevier Scientific, 1982. — xi,318p : ill ; 24cm. — (Developments in aquaculture and fisheries science ; 9)
Includes bibliographies and index
ISBN 0-444-42054-1 : £31.31 : CIP rev.
B81-39217

628.1′62 — Natural resources: Water. Treatment

Belan, F. I.. Water treatment / F.I. Belan ; translated from the Russian by S. Semyonov. — Moscow : Mir ; [London] : distributed by Central Books, 1981. — 232p : ill ; 20cm
Translation of: Vodopodgotovka. —
Bibliography: p229. — Includes index
ISBN 0-7147-1771-1 (pbk) : £3.95 B82-38341

628.1′62 — Water. Purification

Blake, Richard T.. Water treatment for HVAC and potable water systems / Richard T. Blake. — New York ; London : McGraw-Hill, c1980. — x,181p : ill,forms ; 24cm
Includes index
ISBN 0-07-005840-7 : £14.50 B82-37152

Handbook of water purification / editor Walter Lorch. — London : McGraw-Hill, c1981. — xviii,715p : ill,1map ; 26cm
Includes index
ISBN 0-07-084555-7 : £45.00 : CIP rev.
B81-28826

628.1′62 — Water supply. Treatment

Barnes, D.. Chemistry and unit operations in water treatment. — London : Applied Science, Jan.1983. — [300]p
ISBN 0-85334-169-9 : £30.00 : CIP entry
B82-33112

628.1′62′05 — Natural resources: Water. Treatment — *Serials*

Developments in water treatment. — 1-. — London : Applied Science, 1980-. — v. : ill ; 23cm. — (Developments series)
Irregular
ISSN 0263-3736 = Developments in water treatment : £17.00 B82-18538

628.1′66 — Water. Chemical treatment

Benefield, Larry D.. Process chemistry for water and wastewater treatment / Larry D. Benefield and Joseph F. Judkins, Jr. and Barron L. Weand. — Englewood Cliffs ; London : Prentice-Hall, c1982. — xii,510p : ill,1map ; 25cm
Includes bibliographies and index
ISBN 0-13-722975-5 : £22.45 B82-23641

628.1′67 — Water. Desalination

Desalination technology. — London : Applied Science, Feb.1983. — [256]p
ISBN 0-85334-175-3 : £30.00 : CIP entry
B82-39604

Principles of desalination. — 2nd ed. / edited by K.S. Spiegler, A.D.K. Laird. — New York ; London : Academic Press
Previous ed.: published in 1v., 1966. —
Includes bibliographies and index
Pt.B. — 1980. — xi,821p : ill,3maps ; 24cm
ISBN 0-12-656702-6 : Unpriced B82-36744

628.1′6725 — Sewage sludge. Marine disposal — *Conference proceedings*

Disposal of sludge to sea. — Oxford : Pergamon, Mar.1982. — [230]p. — (Water science and technology ; v.14, no.3)
Conference papers
ISBN 0-08-029093-0 : £15.50 : CIP entry
B82-07129

628.1′68 — Coastal waters & fresh waters. Dissolved pollutants. Hydraulic transport

Mixing : in inland and coastal waters / Hugo B. Fischer ... [et al.]. — New York ; London : Academic Press, 1979. — xiv,483p : ill ; 24cm
Bibliography: p459-472. — Includes index
ISBN 0-12-258150-4 : £33.00 B82-24160

628.1′68 — Coastal waters & fresh waters. Dissolved pollutants. Hydraulic transport. Models. Predictive ability — *Conference proceedings*

Symposium on Predictive Ability of Surface Water Flow and Transport Models *(1980 : Berkeley, Calif.)*. Transport models for inland and coastal waters : proceedings of a symposium on predictive ability / edited by Hugo B. Fischer. — New York ; London : Academic Press, 1981. — xv,542p : ill,maps ; 24cm
Proceedings of the Symposium on Predictive Ability of Surface Water Flow and Transport Models, held at the Marriott Inn, Berkeley, California, August 18-20, 1980, under the sponsorship of the International Association for Hydraulic Research, the American Society of Civil Engineers, and the University of California, Berkeley, and with the financial assistance of the National Science Foundation and the Environmental Protection Agency. — Includes bibliographies and index
ISBN 0-12-258152-0 : £26.20 B82-12967

628.1′68 — Great Britain. Fresh waters. Pollution. Biological aspects

Mason, C. F.. Biology of freshwater pollution / C.F. Mason. — London : Longman, 1981. — xi,250p : ill,maps ; 22cm
Bibliography: p209-238. — Includes index
ISBN 0-582-45596-0 (pbk) : £5.50 : CIP rev. B81-28112

628.1′68′01576 — Water. Pollution. Control. Applications of microbiology

Gaudy, Anthony F.. Microbiology for environmental scientists and engineers / Anthony F. Gaudy, Jr., Elizabeth T. Gaudy. — New York ; London : McGraw-Hill, c1980. — xvi,736p : ill ; 25cm. — (McGraw-Hill series in water resources and environmental engineering)
Includes bibliographies and index
ISBN 0-07-023035-8 : £21.75 B82-16876

628.1′686′162 — Oceans. Pollution. Control measures

Patin, S. A.. Pollution and the biological resources of the oceans. — London : Butterworth, Aug.1982. — [300]p
Translation of: Vliīanie zagriaznenīīa na biologicheskie resursy i produktivnost′ morovogo okeana
ISBN 0-408-10840-1 : £30.00 : CIP entry B82-22797

628.1′6861698 — Ground water. Pollution — *Conference proceedings*

Quality of groundwater : proceedings of an international symposium, Noordwijkerhout, The Netherlands, 23-27 March 1981 / edited by W. van Duijvenbooden, P. Glasbergen and H. van Lelyveld. — Amsterdam ; Oxford : Elsevier Scientific, 1981. — xxxiv,1128p : ill,maps ; 25cm. — (Studies in environmental science ; 17)
′A selection of these papers has been published as a special volume of The science of the total environment, volume 21, 1981′. — Includes bibliographies and index
ISBN 0-444-42022-3 : £76.09 B82-08073

628.1′686417 — Ireland *(Republic)*. **Rivers. Pollution**

O′Donnell, C.. Organic micropollutants in Irish waters : results of a pilot study / C. O′Donnell. — Dublin (St. Martin′s House, Waterloo Rd, Dublin 4) : An Foras Forbartha, Water Resources Division, 1980. — 19p : ill,1map ; 21cm. — (WR/G7)
£1.00 (pbk) B82-35371

628.1′688′16337 — Irish Sea. Pollution by petroleum spilled during accident to Christos Bitas *(Ship)*. **Control measures by British Petroleum Company**

The **Christos** Bitas incident : success out of disaster : a report on the oil spill clean-up operations / by BP′s Environmental Control Centre. — London (Britannic House, Moor La., E.C.2) : The Centre, [1979]. — 23p : ill (some col.),col.maps ; 21x30cm
Cover title
Unpriced (pbk) B82-39912

628.1′688′4 — Europe. Coastal waters. Pollution. Control measures. Engineering aspects — *Conference proceedings*

Coastal discharges : engineering aspects and experience : proceedings of the conference organised by the Institution of Civil Engineers and held in London on 7-9 October 1980. — London : Telford for the Institution, 1981. — 216p : ill ; 31cm
ISBN 0-7277-0124-x : £20.00 B82-15392

628.1′688′41 — Great Britain. Seashore. Pollution by petroleum. Control measures

Oil pollution of the coastline : a study for the Department of the Environment. — Lancaster : ISCOL, c1981. — vii,140p(2 folded) : ill ; 30cm
ISBN 0-901699-83-7 (pbk) : Unpriced B82-12659

628.1′688′421 — London. Thames River. Pollution. Control measures, *to 1981*

Wood, Leslie B.. The restoration of the tidal Thames / Leslie B. Wood ; consultant editor D.V. Ager. — Bristol : Hilger, c1982. — 202p : ill,plans,ports ; 24cm
Bibliography: p193-195. — Includes index
ISBN 0-85274-447-1 : £22.50 : CIP rev. B81-33792

628.2 — DRAINAGE, SEWERAGE

628′.2 — Drainage systems. Maintenance

Payne, Rolf. Drain maintenance. — London : Longman, Oct.1982. — [224]p. — (Longman construction site management series)
ISBN 0-582-30513-6 : £9.95 : CIP entry B82-25071

628′.2 — Sewers & sewage pumping systems

Wastewater engineering : collection and pumping of wastewater / Metcalf & Eddy, Inc. ; written and edited by George Tchobanoglous. — New York ; London : McGraw-Hill, c1981. — xvi,432p : ill ; 25cm. — (McGraw-Hill series in water resources and environmental engineering)
Text, ill on lining papers. — Includes bibliographies and index
ISBN 0-07-041680-x : £19.95 B82-00118

628′.2 — Sewers — *Conference proceedings*

Restoration of sewerage systems : proceedings of an international conference organized by the Institution of Civil Engineers, held in London on 22-24 June 1981. — London : Telford, 1982. — 308p : ill ; 31cm
Includes index
ISBN 0-7277-0145-2 : £25.00 B82-36219

628′.21 — Structures. Vertical drainage systems

Vertical drains. — London : Telford, 1982. — 160p : ill ; 26cm
Previously published as a Symposium in print, in Géotechnique, 1981. — Includes bibliographies
ISBN 0-7277-0147-9 : £14.50 B82-36667

628.3 — SEWAGE TREATMENT AND DISPOSAL

628.3 — Sewage. Treatment

Unit processes. — Maidstone (53 London Rd., Maidstone, Kent ME16 8JH) : Institute of Water Pollution Control. — (Manuals of British practice in water pollution control)
Sewage sludge II: Conditioning, dewatering and thermal drying. — 1981. — 124p : ill ; 24cm
Bibliography: p118-122. — Includes index
Unpriced (pbk) B82-24635

628.3 — Sewage. Treatment. Applications of automation — *Conference proceedings*

Practical experiences of control and automation in wastewater treatment and water resources management. — Oxford : Pergamon, Mar.1982. — [846]p. — (Water science and technology)
Conference papers
ISBN 0-08-029086-8 (pbk) : £65.00 : CIP entry B82-03347

628.3 — Waste water. Recycling

Dean, Robert B.. Water reuse : problems and solutions / Robert B. Dean and Ebba Lund. — London : Academic Press, 1981. — xvii,264p : ill ; 24cm
Includes index
ISBN 0-12-208080-7 : £18.40 : CIP rev. B81-31335

628.3 — Waste water. Treatment

Owen, William F.. Energy in wastewater treatment / William F. Owen. — Englewood Cliffs ; London : Prentice-Hall, c1982. — x,373p : ill ; 25cm
Includes index
ISBN 0-13-277665-0 : £26.95 B82-31913

Oxidation ditches in wastewater treatment. — London : Pitman, Jan.1983. — [296]p
ISBN 0-273-08527-1 : £31.50 : CIP entry B82-33720

Water and wastewater engineering systems / D. Barnes ... [et al.]. — London : Pitman, 1981. — xvi,513p : ill ; 24cm. — (A Pitman international text)
Includes index
ISBN 0-273-01138-3 (cased) : Unpriced
ISBN 0-273-01168-5 (pbk) : Unpriced B82-08898

628.3 — Waste water. Treatment — *Conference proceedings*

Physicochemical methods for water and wastewater treatment : proceedings of the third international conference, Lubin, Poland, 21-25 September 1981 / organized under sponsorship of the Federation of European Chemical Societies, by the Polish Chemical Society and the Maria Curie-Sklodowska University ; edited by L. Pawlowski. — Amsterdam ; Oxford : Elsevier Scientific, 1982. — viii,394p : ill ; 25cm. — (Studies in environmental science ; 19)
Includes index
ISBN 0-444-42067-3 : £44.59 : CIP rev. B82-10670

628.3 — Waste water. Treatment. Nitrification

Barnes, D.. Biological control of nitrogen in wastewater treatment. — London : Spon, Feb.1983. — [200]p
ISBN 0-419-12350-4 : £15.00 : CIP entry B82-38301

628.3 — Waste water. Treatment. Use of ozone

Ozonization manual for water and wastewater treatment. — Chichester : Wiley, Sept.1982. — [200]p
ISBN 0-471-10198-2 : £14.00 : CIP entry B82-19527

628.3′51 — Waste water. Biological treatment

Dinges, Ray. Natural systems for water pollution control / Ray Dinges. — New York ; London : Van Nostrand Reinhold, c1982. — xii,252p : ill ; 24cm. — (Van Nostrand Reinhold environmental engineering series)
Includes bibliographies and index
ISBN 0-442-20166-4 : £19.15 B82-13194

Winkler, M. A.. Biological treatment of waste-water / M.A. Winkler. — Chichester : Ellis Horwood, 1981. — 301p : ill ; 23cm
Includes bibliographies and index
ISBN 0-85312-422-1 (pbk) : £9.50 B82-19901

628.3′51 — Waste water. Biological treatment systems. Design — *Manuals*

Benjes, Henry H.. Handbook of biological wastewater treatment : evaluation, performance and cost / Henry H. Benjes, Jr.. — New York ; London : Garland STPM, c1980. — ix,181p : ill ; 24cm. — (Water management series)
Bibliography: p111-112. — Includes index
ISBN 0-8240-7089-5 : Unpriced B82-21235

628.3′51 — Waste water treatment lagoons. Management

Wastewater stabilization lagoon design, performance and upgrading / E. Joe Middlebrooks ... [et al.]. — New York : Macmillan ; London : Collier Macmillan, c1982. — vii,356p : ill,plans ; 25cm
Includes index
ISBN 0-02-949500-8 : £35.00 B82-39391

628.3′54 — Activated sewage sludge. Bulking — *Conference proceedings*

Bulking of activated sludge : preventative and remedial methods / editors B. Chambers and E.J. Tomlinson. — Chichester : Published by Ellis Horwood for the Water Research Centre, 1982. — 279p : ill ; 24cm
Conference papers. — Includes index
ISBN 0-85312-350-0 : £25.00 : CIP rev. B81-36983

628.3′54 — Waste materials. Anaerobic digestion — *Conference proceedings*

International Symposium on Anaerobic Digestion *(2nd : 1981 : Travemünde).* Anaerobic digestion 1981 : proceedings of the second International Symposium on Anaerobic Digestion held in Travemünde, Federal Republic of Germany, on 6-11 September, 1981 / editors D.E. Hughes ... [et al.]. — Amsterdam ; Oxford : Elsevier Biomedical, 1982. — ix,429p : ill ; 24cm
Includes index
ISBN 0-444-80406-4 : £35.90 B82-21020

628.3′54 — Waste materials. Anaerobic digestion — *Serials*

. The Digest : the regular newsletter of the British Anaerobic and Biomass Association Ltd. — No.1 (Mar. 1980)-. — Marlborough (c/o The Secretary, The White House, Little Bedwyn, Marlborough, Wiltshire) : The Association, 1980-. — v. ; 30cm
Three issues yearly. — Description based on: No.5 (Oct. 1981)
ISSN 0262-6349 = Digest (British Anaerobic and Biomass Association Ltd) : £2.50 per issue
Also classified at 662′.6 B82-08458

628.3′623 — Irrigation. Use of municipal waste water — *Conference proceedings*

International Conference on the Status of Knowledge, Critical Research Needs, and Potential Research Facilities Relating to the Cooperative Research Needs for the Renovation and Reuse of Municipal Wastewater in Agriculture *(1980 : Morelos).* Municipal wastewater in agriculture / [proceedings for [i.e. of] the International Conference on the Status of Knowledge, Critical Research Needs, and Potential Research Facilities Relating to the Cooperative Research Needs for the Renovation and Reuse of Municipal Wastewater in Agriculture, held at the Hotel Hacienda Cocoyoc, Morelos, Mexico, December 15-19, 1980] ; edited by Frank M. D'Itri, Jorge Aguirre Martínez, Mauricio Athié Lámbarri. — New York ; London : Academic Press, 1981. — xiv,492p : ill,maps ; 24cm
Includes bibliographies and index
ISBN 0-12-214880-0 : £26.20 B82-39504

628.3′623′0724 — Irrigation. Use of waste water. Mathematical models

Modeling wastewater renovation : land treatment / edited by I.K. Iskandar. — New York ; Chichester : Wiley, c1981. — xv,802p : ill,maps ; 24cm. — (Environmental science and technology)
Includes bibliographies and index
ISBN 0-471-08128-0 : £40.00 B82-01029

628.4 — PUBLIC CLEANSING AND SANITATION

628.4′4 — Solid waste materials. Management

Disposal and recovery of municipal solid waste. — London : Butterworths, Aug.1982. — [200]p
ISBN 0-408-01174-2 : £16.00 : CIP entry B82-15781

628.4′4 — Waste materials. Management

Wilson, David C.. Waste management : planning, evaluation, technologies / David C. Wilson. — Oxford : Clarendon Press, 1981. — xxi,530p : ill ; 23cm. — (Oxford science publications)
Bibliography: p476-507. — Includes index
ISBN 0-19-859001-6 : £45.00 : CIP rev. B81-14909

628.4′4 — Waste materials. Management — *Conference proceedings*

Waste treatment and utilization 2. — Oxford : Pergamon, Dec.1981. — [587]p
Conference papers
ISBN 0-08-024012-7 : £47.50 : CIP entry B81-34222

628.4′4′094 — Europe. Household refuse. Collection & disposal

Household waste management in Europe : economics and techniques / edited by A.V. Bridgwater, K. Lidgren. — New York ; London : Van Nostrand Reinhold, 1981. — xi,249p : ill,maps ; 24cm
Includes bibliographies and index
ISBN 0-442-30464-1 : £16.00 B82-09759

628.4′4′0941 — Great Britain. Solid waste materials. Management — *Serials*

Wastes management : the monthly journal of the Institute of Wastes Management. — Vol.27, no.1 (Jan. 1982)-. — London (28 Portland Place, W1N 4DE) : The Institute, 1982-. — v. : ill(some col.),ports ; 22cm
Continues: Solid wastes
ISSN 0263-8126 = Wastes management : Unpriced B82-33863

628.4′45′094259 — Buckinghamshire. Waste materials. Disposal — *Proposals*

Buckinghamshire. *County Council.* Waste disposal plan / Buckinghamshire County Council. — Aylesbury : County Engineers Department, [1981]. — 141p : ill,maps,2forms ; 30cm
ISBN 0-86059-295-2 (pbk) : Unpriced B82-14620

628.5 — POLLUTION AND INDUSTRIAL SANITATION ENGINEERING

628.5 — Environment. Pollutants. Chemical analysis — *Conference proceedings*

Analytical techniques in environmental chemistry 2. — Oxford : Pergamon, Nov.1982. — [472]p. — (Pergamon series on environmental science ; v.7)
Conference proceedings
ISBN 0-08-028740-9 : £37.50 : CIP entry B82-26869

628.5 — Environment. Pollutants. Chemical properties — *Serials*

Environmental toxicology and chemistry : an international journal. — Vol.1, no.1 (1982)-. — New York ; Oxford : Pergamon, 1982-. — v. : ill ; 26cm
Quarterly
ISSN 0730-7268 = Environmental toxicology and chemistry : Unpriced B82-33874

628.5 — Environment. Pollutants: Chemicals. Short term biological assay — *Conference proceedings*

Symposium on the Application of Short-Term Bioassays in the Fractionation and Analysis of Complex Environmental Mixtures *(2nd : 1980 : Williamsburg).* Short-term bioassays in the analysis of complex environmental mixtures II / [proceedings of the Second Symposium on the Application of Short-Term Bioassays in the Fractionation and Analysis of Complex Environmental Mixtures, held in Williamsburg, Virginia, March 4-7, 1980] ; edited by Michael D. Waters ... [et al.]. — New York ; London : Plenum, [1981]. — xv,524p : ill ; 26cm. — (Environmental science research ; v.22)
Includes bibliographies and index
ISBN 0-306-40890-2 : Unpriced B82-14704

628.5 — Environment. Pollutants. Detection & chemical analysis. Gas chromatography & liquid chromatography

Grob, Robert L.. Environmental problem solving using gas and liquid chromatography / Robert L. Grob, Mary A. Kaiser. — Amsterdam ; Oxford : Elsevier Scientific, 1982. — xiii,240p : ill ; 25cm. — (Journal of chromatography library ; v.21)
Includes index
ISBN 0-444-42065-7 : £27.08 B82-23540

628.5 — Environment. Pollution. Control measures

Jørgensen, S. E.. Principles of environmental science and technology / by S.E. Jørgensen and I. Johnsen. — Amsterdam ; Oxford : Elsevier Scientific, 1981. — xi,516p : ill ; 25cm. — (Studies in environmental science ; 14)
Bibliography: p487-506. — Includes index
ISBN 0-444-99721-0 : Unpriced B82-05982

Lowe, Julian. Total environmental control. — Oxford : Pergamon, Oct.1982. — [126]p
ISBN 0-08-026276-7 (pbk) : £10.65 : CIP entry B82-24951

628.5 — Great Britain. Coastal regions. Pollutants: Petroleum. Clearance — *Manuals*

Oil spill cleanup of the coastline : a technical manual / prepared on behalf of the Department of the Environment. — Stevenage : Warren Spring Labroatory, 1982. — v,72p : ill (some col.) ; 21cm
Includes index
ISBN 0-85624-262-4 (spiral) : Unpriced B82-25288

628.5′028 — Environment. Pollutants. Chromatography

Chromatography of environmental hazards. — Amsterdam ; Oxford : Elsevier Scientific
Vol.4: Drugs of abuse / Lawrence Fishbein. — 1982. — vii,496p : ill ; 25cm
Includes index
ISBN 0-444-42024-x : £47.67 : CIP rev. B81-28176

628.5′3 — Air. Quality control. Applications of mathematical models — *Conference proceedings*

Mathematical models for planning & controlling air quality. — Oxford : Pergamon, Aug.1982. — [255]p. — (IIASA proceedings series ; v.17)
ISBN 0-08-029950-4 : £25.00 : CIP entry B82-20745

628.5′3 — Atmosphere pollution control equipment

Air pollution control equipment : selection, design, operation and maintenance / Louis Theodore and Anthony J. Buonicore editors. — Englewood Cliffs ; London : Prentice-Hall, c1982. — xv,429p : ill ; 24cm
Includes index
ISBN 0-13-021154-0 : £28.50 B82-16848

628.5′32 — Atmosphere. Combustion-generated pollutants: Carbon dust — *Conference proceedings*

Particulate carbon : formation during combustion / [proceedings of an international symposium on particulate carbon-formation during combustion, held October 15-16, 1980, at the General Motors Research Laboratory, Warren, Michigan] ; edited by Donald C. Siegla and George W. Smith. — New York ; London : Plenum, c1981. — x,505p : ill,1port ; 26cm
Includes index
ISBN 0-306-40881-3 : Unpriced B82-14547

628.5′4 — Great Britain. Medical institutions. Clinical waste materials. Disposal. Safety measures

The **Safe** disposal of clinical waste / Health and Safety Commission, Health Services Advisory Committee. — London : H.M.S.O., 1982. — 7p ; 30cm
ISBN 0-11-883641-2 (unbound) : £1.50 B82-39981

628.5′4 — Great Britain. Waste materials: Toxic industrial chemicals. Disposal — *Conference proceedings*

The **Management** of toxic waste from the cradle to the grave, 11 November 1981 London. — [London] : Scientific and Technical Studies, c1981. — iiileaves,87p : ill ; 30cm
Conference papers
ISBN 0-907822-00-2 (pbk) : Unpriced : CIP rev. B82-06066

628.5′4′091724 — Developing countries. Industrial waste water. Treatment & disposal — *Conference proceedings*

Management of industrial wastewater in developing nations : proceedings of the international symposium, Alexandria, March 1981 / sponsored by the High Institute of Public Health, Alexandria University, and the Academy of Scientific Research and Technology, Egypt ; edited by David Stuckey and Ahmed Hamza. — Oxford : Pergamon, 1982. — x,500p : ill ; 24cm
Includes bibliographies and index
ISBN 0-08-026286-4 : £35.00 : CIP rev. B82-14354

628.7 — RURAL SANITARY ENGINEERING

628'.7446 — Livestock: Dairy cattle. Liquid waste materials. Treatment. Use of barrier ditches — *Manuals*

Farm waste management : barrier ditches / ADAS. — Amended [ed.]. — Pinner : Ministry of Agriculture, Fisheries and Food, 1980. — 19p : ill ; 21cm. — (Booklet / Ministry of Agriculture, Fisheries and Food ; 2199)
Cover title. — Previous ed.: 1975. — "Formerly STL 172"
Unpriced (pbk) B82-15574

628.92 — FIRE FIGHTING TECHNOLOGY

628.9'2 — Buildings. Fire protection & fire fighting equipment

Bryan, John L.. Fire suppression and detection systems / John L. Bryan. — 2nd ed. — New York : Macmillan ; London : Collier Macmillan, c1982. — x,518p : ill,plans ; 25cm. — (Macmillan's fire science series)
Previous ed.: Beverly Hills : Glencoe, 1974. — Includes bibliographies and index
ISBN 0-02-471300-7 : Unpriced B82-35272

628.9'2 — Hospitals. Fire prevention & fire fighting — *Manuals*

St. Helens and Knowlsey Area Health Authority. Fire! / St. Helens and Knowlsey Area Health Authority. — [St. Helens] ([Administrative HQ, Cowley Hill Lane, St. Helens]) : The Authority, [1981?]. — 36p : ill(some col.) ; 15cm
Cover title. — Prepared by: E. Reynolds
Unpriced (pbk) B82-04941

628.9'2'072041 — Great Britain. Fire prevention & fire fighting. Research by Great Britain. *Home Office. Scientific Advisory Branch — Serials*

Fire research news : news of Home Office fire research for the fire service. — Issue 1-. — London (Horseferry House, Dean Ryle St., SW1P 2AW) : Home Office Scientific Advisory Branch, [1981]-. — v. : ill,ports ; 30cm
Two issues yearly
ISSN 0261-1589 = Fire research news : Unpriced B82-04898

628.9'2'0941 — Great Britain. Fire prevention & fire fighting — *Inquiry reports*

Review of fire policy : an examination of the deployment of resources to combat fire / Home Office. — London : Home Office, 1980. — 432p : ill ; 25cm
ISBN 0-903727-87-0 (pbk) : £6.50 B82-36977

628.9'22'0941 — Great Britain. Fire protection. Policies — *Proposals*

Rudd, G. T.. Fire policy reviewed / speaker G.T. Rudd ; introductory address by Lord Belstead. — [Dorking?] ([c/o Fire Service Staff College, Dorking, Surrey]) : [Fire Service Research and Training Trust?], [1980]. — vii,43p ; 25cm. — (Lecture / Fire Service Research and Training Trust ; 1980)
Lecture given at Fire Service Staff College, Dorking, Surrey, 4th July 1980
Unpriced (pbk) B82-37305

628.9'22'0941 — Great Britain. Fire protection — *Serials*

[Fire news *(London)*]. Fire news / British Safety Council. — Aug. 1981-. — London (62 Chancellor's Rd. W6 9RS) : The Council, 1981-. — v. : ill,ports ; 38cm
Quarterly
ISSN 0262-4451 = Fire news (London) : £6.00 per year B82-03396

628.9'225 — Buildings. Fire alarms. Design & installation

Traister, John E.. Design and application of security/fire-alarm systems / John E. Traister. — New York ; London : McGraw-Hill, c1981. — viii,176p : ill,plans,forms ; 24cm
Includes index
ISBN 0-07-065114-0 : £12.50
Also classified at 690 B82-00530

628.9'25 — Fire engines, *to 1980*

Mallet, J.. Fire engines of the world. — London : Osprey, June 1982. — [224]p
Translation of: Les véhicules d'incendie dans le monde
ISBN 0-85045-458-1 : £12.95 : CIP entry B82-09842

628.9'25 — Fire fighting — *For children*

Milburn, Constance. The fire service / Constance Milburn ; illustrated by David T. Gray. — [Glasgow] : Blackie, [1981]. — 32p : col.ill ; 22cm
Includes index
ISBN 0-216-91036-6 (pbk) : £0.95 B82-05308

629 — TRANSPORT ENGINEERING, AUTOMATIC CONTROL SYSTEMS, ETC

629.04 — Transport engineering

Paquette, Radnor J.. Transportation engineering : planning and design / Radnor J. Paquette, Norman J. Ashford, Paul H. Wright. — 2nd ed. — New York ; Chichester : Wiley, c1982. — vii,679p : ill,maps ; 25cm
Previous ed.: New York : Ronald Press, 1972. — Includes index
ISBN 0-471-04878-x : Unpriced B82-40523

Transportation and traffic engineering handbook / Institute of Transportation Engineers. — 2nd ed. / Wolfgang S. Homburger, editor ; Louis E. Keefer and William R. McGrath, associate editors. — Englewood Cliffs ; London : Prentice-Hall, c1982. — xii,883p : ill,forms,maps ; 29cm
Previous ed.: 1976. — Includes bibliographies and index
ISBN 0-13-930362-6 : Unpriced B82-39706

Yu, Jason C.. Transportation engineering : introduction to planning, design, and operations / Jason C. Yu. — New York ; Oxford : Elsevier, c1982. — xiv,462p : ill ; 27cm
Includes bibliographies and index
ISBN 0-444-00564-1 : £25.53 B82-30540

629.04'074'0941 — Great Britain. Transport museums — *Directories*

AAA guide to light railway and industrial preservation / edited by Geoffrey Body, Ian G. Body. — Weston-super-Mare : Avon-AngliA, c1982. — 52p : ill,1map ; 22cm
Cover title: Light railways transport and industrial presentation
ISBN 0-905466-45-4 (pbk) : £0.85
Primary classification 385'.5'02541 B82-26988

Garvey, Jude. A guide to the transport museums of Great Britain / Jude Garvey. — London : Pelham, 1982. — 238p : ill,1map ; 24cm
Map on lining papers. — Includes index
ISBN 0-7207-1404-4 : £9.95 : CIP rev. B82-09831

629.04'6 — Fast vehicles — *For children*

Supermachines / editor Toni Palumbo. — London : Marshall Cavendish Children's Books, 1978 (1979 [printing]). — 61p : col.ill ; 30cm. — (Woodpecker books)
Text and ill on lining papers. — Includes index
ISBN 0-85685-337-2 : Unpriced B82-11164

629.04'6 — Vehicles — *For children*

Humberstone, Eliot. Finding out about things that go / written by Eliot Humberstone ; illustrated by Basil Arm ... [et al.]. — London : Usborne, 1981. — 32p : col.ill ; 21cm. — (Usborne explainers)
Includes index
ISBN 0-86020-493-6 (pbk) : £0.99 B82-34562

629.04'9 — Guided land transport. Control systems — *Conference proceedings*

International Conference on Automated Guided Vehicle Systems *(1st : 1981 : Stratford-upon-Avon)*. Proceedings of the 1st International Conference on Automated Guided Vehicle Systems June 2-4, 1981 Stratford-upon-Avon, U.K. : an international event sponsored and organised by IFS (Conferences) Ltd. — Kempston : IFS, c1981. — vi,231p : ill ; 30cm
ISBN 0-903608-18-9 (pbk) : Unpriced B82-40534

629.049 — High speed guided land transport. Applications of magnetic levitation

Rhodes, R. G.. Magnetic levitation for rail transport / R.G. Rhodes and B.E. Mulhall. — Oxford : Clarendon, 1981. — ix,103p : ill ; 24cm. — (Monographs on cryogenics)
Bibliography: p97-100. — Includes index
ISBN 0-19-854802-8 : £15.00 : CIP rev. B81-15835

629.1 — AEROSPACE ENGINEERING

629.1'03'21 — Aerospace engineering — *Encyclopaedias*

Gunston, Bill. Jane's aerospace dictionary / Bill Gunston. — London : Jane's, 1980. — 493p ; 25cm
ISBN 0-7106-0048-8 : £15.00 B82-20808

629.1'05 — Aerospace engineering — *Serials*

Aerospace dynamics : the technical journal of British Aerospace Dynamics Group. — Issue 1 (1979)-. — Stevenage (P.B. 600, Six Hills Way, Stevenage, Herts. SG1 2DA) : The Group, 1979-. — v. : ill(some col.) ; 30cm
Three issues yearly. — Description based on: Issue 7 (Jan. 1982)
ISSN 0263-2012 = Aerospace dynamics : Unpriced B82-28120

Progress in aerospace sciences. — Vol.19. — Oxford : Pergamon, Dec.1981. — [320]p
ISBN 0-08-029098-1 : £61.00 : CIP entry B81-33854

629.1'2 — Aerospace vehicles. Materials. Mechanics

Nica, Alexandru. Mechanics of aerospace materials / Alexandru Nica. — Amsterdam ; Oxford : Elsevier Scientific, 1981. — 346p : ill ; 25cm. — (Materials science monographs ; 9)
Based on: Mecanica materialelor pentru construcţiile aerospaţiale / Şt. Ispas, Alex. Nica and Alex. Morţun. — Includes index
ISBN 0-444-99729-6 : £34.71 : CIP rev. B81-25318

629.13 — AERONAUTICS

629.13 — Aviation

Robertson, Bruce. Aviation enthusiasts' data book / Bruce Robertson. — Cambridge : Stephens, 1982. — 153p : ill ; 25cm
Ill on lining papers. — Bibliography: p130-133. — Includes index
ISBN 0-85059-500-2 : £7.95 : CIP rev. B82-01423

629.13'009 — Aviation, *to 1977 — Readings from contemporary sources*

The **Best** of Flying / compiled by the editors of Flying magazine. — New York ; London : Van Nostrand, 1977 (1981 [printing]). — 352p : ill (some col.),col.facsims,ports ; 27cm
Includes index
ISBN 0-442-22478-8 (pbk) : £12.70 B82-16328

629.13'0094147 — Scotland. Dumfries and Galloway Region. Aeronautics, *1825-1914*

Connon, Peter. In the shadow of the eagle's wing : a history of aviation in the Cumbria, Dumfries and Galloway region, 1825 to 1914. — Cumbria (52 King St., Penrith, Cumbria) : St. Patrick's Press, Sept.1982. — [160]p
ISBN 0-9508287-0-x : £8.95 : CIP entry
Primary classification 629.13'0094278 B82-26712

629.13'0094278 — Cumbria. Aeronautics, *1825-1914*

Connon, Peter. In the shadow of the eagle's wing : a history of aviation in the Cumbria, Dumfries and Galloway region, 1825 to 1914. — Cumbria (52 King St., Penrith, Cumbria) : St. Patrick's Press, Sept.1982. — [160]p
ISBN 0-9508287-0-x : £8.95 : CIP entry
Also classified at 629.13'0094147 B82-26712

629.13'09 — Aviation. Mysteries, *to 1981*

Beaty, David. Strange encounters : mysteries of the air. — London : Methuen, Oct.1982. — [180]p
ISBN 0-413-39760-2 : £7.95 : CIP entry B82-24475

629.13′09′04 — Aviation, *1945-1980*

Jackson, Robert, *1941-*. The jet age : true tales of the air since 1945 / Robert Jackson. — London : Barker, c1980. — 157p ; 22cm
ISBN 0-213-16778-6 : £5.95 B82-22279

629.13′09111 — Flights across North Atlantic Ocean by aircraft, *1977:* Hot air balloons: Double Eagle *(Balloon)*

McCarry, Charles. Double Eagle / Charles McCarry ; with an introduction by Chris Bonington. — Large print ed. — Leicester : Ulverscroft, 1982, c1979. — 441p ; 23cm. — (Ulverscroft large print)
Originally published: Boston, Mass. : Little, Brown, 1979 ; London : W.H Allen, 1980
ISBN 0-7089-0812-8 : Unpriced : CIP rev.
Primary classification 629.13′09111
B82-18552

629.13′09111 — Flights across North Atlantic Ocean by aircraft, *1978:* Hot air balloons: Double Eagle II *(Balloon)*

McCarry, Charles. Double Eagle / Charles McCarry ; with an introduction by Chris Bonington. — Large print ed. — Leicester : Ulverscroft, 1982, c1979. — 441p ; 23cm. — (Ulverscroft large print)
Originally published: Boston, Mass. : Little, Brown, 1979 ; London : W.H Allen, 1980
ISBN 0-7089-0812-8 : Unpriced : CIP rev.
Also classified at 629.13′09111 B82-18552

629.13′092′4 — Aeroplanes. Flying. Lindbergh, Charles A. — *Biographies*

Lindbergh, Charles A.. Autobiography of values / Charles A. Lindbergh ; editor William Jovanovich ; coeditor Judith A. Schiff. — New York ; London : Harcourt Brace Jovanovich, c1978. — xxi,423p,[40]p of plates : ill,maps,1facsim,ports,1geneal.table ; 24cm
Bibliography: p407-411. — Includes index
ISBN 0-15-110202-3 : £8.50 B82-11530

629.13′092′4 — Aeroplanes. Flying — *Personal observations*

Penrose, Harald. Airymouse / Harald Penrose ; illustrated by Philip Trevor. — Shrewsbury : Airlife, 1982. — 162p : ill ; 22cm
Originally published: London : Vernon and Yates, 1967
ISBN 0-906393-16-7 : £6.95 B82-23633

629.13′092′4 — Aeroplanes. Flying. Shuttleworth, Richard — *Biographies*

Desmond, Kevin. Richard Shuttleworth : an illustrated biography / Kevin Desmond. — London : Jane′s, 1982. — 190p : ill,facsims,ports ; 29cm
ISBN 0-7106-0185-9 : £10.00 B82-37220

629.13′092′4 — Flights to Australia by aircraft, *1930 — Personal observations*

Chichester, Francis. Solo to Sydney / by Francis Chichester ; with a foreword by Lady Chichester ; and an introduction by the Baron von Zedlitz. — Greenwich : Conway Maritime, 1982. — 208p,[9]p of plates : ill,facsims,1port ; 23cm
Originally published: London : John Hamilton, 1930
ISBN 0-85177-254-4 : £5.95 B82-19942

629.13′09416 — Northern Ireland. Aviation, *to 1980*

Corlett, John. Aviation in Ulster / John Corlett. — Belfast : Blackstaff, c1981. — xi,136p : ill,facsims,ports ; 24cm
Bibliography: p134. — Includes index
ISBN 0-85640-252-4 (pbk) : £6.95 : CIP rev.
B81-32016

629.13′09422′145 — Surrey. Brooklands. Aircraft. Flying, *1907-1981*

Johnson, Howard, *1916-*. Wings over Brooklands : the story of the birthplace of British aviation / Howard Johnson ; with a foreword by Sir Thomas Sopuith. — Weybridge : Whittet, 1981. — 157p : ill,maps,2facsims,ports ; 26cm
Bibliography: p153. — Includes index
ISBN 0-905483-20-0 : £8.95 : CIP rev.
ISBN 0-905483-21-9 (pbk) : £4.95
Also classified at 338.4′762913′09422145
B81-27990

629.13′09425′5 — Northamptonshire. Aviation, *to 1981*

Gibson, Michael L.. Aviation in Northamptonshire : an illustrated history / by Michael L. Gibson. — Northampton : Northamptonshire Libraries, c1982. — vii,360p : ill,facsims,maps,ports ; 29cm
Bibliography: p354. — Includes index
ISBN 0-905391-08-x : £8.50 B82-32344

629.13′09428′1 — Yorkshire. Aeroplanes. Flights, *to 1919*

Redman, Ronald Nelson. Yorkshire′s early flying days : a pictorial history / by Ronald Nelson Redman. — Clapham : Dalesman, 1981. — 80p : ill,ports ; 18x22cm. — (Dalesman heritage)
ISBN 0-85206-646-5 (pbk) : £3.25 B82-08803

629.132 — Aeroplanes. Flight — *For children*

Sheahan, Denis. Aeroplanes / Denis Sheahan ; illustrated by John Shackell. — London : Black, c1982. — 32p : ill ; 23cm. — (Science explorers)
Includes index
ISBN 0-7136-2149-4 : £2.95 : CIP rev.
B81-33848

629.132 — Flight — *For children*

Asimov, Isaac. How we found out about outer space / Isaac Asimov. — Harlow : Longman, 1982. — 55p : ill ; 23cm. — (How we found out about series ; 1)
Includes index
ISBN 0-582-39147-4 : £2.75 B82-29317

629.132′3 — Aeroplanes. Aerodynamics

Houghton, E. L.. Aerodynamics for engineering students. — 3rd ed., E.L. Houghton, N.B. Carruthers. — London : Arnold, 1982. — viii,696p : ill ; 23cm
Previous ed.: 1970. — Bibliography: p676. — Includes index
ISBN 0-7131-3433-x (pbk) : £18.00
B82-40500

629.132′3 — Aircraft. Aerodynamics

Dole, Charles E.. Flight theory and aerodynamics : a practical guide for operational safety / Charles E. Dole. — New York ; Chichester : Wiley, c1981. — xiv,299p : ill ; 25cm
Bibliography: p293-294. — Includes index
ISBN 0-471-09152-9 : £25.85 B82-09881

629.132′3′0072073 — United States. Aircraft. Aerodynamics. Research, *to 1935*

Hanle, Paul A.. Bringing aerodynamics to America / Paul A. Hanle. — Cambridge, Mass. ; London : MIT, c1982. — xiv,184p : ill,1plan,ports ; 22cm
Includes index
ISBN 0-262-08114-8 : £14.00 B82-37513

629.132′36 — Aeroplanes. Flight. Stability

Etkin, Bernard. Dynamics of flight : stability and control / Bernard Etkin. — 2nd ed. — New York ; Chichester : Wiley, c1982. — xiii,370p : ill ; 25cm
Previous ed.: New York : Wiley ; London : Chapman & Hall, 1958. — Includes index
ISBN 0-471-08936-2 : £19.15 B82-24217

629.132′52 — Aircraft. Flight-decks. Management

Owens, Charles A.. Flight operations. — London : Granada, July 1982. — [208]p
ISBN 0-246-11643-9 : £10.00 : CIP entry
B82-12229

629.132′52′023 — Aeroplanes. Flying — *Career guides*

Jerram, Michael F.. To be a pilot / Mike Jerram. — Shrewsbury : Airlife, 1982. — 116p,[20]p of plates : ill ; 22cm
Bibliography: p113-114
ISBN 0-906393-11-6 : Unpriced B82-23632

629.132′52′0285404 — Aeroplanes. Flying. Applications of microcomputer systems

Garrison, Paul. Cockpit computers / Paul Garrison. — New York ; London : McGraw-Hill, c1982. — vi,249p : ill,facsims ; 25cm. — (McGraw-Hill series in aviation)
Includes index
ISBN 0-07-022893-0 : £18.95 B82-27569

629.132′521′05 — Aeroplanes. Flying — *Serials*

Pilot yearbook. — No.1 (1982)-. — New Malden (88 Burlington Rd, New Malden, Surrey KT3 4NT) : Lernhurst Publications, 1982-. — v. : ill(some col.),ports(some col.) ; 28cm
Annual
ISSN 0263-6905 = Pilot yearbook : £1.00
B82-30483

629.132′5213 — Aeroplanes. Flying. Landing procedures — *Manuals — For pilots*

Bramson, Alan. Make better landings. — London : Martin Dunitz, Aug.1982. — [252]p
ISBN 0-906348-38-2 : £8.95 : CIP entry
B82-17231

629.132′5217 — Aeroplanes. Flying — *Manuals — For private pilots*

Taylor, S. E. T.. Private pilot studies / S.E.T. Taylor, H.A. Parmar. — 4th ed. — Berkhamsted : Poyser, 1979. — 224p : ill ; 23cm
Previous ed.: 1977. — Includes index
ISBN 0-85661-024-0 : £5.60 B82-06366

629.132′5217 — Light aircraft. Flying — *Manuals*

Taylor, Richard L.. Fair-weather flying / Richard L. Taylor. — 2nd ed. — New York : Macmillan ; London : Collier Macmillan, c1981. — xi,353p : ill,1chart ; 22cm
Previous ed.: 1974. — Includes index
ISBN 0-02-616730-1 : £9.95 B82-26205

629.132′5217 — Light aircraft. Flying — *Manuals — For private pilots*

Farr, Geoff. Country flying : how to fly from a private field and operate a group aircraft / by Geoff Farr. — England : Pooley, c1981. — 76p : ill,2maps,2forms ; 20cm
ISBN 0-902037-06-4 : Unpriced B82-35535

629.132′5441′05 — Great Britain. Aeroplanes. Flying — *Practical information — For private pilots — Serials*

Pooley′s pilots information guide / compiled with the assistance of the Civil Aviation Authority and National Air Traffic Services. — 1st ed. (Apr. 1982)-. — [Elstree] (Elstree Aerodrome, Herts.) : Robert Pooley Ltd., 1982-. — v. : ill (some col.),col.maps ; 20cm
Issued every two years
ISSN 0263-6972 = Pooley′s pilots information guide : Unpriced B82-31708

629.133 — Aircraft — *For children*

Cave, Ronald G.. Aircraft / Ron and Joyce Cave ; illustrated by David West, Roy Coombs and Paul Cooper. — London : Watts, 1982. — 30p : col.ill ; 22cm. — (What about?) (A Franklin Watts question and answer book)
Includes index
ISBN 0-85166-979-4 : £2.99 B82-23405

629.133 — Aircraft — *Identification manuals*

Tryatt, Nigel. Cars, motorbikes & planes / written by Nigel Tryatt, David Minton, Alan Wright ; photographs by Peter Hawksby ... [et al.] ; artwork illustrations by Tony Gibbons ... [et al.] ; designed by Kim Blundell ; edited by Lisa Watts and Helen Davies. — London : Usborne, 1980. — 192p : ill(some col.),forms ; 18cm. — (Spotter′s handbook)
Includes index
ISBN 0-86020-419-7 (pbk) : £2.99
Primary classification 629.2 B82-24648

629.133 — Large aircraft, *to 1980*

Taylor, Michael J. H.. Giants in the sky / Michael J.H. Taylor and David Monday. — London : Jane′s, 1982. — 224p : ill ; 27cm
ISBN 0-7106-0190-5 : £8.95 B82-31346

629.133 — Unmanned aircraft, *to 1978*

Reed, Arthur. Brassey′s unmanned aircraft / Arthur Reed. — London : Brassey′s, 1979. — ix,110p : ill ; 24cm
Includes index
ISBN 0-904609-32-4 : Unpriced B82-28012

629.133'0212 — Aircraft — *Technical data*
Green, William, *1927-*. The observer's book of aircraft / compiled by William Green ; with silhouettes by Dennis Punnett. — 31st ed. — London : Warne, 1982. — 256p : ill ; 15cm. — (The Observer's series ; 11)
Previous ed.: 1981. — Includes index
ISBN 0-7232-1626-6 : £1.95
ISBN 0-7232-1618-5 B82-19398

629.133'025'41 — Great Britain. Crashed aircraft & preserved aircraft — *Directories*
Wrecks & relics : the biennial survey of preserved, instructional and derelict airframes in the U.K. and Eire / compiled by Ken Ellis. — 8th ed. — Liverpool : Merseyside Aviation Society, 1982. — 193p : ill ; 21cm
Previous ed.: 1980. — Ill on inside covers. — Bibliography: p175-180. — Includes index
ISBN 0-902420-39-9 (pbk) : £4.95 B82-36345

629.133'025'422 — Southern England. Crashed aircraft & preserved aircraft — *Directories*
Cooksley, Peter. Aviation enthusiasts' guide to London and the South-east. — Cambridge : Patrick Stephens, Apr.1982. — [184]p. — (Action stations)
ISBN 0-85059-533-9 : £8.95 : CIP entry B82-04985

629.133'03'21 — Aircraft, *to 1982* — *Encyclopaedias*
The **Illustrated** encyclopedia of aircraft. — London : Orbis, c1981-[1983?]. — 156v. : ill (some col.) ; 29cm
Cover title
£0.65 per issue (pbk) B82-12962

629.133'05 — Preserved aircraft — *Serials*
FlyPast. — No.1 (May/June 1981)-. — Stamford (1 Wothorpe Rd, Stamford, Lincs. PE9 2JR) : Key Pub. Ltd., 1981-. — v. : ill(some col.),maps,ports ; 30cm
Monthly. — Description based on: No.7 (Feb. 1982)
ISSN 0262-6950 = FlyPast : £14.50 per year B82-18493

629.133'074'02657 — Cambridgeshire. Duxford. Museums: Duxford Airfield. Stock: Aircraft — *Catalogues*
Imperial War Museum. Duxford handbook / Imperial War Museum. — [London] ([Lambeth Rd, SE1 6HZ]) : The Museum, 1981. — 72p : ill,ports ; 20x21cm
Unpriced (pbk) B82-03980

629.133'09 — Unusual aircraft, *to 1980*
Taylor, Michael J. H.. Fantastic flying machines / Michael J.H. Taylor. — London : Jane's, 1981. — 142p : ill(some col.) ; 27cm
ISBN 0-7106-0125-5 : £6.95 B82-03291

629.133'0941 — Great Britain. Aircraft — *Lists*
Widdowson, Kevin P.. Airguide Britain / Kevin P. Widdowson. — [Manchester] ([191 Manor Rd., Droylsden, Manchester M35 6JA]) : [K.P. Widdowson], [1982]. — 51p : ill ; 22cm
Cover title
Unpriced (pbk) B82-32987

629.133'1 — Model aircraft
Encyclopedia of model aircraft / general editor Vic Smeed ; foreword by Henry J. Nicholls. — London : Octopus, 1979. — 225p : ill(some col.) ; 31cm
Ill on lining papers. — Includes index
ISBN 0-7064-0988-4 : £6.95 B82-03927

629.133'1 — Model aircraft. Conversion, painting & detailing, *1918-1965* — *Manuals*
Hall, Alan W.. Aircraft : from the pages of 'Airfix magazine' / Alan W. Hall ; drawings by Richard L. Ward. — Old Woking : Gresham, 1979. — 32p : ill ; 24cm
ISBN 0-905418-71-9 (pbk) : £1.35 B82-03978

629.133'133 — Radio controlled model gliders. Construction & flying — *Manuals*
Stringwell, George. Radio control thermal soaring / by George Stringwell. — Guildford ([P.O. Box 81, Guildford, Surrey GU1 3RL]) : RM Books, 1981. — 341p : ill,ports ; 21cm
Unpriced (pbk) B82-01779

629.133'134 — Model aeroplanes. Construction & flying — *Manuals*
McEntee, Howard G.. The model aircraft handbook / revised by Howard G. McEntee. — 2nd rev. ed. / British edition by Ron Moulton. — London : Hale, 1982. — 228p : ill ; 23cm
Previous ed.: 1970. — Bibliography: p219-221. — Includes index
ISBN 0-7091-8767-x : £7.50 B82-28961

629.133'2'0941 — Great Britain. Lighter than air aircraft, *1950-1981* — *Lists*
Baker, John A.. British balloons : a register of all balloons and airships built or registered in the British Isles since 1950 / John A. Baker and Peter J. Bish. — [Binfield] : [J.A. Baker and P.J. Bish], [1981]. — 239p : ill(some col.),ports ; 16x22cm
Includes index
ISBN 0-9507797-0-9 (cased) : £6.95
ISBN 0-9507797-1-7 (pbk) : £4.95 B82-08644

629.133'24'09 — Airships, *to 1980*
Hall, George, *1941-*. Blimp / photography by George Hall and Baron Wolman ; text by George Larson ; design by Neil Shakery. — New York ; London : Van Nostrand Reinhold, c1981. — 128p : ill(some col.),1map,ports ; 29cm
Includes index
ISBN 0-442-29608-8 : £10.95 B82-17641

629.133'24'0922 — Airships, *1900-1962* — *Personal observations* — *Collections*
Ventry, Arthur Frederick Daubeney Olav Eveleigh de Moleyns, *Baron*. An airship saga. — Poole : Blandford Press, Apr.1982. — [160]p
ISBN 0-7137-1001-2 : £8.95 : CIP entry B82-06244

629.133'25 — Rigid airships: R.101 *(Airship)*
Masefield, *Sir* **Peter G.**. To ride the storm : the story of the airship R.101 / Sir Peter G. Masefield. — London : Kimber, 1982. — 560p,[29]p of plates : ill,facsims,maps,2plans,ports ; 25cm
Includes index
ISBN 0-7183-0068-8 : £15.00 B82-32401

629.133'3 — Remotely piloted aircraft — *Conference proceedings*
Remotely piloted vehicles : international conference, Bristol, UK, 3-5 September 1979 / sponsored jointly by the Royal Aeronautical Society and the Department of Aeronautical Engineering of the University of Bristol. — [Bristol] : [Department of Aeronautical Engineering, University of Bristol], [1979]. — 2v. : ill ; 30cm
Spine title: RPVs Conference, Bristol, 1979
ISBN 0-906515-46-7 (pbk) : £10.00 B82-02854

Remotely piloted vehicles : second international conference, Bristol, UK, 6-8 April 1981 / sponsored jointly by the Royal Aeronautical Society and the University of Bristol. — [Bristol] : [Department of Extra-Mural Studies, University of Bristol], [1981]. — 2v. : ill ; 30cm
Spine title: RPVs Conference, Bristol, 1981
ISBN 0-906515-90-4 (pbk) : £20.00 B82-02855

629.133'3'07402 — Great Britain. Museums. Exhibits: Heavier than air aircraft — *Lists*
Riley, Gordon, *1950-*. Aircraft museums directory : British edition / by Gordon Riley. — 4th ed. — London : Battle of Britain Prints International, c1980. — 32p : ill ; 18cm
Previous ed.: 1978. — Ill on inside front cover
ISBN 0-900913-21-5 (pbk) : £0.85 B82-35700

629.133'33 — Gliders
Hardy, M. J.. Gliders & sailplanes of the world / Michael Hardy. — London : Ian Allan, 1982. — 176p : ill ; 23cm
Includes index
ISBN 0-7110-1152-4 : £6.95 B82-39076

629.133'34 — Aeroplanes. Ageing — *Conference proceedings*
Long-life aircraft structures : 1980 : spring convention 14-15 May / jointly organised by the Royal Aeronautical Society and The Society of Licensed Aircraft Engineers and Technologists. — London : 4 Hamilton Place, W1V 0BQ : The Royal Aeronautical Society, [1980?]. — 1v.(various pagings) : ill ; 30cm
Unpriced (pbk) B82-07064

629.133'34 — Avro aeroplanes, *to 1981*
Hardy, M. J.. Avro / M.J. Hardy. — Cambridge : Stephens, 1982. — 89p : ill,2ports ; 25cm. — (World aircraft)
Ill on lining papers
ISBN 0-85059-506-1 : £5.95 : CIP rev. B82-01452

629.133'34 — Boeing aeroplanes, *to 1981*
Hardy, M. J.. Boeing / M.J. Hardy. — Cambridge : Stephens, 1982. — 86p : ill ; 25cm. — (World aircraft)
Ill on lining papers
ISBN 0-85059-507-x : £5.95 : CIP rev. B82-01451

Taylor, Michael J. H.. Boeing / Michael J.H. Taylor. — London : Jane's, 1982. — 210p : ill ; 27cm. — (Planemakers ; 1)
Includes index
ISBN 0-7106-0133-6 : Unpriced B82-23729

629.133'34 — Civil aircraft — *For children*
Gunston, Bill. Airliners. — London : Granada, Aug.1982. — [64]p. — (Granada guide series ; 21)
ISBN 0-246-11891-1 : £1.95 : CIP entry B82-15709

629.133'34 — Grumman Gulfstream aeroplanes, *to 1979*
Knight, Fred J.. The story of the Grumman Gulfstreams / by Fred J. Knight. — [Worthing] ([31 Lavington Rd, Worthing, W. Sussex BN14 7SL]) : [Henfield Press], [1979]. — 183p : ill,1facsim,ports ; 22cm
ISBN 0-9506753-0-x (cased) : £5.95
ISBN 0-9506753-1-8 (pbk) : Unpriced B82-04000

629.133'34 — Lockheed aeroplanes, *to 1980*
Francillon, René J.. Lockheed aircraft since 1913. — London : Putnam, May 1982. — [600]p
ISBN 0-370-30329-6 : £20.00 : CIP entry B82-06734

629.133'34 — Westland aircraft, *to 1981*
Mondey, David. Westland / David Mondey. — London : Jane, 1982. — 162p : ill ; 27cm. — (Planemakers ; 2)
Includes index
ISBN 0-7106-0134-4 : Unpriced B82-23730

629.133'34'0321 — Civil aircraft — *Encyclopaedias*
The **Encyclopedia** of the world's civil aircraft / compiler David Mondey. — London : Hamlyn-Aerospace, 1981. — 254p : ill(some col.) ; 31cm
Includes index
ISBN 0-600-34979-9 : £9.95 B82-04441

629.133'340422 — Home-built aircraft — *Technical data*
Thurston, David B.. Homebuilt aircraft / David B. Thurston. — New York ; London : McGraw-Hill, c1982. — xiv,210p : ill,ports ; 25cm. — (McGraw-Hill series in aviation)
Ill on lining papers. — Includes index
ISBN 0-07-064552-3 : £17.50 B82-02501

629.133'340422 — United States. Light aircraft. Use by small firms — *Manuals*
Hansen, Paul E.. Business flying : the profitable use of personal aircraft / Paul E. Hansen. — New York ; London : McGraw-Hill, c1982. — x,253p : ill,1facsim,1port ; 24cm. — (AOPA/McGraw-Hill series in general aviation)
Bibliography: p239. — Includes index
ISBN 0-07-026071-0 : £13.95 B82-02516

629.133′340423 — Commercial passenger aeroplanes

McAllister, Chris. Jet liners / Chris McAllister. — London : Batsford, 1982. — 64p : ill(some col.) ; 20cm. — (A Batsford paperback)
Includes index
ISBN 0-7134-4162-3 (pbk) : £2.25 B82-33825

629.133′340423′0973 — United States. Commercial aircraft, *to 1981* — *Illustrations*

Munson, Kenneth. US commercial aircraft / Kenneth Munson. — London : Jane's, 1982. — 223p : ill ; 27cm
Includes index
ISBN 0-7106-0120-4 : £8.95 B82-38001

629.133′34′09 — Aeroplanes, *to 1980*

Jerram, Michael F.. The world's classic aircraft / Mike Jerram. — London : Muller, 1981. — 189p : ill(some col.),ports ; 29cm. — (A Charles Herridge Book)
Ill on lining papers. — Bibliography: p189
ISBN 0-584-97076-5 : £7.95 B82-00807

629.133′34′0944 — French aeroplanes, *1945-1979*

Chillon, J.. French postwar transport aircraft / J. Chillon, J-P. Dubois and J. Wegg. — Tonbridge : Air-Britain, c1980. — 176p,[56]p of plates : ill,2 maps ; 24cm
Preface in English and French. — Text, map on inside cover
ISBN 0-85130-078-2 (pbk) : Unpriced
B82-38643

629.133′34′0971 — Canadian aeroplanes, *to 1981*

Molson, K. M.. Canadian aircraft since 1909 / K.M. Molson and H.A. Taylor. — London : Putnam, 1982. — 530p : ill,ports ; 23cm
ISBN 0-370-30095-5 : £20.00 : CIP rev.
B81-30345

629.133′349 — Jet aeroplanes — *For children*

Chant, Christopher. Jetliner : from takeoff to touchdown / Chris Chant. — [London] : Collins, 1982. — 37p : col.ill,col.maps ; 30cm. — (The Inside story)
Ill on lining papers. — Includes index
ISBN 0-00-195374-5 : £2.95 B82-20813

629.133′349 — Jet Commander IAI aeroplanes & Westwind IAI aeroplanes, *to 1978*

Hartoch, Noam. Jet Commander — Westwind / Noam Hartoch. — Tonbridge : Air-Britain, c1979. — 51p,[6]p of plates : ill ; 24cm
ISBN 0-85130-075-8 (pbk) : Unpriced
B82-40738

629.133′349′0941 — Great Britain. Jet aeroplanes, *1942-1981*

Vicary, Adrian. British jet aircraft. — Cambridge : Patrick Stephens, Aug.1982. — [112]p
ISBN 0-85059-589-4 : £6.95 : CIP entry
B82-17214

629.133′35 — Autogiros — *Technical data*

Taylor, Michael J. H.. Helicopters of the world. — [3rd ed.] / Michael J.H. Taylor. — London : Ian Allan, 1981. — 112p : ill ; 23cm
Previous ed.: 1978. — Includes index
ISBN 0-7110-1131-1 : £5.95
Primary classification 629.133′352′0212
B82-01612

629.133′352 — Helicopters — *Conference proceedings*

European Rotorcraft & Powered Lift Aircraft Forum *(6th : 1980 : Bristol)*. Sixth European rotorcraft & powered lift aircraft forum : Bristol UK, 16-19 September 1980. — [Bristol] ([Department of Extra-Mural Studies, 32 Tyndall's Park Rd., Bristol BS8 1HR]) : [University of Bristol], c1980. — 2v.((looseleaf)) : ill ; 32cm
Conference proceedings
Unpriced B82-41073

629.133′352′0212 — Helicopters — *Technical data*

Taylor, Michael J. H.. Helicopters of the world. — [3rd ed.] / Michael J.H. Taylor. — London : Ian Allan, 1981. — 112p : ill ; 23cm
Previous ed.: 1978. — Includes index
ISBN 0-7110-1131-1 : £5.95
Also classified at 629.133′35 B82-01612

629.133′352′09 — Helicopters, *to 1981*

Watts, Anthony J.. A source book of helicopters and vertical take-off aircraft. — London : Ward Lock, Oct.1982. — 1v.
ISBN 0-7063-5897-x : £3.50 : CIP entry
B82-27199

629.134′1 — Aeroplanes. Design

Stinton, Darrol. The design of the aeroplane. — London : Granada, Sept.1982. — [650]p
ISBN 0-246-11328-6 : £30.00 : CIP entry
B82-19819

629.134′31 — Airframes

Cutler, John. Understanding aircraft structures / John Cutler. — London : Granada, 1981. — v,170p : ill ; 26cm
Includes index
ISBN 0-246-11310-3 : Unpriced : CIP rev.
B81-25784

Peery, David J.. Aircraft structure. — 2nd ed. / David J. Peery, J.J. Azar. — New York ; London : McGraw-Hill, c1982. — ix,454p : ill ; 25cm
Previous ed.: 1950. — Includes index
ISBN 0-07-049196-8 : £25.95 B82-37797

629.134′35 — Helicopters. Refuelling

Helicopter refuelling handbook : a reference for those with refuelling responsibilities on offshore installations / Petroleum Industry Training Board. — Aylesbury (Kingfisher House, Walton St., Aylesbury, Bucks. HP21 7TQ) : The Board, 1981. — 66p : ill,forms ; 30cm
Unpriced (pbk) B82-11211

629.134′35′0228 — Model aircraft. Model engines, *1948-1960* — *Technical data*

Model engine tests of yesteryear / compiled by Geoff Clarke. — London : Double M. Publishing, c1981. — 148p : ill ; 25cm
Includes index
ISBN 0-9507615-0-8 (pbk) : Unpriced
B82-19127

629.134′36 — Helicopters. Transmission systems — *Conference proceedings*

Helicopter transmissions : Rotorcraft Section all-day symposium, Wednesday 6 February 1980 / presented at the Royal Aeronautical Society. — London (4, Hamilton Pl., W1V 0BQ) : [Royal Aeronautical Society], [1981?]. — 118p in various pagings : ill ; 30cm
Unpriced (pbk) B82-08689

629.134′6 — Light aircraft. Maintenance & repair — *Amateurs' manuals*

Thomas, Kas. Personal aircraft maintenance : a do-it-yourself guide for owners and pilots / Kas Thomas. — New York ; London : McGraw-Hill, c1981. — viii,246p : ill ; 25cm. — (McGraw-Hill series in aviation)
Bibliography: p229-239. — Includes index
ISBN 0-07-064241-9 : £15.50 B82-31694

629.135 — Great Britain. Civil aircraft. Radio equipment — *Standards*

Airborne radio apparatus. — London : Civil Aviation Authority. — (CAP ; 208)
Vol.1: Minimum performance requirements. — 1978. — 1v.(loose-leaf) : ill ; 32cm
Originally published: / Great Britain. Board of Trade. London: H.M.S.O., 1970
ISBN 0-86039-058-6 : £8.70 B82-24284

Airborne radio apparatus. — London : Civil Aviation Authority. — (CAP ; 208)
Vol.2: Operational classification of radio apparatus approved for use in United Kingdom registered civil aircraft. — 1977. — 1v.(loose-leaf) : ill ; 32cm
Originally published: / Great Britain. Board of Trade. London: H.M.S.O., 1970
ISBN 0-86039-049-7 : £8.00 B82-24285

629.135 — Great Britain. Flight engineers. Licensing. Examinations — *Practical information*

Civil Aviation Authority. The Flight Engineer's Licence. — 3rd ed. / [Civil Aviation Authority]. — London : The Authority, 1981. — v,23p ; 22cm. — (CAP ; 50)
Previous ed.: 1979
ISBN 0-86039-809-6 (pbk) : £0.70 B82-05694

629.135′5 — Aeroplanes. Digital electronic equipment — *Coference proceedings*

Digital avionics : promise and practice : Joint RAES/IEE symposium Thursday, 20th March 1980. — London : Royal Aeronautical Society, [1980?]. — [89p] : ill ; 30cm
Unpriced (pbk) B82-07065

629.136′6 — Great Britain. Aerodromes. Birds. Control measures

Bird control on aerodromes. — 2nd ed. — London : Civil Aviation Authority, 1981. — iv,24p : ill ; 31cm + 1 sheet(ill ; 60x42cm folded to 30x21cm). — (CAP ; 384)
At head of title: Directorate of Aerodrome Standards. — Previous ed.: 1976. — Folded sheet and form in inside back pocket
ISBN 0-86039-136-1 (pbk) : £1.50 B82-39983

629.136′6 — Great Britain. Air services. Organisations: Civil Aviation Authority. Radar systems. Replacement. Great Britain. *Parliament. House of Commons. Industry and Trade Committee.* First report ... session 1980-81 — *Critical studies*

Great Britain. First special report from the Industry and Trade Committee, session 1980-81 : Civil Aviation Authority radar replacement programme : observations by the government on the second report of the committee in session 1979-80. — London : H.M.S.O., [1980]. — viip ; 25cm. — ([HC] ; 33)
ISBN 0-10-203381-1 (unbound) : £1.10
B82-10330

629.136′6′0941 — Great Britain. Air traffic. Control — *Manuals*

Air traffic control training manual. — London : Civil Aviation Authority, 1981. — (CAP ; 390)
Section 4: Radar theory. — 3rd ed. — vii,100p : ill ; 21cm
Previous ed.: 1977. — Includes index
ISBN 0-86039-119-1 (pbk) : Unpriced
B82-09802

629.2 — MOTOR VEHICLES

629.2 — Motor vehicle engineering — *For technicians*

Kett, P. W.. Motor vehicle science. — London : Chapman and Hall, Sept.1981
Part 1. — [220]p
ISBN 0-412-23590-0 (cased) : £9.50 : CIP entry
ISBN 0-412-22100-4 (pbk) : £4.50 B81-23909

Kett, P. W.. Motor vehicle science. — London : Chapman & Hall
Part 2. — Dec.1981. — [300]p
ISBN 0-412-23600-1 (cased) : £10.00 : CIP entry
ISBN 0-412-23610-9 (pbk) : £5.00 B81-31711

Nunney, M. J.. Vehicle technology 2 / M.J. Nunney. — Sevenoaks : Butterworths, 1982. — 134p : ill ; 25cm. — (Butterworths TEC technical series)
ISBN 0-408-00594-7 (pbk) : Unpriced : CIP rev.
B81-31423

Preceptor. Simple mechanics / by Preceptor. — [Great Britain] : Published by Commercial Motor in association with Renault Trucks & Buses
Vol.1. — [1980?]. — 32p : ill ; 31cm
Cover title
ISBN 0-617-00338-6 (pbk) : £0.75 B82-20141

629.2 — Motor vehicles — *For children*

Fletcher, John, *1952-*. Cars and trucks / by John Fletcher ; editor Jacqui Bailey. — London : Pan, 1982. — 91p : ill(some col.) ; 18cm. — (A Piccolo factbook)
Includes index
ISBN 0-330-26619-5 (pbk) : £1.35 B82-22222

629.2 — Motor vehicles — *Identification manuals*

Tryatt, Nigel. Cars, motorbikes & planes / written by Nigel Tryatt, David Minton, Alan Wright ; photographs by Peter Hawksby ... [et al.] ; artwork illustrations by Tony Gibbons ... [et al.] ; designed by Kim Blundell ; edited by Lisa Watts and Helen Davies. — London : Usborne, 1980. — 192p : ill(some col.),forms ; 18cm. — (Spotter's handbook)
Includes index
ISBN 0-86020-419-7 (pbk) : £2.99
Also classified at 629.133 B82-24648

629.2′022′1 — Motor vehicles. Technical drawings. Draftsmanship — *For technicians*
Zammit, Saviour J.. Motor vehicle engineering drawing for technicians : level 1 / S.J. Zammit. — London : Longman, 1980. — iv,107p : ill ; 28cm. — (Longman technician series. Mechanical and production engineering)
Includes index
ISBN 0-582-41178-5 (pbk) : £4.50 : CIP rev. B80-05924

Zammit, Saviour J.. Motor vehicle engineering drawing for technicians : level 2 / S.J. Zammit. — London : Longman, 1980. — iv,39p : ill ; 28cm. — (Longman technician series. Mechanical and production engineering)
Includes index
ISBN 0-582-41586-1 (pbk) : £2.50 : CIP rev. B80-13399

629.2′07 — Great Britain. Motor vehicle trades. Apprentices. Training
Training of apprentices in motor vehicle trades. — Gloucester (Barton House, Barton St., Gloucester GL1 1QQ) : Food, Drink and Tobacco Industry Training Board, 1978. — 10p : ill ; 30cm
Cover title
Unpriced (pbk) B82-26130

629.22 — MOTOR VEHICLES. SPECIAL TYPES

629.2′2 — Heavy road vehicles
Leeming, David J.. Heavy Vehicle technology / D.J. Leeming and R. Hartley. — 2nd ed. — London : Hutchinson, 1981. — 260p : ill ; 25cm
Previous ed.: 1976. — Includes index
ISBN 0-09-144690-2 (cased) : £12.00 : CIP rev.
ISBN 0-09-144691-0 (pbk) : £5.95 B81-02085

629.2′2 — Volvo motor vehicles, *to 1981*
Creighton, John. Volvo / by John Creighton. — Hornchurch : Ian Henry, 1982. — 64p : ill ; 24cm. — (The 64 transport series ; 5)
ISBN 0-86025-838-6 : £4.25 B82-24883

629.2′21 — Lesney Matchbox model motor vehicles — *Lists*
Leake, Geoffrey. A concise catalogue of 1-75 series 'Matchbox' toys / compiled by Geoffrey Leake. — 2nd ed. — Worcester : G.H.B. Leake, 1981. — 104p ; 21cm
Cover title. — Previous ed.: 1979. — Bibliography: p104
ISBN 0-9507616-0-5 (pbk) : £3.50 B82-09132

629.2′21′0941 — British die-cast model motor vehicles — *Collectors' guides*
Thompson, G. M. K.. British diecasts : a collectors guide to 'toy' cars, vans & trucks / G.M.K. Thompson. — [Yeovil] : Foulis, 1980. — 160p : ill(some col.) ; 25cm
ISBN 0-85429-264-0 (corrected) : £8.50 B82-18932

629.2′2122 — Model cars. Construction — *Manuals*
Scarborough, Gerald. How to go car modelling / Gerald Scarborough. — Cambridge : Stephens, 1981. — 152p : ill ; 24cm
ISBN 0-85059-454-5 : £6.95 : CIP rev. B81-30193

629.2′2122′0924 — Model cars. Construction. Wingrove, Gerald A. — *Biographies*
Wingrove, Gerald A.. The model cars of Gerald Wingrove. — [London] : New Cavendish, c1979. — 111p : ill(some col.) ; 25x30cm
Ill on lining papers. — Includes index
ISBN 0-904568-12-1 : £18.50 B82-22177

629.2′218 — Model racing cars. Construction — *Manuals*
Fairhurst, Peter. Making model racing cars / written and illustrated by Peter Fairhurst. — London : Carousel, 1982. — 95p : ill,plans ; 20cm
ISBN 0-552-54197-4 (pbk) : £0.85 B82-14557

629.2′222 — Alfa-Romeo Spiders, *to 1981*
Owen, David. Alfa Romeo Spiders. — London : Osprey, July 1982. — [136]p. — (Osprey autoHistory)
ISBN 0-85045-462-x : £6.95 : CIP entry B82-13270

629.2′222 — Aston Martin cars, *to 1981*
Aston Martin / compiled by Peter Garnier from the archives of Autocar. — London : Hamlyn, 1982. — 160p : ill(some col.),facsims,plans,ports ; 31cm
ISBN 0-600-35023-1 : £7.95 B82-27141

629.2′222 — Austin 7 cars, *to 1939*
Wyatt, R. J.. The Austin Seven. — 3rd ed. — Newton Abbot : David & Charles, Nov.1982. — [216]p
Previous ed.: 1972
ISBN 0-7153-8394-9 : £8.95 : CIP entry B82-26400

629.2′222 — Austin-Healey sports cars, *to 1980*
Robson, Graham. The big Healeys : a collector's guide / by Graham Robson. — London : Motor Racing Publications, 1981. — 128p : ill ; 19x24cm
ISBN 0-900549-55-6 : £7.95 B82-40528

629.2′222 — Austin mini Metro cars, *to 1981*
Robson, Graham. Metro. — Cambridge : Stephens, Oct.1982. — [192]p
ISBN 0-85059-593-2 : £8.95 : CIP entry B82-25944

629.2′222 — BMW cars, *1945-1980*
Busenkell, Richard L.. BMW since 1945 / Richard L. Busenkell. — Cambridge : Stephens, 1981. — 111p : ill ; 17x25cm
ISBN 0-85059-574-6 : £6.95 B82-18331

629.2′222 — British Leyland Mini Cooper & Mini S cars, *to 1980*
Walton, Jeremy. Mini-Cooper and S : 997 & 998 Cooper : 970, 1071 & 1275S / Jeremy Walton. — London : Osprey, 1982. — 135p,[8]p of plates : ill(some col.),ports ; 23cm. — (Osprey autohistory)
Includes index
ISBN 0-85045-438-7 : £6.95 : CIP rev. B82-04979

629.2′222 — British sports cars & specialist saloon cars, *1955-1960*
Hudson, Bruce A.. Post-war British thoroughbreds and specialist cars / Bruce A. Hudson. — Yeovil : Foulis : Haynes, 1981. — 264p : ill ; 24cm. — (A Foulis motoring book)
Bibliography: p264
ISBN 0-85429-268-3 : Unpriced B82-03209

629.2′222 — British sports cars, *1945-1981*
Fryatt, Nigel. British sports cars : road tests / Nigel Fryatt. — London : Hamlyn, c1982. — 128p : ill(some col.) ; 29cm
ISBN 0-600-34977-2 : £6.95 B82-37093

629.2′222 — Bugatti cars, *to 1947*
Borgeson, Griffith. Bugatti by Borgeson : the dynamics of mythology / Griffith Borgeson. — London : Osprey, 1981. — 223p : ill,facsims,ports ; 26cm
Bibliography: p218-219. — Includes index
ISBN 0-85045-414-x : £9.95 : CIP rev. B81-18094

629.2′222 — Cars
AA book of the car. — 3rd ed., repr. with amendments. — London : Drive Publications for the Automobile Association, 1980, c1976. — 408p : ill(some col.) ; 27cm
Includes index
£10.95 B82-28985

Mennem, Patrick. Motoring mirror : new models, maintenance, money saving tips : an all-in guide to autumn motoring / by Patrick Mennem. — [London] : [Mirror Books], [c1981]. — 26p : ill(some col.),ports ; 37cm. — (A Daily Mirror motoring special)
ISBN 0-85939-285-6 (unbound) : £0.50 B82-06349

629.2′222 — Cars — *For children*
Cave, Ronald G.. Motorcars / Ron and Joyce Cave ; illustrated by David West, Peter Hutton and Paul Cooper. — London : Watts, 1982. — 30p : col.ill ; 22cm. — (What about?) (A Franklin Watts question and answer book)
Includes index
ISBN 0-85166-980-8 : £2.99 B82-23407

Fletcher, John, *1952-*. Cars and trucks / by John Fletcher ; editor Jacqui Bailey. — London : Kingfisher, 1982. — 91p : ill(some col.) ; 19cm. — (A Kingfisher factbook)
Includes index
ISBN 0-86272-031-1 : £2.50 : CIP rev.
Also classified at 629.2′24 B82-00369

Wildig, Alan W.. The motor car / Alan W. Wildig ; with illustrations by Gerald Witcomb. — Rev. ed. — Loughborough : Ladybird, c1982. — 51p : col.ill ; 18cm. — (How it works)
Previous ed.: ca. 1980. — Includes index
ISBN 0-7214-0744-7 : £0.60 B82-37071

629.2′222 — Cars. Items associated with cars — *Collectors' guides*
Gardiner, Gordon. The price guide and identification of automobilia. — Woodbridge : Antique Collectors' Club, June 1982. — [270]p
ISBN 0-907462-15-4 : £19.50 : CIP entry B82-10901

629.2′222 — Chauffeurs, *to 1980*
Montagu of Beaulieu, Edward Douglas-Scott-Montagu, *Baron*. Home James : the chauffeur in the golden age of motoring / Lord Montagu of Beaulieu and Patrick Macnaghten. — London : Weidenfeld and Nicolson, c1982. — 177p,[24]p of plates : ill,ports ; 24cm
ISBN 0-297-78040-9 : £9.50 B82-13967

629.2′222 — Citröen 2CV cars, *to 1981*
MacQueen, Bob. The life and times of the 2CV. — Cambridge : Great Ouse Press, Nov.1982. — [160]p
ISBN 0-907351-07-7 : £7.95 : CIP entry B82-36164

629.2′222 — Customised cars — *Illustrations*
Car culture. — London : Plexus, Nov.1982. — [128]p
ISBN 0-85965-033-2 (cased) : £8.95 : CIP entry
ISBN 0-85965-032-4 (pbk) : £4.95 B82-29144

629.2′222 — DeTomaso cars, *to 1981*
Wyss, Wallace A.. De Tomaso automobiles / Wallace A. Wyss. — London : Osprey, 1981. — 224p : ill,ports ; 26cm
Includes index
ISBN 0-85045-440-9 : £10.95 : CIP rev. B81-30264

629.2′222 — Ferrari 250 GTO cars
Harvey, Chris. Ferrari 250 GTO / Chris Harvey. — [Yeovil] : Foulis : Haynes, 1982. — 56p : ill (some col.),1port ; 28cm. — (Super profile) (A Foulis motoring book)
Ill on lining papers
ISBN 0-85429-308-6 : £3.95 B82-17864

629.2′222 — Ferrari 275 GTB & 275 GTS cars, *to 1968*
Webb, Ian. Ferrari 275GTB & GTS : 2-cam, 4-cam ; 'Competizione' ; Spider / Ian Webb. — London : Osprey, 1981. — 135p : ill(some col.) ; 22cm. — (Osprey autohistory)
Includes index
ISBN 0-85045-402-6 : £5.95 : CIP rev. B81-27962

629.2′222 — Ferrari 308 cars, *to 1981*
Willoughby, Geoff. Ferrari 308. — London : Osprey, Oct.1982. — [136]p. — (AutoHistory)
ISBN 0-85045-454-9 : £6.95 : CIP entry B82-24251

629.2′222 — Ferrari cars, *1957-1980*
Rasmussen, Henry. Ferraris for the road / by Henry Rasmussen. — Yeovil : Haynes, 1981, c1980. — [128]p : ill(some col.),ports(some col.) ; 23x29cm. — (The Survivors series)
Originally published: Osceolo, Wis. : Motorbooks, 1980
ISBN 0-85429-300-0 : Unpriced B82-03207

629.2′222 — Ferrari cars, *to 1979*
Ferrari : the man, the machines / edited and with an introduction by Stan Grayson ; with chapters by Griffith Borgeson ... [et al.]. — London : Muller, [1982], c1975. — 347p : ill (some col.),ports ; 22x25cm. — (An Automobile quarterly library series book)
Originally published: Kutztown, Pa. : Automobile Quarterly Publications, 1975. — Ill on lining papers. — Includes index
ISBN 0-584-95027-6 : £15.95 B82-32338

629.2′222 — Fiat X1/9 cars, *to 1981*
Walton, Jeremy. Fiat X1/9. — London : Osprey, Oct.1982. — [136]p. — (AutoHistory)
ISBN 0-85045-456-5 : £6.95 : CIP entry B82-24252

629.2′222 — Ford Escort RS cars, *to 1980*
Robson, Graham. Ford Escort RS : twin cam ; RS 1600, 1800, 2000 ; Mexico / Graham Robson. — London : Osprey, 1981. — 135p : ill(some col.),ports ; 22cm. — (Osprey autohistory)
Includes index
ISBN 0-85045-401-8 : £5.95 : CIP rev. B81-27963

629.2′222 — Four-wheel-drive off-road cars — *Illustrations*
Morland, Andrew. Off road : four wheel drive vehicles in colour / Andrew Morland. — London : Osprey, 1982. — 128p : chiefly col.ill ; 23cm
ISBN 0-85045-446-8 (pbk) : £5.95 : CIP rev. B82-09841

629.2′222 — Gran turismo cars, *to 1981*
Owen, David. GT car. — London : Osprey, Nov.1982. — [240]p
ISBN 0-85045-468-9 : £9.95 : CIP entry B82-26420

629.2′222 — Great Britain. Customised cars, *1955-1975*
Nichols, Richard. Custom cars / Richard Nichols, Julian Basten. — London : W.H. Allen, 1981. — 127p : ill(chiefly col.) ; 29cm. — (A star book)
ISBN 0-352-31001-4 (pbk) : £4.95 B82-07898

629.2′222 — Jaguar cars, *to 1981*
Harvey, Chris. Jaguar / Chris Harvey ; foreword by Stirling Moss ; general editor John Blunsden. — London : Octopus, 1982. — 80p : ill(some col.) ; 33cm. — (Great Marques)
Ill on lining papers. — Includes index
ISBN 0-7064-1687-2 : £3.95 B82-34477

629.2′222 — Jaguar E-type cars, *to 1976*
Jenkinson, Denis. Jaguar E type : 3.8 & 4.2 6-cylinder : 5.3 V12 / Denis Jenkinson. — London : Osprey, 1982. — 134p,[8]p of plates : ill(some col.),ports ; 22cm. — (Osprey autohistory)
Bibliography: p132. — Includes index
ISBN 0-85045-437-9 : £6.95 : CIP rev. B82-04978

629.2′222 — Jaguar Mk2 saloon cars
Skilleter, Paul. Jaguar Mk 2 saloons : 2.4, 3.4 & 3.8-litre / Paul Skilleter. — [Yeovil] : Foulis : Haynes, 1982. — 56p : ill(some col.),facsims ; 28cm. — (Super profile) (A Foulis motoring book)
ISBN 0-85429-307-8 : £3.95 B82-17865

629.2′222 — Lamborghini cars, *to 1980 — Illustrations*
Box, Rob de la Rive. Lamborghini : the cars from Sant′ Agata Bolognese / Rob de la Rive Box & Richard Crump. — London : Osprey, 1981. — 213p : ill(some col.),1map,facsims,ports ; 23x24cm
ISBN 0-85045-408-5 : £12.95 : CIP rev. B81-20508

629.2′222 — Lamborghini: Miura cars, *to 1981*
Marchet, Jean-François. Lamborghini Miura. — London : Osprey, Sept.1982. — [192]p
ISBN 0-85045-469-7 : £9.95 : CIP entry B82-19801

629.2′222 — Lotus Esprit cars, *to 1981*
Walton, Jeremy. Lotus Esprit. — London : Osprey, July 1982. — [136]p
ISBN 0-85045-460-3 : £6.95 : CIP entry B82-13084

629.2′222 — Lotus Seven cars, *to 1980*
Ortenburger, Dennis. The legend of the Lotus Seven. — London : Osprey, Nov.1981. — [224]p
ISBN 0-85045-411-5 : £11.95 : CIP entry B81-38842

629.2′222 — Maserati Bora cars, *to 1981*
Norbye, Jan. Maserati Bora and Merak. — London : Osprey, Oct.1982. — [136]p. — (AutoHistory)
ISBN 0-85045-471-9 : £6.95 : CIP entry
Also classified at 629.2′222 B82-24253

629.2′222 — Maserati Merak cars, *to 1981*
Norbye, Jan. Maserati Bora and Merak. — London : Osprey, Oct.1982. — [136]p. — (AutoHistory)
ISBN 0-85045-471-9 : £6.95 : CIP entry
Primary classification 629.2′222 B82-24253

629.2′222 — Mercedes-Benz cars, *to 1980*
Robson, Graham. Magnificent Mercedes : the complete history of the marque / Graham Robson. — Yeovil : Foulis, 1981. — 224p : ill (some col.),ports ; 32cm. — (A Foulis motoring book)
Ill on lining papers. — Includes index
ISBN 0-85429-316-7 : Unpriced B82-05265

629.2′222 — MG cars, *to 1978*
Robson, Graham. The mighty MGs : the twin-cam MGC and MGB GT V8 stories / Graham Robson. — Newton Abbot : David & Charles, c1982. — 223p : ill ; 25cm
Includes index
ISBN 0-7153-8226-8 : £10.50 : CIP rev. B82-09620

629.2′222 — MG Midget cars & Austin-Healey Sprite cars
Dymock, Eric. The Sprites and Midgets : a collector′s guide / by Eric Dymock. — London : Motor Racing Publications, 1981. — 112p : ill ; 19x24cm
ISBN 0-900549-53-x : £7.95 B82-33641

629.2′222 — MG Midget T series cars, *to 1955*
Robson, Graham. The T-Series MGs : a collector′s guide / by Graham Robson. — London : Motor Racing, 1980. — 128p : ill,1port ; 19x24cm
ISBN 0-900549-51-3 : £7.95 B82-28789

629.2′222 — MG sports cars, *to 1979*
Harvey, Chris. The MGA, B and C / Chris Harvey. — Oxford : Oxford Illustrated Press, 1980. — 232p,[16]p of plates : ill(some col.),ports ; 26cm
Includes index
ISBN 0-902280-69-4 : £14.95 B82-02768

629.2′222 — MGB cars
Porter, Lindsay. MGB / Lindsay Porter. — [Yeovil] : Foulis : Haynes, 1982. — 56p : ill (some col.) ; 28cm. — (Super profile) (A Foulis motoring book)
Ill on lining papers
ISBN 0-85429-305-1 : £3.95 B82-17869

629.2′222 — MGB cars, *to 1980*
McComb, F. Wilson. MGB. — London : Osprey, July 1982. — [136]p. — (Osprey autoHistory)
ISBN 0-85045-455-7 : £6.95 : CIP entry B82-13269

629.2′222 — Morris Minor 1000 cars, *to 1980*
Skilleter, Paul. Morris Minor : the world′s supreme small car / Paul Skilleter. — London : Osprey, 1981. — 224p : ill,ports ; 26cm
Includes index
ISBN 0-85045-344-5 : £8.95 : CIP rev. B81-12818

629.2′222 — Morris Minor 1000 cars, *to 1981*
Skilleter, Paul. Morris Minor. — 2nd ed. — London : Osprey, Oct.1982. — [208]p
Previous ed.: 1981
ISBN 0-85045-494-8 : £8.95 : CIP entry B82-25737

629.2′222 — Porsche 911 cars, *to 1980*
Cotton, Michael, *1938-*. The Porsche 911 and derivatives : a collector′s guide / by Michael Cotton. — London : Motor Racing Publications, 1980 (1981 [printing]). — 128p : ill,ports ; 19x24cm
ISBN 0-900549-52-1 : £7.95 B82-03276

629.2′222 — Porsche 911 Turbo cars, *to 1980*
Cotton, Michael, *1938-*. Porsche 911 turbo : 3 and 3.3 litre ; project no.930 / Michael Cotton. — London : Osprey, 1981. — 135p : ill ; 22cm. — (Osprey autohistory)
Includes index
ISBN 0-85045-400-x : £5.95 : CIP rev. B81-27961

629.2′222 — Porsche 924, 928 & 944 cars, *to 1980*
Sloniger, Jerrold E.. Porsche 924, 928, 944 : the new generation / Jerry Sloniger. — London : Osprey, 1981. — 168p : ill(some col.) ; 26cm
Includes index
ISBN 0-85045-415-8 : £9.95 : CIP rev. B81-28820

629.2′222 — Porsche cars, *to 1980*
Rasmussen, Henry. Porsches for the road / Henry Rasmussen. — Yeovil : Haynes, 1981. — [128]p : ill(some col.),ports ; 23x29cm. — (The Survivors series) (A Foulis motoring book)
Originally published: Osceola, Wis. : Motorbooks International, 1981
ISBN 0-85429-318-3 : £19.95 B82-16396

629.2′222 — Rolls-Royce cars, *to 1981 — Readings from contemporary sources*
Rolls-Royce / compiled by Peter Garnier and Warren Allport from the archives of Autocar. — 2nd (enl.) ed. — London : Hamlyn, 1981. — 296p : ill(some col.),ports ; 31cm
Previous ed.: i.e. 2nd ed. 1978. — Facsim reprints. — Includes index
ISBN 0-600-34981-0 : £9.95 B82-08161

629.2′222 — Sports & GT cars, *1945-1960 — Technical data*
Robson, Graham. An encyclopaedia of European sports and GT cars : 1945 to 1960 / Graham Robson. — Yeovil : Foulis, 1981. — 328p,[8]p of plates : ill(some col.) ; 25cm. — (A Foulis motoring book)
Includes index
ISBN 0-85429-281-0 : Unpriced B82-03206

629.2′222 — Sports cars, *to 1980*
Ward, Ian, *1949-*. The sports car / Ian Ward ; photography by Jasper Spencer-Smith. — Poole : Blandford, 1982. — 160p : ill(some col.) ; 26cm
Includes index
ISBN 0-7137-1072-1 : £8.95 : CIP rev. B82-20364

629.2′222 — Sunbeam sports cars, *1950-1980*
Langworth, Richard M.. Tiger, Alpine, Rapier : sporting cars from the Rootes group / Richard Langworth. — London : Osprey, 1982. — 175p : ill,facsims,1form,ports ; 26cm
Bibliography: p172. — Includes index
ISBN 0-85045-443-3 : £9.95 : CIP rev. B82-07611

629.2′222 — Triumph Spitfire & GT6 cars, *to 1981*
Robson, Graham. Triumph Spitfire and GT6 : Spitfire 1, 2, 3, IV, 1500 : GT6 1, 2, 3 / Graham Robson. — London : Osprey, 1982. — 192p : ill,ports ; 26cm. — (Osprey classic library)
Includes index
ISBN 0-85045-452-2 : £9.95 : CIP rev. B82-10878

629.2′222 — Volkswagen Beetle cars, *to 1980*
Boddy, William. VW Beetle. — London : Osprey, Mar.1982. — [136]p. — (Osprey autoHistory)
ISBN 0-85045-439-5 : £5.95 : CIP entry B82-01561

629.2'222'0212 — Cars — *Technical data*

Blunsden, John. The observer's book of automobiles / compiled by John Blunsden. — 25th ed. — London : Warne, 1982. — 192p : ill ; 15cm. — (The Observer's series ; 21)
Previous ed.: 1981
ISBN 0-7232-1627-4 : £1.95 B82-19399

Stobbs, Williams. The best cars : a new computerized guide to performance and efficiency / William and Michael Stobbs. — London : Pelham, 1981. — 256p : ill ; 29cm
Includes index
ISBN 0-7207-1376-5 : £12.50 : CIP rev. B81-30394

629.2'222'0222 — Cars — *Illustrations — For children*

Campbell, Rod. Wheels. — London : Abelard-Schuman, Sept.1982. — [6]p
ISBN 0-200-72778-8 (pbk) : £2.95 : CIP entry B82-18961

629.2'222'0289 — Cars. Safety aspects — *Conference proceedings*

Towards safer passenger cars : conference / sponsored by the Automobile Division of the Institution of Mechanical Engineers, Institution Headquarters 17-18 June, 1980. — London : Published by Mechanical Engineering Publications for the Institution of Mechanical Engineers, 1980. — 119p : ill ; 30cm. — (I Mech E conference publications ; 1980-3)
ISBN 0-85298-464-2 (pbk) : £16.00 B82-36199

629.2'222'05 — Cars — *Serials*

Classic and sportscar. — Vol.1, no.1 (Apr. 1982)-. — Teddington : Haymarket, 1982-. — v. : ill(some col.),ports ; 30cm
Monthly. — Continues: Old motor
ISSN 0263-3183 = Classic and sportscar : £12.00 per year B82-23583

629.2'222'09 — Cars, *to 1977*

Ward, Ian, *1949-*. Motoring for the millions / Ian Ward ; photography Jasper Spencer-Smith. — Poole : Blandford, 1981. — 160p : ill(some col.) ; 26cm
Includes index
ISBN 0-7137-1071-3 : £8.95 : CIP rev. B81-22535

629.2'222'09 — Cars, *to 1979 — For children*

Posthumus, Cyril. Motor cars / Cyril Posthumus. — Hove : Wayland, 1982. — 64p : ill(some col.),3ports(1col.) ; 24cm. — (Transport and society)
Bibliography: p62. — Includes index
ISBN 0-85340-934-x : £4.25 B82-28028

629.2'222'0904 — Cars, *1945-1978*

White, Mark. The observer's book of classic cars : after 1945 / Mark White ; with a foreword by Michael Bowler. — London : Warne, 1982. — 184p : ill(some col.),ports ; 15cm. — (The Observer's pocket series)
Bibliography: p179-180. — Includes index
ISBN 0-7232-1614-2 : £1.95 B82-24564

629.2'222'0904 — Cars, *to 1939*

White, Mark. The observer's book of vintage cars : and pre-war classics / Mark White ; with a foreword by Lord Montagu of Beaulieu. — London : Warne, 1982. — 184p : ill(some col.),ports ; 15cm. — (The Observer's pocket series)
Bibliography: p179-180. — Includes index
ISBN 0-7232-1615-0 : £1.95 B82-24565

629.2'222'0973 — American cars, *1950-1970*

Martinez, Alberto. American follies : American cars of the fifties and sixties. — London : Osprey, Sept.1982. — [192]p
Translation of: Les folles américaines
ISBN 0-85045-461-1 : £9.95 : CIP entry B82-20487

629.2'222'0973 — American cars, *1970-1979*

American cars of the seventies / [compiled by] Albert R. Bochroch. — London : Warne, 1982. — 63p : ill ; 19x25cm. — (Warne's transport library)
ISBN 0-7232-2870-1 : £4.95 B82-34772

629.2'2233 — AEC buses, *to 1979 — Illustrations*

Hannay, R. N.. AEC buses in camera / Robin Hannay. — London : Ian Allan, 1982. — 112p : ill ; 24cm
ISBN 0-7110-1160-5 : £5.95 B82-17810

629.2'2233 — Leyland buses, *to 1981*

Booth, Gavin. Leyland : buses in camera / Gavin Booth. — London : Ian Allan, 1981. — 128p : ill ; 24cm
ISBN 0-7110-1149-4 : £6.95 B82-01615

629.2'2233 — London. Routemaster buses, *to 1981*

Curtis, Colin H.. The Routemaster bus : a comprehensive history of a highly successful London bus type from its design, development and introduction into the fleet / by Colin H. Curtis. — Tunbridge Wells : Midas, 1981. — 94p : ill,2facsims,1port ; 31cm. — (Midas transport history series)
Includes index
ISBN 0-85936-281-7 : Unpriced B82-14609

629.2'2233'0212 — Buses — *Technical data*

Moses, Derek. Buses of the world / Derek Moses. — London : Ian Allan, 1982. — 144p : ill ; 23cm
ISBN 0-7110-1124-9 : £6.95 B82-14462

629.2'2233'0222 — Buses & motor coaches — *Illustrations*

Fenton, Mike. British buses around the world. — Cambridge : Patrick Stephens, July 1982. — [88]p
ISBN 0-85059-594-0 : £6.95 : CIP entry B82-13086

629.2'2233'09 — Buses, *to 1975 — For schools*

Booth, Gavin. Buses / Gavin Booth. — Hove : Wayland, 1982. — 64p : ill(some col.) ; 24cm. — (Transport and society)
Bibliography: p62. — Includes index
ISBN 0-85340-959-5 : £4.25 B82-34831

629.2'2233'09 — Buses, *to 1980*

Bruce, J. Graeme. A source book of buses / J. Graeme Bruce. — London : Ward Lock, 1981. — 127p : ill ; 12x17cm. — (Source books)
Includes index
ISBN 0-7063-6054-0 : £2.95 : CIP rev. B81-28066

629.2'2233'0941 — Great Britain. Albion & Crossley buses, *to 1970 — Illustrations*

Brown, Stewart J.. Albion and Crossley buses in camera / Stewart J. Brown. — London : Ian Allan, 1982. — 112p : ill ; 25cm
ISBN 0-7110-1191-5 : £5.95 B82-40520

629.2'2233'0941 — Great Britain. Buses, *1935-1980*

Hilditch, G. G.. A further look at buses / G.G. Hilditch. — London : Ian Allan, 1981. — 128p : ill ; 24cm
ISBN 0-7110-1148-6 : £5.95 B82-11216

Vintage bus album / edited by Ken Blacker. — London : Warne. — (An MHB book)
No.2. — 1982. — 95p : ill ; 31cm
Includes index
ISBN 0-7232-2873-6 : Unpriced B82-35432

629.2'2233'09421 — London. Public transport services: London Transport. Buses. Serial numbers — *Lists*

The **Vehicles** of London Transport and its predecessors : the 'STL' class. — London (52, Old Park Ridings, N21 2ES) : Published jointly by the P.S.V. Circle and the Omnibus Society. — (Fleet history ; LT 10)
Pt.1 — 1932 to 1936. — 1982. — 72p,[4]p of plates : ill ; 30cm
Unpriced (pbk) B82-27452

629.2'2233'09425 — England. East Midlands. Bus services: Barton Transport. Buses, *to 1982 — Illustrations*

Barton past and present / [compiled by] D.G. Bell. — Norwich : Becknell, 1982. — 64p : chiefly ill ; 24cm
ISBN 0-907087-12-4 (pbk) : £4.50 B82-26193

629.2'2233'0942558 — Northamptonshire. Wellingborough. Bus services: Wellingborough Motor Omnibus Company. Buses, *to 1921 — Illustrations*

Leylands of the Wellingborough Motor Omnibus Company Limited / [compiled] by Roger M. Warwick. — Northampton (101 Broadway East, Northampton NN3 2PP) : R.M. Warwick, c1981. — 36p : chiefly ill,ports ; 30cm
ISBN 0-9505980-5-4 (pbk) : Unpriced B82-02320

629.2'2233'09426 — East Anglia. Bus services: Eastern Counties Omnibus Company. Buses, *to 1981 — Illustrations*

Eastern Counties past and present / [compiled by] D.G. Bell. — Norwich : Becknell, 1981. — 64p : chiefly ill ; 24cm
ISBN 0-907087-07-8 (pbk) : £4.50 B82-11902

629.2'2233'09426 — East Anglia. Bus services: Eastern Counties Omnibus Company. Buses, *to 1981*

Eastern Counties Omnibus Company Limited. — London (52 Old Park Ridings, N21 2ES) : The P.S.V. Circle, [1981]. — 269p,16p of plates : ill ; 30cm. — (Fleet history ; 2PF1)
Unpriced (pbk) B82-05593

629.2'2233'094281 — West Yorkshire *(Metropolitan County).* **Public transport services: West Yorkshire Passenger Transport Executive. Buses,** *to 1979 — Illustrations*

Mack, Robert F.. An album of West Yorkshire P.T.E. buses / Robert F. Mack. — Sheffield : Turntable, 1980. — 48p : chiefly ill ; 21cm
ISBN 0-902844-56-3 (pbk) : £1.50 B82-41105

629.2'23 — Customised motor vans

Martinez, Alberto. Vans : customized vans in colour / photography by Alberto Martinez ; text by Jean Loup Nory. — London : Osprey, 1981. — 187p : chiefly ill(some col.) ; 31cm
Translation of: Les vans
ISBN 0-85045-441-7 : £8.95 : CIP rev. B81-30580

629.2'24 — AEC lorries, *to 1979*

Kennett, Pat. AEC / Pat Kennett. — Cambridge : Stephens, 1980. — 87p : ill ; 26cm. — (World trucks ; no.10)
Ill on lining papers
ISBN 0-85059-398-0 : £4.50 : CIP rev. B80-09279

629.2'24 — Bedford commercial vehicles — *Serials*

Bedford operator. — Vol.1, no.1 (Oct. 1981)-. — Luton (Luton LU2 0SY) : Vauxhall Motors, 1981-. — v. : ill ; 30cm
Quarterly
ISSN 0263-0052 = Bedford operator : Unpriced B82-12469

629.2'24 — Daf lorries, *to 1978*

Gibbins, Eric. DAF / Eric Gibbins. — London : Motor Racing Publications, c1981. — 128p : ill ; 14x24cm. — (Trucks today)
ISBN 0-900549-60-2 : £6.95 B82-31249

629.2'24 — Heavy commercial vehicles, *to 1981*

Park, Chris. Heavy truck. — London : Osprey, June 1982. — [192]p
ISBN 0-85045-464-6 : £9.95 : CIP entry B82-14387

629.2'24 — Lorries — *For children*

Cave, Ronald G.. Trucks / Ron and Joyce Cave ; illustrated by David West, Denis Bishop and Paul Cooper. — London : Watts, 1982. — 30p : col.ill ; 22cm. — (What about?) (A Franklin Watts question and answer book)
Includes index
ISBN 0-85166-982-4 : £2.99 B82-23408

Fletcher, John, *1952-*. Cars and trucks / by John Fletcher ; editor Jacqui Bailey. — London : Kingfisher, 1982. — 91p : ill(some col.) ; 19cm. — (A Kingfisher factbook)
Includes index
ISBN 0-86272-031-1 : £2.50 : CIP rev.
Primary classification 629.2'222 B82-00369

629.2′24 — Scammell lorries, *to 1978*
Reed, John, *1934-*. Scammell / John Reed. — London : Ian Allan, 1982. — 95p : ill ; 25cm. — (Trucks in camera)
ISBN 0-7110-1173-7 : £5.95 B82-30639

629.2′24 — Scania lorries, *to 1977*
Gibbins, Eric. Scania : Eric Gibbins. — Chiswick : Motor Racing Publications, 1980. — 111p : ill ; 19x24cm. — (Trucks today)
ISBN 0-900549-58-0 : £6.95 B82-29479

629.2′24′0212 — Commercial vehicles — *Technical data*
The **Observer's** book of commercial vehicles / compiled by Nick Baldwin. — New ed. — London : Warne, 1981. — 192p : ill ; 15cm
Previous ed.: 1978
ISBN 0-7232-1619-3 : £1.95 B82-35690

629.2′24′0294 — Commercial vehicles — *Buyers' guides — Serials*
Shell commercial vehicle and PSV buyer's guide. — 6. — London : Kogan Page, May 1982. — [350]p
Continues: Commercial vehicle buyer's guide
ISBN 0-85038-547-4 (pbk) : £8.95 : CIP entry B82-12826

629.2′24′0321 — Commercial vehicles, *to 1981 — Encyclopaedias*
Miller, Denis N.. The illustrated encyclopedia of trucks and buses / Denis Miller assisted by Stephanie Hutton / Arthur Ingram. — London : Hamyln, c1982. — 320p : ill(some col.),ports ; 30cm. — (A Quarto book)
Ill on lining papers
ISBN 0-600-38820-4 : £9.95 B82-28823

629.2′24′09 — Lorries — *History — Serials*
Vintage lorry annual. — No.1-. — London : Marshall, Harris & Baldwin ; Dorking : Warne [distributor], 1979. — 1v. : ill,ports ; 31cm
Continued by: Vintage lorry album. — Only one issue published under this title
ISSN 0263-3779 = Vintage lorry annual : £6.95 B82-23593

629.2′24′09 — Lorries, *to 1975 — For schools*
Thomas, Alan, *1936-*. Lorries, vans and trucks / Alan Thomas. — Hove : Wayland, 1982. — 63p : ill(some col.) ; 24cm. — (Transport and society)
Bibliography: p62. — Includes index
ISBN 0-85340-957-9 : £4.25 B82-34830

629.2′24′0941 — British lorries, *ca 1950*
Baldwin, Nick. Lorries & vans / Nick Baldwin. — London : Marshall Harris & Baldwin, 1979. — [96]p : ill,facsims ; 31cm
Facsims on lining papers. — Includes index
ISBN 0-906116-05-8 : £6.95 B82-07750

629.2′24′097 — North America. Lorries — *Illustrations*
Jacobs, David, *1952-*. American trucks 2 : More colour photographs of trucks and trucking / David Jacobs. — London : Osprey, 1982. — 128p : chiefly col.ill,col.ports ; 23cm
ISBN 0-85045-442-5 (pbk) : £5.95 : CIP rev. B82-07610

629.2′24′0973 — American lorries, *1970-1979*
Kahn, Elliott. American trucks of the seventies / compiled by Elliott Kahn ; edited by G.N. Georgano. — London : Warne, 1981. — 62p : ill ; 20x25cm. — (Warne's transport library)
Includes index
ISBN 0-7232-2765-9 : £4.95 B82-00872

629.2′25 — Agricultural tractors — *Serials*
Vintage tractor magazine. — 1981-. — Perth (14 Balhouse St., Perth, PH1 5HJ) : Vintage Tractor Publications, 1981-. — v. : ill,maps ; 22cm
Quarterly
ISSN 0263-7529 = Vintage tractor magazine : £3.20 per year B82-32134

629.2′25 — Agricultural tractors, *to 1959*
Cawood, Charles L.. Vintage tractors / Charles L. Cawood. — Aylesbury : Shire, 1980. — 32p : ill ; 21cm. — (Shire album ; 48)
Text on inside cover
ISBN 0-85263-499-4 (pbk) : £0.75 B82-40936

629.2′25 — Agricultural tractors, *to 1973*
Williams, Michael, *1935 Nov.4-*. Great tractors / Michael Williams ; photography Andrew Morland. — Poole : Blandford, 1982. — vi,160p : ill(some col.) ; 26cm
Includes index
ISBN 0-7137-1205-8 : £8.95 : CIP rev. B82-01201

629.2′25 — Allis-Chalmers tractors, *to 1965 — Illustrations*
Huxley, Bill. Allis-Chalmers album / Bill Huxley, Allan T. Condie. — [Perth] : [Allan T. Condie Vintage Tractor Publications], c1980. — 76p : chiefly ill ; 22cm. — (A.T.C. vintage tractor monographs)
Cover title
£3.30 (pbk) B82-23150

629.2′25 — American agricultural tractors
Jones, Fred R.. Farm power and tractors. — 5th ed. / Fred R. Jones, William H. Aldred. — New York ; London : McGraw-Hill, c1980. — viii,466p : ill ; 24cm. — (McGraw-Hill publications in the agricultural sciences)
Previous ed.: published as Farm gas engines and tractors, 1963. — Bibliography: p451-454. — Includes index
ISBN 0-07-032781-5 : £18.95 B82-14031

629.2′25 — Ferguson tractors, *to 1962 — Illustrations*
Booth, Colin E.. Ferguson album / Colin E. Booth. — Perth : Allan T. Condie Vintage Tractor Publications, c1981. — [68]p : chiefly ill,1port ; 21cm. — (A.T.C. vintage tractor monographs)
Cover title
£3.30 (pbk) B82-23147

629.2′25 — Fordson tractors, *to 1968 — Illustrations*
Condie, Allan T.. Fordson album number one / Allan T. Condie. — Perth : Allan T. Condie Vintage Tractor Publications, c1981. — [68]p : chiefly ill ; 21cm. — (A.T.C. vintage tractor monographs)
Cover title
£3.30 (pbk) B82-23144

Condie, Allan T.. Fordson album number three / Allan T. Condie. — Perth : Allan T. Condie Vintage Tractor Publications, c1981. — [68]p : chiefly ill ; 21cm. — (A.T.C. vintage tractor monographs)
Cover title
ISBN 0-907742-09-2 (pbk) : £3.30 B82-26174

Condie, Allan T.. Fordson album number two / Allan T. Condie. — Perth : Allan T. Condie Vintage Tractor Publications, c1981. — 72p : chiefly ill ; 21cm. — (A.T.C. vintage tractor monographs)
Cover title
£3.30 (pbk) B82-23145

Condie, Allan T.. Fordson tractors : an anatomy 1917-52 / Allan T. Condie. — 2nd ed. — Perth : Allan T. Condie Vintage Tractor Publications, c1981. — [56]p : chiefly ill ; 22cm. — (A.T.C. vintage tractor monographs)
Cover title. — Previous ed.: 1979
ISBN 0-907742-07-6 (pbk) : £1.95 B82-23143

629.2′25 — International Harvester tractors, *to 1959 — Illustrations*
Condie, Allan T.. International album / Allan T. Condie & John Melloy. — Perth : Allan T. Condie Vintage Tractor Publications, c1982. — [68]p : chiefly ill ; 21cm. — (A.T.C. vintage tractor monographs ; no.10)
Cover title
ISBN 0-907742-10-6 (pbk) : £3.30 B82-23149

629.2′25 — Marshall tractors, *to 1977 — Illustrations*
Condie, Allan T.. Marshall supplement / Allan T. Condie. — Perth : Allan T. Condie Vintage Tractor Publications, c1980. — [36]p : chiefly ill ; 21cm. — (A.T.C. vintage tractor monographs)
Cover title
£1.65 (pbk) B82-23142

629.2′25 — Nuffield tractors, *to 1968 — Illustrations*
Melloy, John. Nuffield album / John Melloy. — Perth : Allan T. Condie Vintage Tractor Publications, c1981. — [32]p : chiefly ill,1port ; 21cm. — (A.T.C. vintage tractor monographs)
Cover title
£1.65 (pbk) B82-23148

629.2′25 — Roadless tractors, *to 1963 — Illustrations*
Condie, Allan T.. Roadless album / Allan T. Condie. — Perth : Allan T. Condie Vintage Tractor Publications, c1981. — [56]p : chiefly ill ; 21cm. — (A.T.C. vintage tractor monographs)
Cover title
ISBN 0-907742-08-4 (pbk) : £2.25 B82-23141

629.2′25 — Turner tractors, *to 1957 — Illustrations*
Condie, Allan T.. The Turner Yeoman of England / Allan T. Condie. — Perth : Allan T. Condie Vintage Tractor Publications, c1982. — [20]p : ill ; 21cm. — (Vintage tractor profile ; no.1)
Cover title
ISBN 0-907742-12-2 (pbk) : £0.95 B82-23140

629.2′272 — Bicycles — *For children*
Osman, Tony. The complete bicycle book / Tony Osman & Nicola McLaughlin. — London : Sparrow Books, 1982. — 122p : ill ; 18cm
ISBN 0-09-928000-0 (pbk) : £0.95 B82-31203

629.2′272 — Bicycles — *Manuals*
Knottley, Peter. You and your bicycle. — London : Ward Lock, Sept.1981. — [96]p
ISBN 0-7063-5960-7 (cased) : £3.95 : CIP entry
ISBN 0-7063-5961-5 (pbk) : £2.50 B81-25873

629.2′272′0750924 — England. Bicycles. Collecting — *Personal observations*
Smith, Colin, *1930-*. Back to the good old bike / by Colin Smith. — [Hornchurch] ([205 Southend Arterial Rd, Hornchurch]) : Hobby Horse, 1982. — 8p : ill ; 15cm
Limited ed. of 250 copies
£0.10 (unbound) B82-22580

629.2′275 — American racing motorcycles, *to ca 1970*
Hatfield, Jerry H.. American racing motorcycles / Jerry H. Hatfield. — Yeovil : Haynes, 1982. — 224p : ill,ports ; 24cm
Bibliography: p223-224
ISBN 0-85429-291-8 : £9.50 B82-33073

629.2′275 — BMW motorcycles, *to 1981*
Bacon, Roy H.. BMW twins & singles. — London : Osprey, Sept.1982. — [224]p. — (Osprey collector's library)
ISBN 0-85045-470-0 : £7.95 : CIP entry B82-20488

Croucher, Robert M.. The story of BMW motor cycles. — Cambridge : Stephens, Nov.1982. — [128]p. — (Motor cycles marque histories series)
ISBN 0-85059-416-2 : £8.95 : CIP entry B82-26053

629.2′275 — BSA single cylinder motorcycles, *1945-1980*
Bacon, Roy H.. BSA Gold Star : and other singles : the postwar Gold Star, "B", "M", "C", ranges, Bantam, unit singles / Roy Bacon. — London : Osprey, 1982. — 192p : ill,ports ; 22cm. — (Osprey collector's library)
ISBN 0-85045-447-6 : £7.95 : CIP rev. B82-04980

629.2′275 — Douglas motorcycles, *to 1957*
Carrick, Peter. Douglas. — Cambridge : Stephens, Apr.1982. — [883]p. — (World motorcycles ; 2)
ISBN 0-85059-512-6 : £5.50 : CIP entry B82-04982

629.2′275 — Harley-Davidson motorcycles, *to 1981*
Foster, Gerald. Cult of the Harley-Davidson. — London : Osprey, Oct.1982. — [128]p. — (Osprey colour series)
ISBN 0-85045-463-8 (pbk) : £5.95 : CIP entry B82-24743

629.2'275 — Lightweight motorcycles
Hudson-Evans, Richard. The lightweight bike book / Richard Hudson-Evans. — London : Batsford, 1981. — 112p : ill ; 25cm
Includes index
ISBN 0-7134-1972-5 (cased) : Unpriced
ISBN 0-7134-1973-3 (pbk) : Unpriced
B82-03475

629.2'275 — Motorcycles
Forsdyke, G.. Motor cycles. — 2nd ed. — London : Newnes Technical Books, Mar.1982. — [128]p. — (Questions & answers)
Previous ed.: 1976
ISBN 0-408-01144-0 (pbk) : £1.95 : CIP entry
B82-03360

Woollett, Mick. Superbikes / Mick Woollett. — London : Batsford, 1982. — 64p : ill(some col.),ports(some col.) ; 20cm
Includes index
ISBN 0-7134-4172-0 (pbk) : £2.25 B82-33827

629.2'275 — Motorcycles — *For children*
Cave, Ronald G.. Motorcycles / Ron and Joyce Cave ; illustrated by David West and Peter Hutton. — London : Watts, 1982. — 30p : col.ill ; 22cm. — (What about?) (A Franklin Watts question and answer book)
Includes index
ISBN 0-85166-981-6 : £2.99 B82-23406

629.2'275 — Motorcycles. Road tests — *Collections*
Sanderson, Graham, *1954-*. Superbike road tests / Graham Sanderson. — London : Hamlyn, c1982. — 128p : ill(some col.) ; 29cm
ISBN 0-600-34982-9 : £5.95 B82-15249

Willoughby, Vic. Exotic motorcycles : a tester's privilege / Vic Willoughby. — London : Osprey, 1982. — 190p : ill,ports ; 24cm
Includes index
ISBN 0-85045-322-4 : £9.95 : CIP rev.
B82-04975

629.2'275 — Norton twin cylinder motorcycles, *1948-1980*
Bacon, Roy H.. Norton twins : the postwar 500, 600, 650, 750, 850 and lightweight twins / Roy Bacon. — London : Osprey, 1981. — 191p : ill,ports ; 22cm. — (Osprey collector's library)
ISBN 0-85045-423-9 : £7.95 : CIP rev.
B81-20466

629.2'275 — Royal Enfield motorcycles, *to 1970*
Hartley, Peter, *1933-*. The story of Royal Enfield motor cycles / Peter Hartley. — Cambridge : Stephens, 1981. — 128p : ill,facsims,ports ; 25cm
Includes index
ISBN 0-85059-467-7 : £7.95 : CIP rev.
B81-27991

629.2'275 — Royal Enfield motorcycles, *to 1981*
Bacon, Roy H.. Royal Enfield. — London : Osprey, Sept.1982. — [224]p. — (Osprey collector's library)
ISBN 0-85045-459-x : £7.95 : CIP entry
B82-20486

629.2'275 — Vincent HRD motorcycles, *to 1966*
Carrick, Peter. Vincent HRD. — Cambridge : Stephens, Apr.1982. — [88]p. — (World motorcycles)
ISBN 0-85059-513-4 : £5.50 : CIP entry
B82-04983

629.2'275 — Vincent HRD V twin cylinder motorcycles, *to 1955*
Harper, Roy. Vincent vee-twins : the famous 1000 series, plus 500 singles / Roy Harper. — London : Osprey, 1982. — 187p : ill,facsims,ports ; 22cm. — (Osprey collector's library)
Bibliography: p187
ISBN 0-85045-435-2 : £7.95 : CIP rev.
B82-04976

629.2'275'0212 — Motorcycles — *Technical data*
Croucher, Robert M.. The observer's book of motorcycles / Robert M. Croucher. — 4th ed. — London : Warne, 1982. — 192p : ill ; 15cm. — (The Observer's series ; 61)
Previous ed.: 1980
ISBN 0-7232-1628-2 : £1.95 B82-19400

629.2'275'05 — Motorcycles — *Serials*
Daily mail motorcycle review. — 1982-. — London : Harmsworth for Associated Newspapers Group, 1982-. — v. : ill ; 30cm
Annual. — Continues: Daily mail motorcycle show review
ISSN 0263-3914 = Daily Mail motorcycle review : £0.80 B82-24766

[Mechanics *(Peterborough)*]. Mechanics. — July 1982-. — Peterborough (Bushfield House, Orton Centre, Peterborough, PE2 OUW) : EMAP National Publications. — v. : ill(some col.) ; 29cm
Monthly. — Continues: Motorcycle mechanics fortnightly
ISSN 0263-8274 = Mechanics (Peterborough) : £18.00 per year B82-32145

629.2'275'09 — Motorcycles, *1939-1968*
Golden oldies : Classic bike road tests / edited by Mike Nicks ; tests by Mike Nicks ... [et al.]. — Cambridge : Stephens, 1981. — 160p : ill ; 25cm
ISBN 0-85059-571-1 : £7.95 B82-08777

629.2'275'09 — Motorcycles, *to 1981*
Willoughby, Vic. Classic motor cycles / Vic Willoughby. — 2nd ed. — London : Hamlyn, 1982. — 208p : ill(some col.),ports ; 30cm
Previous ed.: 1975
ISBN 0-600-34961-6 : £7.95 B82-40637

629.2'275'0941 — British motorcycles, *1950-1980*
Ayton, C. J.. The Hamlyn guide to postwar British motor cycles / C.J. Ayton. — London : Hamlyn, 1982. — 165p : ill(some col.) ; 20cm
Includes index
ISBN 0-600-38461-6 : £3.99 B82-37380

Wilson, Steve. British motor cycles since 1950 : AJW, Ambassador, AMC (AJS & Matchless) and Ariel: roadsters of 250cc and over / Steve Wilson. — Cambridge : Stephens
Vol.1. — 1982. — 127p : ill,ports ; 25cm
ISBN 0-85059-516-9 : £8.95 : CIP rev.
B82-04984

629.2'275'0941 — British motorcycles, *1960-1969*
Currie, Bob. Great British motor cycles of the sixties / Bob Currie. — London : Hamlyn, c1981. — 144p : ill(some col.),ports ; 27cm
ISBN 0-600-34980-2 : £5.95 B82-00695

629.2'275'0952 — Japanese motorcycle, *1960-1981*
Ayton, C. J.. The Hamlyn guide to Japanese motor cycles / C.J. Ayton. — London : Hamlyn, 1982. — 164p : ill(some col.) ; 20cm
Includes index
ISBN 0-600-38462-4 : £3.99 B82-37379

629.2'275'0952 — Japanese motorcycles, *1945-1981*
Ayton, Cyril. Japanese motorcycles / Cyril Ayton. — London : Muller, 1981. — 188p : ill (some col.),ports(some col.) ; 29cm. — (A Charles Herridge Book)
Ill on lining papers
ISBN 0-584-97075-7 : £7.95 B82-00806

629.2'28 — Cooper racing cars, *to 1981*
Nye, Doug. Cooper cars. — London : Osprey, Nov.1982. — [208]p
ISBN 0-85045-488-3 : £11.95 : CIP entry
B82-26424

629.2'28 — Lotus racing cars, *to 1978*
Harvey, Chris. Lotus : the complete story / Chris Harvey. — Yeovil : Foulis, 1982. — 136p : ill,ports ; 24cm. — (Foulis mini marque history series)
ISBN 0-85429-298-5 : £5.95 B82-27700

629.2'28 — Racing cars — *For children*
Desmond, Kevin. Racing cars. — London : Granada, Apr.1982. — [64]p. — (Granada guide series ; 9)
ISBN 0-246-11640-4 : £1.95 : CIP entry
B82-06497

Rutland, Jonathan. The young engineer book of supercars / [written by Jonathan Rutland]. — London : Usborne, 1979. — 32p : ill(some col.) ; 29cm
Bibliography: p32. — Includes index
ISBN 0-86020-204-6 : £3.50 B82-07756

629.2'28'09045 — Racing sports cars, *1950-1972*
Bowler, Michael. Track tests : sports cars : thoroughbred & classic cars / Michael Bowler. — London : Hamlyn, 1981. — 144p : ill(some col.) ; 29cm
Includes index
ISBN 0-600-32205-x : £6.95 B82-02719

629.2'292'0941 — Great Britain. Traction engines, *to 1960 — Illustrations*
Traction engines in focus / [compiled] by John Crawley. — Turvey : Crawley, 1982. — [96]p : chiefly ill ; 25cm
ISBN 0-9508046-0-6 : £6.95 B82-35857

629.2'293 — Battery operated road vehicles. Development — *Conference proceedings*
Electric Vehicle Development Group. *International Conference (4th : 1981 : London)*. Hybrid, dual mode and tracked systems : Electric Vehicle Development Group Fourth International Conference / the meeting was organised by the Electric Vehicle Development Group with the support of European Electric Road Vehicle Association ... [et al.]. — Stevenage : Peregrinus, c1981. — 179p : ill,maps,ports ; 30cm. — (PPL conference publication ; no.18)
ISBN 0-906048-65-6 (pbk) : Unpriced
B82-10994

629.2'293 — Electric road vehicles
Unnewehr, L. E.. Electric vehicle technology / L.E. Unnewehr, S.A. Nasar. — New York ; Chichester : Wiley, c1982. — xi,256p : ill ; 24cm
Includes index
ISBN 0-471-08378-x : £35.00 B82-37199

629.23 — MOTOR VEHICLES. CONSTRUCTION

629.2'31 — Motor vehicles. Aerodynamics — *Conference proceedings*
Impact of aerodynamics on vehicle design. — St Helier : Interscience Enterprises, Jan.1983. — [516]p. — (Proceedings of the International Association for Vehicle Design : Technological advances in vehicle design ; SP3)
Conference proceedings
ISBN 0-907776-01-9 (pbk) : £60.00 : CIP entry
B82-39304

629.2'31'0289 — Motor vehicles. Design. Safety aspects
Limpert, Rudolf. Vehicle system components : design and safety / Rudolf Limpert. — New York ; Chichester : Wiley, c1982. — xii,144p : ill ; 24cm
Bibliography: p135. — Includes index
ISBN 0-471-08133-7 : Unpriced B82-38321

629.2'34 — Cars. Manufacture — *Conference proceedings*
Automotive Manufacturing Update '81 *(Conference : London)*. Automotive Manufacturing Update '81 : conference / sponsored by the Automobile Division and the Engineering Manufacturing Industries Division of the Institution of Mechanical Engineers under the patronage of Fédération internationale des sociétés d'ingénieurs des techniques de l'automobile (FISITA), 1-2 December 1981, Institution Headquarters ... London. — London : Published by Mechanical Engineering Publications for the Institution of Mechanical Engineers, 1981. — 200p : ill ; 30cm. — (I Mech E conference publications ; 1981-13)
ISBN 0-85298-479-0 (pbk) : Unpriced
B82-12024

629.2'34 — Cars. Manufacture — *For children*
Young, Frank, *19---*. Automobile : from prototype to scrapyard / Frank Young. — [London] : Collins, 1982. — 37p : col.ill,1col.map ; 30cm. — (The Inside story)
Ill on lining papers. — Includes index
ISBN 0-00-195375-3 : £2.95 B82-20812

629.24/7 — MOTOR VEHICLES. PARTS

629.2′44 — Motor vehicles. Hydrostatic transmission systems — *Conference proceedings*

Hydrostatic transmissions for vehicle application : European conference sponsored by the Manufacturing Industries Division of the Institution of Mechanical Engineers, Svenska Mekanisters Forening in association with Verein Deutscher Ingenieure under the patronage of Fédération internationale des societés d′ingenieurs des techniques de l′automobile (FISITA). — London : Published by Mechanical Engineering Publications for the Institution of Mechanical Engineers, 1981. — 152p : ill ; 30cm. — (I Mech E conference publications ; 1981-8)
ISBN 0-85298-476-6 (pbk) : Unpriced
B82-02692

629.2′46 — Cars. Braking systems

Newcomb, T. P.. Automobile brakes and braking. — 2nd ed. — Sevenoaks : Newnes Technical, Jan.1983. — [112]p. — (Questions & answers)
Previous ed.: 1977
ISBN 0-408-01317-6 (pbk) : £1.95 : CIP entry
B82-34439

629.2′482′0288 — Lorries. Tyres. Maintenance & repair — *Manuals*

Service manual for truck tyres. — London (90-91 Tottenham Court Rd., W1P 0BR) : British Rubber Manufacturers′ Association, [1980?]. — 91p : ill ; 30cm
Cover title
£3.80 (spiral) B82-35934

629.2′5 — Cars. Engines

Crouse, Williams H.. Automotive engines. — 6th ed. / William H. Crouse, Donald L. Anglin. — New York ; London : Gregg Division, McGraw-Hill, c1981. — ix,422p : ill ; 28cm
Previous ed.: 1977. — Includes index
ISBN 0-07-014825-2 (pbk) : £10.15
B82-00416

629.2′5′028 — Motor vehicles. Engines. Plastics components

Scott, P.. Plastics under the bonnet / P. Scott. — Shrewsbury (Shawbury, Shrewsbury, Shropshire, SY4 4NR) : RAPRA, [1981]. — 33p ; 30cm. — (Business report ; no.1)
Bibliography: p33
Unpriced (pbk) B82-19757

629.2′504 — Cars. Petrol engines. Tuning — *Amateurs′ manuals*

Campbell, Colin, *1913-*. Tuning for economy / Colin Campbell. — London : Chapman and Hall, 1981. — 143p : ill ; 22cm
Includes index
ISBN 0-412-23480-7 (cased) : Unpriced : CIP rev.
ISBN 0-412-23490-4 (pbk) : £3.95 B81-31710

629.2′504 — Formula 1 racing cars. Cosworth-Ford engines, *to 1980*

Geary, L.. Ford Formula One racing cars : ten years plus / by L. Geary. — Hornchurch : Henry, 1982. — 64p : ill,ports ; 24cm. — ([64 transport series] ; [6])
ISBN 0-86025-855-6 : £4.25 B82-28073

629.2′504 — Vehicles. Two-stroke engines. Tuning - *Amateurs′ manuals*

Bacon, Roy. Two-stroke tuning. — Isleworth : Transport Bookman Publications, May 1981. — 1v.
ISBN 0-85184-039-6 (pbk) : £4.25 : CIP entry
B81-13840

629.2′53 — Industries. Motor vehicles. Fleets. Fuel. Conservation

6 ways to cut fuel costs : transport fleets. — Dublin : Produced by the Department of Industry and Energy in association with the Confederation of Irish Industry, [1982?]. — [16]p : ill ; 21cm
Unpriced (unbound) B82-41142

629.2′53 — Lorries. Fuel. Consumption. Measurement — *Standards*

Vehicle fuel consumption test procedure type 1 : recommended practices. — London (1, Cromwell Place, SW7 2JF) : Institute of Road Transport Engineers, 1982. — 14p : ill,3forms,1map ; 30cm
Cover title
Unpriced (pbk) B82-31012

Vehicle fuel consumption test procedure type II : recommended practices. — London (1, Cromwell Place, SW7 2JF) : Institute of Road Transport Engineers, 1982. — 10p : ill,2forms ; 30cm
Cover title
Unpriced (pbk) B82-31013

629.2′54′0288 — Cars. Ignition ststems. Maintenance & repair

Derato, Frank C.. Automotive ignition systems : diagnosis and repair / Frank C. Derato. — New York ; London : McGraw-Hill, c1982. — ix,262p : ill ; 28cm
Includes index
ISBN 0-07-016501-7 (pbk) : £10.50
B82-16287

629.2′6 — Cars. Bodywork. Design

Modern automotive structural analysis / Martin R. Barone ... [et al.] ; edited by Mounir M. Kamal and Joseph A. Wolf, Jr.. — New York ; London : Van Nostrand Reinhold, c1982. — x,458p : ill ; 24cm
Includes index
ISBN 0-442-24839-3 : £29.35 B82-23710

629.2′6 — Cars. Bodywork. Design. Mathematical models. Applications of digital computer systems

The Use of the finite element method to develop lighter structures for automotive use / L.J. Page ... [et al.]. — [Loughborough] : Department of Transport Technology, Loughborough University of Technology, 1981. — 7p : ill ; 30cm
Unpriced (pbk) B82-21607

629.2′6′0288 — Motor vehicles. Bodywork. Maintenance & repair — *Serials*

Body shop news. — Mar. 1981-. — Leeds (Belmont House, Finkle La., Gildersome, Leeds LS27 7TW) : Vehicle Builders & Repairers Association, 1981-. — v. : ill ; 42cm
Two issues yearly. — Description based on: Aug./Sept. 1981
ISSN 0262-9070 = Body shop news : Unpriced
B82-11150

629.2′7 — Cars. Accessories. Installation — *Manuals*

The Total book of car improvements and accessories. — London : Marshall Cavendish, 1980. — 245p : col.ill ; 31cm
Includes index
ISBN 0-85685-764-5 : £8.95 B82-06136

629.2′7 — Cars. Electronic equipment. Projects — *Amateurs′ manuals*

Penfold, R. A.. Electronic projects for cars and boats / by R.A. Penfold. — London : Babani, 1981. — 85p : ill ; 18cm. — (Bernard Babani ; BP94)
ISBN 0-85934-069-4 (pbk) : £1.95 : CIP rev.
Also classified at 623.8′504 B81-30192

629.2′7 — Motor vehicles. Electronic equipment — *Conference proceedings*

International Conference on Automotive Electronics *(3rd : 1981 : London)*. Third International Conference on Automotive Electronics : 20-23 October 1981, The Institution of Electrical Engineers, London / conference sponsored by the Automobile Division of the Institution of Mechanical Engineers, Computing and Control and the Electronics Division of the Institution of Electrical Engineers. — London : Mechanical Engineering Publications Limited for the Institution of Mechanical Engineers, 1981. — 354p : ill ; 30cm. — (I Mech E conference publications ; 1981-10)
ISBN 0-85298-477-4 (pbk) : Unpriced
B82-06141

629.2′73 — Great Britain. Commercial vehicles. Tachographs

Soye, David P.. The transport manager′s guide to the tachograph / David P. Soye. — London : Kogan Page, 1979. — 96p : ill ; 23cm
ISBN 0-85038-236-x (cased) : £4.95
ISBN 0-85038-237-8 (pbk) : Unpriced
B82-07388

629.2′77 — Cars. Air conditioning equipment. Maintenance & repair — *Manuals*

Samuels, Clifford L.. Automotive air conditioning / Clifford L. Samuels. — Englewood Cliffs ; London : Prentice-Hall, c1981. — xiv,226p : ill ; 28cm
Includes index
ISBN 0-13-054213-x (pbk) : £10.45
B82-07788

629.28 — MOTOR VEHICLES. OPERATION AND MAINTENANCE

629.28′24 — Enduro motorcycles. Track tests — *Personal observations*

Melling, Frank. Enduro motorcycles : track tests of the world′s greatest / Frank Melling. — London : Osprey, 1981. — 143p : ill(some col.) ; 23cm
ISBN 0-85045-406-9 (pbk) : £5.95 : CIP rev.
B81-30615

629.28′3′07041 — Great Britain. Motor vehicles. Driving. Teaching — *Manuals*

Autodriva training system. — Ilkeston (313 Godfrey Drive, Ilkeston, Derbys. DE7 4HU) : Driver Instructor Training Services, c1981. — 323leaves in various foliations : ill,forms ; 30cm
Unpriced (pbk) B82-14559

629.28′32 — Cars. Driving — *Manuals*

Advanced motoring : an exposition of the basis of advanced motoring techniques / compiled by the Institute of Advanced Motorists. — Rev. and updated. — London : Queen Anne Press with the Institute of Advanced Motorists, 1982. — 143p : ill(some col.) ; 22cm
Previous ed.: 1978
ISBN 0-356-08543-0 : £6.95 B82-35689

Advanced motoring : an exposition of the basis of advanced motoring techniques / compiled by the Institute of Advanced Motorists. — Rev. and updated. — London : Macdonald and Co. with the Institute of Advanced Motorists, 1982. — 143p,[7]p of plates : ill(some col.) ; 21cm
Previous ed.: 1976
ISBN 0-356-08544-9 (pbk) : £4.95 B82-30653

Johnson, Felix. Drive in 6 easy lessons / Felix Johnson. — London : Sphere, 1982. — 158p : ill ; 18cm
ISBN 0-7221-5072-5 (pbk) : £1.95 B82-24543

629.28′32 — Cars. High speed driving — *Manuals*

Wherrett, Peter. [Motoring skills & tactics]. Drive it! : the complete book of high speed driving on road & track / Peter Wherrett. — [Yeovil] : Foulis, 1981, c1975. — 108p : ill ; 28cm. — (A Foulis motoring book ; F297)
Originally published: Sydney : Ure Smith, 1975
ISBN 0-85429-297-7 : £4.95 B82-06978

629.28′32′07041 — Great Britain. Cars. Driving. Teaching — *Manuals*

Miller, John, *1938-*. The driving instructor′s handbook : a reference and training manual / John Miller and Nigel Stacey. — London : Kogan Page, 1982. — 237p : ill,facsims,forms ; 23cm
Includes index
ISBN 0-85038-570-9 : £11.95 : CIP rev.
B82-08103

629.28′44 — Heavy commercial vehicles. Driving — *Manuals*

Soye, David P.. The HGV driver′s handbook 1982-83 / David P. Soye. — 2nd ed. — London : Kogan Page, 1982. — xi,209p : ill ; 21cm
Previous ed.: 1979
ISBN 0-85038-556-3 (cased) : Unpriced : CIP rev.
ISBN 0-85038-558-x (pbk) : £3.95 B82-10674

629.28′475 — Motorcycles. Riding — *Manuals*

Advanced motorcycling : the art of better motorcycle riding and advanced motorcycling techniques / compiled by the Institute of Advanced Motorists. — Rev. and updated. — London : Queen Anne Press with the Institute of Advanced Motorists, 1982. — 143p : ill (some col.) ; 22cm
Previous ed.: London : Macdonald & Jane's, 1977
ISBN 0-356-08541-4 (cased) : £6.95
ISBN 0-356-08542-2 (pbk) : £4.95 B82-21334

Monaghan, Tim. Sorry mate, I didn't see you! : or, a survivors' guide to motorcycyling / Tim Monaghan. — London : British Broadcasting Corporation, 1982. — 88p : ill ; 21cm
"Published in conjunction with the BBC Continuing Education Television series, 'Sorry mate, I didn't see you!'" — t.p. verso
ISBN 0-563-16498-0 (pbk) : £1.50 B82-22282

Robinson, John, *1945-*. Pass your motorcycle L test / by John Robinson. — Kingswood : Elliot Right Way, c1982. — 127p : ill ; 18cm. — (Paperfronts)
Includes index
ISBN 0-7160-0677-4 (pbk) : £0.75 B82-23916

Wallach, Theresa. Easy motorcycle riding / by Theresa Wallach ; illustrated by Maggie MacGowan. — Enl. ed. — New York : Sterling ; London : Oak Tree, c1978. — 160p : ill,1port ; 23cm
Previous ed.: New York : Bantam, 1971. — Includes index
ISBN 0-7061-2591-6 : £4.95 B82-24535

629.28′6′068 — Great Britain. Garage services. Management — *Manuals*

Galiegue, B. F.. Service management in the retail motor industry / B.F. Galiegue. — London : Heinemann, 1982. — 159p : ill,1map,plans,forms ; 22cm
Bibliography: p156. — Includes index
ISBN 0-434-90650-6 (pbk) : £5.95 B82-16129

629.28′7 — Diesel vehicles. Maintenance & repair — *Manuals*

Schulz, Erich J.. Diesel equipment / Erich J. Schulz. — New York ; London : McGraw-Hill, c1982
Includes index
1: Lubrication, hydraulics, brakes, wheels, tires. — viii,424p : ill ; 28cm
ISBN 0-07-055716-0 (pbk) : £13.25
B82-00532

629.28′7′07041 — Great Britain. Ceramics industries. Motor vehicle repair services. Personnel. Training

Ridley, M. A. W.. Motor vehicle trades craft training : guide notes for companies / [M.A.W. Ridley, W.G. Patrick, J.A. Crew]. — [Harrow] ([Bovis House, Northolt Rd., Harrow, Middx]) : Ceramics, Glass and Mineral Products Industry Training Board, c1982. — 12p ; 21x30cm
Unpriced (pbk) B82-40440

629.28′722 — Cars. Maintenance & repair — *Amateurs' manuals*

All about motoring breakdowns : a glovebox guide to running repairs / [editor Barry Francis] ; [technical photography John Couzins] ; [contributors Iain Colquhoun, Charles Surridge, David Rowlands]. — Basingstoke : Aubomobile Association, c1982. — 128p : ill ; 22x24cm
Ill, text on inside covers. — Includes index
ISBN 0-86145-064-7 (pbk) : £3.95 B82-35563

Looking after your car. — 2nd ed. — London : Reader's Digest, c1978 (1982 [printing]). — 56p : ill(some col.) ; 27cm. — (Reader's digest basic guide)
Previous ed.: 1975
Unpriced (pbk) B82-38475

Looking after your car. — 2nd ed., reprinted with amendments. — London : Reader's Digest Association, 1981, c1975. — 56p : ill(some col.) ; 27cm. — (Reader's Digest basic guide)
Previous ed.: 1978. — 'Text and illustrations in this book are taken from Reader's Digest repair manual and Reader's Digest/AA new book of the road'
ISBN 0-276-00163-x (pbk) : £1.25 B82-04173

RAC motorists' easy guide to car care and repair. — London : Royal Automobile Club
3: Diagnosis and repair of ignition and carburettor faults. — 1982. — 38p : ill ; 21cm
Includes index
ISBN 0-902628-33-x (pbk) : £1.00 B82-32417

Williams, Roy. Understanding your car : a light-hearted guide for buyers and drivers / Roy Williams ; cartoons by Ross. — London : Evans, 1982. — 95p : ill ; 18cm
ISBN 0-237-45675-3 (pbk) : £1.65 B82-39020

629.28′722 — Chrysler Horizon cars. Maintenance & repair — *Amateurs' manuals*

Mead, John S.. Horizon owners workshop manual / John S. Mead. — Yeovil : Haynes, c1981. — 219p : ill ; 28cm
Includes index
ISBN 0-85696-473-5 : £5.95 B82-08637

629.28′722 — Datsun 140J, 160J & 510 cars. Maintenance & repair — *Amateurs' manuals*

Russek, Peter. Datsun A. 10, Datsun 510, Violet 140J-160J / by Peter Russek. — Marlow : P. Russek, c1979. — 216p : ill ; 20cm. — (Pocket mechanic) (Peter Russek manuals)
'A 10' (1 folded sheet) as insert
ISBN 0-904509-00-1 (pbk) : £3.30 B82-17119

629.28′722 — Datsun 810 cars. Maintenance & repair — *Amateurs' manuals*

Russek, Peter. Datsun 810 : 180B, Saloon, Estate and SSS Coupe / by Peter Russek. — Marlow : P. Russek, c1979. — 210p : ill ; 21cm. — (Pocket mechanic) (Peter Russek manuals)
'Wiring system for Datsun 810 (180B)' (2 folded sheets) as insert
ISBN 0-904509-88-5 (cased) : Unpriced
ISBN 0-904509-83-4 (pbk) : £3.30 B82-17121

629.28′722 — Datsun 1207 & 1407 cars. Maintenance & repair — *Amateurs' manuals*

Russek, Peter. Datsun B310, 120Y-140Y to 1979 / by Peter Russek. — Marlow : P. Russek, c1979. — 203p : ill ; 20cm. — (Pocket mechanic) (Peter Russek manuals)
'B.310' (1 folded sheet) as insert
ISBN 0-904509-03-6 (pbk) : £3.30 B82-17124

629.28′722 — Datsun Cherry cars. Maintenance & repair — *Amateurs' manuals*

Coomber, Ian. Datsun owners workshop manual / Ian Coomber. — Yeovil : Haynes, c1982. — 286p : ill ; 28cm
Includes index
ISBN 0-85696-679-7 : £5.95 B82-21949

629.28′722 — Fiat 124 cars. Maintenance & repair — *Amateurs' manuals*

Haynes, J. H.. Fiat 124 owners workshop manual / by J.H. Haynes and D.H. Stead. — Yeovil : Haynes, c1979. — 223p : ill(some col.) ; 28cm. — (Owners workshop manual ; 080)
Includes index
ISBN 0-85696-508-1 : £5.95 B82-05254

629.28′722 — Fiat 126 cars. Maintenance & repair — *Amateurs' manuals*

Fiat 126 1972-82 autobook : Fiat 126 1972-1977, Fiat 126 L 1972-1975, Fiat 126 de Ville 1976-77, Fiat 126/650 1977-1982, Fiat 126/650 de Ville 1977-1982. — [4th ed. fully rev.] / by the Autobooks Team of Writers and Illustrators. — Wakefield : Autobooks, [1980] ([1982 printing]). — 129p : ill ; 25cm. — (Autobooks owners workshop manuals ; 853)
Previous ed.: published as Fiat 126 1972-77 autobook / by Kenneth Ball and the Autobooks Team of Technical Writers, 1977. — Includes index
ISBN 0-85146-215-4 : Unpriced B82-32658

629.28′722 — Fiat 127 cars. Maintenance & repair — *Amateurs' manuals*

Fiat 127 1971-81 autobook / by the Autobooks team of writers and illustrators. — [6th ed. fully rev.]. — Wakefield : Autobooks, [1981]. — 136p : ill ; 25cm. — (Autobooks owners workshop manual ; 737)
Previous ed.: published as Fiat 127 1971-79 autobook, 1979. — Includes index
ISBN 0-85146-188-3 : Unpriced B82-23809

629.28′722 — Fiat 132 cars. Maintenance & repair — *Amateurs' manuals*

Methuen, P. M.. Fiat 132 owners workshop manual / P.M. Methuen. — Yeovil : Haynes, c1982. — 239p : ill ; 28cm
Includes index
ISBN 0-85696-602-9 : Unpriced B82-17562

629′.28′722 — Ford Capri 1300 & 1600 OHV cars. Maintenance & repair — *Amateurs' manuals*

Haynes, J. H.. Ford Capri 1300 & 1600 ohv : owners workshop manual / by J.H. Haynes and J.R.S. Hall. — Yeovil : Haynes, c1979. — 200p : ill(some col.) ; 28cm
Includes index
ISBN 0-85696-542-1 : £6.95 B82-17614

629.28′722 — Ford Cortina Mk 4 cars. Maintenance & repair — *Amateurs' manuals*

Ford Cortina Mk 4 1976-80 autobook / by the Autobooks team of writers and illustrators. — [5th ed., fully rev.]. — Wakefield : Autobooks, [1981]. — 192p : ill ; 25cm. — (Autobooks owners workshop manual ; 922)
Previous ed.: published as Ford Cortina Mk 4 1976-79 autobook, 1980. — Includes index
ISBN 0-85146-189-1 : Unpriced B82-23808

629.28′722 — Ford Cortina Mk5 cars. Maintenance & repair — *Amateurs' manuals*

Ford Cortina Mk5 : 1979-82 autobook / by the Autobooks team of writers and illustrators. — Wakefield : Autobooks, 1982. — 192p : ill ; 25cm. — (Owners workshop manual ; 992)
Includes index
ISBN 0-85146-181-6 : Unpriced B82-25648

629.28′722 — Ford Granada cars. Maintenance & repair — *Amateurs' manuals*

Ford Granada 1977-81 autobook : Ford Granada 2.0L, GL 1977-81, Ford Granada 2.3L, GL 1977-81, Ford Granada 2.3 Ghia 1980-81, Ford Granada 2.8GL, Ghia 1977-81, Ford Granada 2.8iGL, S 1977-78, Ford Granada 2.8iGLS 1978-81, Ford Granada 2.8i Ghia, S 1977-81 / by the autobooks team of writers and illustrators. — [4th ed., fully rev.]. — Wakefield : Autobooks, [1981]. — 192p : ill ; 25cm. — (The Autobook series of workshop manuals)
Previous ed.: published as Ford Granada 1977-80 autobook. 1980. — Includes index
ISBN 0-85146-198-0 : Unpriced B82-22518

629.28′722 — Hillman Hunter cars. Maintenance & repair — *Amateurs' manuals*

Chrysler Hillman Hunter 1966-79 autobook : Chrysler Hunter, Super 1977-79, Hillman Hunter, Super, GL, GLS, GT 1966-77, Hillman GT 1969-70, Humber Sceptre 1967-76, Singer Vogue 1966-70, Sunbeam Rapier H120 1967-76, Sunbeam Alpine, GT 1969-75, Sunbeam Arrow 1969-72 / by the autobooks team of writers and illustrators. — Wakefield : Autobooks, [1981]. — 160p : ill ; 25cm. — (The Autobook series of workshop manuals)
Previous ed.: / by Kenneth Ball and the Autobooks team of technical writers. 1978. — Includes index
ISBN 0-85146-184-0 : Unpriced B82-22517

629.28′722 — Honda Civic cars. Maintenance & repair — *Amateurs' manuals*

Jones, Alec J.. Honda Civic owners workshop manual / Alec J. Jones. — Yeovil : Haynes, c1982. — 264p : ill ; 28cm. — (Owners workshop manual ; 633)
Includes index
ISBN 0-85696-633-9 : £6.95 B82-34790

629.28′722 — Honda Prelude cars. Maintenance & repair — *Amateurs' manuals*

Jones, Ray M.. Honda Prelude owners workshop manual / Ray M. Jones. — Yeovil : Haynes, c1981. — 253p : ill(some col.) ; 28cm. — (Owners workshop manual ; 601)
Includes index
ISBN 0-85696-601-0 : £5.95 B82-02524

629.28′722 — Mazda 626 cars & Mazda Montrose cars. Maintenance & repairs — *Amateurs' manuals*

Legg, A. K.. Mazda owners workshop manual / A.K. Legg. — Yeovil : Haynes, c1982. — 201p : ill(some col.) ; 28cm
Includes index
ISBN 0-85696-648-7 : Unpriced B82-23517

629.28′722 — Mazda 626 cars. Maintenance & repair — *Amateurs′ manuals*

Russek, Peter. Mazda 626 Montrose : 1.6, 1.8 & 2.0 litres / by Peter Russek. — Marlow : P. Russek, c1979. — 210p : ill ; 20cm. — (Pocket mechanic) (Peter Russek manuals)
′Wiring diagram for Mazda 626 - Montrose R.H.D. models′ (1 folded sheet) as insert
ISBN 0-904509-02-8 (pbk) : £3.30 B82-17120

629.28′722 — Mazda 808 & 818 cars. Maintenance & repair — *Amateurs′ manuals*

Mazda 808, 818 1972-79 Autobook : Mazda 808 1972-1977, Mazda 818 1972-1979 / by the Autobooks team of writers and illustrators. — 5th rev. ed. — Wakefield : Autobooks, 1981. — 146p : ill ; 25cm. — (Autobooks owners workshop manual ; 877)
Previous ed.: 1979. — Includes index
ISBN 0-85146-185-9 : £5.95 B82-02824

629.28′722 — Mazda RX-7 cars. Maintenance & repair — *Amateurs′ manuals*

Mauck, Scott. Mazda RX-7 owner′s workshop manual / Scott Mauck. — Newbury Park, Calif. : Sparkford, Haynes, c1980. — 251p : ill ; 28cm
Includes index
ISBN 0-85696-460-3 : £5.95 B82-16167

629.28′722 — MGB cars. Maintenance & repair — *Amateurs′ manuals*

MGB 1969-81 autobook : MG MGB Mk2 1969-71, MG MGB GT Mk2 1969-71, MG MGB Mk3 1971-81, MG MGB GT Mk3 1971-81 / by the Autobooks team of writers and illustrators. — [11th ed., fully rev.]. — Wakefield : Autobooks, [1980, c1981] ([1981 printing]). — 192p : ill ; 25cm. — (The Autobook series of workshop manuals)
Previous ed.: 1979. — Includes index
ISBN 0-85146-172-7 : Unpriced B82-25833

Russek, Peter. MGB : GT Tourer / by Peter Russek. — Marlow : P. Russek, c1979. — 210p : ill ; 20cm. — (Pocket mechanic) (Peter Russek manuals)
′Key to the wiring diagram - 1977, UK specification′ (1 folded sheet) as insert
ISBN 0-904509-98-2 (pbk) : £3.30 B82-17123

629.28′722 — Morgan Four cars. Maintenance & repair — *Amateurs′ manuals*

Morgan four 1936-81 autobook / by the Autobooks team of writers and illustrators. — [5th ed. fully rev.]. — Wakefield : Autobooks, [1979] ([1982 printing]). — 185p : ill ; 25cm. — (Autobooks owners workshop manual ; 796)
Previous ed.: published as Morgan four 1936-79 autobook / by R. Clarke, 1977. — Includes index
ISBN 0-85146-187-5 : Unpriced B82-23810

629.28′722 — Morris Ital 1.3 cars. Maintenance & repair — *Amateurs′ manuals*

Mead, John S.. Morris Ital owners workshop manual / John S. Mead. — Yeovil : Haynes, c1982. — 195p : ill(some col.),plans ; 28cm
Includes index
ISBN 0-85696-705-x : £5.95 B82-29344

629.28′722 — Morris Ital cars. Maintenance & repair — *Amateurs′ manuals*

Ital 1.3, 1.7, 2.0 : 1980-82 autobook : Morris Ital 1.3L, HL, HLS saloons and estates 1980-82, Morris Ital 1.7L, HL, HLS saloons and estates 1980-82, Morris Ital 2.0 HLS saloon and estate 1980-82, Morris 440, 440L van 1980-82, Morris 575, 575L van 1980-82, Morris 575 pick-up 1980-82 / by the Autobooks team of writers and illustrators. — Wakefield : Autobooks, 1982. — 183p : ill ; 25cm. — (Owners workshop manual ; OWM 991)
Includes index
ISBN 0-85146-180-8 : Unpriced B82-37281

Mead, John S.. Morris Ital owners workshop manual / John S. Mead. — Yeovil : Haynes, 1982. — 198p : ill(some col.) ; 28cm. — (Owners workshop manual ; 714)
Includes index
ISBN 0-85696-714-9 : £6.95 B82-31404

629.28′722 — Morris Marina cars. Maintenance & repair — *Amateurs′ manuals*

Marina 1300, 1700 1978-81 autobook : Morris Marina 1300, 1300L, 1300HL 1978-80, Morris Marina 1700, 1700L, 1700HL 1978-80, Morris 1100 440 Van 1978-79, Morris 1300 440, L Van 1978-81, Morris 525, L Van 1978-81, Morris 575 Pick-up 1978-81 / by the Autobooks team of writers and illustrators. — [2nd ed., fully rev.]. — Wakefield : Autobooks, [1982]. — 186p : ill ; 25cm. — (The Autobook series of workshop manuals)
Previous ed.: published as Marina 1300, 1700 1978-79 autobook. 1979. — Includes index
ISBN 0-85146-193-x : Unpriced B82-22519

629.28′722 — Opel Kadett cars. Maintenance & repair — *Amateurs′ manuals*

Strasman, Peter G.. Opel Kadett owners workshop manual / Peter G. Strasman. — Yeovil : Haynes, c1982. — 228p : ill ; 28cm
Includes index
ISBN 0-85696-634-7 : £5.95 B82-15271

629.28′722 — Peugeot 104 cars. Maintenance & repair — *Amateurs′ manuals*

Peugeot 104 1973-80 autobook / by the Autobooks team of writers and illustrators. — [5th ed. fully rev.]. — Wakefield : Autobooks, [1980]. — 144p : ill ; 25cm. — (Autobooks owners workshop manual ; 809)
Previous ed.: published as Peugeot 104 1973-79 autobook, 1979. — Includes index
ISBN 0-85146-170-0 : Unpriced B82-23807

629.28′722 — Peugeot 504 cars. Maintenance & repair — *Amateurs′ manuals*

Peugeot 504 1968-82 autobook ... — [9th ed., fully rev.] / by the Autobooks team of writers and illustrators. — Wakefield : Autobooks, [1982]. — 185p : ill ; 25cm. — (Owners workshop manual ; 783)
Previous ed.: 1979. — Includes index
ISBN 0-85146-203-0 : Unpriced B82-27877

629.28′722 — Range Rover cars. Maintenance & repair — *Amateurs′ manuals*

Methuen, P. M.. Range Rover owners workshop manual : all standard production models of the Range Rover with 3528cc V8 engine / Philip Methuen and Ian Coomber. — Yeovil : Haynes, c1982. — 225p : ill ; 28cm
Includes index
ISBN 0-85696-606-1 : £5.95 B82-20091

Range Rover 1970-81 autobook / by the Autobooks team of writers and illustrators. — [5th ed. fully rev.]. — Wakefield : Autobooks, [1981]. — 161p : ill ; 25cm. — (Autobooks owners workshop manual ; 787)
Previous ed.: published as Range Rover 1970-79 autobook, 1979. — Includes index
ISBN 0-85146-191-3 : Unpriced B82-23806

629.28′722 — Reliant Robin cars. Maintenance & repair — *Amateurs′ manuals*

Reliant Robin : 1973-82 autobooks : Reliant Robin 750 saloon, van 1973-75, Reliant Robin 750 super saloon, van 1973-75, Reliant Robin 850 saloon, van 1975-82, Reliant Robin 850 super saloon 1975-82, Reliant Robin 850 super estate 1976-82, Reliant Robin 850 super van 1975-77, Reliant Robin 850 estate 1977-82, Reliant Robin 850 'Jubilee' saloon, estate 1977, Reliant Robin 850 GB special saloon 1977 / by the Autobooks team of writers and illustrators. — Wakefield : Autobooks, 1982. — 143p : ill ; 25cm. — (Owners workshop manual ; OWM 894)
Includes index
ISBN 0-85147-655-4 : Unpriced B82-37282

629.28′722 — Renault 5GTL & 5TS cars. Maintenance & repair — *Amateurs′ manuals*

Russek, Peter. Renault 5 to 1980 : TS, GTL, Gordini and Le Car / by Peter Russek. — Up-dated. — Marlow : P. Russek, c1979. — 210p : ill ; 20cm. — (Pocket mechanic) (Peter Russek manuals)
"Wiring diagram - Renault 5 - since 1978" (1 folded sheet) as insert
ISBN 0-904509-87-7 (pbk) : £3.30 B82-17117

629.28′722 — Renault 5L & 5TL cars. Maintenance & repair — *Amateurs′ manuals*

Russek, Peter. Renault 5L & 5TL : (includes 1980 1108c.c. engine) / by Peter Russek. — Rev. — Marlow : P. Russek, c1979. — 192,[11]p : ill ; 20cm. — (Pocket mechanic) (Peter Russek manuals)
One folded sheet as insert
ISBN 0-904509-93-1 (pbk) : £3.30 B82-17122

629.28′722 — Renault 12 cars. Maintenance & repair — *Amateurs′ manuals*

Haynes, J. H.. Renault 12 owners workshop manual : models covered : all Renault 12 models, 1289cc, Saloon L, TL, TS and TR, Estate TN and TL / by J.H. Haynes and Tim Parker. — Yeovil : Haynes, c1981. — 204p : ill (some col.) ; 28cm. — (Owners workshop manual ; 097)
Includes index
ISBN 0-85696-503-0 : £5.95 B82-05253

629.28′722 — Renault 14 cars. Maintenance & repair — *Amateurs′ manuals*

Russek, Peter. Renault 14TL-GTL to 1980 / by Peter Russek. — Up-dated. — Marlow : P. Russek, c1980. — 186p : ill ; 20cm. — (Pocket mechanic) (Peter Russek manuals)
Previous ed.: 1978. — ′Renault 14′ (1 folded sheet) as insert
ISBN 0-904509-67-2 (pbk) : £3.30 B82-17126

629.28′722 — Renault 16 cars. Maintenance & repair — *Amateurs′ manuals*

Haynes, J. H.. Renault 16 owners workshop manual / by J.H. Haynes and Peter G. Strasman. — Yeovil : Haynes, c1979. — 271p : ill(some col.) ; 28cm. — (Owners workshop manual ; 081)
Includes index
ISBN 0-85696-504-9 : £5.95 B82-05257

629.28′722 — Renault 18 cars. Maintenance & repair — *Amateurs′ manuals*

Fowler, John, *1930-*. Renault 18 owners workshop manual / John Fowler. — Sparkford : Haynes, c1982. — 187p : ill(some col.) ; 28cm
Includes index
ISBN 0-85696-598-7 : £6.95 B82-33032

Renault 18 : 1978-81 autobook : Renault 1397cc, TL and GTL 1978-81, Renault 1647cc, TS, GTS and Auto 1978-81, Renault 1397cc, TL Estate 1979-81, Renault 1647cc, TS, LS, Auto Estate 1979-81 / by the Autobooks team of writers and illustrators. — Wakefield : Autobooks, 1981. — 176p : ill ; 25cm. — (The Autobook series of workshop manuals ; 987)
Includes index
ISBN 0-85146-178-6 : Unpriced B82-14411

629.28′722 — Rover 3500 cars. Maintenance & repair — *Amateurs′ manuals*

Rover 3500 1976-80 autobook / by the Autobooks team of writers and illustrators. — [3rd ed. fully rev.]. — Wakefield : Autobooks, 1980. — 184p : ill ; 25cm. — (Autobooks owners workshop manual ; 921)
Previous ed.: published as Rover 3500 SD1 1976-79 autobook, 1979. — Includes index
ISBN 0-85146-146-8 : Unpriced B82-23805

629.28′722 — Skoda Estelle cars. Maintenance & repair — *Amateurs′ manuals*

Russek, Peter. Škoda Estelle : 105S, 105L, 120L, 120LS / by Peter Russek. — Marlow : P. Russek, c1979. — 191p : ill ; 21cm. — (Pocket mechanic) (Peter Russek manuals)
′Wiring diagram for Skoda 105 and 120 series′ (1 folded sheet) as insert
ISBN 0-904509-99-0 (cased) : Unpriced
ISBN 0-904509-89-3 (pbk) : £3.30 B82-17125

629.28′722 — Talbot Avenger cars. Maintenance & repair — *Amateurs′ manuals*

Talbot Chrysler Avenger 1970-81 autobook / by the Autobooks team of writers and illustrators. — [9th ed. fully rev.]. — Wakefield : Autobooks, [1982]. — 184p : ill ; 25cm. — (Autobooks owners workshop manual ; 820)
Cover title: Talbot Avenger. — Previous ed.: published as Chrysler Hillman Avenger 1970-79 autobook, 1979. — Includes index
ISBN 0-85146-199-9 : Unpriced B82-23802

629.28'722 — Toyota Carina cars & Toyota Celica cars. Maintenance & repair — *Amateurs' manuals*

Russek, Peter. Carina B Celica / by Peter Russek. — Marlow : P. Russek, c1979. — 208p : ill,1facsim ; 20cm. — (Pocket mechanic) (Peter Russek manuals)
'Wiring diagram for Toyota Celica and Carina (except U.S.A. and Canada)' (1 folded sheet) as insert
ISBN 0-904509-92-3 (pbk) : £3.30 B82-17118

629.28'722 — Triumph Dolomite 1300 & 1500 cars. Maintenance & repair — *Amateurs' manuals*

Dolomite 1300, 1500 1976-1981 autobook : triumph dolomite 1300 1976-1981, triumph dolomite 1500 1976-1981, triumph dolomite 1500 HL 1976-1981, triumph dolomite 1500 SE 1979. — [3rd ed. fully rev.] / by the Autobooks Team of Writers and Illustrators. — Wakefield : Autobooks, [1979] ([1982 printing]). — 176p : ill ; 25cm. — (Autobooks owners workshop manual ; 907)
Previous ed.: Published as Dolomite 1300, 1500 1976-1978 autobook / by Kenneth Ball and the Autobooks Team of Technical Writers, 1978. — Includes index
ISBN 0-85146-209-x : Unpriced B82-32656

629.28'722 — Triumph Dolomite 1850 cars. Maintenance & repair — *Amateurs' manuals*

Dolomite 1850 1972-81 autobook : Triumph Dolomite 1850 1972-76, Triumph Dolomite 1850HL 1976-81 / by the Autobooks team of writers and illustrators. — 7th ed., fully rev. — Wakefield : Autobooks, 1982. — 207p : ill ; 25cm. — (Owners workshop manual ; OWM 762)
Previous ed.: 1980. — Includes index
ISBN 0-85146-216-2 : Unpriced B82-37283

629.28'722 — Triumph Dolomite cars & Triumph Dolomite Sprint cars. Maintenance & repair — *Amateurs' manuals*

Haynes, J. H.. Triumph Dolomite & Dolomite Sprint owners workshop manual : models covered : Triumph Dolomite Saloon and Saloon HL, 1854cc, Triumph Dolomite Sprint Saloon, 1998cc / by J.H. Haynes and Peter Ward. — Yeovil : Haynes, c1981. — 268p : ill (some col.) ; 28cm. — (Owners workshop manual ; 158)
Includes index
ISBN 0-85696-502-2 : £5.95 B82-05255

629.28'722 — Triumph Spitfire cars. Maintenance & repair — *Amateurs' manuals*

Triumph spitfire mk.3, 4, 1500 1969-80 autobook : triumph spitfire mk.3 1969-70, triumph spitfire mk.4 1970-75, triumph spitfire 1500 1975-1980. — [9th ed. fully rev.] / by the Autobooks Team of Writers and Illustrators. — Wakefield : Autobooks, [1980] ([1982 printing]). — 185p : ill ; 25cm. — (Autobooks owners workshop manual ; 711)
Previous ed.: 1979. — Includes index
ISBN 0-85146-138-7 : Unpriced B82-32657

629.28'722 — Vauxhall Astra cars. Maintenance & repair — *Amateurs' manuals*

Strasman, Peter G.. Vauxhall Astra owners workshop manual / Peter G. Strasman. — Yeovil : Haynes, c1982. — 228p : ill ; 28cm
Includes index
ISBN 0-85696-635-5 : £5.95 B82-15270

629.28'722 — Vauxhall Cavalier cars. Maintenance & repair — *Amateurs' manuals*

Cavalier 1975-81. — [5th ed., fully rev.] / by the Autobooks team of writers and illustrators. — Wakefield : Autobooks, [1982]. — 186p : ill ; 25cm. — (Owners workshop manual ; 884)
Previous ed.: 1980. — Includes index
ISBN 0-85146-195-6 : Unpriced B82-27876

Haynes, J. H.. Vauxhall Cavalier owners workshop manual : models covered : Vauxhall Cavalier 1600, 1900 and 2000 ; saloon coupe and sports hatch, with 1584, 1897 and 1979cc ohc engines / by J.H. Haynes and Marcus Daniels. — Yeovil : Haynes, c1981. — 214p : ill(some col.) ; 28cm
New ed. — Previous ed.: 1979. — Includes index
ISBN 0-85696-599-5 : £5.95 B82-29172

629.28'722 — Vauxhall Chevette cars. Maintenance & repair — *Amateurs' manuals*

Chevette 1975-81 autobook : Vauxhall Chevette 1975-76, Vauxhall Chevette E, L 1975-81, Vauxhall Chevette GL, GLS 1976-81. — [5th ed., fully rev.] / by the Autobooks team of writers and illustrators. — Wakefield : Autobooks, [1981]. — 144p : ill ; 25cm
Previous ed.: published as Chevette 1975-80 autobook. 1980. — Includes index
ISBN 0-85146-186-7 : Unpriced B82-06447

629.28'722 — Volkswagen Derby cars. Maintenance & repair — *Amateurs' manuals*

Russek, Peter. VW Derby to 1980 / by Peter Russek. — Marlow : P. Russek, c1978. — 194p : ill ; 21cm. — (Pocket mechanic) (Peter Russek manuals)
'Derby' (2 folded sheets) as insert
ISBN 0-904509-78-8 (cased) : Unpriced
ISBN 0-904509-79-6 (pbk) : £3.30 B82-17114

629.28'722 — Volkswagen Golf cars & Volkswagen Scirocco cars. Maintenance & repair — *Amateurs' manuals*

Russek, Peter. VW Golf, VW Scirocco to 1979 / by Peter Russek. — Marlow : P. Russek, c1979. — 216p : ill ; 20cm. — (Pocket mechanic) (Peter Russek manuals)
'Wiring diagram - VW Golf and Scirocco - after 1977' (1 folded sheet) as insert
ISBN 0-904509-97-4 (pbk) : £3.00 B82-17116

629.28'722 — Volkswagen Golf cars, Volkswagen Rabbit cars & Volkswagen Scirocco cars. Maintenance & repair — *Amateurs' manuals*

Golf, Scirocco, Rabbit 1974-82 autobook ... / by the Autobooks team of writers and illustrators. — 5th ed., fully rev. — Wakefield : Autobooks, 1982. — 232p : ill ; 25cm. — (The Autobook series of workshop manuals)
Previous ed.: 1980. — Includes index
ISBN 0-85146-204-9 : Unpriced B82-39885

629.28'73 — Ford Transit motor vans. Maintenance & repair — *Amateurs' manuals*

Coomber, Ian. Ford Transit owners workshop manual / I.M. Coomber. — Sparkford : Haynes, c1982. — 239p : ill(some col.) ; 28cm
Includes index
ISBN 0-85696-719-x : £6.55 B82-39475

Hawes, R. G. O.. Ford Transit : all petrol and diesel engine models from 1965 to 1978 (does not cover 'New Transit' models introduced 1978) : owner's handbook/servicing guide / by R.G.O. Hawes. — Yeovil : Haynes, c1980. — 127p : ill ; 24cm
Includes index
ISBN 0-85696-447-6 (pbk) : £1.95 B82-40806

629.28'73 — Mazda pick-up trucks. Maintenance & repair — *Amateurs' manuals*

Russek, Peter. Mazda B1600-1800 / by Peter Russek. — Marlow : P. Russek, c1978. — 210p : ill,1facsim ; 21cm. — (Pocket mechanic) (Peter Russek manuals)
'Mazda pick-up' (1 folded leaf) as insert
ISBN 0-904509-84-2 (cased) : Unpriced
ISBN 0-904509-74-5 (pbk) : £3.30 B82-17115

629.28'74 — Commercial vehicles. Preservation

Jenkinson, Keith A.. Preserving commercial vehicles / Keith A. Jenkinson. — Cambridge : Stephens, 1982. — 152p : ill ; 24cm
Ill on lining papers
ISBN 0-85059-502-9 : £7.95 : CIP rev.
B81-35838

629.28'772 — Bicycles & mopeds. Maintenance & repair — *Amateurs' manuals*

The **Maintenance** of bicycles and mopeds. — London : Readers Digest Association, 1975 (1981 [printing]). — 40p : col.ill ; 27cm. — (Reader's Digest basic guide)
'Text and illustrations in this book are taken from Reader's Digest repair manual', 1972
ISBN 0-276-00087-0 (pbk) : £1.25 B82-04171

629.28'772 — Yamaha Passola mopeds. Maintenance & repair — *Amateurs' manuals*

Shoemark, Pete. Yamaha Passola owners workshop manual : models covered SA50M Passola. 49.9cc introduced May 1980 / by Pete Shoemark. — Yeovil : Haynes, c1981. — 112p : ill(some col.) ; 27cm + 1sheet (54x41cm folded to 27x21cm)
Includes index
ISBN 0-85696-733-5 (pbk) : Unpriced
B82-19415

629.28'775 — Honda CB250RS motorcycles. Maintenance & repair — *Amateurs' manuals*

Shoemark, Pete. Honda CB250RS owners workshop manual : models covered CB250RS introduced UK 1980 / by Pete Shoemark. — Yeovil : Haynes, c1981. — 144p : ill(some col.) ; 27cm. — (Owners workshop manual)
'Routine maintenance guide' (1 folded sheet) as insert. — Includes index
ISBN 0-85696-732-7 (pbk) : £4.50 B82-09481

629.28'775 — Honda CD185/200 & CM185/200 motorcycles. Maintenance & repair — *Amateurs' manuals*

Meek, Martyn. Honda CD185/200 and CM185/200 owners workshop manual / Martyn Meek. — Yeovil : Haynes, c1981. — 148p : ill(some col.) ; 27cm + 1sheet(54x40cm folded to 27x20cm)
Includes index
ISBN 0-85696-572-3 (pbk) : £2.95 B82-05525

629.28'775 — Honda Gold Wing GL1100 motorcycles. Maintenance & repair — *Amateurs' manuals*

Rogers, Chris. Honda GL1100 Gold Wing owners workshop manual / by Chris Rogers. — Yeovil : Haynes, c1981. — 180p : ill(some col.) ; 27cm
Includes index
ISBN 0-85696-669-x (pbk) : £4.50 B82-08636

629.28'775 — Honda XL/XR 250 & 500 motorcycles. Maintenance & repair — *Amateurs' manuals*

Shoemark, Peter. Honda XL/XR 250 & 500 owners workshop manual / by Peter Shoemark. — Yeovil : Haynes, c1981. — 148p : ill(some col.) ; 27cm + 1sheet(54x40cm folded to 27x20cm)
Includes index
ISBN 0-85696-567-7 (pbk) : £2.95 B82-05526

629.28'775 — Laverda 650, 750, 1000 & 1200 motorcycles. Maintenance & repair — *Amateurs' manuals*

Parker, Tim. Laverda twin & triple repair & tune-up guide : (incorporating the 650/750 twins and the 1000/1200 triples) / Tim Parker. — Ware : Ampersand, 1979. — 175p : ill ; 27cm
ISBN 0-906613-00-0 (pbk) : Unpriced : CIP rev. B79-14797

629.28'775 — Motorcycles. Maintenance & repair — *Amateurs' manuals*

The **Complete** motorcycle workshop / consultant editor David Buxton. — London : Enigma, 1981. — 217p : col.ill ; 31cm
Includes index
ISBN 0-85685-940-0 : Unpriced B82-06104

629.28'775 — Motorcycles. Maintenance & repair — *Manuals*

Crouse, William H.. Motorcycle mechanics / William H. Crouse, Donald L. Anglin. — New York ; London : Gregg Division, McGraw-Hill, c1982. — viii,360p : ill ; 28cm
Includes index
ISBN 0-07-014781-7 (pbk) : £12.25
B82-25221

629.28'775 — Suzuki GP100 & 125 motorcycles. Maintenance & repair — *Amateurs' manuals*

Rogers, Chris. Suzuki GP 100 & 125 owners workshop manual / by Chris Rogers. — Yeovil : Haynes, c1982. — 167p : ill ; 27cm
One folded sheet (checklist) as insert. — Includes index
ISBN 0-85696-576-6 (pbk) : £4.50 B82-35836

629.28′775 — Suzuki GS 250, GS 400, GSX 250 & GSX 400 motorcycles. Maintenance & repair — *Amateurs′ manuals*
Rogers, Chris. Suzuki GS & GSX 250 and 400 Twins owners workshop manual / by Chris Rogers. — Yeovil : Haynes, c1982. — 192p : ill(some col.) ; 27cm + 1 sheet(ill ; 54x40cm folded to 27x20cm)
Includes index
ISBN 0-85696-736-x (pbk) : Unpriced
B82-27439

629.28′775 — Suzuki trail motorcycles. Maintenance & repair — *Amateurs′ manuals*
Darlington, Mansur. Suzuki trail bikes : owners workshop manual / Mansur Darlington. — Yeovil : Haynes, c1979. — 176p : ill(some col.) ; 27cm
Originally published: 1975. — Includes index
ISBN 0-85696-520-0 (pbk) : Unpriced
B82-24531

629.28′775 — Yamaha 250 & 350 twin cylinder motorcycles. Maintenance & repair — *Amateurs′ manuals*
Shoemark, Pete. Yamaha RD250 & 350 LC owners workshop manual / by Pete Shoemark. — Yeovil : Haynes, c1982. — 176p : ill(some col.) ; 27cm + routine maintenance guide sheet(ill; 53x41cm folded to 27x21cm)
Includes index. — 'Models covered RD250 LC.247cc. Introduced May 1980. RD350 LC. 347cc. Introduced June 1980'
ISBN 0-85696-803-x (pbk) : Unpriced
B82-37953

629.3 — HOVERCRAFT

629.3 — Light hovercraft. Design & construction
Light hovercraft handbook. — Re-written and up-dated. — [Cranfield] ([c/o Information Officer, 5 Lordsmead, Cranfield, Bedford MK43 3HP]) : Hover Club of Great Britain, 1976 (1982 [printing]). — 92p : ill ; 22cm
Previous ed.: i.e. repr. and extended. 1975
Unpriced (pbk) B82-27470

629.4 — ASTRONAUTICS

629.4 — Astronautics — *Conference proceedings*
International Astronautical Congress *(32nd : 1981 : Rome)*. Space : mankind′s fourth environment : selected papers from the XXXII International Astronautical Congress, Rome, 6-12 September 1981 / edited by L.G. Napolitano. — Oxford : Pergamon, 1982. — viii,558p : ill,maps ; 26cm
Includes bibliographies
ISBN 0-08-028708-5 : £45.00 : CIP rev.
B82-01702

629.4′1′0947 — Soviet space flight, *to 1980*
Oberg, James E.. Red star in orbit / James E. Oberg. — London : Harrap, 1981. — 272p,[16]p of plates : ill,ports ; 23cm
Originally published: New York : Random House, 1981. — Bibliography: p256-259. — Includes index
ISBN 0-245-53809-7 : £7.95 B82-01816

629.43′54′09 — Outer space. Unmanned space flight, *to 1978*
Powers, Robert M.. Planetary encounters / Robert M. Powers. — London : Sidgwick & Jackson, 1982, c1979. — 368p : ill,3ports ; 21cm
Originally published: Harrisburg : Stackpole, 1978. — Bibliography: p357-359. — Includes index
ISBN 0-283-98764-2 : £8.50 B82-19469

629.44′1 — Space shuttles — *For children*
Furniss, Tim. The story of the space shuttle / Tim Furniss. — 2nd rev. ed. — London : Hodder and Stoughton, 1982. — 105p : ill (some col.),ports(some col.) ; 25cm
Previous ed.: 1979
ISBN 0-340-27967-2 (pbk) : Unpriced : CIP rev.
ISBN 0-340-28216-9 (pbk) : £3.95 B81-36369

629.45′009 — Manned space flight, *to 1981*
Baker, David, *1944-*. The history of manned space flight / David Baker. — London : New Cavendish, c1981. — 544p : ill(some col.),maps,ports(some col.) ; 35cm
Includes index
ISBN 0-904568-30-x : Unpriced B82-17561

Bedford, Ronald. The shuttle story : countdown to the age of the space train — / by Ronald Bedford. — London : Mirror Books, 1981. — [28]p : ill,maps,ports ; 36cm. — (A Daily mirror space special)
At head of title: Space Mirror
ISBN 0-85939-294-5 (unbound) : £0.50
B82-03022

629.47 — Artificial satellites. Observation — *Amateurs′ manuals*
King-Hele, Desmond. Observing earth satellites. — London : Macmillan, June 1982. — [176]p
ISBN 0-333-33041-2 : £7.95 : CIP entry
B82-10001

629.47 — Artificial satellites — *Tables*
The **RAE** table of earth satellites, 1957-1980 / compiled by D.G. King-Hele ... [et al.]. — London : Macmillan, 1981. — xvi,656p : ill ; 31cm. — (Macmillan reference books)
Includes index
ISBN 0-333-32234-7 : £30.00 B82-00574

629.47′42 — Space vehicles. Attitude. Control — *Conference proceedings*
Spacecraft attitude determination and control / edited by James R. Wertz ; written by members of the technical staff Attitude Systems Operation, Computer Sciences Corporation ... — Dordrecht ; London : Reidel, c1980, c1978. — xvi,858p : ill,charts ; 25cm. — (Astrophysics and space science library ; v.73)
Includes index
ISBN 90-277-0959-9 (cased) : Unpriced
ISBN 90-277-1204-2 (pbk) : Unpriced
B82-39096

629.47′5 — Aerospace vehicles: Rockets — *For children*
Guston, Bill. Rockets and missiles. — London : Granada, Apr.1982. — [64]p. — (Granada guide series ; 12)
ISBN 0-246-11639-0 : £1.95 : CIP entry
B82-05386

629.8 — AUTOMATIC CONTROL SYSTEMS

629.8 — Automatic control systems
Bretschi, Jürgen. Automatic inspection systems for industry. — Kempston (35 High St., Kempston, Bedford MK42 7BT) : IFS Publications, Dec.1981. — [230]p
Translation of: Intelligente Messsysteme zur Automatisierung technischer Prozesse
ISBN 0-903608-20-0 (pbk) : £23.00 : CIP entry
B81-32055

Kuo, Benjamin C.. Automatic control systems / Benjamin C. Kuo. — 4th ed. — Englewood Cliffs ; London : Prentice-Hall, c1982. — xi,721p : ill ; 25cm
Previous ed.: 1975. — Includes index
ISBN 0-13-054817-0 : Unpriced B82-20162

Morris, Noel M.. Control engineering. — 3rd ed. — London : McGraw-Hill, Feb.1983. — [256]p
Previous ed.: 1974
ISBN 0-07-084666-9 (pbk) : £6.95 : CIP entry
B82-36433

Ramsay, D. C.. Engineering instrumentation and control / D.C. Ramsay. — Cheltenham : Stanley Thornes, 1981. — 262p : ill ; 24cm. — (ST(P) Technology today)
Includes index
ISBN 0-85950-439-5 (pbk) : £4.75
Primary classification 620′.0044 B82-01263

Sutton, H. B.. Engineering instrumentation and control 4 checkbook / H.B. Sutton. — London : Butterworth Scientific, 1982. — viii,191p : ill ; 20cm. — (Butterworths technical and scientific checkbooks)
Includes index
ISBN 0-408-00680-3 (cased) : £8.95 : CIP rev.
ISBN 0-408-00617-x (pbk)
Primary classification 620′.0044 B82-10483

629.8 — Automatic control systems — *Conference proceedings*
International Federation of Automatic Control. *Triennial World Congress (8th : 1981 : Kyoto)*. Control science & technology for the progress of society. — Oxford : Pergamon, Apr.1982. — 7v.. — (IFAC proceedings series)
ISBN 0-08-027580-x : £375.00 : CIP entry
B82-03731

629.8 — Control systems — *For technicians*
Haslam, J. A.. Engineering instrumentation and control / J.A. Haslam, G.R. Summers, D. Williams. — London : Edward Arnold, 1981. — ix,310p : ill ; 22cm
Bibliography: p303. — Includes index
ISBN 0-7131-3431-3 (pbk) : £6.50 : CIP rev.
Primary classification 620′.0044 B81-27979

629.8 — Multipass systems
Edwards, J. B.. Analysis and control of multipass processes / J.B. Edwards and D.H. Owens. — Chichester : Research Studies Press, c1982. — xix,298p : ill ; 24cm. — (Electronic & electrical engineering research studies. Control theory and applications studies series ; 2)
Bibliography: p285-289. — Includes index
ISBN 0-471-10163-x : Unpriced : CIP rev.
B82-01107

629.8′3 — Digital control systems
Katz, Paul, *1934-*. Digital control using microprocessors / Paul Katz. — Englewood Cliffs ; London : Prentice-Hall, c1981. — ix,293p : ill ; 24cm
Bibliography: p286-288. — Includes index
ISBN 0-13-212191-3 : £16.95 : CIP rev.
B81-14384

629.8′3 — Feedback systems
Ashworth, M. J.. Feedback design of systems with significant uncertainty / M.J. Ashworth. — Chichester : Research Studies Press, c1982. — xvi,246p : ill ; 24cm. — (Mechanical engineering research studies) (Engineering dynamics and control monograph series ; 1)
Includes index
ISBN 0-471-10213-x : £15.50 : CIP rev.
B82-06507

629.8′312 — Automatic control systems. Identification & parameter estimation — *Conference proceedings*
Identification and system parameter estimation : proceedings of the fifth IFAC symposium, Darmstadt, Federal Republic of Germany, 24-28 September 1979 / edited by R. Isermann. — Oxford : Published for the International Federation of Automatic Control by Pergamon, 1980. — 2v.(xxix,1347p) : ill ; 31cm
Includes bibliographies and index
ISBN 0-08-024451-3 : £87.00 : CIP rev.
B80-06968

629.8′312 — Automatic control systems. Mathematical models. System identification — *Conference proceedings*
IFAC Symposium on Identification and System Parameter Estimation *(6th : 1982 : Washington, D.C.)*. Identification and system parameter estimation. — Oxford : Pergamon. — (IFAC proceedings series)
Vol.1. — Feb.1983. — [1700]p
ISBN 0-08-029344-1 : £212.50 : CIP entry
B82-40886

629.8′312 — Control systems. Design
Design of modern control systems / editors D.J. Bell, P.A. Cook, N. Munro. — Stevenage : Peregrinus on behalf of the Institution of Electrical Engineers, 1982. — 332p : ill ; 23cm. — (IEE control engineering series ; 20)
Includes index
ISBN 0-906048-74-5 (pbk) : Unpriced : CIP rev.
B82-07834

629.8′312 — Control systems. Mathematics
Systems modelling and optimization / edited by Peter Nash. — Stevenage : Peregrinus on behalf of the Institution of Electrical Engineers, c1981. — xii,201p : ill ; 23cm. — (IEE control engineering series ; 16)
Bibliography: p197-198. — Includes index
ISBN 0-906048-63-x (pbk) : Unpriced : CIP rev.
B81-27474

629.8'312 — Control theory

Leigh, J. R.. Applied control theory / J.R. Leigh. — Stevenage : Peregrinus on behalf of the Institution of Electrical Engineers, c1982. — x,163p : ill ; 24cm. — (IEE control engineering series ; 18)
Bibliography: p156-160. — Includes index
ISBN 0-906048-72-9 : Unpriced : CIP rev.
B82-07131

629.8'312 — Control theory. Applications of Laplace transforms

Bogart, Theodore F.. Laplace transforms and control systems theory for technology : including microprocessor-based control systems / Theodore F. Bogart, Jr.. — New York ; Chichester : Wiley, c1982. — xiv,541p : ill ; 24cm. — (Electronic technology series)
Includes index
ISBN 0-471-09044-1 : £15.35 B82-28079

629.8'312 — Control theory — *Conference proceedings*

IMA Conference on Control Theory *(3rd : 1980 : University of Sheffield)*. Third IMA Conference on Control Theory : based on the proceedings of a conference on control theory / organised by the Institute of Mathematics and its Applications and held at the University of Sheffield 9-11 September, 1980 ; edited by J.E. Marshall ... [et al.]. — London : Academic Press, 1981. — xi,922p : ill ; 24cm. — (The Institute of Mathematics and its Applications conference series)
Includes bibliographies and index
ISBN 0-12-473960-1 : £42.00 : CIP rev.
B81-34409

629.8'312 — Feedback systems. Design

Hostetter, Gene H.. Design of feedback control systems / Gene H. Hostetter, Clement J. Savant, Jr., Raymond T. Stefani. — New York ; London : Holt, Rinehart and Winston, c1982. — xvi,541p : ill ; 24cm. — (HRW series in electrical and computer engineering)
Includes index
ISBN 0-03-057593-1 : £23.95
ISBN 4-8337-0010-7 (International Edition) : £8.50 B82-23122

629.8'312 — Multivariable systems

Patel, Rajnikant V.. Multivariable system theory and design / by Rajnikant v. Patel and Neil Munro. — Oxford : Pergamon, 1982. — xii,374p : ill ; 24cm. — (International series on systems and control ; v.4) (Pergamon international library)
Includes index
ISBN 0-08-027297-5 (cased) : Unpriced : CIP rev.
ISBN 0-08-027298-3 (pbk) : £9.50 B81-32038

629.8'312 — Multivariable systems & optimal systems

Owens, D. H.. Multivariable and optimal systems / D.H. Owens. — London : Academic, 1981. — ix,300p : ill ; 24cm
Bibliography: p292-296. — Includes index
ISBN 0-12-531720-4 (cased) : £22.80 : CIP rev.
ISBN 0-12-531722-0 (pbk) : £8.00 B81-31345

629.8'312 — Multivariable systems — *Conference proceedings*

Multivariable technological systems : proceedings of the Symposium / organised by the Institute of Measurement and Control ; under the aegis of UKAC on behalf of the International Federation of Automatic Control, 16-19 September, 1974, University of Manchester, U.K.. — London (20 Peel St., W.8.) : The Institute, c1975. — 500p in various pagings : ill ; 30cm
Unpriced (pbk) B82-37308

629.8'312 — Optimal control theory

Kalaba, Robert. Control, identification, and input optimization / Robert Kalaba and Karl Spingarn. — New York ; London : Plenum, c1982. — xi,431p ; 24cm. — (Mathematical concepts and methods in science and engineering)
Includes bibliographies and index
ISBN 0-306-40847-3 : Unpriced B82-30269

Knowles, Greg. An introduction to applied optimal control / Greg Knowles. — New York ; London : Academic Press, 1981. — x,180p : ill ; 24cm. — (Mathematics in science and engineering ; v.159)
Includes index
ISBN 0-12-416960-0 : Unpriced B82-27994

Ryan, E. P.. Optimal relay and saturating control system synthesis / E.P. Ryan. — Stevenage : Peregrinus on behalf of the Institution of Electrical Engineers, c1982. — x,340p : ill ; 24cm. — (IEE control engineering series ; 14)
Includes index
ISBN 0-906048-56-7 : Unpriced : CIP rev.
B81-20496

629.8'312 — Stochastic control theory. Applications of functional analysis

Bensoussan, Alain. Stochastic control by functional analysis methods / Alain Bensoussan. — Amsterdam ; Oxford : North Holland, 1982. — xv,410p ; 23cm. — (Studies in mathematics and its applications ; v.11)
Bibliography: p399-410
ISBN 0-444-86329-x : Unpriced B82-25696

629.8'312 — Stochastic control theory. Applications of variational inequalities

Bensoussan, Alain. Applications of variational inequalities in stochastic control / Alain Bensoussan, Jacques-Louis Lions. — Amsterdam ; Oxford : North Holland, 1982. — xi,564p ; 23cm. — (Studies in mathematics and its applications ; v.12)
Translation of: Applications des inéquations variationnelles en contrôle stochastique. — Bibliography: p559-564
ISBN 0-444-86358-3 : Unpriced B82-25697

629.8'312'03 — Control theory — *Polyglot dictionaries*

Multilingual glossary of automatic control technology : English - French - German - Russian - Italian - Spanish - Japanese / editors David T. Broadbent ... [et al.]. — Oxford : Published for the International Federation of Automatic Control by Pergamon, 1981. — 208p in various pagings ; 26cm
Includes index
ISBN 0-08-027607-5 : £22.50 : CIP rev.
B81-21593

629.8'32 — Discrete linear control systems. Algebra. Polynomials

Blomberg, H.. Algebraic theory for multivariable linear systems. — London : Academic Press, Dec.1982. — [380]p. — (Mathematics in science and engineering)
ISBN 0-12-107150-2 : CIP entry B82-29873

629.8'32 — Discrete linear control systems. States. Analysis. State space methods

Strejc, Vladimír. State space theory of discrete linear control / Vladimír Strejc. — Chichester : Wiley, c1981. — 426p : ill ; 25cm
Translated from the Czech. — Bibliography: p407-421. — Includes index
ISBN 0-471-27594-8 : £17.25 B82-03750

629.8'36 — Adaptive control systems

International Workshop on Applications of Adaptive Control *(1979 : Yale University)*. Applications of adaptive control / [papers included in this book were presented at the International Workshop on Applications of Adaptive Control held at Yale University, August 23-25, 1979] ; edited by Kumpati S. Narendra, Richard V. Monopoli. — New York ; London : Academic Press, 1980. — xiii,554p : ill ; 24cm
ISBN 0-12-514060-6 : £22.20 B82-40723

Self-tuning and adaptive control : theory and applications / edited by C.J. Harris and S.A. Billings. — Stevenage : Peregrinus on behalf of the Institution of Electrical Engineers, c1981. — xv,333p : ill ; 23cm. — (IEE control engineering series ; 15)
Includes index
ISBN 0-906048-62-1 (pbk) : Unpriced : CIP rev.
B81-27475

629.8'36 — Nonlinear control systems

Atherton, Derek P.. Nonlinear control engineering / by Derek P. Atherton. — Student ed. — London : Van Nostrand Reinhold, 1982, c1975. — xvii,470p : ill ; 24cm
Previous ed.: 1975. — Includes bibliographies and index
ISBN 0-442-30486-2 (pbk) : £8.95 B82-30347

629.8'92 — Industrial robots

Great Britain. *Department of Industry*. Robots : government support for industrial robots / Department of Industry. — London (Room 420, 123 Victoria St., SW1E 6RB) : Department of Industry, Mechanical and Electrical Engineering Division, [1982?]. — [8]p : col.ill ; 30cm. — (It)
Cover title. — Text on inside cover
Unpriced (pbk) B82-40104

Warnecke, H.-J.. Industrial robots : application experience. — Bedford (35-39 High St., Kempston, Bedford MK42 7BT) : IFS Publications, Apr.1982. — [300]p
Translation of: Industrieroboter
ISBN 0-903608-21-9 (pbk) : £24.00 : CIP entry
B82-06266

629.8'92 — Industrial robots — *Conference proceedings*

Colloquium on Robotics *(1978)*. Colloquium on Robotics, 30-31 March 1978. — Glasgow : National Engineering Laboratory, c1978. — 115p in various pagings : ill ; 30cm
Unpriced (spiral) B82-05797

629.8'92 — Industrial robots. Manipulators. Control. Applications of digital computer systems

Paul, Richard P.. Robot manipulators : mathematics, programming, and control : the computer control of robot manipulators / Richard P. Paul. — Cambridge, Mass. ; London : MIT, c1981. — 279p : ill ; 24cm. — (The MIT Press series in artificial intelligence)
Includes bibliographies and index
ISBN 0-262-16082-x : £17.50 B82-21012

629.8'92 — Industrial robots. Visual perception units — *Conference proceedings*

International Conference on Robot Vision and Sensory Controls *(1st : 1981 : Stratford-upon-Avon)*. Proceedings of the 1st International Conference on Robot Vision and Sensory Controls, April 1-3, 1981. Stratford-upon-Avon, UK : an international event sponsored and organised by IFS (Conferences) Ltd. — Kempston : IFS, c1981. — iv,347p : ill ; 30cm
ISBN 0-903608-15-4 (pbk) : Unpriced
B82-40535

629.8'92 — Robots

Henson, Hilary. Robots. — London (Elsley Court, 20 Great Titchfield St., W1P 7AD) : Kingfisher, Sept.1981. — [80]p
ISBN 0-86272-003-6 : £3.95 : CIP entry
B81-20165

629.8'92 — Robots — *For children*

Kerrod, Robin. Robots. — London : Granada, Aug.1982. — [64]p. — (Granada guide series ; 22)
ISBN 0-246-11893-8 : £1.95 : CIP entry
B82-15710

629.8'95 — Automatic control. Applications of digital computer systems — *Conference proceedings*

Theory & application of digital control. — Oxford : Pergamon, July 1982. — [670]p. — (IFAC proceedings)
ISBN 0-08-027618-0 : £75.00 : CIP entry
B82-14222

629.8'95 — Automatic control. Applications of microprocessors

Thompson, J. F. A.. Microprocessors and control. — London : Longman, Nov.1982. — [176]p. — (Longman technician series. Mathematics and sciences)
ISBN 0-582-41260-9 (pbk) : £4.95 : CIP entry
B82-26534

629.8′95 — Automatic control systems. Applications of microprocessors — *Conference proceedings*
Application of Microprocessors in Devices for Instrumentation and Automatic Control *(Conference : 1980 : London).* Application of micoprocessors in devices for instrumentation and automatic control : [collected papers from a symposium, 'Application of Micoprocessors in Devices for Instrumentation and Automatic Control', in London, 18-20 November 1980] / [The Institute of Measurement and Control ... organised the symposium]. — [London] : [The Institute], c1980. — 404p : ill ; 30cm
Unpriced (pbk)
Primary classification 620′.0044 B82-09380

629.8′95 — Distributed digital control systems — *Conference proceedings*
Distributed computer control systems — III. — Oxford : Pergamon, May 1982. — [176]p. — (IFAC proceedings series)
Conference papers
ISBN 0-08-028672-0 : £25.00 : CIP entry B82-09186

629.8′95 — On-line digital control systems — *Conference proceedings*
International Conference on Trends in On-Line Computer Control Systems *(4th : 1982 : University of Warwick).* Fourth International Conference on Trends in On-Line Computer Control Systems : 5-8 April 1982 / organised by the Computing and Control Division of the Institution of Electrical Engineers in association with the British Computer Society ... [et al.] ; venue University of Warwick, UK. — London : Institution of Electrical Engineers, c1982. — vi,124p : ill,1map ; 30cm. — (IEE conference publication ; no.208)
Cover title: Trends in on-line computer control systems
ISBN 0-85296-256-8 (pbk) : Unpriced B82-27686

629.8′95 — Programmable automatic control systems — *Conference proceedings*
New frontiers in PC systems : international conference at Mount Royal Hotel, London, 19th & 20th November 1981. — [London] ([2 Serjeant's Inn, Fleet Street, London EC4]) : Automation & Engineers' Digest, [1982]. — [160]p : ill ; 30cm. — (Automation technical conferences)
Unpriced (spiral) B82-13458

629.8′95′0289 — Automatic control systems. Applications of computer systems. Safety aspects — *Conference proceedings*
Safety of computer control systems : proceedings of the IFAC workshop, Stuttgart, Federal Republic of Germany, 16-18 May 1979 / edited by R. Lauber. — Oxford : Published for the International Federation of Automatic Control by Pergamon, 1980. — ix,219p : ill ; 31cm
Includes index
ISBN 0-08-024453-x : £25.00 : CIP rev. B80-05444

630 — AGRICULTURE

630 — Agriculture — *For children*
Hollyer, Belinda. Farms and farming / Belinda Hollyer ; [editor John Morton] ; [illustrators Rudolph Britto, Edward Carr, David Gifford]. — London : Macdonald Educational, 1982. — 45p : ill(some col.),1col.map ; 25cm. — (Macdonald new reference library)
Bibliography: p44. — Includes index
ISBN 0-356-05829-8 : £2.95 B82-35489

630 — England. Agriculture. Organic methods
Vine, Anne. Organic farming systems in England and Wales : practice, performance and implications / by Anne Vine and David Bateman. — Aberystwyth : Department of Agricultural Economics, University College of Wales, 1981. — 210p : ill ; 21cm
Bibliography: p209-210
£5.00 (pbk) B82-22443

630 — Europe. Food. Production. Effects of climatic change — *Conference proceedings*
Climatic change and European agriculture : seminar 1977 / edited by S.W. Burrage, M.K.V. Carr. — Ashford, Kent : Wye College, c1981. — iii,118p : ill ; 30cm. — (Seminar papers, ISSN 0307-1111 ; no.12)
Includes bibliographies
ISBN 0-905378-39-3 (pbk) : £8.50 B82-09800

630 — Food. Production. Effects of climate — *Conference proceedings*
Food-climate interactions : proceedings of an International Workshop held in Berlin (West), December 9-12, 1980 / edited by Wilfrid Bach, Jürgen Pankrath and Stephen H. Schneider. — Dordrecht ; London : Reidel, c1981. — xxxi,504p : ill,charts,maps ; 25cm
Includes index
ISBN 90-277-1353-7 (cased) : Unpriced
ISBN 90-277-1354-5 (pbk) : Unpriced B82-11233

Food, nutrition and climate / [International Symposium organised by the Rank Prize Funds and held at the Dormy Hotel, Ferndown, Dorset, U.K., on 5-9 April, 1981] ; edited by Sir Kenneth Blaxter and Leslie Fowden. — London : Applied Science, c1982. — ix,422p : ill,maps ; 23cm
Includes bibliographies and index
ISBN 0-85334-107-9 : £36.00 : CIP rev. B82-01412

630 — Food. Production — *Encyclopaedias*
Food and food production encyclopedia / Douglas M. Considine editor-in-chief, Glenn D. Considine, managing editor. — New York ; London : Van Nostrand Reinhold, c1982. — xvi,2305p,[6]p of plates : ill(some col.),maps ; 29cm
Includes bibliographies and index
ISBN 0-442-21612-2 : £165.00 B82-35486

630 — Food. Production — *Manuals*
Robinson, R. K.. The vanishing harvest. — Oxford : Oxford University Press, Jan.1983. — [300]p
ISBN 0-19-854713-7 : £15.00 : CIP entry B82-33483

630 — Great Britain. Agricultural industries. Smallholdings — *Manuals*
Seymour, John, *1914-*. The lore of the land / John Seymour ; with illustrations by Sally Seymour. — Weybridge : Whittet, 1982. — 159p : ill ; 26cm
Includes index
ISBN 0-905483-23-5 : £8.50 : CIP rev. B82-05777

630 — Ireland *(Republic).* **Agricultural industries. Energy. Conservation** — *Manuals*
Farmers : hints to save fuel and your money / ACOT. — [Blackrock] ([Frascati Rd., Blackrock, Co. Dublin]) : [ACOT], [1981?]. — [8]p : col.ill,1map ; 21cm
Unpriced (unbound) B82-05190

630′.2′0122 — Cornwall. St Agnes. Agricultural industries. Farms: Jennings Farm, *1976-1980* — *Illustrations*
Inglis, Nigel. Nigel Inglis : photographs : Jennings farm 1976-1980. — [Penzance] : Newlyn Orion, Newlyn Art Gallery, [1980?]. — [4]leaves : ill ; 30cm
Produced to accompany a touring exhibition
Unpriced (unbound) B82-05836

630′.2′0341 — Great Britain. Agriculture — *Career guides*
Careers in agriculture. — [Beckenham] : Agricultural Training Board on behalf of the Joint Working Party on Careers Literature, 1981. — [8]p : ill ; 21cm
Unpriced (unbound) B82-19775

Mister, Alan A.. Working on a farm / Alan A. Mister. — London : Batsford Academic and Educational, 1982. — 105p,[8]p of plates : ill ; 23cm
Includes index
ISBN 0-7134-3962-9 : £5.95 : CIP rev. B82-01214

Work on the land. — [Beckenham] : Agricultural Training Board, [198-?]. — 7p ; 21cm
Unpriced (unbound) B82-19772

630′.274 — Agriculture. Efficiency. Biological aspects
Spedding, C. R. W.. Biological efficiency in agriculture / C.R.W. Spedding, J.M. Walsingham, and A.M. Hoxey. — London : Academic Press, 1981. — x,383p : ill ; 24cm
Includes bibliographies and index
ISBN 0-12-656560-0 : £18.40 : CIP rev. B81-06044

630′.2′76 — Agricultural microbiology
Advances in agricultural microbiology. — London : Butterworths, Oct.1982. — [726]p
ISBN 0-408-10848-7 : £40.00 : CIP entry B82-25188

630′.2′76 — Fermented food. Production. Microbiological aspects
Fermented foods. — London : Academic Press, June 1982. — [370]p. — (Economic microbiology ; v.7)
ISBN 0-12-596557-5 : CIP entry B82-12131

630′.5 — Agriculture — *Serials*
Advances in applied biology. — Vol.6-. — London : Academic Press, 1981-. — v. : ill,maps ; 24cm
Continues: Applied biology
Unpriced B82-07634

Advances in applied biology. — Vol.7. — London : Academic Press, Nov.1982. — [438]p
ISBN 0-12-040907-0 : CIP entry
ISSN 0309-1791 B82-26859

630′.6′042 — England. Agriculture. Organisations: National Federation of Young Farmers' Clubs — *Serials*
The **New** young farmer : the official magazine of the National Federation of Young Farmers' Clubs. — Vol.1, no.1 (Apr. 1982)-. — Kenilworth (YFC Centre, National Agricultural Centre, Kenilworth, Warwickshire, CV8 2LG) : The Federation, 1982-. — ill,ports ; 30cm
Continues: National news (National Federation of Young Farmers' Clubs)
ISSN 0263-6921 = New young farmer : Unpriced B82-30484

630′.6′042 — England. Agriculture. Organisations: National Federation of Young Farmers' Clubs, *to 1980*
Fifty years young. — Kenilworth : National Federation of Young Farmers' Clubs, 1982. — 99p : ill,facsims,ports ; 21x15cm
ISBN 0-906863-01-5 (pbk) : Unpriced B82-31746

Shields, Tanner. Youthful forward thinking : young farmers clubs of England and Wales : their past, present and future / by Tanner Shields. — 2nd ed. — [Kenilworth] : National Federation of Young Farmers' Clubs, [198-?]. — iv,51p : ill,ports ; 21cm
ISBN 0-906863-00-7 (pbk) : Unpriced B82-26358

630′.68 — Agricultural industries. Management
Dalton, G. E.. Managing agricultural systems. — London : Applied Science, Nov.1982. — [160]p
ISBN 0-85334-165-6 : £19.00 : CIP entry B82-26318

630′.68 — Agricultural industries. Management — *Serials*
Research in domestic and international agribusiness management : a research annual. — Vol.1 (1980)-. — Greenwich, Conn. : JAI Press ; London (3 Henrietta St., WC2E 8LU) : Distributed by JAICON Press, 1980-. — v. ; 24cm
£22.85 B82-02356

630′.68 — Great Britain. Agricultural industries. Farms. Management. Applications of digital computer systems
Jarrett, Dennis. Business systems handbook for farmers. — London (55 Charterhouse St., EC1M 6HD) : New Technology Press, Sept.1982. — [150]p
ISBN 0-86330-205-x (pbk) : £12.50 : CIP entry B82-28605

630'.68 — Great Britain. Agricultural industries. Farms. Management — *Manuals*

An introduction to farm business management / Ministry of Agriculture, Fisheries and Food. — London : H.M.S.O., 1980. — 137p : ill,forms ; 25cm. — (Reference book ; 381)
ISBN 0-11-241177-0 (pbk) : £6.50 B82-15567

Nix, John. Farm management pocketbook / by John Nix with Paul Hill. — 12th ed. — Ashford : Wye College (University of London), School of Rural Economics, Farm Business Unit, 1981. — viii,160 ; 22cm
Previous ed.: 1980. — Includes index
ISBN 0-901859-95-8 (pbk) : £2.90 B82-00964

630'.68'1 — Great Britain. Agricultural industries. Farms. Financial management

Sturrock, F. G.. Farm accounting and management / Ford Sturrock. — 7th ed. — London : Pitman, 1982. — xii,300p : ill,plans ; 23cm
Previous ed.: 1971. — Includes index
ISBN 0-273-01788-8 (cased) : Unpriced : CIP rev.
ISBN 0-273-01765-9 (pbk) : Unpriced
B82-04323

630'.68'1 — Tropical regions. Agricultural industries. Financial management

Coy, David V.. Accounting and finance for managers in tropical agriculture. — London : Longman, Aug.1982. — [132]p. — (Intermediate tropical agriculture series)
ISBN 0-582-77502-7 (pbk) : £2.95 : CIP entry
B82-14942

630'.68'4 — Agricultural industries. Project management. Teaching aids — *Case studies*

Potts, D. J.. The tomato concentrate project : a teaching case study in the planning and appraisal of an agro-industrial project / by D.J. Potts and R.L. Kitchen ; produced by the Teaching Materials Development Group, Project Planning Centre for Developing Countries, University of Bradford. — [Bradford] : The Centre, 1981. — 1portfolio : ill,forms ; 34cm. — (Teaching materials series, ISSN 0262-5164 ; no.2)
ISBN 0-901945-43-9 : Unpriced B82-23564

630'.68'8 — Great Britain. Agricultural products. Marketing

A Directors' guide to practical marketing. — [London] ([Market Towers, New Covent Garden Market SW8 5NQ]) : CCAHC, [1982]. — 48p : ill,1map ; 21cm
Cover title
Unpriced (pbk) B82-34561

630'.7 — Agriculture. Information sources

Guide to sources for agricultural and biological research / edited by J. Richard Blanchard and Lois Farrell ; sponsored by the United States National Agricultural Library United States Department of Agriculture, Beltsville, Maryland. — Berkeley, [Calif.] ; London : University of California Press, c1981. — xi,735p ; 29cm
Includes index
ISBN 0-520-03226-8 : Unpriced
Also classified at 574'.07 B82-28301

630'.7'0417 — Ireland *(Republic).* **Education. Curriculum subjects: Agriculture**

General guide to agricultural education. — Blackrock (Frascati Rd., Blackrock, Co. Dublin) : ACOT, [1981?]. — 12p : ill ; 22cm
Cover title. — Text on inside cover
Unpriced (pbk) B82-01595

630'.7'1 — Great Britain. Agricultural industries. Apprentices. Training — *Manuals*

Giving instruction : notes for employers and instructors of apprentices. — [Beckenham] : Agricultural Training Board, 1979. — 1folded sheet([6]p) : ill ; 22cm
Unpriced B82-19771

630'.7'1 — Great Britain. Agricultural industries. Apprentices. Training schemes: Apprenticeship and Croft Training Scheme

Apprenticeship. — Beckenham : Agricultural Training Board, [c1981]. — 28p ; 21cm
Unpriced (pbk) B82-19770

630'.7'1 — Great Britain. Agriculture industries. Training — *For trainees*

What next after work experience?. — [Beckenham] : Agricultural Training Board, 1981. — 7p : col.ill ; 21cm
Unpriced (unbound) B82-19769

630'.7'11417 — Ireland *(Republic).* **Further education institutions & higher education institutions. Curriculum subjects: Agriculture** — *Inquiry reports*

Report of the ACOT expert group on agricultural education and training. — Blackrock : ACOT, 1981. — xi,171p : ill,1map ; 21cm
ISBN 0-907816-00-2 (pbk) : £4.00
Also classified at 331.25'92 B82-08856

630'.7'1501724 — Developing countries. Agricultural industries. Extension services

Adams, M. E.. Agricultural extension in developing countries. — London : Longman, May 1982. — [192]p. — (Intermediate tropical agriculture series)
ISBN 0-582-65025-9 (pbk) : £2.50 : CIP entry
B82-10860

630'.7'154096711 — Cameroon. Farmers. Training. Correspondence courses

Jenkins, Janet. Training farmers by correspondence in Cameroon / Janet Jenkins and Hilary Perraton. — Cambridge : International Extension College, 1982. — viii,42p : ill,maps ; 30cm
Bibliography: p42
ISBN 0-903632-22-5 (pbk) : Unpriced
B82-36037

630'.72 — Agriculture. Research. Applications of nuclear technology

Vose, Peter B.. Introduction to nuclear techniques in agronomy and plant biology / by Peter B. Vose. — Oxford : Pergamon, 1980. — xiii,391p : ill ; 25cm. — (Pergamon international library of science, technology, engineering and social studies)
Includes bibliographies and index
ISBN 0-08-024924-8 (cased) : Unpriced : CIP rev.
ISBN 0-08-024923-x (pbk) : £11.95
Also classified at 581'.072 B79-34938

630'.7'20134 — Developing countries. Agriculture. Research & technological innovation. Economic aspects

Pinstrup-Anderson, Per. Agricultural research and technology in economic development. — London : Longmans, Apr.1982. — [220]p
ISBN 0-582-46048-4 : £17.50 : CIP entry
B82-06511

630'.720171241 — Commonwealth countries. Agriculture. Research organisations: Commonwealth Agricultural Bureaux — *Conference proceedings*

Commonwealth Agricultural Bureaux. *Review Conference (1980 : London).* Commonwealth Agricultural Bureaux Review Conference, London 1980 : report of proceedings. — London : H.M.S.O., [1981]. — viii,64p : ill ; 25cm. — (Cmnd. ; 8411)
ISBN 0-10-184110-8 (pbk) : £4.75 B82-12497

630'.72041 — Great Britain. Hilly regions. Agriculture. Research organisations: Hill Farming Research Organisation, *to 1979*

Science and hill farming : twenty-five years of work at the Hill Farming Research Organisation 1954-1979. — [Penicuick] : Hill Farm Research Organisation, 1979. — v,184p,[9]leaves of plates : ill(some col.) ; 24cm
Includes bibliographies
ISBN 0-7084-0117-1 : Unpriced B82-07919

630'.76 — England. Agricultural industries. Personnel. Proficiency. Testing

Lambert, Elaine. The testing of farm skills : report of a postal survey concerning individuals involved in proficiency testing in agriculture and horticulture in England and Wales / Elaine Lambert. — Beckenham (Bourne House, 32-34 Beckenham Rd., Beckenham, Kent BRO 4PB) : Agricultural Training Board, 1980. — 119p : ill ; 30cm. — (ATB research report)
Bibliography: p119
£2.00 (pbk) B82-25785

The **Testing** of farm skills : a report and recommendations for action. — Beckenham (Bourne House, 32-34 Beckenham Rd., Beckenham, Kent BRO 4PB) : Agricultural Training Board, 1981. — 30p : ill ; 30cm
Cover title
Unpriced (pbk) B82-25786

630.9 — AGRICULTURE. HISTORICAL AND GEOGRAPHICAL TREATMENT

630'.9 — Agriculture. Geographical aspects

Bayliss-Smith, T. P.. The ecology of agricultural systems. — Cambridge : Cambridge University Press, Oct.1982. — [106]p. — (Cambridge topics in geography series)
ISBN 0-521-23125-6 (cased) : £6.95 : CIP entry
ISBN 0-521-29829-6 (pbk) : £3.25 B82-23328

630'.913 — Tropical regions & subtropical regions. Agriculture

Agricultural compendium : for rural development in the tropics and subtropics / produced and edited by ILACO B.V., International Land Development Consultants, Arnheim, The Netherlands ; commissioned by the Ministry of Agriculture and Fisheries, The Hague, The Netherlands. — Amsterdam ; Oxford : Elsevier Scientific, 1981. — xxxvii,739p : ill,maps ; 21cm
Includes bibliographies and index
ISBN 0-444-41952-7 : £21.69 : CIP rev.
B81-11912

630'.913 — Tropical regions. Agriculture

Wrigley, Gordon. Tropical agriculture. — 4th ed. — London : Longman, Apr.1982. — [400]p
Previous ed.: London : Faber, 1971
ISBN 0-582-46037-9 : £17.00 : CIP entry
B82-04619

630'.913 — Tropical regions. Agriculture — *For West African students*

Uguru, O. O.. An introduction to agricultural science for tropical areas / O.O. Uguru ; [drawings and diagrams by Linda Alexander, Colin Stone and Geoff Wilson] ; [maps by Nick Skelton]. — Walton-on-Thames : Nelson, 1981. — 384p : ill,maps,1facsim,ports ; 28cm
Bibliography: p378-379. — Includes index
ISBN 0-17-511085-9 (pbk) : £4.50 B82-03884

630'.9182'1 — Caribbean region. Agriculture — *For Caribbean students*

Persad, Ralph S.. Agricultural science for Caribbean primary schools / Ralph Persad and Dipwatee Maharaj. — Walton-on-Thames : Nelson
Book 1. — 1981. — 96p : ill(some col.) ; 25cm
ISBN 0-17-566309-2 (pbk) : £1.65 B82-13914

Ramharacksingh, R.. Caribbean primary agriculture / R. Ramharacksingh ; illustrated by G.J. Galsworthy. — London : Cassell
Bk.4. — 1982. — 95p : ill(some col.) ; 25cm
ISBN 0-304-30867-6 (pbk) : £2.25 B82-35514

Ramharacksingh, R.. Caribbean primary agriculture / R. Ramharacksingh ; illustrated by G.J. Galsworthy. — London : Cassell
Workbook 4. — 1982. — 64p : ill,forms ; 25cm
ISBN 0-304-30868-4 (pbk) : £1.15 B82-40399

630'.9182'1 — Caribbean region. Agriculture — *Questions & answers — For Caribbean students*

Persad, Ralph S.. Agricultural science for Caribbean primary schools / Ralph Persad and Dipwatee Maharaj. — Walton-on-Thames : Nelson Caribbean
Workbook 1. — 1981. — 43p ; 25cm
ISBN 0-17-566311-4 (pbk) : £0.50 B82-04690

630'.92'4 — Scotland. Orkney. Egilsay. Agricultural industries. Smallholdings. Self-sufficiency, *1974-1980 — Personal observations*

Coleman, Vicki. Living on an island / Vicki Coleman and Ruth Wheeler. — Findhorn : Thule Press, 1981. — 127p : 1map ; 21cm
ISBN 0-906191-55-6 (pbk) : £2.50
Primary classification 630'.92'4 B82-04004

630'.92'4 — Scotland. Shetland. Papa Stour. Agricultural industries. Smallholdings. Self-sufficiency, *1972-1980 — Personal observations*

Coleman, Vicki. Living on an island / Vicki Coleman and Ruth Wheeler. — Findhorn : Thule Press, 1981. — 127p : 1map ; 21cm
ISBN 0-906191-55-6 (pbk) : £2.50
Also classified at 630'.92'4 B82-04004

630'.92'4 — Welsh Marches. Agriculture — *Personal observations*

Holgate, John, *1924-*. Make a cow laugh : a first year in farming / John Holgate. — London : Pan in association with Peter Davies, 1979, c1977 (1981 printing). — 220p ; 18cm
Originally published: London : P. Davies, 1977
ISBN 0-330-25780-3 (pbk) : £1.25 B82-00393

630'.936 — Europe. Prehistoric agriculture

Early European agriculture : its foundations and development. — Cambridge : Cambridge University Press, Aug.1982. — [304]p
ISBN 0-521-24359-9 : £25.00 : CIP entry
B82-26241

630'.941 — Great Britain. Agriculture — *For children*

Crabtree, Vickie. Farming today / Vickie Crabtree. — London : Muller, 1982. — 155p : ill,maps,1plan ; 21cm
Includes index
ISBN 0-584-10412-x : £6.95 : CIP rev.
B81-32002

630'.941 — Great Britain. Agriculture. Information systems

Woodward, A. M. (Anthony Michael). Strategies for agricultural information reviews and grey literature : report to British Library Research and Development Department : project SI/CT/76 / by A.M. Woodward. — [London] : [British Library Research and Development Department], 1982. — 31p ; 29cm. — (BL R & D report ; 5685)
Bibliography: p29-30
Unpriced (pbk) B82-17703

630'.941 — Great Britain. Agriculture — *Manuals*

McConnell, Primrose. Primrose McConnell's The agricultural notebook. — 17th ed. / edited by R.J. Halley. — London : Butterworth Scientific, 1982. — xviii,683p : ill ; 26cm
Previous ed.: London : Newnes-Butterworth, 1976. — Includes bibliographies and index
ISBN 0-408-10701-4 : Unpriced : CIP rev.
B82-12323

630'.941 — Great Britain. Agriculture - *Serials*

Agriculture. — 1978-79. — London : Health & Safety Executive, July 1981. — [30]p
ISBN 0-11-883436-3 (pbk) : CIP entry
B81-14937

630'.942 — England. Agriculture, *1837-1936 — Illustrations*

Victorian and Edwardian farming from old photographs / [compiled by] Edward Hart. — London : Batsford, 1981. — 120p : chiefly ill,facsims,1plan ; 26cm
ISBN 0-7134-3799-5 : £6.95 B82-05158

630'.9422'74 — Hampshire. Butser Hill. Replica Iron Age farms. Projects: Butser Ancient Farm Research Project

Reynolds, Peter J.. Butser Ancient Farm impressions / by Peter J. Reynolds. — Petersfield (Lyndum House, Petersfield, Hants.) : Archaeological Research, c1980. — 45 [i.e.90]p : ill ; 22cm
Unpriced (pbk) B82-13907

630'.9428'1 — Yorkshire. Agriculture — *Serials*

The **York** farmers' journal. — Vol.23, no.2 (Feb. 1982)-. — Dorchester (5 High East St., Dorchester, Dorset) : N.F.U. County Publications, 1982-. — v. : ill ; 24cm
Monthly. — Journal of: National Farmers' Union. York County Branch. — Continues: North Riding farmer
ISSN 0263-2519 = York farmers' journal : Unpriced B82-22656

630'.9429'82 — West Glamorgan. Gower. Agricultural industries. Farms — *Walkers' guides*

Howells, Roscoe. Gower farm trail / written by Roscoe Howells. — [Swansea] ([The Guildhall, Swansea]) : Planning Department, West Glamorgan County Council, [1980]. — 20p : ill,maps ; 21cm
Cover title. — Bibliography: p20
Unpriced (pbk) B82-16039

631 — CROPS, AGRICULTURAL EQUIPMENT AND OPERATIONS

631 — Crops

Langer, R. H. M.. Agricultural plants / R.H.M. Langer, G.D. Hill ; illustrations by Karen Mason. — Cambridge : Cambridge University Press, 1982. — vii,344p : ill ; 24cm
Includes bibliographies and index
ISBN 0-521-22450-0 (cased) : £20.00 : CIP rev.
B81-33619

Plant science : an introduction to world crops / Jules Janick ... [et al.]. — 3rd ed. — Oxford : W.H. Freeman, c1981. — viii,868p : ill,maps,ports ; 25cm
Previous ed.: 1974. — Includes bibliographies and index
ISBN 0-7167-1261-x : £15.60 B82-05553

631 — Great Britain. Crops: Outdoor plants. Production — *Career guides*

Working in outdoor vegetable, flower and bulb production. — [Beckenham] ([32 Beckenham Rd, Beckenham, Kent BR3 4PB]) : Agricultural Training Board on behalf of the Joint Working Party on Careers Literature, 1981. — [4]p : ill ; 21cm. — (Careers in horticulture) (Job leaflet)
Unpriced (unbound) B82-19446

631 — Post-harvest food crops. Physiology

Burton, W. G.. Post-harvest physiology of food crops / W.G. Burton. — London : Longman, 1982. — 339p : ill ; 23cm
Bibliography: p270-310. — Includes index
ISBN 0-582-46038-7 : £16.00 : CIP rev.
B82-10760

631.2 — FARM BUILDINGS AND STRUCTURES

631.2'0941 — Great Britain. Agricultural industries. Farms. Buildings, *to ca 1900*

Peters, J. E. C.. Discovering traditional farm buildings / J.E.C. Peters. — Princes Risborough : Shire, 1981. — 80p : ill,plans ; 18cm
Includes index
ISBN 0-85263-556-7 (pbk) : £1.50 B82-31001

631.2'0941 — Great Britain. Agricultural industries. Farms. Traditional buildings

Brunskill, R. W.. Traditional farm buildings of Britain / R.W. Brunskill. — London : Gollancz in association with Peter Crawley, 1982. — 160p : ill,plans ; 26cm
Bibliography: p154-156. — Includes index
ISBN 0-575-03117-4 : £10.95 : CIP rev.
B82-12982

631.2'09429'3 — Clwyd. Agricultural industries. Farms. Vernacular buildings, *to 1900*

Wiliam, Eurwyn. Traditional farm buildings in north-east Wales 1550-1900 / Eurwyn Wiliam. — [Cardiff] : National Museum of Wales, Welsh Folk Museum, 1982. — 334p : ill,maps,plans ; 25cm
Bibliography: p296-301. — Includes index
ISBN 0-85485-049-x : Unpriced B82-24164

631.2'7 — Hedging — *Manuals*

Hart, Edward. Hedge laying and fencing : the countryman's art explained / by Edward Hart. — Wellingborough : Thorsons, 1981. — 128p : ill ; 22cm
Bibliography: p126. — Includes index
ISBN 0-7225-0701-1 (cased) : Unpriced : CIP rev.
ISBN 0-7225-0700-3 (pbk) : £2.95
Also classified at 690'.18 B81-30487

631.3 — AGRICULTURAL MACHINERY AND IMPLEMENTS

631.3 — Agricultural industries. Farms. Machinery. Use. Management

Butterworth, Bill. Farm mechanisation for profit. — London : Granada, Sept.1982. — [288]p
ISBN 0-246-11562-9 (pbk) : £9.95 : CIP entry
B82-18851

631.3 — Aquaculture. Engineering aspects — *Serials*

Aquacultural engineering : an international journal. — Vol.1, no.1 (Jan. 1982)-. — London : Applied Science, 1982-. — v. : ill,maps ; 25cm
Quarterly
ISSN 0144-8609 = Aquacultural engineering : £43.00 per year B82-22679

631.3 — British horse-drawn agricultural machinery, *ca 1800-ca 1900 — Early works — Facsimiles*

Horse-drawn farm implements. — Fleet : J. Thompson
Part 2: Preparing the soil / [compiled and introduced by John Thompson]. — 1979. — 82p : ill,facsims ; 25cm
Facsims on inside covers
ISBN 0-9505775-7-x (pbk) : Unpriced
ISBN 0-9505775-5-3 (set) : Unpriced
B82-10314

Horse-drawn farm implements. — Fleet : J. Thompson
Part 3: Sowing and haymaking : a source book / [compiled] by John Thompson. — 1978. — 78p : ill,facsims ; 25cm
Facsims on inside covers
ISBN 0-9505775-8-8 (pbk) : Unpriced
ISBN 0-9505775-5-3 (set) : Unpriced
B82-10315

Horse-drawn farm implements. — Fleet : J. Thompson
Part 4: Harvesting : a source book / [compiled] by John Thompson. — 1979. — 68p : ill,facsims ; 25cm
Ill on inside covers
ISBN 0-9505775-9-6 (pbk) : Unpriced
ISBN 0-9505775-5-3 (set) : Unpriced
B82-10316

631.3 — Scotland. Agricultural engineering. Research organisations: Scottish Institute of Agricultural Engineering — *Serials*

Scottish Institute of Agricultural Engineering. Biennial report / Scottish Institute of Agricultural Engineering. — 1974-1976-. — Penicuik (Bush Estate, Penicuik, Midlothian EH26 0PH) : SIAE, 1976-. — v. : ill ; 24cm
Description based on: Apr. 1978-Mar. 1980 issue
ISSN 0144-6584 = Biennial report - Scottish Institute of Agricultural Engineering : £2.50
B82-18530

631.3'023'41 — Great Britain. Agricultural equipment. Operation — *Career guides*

Working with machinery. — [Beckenham] ([32 Beckenham Rd, Beckenham, Kent BR3 4PB]) : Agricultural Training Board on behalf of the Joint Working Party on Careers Literature, 1980. — 1folded sheet(6p) ; 21cm. — (Careers in agriculture) (Job leaflet)
Unpriced (unbound) B82-19441

631.3'05 — Welfare work. Applications of behavioural sciences — *Serials*

International journal of behavioural social work & abstracts. — Vol.1, no.1 (1981)-. — Oxford : Pergamon, 1981-. — v. : ill ; 25cm
Three issues yearly
ISSN 0271-5171 = International journal of behavioural social work and abstracts : £20.45 per year (£10.00 to members of the British Association for Behavioural Psychotherapy)
B82-01068

631.3'0941 — Great Britain. Agricultural equipment, *ca 1880-1940* **—** *Illustrations*

Lawson, Douglas. Hand to the plough : old farm tools and machinery in pictures / Douglas Lawson ; captions by Henry Jackson ; foreword by Bernard Price. — Sevenoaks : Ashgrove, c1982. — [120]p : chiefly ill ; 29cm
ISBN 0-906798-05-1 (cased) : £9.50
ISBN 0-906798-06-x (pbk) : Unpriced
B82-36510

631.3'71 — Agricultural equipment: Electric pumping systems. Design

Farm-electric pumping and irrigation : a guide to the design of simple pumping systems. — Stoneleigh (National Agricultural Centre, Stoneleigh, Kenilworth, Warwickshire, CV8 2LS) : Electricity Council, Farm-Electric Centre, [1980?]. — 61p : ill(some col.),1col.map ; 30cm. — (A farmelectric handbook)
Unpriced (pbk) B82-40739

631.4 — AGRICULTURE. SOILS

631.4 — Agricultural land. Soils. Conservation. Engineering aspects

Soil and water conservation engineering. — 3rd ed. / Glenn O. Schwab ... [et al.]. — New York ; Chichester : Wiley, c1981. — xv,525p : ill,maps ; 24cm
Previous ed.: / by Richard K. Frevert ... [et al.], 1966. — Includes bibliographies and index
ISBN 0-471-03078-3 : £24.40
Also classified at 631.7 B82-04187

631.4 — Agriculture. Field engineering

Hudson, N. W.. Field engineering for agricultural development. — Oxford : Clarendon Press, Nov.1982. — [240]p. — (Oxford tropical handbooks)
Originally published: 1975
ISBN 0-19-442375-1 (pbk) : £2.95 : CIP entry
B82-26214

631.4 — Soil science

Duchaufour, Philippe. Pedology : pedogenesis and classification. — London : Allen & Unwin, Oct.1982. — [480]p
Translation of: Pédologie. Pédogenèse et classification
ISBN 0-04-631015-0 (cased) : £25.00 : CIP entry
ISBN 0-04-631016-9 (pbk) : £13.95
B82-23095

Gerrard, John. Soils and landforms : an integration of geomorphology and pedology / A.J. Gerrard. — London : Allen & Unwin, 1981. — xviii,219p : ill ; 24cm
Bibliography: p191-120. — Includes index
ISBN 0-04-551048-2 (cased) : Unpriced : CIP rev.
ISBN 0-04-551049-0 (pbk) : Unpriced
Primary classification 631.4 B81-26737

631.4 — Soil science — *For geography*

Fenwick, I. M.. Soils process & response. — London : Duckworth, Nov.1981. — [208]p
ISBN 0-7156-1394-4 : £18.00 : CIP entry
B81-30262

631.4 — Soils

Bonneau, M.. Constituents and properties of soils / M. Bonneau and B. Souchier ; V.C. Farmer, translation editor. — London : Academic Press, 1982. — xix,496p : ill,maps ; 24cm
Translation of: Constituents et propriétés du sol. — Includes bibliographies and index
ISBN 0-12-114550-6 : £36.20 : CIP rev.
B82-04138

631.4 — Soils. Cultivation

Davies, D. B.. Soil management / D.B. Davies, D.J. Eagle and J.B. Finney. — 3rd rev ed. — Ipswich : Farming Press, 1977 (1979 [printing]). — 268p,[1]folded p of plates : ill (some col.),2maps ; 23cm
Previous ed.: 1975. — Includes index
ISBN 0-85236-077-0 : £7.00 B82-26302

631.4 — Soils — *For children*

Jennings, Terry. Rocks and soil / Terry Jennings ; illustrated by Norma Burgin. — Oxford : Oxford University Press, 1982. — 32p : ill (chiefly col.) ; 29cm. — (The Young scientist investigates)
ISBN 0-19-918045-8 (cased) : Unpriced
ISBN 0-19-918039-3 (pbk) : £1.50
Primary classification 552 B82-29523

Leutscher, Alfred. Earth. — London : Methuen/Walker, Oct.1982. — [32]p. — (The Elements ; 3)
ISBN 0-416-06450-7 : £3.50 : CIP entry
B82-24481

631.4 — Soils — *For schools*

Principles and applications of soil geography / edited by E.M. Bridges and D.A. Davidson. — London : Longman, 1982. — xii,297p : ill,maps ; 24cm
Bibliography: p275-292. — Includes index
ISBN 0-582-30014-2 (pbk) : £6.95 : CIP rev.
B81-30185

631.4 — Soils. Formation. Effects of landforms

Gerrard, John. Soils and landforms : an integration of geomorphology and pedology / A.J. Gerrard. — London : Allen & Unwin, 1981. — xviii,219p : ill ; 24cm
Bibliography: p191-120. — Includes index
ISBN 0-04-551048-2 (cased) : Unpriced : CIP rev.
ISBN 0-04-551049-0 (pbk) : Unpriced
Also classified at 631.4 B81-26737

631.4'1 — Soils. Chemical properties

Soil chemistry. — Amsterdam ; Oxford : Elsevier Scientific
B: Physico-chemical models / edited by G.H. Bolt ; contributing authors J. Beek ... [et al.]. — 2nd rev. ed. — 1982. — xxii,527p : ill ; 25cm. — (Developments in soil science ; 5B)
Previous ed.: 1979. — Includes bibliographies and index
ISBN 0-444-42060-6 : £38.38 B82-24666

631.4'1'028 — Soils. Analysis. Use of electro-ultrafiltration

International Symposium on the Application of Electro-Ultrafiltration in Agricultural Production *(1st : 1980 : Budapest)*. Application of electro-ultrafiltration (EUF) agricultural production : proceedings of the First International Symposium on the Application of Electro-Ultrafiltration in Agricultural Production, organised by the Hungarian Ministry of Agriculture and the Central Research Institute for Chemistry of the Academy of Sciences, Budapest, May 6-10, 1980 / edited by K. Németh. — The Hague ; London : Nijhoff, 1982. — 138p : ill ; 24cm
Includes bibliographies
ISBN 90-247-2641-7 (pbk) : Unpriced
B82-25293

631.4'1'028 — Soils. Analysis. Use of electron microscopy

Smart, Peter. Electron microscopy of soils and sediments / Peter Smart and N. Keith Tovey. — Oxford : Clarendon Press. — (Oxford science publications)
Examples. — 1981. — viii,177p : ill ; 26cm
Bibliography: p170-171. — Includes index
ISBN 0-19-854515-0 : £30.00 : CIP rev.
Also classified at 551.3'04'028 B81-15841

631.4'16 — Soils. Copper — *Conference proceedings*

Copper in soils and plants : proceedings of the Golden Jubilee International Symposium on 'Copper in Soils and Plants' held at Murdoch University, Perth, Western Australia on May 7-9, 1981 under the sponsorship of the Australian Academy of Technological Sciences / edited by J.F. Loneragan, A.D. Robson, R.D. Graham. — Sydney ; London : Academic Press, 1981. — xv,380p : ill ; 24cm
Includes bibliographies and index
ISBN 0-12-455520-9 : £16.00
Also classified at 581.1'3356 B82-07560

631.4'16 — Soils. Salinity — *Conference proceedings*

Land and stream salinity : an international seminar and workshop held in November 1980 in Perth, Western Australia / edited by J.W. Holmes and T. Talsma. — Amsterdam ; Oxford : Elsevier Scientific, 1981. — 392p : ill,maps ; 25cm. — (Developments in agricultural engineering ; 2)
"Reprinted from Agricultural water management V.4. no.1,2,3(1981)" — Half t.p. verso. — Includes bibliographies and index
ISBN 0-444-41999-3 : Unpriced : CIP rev.
Also classified at 551.48 B81-24632

631.4'17 — Humus. Chemical properties

Stevenson, F. J.. Humus chemistry : genesis, composition, reactions / F.J. Stevenson. — New York ; Chichester : Wiley, c1982. — xiii,443p : ill ; 24cm
Includes index
ISBN 0-471-09299-1 : £27.75 B82-26476

631.4'4 — Soils. Classification

Oliver, Margaret A.. Contrasting approaches to soil classification / Margaret A. Oliver. — Birmingham : Department of Geography, University of Birmingham, 1980. — 14p ; 30cm. — (Working paper series / University of Birmingham. Department of Geography ; 2)
Bibliography: p10-14
ISBN 0-7044-0557-1 (pbk) : £0.30 B82-23560

631.4'4'0942 — England. Soils. Classification. Great Britain. *Ministry of Agriculture, Fisheries and Food.* **Agricultural Land Classification —** *Critical studies*

Worthington, Tom. Agricultural land : Grade 3 — third class? / by Tom Worthington. — Wallingford : Reading Agricultural Consultants, 1981. — 42p ; 20cm
ISBN 0-9507931-0-8 (pbk) : Unpriced
B82-29203

631.4'4'0942 — England. Soils — *Classification schedules*

Avery, B. W.. Soil classification for England and Wales : (higher categories) / B.W. Avery. — Harpenden (Rothamsted Experimental Station, Harpenden, Herts. AL5 2JQ) : Soil Survey of England and Wales, 1980. — 67p : ill ; 21cm. — (Soil Survey technical monograph ; no.14)
Bibliography: p63-64
£1.00 (pbk) B82-31841

631.4'4'0966 — West Africa. Soils. Classification

Characterization of soils : in relation to their classification and management for crop production : examples from some areas of the humid tropics / edited by D.J. Greenland. — Oxford : Clarendon, 1981. — xiv,446p,[16]p of plates : ill ; 24cm
Includes bibliographies and index
ISBN 0-19-854538-x : £35.00 : CIP rev.
B80-02086

631.4'5 — Soils. Erosion

Zachar, Dušan. Soil erosion / Dušan Zachar. — Amsterdam ; Oxford : Elsevier Scientific, 1982. — 547p : ill(some col.),maps ; 25cm. — (Developments in soil science ; 10)
Translation of: Erózia pôdy. — Bibliography: p483-514. — Includes index
ISBN 0-444-99725-3 : Unpriced : CIP rev.
B81-31614

631.4'7 — Soils. Surveying

Brink, A. B. A.. Soil survey for engineering / A.B.A. Brink, T.C. Partridge, and A.A.B Williams. — Oxford : Clarendon, 1982. — x,378p,[20]p of plates : ill(some col.),maps ; 22cm. — (Monographs on soil survey) (Oxford science publications)
Bibliography: p358-364. — Includes index
ISBN 0-19-854537-1 : £35.00 : CIP rev.
B81-15920

Dent, David. Soil survey and land evaluation / David Dent and Anthony Young. — London : Allen & Unwin, 1981. — xiii,278p,4folded p of plates : ill,maps ; 24cm
Bibliography: p263-269. — Includes index
ISBN 0-04-631013-4 (cased) : Unpriced : CIP rev.
ISBN 0-04-631014-2 (pbk) : Unpriced
Also classified at 526.9 B81-26738

631.4′913 — Tropical regions. Soils
Eden, T.. Elements of tropical soil science / T. Eden. — 2nd ed. — London : Macmillan, 1964 (1979 [printing]). — ix,164p : ill ; 19cm
Previous ed.: 1947. — Includes index
ISBN 0-333-04261-1 (pbk) : £2.95 : CIP rev. B79-05788

631.4′941 — Great Britain. Soils
Illsley, T. W. B.. Soil / T.W.B. Illsley. — London (16 Strutton Ground, SW1P 2HP) : Association of Agriculture, 1981. — 47p,[4]p of plates : ill ; 21cm. — (Modern agriculture series)
Text on inside back cover. — Bibliography: p47
Unpriced (pbk) B82-33666

Simpson, Ken. Soil. — London : Longman, Mar.1982. — [230]p. — (Longman handbooks in agriculture)
ISBN 0-582-44641-4 (pbk) : £8.00 : CIP entry B82-07817

631.4′9423′5 — Devon. Soils
Soils in Devon. — Harpenden : Soil Survey
6: Sheet SS 63 (Brayford) / D.V. Hogan. — 1981. — viii,134p : ill,maps ; 21cm + 2 folded sheets(col.maps). — (Soil survey record ; no.71)
Book and maps in plastic wallet. — Text on inside covers. — Includes index
ISBN 0-7084-0199-6 (pbk) : £6.00
ISBN 0-7084-0200-3 (without maps) : £2.00 B82-24696

631.4′94241 — Gloucestershire. Soils
Soils in Gloucestershire. — Harpenden : Soil Survey of England and Wales. — (Soil survey record ; no.73)
3: Sheet SO61 (Cinderford) / G.J.N. Colborne. — 1981. — ix,231p,[1]folded leaf of plates : ill,maps ; 22cm + 1map(67x74cm folded to 17x15cm)
In slip case. — Bibliography: p208-211. — Includes index
£4.00 with map (£2.00 without map) (pbk) B82-32346

631.4′9425′2 — Nottinghamshire. Soils
Soils in Nottinghamshire. — Harpenden : Soil Survey
4: Sheet SK 78N/79S (Gringley on the Hill) / M.J. Reeve and A.J. Thomasson. — 1981. — ix,138p : ill,maps ; 21cm + 2 folded sheets (col.maps). — (Soil survey record ; no.72)
Bibliography: p87-88. — Includes index
ISBN 0-7084-0201-1 (pbk) : £6.00
ISBN 0-7084-0202-x (without maps) : £2.00 B82-24697

631.4′9426′5 — Cambridgeshire. Soils
Soils in Cambridgeshire. — Harpenden (Rothamsted Experimental Station, Harpenden, Herts. AL5 2JQ) : Soil Survey
2: Sheet TF 00E/10W (Barnack) / R.G.O. Burton. — 1981. — viii,175p : ill,maps ; 21cm + 2 folded sheets(col.maps). — (Soil survey record ; no.69)
Book and maps in plastic wallet. — Text on inside covers. — Bibliography: p162-164. — Includes index
£6.00 (£2.00 without maps) (pbk) B82-24695

631.4′94284 — North Yorkshire. Soils
Soils in North Yorkshire. — Harpenden : Soil Survey of England and Wales. — (Soil survey record ; no.68)
6: Sheet SE39 (Northallerton) / J.W. Allison and R. Hartnup. — 1981. — viii,132p : ill ; 21cm + 2 folded sheets(col.maps)
Also available without maps. — Bibliography: p113-114. — Includes index
£6.00 (pbk) (Without maps) : £2.00 B82-06341

631.4′94296 — Dyfed. Soils
Soil in Dyfed = Priddoedd yn Nyfed. — Harpenden : Soil Survey of England and Wales. — (Soil survey record ; no.74)
6: Sheet SN72 (Llangadog) = Tudalen SN 72 (Llangadog) / P.S. Wright. — 1981. — x,142p : ill(some col.),maps(some col.) ; 21cm + 1folded sheet(col.map ; 56x72cm folded to 14x18cm)
Bibliography: p124-125. — Includes index
ISBN 0-7084-0205-4 (pbk) : £4.00 with maps
ISBN 0-7084-0206-2 (without maps) : £2.00 B82-40448

631.5 — AGRICULTURE. CULTIVATION AND HARVESTING

631.5 — Plants. Cultivation — *Manuals* — *For children*
Pavord, Anna. Growing things / Anna Pavord ; illustrated by Kathleen McDougall. — [London] : Macmillan Children's, 1982. — 32p : ill(some col.) ; 29cm. — (Help yourself books)
ISBN 0-333-30858-1 : £2.95 : CIP rev. B81-35784

631.5′09417 — Ireland *(Republic).* **Crops. Production**
O'Loan, Arthur. Farm plants / Arthur O'Loan. — [Blackrock] ([Frascati Rd., Blackrock, Co. Dublin]) : ACOT, c1981. — 66p : ill(some col.),maps ; 30cm
Unpriced (pbk) B82-05193

631.5′21 — Seeds. Protein content — *Conference proceedings*
Seed proteins. — London : Academic Press, Dec.1982. — [350]p. — (Annual proceedings of the Phytochemical Society of Europe, ISSN 0309-9393 ; no.20)
ISBN 0-12-204380-4 : CIP entry B82-29879

631.5′21′07 — Great Britain. Seed processing industries. Personnel. Training
Production training manual for seedsmen. — Gloucester (Barton House, Barton St., Gloucester GL1 1QQ) : Food, Drink and Tobacco Industry Training Board, [1979]. — 1v(loose leaf) ; 32cm
£2.50 B82-26128

631.5′3 — Crops. Breeding. Environmental factors
Breeding plants for less favorable environments / edited by M.N. Christiansen, Charles F. Lewis. — New York ; Chichester : Wiley, c1982. — viii,459p : ill,maps ; 24cm
Includes bibliographies and index
ISBN 0-471-04483-0 : Unpriced B82-19713

631.5′3 — Plants. Propagation — *Manuals*
Guyton, Anita. The pocket book of propagation / Anita Guyton. — London : Evans, 1981. — 111p : ill ; 17cm
Includes index
ISBN 0-237-45556-0 (pbk) : £1.95 : CIP rev. B81-04240

631.5′4 — Crops. Growth. Regulation. Use of chemicals
Fletcher, W. W.. Herbicides and plant growth regulators. — London : Granada, June 1982. — [400]p
ISBN 0-246-11266-2 : £25.00 : CIP entry B82-09985

631.5′4 — Crops. Growth. Regulation. Use of chemicals — *Conference proceedings*
Chemical manipulation of crop growth and development / [edited by] J.S. McLaren. — London : Butterworth Scientific, 1982. — xiii,564p : ill ; 24cm
Conference proceedings. — Includes bibliographies and index
ISBN 0-408-10767-7 : Unpriced : CIP rev. B82-01969

631.5′84 — Crops. Organic cultivation
Biological husbandry : a scientific approach to organic farming / [edited by] B. Stonehouse. — London : Butterworths, 1981. — xiii,352p : ill ; 25cm
Conference proceedings
ISBN 0-408-10726-x : Unpriced : CIP rev. B81-23905

631.5′85 — Plants. Cultivation. Nutrient film
Commercial applications of NFT. — 2nd ed. — London : Grower, 1982. — 93p : ill ; 21cm
Previous ed.: 1978
ISBN 0-901361-69-0 (pbk) : Unpriced B82-24929

631.6 — AGRICULTURE. LAND RECLAMATION AND DRAINAGE

631.6′2 — Agricultural land. Drainage systems. Filters
Dennis, C. W.. Field drainage pipes and filters : report of a study tour undertaken in Canada and USA 23 August-5 September 1981 / C.W. Dennis. — [London] ([Great Westminster House, Horseferry Rd., SW1P 2AE]) : ADAS, 1982. — 15p : 1ill ; 30cm. — (ADAS overseas study tour programme ; 1981/82)
Cover title
Unpriced (pbk) B82-40444

631.6′2′09426 — East Anglia. Fens. Agricultural land. Drainage. Political aspects, *1626-1719*
Lindley, Keith. Fenland riots and the English Revolution / Keith Lindley. — London : Heinemann Educational, 1982. — ix,276p : ill,maps ; 23cm
Includes index
ISBN 0-435-32535-3 : £16.50 : CIP rev. B82-01114

631.6′2′0942619 — Norfolk. South Norfolk *(District).* **Agricultural land. Drainage,** *1800-1899*
Burgess, Ben. Nineteenth century tile drainage : and the specialist tools of south Norfolk / Ben Burgess. — Norwich (King St., Norwich) : B.B. & Co., [1982?]. — 12p : ill ; 22cm
Cover title. — Text, ill on inside covers
Unpriced (pbk) B82-38944

631.7 — AGRICULTURE. IRRIGATION

631.7 — Agricultural land. Small scale irrigation — *Manuals*
Stern, Peter H.. Small scale irrigation : a manual of low-cost water technology / Peter H. Stern. — London : Intermediate Technology, 1979 (1980 [printing]). — 152p : ill ; 22cm
£4.50 (pbk) B82-11185

631.7 — Agricultural land. Water. Conservation. Engineering aspects
Soil and water conservation engineering. — 3rd ed. / Glenn O. Schwab ... [et al.]. — New York ; Chichester : Wiley, c1981. — xv,525p : ill,maps ; 24cm
Previous ed.: / by Richard K. Frevert ... [et al.], 1966. — Includes bibliographies and index
ISBN 0-471-03078-3 : £24.40
Primary classification 631.4 B82-04187

631.7′072 — Agricultural land. Irrigation. Management. Applications of action research
Bottrall, Anthony. The action research approach to problem solving, with illustrations from irrigation management / Anthony F. Bottrall. — London : Overseas Development Institute, 1982. — 20p ; 30cm. — (ODI working paper ; no.9)
Bibliography: p19-20
ISBN 0-85003-083-8 (pbk) : Unpriced B82-35795

631.7′0722 — China. Agricultural land. Irrigation — *Case studies*
Water management organization in the People's Republic of China / edited with an introduction by James E. Nickum. — Armonk, N.Y. : Sharpe ; London : distributed by Eurospan, c1981. — xvi,269p : ill,maps ; 24cm. — (The China book project)
Translation from the Chinese
ISBN 0-87332-140-5 : £14.95 B82-17302

631.8 — AGRICULTURE. FERTILISERS

631.8′1 — Agricultural land. Fertilisers. Environmental aspects
Fertilisers and our environment. — London : Fertiliser Manufacturers Association, c1981. — 22p ; 21cm
£1.00 (pbk) B82-21418

631.8′1 — Fertilisers
Cooke, G. W.. Fertilizing for maximum yield. — 3rd ed. — London : Granada, Sept.1982. — [480]p
Previous ed.: London : Crosby Lockwood Staples, 1975
ISBN 0-246-11788-5 : £10.00 : CIP entry B82-18861

631.8′4 — Nitrogenous fertilisers — *Conference proceedings*

International Conference on Fertilizer Technology *(4th : 1981 : London).* Fertilizer nitrogen : facing the challenge of more expensive energy : proceedings of the British Sulphur Corporation's fourth International Conference on Fertilizer Technology, London, 19-21 January 1981 / editor: A.I. More. — London : The Corporation, 1982. — xiv,692p : ill ; 22cm
ISBN 0-902777-55-6 : Unpriced B82-33171

631.8′6 — Fertilisers: Industrial waste materials. Constituents: Antibiotics

Bewick, M. W. M.. Considerations on the use of antibiotic fermentation wastes as fertilizers : a review of their past use and potential effects on the soil ecosystem / M.W.M. Bewick. — Slough : Commonwealth Agricultural Bureaux, 1977. — 20p ; 25cm. — (Special publication / Commonwealth Bureau of Soils ; no.4)
Bibliography: p11-20
ISBN 0-85198-396-0 (pbk) : Unpriced
B82-10723

632 — AGRICULTURE. PLANT INJURIES, DISEASES, PESTS

632 — Crops. Airborne pests & diseases. Meteorological aspects

Pedgley, David E.. Windborne pests and diseases. — Chichester : Ellis Horwood, June 1982. — [240]p
ISBN 0-85312-312-8 : £22.50 : CIP entry
B82-17215

632 — Crops. Pathogens. Biological control — *Conference proceedings*

Biological control in crop production : invited papers presented at a symposium held May 18-21, 1980, at the Beltsville Agricultural Research Center (BARC), Beltsville, Maryland 20705 / [general editor George C. Papavizas] ; organized by The BARC Symposium V Committee ; sponsored by The Beltsville Agricultural Research Center. — Totowa : Allenheld, Osmun ; London : Granada, 1981. — ix,461p : ill ; 25cm. — (Beltsville symposia in agricultural research ; 5)
Includes bibliographies and index
ISBN 0-246-11512-2 : Unpriced
Primary classification 632′.96 B82-24199

632′.05 — Crops. Protection — *Serials*

Crop protection : an international journal of pest, disease and weed control. — Vol.1, no.1 (Mar. 1982)-. — Guildford : Butterworth Scientific, 1982-. — v. : ill ; 25cm
Quarterly
ISSN 0261-2194 = Crop protection : £45.00 per year B82-24759

632′.0913 — Subtropical regions & tropical regions. Crops. Diseases & pests

Cook, Allyn Austin. Diseases of tropical and subtropical field, fiber and oil plants / Allyn Austin Cook. — New York : Macmillan ; London : Collier Macmillan, c1981. — xiv,450p : ill ; 25cm
Includes bibliographies and index
ISBN 0-02-949300-5 : £30.00 B82-39390

632′.0913 — Tropical regions. Crops. Diseases & pests

Hill, D. S.. Pests and diseases of tropical crops / D.S. Hill, J.M. Waller. — London : Longman. — (Intermediate tropical agriculture series)
Vol.1: Principles and methods of control. — 1982. — xvi,175p : ill,1form,1map ; 22cm
Includes bibliographies and index
ISBN 0-582-60614-4 (pbk) : Unpriced : CIP rev. B81-10438

632′.0941 — Great Britain. Crops. Diseases & pests. Control measures

The **Fight** for food. — London (Alembic House, 93 Albert Embankment, SE1 7TU) : British Agrochemicals Association Ltd., [1982?]. — 15p : col.ill ; 30cm
Unpriced (pbk) B82-28381

632′.09411 — Scotland. Crops. Protection — *Conference proceedings — Serials*

Crop protection in Northern Britain. — 1981-. — [s.l.] ([c/o R.A. Fox, Scottish Crop Research Institute, Invergowrie, Dundee DD2 5DA]) : [s.n.], 1981-. — v. ; 20cm
Annual
ISSN 0260-485x = Crop protection in Northern Britain : Unpriced B82-03397

632.3 — AGRICULTURE. PLANT DISEASES

632′.3 — Plants. Diseases. Control

Phillips, D. H.. International plant health controls : conflicts, problems & cooperation : a European experience / D.H. Phillips ; prepared for the Eleventh Commonwealth Forestry Conference, Trinidad, September 1980. — Edinburgh : Forestry Commission, 1980. — 20p ; 21cm. — (Forestry Commission R & D paper ; 125)
Cover title. — Bibliography: p18-20
ISBN 0-85538-080-2 (pbk) : Unpriced
B82-37884

Vanderplank, J. E.. Host-pathogen interactions in plant disease / J.E. Vanderplank. — New York ; London : Academic Press, 1982. — xii,207p : ill ; 24cm
Bibliography: p187-201. — Includes index
ISBN 0-12-711420-3 : £17.20 B82-29597

632′.3 — Plants. Diseases. Vectors. Control

Pathogens, vectors and plant diseases : approaches to control / edited by Kerry F. Harris, Karl Maramorosch. — New York : London : Academic Press, 1982. — xii,310p : ill ; 24cm
Includes bibliographies and index
ISBN 0-12-326440-5 : £31.80 B82-34856

632.4 — AGRICULTURE. FUNGUS DISEASES

632′.452 — Crops. Downy mildews

The **Downy** mildews / edited by D.M. Spencer. — London : Academic, 1981. — xxi,636p : ill,maps ; 24cm
Includes bibliographies and index
ISBN 0-12-656860-x : £49.60 : CIP rev.
B81-27353

632.5 — AGRICULTURE. HARMFUL PLANTS

632′.58 — Crops. Diseases & pests. Ecology. Role of weeds — *Conference proceedings*

Pests pathogens and vegetation : the role of weeds and wild plants in the ecology of crop pests and diseases : the outcome of a meeting arranged at the University of York 15-17 April 1980 in collaboration with the British Ecological Society and the Federation of British Plant Pathologists / edited by J.M. Thresh ; associate editors J.E. Crosse ... [et al.]. — Boston, Mass. ; London : Pitman Advanced Publishing Program, c1981. — x,517p : ill,maps ; 24cm. — (The Pitman series in applied biology)
At head of title: Association of Applied Biologists. — Includes bibliographies and index
ISBN 0-273-08498-4 : Unpriced B82-03564

632′.58 — Weeds. Control measures

Stephens, R. J.. Theory and practice of weed control / R.J. Stephens. — London : Macmillan, 1982. — viii,215p : ill ; 22cm. — (Science in horticulture series)
Includes bibliographies and index
ISBN 0-333-31950-8 (cased) : Unpriced
ISBN 0-333-21294-0 (pbk) : £8.95 B82-20941

632′.58′0941 — Great Britain. Weeds. Control measures — *Manuals*

British Crop Protection Society. Weed control handbook. — 7th ed. — Oxford : Blackwell Scientific, Nov.1982. — [549]p
Previous ed.: 1977
ISBN 0-632-01018-5 : £20.00 : CIP entry
B82-32293

632′.58′0973 — United States. Weeds. Control measures

Klingman, Glenn C.. Weed science : principles and practices. — 2nd ed. / Glenn C. Klingman, Floyd M. Ashton with the editorial assistance of Lyman J. Noordhoff. — New York ; Chichester : Wiley, c1982. — viii,449p : ill ; 24cm
Previous ed.: 1975. — Includes bibliographies and index
ISBN 0-471-08487-5 : £19.00 B82-39650

632.6 — AGRICULTURE. ANIMAL PESTS

632′.654 — Stored tropical crops. Pests: Arachnida

Haines, C. P.. Insects and arachnids from stored products : a report on specimens received by the Tropical Stored Products Centre 1973-77 / C.P. Haines. — London : Tropical Products Institute, 1978. — iv,73p ; 30cm
English text, French and Spanish summaries. — At head of title: Tropical Products Institute. — Bibliography: p61-65
ISBN 0-85954-133-9 (pbk) : £6.15
Primary classification 632′.7 B82-04212

632′.69322 — New Zealand. Pests: Rabbits. Control

McKillop, I. G.. Rabbit research and rabbit control : report of a visit to New Zealand July-August 1981 / I.G. McKillop. — [London] : ADAS, [1982]. — 18p ; 30cm
Unpriced (pbk) B82-21198

632.7 — AGRICULTURE. INSECT PESTS

632′.7 — Crops. Pests: Insects. Natural resistance

Panda, Niranjan. Principles of host-plant resistance in insect pests / Niranjan Panda. — Delhi : Hindustan Publishing ; Chichester : Packard, c1979. — xix,386p : ill ; 25cm
Includes bibliographies and index
ISBN 0-906527-11-2 : Unpriced B82-08135

632′.7 — Pests: Insects. Biological control

Van den Bosch, Robert. An introduction to biological control. — Rev. version / Robert van den Bosch, P.S. Messenger, A.P. Gutierrez. — New York ; London : Plenum, c1982. — xiv,247p : ill ; 24cm
Previous ed.: published as Biological control. New York : Intext ; Aylesbury : Intertext, 1973. — Includes bibliographies and index
ISBN 0-306-40706-x : Unpriced B82-25809

632′.7 — Pests: Insects. Biological control — *Conference proceedings*

Emmett, B. J.. Report on International Symposium on Insect Control of Tomorrow, Wageningen, Holland, 14-16 September 1981 / B.J. Emmett. — [London] ([Great Westminster House, Horseferry Rd., SW2P 2AE]) : ADAS, [1981]. — 6p ; 30cm
Cover title
Unpriced (pbk) B82-11661

632′.7 — Pests: Insects. Control

Perkins, John H.. Insects, experts and the insecticide crisis : the quest for new pest management strategies / John H. Perkins. — New York ; London : Plenum, c1982. — xviii,304p : ill,2maps ; 23cm
Includes index
ISBN 0-306-40770-1 : Unpriced B82-28647

632′.7 — Stored tropical crops. Pests: Insects

Haines, C. P.. Insects and arachnids from stored products : a report on specimens received by the Tropical Stored Products Centre 1973-77 / C.P. Haines. — London : Tropical Products Institute, 1978. — iv,73p ; 30cm
English text, French and Spanish summaries. — At head of title: Tropical Products Institute. — Bibliography: p61-65
ISBN 0-85954-133-9 (pbk) : £6.15
Also classified at 632′.654 B82-04212

632′.726 — Pests: Desert locusts. Migration. Forecasting — *Manuals*

Desert Locust forecasting manual / edited by D. Pedgley. — London : Centre for Overseas Pest Research, 1981. — 2v. : ill,maps(some col.) ; 31cm
Bibliography: p248-253. — Includes index
ISBN 0-85135-121-2 : Unpriced B82-22257

632'.726 — Thailand. Pests: Locusts & grasshoppers

Roffey, Jeremy. Locusts and grasshoppers of economic importance in Thailand / Jeremy Roffey. — London : Centre for Overseas Pest Research, 1979. — 200p : ill,maps ; 30cm. — (Anti-locust memoir, ISSN 0373-8906 ; 14)
Bibliography: p139-150
ISBN 0-85135-104-2 (pbk) : £16.15
B82-28894

632.9 — AGRICULTURE. PEST CONTROL

632'.9 — Crops. Pests. Control

Martin, Hubert. The scientific principles of crop protection. — 7th ed. — London : Edward Arnold, July 1982. — [416]p
Previous ed.: 1973
ISBN 0-7131-3467-4 : £30.00 : CIP entry
B82-13017

632'.9'0913 — Tropical regions. Pests. Control measures

Natural products for innovative pest management . — Oxford : Pergamon, Jan.1983. — [550]p. — (Current themes in tropical science ; v.2)
ISBN 0-08-028893-6 : £65.00 : CIP entry
B82-33612

632'.93'094 — Europe. Imports: Plants. Quarantine — *Conference proceedings*

EPPO conference on pest and disease risks from imported exotic material : report of a visit to Denmark 25-27 November 1980 / P. Aitkenhead ... [et al.]. — [London] ([Great Westminster House, Horseferry Rd., SW1P 2AE]) : ADAS, [1982]. — 12p in various pagings ; 30cm
Cover title
Unpriced (pbk)
B82-40873

632'.94 — Crops. Pests. Control measures: Spraying. Techniques

Matthews, G. A.. Pesticide application methods / G.A. Matthews. — London : Longman, 1979 (1982 [printing]). — 336p : ill ; 24cm
Originally published: 1979. — Bibliography: p309-325. — Includes index
ISBN 0-582-46351-3 (pbk) : £7.95 : CIP rev.
B82-00239

632'.95 — Crops. Pesticides — *Conference proceedings*

Crop protection chemicals : directions of future development : a Royal Society discussion held on 18 and 19 February 1981 / organized by L. Fowden, and I.J. Graham-Bryce. — London : Royal Society, 1981. — 212p : ill ; 31cm
"First published in Philosophical transactions of the Royal Society of London series B, V.295 (no.1076), p 1-212" — Title page verso. — Includes bibliographies
ISBN 0-85403-175-8 : £23.30
B82-03933

632'.95'0289 — Pesticides. Use. Safety measures

International Association on Occupational Health *. Scientific Committee on Pesticides. International workshop (6th : 1981 : Buenos Aires and San Carlos de Bariloche)*. Education and safe handling in pesticide application : proceedings of the Sixth International Workshop of the Scientific Committee on Pesticides of the International Association on Occupational Health, Buenos Aires and San Carlos de Bariloche, Argintina, March 12-18, 1981 / edited by E.A.H. van Heemstra-Lequin, W.F. Tordoir. — Amsterdam ; Oxford : Elsevier Scientific, 1982. — xiv,302p : ill ; 25cm. — (Studies in environmental science ; 18)
ISBN 0-444-42041-x : £31.78 : CIP rev.
B81-34009

632'.95042 — Pesticides: Pentachlorophenol. Toxic effects

Great Britain. *Health and Safety Executive*. Pentachlorophenol. — London : H.M.S.O., Apr.1982. — [30]p. — (Toxicity review ; 5)
ISBN 0-11-883630-7 (pbk) : CIP entry
B82-14053

632'.95'0913 — Tropical regions. Crops. Pesticides — *Lists* — *Serials*

Tropical pest management pesticide index : an index of chemical, common and trade names of pesticides. — 1981 ed.-. — London : Centre for Overseas Pest Research, 1981-. — v. ; 30cm
Irregular. — Continues: PANS pesticide index
ISSN 0262-5105 = Tropical Pest Management pesticide index : £2.50
B82-04895

632'.954 — Herbicides: 2,4,5-trichlorophenoxyacetic acid

Cook, Judith. Portrait of a poison : the 2, 4, 5-T story / Judith Cook and Chris Kaufman. — London : Pluto, 1982. — xi,100p ; 20cm. — (The Politics of health)
Bibliography: p94-96
ISBN 0-86104-324-3 (pbk) : £2.95 : CIP rev.
B82-14926

632'.96 — Crops. Pests. Biological control — *Conference proceedings*

Biological control in crop production : invited papers presented at a symposium held May 18-21, 1980, at the Beltsville Agricultural Research Center (BARC), Beltsville, Maryland 20705 / [general editor George C. Papavizas] ; organized by The BARC Symposium V Committee ; sponsored by The Beltsville Agricultural Research Center. — Totowa : Allenheld, Osmun ; London : Granada, 1981. — ix,461p : ill ; 25cm. — (Beltsville symposia in agricultural research ; 5)
Includes bibliographies and index
ISBN 0-246-11512-2 : Unpriced
Also classified at 632
B82-24199

633 — AGRICULTURE. FIELD CROPS

633'.00941 — Great Britain. Field crops. Cultivation — *Serials*

[The Agronomist *(Ipswich)*]. The Agronomist : the BASF magazine for the progressive arable farmer. — Spring 1982-. — Ipswich (325 London Rd, Ipswich, Suffolk) : Grigsmore Ltd. for BASF United Kingdom Agrochemical Division, 1982-. — v. : ill(chiefly col.) ; 30cm
Two issues yearly. — Continues: Agricultural news
ISSN 0263-9882 = Agronomist (Ipswich) : Unpriced
B82-40044

633.1 — AGRICULTURE. CEREAL CROPS

633.1'0493 — Cereals. Diseases

Hessayon, D. G.. The cereal disease expert / D.G. Hessayon. — Waltham Cross : pbi, c1982. — 32p : col.ill,col.maps ; 28cm
ISBN 0-903505-16-9 (pbk) : £2.00
B82-21137

633.1'0494 — Cereals. Take-all disease

Biology and control of take-all / edited by M.J.C. Asher and P.J. Shipton. — London : Academic Press, 1981. — xv,538p : ill ; 24cm
Bibliography: p453-507. — Includes index
ISBN 0-12-065320-6 : £41.40 : CIP rev.
B81-06621

633.1'04995'0941 — Great Britain. Cereals. Pesticides

Hughes, R. G. (Roy Gilbert). Ciba-Geigy pesticide briefing : report of a visit to West Germany 11-14 June 1981 / R.G. Hughes. — [London] ([Great Westminster House, Horseferry Rd., SW1P 2AE]) : ADAS, [1982]. — 5p ; 30cm
Cover title
Unpriced (pbk)
B82-40878

633.1'1 — Crops: Wheat

Kihara, Hitoshi. Wheat studies : retrospect and prospects / by Hitoshi Kihara. — Tokyo : Kodansha ; Amsterdam ; Oxford : Elsevier Scientific, 1982. — xviii,308p : ill,1facsim,maps,ports ; 24cm. — (Developments in crop science ; v.3) (Kodansha scientific book)
Includes index
ISBN 0-444-99695-8 : £34.95 : CIP rev.
ISBN 0-444-41617-x (set)
B82-06830

633.1'1'0941 — Great Britain. Winter wheat. Production — *Manuals*

Winter wheat — husbandry and growing systems / ADAS. — Pinner : Ministry of Agriculture, Fisheries and Food, 1980. — ii,41p : ill ; 21cm. — (Booklet / Ministry of Agriculture, Fisheries and Food ; 2291)
Cover title. — Bibliography: p41
Unpriced (pbk)
B82-15570

633.1'5'094 — Europe. Maize. Production & use — *Conference proceedings*

Euromais 1979 *(Conference : Cambridge)*. Production and utilization of the maize crop : proceedings of the First European Maize Congress, Euromais 1979, September 3-7, 1979, Cambridge, England / edited for the Maize Development Association by E.S. Bunting. — Ely : Hereward & Stourdale in association with Packard, 1980. — xix,401p : ill ; 25cm. — (World crops ; 1)
Includes bibliographies
ISBN 0-905996-18-6 : Unpriced
B82-08127

633.1'6 — Barley. Cultivation — *Conference proceedings*

International Barley Genetics Symposium *(4th : 1981 : Edinburgh)*. Barley genetics IV. — Edinburgh (Pentlandfield, Roslin, Midlothian, EH25 9RF) : Scottish Crop Research Institute, Nov.1982. — [970]p
ISBN 0-9508016-0-7 : £25.00 : CIP entry
B82-32886

633.1'69'09411 — Scotland. Spring barley. Damage. Control measures — *Manuals*

Blackett, G. A.. Problems of spring barley / [compiled by G.A. Blackett]. — Edinburgh (West Mains, Edinburgh EH9 3JG) : The East of Scotland College of Agriculture, 1982. — 36p ; 21cm. — (Publication, ISSN 0308-5708 ; no.87)
Cover title. — Text on inside covers
Unpriced (pbk)
B82-12511

633.1'8 — Rice. Nutrients: Zinc. Deficiency

Mikkelsen, D. S.. Zinc fertilization and behavior in flooded soils / D.S. Mikkelsen and Shiou Kuo. — Slough : Commonwealth Agricultural Bureaux, 1977. — 59p : ill ; 25cm. — (Special publication / Commonwealth Bureau of Soils ; no.5)
Bibliography: p47-59
ISBN 0-85198-397-9 (pbk) : Unpriced
B82-10725

633.2/3 — AGRICULTURE. FORAGE CROPS

633.2 — Great Britain. Grassland. Fertilisers: Phosphates & potash

Phosphate and potash for grassland / ADAS. — Pinner : Ministry of Agriculture, Fisheries and Food, 1980. — 7p ; 22cm. — (Grassland practice ; no.4) (Booklet / Ministry of Agriculture, Fisheries and Food ; 2044)
Cover title. — 'incorporates Booklet 2045'
Unpriced (pbk)
B82-15516

633.2 — Hay. Production — *For children*

Patterson, Geoffrey. The story of hay / Geoffrey Patterson. — [London] : Deutsch, 1982. — 32p : col.ill ; 20x26cm
Includes index
ISBN 0-233-97356-7 : £4.50 : CIP rev.
B81-14813

633.2'0072042 — England. Forage crops. Cultivation. Research by Agricultural Development and Advisory Service. *Agriculture Service* — *Serials*

Agricultural Development and Advisory Service. *Agriculture Service*. Grassland, fodder conservation and forage crops : results of Agriculture Service experiments. — 1978-. — [London] ([Great Westminster House, Horseferry Rd, SW1P 2AE]) : ADAS, [1979?]-. — v. ; 21cm
Annual. — Continues: Agricultural Development and Advisory Service. Agriculture Service. Fodder crops, grassland and fodder conservation
ISSN 0263-1695 = Grassland, fodder conservation and forage crops : Unpriced
B82-22687

633.2'00941 — Great Britain. Grassland. Agriculture

Soper, M. H. R.. Grassland / M.H.R. Soper. — London (16 Strutton Ground, SW1P 2HP) : Association of Agriculture, 1982. — 43p,[4]p of plates : ill,1map ; 21cm. — (Modern agriculture series)
Bibliography: p43
Unpriced (pbk) B82-33665

633.2'00942 — England. Agricultural industries. Farms. Grassland

Green, J. O.. A sample survey of grassland in England and Wales 1970-72 : physical features of the grassland, and their relation to age-structure and botanical composition / J.O. Green. — Maidenhead : Grassland Research Institute, c1982. — 39p : ill(some col.),1map ; 30cm
Bibliography: p33
ISBN 0-7084-0227-5 (pbk) : Unpriced
B82-31330

633.2'02 — Scotland. Crops: Grasses. Varieties

Seed mixtures for Scotland. — Edinburgh (West Mains Rd., Edinburgh EH9 3JG) : East of Scotland College of Agriculture, 1982. — 12p ; 21cm. — (Publication / Scottish Agricultural Colleges, ISSN 0308-5708 ; no.86)
Unpriced (unbound)
Also classified at 633.3'27'09411 B82-20476

633.2'55'094 — Europe. Forage crops: Maize

Forage maize : production and utilisation / editors E.S. Bunting ... [et al.]. — London : Agricultural Research Council, 1978. — xv,346p,[8]p of plates : ill(some col.),maps ; 22cm
Includes bibliographies and index
ISBN 0-7084-0082-5 (pbk) : Unpriced
B82-08007

633.3'0913 — Tropical regions. Crops: Legumes

Kay, Daisy E.. Food legumes / Daisy E. Kay. — London : Tropical Products Institute, c1979. — xvi,435p ; 21cm. — (TPI crop and product digest ; no.3)
Includes bibliographies and index
ISBN 0-85954-085-5 (pbk) : £6.50 B82-04108

633.3'27'09411 — Scotland. Crops: Clover. Varieties

Seed mixtures for Scotland. — Edinburgh (West Mains Rd., Edinburgh EH9 3JG) : East of Scotland College of Agriculture, 1982. — 12p ; 21cm. — (Publication / Scottish Agricultural Colleges, ISSN 0308-5708 ; no.86)
Unpriced (unbound)
Primary classification 633.2'02 B82-20476

633.3'68976 — Gambia. Groundnuts. Infestation by Caryedon serratus

Friendship, R.. A preliminary investigation of field and secco infestation of Gambian groundnuts by Caryedon serratus (01) / R. Friendship. — London : Tropical Products Institute, 1974. — iv,14p : ill ; 30cm
English text, English, French and Spanish summaries. — At head of title: Tropical Products Institute
ISBN 0-85954-029-4 (pbk) : £0.30 B82-07463

633.4 — AGRICULTURE. ROOT AND TUBER CROPS

633'.491 — Crops: Potatoes. Growth. Environmental factors

Steward, F. C.. Growth, form and composition of potato plants as affected by environment / F.C. Steward, Ulises Moreno, W.M. Roca. — London : Academic Press for the Annals of Botany Company, 1981. — 45p : ill ; 26cm
Reprinted from Supplement 2 (pp.1-45) to Annals of Botany, volume 48, 1981. — Bibliography: p43-45
ISBN 0-12-670380-9 (pbk) : £5.80 B82-21295

633'.491'09441 — France. Brittany. Early potatoes. Production

Cromack, H. T. H.. Early potato production : report of a study tour undertaken in France and Spain 2-7 May 1981 / H.T.H. Cromack. — [London] ([Great Westminster House, Horseferry Rd., SW1P 2AE]) : ADAS, [1982]. — 18p ; 30cm
Cover title
Unpriced (pbk)
Also classified at 633'.491'094676 B82-40876

633'.491'094676 — Spain. Valencia *(Region)*. Early potatoes. Production

Cromack, H. T. H.. Early potato production : report of a study tour undertaken in France and Spain 2-7 May 1981 / H.T.H. Cromack. — [London] ([Great Westminster House, Horseferry Rd., SW1P 2AE]) : ADAS, [1982]. — 18p ; 30cm
Cover title
Unpriced (pbk)
Primary classification 633'.491'09441
B82-40876

633'.4915'0941 — Great Britain. Potatoes. Damage by harvesting

Balls, R. C.. Report on the National Potato Damage Awareness Campaign : 1981 / a joint project by the Potato Marketing Board and the Agricultural Development and Advisory Service with the co-operation of the East of Scotland College of Agriculture and the North of Scotland College of Agriculture ; report prepared by R.C. Balls, J.S. Gunn, A.J. Starling. — [London] ([50 Hans Cres., SW1X 0HD]) : [Potato Marketing Board], 1982. — 32p : forms ; 21cm
Unpriced (pbk) B82-30914

633'.49168'028 — Great Britain. Potatoes. Indoor storage. Materials handling equipment

Handling equipment for indoor potato storage / ADAS. — Revised [ed.]. — Pinner : Ministry of Agriculture, Fisheries and Food, 1980. — 12p : ill ; 21cm. — (Booklet / Ministry of Agriculture, Fisheries and Food ; 2290)
Cover title. — Previous ed.: 1977. — "Formerly STL 128"
Unpriced (pbk) B82-15568

633.6 — AGRICULTURE. SUGAR AND STARCH PLANTS

633.6'3'072042 — England. Crops: Sugar beet. Cultivation. Research by Agricultural Development and Advisory Service. *Agriculture Service — Serials*

Agricultural Development and Advisory Service. *Agriculture Service.* Sugar beet, oilseed rape and minor cash crops : research and development reports / Agriculture Service. — [197-]-. — [London] ([Great Westminster House, Horseferry Rd, SW1P 2AE]) : ADAS, [between 1978 and 1980]-. — v. ; 21cm
Annual. — Description based on: 1979 issue
ISSN 0263-0737 = Sugar beet, oilseed rape and minor cash crops : Unpriced
Also classified at 633.8'53'072042 B82-15154

633.6'3'0941 — Great Britain. Sugar beet. Cultivation

Sugar beet : a grower's guide / Sugar Beet Research and Education Committee. — 1982 ed. — Bury St. Edmunds (Broom's Barn Experimental Station, Higham, Bury St. Edmunds, IP28 6NP) : [The committee], 1982. — 72p : ill(some col.) ; 21cm
Cover title. — Previous ed.: 1980. — Text on inside covers. — Includes bibliographies
£1.75 (pbk) B82-17423

633.6'35'028 — Great Britain. Sugar beet harvesters. Use & performance

Sugar beet harvesting / ADAS. — Revised [ed.]. — Pinner : Ministry of Agriculture, Fisheries and Food, 1979. — 25p : ill ; 21cm. — (Mechanisation booklet ; 9) (Booklet / Ministry of Agriculture, Fisheries and Food ; 2109)
Cover title. — "Formerly ML9"
Unpriced (pbk) B82-15573

633.8 — AGRICULTURE. PLANTS FOR PERFUMES, FLAVOURINGS, MEDICINAL PURPOSES, ETC

633.8'5 — European Community countries. Crops: Oilseeds. Proteins — *Conference proceedings*

Production and utilization of protein in oilseed crops : proceedings of a seminar in the EEC Programme of Coordination of Research on the Improvement of the Production of Plant Proteins, organised by the Institut für Pflanzenbau und Pflanzenzüchting at Braunschweig, Federal Republic of Germany, 8-10 July 1980 / sponsored by the Commission of the European Communities Directorate-General for Agriculture, Coordination of Agricultural Research ; edited by E.S. Bunting. — The Hague ; London : Nijhoff for the Commission of the European Communities, 1981. — xiv,382p : ill ; 25cm. — (World crops)
Includes bibliographies
ISBN 90-247-2532-1 : Unpriced B82-03459

633.8'53'072042 — England. Crops: Oilseed rape. Cultivation. Research by Agricultural Development and Advisory Service. *Agriculture Service — Serials*

Agricultural Development and Advisory Service. *Agriculture Service.* Sugar beet, oilseed rape and minor cash crops : research and development reports / Agriculture Service. — [197-]-. — [London] ([Great Westminster House, Horseferry Rd, SW1P 2AE]) : ADAS, [between 1978 and 1980]-. — v. ; 21cm
Annual. — Description based on: 1979 issue
ISSN 0263-0737 = Sugar beet, oilseed rape and minor cash crops : Unpriced
Primary classification 633.6'3'072042
B82-15154

633.8'8'0942 — England. National Trust properties. Gardens. Medicinal plants — *Lists*

National Trust. A short guide to herbs and medicinal plants in National Trust gardens. — [London] : [National Trust], [1982?]. — 32p : ill(some col.) ; 21cm
Cover title. — Ill on inside covers
Unpriced (pbk)
Primary classification 635'.7'0942 B82-33072

634 — FRUIT. CULTIVATION

634 — Fruit. Cultivation

Fruit and vegetables from seed. — Exeter : Webb & Bower, Oct.1982. — [208]p
ISBN 0-906671-45-0 : £9.95 : CIP entry
Also classified at 635 B82-24596

634 — Gardens. Fruit. Cultivation — *Manuals*

Spiller, Mary. Growing fruit / Mary Spiller ; drawings by Andrew Ingham. — Harmondsworth : Penguin, 1982, c1980. — 319p : ill ; 20cm
Originally published: London : Allen Lane, 1980. — Includes index
ISBN 0-14-046319-4 (pbk) : £2.95 B82-18145

634 — Gardens. Fruit trees. Cultivation — *Manuals*

Bloom, Adrian. Adrian Bloom's Guide to tree fruit / text by Peter Blackburne-Maze. — Norwich : Jarrold Colour, c1982. — 32p : ill (some col.),1port ; 20cm. — (A Jarrold garden series)
Port on inside cover
ISBN 0-7117-0023-0 (pbk) : Unpriced
B82-35084

634 — Post-harvest fruit. Physiology

Recent advances in the biochemistry of fruits and vegetables / edited by J. Friend and M.J.C. Rhodes. — London : Academic Press, 1981. — xiii,275p : ill ; 24cm. — (Annual proceedings of the Phytochemical Society of Europe, ISSN 0309-0393 ; no.19)
Includes bibliographies and index
ISBN 0-12-268420-6 : £24.00 : CIP rev.
Also classified at 635 B81-33868

634'.0468 — Fruit. Storage

Snowdon, Anna L.. The storage and transport of fresh fruit and vegetables / by Anna L. Snowdon and Awad H.M. Ahmed. — London (308 Seven Sisters Rd., Finsbury Park, N4 2BN) : National Institute of Fresh Produce in association with the Food, Drink and Tobacco Industry Training Board, c1981. — 32p : ill ; 21cm
Bibliography: p18
£5.00 (pbk)
Primary classification 635'.0468 B82-27917

634'.047'0941 — Great Britain. Fruit. Varieties. Trials — *Serials*

Agricultural Development and Advisory Service. *Agriculture Service.* Fruit and hops : research and development reports / Agriculture Service. — 1979-. — [London] ([Great Westminster House, Horseferry Rd, SW1P 2AE]) : ADAS, [1980?]-. — v. ; 21cm
Annual. — Continues: Agricultural Development and Advisory Service. Agriculture Service. Fruit crops. — Description based on: 1980 issue
ISSN 0263-192X = Fruit and hops : Unpriced B82-22658

634'.068'8 — Great Britain. Fruit. Marketing

Marketing home grown fresh produce. — London (308 Seven Sisters Rd., Finsbury Park, N4 2BN) : National Institute of Fresh Produce in association with the Food, Drink and Tobacco Industry Training Board, c1981. — 36p : ill ; 21cm
Cover title. — Text on inside covers
£2.00 (pbk)
Primary classification 635'.068'8 B82-27920

634'.068'8 — Great Britain. Imports: Fruit. Marketing

Marketing imported fresh produce. — London (308 Seven Sisters Rd., Finsbury Park, N4 2BN) : National Institute of Fresh Produce in association with the Food, Drink and Tobacco Industry Training Board, c1981. — 40p : ill ; 21cm
Cover title. — Text on inside covers
£2.00 (pbk)
Primary classification 635'.068'8 B82-27918

634'.072042 — England. Crops: Fruit. Cultivation. Research by Agricultural Development and Advisory Service. *Agriculture Service* — *Serials*

Agricultural Development and Advisory Service. *Agriculture Service.* Fruit crops : results of experiments at the Experimental Horticulture Stations. — 1976-1978. — [London] ([Great Westminster House, Horseferry Rd, SW1P 2AE]) : ADAS, [1977?]-[1979?]. — 3v. ; 21cm
Annual. — Reports results of experiments carried out by: Agriculture Service of ADAS. — Continued by: Agricultural Development and Advisory Service. Agriculture Service. Fruit and hops
Unpriced B82-22690

634'.11 — Apples. Production

Turnbull, J.. Orchard systems : report of a study tour undertaken in Holland and Belgium 16-21 August 1981 / J. Turnbull & M.J. Marks. — [London] ([Great Westminster House, Horseferry Rd., SW1P 2AE]) : ADAS, 1982. — 26p : ill ; 30cm. — (ADAS overseas study tour programme ; 1981/82)
Cover title
Unpriced (pbk) B82-40447

634'.7'02341 — Great Britain. Crops: Soft fruit. Production — *Career guides*

Working in tree and soft fruit production. — [Beckenham] ([32 Beckenham Rd, Beckenham, Kent BR3 4PB]) : Agricultural Training Board on behalf of the Joint Working Party on Careers Literature, 1981. — 1 : sheet,1ill ; 21cm. — (Careers in horticulture) (Job leaflet)
Unpriced (unbound) B82-19445

634'.71'0941 — Great Britain. Cane fruit. Cultivation — *Manuals*

Cane fruit. — [6th ed.]. — London : Grower, 1982. — 89p,viiip of plates : ill(some col.) ; 21cm. — (ADAS/MAFF reference book ; 156)
Previous ed.: 1975. — Includes index
ISBN 0-901361-67-4 (pbk) : £4.50 B82-30664

634'.772 — Bananas. Production

Simmonds, N. W.. Bananas / N.W. Simmonds. — 2nd ed. — London : Longman, 1966 (1982 [printing]). — 512p : ill,maps ; 22cm. — (Tropical agriculture series)
Originally published: London : Longmans, 1959. — Includes bibliographies and index
ISBN 0-582-46355-6 (pbk) : £12.95 : CIP rev. B82-23355

634'.8'0942 — England. Vineyards. Grapes. Cultivation

Bedford, John R.. Discovering English vineyards / John R. Bedford. — Princes Risborough : Shire, 1982. — 56p : ill,1map ; 18cm. — (The Discovering series ; 269)
Bibliography: p56
ISBN 0-85263-604-0 (pbk) : £1.25 B82-39400

Grapes for wine / Ministry of Agriculture, Fisheries and Food. — London : H.M.S.O., 1980. — vi,46p,viiip of plates : ill(some col.),1map ; 25cm. — (Reference book ; 322)
ISBN 0-11-240332-8 (pbk) : £4.50 B82-15566

Pearkes, Gillian. Vinegrowing in Britain / Gillian Pearkes ; with illustrations by the author. — London : Dent, 1982. — xii,324p : ill,2maps ; 25cm
Bibliography: p316-317. — Includes index
ISBN 0-460-04393-5 : £10.50 : CIP rev. B82-09708

634.9 — FORESTRY

634.9 — Forestry

Introduction to forest science / Raymond A. Young editor. — New York ; Chichester : Wiley, c1982. — xvii,554p : ill,maps ; 25cm
Text and ill on lining papers. — Includes index
ISBN 0-471-06438-6 : £17.50 B82-36952

634.9'06'041 — Great Britain. Forestry. Organisations: Royal Forestry Society of England, Wales and Northern Ireland, *to 1981*

James, N. D. G.. A forestry centenary : the history of the Royal Forestry Society of England, Wales and Northern Ireland. — Oxford : Basil Blackwell, May 1982. — [224]p
ISBN 0-631-13015-2 : £12.50 : CIP entry B82-06943

634.9'072 — Forestry. Research projects. Planning

Johnston, D. R.. The formulation of research programmes / D.R. Johnston ; prepared for the Eleventh Commonwealth Forestry Conference, Trinidad, September 1980. — Edinburgh : Forestry Commission, c1980. — 16p ; 21cm. — (Forestry Commission R & D paper ; 126)
Cover title
ISBN 0-85538-081-0 (pbk) : Unpriced B82-37886

634.9'0913 — Tropical regions. Forestry

Evans, Julian. Plantation forestry in the tropics / Julian Evans. — Oxford : Clarendon, 1982. — xv,472p : ill,1map,1plan ; 24cm. — (Oxford science publications)
Bibliography: p430-452. — Includes index
ISBN 0-19-859464-x : £35.00 : CIP rev. B81-36229

634.9'0941 — Great Britain. Forestry

James, N. D. G.. The forester's companion. — 3rd ed. — Oxford : Blackwell, Oct.1981. — [400]p
ISBN 0-631-12796-8 (cased) : £15.00 : CIP entry
ISBN 0-631-12797-6 (pbk) : £5.95 B81-28014

634.9'28 — Tropical forests. Management. Socioeconomic aspects — *Conference proceedings*

Socio-economic effects and constraints in tropical forest management. — Chichester : Wiley, Dec.1982. — [250]p
Conference papers
ISBN 0-471-10375-6 : £14.75 : CIP entry B82-30825

634.9'3 — Great Britain. Forests. Roads. Planning

Granfield, E. F.. Developments in forest road planning / E.F. Granfield, C.D. MacMahon, D.A. Mithen ; prepared for the Eleventh Commonwealth Forestry Conference, Trinidad, September 1980. — Edinburgh : Forestry Commission, c1980. — 24p : ill,2maps ; 21cm. — (Forestry Commission R & D paper ; 127)
Cover title. — Folded leaf attached to inside cover. — Bibliography: p18
ISBN 0-85538-082-9 (pbk) : Unpriced B82-37885

634.9'5 — Forestry. Applications of plant ecology

Application of vegetation science to forestry / edited by G. Jahn. — The Hague ; London : Junk, 1982. — xi,405p : ill,maps,1port ; 25cm
Includes some summaries in German. — Includes bibliographies and index
ISBN 90-619-3193-2 : Unpriced B82-21458

634.9'5 — Great Britain. Trees. Requirements: Rainwater

Binns, W. O.. Trees and water / W.O. Binns ; prepared for the Department of the Environment by the Forestry Commission. — [London] : H.M.S.O., 1980. — 19p : ill(some col.). — (Arboricultural leaflet ; 6)
Bibliography: p19
ISBN 0-11-751473-x (21cmunbound) : £2.00
Also classified at 634.9'5 B82-15517

634.9'5 — Great Britain. Trees. Requirements: Soil water

Binns, W. O.. Trees and water / W.O. Binns ; prepared for the Department of the Environment by the Forestry Commission. — [London] : H.M.S.O., 1980. — 19p : ill(some col.). — (Arboricultural leaflet ; 6)
Bibliography: p19
ISBN 0-11-751473-x (21cmunbound) : £2.00
Primary classification 634.9'5 B82-15517

634.9'5'072041 — Great Britain. Silviculture. Research — *Conference proceedings*

Research strategy for silviculture : proceedings of a discussion meeting, Cumbria College of Agriculture and Forestry, Newton Rigg, Penrith, 28-30 March 1980 / edited by D.C. Malcolm. — Edinburgh : Institute of Foresters of Great Britain, [1980]. — 109p : 1ill ; 21cm
Cover title. — Includes bibliographies
ISBN 0-907284-00-0 (pbk) : Unpriced B82-35372

634.9'56 — Forestry. Applications of plant tissue culture

Tissue culture in forestry / edited by J.M. Bonga and D.J. Durzan. — The Hague ; London : Nijhoff, 1982. — xi,420p : ill ; 25cm. — (Forestry sciences)
Includes bibliographies and index
ISBN 90-247-2660-3 : Unpriced B82-37029

634.9'56 — Forestry. Applications of quantitative methods of genetics

Namkoong, Gene. Introduction to quantitative genetics in forestry / Gene Namkoong. — Tunbridge Wells : Castle House, c1981. — viii,342p : ill ; 24cm
Bibliography: p321-342
ISBN 0-7194-0067-8 (cased) : £15.00
ISBN 0-7194-0068-6 (pbk) : Unpriced B82-14465

634.9'56'09413 — Scotland. Central Lowlands. Afforestation — *Proposals*

Central Scotland Woodlands Project. *Steering Group.* Central Scotland Woodlands Project : report of the Steering Group. — Edinburgh (12 St. Giles St., Edinburgh 1) : Lothian Regional Council, Department of Physical Planning, 1978. — 43p : maps ; 30cm
Text and ill on inside covers
Unpriced (pbk) B82-20918

634.9'56'09413 — Scotland. Central Lowlands. Afforestation — *Serials*

Central Scotland Woodlands Project. Interim report / Central Scotland Woodland[s] Project. — 1st (Feb. 1979-Jan. 1980)-. — [Falkirk] ([St. Crispins Place, Falkirk FK1 1QF]) : [The Project], 1980-. — v. : ill,maps ; 30cm
Annual. — Description based on: 2nd (Feb. 1980-Jan. 1981)
ISSN 0263-0656 = Interim report - Central Scotland Woodland Project : Unpriced B82-14787

634.9'618'0973 — United States. Forests. Fire prevention & fire fighting, *to 1981*. Cultural aspects

Pyne, Stephen J.. Fire in America : a cultural history of wildland and rural fire / Stephen J. Pyne. — Princeton, N.J. ; Guildford : Princeton University Press, c1982. — xvi,654p : ill ; 25cm
Bibliography: p618-626. — Includes index
ISBN 0-691-08300-2 : £24.70 B82-39891

634.9'63 — Trees. Diseases. Diagnosis. Laboratory techniques

Blanchard, Robert O.. Field and laboratory guide to tree pathology / Robert O. Blanchard, Terry A. Tattar. — New York ; London : Academic Press, 1981. — xv,285p : ill ; 25cm
Includes bibliographies and index
ISBN 0-12-103980-3 : £15.60 B82-10148

634.9'695'0941 — Great Britain. Forests. Pesticides

Great Britain. *Forestry Commission.* The use of chemicals in the Forestry Commission. — Edinburgh : The Commission, 1979. — ii,98p ; 21cm
'Guide to use of herbicides in the forest' (1 folded sheet) as insert. — Includes index
ISBN 0-85538-072-1 (pbk) : Unpriced B82-15524

634.9'75 — Forests. Timber trees: Conifers. Use

Richards, E. G. (Ernest Glenesk). Developments towards whole tree utilization of softwoods / E.G. Richards ; prepared for the Eleventh Commonwealth Forestry Conference, Trinidad, September 1980. — Edinburgh : Forestry Commission, c1980. — 14p ; 21cm. — (Forestry Commission R & D paper ; 128)
Cover title. — Bibliography: p12-14
ISBN 0-85538-086-1 (pbk) : Unpriced B82-37883

634.9'754 — Douglas fir trees. Growth. Effects of thinning

Adlard, P. G.. Growth and growing space : results from an individual-tree thinning experiment in a 20-year-old Douglas Fir plantation / by P.G. Adlard and J.P. Smith. — Oxford : Commonwealth Forestry Institute, Oxford University, 1981. — ii,28p : ill ; 30cm. — (CFI occasional papers, ISSN 0141-8181 ; no.14)
Bibliography: p26-28
Unpriced (pbk) B82-11341

634.9'8'0913 — Tropical regions. Trees. Crops

Opeke, Lawrence K.. Tropical tree crops / Lawrence K. Opeke. — Chichester : Wiley, c1982. — xvii,312p : ill ; 24cm
Includes bibliographies and index
ISBN 0-471-10060-9 : £17.25 : CIP rev.
ISBN 0-471-10066-8 (pbk) : Unpriced B82-09698

635 — GARDENING

635 — Allotments. Plants. Cultivation — *Manuals*

Titchmarsh, Alan, *1949-*. The allotment gardener's handbook. — London : Severn House, Sept.1982. — [176]p
ISBN 0-7278-2026-5 : £7.95 : CIP entry B82-20398

635 — Crops: Vegetables. Cultivation

Hardy, Frank. Commercial vegetable growing. — London : Muller, Sept.1982. — [272]p
ISBN 0-584-11016-2 : £9.95 : CIP entry B82-21977

635 — Crops: Vegetables. Cultivation — *Conference proceedings*

International Symposium on Timing of Field Production of Vegetables *(4th : 1981 : Nyborg)*. Report on the International Society for Horticultural Science 4th International Symposium on Timing of Field Production of Vegetables, Nyborg, Denmark 27-31 July 1981 / J.D. Whitwell, N.T. Weatheritt. — [London] : ADAS, 1982. — 13p ; 30cm
Cover title
Unpriced (pbk) B82-21812

635 — Gardening

Gardeners' question time / Ken Ford ... [et al.]. — Harmondsworth : Penguin, 1982, c1981. — 264p ; 18cm
Originally published: London : Robson, 1981
ISBN 0-14-046511-1 (pbk) : £1.50 B82-18152

Hamilton, Geoff. The Gardeners' world cottage garden / Geoff Hamilton ; drawings by Lorna Turpin. — London : British Broadcasting Corporation, 1982. — 176p : ill(some col.),plans ; 23cm. — (The Small garden guide)
Includes index
ISBN 0-563-20059-6 (pbk) : £4.75 B82-31754

Hellyer, A. G. L.. Gardening through the year / Arthur Hellyer. — Rev. — London : Hamlyn, 1981. — 224p : ill(some col.) ; 29cm
Previous ed.: i.e. 4th ed. published as Your garden week by week, 1977. — Ill on lining papers. — Includes index
ISBN 0-600-30514-7 : £8.95 B82-00694

Jekyll, Gertrude. A gardener's testament. — Woodbridge : Antique Collectors' Club, Oct.1982. — [400]p
Originally published: London : Country Life, 1937
ISBN 0-907462-29-4 : £12.50 : CIP entry B82-25750

Jekyll, Gertrude. Home and garden. — Woodbridge : Antique Collectors' Club, Apr.1982. — [360]p
Originally published: London : Longmans, 1900
ISBN 0-907462-18-9 : £12.50 : CIP entry B82-14195

Loads, Fred. Fred Load's gardening tips of a lifetime. — London : Hamlyn Paperbacks, 1982, c1980. — 207p : ill ; 20cm
Originally published: 1980. — Includes index
ISBN 0-600-20500-2 (pbk) : £1.50 B82-12391

McHoy, Peter. The gardener's diary. — Poole : Blandford Press, Dec.1982. — 1v.
ISBN 0-7137-1267-8 : £9.95 : CIP entry B82-30213

The **Observer** good gardening guide. — Exeter : Webb & Bower, Feb.1983. — [256]p
ISBN 0-906671-54-x : £15.00 : CIP entry B82-39813

Smith, Geoffrey. Mr Smith's favourite garden / by Geoffrey Smith ; illustrated by Maggie Raynor ; edited by Brian Davies. — London : British Broadcasting Corporation, 1982. — 80p : ill ; 21cm
Includes index
ISBN 0-563-16482-4 (pbk) : £1.50 B82-13681

Step-by-step gardening. — London : Collins, Aug.1982. — [288]p
ISBN 0-00-218080-4 : £8.95 : CIP entry B82-21074

Ward Lock's complete home gardener. — London : Ward Lock, Sept.1982. — [288]p
ISBN 0-7063-6125-3 : £9.95 : CIP entry B82-20011

The **Wisley** book of gardening : a guide for enthusiasts / foreword by Lord Aberconway ; editor Robert Pearson ; consultant editor Elspeth Napier ; with contributions by C.D. Brickell ... [et al.] ; line drawings by Charles Stitt. — Feltham : Royal Horticultural Society in association with Collingridge, 1981. — 352p,32p of plates : ill(some col.),plans ; 26cm
Includes index
ISBN 0-600-36778-9 : £15.00 B82-00753

635 — Gardens. Plants

Bloom, Adrian. Adrian Bloom's guide to garden plants. — Norwich : Jarrold. — (A Jarrold garden series)
Bk.10: Annual & bedding plants / text by Bob Hopkins. — 1981. — [32]p : col.ill,1port ; 20cm
Text, port on inside covers
ISBN 0-85306-937-9 (pbk) : Unpriced B82-01364

635 — Gardens. Plants. Cultivation

Foster, Raymond. The gardener's guide to rare, exotic and difficult plants. — Newton Abbot : David & Charles, Sept.1982. — [192]p
ISBN 0-7153-8293-4 : £10.50 : CIP entry B82-20376

635 — Gardens. Vegetables. Cultivation — *Manuals*

Bleasdale, J. K. A.. Know & grow vegetables 2 / J.K.A. Bleasdale, P.J. Salter and others. — Oxford : Oxford University Press, 1982. — 202p : ill ; 21cm
Includes index
ISBN 0-19-217727-3 (cased) : Unpriced : CIP rev.
ISBN 0-19-286017-8 (pbk) : £2.95 B81-34376

Growing vegetables. — London : Readers Digest Association, 1978 (1981 [printing]). — 56p : col.ill ; 27cm. — (Reader's Digest basic guide)
'Text and illustrations in this book are taken from Reader's Digest illustrated guide to gardening', 1975
ISBN 0-276-00169-9 (pbk) : £1.25 B82-04168

Home produce : vegetables and herbs. — London : Reader's Digest, c1978 (1982 [printing]). — 56p : ill ; 27cm. — (Reader's digest basic guide)
Unpriced (pbk) B82-34675

635 — Horticultural industries. Nursery stock. Cultivation

Dick, Lila. An introduction to modern nursery stock production. — London : Muller, May 1981. — [192]p
ISBN 0-584-10410-3 (cased) : £6.95 : CIP entry
ISBN 0-584-10411-1 (pbk) : £3.50 B81-12825

635 — Post-harvest vegetables. Physiology

Recent advances in the biochemistry of fruits and vegetables / edited by J. Friend and M.J.C. Rhodes. — London : Academic Press, 1981. — xiii,275p : ill ; 24cm. — (Annual proceedings of the Phytochemical Society of Europe, ISSN 0309-0393 ; no.19)
Includes bibliographies and index
ISBN 0-12-268420-6 : £24.00 : CIP rev.
Primary classification 634 B81-33868

635 — Vegetables. Cultivation

Fruit and vegetables from seed. — Exeter : Webb & Bower, Oct.1982. — [208]p
ISBN 0-906671-45-0 : £9.95 : CIP entry
Primary classification 634 B82-24596

635'.023'41 — Great Britain. Commercial nurseries — *Career guides*

Working in a plant nursery. — [Beckenham] ([32 Beckenham Rd, Beckenham, Kent BR3 4PB]) : Agricultural Training Board on behalf of the Joint Working Party on Careers Literature, 1981. — [4]p : ill ; 21cm. — (Careers in horticulture) (Job leaflet)
Unpriced (unbound) B82-19442

635'.023'41 — Great Britain. Horticulture — *Career guides*

Careers in horticulture. — [Beckenham] ([32 Beckenham Rd, Beckenham, Kent BR3 4PB]) : Agricultural Training Board on behalf of the Joint Working Party on Careers Literature, 1980. — 8p : ill ; 21cm
Unpriced (unbound) B82-19448

635'.028'8 — Garden equipment. Maintenance & repair — *Amateurs' manuals*

Looking after your garden. — London : Readers Digest Association, 1978 (1980 [printing]). — 64p : col.ill ; 27cm. — (Reader's Digest basic guide)
'Text and illustrations in this book are taken from Reader's Digest repair manual', 1972
ISBN 0-276-00173-7 (pbk) : £0.95 B82-04170

635'.03'21 — Gardening — *Encyclopaedias*

Everett, Thomas H.. The New York Botanical Garden illustrated encyclopedia of horticulture / Thomas H. Everett. — New York ; London : Garland
Vol.6: Id-Ma. — c1981. — xx,p1777-2130,[14]p of plates : ill(some col.) ; 31cm
ISBN 0-8240-7236-7 : Unpriced B82-02777

Everett, Thomas H.. The New York Botanical Garden illustrated encyclopedia of horticulture / Thomas H. Everett. — New York ; London : Garland
Vol.7: Ma-Par. — c1981. — xxp,p2131-2492,[16]p of plates : ill(some col.) ; 32cm
ISBN 0-8240-7237-5 : £63.53 B82-11470

635'.03'21 — Gardening — *Encyclopaedias continuation*

Everett, Thomas H.. The New York Botanical Garden illustrated encyclopedia of horticulture / Thomas H. Everett. — New York ; London : Garland
Vol.8: Par-Py. — c1981. — xxp,p2493-2862,[16]p of plates : ill(some col.) ; 32cm
ISBN 0-8240-7238-3 : Unpriced B82-14533

Everett, Thomas H.. The New York Botanical Garden illustrated enyclopedia of horticulture / Thomas H. Everett. — New York ; London : Garland
Ill on front lining papers
Vol.9: Q-Sta. — c1982. — xx,2963-3224p,[16]p of plates : ill(some col.) ; 32cm
ISBN 0-8240-7239-1 : Unpriced B82-35125

Huxley, Anthony. The Penguin encyclopedia of gardening / Anthony Huxley ; illustrations by Vana Haggerty. — London : Allen Lane, 1981. — 373p,[16]p of plates : ill(some col.) ; 25cm
Ill on lining papers
ISBN 0-7139-1141-7 : £9.95 B82-03893

635'.03'21 — Gardens. Plants — *Encyclopaedias*

Reader's Digest encyclopaedia of garden plants and flowers. — 2nd ed, repr. with amendments. — London : Reader's Digest, 1981. — 800p : ill(some col.) ; 27cm
Previous ed.: ie. 2nd ed. 1978
£12.95 B82-06070

Reader's digest encyclopaedia of garden plants and flowers. — 2nd ed., repr. with amendments. — London : Reader's Digest Association, 1982, c1978. — 800p : ill(some col.) ; 27cm
£12.95 B82-31555

635'.043 — Gardens. Plants. Propagation

Toogood, Alan R.. Propagation / Alan Toogood. — London : Dent, 1980 (1982 [printing]). — 320p : ill ; 24cm
Bibliography: p305. — Includes index
ISBN 0-460-02235-0 (pbk) : £3.95 B82-23938

635'.043 — Gardens. Plants. Propagation — *Manuals*

The **Hamlyn** guide to plant propagation / edited by Susanne Mitchell and Barbara Haynes. — London : Hamlyn, c1982. — 128p : ill(some col.) ; 23cm
Includes index
ISBN 0-600-30516-3 : £3.99 B82-17611

635'.0468 — Vegetables. Storage

Snowdon, Anna L.. The storage and transport of fresh fruit and vegetables / by Anna L. Snowdon and Awad H.M. Ahmed. — London (308 Seven Sisters Rd., Finsbury Park, N4 2BN) : National Institute of Fresh Produce in association with the Food, Drink and Tobacco Industry Training Board, c1981. — 32p : ill ; 21cm
Bibliography: p18
£5.00 (pbk)
Also classified at 634'.0468 B82-27917

635'.047'0941 — Great Britain. Gardens. Vegetables. Varieties

Chowings, J. W.. Vegetable varieties for the gardener / [J.W. Chowings, W.M. French]. — Cambridge ([Huntingdon Rd., Cambridge CB3 0LE]) : National Institute of Agricultural Botany, [1982?]. — 32p ; 21cm
Text on inside covers
£0.75 (pbk) B82-32954

635'.0483 — England. Greenhouses. Vegetables. Cultivation. Research by Agricultural Development and Advisory Service. *Agriculture Service* **—** *Serials*

Agricultural Development and Advisory Service. *Agriculture Service.* Protected crops. Vegetables : research and development reports / Agriculture Service. — 1977-. — [London] ([Great Westminster House, Horseferry Rd, SW1P 2AE]) : ADAS, [1978?]-. — v. ; 21cm
Annual. — Description bases on: 1980 issue
ISSN 0263-0753 = Protected crops. Vegetables : Unpriced B82-15153

635'.0483 — Great Britain. Greenhouse horticulture — *Career guides*

Working in glasshouses. — [Beckenham] ([32 Beckenham Rd, Beckenham, Kent BR3 4PB]) : Agricultural Training Board on behalf of the Joint Working Party on Careers Literature, 1981. — [4]p : ill ; 21cm. — (Careers in horticulture) (Job leaflet)
Unpriced (unbound) B82-19447

635'.0483 — Great Britain. Greenhouses. Vegetables. Cultivation

Vegetables under glass. — London : Grower, 1982. — 77p : ill ; 21cm. — (Grower guide ; no.26)
ISBN 0-901361-64-x (pbk) : £3.75 B82-21122

635'.0483 — Greenhouses. Plants. Cultivation — *Manuals*

Hellyer, A. G. L.. The Dobies book of greenhouses / Arthur Hellyer ; drawings by Debbie Kartun. — London : published in collaboration with Dobie [by] Heinemann, 1981. — 149p : col.ill ; 25cm
Includes index
ISBN 0-434-32626-7 (pbk) : £4.95 B82-02604

635'.0483 — Greenhouses. Vegetables. Commercial cultivation — *Manuals*

Walls, Ian. Modern greenhouse methods : vegetables. — London : Muller, Nov.1981. — [160]p
ISBN 0-584-10388-3 : £9.95 : CIP entry B81-30533

635'.0483 — Horticultural greenhouses. Ventilation — *Manuals*

Greenhouse ventilation / ADAS. — Revised [ed.]. — Pinner : Ministry of Agriculture, Fisheries and Food, 1979. — ii,24p : ill ; 21cm. — (Mechanisation booklet ; 5) (Booklet / Ministry of Agriculture, Fisheries and Food ; 2105)
Cover title. — "Formerly ML5"
Unpriced (pbk) B82-15569

635'.0483 — Solar growers — *Manuals*

Pierce, John H.. Home solar gardening / John H. Pierce. — Toronto ; London : Van Nostrand Reinhold, c1981. — xi,164p : ill ; 24cm
Bibliography: p157-159. — Includes index
ISBN 0-442-29680-0 (cased) : £12.70
ISBN 0-442-29679-7 (pbk) : £7.60 B82-26172

635'.068'8 — Great Britain. Imports: Vegetables. Marketing

Marketing imported fresh produce. — London (308 Seven Sisters Rd., Finsbury Park, N4 2BN) : National Institute of Fresh Produce in association with the Food, Drink and Tobacco Industry Training Board, c1981. — 40p : ill ; 21cm
Cover title. — Text on inside covers
£2.00 (pbk)
Also classified at 634'.068'8 B82-27918

635'.068'8 — Great Britain. Vegetables. Marketing

Marketing home grown fresh produce. — London (308 Seven Sisters Rd., Finsbury Park, N4 2BN) : National Institute of Fresh Produce in association with the Food, Drink and Tobacco Industry Training Board, c1981. — 36p : ill ; 21cm
Cover title. — Text on inside covers
£2.00 (pbk)
Also classified at 634'.068'8 B82-27920

635'.072042 — England. Crops: Vegetables. Cultivation. Research by Agricultural Development and Advisory Service. *Agriculture Service* **—** *Serials*

Agricultural Development and Advisory Service. *Agriculture Service.* Field vegetables : results of experiments / Agriculture Service. — 1978-. — [London] ([Great Westminster House, Horseferry Rd, SW1P 2AE]) : ADAS, [1979?]-. — v. ; 21cm
Annual
ISSN 0263-0729 = Field vegetables : Unpriced B82-15144

635'.072042275 — Horticulture. Research organisations: Efford Experimental Horticulture Station — *Serials*

Efford Experimental Horticulture Station. Annual review / Efford Experimental Horticulture Station. — 1979-. — Lymington (Lymington, Hants. SO4 0LZ) : The Station, 1980-. — v. : ill ; 21cm
Continues: Efford Experimental Horticulture Station. Annual report. — Description based on: 1980 issue
ISSN 0263-0281 = Annual review - Efford Experimental Horticulture Station : Unpriced B82-32156

635'.072042489 — Horticulture. Research organisations: Luddington Experimental Horticulture Station — *Serials*

Luddington Experimental Horticulture Station. Annual review / Luddington Experimental Horticulture Station. — 1979-. — Stratford-upon-Avon (Stratford-upon-Avon, Warwickshire CV37 9SJ) : The Station, 1980-. — v. : ill ; 21cm
Continues: Luddington Experimental Horticulture Station. Annual report
ISSN 0263-0508 = Annual review - Luddington Experimental Horticulture Station : Unpriced B82-32155

635'.074'02134 — London. Kensington and Chelsea *(London Borough).* **Horticultural shows: Chelsea Flower Show,** *to 1975*

Whiten, Faith. The Chelsea Flower Show / Faith and Geoff Whiten ; with photographs by Derek Goard. — London : Elm Tree in association with the Royal Horticultural Society, 1982. — 127p,[8]p of plates : ill(some col.),facsims,1plan,ports(some col.) ; 25cm
Includes index
ISBN 0-241-10744-x : £8.95 : CIP rev. B82-09283

635'.088042 — Great Britain. Women gardeners, *to ca 1980*

MacLeod, Dawn. Down-to-earth women : those who care for the soil / Dawn MacLeod. — Edinburgh : Blackwood, 1982. — xx,186p,[28]p of plates : ill,1fascim,ports ; 23cm
Bibliography: p177-179. — Includes index
ISBN 0-85158-158-7 : £7.95 B82-28837

635'.092'4 — Gardening — *Personal observations*

Cragoe, Elizabeth. The untidy gardener / by Elizabeth Cragoe. — London : Hamilton, 1982. — 186p : 1plan ; 23cm
ISBN 0-241-10759-8 : £8.95 : CIP rev. B82-12568

635'.092'4 — Great Britain. Gardening. Robinson, William, *1838-1935* **—** *Biographies*

Allan, Mea. William Robinson 1838-1935 : father of the English flower garden / by Mea Allan. — London : Faber, 1982. — 255p : ill,ports ; 24cm
Bibliography: p238-241. — Includes index
ISBN 0-571-11865-8 : £10.50 : CIP rev. B82-10764

635'.0941 — Great Britain. Gardening

Jekyll, Gertrude. Wood and garden : notes and thoughts, practical and critical, of a working amateur / by Gertrude Jekyll. — [Woodbridge] : Antique Collectors' Club, c1981. — 377p : ill (some col.) ; 22cm
Originally published: London : Longmans, Green, 1899. — Includes index
ISBN 0-907462-11-1 : £12.50 : CIP rev. B81-36999

Scott, Amoret. The garden diary / by Amoret Scott. — Yeovil : Oxford Illustrated Press, c1982. — 64p : ill ; 28cm
ISBN 0-902280-86-4 : £3.95 B82-26761

635'.09417 — Ireland *(Republic).* **Gardens. Plants —** *Serials*

Moorea : the journal of the Irish Garden Plant Society. — Vol.1 (Mar. 1982)-. — Dublin (c/o National Botanic Gardens, Glasnevin, Dublin 9) : The Society, 1982-. — v. : ports ; 30cm
£5.00 B82-27659

635'.09422'74 — Hampshire. Selborne. Gardening — *Correspondence, diaries, etc.*

White, Gilbert. [The Garden kalendar. Selections]. Gilbert White's year : passages from 'The garden kalendar' & 'The naturalist's journal' / selected by John Commander ; introduction by Richard Mabey. — Oxford : Oxford University Press, 1982. — 134p : ill ; 20cm. — (Oxford paperbacks)
Originally published: London : Scolar Press, 1979
ISBN 0-19-281354-4 (pbk) : £2.95 : CIP rev.
Primary classification 508.422'74 B82-10434

635'.0944'5 — France. Loire Valley. Horticultural industries. Nursery stock. Cultivation

Rowell, D. J.. Nursery stock production in the Loire Valley : report of a study tour undertaken in France 6-11 September 1981 / D.J. Rowell. — [London] ([Great Westminster House, Horseferry Rd., SW1P 2AE]) : ADAS, 1982. — 14p : 1map ; 30cm
Cover title. — Text on inside cover
Unpriced (pbk) B82-18707

635'.23'0966 — West Africa. Food crops: Yams - *Conference proceedings*

Yams = Ignames. — Oxford : Clarendon Press, Aug.1981. — 1v.
Conference papers
ISBN 0-19-854557-6 : £15.00 : CIP entry
B81-16356

635'.35 — Crops: Cauliflowers. Production

Cauliflowers. — London : Grower, 1982. — 87p,16p of plates : ill(some col.) ; 21cm. — (ADAS/MAFF reference book ; 131)
Includes index
ISBN 0-901361-66-6 (pbk) : £4.50 B82-24652

635'.642'09492 — Netherlands. Tomatoes. Nurseries

Charlesworth, R. R.. Visit by the West Sussex Tomato Working Party to nurseries of prominent growers : report of a visit to Holland 18-19 September 1981 / R.R. Charlesworth, A.P. Wareing. — [London] ([Great Westminster House, Horseferry Rd., SW1P 2AE]) : ADAS, [1982]. — 5p ; 30cm
Cover title
Unpriced (pbk) B82-40877

635'.7 — Gardens. Herbs. Cultivation — *Manuals*

Bonar, Ann. Book of herbs and herb gardening / Ann Bonar. — Poole : Blandford, [1981]. — 95p : ill(some col.),1port ; 15cm
Includes index
ISBN 0-7137-1053-5 (pbk) : £1.95 B82-20226

635'.7'0941 — Great Britain. Gardens. Herbs. Cultivation from seeds

McEwan, Helen. Seed growers guide to herbs & wild flowers / by Helen McEwan. — Sudbury : Suffolk Herbs, c1982. — 47p : ill ; 21cm
ISBN 0-9508022-0-4 (pbk) : Unpriced
Also classified at 635.9'42'0941 B82-20346

635'.7'0942 — England. National Trust properties. Gardens. Herbs — *Lists*

National Trust. A short guide to herbs and medicinal plants in National Trust gardens. — [London] : [National Trust], [1982?]. — 32p : ill(some col.) ; 21cm
Cover title. — Ill on inside covers
Unpriced (pbk)
Also classified at 633.8'8'0942 B82-33072

635'.8 — Mushrooms. Cultivation — *Manuals*

Genders, Roy. Mushroom growing for everyone / Roy Genders. — Rev. ed. — London : Faber, 1982. — 216p : ill ; 20cm
Previous ed.: 1969. — Includes index
ISBN 0-571-11806-2 (pbk) : £2.95 : CIP rev.
B82-00205

635.9 — GARDENING. FLOWERS AND ORNAMENTAL PLANTS

635.9 — England. Plants. Nurseries. Hardy ornamental plants. Cultivation. Research by Agricultural Development and Advisory Service. *Agriculture Service — Serials*

Agricultural Development and Advisory Service. *Agriculture Service*. Hardy ornamental nursery stock : research and development reports / Agriculture Service. — 1977-. — [London] ([Great Westminster House, Horseferry Rd, SW1P 2AE]) : ADAS, [1978?]-. — v. ; 21cm
Annual. — Description based on: 1980 issue
ISSN 0263-0761 = Hardy ornamental nursery stock : Unpriced B82-15147

635.9 — Gardens. Ornamental flowering plants. Cultivation — *Manuals*

Bonar, Ann. Book of flower gardening / Ann Bonar. — Poole : Blandford, [1982]. — 95p : ill(some col.),1port ; 15cm. — ('How to')
Includes index
ISBN 0-7137-1052-7 (pbk) : £1.95 B82-20221

635.9 — Gardens. Ornamental plants

Johnson, Hugh. The Mitchell Beazley pocket guide to garden plants / Hugh Johnson and Paul Miles. — London : Mitchell Beazley, c1981 (1982 [printing]). — 168p : col.ill,1col.map ; 20cm
Includes index
ISBN 0-85533-289-1 : £3.95 B82-33575

635.9 — Great Britain. Buildings. Grounds. Construction & maintenance. Standard costs — *Lists*

Schedule of rates for grounds maintenance, 1981 / Department of the Environment, Property Services Agency. — 2nd ed. — London : H.M.S.O., 1981. — v,29p ; 30cm
Previous ed.: published as Schedule of rates for the preparation and maintenance of land, 1973. — Includes index
ISBN 0-11-671077-2 (pbk) : £3.50 B82-10957

635.9'072042 — England. Crops: Ornamental flowering plants. Cultivation. Research by Agricultural Development and Advisory Service. *Agriculture Service — Serials*

Agricultural Development and Advisory Service. *Agriculture Service*. Protected crops. Ornamentals : research and development reports / Agriculture Service. — 1977-. — [London] ([Great Westminster House, Horseferry Rd, SW1P 2AE]) : ADAS, [1978?]-. — v. ; 21cm
Annual. — Description bases on: 1980 issue
ISSN 0263-0745 = Protected crops. Ornamentals : Unpriced B82-15152

635.9'094 — Europe. Gardens. Flowering plants — *Early works*

Curtis, William, *1746-1799*. Curtis's flower garden displayed : 120 plates from the years 1787-1807 / with new descriptions by Tyler Whittle and Christopher Cook. — Oxford : Oxford University Press, 1981, c1979. — 258p (some folded) : col.ill ; 27cm
Originally published: Bern : Colibri, AG, 1979. — Includes index
ISBN 0-19-217715-x : £19.50 : CIP rev.
B81-28020

635.9'0941 — Great Britain. Country gardens. Plants

McFadyen, David. A cottage flora. — Exeter : Webb & Bower, Oct.1982. — [112]p
ISBN 0-906671-64-7 : £6.95 : CIP entry
B82-24598

635.9'0941 — Great Britain. Gardens. Ornamental plants — *Encyclopaedias*

Herwig, Rob. The gardener's guide to flowers, trees and shrubs / Rob Herwig. — Newton Abbot : David & Charles, c1980. — 200p : col.ill,1col.port ; 24cm
Translation of: 350 tuinflanten en hun toepassing. — Includes index
ISBN 0-7153-8280-2 : £6.95 : CIP rev.
B82-04874

635.9'32'0321 — Gardens. Perennial plants — *Encyclopaedias*

Thomas, Graham Stuart. Perennial garden plants, or, The modern florilegium. — 2nd ed. — London : Dent for the Royal Horticultural Society, May 1982. — [389]p
Previous ed.: 1976
ISBN 0-460-04575-x : £15.00 : CIP entry
B82-07977

635.9'32'091814 — Southern hemisphere. Gardens. Perennial ornamental flowering plants — *Encyclopaedias*

Bulbs and perennials : a Southern Hemisphere garden book. — [Rev. ed.] / [compiled by] Richmond E. Harrison. — Wellington ; London : A.H. & A.W. Reed, [1977]. — 214p : chiefly col.ill ; 29cm. — (Know your garden flowers)
Photographs chiefly by Charles Harrison. — Previous ed.: Richmond E. Harrison, Charles R. Harrison, 1967. — Includes index
ISBN 0-589-01004-2 : £13.75 B82-13545

635.9'33111 — Gardens. Waterlilies

Swindells, Philip. Waterlilies. — London : Croom Helm, Feb.1983. — [224]p
ISBN 0-7099-2357-0 : £7.95 : CIP entry
B82-38896

635.9'33152 — Gardens. Perpetual-flowering carnations. Cultivation

Bailey, Steven. Carnations : perpetual-flowering carnations, borders and pinks / Steven Bailey. — Poole : Blandford, 1982. — 215p,[16]p of plates : ill(some col.) ; 23cm
Includes index
ISBN 0-7137-1187-6 : £8.95 : CIP rev.
B82-06248

635.9'33216 — Gardens. Erodiums. Cultivation

Clifton, R. T. F.. Erodiums in cultivation / prepared by R.T.F. Clifton. — Westcliff-on-Sea (47, Gainsborough Drive, Westcliff-on-Sea, Essex) : R.T.F. Clifton, 1981. — [4]p ; 21cm
At head of title: British Pelargonium and Geranium Society
£0.10 (unbound) B82-01379

635.9'33216'05 — Gardens. Geraniaceae — *Serials*

Geraniaceae Group news : Pelargonium, Geranium, Erodium, Sarcocaulon, Monsonia / the British Pelargonium and Geranium Society. — No.1 (Spring 1981)-. — Uxbridge (c/o D. Griffiths, 11 Malcolm Rd., Ickenham, Uxbridge, Middx) : The Group, 1981-. — v. : ill ; 21cm
Sheet (col.ill ; 24x15cm) with every Spring issue
ISSN 0262-687x = Geraniaceae Group news : Unpriced B82-10356

635.9'33372 — Gardens. Roses

Gibson, Michael. Shrub roses, climbers and ramblers / Michael Gibson ; illustrated with colour photographs by the author. — London : Collins, 1981. — 192p,[16]p of plates : ill(some col.) ; 22cm
Includes index
ISBN 0-00-219013-3 : £8.95 B82-05709

Jekyll, Gertrude. Roses for English gardens. — Woodbridge : Antique Collectors' Club, Oct.1982. — [390]p
Originally published: London : Country Life, 1902
ISBN 0-907462-24-3 : £12.50 : CIP entry
B82-25749

Krüssmann, Gerd. Roses / Gerd Krüssmann ; translated by Gerd Krüssmann and Nigel Raban. — London : Batsford, 1982, c1981. — xii,436p,14p of plates : ill,maps,ports ; 29cm
Translation of : Rosen, Rosen, Rosen. — Originally published: Portland : Timber Press, 1981. — Includes bibliographies and index
ISBN 0-7134-4475-4 : £25.00 B82-22242

635.9'33372 — Gardens. Roses. Varieties

McGredy, Sam. Look to the rose / by Sam McGredy ; paintings by Joyce Blake. — London : Collins in association with David Bateman, 1982. — 112p : ill(some col.) ; 30cm
Ill on lining papers. — Includes index
ISBN 0-00-219250-0 : £9.95 B82-09965

635.9′3344 — Fuchsias. Cultivation

Clapham, Sidney. Fuchsias : for house and garden / Sidney Clapham. — Newton Abbot : David & Charles, c1982. — 184p : ill(some col.) ; 25cm
Includes index
ISBN 0-7153-8217-9 : £8.95 : CIP rev. B82-15837

635.9′3344 — Gardens. Fuchsias. Varieties — *Lists*

Ewart, Ron. Fuchsia lexicon / Ron Ewart. — Poole : Blandford, 1982. — 336p : ill(some col.) ; 24cm
Bibliography: p331. — Includes index
ISBN 0-7137-1078-0 : £10.95 : CIP rev. B82-06247

635.9′3355 — Gardens. Chrysanthemums — *Manuals*

Randall, Harry. Growing chrysanthemums. — London : Croom Helm, Feb.1983. — [224]p
ISBN 0-7099-2225-6 : £7.95 : CIP entry B82-38895

635.9′3362 — Gardens. Azaleas & rhododendrons

Kessell, Mervyn S.. Rhododendrons and azaleas / Mervyn S. Kessell. — Poole : Blandford, 1981. — 176p,[32]p of plates : ill(some col.) ; 23cm
Bibliography: p168-170. — Includes index
ISBN 0-7137-1076-4 : £8.95 : CIP rev. B81-30310

635.9′3362 — Hampshire. Exbury. Country houses: Exbury House. Gardens. Rhododendrons

Phillips, C. E. Lucas. The Rothschild rhododendrons : a record of the gardens at Exbury / C.E. Lucas Phillips and Peter N. Barber ; drawings by Gillian Kenny ; photography by Harry Smith ; with a foreword by the Lord Aberconway. — 2nd rev. ed. — London : Cassell, 1979. — xviii,138p,65leaves of plates : ill(some col.),1map,plans,1port ; 32cm
Previous ed.: 1967. — Bibliography: p131. — Includes index
ISBN 0-304-30436-0 : £30.00 B82-23386

635.9′33672 — Gardens. Cyclamen. Cultivation — *Manuals*

Nightingale, Gay. Growing cyclamen. — London : Croom Helm, Oct.1982. — [144]p
ISBN 0-7099-1805-4 : £7.95 : CIP entry B82-23192

635.9′3381 — Pot plants: African violets. Cultivation

Robey, Melvin J.. African violets : queens of the indoor gardening kingdom / Melvin J. Robey ; illustrated by Nanci P. Robey. — San Diego : Barnes ; London : Tantivy, c1980. — 199p,[4]p of plates : ill(some col.) ; 25cm
Includes index
ISBN 0-498-02349-4 : £7.50 B82-31486

635.9′3415 — Indoor plants: Orchids. Cultivation

An **Illustrated** guide to growing your own orchids : easy-to-follow instructions for growing 150 of the world's most beautiful flowers / edited by Wilma Rittershausen. — London : Salamander, c1982. — 160p : ill(some col.) ; 23cm
Ill on lining papers. — Bibliography: p157
ISBN 0-86101-117-1 : £3.95 B82-22270

635.9′3415 — Orchids. Cultivation

Richter, Walter. Orchid care : a guide to cultivation and breeding / Walter Richter ; translated and adapted by Edmund Launert and P. Francis Hunt ; line drawings by Hans Preusse. — New York ; London : Van Nostrand Reinhold, 1977, c1972 (1982 [printing]). — 212p : ill ; 24cm
Translation of: Orchideen pflegen, vermehren, züchten. — Originally published: London : Studio Vista, 1972. — Bibliography: p206-207. — Includes index
ISBN 0-442-26873-4 (pbk) : £8.45 B82-34328

635.9′3415′0994 — Australia. Orchids. Cultivation

Rentoul, J. N.. Growing orchids : cymbidiums and slippers / J.N. Rentoul. — Seattle ; London : University of Washington Press, c1980. — 170p : ill(some col.) ; 26cm
Bibliography: p170. — Includes index
ISBN 0-295-95839-1 : Unpriced B82-19573

635.9′3424 — Gardens. Irises

Cassidy, G. E.. Growing irises / G.E. Cassidy and S. Linnegar. — London : Croom Helm, c1982. — 160p,[8]p of plates : ill(some col.),1map ; 24cm
Bibliography: p152. — Includes index
ISBN 0-7099-0706-0 : £7.95 : CIP rev. B81-34311

635.9′3425 — Amaryllis. Cultivation

Growing amaryllis / by staff members at the Aalsmeer, Naaldwijk and Lisse Research stations in Holland. — London : Grower Books, 1981. — 57p : ill ; 21cm. — (Grower guide ; 23)
ISBN 0-901361-60-7 (pbk) : £3.75 B82-01229

635.9′34324 — Gardens. Lilies

Jekyll, Gertrude. Lilies for English gardens. — Woodbridge : Antique Collectors' Club, Sept.1982. — [150]p
Originally published: London : Country Life, 1901
ISBN 0-907462-28-6 : £12.50 : CIP entry B82-25943

635.9′42′0941 — Great Britain. Gardens. Flowers. Cultivation from seeds

McEwan, Helen. Seed growers guide to herbs & wild flowers / by Helen McEwan. — Sudbury : Suffolk Herbs, c1982. — 47p : ill ; 21cm
ISBN 0-9508022-0-4 (pbk) : Unpriced
Primary classification 635′.7′0941 B82-20346

635.9′44 — Gardens. Flowering bulbs

Rix, Martyn. The bulb book : a photographic guide to over 800 hardy bulbs / by Martyn Rix and Roger Phillips ; edited by Brian Mathew. — London : Pan, 1981. — 192p : col.ill ; 28cm. — (Pan original)
Bibliography: p188. — Includes index
ISBN 0-330-26481-8 (pbk) : £6.95 B82-01876

635.9′44 — Gardens. Flowering bulbs, flowering corms & flowering tubers

Fogg, H. G. Witham. Beautiful bulbs / H.G. Witham Fogg. — London : Octopus, 1982, c1980. — 80p : col.ill ; 29cm. — (Colour in your garden)
Originally published: London : Sundial, 1980. — Ill on lining papers. — Includes index
ISBN 0-7064-1776-3 : £2.95 B82-20823

635.9′44′072042 — England. Crops: Flowering bulbs. Cultivation. Research by Agricultural Development and Advisory Service. *Agriculture Service* — *Serials*

Agricultural Development and Advisory Service. *Agriculture Service*. Bulbs and allied flower crops : research and development reports / Agriculture Service. — 1978-. — [London] ([Great Westminster House, Horseferry Rd, SW1P 2AE]) : ADAS, [1979?]-. — v. ; 21cm
Annual. — Description based on: 1980 issue
ISSN 0263-0702 = Bulbs and allied flower crops : Unpriced B82-15146

635.9′51′795 — Pacific Northwest. Native flowering plants. Cultivation

Kruckeberg, Arthur R.. Gardening with native plants of the Pacific Northwest : an illustrated guide / by Arthur R. Kruckeberg. — Seattle ; London : University of Washington Press, c1982. — 252p : ill,maps ; 27cm
Bibliography: p244-246. — Includes index
ISBN 0-295-95893-6 : Unpriced B82-38560

635.9′55 — Great Britain. Gardens. Plants flourishing in damp conditions

Chatto, Beth. The damp garden / Beth Chatto ; drawings by Margaret Davies. — London : Dent, 1982. — 336p,[8]p of plates : ill(some col.) ; 25cm
Bibliography: p319. — Includes index
ISBN 0-460-04551-2 : £9.95 : CIP rev. B82-06846

635.9′6 — Gardens. Wall plants. Cultivation

Rose, Peter Q.. Climbers and wall plants. — Poole : Blandford Press, Oct.1982. — [160]p
ISBN 0-7137-1179-5 : £8.95 : CIP entry
Primary classification 635.9′74 B82-22995

635.9′62 — Gardens. Raised flower beds. Plants. Cultivation

Thear, Katie. Raised bed cultivation. — Wellingborough : Thorsons, Sept.1982. — [128]p
ISBN 0-7225-0747-x (pbk) : £3.50 : CIP entry B82-20392

635.9′62′0941 — Great Britain. Bedding plants. Cultivation — *Manuals*

Bedding plants. — London : Grower, 1981. — 88p : ill ; 21cm. — (Grower guide ; no.24)
ISBN 0-901361-61-5 (pbk) : £3.75 B82-01467

635.9′64′0941 — Great Britain. Rural regions. Recreation land: Grassland. Cultivation

Grassland establishment for countryside recreation. — Chleltenham : Countryside Commission, 1980. — 48p : ill ; 22cm. — (Advisory series, ISSN 0140-5357 ; no.13)
Bibliography: p47-48
ISBN 0-86170-009-0 (pbk) : Unpriced B82-31839

635.9′642′0288 — Great Britain. Recreation land. Turf. Maintenance — *Serials*

Turf management : for sports and leisure. — Vol.1, no.1 (Jan. 1982)-. — London (Millstream House, 41 Maltby St., SE1 3PA) : Golf World Ltd., 1892-. — v. : ill,ports ; 30cm
Monthly
ISSN 0262-0669 = Turf management : £1.50 per issue B82-18506

635.9′647 — Gardens. Lawns. Cultivation — *Manuals*

Bloom, Adrian. Adrian Bloom's guide to lawns / text by David Mann. — Norwich : Jarrold, c1981. — 32p : col.ill,1port ; 20cm. — (A Jarrold garden series ; bk.9)
Text, port on inside covers
ISBN 0-85306-938-7 (corrected : pbk) : Unpriced B82-03483

Hessayon, D. G.. The lawn expert / D.G. Hessayon. — Enl. ed. — Waltham Cross : pbi, c1982. — 104p : col.ill ; 24cm
Previous ed.: published as Be your own lawn expert. 1961. — Includes index
ISBN 0-903505-15-0 (pbk) : Unpriced B82-21138

635.9′65 — Flowering indoor plants & flowering pot plants. Cultivation

Flowering pot plants. — London : Grower, 1980. — 71p : ill ; 21cm. — (Grower guide ; no.17)
ISBN 0-901361-45-3 (pbk) : Unpriced B82-37887

Flowering pot plants. — London : Grower 2. — 1982. — 73p : ill ; 21cm. — (Grower guide ; no.27)
ISBN 0-901361-65-8 (pbk) : £3.75 B82-17546

635.9′65 — Gardening in containers

Squire, David. Window-boxes, pots and tubs. — Newton Abbot : David & Charles, Feb.1983. — [168]p
ISBN 0-7153-8385-x : £8.95 : CIP entry B82-39453

635.9′65 — Indoor foliage plants

Perry, Frances. [Beautiful leaved plants]. Grown for their leaves / Frances Perry ; with a note on Benjamin Fawcett by Ray Desmond. — London : Scolar, 1979 (1982 [printing]). — xiv,141p : col.ill ; 26cm
Originally published: 1979. — Includes index
ISBN 0-85967-661-7 (pbk) : £4.95 : CIP rev. B82-04821

635.9′65 — Indoor gardening — *Manuals*

Genders, Roy. Indoor gardening for profit / Roy Genders. — London : Hale, 1982. — 207p : ill ; 23cm
Includes index
ISBN 0-7091-9479-x : £8.50 B82-13052

635.9'65 — Indoor plants

Davidson, William, *19---*. The houseplant survival manual : how to keep your houseplants healthy / William Davidson ; photography by Ian Howes. — London : Hamlyn, 1982. — 192p : ill(some col.) ; 26cm. — (A QED book)
Includes index
ISBN 0-600-38470-5 : £6.95 B82-30962

635.9'65 — Indoor plants. Cultivation — *For children*

Janus Hertz, Grete. Flowerpot gardening / written by Grete Janus Hertz ; photographs by Mogens Hertz. — London : Longman, 1980. — 22p : col.ill ; 25cm
ISBN 0-582-39070-2 : £2.95 B82-26921

635.9'65 — Indoor plants. Cultivation — *Manuals*

Indoor gardening. — London : Reader's Digest Association, 1977 (1980 [printing]). — 48p : ill (some col.) ; 27cm. — (Reader's Digest basic guide)
'Text and illustrations in this book are taken from Reader's Digest illustrated guide to gardening', 1975. — Includes index
ISBN 0-276-00159-1 (pbk) : £0.95 B82-04174

Payne, Christina. Houseplants : care and management / Christina Payne and Hazel Dodgson. — London : Batsford, 1982. — 64p : ill(some col.) ; 20cm. — (A Batsford paperback)
Includes index
ISBN 0-7134-4166-6 (pbk) : £2.25 B82-33828

Wickham, Cynthia. The house plant book : a complete guide to creative indoor gardening / Cynthia Wickham. — London : Collins, 1982, c1977. — 256p : ill(some col.),1col.map ; 30cm
Originally published: London : Marshall, Cavendish, 1977. — Bibliography: p242. — Includes index
ISBN 0-00-411652-6 : £10.95 B82-36536

635.9'65 — Indoor plants — *Field guides*

Jacobi, K.. Ward Lock's guide to houseplants / K. Jacobi. — London : Ward Lock, 1982. — 190p : ill(some col.) ; 24cm
Translation of: Das farbige Hausbuch der Zimmerpflanzen. — Includes index
ISBN 0-7063-6177-6 (cased) : Unpriced : CIP rev.
ISBN 0-7063-6178-4 (pbk) : Unpriced B82-02633

635.9'672 — Gardens. Rock plants: Alpine plants

Foster, Raymond. Rock garden & alpine plants / Raymond Foster. — Newton Abbot : David & Charles, c1982. — 256p : ill(some col.) ; 24cm
Bibliography: p249. — Includes index
ISBN 0-7153-8203-9 : £12.50 : CIP rev. B81-31808

635.9'672 — Small gardens. Rock plants. Cultivation — *Manuals*

Heath, Royton E.. Rock plants for small gardens / Royton E. Heath. — 3rd ed. — [London] : Collingridge, 1982. — 144p,[24]p of plates : ill (some col.) ; 23cm
Previous ed.: 1969. — Includes index
ISBN 0-600-36811-4 : £7.95 B82-21772

635.9'672'0321 — Gardens. Rock plants: Alpine plants — *Encyclopaedias*

Ingwersen, Will. Rock gardening / Will Ingwersen. — London : Ward Lock, 1982. — 108p,12p of plates : ill(some col.) ; 20cm
Includes index
ISBN 0-7063-6085-0 (pbk) : £2.95 : CIP rev. B82-04614

635.9'68 — Gardens. Scented plants

Sanecki, Kay N., *1922-*. The fragrant garden / Kay N. Sanecki ; line drawings by Rosemary Wise. — London : Batsford, 1981. — 166p,[4]p of plates : ill(some col.) ; 26cm
Bibliography: p159. — Includes index
ISBN 0-7134-2373-0 : £9.95 B82-06215

635.9'74 — Gardens. Climbing plants. Cultivation

Rose, Peter Q.. Climbers and wall plants. — Poole : Blandford Press, Oct.1982. — [160]p
ISBN 0-7137-1179-5 : £8.95 : CIP entry
Also classified at 635.9'6 B82-22995

635.9'76 — Gardens. Shrubs

Evison, J. R. B.. Beautiful shrubs / J.R.B. Evison. — London : Octopus, 1982, c1979. — 95p : col.ill ; 29cm. — (Colour in your garden)
Originally published: London : Sundial, 1979. — Ill on lining papers. — Includes index
ISBN 0-7064-1775-5 : £2.95 B82-20824

635.9'76'0321 — Gardens. Shrubs — *Encyclopaedias*

Hellyer, A. G. L.. Garden shrubs / Arthur Hellyer ; drawings by Nicholas Parlett. — London : Dent, 1982. — 248p,[8]p of plates : ill(some col.) ; 26cm
Bibliography: p243. — Includes index
ISBN 0-460-04474-5 : £12.00 : CIP rev. B81-04203

Hillier's manual of trees & shrubs. — 5th ed. — Newton Abbot : David & Charles, c1981. — 575p,[16]p of plates : ill(some col.) ; 22cm
Previous ed.: 1977. — Bibliography: p5
ISBN 0-7153-8302-7 : £9.50 : CIP rev.
Primary classification 635.9'77'0321 B81-31236

635.9'77'0321 — Gardens. Trees — *Encyclopaedias*

Hillier's manual of trees & shrubs. — 5th ed. — Newton Abbot : David & Charles, c1981. — 575p,[16]p of plates : ill(some col.) ; 22cm
Previous ed.: 1977. — Bibliography: p5
ISBN 0-7153-8302-7 : £9.50 : CIP rev.
Also classified at 635.9'76'0321 B81-31236

635.9'77'0941 — Great Britain. Gardens. Trees

Mitchell, Alan, *1922-*. The gardener's book of trees / Alan Mitchell ; illustrated by Joanna Langhorne. — London : Dent, 1981. — 216p,[8]p of plates : ill(some col.) ; 26cm
Includes index
ISBN 0-460-04403-6 : £14.95 : CIP rev. B81-20146

635.9'77'0941 — Great Britain. Gardens. Trees. Selection & cultivation

Helliwell, Rodney. Garden trees. — Chichester : Wiley, May 1982. — [112]p. — (Forestry research studies series)
ISBN 0-471-10382-9 (pbk) : £10.00 : CIP entry B82-07666

635.9'772 — Bonsai. Cultivation — *Manuals*

Stewart, Christine. Bonsai / Christine Stewart. — London : Orbis, c1981. — 112p : ill(some col.) ; 30cm
Bibliography: p110. — Includes index
ISBN 0-85613-066-4 : £7.95 B82-20547

Swinton, Anne. The Collingridge handbook of bonsai / Anne Swinton ; with a preface by Anthony Huxley ; photographs by Dick Robinson ; and line drawings by Ron Hayward. — London : Collingridge, 1982. — 192p : ill(some col.) ; 24cm
Text on lining papers. — Includes index
ISBN 0-600-36816-5 : £7.95 B82-28935

635.9'773114 — Gardens. Magnolias

Treseder, Neil G.. The book of magnolias / by Neil G. Treseder ; with paintings by Marjorie Blamey. — London : Collins, 1981. — 96p : ill (some col.) ; 37cm
ISBN 0-00-219535-6 : £25.00 B82-00684

635.9'823 — Greenhouses. Flowering plants. Commercial cultivation — *Manuals*

Walls, Ian. Modern greenhouse methods : flowers and plants. — London : Muller, Nov.1981. — [224]p
ISBN 0-584-10386-7 : £10.50 : CIP entry B81-32003

635.9'86 — Plant containers. Plants. Cultivation — *Manuals*

Green, Madge. Hanging baskets, window boxes & patios / by Madge Green. — London : Foulsham, c1981. — 96p : ill(some col.) ; 24cm
Includes index
ISBN 0-572-01035-4 : £4.95 B82-04240

636 — LIVESTOCK, PETS

636 — Developing countries. Livestock. Intensive production — *Conference proceedings*

Intensive animal production in developing countries : proceedings of a symposium organized by the British Society of Animal Production and held at Harrogate in November 1979 / edited by A.J. Smith and R.G. Gunn. — Thames Ditton (c/o Milk Marketing Board, Thames Ditton, Surrey KT7 0EL) : BSAP, 1981. — 481p : ill,1map ; 25cm. — (BSAP occasional publication ; no.4)
Conference papers. — Text on inside front cover and back cover. — Includes bibliographies and index
Unpriced (pbk) B82-37941

636 — Great Britain. Livestock. Intensive production. Welfare aspects

Sense or sentiment? : the debate on farm animal welfare. — London (Agriculture House, Knightsbridge SW1X 7NJ) : National Farmers' Union of England and Wales, [1980]. — [12]p : ill ; 21x31cm
Unpriced (unbound) B82-32201

636 — Livestock. Intensive production — *Conference proceedings*

Watson, W.. Symposium on managerial and economic aspects of large livestock holdings, and technical, economic and sanitary aspects of buildings and equipment : report of a visit to Spain 19-23 October 1981 / W. Watson & D. Sisson. — [London] ([Great Westminster House, Horseferry Rd., SW1P 2AE]) : ADAS, 1982. — 17p ; 30cm
Cover title
Unpriced (pbk) B82-40445

636 — Livestock — *Manuals*

McNitt, J. I.. Livestock husbandry techniques. — London : Granada, Jan.1983. — [192]p
ISBN 0-246-11871-7 (pbk) : £3.95 : CIP entry B82-33711

636 — Livestock. Non-intensive production

Alternatives to intensive husbandry systems : proceedings of a symposium held at Wye College (University of London), Ashford, Kent. 13th, 14th, and 15th july, 1981 / [Universities Federation for Animal Welfare]. — Potters Bar : The Federation, c1981. — 104p : ill,plans ; 21cm. — (Proceedings of UFAW Symposia)
Includes bibliographies
ISBN 0-900767-25-1 (pbk) : £3.65 B82-21897

Carnell, Paul. Alternatives to factory farming. — London (258 Pentonville Rd., N1 9JY) : Earth Resources Research, Nov.1982. — 1v.
ISBN 0-946281-01-7 (pbk) : £3.00 : CIP entry B82-31326

636 — Livestock. Production. Biochemical aspects

Dynamic biochemistry of animal production. — Oxford : Elsevier Scientific, Sept.1982. — [400] p. — (World animal science ; A3)
ISBN 0-444-42052-5 : CIP entry B82-20633

636'.0028'54 — Great Britain. Livestock. Production. Applications of computer systems

Computers in animal production : proceedings of a symposium organized by the British Society of Animal Production and held at Harrogate in November 1980 / edited by G.M. Hillyer, C.T. Whittemore and R.G. Gunn. — Thames Ditton (c/o Milk Marketing Board, Thames Ditton, Surrey KT7 0EL) : BSAP, 1981. — 155p : ill ; 25cm. — (BSAP occasional publication ; no.5)
Conference papers. — Text on inside front cover and back cover. — Includes bibliographies
Unpriced (pbk) B82-37942

636'.0068'1 — Great Britain. Agricultural industries. Farms. Livestock. Production. Profitability. Improvement — *Conference proceedings*

Profits from livestock and ways to achieve them : proceedings of the Thirteenth Annual Conference of the Reading University Agricultural Club 1979 / edited by the Conference Committee. — Reading : The Club, 1979. — 32p : ill ; 30cm
Includes bibliographies
ISBN 0-7049-0307-5 (pbk) : Unpriced B82-12115

636'.0094 — Europe. Livestock. Production

Livestock production in Europe : perspectives and prospects / a long range study of the European Association for Animal Production compiled and edited by studygroups ; edited by R.D. Politiek and J.J. Bakker. — Amsterdam ; Oxford : Elsevier Scientific, 1982. — xviii,335p : ill,maps ; 25cm. — (Developments in animal and veterinary sciences ; 8) (EAAP publication ; no.28)
'Reprinted from Livestock production science, Vol.9 nos.1, 2'. — Includes bibliographies
ISBN 0-444-42105-x : Unpriced B82-39857

636'.00941 — Great Britain. Royal families. Livestock

Brown, Michele. The royal animals / Michele Brown. — London : W.H. Allen, 1981. — 94p : ill(some col.),coats of arms(some col.),2facsims,ports(some col.) ; 27cm
ISBN 0-352-31172-x (pbk) : £2.50 B82-39760

636.08'2 — Livestock. Breeding

Hammond, *Sir* **John**. Hammond's farm animals. — 5th ed. — London : Edward Arnold, Aug.1982. — [320]p
Previous ed.: 1971
ISBN 0-7131-2848-8 (pbk) : £10.00 : CIP entry B82-17209

New technologies in animal breeding / edited by Benjamin G. Brackett, George E. Seidel Jr, Sarah M. Seidel. — New York ; London : Academic Press, 1981. — xiv,268p : ill ; 24cm
Includes bibliographies and index
ISBN 0-12-123450-9 : £24.80 B82-38382

636.08'21 — Livestock. Breeding. Genetic aspects

Gordon, Ian. Controlled breeding in farm animals. — Oxford : Pergamon, Oct.1982. — [400]p
ISBN 0-08-024410-6 (cased) : £29.00 : CIP entry
ISBN 0-08-024409-2 (pbk) : £14.50 B82-24947

Maciejowski, Janusz. Genetics and animal breeding. — Oxford : Elsevier Scientific. — (Developments in animal veterinary sciences ; 10)
Part B: Stock improvement methods. — Oct.1981. — [230]p
ISBN 0-444-99732-6 : £35.00 : CIP entry B81-25290

Maciejowski, Janusz. Genetics and animal breeding. — Oxford : Elsevier. — (Developments in animal and veterinary sciences ; 10)
Translation and revision of: Genetyka i ogólna hodowla zwierzat. t.1
Pt.A: Biological and genetics foundations of animal breeding. — Apr.1982. — [300]p
ISBN 0-444-99696-6 : £35.00 : CIP entry B82-03585

636.08'3 — Great Britain. Livestock. Management. Welfare aspects. Great Britain. ***Parliament House of Commons. Agriculture Committee.*** **First report ... session 1980-81** — *Critical studies*

Great Britain. Animal welfare in poultry, pig and veal calf production : response of the Government to the first report from the Agriculture Committee 1980-81 session. — London : H.M.S.O., 1981. — 9p ; 25cm. — (Cmnd. ; 8451)
ISBN 0-10-184510-3 (unbound) : £1.50 B82-13808

Great Britain. *Ministry of Agriculture, Fisheries and Food*. Second special report from the Agriculture Committee, session 1980-81, animal welfare in poultry, pig and veal calf production : observations by the Minister of Agriculture, Fisheries and Food on the First report from the Agriculture Committee 1980-81 (HC (1980-81)406). — London : H.M.S.O., [1981]. — vip ; 25cm. — ([H.C.] ; 474)
ISBN 0-10-247481-8 (unbound) : £1.15 B82-06338

636.08'3 — Livestock. Care & management — *Manuals*

Ewer, T. K.. Practical animal husbandry / T.K. Ewer. — Bristol : Wright Scientechnica, 1982. — vii,257p : ill,plans ; 24cm
Includes bibliographies and index
ISBN 0-85608-026-8 (pbk) : Unpriced : CIP rev. B82-09309

636.08'3 — Livestock. Pests: Blackflies. Biological control measures

Blackflies : the future for biological methods in integrated control / editor Marshall Laird ; sponsored by International Development Research Centre. — London : Academic Press, 1981. — xii,399p : ill,maps ; 26cm
Bibliography: p341-387. — Includes index
ISBN 0-12-434060-1 : £28.20 : CIP rev. B81-13443

636.08'3'02341 — Great Britain. Livestock. Care — *Career guides*

Working with livestock. — [Beckenham] ([32 Beckenham Rd, Beckenham, Kent BR3 4PB]) : Agricultural Training Board on behalf of the Joint Working Party on Careers Literature, 1980. — [8]p : ill ; 21cm. — (Careers in agriculture) (Job leaflet)
Unpriced (unbound) B82-19439

636.08'3'0924 — Livestock. Training. Woodhouse, Barbara — *Biographies*

Woodhouse, Barbara. Just Barbara : an autobiography / by Barbara Woodhouse. — London : Michael Joseph and Rainbird, 1981. — 192p : ill,facsims,ports ; 24cm
Includes index
ISBN 0-7181-2012-4 : £8.50 B82-01293

636.08'3'0994 — Australia. Arid regions. Livestock. Management

Squires, Victor. Livestock management in the arid zone / Victor Squires. — Melbourne ; London : Inkata, 1981. — 271p : ill,maps,plans ; 25cm
Bibliography: p256-266. — Includes index
ISBN 0-909605-23-8 : Unpriced B82-37020

636.08'31 — Great Britain. Agricultural industries. Farms. Animal housing — *Conference proceedings*

Environmental aspects of housing for animal production / [edited by] J.A. Clark. — London : Butterworths, 1981. — xvi,511p : ill ; 25cm
Conference papers. — Includes bibliographies and index
ISBN 0-408-10688-3 : £39.50 : CIP rev. B81-23916

636.08'4 — Livestock. Feeding & nutrition

A **Guide** to livestock feeding 1980. — [Ireland] : Irish Sugar Company Ltd., [1980?]. — 50p : ill (some col.) ; 21cm
Cover title
Unpriced (pbk) B82-30396

636.08'52 — Livestock. Nutrition

McDonald, Peter, *1926-*. Animal nutrition / P. McDonald, R.A. Edwards, J.F.D. Greenhalgh. — 3rd ed. — London : Longman, 1981. — vii,479p : ill ; 24cm
Previous ed: 1973. — Includes bibliography and index
ISBN 0-582-44399-7 (pbk) : £11.95 : CIP rev. B81-15943

636.08'52'05 — Livestock. Nutrition — *Serials*

Recent advances in animal nutrition. — 1981. — London : Butterworths, Dec.1981. — [192]p. — (Studies in the agricultural and food sciences)
ISBN 0-408-71014-4 : £17.00 : CIP entry B81-31718

Recent advances in animal nutrition. — 1982. — London : Butterworth, Oct.1982. — [224]p. — (Studies in the agricultural and food sciences)
ISBN 0-408-71015-2 : £18.00 : CIP entry B82-24472

636.08'552'09417 — Ireland ***(Republic).*** **Silage. Production** — *Manuals*

Wondering when to cut that silage field?. — [Blackrock] ([Frascati Rd., Blackrock, Co. Dublin]) : ACOT, [1981?]. — [4]p : ill(some col.) ; 30cm
Unpriced (unbound) B82-05194

636.08'77 — Livestock. Nutrients: Minerals

Georgievskiĭ, V. I.. Mineral nutrition of animals / V.I. Georgievskii, B.N. Annenkov, V.T. Samokhin ; under the general editorship of Professor Georgievskii ; translated by Freund Publishing House, Israel ; English translation verified by H. Brookes. — London : Butterworths, 1982, c1981. — viii,475p : ill ; 25cm. — (Studies in the agricultural and food sciences)
Translation of: Mineral'noe pitanie zhivotnykh. — Includes bibliographies and index
ISBN 0-408-10770-7 : Unpriced : CIP rev. B81-31716

636.08'83 — Livestock: Animals reared for meat. Production

Development of animal production systems. — Oxford : Elsevier Scientific, Oct.1982. — [350] p. — (World animal sciences ; A2)
ISBN 0-444-42050-9 : CIP entry B82-24013

636.08'85 — Laboratory animals

A **Guide** to laboratory animal technology / Martin D. Buckland ... [et al.]. — London : Heinemann Medical, 1981. — viii,229p : ill ; 22cm
Bibliography: p213-217. — Includes index
ISBN 0-433-04590-6 (pbk) : £6.50 B82-07758

636.08'85 — Laboratory animals. Care. Microbiological aspects

Roe, F. J. C.. Microbiological standardisation of laboratory animals. — Chichester : Ellis Horwood, Jan.1983. — [112]p
ISBN 0-85312-556-2 : £16.50 : CIP entry B82-39302

636.08'85 — Laboratory animals. Immunological deficiency — *Conference proceedings*

Immunologic defects in laboratory animals. — New York ; London : Plenum
Conference papers. — Includes bibliographies and index
[Vol.]1 / edited by M. Eric Gershwin and Bruce Merchant. — c1981. — xx,360p : ill ; 26cm
ISBN 0-306-40668-3 : Unpriced B82-05803

Immunologic defects in laboratory animals / edited by M. Eric Gershwin and Bruce Merchant. — New York ; London : Plenum
2. — c1981. — xx,382p : ill ; 26cm
Includes bibliographies and index
ISBN 0-306-40673-x : Unpriced B82-08346

636.08'85 — Laboratory animals: Mammals. Blood. Cells. Anatomy — *Illustrations*

Sanderson, J. H.. An atlas of laboratory animal haematology / J.H. Sanderson, Christine E. Phillips. — Oxford : Clarendon Press, 1981. — 473p : chiefly ill(some col.) ; 31cm. — (Oxford science publications)
Bibliography: p473
ISBN 0-19-857520-3 : £75.00 : CIP rev. B81-07455

636.08'85'0289 — Great Britain. Laboratory animals. Safety measures

Safety in the animal house. — 2nd rev. ed., edited by J.H. Seamer & Margery Wood. — London : Laboratory Animals Ltd., 1981. — 106p ; 23cm. — (Laboratory animals handbook ; 5)
Previous ed.: 1972. — Includes bibliographies
ISBN 0-901334-09-x (pbk) : Unpriced B82-40286

636.08'87 — Pets

Isaac, Peter, *1932-*. Which pet?. — London : Norman & Hobhouse, Sept.1982. — [176]p
ISBN 0-906908-56-6 : £6.95 : CIP entry B82-21578

Mountfield, Anne. Pets / Anne Mountfield. — London : Harrap, 1982. — 39p : ill ; 19cm. — (The Reporters series)
ISBN 0-245-53654-x (pbk) : £0.90 B82-33507

636.08'87 — Pets. Care — *For children*

Creatures : a pet book with a difference / written and produced by McPhee Gribble Publishers ; illustrated by David Lancashire. — Harmondsworth : Puffin, 1980. — [32]p : ill (some col.) ; 19cm. — (Practical puffin ; no.18)
ISBN 0-14-049166-x (pbk) : £0.80 B82-35154

636.08′87 — Pets. Care — *For children* *continuation*

Looking after animals / illustrated by Dieter Jonas. — London : Ward Lock, c1981. — 47p : col.ill ; 30cm
Translation of: Haustierbuch fuer Kinder
ISBN 0-7063-6082-6 : £2.95 : CIP rev. B81-12890

Pitt, Valerie, *1939-*. Pets / by Valerie Pitt ; illustrated by Frankie Coventry. — London : Watts, c1980. — 48p : ill(some col.) ; 22cm. — (A First look book)
Includes index
ISBN 0-85166-855-0 : £2.99 B82-13177

636.08′87 — Pets: Small animals. Care — *Manuals*

Allcock, James. Small pets of your own. — London : Sheldon, Jan.1983. — [80]p. — (The British Veterinary Association pet care series)
ISBN 0-85969-366-x (pbk) : £1.95 : CIP entry B82-33119

636.08′87′0924 — Pets. Behaviour — *Personal observatoins*

Paling, John. Snowy & Co. : insights into pet behaviour / John Paling ; colour illustrations by Oxford Scientific Films Ltd. ; line drawings by Joan Sellwood, The Garden Studio. — London : Collins, 1981. — 189p,[16]p of plates : ill(some col.) ; 23cm
ISBN 0-00-216872-3 : £7.95 B82-05563

636.089 — VETERINARY MEDICINE

636.089 — Veterinary medicine — *For children*

Lenga, Rosalind. Let′s go to the vet / Rosaliind Lenga ; general editor Henry Pluckrose ; photography by Marc Henrie. — London : Watts, c1979 (1982 [printing]). — 32p : col.ill ; 22cm. — (Let′s go series)
ISBN 0-85166-743-0 : £2.99 B82-23409

Swayne, Dick. I am a vet. — London : Dent, Sept.1982. — [32]p
ISBN 0-460-06088-0 : £3.50 : CIP entry B82-19704

636.089 — Zoos. Veterinary medicine

Klös, Heinz-Georg. Handbook of zoo medicine : disease and treatment of wild animals in zoos, game parks, circuses and private collections / authors Heinz-Georg Klös, Ernst M. Lang ; contributors H.-P. Brandt ... [et al.] ; editors Reinhard Göltenboth, Dietmar Jarofke ; English text Günter Speckmann ; translation G. Speckmann. — New York ; London : Van Nostrand Reinhold, c1982. — xvii,453p : ill ; 24cm
Bibliography: p388-420. — Includes index
ISBN 0-442-21367-0 : £42.10 B82-07880

636.089′024613 — Livestock: Small animals. Veterinary aspects — *For nursing*

Jones, Bruce V.. Jones′s Animal nursing. — 3rd ed. / edited by D.R. Lane for the British Small Animal Veterinary Association, with contributions from twenty-four authors. — Oxford : Pergamon, 1980. — xii,606p : ill ; 26cm. — (Pergamon international library)
Previous ed.: 1976. — Includes bibliographies and index
ISBN 0-08-024945-0 (cased) : £30.00 : CIP rev.
ISBN 0-08-022944-2 (pbk) : £16.00 B80-02822

636.089′03′21 — Veterinary medicine — *Dictionaries*

Black′s veterinary dictionary. — 14th ed. — London : A. & C. Black, July 1982. — [928]p
Previous ed.: 1979
ISBN 0-7136-2226-1 : £9.95 : CIP entry B82-13060

636.089′05 — Veterinary medicine — *Serials*

Animal pharm : world animal health news. — Special issue (Nov. 23rd 1981) ; No.1 (1982)-. — Richmond (18 Hill Rise, Richmond, Surrey TW10 6UA) : V&O Publications, 1981-. — v. ; 30cm
Fortnightly
ISSN 0262-2238 = Animal pharm : £150.00 per year B82-33868

The **Veterinary** annual. — 22nd issue. — Bristol : Wright, Jan.1982. — [400]p
ISBN 0-85608-035-7 : £15.00 : CIP entry
ISSN 0083-5870 B81-35030

636.089′092′4 — Great Britain. Veterinary medicine. McFadyean, John — *Biographies*

Pattison, Iain. John McFadyean : a great British veterinarian / by Iain Pattison. — London : J.A. Allen, 1981. — 240p : 1port ; 23cm
Includes index
ISBN 0-85131-352-3 : Unpriced : CIP rev. B81-30467

636.089′092′4 — Great Britain. Veterinary medicine. Straiton, Eddie — *Biographies*

Straiton, Eddie. A vet at large / Eddie Straiton. — London : Severn House, 1982, c1981. — 217p ; 21cm
Originally published: London : Arrow, 1981
ISBN 0-7278-0767-6 : £6.95 B82-21156

636.089′092′4 — Veterinary medicine. Herriot, James — *Biographies*

Herriot, James. If only they could talk ; It shouldn′t happen to a vet ; Let sleeping vets lie ; Vet in harness ; Vets might fly ; Vet in a spin / James Herriot. — London : Heinemann/Octopus, 1982. — 829p ; 24cm
ISBN 0-905712-58-7 : £7.95 B82-22524

Herriot, James. The Lord God made them all. — Large print ed. — Anstey : Ulverscroft, Aug.1982. — [528]p. — (Ulverscroft large print series)
Originally published: London : Joseph, 1981
ISBN 0-7089-0840-3 : £5.00 : CIP entry B82-27002

636.089′092′4 — Zoos. Veterinary medicine — *Personal observations*

Taylor, David, *1934-*. Next panda, please! : further adventures of a wildlife vet / David Taylor. — London : Allen & Unwin, 1982. — 196p ; 23cm
ISBN 0-04-925021-3 : £6.50 : CIP rev. B82-07237

636.089′1018 — Livestock. Histology

Banks, William J.. Applied veterinary histology / William J. Banks ; illustrated by Biomedical Media, College of Veterinary Medicine and Biomedical Sciences, Colorado State University. — [Rev., rewritten and updated]. — Baltimore ; London : Williams & Wilkins, c1981. — xv,572p : ill(some col.) ; 29cm
Previous ed.: published as Histology and comparative organology. 1973. — Includes bibliographies and index
ISBN 0-683-00410-7 : Unpriced B82-07786

636.089′26 — Livestock. Reproduction

Arthur, Geoffrey H.. Veterinary reproduction and obstetrics. — 5th ed. — London : Bailliére Tindall, Sept.1982. — [520]p
Previous ed.: 1975
ISBN 0-7020-0923-7 : £19.50 : CIP entry
Primary classification 636.089′82 B82-20006

Hunter, R. H. F.. Reproduction of farm animals. — London : Longman, Nov.1982. — [150]p. — (Longman handbooks in agriculture)
ISBN 0-582-45085-3 (pbk) : £5.95 : CIP entry B82-26538

636.089′4 — Animals. Slaughtering. Humane techniques. Organisations: Council of Justice to Animals and Humane Slaughter Association — *Serials*

CJA and HSA newsletter. — No.1 (May. 1979-). — Potters Bar (34 Blanche La., Potters Bar, Herts EN6 3PA) : Council of Justice to Animals and Humane Slaughter Association, 1979-. — v. ; 37x26cm
Annual. — Description based on: No.3 (Mar. 1981)
ISSN 0263-1407 = CJA and HSA newsletter : Unpriced B82-18523

636.089′4 — Great Britain. Livestock. Slaughtering. Techniques — *Conference proceedings*

Report of a seminar held between April 16-18th 1980 at Ammerdown, Radstock nr. Bath on the transport and slaughter of farm animals. — Bristol ([c/o] Alastair Mews, University of Bristol, School of Veterinary Sciences, Langford House, Langford, Bristol BS18 7DU) : Ammerdown Group, c1980. — 20p ; 21cm
Cover title
£1.00 (pbk) B82-11410

636.089′4 — Livestock. Slaughtering. Islamic techniques

Khan, Ghulam Mustafa. Al-Zabah : slaying animals for food the Islamic way. — 2nd ed. — London (68a Delancey St., NW1 7RY) : Ta-Ha Publishers, Feb.1982. — [128]p
Previous ed.: London : Green Link Ltd., 197-?
ISBN 0-907461-14-x (pbk) : £1.25 : CIP entry B82-07821

636.089′5 — Veterinary medicine. Pharmacology & therapeutics

Daykin, P. W.. Veterinary applied pharmacology and therapeutics. — 4th ed. — London : Baillière Tindall, July 1982. — [544]p
Previous ed.: 1977
ISBN 0-7020-0871-0 : £17.00 : CIP entry B82-12997

636.089′59 — Veterinary medicine. Toxicology

Clarke, Myra L.. Veterinary toxicology. — 2nd ed. — London : Baillière Tindall, July 1981. — [336]p
Previous ed.: 1975
ISBN 0-7020-0862-1 : £14.50 : CIP entry B81-13459

636.089′6′00941 — Great Britain. Livestock. Diseases — *Serials*

Return of proceedings under the Animal Health Act 1981 / Ministry of Agriculture, Fisheries and Food, Department of Agriculture and Fisheries for Scotland, Welsh Office, Agriculture Department. — 1981-. — London : H.M.S.O., 1982-. — v. ; 25cm
Annual. — Continues: Return of proceedings under the Diseases of Animals Act, 1950
ISSN 0263-4090 = Return of proceedings under the Animal Health Act 1981 : £1.90 B82-24754

636.089′60252 — Animals. First aid — *Manuals*

Jordan, W. J.. Care of the wild : family first aid for birds and other animals / W.J. Jordan and John Hughes. — London : Macdonald, 1982. — 198p : ill ; 22cm
Includes index
ISBN 0-356-08538-4 (cased) : £7.95
ISBN 0-356-08556-2 (pbk) : Unpriced B82-16942

636.089′6042 — Livestock. Genetic disorders

Hámori, D.. Constitutional disorders and hereditary diseases in domestic animals. — Oxford : Elsevier Scientific, Jan.1983. — [600] p. — (Developments in animal and veterinary sciences ; 11)
Translation of: Háziállatok öröklödö alkati hibái és betegségei
ISBN 0-444-99683-4 : £50.00 : CIP entry B82-34599

636.089′607 — Livestock: Small animals. Pathology

Kelly, D. F.. Notes on pathology for small animal clinicians. — Bristol : Wright, Feb.1982. — [112]p. — (A Veterinary practitioner handbook)
ISBN 0-85608-037-3 (pbk) : £7.50 : CIP entry B81-37597

636.089'6079 — European Community countries. Livestock. Mucous membranes. Diseases. Immunological aspects — *Conference proceedings*

The **mucosal** immune system : proceedings of a seminar in the EEC Programme of Coordination of Agricultural Research on Protection of the Young Animal against Perinatal Diseases, held at the University of Bristol, School of Veterinary Science, Langford, Nr. Bristol, United Kingdom on September 9-11, 1980 : sponsored by the Commission of the European Communities, Directorate-General for Agriculture, Coordination of Agricultural Research / edited by F.J. Bourne. — The Hague ; London : Nijhoff for Commission of the European Communities, 1981. — ix,560p : ill ; 25cm. — (Current topics in veterinary medicine and animal science ; v.12)
Includes bibliographies
ISBN 90-247-2528-3 : Unpriced B82-03859

636.089'6079'05 — Veterinary medicine. Immunology — *Serials*

Advances in veterinary immunology. — 1981-. — Amsterdam ; Oxford : Elsevier Scientific, 1982-. — v. : ill ; 25cm. — (Developments in animal and veterinary sciences)
£25.26 B82-23596

636.089'68 — Laboratory animals: Brain damaged mammals. Recovery — *Conference proceedings*

Functional recovery from brain damage / edited by M.W. van Hof and G. Mohn. — Amsterdam ; Oxford : Elsevier/North-Holland Biomedical, 1981. — ix,449p : ill,1port ; 25cm. — (Developments in neuroscience ; v.13)
Conference papers. — Includes bibliographies and index
ISBN 0-444-80394-7 : £37.45
Primary classification 616.8 B82-13437

636.089'692 — Livestock. Theileriosis. Control — *Conference proceedings*

Advances in the control of theileriosis : proceedings of an international conference held at the International Laboratory for Research on Animal Diseases in Nairobi, 9-13th February, 1981 / edited by A.D. Irvin, M.P. Cunningham, A.S. Young. — The Hague ; London : Nijhoff, 1981. — xiii,427p : ill ; 25cm. — (Current topics in veterinary medicine and animal science ; v.14)
Includes bibliographies
ISBN 90-247-2575-5 : Unpriced B82-03857

636.089'6925 — Livestock. Virus diseases

Virus diseases of food animals : a world geography of epidemiology and control / edited by E.P.J. Gibbs. — London : Academic Press, 1981. — 2v.(xvi,786p) : ill ; 24cm
Includes bibliographies and index
ISBN 0-12-282201-3 : Unpriced : CIP rev.
ISBN 0-12-282202-1 (v.2) : £33.80 B81-28792

636.089'6927'00720431 — East Germany. Veterinary medical institutions. Visits by British veterinary surgeons: Visits concerning research on salmonella pathogens of livestock — *Personal observations*

Wray, C.. British Council cultural exchange programme between Britain and the German Democratic Republic : report of a visit to the German Democratic Republic 7-20 September 1981 / C. Wray. — [London] ([Whitehall Place, SW1]) : ADAS, [1982]. — 12p ; 30cm
Unpriced (unbound) B82-16554

636.089'6962 — Livestock. Helminthic diseases

Soulsby, E. J. L.. Helminths, arthropods and protozoa of domesticated animals. — 7th ed. — London : Baillière Tindall, July 1982. — [768]p
Previous ed.: 1968
ISBN 0-7020-0820-6 : £20.00 : CIP entry B82-12995

636.089'82 — Livestock. Obstetrics

Arthur, Geoffrey H.. Veterinary reproduction and obstetrics. — 5th ed. — London : Baillière Tindall, Sept.1982. — [520]p
Previous ed.: 1975
ISBN 0-7020-0923-7 : £19.50 : CIP entry
Also classified at 636.089'26 B82-20006

636.1 — LIVESTOCK. HORSES

636.1 — Livestock: Horses

The **Book** of horses / edited by Fred Urquhart. — London : Secker & Warburg, 1981. — ix,244p,[16]p of plates : ill(some col.),ports ; 29cm
Includes index
ISBN 0-436-54935-2 : £12.50 B82-02608

The **Complete** book of the horse. — Revised ed. — London : Ward Lock, Oct.1982. — [344]p
Previous ed.: 1973
ISBN 0-7063-6123-7 : £9.95 : CIP entry B82-23184

The **Country** life book of the horse / edited by Robert Owen. — [Feltham] : Country life, 1979. — 231p : ill(some col.),ports(some col.) ; 27cm
Includes index
ISBN 0-600-34577-7 : £7.95 B82-04364

Hartley Edwards, Elwyn. The family library of horses / Elwyn Hartley Edwards. — London : Octopus, 1982, c1981. — 80p : ill(chiefly col.),col.ports ; 33cm
Ill on lining papers. — Includes index
ISBN 0-7064-1458-6 : £2.95 B82-30160

636.1 — Livestock: Horses. Behaviour — *For training*

Ledger, Val. Horse problems and vices explained / Val Ledger. — London : Ward Lock, 1982. — 104p : ill(some col.) ; 20cm. — (Horseman's handbooks)
ISBN 0-7063-6119-9 (pbk) : £2.95 : CIP rev. B82-07110

636.1 — Livestock: Horses. Breeding, training & care — *Manuals*

An **Illustrated** guide to horse and pony care : a comprehensive guide to riding, schooling and caring for your horse / compiled by Jane Kidd. — London : Salamander, c1981. — 200p : ill (some col.) ; 23cm
Ill on lining papers. — Includes index
ISBN 0-86101-091-4 : £3.95 B82-07993

636.1 — Livestock: Horses — *Field guides*

Spector, Joanna. Spotter's guide to horses & ponies / Joanna Spector ; illustrated by David Wright, Elaine Keenan & Malcolm McGregor ; with additional illustrations by Ed Roberts and Andy Martin. — London : Usborne, 1979. — 64p : ill(some col.) ; 19cm. — (Spotter's Guides) (Usborne pocketbooks)
Bibliography: p61. — Includes index
ISBN 0-86020-254-2 : £1.85 B82-05599

636.1'0023 — Occupations involving horses — *Career guides*

Harvey, Rex. Working with horses. — London : Batsford, July 1982. — [112]p
ISBN 0-7134-4461-4 : £5.95 : CIP entry B82-13059

Mortimer, Monty. Careers working with horses. — London : Kogan Page, Jan.1983. — [100]p. — (Kogan Page careers series)
ISBN 0-85038-639-x (cased) : £6.95 : CIP entry
ISBN 0-85038-640-3 (pbk) : £2.50 B82-37464

636.1'003'21 — Livestock: Horses — *Encyclopaedias*

Owen, Robert, *1918-*. The Beaver horse and pony dictionary / Robert Owen ; illustrated by Christine Bousfield. — London : Beaver, 1981. — 123p : ill ; 18cm
ISBN 0-600-20366-2 (pbk) : £0.95 B82-02844

636.1'00941 — Great Britain. Livestock: Horses — *Practical information*

Popescu, Lucy. Pony holiday book / Lucy Popescu ; illustrated by Peter Clark. — London : Granada, 1982. — 90p : ill ; 18cm. — (A Dragon book)
ISBN 0-583-30420-6 (pbk) : £0.85 B82-22056

636.1'08'1 — Livestock: Horses. Purchase — *Amateurs' manuals*

Macdonald, Janet W.. The right horse : an owners' and buyers' guide. — London : Methuen, Oct.1982. — [128]p
ISBN 0-413-51080-8 : £6.95 : CIP entry B82-24480

636.1'082 — Livestock: Horses. Breeding. Veterinary aspects

Rossdale, Peter. Equine stud farm medicine / P.D. Rossdale, S.W. Ricketts. — 2nd ed. — London : Baillière Tindall, 1980. — viii,564p : ill ; 24cm
Previous ed.: published as Practice of equine stud medicine. 1974. — Includes bibliographies and index
ISBN 0-7020-0754-4 : £19.50 : CIP rev. B80-17804

636.1'082'09415 — Ireland. Livestock: Horses. Breading, *1886-1903*

Lewis, Colin A.. Horse breeding in Ireland : and the role of the Royal Dublin Society's horse breeding schemes, 1886-1903 / Colin A. Lewis. — London : J.A. Allen, 1980. — 232p : ill,maps,ports ; 25cm
Includes index
ISBN 0-85131-315-9 : £12.50 : CIP rev. B79-08061

636.1'083 — Livestock: Horses. Care — *Manuals*

Saunders, Ray. Ownership, stabling & feeding / Ray Saunders. — London : Muller, 1982. — 106p,[8]p of plates : ill(some col.) ; 22cm. — (Horsekeeping)
Includes index
ISBN 0-584-95009-8 (cased) : Unpriced
ISBN 0-584-95010-1 (pbk) : £3.95 B82-39967

Walrond, Sallie. Your problem horse. — London : Pelham, Nov.1982. — [128]p. — (Pelham horsemaster series)
ISBN 0-7207-1408-7 : £5.95 : CIP entry B82-26406

636.1'0837 — Tack

Horse tack : the complete equipment guide for riding and driving / edited by Julie Richardson. — London : Pelham, c1982. — 192p : ill(some col.) ; 29cm. — (A London Editions book)
Includes index
ISBN 0-7207-1377-3 : £10.95 B82-14884

636.1'0888 — Livestock: Horses. Showing

Skelton, E. C.. Ringcraft / Elizabeth Skelton. — London : Pelham, 1978 (1980 [printing]). — 96p,[8]p of plates : ill,ports ; 21cm. — (Pelham horsemaster series)
Originally published: Walton-on-Thames : Nelson, 1970. — Includes index
ISBN 0-7207-1083-9 : £5.50 B82-25602

636.1'089 — Livestock: Horses. Veterinary aspects

Vogel, Colin. Horse ailments and health care. — London : Ward Lock, Sept.1982. — [96]p. — (Practical horse guide)
ISBN 0-7063-6199-7 : £4.95 : CIP entry B82-21387

636.1'089746 — Livestock: Horses. Urogenital system. Surgery

Walker, D. F.. Bovine and equine urogenital surgery / D.F. Walker, J.T. Vaughan. — Philadelphia : Lea & Febiger ; London : Baillière Tindall, 1980. — x,277p : ill ; 27cm
Includes bibliographies and index
ISBN 0-8121-0284-3 : £18.00
Also classified at 636.2'089746 B82-38425

636.1'2 — Racehorses. Breeding — *French & English dictionaries*

Kearney, Mary-Louise. A glossary of French bloodstock terminology / Mary-Louise Kearney. — London : J.A. Allen, 1981. — 48p : ill ; 18cm
ISBN 0-85131-354-x (pbk) : £2.00 : CIP rev.
Also classified at 798.4'003'41 B81-13553

636.1'2 — Racehorses. Breeding — *Manuals*

Leicester, *Sir* **Charles**. Bloodstock breeding. — 2nd ed. — London : J.A. Allen, Feb.1983. — 1v.
Previous ed.: 1964
ISBN 0-85131-349-3 : £20.00 : CIP entry B82-39592

636.1′2 — Racehorses. Racing. Races. Winners, *1960-1980.* **Pedigrees** - *Collections*

Pickering, Martin. Pedigrees of leading winners, 1960-1980. — London : J.A. Allen, July 1981. — [200]p
ISBN 0-85131-372-8 : £25.00 : CIP entry
B81-19217

636.1′2′0924 — Great Britain. Racehorses. Ownership. Sangster, Robert — *Biographies*

Poole, Christopher. Classic treble : the Sangster-Piggott-O′Brian partnership / Christopher Poole. — London : Queen Anne, 1982. — 192p : ill,ports ; 24cm
ISBN 0-356-08566-x : £8.95 B82-25788

636.1′2′0924 — Great Britain. Racehorses. Training. Dingwall, Louie — *Biographies*

Bennett, Alan R.. Horsewoman : the extraordinary Mrs D : a biography of Louie Dingwall, Dorset′s racehorse trainer / by Alan R. Bennett ; with a foreword by Brough Scott. — Sherborne : Dorset Publishing, 1979. — 207p : ill,facsims,ports ; 23cm
Includes index
£7.95 B82-08901

636.1′2′0924 — Great Britain. Racehorses. Training. Price, Ryan — *Biographies*

Bromley, Peter. The price of success. — London : Paul, Oct.1982. — [260]p
ISBN 0-09-149880-5 : £7.95 : CIP entry
B82-25532

636.1′32 — Great Britain. Stud farms. Thoroughbred horses: Stallions — *Lists* — *Serials*

Thoroughbred. Supplement. — [No.1]-. — [London] ([Suite 53, 26 Charing Cross Rd, WC2H ODJ]) : [Sagittarius Bloodstock Agency], [1982]-. — v. ; 30cm
Irregular. — Supplement to: Thoroughbred
ISSN 0263-3027 = Thoroughbred. Supplement : Unpriced B82-22685

636.1′32 — Great Britain. Thoroughbred horses: Stallions. Breeding — *Serials*

Thoroughbred. — Jan. 1982-. — London (Suite 53, 26 Charing Cross Rd, WC2H ODJ) : Sagittarius Bloodstock Agency, 1982-. — v. : ill ; 30cm
Four issues yearly. — Supplement: Thoroughbred. Supplement
ISSN 0263-3019 = Thoroughbred : £10.00 per year B82-22686

636.1′32 — Thoroughbred horses. Breeding. Genetic aspects

Robertson, J. B.. The principles of heredity applied to the racehorse. — London : J.A. Allen, July 1981. — [43]p
ISBN 0-85131-374-4 : £5.00 : CIP entry
B81-25699

636.1′4 — Harness horses. Breaking to harness — *Manuals*

Walrond, Sallie. Breaking a horse to harness : a step-by-step guide / Sallie Walrond. — London : Pelham, 1981. — 136p : ill,ports ; 22cm
ISBN 0-7207-1369-2 : £7.50 : CIP rev.
B81-30363

636.1′4 — Harness horses. Harnessing — *Manuals*

Spruytte, J.. Early harness systems. — London : J.A. Allen, Jan.1983. — [144]p
Translation of: Etudes experimentales sur l′attelage
ISBN 0-85131-376-0 : £10.50 : CIP entry
B82-33106

636.1′5 — British carthorses. Showing

Hart, Edward. Care and showing of the heavy horse / Edward Hart. — London : Batsford, 1981. — 144p,[4]p of plates : ill(some col.),ports ; 26cm
Bibliography: p140. — Includes index
ISBN 0-7134-3494-5 : £9.95 B82-03474

636.1′5 — Clydesdale horses

Baird, Eric. The Clydesdale horse / Eric Baird. — London : Batsford, 1982. — 128p,[16]p of plates : ill,ports ; 24cm
Bibliography: p119. — Includes index
ISBN 0-7134-4041-4 : £8.95 B82-31560

636.1′6 — Livestock: Ponies. Care — *Manuals* — *For children*

Allen, Jane, *1942-*. Hello to ponies / Jane Allen and Mary Danby ; illustrated by Alison Prince. — London : Armada, 1982, c1979. — 96p : ill ; 20cm
Originally published: London : Heinemann, 1979. — Includes index
£0.90 (pbk) B82-15118

636.1′6 — Livestock: Ponies — *For children*

Henschel, Georgie. All about your pony / Georgie Henschel. — London : Ward Lock, 1981. — 104p : ill(some col.) ; 20cm. — (Horseman′s handbooks)
ISBN 0-7063-6122-9 (pbk) : £2.95 : CIP rev.
B81-12313

636.1′6 — Livestock: Ponies. Training & care — *Manuals*

Woodhouse, Barbara. Barbara Woodhouse′s book of ponies. — Harmondsworth : Puffin, 1982, c1954. — 95p,[12]p of plates : ill ; 20cm. — (Puffin plus)
Originally published: London : Hulton, 1957
ISBN 0-14-031447-4 (pbk) : £1.00 B82-30178

636.1′8 — Livestock: Donkeys

Borwick, Robin. The book of the donkey / Robin Borwick. — London : Pelham, 1981. — 256p : ill ; 25cm
Bibliography: p245. — Includes index
ISBN 0-7207-1362-5 : £9.95 B82-05174

636.2 — LIVESTOCK. RUMINANTS, CATTLE

636.2′084 — Livestock: Ruminants. Feeding & nutrition

The **Nutrient** requirements of ruminant livestock : technical review by an Agricultural Research Council working party. — Slough : Published on behalf of the Agricultural Research Council by Commonwealth Agricultural Bureaux, c1980. — xvi,351p ; 24cm
Bibliography. — Includes index
ISBN 0-85198-459-2 : Unpriced B82-24302

Wilson, P. N.. Improved feeding of cattle and sheep : a practical guide to modern concepts of ruminant nutrition / P.N. Wilson and T.D.A. Brigstocke. — London : Granada, 1981. — 238p : ill ; 24cm
Bibliography: p228-231. — Includes index
ISBN 0-246-11210-7 (pbk) : Unpriced : CIP rev. B81-34152

636.2′0852 — Livestock: Cattle. Feedingstuffs. Constituents: Nitrogen & proteins. Sources — *Conference proceedings*

Protein contribution of feedstuffs for ruminants : application to feed formulation / editors E.L. Miller and I.H. Pike in association with A.J.H. Van Es. — London : Butterworth Scientific, 1982. — 160p : ill ; 24cm. — (Studies in the agricultural and food sciences)
Includes index
ISBN 0-408-11151-8 : £15.00 : CIP rev.
B82-04042

636.2′0852 — Livestock: Ruminants. Nutrition. Proteins

Ørskov, E. R.. Protein nutrition in ruminants / O. [i.e.E.]R. Ørskov. — London : Academic Press, 1982. — viii,160p : ill ; 24cm
Includes bibliographies and index
ISBN 0-12-528480-2 : £11.80 : CIP rev.
B82-10422

636.2′0852 — Livestock: Ruminants. Nutrition. Proteins — *Conference proceedings*

Protein and energy supply for high production of milk and meat : proceedings of a symposium of the Committee on Agricultural Problems of the Economic Commission for Europe and the Food and Agriculture Organisation, Geneva, Switzerland, 12-15 January 1981. — Oxford : Published for the United Nations by Pergamon, 1982. — xii,191p : ill ; 26cm
Includes 2 chapters in French. — Includes bibliographies
ISBN 0-08-028909-6 : £15.00 : CIP rev.
B81-38300

636.2′08962′0094 — European Community countries. Livestock: Cattle. Respiratory system. Diseases — *Conference proceedings*

Respiratory diseases in cattle : a seminar in the EEC programme of coordination of research on beef production held at Edinburgh, Nov.8-10, 1977 : sponsored by the Commission of the European Communities, Directorate-General for Agriculture, Coordination of Agricultural Research / edited by W.B. Martin. — The Hague ; London : Nijhoff for the Commission of European Communities, 1978. — xii,562p : ill ; 24cm. — (Current topics in veterinary medicine ; v.3)
ISBN 90-247-2134-2 : Unpriced B82-12873

636.2′08967 — Livestock: Cattle. Lameness

Greenough, Paul R.. Lameness in cattle / Paul R. Greenough, Finlay J. MacCallum, A. David Weaver. — 2nd ed. / edited by A. David Weaver. — Bristol : John Wright, 1981. — vii,471p : ill ; 24cm
Previous ed.: Edinburgh : Oliver and Boyd, 1972. — Includes index
ISBN 0-85608-030-6 : Unpriced : CIP rev.
B81-21550

636.2′0896965 — European Community countries. Livestock: Cattle. Nematodiasis — *Conference proceedings*

Epidemiology and control of nematodiasis in cattle : an animal pathology in the CEC Programme of Coordination of Agricultural Research, held at the Royal Veterinary and Agricultural University, Copenhagen, Denmark, February 4-6, 1980 / sponsored by the Commission of the European Communities, Directorate-General for Agriculture, Coordination of Agricultural Research ; edited by P. Nansen, R. Jess Jørgensen, E.J.L. Soulsby. — The Hague ; London : Nijhoff for the Commission of the European Communities, 1981. — x,606p : ill ; 25cm. — (Current topics in veterinary medicine and animal science ; v.9)
Includes bibliographies
ISBN 90-247-2502-x : Unpriced B82-03457

636.2′089699419 — Livestock: Cattle. Leukaemia — *Conference proceedins*

International Symposium on Bovine Leukosis *(4th : 1980 : Bologna).* Fourth International Symposium on Bovine Leukosis : a seminar in the EEC programme of coordination of research on animal pathology organised by O.C. Straub and G. Gentile, and held in Bologna, 5-7 November 1980 / sponsored by the Commission of the European Communities, Directorate-General for Agriculture, Coordination of Agricultural Research ; edited by O.C. Straub. — The Hague ; London : Nijhoff for the Commission of the European Communities, 1982. — xii,614p : ill ; 25cm. — (Current topics in veterinary medicine and animal science ; v.15)
Includes bibliographies
ISBN 90-247-2604-2 : Unpriced B82-17267

636.2′089746 — Livestock: Cattle. Urogenital system. Surgery

Walker, D. F.. Bovine and equine urogenital surgery / D.F. Walker, J.T. Vaughan. — Philadelphia : Lea & Febiger ; London : Baillière Tindall, 1980. — x,277p : ill ; 27cm
Includes bibliographies and index
ISBN 0-8121-0284-3 : £18.00
Primary classification 636.1′089746
B82-38425

636.2′089819 — Livestock: Cattle: Cows. Udders. Mastitis. Control measures

Mastitis control and herd management : the proceedings of a course organized by the National Institute for Research in Dairying, on 22, 23 and 24 September 1980, for the British Cattle Veterinary Association / course organized and papers edited by A.J. Bramley, F.H. Dodd & T.K. Griffin. — Reading : The Institute, 1981. — 290p : ill(some col.),forms (some col.) ; 21cm. — (Technical bulletin ; 4)
Includes bibliographies and index
ISBN 0-7084-0195-3 (pbk) : Unpriced
B82-14482

636.2'0898923427075 — Livestock: Newborn calves. Diarrhoeal diseases. Diagnosis. Laboratory techniques — *Conference proceedings*

Laboratory diagnosis in neonatal calf and pig diarrhoea : proceedings of a workshop on diagnostic techniques for enteropathogenic agents associated with neonatal diarrhoea in calves and pigs, held at the Central Veterinary Institute, Department of Virology, Lelystad, The Netherlands, June 3-5, 1980 / sponsored by the Commission of the European Communities Directorate-General for Agriculture, Co-ordination of Agricultural Research ; edited by P. W. de Leeuw and P.A.M. Guinée. — The Hague ; London : Nijhoff for the Commission of the European Communities, 1981. — x,200p : ill ; 25cm. — (Current topics in veterinary medicine and animal science ; v.13)
Includes index
ISBN 90-247-2527-5 : Unpriced
Also classified at 636.4'0898923427075
B82-00483

636.2'13 — Denmark. Livestock: Beef cattle: Bulls. Feedingstuffs: Grass silage

Lawrence, N. G.. The storage feeding of grass silage to bull beef / N.G. Lawrence. — [London] ([Great Westminster House, Horseferry Rd., SW1P 2AE]) : ADAS, [1981]. — i,24p ; 30cm. — (ADAS overseas study tour programme ; 1981/82)
"Report of a study tour undertaken in Denmark, 11-18 July 1981". — Cover title
Unpriced (pbk) B82-11659

636.2'13 — Great Britain. Livestock: Beef cattle. Suckler cows. Production — *Conference proceedings*

Report on suckler cow workers meeting, Grange, Dunsany, Republic of Ireland 9-12 June 1981 / [edited by] J.R. Noble, J. MacLeod. — [Cambridge] (Block C, Brooklands Ave, Cambridge, CB2 2DR]) : [ADAS, Ministry of Agriculture, Fisheries and Food], [1981]. — i,18p ; 30cm
Conference papers. — Cover title
Unpriced (pbk) B82-15999

636.2'13 — Livestock: Beef cattle. Feeding & nutrition

Blueprints for beef / MLC Beef Improvement Services. — Bletchley (P.O. Box 44, Queensway House, Bletchley MK2 2EF) : Meat and Livestock Commission, [1982]. — 36p ; 21cm
Cover title
£2.00 (pbk) B82-38435

636.2'13'072042 — Great Britain. Livestock: Beef cattle. Production. Research by Agricultural Development and Advisory Service. *Agriculture Service* — *Serials*

Agricultural Development and Advisory Service. *Agriculture Service.* Beef : research and development reports / Agriculture Service. — 1980-. — [London] ([Great Westminster House, Horseferry Rd, SW1P 2AE]) : ADAS, [1982]-. — v. ; 21cm
Annual. — Continues: Agricultural Development and Advisory Service. Agriculture Service. Beef cattle
ISSN 0263-8037 = Beef (London) : Unpriced
B82-36718

636.2'13'0941 — Great Britain. Livestock: Beef cattle. Production — *Statistics* — *Serials*

Commercial beef production yearbook / MLC Economics, Livestock and Marketing Services. — 1980-81-. — Bletchley (PO Box 44, Queensway House, Bletchley MK2 2EF) : Meat and Livestock Commission, 1981-. — v. : ill,maps ; 30cm
ISSN 0262-9100 = Commercial beef production yearbook : £3.00 B82-11812

636.2'142 — Dairy farming — *Conference proceedings*

Moorepark farmers' conference : May 1982. — Dublin (19 Sandymount Ave., Dublin 4) : An Foras Talúntais, [1982]. — 140p : ill ; 21cm
Includes bibliographies
£2.00 (pbk) B82-33662

636.2'142 — Devon. Dairy farming. Robertson, James, *1945-* — *Biographies*

Robertson, James, *1945-*. Any fool can be a dairy farmer / James Robertson ; drawings by Charles Gore. — London : Corgi, 1982, c1980. — 188p : ill ; 18cm
Originally published: Ipswich : Farming Press, 1980
ISBN 0-552-12014-6 (pbk) : £1.50 B82-40192

636.2'142 — England. Livestock: Dairy cattle. Research by Agricultural Development and Advisory Service. *Agriculture Service* — *Serials*

Agricultural Development and Advisory Service. *Agriculture Service.* Dairy cattle : results of Agriculture Service experiments. — 1978-. — [London] ([Great Westminster House, Horseferry Rd, SW1P 2AE]) : ADAS, [1979?]-. — v. ; 21cm
Annual. — Continues in part: Agricultural Development and Advisory Service. Agriculture Service. Dairy cattle, pigs and poultry
ISSN 0263-1733 = Dairy cattle : Unpriced
B82-22688

636.2'142 — Great Britain. Livestock: Diary cattle. Tuberculosis. Transfer from badgers

Zuckerman, Solly Zuckerman, *Baron*. Badgers, cattle and tuberculosis : report to the Right Honourable Peter Walker, MBE MP / by Lord Zuckerman. — London : H.M.S.O., 1980. — 106p : ill,maps ; 25cm
Includes bibliographies
ISBN 0-11-240355-7 (pbk) : £5.20 B82-16411

636.2'142 — Livestock: Cattle: Cows — *For children*

Ingves, Gunilla. Cows. — London : A. & C. Black, Sept.1982. — [32]p. — (Farm animals)
Translation of: Kor
ISBN 0-7136-2238-5 : £3.50 : CIP entry
B82-20358

636.2'142 — Livestock: Dairy cattle: Cows — *For children*

Whitlock, Ralph. Dairy cows / Ralph Whitlock ; illustrated by Anna Jupp. — Hove : Wayland, 1982. — 32p : col.ill ; 20x22cm. — (Farm animals)
Includes index
ISBN 0-85340-909-9 : £3.50 B82-18428

636.2'142 — Livestock: Dairy cattle. Diseases

Barron, Norman. The dairy farmer's veterinary book / Norman Barron. — 10th ed. (rev.). — Ipswich : Farming Press, 1979, c1976. — 256p,[41]p of plates : ill ; 23cm
Previous ed.: 1976. — Includes index
ISBN 0-85236-099-1 : Unpriced B82-06379

636.2'142 — Surrey. Dairy farming. Caddey, Avril D. — *Biographies*

Caddey, Avril D.. Four score years : (dedicated to the dairy cow) / some reminiscences of Avril D. Caddey. — Market Harborough (5 St. Mary's Rd., Market Harborough, Leics. LE16 7DS) : Green, c1981. — 181p,[8]p of plates : ill,ports ; 21cm
£4.00 (pbk) B82-33137

636.2'342 — Wiltshire. Chippenham. Livestock: Dairy cattle: Friesian bulls. Rearing. Organisations: Milk Marketing Board. *Bull Rearing Unit*

Chippenham bull rearing unit. — Chippenham (Malmesbury Rd, Kington Langley, Chippenham, Wilts. SN15 5PZ) : MMB Bull Rearing Unit, 1980. — [8]p : ill ; 30cm
Cover title. — Text, ill on inside covers
Unpriced (pbk) B82-36812

636.2'94 — United States. Livestock: Deer. Management

Dasmann, William. Deer range : improvement and management / by William Dasmann. — Jefferson, N.C. ; London : McFarland ; Folkestone : Distributed in Great Britain by Bailey Bros & Swinfen, 1981. — viii,168p : ill ; 24cm
Bibliography: p141-164. — Includes index
ISBN 0-89950-027-7 : Unpriced B82-21034

636.3 — LIVESTOCK. SHEEP AND GOATS

636.3 — Livestock: Sheep — *For children*

Whitlock, Ralph. Sheep / Ralph Whitlock ; illustrated by Anna Jupp. — Hove : Wayland, 1982. — 32p : col.ill ; 20x22cm. — (Farm animals)
Includes index
ISBN 0-85340-910-2 : £3.50 B82-18427

636.3 — Livestock: Sheep. Production

Sheep and goat production. — Oxford : Elsevier Scientific, Feb.1982. — [350]p. — (World animal science. C ; 1)
ISBN 0-444-41989-6 : CIP entry
Also classified at 636.3'9 B81-35707

636.3'0072042 — England. Livestock: Pigs. Research by Agricultural Development and Advisory Service. *Agriculture Service* — *Serials*

Agricultural Development and Advisory Service. *Agriculture Service.* Pigs and poultry : results of Agriculture Service experiments. — 1978-. — [London] ([Great Westminster House, Horseferry Rd, SW1P 2AE]) : ADAS, [1979?]-. — v. ; 21cm
Annual. — Continues in part: Agricultural Development and Advisory Service. Agriculture Service. Dairy cattle, pigs and poultry
ISSN 0263-1741 = Pigs and poultry : Unpriced
Primary classification 636.5'0072042
B82-22689

636.3'009 — Livestock: Sheep, *to 1981*

Ryder, M. L.. Sheep and man. — London : Duckworth, Jan.1983. — [700]p
ISBN 0-7156-1655-2 : £28.00 : CIP entry
B82-32615

636.3'00913 — Tropical regions. Livestock: Sheep. Production

Devendra, C.. Goat and sheep production in the tropics. — London : Longman, Nov.1982. — [269]p. — (Intermediate tropical agriculture series)
ISBN 0-582-60935-6 (pbk) : £3.50 : CIP entry
Primary classification 636.3'9'00913
B82-26541

636.3'00913 — Tropical regions. Livestock: Sheep. Production — *Manuals*

Carles, A. B.. Sheep production in the tropics. — Oxford : Oxford University Press, Nov.1982. — [200]p. — (Oxford tropical handbooks)
ISBN 0-19-859449-6 (cased) : £12.00 : CIP entry
ISBN 0-19-859485-2 (pbk) : £5.95 B82-26885

636.3'00941 — Great Britain. Livestock: Sheep. Production — *Manuals*

Cooper, M. McG.. Profitable sheep farming / M. McG. Cooper and R.J. Thomas. — 4th rev ed. — Ipswich : Farming Press, 1979. — 164p,[7]p of plates : ill ; 23cm
Previous ed.: 1975. — Includes index
ISBN 0-85236-100-9 : Unpriced B82-26301

636.3'0885 — Laboratory animals: Sheep

Hecker, J. F.. The sheep as an experimental animal. — London : Academic Press, Jan.1983. — [250]p
ISBN 0-12-336050-1 : CIP entry B82-33462

636.3'08982 — Livestock: Ewes. Lambing

Bird, A. F.. United States Sheep Experimental Station : report of a visit to the USA, 21-24 September 1981 / A.F. Bird. — [London] ([Great Westminster House, Horseferry Rd., SW1P 2AE]) : ADAS, 1982. — 8p : 2ill,maps ; 30cm
Cover title
Unpriced (pbk) B82-40446

636.3'13'0941 — Great Britain. Livestock: Lambs. Production

Lamb carcase production : planning to meet your market. — Bletchley (PO Box 44, Queenway Hse., Bletchley MK2 2EF) : Meat and Livestock Commission, [1981]. — 11p : ill (some col.) ; 20cm
Cover title
£0.50 (pbk) B82-17320

636.3'142 — Dairy sheep. Management
Mills, Olivia. Practical sheep dairying : the care and milking of the dairy ewe / by Olivia Mills ; line drawings by John Harman. — Wellingborough : Thorsons, 1982. — 224p : ill,2forms,1plan ; 22cm
Bibliography: p219-220. — Includes index
ISBN 0-7225-0731-3 (pbk) : £5.95 : CIP rev. B82-09837

636.3'2 — Great Britain. Livestock: Sheep. Breeds
British sheep. — Rev. ed. — [Tring] ([Cholesbury, Tring, Herts.]) : National Sheep Association, 1979. — 195p : ill,1map ; 22cm
Previous ed.: 1976
Unpriced (pbk) B82-22203

636.3'2 — Livestock: Welsh sheep. Breeds
Williams-Davies, John. Welsh sheep and their wool / John Williams-Davies. — Llandysul : Gomer, 1981. — 74p : ill ; 22cm
Bibliography: p73-74
ISBN 0-85088-964-2 (pbk) : £1.25
Also classified at 338.4'767731'09429 B82-10705

636.3'9 — Livestock: Goats. Production
Goat production / edited by C. Gall. — London : Academic Press, 1981. — xix,619p : ill,1map ; 24cm
Includes bibliographies and index
ISBN 0-12-273980-9 : £41.40 : CIP rev. B81-18087

Sheep and goat production. — Oxford : Elsevier Scientific, Feb.1982. — [350]p. — (World animal science. C ; 1)
ISBN 0-444-41989-6 : CIP entry
Primary classification 636.3 B81-35707

636.3'9'00913 — Tropical regions. Livestock: Goats. Production
Devendra, C.. Goat and sheep production in the tropics. — London : Longman, Nov.1982. — [269]p. — (Intermediate tropical agriculture series)
ISBN 0-582-60935-6 (pbk) : £3.50 : CIP entry
Also classified at 636.3'00913 B82-26541

636.3'9083 — Livestock: Goats. Care & management — *Amateurs' manuals*
Halliday, John, *1943-*. Practical goat-keeping / John & Jill Halliday. — London : Ward Lock, 1982. — 104p : ill ; 23cm
Bibliography: p99-100. — Includes index
ISBN 0-7063-6084-2 : £5.95 : CIP rev. B82-00219

636.4 — LIVESTOCK. PIGS

636.4 — Livestock: Pigs. Production
Krider, J. L.. Swine production. — 5th ed. / J.L. Krider, J.H. Conrad, W.E. Carroll. — New York ; London : McGraw-Hill, c1982. — viii,679p : ill,plans ; 24cm. — (McGraw-Hill publications in the agricultural sciences)
Previous ed.: 1971. — Includes bibliographies and index
ISBN 0-07-035503-7 : £22.95 B82-29271

636.4'00942 — England. Livestock: Pigs
Thomas, W. J. K.. The structure of pig production in England and Wales / W.J.K. Thomas. — Exeter (Lafrouda House, St. German's Rd., Exeter EX4 6TL) : University of Exeter Agricultural Economics Unit, 1981. — 13p : ill ; 30cm. — (Occasional paper / University of Exeter Agricultural Economics Unit ; no.3)
£0.50 (pbk) B82-40974

636.4'009426'13 — Norfolk. Terrington St Clement. Agricultural industries. Experimental farms: Terrington Experimental Husbandry Farm. Pig production — *Serials*
Terrington Experimental Husbandry Farm. Pig review / Terrington Experimental Husbandry Farm. — 4th (1981)-. — Terrington St Clement (Terrington St Clement, King's Lynn, Norfolk PE34 4PW) : The Farm, 1981-. — v. : ill ; 21cm
Irregular. — Continues: Terrington Experimental Husbandry Farm. Annual pig review
ISSN 0262-3757 = Pig review : Unpriced B82-02358

636.4'0852 — Livestock: Pigs. Nutrition
Whittemore, Colin T.. Practical pig nutrition / C.T. Whittemore and F.W.H. Elsley. — 2nd impression (with amendments). — Ipswich : Farming Press, 1979. — 190p : ill ; 23cm
Previous ed.: 2nd. 1977. — Includes index
ISBN 0-85236-074-6 : Unpriced B82-26300

636.4'08926 — Livestock: Pigs. Reproduction — *Conference proceedings*
Control of pig reproduction. — London : Butterworth Scientific, May 1982. — [450]p
Conference papers
ISBN 0-408-10768-5 : £33.00 : CIP entry B82-06743

636.4'0896 — Livestock: Pigs. Diseases
Taylor, D. J.. Pig diseases / D.J. Taylor. — [Glasgow] ([31 North Birbiston Rd., Lennoxtown, Glasgow]) : [D.J. Taylor], 1979. — 176p ; 22cm
Unpriced (pbk) B82-33508

Taylor, D. J.. Pig diseases / D.J. Taylor. — 2nd ed. — [Glasgow] : [D.J. Taylor], 1981. — 200p ; 21cm
Previous ed.: 1979
ISBN 0-9506932-1-9 (pbk) : Unpriced B82-33509

636.4'0898923427075 — Livestock: Newborn pigs. Diarrhoeal diseases. Diagnosis. Laboratory techniques — *Conference proceedings*
Laboratory diagnosis in neonatal calf and pig diarrhoea : proceedings of a workshop on diagnostic techniques for enteropathogenic agents associated with neonatal diarrhoea in calves and pigs, held at the Central Veterinary Institute, Department of Virology, Lelystad, The Netherlands, June 3-5, 1980 / sponsored by the Commission of the European Communities Directorate-General for Agriculture, Co-ordination of Agricultural Research ; edited by P. W. de Leeuw and P.A.M. Guinée. — The Hague ; London : Nijhoff for the Commission of the European Communities, 1981. — x,200p : ill ; 25cm. — (Current topics in veterinary medicine and animal science ; v.13)
Includes index
ISBN 90-247-2527-5 : Unpriced
Primary classification 636.2'0898923427075 B82-00483

636.5 — LIVESTOCK. POULTRY

636.5 — Poultry
Physiology and biochemistry of the domestic fowl . — London : Academic Press
Vol.4. — Feb.1983. — [430]p
ISBN 0-12-267104-x : CIP entry B82-36571

636.5 — Poultry — *Conference proceedings*
Groom, C. M.. 1) Jubilee symposium on 'The World's Poultry Production', 2) 5th Symposium on Quality of Poultry Meat & 3) 1st Symposium on Egg Quality, the Netherlands, 17-23 May 1981 / C.M. Groom, N.D. Overfield, F.H. Whaley. — [London] ([Great Westminster House, Horseferry Rd., SW1P 2AE]) : ADAS, [1982]. — 14,6p : 1map ; 30cm
Cover title
Unpriced (pbk) B82-40874

636.5'0023'41 — Great Britain. Poultry. Production — *Career guides*
Careers in poultry husbandry. — [Beckenham] : Agricultural Training Board on behalf of the Joint Working Party on Careers Literature, 1979. — 7p : ill ; 21cm
Unpriced (unbound) B82-19774

636.5'0072042 — England. Poultry. Research by Agricultural Development and Advisory Service. Agriculture Service — *Serials*
Agricultural Development and Advisory Service. *Agriculture Service*. Pigs and poultry : results of Agriculture Service experiments. — 1978-. — [London] ([Great Westminster House, Horseferry Rd, SW1P 2AE]) : ADAS, [1979?]-. — v. ; 21cm
Annual. — Continues in part: Agricultural Development and Advisory Service. Agriculture Service. Dairy cattle, pigs and poultry
ISSN 0263-1741 = Pigs and poultry : Unpriced
Also classified at 636.3'0072042 B82-22689

636.5'0072042523 — England. Poultry. Research by Gleadthorpe Experimental Husbandry Farm
Gleadthorpe : experimental husbandry farm / ADAS. — [London] : Ministry of Agriculture, Fisheries and Food, 1981. — lii,43p : ill,1map ; 21cm. — (Poultry booklet ; no.8)
Cover title
Unpriced (pbk) B82-32225

636.5'00941 — Great Britain. Poultry. Breeds. Standards
British poultry standards. — 4th ed. — London : Butterworth Scientific, May 1982. — [334]p
Previous ed.: London : Iliffe, 1981
ISBN 0-408-70952-9 : £17.50 : CIP entry B82-06744

636.5'00941 — Great Britain. Poultry. Fancying — *Serials*
Fancy fowl. — Vol.1, no.1 (Oct. 1981)-. — Highclere (Crondall Cottage, Highclere, Newbury, Berks.) : Fancy Fowl, 1981-. — v. : ill ; 30cm
Six issues yearly
ISSN 0262-3846 = Fancy fowl : £5.00 per year B82-04910

636.5'083 — Poultry. Care & management — *Amateurs' manuals*
Laud, Peter. Keeping your own poultry : advice for the small-scale beginner / by Peter Laud ; illustrations by Peter Averis. — Wellingborough : Thorsons, 1982. — 128p : ill ; 22cm
Includes index
ISBN 0-7225-0712-7 (pbk) : Unpriced : CIP rev. B81-35847

Sturges, T. W.. Poultry culture for profit : a guide to the general management of poultry / by T.W. Sturges. — 8th ed. / completely revised by editorial staff of Saiga Publishing Co. Ltd.. — Hindhead : Saiga, c1981. — viii,115p,[1]leaf of plates : ill(some col.) ; 23cm. — (Spur Publications poultry fanciers' library)
Previous ed.: Liss : Spur, 1976. — Includes index
ISBN 0-904558-98-3 : £6.00 B82-08703

Walters, John, *1944-*. Keeping chickens. — 2nd ed. — London : Pelham Books, Sept.1982. — [128]p
Previous ed.: 1976
ISBN 0-7207-1435-4 (pbk) : £2.95 : CIP entry B82-19824

Walters, John, *1944-*. Keeping ducks, geese and turkeys. — 2nd ed. — London : Pelham Books, Sept.1982. — [128]p
Previous ed.: 1976
ISBN 0-7207-1437-0 (pbk) : £2.95 : CIP entry
Also classified at 636.5'92'083 ; 636.5'97 ; 636.5'98 B82-19826

636.5'0896 — Poultry. Diseases
Coutts, G. S.. Poultry diseases under modern management. — 2nd ed. / by G.S. Coutts. — Hindhead : Saiga, c1981. — viii,245p,8p of plates : ill(some col.) ; 24cm
Previous ed.: / by 'Poultry World' veterinary adviser. London : Iliffe, 1961. — Includes index
ISBN 0-904558-80-0 : £10.00 B82-08711

Poultry diseases. — 2nd ed. — London : Baillière Tindall, July 1982. — [384]p
Previous ed.: 1977
ISBN 0-7020-0907-5 : £15.00 : CIP entry B82-12998

636.5'13 — Saudi Arabia. Taif. Broiler production industries: Fakieh Farms. Livestock: Broilers. Veterinary aspects
Cullen, G. A.. Report of a visit to Fakieh farms, Taif, Saudia Arabia 20-26 November 1981 / G.A. Cullen. — [London] ([Whitehall Place, SW1]) : ADAS, [1982]. — 21p ; 30cm
Unpriced (unbound) B82-16555

636.5'142 — Poultry. Eggs. Production. Battery system
The **Battery** cage. — Petersfield (20 Lavant St, Petersfield, Hants. GU32 3EW) : Compassion in World Farming, [1982]. — [4]p : ill ; 21cm
Accompanied by two leaflets and an area contact list
Unpriced (unbound) B82-31747

636.5′142 — Poultry. Eggs. Production — *Serials*

[**Technical bulletin** *(Eggs Authority)*]. Technical bulletin / the Eggs Authority. — No.1 (Nov. 1977)-. — Tunbridge Wells (Union House, Eridge Rd, Tunbridge Wells, Kent TN4 8HF) : The Authority, 1977-. — v. : ill ; 20cm
Three issues yearly. — Description based on: No.12 (May 1982)
ISSN 0263-5178 = Technical bulletin - Eggs Authority : Unpriced B82-40066

636.5′142 — Poultry. Laying stock

The **Laying** hen and its environment : a seminar in the EEC Programme of Coordination of Research on Animal Welfare / organised by R. Moss and V. Fischbach and held at Luxembourg, March 11-13, 1980 ; sponsored by the Commission of the European Communities, Directorate-General for Agriculture, Coordination of Agricultural Research ; edited by R. Moss. — The Hague ; London : Nijhoff for the Commission of the European Communities, 1980. — viii,333p : ill ; 25cm. — (Current topics in veterinary medicine and animal science ; v.8)
Includes bibliographies
ISBN 90-247-2423-6 : Unpriced B82-39115

636.5′8 — Australian game fowls

Marshall, Mark. The king of fowls / by Mark Marshall ; foreword by Athol Giles ; edited by 'Duckwing'. — 2nd ed. — Hindhead : Saiga, c1981. — xxii,58p,[11]leaves of plates : ill(some col.) ; 23cm
Previous ed.: 1958
ISBN 0-904558-96-7 : £7.50 B82-08706

636.5′92′083 — Livestock: Turkeys. Care & management — *Amateurs' manuals*

Walters, John, *1944-*. Keeping ducks, geese and turkeys. — 2nd ed. — London : Pelham Books, Sept.1982. — [128]p
Previous ed.: 1976
ISBN 0-7207-1437-0 (pbk) : £2.95 : CIP entry
Primary classification 636.5′083 B82-19826

636.5′96 — Pigeons

Physiology and behaviour of the pigeon. — London : Academic Press, Dec.1982. — [370]p
ISBN 0-12-042950-0 : CIP entry B82-29871

636.5′96 — Racing pigeons — *Manuals*

Belding, D. V.. Racing pigeons : including the management of a small team / by D.V. Belding. — Hindhead : Saiga, c1981. — viii,194p : ill,1plan ; 24cm
Includes index
ISBN 0-86230-014-2 : £7.50 B82-08712

Robinson, David, *1947-*. The right way to keep pigeons / by David Robinson. — Kingswood : Paperfronts, c1981. — 124p : ill,1plan ; 19cm
Includes index
ISBN 0-7160-0671-5 (pbk) : £0.75 B82-01803

636.5′96 — Racing pigeons. Veterinary aspects — *Amateurs' manuals*

Whitney, Leon F.. Keep your pigeons flying. — 2nd ed. — London : Faber, Jan.1983. — [256]p
Originally published: 1968
ISBN 0-571-11541-1 (pbk) : £4.00 : CIP entry B82-34093

636.5′97 — Buckinghamshire. Aylesbury Vale *(District)*. **Livestock: Aylesbury ducks. Production**, *to 1950*

Cole, Alison. The Aylesbury duck / Alison Cole. — Aylesbury : Buckinghamshire County Museum, c1982. — 40p : ill,ports ; 20cm
Bibliography: p40
ISBN 0-86059-266-9 (pbk) : £1.11 B82-37589

636.5′97 — Livestock: Ducks. Care & management — *Amateurs' manuals*

Walters, John, *1944-*. Keeping ducks, geese and turkeys. — 2nd ed. — London : Pelham Books, Sept.1982. — [128]p
Previous ed.: 1976
ISBN 0-7207-1437-0 (pbk) : £2.95 : CIP entry
Primary classification 636.5′083 B82-19826

636.5′98 — Livestock: Geese. Care & management — *Amateurs' manuals*

Walters, John, *1944-*. Keeping ducks, geese and turkeys. — 2nd ed. — London : Pelham Books, Sept.1982. — [128]p
Previous ed.: 1976
ISBN 0-7207-1437-0 (pbk) : £2.95 : CIP entry
Primary classification 636.5′083 B82-19826

636.6 — LIVESTOCK. BIRDS(OTHER THAN POULTRY)

636.6 — Pets: Birds. Care — *Manuals*

Allcock, James. A pet bird of your own / James Allcock ; illustrated by Mike Morris. — London : Sheldon, 1981. — 68p : ill ; 22cm
Includes index
ISBN 0-85969-344-9 (pbk) : £1.95 B82-08477

636.6 — Pets: Young birds. Hand feeding

Cooper, Jo. Handfeeding baby birds / Jo Cooper. — Neptune, N.J. ; Reigate : T.F.H., c1979. — 93p : ill(some col.),ports(some col.) ; 21cm
Ill on lining papers
ISBN 0-87666-992-5 : Unpriced B82-08308

636.6′0941 — Great Britain. Birds in captivity

British birds in aviculture / edited by Peter Lander ; with specialist contributors ; foreword by John Hargreaves. — Hindhead : Saiga, issued by the British Bird Council, c1981. — xiii,206p,12p of plates : ill(some col.) ; 25cm. — (Cage and aviary series)
Includes index
ISBN 0-86230-035-5 : £8.50 B82-10836

636.6′8 — Ornamental wildfowl — *Field guides*

Kolbe, Hartmut. Ornamental waterfowl / Hartmut Kolbe. — [English ed.] / [translated from the German by Ilse Lindsay] ; [revised by Aloys Hüttermann]. — Old Woking : Gresham, 1979. — 258p : ill(some col.),maps ; 25cm
Translated from the German. — Bibliography: p255-256. — Includes index
ISBN 0-905418-49-2 : £8.50 B82-08071

636.6′86 — Bird cages & aviaries

Enehjelm, Curt af. Cages and aviaries / Curt af Enehjelm ; translated by U. Erich Friese. — Neptune, N.J. ; Reigate : T.F.H., 1981. — 155p : ill(some col.) ; 21cm
Translation of: Kafige und Volieren. — Ill on lining papers. — Includes index
ISBN 0-87666-840-6 : £4.95 B82-10813

636.6′86 — Cage birds & aviary birds: Soft-billed birds. Care

Martin, Richard Mark. How to keep softbilled birds in cage or aviary / Richard Mark Martin ; with illustrations by Michael Stringer. — Edinburgh : Bartholomew, 1980. — 96p : ill (some col.) ; 19cm
Includes index
ISBN 0-7028-8010-8 (pbk) : £1.25 : CIP rev. B80-04861

636.6′86 — Cage birds. Care

Alderton, David. Looking after cage birds. — London : Ward Lock, Oct.1982. — [128]p
ISBN 0-7063-6196-2 : £6.95 : CIP entry B82-23186

636.6′862 — Pets: Australian finches. Breeding & care

Enehjelm, Curt af. Australian finches / Curt af Enehjelm ; translated by V. Erich Friese. — Neptune, N.J. : T.F.H. Publications, c1979 ; Reigate : T.F.H. (Great Britain). — 124p : ill (some col.) ; 21cm
Translation of: Australische Prachtfinken. — Col.ill on lining papers
ISBN 0-87666-987-9 : Unpriced B82-40702

636.6′862 — Pets: Border canaries

Bracegirdle, Joe. The border canary / by Joe Bracegirdle ; with colour illustrations by Michael Stringer. — Hindhead : Saiga, [1980?]. — ix,145p,[2]p of plates : ill(some col.) ; 25cm. — (Cage and aviary series)
Includes index
ISBN 0-904558-95-9 : £7.50 B82-08704

636.6′862 — Pets: Society finches. Care

Roberts, Mervin F.. Society finches / by Mervin F. Roberts. — Hong Kong : T.F.H. ; Reigate : distributed by T.F.H., c1979. — 93p : ill(some col.) ; 21cm
Ill on lining papers
ISBN 0-87666-990-9 : Unpriced B82-24626

636.6′864 — Pets: Budgerigars. Breeding & care

Scoble, John. The complete book of budgerigars / John Scoble. — Poole : Blandford, 1982, c1981. — 144p : ill(some col.),1map,plans,facsims ; 29cm
Originally published: Sydney : Lansdowne, 1981. — Includes index
ISBN 0-7137-1262-7 : £8.95 B82-20227

636.6′864 — Pets: Budgerigars. Breeding, *to 1980*

Rogers, Cyril H.. The world of budgerigars / by Cyril H. Rogers. — Hindhead : Saiga, c1981. — ix,133p,8p of plates : ill(some col.),ports ; 24cm. — (Cage and aviary series)
Bibliography: p133
ISBN 0-86230-036-3 : £9.50 B82-08710

636.6′864 — Pets: Talking birds: Budgerigars. Training — *Manuals*

Dunigan, Opal. Training budgerigars to talk / Opal Dunigan. — Neptune, N.J. ; Reigate : T.F.H., c1981. — 125p : ill(some col.),1port ; 21cm
Ill on lining papers
£3.50 B82-10816

636.6′865 — Pets: Amazon parrots. Care

Teitler, Risa. Taming and training Amazon parrots / by Risa Teitler. — Neptune, N.J. : T.F.H. ; Reigate : T.F.H. (Gt. Britain) [distributor], c1979. — 92p : ill(some col.) ; 21cm
Ill on lining papers
ISBN 0-87666-881-3 : Unpriced B82-08227

636.6′865 — Pets: Australian parrots. Breeding & care

Harman, Ian. Australian parrots : in bush and aviary / Ian Harman. — Newton Abbot : David & Charles, c1981. — 200p : ill(chiefly col.) ; 25cm
Bibliography: p199. — Includes index
ISBN 0-7153-8259-4 : £12.50 B82-11726

636.6′865 — Pets: Lovebirds. Training — *Manuals*

Teitler, Risa. Taming & training lovebirds / by Risa Teitler. — Neptune, N.J. ; Reigate : T.F.H., c1979. — 93p : ill(some col.),1col.port ; 21cm
Ill. on lining papers
ISBN 0-87666-988-7 : Unpriced B82-01476

636.6′865 — Pets: Parrots. Care

De Grahl, Wolfgang. Parrots. — London : Ward Lock, Apr.1981. — [160]p
Translation of the German
ISBN 0-7063-6080-x : £7.95 : CIP entry B81-07485

Vriends, Matthew M.. Parrots / Matthew M. Vriends and Herbert R. Axelrod. — Neptune, N.J. : T.F.H. ; Reigate : T.F.H. (Gt. Britain) [distributor], c1979. — 93p : ill(some col.) ; 21cm
Ill on lining papers
ISBN 0-87666-995-x : Unpriced B82-08228

636.7 — LIVESTOCK. DOGS

636.7 — Livestock: Dogs — *Field guides*

Glover, Harry. Spotter's guide to dogs / Harry Glover ; illustrated by John Francis and Andy Martin. — London : Usborne, 1979 (1981 [printing]). — 64p : ill(some col.),1col.map ; 18cm. — (Usborne pocketbooks)
Bibliography: p60. — Includes index
ISBN 0-86020-253-4 (pbk) : £1.25 B82-04192

636.7 — Livestock: Dogs — *For children*

Feder, Jan. The life of a dog / Jan Feder ; illustrated by Tilman Michalski ; translated by Anthea Bell. — London : Hutchinson, 1982. — 32p : col.ill ; 25cm. — (Animal lives)
ISBN 0-09-145420-4 : £2.95 : CIP rev. B81-22557

636.7 — Livestock: Dogs — *For children*
continuation
Lambert, David. Dogs. — London : Granada, Apr.1982. — [64]p. — (Granada guide series ; 11)
ISBN 0-246-11637-4 : £1.95 : CIP entry
B82-06495

636.7 — Livestock: Dogs — *Stories, anecdotes*
Newman, Nanette. The dog lover's coffee-table book. — London : Collins, Oct.1982. — [48]p
ISBN 0-00-216463-9 : £2.95 : CIP entry
B82-23070

636.7 — Pets: Dogs
Boorer, Wendy. The family library of dogs / Wendy Boorer. — London : Octopus, 1982, c1981. — 80p : col.ill,1col.map ; 33cm
Ill on lining papers. — Includes index
ISBN 0-7064-1460-8 : £2.95 B82-30161

636.7 — Pets: Mongrel dogs — *Stories, anecdotes*
Cooper, Jilly. Intelligent and loyal : a celebration of the mongrel / Jilly Cooper ; with photographs by Graham Wood. — London : Eyre Methuen, 1981. — 221p : ill(some col.) ; 26cm
Facsims and ill on lining papers
ISBN 0-413-48000-3 : £7.50 B82-17543

636.7'006'0411 — Scotland. Livestock: Dogs. Organisations: Scottish Kennel Club, *to 1880*
Leiper, Sally M.. A kennel club for Scotland. — Aberdeen : Aberdeen University Press, May 1981. — [72]p
ISBN 0-08-025752-6 (cased) : £5.25 : CIP entry
ISBN 0-08-025753-4 (pbk) : £3.75 B81-06042

636.7'0092'4 — Gwynedd. Ynys Môn. Pets: Dogs — *Personal observations*
Stranger, Joyce. Two for Joy / Joyce Stranger. — London : Joseph, 1982. — 197p,[8]p of plates : ill ; 23cm
ISBN 0-7181-2156-2 : £7.95 B82-35034

636.7'0092'4 — Pets: Dogs — *Personal observations*
Whatley, Allan. Whiskey, the left-handed dog / Allan Whatley. — Bognor Regis : New Horizon, c1982. — 53p,[5]leaves of plates : ill ; 21cm
ISBN 0-86116-526-8 : £3.25 B82-22240

636.7'01'0924 — England. Pets: Dogs. Boarding establishments — *Personal observations*
Cooper, Diana, *1919-*. Up to scratch / Diana Cooper. — London : Corgi, 1982, c1981. — 288p ; 18cm
Originally published: London : Joseph, 1981
ISBN 0-552-11993-8 (pbk) : £1.50 B82-35478

636.7'082 — Livestock: Dogs. Breeding — *Manuals*
White, Kay. Dog breeding : a guide to mating and whelping / Kay White. — Edinburgh : Bartholomew, 1980. — 92p : col.ill,1col.form ; 19cm
Includes index
ISBN 0-7028-1059-2 (pbk) : £1.25 : CIP rev.
B80-09752

636.7'082 — Livestock: Dogs. Reproduction
Christiansen, Ib J.. Reproduction in the dog and cat. — London : Baillière Tindall, Sept.1982. — [208]p
ISBN 0-7020-0918-0 (pbk) : £8.50 : CIP entry
Also classified at 636.8'082 B82-20005

636.7'082 — Pets: Dogs. Breeding
Gwynne-Jones, Olwen. The popular guide to puppy-rearing / Olwen Gwynne-Jones. — 11th ed. — London : Popular Dogs, 1981. — 107p : ill ; 19cm
Previous ed.: 1977. — Includes index
ISBN 0-09-143701-6 (pbk) : £2.95
Primary classification 636.7'0887 B82-22940

636.7'08'21 — Pets: Dogs. Breeding. Genetic factors
Robinson, Roy. Genetics for dog breeders. — Oxford : Pergamon, May 1982. — [175]p
ISBN 0-08-025917-0 : £8.95 : CIP entry
B82-07242

636.7'0824 — Livestock: Dogs. Reproduction. Veterinary aspects
Joshua, Joan O.. Reproductive clinical problems in the dog. — Bristol : Wright, Feb.1982. — [176]p. — (A Veterinary practitioner handbook)
ISBN 0-85608-036-5 : £9.00 : CIP entry
B81-37598

636.7'083 — Pets: Dogs. Care
Bunting, Marjorie. Caring for your dog / Marjorie Bunting ; illustrated by Vanessa Pancheri. — [London] : Hodder and Stoughton, 1980. — 168p,[4]p of plates : ill ; 20cm. — (Teach yourself books)
Includes index
ISBN 0-340-25113-1 (pbk) : £1.50 B82-35367

Hawkins, Colin. How to look after your dog / Colin Hawkins. — London : Evans, 1982. — [28]p : col.ill ; 17cm
ISBN 0-237-45595-1 : £2.25 B82-36645

636.7'08'3 — Pets: Dogs. Care
Holmes, John. Looking after your dog. — London : Ward Lock, Sept.1981. — [128]p
ISBN 0-7063-6144-x : £4.95 : CIP entry
B81-23839

636.7'0852 — Pets: Dogs. Nutrition
Dog and cat nutrition. — Oxford : Pergamon, June 1982. — [124]p
ISBN 0-08-028891-x (cased) : £12.50 : CIP entry
ISBN 0-08-028890-1 (pbk) : £6.00
Also classified at 636.8'0852 B82-10602

636.7'0882 — Dogs. Backpacking — *Manuals*
Riley, Alan. Taking your dog backpacking / by Alan and Joann Riley. — Neptune, N.J. : T.F.H. ; Reigate : T.F.H. (Gt. Britain) [distributor], c1979. — 125p : ill(some col.) ; 21cm
Ill on lining papers
ISBN 0-87666-675-6 : Unpriced B82-08229

636.7'0887 — Pets: Puppies. Care
Gwynne-Jones, Olwen. The popular guide to puppy-rearing / Olwen Gwynne-Jones. — 11th ed. — London : Popular Dogs, 1981. — 107p : ill ; 19cm
Previous ed.: 1977. — Includes index
ISBN 0-09-143701-6 (pbk) : £2.95
Also classified at 636.7'082 B82-22940

White, Robert C.. The care of the family puppy / Robert C. White. — Rev. ed. — London : Popular Dogs, 1982. — 104p : ill ; 19cm
Previous ed.: 1972. — Includes index
ISBN 0-09-147971-1 (pbk) : £2.95 B82-37026

636.7'0888 — Great Britain. Dog shows. Agility tests
Lewis, Peter, *1935-*. The agility dog / Peter Lewis ; training photographs Jon Stainton-Ellis ; illustrations Peter Lewis & Ted Groome. — Portsmouth : Canine Publications, c1981. — 126p,[16]p of plates : ill,ports,forms ; 23cm
ISBN 0-906422-04-3 : Unpriced B82-10835

636.7'0888 — Livestock: Dogs. Showing — *Manuals*
Nicholas, Anna Katherine. Successful dog show exhibiting / by Anna Katherine Nicholas. — Neptune, N.J. ; Reigate : T.F.H., c1981. — 381p : ill(some col.),ports(some col.) ; 21cm
Ill on lining papers. — Includes index
ISBN 0-87666-676-4 : £8.95 B82-10814

636.7'08960252 — Livestock: Dogs. First aid — *Manuals*
Edgson, F. Andrew. First-aid and nursing for your dog / F. Andrew Edgson and Olwen Gwynne-Jones. — 8th ed. — London : Popular Dogs, 1982. — 128p,[4]p of plates : ill ; 19cm
Previous ed.: 1979. — Includes index
ISBN 0-09-147961-4 (pbk) : £2.95 B82-32086

Rubin, Sheldon. Emergency first aid for dogs / Sheldon Rubin ; edited by W.I. Atkinson. — London : Muller, 1982, c1981. — 96p : ill ; 28cm
Includes index
ISBN 0-584-95016-0 (pbk) : £3.95 B82-39491

636.7'089607 — Livestock: Dogs. Pathology
Kelly, D. F.. Notes on pathology for small animal clinicians / D.F. Kelly, V.M. Lucke, C.J. Gaskell. — Bristol : John Wright, 1982. — viii,118p : ill,forms ; 22cm. — (A Veterinary practitioner handbook)
Includes bibliographies and index
ISBN 0-7236-0657-9 (pbk) : Unpriced
Also classified at 636.8'089607 B82-21318

636.7'08966 — Livestock: Dogs. Reproductive system. Veterinary aspects
Jones, D. Edwards. Reproductive clinical problems in the dog / D. Edward Jones, Joan O. Joshua. — Bristol : John Wright, 1982. — vii,198p : ill ; 22cm. — (A Veterinary practitioner handbook)
Includes bibliographies and index
ISBN 0-7236-0656-0 (pbk) : Unpriced
B82-21319

636.7'0897'371 — Livestock: Dogs. Head & neck. Surgery — *Manuals*
Lane, J. G.. ENT and oral surgery of the dog and cat. — Bristol : J. Wright, Oct.1982. — [288]p. — (A Veterinary practitioner handbook)
ISBN 0-7236-0659-5 (pbk) : £8.50 : CIP entry
Also classified at 636.8'0897'371 B82-27215

636.7'1 — Livestock: Dogs. Breeds
Bengtson, Bo. The dogs of the world. — 2nd ed. — Newton Abbot : David & Charles, Oct.1982. — [304]p
Translation of: All världens hundar. — Previous ed.: 1977
ISBN 0-7153-8431-7 : £6.95 : CIP entry
B82-24737

636.7'1 — Pets: Dogs. Breeds
Boorer, Wendy. Dogs. — London (Elsley Court, 20 Great Titchfield St., W1P 7AD) : Kingfisher, Oct.1981. — [128]p. — (Kingfisher guides)
ISBN 0-86272-005-2 : £2.50 : CIP entry
B81-27446

636.7'2 — Bulldogs
Bulldogs / edited by the staff of T.F.H.. — Neptune, N.J. : T.F.H. Publications, c1980 ; Reigate : T.F.H. (Great Britain) [distributor]. — 125p : ill(some col.) ; 21cm
Ill on lining papers
ISBN 0-87666-714-0 : £1.00 B82-36973

636.7'2 — Poodles
Donnelly, Kerry. Poodles / by Kerry Donnelly. — Neptune, N.J. : T.F.H. Publications, c1979 ; Reigate : Distributed by T.F.H. (Gt. Britain). — 125p : ill(some col.) ; 21cm
Ill on lining papers
ISBN 0-87666-699-3 : £1.00 B82-36976

Sheldon, Margaret. All about poodles. — London : Pelham, Jan.1983. — [240]p
ISBN 0-7207-1440-0 : £7.95 : CIP entry
B82-32626

636.7'3 — Bearded collies
Shiel. The bearded collie / 'Shiel' ; illustrations by Sheila Smith. — Edinburgh : Bartholomew, 1981. — 96p : ill ; 19cm. — (Bartholomew pet care guides)
Bibliography: p88-89. — Includes index
ISBN 0-7028-8400-6 (pbk) : Unpriced : CIP rev. B80-04277

636.7'3 — Boxer dogs. Care
Pisano, Beverly. Boxers / by Beverly Pisano. — Neptune, N.J. : T.F.H. ; Reigate : T.F.H. (Gt. Britain) [distributor], c1979. — 125p : ill(some col.) ; 21cm
Ill on lining papers
ISBN 0-87666-688-8 : Unpriced B82-08226

636.7'3 — Collies. Breeding, training & care — *Manuals*
Keith, Shirley L.. Collies : the rough and and the smooth / by Shirley L. Keith. — Selby (["Aberhill", Garmancarr La.], Wistow, Selby, N. Yorks. YO8 0UW) : Andrew Toothill
Vol.1. — 1981. — 180p : ill ; 22cm
Unpriced B82-20541

636.7'3 — Dobermanns

Donnelly, Kerry. Doberman [sic] Pinschers / by Kerry Donnelly. — Neptune, N.J. : T.F.H. Publications, c1979 ; Reigate : Distributed by T.F.H. (Gt. Britain). — 125p : ill(some col.) ; 21cm
Ill on lining papers
ISBN 0-87666-698-5 : £1.00 B82-36974

636.7'3 — Great Danes — *Personal observations*

Woodhouse, Barbara. Almost human / Barbara Woodhouse. — Harmondsworth : Penguin, 1981, c1976. — 155p,[16]p of plates : ill,ports ; 18cm
Originally published: Rickmansworth : B. Woodhouse, 1976
ISBN 0-14-006029-4 (pbk) : £1.25 B82-07288

636.7'3 — Livestock: Sheepdogs. Working trials

Halsall, Eric. Sheepdog trials. — Cambridge : Patrick Stephens, Aug.1982. — [200]p
ISBN 0-85059-565-7 : £8.95 : CIP entry B82-16655

636.7'3 — Rough coated collies

Shiel. The rough collie / Shiel ; illustrations by Sheila Smith. — Edinburgh : Bartholomew, 1981. — 96p : ill ; 19cm. — (Bartholomew pet care guides)
Bibliography: p87-88. — Includes index
ISBN 0-7028-8410-3 (pbk) : Unpriced : CIP rev. B80-04278

636.7'3 — Welsh corgis

Cole, Margaret A.. The Welsh corgi / Margaret A. Cole ; illustrations by Ken Hunter. — Edinburgh : Bartholomew, 1981. — 96p : ill ; 19cm. — (Bartholomew pet care guides)
Bibliography: p90. — Includes index
ISBN 0-7028-8490-1 (pbk) : Unpriced B82-03526

636.7'52 — Cocker spaniels

McCarthy, Dennis. The cocker spaniel / Dennis McCarthy ; illustrations by Sheila Smith. — Edinburgh : Bartholomew, 1980. — 96p : ill ; 19cm
Bibliography: p93. — Includes index
ISBN 0-7028-8370-0 (pbk) : Unpriced : CIP rev. B80-04280

636.7'52 — Cocker spaniels. Care

King, Bart. Cocker spaniels / by Bart King. — Neptune, N.J. ; Reigate : T.F.H., c1979. — 125p : ill(some col.) ; 21cm
Ill on lining papers. — Bibliography: p125
ISBN 0-87666-692-6 : Unpriced B82-08309

636.7'52 — Guide dogs: Labradors — *Stories, anecdotes*

Hocken, Sheila. Emma's story / Sheila Hocken ; illustrated by Janet Kerr. — London : Gollancz, 1981. — 110p : ill ; 21cm
ISBN 0-575-02890-4 : £5.50 B82-02213

636.7'52 — Gun dogs. Training — *Manuals*

Douglas, James. Gundog training. — Newton Abbot : David & Charles, Feb.1983. — [144]p
ISBN 0-7153-8336-1 : £6.95 : CIP entry B82-39444

Hutchinson, W. N.. Dog breaking : the most expeditious, certain and easy method : whether great excellence or only mediocrity be required : with odds and ends for those who love the dog and gun / by W.N. Hutchinson. — [Ballindalloch] : [D.G. Argue], [1979]. — xl,359p : ill ; 20cm
Cover title. — Facsim of: 10th ed. London : John Murray, 1898. — Includes index
Unpriced (pbk) B82-07925

Stephens, Wilson. Gundog sense and sensibility / Wilson Stephens ; sketches by Mary Beattie Scott. — London : Pelham, 1982. — 224p : ill ; 23cm
Includes index
ISBN 0-7207-1407-9 : £8.95 : CIP rev. B82-13078

636.7'52 — Irish setters. Care

Holvenstot, Luz. Irish setters / by Luz Holvenstot. — Neptune, N.J. ; Reigate : T.F.H., c1979. — 125p : ill(some col.),ports ; 22cm
Ill on lining papers
ISBN 0-87666-691-8 : Unpriced B82-08307

636.7'53 — Bassets

Wells-Meacham, Joan. The Basset hound / Joan Wells-Meacham ; illustrations by Ishbel Macdonald. — Edinburgh : Bartholomew, 1980. — 76p : ill ; 19cm
Bibliography: p75. — Includes index
ISBN 0-7028-8390-5 (pbk) : Unpriced : CIP rev. B80-04281

636.7'53 — England. Lurchers — *Personal observations*

Plummer, David Brian. Merle : the start of a dynasty. — Woodbridge : Boydell & Brewer, Sept.1982. — [160]p
ISBN 0-85115-171-x : £8.95 : CIP entry B82-20496

636.7'53 — Foxhounds - *Early works*

Beckford, Peter. Thoughts on hunting. — London : J.A. Allen, June 1981. — [244]p
ISBN 0-85131-367-1 : £6.75 : CIP entry B81-12797

636.7'53 — Irish wolfhounds. Breeding, training & care — *Manuals*

Hudson, D. E. S.. The Brabyns handbook on Irish wolfhounds / by D.E.S. Hudson. — [Ewhurst] : [Irish Wolfhound Magazine], c1981. — 74p : ill,1port ; 22cm
ISBN 0-9507770-0-5 (pbk) : Unpriced B82-14297

636.7'53 — Lurchers

Tottenham, Katharine. All about the lurcher. — London : Pelham, Jan.1983. — [144]p
ISBN 0-7207-1441-9 : £7.95 : CIP entry B82-32627

636.7'55 — Edinburgh. Skye terriers: Greyfriars Bobby — *Stories, anecdotes*

Atkinson, Eleanor. Greyfriars Bobby / Eleanor Atkinson. — Harmondsworth : Puffin, 1962 (1982 [printing]). — 218p ; 18cm
ISBN 0-14-030166-6 (pbk) : £1.10 B82-18154

636.7'55 — Jack Russell terriers

Tottenham, Katherine. The Jack Russell terrier / Katherine Tottenham. — Newton Abbot : David & Charles, c1982. — 159p : ill,1port ; 23cm
Includes index
ISBN 0-7153-8156-3 : £7.50 : CIP rev. B81-33821

636.7'55 — Staffordshire bull terriers

Morley, W. M.. The Staffordshire bull terrier / W.M. Morley. — Newton Abbot : David & Charles, c1982. — 176p : ill,forms,ports ; 23cm
Includes index
ISBN 0-7153-8232-2 : £6.95 : CIP rev. B81-33817

636.7'55 — West Highland white terriers

Dennis, D. Mary. The West Highland white terrier / D. Mary Dennis. — 6th ed. rev. / revised by Catherine Owen. — London : Popular Dogs, 1982, c1981. — 182p,[16]p of plates : ill,ports ; 23cm. — (Popular Dogs' breed series)
Previous ed.: i.e. 5th ed. rev. 1979. — Includes index
ISBN 0-09-145450-6 : £7.95 : CIP rev. B81-13497

636.7'6 — Pugs

Pugs / edited by the staff of T.F.H.. — Neptune, N.J. ; Reigate : T.F.H., c1981. — 125p : ill (some col.) ; 21cm
Ill on lining papers
ISBN 0-87666-725-6 : £1.25 B82-10819

636.7'6 — Shih tzus

Collins, Gerarda M.. Shih Tzu / Gerarda M. Collins, Robert P. Parker. — Neptune, N.J. ; Reigate : T.F.H., c1981. — 125p : ill(some col.) ; 21cm
Ill on lining papers
ISBN 0-87666-703-5 : £1.25 B82-10818

636.7'6 — Yorkshire terriers. Care — *Manuals*

Donnelly, Kerry. Yorkshire terriers / Kerry Donnelly. — Neptune, N.J. : T.F.H. Publications, c1979 ; Reigate : Distributed by T.F.H. (Gt. Britain). — 125p : ill(some col.) ; 21cm
Ill on lining papers
ISBN 0-87666-696-9 : £1.00 B82-36975

636.8 — PETS. CATS

636.8 — Pets: Cats

Frazier, Anitra. The natural cat. — Wellingborough : Thorsons, Sept.1982. — [216]p
Originally published: San Francisco : Harbor, 1981
ISBN 0-7225-0777-1 (pbk) : £3.50 : CIP entry B82-21102

Sayer, Angela. The encyclopedia of the cat / Angela Sayer ; Pauline Thompson, US consultant editor ; Michael Findlay, veterinary consultant editor. — London : Octopus, 1979. — 224p : ill(some col.) ; 31cm
Ill on lining papers. — Includes index
ISBN 0-7064-0987-6 : £6.95 B82-03926

636.8 — Pets: Cats. Behaviour

Baerends-van Roon, J. M.. The morphogenesis of the behaviour of the domestic cat : with a special emphasis on the development of prey-catching / J.M. Baerends-van Roon en G.P. Baerends. — Amsterdam ; Oxford : North-Holland, 1979. — 115p : ill ; 26cm. — (Verhandelingen der Koninklijke Nederlandse Akademie)
ISBN 0-7204-8480-4 (pbk) : Unpriced B82-05807

636.8 — Pets: Cats — *For children*

Feder, Jan. The life of a cat / Jan Feder ; illustrated by Tilman Michalski ; translated by Anthea Bell. — London : Hutchinson, 1982. — 32p : col.ill ; 25cm. — (Animal lives)
ISBN 0-09-145010-1 : £2.95 : CIP rev. B81-12328

636.8 — Pets: Cats. Pure breeds

The **Whiskas** guide to pedigree cats. — Melton Mowbray (Melton Mowbray, Leicestershire) : Pedigree Petfoods, [1982]. — [8]p : col.ill,1col.port ; 21cm
Unpriced (unbound) B82-15267

636.8 — Pets: Kittens. Birth & growth — *For children*

Fischer-Nagel, Andreas. Birth of a kitten. — London : Dent, Oct.1982. — [40]p
ISBN 0-460-06123-2 : £4.95 : CIP entry B82-23323

636.8'0092'4 — Leicestershire. Pets: Cats — *Personal observations*

Bourne, Renee. The cats in my life / by Renee Bourne. — [Great Britain] : [S.n.], c1980 (Market Harborough : Green & Co.). — 48p : ill ; 21cm
Unpriced (pbk) B82-12374

636.8'0092'4 — Pets: Cats — *Personal observations*

Arnold, Jeannette. Septimus Bumble / Jeannette Arnold. — Ilfracombe : Stockwell, 1982. — 47p ; 19cm
ISBN 0-7223-1567-8 (pbk) : £1.99 B82-21487

Atkins, Barbara J.. Living with Marcus and friends / Barbara J. Atkins. — Ilfracombe : Stockwell, 1982. — 56p : ill ; 19cm
ISBN 0-7223-1579-1 (pbk) : £1.75 B82-30970

Stokes, Zoë. Zöe's cats / Zoë Stokes. — London : Thames and Hudson, c1982. — 62p : ill(some col.) ; 22cm
ISBN 0-500-01273-3 : £5.95 B82-39543

636.8'08 — Pets: Cats. Breeding & care

Tottenham, Katharine. Looking after your cat : keep and care / Katharine Tottenham. — London : Ward Lock, c1981. — 96p : ill ; 26cm
Includes index
ISBN 0-7063-6143-1 : £4.95 : CIP rev. B81-16939

636.8′082 — Cats. Reproduction

Christiansen, Ib J.. Reproduction in the dog and cat. — London : Baillière Tindall, Sept.1982. — [208]p
ISBN 0-7020-0918-0 (pbk) : £8.50 : CIP entry
Primary classification 636.7′082 B82-20005

636.8′083 — Pets: Cats. Care

Bush, Barry. The Cat care question and answer book / Barry Bush. — London : Orbis, 1981. — 240p : ill ; 24cm
Includes index
ISBN 0-85613-327-2 : £5.95 B82-01457

636.8′0852 — Pets: Cats. Nutrition

Dog and cat nutrition. — Oxford : Pergamon, June 1982. — [124]p
ISBN 0-08-028891-x (cased) : £12.50 : CIP entry
ISBN 0-08-028890-1 (pbk) : £6.00
Primary classification 636.7′0852 B82-10602

636.8′08960252 — Pets: Cats. First aid — *Manuals*

Rubin, Sheldon. Emergency first aid for cats / Sheldon Rubin ; edited by W.I. Atkinson. — London : Muller, 1982, c1981. — 96p : ill ; 28cm
Includes index
ISBN 0-584-95017-9 (pbk) : £3.95 B82-32698

636.8′089607 — Pets: Cats. Pathology

Kelly, D. F.. Notes on pathology for small animal clinicians / D.F. Kelly, V.M. Lucke, C.J. Gaskell. — Bristol : John Wright, 1982. — viii,118p : ill,forms ; 22cm. — (A Veterinary practitioner handbook)
Includes bibliographies and index
ISBN 0-7236-0657-9 (pbk) : Unpriced
Primary classification 636.7′089607
B82-21318

636.8′0897′371 — Livestock: Cats. Head & neck. Surgery — *Manuals*

Lane, J. G.. ENT and oral surgery of the dog and cat. — Bristol : J. Wright, Oct.1982. — [288]p. — (A Veterinary practitioner handbook)
ISBN 0-7236-0659-5 (pbk) : £8.50 : CIP entry
Primary classification 636.7′0897′371
B82-27215

636.9 — LIVESTOCK. RABBITS, GUINEA PIGS, ETC

636.9′09411′5 — Scotland. Moray Firth region. Nature conservation. Implications of proposed utilisation of wave power

Probert, P. K.. Nature conservation implications of siting wave energy converters off the Moray Firth / by P.K. Probert and R. Mitchell ; a report for Technical Advisory Group 7 (Wave Energy Steering Committee) by the Nature Conservancy Council ... — [Shrewsbury] : Nature Conservancy Council, 1980. — 68p,[5] leaves of plates : ill,maps ; 30cm
Bibliography: p47-54
ISBN 0-86139-146-2 (spiral) : Unpriced
B82-02085

636′.9322 — Great Britain. Livestock: Rabbits. Production

Portsmouth, John. Commercial rabbit meat production / J.I. Portsmouth. — 2nd. ed. — Hindhead : Saiga, 1979. — viii,142p,[12]p of plates : ill ; 23cm
Previous ed.: London : Iliffe, 1962. — Includes index
ISBN 0-904558-31-2 : £6.00 B82-19495

636′.9322 — Great Britain. Livestock: Rabbits — *Serials*

[Fur & feather *(1982)*]. Fur & feather : incorporating Rabbits : [official journal of the British Rabbit Council]. — No.1 (Thursday 14 Jan. 1982)-. — Preston (1a East Cliff, Preston, Lancs. PR1 3JE) : Winckley Publishing, 1982-. — v. : ports ; 30cm
Fortnightly. — Continues: Rabbits (Idle)
ISSN 0262-6489 = Fur & feather (1982) : £16.00 per year B82-33864

636′.93233 — Laboratory animals: Mice. Cells & tissues — *Illustrations*

Gude, William D.. Histological atlas of the laboratory mouse / William D. Gude, Gerald E. Cosgrove and Gerald P. Hirsch. — New York ; London : Plenum, c1982. — ix,151p : col.ill ; 19x26cm
Bibliography: p145. — Includes index
ISBN 0-306-40686-1 (spiral) : Unpriced
B82-31926

636′.93234 — Exhibition guinea pigs — *Manuals*

Turner, Isabel. Exhibition and pet cavies / by Isabel Turner. — 2nd ed. — Hindhead : Saiga, 1981. — vii,151p,[4]p of plates : ill(some col.),2forms ; 23cm. — (Exhibition and family pets series)
Previous ed.: 1977. — Bibliography: p152
ISBN 0-904558-48-7 : £5.50 B82-08694

636′.961′0924 — Burma. Livestock. Elephants, *1920-1945* — *Personal observations*

Williams, J. H.. Elephant Bill / J.H. Williams ; with a foreword by Sir William Slim. — London : Granada, 1982, c1950. — 249p : ill ; 18cm. — (A Panther book)
Originally published: London : Hart Davis, 1950
ISBN 0-586-04912-6 (pbk) : £1.50 B82-22055

636′.9744287 — Wildlife reserves. Felidae. Care — *Conference proceedings*

Association of British Wild Animal Keepers. *Symposium (4th : 1979 : Zoological Society of London).* Management of wild cats in captivity : proceedings of Symposium 4 of the Association of British Wild Animal Keepers / [edited by Jon Barzdo]. — Dunstable (c/o Hon. Sec., 5 Chequers Cottages, Whipsnade, Dunstable, Beds. LU6 2LJ) : The Association, c1980. — 50p : ill,2plans ; 21cm
Includes bibliographies
Unpriced (pbk) B82-31262

636.9′772 — Bonsai. Cultivation — *Amateurs′ manuals*

Adams, Peter D.. The art of Bonsai. — London : Ward Lock, Sept.1981. — [176]p
ISBN 0-7063-5860-0 : £6.95 : CIP entry
B81-23836

637 — DAIRY PRODUCTS

637′.01′543 — Dairy products. Chemical analysis — *Serials*

Developments in dairy chemistry. — 1. — London : Applied Science, Aug.1982. — [400] p. — (The Developments series)
ISBN 0-85334-142-7 : £36.00 : CIP entry
B82-16662

637′.01′576 — Dairy products. Microbiological aspects

Hayes, Susan, *1953-*. Dairy microbiology / [Susan Hayes]. — London : National Dairy Council, 1981. — 71p : ill(same col.) ; 26cm
ISBN 0-902748-27-0 (pbk) : Unpriced
B82-05809

637′.01′576 — Dairy products. Microorganisms

Dairy microbiology / edited by R.K. Robinson. — London : Applied Science, c1981. — 2v. : ill ; 23cm
Includes bibliographies and index
ISBN 0-85334-948-7 : Unpriced : CIP rev.
ISBN 0-85334-961-4 (v.2) : £23.00 B81-13733

637′.028 — Great Britain. Dairy equipment. Fitting — *Manuals*

Instruction manual for dairy industry fitters. — Gloucester (Barton House, Barton St., Gloucester GL1 1QQ) : Food, Drink and Tobacco Industry Training Board in association with the Dairy Industry Training and Education Committee with the agreement of the Engineering Industry Training Board, c1981. — 223p : ill ; 31cm + Supplement : liquid milk FDT 2(149p : ill, 31cm)
Unpriced (spiral) B82-27620

637′.1 — Ireland *(Republic)*. **Milk. Chemical composition**

Chemical composition of milk in Ireland. — [Dublin] : An Foras Talúntais, 1981. — ii,347p ; 20cm
Cover title. — At head of title: An Foras Talúntais
Unpriced (pbk) B82-20680

637′.1′01576 — Milk. Microorganisms — *For children*

Jansen, Mogens. Micro-life in milk / written by Morgens [i.e. Mogens] Jansen ; translated by E. Meyland-Smith ; edited by Su Swallow. — Harlow : Longman, 1981. — 31p : col.ill ; 23cm. — (A First look at microbiology)
Translated from the Danish
ISBN 0-582-39132-6 : £2.50 B82-21054

637′.1′0942 — England. Milk. Production — *Serials*

Milk production / Ministry of Agriculture, Fisheries and Food. — 1980/81-. — London : H.M.S.O., 1982-. — v. ; 21cm
Issued every four years
ISSN 0263-3035 = Milk production : £4.20
B82-22691

637′.125 — Milking machines

Machine milking and milking facilities / E. O′Callaghan ... [et al.]. — Dublin : An Foras Talúntais, 1982. — iii,51p : ill,2forms,plans ; 30cm. — (An Foras Talúntais handbook series ; no.19)
ISBN 0-905442-59-8 (pbk) : Unpriced
B82-35406

637′.127 — Great Britain. Milk. Quality

The Quality of milk / [National Dairy Council]. — London (John Princes St., W1M 0AP) : National Dairy Council, [1982]. — 16p : ill ; 21cm
Bibliography: p16
£0.10 (unbound) B82-35780

637′.352 — Soft cheeses. Making — *Manuals*

Pike, Mary Ann. Soft cheese craft : and other recipes for the aspiring dairymaid / by Mary Ann Pike. — Weybridge : Whittet, 1982. — 125p : ill,facsims,1plan ; 23cm
Bibliography: p125
ISBN 0-905483-24-3 : £5.95 : CIP rev.
B82-05778

638 — INSECT CULTURE

638′.1 — Bee-keeping

Gedde, John. A new discovery of an excellent method of bee-houses & colonies / John Gedde. — London : International Bee Research Association, c1982. — 16leaves ; 30cm. — (Texts of early beekeeping books ; no.5)
Originally published: London : J. Gedde, 1675
ISBN 0-86098-110-x (pbk) : Unpriced : CIP rev. B82-11971

Hill, Thomas, *fl.1590*. A profitable instruction of the perfect ordering of bees / Thomas Hill. — 2nd ed. — London : International Bee Research Association, c1981. — 46leaves ; 30cm. — (Texts of early beekeeping books ; no.4)
Originally published: London : H.B., 1608
ISBN 0-86098-092-8 (pbk) : Unpriced : CIP rev. B81-21552

Southerne, Edmund. A treatise concerning the right use and ordering of bees / Edmund Southerne. — London : International Bee Research Association, c1981. — 24leaves : ill ; 30cm. — (Texts of early beekeeping books ; no.1)
Originally published: London : Thomas Orwin for Thomas Woodcocke, 1593
ISBN 0-86098-088-x (pbk) : Unpriced : CIP rev. B82-03128

638′.1 — Bee-keeping — *Manuals*

Aebi, Ormond. [The Art and adventure of beekeeping]. Mastering the art of beekeeping / by Ormond and Harry Aebi ; illustrations by Eric Mathes. — Dorchester : Prism
Vol.1. — 1982. — 184p : ill,1plan ; 23cm
Originally published: as The art and adventure of beekeeping. Santa Cruz : Unity, 1975. — Includes index
ISBN 0-907061-22-2 (cased) : £6.95
ISBN 0-907061-24-9 (pbk) : £2.95 B82-21135

638'.1 — Bee-keeping — *Manuals*
continuation

Aebi, Ormond. Mastering the art of beekeeping / by Ormond and Harry Aebi ; illustrations by Eric Mathes. — Dorchester : Prism
Vol.2. — 1982. — 283p : ill,music,1plan ; 23cm
Originally published: Santa Cruz : Unity, 1979. — Includes index
ISBN 0-907061-23-0 (cased) : £7.95
ISBN 0-907061-25-7 (pbk) : £2.95 B82-21136

Beckley, Peter. Keeping bees. — 2nd ed. — London : Pelham Books, Sept.1982. — [125]p
Previous ed.: 1977
ISBN 0-7207-1436-2 (pbk) : £2.95 : CIP entry B82-19825

Meyer, Owen. The beekeeper's handbook : a practical manual of bee management / by Owen Meyer. — Wellingborough : Thorsons, 1981. — 253p : ill ; 22cm
Bibliography: p239-240. — Includes index
ISBN 0-7225-0669-4 (pbk) : £4.95 : CIP rev. B81-21513

638'.1'0251724 — Developing countries. Bee-keeping. Voluntary personnel. Agencies — *Directories*

International Bee Research Association. Sources of voluntary workers for apicultural development. — Gerrards Cross : International Bee Research Association, Apr.1982. — [4]p. — (Source materials for apiculture ; no.5)
ISBN 0-86098-115-0 (pbk) : £1.00 : CIP entry B82-16203

638'.1'06 — Developing countries. Bee-keeping. Organisations — *Directories*

Directory of institutions in developing countries known to be concerned with apiculture. — London : International Bee Research Association, Jan.1982. — 1v.. — (IBRA publication ; L17)
ISBN 0-86098-105-3 : £10.00 : CIP entry B82-03383

638'.1'0701724 — Developing countries. Bee-keeping. Information sources — *Lists*

International Bee Research Association. Obtaining apicultural information for use in developing countries. — Gerrards Cross : International Bee Research Association, Apr.1982. — [6]p. — (Source materials for apiculture ; no.7)
ISBN 0-86098-117-7 (pbk) : £1.00 : CIP entry B82-16201

638'.1'071 — Educational institutions. Curriculum subjects: Bee-keeping. Courses — *Directories*

International Bee Research Association. Opportunities for training in apiculture world-wide. — Gerrards Cross : International Bee Research Association, Apr.1982. — [10]p. — (Source materials for apiculture ; no.4)
ISBN 0-86098-114-2 (pbk) : £1.00 : CIP entry B82-16204

638'.1'078 — Bee-keeping. Teaching aids — *Lists*

International Bee Research Association. Educational aids on apiculture. — Gerrards Cross : International Bee Research Association, Apr.1982. — [6]p. — (Source materials for apiculture ; no.9)
ISBN 0-86098-119-3 (pbk) : £1.00 : CIP entry B82-14043

638'.1'09 — Bee-keeping. Archaeological investigation, *to 1982*

Crane, Eva. The archaeology of beekeeping. — London : Duckworth, Jan.1983. — [384]p
ISBN 0-7156-1681-1 : £18.00 : CIP entry B82-32618

638'.1'0913 — Tropical regions. Bee-keeping — *Conference proceedings*

Conference on Apiculture in Tropical Climates *(1st : 1976 : London)*. Apiculture in tropical climates : full report of the First Conference on Apiculture in Tropical Climates / edited by Eva Crane. — London : International Bee Research Association, 1976, c1981 (1981 [printing]). — x,207p : ill,maps ; 30cm
Includes index
ISBN 0-86098-100-2 (pbk) : Unpriced : CIP rev. B81-32004

638'.13 — Great Britain. Gardens. Plants useful to bees — *Lists*

Garden plants valuable to bees / by International Bee Research Association ; principal collaborators Mary F. Mountain ... [et al.]. — London : The Association, 1981. — 52p ; 21cm
Bibliography: p52
ISBN 0-86098-104-5 (pbk) : Unpriced : CIP rev. B82-00180

638'.142'025 — Suppliers of bee-keeping equipment — *Directories*

Directory of suppliers of beekeeping equipment world-wide. — Gerrards Cross : International Bee Research Association, Aug.1982. — [13]p. — (IBRA publication ; 18)
ISBN 0-86098-122-3 (pbk) : £10.00 : CIP entry B82-28600

International Bee Research Association. Suppliers of beekeeping equipment for tropical and subtropical beekeeping. — Gerrards Cross : International Bee Research Association, Apr.1982. — [6]p. — (Source materials for apiculture ; no.1)
ISBN 0-86098-111-8 (pbk) : £1.00 : CIP entry B82-14046

638'.15 — Honey-bees. Diseases

Bailey, L.. Honey bee pathology / Leslie Bailey. — London : Academic Press, 1981. — viii,124p,[8]p of plates : ill ; 24cm
Bibliography: p107-115. — Includes index
ISBN 0-12-073480-x : £9.40 : CIP rev. B81-31332

638'.15 — Honey-bees. Poisoning by chemicals

Johansen, Carl A.. Honeybee poisoning by chemicals : signs, contributing factors, current problems and prevention / by Carl A. Johansen. — Gerrards Cross : International Bee Research Association, [1979?]. — 19p ; 21cm. — (International Bee Research Association reprint ; M100)
Reprinted from Bee world 60(3): 109-127 (1979). — Bibliography: p16-19
ISBN 0-86098-080-4 (pbk) : Unpriced B82-03443

638'.2'09548 — Southern India *(Republic)*. Silkworms. Culture

Charsley, S. R.. Culture and sericulture. — London : Academic Press, May 1982. — [220] p. — (Studies in anthropology)
ISBN 0-12-169380-5 : CIP entry B82-07264

638'.5722'0724 — Laboratory animals: Cockroaches. Experiments — *Manuals*

Bell, William J.. The laboratory cockroach : experiments in cockroach anatomy, physiology and behaviour / William J. Bell. — London : Chapman and Hall, 1981. — 161p : ill ; 30cm
Includes bibliographies and index
ISBN 0-412-23990-6 (spiral) : £6.95 : CIP rev. B81-31712

639 — HUNTING, TRAPPING, FISHING

639'.09162 — Aquaculture

Recent advances in aquaculture. — London : Croom Helm, Mar.1982. — [352]p
ISBN 0-7099-0303-0 : £22.50 : CIP entry B82-02627

639'.09162 — Japan. Aquaculture

Modern methods of aquaculture in Japan. — Oxford : Elsevier Scientific, Jan.1983. — [300] p. — (Developments in aquaculture and fisheries science ; 11)
ISBN 0-444-99674-5 : £40.00 : CIP entry B82-33340

639.2 — FISHING, WHALING, SEALING

639'.22 — Oceans. Fisheries. Resources. Effects of climate

Cushing, D. H.. Climate and fisheries. — London : Academic Press, Dec.1982. — [320]p
ISBN 0-12-199720-0 : CIP entry B82-29878

639'.22 — Oceans. Fisheries. Resources. Management

Laevastu, Taivo. Fisheries oceanography and ecology / Taivo Laevastu and Murray L. Hayes. — Farnham, Surrey : Fishing News Books, [1981?]. — xiv,199p : ill,charts,maps ; 26cm
Bibliography: p175-186. — Includes index
ISBN 0-85238-117-4 : £19.50 : CIP rev. B81-30623

Study of the sea : the development of marine research under the auspices of the International Council for the Exploration of the Sea / edited by E.M. Thomasson. — Farnham : Fishing News, c1981. — xiv,256p : ill,charts,ports ; 26cm
Includes bibliographies and index
ISBN 0-85238-112-3 : Unpriced : CIP rev.
Primary classification 551.46 B81-16893

639'.22 — Sea fishing

Avery, Rob. The complete book of seafood fishing / Rob Avery ; illustrated by Paul Dadds. — Dorchester : Prism, 1982. — 162p : ill ; 27cm
Includes index
ISBN 0-904727-82-3 (cased) : Unpriced
ISBN 0-907061-10-9 (pbk) : £4.95 B82-33007

639'.22'028 — Great Britain. Sea fishing equipment — *Encyclopaedias*

Glossary of United Kingdom fishing gear terms / compiled by J.P. Bridger ... [et al.]. — Farnham : Fishing News, c1981. — xi,115p : ill ; 26cm
ISBN 0-85238-119-0 : £15.00 : CIP rev. B81-36992

639'.22'028 — Sea fishing equipment: Nets. Materials

Klust, Gerhard. Netting materials for fishing gear / by Gerhard Klust. — 2nd ed. — Farnham, Surrey : Published by arrangement with the Food and Agriculture Organization of the United Nations by Fishing News Books, 1982. — xiii,175p : ill ; 24cm. — (FAO fishing manuals)
Previous ed.: 1973. — Bibliography: p171-175
ISBN 0-85238-118-2 (pbk) : £8.00 : CIP rev. B81-38826

639'.28'0904 — Whaling, *ca 1850-1978*

Tønnessen, J. N.. The history of modern whaling / J.N. Tønnessen, A.O. Johnsen ; translated from the Norwegian by R.I. Christophersen. — London : Hurst, c1982. — xx,798p : ill,maps,ports ; 25cm
Translation of: Den moderne hvalfangsts historie. — Bibliography: p756-773. — Includes index
ISBN 0-905838-23-8 : £19.50 : CIP rev. B79-34300

639'.28'091632 — Arctic Ocean. Whaling. Voyages by sailing ships, *1806*: Resolution *(Ship)*. Logs — *Texts — Facsimiles*

Scoresby, William, *1789-1857*. The 1806 log book : concerning the Arctic voyage of Captain William Scoresby / kept by William Scoresby, Junior ; foreword by J.G. Graham. — Whitby : Caedmon of Whitby by arrangement with the Whitby Literary and Philosophical Society, c1981. — [43]leaves : ill ; 27cm
Facsim. of: Whitby Museum manuscript entitled A journal of the fourth voyage of the ship Resolution from Whitby towards Greenland 1806
ISBN 0-905355-24-5 : £12.50 B82-09044

639'.28'09415 — Ireland. Coastal waters. Whaling, *to 1976*

Fairley, James. Irish whales and whaling / James Fairley. — Belfast : Blackstaff, c1981. — 218p : ill,maps,ports ; 22cm
Bibliography: p205-212. — Includes index
ISBN 0-85640-232-x : £8.95 : CIP rev.
Primary classification 599.5 B80-21929

639.3 — FISH CULTURE, FISH AS PETS

639.3′11 — Garden features: Ponds. Cold water fish — *Amateurs′ manuals*

Pinks, Roy. Coldwater fish in aquaria and garden ponds / Roy Pinks ; illustrations by Rex Nicholls. — Edinburgh : Bartholomew, 1981. — 96p : ill ; 19cm
Bibliography: p93. — Includes index
ISBN 0-7028-8360-3 (pbk) : Unpriced : CIP rev.
Primary classification 639.3′4 B80-11516

639.3′11′05 — Fish farming — *Serials*

Fish farmer : a Farmers weekly publication. — Vol.1, no.1 (Nov. 1977)-. — Sutton (1 Throwley Way, Sutton, Surrey SM1 4QQ) : IPC Agricultural Press, 1977-. — v. : ill,maps,ports ; 30cm
Seven issues yearly. — Description based on: Vol.5, no.2 (Jan. 1982)
ISSN 0262-9615 = Fish farmer : £18.50 per year B82-27648

639.3′11′095694 — Israel. Fish farming

Hepher, Balfour. Commercial fish farming : with special reference to fish culture in Israel / Balfour Hepher, Yoel Pruginin. — New York ; Chichester : Wiley, c1981. — ix,261p,[2]p of plates : ill,plans,2forms ; 24cm
Bibliography: p239-251. — Includes index
ISBN 0-471-06264-2 : £24.00 B82-05816

639.3′4 — Aquariums

Hunnam, Peter. The living aquarium. — London : Ward Lock, Oct.1981. — [240]p
ISBN 0-7063-6127-x : £15.00 : CIP entry B81-28040

639.3′4 — Aquariums — *Amateurs′ manuals*

The **Macdonald** encyclopedia of aquaria. — London : Macdonald, 1982, c1977. — 47,[335]p : col.ill ; 19cm
Translated from the Italian. — Includes index
ISBN 0-356-07914-7 (pbk) : £4.95 B82-39683

639.3′4 — Aquariums. Cold water fish — *Amateurs′ manuals*

Pinks, Roy. Coldwater fish in aquaria and garden ponds / Roy Pinks ; illustrations by Rex Nicholls. — Edinburgh : Bartholomew, 1981. — 96p : ill ; 19cm
Bibliography: p93. — Includes index
ISBN 0-7028-8360-3 (pbk) : Unpriced : CIP rev.
Also classified at 639.3′11 B80-11516

639.3′4 — Brackish water aquariums

Gos, Michael W.. Brackish aquariums / Michael W. Gos. — Neptune, N.J. ; Reigate : T.F.H., c1979. — 93p : ill(some col.) ; 21cm
Ill on lining papers
ISBN 0-87666-519-9 : Unpriced B82-08312

639.3′4 — Freshwater aquariums. Fish

Gosse, J. P.. Freshwater aquarium fish. — Newton Abbot : David & Charles, Feb.1983. — [184]p
Translation of: Guides des poissons d′aquarium (eau douce)
ISBN 0-7153-8399-x : £6.95 : CIP entry B82-39454

639.3′4 — Laboratory animals: Fish. Care

Aquarium systems / edited by A.D. Hawkins. — London : Academic Press, 1981. — x,452p : ill ; 24cm
Includes bibliographies and index
ISBN 0-12-333380-6 : £27.80 : CIP rev. B81-18130

639.3′4 — Tropical aquariums. Fish — *Amateurs′ manuals*

Walker, Braz. Tropical fish in colour / by Braz Walker. — Poole : Blandford, 1971 (1981 [printing]). — 256p : col.ill ; 14cm
Adaptation of: Bunt Welt der Tropenfische / by Waldtraud Weiss. — Includes index
ISBN 0-7137-1247-3 (pbk) : £2.95 B82-21867

639.3′4′03 — Aquariums. Fish — *Encyclopaedias*

The **aquarium** lexicon. — Poole : Blandford, Sept.1981. — [600]p
Translation of: Lexicon der Aquaristik und Ichthyologie
ISBN 0-7137-1146-9 : CIP entry B81-22677

639.3′44 — Aquariums. Tropical freshwater fish — *Encyclopaedias*

The **Complete** aquarium encyclopedia of tropical freshwater fish / managing editor J.D. van Ramshorst ; photos by A. van den Nieuwenhuizen. — Oxford : Phaidon, 1980, c1978. — 391p : ill(some col.) ; 28cm
Originally published: Oxford : Elsevier Phaidon, 1978. — Bibliography: p390-391. — Includes index
ISBN 0-7148-2156-x (pbk) : £12.50 B82-39106

Exotic tropical fishes / Herbert R. Axelrod ... [et al.]. — Expanded ed. — Neptune, N.J. ; Reigate : T.F.H., c1980. — 1302p : ill(some col.) ; 23cm
Previous ed.: 1977. — Includes index
ISBN 0-87666-543-1 (pbk) : £18.75
ISBN 0-87666-537-7 (loose-leaf) B82-40388

Popular tropical fish for your aquarium / edited by Cliff Harrison. — London : Foulsham, c1982. — 104p : ill(some col.) ; 22cm
Includes index
ISBN 0-572-01162-8 (pbk) : £2.95 B82-25818

639.3′7 — Zoos. Amphibians. Care — *Conference proceedings*

Association of British Wild Animal Keepers. *Symposium (6th : 1981)*. Management of reptiles and amphibians : the sixth specialist symposium of the Association of British Wild Animal Keepers ... with the International Herpetological Society of Chester Zoo on 21st March 1981 ... / [edited by Jon Barzdo]. — Dunstable (c/o Graham Lucas, 5 Chequers Cottages, Whipsnade, Dunstable, Beds. LU6 2LJ) : The Association, c1981. — 42p : ill ; 21cm
Text on inside cover. — Includes bibliographies
£1.65 (pbk)
Primary classification 639.3′9 B82-05652

639.3′753 — Aquariums. Killifish. Breeding & care — *Amateurs′ manuals*

Turner, Bruce J.. Enjoy your killifish / by Bruce J. Turner and John W. Pafenyk ; Earl Schneider, editor. — Harrison, N.J. : Pet Library, [1981?] ; London : Pet Library (London) [distributor]. — 32p : col.ll ; 21cm
Unpriced (pbk) B82-06969

639.3′755 — Salmon farming

Sedgwick, S. Drummond. The salmon handbook. — London : Deutsch, Apr.1982. — [256]p
ISBN 0-233-97331-1 : £8.95 : CIP entry B82-04726

639.376/8 — CULTURE OF AMPHIBIANS

639.3′76 — Captive amphibians. Care

Mattison, Christopher. The care of reptiles and amphibians in captivity / Christopher Mattison. — Poole : Blandford, 1982. — 304p : ill(some col.) ; 23cm
Bibliography: p295-298. — Includes index
ISBN 0-7137-1158-2 : £8.95 : CIP rev.
Also classified at 639.3′9 B82-15829

639.3′76 — Pets: Amphibians. Care — *For children*

Crush, Margaret. Handy homes for creepy crawlies / Margaret Crush ; illustrated by Sally Kindberg. — London : Granada, 1982. — 126p : ill ; 18cm. — (A Dragon book)
ISBN 0-583-30484-2 (pbk) : £0.95
Primary classification 639′.4 B82-22247

639.39 — CULTURE OF REPTILES

639.3′9 — Captive reptiles. Care

Mattison, Christopher. The care of reptiles and amphibians in captivity / Christopher Mattison. — Poole : Blandford, 1982. — 304p : ill(some col.) ; 23cm
Bibliography: p295-298. — Includes index
ISBN 0-7137-1158-2 : £8.95 : CIP rev.
Primary classification 639.3′76 B82-15829

639.3′9 — Pets: Reptiles. Care — *For children*

Crush, Margaret. Handy homes for creepy crawlies / Margaret Crush ; illustrated by Sally Kindberg. — London : Granada, 1982. — 126p : ill ; 18cm. — (A Dragon book)
ISBN 0-583-30484-2 (pbk) : £0.95
Primary classification 639′.4 B82-22247

639.3′9 — Zoos. Reptiles. Care — *Conference proceedings*

Association of British Wild Animal Keepers. *Symposium (6th : 1981)*. Management of reptiles and amphibians : the sixth specialist symposium of the Association of British Wild Animal Keepers ... with the International Herpetological Society of Chester Zoo on 21st March 1981 ... / [edited by Jon Barzdo]. — Dunstable (c/o Graham Lucas, 5 Chequers Cottages, Whipsnade, Dunstable, Beds. LU6 2LJ) : The Association, c1981. — 42p : ill ; 21cm
Text on inside cover. — Includes bibliographies
£1.65 (pbk)
Also classified at 639.3′7 B82-05652

639.4/7 — CULTURE OF INVERTEBRATES

639′.4 — Pets: Invertebrates. Care — *For children*

Crush, Margaret. Handy homes for creepy crawlies / Margaret Crush ; illustrated by Sally Kindberg. — London : Granada, 1982. — 126p : ill ; 18cm. — (A Dragon book)
ISBN 0-583-30484-2 (pbk) : £0.95
Also classified at 639.3′9 ; 639.3′76 B82-22247

639′.4 — Pets: Land invertebrates

Murphy, Frances. Keeping spiders, insects and other land invertebrates in captivity / Frances Murphy ; with illustrations by Denise Finney. — Edinburgh : Bartholomew, 1980. — 96p : col.ill ; 19cm. — (Bartholomew pet series)
Includes index
ISBN 0-7028-8020-5 (pbk) : £1.25 : CIP rev. B80-04282

639′.42′0942 — England. Marine mussels. Culture

Dare, P. J.. Mussel cultivation in England and Wales / P.J. Dare. — Lowestoft ([Fisheries Laboratory, Pakefield, Lowestoft, Suffolk.]) : Ministry of Agriculture, Fisheries and Food, Directorate of Fisheries Research, 1980. — 18p : ill,1map ; 30cm
Cover title. — Bibliography: p17-18
Unpriced (pbk) B82-40693

639′.4811 — England. Scallops. Fishing

Franklin, A.. The scallop and its fishery in England and Wales / A. Franklin, G.D. Pickett, P.M. Connor. — Lowestoft ([Fisheries Laboratory, Pakefield Rd., Lowestoft, Suffolk]) : Ministry of Agriculture, Fisheries and Food, Directorate of Fisheries Research, c1980. — 19p : ill,1map ; 30cm. — (Laboratory leaflet, ISSN 0143-8018 ; 51)
Cover title. — Bibliography: p18-19
Unpriced (pbk) B82-36200

639′.4858 — Squid-jigging — *Manuals*

Hamabe, Mototsugu. Squid jigging from small boats. — Farnham : Fishing News Books, Aug.1982. — [84]p. — (FAO fishing manuals)
ISBN 0-85238-122-0 (pbk) : £6.00 : CIP entry B82-22791

639′.54′3 — Prawns. Culture — *Conference proceedings*

Giant Prawn *(Conference : 1980 : Bangkok)*. Giant prawn farming. — Oxford : Elsevier Scientific, June 1982. — [650]p. — (Developments in aquaculture and fisheries science ; v.10)
ISBN 0-444-42093-2 : CIP entry B82-17202

639.9 — WILDLIFE CONSERVATION

639.9 — Aquatic organisms. Conservation — *Serials*

The **Underwater** Conservation Society newsletter. — [June 1980?]-. — Kempley (c/o Dr. R. Earll, Candle Cottage, Kempley, Glos.) : UCS, [1980?]. — v. : ill,maps ; 30cm
Description based on: June 1981 issue
ISSN 0262-2157 = Underwater Conservation Society newsletter : Available to members only B82-23581

639.9'07'1041 — Great Britain. Schools. Curriculum subjects: Nature conservation — *Serials*

Conservation education : a bulletin for teachers and youth leaders. — Issue no.1 (1981)-. — Guildford (19 Quarry St., Guildford, Surrey GU1 3EH) : Young People's Trust for Endangered Species, 1981-. — v. : ill ; 30cm
Three issues yearly. — Description based on: Issue no.2 (Autumn 1981)
ISSN 0262-2203 = Conservation education : Unpriced B82-13419

639.9'0722 — Wildlife. Conservation — *Case studies*

Stonehouse, Bernard. Saving the animals : the World Wildlife Fund book of conservation / Bernard Stonehouse ; foreword by the Duke of Edinburgh ; introduction by Sir Peter Scott. — London : Weidenfeld & Nicolson, c1981. — 224p : ill(some col.),maps ; 29cm
Ill on lining papers. — Includes index
ISBN 0-297-77931-1 : £9.95 B82-03023

639.9'092'4 — Hereford and Worcester. Malvern Hills *(District).* **Nature reserves: Ravenshill Woodland Reserve. Organisation** — *Personal observations*

Barling, Elizabeth. Birth of a nature reserve / Elizabeth Barling. — Lincoln : Royal Society for Nature Conservation, 1982. — 193p,[32]p of plates : ill,maps,ports ; 23cm
Maps on lining papers
ISBN 0-902484-03-6 : £8.00 B82-36897

639.9'092'4 — Kenya. Wildlife. Conservation. Adamson, Joy — *Biographies*

Adamson, Joy. The searching spirit : an autobiography / Joy Adamson. — Large print ed. — Leicester : Ulverscroft, 1982, c1978. — 369p ; 23cm. — (Ulverscroft large print)
Originally published: London : Collins, 1978
ISBN 0-7089-0826-8 : Unpriced : CIP rev. B82-15965

639.9'092'4 — Ontario. Wildlife. Conservation — *Personal observations*

Lawrence, R. D.. The zoo that never was / R.D. Lawrence. — Large print ed. — South Yarmouth, Mass. : Curley ; Skipton : Magna Print [distributor], c1981. — 541p ; 22cm
Originally published: New York : Holt, Rinehart and Winston, 1981
ISBN 0-89340-388-1 : Unpriced B82-29229

639.9'0941 — Great Britain. Nature conservation

Rose, Chris. Cash or crisis : a report on the imminent failure of the Wildlife and Countryside Act / Chris Rose and Charles Secrett for the British Association of Nature Conservationists and the Friends of the Earth. — [London] ([377 City Rd. EC1V 1NA]) : [Friends of the Earth], 1982. — 22p ; 30cm
£2.50 (pbk) B82-28936

639.9'09411'65 — Scotland. Highland Region. Inchnadamph. Nature reserves: Inchnadamph National Nature Reserve

Nature Conservancy Council. Inchnadamph National Nature Reserve / Nature Conservancy Council. — Inverness : Nature Conservancy Council, North West Scotland Region, c1980. — [4]p : 1map ; 21cm
ISBN 0-86139-101-2 (unbound) : Unpriced B82-17441

639.9'09411'75 — Scotland. Highland Region. Glen Strathfarrar. Nature reserves: Strathfarrar National Nature Reserve

Nature Conservancy Council. Strathfarrar National Nature Reserve / Nature Conservancy Council. — Inverness : Nature Conservancy Council, North West Scotland Region, c1980. — [4]p : 1ill,1map ; 21cm
ISBN 0-86139-104-7 (unbound) : Unpriced B82-17443

639.9'09412'4 — Scotland. Grampian Region. Muir of Dinnet. Nature reserves: Muir of Dinnet National Nature Reserve

Nature Conservancy Council. Muir of Dinnet National Nature Reserve / Nature Conservancy Council. — Aberdeen : Nature Conservancy Council, North East Scotland Region, c1979. — [4]p : (1col.map) ; 21cm
ISBN 0-86139-078-4 (unbound) : Unpriced B82-35376

639.9'09413'5 — Scotland. Lothian Region. Midlothian *(District).* **Nature reserves: Gladhouse Local Nature Reserve**

Gladhouse Local Nature Reserve : descriptive report. — [Edinburgh] ([12 St. Giles St., Edinburgh EH1 1PT]) : Lothian Regional Council, Dept. of Physical Planning, [1981]. — 68p : ill,maps ; 30cm
Cover title
Unpriced (pbk) B82-14190

639.9'09413'5 — Scotland. Lothian Region. Midlothian *(District).* **Nature reserves: Gladhouse Local Nature Reserve. Planning** — *Proposals*

Gladhouse Local Nature Reserve : management plan 1982-86. — [Edinburgh] ([12 St. Giles St., Edinburgh EH1 1PT]) : Lothian Regional Council, Dept. of Physical Planning, [1981]. — 25,viiip : plans ; 30cm
Cover title. — Prepared by a management group set up under the chairmanship of the Regional Director of Physical Planning
Unpriced (pbk) B82-14189

639.9'0941423 — Scotland. Strathclyde Region. Bonawe. Nature reserves: Glen Nant National Nature Reserve

Nature Conservancy Council. Glen Nant National Nature Reserve and Bonawe furnace / Nature Conservancy Council. — Balloch : Nature Conservancy Council, South West Scotland Region, c1980. — [4]p : ill,1map ; 21cm
ISBN 0-86139-096-2 (unbound) : Unpriced B82-17442

639.9'09416 — Northern Ireland. Nature conservation — *Serials*

The **Irish** hare : newsletter of the Ulster Trust for Nature Conservation. — No.1 (1978)-. — [Belfast] ([UTNC Conservation Centre, 11A Stranmillis Rd, Belfast BT9 5AF]) : The Trust, 1978-. — v. : ill ; 30cm
Three issues yearly. — Description based on: No.4 (Mar. 1980)
ISSN 0260-986x = Irish hare : £0.30 per issue (Free to Trust members) B82-05974

639.9'09423'19 — Wiltshire. Ebbesbourne Wake. Nature reserves: Prescombe Down National Nature Reserve

Nature Conservancy Council. Prescombe Down National Nature Reserve / Nature Conservancy Council. — Newbury : Nature Conservancy Council, Southern Region, c1980. — [4]p : 1ill,1map ; 21cm
ISBN 0-86139-102-0 (unbound) : Unpriced B82-35378

639.9'09423'19 — Wiltshire. Wylye. Nature reserves: Wylye Down National Nature Reserve

Nature Conservancy Council. Wylye Down National Nature Reserve / Nature Conservancy Council. — Newbury : Nature Conservancy Council, South Region, c1980. — [9]p : 1map ; 21cm
ISBN 0-86139-100-4 (unbound) : Unpriced B82-39679

639.9'09423'55 — Devon. Bovey Tracey. Nature reserves: Bovey Valley Woodlands National Nature Reserve

Nature Conservancy Council. Bovey Valley Woodlands National Nature Reserve / Nature Conservancy Council. — Taunton : [Nature Conservancy Council], South West Region, c1980. — [4]p : 1ill,1map ; 21cm
ISBN 0-86139-089-x (unbound) : Unpriced B82-17439

639.9'09423'76 — Corwnall. Lizard Peninsula. Nature reserves: Lizard National Nature Reserve

Nature Conservancy Council. The Lizard National Nature Reserve / Nature Conservancy Council. — Taunton : [Nature Conservancy Council], South West Region, c1980. — [4]p : 1ill,1map ; 21cm
ISBN 0-86139-088-1 (unbound) : Unpriced B82-17438

639.9'09424 — England. Severn Estuary. Nature conservation. Implications of proposed tidal power barrages

Nature conservation : Severn tidal power / R. Mitchell ... [et al.] ; report ... commissioned by the United Kingdom Atomic Energy Authority ... — [Shrewsbury] : Nature Conservancy Council, 1981. — 50p in various pagings : maps ; 30cm
Bibliography: p22
ISBN 0-86139-147-0 (spiral) : Unpriced B82-02083

639.9'09426'17 — Norfolk Broads. Organisms. Conservation

Nature conservation in Broadland / Nature Conservancy Council. — Norwich : Nature Conservancy Council, East Anglia Region, [1980]. — [16]p : ill,maps(1col.) ; 21cm
ISBN 0-86139-091-1 (unbound) : £0.20 B82-35375

639.9'09427'16 — Cheshire. Rostherne. Nature reserves: Rostherne Mere National Nature Reserve

Nature Conservancy Council. Rostherne Mere National Nature Reserve / Nature Conservancy Council. — Shrewsbury : Nature Conservancy Council, West Midlands Region, c1980. — [4]p : 1ill,1map ; 21cm
ISBN 0-86139-105-5 (unbound) : Unpriced B82-35379

639.9'09428'81 — Northumberland. Tynedale *(District).* **Nature reserves: Coom Rigg Moss National Nature Reserve**

Nature Conservancy Council. Coom Rigg Moss National Nature Reserve / Nature Conservancy Council. — Newcastle-upon-Tyne : [Nature Conservancy Council], North East Region, c1980. — [4]p : 1ill,1map ; 21cm
ISBN 0-86139-087-3 (unbound) : Unpriced B82-35374

639.9'09428'89 — Northumberland. Holy Island. Nature reserves: Lindisfarne National Nature Reserve

Nature Conservancy Council. Lindisfarne National Nature Reserve / Nature Conservancy Council. — Newcastle-upon-Tyne : Nature Conservancy Council, North East Region, c1979. — [4]p : 1ill,(1col.map) ; 21cm
ISBN 0-86139-077-6 (unbound) : Unpriced B82-35377

639.9'09429'29 — Gwynedd. Aberdyfi. Nature reserves: Dyfi National Nature Reserve. Ynyslas dunes

Nature Conservancy Council. Ynyslas Dunes : Dyfi National Nature Reserve / Nature Conservancy Council/Cyngor Gwarchod Natur. — Aberystwyth : Nature Conservancy Council, Dyfed-Powys Region, c1979. — [6]p : 1ill,1plan ; 21cm
ISBN 0-86139-068-7 (unbound) : Unpriced B82-17446

639.9'09429'82 — West Glamorgan. Gower. Nature conservation

Nature conservation and field studies in Gower / Nature Conservancy Council/Cyngor Gwarchod Natur. — Cardiff : Nature Conservancy Council, South Wales Region, c1980. — [12]p : ill(some col.) ; 21cm
Bibliography: p9-10
ISBN 0-86139-098-9 (unbound) : Unpriced B82-17444

639.9'5'0924 — England. Gamekeeping. Mursell, Norman — *Biographies*

Mursell, Norman. Come dawn, come dusk : fifty years a gamekeeper / Norman Mursell ; illustrated by Rodger McPhail. — London : Allen & Unwin, 1981. — 149,[8]p of plates : ill,1facsim,ports ; 25cm
ISBN 0-04-799014-7 : Unpriced : CIP rev. B81-13771

639.9'5'0924 — England. Gamekeeping. Rogers, Evan — *Biographies*

Rogers, Evan. A funny old Quist : recorded March 27th to April 6th and May 27th to May 29th, 1978 / Evan Rogers. — London : Dobson, 1981. — 215p ; 22cm. — (Ordinary lives ; 5)
ISBN 0-234-72258-4 : £6.95 B82-14702

639.9′5′0941 — Great Britain. Gamekeeping — *Amateurs′ manuals*

Smith, Guy N.. Gamekeeping and shooting for amateurs / by Guy N. Smith ; drawings by Bob Sanders. — 2nd ed. — Hindhead : Saiga, c1981. — vii,209p : ill ; 23cm. — (Field sports library)
Previous ed.: Liss : Spur, 1976
ISBN 0-904558-93-2 : £6.00
Primary classification 799.2′13′0941
B82-08705

639.9′6 — Great Britain. Pests. Trapping — *Manuals*

Smith, Guy N.. Ferreting and trapping for amateur gamekeepers / by Guy N. Smith ; photographs by Lance Smith ; drawings by Pat Larkin. — 2nd ed. — Hindhead : Spur, 1979. — 159p : ill,1plan ; 23cm
Previous ed.: 1978. — Includes index
ISBN 0-904558-73-8 : £5.50
Primary classification 799.2′3 B82-08776

639.9′6 — Wildlife. Conservation. Effects of diseases — *Conference proceedings*

Animal disease in relation to animal conservation : (the proceedings of a symposium held at the Zoological Society of London on 26 and 27 November 1981) / edited by Marcia A. Edwards and Unity McDonnell. — London : Published for the Zoological Society of London by Academic Press, 1982. — xviii,336p : ill,maps ; 24cm. — (Symposia of the Zoological Society of London ; no.50)
Includes bibliographies and index
ISBN 0-12-613350-6 : £26.40 : CIP rev.
B82-15928

639.9′78′0924 — Great Britain. Birds. Conservation — *Personal observations*

Robinson, Peter, *1939-*. Bird detective / by Peter Robinson ; with a foreword by H.R.H. The Prince of Wales. — London : Elm Tree Books in association with the Royal Society for the Protection of Birds, 1982. — xxx,159p,[8]p of plates : ill ; 23cm
Includes index
ISBN 0-241-10709-1 : £7.95 : CIP rev.
B81-36388

639.9′782941 — Great Britain. Bird sanctuaries

Dougall, Robert. Birdwatch round Britain : with Robert Dougall and Herbert Axell : a personal selection of Britain′s bird reserves / foreword by Ian Prestt. — London : Collins and Harvill, 1982. — 191p,[8]p of plates : ill(some col.),maps ; 25cm
Includes index
ISBN 0-00-262256-4 : £8.95 : CIP rev.
B82-03700

639.9′79 — Large mammals. Management

Riney, Thane. Study and management of large mammals / Thane Riney. — Chichester : Wiley, c1982. — ix,552p : ill,forms,1map ; 24cm
Bibliography: p533-540. — Includes index
ISBN 0-471-10062-5 : £26.50 : CIP rev.
B82-09699

639.9′7974428 — Derbyshire. Derby region. Stray cats. Conservation. Organisations: Cats′ Protection League. ***Derby & District Branch —*** *Serials*

[Derby & District Branch news *(Cats′ Protection League)*]. Derby & District Branch news / The Cats′ Protection League. — Magazine no.15 (Mar.-Apr. 1982)-. — Derby (c/o Mrs J. Priestley, 21 Askerfield Ave, Allestree, Derby DE3 2SU) : The Branch, 1982-. — v. ; 21cm
Six issues yearly. — Continues: Waifarers
ISSN 0263-3795 = Derby & District Branch news - Cats′ Protection League : Unpriced
B82-24753

639.9′7974447 — Great Britain. Common otters. Conservation

King, Angela. A guide to otter conservation for water authorities / Angela King and Angela Potter for the Otter Haven Project. — London (21 Bury St. EC3A 5AU) : Vincent Wildlife Trust, 1980. — iii,20p : ill ; 20cm
Cover title. — Ill on inside covers. —
Bibliography: p19-20
Unpriced (pbk) B82-24300

640 — HOUSEHOLD MANAGEMENT

640 — Great Britain. Rural regions. Households. Self-sufficiency — *Manuals*

Fuller, Richard R.. Small scale self-sufficiency / Richard R. Fuller. — St. Ives, Cornwall : United Writers, c1981. — 78p : ill ; 22cm
ISBN 0-901976-60-1 : £4.95 B82-20113

640 — Home economics — *For Irish students*

Murphy, Eileen. Post primary home economics / Eileen Murphy. — Dublin : Educational Company, 1977-1978. — 2v. : ill ; 21cm
Includes index
£4.42 (pbk) B82-23736

640 — Home economics — *For schools*

Bagshaw, Mary. Science in home economics / Mary Bagshaw. — Edinburgh : Oliver & Boyd, c1982. — 156p : ill,1map ; 23cm
Includes index
ISBN 0-05-003254-2 (pbk) : Unpriced
B82-36002

Hampson, Margaret. Foundation home economics / Margaret Hampson, Bob McDuell. — Walton-on-Thames : Nelson, 1982. — 160p : ill ; 25cm
Includes index
ISBN 0-17-438204-9 (pbk) : Unpriced
B82-26907

Nuffield home economics / [general editors Harry Faulkner, Sharon M. Mansell] ; [consultant editor Marie Edwards]. — London : Published for the Nuffield-Chelsea Curriculum Trust by Hutchinson Education, 1982
The basic course. — vi,185p : ill,1map,1facsim ; 24cm
Includes index
ISBN 0-09-145601-0 (pbk) : Unpriced : CIP rev. B81-12326

640 — Home economics - *For schools*

Nuffield home economics. — London : Hutchinson Educational, July 1981
Masters for worksheets and OHP′s for the basic course. — [64]p
ISBN 0-09-145581-2 : £15.00 : CIP entry
B81-13499

640 — Home economics — *For schools*

Nuffield home economics / [general editors Harry Faulkner, Sharon M. Mansell] ; [consultant general editor Marie Edwards]. — London : Published for the Nuffield-Chelsea Curriculum Trust by Hutchinson Education, 1982
Teacher′s guide to the basic course. — xiv,402p : ill ; 24cm
Includes index
ISBN 0-09-145591-x (pbk) : Unpriced : CIP rev. B81-12327

640 — Home economics — *Practical information*

Chevallier, Ginette. [1000 things you ought to know]. Ginette Chevallier′s book of 1000 things you ought to know / illustrated by Malcolm Bird. — London : Futura, [1982], c1980. — 192p : ill ; 21cm
Originally published: London : Jill Norman, 1980. — Includes index
ISBN 0-7088-2075-1 (pbk) : £2.95 B82-12753

Hopcraft, Jan. Tips and tricks for the kitchen. — London : Methuen, Oct.1982. — [112]p
ISBN 0-413-50380-1 : £3.95 : CIP entry
B82-24478

640 — Household management — *For schools*

Gray, Christine. Basic home economics / Christine Gray ; edited by Janet Harvey. — London : Edward Arnold, 1980. — 108p : ill ; 30cm
Originally published: Sydney : Cleary, 1975
ISBN 0-7131-0438-4 (pbk) : £2.50 : CIP rev.
B80-02488

640 — Household management — *Manuals*

Ager, Stanley. [Ager′s way to easy elegance]. The Butler′s guide : to clothes care, managing the table, running the home and other graces / Stanley Ager and Fiona St. Aubyn ; produced by James Wagenvoord. — London : Macmillan, 1982, c1980. — 191p : ill ; 24cm. — (Papermac)
Originally published: New York : Bobbs-Merrill, 1980. — Includes index
ISBN 0-333-32911-2 (pbk) : £3.95 B82-20900

Beaumont, Elizabeth. In grandmother′s footsteps : a treasury of household hints from the past / Elizabeth Beaumont ; with a foreword by Jilly Cooper. — London : Corgi, 1982, c1980. — 94p ; 18cm
Originally published: London : Bodley Head, 1980. — Includes index
ISBN 0-552-11894-x (pbk) : £1.00 B82-25631

Beeton, *Mrs.* [Mrs Beeton′s cookery and household management]. Mrs Beeton′s everyday cookery. — London : Ward Lock, Oct.1982. — [632]p
ISBN 0-7063-6224-1 : £9.95 : CIP entry
Also classified at 641.5 B82-23187

640 — Household management - *Manuals*

Chandler, Barbara. How to cope at home. — London : Ward Lock, June 1981. — [160]p
ISBN 0-7063-5918-6 : £6.95 : CIP entry
B81-12842

640 — Household management — *Manuals*

Collins practical dictionary of household hints / [editor, Dorothy Darrell Ward] ; [contributing editors, Barbara Croxford, Jill Blake, Mike Lawrence] ; [illustrators, Anne Morrow ... et al.]. — London : Collins, 1982. — 318p : ill ; 22cm
Includes index
ISBN 0-00-411636-4 : £7.95 B82-08811

Davies, Hilary, *1949-*. Household hints / Hilary Davies. — [London] : Fontana Paperbacks, 1981. — 158p : ill ; 18cm
Includes index
ISBN 0-00-636323-7 (pbk) : £1.25 B82-07928

King, Sally. Setting up home. — London : Muller, Sept.1982. — [160]p
ISBN 0-584-11015-4 : £6.95 : CIP entry
Primary classification 643′.7 B82-20278

640 — Household management — *Practical information*

Grunfeld, Nina. The complete book of household lists. — Loughton : Piatkus, Oct.1982. — [304]p
ISBN 0-86188-170-2 : £6.95 : CIP entry
B82-24575

Pinkham, Mary Ellen. Mary Ellen′s best of helpful hints / Mary Ellen Pinkham and Pearl Higginbotham ; illustrations by Lynn Johnston. — Rev. ed. — London : New English Library, 1981, c1979. — 159p : ill ; 18cm
Previous ed.: New York : Warner, 1979. — Includes index
ISBN 0-450-05189-7 (pbk) : £1.25 B82-39704

640 — Self-sufficiency — *Manuals*

Urquhart, Judy. Living off nature / Judy Urquhart ; illustrations by Vana Haggerty. — Harmondsworth : Penguin, 1982, c1980. — vii,396p : ill ; 22cm
Originally published: London : Allen Lane, 1980. — Bibliography: p385-392
ISBN 0-14-005107-4 (pbk) : £5.95 B82-30516

640 — Western Mayo *(County)*. **Self-sufficiency —** *Personal observations*

Viney, Michael. Another life again / Michael & Ethna Viney. — Dublin : Irish Times, 1981. — 185p : ill ; 22cm
ISBN 0-907011-06-3 (cased) : £7.50
ISBN 0-907011-05-5 (pbk) : £4.50 B82-29835

640′.242 — Household management — *Manuals —* *For Christians*

Longacre, Doris Janzen. Living more with less. — London : Hodder & Stoughton, June 1982. — [304]p
ISBN 0-340-27236-8 (pbk) : £4.95 : CIP entry
B82-10012

640′.321 — Home economics — *Encyclopaedias — For schools*

Brown, Philomena. A basic dictionary of home economics. — London : Bell & Hyman, Apr.1982. — [64]p. — (Basic dictionary series)
ISBN 0-7135-1317-9 (pbk) : £1.75 : CIP entry
B82-04494

640′.46′088042 — Uited States. Women. Domestic service, *1865-1918*

Katzman, David M.. Seven days a week : women and domestic service in industrializing America / David M. Katzman. — Urbana ; London : University of Illinois Press, 1981, c1978. — xviii,374p : ill ; 21cm
Originally published: New York : Oxford University Press, 1978. — Includes index
ISBN 0-252-00882-0 (pbk) : £6.30 B82-05727

640′.46′088042 — United States. Women. Domestic service, *1800-1920*

Sutherland, Daniel E.. Americans and their servants : domestic service in the United States from 1800 to 1920 / Daniel E. Sutherland. — Baton Rouge ; London : Louisiana State University Press, c1981. — xv,229p : ill,2plans ; 24cm
Bibliography: p201-222. — Includes index
ISBN 0-8071-0860-x : £14.00 B82-15447

640′.46′0924 — England. Butlers: Russell, Peter, *1933-* — *Biographies*

Russell, Peter, *1933-*. Butler royal / Peter Russell. — London : Hutchinson, 1982. — 205p,[8]p of plates : ill,ports ; 23cm
ISBN 0-09-147850-2 : £7.95 : CIP rev.
B82-11291

640′.46′0924 — England. Domestic service. Gibbs, Rose — *Biographies*

Gibbs, Rose. In service : Rose Gibbs remembers. — Bassingbourn (History Department, Bassingbourn Village College, Bassingbourn, Cambs. nr. Royston, Herts.) : Archives for Bassingbourn & Comberton Village Colleges, c1981. — 15p : ill,ports ; 21cm
Ill and text on inside covers. — Limited ed. of 500 numbered copies
Unpriced (pbk) B82-12121

640′.46′0924 — Great Britain. Country houses. Domestic service, *ca 1930-1950* — *Personal observations*

Balderson, Eileen. Backstairs life in a country house / Eileen Balderson with Douglas Goodlad. — Newton Abbot : David & Charles, c1982. — 127p ; 23cm
Includes index
ISBN 0-7153-8021-4 : £5.95 : CIP rev.
B82-04864

640′.5 — Home economics — *Serials*

[The Home economist *(Bristol)*]. The Home economist : journal of the Association of Home Economists. — Vol.1, no.1 (July 1981)-. — Bristol : John Wright & Sons, 1981-. — v. : ill,maps ; 25cm
Quarterly
ISSN 0261-1384 = Home economist (Bristol) : £9.00 per year B82-10354

640′.7′1241 — Great Britain. Middle schools. Curriculum subjects: Home economics. Teaching

Home and family 8-13 / Schools Council Project, Home Economics in the Middle Years. — London : Forbes for the Schools Council, 1979. — 1case : ill ; 25cm
ISBN 0-901762-31-8 : Unpriced
ISBN 0-901762-32-6 (Development guide)
ISBN 0-901762-35-4 (Interdependence guide)
ISBN 0-901762-34-2 (Management guide)
ISBN 0-901762-35-0 (Nutrition guide)
ISBN 0-901762-36-9 (Protection guide)
ISBN 0-901762-37-7 (Planning bk) B82-33249

640′.73 — Great Britain. Consumer durables. Faults

Faulty goods / [National Consumer Council]. — London : The Council, 1981. — 26p ; 30cm. — (Occasional paper)
Based on a survey carried out for the National Consumer Council by Research Services Limited
ISBN 0-905653-32-7 (unbound) : Unpriced
B82-02422

640′.73 — Great Britain. Second-hand goods. Purchase — *Practical information*

Ball, Richard, *1947-*. How to buy secondhand : (almost anything) / Richard Ball. — London : Astragal, 1981. — 216p : ill ; 23cm
Bibliography: p212-216
ISBN 0-906525-21-7 : £7.95 : CIP rev.
B81-20587

640′.76 — Home economics - *Questions & answers - For schools*

Creese, Angela. 1050 questions and answers in home economics. — 2nd ed. — London : Bell & Hyman, July 1981. — [183]p
Previous ed.: London : Mills & Boon, 1970
ISBN 0-7135-2061-2 (pbk) : £1.95 : CIP entry
B81-15909

641 — FOOD AND DRINK, NUTRITION

641′.01′30941 — Great Britain. Gastronomy

Harrison, Alan F.. Gastronomy / by Alan F. Harrison. — Bognor Regis : New Horizon, 1982. — x,280p : ill,forms ; 22cm
Bibliography: p240-254, p266-277. — Includes index
ISBN 0-86116-693-0 : Unpriced B82-23284

641′.0944 — France. Food & drinks, *1700-1800* — *Correspondence, diaries, etc. — French texts*

Lettre d'un pâtissier anglais : et autres contributions à une polemique gastronomique du xviiième siecle / edition préparée par Stephen Mennell. — [Exeter] : University of Exeter, 1981. — xxxi,64p : ill ; 22cm. — (Textes littéraires, ISSN 0309-6998 ; 42)
ISBN 0-85989-172-0 (pbk) : Unpriced
B82-00686

641.1 — Food. Chemical constituents & properties

Fox, Brian A.. Food science : a chemical approach / Brian A. Fox, Allan G. Cameron. — 4th ed. — London : Hodder and Stoughton, 1982. — xi,370p : ill ; 22cm
Previous ed.: 1977. — Bibliography: p354-355. — Includes index
ISBN 0-340-27863-3 (pbk) : £4.95 : CIP rev.
B82-07441

641.1 — Food. Colloids

Dickinson, Eric. Colloids in food. — London : Applied Science, Sept.1982. — [544]p
ISBN 0-85334-153-2 : £45.00 : CIP entry
B82-18777

641.1 — Food. Fibre — *Tables*

Keating, Leslie. The fibre and calorie content. — Havant : Mason, Aug.1982. — [32]p
ISBN 0-85937-290-1 (pbk) : £0.30 : CIP entry
Also classified at 641.1′042 B82-23841

641.1 — Food science

Charley, Helen. Food science / Helen Charley. — 2nd ed. — New York ; Chichester : Wiley, c1982. — 564p : ill ; 25cm
Previous ed.: New York : Ronald Press, 1970. — Includes index
ISBN 0-471-06206-5 : £15.50 B82-13292

Pyke, Magnus. Food science & technology / Magnus Pyke ; with a foreword by John Hawthorn. — 4th ed. / revised and enlarged by Lelio Parducci. — London : John Murray, 1981. — xiii,304p : ill ; 22cm
Previous ed.: 1970. — Includes index
ISBN 0-7195-3850-5 : £7.50 : CIP rev.
Also classified at 664 B81-14897

641.1′042 — Food. Calorific values - *Lists*

Fielding, Jean. Calorie controlled meals. — Havant : Mason, Aug.1981. — [32]p
Originally published: 1974
ISBN 0-85937-103-4 (pbk) : £0.20 : CIP entry
B81-18048

641.1′042 — Food. Calorific values — *Tables*

Deutsch, Ronald M.. The fat counter guide / Ronald M. Deutsch. — Palo Alto : Bull ; London : Distributed by Eurospan, c1978. — 131p ; 18cm
ISBN 0-915950-16-2 (pbk) : Unpriced
B82-36775

Keating, Leslie. Count your calories. — 7th rev. ed. — Havant : K. Mason, Mar.1982. — [32]p
Previous ed.: 1980
ISBN 0-85937-285-5 (pbk) : £0.20 : CIP entry
B82-07832

Keating, Leslie. The fibre and calorie content. — Havant : Mason, Aug.1982. — [32]p
ISBN 0-85937-290-1 (pbk) : £0.30 : CIP entry
Primary classification 641.1 B82-23841

641.1′2 — Food. Proteins — *Conference proceedings*

Food proteins. — London : Applied Science, July 1982. — [368]p
Conference papers
ISBN 0-85334-143-5 : £40.00 : CIP entry
B82-13140

641.1′2′05 — Food. Proteins — *Serials*

Developments in food proteins. — 1-. — London : Applied Science, 1982-. — v. ; 23cm. — (Developments series)
Irregular
ISSN 0263-4708 = Developments in food proteins : £35.00 B82-26157

641.1′3 — Food. Carbohydrates

Developments in food carbohydrate. — London : Applied Science Publishers
3: Disaccharidases / edited by C.K. Lee and M.G. Lindley. — c1982. — xii,217p : ill ; 24cm
Includes index
ISBN 0-85334-996-7 : £26.00 : CIP rev.
B81-33784

641.2′1′094 — European wines & spirits

Millon, Marc. The wine and food of Europe. — Exeter : Webb & Bower, Sept. 1982. — [224]p
ISBN 0-906671-35-3 : £9.95 : CIP entry
Also classified at 641.594 B82-21573

641.2′2 — Fortified wines: Port

Robertson, George, *1918-*. Port / George Robertson. — Rev. ed. — London : Faber, 1982. — 188p : ill,maps ; 22cm
Previous ed.: 1978. — Bibliography: p179-180. — Includes index
ISBN 0-571-11766-x (pbk) : £3.50 : CIP rev.
B81-33802

641.2′2 — Sherry

Jeffs, Julian. Sherry / Julian Jeffs. — 3rd ed. — London : Faber, 1982. — 314p : ill,maps ; 23cm
Previous ed.: 1970. — Bibliography: p293-299. — Includes index
ISBN 0-571-18047-7 (cased) : £7.95 : CIP rev.
ISBN 0-571-11799-6 (pbk) : Unpriced
B82-09300

641.2′2 — Wines

André Simon's wines of the world. — 2nd ed. / by Serena Sutcliffe. — London : Macdonald Futura, 1981. — 639p,56p of plates : col.ill,maps ; 28cm
Previous ed.: Maidenhead : McGraw-Hill, 1972. — Ill on lining papers. — Bibliography: p627-628. — Includes index
ISBN 0-354-04631-4 : £17.50 B82-03493

Cooper, Rosalind. The wine book. — London : Collins, Aug.1982. — [96]p
ISBN 0-00-218095-2 : £5.95 : CIP entry
B82-21075

Ensrud, Barbara. The pocket guide to wine / Barbara Ensrud. — Rev. ed. — London : Muller, 1982. — 138p : ill(some col.),col.maps ; 24x12cm
Originally published: New York : Putnam, 1982
ISBN 0-584-95032-2 (cased) : £4.95 : CIP rev.
ISBN 0-584-95035-7 (pbk) : £2.95 B82-26570

Harveys pocket guide to wine. — London : Octopus, 1981. — 160p : ill,col.maps ; 19cm
ISBN 0-7064-1524-8 : £2.95 B82-08369

641.2′2 — Wines. Judging — *Manuals*

National Guild of Wine and Beer Judges. Judging wine and beer. — 6th ed. — Petersfield (c/o V.H. Goffen, 13 Monks Orchard, Petersfield, Hants. GU30 2JJ) : The Guild, Nov.1982. — 1v. Previous ed.: 1978 ISBN 0-9508294-0-4 (pbk) : CIP entry *Also classified at 641.2′3* B82-34100

641.2′2 — Wines. Selection & serving

Forest, Louis. Wine album. — London : Gollancz, Oct.1982. — [160]p Translation and adaptation of: Monseigneur Le Vin ISBN 0-575-03221-9 : £6.95 : CIP entry B82-23353

641.2′2 — Wines. Tasting — *Manuals*

Broadbent, J. M.. [Wine tasting]. Michael Broadbent′s pocket guide to wine tasting. — London : Mitchell Beazley in association with Christie′s Wine Publications, c1982. — 144p : col.ill ; 20x9cm Originally published: London : Wine & Spirit Publications, 1968. — Bibliography: p130-137. — Includes index ISBN 0-85533-373-1 : £3.95 B82-27321

641.2′2′0294 — Wines — *Buyers′ guides*

Johnson, Hugh, *1939-*. Understanding wine / Hugh Johnson. — Cambridge : Published for J. Sainsbury Ltd. by Woodhead-Faulkner, 1980 (1981 [printing]). — 40p : ill,1map,facsims ; 21cm. — (Sainsbury′s food guides ; no.7) Cover title £0.30 (pbk)

Peppercorn, David. Drinking wine : a complete guide for the buyer & consumer / David Peppercorn, Brian Cooper, Elwyn Blacker. — Rev. ed. — London : Macdonald, 1982, c1979. — 256p : ill(some col.),maps(some col.) ; 26cm Previous ed.: 1979. — Bibliography: p234-235. — Includes index ISBN 0-356-07894-9 : £9.95 B82-21338

641.2′2′0943 — German wines

Hallgarten, S. F.. German wines / S.F. Hallgarten. — [2nd ed.]. — London : Publivin, c1981. — 399p : ill,maps ; 23cm Previous ed.: London : Faber, 1976. — Bibliography: p383-385. — Includes index ISBN 0-9507410-0-0 : Unpriced B82-08860

641.2′2′0945 — Italian wines — *Encyclopaedias*

Ray, Cyril. The new book of Italian wines / Cyril Ray. — London : Sidgwick & Jackson, 1982. — 158p,[8]p of plates : col.ill ; 24cm Maps on lining papers ISBN 0-283-98745-6 : £10.00 B82-31389

641.2′2′0946 — Spanish wines

Read, Jan. The wines of Spain. — London : Faber, Oct.1982. — [272]p ISBN 0-571-11937-9 (cased) : £5.95 : CIP entry ISBN 0-571-11938-7 (pbk) : £3.25 B82-28471

641.2′2′09469 — Portuguese wines

Read, Jan. The wines of Portugal. — London : Faber, Oct.1982. — 1v. ISBN 0-571-11951-4 (cased) : £5.95 : CIP entry ISBN 0-571-11952-2 (pbk) : £2.95 B82-28472

641.2′22′09444 — Burgundies

Hanson, Anthony, *1945-*. Burgundy / Anthony Hanson. — London : Faber, 1982. — 378p : ill,maps ; 23cm Bibliography: p347-351. — Includes index ISBN 0-571-11797-x (cased) : £12.50 : CIP rev. ISBN 0-571-11798-8 (pbk) : Unpriced B82-09297

641.2′22′094471 — Bordeaux wines

Peppercorn, David. Bordeaux / David Peppercorn. — London : Faber, 1982. — 428p : ill,maps ; 23cm Bibliography: p415-416. — Includes index ISBN 0-571-11751-1 (cased) : £12.50 : CIP rev. ISBN 0-571-11758-9 (pbk) : Unpriced B82-06856

641.2′223′094471 — Red Bordeaux wines, *to 1978*

Coates, Clive. Claret. — London : Century Publishing, Oct.1982. — [384]p ISBN 0-7126-0009-4 : £14.95 : CIP entry B82-23881

641.2′3 — Beers

Jackson, Michael, *1942-*. The pocket guide to beer / Michael Jackson. — London : Muller, 1982. — 138p : maps ; 24x12cm Includes index ISBN 0-584-95013-6 (cased) : Unpriced ISBN 0-584-95015-2 (pbk) : £2.95 B82-27435

641.2′3 — Beers. Judging — *Manuals*

National Guild of Wine and Beer Judges. Judging wine and beer. — 6th ed. — Petersfield (c/o V.H. Goffen, 13 Monks Orchard, Petersfield, Hants. GU30 2JJ) : The Guild, Nov.1982. — 1v. Previous ed.: 1978 ISBN 0-9508294-0-4 (pbk) : CIP entry *Primary classification 641.2′2* B82-34100

641.2′3 — England. Cider, *to 1981*

French, R. K.. The history and virtues of cyder / R.K. French. — New York : St. Martin′s ; London : Hale, 1982. — 200p : ill ; 23cm Includes index ISBN 0-7091-9147-2 : £7.95 B82-14580

641.2′52 — Scotch whiskies — *Collectors′ guides*

Daiches, David. Let′s collect Scotch whisky / with text by David Daiches. — Norwich : Jarrold, 1981. — [32]p : ill(some col.),2col.maps,1port ; 20cm. — (Jarrold collectors series) Text, ill, port on inside covers ISBN 0-85306-969-7 (pbk) : Unpriced B82-01363

641.2′52 — Scotch whiskies, *to 1974*

Lockhart, *Sir* **Robert Bruce.** Scotch. — 5th ed. — London : Putnam, Sept.1981. — [184]p Originally published: 1974 ISBN 0-370-30910-3 : £4.95 : CIP entry B81-21648

641.3 — Food

Freud, Clement. Below the belt. — London : Robson, Sept.1982. — [208]p ISBN 0-86051-199-5 : £6.50 : CIP entry B82-20871

641.3 — Food — *For children*

Food. — [London] : Save the Children Fund, 1981. — 31p : col.ill,col.maps ; 27cm. — (Round the world) ISBN 0-333-30676-7 : £1.95 B82-07008

641.3 — Food — *For schools*

Bennett, Olivia. Food for life / Olivia Bennett. — London : Macmillan Education in association with the Save the Children Fund and the Commonwealth Institute, 1982. — 48p : col.ill ; 26cm. — (Patterns of living) Text on lining papers. — Includes index ISBN 0-333-31197-3 : Unpriced B82-33386

Crystal, David. Food. — London : Edward Arnold, May 1982. — [24]p. — (Databank) ISBN 0-7131-0631-x (pbk) : £0.90 : CIP entry B82-06908

641.3′003′21 — Food — *Encyclopaedias*

Hering, Richard. Hering′s dictionary of classical and modern cookery : and practical reference manual for the hotel, restaurant and catering trade : brief recipes, professional knowledge concerning wine, cocktails and other drinks, menu knowledge and table service. — 7th English ed. / by Walter Bickel. — London : Virtue, c1981. — 852p,[2]leaves ; 19cm Translation of: Lexikon der Küche. — English text, vocabulary in English, French, German, Italian and Spanish. — Previous ed.: 1974. — Includes index ISBN 3-8057-0244-2 : Unpriced B82-08953

641.3′005 — Food — *Serials*

Food world news : the international news magazine of the food and drink, food ingredients and process plant industries. — 1-. — London (130 Wigmore St., W1H 0AT) : World News Publications, 1981-. — v. : ill ; 33cm Six issues yearly. — Description based on: 2 ISSN 0260-1974 = Food world news : £20.00 per year B82-03400

641.3′007′1041 — Great Britain. Schools. Students, 5-14 years. Curriculum subjects: Food — *For teaching*

Batty, Mervyn. Cooking and what we eat / Mervyn Batty and Dorothy Smith. — Basingstoke : Globe Education, 1982. — 45p : ill,forms ; 36cm. — (Science horizons. Level 1) Published for West Sussex County Council ISBN 0-333-32156-1 (pbk) : Unpriced B82-38808

641.3′0094 — Food: Western European dishes — *Polyglot dictionaries*

The **Pocket** gourmet : instant menu translator. — London : Foulsham, c1982. — 128p ; 16cm Contents: France / Catherine Manac′h — Germany / Hans & Gabbi Jacobi — Italy / Simonetta Vigni — Spain / Consuelo de Urcola ISBN 0-572-01164-4 (pbk) : £1.75 B82-26930

641.3′009411 — Food: Scottish dishes

Fisher, Joan. Food and drink / Joan Fisher ; drawings by John M. Laing. — Edinburgh : Spurbooks, c1982. — 64p : ill ; 19cm. — (Introducing Scotland) Bibliography: p63. — Includes index ISBN 0-7157-2080-5 (pbk) : £1.25 B82-20596

641.3′00944 — Food: French dishes

Reader′s Digest/Perrier guide to the French menu / contributor and advisor Silvino Trompetto ; contributing editor Lizzie Boyd. — London : Reader′s Digest Association, c1982. — 63p : ill(some col.),1col.map,1col.port ; 21cm ISBN 0-340-28531-1 (pbk) : £2.50 B82-40756

641.3′00944 — Food: French dishes — *Encyclopaedias*

Sharman, Fay. The taste of France : a dictionary of French food & wine / Fay Sharman ; consultant editors Brian Chadwick and Klaus Boehm ; designed and illustrated by Bryan Reading. — [London] : Macmillan Reference Books, 1982. — 320p : ill(some col.),maps ; 23cm Maps on lining papers ISBN 0-333-32006-9 : £5.95 B82-37757

641.3′00945 — Food: Italian dishes

Reader′s Digest/Perrier guide to the Italian menu / contributor and advisor Simone Lavarini ; contributing editor Lizzie Boyd. — London : Reader′s Digest Association, c1982. — 63p : ill (some col.),1col.map,1col.port ; 21cm ISBN 0-340-28530-3 (pbk) : £2.50 B82-40757

641.3′009495 — Food: Greek dishes

Reader′s Digest/Perrier guide to the Greek menu / contributor Claudia Roden ; contributing editor Lizzie Boyd. — London : Reader′s Digest Association, c1982. — 63p : ill(some col.),1col.port ; 21cm ISBN 0-340-28532-x (pbk) : £2.50 B82-40754

641.3′00951 — Food: Chinese dishes

Reader′s Digest/Perrier guide to the Chinese menu / contributor and advisor Kenneth Lo ; contributing editor Lizzie Boyd. — London : Reader′s Digest Association, c1982. — 63p : ill (some col.,1col.port ; 21cm ISBN 0-340-28534-6 (pbk) : £2.50 B82-40755

641.3′00954 — Food: Indian dishes

Reader′s Digest/Perrier guide to the Indian menu / contributor and advisor Madhur Jaffrey ; contributing editor Lizzie Boyd. — London : Reader′s Digest Association, c1982. — 63p : ill (some col.),1col.port ; 21cm ISBN 0-340-28533-8 (pbk) : £2.50 B82-40758

641.30'2 — Spirulina. Nutritional aspects
Hanssen, Maurice. Spirulina. — Wellingborough : Thorsons, Nov.1981. — [64]p
ISBN 0-7225-0742-9 (pbk) : £0.75 : CIP entry B81-34210

641.3'31 — Bread — *For children*
Rutland, Jonathan. Bread / J.P. Rutland ; illustrations Robery [i.e. Robert] Geary. — New ed. — London : Watts, c1982. — 48p : col.ill ; 22cm. — (Focus on food)
Previous ed.: published as A first look at bread. 1972. — Includes index
ISBN 0-85166-966-2 : £2.99 B82-23298

641.3'36 — Sugar — *For children*
Lucas, Angela. A spoonful of sugar / Angela and Derek Lucas. — Hove : Wayland, 1982. — 32p : col.ill ; 19x24cm. — (Origins)
ISBN 0-85340-940-4 : £3.25 B82-31031

Pitt, Valerie, *1939-*. Sugar / Valerie Pitt ; illustrations Anne Knight. — New ed. — London : Watts, c1982. — 48p : col.ill,2col.maps ; 22cm. — (Focus on food)
Previous ed.: 1974. — Includes index
ISBN 0-85166-975-1 : £2.99 B82-23299

641.3'36 — Sweeteners — *Conference proceedings*
Nutritive sweeteners / edited by G.G. Birch and K.J. Parker. — London : Applied Science, c1982. — ix,316p : ill ; 23cm
Conference papers. — Includes index
ISBN 0-85334-997-5 : £29.00 : CIP rev. B81-34787

641.3'372 — Tea
Anderson, Kenneth, *19---*. The pocket guide to coffees and teas / Kenneth Anderson. — London : Muller, 1982. — 136p : ill,maps ; 23cm
Includes index
ISBN 0-584-95014-4 (pbk) : £2.95
Also classified at 641.3'373 B82-32701

Wright, Carol. The pocket book of tea and coffee / Carol Wright. — London : Evans, 1982. — 125p : ill ; 17cm
Includes index
ISBN 0-237-45586-2 (pbk) : £1.95 : CIP rev.
Also classified at 641.3'373 B81-25781

641.3'372 — Tea — *For children*
Langley, Andrew. A cup of tea / Andrew Langley. — Hove : Wayland, 1982. — 32p : col.ill,1col.map ; 19x24cm. — (Origins)
Bibliography: p32
ISBN 0-85340-942-0 : £3.25 B82-28026

Smith, Michael, *1929-*. Tea / by Michael Smith ; illustrated by David Palmer and Roger Hall. — Loughborough : Ladybird, c1981. — 51p : col.ill,1col.map ; 18cm. — (A Ladybird leader)
Text and col. ill on lining papers. — Includes index
ISBN 0-7214-0652-1 : £0.50 B82-16032

641.3'373 — Coffee
Anderson, Kenneth, *19---*. The pocket guide to coffees and teas / Kenneth Anderson. — London : Muller, 1982. — 136p : ill,maps ; 23cm
Includes index
ISBN 0-584-95014-4 (pbk) : £2.95
Primary classification 641.3'372 B82-32701

Wright, Carol. The pocket book of tea and coffee / Carol Wright. — London : Evans, 1982. — 125p : ill ; 17cm
Includes index
ISBN 0-237-45586-2 (pbk) : £1.95 : CIP rev.
Primary classification 641.3'372 B81-25781

641.3'383 — Spices
Heal, Carolyn. Cooking with spices. — Newton Abbot : David & Charles, Feb.1983. — [208]p
ISBN 0-7153-8369-8 : £8.95 : CIP entry B82-39446

Spices. — London : Longman, Apr.1981. — (Tropical agriculture series)
Vol.1. — [560]p
ISBN 0-582-46811-6 : £33.00 : CIP entry B81-03827

Spices / J.W. Purseglove ... [et al.]. — London : Longman. — (Tropical agriculture series)
Vol.2. — 1981. — p.447-813 : ill ; 23cm
Includes bibliographies and index
ISBN 0-582-46342-4 : £20.00 : CIP rev. B81-03826

641.3'526 — Garlic
Richardson, Rosamond. The little garlic book. — Loughton : Piatkus, Nov.1982. — [64]p
ISBN 0-86188-211-3 : £1.95 : CIP entry B82-26064

641.3'5643 — Capsicums
Berriedale-Johnson, Michelle. The little pepper book. — Loughton : Piatkus, Nov.1982. — [64]p
ISBN 0-86188-215-6 : £1.95 : CIP entry B82-26063

641.3'5'7 — Herbs
Rutherford, Meg. A pattern of herbs. — London : Allen & Unwin, May 1981. — [152]p
Originally published: 1975
ISBN 0-04-635011-x (pbk) : £2.95 : CIP entry B81-04348

641.3'57 — Herbs
Sanecki, Kay N., *1922-*. Discovering herbs / Kay N. Sanecki. — 3rd ed. — Princes Risborough : Shire, 1982. — 64p ; 18cm
Previous ed.: 1973. — Includes index
ISBN 0-85263-586-9 (pbk) : £1.25 B82-31008

641.3'57 — Herbs — *Quotations — Collections*
A Calendar of herbs : a diary for every year / compiled and illustrated by Yvonne Skargon. — London : Scolar, 1978 (1979 [printing]). — [77]p : ill ; 21cm
ISBN 0-85967-556-4 : £2.25 B82-24189

641.3'57 — Herbs. Use
Eagle, Robert. Herbs, useful plants / Robert Eagle. — London : BBC, 1981. — 96p : ill,ports ; 21cm
"This book is published in conjunction with the BBC radio series Herbs, useful plants, first broadcast on Radio 4 in Autumn 1981" - t.p. verso. — Bibliography: p93-94. — Includes index
ISBN 0-563-16497-2 (pbk) : £2.50 B82-01468

Painter, Gillian. A garden of old-fashioned and unusual herbs. — London : Hodder & Stoughton, Sept.1982. — [268]p
ISBN 0-340-27224-4 : £14.95 : CIP entry B82-18791

641.3'57 — Herbs. Use — *Manuals*
Law, Donald. The concise herbal encyclopedia. — Edinburgh : Bartholomew, Jan.1982. — [256]p
Originally published: 1973
ISBN 0-7028-8091-4 (pbk) : £4.95 : CIP entry B81-38290

641.3'7 — Dairy products
A Handbook of dairy foods / [National Dairy Council]. — 5th ed. — London : National Dairy Council, 1982. — 67p : ill(some col.) ; 26cm
Previous ed.: 1979. — Text on inside front cover. — Bibliography: p67
ISBN 0-902748-30-0 (pbk) : Unpriced B82-35781

641.3'71 — Milk — *For children*
Rutland, Jonathan. Milk / J.P. Rutland ; illustrations Norma Crockford. — New ed. — London : Watts, c1982. — 48p : ill(some col.) ; 22cm. — (Focus on food)
Previous ed.: published as A first look at milk. 1972. — Includes index
ISBN 0-85166-973-5 : £2.99 B82-23295

641.3'72 — Butter — *For children*
Hinds, Lorna. Butter and margarine / Lorna Hinds ; illustrations Lorraine Calaora. — New ed. — London : Watts, c1982. — 489p : ill (some col.),2col.ports ; 22cm. — (Focus on food)
Previous ed: 1977. — Includes index
ISBN 0-85166-967-0 : £2.99
Also classified at 664'.32 B82-23296

641.3'73 — Cheeses — *For children*
Pitt, Valerie, *1939-*. Cheese / Valerie Pitt ; illustrations Christine Sharr. — New ed. — London : Watts, c1982. — 47p : col.ill,1map ; 22cm. — (Focus on food)
Previous ed.: published as A first look at cheese. 1973. — Includes index
ISBN 0-85166-968-9 : £2.99 B82-23294

641.3'73'0321 — Cheeses — *Encyclopaedias*
Carr, Sandy. The Mitchell Beazley pocket guide to cheese / Sandy Carr. — London : Mitchell Beazley, 1981. — 144p : ill,maps ; 20cm
Includes index
ISBN 0-85533-359-6 : £3.95 B82-01924

Ensrud, Barbara. The pocket guide to cheese / Barbara Ensrud. — London : Muller, 1981. — vi,138p : col.ill,maps ; 23cm
Includes index
ISBN 0-584-95002-0 (pbk) : £2.95 B82-08810

641.3'73'0942 — English cheeses
Rance, Patrick. The great British cheese book / Patrick Rance ; [illustrations by Chris and Hilary Evans]. — London : Macmillan, 1982. — viii,168p : ill,maps ; 23cm
Bibliography: p161-162. — Includes index
ISBN 0-333-28840-8 : £8.95 B82-39993

641.3'7541 — Food: Eggs — *For children*
Hinds, Lorna. Eggs / Lorna Hinds. — New ed. — London : Watts, c1982. — 48p : ill(some col.) ; 22cm. — (Focus on food)
Previous ed.: 1975. — Includes index
ISBN 0-85166-971-9 : £2.99 B82-23297

641.4 — Food. Preservation
Developments in food preservation. — London : Applied Science, c1981. — (The Developments series)
1 / edited by Stuart Thorne. — Oct.1981. — xii,272p : ill ; 23cm
Includes index
ISBN 0-85334-979-7 : £30.00 : CIP rev. B81-25842

641.4 — Food. Preservation — *Amateurs' manuals*
Dewey, Mariel. 12 months harvest / basic research and text, Mariel Dewey ; coordinating editor, A. Cort Sinnes ; photography, Clyde Childress ; special consultants Janeth Nix and Lawrence Siegel. — Edinburgh : Bartholomew, 1980, c1975. — 95p : col.ill,col.ports ; 29cm
Originally published: San Francisco : Ortho Books, C1975. — Includes index
ISBN 0-7028-8300-x : £6.95 : CIP rev. B80-04286

641.4'53 — Food. Deep freezing. Use of small freezers — *Amateurs' manuals*
Norwak, Mary. Mary Norwak's guide to home freezing. — London : Ward Lock, 1982. — 224p,[32]p of plates : ill(some col.) ; 26cm
Includes index
ISBN 0-7063-6194-6 : £7.95 : CIP rev. B82-04617

641.5 — COOKERY

641.5 — Cookery — *For African students*
Ndungi, Harriet Karura. Food and nutrition for schools and colleges / Harriet Karura Ndungi ; edited by S.M. Passmore and V. Williams. — London : Evans, 1982. — vi,218p : ill ; 22cm
Includes index
ISBN 0-237-50460-x (pbk) : Unpriced B82-11013

641.5 — Cookery — *Manuals*
Allison, Sonia. A pleasure to cook. — London : Hamilton, Sept.1982. — [256]p
ISBN 0-241-10843-8 : £8.95 : CIP entry B82-18836

Aziz, Khalid, *1953-*. Cooking with Khalid : from Look north / Khalid Aziz. — London : British Broadcasting Corporation, 1981. — 64p : ill ; 20cm
ISBN 0-563-20010-3 (pbk) : £1.25 B82-00831

641.5 — Cookery — *Manuals* *continuation*

Beard, James. James Beard's Theory and practice of good cooking / in collaboration with José Wilson ; illustrations by Karl Stueckle n. — Harmondsworth : Penguin, 1981, c1977. — 430p : ill ; 20cm. — (Penguin handbooks)
Originally published: New York : Knopf, 1977. — Includes index
ISBN 0-14-046331-3 (pbk) : £3.95 B82-07290

Cadogan, Mary. Prepare to cook : basic cooking skills illustrated step by step / Mary Cadogan. — [London] : Peter Lowe, 1981. — 196p : ill (some col.) ; 28cm
Includes index
ISBN 0-85654-632-1 : £6.95 B82-26978

Follows, Eileen. First steps in kitchencraft / Eileen Follows. — Newton Abbot : David & Charles, c1982. — 48p : ill ; 21cm
ISBN 0-7153-8131-8 (pbk) : £1.95 : CIP rev. B82-01181

Hemming, Sukie. Cooking for profit. — London : Norman & Hobhouse, June 1982. — [196]p
ISBN 0-906908-68-x (pbk) : £3.95 : CIP entry B82-17234

Waldegrave, Caroline. Basic cooking skills / Caroline Waldegrave ; with an introduction by Prue Leith. — Cambridge : Published for J. Sainsbury Ltd. by Woodhead-Faulkner, c1981. — 40p : ill ; 21cm. — (Sainsbury's food guides ; no.9)
Cover title
£0.30 (pbk) B82-00832

641.5 — Cookery — *Manuals — For schools*

Creese, Angela. Revision notes for 'O' Level and CSE cookery. — 3rd ed. — London : Bell & Hyman, Oct.1981. — [96]p. — (Allman revision notes)
Previous ed.: 1974
ISBN 0-7135-2207-0 (pbk) : £1.50 : CIP entry B81-30464

Forsyth, Anne. Beginning cookery. — London : Bell & Hyman, Nov.1981. — [80]p
ISBN 0-7135-1275-x (pbk) : £2.95 : CIP entry B81-30387

McGrath, Helen. All about food : practical home economics / Helen McGrath. — Oxford : Oxford University Press, 1982. — 224p : ill ; 25cm
Bibliography: p221. — Includes index
ISBN 0-19-832713-7 (pbk) : £3.25 B82-18413

Williams, Joy, *1955-*. Feeding the family : recipes and presentation of meals / Joy Williams. — London : Batsford Academic and Educational, 1982. — 72p : ill ; 26cm
Includes index
ISBN 0-7134-4081-3 : £5.50 : CIP rev. B82-01208

641.5 — Cookery. Styles — *Conference proceedings*

Oxford symposium 1981 : national & regional styles of cookery : proceedings / [editor Alan Davidson]. — London : Prospect Books, c1981. — 3v. : ill ; 29cm
ISBN 0-907325-07-6 (pbk) : Unpriced
ISBN 0-907325-08-4 (2)
ISBN 0-907325-09-2 (3) B82-03062

641.5 — Cookery. Techniques — *Manuals*

Masterclass : expert lessons in kitchen skills. — London : Norman & Hobhouse, July 1982. — [160]p
ISBN 0-906908-46-9 (cased) : £6.50 : CIP entry
ISBN 0-906908-80-9 (pbk) : £3.95 B82-16235

641.5 — Food: Dishes for picnics — *Recipes*

Gurney, Jackie. The National Trust book of picnics / Jackie Gurney. — Newton Abbot : David & Charles, c1982. — 96p : ill,1facsim,2ports ; 22cm
Includes index
ISBN 0-7153-8099-0 : £4.50 : CIP rev. B82-04865

641.5 — Food — *Recipes*

Allen, Myrtle. The Ballymaloe cookbook / by Myrtle Allen ; drawings by Mel Calman ; introduction by Len Deighton. — London : Eyre Methuen, 1981, c1977. — 175p : ill ; 20cm
Originally published: Ireland : Agri, 1977. — Includes index
ISBN 0-413-48940-x (pbk) : £3.95 B82-17574

Anthony, Patrick. Patrick's pantry : recipes to remember — / by Patrick Anthony. — Norwich : Published by Jarrold Colour Publications for Anglia Television, c1981. — 16p ; 18x21cm
Cover title
ISBN 0-7117-0009-5 (pbk) : £1.00 B82-14883

The **Art** of home cooking / [created and written by the Stork Cookery Service]. — Burgess Hill (Sussex House, Civic Way, Burgess Hill, West Sussex) : Stork Cookery Service, [1982]. — 174p : ill(some col.) ; 21cm
Cover title. — Includes index
Unpriced (pbk) B82-25551

Beeton, *Mrs*. [Mrs Beeton's cookery and household management]. Mrs Beeton's everyday cookery. — London : Ward Lock, Oct.1982. — [632]p
ISBN 0-7063-6224-1 : £9.95 : CIP entry
Primary classification 640 B82-23187

Beeton, *Mrs*. Mrs Beeton's cookery for all / [edited by Susan Dixon]. — London : Ward Lock, 1982. — 455p,[2]p of plates : ill(some col.) ; 26cm
Includes index
ISBN 0-7063-6135-0 : £6.95 : CIP rev. B82-12906

Berry, Mary, *1935-*. Mary Berry's recipes from home & abroad. — London : Thames Macdonald, 1981. — 64p : ill(some col.) ; 27cm
Includes index
ISBN 0-356-07760-8 (pbk) : £2.25 B82-04273

Black, Maggie. The wholesome food cookbook. — Newton Abbot : David & Charles, Sept.1982. — [276]p
ISBN 0-7153-8229-2 : £9.95 : CIP entry B82-20379

Boxer, Arabella. First slice your cookbook / Arabella Boxer ; with decorations by Alan Cracknell. — New rev. ed. / wines recommended by Hugh Johnson. — [London] : Fontana, 1979. — [166]p : ill ; 30cm
Previous ed. Edinburgh : Nelson, 1964. — In slipcase. — Each page cut horizontally to form 3 sections. — Includes index
ISBN 0-00-635425-4 (spiral) : £7.59 B82-09528

Boxer, Arabella. Summer & winter cookbook / Arabella Boxer and Tessa Traeger. — London : Beazley, c1980. — 128,128p : ill(some col.) ; 30cm
Spine title. — Includes index. — Contents: The Vogue summer cookbook — The Vogue winter cookbook
ISBN 0-85533-216-6 : £12.50 B82-21517

Carrier, Robert. Cooking with Robert Carrier. — London : Hamlyn, c1982. — 432p : ill(some col.) ; 27cm
Includes index
ISBN 0-600-32301-3 : £10.95 B82-38005

Chaliand, Gerard. Food without frontiers / Gerard Chaliand ; with an introduction by Claudia Roden. — London : Pluto, 1981. — 120p ; 20cm. — (A Big red cookbook)
Includes index
ISBN 0-86104-351-0 (pbk) : £2.50 B82-20696

Chatto, James. The seducer's cookbook / James Chatto ; cartoons by Ffolkes. — Newton Abbot : David & Charles, c1981. — 63p : ill ; 22cm
Includes index
ISBN 0-7153-8201-2 : £3.95 : CIP rev. B81-28126

Christian, Glynn. The LBC radio cookbook. — London : Jill Norman and Hobhouse, Nov.1981. — [80]p
ISBN 0-906908-77-9 (pbk) : £1.95 : CIP entry B81-33634

Collins colour cookery. — London : Collins, 1982. — 144p : col.ill ; 21cm
Includes index
ISBN 0-00-411227-x (corrected) : £4.95 B82-39541

Connolly, M.. Hearty and crafty cooking / by M. Connolly & M. Blackburn. — [Manchester] ([53 Sunningdale Drive, Irlam, Manchester M30 6NJ]) : [Irlam Cadishead and District Local History Society], [c1981]. — 19leaves : ill ; 30cm
£0.20 (unbound) B82-16345

Davenport, Philippa. Cooking for family and friends. — London : Norman & Hobhouse, Oct.1982. — [288]p
ISBN 0-906908-32-9 : £7.95 : CIP entry B82-24608

Davenport, Philippa. Davenport's dishes. — London : Jill Norman, July 1981. — [160]p
ISBN 0-906908-47-7 (cased) : £6.50 : CIP entry
ISBN 0-906908-48-5 (pbk) : £3.50 B81-15898

The **Devonair** cookbook. — Exeter : Webb & Bower, Nov.1982. — [64]p
ISBN 0-906671-31-0 (pbk) : £0.99 : CIP entry B82-26715

Ellis, Audrey. The great little cookbook : all you need to know about cooking in one book / Audrey Ellis. — London : Corgi, c1982. — 185p ; 18cm
Includes index
ISBN 0-552-11912-1 (pbk) : £1.25 B82-21600

Ellison, J. Audrey. [Colman's book of traditional British cookery]. Traditional British cookery. — London : Ward Lock, Sept.1982. — [104]p
Originally published: 1980
ISBN 0-7063-6228-4 (pbk) : £2.95 : CIP entry B82-19806

Friends of Eden Court recipe book. — Inverness (Eden Court Theatre, Inverness) : Friends of Eden Court, [1982?]. — 48p : ill ; 15x21cm
£1.00 (pbk) B82-23372

From Woman's weekly's kitchen. — London (King's Reach Tower, Stamford St., SE1 9LS) : IPC Magazines, c1982. — 192p : ill ; 17cm
Includes index
£0.60 (pbk) B82-23826

Gillie, Cecilia. Cecilia's cookbook. — London : Norman & Hobhouse, Aug.1982. — [224]p
ISBN 0-906908-67-1 : £6.95 : CIP entry B82-19292

Gillon, Jack. Le menu gastronomique : an interpretation of nouvelle cuisine / Jack Gillon. — Edinburgh : Macdonald, c1981. — 167p : ill ; 23cm
Bibliography: p162. — Includes index
ISBN 0-904265-60-9 : £7.95 B82-05917

Glayva clans cook book : favourite family recipes of Scotland's clan chiefs / compiled by Wendy Jones ; foreword by the Earl of Elgin and Kincardine. — Edinburgh : Macdonald Publishers, c1981. — 144p : ill(some col.) ; 28cm
Includes index
ISBN 0-904265-47-1 : £8.95 B82-05323

Hambro, Nathalie. Particular delights. — London : Jill Norman, Oct.1981. — [144]p
ISBN 0-906908-34-5 : £6.95 : CIP entry B81-27460

641.5 — Food — *Recipes* *continuation*

Harlech, Pamela. Practical guide to cooking, entertaining and household management / Pamela Harlech. — London : Macmillan, 1981. — xii,436p : ill ; 24cm
Bibliography: p420-422. — Includes index
ISBN 0-333-31002-0 : £9.95 B82-06696

Henrietta Barnett School book of favourite recipes / ... produced by the Class ′77 Committee of the Henrietta Barnett School PTA. — [London] ([London NW11]) : [The Committee], [1981]. — 55p : ill ; 30cm
Unpriced (spiral) B82-11078

Knott, Claire. Good food with menus planned / by Claire Knott ; illustrations by Olive Rollings. — Guildford (6, Hipley Court, Warren Rd., Guildford) : C. Knott, [1981]. — 170p : ill ; 27cm
Includes index
ISBN 0-9507795-0-4 : Unpriced B82-08155

The **Land** of spices : international cook book / edited by Oonagh Goode ; illustrated by Susan Hsuan (from early Christian manuscripts and mosaics). — Watford : St. Lukes Church, 1981. — 56p : ill ; 15x22cm
Limited ed. of 500 copies. — Includes index
ISBN 0-9507765-0-5 (spiral) : £1.25
B82-03056

Lane, Margaret, *1907-*. The Beatrix Potter country cookery book / Margaret Lane. — London : Warne, 1981. — 120p : ill(some col.) ; 19cm
Includes index
ISBN 0-7232-2777-2 : £4.95 B82-00862

Leith, Prudence. The best of Prue Leith / Prue Leith and Jean-Baptiste Reynaud. — London : Sphere, 1982, c1979. — 189p ; 20cm
Originally published: London : Dent, 1979. — Includes index
ISBN 0-7221-5471-2 (pbk) : £1.95 B82-33811

Leith, Prudence. Leith′s cookery course / Prudence Leith and Caroline Waldegrave. — [London] : Fontana
1: [Basic]. — 1979. — 512p : ill ; 20cm
Includes index
ISBN 0-00-636533-7 (pbk) : £2.95 B82-24419

Leith, Prudence. Leith′s cookery course / Prudence Leith and Caroline Waldegrave. — [London] : Fontana
2: [Intermediate]. — 1980 (1982 [printing]). — 349p : ill ; 20cm
Includes index
ISBN 0-00-636534-5 (pbk) : £2.50 B82-24422

Leith, Prudence. Leith′s cookery course / Prudence Leith and Caroline Waldegrave. — [London] : Fontana
3: [Advanced]. — 1980. — 364p : ill ; 20cm
Includes index
ISBN 0-00-636535-3 (pbk) : £2.95 B82-24420

Mercia mouth waterers / edited by Cate Bradford ; graphics by Sophie Gibberd. — Coventry : Midland Community Radio, 1981. — 128p : ill,1port ; 19cm
Includes index
ISBN 0-907873-00-6 (pbk) : Unpriced
B82-12964

Meredith, Mary. Cook with us / an invitation to excellence from Mary Meredith and her Cordon Bleu team ; recipes tested in the Woman and Home kitchen. — London : IPC Magazines, c1981. — 112p : ill(some col.) ; 30cm
Includes index
£0.75 (pbk) B82-14695

Mosimann, Anton. Cuisine à la carte / Anton Mosimann ; introduction by Quentin Crewe. — London : Northwood, 1981. — 304p,20p of plates : ill(some col.),ports(some col.) ; 26cm
Includes index
ISBN 0-7198-2814-7 : £12.95 B82-15203

Norman, Ursel. Super suppers : soup, salad and pasta / a collection of recipes by Ursel Norman ; designed and illustrated by Derek Norman. — London : Collins, 1982. — 176p : ill(chiefly col.) ; 28cm
Includes index
ISBN 0-00-411250-4 : £8.95
Also classified at 641.8′13 ; 641.8′3 ; 641.8′22
B82-38769

Parkes, Antoinette. The country weekend cookbook / Antoinette Parkes ; foreword by Margaret Lane ; drawings by John Bigg. — London : Collins, 1981. — 224p : ill ; 26cm
Includes index
ISBN 0-00-216318-7 : £12.00 : CIP rev.
B81-24586

Recipes from Charlwood : on the occasion of the 900th anniversary / edited by Helen de Courcy ; illustrated by Merida Drysdale ; introduction by Jean B. Coggan. — [Charlwood] : Charlwood Festival Committee, 1979 (1980 [printing]). — vi,89p : ill ; 21cm
ISBN 0-9506617-0-8 (pbk) : Unpriced
B82-01264

Rose, Evelyn. Quick, easy and delicious recipes for the first time cook. — London : Robson, Oct.1982. — [192]p
ISBN 0-86051-184-7 : £5.95 : CIP entry
B82-24139

Rosenthal, Sylvia. How cooking works : the indispensable kitchen handbook / Sylvia Rosenthal and Fran Shinagel ; illustrated by Cal Sacks and Ray Skibinski. — New York : Macmillan ; London : Collier Macmillan, c1981. — viii,600p : ill ; 25cm. — (A Tree Communications edition)
Includes index
ISBN 0-02-605090-0 : £9.95 B82-26387

Scottish eco cook book / Friends of the Earth Scotland. — 2nd ed. — Edinburgh : F.O.E. (Scotland), 1980. — 53p : ill ; 22cm
Cover title. — Previous ed.: 1978. — Text on inside covers. — Bibliography: p53
£0.50 (pbk) B82-25335

Skinner, Zena. Zena Skinner′s down to earth cookbook. — London : Robson, 1982. — 256p,[12]p of plates : ill(some col.) ; 24cm
ISBN 0-86051-159-6 : £7.95 : CIP rev.
B82-00341

Smith, Mari. Simple kitchen skills and recipes. — London : Edward Arnold, Jan.1982. — [64]p
ISBN 0-7131-0566-6 (pbk) : £1.75(non-net) : CIP entry B81-33886

Star recipes. — [Newcastle upon Tyne] ([Front St., Longbenton, Newcastle upon Tyne, NE12 8AE]) : Longbenton C. of E. First School, [1981?]. — 12p ; 30cm
Cover title
£0.50 (pbk) B82-07539

Tovey, John, *1933-*. Table talk with Tovey : a cook′s tour of his cullinary [sic] education / John Tovey ; photographs by Mick Duff ; drawings by Lorna Turpin. — London : Macdonald, 1981. — 191p,[16]p of plates : ill (some col.) ; 27cm
Includes index
ISBN 0-354-04722-1 : £9.95 B82-03492

West, Elizabeth. Kitchen in the hills : the hovel cookbook / Elizabeth West ; with line drawings by Una Lindsay. — London : Faber, 1981. — 184p : ill ; 23cm
Includes index
ISBN 0-571-11709-0 : £6.25 : CIP rev.
B81-28029

Whitlock, Kathleen. The compass cookbook / Kathleen Whitlock. — Bristol : Redcliffe, 1980. — 48p ; 18cm
ISBN 0-905459-33-4 (pbk) : £0.75 B82-21816

Whitlock, Kathleen. The new compass cookbook / Kathleen Whitlock. — Bristol : Redcliffe, 1981. — 47p : ill ; 18cm
ISBN 0-905459-40-7 (pbk) : £0.90 B82-21815

Wolter, Annette. Family cooking / Annette Wolter. — London : Hamlyn, c1982. — 79p : col.ill ; 26cm. — (Hamlyn kitchen shelf)
Translation of: Gesunde Küche für jeden Tag. — Includes index
ISBN 0-600-32284-x : £2.50 B82-32756

641.5 — Food — *Recipes — For children*

Burrow, Jackie. Fred′s round the world cook book / recipes by Jackie Burrow ; illustrated by Charlie Starkey. — London : Transworld, 1981. — [32]p : col.ill ; 28cm. — (A Carousel book)
Text and ill on inside covers. — Includes index
ISBN 0-552-54195-8 (pbk) : £0.95 B82-10268

Félix, Monique. Cookery : a first cook book / Monique Félix. — London : Evans, c1982. — 32p : chiefly col.ill ; 22cm. — (Busy books)
ISBN 0-237-45601-x : £2.25 B82-26261

First steps in cooking / illustrated by Dorothea Desmarowitz. — London : Ward Lock, c1981. — 47p : col.ill ; 30cm
Translation of: Kochbuch fuer Kinder. — Includes index
ISBN 0-7063-6081-8 : £2.95 : CIP rev.
B81-12879

John, Sue. How and why. — London : Methuen/Walker, Sept.1982. — [32]p
ISBN 0-416-06410-8 : £3.95 : CIP entry
B82-19238

John, Sue. Time to eat. — London : Methuen/Walker, Sept.1982. — [32]p
ISBN 0-416-06420-5 : £3.95 : CIP entry
B82-19239

Ridgway, Judy. 101 fun foods to make / Judy Ridgway ; illustrated by Gillian Chapman. — London : Hamlyn, 1982. — 157p : col.ill ; 22cm
ISBN 0-600-36647-2 : £2.95 B82-35838

Sewell, Elizabeth, *19---*. [My first cookbook]. My first ‘show me how’ cookbook / written by Elizabeth Sewell ; illustrated by Jan Howarth. — London : Dean : 1981, c1973. — 45p : ill ; 26cm
Originally published: 1975
ISBN 0-603-00257-9 : Unpriced B82-26756

Walt Disney′s Mickey Mouse cookbook. — London : W.H. Allen, 1981, c1975. — 70p : col.ill ; 29cm
ISBN 0-491-02994-2 : £4.95 B82-00114

641.5 — Food — *Recipes — For schools*

King, Aileen. Better cookery. — London : Bell & Hyman, Sept.1981. — [512]p
ISBN 0-7135-2053-1 (cased) : £4.95 : CIP entry
ISBN 0-7135-2055-8 (pbk) : £3.90 B81-28205

Silverton, Norma. Looking and cooking : simple step-by-step recipes / Norma Silverton. — London : Edward Arnold, 1981. — 30leaves : ill ; 28cm
Spirit duplicator masters
ISBN 0-7131-0575-5 (pbk) : £9.00 B82-08393

641.5′03′21 — Cookery — *Encyclopaedias*

Stobart, Tom. The cook′s encyclopaedia : ingredients & processes / Tom Stobart. — London : Papermac, 1982, c1980. — 463p ; 25cm
Originally published: London : Batsford, 1980
ISBN 0-333-33036-6 (pbk) : £5.95 B82-32228

641.5′0941 — Great Britain. Restaurants. Food — *Recipes*

The **Master** chefs of Britain recipe book : over 250 recipes from the Great Chefs of Britain / compiled with the cooperation of Carte Blanche. — Newton Abbot : David & Charles, c1981. — 192p,[16]p of plates : ill(some col.) ; 29cm
″A publication of the Master Chefs Institute″. — Includes index
ISBN 0-7153-8240-3 : £9.50 B82-07068

641.5'0941 — Great Britain. Rural regions. Restaurants. Food — *Recipes*

Kent, Elizabeth. Country cuisine : cooking with country chefs / Elizabeth Kent ; wines chosen by Jancis Robinson ; special illustrations by Jane Jamieson. — [London] : Fontana Paperbacks, 1981, c1980. — 415p : ill ; 20cm
Originally published: London : Sidgwick and Jackson, 1980. — Bibliography: p406. — Includes index
ISBN 0-00-635713-x (pbk) : £3.95 B82-02217

641.5'3 — Luncheons — *Recipes*

Berry, Mary. The perfect Sunday lunch. — London : Century Publishing, Oct.1982. — [224]p
ISBN 0-7126-0040-x : £6.95 : CIP entry
B82-23884

641.5'3 — Suppers — *Recipes*

Berry, Mary 19---. Fast suppers / by Mary Berry. — Loughton : Piatkus, 1982. — 192p : col.ill ; 26cm
Includes index
ISBN 0-86188-199-0 : £7.95 : CIP rev.
B82-21551

641.5'55 — Food: Dishes for deep freezing — *Recipes*

The **Freezer** cookbook / edited by Gill Edden & Wendy James ; home economist Gilly Cubitt. — London : Orbis, 1981. — 189p : col.ill ; 29cm
Includes index
ISBN 0-85613-353-1 (pbk) : Unpriced
B82-16627

641.5'55 — Food: Time-saving dishes — *Recipes*

Downing, Beryl. Quick cook : recipes in thirty minutes and under / Beryl Downing. — Harmondsworth : Penguin, 1981. — xviii,222p ; 20cm
Includes index
ISBN 0-14-046453-0 (pbk) : £1.50 B82-08033

Smith, Beverley Sutherland. A taste in time : Beverley Sutherland Smith's 60 minute menus / photographer Ray Joyce. — [London] : Windward, 1982, c1981. — 126p : col.ill ; 29cm
Includes index
ISBN 0-7112-0248-6 : £4.95 B82-28831

Stewart, Katie. Short cut cookbook / Katie Stewart. — London : Pan, 1981. — 203p : ill ; 20cm
Originally published: London : Hamlyn, 1979. — Includes index
ISBN 0-330-26507-5 (pbk) : £1.95 B82-04253

Wolter, Annette. Quick dishes / Annette Wolter. — London : Hamlyn, c1982. — 79p : col.ill ; 26cm. — (Hamlyn kitchen shelf)
Translation of: Die Raffinierte Schnellküche. — Originally published: in English as A meal in a minute. London : Nelson, 1974. — Includes index
ISBN 0-600-32286-6 : £2.50 B82-32757

641.5'55'0954 — Food: Indian time-saving dishes — *Recipes*

Pandya, Michael. Indian quick meals / Michael Pandya. — Cardiff : Preeti, c1981. — 56p : ill (some col.) ; 21cm
Includes index
ISBN 0-9507595-1-1 (pbk) : £2.25 B82-01466

641.5'622 — Children. Food — *Recipes*

Richardson, Rosamond. Cooking for kids / Rosamond Richardson ; illustrated by John Verney. — London : Norman, 1981. — 144p : ill ; 23cm
Includes index
ISBN 0-906908-40-x : £5.95 B82-36210

641.5'622 — Children. Food — *Recipes — For children*

Bouhuys, Mies. What's cooking in Spoon Street? / Mies Bouhuys ; illustrated by Tineke Schinkel ; translated by Marianne Velmans. — Harmondsworth : Puffin, 1982. — 91p : ill ; 18cm
Translation of: Alles kan in de Lepelstraat. — Includes index
ISBN 0-14-031211-0 (pbk) : £0.90 B82-22484

641.5'622 — Children, to 5 years. Food — *Recipes*

Growing up with good food / edited by Catherine Lewis ; foreword by Penelope Leach. — London : Unwin, 1982. — 124p ; 20cm
Originally published: Leeds : National Childbirth Trust, 1978. — Bibliography: p116-118. — Includes index
ISBN 0-04-641040-6 (pbk) : £1.95 : CIP rev.
B82-01534

641.5'63 — Chldren. Food — *Recipes — For dental health*

Recipes for healthier teeth / from the National Dairy Council in association with the General Dental Council. — London (John Princes St., W1M 0AP) : National Dairy Council in association with the General Dental Council, [1981]. — 19p : ill(some col.) ; 21cm
Cover title
Unpriced (pbk) B82-05806

641.5'63 — Food allergic persons. Food — *Recipes*

Carter, Patricia. An allergy cookbook : recipes free from eggs, milk, cheese, butter, wheat flour, chocolate, salt, sugar, baking powder and cornflour / by Patricia Carter. — Hornchurch : Ian Henry, 1981. — x,139p ; 21cm
Includes index
ISBN 0-86025-852-1 : £4.95 B82-11916

641.5'631 — Heart disease victims & multiple sclerosis victims. Food: Low fat dishes — *Recipes*

Forsythe, Elizabeth. The low-fat gourmet : a doctor's cookbook for heart disease and multiple sclerosis / Elizabeth Forsythe ; illustrations by Susan Neale. — London : Sphere, 1982, c1980. — 154p : ill ; 18cm
Originally published: London : Pelham, 1980. — Includes index
ISBN 0-7221-3604-8 (pbk) : £1.75 B82-36548

641.5'631 — Migraine sufferers. Food — *Recipes*

Wentworth, Josie A.. The migraine guide & cookbook / Josie A. Wentworth ; with an introduction by Katharina Dalton. — London : Corgi, 1982, c1981. — 220p : ill ; 18cm
Originally published: London : Sidgwick & Jackson, 1981. — Bibliography: p210-212. — Includes index
ISBN 0-552-11897-4 (pbk) : £1.50
Also classified at 616.8'57071 B82-18418

641.5'6314 — Diabetics. Food — *Recipes*

Budd, Martin. Diets to help diabetics. — Wellingborough : Thorsons, Feb.1983. — [64]p
ISBN 0-7225-0733-x (pbk) : £0.95 : CIP entry
B82-39276

Mann, Jim. The diabetics' diet book. — London : Martin Dunitz, Aug.1982. — [128]p. — (Positive health guide)
ISBN 0-906348-34-x (cased) : £5.95 : CIP entry
ISBN 0-906348-35-8 (pbk) : £2.95 B82-17230

641.5'6314'095 — Diabetics. Food: Oriental dishes — *Recipes*

Revell, Dorothy. Oriental cooking for the diabetic / Dorothy Revell. — Tokyo : Japan Publications ; Hemel Hempstead : International Book Distributors [distributor], 1981. — 160p ; 26cm
Includes index
ISBN 0-87040-492-x (pbk) : £5.93 B82-00032

641.5'632 — Food: Milkless dishes — *Recipes*

Zukin, Jane. Milk-free diet cookbook : cooking for the lactose intolerant / Jane Zukin ; foreword by Eugene A. Gelzayd. — New York : Sterling ; Poole (distributed by Blandford), c1982. — 155p ; 24cm
Includes index
ISBN 0-8069-5566-x (cased) : £7.95
ISBN 0-8069-5567-8 (lib.bdg)
ISBN 0-8069-7544-x (pbk) : £3.50 B82-21879

641.5'635 — Food: Low calorie dishes — *Recipes*

Prince, Francine. The dieter's gourmet cookbook : no sugar, no salt, low fat, low cholesterol / by Francine Prince. — London : Foulsham, c1981. — 160p,[8]p of plates : ill(some col.) ; 23cm
Originally published: New York : Cornerstone Library, 1979. — Includes index
ISBN 0-572-01142-3 : £6.95 B82-11864

Weight Watchers International cookbook / introduction by Jean Nidetch. — [London] : New English Library, c1977. — v,397p,[32]p of plates : col.ill ; 24cm
Includes index
ISBN 0-450-04868-3 : £6.95 B82-23387

Wolter, Annette. Low-calorie cooking / Annette Wolter. — London : Hamlyn, c1982. — 79p : col.ill ; 26cm. — (Hamlyn kitchen shelf)
Translation of: Die Mini-Kalorien-Küche. — Text on lining paper. — Includes index
ISBN 0-600-32285-8 : £2.50 B82-39411

641.5'635 — Slimmers. Food — *Recipes*

Pappas, Lou Seibert. [Gourmet cooking]. The slim gourmet / Lou Seibert Pappas. — Feltham : Hamlyn, 1982, c1977. — 185p : ill ; 18cm. — (Hamlyn kitchen library)
Originally published as: Gourmet cooking. Reading, Mass. : Addison-Wesley, 1977 ; London : Evans, 1980. — Includes index
ISBN 0-600-20449-9 (pbk) : £1.50 B82-31645

Raymond, Julie. Eat and grow slim / Julie Raymond. — Staplehurst : Juniper, c1982. — 34p ; 15cm
Cover title
ISBN 0-9508051-0-6 (pbk) : Unpriced
B82-40012

Yudkin, John. Eat well, slim well / John Yudkin. — London : Collins with Davis-Poynter, 1982. — 64p ; 22cm
ISBN 0-00-216396-9 (pbk) : £2.25 : CIP rev.
B82-01701

641.5'636 — Vegans. Food — *Recipes*

Leneman, Leah. Vegan cooking. — Wellingborough : Thorsons, Oct.1982. — [128]p
ISBN 0-7225-0753-4 (pbk) : £1.50 : CIP entry
B82-24241

641.5'636 — Vegetarians. Food: Dishes using natural foods — *Recipes*

Shulman, Martha Rose. The vegetarian feast / by Martha Rose Shulman ; illustrations by Beverly Leathers. — Wellingborough : Thorsons, 1982, c1979. — xii,319p : ill ; 22cm
Includes index
ISBN 0-7225-0758-5 (pbk) : £3.95 : CIP rev.
B82-07605

641.5'636 — Vegetarians. Food — *Recipes*

Elliot, Rose. [Vegetarian dishes of the world]. A foreign flavour : vegetarian dishes of the World / Rose Elliot. — [London] : Fontana, 1982, c1981. — 352p ; 20cm
Originally published: London : Collins, 1981. — Includes index
ISBN 0-00-635728-8 (pbk) : £2.95 B82-39015

Garber, Sonja. A taste of health : a vegetarian recipe book / Sonja Garber. — London : Hale, 1981. — 168p ; 22cm
ISBN 0-7091-9196-0 : £5.25 B82-03290

Ridge, Judy. The vegetarian gourmet / Judy Ridgway. — London : Ward Lock, 1979 (1982 [printing]). — 167p : ill(some col.) ; 25cm
Bibliography: p163. — Includes index
ISBN 0-7063-6176-8 (pbk) : £3.95 B82-21365

Sherman, Kay Lynne. The Findhorn family cook book : a vegetarian cookbook which celebrates the wholeness of life / by Kay Lynne Sherman. — Findhorn : Findhorn Publications, 1981. — 152p : ill,ports ; 24cm
Includes index
ISBN 0-905249-50-x (pbk) : £3.50 B82-09518

Thorpe, Susan. The four seasons wholefood cookbook. — Wellingborough : Thorsons, Oct.1982. — [160]p
ISBN 0-7225-0748-8 : £7.95 : CIP entry
B82-25767

641.5636'09495 — Vegetarians. Food: Greek dishes — *Recipes*

Chaitow, Alkmini. Greek vegetarian cooking. — Wellingborough : Thorsons, Aug.1982. — [128]p
ISBN 0-7225-0725-9 (pbk) : £3.50 : CIP entry
B82-15848

641.5′637 — Food: Dishes using natural foods — *Recipes*

Evans, Brenda. Wholefood for beginners : easy recipes and hints / by Brenda Evans. — Oulton : Teecoll, 1980. — 81p : ill ; 22cm
Includes index
ISBN 0-7109-0002-3 : Unpriced B82-36934

Hunt, Janet, *1942-*. Simple and speedy whole food cookery. — Wellingborough : Thorsons, Oct.1982. — [128]p
ISBN 0-7225-0752-6 (pbk) : £1.50 : CIP entry B82-23030

Pfeiffer, Carl C.. [Dr. Pfeiffer′s total nutrition]. Total nutrition / Carl C. Pfeiffer and Jane Banks. — London : Granada, 1982, c1980. — 161p ; 21cm
Originally published: New York : Simon and Schuster, 1980. — Includes index
ISBN 0-246-11686-2 : £4.95 : CIP rev.
Primary classification 613.2′8 B81-35797

641.5′637 — Food: High-fibre dishes — *Recipes*

Westland, Pamela. The high-fibre cookbook : recipes for good health. — London : Dunitz, June 1982. — [160]p. — (Positive health guide)
Also published as: Recipes for good health. London : Dunitz, 1982
ISBN 0-906348-33-1 (pbk) : £2.50 : CIP entry B82-10893

Westland, Pamela. Recipes for good health : the high-fibre cookbook. — London : Dunitz, June 1982. — [160]p. — (Positive health guide)
Also published as: The high-fibre cookbook. London : Dunitz, 1982
ISBN 0-906348-32-3 : £9.95 : CIP entry B82-10892

641.5′637 — Health food breakfasts — *Recipes*

Holme, Rachael. Better breakfasts : a healthy wholefood start to the day / by Rachael Holme ; illustrated by Clive Birch. — Wellingborough : Thorsons, 1982. — 160p : ill ; 22cm. — (A Thorsons wholefood cookbook)
Includes index
ISBN 0-7225-0710-0 (pbk) : £3.50 : CIP rev. B82-13079

641.5′637 — Health food dishes — *Recipes*

Burrow, Jackie. Health food cookbook / Jackie Burrow & Mary Norwak. — London : Octopus, 1979. — 160p : ill(some col.) ; 29cm
Ill on lining papers. — Includes index
ISBN 0-7064-0937-x : £3.95 B82-08625

Canter, David. The Cranks recipe book. — London : Dent, Sept.1982. — [224]p
ISBN 0-460-04416-8 : £12.95 : CIP entry B82-19697

Forsythe, Elizabeth. The high-fibre gourmet. — London : Pelham, Jan.1983. — [156]p
ISBN 0-7207-1420-6 : £7.95 : CIP entry B82-32625

Recipes : eating for a healthy life / [prepared by Health Service dieticians in the Oxfordshire area]. — [Great Britain] : [Oxford Area Health Authority?], [1982?]. — 1folded sheet([8]p) ; 21cm
Unpriced (unbound) B82-21817

641.5′64 — Food: Seasonal dishes — *Recipes*

The **Cookery** year. — London : Reader′s Digest, c1973 (1982 [printing]). — 439p : ill(some col.) ; 22x27cm
Text on lining papers. — Includes index
£11.95 B82-31585

Duff, Gail. The countryside yearbook : a cook′s calendar / Gail Duff ; illustrated by Linda Garland ; with line illustrations by Roger Garland. — Dorchester : Prism, 1982. — 191p : ill(some col.) ; 26cm
ISBN 0-907061-28-1 : £5.95
Primary classification 641.6 B82-21267

Ellis, Audrey. Cooking through the year / Audrey Ellis. — London : Hamlyn, c1982. — 192p : ill(some col.) ; 29cm
Includes index
ISBN 0-600-32276-9 : £7.95 B82-36862

Payne, Clare. Seasonal menus for home entertaining / Clare Payne. — Cambridge : Woodhead-Faulkner for J. Sainsbury, c1982. — 96p : ill(chiefly col.),1port ; 19cm. — (A Sainsbury cookbook)
£0.75 (pbk) B82-29519

641.5′66 — Food: Christmas dishes — *Recipes*

Dimbleby, Josceline. Cooking for Christmas / Josceline Dimbleby. — Cambridge : Woodhead-Faulkner for J. Sainsbury Limited, 1980, c1978. — 96p : ill(some col.),1port ; 19cm. — (A Sainsbury cookbook)
ISBN 0-85941-101-x (pbk) : £0.75 B82-09157

Holder, Judith. Christmas fare. — Exeter : Webb & Bower, Nov.1981. — [64]p
ISBN 0-906671-34-5 : £3.95 : CIP entry
Primary classification 769.5 B81-30976

641.5′66 — Food — *Recipes* — *For church year*

The **Christian** year cookbook : a collection of recipes for home and parish use / compiled by Félicité Nesham and Helen Kilminster ; with illustrations by Barbara Cooper. — London : Mowbray, 1980. — 70p : ill ; 21cm
Includes index
ISBN 0-264-66735-2 (pbk) : £1.95 B82-17997

641.5′676 — Food: Kosher dishes — *Recipes*

Greenberg, Florence. Florence Greenberg′s Jewish cookbook. — Rev. and updated ed. — London : Published in association with the Jewish Chronicle [by] Hamlyn, 1980 (1982 [printing]). — 213p ; 20cm. — (Hamlyn Kitchen library)
Includes index
ISBN 0-600-20460-x (pbk) : £1.50 B82-14162

641.5′68 — Food: Dishes for buffets — *Recipes*

Teubner, Christian. The best of salads and buffet cookery / Christian Teubner and Annette Wolter ; photography by Christian Teubner. — London : Hamlyn, 1982. — 240p : ill(some col.) ; 29cm
Translation of: Kalte Köstlichkeiten wie noch nie. — Includes index
ISBN 0-600-32281-5 : £8.95 B82-32787

641.5′68 — Food: Dishes for dinner parties & dishes for supper parties — *Recipes*

Hume, Rosemary. Cordon bleu cookbook : recipes for freezing and entertaining / by Rosemary Hume and Muriel Downes. — London : Macdonald, 1982, c1977. — 128p : col.ill ; 31cm
Includes index
ISBN 0-356-08693-3 : £4.95 B82-38004

641.5′68 — Food: Dishes for seasonal festivals — *Recipes*

Paston-Williams, Sara. The National Trust book of Christmas & festive day recipes / Sara Paston-Williams. — Newton Abbot : David & Charles, c1981. — 128p : ill ; 22cm
Includes index
ISBN 0-7153-8100-8 : £4.50 : CIP rev. B81-22503

641.5′68 — Food: Dishes for special occasions — *Recipes*

Allison, Sonia. Making gifts with food. — Newton Abbot : David & Charles, Oct.1982. — [64]p
ISBN 0-7153-8264-0 : £2.95 : CIP entry B82-23009

641.5′68 — Food: Dishes for special occasions — *Recipes* — *For children*

John, Sue. Special days. — London : Methuen/Walker, May 1982. — [32]p
ISBN 0-416-06390-x : £3.95 : CIP entry B82-06751

641.5′68 — Food: Party dishes — *Recipes*

Leith, Prudence. Cooking for friends. — Sevenoaks : New English Library, Jan.1983. — [256]p
ISBN 0-450-05371-7 (pbk) : £1.75 : CIP entry B82-36136

Rose, Evelyn. The entertaining cookbook / Evelyn Rose. — [London] : Fontana, 1982, c1980. — 606p ; 20cm
Originally published: London : Robson, 1980. — Includes index
ISBN 0-00-635502-1 (pbk) : £3.95 B82-24421

641.5′68 — Food: Time-saving party dishes — *Recipes*

Pizzey, Erin. The slut′s cook book / Erin Pizzey ; illustrations by Anny White. — London : Macdonald, 1981. — 153p : ill ; 22cm
Includes index
ISBN 0-354-04724-8 : £6.95 B82-01022

641.5′7 — Cookery — *Manuals* — *For chefs*

Wolfe, Kenneth C.. Cooking the professional way / Kenneth C. Wolfe. — Rev. ed. — New York ; London : Van Nostrand Reinhold, 1982. — viii,358p,[8]p of plates : ill(some col.) ; 24cm
Previous ed.: published as Cooking for the professional chef. New York ; London : Van Nostrand Reinhold, 1976. — Includes index
ISBN 0-442-23887-8 : £14.40 B82-24924

641.5′75 — Food: Dishes for travellers — *Recipes*

Holt, Geraldene. Geraldene Holt′s Travelling food : a practical guide to over 200 movable feasts / illustrations by Prue Theobalds. — London : Hodder and Stoughton, 1982. — 224p : ill ; 22cm
Includes index
ISBN 0-340-27222-8 (pbk) : £4.95 : CIP rev. B82-04700

641.5′78 — Outdoor cookery - *Manuals*

Roden, Claudia. Picnic. — London : 90 Great Russell St., WC1B 3PY : J.U. Norman, Apr.1981. — [352]p
ISBN 0-906908-11-6 : CIP entry B81-04309

641.5′78 — Outdoor dishes — *Recipes*

Roden, Claudia. Picnic : the complete guide to outdoor food / Claudia Roden ; illustrated by Linda Kitson. — Harmondsworth : Penguin, 1982, c1981. — 381p : ill ; 20cm. — (Penguin handbooks)
Originally published: London : J.U. Norman, 1981. — Bibliography: p367-369. — Includes index
ISBN 0-14-046323-2 (pbk) : £2.95 B82-30256

641.5′782′0243694 — Camping. Cookery — *Manuals* — *For scouting*

Hazlewood, Rex. Camp catering and cooking / by Rex Hazlewood ; with drawings by Anthony Birch. — 4th ed. — Glasgow : Brown, Son & Ferguson, 1982. — viii,70p : ill ; 17cm
Previous ed.: 1977. — Includes index
ISBN 0-85174-423-0 (pbk) : £2.50 B82-24303

641.5′8 — Cookery. Influence of use of coal

Roberts, Hugh D.. Downhearth to bar grate : an illustrated account of the evolution in cooking due to the use of coal instead of wood / Hugh D. Roberts. — Avebury : Wiltshire Folk Life Society, c1981. — 84p : ill ; 24cm
Cover title. — Bibliography: p81. — Includes index
ISBN 0-907756-00-x (pbk) : £3.00 B82-08050

641.5′8 — Food: Dishes prepared using woks — *Recipes*

Solomon, Charmaine. Wok cookbook / text and recipes by Charmaine Solomon ; photographs by Reg Morrisson. — Leicester : Windward, 1981 (1982 [printing]). — 128p : ill(some col.) ; 29cm
Includes index
ISBN 0-7112-0210-9 : £3.95 B82-21259

641.5′87 — Food: Dishes prepared using pressure cookers — *Recipes*

Todd, Jane. The Hamlyn pressure cookbook / Jane Todd. — [London] : Hamlyn Paperbacks, 1979, c1976. — 171p : ill ; 18cm. — (Hamlyn kitchen library)
Originally published: Feltham : Hamlyn, 1976. — Includes index
ISBN 0-600-37229-4 (pbk) : £0.85 B82-05564

Yates, Annette. The Tower pressure cook book / by Annette Yates. — [New ed.]. — London : Foulsham, c1981. — 120p : ill(some col.) ; 23cm. — ([Know-how books])
Previous ed.: 1977. — Includes index
ISBN 0-572-01146-6 : £4.50 B82-11865

641.5′88 — Food: Dishes prepared using infrared grills — *Recipes*

Jones, Bridget. Contact grill / Bridget Jones. — London : Hamlyn, c1982. — 128p : ill(some col.) ; 23cm
Includes index
ISBN 0-600-32275-0 : £3.50 B82-17609

641.5′882 — Food: Dishes prepared using microwave ovens — *Recipes*

Collins, Val. The beginner's guide to microwave cookery. — Newton Abbot : David & Charles, Oct.1982. — [120]p
ISBN 0-7153-8316-7 (pbk) : £3.95 : CIP entry B82-23010

Methven, Barbara. Microwave cooking for one & two from Litton / [author Barbara Methven]. — Minneapolis : Litton Microwave Cooking Products ; [New York] ; [London] : [Van Nostrand Reinhold], c1981. — 160p : col.ill ; 29cm
'Microwave oven power level setting guide' (1 sheet). — Includes index
ISBN 0-442-25634-5 : £11.00 B82-30344

Microwave cooking / [Litton Microwave Cooking Center]. — Minneapolis : Litton Microwave Cooking Products ; London : Van Nostrand Reinhold
'Microwave oven power level setting guide' (1 folded sheet) as insert. — Includes index
[Vol.9]: Holidays & parties. — c1981. — 169p : col.ill ; 29cm
ISBN 0-442-24572-6 : £11.00 B82-13224

Norman, Cecilia. Cecilia Norman's Microwave cookery course. — London : Granada, 1981. — 304p : 1ill ; 18cm. — (A Mayflower book)
Includes index
ISBN 0-583-13544-7 (pbk) : £1.50 B82-11163

Norman, Cecilia. Faster cooking with microwave and magimix : recipes written for food processors / by Cecilia Norman. — Sunbury : ICTC, 1981. — 32p : 1port ; 15x22cm
Cover title. — Text, port on inside covers
ISBN 0-9506518-9-3 (spiral) : Unpriced
Primary classification 641.5′89 B82-08926

Rosier, Annemarie. The Toshiba book of microwave cookery / Annemarie Rosier. — Repr. with revisions. — Cambridge : Woodhead-Faulkner, 1980. — 96p,8p of plates : ill(some col.) ; 18cm
Originally published: 1978. — Includes index
ISBN 0-85941-074-9 (pbk) : £1.50 B82-09158

Spencer, Jill. Microwave cookbook : the complete guide to a new way of cooking / Jill Spencer. — Feltham : Hamlyn Paperbacks, 1978 (1981 [printing]). — 176p : ill ; 18cm
Includes index
ISBN 0-600-20499-5 (pbk) : £1.25 B82-08549

Weale, Margaret. Good Housekeeping microwave handbook / Margaret Weale. — London : Ebury Press, 1982. — 104p : ill(some col.) ; 25cm
Includes index
ISBN 0-85223-222-5 (cased) : £5.95
ISBN 0-85223-230-6 (pbk) : £3.95 B82-31183

641.5′882′0951 — Food: Chinese dishes: Dishes prepared using microwave ovens — *Recipes*

Chen, Lillian. The microwave Chinese cookbook / Lillian Chen, Edith Nobile. — New York ; London : Van Nostrand Reinhold, c1981. — 157p,[8]p of plates : ill(some col.) ; 24cm
Includes index
ISBN 0-442-22096-0 : £9.30 B82-13192

641.5′884 — Food: Dishes prepared using crock-pots — *Recipes*

Yates, Annette. The Tower slo-cook book / by Annette Yates. — [New ed.]. — London : Foulsham, c1981. — 120p : ill(some col.) ; 23cm. — ([Know-how books])
Previous ed.: 1978. — Includes index
ISBN 0-572-01145-8 : £3.95 B82-11866

641.5′89 — Food: Dishes prepared using food processors — *Recipes*

Allison, Sonia. Sonia Allison's food processor cookbook / written with Patricia Hudson. — [London] : Fontana, 1982, c1980. — x,209p ; 20cm
Originally published: Loughton : Piatkus, 1980. — Includes index
ISBN 0-00-636452-7 (pbk) : £1.95 B82-24418

The **Food** processor cookbook / edited by Norma Miller. — London : Octopus, 1979. — 92p : ill (some col.) ; 27cm
Ill on lining papers. — Includes index
ISBN 0-7064-1071-8 : £1.99 B82-19971

Street, Myra. The Kitchen Wizz cookbook : a guide to using food processors / Myra Street. — Cambridge : Martin Books in association with Breville Europe, 1981. — 96p : col.ill ; 18cm. — (A Martin book)
ISBN 0-85941-148-6 (pbk) : £1.50 B82-36347

641.5′89 — Food: Dishes prepared using Magimix food processors — *Recipes*

Hanbury Tenison, Marika. Magimix cookery / Marika Hanbury Tenison. — Isleworth : ICTC, 1982. — 311p : ill(some col.) ; 26cm
Ill on lining papers. — Includes index
ISBN 0-907642-04-7 : £7.95 : CIP rev. B82-06065

Norman, Cecilia. Faster cooking with microwave and magimix : recipes written for food processors / by Cecilia Norman. — Sunbury : ICTC, 1981. — 32p : 1port ; 15x22cm
Cover title. — Text, port on inside covers
ISBN 0-9506518-9-3 (spiral) : Unpriced
Also classified at 641.5′882 B82-08926

641.5′89 — Food: One-pot dishes — *Recipes*

Allison, Sonia. Pot luck. — Loughton : Piatkus, Nov.1982. — [192]p
ISBN 0-86188-204-0 : £7.95 : CIP entry B82-29420

641.59 — Food: Foreign dishes — *Recipes*

Patten, Marguerite. 500 recipes from around the world / by Marguerite Patten. — London : Hamlyn, 1962 (1982 [printing]). — 96p ; 24cm
Includes index
ISBN 0-600-32300-5 (pbk) : £0.99 B82-39408

641.59 — Food: Regional dishes — *Recipes*

Symposium fare : recipes from the Oxford symposium 1981 on national and regional styles of cookery / edited by Dorothy Brown. — London : Prospect, 1981. — 76p : ill,1port ; 21cm
Bibliography: p8. — Includes index
ISBN 0-907325-10-6 (spiral) : £2.25 B82-12081

641.59′1821 — Food: Caribbean dishes — *Recipes*

Aziz, Khalid. The Khalid Aziz book of simple Caribbean cooking / by Khalid Aziz ; illustrated by Robin Laurie. — London : Pepper Press, 1982. — 48p : ill(some col.) ; 21cm
Ill on lining papers. — Includes index
ISBN 0-237-45622-2 : £2.95 B82-33543

641.59′2′927 — Food: Arab dishes — *Recipes*

Der Haroutunian, Arto. Complete Arab cookery / Arto der Haroutunian. — London : Granada, 1982. — 299p ; 18cm. — (A Mayflower book)
Includes index
ISBN 0-583-13559-5 (pbk) : £1.50 B82-40720

641.593/9 — COOKERY AND RECIPES OF SPECIAL COUNTRIES

641.594 — Food: European dishes

Millon, Marc. The wine and food of Europe. — Exeter : Webb & Bower, Sept. 1982. — [224]p
ISBN 0-906671-35-3 : £9.95 : CIP entry
Primary classification 641.2′1′094 B82-21573

641.5941 — Food: British dishes — *Recipes*

Arbib, Helen. The London cookbook / concept, text and design by Helen Arbib ; drawings by Ray Evans. — London : Collins, 1982. — 64p : ill ; 25cm. — (Minimum effort maximum effect)
Includes index
ISBN 0-00-411236-9 : £2.95 B82-37315

British cookery : a complete guide to culinary practice in the British Isles : based on research undertaken for the British Farm Produce Council and the British Tourist Authority by the University of Strathclyde / [edited by Lizzie Boyd]. — New ed. — London : Croom Helm, 1977. — 640p,[8]p of plates : ill(some col.) ; 26cm
Originally published: 1976. — Includes index
ISBN 0-85664-851-5 : £6.95 : CIP rev. B78-29716

Hanbury Tenison, Marika. The best of British cooking / Marika Hanbury Tenison. — London : Granada, 1981, c1976. — 271p ; 18cm
Originally published: London : Hart-Davis MacGibbon, 1976. — Includes index
ISBN 0-583-13485-8 (pbk) : £1.50 B82-04012

641.5942 — Food. English dishes, *ca 1390 - Recipes*

Knight, Katherine. Fit for a king. — London : Evans Bros, Aug.1981. — [160]p
ISBN 0-237-45548-x : £7.25 : CIP entry B81-16886

641.5942 — Food: English dishes — *Recipes*

Campbell, Susan. English cookery new and old / Susan Campbell. — London : Consumers' Association, c1981. — 272p : ill ; 26cm
Bibliography: p269. — Includes index
ISBN 0-340-26630-9 : Unpriced B82-05264

Webber, Kathie. Traditional English cooking : a book of country recipes / Kathie Webber. — London : Batsford, 1981. — 137p : ill ; 26cm
Includes index
ISBN 0-7134-3887-8 : £7.95 B82-06216

641.59423 — Food: South-west English dishes — *Recipes*

Fitzgibbon, Theodora. Traditional West Country cookery / Theodora Fitzgibbon. — [London] : Fontana, 1982. — 256p ; 20cm
Includes index
ISBN 0-00-635985-x (pbk) : £2.50 B82-22559

641.59423′7 — Food: Cornish dishes — *Recipes*

Graham, Jean M.. The Poldark cookery book / Jean M. Graham ; with a foreword by Winston Graham. — [St. Albans] : Triad, 1981. — 160p : ill ; 18cm
Includes index
ISBN 0-583-13490-4 (pbk) : £1.50 B82-11162

641.59427 — Food: Northern English dishes — *Recipes*

Dutton, Dave. The Cloggies cookbook / Dave Dutton and Hal Dootson ; illustrated by Bill Tidy. — [London] : Star, 1981. — 123p : ill ; 20cm
ISBN 0-352-30571-1 (pbk) : £1.50 B82-14170

641.59429 — Food: Welsh dishes — *Recipes*

Roberts, Enid. Food of the bards 1350-1650 / by Enid Roberts. — Cardiff : Image, c1982. — [24]p : ill ; 20cm
Translation of: Bwyd y beirdd
ISBN 0-9507254-3-9 (pbk) : Unpriced : CIP rev.
Also classified at 891.6′611′080355 B82-11969

Welsh recipes : a collection of the traditional dishes of Wales. — Cardiff : John Jones, [198-?]. — 48p : ill ; 11x16cm
£0.30 (pbk) B82-21332

641.59429′3 — Food: Clwyd dishes — *Recipes*

Clwyd archives cookbook / compiled by Elizabeth L. Pettitt. — Hawarden : Clwyd Record Office, 1980. — 32p : ill,facsims ; 15x21cm
Includes index
ISBN 0-904444-41-4 (pbk) : £0.90 B82-16038

641.5944 — Food: French dishes — *Recipes*

Bertholle, Louisette. French cooking for all / Louisette Bertholle ; translated and edited by Maggie Black ; illustrations by Earl Thollander. — London : Weidenfeld & Nicolson, 1981. — ix,431p : ill ; 25cm
Translation of: Une grande cuisine pour tous. — Includes index
ISBN 0-297-77803-x : £12.95 B82-01458

Bjorklund, Gertrude. Menus plaisirs. — London : Burke, May 1981. — 1v
ISBN 0-222-00803-2 : £6.50 : CIP entry B81-04334

Bourne, Patricia. The Tante Marie book of traditional French cookery. — London : Collins, Oct.1982. — [240]p
ISBN 0-00-218084-7 : £14.95 : CIP entry B82-23074

McDouall, Robin. Recipes from a château in Champagne. — London : Gollancz, Oct.1982. — [160]p
ISBN 0-575-03177-8 : £9.95 : CIP entry B82-23345

The **Master** chefs of France recipe book : recipes from 300 great restaurants of France / compiled with the cooperation of Carte Blanche ; edited and with an introduction by Robert J. Courtine. — Newton Abbot : David & Charles, c1982. — 191p,[16]p of plates : ill (some col.) ; 29cm
Translated from the French. — Includes index
ISBN 0-7153-8241-1 : £9.50 B82-39632

Olney, Richard. Simple French food. — London : Jill Norman & Hubhouse, Oct.1981. — [336]p
Originally published: New York : Atheneum, 1975
ISBN 0-906908-22-1 : £7.95 : CIP entry B81-28120

Pellaprat, Henri-Paul. Modern French culinary art : the Pellaprat of the 20th century / Henri-Paul Pellaprat. — Rev. ed. / edited by John Fuller. — London ([c/o 25 Breakfield, Coulsdon, Surrey CR3 2UE]) : Virtue, 1979. — xvi,952,69p : ill(some col.) ; 27cm
Translation of: L'art culinaire moderne. — Previous ed.: s.l. : s.n., 197?. — Includes index
Unpriced B82-00132

Pellaprat, Henri-Paul. Modern French culinary art. — Revised ed. — Coulsdon : Virtue and Co., July 1981. — [1037]p
ISBN 0-900778-07-5 : £30.00 : CIP entry B81-17524

641.5944 — Food: French regional dishes — *Recipes*

Willan, Anne. French regional cooking / Anne Willan & l'Ecole de Cuisine La Varenne, Paris. — London : Hutchinson, 1981. — 320p : ill (some col.),col.maps ; 30cm
Bibliography: p320. — Includes index
ISBN 0-09-146210-x : £12.95 : CIP rev. B81-26765

641.5944 — France. Restaurants. Food: French dishes — *Recipes*

Bertholle, Louisette. Secrets of the great French restaurants : nearly 400 recipes from famous restaurants starred in the Michelin guide / selected and edited by Louisette Bertholle, author of the introduction, appendices and glossary ; translated by Carole Fahy and Bud MacLennan. — [London] : Papermac, 1982, c1973. — 374p : ill,maps ; 24cm
Translation of: Les recettes secrètes des meilleurs restaurants de France. — Originally published: London : Weidenfeld and Nicolson, 1973. — Includes index
ISBN 0-333-33459-0 (pbk) : £5.95 B82-37761

641.5945 — Food: Italian dishes — *Recipes*

Alden, Zita. Italian recipes / Zita Alden. — London (36 Park St., W1Y 4DE) : Albany, 1979. — 93p : ill(some col.) ; 29cm
Ill on lining papers. — Includes index
Unpriced B82-34667

Easy Italian cookery. — London : Ward Lock, Sept.1982. — [80]p
ISBN 0-7063-6207-1 : £4.95 : CIP entry B82-20015

The **Encyclopedia** of Italian cooking / general editor Jeni Wright. — London : Octopus, 1981. — 192p : col.ill,1map ; 31m
Translated from the Italian. — Ill on lining papers. — Includes index
ISBN 0-7064-1399-7 : £7.95 B82-03929

Gioco, Giorgio. [Italian cookery]. Cuisine of Italy / Giorgio Gioco. — London : W.H. Allen, 1981, c1972. — 190p : col.ill ; 28cm
Translation from the Italian. — Originally published: London : Collins, 1973. — Includes index
ISBN 0-491-02766-4 : £6.95 B82-05268

Hazan, Marcella. The second classic Italian cookbook. — Rev. & metricated ed. — London : Jill Norman & Hobhouse, Mar.1982. — [360]p
Previous ed. published as: More classic Italian cooking. New York : Knopf, 1978
ISBN 0-906908-66-3 : £9.95 : CIP entry B82-01408

Santini, Amelia. The Italian commonsense cookery book / Amelia Santini ; photographs by John Clutterbuck. — London : Angus & Robertson, 1981. — x,133p,[10]p of plates : col.ill ; 26cm
Includes index
ISBN 0-207-14117-7 : Unpriced B82-09961

641.5947 — Food: Russian dishes — *Recipes*

Chamberlain, Lesley. The food and cooking of Russia / Lesley Chamberlain. — London : Allen Lane, 1982. — 330p : ill ; 23cm
Bibliography: p318-319. — Includes index
ISBN 0-7139-1468-8 : £9.95 B82-33655

641.595 — Food: Oriental dishes — *Recipes*

Easy Chinese and Far Eastern cookery. — London : Ward Lock, Sept.1982. — [80]p
ISBN 0-7063-6205-5 : £4.95 : CIP entry
Primary classification 641.5951 B82-20013

Wickramasinghe, Priya. Oriental cookbook / Priya Wickramasinghe. — London : Dent, 1982. — 301p ; 24cm
Includes index
ISBN 0-460-04510-5 : £7.50 : CIP rev. B82-06845

641.595 — Restaurants. Food: Oriental dishes — *Lists*

Ohliger, Lori. Eating out oriental. — Newton Abbot : David & Charles, Feb.1983. — [96]p
ISBN 0-7153-8345-0 : £2.50 : CIP entry B82-39445

641.5951 — Food: Chinese dishes — *Recipes*

Chang, Constance D.. Chinese cooking lessons / by Constance D. Chang ; [illustrations by Bunji Yoshinaga]. — Newton Abbot : David & Charles, 1982. — 122p : ill(some col.),1map,1port ; 27cm
Originally published: Tokyo : Shufunotomo, 1976. — Includes index
ISBN 0-7153-8360-4 : £5.95 B82-39409

Easy Chinese and Far Eastern cookery. — London : Ward Lock, Sept.1982. — [80]p
ISBN 0-7063-6205-5 : £4.95 : CIP entry
Also classified at 641.595 B82-20013

Kinsman, Lisa. Chinese delights. — London : Norman & Hobhouse, Sept.1982. — [132]p
ISBN 0-906908-75-2 : £6.95 : CIP entry B82-21579

Lin, Hsiang-ju. Chinese gastronomy. — London : Jill Norman and Hobhouse, June 1982. — [208]p
ISBN 0-906908-78-7 (pbk) : £4.95 : CIP entry B82-10898

Lo, Kenneth. Memories of China cookbook. — Weybridge : Whittet Books, Oct.1982. — [160]p
ISBN 0-905483-22-7 : £6.95 : CIP entry B82-24599

641.5951 — Food: Chinese regional dishes — *Recipes*

Leeming, Margaret. Chinese regional cookery. — London : Rider, Jan.1983. — [192]p
ISBN 0-09-150981-5 (pbk) : £4.95 : CIP entry B82-37648

641.5952 — Food: Japanese dishes — *Recipes*

Scott, David, *1944-*. The Japanese cookbook / David Scott ; line drawings by Steve Hardstaff. — Abridged ed. — London : Granada, 1981. — xi,208p : ill ; 18cm. — (A Mayflower book)
Full ed.: London : Barrie and Jenkins, 1978. — Includes index
ISBN 0-583-13218-9 (pbk) : £1.50 B82-00796

641.5954 — Food: Indian dishes — *Recipes*

Aziz, Khalid, *1953-*. The Khalid Aziz book of simple Indian cooking / illustrated by Robin Lawrie. — Leeds : Pepper, 1981. — 48p : ill (some col.),1col.port ; 21cm
Includes index
ISBN 0-560-74521-4 : £2.95 B82-01775

Day, Harvey. Indian curries. — Wellingborough : Thorsons, Oct.1982. — [128]p
ISBN 0-7225-0781-x (pbk) : £1.50 : CIP entry B82-24245

Wickramasinghe, Priya. Spicy and delicious. — London : Coronet, July 1981. — [192]p
Originally published: London : Dent, 1979
ISBN 0-340-26676-7 (pbk) : £1.25 : CIP entry
Also classified at 641.59549'3 B81-14953

641.5954'05 — Food: Indian dishes — *Serials*

The **Curry** magazine. — Spring 1982-. — Haslemere (P.O. Box 7, Haslemere, Surrey GU27 1EP) : Curry Club, 1982-. — v. : ill,ports ; 27cm
Quarterly
ISSN 0263-9866 = Curry magazine : Unpriced B82-40034

641.59549'3 — Food: Sri Lanka dishes — *Recipes*

Wickramasinghe, Priya. Spicy and delicious. — London : Coronet, July 1981. — [192]p
Originally published: London : Dent, 1979
ISBN 0-340-26676-7 (pbk) : £1.25 : CIP entry
Primary classification 641.5954 B81-14953

641.59593 — Food: Thai dishes — *Recipes*

Brennan, Jennifer. Thai cooking. — London : Jill Norman & Hobhouse, Oct.1981. — [224]p
Revision of: The original Thai cookbook. New York : Marek, 1981
ISBN 0-906908-63-9 : £7.95 : CIP entry B81-28006

641.59594 — Food: Laotian dishes — *Recipes*

Sing, *Phayā*. Traditional recipes of Laos : being the manuscript recipe book of the late Phia Sing, from the Royal Palace at Luang Prabang, reproduced in facsimile and furnished with an English translation / translators Phouangphet Vannithone and Boon Song Klausner ; editors Alan and Jennifer Davidson ; drawings by Thao Soun Vannithone. — London : Prospect, 1981. — 318p : ill,1map,facsims,1port ; 24cm
Parallel Laotian text and English translation, introduction, notes, bibliography. — Bibliography: p313-314. — Includes index
ISBN 0-907325-02-5 (pbk) : £6.95 B82-10318

641.596 — Food: African dishes

Van der Post, Laurens. First catch your eland. — Large print ed. — Anstey : Ulverscroft, Oct.1982. — [448]p. — (Ulverscroft large print series)
Originally published: London : Hogarth Press, 1977
ISBN 0-7089-0868-3 : £5.00 : CIP entry B82-27017

641.59669 — Food: Nigerian dishes — *Recipes*

Anthonio, H. O.. Nigerian cookbook / H.O. Anthonio, M. Isoun. — London : Macmillan, 1982. — vii,216p,[8]p of plates : ill(some col.) ; 23cm
Bibliography: p209. — Includes index
ISBN 0-333-32698-9 (pbk) : Unpriced B82-33848

641.59729 — Food: West Indian dishes — *Recipes*

Captain Blackbeard's beef creole : and other Caribbean recipes. — London : Peckham Publishing Project, c1981. — 72p : ill ; 15x21cm
Includes index
ISBN 0-906464-01-3 (pbk) : Unpriced B82-21687

641.59969 — Food: Hawaiian dishes — *Recipes*

Schindler, Roana. [Hawaii Kai cookbook]. Hawaiian cookbook / by Roana and Gene Schindler. — New York : Dover ; London : Constable, 1981, c1970. — 272p : ill ; 22cm
Originally published: New York : Hearthside Press, 1970. — Includes index
ISBN 0-486-24185-8 (pbk) : £3.00 B82-24095

641.6 — COOKERY AND RECIPES BASED ON SPECIAL MATERIALS

641.6 — Food: Dishes using wild plants — *Recipes*

Duff, Gail. The countryside cook book : recipes & remedies / Gail Duff ; illustrated by Linda Garland ; with line illustrations by Roger Garland. — Dorchester : Prism, 1982. — 191p : ill(some col.) ; 26cm
Bibliography: p187. — Includes index
ISBN 0-907061-21-4 : £8.95
Also classified at 615′.321 B82-21266

Duff, Gail. The countryside yearbook : a cook's calendar / Gail Duff ; illustrated by Linda Garland ; with line illustrations by Roger Garland. — Dorchester : Prism, 1982. — 191p : ill(some col.) ; 26cm
ISBN 0-907061-28-1 : £5.95
Also classified at 641.5′64 B82-21267

Scott, Amoret. Hedgerow harvest : conserves, chutneys, jams, jellies, pickles, preserves, relishes, wines, cheeses, soups and surprises / Amoret Scott. — Oxford : Oxford Illustrated Press, 1979. — 124p : ill ; 23cm
Bibliography: p117-118. — Includes index
ISBN 0-902280-70-8 : £4.95 B82-05938

641.6′16 — Chutneys & pickles — *Recipes*

McNair, James K.. All about pickling / [coordinating editor and manuscript James K. McNair] ; [photography Clyde Childress]. — Edinburgh : Bartholomew, 1980. — 96p : col.ill ; 29cm
Originally published: San Francisco : Orth Books, c1975. — Includes index
ISBN 0-7028-8310-7 : £6.95 : CIP rev. B80-04294

641.6′2 — Food: Dishes using alcoholic drinks — *Recipes*

Allison, Sonia. Spirited cooking : with liqueurs, spirits and wine / Sonia Allison. — Newton Abbot : David & Charles, c1981. — 136p : ill (some col.) ; 25cm
Includes index
ISBN 0-7153-8015-x : £7.50 : CIP rev. B81-30332

641.6′23 — Food: Dishes using cider — *Recipes*

Harrison, Shirley. A taste of cider / Shirley Harrison ; illustrations by Graeme Jenner. — Newton Abbot : David & Charles, c1982. — 96p : ill ; 23cm
Includes index
ISBN 0-7153-8216-0 : £4.50 : CIP rev. B82-09619

641.6′318 — Food: Rice dishes — *Recipes*

Ridgway, Judy. Making the most of rice. — Newton Abbot : David & Charles, Feb.1983. — [48]p
ISBN 0-7153-8374-4 (pbk) : £1.50 : CIP entry B82-39450

641.6′382 — Food: Seasonal dishes using mayonnaise — *Recipes*

Hellmann's real mayonnaise seasonal cookbook. — Esher (Claygate House, Esher, Surrey KT10 9PN) : Hellmann's Real Mayonnaise CPC (United Kingdom) Ltd, [1982?]. — 20p : col.ill ; 21cm
Includes index
Unpriced (unbound) B82-23047

641.6′383 — Food: Dishes using spices — *Recipes*

Mességué, Maurice. A kitchen herbal. — London : Collins, Oct.1982. — [200]p
Translation of: Mon herbier de cuisine
ISBN 0-00-216395-0 : £7.95 : CIP entry
Primary classification 641.6′57 B82-23069

641.6′383′09429 — Food: Welsh dishes using spices — *Recipes*

Jones, Gwen Pritchard. Welsh recipes with herbs and spices / [compiled and tested by Gwen Pritchard Jones]. — Cardiff : John Jones, c1978. — 45p : ill ; 11x156cm
ISBN 0-902375-47-4 (pbk) : £0.30
Primary classification 641.6′57′09429 B82-21333

641.6′384 — Food: Curried dishes — *Recipes*

Pandya, Michael. Indian curries / Michael Pandya. — Cardiff : Preeti, c1982. — 48p : ill ; 21cm
Text on inside covers. — Includes index
ISBN 0-9507595-3-8 (pbk) : £1.25 B82-21302

641.6′4 — Food: Dishes using dried fruit — *Recipes*

Dark, Robert. Dried fruit. — Wellingborough : Thorsons, Oct.1982. — [96]p
ISBN 0-7225-0682-1 (pbk) : £0.95 : CIP entry B82-23029

641.6′4 — Food: Fruit dishes: Dishes prepared using microwave ovens — *Recipes*

Collins, Val. The microwave fruit & vegetable cookbook / Val Collins. — Newton Abbot : David & Charles, c1981. — 120p : ill(some col.) ; 28cm
Includes index
ISBN 0-7153-8199-7 : £5.95 : CIP rev.
Also classified at 641.6′5 B81-27948

641.6′4 — Food: Fruit dishes — *Recipes*

Berry, Mary, *1935-*. Fruit fare / by Mary Berry. — Loughton : Piatkus, 1982. — 192,[8]p of plates : ill(some col.) ; 23cm
Includes index
ISBN 0-86188-080-3 : £7.95 : CIP rev. B82-00351

Grigson, Jane. Jane Grigson's fruit book / illustrated by Yvonne Skargon. — London : Joseph, 1982. — xiii,508p : ill ; 24cm
Includes index
ISBN 0-7181-2125-2 : £12.95 B82-27038

641.6′446 — Food: Dishes using carob — *Recipes*

Whiteside, Lorraine. The carob cookbook / Lorraine Whiteside. — Wellingborough : Thorsons, 1981. — 95p : ill ; 18cm
Includes index
ISBN 0-7225-0726-7 (pbk) : £0.95 : CIP rev. B81-30586

641.6′4653 — Food: Avocado dishes — *Recipes*

Doeser, Linda. The little green avocado book / Linda Doeser. — Loughton : Piatkus, 1981. — 60p : ill ; 16cm
ISBN 0-86188-125-7 : £1.95 : CIP rev. B81-27472

641.6′5 — Food: Vegetable dishes: Dishes prepared using microwave ovens — *Recipes*

Collins, Val. The microwave fruit & vegetable cookbook / Val Collins. — Newton Abbot : David & Charles, c1981. — 120p : ill(some col.) ; 28cm
Includes index
ISBN 0-7153-8199-7 : £5.95 : CIP rev.
Primary classification 641.6′4 B81-27948

641.6′5 — Food: Vegetable dishes — *Recipes*

[The Green thumb cookbook]. Vegetables / [editors Anne Moyer and Gillian Andrews]. — Aylesbury : Rodale Press, 1982. — 255p,[16]p of plates : ill(some col.) ; 27cm. — (Rodale's good food kitchen)
Originally published: Emmaus, Pa. : Rodale Press, 1977. — Includes index
ISBN 0-87857-392-5 : Unpriced B82-35784

Hanbury Tenison, Marika. Cooking with vegetables : original recipes / by Marika Hanbury Tenison ; illustrations by John Miller. — [St Albans] : Triad, 1982, c1980. — 381p : ill ; 18cm
Originally published: London : Cape, 1980. — Includes index
ISBN 0-583-13424-6 (pbk) : £1.95 B82-29735

Stone, Marie. The Covent Garden cookbook / Marie Stone. — London : Allison and Busby, c1974 (1981 [printing]). — 253p : ill,maps,facsims,ports ; 21cm
Bibliography: p240. — Includes index
ISBN 0-85031-440-2 : £4.95 B82-01759

641.6′521 — Food: Potato dishes — *Recipes*

Ridgway, Judy. Making the most of potatoes. — Newton Abbot : David & Charles, Feb.1983. — [48]p
ISBN 0-7153-8372-8 (pbk) : £1.50 : CIP entry B82-39448

641.6′565 — Vegetarians. Food: Dishes using pulses — *Recipes*

Dixon, Pamela. The bean & lentil cookbook : colourful, inexpensive and highly nutritious pulse recipes : includes sweet dishes / by Pamela Dixon ; illustrated by Clive Birch. — Wellingborough : Thorsons, 1982, c1980. — 128p : ill ; 22cm
Originally published as: Pulse cookery, 1980. — Includes index
ISBN 0-7225-0757-7 (pbk) : £3.50 : CIP rev. B82-07604

641.6′5655 — Food: Dishes using textured vegetable proteins — *Recipes*

Forster, Dorothy H.. Cooking with Tvp : exciting, nutritious and economic dishes using textured soya protein / by Dorothy H. Forster. — Wellingborough : Thorsons, 1981. — 95p : ill ; 18cm
Includes index
ISBN 0-7225-0720-8 (pbk) : £0.95 : CIP rev. B81-30585

641.6′57 — Food: Dishes using herbs — *Recipes*

Mességué, Maurice. A kitchen herbal. — London : Collins, Oct.1982. — [200]p
Translation of: Mon herbier de cuisine
ISBN 0-00-216395-0 : £7.95 : CIP entry
Also classified at 641.6′383 B82-23069

641.6′57′09429 — Food: Welsh dishes using herbs — *Recipes*

Jones, Gwen Pritchard. Welsh recipes with herbs and spices / [compiled and tested by Gwen Pritchard Jones]. — Cardiff : John Jones, c1978. — 45p : ill ; 11x156cm
ISBN 0-902375-47-4 (pbk) : £0.30
Also classified at 641.6′383′09429 B82-21333

641.6′6 — Food: Meat dishes — *Recipes*

Berry, Mary, *1935-*. The new book of meat cookery / Mary Berry. — London : Queen Anne Press, published in association with Oxo, c1981. — 215p : col.ill ; 27cm
Includes index
ISBN 0-362-00559-1 : £7.95 B82-03491

641.6′6 — Food: Minced meat dishes — *Recipes*

Dimbleby, Josceline. Marvellous meals with mince / Josceline Dimbleby. — Cambridge (17 Market St., Cambridge CB2 3PA) : Woodhead-Faulkner for J. Sainsbury Limited, 1982. — 96p : col.ill,1port ; 19cm. — (A Sainsbury cookbook)
£0.75 (pbk) B82-17587

641.6′6 — Pâtés & terrines — *Recipes*

Binns, Brian. Pâtés and terrines with Magimix / recipes written by Brian and Vanessa Binns for food processors. — Sunbury : ICTC, 1982. — 33p : ports ; 15x22cm
Cover title. — Text, ports on inside covers
ISBN 0-907642-03-9 (spiral) : Unpriced B82-30118

641.6′73 — Food: Cheese dishes — *Recipes*

Ridgway, Judy. Making the most of cheese. — Newton Abbot : David & Charles, Feb.1983. — [48]p
ISBN 0-7153-8376-0 (pbk) : £1.50 : CIP entry B82-39452

641.6′75 — Food: Egg dishes — *Recipes*

Ridgway, Judy. Making the most of eggs. — Newton Abbot : David & Charles, Feb.1983. — [48]p
ISBN 0-7153-8375-2 (pbk) : £1.50 : CIP entry B82-39451

641.6′9 — Food: Seafood dishes — *Recipes*

Fish and shell-fish / editor A.E. Simms ; assistant editor Mabel Quin ; preface John Fuller. — 2nd rev. ed. — Coulsdon (25 Breakfield, Coulsdon, Surrey) : Virhie and Company, 1979, c1973. — xx,504p : ill ; 27cm
Previous ed.: 1973. — Includes index
Unpriced B82-03487

641.6′92 — Food: Fish dishes — *Recipes*

Patten, Marguerite. 500 recipes for fish dishes / by Marguerite Patten. — London : Hamlyn, 1965 (1982 [printing]). — 96p ; 24cm
Includes index
ISBN 0-600-32305-6 (pbk) : £0.99 B82-37381

641.7 — COOKERY. SPECIAL PROCESSES AND TECHNIQUES

641.7′1 — Baking — *Recipes*

Teubner, Christian. Baking at home / Christian Teubner. — London : Hamlyn, c1982. — 79p : col.ill ; 26cm. — (Hamlyn kitchen shelf)
Translation of: Back-Vergnugen leicht gemacht. — Text on lining paper. — Includes index
ISBN 0-600-32283-1 : £2.50 B82-39410

641.8 — COOKERY. COMPOSITE DISHES

641.8 — Pancakes, crepes & waffles — *Recipes*

Lomask, Martha. Pancakes, crepes & waffles. — Loughton : Piatkus, Feb.1983. — [96]p
ISBN 0-86188-200-8 : £3.95 : CIP entry B82-39806

641.8 — Vegetarians. Food: Flans — *Recipes*

Hunt, Janet, *1942-*. Quiches and flans / by Janet Hunt ; illustrated by Clive Birch. — Wellingborough : Thorsons, 1982. — 128p : ill ; 20cm
Includes index
ISBN 0-7225-0722-4 (pbk) : £1.50 : CIP rev. B82-07599

641.8 — Vegetarians. Food: Pancakes & pizzas — *Recipes*

Hunt, Janet, *1942-*. Pizzas and pancakes / by Janet Hunt ; illustrated by Clive Birch. — Wellingborough : Thorsons, 1982. — 128p : ill ; 20cm
Includes index
ISBN 0-7225-0723-2 (pbk) : £1.50 : CIP rev. B82-07600

641.8′12 — Food: Savoury dishes — *Recipes*

FitzGibbon, Theodora. Savouries. — London : Century Publishing, Oct.1982. — [64]p
ISBN 0-7126-0005-1 : £3.95 : CIP entry B82-23873

641.8′12 — Food: Starters: Dishes using natural food — *Recipes*

Greer, Rita. Superb soups and starters : easy to make and full of goodness / by Rita Greer. — Wellingborough : Thorsons, 1981. — 128p : ill ; 22cm. — (A Thorsons wholefood cookbook)
Includes index
ISBN 0-7225-0691-0 (pbk) : £2.95 : CIP rev.
Primary classification 641.8′13 B81-22561

641.8′12 — Food: Starters prepared using Magimix food processors — *Recipes*

Cox, Nicola. Starters with magimix : recipes written for food processors / by Nicola Cox. — Sunbury : ICTC, 1981. — 26p : 1port ; 15x22cm
Cover title. — Text, port on inside covers
ISBN 0-907642-01-2 (spiral) : Unpriced B82-08927

641.8′12 — Snacks — *Recipes*

Cocktails and snacks. — London : Ward Lock, Oct.1982. — [96]p
ISBN 0-7063-6204-7 : £5.95 : CIP entry
Primary classification 641.8′74 B82-23185

641.8′13 — Soups: Dishes using natural food — *Recipes*

Greer, Rita. Superb soups and starters : easy to make and full of goodness / by Rita Greer. — Wellingborough : Thorsons, 1981. — 128p : ill ; 22cm. — (A Thorsons wholefood cookbook)
Includes index
ISBN 0-7225-0691-0 (pbk) : £2.95 : CIP rev.
Also classified at 641.8′12 B81-22561

641.8′13 — Soups — *Recipes*

Law, Digby. A Soup cookbook. — London : Hodder & Stoughton, Aug.1982. — [239]p
ISBN 0-340-27992-3 : £7.95 : CIP entry B82-15732

Norman, Ursel. Super suppers : soup, salad and pasta / a collection of recipes by Ursel Norman ; designed and illustrated by Derek Norman. — London : Collins, 1982. — 176p : ill(chiefly col.) ; 28cm
Includes index
ISBN 0-00-411250-4 : £8.95
Primary classification 641.5 B82-38769

641.8′15 — Bread — *Recipes*

Bateman, Michael. The Sunday Times book of real bread / Michael Bateman and Heather Maisner. — Aylesbury : Rodale, 1982. — 336p : ill(some col.),ports ; 26cm
Includes index
ISBN 0-87857-368-2 : £12.95 B82-23634

Ridgway, Judy. Making the most of bread. — Newton Abbot : David & Charles, Feb.1983. — 1v.
ISBN 0-7153-8371-x (pbk) : £1.50 : CIP entry B82-39447

641.8′15 — Bread — *Recipes — For children*

John, Sue. Bread basket. — London : Methuen/Walker, May 1982. — [32]p
ISBN 0-416-06400-0 : £3.95 : CIP entry B82-06752

641.8′2 — Main courses — *Recipes*

Conil, Jean. Variations on a main course : how to create your own original dishes / Jean Conil and Hugh Williams. — London : New English Library, 1981. — 144p : ill ; 20cm. — (New English Library books for cooks)
Originally published: Loughton : Piatkus, 1981. — Includes index
ISBN 0-450-05204-4 (pbk) : £1.25 B82-04766

641.8′22 — Food: Pasta dishes — *Recipes*

Norman, Ursel. Super suppers : soup, salad and pasta / a collection of recipes by Ursel Norman ; designed and illustrated by Derek Norman. — London : Collins, 1982. — 176p : ill(chiefly col.) ; 28cm
Includes index
ISBN 0-00-411250-4 : £8.95
Primary classification 641.5 B82-38769

Ridgway, Judy. Making the most of pasta. — Newton Abbot : David & Charles, Feb.1983. — [48]p
ISBN 0-7153-8373-6 (pbk) : £1.50 : CIP entry B82-39449

Street, Myra. Pasta cookbook / Myra Street. — London : Hamlyn, 1974 (1981 [printing]). — 80p : ill(some col.),1map ; 26cm
Includes index
ISBN 0-600-32292-0 : £2.95 B82-08154

641.8′22 — Vegetarians. Food: Pasta dishes — *Recipes*

Hunt, Janet, *1942-*. Pasta dishes / by Janet Hunt ; illustrated by Clive Birch. — Wellingborough : Thorsons, 1982. — 128p : ill ; 20cm
Includes index
ISBN 0-7225-0750-x (pbk) : £1.50 : CIP rev. B82-07602

641.8′3 — Food: Salad dishes — *Recipes*

Denny, Roz. Salads for every season / Roz Denny. — Cambridge : Martin, 1982. — 96p : col.ill ; 19cm
Includes index
ISBN 0-85941-187-7 (pbk) : £1.50 B82-21336

Hine, Jacqui. Book of salads and summer dishes / Jacqui Hine. — Poole : Blandford, [1982]. — 95p : ill(some col.),1port ; 15cm. — ('How to')
Includes index
ISBN 0-7137-1055-1 (pbk) : £1.95 B82-20222

Norman, Ursel. Super suppers : soup, salad and pasta / a collection of recipes by Ursel Norman ; designed and illustrated by Derek Norman. — London : Collins, 1982. — 176p : ill(chiefly col.) ; 28cm
Includes index
ISBN 0-00-411250-4 : £8.95
Primary classification 641.5 B82-38769

641.8′4 — Toasted sandwiches — *Recipes*

Ridgway, Judy. The Breville toasted sandwiches book / Judy Ridgway. — Cambridge : Martin books in association with Breville Europe, 1982. — 96p : col.ill ; 18cm
ISBN 0-85941-189-3 (pbk) : £1.50 B82-23403

641.8′52 — Preserves. Making — *Amateurs′ manuals*

Nice, Jill. Home-made preserves : the complete guide to making jams, jellies, pickles, chutneys, conserves and ketchups / Jill Nice. — London : Collins, 1982. — 384p : ill ; 26cm
Includes index
ISBN 0-00-411234-2 : £9.95 B82-22831

641.8′52 — Preserves using honey — *Recipes*

Geiskopf, Susan. The sunshine larder : using honey to preserve the natural goodness of summer′s bounty / by Susan Geiskopf. — Wellingborough : Thorsons, 1981, c1979. — 157p : ill ; 22cm
Originally published: Ashland, Or. : Quicksilver, 1979. — Includes index
ISBN 0-7225-0696-1 (pbk) : £3.50 : CIP rev. B81-22560

641.8′53 — Chocolates — *Recipes*

Rubinstein, Helge. The chocolate book / Helge Rubinstein. — London : Macdonald, 1981. — 214p : ill,facsims ; 22cm
Bibliography: p212. — Includes index
ISBN 0-354-04601-2 : £7.95 B82-01813

641.8′53 — Confectionery: Sweets — *Recipes*

Allison, Sonia. Sonia Allison′s sweets book. — Loughton : Piatkus, June 1982. — [96]p
ISBN 0-86188-167-2 : £2.95 : CIP entry B82-11121

641.8′6 — Desserts: Cold sweets — *Recipes*

Allday, Jenny. Ice creams, sorbets, mousses & parfaits : the delicious natural way / by Jenny Allday ; illustrated by Paul Turner. — Wellingborough : Thorsons, 1982. — 128p : ill ; 22cm. — (A Thorsons wholefood cookbook)
Includes index
ISBN 0-7225-0729-1 (pbk) : £3.50 : CIP rev. B82-09836

641.8′6 — Desserts: Dishes using natural foods — *Recipes*

Wholefood desserts. — Sheffield (Townhead, Dunford Bridge, Sheffield, S30 6TG) : Lifespan Community Collective, c1980. — 13p : ill ; 22cm
Includes index
£0.25 (pbk) B82-26488

641.8'6 — Desserts — *Recipes*

Bowen, Carol. Hamlyn all colour book of puddings & desserts / Carol Bowen. — London : Hamlyn, 1982. — 124p : ill(some col.) ; 31cm
Ill on lining papers. — Includes index
ISBN 0-600-32271-8 : £3.99 B82-30755

Conil, Jean. Variations on a dessert. — London : New English Library, Feb.1982. — [144]p
Originally published: Loughton : Piatkus, 1981
ISBN 0-450-05205-2 (pbk) : £1.25 : CIP entry B81-36206

Norwak, Mary. English puddings : sweet and savoury / Mary Norwak. — London : Batsford, 1981. — 120p : ill ; 25cm
Includes index
ISBN 0-7134-1927-x : £7.95 B82-01684

Smith, Michael, *1929-*. Just desserts / Michael Smith. — London : British Broadcasting Corporation, 1982. — 56p ; 18cm
ISBN 0-563-20050-2 (pbk) : £1.25 B82-26486

641.8'65 — Pastries: Dishes prepared using Magimix food processors — *Recipes*

Barber, Lucille. Yeast cookery with Magimix / recipes written by Lucille Barber for food processors. — Sunbury : ICTC, 1982. — 35p : 1port ; 15cm
Cover title. — Port on inside cover
ISBN 0-907642-02-0 (spiral) : Unpriced B82-28483

641.8'65 — Pastries — *Recipes*

Barker, William, *b. 1908 Oct.8*. The modern pâtissier : a complete guide to pastry cookery / William Barker. — 2nd ed. — London : Northwood, 1978. — viii,285p,[12]p of plates : ill(some col.) ; 26cm. — (A Catering Times book)
Previous ed.: 1974. — Includes index
ISBN 0-7198-2654-3 : £8.50 B82-26920

Orsini, Elisabeth. The book of pies / Elisabeth Orsini. — London : Pan, 1981. — 191p : ill ; 30cm. — (Pan original)
Bibliography: p178-179. — Includes index
ISBN 0-330-26508-3 (pbk) : £1.95 B82-04252

Wadey, Rosemary. The pastry book. — Newton Abbot : David & Charles, Oct.1982. — [168]p
ISBN 0-7153-8344-2 : £7.95 : CIP entry B82-23013

641.8'653 — Cakes. Decoration — *Amateurs' manuals*

Cake decorating / edited by Mary Morris. — London : Octopus, 1981. — 76p : ill(some col.) ; 27cm
Ill on lining papers. — Includes index
ISBN 0-7064-1509-4 : £1.99 B82-01011

May, Bill. Cake designs and ideas / designed and projected by Bill May and Kathleen Metcalfe. — [Preston] : [Felicity Clare], c1982. — 141p : col.ill ; 29cm
ISBN 0-9507899-0-9 : Unpriced B82-21231

Spencer, Louise. Cake decorating ideas & designs / Louise Spencer. — New York : Sterling ; London : Oak Tree, c1981. — 176p,[8]p of plates : ill(some col) ; 26cm
Includes index
ISBN 0-7061-2794-3 : £7.95 B82-21877

641.8'653 — Cakes — *Recipes*

Asher, Jane. Party cakes. — London : Pelham, Oct.1982. — [112]p
ISBN 0-7207-1412-5 : £7.95 : CIP entry B82-23027

Maher, Barbara. Cakes. — London : Norman & Hobhouse, Sept. 1982. — [320]p
ISBN 0-906908-14-0 : £7.95 : CIP entry B82-21577

Segal, Vera. Traditional cakes / collected by Vera Segal. — London : Cottage, 1981. — 32p : ill ; 15cm
ISBN 0-907782-00-0 (pbk) : Unpriced B82-22530

Wadey, Rosemary. Cakes and cake decorating / Rosemary Wadey. — London : Octopus, 1982, c1979. — 159p : ill(some col.) ; 28cm
Originally published: 1979. — Includes index
ISBN 0-7064-1817-4 (pbk) : £2.99 B82-38157

641.8'654 — Biscuits — *Recipes*

Allison, Sonia. Sonia Allison's biscuit book. — Loughton : Piatkus, 1981. — 95p ; 12x18cm
Includes index
ISBN 0-86188-126-5 : £2.95 : CIP rev. B81-30377

The **Book** of biscuits. — London : WI Books, Sept.1982. — [96]p
ISBN 0-900556-76-5 (pbk) : £2.25 : CIP entry B82-28606

Segal, Vera. Traditional biscuits / collected by Vera Segal. — London : Cottage, 1982. — 32p : ill ; 15cm
ISBN 0-907782-01-9 (pbk) : Unpriced B82-22529

641.87 — PREPARATION OF BEVERAGES

641.8'72 — Wines. Additives. Use — *Amateurs' manuals*

Chant, Maurice. Additives for winemaking / Maurice Chant. — [Bristol] ([519 Fishponds Rd, Fishponds, Bristol BS16 3AJ]) : M. Chant, [c1981]. — [9]p ; 22cm
Cover title. — Includes index
Unpriced (pbk) B82-00960

641.8'72 — Wines. Making — *Amateurs' manuals*

Austin, Cedric. Whys and wherefores of wine-making / [Cedric Austin]. — Andover : Amateur Winemaker, 1970 (1978 [printing]). — 120p ; 18cm
Includes index
ISBN 0-900841-15-x (pbk) : £0.60 B82-25850

Bennetts, Ben. Quickie table wines : an easy-to-follow guide to making your own table wines from fresh or tinned fruit / 'Ben' Bennetts. — 3rd ed. — [Andover] ([South St, Andover, Hants]) : [The Amateur Winemaker], 1981, c1977. — 13p : ill(some col.) ; 21cm
Cover title. — Previous ed.: 197-?
Unpriced (pbk) B82-23040

Leverett, Brian. Basic winemaking / by Brian Leverett. — Dorchester, Dorset : Gavin Press, 1982. — viii, : ill ; 22cm
Includes index
ISBN 0-905868-10-2 (pbk) : £1.00 B82-37701

Mackay, Muriel Hooker. Country winemaking and wine cookery. — Newton Abbot : David & Charles, Nov.1982. — [144]p
ISBN 0-7153-8368-x : £4.95 : CIP entry B82-26399

Mitchell, J. R. (John Richard). Scientific winemaking made easy / by J.R. Mitchell. — Andover : Amateur Winemaker, 1969 (1979 [printing]). — 246p,[4]p of plates : ill ; 18cm
Includes index
ISBN 0-900841-42-7 (pbk) : £1.50 B82-22883

Tayleur, W. H. T.. The Penguin book of home brewing and wine-making / W.H.T. Tayleur ; drawings by Michael Spink. — 2nd ed. — Harmondsworth : Penguin, 1982. — 343p : ill ; 20cm. — (Penguin handbooks)
Previous ed.: 1973. — Includes index
ISBN 0-14-046190-6 (pbk) : £2.95
Primary classification 641.8'73 B82-25120

641.8'72'05 — Wines. Making — *Amateurs' manuals — Serials*

Practical winemaking and brewing. — No.1 (Summer 1981)-. — Bournemouth (12 Poole Hill, Bournemouth, Dorset) : M.R.T. Consultants, 1981-. — v. : ill ; 30cm
Six issues yearly
ISSN 0263-2314 = Practical winemaking and brewing : £4.50 per year
Also classified at 641.8'73'05 B82-19849

641.8'73 — Brewing — *Amateurs' manuals*

Foster, Charles. Home winemaking, brewing and other drinks. — London : Ward Lock, Mar.1982. — [80]p
ISBN 0-7063-5941-0 : £3.50 : CIP entry B82-02630

Miller, David G.. Home brewing for Americans : mastering the art of brewing American and European type beers at home / by David G. Miller. — Andover : Amateur Winemaker, 1981. — 110p : ill ; 22cm
Includes index
ISBN 0-900841-61-3 (pbk) : £1.50 B82-39016

Tayleur, W. H. T.. The Penguin book of home brewing and wine-making / W.H.T. Tayleur ; drawings by Michael Spink. — 2nd ed. — Harmondsworth : Penguin, 1982. — 343p : ill ; 20cm. — (Penguin handbooks)
Previous ed.: 1973. — Includes index
ISBN 0-14-046190-6 (pbk) : £2.95
Also classified at 641.8'72 B82-25120

641.8'73'05 — Brewing — *Amateurs' manuals — Serials*

Practical winemaking and brewing. — No.1 (Summer 1981)-. — Bournemouth (12 Poole Hill, Bournemouth, Dorset) : M.R.T. Consultants, 1981-. — v. : ill ; 30cm
Six issues yearly
ISSN 0263-2314 = Practical winemaking and brewing : £4.50 per year
Primary classification 641.8'72'05 B82-19849

641.8'74 — Cocktails — *Recipes*

A to Z of cocktails / introduction by John Doxat. — London : Ward Lock, 1980. — 120p : col.ill ; 28cm
Includes index
ISBN 0-7063-5831-7 : £4.95 : CIP rev. B79-25805

Chester, Helen. Cocktails. — London : Ward Lock, Oct.1982. — [80]p
ISBN 0-7063-6203-9 (pbk) : £3.50 : CIP entry B82-27198

Cocktails and snacks. — London : Ward Lock, Oct.1982. — [96]p
ISBN 0-7063-6204-7 : £5.95 : CIP entry
Also classified at 641.8'12 B82-23185

641.8'74 — England. Licensed premises. Bar work — *Manuals*

Coombs, James H.. Bar service / James H. Coombs ; with a foreword by J.G. Miles ; drawings by Bill Hooper. — 2nd ed. — London : Hutchinson, 1982, c1975. — 182p : ill ; 22cm. — (Catering and hotel management books)
Originally published: London : Barrie and Jenkins, 1975
ISBN 0-09-147541-4 (pbk) : £4.95 B82-31831

641.8'74 — Man. Hangovers. Remedies

Outerbridge, David. The hangover handbook : the definitive guide to the causes and cures of man's oldest affliction / David Outerbridge ; cartoons by Gray Jolliffe. — London : Pan, 1981. — 96p : ill ; 20cm. — (Pan original)
ISBN 0-330-26535-0 (pbk) : £1.25 B82-01583

641.8'75 — Soft drinks — *Recipes*

Honey, Babs. Drinks for all seasons / Babs Honey. — Wakefield : EP, 1982. — 96p : ill (some col.) ; 25cm
Includes index
ISBN 0-7158-0739-0 (pbk) : £2.95 B82-39675

642 — FOOD AND MEAL SERVICE

642'.3 — Expeditions by school parties. Food. Planning — *Manuals*

Expedition food and rations planning manual / Young Explorers' Trust. — London (1 Kensington Gore, SW7 2AR) : Young Explorers' Trust at the Royal Geographical Society, 1976 (1980 [printing]). — 17,[24]p,[4]p of plates : ill ; 21cm
Bibliography: p16-17
Unpriced (pbk) B82-11881

642′.4 — Hotels. Banquets. Salesmanship — *Manuals*

Taylor, Derek, *1932-*. How to sell banquets : the key to conference and function promotion / Derek Taylor. — London : Northwood, 1979. — 176p : ill ; 26cm. — (A Catering times book)
Includes index
ISBN 0-7198-2734-5 : £5.95 B82-01453

642′.5 — Great Britain. Hospitals. Catering services. Evaluation — *Study examples: Frimley Park Hospital*

Evaluation of the best buy hospitals catering department, March 1978. — [London] (Room 538, Euston Tower, 286 Euston Rd., NW1 3DN) : DHSS, 1980. — [4],39p ; 30cm
Cover title: Best buy hospitals mark I evaluation report
£1.75 (pbk)
Also classified at 642′.5 B82-17768

642′.5 — Great Britain. Hospitals. Catering services. Evaluation — *Study examples: West Suffolk Hospital*

Evaluation of the best buy hospitals catering department, March 1978. — [London] (Room 538, Euston Tower, 286 Euston Rd., NW1 3DN) : DHSS, 1980. — [4],39p ; 30cm
Cover title: Best buy hospitals mark I evaluation report
£1.75 (pbk)
Primary classification 642′.5 B82-17768

642′.6 — Great Britain. Catering. Waitering — *Manuals*

Houston, Joseph. The professional service of food and beverage / Joseph Houston and Neil Glenesk. — London : Batsford Academic and Educational, 1982. — 143p : ill,forms ; 22cm
Includes index
ISBN 0-7134-3529-1 (pbk) : £4.95 B82-27499

643 — THE HOME AND ITS EQUIPMENT

643 — Great Britain. Residences. Security measures — *Amateurs′ manuals*

Waters, Tony. Home protection. — London : Newnes Technical Books, Mar.1982. — [112]p
ISBN 0-408-00576-9 (pbk) : £3.45 : CIP entry B82-00909

643 — Residences — *For children*

Testa, Fulvio. The ideal home / Fulvio Testa. — London : Abelard, 1982. — [24]p : col.ill ; 25cm
ISBN 0-200-72768-0 : £4.95 : CIP rev. B81-26757

643 — Residences — *Forecasts* — *For children*

Ardley, Neil. Tomorrow′s home / Neil Ardley. — London : Watts, [1981]. — 37p : col.ill ; 30cm. — (World of tommorow)
ISBN 0-85166-931-x : £3.99 B82-05551

643′.022′2 — Household objects — *Illustrations* — *For children*

Daniels, Meg. Indoors. — London : Blackie, Feb.1982. — [12]p. — (Blackie concertina books)
ISBN 0-216-91129-x : £0.95 : CIP entry B81-36033

643′.028′9 — Great Britain. Residences. Safety measures & security measures

Hasler, Gordon. Protect your property and defend yourself / Gordon Hasler ; illustrated by Jo Whitley. — Harmondsworth : Penguin, 1982. — 171p : ill ; 20cm. — (Penguin handbooks)
Includes index
ISBN 0-14-046486-7 (pbk) : £2.25 B82-35262

Home safety : what′s it all about? : a guide for professional officers, policymakers, speakers and students. — Birmingham : RoSPA, c1982. — 11p : ill ; 30cm
ISBN 0-900635-57-6 (unbound) : £0.75 B82-34547

643′.028′9 — Great Britain. Residences. Safety measures — *Manuals*

Accident action : the essential family guide to home safety and first aid. — London : Macmillan, c1978. — 117p : ill ; 27cm
Text on lining papers. — Includes index
ISBN 0-333-25266-7 : £3.95 : CIP rev.
Primary classification 616.02′52 B78-27385

643′.028′9 — Residences. Safety measures - *Amateurs′ manuals*

Creese, Angela. Safety for your family. — 2nd ed. — London : Bell & Hyman, Aug.1981. — [281]p
Previous ed.: London : Mills & Boon, 1968
ISBN 0-7135-2070-1 (pbk) : CIP entry
Also classified at 616.02′52′024649 B81-16361

643′.16 — Great Britain. Residences. Burglary. Prevention — *Manuals*

Walker, Brian. Household security. — London : Newnes Technical, Jan.1983. — [120]p. — (Questions & answers)
ISBN 0-408-01201-3 (pbk) : £1.95 : CIP entry B82-34438

643′.16 — Residences. Security equipment

Securing your home / [edited by Edith Rudinger]. — London : Consumers′ Association, c1981. — 122p : ill ; 21cm
Includes index
ISBN 0-85202-207-7 (pbk) : Unpriced
ISBN 0-340-27485-9 (Hodder & Stoughton) B82-05307

643′.5 — Houses. Lofts. Conversion — *Amateurs′ manuals*

Tattersall, Robert, *1927-*. Room at the top : a D.I.Y. guide to loft conversions / Robert Tattersall. — London : Stanley Paul, 1982. — 123p : ill ; 22cm
Includes index
ISBN 0-09-146851-5 (pbk) : £4.95 : CIP rev. B82-00282

643′.55 — Great Britain. Houses. Garden rooms, *ca 1750-1950* — *Illustrations*

Boniface, Priscilla. The garden room / Priscilla Boniface ; general editor Peter Fowler. — London : H.M.S.O., 1982. — vi,[70]p : chiefly ill,1port ; 25cm. — (National Monuments Record photographic archives)
"Royal Commission on Historical Monuments England". — Ill on inside cover. — Bibliography on title page verso. — Includes index
ISBN 0-11-701127-4 (pbk) : £4.95 B82-35527

643′.6 — Household electric equipment. Maintenance & repair — *Amateurs′ manuals*

Understanding practical electrics. — London : Reader′s Digest Association, 1977 (1981 [printing]). — 48p : ill(some col.) ; 27cm. — (Reader′s Digest basic guide)
′Text and illustrations in this book are taken from Reader′s Digest repair manual′, 1972
ISBN 0-276-00107-9 (pbk) : £1.25 B82-04172

643′.6 — Household equipment — *For children*

Humberstone, Eliot. Finding out about things at home / written by Eliot Humberstone ; illustrated by Basil Arm ... [et al.]. — London : Usborne, 1981. — 32p : col.ill ; 21cm. — (Usborne explainers)
Includes index
ISBN 0-86020-501-0 (pbk) : £0.99 B82-34563

643′.604 — Great Britain. Household equipment for physically handicapped persons — *Buyers′ guides*

Home management : October 1981. — 5th ed / compiler E.R. Wilshere ; editors G.M. Cochrane, E.R. Wilshere. — [Oxford] : Oxford Area Health Authority (Teaching), c1981. — 58p : ill ; 30cm. — (Equipment for the disabled)
Previous ed.: 1976. — Bibliography: p50. — Includes index
£3.00 (pbk) B82-05692

643′.6′074042815 — West Yorkshire *(Metropolitan County)*. **Wakefield. Museums: Clarke Hall. Stock: English household equipment,** *1600-1700*. **Terminology** — *For schools*

Widdowson, J. D. A.. A century of words : a hundred items to be found at Clarke Hall, Wakefield / [text J.D.A. Widdowson] ; [design & illustrations Steve Denham]. — [Wakefield] : School Museum and Research Service. (Yorkshire Consortium for Education Joint Services), c1982. — 40p : ill ; 15x21cm
Includes index
ISBN 0-86169-009-5 (pbk) : Unpriced B82-23973

643′.7 — Houses. Improvement — *Amateurs′ manuals*

The Knack. — London : Marshall Cavendish, Feb.1982. — 24v.
ISBN 0-85685-999-0 : CIP entry B81-37580

643′.7 — Houses. Renovation — *Amateurs′ manuals*

Turner, Stuart. Buying and renovating a cottage. — Cambridge : Patrick Stephens, July 1982. — [184]p
ISBN 0-85059-592-4 : £8.95 : CIP entry B82-13085

643′.7 — Residences. Conversion & improvement — *Manuals*

King, Sally. Setting up home. — London : Muller, Sept.1982. — [160]p
ISBN 0-584-11015-4 : £6.95 : CIP entry
Also classified at 640 B82-20278

643′.7 — Residences. Decorating — *Amateurs′ manuals*

Home decorating. — London : Reader′s Digest, c1975 (1982 [printing]). — 47p : ill(some col.) ; 27cm. — (Reader′s digest basic guide)
Unpriced (pbk) B82-34674

Home decorating. — Reprinted with amendments. — London : Readers Digest Association, 1981, c1975. — 48p : col.ill ; 27cm. — (Reader′s Digest basic guide)
Previous ed.: 1978. — ′Text and illustrations in the book are taken from the Reader′s Digest complete do-it-yourself manual′, 1972
ISBN 0-276-00124-9 (pbk) : £1.25 B82-04167

643′.7 — Residences. Exteriors. Maintenance & repair — *Amateurs′ manuals*

King, Harold, *1927-*. Exterior house maintenance / Harold and Elizabeth King. — London : Pelham, 1981. — 136p : ill ; 21cm. — (Tricks of the trade)
Includes index
ISBN 0-7207-1325-0 : £5.50 B82-13543

643′.7 — Residences. Interiors. Decorating — *Amateurs′ manuals*

Dickson, Elizabeth. The Laura Ashley book of home decorating / Elizabeth Dickson and Margaret Colvin ; foreword by Laura Ashley. — London : Octupus, 1982. — 160p : ill(some col.) ; 29cm
Includes index
ISBN 0-7064-1478-0 : £7.95
Primary classification 747 B82-24563

Phipps, Diana. Diana Phipps′s Affordable splendour : an ingenious guide to decorating elegantly, inexpensively and doing most of it yourself / with illustrations by the author. — London : Weidenfeld and Nicolson, c1982. — 276p,[32]p of plates : ill(some col.),plans ; 24cm
Includes index
ISBN 0-297-78100-6 : £10.95 B82-31053

643′.7 — Residences. Maintenance & repair — *Amateurs′ manuals*

Good Housekeeping quick home repairs / Good Housekeeping Institute. — London : Ebury, 1982. — 127p : ill ; 22cm
Includes index
ISBN 0-85223-220-9 (cased) : £5.95
ISBN 0-85223-216-0 () : £2.95 B82-33381

Grace, Ron. The quick and easy guide to home repairs / Ron Grace. — London : Octopus, 1982, c1979. — 96p : col.ill ; 29cm
Originally published: London : Sundial, 1979. — Ill on lining papers. — Includes index
ISBN 0-7064-1780-1 : £2.95 B82-20822

643′.7 — Residences. Maintenance & repair — *Amateurs′ manuals* *continuation*

Keegan, Patrick. The reluctant handyman / Patrick Keegan and Ian Layzell. — [Weybridge] : Whittet ; [London] : Windward, 1981. — 191p : ill ; 25cm
Includes index
ISBN 0-7112-0204-4 : £5.95 : CIP rev. B81-28067

Looking after your house. — Reprinted with amendments. — London : Reader′s Digest Association, 1981, c1977. — 48p : ill(some col.) ; 27cm. — (Reader′s Digest basic guide)
Previous ed.: 1977. — ′Text and illustrations in this book are taken from Reader′s Digest repair manual′, 1972
ISBN 0-276-00167-2 (pbk) : £0.95 B82-04176

The **Which?** book of do-it-yourself. — London : Consumers′ Association and Hodder & Stoughton, c1981. — 320p : ill(some col.) ; 26cm
Includes index
ISBN 0-340-26237-0 : £11.95 B82-02590

643′.7 — Residences. Maintenance, repair & improvement — *Amateurs′ manuals*

Abbey National book of the home. — London : Octopus, 1982. — 205p : col.ill ; 29cm
Includes index
ISBN 0-7064-1725-9 : £6.95 B82-36508

The **Knack** : the complete manual of DIY skills, projects and home ideas. — London : Marshall Cavendish, c1982. — 98v.(various pagings) : ill (some col.) ; 28cm
Includes index
£0.55 per vol. (unbound) B82-35752

The **New** home owner manual. — London : Hamlyn, 1982. — 880p : ill,plans ; 20cm
Originally published: 1975. — Includes index
ISBN 0-600-34991-8 : £4.95 B82-27146

643′.7 — Stone buildings. Renovation — *Amateurs′ manuals*

Harrison, J. A. C.. Old stone buildings : buying, extending, renovating / J. A. C. Harrison. — Newton Abbot : David & Charles, c1982. — 191p : ill,plans ; 25cm
Bibliography: p186. — Includes index
ISBN 0-7153-8125-3 : £10.95 : CIP rev. B82-07582

643′.7′094294 — South Wales, Old persons. Residences. Improvement. Projects: Ferndale Project

Morton, Jane. Ferndale : a caring repair service for elderly home owners. — London : Shelter, Sept.1982. — [24]p
ISBN 0-901242-63-2 (pbk) : £2.25 : CIP entry B82-29399

644 — HOUSEHOLD UTILITIES

644 — Great Britain. Energy resources. Conservation by households — *Manuals* **—** *Serials*

Practical alternatives : a magazine of ways of saving resources in everyday life, and newsletter of Ecological Life Style Ltd. — No.1 (July 1981)-. — Radlett (11 Lodge End, Radlett, Herts.) : David Stephens and Associates, 1981-. — v. ; 21cm
Absorbed: Newsletter (Ecological Life Style Ltd)
ISSN 0262-4540 = Practical alternatives : Unpriced B82-04904

644 — Ireland *(Republic)*. **Farmhouses. Energy. Conservation —** *Manuals*

Protect your home against heat loss and save money / ACOT. — [Blackrock] ([Frascati Rd., Blackrock, Co. Dublin]) : Farm House Management Advisory Service, [ACOT], [1981?]. — 8p : col.ill ; 22cm
Unpriced (unbound) B82-05188

644 — Residences. Energy. Consumption & conservation

Kirk, David. Services, heating and equipment for home economists. — Chichester : Ellis Horwood, July 1982. — [360]p. — (Ellis Horwood series in food science & technology)
ISBN 0-85312-134-6 : £22.50 : CIP entry B82-20652

644′.1 — Great Britain. Residences. Communal heating systems. Evaporative radiator metering

Fisk, D. J.. Field performance of evaporative heat metering in district heating schemes / D.J. Fisk and A.S. Eastwell. — London : H.M.S.O., 1981. — iv,23p : ill ; 30cm. — (Building Research Establishment report)
"Department of the Environment Building Research Establishment"
ISBN 0-11-670775-5 (pbk) : £2.80 B82-02406

644′.1 — Great Britain. Residences. Heating. Costs. Reduction

Makkar, Lali. How to cut your fuel bills. — London : Kogan Page, Sept.1982. — [150]p
ISBN 0-85038-580-6 : £6.95 : CIP entry B82-22813

644′.6 — Great Britain. Residences. Hot water heating systems. Energy. Conservation

Energy conservation in the production of domestic hot water. — London : H.M.S.O., 1981. — vii,15p ; 25cm. — (Energy paper / Department of Energy ; no.48) (Paper / Advisory Council on Energy Conservation ; 12)
Prepared by the Buildings Working Group of the Advisory Council on Energy Conservation
ISBN 0-11-411022-0 (pbk) : £2.80 B82-06093

645 — HOUSEHOLD FURNISHINGS

645′.4 — Upholstered furniture. Restoration — *Amateurs′ manuals*

Mack, Lorrie. Restoring upholstered furniture / Lorrie Mack with Geoffrey Hayley ; drawings by Wendy Jones. — London : Orbis, 1981. — 112p : ill(some col.) ; 30cm
Bibliography: p112. — Includes index
ISBN 0-85613-329-9 : Unpriced B82-08006

645′.4 — Upholstering — *Amateurs′ manuals*

Brock, Anne. Upholstery properly explained / by Anne Brock. — Kingswood : Elliot Right Way, c1982. — 157p : ill ; 18cm. — (Paperfronts)
Includes index
ISBN 0-7160-0673-1 (pbk) : £0.75 B82-23919

Edwards, Margaret. Upholstery and canework. — London : Pelham, Nov.1982. — [128]p. — (Tricks of the trade)
ISBN 0-7207-1418-4 : £5.50 : CIP entry
Also classified at 684.1′3 B82-26408

Ward, Kitty. Upholstery : a beginner′s guide / Kitty Ward ; black and white photographs by Timothy Ward. — London : Stanley Paul, 1981. — 212p,[8]p of plates : ill ; 22cm
Bibliography: p210. — Includes index
ISBN 0-09-145681-9 (pbk) : £5.50 : CIP rev. B81-22615

646 — CLOTHING, SEWING, ETC

646.2 — Sewing — *Amateurs′ manuals*

Speller, Betty. The reluctant needle-worker. — Weybridge : Whittet Books, Oct.1982. — [96]p
ISBN 0-905483-25-1 : £5.95 : CIP entry B82-24600

646.2 — Sewing — *For children*

Barber, Janet. The Beaver book of sewing / Janet Barber ; illustrated by Virginia Lister. — London : Hamlyn, 1982. — 159p : ill ; 18cm. — (Beaver books)
ISBN 0-600-20323-9 (pbk) : £1.10 B82-10286

Wallis, Jill. [My first sewing book]. My first ‘show me how’ sewing book / written by Jill Wallis ; illustrated by Lindal Mann. — London : Dean, 1981, c1973. — 45p : col.ill ; 26cm
Originally published: 1975
ISBN 0-603-00258-7 : Unpriced B82-26754

646.2 — Sewing — *Manuals*

Stitch by stitch : the illustrated encyclopedia of sewing, knitting & crochet. — London : Marshall Cavendish, Feb.1982. — 20v.
ISBN 0-85685-768-8 : CIP entry
Also classified at 746.43 B82-02469

646.2′044 — Sewing machines, *to ca 1900*

Head, Carol. Old sewing machines / Carol Head. — Princes Risborough : Shire, 1982. — 32p : ill ; 21cm. — (Shire album ; 84)
Bibliography: p32
ISBN 0-85263-591-5 (pbk) : £0.95 B82-39393

646.2′1 — Household soft furnishings. Making — *Manuals*

Fishburn, Angela. The Batsford book of home furnishings / Angela Fishburn. — London : Batsford, 1982. — 144p,[4]p of plates : ill(some col.) ; 26cm
Bibliography: p141. — Includes index
ISBN 0-7134-3466-x : £7.95 B82-22166

646.2′1 — Soft furnishings: Curtains & blinds. Making — *Manuals*

O′Leary, Helen. Curtains and blinds. — London : Pelham, Oct.1982. — [128]p. — (Tricks of the trade)
ISBN 0-7207-1419-2 : £5.50 : CIP entry B82-23028

646.2′13 — Soft furnishings: Loose covers. Making — *Manuals*

Davies, Mary. Tailored loose covers. — London : Paul, Oct.1981. — 1v.
ISBN 0-09-145660-6 (cased) : £6.95 : CIP entry
ISBN 0-09-145661-4 (pbk) : £4.95 B81-26770

646′.3 — Dressing-up — *Manuals* **—** *For children*

Stoker, Diana S.. Dressing-up / Diana Stoker, Stephanie Connell ; illustrated by Joan Hickson. — London : Methuen Children′s in association with Thames Television International, 1981. — [32]p : col.ill ; 19cm. — (Rainbow things to do) (A Thames/Magnet book)
Also published in one volume with ′Puppets′ and ′Messy things′
ISBN 0-423-00090-x (pbk) : £0.85 B82-17594

Tanaka, Béatrice. Disguise workshop / Béatrice Tanaka ; translated by Anthea Bell. — [London] : Pepper, 1982. — 47p : ill(some col.) ; 28cm
Translation of: Aktionsbuch
ISBN 0-237-45634-6 : £4.25 B82-27666

646′.31 — Physically handicapped persons′ clothing

Goldsworthy, Maureen. Clothes for disabled people / Maureen Goldsworthy. — London : Batsford, 1981. — 117p : ill ; 25cm
Bibliography: p117
ISBN 0-7134-3928-9 (cased) : Unpriced
ISBN 0-7134-3929-7 (pbk) : £4.95 B82-05157

646′.34 — Women′s clothing. Selection — *Manuals*

Hogg, Kate. More dash than cash. — London : Hutchinson, Sept.1982. — 1v.
ISBN 0-09-149470-2 : £9.95 : CIP entry B82-22414

Perceval, Sara. Star image / Sara Perceval. — London : Unwin, 1981. — 132p,[12]p of plates : ill,ports ; 20cm
ISBN 0-04-391005-x (pbk) : £2.50 : CIP rev. B81-28153

646.4 — Clothing. Making — *Manuals*

Christensen, Olive. Concise needlecraft / Olive Christensen. — New ed. — Exeter : Wheaton, 1982, c1977. — vii,71p : ill(some col.) ; 30cm
Previous ed.: 1977. — Includes index
ISBN 0-08-027911-2 (pbk) : Unpriced B82-33785

Ladbury, Ann. Weekend wardrobe / Ann Ladbury ; designs by Caroline Charles. — London : British Broadcasting Corporation, 1982. — 72p : ill(some col.) ; 30cm
Published to accompany the BBC television series. — Patterns in pocket
ISBN 0-563-16490-5 (pbk) : £4.95 B82-21343

646.4′04 — Maternity clothing. Designs — *Patterns*

Cardy, Lynn. Maternity clothes. — London : Bell & Hyman, June 1982. — [128]p
ISBN 0-7135-1312-8 (cased) : £7.95 : CIP entry
ISBN 0-7135-1313-6 (pbk) : £4.95 B82-09605

646.4'04 — Women's clothing. Sewing — *Amateurs' manuals*
Shaeffer, Claire B.. The complete book of sewing short cuts / Claire B. Shaeffer. — New York : Sterling ; Poole : Blandford [distributor], c1981. — 256p : ill ; 27cm
Includes index
ISBN 0-8069-5432-9 (cased) : £10.95
ISBN 0-8069-7564-4 (pbk) : Unpriced B82-21868

The **Vogue** sewing book. — Rev. metricated ed. / [Elizabeth J. Musheno : editor] ; [Tony Serino : art director]. — Poole : Blandford Press, 1978 (1981 [printing]). — 464p,[60]p of plates : ill (some col.),ports ; 26cm
Includes index
ISBN 0-7137-1257-0 : £12.50 B82-39941

646.4'06 — Children's clothing. Making — *Manuals*
Benton, Kitty. Sewing classic clothes for children / Kitty Benton. — London : Hamlyn, 1981. — 192p : ill(some col.),ports ; 29cm
Originally published: New York : Hearst, 1981. — Includes index
ISBN 0-600-38463-2 : £9.95 B82-08123

646.4'06 — Clothing for children, to 11 years. Making — *Patterns*
Cardy, Lynn. Kid's clothes. — London : Bell & Hyman, Oct.1981. — [128]p
ISBN 0-7135-1295-4 (cased) : £7.95 : CIP entry
ISBN 0-7135-1296-2 (pbk) : £4.95 B81-24654

646.4'07 — Clothing. Aran knitting — *Patterns*
Hollingworth, Shelagh. The complete book of traditional Aran knitting / Shelagh Hollingworth ; with a foreword by Heinz Edgar Kiewe. — London : Batsford, 1982. — 144p : ill ; 26cm
Bibliography: p142. — Includes index
ISBN 0-7134-2570-9 : £7.95 B82-31188

646.4'07 — Clothing. Fair Isle knitting — *Patterns*
Don, Sarah. Fair Isle knitting. — London : Bell & Hyman, Apr.1982. — [126]p
Originally published: London : Mills and Boon, 1979
ISBN 0-7135-2019-1 : £6.50 : CIP entry B82-09192

Traditional Fair Isle knitting patterns. — Edinburgh (5 Charlotte Sq., Edinburgh EH2 4DU) : National Trust for Scotland, [1981]?. — [12]p : col.ill ; 30cm
£1.50 (unbound) B82-00578

646.4'07 — Clothing. North American Indian designs — *Patterns*
Wood, Margaret, *1950-*. Native American fashion : modern adaptations of traditional designs / Margaret Wood ; photographs by DeCastro Studios ; illustrations by Susan Raudman and Charles Wood. — New York ; London : Van Nostrand Reinhold, c1981. — 128p : ill,1map ; 29cm
Bibliography: p123-126. — Includes index
ISBN 0-442-20756-5 : £13.55 B82-13197

646.4'072 — Clothing. Knitting. Designs — *Manuals*
Stanley, Montse. Knitting : your own designs for a perfect fit / Montse Stanley. — Newton Abbot : David & Charles, c1982. — 176p : ill (some col.) ; 31cm
Includes index
ISBN 0-7153-8227-6 : £8.95 : CIP rev. B82-09621

646.4'204 — Lingerie. Making — *Manuals*
Lingerie : original designs for you to make / edited by Jack Angell. — Newton Abbot : David & Charles, c1981. — 135p : ill(some col.) ; 30cm
ISBN 0-7153-8174-1 : £9.50 : CIP rev. B81-27949

646.4'3'04 — Dressmaking — *For schools*
Goldsworthy, Maureen. Knowing your sewing. — London : Bell & Hyman, July 1981. — [64]p
Originally published: London : Mills & Boon, 1978
ISBN 0-7135-2002-7 (pbk) : £3.00 : CIP entry B81-21501

646.4'304 — Women's clothing. Knitting — *Patterns*
Probert, Christina. Knitting in Vogue : patterns from the '30s to the '80s to knit now. — Newton Abbot : David & Charles, Sept.1982. — [176]p
ISBN 0-7153-8208-x : £10.95 : CIP entry B82-20378

646.4'3204 — Dressmaking. Fitting — *Amateurs' manuals*
Hall, Gerald Marshall. Fitting / Gerald Marshall Hall ; illustrations by Barbara Firth. — London : Warne, 1982. — 69p : ill ; 22cm. — (Making clothes ; stage 4) (An Observer's guide)
ISBN 0-7232-2889-2 (pbk) : £1.95 B82-36615

646.4'3204 — Dressmaking — *Manuals*
Encyclopedia of advanced dressmaking / [edited by Annie Woolridge] ; [photography by John Carter ... [others] ; [illustrations Terry Evans, Barbara Firth, Garry Shewring]. — London : Marshall Cavendish, 1978. — 247p : ill(some col.) ; 30cm
Originally published: in Golden hands monthly and Fashion maker. — Ill on lining papers. — Includes index
ISBN 0-85685-452-2 : £6.95 B82-03278

646.4'3204 — Dressmaking — *Patterns*
Foster, Betty. Betty Foster dressmaking course : for fashion that fits. — London : Independent Television Books, 1982. — 60p : ill(some col.),1port ; 30cm
Cover title
ISBN 0-900727-94-2 (pbk) : £1.45 B82-30099

646.4'3204 — Dressmaking. Patterns. Cutting
Stanley, Helen. Modelling and flat cutting for fashion. — London : Hutchinson Education 2. — May 1982. — [120]p
ISBN 0-09-147480-9 (cased) : £12.00 : CIP entry
ISBN 0-09-147481-7 (pbk) : £6.95 B82-07256

Stanley, Helen. Modelling and flat cutting for fashion. — London : Hutchinson Education 3. — May 1982. — [120]p
ISBN 0-09-147490-6 (cased) : £12.00 : CIP entry
ISBN 0-09-147491-4 (pbk) : £6.95 B82-07258

646.4'3204 — Dressmaking. Patterns. Cutting — *Manuals*
Naldrett, Toni. Cutting out / Toni Naldrett ; illustrated by Barbara Firth. — London : Warne, 1982. — 45p : ill,forms ; 22cm. — (Making clothes ; stage 1) (An Observer's guide)
ISBN 0-7232-2892-2 (pbk) : £1.95 B82-36616

Shoben, Martin. Pattern cutting and making up : the professional approach / Martin Shoben and Janet Ward. — London : Batsford
1: Basic techniques and sample development. — 1980. — 144p : ill(some col.) ; 25cm
Includes index
ISBN 0-7134-3338-8 (cased) : £12.95
ISBN 0-7134-3339-6 (pbk) : £7.95 B82-21350

646.4'3204 — Dressmaking. Patterns. Design — *Manuals*
Aldrich, Winifred. Metric pattern cutting. — London : Bell & Hyman, Feb.1982. — [144]p
Originally published: London : Mills and Boon, 1979
ISBN 0-7135-2007-8 : £5.95 : CIP entry B81-40238

Wolfe, Mary Gorgen. Clear-cut pattern making : by the flat-pattern method / Mary Gorgen Wolfe. — New York ; Chichester : Wiley, c1982. — x,221p : ill ; 28cm
Includes index
ISBN 0-471-09937-6 (spiral) : £13.20 B82-36947

646.4'3204 — Dressmaking. Pressing — *Amateurs' manuals*
Hall, Gerald Marshall. Pressing / Gerald Marshall Hall ; illustrations by Barbara Firth. — London : Warne, 1982. — 63p : ill ; 22cm. — (Making clothes ; stage 3) (An Observer's guide)
ISBN 0-7232-2890-6 (pbk) : £1.95 B82-36618

646.4'3204 — Dressmaking. Sewing machines. Techniques
Naldrett, Toni. The sewing machine / Toni Naldrett ; illustrations by Barbara Firth. — London : Warne, 1982. — 63p : ill ; 22cm. — (Making clothes ; stage 2) (An Observer's guide)
ISBN 0-7232-2891-4 (pbk) : £1.95 B82-36617

646.4'3204'0321 — Dressmaking — *Encyclopaedias*
Ladbury, Ann. The dressmaker's dictionary / Ann Ladbury ; illustrations by Jil Shipley and others. — London : Batsford, 1982. — 358p : ill ; 26cm
ISBN 0-7134-1823-0 : £9.95 B82-33823

646.4'54 — Sweaters. Knitting — *Manuals*
The **Sweater** book. — London (9 Henrietta St., WC2E 8PS) : Dorling Kindersley, Oct.1982. — [144]p
ISBN 0-86318-006-x : £7.95 : CIP entry B82-24616

646.4'5406 — Children's sweaters. Knitting. Chinese designs — *Patterns*
Gross, Judith. Patterns from China : sweater ideas for children / Judith Gross. — New York ; London : Van Nostrand Reinhold, c1982. — 96p,[4]p of plates : ill(some col.) ; 29cm
Bibliography: p93. — Includes index
ISBN 0-442-20399-3 : £15.25 B82-16310

646.4'7 — Wedding dresses, *1260-1900.* **Sewing -** *Patterns*
Bullen, Nicholas. Making classic wedding dresses. — London : Bell & Hyman, July 1981. — [80]p
ISBN 0-7135-1283-0 (pbk) : £5.95 : CIP entry B81-18107

646.5'04 — Women's hats. Making — *Manuals*
Morgan, Peter, *1942-*. Making hats / Peter Morgan. — London : Batsford, 1971 (1978 [printing]). — 95p : ill ; 20cm
ISBN 0-7134-1078-7 (pbk) : £4.95 B82-06212

646.7 — MANAGEMENT OF PERSONAL AND FAMILY LIVING, GROOMING

646.7'088042 — Adolescent girls. Beauty care & cleanliness — *Manuals*
Shure, Jan. Girl : a complete guide to looking and feeling good. — Loughton : Piatkus, Oct.1982. — [128]p
ISBN 0-86188-210-5 (cased) : £6.95 : CIP entry
ISBN 0-86188-213-x (pbk) : £3.95 B82-24578

646.7'088042 — Women. Beauty care & cleanliness — *Manuals*
Clark, Felicity. Vogue guide to skin care, hair care and make up / Felicity Clark. — London : Allen Lane, 1982, c1981. — 256p,[32]p of plates : ill(some col.) ; 21cm
'First published in three separate volumes by Penguin Books 1981' — t.p verso. — Includes index
ISBN 0-7139-1489-0 : £7.95 B82-30102

Spoiling yourself / [text by Sarah Collins ... et al.] ; [illustrations by Roberta Colegate-Stone, Pat Ludlow, Belinda Lyon]. — [Kettering] ([Newtown St., Woodford, Kettering, Northants. NN14 4HW]) : Kingfisher, c1981. — 28p : ill(some col.),ports(some col.) ; 21cm. — (The New you beauty programme)
Cover title. — Text on inside covers
Unpriced (pbk) B82-11332

646.7'2 — Women. Beauty care. Use of herbs — *Manuals*
Little, Kitty, *1949-*. Kitty Little's book of herbal beauty / illustrated by John Dodson. — Harmondsworth : Penguin, 1981, c1980. — 240p,8p of plates : ill(some col.) ; 21cm
Originally published: London : Jill Norman, 1980. — Bibliography: p236-237. — Includes index
ISBN 0-14-046355-0 (pbk) : £2.95 B82-08146

646.7'2 — Women. Beauty care. Use of natural food

Meredith, Bronwen. Vogue natural health and beauty / Bronwen Meredith. — Harmondsworth : Penguin, 1981, c1979. — 300p,[16]p of plates : ill(some col.),facsims ; 25cm
Originally published: London : Allen Lane, 1979. — Includes index
ISBN 0-14-005040-x (pbk) : £4.95
Primary classification 613.2'6 B82-07285

646.7'2 — Women. Face. Beauty care — *Manuals*

Cartland, Barbara. Keep young and beautiful / Barbara Cartland & Elinor Glyn. — London : Duckworth, 1982. — x102p : ill ; 21cm. — (Paperduck)
ISBN 0-7156-1496-7 (pbk) : £1.95 B82-28827

646.7'2'023 — Beauty care — *Career guides*

Morris, Joy. Working in the world of beauty / Joy Morris. — London : Batsford Academic and Educational, 1982. — 88p,[8]p of plates : ill ; 22cm
Includes index
ISBN 0-7134-4077-5 : £5.95 B82-14096

646.7'2'088042 — Negro women. Beauty care — *Serials*

Black beauty & hair : for the beauty conscious black woman. — Summer 1982-. — Sutton (Quadrant House, The Quadrant, Sutton, Surrey) : IPC Consumer Industries Press, 1982-. — v. : ill(some col.),ports ; 29cm
Quarterly
ISSN 0263-3213 = Black beauty & hair : £1.00 B82-33855

646.7'2'088042 — Pregnant women. Beauty care — *Manuals*

Gates, Wende Devlin. Newborn beauty : a complete beauty, health and energy guide to the nine months of pregnancy and the nine months after / by Wende Devlin Gates and Gail McFarland Meckel ; with a preface by Gideon G. Panter ; photographs by Michael Pateman ; illustrations by Durell Godfrey. — Toronto ; London : Bantam, 1981, c1980. — xiii,352p : ill,ports ; 24cm
Originally published: New York : Viking Press, 1980
ISBN 0-553-01341-6 (pbk) : £3.95 B82-21603

Natale, Gloria. The pregnant woman's beauty book. — London : New English Library, Mar.1982. — [144]p
ISBN 0-450-05367-9 (pbk) : £1.25 : CIP entry B82-01986

646.7'2'088042 — Women. Beauty care — *Manuals*

The **24** hour look / [text by Sarah Collins et al.] ; [illustrations by Roberta Colegate-Stone et al.]. — [Kettering] ([Newtown St, Woodford, Kettering, Northants. NN14 4HW]) : Kingfisher, c1981. — 28p : ill(some col.) ; 21cm. — (The New you beauty programme)
Cover title. — Text on inside covers
Unpriced (pbk) B82-03241

Baker, Oleda. How to renovate yourself from head to toe / Oleda Baker ; illustrated by Mona Mark. — London : Severn House, 1982, c1980. — x,209p : ill ; 21cm
Originally published: Garden City, N.Y. : Doubleday, 1980. — Includes index
ISBN 0-7278-2015-x : £7.95 : CIP rev. B81-21516

Blueprint for beauty. — [Kettering] ([Newtown St., Woodford, Kettering, Northants. NN14 4HW]) : Kingfisher
Pt.2. — c1981. — 27p : ill(some col.) ; 21cm. — (The New you beauty programme)
Text on inside covers
Unpriced (pbk) B82-11331

Collins, Sarah. A woman for all seasons / [text by Sarah Collins, Mundy Ellis, Norma Knox] ; [illustrations by Terry Evans, Pat Ludlow, Belinda Lyon]. — [Great Britain] : Kingfisher, c1982. — 28p : ill(some col.) ; 21cm. — (The New you beauty programme)
Cover title. — Text, ill on inside covers
Unpriced (pbk) B82-33988

The **Face** and body book / general editor Miriam Stoppard. — London : Pan, 1981, c1980. — 256p : ill(some col.),ports ; 27cm
Originally published: London : Windward, 1980. — Includes index
ISBN 0-330-26565-2 (pbk) : Unpriced B82-01585

Meredith, Bronwen. Vogue young beauty / Bronwen Meredith. — London : Allen Lane, c1982. — 207p,[16]p of plates : ill(some col.) ; 28cm
Includes index
ISBN 0-7139-1346-0 : £9.95 B82-30101

Natural beauty / [text by Nina Ridgewell ... [et al.] ; illustrations by Norman Livingstone ... [et al.]. — [Great Britain] : Kingfisher, c1982. — 28p : ill(some col.) ; 21cm. — (The New you beauty programme)
Cover title. — Text, ill on inside covers
Unpriced (pbk) B82-33987

Tiegs, Cheryl. The way to natural beauty / Cheryl Tiegs with Vicki Lindner. — London : Orbis, 1982, c1980. — 284p : ill,ports ; 24cm
Originally published: New York : Simon and Schuster, c1980
ISBN 0-85613-406-6 (pbk) : £4.95 B82-24029

Top to toe beauty / [text by Caroline Richards et al.] ; [illustrations by Pat Ludlow, Belinda Lyon]. — [Kettering] ([Newtown St, Woodford, Kettering, Northants. NN14 4HW]) : Kingfisher, c1981. — 28p : ill(some col.) ; 21cm. — (The New you beauty programme)
Cover title. — Text on inside covers
Unpriced (pbk) B82-03240

Vogue stay young / editor Alexandra Penney ; associate editor Diana Edkins ; design Miki Denhof. — London : Macmillan, c1981. — 256p : ill(some col.),ports ; 28cm
Originally published: New York : St. Martin's Press, 1981. — Includes index
ISBN 0-333-32727-6 : £9.95 B82-06961

646.7'24 — Man. Facial hair. Removal by electrolysis

Gallant, Ann. Principles and techniques for the electrologist. — Cheltenham : Thornes, June 1982. — [352]p
ISBN 0-85950-489-1 (pbk) : £6.95 : CIP entry B82-11789

646.7'24 — Man. Hair. Care

Young, Marc. The complete book of hair care. — London : Severn House, Oct.1982. — [128]p
ISBN 0-7278-2023-0 : £6.95 : CIP entry B82-24247

646.7'24'068 — Hairdressing businesses. Management

Palladino, Leo. Hairdressing management. — Cheltenham : Stanley Thornes, Sept.1982. — [352]p
ISBN 0-85950-338-0 (pbk) : £7.50 : CIP entry B82-20845

646.7'24'088042 — Women. Hair. Beauty care — *Manuals*

Heading for a change / [text by Marion Matthews ... et al.] ; [illustrations by Terry Evans ... et al.]. — [Great Britain] : Kingfisher, c1982. — 28p : ill(some col.) ; 21cm. — (The New you beauty programme)
Cover title. — Text, ill on inside covers
Unpriced (pbk) B82-33986

Stunning hair styles / [text by Caroline Richards et al.] ; [illustrations by Terry Evans et al.]. — [Kettering] ([Newtown St, Woodford, Kettering, Northants. NN14 4HW]) : Kingfisher, c1981. — 28p : ill(some col.),2ports ; 21cm. — (The New you beauty programme)
Cover title. — Text on inside covers
Unpriced (pbk) B82-03243

646.7'242'015 — Hairdressing. Scientific aspects

Bennett, Ruth. The science of hairdressing / Ruth Bennett. — 2nd ed. — London : Edward Arnold, 1982. — viii,211p : ill ; 25cm
Previous ed.: 1975. — Bibliography: p203. — Includes index
ISBN 0-7131-0628-x (pbk) : £5.75 : CIP rev. B82-06907

Openshaw, Florence. Advanced hairdressing science / Florence Openshaw. — London : Longman, 1981. — 233p : ill ; 22cm
Includes index
ISBN 0-582-41583-7 (pbk) : £4.95 : CIP rev. B81-25729

646.7'242'015 — Hairdressing. Scientific aspects — *Questions & answers*

Hampson, J.. Objective tests in hairdressing science. — London : Longman, Sept.1981. — [96]p. — (Longman objective tests)
ISBN 0-582-41238-2 (pbk) : £1.95 : CIP entry B81-28203

646.7'242'0207 — Hairdressing — *Humour* — *Early works* — *Facsimiles*

Moor, John. Useful advice to hair-dressers, barbers, &c. &c. &c. / by John Moor. — St. Peter Port : Toucan, 1982. — 24p : 1ill ; 20cm
Facsim of ed. published: London : J. Bailey, 1810
ISBN 0-85694-260-x (pbk) : £2.10 B82-17407

646.7'242'068 — Hairdressing services. Organisation — *Manuals*

Jeremiah, R. W.. How you can make money in the hairdressing business / by R.W. Jeremiah. — Cheltenham : Thornes, 1982. — vii,114p : ill,1plan,forms ; 21cm
Includes index
ISBN 0-85950-330-5 (pbk) : £2.75 : CIP rev. B81-34786

646.7'242'096 — Africa. Hairdressing, *to 1981*

Sagay, Esi. African hairstyles : styles of yesterday and today. — London : Heinemann Educational, July 1982. — [120]p
ISBN 0-435-89830-2 (pbk) : £3.95 : CIP entry B82-16226

646.7'26 — Man. Skin. Care

Klein, Arnold W.. The skin book : looking and feeling your best through proper skin care / Arnold W. Klein, James H. Sternberg, and Paul Bernstein. — New York : Collier Books ; London : Collier Macmillan, c1981, c1980. — vii,184p : ill ; 24cm
Originally published: New York : Macmillan, 1980. — Includes index
ISBN 0-02-080750-3 (pbk) : £2.95 B82-26201

Murray, David, *1943-*. Scientific skin care. — London : Arlington Books, May 1982. — [224]p
ISBN 0-85140-573-8 : £9.95 : CIP entry B82-07019

646.7'26 — Women. Suntanning — *Manuals*

Helena Rubinstein's Book of the sun / edited by Laura Torbet. — London : Angus and Robertson, 1980, c1979. — 186p : ill ; 29cm
Originally published: New York : Times Books, 1979
ISBN 0-207-95862-9 : £6.95 B82-03045

646.7'26'088042 — Women. Skin. Beauty care — *Manuals*

Harris, Anthony, *1937-*. Your skin : its nature, care and beauty / Anthony Harris. — Sevenoaks : New English Library, 1982. — 207p : ill ; 19cm
ISBN 0-450-05303-2 (pbk) : £1.75 : CIP rev. B82-09295

Perfect skin / [text by Alix Kirsta et al.] ; [illustrations by Valerie Hill et al.]. — [Kettering] ([Newtown St, Woodford, Kettering, Northants. NN14 4HW]) : Kingfisher, c1981. — 28p : ill(some col.),2col.port ; 22cm. — (The New you beauty programme)
Cover title. — Text on inside covers
Unpriced (pbk) B82-03242

646.7'5 — Women. Physical fitness. Slimming. Exercises

Filson, Sidney. Shaping up. — London : Hodder and Stoughton, Apr.1982. — [224]p. — (Coronet books)
Originally published: Boston : Little, Brown, 1980
ISBN 0-340-26872-7 (pbk) : £1.50 : CIP entry B82-06499

646.7'7 — Women. Sex relations. Seduction — *Manuals*

Nichols, Richard. Do you come here often? / Richard Nichols. — [London] : Star, 1982. — 182p : ill ; 18cm
ISBN 0-352-31173-8 (pbk) : £1.50 B82-41127

Owens, Tuppy. Take me I'm yours : a guide to female psychology / Tuppy Owens. — Edinburgh : Harris, 1980. — x,180p ; 23cm
Bibliography: p180
ISBN 0-904505-73-1 : £4.95 B82-24066

646.7'9 — Great Britain. Retirement. Planning — *Manuals*

Open University. Planning retirement. — Milton Keynes : Open University Press, Nov.1982. — [256]p
ISBN 0-906139-09-0 : £25.00 : CIP entry
B82-36330

646.7'9 — Retirement. Planning — *Manuals*

Erskine, Aleda. The time of your life : a handbook for retirement / [written by Aleda Erskine] ; [edited by Susanna Johnston]. — London : Help the Aged in association with the Health Education Council, c1979. — 96p : ill(some col.),ports ; 30cm
Includes bibliographies
ISBN 0-905852-06-0 (pbk) : £1.95 B82-00131

Erskine, Aleda. The time of your life : a handbook for retirement / [written by Aleda Erskine] ; [edited by Susanna Johnston]. — Rev. 2nd ed. — London : Help the Aged in association with The Health Education Council, 1981. — 96p : ill(some col.),ports ; 30cm
Previous ed.: 1979. — Includes bibliographies and index
ISBN 0-905852-11-7 (pbk) : £2.95 B82-26851

646.7'9'0941 — Great Britain. Retirement — *Practical information*

Kay, Isabel. Your hopeful future : how to live well financially, medically and emotionally during retirement, unemployment or disablement / Isabel and Ernest Kay. — London : Macdonald, 1982. — 192p ; 23cm
Bibliography: p186-188. — Includes index
ISBN 0-356-08604-6 (cased) : £7.95
ISBN 0-356-08605-4 (pbk) : Unpriced
Primary classification 362.4'0941 B82-37218

647 — INSTITUTIONAL MANAGEMENT

647'.6 — Great Britain. Hotel industries. Receptionists. Duties

White, Paul B.. Hotel reception / Paul B. White, Helen Beckley. — 4th ed. — London : Edward Arnold, 1982. — vi,195p : ill,forms ; 22cm
Previous ed.: 1978. — Bibliography: p191. — Includes index
ISBN 0-7131-0718-9 (pbk) : Unpriced : CIP rev.
B82-11130

647'.6 — Great Britain. Hotel industries. Receptionists. Duties — *Questions & answers*

Bull, Jean. Questions in hotel reception / Jean Bull and Gordon Bull. — Cheltenham : Thornes, 1981. — 84p : ill,forms ; 24cm
Bibliography: p84
ISBN 0-85950-310-0 (pbk) : £1.85 : CIP rev.
B81-33772

647'.9 — Residential institutions. Household management — *Manuals*

Branson, Joan C.. Hotel, hostel and hospital housekeeping / Joan C. Branson, Margaret Lennox. — 4th ed. — London : Edward Arnold, 1982. — 310p : ill,plans ; 22cm
Previous ed.: 1976. — Includes index
ISBN 0-7131-0581-x (pbk) : £4.95 : CIP rev.
B81-35835

647'.9'076 — Residential institutions. Household management — *Questions & answers*

Branson, Joan C.. Questions on hotel, hostel and hospital housekeeping / Joan C. Branson, Margaret Lennox. — London : Edward Arnold, 1982. — vi,74p : ill,plans ; 22cm
ISBN 0-7131-0714-6 (pbk) : £2.75 : CIP rev.
B82-06917

647.94 — HOTELS, INNS, VACATION ACCOMMODATION, ETC

647'.94 — Hotels — *Directories — Serials*

Financial times world hotel directory. — 1982/83. — London : Longman, Sept.1982. — [880]p. — (Financial times international year books : information to business)
ISBN 0-582-90314-9 : £23.00 : CIP entry
ISSN 0308-8464 B82-25726

647'.94 — Hotels — *For children*

Mattock, Kate. Hotel / Kate Mattock. — London : Evans, 1982. — 48p : ill(some col.) ; 21cm. — (Talking shop)
ISBN 0-237-29253-x (pbk) : Unpriced
B82-16621

647'.94'023 — Great Britain. Hotels — *Career guides*

Ludlow, Diane. Working in a hotel / by Diane Ludlow ; photography by Christopher Fairclough. — Hove : Wayland, 1982. — 94p : ill,ports ; 25cm. — (People at work)
Includes index
ISBN 0-85340-955-2 (pbk) : £4.95 B82-33431

647'.94'02341 — Great Britain. Hotel industries — *Career guides*

Carabok, Miriam. Careers in catering and hotel management. — London : Kogan Page, Mar.1982. — [100]p
ISBN 0-85038-528-8 (cased) : £5.95 : CIP entry
ISBN 0-85038-529-6 (pbk) : £2.50 B82-02641

Hotels & catering / [written, designed and produced by SGS Education]. — Walton on Thames : Nelson, 1982. — 15p : ill ; 28cm. — (Career profiles ; 21)
ISBN 0-17-438369-x (unbound) : Unpriced
Primary classification 647'.95'02341
B82-27847

647'.94'068 — Bed & breakfast accommodation. Management

Vellacott, Audrey. Doing bed & breakfast / Audrey Vellacott and Liz Christmas. — Newton Abbot : David & Charles, c1982. — 96p : ill ; 23cm
Includes index
ISBN 0-7153-8236-5 : £4.95 : CIP rev.
B82-01182

647'.94'068 — Hereford and Worcester. Herefordshire. Vacation accomodation: Farmhouses. Management — *Stories, anecdotes*

Cox, Evelyn. Holiday farm / Evelyn Cox ; illustrations by Rodney Shackell. — London : Hodder and Stoughton, 1982. — 192p : ill ; 23cm
Ill on lining papers
ISBN 0-340-27835-8 : £6.95 : CIP rev.
B82-10016

647'.94'0683 — Hotel industries. Personnel management

Boella, M. J.. Personnel management in the hotel and catering industry. — 3rd ed. — London : Hutchinson Education [Oct.1982]. — [192]p
Previous ed.: 1980
ISBN 0-09-150101-6 (pbk) : £6.50 : CIP entry
Also classified at 647'.95'0683 B82-24970

647'.94'0688 — Hotels. Occupancy. Salesmanship — *Manuals*

Taylor, Derek, *1932-*. Profitable hotel reception. — Oxford : Pergamon, July 1982. — [260]p. — (International series in hospitality management)
ISBN 0-08-026769-6 (cased) : £15.00 : CIP entry
ISBN 0-08-026768-8 (pbk) : £7.50 B82-12412

647'.9441 — Great Britain. Conference centres & vacation accommodation — *Directories — For youth groups*

Holiday and conference centres guide. — [Leicester] ([17 Albion St., Leicester LE1 6GD]) : [National Youth Bureau], 1982. — 50p ; 30cm
Cover title
ISBN 0-86155-055-2 (pbk) : £1.50 B82-34497

647'.9441 — Great Britain. Conference centres — *Directories — Serials*

Training and consultancy register. — 1981-. — [Creaton] ([Grooms La., Creaton, Northampton NN6 8NS]) : Hamilton House, 1981-. — v. : ill ; 30cm
Annual
ISSN 0262-1177 = Training and consultancy register : £10.00 B82-02378

647'.9441 — Great Britain. Self-catering vacation accommodation — *Directories*

[AA guide to holiday houses, cottages and chalets]Self catering in Britain / editor Patricia Kelly ; compiled by Publicatons Research Unit ; disgned by Turnergraphic Ltd ; maps by Cartographic Department. — [Basingstoke] : A.A. ; London : Distributed by Hutchinson, [c1980]. — 272p : ill,col.maps,1form ; 22cm
Originally published: 1978
ISBN 0-86145-009-4 (pbk) : £2.50 B82-12103

647'.944101 — Great Britain. Hotels adjacent to golf courses — *Directories — Serials*

Golf — where to play and where to stay : a golfers guide to hotels and courses in the United Kingdom and Ireland. — 4th. ed.-. — [Macclesfield] ([Charles Roe House, Chestergate, Macclesfield, Cheshire]) : [McMillan Martin Ltd], 1980-. — v. : ill,maps ; 21cm
Annual. — Continues: Where to stay and where to play
ISSN 0263-4066 = Golf, where to play and where to stay : £1.95
Primary classification 796.352'06'841
B82-19862

647'.944101'0288 — Great Britain. Hotels. Maintenance

Hurst, Rosemary. Services and maintenance for hotels and residential establishments / Rosemary Hurst. — London : Heinemann, 1971 (1982 [printing]). — viii,144p : ill ; 22cm
Includes index
ISBN 0-434-90793-6 (pbk) : £4.50 B82-36874

647'.944101'05 — Great Britain. Hotels — *Directories — Serials*

[Holidays in Britain *(Teddington)*]. Holidays in Britain. — 1977-. — Teddington : Haymarket Pub., 1977-. — v. : ill,maps ; 21cm
Annual. — Continues: British holiday guide
ISSN 0263-9173 = Holidays in Britain (Teddington) : £1.00 per issue B82-36704

647'.944108 — Great Britain. Camping & caravanning. Sites — *Directories*

Great Britain and Ireland caravan and camping sites / inspected and recognised by the RAC. — Rev ed. — Croydon : Published for the Royal Automobile Club by RAC Motoring Services, 1982. — 223p ; 21cm
Previous ed.: 1973
ISBN 0-86211-037-8 (pbk) : £2.25 B82-34866

Rowlands, David, *1946-*. Camping and caravanning : Britain's best sites / [text by David Rowlands]. — 2nd rev. ed. — Basingstoke : Automobile Association, c1982. — 80p : col.ill,col.maps ; 30cm. — (AA activity guide)
Previous ed.: 1981
ISBN 0-86145-036-1 (pbk) : £1.99 B82-34475

647'.944121 — Scotland. Grampian Region. Self-catering vacation accommodation — *Directories — Serials*

Go Grampian : self-catering holidays in Scotland's North East. — 1982-. — Aberdeen (Woodhill House, Ashgrove Rd. West, Aberdeen AB9 2LU) : Department of Leisure, Recreation and Tourism, Grampian Regional Council, [1982]-. — v. : ill,maps ; 21cm
ISSN 0263-4651 = Go Grampian : Unpriced
B82-24765

647'.9442 — England. Bed & breakfast accommodation — *Directories — Serials*

Where to stay. Farmhouses and bed & breakfast in England. — '80-. — London (4 Grosvenor Gdns, SW1W ODU) : English Tourist Board, 1980-. — v. : ill(some col.),maps ; 21cm
Annual. — Continues in part: Where to stay. Hotels in England. — Description based on: '81 issue
ISSN 0263-3744 = Where to stay. Farmhouses and bed & breakfast in England : £1.25
B82-18711

647'.944201 — England. Hotels — *Visitors' guides*

Gundrey, Elizabeth. Staying off the beaten track : a unique selection of modestly priced inns, small hotels, farms and country houses in England / Elizabeth Gundrey. — Feltham : Hamlyn, 1982. — 271p : ill,1map ; 20cm
At head of title: The Observer
ISBN 0-600-20527-4 (pbk) : £2.95 B82-22281

647'.944201'09 — England. Inns, *1066-1982*

Bruning, Ted. The David & Charles book of historic English inns / Ted Bruning & Keith Paulin. — Newton Abbot : David & Charles, c1982. — 253p : ill,1map ; 22cm
Includes index
ISBN 0-7153-8178-4 : £9.50 : CIP rev.
B82-01172

647'.94421 — London. Hostels for women — *Directories*

Austerberry, Helen. A guide to women's hostels in London : compiled by Helen Austerberry and Sophie Watson / photography Ian Forsyth. — London : SHAC, 1982. — 32p : ill ; 30cm
Text on inside back cover. — Includes index
Unpriced (pbk) B82-33669

647'.944219401'0222 — London. Kingston upon Thames *(London Borough)*. **Hotels & inns,** *1835-1930 — Illustrations*

Local inns and hotels. — [Kingston upon Thames] : Royal Borough of Kingston upon Thames, [1982?]. — 1portfolio : ill(some col.) ; 31cm
Includes bibliography
ISBN 0-903183-09-9 : Unpriced B82-28816

647'.94423501'068 — Devon. Bed & breakfast hotels. Management — *Stories, anecdotes*

Brickell, Hammond. B&B, h&c / Hammond Brickell. — St. Ives, Cornwall : United Writers, c1981. — 149p ; 22cm
ISBN 0-901976-68-7 : £5.20 B82-20115

647'.94423595 — Devon. Torquay. Hotels: Imperial Hotel *(Torquay), to 1981*

Denes, Gabor. The story of the Imperial : the life and times of Torquay's great hotel / Gabor Denes. — Newton Abbot : David & Charles, c1982. — 158p : ill,ports ; 24cm
Bibliography: p155. — Includes index
ISBN 0-7153-8051-6 : £8.50 : CIP rev.
B81-33824

647'.9442656 — Cambridgeshire. Ely. Inns: Cutter Inn, *to 1980*

Holmes, Reg. Cutter Inn Ely / by Reg Holmes. — Ely : EARO, c1981. — [12]p : ill,1map ; 21cm
ISBN 0-904463-81-8 (pbk) : £0.25 B82-30534

647'.94426712 — Essex. Stansted Airport region. Hotels — *Proposals*

Stansted Airport hotel requirements / joint report by British Airports Authority ... [et al.] ; based on information supplied by researchers of the above bodies and prepared by the Planning and Research Services Branch of the English Tourist Board. — [London] ([4 Grosvenor Gardens SW1W 3DU]) : English Tourist Board, 1981. — 43leaves : maps ; 30cm
Unpriced (spiral) B82-21484

647'.944273 — Greater Manchester *(Metropolitan County)*. **Conference centres** — *Directories*

Greater Manchester : the natural conference venue at the heart of Britain / [Greater Manchester Conference and Exhibitions Office]. — London : Burrow, 1981. — 64p : ill(some col.),3 col.maps ; 30cm
Unpriced (pbk) B82-14566

647'.94595701'09 — Singapore. Hotels: Raffles Hotel, *to 1980*

Sharp, Ilsa. There is only one Raffles : the story of a grand hotel / Ilsa Sharp. — London : Souvenir, 1981. — 143p,[8]p of plates : ill(some col.),facsims,ports ; 23cm
Bibliography: p139-140
ISBN 0-285-62383-4 : £8.95 B82-14579

647'.947301'068 — United States. Hotel industries. Management — *Case studies*

Wyckoff, D. Daryl. The U.S. lodging industry / D. Daryl Wyckoff, W. Earl Sasser. — Lexington, Mass. : Lexington Books, c1981 ; [Aldershot] : Gower [distributor], 1982. — lxix,255p : ill,maps,facsims,1plan ; 24cm. — (Lexington casebook series in industry analysis)
ISBN 0-669-02819-3 : £20.00 B82-12107

647.95 — CATERING INSTITUTIONS, RESTAURANTS, PUBLIC HOUSES, ETC

647'.95'0212 — Catering equipment — *Technical data*

Scriven, Carl. Food equipment facts : a handbook for the food service industry / Carl Scriven & James Stevens. — New York ; Chichester : Wiley, c1982. — xi,429p : ill,forms ; 23cm
Originally published: Troy, N.Y. : Conceptual Design, 1980. — Includes index
ISBN 0-471-86819-1 (pbk) : £8.95 B82-27724

647'.95'02341 — Great Britain. Catering industries — *Career guides*

Hotels & catering / [written, designed and produced by SGS Education]. — Walton on Thames : Nelson, 1982. — 15p : ill ; 28cm. — (Career profiles ; 21)
ISBN 0-17-438369-x (unbound) : Unpriced
Also classified at 647'.94'02341 B82-27847

647'.95'0285404 — Catering industries. Applications of microcomputer systems

Implications of microcomputers in small and medium hotel and catering firms / prepared for the Hotel and Catering Industry Training Board by the Department of Hotel, Catering & Tourism Management, University of Surrey, Guildford. — [Wembley] : [The Board], [1980] ([1982 printing]). — ix,157p : ill ; 30cm. — (Research report / HCITB)
Bibliography: p123-129
ISBN 0-7033-0023-7 (pbk) : Unpriced
B82-36509

647'.95'068 — Catering industries. Management

The **Management** of hospitality. — Oxford : Pergamon, Nov.1982. — [236]p. — (International series in hospitality management)
Conference papers
ISBN 0-08-028107-9 : £11.25 : CIP entry
B82-31280

647'.95'068 — Great Britain. Catering industries. Home-based small firms. Organisation — *Manuals*

Ridgway, Judy. Home cooking for money. — Loughton : Piatkus, Nov.1982. — [256]p
ISBN 0-86188-221-0 : £6.95 : CIP entry
B82-26065

647'.95'068 — Great Britain. Catering industries. Management — *Serials*

International journal of hospitality management. — Vol.1, no.1 (1982)-. — Oxford : Pergamon with the support of the International Association of Hotel Management Schools, 1982-. — v. : ill ; 30cm
Three issues yearly
Unpriced B82-28109

647'.95'068 — Great Britain. Restaurants. Management — *Manuals*

Johnson, R. H. (Reginald Herbert). Running your own restaurant / R.H. Johnson. — 2nd ed. — London : Hutchinson, 1982. — xiv,185p ; 24cm. — (Catering and hotel management books)
Previous ed.: London : Barrie & Jenkins, 1976. — Bibliography: p185
ISBN 0-09-149231-9 (pbk) : £5.95 : CIP rev.
B82-07260

647'.95'068 — Restaurants. Management — *Manuals*

Fuller, John, *1916-*. Modern restaurant service. — London : Hutchinson Education, Mar.1982. — [376]p
ISBN 0-09-146830-2 (cased) : £12.00 : CIP entry
ISBN 0-09-146831-0 (pbk) : £6.00 B82-00268

647'.95'0683 — Catering industries. Personnel management

Boella, M. J.. Personnel management in the hotel and catering industry. — 3rd ed. — London : Hutchinson Education [Oct.1982]. — [192]p
Previous ed.: 1980
ISBN 0-09-150101-6 (pbk) : £6.50 : CIP entry
Primary classification 647'.94'0683 B82-24970

647'.95'0688 — Marketing by catering industries

Creative marketing for the foodservice industry : a practitioner's handbook / edited by William P. Fisher. — New York ; Chichester : Wiley, c1982. — ix,296p : ill ; 24cm
ISBN 0-471-08111-6 : £23.25 B82-36685

647'.95'0688 — Marketing by public houses — *Manuals*

Marketing for publicans : designed to assist licensees to increase the business potential of their house by adopting a marketing approach to running their business : a licensed trade self-help guide from the Small Business Service of the Hotel and Catering Industry Training Board. — [Wembley] : [The Board], [1982]. — 51p : ill,2maps ; 21cm
ISBN 0-7033-0014-8 (pbk) : Unpriced
B82-14402

647'.9541 — Great Britain. Transport cafés — *Directories — Serials — For lorry drivers*

What's new guide to transport cafes. — Summer 1982-. — Northampton (Grooms La., Creaton, Northants.) : Hamilton House, 1982-. — v. : col.ill,maps ; 21cm
ISSN 0263-7596 = What's new guide to transport cafes : £0.95 B82-32356

647'.954121 — Scotland. Grampian Region. Catering establishment — *Directories*

Eating out in the Grampian region : restaurant & bar meals, morning coffee, afternoon tea, specialities of the region. — Aberdeen ([Woodhill House, Ashgrove Rd. West, Aberdeen, AB9 2LU]) : Department of Leisure, Recreation and Tourism, Grampian Regional Council, [1982?]. — [44]p : ill,1map ; 10x20cm
Cover title
Unpriced (pbk) B82-30030

647'.954134 — Edinburgh. Public houses & restaurants — *Directories*

Eating and drinking in Edinburgh : and round about. — 5th rev. ed. — Edinburgh : Ramsay Head, c1981. — 71p : ill ; 19cm
Previous ed.: 1980
ISBN 0-902859-74-9 (pbk) : £0.75 B82-25652

647'.954134 — Edinburgh. Public houses selling unpressurised beers — *Directories*

Real ale in Edinburgh / [Campaign for Real Ale, Edinburgh and S.E. Scotland Branch]. — Updated. — Edinburgh (1 Upper Bow, Lawnmarket, Edinburgh EH1 2JN) : The Branch, c1980. — 28p : 1map ; 21cm
Cover title
£0.30 (pbk) B82-21518

647'.9542 — England. Vegetarian restaurants — *Directories*

Nelson, Lesley. Vegetarian restaurants in England / Lesley Nelson. — Harmondsworth : Penguin, 1982. — 202p ; 30cm. — (Penguin handbooks)
ISBN 0-14-046466-2 (pbk) : £2.50 B82-33147

647'.95421 — London. Restaurants — *Visitors' guides*

Streich, Corrine. Let's lunch in London / Corrine Streich (with Lori Streich). — London : Macmillan, 1982. — vii,208p : maps ; 20cm
Includes index
ISBN 0-333-33392-6 (pbk) : £3.95 B82-38784

647'.95421'05 — London. Restaurants — *Serials*

Best of London eating. — Issue no.1 (Winter 1981)-. — Bracknell (3M House, P.O. Box 1, Bracknell, Berks. RG12 1JU) : 3M United Kingdom PLC, 1981-. — v. : ill ; 28cm
Quarterly
ISSN 0262-5016 = Best of London eating : £1.50 per issue
B82-14261

647'.9542192 — London. Sutton *(London Borough).* **Public houses,** *to 1980*
Crowe, A. J.. Inns, taverns & pubs of the London Borough of Sutton : their history & architecture, with 61 original drawings / by A.J. Crowe. — [Sutton] : London Borough of Sutton Libraries & Arts Services, 1980. — 122p : ill,maps ; 15x21cm
ISBN 0-907335-00-4 (pbk) : £2.45 B82-17501

647'.9542233 — Kent. Faversham. Public houses — *Visitors' guides*
Haley, Frank. The inns and taverns of Faversham / by Frank Haley. — Faversham : Faversham Society, 1982. — viii,86p ; 26cm. — (Faversham papers, ISSN 0014-892x ; no.19)
ISBN 0-900532-31-9 (pbk) : Unpriced
B82-32712

647'.95422357 — Kent. Ramsgate. Public houses, *to 1980*
Mirams, Michael David. Old Ramsgate pubs / by Michael David Mirams. — [Margate] ([11 Ulster Rd, Margate, Kent CT9 5RZ]) : M.D. Mirms and H.R. Hart, c1981. — 56p : ill,plans ; 21cm
£1.60 (pbk) B82-04188

647'.954227 — Hampshire. Restaurants — *Directories*
Where to eat in Hampshire. — Newbury (11 Swan St., Kingsclere, Newbury, Berks.) : Kingsclere, 1979. — 48p : ill ; 19cm
£0.30 (pbk) B82-00470

647'.954231 — Wiltshire. Public houses selling unpressurised beers — *Directories*
Real ale in Wiltshire / [Campaign for Real Ale]. — 5th ed. — Swindon (Old Estate House, Foxhill, Swindon SN4 0BR) : CAMRA, c1980. — 54p : ill ; 21cm
Previous ed.: 1979. — Text on inside front cover
£0.75 (pbk) B82-25357

647'.954231 — Wiltshire. Public houses with facilities for children — *Directories*
Litherland, Barbara Anne. A guide to over 500 public houses with facilities for children : Wiltshire and Gloucestershire / [compiled and edited by Barbara Anne Litherland]. — [Bradford-on-Avon] : Children's Corner, 1982. — 40p : ill,2maps ; 21cm
Cover title
ISBN 0-946016-00-3 (pbk) : £0.95
Also classified at 647'.954241 B82-34566

647'.954241 — Gloucestershire. Public houses with facilities for children — *Directories*
Litherland, Barbara Anne. A guide to over 500 public houses with facilities for children : Wiltshire and Gloucestershire / [compiled and edited by Barbara Anne Litherland]. — [Bradford-on-Avon] : Children's Corner, 1982. — 40p : ill,2maps ; 21cm
Cover title
ISBN 0-946016-00-3 (pbk) : £0.95
Primary classification 647'.954231 B82-34566

647'.9542517 — Derbyshire. Derby. Public houses, *to 1981*
Taverns in the town : pubs of bygone Derby. — Derby : Breedon Books, 1982. — 32p : chiefly ill,2facsims ; 21cm
ISBN 0-907969-00-3 (pbk) : Unpriced
B82-35533

647'.954254 — Leicestershire. Public houses selling unpressurised beers — *Directories*
Real ale in Leicestershire and Rutland. — 4th ed. / editor Dave Flatters ; asst editor Martin Wilson. — [Loughborough] : Leicester & Loughborough Branches of CAMRA, 1981. — 96p : ill,maps ; 22cm
Previous ed.: published as A real ale guide to Leicestershire and Rutland / editor Mike Scott
ISBN 0-9506069-2-8 (pbk) : £1.00 B82-26665

647'.9542732 — Greater Manchester *(Metropolitan County).* **Eccles. Public houses,** *to 1980*
Flynn, Tony, *1950-.* A history of the pubs of Eccles / by Tony Flynn. — Swinton : Neil Richardson, [1982?]. — 40p : ill,facsims,maps ; 30cm
Cover title. — Text, ill on inside covers
ISBN 0-907511-02-3 (pbk) : £1.50 B82-40230

647'.9542732 — Greater Manchester *(Metropolitan County).* **Swinton & Pendlebury. Public houses,** *to 1980*
Richardson, Neil, *1948-.* The pubs of Swinton & Pendlebury : (including Clifton and Newtown) / Neil Richardson & Roger Hall. — Swinton (375 Chorley Rd., Swinton M27 2AY) : N. Richardson, [1981?]. — 51p : ill,maps,facsims,plans,ports ; 30cm
£2.00 (pbk)
B82-08871

647'.9542738 — Greater Manchester *(Metropolitan County).* **Prestwich. Public houses,** *to 1980*
Rowlinson, David. A history of Prestwich pubs / by David Rowlinson. — Swinton (375 Chorley Rd., Swinton M27 2AY) : Neil Richardson, [1981?]. — 27p : ill,coats of arms,facsims,ports ; 30cm
Cover title. — Text, ill on covers
£1.50 (pbk) B82-12961

647'.954281 — Yorkshire. Public houses serving food — *Directories*
Ramkin, Harry. Guide to pub food (and budget eating) in Yorkshire & Humberside / by Harry Ramkin. — York (312 Tadcaster Rd., York, YO2 2HF) : Yorkshire & Humberside Tourist Board, c1982. — 72p : 1map ; 21cm
Text on inside covers
£0.90 (pbk) B82-40438

647'.9542'82 — South Yorkshire *(Metropolitan County).* **Public houses selling unpressurised beers** — *Directories*
Real beer in South Yorkshire / produced by the South Yorkshire Branches of CAMRA. — [Sheffield] ([c/o D.R. Grey, 43 Endcliffe Hall Ave., Sheffield, S10 3EL]) : [CAMRA Sheffield and District Branch], c1982. — 82p : ill,maps ; 22cm
Text on inside back cover
ISBN 0-9504393-1-2 (pbk) : £0.75 B82-31184

647'.9542981 — West Glamorgan. Port Talbot. Public houses, *to 1979*
Jones, Sally, *1935-.* Welcome to town / a brief account of Port Talbot's inns ; by Sally Jones. — Port Talbot : Alun Books, 1980. — 27p : ill,1map ; 22cm
Includes index
ISBN 0-907117-01-5 (pbk) : Unpriced
B82-03489

647'.95442 — France. Normandy. Restaurants — *Directories*
Wear, Victor. Bon appétit in Normandy / by Victor Wear. — London (2A Chester Close, Chester St., SW1X 7BQ) : Time Off, 1980. — 48p : ill,2maps ; 21cm
Cover title
£1.35 (pbk) B82-17626

647'.954427 — France. Boulogne region. Restaurants — *Directories*
Wear, Victor. Bon appétit in Opal Coast / by Victor Wear. — London (2A Chester Close, Chester St., SW1X 7BQ) : Time Off, 1971 (1980 [printing]). — 52p : ill,1map ; 21cm
Cover title
£1.35 (pbk) B82-17627

648 — HOUSEKEEPING

648 — Housework — *Manuals*
Aslett, Don. Is there life after housework?. — Watford : Exley, June 1982. — [144]p
ISBN 0-905521-61-7 : £4.95 : CIP entry
B82-18594

648'.0941 — Great Britain. Women. Housework, *1650-1950*
Davidson, Caroline. A woman's work is never done. — London : Chatto & Windus, Sept.1982. — [288]p
ISBN 0-7011-3901-3 : £9.50 : CIP entry
B82-20002

648'.1 — Clothing. Pressing — *Manuals*
Bratt, Jack. Garment pressing. — [Great Britain] : Guild of Cleaners & Launderers, [1982]. — 27p : ill(some col.) ; 21x30cm + 'About the author'(1sheet : 1ill ; 19x29cm). — (A training manual / Guild of Cleaners and Launderers)
By Jack Bratt
Unpriced (pbk) B82-37227

648'.1 — Laundering - *For schools*
Ling, E. M.. Modern household science. — 4th ed. — London : Bell & Hyman, July 1981. — [258]p
Previous ed.: London : Mills & Boon, 1979
ISBN 0-7135-2073-6 (pbk) : £2.95 : CIP entry
Primary classification 677 B81-15910

648'.5'028 — Household materials. Cleaning. Techniques — *Manuals*
Polish and shine : recipes of Women's Institute members and their ancestors / edited by Gwynedd Lloyd. — New ed. — London : WI Books, 1981. — 39p : 1ill ; 21cm. — (WI reference & guides)
Previous ed.: 1957
ISBN 0-900556-69-2 (pbk) : Unpriced
B82-15217

Wylie, Harriet. Clean as a whistle / by Harriet Wylie. — London : Ernest Benn, 1980. — 96p : ill ; 23cm
Includes index
ISBN 0-510-00056-8 : £3.50 B82-21429

649.1 — HOME CARE OF CHILDREN

649'.1 — Children. Home care — *For nursery nursing*
Geraghty, Patricia. Caring for children : a textbook for nursery nurses / Patricia Geraghty ; with a foreword by James W. Farquhar. — London : Baillière Tindall, 1981. — x,486p : ill ; 22cm
Includes bibliographies and index
ISBN 0-7020-0887-7 (pbk) : £9.50 : CIP rev.
B81-28818

649'.1 — Children. Home care — *Manuals* — *For parents*
Burstein, A. Joseph. Dr. Burstein's book on children. — Poole : Blandford Press, Sept.1982. — [224]p
ISBN 0-7137-1273-2 : £6.95 : CIP entry
B82-21983

Hauck, Paul. [The rational management of children]. How to bring up your child successfully. — London : Sheldon, Oct.1982. — [200]p. — (Overcoming common problems)
Originally published: New York : Libra, 1967
ISBN 0-85969-371-6 (pbk) : £2.95 : CIP entry
B82-25742

649'.1 — Children, to 10 years. Home care — *Manuals*
Reader's Digest Mothercare book. — Rep. with amendments. — London (25 Berkeley Square, W1X 6AB) : Reader's Digest Association in conjunction with Mothercare, 1979 (1982 [printing]). — 288p : ill ; 22cm
Includes index
£4.95 B82-23783

649'.1'019 — Children. Home care. Psychological aspects
Teele, James E.. Mastering stress in child rearing : a longitudinal study of coping and remission / James E. Teele. — Lexington, Mass. : Lexington Books ; Aldershot : Gower [distributor], 1982, c1981. — xxiv,287p ; 24cm
Includes index
ISBN 0-669-03622-6 : £19.50 B82-08991

649'.1'0248 — Avon. Childminding — *Manuals*
Your guide to sponsored childminding in Avon / Avon County Council, Social Services Department. — 2nd ed. — Bristol : County Public Relations and Publicity Department, 1981. — 25p : ill ; 21cm
Cover title. — Previous ed.: 197-?. — Includes index
ISBN 0-86063-126-5 (pbk) : Unpriced
B82-01873

649'.1'0712 — Secondary schools. Curriculum subjects: Home care of children — *For teaching*
Whitfield, Richard C.. Education for family life : some new policies for child care / Richard C. Whitfield. — London : Hodder and Stoughton, 1980. — xiv,161p : ill ; 22cm
Bibliography: p158-159. — Includes index
ISBN 0-340-25524-2 (pbk) : £3.25 : CIP rev.
B80-08842

649'.1'0903 — Children. Home care. Theories, *1750-1981*
Hardyment, Christina. Dream babies. — London : Cape, Jan.1983. — [256]p
ISBN 0-224-01910-4 : £8.95 : CIP entry
B82-33496

649'.122 — Babies, to 1 year. Home care — *Manuals*
The **First** wondrous year : you and your baby / edited by Richard A. Chase and Richard R. Rubin. — New York : Collier ; London : Collier Macmillan, c1979. — 410p : ill(some col.) ; 28cm. — (Johnson & Johnson child development publications)
Includes index
ISBN 0-02-077100-2 (pbk) : £6.95 B82-40746

649'.122 — Children, 1-5 years. Home care — *Manuals*
The **Baby** book / editor Catherine Munnion ; with contributions by Anne Lawrence ... [et al.]. — London : Hamlyn, 1982. — 208p : ill (some col.) ; 26cm
Includes index
ISBN 0-600-30510-4 : £5.95 B82-36860

649'.122 — Children, to 3 years. Home care
Stoppard, Miriam. Miriam Stoppard's book of babycare. — London : Futura, 1979, c1977. — 158p : ill ; 22cm
Originally published: London : Weidenfeld & Nicolson, 1977. — Includes index
ISBN 0-7088-1484-0 (pbk) : £1.50 B82-12502

649'.122'028 — Babies' supplies — *For mothers*
Junor, Penny. Babyware / Penny Junor. — London : Sidgwick & Jackson, 1982. — 159p : ill ; 23cm
Includes index
ISBN 0-283-98868-1 : £6.95 B82-34990

649'.122'05 — Children, to 5 years. Home care — *Serials*
LLLGB newsletter : news & views from La Leche League Great Britain. — No.1 ([198-?])-. — [London] ([BM 3424, WC1V 6XX]) : The League, [198-?]-. — v. : ill ; 21cm
Description based on: No.10 (May/June '82
ISSN 0263-6220 = LLLGB newsletter : Free to League members B82-28111

649'.122'0926 — Babies. Home care — *Case studies*
Robertson, James, *1911-*. A baby in the family : loving and being loved / James and Joyce Robertson. — Harmondsworth : Penguin, 1982. — 127p : ill ; 21cm. — (A Penguin handbook)
ISBN 0-14-046499-9 (pbk) : £2.95 B82-18139

649'.124 — Children, 5-10 years. Home care — *Manuals*
Living with children 5-10 : a parent's guide / The Open University in association with the Health Education Council ; [Open University course team : Monica Darlington ... et al.] ; [editor : Denise Winn]. — London : Harper & Row, c1981. — ix,252p : ill(some col.),plans,forms (some col.) ; 29cm
Bibliography: p250-251
ISBN 0-06-318216-5 : Unpriced B82-20548

649'.125 — Adolescents. Development. Role of parents
Parents and teenagers. — London : Harper & Row, Sept.1982. — [224]p
ISBN 0-06-318243-2 (pbk) : £6.95 : CIP entry
B82-26211

649'.151 — Multi-handicapped children. Home care — *Manuals*
The **Next** step on the ladder : assessment and management of the multi-handicapped child / revised by G.B. Simon ; foreword Peter Mittler ; illustrations David Baird. — 3rd ed. — [Kidderminster] : [British Institute of Mental Handicap], 1981. — ii,144p : ill,2forms ; 27cm + Assessment chart([4]p : 2 forms ; 30cm)
Previous ed.: 1974. — Includes "NSL development assessment scale" as insert. —
Bibliography: p143-144
ISBN 0-906054-27-3 (cased) : Unpriced
ISBN 0-906054-26-5 (pbk) : Unpriced
ISBN 0-906054-36-2 (Assessment chart)
B82-36857

649'.3 — Babies. Breast feeding
Helsing, Elisabet. Breast-feeding in practice : a manual for health workers / Elisabet Helsing with F. Savage King. — Oxford : Oxford University Press, 1982. — xvi,271p : ill ; 22cm. — (Oxford medical publications)
Bibliography: p252-265. — Includes index
ISBN 0-19-261298-0 (pbk) : £5.95 : CIP rev.
B81-33825

649'.3 — Great Britain. Babies. Breast feeding. Organisations: La Leche League Great Britain — *Serials*
[Feedback *(Burwell, Cambs.)*]. Feedback / leader letter of La Leche League of Great Britain. — 1980-. — Burwell (c/o Rachel O'Leary, 27 Mason Rd, Burwell, Cambs. CB5 0B6) : The League, 1980-. — v. ; 30cm
Six issues yearly. — Description based on: Mar./Apr. 1982 issue
ISSN 0263-6689 = Feedback (Burwell, Cambs.) : £2.00 per year B82-28877

649'.3 — Great Britain. Babies, to 1 year. Feeding — *Inquiry reports*
Martin, Jean. Infant feeding 1980 : a survey carried out on behalf of the Department of Health and Social Security and the Scottish Home and Health Department / Jean Martin, Janet Monk. — [London] : Office of Population Censuses and Surveys, Social Survey Division, [1982]. — xii,73p : ill,forms ; 30cm
ISBN 0-903933-07-1 (pbk) : £3.00 B82-30868

649'.4 — Babies. Massage — *Manuals*
Auckett, Amelia. Baby massage. — Wellingborough : Thorsons, Aug.1982. — [80]p
ISBN 0-7225-0776-3 (pbk) : £2.75 : CIP entry
B82-15849

649'.5 — Children. Play
Biology of play / edited by Barbara Tizard and David Harvey. — [Great Britain] : Spastics International Medical, 1977. — vi,217p : ill ; 25cm. — (Clinics in developmental medicine, ISSN 0069-4835 ; no.62)
Includes bibliographies and index
ISBN 0-433-32376-0 : £7.00 B82-17281

Prendergast, Muriel. Play in a small space / [Muriel Prendergast]. — London (68 Chalton St., NW1 1JR) : COPE(UK), 1982. — 14p ; 21cm
Cover title
£0.50 (pbk) B82-27459

649'.5'0941 — Great Britain. Children. Play — *Conference proceedings*
Healthy play — healthy children : reports of a conference held in July 1979 / Alfred Boom editor ; organised by Bulmershe College of Higher Education and West Berkshire Community Health Council. — Reading (William Smith (Booksellers) Ltd., 35-39 London St., Reading) : Distributed by The London Street Bookshop for Bulmershe College of Higher Education, 1981. — 33p ; 21cm
Unpriced (pbk) B82-12126

649'.55'0880816 — Great Britain. Handicapped children. Play. Teaching aids: Toys
Aids to play : a booklet for the handicapped / prepared and compiled by Junior Chamber Aberdeen. — [Aberdeen] ([15 Union Terrace, Aberdeen]) : [Junior Chamber, Aberdeen], [1982?]. — 47p : ill ; 21cm
Cover title
Unpriced (pbk) B82-17800

649'.64 — Children. Behaviour modification — *Serials*
Behaviour modification with children : the quarterly journal of the Association for Behaviour Modification with Children. — Vol.4, no.1 (Mar. 1980)-v.5, no.1 (Mar. 1981). — [Hartlepool] (c/o S. Winter [Burn Valley Centre, Elwick Rd, Hartepool, Cleveland]) : The Association, 1980-1981. — 2v. ; 21cm
Continued by: Behavioural approaches with children. — Continues: Newsletter of the Association for Behaviour Modification with Children. — Description based on: Vol.5, no.1 (Mar. 1981)
Unpriced B82-29049

649'.64 — Children, to 7 years. Behaviour modification — *Manuals* — *For parents*
Dobson, James. Hide or seek. — London : Hodder and Stoughton, Sept.1982. — [192]p
ISBN 0-340-28198-7 : £1.75 : CIP entry
B82-18796

649'.64 — New Zealand. Children. Corporal punishment
Ritchie, Jane. Spare the rod. — London : Allen & Unwin, Dec.1981. — [155]p
ISBN 0-86861-107-7 : £10.00 : CIP entry
B81-31639

649'.64 — Young persons. Behaviour modification — *Manuals* — *For Christian parents*
Dobson, James, *1936-*. Dare to discipline / James Dobson. — New ed. — Eastbourne : Kingway, 1975, c1970 (1981 [printing]). — 206p : ill ; 18cm
Previous ed.: 1971
ISBN 0-902088-27-0 (pbk) : £1.60 B82-10519

649'.65 — Children. Sex education — *For parents*
Pickering, Lucienne. Parents listen / Lucienne Pickering. — London : Chapman, 1981. — 90p : ill ; 21cm
ISBN 0-225-66311-2 (pbk) : Unpriced : CIP rev. B81-20121

649'.68 — Children. Home-based education — *Manuals*
Holt, John, *1923-*. Teach your own : a hopeful path for education / John Holt. — Brightlingsea : Lighthouse, c1981. — 369p ; 23cm
Includes index
ISBN 0-907637-00-0 (pbk) : £5.95 B82-22474

649.8 — HOME NURSING

649.8 — Dementia patients. Home care — *Manuals*
Mace, Nancy L.. The 36-hour day : a family guide to caring for persons with Alzheimer's disease, related dementing illnesses, and memory loss in later life / Nancy L. Mace, Peter V. Rabins. — Baltimore ; London : Johns Hopkins University Press, c1981. — xvii,253p ; 24cm
Bibliography: p233-236. — Includes index
ISBN 0-8018-2659-4 (cased) : £11.25
ISBN 0-8018-2660-8 (pbk) : Unpriced
B82-34343

649.8 — Diabetic children. Home care — *For parents*
Craig, Oman. Childhood diabetes. — Oxford : Oxford University Press, July 1982. — [125]p. — (Oxford medical publications)
ISBN 0-19-261330-8 : £5.95 : CIP entry
B82-14356

649.8 — Great Britain. Old persons. Home care — *Manuals*
Hooker, Susan. Caring for elderly people : understanding and practical help / Susan Hooker. — 2nd ed. — London : Routledge & Kegan Paul, 1981. — xiv,197p : ill ; 22cm
Previous ed.: 1976. — Bibliography: p185-187. — Includes index
ISBN 0-7100-0890-2 (pbk) : £3.95 B82-05668

649.8 — Stroke victims. Home care — *Practical information*
Recovery from a stroke. — London (57 Gloucester Place, W1H 4DH) : British Heart Foundation, 1980. — 23p ; 18cm. — (Heart research series ; no.3)
Unpriced (unbound) B82-19759

650 — BUSINESS PRACTICES

650 — Business practices — *For schools*
Johnson, Katherine. Practical business studies. — London : Bell and Hyman, June 1982. — [160]p
ISBN 0-7135-1310-1 (pbk) : £3.95 : CIP entry
B82-09604

650'.076 — Busines practices — *Questions & answers* — *For schools*
Aremu, E. A.. Objective tests : O-Level business methods / E.A. Aremu. — Harlow : Longman, 1981. — 44p : ill ; 22cm. — (Study for success)
ISBN 0-582-65511-0 (pbk) : £0.75 B82-03301

650′.076 — Business practices — *Questions & answers*
Glew, Matthew. Cross modular assignments for BEC national. — London : Heinemann Educational, Nov.1982. — [96]p
ISBN 0-435-45049-2 (pbk) : £2.95 : CIP entry B82-27505

650′.076 — Business practices — *Questions & answers — For West African students*
Omotosho, Jacob 'Niyi. Multiple choice tests in business methods / Jacob 'Niyi Omotosho. — London : Macmillan Education, 1981. — 121p : ill,forms ; 25cm
ISBN 0-333-30507-8 (pbk) : £1.10 B82-06960

650′.094 — European Community countries. Business practices — *For foreign businessmen*
Drew, John, *1936-*. Doing business in the European Community. — 2nd ed. — London : Butterworth Scientific, Nov.1982. — [288]p
Previous ed.: 1979
ISBN 0-408-10836-3 : £18.50 : CIP entry B82-28271

650′.0941 — Great Britain. Business practices
Anstis, R. D.. Practical business education : an integrated approach / R.D. Anstis, S.H.E. Fishlock, C.E. Stafford. — Plymouth : MacDonald & Evans. — (M & E BEC books)
Bk.1. — 1978. — viii,280p : ill,forms
ISBN 0-7121-2336-9 (pbk) : £3.50 B82-39570

650.1 — Business enterprise. Success — *Manuals*
Farnsworth, Terry. On the way up : the executive's guide to company politics. — London : McGraw-Hill, Apr.1982. — [176]p
Originally published: 1976
ISBN 0-07-084585-9 (pbk) : £5.95 : CIP entry B82-14353

650.1 — Business enterprise. Success — *Proposals*
Dunne, John. 39 steps to money making / by John Dunne. — Claygate Esher (61 Hare La., Claygate Esher, Surrey KT10 0QK) : Clearway Promotions, [1981?]. — 54p ; 30cm
Cover title
Unpriced (spiral) B82-00683

650.1′3 — Business firms. Personnel. Interpersonal relationships. Listening
Burley-Allen, Madelyn. Listening : the forgotten skill / Madelyn Burley-Allen. — New York ; Chichester : Wiley, c1982. — vi,153p : ill
Bibliography: p152. — Includes index
ISBN 0-471-08776-9 (pbk) : Unpriced B82-37963

650.1′4 — Job hunting. Interviews — *Manuals*
Davey, D. Mackenzie. How to be interviewed / D. Mackenzie Davey & P. McDonnell ; illustrated by Peter Kneebone. — London : British Institute of Management Foundation, 1980. — 67p : ill ; 21cm
Bibliography: p67
ISBN 0-85946-107-6 (pbk) : £3.30 B82-13743

650.1′4 — Job hunting — *Manuals*
Bax, Kris. How to succeed at an interview : and how to survive if you don't : a guide to successful preparation for job applications and interviews (and a brief survival kit for unemployment) / Kris Bax & Don Cole. — Wakefield : EP, 1982. — 56p ; 19cm
ISBN 0-7158-0819-2 (cased) : Unpriced
ISBN 0-7158-0820-6 (pkk) : £1.50 B82-34877

Dowding, Howard. Getting the job you want / Howard Dowding and Sheila Boyce. — Rev. ed. — London : Ward Lock, 1982. — 95p : ill ; 19cm
Previous ed.: 1979. — Bibliography: p90
ISBN 0-7063-6202-0 (pbk) : £2.50 B82-21425

Job stalker / produced by Tecmedia. — London : JMK Associates, 1981. — 1portfolio : ill,forms ; 32cm
ISBN 0-9507952-0-8 : Unpriced B82-28304

Robertson, John P.. You and your next job / John P. Robertson. — London : British Institute of Management Foundation, c1982. — 132p ; 21cm
Bibliography: p131-132
ISBN 0-85946-122-x (pbk) : Unpriced B82-40540

650.1′4 — Occupations. Application forms. Filling — *Manuals*
Chudley, Philippa. How to write job applications / Philippa Chudley. — Northampton : Hamilton House, 1982. — 32p. — (Careerscope ; 9)
ISBN 0-906888-28-x (pbk) : Unpriced B82-17431

650.1′4 — Personnel. Selection. Interviewing — *Manuals — For interviewees*
Higham, Martin. Coping with interviews. — London : New Opportunity Press, Dec.1981. — [111]p
ISBN 0-86263-019-3 (cased) : £5.95 : CIP entry
ISBN 0-86263-016-9 (pbk) : £2.75 B82-00174

650′.76 — Business practices — *Questions & answers*
Clough, D.. Cross modular assignments for BEC Higher / Danny Clough, William Green and Anthony Amrit Nasta. — London : Heinemann Educational, 1980
Teacher's book. — viii,65p : plans ; 21cm
ISBN 0-435-45071-9 (pbk) : Unpriced B82-05071

651 — OFFICE PRACTICES

651 — Great Britain. Office practices. Automation
Doswell, Andrew. Office automation. — Chichester : Wiley, Feb.1983. — [280]p. — (Wiley series in information processing)
ISBN 0-471-10457-4 : £14.00 : CIP entry B82-38710

Wilson, P. A.. Office technology benefits. — Manchester : NCC Publications, Nov.1982. — [170]p
ISBN 0-85012-362-3 (pbk) : £12.50 : CIP entry B82-26411

651 — Great Britain. Offices. Automation — *Serials*
Office automation report. — Vol.1, issue 1 (Nov. 1981)- v.1, issue 3 (Jan. 1982)-. — London (39 North Rd, N7 9DP) : Paradox Publications, 1981-1982. — 1v. : ill,ports ; 30cm
Monthly
ISSN 0261-8451 = Office automation report : £80.00 per year B82-18519

651 — Office practices
Bailey, Paul, *1937 Dec.29-*. Mastering office practice / P. Bailey. — London : Macmillan, 1982. — xiv,320p : ill,forms ; 23cm. — (Macmillan master series)
Includes index
ISBN 0-333-27000-2 : Unpriced
ISBN 0-333-27199-8 (pbk) : Unpriced
ISBN 0-333-29522-6 (export ed.) : Unpriced B82-17298

Denyer, J. C.. Office administration / J.C. Denyer. — 4th ed. / revised by A.L. Mugridge. — Plymouth : Macdonald and Evans, 1982. — ix,214p ; 19cm. — (The M & E handbook series)
Previous ed.: 1978. — Bibliography: p202-203. — Includes index
ISBN 0-7121-1540-4 (pbk) : £2.50 B82-34865

Shaw, Josephine. Office practice / Josephine Shaw. — 2nd ed. — [Sevenoaks] : Teach Yourself Books, 1981. — viii,198p : ill,forms ; 18cm. — (Teach yourself books)
Previous ed.: 1972. — Includes index
ISBN 0-340-26832-8 (pbk) : £1.95 : CIP rev. B81-26731

651 — Office practices. Automation
Electronic office monitor. — Aldershot : Gower, Aug.1982. — 1v.(loose-leaf)
ISBN 0-566-03413-1 : £120.00 (to include 3 quarterly updates) : CIP entry B82-21764

International Workshop on Office Information Systems *(2nd : 1981 : Couvent royal de Saint-Maximin)*. Office information systems : proceedings of the Second International Workshop on Office Information Systems, Couvent Royal de Saint-Maximin, France, 13-15 October 1981 / [organized by Agence de l'informatique and Institut national de recherche en informatique et en automatique) ; edited by Najah Naffah. — Amsterdam ; Oxford : North-Holland, 1982. — xiii,656p : ill,forms ; 23cm
ISBN 0-444-86398-2 : £38.30 B82-30541

Jarrett, Dennis. The electronic office : a management guide to the office of the future / Dennis Jarrett. — Aldershot : Gower with Philips Business Systems, c1982. — 165p : ill (some col.) ; 24cm
Bibliography: p157-159. — Includes index
ISBN 0-566-03409-3 : Unpriced : CIP rev. B82-02452

Peltu, Malcolm. A guide to the electronic office / by Malcolm Peltu ; based on a study by the UK Computing Services Association. — London : Associated Business Press, 1981. — x,185p,[4]p of plates : ill ; 23cm
Includes index
ISBN 0-85227-267-7 : Unpriced B82-20160

651 — Office practices. Automation. Management
The **Advanced** automated office. — London (2 St Bride St., EC4 4HR) : Binder Hamlyn Fry & Co, c1981. — 25p : ill ; 30cm. — (Executive guide)
£3.00 (free to clients) (unbound) B82-30632

Lieberman, Mark A.. Office automation : a manager's guide for improved productivity / Mark A. Lieberman, Gad J. Selig, John J. Walsh. — New York ; Chichester : Wiley, c1982. — xxi,331p : ill ; 24cm
Bibliography: p302-304. — Includes index
ISBN 0-471-07983-9 : Unpriced B82-38323

Rosen, Arnold. Administrative procedures for the electronic office / Arnold Rosen, Eileen Feretic Tunison, Margaret Hilton Bahniuk. — New York ; Chichester : Wiley, c1982. — xvi,520p : ill(some col.),facsims ; 25cm
Text on lining papers. — Bibliography: p490-491. — Includes index
ISBN 0-471-08700-9 : £12.15 B82-26453

651 — Office practices. Automation. Management. Role of personnel management
Managing office automation : office automation for personnel managers. — Slough : Urwick Nexos, [1981?]. — ii,51p : ill,forms ; 30cm. — (Urwick Nexos report series ; 6)
ISBN 0-907535-07-0 (pbk) : Unpriced B82-13804

651 — Office practices. Automation. Organisation — *Manuals*
Checklists for action : setting up a working party / Urwick Nexos. — Slough : Urwick Nexos Limited, [1981?]. — iii,33[i.e.44]leaves : ill ; 30cm. — (Managing office automation) (Urwick Nexos report series ; 1)
ISBN 0-907535-01-1 (pbk) : Unpriced B82-05203

Derrick, John. A handbook of new office technology. — London : Kogan Page, June 1982. — [250]p
ISBN 0-85038-584-9 : £11.95 : CIP entry B82-14921

Planning for the office of the future / edited by Alan Simpson. — Aldershot : Gower, c1982. — vi,140p : ill ; 22cm. — (The Office of the future ; no.1)
Bibliography: p139-140
ISBN 0-566-03404-2 (pbk) : Unpriced : CIP rev. B81-30532

Pritchard, J. A. T.. Planning office automation : electronic message systems / J.A.T. Pritchard and P.A. Wilson. — Manchester : NCC, 1982. — 242p : ill ; 21cm
Bibliography: p231-232. — Includes index
ISBN 0-85012-331-3 (pbk) : Unpriced : CIP rev. B81-34578

651 — Office practices — *For West African students*

Harrison, John, *1931-*. Secretarial duties / John Harrison. — West African ed. / E. Ifeanyi Odina, Dan Fosu. — London : Pitman Education, 1979 (1980 [printing]). — v,305p : ill ; 23cm. — (Pitmans African business series)
Includes index
ISBN 0-273-01273-8 (pbk) : Unpriced
B82-30553

651 — Office practices — *Manuals*

Bartholomew, Stanley N.. Basic office practice terms and exercises / S.N. Bartholomew. — London : Edward Arnold, 1980. — viii,136p : ill,forms ; 22cm
Includes index
ISBN 0-7131-0359-0 (pbk) : £2.75 : CIP rev.
B80-13894

Chanin, J. B.. Secretarial office solutions. — Maidenhead : McGraw-Hill, Dec.1982. — [176]p
ISBN 0-07-084651-0 (pbk) : £4.25 : CIP entry
B82-30306

Watcham, Maurice. Watcham's office practice. — 3rd ed. — London : McGraw-Hill
Bk.1 / Margaret Rees-Boughton assisted by Elizabeth Taylor. — c1979. — xii,236p : ill,forms ; 25cm
Previous ed.: published as Office practice. 1972. — Includes index
ISBN 0-07-084612-x (pbk) : £2.75 : CIP rev.
B79-23349

651'.023 — Office work — *Career guides*

Stace, Alexa. Careers in secretarial and office work. — 2nd ed. — London : Kogan Page, Feb.1983. — [100]p. — (Kogan Page careers series)
Previous ed.: 1980
ISBN 0-85038-660-8 (cased) : £6.95 : CIP entry
ISBN 0-85038-661-6 (pbk) : £2.50 B82-39285

651'.023'41 — Great Britain. Office work — *Career guides*

Office work : secretarial and administrative / [written, designed and produced by SGS Education]. — Walton on Thames : Nelson, 1982. — 15p : ill,facsims ; 28cm. — (Career profiles ; 28)
ISBN 0-17-438361-4 (unbound) : Unpriced
B82-27851

Offices / [prepared by COIC and the Central Office of Information]. — [London] : [Manpower Services Commission], [1982]. — 11v. : col.ill ; 30cm. — (Close-up)
Unpriced B82-40363

651'.076 — Office practices — *Questions & answers* — *For schools*

Greig, R. A.. Multiple choice questions on office practice and secretarial duties / R.A. Greig. — London : Edward Arnold, 1982. — iv,108p : ill,forms ; 22cm
ISBN 0-7131-0629-8 (pbk) : £2.50 : CIP rev.
B81-33900

Norman, Susan. Office practice / Susan Norman. — Harlow : Longman, 1982. — 46p : ill,forms,2plans ; 23cm. — (World at work)
ISBN 0-582-74844-5 (pbk) : Unpriced
B82-31767

651'.0973 — United States. Office practices — *Manuals*

Thompson, Margaret H.. Revised standard reference for secretaries and administrators / Margaret H. Thompson, J. Harold Janis. — [Rev. ed.]. — New York : Macmillan ; London : Collier Macmillan, c1980. — xii,763p : ill,forms ; 25cm
Previous ed.: published as New Standard reference for secretaries and administrative assistants. 1972. — Text on lining papers. — Includes index
ISBN 0-02-420660-1 : £9.50 B82-14133

651.2 — Business equipment

Dew, Gladys D.. Office machinery and equipment. — London : McGraw-Hill, Jan.1983
Teacher's handbook. — [200]p
ISBN 0-07-084629-4 (unbound) : £10.95 : CIP entry B82-36307

651'.2 — Electronic office equipment — *For law*

James, Keith R.. Computers and word processors : a guide to the electronic office for practising lawyers / [by Keith R. James and Neil M. Maybury]. — Abingdon : Society for Computers and Law, [1981]. — 27p : ill ; 21cm
ISBN 0-906122-09-0 (pbk) : £1.00 B82-01523

651'.2 — Office equipment — *For schools*

Dew, Gladys D.. Office machinery and equipment / Gladys D. Dew. — London : McGraw-Hill. — (McGraw-Hill business education courses)
Students' text. — c1982. — 141p : ill,facsims,forms,1plan ; 25cm
Includes index
ISBN 0-07-084622-7 (pbk) : £4.25 : CIP rev.
B82-07656

651'.2 — Office equipment. Selection — *Manuals*

Cordon, M. A.. Office workstations. — Manchester : NCC Publications, Dec.1982. — [102]p. — (Office technology in the '80s ; v.6)
ISBN 0-85012-387-9 (pbk) : £6.50 : CIP entry
B82-37505

651'.2 — Offices. Effects of automation — *Forecasts*

Office of the future. — Aldershot : Gower
No.4: Planning for telecommunications. — July 1982. — [144]p
ISBN 0-566-03415-8 (pbk) : £9.50 : CIP entry
B82-12976

651'.29 — Office stationery: Forms. Design — *For distributive trades*

Clerical forms / [Distributive Industry Training Board]. — Manchester (MacLaren House, Talbot Rd., Stretford, Manchester M32 0FP) : The Board, [1981?]. — 15leaves : forms ; 21cm
Cover title
Unpriced (spiral) B82-17325

651.3 — Offices. Layout

Klein, Judy Graf. The office book. — London : Muller, Oct.1982. — [288]p
ISBN 0-584-95031-4 : £21.95 : CIP entry
B82-23213

Planning and designing the office environment / David A. Harris ... [et al.]. — New York ; London : Van Nostrand Reinhold, c1981. — xiii,194p : ill(some col.),plans ; 29cm
Includes index
ISBN 0-442-28418-7 (corrected) : £23.40
B82-02405

651'.3 — Offices. Management

Brealey, Ronald. An activity course in office administration. — 2nd ed. — London : Longman, Nov.1982. — [192]p
Previous ed.: 1976
ISBN 0-582-41314-1 (pbk) : £4.95 : CIP entry
B82-26535

651'.3 — Offices. Management — *Manuals*

Walley, B. H.. Handbook of office management. — 2nd ed. — London : Business Books, July 1982. — [288]p
Previous ed.: published as : Office administration handbook. 1975
ISBN 0-09-147440-x : £17.50 : CIP entry
B82-12421

651.3 — Sales offices. Management

Forsyth, Patrick. Running an effective sales office / Patrick Forsyth. — Farnborough, Hants. : Gower, c1980. — xii,142p : ill,forms ; 31cm
Bibliography: p138-139. — Includes index
ISBN 0-566-02185-4 : £12.50 : CIP rev.
B80-11528

651.3'7 — Great Britain. Distributive trades. Office practices: Clerical procedures. Work measurement

Clerical work measurement. — Manchester : Distributive Industry Training Board, [1981?]. — 28leaves ; 20cm. — (Clerical work control aids)
Cover title
Unpriced (spiral) B82-17314

651.3'7 — Office practices: Clerical procedures

Foster, Thelma J.. Office skills / Thelma J. Foster. — Cheltenham : Stanley Thornes, 1981. — xii,382p : ill,forms ; 24cm
Includes index
ISBN 0-85950-459-x (pbk) : £3.95 : CIP rev.
B81-22502

Foster, Thelma J.. Office skills answer book. — Cheltenham : Thornes, June 1982. — [76]p
ISBN 0-85950-383-6 (pbk) : £2.50 : CIP entry
B82-20781

651.3'7 — Office practices: Clerical procedures — *Manuals*

Brealey, Ronald. Clerical duties activity course : a teacher's manual : keys to activities in workbook / Ronald Brealey. — London : Longman, 1980. — [78]p : ill,forms ; 30cm
ISBN 0-582-41198-x (unbound) : £4.95 : CIP rev. B79-19380

651.3'741 — Great Britain. Clubs. Secretaryship — *Manuals*

Quinn, Hestia. The club secretary's guide / Hestia Quinn. — Newton Abbot : David & Charles, 1982. — vi,97p : ill,facsims,forms ; 19cm
Originally published: Wellington : Reed, 1982
ISBN 0-7153-8284-5 : £3.95 : CIP rev.
B82-10695

651.3'741 — Secretaryship — *Manuals*

Austin, Evelyn. Secretarial services / Evelyn Austin. — Plymouth : Macdonald & Evans, 1982. — viii,197p : ill ; 22cm. — (The M & E BEC book series)
Includes index
ISBN 0-7121-1984-1 (pbk) : £3.50 B82-39708

Lee, Dorothy E.. Secretarial office procedures / Dorothy E. Lee, Walter A. Brower. — 2nd ed. — New York ; London : McGraw-Hill, 1981, c1960. — vii,211,169p : ill,forms ; 28cm
Previous ed.: 1976. — Includes index
ISBN 0-07-037037-0 (pbk) : £9.50 B82-05069

651.3'743 — United States. Hospitals. Ward clerks. Duties — *Manuals*

Willson, Myra S.. A textbook for ward clerks and unit secretaries / Myra S. Willson. — St. Louis, Mo. ; London : Mosby, 1979. — xi,174p : ill,forms ; 26cm
Includes index
ISBN 0-8016-5593-5 (pbk) : Unpriced
B82-19929

651.5 — Accounting. Records management

Grimsley, Bob. Management accounting systems and records. — 2nd ed. — Aldershot : Gower, Oct.1981. — [125]p
Previous ed.: 1972
ISBN 0-566-02339-3 : £12.50 : CIP entry
B81-24619

651.5'042 — Devon. Nursery schools. Students, 3-5 years. Personal records — *Proposals*

Records 3-5 : a handbook of guidance / Devon County Council Education Department. — Exeter : The Department, c1981. — 22p ; 30cm
Bibliography: p21
ISBN 0-86114-340-x (spiral) : Unpriced
B82-14761

651.5'042 — England. Primary schools. Students. Personal records. Records management

Clift, Philip. Record keeping in primary schools / Philip Clift, Gaby Weiner, Edwin Wilson. — Basingstoke : Macmillan Education, 1981. — x,310p : ill,forms ; 24cm. — (Schools Council research studies)
ISBN 0-333-30945-6 (pbk) : £7.95 : CIP rev.
B81-13810

651.5′9 — Great Britain. Medical records. Records management. Applications of digital computer systems: Master Patient Index

The **Tayside** master patient index. — [Dundee] ([P.O. Box 75, Vernonholme, Riverside Drive, Dundee DD1 9NL]) : Tayside Health Board, 1978. — v,62p : ill ; 21cm
£1.00 (pbk) B82-11040

651.5′9 — Great Britain. Organisations. Personnel. Records. Records management. Applications of digital computer systems

Bilsland, Isabel. Computerizing personnel systems : how to choose and where to go / IPM Information Services. — [London] : Institute of Personnel Management, 1982. — 51p ; 30cm
Compiled by Isabel Bilsland. — Bibliography: p49-51
ISBN 0-85292-311-2 (spiral) : Unpriced : CIP rev. B82-07119

651.5′9 — Offices. Records. Records management. Automation

Newton, S. C.. Office automation and records management : report of a working party / Society of Archivists Records Management Group. — Sheffield : Society of Archivists, 1981. — 21p : 1ill ; 30cm. — (Records Management Group occasional papers ; 1)
Author: S.C. Newton
ISBN 0-902886-05-3 (pbk) : Unpriced B82-16732

651.7 — Business practices. Communication — *Manuals*

Bittleston, John. The book of business communications checklists / by John Bittleston and Barbara Shorter. — London : Associated Business Press, 1981. — 152p ; 23cm
Includes index
ISBN 0-85227-263-4 : Unpriced B82-20161

Evans, Desmond W.. Communication at work / Desmond W. Evans. — London : Pitman, 1982. — iv,188p : ill ; 30cm
ISBN 0-273-01734-9 (pbk) : Unpriced B82-30556

651.7 — Electronic mail

Connell, Stephen. The electronic mail handbook. — London : Kogan Page, Sept.1982. — [200]p
ISBN 0-85038-589-x : £11.95 : CIP entry B82-23860

Managing office automation : electronic mail and message systems / Urwick Nexos. — Slough : Urwick Nexos, [1981?]. — ii,44leaves : ill ; 30cm. — (Urwick Nexos report series ; 5)
ISBN 0-907535-06-2 (pbk) : Unpriced B82-09804

Planning for electronic mail / edited by Alan Simpson. — Aldershot : Gower, c1982. — vi,133p ; 22cm. — (The Office of the future ; no.2)
ISBN 0-566-03406-9 (pbk) : Unpriced B82-22735

Welch, J. A.. Electronic mail systems : a practical evaluation guide / J.A. Welch and P.A. Wilson. — Manchester : National Computing Centre, 1981. — 78,48p : forms ; 20cm. — (Office technology in the '80's)
ISBN 0-85012-350-x (pbk) : Unpriced : CIP rev. B81-39238

651.7′0722 — Business practices. Communication — *Case studies*

Jones, Alwyn. The AZTEC file : a business communications course / Alwyn Jones. — Cheltenham : Stanley Thornes, 1981. — viii,56p : ill ; 29cm
ISBN 0-85950-499-9 (pbk) : £1.95 : CIP rev. B81-16904

651.7′5 — Great Britain. Personnel management. Legal aspects. Correspondence — *Forms & precedents*

Janner, Greville. Janner's handbook of draft letters of employment law for employers and personnel managers / Greville Janner ; illustrations by Tobi. — 2nd ed. — London : Business Books, 1981. — xxx,381p : ill ; 23cm
Previous ed.: published as The employer's and personnel manager's handbook of draft letters of employment law. 1977. — Includes index
ISBN 0-09-145730-0 : Unpriced : CIP rev. B81-20561

651.8 — Great Britain. Business firms. Word processing equipment — *Buyers' guides*

Harris, Helen. So you want to buy a word processor?. — London : Business Books, Oct.1982. — [152]p
ISBN 0-09-150350-7 (cased) : £15.00 : CIP entry
ISBN 0-00-150351-5 (pbk) : £8.50 B82-24976

651.8 — Great Britain. Solicitorship. Practices. Applications of word processing systems

Townsend, Kevin. Word processing for solicitors. — Aldershot : Gower, Nov.1982. — [150]p
ISBN 0-566-03450-6 : £15.00 : CIP entry B82-26555

651.8 — Office practice. Word processing

Bradshaw, M. E.. Word processing. — London : Edward Arnold, Nov.1982. — [64]p
ISBN 0-7131-0803-7 (pbk) : £2.50 : CIP entry B82-23031

651.8 — Offices. Word processing systems

Chambers, Harry T.. Making the most of word-processing. — London : Business Books, Aug.1982. — [192]p
ISBN 0-09-147420-5 : £12.00 : CIP entry B82-15659

Planning for word processing / edited by Alan Simpson. — Aldershot : Gower, c1982. — vi,150p ; 22cm. — (The Office of the future ; no.3)
ISBN 0-566-03414-x (pbk) : Unpriced : CIP rev. B82-01548

Will, Mimi. Concepts in word processing : the challenge of change / Mimi Will, Donette Dake. — Boston [Mass.] ; London : Allyn and Bacon, c1982. — vi,345p : ill,facsims,forms ; 24cm
Includes index
ISBN 0-205-07654-8 (pbk) : Unpriced B82-17748

651.8 — United States. Office practices. Word processing

Rosen, Arnold. Word processing / Arnold Rosen, Rosemary Fielden. — 2nd ed. — Englewood Cliffs ; London : Prentice-Hall, c1982. — xvii,430p : ill,forms,ports ; 24cm
Previous ed.: 1977. — Bibliography: p421-423. — Includes index
ISBN 0-13-963488-6 : £14.20 B82-16853

651.8 — Word processing equipment

Skelcher, Derek. Word processing : equipment survey / [by Derek Skelcher on behalf of Online Conferences Limited]. — Northwood Hills : Online Conferences, c1980. — vii,222p ; 29cm
ISBN 0-903796-56-2 (pbk) : Unpriced B82-03327

651.8 — Word processing equipment — *Manuals*

Rosen, Arnold. Word processing : keyboarding applications and exercises / Arnold Rosen, William Hubbard. — New York ; Chichester : Wiley, c1981. — viii,291p : ill,facsims,forms ; 28cm
Includes index
ISBN 0-471-07746-1 (spiral) : £12.55 B82-02489

651.8 — Word processing — *Manuals*

Pigott, Janet. Word processing experience. — Cheltenham : Stanley Thornes, Sept.1982. — [216]p
ISBN 0-85950-386-0 (spiral) : £3.50 : CIP entry B82-20200

Pigott, Janet. Word processing experience. — Cheltenham : Stanley Thornes
Teacher's handbook and solutions. — Sept.1982. — [224]p
ISBN 0-85950-393-3 (pbk) : £8.50 : CIP entry B82-31312

651.8 — Word processing systems

Bradshaw, M. E.. Word processing. — London : Edward Arnold, Nov.1982. — [80]p
ISBN 0-7131-0815-0 (pbk) : £2.75 : CIP entry B82-27958

Glatzer, Hal. Introduction to word processing / Hal Glatzer. — Berkeley, Calif. : Sybex ; Birmingham : the Computer Bookshop [distributor], 1981. — xiv,210p : ill,facsims ; 22cm
Bibliography: p167-177. — Includes index
ISBN 0-89588-076-8 (pbk) : Unpriced B82-27397

Morgan, Richard, *1938-*. Word processing / Richard Morgan, Brian Wood. — London : Longman, 1982. — viii,152p : ill ; 22cm
Originally published: London : Oyez, 1981. — Includes index
ISBN 0-582-41318-4 (pbk) : £4.95 : CIP rev. B82-14379

Simons, G. L.. Introducing word processing / G.L. Simons. — Manchester : NCC, 1981. — 228p : ill ; 21cm
Bibliography: p171-181. — Includes index
ISBN 0-85012-320-8 (pbk) : Unpriced : CIP rev. B81-28133

651.8 — Word processing systems — *For businessmen*

Townsend, Kevin. Choosing and using a word processor / Kevin and Kate Townsend. — Aldershot : Gower, c1981. — 225p : ill ; 22cm
Includes index
ISBN 0-566-03408-5 : Unpriced : CIP rev. B81-35875

651.8 — Word processing systems. Purchase

Bruley, Karina. Guide to implementing word processing systems / [Karina Bruley]. — [2nd ed.]. — [Guildford] : [K. Bruley], [1982]. — 19leaves ; 30cm
Previous ed.: 1981?
ISBN 0-9507929-0-x (spiral) : £3.00 B82-13207

651.8 — Word processing systems. Security aspects

Doswell, R.. Word processing : security guidelines. — Manchester : NCC Publications, Sept.1982. — [303]p
ISBN 0-85012-361-5 : £4.50 : CIP entry B82-30607

651.8 — Word processing systems. Teaching — *Manuals*

Dake, Donette. Instructor's manual for Concepts in word processing, the challenge of change / by Donette Dake, Mimi Will. — Boston ; London : Allyn and Bacon, 1982. — vi,320p ; 28cm
ISBN 0-205-07655-6 (pbk) : Unpriced B82-31100

651.8′4 — Business practices. Applications of digital computer systems

Organizations in the computer age. — Aldershot : Gower, Jan.1983. — [284]p
ISBN 0-566-00488-7 : £15.00 : CIP entry B82-32433

Orilia, Lawrence S.. Introduction to business data processing / Lawrence S. Orilia. — 2nd ed. — New York ; London : McGraw-Hill, c1982. — xxiii,683,[30]p : ill,2ports ; 24cm
Previous ed.: 1979. — Includes index
ISBN 0-07-047835-x : £14.50 B82-22481

Shave, M. J. R.. Computer science applied to business systems. — London : Addison-Wesley, May 1982. — [288]p. — (International computer science series ; 2)
ISBN 0-201-13794-1 (pbk) : £6.95 : CIP entry B82-07527

651.8′4 — Electronic office equipment — *Buyers' guides*

Derrick, John. New office technology : a buyer's guide. — London : Kogan Page, Aug.1982. — [200]p
ISBN 0-85038-586-5 : £11.95 : CIP entry B82-19275

651.8′4 — Great Britain. Business firms. Data transmission systems

Data communications in retailing 1982-86. — [Brighton] : [Retail Management Development Programme], [1982]. — 107p : ill,maps ; 30cm. — (Retail management handbook ; 4)
ISBN 0-907923-03-8 (pbk) : Unpriced B82-29833

651.8′404 — Great Britain. Solicitorship. Practices. Applications of microcomputer systems

Edge, C. T.. Microcomputers for solicitors. — Aldershot : Gower, Dec.1982. — [200]p
ISBN 0-566-03442-5 : £15.00 : CIP entry B82-30058

651.8′4′0973 — United States. Business firms. Digital computer systems

Fink, Stuart S.. Business data processing. — 2nd ed. / Barbara J. Burian, Stuart S. Fink. — Englewood Cliffs ; London : Prentice-Hall, c1982. — xviii,494p : ill ; 25cm
Previous ed.: New York : Appleton-Century-Crofts, 1974. — Includes index
ISBN 0-13-094045-3 : £14.20 B82-16851

651.8′423 — Business practices. Applications of digital computer systems. Programming. Flowcharts

Singelmann, Jay. Business programming logic : a structured approach / Jay Singelmann, Jean Longhurst. — 2nd ed. — Englewood Cliffs ; London : Prentice-Hall, c1982. — viii,279p : ill,2forms ; 28cm
Previous ed.: 1978. — Includes index
ISBN 0-13-107623-x (pbk) : £11.95 B82-24094

651′.961′0973 — United States. Medicine. Office practices

Bredow, Miriam. Medical office procedures / Miriam Bredow, Karonne J. Becklin, Edith M. Sunnarborg. — 2nd ed. — New York ; London : Gregg Division/McGraw-Hill, c1981. — vi,201,WP211p : ill,forms ; 28cm. — (College series)
Previous ed.: 1973. — Bibliography: p194-196. — Includes index
ISBN 0-07-007441-0 (pbk) : £11.75 B82-08067

Fordney, Marilyn Takahashi. Administrative medical assisting / Marilyn Takahashi Fordney, Joan Johnson Follis. — New York ; Chichester : Wiley, c1982. — xii,629p : ill,facsims,forms ; 28cm
ISBN 0-471-06380-0 (spiral) : £14.75 B82-18064

652.3 — TYPING

652.3 — Typing — *Manuals*

Body, Edna. QWERTY plus : a short course in keyboard skills / Edna Body. — London : Edward Arnold, 1982. — 45p : ill ; 30cm
ISBN 0-7131-0712-x (pbk) : £2.00 : CIP rev. B82-06916

Davis, Margaret, *1912-*. Practical typewriting : made simple / Margaret Davis. — London : Heinemann, c1981. — 144p : ill,forms ; 23cm. — (Made simple books)
Bibliography: p134-135
ISBN 0-434-98527-9 (cased) : £5.95
ISBN 0-434-98465-5 (pbk) : £1.95 B82-12875

Drummond, A. M. (Archibald Manson). Typing first course / Archie Drummond, Anne Coles-Mogford, with Ida Scattergood. — 4th ed. — London : McGraw-Hill, c1982
Previous ed.: 1977
Handbook and solutions. — vi,229p : forms ; 30cm
ISBN 0-07-084648-0 (unbound) : £6.95 B82-31695

Mackay, Edith. Universal typing / Edith Mackay. — London : Pitman
Two-way paging
Graded production tasks
Elementary. — 1981. — 64p ; 21x30cm
ISBN 0-273-01663-6 (pbk) : Unpriced B82-11025

Mackay, Edith. Universal typing / Edith Mackay. — London : Pitman
Two-way paging
Graded production tasks
Intermediate. — 1981. — 64p ; 21x30cm
ISBN 0-273-01664-4 (pbk) : Unpriced B82-11026

Thomas, D. J.. A first course in typewriting. — London : Bell & Hyman, Sept.1982. — [192]p
ISBN 0-7135-1326-8 (spiral) : £3.95 : CIP entry B82-21747

652.3′0076 — Typing — *Questions & answers*

Drummond, A. M. (Archibald Manson). Typing : first course. — 4th ed. / Archie Drummond, Anne Coles-Mogford, with Ida Scattergood. — New York ; London : McGraw-Hill, c1982. — x,181p : ill(some col.),facsims,forms ; 21x30cm
Previous ed.: 1977. — Notebook format. — Two-way paging. — Includes index
ISBN 0-07-084647-2 : £3.25 B82-27225

Levine, Nathan. Typing made simple. — 3rd rev. ed. — London : Heinemann, Jan.1983. — [170] p. — (Made simple books)
Originally published: London : W.H. Allen, 1974
ISBN 0-434-98466-3 (pbk) : £2.50 : CIP entry B82-34581

652.3′007′7 — Typing — *Manuals* — *Programmed instructions*

Meyer, Lois. Machine transcription in modern business / Lois Meyer, Ruth Moyer. — 2nd ed. — New York ; Chichester : Wiley, c1982. — xi,220p : ill,forms ; 29cm. — (Wiley word processing series)
Previous ed.: 1978
ISBN 0-471-08260-0 (spiral) : £11.05 B82-16017

652.3′07 — Timed typing — *Questions & answers*

Grubbs, Robert L.. Sustained timed writings / Robert L. Grubbs, James L. White. — 4th ed. — New York ; London : Gregg Division, McGraw-Hill, c1982. — vi,90p ; 22x29cm
Previous ed.: 1971?
ISBN 0-07-025063-4 (spiral) : Unpriced B82-36041

653 — SHORTHAND

653′.07 — Shorthand. Teaching methods

Crank, Doris H.. Methods of teaching shorthand and transcription / Doris H. Crank, Ruth I. Anderson, John C. Peterson. — New York ; London : McGraw-Hill, c1982. — 426p : ill ; 24cm
Includes index
ISBN 0-07-013465-0 : £11.95 B82-03533

653′.076 — Shorthand — *Questions & answers*

Quint, Marie. Progressive shorthand passages / Marie Quint. — London : Longman. — (Longman secretarial studies series)
Book 1: Speed development 0-80 wpm. — 1981. — 22p ; 22cm
ISBN 0-582-41589-6 (pbk) : £1.75 : CIP rev. B81-32593

Quint, Marie. Progressive shorthand passages / Marie Quint. — London : Longman. — (Longman secretarial studies series)
Book 2: Speed development 0-80 wpm. — 1982. — 24p ; 21cm
ISBN 0-582-41588-8 (pbk) : £1.75 B82-22762

Quint, Marie. Progressive shorthand passages / Marie Quint. — London : Longman. — (Longman secretarial studies series)
Book 3: Speed development 80-120 wpm. — 1981. — 27p ; 22cm
ISBN 0-582-41590-x (pbk) : £1.75 : CIP rev. B81-32594

Quint, Marie. Progressive shorthand passages / Marie Quint. — London : Longman. — (Longman secretarial studies series)
Book 4: Speed development 120-150 wpm. — 1982. — 22p ; 21cm
ISBN 0-582-41591-8 (pbk) : £1.75 : CIP rev. B82-08418

653′.18 — Shorthand — *For medical secretaries*

Kerr, Janice. Medical words and phrases / Janice Kerr. — London : Pitman, c1980. — vii,132p ; 22cm. — (Pitman 2000 shorthand)
ISBN 0-273-01203-7 (pbk) : £6.50 B82-37788

653′.4242 — Pitman 2000 shorthand — *Manuals*

Pitman 2000 shorthand. — London : Pitman
Dictation practice / B.W. Canning. — 2nd ed. — 1982. — v,79p ; 22cm + 2 workbooks
Previous ed.: 1975
ISBN 0-273-01803-5 (pbk) : £3.25
ISBN 0-273-01804-3 (Workbook pt.1) : £2.25
ISBN 0-273-01805-1 (Workbook pt.2) : £2.25 B82-30361

Pitman 2000 shorthand. — London : Pitman
First course. — 2nd ed. — 1982. — xxiii,151p ; 22cm
Previous ed.: 1975. — Includes index
ISBN 0-273-01800-0 (pbk) : £3.25 B82-30362

Pitman 2000 shorthand. — London : Pitman
First course facility drills / Bryan Coombs. — 2nd ed. — 1982. — iii,58p ; 21cm
Previous ed.: 1975
ISBN 0-273-01806-x (pbk) : £1.50 B82-30365

Pitman 2000 shorthand. — London : Pitman
First course graded exercises / Bryan Coombs. — 2nd ed. — 1982. — v,88p : ill ; 22cm
Previous ed.: 1977. — Includes index
ISBN 0-273-01807-8 (pbk) : £2.50 B82-30363

Pitman 2000 shorthand. — London : Pitman
First course review / Bryan Coombs. — 2nd ed. — 1982. — vi,90p ; 22cm
Previous ed.: 1976
ISBN 0-273-01801-9 (pbk) : £2.95 B82-30366

Pitman 2000 shorthand. — London : Pitman
Key to first course, 2nd ed. — 1982. — 38p ; 22cm
ISBN 0-273-01808-6 (pbk) : £1.50 B82-30364

Pitman 2000 shorthand. — London : Pitman
Phrase book (formerly skill book) / Bryan Coombs. — 2nd ed. — 1982. — vi,119p ; 22cm
Previous ed.: 1976
ISBN 0-273-01802-7 (pbk) : £3.50 B82-30367

653′.4242 — Pitman 2000 shorthand. Reading books. Special subjects: Short stories in English. Australian writers, *1900-* — *Anthologies*

Australian short stories / edited by Gwen M. Williams. — Carlton, Vic. ; London : Pitman, 1979. — vi,87p ; 19cm. — (Pitman 2000)
ISBN 0-85896-616-6 (pbk) : £3.50 B82-07156

653′.4242′0321 — Pitman 2000 shorthand — *Dictionaries*

Pitman 2000 dictionary of English and shorthand / [based on the work of] Isaac Pitman. — London : Pitman, c1982. — 858p in various pagings ; 23cm. — (Pitman 2000 shorthand)
ISBN 0-273-01618-0 : £12.95 B82-30368

653′.4242′076 — Pitman 2000 shorthand — *Questions & answers*

Pitman, Isaac. 700 common-word reading and dictation exercises : the 700 most frequently recurring shorthand outlines with specially selected derivatives, followed by reading and dictation exercises using outlines listed / Isaac Pitman. — London : Pitman, c1979. — ix,181p ; 22cm
ISBN 0-273-01255-x (pbk) : £2.25 B82-00094

Reporting style. — London : Pitman, c1979. — viii,264p ; 23cm. — (Pitman 2000 shorthand)
ISBN 0-273-01415-3 : Unpriced B82-06592

653'.4242'0924 — Pitman shorthand. Pitman, Isaac — *Biographies*

Baker, Alfred. The life of Sir Isaac Pitman : (inventor of phonography) / by Alfred Baker. — Centenary ed. — London : Pitman, 1913 (1980 [printing]). — xviii,392p,[34]p of plates (1folded) : ill,facsims,music,ports ; 23cm
Previous ed.: 1908. — Bibliography: p355-380. — Includes index
ISBN 0-273-01587-7 : £7.95 B82-40700

653'.428 — Teeline — *Dictionaries*

Hill, I. C.. Teeline word list / I.C. Hill. — London : Heinemann Educational, 1981. — ix,163p ; 21cm
ISBN 0-435-45344-0 (pbk) : £2.95 : CIP rev. B81-25861

653'.428 — Teeline — *Manuals*

Butler, Harry, *1913-*. Teeline shorthand made simple / Harry Butler. — London : Heinemann, c1982. — xii,306p ; 23cm. — (Made simple books)
Includes bibliographies and index
ISBN 0-434-98497-3 (cased) : £5.95
ISBN 0-434-98500-7 (pbk) : £2.50 B82-37746

653'.428 — Teeline — *Questions & answers*

Hill, I. C.. Teeline. — 2nd ed. — London : Heinemann Educational, Jan.1983. — [232]p
Previous ed.: 1977
ISBN 0-435-45327-0 (pbk) : £2.95 : CIP entry B82-34584

657 — ACCOUNTING

657 — Accounting

Beams, Floyd A.. Advanced accounting / Floyd A. Beams. — 2nd ed. — Englewood Cliffs ; London : Prentice-Hall, c1982. — xvii,904p : ill ; 25cm
Previous ed.: 1979. — Includes bibliographies and index
ISBN 0-13-010157-5 : £20.20 B82-20084

Davidson, Sidney. Intermediate accounting : concepts, methods and uses / Sidney Davidson, Clyde P. Stickney, Roman L. Weil. — 3rd ed. — Chicago ; London : Dryden Press, c1982. — [1100]p ; 25cm. — (The Dryden Press series in accounting)
Previous ed.: 1981. — Text on lining papers. — Includes index
ISBN 0-03-058916-9 : £24.95 B82-38753

Dixon, Robert L.. The executive's accounting primer / Robert L. Dixon. — 2nd ed. — New York ; London : McGraw-Hill, c1982. — xv,395p ; 24cm
Previous ed. 1971. — Includes index
ISBN 0-07-017079-7 : £19.50 B82-27412

Dixon, Robert L.. The McGraw-Hill 36-hour accounting course / Robert L. Dixon. — 2nd ed. — New York ; London : McGraw-Hill, c1982. — xxiii,412p ; 24cm
Previous ed.: 1976. — Includes index
ISBN 0-07-017091-6 : £22.95 B82-27411

Glautier, M. W. E.. Accounting theory and practice. — 2nd. — London : Pitman, June 1982. — [653]p
Previous ed.: 1976
ISBN 0-273-01541-9 (pbk) : £8.95 : CIP entry B82-09994

Glautier, M. W. E.. Basic accounting practice / M.W.E. Glautier, B. Underdown and A.C. Clark. — 2nd ed. — London : Pitman. — (A Pitman international text)
Previous ed.: 1979
Teacher's guide. — 1980. — 243p ; 25cm
ISBN 0-273-01521-4 (pbk) : £5.95 B82-07319

Haried, Andrew A.. Advanced accounting / Andrew A. Haried, Leroy F. Imdieke, Ralph E. Smith. — 2nd ed. — New York ; Chichester : Wiley, c1982. — xxiv,912p ; 25cm
Previous ed.: 1979. — Includes index
ISBN 0-471-08717-3 : £19.50 B82-18155

McCullers, Levis D.. Accounting theory : text and readings / Levis D. McCullers, Richard G. Schroeder. — 2nd ed. — New York ; Chichester : Wiley, c1982. — xii,686p : ill ; 24cm
Previous ed.: 1978. — Includes bibliographies and index
ISBN 0-471-06029-1 : £20.70 B82-19892

Mosich, A. N.. Intermediate accounting. — 5th ed. / A.N. Mosich, E. John Larsen. — New York ; London : McGraw-Hill, c1982. — xxii,1114p ; 25cm
Previous ed.: / by Walter B. Meigs, A.N. Mosich, Charles E. Johnson. 1978. — Text on lining papers. — Includes index
ISBN 0-07-041580-3 : £21.95 B82-16375

Norkett, P. T. C.. Financial accounting / Paul Norkett. — Harlow : Longman, 1981. — xvi,335p : ill ; 22cm. — (Accountancy for non-accountants ; v.1)
Includes index
ISBN 0-582-41207-2 (pbk) : £4.95 B82-08747

Pickles, William. Accountancy. — 5th ed. — London : Pitman, Sept.1982. — [1568]p
Previous ed.: 1974
ISBN 0-273-01256-8 (pbk) : £8.95 : CIP entry B82-30568

Stott, J. Randall. Mastering principles of accounts / J. Randall Stott. — London : Macmillan, 1982. — 237p ; 23cm. — (Macmillan master series)
Includes index
ISBN 0-333-31289-9 (cased) : £8.95
ISBN 0-333-30446-2 (pbk) : Unpriced B82-17106

Wilkinson-Riddle, G. J.. Accounting Level III / G.J. Wilkinson-Riddle. — Plymouth : Macdonald and Evans, 1982. — viii,261p : ill ; 22cm. — (The M & E BEC book series)
Includes index
ISBN 0-7121-0175-6 (pbk) : £5.75 B82-37771

657 — Accounting, *1500-1850*. Early works

Bywater, M. F.. Historic accounting literature : a companion guide / M.F. Bywater and B.S. Yamey. — London : Scolar, 1982. — 255p ; 22cm. — (Historic accounting literature)
Bibliography: p242-249. — Includes index
ISBN 0-85967-647-1 : Unpriced : CIP rev. B82-01341

657 — Accounting — *For Caribbean students*

Wood, Frank. Principles of accounts for the Caribbean / Frank Wood with educational and technical advice from Gloria Hamilton and Mahadeo Narine. — Harlow : Longman, 1982. — 312p : forms ; 22cm
Includes index
ISBN 0-582-76596-x (pbk) : Unpriced B82-37164

657 — Accounting — *For schools*

Smyth, W. M.. Junior accounting / W.M. Smyth. — Rev. ed. — Christchurch ; London : Whitcoulls, 1979, c1977. — 137p : ill,facsims ; 22cm
Includes index
ISBN 0-7233-0593-5 : Unpriced B82-05543

Smyth, W. M.. School certificate accounting / W.M. Smyth and R.B. Wheeler. — Christchurch ; London : Whitcoulls, 1982. — 271p : ill ; 22cm
Includes index
ISBN 0-7233-0681-8 : Unpriced B82-38399

Turner, D. E.. Accounting for 'O' level / D.E. Turner and P.H. Turner. — London : Edward Arnold, 1982. — ix,303p : ill ; 22cm
Includes index
ISBN 0-7131-0719-7 (pbk) : £4.95 : CIP rev. B82-13514

657 — Accounting. Information systems

Page, John, *1949-*. Accounting and information systems / John Page, Paul Hooper. — 2nd ed. — Englewood Cliffs ; London : Prentice-Hall, c1982. — xiii,607p : ill,forms ; 24cm
Previous ed.: 197-?. — Includes index
ISBN 0-8359-0095-9 (pbk) : Unpriced B82-33701

657 — Accounting — *Manuals*

Garbutt, Douglas. Accounting foundations : an introductory textbook / by Douglas Garbutt. — London : Pitman, 1980. — xiii,439p : ill ; 25cm
Includes index
ISBN 0-273-01369-6 (pbk) : Unpriced B82-30555

Johnson, Harry, *1931-*. A practical foundation in accounting / by Harry Johnson and Austin Whittam. — London : Allen & Unwin, 1982. — xi,447p ; 24cm
Includes index
ISBN 0-04-332082-1 (cased) : Unpriced : CIP rev.
ISBN 0-04-332083-x (pbk) : Unpriced B82-07228

Longman audit and accountancy practice manual. — London : Longman, June 1982. — [160]p
ISBN 0-582-29588-2 (pbk) : £9.50 : CIP entry B82-09445

Millmore, Lionel. Accounting through numeracy / Lionel Millmore, Stephen Flowers. — Walton-on-Thames : Nelson, 1982. — 188p : ill ; 25cm. — (Nelson BEC books)
Includes index
ISBN 0-17-741131-7 (pbk) : £4.25 B82-31034

657 — Accounting. Quantitative methods

Lucey, T.. Quantitative techniques : an instructional manual for business and accountancy students / T. Lucey. — Winchester : D.P. Publications, 1979, c1980 (1980 [printing]). — iv,339p : ill ; 22cm
Includes index
ISBN 0-905435-09-5 (pbk) : Unpriced B82-05270

657 — Accounts — *For Asian students*

Li, Betsy. Principles of accounts / Betsi Li, Tan Sai Kim, Goh Ling Chin. — Kuala Lumpur ; Oxford : Oxford University Press, 1978. — iv,168p ; 26cm. — (Modern certificate guides)
ISBN 0-19-581147-x (pbk) : £1.95 B82-35164

657 — Organisations. Accounting systems

Gee, Kenneth P.. Financial control / Kenneth P. Gee. — [Salford] : University of Salford, [1980?]. — [14]p : ill ; 21cm. — (Inaugural lecture)
Unpriced (pbk) B82-30529

657'.0218 — Accounting. Standards

Blake, John, *1950-*. Accounting standards / John Blake. — London : Longman, 1981. — 276p : ill ; 22cm. — (Longman professional education series)
Includes index
ISBN 0-582-41211-0 (pbk) : £4.95 B82-08897

657'.023 — Accountancy — *Career guides*

Taylor, Felicity. Careers in accountancy. — London : Kogan Page, Feb.1982. — [100]p
ISBN 0-85038-520-2 (cased) : £5.95 : CIP entry
ISBN 0-85038-521-0 (pbk) : £2.50 B82-00150

657'.023'41 — Great Britain. Accountancy — *Career guides — For graduates*

The **DOG** guide to accountancy & finance / [editor Iris Rosier]. — [London] : [VNU Business Publications], [1981?]. — 52p : ill ; 25cm
Cover title
ISBN 0-86271-017-0 (corrected : pbk) : Unpriced
Primary classification 332'.023'41 B82-05187

657'.023417 — Ireland *(Republic)*. Accountancy — *Career guides*

Chartered accountant 80. — [Dublin] ([7 Fitzwilliam Pl., Dublin 2]) : The Institute of Chartered Accountants in Ireland, [1980?]. — 68p : ill(some col.),ports ; 21cm
Unpriced (pbk) B82-30397

657'.023'42 — England. Accountancy — *Career guides*

The **Chartered** accountant's world. — London (P.O. Box 433, Chartered Accountant's Hall, Moorgate Place, EC2P 2BJ) : Institute of Chartered Accountants in England and Wales, [1980?]. — 16p : col.ill ; 30cm
Unpriced (pbk) B82-19341

657'.024332 — Accounting — *For banking*

Egginton, Don A.. Accounting for the banker. — 2nd ed. — London : Longman, Nov.1982. — [320]p
Previous ed.: 1977
ISBN 0-582-29633-1 : £6.95 : CIP entry B82-26528

657'.02434 — Accountancy — *For law*

Berger, Robert O.. Practical accounting for lawyers / Robert O. Berger, Jr.. — New York ; Chichester : Wiley, c1981. — xiv,357p ; 24cm. — (Modern accounting perspectives and practices series)
Bibliography: p345-346. — Includes index
ISBN 0-471-08486-7 : £25.85 B82-05799

657'.024658 — Accounting — *For business studies*

Claret, Jake. Accounting 2 : a practical approach / Jake Claret. — London : McGraw-Hill, c1981. — xiv,290p : ill,forms ; 25cm. — (McGraw-Hill business education courses)
Includes index
ISBN 0-07-084621-9 (pbk) : £4.65 : CIP rev. B81-14461

Counsell, Robert E.. Accounting II / Robert E. Counsell. — London : Cassell, 1982. — 281p ; 22cm. — (Cassell BEC series. National level)
ISBN 0-304-30337-2 (pbk) : Unpriced B82-14791

Francis, D. Pitt. Accounting concepts and methods : accounting 2 / D. Pitt Francis. — London : Holt, Rinehart and Winston, c1982. — xi,354p : ill,forms ; 22cm. — (Holt business texts)
Includes index
ISBN 0-03-910342-0 (pbk) : £4.95 : CIP rev. B81-33926

Turner, D. E.. Accounting and numeric methods for business studies students / D.E. Turner and P.H. Turner. — London : Edward Arnold, 1981. — ix,278p : ill ; 22cm
Includes index
ISBN 0-7131-0590-9 (corrected : pbk) : £4.95 : CIP rev. B81-22517

657'.025'41 — Great Britain. Accountancy — *Directories* — *Serials*

[Training opportunities *(Institute of Chartered Accountants in England and Wales)***]**. Training opportunities / the Institute of Chartered Accountants in England and Wales. — 1982-. — London : The Institute, [1981]-. — v. ; 21cm
Annual. — Merger of: Directory of firms with training opportunities for non-graduates ; and, Directory of firms with training opportunities for graduates of universities in Great Britain and holders of CNAA degrees
ISSN 0262-2882 = Training opportunities - Institute of Chartered Accountants in England and Wales : Unpriced B82-01074

657'.028'54 — Accounting. Information systems. Applications of digital computer systems

Robinson, Leonard A.. Accounting information systems : a cycle approach / Leonard A. Robinson, James R. Davis, C. Wayne Alderman. — New York ; London : Harper & Row, c1982. — xv,584p : ill,forms ; 24cm
Ill on lining papers. — Includes bibliographies and index
ISBN 0-06-045509-8 : £16.95 B82-32832

Wilkinson, Joseph W.. Accounting and information systems / Joseph W. Wilkinson. — New York Chichester : Wiley, c1982. — xvi,845p : ill ; 25cm
Includes bibliographies and index
ISBN 0-471-04986-7 : £21.40 B82-18212

657'.028'54 — Accounting. Information systems. Applications of digital computer systems — *Questions & answers*

Moscove, Stephen A.. Instructor's manual to accompany Accounting information systems — concepts and practice for effective decision making / Stephen A. Moscove, Mark G. Simkin. — New York ; Chichester : Wiley, c1981. — 467,[100]p : ill,facsims,forms ; 28cm
ISBN 0-471-03371-5 (pbk) : £50.85 B82-38981

657'.03'21 — Accountancy — *Encyclopaedias*

March, Robert T.. [Running Press glossary of accounting language]. The language of accountancy / Robert T. March. — London : W.H. Allen, 1981, c1978. — 77p ; 20cm. — (A Star book)
Originally published: Philadelphia : Running Press, 1978
ISBN 0-352-30957-1 (pbk) : £1.50 B82-03039

Robb, Alan J.. A dictionary of accounting terms / Alan J. Robb. — Christchurch, [N.Z.] ; London : Whitcoulls, 1981. — 72p ; 21cm
ISBN 0-7233-0665-6 (pbk) : Unpriced B82-01253

657'.03'927 — Accountancy — *Arabic & English dictionaries*

Abdeen, Adnan. English-Arabic dictionary of accounting and finance : with an Arabic-English glossary / Adnan Abdeen. — Chichester : Wiley, c1981. — xi,226p,[42]p : forms ; 25cm
Parallel English and Arabic text
ISBN 0-471-27673-1 : £9.75 : CIP rev. B80-08845

657'.06'01 — Accountancy. Organisations: Association of Certified Accountants — *For accountancy students*

Association of Certified Accountants. Certified accountants students' handbook / Association of Certified Accountants. — [London] ([29 Lincoln's Inn Fields, WC2A 3EE]) : [The Association], [1982]. — 64p ; 21cm
Cover title. — Includes index
£1.00 (pbk) B82-19471

657'.068'3 — England. Trainee accountants. Recruitment & selection

Student recruitment and selection. — London : Institute of Chartered Accountants in England and Wales, 1982. — 20p : forms ; 30cm
Cover title
£2.00 (pbk) B82-25782

657'.07'11 — Universities. Curriculum subjects: Accounting

Perks, R. W.. Accounting as a university subject : an inaugural lecture delivered before the Queen's University of Belfast on 13 October 1981. — [Belfast] : Queen's University of Belfast, c1982. — 18p ; 21cm. — (New lecture series ; no.130)
ISBN 0-85389-209-1 (pbk) : £0.40 B82-34653

657'.07'1141 — Great Britain. Higher education institutions. Curriculum subjects: Accountancy. Degree courses — *Directories* — *Serials*

Approved courses for accountancy education. — 1981 ed.-. — [London] ([11 Copthall Ave, EC2P 2BJ]) : [Accounting Education Consultative Board], [1981?]-. — v. ; 30cm
Annual. — Continues: Degree studies and the accountancy profession
ISSN 0263-1768 = Approved courses for accountancy education : Unpriced B82-18543

657'.076 — Accounting — *Questions & answers*

Chahin, M.. Key to Favell's Practical bookkeeping and accounts / by M. Chahin. — 2nd ed. — Slough : University Tutorial Press, 1980. — 218p ; 22cm
Previous ed.: 1972
ISBN 0-7231-0804-8 (pbk) : £5.00 B82-31263

Daff, Trevor. Accounting workbook 2 / T. Daff and G. Blake. — London : Pitman, 1982. — 187p ; 22cm
ISBN 0-273-01730-6 (pbk) : Unpriced B82-26735

Garbutt, Douglas. Guide to accounting foundations / Douglas Garbutt, Cedric McCallum, Elaine D. Rennie. — London : Pitman, 1980. — xi,348p : ill ; 25cm
ISBN 0-273-01370-x (pbk) : Unpriced B82-30554

Johnson, Harry, *1931-*. A practical foundation in accounting : a student's solution guide / Harry Johnson and Austin Whittam. — London : Allen & Unwin, 1982. — 202p ; 24cm
ISBN 0-04-332085-6 (pbk) : Unpriced : CIP rev. B82-10577

Langley, F. P.. Workbook in accounting / F.P. Langley and D.A. Caldicott. — 3rd ed. — London : Butterworths, 1981. — 273p : ill ; 25cm + Teachers' guide(52p ; 25cm)
Previous ed.: 1975
ISBN 0-408-10680-8 (pbk) : Unpriced : CIP rev.
ISBN 0-408-10823-1 (Teachers' guide) : Unpriced B81-30460

Person, Samuel. Intermediate accounting / Samuel Person, Daniel Wolinsky ; technical editor Robert Beekman. — 1981/82 ed. — Chicago ; London : Dryden, c1982. — xv,151p ; 28cm. — (CPA exam supplement)
ISBN 0-03-059793-5 (pbk) : £6.95 B82-23305

657'.076 — Accounting — *Questions & answers* — *For Irish students*

Accounting 1981 (Ordinary and Higher Level). — [Dublin] : Folens
Solutions / John O'Connor. — [1981?]. — 32p ; 25cm
Cover title
£1.00 (pbk) B82-18013

657'076 — Accounting — *Questions & answers* — *For Irish students*

O'Connor, John, *1949-*. Accounting assignments / John O'Connor. — [Dublin] : Folens, [1979?]. — (Leaving certificate)
Cover title
1: Ordinary level. — 48p ; 25cm + Key(67p ; 25cm)
ISBN 0-86121-054-9 (pbk) : Unpriced B82-01228

657'.076 — Accounting — *Questions & answers* — *For schools*

Cooper, J. M.John Macneill. Objective tests in accounts 1 / J.M. Cooper. — London : Longman, 1981. — 81p ; 20cm. — (Longman objective tests series)
ISBN 0-582-41577-2 (pbk) : £1.50 B82-01699

657'.076 — Accounting — *Questions & answers* — *For West African students*

Wood, Frank. Business accounting 1. — West African ed. / Frank Wood, J.O. Omuya. — Harlow : Longman, 1982. — 424p ; 22cm
British ed.: 1967. — Includes index
ISBN 0-582-65602-8 (pbk) : £2.65 B82-21793

657'.076 — England. Accountants. Professional education. Practical experience. Self-assessment — *Manuals* — *For trainee accountants*

Students's training record file / Institute of Chartered Accountants in England and Wales. — [London] : [The Institute], [1981?]. — 1v.(loose-leaf) : forms ; 32cm
Unpriced B82-07138

657'.076 — United States. Accountants. Professional education. C.P.A. examinations

Stenzel, Alvin M.. Approaching the CPA examination : a personal guide to examination preparation / Alvin M. Stenzel, Jr.. — New York ; Chichester : Wiley, 1981. — 102p ; 23cm
Bibliography: p97-102
ISBN 0-471-08699-1 (pbk) : £3.80 B82-01033

657′.094 — Europe. Accounting — *Polyglot dictionaries*

Percival, C. T. Glossary of European accounting charts : European charts of accounts with English translation / C.T. Percival, P.J. Donaghy, J. Laidler. — Durham : Flambard (European)
Vol.1: France, Plan Comptable Général [PCG], Germany BDI Industrie-Kontenrahmen (IKR), Spain, Plan General de Contabilidad (PGC). — c1982. — ii,170p ; 30cm
Includes index
ISBN 0-9507949-0-2 (spiral) : £17.50 B82-20961

657′.094 — Western Europe. Accounting

Oldham, K. Michael. Accounting systems and practice in Europe / K. Michael Oldham. — 2nd ed. — Aldershot : Gower, 1981, c1975. — xiv,271p ; 26cm
Previous ed.: 1975. — Bibliography: p263-264. — Includes index
ISBN 0-566-02147-1 : Unpriced : CIP rev. B81-16368

657′.0941 — Great Britain. Accounting. Standards. Formulation. Proposals: Accounting Standards Committee, *1970-1980*

British accounting standards : the first 10 years / edited by Sir Ronald Leach and Edward Stamp. — Cambridge : Woodhead-Faulkner, 1981. — viii,247p : ports ; 24cm
Bibliography: p81-84
ISBN 0-85941-149-4 : £12.50 B82-21062

657′.09931 — New Zealand. Accounting

Wheeler, R. B.. Advanced accounting in New Zealand / R.B. Wheeler and R.H. Boyan. — 2nd ed. — Christchurch ; London : Whitcoulls, 1978. — 436p ; 25cm
Previous ed.: 1973. — Includes index
ISBN 0-7233-0560-9 : Unpriced B82-29703

657′.2 — Book-keeping

Johnson, G. B.. Bookkeeping / [G.B. Johnson]. — 5th ed. — [London] : Pitman in association with Michael Benn & Associates. — 2v ; 10x16cm. — (Pitman revision cards)
Previous ed.: 1979
ISBN 0-904096-86-6 (spiral) : Unpriced
ISBN 0-904096-87-4 (v.2) : Unpriced B82-01669

657′.2 — Book-keeping — *For East African students*

Mutabiirwa, D. E. R.. Book-keeping and accounts for East Africa / D.E.R. Mutabiirwa and W. Barber. — Walton-on-Thames : Nelson, 1981. — 186p : forms ; 25cm. — (Nelson Africa business studies)
Includes index
ISBN 0-17-511491-9 (pbk) : £2.20 B82-03275

657′.2 — Book-keeping - *Manuals*

Kellock, John. A manual of basic bookkeeping. — London : Bell & Hyman, July 1981. — [160]p
ISBN 0-7135-1285-7 (pbk) : £2.50 : CIP entry B81-15911

657′.2 — Great Britain. Small firms. Book-keeping — *Manuals*

Kellock, John. A practical guide to good bookkeeping and business systems / John Kellock. — London : Business Books, 1982. — 206p : ill,facsims,forms ; 31cm
ISBN 0-09-147410-8 : Unpriced : CIP rev. B82-08432

Whitehead, Geoffrey. Simplified book-keeping for small businesses / Geoffrey Whitehead. — 2nd ed.(rev. and enl.). — Holmfirth : Vyner, 1981, c1978. — 182p : ill,forms ; 22cm
Previous ed.: 1978. — Includes index
ISBN 0-906628-00-8 (pbk) : £3.00 B82-03277

657′.2′024344 — Book-keeping — *For solicitors*

Halberstadt, Richard. Basic book-keeping for solicitors. — 2nd ed. — London : Sweet & Maxwell, Sept.1982. — [250]p
Previous ed.: 1979
ISBN 0-421-29760-3 (pbk) : £8.25 : CIP entry B82-19667

657′.3 — Balance sheets

How a banker looks at a balance sheet. — London (10 Lombard St., EC3V 9AT) : BES, 1979. — 19p ; 21cm. — (Study booklet series ; 10)
Cover title
Unpriced (pbk) B82-16265

657′.3 — Companies. Deferred corporation tax. Financial statements

Hoepen, M. A. van. Anticipated and deferred corporate income tax in companies′ financial statements / by M.A. van Hoepen. — Deventer ; London : Kluwer, 1981. — xi,295p ; 25cm
Bibliography: p291-295
ISBN 90-654-4008-9 : Unpriced B82-10140

657′.3′0973 — United States. Companies. Financial statements

Costales, S. B.. The guide to understanding financial statements : a revised edition of Financial statements of small business / S.B. Costales. — Rev ed. — New York ; London : McGraw-Hill, c1979. — viii,166p ; 24cm
Previous ed.: published as Financial statements of small business. 1970. — Includes index
ISBN 0-07-013190-2 : £9.50 B82-07449

657′.33 — Companies. Financial statements. Interpretation

Parker, R. H.. Understanding company financial statements / R.H. Parker. — 2nd ed. — Harmondsworth : Penguin, 1982. — 176p : ill ; 20cm. — (Pelican library of business and management)
Previous ed.: 1972. — Bibliography: p100-105. — Includes index
ISBN 0-14-022421-1 (pbk) : £2.50 B82-26790

657′.33′019 — Companies. Financial statements. Use by investors. Psychological aspects

Taffler, R. J.. Improving man′s ability to use accounting information : a cognitive synegesis / by R.J. Taffler. — London (Basinghall St., EC2V 5AH) : City University Business School, c1981. — 34leaves : ill ; 30cm. — (Working paper, ISSN 0140-1041 ; no.32)
Bibliography: leaves 31-34
Unpriced (pbk) B82-14182

657′.33′02854 — Companies. Financial statements. Interpretation. Applications of digital computer systems

Smith, G. M.. Improving the communication function of published accounting statements / by G.M. Smith and R.J. Taffler. — London (Gresham College, Basinghall St., EC2V 5AH) : City University Business School, c1982. — 25leaves : ill ; 30cm. — (Working paper series / City University Business School, ISSN 0140-1041 ; no.38)
Bibliography: leaves 17-19
Unpriced (pbk) B82-27449

657′.42 — Cost accounting

Information for decision making : readings in cost and managerial accounting / edited by Alfred Rappaport. — 3rd ed. — Englewood Cliffs ; London : Prentice-Hall, c1982. — 412p : ill ; 23cm
Previous ed.: 1975. — Includes bibliographies
ISBN 0-13-464354-2 (pbk) : £14.95
Also classified at 658.1′511 B82-35162

Roche, A.. Accountancy control systems / A. Roche. — London : Longman, 1982. — 283p : ill ; 22cm. — (Longman professional education series)
Includes index
ISBN 0-582-40002-3 (pbk) : £4.95 : CIP rev. B81-13824

657′.42′076 — Cost accounting — *Questions & answers*

Hazzard, Peter A.. How to pass examinations in cost accounting / P.A. Hazzard. — London : Cassell, 1982. — xi,196p ; 22cm
Includes index
ISBN 0-304-30924-9 (pbk) : £4.25 B82-31656

Walker, C. J.. Key to Principles of cost accounting / C.J. Walker. — 2nd ed. — Plymouth : Macdonald and Evans, 1979. — 196p : ill,forms ; 22cm
Previous ed.: 1970
ISBN 0-7121-1102-6 (pbk) : £4.25 B82-12179

657′.42′0973 — United States. Cost accounting — *Questions & answers*

Person, Samuel. Cost accounting / Samuel Person, Daniel Wolinsky ; technical editor Robert Beekman. — Chicago ; London : Dryden, c1982. — xv,138p : ill ; 28cm. — (CPA exam supplement)
ISBN 0-03-059797-8 (pbk) : £6.95 B82-19055

657′.45 — Auditing

De Paula, F. Clive. Auditing : principles and practice. — 16th ed. / F. Clive de Paula and Frank A. Attwood. — London : Pitman, 1982. — 420p : ill,forms ; 23cm
Previous ed.: 1976. — Includes index
ISBN 0-273-01778-0 (pbk) : Unpriced : CIP rev. B82-23481

Howard, Leslie R.. Auditing / Leslie R. Howard. — 7th ed. — Plymouth : Macdonald and Evans, c1982. — xiii,332p ; 18cm. — (The M & E handbook series)
Previous ed.: 1978. — Includes index
ISBN 0-7121-0178-0 (pbk) : £3.95 B82-32745

Pratt, M. J. (Michael John). Auditing / Michael J. Pratt. — London : Longman, 1982. — xii,507p : ill,forms ; 24cm
Includes index
ISBN 0-582-29527-0 (pbk) : £8.95 : CIP rev. B81-25879

Stettler, Howard F.. Auditing principles : a systems-based approach / Howard F. Stettler. — 5th ed. — Englewood Cliffs ; London : Prentice-Hall, c1982. — xvii,682p : ill ; 24cm. — (Prentice-Hall series in accounting)
Previous ed.: 1977. — Includes index
ISBN 0-13-051722-4 : £20.20 B82-29230

Taylor, Donald H. Auditing : integrated concepts and procedures / Donald H. Taylor, G. William Glezen. — 2nd ed. — New York ; Chichester : Wiley, c1982. — xxvi,931p : ill ; 24cm
Previous ed.: 1979. — Includes bibliographies and index
ISBN 0-471-08166-3 : £19.20 B82-18220

Woolf, Emile. Auditing today / Emile Woolf. — 2nd ed. — Englewood Cliffs ; London : Prentice-Hall, c1979 [i.e. 1982]. — xvii,534p : ill,forms ; 23cm
Previous ed.: 1979. — Includes index
ISBN 0-13-052159-0 (pbk) : £10.95 : CIP rev. B81-35791

657′.45 — Auditing. Implications of amounts derived from previous financial statements

Exposure draft : auditing guideline : amounts derived from the preceding financial statements / APC, CCAB. — [London] ([P.O. Box 433, Moorgate Place, EC29 2BJ]) : Auditing Practices Committee, c1981. — 10p ; 21cm
Unpriced (unbound) B82-02538

657′.45 — Great Britain. Manufacturing companies. Auditing. Costs. Determination

Taffler, R. J.. The determinants of the audit fee in the U.K. : an exploratory study / by R.J. Taffler and K.S. Ramalinggam. — London (Gresham College, Basinghall St., EC2V 5AH) : City University Business School, c1982. — 23leaves ; 30cm. — (Working paper series / City University Business School, ISSN 0140-1041 ; no.37)
Unpriced (pbk) B82-27450

657′.45 — Great Britain. Value for money auditing — *Conference proceedings*

Value for money audits : proceedings of a one-day seminar organised by Peat, Marwick, Mitchell & Co. in association with the Royal Institute of Public Administration. — London : Royal Institute of Public Administration, 1982. — 44p ; 21cm
ISBN 0-900628-26-x (pbk) : £2.50 B82-37587

657′.45′0151952 — Auditing. Applications of statistical sampling

Arens, Alvin A.. Applications of statistical sampling to auditing / Alvin A. Arens, James K. Loebbecke. — Englewood Cliffs ; London : Prentice-Hall, c1981. — xiii,370p : ill ; 24cm
Includes index
ISBN 0-13-039156-5 : £19.45 B82-04530

657'.45'0151952 — Auditing. Statistical mathematics. Sampling

Arkin, Herbert. Sampling methods for the auditor : an advanced treatment / Herbert Arkin. — New York ; London : McGraw-Hill, c1982. — x,251p : ill ; 24cm
Includes index
ISBN 0-07-002194-5 : £18.95 B82-16373

657'.45'0722 — Auditing — *Case studies*

Cases in auditing practice. — 3rd ed. / edited by J. Innes, T.A. Lee, F. Mitchell. — London : Institute of Chartered Accountants in England and Wales, 1981. — vi,282p : ill,forms ; 24cm + Solutions manual(v,128p : ill,forms ; 24cm)
Previous ed.: published as A casebook on auditing procedures / by Peter Bird. 1971
ISBN 0-85291-293-5 (pbk) : Unpriced
ISBN 0-85291-294-3 (Solutions manual) : Unpriced B82-11623

657'.45'076 — Auditing — *Questions & answers*

Childs, L. R.. Objective tests in auditing / L.R. Childs, A.R. Leal. — London : Longman, 1981. — 106p ; 20cm. — (Longman objective tests series)
ISBN 0-582-41594-2 (pbk) : £1.95 B82-04939

Person, Samuel. Auditing : CPA exam supplement / Samuel Person, Daniel Wolinsky ; technical editor Robert Beekman. — Chicago ; London : Dryden, c1982. — xiii,145p ; 28cm
ISBN 0-03-059794-3 (pbk) : Unpriced B82-27780

Stein, Neil D.. How to pass examinations in auditing / Neil D. Stein. — London : Cassel, 1982. — 154p : ill ; 22cm. — (Cassell's how to pass exams)
Includes index
ISBN 0-304-30947-8 (pbk) : £3.95 B82-38957

657'.45'0941 — Great Britain. Auditing

Crowhurst, John. Auditing : a guide to principles and practice / John Crowhurst. — London : Cassell, 1982. — x,352p : ill ; 22cm. — (A Cassell professional handbook)
Includes index
ISBN 0-304-30905-2 (pbk) : £6.95 B82-22208

657'.45'0941 — Great Britain. Companies. Auditing

Lee, Tom. Company auditing / Tom Lee. — 2nd ed. — [London] : Published for The Institute of Chartered Accountants of Scotland by Gee & Co, 1982. — x,195p ; 21cm
Previous ed.: Edinburgh : Accountants Publishing Co., 1972. — Includes index
ISBN 0-85258-221-8 (pbk) : £6.00 B82-31257

657'.453 — Computerised accounts. Auditing

Davis, Keagle W.. Auditing computer applications : a basic systematic approach / Keagle W. Davis, William F. Perry. — New York ; Chichester : Wiley, c1982. — xvi,601p : ill,forms ; 29cm
ISBN 0-471-05482-8 : £27.25 B82-38979

Douglas, I. J.. Audit and control of mini- and microcomputers. — Manchester : NCC Publications, Nov.1982. — [85]p
ISBN 0-85012-368-2 (pbk) : £9.50 : CIP entry B82-26412

Weber, Ron. EDP auditing : conceptual foundations and practice / Ron Weber. — New York ; London : McGraw-Hill, c1982. — xiv,642p : ill,1plan,forms ; 25cm. — (McGraw-Hill series in management information systems)
Includes bibliographies and index
ISBN 0-07-068830-3 : £21.50 B82-15980

657'.458 — Companies. Internal auditing

Chambers, A.. Internal auditing. — London : Pitman, Oct.1981. — [360]p
ISBN 0-273-01632-6 : £11.95 : CIP entry B81-30256

657'.48 — Financial accounting

Bowman, Robert. Basic financial accounting. — London : Arnold, Aug.1982. — [388]p
ISBN 0-7131-0729-4 (pbk) : £6.95 : CIP entry B82-15916

Davidson, Sidney. Financial accounting : an introduction to concepts, methods, and uses / Sidney Davidson, Clyde P. Stickney, Roman L. Weil. — 3rd ed. — Chicago ; London : Dryden, c1982. — 773p : ill ; 25cm
Previous ed.: 1979. — Includes index
ISBN 0-03-059871-0 : £17.50 B82-15354

Huefner, Ronald J.. Advanced financial accounting / Ronald J. Huefner, James A. Largay III. — Chicago ; London : Dryden, c1982. — xix,821p ; 25cm
Includes index
ISBN 0-03-052641-8 : £19.95 B82-16907

Pizzey, Alan. Financial accounting techniques : a practical approach / Alan Pizzey, Alan Jennings. — London : Holt, Rinehart and Winston, c1982. — xiii,418p ; 25cm
Includes index
ISBN 0-03-910367-6 (pbk) : £4.95 : CIP rev. B82-10776

Samuels, John. Advanced financial accounting / John Samuels, Colin Rickwood and Andrew Piper. — London : McGraw-Hill, c1981. — viii,341p ; 25cm
Includes bibliographies and index
ISBN 0-07-084571-9 (pbk) : £9.95 : CIP rev. B81-21602

657'.48 — Financial accounting — *Manuals*

Stilling, P. J.. Manual of financial reporting and accounting / P.J. Stilling, R.A. Wyld, A.W. Guida. — London : Butterworths, 1982. — ix,343p ; 24cm
Includes index
ISBN 0-406-40190-x (pbk) : Unpriced B82-38726

657'.48 — Netherlands. Replacement-value accounting

Ashton, R. K.. The use and extent of replacement value accounting in the Netherlands / R.K. Ashton. — London : Institute of Chartered Accountants in England and Wales, 1981. — 207p ; 26cm
ISBN 0-85291-309-5 (pbk) : Unpriced B82-02024

657'.48 — Price-level accounting

Farmer, E. R.. Accounting for inflation and price level changes : (including SSAP 16) : a guide for students / E.R. Farmer. — 2nd ed. — London : Gee, 1980. — 113p ; 25cm. — (A Gee's study book)
Previous ed.: 1979
ISBN 0-85258-199-8 (pbk) : £3.95 B82-41046

Lucas, Timothy S.. Understanding inflation accounting / by Timothy S. Lucas. — [Stamford, Conn.] : Financial Accounting Standards Board ; New York ; London : Distributed by McGraw-Hill, c1981. — v,82p ; 23cm
Bibliography: p81-82
ISBN 0-07-020830-1 (pbk) : £6.50 B82-13537

Scapens, Robert W.. Accounting in an inflationary environment / Robert W. Scapens. — 2nd ed. — London : Macmillan, 1981. — xii,183p : ill ; 23cm. — (Macmillan series in finance and accounting)
Previous ed.: 1977. — Includes index
ISBN 0-333-31899-4 (cased) : Unpriced
ISBN 0-333-31900-1 (pbk) : Unpriced B82-06647

Whittington, Geoffrey. Inflation accounting. — Cambridge : Cambridge University Press, Feb.1983. — [244]p. — (Management and industrial relations series)
ISBN 0-521-24903-1 (cased) : £15.00 : CIP entry
ISBN 0-521-27055-3 (pbk) : £5.95 B82-40900

657'.48 — Price-level accounting — *For management*

Current cost accounting : an outline for managers. — [London] : CBI, 1981. — 36p ; 30cm
£3.00 (pbk) B82-02215

657'.48'0218 — Financial accounting. Standards. Formulation

Macve, Richard. A conceptual framework for financial accounting and reporting : the possibilities for an agreed structure : a report prepared at the request of the Accounting Standards Committee / Richard Macve. — London : Institute of Chartered Accountants in England and Wales, 1981. — 175p : ill ; 25cm
ISBN 0-85291-311-7 (pbk) : Unpriced B82-08693

657'.48'02854 — Financial accounting. Estimates. Statistical methods. Applications of digital computer systems

Newman, Maurice S.. Accounting estimates by computer sampling / Maurice S. Newman. — 2nd ed. — New York ; Chichester : Wiley, c1982. — xiii,279p : ill ; 24cm. — (Systems and controls for financial management series)
Previous ed.: published as Financial accounting estimates through statistical sampling by computer. 1976. — Includes index
ISBN 0-471-09147-2 : £22.00 B82-16545

657'.48'076 — Financial accounting — *Questions & answers*

Person, Samuel. Financial accounting / Samuel Person, Daniel Wolinsky ; technical editor Robert Beekman. — Chicago ; London : Dryden, c1982. — xiv,110p ; 28cm. — (CPA exam supplement)
ISBN 0-03-059798-6 (pbk) : £6.95 B82-23304

657'.61'0973 — United States. Accounting. C.P.A. practice — *Manuals*

Langenderfer, Harold Q.. C.P.A. examination : a comprehensive review / Harold Q. Langenderfer, E. Ben Yager. — Columbus, Ohio ; London : Merrill
Previous ed.: 1974
Vol.1: Problems. — 3rd ed. — c1979. — xii,1089p : ill ; 26cm
ISBN 0-675-08298-6 : £16.50 B82-05723

Langenderfer, Harold Q.. C.P.A. examination : a comprehensive review / Harold Q. Langenderfer, E. Ben Yager. — 3rd ed. — Columbus, Ohio ; London : Merrill
Previous ed.: Columbus, Ohio : Merrill, 1974
Vol.2: Solutions. — c1979. — vi,566p ; 25cm
ISBN 0-675-08297-8 (pbk) : £16.50 B82-37329

657'.8327 — Great Britain. Colleges of further education. Auditing

Colleges of further education guide to the measurement of resource efficiency : district audit. — [Great Britain] : [s.n.], 1981. — 46p : forms ; 30cm
£4.00 (spiral) B82-34003

657'.833 — Great Britain. Building societies. Auditing

Auditing guideline building societies : exposure draft. — London (P.O Box 433, Moorgate Place, EC2P 2BJ) : Auditing Practices Committee, 1980. — 31p ; 21cm
Unpriced (unbound) B82-21701

657'.833 — United States. Banks. Internal auditing

Shont, Esther M.. Internal bank auditing / Esther M. Shont. — New York ; Chichester : Wiley, c1982. — xiv,249p : ill ; 24cm
Bibliography: p244-245. — Includes index
ISBN 0-471-08918-4 : £19.50 B82-35308

657'.834 — United States. Libraries. Cost accounting

Mitchell, Betty Jo. Cost analysis of library functions : a total system approach / Betty Jo Mitchell, Norman E. Tanis, Jack Jaffe. — Greenwich, Conn. : Jai Press ; London : distributed by Jaicon Press, 1978. — xiii,192p : ill,forms ; 24cm. — (Foundations in library and information science ; v.6)
Five microfiche in pocket. — Includes index
ISBN 0-89232-072-9 : £22.85 B82-02009

657'.83702 — Hotel & catering industries. Book-keeping

Kotas, Richard. Book-keeping in the hotel and catering industry / Richard Kotas. — 4th ed. — London : International Textbook, 1982. — 152p : forms ; 25cm
Previous ed.: 1972. — Includes index
ISBN 0-7002-0281-1 (pbk) : £6.25 : CIP rev. B82-09302

657'.839'00935 — Ancient Mesopotamia. Merchants. Accounts

Snell, Daniel C.. Ledgers and prices : early Mesopotamian merchant accounts / Daniel C. Snell. — New Haven ; London : Yale University Press, c1982. — xx,282p,xliiplates : ill ; 25cm. — (Yale Near Eastern researches ; 8)
Bibliography: p279-282
ISBN 0-300-02517-3 : Unpriced : CIP rev.
B82-13491

657'.863'002854 — Great Britain. Agricultural industries. Farms. Accounting. Applications of digital computer systems — *Conference proceedings*

Effective use of computing for farm accounting : report of a Gower conference held in April 1981 / edited by Ann Foster. — Aldershot : Gower, c1981. — 72p : ill ; 30cm. — (Computing in business report)
ISBN 0-566-03028-4 (pbk) : Unpriced : CIP rev.
B81-35874

657'.86302'0941 — Great Britain. Agricultural industries. Farms. Book-keeping — *Manuals*

Mordaunt, F. D. Cash recording : the first step to financial control. — Edinburgh (6 South Oswald Rd., Edinburgh EH9 2HH) : Farm Business Management Unit, East of Scotland College of Agriculture, 1981. — 14p : ill,forms ; 21cm. — (Advisory leaflet, ISSN 0308-8278 ; 119)
Authors: F.D. Mordaunt, J.D. Rowbottom
Unpriced (unbound)
B82-01505

657'.9042'0941 — Great Britain. Small firms. Accounting

Wheeler, Bernard F.. Making the best use of your company's accountant / by Bernard F. Wheeler. — London : Institute of Chartered Accountants in England and Wales, 1981. — 12p ; 21cm. — (Notes for businessmen)
£0.75 (pbk)
B82-27222

657'.95 — Companies. Accounts

Reid, Walter. The meaning of company accounts / Walter Reid and D.R. Myddleton. — 3rd ed. — Aldershot : Gower, c1982. — ix,353p : forms ; 21x30cm. — (A Gower workbook)
Previous ed.: 1974. — Includes index
ISBN 0-566-02284-2 (cased) : Unpriced : CIP rev.
ISBN 0-566-02285-0 (pbk) : Unpriced
B81-28192

657'.95'094 — Western Europe. Companies. Accounting

European financial reporting. — London : Institute of Chartered Accountants in England and Wales
5: Spain / P.J. Donaghy, J. Laidler. — [1982]. — iii,181p : 1form ; 30cm
Includes Spanish text in appendix, and Spanish-English and English-Spanish glossaries. — Bibliography: p175-177. — Includes index
ISBN 0-85291-314-1 (pbk) : Unpriced
B82-32499

657'.95'0941 — Great Britain. Companies. Accounting — *Manuals*

Companies Act 1981 : a guide to the preparation of accounts. — London : Binder Hamlyn, [1982]. — 121p ; 30cm
Unpriced (pbk)
B82-36400

657'.95'0941 — Great Britain. Companies. Accounts

Flint, David. A true and fair view in company accounts / by David Flint. — London : Published for the Institute of Chartered Accountants of Scotland by Gee, 1982. — vi,47p ; 21cm
Bibliography: p46-47
ISBN 0-85258-223-4 (pbk) : £4.30
B82-35328

Warren, Roy. How to understand and use company accounts. — London : Business Books, Jan.1983. — [224]p
ISBN 0-09-145890-0 : £15.00 : CIP entry
B82-33630

657'.96'0941 — Great Britain. Companies. Groups. Accounting — *Questions & answers*

Frankel, M. R.. The preparation of group accounts / M.R. Frankel. — London : Financial Training with HFL (Publishers), 1979. — 259p ; 30cm
Includes index
ISBN 0-372-30031-6 (pbk) : £4.95
B82-17615

658 — MANAGEMENT

658 — ASEAN countries. Business opportunities — *For British businessmen*

The **Asean** countries : Indonesia, Malaysia, Philippines, Singapore, Thailand : business opportunities in the 1980s / compiled and published by Metra Consulting. — London : Metra Consulting, c1979. — vi,364p : maps ; 30cm
Unpriced (spiral)
B82-14988

658 — Business firms. Management

Koontz, Harold. Essentials of management. — 3rd ed. / Harold Koontz, Cyril O'Donnell, Heinz Weihrich. — New York ; London : McGraw-Hill, c1982. — xix,553p : ill,1form ; 24cm. — (McGraw-Hill series in management)
Previous ed.: 1978. — Includes index
ISBN 0-07-035419-7 (pbk) : £12.50
B82-27154

Pitfield, Ronald R.. Administration in business made simple. — London : Heinemann, Nov.1982. — [240]p. — (Made simple books)
Originally published: London: W.H. Allen, 1980
ISBN 0-434-98562-7 (pbk) : £2.95 : CIP entry
B82-31294

658 — Business firms. Management — *For business studies*

Shaw, Josephine. Administration in business / Josephine Shaw. — Plymouth : Macdonald and Evans, 1982. — xiv,337p : ill ; 22cm. — (The M & E BECbook series)
Includes index
ISBN 0-7121-0152-7 (pbk) : £4.75
B82-22252

658 — Business opportunities — *Serials*

Worldwide business opportunities : international trade leads and ideas. — Vol.1, no.2 (May 1982)-. — Oxford (P.O. Box 125, Oxford) : Oxford Research Association, 1982-. — v. ; 30cm
Monthly. — Merger of: Mail order trader; and, International trader
ISSN 0263-3531 = Worldwide business opportunities : Unpriced
B82-32177

658 — China. Business opportunities — *For British businessmen*

China : business opportunities in the 1980s : consultants appraisal of a new world market / compiled and published by Metra Consulting. — London : Metra Consulting, c1979. — 287p : ill,maps ; 30cm
ISBN 0-902231-14-6 (spiral) : Unpriced
B82-12393

658 — Management

Boyatzis, Richard E.. The competent manager : a model for effective performance / Richard E. Boyatzis. — New York ; Chichester : Wiley, c1982. — xiv,308p : ill ; 24cm
Bibliography: p261-266. — Includes index
ISBN 0-471-09031-x : £21.75
B82-18245

Carlisle, Howard M.. Management essentials concepts and applications / Howard M. Carlisle. — Chicago ; Henley-on-Thames : Science Research Associates, c1979. — xiv,489p : ill ; 25cm
Includes bibliographies and index
ISBN 0-574-19370-7 : £10.30
B82-02117

Davidmann, M.. Style of management and leadership / M. Davidmann. — [Stanmore] : Social Organisation Ltd., [c1981]. — 60leaves : ill ; 30cm. — (Community leadership and management)
ISBN 0-85192-016-0 (pbk) : £4.95
B82-17850

Eyre, E. C.. Mastering basic management / E.C. Eyre. — [London] : Macmillan, 1982. — xv,266p : ill ; 23cm. — (Macmillan master series)
Includes index
ISBN 0-333-31296-1 (cased) : £8.95
ISBN 0-333-30902-2 (pbk) : Unpriced
B82-17109

The **Gower** handbook of management. — Aldershot : Gower, Feb.1983. — [1200]p
ISBN 0-566-02333-4 : £25.00 : CIP entry
B82-38722

Hall, Jay. The competence process : managing for commitment and creativity / by Jay Hall. — The Woodlands, Tex. : Teleometrics ; Bromley : Chartwell-Bratt, 1980. — xvi,275p : ill(some col.) ; 24cm
ISBN 0-86238-014-6 : Unpriced
B82-36837

Management bibliographies and reviews. — Bradford : MCB
Vol.6 / edited by Barrie O. Pettman. — c1980. — 256p : ill ; 25cm
Bibliography: p229-255. — Includes index
ISBN 0-86176-096-4 : Unpriced
B82-01378

Models for management : the structure of competence / edited by John A. Shtogren. — The Woodlands, Tex. : Teleometrics ; Bromley : Chartwell-Bratt, 1980. — xi,520p : ill ; 23cm
ISBN 0-86238-013-8 (pbk) : Unpriced
B82-36838

Schermerhorn, John R.. Managing organizational behavior / John R. Schermerhorn, Jr., James G. Hunt, Richard N. Osborn. — New York ; Chichester : Wiley, c1982. — xxii,622p : ill (some col.) ; 24cm
Includes index
ISBN 0-471-04497-0 : £17.00
B82-25867

Sheikh, M. Saeed. Managerial challenge to change. — Chelmsford (3 Lucas Ave., Chelmsford, Essex CM2 9JJ) : Chelmer Management Consultancy, Dec.1982. — [150]p
ISBN 0-946144-02-8 (pbk) : £6.95 : CIP entry
B82-29159

Stewart, Rosemary. Choices for the manager : a guide to managerial work and behaviour / Rosemary Stewart. — London : McGraw-Hill, c1982. — x,165p : ill,1form ; 24cm
Bibliography: p159-160. — Includes index
ISBN 0-07-084573-5 : £10.50 : CIP rev.
B82-00915

658'.001 — Administration. Theories

Dunsire, Andrew. Administration. — Oxford : Robertson, Apr.1981. — [262]p
Originally published: 1973
ISBN 0-85520-020-0 (pbk) : £4.95 : CIP entry
B81-09979

658'.001'9 — Management. Psychosocial aspects

Weick, Karl E.. The social psychology of organizing / Karl E. Weick. — 2nd ed. — Reading, Mass. ; London : Addison-Wesley, c1979. — ix,294p : ill ; 24cm. — (Topics in social psychology)
Previous ed.: 1969. — Bibliography: p265-283. — Includes index
ISBN 0-201-08591-7 (pbk) : £6.40
B82-31149

658'.0024092 — Management — *For librarianship*

Rizzo, John R.. Management for librarians : fundamentals and issues / John R. Rizzo. — London : Aldwych, 1980. — xv,339p : ill ; 25cm
Includes bibliographies and index
ISBN 0-86172-009-1 : £27.50
B82-31084

658'.0024616 — Management — *For doctors*

Management for clinicians. — London : Pitman, Apr.1982. — [300]p
ISBN 0-272-79646-8 : £17.50 : CIP entry
B82-04322

658'.002462 — Management — *For engineering*

Badawy, M. K.. Developing managerial skills in engineers and scientists : succeeding as a technical manager / M.K. Badawy. — New York ; London : Van Nostrand Reinhold, c1982. — xiv,368p : ill ; 24cm. — (Van Nostrand Reinhold series in managerial skill development in engineering and science)
Bibliography: p349-361. — Includes index
ISBN 0-442-20481-7 : £25.16 B82-30758

658'.003'21 — Management — *Encyclopaedias*

The **Encyclopedia** of management / edited by Carl Heyel. — 3rd ed. — New York ; London : Van Nostrand Reinhold, c1982. — xxx,1371p : ill,facsims,forms,maps ; 26cm
Previous ed.: 1973. — Includes bibliographies and index
ISBN 0-442-25165-3 : £48.90 B82-28149

A **Glossary** of management terms. — Loughborough : Centre for Library and Information Management, Department of Library and Information Studies, Loughborough University, 1981. — 19p ; 21cm. — (British Library research and development reports, ISSN 0308-2385 ; no.5662) (Report / CLAIM, ISSN 0261-0302 ; no.10)
Includes index
ISBN 0-904924-30-0 (pbk) : Unpriced B82-05459

658'.005 — Business firms. Management — *Serials*

[Administrator *(London)***]**. Administrator : [the journal of the Institute of Chartered Secretaries and Administrators]. — Vol.2, no.1 (Jan. 1982)-. — London (16 Park Cres., W1N 4AH) : The Institute, 1982-. — v. : ill(some col.),ports ; 29cm
Monthly. — Continues: Professional administration. — Supplement: Local government administrator. — Description based on: Vol.2, no.2 (Feb. 1982)
ISSN 0263-3868 = Administrator (London) : £9.75 per year (free to members of the ICSA) B82-25473

658'.007 — Management. Information sources — *Lists*

Brownstone, David M.. Where to find business information : a worldwide guide for everyone who needs the answers to business questions / David M. Brownstone, Gorton Carruth. — 2nd ed. — New York ; Chichester : Wiley, c1982. — xiii,5108p ; 29cm
Previous ed.: 1979
ISBN 0-471-08736-x : £33.30 B82-27720

658'.007'11 — Managers. Professional education

Management education : issues in theory, research and practice / edited by Richard D. Freedman, Cary L. Cooper, Stephen A. Stumpf. — Chichester ; New York : Wiley, c1982. — ix,278p : ill ; 24cm
Includes bibliographies and index
ISBN 0-471-10078-1 : £15.50 : CIP rev. B82-09700

658'.007'1141 — Great Britain. Business schools *compared with* **business schools in France**

Whitley, Richard. Masters of business?. — London : Tavistock, Dec.1981. — [220]p. — (Tavistock studies in sociology)
ISBN 0-422-76500-7 : £10.50 : CIP entry
Also classified at 658'.007'1144 B81-31703

658'.007'1141 — Great Britain. Higher education institutions. Curriculum subjects: Business studies. Council for National Academic Awards courses: Postgraduate courses

Courses for managers : guidelines for courses of study leading to CNAA postgraduate awards in business and management education / CNAA. — London (344 Grays Inn Rd., WC1X 8BP) : Council for National Academic Awards, [1979]. — 12p ; 21cm
Cover title. — Text on inside cover
Unpriced (pbk) B82-32773

658'.007'1141 — Great Britain. Higher education institutions. Curriculum subjects: Management. Diploma in Management Studies courses — *Serials*

DMS bulletin / CNAA. — [No.1 (197-)?]-. — London (344 Gray's Inn Rd, WC1X 8BP) : Council for National Academic Awards, [197-]-. — v. ; 30cm
Irregular. — Description based on: No.9 (Nov. 1978)
ISSN 0263-8061 = DMS bulletin : Unpriced B82-36690

658'.007'11411 — Scotland. Higher education institutions. Curriculum subjects: Management. Diploma in Management Studies courses

Guidelines for the conduct of DMS courses offered by institutions in Scotland. — London (344 Gray's Inn Rd., WC1X 8BP) : Council for National Academic Awards, 1976. — 16p ; 21cm
Unpriced (pbk) B82-32767

658'.007'1142 — England. Higher education institutions. Curriculum subjects: Management. Diploma in Management Studies courses

Guidelines for the conduct of DMS courses offered by institutions in England, Wales and Northern Ireland. — London (344 Gray's Inn Rd., WC1X 8BP) : Council for National Academic Awards, 1976. — 24p ; 21cm
Unpriced (pbk) B82-32774

658'.007'1144 — France. Business schools *compared with* **business schools in Great Britain**

Whitley, Richard. Masters of business?. — London : Tavistock, Dec.1981. — [220]p. — (Tavistock studies in sociology)
ISBN 0-422-76500-7 : £10.50 : CIP entry
Primary classification 658'.007'1141 B81-31703

658'.007'1173 — United States. Business schools. Curriculum subjects: Management — *Forecasts*

Management for the XXI century : education and development / the American Assembly of Collegiate Schools of Business and the European Foundation for Management Development. — Boston, Mass. ; London : Kluwer Nijhoff, c1982. — xvii,210p : ill ; 24cm
ISBN 0-89838-097-9 : Unpriced
ISBN 0-89838-098-7 (pbk) : Unpriced B82-31279

658'.007'117444 — Massachusetts. Cambridge. Business schools. French graduates. Organisations: Harvard Business School. *Club de France* — *Serials*

Harvard Business School. *Club de France*. Annuaire / Harvard Business School Club de France. — 1981-. — London (9 Courtleigh Gardens, NW11 9JX) : A.P. Books, 1981-. — v. ; 21cm
Continues: Harvard Business School. Association. French directory
ISSN 0260-8227 = Annuaire - Harvard Business School Club de France : Unpriced B82-10129

658'.0072 — Management. Research

Hesseling, Pjotr. Effective organization research for development / by Pjotr Hesseling. — Oxford : Pergamon, 1982. — xix,219p : ill ; 22cm
Bibliography: p199-214. — Includes index
ISBN 0-08-024082-8 : £9.95 : CIP rev. B81-34571

658'.0072 — Management. Research — *Serials*

Applications of management science : a research annual. — Vol.1 (1981)-. — Greenwich, Conn. : JAI Press ; London (3 Henrietta St., WC2E 8LU) : Distributed by JAICON Press, 1981-. — v. ; 24cm
£28.10 B82-02354

658'.00722 — Management. Case studies

Easton, Geoff. Learning from case studies / Geoff Easton. — Englewood Cliffs ; London : Prentice-Hall, c1982. — xiii,203p : ill ; 22cm
Bibliography: p198-199. — Includes index
ISBN 0-13-527416-8 (pbk) : £6.95 : CIP rev. B82-08436

658'.00722 — Management — *Case studies*

Heyel, Carl. The manager's bible : how to resolve 127 classic management dilemmas / Carl Heyel. — New York : Free Press ; London : Collier Macmillan, c1981. — xi,320p ; 25cm
Includes index
ISBN 0-02-914680-1 : £9.95 B82-18006

658'.00941 — Great Britain. Business firms. Management — *Manuals*

The **Complete** guide to managing your business / [editor Maggi McCormick]. — London : Eaglemoss, 1979 (1978 [printing]). — 1v.(loose-leaf) : ill,maps ; 24x28cm
Includes index
ISBN 0-906788-00-5 : Unpriced B82-18053

658'.00941 — Great Britain. Companies. Management — *Manuals*

Company administration handbook. — 5th ed. — Aldershot : Gower, Aug.1982. — [800]p
Previous ed.: 1980
ISBN 0-566-02352-0 : £25.00 : CIP entry B82-15887

658'.00941 — Great Britain. Management — *Serials*

West Midlands Regional Management Centre review. — Vol.1, no.1 (Autumn 1981)-. — Stoke-on-Trent (North Staffordshire Polytechnic, College Rd, Stoke-on-Trent, Staffs ST4 2DE) : The Centre, 1981-. — v. : ill ; 30cm
Three issues yearly
ISSN 0260-6224 = West Midlands Regional Management Centre review : £12.00 per year (£20.00 to institutions) B82-18514

658'.009417 — Ireland *(Republic)*. **Industries. Management**

Bourke, Philip. Production and distribution / Philip Bourke and Aidan Kelly. — Dublin : Gill and Macmillan, 1981. — 39p : 1ill ; 22cm. — (Topics in business organisation series)
ISBN 0-7171-0879-1 (pbk) : £1.10 B82-13467

658'.00945 — Italy. Industries. Management

Derossi, Flavia. The technocratic illusion : a study of managerial power in Italy / Flavia Derossi ; with a foreword by Harold J. Leavitt ; translated by Susan LoBello. — New York : Sharpe ; London : distributed by Eurospan, c1982. — xii,235p : ill ; 24cm
Translation of: L'illusione tecnocratica
ISBN 0-87332-185-5 : £22.50 B82-26729

658'.00952 — Japan. Business firms. Management *compared with* **management of business firms in United States**

Pascale, Richard Tanner. The art of Japanese management / Richard Tanner Pascale, Anthony G. Athos. — London : Allen Lane, 1982, c1981. — 221p : ill ; 23cm
Originally published: New York : Simon & Schuster, 1981
ISBN 0-7139-1459-9 : £7.50
Also classified at 658'.00973 B82-14552

658'.00952 — Japan. Business firms. Management — *For Western businessmen*

Ohmae, Kenichi. The mind of the strategist : the art of Japanese business / Kenichi Ohmae. — New York ; London : McGraw-Hill, c1982. — xiii,283p : ill ; 21cm
Includes index
ISBN 0-07-047595-4 : Unpriced B82-40609

658'.00973 — United States. Business firms. Management

Boone, Louis E.. Contemporary business / Louis E. Boone, David L. Kurtz. — 3rd ed. — Chicago ; London : Dryden, c1982. — vii,641,[47]p : ill(some col.),maps,plans ; 26cm
Previous ed.: 1979. — Bibliography: pA1-A3. — Includes index
ISBN 0-03-059752-8 : £14.95 B82-15362

658'.00973 — United States. Business firms. Management *compared with* **management of business firms in Japan**

Pascale, Richard Tanner. The art of Japanese management / Richard Tanner Pascale, Anthony G. Athos. — London : Allen Lane, 1982, c1981. — 221p : ill ; 23cm
Originally published: New York : Simon & Schuster, 1981
ISBN 0-7139-1459-9 : £7.50
Primary classification 658'.00952 B82-14552

658′.022 — Great Britain. Home-based employment — *Manuals*

Gray, Marianne. Working from home : 201 ways to earn money. — Loughton : Piatkus, June 1982. — [224]p
ISBN 0-86188-152-4 : £5.95 : CIP entry B82-10250

658′.022 — Small firms. Organisation — *Manuals*

Silverstone, E.. Planning and running a small business. — London (Henrietta House, 9 Henrietta Place W1M 9AG) : Action Resource Centre, May 1982. — [45]p
ISBN 0-946100-00-4 (unbound) : £2.50 : CIP entry B82-17889

658′.022′0285404 — Small firms. Applications of microcomputer systems

Pannell, B. K.. Make a success of micro-computing in your business / B.K. Pannell, D.C. Jackson and S.B. Lucas. — Manchester : Enterprise, 1981. — viii,120p : ill ; 24cm
ISBN 0-906896-05-3 (pbk) : Unpriced : CIP rev. B81-30277

658′.022′0941 — Great Britain. Home-based small firms. Organisation — *For women* — *Serials*

Creative woman : the monthly report for the homebased businesswoman. — No.1 (July 1982)-. — Oxford (151 Harefields, Oxford OX2 8NR) : Oxford Research Associates, 1982-. — v. ; 30cm
ISSN 0264-0554 = Creative woman : Unpriced B82-40064

658′.022′0941 — Great Britain. Small firms. Organisation — *Manuals*

Hillman, Judy. Start your own business. — London (69 Cannon St., EC4N 5AB London) : Enterprise Agency, Nov.1982. — [72]p
ISBN 0-901902-57-8 (pbk) : £2.50 : CIP entry B82-30585

Jones, Derek. How to start your own business. — Brighton : Harvester, Dec.1982. — [160]p
ISBN 0-7108-0159-9 : CIP entry
ISBN 0-7108-0200-5 (pbk) B82-30295

Knightley, M.. How to set up a business of your own / M. Knightley. — 5th ed. — London : Malcolm Stewart, 1982. — 70p ; 25cm. — (Kingfisher business guides)
Previous ed.: 1979. — Includes index
ISBN 0-904132-60-9 (pbk) : £3.50 B82-37097

Knightley, M.. Your own first business : the wise way / M. Knightley. — 2nd ed. — London : Malcolm Stewart, 1982. — 66p ; 25cm. — (Kingfisher business guides)
Previous ed.: London : Kingfisher, 1976. — Includes index
ISBN 0-904132-58-7 (pbk) : £3.50 B82-17184

Sproxton, Alan. Starting and running a small business / Alan Sproxton ; drawings by Jack Pountney. — Rev. ed. — St. Ives : United Writers, 1981. — 156p : ill ; 22cm
Previous ed.: i.e. new and rev. ed. 1979
ISBN 0-901976-69-5 : £5.20 B82-34992

658′.022′09428 — North-east England. Small firms. Organisation — *Manuals*

Make your own job : a guide / [compiled by Project North East]. — [Gosforth] ([51 Rectory Ave., Gosforth, Newcastle upon Tyne]) : [Project North East], [1981]. — 18p : ill ; 30cm
Cover title. — Text, ill on inside cover
Unpriced (pbk) B82-08036

658′.022′0973 — United States. Small firms. Management

Hodgetts, Richard M.. Effective small business management / Richard M. Hodgetts. — New York ; London : Academic Press, c1982. — xv,496p : ill ; 25cm
Includes index
ISBN 0-12-351050-3 : £13.20 B82-07717

658′.022′0973 — United States. Small firms. Management — *Manuals*

Edmunds, Stahrl W.. Performance measures for growing business : a practical guide to small business management / Stahrl W. Edmunds. — New York ; London : Van Nostrand Reinhold, c1982. — vii,247p : ill ; 24cm
Includes index
ISBN 0-442-22605-5 : £16.95 B82-13191

658′.022′0973 — United States. Small firms. Organisation & management

Kishel, Gregory F.. How to start, run, and stay in business / Gregory F. Kishel and Patricia Gunter Kishel. — New York ; Chichester : Wiley, c1981. — viii,200p : ill,forms ; 21cm
Bibliography: p197-198. — Includes index
ISBN 0-471-08274-0 (pbk) : £5.90 B82-09884

658′.022′0973 — United States. Small firms. Organisation & management — *Manuals*

Baca Smith, Randy. Setting up shop : the do′s and dont′s of starting a small business / Randy Baca Smith. — New York ; London : McGraw-Hill, c1982. — xiii,274p : forms ; 24cm
Bibliography: p261. — Includes index
ISBN 0-07-058531-8 : £14.95 B82-15983

Curtin, Richard T.. Running your own show : mastering the basics of small business / Richard T. Curtin. — New York ; Chichester : Wiley, c1982. — ix,226p : forms ; 24cm. — (Wiley series on small business management, ISSN 0271-6054)
Includes index
ISBN 0-471-86074-3 : £13.25 B82-26469

658′.041 — Great Britain. Home-based industries

Filbee, Marjorie. Cottage industries. — Newton Abbot : David & Charles, Nov.1982. — [192]p
ISBN 0-7153-8286-1 : £8.95 : CIP entry B82-26396

658′.041 — Great Britain. Self-employment — *Case studies*

Pettit, Rosemary. Occupation, self employed. — London : Wildwood House, Sept.1981. — [208]p
Originally published: 1977
ISBN 0-7045-0432-4 (pbk) : £4.50 : CIP entry B81-25126

658′.041 — Self-employment — *For school leavers*

Starting up : they couldn′t find jobs — so they got it together themselves. — [Cambridge] : Basic Skills Unit, c1981. — [12]p : ill ; 30cm
Bibliography: p[12]
ISBN 0-86082-303-2 (unbound) : Unpriced B82-38997

658′.041 — Self-employment — *Manuals*

Golzen, Godfrey. Working for yourself : the Daily telegraph guide to self-employment / Godfrey Golzen. — 5th ed. — London : Kogan Page, 1982. — 288p : ill ; 23cm
Previous ed.: 1981. — Bibliography: p266-273. — Includes index
ISBN 0-85038-542-3 (cased) : Unpriced : CIP rev.
ISBN 0-85038-543-1 (pbk) : £4.95 B82-12841

658′.041′023 — Self-employment — *Career guides*

Attwood, Tony. Create your own job : how to survive the recession / Tony Attwood. — Northampton : Hamilton House, 1982. — 71p ; 21cm. — (Careerscope ; 8)
Bibliography: p68-70
ISBN 0-906888-27-1 (pbk) : Unpriced B82-17432

658′.041′0941 — Great Britain. Self-employment — *Manuals*

Milne, T.. Be your own boss : a practical guide / by T. Milne. — [Buckie] : [T. Milne], c1982. — 72p ; 21cm
Cover title
ISBN 0-9508189-0-9 (pbk) : Unpriced B82-38850

658′.041′0941 — Great Britain. Self-employment — *Serials*

[Enterprise *(Oxford)*]. Enterprise : a monthly report on the art of self-employment and survival. — Vol.1, no.1 (Jan. 1981)-. — [Oxford] ([P.O. Box 125, Oxford]) : [Research Associates], 1981-. — v. ; 30cm
Description based on: Vol.1, no.11 (Nov. 1981)
ISSN 0262-4907 = Enterprise (Oxford) : £24.50 per year B82-13415

658′.048′0973 — United States. Non-profit making organisations. Management — *Manuals*

The **Nonprofit** organization handbook / Tracy Daniel Connors, editor in chief. — New York ; London : McGraw-Hill, c1980. — 1v.(various pagings) : ill,facsims,forms ; 24cm
Includes index
ISBN 0-07-012422-1 : £24.50 B82-02520

658′.049 — Great Britain. Japanese business enterprises. Management

White, Michael. Under Japanese management. — London : Heinemann Educational, Jan.1983. — [192]p. — (Policy studies Institute series)
ISBN 0-435-83935-7 : £13.50 : CIP entry B82-36300

658′.054 — Business firms. Applications of digital computer systems

Clifton, H. D.. Business data systems. — 2nd ed. — London : Prentice-Hall, Jan.1983. — [400]p
Previous ed.: 1978
ISBN 0-13-094078-x (pbk) : £7.95 : CIP entry B82-33468

658′.054 — Business firms. Applications of digital computer systems — *Buyers′ guides*

Derrick, John. Micro- and mini-computers for business : a buyer′s guide. — London : Kogan Page, Aug.1982. — [150]p
ISBN 0-85038-585-7 : £11.95 : CIP entry B82-19274

658′.054 — Business firms. Management. Applications of computer systems

Carter, Roger. Business administration : a textbook for the computer age / Roger Carter. — London : Heinemann, 1982. — viii,200p : ill,forms ; 25cm
Includes index
ISBN 0-434-90219-5 (pbk) : £7.95 B82-37290

658′.054 — Management. Applications of digital computer systems

Rowan, T. G.. Managing with computers / T.G. Rowan. — London : Pan in association with Heinemann, 1982. — 299p : ill ; 18cm
Includes index
ISBN 0-330-26512-1 (pbk) : £2.50 B82-15115

658′.054 — Organisations. Management. Applications of digital computer systems

Rowan, T. G.. Managing with computers / T.G. Rowan. — London : Heinemann, 1982. — 219p : ill ; 23cm
Includes index
ISBN 0-434-91760-5 : £8.95 B82-25632

658′.054 — Small firms. Applications of digital computer systems

Best, Peter J.. Small business computer systems / Peter J. Best. — Sydney ; London : Prentice-Hall, c1980. — xii,296p : ill ; 24cm
Bibliography: p292. — Includes index
ISBN 0-7248-1136-2 (pbk) : £8.40 B82-02232

The **Small** business computer guide / Australian Computer Society. — Sydney : Prentice-Hall of Australia ; London : Prentice-Hall, c1981. — xiii,112p ; 25cm
ISBN 0-7248-1134-6 : £9.70 B82-24414

Tampoe, F. M. K.. Successful business computing. — London : Butterworth, Oct.1982. — [128]p
ISBN 0-408-01217-x : £7.00 : CIP entry B82-24469

658′.05404 — Business firms. Applications of microcomputer systems — *For management*

Planning for office microcomputers. — Aldershot : Gower, Nov.1982. — [180]p. — (The Office of the future ; no.5)
ISBN 0-566-03416-6 : £9.50 : CIP entry B82-26554

658′.05404 — Business firms. Applications of microcomputer systems. Management aspects

Edwards, Chris, *1947-*. Developing micro-computer based business systems / Chris Edwards. — Englewood Cliffs ; London : Prentice-Hall, c1982. — x,202p : ill ; 23cm
Bibliography: p196-198. — Includes index
ISBN 0-13-204560-5 (cased) : Unpriced : CIP rev.
ISBN 0-13-204552-4 (pbk) : £5.95 B81-38306

658′.05404 — Business firms. Applications of microcomputer systems — *Serials*

Micro decision : the new idea in computer magazines. — No.1 (Oct. 1981)-. — London : VNU Business Publications, 1981-. — v. : ill,ports ; 30cm
Monthly. — Description based on: No.5 (Mar. 1982)
ISSN 0261-5142 = Micro decision : £9.60 per year B82-18715

658′.054′04 — Business firms. Management. Applications of microcomputer systems

Lewis, Colin. Managing with microcomputers. — Oxford : Blackwell, Oct.1982. — [280]p
ISBN 0-631-13136-1 : £9.50 : CIP entry B82-23170

658′.054′04 — Business firms. Small digital computer systems. Selection — *Manuals*

Bennett, W. E.. Choosing a small computer : a checklist guide / W.E. Bennett. — Rev. UK ed. — London : British Institute of Management Foundation, 1981, c1980. — 36p ; 21cm
Previous ed.: published as Checklist/guide to selecting a small computer. New York : Pilot, 1980. — Bibliography: p35-36
ISBN 0-85946-120-3 (pbk) : Unpriced B82-23139

658′.05404 — Industries. Management. Applications of microcomputer systems — *For schools*

Industry in the 80s. — Manchester : NCC Publications, Mar.1982
Module 1: Industrial appreciation. — [270]p
ISBN 0-85012-352-6 (spiral) : £11.00 : CIP entry B82-07795

Industry in the 80s. — Manchester : NCC Publications, Mar.1982
Module 2: Computers, monitoring and decision making. — [144]p
ISBN 0-85012-353-4 (spiral) : £7.00 : CIP entry B82-07796

Industry in the 80s. — Manchester : NCC Publications
Module 3: Project progress and control. — Mar.1982. — [48]p
ISBN 0-85012-354-2 (spiral) : £8.00 : CIP entry B82-08114

Industry in the 80s. — Manchester : NCC Publications, Mar.1982
Module 4: Modular electronics. — [45]p
ISBN 0-85012-355-0 (spiral) : £8.00 : CIP entry B82-07798

Industry in the 80s. — Manchester : NCC Publications, Mar.1982
Module 5: Process control in practice. — [60]p
ISBN 0-85012-356-9 (spiral) : £6.00 : CIP entry B82-07799

Industry in the 80s. — Manchester : NCC Publications
Module 6: Projects with industry. — Mar.1982. — [55]p
ISBN 0-85012-357-7 (spiral) : £5.00 : CIP entry B82-08115

658′.054′04 — Small firms. Small digital computer systems. Selection

Isshiki, Koichiro R.. Small business computers : a guide to evaluation and selection / Koichiro R. Isshiki. — Englewood Cliffs ; London : Prentice-Hall, c1982. — xvi,478p : ill,facsims,forms ; 25cm. — (Prentice-Hall series in data processing management)
Includes index
ISBN 0-13-814152-5 : £20.20 B82-23644

658′.054′07 — Great Britain. Business firms. Data processing services. Personnel. Training — *Serials*

DOT plus : Directory of training update & advisory service : your up-to-date link with DP education & training. — Mar. 1982-. — Henley-on-Thames (Enterprise House, Badgemore Park, Henley-on-Thames, Oxon. RG9 4NR) : Directory of Training, 1982-. — v. : ill,port ; 29cm
Supplement to: Directory of training (Henley-on-Thames)
ISSN 0263-6034 = DOT plus : £10.00 per year B82-29045

658′.05424 — Business firms. Management. Applications of programs written in Basic language

Alonso, J. R. F.. SIMPLE : BASIC programs for business applications / J.R.F. Alonso. — Englewood Cliffs ; London : Prentice-Hall, c1981. — xii,297p : ill ; 29cm. — (A Spectrum book)
Bibliography: p289-290
ISBN 0-13-809897-2 (cased) : Unpriced
ISBN 0-13-809889-1 (pbk) : £9.70 B82-16847

658.1 — COMPANY ORGANISATION AND FINANCE

658.1 — Business firms. Organisation structure

The **Business** context. — Eastbourne : Holt-Saunders, Jan.1983. — [432]p
ISBN 0-03-910306-4 (pbk) : £6.95 : CIP entry B82-33592

658.1′1 — Business firms. Organisation

Davidmann, M.. Organising / M. Davidmann. — [Stanmore] : Social Organisation Ltd., [c1981]. — 32leaves : ill ; 30cm. — (Community leadership and management)
ISBN 0-85192-017-9 (pbk) : £2.90 B82-17849

658.1′5 — Business firms. Financial management

Basic financial management / J. William Petty ... [et al.]. — 2nd ed. — Englewood Cliffs ; London : Prentice-Hall, c1982. — xix,684p : ill (some col.) ; 24cm
Previous ed.: 1979. — Includes bibliographies and index
ISBN 0-13-060525-5 : £17.95 B82-33771

Gitman, Lawrence J.. Principles of managerial finance / Lawrence J. Gitman. — 3rd ed. — Cambridge, [Mass.] ; London : Harper & Row, c1982. — xxii,724,G-25,I-12p : ill ; 24cm
Previous ed.: 1979. — Text on lining papers. — Includes index
ISBN 0-06-042334-x : Unpriced B82-34021

Morine, F. John. [Bigger profits in the 80′s]. Riding the recession : how to cope now with shrinking markets and high inflation / by F. John Morine. — London : Business Books, 1981, c1980. — xi,159p ; 22cm
Originally published: New Zealand : Management Publications, 1980
ISBN 0-09-145870-6 (cased) : Unpriced : CIP rev.
ISBN 0-09-145871-4 (pbk) : Unpriced B81-27371

Moss, Scott J.. An economic theory of business strategy : an essay in dynamics without equilibrium / Scott J. Moss. — Oxford : Martin Robertson, 1981. — xi,223p ; 23cm
Bibliography: p214-218. — Includes index
ISBN 0-85520-386-2 (cased) : £15.00 : CIP rev.
ISBN 0-85520-394-3 (pbk) : Unpriced B81-13751

Weston, J. Fred. Essentials of managerial finance / J. Fred Weston, Eugene F. Brigham. — 6th ed. — Chicago ; London : Dryden Press, c1982. — ix,741p : ill(some col.) ; 25cm
Previous ed.: 1979. — Text on lining papers. — One folded sheet as insert. — Includes index
ISBN 0-03-059548-7 (cased) : £17.95
ISBN 4-8337-0071-9 (pbk) : Unpriced B82-26825

658.1′5 — Business firms. Financial management. Long-range planning. Techniques

Financial planning for business management : a practical guide. — [Stamford] : [Adlink], [1982]. — 66leaves ; 30cm
Cover title
ISBN 0-907979-00-9 (spiral) : Unpriced B82-28991

658.1′5 — Companies. Financial management

Financial management handbook. — 2nd ed. — Aldershot : Gower, Jan.1983. — [350]p
Previous ed.: 1972
ISBN 0-566-02175-7 : £20.00 : CIP entry B82-32441

Paish, F. W.. Business finance. — 6th ed. — London : Pitman, May 1982. — [175]p
Previous ed.: 1978
ISBN 0-273-01768-3 (pbk) : £6.50 : CIP entry B82-07418

Samuels, J. M.. Management of company finance / J.H. Samuels and F.M. Wilkes. — 3rd ed. — Walton-on-Thames : Nelson, 1980. — x,497p : ill ; 25cm
Previous ed.: 1975. — Includes index
ISBN 0-17-761092-1 (cased) : £14.95 : CIP rev.
ISBN 0-17-771091-8 (pbk) : £7.95 B80-09769

658.1′5 — Corporate planning. Financial aspects. Models

Corporate strategy : the integration of corporate planning models and economics / edited by Thomas H. Naylor. — Amsterdam ; Oxford : North-Holland, 1982. — viii,210p : ill ; 23cm. — (Studies in management science and systems ; v.8)
Includes bibliographies
ISBN 0-444-86331-1 : £18.05 B82-28560

658.1′5 — Factories. Financial management

Monaghan, M. W.. Basic factory accounting and administration. — Aldershot : Gower, Mar.1982. — [270]p
ISBN 0-566-02281-8 : £12.50 : CIP entry B82-00198

658.1′5 — Financial management

Gibbs, John, *1943-*. A practical approach to financial management / John Gibbs. — 2nd ed. — London : Financial Training, 1980. — xi,291p : ill,forms ; 22cm
Previous ed.: 1978. — Includes index
ISBN 0-372-30051-0 (pbk) : £6.95 B82-11923

Readings in financial management / [edited by] David F. Scott ... [et al.]. — New York ; London : Academic Press, c1982. — x,246p ; 24cm
Includes bibliographies
ISBN 0-12-633320-3 (pbk) : £6.60 B82-29975

Spiro, Herbert T.. Finance for the nonfinancial manager / Herbert T. Spiro. — 2nd ed. — New York ; Chichester : Wiley, c1982. — xviii,278p : ill,facsims ; 27cm
Previous ed.: 1977. — Includes index
ISBN 0-471-09732-2 : £14.75 B82-26474

658.1′5 — Financial management. Implications of inflation — *For engineering*

Jones, Byron W.. Inflation in engineering economic analysis / Byron W. Jones. — New York ; Chichester : Wiley, c1982. — xiii,216p : ill ; 24cm
Includes index
ISBN 0-471-09048-4 : Unpriced B82-23943

658.1′5 — Marketing. Decision making. Financial aspects

Financial dimensions of marketing : a source book / compiled by Richard M.S. Wilson. — [London] : Macmillan in associat[i]on with the Institute of Cost and Management Accountants, 1981. — 2v.(xxvi,543p) : ill ; 25cm. — (Macmillan/I.C.M.A. series)
Bibliography: p455-519. — Includes index
ISBN 0-333-25741-3 : Unpriced : CIP rev.
ISBN 0-333-25742-1 (v.2) : £20.00 B80-20838

658.1′5 — United States. Business firms. Financial management. Implications of inflation

Bierman, Harold. Financial management and inflation / Harold Bierman, Jr. ; with epigraphs by Florence M. Kelso. — New York : Free Press ; London : Collier Macmillan, c1981. — viii,175p : ill ; 25cm
Includes bibliographies and index
ISBN 0-02-903570-8 : £10.95 B82-20408

658.1′5′02462 — Financial management — *For engineering*

Leech, D. J.. Economic and financial studies for engineers. — Chichester : Horwood, Sept.1982. — [256]p
ISBN 0-85312-484-1 : £20.00 : CIP entry B82-28587

Riggs, James L.. Engineering economics / James L. Riggs. — 2nd ed. — New York ; London : McGraw-Hill, c1982. — xviii,789p : ill,forms ; 25cm. — (McGraw-Hill series in industrial engineering and management science)
Previous ed.: 1977. — Bibliography: p741-743. — Includes index
ISBN 0-07-052862-4 : £19.95 B82-27149

Riggs, James L.[Engineering economics. *Selections*]. Essentials of engineering economics / James L. Riggs. — New York ; London : McGraw-Hill, c1982. — xv,557p : ill,forms ; 25cm. — (McGraw-Hill series in industrial engineering and management science)
Bibliography: p511-513. — Includes index. — Contains the first nineteen chapters of the author′s "Engineering economics". 2nd ed., 1982
ISBN 0-07-052864-0 : £16.75 B82-27148

658.1′5′02854 — Financial management. Applications of microcomputer systems

Drew, Rodney. Microcomputers for financial planning. — Aldershot : Gower, Dec.1982. — [200]p
ISBN 0-566-03443-3 : £15.00 : CIP entry B82-30059

658.1′5′0724 — Companies. Financial management. Mathematical models

Financial modelling in corporate management / edited by James W. Bryant. — Chichester : Wiley, c1982. — xiv,455p : ill ; 24cm
Includes bibliographies and index
ISBN 0-471-10021-8 : £13.90 : CIP rev. B81-34490

658.1′5′0941 — Great Britain. Business firms. Financial management. Techniques

Prescott, Jeremy. How to survive the recession : a guide to basic business controls, designed to ensure that your business will survive the recession / Jeremy Prescott. — [London] : Institute of Chartered Accountants, 1982. — 152p : ill,forms ; 26cm
ISBN 0-906322-12-x (pbk) : Unpriced B82-26361

658.1′5′0941 — Great Britain. Companies. Financial management

Hargreaves, Richard L.. Managing your company′s finances / Richard L. Hargreaves and Robert H. Smith ; foreword by Viscount Caldecote. — London : Heinemann published in association with ICFC Industrial and Commercial Finance Corporation Limited, 1981. — xiv,190p ; 23cm. — (The Heinemann accountancy and administration series)
Includes index
ISBN 0-434-90686-7 : £8.95 B82-09150

Vause, R.. Finance for managers / R. Vause and N. Woodward. — 2nd ed. — London : Macmillan, 1981. — xi,208p : ill ; 23cm
Previous ed.: published as Finance for non-financial managers. 1975. — Bibliography: p200-201. — Includes index
ISBN 0-333-30810-7 (cased) : £12.00
ISBN 0-333-30651-1 (pbk) : Unpriced B82-21630

658.1′5′0941 — Great Britain. Companies. Financial management — *Serials*

Finance confidential. — No.1 (Nov. 1981)-. — London (13 Golden Sq., W1) : Stonehart Publications, 1981-. — v. ; 27cm
Monthly
ISSN 0262-5695 = Finance confidential : Unpriced B82-06174

658.1′5′0941 — Great Britain. Financial management

Gee, Kenneth P.. Financial control : inaugural lecture delivered on 19th November 1980 / Kenneth P. Gee. — [Salford] ([Salford, Lancs. M5 4WT]) : University of Salford, [1981?]. — [12]p : ill ; 21cm
Bibliography: p[12]
Unpriced (pbk) B82-19965

658.1′5′0973 — United States. Business firms. Financial management — *Question & answers*

Aragon, George A.. Study guide to accompany Johnson and Melicher′s Financial management, 5th edition / George Aragon. — Boston ; London : Allyn and Bacon, c1982. — 201p : ill ; 24cm
ISBN 0-205-07822-2 (pbk) : Unpriced B82-27101

Huang, Roger D.. Test manual to accompany Johnson and Melicher′s Financial management, 5th ed. / Roger D. Huang. — Boston, [Mass] ; London : Allyn and Bacon, c1982. — 179p ; 24cm
ISBN 0-205-07812-5 (pbk) : Unpriced B82-27102

658.1′5′0973 — United States. Companies. Financial management

Brigham, Eugene F.. Financial management : theory and practice / Eugene F. Brigham. — 3rd ed. — Chicago ; London : Dryden, c1982. — xviii,875p : ill(some col.) ; 25cm
Previous ed.: 1979. — Text on lining paper. — Tables (1 folded sheet) as insert. — Includes bibliographies and index
ISBN 0-03-059593-2 : Unpriced
ISBN 4-8337-0076-x (International Edition) : £10.50 B82-20603

Readings in strategy for corporate investment / [edited by] Frans G.J. Derkinderen, Roy L. Crum. — Boston, [Mass.] ; London : Pitman, c1981. — iv,219p : ill ; 24cm
Includes bibliographies
ISBN 0-273-01635-0 (pbk) : Unpriced B82-16073

Sathe, Vijay. Controller involvement in management / Vijay Sathe with the research assistance of Srinivasan Umapathy. — Englewood Cliffs ; London : Prentice-Hall, c1982. — xviii,189p : ill ; 24cm
Bibliography: p177-182. — Includes index
ISBN 0-13-171660-3 : £17.20 B82-20086

658.1′51 — Business firms. Financial management. Decision making

Koutsoyiannis, A.. Non-price decisions : the firm in a modern context / A. Koutsoyiannis. — London : Macmillan, 1982. — xxiii,671p : ill ; 25cm
Bibliography: p642-653. — Includes index
ISBN 0-333-26587-4 (cased) : Unpriced
ISBN 0-333-26588-2 (pbk) : Unpriced B82-26769

658.1′51 — Financial management. Decision making

Carsberg, Bryan. Economics of business decisions / Bryan Carsberg. — London : Pitman, 1979, c1975. — 328p : ill ; 23cm
Originally published: Harmondsworth : Penguin, 1975. — Bibliography: p317-324. — Includes index
ISBN 0-273-01459-5 : Unpriced B82-01756

658.1′51 — Financial management. Decision making. Simulations. Applications of digital computer systems

Bhaskar, Krish. Financial modelling with computers : a guide for management / by Krish Bhaskar, Peter Pope and Richard Morris. — London (Spencer Hse., 27 St James′s Pl., SW1 1NT) : Economist Intelligence Unit, 1982. — 139p : ill ; 30cm. — (EIU special report ; no.120)
Includes bibliographies
Unpriced (pbk) B82-27737

658.1′511 — Management accounting

Arnold, John. Accounting for management decisions. — London : Prentice Hall, Feb.1983. — [400]p
ISBN 0-13-001982-8 (pbk) : £8.95 : CIP entry B82-36605

Chenhall, Robert H.. The organizational context of management accounting / Robert H. Chenhall, Graeme L. Harrison, David J.H. Watson. — Boston [Mass.] ; London : Pitman, c1981. — xxv,398p : ill ; 24cm
Bibliography: p393-398
ISBN 0-273-01644-x : Unpriced B82-00064

DeCoster, Don T.. Management accounting : a decision emphasis / Don T. DeCoster, Eldon L. Schafer. — 3rd ed. — New York ; Chichester : Wiley, c1982. — x,720p : ill ; 25cm
Previous ed.: 1979. — Includes index
ISBN 0-471-09811-6 : £19.95 B82-28081

Grimsley, Bob. Management accounting systems and records / Bob Grimsley. — 2nd ed / M.W. Monaghan. — Aldershot : Gower, 1981. — xi,117p : ill ; 26cm
Previous ed.: 1972. — Includes index
ISBN 0-566-02349-0 : Unpriced B82-17875

Information for decision making : readings in cost and managerial accounting / edited by Alfred Rappaport. — 3rd ed. — Englewood Cliffs ; London : Prentice-Hall, c1982. — 412p : ill ; 23cm
Previous ed.: 1975. — Includes bibliographies
ISBN 0-13-464354-2 (pbk) : £14.95
Primary classification 657′.42 B82-35162

Kaplan, Robert S.. Advanced management accounting / Robert S. Kaplan. — Englewood Cliffs ; London : Prentice-Hall, c1982. — xvi,655p : ill ; 25cm. — (Prentice-Hall series in accounting)
Includes bibliographies and index
ISBN 0-13-011403-0 : £22.45 B82-34458

Management accounting guidelines. — London : Institute of Cost and Management Accountants
1: Iner-unit transfer pricing. — 1981. — iv,26p ; 21cm
ISBN 0-901308-61-7 (pbk) : Unpriced B82-08870

Mearns, Ian. Fundamentals of cost and management accounting / Ian Mearns. — London : Longman, 1981. — vii,319p : ill,forms ; 22cm. — (Longman professional education series)
Includes index
ISBN 0-582-41575-6 (pbk) : £4.50 : CIP rev. B81-13826

Norkett, P. T. C.. Management accounting / Paul Norkett. — Harlow : Longman, 1982. — xx,506p : ill,forms ; 22cm. — (Accountancy for non-accountants ; v.2)
Includes index
ISBN 0-582-41208-0 (pbk) : £8.50 B82-39673

Sizer, John. An insight into management accounting / John Sizer. — 2nd ed. — London : Pitman, 1979. — 525p : ill ; 23cm
Previous ed.: Harmondsworth : Penguin, 1969. — Includes bibliographies and index
ISBN 0-273-01463-3 : Unpriced B82-09791

658.1′511 — Management accounting — *For executives*

Droms, William G.. Finance and accounting for nonfinancial managers / William G. Droms. — Reading, Mass. ; London : Addison-Wesley, c1979. — ix,198p : ill ; 24cm
Includes bibliographies
ISBN 0-201-01392-4 (pbk) : £6.40 B82-33446

Walker, T. M.. Management accountancy for the company executive / by T.M. Walker. — London : Institute of Cost and Management Accountants, 1981. — 93p : ill ; 21cm
Includes index
ISBN 0-901308-60-9 (pbk) : Unpriced B82-08867

658.1′511′0722 — Management accounting — *Case studies*
Clinton, G. S.. Case studies in management accounting / G.S. Clinton. — London : Institute of Cost and Management Accountants, 1982. — v,81p : ill,1map ; 30cm
Facsims of: studies originally published in Management accounting, 1978-1980
ISBN 0-901308-63-3 (pbk) : Unpriced
B82-31487

Ray, Graham H.. Hardy Developments Ltd. : text and cases in management accounting / Graham Ray, Joe Smith. — Aldershot : Gower, c1982. — x,413p : ill ; 23cm
Bibliography: p413
ISBN 0-566-02251-6 (cased) : Unpriced : CIP rev.
ISBN 0-566-02252-4 (pbk) : Unpriced
B81-25824

Shank, John. Contemporary managerial accounting : a casebook / John Shank. — Englewood Cliffs ; London : Prentice-Hall, c1981. — xii,335p : ill ; 24cm
ISBN 0-13-170357-9 (pbk) : £11.20
B82-05547

658.1′511′076 — Management accounting — *Questions & answers — For business studies*
Fred, J. David. Study guide to accompany Schattke and Jensen′s Managerial accounting, concepts and uses, second ed. / prepared by J. David Fred. — Boston, Mass. ; London : Allyn and Bacon, c1981. — 193p : ill ; 28cm
ISBN 0-205-07322-0 (pbk) : £2.50 B82-17844

658.1′511′0941 — Great Britain. Management accounting — *Conference proceedings*
Managing for profit / editor Patrick Mills. — London : McGraw Hill, c1982. — 142p : ill ; 24cm
ISBN 0-07-084575-1 : £10.50 : CIP rev.
B81-38837

658.1′512 — Great Britain. Public companies. Financial information. Use by institutional shareholders
Lee, T. A.. The institutional investor and financial information : a report sponsored by the Research Committee of the Institute of Chartered Accountants in England and Wales / T.A. Lee, D.P. Tweedie. — London : The Institute, 1981. — x,209p : forms ; 22cm
Bibliography: p209
ISBN 0-85291-301-x : Unpriced B82-08691

658.1′52 — Capital investment by business firms. Decision making
Levy, Haim. Capital investment and financial decisions / Haim Levy & Marshall Sarnat. — 2nd ed. — Englewood Cliffs ; London : Prentice-Hall, c1982. — x,598p : illl ; 24cm
Previous ed.: 1978. — Includes bibliographies and index
ISBN 0-13-113589-9 : £10.95 : CIP rev.
B81-33978

658.1′52 — Capital investment by companies. Decision making. Mathematical models
Manners, George E.. Managing return on investment : implications for pricing, volume, and funds flow / George E. Manners, Joseph G. Louderback. — Lexington : Lexington Books, c1981 ; [Aldershot] : Gower [[distributor]], 1982. — xvi,172p ; 24cm
Includes index
ISBN 0-669-04383-4 : £16.50 B82-21268

658.1′52 — Capital investment. Decision making
Bromwich, Michael. The economics of capital budgeting / Michael Bromwich. — London : Pitman, 1979, c1976. — 395p : ill ; 23cm
Originally published: Harmondsworth : Penguin, 1976. — Bibliography: p383-390. — Includes index
ISBN 0-273-01460-9 : Unpriced B82-01755

658.1′52 — Great Britain. Capital investment by companies. Appraisal. Management aspects
Mott, Graham. Investment appraisal for managers / Graham Mott. — London : Macmillan, 1982. — 156p : ill ; 23cm
Includes index
ISBN 0-333-34060-4 : £15.00 B82-38785

658.1′522 — Great Britain. Companies. Assets. Life cycle costing
De la Mare, R. F.. Manufacturing systems economics : the life-cycle costs and benefits of industrial assets / R.F. de la Mare. — London : Holt, Rinehart and Winston, c1982. — xiii,546p : ill ; 25cm
Includes index
ISBN 0-03-910363-3 (pbk) : £9.50 : CIP rev.
B82-07223

658.1′522 — Great Britain. Small firms. Capital. Sources. Management aspects
Money for business : a guide / prepared by the Bank of England and the City Communications Centre. — 3rd ed. — London : Industrial Finance Division, Bank of England, 1981. — viii,126p ; 24cm
Previous ed.: 1978
ISBN 0-903312-40-9 (pbk) : Unpriced
B82-05047

658.1′522 — Great Britain. Small firms. Finance. Sources — *Manuals*
Finding money for your business : a guide to finance for the smaller business / CBI. — London : Confederation of British Industry, 1982. — 60p ; 20x21cm
Bibliography: p57-58
£3.50 (pbk) B82-21683

658.1′522 — Great Britain. Small firms. Financial management. Capital. Raising
Woodcock, Clive. Raising finance for the small business. — London : Kogan Page, Aug.1982. — [180]p
ISBN 0-85038-544-x (cased) : £9.95 : CIP entry
ISBN 0-85038-553-9 (pbk) : £4.95 B82-17978

658.1′5224 — Denmark. Business firms. Capital. External sources: International capital & money markets
Stonehill, Arthur I.. Internationalizing the cost of capital in theory and practice. — Chichester : Wiley, Dec.1982. — [157]p
ISBN 0-471-90127-x : £12.00 : CIP entry
B82-37506

658.1′5242 — United States. Industrial equipment. Leasing
Bierman, Harold. The lease versus buy decision / Harold Bierman, Jr. — Englewood Cliffs, N.J. ; London : Prentice-Hall, c1982. — xii,111p : ill ; 24cm. — (Prentice-Hall foundations of finance series)
Bibliography: p107-108. — Includes index
ISBN 0-13-527994-1 (cased) : Unpriced
ISBN 0-13-527986-0 (pbk) : £8.20 B82-33774

658.1′526′0941 — Great Britain. Business firms. Debtors — *Conference proceedings*
How to protect your business from insolvent and fraudulent debtors : report of a conference held in May 1981 / contributors W.V. Adams ... [et al.] ; editor W.V. Adams. — Aldershot : Gower, c1981. — 67p ; 30cm. — (Gower executive report)
ISBN 0-566-03029-2 (pbk) : Unpriced
B82-22961

658.1′53 — Great Britain. Business firms. Tax avoidance — *Manuals*
Apsion, Gordon. UK corporate tax shelters / by Gordon Apsion. — London : Economist Intelligence Unit, 1981. — 89p ; 30cm. — (EIU special report ; no.109)
Unpriced (pbk) B82-03984

658.1′53 — Great Britain. Companies. Tax avoidance — *Manuals*
Eastaway, Nigel A.. Utilising company tax losses and reliefs / by Nigel A. Eastaway and Edward P. Magrin. — 2nd ed. — London : Institute of Chartered Accountants in England and Wales, 1982. — xxxiv,321p ; 21cm. — (Chartac taxation guides)
Previous ed.: 1979. — Includes index
ISBN 0-85291-313-3 (pbk) : Unpriced
B82-24570

658.1′53 — Great Britain. Tax avoidance — *For family firms*
Tax saving for the family business / Coopers & Lybrand. — London : Harrap, 1982, c1981. — 60p ; 22cm
Includes index
ISBN 0-245-53866-6 (pbk) : £1.95 B82-16977

658.1′53 — United States. Deferred gifts. Financial management by non-profit making organisations
Fink, Norman S.. The costs and benefits of deferred giving / Norman S. Fink, Howard C. Metzler ; prepared for the Lilly Endowment, Inc.. — New York ; Guildford, Surrey : Columbia University Press, 1982. — xiv,255p ; 24cm
Bibliography: p247-251. — Includes index
ISBN 0-231-05478-5 : £14.85 B82-36481

658.1′54 — Business firms. Financial management. Zero-based budgeting
Zero based budgeting. — London (2 St Bride St., EC4A 4HR) : Binder Hamlyn Fry & Co., c1982. — 13p : forms ; 30cm. — (Executive guide)
£3.00 (free to clients) (unbound) B82-30633

658.1′54 — Capital expenditure. Budgeting
Herbst, Anthony F.. Capital budgeting : theory, quantitative methods, and applications / Anthony F. Herbst. — New York ; London : Harper & Row, c1982. — xiv,398p : ill ; 25cm
Includes bibliographies and index
ISBN 0-06-042795-7 : £17.95 B82-26279

658.1′552 — Business firms. Financial services. Costs. Reduction — *Conference proceedings*
Cutting the costs of financial services : report of a conference / contributors Richard Heseltine ... [et al.]. — Aldershot : Gower, c1981. — vi,83p ; 30cm. — (Gower executive report)
ISBN 0-566-03027-6 (pbk) : Unpriced : CIP rev.
B81-31241

658.1′552 — Financial management. Costing
Whitehead, Geoffrey. Success in accounting and costing. — London : J. Murray, Oct.1982. — [472]p
ISBN 0-7195-3835-1 (pbk) : £4.50 : CIP entry
B82-23017

658.1′552 — Financial management. Costing — *Questions & answers*
Whitehead, Geoffrey. Success in accounting and costing: problems and projects. — London : J. Murray, Oct.1982. — [368]p
ISBN 0-7195-3836-x (pbk) : £3.95 : CIP entry
B82-23018

658.1′552 — Financial management. Estimating
Stewart, Rodney D.. Cost estimating / Rodney D. Stewart. — New York ; Chichester : Wiley, c1982. — xvii,307p : ill ; 24cm
Bibliography: p263-264. — Includes index
ISBN 0-471-08175-2 : £23.25 B82-18200

658.1′552 — Industries. Costs. Control — *Manuals*
Wilson, R. M. S.. Cost control handbook. — 2nd ed. — Aldershot : Gower, May 1982. — [500] p. — (A Gower handbook)
Previous ed.: 1975
ISBN 0-566-02250-8 : £18.50 : CIP entry
B82-06855

658.1′552′076 — Costing — *Questions & answers*
Childs, L. R.. Objective tests in costing / L.R. Childs, A.R. Leal. — London : Longman, 1982. — 79p ; 20cm. — (Longman objective test series)
ISBN 0-582-41240-4 (pbk) : £1.50 : CIP rev.
B82-10780

658.1′554 — Business firms. Profits. Improvement. Techniques
Goodman, Sam R.. Increasing corporate profitability : financial techniques for marketing, manufacturing, planning and control / Sam R. Goodman. — New York ; Chichester : Wiley, c1982. — xix,300p : ill,forms ; 24cm. — (Systems and controls for financial management series)
Text on lining papers. — Includes index
ISBN 0-471-09161-8 : Unpriced B82-38317

658.1′592 — Small firms. Financial management
Bates, James. The financing of small business. — 3rd ed. — London : Sweet and Maxwell, Nov.1982. — [224]p
Previous ed.: 1971
ISBN 0-421-29200-8 : £23.00 : CIP entry
B82-28280

658.1′592′0924 — Great Britain. Small firms. Financial management — *Personal observations*

Kinross, John, *1904-*. Fifty years in the City : financing small business / John Kinross. — London : Murray, c1982. — xiv,238p,[8]p of plates : ill,ports ; 23cm
Includes index
ISBN 0-7195-3937-4 : £12.50 B82-23628

658.1′599 — Multinational companies. Financial management

The **Essentials** of treasury management / edited by Richard Ensor and Peter Muller. — London : Euromoney Publications, c1981. — ix,259p : ill ; 30cm
ISBN 0-903121-24-7 (pbk) : Unpriced B82-15006

Shapiro, Alan C.. Multinational financial management / Alan C. Shapiro. — Boston [Mass.] ; London : Allyn and Bacon, c1982. — xv,608p : ill ; 25cm
Text on lining papers. — Includes index
ISBN 0-205-07617-3 : Unpriced B82-26762

658.1′6 — Great Britain. Companies. Acquisition. Management aspects

Jones, C. Stuart. Successful management of acquisitions / by C. Stuart Jones. — London : Derek Beattie, 1982. — xviii,173p ; 23cm
Includes index
ISBN 0-907591-02-7 : Unpriced B82-40209

658.1′6 — Great Britain. Companies. Buy-outs by managers

Management buy-outs : a guide for sellers, managers and investers. — London : Economist Intelligence Unit, 1982. — 132p ; 30cm. — (EIU special report ; no.115)
Unpriced (pbk) B82-19618

658.1′6 — United States. Business firms. Acquisition. Management aspects

Bradley, James W.. Acquisition and corporate development : a contemporary perspective for the manager / James W. Bradley, Donald H. Korn. — Lexington, [Mass.] : Lexington Books, 1981 ; [Aldershot] : Gower [distributor], 1982. — xiv,252p : ill ; 24cm. — (Arthur D. Little books)
Includes bibliographies and index
ISBN 0-669-03170-4 : £18.50 B82-11705

658.1′6′0941 — Great Britain. Companies. Mergers & take-overs. Management aspects

Johannsen, H.. Buying a company : a checklist guide to successful acquisitions for the smaller company / [adapted and edited by H. Johannsen for the British Institute of Management Foundation]. — London : British Institute of Management, c1982. — 37p ; 21cm
Originally published: as A checklist guide to successfull acquisitions / by Victor Harold. United States : Pilot Industries, 1980. — Bibliography: p35-37
ISBN 0-85946-121-1 (corrected : pbk) : Unpriced B82-18323

658.1′8 — Multinational companies. Cooperation. Management

Moran, Robert T.. Managing cultural synergy / Robert T. Moran, Philip R. Harris. — Houston ; London : Gulf, c1982. — xiii,399p ; 24cm. — (The International management productivity series ; v.2)
Bibliography: p368-385. — Includes index
ISBN 0-87201-827-x : Unpriced B82-39860

658.1′8 — Technology transfer. International licensing

Contractor, Farok J.. International technology licensing : compensation, costs, and negotiation / Farok J. Contractor. — Lexington : Lexington Books, c1981 ; [Aldershot] : Gower [distributor], 1982. — xiv,193p ; 24cm
Bibliography: p185-189. — Includes index
ISBN 0-669-04359-1 : £22.50 B82-18256

658.2 — PLANT MANAGEMENT

658.2 — Energy resources. Conservation by distribution trades

Energy saving in distribution / edited by Peter N.C. Cooke. — Aldershot : Gower, c1981. — xviii,262p : ill ; 23cm
Bibliography: p247-252. — Includes index
ISBN 0-566-02155-2 : Unpriced B82-17822

658.2′02 — Buildings. Maintenance. Management

Chartered Institute of Building. Maintenance management. — 2nd ed. — Ascot : Chartered Institute of Building, Apr.1982. — 1v.
Previous ed.: 1975
ISBN 0-906600-55-3 (pbk) : CIP entry B82-13479

658.2′1′0941 — Great Britain. Industrial buildings. Choice — *For small firms*

Taking new premises : a guide to industrialists / [prepared by the Planning & Development Division, the Royal Institution of Chartered Surveyors]. — London : Published on behalf of the Royal Institution of Chartered Surveyors by Surveyors Publication, c1981. — 23p ; 15x21cm
ISBN 0-85406-137-1 (pbk) : Unpriced B82-07761

658.2′6 — Great Britain. Industries. Energy. Conservation. Management — *Manuals*

Murphy, W. R.. Energy management / W.R. Murphy, G. McKay. — London : Butterworths, 1982. — ix,374p : ill ; 24cm
Includes bibliographies and index
ISBN 0-408-00508-4 : Unpriced : CIP rev. B81-31734

658.2′6 — Industries. Energy. Conservation. Management

Energy management handbook / edited by Wayne C. Turner. — New York ; Chichester : Wiley, c1982. — xxiii,714p : ill,forms,maps ; 24cm
Includes bibliographies and index
ISBN 0-471-08252-x : £36.60 B82-28082

O′Callaghan, Paul W.. Design and management for energy conservation : a handbook for energy managers, plant engineers and designers / Paul W. O′Callaghan. — Oxford : Pergamon, 1981. — xvi,344p : ill,1port ; 24cm
Bibliography: p260-262. — Includes index
ISBN 0-08-027287-8 : £15.00 : CIP rev. B81-31743

658.2′8 — Great Britain. Workplaces. Cloakroom accommodation & washing facilities. Provision

Cloakroom accommodation and washing facilities. — London : H.M.S.O., 1980. — 27p : ill ; 21cm. — (Health & safety series booklet ; HS (G) 10)
ISBN 0-11-883295-6 (pbk) : £1.00 : CIP rev. B79-30749

658.3 — PERSONNEL MANAGEMENT

658.3 — Personnel management

Burack, Elmer H.. Personnel management : a human resource system approach / Elmer H. Burack, Robert D. Smith. — New York ; Chichester : Wiley, c1982. — xxvii,609p : ill,forms ; 25cm. — (Wiley series in management)
Includes bibliographies and index
ISBN 0-471-09283-5 : £19.95 B82-21443

Humphrey, Peter. How to be your own personnel manager. — London : Institute of Personnel Management, June 1981. — [160]p
ISBN 0-85292-273-6 (pbk) : £1.95 : CIP entry B81-12894

Hunt, John W.. Managing people at work : a manager′s guide to behaviour in organizations / John Hunt. — London : Pan, 1981, c1979. — 279p : ill ; 18cm. — (Pan business / management)
Originally published: London : McGraw-Hill, 1979. — Includes bibliographies and index
ISBN 0-330-26259-9 (pbk) : £1.95 B82-01596

Making organizations humane and productive : a handbook for practitioners / edited by H. Meltzer, Walter R. Nord. — New York ; Chichester : Wiley, c1981. — xiv,510p : ill ; 25cm
Includes index
ISBN 0-471-07813-1 : £20.70 B82-01051

Robbins, Stephen P.. Personnel : the management of human resources / Stephen P. Robbins. — 2nd ed. — Englewood Cliffs ; London : Prentice-Hall, c1982. — xxiii,520p : ill,1form ; 25cm
Previous ed.: 1978. — Includes bibliographies and index
ISBN 0-13-657825-x : £17.20 B82-23231

Thomason, George F.. A textbook of personnel management / George F. Thomason. — 4th ed. — [London] : Institute of Personnel Management, 1981. — xviii,619p : ill ; 22cm. — (Management in perspective)
Previous ed.: 1978. — Bibliography: p565-603. — Includes index
ISBN 0-85292-301-5 (pbk) : Unpriced : CIP rev. B81-20531

Using personnel research. — Aldershot : Gower, Aug.1982. — [350]p
ISBN 0-566-02264-8 : £15.00 : CIP entry B82-15884

658.3 — Personnel management — *Manuals*

Armstrong, Michael. Personnel management. — London : Kogan Page, Feb.1981. — [200]p
ISBN 0-85038-504-0 : £11.00 : CIP entry B82-03121

Torrington, Derek. Face to face in management. — London : Prentice-Hall, Sept.1982. — [200]p
ISBN 0-13-299099-7 (pbk) : £8.95 : CIP entry B82-21382

Tyson, Shaun. Personnel management made simple / Shaun Tyson, Alfred York. — London : Heinemann, c1982. — xii,350p : ill,forms ; 23cm. — (Made simple books)
Includes bibliographies and index
ISBN 0-434-98510-4 (cased) : £5.95
ISBN 0-434-98511-2 (pbk) : £2.95 B82-20420

658.3′0028′54 — Great Britain. Personnel management. Applications of digital computer systems — *Conference proceedings*

National Conference and Exhibition on Computers in Personnel *(1st : 1982 : London)*. Computers in personnel : papers for presentation to the First National Conference and Exhibition on Computers in Personnel, London 22-24 June 1982 / edited by Terry Page. — Brighton : Institute of Manpower Studies, c1982. — 163p : ill,1map ; 30cm. — (IMS report ; no.53)
£10.00 (£8.00 to IPM members and IMS subscribers) (pbk) B82-40453

658.3′0028′54 — Personnel management. Applications of digital computer systems

Ive, Tony. Personnel computer systems / Tony Ive. — London : McGraw-Hill : c1982. — 199p ; 24cm
Includes index
ISBN 0-07-084572-7 : £9.95 : CIP rev. B81-28779

658.3′003 — Personnel management — *Polyglot dictionaries*

An International dictionary of personnel terms / European Association of [i.e. for] Personnel Management. — 2nd ed. — London : Institute of Personnel Management on behalf of the Association, c1980. — 157p ; 20cm
Previous ed.: 197-?. — Includes index
ISBN 0-85292-285-x (pbk) : £6.95 B82-40480

658.3′00722 — United States. Personnel management — *Case studies*

Foulkes, Fred K.. Human resources management : text and cases / Fred K. Foulkes, E. Robert Livernash. — Englewood Cliffs ; London : Prentice-Hall, c1982. — xiii,448p : ill,1plan,forms ; 25cm
Includes bibliographies
ISBN 0-13-446310-2 (cased) : Unpriced
ISBN 0-13-446302-1 (pbk) : £11.95 B82-20082

658.3′00941 — Great Britain. Personnel management

McIlwee, Terry. Personnel management in context. — Buckden (45 Park Rd., Buckden, Cambs PE18 9SL) : Elm Publications, Oct.1982. — [320]p
ISBN 0-9505828-8-3 (pbk) : £7.90 : CIP entry
B82-29415

The **Personnel** and training databook 1982 / consultant editor Michael Armstrong. — London : Kogan Page, 1981. — x,422p ; 23cm
Bibliography: p151-157. — Includes index
ISBN 0-85038-493-1 : £14.95 : CIP rev.
B81-33638

Pratt, K. J.. How to pass examinations in personnel management / K.J. Pratt and S.G. Bennett. — London : Cassell, 1982. — 118p ; 22cm
Bibliography: p118
ISBN 0-304-30961-3 (pbk) : £3.95 B82-31657

658.3′00941 — Great Britain. Personnel management — *Forms*

Janner, Greville. Janner′s Employment forms / Greville Janner. — 2nd ed. — London : Business Books, 1982. — xv,423p : chiefly forms ; 31cm
Previous ed.: 1979. — Includes index
ISBN 0-09-147390-x : Unpriced : CIP rev.
B82-10415

658.3′00941 — Great Britain. Personnel management — *Serials*

Personnel and training databook. — 2nd ed. (1983). — London : Kogan Page, Nov.1982. — [420]p
ISBN 0-85038-567-9 : £16.95 : CIP entry
ISSN 0261-9245 B82-26417

658.3′00973 — United States. Personnel management

Stone, Thomas H.. Understanding personnel management / Thomas H. Stone. — Chicago ; London : Dryden, c1982. — 528p : ill ; 25cm
Includes index
ISBN 0-03-045671-1 : £16.95 B82-25377

658.3′00973 — United States. Personnel management. Forms

Famularo, Joseph J.. Handbook of personnel forms, records, and reports / by Joseph J. Famularo. — New York ; London : McGraw-Hill, c1982. — xxiii,624p : ill,forms ; 31cm
Includes index
ISBN 0-07-019913-2 : Unpriced B82-41111

658.3′01 — Manpower planning. Management aspects

Bramham, John. Practical manpower planning. — 3rd ed. — London : Institute of Personnel Management, July 1982. — [206]p
Previous ed.: 1978
ISBN 0-85292-313-9 : £5.50 : CIP entry
B82-21958

658.3′02 — Management. Supervision

Broadwell, Martin M.. The new supervisor / Martin M. Broadwell. — 2nd ed. — Reading, Mass. ; London : Addison-Wesley, c1979. — xv,172p : ill ; 21cm
Previous ed.: 1972. — Includes index
ISBN 0-201-00565-4 (pbk) : £0.80 B82-31152

Fulmer, Robert M.. Supervision : principles of professional management / Robert M. Fulmer, Stephen G. Franklin. — 2nd ed. — New York : Macmillan ; London : Collier Macmillan, c1982. — viii,360p : ill,forms ; 26cm
Previous ed.: 1976. — Includes index
ISBN 0-02-479660-3 : £13.95 B82-19513

658.3′02 — Management. Supervision — *Manuals*

Administrator′s guide for Management-minded supervision : a self-study training program / prepared by Coastline Community College, Coast Community College District as supplementary instructional material for use with the adaptation of Bradford B. Boyd′s Management-minded supervision, second edition. — New York ; London : McGraw-Hill, c1979. — 1v.(looseleaf) : forms ; 29cm
ISBN 0-07-006944-1 : £39.95 B82-28981

658.3′03′07 — Small firms. Management. Professional education

Education and assistance for the entrepreneur. — Aldershot : Gower, July 1982. — [228]p
ISBN 0-566-00381-3 : £10.50 : CIP entry
B82-14077

658.3′041 — Great Britain. Expatriate personnel. Employment. Management aspects

The **Management** of expatriates. — London : Institute of Personnel Management, June 1982. — [368]p
ISBN 0-85292-304-x (pbk) : £39.00 : CIP entry
B82-12847

658.3′06 — Job analysis. Questionnaires — *Texts*

Job components inventory mark II / authors M.H. Banks ... [et al.]. — Sheffield : Training Services, Manpower Services Commission, 1982. — 130p in various pagings : ill ; 30cm + Response sheets([32]leaves : 30cm). — (MSC training studies)
ISBN 0-905932-48-x (spiral) : Unpriced
B82-40852

658.3′06 — Job design

Bailey, John. Job design and work organization. — London : Prentice Hall, Feb.1983. — [280]p
ISBN 0-13-509919-6 (pbk) : £8.50 : CIP entry
B82-36606

658.3′11 — Personnel. Recruitment & selection

Recruitment handbook. — 3rd ed. — Aldershot : Gower, Mar.1982. — [330]p
Previous ed.: 1975
ISBN 0-566-02192-7 : £17.50 : CIP entry
B82-00197

658.3′11 — Personnel. Recruitment & selection — *Manuals*

Hackett, Penny. The Daily telegraph recruitment handbook. — 2nd ed. — London : Kogan Page, Nov.1981. — [244]p
Previous ed.: 1979
ISBN 0-85038-488-5 : £12.50 : CIP entry
B81-34961

Hackett, Penny. The Daily telegraph recruitment handbook. — 2nd ed. — London : New Opportunity Press, Dec.1981. — [224]p
Previous ed.: London : Kogan Page, 1979
ISBN 0-903578-95-6 : £8.50 : CIP entry
B81-40251

658.3′11 — Salesmen. Recruitment & selection

Lidstone, John. How to recruit and select successful salesmen. — Aldershot : Gower, Aug.1982. — [220]p
ISBN 0-566-02325-3 : £17.50 : CIP entry
B82-15885

658.3′111 — Scotland. Young persons. Recruitment. Attitudes of employers

Hunt, Janice. Employing young people : a study of employers′ attitudes, policies and practice / Janice Hunt and Peter Small. — Edinburgh : Scottish Council for Research in Education, c1981. — v,42p ; 30cm
Bibliography: p41-42
ISBN 0-901116-32-7 (pbk) : Unpriced
B82-11854

658.3′112 — Great Britain. Warehouses. Personnel. Selection

Warehouse staff training. — Stretford : Distributive Industry Training Board, [1981?]. — 28p : col.ill,1map,forms ; 20x21cm. — (A DITB training guide)
Cover title. — Text on inside cover
ISBN 0-903416-23-9 (pbk) : Unpriced
Primary classification 658.7′85′07041
B82-17428

658.3′1124 — Personnel. Interviewing — *Manuals*

Goodale, James G.. The fine art of interviewing / James G. Goodale. — Englewood Cliffs ; London : Prentice-Hall, c1982. — xv,201p ; 24cm
Includes index
ISBN 0-13-317008-x : Unpriced B82-37729

658.3′1124 — Personnel. Interviewing — *Questions & answers*

Hackett, Penny. Interview skills training : practice packs for trainers / Penny Hackett. — Rev. ed. — London : Institute of Personnel Management, 1981. — v.(loose-leaf) : forms ; 31cm
Previous ed.: / published as Interviewing skills training. 1978
ISBN 0-85292-299-x : £25.00 : CIP rev.
B81-25118

658.3′1124 — Personnel. Selection. Interviewing — *Manuals*

Goodworth, Clive T.. Effective interviewing for employment selection. — London : Business Books, Jan.1983. — [156]p
Originally published: 1979
ISBN 0-09-150330-2 (cased) : £12.00 : CIP entry
ISBN 0-09-150331-0 (pbk) : £5.25 B82-33456

Olson, Richard Fischer. Managing the interview / Richard Fischer Olson. — New York ; Chichester : Wiley, c1980. — vii,183p : ill ; 26cm. — (Wiley self-teaching guides)
Bibliography: p179. — Includes index
ISBN 0-471-04859-3 (pbk) : £5.30 B82-11556

658.3′122 — Great Britain. Personnel. Sickness. Self certification. Management aspects

Bilsland, Isabel. Self certification : a guide / compiled by Isabel Bilsland and Deirdre Gill. — London : Information Services, Institute of Personnel Managment, 1982. — 55p : ill,forms ; 30cm
Bibliography: p54-55
ISBN 0-85292-317-1 (spiral) : Unpriced : CIP rev. B82-14395

Howard, Gillian. A guide to self-certification / by Gillian Howard. — London : The Industrial Society, 1982. — 47p : forms ; 22cm
ISBN 0-85290-213-1 (pbk) : £3.50 B82-33060

658.3′124 — Industrial training. Learning curves & progress functions

Industrial applications of learning curves and progress functions. — London : Institution of Electronic and Radio Engineers, c1981. — 159p : ill ; 30cm. — (Proceedings / Institution of Electronic and Radio Engineers ; no.52)
Conference papers
ISBN 0-903748-47-9 (pbk) : Unpriced
B82-20473

658.3′124 — Organisations. Personnel. Training

Warren, Malcolm W.. Training for results : a systems approach to the development of human resources in industry / Malcolm W. Warren. — 2nd ed. — Reading, Mass. ; London : Addison-Wesley, c1979. — xviii,269p : ill ; 24cm
Previous ed.: 1969. — Bibliography: p263-266. — Includes index
ISBN 0-201-08504-6 (pbk) : £8.00 B82-12652

658.3′124 — Organisations. Personnel. Training — *Manuals*

Development at work. — [Gloucester] ([Barton House, Barton St., Gloucester GL1 1QQ]) : [Food, Drink and Tobacco Industry Training Board], [1978?]. — 2v : ill ; 32cm
£10.00 B82-27618

People and organisations. — Aldershot : Gower, July 1982. — [144]p
ISBN 0-566-00373-2 : £10.00 : CIP entry
B82-12970

Robinson, Kenneth R.. A handbook of training management / Kenneth R. Robinson. — London : Kogan Page, 1981. — 231p : ill ; 23cm
Includes index
ISBN 0-85038-527-x : £13.50 : CIP rev.
B81-38851

658.3′124 — Personnel. Training — *Manuals*

Dickenson, Arthur. You′ll soon get the hang of it : the technique of one-to-one training / written by Arthur Dickenson and Tina Tietjen ; illustrated by Carlo Roberto. — London : Video Arts, 1981. — 31p : ill ; 21cm
Cover title
ISBN 0-906607-17-5 (pbk) : Unpriced
B82-35604

658.3'124 — Small firms. Personnel. Training — *Manuals*

Training your staff : a guide for managers, supervisor and small business proprietors. — Wembley : Hotel and Catering Industry Training Board, 1982. — vii,48p : ill,forms ; 21cm
ISBN 0-7033-0020-2 (pbk) : Unpriced
B82-30837

658.3'12404 — Great Britain. Industrial training. Programmes. Design — *Manuals*

How to produce a simple modular training scheme : a guide for managers and training officers. — Gloucester (Barton House, Barton St., Gloucester GL1 1QQ) : Food, Drink and Tobacco Industry Training Board, [1977]. — 16p : ill ; 30cm
Cover title. — Originally published: 1976
£2.00 (pbk) B82-27615

658.3'12404 — Great Britain. Training officers. Training — *Proposals*

Great Britain. *Training of Trainers Committee.* Direct trainers : second report of the Training of Trainers Committee. — [London] : Training Services Division, Manpower Services Commission, 1980. — 32p ; 30cm
ISBN 0-11-888510-3 (pbk) : £2.50 B82-18617

658.3'124'0941 — Great Britain. Personnel. Training. Effects of digital computer systems — *Conference proceedings*

The **Impact** of new technology on training : a report of a seminar / organised jointly by Training Division CSD and the Civil Service College, held at Sunningdale on 9-11 February 1981. — Ascot, Berks. (Sunningdale Park, Ascot, Berks.) : Civil Service College, [1982?]. — iii,39p : ports ; 30cm
Unpriced (spiral) B82-17687

658.3'1242'0941 — Great Britain. Personnel. Induction training — *Manuals*

The **Introduction** of new staff. — London (308 Seven Sisters Rd., Finsbury Park, N4 2BN) : National Institute of Fresh Produce in association with the Food, Drink and Tobacco Industry Training Board, [1980]. — [8]p : ill ; 21cm
£0.60 (pbk) B82-27911

658.3'1243 — Great Britain. Unemployed persons: Professional personnel. Retraining. Transfer of Employment courses

Davison, Robert. Transfer of employment (TOE) courses : a follow-up study / Robert Davison. — Sheffield : Training Services, Manpower Services Commission, [1982]. — 41p : ill ; 30cm. — (MSC training studies)
Unpriced (spiral) B82-31235

658.3'1244 — Great Britain. Industries. Personnel. Industrial training. Curriculum subjects: Industrial health & industrial safety

Training for health & safety at work / [prepared by the Working Party on Health and Safety Training of the Food, Drink and Tobacco Industry Training Board]. — Gloucester (Barton House, Barton St., Gloucester GL1 1QQ) : The Board, 1975 (1976 [printing]). — 40p : 1ill ; 30cm
Cover title. — Text on inside cover
£1.50 (pbk) B82-23755

Training for health & safety at work : package / produced by the Food, Drink and Tobacco Industry Training Board. — [Gloucester] ([Barton House, Barton St., Gloucester GL1 1QQ]) : [The Board], [1982?]. — 1v(loose-leaf) : col.ill ; 32cm
Eight-nine colour slides in envelope as insert
Unpriced B82-23756

658.3'1244 — Industrial training. Curriculum subjects: Conflict studies. Teaching — *Manuals*

Hart, Lois Barland. Learning from conflict : a handbook for trainers and group leaders / Lois Barland Hart. — Reading, Mass. ; London : Addison-Wesley, c1981. — xvii,218p : ill ; 28cm
ISBN 0-201-03144-2 (pbk) : £7.20 B82-39896

658.3'1245 — Great Britain. Commercial travellers. Training

Van sales training. — Croydon (Leon House, High St., Croydon CR9 3RT) : Food, Drink and Tobacco Industry Training Board, [1978?]. — 33p : ill,forms ; 30cm
Bibliography: p33
£1.00 (pbk) B82-26125

658.3'125 — Personnel. Assessment

Judging people : a guide to orthodox and unorthodox methods of assessment / edited by D. Mackenzie Davey and Marjorie Harris. — London : McGraw-Hill, c1982. — xiii,150p : ill,facsims ; 24cm
Includes index
ISBN 0-07-084581-6 : £7.95 : CIP rev.
B82-12711

658.3'125 — Personnel. Performance. Appraisal

Performance appraisal on the line / David L. Devries ... [et al.]. — New York ; Chichester : Wiley, c1981. — x,160p : ill,forms ; 24cm
Bibliography: p140-149. — Includes index
ISBN 0-471-09254-1 : £14.00 B82-04546

658.3'125 — Personnel. Performance. Appraisal — *Manuals*

Latham, Gary P.. Increasing productivity through performance appraisal / Gary P. Latham, Kenneth N. Wexley. — Reading, Mass. ; London : Addison-Wesley, c1981. — x,262p : ill ; 21cm. — (Addison-Wesley series on managing human resources)
Bibliography: p239-256. — Includes index
ISBN 0-201-04217-7 (pbk) : £6.40 B82-33448

658.3'125 — Personnel. Performance. Effects of expectations of managers

Batten, Joe. Expectations and possibilities / Joe Batten. — Reading, Mass. ; London : Addison-Wesley, c1981. — ix,213p : ill,forms ; 25cm
Bibliography: p209-213
ISBN 0-201-00093-8 : £8.80 B82-32916

658.3'13 — United States. Personnel. Dismissal

Coulson, Robert. The termination handbook / Robert Coulson. — New York : Free Press ; London : Collier Macmillan, c1981. — viii,323p ; 25cm
Bibliography: p223-227. — Includes index
ISBN 0-02-906700-6 : £10.95 B82-18905

658.3'134 — Great Britain. Personnel. Redundancy. Personal adjustment — *Manuals*

How to survive redundancy!. — Cardiff : Welsh Consumer Council, 1981. — 52p in various pagings : ill ; 22cm
Cover title
ISBN 0-907749-02-x (pbk) : Unpriced
B82-04427

Kemp, Fred. Coping with redundancy. — London : Kogan Page, Nov.1981. — [250]p
ISBN 0-85038-526-1 : £7.95 : CIP entry
B81-33639

Kemp, Fred. [Focus on redundancy]. Coping with redundancy / Fred Kemp, Bernard Buttle & Derek Kemp. — London : Hamlyn Paperbacks, 1981. — 224p : ill,1map ; 18cm
Originally published: London : Kogan Page, 1980. — Bibliography: p219-220. — Includes index
ISBN 0-600-20549-5 (pbk) : £1.50 B82-00974

658.3'134'0973 — United States. Companies. Personnel. Redundancy. Policies of companies

Cross, Michael. U.S. corporate personnel reduction policies : an edited collection of manpower layoff, reduction and termination policies / Michael Cross. — Aldershot : Gower, 1981. — ix,134p : forms ; 23cm
ISBN 0-566-00501-8 : Unpriced : CIP rev.
B81-31609

658.3'14 — Great Britain. Personnel. Absenteeism. Management aspects

Barlow, David H. (David Henry). An employer's guide to absenteeism and sick-pay / David H. Barlow. — London : Kogan Page, 1982. — 174p : ill,forms ; 23cm
Includes index
ISBN 0-85038-582-2 : £11.95 : CIP rev.
B82-17982

658.3'14 — Great Britain. Personnel. Discipline. Procedure. Psychosocial aspects

Salamon, M. W.. Industrial discipline : the formal disciplinary process / M.W. Salamon. — Bristol : South West Regional Management Centre, 1981. — 32p ; 29cm. — (Occasional paper series / South West Regional Management Centre ; v.II, no.1)
At head of title: South West Regional Management Centre
ISBN 0-904951-18-9 (spiral) : Unpriced
B82-17706

658.3'14 — Industries. Productivity. Improvement. Applications of psychology

Gruneberg, Michael M.. Industrial productivity : a psychological perspective / Michael M. Gruneberg and David J. Oborne. — London : Macmillan, 1982. — 219p : ill ; 23cm
Bibliography: p187-209. — Includes index
ISBN 0-333-28160-8 : £15.00 B82-28529

658.3'14 — Personnel. Attitudes. Surveys. Techniques

Reeves, Tom Kynaston. Surveys at work : practitioner's guide / Tom Kynaston Reeves and Don Harper. — London : McGraw-Hill, c1981. — xviii,259p : ill,forms ; 24cm + student project manual(xvi,259p : ill, forms ; 23cm)
Bibliography: p250-253. — Includes index
ISBN 0-07-084563-8 : £15.95 : CIP rev.
ISBN 0-07-084568-9 (Student project manual) : £6.95 B81-20549

658.3'14 — Personnel. Motivation

Davidmann, M.. The will to work, remuneration, job satisfaction and motivation, what people strive to achieve, struggle for independence and good life / M. Davidmann. — [Stanmore] : Social Organisation Ltd., [c1981]. — 27leaves : ill ; 30cm. — (Community leadership and management)
ISBN 0-85192-020-9 (pbk) : £2.90 B82-17851

658.3'14 — Personnel. Motivation — *For management*

Rosenbaum, Bernard L.. How to motivate today's workers : motivational models for managers and supervisors / Bernard L. Rosenbaum. — New York ; London : McGraw-Hill, c1982. — xiv,201p : ill ; 21cm
Bibliography: p195-196. — Includes index
ISBN 0-07-053711-9 : £11.50 B82-02327

658.3'14 — Personnel. Motivation. Management

Hersey, Paul. Management of organizational behavior : utilizing human resources / Paul Hersey, Kenneth H. Blanchard. — 4th ed. — Englewood Cliffs ; London : Prentice-Hall, c1982. — xviii,343p : ill ; 24cm
Previous ed.: 1977. — Bibliography: p313-334. — Includes index
ISBN 0-13-549618-7 (cased) : Unpriced
ISBN 0-13-549600-4 (pbk) : £11.20
B82-16838

658.3'14 — Personnel. Poor performance. Improvement — *For management*

Stewart, Valerie. Managing the poor performer / Valerie Stewart, Andrew Stewart. — Aldershot : Gower, c1982. — viii,178p ; 23cm
Bibliography: p175-176. — Includes index
ISBN 0-566-02248-6 : Unpriced : CIP rev.
B81-32017

658.3'14 — Productivity. Improvement — *Manuals*

Bain, David, *1939-*. The productivity prescription : the manager's guide to improving productivity and profits / David Bain. — New York ; London : McGraw-Hill, c1982. — xii,308p : ill,forms ; 24cm
Bibliography: p299-300. — Includes index
ISBN 0-07-003235-1 : £15.50 B82-40608

658.3'14 — United States. Personnel. Discipline — *Manuals*

Grote, Richard C.. Positive discipline / Richard C. Grote. — New York ; London : McGraw-Hill, c1979. — 1v.(loose-leaf) : forms ; 29cm + leaders guide(loose-leaf: 29cm)
ISBN 0-07-025006-5 : £22.40 B82-25018

658.31'4'0941 — Great Britain. Personnel. Discipline. Procedure

Croner's guide to discipline / written and compiled by Croner's Employment Law Editorial Department. — New Malden : Croner, 1982. — 92p ; 18cm
Includes index
ISBN 0-900319-26-7 (pbk) : £1.40 B82-19310

658.3'1422 — Business firms. Personnel. Job satisfaction. Effects of installation of computer systems — *Case studies*

Munford, Enid. Values, technology and work / by Enid Munford. — The Hague ; London : Nijhoff, 1981. — x,318p : ill ; 25cm. — (Sijthoff & Noordhoff series on information systems ; v.3)
Bibliography: p302-312. — Includes index
ISBN 90-247-2562-3 : Unpriced B82-00477

658.3'1422 — Job satisfaction

Hankin, Barclay. Managing job satisfaction : a practical guide / by Barclay Hankin. — London : Hillbex, 1982. — v,137p : ill ; 21cm
ISBN 0-9507838-0-3 (pbk) : £3.00 : CIP rev.
B81-35020

658.3'1422 — Job satisfaction. Improvement. Use of job redesign

Kelly, J. E.. Scientific management, job redesign, and work performance. — London : Academic Press, Aug.1982. — [300]p. — (Organizational and occupational psychology)
ISBN 0-12-404020-9 : CIP entry B82-15668

658.31'422'09417 — Ireland *(Republic)*. Job satisfaction. Attitudes of personnel

Whelan, Christopher T.. Employment conditions and job satisfaction : the distribution, perception and evaluation of job rewards / Christopher T. Whelan. — Dublin : Economic and Social Research Institute, 1980. — ix,171p : ill ; 25cm. — (Paper / Economic and Social Research Institute ; no.101)
Bibliography: p136-141
ISBN 0-7070-0034-3 (pbk) : £5.50 (Irish) (£2.75 for students)
Primary classification 331.2'1'09417
B82-41045

658.3'15 — Industrial relations. Management

Conflict management and industrial relations / edited by Gerard B.J. Bomers, Richard B. Peterson. — Boston ; London : Kluwer, c1982. — x,454p ; 24cm. — (Nijenrode studies in business)
Includes bibliographies
ISBN 0-89838-068-5 : Unpriced B82-39053

658.3'15 — Organisations. Information. Disclosure to personnel. Team briefing — *Manuals*

McDougall, Ian, *1949-*. A guide to team briefing / Ian McDougall. — London : Industrial Society, 1981. — 20p : ill,1form ; 21cm
ISBN 0-85290-208-5 (pbk) : £1.00 B82-11953

658.3'15 — Organisations. Personnel suggestion schemes

Smith, Paul I. Slee. Employee suggestion schemes / Paul I. Slee Smith. — London : British Institute of Management Foundation, c1981. — 136p : ill,forms ; 21cm
Bibliography: p134-135
ISBN 0-85946-119-x (pbk) : Unpriced
B82-01471

658.3'15'0941 — Great Britain. Industrial relations. Management

Marchington, Mick. Managing industrial relations / Mick Marchington. — London : McGraw-Hill, c1982. — xii,189p ; 23cm
Bibliography: p177-185. — Includes index
ISBN 0-07-084580-8 (pbk) : £8.95 : CIP rev.
B82-12447

658.3'152 — European Community countries. American multinational companies. Management. Participation of personnel

DeVos, Ton. U.S. multinationals and worker participation in management : the American experience in the European community / Ton DeVos. — London : Aldwych, 1981. — xv,229p : ill ; 25cm
Bibliography: p215-223. — Includes index
ISBN 0-86172-022-9 : £21.75 B82-30921

658.3'152 — North-west England. Manufacturing industries. Management. Participation of personnel. Attitudes of managers

Employee participation in manufacturing industry : management attitudes / M.J. Dowling ... [et al.]. — Manchester (P.O. Box 88, Manchester M60 1QD) : Department of Management Sciences, University of Manchester Institute of Science and Technology, 1981. — 24p ; 31cm. — (Occasional paper / Department of Management Sciences, University of Manchester Institute of Science and Technology ; no.8110)
Unpriced (pbk) B82-27239

658.3'152 — North-west England. Manufacturing industries. Management. Participation of personnel. Attitudes of trade unions

Employee participation in manufacturing industry : trade union attitudes / M.J. Dowling ... [et al.]. — Manchester (P.O. Box 88, Manchester M60 1QD) : Department of Management Sciences, University of Manchester Institute of Science and Technology, 1981. — 26p ; 31cm. — (Occasional paper / Department of Management Sciences, University of Manchester Institute of Science and Technology ; no.8111)
Unpriced (pbk) B82-27238

658.3'152'0941 — Great Britain. Companies. Management. Participation of personnel

Current employee involvement practice in British business. — London (Centre Point, 103 New Oxford St., WC1A 1DU) : CBI, 1981. — 32p : ill ; 20cm
£5.00 (pbk) B82-09088

658.3'152'0941 — Great Britain. Industries. Management. Participation of personnel

What do the British want from participation and industrial democracy? / by Frank Heller ... [et al.]. — London : Anglo-German Foundation for the Study of Industrial Society, c1979. — iv,103p : ill ; 21cm. — (Series A ; 0679)
ISBN 0-905492-18-8 (pbk) : £7.95 B82-01283

658.3'152'0941 — Great Britain. Organisations. Management. Participation of personnel

Practical participation and involvement. — London : Institute of Personnel Management
2: Representative structures. — 1981. — vi,230p : ill ; 30cm
Bibliography: p227-230
ISBN 0-85292-289-2 (pbk) : £12.00
B82-09020

Practical participation and involvement. — London : Institute of Personnel Management
3: The individual and the job / [compiled and written by Alastair Evans]. — 1982. — v,197p : ill ; 30cm
Bibliography: p194-197
ISBN 0-85292-290-6 (pbk) : £16.60
B82-33058

Practical participation and involvement. — London : Institute of Personnel Management
4: Meeting education and training needs. — 1982. — v,144p : ill ; 29cm
Bibliography: p142-144
ISBN 0-85292-292-2 (pbk) : £15.00
B82-33057

658.3'152'09427 — North-west England. Manufacturing industries. Management. Participation of personnel

Employee participation in manufacturing industry : themes and implications / M.J. Dowling ... [et al.]. — Manchester (P.O. Box 88, Manchester M60 1QD) : Department of Management Sciences, University of Manchester Institute of Science and Technology, 1981. — 27p ; 31cm. — (Occasional paper / Department of Management Sciences, University of Manchester Institute of Science and Technology ; no.8112)
Bibliography: p26-27
Unpriced (pbk) B82-27237

658.3'152'094585 — Malta. Industries. Management. Participation of personnel

Kester, Gerard. Transition to workers' self-management : its dynamics in the decolonizing economy of Malta / Gerard Kester. — The Hague : Institute of Social Studies ; Nottingham : Spokesman Books, 1980. — xii,255p ; 24cm. — (Research report series ; no.7)
Bibliography: p245-255
ISBN 90-649-0001-9 (pbk) : £3.50 B82-33526

658.3'2'0941 — Great Britain. Industries. Personnel. Remuneration. Management aspects

Handbook of salary and wage systems. — 2nd ed. — Farnborough : Gower, Oct.1981. — [430]p
Previous ed.: 1975
ISBN 0-566-02261-3 : £17.50 : CIP entry
B81-25825

658.3'2'0941 — Great Britain. Personnel. Remuneration. Management aspects

Genders, Peter. Wages and salaries : managing pay effectively / Peter Genders. — [London] : Institute of Personnel Management, 1981. — 236p ; 19cm. — (Management paperbacks)
Bibliography: p231-233. — Includes index
ISBN 0-85292-275-2 (pbk) : £6.95 : CIP rev.
B81-31107

658.3'2'0941 — Great Britain. Personnel. Remuneration. Management aspects — *Serials*

Payroll manager : the magazine of Peterborough Data Processing Services Limited. — Issue 1 (June 1981)-. — Peterborough (Borough House, Newark Rd., Peterborough PE1 5YJ) : Peterborough Data Processing Services, 1981-. — v. : ill ; 30cm
Quarterly. — Description based on: Issue 2 (Dec. 1981)
ISSN 0262-981x = Payroll manager : Unpriced B82-13414

658.3'21 — Remuneration. Payment. Methods. Management aspects

Lupton, Tom. Wages and salaries. — 2nd ed. — Aldershot : Gower, Jan.1983. — [200]p
Previous ed.: Harmondsworth: Penguin, 1974
ISBN 0-566-02368-7 (cased) : £15.00 : CIP entry
ISBN 0-566-02375-x (pbk) : £6.50 B82-32444

658.3'253 — Great Britain. Superannuation schemes. Trusteeship

Pension Scheme Trusteeship. — [Croydon] : [National Association of Pension Funds], [1982]. — (An N.A.P.F. publication)
Cover title. — Text on inside covers
Booklet C: Secretarial/administration. — 12p ; 21cm
ISBN 0-905796-23-3 (pbk) : Unpriced
ISBN 0-905796-20-9 (set) : Unpriced
B82-28323

Pension Scheme Trusteeship. — [Croydon] : [National Association of Pension Funds], [1982]. — (An N.A.P.F. publication)
Cover title
Booklet D: Discretionary powers. — 12p ; 21cm
ISBN 0-905796-24-1 (pbk) : Unpriced
ISBN 0-905796-20-9 (set) : Unpriced
B82-28321

Pension Scheme Trusteeship. — [Croydon] : [National Association of Pension Funds], [1982]. — (An N.A.P.F. publication)
Cover title. — Text on inside covers
Booklet A: Legal. — 16p ; 21cm
ISBN 0-905796-21-7 (pbk) : Unpriced
ISBN 0-905796-20-9 (set) : Unpriced
B82-28320

Pension Scheme Trusteeship. — [Croydon] : [National Association of Pension Funds], [1982]. — (An N.A.P.F. publication)
Cover title. — Text on inside covers
Booklet B: Actuarial. — 16p ; 21cm
ISBN 0-905796-22-5 (pbk) : Unpriced
ISBN 0-905796-20-9 (set) : Unpriced
B82-28322

658.3'253 — Great Britain. Superannuation schemes. Trusteeship *continuation*

Pension Scheme Trusteeship. — [Croydon] : [National Association of Pension Funds], [1982]. — (An N.A.P.F. publication)
Cover title. — Text on inside covers
Booklet E: Report and accounts. — 14p ; 18cm
ISBN 0-905796-25-x (pbk) : Unpriced
ISBN 0-905796-20-9 (set) : Unpriced
B82-28324

Pension Scheme Trusteeship. — [Croydon] : [National Association of Pension Funds], [1982]. — (An N.A.P.F. publication)
Cover title. — Text on inside covers
Booklet F: Investments. — 12p ; 21cm
ISBN 0-905796-26-8 (pbk) : Unpriced
ISBN 0-905796-20-9 (set) : Unpriced
B82-28325

Pension Scheme Trusteeship. — [Croydon] : [National Association of Pension Funds], [1982]. — (An N.A.P.F. publication)
Cover title. — Text on inside covers
Booklet G: Member participations and pension communication. — 8p ; 21cm
ISBN 0-905796-27-6 (pbk) : Unpriced
ISBN 0-905796-20-9 (set) : Unpriced
B82-28326

658.3'8'0973 — United States. Industrial welfare services

Masi, Dale A.. Human services in industry / Dale A. Masi. — Lexington, Mass. : Lexington Books ; [Aldershot] : Gower [distributor], 1982. — xvi,247p : ill,1form ; 24cm
Includes index
ISBN 0-669-05104-7 : £19.50 B82-28662

658.3'82 — Great Britain. Industries. Safety representatives — *For safety representatives*

LRD guide for safety representatives / Labour Research Department. — London : LRD Publications, 1979. — 43p ; 22cm
Bibliography: p39-43
£0.50 (unbound) B82-02736

658.3'82 — Great Britain. Manufacturing industries. Safety committees. Effectiveness

The **Determinants** of effective joint health and safety committees : a report of a project funded by The Leverhulme Trust / P.B. Beaumont ... [et al.]. — Glasgow : University of Glasgow, Centre for Research in Industrial Democracy and Participation, 1982. — 22p ; 30cm
Bibliography: p21-22
Unpriced (pbk) B82-26457

658.3'82 — Great Britain. Safety representatives & safety committees

Training for health & safety at work : safety representatives & safety committees / [prepared by the Working Party on Health and Safety Training of the Food, Drink and Tobacco Industry Training Board]. — Gloucester (Barton House, Barton St., Gloucester GL1 1QQ) : The Board, 1977. — 12p : 1ill ; 30cm
Cover title. — Text on inside cover
£1.00 (pbk) B82-23753

658.3'82 — Personnel. Stress. Management aspects

Warshaw, Leon J.. Managing stress / Leon J. Warshaw. — Reading, Mass. ; London : Addison-Wesley, c1979. — xi,212p ; 21cm. — (Addison-Wesley series on occupational stress)
Bibliography: p201-202. — Includes index
ISBN 0-201-08299-3 (pbk) : £5.50 B82-37177

658.3'82'0941 — Great Britain. Industrial health & industrial safety. Role of management

Managing safety : a review of the role of management in occupational health & safety / by the Accident Prevention Unit of HM Factory Inspectorate. — London : H.M.S.O., 1981. — 35p ; 21cm. — (HSE occasional paper series ; OP3)
Bibliography: p34-35
ISBN 0-11-883443-6 (pbk) : £2.25 B82-04387

658.3'822 — Great Britain. Personnel. Alcoholism. Treatment. Policies

The **Problem** drinker at work : guidance in joint management and trade union co-operation to assist the problem drinker / [prepared jointly by the Health and Safety Executive ... [et al.]. — London : H.M.S.O., 1981. — 15p ; 21cm. — (HSE occasional paper series ; OP1)
Text on inside covers. — Bibliography: p10
ISBN 0-11-883428-2 (pbk) : £1.50 : CIP rev.
B81-13864

658.3'83 — Great Britain. Personnel. Ridesharing. Management — *Proposals*

Travel to work : opportunities for employers in the 1980 Transport Act. — [London] ([2 Marsham St., SW1 3EP]) : Department of Transport, [c1980]. — 10p ; 21cm
Cover title
Unpriced (pbk) B82-38482

658.4 — EXECUTIVE MANAGEMENT

658.4 — Executive management

Drucker, Peter F.. The changing world of the executive / Peter F. Drucker. — London : Heinemann, 1982. — xiv,271p ; 24cm
Includes index
ISBN 0-434-90406-6 : £10.95 B82-25633

Lundborg, Louis B.. The art of being an executive / Louis B. Lundborg. — New York : Free Press ; London : Collier Macmillan, c1981. — xvi,262p ; 25cm
Includes index
ISBN 0-02-919300-1 : £10.95 B82-18009

658.4 — Management. Quantitative methods

Levin, Richard I.. Quantitative approaches to management. — 5th ed. / Richard I. Levin, Charles A. Kirkpatrick, David S. Rubin. — New York ; London : McGraw-Hill, c1982. — xix,763p : col.ill,forms ; 24cm
Previous ed.: 1978. — Includes bibliographies and index
ISBN 0-07-037436-8 : £18.95 B82-27908

Render, Barry. Cases and readings in quantitative analysis for management / Barry Render, Ralph M. Stair, Jr. — Boston, Mass. ; London : Allyn and Bacon, c1982. — xvi,301p : ill,1facsim ; 24cm
ISBN 0-205-07754-4 (pbk) : Unpriced
B82-28490

658.4 — Management. Techniques

Carlson, Dick. Modern management : principles and practices / Dick Carlson. — Nigeria ; London : Macmillan, 1982, c1962. — ix,137p : ill,forms ; 24cm. — (Macmillan international college editions)
Originally published: Paris : O.E.C.D, 1962
ISBN 0-333-33533-3 (pbk) : Unpriced
B82-39994

Flippo, Edwin B.. Management / Edwin B. Flippo, Gary M. Munsinger. — 5th ed. — Boston, Mass. ; London : Allyn and Bacon, c1982. — xiv,604p : ill ; 25cm
Previous ed.: 1978. — Includes bibliographies and index
ISBN 0-205-07681-5 : Unpriced B82-28778

Hodgetts, Richard M.. Management : theory, process and practice / Richard M. Hodgetts. — 3rd ed. — Chicago ; London : Dryden, c1982. — xvii,542p : ill(some col.) ; 25cm. — (The Dryden press series in management)
Previous ed. published: Philadelphia : Saunders, 1979. — Includes bibliographies and index
ISBN 0-03-059881-8 : £17.95 B82-15355

Newman, William H.. The process of management : strategy, action, results. — 5th ed / William H. Newman, E. Kirby Warren, Jerome E. Schnee. — Englewood Cliffs ; London : Prentice-Hall, c1982. — xv,578p : ill (some col.),1col.map ; 25cm
Previous ed.: 1977. — Includes bibliographies and index
ISBN 0-13-723445-7 : £17.20 B82-23647

Stoner, James A. F.. Management / James A.F. Stoner. — 2nd ed. — London : Prentice-Hall, c1982. — xx,683p : ill(some col.) ; 24cm
Previous ed.: 1978. — Bibliography: p671. — Includes index
ISBN 0-13-549642-x (pbk) : £8.95 B82-16704

Tosi, Henry L.. Management / Henry L. Tosi, Stephen J. Carroll. — 2nd ed. — New York ; Chichester : Wiley, c1982. — xxiv,587p : ill (some col.) ; 25cm
Previous ed.: Chicago : St. Clair Press, 1976. — Includes index
ISBN 0-471-07884-0 : £17.75 B82-13295

658.4 — Management. Techniques — *Manuals*

Crosby, Philip B.. The art of getting your own sweet way / Philip B. Crosby. — 2nd ed. — New York ; London : McGraw-Hill, c1981. — ix,230p : ill ; 21cm
Previous ed.: 1972. — Text on lining papers. — Includes index
ISBN 0-07-014515-6 : £9.95 B82-02518

658.4 — Organisations. Crises. Management

De Greene, Kenyon B.. The adaptive organization : anticipation and management of crisis / Kenyon B. De Greene. — New York ; Chichester : Wiley, c1982. — xvii,394p ; 24cm
Bibliography: p373-381. — Includes index
ISBN 0-471-08296-1 : £24.75 B82-18226

658.4 — Organisations. Management

Moore, Franklin G.. The management of organizations / Franklin G. Moore. — New York ; Chichester : Wiley, c1982. — 592p ; 27cm. — (Wiley series in management)
Includes bibliographies and index
ISBN 0-471-87691-7 : £16.00 B82-27764

658.4 — Organisations. Management — *For business studies*

Capey, J. G.. People and work organizations / J.G. Capey, N.R. Carr. — London : Holt, Rinehart and Winston, c1982. — viii,255p : ill,1form ; 25cm. — (Holt business texts)
Includes index
ISBN 0-03-910365-x (pbk) : Unpriced : CIP rev.
B82-11747

Fearns, Peter. Business studies : an integrated approach / Peter Fearns. — London : Hodder and Stoughton, c1980. — x,243p : ill ; 24cm
Includes index
ISBN 0-340-25570-6 (pbk) : £3.95 : CIP rev.
B80-09308

658.4 — United States. Business firms. Crises. Management — *Manuals*

Bibeault, Donald B.. Corporate turnaround : how managers turn losers into winners / Donald B. Bibeault. — New York ; London : McGraw-Hill, c1982. — xix,406p ; 24cm
Bibliography: p373-392. — Includes index
ISBN 0-07-005190-9 : £17.50 B82-02283

Kibel, H. Ronald. How to turn around a financially troubled company / H. Ronald Kibel. — New York ; London : McGraw-Hill, c1982. — vii,182p : ill,forms ; 24cm
Includes index
ISBN 0-07-034540-6 : Unpriced B82-40610

658.4'032 — Personnel management. Systems design

Kaumeyer, Richard A.. Planning and using a total personnel system / Richard A. Kaumeyer, Jr. — New York ; London : Van Nostrand Reinhold, c1982. — xi,195p : ill,forms ; 24cm
Includes index
ISBN 0-442-21370-0 : £13.55 B82-14010

658.4'01 — Management. Policies

Steiner, George A.. Management policy and strategy / George A. Steiner, John B. Miner. — 2nd ed. — New York : Macmillan ; London : Collier Macmillan, c1982. — x,357p : ill ; 24cm
Previous ed.: 1977. — Bibliography: p317-342. — Includes index
ISBN 0-02-416790-8 (pbk) : Unpriced
B82-33693

658.4'012 — Business firms. Management. Long-range planning — *Conference proceedings*

Implementation of strategic planning / [edited by] Peter Lorange. — Englewood Cliffs ; London : Prentice-Hall, c1982. — vi,231p : ill ; 24cm
Based on conference proceedings. — Includes index
ISBN 0-13-451815-2 : £16.45 B82-16992

658.4'012 — Business firms. Planning

Shaw, W. C.. How to do a company plan and put it into action : a step-by-step guide for managers / W.C. Shaw. — London : Business Books, 1981. — 220p : ill,forms ; 25cm
Includes index
ISBN 0-09-145980-x : Unpriced : CIP rev.
B81-27370

658.4'012 — Companies. Management. Planning. Effectiveness. Improvement

Allen, Louis A.. Making managerial planning more effective / Louis A. Allen. — New York ; London : McGraw-Hill, c1982. — xvi,307p : ill ; 24cm
Bibliography: p283-290. — Includes index
ISBN 0-07-001078-1 : £18.95 B82-21128

658.4'012 — Corporate planning

Chandler, John. Techniques of scenario planning / John Chandler and Paul Cockle. — London : McGraw-Hill, c1982. — v,170p : ill ; 24cm
Includes index
ISBN 0-07-084570-0 : £13.95 : CIP rev.
B81-27378

Hussey, D. E.. Corporate planning theory and practice / by D.E. Hussey. — 2nd ed. — Oxford : Pergamon, 1982. — xvii,523p,[1] folded leaf of plates : ill ; 24cm
Previous ed.: 1974. — Includes bibliographies and index
ISBN 0-08-024073-9 : £17.50 : CIP rev.
B81-13451

Taylor, Bernard, *1931-*. The realities of planning / by Bernard Taylor and David Hussey with contributions from A. Pettigrew ... [et al.]. — Oxford : Pergamon, 1982. — x,252p : ill ; 24cm
Includes bibliographies and index
ISBN 0-08-022226-9 : £15.50 : CIP rev.
B81-23745

658.4'012 — Corporate planning — *Manuals*

Jones, Harry, *1911-*. Preparing company plans : a workbook for effective corporate planning. — 2nd ed. — Aldershot : Gower Press, Aug.1982. — [270]p. — (A Gower workbook)
Previous ed.: 1974
ISBN 0-566-02324-5 : £19.50 : CIP entry
B82-15886

658.4'012 — Great Britain. Business firms. Planning. Data

British planning databook. — Oxford : Pergamon, Nov.1982. — [169]p
ISBN 0-08-028170-2 : £20.00 : CIP entry
B82-40884

658.4'012 — Management. Planning

Davidmann, M.. Directing, adapting to change, deciding what needs to be done, planning ahead, getting results, evaluating progress / M. Davidmann. — [Stanmore] : Social Organisation Ltd., [c1981]. — 24leaves : ill ; 30cm. — (Community leadership and management)
ISBN 0-85192-015-2 (pbk) : £2.90 B82-17848

Nadler, Gerald. The planning and design approach / Gerald Nadler. — New York ; Chichester : Wiley, c1981. — xi,394p : ill ; 29cm
Includes index
ISBN 0-471-08102-7 : £33.00
Also classified at 658.4'032 B82-01030

658.4'012 — Management. Policies. Formulation

Paine, Frank T.. Organizational strategy and policy : text and cases / Frank T. Paine, William Naumes. — 3rd ed. — Chicago ; London : Dryden, c1982. — xiv,618p : ill,1map ; 25cm
Previous ed.: Philadelphia ; London : Saunders, 1978. — Includes index
ISBN 0-03-060067-7 : £17.95 B82-25409

658.4'012'024657 — Business firms. Corporate planning — *For accounting*

Hussey, D. E.. Corporate planning : an introduction for accountants / D.E. Hussey. — London : Institute of Chartered Accountants in England and Wales, c1981. — viii,102p : ill ; 22cm. — (The Accountant in industry and commerce)
Bibliography: p100-102
ISBN 0-85291-299-4 (pbk) : Unpriced
B82-08692

658.4'012'05 — Business firms. Policies. Social aspects — *Serials*

Research in corporate social performance and policy : an annual compilation of research. — Vol.1 (1978)-. — Greenwich, Conn. : JAI Press ; London (3 Henrietta St., WC2E 8LU) : Distributed by JAICON Press, 1978-. — v. ; 24cm
ISSN 0191-1937 = Research in corporate social performance and policy : £24.50
B82-02339

658.4'012'0722 — United States. Business firms. Management. Policies. Formulation — *Case studies*

Schellenberger, Robert E.. Policy formulation and strategy management : text and cases / Robert E. Schellenberger, Glenn Boseman. — 2nd ed. — New York ; Chichester : Wiley, c1982. — xvi,760p : ill,maps,plans ; 25cm. — (Wiley series in management, ISSN 0271-6046)
Previous ed.: 1978. — Includes bibliographies and index
ISBN 0-471-08215-5 : £19.20 B82-13288

658.4'012'0722 — United States. Management. Planning — *Case studies*

Hosmer, LaRue T.. Strategic management : text and cases on business policy / LaRue T. Hosmer. — Englewood Cliffs ; London : Prentice-Hall, c1982. — xviii,758p : ill,maps ; 25cm
ISBN 0-13-851063-6 : £17.20 B82-20089

658.4'012'0941 — Great Britain. Companies. Corporate planning

Corporate renewal or decline : some recent examples. — London (24 Buckingham Gate, S.W.1) : Corporate Consulting Group, [1982?]. — 32p ; 26cm
Unpriced (pbk) B82-21783

658.4'012'0973 — United States. Business firms. Policies. Formulation

Readings in business policy strategy from Business week. — 2nd ed. / edited by William F. Glueck, Neil H. Snyder. — New York ; London : McGraw-Hill, c1982. — xxii,263p : ill,1map,ports ; 28cm. — (McGraw-Hill series in management)
Previous ed.: published as Readings in business policy from Business week. 1978
ISBN 0-07-059540-2 (pbk) : £9.25 B82-29324

658.4'02 — Organisations. Teams. Management — *Manuals*

Woodcock, Mike. Organisation development through teambuilding : planning a cost effective strategy / Mike Woodcock and Dave Francis. — Aldershot : Gower, c1981. — ix,157p : ill ; 24cm
ISBN 0-566-02320-2 : Unpriced : CIP rev.
B81-28048

658.4'03 — Business enterprises. Risks. Management

Hertz, David B.. Risk analysis and its applications. — Chichester : Wiley, Sept.1982. — [250]p
ISBN 0-471-10145-1 : £15.00 : CIP entry
B82-19522

658.4'03 — Business firms. Management. Decision making. Quantitative methods

Seddon, V. J.. A first course in business analysis / V.J. Seddon, J.H. Butel. — London : Holt, Rinehart and Winston, c1982. — x,230p : ill ; 25cm. — (Holt business texts)
Includes index
ISBN 0-03-910353-6 (pbk) : £4.95 : CIP rev.
B82-10774

658.4'03 — Companies. Management auditing

Flesher, Dale L.. Independent auditor's guide to operational auditing / Dale L. Flesher, Stewart Siewert. — New York ; Chichester : Wiley, c1982. — ix,265p : ill ; 24cm. — (Modern accounting perspectives and practice)
Includes index
ISBN 0-471-09368-8 : £27.25 B82-35993

658.4'03 — Great Britain. Business firms. Information services. Management

Planning for information handling. — Aldershot : Gower, Dec.1982. — [180]p. — (The Office of the future ; no.6)
ISBN 0-566-03417-4 : £9.50 : CIP entry
B82-30057

658.4'03 — Management. Decision making

Jolly, W. P.. Management forecasting. — London : Teach Yourself Books, Nov.1982. — [160]p. — (Teach yourself books)
ISBN 0-340-26284-2 (pbk) : £2.75 : CIP entry
B82-28728

Leigh, Andrew. Decisions, decisions. — London : Institute of Personnel Management, Jan.1983. — [224]p
ISBN 0-85292-315-5 (pbk) : £7.95 : CIP entry
B82-39301

658.4'03 — Management. Decision making & problem solving

Adair, John, *1934-*. Training for decisions / John Adair. — Farnborough : Gower, 1978, c1971 (1979 [printing]). — 166p : ill ; 23cm
Originally published: London : Macdonald, 1971. — Includes index
ISBN 0-566-02111-0 : Unpriced : CIP rev.
B78-25795

Plunkett, Lorne C.. The proactive manager : the complete book of problem solving and decision making / Lorne C. Plunkett, Guy A. Hale. — New York ; Chichester : Wiley, c1982. — xii,221p : ill,1plan,forms ; 25cm
Bibliography: p201. — Includes index
ISBN 0-471-08509-x : £17.75 B82-13358

658.4'03 — Management. Decision making. Quantitative methods

Powell, John, *1945-*. Quantitative decision making / John Powell and John Harris. — Harlow : Longman, 1982. — viii,224p : ill ; 24cm. — (Understanding business)
Includes index
ISBN 0-582-35545-1 (pbk) : £4.50 B82-36090

Render, Barry. Quantitative analysis for management / Barry Render, Ralph M. Stair, Jr. — Boston [Mass.] ; London : Allyn and Bacon, c1982. — xiv,674p : ill ; 25cm + Instructor's manual(363p : ill ; 28cm : pbk)
Includes index
ISBN 0-205-07619-x : Unpriced
ISBN 0-205-07620-3 (Instructor's manual)
B82-26767

658.4'03 — Management. Decision making. Quantitative methods — *Questions & answers*

Harpell, John L.. Study guide to accompany Render and Stair's Quantitative analysis for management / John L. Harpell. — Boston ; London : Allyn and Bacon, c1982. — 261p : ill ; 24cm
ISBN 0-205-07621-1 (pbk) : Unpriced
B82-26937

658.4'03 — Management. Problem solving

De Bono, Edward. Edward De Bono's atlas of management thinking. — London : Temple Smith, Sept.1981. — [224]p
ISBN 0-85117-213-x : £9.95 : CIP entry
B81-26687

658.4'03 — Organisations. Management. Decision making

Heirs, Ben. The mind of the organization / Ben Heirs and Gordon Pehrson. — Rev. ed. — New York ; London : Harper & Row, 1982. — xxii,140p ; 22cm
Previous ed.: 1977
ISBN 0-06-337026-3 : £6.95 B82-31811

658.4'03 — Organisations. Management. Decision making *continuation*
McLaren, Robert I.. Organizational dilemmas / Robert I. McLaren. — Chichester : Wiley, c1982. — ix,130p : ill ; 24cm
Includes index
ISBN 0-471-10155-9 : £9.50 : CIP rev.
B82-03609

658.4'03 — Organisations. Management. Decision making. Quantitative methods
Saaty, Thomas L.. The logic of priorities : applications in business, energy, health and transportation / Thomas L. Saaty, Luis G. Vargas. — Boston ; London : Kluwer-Nijhoff, c1982. — xiv,299p : ill ; 24cm. — (International series in management science/operations research)
Includes bibliographies and index
ISBN 0-89838-071-5 (cased) : Unpriced
ISBN 0-89838-078-2 (pbk) : Unpriced
B82-16392

658.4'03 — Risks. Assessment — *Conference proceedings*
Measurement of Risks *(Conference : 1980 : University of Rochester)*. Measurement of risks / [proceedings of the Thirteenth Rochester International Conference on Environmental Toxicity, entitled Measurement of Risks, held June 2-4, 1980, at the University of Rochester, Rochester, New York] ; edited by George G. Berg and H. David Maillie. — New York ; London : Plenum, c1981. — x,550p : ill,ports ; 26cm. — (Environmental science research ; v.21)
Includes index
ISBN 0-306-40818-x : Unpriced B82-13920

658.4'03'018 — Risks. Management. Decision making. Methodology
Acceptable risk / Baruch Fischoff ... [et al.]. — Cambridge : Cambridge University Press, 1981. — xv,185p : ill ; 24cm
Bibliography: p172-181. — Includes index
ISBN 0-521-24164-2 : £15.00 B82-36429

658.4'03'028 — Business firms. Management. Decision making. Techniques
Park, William R.. Strategic analysis for venture evaluation : the SAVE approach to business decisions / W.R. Park, J.B. Maille. — New York ; London : Van Nostrand Reinhold, c1982. — xv,179p : ill ; 24cm
Includes index
ISBN 0-442-24507-6 : £16.95 B82-07881

658.4'03'02854 — Management. Decision making. Applications of digital computer systems
Decision support systems : issues and challenges : proceedings of an international task force meeting June 23-25, 1980 / Göran Fick, Ralph H. Sprague Jr., editors. — Oxford : Pergamon, 1980. — viii,189p : ill ; 26cm. — (IIASA proceedings series ; v.11)
Includes bibliographies
ISBN 0-08-027321-1 : £12.50 : CIP rev.
B80-35218

Sprague, Ralph H.. Building effective decision support systems / Ralph H. Sprague, Jr., Eric D. Carlson. — Englewood Cliffs ; London : Prentice-Hall, c1982. — xx,329p : ill ; 24cm
Includes bibliographies and index
ISBN 0-13-086215-0 : £18.70 B82-33773

658.4'03'0722 — Management. Decision making — *Case studies*
Dyer, James S.. Management science/operations research : cases and readings / James S. Dyer, Roy D. Shapiro. — New York ; Chichester : Wiley, c1982. — xiii,388p : ill,maps ; 24cm
ISBN 0-471-09757-8 (pbk) : £11.50
B82-22639

658.4'032 — Business firms. Systems design
Jackson, Michael. System development. — London : Prentice-Hall, Jan.1983. — [368]p
ISBN 0-13-880328-5 : £15.95 : CIP entry
B82-33472

658.4'032 — Critical path analysis
Palmer, Colin F.. Network planning and control / by Colin F. Palmer. — London : Gee, 1980. — 60p : ill ; 24cm. — (A Gee study book)
ISBN 0-85258-193-9 (corrected : pbk) : £3.25
B82-12113

658.4'032 — Critical path analysis — *Programmed instructions*
Paice, D. A.. Critical path analysis : basic techniques : a programmed text / D.A. Paice. — London : Longman, 1982. — vi,65p : ill ; 21cm
ISBN 0-582-41304-4 (pbk) : £1.95 : CIP rev.
B82-06928

658.4'032 — Management. Decision making. Use of stochastic networks
Lee, Sang M.. Network analysis for management decisions : a stochastic approach / Sang M. Lee, Gerald L. Moeller, Lester A. Digman. — Boston, [Mass.] ; London : Kluwer-Nijhoff, c1982. — vii,320p : ill ; 24cm. — (International series in management science/operations reseach)
Bibliography: p311-313. — Includes index
ISBN 0-89838-077-4 : Unpriced B82-15434

658.4'032 — Management. Systems analysis
Smith, August W.. Management systems : analyses and applications / August W. Smith. — Chicago ; London : Dryden, c1982. — 429p : ill ; 25cm
Bibliography: p398-407. — Includes index
ISBN 0-03-056731-9 : £19.95 B82-29500

658.4'032 — Management. Systems design
Nadler, Gerald. The planning and design approach / Gerald Nadler. — New York ; Chichester : Wiley, c1981. — xi,394p : ill ; 29cm
Includes index
ISBN 0-471-08102-7 : £33.00
Primary classification 658.4'012 B82-01030

658.4'032 — Work study
Grant, Alan. Against the clock. — London : Pluto Press, Feb.1983. — [176]p. — (Workers' handbooks)
ISBN 0-86104-369-3 (pbk) : £4.95 : CIP entry
B82-39287

658.4'033 — Management. Decision making. Mathematical models
Byrd, Jack. Decision models for management / Jack Byrd, Jr., L. Ted Moore. — New York ; London : McGraw-Hill, c1982. — xvi,407p : ill,1form ; 25cm. — (McGraw-Hill series in quantitative methods for management)
Includes index
ISBN 0-07-009511-6 : £18.95 B82-22765

658.4'033 — Management. Decision making. Use of mathematical models
Dunn, Robert A.. Management science : a practical approach to decision making / Robert A. Dunn, Kenneth D. Ramsing. — New York : Macmillan ; London : Collier Macmillan, c1981. — x,527p : ill ; 25cm
Includes bibliographies and index
ISBN 0-02-977550-7 (pbk) : Unpriced
B82-33690

Pinney, William E.. Management sciences : an introduction to quantitative analysis for management / William F. Pinney, Donald B. McWilliams. — New York ; London : Harper & Row, c1982. — xxi,568p : ill ; 24cm
Bibliography: p549-553. — Includes index
ISBN 0-06-045222-6 : Unpriced B82-02194

658.4'033 — Management. Mathematical models
Quantitative planning and control : essays in honor of William Wager Cooper on the occasion of his 65th birthday / edited by Yuji Ijiri, Andrew B. Whinston. — New York ; London : Academic Press, 1979. — xxx,344p : ill ; 24cm
Includes bibliographies
ISBN 0-12-370450-2 : £24.80 B82-07737

Randall, K. V.. Managerial economics / Ken Randall. — London : Heinemann Educational, 1982. — 184p : ill ; 25cm
Bibliography: p177-179. — Includes index
ISBN 0-435-84540-3 (pbk) : £4.95 : CIP rev.
B81-27435

658.4'033 — Management. Multiple objective decision making. Mathematical models
Zeleny, Milan. Multiple criteria decision making / Milan Zeleny. — New York ; London : McGraw-Hill, c1982. — xxii,563p : ill ; 25cm. — (McGraw-Hill series in quantitative methods for management)
Includes bibliographies and index
ISBN 0-07-072795-3 : £15.95 B82-00528

658.4'034 — Management. Operations research
Harper, W. M.. Operational research. — 2nd ed. / W.M. Harper, H.C. Lim. — Plymouth : Macdonald & Evans, 1982. — x,310p ; 18cm. — (The M & E handbook series)
Previous ed.: 1975. — Includes index
ISBN 0-7121-1539-0 (pbk) : £3.95 B82-35428

658.4'0352 — Industries. Management. Simulation games: MANSYM — *Manuals*
Schellenberger, Robert E.. Mansym III : a dynamic management simulator with decision support system / Robert Schellenberger, Glenn Boseman, Brian T. Schellenberger. — Rev. — New York ; Chichester : Wiley, 1982. — 94p : forms ; 28cm
Previous ed.: i.e. 2nd ed.: Wayne, Pa. : Management Development Institute, 1969
ISBN 0-471-08581-2 (pbk) : £8.85 B82-13390

658.4'0353 — Management. Simulation games
Elgood, Chris. Handbook of management games / Chris Elgood. — 2nd ed. — Aldershot : Gower, 1981. — viii,246p : ill ; 23cm
Previous ed.: 1976
ISBN 0-566-02229-x : Unpriced : CIP rev.
B81-28847

658.4'0353 — Management. Simulation games — *Conference proceedings*
Simulation in management and business education. — London : Kogan Page, July 1982. — [160]p. — (Perspectives on academic gaming ; 7)
Conference proceedings
ISBN 0-85038-583-0 : £14.50 : CIP entry
B82-21108

658.4'0354 — Decision analysis
Buchanan, J. T.. Discrete and dynamic decision analysis. — Chichester : Wiley, July 1982. — [288]p
ISBN 0-471-10130-3 (cased) : £16.00 : CIP entry
ISBN 0-471-10131-1 (pbk) : £7.90 B82-13249

Multiple criteria analysis : operational methods / edited by Peter Nijkamp and Jaap Spronk. — Aldershot : Gower, c1981. — xii,271p : ill ; 24cm
Conference papers. — Includes bibliographies
ISBN 0-566-00412-7 : Unpriced B82-18029

658.4'0354'0245 — Decision analysis — *For science and technology*
Bunn, Derek W.. Analysis for optimal decisions. — Chichester : Wiley, Sept.1982. — [272]p
ISBN 0-471-10132-x (cased) : £15.00 : CIP entry
ISBN 0-471-10133-8 (pbk) : £8.75 B82-19521

658.4'038 — Business firms. Information services — *For management*
Pritchard, J. A. T.. Planning office automation — information management systems. — Manchester : NCC Publications, Oct.1982. — [260]p
ISBN 0-85012-366-6 (pbk) : £12.50 : CIP entry
B82-24269

658.4'038 — Organisations. Information services. Management aspects — *Conference proceedings*
Information management and organisational change / [proceedings of an ASLIB conference held at the London Tara Hotel on 6-8 April 1981] ; edited by Heather Taylor. — London : ASLIB, [1981]. — 113p : ill ; 30cm
Bibliography: p109-113
ISBN 0-85142-148-2 (pbk) : Unpriced
B82-17733

658.4'0383 — Systems design. Security aspects
Squires, T.. Security in systems design. — Manchester : NCC Publications, Apr.1981. — [54]p
ISBN 0-85012-304-6 (pbk) : CIP entry
B81-12393

658.4'0388 — Business firms. Information systems. Management

Synnott, William R.. Information resource management : opportunities and strategies for the 1980s / William R. Synnott, William H. Gruber. — New York ; Chichester : Wiley, c1981. — ix,356p : ill,forms ; 25cm
Includes index
ISBN 0-471-09451-x : £18.50 B82-12294

658.4'0388 — Great Britain. Business firms. Management. Information systems. Applications of digital computer systems — *Serials*

Business information technology. — Issue 1 (1981)-. — Ruislip (Audit House, Field End Rd, Ruislip, Middx HA4 9LT) : Business Publication[s], 1981-. — v. : ill ; 30cm
Monthly. — Description based on: Issue 6 (Jan. 1982)
ISSN 0263-175x = Business information technology : £18.00 per year B82-18547

658.4'0388 — Management. Information systems

Lucas, Henry C.. Information systems concepts for management / Henry C. Lucas, Jr. — 2nd ed. — New York ; London : McGraw-Hill, c1982. — 515p : ill ; 25cm. — (McGraw-Hill series in management information systems)
Previous ed.: 1978. — Bibliography: p503-507. — Includes index
ISBN 0-07-038924-1 : £19.75 B82-22878

McCosh, Andrew M.. Developing managerial information systems / Andrew M. McCosh, Mawdudur Rahman and Michael J. Earl. — London : Macmillan, 1981. — xi,387p : ill ; 23cm
Includes bibliographies and index
ISBN 0-333-23374-3 : £25.00 : CIP rev. B80-18414

McLeod, Raymond. Management information systems / Raymond McLeod, Jr.. — Chicago ; Henley-on-Thames : Science Research Associates, c1979. — xvii,510p : ill,forms ; 25cm
Bibliography: p501-506. — Includes index
ISBN 0-574-21245-0 : £12.05 B82-02118

658.4'0388 — Management. Information systems. Systems analysis

Tricker, R. I.. Management information and control systems. — 2nd ed. — Chichester : Wiley, Nov.1982. — [400]p
Previous ed.: 1976
ISBN 0-471-10450-7 (cased) : £15.00 : CIP entry
ISBN 0-471-90020-6 (pbk) : £8.75 B82-27548

658.4'0388 — Organisations. Management. Information systems. Long-range planning

Long, Larry E.. Design and strategy for corporate information services : MIS long-range planning / Larry E. Long. — Englewood Cliffs, N.J. ; London : Prentice-Hall, c1982. — xii,186p : ill,forms ; 25cm
Includes index
ISBN 0-13-201707-5 : Unpriced B82-28344

658.4'0388 — Small firms. Management. Information systems: Microcomputer systems

Haueisen, William D.. Business systems for microcomputers : concepts, design, and implementation / William D. Haueisen, James L. Camp. — Englewood Cliffs ; London : Prentice-Hall, c1982. — xvi,416p : ill ; 25cm. — (Prentice-Hall series in data processing management)
Includes index
ISBN 0-13-107805-4 : Unpriced B82-37731

658.4'0388'02854 — Business firms. Management. Information systems. Applications of digital computer systems

McLeod, Raymond. Computerized business information systems : an introduction to data processing / Raymond McLeod, Jr, Irvine Forkner. — New York ; Chichester : Wiley, c1982. — xxii,583p : il(some col.),forms ; 25cm
Includes index
ISBN 0-471-02575-5 : £15.30 B82-18058

658.4'04 — Data processing systems. Project management

Bentley, Colin. Computer project management / Colin Bentley. — London : Heyden, c1982. — ix,110p : ill,forms ; 25cm. — (Computing science series)
Includes index
ISBN 0-85501-713-9 : £13.00 : CIP rev. B82-03125

658.4'04 — Project management

The **Implementation** of project management : the professional's handbook / edited by Linn C. Stuckenbruck. — Reading, Mass. ; London : Addison-Wesley, 1981. — xii,254p : ill ; 29cm
Title page: Project Management Institute. — Includes bibliographies and index
ISBN 0-201-07260-2 : £20.00 B82-37945

Kerzner, Harold. Project management for executives / Harold Kerzner. — New York ; London : Van Nostrand Reinhold, c1982. — xiv,716p : ill,forms ; 24cm
Bibliography: p667-682. — Includes index
ISBN 0-442-25920-4 : £24.25 B82-18923

Lester, A.. Project planning and control. — London : Butterworths, Sept.1982. — [240]p
ISBN 0-408-01164-5 (pbk) : £12.00 : CIP entry B82-19217

Turner, W. S.. Project auditing methodology / W.S. Turner III. — Amsterdam ; Oxford : North-Holland Publishing, 1980. — xv,454p : ill,forms ; 23cm
Bibliography: p432-446. — Includes index
ISBN 0-444-86018-5 : £19.11 B82-40701

658.4'04 — Project management. Failure — *Case studies*

Kharbanda, O. P.. How to learn from project disasters. — Aldershot : Gower, Apr.1982. — [270]p
ISBN 0-566-02340-7 : £15.00 : CIP entry B82-03624

658.4'04'078 — Project management. Teaching aids — *Case studies*

MacArthur, J. D.. Case studies in teaching project analysis : experience from the project planning centre / by J.D. MacArthur, D.J. Potts and F.A. Wilson. — [Bradford] : University of Bradford Project Planning Centre for Developing Countries, 1981. — 29p ; 30cm. — (Teaching materials series, ISSN 0262-5164 ; no.1)
Bibliography: p29
ISBN 0-901945-42-0 (pbk) : Unpriced B82-23562

658.4'06 — Business firms. Innovation. Management

Vedin, Bengt-Arne. Creativity management in media industry applied to technology / Bengt-Arne Vedin. — Lund : Studentlitteratur ; Bromley : Chartwell-Bratt, 1980. — 97p : ill ; 23cm
ISBN 0-86238-002-2 (pbk) : Unpriced B82-36841

Vedin, Bengt-Arne. Innovation organization : from practice to theory and back / Bengt-Arne Vedin. — Lund : Studentlitteratur ; Bromley : Chartwell-Bratt, 1980. — 92p : ill ; 23cm
ISBN 0-86238-005-7 (pbk) : Unpriced B82-36842

Vedin, Bengt-Arne. Large company organization and radical product innovation / Bengt-Arne Vedin. — Lund : Studentlitteratur ; Bromley : Chartwell-Bratt, 1980. — 129p : ill ; 23cm
ISBN 0-86238-004-9 (pbk) : Unpriced B82-36840

658.4'06 — Companies. Organisational change. Management

Asplund, Gisèle. An integrated development strategy / Gisèle Asplund and Göran Asplund. — Chichester : Wiley, c1982. — x,131p : ill ; 24cm
Bibliography: p127. — Includes index
ISBN 0-471-10075-7 : £11.00 : CIP rev. B82-01106

658.4'06 — Organisation development

Harvey, Donald F.. An experiential approach to organization development / Donald F. Harvey, Donald R. Brown. — 2nd ed. — Englewood Cliffs ; London : Prentice-Hall, c1982. — xviii,477p : ill ; 24cm
Previous ed.: 1976. — Includes index
ISBN 0-13-295360-9 (pbk) : £14.95 B82-33769

Organization development : progress and perspectives / edited by Daniel Robey, Steven Altman. — New York : Macmillan ; London : Collier Macmillan, c1982. — vi,457p : ill ; 24cm
Includes bibliographies
ISBN 0-02-471540-9 (pbk) : £10.95 B82-19511

658.4'06 — Organisational change. Management aspects

Fordyce, Jack K.. Managing with people : a manager's handbook of organization development methods / Jack K. Fordyce, Raymond Weil. — 2nd ed. — Reading, Mass. ; London : Addison-Wesley, c1979. — xiii,206p : ill ; 24cm
Previous ed.: 1971
ISBN 0-201-02031-9 (pbk) : Unpriced B82-27982

Organization development in transition : evidence of an evolving profession / A.J. McLean ... [et al.]. — Chichester : Wiley, c1982. — vii,131p : 1ill ; 24cm
Includes bibliographies and index
ISBN 0-471-10142-7 : £9.75 : CIP rev. B82-03608

658.4'06 — Organisations. Development. Assessment

Carnall, Colin. The evaluation of organisation change. — Aldershot : Gower, June 1982. — [136]p
ISBN 0-566-00519-0 : £12.50 : CIP entry B82-09731

658.4'062 — Business firms. Applications of microelectronic devices. Management aspects

The **Managerial** implications of microelectronics / edited by Brian C. Twiss. — London : Macmillan, 1981. — xix,216p : ill ; 23cm
Includes bibliographies and index
ISBN 0-333-28090-3 : £20.00 B82-10809

658.4'063'0973 — United States. Industries. Technological innovation. Management aspects

Readings in the management of innovation / [edited by] Michael L. Tushman, William L. Moore. — Boston, [Mass.] ; London : Pitman, c1982. — xiii,652p : ill ; 24cm
Includes bibliographies and index
ISBN 0-273-01786-1 (pbk) : £15.00 B82-33658

658.4'07111 — Executives. Recruitment. Role of executive search firms

McKinnon, Robert. Head hunters / Robert McKinnon. — Newbury : Scope, 1982. — 172p ; 23cm
ISBN 0-906619-10-6 : £9.75 : CIP rev. B82-06534

658.4'07111'0941 — Great Britain. Executives. Recruitment — *Serials*

The **Journal** of executive recruitment. — Vol.1, no.1 (Jan 1982)-. — London (85 Jermyn St, SW1Y 6JD) : Baird Pub., 1982-. — v. : ill,ports ; 30cm
Monthly. — Description based on: Vol. 1, no.6 (June 1982)
ISSN 0262-4370 = Journal of executive recruitment : £60.00 per year B82-38523

658.4'07124 — Great Britain. Women managers. Training — *Conference proceedings*

Seminar-workshop on how management training can meet the needs of women and the complementary needs of employers operating an equal opportunity policy : held at Danbury Park Essex 31 October-2 November 1980 / report by Ian Cunningham and Virginia Novarra. — [Chelmsford] ([Danbury Park, Danbury, Chelmsford, Essex, CM3 4AT]) : Anglian Regional Management Centre, [1982?]. — 38leaves ; 30cm
Unpriced (pbk) B82-16597

658.4'07124 — Management assessment centres

Wilkinson, Brian. The role of assessment centres in a manager's development / Brian Wilkinson. — Bristol : South West Regional Management Centre, 1978. — 17p : ill ; 29cm. — (Occasional paper series / South West Regional Management Centre ; v.I, no.2)
At head of title: South West Regional Management Centre. — Bibliography: p15-17
ISBN 0-904951-16-2 (spiral) : Unpriced
B82-17704

658.4'07124 — Managers. Training

Management development : context and strategies / edited by John Burgoyne and Roger Stuart. — Farnborough : Gower, c1978. — xi,142p : ill ; 23cm. — (A Personnel review monograph)
Includes bibliographies
ISBN 0-566-02101-3 : Unpriced : CIP rev.
B78-21332

New approaches to management development / edited by Bruce Nixon. — Aldershot : Gower for the Association of Teachers of Management, c1981. — xviii,111p : ill ; 23cm
ISBN 0-566-02290-7 : Unpriced : CIP rev.
B81-31820

Revans, R. W.. The origins and growth of action learning / Reginald W. Revans. — Lund : Studentlitteratur ; Bromley : Chartwell-Bratt, 1982. — xi,846p : ill ; 23cm
Bibliography: p818-819. — Includes index
ISBN 0-86238-020-0 : Unpriced B82-36835

658.4'07124 — Managers. Training. Self-development

Tack, Alfred. Executive development / Alfred Tack. — Tadworth : World's Work, c1981. — 175p ; 19cm. — (Cedar books)
Includes index
ISBN 0-437-95162-6 (pbk) : £2.50 B82-09262

658.4'07124'019 — Managers. Training. Use of Bender Gestalt Test

Clark, Neil. The Gestalt approach : an introduction for managers and trainers / Neil Clark and Tony Fraser. — Horsham : Roffey Park Management College, [1982]. — 42p : ill ; 21cm
Bibliography: p40-42
ISBN 0-907416-01-2 (pbk) : Unpriced
B82-22879

658.4'07124'05 — Management skills. Development — *Serials*

The Journal of management development. — Vol.1, no.1 (1982)-. — Bradford : MCB Publications, 1982-. — v. : ill ; 25cm
Quarterly
ISSN 0262-1711 = Journal of management development : Unpriced B82-31719

658.4'07124'0941 — Great Britain. Industries. Managers. Training & development — *Forecasts*

Development managers for the 1980s / edited by Cary L. Cooper. — London : Macmillan, 1981. — xxxvii,149p : ill ; 23cm
Includes index
ISBN 0-333-25510-0 : £15.00
Also classified at 658.4'07124'0973 B82-11867

658.4'07124'0973 — United States. Industries. Managers. Training & development — *Forecasts*

Development managers for the 1980s / edited by Cary L. Cooper. — London : Macmillan, 1981. — xxxvii,149p : ill ; 23cm
Includes index
ISBN 0-333-25510-0 : £15.00
Primary classification 658.4'07124'0941
B82-11867

658.4'071244 — Great Britain. Managers. Industrial training. Curriculum subjects: Industrial relations

Industrial relations training : methods guide. — Gloucester (Barton House, Barton St., Gloucester GK1 1QQ) : Food, Drink and Tobacco Industry Training Board, [198-?]. — 32p ; 30x21cm
Cover title
£2.00 (pbk) B82-27616

Industrial relations training : a systematic approach. — Gloucester (Barton House, Barton St., Gloucester GL1 1QQ) : Food, Drink and Tobacco Industry Training Board, [198-?]. — 16p ; 30cm
£2.00 (unbound) B82-27617

658.4'071245 — Great Britain. Hotel & catering industries. Managers. Training requirements

Training guidelines for employee relations / HCITB. — Wembley : HCITB, 1982. — 32p : 1map ; 21cm
ISBN 0-7033-0019-9 (pbk) : Unpriced
B82-27285

658.4'07125 — Multinational companies. Managers. Evaluation

Miller, Elwood L.. Responsibility accounting and performance evaluations / Elwood L. Miller. — New York ; London : Van Nostrand Reinhold, c1982. — xiii,238p : ill ; 24cm
Bibliography: p223-227. — Includes index
ISBN 0-442-28818-2 : £16.95 B82-18926

658.4'07125 — Potential managers. Assessment

Cox, Philip S.. Psychological measurement and management potential : a review / Philip S. Cox. — Bristol : South West Regional Management Centre, 1978. — 23,14p ; 29cm. — (Occasional paper series / South West Regional Management Centre ; v.I, no.1)
At head of title: South West Regional Management Centre. — Bibliography: p14
ISBN 0-904951-17-0 (spiral) : Unpriced
B82-17705

658.4'08 — Business firms. Social responsibility

Davidmann, M.. Social responsibility, profits and social accountability, incidents, disasters and catastrophes, the world-wide struggle for social accountability, community aims and community leadership / M. Davidmann. — [Stanmore] : Social Organisation Ltd., [c1981]. — 57leaves ; 30cm. — (Community leadership and management)
ISBN 0-85192-021-7 (pbk) : £4.95 B82-17854

658.4'08'0973 — United States. Companies. Social responsibility

Molander, Earl A.. Responsive capitalism : case studies in corporate social conduct / Earl A. Molander with the assistance of David L. Arthur. — New York ; London : McGraw-Hill, c1980. — xiv,299p : ill,maps ; 24cm
Bibliography: p284-291. — Includes index
ISBN 0-07-042658-9 (pbk) : Unpriced
B82-39545

Steckmest, Francis W.. Corporate performance : the key to public trust / by Francis W. Steckmest with a resource and review committee for the Business Roundtable. — New York ; London : McGraw-Hill, c1982. — xxi,295p ; 24cm
Includes index
ISBN 0-07-009306-7 : £12.95 B82-24554

658.4'08'0973 — United States. Industries. Social responsibility — *For management*

Social forces and the manager : readings and cases / [compiled by] Willliam R. Allen, Louis K. Bragaw, Jr. — New York ; Chichester : Wiley, c1982. — xiv,502p : ill ; 24cm. — (Wiley series in management)
Includes bibliographies
ISBN 0-471-08611-8 (pbk) : £11.75
B82-13988

658.4'09 — Business firms. Managers. Self-development

Woodcock, Mike. The unblocked manager : a practical guide to self-development / Mike Woodcock and Dave Francis. — Aldershot : Gower, c1982. — ix,241p : ill,forms ; 24cm
Includes bibliographies
ISBN 0-566-02373-3 : Unpriced : CIP rev.
B82-02662

658.4'092 — Managers. Leadership. Self-appraisal — *Programmed instructions*

Fiedler, Fred E.. Improving leadership effectiveness : the leader match concept / Fred E. Fiedler, Martin M. Chemers with Linda Mahar. — Rev ed. — New York ; London : Wiley, c1977. — viii,219p : ill ; 26cm. — (A Self-teaching guide)
Previous ed.: 1976
ISBN 0-471-25811-3 (pbk) : Unpriced
B82-16013

658.4'093 — Industries. Managers. Time. Allocation — *Manuals*

White, T. Kenneth. The technical connection : the how to's of time management for the technical manager / T. Kenneth White. — New York ; Chichester : Wiley, c1981. — xi,203p ; 24cm
ISBN 0-471-94034-8 : £18.50 B82-11584

658.4'093 — Organisations. Executives. Time. Allocation — *Manuals*

Januz, Lauren Robert. Time-management for executives : a handbook from the editors of Execu time / Lauren Robert Januz and Susan K. Jones. — London : Sidgwick & Jackson, 1982. — 232p ; 22cm
Originally published: New York : Scribner, 1981. — Bibliography: p227-232
ISBN 0-283-98851-7 : £7.95 B82-20332

658.4'093 — Organisations. Managers. Time. Allocation — *Manuals*

Pernet, Roy. Effective use of time / Roy Pernet. — London : Industrial Society, 1979 (1980 [printing]). — 39p : ill ; 21cm. — (Notes for managers ; no.31)
Bibliography: p37
ISBN 0-85290-173-9 (pbk) : Unpriced
B82-17401

Reynolds, Helen. Executive time management : getting 12 hours' work out of an 8-hour day / Helen Reynolds & Mary E. Tramel. — Aldershot : Gower, [198-]. — xiv,174p : ill ; 24cm
Originally published: Englewood Cliffs : Prentice-Hall, 1979
ISBN 0-566-02297-4 : Unpriced : CIP rev.
B81-14883

658.4'094 — Managers. Assertive behaviour — *Manuals*

Back, Ken. Assertiveness at work : a practical guide to handling awkward situations / Ken and Kate Back. — London : McGraw-Hill, c1982. — x,150p ; 24cm
Includes index
ISBN 0-07-084576-x : £8.95 : CIP rev.
B82-08431

658.4'2 — Business firms. Managing directors. Role

Copeman, George. The managing director. — 2nd ed. — London : Business Books, July 1982. — [276]p
Previous ed.: Newton Abbot : David and Charles, 1978
ISBN 0-09-147280-6 : £12.00 : CIP entry
B82-12420

658.4'2'088042 — United States. Companies. Women managers. Discrimination by companies

Fernandez, John P.. Racism and sexism in corporate life : changing values in American business / John P. Fernandez. — Lexington, Mass. : Lexington Books, c1981 ; [Aldershot] : Gower [distributor], 1982. — xxiii,359p : ill ; 24cm
Bibliography: p333-346. — Includes index
ISBN 0-669-04477-6 : £19.50
Primary classification 658.4'2'089 B82-08794

658.4'2'089 — United States. Companies. Ethnic minority managers. Discrimination by companies

Fernandez, John P.. Racism and sexism in corporate life : changing values in American business / John P. Fernandez. — Lexington, Mass. : Lexington Books, c1981 ; [Aldershot] : Gower [distributor], 1982. — xxiii,359p : ill ; 24cm
Bibliography: p333-346. — Includes index
ISBN 0-669-04477-6 : £19.50
Also classified at 658.4'2'088042 B82-08794

658.4'2'0941 — Great Britain. Companies. Non-executive directors. Role

The **Non-executive** director in the U.K.. — London (4 Buckingham Gate, SW1) : Corporate Consulting Group, [1982?]. — 19p ; 26cm
Unpriced (pbk) B82-21845

658.4'2'0941 — Great Britain. Managers

Managers in focus : the British manager in the early 1980's / Michael Poole ... [et al.]. — Aldershot : Gower, c1981. — viii,184p : ill,1form ; 23cm
Bibliography: p169-178. — Includes index
ISBN 0-566-00468-2 : Unpriced : CIP rev. B81-34280

658.4'22 — Companies. Boards of directors. Accountability

Management accountability and corporate governance : selected readings / edited by Kenneth Midgley. — London : Macmillan, 1982. — xvii,229p ; 23cm
Conference papers. — Includes index
ISBN 0-333-31200-7 : £20.00 B82-28526

658.4'22 — Great Britain. Companies. Boards of directors. Professional conduct

Guidelines for directors : recommendations and guidance on boardroom practice / prepared under the supervision of the Company Affairs Committee of the Institute of Directors, under the chairmanship of Sir Philip de Zulueta ; with a foreword by Lord Erroll of Hale. — New ed. — [London] : Institute of Directors, 1982. — 72p ; 22cm
Previous ed.: i.e. Repr. with revisions. 1980. — Bibliography: p70-72
£5.95 (pbk) B82-21419

658.4'22'0973 — United States. Companies. Boards of directors

The **Changing** boardroom : making policy and profits in an age of corporate citizenship / edited by George C. Greanias and Duane Windsor. — Houston ; London : Gulf, c1982. — ix,148p ; 22cm
Conference papers. — Includes index
ISBN 0-87201-103-8 : Unpriced B82-29167

658.4'5 — Great Britain. Business firms. Relations with mass media — *Manuals — For businessmen*

The **Headline** business : a businessman's guide to working with the media / [compiled by Squire Barraclough for the CBI Information Directorate]. — [London] : Confederation of British Industry in association with Abbey Life Assurance Co. Ltd., c1981. — 112p : ill ; 21cm
Cover title
£2.50 (pbk)
Also classified at 302.2'34'0941 B82-06373

658.4'5 — Management. Communication

Without bias : a guidebook for non-discriminatory communication / International Association of Business Communicators. — 2nd ed. — New York ; Chichester : Wiley, c1982. — viii,200p : ill ; 22cm
Editor: Judy E. Pickens. — Previous ed.: San Francisco : International Association of Business Communicators, 1977. — Bibliography: p184-192. — Includes index
ISBN 0-471-08561-8 : £8.00 B82-16533

658.4'5 — Management. Negotiation — *For industrial training — For hotel & catering industries*

Tutor's manual for training in negotiating and the development of influencing skills. — Wembley : HCITB, 1981. — 1v.(loose-leaf) : ill ; 33cm + Workshop documentation(25 sheets ; 19cm)
Cover title: Getting a good deal. — 7 cards in pocket
ISBN 0-7033-0008-3 : £40.00 B82-09021

658.4'5 — Organisations. Communication

Phillips, Gerald M.. Communicating in organizations / Gerald M. Phillips. — New York : Macmillan ; London : Collier Macmillan, c1982. — xii,366p : ill ; 25cm
Includes bibliographies and index
ISBN 0-02-395160-5 : Unpriced B82-35273

658.4'5 — Organisations. Management. Communication

Adair, John, *1934-*. Training for communication / John Adair. — Aldershot : Gower, 1978, c1973 (1981 [printing]). — 205p ; 23cm
Originally published: London : Macdonald, 1973. — Includes bibliographies and index
ISBN 0-566-02112-9 : Unpriced B82-28765

May, John, *19---*. How to make effective business presentations : and win!. — London : McGraw-Hill, Feb.1983. — [160]p
ISBN 0-07-084587-5 (pbk) : £7.95 : CIP entry B82-37663

Myers, Michele Tolela. Managing by communication : an organizational approach / Michele Tolela Myers, Gail E. Myers. — New York ; London : McGraw-Hill, c1982. — xvii,478p : ill,forms ; 24cm
Bibliography: p302-309. — Includes index
ISBN 0-07-044235-5 (pbk) : £11.95 B82-15981

Rosenblatt, S. Bernard. Communication in business / S. Bernard Rosenblatt, T. Richard Cheatham, James T. Watt. — 2nd ed. — Englewood Cliffs ; London : Prentice-Hall, c1982. — xii,403p : ill,forms ; 24cm
Previous ed.: 1977. — Includes bibliographies and index
ISBN 0-13-153478-5 : £14.20 B82-24091

658.4'56'0941 — Great Britain. National Federation of Women's Institutes. Meetings. Procedure

National Federation of Women's Institutes. Procedure at meetings. — 11th ed. — London : The Federation, Apr.1982. — [64]p
Previous ed.: 19-?
ISBN 0-900556-67-6 : £1.00 : CIP entry B82-12809

658.4'563 — Committees. Procedure — *Manuals — Welsh texts*

Owen, Gwilym B.. Llawlyfr pwyllgorau : a chyrff cyffelyb / gan G.B. Owen. — Dinbych [Denbigh] : Gwasg Gee, c1981. — 126p ; 14cm
Includes index
Unpriced (pbk) B82-13763

658.4'563 — Meetings. Organisation — *Manuals*

The **Conduct** of meetings. — 22nd ed. / edited by John Yelland. — Bristol : Rose-Jordan, 1982. — xvii,206p ; 22cm
Previous ed.: by T.P.E. Curry, J. Richard Sykes and Philip L. Heslop. 1975. — Includes index
ISBN 0-907313-01-9 (pbk) : £6.00 B82-31401

658.4'6 — Business firms. Evaluation. Techniques — *For consultants*

Reeves, Tom Kynaston. Surveys at work. — London : McGraw-Hill, Sept.1981
Student project manual. — [288]p
ISBN 0-07-084568-9 (pbk) : £7.95 : CIP entry B81-21572

658.4'6'02341 — Great Britain. Management services — *Career guides*

Management services : computer work, work study, organisation and methods, operational research / [written, designed and produced by SGS Education ; photographs by André Gordon ; illustrations by Barrie Thorpe and John Plumb ; careers adviser Brian Heap]. — Walton on Thames : Nelson, 1981. — 15p : ill,1map,ports ; 28cm. — (Career profiles ; 29)
ISBN 0-17-438363-0 (unbound) : Unpriced B82-14314

658.4'7'0941 — Great Britain. Business firms. Security measures. Management

Hill, D. A.. Security : its management and control / D.A. Hill and L.E. Rockley. — London : Business Books, 1981. — xiv,210p : ill ; 24cm
Includes index
ISBN 0-09-143010-0 : Unpriced B82-08365

658.4'72 — Industrial espionage

Heims, Peter A.. Countering industrial espionage / by Peter A. Heims. — Leatherhead : 20th Century Security Education, c1982. — xii,290p : ill ; 23cm
Bibliography: p221-226. — Includes index
ISBN 0-905961-03-x : Unpriced B82-40223

658.4'78 — Computer systems. Security measures

Computer systems security. — Maidenhead : Pergamon Infotech, c1981. — iv,448p : ill,ports ; 31cm. — (Infotech state of the art report. series 9 ; no.5)
Edited by Ray Ellison and Ken Wong. — Bibliography: p399-425. — Includes index
ISBN 0-08-028558-9 : Unpriced B82-01461

Schweitzer, James A.. Managing information security : a program for the electronic information age / James A. Schweitzer. — Boston, [Mass.] ; London : Butterworth, c1982. — 133p : ill,forms ; 24cm
Bibliography: p126-127. — Includes index
ISBN 0-409-95055-6 : Unpriced B82-21269

Wood, Michael B.. Introducing computer security. — Manchester : NCC Publications, Dec.1982. — [160]p
ISBN 0-85012-340-2 (pbk) : £8.50 : CIP entry B82-32298

658.4'78 — Computer systems. Security measures. Management aspects

Fernandez, Eduardo B.. Database security and integrity / Eduardo B. Fernandez, Rita. C. Summers, Christopher Wood. — Reading, Mass. ; London : Addison-Wesley, c1981. — xiv,320p : ill ; 25cm. — (The Systems programming series)
Ill on lining papers. — Includes bibliographies and index
ISBN 0-201-14467-0 : Unpriced B82-20558

658.4'78 — Great Britain. Civil service. Digital computer systems. Security measures

Protection of information in computer systems / Civil Service Department, Central Computer Agency. — [London] : Civil Service Department, [1982?]. — 23p ; 30cm
Cover title
Unpriced (pbk) B82-33402

658.4'78'05 — Digital computer systems. Security measures. Management — *Serials*

Advances in computer security management. — Vol.1-. — Philadelphia ; London : Heyden, 1980-. — v. : ill ; 24cm
Annual
ISSN 0197-1514 = Advances in computer security management : £15.50 B82-11800

658.5 — PRODUCTION MANAGEMENT

658.5 — Industrial engineering

Handbook of industrial engineering / edited by Gavriel Salvendy. — New York ; Chichester : Wiley, c1982. — 1v.((various pagings)) : ill,forms ; 24cm
Includes bibliographies and index
ISBN 0-471-05841-6 : £50.00 B82-37198

658.5 — Manufacturing industries. Management

Amrine, Harold T.. Manufacturing organization and management / Harold T. Amrine, John A. Ritchey, Oliver S. Hulley. — 4th ed. — Englewood Cliffs ; London : Prentice-Hall, c1982. — xiv,529p : ill,forms ; 24cm
Previous ed.: 1975. — Includes index
ISBN 0-13-555748-8 : £14.95 B82-16845

658.5 — Production management

Adam, Everett E.. Production and operations management : concepts, models and behavior / Everett E. Adam, Ronald J. Ebert. — 2nd ed. — Englewood Cliffs ; London : Prentice-Hall, c1982. — 698p : ill ; 24cm
Previous ed.: 1978. — Includes bibliographies and index
ISBN 0-13-724971-3 : £19.45 B82-16719

Barndt, Stephen E.. Essentials of operations management / Stephen E. Barndt, Davis W. Carvey. — Englewood Cliffs ; London : Prentice-Hall, c1982. — xv,160p : ill ; 23cm. — (Prentice-Hall essentials of management series)
Includes bibliographies and index
ISBN 0-13-286534-3 (cased) : Unpriced
ISBN 0-13-286526-2 (pbk) : £8.20 B82-23236

658.5 — Production management
continuation

Mayer, Raymond R.. Production and operations management / Raymond R. Mayer. — 4th ed. — New York ; London : McGraw-Hill, c1982. — xvii,654p : ill,plans,forms ; 25cm. — (McGraw-Hill series in management)
Previous ed.: 1975. — Includes bibliographies and index
ISBN 0-07-041025-9 : £18.25 B82-15982

Monks, Joseph G.. Operations management : theory and problems / Joseph G. Monks. — 2nd ed. — New York ; London : Collier Macmillan, c1982. — xv,725,[38]p : ill ; 25cm. — (McGraw-Hill series in management)
Previous ed.: 1977. — Includes bibliographies and index
ISBN 0-07-042720-8 : £18.95 B82-30022

658.5′00722 — Production management — *Case studies*

Cases in production and operations management / Robert C. Meier ... [et al.]. — Englewood Cliffs ; London : Prentice-Hall, c1982. — xv,319p : ill,2maps ; 23cm
ISBN 0-13-118950-6 (pbk) : £11.95
B82-20076

658.5′00722 — United States. Business firms. Production management — *Case studies*

Chen, Gordon K. C.. Productivity management text & cases / Gordon K.C. Chen, Robert E. McGarrah. — Chicago ; London : Dryden, c1982. — xii,542p : ill,2maps,plans ; 25cm
Includes index
ISBN 0-03-048901-6 : Unpriced B82-23123

658.5′00724 — Production management. Mathematical models

Bestwick, Paul F.. Quantitative production management : solutions manual / Paul F. Bestwick and Keith Lockyer. — London : Pitman, 1982. — 366p : ill ; 25cm
ISBN 0-273-01613-x (pbk) : Unpriced : CIP rev. B81-35779

Bestwick, Paul F.. Quantitative production management / Paul F. Bestwick and Keith Lockyer. — London : Pitman, 1982. — xiii,442p : ill ; 24cm
Bibliography: p430-437. — Includes index
ISBN 0-273-01614-8 : Unpriced : CIP rev.
B81-35778

658.5′1 — Commonwealth developing countries. Products. Standardisation

Commonwealth Regional Programme on Standardization and Quality Control. *Steering Committee. Meeting (1st : 1979 : Nairobi).* Commonwealth Regional Programme on Standardization and Quality Control / report on the First Meeting of the Steering Committee 15-19 January 1979, Nairobi, Kenya. — London (Marlborough House, Pall Mall, SW1Y 5HX) : Commonwealth Science Council, 1979. — 46p ; 30cm
Unpriced (pbk)
Also classified at 658.5′62′09171241
B82-40577

658.5′3 — Production management. Scheduling

French, Simon, *1950-*. Sequencing and scheduling : an introduction to the mathematics of the job-shop / Simon French. — Chichester : Ellis Horwood, 1982. — x,245p : ill ; 24cm. — (Ellis Horwood series in mathematics and its applications)
Bibliography: p230-237. — Includes index
ISBN 0-85312-299-7 (cased) : Unpriced : CIP rev.
ISBN 0-85312-364-0 (pbk) : Unpriced
B81-13862

658.5′3 — Scheduling. Mathematical aspects

Bellman, R.. Mathematical aspects of scheduling and applications. — Oxford : Pergamon, Sept.1982. — [300]p. — (International series in modern applied mathematics and computer science ; v.4)
ISBN 0-08-026477-8 (cased) : £15.50 : CIP entry
ISBN 0-08-026476-x (pbk) : £8.90 B82-19093

658.5′3 — Scheduling. Mathematical models

NATO Advanced Study and Research Institute on Theoretical Approaches to Scheduling Problems *(1981 : Durham)*. Deterministic and stochastic scheduling : proceedings of the NATO Advanced Study and Research Institute on Theoretical Approaches to Scheduling Problems held in Durham, England, July 6-17, 1981 / edited by M.A.H. Dempster, J.K. Lenstra and A.H.G. Rinnooy Kan. — Dordrecht ; London : Published in cooperation with NATO Scientific Affairs Division [by] Reidel, c1982. — xii : ill ; 25cm. — (NATO advanced study institute series. Series C, Mathematical and physical sciences ; v.84)
Includes bibliographies and index
ISBN 90-277-1397-9 : Unpriced B82-28047

658.5′6 — Production control — *Manuals*

Tooley, Desmond F.. Production control systems & records / Desmond F. Tooley. — 2nd ed. — Aldershot : Gower, 1981. — 151p : ill,forms ; 26cm
Previous ed.: 1972. — Includes index
ISBN 0-566-02253-2 : Unpriced : CIP rev.
B81-04258

658.5′6′02854 — Production control systems using digital computer systems

Bedworth, David D.. Integrated production control systems : management, analysis, design / David D. Bedworth, James E. Bailey. — New York ; Chichester : Wiley, c1982. — x,433p : ill ; 25cm
Includes index
ISBN 0-471-06223-5 : £16.00 B82-21797

658.5′62 — Quality control

Broh, Robert A.. Managing quality for higher profits : a guide for business executives and quality managers / Robert A. Broh. — New York ; London : McGraw-Hill, c1982. — viii,200p : ill ; 24cm
Includes index
ISBN 0-07-007975-7 : £12.50 B82-37580

Caplen, Rowland. A practical approach to quality control / Rowland Caplen. — 4th ed. — London : Business Books, 1982. — ix,326p : ill,1facsim,forms ; 22cm
Previous ed.: 1978. — Includes index
ISBN 0-09-147451-5 (pbk) : £6.95 : CIP rev.
B82-12422

Juran, J. M.. Quality planning and analysis : from product development through use / J.M. Juran, Frank M. Gryna, Jr.. — 2nd ed. — New York ; London : McGraw-Hill, c1980. — xvii,629p : ill ; 25cm
Previous ed.: 1970. — Includes bibliographies and index
ISBN 0-07-033178-2 : £21.50 B82-16883

Robson, Mike. An introduction to quality circles. — Aldershot : Gower, July 1982. — [150]p
ISBN 0-566-02343-1 : £12.50 : CIP entry
B82-12975

658.5′62 — Quality control. Applications of microscopy — *Conference proceedings*

Quality control using microscopical techniques. — [London] ([120 Wigmore St., W1H OHS]) : Scientific Symposia Ltd, [1982?]. — [34]leaves ; 30cm
Abstracts of conference proceedings. — Includes bibliographies
Unpriced (pbk) B82-27924

658.5′62′09171241 — Commonwealth developing countries. Quality control

Commonwealth Regional Programme on Standardization and Quality Control. *Steering Committee. Meeting (1st : 1979 : Nairobi).* Commonwealth Regional Programme on Standardization and Quality Control / report on the First Meeting of the Steering Committee 15-19 January 1979, Nairobi, Kenya. — London (Marlborough House, Pall Mall, SW1Y 5HX) : Commonwealth Science Council, 1979. — 46p ; 30cm
Unpriced (pbk)
Primary classification 658.5′1 B82-40577

658.5′62′0941 — Great Britain. Manufacturing industries. Quality control *compared with* Japanese quality control

Quality management & product liability including the lesson from Japan / M.P. Cumbers (editor), H.A.J. Prentice, A.O. Jakubovic. — Sheffield : Yorkshire & Humberside Regional Management Centre, 1981. — 50leaves ; 30cm
ISBN 0-903761-46-7 (pbk) : £8.00
Also classified at 658.5′62′0952 B82-17280

658.5′62′09417 — Ireland *(Republic)*. Manufacturing industries. Quality control

Roche, John G.. National survey of quality control in manufacturing industry 1980 / John G. Roche. — Dublin : National Board for Science and Technology, 1981. — 52p ; 30cm
ISBN 0-86282-012-x (pbk) : Unpriced
B82-29244

658.5′62′0952 — Japan. Manufacturing industries. Quality control *compared with* British quality control

Quality management & product liability including the lesson from Japan / M.P. Cumbers (editor), H.A.J. Prentice, A.O. Jakubovic. — Sheffield : Yorkshire & Humberside Regional Management Centre, 1981. — 50leaves ; 30cm
ISBN 0-903761-46-7 (pbk) : £8.00
Primary classification 658.5′62′0941
B82-17280

658.5′68 — Management. CuSum charts & Shewhart charts

Bissell, A. F.. An introduction to Cusum charts / by A.F. Bissell. — [Bury St. Edmunds] : Institute of Statisticians, [1982?]. — 17p : ill ; 22cm
Cover title. — Bibliography: p17
£0.50 (pbk) B82-31965

658.5′7 — Industries. Technological innovation. Management

Parker, R. C.. The management of innovation. — Chichester : Wiley, Jan.1983. — [272]p
ISBN 0-471-10421-3 : £12.75 : CIP entry
B82-34619

658.5′7 — United States. Industries. Technological innovation. Creativity

Carney, Thomas P.. False profits : the decline of industrial creativity / Thomas P. Carney. — Notre Dame ; London : University of Notre Dame Press, c1981. — viii,184p ; 24cm
Includes index
ISBN 0-268-00851-5 : £13.30 B82-13564

658.5′75 — Industries. Technological innovation. Management

Woodward, J. F.. Science in industry : science of industry. — Aberdeen : Aberdeen University Press, June 1982. — [208]p
ISBN 0-08-028451-5 (cased) : £11.00 : CIP entry
ISBN 0-08-028452-3 (pbk) : £5.00 B82-09417

658.5′75 — New products. Management

Pessemier, Edgar A.. Product management : strategy and organization / Edgar A. Pessemier. — 2nd ed. — New York ; Chichester : Wiley, c1982. — xix,668p : ill,forms ; 24cm. — (Wiley series in marketing)
Previous ed.: 1977. — Includes index
ISBN 0-471-05718-5 : £20.65 B82-13968

658.7 — MATERIALS MANAGEMENT

658.7 — Materials management

Baily, Peter. Materials management handbook / Peter Baily and David Farmer. — Aldershot : Gower, c1982. — xvi,300p : ill ; 24cm. — (A Gower handbook)
Includes bibliographies and index
ISBN 0-566-02272-9 : Unpriced : CIP rev.
B81-30960

658.7′2 — Purchasing by organisations

Aljian's purchasing handbook / formerly edited by George W. Aljian. — 4th ed. / sponsored by the National Association of Purchasing Management ; coordinating editor Paul V. Farrell. — New York ; London : McGraw-Hill, c1982. — 845p in various pagings : ill,forms ; 24cm
Previous ed.: New York : McGraw-Hill, 1973. — Bibliography: 26p. — Includes index
ISBN 0-07-045899-5 : £34.95 B82-14015

658.7′2 — Purchasing by organisations *continuation*

Lysons, C. K.. Purchasing / C.K. Lysons. — Plymouth : Macdonald & Evans, 1981. — viii,211p : ill ; 18cm. — (The M & E handbook series)
Includes index
ISBN 0-7121-1752-0 (pbk) : £3.75 B82-07283

658.7′2 — Stock control. Purchasing
Baily, Peter. Purchasing principles and management / Peter Baily, David Farmer. — 4th ed. — London : Pitman, 1981. — ix,337p ; 23cm
Previous ed.: published as Purchasing principles and techniques. 1977. — Includes bibliographies and index
ISBN 0-273-01719-5 (pbk) : Unpriced : CIP rev. B81-30155

658.7′2 — Stock control. Purchasing. Planning
Baily, Peter. Purchasing systems and records. — 2nd ed. — Aldershot : Gower, July 1982. — [170]p
Previous ed. published as: Design of purchasing systems and records. 1970
ISBN 0-566-02337-7 : £15.00 : CIP entry B82-14377

Parsons, W. J.. Improving purchasing performance / W.J. Parsons. — Aldershot : Gower, c1982. — xiii,169p : ill ; 23cm
Includes index
ISBN 0-566-02271-0 : Unpriced : CIP rev. B81-21561

658.7′2′05 — Purchasing by organisations — *Serials*
[Purchasing *(London)*]. Purchasing : the journal of commercial and industrial purchasing. — Vol.17, no.8 (Apr. 1982)-. — London (30 Calderwood St., SE18 6QH) : Morgan-Grampian, 1982-. — v. : ill(some col.),ports ; 29cm
Monthly. — Merger of: Industrial purchasing news; and, Modern purchasing (London)
ISSN 0263-8851 = Purchasing (London) : £25.00 per year B82-32360

658.7′2′094 — Western Europe. Industrial purchasing
International marketing and purchasing of industrial goods : an interaction approach / by IMP Project Group ; editor Håkan Håkansson. — Chichester : Wiley, c1982. — x,406p ; 23cm
Bibliography: p395-401. — Includes index
ISBN 0-471-27987-0 : £17.75 : CIP rev.
Primary classification 658.8′0094 B81-36235

658.7′81′01 — Materials handling. Management. Applications of systems theory
Gledstone, C.. Materials handling : the systems approach / authors C. Gledstone, W. Hesketh ; edited by R.H. Hollier. — London : H.M.S.O., 1982. — iv,222p : ill ; 25cm
At head of title: Department of Industry, Committee for Materials Handling (Management and Technology). — Includes bibliographies
ISBN 0-11-511748-2 (pbk) : £9.95 B82-40753

658.7′85 — Warehouses. Management
Burton, J. A. (John Antony). Effective warehousing / J.A. Burton. — 3rd ed. — Plymouth : Macdonald and Evans, 1981. — xi,352p : ill,2maps,forms ; 22cm
Previous ed.: 1979. — Bibliography: p346-347. — Includes index
ISBN 0-7121-0591-3 (pbk) : £5.95 B82-10615

658.7′85′07041 — Great Britain. Warehouses. Personnel. Training
Warehouse staff training. — Stretford : Distributive Industry Training Board, [1981?]. — 28p : col.ill,1map,forms ; 20x21cm. — (A DITB training guide)
Cover title. — Text on inside cover
ISBN 0-903416-23-9 (pbk) : Unpriced
Also classified at 658.3′112 B82-17428

658.7′85′0942733 — Greater Manchester *(Metropolitan County)*. Manchester. Warehouses, *to 1981*
Wilkinson, Stephen. Manchester's warehouses : their history and architecture / by Stephen Wilkinson. — Manchester : Richardson, [1982]. — 12p : ill,maps,plans ; 30cm
Cover title. — Text and ill on inside cover
ISBN 0-9506257-9-5 (pbk) : £1.00 B82-32069

658.7′87 — Great Britain. Retail trades. Goods. Bar marking codes. Location — *Manuals*
Guideline on the location of bar code symbols / Article Number Association (UK) Limited. — London (6 Catherine St., WC2B 5JJ) : The Association, 1980. — 14leaves,[11]leaves of plates : ill ; 30cm
Unpriced (spiral) B82-31980

658.7′87 — Stock control
The **Economics** and management of inventories / edited by Attila Chikán. — Amsterdam ; Oxford : Elsevier Scientific, 1981. — 2v. : ill ; 25cm. — (Studies in production and engineering economics ; v.2)
Conference papers. — Includes bibliographies and index
ISBN 0-444-99718-0 : £81.88 : CIP rev.
ISBN 0-444-99720-2 (pt.A)
ISBN 0-444-99719-9 (pt.B) B81-30411

658.7′87′0973 — United States. Companies. Stock control. Use of inventories
Tersine, Richard J.. Principles of inventory and materials management / Richard J. Tersine. — 2nd ed. — New York ; Oxford : North-Holland, c1982. — xii,477p : ill ; 24cm
Previous ed.: published as Materials management and inventory systems. New York : North-Holland, 1976. — Bibliography: p461-465. — Includes index
ISBN 0-444-00641-9 : Unpriced B82-17465

658.7′88′0285 — Goods. Physical distribution. Management. Applications of data processing systems — *Conference proceedings*
Data processing in physical distribution management. — [Uxbridge] : [Online Conferences], [c1978]. — viii,176p : ill,maps ; 29cm
Conference papers
ISBN 0-903796-24-4 (pbk) : Unpriced B82-03323

658.7′88′0724 — Goods. Physical distribution. Mathematical models — *For schools*
Loads of problems. — Cheltenham : Thornes, Sept.1982. — [56]p. — (Mathematics towards relevance)
ISBN 0-85950-361-5 (pbk) : £1.85 : CIP entry B82-30712

Loads of problems. — Cheltenham : Thornes. — (Mathematics towards relevance)
2: Diagrams and tables. — Aug.1982. — [48]p
ISBN 0-85950-392-5 (pbk) : £1.50 : CIP entry B82-22790

Loads of problems. — Cheltenham : Thornes, Sept.1982. — (Mathematics towards relevance)
Tutor's notes. — [1v.]
ISBN 0-85950-364-x (pbk) : £1.85 : CIP entry B82-30709

658.7′882 — Retail trades. Goods. Physical distribution. Management
Handbook of physical distribution management. — 3rd ed. — Aldershot : Gower, Sept.1982. — [540]p
Previous ed.: 1976
ISBN 0-566-02219-2 : £19.50 : CIP entry B82-19545

658.8 — MARKETING

658.8 — Marketing
Evans, Joel R.. Marketing / Joel R. Evans, Barry Berman. — London : Macmillan, c1982. — xxvi,723,64p : ill(some col.) ; 24cm
Text on lining papers. — Includes index
ISBN 0-02-334500-4 : £9.95 B82-26291

Foster, Douglas. Mastering marketing / Douglas Foster. — [London] : Macmillan, 1982. — 325p : ill ; 23cm. — (Macmillan master series)
Bibliography: p314. — Includes index
ISBN 0-333-31779-3 (cased) : £8.95
ISBN 0-333-31780-7 (pbk (home ed.)) : Unpriced
ISBN 0-333-31781-5 (pbk (export ed.)) B82-39154

Foxall, Gordon R.. Strategic marketing management / Gordon R. Foxall. — London : Croom Helm, c1981. — 273p : ill ; 23cm. — (A Halsted Press book)
Includes bibliographies and index
ISBN 0-7099-1002-9 (cased) : £12.50
ISBN 0-7099-1003-7 (pbk) : Unpriced B82-07150

Guiltinan, Joseph P.. Marketing management : strategies and programs / Joseph P. Guiltinan, Gordon W. Paul. — New York ; London : McGraw-Hill, c1982. — xvi,412p : ill ; 25cm. — (McGraw-Hill series in marketing)
Includes bibliographies and index
ISBN 0-07-048920-3 : £17-25 B82-27226

Hadsell, Antonia McGinley. Study guide to accompany Schoell and Ivy's Marketing : contemporary concepts and practices / Antonia McGinley Hadsell, August Charles Drubel. — Boston, [Mass.] ; London : Allyn and Bacon, c1982. — 345p ; 24cm
ISBN 0-205-07659-9 (pbk) : Unpriced B82-27107

McDaniel, Carl. Marketing / Carl McDaniel, Jr.. — 2nd ed. — New York ; London : Harper & Row, c1982. — 19xix,752,[26]p : ill(some col.) ; 25cm
Previous ed.: 1979. — Includes index
ISBN 0-06-044359-6 : £15.95 B82-26280

Majaro, Simon. Marketing in perspective / Simon Majaro. — London : Allen & Unwin, 1982. — xvi,236p : ill ; 23cm
Bibliography: p229-231. — Includes index
ISBN 0-04-658234-7 (cased) : Unpriced : CIP rev.
ISBN 0-04-658235-5 (pbk) : Unpriced B82-10583

Markin, Rom J.. Marketing : strategy and management / Rom Markin. — 2nd ed. — New York ; Chichester : Wiley, c1982. — xv,672p : ill(some col.),col.maps,facsims,1form ; 25cm. — (The Wiley series in marketing)
Previous ed.: 1979. — Includes index
ISBN 0-471-08522-7 : £14.70 B82-13294

Nickels, Williams G.. Marketing principles / William G. Nickels. — 2nd ed. — Englewood Cliffs ; London : Prentice-Hall, c1982. — xxiii,648p : ill,facsims ; 25cm
Previous ed.: 1978. — Includes index
ISBN 0-13-558197-4 : £18.70 B82-27564

Schoell, William F.. Marketing : contemporary concepts and practices / William F. Schoell and Thomas T. Ivy. — Boston ; London : Allyn and Bacon, c1982. — xv,685p : ill(some col.),facsims ; 25cm + Instructor's manual (427,T1-T78p ; 29cm) + Test bank manual (ca.300leaves ; 28cm)
Includes index
ISBN 0-205-07656-4 : Unpriced
ISBN 0-205-07657-2 (instructor's manual)
ISBN 0-205-07658-0 (test bank manual) B82-26933

Strategic market decisions : a reader / edited by Keith K. Cox, Vern J. McGinnis. — Englewood Cliffs ; London : Prentice-Hall, c1982. — xii,323p : ill ; 24cm
ISBN 0-13-851022-9 (pbk) : £11.20 B82-31911

658.8 — Marketing. Applications of behavioural sciences
Williams, Keith C.. Behavioural aspects of marketing / Keith C. Williams. — London : Heinemann on behalf of the Institute of Marketing and the CAM Foundation, 1981. — ix,235p : ill ; 24cm
Includes index
ISBN 0-434-92300-1 (pbk) : £6.95 B82-03894

658.8 — Marketing auditing
Wilson, Aubrey. Aubrey Wilson's marketing audit check lists : a guide to effective marketing resource realization. — London : McGraw-Hill, c1982. — xi,215p : ill ; 25cm
Includes index
ISBN 0-07-084574-3 : £14.50 : CIP rev. B82-00307

658.8 — Marketing by multinational companies
Beharrell, Brian. Problems in marketing management in a changing environment for large corporations / Brian Beharrell, Howard Lyons. — [Sheffield] : Sheffield City Polytechnic, 1982. — 19p ; 30cm
Bibliography: p19
ISBN 0-903761-43-2 (pbk) : Unpriced B82-29916

658.8 — Marketing by non-profit making organisations
Kotler, Philip. Marketing for nonprofit organizations / Philip Kotler. — 2nd ed. — Englewood Cliffs ; London : Prentice Hall, c1982. — xv,528p : ill ; 24cm. — (The Prentice-Hall series in marketing)
Previous ed.: 1975. — Includes index
ISBN 0-13-556142-6 : £19.45 B82-29237

658.8 — Marketing by small firms — *Manuals*
Lace, Geoffrey. Effective marketing for the smaller business : a practical guide / by Geoffrey Lace. — Newbury : Scope, 1982. — 221p : ill,forms ; 23cm
Includes index
ISBN 0-906619-13-0 : £12.00 : CIP rev. B82-07695

658.8 — Marketing — *Manuals*
Morse, Stephen. Management skills in marketing / Stephen Morse. — London : McGraw-Hill, c1982. — xi,150p : ill,forms ; 24cm
Includes index
ISBN 0-07-084577-8 : £8.95 : CIP rev. B82-08074

658.8′001 — Marketing. Theories. Construction
Zaltman, Gerald. Theory construction in marketing : some thoughts on thinking / Gerald Zaltman, Karen Lemasters, Michael Heffring. — New York ; Chichester : Wiley, c1982. — xxii,209p : ill ; 24cm. — (Theories in marketing series, ISSN 0273-2955)
Bibliography: p199-203. — Includes index
ISBN 0-471-98127-3 : £20.20 B82-40416

658.8′0023 — Marketing — *Career guides — Serials — For graduates*
Graduate careers in sales and marketing for graduates and postgraduates. — 1980-81 ed. — London : New Opportunity Press, 1980-. — v. : maps ; 21cm
Annual. — Continues: Graduate careers in sales & marketing. — Description based on: 1981-82 ed
ISSN 0260-0706 = Graduate careers in sales and marketing for graduates and postgraduates : £2.50 B82-18719

658.8′00722 — Marketing — *Case studies*
Strategy and marketing : a case approach / Kenneth Simmonds (editor). — Oxford : Philip Allan, 1982. — xiii,321p : ill,maps,facsims ; 31cm
ISBN 0-86003-516-6 (cased) : Unpriced : CIP rev.
ISBN 0-86003-615-4 (pbk) : Unpriced B81-38822

658.8′00722 — Marketing — *Case studies — For business studies*
Strategy and marketing. — Oxford : Philip Allan, Jan.1982
Instructor′s manual. — [432]p
ISBN 0-86003-616-2 (pbk) : £8.50 : CIP entry B81-38823

658.8′0094 — Western Europe. Industrial marketing
International marketing and purchasing of industrial goods : an interaction approach / by IMP Project Group ; editor Håkan Håkansson. — Chichester : Wiley, c1982. — x,406p ; 23cm
Bibliography: p395-401. — Includes index
ISBN 0-471-27987-0 : £17.75 : CIP rev.
Also classified at 658.7′2′094 B81-36235

658.8′00941 — Great Britain. Marketing — *Manuals — For hotel & catering industries*
Shepherd, John W.. Marketing practice in the hotel and catering industry / John W. Shepherd. — London : Batsford Academic and Education, 1982. — 144p : ill,forms ; 22cm
Bibliography: p6. — Includes index
ISBN 0-7134-0498-1 (pbk) : £4.95 : CIP rev. B82-04490

658.8′02 — Industrial marketing. Techniques. Effects of competition
Mathur, Shiv Sahai. Strategic industrial marketing : transaction shifts and competitive response / by Shiv Sahai Mathur. — London (Basinghall St, EC2V 5AH) : Gresham College, c1981. — 25leaves ; 30cm. — (Working paper / City University Business School, ISSN 0140-1041 ; no.33)
Bibliography: leaf 25
Unpriced (pbk) B82-16003

658.8′02 — Marketing. Decision making. Mathematical models
Marketing decision models / edited by Randall L. Schultz, Andris A. Zoltners. — New York ; Oxford : North Holland, c1981. — xii,298p : ill ; 24cm
Includes bibliographies and index
ISBN 0-444-00426-2 : Unpriced B82-00802

658.8′02 — Marketing. Planning
Bureau, J. R.. Brand management : planning and control / J.R. Bureau. — London : Macmillan, 1981. — xiii,250p : ill ; 23cm. — (Macmillan studies in marketing management)
Bibliography: p244-245. — Includes index
ISBN 0-333-31902-8 (cased) : Unpriced
ISBN 0-333-31903-6 (pbk) : Unpriced B82-15252

McDonald, M. H. B.. Handbook of marketing planning / by M.H.B. McDonald. — Bradford : MCB Publications, c1980. — 128p : ill ; 30cm
ISBN 0-905440-95-1 (pbk) : Unpriced B82-36895

Readings in marketing strategies and programs / [edited by] Joseph P. Guiltinan, Gordon W. Paul. — New York ; London : McGraw-Hill, c1982. — xii,591p : ill ; 24cm. — (McGraw-Hill series in marketing)
Includes bibliographies
ISBN 0-07-048922-x (pbk) : £12.25 B82-29268

Stapleton, John. How to prepare a marketing plan / John Stapleton. — 3rd ed. — Aldershot : Gower, 1982, c1974. — 299p : ill ; 20x24cm
Previous ed.: 1974. — Includes index
ISBN 0-566-02288-5 : Unpriced : CIP rev. B81-31610

658.81 — SALES MANAGEMENT

658.8′1 — Sales management
Dalrymple, Douglas J.. Sales management : concepts and cases / Douglas J. Dalrymple. — New York ; Chichester : Wiley, c1982. — xvi,485p : ill,forms,maps ; 25cm
Includes index
ISBN 0-471-07867-0 : £18.45 B82-28084

Wilson, M. T.. Managing a sales force. — 2nd ed. — Aldershot : Gower, Nov.1982. — [200]p
Previous ed.: 1970
ISBN 0-566-02377-6 : £16.50 : CIP entry B82-26551

658.8′1 — Sales management — *Manuals*
Senton, David. Improving sales productivity. — Aldershot : Gower, Nov.1982. — [170]p
ISBN 0-566-02379-2 : £15.00 : CIP entry B82-26552

658.8′102 — Salesmanship. Teams. Management — *Manuals*
Sweeney, Neil R.. Managing a sales team : techniques for field sales managers / Neil R. Sweeney. — London : Kogan Page, 1982, c1979. — xvii,252p : ill,forms ; 23cm
Originally published: New York : Lebhar-Friedman, 1979
ISBN 0-85038-539-3 : £11.95 : CIP rev. B81-40246

658.8′12 — Salesmanship. Use of telephones — *Manuals*
Shafiroff, Martin D.. Successful telephone selling in the ′80s / Martin D. Shafiroff and Robert L. Shook. — New York ; London : Harper & Row, c1982. — xv,171p ; 22cm
Includes index
ISBN 0-06-014952-3 : Unpriced B82-18398

658.82 — SALES PROMOTION

658.8′2 — Great Britain. Sponsorship by business firms — *For marketing*
Head, Victor. Sponsorship : the newest marketing skill / Victor Head. — Cambridge : Woodhead Faulkner in association with the Institute of Marketing, 1981. — ix,116p : 2ill ; 25cm
Includes index
ISBN 0-85941-151-6 : £9.75 B82-00070

658.8′2 — Retail trades. Sales promotion — *Manuals*
Guberman, Reuben. Handbook of retail promotion ideas / by Reuben Guberman. — Reading, Mass. ; London : Addison-Wesley, c1981. — xii,258p : ill,forms ; 29cm
Includes index
ISBN 0-201-02720-8 : £20.00 B82-34282

658.8′2 — Sales promotion
Stanley, Richard E.. Promotion : advertising, publicity, personal selling, sales promotion / Richard E. Stanley. — 2nd ed. — Englewood Cliffs ; London : Prentice-Hall, c1982. — xxii,389p : ill ; 24cm
Previous ed.: 1977. — Includes bibliographies and index
ISBN 0-13-730895-7 : £17.20 B82-34457

658.8′2′0941 — Great Britain. Sales promotion
Gentry, Susan. How British industry promotes / by Susan Gentry and Leslie Rodger. — London : Industrial Market Research, 1978. — v,88p ; 21x30cm. — (Reports / Industrial Market Research Limited ; 3)
ISBN 0-906142-00-8 (spiral) : £7.50 B82-40745

658.83 — MARKET RESEARCH AND ANALYSIS

658.8′3 — Marketing. Research
Applied marketing and social research / edited by Ute Bradley. — New York ; London : Van Nostrand Reinhold, c1982. — xiii,314p : ill,forms ; 24cm
Includes bibliographies
ISBN 0-442-30437-4 (cased) : Unpriced
ISBN 0-442-30438-2 (pbk) : £5.50 B82-34327

Marketing research. — 6th ed / David J. Luck ... [et al.]. — Englewood Cliffs ; London : Prentice-Hall, c1982. — xviii,616p : ill,maps ; 25cm
Previous ed.: 1978. — Bibliography: p591-599. — Includes index
ISBN 0-13-557652-0 : £20.75 B82-39738

Marketing research : applications and problems / edited by Arun K. Jain, Christian Pinson, Brian T. Ratchford. — Chichester : Wiley, 1982. — xiv,555p : ill ; 24cm
Includes bibliographies and index
ISBN 0-471-10081-1 : Unpriced : CIP rev. B82-06834

658.8′3 — Marketing. Research — *Manuals*
Breen, George Edward. Do-it-yourself marketing research. — 2nd ed., George Edward Breen, A.B. Blankenship, illustrated by Howard Munce. — New York ; London : McGraw-Hill, c1982. — x,303p : ill,facsims,forms ; 24cm
Previous ed.: 1977. — Includes index
ISBN 0-07-007446-1 : £18.95 B82-40611

658.8′3 — New products. Marketing. Forecasting. Mathematical models
New-product forecasting : models and applications / edited by Yoram Wind, Vijay Mahajan, Richard N. Cardozo. — Lexington : Lexington Books, c1981 ; [Aldershot] : Gower [[distributor]], 1982. — x,564p : ill ; 24cm
Includes bibliographies and index
ISBN 0-669-04102-5 : £27.50 B82-21260

658.8′3′05 — Marketing. Research — *Serials*
Research in marketing : an annual compilation of research. — Vol.1 (1978)-. — Greenwich, Conn. : JAI Press ; London (3 Henrietta St., WC2E 8LU) : Distributed by JAICON Press, 1978-. — v. : ill ; 24cm
ISSN 0191-3026 = Research in marketing : £24.50 B82-02346

658.8'3'0722 — United States. Market research — *Case studies*

Zikmund, William G.. Cases in marketing research / William G. Zikmund, William J. Lundstrom, Donald Sciglimpaglia. — Chicago ; London : Dryden, c1982. — 344p : ill,facsims ; 24cm
ISBN 0-03-057636-9 (pbk) : £8.50 B82-25411

658.8'3'076 — Marketing. Research — *Questions & answers*

Sciglimpaglia, Donald. Applied marketing research / Donald Sciglimpaglia. — Chicago ; London : Dryden, c1983. — xi,335p : forms ; 23cm
ISBN 0-03-057634-2 (pbk) : £6.95 B82-33818

658.8'3'0973 — United States. Marketing. Research

Zikmund, William G.. Exploring marketing research / William G. Zikmund. — Chicago ; London : Dryden, c1982. — xxv,657p : ill ; 25cm
Includes index
ISBN 0-03-056227-9 : £13.95 B82-22249

658.8'342 — Consumer behaviour

Engel, James F.. Consumer behavior / James F. Engel, Roger D. Blackwell. — 4th ed. — Chicago ; London : Dryden, c1982. — 690p : ill ; 25cm
Previous ed.: 1978. — Includes index
ISBN 0-03-059242-9 : £17.50 B82-25415

658.8'342'018 — Consumer behaviour. Methodology — *Case studies*

Prince, Melvin. Consumer research for management decisions / Melvin Prince with the collaboration of Irene A. Silbert. — New York ; Chichester : Wiley, c1982. — xiii,210p : ill ; 24cm. — (Ronald series on marketing management, ISSN 0275-875x)
Bibliography: p202-208. — Includes index
ISBN 0-471-09715-2 : £22.00 B82-26475

658.84 — MARKETING. CHANNELS OF DISTRIBUTION

658.8'4 — Auctions. Purchase & sale — *Manuals*

Ketchum, William C.. Auction! / by William C. Ketchum, Jr. — New York : Sterling ; Poole : Distributed by Blandford Press, c1980 (1982 printing). — 192p : ill,forms ; 23cm
Includes index
ISBN 0-8069-7568-7 (pbk) : £3.95 B82-39882

658.8'4'0973 — United States. Marketing. Channels of distribution

Stern, Louis W.. Marketing channels / Louis W. Stern, Adel I. El-Ansary. — 2nd ed. — Englewood Cliffs ; London : Prentice-Hall, c1982. — xx,588p : ill ; 25cm. — (The Prentice-Hall series in marketing) (Prentice-Hall international series in management)
Previous ed.: 1977. — Includes index
ISBN 0-13-557173-1 : £18.70 B82-21676

658.8'48 — Exporting — *Manuals*

Piercy, Nigel. Export strategy. — London : Allen & Unwin, Nov.1982. — [272]p
ISBN 0-04-382037-9 (cased) : £15.00 : CIP entry
ISBN 0-04-382038-7 (pbk) : £6.95 B82-27815

658.8'48 — Exports. Marketing

Case studies in international marketing / edited by Peter Doyle and Norman A. Hart. — London : Heinemann published on behalf of the CAM Foundation and the Institute of Marketing, 1982. — vii,391p : ill ; 24cm
ISBN 0-434-90370-1 (pbk) : £7.95 B82-37289

Majaro, Simon. International marketing. — Revised ed. — London : Allen & Unwin, Nov.1982. — [320]p
Previous ed.: 1977
ISBN 0-04-658240-1 : £7.95 : CIP entry B82-27823

Walsh, L. S.. International marketing / L.S. Walsh. — 2nd ed. — Plymouth : Macdonald and Evans, 1981. — xvi,252p : ill ; 19cm. — (The M & E handbook series)
Previous ed.: 1978. — Bibliography: p229-230. — Includes index
ISBN 0-7121-0968-4 (pbk) : £3.25 B82-00720

658.8'48 — Great Britain. Exports. Marketing. Use of foreign languages — *Conference proceedings*

The **Language** key in export strategy : report of a conference held in Birmingham on Monday 12 January 1981 at the Birmingham Chamber of Industry and Commerce / conference chairmen Lord Limerick, Sir Adrian Cadbury. — Birmingham ([Gosta Green, Birmingham B4 7ET]) : Department of Modern Languages, University of Aston in Birmingham, 1981. — 65p : ill ; 30cm
Bibliography: p59-65
Unpriced (pbk) B82-16352

658.8'48'05 — Exports. Marketing — *Serials*

Journal of international marketing. — Vol.1, no.1 (1981)-. — Bradford : MCB Publications, 1981-. — v. ; 25cm
Three issues yearly. — Each issue has a distinctive title
ISSN 0262-1703 = Journal of international marketing : Unpriced B82-15140

658.8'48'076 — Exporting — *Questions & answers — For schools*

Hollett, Vicki. Import export / Vicki Hollett. — Harlow : Longman, 1982. — 48p : ill,2forms,1map ; 23cm. — (World at work)
Text on inside cover
ISBN 0-582-74850-x (pbk) : Unpriced B82-31768

658.8'48'0941 — Great Britain. Exporting. Marketing

How British and German industry exports. — London : Industrial Market Research, 1978. — xiv,158p ; 21x30cm. — (Reports / Industrial Market Research Limited ; 6)
ISBN 0-906142-03-2 (spiral) : £20.00
Also classified at 658.8'48'0943 B82-40744

How British industry exports. — London : Industrial Market Research, 1978. — xiv,154p ; 21x30cm. — (Reports / Industrial Market Research Limited ; 4)
ISBN 0-906142-01-6 (spiral) : £15.00 B82-40742

658.8'48'0941 — Great Britain. Exporting to European Community countries

The **EEC** as an expanded home market for the United Kingdom and the Federal Republic of Germany : a report / prepared for The Anglo-German Foundation for the Study of Industrial Society by Arthur D. Little Ltd. — London : The Foundation, 1979, c1980. — 134p : ill ; 30cm
English text, German summary
ISBN 0-905492-29-3 (pbk) : £15.00
Also classified at 658.8'48'0943 B82-01286

658.8'48'0941 — Great Britain. Exporting to Western Europe — *Manuals*

Selling to Western Europe. — 2nd ed. — [London] : H.M.S.O., 1982. — 126p : ill ; 21cm
Previous ed.: 1981. — Includes index
ISBN 0-11-513573-1 (pbk) : Unpriced B82-30856

658.8'48'0943 — West Germany. Exporting. Marketing

How British and German industry exports. — London : Industrial Market Research, 1978. — xiv,158p ; 21x30cm. — (Reports / Industrial Market Research Limited ; 6)
ISBN 0-906142-03-2 (spiral) : £20.00
Primary classification 658.8'48'0941 B82-40744

How German industry exports. — London : Industrial Market Research, 1978. — vi,150p ; 21x30cm. — (Reports / Industrial Market Research Limited ; 5)
ISBN 0-906142-02-4 (spiral) : £20.00 B82-40743

658.8'48'0943 — West Germany. Exporting to European Community countries

The **EEC** as an expanded home market for the United Kingdom and the Federal Republic of Germany : a report / prepared for The Anglo-German Foundation for the Study of Industrial Society by Arthur D. Little Ltd. — London : The Foundation, 1979, c1980. — 134p : ill ; 30cm
English text, German summary
ISBN 0-905492-29-3 (pbk) : £15.00
Primary classification 658.8'48'0941 B82-01286

658.85 — SALESMANSHIP

658.8'5 — Auctions. Purchase & selling — *Manuals*

Hildesley, Hugh. Sotheby's guide to buying & selling at auction. — London : Dent, Oct.1982. — [256]p
ISBN 0-460-04568-7 : £8.95 : CIP entry B82-23992

658.8'5 — Salesmanship

Young, James R.. Personal selling : function, theory, and practice / James R. Young, R. Wayne Mondy. — 2nd ed. — Chicago ; London : Dryden, c1982. — 536p : ill ; 25cm
Previous ed.: 1978. — Includes index
ISBN 0-03-060291-2 : Unpriced B82-20714

658.8'5 — Salesmanship — *Manuals*

Gillam, Alan. The principles and practice of selling / Alan Gillam. — London : Heinemann on behalf of the Institute of Marketing, 1982. — 160p ; 22cm
Bibliography: p154. — Includes index
ISBN 0-434-90661-1 (pbk) : £5.95 B82-32246

Kossen, Stan. Creative selling today / Stan Kossen. — 2nd ed. — New York ; London : Harper & Row, c1982. — xvii,493p : ill,facsims,forms ; 24cm
Previous ed.: San Francisco : Canfield Press, 1977. — Text on lining papers. — Includes index
ISBN 0-06-043767-7 : £14.50 B82-30759

Russell, Frederic A.. Selling : principles and practices / Frederic A. Russell, Frank H. Beach, Richard H. Buskirk. — 11th ed. — New York ; London : McGraw-Hill, c1982. — xvi,560p : ill ; 24cm. — (McGraw-Hill series in marketing)
Previous ed.: published as Textbook of salesmanship, 1978. — Includes index
ISBN 0-07-054353-4 : £18.25 B82-27902

Shinn, George. Introduction to professional selling / George Shinn. — New York ; London : Gregg Division, McGraw-Hill,, c1982. — ix,406p : ill(some col.),forms,ports ; 24cm. — (The Gregg/McGraw-Hill marketing series)
Includes index
ISBN 0-07-056906-1 : £11.25 B82-24552

Tack, Alfred. Sell your way to success / by Alfred Tack. — 6th ed., rev. 2nd impression. — London : Business Books, 1978. — 256p ; 23cm
Previous ed.: 1959. — Includes index
ISBN 0-220-66365-3 (cased) : £5.95
ISBN 0-220-66366-1 (pbk) : Unpriced B82-36647

658.8'5'0973 — United States. Salesmanship — *Manuals*

Lambert, Clark. Field selling skills / Clark Lambert. — New York ; Chichester : Wiley, c1981. — xiii,271p : ill,forms ; 24cm
Bibliography: p267-268. — Includes index
ISBN 0-471-08012-8 : £14.75 B82-03904

658.87 — RETAILING

658.8'7 — Retailing

Bolen, William H.. Contemporary retailing / William H. Bolen. — 2nd ed. — Englewood Cliffs ; London : Prentice-Hall, c1982. — xxi,561p : ill ; 25cm
Previous ed.: 1978. — Includes index
ISBN 0-13-170266-1 : £19.95 B82-37727

658.8'7 — Retailing — *Manuals*

Foster, Ann. The retail handbook : a practical guide to running a successful small retail business / Ann Foster and Bill Thomas. — London : McGraw-Hill, c1981. — xii,158p : ill ; 23cm
Includes index
ISBN 0-07-084565-4 (pbk) : £5.95 : CIP rev. B81-20548

658.8'7 — Shopkeeping — *For children*

Turner, Dorothy. A day with a shopkeeper / Dorothy Turner and Tim Humphrey. — Hove : Wayland, 1982. — 55p : ill ; 24cm. — (A Day in the life)
Bibliography: p55
ISBN 0-85340-967-6 : £3.25 B82-33429

658.8'7'002341 — Great Britain. Retailing — *Career guides*

Working in a shop. — Cambridge : National Extension College, c1980. — 16p + tutors notes([2]p ; 30cm) : ill,facsims,forms ; 30cm
Cover title. — Title page: Basic Skills Unit. — Text on inside covers
ISBN 0-86082-232-x (pbk) : Unpriced B82-39000

658.8'7'00285 — Retailing. Applications of data processing systems — *Conference proceedings*

Retailing in the 80's : automation for profit. — Uxbridge : Online Conferences, c1979. — x,127p : ill,1form ; 29cm. — (The Online series)
Conference papers
ISBN 0-903796-48-1 (pbk) : Unpriced B82-38994

658.8'7'002853 — Retailing. Automation — *Serials*

Retail automation. — Vol.1 no.1 (Sept./Oct. 1981)-. — Brighton (5 East St., Brighton, Sussex [BN1 1HP]) : Retail Management Development Programme, 1981-. — v. : ill ; 30cm
Six issues yearly. — Description based on: Vol.1 no.2 (Nov./Dec. 1981)
ISSN 0263-1377 = Retail automation : £48.00 per year B82-18518

658.8'7'00941 — Great Britain. Retailing — *Statistics*

Eassie, Richard. British retailing facts and trends 1980 / by Richard Eassie, Pamela Robertson. — London (20 Buckingham St., WC2N 6EE) : Mintel Publications, [1980]. — 275p,[6]leaves of plates : col.ill ; 29cm. — (Market intelligence reports)
£495.00 (pbk) B82-35362

658.8'7'00941 — Great Britain. Urban regions. Retailing

Potter, Robert B.. Urban retailing system. — Aldershot : Gower, Aug.1982. — [264]p
ISBN 0-566-00458-5 : £12.50 : CIP entry B82-18576

658.8'701 — Great Britain. Community shops. Organisation — *Manuals*

Gwilliam, Sue. If the village shop closes — : a handbook on community shops / Sue Gwilliam. — [Oxford] ([101 Banbury Rd., Oxford]) : Oxfordshire Rural Community Council in association with the Development Commission, c1981. — 71p : ill,1facsim ; 30cm
Unpriced (pbk) B82-10324

658.8'7'023'41 — Great Britain. Retailing — *Career guides*

Stace, Alexa. Careers in retailing. — London : Kogan Page, Feb.1982. — [100]p
ISBN 0-85038-466-4 (cased) : £5.95 : CIP entry
ISBN 0-85038-467-2 (pbk) : £2.50 B82-00145

658.8'708'05 — Franchises — *Serials*

Franchise reporter. — Nov. 1981-. — London (37 Nottingham Rd, SW17 7EA) : Franchise Publications, 1981-. — v. ; 30cm
Eight issues yearly. — Description based on: May 1982 issue
ISSN 0263-8053 = Franchise reporter : £15.00 per year B82-32166

658.8'708'0941 — Great Britain. Franchising

Adams, John, *19---*. Franchising : practice and precedents in business format franchising / John Adams, K.V. Prichard Jones. — London : Butterworths, 1981. — xxvi,324p : ill ; 26cm
Includes index
ISBN 0-406-10115-9 : Unpriced B82-16615

Mendelsohn, M.. The guide to franchising / by M. Mendelsohn. — 3rd ed. — Oxford : Pergamon, 1982. — xv,275p ; 22cm
Previous ed.: 1979. — Includes index
ISBN 0-08-025845-x : £12.50 : CIP rev. B81-34468

658.8'71'0973 — United States. Department stores. British consumer goods. Marketing — *For British businessmen*

Doing business with American department stores / [prepared by the British Overseas Trade Board and the Central Office of Information]. — London : British Overseas Trade Board, 1980. — 18p ; 22cm
Text on inside cover
Unpriced (pbk) B82-16035

658.8'72'0941 — Great Britain. Direct-mail marketing

Fairlie, Robin. Direct mail : principles and practice / Robin Fairlie. — London : Kogan Page, 1979. — 222p : ill ; 23cm
Bibliography: p212-213. — Includes index
ISBN 0-85038-249-1 : £12.50 B82-13309

658.8'72'0941 — Great Britain. Home mail-order — *Serials*

Mail order trader : a monthly report on the art of selling by mail. — Vol.1, no.1 (Feb. 1982). — Oxford (P.O. Box 125, Oxford) : Oxford Research Associates for the Enterprise Association, 1982-1982. — 1v. ; 30cm
Monthly. — Merged with: International trader to become: Worldwide business opportunities
ISSN 0263-1482 = Mail order trader : Available only to Association members B82-18716

658.8'72'0973 — United States. Direct-mail marketing — *Manuals*

Nash, Edward L.. Direct marketing : strategy, planning, execution / Edward L. Nash. — New York ; London : McGraw-Hill, c1982. — xxii,423p : ill ; 24cm
Includes index
ISBN 0-07-046019-1 : £18.95 B82-25986

658.8'72'0973 — United States. Mail-order firms. Organisation — *Manuals*

Cohen, William A.. Building a mail order business : a complete manual for success / William A. Cohen. — New York ; Chichester : Wiley, c1982. — xiv,442p : ill,facsims,forms ; 25cm
Includes index
ISBN 0-471-08803-x : £13.30 B82-27725

658.88 — CREDIT MANAGEMENT

658.8'8'0941 — Great Britain. Small firms. Credit management — *Manuals*

Lewis, Mel. How to collect money that is owed to you / Mel Lewis. — London : McGraw-Hill, c1982. — 130p : ill,forms ; 24cm
Bibliography: p121-125. — Includes index
ISBN 0-07-084578-6 : £8.95 : CIP rev. B82-03728

659.1 — ADVERTISING

659.1 — Advertising

Aaker, David A.. Advertising management / David A. Aaker, John G. Myers. — 2nd ed. — Englewood Cliffs ; London : Prentice-Hall, c1982. — xiii,560p : ill,facsims,ports ; 24cm. — (Prentice-Hall international series in management)
Previous ed.: 1975. — Includes index
ISBN 0-13-016006-7 : £18.70 B82-23239

Dyer, Gillian. Advertising as communication. — London : Methuen, Oct.1982. — [160]p. — (Studies in communication)
ISBN 0-416-74520-2 (cased) : £8.00 : CIP entry
ISBN 0-416-74530-x (pbk) : £3.95 B82-23986

Fulop, Christina. Advertising, competition and consumer behaviour : public policy and the market / Christina Fulop. — London : Holt, Rinehart and Winston with the Advertising Association, c1981. — x,176p ; 25cm
Bibliography: p167-171. — Includes index
ISBN 0-03-910295-5 : £12.50 : CIP rev. B81-31206

Wright, John S.. Advertising. — 5th ed. / John S. Wright, Willis L. Winter, Jr., Sherilyn K. Zeigler. — New York ; London : McGraw-Hill, c1982. — xiv,545p,[16]p of plates : ill(some col.),facsims,forms,maps,ports ; 27cm. — (McGraw-Hill series in marketing)
Previous ed.: 1977. — Ill on lining papers. — Includes bibliographies and index
ISBN 0-07-072069-x : £17.50 B82-27230

659.1 — Advertising — *Manuals*

Switkin, Abraham. Ads : design & make your own / Abraham Switkin. — New York ; London : Van Nostrand Reinhold, c1981. — 160p : ill,facsims ; 29cm
Bibliography: p157. — Includes index
ISBN 0-442-24342-1 : £13.55 B82-00749

White, Roderick. Advertising. — Maidenhead : McGraw-Hill, Dec.1982. — [256]p
Originally published: 1980
ISBN 0-07-084589-1 (pbk) : £7.50 : CIP entry B82-39258

659.1 — Advertising. Positioning

Crosier, Keith. Ladders in the mind : report on a new marketing strategy for successfully communicating with an over-communicated audience / by Keith Crosier. — Glasgow (2 Blythswood Sq., Glasgow G2 4UB) : Struthers Advertising Group, c1981. — 26p : ill ; 21cm
Unpriced (pbk) B82-25685

659.1 — Great Britain. Women. Portrayal by advertising media. Attitudes of women consumers

Hamilton, Robert, *1937-*. Adman and Eve : an empirical study of the relative marketing effectiveness of traditional and modern portrayals of women in certain mass-media advertisements / carried out in June-October 1981 for the Equal Opportunities Commission ; by Robert Hamilton, Brian Haworth, Nazli Sardar ; of the Marketing Consultancy and Research Services of the Department of Marketing in the Lancaster University School of Management and Organisational Sciences. — Manchester : Equal Opportunities Commission, 1982. — ii,41leaves ; 30cm
Bibliography: p40-41
ISBN 0-905829-52-2 (spiral) : Unpriced B82-26637

659.1'023'41 — Great Britain. Advertising — *Career guides*

Attwood, Tony. Careers in advertising / Tony Attwood. — Totnes : Hamilton House, 1981. — 24p ; 21cm. — (Careerscope ; 1)
ISBN 0-906888-18-2 (pbk) : Unpriced B82-03068

659.1'042'0973 — United States. Social change. Role of advertising

Berman, Ronald. Advertising and social change / Ronald Berman. — Beverly Hills ; London : Sage, c1981. — 159p ; 23cm. — (The Sage commtext series ; v.8)
Bibliography: p151-154. — Includes index
ISBN 0-8039-1737-6 (cased) : Unpriced
ISBN 0-8039-1738-4 (pbk) : £4.95 B82-11693

Ewen, Stuart. Channels of desire : mass images and the shaping of American consciousness / Stuart Ewen and Elizabeth Ewen. — New York ; London : McGraw-Hill, 1982. — viii,312p ; 21cm
Includes index
ISBN 0-07-019850-0 (cased) : Unpriced
ISBN 0-07-019848-9 (pbk) : £9.95 B82-40607

659.1'05 — Advertising — *Serials*

Creative review. — Vol.1, no.1 (May 1980)-. — London (60 Kingly St., W1R 5LH) : Marketing Week Communications, 1980-. — v. : ill(some col.),ports ; 28cm
Quarterly (1980-1981), monthly (Sept. 1981-). — Description based on: Vol.2, no.1 (Sept. 1981)
ISSN 0262-1037 = Creative review : £15.00 per year B82-09077

659.1′068 — Advertising industries. Management
Patti, Charles H.. Advertising management : cases and concepts / Charles H. Patti, John H. Murphy. — New York ; Chichester : Wiley, c1978. — xiv,298p : ill,facsims,plans ; 24cm. — (Wiley series in marketing)
Includes bibliographies and index
ISBN 0-471-86999-6 : £15.50 B82-36686

659.1′0941 — Great Britain. Advertising, *to 1979*
Nevett, T. R.. Advertising in Britain. — London : Scolar Press, May 1981. — [288]p
ISBN 0-85967-598-x (cased) : £15.00 : CIP entry
ISBN 0-85967-632-3 (pbk) : £6.95 B81-08808

659.1′0941 — Great Britain. Advertising, *to 1981*
Nevett, T. R.. Advertising in Britain : a history / T.R. Nevett. — London : Heinemann on behalf of the History of Advertising Trust, 1982. — xiii,231p,[32]p of plates : ill(some col.),facsims,ports(some col.) ; 25cm
Bibliography: p218-225. — Includes index
ISBN 0-434-49642-1 : £12.50 B82-17171

659.1′0973 — United States. Advertising
Dunn, S. Watson. Advertising : its role in modern marketing. — 5th ed. / S. Watson Dunn, Arnold M. Barban. — Chicago ; London : Dryden, c1982. — xxi,710p,[8]p of plates : ill(some col.),1col.map,music,facsims (some col.),ports ; 25cm. — (Dryden Press series in marketing)
Previous ed.: 1978. — Includes bibliographies and index
ISBN 0-03-060049-9 : Unpriced B82-20606

659.1′125′0941 — Great Britain. Advertising agencies. Attitudes of Scottish advertisers
Crosier, Keith. The advertising iceberg : report on an investigation into Scottish advertisers′ expectations of advertising agencies / by Keith Crosier. — Glasgow (2 Blythswood Sq., Glasgow G2 4UB) : Struthers Advertising Group, c1980. — 60p ; 21cm
Unpriced (pbk) B82-28338

659.13′094 — Western Europe. Advertising media — *Statistics — Serials*
European media guide / JWT/Campaign Europe. — 1982-. — [London] ([22 Lancaster Gate, W2 3LY]) : Campaign Europe, [1981]-. — v. : ill,maps ; 28cm
Unpriced B82-11814

659.13′14 — Tobacco. Pictorial advertising — *Illustrations*
Pipe dreams : early advertising art from the Imperial Tobacco Company / edited by Mike Dempsey ; introduced by Tim Shackleton. — London : Pavilion Books, 1982. — 94p : chiefly ill(some col.),facsims ; 30cm
ISBN 0-907516-12-2 (pbk) : £6.95 : CIP rev. B82-05791

659.13′22 — Slogans in English — *Anthologies*
Rees, Nigel. Slogans. — London : Allen & Unwin, July 1982. — [176]p
ISBN 0-04-827064-4 : £7.50 : CIP entry B82-12424

659.13′23 — Commercial photography
Advertising photography / [edited and compiled] by Allyn Salomon. — London : Thames and Hudson, c1982. — 175p : ill(some col.),ports (some col.) ; 32cm
Originally published: New York : Amphoto Books, 1982
ISBN 0-500-54081-0 : £12.00 B82-34981

659.13′23 — Rock music. Promotional material. Design. Techniques
Thorgerson, Storm. The goodbye look. — London : Vermilion, Nov.1982. — [128]p
ISBN 0-09-150641-7 (pbk) : £7.95 : CIP entry B82-29418

659.13′3 — Great Britain. Direct-mail advertising — *Manuals*
A **Guide** to effective direct mail. — London (Marketing Dept., Postal headquarters, St. Martins-le-Grand EC1A 1HQ) : Post Office, [1982?]. — 27p : col.ill,facsims(some col.) ; 21x30cm
Unpriced (pbk) B82-19583

659.13′4 — Great Britain. Advertising posters. Sites
Poster advertising site evaluation in Great Britain : a study of advertisers′ and agents′ attitudes / prepared for Malcrest Advertising Ltd. — London : Economist Intelligence Unit. — (E.I.U. report)
Vol.2: Findings and conclusions. — 1981. — 53,xivleaves : ill ; 30cm
Unpriced (spiral) B82-02542

659.13′42 — British enamel advertising signs, *to ca 1950*
Baglee, Christopher. Street jewellery : a history of enamel advertising signs / by Christopher Baglee & Andrew Morley. — London : New Cavendish, 1978 (1979 [printing]). — 87p : ill (some col.),1map,facsims ; 29cm
Bibliography: p84. — Includes index
ISBN 0-904568-16-4 (pbk) : £3.50 B82-00679

659.1′5 — Libraries. Displays — *Manuals*
Kohn, Rita. Experiencing displays / by Rita Kohn. — Metuchen ; London : Scarecrow, 1982. — xvi,220p : ill,forms ; 28cm
Includes index
ISBN 0-8108-1534-6 (pbk) : £11.60 B82-32089

659.1′5 — Retailing. Display work — *Manuals*
Mills, Kenneth H.. [Create distinctive displays]. Applied visual merchandising / Kenneth H. Mills, Judith E. Paul. — Englewood Cliffs ; London : Prentice-Hall, c1982. — xii,224p,[4]p of plates : ill(some col.),forms ; 25cm
Originally published: 1974. — Bibliography: p213-214. — Includes index
ISBN 0-13-043331-4 : £14.95 B82-24092

659.1′52 — Exhibitions. Design — *Manuals*
The **Design** of educational exhibits. — London : Allen & Unwin, Nov.1982. — [208]p
ISBN 0-04-069002-4 : £19.95 : CIP entry B82-28995

659.1′52 — Exhibitions. Displays — *Amateurs′ manuals*
A **Simple** guide to display. — Slough (375 Bath Rd., Slough, Berks. SL1 5QD) : SD Systems Ltd, [1981?]. — [8]p : ill ; 22cm
Unpriced (unbound) B82-04363

659.1′52 — United States. Advertising & fashion. Modelling — *Career guides*
Hunt, Cecily. How to get work & make money in commercials & modeling / by Cecily Hunt. — New York ; London : Van Nostrand Reinhold, c1982. — 176p : ill,ports ; 29cm
Includes index
ISBN 0-442-23643-3 (cased) : Unpriced
ISBN 0-442-23644-1 (pbk) : £11.00 B82-38588

659.1′52 — Women fashion models — *Interviews*
Lopez, Antonio. Antonio′s girls / Antonio Lopez ; text by Christopher Hemphill ; designed by Juan Ramos ; devised and edited by Karen Amiel. — London : Thames and Hudson, 1982. — 128p : ill(some col.),ports(some col.) ; 29cm
ISBN 0-500-27265-4 (pbk) : £8.95
Primary classification 746.9′2 B82-24935

659.1′52′025 — Trade exhibitions — *Directories — Serials*
The **Exhibition** trade′s directory. — 1982/83. — London : Kogan Page, Sept.1982. — [300]p
ISBN 0-85038-545-8 : £18.00 : CIP entry B82-22812

659.1′9374841 — Great Britain. Adult education institutions. Publicity — *Manuals*
Reaching the public. — [London] ([Chequer Centre, Chequer St., Bunhill Row, EC1Y 8PL]) : Educational Centres Association, [1982?]. — [4]p ; 21cm. — (ECA advisory leaflet ; no.6)
Unpriced (unbound) B82-29617

659.2 — PUBLIC RELATIONS

659.2 — Business firms. Public relations
Kopel, Ellis. Financial and corporate public relations. — London : McGraw-Hill, July 1982. — [128]p
ISBN 0-07-084586-7 : £12.95 : CIP entry B82-17963

659.2 — Public relations
Coulson-Thomas, Colin. Public relations is your business : a guide for every manager / Colin Coulson-Thomas. — London : Business Books, 1981. — 273p : ill ; 24cm
Includes index
ISBN 0-09-142960-9 : Unpriced : CIP rev. B81-17516

Cutlip, Scott M.. Effective public relations / Scott M. Cutlip, Allen H. Center. — Rev. 5th ed. — Englewood Cliffs ; London : Prentice-Hall, c1982. — xvii,612p : ill,facsims,ports ; 24cm
Previous ed.: 1978. — Includes bibliographies and index
ISBN 0-13-245068-2 : £15.75 B82-27565

Jefkins, Frank. Public relations made simple / Frank Jefkins. — London : Heinemann, c1982. — xiv,271p : ill ; 23cm. — (Made simple books)
Bibliography: p261-262. — Includes index
ISBN 0-434-98518-x (cased) : £6.95
ISBN 0-434-98506-6 (pbk) : £2.95 B82-32241

The **Practice** of public relations / edited by Wilfred Howard. — London : Heinemann, 1982. — xxi,250p,[4]p of plates : ill ; 24cm
Includes index
ISBN 0-434-90766-9 (pbk) : £7.95 B82-21671

659.2′0973 — United States. Business firms. Public relations, *1900-1950*
Tedlow, Richard S.. Keeping the corporate image : public relations and business, 1900-1950 / by Richard S. Tedlow. — Greenwich, Conn. : Jai Press ; London : distributed by Jaicon Press, c1979. — xx,233p ; 24cm. — (Industrial development and the social fabric ; v.3)
Bibliography: p213-227. — Includes index
ISBN 0-89232-095-8 : £21.10 B82-02012

659.2′0973 — United States. Public relations
Lovell, Ronald P.. Inside public relations / Ronald P. Lovell. — Boston, Mass. ; London : Allyn and Bacon, c1982. — xv,415p : ill,facsims,ports ; 25cm
Bibliography: p405-407. — Includes index
ISBN 0-205-07741-2 : £21.95 B82-31686

659.2′0973 — United States. Publicity — *Amateurs′ manuals*
Winston, Martin Bradley. Getting publicity / Martin Bradley Winston. — New York ; Chichester : Wiley, c1982. — x,193p : ill ; 23cm
Includes index
ISBN 0-471-08225-2 (pbk) : £6.65 B82-32737

659.2′93632′0973 — United States. Police. Relations with community
Johnson, Thomas A. (Thomas Alfred). The police and society : an environment for collaboration and confrontation / Thomas A. Johnson, Gordon E. Misner, Lee P. Brown. — Englewood Cliffs ; London : Prentice-Hall, c1981. — xi,404p ; 24cm. — (Prentice-Hall series in criminal justice)
Includes index
ISBN 0-13-684076-0 : £13.45 B82-07543

659.2′9371′00973 — United States. Schools. Public relations
Hilldrup, Robert P.. Improving school public relations / Robert P. Hilldrup. — Boston, Mass. ; London : Allyn and Bacon, c1982. — xi,225p ; 25cm
ISBN 0-205-07738-2 : £18.95 B82-31550

659.2′93805′0941 — Great Britain. Transport services. Public relations
Wragg, David W.. Publicity and customer relations in transport management / David W. Wragg. — Aldershot : Gower, c1981. — xiii,144p ; 23cm. — (Gower Pegasus transport library)
Bibliography: p137-138. — Includes index
ISBN 0-566-00442-9 (cased) : Unpriced : CIP rev.
ISBN 0-566-00516-6 (pbk) : Unpriced B81-30561

659.2′963′09411 — Scotland. Agricultural industries. Farms. Open days. Attitudes of visitors

Lee, T. R.. The educational effectiveness of the farm open day / T.R. Lee, D.L. Uzzell ; commissioned by the Countryside Commission for Scotland. — Perth : The Commission, c1980. — 53p : ill ; 30cm
Bibliography: p48
ISBN 0-902226-49-5 (pbk) : Unpriced
B82-32200

659.2′96748′0973 — United States. Timber products industries. Public relations

Sonnenfeld, Jeffrey A.. Corporate views of the public interest : perceptions of the forest products industry / Jeffery A. Sonnenfeld. — Boston, Mass. : Auburn House ; London : distributed by Eurospan, c1981. — xvi,285p : ill ; 25cm
Includes index
ISBN 0-86569-060-x : £16.25 B82-13428

659.2′99142 — England. Tourism. Promotion by local authorities

Tourism enterprise by local authorities : a review of new developments : based on an assessment by Michael Dower of the entries for the first series of Sir Mark Henig awards / English Tourist Board. — London : English Tourist Board, [1982?]. — 37p : ill(some col.),1col.map,ports(some col.) ; 20x21cm
Cover title
£5.00 (pbk) B82-30848

659.2′9914228 — Isle of Wight. Tourism. Promotion — *Proposals*

Isle of Wight tourism study / prepared by English Tourist Board Planning and Research Services Branch ; for Isle of Wight Tourist Board, English Tourist Board, Southern Tourist Board. — London : English Tourist Board, 1981. — v,64p : ill,maps ; 30cm
List no.: 7813
£3.50 (spiral) B82-05052

660 — CHEMICAL TECHNOLOGY

660 — Chemical technology — *Case studies — For schools*

Harrison, W.. Industrial chemistry. — London : Edward Arnold, Jan.1982. — 1v.
ISBN 0-7131-0588-7 (pbk) : CIP entry
B81-34581

660′.03′21 — Chemical technology — *Encyclopaedias*

Encyclopedia of chemical technology / editorial board Herman F. Mark ... [et al.]. — 3rd ed. — New York ; Chichester : Wiley
Vol.15: Matches to n-nitrosamines / executive editor Martin Grayson ; associate editor David Eckroth. — c1981. — xxvi,996p : ill ; 27cm
At head of title: Kirk-Othmer. — Previous ed.: / by Raymond Eller Kirk and Donald Frederick Othmer, 1963-1972
ISBN 0-471-02068-0 : £70.00 B82-02488

Encyclopedia of chemical technology / editorial board Herman F. Mark ... [et al.]. — 3nd ed. — New York ; Chichester : Wiley
Previous ed.: / by Raymond Eller Kirk and Donald Frederick Othmer. 1963-1972
Vol.16: Noise pollution to perfumes / executive editor Martin Grayson ; associate editor David Eckroth. — c1981. — xxvi,971p : ill ; 27cm
At head of title: Kirk-Othmer
ISBN 0-471-02069-9 : £70.00 B82-13291

Encyclopedia of chemical technology / [editorial board Herman F. Mark ... et al.]. — 3rd ed. — New York ; Chichester : Wiley
Previous ed.: / by Kirk and Othmer. New York : London : Interscience, 1963-72
Vol.18: Plant-growth substances to potassium compounds / executive editor Martin Grayson ; associate editor David Eckroth. — c1982. — xxvi,950p : ill ; 27cm
At head of title: Kirk-Othmer
ISBN 0-471-02071-0 : £95.00 B82-36948

Encyclopedia of chemical technology. — 3rd ed. — New York ; Chichester : Wiley
At head of title: Kirk-Othmer. — Previous ed.: / by Kirk and Othmer
Index : volumes 13 to 16 : hydrogen-ion activity to perfumes. — 1982. — 245p ; 26cm
ISBN 0-471-02070-2 (pbk) : Unpriced
B82-31102

Encyclopedia of chemical technology. — 3rd ed. — New York ; Chichester : Wiley
At head of title: Kirk-Othmer. — Previous ed.: / by Kirk and Othmer. 1963-1972
Index : volumes 13 to 16 : hydrogen-ion activity to perfumes. — c1982. — 245p ; 26cm
ISBN 0-471-02070-2 (pbk) : Unpriced
B82-28031

660′.041 — Solids. Processing

Bridgwater, J.. New territory : the chemical processing of solids / J. Bridgwater. — [Birmingham] : University of Birmingham, 1981. — 19p : ill ; 22cm
Cover title
ISBN 0-7044-0580-6 (pbk) : Unpriced
B82-08491

660.2 — CHEMICAL ENGINEERING

660.2 — Chemical engineering

Coulson, J. M.. Chemical engineering. — Oxford : Pergamon. — (Pergamon international library)
Vol.6: Design. — Sept.1982. — [720]p
ISBN 0-08-022969-7 (cased) : £35.00 : CIP entry
ISBN 0-08-022970-0 (pbk) : £12.50
B82-19088

660.2 — Chemical engineering. Calculations

Himmelblau, David M.. Basic principles and calculations in chemical engineering / David M. Himmelblau. — 4th ed. — Englewood Cliffs ; London : Prentice-Hall, c1982. — xii,628p : ill ; 25cm. — (Prentice-Hall international series in the physical and chemical engineering sciences)
Previous ed.: 1974. — One folded sheet in pocket. — Includes index
ISBN 0-13-066498-7 : £23.95 B82-37725

660.2 — Chemical engineering — *Conference proceedings*

A **Century** of chemical engineering / [based on the proceedings of an international symposium on the history of chemical engineering, held August 24-29, 1980, at the 108th meeting of the Chemical Society, in Las Vegas, Nevada] ; edited by William F. Furter. — New York ; London : Plenum, c1982. — viii,463p : ill,1map,ports ; 26cm
Includes bibliographies and index
ISBN 0-306-40895-3 : Unpriced B82-31528

In-house or sub-contracted resources for process engineering projects? : January 21st 1981 / edited by B.D. Willson. — Manchester : Institution of Chemical Engineers, North Western Branch, c1982. — 47p in various pagings : ill ; 30cm. — (Symposium papers 1981 ; no.1)
Conference proceedings
ISBN 0-906636-09-4 (pbk) : £6.00 (£5.00 to members of the Institution) B82-34401

660.2′05 — Chemical engineering — *Serials*

Chemical engineering bulletin. — Issue 1 (1976)-issue 11 (1981). — Bracknell (Easthampstead Rd, Bracknell, Berks. RG12 1NS) : Technical Indexes Ltd., 1976-1981. — 11v. : ill ; 30cm
Two issues yearly. — Supplement to: Chemical engineering index. — Description based on: Issue 10 (Feb. to July 1981)
ISSN 0262-2564 = Chemical engineering bulletin : Unpriced B82-26139

660.2′07 — Great Britain. Chemical engineering industries. Personnel. Training

The **Training** and further education of craftsmen and technicians for the process industries / [a report by the Working Party on Craft and Technician Training and Education for the Process Industries Manpower Group]. — [Great Britain] : Ceramics, Glass and Mineral Products Industry Training Board, c1982. — 14p : 1ill ; 30cm
Unpriced (unbound) B82-30862

660.2′07′114 — Western Europe. Higher education institutions. Curriculum subjects: Chemical engineering — *Conference proceedings*

Chemical engineering education : organised by the Institution of Chemical Engineers in London, 16/18 September 1981. — Rugby : The Institution, c1981. — 212p ; 22cm. — (EFEC publication series ; no.18) (The Institution of Chemical Engineers symposium series ; no.70)
ISBN 0-85295-143-4 : Unpriced B82-39510

660.2′07′1141 — Great Britain. Higher education institutions. Curriculum subjects: Chemical engineering. Courses — *Directories*

A **Guide** to chemical engineering education : university, polytechnic and college courses / compiled and edited by Gordon S.G. Beveridge and J. Harry Bowen. — Rugby : Institution of Chemical Engineers, c1980. — 110p ; 21cm
ISBN 0-85295-139-6 (pbk) : £4.00 B82-17145

660.2′8 — Chemical engineering plants. Reliability. On-line monitoring — *Conference proceedings*

On-line surveillance and monitoring of plant reliability : papers presented at a conference sponsored by the Society of Chemical Industry and held at Imperial College, London, England, 23-25 September 1980. — London : Society of Chemical Industry, 1981. — 349p : ill ; 30cm
Includes index
ISBN 0-901001-67-8 (pbk) : Unpriced
B82-23569

660.2′8′00153111 — Chemical engineering plants. Dynamics

Mohilla, Rezsö. Chemical process dynamics / by Rezsö Mohilla and Béla Ferencz. — Amsterdam ; Oxford : Elsevier Scientific, 1982. — 299p : ill ; 25cm. — (Fundamental studies in engineering ; 4)
Translation of: Vegyipari folyamatok dinamikája. — Bibliography: p295-296. — Includes index
ISBN 0-444-99730-x : Unpriced : CIP rev.
B81-33863

660.2′8′003 — Chemical engineering equipment — *Polyglot dictionaries*

Illustrated glossary of process equipment = Glossaire illustré des équipements de procédé = Glosario ilustrado de equipos de proceso / Bernard H. Paruit editor. — Houston ; London : Gulf, c1982. — xxvii,318p : ill ; 22cm
English, French and Spanish text
ISBN 0-87201-691-9 : Unpriced B82-29164

660.2′804 — Chemical engineering plants. Dusts. Explosions. Safety measures

Cross, Jean. Dust explosions / Jean Cross and Donald Farrer. — New York ; London : Plenum, c1982. — ix,248p : ill ; 24cm
Bibliography: p231-245. — Includes index
ISBN 0-306-40871-6 : Unpriced B82-39081

660.2′804 — Factories. Ducts. Explosion reliefs

Flame arresters and explosion reliefs / Health and Safety Executive. — London : H.M.S.O., 1980. — 44p ; ill ; 21cm. — (Health and safety series booklet ; HS(G)11)
Bibliography: p44
ISBN 0-11-883258-1 (pbk) : £1.25 : CIP rev.
Primary classification 660.2′804 B80-06993

660.2′804 — Factories. Piping systems. Flame arresters

Flame arresters and explosion reliefs / Health and Safety Executive. — London : H.M.S.O., 1980. — 44p ; ill ; 21cm. — (Health and safety series booklet ; HS(G)11)
Bibliography: p44
ISBN 0-11-883258-1 (pbk) : £1.25 : CIP rev.
Also classified at 660.2′804 B80-06993

660.2′804 — Flame arresters. Testing — *Manuals*

Rogowski, Z. W.. Manual for testing flame arresters / Z.W. Rogowski. — Borehamwood (Borehamwood, Hertfordshire WD6 2BL) : Dept, of the Environment, Building Research Establishment, Fire Research Station, 1978. — 11p : ill ; 30cm
£1.00 (pbk) B82-25803

660.2′804 — Great Britain. Chemical engineering plants. Hazards

Lihou, D. A.. Hazard identification and control in the process industries / [a report prepared by D.A. Lihou from the proceedings of a conference organised by the Scientific and Technical Studies Division of Oyez International Business Communications Ltd in London in 1980]. — [London] : Oyez, [1981]. — 139leaves : ill ; 30cm. — (Oyez intelligence reports)
ISBN 0-85120-576-3 (spiral) : Unpriced
B82-00035

660.2′83 — Chemical engineering equipment. Electrostatic precipitators

Böhm, Jaroslav. Electrostatic precipitators / Jaroslav Böhm. — Amsterdam ; Oxford : Elsevier Scientific, 1982. — 366p : ill ; 25cm. — (Chemical engineering monographs ; v.14)
Translation of: Elektrické odlučovaće. — Bibliography: p348-359. — Includes index
ISBN 0-444-99764-4 : Unpriced : CIP rev.
B81-31612

660.2′83 — Chemical engineering equipment: Reactors. Design

Rose, L. M.. Chemical reactor design in practice / L.M. Rose. — Amsterdam ; Oxford : Elsevier Scientific, 1981. — xxii,378p : ill ; 25cm. — (Chemical engineering monographs ; 13)
Includes bibliographies and index
ISBN 0-444-42018-5 : Unpriced : CIP rev.
B81-28196

660.2′83 — Chemical engineering equipment. Silencers & acoustic enclosures — *Standards — For petroleum industries*

Acoustic insulation of pipes, valves and flanges. — Chichester : Wiley, Dec.1982. — [22]p. — (Specification / Oil Companies Materials Association ; no.NWG-5)
ISBN 0-471-26246-3 : £10.00 : CIP entry
B82-37669

General specification for silencers and acoustic enclosures. — London : Heyden on behalf of the Institute of Petroleum in association with the Oil Companies Materials Association, 1979. — iii,16p : form ; 30cm. — (Specification / Oil Companies Materials Association ; no.NWG-4)
Cover title
ISBN 0-85501-397-4 (pbk) : £4.80 B82-00773

660.2′83 — Chemical engineering. Instrumentation

Andrew, W. G.. Applied instrumentation in the process industries. — 2nd ed. — Houston ; London : Gulf Publishing
Previous ed.: 1974
Vol.2: Practical guidelines / W.G. Andrew, H.B. Williams. — 1980. — viii,312p : ill,forms ; 29cm
Includes index
ISBN 0-87201-383-9 : £21.50 B82-35681

660.2′83 — Great Britain. Chemical engineering equipment: Reactors. Venting — *Conference proceedings*

The **Safe** venting of chemical reactors : March 6-7, 1979 / [a symposium organised by the Chester Centre of the N.W. Branch of the Institution of Chemical Engineers on Tuesday 6th and Wednesday 7th March 1979] ; edited by C. Minors. — Manchester : The Branch, c1979. — 122p in various pagings : ill ; 30cm. — (Symposium papers 1979 ; no.2)
ISBN 0-906636-01-9 (pbk) : £12.50 (£10.00 to Institution members) B82-40933

660.2′842 — Chemical engineering. Separation

King, C. Judson. Separation processes / C. Judson King. — 2nd ed. — New York ; London : McGraw-Hill, c1980. — xxvi,850p : ill ; 25cm. — (McGraw-Hill chemical engineering series)
Previous ed.: 1971. — Includes bibliographies and index
ISBN 0-07-034612-7 : £24.75 B82-22466

660.2′842 — Chemical engineering. Transport phenomena

Bennett, C. O.. Momentum, heat, and mass transfer / C.O. Bennett, J.E. Myers. — 3rd ed. — New York ; London : McGraw-Hill, c1982. — xii,832p : ill ; 25cm. — (McGraw-Hill chemical engineering series)
Previous ed.: 1974. — Text on lining papers. — Includes index
ISBN 0-07-004671-9 : £26.75 B82-29456

660.2′842 — Solid materials. Separation from liquid materials

Solid-liquid separation / editor Ladislav Svarovsky. — 2nd ed. — London : Butterworths, 1981. — xiii,556p : ill ; 25cm. — (Butterworths monographs in chemistry and chemical engineering)
Previous ed.: 1977. — Includes index
ISBN 0-408-70943-x : Unpriced : CIP rev.
B81-31182

660.2′842′05 — Chemical engineering. Separation - *Serials*

Progress in filtration and separation. — Vol.2. — Oxford : Elsevier Scientific, July 1981. — [350]p
ISBN 0-444-42006-1 : CIP entry
Primary classification 660.2′8424′05
B81-19137

660.2′8423 — Chemical engineering. Absorption — *Conference proceedings*

What′s new in absorption with chemical reaction? : Manchester, 16th December 1981 / edited by J.E. Gillett. — [Manchester] : Institution of Chemical Engineers, North Western Branch, c1982. — 1v.(various pagings) : ill ; 30cm. — (Symposium papers 1981 ; no.6)
Conference proceedings
ISBN 0-906636-13-2 (pbk) : £12.00 (£10.00 to members) B82-34245

660.2′8424 — Filtration

Percolation structures and processes. — Bristol : Hilger, Nov.1982. — [250]p. — (Annals of the Israel Physical Society, ISSN 0309-8710 ; v.5)
ISBN 0-85274-477-3 : £25.00 : CIP entry
B82-28755

660.2′8424′05 — Filtration - *Serials*

Progress in filtration and separation. — Vol.2. — Oxford : Elsevier Scientific, July 1981. — [350]p
ISBN 0-444-42006-1 : CIP entry
Also classified at 660.2′842′05 B81-19137

660.2′8425 — Chemical engineering. Multicomponent distillation

Holland, Charles D.. Fundamentals of multicomponent distillation / Charles D. Holland. — New York ; London : McGraw-Hill, c1981. — xiv,626p : ill ; 25cm. — (McGraw-Hill chemical engineering series)
Includes bibliographies and index
ISBN 0-07-029567-0 : £27.95 B82-24903

660.2′8425 — Continuous distillation plants. Automatic control — *Conference proceedings*

Automatic control in desalination and the oil industry. — Oxford : Pergamon Press, Mar.1982. — [231]p
Conference papers
ISBN 0-08-028698-4 : £22.50 : CIP entry
B82-01537

660.2′8425 — Solar stills

Solar distillation : a practical study of a wide range of stills and their optimum design, construction and performance / by M.A.S. Malik ... [et al.]. — Oxford : Pergamon, 1982. — x,175p : ill,1plan ; 24cm
Bibliography: p131-170. — Includes index
ISBN 0-08-028679-8 : £12.50 : CIP rev.
B82-07244

660.2′8425′0681 — Distillation plants. Cost-effectiveness — *Conference proceedings*

Cost savings in distillation : a symposium organised by the Yorkshire Branch and Fluid Separation Processes Group of the Institution of Chemical Engineers. — Rugby : Institution of Chemical Engineers, c1981. — 177p : ill ; 22cm. — (Institution of Chemical Engineers symposium series ; no.61)
Bibliography: p175-176
ISBN 0-85295-141-8 : Unpriced B82-04457

660.2′8426 — Evaporating ovens. Safety measures

Evaporating and other ovens. — London : Health & Safety Executive, July 1981. — [56]p. — (HS(G))
ISBN 0-11-883433-9 (pbk) : CIP entry
B81-13505

660.2′8426 — Solids. Thermal drying

Drying ′82 / edited by Arun S. Mujumder. — Washington [D.C.] ; London : Hemisphere ; London : McGraw-Hill [[distributor]], c1982. — ix,254p : ill ; 29cm
Includes index
ISBN 0-07-043982-6 : Unpriced B82-40605

660.2′84292 — Industrial chemicals: Liquids. Heats of mixing — *Tables*

Christensen, James J.. Handbook of heats of mixing / James J. Christensen, Richard W. Hanks, Reed M. Izatt. — New York ; Chichester : Wiley, c1982. — xiv,1586p ; 29cm
Includes index
ISBN 0-471-07960-x : Unpriced B82-38978

660.2′84292 — Mixtures. Mixing — *Conference proceedings*

European Conference on Mixing *(3rd : 1979 : University of York)*. Proceedings of the third European Conference on Mixing : held at the University of York, England, April 4th-6th, 1979 / organised by BHRA Fluid Engineering in conjunction with the Institution of Chemical Engineers. — Cranfield : BHRA Fluid Engineering, c1979. — 2 : v.,ill ; 30cm
Includes index
ISBN 0-906085-31-4 (pbk) : Unpriced : CIP rev.
ISBN 0-906085-32-2 (v.1) : Unpriced
ISBN 0-906085-33-0 (v.2) : Unpriced
B79-12503

European Conference on Mixing *(4th : 1982 : Noordwijkerhout)*. Papers presented at the Fourth European Conference on Mixing : held at Noordwijkerhout, Netherlands, September 15-17, 1982 / conference sponsored and organised by BHRA Fluid Engineering ; [editors H.S. Stephens and D.H. Goodes]. — Cranfield : BHRA Fluid Engineering, [1982]. — viii,476p : ill ; 30cm
ISBN 0-906085-66-7 (pbk) : Unpriced
B82-34999

660.2′84298 — Industrial chemicals. Crystallisation — *Conference proceedings*

Symposium on Industrial Crystallization *(8th : 1981 : Budapest)*. Industrial crystallization 81 : proceedings of the 8th Symposium on Industrial Crystallization, Budapest, Hungary, 28-30 September, 1981 / sponsored by the Working Party on Crystallization of the European Federation of Chemical Engineering ; edited by S.J. Jančić, E.J. De Jong. — Amsterdam ; Oxford : North-Holland, c1982. — xiv,394p : ill ; 27cm
Includes index
ISBN 0-444-86402-4 : £31.65 B82-38190

660.2′8449 — Industrial fermentation

Mixed culture fermentations / edited by M.E. Bushell and J.H. Slater. — London : Published for the Society for General Microbiology by Academic Press, 1981. — xi,175p : ill ; 24cm. — (Special publications of the Society for General Microbiology ; 5)
Includes bibliographies and index
ISBN 0-12-147480-1 : £12.00 : CIP rev.
B81-28784

660.2′94515′0287 — Aerosol containers. Testing — *Standards*

Standard test methods / [British Aerosol Manufacturers′ Association]. — London (93 Albert Embankment, SE1 7TU) : The Association, 1980. — 68p : ill ; 25cm
£3.00 (pbk) B82-13323

660.2′97 — Industrial electrochemistry — *Conference proceedings*

Prospects for industrial electrochemistry : a Royal Society discussion held on 10 and 11 December 1980 / organized by G.B.R. Feilden, G.T. Rogers and W.J. Albery. — London : Royal Society, 1981. — vi,165p,[2]leaves of plates : ill ; 31cm
"First published in Philosophical transactions of the Royal Society of London, series A. V.302(no.1468), p217-383". — Title page verso. — Includes bibliographies
ISBN 0-85403-174-x : £19.50 B82-03936

660.2′9723 — Materials. Implantation of ions — *Conference proceedings*

Materials Research Society. *Meeting (1981 : Boston, Mass.).* Metastable materials formation by ion implantation : proceedings of the Materials Research Society annual meeting, November 1981, Boston Park Plaza Hotel, Boston, Massachusetts, USA / editors S. Thomas Picraux and W.J. Choyke. — New York ; Oxford : North-Holland, c1982. — xiii,446p : ill ; 24cm. — (Materials Research Society symposia proceedings ; v.7)
Includes index
ISBN 0-444-00692-3 : £37.47 B82-36635

660.2′993 — Industrial chemicals: Polymer dispersions — *Conference proceedings*

The **Effect** of polymers on dispersion properties / [based on the proceedings of an international symposium of the Colloid and Surface Chemistry Group of the Society for [i.e. of] Chemical Industry held at University College, London, from 21-23 September, 1981] ; edited by Th. F. Tadros. — London : Academic Press, 1982. — viii,423p : ill ; 24cm
Includes bibliographies and index
ISBN 0-12-682620-x : £19.20 : CIP rev. B81-40233

660.2′995 — Industrial chemicals: Heterogeneous catalysts. Characterisation

Characterisation of catalysts / edited by J.M. Thomas and R.M. Lambert. — Chichester : Wiley, c1980. — xiv,283p : ill ; 24cm
ISBN 0-471-27874-2 : £16.50 : CIP rev. B80-25910

660.6 — INDUSTRIAL BIOLOGY

660′.6 — Industrial biology

Biotechnology : a review and annotated bibliography / Technology Policy Unit, University of Aston, Birmingham ; prepared by Harry Rothman ... [et al.]. — London : Pinter, 1980, c1981. — xii,141p ; 22cm
ISBN 0-903804-74-3 : £11.00 B82-02114

Investing in biotechnology. — London : Scientific & Technical Services, Sept.1982. — [150]p
ISBN 0-907822-13-4 (pbk) : £75.00 : CIP entry B82-29152

Moses, V.. Biotechnology : a guide for investors / by Vivian Moses and Bob Rabin. — London : Economist Intelligence Unit, 1982. — 115p : ill ; 30cm. — (EIU special report ; no.124)
Unpriced (pbk) B82-32208

Principles of biotechnology. — Glasgow : Surrey University Press, Sept.1982. — [216]p
ISBN 0-903384-32-9 : £10.00 : CIP entry B82-25085

Smith, John E. (John Edward). Biotechnology / John E. Smith. — London : Edward Arnold, 1981. — 75p : ill ; 22cm. — (The Institute of Biology's studies in biology, ISSN 0537-9024 ; no.136)
Bibliography: p75. — Includes index
ISBN 0-7131-2835-6 (pbk) : £2.60 : CIP rev. B81-31557

660′.6 — Industrial biology — *Conference proceedings*

Microbial aspects of biotechnology / proceedings of a joint meeting held at the Royal Irish Academy, 27th April 1981 ; sponsored by Royal Irish Academy, National Board for Science and Technology, Society for General Microbiology (Irish Branch) ; and arranged under the auspices of Royal Irish Academy National Commission for Microbiology. — [Dublin] ([Academy House, 19 Dawson St., Dublin 2]) : [Royal Irish Academy], [1982]. — 119p : ill ; 29cm
Includes bibliographies
Unpriced (pbk) B82-27486

660′.6 — Industrial biology. Use of hydrocarbons — *Conference proceedings*

Hydrocarbons in biotechnology : proceedings of a meeting organized by the Institute of Petroleum and held at the University of Kent at Canterbury, UK, 25-26 September 1979 / edited by D.E.F. Harrison, I.J. Higgins and R. Watkinson. — London : Published by Heyden on behalf of the Institute of Petroleum, c1980. — ix,201p : ill ; 24cm
Includes bibliographies and index
ISBN 0-85501-325-7 : £18.00 B82-40784

660′.6′05 — Industrial biology — *Serials*

Biotech news : advances in biotechnology news bulletin. — Vol.1 no.1 (1982)-. — Alton, Hants. (P.O. Box 3, Newman La., Alton, Hants. GU34 2PG) : Microinfo, 1982-. — v. ; 30cm
Monthly. — Description based on: Vol.1 no.3 (May 1982)
ISSN 0263-8029 = Biotech news : Unpriced B82-32160

Biotech quarterly : official bulletin of the British Co-ordinating Committee for Biotechnology. — Vol.1, no.1 (Mar. 1982)-. — Kew (12 Clarence Rd, Kew, Surrey TW9 3NL) : Published on behalf of the Committee by Science & Technology Letters, 1982-. — v. ; 30cm
ISSN 0262-2963 = Biotech quarterly : £12.00 per year B82-28124

Biotechnology bulletin. — Charter issue (Jan. 1982) ; Vol.1, no.1 (Feb. 1982)-. — London (11 Norwich St, EC4A 1AB) : Scientific and Technical Studies, 1982-. — v. ; 30cm
Monthly. — Supplement: Biotechnology reports. — Description based on: Vol.1, no.5 (June 1982)
ISSN 0261-6904 = Biotechnology bulletin : £80.00 per year B82-38543

Biotechnology bulletin. Report. — No.1 (1982)-no.4 (June 1982)-. — London (11 Norwich St, EC4A 1AB) : Scientific & Technology [ie Technical] Studies, 1982-1982. — 4v. ; 30cm
Twenty-four issues yearly. — Continued by: Biotechnology reports. — Supplement to: Biotechnology bulletin. — Description based on: No.3 (June 1982)
£48.00 per year B82-38544

Biotechnology reports. — 5 & 6 (July 1982)-. — London (11 Norwich St, EC4A 1AB) : Scientific & Technical Studies, 1982-. — v. ; 30cm
Twenty-four issues yearly. — Continues: Biotechnology bulletin. Report. — Supplement to: Biotechnology bulletin
ISSN 0264-0384 = Biotechnology reports : Unpriced B82-38542

Practical biotechnology. — Apr. 1981-. — Harpenden (4 Woodlands, Harpenden, Herts.) : R. Hardman, 1981-. — v. ; 30cm
Six issues yearly
ISSN 0262-7884 = Practical biotechnology : £90.00 per year B82-08461

660′.6′07041 — Great Britain. Education. Curriculum subjects: Industrial biology

Biotechnology and education : the report of a working group. — [London] : Royal Society, 1981. — x,39p ; 21cm
Bibliography: p39
£1.00 (unbound) B82-18927

660′.62 — Chemical engineering. Applications of genetic engineering of microorganisms — *Conference proceedings*

Genetic engineering of microogranisms for chemicals / [proceedings of a symposium on genetic engineering of microorganisms for chemicals, held May 26-29, 1981, at the University of Illinois at Champaign-Urbana] ; edited by Alexander Hollaender and Ralph D. DeMoss ... [et al.]. — New York ; London : Plenum, c1982. — xiii,485p : ill ; 26cm. — (Basic life sciences ; v.19)
Includes bibliographies and index
ISBN 0-306-40912-7 : Unpriced B82-22014

660′.62 — Industrial microbiology

Bioactive microbial products : search and discovery / edited by J.D. Bu'Lock, L.J. Nisbet, D.J. Winstanley. — London : Published for the Society for General Microbiology by Academic Press, 1982. — 148p : ill ; 24cm. — (Special publications of the Society for General Microbiology ; 6)
Conference papers. — Includes bibliographies and index
ISBN 0-12-140750-0 : £10.00 : CIP rev. B82-04134

Prescott, Samuel Cate. Prescott & Dunn's industrial microbiology. — 4th ed., edited by Gerald Reed. — Westport, Conn. : Avi Publishing ; [London] : Macmillan, 1982. — xii,883p : ill ; 23cm
Previous ed.: New York, London : McGraw-Hill, 1959. — Includes bibliographies and index
ISBN 0-333-33630-5 : Unpriced B82-40018

660′.62′05 — Industrial microbiology — *Serials*

Progress in industrial microbiology. — Vol.16. — Oxford : Elsevier Scientific, Nov.1981. — [375]p
ISBN 0-444-42037-1 : CIP entry B81-32019

661 — INDUSTRIAL CHEMICALS

661 — Speciality industrial chemicals: Inorganic compounds — *Conference proceedings*

Speciality inorganic chemicals : the proceedings of a symposium organised by the Inorganic Chemicals Group, the Fine Chemicals and Medicinals Group, and the N.W. Region of the Industrial Division of the Royal Society of Chemistry, in association with the Dalton Division, University of Salford, September 10th-12th 1980 / edited by R. Thompson. — London : Royal Society of Chemistry, c1981. — viii,497p : ill ; 21cm. — (Special publication / Royal Society of Chemistry, ISSN 0260-6291 ; no.40)
Conference papers. — Includes index
ISBN 0-85186-835-5 (pbk) : Unpriced : CIP rev. B81-30208

661′.005 — Industrial chemicals — *Serials*

Industrial chemistry bulletin. — Vol.1, no.1 (Feb. 1982)-. — London : Royal Society of Chemistry, 1982-. — v. : ill ; 30cm
Six issues yearly. — Description based on: Vol.1, no.2 (Apr. 1982)
ISSN 0261-9253 = Industrial chemistry bulletin : £30.00 per year (£8.00 to members) B82-32140

661′.8 — Industrial chemicals: Enzymes — *Serials*

Topics in enzyme and fermentation biotechnology . — 6. — Chichester : Ellis Horwood, Nov.1981. — [256]p
ISBN 0-85312-372-1 : £19.50 : CIP entry
ISSN 0140-0835 B81-32012

Topics in enzyme and fermentation biotechnology . — 7. — Chichester : Ellis Horwood, Dec.1982. — [280]p
ISBN 0-85312-465-5 : £30.00 : CIP entry
ISSN 0140-0835 B82-30313

661′.8 — Industrial chemicals: Polysaccharides — *Serials*

Carbohydrate polymers. — Vol.1, no.1 (Sept. 1981)-. — London : Applied Science, 1981-. — v. : ill ; 24cm
Quarterly
ISSN 0144-8617 = Carbohydrate polymers : Unpriced B82-06776

661'.803 — Industrial chemicals. Conversion of coal

Chemical feedstocks from coal / edited by Jürgen Falbe ; [contributors] E. Ahland ... [et al.] ; translated by Alexander Mullen. — New York ; Chichester : Wiley, c1982. — xii,647p : ill ; 24cm. — (A Wiley inter-science publication)
Translation of: Chemierohstoffe aus Kohle. — Includes index
ISBN 0-471-05291-4 : £60.00 B82-18214

661'.807 — Industrial chemicals: Chlorinated solvents. Use — *Serials*

Solvents news : a digest of methods to achieve the safe and efficient use of chlorinated solvents. — 1-. — Runcorn (PO Box 13, The Heath, Runcorn, Cheshire WA7 4QF) : Imperial Chemical Industries, Mond Division, [1978]-. — v. : ill ; 30cm
Quarterly
ISSN 0262-1150 = Solvents news : Unpriced B82-02376

661'.807 — Solvents

Safe use of solvents. — London : Academic Press, Aug.1982. — [400]p
ISBN 0-12-181250-2 : CIP entry B82-19250

661'.808 — Photographic materials. Chemical properties

Hoffman, A.. Thermodynamic theory of latent image formation. — London : Focal Press, July 1982. — [94]p. — (Progress reports in imaging science)
ISBN 0-240-51200-6 (pbk) : £12.00 : CIP entry B82-22398

661'.81 — Hydrocarbon processing industries. Control systems. Optimisation

Process control and optimization handbook for the hydrocarbon processing industries / compiled by Les A. Kane. — Houston ; London : Gulf Publishing, c1980. — vi,247p : ill ; 28cm
ISBN 0-87201-144-5 (pbk) : £9.25 B82-35011

661'.81 — Hydrocarbon processing plants. Environmental aspects

Environmental management handbook for the hydrocarbon processing industries / compiled by James D. Wall. — Houston ; London : Gulf Publishing, c1980. — vi,227p : ill ; 28cm
ISBN 0-87201-265-4 (pbk) : £9.25 B82-35008

661'.81'02854 — Industrial chemicals: Hydrocarbons. Processing. Simulations. Applications of programmable electronic calculators

Calculator programs for the hydrocarbon processing industries. — Houston ; London : Gulf
Vol.1 / S. Jagannath. — 1980. — xi,224p : ill ; 22cm
Includes index
ISBN 0-87201-091-0 : £10.75 B82-35624

Jagannath, S.. Calculator programs for the hydrocarbon processing industries / S. Jagannath. — Houston ; London : Gulf
Vol.2. — c1982. — xiii,416p : ill ; 22cm
Includes index
ISBN 0-87201-092-9 : Unpriced B82-29165

661'.816 — Industrial chemicals: Toluenes & xylenes

Toluene, the xylenes and their industrial derivatives / edited by E.G. Hancock. — Amsterdam ; Oxford : Elsevier Scientific, 1982. — xxii,551p : ill ; 25cm. — (Chemical engineering monographs ; v.15)
Includes index
ISBN 0-444-42058-4 : £63.62 : CIP rev. B82-02667

662.5 — MATCHES

662'.5 — Matches

Finch, C. A.. Matchmaking. — Chichester : Ellis Horwood, Dec.1982. — [216]p
ISBN 0-85312-315-2 : £22.50 : CIP entry B82-32309

662.6 — FUELS

662'.6 — Biomass fuels

White, L. P.. Biomass as fuel / L.P. White and L.G. Plaskett. — London : Academic Press, 1981. — x,211p : ill ; 24cm
Bibliography: p191-203. — Includes index
ISBN 0-12-746980-x : £14.20 : CIP rev. B81-31351

662'.6 — Biomass fuels. Production

Biomass conversion processes for energy and fuels / edited by Samir S. Sofer and Oskar R. Zaborsky. — New York ; London : Plenum, c1981. — xvi,420p : ill ; 24cm
Includes index
ISBN 0-306-40663-2 : Unpriced B82-14754

662'.6 — Developing countries. Energy sources: Biomass

Hall, D. O.. Biomass for energy in the developing countries : current role, potential, problems, prospects / by D.O. Hall, G.W. Barnard and P.A. Moss. — Oxford : Pergamon, 1982. — xxxiii,220p : ill ; 24cm
Includes bibliographies
ISBN 0-08-029313-1 (cased) : Unpriced : CIP rev.
ISBN 0-08-028689-5 (pbk) : £10.00 B82-05382

662'.6 — Energy sources: Biomass — *Conference proceedings*

EC Contractors' Meeting *(1981 : Copenhagen)*. Energy from biomass : proceedings of the EC Contractors' Meeting held in Copenhagen, 23-24 June 1981 / edited by P. Chartier and W. Palz. — Dordrecht ; London : Reidel for the Commission of the European Communities, c1981. — x,220p : ill ; 24cm. — (Solar energy R & D in the European Community ; V.1)
ISBN 90-277-1348-0 : Unpriced B82-04417

International Conference on Biomass *(1982 : Berlin)*. Energy from biomass. — London : Applied Science, Jan.1983. — [1150]p
ISBN 0-85334-196-6 : £50.00 : CIP entry B82-40301

662'.6 — Energy sources: Biomass. Research projects — *Lists*

Inventory of national and international biomass R&D research programs / prepared by the Information Technology Group of the Institute for Industrial Research and Standards — Ireland, in conjunction with the National Board for Science and Technology. — [Dublin?] : IEA Biomass Conversion Technical Information Service, 1981. — 2v.(1258p) ; 30cm
Includes index
Unpriced (pbk) B82-27881

662'.6 — Energy sources: Biomass — *Serials*

Biomass : an international journal. — Vol.1, no.1 (Sept. 1981)-. — London : Applied Science, 1981-. — v. ; 24cm
Quarterly
ISSN 0144-4565 = Biomass : Unpriced B82-04919

Biomass bulletin. — Vol.1, no.1 (Sept. 1981)-. — London (42 New Broad St., EC2M 1QY) : Multi-Science Pub. Co., 1981-. — v. ; 29cm
Quarterly
ISSN 0262-7183 = Biomass bulletin : £48.00 per year B82-10130

. The Digest : the regular newsletter of the British Anaerobic and Biomass Association Ltd. — No.1 (Mar. 1980)-. — Marlborough (c/o The Secretary, The White House, Little Bedwyn, Marlborough, Wiltshire) : The Association, 1980-. — v. ; 30cm
Three issues yearly. — Description based on: No.5 (Oct. 1981)
ISSN 0262-6349 = Digest (British Anaerobic and Biomass Association Ltd) : £2.50 per issue
Primary classification 628.3'54 B82-08458

662'.6 — Energy sources: Fossil fuels

New sources of oil & gas. — Oxford : Pergamon, July 1982. — [120]p
ISBN 0-08-029335-2 : £12.50 : CIP entry B82-17964

662'.6 — Energy sources: Fossil fuels. Chemical analysis — *Conference proceedings*

American Nuclear Society Conference on Atomic and Nuclear Methods in Fossil Fuel Energy Research *(1980 : Mayaguez)*. Atomic and nuclear methods in fossil energy research / [proceedings of the American Nuclear Society Conference on Atomic and Nuclear Methods in Fossil Fuel Energy Research held December 1-4, 1980 in Mayaguez, Puerto Rico] ; edited by Royston H. Filby ; associate editors B. Stephen Carpenter and Richard C. Ragaini. — New York ; London : Plenum, c1982. — xii,506p : ill,1map ; 26cm
Includes bibliographies and index
ISBN 0-306-40899-6 : Unpriced B82-38667

662'.6 — Energy sources: Fossil fuels — *For children*

Rice, Dale. Energy from fossil fuels. — Oxford : Blackwell Raintree, Nov.1982. — [42]p. — (A Look inside)
ISBN 0-86256-069-1 : £3.25 : CIP entry B82-26074

662.6'2'072041 — Great Britain. Coal technology. Research projects — *Directories*

Coal research projects - United Kingdom / [IEA Coal Research, Technical Information Service]. — London : IEA Coal Research, 1981. — 163p ; 30cm
Includes index
ISBN 92-902905-7-9 (pbk) : Unpriced B82-01492

662.6'2'0941 — Great Britain. Coal products. Production

Gibson, J.. Chemical feedstocks and synthetic products from coal : a memorial lecture delivered at the University of Bradford on 5 March 1981 / by J. Gibson. — [Bradford] : [Bradford University Press], [1981]. — 20p : ill ; 21cm. — (Eleventh Professor Moore memorial lecture)
ISBN 0-901945-41-2 (pbk) : Unpriced B82-05181

662.6'23 — Coal. Carbonization — *Conference proceedings*

British Carbonization Research Association. *Associate Members' Conference (1981 : Chesterfield)*. Report of the Associate Members' Conference, 24-25 June 1981. — Chesterfield : British Carbonization Research Association, 1981. — 24p,[4]p of plates : ill,ports ; 30cm. — (Special publication / British Carbonization Research Association ; 26)
Unpriced (pbk) B82-28895

662'.65 — Fuels: Wood. Combustion

Tillman, David A.. Wood combustion : principles, processes, and economics / David A. Tillman, Amadeo J. Rossi, William D. Kitto. — New York ; London : Academic Press, 1981. — x,208p : ill ; 24cm
Includes bibliographies and index
ISBN 0-12-691240-8 : £13.00 B82-30129

662'.66 — Synthetic fuels. Production

Probstein, Ronald F.. Synthetic fuels / Ronald F. Probstein, R. Edwin Hicks. — New York ; London : McGraw-Hill, c1982. — xiv,490p : ill ; 24cm. — (McGraw-Hill chemical engineering series)
Includes index
ISBN 0-07-050908-5 : £22.50 B82-02329

662'.6622 — Coal. Liquefaction

Olliver, Dick. Oil and gas from coal / Dick Olliver ; editorial consultant Bruce Andrews ; [illustrations prepared by Martyn Barnes]. — London : Financial Times Business Information Ltd, c1981. — ix,239p : ill,1map ; 30cm
Bibliography: p225-233
ISBN 0-903199-48-3 (spiral) : Unpriced
Primary classification 665.7'72 B82-37774

662'.6622 — Coal. Liquefaction — *Conference proceedings*
Symposium on the Gasification and Liquefaction of Coal *(1979 : Katowice)*. Oils and gases from coal : a review of the state-of-the-art in Europe and North America : based on the work of the Symposium on the Gasification and Liquefaction of Coal held under the auspices of the United Nations Economic Commission for Europe, Katowice, Poland, 23-27 April 1979. — Oxford : Published for the United Nations by Pergamon, 1980. — vii,305p : ill ; 26cm
ISBN 0-08-025678-3 : £24.50 : CIP rev.
Also classified at 665.7'72 B80-06499

662'.72'028 — Coke manufacturing plants. Ovens. Electric equipment. Installation — *Standards*
Guide to electrical installations on coke-oven machines / prepared by the Coke-oven Plant Electrical Committee. — Chesterfield : British Carbonization Research Association, 1981. — 20p ; 21cm. — (Special publication / British Carbonization Research Association ; 25)
Unpriced (pbk) B82-28897

663 — BEVERAGE MANUFACTURES

663 — Energy & materials. Consumption by drinks containers manufacturing industries
Boustead, I.. Energy and packaging / I. Boustead, G.F. Hancock. — Chichester : Ellis Horwood, 1981. — 519p : ill ; 24cm. — (Ellis Horwood series in energy and fuel science)
Includes index
ISBN 0-85312-206-7 : £45.00 : CIP rev.
ISBN 0-470-27269-4 (Halsted) B81-28021

663'.1'07 — Great Britain. Wines & spirits trades. Personnel. Induction training
The **Introduction** of new staff to the wine and spirit trade. — London (Five Kings House, Kennet Wharf Lane, Upper Thames St., EC4V 3BH) : Wine and Spirit Association of Great Britain and Northern Ireland in association with the Food, Drink and Tobacco Industry Training Board, [1981]. — [8]p : ill ; 21cm
Cover title
Unpriced (pbk) B82-27915

663'.19'07 — Great Britain. Wines & spirits bottling industries. Manual personnel. Training — *Manuals*
Training manual for bottling hall operatives / this manual was produced jointly by the Food, Drink and Tobacco Industry Training Board and Grants of St James's Limited. — Gloucester (Barton House, Barton St., Gloucester GL1 1QQ) : Food, Drink and Tobacco Industry Training Board, c1981. — 9p,44leaves : ill ; 32cm
£20.00 (unbound) B82-27619

663'.3 — Brewing
Malting and brewing science. — 2nd ed. — London : Chapman and Hall
Previous ed.: 1971
Vol.2: Hopped wort and beer. — July 1982. — [300]p
ISBN 0-412-16590-2 : £17.50 : CIP entry B82-13237

663'.3 — Brewing & malting
Malting and brewing science. — 2nd ed. — London : Chapman and Hall
Previous ed.: 1971
Part 1: Malt and sweet wort. — Oct.1981. — [300]p
ISBN 0-412-16580-5 : £15.00 : CIP entry B81-27938

663'.3 — Brewing — *Conference proceedings*
European Brewery Convention. *Congress (18th : 1981 : Copenhagen)*. European Brewery Convention. — Eynsham (1 Abbey St., Eynsham, Oxford OX8 1JJ) : IRL Press, Oct.1981. — [800]p
Conference papers
ISBN 0-904147-30-4 : £36.00 : CIP entry B81-31093

663'.32'07 — Great Britain. Malting industries. Personnel. Training
Production training manual for maltsters. — Gloucester (Barton House, Barton St., Gloucester GL1 1QQ) : Food, Drink and Tobacco Industry Training Board, [1980]. — 1 (loose leaf) ; 32cm
£5.00 B82-26126

663'.6 — Soft drinks. Production - *Serials*
Developments in soft drinks technology. — London : Applied Science, July 1981. — (Developments series)
2. — [288]p
ISBN 0-85334-962-2 : £23.00 : CIP entry B81-13734

664 — FOOD MANUFACTURES

664 — Food & drinks. Flavours
Food flavours / edited by I.D. Morton, A.J. Macleod. — Amsterdam ; Oxford : Elsevier Scientific. — (Developments in food science ; 3A)
Part A: Introduction. — 1982. — xiii,473p : ill ; 25cm
Includes bibliographies and index
ISBN 0-444-41857-1 : £58.64 : CIP rev. B80-19317

664 — Food & drinks. Flavours — *Conference proceedings*
International Flavor Conference *(2nd : 1981 : Athens)*. The quality of foods and beverages : chemistry and technology / [proceedings of a symposium of the Second International Flavor Conference held July 20-21, 1981, Athens, Greece] ; edited by George Charalambous, George Inglett. — New York ; London : Academic Press
Vol.1. — 1981. — xviii,443p : ill ; 24cm
Includes bibliographies and index
ISBN 0-12-169101-2 : £19.60 B82-02203

664 — Food & drinks. Flavours. Heterocyclic compounds
Chemistry of heterocyclic compounds in flavours and aromas / editor G. Vernin. — Chichester : Horwood, 1982. — 375p : ill ; 24cm
Includes bibliographies and index
ISBN 0-85312-263-6 : £32.50 : CIP rev. B82-11489

664 — Food technology
Pyke, Magnus. Food science & technology / Magnus Pyke ; with a foreword by John Hawthorn. — 4th ed. / revised and enlarged by Lelio Parducci. — London : John Murray, 1981. — xiii,304p : ill ; 22cm
Previous ed.: 1970. — Includes index
ISBN 0-7195-3850-5 : £7.50 : CIP rev.
Primary classification 641.1 B81-14897

664'.00321 — Food. Processing — *Encyclopaedias*
Bender, Arnold E.. Dictionary of nutrition and food technology. — 5th ed. — London : Butterworths, Nov.1982. — [320]p
Previous ed.: London : Newnes-Butterworths, 1975
ISBN 0-408-10855-x : £15.00 : CIP entry
Primary classification 613.2'03'21 B82-28273

664'.0068'3 — Great Britain. Food & drinks industries. Management. Supervision
Developing effective supervision for the future. — Gloucester (Barton House, Barton St., Gloucester GL1 1QQ) : Food, Drink and Tobacco Industry Training Board, [1981?]. — 37p : ill(some col.),forms ; 30cm
£2.00 (pbk)
Also classified at 679'.7'0683 B82-11170

664'.0068'3 — Great Britain. Food & drinks industries. Personnel. Job analysis
How to use job analysis for profitable training / [issued by the Food, Drink and Tobacco Industry Training Board]. — Croydon (Leon House, High St., Croydon, CR9 3NT) : [The Board], [1982?]. — 31p : ill ; 30cm. — (Systematic training guide ; no.2)
Cover title. — Text on inside cover. — 'Example A,B,C' as insert. — Bibliography: p31
£0.65 (pbk)
Also classified at 679'.7'0683 B82-24291

664'.0068'3 — Great Britain. Food & drinks industries. Training officers
The **Development** of training staff / [issued by the Food, Drink and Tobacco Industry Training Board]. — Croydon (Leon House, High St., Croydon, CR9 3NT) : [The Board], [1982?]. — 28p ; 30cm. — (Systematic training guide ; no.5)
Cover title. — Text on inside cover
£0.65 (pbk)
Also classified at 679'.7'0683 B82-24292

664'.0068'3 — Great Britain. Foods & drinks industries. Management. Participation of personnel
Employee participation : sources of help available to companies introducing employee participation. — Gloucester (Barton House, Barton St., Gloucester GL1 1QQ) : Food, Drink and Tobacco Industry Training Board, 1980. — 17p ; 30cm
Cover title
£2.00 (pbk)
Also classified at 679'.7'0683 B82-26131

664'.007 — Great Britain. Food & drinks industries. Personnel: Technicians. Training
Creating a training programme for technicians / [issued by Food, Drink and Tobacco Industry Training Board]. — Croydon (Leon House, High St., Croydon, CR9 3NT) : [The Board], [1982?]. — 24p : forms ; 30cm. — (Training recommendations ; no.2)
Cover title. — Text on inside cover
£0.65 (pbk)
Also classified at 679'.7'07 B82-24288

664'.007 — Great Britain. Food & drinks industries. Personnel. Training. Effectiveness. Evaluation
Reviewing the effectiveness of training. — Gloucester (Barton House, Barton St., Gloucester GL1 1QQ) : Food, Drink and Tobacco Industry Training Board, [1982?]. — 23p : ill,2forms ; 30cm. — (Systematic training guide ; no.4)
Cover title. — Text on inside cover
£0.50 (pbk)
Also classified at 679'.7'07 B82-24283

664'.007 — Great Britain. Food & drinks industries. Personnel. Training. Planning
How to prepare training plans and programmes / [issued by the Food, Drink and Tobacco Industry Training Board]. — Croydon (Leon House, High St., Croydon, CR9 3NT) : [The Board], [1982?]. — 32p : ill ; 30cm + Planning an induction training programme(14p ill; 29cm). — (Systematic training guide ; no.3)
Cover title. — Text on inside cover
£0.70 (pbk)
Primary classification 679'.7'07 B82-24293

664'.007 — Great Britain. Food & drinks industries. Personnel. Training. Requirements. Assessment
Assessing your company's training needs / [issued by the Food, Drink and Tobacco Industry Training Board]. — Croydon (Leon House, High St., Croydon, CR9 3NT) : [The Board], [1982?]. — 40p ; 30cm. — (Systematic training guide ; no.1)
Cover title. — Text on inside cover
£0.50 (pbk)
Also classified at 679'.7'07 B82-24289

664'.007 — Great Britain. Food & drinks industries. Personnel. Training. Requirements — *For management*
Training individual managers : a programme to help managers to identify and tackle training needs / developed by the Food, Drink and Tobacco Industry Training Board. — Gloucester (Barton House, Barton St., Gloucester GL1 1QQ) : Food, Drink and Tobacco Industry Training Board, [1979]. — 1v(loose leaf) ; 32cm
Bibliography: p86-87
£5.00
Also classified at 679'.7'07 B82-26127

664'.02 — Food. Processing: Maillard reactions
Maillard reactions in food. — Oxford : Pergamon, June 1981. — [500]p. — (Progress in food and nutrition science ; v.5)
ISBN 0-08-025496-9 : £65.00 : CIP entry B81-19210

664'.028'072041 — Great Britain. Food. Preservation. Research organisations: Campden Food Preservation Research Association
Campden Food Preservation Research Association. Research facilities and services. — Chipping Campden (Chipping Campden, Gloucestershire, GL55 6LD) : Campden Food Preservation Research Association, [1980]. — [18]p : ill ; 30cm
Cover title
Unpriced (pbk) B82-14888

664'.028'072042417 — Great Britain. Food. Preservation. Research organisations: Campden Research Station, ***1919-1965***

Adam, W. B.. A history of the Campden Research Station 1919-1965 / by W.B. Adam. — [Chipping Campden] ([Chipping Campden, Gloucestershire, GL55 6LD]) : Campden Food Preservation Research Association, [1980]. — 84p ; 30cm
Unpriced (pbk) B82-14191

664'.0288 — Food. Irradiation

Food irradiation now : proceedings of a symposium held in Ede, the Netherlands, 21 October 1981 / sponsored by Gammaster. — The Hague ; London : Nijhoff, 1982. — ix,157p : ill ; 25cm. — (Nutrition sciences ; v.1)
ISBN 90-247-2703-0 : Unpriced B82-39762

664'.06 — Food. Additives: Gums

Gums and stabilisers for the food industry. — Oxford : Pergamon, Apr.1982. — [420]p. — (Progress in food and nutrition science ; 6)
ISBN 0-08-026843-9 : £45.00 : CIP entry B82-11261

664'.06 — Food. Colouring agents: Anthocyanins

Anthocyanins as food colors / edited by Pericles Markakis. — New York ; London : Academic Press, 1982. — xii,263p : ill ; 24cm. — (Food science and technology)
Includes bibliographies and index
ISBN 0-12-472550-3 : £23.20 B82-38386

664'.06 — Food. Preservatives — *Serials*

Developments in food preservatives. — 1-. — London : Applied Science, 1980-. — v. ; 23cm. — (Developments series)
Irregular
ISSN 0263-3728 = Developments in food preservatives : £14.50 B82-18540

664'.07 — Food & drinks. Flavours. Research — *Conference proceedings*

The **Quality** of foods and beverages / [proceedings of a symposium of the Second International Flavor Conference, held July 20-21, 1981, Athens, Greece]. — New York ; London : Academic Press
Vol.2: Chemistry and technology / edited by George Charalambous, George Inglett. — 1981. — xviii,390p : ill ; 24cm
Includes bibliographies and index
ISBN 0-12-169102-0 : £17.60 B82-04334

664'.07 — Food & drinks. High pressure liquid chromatography

HPLC in food analysis. — London : Academic Press, Dec.1982. — [350]p. — (Food and science technology)
ISBN 0-12-464780-4 : CIP entry B82-30587

664'.07 — Food & drinks. High pressure liquid chromatography — *Conference proceedings*

Liquid chromatographic analysis of food and beverages / [proceedings of a symposium on the Analysis of Food and Beverages by HPLC, held in Honolulu, Hawaii, April 1-6, 1979] ; edited by George Charalambous. — New York ; London : Academic Press
Includes index
Vol.2. — 1979. — xiip, p237-563 : ill ; 24cm
ISBN 0-12-169002-4 : £21.80 B82-16608

664'.07 — Food. Chemical analysis

Pearson, David, *1919-77.* Pearson's chemical analysis of foods. — 8th ed. / Harold Egan, Ronald S. Kirk, Ronald Sawyer. — Edinburgh : Churchill Livingstone, 1981. — vi,591p : ill ; 24cm
Previous ed.: published as The chemical analysis of foods. 1976. — Includes bibliographies and index
ISBN 0-443-02149-x : Unpriced : CIP rev. B81-16408

664'.07 — Food. Quality control

Earle, R. L.. Unit operations in food processing. — 2nd ed. — Oxford : Pergamon, Nov.1982. — [220]p. — (Pergamon international library)
Previous ed.: 1966
ISBN 0-08-025537-x (cased) : £15.00 : CIP entry
ISBN 0-08-025536-1 (pbk) : £8.00 B82-27831

664'.07 — Food. Quality control. Applications of microprocessor systems — *Conference proceedings*

Smith, D. (David), *1939-.* The impact of microprocessors on the control of food quality : a paper presented at a symposium organised by CFPRA, held at the Lygon Arms Hotel, Broadway, on 11th March 1981 / by D. Smith. — Chipping Campden (Chipping Campden, Gloucestershire, GL55 6LD) : Campden Food Preservation Research Association, [1981]. — 22p : ill ; 30cm
Unpriced (pbk) B82-14885

664'.07 — Food. Quality. Effects of techniques in agriculture — *Conference proceedins*

Agricultural practices and food quality : proceedings of a seminar 28-29 February 1980. — Dublin : Royal Irish Academy, 1980. — viii,120p : ill ; 21cm
Conference papers. — Includes bibliographies
ISBN 0-901714-16-x (pbk) : Unpriced B82-25256

664'.092'05 — Food. Packaging — *Serials*

Developments in food packaging. — 1-. — London : Applied Science, 1980-. — v. : ill ; 23cm. — (Developments series)
Irregular
ISSN 0263-3752 = Developments in food packaging : £18.00 B82-19876

664'.096 — Food industries. Waste materials. Disposal & recovery — *Conference proceedings*

Food industry wastes : disposal and recovery / edited by A. Herzka and R.G. Booth. — London : Applied Science, c1981. — viii,246p : ill ; 23cm
Conference papers. — Includes index
ISBN 0-85334-957-6 : £20.00 : CIP rev. B81-30419

664'.1 — Sugar. Production

Deerr, Noël. Noël Deerr : classic papers of a sugar cane technologist. — Oxford : Elsevier Scientific, Jan.1983. — 1v.. — (Sugar cane series ; 5)
ISBN 0-444-42149-1 : CIP entry B82-39295

664'.122 — Cane sugar. Processing

Baikow, V. E.. Manufacture and refining of raw cane sugar / V.E. Baikow. — 2nd, completely rev. ed. — Amsterdam ; Oxford : Elsevier Scientific, 1982. — 588p : ill ; 25cm. — (Sugar series ; 2)
Previous ed.: 1967. — Includes bibliographies and index
ISBN 0-444-41896-2 : £78.95 : CIP rev. B81-32090

Payne, John Howard. Unit operations in cane sugar production. — Oxford : Elsevier Scientific, July 1982. — [220]p. — (Sugar series ; 4)
ISBN 0-444-42104-1 : CIP entry B82-21370

664'.19 — Cane sugar industries. Waste materials. Recycling

Paturau, J. Maurice. By-products of the cane sugar industry : an introduction to their industrial utilization / J. Maurice Paturau. — 2nd completely rev. ed. — Amsterdam ; Oxford : Elsevier Scientific, 1982. — xi,366p : ill ; 25cm. — (Sugar series ; 3)
Previous ed.: 1969. — Includes index
ISBN 0-444-42034-7 : Unpriced : CIP rev. B81-32025

664'.32 — Margarine — *For children*

Hinds, Lorna. Butter and margarine / Lorna Hinds ; illustrations Lorraine Calaora. — New ed. — London : Watts, c1982. — 489p : ill (some col.),2col.ports ; 22cm. — (Focus on food)
Previous ed: 1977. — Includes index
ISBN 0-85166-967-0 : £2.99
Primary classification 641.3'72 B82-23296

664'.32'0941 — Great Britain. Margarine. Standards — *Proposals*

Great Britain. *Food Standards Committee.* Report on margarine and other table spreads / Food Standards Committee. — London : H.M.S.O., 1981. — 20p ; 25cm
ISBN 0-11-240655-6 (pbk) : £2.60 B82-02752

664'.53 — Spices. Processing

Pruthi, J. S.. Spices and condiments : chemistry, microbiology, technology / J.S. Pruthi. — New York ; London : Academic Press, 1980. — xiv,449p : ill ; 24cm. — (Advances in food research ; suppl.4)
Bibliography: p365-434. — Includes index
ISBN 0-12-016464-7 : £22.20 B82-35948

664'.64 — Protein enriched food. Production

New protein foods. — New York ; London : Academic Press. — (Food science and technology)
Vol.4: Animal protein supplies / edited by Aaron M. Altschul, Harold L. Wilcke
Pt.B. — c1981. — xix,378p : ill ; 24cm
Includes bibliographies and index
ISBN 0-12-054804-6 : £32.40 B82-30133

664'.7'03 — Cereals. Processing — *Polyglot dictionaries*

Dictionary of cereal processing and cereal chemistry : in English, German, French, Latin and Russian / compiled by R. Schneeweiss. — [Vienna] : International Association for Cereal Chemistry ; Amsterdam ; Oxford : Elsevier Scientific, 1982. — 520p ; 25cm
ISBN 0-444-42049-5 : £60.38 B82-38134

664'.7207 — Norfolk. Flour milling windmills

Smith, Arthur C. (Arthur Carlton). Corn windmills in Norfolk : a contemporary survey / by Arthur C. Smith. — Stevenage : Stevenage Museum, c1982. — 51p : ill ; 30cm
Bibliography: p49-50
ISBN 0-9504239-7-1 (pbk) : Unpriced B82-26483

664'.72272'072041 — Great Britain. Wheat flour. Research organisations: Flour Milling and Baking Research Association — *Serials*

Chorleywood digest. — No.1 (Jan. 1982)-. — Chorleywood (Chorleywood, Rickmansworth, Herts. WD3 5SH) : Flour Milling and Baking Research Association, 1982-. — v. : ill,ports, ; 30cm
Monthly. — Continues in part: Bulletin (Flour Milling and Baking Research Association)
ISSN 0263-2632 = Chorleywood digest : Free to Association members only B82-22673

664'.7523 — Bread. Manufacture

Fance, Wilfred James. The student's technology of breadmaking and flour confectionery / by Wilfred James Fance. — 2nd ed. — London : Routledge and Kegan Paul, 1966 (1981 [printing]). — xx,443p,[32]p of plates : ill ; 22cm
Previous ed.: 1960. — Bibliography: p435-436. — Includes index
ISBN 0-7100-1363-9 (cased) : Unpriced
ISBN 0-7100-9046-3 (pbk) : £8.95
Also classified at 664'.7525 B82-07738

664'.7525 — Confectionery using flour. Manufacture

Fance, Wilfred James. The student's technology of breadmaking and flour confectionery / by Wilfred James Fance. — 2nd ed. — London : Routledge and Kegan Paul, 1966 (1981 [printing]). — xx,443p,[32]p of plates : ill ; 22cm
Previous ed.: 1960. — Bibliography: p435-436. — Includes index
ISBN 0-7100-1363-9 (cased) : Unpriced
ISBN 0-7100-9046-3 (pbk) : £8.95
Primary classification 664'.7523 B82-07738

Hanneman, L. J.. Bakery : flour confectionery / L.J. Hanneman. — London : Heinemann, 1981. — xi,304p : ill ; 24cm
Includes index
ISBN 0-434-90710-3 : £10.50 B82-09550

664'.76 — Feedingstuffs. Data. Organisations: International Network of Feed Information Centres

Barber, W. P.. The international network of feed information centres : report of a study tour undertaken in USA, June 1981 / W.P. Barber. — [London] ([Great Westminster House, Horseferry Rd., SW1P 2AE]) : ADAS, 1982. — i,22p : 1form ; 30cm. — (ADAS study tour programme / Ministry of Agriculture, Fisheries and Food ; 1981/82)
Cover title
Unpriced (pbk) B82-18706

664'.9'001576 — Meat products. Microbiological aspects

Meat microbiology. — London : Applied Science, Aug.1982. — [576]p
ISBN 0-85334-138-9 : £48.00 : CIP entry
B82-16661

664.9'0023'41 — Great Britain. Meat industries & trades — *Career guides*

A **Career** in the meat industry. — London (Boundary House, 91-93 Charterhouse St., EC1M 6HR) : Institute of Meat in association with the Food, Drink and Tobacco Industry Training Board, [1981]. — 1folded sheet([6]p) : ill ; 21cm
Unpriced B82-27921

664'.9'007 — Great Britain. Meat industries. Manual personnel. Training — *Manuals*

Training for manual skills in the meat industry : handbook for managers and instructors. — Gloucester (Barton House, Barton St., Gloucester GL1 1QQ) : Food, Drink and Tobacco Industry Training Board, [1979?]. — 38,xp : ill,forms ; 30cm + 5 sheets(training plans: 30x42cm folded to 30x21cm)
Unpriced (pbk) B82-26129

664'.907 — Great Britain. Meat & meat products. Quality control

Meat and meat products : factors affecting quality control / edited by N.R.P. Wilson in collaboration with E.J. Dyett, R.B. Hughes, C.R.V. Jones. — London : Applied Science, c1981. — ix,207p : ill ; 23cm
Includes index
ISBN 0-85334-951-7 : £16.00 : CIP rev.
B81-04250

664'.92 — European Community countries. Beef. Quality. Effects of pre-slaughter stress — *Conference proceedings*

The **Problem** of dark-cutting in beef : a seminar in the EEC Programme of Coordination of Research on Animal Welfare, organised by D.E. Hood and P.V. Tarrant, and held in Brussels, October 7-8, 1980 : sponsored by the Commission of the European Communities, Directorate-General for Agriculture, Coordination of Agricultural Research / edited by D.E. Hood and P.V. Tarrant. — The Hague ; London : Nijhoff for Commission of the European Communities, c1981. — xi,504p : ill ; 25cm. — (Current topics in veterinary medicine and animal science)
Includes bibliographies
ISBN 90-247-2522-4 : Unpriced B82-03856

664'.92'07041 — Great Britain. Supermarkets. Butchers. Training — *Manuals*

One man's meat : a guide to the training of supermarket butchers. — Manchester : Distributive Industry Training Board, [1981?]. — 24p : ill(some col.) ; 20cm. — (A DITB training guide)
Cover title
ISBN 0-903416-25-5 (pbk) : Unpriced
B82-17318

664'.94 — Fish products

Windsor, Malcolm. Introduction to fishery by-products / by Malcolm Windsor and Stuart Barlow. — Farnham : Fishing News, 1981. — xv,187p : ill ; 23cm
Bibliography: p133. — Includes index
ISBN 0-85238-115-8 : £13.50 : CIP rev.
B81-18082

664'.94 — Food: Fish. Processing

Fish handling & processing. — 2nd ed. / editors A. Aitken ... [et al.]. — [Aberdeen] : Torry Research Station, 1982. — v,191p : ill ; 26cm
Previous ed.: Edinburgh : H.M.S.O., 1965. — Includes index
ISBN 0-11-491741-8 : Unpriced B82-38434

665 — INDUSTRIAL OILS, FATS, WAXES, GASES

665 — Industrial chemicals: Fats & oils

Bailey, Alton Edward. Bailey's industrial oil and fat products / edited by Daniel Swern. — 4th ed. — New York ; Chichester : Wiley
Previous ed.: published in 1 v. as Industrial oil and fat products. New York ; London : Interscience, 1964
Vol.2 / authors Robert R. Allen ... [et al.]. — c1982. — xi,603p : ill ; 24cm
Includes index
ISBN 0-471-83958-2 : £44.00 B82-19893

665.4 — MINERAL OILS AND WAXES

665'.4 — Process oils

An **Introduction** to process oils. — [London] : British Petroleum, [1982?]. — 8p : ill ; 30cm + 1sheet(28x21cm)
1 sheet 'Potential applications for BP process oils' in pocket
Unpriced (pbk) B82-39895

665'.4 — Waste mineral oils. Recycling — *Conference proceedings*

European Congress on the Recycling of Used Oils *(2nd : 1980 : Paris)*. Recycling of used oils : Second European Congress on the Recycling of Used Oils = Zweiter Europäischer Grebrauchtöl-Recycling Kongress = Deuxième Congrès Européen sur le recyclage des huiles usagées = Secondo Congresso Europeo sul riciclaggio degli oli usati : Paris, September 30-October 2, 1980 / supported by the Commission of the European Communities and organized by the European Commission for Regeneration of the European Union of Independent Lubricant Manufacturers. — Dordrecht ; London : Reidel, c1981. — xvi,366p : ill ; 24cm
Includes papers in English, French, German and Italian
ISBN 90-277-1369-3 : Unpriced B82-17290

665.5 — PETROLEUM

665.5 — Natural gas & petroleum. Chemical properties

Neumann, Hans-Joachim. Composition and properties of petroleum / Hans-Joachim Neumann, Barbara Paczyńska-Lahme, Dieter Severin ; [translation Dagmar Meyer]. — New York : Halsted ; Chichester : Wiley, c1981. — ix,137p : ill ; 23cm. — (Geology of petroleum, ISSN 0720-8863 ; v.5)
Translation from the German. — Bibliography: p127-131. — Includes index
ISBN 0-471-09993-7 (pbk) : £9.50 B82-12047

665.5'023'41 — Great Britain. Petroleum industries — *Career guides*

Algar, Philip. Careers in oil and gas. — London : Kogan Page, Feb.1983. — [100]p. — (Kogan Page careers series)
ISBN 0-85038-563-6 (cased) : £6.95 : CIP entry
ISBN 0-85038-564-4 (pbk) : £2.50
Also classified at 665.7'023'41 B82-39278

665.5'028'9 — Great Britain. Petroleum refining industries. Safety measures — *Standards*

Institute of Petroleum. Refining safety code. — 3rd ed. — London : Heyden, Oct.1981. — [200]p
Previous ed.: 1965
ISBN 0-85501-663-9 : £20.00 : CIP entry
B81-25738

665.5'38 — Paraffin products

Paraffin products. — Oxford : Elsevier Scientific, Jan.1982. — [320]p. — (Developments in petroleum science ; 14)
Translation of: Köolaj paraffinok
ISBN 0-444-99712-1 : £50.00 : CIP entry
B81-34492

665.5'38 — Petroleum products. Chemical analysis — *Conference proceedings*

Petroanalysis '81. — Chichester : Wiley, Oct.1982. — [416]p. — (Proceedings of the Institute of Petroleum ; 2)
Conference papers
ISBN 0-471-26217-x : £25.00 : CIP entry
B82-29406

665.5'38'0287 — Petroleum products. Measurement — *Standards*

Institute of Petroleum. Petroleum measurement manual. — Revised ed. — London : Heyden, Apr.1982
Previous ed.: 1971
Part 5: Automatic tank gauging. — [50]p
ISBN 0-85501-544-6 (pbk) : CIP entry
B82-07823

665.5'388 — Bitumen. Safety measures

Institute of Petroleum. Bitumen safety code / Institute of Petroleum. — London : Heyden on behalf of the Institute of Petroleum, 1979 (1980 [printing]). — xi,23p ; 31cm. — (Institute of Petroleum model code of safe practice in the petroleum industry ; pt.11)
ISBN 0-85501-319-2 : Unpriced B82-08399

665.5'44'05 — Petroleum pipelines — *Serials*

Oil & gas pipeline news. — Vol.1, no.1 (5 Apr. 1982)-. — London (11 Norwich St., EC4A 1AB) : Scientific & Technical Studies, 1982-. — v. ; 30cm
Fortnightly
ISSN 0262-7906 = Oil & gas pipeline news : £135.00 per year
Also classified at 665.7'44'05 B82-36733

665.7/8 — INDUSTRIAL GASES

665.7 — Ethane. Solubility — *Tables*

Ethane. — Oxford : Pergamon, Oct.1982. — [286]p. — (Solubility data series ; v.9)
ISBN 0-08-026230-9 : £50.00 : CIP entry
B82-25508

665.7'023'41 — Great Britain. Gas industries — *Career guides*

Algar, Philip. Careers in oil and gas. — London : Kogan Page, Feb.1983. — [100]p. — (Kogan Page careers series)
ISBN 0-85038-563-6 (cased) : £6.95 : CIP entry
ISBN 0-85038-564-4 (pbk) : £2.50
Primary classification 665.5'023'41 B82-39278

665.7'4 — Gas supply — *For children*

Lucas, Angela. The gas in your home / Angela and Derek Lucas. — Hove : Wayland, 1982. — 32p : col.ill ; 19x24cm. — (Origins)
Bibliography: p32
ISBN 0-85340-938-2 : £3.25 B82-18432

665.7'4'0289 — Great Britain. Gas supply. Safety aspects — *For consumers*

Help yourself to gas safety. — [London] ([152 Grosvenor Rd., SW1V 3JT]) : British Gas, 1981. — 11p : col.ill ; 21cm
Unpriced (unbound) B82-23793

665.7'4'0941 — Great Britain. Gas supply — *For consumers*

Help & advice from the Gas Consumers' Council / [prepared by the National Gas Consumers' Council]. — London (Estate House, 130 Jermyn St., SW1Y 4UJ) : National Gas Consumers' Council, 1981. — [14]p : ill(some col.) ; 15x21cm
Unpriced (unbound) B82-23795

665.7'44'05 — Natural gas pipelines — *Serials*

Oil & gas pipeline news. — Vol.1, no.1 (5 Apr. 1982)-. — London (11 Norwich St., EC4A 1AB) : Scientific & Technical Studies, 1982-. — v. ; 30cm
Fortnightly
ISSN 0262-7906 = Oil & gas pipeline news : £135.00 per year
Primary classification 665.5'44'05 B82-36733

665.7'72 — Coal. Gasification

Olliver, Dick. Oil and gas from coal / Dick Olliver ; editorial consultant Bruce Andrews ; [illustrations prepared by Martyn Barnes]. — London : Financial Times Business Information Ltd, c1981. — ix,239p : ill,1map ; 30cm
Bibliography: p225-233
ISBN 0-903199-48-3 (spiral) : Unpriced
Also classified at 662'.6622 B82-37774

665.7'72 — Coal. Gasification — *Conference proceedings*
Symposium on the Gasification and Liquefaction of Coal *(1979 : Katowice)*. Oils and gases from coal : a review of the state-of-the-art in Europe and North America : based on the work of the Symposium on the Gasification and Liquefaction of Coal held under the auspices of the United Nations Economic Commission for Europe, Katowice, Poland, 23-27 April 1979. — Oxford : Published for the United Nations by Pergamon, 1980. — vii,305p : ill ; 26cm
ISBN 0-08-025678-3 : £24.50 : CIP rev.
Primary classification 662'.6622 B80-06499

665.7'73 — Liquefied petroleum gas
Williams, A. F.. Liquefied petroleum gases : guide to properties, applications and uses / A.F. Williams and W.L. Lom. — 2nd ed., rev. and extended. — Chichester : Horwood, 1982. — xix,522p : ill ; 23cm. — (Ellis Horwood series in energy and fuel science)
Previous ed.: 1974. — Includes index
ISBN 0-85312-360-8 : £45.00 : CIP rev.
ISBN 0-470-27275-9 (Halstead Press)
B81-28171

665.7'73 — Liquefied petroleum gas. Flow meters. Safety measures
Liquid measuring systems for LPG. — London : LPGITA, 1982. — 24p : ill ; 21cm. — (Code of practice ; 19)
Cover title
ISBN 0-900323-51-5 (pbk) : Unpriced
B82-34243

665.7'76 — Fuels: Methane. Production. Use of sewage. Use of anaerobic digesters
Meynell, Peter-John. Methane : planning a digester / by Peter-John Meynell. — 2nd rev. ed. — Dorchester, Dorset : Prism, 1982. — 163p : ill,forms ; 23cm
Previous ed.: 1976. — Bibliography: p159-161. — Includes index
ISBN 0-907061-14-1 (cased) : Unpriced
ISBN 0-907061-15-x (pbk) : Unpriced
B82-26794

665.7'8 — Industrial chemicals: Gases. Dispersants: Water
The **Containment** and dispersion of gases by water sprays : November 11th, 1981 / edited by D.V. Greenwood. — [Manchester] : Institute of Chemical Engineers, North Western Branch, c1982. — 1v.(various pagings) : ill ; 30cm
ISBN 0-906636-12-4 (pbk) : £12.00 (£10.00 to members) B82-34244

665.8'1 — Fuels: Hydrogen. Storage. Use of metal hydrides — *Conference proceedings*
Miami International Symposium on Metal-Hydrogen Systems *(1981)*. Metal-hydrogen systems. — Oxford : Pergamon, Jan.1982. — [1750]p
ISBN 0-08-027311-4 : £75.00 : CIP entry
B81-37532

666 — CERAMICS AND RELATED TECHNOLOGIES

666 — Ceramic products. Raw materials
Worrall, W. E.. Ceramic raw materials. — 2nd rev. ed. — Oxford : Pergamon, May 1982. — [120]p. — (Institute of Ceramics textbook series) (Pergamon international library)
Previous ed. published as: Raw materials. London : Maclaren, 1969
ISBN 0-08-028710-7 (cased) : £9.00 : CIP entry
ISBN 0-08-028711-5 (pbk) : £3.95 B82-07245

666 — Ceramics
McColm, I. J.. Ceramics science for materials technologists. — Glasgow : Leonard Hill, Feb.1983. — [272]p
ISBN 0-249-44163-2 : £22.75 : CIP entry
B82-39274

666 — Ceramics, *1900-1980*
Préaud, Tamara. Ceramics of the twentieth century. — Oxford : Phaidon, Oct.1982. — [224]p
Translation of: La céramique art du XXe siècle
ISBN 0-7148-8000-0 : £40.00 : CIP entry
B82-23005

666'.07 — Great Britain. Ceramics industries. Professional personnel. Training
A **Guide** to the training and development of professional and administrative staff. — [Great Britain] : Ceramics, Glass and Mineral Products Industry Training Board, c1982. — 48p : ill ; 21cm
Cover title
Unpriced (pbk) B82-30861

666'.07'041 — Great Britain. Ceramics industries. Personnel. Training
Ridley, M. A. W.. Engineering craft training the module system : guide notes for companies / [M.A.W. Ridley, W.G. Patrick, J.A. Crew]. — [Harrow] ([Bovis House, Northolt Rd., Harrow, Middx]) : Ceramics, Glass and Mineral Products Industry Training Board, [1982?]. — 12p : ill ; 21x30cm
Two sheets in inside back pocket
Unpriced (pbk) B82-40439

666'.1 — Glass
Hlaváč, Jan. The technology of glass and ceramics. — Oxford : Elsevier Scientific, Oct.1982. — [300]p. — (Glass science and technology ; 4)
ISBN 0-444-99688-5 : £40.00 : CIP entry
B82-24016

666'.1'02493 — Glass — *For archaeology*
Frank, Susan. Glass and archaeology / Susan Frank. — London ; New York : Academic Press, 1982. — xi,155p : ill,maps,plans ; 24cm. — (Studies in archaeological science)
Includes bibliographies and index
ISBN 0-12-265620-2 : £12.20 : CIP rev.
B82-10420

666'.1042 — Glass. Chemical properties
Paul, A. (Amal). Chemistry of glasses / A. Paul. — London : Chapman and Hall, 1982. — ix,293p : ill ; 25cm
Includes index
ISBN 0-412-23020-8 : Unpriced : CIP rev.
B82-06223

666'.1'0684 — Organisational change — *Study examples: Emmaboda Glasverk*
Berg, Per-Olof. Emotional structures in organization : a study of the process of change in a Swedish company / Per-Olof Berg. — 2nd ed. — Lund : Studentlitteratur ; Bromley : Chartwell-Bratt, 1981, c1979. — 287p : ill ; 23cm
Previous ed.: 1979. — Bibliography: p280-287
ISBN 0-86238-022-7 (pbk) : Unpriced
B82-36843

666'.1'07 — Great Britain. Glass industries. Personnel. Training
Education and training in materials engineering for the glass and other materials processing industries. — [Great Britain] : Ceramics, Glass and Mineral Products Industry Training Board, c1981. — 12p ; 30cm
Cover title
Unpriced (pbk) B82-30863

Education and training in materials engineering for the materials processing industries. — [Great Britain] : Ceramics, Glass and Mineral Products Industry Training Board, [1982?]. — 13p ; 30cm
Cover title. — Text on inside back cover
Unpriced (pbk) B82-30864

A **Guide** to the initial and further training of manufacturing process operatives in the glass industry. — [Great Britain] : Glass Manufacturers' Federation, [1982?]. — 40p : ill ; 30cm
Cover title
Unpriced (pbk) B82-30858

666'.3'2341 — Great Britain. Pottery & porcelain industries — *Career guides*
Careers in the pottery industry. — [Harrow] ([Bovis House, Northolt Rd., Harrow, Middx]) : Ceramics, Glass and Mineral Products Industry Training Board, c1981. — 25p : ill (some col.) ; 21cm
Cover title. — Text on inside covers
Unpriced (pbk) B82-04951

666'.8 — Concrete
Ramachandran, V. S.. Concrete science. — London : Heyden, Nov.1981. — [400]p
ISBN 0-85501-703-1 : CIP entry B81-30625

666'.893 — Concrete
Jones, T. F.. Concrete technology 4 checkbook / T.F. Jones. — London : Butterworth Scientific, 1982. — (Butterworths technical and scientific checkbooks)
Vol. 1: Properties and materials. — vi,114p : ill,forms ; 20cm
Bibliography: p110-111. — Includes index
ISBN 0-408-00673-0 : Unpriced : CIP rev.
ISBN 0-408-00643-9 (pbk) : Unpriced
B82-04031

Ropke, John C.. Concrete problems : causes and cures / John C. Ropke. — New York ; London : McGraw-Hill, c1982. — xvii,187p : ill ; 24cm
Includes index
ISBN 0-07-053609-0 : £17.50 B82-15973

666'.893 — Demolition waste materials: Concrete. Recycling — *Conference proceedings*
NATO Advanced Research Institute on Adhesion Problems in the Recycling of Concrete *(1980 : Saint-Rémy-les-Chevreuse)*. Adhesion problems in the recycling of concrete / [proceedings of a NATO Advanced Research Institute on Adhesion Problems in the Recycling of Concrete, held November 25-28, 1980, in Saint-Remy-les-Chevreuse, France] ; edited by Pieter C. Kreijger. — New York ; London : Plenum in co-operation with the NATO Scientific Affairs Division, c1981. — xi,419p : ill ; 26cm. — (NATO conference series. VI, Materials science ; v.4)
Includes index
ISBN 0-306-40817-1 : Unpriced B82-13952

666'.895 — Autoclaved aerated concrete — *Conference proceedings*
Autoclaved aerated concrete, moisture and properties. — Oxford : Elsevier Scientific, Sept.1982. — [370]p. — (Developments in civil engineering ; v.6)
Conference papers
ISBN 0-444-42117-3 : CIP entry B82-26694

666'.94 — Portland cement
Bye, G. C.. Portland cement. — Oxford : Pergamon, Jan.1983. — [120]p. — (Institute of Ceramics textbook series)
ISBN 0-08-029965-2 (cased) : £10.00 : CIP entry
ISBN 0-08-029964-4 (pbk) : £4.95 B82-33610

Ghosh, S. N.**Advances** in cement technology. — Oxford : Pergamon, Aug.1982. — [600]p
ISBN 0-08-028670-4 : £50.00 : CIP entry
B82-15656

666'.94 — Wood wool cement slabs. Raw materials: Eucalyptus grandis & Pinus kesiya. Testing
Hawkes, A. J.. The suitability of Eucalyptus grandis and two provenances of Pinus kesiya for wood wool-cement slab manufacture / A.J. Hawkes and A.P. Robinson. — London : Tropical Products Institute, 1978. — iii,32p : ill ; 30cm
English text, French and Spanish summaries. — At head of title: Tropical Products Institute. — Bibliography: p12
ISBN 0-85954-086-3 (pbk) : £0.80 B82-04210

667 — CLEANING, DYEING, INKS, COATINGS

667'.12 — Dry cleaning
Intermediate drycleaning technology. — [London?] : [Guild of Cleaners and Launderers], c1981. — 201p : ill ; 21cm
Cover title. — Guild of Cleaners and Launderers
Unpriced (spiral) B82-35702

667'.12 — Textiles. Stains. Removal
Stain removal. — [S.l.] : Guild of Cleaners & Launderers, [1980?]. — 88p ; 21cm. — (Technical monographs)
Cover title
Unpriced (spiral) B82-40478

667′.13 — Laundering
An **Introduction** to laundry chemistry. — [England] : Guild of Cleaners & Launderers, [1980?]. — 46leaves : 1ill. — (Technical monographs)
Cover title
Unpriced (spiral) B82-40477

667′.2 — Fluorescent brightening agents
Zahradník, Miloš. The production and application of fluorescent brightening agents. — Chichester : Wiley, Sept.1982. — [162]p
ISBN 0-471-10125-7 : £13.00 : CIP entry
B82-19519

667′.26 — Natural dyes. Making — *Manuals*
Schultz, Kathleen. Create your own natural dyes / Kathleen Schultz. — New York : Sterling ; Poole : Distributed by Blandford Press, c1975 (1982 printing). — 96p : ill(some col.) ; 23cm
Includes index
ISBN 0-8069-7576-8 (pbk) : £3.95 B82-39881

667′.29 — Liquids. Powders. Dispersion — *Study examples: Pigments*
Dispersion of powders in liquids : with special reference to pigments / edited by G.D. Parfitt. — 3rd ed. — London : Applied Science Publishers, 1981. — xv,518p : ill ; 23cm
Previous ed.: 1973. — Includes index
ISBN 0-85334-990-8 : £38.00 : CIP rev.
B81-30423

667′.3 — Great Britain. Dyeing industries. Energy. Conservation. Demonstration projects
Demonstration of the improved energy efficiency of a chemical plant by heat and process integration : demonstration project at Clayton Aniline Ltd., Manchester. — Harwell ([Building 156, AERE, Harwell, Oxon. OX11 0RA]) : Energy Technology Support Unit on behalf of the Departments of Energy and Industry, [1981?]. — 25p,[2]leaves of plates : ill (some col.) ; 30cm
Energy Conservation Demonstration Projects Scheme
Unpriced (spiral) B82-38374

667′.3 — Textiles. Foam dyeing — *Conference proceedings*
Foam processing for dyeing and finishing : papers presented at a Shirley Institute conference on 15 April 1981. — Manchester : The Institute, c1981. — 38p : ill ; 30cm. — (Shirley Institute publication, ISSN 0306-5154 ; s.42)
ISBN 0-903669-38-2 (pbk) : £16.00 (£12.00 to members of the Institute) : CIP rev.
Primary classification 677′.02825 B81-28802

667′.3′0321 — Textile fibres. Dyeing — *Encylopaedias*
Ponting, Ken. A dictionary of dyes and dyeing. — London : Bell & Hyman, Apr.1982. — [212]p
Previously published: London : Mills & Boon, 1980
ISBN 0-7135-1311-x (pbk) : £4.95 : CIP entry
B82-04493

667′.318 — Coir. Dyeing. Black dyes. Testing
Black dyes for coir fibre. — London : Tropical Products Institute
2: Evaluation of selected dyes / A.J. Canning, C.G. Jarman and S.M. Mykoluk. — 1979. — v,36p : ill ; 30cm
English text, French and Spanish summaries. — Bibliography: p36
ISBN 0-85954-095-2 (pbk) : £1.15 B82-04213

667′.331 — Wool. Dyeing. Use of plant dyes — *Amateurs′ manuals*
Rippengal, Joan. How to dye in your kitchen : basic information on using natural dyes / [Joan Rippengal]. — [Eastbourne] ([25 Freeman Ave., Hampden Park, Eastbourne, E. Sussex BN22 9NU]) : [J. Rippengal], c1980. — 17p ; 21cm
Bibliography: p17
Unpriced (pbk) B82-11041

667′.5 — Printing inks
The **Printing** ink manual. — 3rd ed. / by D.E. Bisset ... [et al.]. — London : Northwood, 1979. — xv,488p : ill ; 25cm
Previous ed.: Cambridge : Heffer, 1969. — Bibliography: p465-474. — Includes index
ISBN 0-7198-2559-8 : £20.00 B82-31075

667′.6 — Paints
Morgans, W. M.. Outlines of paint technology / W.M. Morgans. — 2nd ed. — London : Griffin
Previous ed.: in one vol. 1969
Vol.1: Materials. — 1982. — ix,298p : ill ; 25cm
Includes index
ISBN 0-85264-259-8 : £24.00 : CIP rev.
B82-07114

667′.9 — Coatings
Paint handbook / edited by Guy E. Weismantel. — New York ; London : McGraw-Hill, c1981. — 1v.(various pagings) : ill ; 24cm
Includes bibliographies and index
ISBN 0-07-069061-8 : £28.50 B82-27413

667′.9 — Coatings. Curing. Use of ultraviolet photopolymerisation
Roffey, C. G.. Photopolymerization of surface coatings / C.G. Roffey. — Chichester : Wiley, c1982. — xvii,353p : ill ; 24cm
Includes index
ISBN 0-471-10063-3 : £20.00 : CIP rev.
B82-06833

667′.9 — Waterborne powder coatings
Chandler, R. H.. Aqueous powder coatings : (and powder electropaints) / R.H. Chandler and J.I. Chandler. — Braintree : R.H. Chandler, 1981. — 46p : ill ; 30cm. — (Bibliographies in paint technology ; no.37)
Text on inside cover
Unpriced (pbk) B82-07778

667′.9′0212 — Coatings — *Technical data*
Ash, Michael. A formulary of paints and other coatings / compiled by Michael and Irene Ash. — London : Godwin
Vol.2. — 1982. — 399p ; 23cm
Includes index
ISBN 0-7114-5514-7 : £18.50 B82-33146

668.1 — SURFACE ACTIVE AGENTS

668′.1 — Surface-active agents
Attwood, D.. Surfactant systems. — London : Chapman and Hall, Aug.1982. — [700]p
ISBN 0-412-14840-4 : £35.00 : CIP entry
B82-15784

Surface active agents : a symposium held at Nottingham University, England, 26-28 September 1979, by the Society of Chemical Industry Colloid and Surface Chemistry Group in collaboration with the Chemical Society — Faraday Division Colloid and Interface Science Group. — London : SCI, 1979. — iv,323p : ill ; 21cm
Conference papers
ISBN 0-901001-59-7 (pbk) : Unpriced
B82-31248

668′.1′094 — Europe. Surface-active agents — *Lists*
Surfactants Europa : a directory of surface active agents available in Europe. — London : George Godwin
Vol.1. — Jan.1982. — [390]p
ISBN 0-7114-5736-0 (pbk) : £30.00 : CIP entry
B81-35901

668′.1′0941 — Great Britain. Surface-active agents — *Lists*
Stroud, Marion. The gift of marriage / written and compiled by Marion Stroud ; produced in conjunction with Pictor International. — London : Lion, 1982. — [60]p : col.ill ; 25cm
ISBN 0-85648-398-2 : £4.95 B82-32938

668′.14 — Detergents. Quality control. Chemical analysis
Milwidsky, B. M.. Detergent analysis : a handbook for cost-effective quality control / B.M. Milwidsky and D.M. Gabriel. — London : Godwin, 1982. — xi,291p ; 24cm
Bibliography: p276. — Includes index
ISBN 0-7114-5735-2 : Unpriced : CIP rev.
B81-35031

668.3 — ADHESIVES AND RELATED PRODUCTS

668′.3 — Adhesives
Wahe, William C.. Adhesion and the formualtion of adhesives. — 2nd ed. — London : Applied Science, July 1982. — [352]p
Previous ed.: 1976
ISBN 0-85334-134-6 : £30.00 : CIP entry
Primary classification 541.3′453 B82-13138

668′.3 — Adhesives - *Serials*
Developments in adhesives. — London : Applied Science, May 1981. — (The developments series)
2. — [284]p
ISBN 0-85334-958-4 : £24.00 : CIP entry
B81-06628

668′.37 — Water soluble gums & water soluble resins
Handbook of water-soluble gums and resins / Robert L. Davidson, editor in chief. — New York ; London : McGraw-Hill, c1980. — 672p in various pagings : ill,ports ; 24cm
Bibliography: p24.30-24.31. — Includes index
ISBN 0-07-015471-6 : £20.50 B82-07357

668.4 — PLASTICS

668.4 — Bulk plastics. Pneumatic transport & storage
Plastics pneumatic conveying and bulk storage / edited by G. Butters. — London : Applied Science, c1981. — xi,296p : ill ; 23cm
Includes index
ISBN 0-85334-983-5 : £27.00 : CIP rev.
B81-25720

668.4 — Plastics
Birley, Arthur W.. Plastics materials : properties and applications / Arthur W. Birley and Martyn J. Scott. — Glasgow : Leonard Hill, 1982. — viii,167p : ill ; 23cm
Includes index
ISBN 0-249-44162-4 : £18.95 : CIP rev.
ISBN 0-249-44161-6 (pbk) : £8.95 B82-10686

Brydson, J. A.. Plastics materials. — 4th ed. — London : Butterworth Scientific, June 1982. — [840]p
Previous ed: London : Newnes-Butterworths, 1975
ISBN 0-408-00538-6 : £35.00 : CIP entry
B82-10486

Schwartz, Seymour S.. Plastics materials and processes / Seymour S. Schwartz, Sidney H. Goodman. — New York ; London : Van Nostrand Reinhold, c1982. — xiv,965p : ill ; 29cm
Includes bibliographies and index
ISBN 0-442-22777-9 : £76.00 B82-36987

668.4 — Plastics — *For schools*
Plastics. — Cambridge : Cambridge University Press in association with the Inner London Education Authority Learning Materials Service. — (Innovation in craft)
Plastics identified. — 1979. — 17p : ill ; 21x30cm
Originally published: London : ILEA, 1975. — Bibliography: p16
ISBN 0-521-21971-x (pbk) : £0.95 B82-26369

668.4 — Plastics. Manufacture & applications
Crawford, R. J.. Plastics engineering. — Oxford : Pergamon, Sept.1981. — [360]p. — (Progress in polymer science ; v.7)
ISBN 0-08-026262-7 (cased) : £31.25 : CIP entry
ISBN 0-08-026263-5 (pbk) : £10.50
B81-21555

668.4 — Plastics. Manufacture — *For children*
Althea. Making plastics / by Althea ; illustrated by Tim Hunkin. — Over : Dinosaur, c1981. — 24p : col.ill ; 16x19cm. — (Dinosaur′s Althea books)
ISBN 0-85122-277-3 (cased) : £2.25
ISBN 0-85122-261-7 (pbk) : £0.70 B82-08270

668.4 — Plastics. Processing
Coates, P. D.. Interplas '81 / P.D. Coates. — London (3 Charing Cross Rd., WC2H 0HW) : Science and Engineering Research Council, Polymer Engineering Directorate
Pt.1: Robotic handling devices. — [1982]. — 3,[7]leaves : ill ; 30cm
'Report on robotic handling displayed at Interplas '81'
Unpriced (pbk) B82-31521

Coates, P. D.. Interplas '81 / P.D. Coates. — London (3 Charing Cross Rd., WC2H 0HW) : Science and Engineering Research Council, Polymer Engineering Directorate
Pt.2: Microprocessors in plastics processing. — [1982]. — 9,[13]leaves : ill ; 30cm
'Report on microprocessors in plastics processing equipment displayed at Interplas '81'
Unpriced (pbk) B82-31522

668.4'03 — Plastics — *Polyglot dictionaries*
Kaliske, Gisbert. Dictionary of plastics technology. — Oxford : Elsevier Scientific, Oct.1982. — [380]p
ISBN 0-444-99687-7 : £50.00 : CIP entry
B82-24015

668.4'05 — Plastics — *Serials*
Developments in plastics technology. — 1. — London : Applied Science, Oct.1982. — [256]p. — (The Developments series)
ISBN 0-85334-155-9 : £30.00 : CIP entry
B82-24259

668.4'1 — Plastics. Surface treatment
Surface analysis and pretreatment of plastics and metals / edited by D.M. Brewis. — London : Applied Science, c1982. — xvi,268p : ill ; 23cm
Includes index
ISBN 0-85334-992-4 : £24.00 : CIP rev.
Also classified at 671.7 B81-31516

668.4'1 — Polymers. Stabilisation
Developments in polymer stabilisation / edited by Gerald Scott. — London : Applied Science. — (Developments series)
5. — c1982. — x,240p : ill ; 23cm
Includes index
ISBN 0-85334-967-3 : £29.00 : CIP rev.
B81-20545

668.4'12 — Plastics mouldings. Design
Greenwood, D. P.. Modern design in plastics. — London : J. Murray, July 1982. — [96]p
ISBN 0-7195-3966-8 (pbk) : £4.95 : CIP entry
B82-13076

668.4'13 — Polymers. Extrusion — *Conference proceedings*
Polymer Extrusion II *(Conference : 1982 : London)*. Conference : Polymer Extrusion II : 12 May and 13 May 1982 : the Rainbow Suite, London. — London (11 Hobart Place, SW1W 0HL) : Plastics and Rubber Institute, [1982]. — 115p in various pagings : ill ; 21cm
Cover title. — Spine title: Polymer Extrusion II — May 1982
£15.00 (pbk) B82-26609

668.4'197 — Molten plastics. Rheometry. Techniques
Dealy, John M.. Rheometers for molten plastics : a practical guide to testing and property measurement / John M. Dealy ; sponsored by the Society of Plastics Engineers. — New York ; London : Van Nostrand Reinhold, c1982. — xviii,302p : ill ; 24cm
Includes index
ISBN 0-442-21874-5 : £31.45 B82-16308

668.4'197 — Plastics. Testing — *Standards*
Handbook of plastics test methods. — 2nd ed. — London : Godwin, Sept.1981. — [430]p
Previous ed.: / by G.C. Ives, J.A. Mead and M.M. Riley. London : Iliffe, 1971
ISBN 0-7114-5618-6 : £28.50 : CIP entry
B81-23852

668.4'2 — Polytetrahydrofuran
Dreyfuss, P.. Poly(tetrahydrofuran) / P. Dreyfuss. — New York ; London : Gordon and Breach, c1982. — xiii,306p : ill ; 23cm. — (Polymer monographs ; v.8)
Includes index
ISBN 0-677-03330-3 : Unpriced B82-26959

668.4'22 — Thermosetting plastics. Applications
Thermosetting plastics. — London : Godwin, Sept.1981. — [216]p
ISBN 0-7114-5617-8 : £16.00 : CIP entry
B81-20464

668.4'22 — Thermosetting plastics. Injection moulding — *Conference proceedings*
Thermosets Injection — High Performance at Low Cost *(Conference : 1982 : Solihull)*. Conference Thermosets Injection — High Performance at Low Cost : 2 and 3 March 1982 : Library Theatre, Solihull, West Midlands. — London (11 Hobart Place SW1W 0HL) : The Plastics and Rubber Institute, c1982. — 1v(various pagings) : ill ; 21cm
Unpriced (pbk) B82-20152

668.4'22 — Thermosetting power coatings
Thermoset powder coatings / editorial director Derek Eddowes ; editor John Ward. — Redhill : Fuel & Metallurgical Journals, c1982. — 140p : ill(some col.) ; 21cm
ISBN 0-86108-106-4 (pbk) : Unpriced
B82-26925

668.4'225 — Polyester elastomers
Hepburn, C.. Polyurethane elastomers. — London : Applied Science, July 1982. — [400]p
ISBN 0-85334-127-3 : £35.00 : CIP entry
B82-16491

668.4'23 — Short fibre reinforced thermoplastics
Folkes, M. J.. Short fibre reinforced thermoplastics / M.J. Folkes. — Chichester : Research Studies Press, c1982. — x,176p : ill ; 24cm. — (Polymer engineering research studies series ; 1)
Includes bibliographies and index
ISBN 0-471-10209-1 : £13.50 : CIP rev.
B82-03612

668.4'23 — Thermoplastics. Injection moulding
Developments in injection moulding. — London : Applied Science. — (The Developments series)
2: Improving efficiency / edited by A. Whelan and J.L. Craft. — c1981. — x,349p : ill ; 23cm
Includes index
ISBN 0-85334-968-1 : £36.00 : CIP rev.
B81-20544

Whelan, A.. Injection moulding materials / A. Whelan. — London : Applied Science Publishers, c1982. — ix,398p : ill ; 24cm
Includes bibliographies and index
ISBN 0-85334-993-2 : Unpriced : CIP rev.
B81-33786

668.4'234 — Polyolefine stabilizers — *Lists*
World index of polyolefine stabilizers. — London : Kogan Page, July 1981. — [250]p
ISBN 0-85038-462-1 : £55.00 : CIP entry
B81-20648

668.4'236 — Polyvinyl acetate. Emulsion polymerisation
Emulsion polymerization of vinyl acetate / edited by Mohamed S. El-Aasser and John W. Vanderhoff. — London : Applied Science, c1981. — xiv,290p : ill ; 23cm
Conference papers. — Includes index
ISBN 0-85334-971-1 : £24.00 : CIP rev.
B81-20542

668.4'236 — Polyvinyl chloride
Particulate nature of PVC : formation, structure and processing / edited by G. Butters. — London : Applied Science, c1982. — xv,240p : ill ; 23cm
Includes index
ISBN 0-85334-120-6 : £20.00 : CIP rev.
B82-09876

668.4'236 — Polyvinyl chloride. Plasticisation
Sears, J. Kern. The technology of plasticizers / J. Kern Sears and Joseph R. Darby. — New York ; Chichester : Wiley, c1982. — xi,1166p : ill ; 27cm. — (SPE monographs)
Includes bibliographies and index
ISBN 0-471-05583-2 : £97.50 B82-30696

668.4'237 — Polyvinyl chloride. Manufacture
Manufacture and processing of PVC / edited by R.H. Burgess. — London : Applied Science, c1982. — xviii,276p : ill ; 23cm
Includes index
ISBN 0-85334-972-x : £22.00 : CIP rev.
B81-20541

668.4'93 — Flexible polyurethane foams
Woods, George. Flexible polyurethane foams : chemistry and technology / George Woods. — London : Applied Science Publishers, c1982. — xii,334p : ill ; 24cm
Includes index
ISBN 0-85334-981-9 : £28.00 : CIP rev.
B81-25718

668.4'94'05 — Reinforced plastics — *Serials*
Developments in reinforced plastics. — 2. — London : Applied Science, May 1982. — [200] p. — (The Developments series)
ISBN 0-85334-125-7 : £21.00 : CIP entry
ISSN 0260-9185 B82-07028

668.5 — PERFUMES AND COSMETICS

668'.5 — Cosmetics & toiletries. Manufacture
Harry, Ralph G.. Harry's cosmeticology. — 7th ed. / edited by J.B. Wilkinson, R.J. Moore. — London : Godwin, 1982. — xv,934p : ill ; 35cm
Previous ed.: London : Hill, 1973. — Includes index
ISBN 0-7114-5679-8 : Unpriced : CIP rev.
B82-01207

668'.5 — Cosmetics, perfumes & toiletries. Making — *Manuals*
Lotions and potions. — London : WI Books, June 1982. — [32]p
Originally published: 1955
ISBN 0-900556-63-3 (unbound) : £0.95 : CIP entry
Primary classification 615.5'35 B82-19269

668.6 — AGRICULTURAL CHEMICALS

668'.62 — Great Britain. Fertiliser industries. Energy. Conservation — *Proposals*
Brookes, G.. The fertilizer industry : energy consumption and conservation in the fertilizer industry : a report / prepared for the Department of Energy by G. Brookes. — [London] : Issued jointly by the Department of Energy and Department of Industry, [1981]. — vi,72p : ill,maps ; 30cm. — (Energy audit series ; no.13)
Unpriced (pbk) B82-10174

668'.65'0218 — Pesticides. Standards
Lovett, J. F.. FAO Panel of Experts on Pesticide Specifications, Registration Requirements and Applications Standards : report of a visit to Italy 5-9 October 1981 / J.F. Lovett. — [London] ([Great Westminster House, Horseferry Rd., SW1P 2AE]) : ADAS, [1982]. — 16p ; 30cm
Cover title
Unpriced (pbk) B82-40875

668.9 — INDUSTRIAL POLYMERS

668.9 — Polymers. Degradation & stabilisation — *Serials*
Developments in polymer degradation. — 4. — London : Applied Science, July 1982. — [296] p. — (The Developments series)
ISBN 0-85334-132-x : £29.00 : CIP entry
B82-13136

668.9 — Polymers. Processing. Multiphase flow
Han, Chang Dae. Multiphase flow in polymer processing / Chang Dae Han. — New York ; London : Academic Press, 1981. — xv,459p : ill ; 24cm
Includes index
ISBN 0-12-322460-8 : £44.40 B82-21248

668.9 — Polymers. Processing. Rheology
Cogswell, F. N.. Polymer melt rheology : a guide for industrial practice / F.N. Cogswell. — London : Godwin in association with the Plastics and Rubber Institute, 1981. — x,178p : ill ; 24cm
Bibliography: p129-130 . — Includes index
ISBN 0-7114-5608-9 : Unpriced B82-38489

668.9 — Polymers. Stabilisation — *Serials*

Developments in polymer stabilisation. — 6. — London : Applied Science, Jan.1983. — [352]p. — (The Developments series)
ISBN 0-85334-168-0 : £40.00 : CIP entry
B82-33110

669 — METALLURGY

669 — Extractive metallurgy — *Conference proceedings*

Extraction metallurgy ′81 : papers presented at a symposium organized by the Institution of Mining and Metallurgy in collaboration with Gesellschaft Deutscher Metallhütten- und Bergleute, Benelux Métallurgie and Société Francaise de Métallurgie and held in London from 21 to 23 September 1981. — London : The Institution of Mining and Metallurgy, c1981. — 441p : ill ; 30cm
ISBN 0-900488-59-x (pbk) : Unpriced
B82-15423

669 — Metals

Venet͡skiĭ, S. I.. Tales about metals / S.I. Venetsky ; translated from the Russian by N.G. Kittell. — Moscow : Mir ; [London] : Distributed by Central Books, 1981. — 210p : col.ill ; 23cm
Translation of: Rasskazy o metallakh
ISBN 0-7147-1741-x : £3.50 B82-40111

669′.00212 — Metals — *Technical data*

Smithells, Colin James. Smithells metals reference book. — 6th ed. — London : Butterworth Scientific, June 1982. — [1600]p
Previous ed.: 1976
ISBN 0-408-71053-5 : £80.00 : CIP entry
B82-10497

669′.009 — Metallurgy, *to 1980*

Waldron, M. B.. Metals : a key to civilisation / M.B. Waldron. — [Guildford] ([Guildford, Surrey GU2 5XH]) : [University of Surrey], [1978?]. — 31p : ill ; 21cm. — (University of Surrey university lecture)
Cover title
Unpriced (pbk) B82-26656

669′.00951′5 — Tibet. Metallurgy, *to 1980*

Aspects of Tibetan metallurgy / edited by W.A. Oddy and W. Zwalf. — London : British Museum, 1981. — v,137p : ill,1map ; 30cm. — (Occasional paper / British Museum, ISSN 0142-4815 ; no.15)
Bibliography: p125-137
ISBN 0-86159-014-7 (pbk) : Unpriced
B82-05609

669′.022462 — Metallurgy — *For engineering*

Higgins, Raymond A.. Engineering metallurgy. — 5th ed. — London : Hodder and Stoughton
Previous ed.: London : English Universities Press, 1973
Part 1: Applied physical metallurgy. — July 1982. — [480]p
ISBN 0-340-28524-9 (pbk) : £5.95 : CIP entry
B82-18569

669′.0951 — China. Metals. Production — *Serials*

RLC : Roskill′s letter from China = Zhongguo youse jinshu gongye kuaibao. — No.1 (1981)-. — London (2 Clapham Rd, SW9 0JA) : Roskill Information Services, 1981-. — v. : ill ; 30cm
Quarterly. — Description based on: No.2 (Summer 1981)
ISSN 0261-1724 = RLC. Roskill′s letter from China : Unpriced B82-11146

669.1 — METALLURGY OF FERROUS METALS

669′.1 — Iron & steel industries. Quality control — *Conference proceedings*

Steel Casting Research and Trade Association. *Conference (25th : 1980 : Harrogate).* Metallurgy and quality : proceedings of the 25th annual conference, Harrogate, 24-25 April 1980 / Steel Casting Research and Trade Association. — Sheffield : The Association, 1981. — 163p in various pagings : ill,1plan,forms ; 30cm
£12.50 (£6.25 to members of SCRATA) (pbk)
B82-02862

669′.1 — Iron & steel. Production

Peters, A. T.. Ferrous production metallurgy / A.T. Peters. — New York ; Chichester : Wiley, c1982. — xvi,299p : ill ; 25cm
Bibliography: p292-293. — Includes index
ISBN 0-471-08597-9 : £35.00 B82-16543

669′.142 — Steel. Production

Small-scale steelmaking. — London : Applied Science, Feb.1983. — [192]p
ISBN 0-85334-181-8 : £24.00 : CIP entry
B82-39607

669′.142′0212 — Steel — *Technical data* — *For design*

An Introduction to steel selection. — [Oxford] : Published for the Design Council, the British Standards Institution, and the Council of Engineering Institutions by Oxford University Press. — (Engineering design guides ; 43)
Pt.2: Stainless steels / D. Elliott and S.M. Tupholme. — c1981. — 30p : ill ; 30cm
Bibliography: p30
ISBN 0-19-859179-9 (pbk) : £4.95 : CIP rev.
B81-16383

669′.142′0684 — Great Britain. Steel industries. Managers. Development

Manager development for a modern steel industry . — London (190 Fleet St., EC4A 2AH) : Iron and Steel Industry Training Board, 1981. — 16p ; 30cm
Cover title
Unpriced (pbk) B82-04946

669′.1424 — Electroslag refining

Hoyle, G.. Electroslag processes. — London : Applied Science, Nov.1982. — [232]p
ISBN 0-85334-164-8 : £27.00 : CIP entry
B82-26317

669.2/7 — METALLURGY OF NONFERROUS METALS

669′.2 — Precious metals — *Conference proceedings*

International Precious Metals Institute. *Conference (5th : 1981 : Providence, R.I.).* Precious metals 1981 / [proceedings of the Fifth International Precious Metals Institute Conference, held in Providence, Rhode Island, June 2-5, 1981] ; edited by E.D. Zysk. — Toronto ; Oxford : Pergamon, c1982. — xiv,461p : ill ; 26cm
Includes bibliographies and index
ISBN 0-08-025392-x : £32.50 B82-30620

669′.22 — Gold

Weston, Rae. Gold. — London : Croom Helm, Jan.1983. — [384]p
ISBN 0-7099-0202-6 : £14.95 : CIP entry
B82-32550

669′.22′09 — Gold, *to 1980*

Kettell, Brian. Gold. — London : Graham & Trotman, Sept.1981. — [250]p
ISBN 0-86010-257-2 : £9.75 : CIP entry
B81-28145

669′.24 — Platinum metals

McDonald, Donald. A history of platinum and its allied metals. — London : Johnson Matthey ; London : Europa [distributor], July 1982. — [460]p
ISBN 0-905118-83-9 : CIP entry B82-22399

669′.3 — Copper

West, E. G.. Copper and its alloys. — Chichester : Horwood, July 1982. — [192]p. — (Ellis Horwood series in industrial metals)
ISBN 0-85312-505-8 : £18.50 : CIP entry
B82-20654

669′.3′0901 — Copper. Prehistoric metallurgy

Scientific studies in early mining and extractive metallurgy / edited by P.T. Craddock. — London : British Museum, 1980. — 173p : ill,maps,plans ; 30cm. — (Occasional paper, ISSN 0142-4815, ISSN no.20)
Conference papers. — Includes bibliographies
ISBN 0-86159-019-8 (pbk) : Unpriced
Also classified at 622′.343′0901 B82-36198

669′.733 — Cobalt & cobalt alloys

Betteridge, W.. Cobalt and its alloys / W. Betteridge. — Chichester : Horwood, 1982. — 159p : ill ; 24cm. — (Industrial metals)
Text on lining papers. — Includes index
ISBN 0-85312-451-5 : £16.50 : CIP rev.
B82-07840

669.9 — PHYSICAL AND CHEMICAL METALLURGY

669′.9 — Metals. Heat transfer & mass transfer — *Conference proceedings*

Heat and mass transfer in metallurgical systems / edited by D. Brian Spalding and N.H. Afgan. — Washington ; London : Hemisphere, c1981. — x,758p : ill ; 25cm. — (Proceedings of the International Centre for Heat and Mass Transfer ; 11)
Conference papers. — Includes index
ISBN 0-89116-169-4 : £72.50 B82-15971

669′.9 — Metals. Recrystallisation

Gorelik, S. S.. Recrystallization in metals and alloys / S.S. Gorelik ; translated from the Russian by V. Afanasyev. — Moscow : MIR ; [London] : distributed by Central, 1981. — 479p : ill ; 23cm
Translation of: Rekristallizat͡sii͡a metallov i splavov. — Includes index
ISBN 0-7147-1692-8 : £5.95 B82-29292

669′.95 — Metallography

Mehrotra, R. C.. Metal carboxylates. — London : Academic Press, Feb.1983. — [380]p
ISBN 0-12-488160-2 : CIP entry B82-36580

669′.95′028 — Metals. Interfaces & surfaces. Spectroscopy

Electron and positron spectroscopies in materials science and engineering / edited by Otto Buck, John K. Tien, Harris L. Marcus. — New York ; London : Academic Press, 1979. — xv,340p : ill ; 23cm. — (Materials science and technology)
Includes bibliographies and index
ISBN 0-12-139150-7 : £33.80 B82-24159

669′.967322 — Titanium & titanium alloys. Structure & properties — *Conference proceedings*

International Conference on Titanium *(3rd : 1976 : Moscow).* Titanium and titanium alloys : scientific and technological aspects / [proceedings of the Third International Conference on Titanium, organized by the Academy of Sciences of the USSR, in association with The Metallurgical Society of AIME ... [et al.], in Moscow, on May 18-21 1976] ; edited by J.C. Williams and A.F. Belov ; associate editors N.F. Anoshkin ... [et al.]. — New York ; London : Plenum, c1982. — 3v.(xxxii,2467p) : ill ; 26cm
Includes bibliographies and index
ISBN 0-306-40191-6 : Unpriced B82-28221

670 — MANUFACTURES

670 — Manufacture

Fundamentals of manufacturing engineering / V.M. Kovan ... [et al.] ; V.S. Korsakov, general editor ; translated from the Russian by F. Palkin and V. Palkin. — Moscow : Mir, 1979 ; [London] : Distributed by Central Books. — 422p : ill ; 22cm
Translation of: Osnovy tekhnologii mashinostroenii͡a. — Bibliography: p419. — Includes index
ISBN 0-7147-1744-4 : £5.50 B82-39312

670′.212 — Manufactured goods. Certification. International schemes

International certification and approval schemes : a guide to the scope and operation of selected schemes and organisations. — 2nd (rev.) ed. — Hemel Hempstead : Technical Help to Exporters, British Standards Institution, 1981. — vi,90p : ill ; 21cm
Previous ed.: 1978. — Bibliography: p89-90
ISBN 0-905877-65-9 (pbk) : Unpriced
B82-16394

670.42 — Production engineering — *For technicians*

Pritchard, R. T.. Technician manufacturing technology III. — London : Hodder & Stoughton, July 1982. — [208]p
ISBN 0-340-24353-8 (pbk) : £3.45 : CIP entry
B82-14511

670.42′023′41 — Great Britain. Factory work — *Career guides*

Factories / [prepared jointly by COIC and the Central Office of Information]. — [London] : [Manpower Services Commission], [1982?]. — 8v. : col.ill ; 30cm. — (Close-up)
ISBN 0-86110-175-8 : Unpriced
ISBN 0-86110-178-2 (CU75)
ISBN 0-86110-177-4 (CU76)
ISBN 0-86110-182-0 (CU77)
ISBN 0-86110-180-4 (CU78)
ISBN 0-86110-183-9 (CU79)
ISBN 0-86110-176-6 (CU80)
ISBN 0-86110-181-2 (CU81) B82-40362

670.42′028′54 — Manufacturing industries. Products. Design & manufacture. Applications of computer systems

Simons, G. L.. Computers in engineering and manufacture / G. L. Simons. — Manchester : N.C.C., 1982. — 358p : ill ; 22cm
Bibliography: p297-334. — Includes index
ISBN 0-85012-347-x : Unpriced : CIP rev. B82-08448

670.42′3 — Materials. Abrasive machinery

McKee, Richard L.. Machining with abrasives / Richard L. McKee. — New York ; London : Van Nostrand Reinhold, c1982. — ix,304p : ill ; 24cm
Includes index
ISBN 0-442-25281-1 : £16.95 B82-21853

670.42′3 — Materials. Machining — *Conference proceedings*

New tool materials metal cutting & forming : international conference at Mount Royal Hotel, London 26 & 27 March 1981. — [London] ([120 Wigmore St., W1H 0HS]) : [Engineers′ Digest], [1982?]. — 1v.(various pagings) : ill ; 30cm. — (Engineers′ digest technical conferences)
Cover title
Unpriced (spiral) B82-27927

670.42′3 — Workshop practice

Kibbe, Richard R.. Machine tool practices. — 2nd ed. / Richard R. Kibbe, John E. Neely ; contributing co-authors Roland O. Meyer, Warren T. White. — New York ; Chichester : Wiley, c1982. — xiv,806p : ill ; 29cm
Previous ed.: i.e. New ed. 1979. — Includes index
ISBN 0-471-05788-6 : £19.95 B82-18063

Neely, John E.. Practical machine shop / John E. Neely. — New York ; Chichester : Wiley, c1982. — xi,675p : ill ; 29cm
Includes index
ISBN 0-471-08000-4 : £16.00 B82-18216

670.42′3 — Workshop practice — *For technicians*

Shotbolt, C. R.. Technician workshop processes and materials 1. — 2nd (rev.) ed. — London : Cassell, Sept.1982. — [256]p
Previous ed.: 1977
ISBN 0-304-30957-5 (pbk) : £5.50 : CIP entry B82-29002

Timings, R. L.. Workshop processes and materials 1 checkbook. — London : Butterworth Scientific, Jan.1983. — [192]p. — (Butterworths technical and scientific checkbooks)
ISBN 0-408-00679-x (cased) : £7.95 : CIP entry
ISBN 0-408-00621-8 (pbk) : £3.95 B82-34425

670.42′7 — Industries. Process control. Applications of digital computer systems

Computer control of industrial processes / editors S. Bennett, & D.A. Linken. — Stevenage : Peregrinus on behalf of the Institution of Electrical Engineers, c1982. — xiv,208p : ill ; 23cm. — (IEE control engineering series ; 21)
Conference papers. — Includes index
ISBN 0-906048-80-x (pbk) : Unpriced : CIP rev. B82-12889

670.42′7 — Industries. Process control. Instrumentation

Johnson, Curtis D.. Process control instrumentation technology / Curtis D. Johnson. — 2nd ed. — New York ; Chichester : Wiley, c1982. — xiv,497p : ill ; 24cm. — (Electronic technology series, ISSN 0422-910x)
Previous ed.: 1977. — Includes index
ISBN 0-471-05789-4 : £18.45 B82-18203

670.42′7 — Process control. Applications of microcomputer systems

Holland, R. C.. Microcomputers for process control. — Oxford : Pergamon, Feb.1983. — [300]p. — (Materials engineering practice)
ISBN 0-08-029957-1 (cased) : £10.00 : CIP entry
ISBN 0-08-029956-3 (pbk) : £5.50 B82-36467

670.42′7 — Process control — *Conference proceedings*

PROMECON/81 *(Conference : London)*. PROMECON : proceedings of PROMECON/81, Process Measurement and Control Conference, 16-18 June 1981, London, United Kingdom / programmed jointly by the Institute of Measurement and Control, Instrument Society of America. — London : Institute of Measurement and Control
Vol.1. — c1981. — 223,10p : ill ; 28cm
Includes index
ISBN 0-87664-530-9 (pbk) : £19.20 B82-08865

670.42′7′068 — Industries. Automation. Management aspects — *Conference proceedings*

The **Management** of automation : proceedings of the British Management Data Foundation conferences on 2nd, 3rd December 1980 and 14th April 1981 with addenda. — London : British Management Data Foundation, c1981. — 80p : ill,3plans ; 30cm
ISBN 0-9507129-1-4 (pbk) : Unpriced B82-19486

670′.68′4 — Great Britain. Manufacturing industries. Use of microelectronic devices. Management aspects

Applying microelectronics in manufacturing industry — a guide for management : (based on a study by the Computing Services Association). — London (Room 524, Dean Bradley House, 52 Horseferry Rd., SW1P 4AG) : Department of Industry MAP, [1982]. — 1portfolio ; 32cm
£3.50 B82-38327

671 — METAL MANUFACTURES

671 — Metals. Industrial processes — *For technicians*

Flood, C. R. (Charles Richard). Fabrication, welding & metal joining processes : a textbook for technicians and craftsmen / C.R. Flood. — London : Butterworths, 1981. — 81p : ill ; 25cm
ISBN 0-408-00448-7 (pbk) : £5.95 : CIP rev. B81-16923

Monks, H. A.. Technician metallurgical process technology 2 / H.A. Monks, D.C. Rochester. — London : Cassell, 1980. — 332p : ill ; 22cm. — (Cassell′s TEC series)
ISBN 0-304-30290-2 (pbk) : £4.95 B82-34650

671.2 — Foundry work — *Conference proceedings*

Foundry 81 Conference *(National Exhibition Centre, Birmingham)*. Founding tomorrow : progress in plant & process technology : Metropole Hotel, National Exhibition Centre, Birmingham, Tuesday 24 and Wednesday 25 March 1981 : held concurrently with Foundry 81 International Exhibition, Hall 5, 19-21 March 1981. — [Birmingham] : [Foundry 81 Conference]
Vol.1: Moulding & coremaking. — [1981]. — 246p in various pagings : ill ; 30cm
Cover title. — At head of cover title: Foundry 81 Conference
Unpriced (spiral) B82-11079

Foundry 81 Conference *(National Exhibition Centre, Birmingham)*. Founding tomorrow : progress in plant & process technology : Metropole Hotel, National Exhibition Centre, Birmingham, Tuesday 24 and Wednesday 25 March 1981 : held concurrently with Foundry 81 International Exhibition, Hall 5, 19-21 March 1981. — [Birmingham] : [Foundry 81 Conference]
Vol.2: Metal melting & treatment. — [1981]. — 214p in various pagings : ill ; 30cm
Cover title. — At head of cover title: Foundry 81 Conference
Unpriced (spiral) B82-11080

671.2 — Small scale foundries

Harper, J. D.. Small scale foundries for developing countries : a guide to process selection / J.D. Harper. — London : Intermediate Technology Publications, c1981. — iv,66p : ill ; 26cm
Bibliography: p58-59
ISBN 0-903031-78-7 (pbk) : Unpriced B82-18294

671.2′07′1 — Schools. Curriculum subjects: Foundry work — *For teaching*

Bolan, John. Casting and moulding : foundry techniques for schools / John Bolan. — London : Heinemann Educational, 1982. — 71p : ill ; 26cm
ISBN 0-435-75090-9 : £5.95 : CIP rev. B81-27957

671.2′53 — Die casting

Kaye, Alan. Die casting metallurgy. — London : Butterworths, July 1982. — [304]p. — (Butterworths monographs in materials)
ISBN 0-408-10717-0 : £20.00 : CIP entry B82-12326

671.2′53 — Pressure die casting

Allsop, D. F.. Pressure diecasting. — Oxford : Pergamon. — (The Pergamon materials engineering practice series)
Pt.2: The technology of the casting and the die. — Nov.1982. — [200]p
ISBN 0-08-027615-6 (cased) : £13.50 : CIP entry
ISBN 0-08-027614-8 (pbk) : £5.50 B82-27833

Upton, B.. Pressure diecasting. — Oxford : Pergamon. — (The Pergamon materials engineering practice series)
Pt.1: Metals, machines, furnaces / B. Upton. — 1982. — vii,158p : ill ; 24cm
Includes index
ISBN 0-08-027621-0 (cased) : Unpriced : CIP rev.
ISBN 0-08-027622-9 (pbk) : £4.95 B81-35935

671.3 — Metal engineering components. Forming. Use of numerical control machine tools — *Conference proceedings*

Numerical methods in industrial forming processes. — Swansea (91 West Cross La., West Cross, Swansea) : Pineridge Press, July 1982. — [600]p
Conference papers
ISBN 0-906674-20-4 : CIP entry B82-13171

671.3′2 — Sheet metal folding machines. Construction — *Manuals*

Hitchings, Rob. How to make a folding machine for sheet metal work / designed and writen by Rob Hitchings. — London : Intermediate Technology Publications, c1981. — 31p : ill,plans ; 26cm
ISBN 0-903031-76-0 (pbk) : Unpriced B82-18295

671.3′5 — Metals. Grinding

Challis, Harry. Grinding : research on the problems of grinding technology / prepared for the Science and Engineering Research Council by Harry Challis and Chris Stanton in cooperation with Ray Palmer. — Swindon : The Council, 1982. — 44p : ill ; 30cm
ISBN 0-901660-48-5 (pbk) : Unpriced B82-23762

Loskutov, V. V.. Grinding of metals / V.V. Loskutov ; translated from the Russian by I. Savin. — Moscow : Mir ; [London] : Distributed by Central Books, 1981. — 300p : ill ; 21cm
Translation of: Shlifovanie metallov. — Added t.p. in Russian. — Includes index
ISBN 0-7147-1654-5 : £2.95 B82-02701

671.3′6 — Metals. Heat treatment

Hackworth, E.. Materials and heat treatment / E. Hackworth. — London : Cassell, 1982. — 111p : ill ; 25cm. — (Cassell′s technical craft series)
Includes index
ISBN 0-304-30929-x (pbk) : Unpriced B82-28812

671.3′6 — Valves. Springs. Heat treatment: Shot peening — *Conference proceedings*

Shot peening. — Oxford : Pergamon, Mar.1982. — [560]p
Conference papers
ISBN 0-08-027599-0 : £32.50 : CIP entry
B82-00287

671.3′6′0289 — Metals. Heat treatment. Safety measures

Guidelines for safety in heat treatment. — [Birmingham] : [Wolfson Heat Treatment Centre]
Part 1: Use of molten salt baths. — c1981. — 24p : ill ; 30cm
At head of title: Wolfson Heat Treatment Centre, Engineering Group. — Text on inside cover
ISBN 0-9507768-0-7 (pbk) : £13.00 (£10.00 to members of the Wolfson Heat Treatment Centre) B82-08599

671.3′73 — Hardmetals

Brookes, Kenneth J. A.. World directory and handbook of hardmetals / by Kenneth J.A. Brookes. — [London] (120 Wigmore St., W1) : [Engineers′ digest], c1975. — 224p : ill ; 30cm. — (An Engineers′ digest publication)
Includes index
Unpriced B82-37156

Brookes, Kenneth J. A.. World directory and handbook of hardmetals / by Kenneth J.A. Brookes. — 2nd ed., completely rev. and enl. — London : Engineers′ digest in association with International Carbide Data, 1979. — 296p : ill ; 30cm. — (An Engineers′ digest publication)
Previous ed.: London : Engineers′ digest, 1975. — Includes index
ISBN 0-9504931-1-2 : Unpriced B82-37157

671.3′73 — Sintering — *Conference proceedings*

International Round Table Conference on Sintering *(5th : 1981 : Portorož)*. Sintering. — Oxford : Elsevier Scientific, Oct.1982. — [654] p. — (Materials science monographs ; v.14)
ISBN 0-444-42122-x : CIP entry B82-30601

Synthetic materials for electronics : proceedings of the second international summer school, Jachranka near Warsaw, October 8-10, 1979 / edited by B. Jakowlew, A. Szymański, W. Włosiński. — Amsterdam ; Oxford : Elsevier Scientific, 1981. — ix,349p : ill ; 24cm. — (Materials science monographs ; 8)
ISBN 0-444-99741-5 : Unpriced : CIP rev.
B81-05159

671.5′2 — Explosive welding

Explosive welding, forming and compaction. — London : Applied Science, Dec.1982. — [400]p
ISBN 0-85334-166-4 : £45.00 : CIP entry
B82-30719

671.5′2 — Welded structures. Design

Gray, T. G. F.. Rational welding design. — 2nd ed. — London : Butterworth, Jan.1983. — [312]p
Previous ed.: 1975
ISBN 0-408-01200-5 (cased) : £13.00 : CIP entry
ISBN 0-408-01198-x (pbk) : £8.95 B82-34431

671.5′20422 — Welded structures. Deformation & stresses

Masubuchi, Koichi. Analysis of welded structures : residual stresses, distortion and their consequences / by Koichi Masubuchi. — Oxford : Pergamon, 1980. — xi,642p : ill ; 26cm. — (Pergamon international library) (International series on materials science and technology ; v.33)
Includes index
ISBN 0-08-022714-7 (cased) : £50.00 : CIP rev.
ISBN 0-08-026129-9 (pbk) : £18.00
B80-00268

671.5′212 — Arc welding

Leake, K.. Electric arc welding : questions & answers / K. Leake and N.J. Henthorne. — 3rd ed. — Sevenoaks : Newnes Technical, c1981. — 135p : ill ; 17cm. — (Questions & answers)
Previous ed.: published as Questions and answers on electric arc welding. 1974. — Includes index
ISBN 0-408-01128-9 (pbk) : Unpriced : CIP rev. B81-16926

671.5′212 — Gas-shielded arc welding

Henthorne, N. J.. Gas shielded arc welding. — London : Newnes Technical, Oct.1982. — [144]p. — (Questions & answers)
ISBN 0-408-01182-3 (pbk) : £1.95 : CIP entry
B82-24468

671.5′212′028 — Arc welding equipment — *Technical data*

The **Guide** to British arc welding electrodes and consumables. — Rev. ed. / prepared by the Arc Welding Consumables Section. — London : Welding Manufacturers′ Association, 1979. — 80p ; 21cm. — (WMA publication ; no.180)
Previous ed.: 197-
Unpriced (spiral) B82-40798

671.5′22 — Oxyacetylene welding

Bourbousson, P. H. M.. Gas welding and cutting. — 2nd ed. — London : Newnes Technical Books, May 1982. — [128]p. — (Questions & answers)
Previous ed.: 1973
ISBN 0-408-01180-7 (pbk) : £1.95 : CIP entry
B82-06740

671.5′22′0289 — Metals. Welding. Use of compressed gases. Safety measures

Welding and flame-cutting using compressed gases / Health and Safety Executive. — London : H.M.S.O., 1977 (1980 [printing]). — 18p ; 21cm. — (Health & safety at work ; 50)
ISBN 0-11-883366-9 (pbk) : £1.00
Also classified at 671.5′3 B82-16634

671.5′29 — Metals. Explosive welding

Crossland, Bernard. Explosive welding of metals and its application / by Bernard Crossland. — Oxford : Clarendon, 1982. — viii,233p : ill ; 25cm. — (Oxford series on advanced manufacturing ; 2)
Includes index
ISBN 0-19-859119-5 : £20.00 : CIP rev.
B82-04289

671.5′3 — Metals. Flame cutting. Use of compressed gases. Safety measures

Welding and flame-cutting using compressed gases / Health and Safety Executive. — London : H.M.S.O., 1977 (1980 [printing]). — 18p ; 21cm. — (Health & safety at work ; 50)
ISBN 0-11-883366-9 (pbk) : £1.00
Primary classification 671.5′22′0289
B82-16634

671.5′6 — Brazing & soldering

Thwaites, C. J.. Capillary joining : brazing and soft-soldering / C.J. Thwaites. — Chichester : Research Studies Press, 1982. — xii,211p : ill ; 24cm. — (Materials science research studies series)
Includes index
ISBN 0-471-10167-2 : £10.50 : CIP rev.
B82-02665

671.5′6 — Soldering

Manko, Howard H.. Solders and soldering : materials, design, production and analysis for reliable bonding / Howard H. Manko. — 2nd ed. — New York ; London : McGraw-Hill, c1979. — xv,350p : ill ; 24cm
Previous ed.: 1964. — Includes index
ISBN 0-07-039897-6 : £21.66 B82-14030

671.5′6′05 — Soldering — *Serials*

Brazing & soldering. — No.1 (Autumn 1981)-. — Ayr (29 Barns St., Ayr KA7 1XB) : Wela Publications in association with the British Association for Brazing and Soldering, 1981-. — v. : ill,ports ; 30cm
Two issues yearly
ISSN 0263-0060 = Brazing & soldering : £11.70 per year B82-12471

671.7 — Metals. Surface treatment

Surface analysis and pretreatment of plastics and metals / edited by D.M. Brewis. — London : Applied Science, c1982. — xvi,268p : ill ; 23cm
Includes index
ISBN 0-85334-992-4 : £24.00 : CIP rev.
Primary classification 668.4′1 B81-31516

671.7′32 — Hard chromium electroplating

Greenwood, J. David. Hard chromium plating : a handbook of modern practice / by J. David Greenwood. — 3rd ed. — Redhill : Portcullis, 1981. — 217p : ill,1port ; 24cm
Previous ed.: Teddington : Draper, 1971. — Includes index
ISBN 0-86108-088-2 : Unpriced B82-10261

671.8′3 — Double-seamed cans. Manufacture. Applications of microcomputer systems — *Conference proceedings*

Baria, C. N.. Double seam analysis by micro-computer : papers presented at a symposium organised by CFPRA, held at the Lygon Arms Hotel, Broadway, on 11th March 1981 / by C.N. Baria and R. Hannah. — Chipping Campden (Chipping Campden, Gloucestershire, GL55 6LD) : Campden Food Preservation Research Association, [1981]. — 24p in various pagings : ill,facsims ; 30cm
Unpriced (pbk) B82-14886

672 — FERROUS METALS MANUFACTURES

672 — Great Britain. Iron products & steel products. Transport

The **Handling** of iron and steel products. — London : Published and distributed on behalf of the Technical Committee of the United Kingdom Section of ICHCA by the ICHCA Central Office, 1982. — 67p : ill ; 30cm. — (Briefing pamphlet (International Cargo Handling Co-ordination Association. United Kingdom) ; no.4)
ISBN 0-906297-20-6 (pbk) : £10.00 (£5.00 to members) B82-20707

672′.068′3 — Great Britain. Iron & steel industries. Management. Supervision

Effective supervision : a package of ideas for helping managers and supervisors develop effective working relationships. — London (190 Fleet Street, EC4A 2AH) : Iron and Steel Industry Training Board, 1981. — 50p : ill,forms ; 30cm
Unpriced (spiral) B82-11175

672.5′21 — Mild steel & low alloy steel. Welding. Flux

Davis, Louise. An introduction to welding fluxes for mild and low alloy steels / Louise Davis. — Cambridge : Welding Institute, c1981. — 16p : ill(some col.) ; 30cm
Bibliography: p14-15
ISBN 0-85300-145-6 (pbk) : £5.40 B82-01260

672.7′33 — Galvanizing — *Conference proceedings*

International Galvanizing Conference *(12th : 1979 : Paris)*. 12th International Galvanizing Conference, Paris 1979 : edited proceedings / edited by Zinc Development Association. — Redhill : Portcullis, c1981. — 361p : ill ; 30cm
Cover title: Intergalva 79
ISBN 0-86108-091-2 (pbk) : Unpriced
B82-13636

672.8 — Steel structural components. Manufacture

Davies, B. J.. Structural steelwork fabrication / by B.J. Davies and E.J. Crawley. — London (92-96 Vauxhall Bridge Rd, SW1V 2RL) : British Constructional Steelwork Association
Vol.1. — [1981?]. — 111p : ill(some col.) ; 30cm. — (BCSA publication ; no.7/80)
Includes index
Unpriced (pbk) B82-09476

672.8′3 — Engineering components: Iron & steel rods & bars. Manufacture — *Conference proceedings*

Rod and bar production in the 1980s : proceedings of an international conference organized by the Metals Society and held at the Royal Lancaster Hotel, London on 13-14 May, 1981. — London : Metals Society, c1981. — vii,179p : ill ; 31cm
Includes index
ISBN 0-904357-40-6 : Unpriced B82-19768

673 — NONFERROUS METALS MANUFACTURES

673'.52253 — Zinc alloy die castings — *Technical data — For design*

Chivers, A. R. L.. Zinc diecasting / A.R.L. Chivers. — [Oxford] : Published for the Design Council, the British Standards Institution, and the Council of Engineering Institutions by Oxford University Press, c1981. — 28p : ill ; 30cm. — (Engineering design guides ; 41)
Bibliography: p27-28
ISBN 0-19-859180-2 (pbk) : £5.95 : CIP rev. B81-05121

673'.722732 — Aluminium & aluminium alloys. Anodising

Henley, V. F.. Anodic oxidation of aluminium and its alloys / V.F. Henley. — Oxford : Pergamon, 1982. — x,170p : ill ; 24cm. — (The Pergamon materials engineering practice series)
Bibliography: p161-162. — Includes index
ISBN 0-08-026726-2 (cased) : Unpriced : CIP rev.
ISBN 0-08-026725-4 (pbk) : £4.95 B81-35933

674 — TIMBER MANUFACTURES

674'.88 — Wooden tableware. Making — *Manuals*

Sainsbury, John A.. Sainsbury's woodturning projects for dining. — New York : Sterling ; London : Oak Tree, c1981. — 191p : ill ; 27cm
Includes index
ISBN 0-7061-2790-0 : £7.95 B82-21876

675 — LEATHER AND FUR PROCESSING

675'.29 — Leather. Fibres

Haines, B. M.. The fibre structure of leather / [B.M. Haines]. — London (9 St. Thomas St., SE1 9SA) : Leather Conservation Centre, 1981. — i,36p : ill ; 30cm
Unpriced (pbk) B82-22323

676 — PULP AND PAPER TECHNOLOGY

676'.121 — Coconut palms. Pulping properties

Palmer, E. R.. Pulping trials on the wood from the trunk of coconut (Cocos nucifera) / E.R. Palmer and J.A. Gibbs. — London : Tropical Products Institute, 1979. — iv,23p ; 30cm
English text, French and Spanish summaries. — At head of title: Tropical Products Institute. — Includes Bibliographies
ISBN 0-85954-106-1 (pbk) : £2.05 B82-04211

676'.121 — Cuba. Pinus caribaea. Pulping properties

Palmer, E. R.. The pulping characteristics of two samples of Pinus caribaea var caribaea from Cuba / E.R. Palmer and J.A. Gibbs. — London : Tropical Products Institute, 1975. — iv,24p ; 30cm
English text, English, French and Spanish summaries. — At head of title: Tropical Products Institute
ISBN 0-85954-038-3 (pbk) : £0.45 B82-07461

676'.121 — Fiji. Pinus caribaea. Pulping properties. Effects of growth

Palmer, E. R.. Pulping characteristics of Pinus caribaea from Fiji : the effect of rate of growth / E.R. Palmer and J.A. Gibbs. — London : Tropical Products Institute, 1977. — iv,15p : ill ; 30cm
English text, English, French and Spanish summaries. — At head of title: Tropical Products Institute
ISBN 0-85954-075-8 (pbk) : £0.60 B82-07460

676'.121 — Zambia. Pinus kesiya & Eucalyptus grandis. Pulping properties

Palmer, E. R.. Pulping characteristics of Pinus kesiya and Eucalyptus grandis from Zambia / E.R. Palmer and J.A. Gibbs. — London : Tropical Products Institute, 1977. — iv,23p ; 30cm
English text, English, French and Spanish summaries. — At head of title: Tropical Products Institute
£0.90 (pbk) B82-07464

676'.183 — Medium density fibre boards

Medium density fibreboard : basic properties and performance. — Stevenage : Furniture Industry Research Association, 1980. — 39p : ill ; 30cm. — (FIRA handbook ; no.1)
Unpriced (pbk) B82-11052

676'.2 — Paper — *For children*

Langley, Andrew. The paper in your home / Andrew Langley. — Hove : Wayland, 1982. — 32p : col.ill,1col.map ; 19x24cm. — (Origins)
Bibliography: p32
ISBN 0-85340-939-0 : £3.25 B82-18431

676'.2 — Paper. Manufacture

Handbook of paper science : the science and technology of papermaking, paper properties and paper usage / edited by H.F. Rance. — Amsterdam ; Oxford : Elsevier Scientific
Vol.2: The structure and physical properties of paper. — 1982. — xii,288p : ill ; 25cm
Includes index
ISBN 0-444-41974-8 : Unpriced : CIP rev. B81-30373

676'.2'072041 — Great Britain. Paper. Manufacture. Research organisations: Pira. *Information and Training Division*

Management's guide to problem solving. — Leatherhead (Randalls Rd., Leatherhead, Surrey KT22 7RU) : Pira, Information and Training Division, [1980?]. — [12],[1]leaf of plates : 1ill ; 30cm
Cover title
Unpriced (spiral) B82-17512

676'.2'072041 — Great Britain. Paper. Manufacture. Research organisations: Pira — *Serials*

Pira. Annual review of research & services / Pira. — 1977/78. — [Leatherhead] ([Randalls Rd, Leatherhead, Surrey KT22 7RU]) : Pira, 1978-. — v. : ill,ports ; 30cm
Continues: Pira. Review of research & services. — Description based on: 1980/81 issue
ISSN 0262-8600 = Annual review of research & services - Pira : Free to Pira members B82-10119

676'.28027 — Paper. American watermarks, *1690-1835* — *Lists*

Gravell, Thomas L.. A catalogue of American watermarks 1690-1835 / Thomas L. Gravell, George Miller. — New York ; London : Garland, 1979. — xxiii,230p : facsims ; 29cm. — (Garland reference library of the humanities ; v.151)
Bibliography: p215-217. — Includes index
ISBN 0-8240-9791-2 : Unpriced B82-31979

677 — TEXTILE MANUFACTURES

677 — Textiles

Lyle, Dorothy Siegert. Modern textiles / Dorothy Siegert Lyle. — 2nd ed. — New York ; Chichester : Wiley, c1982. — xxiii,513p,[8]p of plates : ill(some col.) ; 29cm
Previous ed.: 1976. — Bibliography: p483-499. — Includes index
ISBN 0-471-07805-0 : £19.25 B82-36946

Tortora, Phyllis G.. Understanding textiles / Phyllis G. Tortora. — 2nd ed. — London : Macmillan, c1982. — ix,454p : ill ; 25cm
Previous ed.: 1978. — Bibliography: p413-420. — Includes index
ISBN 0-02-420870-1 : £12.95 B82-26284

677 — Textiles - *For schools*

Ling, E. M.. Modern household science. — 4th ed. — London : Bell & Hyman, July 1981. — [258]p
Previous ed.: London : Mills & Boon, 1979
ISBN 0-7135-2073-6 (pbk) : £2.95 : CIP entry
Also classified at 648'.1 B81-15910

677'.003'21 — Textiles — *Encyclopaedias*

Burnhan, Dorothy K.. [Warp and weft]. A textile terminology : warp and weft / Dorothy K. Burnham. — London : Routledge & Kegan Paul, 1981, c1980. — xiv,216p : ill ; 29cm
English text, with technical terms in various languages. — Adapted and expanded from: The vocabulary of technical terms, 1964, with permission of the Centre international d'étude des textiles anciens. — Originally published: Toronto : Royal Ontario Museum 1980. — Bibliography: p206-216
ISBN 0-7100-0955-0 : £16.95 : CIP rev. B81-21478

677'.0076 — Textiles — *Questions & answers — For schools*

Hartley, K. M.. Topics and questions in textiles / K.M. Hartley and J.M. Roe ; illustrated by Jane Lewington. — London : Heinemann Educational, 1982. — 74p : ill ; 25cm + Teacher's book(42p : ill ; 25cm)
ISBN 0-435-42834-9 (pbk) : £2.25 : CIP rev. B81-12342

677'.0076 — Textiles - *Questions & answers - For schools*

Hartley, Kathleen. Topics and questions in textiles. — London : Heinemann Educational, June 1981
Teacher's book. — [64]p
ISBN 0-435-42833-0 (pbk) : £3.95 : CIP entry B81-12355

677'.028242 — Weaving

Lord, P. R.. Weaving : conversion of yarn to fabric / P.R. Lord, M.H. Mohamed. — Shildon : Merrow, c1982. — viii,394p : ill ; 21cm. — (Merrow technical library. Textile technology)
Previous ed.: 1973. — Includes index
ISBN 0-900541-78-4 (pbk) : £9.50 B82-34376

677'.028245 — Weft knitting — *Serials*

Knitting industry technical review / Hatra. — Vol.1, no.1 (Apr. 1981)-. — Nottingham (7 Gregory Boulevard, Nottingham NG7 6LD) : Hatra, 1981-. — v. : ill(some col.),ports ; 30cm
Six issues yearly. — Merger of: Hatranews ; and, Hosiery abstracts ; and, Knit knacks
ISSN 0260-8553 = Knitting industry technical review : £25.00 per year B82-01070

677'.02825 — Textiles. Foam finishing — *Conference proceedings*

Foam processing for dyeing and finishing : papers presented at a Shirley Institute conference on 15 April 1981. — Manchester : The Institute, c1981. — 38p : ill ; 30cm. — (Shirley Institute publication, ISSN 0306-5154 ; s.42)
ISBN 0-903669-38-2 (pbk) : £16.00 (£12.00 to members of the Institute) : CIP rev.
Also classified at 667'.3 B81-28802

677'.02832 — Textile fibres

Needles, Howard L.. Handbook of textile fibers, dyes and finishes / Howard L. Needles. — New York ; London : Garland STPM, c1981. — xii,170p : ill ; 24cm
Includes index
ISBN 0-8240-7046-1 : Unpriced B82-28354

677'.0285 — Textile machinery

Contemporary textile engineering. — London : Academic Press, Dec.1982. — [550]p
ISBN 0-12-323750-5 : CIP entry B82-29881

Ormerod, A.. Modern preparation and weaving machinery. — London : Butterworth, Jan.1983. — [320]p
ISBN 0-408-01212-9 : £20.00 : CIP entry B82-34432

677'.02862 — Knitting yarns

Lorant, Tessa. Yarns for the knitter / Tessa Lorant. — Wells : Thorn, 1980. — 64p : ill ; 22cm. — (Profitable knitting series)
Cover title
ISBN 0-906374-12-x (pbk) : £1.35 B82-16041

677′.02864 — Fabrics — *For schools*

Piper, Brenda. Fibres and fabrics / Brenda Piper ; drawings by Peter Kesteven. — 2nd ed. — Harlow : Longman, 1981. — vi,82p : ill ; 21cm. — (Longman housecraft series)
Previous ed.: 1968. — Bibliography: p78. — List of films: p78-79. — Includes index
ISBN 0-582-22174-9 (pbk) : Unpriced
B82-05236

677′.02864 — Great Britain. Art galleries & museums. Exhibits: Fabrics manufactured by Warner & Sons, ***1850-1980*** **—** ***Catalogues***

Bury, Hester. A choice of design 1850-1980 : fabrics by Warner & Sons Ltd.. — London (7 Noel St., W.1.) : Warner & Sons, Sept.1981. — [116]p
ISBN 0-9506587-1-5 (pbk) : £5.50 : CIP entry
B81-28403

677′.0287 — Yarns. Evenness. Testing

Evenness testing in yarn production. — Manchester : Textile Institute. — (Manual of textile technology) (Quality control and assessment series)
Part 1 / R. Furter ; preface by S.L. Anderson. — c1982. — 86p : ill ; 30cm
Bibliography: p86
ISBN 0-900739-48-7 (pbk) : Unpriced
B82-34971

677′.2121 — Cotton. Spinning. Cardroom processes. Safety measures

Great Britain. *Health and Safety Executive*. Cardroom processes : cotton and allied fibres. — London : H.M.S.O., Dec.1982. — [50]p. — (HS(G) ; 21)
ISBN 0-11-883449-5 (unbound) : CIP entry
B82-29900

677′.2122 — Cotton. Spinning. Opening processes. Safety measures

Opening processes : cotton and allied fibres : safety in the cotton and allied fibres industry / Health and Safety Executive. — Revised [ed.]. — London : H.M.S.O., 1980. — 27p : ill ; 21cm. — (Health and safety series booklet ; HS (G)14)
Previous ed.: published as Safety in the cotton & allied fibres industry — opening processes. 1974
ISBN 0-11-883269-7 (pbk) : £2.50 : CIP rev.
B80-11536

677′.31 — Wool — *For children*

Watson, Tom. Wool / Tom and Jenny Watson. — Hove : Wayland, 1980 (1981 [printing]). — 72p : ill,1map ; 20x22cm. — (World resources)
Bibliography: p81. — Includes index
ISBN 0-85340-756-8 : £3.95 B82-25812

677′.31 — Wool. Production — *For children*

Watson, Tom. Wool for warmth / Tom and Jenny Watson. — Hove : Wayland, 1982. — 32p : col.ill,3col.maps ; 19x24cm. — (Origins)
Bibliography: p32
ISBN 0-85340-937-4 : £3.25 B82-28029

677′.4745 — Polypropylene textile fibres

Ahmed, M.. Polypropylene fibers. — Oxford : Elsevier Scientific, June 1982. — [400]p. — (Textile science and technology ; 5)
ISBN 0-444-42090-8 : CIP entry B82-16496

677′.4745 — Polypropylene textile fibres — *Conference proceedings*

Polypropylene fibres and textiles : second international conference, 26-28 September 1979 : University of York. — London : Plastics and Rubber Institute, [c1979]. — 410p in various pagings : ill,maps,1plan,ports ; 21cm
Cover title. — Includes bibliographies
ISBN 0-903107-18-x (pbk) : Unpriced
B82-08004

Polypropylene textiles. — Manchester : Shirley Institute, Sept.1982. — [66]p. — (Shirley Institute publications, ISSN 0306-5154 ; S.44)
Conference papers
ISBN 0-903669-39-0 : £16.00 : CIP entry
B82-31317

678 — ELASTOMERS AND ELASTOMER PRODUCTS

678 — Textile fibre reinforced elastomers

Textile reinforcement of elastomers / edited by William C. Wake and David B. Wootton. — London : Applied Science, c1982. — xiii,271p : ill ; 23cm
Includes index
ISBN 0-85334-998-3 : £24.00 : CIP rev.
B81-35856

678′.05 — Elastomers & rubber — *Serials*

Developments in rubber technology. — 3. — London : Applied Science, July 1982. — [240] p. — (The Developments series)
ISBN 0-85334-135-4 : £24.00 : CIP entry
B82-13139

678.2/4 — RUBBER TECHNOLOGY

678′.2 — Rubber — *For children*

Gibbs, Richard. Rubber tyres on your bike / Richard Gibbs. — Hove : Wayland, 1982. — 32p : col.ill,1col.map ; 19x24cm. — (Origins)
ISBN 0-85340-945-5 : £3.25 B82-31030

678′.2 — Rubber. Processing

Evans, Colin W.. Practical rubber compounding and processing / Colin W. Evans. — London : Applied Science, c1981. — xiii,205p : ill ; 23cm
Includes index
ISBN 0-85334-901-0 : £17.00 : CIP rev.
B80-11978

Rubber technology and manufacture. — 2nd ed. — London : Butterworths, Apr.1982. — [509]p
Previous ed.: London : Newnes Butterworths, 1971
ISBN 0-408-00587-4 : £23.00 : CIP entry
B82-04028

678′.2′05 — Rubber & rubber products — *Serials*

Developments in rubber and rubber composites. — 2. — London : Applied Science, Feb.1983. — [200]p. — (The Developments series)
ISBN 0-85334-173-7 : £26.00 : CIP entry
B82-39601

678′.2′05 — Rubber — *Serials*

Progress of rubber technology. — Vol.44 (1981). — London : Applied Science, Nov.1981. — [148]p
ISBN 0-85334-984-3 : £18.00 : CIP entry
B81-30418

678′.21′0289 — Great Britain. Rubber industries. Industrial chemicals. Safety measures — *Standards*

Toxicity and safe handling of rubber chemicals : B.R.M.A. code of practice 1978. — Birmingham (Health Research Unit, Scala House, Holloway Circus, Birmingham 1) : British Rubber Manufacturers′ Association, [1978]. — 1v. ; 23cm
Bibliography: p47-51. — Includes index
£10.00 (loose-leaf) B82-37155

678′.27 — Rubber. Compression moulding & transfer moulding

An Introduction to compression and transfer moulding of rubber. — Brentford (950 Great Western Rd., Brentford, Middx) : Rubber & Plastics Processing Industry Training Board, c1980. — 31p : ill(some col.) ; 15x21cm
Cover title
Unpriced (pbk) B82-13321

678.6 — NATURAL ELASTOMERS

678′.61 — Natural latex concentrates

Pendle, T. D.. Current uses of natural latex concentrate / T.D. Pendle. — Hertford (Tun Abdul Razak Laboratory, Brickendonbury SG13 8NL) : Malaysian Rubber Producers′ Research Association, [1980?]. — [8]p : ill,1port ; 30cm. — (NR background ; 3)
Cover title
Unpriced (pbk) B82-34312

678′.62′09595 — Malaysian natural rubber

Bristow, G. M.. Market grades of Malaysian natural rubber / G.M. Bristow and I.G. Rose. — [Brickendonbury] : Malaysian Rubber Producers′ Research Association, [1982?]. — 8p : ill,2ports ; 30cmcm. — (NR background, ISSN 0144-7734 ; 4)
Cover title
Unpriced (pbk) B82-38739

678.7 — SYNTHETIC ELASTOMERS

678′.71 — Synthetic latexes

Polymer lattices and their applications / edited by K.O. Calvert. — London : Applied Science, c1982. — xi,262p : ill ; 23cm
Includes bibliographies and index
ISBN 0-85334-975-4 : £18.00 : CIP rev.
B81-20163

678′.72 — Isoprene

Ceausescu, Elena. Stereospecific polymerization of isoprene. — Oxford : Pergamon, Dec.1982. — [300]p
Translation of: Polymerizarea stereospecifică a izoprenului
ISBN 0-08-029987-3 : £30.00 : CIP entry
B82-30595

679 — MANUFACTURES. IVORY, FEATHER, FIBRE, BRISTLE, TOBACCO AND OTHER PRODUCTS

679 — Wigs. Manufacture, ***to 1776*** **—** ***Early works***

The **Wigmaker′s** art in the 18th century : a translation of the section on wigmaking in the 3rd edition (1776) of the Encyclopedie of Denis Diderot & Jean D′Alembert / edited by J. Stevens Cox. — 2nd ed. — St Peter Port : Toucan, 1980. — 30p,7p of plates : ill ; 25cm
Translated from French. — Previous ed.: 1965
ISBN 0-85694-221-9 (pbk) : Unpriced
B82-19931

679′.7′0683 — Great Britain. Tobacco industries. Management. Participation of personnel

Employee participation : sources of help available to companies introducing employee participation. — Gloucester (Barton House, Barton St., Gloucester GL1 1QQ) : Food, Drink and Tobacco Industry Training Board, 1980. — 17p ; 30cm
Cover title
£2.00 (pbk)
Primary classification 664′.0068′3 B82-26131

679′.7′0683 — Great Britain. Tobacco industries. Management. Supervision

Developing effective supervision for the future. — Gloucester (Barton House, Barton St., Gloucester GL1 1QQ) : Food, Drink and Tobacco Industry Training Board, [1981?]. — 37p : ill(some col.),forms ; 30cm
£2.00 (pbk)
Primary classification 664′.0068′3 B82-11170

679′.7′0683 — Great Britain. Tobacco industries. Personnel. Job analysis

How to use job analysis for profitable training / [issued by the Food, Drink and Tobacco Industry Training Board]. — Croydon (Leon House, High St., Croydon, CR9 3NT) : [The Board], [1982?]. — 31p : ill ; 30cm. — (Systematic training guide ; no.2)
Cover title. — Text on inside cover. — ′Example A,B,C′ as insert. — Bibliography: p31
£0.65 (pbk)
Primary classification 664′.0068′3 B82-24291

679′.7′0683 — Great Britain. Tobacco industries. Training officers

The **Development** of training staff / [issued by the Food, Drink and Tobacco Industry Training Board]. — Croydon (Leon House, High St., Croydon, CR9 3NT) : [The Board], [1982?]. — 28p ; 30cm. — (Systematic training guide ; no.5)
Cover title. — Text on inside cover
£0.65 (pbk)
Primary classification 664′.0068′3 B82-24292

679.7'068'4 — United States. Tobacco industries. Corporate planning. Effects of policies of government

Miles, Robert H.. Coffin nails and corporate strategies / Robert H. Miles in collaboration with Kim S. Cameron. — Englewood Cliffs ; London : Prentice-Hall, c1982. — xxii,298p : ill ; 23cm
Bibliography: p277-286. — Includes index
ISBN 0-13-139816-4 (cased) : Unpriced
ISBN 0-13-139808-3 (pbk) : £8.65 B82-35170

679'.7'07 — Great Britain. Tobacco industries. Personnel: Technicians. Training

Creating a training programme for technicians / [issued by Food, Drink and Tobacco Industry Training Board]. — Croydon (Leon House, High St., Croydon, CR9 3NT) : [The Board], [1982?]. — 24p : forms ; 30cm. — (Training recommendations ; no.2)
Cover title. — Text on inside cover
£0.65 (pbk)
Primary classification 664'.007 B82-24288

679'.7'07 — Great Britain. Tobacco industries. Personnel. Training. Effectiveness. Evaluation

Reviewing the effectiveness of training. — Gloucester (Barton House, Barton St., Gloucester GL1 1QQ) : Food, Drink and Tobacco Industry Training Board, [1982?]. — 23p : ill,2forms ; 30cm. — (Systematic training guide ; no.4)
Cover title. — Text on inside cover
£0.50 (pbk)
Primary classification 664'.007 B82-24283

679'.7'07 — Great Britain. Tobacco industries. Personnel. Training. Planning

How to prepare training plans and programmes / [issued by the Food, Drink and Tobacco Industry Training Board]. — Croydon (Leon House, High St., Croydon, CR9 3NT) : [The Board], [1982?]. — 32p : ill ; 30cm + Planning an induction training programme(14p ill; 29cm). — (Systematic training guide ; no.3)
Cover title. — Text on inside cover
£0.70 (pbk)
Also classified at 664'.007 B82-24293

679'.7'07 — Great Britain. Tobacco industries. Personnel. Training. Requirements. Assessment

Assessing your company's training needs / [issued by the Food, Drink and Tobacco Industry Training Board]. — Croydon (Leon House, High St., Croydon, CR9 3NT) : [The Board], [1982?]. — 40p ; 30cm. — (Systematic training guide ; no.1)
Cover title. — Text on inside cover
£0.50 (pbk)
Primary classification 664'.007 B82-24289

679'.7'07 — Great Britain. Tobacco industries. Personnel. Training. Requirements — *For management*

Training individual managers : a programme to help managers to identify and tackle training needs / developed by the Food, Drink and Tobacco Industry Training Board. — Gloucester (Barton House, Barton St., Gloucester GL1 1QQ) : Food, Drink and Tobacco Industry Training Board, [1979]. — 1v(loose leaf) ; 32cm
Bibliography: p86-87
£5.00
Primary classification 664'.007 B82-26127

680 — CRAFTS

680 — Craft workshops. Organisation — *Manuals*

Setting up a workshop. — [5th ed.] / edited by John Crowe ; [cartoons by Bill Tidy]. — London : Crafts Council, c1982. — 77p : ill ; 21cm
Previous ed.: 1980?. — Bibliography: p76-77
ISBN 0-903798-59-x (pbk) : Unpriced B82-32421

680'.6'041 — Great Britain. Crafts. Organisations: Crafts Council — *Serials*

Crafts Council. The work of the Crafts Council. — 1977-1980-. — London : The Council, [1980]-. — v. : ill,ports ; 30cm
Issued every three years. — Continues: Great Britain. Crafts Advisory Committee. The work of the Crafts Advisory Committee
ISSN 0262-7329 = Work of the Crafts Council : £0.90 B82-12455

680'.7'1 — Schools. Curriculum subjects: Crafts. Designs — *Illustrations*

A **Further** folio of ideas. — [Bristol] ([c/o George Day, 24 Elm Rd., Kingswood, Bristol BS15 2ST]) : The Educational Institute of Design, Craft & Technology, 1981. — [38]p : ill,plans ; 30cm
Cover title
£2.00 (£1.50 to members) (pbk) B82-30860

School crafts : a folio of ideas. — [Bristol] ([c/o George Day, 24 Elm Rd., Kingswood, Bristol BS15 2ST]) : The Educational Institute of Design, Craft & Technology, 1980. — [24]p : ill,plans ; 30cm
Cover title. — Ill on inside front cover
£1.00 (pbk) B82-30859

680'.9415 — Ireland. Rural crafts

Manners, John. Irish crafts and craftsmen. — Belfast : Appletree Press, Apr.1982. — [120]p
ISBN 0-904651-92-4 (pbk) : £3.95 : CIP entry B82-09212

680'.9428'1 — Yorkshire. Craftsmen

Rees, David Morgan. Yorkshire craftsmen at work : a unique photographic survey of a living tradition / by David Morgan Rees. — Clapham, North Yorkshire : Dalesman, 1981. — 96p : ill,ports ; 17x21cm. — (Dalesman heritage)
ISBN 0-85206-656-2 (pbk) : £3.50 B82-14846

681.1 — MANUFACTURES. ANALOGUE AND DIGITAL INSTRUMENTS

681.1'1 — Electronic clocks & watches. Servicing — *Amateurs' manuals*

Weaver, J. D.. Electrical and electronic clocks and watches / J.D. Weaver. — London : Newnes Technical, 1982. — 233p : ill ; 23cm
Includes index
ISBN 0-408-01140-8 : Unpriced : CIP rev. B82-04037

681.1'1'0288 — Clocks & watches. Maintenance & repair — *Manuals*

De Carle, Donald. Clock and watch repairing / by Donald de Carle. — 2nd ed. — London : Hale, 1981. — x,309p : ill ; 23cm
Previous ed.: London : Pitman, 1959. — Includes index
ISBN 0-7091-9436-6 : £8.95 B82-04182

Whiten, A. J.. Repairing old clocks and watches / A.J. Whiten ; illustrations by Joel Degen. — London : NAG, 1979. — viii,280p : ill ; 23cm
Includes index
ISBN 0-7198-2740-x : £5.95 B82-06402

681.1'1'09 — Clocks & watches, *to 1914*

Britten, Frederick James. Britten's old clocks and watches and their makers. — 9th ed. rev. and enl. — London : Eyre Methuen, Sept.1982. — [700]p
Previous ed.: 1973
ISBN 0-413-39720-3 : £60.00 : CIP entry B82-19229

681.1'1'0941457 — Scotland. Strathclyde Region. Hamilton. Clocks & watches. Manufacture, *to 1976*

Wallace, William, *1916-*. Marking time in Hamilton : 300 years of Lanarkshire watches and clocks / by William Wallace. — Hamilton (49 Laburnum Lea, Silvertonhill, Hamilton ML3 7LY) : W. Wallace, 1981. — 32p : ill ; 21cm
Cover title. — Text on inside cover
£0.70 (pbk) B82-04437

681.1'13 — Bracket clocks — *Collectors' guides*

Roberts, Deryck. The bracket clock / Deryck Roberts. — Newton Abbot : David & Charles, c1982. — 192p : ill,music ; 25cm
Includes index
ISBN 0-7153-8261-6 : £12.50 : CIP rev. B82-12934

681.1'13 — British long case clocks, *1658-1835* — *Collectors' guides*

Robinson, Tom, *1915-*. The longcase clock / Tom Robinson. — [Woodbridge] : Antique Collectors' Club, c1981. — 467p : ill(some col.) ; 28cm
Ill on lining papers. — Bibliography: p458-460. — Includes index
ISBN 0-907462-07-3 : £29.50 : CIP rev. B81-34965

681.1'13 — English bracket & mantel clocks, *1650-1900*

Nicholls, Andrew. English bracket and mantel clocks / Andrew Nicholls. — Poole : Blandford, 1981, c1982. — 160p : ill ; 26cm
Bibliography: p158. — Includes index
ISBN 0-7137-1009-8 : £8.95 : CIP rev. B81-22533

681.1'13 — London. Westminster *(London Borough)*. **Government buildings: Palace of Westminster. Big Ben. Clocks. Engineering aspects**

Big Ben : its engineering past and future / the Engineering Sciences Division of the Institution of Mechanical Engineers. — London : Institution of Mechanical Engineers, [1981]. — 59p in various pagings : ill ; 21cm
Cover title
£2.00 (pbk) B82-00864

681.1'13 — Long case clocks. Design & construction — *Manuals*

Williams, Gary. Designing and building a grandfather clock / Gary Williams ; illustrations by the author. — San Diego : Barnes ; London : Tantivy Press, c1980. — 144p : ill ; 25cm
ISBN 0-498-02209-9 : £4.75 B82-39733

681.1'13 — Long case clocks, *to 1900* — *Collectors' guides*

McDonald, John, *1910-*. Longcase clocks / John McDonald. — [London] : Country Life Books ; London : Hamlyn [distributor], 1982. — 128p : ill(some col.) ; 23cm. — (The Country life library of antiques)
Includes index
ISBN 0-600-32103-7 : £6.95 B82-19925

681.1'13'0288 — Clocks *antique*. **Repair** — *Manuals*

Wilding, John, *1924-*. How to repair antique clocks / by John Wilding. — Ashford, Kent : Brant Wright
[Vol.1]. — c1979. — v,94p : ill ; 26cm
ISBN 0-903512-23-8 : £12.75 B82-06186

681.1'13'09 — Clocks, *to 1980*

Tyler, E. J.. Clock types. — London : Longman, Oct.1982. — [160]p
ISBN 0-582-50308-6 : £8.50 : CIP entry B82-23359

681.1'13'0942 — English clocks, *1250-1950* — *Collectors' guides*

Lloyd, H. Alan. Some outstanding clocks over seven hundred years 1250-1950 / H. Alan Lloyd. — [Woodbridge] : Antique Collectors' Club, c1981. — xx,333p : ill,facsims ; 28cm
Originally published: London : L. Hill, 1958. — Ill on lining papers. — Includes index
ISBN 0-907462-04-9 : £29.50 : CIP rev. B81-12381

681.1'13'0942 — English domestic clocks, *to 1700*

Dawson, Percy. Early English clocks. — Woodbridge : Antique Collectors Club, Dec.1982. — [500]p
ISBN 0-902028-59-6 : £45.00 : CIP entry B82-30740

681.1′13′0943 — German clocks, *1550-1650*

Clockwork Universe *(Exhibition) (1980-1981 : Munich and Washington, D.C.).* The clockwork universe : German clocks and automata 1550-1650 / [... catalog of the exhibition the Clockwork Universe shown in Munich from April 15 to September 30, 1980, and in Washington, D.C., from November 7, 1980, to February 15, 1981 ... conceived, planned, and produced jointly by the National Museum of History and Technology, Smithsonian Institution, Washington, D.C., and the Bayerisches Nationalmuseum, Munich] ; edited by Klaus Maurice and Otto Mayr. — Washington, D.C. : Smithsonian Institution ; Bristol : Hilger, 1980. — ix,321p : ill(some col.),ports ; 30cm
Includes index
ISBN 0-85274-542-7 : £27.00 B82-35360

681.1′14 — Watches. Making — *Manuals*

Daniels, George, *1926-.* Watchmaking / George Daniels ; drawings by David Penney. — [London] : Sotheby, 1981. — xv,416p,viiip of plates : ill(some col.) ; 27cm
Ill on lining papers. — Bibliography: p405. — Includes index
ISBN 0-85667-150-9 : Unpriced B82-08515

681.1′14′07402 — England. Burton, Stanley H. Private collections: Watches, *ca 1580-1980*

Burton, Stanley H.. The watch collection of Stanley H. Burton : 'warts and all' / Stanley H. Burton. — London : Batsford, 1981. — 456p : ill(some col.) ; 26cm
Includes index
ISBN 0-7134-3766-9 : £50.00 B82-01600

681.2 — MANUFACTURES. MEASURING INSTRUMENTS

681′.2 — Barometers, *to 1900*

Bolle, Bert. Barometers / Bert Bolle. — Watford : Argus, 1982. — 255p : ill,facsims,ports ; 26cm
Translated from the Dutch. — Bibliography: p248. — Includes index
ISBN 0-85242-710-7 : £12.50 B82-31832

681.4 — MANUFACTURES. OPTICAL EQUIPMENT

681′.413 — Microscopes — *Collectors′ guides*

Turner, Gerard L′E.. Collecting microscopes / Gerard L′E. Turner. — [London] : Studio Vista, 1981. — 120p : ill(some col.),facsims (some col.),1port ; 26cm. — (Christie′s South Kensington collectors series)
Bibliography: p120
ISBN 0-289-70882-6 : £6.95

681′.418 — Cameras, *1957-1964 — Collectors′ guides*

Emanuel, W. D.. Cameras : the facts : a collector′s guide 1957-64 / W.D. Emanuel and Andrew Matheson. — Historical ed. / edited by Leonard Gaunt. — London : Focal, 1981. — 527p : ill ; 23cm
ISBN 0-240-51062-3 : Unpriced : CIP rev. B80-07895

681′.42 — Optical equipment: Lenses. Manufacture

Horne, Douglas F.. Optical production technology. — Rev. ed. — Bristol : Hilger, Dec.1982. — [406]p
Previous ed.: 1972
ISBN 0-85274-350-5 : £40.00 : CIP entry B82-30732

681.6/7 — MANUFACTURES. PRINTING, DUPLICATING AND OTHER SPECIAL-PURPOSE MACHINERY

681′.6′05 — Printing equipment — *Serials*

British Printer dataguide : machinery and equipment for the graphic arts. — No.1 (1978)-. — London (30 Old Burlington St, W1X 2AE) : Maclean-Hunter, 1978-. — v. : ill ; 30cm
Annual. — Continues in part: British Printer specification manual. — Description based on: No.3 (Sept. 1980)
ISSN 0262-9372 = British Printer dataguide : £12.50 B82-38521

681′.75′09 — Scientific instruments, *to ca 1910 — Collectors′ guides*

Curtis, Tony, *1939-.* Instruments / compiled by Tony Curtis. — Galashiels : Lyle, c1982. — 126p : ill ; 16cm. — (Antiques and their values)
Includes index
ISBN 0-86248-034-5 : £2.50 B82-29160

681′.761 — Man. Heart. Cardiac pacemakers. Manufacture — *Standards*

Specific requirements for quality systems for manufacturers of implantable cardiac pacemakers / [compiled by the DHSS, Scientific and Technical Branch]. — London : H.M.S.O., 1981. — 36p ; 30cm
ISBN 0-11-320779-4 (pbk) : £3.95 B82-16796

681′.761 — Pharmaceutical products containers, *1800-1900*

Jackson, W. A.. The Victorian chemist and druggist / W.A. Jackson. — Princes Risborough : Shire, 1981. — 32p : ill ; 21cm. — (Shire album ; 80)
Bibliography: p32
ISBN 0-85263-583-4 (pbk) : £0.95 B82-31136

681′.763′07 — Great Britain. Agricultural machinery trades. Apprentices. Training

Training of apprentices in agricultural machinery. — Gloucester (Barton House, Barton St., Gloucester GL1 1QQ) : Food, Drink and Tobacco Industry Training Board, 1978. — 7p ; 31cm
Unpriced (pbk) B82-26132

682 — BLACKSMITHING

682′.092′4 — Humberside. Hibaldstow. Blacksmithing, *ca 1930-1979 — Personal observations*

Farmer, David K.. Under a spreading chestnut tree : the reminiscences of a village blacksmith / David K. Farmer. — [Hull] : Humberside Leisure Services Department, c1981. — 79p : ill,1port ; 31cm
ISBN 0-904451-20-8 (pbk) : £3.50 B82-17458

683.3 — LOCKS

683′.3′05 — Locksmithing — *Serials*

Keyways : the journal of the Master Locksmiths Association. — Vol.1 no.1 (1979)-. — London (106 Hampstead Rd, NW1 2LS) : Victor Green Publications, 1979-. — v. : ill,ports ; 22cm
Six issues yearly. — Description based on: Vol.3 no.4 (Aug. 1981)
ISSN 0262-4478 = Keyways : £6.00 per year B82-04916

683.4 — FIREARMS

683.4 — Air guns & gas guns

Walter, John. The airgun book / John Walter. — 2nd ed. rev. — London : Arms and Armour, 1982. — 146p : ill ; 26cm
Previous ed.: 1981
ISBN 0-85368-518-5 : £8.50 : CIP rev. B82-04797

683.4 — Firearms. Assembly & disassembly — *Amateurs′ manuals*

Wood, J. B. (Jay Barclay). The Gun digest book of firearms assembly/disassembly / by J.B. Wood. — Northfield, Ill. : DBI Books ; [London] : [Distributed by Arms and Armour Press]
Pt.5: Shotguns. — c1980. — 288p : chiefly ill,1port ; 27cm
Port, ill on inside cover
ISBN 0-910676-11-9 (pbk) : £4.50 B82-13345

683.4 — Firearms. Customising

The **Gun** digest review of custom guns / edited by Ken Warner. — Northfield, Ill. : DBI Books, c1980 ; London : Arms and Armour Press [distributor]. — 256p : ill ; 28cm
Text, ill. on inside covers
ISBN 0-910676-10-0 (pbk) : £4.50 B82-35052

683.4′007 — United States. Police. Training. Curriculum subjects: Use of firearms

Mullin, Timothy John. Training the gunfighter : firearms selection, equipment, and training for the small- and medium-size police or sherriff′s department with helpful hints to the individual law enforcement or military officer, home defender, soldier of fortune, explorer, adventurer, bodyguard, and store operator / by Timothy John Mullin. — Boulder : Paladin Press ; London : Arms and Armour, c1981. — viii,237p : ill,ports ; 29cm
ISBN 0-85368-208-9 : Unpriced B82-02832

683.4′009 — Firearms, *to 1980*

Wilkinson, Frederick. A source book of small arms. — London : Ward Lock, May 1981. — [128]p
ISBN 0-7063-6055-9 : £3.95 : CIP entry B81-07468

683.4′06 — Firearms. Cartridges — *Identification manuals*

Hogg, Ian V.. The cartridge guide : the small arms ammunition identification manual / Ian V. Hogg. — London : Arms and Armour, 1982. — 192p : ill ; 24cm
ISBN 0-85368-468-5 : £8.95 : CIP rev. B81-33779

683.4′06 — Firearms. Cartridges. Loading — *Amateurs′ manuals*

Metallic cartridge reloading / edited by Robert S.L. Anderson ; load tables by Edward Matunas. — London : Arms and Armour Press, c1982. — 320p : ill ; 28cm
ISBN 0-910676-39-9 (pbk) : Unpriced B82-39689

683.4′2′09 — Sporting firearms, *to 1978*

Waterman, Charles F.. The treasury of sporting guns / by Charles F. Waterman ; special photography by J. Barry O′Rourke and Robert J. Kligge. — London : Hamlyn, 1979. — 240p : ill(some col.),ports ; 28cm
Bibliography: p235. — Includes index
ISBN 0-600-34094-5 : Unpriced B82-04359

683.4′26′09 — Shotguns, *to 1980*

Marshall-Ball, Robin. The sporting shotgun : a user′s handbook / by Robin Marshall-Ball. — Hindhead : Saiga, c1981. — x,162p : ill,maps,1port ; 26cm. — (Field sports library)
Bibliography: p159. — Includes index
ISBN 0-86230-037-1 : £8.50 B82-10839

683.8 — MANUFACTURES. HOUSEHOLD EQUIPMENT

683′.8 — English household kitchen equipment, *to ca 1930 — Collectors′ guides*

Curtis, Tony, *1939-.* Kitchen equipment / compiled by Tony Curtis. — Galashiels : Lyle, c1982. — 126p : ill ; 17cm. — (Antiques and their values)
Includes index
ISBN 0-86248-035-3 : £2.50 B82-28675

683′.8 — Household kitchen equipment, *1600-1920 — Collectors′ guides*

Barton, Stuart. Kitchenalia / by Stuart Barton. — Tenterden : MJM, c1982. — 117p : ill ; 22cm. — (Buyer′s price guides)
Includes index
ISBN 0-905879-08-2 : £3.95 B82-33578

683′.8 — Household kitchen equipment — *Catalogues*

Alternative kitchens : 13th September-2nd November, 1980 : Southampton Art Gallery Civic Centre Southampton / the exhibition has been sponsored by Southern Arts Association and Southern Gas. — [Southampton] : Department of Leisure Services, [1980]. — 28p : ill ; 30cm
Unpriced (pbk) B82-35009

683′.88 — Developing countries. Stoves. Intermediate technology — *Serials*

Boiling point / produced by the I.T.D.G. Stoves Team. — No.1 (Jan. 1982)-. — Reading (Shinfield Rd, Reading, Berks.) : Intermediate Technology Development Group, Applied Research Section, Shinfield, 1982-. — v. : ill ; 30cm
ISSN 0263-3167 = Boiling point : Unpriced B82-23585

684 — WOODWORKING, METALWORKING, FURNITURE MAKING, FURNISHINGS

684′.08 — Plywood. Woodworking — *Amateurs′ manuals*

Shea, John G.. Plywood working for everybody / John Gerald Shea. — New York ; London : Van Nostrand Reinhold, 1963 (1981 [printing]). — x,212p : ill ; 28cm
Includes index
ISBN 0-442-26429-1 (pbk) : £8.45 B82-09793

684′.08 — Polyethylene glycol treated green wood. Woodworking. Techniques — *Amateurs′ manuals*

Spielman, Patrick E.. Working green wood with PEG / Patrick Spielman. — New York ; Sterling ; Poole : distributed by Blandford, c1980 (1981 [printing]). — 120p : ill ; 23cm
Includes index
ISBN 0-8069-5416-7 (cased) : Unpriced
ISBN 0-8069-8924-6 (pbk) : Unpriced
ISBN 0-8069-5417-5 (library) : Unpriced
B82-39528

684′.08 — Wood turning — *Amateurs′ manuals*

Underwood, Frank. Beginner′s guide to woodturning / Frank Underwood and Gordon Warr. — Sevenoaks : Newnes Technical, 1981. — 186p : ill ; 19cm
Includes index
ISBN 0-408-00507-6 (pbk) : £3.60 : CIP rev.
B81-30274

684′.08 — Wood turning — *Manuals*

Nish, Dale L.. Artistic woodturning / Dale L. Nish. — London : Stobart, 1981, c1980. — 255p : ill(some col.) ; 28cm
Originally published: Provo, Utah : Brigham Young University Press, 1980. — Includes index
ISBN 0-85442-017-7 (pbk) : £8.95 B82-15286

Wooldridge, W. J.. Woodturning / W.J. Wooldridge. — London : Batsford, 1982. — 160p : ill ; 26cm
Ill on lining papers. — Includes index
ISBN 0-7134-4045-7 : £8.95 B82-17660

684′.08 — Woodworking

Groneman, Chris H.. General woodworking / Chris H. Groneman. — 6th ed. — New York ; London : Webster Division, McGraw-Hill, c1982. — xi,324p,[8]p of plates : ill(some col.) ; 25cm. — (McGraw-Hill publications in industrial education)
Previous ed.: 1976. — Includes index
ISBN 0-07-025003-0 : £11.50 B82-03298

684′.08 — Woodworking — *Amateurs′ manuals*

Endacott, Geoffrey. Fine furniture making and woodworking / Geoffrey Endacott. — Newton Abbot : David & Charles, c1982. — 176p,[4]p of plates : ill(some col.) ; 25cm
Includes index
ISBN 0-7153-8389-2 : £8.95 B82-37690

Hayward, Charles H.. Carpentry / Charles Hayward. — 3rd ed. / rev. by F.E. Sherlock. — London : Teach Yourself Books, 1981. — xvi,199p : ill ; 18cm. — (Teach yourself book)
Previous ed.: 1973. — Includes index
ISBN 0-340-27112-4 (pbk) : £1.50 : CIP rev.
B81-22482

Sherlock, F. E.. Home woodworking / Fred Sherlock. — London : Newnes Technical, 1982. — 101p : ill(some col.) ; 25cm
Text on inside covers. — Includes index
ISBN 0-408-01121-1 (pbk) : £3.95 : CIP rev.
B82-00908

684′.08 — Woodworking — *Amateurs′ manuals — For children*

Lawler, Tony. Beginner′s guide to woodwork / Tony Lawler ; illustrated by Diana McLean. — London : Usborne, 1979. — 64p : ill(chiefly col.) ; 18cm
Includes index
ISBN 0-86020-309-3 (pbk) : £0.85 B82-13394

684′.08 — Woodworking — *For schools*

Stewart, Richard. Adventures with woodwork. — London : Murray, July 1982. — [64]p
ISBN 0-7195-3990-0 (cased) : £4.95 : CIP entry
ISBN 0-7195-3991-9 (pbk) : £2.75 B82-14526

684′.08 — Woodworking — *Manuals*

De Cristoforo, R. J.. Build your own wood toys, gifts & furniture / R.J. De Cristoforo. — New York : Popular Science ; New York ; London : Van Nostrand Reinhold, c1981. — xi,403p : ill ; 24cm. — (A Popular Science book)
ISBN 0-442-21883-4 (corrected) : £21.20
B82-25969

Fine wood working techniques / selected by the editors of Fine Woodworking magazine. — London : Stobart, 1978. — 189p : ill ; 32cm
Includes index
ISBN 0-85442-015-0 : £9.50 B82-15285

Maynard, J.. Craft practice in wood : an introduction to basic techniques / J. Maynard ; photographs by L. Ouseley. — Rev. and new ed. — Amersham : Hulton Educational, 1979. — 87p : ill ; 19x24cm
Previous ed.: published as Woodwork, techniques and constructions. 1966
ISBN 0-7175-0825-0 (pbk) : Unpriced
B82-23926

684′.08 — Woodworking. Projects — *Manuals*

101 projects for woodworkers / the editors of The woodworker′s journal. — London : Stobart, 1981. — viii,247p : ill ; 29cm
ISBN 0-85442-018-5 : £10.95 B82-15287

684′.08′05 — Woodworking — *Serials*

Woodworker planbook. — 1981/82-. — Hemel Hempstead : Model & Allied Publications, [1981]-. — v. : ill ; 21cm
Irregular
ISSN 0262-950x = Woodworker planbook : £0.75 B82-11821

684′.09 — Metalworking

Harris, John Noel. Mechanical working of metals. — Oxford : Pergamon, July 1982. — [275]p. — (International series on materials science and technology ; v.36) (Pergamon international library)
ISBN 0-08-025464-0 (cased) : £20.00 : CIP entry
ISBN 0-08-025463-2 (pbk) : £7.95 B82-12409

684′.09 — Metalworking — *For schools*

Green, J. N.. Metalwork theory for GCE and CSE. — 3rd ed. — London : Bell & Hyman, Sept.1982. — [88]p
Previous ed.: S.l. : s.n., 196-?
ISBN 0-7135-2045-0 (pbk) : £2.95 : CIP entry
B82-22811

Mold, R. A.. Metalwork theory. — 2nd ed. — London : Murray, Oct.1982. — [64]p
Previous ed.: 1979
ISBN 0-7195-4012-7 (pbk) : £1.20 : CIP entry
B82-30570

684′.09 — Metalworking — *Manuals*

Streeter, Donald. Professional smithing : traditional techniques for decorative ironwork, whitesmithing, hardware, toolmaking, and locksmithing / Donald Streeter ; with photographs and drawings by the author. — London : Murray, 1982, c1980. — ix,133p : ill ; 28cm
Originally published: New York : Scribner, 1980. — Includes index
ISBN 0-7195-3904-8 : £7.95 : CIP rev.
B81-30269

684.1 — Furniture. Design

Harris, I.. Drawing office manual / by I. Harris. — Stevenage : Furniture Industry Research Association, 1982. — 96p : ill ; 30cm
£8.50(£5.00 to members of FIRA) (spiral)
B82-29208

684.1 — Furniture. Making — *Amateurs′ manuals*

Johnston, David, *1921-*. The craft of furniture making / David Johnston. — 2nd ed. — London : Batsford, 1981. — 136p,[4]p of plates : ill(some col.) ; 25cm. — (A Batsford craft paperback)
Previous ed.: 1979. — Bibliography: p133. — Includes index
ISBN 0-7134-1547-9 (pbk) : £3.95 B82-01606

684.1′0068′1 — Furniture industries. Costing — *Manuals*

Parker, V.. Product costing / by V. Parker. — Stevenage (Maxwell Road, Stevenage, Hertfordshire, SG1 2EW) : Furniture Industry Research Association, 1981. — 102p : ill ; 30cm
£45.00 (£20.00 to members of FIRA) (spiral)
B82-13964

Parker, V.. Product costing / by V. Parker. — Maxwell Road, Stevenage, Hertfordshire, SG1 2EW Stevenage : Furniture Industry Research Association, 1981. — 102p : ill ; 30cm
£45.00 (£20.00 to members of FIRA) (spiral)
B82-22221

684.1′04 — Cabinet-making — *Manuals*

Karg, Franz. Modern cabinetmaking in solid wood / Franz Karg ; [translated by R.E.K. Meuss]. — London : Bell & Hyman, 1980. — 136p : ill ; 30cm
Translation from the German
ISBN 0-7135-1203-2 : £12.50 : CIP rev.
B80-10157

684.1′04 — Pine furniture. Making

Gilmore, J. W. L.. The business of pine / J.W.L. Gilmore. — [Belfast] ([124 North Rd., Belfast, BTL 3DJ]) : [J.W.L. Gilmore], [1982?]. — 13p : ill ; 33cm
Unpriced (unbound) B82-40022

684.1′04 — Pine furniture. Making — *Manuals*

Gilmore, J. W. L.. Working with Scots pine / J.W.L. Gilmore. — [Belfast] ([124 North Rd., Belfast, BTL 3DJ]) : [J.W.L. Gilmore], [1982?]. — 13p : ill ; 33cm
Unpriced (unbound) B82-40023

684.1′04′088054 — Children′s wooden furniture, *to 1981 — Collectors′ guides*

Gelles, Edward. Nursery furniture : antique children′s, miniature and doll′s house furniture / Edward Gelles. — London : Constable, 1982. — 164p,[2]p of plates : ill(some col.) ; 23cm. — (Medallion collectors′ series)
Includes index
ISBN 0-09-463990-6 : £9.95 B82-27118

684.1′043 — Wooden furniture. Finishing — *Amateurs′ manuals*

Gibbia, S. W.. Wood finishing and refinishing / S.W. Gibbia. — 3rd ed. — New York ; London : Van Nostrand Reinhold, c1981. — 316p : ill ; 24cm
Previous ed.: 1971. — Includes index
ISBN 0-442-24708-7 : £12.70
Also classified at 684.1′0443 B82-09760

Gladstone, Bernard. The complete home guide to furniture finishing and refinishing / Bernard Gladstone ; illustrated by Robert Strimban. — London : Evans, 1982, c1981. — 128p : ill ; 24cm
Originally published: New York : Simon and Schuster, 1981. — Includes index
ISBN 0-237-45647-8 (pbk) : £3.25 B82-36802

684.1′044 — Furniture. Repair — *Amateurs′ manuals*

Mason, David, *19---*. Which? way to repair and restore furniture / [compiled by David Mason]. — London : Consumers′ Association, 1980. — 180p : ill ; 19x21cm
ISBN 0-85202-193-3 (pbk) : Unpriced
ISBN 0-85202-193-3 (Hodder & Stoughton) : Unpriced
Also classified at 749′.0288 B82-40548

684.1′0442 — Wooden furniture. Restoration — *Amateurs′ manuals*

Jackson, Albert, *1943-*. Better than new : a practical guide to renovating furniture / by Albert Jackson and David Day ; edited by Ron Bloomfield. — London : British Broadcasting Corporation, 1982. — 144p : ill(some col.) ; 22cm
Published to accompany a BBC television series. — Includes index
ISBN 0-563-16485-9 (pbk) : £4.75 B82-13973

684.1′0443 — Wooden furniture. Refinishing — *Amateurs′ manuals*

Gibbia, S. W.. Wood finishing and refinishing / S.W. Gibbia. — 3rd ed. — New York ; London : Van Nostrand Reinhold, c1981. — 316p : ill ; 24cm
Previous ed.: 1971. — Includes index
ISBN 0-442-24708-7 : £12.70
Primary classification 684.1′043 B82-09760

684.1′06 — Cane furniture & wicker furniture. Making — *Manuals*

Bausert, John. The complete book of wicker & cane furniture making / by John Bausert. — New York : Sterling ; London : Oak Tree, c1976. — 123p : ill,1port ; 28cm
ISBN 0-8069-8240-3 (pbk) : £4.50 B82-28178

684.1′2 — Upholstering. Techniques — *Manuals*

Clare, Hilary. First steps in upholstery : traditional handmade / Hilary Clare ; line drawings by Dinah Cohen. — London : Warne, 1981. — 91p : ill ; 22cm. — (An Observer′s guide. Art and craft)
Includes index
ISBN 0-7232-2761-6 (pbk) : £1.95 B82-00870

684.1′3 — Chairs & stools. Seats. Cord rushworking & seagrass reshworking — *Manuals*

Maynard, Barbara. Cord & seagrass seating / Barbara Maynard. — Leicester : Dryad, 1979. — 15p : col.ill ; 15x21cm. — (Dryad leaflet ; 524)
ISBN 0-85219-124-3 (unbound) : Unpriced B82-14336

684.1′3 — Chairs. Seats. Caning — *Amateurs′ manuals*

Edwards, Margaret. Upholstery and canework. — London : Pelham, Nov.1982. — [128]p. — (Tricks of the trade)
ISBN 0-7207-1418-4 : £5.50 : CIP entry
Primary classification 645′.4 B82-26408

684.1′3 — Pine coffee tables. Making — *Manuals*

Gilmore, J. W. L.. Design for pine coffee table / J.W.L. Gilmore. — [Belfast] ([124 North Rd., Belfast, BTL 3DJ]) : [J.W.L. Gilmore], [1982?]. — 4p : ill ; 33cm
Unpriced (unbound) B82-40026

684.1′3 — Pine telephone stools & pine coffee tables. Making — *Manuals*

Gilmore, J. W. L.. Design for pine telephone seat and matching modern style coffee table / J.W.L. Gilmore. — [Belfast] ([124 North Rd., Belfast, BTL 3DJ]) : [J.W.L. Gilmore], [1982?]. — 8p : ill ; 33cm
Unpriced (unbound) B82-40030

684.1′3 — Residences. Wooden refectory tables & wooden refectory benches. Making — *Manuals*

Gilmore, J. W. L.. Design for refectory table and benches / J.W.L. Gilmore. — [Belfast] ([124 North Rd., Belfast, BTL 3DJ]) : [J.W.L. Gilmore], [1982?]. — 6p : ill ; 33cm
Unpriced (unbound) B82-40029

684.1′3 — Seating. Ergonomic aspects — *Conference proceedings*

Proceedings of the symposium on sitting posture = sitzhaltung = posture assise / edited by E. Grandjean. — London : Taylor & Francis, 1969 (1976 [printing]). — 253p : ill,plans ; 27cm
Text in English and German. — Includes index
ISBN 0-85066-029-7 : £10.00 B82-31076

684.1′3 — Seating for handicapped children

York-Moore, Rosemary. Management of the physically handicapped child : guidelines to lifting, carrying and seating / by Rosemary York-Moore and Pamela Stewart ; photographs P. Denys Stone, Pamela Stewart. — Kidderminster : British Institute of Mental Handicap, 1982. — ii,16p : ill ; 15x21cm. — (Pamphlet ; no.2)
Bibliography: p15
ISBN 0-906054-24-9 (pbk) : £1.50
Primary classification 362.4′088054 B82-35264

684.1′3 — Seating for physically handicapped persons

Rodger, J.. DHSS aids assessment programme : a comparative assessment of 3 types of moulded body support : summary report / J. Rodger, G.R. Johnson, G.M. Cochrane. — Derby (Derbyshire Royal Infirmary, London Rd., Derby) : Orthotics & Disability Research Centre, 1980, c1981. — 12p : ill ; 30cm
Unpriced (pbk) B82-40862

Sitting comfortably / [text and photographs by members of Chailey Heritage staff]. — North Chailey (North Chailey, Lewes, Sussex) : Chailey Heritage, 1982. — 9p : ill ; 21cm. — (Chailey Heritage information for independence ; 1)
£0.20 (unbound) B82-36552

684.1′6 — Wooden bedside cabinets. Making — *Manuals*

Gilmore, J. W. L.. Design for bedside cabinet / J.W.L. Gilmore. — [Belfast] ([124 North Rd., Belfast, BTL 3DJ]) : [J.W.L. Gilmore], [1982?]. — 8p : ill ; 33cm
Unpriced (unbound) B82-40024

684.1′6 — Wooden corner dressers. Making — *Manuals*

Gilmore, J. W. L.. Design for corner dresser / J.W.L. Gilmore. — [Belfast] ([124 North Rd., Belfast, BTL 3DJ]) : [J.W.L. Gilmore], [1982?]. — 13p : ill ; 33cm
Unpriced (unbound) B82-40025

684.1′6 — Wooden three-door Welsh dressers. Making — *Manuals*

Gilmore, J. W. L.. Design for three door Welsh dresser / J.W.L. Gilmore. — [Belfast] ([124 North Rd., Belfast, BTL 3DJ]) : [J.W.L. Gilmore], [1982?]. — 13p : ill ; 33cm
Unpriced (unbound) B82-40028

684.1′6 — Wooden two-door wall cupboards. Making — *Manuals*

Gilmore, J. W. L.. Design for two door wall cupboard / J.W.L. Gilmore. — [Belfast] ([124 North Rd., Belfast, BTL 3DJ]) : [J.W.L. Gilmore], [1982?]. — 6p : ill ; 33cm
Unpriced (unbound) B82-40021

684.1′6 — Wooden wall shelving. Making — *Manuals*

Gilmore, J. W. L.. Design for wall shelf unit / J.W.L. Gilmore. — [Belfast] ([124 North Rd., Belfast, BTL 3DJ]) : [J.W.L. Gilmore], [1982?]. — 6p : ill ; 33cm
Unpriced (unbound) B82-40031

684.1′6 — Wooden Welsh dressers. Making — *Manuals*

Gilmore, J. W. L.. Design for traditional Welsh dresser / J.W.L. Gilmore. — [Belfast] ([124 North Rd., Belfast, BTL 3DJ]) : [J.W.L. Gilmore], [1982?]. — 10p : ill ; 33cm
Unpriced (unbound) B82-40027

685 — LEATHER, FUR AND RELATED PRODUCTS

685′.1 — Saddlery

Baker, Jennifer. Saddlery and horse clothing. — London : Ward Lock, Sept.1982. — [96]p. — (Practical horse guide)
ISBN 0-7063-6198-9 : £4.95 : CIP entry B82-21386

The **Country** life book of saddlery and equipment / consultant editor Elwyn Hartley Edwards. — Feltham : Country Life Books, c1981. — 255p : ill(some col.) ; 31cm. — (A Quarto book)
Includes index
ISBN 0-600-38429-2 : £10.00 B82-17603

685′.1′0924 — Hereford and Worcester. Hereford. Saddlery. Making, *ca 1920-ca 1940 — Personal observations*

Davis, Sidney A.. The saddler / Sidney A. Davis. — Aylesbury : Shire, c1980. — 64p : ill,ports ; 21cm
Includes index
ISBN 0-85263-527-3 (pbk) : £2.25 B82-15059

685′.3102′068 — Great Britain. Industries. Design. Management — *Study examples: Footwear industries*

Oldham, Stuart W.. Design and design management in the UK footwear industry / Stuart W. Oldham. — London : Design Council, 1982. — 56p : ill ; 30cm
Bibliography: p56
ISBN 0-85072-127-x (pbk) : £5.00 : CIP rev. B81-40243

685′.51′0941 — British handbags & purses, *1600-1980*

Foster, Vanda. Bags and purses / Vanda Foster. — London : Batsford, 1982. — 96p,[4]p of plates : ill(some col.),1facsim,1port ; 26cm. — (The Costume accessories series)
Bibliography: p91. — Includes index
ISBN 0-7134-3772-3 : £6.95 B82-17656

685′.53 — Backpacking equipment. Making — *Amateurs′ manuals*

Nelson, Hugh. Make your own backpack and other wilderness campgear / Hugh Nelson ; with illustrations by Dennis Reed. — Chicago ; London : Swallow, c1981. — 131p : ill ; 28cm
ISBN 0-8040-0355-6 (pbk) : £9.10 B82-15532

686 — PRINTING AND RELATED ACTIVITIES

686 — Books. Design

Trevitt, John. Book design / John Trevitt. — Cambridge : Cambridge University Press, 1980. — iv,34p ; 22cm. — (Cambridge authors′ and publishers′ guides)
ISBN 0-521-29741-9 (pbk) : £1.35 B82-26371

686 — Books. Production

Hobbs the Printers. The newprint bookplan : a system devised for the economic production of books by Hobbs the Printers Ltd of Southampton. — Southampton (Second Ave., Millbrook, Southampton SO9 2UZ) : Hobbs the Printers, [1982?]. — 47p : ill,ports ; 30cm
Ill on inside covers
Unpriced (pbk) B82-35826

686′.0941 — Great Britain. Books. Production, *to 1981 — For schools*

Wilkins, Frances. Books / Frances Wilkins. — London : Batsford Academic and Educational, 1982. — 72p : ill,facsims ; 26cm. — (History in focus)
Bibliography: p70. — Includes index
ISBN 0-7134-4057-0 : £5.95 B82-22244

686.2 — PRINTING

686.2 — Printing — *Amateurs′ manuals*

Green, J. C. R.. Starting in print. — Scotland (P.O. Box 1, Portree, Isle of Skye, Scotland IV51 9BT) : J.C.R. Green Associates, Jan.1983. — [48]p
ISBN 0-907762-00-x (pbk) : £2.50 : CIP entry B82-33248

686.2 — Printing — *Conference proceedings*

International Conference of Printing Research Institutes *(16th : 1981 : Key Biscayne)*. Advances in printing science and technology. — London : Pentech Press, July 1982. — [460]p
ISBN 0-7273-0108-x : £26.00 : CIP entry B82-20775

686.2 — Printing — *For graphic design*

Cray, Peter. Graphic design and reproduction techniques. — 3rd ed. — London : Butterworths, May 1982. — [284]p
Previous ed.: London : Focal Press, 1972
ISBN 0-240-51124-7 : £8.50 : CIP entry
B82-07395

686.2′03 — Printing — *Polyglot dictionaries*

Dictionary of the graphic arts industry : in eight languages English German French Russian Spanish Polish Hungarian Slovak / edited by Wolfgang Müller. — Amsterdam ; Oxford : Elsevier Scientific, 1981. — 1020p ; 25cm
ISBN 0-444-99745-8 : £48.39 B82-11939

686.2′05 — Books. Printing — *Serials*

[Matrix *(Andoversford)***]**. Matrix : a review for printers and bibliophiles. — No.1 (Autumn 1981)-. — Andoversford : Whittington Press, 1981-. — v. : ill ; 29cm
One or two issues yearly
ISSN 0261-3093 = Matrix (Andoversford) : Unpriced B82-28107

686.2′092′4 — France. Paris. Printing, *ca 1735-ca 1760* — *Personal observations* — *French texts*

Le Brun. Anecdotes typographiques : où l'on voit la description des coutumes, moeurs et usages singuliers des Compagnons imprimeurs / by Nicholas Contat dit Le Brun. La misère des apprentis imprimeurs / by Dufresne ; edited with an introduction and notes by Giles Barber. — Oxford : Oxford Bibliographical Society, 1980. — viii,163p,[6]leaves of plates : ill,facsims,ports ; 24cm. — (Oxford Bibliographical Society publications. New series ; v.20)
French text, English introduction and notes. — Anecdotes typographiques. Originally published: Brussels : Pierre Hardy, 1762. — La misère des apprentis imprimeurs. Originally published: s.l. : s.n., 1710
ISBN 0-901420-35-2 : Unpriced B82-10708

686.2′0942 — England. Printing, *to ca 1500*

Hellinga, Lotte. Caxton in focus : the beginning of printing in England. — London : British Library, Reference Division, May 1982. — [94]p
ISBN 0-904654-76-1 : £6.95 : CIP entry
B82-10859

686.2′09428′37 — Humberside. Hull. Printers, *to 1840*

Chilton, C. W.. Early Hull printers and booksellers : an account of the printing, bookselling and allied trades from their beginnings to 1840 / by C.W. Chilton. — [Kingston-upon-Hull] : Kingston-upon-Hull City Council, 1982. — 274,lxxxiii p ; 30cm
Map on inside cover. — Bibliography: p277-274. — Includes index
ISBN 0-904767-07-8 (spiral) : Unpriced
Primary classification 381′.45002′0942837
B82-34756

686.2′0945 — Italy. Printing, *ca 1450-ca 1700*

Rhodes, Dennis E.. Studies in early Italian printing. — London (35 Palace Court, W2 4LS) : Pindar Press, Oct.1981. — [384]p. — (Studies in the history of printing ; 1)
ISBN 0-907132-02-2 : £25.00 : CIP entry
B81-27993

686.2′2′0924 — Typography. Design. Tschichold, Jan — *Catalogues*

Jan Tschichold : typographer and type designer 1902-1974. — Edinburgh : National Library of Scotland, 1982. — 78p : ill,facsims,1port ; 22cm
Published to accompany an exhibition held at the National Library of Scotland, 5 August to 30 October 1982. — Translated from the German. — Bibliography: p64-77
ISBN 0-902220-53-5 (pbk) : Unpriced
B82-40014

686.2′24′0222 — Typefaces — *Illustrations*

The **Designer's** guide to text type / [compiled by] Jean Callan King and Tony Esposito. — New York ; London : Van Nostrand Reinhold, c1980. — 319p : 2ill ; 31cm
ISBN 0-442-25425-3 (pbk) : £18.70
B82-35358

686.2′24′09 — Typefaces, *to 1800*

Updike, Daniel Berkeley. Printing types : their history, forms and use : a study in survivals / by Daniel Berkeley Updike. — 2nd ed. — New York : Dover ; London : Constable, 1980. — 2v. : ill,facsims ; 24cm
Previous ed.: Cambridge, Mass. : Harvard University Press, 1922. — Includes index
ISBN 0-486-23928-4 (pbk) : £11.30
ISBN 0-486-23929-2 (v.2) : Unpriced
B82-41014

686.2′25 — Printing. Composition — *Manuals*

Hart, Horace. Hart's rules for compositors and readers at the University Press, Oxford. — 39th ed. — Oxford : Oxford University Press, Nov.1982. — [196]p
Previous ed.: 1978
ISBN 0-19-212983-x : £4.95 : CIP entry
B82-28999

686.2′25 — Printing. Paste-up techniques — *Manuals*

Hird, Kenneth F.. Paste-up for graphic arts production / Kenneth F. Hird. — Englewood Cliffs ; London : Prentice-Hall, c1982. — x,403p : ill,facsims ; 28cm
Includes index
ISBN 0-13-652875-9 (pbk) : £11.95
B82-21678

686.2′252 — Magazines. Design — *Manuals*

White, Jan V.. Editing by design : a guide to effective word-and-picture communication for editors and designers / by Jan V. White. — 2nd ed. — New York ; London : Bowker, 1982. — xv,248p : ill,facsims ; 28cm
Previous ed.: 1974. — Includes index
ISBN 0-8352-1508-3 (pbk) : Unpriced
B82-38749

686.4 — PHOTOCOPYING

686.4′068′4 — Duplicating services. Small firms. Organisation

Saunders, Mark. Duplication / [Mark Saunders]. — Rev. ed. — Irchester : M. Saunders, 1982. — 41p ; 20cm. — (Castle books)
Previous ed.: 1981
ISBN 0-907877-15-x (pbk) : £1.00 B82-24995

686.4′3′028 — Microform equipment — *Serials*

Microfilm & video systems. — Vol.1, no.1 (Jan. 1982)-. — Guildford (54 Quarry St., Guildford, Surrey GU1 13UF) : G.G. Baker, 1982-. — v. : ill,ports ; 30cm
Six issues yearly
ISSN 0262-0022 = Microfilm & video systems : £15.00 per year B82-14781

687 — MANUFACTURES. CLOTHING

687′.8 — Great Britain. Sewing needles. Manufacture, *to 1960*

Rollins, John G.. Needlemaking / John G. Rollins. — Princes Risborough : Shire, 1981. — 32p : ill ; 21cm. — (Shire album ; 71)
Bibliography: p32
ISBN 0-85263-563-x (pbk) : £0.95 B82-31139

688.4 — MANUFACTURES. SMOKERS' SUPPLIES

688′.42 — Gloucestershire. Clay tobacco pipes, *to 1900*

Peacey, Allan. Clay tobacco pipes in Gloucestershire / by Allan Peacey. — Bristol (The Archaeological Centre, Mark La., Bristol BS1 4XR) : Committee for Rescue Archaeology In Avon, Gloucestershire and Somerset, c1979. — p45-79 : ill,maps ; 30cm. — (Occasional papers ; no.4)
Cover title. — Bibliography: p79
Unpriced (pbk) B82-35982

688.7 — MANUFACTURES. RECREATIONAL EQUIPMENT

688.7′2 — Toys for children, to 7 years

Chetwood, Doreen. Growing up with toys. — London : Heinemann Educational, Mar.1982. — [96]p
ISBN 0-435-42100-x (pbk) : £2.95 : CIP entry
B82-01955

688.7′2 — Toys — *Illustrations* — *For children*

Daniels, Meg. Toys. — London : Blackie, Feb.1982. — [12]p. — (Blackie concertina books)
ISBN 0-216-91127-3 : £0.95 : CIP entry
B81-36032

688.7′2 — Toys — *Lists* — *Serials*

The **Good** toy guide. — 1983. — London : Inter-Action Inprint, Sept.1982. — [240]p
ISBN 0-904571-40-8 (pbk) : £2.95 : CIP entry
B82-21997

688.7′2′09033 — Toys, *ca 1700-ca 1950* — *Collectors' guides*

Dolls & toys / compiled by Tony Curtis. — Galashiels : Lyle, c1981. — 126p : chiefly ill ; 17cm. — (Antiques and their values)
Includes index
ISBN 0-86248-009-4 : £2.50 B82-08191

688.7′221′05 — Dolls — *Serials*

International dollmaking & collecting. — No.1 (Oct./Nov. 1980)-. — London (10 Bloomsbury Way, WC1A 2SH) : Collector Publications, 1980-. — v. : ill ; 21cm
Six issues yearly. — Continues: Living dolls
ISSN 0261-3948 = International dollmaking & collecting : £5.00 per year B82-20890

688.7′54′0942 — English playing cards, *1681-1720*
Special subjects: England, *1588-1720*

Whiting, J. R. S.. A handful of history. — Gloucester : Alan Sutton, Mar.1982. — [202]p
ISBN 0-86299-000-9 : £4.25 : CIP entry
B82-07811

688.7′6 — Recreation facilities. Polymeric playing surfaces

Tipp, G.. Polymeric surfaces for sports and recreation / G. Tipp and V.J. Watson. — London : Applied Science, c1982. — x,405p : ill ; 23cm
Includes bibliographies and index
ISBN 0-85334-980-0 : £24.00 : CIP rev.
B81-25717

688.7′62 — Inflatable play equipment. Construction & use — *Manuals*

Inflatables handbook / written by GASP Community Arts. — [Stafford] : West Midlands Arts, 1978. — 16p : ill ; 30cm. — (West Midlands Arts publication ; no.2)
Material compiled as part of Trinity Arts Playvan Project
Unpriced (pbk) B82-14650

688.7′6358′068 — Cricket pitches. Non-turf wickets

Cricket pitch research / Nottinghamshire County Council, Education Playing Fields Service. — [Nottingham] ([County Hall, West Bridgeford, Nottingham NG2 7QP]) : [The Council], c1978. — 16p : ill ; 30cm + Supplement(18p : ill : ports ; 30cm)
Cover title. — With information sheets [10] leaves as inserts
Unpriced (pbk) B82-05054

688.7′6358′068 — Cricket pitches. Non-turf wickets. Bases. Construction — *Manuals*

The **Construction** of non-turf cricket pitches including 'The Nottinghamshire pitch'. — [Nottingham] ([County Hall, West Bridgford, Nottingham NG2 7QP]) : Nottinghamshire County Council, [1981]. — 18p : ill ; 22cm
Unpriced (unbound) B82-04693

688.7′6358′0680924 — Cricket pitches. Wickets. Maintenance & preparation — *Personal observations*

Fairbrother, Jim. Testing the wicket. — London : Pelham, Aug.1982. — [176]p
ISBN 0-7207-1399-4 : £7.95 : CIP entry
B82-15845

688.7′65 — Expedition equipment — *Manuals*

Equipment manual. — 6th ed. / edited by Tony Lack. — London : Expedition Advisory Centre, 1981. — 63p ; 21cm
Cover title. — Previous ed.: 1980
ISBN 0-907649-00-9 (spiral) : Unpriced
B82-11736

688.7′65 — Expeditions by school parties. Equipment

The Young Explorers′ Trust expedition equipment quide. — 4th ed. — London (The Royal Geographical Society, 1 Kensington Gore, SW7 2AR) : Young Explorers′ Trust, 1978. — 62,9p ; 21cm
Previous ed.: 1977
£1.00 (pbk) B82-11880

688.7′9 — Scottish poaching equipment, *1700-1981*

Hendry, Colin C.. Scottish poaching equipment : an illustrated guide to the poaching collection in the National Museum of Antiquities of Scotland / Colin C. Hendry. — Edinburgh : H.M.S.O., 1982. — 35p : ill ; 15x21cm
ISBN 0-11-492011-7 (pbk) : £1.50 B82-33403

688.7′912 — Fly fishing. Flies. Tying — *Manuals*

Stewart, Tom. [Fifty popular flies and how to tie them]. Two hundred popular flies and how to tie them. — London : A. & C. Black, Dec.1982. — [400]p
Originally published as: Fifty popular flies and how to tie them. Vol.1-4. 1962-1973
ISBN 0-7136-2233-4 : CIP entry B82-30211

688.7′912 — Fly fishing. Flies. Tying. Techniques — *Amateurs′ manuals*

Trout and salmon flies. — London : Pelham Books, Sept.1982. — [128]p
ISBN 0-7207-1396-x : £15.00 : CIP entry B82-20391

688.7′912 — Fly fishing. Flies. Tying. Techniques — *Illustrations*

Andrews, Ted. Basic fly-tying in pictures. — London : Stanley Paul, Jan.1983. — [64]p
ISBN 0-09-149891-0 (pbk) : £2.95 : CIP entry B82-33631

688.8 — PACKAGING TECHNOLOGY

688.8 — Consumer goods containers. Capping, lidding & stoppering

Closures. — [Gloucester] ([Barton House, Barton St., Gloucester GL1 1QQ]) : [Food Drink and Tobacco Industry Training Board], [1981]. — v,106leaves : ill ; 23cm + Test booklet(24p : ill,forms ; 15x21cm). — (Self-instruction manual ; no.12)
Set of 15 35mm col. slides in pockets
Unpriced (spiral) B82-25298

688.8 — Consumer goods containers. Labelling

Labelling - basic principles. — [Gloucester] ([Barton House, Barton St., Gloucester GL1 1QQ]) : [Food Drink and Tobacco Industry Training Board], [1980]. — iv,90leaves : ill ; 23cm + Test booklet(23p : forms ; 15x21cm). — (Self-instruction manual ; no.10)
Set of 18 35mm col. slides in pockets
Unpriced (spiral) B82-25296

Labelling operations. — [Gloucester] ([Barton House, Barton St., Gloucester GL1 1QQ]) : [Food Drink and Tobacco Industry Training Board], [1981]. — v,95leaves : ill ; 23cm + Test booklet(23p : forms ; 15x21cm). — (Self-instruction manual ; no.11)
Set of 16 35mm col. slides in pockets
Unpriced (spiral) B82-25297

688.8 — Consumer goods. Machine-readable labelling

Chartier, Paul. Merchandise marking / ... prepared by Paul Chartier ... in collaboration with RMDP Ltd. — Brighton : Retail Management Development Programme, [1982]. — 162p : facsims ; 30cm. — (The Retail management handbook ; 2)
ISBN 0-907923-01-1 (pbk) : Unpriced B82-39509

688.8 — Liquid consumer goods containers. Filling

Liquid filling. — [Gloucester] ([Barton House, Barton St., Gloucester GL1 1QQ]) : [Food Drink and Tobacco Industry Training Board], [1979]. — iv,96leaves : ill ; 23cm + Test booklet(19p : forms ; 15x21cm). — (Self-instruction manual ; no.8)
Set of 12 35mm col. slides in pockets
Unpriced (spiral) B82-25294

688.8 — Packaging

Fundamentals of packaging / editor F.A. Paine. — Rev. ed. — Stanmore : Institute of Packaging, 1981. — 235p,[3]p of plates : ill,plans ; 21cm
Previous ed.: London : Blackie, 1962
ISBN 0-9507567-0-9 (pbk) : Unpriced B82-11922

688.8 — Solid consumer goods containers. Filling

Solid filling. — [Gloucester] ([Barton House, Barton St., Gloucester GL1 1QQ]) : [Food Drink and Tobacco Industry Training Board], [1980]. — iv,99leaves : ill ; 23cm + Test booklet(19p : forms ; 15x21cm). — (Self-instruction manual ; no.9)
Set of 15 35mm col. slides in pockets
Unpriced (spiral) B82-25295

690 — BUILDINGS. CONSTRUCTION

690 — Buildings. Construction

Barry, R.. Construction of buildings. — London : Granada
Vol.2. — 3rd ed. — Aug.1982. — [136]p
Previous ed.: London : Crosby Lockwood Staples, 1975
ISBN 0-246-11263-8 (pbk) : £4.50 : CIP entry B82-15702

Bowyer, Jack. Building technology / Jack Bowyer ; illustrations prepared by Peter Bowyer. — London : Newnes-Butterworths. — (TEC technician series)
3. — 1980. — [12],91p : ill,plans ; 25cm
Bibliography: p[9-10]
ISBN 0-408-00411-8 (pbk) : £3.25 : CIP rev. B80-07898

Grundy, J. T.. Construction technology / J.T. Grundy. — London : Edward Arnold
Vol. 3. — 1981. — 202p : ill ; 22cm
Includes index
ISBN 0-7131-3419-4 (pbk) : £4.50: CIP rev. B80-13914

690 — Buildings. Construction — *Amateurs′ manuals*

Allen, Edward, *1938-*. Teach yourself to build / Edward Allen and Gale Beth Goldberg. — Cambridge, Mass. ; London : MIT Press, c1979. — 117p : ill ; 28cm
ISBN 0-262-51020-0 (pbk) : £3.90
ISBN 0-262-51021-9 (students ed) : Unpriced B82-09790

690 — Buildings. Construction — *For technicians*

Adams, E. C.. Science in building. — London : Hutchinson Education
1. — 2nd ed. — Jan.1983. — [298]p
Previous ed.: 1965
ISBN 0-09-150291-8 (pbk) : £4.95 : CIP entry B82-33623

Adams, E. C.. Science in building. — London : Hutchinson Education
2. — 2nd ed. — Jan.1983. — [309]p
Previous ed.: 1967
ISBN 0-09-150301-9 (pbk) : £4.95 : CIP entry B82-33624

Adams, E. C.. Science in building. — London : Hutchinson Education
3. — 2nd ed. — Jan.1983. — [355]p
Previous ed.: 1969
ISBN 0-09-150311-6 (pbk) : £4.95 : CIP entry B82-33625

Chudley, R.. Construction technology 2 checkbook / R. Chudley ; illustrated by the author. — London : Butterworths, 1981. — ix,118p ; 20cm. — (Butterworths technical and scientific checkbooks. Level 2)
Includes index
ISBN 0-408-00671-4 (cased) : £6.95 : CIP rev.
ISBN 0-408-00603-x (pbk) : Unpriced B81-31426

Monckton, P. L.. Construction technology for civil engineering technicians. — London : Longman, Jan.1983. — [288]p. — (Longman technician series. Construction and civil engineering)
ISBN 0-582-41221-8 (pbk) : £7.50 : CIP entry B82-32466

690 — Buildings. Construction — *Manuals*

Chudley, R.. Building finishes, fittings and domestic services. — London : Construction Press, Nov.1982. — [228]p
ISBN 0-86095-717-9 (pbk) : £5.95 : CIP entry B82-26352

Clark, George, *1917-*. Construction technology guide / George Clark. — London : Northwood. — (A Building trades journal book)
Vol.1. — 1979. — viii,200p : ill,plans ; 31cm
Includes index
ISBN 0-7198-2750-7 : Unpriced B82-01386

690 — Buildings. Construction. Sites — *Manuals*

Chudley, R.. Building site works, substructure and plant. — London : Construction Press, Nov.1982. — [360]p
ISBN 0-86095-716-0 (pbk) : £7.95 : CIP entry B82-26353

690 — Buildings. Construction. Sites — *Manuals — For supervision*

Ballantyne, J. K.. The resident engineer. — London : Telford, Jan.1983. — [48]p
ISBN 0-7277-0162-2 (pbk) : £2.50 : CIP entry B82-32632

690 — Buildings. Joints. Design & construction — *Manuals*

Ryan, Nicholas M.. Joints and jointing in building / Nicholas M. Ryan. — Dublin : An Foras Forbartha, 1982. — iv,20p : ill ; 30cm
ISBN 0-906120-56-x (pbk) : £2.00 B82-32043

690 — Buildings. Security equipment. Design & installation

Traister, John E.. Design and application of security/fire-alarm systems / John E. Traister. — New York ; London : McGraw-Hill, c1981. — viii,176p : ill,plans,forms ; 24cm
Includes index
ISBN 0-07-065114-0 : £12.50
Primary classification 628.9′225 B82-00530

690 — Buildings. Security measures

Hughes, Denis. The security survey / Denis Hughes and Peter Bowler. — Aldershot : Gower, c1982. — vii,145p ; 23cm
Includes index
ISBN 0-566-02291-5 : Unpriced : CIP rev. B81-36213

690 — Buildings. Structural components. Connectors

Holmes, M.. Analysis and design of connections between structural elements. — Chichester : Ellis Horwood, Dec.1982. — [256]p. — (Ellis Horwood series in civil & mechanical engineering)
ISBN 0-85312-215-6 : £25.00 : CIP entry B82-30309

690′.028′7 — Great Britain. Buildings. Construction. Measurement

SMM7 : further proposals for discussion / Standard Method of Measurement Development Unit. — [London] : Royal Institution of Chartered Surveyors, 1982. — 28p ; 30cm
Cover title
Unpriced (spiral) B82-38173

690′.03 — Buildings. Construction — *Polyglot dictionaries*

Chaballe, L. Y.. Elsevier′s dictionary of building tools and materials. — Oxford : Elsevier Scientific, May1982. — 1v.
ISBN 0-444-42047-9 : CIP entry B82-16214

690′.03′21 — Buildings. Construction — *Dictionaries*

Marsh, Paul. Illustrated dictionary of building. — London : Construction Press, May 1982. — [256]p
ISBN 0-86095-848-5 (cased) : £19.95 : CIP entry
ISBN 0-86095-887-6 (pbk) : £9.95 B82-08452

690′.03′41 — Buildings. Construction — *French & English dictionaries*
Butterworth, Basil. Dictionnaire de la construction : français-anglais, anglais-français = Dictionary of building terms : French-English, English-French / by Basil Butterworth and Janine Flitz. — London : Construction Press, 1981. — xiv,129p ; 24cm
French and English text
ISBN 0-86095-886-8 (pbk) : £12.00 : CIP rev.
B81-13578

690′.068 — Great Britain. Building industries. Management
Butler, John T.. Elements of administration for building students. — 3rd ed. — London : Hutchinson Education, Oct.1982. — [236]p
Previous ed.: 1977
ISBN 0-09-149451-6 (pbk) : £5.50 : CIP entry
B82-24965

690′.068′1 — Buildings. Construction. Sites. Financial management
Gobourne, J.. Site cost control in the construction industry. — London : Butterworth, Sept.1982. — [240]p
ISBN 0-408-01222-6 (cased) : £7.95 : CIP entry
ISBN 0-408-01122-x (pbk) : Unpriced
B82-19214

690′.068′1 — England. Building industries. Cost value reconciliation. Standards. Institute of Chartered Accountants in England and Wales. Stocks and work in progress — *Critical studies*
Barrett, F. R.. Cost value reconciliation / by F.R. Barrett. — Ascot : Chartered Institute of Building, 1981. — 63p : ill ; 29cm
ISBN 0-906600-42-1 (pbk) : Unpriced
B82-06462

690′.068′1 — Great Britain. Buildings. Construction. Cost planning
Cartlidge, Duncan P.. Practical cost planning : a guide for surveyors and architects / Duncan P. Cartlidge and Ian N. Mehrtens. — London : Hutchinson, 1982. — 120p : ill,plans,forms ; 24cm
Includes index
ISBN 0-09-146841-8 (pbk) : £5.50 : CIP rev.
B82-04119

690′.068′1 — Great Britain. Buildings. Construction. Cost planning. Applications of digital computer systems
Construction cost data base : third annual report 1981 / prepared on behalf of PSA by University of Reading Department of Construction Management. — [London] ([2 Marsham St, SW1]) : Directorate of Quantity Surveying Services, Department of the Environment, PSA, [1981?]. — 190p : ill ; 20cm
Cover title
Unpriced (pbk)
B82-25876

Construction cost data base report / prepared on behalf of PSA by University of Reading Department of Construction Management. — [London] ([2 Marsham St, SW1,]) : Directorate of Quantity Surveying Services, Department of the Environment, PSA, [1981?]. — iii,164leaves ; 30cm
Cover title
Unpriced
B82-25875

Cost planning and computers : a research study / conducted for the Property Services Agency by the Department of Construction Management, University of Reading. — [Croydon] (['C' Block, Whitgift Centre, Croydon CR9 3LY]) : [The Agency], 1981. — iii,56p,[1]folded leaf of plates : ill ; 30cm
Unpriced (pbk)
B82-05700

690′.068′1 — Great Britain. Buildings. Construction. Costs. Control — *For quantity surveying*
Pre-contract cost control & cost planning / the Quantity Surveyors Division of the Royal Institution of Chartered Surveyors. — London : Published on behalf of the Royal Institution of Chartered Surveyors by Surveyors Publications, c1982. — 27p : forms ; 30cm. — (Quantity surveyors practice pamphlet, ISSN 0262-9682 ; no.2)
Text on inside covers. — Bibliography: p26-27
ISBN 0-85406-169-x (pbk) : Unpriced
B82-34636

690′.068′4 — Building industries. Project management
Project management in building : (incorporating Education for project management in building) / [the Chartered Institute of Building]. — [Ascot] : [The Institute], c1982. — 36p : ill ; 30cm
Project management in building. Originally published: Ascot : Institute of Building, 1979 — Education for project management in building. Originally published: Ascot : Chartered Institute of Building, 1981
ISBN 0-906600-53-7 (pbk) : Unpriced : CIP rev.
B82-03389

690′.068′4 — United States. Building industries. Small scale projects. Management — *Manuals*
McNulty, Alfred P.. Management of small construction projects / by Alfred P. McNulty. — New York ; London : McGraw-Hill, c1982. — xiii,256p : ill,forms,plans ; 24cm. — (The Engineering news - record series)
Includes index
ISBN 0-07-045685-2 : £18.95
B82-25274

690′.068′5 — Great Britain. Buildings. Construction. Demand. Management aspects
Barnard, R. H.. Survival or success : developing an appropriate response to a fluctuating demand for the building firm / by R.H. Barnard. — Ascot : Chartered Institute of Building, [1981]. — 22p : ill ; 29cm. — (Occasional paper / Chartered Institute of Building, ISSN 0306-6878 ; no.25)
ISBN 0-906600-46-4 (pbk) : Unpriced
B82-06461

690′.068′7 — Buildings. Construction. Sites. Building materials. Materials handling. Management
Wyatt, D. P.. Materials management. — Ascot : Chartered Institute of Building. — (Occasional paper / Chartered Institute of Building, ISSN 0306-6878 ; no.23)
Pt.2. — Mar.1982. — 1v.
ISBN 0-906600-52-9 (pbk) : CIP entry
B82-03388

690′.07′1141 — Great Britain. Building industries. Industrial training. Courses — *Directories*
List of building courses 1981-83. — Ascot : Chartered Institute of Building, c1981. — 58p ; 21x30cm
ISBN 0-906600-47-2 (pbk) : £3.75
B82-06460

690′.0724 — Building science. Experiments
Tyler, H. A.. Experimental building science / H.A. Tyler. — New York ; London : Van Nostrand Reinhold, 1982. — x,182p : ill ; 25cm. — (VNR crafts series)
ISBN 0-442-30468-4 (cased) : £11.95
ISBN 0-442-30469-2 (pbk) : £5.75
B82-14007

690′.076 — Buildings. Construction — *Questions & answers* — *For technicians*
Chudley, R.. Construction technology 3 checkbook / R. Chudley ; illustrated by the author. — London : Butterworth Scientific, 1982. — vi,121p : ill ; 20cm. — (Butterworths technical and scientific checkbooks)
Includes index
ISBN 0-408-00686-2 : Unpriced : CIP rev.
B82-10490

690′.0973 — United States. Buildings. Structural engineering
Ambrose, James. Building structures primer / James Ambrose. — 2nd ed. — New York ; Chichester : Wiley, c1981. — ix,136p : ill ; 26cm
Previous ed.: 1967. — Includes index
ISBN 0-471-08678-9 : £16.30
B82-04434

690′.1 — Buildings. Structural components
Chudley, R.. Building superstructure. — London : Construction Press, Nov.1982. — [400]p
ISBN 0-86095-715-2 (pbk) : £7.95 : CIP entry
B82-26351

690′.1 — Buildings. Trusses. Design
Parker, Harry, *b. 1887*. Simplified design of building trusses for architects and builders / the late Harry Parker. — 3rd ed. / prepared by James Ambrose. — New York ; Chichester : Wiley, c1982. — xiii,301p : ill ; 22cm
Previous ed.: published as Simplified design of roof trusses for architects and builders. 1967. — Text on lining papers. — Includes index
ISBN 0-471-07722-4 : £21.75
B82-35305

690′.18 — Agricultural industries. Farms. Fences. Construction — *Manuals*
Hart, Edward. Hedge laying and fencing : the countryman's art explained / by Edward Hart. — Wellingborough : Thorsons, 1981. — 128p : ill ; 22cm
Bibliography: p126. — Includes index
ISBN 0-7225-0701-1 (cased) : Unpriced : CIP rev.
ISBN 0-7225-0700-3 (pbk) : £2.95
Primary classification 631.2′7
B81-30487

690′.184 — Patios. Construction — *Amateurs' manuals*
Johns, Pat. Success with making your own patio / Pat Johns. — London : Grower Books, 1981. — 41p ; 22cm. — (Grower garden guide ; no.5)
ISBN 0-901361-63-1 (pbk) : £0.95
B82-11686

690′.2 — Buildings. Construction. Inspection — *Manuals*
Liebing, Ralph W.. Systematic construction inspection / Ralph W. Liebing. — New York ; Chichester : Wiley, c1982. — xiii,119p : ill,1plan,forms ; 29cm
Includes index
ISBN 0-471-08065-9 : £18.00
B82-13360

690′.24 — Great Britain. Buildings. Conversion, extension & improvement
Catt, Richard. The conversion, improvement and extension of buildings / by Richard Catt and Sarah Catt. — London : Estates Gazette, 1981. — xii,344p : ill,plans ; 31cm
Includes index
£18.00
B82-10182

690′.24 — Great Britain. Buildings. Defects. Causes
Ransom, W. H.. Building failures : diagnosis and avoidance / W.H. Ransom. — London : Spon, 1981. — viii,174p : ill ; 23cm
Bibliography: p163-166. — Includes index
ISBN 0-419-11750-4 (cased) : Unpriced : CIP rev.
ISBN 0-419-11760-1 (pbk) : £4.50
B81-18154

Symposium on structural failures in buildings : Wednesday, 30 April 1980, Café Royal, London W1. — London (11 Upper Belgrave St., SW1X 8BH) : Institution of Structural Engineers, 1980. — 78p : ill ; 30cm
£12.00 (£8.00 to members of the Institution) (pbk)
B82-34145

690′.24 — Great Britain. Buildings. Maintenance. Standard costs — *Lists* — *Serials*
BMCIS building maintenance price book. — 1982/83. — Kingston upon Thames : Building Maintenance Cost Information Service, Sept.1982. — [170]p
ISBN 0-906182-06-9 (spiral) : £10.00 : CIP entry
ISSN 0261-2933
B82-21571

BMCIS news / Building Maintenance Cost Information Service. — No.1 (Mar. 1977)-. — Kingston-upon-Thames (85 Clarence St., Kingston-upon-Thames, Surrey KT1 1RB) : The Service, 1977-. — v. : ill ; 30cm
Monthly. — Description based on: No.43 (Mar. 1982)
ISSN 0263-2020 = BMCIS news : Unpriced
B82-36693

690′.24 — United States. Buildings. Conversion
New life for old buildings / edited by Mildred F. Schmertz. — New York ; London : McGraw-Hill, c1982. — vii,189p : ill(some col.),plans ; 32cm. — (An Architectural record book)
Includes index
ISBN 0-07-002364-6 : £24.95
B82-28050

690′.26 — Buildings. Demolition

Topliss, Colin. Demolition. — London : Longman, July 1982. — 1v.
ISBN 0-582-41110-6 : £20.00 : CIP entry
B82-16242

690′.54′0289 — Great Britain. Disused industrial buildings. Conversion — *Case studies*

Recycling industrial buildings / by URBED (Urban and Economic Development) Ltd. ; commissioned and funded by the Social Science Research Council. — Edinburgh : Capital Planning Information, 1981. — 54p : ill ; 30cm. — (Planning reviews ; no.1)
Bibliography: p53-54
ISBN 0-906011-11-6 (pbk) : £3.00 : CIP rev.
B81-25121

690′.557 — Scotland. Strathclyde Region. Glasgow. Hospitals: Royal Hospital for Sick Children *(Glasgow)*. **Construction. Defects** — *Inquiry reports*

Great Britain. *Parliament. House of Commons. Committee of Public Accounts*. Twenty-fifth report from the Committee of Public Accounts : together with the proceedings of the committee, the minutes of evidence and appendices : session 1979-80 : Department of Health & Social Security, Scottish Home and Health Department, Welsh Office : cost control of pharmaceutical prescribing in the National Health Service, banking arrangements in the National Health Service, the Royal Hospital for Sick Children, Glasgow. — London : H.M.S.O., [1980]. — xviii,61p ; 25cm. — ([HC] ; 764)
ISBN 0-10-027649-0 (pbk) : £4.90
Primary classification 338.4′33621′0941
B82-09501

690′.65′0942398 — Avon. Bath. Parish churches: All Saints Church *(Weston, Bath)*. **Rebuilding,** *1832*

Messer, Michael. A new church : the story of the rebuilding of the parish church of All Saints, Weston, Bath in 1832 / by Michael Messer. — Bath (All Saints Church, Weston, Bath, Avon) : The Rector and churchwardens, 1982. — 15p : ill ; 22cm
Unpriced (unbound) B82-35820

690′.66 — Cathedrals. Gothic style. Construction — *For children*

Macaulay, David. Cathedral : the story of its construction / David Macaulay. — London : Collins, 1976, c1973 (1982 [printing]). — 77p : ill,1plan ; 31cm
Previous ed.: Boston, Mass. : Houghton, 1973 ; London : Collins, 1974
ISBN 0-00-192142-8 (pbk) : £3.50 B82-15442

690′.8 — Residences. Defects. Causes

Structural failure in residential buildings. — London : Granada

Vol.3: Basements and adjoining land drainage / Erich Schild ... [et al.] ; illustrations by Volker Schnapauff ; [translated from the German by TST Translations]. — 1980. — 154p : ill ; 31cm
Translation of: Schwachstellen Bd.3. — Bibliography: p151. — Includes index
ISBN 0-246-11170-4 : £15.00 : CIP rev.
B79-34965

690′.8 — United States. Underground houses. Construction — *Manuals*

Oehler, Mike. The 50 [dollar] and up underground house book / by Mike Oehler ; illustrations by Chris Royer. — 4th ed. — New York ; London : Mole Publishing, c1981. — 115p,[1]leaf of plates : ill,1form,plans,ports ; 28cm
Previous ed.: 1978?
ISBN 0-442-27311-8 (pbk) : £7.60 B82-23707

690′.8′0973 — United States. Residences. Construction — *Amateurs′ manuals*

McLaughlin, Jack. The housebuilding experience / Jack McLaughlin. — New York ; London : Van Nostrand Reinhold, c1981. — xv,238p : ill,plans ; 24cm
Bibliography: p221-228. — Includes index
ISBN 0-442-25398-2 : £12.70 B82-08237

690′.83 — Houses. Construction — *Amateurs′ manuals*

Van Orman, Halsey. Illustrated handbook of home construction / Halsey Van Orman. — New York ; London : Van Nostrand Reinhold, c1982. — vii,327p : ill,forms,plans ; 29cm
Bibliography: p321. — Includes index
ISBN 0-442-25887-9 (cased) : £18.65
ISBN 0-442-25886-0 (pbk) : £12.70
B82-28148

690′.83 — Houses. Construction — *For children*

Althea. Building a house / by Althea ; illustrated by Colin King. — Over : Dinosaur, c1981. — [24]p : col.ill ; 16x19cm. — (Dinosaur′s Althea books)
ISBN 0-85122-311-7 (cased) : £2.25
ISBN 0-85122-077-0 (pbk) : Unpriced
B82-08272

690′.83 — Houses. Strip foundations — *Manuals*

Barnbrook, G.. Strip foundations for houses / G. Barnbrook. — Slough : Cement and Concrete Association, 1980. — 7p : col.ill ; 30cm. — (Construction guide, ISSN 0143-6880) (Cement and Concrete Association publication ; 48.047)
ISBN 0-7210-1212-4 (unbound) : Unpriced
B82-31850

690′.83′09417 — Ireland *(Republic)*. **Private houses. Construction,** *1976-1980*

Duffy, T. P.. Private housebuilding in Ireland, 1976-1980 / T.P. Duffy. — Dublin : An Foras Forbartha, 1980. — v,60p : ill ; 30cm
ISBN 0-906120-43-8 (pbk) : £3.00 B82-23271

690′.872 — England. Self-catering vacation accommodation. Conversion from farm buildings — *Manuals* — *For farmers*

Bunkhouse barns : a new use for redundant farm buildings : a guide for conversion and management. — Cheltenham : Countryside Commission, c1980. — iv,56p : ill,2maps,plans ; 30cm. — (CCP ; 131)
ISBN 0-86170-016-3 (pbk) : £2.75 B82-13860

691 — BUILDING MATERIALS

691 — Great Britain. Building components. Failure

Addleson, Lyall. Building failures : a guide to diagnosis, remedy and prevention / Lyall Addleson. — London, Architectural Press, 1982. — 117p : ill ; 30cm
ISBN 0-85139-768-9 (pbk) : £12.95
B82-37420

691′.1 — Building materials: Timber. Damage by wood boring insects

Hickin, Norman E.. The woodworm problem / Norman E. Hickin. — 3rd (rev.) ed. — East Grinstead : Rentokil, 1981. — 123p : ill(some col.) ; 24cm. — (The Rentokil library)
Previous ed.: London : Hutchinson, 1972. — Bibliography: p119. — Includes index
ISBN 0-906564-03-4 : £6.50 B82-21936

691′.3 — Building components: Precast concrete blocks. Design

Fisher, B. H.. Guide to the structural design of precast concrete blockwork : in accordance with B55628: Part 1: 1978 / B.H. Fisher. — Slough : Cement and Concrete Association on behalf of the Aggregate Concrete Block Association and the Autoclaved Aerated Concrete Products Association, 1981. — 23p : ill,plans ; 30cm
ISBN 0-7210-1252-3 (pbk) : £2.50 B82-27484

691′.3 — Building materials: Precast concrete

Levitt, M.. Precast concrete : materials, manufacture, properties usage / M. Levitt. — London : Applied Science Publishers, c1982. — ix,233p : ill ; 24cm
Includes index
ISBN 0-85334-994-0 : £24.00 : CIP rev.
B81-34573

692 — BUILDINGS. PLANS, SPECIFICATIONS, ESTIMATING, CONTRACTS

692 — Great Britain. Buildings. Structural conditions. Surveying — *Manuals*

Appraisal of existing structures. — London (11 Upper Belgrave St., SW1X 8BH) : Institution of Structural Engineers, 1980. — 60p : ill ; 30cm
£12.00 (£8.00 to members of the Institution) (pbk) B82-34142

692′.1 — United States. Residences. Blueprints. Draftsmanship & interpretation — *For carpentry*

McDonnell, Leo P.. Blueprint reading and sketching for carpenters : residential. — 3rd ed. / Leo McDonnell, John E. Ball. — New York ; London : Van Nostrand Reinhold, c1981. — vii,151p : ill,plans ; 27cm
Previous ed.: Albany, N.Y. : Delmar Publishers, 1975. — Seven plans on 2 sheets (88x118cm folded to 23x16cm) in pocket. — Includes index
ISBN 0-442-26265-5 : £10.15 B82-14310

692.049 — Road transport engineering. Measurement. Applications of sensors — *Conference proceedings*

Sensors in highway and civil engineering : proceedings of the conference organized by the Institution of Civil Engineers, London, 5 February 1981. — London : Thomas Telford, 1981. — 185p : ill ; 22cm
ISBN 0-7277-0109-6 : £10.00 B82-01690

692′.1′0221 — Buildings. Construction. Technical drawings. Draftsmanship

Greening, J.. Construction drawing 1 checkbook / J. Greening, A. Bowers. — London : Butterworth Scientific, 1982. — vi,122p : ill,plans ; 20cm. — (Butterworths technical and scientific checkbooks)
Bibliography: p120. — Includes index
ISBN 0-408-00672-2 (cased) : Unpriced : CIP rev.
ISBN 0-408-00646-3 (pbk) : Unpriced
B82-04030

692′.2′09421 — London. Buildings. Architectural design. Detail drawings — *Illustrations*

GLC detailing for building construction : a designers′ manual of over 350 standard details / [produced in the Department of Architecture and Civic Design, Greater London Council]. — London : Architectural Press, c1980. — 416p : ill,plans ; 22x30cm
ISBN 0-85139-233-4 (cased) : £19.95
ISBN 0-85139-234-2 (pbk) : £12.95
B82-35013

692′.3 — Great Britain. Buildings. Construction. Standard method of measurement

SMM6 practice handbooks. — London : Godwin
Section F: Concrete work. — Jan.1983. — [160]p
ISBN 0-7114-5674-7 : £9.50 : CIP entry
B82-32557

692′.5 — Buildings. Construction. Bills of quantities. Preambles — *Manuals*

GLC preambles to bills of quantities. — 9th ed. / Greater London Council, Department of Architecture and Civic Design. — London : Architectural Press, 1980. — viii,438p : forms ; 31cm
Previous ed.: London : GLC, 1977
ISBN 0-85139-542-2 : £45.00 B82-32203

692′.5 — Buildings. Construction. Costs — *Conference proceedings*

Building Cost Research Conference *(1982 : Portsmouth Polytechnic)*. Building cost techniques : new directions. — London : Spon, Oct.1982. — [488]p
ISBN 0-419-12940-5 : £20.00 : CIP entry
B82-25925

692′.5 — Buildings. Construction. Estimating

Ashworth, A. A.. Accuracy in estimating. — Ascot : Chartered Institute of Building, Oct.1982. — [25]p. — (Occasional paper / Chartered Institute of Building, ISSN 0306-6878 ; 27)
ISBN 0-906600-57-x (pbk) : £2.00 : CIP entry
B82-32888

692'.5 — Buildings. Construction. Estimating — *Manuals*

Atton, W.. Estimating applied to building / W. Atton. — 5th ed. in accordance with the Standard method of measurement of building works, 6th ed. (August 1978). — London : Godwin, 1982. — 297p ; 23cm
Previous ed.: 1979. — Includes index
ISBN 0-7114-5751-4 : Unpriced : CIP rev.
B82-00299

692'.5 — Buildings. Quantity surveying

Goodacre, Peter. Worked examples in quantity surveying measurement. — London : Chapman and Hall, Nov.1982. — [100]p
ISBN 0-419-12340-7 (spiral) : £9.50 : CIP entry
B82-28253

692'.5 — Great Britain. Buildings. Construction. Standard costs — *Lists* **—** *Serials*

Spon's architects' and builders' price book. — 107th ed. (1982). — London : Spon, Nov.1981. — [560]p
ISBN 0-419-12460-8 : £12.00 : CIP entry
ISSN 0306-3046
B81-31164

Spon's architects' and builders' price book. — 108th ed. (1983). — London : Spon, Dec.1982. — [704]p
ISBN 0-419-12870-0 : £15.00 : CIP entry
ISSN 0306-3046
B82-29790

692'.5'0941 — Great Britain. Construction. Tendering

Tenders and contracts for building. — 2nd ed. — London : Granada, May 1982. — [112]p
Previous ed. published as: Which builder? London : Crosby Lockwood Staples, 1975
ISBN 0-246-11838-5 (pbk) : £5.95 : CIP entry
Also classified at 692'.8'0941
B82-07411

692'.8 — Buildings. Construction. Contracts

Clough, Richard H.. Construction contracting / Richard H. Clough. — 4th ed. — New York ; Chichester : Wiley, c1981. — x,502p : ill,forms ; 26cm
Previous ed.: 1975. — Includes index
ISBN 0-471-08657-6 : £21.50
B82-13621

692'.8 — Buildings. Construction. Contracts. Calculations. Effects of cost variation

Wainwright, W. Howard. Variation and final account procedure. — 4th ed. — London : Hutchinson Education, Jan.1983. — [200]p
Previous ed.: 1979
ISBN 0-09-150091-5 (pbk) : £6.50 : CIP entry
B82-33622

692'.8 — Great Britain. Buildings. Construction. Contracts. Standard conditions, *1834-1980*

Spiers, G. S.. The standard form of contract in times of change, 1834-1980. — Ascot : Chartered Institute of Building, Oct.1982. — 1v.
ISBN 0-906600-58-8 : CIP entry
B82-36163

692'.8 — Great Britain. Buildings. Construction. Contracts. Standard conditions: Joint Contracts Tribunal. Standard form of building contract. 1980 — *Algorithms*

Jones, Glyn P.. A new approach to the [JCT] 1980 standard form of nominated sub-contract / Glyn P. Jones. — London : Construction, 1982. — 215p : ill ; 22x31cm
ISBN 0-86095-001-8 : £30.00 : CIP rev.
B82-04832

692'.8 — Great Britain. Buildings. Construction. Contracts. Standard conditions: Joint Contracts Tribunal. Standard form of building contract. 1980 — *Commentaries*

Joint Contracts Tribunal. Practice note 20 : deciding on the appropriate form of JCT main contract / Joint Contracts Tribunal for the Standard form of building contract. — London : RIBA Publications, c1982. — 6p ; 30cm
Cover title. — At head of title: Standard form of building contract, 1980 edition
Unpriced (pbk)
B82-33406

Joint Contracts Tribunal. Practice notes 9-13 : sub-contracting under the JCT standard form 1980 edition / Joint Contracts Tribunal for the Standard form of building contract. — London : RIBA Publications, c1982. — 16p ; 30cm
Cover title. — At head of title: Standard form of building contract 1980 edition
Unpriced (pbk)
B82-33404

Joint Contracts Tribunal. Practice notes 14-19 / Joint Contracts Tribunal for the Standard form of building contract. — London : RIBA Publications, c1982. — 32p : forms ; 30cm
Cover title. — At head of title: Standard form of building contract 1980 edition
Unpriced (pbk)
B82-33405

692'.8 — Great Britain. Buildings. Construction. Contracts. Standard conditions: Joint Contracts Tribunal. Standard form of building contract. 1980 — *Texts with commentaries*

Dickason, I. J.. JCT80 and the builder. — Ascot : Chartered Institute of Building, June 1982. — [204]p
ISBN 0-906600-56-1 (pbk) : £8.50 : CIP entry
B82-19285

Fellows, R. F.. 1980 JCT standard form of building contract : a commentary for students and practitioners / R.F. Fellows. — London : Macmillan, 1981. — x,165p : ill ; 24cm
Bibliography: p165
ISBN 0-333-32110-3 (pbk) : Unpriced
B82-10193

Parris, John. The standard form of building contract. — London : Granada, Sept.1982. — [208]p
ISBN 0-246-11633-1 : £15.00 : CIP entry
B82-18854

692'.8'0941 — Great Britain. Buildings. Construction. Contracts — *Manuals*

Audas, J. M.. A builder's guide to the agreement for minor building works - January 1980 edition / by J.M. Audas. — Ascot : Chartered Institute of Building, 1981. — 22p ; 30cm
ISBN 0-906600-32-4 (pbk) : Unpriced : CIP rev.
B81-12363

Marsh, P. D. V.. Contracting for engineering and construction projects / P.D.V. Marsh. — 2nd ed. — Aldershot : Gower in association with the Institute of Purchasing and Supply, 1981. — viii,257p : ill ; 23cm
Previous ed.: 1969. — Includes index
ISBN 0-566-02232-x : Unpriced : CIP rev.
Primary classification 624
B81-14815

692'.8'0941 — Great Britain. Buildings. Construction. Contractual arrangements

Cooke, B.. Contract planning and contractual procedures / B. Cooke. — London : Macmillan, 1981. — x,215p : ill,forms ; 25cm. — (Macmillan building and surveying series)
ISBN 0-333-30720-8 : Unpriced
B82-08906

692'.8'0941 — Great Britain. Construction. Contractual arrangements

Tenders and contracts for building. — 2nd ed. — London : Granada, May 1982. — [112]p
Previous ed. published as: Which builder? London : Crosby Lockwood Staples, 1975
ISBN 0-246-11838-5 (pbk) : £5.95 : CIP entry
Primary classification 692'.5'0941
B82-07411

693 — BUILDINGS. CONSTRUCTION IN SPECIAL MATERIALS AND FOR SPECIAL PURPOSES

693 — Lightweight buildings. Construction

Smith, Ronald C.. Principles and practices of light construction / Ronald C. Smith. — 3rd ed. — Englewood Cliffs ; London : Prentice-Hall, c1980. — xi,420p : ill,plans ; 29cm
Previous ed.: 1970. — Includes index
ISBN 0-13-701979-3 : £18.70
B82-13698

693'.1'0924 — South-west England. Stone masonry. Beazer, Cyril H. G. — *Biographies*

Beazer, Cyril H. G.. Random reflections of a West Country master craftsman / Cyril H.G. Beazer. — Bath : C.H.G. Beazer, 1981. — 158p,xxiiip of plates : ill(some col.),ports ; 25cm
Includes index
ISBN 0-9507709-0-6 : Unpriced
B82-04110

693'.21 — Brickwork — *Amateurs' manuals*

Working with bricks, concrete and stone. — Reprinted with amendments. — London : Readers Digest Association, 1981, c1977. — 48p : ill(some col.) ; 27cm. — (Reader's Digest basic guide)
Previous ed.: 1976. — 'Text and illustrations in this book are taken from The Reader's Digest complete do-it-yourself manual', 1975
ISBN 0-276-00155-9 (pbk) : £0.95
B82-04169

693'.4 — Building components: Concrete blocks. Laying — *For West African students*

Obande, M. O.. Blocklaying and concreting / M.O. Obande. — Ikeja ; Harlow : Longman, 1981. — x,115p : ill ; 19x25cm. — (Longman industrial craft series)
ISBN 0-582-65800-4 (pbk) : Unpriced
B82-31769

693'.5 — Great Britain. Cow cubicles. Construction materials: Concrete — *Manuals*

Barnes, Maurice M.. Concrete in cow cubicles / Maurice M. Barnes. — Slough : Cement and Concrete Association, 1982. — [6]p : ill,1map ; 30cm. — (Farm note, ISSN 0307-0352 ; 12)
ISBN 0-7210-1263-9 (unbound) : Unpriced
B82-35981

693'.52 — Steel & concrete composite floors with profiled steel sheeting. Design & construction — *Standards*

European Convention for Constructional Steelwork. *Committee 11*. European recommendations for the design of composite floors with profiled steel sheet / European Convention for Constructional Steelwork Committee 11. — Repr. with corrections to calculations. — Croydon : Constrado, 1976 (1981 [printing]). — v,77leaves : ill ; 30cm
Originally published: 1974?
Unpriced (pbk)
B82-17740

693'.54 — Buildings. Reinforced concrete structural components. Design

Cowan, Henry J.. Design of reinforced concrete structures / Henry J. Cowan. — Englewood Cliffs ; London : Prentice-Hall, c1982. — xiv,286p : ill,1map ; 24cm
Includes index
ISBN 0-13-201376-2 : £17.95
B82-23416

693'.7 — Building components: Cold-formed profiled metal sheets. Testing — *Standards*

European Convention for Constructional Steelwork. *Committee 17*. European recommendations for the testing of profiled metal sheets / Committee 17 - Cold-formed Thin-Walled Sheet Steel in Building, European Convention for Constructional Steelwork. — Croydon : Constrado, 1977. — 44p in various pagings : ill ; 30cm. — (ECCS- XVII-77-2E ; 20)
Unpriced (pbk)
B82-17743

693'.71 — Building components: Cold-formed profiled steel sheeting. Fastenings. Testing — *Standards*

European Convention for Constructional Steelwork. *Committee 17*. European recommendations for the testing of connections in profiled sheeting and other light gauge steel components / Committee 17 - Cold-formed Thin-walled Sheet Steel in Building, European Convention for Constructional Steelwork. — Croydon : Constrado, 1978. — 62p in various pagings : ill ; 30cm. — (ECCS- XVII-77-3E ; 21)
Unpriced (pbk)
B82-17744

693'.71 — Building components: Thin-walled steel claddings & thin-walled steel deckings. Stressed skin diaphragms. Design — *Standards*

European Convention for Constructional Steelwork. *Committee 17.* European recommendations for the stressed skin design of steel structures / Committee 17 - Cold-formed Thin-Walled Sheet Steel in Building, European Convention for Constructional Steelwork. — Croydon : Constrado, 1977 (1980 [printing]). — 196p in various pagings : ill ; 30cm. — (ECCS- XVII-77-IE ; 19)
Unpriced (pbk) B82-17741

693'.71 — Buildings. Steel beams. Webs. Holes. Stresses & strain — *Technical data*

Holes in beam webs : allowable stress design. — Croydon : Constrado, c1977. — 9p : ill ; 30cm
Cover title. — Text on inside covers. — Bibliography: p9
Unpriced (pbk) B82-17736

693'.71 — Buildings. Steel frames. Design

Steel designers' manual. — 4th rev. ed. — London : Granada, Feb.1983. — [1120]p
Previous ed.: 1972
ISBN 0-246-12046-0 (pbk) : £12.50 : CIP entry
B82-37659

693'.71 — Buildings. Steel frames. Plastic design

Plastic design of frames. — Cambridge : Cambridge University Press, 1969 (1980 [printing])
1: Fundamentals / Lord Baker and Jacques Heyman. — vii,227p : ill ; 24cm
Includes index
ISBN 0-521-07517-3 (cased) : Unpriced
ISBN 0-521-29778-8 (pbk) : £7.50 B82-36228

693'.71 — Commercial buildings & industrial buildings. Steel frames. Trusses & columns — *Technical data*

Lazenby, David W.. Design of a stanchion and truss frame / D.W. Lazenby. — Croydon : Constrado, c1981. — 32p : ill ; 30cm
New version of: Design of a stanchion and truss frame / Lewis E. Kent and David W. Lazenby. British Constructional Steelwork Association, 1965
Unpriced (pbk) B82-17737

693'.71 — Great Britain. Buildings. Steel beam-column connections. Construction — *Manuals*

Pask, John W.. Manual on connections : for beam and column construction : conforming with the requirements of BS449 : Part 2 : 1969 / by John W. Pask. — London : British Constructional Steelwork Association, 1982. — 123p : ill ; 30cm
ISBN 0-85073-010-4 (pbk) : Unpriced : CIP rev. B82-00169

693'.71 — Industrial workshops with gantry cranes. Steel structural components — *Technical data*

Bates, William. Workshop with EOT crane / W. Bates. — Croydon : Constrado, c1977. — 36p : ill,plans ; 30cm. — (Design of structural steelwork)
Cover title
Unpriced (pbk) B82-17738

693'.71 — Steel-framed buildings. Steel & concrete composite beams — *Technical data*

Noble, P. W.. Design tables for composite steel and concrete beams for buildings / P.W. Noble and L.V. Leech. — Croydon : Constrado, [197-]. — 68p : ill ; 30cm
New version of: Composite construction for steel framed buildings. Pt.1 / W. Basil Scott. British Constructional Steelwork Association, 1965
Unpriced (pbk) B82-17734

693.8'2 — Fire-resistant buildings. Design

Malhotra, H. L.. Design of fire-resisting structures / H.L. Malhotra. — [Glasgow] : Surrey University Press, 1982. — xiii,226p : ill ; 24cm
Includes index
ISBN 0-903384-28-0 : £18.95 : CIP rev.
B81-36040

693.8'32 — Great Britain. Residences. Thermal insulation — *Proposals*

Improving insulation in existing dwellings : a discussion paper. — London : Electricity Consumers' Council : National Consumer Council, 1981. — 75p ; 30cm
Unpriced (spiral) B82-05831

693.8'32 — Residences. Thermal insulation — *Amateurs' manuals*

Colesby, J. A.. Keeping warm for half the cost / John Colesby and Phil Townsend. — 2nd ed., revised and updated by Bob Lowe, Colin Moorcraft. — Dorchester, Dorset : Prism, 1981. — 122p : ill,1map ; 22cm
Previous ed.: Mountsorrel : J. Colesby, 1976
ISBN 0-907061-09-5 (cased) : Unpriced
ISBN 0-907061-13-3 (pbk) : Unpriced
B82-19048

Johnson, W. H. (William Harold), *1913-.* Domestic heating and insulation / W.H. Johnson. — London : Pelham, 1982. — 135p : ill ; 21cm. — (Tricks of the trade)
Includes index
ISBN 0-7207-1387-0 : £5.50 : CIP rev.
Primary classification 697 B82-00381

693.8'32 — Residences. Thermal insulation — *Practical information*

Campbell, Peter. Home insulation. — London : Newnes Technical Books, Aug.1982. — [128]p. — (Questions & answers)
ISBN 0-408-01142-4 (pbk) : £1.95 : CIP entry
B82-15779

693.8'32'0973 — United States. Residences. Thermal insulation — *Amateurs' manuals*

Knight, Paul A.. The Energy Resources Center illustrated guide to home retrofitting for energy savings / Paul A. Knight ; John M. Porterfield, technical consultant ; Paul S. Galen, technical and editorial assistance. — Washington ; London : Hemisphere, c1981. — xiii,364p : ill ; 29cm
Includes index
ISBN 0-07-019490-4 : £11.50 B82-16372

693.8'34 — Buildings. Noise. Control measures

Noise and the design of buildings and services / edited by Derek J. Croome. — London : Construction, 1982. — 165p : ill,2maps ; 31cm
Conference papers. — Includes index
ISBN 0-86095-877-9 : £19.50 : CIP rev.
B82-10885

693'.97 — United States. Houses. Industrial construction

Lytle, R. J.. Component & modular techniques : a builder's handbook. — 2nd ed. / R.J. Lytle, Robert C. Reschke. — New York ; London : McGraw-Hill, c1982. — 322p : ill,plan ; 29cm
Previous ed.: published as Industrialized builders handbook. Farmington, Mich. : Structures Publishing Co., 1971. — Includes index
ISBN 0-07-039274-9 : £18.95 B82-07870

693'.98 — Air-supported structures

Symposium on air-supported structures : the state of the art : Wednesday, 4 June 1980, Café Royal, London W1. — London (11 Upper Belgrave St., SW1X 8BH) : Institution of Structural Engineers, 1980. — 207p : ill,2charts,ports ; 30cm
£12.00 (pbk) B82-34143

694 — CARPENTRY, JOINERY

694 — Carpentry & joinery

Mitchell, George. Carpentry and joinery. — London : Cassell, Aug.1982. — [256]p. — (Cassell's technical craft series)
ISBN 0-304-30951-6 (pbk) : £6.50 : CIP entry
B82-25526

694 — Carpentry & joinery — *Manuals*

Porter, Brian, *1938-.* Carpentry and joinery / Brian Porter. — London : Edward Arnold, 1982
Includes index
Vol.1. — viii,277p : ill ; 22cm
ISBN 0-7131-3456-9 (pbk) : £4.95 : CIP rev.
B82-06921

694'.076 — Carpentry & joinery — *Questions & answers*

Brett, Peter. Carpentry and joinery for building craft students multiple choice assessment. — London : Hutchinson, Sept.1982. — [80]p
ISBN 0-09-149441-9 (pbk) : £3.95 : CIP entry
B82-19153

694'.6 — Joinery

Foad, E. V.. Purpose-made joinery / E.V. Foad. — New York ; London : Van Nostrand, 1982. — xii,204p : ill ; 25cm. — (VNR crafts series)
Includes index
ISBN 0-442-30470-6 (cased) : £11.50
ISBN 0-442-30472-2 (pbk) : £5.50 B82-16325

695 — ROOFING, AUXILIARY STRUCTURES

695 — Flat roofs. Design & construction — *Manuals*

Flat roofs technical guide / Directorate of Architectural Services. — 2nd ed. — Croydon : Department of the Environment Property Services Agency, 1981. — 94p : ill ; 30cm
Cover title. — Previous ed.: published in 4v. 1979. — Text on inside cover. — Includes index
ISBN 0-86177-079-x (pbk) : £7.00 B82-35521

695 — Great Britain. Cattle housing. Spaced steel sheet roofs — *Case studies*

Spaced steel sheet roofing for farm buildings. — Croydon : Constrado, c1978. — 27p : ill(some col.),plans ; 30cm
Cover title. — Bibliography: p27
Unpriced (pbk) B82-17735

695 — Steel folded plate roofs. Design & construction

Davies, J. M. (John Michael). Light gauge steel folded plate roofs / J.M. Davies. — Croydon : Constrado, c1978. — 12p : ill ; 30cm
Cover title
Unpriced (pbk) B82-17742

696 — PLUMBING, PIPE FITTING, HOT WATER SUPPLY

696 — Buildings. Energy. Conservation

Coad, William J.. Energy engineering and management for building systems / William J. Coad. — New York ; London : Van Nostrand Reinhold, c1982. — xii,275p : ill ; 26cm
Includes index
ISBN 0-442-25467-9 : £23.40 B82-18929

Energy conservation and thermal insulation / edited by R. Derricott, S.S. Chissick. — Chichester : Wiley, c1981. — xxi,785p : ill ; 24cm. — (Properties of materials safety and environmental factors)
Includes bibliographies and index
ISBN 0-471-27930-7 : £37.50 B82-04431

Patrick, Dale R.. Energy management and conservation / Dale R. Patrick, Stephen W. Fardo. — Englewood Cliffs ; London : Prentice-Hall, c1982. — x,229p : ill ; 29cm
Includes index
ISBN 0-13-277657-x : £18.70 B82-34460

696 — Buildings. Energy. Conservation. Applications of digital computer systems

Abba Consultants. Computer based energy management in buildings. — London : Pitman, June 1982. — [600]p
ISBN 0-273-08580-8 : £35.00 : CIP entry
B82-16466

696 — Buildings. Energy. Conservation — *Conference proceedings*

Energy conservation in heating, cooling and ventilating buildings : heat and mass transfer techniques and alternatives / edited by C.J. Hoogendoorn and N.H. Afgan. — Washington ; London : Hemisphere, c1978. — 2v.(xii,901p) : ill ; 25cm. — (Series in thermal and fluids engineering) (A Publication of the International Centre for Heat and Mass Transfer Belgrade)
Conference papers. — Includes index
ISBN 0-89116-094-9 : £52.35
ISBN 0-89116-095-7 (v.2) : Unpriced
B82-39696

696 — Buildings. Energy. Conservation — *Conference proceedings* *continuation*

Experience of energy conservation in buildings / [based on the conference of the same title organised in March 1980 by the Construction Industry Conference Centre Limited in conjunction with the Chartered Institution of Building Services et al.] ; edited by A.F.C. Sherratt. — London : Construction Press, 1981. — 180p : ill ; 31cm
Conference papers. — Includes index
ISBN 0-86095-875-2 : £20.00 : CIP rev.
B81-13521

696 — Buildings. Energy. Conservation — *For architecture*

Gage, Michael. Design and detailing for energy conservation. — London : Architectural Press, June 1982. — [256]p
ISBN 0-85139-169-9 : £50.00 : CIP entry
B82-09865

696 — Buildings. Energy resources. Conservation — *For architectural design*

The **Architecture** of energy / edited by Dean Hawkes and Janet Owers. — Harlow : Construction Press, 1981 [i.e.1982]. — 254p : ill,plans ; 31cm
Conference papers. — At head of title: The Martin Centre for Architectural and Urban Studies, University of Cambridge Department of Architecture. — Includes bibliographies
ISBN 0-86095-897-3 : £16.00 : CIP rev.
B81-37000

696 — Buildings. Engineering services — *For technicians*

Hall, F.. Building services and equipment / F. Hall. — London : Longman. — (Longman technician series. Construction and Civil engineering)
Vol.3. — [1980]. — 141p : ill ; 28cm
Includes index
ISBN 0-582-41179-3 (pbk) : £7.50 : CIP rev.
B79-23954

696 — Buildings. Engineering services. Installation. Supervision

Watts, John W.. The supervision of installation : a guide to the installation of mechanical and electrical plant and services / John W. Watts. — London : Batsford Academic and Educational, 1982. — xiv,162p : ill ; 25cm
Bibliography: p156. — Includes index
ISBN 0-7134-3502-x : £12.50 : CIP rev.
B82-20044

696 — Buildings. Engineering services — *Questions & answers — For technicians*

Hall, F.. Building services and equipment 5 checkbook / F. Hall. — London : Butterworths, 1981. — viii,152p : ill ; 20cm. — (Butterworths technical and scientific checkbooks)
Includes index
ISBN 0-408-00651-x (cased) : Unpriced : CIP rev.
ISBN 0-408-00614-5 (pbk) : Unpriced
B81-16925

696 — Buildings. Engineering services, *to 1981*

Billington, Neville S.. Building services engineering : a review of its development / by Neville S. Billington and Brian M. Roberts. — Oxford : Pergamon, 1982. — xv,537p : ill,plans ; 26cm. — (International series on building environmental engineering ; v.1) (Pergamon international library)
Includes bibliographies and index
ISBN 0-08-026741-6 (cased) : Unpriced : CIP rev.
ISBN 0-08-026742-4 (pbk) : £10.00
B81-20619

696 — Buildings. Use of solar energy — *Conference proceedings*

Solar energy in public buildings : conference organised by the UK section of the International Solar Energy Society (UK-ISES) at the Geological Society, Burlington House, Piccadilly, London, W1, UK on Thursday April 29 1981 / edited by Leslie F. Jesch. — London : UK-ISES, 1982. — 135p : ill,1map ; 30cm. — (UK-ISES conference proceedings, ISSN 0306-7874 ; C29)
ISBN 0-904963-30-6 (pbk) : Unpriced
B82-34634

696 — Great Britain. Agricultural industries. Farms. Energy supply systems, *to 1980*

Weller, John B.. History of the farmstead : the development of energy sources / John Weller. — London : Faber, 1982. — 248p : ill,facsims,plans ; 23cm
Bibliography: p221-228. — Includes index
ISBN 0-571-11804-6 (cased) : £9.95 : CIP rev.
ISBN 0-571-11805-4 (pbk) : Unpriced
B82-10755

696′.1 — Buildings. Plumbing. Design

Nielsen, Louis S.. Standard plumbing engineering design / Louis S. Nielsen. — 2nd ed. — New York ; London : McGraw-Hill, c1982. — xiv,418p : ill ; 24cm
Previous ed.: 1963. — Includes index
ISBN 0-07-046541-x : £19.25 B82-02332

696′.1 — Residences. Plumbing — *Amateurs′ manuals*

Hall, Ernest. The David & Charles manual of home plumbing / Ernest Hall ; line illustrations by Calvin Brett. — Newton Abbot : David & Charles, c1982. — 207p : ill ; 26cm
Includes index
ISBN 0-7153-8146-6 : £8.95 : CIP rev.
B81-35825

Home plumbing. — Reprinted with amendments. — London : Reader′s Digest Association, 1981, c1975. — 48p : col.ill ; 27cm. — (Reader′s Digest basic guide)
Previous ed.: 1975. — ′Text and illustrations in this book are taken from Reader′s Digest repair manual′, 1972
ISBN 0-276-00089-7 (pbk) : £1.25 B82-04175

696′.1′113 — Buildings. Plumbing. Design. Implications of cold climate

Design of water and wastewater services for cold climate communities. — Oxford : Pergamon, Sept.1981. — [190]p
ISBN 0-08-029079-5 : £20.00 : CIP entry
B81-28486

696′.6 — Buildings. Solar energy hot water supply systems. Design & installation — *Case studies*

Carrie, John. The Iona solar energy project / by John Carrie. — [Edinburgh] ([121 George St., Edinburgh EH2 4YN]) : [Society, Religion and Technology Project], [1979?]. — [12]p,[2]folded leaves of plates : ill ; 30cm
Unpriced (pbk) B82-27882

697 — BUILDINGS. HEATING, VENTILATING, AIR-CONDITIONING

697 — Air conditioning, heating & ventilation equipment. Analysis & design

McQuiston, Faye C.. Heating, ventilating, and air conditioning : analysis and design / Faye C. McQuiston, Jerald D. Parker. — 2nd ed. — New York ; Chichester : Wiley, c1982. — xviii,666p : ill,forms ; 25cm
Previous ed.: 1977. — Text on lining papers. — Charts (7 folded sheets) in pocket. — Includes index
ISBN 0-471-08259-7 : £19.20 B82-13290

697 — Buildings. Air conditioning, heating & ventilation equipment

Porges, F.. Handbook of heating, ventilating and air conditioning / F. Porges. — 8th ed. — London : Butterworths, 1982. — 267p[4]p of plates : ill ; 22cm
Previous ed.: 1976. — Includes index
ISBN 0-408-00519-x : Unpriced : CIP rev.
B81-28202

697 — Buildings. Air conditioning, heating & ventilation equipment. Automatic control systems

Letherman, K. M.. Automatic controls for heating and air conditioning : principles and applications / by K.M. Letherman. — Oxford : Pergamon, 1981. — xiv,235p : ill ; 26cm. — (International series in heating, ventilation and refrigeration ; v.15)
Bibliography: p199-205. — Includes index
ISBN 0-08-023222-1 : £12.50 : CIP rev.
B81-07616

697 — Buildings. Heat transfer

Pratt, A. W.. Heat transmission in buildings / A.W. Pratt. — Chichester : Wiley, c1981. — xi,308p : ill ; 24cm
Includes bibliographies and index
ISBN 0-471-27971-4 : £21.80 : CIP rev.
B81-23753

697 — Buildings. Heating engineering. Mathematics — *Questions & answers*

Hall, F.. Plumbing and heating calculations / F. Hall. — London : Longman, 1982. — 211p : ill ; 22cm
Includes index
ISBN 0-582-41268-4 (pbk) : £4.95 : CIP rev.
Primary classification 697′.001′51 B82-12991

697 — Buildings. Heating, ventilation & air conditioning

Havrella, Raymond A.. Heating, ventilating, and air conditioning fundamentals / Raymond A. Havrella. — New York ; London : McGraw-Hill, c1981. — viii,280p : ill,1maps,plans,forms ; 29cm. — (Contemporary construction series)
Includes index
ISBN 0-07-027281-6 : £11.95 B82-04452

697 — Great Britain. Christian church. Buildings. Heating systems — *For architectural design*

Bordass, William. The role of heating in existing churches / William Bordass. — [Newcastle upon Tyne] : Ecclesiastical Architects′ and Surveyors′ Association, c1981. — 20p : ill ; 30cm. — (EASA papers ; 1)
Cover title. — Bibliography: p19
ISBN 0-907866-00-x (pbk) : £1.00 B82-10824

697 — Great Britain. Heating & air conditioning equipment. Installation. Standard costs — *Serials*

Spon′s mechanical and electrical services price book. — 13th ed. (1982). — London : Spon, Nov.1981. — [500]p
ISBN 0-419-12470-5 : £8.25 : CIP entry
ISSN 0305-4543 B81-31166

Spon′s mechanical and electrical services price book. — 14th ed. (1983). — London : Spon, Dec.1982. — [544]p
ISBN 0-419-12880-8 : £18.75 : CIP entry
ISSN 0305-4543 B82-29791

697 — Ireland *(Republic)*. **Residences. Heating systems. Efficiency**

Fuller, T.. Efficiency and energy conservation potential of domestic heating systems / project supported by the Department of Energy ; T. Fuller, P. Minogue. — Dublin : An Foras Forbartha, 1981. — viii,83p : 1map ; 30cm
ISBN 0-906120-47-0 (pbk) : £3.00 B82-15378

697 — Residences. Heating

Total warmth : the complete guide to winter well-being / Geri Harrington ... [et al.]. — New York : Collier Books ; London : Collier Macmillan, 1981. — xiv,210p : ill ; 28cm
Includes index
ISBN 0-02-548460-5 (cased) : Unpriced
ISBN 0-02-080070-3 (pbk) : Unpriced
Also classified at 612′.01426 B82-28916

697 — Residences. Heating systems. Installation — *Amateurs′ manuals*

Johnson, W. H. (William Harold), *1913-*. Domestic heating and insulation / W.H. Johnson. — London : Pelham, 1982. — 135p : ill ; 21cm. — (Tricks of the trade)
Includes index
ISBN 0-7207-1387-0 : £5.50 : CIP rev.
Also classified at 693.8′32 B82-00381

697′.001′51 — Buildings. Plumbing. Mathematics — *Questions & answers*

Hall, F.. Plumbing and heating calculations / F. Hall. — London : Longman, 1982. — 211p : ill ; 22cm
Includes index
ISBN 0-582-41268-4 (pbk) : £4.95 : CIP rev.
Also classified at 697 B82-12991

697′.00941 — Great Britain. Residences. Heating systems — *Comparative studies*
Olliver, Dick. Domestic heating & insulation 1982 / [by Dick Olliver]. — London : Euromonitor Publications, c1982. — 73p ; 30cm
ISBN 0-903706-78-4 (spiral) : Unpriced
B82-28399

697′.22 — Woodburning stoves
Thorpe, Simon J.. Chimneys and fuel for woodstoves / by Simon J. Thorpe. — 2nd ed. — Newcastle Emlyn (New Rd., Newcastle Emlyn, Dyfed) : Simon Thorpe Limited, 1980. — [20]p : ill,1map ; 21cm
Previous ed.: 1979
£1.00 (pbk) B82-27432

697′.54 — District heating. Use of heat from power stations — *Conference proceedings*
Combined production of electric power and heat : proceedings of a seminar / organized by the Committee on Electric Power of the United Nations Economic Commission for Europe, Hamburg, Federal Republic of Germany, 6-9 November 1978. — Oxford : Published for the United Nations by Pergamon, 1980. — xxii,133p : ill,1map ; 26cm
ISBN 0-08-025677-5 : £13.00 : CIP rev.
B80-12916

697′.54′0681 — District heating. Use of heat from power stations. Cost-effectiveness
District heating combined with electricity generation : a study of some of the factors which influence cost-effectiveness / by J.A. Macadam ... [et al.]. — London : Thames House South, Millbank, SW1P 4QJ : Department of Energy, [1981]. — 214p : ill(some col.),1col.map ; 30cm
Includes bibliographies
Unpriced (spiral) B82-17329

697′.54′0941 — Great Britain. District heating. Use of waste heat from power stations — *Forecasts*
England, Glyn. CHP : from debate to practical progress? / based on an address by Glyn England, Chairman of the Central Electricity Generating Board, at the annual open meeting of the District Heating Association in London on 28 January 1982. — London : Central Electricity Generating Board, 1982. — [12]p : 1ill,1port ; 21cm
Unpriced (pbk) B82-21806

697′.78 — Buildings. Heating & air conditioning. Use of solar energy
Harrell, Joe J.. Solar heating and cooling of buildings / Joe J. Harrell, Jr. — New York ; London : Van Nostrand Reinhold, c1982. — xii,365p : ill,forms,lmaps,plans ; 26cm
Includes bibliographies and index
ISBN 0-442-21658-0 : £19.50 B82-38487

697′.78 — Buildings. Heating & air conditioning. Use of solar energy — *Manuals*
Kreider, Jan F.. Solar heating and cooling : active and passive design / Jan F. Kreider, Frank Kreith. — Washington, [D.C] ; London : Hemisphere, c1982. — xiii,479p : ill,maps ; 25cm
Previous ed.: Washington, D.C. : Scripta ; New York ; London : McGraw-Hill, 1976. — Includes index
ISBN 0-07-035486-3 : £22.95 B82-24551

697′.78 — Buildings. Passive solar energy heating systems — *Conference proceedings*
Second U.K. passive solar conference / organised by the UK Section of the International Solar Energy Society (UK-ISES) at the Royal Institution of British Architects (RIBA) 66 Portland Place, London, W1 on Tuesday, November 10, 1981. — London : UK-ISES, c1981. — 81p : ill,plans ; 30cm. — (UK-ISES conference proceedings, ISSN 0306-7874 ; C27)
Includes bibliographies
ISBN 0-904963-28-4 (pbk) : £8.00 (£4.00 to members of the UK-ISES) B82-09136

697′.78 — Buildings. Solar energy heating systems
Kut, David. Applied solar energy. — 2nd ed. — London : Butterworth, Feb.1983. — [176]p
Previous ed.: London : Architectural Press, 1979
ISBN 0-408-01244-7 : £12.95 : CIP entry
B82-38285

697′.78 — Buildings. Solar energy heating systems — *Conference proceedings*
Modelling & monitoring solar thermal systems : conference (C24) at the Geological Society, London, October 1980. — London : UK Section of the International Solar Energy Society, [1980]. — 104p : ill ; 30cm
Cover title
ISBN 0-904963-22-5 (pbk) : £8.00 B82-39539

697′.78 — Buildings. Solar energy heating systems. Design
Kreider, Jan F.. The solar heating design process : active and passive systems / Jan F. Kreider. — New York ; London : McGraw-Hill, c1982. — viii,456p : ill ; 25cm
Includes index
ISBN 0-07-035478-2 : £20.95 B82-16010

697′.78 — Residences. Solar energy heating systems
Montgomery, Richard H.. The solar decision book of homes : a guide to designed and remodeling for solar heating / Richard H. Montgomery with Walter F. Miles. — New York ; Chichester : Wiley, c1982. — xix,332p : ill,plans ; 29cm
Includes index
ISBN 0-471-08280-5 (cased) : £20.25
ISBN 0-471-87523-6 (pbk) : Unpriced
B82-32731

697′.78 — United States. Residences. Passive solar energy heating systems — *Amateurs′ manuals*
Strickler, Darryl J.. Passive solar retrofit : how to add natural heating and cooling to your home / Darryl J. Strickler. — New York ; London : Van Nostrand Reinhold, c1982. — 173p : ill,charts,maps ; 28cm
Includes index
ISBN 0-442-27720-2 (cased) : Unpriced
ISBN 0-442-27719-9 (pbk) : £16.10
B82-30964

697′.78′02472 — Buildings. Heating. Use of solar energy — *For architectural design*
Johnson, Timothy E. (Timothy Edward), *1939-*. Solar architecture : the direct gain approach / Timothy E. Johnson. — New York ; London : McGraw-Hill, c1981. — v,218p : ill,1map,plans ; 25cm. — (An Energy learning systems book)
Includes index
ISBN 0-07-032598-7 : £16.50 B82-27228

697′.78′0973 — United States. Residences. Solar energy heating systems. Attitudes of households
Warkov, Seymour. Solar diffusion and public incentives / Seymour Warkov, Judith W. Meyer. — [Lexington, Mass.] : Lexington Books ; [Aldershot] : Gower [distributor], 1982. — xii,157p ; 24cm
Bibliography: p147-152. — Includes index
ISBN 0-669-04510-1 : £15.50 B82-35425

697′.8 — Great Britain. Industrial buildings. Chimneys. Height. Calculation
Chimney heights / Department of the Environment, Scottish Development Department, Welsh Office. — 3rd ed. of the 1956 Clean Air Act memorandum. — London : H.M.S.O., 1981. — 20p : ill ; 30cm
Previous ed.: 1967
ISBN 0-11-751556-6 (pbk) : £2.40 B82-36815

697.9′2 — Buildings. Air. Infiltration. Design — *Conference proceedings*
Building design for minimum air infiltration : 2nd AIC conference : (held at Royal Institute of Technology, Stockholm, Sweden 21-23 September 1981) : proceedings. — Bracknell : Air Infiltration Centre, c1982. — iv,215p : ill ; 30cm
Part of the work of the IEA Energy Conservation in Buildings & Community Systems Programme
ISBN 0-946075-01-8 (pbk) : Unpriced
B82-37939

697.9′3′0287 — Air conditioning equipment. Testing — *Manuals*
Gladstone, John, *1917-*. Air conditioning : testing/adjusting/balancing : a field practice manual / John Gladstone. — New York ; London : Van Nostrand Reinhold, c1981. — xi,196p : ill ; 24cm
Previous ed.: published as Air conditioning testing and balancing. 1974. — Text and ill on lining papers. — Bibliography: p161-162. — Includes index
ISBN 0-442-22714-0 : £16.10 B82-07879

698 — BUILDINGS. DECORATING, GLAZING, ETC

698 — Great Britain. Buildings. Decorating. Standard costs — *Lists*
Schedule of rates for decoration work 1973 / Department of the Environment, Property Services Agency. — Consolidated ed. — London : H.M.S.O., 1980. — 44p ; 30cm
Previous ed.: 1978. — ′... incorporating Amendments Nos 1 and 2 dated June 1977 and May 1979 respectively′ — t.p. verso
ISBN 0-11-671052-7 (pbk) : £3.25 B82-18626

698′.1 — Buildings. Decorating. Painting — *Manuals*
Beckly, Albert. Handbook of painting & decorating products. — St. Albans : Granada, Feb.1983. — [240]p
ISBN 0-246-11842-3 (pbk) : £12.50 : CIP entry
B82-37830

698′.9′05 — Floor coverings — *Serials*
Floors & flooring : news journal of the flooring trade. — Vol.1, issue 1 (June 1982)-. — Purley (17 Church Hill, Purley, Surrey CR2 3QP) : Maple Printers, 1982-. — v. : ill,ports ; 43cm
Monthly. — Description based on: Vol.1, issue 2 (July 1982)
ISSN 0263-7693 = Floors & flooring : £12.00 per year B82-32180

700 — ARTS

700 — Arts. Attitudes of Fabian socialists, *1884-1918*
Britain, Ian. Fabianism and culture : a study in British socialism and the arts c.1884-1918 / Ian Britain. — Cambridge : Cambridge University Press, 1982. — xii,344p ; 24cm
Bibliography: p310-324. — Includes index
ISBN 0-521-23563-4 : £19.50 : CIP rev.
B82-12698

700 — Arts — *Marxist-Leninist viewpoints*
Marxist-Leninist aesthetics and the arts / [compiled by I.S. Kulikova and A. Ia͡ Zis′] ; [translated from the Russian by Angus Roxburgh]. — Moscow : Progress ; [London] : Distributed by Central, c1980. — 343p ; 21cm
Translation of: Marksistsko-Leninskaia͡ estetika i khudozhestvennoe tvorchestvo
£3.25 B82-21717

700 — Arts. Representation & allegory
Allegory and representation / edited, with a preface, by Stephen J. Greenblatt. — Baltimore ; London : Johns Hopkins University Press, c1981. — xiii,193p : ill ; 21cm. — (Selected papers from the English Institute, 1979-80. New series ; no.5)
ISBN 0-8018-2642-x : £6.00 B82-11842

700 — English arts, *1603-1642*. **Special subjects: Great Britain. Stuart** *(House of)* — *Critical studies*
Parry, Graham. The golden age restor′d : the culture of the Stuart court, 1603-42 / Graham Parry. — Manchester : Manchester University Press, c1981. — xi,276p : ill,ports ; 24cm
Bibliography: p269-271. — Includes index
ISBN 0-7190-0825-5 : £22.50 : CIP rev.
B81-02124

700 — Visual arts
Clark, Kenneth, *1903-*. Moments of vision / Kenneth Clark. — London : John Murray, 1981. — 191p ; 23cm
Includes index
ISBN 0-7195-3860-2 : £9.50 : CIP rev.
B81-21521

Fuller, Peter, *1947-*. Beyond the crisis in art / Peter Fuller. — London : Writers and Readers, 1980. — 267p : ill ; 23cm
ISBN 0-906495-33-4 (cased) : £6.95
ISBN 0-906495-34-2 (pbk) : Unpriced
B82-19593

700′.1 — Arts. Aesthetics
Savile, Anthony. The test of time : an essay in philosophical aesthetics / Anthony Savile. — Oxford : Clarendon, 1982. — xiii,319p ; 23cm
Includes index
ISBN 0-19-824590-4 : £20.00 : CIP rev.
B82-07515

700'.1 — Arts. Aesthetics *continuation*

Wollheim, Richard. Art and its objects / Richard Wollheim. — 2nd ed., with six supplementary essays. — Cambridge : Cambridge University Press, c1980. — xv,270p ; 22cm
Previous ed.: New York : Harper & Row, 1968 ; Harmondsworth : Pelican, 1970. — Bibliography: p241-270
ISBN 0-521-22898-0 (cased) : £14.00
ISBN 0-521-29706-0 (pbk) : £5.50 B82-39484

700'.1 — Arts. Aesthetics — *For teaching — Conference proceedings*

The **Development** of aesthetic experience / edited by Malcolm Ross. — Oxford : Pergamon, 1982. — xiii,210p ; 22cm. — (Curriculum issues in arts education ; v.3)
Conference papers. — Includes bibliographies and index
ISBN 0-08-028908-8 : Unpriced : CIP rev. B82-11288

700'.1 — Arts. Aesthetics — *Sociological perspectives*

Wolff, Janet. Aesthetics and the sociology of art. — London : Allen & Unwin, Nov.1982. — [128]p. — (Controversies in sociology ; 14)
ISBN 0-04-301152-7 (cased) : £10.95 : CIP entry
ISBN 0-04-301153-5 (pbk) : £4.95 B82-26207

700'.1 — Arts. Theories

Sparshott, Francis. The theory of the arts / Francis Sparshott. — Princeton, N.J. ; Guildford : Princeton University Press, c1982. — xiii,726p ; 25cm
Bibliography: p685-711. — Includes index
ISBN 0-691-07266-3 (cased) : £31.80
ISBN 0-691-10130-2 (pbk limited ed) : £10.60 B82-39887

700'.1'9 — Arts. Aesthetics. Psychological aspects

Psychology and the arts / edited by David O'Hare. — Brighton : Harvester, 1981. — 335p : ill,1port ; 23cm
Bibliography: p305-332. — Includes index
ISBN 0-85527-958-3 : £22.50 : CIP rev. B81-30335

700'.5 — Arts — *Critical studies — Serials*

Temenos. — 2. — Dulverton : Watkins, Jan.1982. — [284]p
ISBN 0-7224-0197-3 (pbk) : £5.00 : CIP entry B81-39236

700'.5 — Arts — *Serials*

Intrigue : poetry— art— stories— magazine. — Preview ed.-. — Plymouth (174 Citadel Rd, The Hoe, Plymouth, Devon PL1 3OU) : Pablo Publications, [1981]-. — v. : ill ; 30cm
ISSN 0263-9238 = Intrigue : £0.35 per issues B82-38514

The **Orkney** arts review. — Summer 1980-. — [Kirkwall] ([P.O. Box 12, Kirkwall, Orkney]) : [s.n.], 1980-. — v. ; 21cm
Irregular
ISSN 0263-1601 = Orkney arts review : £0.80 per issue B82-20879

Southern Arts bulletin. — No.1 (Mar./Apr. 1980)-. — [Winchester] ([19 Southgate St., Winchester, Hants. SO23 9EB]) : Southern Arts, 1980-. — v. : ill,ports ; 30cm
Six issues yearly. — Continues: Southern Arts diary. — Description based on: No.10 (Sept.Oct. 1981)
ISSN 0262-1169 = Southern Arts bulletin : Unpriced B82-02377

Temenos : a review devoted to the arts of the imagination. — 1-. — Dulverton : Watkins, 1981-. — v. : ill ; 22cm
Two issues yearly
ISSN 0262-4524 = Temenos : £5.00 B82-04909

700'.7'1 — Educational institutions. Curriculum subjects: Arts — *Serials*

Journal of art & design education. — Vol.1, no.1 (1982)-. — Abingdon (P.O. Box 25, Abingdon, Oxfordshire OX14 1RW) : Published for the National Society for Art Education by Carfax Pub. Co., 1982-. — v. : ill,ports ; 25cm
Three issues yearly. — Continues: Journal (National Society for Art Education)
ISSN 0260-9991 = Journal of art & design education : Unpriced B82-26142

700'.7'1041 — Great Britain. Educational institutions. Curriculum subjects: Arts

The **Aesthetic** imperative : relevance and responsibility in arts education / edited by Malcolm Ross. — Oxford : Pergamon Press, 1981. — xiii,177p ; 22cm. — (Curriculum issues in arts education ; v.2)
Conference papers. — Includes bibliographies and index
ISBN 0-08-026766-1 : £8.75: CIP rev. B81-20566

700'.7'1073 — United States. Schools. Curriculum subjects: Arts

Remer, Jane. Changing schools through the arts : the power of an idea / Jane Remer ; foreword by John I. Goodlad ; sponsored by, The Exxon Education Foundation, The JDR 3rd Fund ; with administrative support from, The New York Foundation for the Arts. — New York ; London : McGraw-Hill, c1982. — xvi,165p ; 24cm
Bibliography: p155-157. — Includes index
ISBN 0-07-051847-5 : £9.50 B82-16291

700'.7'1141 — Great Britain. Further education institutions. Curriculum subjects: Arts

Shaw, *Sir* Roy. The arts and further education / by Sir Roy Shaw. — Sheffield (c/o Hon Sec., Sheffield City Polytechnic, Pond St., Sheffield S1 1WB) : Association of Colleges for Further and Higher Education, [1982]. — 7p ; 21cm
Conference paper from ACFHE annual general meeting 25-26 February 1982
£0.75 (unbound) B82-24392

700'.7'15 — England. Adult education. Curriculum subjects: Arts. Provision

Adkins, Geoffrey. The arts and adult education / by Geoffrey Adkins. — Leicester : ACACE, 1981. — xi,164p ; 21cm
ISBN 0-906436-11-7 (pbk) : £3.00 B82-39501

700'.7'15 — Great Britain. Adult education. Curriculum subjects: Arts

Adult education and the arts / edited D.J. Jones and A.F. Chadwick. — [Nottingham] : Department of Adult Education, University of Nottingham, c1981. — 82p ; 20cm. — (Nottingham working papers in the education of adults ; 2)
ISBN 0-902031-54-6 (pbk) : £3.30 B82-17072

700'.79 — Europe. Arts. Patronage, *1453-1517*

Patronage in the Renaissance / edited by Guy Fitch Lytle and Stephen Orgel. — Princeton ; Guildford : Princeton University Press, c1981. — xiv,389p : ill,plans ; 25cm. — (Folger Institute essays)
Includes index
ISBN 0-691-05338-3 (cased) : £26.00
ISBN 0-691-10125-6 (pbk) : £10.30 B82-32654

700'.79 — Great Britain. Arts. Patronage. Organisations: Arts Council of Great Britain, *to 1980*

Hutchison, Robert. The politics of the Arts Council / Robert Hutchison. — London : Sinclair Browne, 1982. — 186p : ill ; 23cm
ISBN 0-86300-016-9 (cased) : £7.95 : CIP rev.
ISBN 0-86300-017-7 (pbk) : £3.50 B82-04704

The **State** and the arts / edited by John Pick. — Eastbourne : Offord, 1980. — 160p : ill ; 22cm. — (City arts series)
Includes index
ISBN 0-903931-30-3 : £6.95 B82-27064

700'.7'9 — Great Britain. Arts. Sponsorship by business firms — *Serials*

Sponsorship news : a monthly update of sponsorship news in sport and the arts. — Vol.1, issue 1 (Feb. 1982)-. — [Wokingham] ([31A Rose St., Wokingham, Berks. RG11 1XS]) : [Charterhouse Business Publications], 1982-. — v. : ill,ports ; 30cm
ISSN 0263-3809 = Sponsorship news : £24.00 per year
Also classified at 796'.079 B82-24751

700'.79 — Russia. Arts. Patronage, *1900-1917*

Kean, Beverly Whitney. All the empty palaces : the great merchant patrons of modern art in pre-revolutionary Russia. — London : Barrie & Jenkins, Sept.1982. — [336]p
ISBN 0-09-147980-0 : £12.95 : CIP entry B82-19108

700'.79 — Scotland. Arts. Patronage. Organisations: Scottish Arts Council — *Serials*

[**Bulletin** *(Scottish Arts Council)*]. Bulletin / Scottish Arts Council. — No.1 (May 1980)-. — Edinburgh (19 Charlotte Sq., Edinburgh EH2 4DF) : The Council, 1980-. — v. : ill,ports ; 30cm
Six issues yearly. — Description based on: No.8 (July 1981)
ISSN 0144-2821 = Bulletin - Scottish Arts Council : Unpriced B82-15763

700'.88042 — American arts. Role of women, *1970-1980*

Women's culture : the women's renaissance of the seventies / edited by Gayle Kimball. — Metuchen, N.J. ; London : Scarecrow, 1981. — 296p : ill,ports ; 23cm
Includes bibliographies and index
ISBN 0-8108-1455-2 : £12.80 B82-05353

700'.899275694 — Palestinian Arab arts. Political aspects

Ataöv, Türkkaya. The independent personality of the Palestinians through their arts / by Türkkaya Ataöv. — London (35 Ludgate Hill, EC4M 7JN) : International Organisation for the Elimination of All Forms of Racial Discrimination, [1981]. — 16p ; 21cm. — (Paper / International Organisation for the Elimination of All Forms of Racial Discrimination ; no.19)
£0.30 (unbound) B82-07743

700'.9 — Arts, *to 1977.* **Social aspects**

Literary taste, culture and mass communication / edited by Peter Davison, Rolf Meyersohn, Edward Shils. — Cambridge : Chadwyck-Healey
Vol.14: The cultural debate. — c1980
Pt.2. — xii,262p : ill ; 25cm
Facsim reprints. — Includes index
ISBN 0-85964-049-3 : Unpriced : CIP rev. B78-05340

700'.9 — Arts, *to 1979*

Cornell, Sara. Art : a history of changing style. — Oxford : Phaidon, Apr.1982. — [456]p
ISBN 0-7148-2190-x : £14.95 : CIP entry B82-04507

700'.9 — Arts, *to ca 1970 — Critical studies*

Wind, Edgar. The eloquence of symbols. — Oxford : Clarendon Press, Nov.1982. — [192]p
ISBN 0-19-817341-5 : £25.00 : CIP entry B82-26884

700'.9'03 — European arts, *1750-1982.* **Symbolism** — *Critical studies*

Landow, George P.. Images of crisis : literary iconology, 1750 to the present / George P. Landow. — Boston, Mass. ; London : Routledge & Kegan Paul, 1982. — xii,234p,[16]p of plates : ill,1plan ; 22cm
Includes index
ISBN 0-7100-0818-x : £17.50 B82-24904

700'.9'034 — Arts. Modernism, *1880-1950*

Modern art and modernism. — London : Harper & Row, Oct.1982. — [336]p
ISBN 0-06-318234-3 (cased) : £11.95 : CIP entry
ISBN 0-06-318233-5 (pbk) : £5.95 B82-24945

700'.9'04 — Arts, *ca 1900-1980 — Critical studies*
Dipped in vitriol / edited by Nicholas Parsons. — London : Pan, 1981. — xii,226p : ill ; 20cm
Bibliography: p223-226
ISBN 0-330-26556-3 (pbk) : £1.50 B82-08251

700'.9'04 — Western avant garde arts, *ca 1965-1981 — Critical studies*
Wollen, Peter. Readings and writings. — London : Verso/NLB, Oct.1982. — [256]p
ISBN 0-86091-055-5 (cased) : £14.50 : CIP entry
ISBN 0-86091-755-x (pbk) : £4.95 B82-28596

700'.92'2 — English arts. Pre-Raphaelite Brotherhood
Bell, Quentin. A new and noble school : the Pre-Raphaelites / Quentin Bell. — London : Macdonald, 1982. — 192p,16p of plates : ill (some col.),ports ; 25cm
Bibliography: p188. — Includes index
ISBN 0-356-08546-5 : £10.95 B82-32937

700'.92'4 — English arts. James, Edward, *1907- — Biographies*
James, Edward, *1907-*. Swans reflecting elephants : my early years / Edward James ; edited by George Melly. — London : Weidenfeld and Nicolson, c1982. — 178p,[8]p of plates : ports ; 23cm
Includes index
ISBN 0-297-77988-5 : £8.95 B82-32809

700'.941 — Great Britain. Society. Role of arts
Baldry, H. C.. The case for the arts / Harold Baldry. — London : Secker & Warburg, 1981. — 173p ; 23cm
Bibliography: p165-168. — Includes index
ISBN 0-436-03190-6 (cased) : £7.95
ISBN 0-436-03191-4 (pbk) : £2.95 B82-02606

700'.9415 — Irish arts, *to 1970 — Chronologies*
Fitz-Simon, Christopher. The arts in Ireland : a chronology / Christopher Fitz-Simon. — Dublin : Gill and Macmillan, 1982. — xiv,257p : ill,1map,music,facsims,ports ; 24cm
Bibliography: p248-250. — Includes index
ISBN 0-7171-1142-3 : £17.25 B82-21322

700'.942 — English arts, *ca 1890-1900 — Critical studies — Serials — Early works — Facsimiles*
The **Quarto** 1896-1898 / with an introduction by Rodney Shewan. — New York ; London : Garland, 1979. — 4v. in 2 : ill,music ; 29cm. — (The Aesthetic movement and the arts & crafts movement. Periodicals)
Facsim reprints
ISBN 0-8240-3622-0 : Unpriced B82-15184

700'.9794'6 — California. San Francisco Bay. Conceptual art, *1970-1980*
Foley, Suzanne. Space, time, sound : conceptual art in the San Francisco Bay area : the 1970's / by Suzanne Foley ; chronology by Constance Lewallen. — San Francisco : San Francisco Museum of Modern Art ; London : University of Washington Press [distributor], c1981. — 208p : ill ; 28cm
Published to accompany an exhibition at the San Francisco Museum of Modern Art, 1979-1980. — Includes index
ISBN 0-295-95879-0 (pbk) : £9.10 B82-24211

701 — VISUAL ARTS. PHILOSOPHY AND THEORY

701'.03 — Visual arts. Social aspects
Becker, Howard S.. Art worlds / Howard S. Becker. — Berkeley ; London : University of California Press, c1982. — xiv,392p : ill,facsims,ports ; 25cm
Bibliography: p373-384. — Includes index
ISBN 0-520-04386-3 : £18.75 B82-34360

701'.03'094551 — Italy. Florence. Visual arts, *1420-1530.* **Socioeconomic aspects**
Wackernagel, Martin. The world of the Florentine Renaissance artist : projects and patrons, workshop and art market / Martin Wackernagel ; translated by Alison Luchs. — Princeton ; Guildford : Princeton University Press, c1981. — xxx,447p ; 25cm
Bibliography: p371-403. — Includes index
ISBN 0-691-03966-6 (cased) : £26.40
ISBN 0-691-10117-5 (pbk) : £10.20
B82-14538

701'.1'5 — Visual arts. Perception. Psychoanalytical aspects
Fuller, Peter, *1947-*. Art and psychoanalysis / Peter Fuller. — London : Writers and Readers, 1980. — 250p : ill,ports ; 23cm
ISBN 0-906495-24-5 (cased) : £5.95
ISBN 0-906495-32-6 (pbk) : Unpriced
B82-01374

701'.1'5 — Visual arts *related to* **visual perception**
Gambrich, E. H.. The image and the eye : further studies in the psychology of pictorial representation. — Oxford : Phaidon, May 1982. — [320]p
ISBN 0-7148-2245-0 : £15.00 : CIP entry
B82-12823

701'.8 — Proportions. Aesthetic aspects
Doczi, György. The power of limits : proportional harmonies in nature, art and architecture / György Doczi. — Boulder ; London : Shambhala, 1981 ; London : Distributed by Routledge & Kegan Paul. — 150p : ill,facsims,plans,ports ; 25x27cm
Includes index
ISBN 0-87773-194-2 (cased) : Unpriced
ISBN 0-87773-193-4 (pbk) : £6.50 B82-03280

701'.8 — Visual arts. Colour *— Early works*
Chevreul, M. E.. The principles of harmony and contrast of colors and their applications to the arts / by M.E. Chevreul ... ; with a special introduction and explanatory notes by Faber Birren. — New York ; London : Van Nostrand Reinhold, 1981. — 224p : ill,facsims,ports ; 29x31cm
'Based on the first English edition of 1854 as translated from the first French edition of 1839: De la loi du contraste simultane des couleurs'. — Translation of: De la loi du contraste simultane des couleurs. — Facsim. of ed. published: London : Bohn, 1854. — Includes index
ISBN 0-442-21212-7 (pbk) : £16.95
B82-00742

701'.8 — Visual arts. Spatial representation
Arnheim, Rudolf. The power of the center : a study of composition in the visual arts / Rudolf Arnheim. — Berkeley ; London : University of California Press, c1982. — xii,227p : 1port ; 24cm
Bibliography: p221-223. — Includes index
ISBN 0-520-04426-6 : £14.25 B82-40469

702 — VISUAL ARTS. MISCELLANY

702'.3'41 — Great Britain. Visual arts *— Career guides*
Christie, Catherine. Careers in art and design / Catherine Christie. — Northampton : Hamilton House, 1981. — 32p ; 21cm. — (Careerscope ; 5)
ISBN 0-906888-24-7 (pbk) : Unpriced
B82-03066

702'.5'4249 — England. West Midlands. Visual arts *— Directories*
Artists, craftsmen, photographers : in the West Midlands. — Stafford : West Midland Arts, c1977. — [113]p : ill ; 29x13cm
Includes index
ISBN 0-9504364-2-9 (pbk) : Unpriced
B82-15336

702'.8 — Patterns. Making *— Manuals — For children*
Foster, Maureen. Creating patterns from grasses, seedheads and cones. — London : Pelham Books, July 1982. — [48]p
ISBN 0-7207-1397-8 : £4.95 : CIP entry
B82-13077

702'.8 — Visual arts. Techniques
Understanding art : an introduction to painting and sculpture / [chief contributor and general editor David Piper] ; [editor Jack Tresidder]. — London : Mitchell Beazley, 1981. — 223p : ill(some col.) ; 30cm. — (The Mitchell Beazley library of art ; v.1)
Includes index
ISBN 0-85533-355-3 : £13.95
ISBN 0-85533-177-1 (set) : Unpriced
B82-03762

702'.8 — Visual arts. Tools *— Encyclopaedias*
Handtools of arts and crafts : the encyclopaedia of the fine, decorative and applied arts / the Diagram Group. — London : Harrap, 1981. — 319p : ill(some col.),ports ; 29cm
Originally published: New York : St. Martin's Press, 1981. — Ill on lining papers. — Bibliography: p310-311. — Includes index
ISBN 0-245-53823-2 : £12.50 B82-01811

702'.8'12 — Collages. Techniques *— Manuals*
Mills, John FitzMaurice. Materials & techniques of collage / John FitzMaurice Mills. — London : Warne, 1981. — 63p : ill(some col.) ; 22cm. — (An Observer's guide. Art and craft)
ISBN 0-7232-2478-1 (pbk) : £2.50 B82-00868

703 — VISUAL ARTS. DICTIONARIES, ENCYCLOPAEDIAS, CONCORDANCES

703'.21 — Visual arts *— Encyclopaedias*
Art and artists : the dictionary of painting and sculpture / [chief contributor and general editor David Piper] ; [editor Jane Crawley]. — London : Mitchell Beazley, 1981. — 192p : ill,ports ; 30cm. — (The Mitchell Beazley library of art ; v.4)
ISBN 0-85533-358-8 : £13.95
ISBN 0-85533-177-1 (set) : Unpriced
B82-03765

Reynolds, Kimberley. Illustrated dictionary of art terms : a handbook for the artist and art lover / Kimberley Reynolds with Richard Seddon. — London : Ebury, 1981. — 190p : ill,ports ; 24cm
Bibliography: p187-189
ISBN 0-85223-207-1 : £8.95 B82-04249

Thomas, Denis. Dictionary of fine arts / Denis Thomas. — London : Hamlyn, 1981. — 199p : ill,ports ; 25cm
ISBN 0-600-32995-x : £6.95 B82-03204

703'.41 — Art objects *— Encyclopaedias — French texts — Facsimiles*
Bosc, Ernest. Dictionnaire de l'art de la curiosité et du bibelot / Ernest Bosc. — New York ; London : Garland, 1979. — xvi,695p,[3]leaves of plates : ill,ports ; 27cm. — (A Dealers' and collectors' bookshelf. Ceramics and glass)
Facsim. of: ed. published Paris : Librairie de firmin-didot, 1883
ISBN 0-8240-3387-6 : Unpriced B82-14682

704 — VISUAL ARTS. SPECIAL ASPECTS

704.9'42 — British persons, *to 1979.* **Portraits** *— Lists*
Dictionary of British portraiture : in four volumes / edited by Richard Ormond and Malcolm Rogers ; with a foreword by John Hayes. — London : Batsford in association with the National Portrait Gallery
Vol.3: The Victorians : historical figures born between 1800 and 1860 / compiled by Elaine Kilmurray. — 1981. — 228p ; 26cm
ISBN 0-7134-1472-3 : £37.50 B82-18944

Dictionary of British portraiture : in four volumes / edited by Richard Ormond and Malcolm Rogers ; with a foreword by John Hayes. — London : Batsford in association with the National Portrait Gallery
Vol.4: The twentieth century : historical figures born before 1900 / compiled by Adriana Davies. — 1981. — 176p ; 26cm
Includes index
ISBN 0-7134-1474-x : £37.50 B82-18943

704.9'42 — Visual arts. Special subjects: Face, *to 1980 — Critical studies — For children*
Waterfield, Giles. Faces / Giles Waterfield ; consultant editor Ronald Parkinson. — Hove : Wayland, 1982. — 47p : ill(some col.),ports ; 27cm. — (Looking at art)
Includes index
ISBN 0-85340-893-9 : £4.95 B82-16416

704.9′42 — Visual arts. Special themes: Androgyny

Zolla, Elémire. The androgyne : fusion of the sexes / Elémire Zolla. — London : Thames and Hudson, c1981. — 96p : ill(some col.),ports ; 28cm
Bibliography: p96
ISBN 0-500-81028-1 (pbk) : £3.95 B82-08017

704.9′423 — Visual arts. Special subjects: English poets, *ca 1590-ca 1890 — Critical studies*

Piper, David. The image of the poet. — Oxford : Clarendon, June 1982. — [240]p
ISBN 0-19-817365-2 : £20.00 : CIP entry B82-25899

704.9′423′07402132 — London. Westminster *(London Borough).* **Art galleries: Institute of Contemporary Arts. Exhibits: Visual arts. Women artists. Special subjects: Men —** *Catalogues*

Women's Images of Men *(1980-1981).* Women's images of men. — London : Institute of Contemporary Arts, c1980. — [55]p : ill(some col.),ports ; 30cm
ISBN 0-905263-07-3 (pbk) : Unpriced B82-11336

704.9′424 — British visual arts. Special subjects: Godiva, *Countess of Mercia — Critical studies*

Clarke, Ronald Aquilla. Lady Godiva : images of a legend in art & society / by Ronald Aquilla Clarke & Patrick A.E. Day. — Coventry : City of Coventry Leisure Services, Arts and Museums Division, 1982. — 38p : ill(some col.),facsims,ports(some col.) ; 30cm
Published to accompany an exhibition held at the Herbert Art Gallery and Museum, Coventry, 1982. — Bibliography: p38
ISBN 0-901606-51-0 (pbk) : Unpriced B82-38915

704.9′428′0937 — Ancient Roman erotic visual arts *— Critical studies*

Johns, Catherine. Sex or symbol : erotic images of Greece and Rome. — London : British Museum Publications, Sept.1982. — [160]p. — (A Colonnade book)
ISBN 0-7141-8042-4 : £12.95 : CIP entry
Primary classification 704.9′428′0938 B82-20366

704.9′428′0938 — Ancient Greek erotic visual arts *— Critical studies*

Johns, Catherine. Sex or symbol : erotic images of Greece and Rome. — London : British Museum Publications, Sept.1982. — [160]p. — (A Colonnade book)
ISBN 0-7141-8042-4 : £12.95 : CIP entry
Also classified at 704.9′428′0937 B82-20366

704.9′428′095 — Oriental erotic visual arts — *Critical studies*

Rawson, Philip. Oriental erotic art / Philip Rawson. — London : Quartet, 1981. — 176p : ill(some col.) ; 29cm
Includes index
ISBN 0-7043-2291-9 : £15.00 B82-01061

704.9′44 — Hertfordshire. St Albans. Cathedrals: St Albans Cathedral. Exhibits: English visual arts, *1700-1900.* **Special subjects: St Albans Cathedral —** *Catalogues*

Photographs, prints, drawings, & paintings of the Abbey 1700-1900 : exhibition 15 July-15 September 1979 in the cathedral nave : catalogue / [written by J.G.E. Cox]. — [S.l.] : [s.n.], c1979 (St. Albans : Campfield Press). — [40]p : ill ; 20cm
Cover title. — At head of title: St Albans Cathedral Appeal
Unpriced (pbk) B82-15337

704.9′46 — French visual arts, *1800-1900.* **Special subjects: Fools. Symbolic aspects**

Fletcher, Dennis. Praise of folly : an inaugural lecture / by Dennis Fletcher. — [Durham] ([Old Shire Hall, Durham DH1 3HP]) : University of Durham, 1981. — 19p ; 22cm
£0.60 (pbk)
Primary classification 840.9′27 B82-07759

704.9′48 — Eastern Orthodox Churches. Religious visual arts, *to 1400*

Walter, Christopher. Art and ritual of the Byzantine Church. — London : Variorum, Sept.1982. — [302]p. — (Birmingham Byzantine series ; 1)
ISBN 0-86078-104-6 : £28.00 : CIP entry B82-21398

704.94′930685′09 — Visual arts. Special subjects: Family life, *ca 1430-1957 — Critical studies — For children*

Conner, Patrick. People at home / Patrick Conner ; consultant editor Ronald Parkinson. — Hove : Wayland, 1982. — 47p : ill(some col.),ports ; 27cm. — (Looking at art)
Includes index
ISBN 0-85340-891-2 : £4.95 B82-16415

704.9′493317 — Visual arts. Special subjects: Working life, *to 1980 — Critical studies — For children*

Conner, Patrick. People at work / Patrick Conner ; consultant editor Ronald Parkinson. — Hove : Wayland, 1982. — 47p : col.ill ; 27cm. — (Looking at art)
Includes index
ISBN 0-85340-889-0 : £4.95 B82-16417

704.9′4961689 — European visual arts, *1200-1900.* **Special subjects: Insanity —** *Critical studies*

Gilman, Sander L.. Seeing the insane : a cultural history of madness and art in the western world ... / by Sander L. Gilman. — New York ; Chichester : Wiley in association with Brunner-Mazel, c1982. — xiii,241p : ill ; 32cm
Bibliography: p235-236. — Includes index
ISBN 0-471-86722-5 : Unpriced B82-28140

704.9′4997802 — American visual arts, *1850-1900.* **Special subjects: United States. Western states —** *Critical studies*

Taft, Robert. Artists and illustrators of the Old West 1850-1900 / by Robert Taft. — Princeton ; Guildford : Princeton University Press, 1982, c1953. — xvii,400p,[77]p of plates : ill,maps ; 26cm
Originally published: New York : Scribner, 1953. — Includes index
ISBN 0-691-03995-x (cased) : Unpriced
ISBN 0-691-00343-2 (pbk) : £7.05 B82-30378

705 — VISUAL ARTS. SERIALS

705 — Visual arts — *For art school students — Serials*

AX5 : the student art magazine. — [No.1]-. — London (52a Walham Grove, Fulham SW6) : Byam Shaw School of Art, [1981]-. — v. : ill,ports ; 21cm
Three issues yearly. — Description based on: [No.2]
ISSN 0262-7051 = AX5 : Unpriced B82-06779

705 — Visual arts — *Serials*

Christie's review of the season. — 1982. — London : Christie, Manson and Woods ; Oxford : Phaidon [distributor], Nov.1982. — [504]p
ISBN 0-7148-8002-7 : £25.00 : CIP entry B82-26394

707 — VISUAL ARTS. STUDY AND TEACHING

707′.1 — Schools. Curriculum subjects: Visual arts. Teaching

Tritten, Gottfried. Teaching color and form / Gottfried Tritten ; translated by Alba and Ernest H. Lorman. — New York ; London : Van Nostrand Reinhold, c1981. — 408p : ill (some col.) ; 31cm
Translation of: Erziehung durch Farbe und Form. — Bibliography: p408
ISBN 0-442-25037-1 : £30.55 B82-08348

707′.1042 — England. Educational institutions. Curriculum subjects: Visual arts. Courses — *National Association of Teachers in Further and Higher Education viewpoints*

National Association of Teachers in Further and Higher Education. Art and design education : a policy statement / NATFHE. — [London] : [National Association of Teachers in Further and Higher Education], 1978. — 11p ; 21cm
Cover title
£0.30 (pbk) B82-08490

707′.1141 — Great Britain. Higher education institutions. Curriculum subjects: Visual arts

The **Pull** of the future : a collection of occasional papers by staff of the Department of Art Education and Foundation Studies / edited by H. Loeb. — Birmingham (Margaret St., Birmingham B3 3BX) : City of Birmingham Polytechnic, Faculty of Art & Design, 1981. — ii,90p,[4]leaves of plates : ill(some col.),1facsim,1col.plan ; 30cm
Bibliography: p32
Unpriced (pbk) B82-05304

707′.1142189 — London. Enfield *(London Borough).* **Art schools: Middlesex Polytechnic.** *Faculty of Art and Design, to 1982*

Ashwin, Clive. A century of art education 1882-1982 / Clive Ashwin. — [London] : Middlesex Polytechnic, 1982. — 59p : ill,facsims,ports ; 20cm
Published to accompany an exhibition to mark the centenary of the foundation of Hornsey School of Art, held at the New Gallery, Hornsey Library March 9-April 3 1982
ISBN 0-904804-15-1 (pbk) : Unpriced B82-23497

707′.1142615 — Norfolk. Norwich. Art schools: Norwich School of Art, *to 1982*

Allthorpe-Guyton, Marjorie. A happy eye : a school of art in Norwich 1845-1982 / Marjorie Allthorpe-Guyton with John Stevens. — Norwich : Jarrold, 1982. — 144p : ill,facsims,ports ; 25cm
Ill on inside covers. — Bibliography: p143-144
ISBN 0-7117-0028-1 (pbk) : Unpriced B82-31097

707′.1142733 — Greater Manchester *(Metropolitan County).* **Manchester. Polytechnics. Art schools: Manchester Polytechnic.** *School of Art, to 1980*

Jeremiah, D.. A hundred years and more / D. Jeremiah. — [Manchester] : Manchester Polytechnic, 1980. — 63p : ill,1plan,ports ; 25cm
Ill on lining papers
Unpriced (pbk) B82-10974

707′.1241 — Great Britain. Secondary schools. Curriculum subjects: Visual arts. History. Teaching — *Conference proceedings*

History of art in secondary education : report of a conference held at the Institute of Education on Friday 7th November 1980 and presented by the Art Department of the Institute in conjunction with the Association of Art Historians / compiled and edited by Anthony Dyson. — [London] : Art Department, University of London Institute of Education, 1981. — 22p ; 30cm
ISBN 0-85473-106-7 (pbk) : £0.50 B82-09554

707′.5′0924 — Europe. Art objects. Plunder by Hitler, Adolf, *1938-1945*

De Jaeger, Charles. The Linz file : Hitler's plunder of Europe's art / Charles de Jaeger. — Exeter : Webb & Bower, 1981. — 192p : ill,plans,ports ; 24cm
Bibliography: p181-185. — Includes index
ISBN 0-906671-30-2 : £7.95 : CIP rev. B81-19202

707.5′092′4 — Visual arts. Collecting, *1848-1861 — Personal observations — Correspondence, diaries, etc.*

Hertford, Richard Seymour-Conway, *Marquess of*. The Hertford Mawson letters : the 4th Marquess of Hertford to his agent Samuel Mawson / edited by John Ingamells. — London : Trustees of the Wallace Collection, 1981. — 143p : ill,facsims,ports,1geneal.table ; 24cm
At head of title: Wallace Collection. — Includes index
Unpriced (pbk) B82-13798

707′.9 — Great Britain. Visual arts. Patronage by government, *1760-1981*

Pearson, Nicholas M.. The state and the visual arts. — Milton Keynes : Open University Press, Aug.1982. — [136]p
ISBN 0-335-10109-7 (pbk) : £5.95 : CIP entry B82-22404

708 — VISUAL ARTS. GALLERIES, MUSEUMS, PRIVATE COLLECTIONS

708′.0025 — Art galleries — *Directories*

Langdon, Helen. The Mitchell Beazley pocket art gallery guide : a guide to collections of Western art from the early Renaissance to the present day / Helen Langdon. — London : Mitchell Beazley, 1981. — 184p : col.ill ; 20cm
Includes index
ISBN 0-85533-318-9 : £3.95 B82-01923

708′.0025′41 — Great Britain. Art galleries - *Directories - Serials*

Libraries, museums and art galleries year book. — 1978-1979. — Cambridge : James Clarke, May 1981. — [272]p
ISBN 0-227-67835-4 : £23.00 : CIP entry
ISSN 0075-899x
Primary classification 027′.0025′41 B81-14963

708.147′1 — New York *(City).* **Art galleries** — *Directories*

New York art guide. — London (89 Notting Hill Gate, W11 3JZ) : Art Guide Publications, Mar.1982. — [128]p
ISBN 0-9507160-4-9 (pbk) : £2.95 : CIP entry B82-09313

708.2 — England. Knight, Richard Payne. Private collections: Visual arts — *Critical studies*

The **Arrogant** connoisseur : Richard Payne Knight 1751-1824 : essays on Richard Payne Knight together with a catalogue of works exhibited at the Whitworth Art Gallery, 1982 / editors Michael Clarke & Nicholas Penny. — [Manchester] : Manchester University Press, c1982. — x,189p,[8]p of plates : ill(some col.),ports(some col.) ; 26cm
Bibliography: p120-124
ISBN 0-7190-0871-9 (cased) : Unpriced : CIP rev.
ISBN 0-7190-0872-7 (pbk) : £9.50 B82-00386

708.2 — Great Britain. Art objects. Retention in Great Britain. Great Britain. *Parliament. House of Commons. Education, Science and Arts Committee.* **Third report ... session 1980-81** — *Critical studies*

Great Britain. Retention of works of art in Britain and their acquisition for the nation : observations by the Government on the third report from the Education, Science and Arts Committee, session 1980/81. — London : H.M.S.O., [1982?]. — 6p ; 25cm. — (Cmnd. ; 8538)
ISBN 0-10-185380-7 (unbound) : £1.15 B82-24698

708.2 — Great Britain. Visual arts. Collections

Britain : a fine art guide. — [London] : British Tourist Authority, c1982. — 68p : ill(some col.),1map,ports
ISBN 0-7095-1025-x (pbk) : Unpriced B82-12728

708.2′1 — London. Art galleries. Exhibits — *Serials*

Arts London review : trade paper of the artist. — Vol.1, no.1 (15 Jan. 1981)-. — London (16 Woodstock St., W1) : Woodstock Gallery Press, 1981-. — v. : ill ; 30cm
Monthly
ISSN 0260-6801 = Arts London review : £0.30 per issue B82-08463

708.2′132 — London. Westminster *(London Borough).* **Art galleries: Royal Academy of Arts,** *to 1980*

Royal Academy of Arts. The genius of the Royal Academy / Eric Shanes. — [London] : Royal Academy, c1981. — 86p : ill(some col.),ports (some col.) ; 21cm
ISBN 0-7195-3919-6 (pbk) : £2.25 B82-00670

708.2′132′005 — London. Westminster *(London Borough).* **Art galleries: Royal Academy** — *Serials*

Royal Academy. Royal Academy (year book). — 1981. — Henley-on-Thames : A. Ellis, Oct.1981. — [192]p
ISBN 0-85628-108-5 : £10.00 : CIP entry B81-28046

708.2′134 — London. Kensington and Chelsea *(London Borough).* **Museums: Victoria and Albert Museum,** *to 1980*

Cocks, Anna Somers. The Victoria and Albert Museum : the making of the collection / Anna Somers Cocks ; designed by Philip Clucas ; produced by Ted Smart and David Gibbon ; featuring the photography of Clive Friend. — [Leicester] : Windward, 1980. — 186p : col.ill ; 33cm
Bibliography: p182-183. — Includes index
ISBN 0-7112-0042-4 : £9.95 B82-36863

708.2′134 — London. Kensington and Chelsea *(London Borough).* **Museums: Victoria and Albert Museum,** *to 1981*

Physick, John. The Victoria and Albert Museum : the history of its building. — Oxford : Phaidon, Nov.1982. — [304]p
ISBN 0-7148-8001-9 : £20.00 : CIP entry B82-26393

708.2′276 — Hampshire. Southampton. Art galleries: Southampton Art Gallery. Stock: Visual arts — *Catalogues*

Southampton Art Gallery. Southampton Art Gallery collection : illustrated inventory of paintings, drawings and sculpture. — Southampton (Department of Leisure Services, Civic Centre, Southampton SO9 4XF) : The Gallery, c1980. — 96p : ill(some col.),ports (some col.) ; 30cm
Text, ill on inside back cover
Unpriced (pbk) B82-12042

708.2′54 — Leicestershire. Educational institutions. Stock: Visual arts

Growing up with art : the Leicestershire collection for schools and colleges. — London : Arts Council of Great Britain, c1980. — 32p : ill ; 27cm
An exhibition organised by the Arts Council of Great Britain and the Whitechapel Art Gallery
ISBN 0-7287-0249-5 (pbk) : Unpriced B82-17506

708.2′821 — South Yorkshire *(Metropolitan County).* **Sheffield. Art galleries: Sheffield City Art Galleries. Stock: Visual arts** — *Catalogues*

Sheffield City Art Galleries. Concise catalogue of works by artists born after 1850 / Sheffield City Art Galleries. — Sheffield : The Galleries, 1981. — 77p : ill,ports ; 30cm
Includes index
ISBN 0-900660-57-0 (pbk) : Unpriced B82-06586

708.2′929 — Wales. Art galleries

Pearson, Nicholas M.. Art galleries and exhibition spaces in Wales : a report commissioned by the Welsh Arts Council 1980/81 / Nicholas Pearson. — Cardiff : Welsh Arts Council, 1981. — 207p : 1map ; 21cm
Includes index
ISBN 0-905171-90-x (pbk) : £3.00 B82-14686

708.7′453 — Russia *(RSFSR).* **Leningrad. Museums: Ermitazh,** *to 1981*

Piotrovsky, Boris. The Hermitage. — London : Granada, Dec.1982. — [216]p
Translation of: Ermitazh
ISBN 0-246-12011-8 : £30.00 : CIP entry B82-29635

709 — VISUAL ARTS. HISTORICAL AND GEOGRAPHICAL TREATMENT

709 — Visual arts — *Critical studies*

Lynton, Norbert. Looking at art. — London (Elsley Court, 20 Great Titchfield St., W1P 7AD) : Kingfisher, Oct.1981. — [180]p
ISBN 0-86272-004-4 : £6.95 : CIP entry B81-27447

709 — Visual arts, *to 1977*

Janson, H. W.. History of art : for young people / H.W. Janson with Samuel Cauman. — 2nd ed. revised by Anthony F. Janson. — London : Thames and Hudson, 1982, c1971. — 410p : ill (some col.),maps ; 27cm
Previous ed. published: New York : Abrams, 1971 ; London : Thames and Hudson, 1973. — Bibliography: p394-397. — Includes index
ISBN 0-500-23353-5 : £10.50 B82-24510

709 — Visual arts, *to ca 1700* — *Critical studies*

Kurz, Otto. Selected studies. — London (66 Lyncroft Gardens, NW6 1JY) : Pindar Press Vol.2. — Mar.1982. — [272]p
ISBN 0-907132-07-3 : £40.00 : CIP entry B82-01161

709 — Western visual arts, *to 1789*

Great traditions : the history of painting and sculpture / [chief contributor and general editor David Piper] ; [editor Paul Holberton]. — London : Mitchell Beazley, 1981. — 272p : ill(some col.),col.maps,ports(some col.) ; 30cm. — (The Mitchell Beazley library of art ; v.2)
Includes index
ISBN 0-85533-356-1 : £13.95
ISBN 0-85533-177-1 (set) : Unpriced B82-03763

709′.01 — Visual arts, *to ca 400* — *Critical studies*

Art in the ancient world : a handbook of styles and forms : Iran, Mesopotamia, The Levant, Egypt, Greece, Etruria, Rome / by Pierre Amiet ... [et al.] ; translated by Valerie Bynner. — London : Faber, 1981. — 567p : ill,maps,plans ; 22cm
Includes bibliographies
ISBN 0-571-11743-0 : £20.00 : CIP rev. B81-12897

709′.01′107402542 — Leicestershire. Leicester. Museums: Leicester Museum & Art Gallery. Exhibits: Tribal artefacts — *Catalogues*

Attenborough, David. Tribal encounters : an exhibition of ethnic objects collected by David Attenborough. — [Leicester] : Leicestershire Museums, Art Galleries and Records Service, c1981. — iii,90p : col.ill ; 20cm. — (Leicestershire Museums publication ; no.29)
ISBN 0-85022-101-3 (pbk) : Unpriced B82-14648

709′.02 — Byzantine visual arts. Influence of Greek literature, *500-1000*

Maguire, Henry. Art and eloquence in Byzantium / Henry Maguire. — Princeton, N.J. ; Guildford : Princeton University Press, c1981. — xxii,148p,[72]p of plates : ill ; 27cm
Includes index
ISBN 0-691-03972-0 : £22.80 B82-15369

709′.02 — Christian visual arts, *300-1500*

Art in the Christian world, 300-1500. — London : Faber, Aug.1982. — [560]p
Translation from the French
ISBN 0-571-11941-7 : CIP entry B82-16647

709′.02 — European visual arts, *1050-1500* — *Critical studies*

Shaver-Crandell, Anne. The Middle Ages / Anne Shaver-Crandell. — Cambridge : Cambridge University Press, 1982. — 122p : ill(some col.),1map,plans ; 25cm. — (Cambridge introduction to the history of art ; 2)
Bibliography: p120. — Includes index
ISBN 0-521-23209-0 (cased) : Unpriced : CIP rev.
ISBN 0-521-29870-9 (pbk) : Unpriced B81-32530

709′.02′1 — European visual arts. Influence of Byzantine visual arts, *500-1200*

Weitzmann, Kurt. Art in the medieval west and its contacts with Byzantium / Kurt Weitzmann. — London : Variorum Reprints, 1982. — 322p in various pagings : ill,1port ; 31cm. — (Collected studies series ; CS148)
Includes 4 papers in German. — Facsimile reprints. — Includes index
ISBN 0-86078-095-3 : £67.50 : CIP rev. B82-01567

709′.02′4 — European visual arts, *1400-1600* — *Critical studies*

White, John. Studies in Renaissance art. — London (66 Lyncroft Gardens, NW6 1JY) : Pindar Press, Mar.1982. — [384]p
ISBN 0-907132-06-5 : £50.00 : CIP entry B82-01167

709.02'4 — London. Camden *(London Borough).* **Museums: British Museum. Exhibits: Western European art objects,** *1400-1600.* **Collections: Waddesdon Bequest**

Tait, Hugh. The Waddesdon Bequest. — London : British Museum Publications, Sept.1981. — [128]p
ISBN 0-7141-1357-3 (pbk) : £4.95 : CIP entry B81-23830

709'.03 — Great Britain. Arts. Patronage. Organisations: Arts Council of Great Britain. Exhibits: European visual arts, *1634-1979 — Catalogues*

More than a glance : an Arts Council exhibition showing at Sheffield, Graves Art Gallery, 4 October to 2 November 1980, Cheltenham, Cheltenham Art Gallery and Museum, 8 November to 6 December 1980, Swansea, Glynn Vivian Art Gallery and Museum, 13 December to 24 January 1981, Southampton, Southampton Art Gallery, 7 February to 8 March 1981, Wakefield, the Elizabethan Exhibition Gallery, 14 March to 19 April 1981. — [London] : Arts Council of Great Britain, [1980]. — 40p : ill,ports ; 21x30cm
Catalogue to accompany the exhibitions
Unpriced (pbk) B82-22450

709'.03'42 — Western visual arts. Romanticism, *ca 1790-ca 1860 — Critical studies*

Honour, Hugh. Romanticism / Hugh Honour. — Harmondsworth : Penguin, 1981, c1979. — 415p : ill,ports ; 24cm
Originally published: London : Allen Lane, 1979. — Includes index
ISBN 0-14-022306-1 (pbk) : £5.95 B82-07300

709'.03'49 — Art objects. Art nouveau style — *Collectors' guides*

Art nouveau-deco / compiled by Tony Curtis. — Galashiels : Lyle, c1981. — 126p : chiefly ill ; 17cm. — (Antiques and their values)
Includes index
ISBN 0-86248-011-6 : £2.50
Also classified at 709'.04'012 B82-08193

Brunger, Stuart M.. Art Nouveau / compiled and edited by Stuart M. Brunger ; consultant editor Judith H. Miller. — Tenterden : MJM, [1982?]. — 91p : ill ; 22cm. — (Buyer's price guides)
Includes index
ISBN 0-905879-18-x : £2.95 B82-33574

709'.04 — Avant garde visual arts *— Catalogues*

Crossroads Parnass : international avant-garde at Galerie Parnass, Wuppertal 1949-1965 / [editing of catalogue Günter Bär ... et al.] ; [translations Eileen Martin, Christa Merkes]. — London : Goethe-Institut, 1982. — 92p : ill (some col.) ; 30cm
Published to accompany an exhibition of the Goethe Institute, 1982. — Translated from the German. — Cover title: Treffpunkt Parnass, Wuppertal 1949-1965
ISBN 2-85527-001-4 (pbk) : £2.00 B82-35143

709'.04 — Jewish visual arts, *1900-1980 — Critical studies*

Kampf, Avram. Jewish experience in the art of the twentieth century. — Oxford : Phaidon, Oct.1981. — [224]p
ISBN 0-7148-2154-3 : £15.00 : CIP entry B81-27945

709'.04 — Visual arts, *1860-1980*

Russell, John, *1919-*. The meanings of modern art / John Russell. — London : Thames and Hudson, 1981. — 429p : ill(some col.),ports ; 26cm
Bibliography: p406-416. — Includes index
ISBN 0-500-23335-7 : £18.00 B82-03495

709'.04 — Visual arts, *1900-1980 — Encyclopaedias*

The **Oxford** companion to twentieth-century art / edited by Harold Osborne. — Oxford : Oxford University Press, 1981. — x,656p,[128]p of plates : ill(some col.) ; 24cm
Bibliography: p601-648
ISBN 0-19-866119-3 : £19.50 : CIP rev. B81-26761

709'.04 — Visual arts, *1910-1945 — Catalogues*

Beckett, Jane. Collages and reliefs 1910-1945 / essays by Jane Beckett. and, Hiller-heliographs / essay by Andrei Nakov : 30 June-2 October, 1982. — London (11 Tottenham Mews, W1P 9PJ) : Annely Juda Fine Art, c1982. — 119p : ill(some col.),ports ; 24cm
Published to accompany an exhibition at Annely Juda Fine Art, London, 1982
Unpriced (pbk) B82-37620

709'.04 — Visual arts, *1914-1939*

David, Jean-Luc. Avant-garde art 1914-1939 / by Jean-Luc Daval. — Geneva : Skira ; London : Macmillan, 1981, c1980. — 223p : ill(some col.),ports ; 35cm
In slip case. — Includes index
ISBN 0-333-31473-5 : Unpriced B82-01942

709'.04 — Visual arts. Movements, *1900-1980 — Critical studies*

Concepts of modern art. — Rev. and enl. ed. / edited by Nikos Stangos. — London : Thames and Hudson, c1981. — 384p : ill ; 22cm
Previous ed.: Harmondsworth : Penguin, 1974. — Bibliography: p373-377. — Includes index
ISBN 0-500-18186-1 : £7.95 B82-03494

709'.04 — Western arts, *1900-1980.* **Representation**

Albright, Daniel. Representation and the imagination : Beckett, Kafka, Nabokov, and Schoenberg / Daniel Albright. — Chicago ; London : University of Chicago Press, 1981. — viii,221p,[17]p of plates : ill,ports ; 23cm. — (Chicago originals)
Includes index
ISBN 0-226-01252-2 (pbk) : £9.95 B82-09668

709'.04 — Western visual arts, *1789-ca 1980*

New horizons : the history of painting and sculpture / [chief contributor and general editor David Piper] ; [editor Paul Holberton]. — London : Mitchell Beazley, 1981. — 272p : ill(some col.),col.maps,ports(some col.) ; 30cm. — (The Mitchell Beazley library of art ; v.3)
Includes index
ISBN 0-85533-357-x : £13.95
ISBN 0-85533-177-1 (set) : Unpriced
Also classified at 709'.5 B82-03764

709'.04 — Western visual arts. Influence of Japanese visual arts, *1858-1979*

Wichmann, Siegfried. Japonisme : the Japanese influence on Western art since 1858 / Siegfried Wichmann. — London : Thames and Hudson, 1981. — 432p : ill(some col.),ports(some col.) ; 31cm
Translation of: Japonismus. — Bibliography: p417-419. — Includes index
ISBN 0-500-23341-1 : £30.00 B82-02825

709'.04'007402 — Great Britain. Arts. Patronage. Organisations: Arts Council of Great Britain. Exhibits: Visual arts, *1923-1980 — Catalogues*

Constructed images : an Arts Council exhibition ... — London : Arts Council of Great Britain, c1981. — [4]p : ill ; 30cm. — (Approaches to modern art)
Catalogue of an exhibition
ISBN 0-7287-0288-6 (unbound) : Unpriced B82-13039

709'.04'012 — Art objects. Art deco style — *Collectors' guides*

Art nouveau-deco / compiled by Tony Curtis. — Galashiels : Lyle, c1981. — 126p : chiefly ill ; 17cm. — (Antiques and their values)
Includes index
ISBN 0-86248-011-6 : £2.50
Primary classification 709'.03'49 B82-08193

Barton, Stuart. Art Deco / compiled and edited by Stuart Barton ; consultant editor Martin Miller. — Tenterden : MJM, [1982?]. — 89p : ill ; 22cm. — (Buyer's price guides)
Includes index
ISBN 0-905879-17-1 : £2.95 B82-33573

709'.04'074013 — United States. Rockefeller, Nelson A.. Private collections: Visual arts, *1900-1975*

Masterpieces of modern art : the Nelson A. Rockefeller collection / photographs by Lee Boltin ; text by William S. Lieberman ; introduction by Nelson A. Rockefeller ; essay by Alfred H. Barr, Jr. ; edited and with preface by Dorothy Canning Miller. — London : Orbis, 1982. — 255p : ill(some col.),1port ; 31cm
Bibliography: p248-252. — Includes index
ISBN 0-85613-405-8 : £25.00 B82-20151

709'.04'1 — Western visual arts, *1884-1914 — Critical studies*

Daval, Jean-Luc. Modern art : the decisive years, 1884-1914 / by Jean-Luc Daval ; [translated from the French by Helga Harrison]. — London : Macmillan, 1979. — 221p : ill(some col.) ; 35cm
In slip case. — Includes index
ISBN 0-333-26559-9 : £35.00 B82-20255

709'.04'60740355 — West Germany. Mönchengladbach. Museums: Städtisches Museum, Mönchengladbach. Exhibits: European avant garde visual arts, *1955-1970 — Catalogues*

Städtisches Museum, Mönchengladbach. The avant-garde in Europe, 1955-70 : the collection of the Staedtisches Museum Moenchengladbach. — Edinburgh : Scottish National Gallery of Modern Art, [1981?]. — 41p : ill ; 30cm
Unpriced (unbound) B82-02872

709'.04'7 — Northern England. Art galleries. Exhibits: Western visual arts, *1970-1980 — Catalogues*

Artist and Camera. — [London] : Arts Council of Great Britain, c1980. — 60p : ill ; 21x23cm
Catalogue of an exhibition. — Bibliography: p60
ISBN 0-7287-0259-2 (pbk) : Unpriced B82-21519

709'.04'8 — Urban regions. Public places. Visual arts *— Illustrations*

Redstone, Louis G.. Public art : new directions / Louis G. Redstone with Ruth R. Redstone. — New York ; London : McGraw-Hill, c1981. — viii,216p : chiefly ill(some col.) ; 29cm
Includes index
ISBN 0-07-051345-7 : £26.50 B82-14022

709'.17'671 — Islamic visual arts *— Serials*

Art east : a review of Islamic and Asiatic art. — No.1 (1982)-. — London (193a Shirland Rd, W9 2EU) : Hali Publications, 1982-. — v. : ill(some col.) ; 30cm
ISSN 0263-3892 = Art east : £3.00 per issue
Primary classification 709'.5 B82-25479

709'.2'2 — United States. Visual arts. Women artists *— Interviews*

Lives and works : talks with women artists / [compiled and edited by] Lynn F. Miller, Sally S. Swenson. — Metuchen ; London : Scarecrow, 1981. — vii,244p : ill,ports ; 23cm
ISBN 0-8108-1458-7 : Unpriced B82-10200

709'.2'2 — Visual arts *— Biographies — Serials*

International directory of exhibiting artists. — Oxford : Clio Press, May 1982. — 2v.([496 ; 324]p.)
ISBN 0-903450-61-5 : £35.00 : CIP entry B82-21114

709'.2'2 — Visual arts. Criticism. Women writers, *1820-1979*

Women as interpreters of the visual arts, 1820-1979 / edited by Claire Richter Sherman with Adele M. Holcomb. — Westport ; London : Greenwood Press, 1981. — xxiv,487p : ill,ports ; 25cm. — (Contributions in women's studies, ISSN 0147-104x ; no.18)
Bibliography: p441-457. — Includes index
ISBN 0-313-22056-5 : Unpriced B82-02243

709′.2′2 — Visual arts. Women artists, *ca 1970-1980*

Issue : social strategies by women artists : an exhibition / selected by Lucy R. Lippard. — London : Institute of Contemporary Arts, c1980. — [67]p : chiefly ill,facsims,1form,ports ; 30cm
Accompanies on exhibition held at ICA, 14 Nov. -21 Dec. 1980. — Includes bibliographies
ISBN 0-905263-09-x (pbk) : Unpriced
B82-19923

709′.2′2 — Visual arts. Women artists. Historiology — *Feminist viewpoints*

Parker, Rozsika. Old mistresses : women, art and ideology / Rozsika Parker and Griselda Pollock. — London : Routledge & Kegan Paul, 1981. — xxi,184p : ill,facsims,ports ; 25cm
Bibliography: p171-175. — Includes index
ISBN 0-7100-0879-1 (cased) : £12.95 : CIP rev.
ISBN 0-7100-0911-9 (pbk) : £5.95 B81-30600

709′.2′4 — American visual arts. Irwin, Robert, *1928- — Biographies*

Weschler, Lawrence. Seeing is forgetting the name of the thing one sees : a life of contemporary artist Robert Irwin / by Lawrence Weschler. — Berkeley ; London : University of California Press, c1982. — xiv,212p,[8]p of plates : ill,1plan,ports ; 24cm
Bibliography: p205-208. — Includes index
ISBN 0-520-04595-5 : £11.25 B82-37066

709′.2′4 — Cornwall. Newlyn. Art galleries: Newlyn Art Gallery. Exhibits: English visual arts. Carrick, Ian — *Catalogues*

Carrick, Ian. Ian Carrick : sculpture. — Penzance : Newlyn Orion, 1981. — [4]p : ill ; 21x30cm
Produced to accompany an exhibition at Newlyn Art Gallery, 20 May-20th June 1981. — One sheet (catalogue of exhibition) as insert
Unpriced (unbound) B82-05966

709′.2′4 — Cumbria. Carlisle *(District)*. **Brampton. Art galleries: LYC Museum and Art Gallery. Exhibits: English experimental arts. Upton, Lawrence** — *Catalogues*

81 November 7 / Kate Nicholson, Harvey Shields, Lawrence Upton. — Brampton (Banks, Brampton, Cumbria CA8 2JH) : LYC Museum & Art Gallery, c1981. — [45]p : ill,2ports ; 14cm
ISBN 0-9504571-1-6 (unbound) : Unpriced
Primary classification 759.2 B82-08952

709′.2′4 — Dutch visual arts. Elk, Ger van — *Critical studies*

Elk, Ger van. Ger Van Elk : recent painting and sculpture and a selection of earlier work : Fruit Market Gallery, Edinburgh 14 November-19 December 1981, Serpentine Gallery, London 30 January-7 March 1982, Arnolfini, Bristol 3 April-15 May 1982. — [London] : Arts Council of Great Britain, [1981?]. — [4]p : ill ; 30cm
Unpriced (unbound) B82-13031

709′.2′4 — England. Art galleries. Exhibits: American visual arts. Masi, Denis — *Catalogues*

Masi, Denis. Denis Masi : Angela Flowers Gallery, 11 Tottenham Mews, London W1, May 5-May 30 1981 : Spacex Gallery, 45 Preston Street, Exeter, October 9-Novemeber 7 1981 : Bluecoat Gallery, School Lane, Liverpool L1 3BX January 9-February 5 1982. — Exeter : Spacex Gallery, 1981. — 40p : ill ; 21cm
ISBN 0-9507516-0-x (pbk) : Unpriced
B82-09031

709′.2′4 — English experimental visual arts. Atkinson, Conrad. Special subjects. Great Britain. Political events, *1970-1981 — Critical studies*

Atkinson, Conrad. Conrad Atkinson : picturing the system / edited by Sandy Nairne and Caroline Tisdall ; essay by Lucy R. Lippard and Timothy Rollins. — London : Pluto, 1981. — 83p : ill,ports ; 30cm
ISBN 0-86104-358-8 (pbk) : £3.95 B82-20693

709′.2′4 — English visual arts. Craig-Martin, Michael — *Critical studies*

Craig-Martin, Michael. Michael Craig-Martin : fifth Triennale India, New Delhi, 15 March-7 April 1982. — London : Fine Arts Department, the British Council, c1982. — 16p : ill(some col.) ; 20x21cm
ISBN 0-901618-72-1 (pbk) : Unpriced
B82-23048

709′.2′4 — English visual arts. Dannatt, George — *Illustrations*

Dannatt, George. George Dannatt : paintings, drawings and constructions 1960-1981. — Newlyn ([Newlyn, Cornwall]) : Newlyn Orion, c1981. — [24]p : ill(some col.),1port ; 21cm
Accompanies an exhibition held at the Newlyn Art Gallery, Cornwall, 20 May-20 June 1981
ISBN 0-9506579-2-1 (pbk) : Unpriced
B82-05469

709′.2′4 — English visual arts. Gregory, Robert — *Festschriften*

Robert Gregory 1881-1918 : a centenary tribute / with a foreword by his children ; edited by Colin Smythe. — Gerrards Cross : Smythe, 1981. — 40p : ill,1facsim,ports ; 22cm
ISBN 0-86140-108-5 (pbk) : £3.25
ISBN 0-86140-114-x (special ed) B82-01751

709′.2′4 — English visual arts. Jones, David, *1895-1974 — Critical studies*

Pacey, Philip. David Jones and other wonder voyagers. — Bridgend : Poetry Wales Press, Dec.1982. — [136]p
ISBN 0-907476-14-7 : £8.95 : CIP entry
B82-33369

709′.2′4 — English visual arts. Morris, William, *1834-1896 — Critical studies*

William Morris & Kelmscott. — London : Design Council, 1981. — 190p : ill(some col.),facsims,ports(some col.) ; 21cm
ISBN 0-85072-121-0 (pbk) : £7.00 : CIP rev.
B81-30612

709′.2′4 — English visual arts. Morris, William, *1834-1896 — Critical studies — Conference proceedings*

William Morris : aspects of the man and his work : proceedings of the 1977 Conference on William Morris held at Loughborough University of Technology, March 1977 / edited by Peter Lewis. — Loughborough : Loughborough Victorian Studies Group, [c1978]. — vii,119p,[6]leaves,[7]leaves of plates : ill ; 30cm
ISBN 0-904641-09-0 (pbk) : Unpriced
B82-11594

709′.2′4 — English visual arts. Ricketts, Charles — *Correspondence, diaries, etc.*

Ricketts, Charles. Letters from Charles Ricketts to 'Michael Field' (1903-1913) / edited sby J.G. Paul Delaney. — Edinburgh : Tragara, c1981. — 30p ; 24cm
Limited ed. of 145 numbered copies
ISBN 0-902616-72-2 (pbk) : £9.50
Also classified at 821′.8 B82-01388

709′.2′4 — English visual arts. Sedgley, Peter — *Critical studies*

Sedgley, Peter. Painting, objects, installations : 1963-1980 / Peter Sedgley ; text by Cyril Barrett. — London : Kelpra-Studios, [1980]. — [39]p : ill(some col.) ; 30cm
English and German text
ISBN 0-9507266-0-5 (pbk) : Unpriced
B82-02919

709′.2′4 — European visual arts. Surrealism — *Personal observations*

Colquhoun, Ithell. Surrealism : paintings, drawings, collages, 1936-1976 / Ithell Colquhoun. — [Newlyn] ([Newlyn, Cornwall]) : Newlyn Orion Galleries, 1976. — [12]p : ill,1port ; 22cm
Accompanies an exhibition mounted by the Newlyn Orion Galleries, Cornwall
Unpriced (unbound) B82-05473

709′.2′4 — French visual arts. Duchamp, Marcel — *Catalogues*

Marcel Duchamp's travelling box : published to accompany the exhibition organised by the Centre national d'art et de culture Georges-Pompidou, Paris and presented by the Arts Council of Great Britain. — [London] : Arts Council, c1982. — 24p : ill,port ; 15cm
ISBN 0-7287-0308-4 (pbk) : £1.50 B82-29329

709′.2′4 — German experimental visual arts. Beuys, Joseph — *Catalogues*

Tisdall, Caroline. Joseph Beuys : dernier espace avec introspecteur 1964-1982 / text and photographs by Caroline Tisdall. — London (7 and 23 Dering St., W1) : Anthony d'Offay Gallery, 1982. — [41]p : ill ; 19cm
Published to accompany an exhibition at the Anthony d'Offay Gallery, London, March-May 1982
(pbk) B82-31365

709′.2′4 — Irish visual arts. Cragg, Tony — *Critical studies*

Cragg, Tony. Tony Cragg : fifth Triennale India, New Delhi, 15 March-7 April 1982. — London : Fine Arts Department, the British Council, c1982. — 16p : ill(some col.) ; 20x21cm
ISBN 0-901618-71-3 (pbk) : Unpriced
B82-23049

709′.2′4 — London. Westminster *(London Borough)*. **Art galleries: Leinster Fine Art. Exhibits: German visual arts. Schad, Christian** — *Catalogues*

Schad, Christian. Christian Schad : etchings, woodcuts, schadographs : 1 December-19 December 1981. — London (9 Hereford Rd., W2 4AB) : Leinster Fine Art, [1981]. — 1folded sheet([8]p) : ill,1port ; 21cm
Bibliography: 1p
Unpriced B82-09117

709′.2′4 — London. Westminster *(London Borough)*. **Art galleries: Marlborogh Fine Art (London) Limited. Exhibits: German visual arts. Schwitters, Kurt** — *Catalogues*

Schwitters, Kurt. Kurt Schwitters in exile : the late work 1937-1948 = Kurt Schwitters im Exil : das Spätwerk 1937-1948 : 2-31 October 1981. — London : Marlborough Fine Art (London), c1981. — 160p : ill(some col.),1map,facsims,ports(some col.) ; 30cm
Text in English and German. — Bibliography: p158-159
ISBN 0-900955-20-1 (pbk) : Unpriced
B82-02182

709′.2′4 — London. Westminster *(London Borough)*. **Art galleries: Serpentine Gallery. Exhibits: American visual arts. Sommer, Frederick** — *Catalogues*

Sommer, Frederick. Frederick Sommer : photographs, drawings and musical scores : 17 October-22 November 1981, Serpentine Gallery, Kensington Gardens, London / exhibition organised by the Art Musuem and Galleries, California State University, Long Beach. — [London] : Arts Council of Great Britain, [1981?]. — [16]p : ill ; 21cm
Unpriced (unbound) B82-13030

709′.2′4 — Merseyside *(Metropolitan County)*. **Liverpool. Art galleries: Bluecoat Gallery. Exhibits: English visual arts. Grant, Duncan** — *Catalogues*

Grant, Duncan. Duncan Grant : designer : an exhibition devised and organized by Richard Shone with the assistance of Judith Collins for the Bluecoat Gallery, Liverpool / sponsored by the Liverpool daily post & echo with additional financial assistance from the Arts Council of Great Britain. — [Liverpool] ([School La., Liverpool L1 3BX]) : [The Gallery], [1981?]. — 40p : ill,1port ; 21x22cm
Unpriced (pbk) B82-09037

709′.2′4 — Merseyside *(Metropolitan County).* **Liverpool. Art galleries: Bluecoat Gallery. Exhibits: English visual arts. Kenny, Michael,** *1941 — Catalogues*

Kenny, Michael, *1941-*. Michael Kenny : sculpture & drawings : Bluecoat Gallery, School Lane, Liverpool L1 3BX, 5-28 February 1981 : Newcastle Polytechnic Art Gallery Library Building, Sandyford Road, Newcastle-upon-Tyne NE1 8ST 10 November-4 December 1981. — Liverpool (School La., Liverpool L1 3BX) : Bluecoat Gallery, [1981?]. — [18]p : ill ; 19cm
£0.50 (pbk) B82-09034

709′.2′4 — Merseyside *(Metropolitan County).* **Liverpool. Art galleries: Walker Art Gallery. Exhibits: English visual arts. McKeever, Ian —** *Catalogues*

McKeever, Ian. Islands and night flak / Ian McKeever. — Liverpool ([William Brown St, Liverpool L3 8EL]) : Walker Art Gallery, 1981. — 23p : ill(some col.) ; 19cm
Published to accompany an exhibition at the Walker Art Gallery. — Limited ed. of 1000 copies
£1.00 (pbk) B82-02889

709′.2′4 — Scotland. Art galleries. Exhibits: English visual arts. Ayrton, Michael — *Catalogues*

Ayrton, Michael. Michael Ayrton : paintings, sculptures, drawings, etchings, theatre designs, prints. — [Aberdeen] ([37, Belmont St, Aberdeen AB1 1JS]) : [Artspace], [1981]. — 29p : ill,1port ; 19cm
Published to accompany an exhibition at Artspace Galleries [Aberdeen] Ltd ; Collins Exhibition Hall, Glasgow ; City Art Centre, Edinburgh, 1981-1982. — Bibliography: p26-27
Unpriced (pbk) B82-05319

709′.2′4 — Swiss visual arts. Gerstner, Karl — *Critical studies*

The **Art** of Karl Gerstner : nine picture chapters and selected essays / edited by Henri Stierlin ; translated from the German by Dennis Q. Stephenson ; foreword by Grace Glueck ; contributions by François Fricker and Max Lüscher. — Cambridge, Mass. ; London : MIT Press, [c1981]. — 225p : ill(some col.) ; 25cm
Translation of: Der Geist der Farbe. — Half title page title: The spirit of colors. — In slip case
ISBN 0-262-07084-7 : £28.00 B82-13701

709′.2′4 — Visual arts. Criticism. Ruskin, John — *Critical studies*

The **Ruskin** polygon : essays on the imagination of John Ruskin / John Dixon Hunt, Faith M. Holland, editors. — Manchester : Manchester University Press, c1982. — xii,284p : ill,facsims,ports ; 25cm
Facsims on lining papers. — Includes index
ISBN 0-7190-0834-4 : £30.00 : CIP rev.
Primary classification 828′.809 B81-19160

709′.2′4 — Visual arts — *Personal observations*

Berger, John. Permanent red : essays in seeing / by John Berger. — London : Writers and Readers, 1979, c1960. — 223p ; 21cm
Originally published: London : Methuen, 1960. — Includes index
ISBN 0-906495-07-5 : £4.95 B82-01373

709′.37 — Ancient Roman visual arts

Andreae, Bernard. The art of Rome / Bernard Andreae ; translated from the German by Robert Erich Wolf. — London : Macmillan, 1978. — 655p : ill(some col.),plans ; 32cm
Ill on lining paper. — Bibliography: p632-645. — Includes index
ISBN 0-333-25689-1 : £40.00 : CIP rev. B78-23560

709′.37 — Ancient Roman visual arts — *Critical studies*

A **Handbook** of Roman art. — Oxford : Phaidon, Oct.1982. — [320]p
ISBN 0-7148-2214-0 (pbk) : £10.00 : CIP entry B81-24659

Woodford, Susan. The art of Greece and Rome / Susan Woodford. — Cambridge : Cambridge University Press, 1982. — 122p : ill(some col.),plans ; 25cm. — (Cambridge introduction to the history of art ; 1)
Bibliography: p120. — Includes index
ISBN 0-521-23222-8 (cased) : £7.25 : CIP rev.
ISBN 0-521-29873-3 (pbk) : Unpriced
Primary classification 709′.38 B81-32531

709′.38 — Ancient Greek visual arts, *B.C.323-B.C.31*

Havelock, Christine Mitchell. Hellenistic art : the art of the classical world from the death of Alexander the Great to the Battle of Actium / by Christine Mitchell Havelock. — 2nd ed. — New York ; London : Norton, c1981. — 283p : ill,1map,plans ; 20cm
Previous ed.: London : Phaidon, 1971. — Bibliography: p273-275. — Includes index
ISBN 0-393-01400-2 (cased) : £14.25
ISBN 0-393-95133-2 (pbk) : Unpriced B82-35678

709′.38 — Ancient Greek visual arts, *ca. B.C. 1550-ca B.C. 600*

Hampe, Roland. The birth of Greek art : from the Mycenaean to the Archaic period / Roland Hampe, Erika Simon ; foreword by John Boardman. — London : Thames and Hudson, 1981, c1980. — 318p : ill(some col.),maps,plans ; 32cm
Bibliography: p285-309. — Includes index
ISBN 0-500-23342-x : £35.00 B82-01310

709′.38 — Ancient Greek visual arts — *Critical studies*

Woodford, Susan. The art of Greece and Rome / Susan Woodford. — Cambridge : Cambridge University Press, 1982. — 122p : ill(some col.),plans ; 25cm. — (Cambridge introduction to the history of art ; 1)
Bibliography: p120. — Includes index
ISBN 0-521-23222-8 (cased) : £7.25 : CIP rev.
ISBN 0-521-29873-3 (pbk) : Unpriced
Also classified at 709′.37 B81-32531

709′.38′5 — Ancient Athenian visual arts — *Festschriften*

The **Eye** of Greece : studies in the art of Athens. — Cambridge : Cambridge University Press, Sept.1982. — [216]p
ISBN 0-521-23726-2 : £29.50 : CIP entry B82-29363

709′.4 — European visual arts, *1000-1880 — Critical studies*

Ruskin, John. The lamp of beauty : writings on art / by John Ruskin ; selected and edited by Joan Evans. — 2nd ed. — Oxford : Phaidon, 1980. — 342p,[79]p of plates : ill,1port ; 21cm. — (Landmarks in art history)
Previous ed.: 1959. — Includes index
ISBN 0-7148-2104-7 (pbk) : £5.95 : CIP rev. B80-11985

709′.4 — European visual arts, *to ca 1790 — Early works*

Reynolds, *Sir* **Joshua**. Discourse on art. — London : Yale University Press, Sept.1981. — [384]p
Originally published: 1975
ISBN 0-300-02775-3 : £5.95 : CIP entry B81-30244

709′.41 — British visual arts. Artists, *ca 1900-1930 - Directories*

Dolman, Bernard. Dictionary of contemporary British artists. — Woodbridge : Antique Collectors′ Club, May 1981. — 1v.
Originally published: 1929
ISBN 0-902028-99-5 : £19.50 : CIP entry B81-12358

709′.41 — Great Britain. Visual arts

Layzell, Richard. The artist′s directory. — London (Notting Hill Gate, W11 3JZ) : Art Guide Publications, Mar.1982. — [250]p
ISBN 0-9507160-5-7 (pbk) : £5.95 : CIP entry B82-09314

709′.41 — Great Britain. Visual arts — *Serials*

AN : artists newsletter. — Sept. 1980-. — Sunderland (c/o 17 Shakespeare Terrace, Sunderland, Tyne & Wear SR2 7JG) : Artic Producers, 1980-. — v. : ill ; 30cm
Monthly. — Description based on: June 1981
ISSN 0261-3425 = AN. Artists newsletter : £8.00 per year B82-10351

709′.41′074 — British visual arts — *Catalogues*

Inner worlds : an Arts Council Collection exhibition of sculptures, paintings and drawings / selected by Paul Overy. — London : Arts Council of Great Britain, c1982. — [24]p : ill ; 21cm
ISBN 0-7287-0313-0 (pbk) : Unpriced B82-29332

709′.41′07402 — Great Britain. Arts. Patronage. Organisations: Arts Council of Great Britain. Exhibits: British visual arts, *ca 1955-1980 — Catalogues*

Spalding, Julian. Fragments against ruin : a journey through modern art. — London : Arts Council of Great Britain, c1981. — [87]p : ill ; 10x21cm
Published to accompany an Arts Council collection touring exhibition, held at 8 different centres, 11 April 1981-6 March 1982. — Author: Julian Spalding
ISBN 0-7287-0278-9 (pbk) : £2.25 B82-06152

709′.41′07402659 — Cambridgeshire. Cambridge. Art galleries: Kettle′s Yard Gallery. Exhibits: British visual arts, *1934-1940 — Catalogues*

Circle : constructive art in Britain 1934-40 / edited by Jeremy Lewison. — Cambridge : Kettle′s Yard Gallery, c1982. — 88p : ill ; 30cm
Published to accompany the exhibition ′Circle′, held at Kettle′s Yard Gallery from 20 February to 28 March 1982
ISBN 0-907074-12-x (pbk) : Unpriced B82-20821

709′.415 — Irish visual arts

Knowles, Roderic. Contemporary Irish art. — Dublin : Wolfhound Press, Oct.1982. — [128]p
ISBN 0-86327-001-8 : £25.00 : CIP entry B82-29147

709′.415′07402915 — Ireland. Art galleries. Exhibits: Irish visual arts, *1970-1980 — Catalogues*

Hibernian inscape / the Douglas Hyde Gallery, Trinity College, Dublin, the Arts Council of Northern Ireland. — Dublin : Douglas Hyde Gallery, Trinity College, [1980]. — [31]p : ill,2ports ; 24cm
Published to accompany the ad hoc exhibitions held from 2nd Dec., 1980 to October 1981
Unpriced (pbk) B82-23578

709′.42 — England. Anglo-Saxon visual arts — *Readings from contemporary sources — Critical studies*

Dodwell, C. R.. Anglo-Saxon art : the literary perspective. — Manchester : Manchester University Press, Apr.1982. — [312]p
ISBN 0-7190-0861-1 : £17.50 : CIP entry B82-04880

709′.42 — English visual arts, *1888-1891 — Serials — Early works — Facsimiles*

Transactions of the National Association for the Advancement of Art and its Application to Industry 1888-1891. — New York ; London : Garland, 1979. — 3v. ; 24cm. — (The Aesthetic movement and the arts & crafts movement. Periodicals)
Facsim reprints. — Includes index
ISBN 0-8240-3617-4 : Unpriced B82-15182

709′.42 — English visual arts, *1894-1897 — Readings from contemporary sources*

The **Yellow** book. — Woodbridge : Boydell Press, Sept.1982. — [320]p
ISBN 0-85115-207-4 (pbk) : £4.95 : CIP entry
Primary classification 820.8′008 B82-18775

709′.42 — English visual arts, *1974-1977 — Illustrations*
Peter Joseph, Richard Long, David Tremlett in Newlyn. — [Penzance] : Newlyn Orion Galleries, 1978. — 1portfolio : ill ; 23x27cm
Produced to accompany an exhibition at the Newlyn Art Gallery in 1978
Unpriced
Also classified at 741.942 ; 759.2 ; 779′.092′4
B82-05968

709′.42′074 — English visual arts — *Catalogues*
82 June 5 : LYC Gallery / paintings by Harry McArdle, Jack Shotbolt ; sculpture by Charles Monkhouse ; photographs by Julia Szoka. — Brampton, Cumbria : Lyc Press, c1982. — [36]p : ill,ports ; 14cm
£0.35 (pbk) B82-40589

82 May 1 / Alan Tinley ... [et al.]. — Brampton : LYC Museum & Art Gallery, c1982. — [44]p : ill,ports ; 14cm
Cover title
ISBN 0-9504571-1-6 (pbk) : Unpriced
B82-28406

LYC August exhibition 1982. — Brampton (Banks, Brampton, Cumbria CA8 JJH) : LYC, c1982. — [48]p : ill ; 14cm
Unpriced (pbk) B82-40976

A **Mansion** of many chambers : Beauty and other works : an Arts Council Collection exhibition of special purchases and loans / selected by David Brown. — London : Arts Council of Great Britain, c1981. — [14]p : ill(some col.) ; 30x14cm
ISBN 0-7287-0306-8 (unbound) : £1.15
B82-29333

709′.42′07402 — Great Britain. Arts. Patronage. Organisations: Arts Council of Great Britain. Stock: English visual arts, *1954-1979 — Catalogues*
Arts Council of Great Britain. From object to object : an Arts Council Collection exhibition. — London : Arts Council of Great Britain, c1980. — [24]p : ill ; 16x21cm + 1card(2p : ill; 16x21cm)
ISBN 0-7287-0268-1 (pbk) : £1.10 B82-06149

709′.42′07402789 — Cumbria. Carlisle *(District).* **Brampton. Art galleries: LYC Museum & Art Gallery. Exhibits: English visual arts,** *1978-1981 — Catalogues*
82 January 2 / Richard Bray ... [et al.]. — Brampton : LYC Museum & Art Gallery, c1981. — [36]p : ill,ports ; 14cm
Cover title
ISBN 0-9504571-1-6 (pbk) : £0.35 B82-13877

709′.42′07402789 — Cumbria. Carlisle *(District).* **Brampton. Art galleries: LYC Museum and Art Gallery. Exhibits: English visual arts,** *1970-1980 — Catalogues*
81 December 5 : Rod Bugg, John C.M. Lyons, Alan Ball / LYC Museum & Art Gallery. — Brampton : LYC Press, c1981. — [40]p : chiefly ill,3ports ; 14cm
ISBN 0-9504571-1-6 (unbound) : Unpriced
B82-15004

709′.42′07402789 — Cumbria. Carlisle *(District).* **Brampton. Art galleries: LYC Museum and Gallery. Exhibits: English visual arts,** *ca 1965-1981 — Catalogues*
Barber, Wendy. 1982 April 03 / Wendy Barber, Doug Cocker, Barbara Gray. — Brampton : LYC Museum & Art Gallery, c1982. — [50]p : chiefly ill,2ports ; 14cm
ISBN 0-9504571-1-6 (unbound) : £0.35
B82-27621

709′.424′48 — Hereford and Worcester. Worcester. Cathedrals: Worcester Cathedral. Visual arts, *1000-1500*
Medieval art and architecture at Worcester Cathedral. — [London] ([61 Old Park Ridings, N21 2ET]) : British Archaeological Association], 1978. — vii,189p xxviiip of plates : ill,plans ; 26cm. — (Conference transactions / British Archaeological Association ; 1975, 1)
Editor: Glenys Popper. — Bibliography: p196-189
Unpriced
Primary classification 726′.6′0942448
B82-16313

709′.43 — German experimental visual arts — *Catalogues*
Hundertmark, Armin. Edition Hundertmark : Berlin/Köln / [responsible for the catalogue Armin Hundertmark] ; [translation Hildegard Gräven]. — London : Goethe Institut, 1981. — 64p : ill(some col.) ; 21cm
Translated from the German
£0.80 (pbk) B82-35139

709′.436′13 — Austrian visual arts: Viennese visual arts, *1898-1918*
Vergo, Peter. Art in Vienna 1898-1918 : Klimt, Kokoschka, Schiele and their contemporaries / Peter Vergo. — 2nd ed. — Oxford : Phaidon, 1981, c1975. — 256p : ill(some col.),ports ; 29cm
Previous ed.: 1975. — Bibliography: p250-252. — Includes index
ISBN 0-7148-2222-1 (cased) : £12.95 : CIP rev.
ISBN 0-7148-2224-8 (pbk) : Unpriced
B81-21483

709′.437′1 — Bohemian visual arts, *1500-1600 — Critical studies*
Renaissance art in Bohemia / text by Jiřina Hořejší ... [et al.]. — London : Hamlyn, [1980?]. — 245p : ill(some col.),maps,plans, ports(some col.) ; 32cm
Translated from Czech. — Ill on lining paper. — Bibliography: p222-234. — Includes index
ISBN 0-600-37573-0 : £20.00 B82-25021

709′.44 — France. Visual arts. Influence of political events, *1848-1851*
Clark, T. J.. The absolute bourgeois : artists and politics in France 1848-1851 / T.J. Clark ; with 109 illustrations. — London : Thames and Hudson, c1973 (1982 [printing]). — 224p : ill,2facsims,2ports ; 24cm
Bibliography: p209-218. — Includes index
ISBN 0-500-27246-8 (pbk) : £4.95 B82-20412

709′.44′07402132 — London. Westminster *(London Borough).* **Art galleries: Wallace Collection. Exhibits: French visual arts,** *1700-1800.* **Orientalism**
Hughes, Peter. Eighteenth-century France and the East / by Peter Hughes. — London (Manchester Sq, W1M 6BN) : Trustees of the Wallace Collection, 1981. — 32p,xip of plates : ill(some col.) ; 18cm. — (Wallace Collection monographs ; 4)
Unpriced (pbk) B82-03305

709′.45′074 — Italian visual arts, *1400-1600 — Catalogues*
Splendours of the Gonzaga : catalogue / edited by David Chambers & Jane Martineau. — London (Exhibition Rd, South Kensington, SW7) : Victoria & Albert Museum, c1981. — xxiii,248p : ill,1geneal.table,2maps,3plans(some col.),ports(some col.) ; 27cm
Exhibition held 4 November 1981-31 January 1982. — Bibliography: pix-xvi
Unpriced (pbk) B82-39640

709′.46′07402132 — London. Westminster *(London Borough).* **Art galleries: National Gallery. Exhibits: Spanish visual arts,** *1542-1828 — Catalogues*
Braham, Allan. El Greco to Goya : the taste for Spanish paintings in Britain and Ireland / introduction and catalogue by Allan Braham. — London : National Gallery, 1981. — 120p,[6]p of plates : ill(some col.),1map,ports (some col.) ; 25cm
Catalogue of the exhibition held at National Gallery 16th September-29th November, 1981. — Bibliography: p117-119. — Includes index
ISBN 0-901791-74-1 (pbk) : Unpriced
B82-04223

709′.47′07407312 — Russia *(RSFSR).* **Moscow. Art galleries: Gosudarstvennaīa Tre′iakovskaīa galleriīa. Exhibits: Russian avant garde visual arts,** *1900-1920.* **Collections: George Costakis Collection** *— Catalogues*
Russian avant-garde art : the George Costakis Collection / [general editor Angelica Zander Rudenstine] ; [introduction by S. Frederick Starr]. — [London] : [Thames and Hudson], [1981]. — 527p : ill(some col.),1facsim,ports ; 30cm
Ill on lining papers. — Includes index
ISBN 0-500-23345-4 : £28.00 B82-08560

709′.5 — Asian visual arts — *Serials*
Art east : a review of Islamic and Asiatic art. — No.1 (1982)-. — London (193a Shirland Rd, W9 2EU) : Hali Publications, 1982-. — v. : ill(some col.) ; 30cm
ISSN 0263-3892 = Art east : £3.00 per issue
Also classified at 709′.17′671 B82-25479

709′.5 — Far Eastern visual arts
New horizons : the history of painting and sculpture / [chief contributor and general editor David Piper] ; [editor Paul Holberton]. — London : Mitchell Beazley, 1981. — 272p : ill(some col.),col.maps,ports(some col.) ; 30cm. — (The Mitchell Beazley library of art ; v.3)
Includes index
ISBN 0-85533-357-x : £13.95
ISBN 0-85533-177-1 (set) : Unpriced
Primary classification 709′.04 B82-03764

709′.51 — Chinese visual arts, *ca B.C.1600-A.D.1912*
Watson, William, *1917 Dec.9-*. Art of dynastic China / William Watson. — London : Thames and Hudson, 1981. — 633p : ill(some col.),col.maps,plans ; 33cm
Translation of: L′Art de l′ancienne Chine. — Bibliography: p613-620. — Includes index
ISBN 0-500-23347-0 : £60.00 B82-13790

709′.51 — Chinese visual arts, *to 1980*
Juliano, Annette. Treasures of China / Annette Juliano. — London : Allen Lane, 1981. — 192p : col.ill,maps,plans ; 29cm
Ill on lining papers. — Bibliography: p186-188. — Includes index
ISBN 0-7139-1410-6 : £12.95 B82-01906

709′.52 — Japanese visual arts, *to 1868 — Critical studies*
Swann, Peter C.. A concise history of Japanese art / Peter C. Swann. — [Rev. ed.]. — Tokyo : Kodansha International ; Oxford : Phaidon [distributor], 1979. — 332p : ill(some col.) ; 19cm
Previous ed: published as ′An introduction to the arts of Japan′. Oxford : Cassirer, 1958. — Bibliography: p323-325. — Includes index
ISBN 0-87011-377-1 : £8.95 B82-02057

709′.52′07402132 — London. Westminster *(London Borough).* **Art galleries: P. and D. Colnaghi and Co.. Exhibits: Japanese visual arts,** *900-1900 — Catalogues*
One thousand years of art in Japan / Colnaghi Oriental in association with Shirley Day Ltd. — London (14 Old Bond St., W1X 4JL) : Colnaghi Oriental, [1981]. — 97p,[6]fold leaves of plates : ill(some col.) ; 30cm
Bibliography: p13-14
Unpriced (pbk) B82-07269

709′.52′07402132 — London. Westminster *(London Borough).* **Art galleries: Royal Academy of Arts. Exhibits: Japanese visual art,** *1600-1868 — Catalogues*
Great Japan Exhibition *(1981-1982 : Royal Academy of Arts).* The Great Japan Exhibition : art of the Edo period 1600-1868 : Royal Academy of Arts London 1981-2 / edited by William Watson. — [London] : [The Academy] in association with Weidenfeld and Nicolson, c1981. — 365p : ill(some col.),1map,1port ; 29cm
Bibliography: p351. — Includes index
ISBN 0-297-78027-1 (cased) : £17.50
ISBN 0-297-78035-2 (pbk) : £9.95 B82-05252

709′.53 — Arabian visual arts — *Serials — Arabic texts*
Funūn ʻArabiyyah : mağallah fikriyyah tuʻnī ibi-l-fann fi l-watan al-ʻArabī. — 1981, 1-. — London (Achilles House, Western Ave., W3 0RX) : Pan Middle East Graphics and Publishing (UK) Ltd., 1981-. — v. : ill(some col.),ports ; 30cm
Quarterly
ISSN 0263-3116 = Funūn ʻArabiyyah : £12.00 per year B82-23590

709′.54 — Indian visual arts, *to 1980*
The **Arts** of India / edited by Basil Gray. — Oxford : Phaidon, 1981. — 224p : ill(some col.) ; 29cm
Bibliography: p217-220. — Includes index
ISBN 0-7148-2150-0 : £25.00 : CIP rev.
B81-30469

709'.54 — Indian visual arts, *to 1980*
continuation

In the image of man : the Indian perception of the universe through 2000 years of painting and sculpture : Hayward Gallery, London 25 March-13 June 1982. — London : Published in association with the Arts Council of Great Britain [by] Weidenfeld and Nicolson, c1982. — 231p : ill(some col.),1map ; 29cm
Bibliography: p229
ISBN 0-297-78071-9 (cased) : £12.95
ISBN 0-297-78124-3 (pbk) : £7.95 B82-24212

709'.54'074 — Indian visual arts, *1500-1800 — Catalogues*

The **Indian** heritage : court life & arts under Mughal rule : Victoria & Albert Museum 21 April-22 August 1982. — [London] : [Victoria and Albert Museum], [1982]. — 176p : ill(some col.),1map,ports ; 27cm
Bibliography: p172-176
ISBN 0-905209-20-6 (pbk) : Unpriced
B82-27709

709'.54'074 — Indian visual arts, *to 1900 — Catalogues*

In the image of man : the Indian perception of the universe through 2000 years of painting and sculpture : Hayward Gallery, London 25 March-13 June 1982. — London : Arts Council of Great Britain in association with Weidenfeld and Nicolson, c1982. — 231p : ill (some col.),1map,plans ; 28cm
Bibliography: p229
ISBN 0-7287-0311-4 (pbk) : £7.50 B82-29335

Narain, L. A.. In the image of man : the Indian perception of the universe through 2000 years of painting and sculpture : Hayward Gallery, London, 25 March-13 June 1982 / [written by L.A. Narain with the assistance of others]. — [London] : Arts Council of Great Britain, 1982. — 24p : ill,1map,plans ; 25cm
Text, plans on inside covers
ISBN 0-7287-0318-1 (pbk) : £0.75 B82-29334

709'.5645 — Cypriot visual arts, *to 1570 — Critical studies*

British Museum. Cypriote art : in the British Museum / edited B.F. Cook. — London : Published for the Trustees of the British Museum by British Museum Publications Ltd., c1979. — 64p : ill ; 24cm
Ill on inside covers. — Bibliography: p63-64
ISBN 0-7141-1268-2 (pbk) : Unpriced
B82-18054

709'.593 — Thai visual arts, *ca 1250-1450*

Stratton, Carol. The art of Sukhothai : Thailand's golden age : from the mid-thirteenth to the mid-fifteenth centuries : a cooperative study / written and researched by Carol Stratton, Miriam McNair Scott ; photographs by Robert Stratton, Robert McNair Scott ; drawing by Turachai Kambhu na Ayudhaya. — Kuala Lumpur ; Oxford : Oxford University Press, 1981. — xxviii,163p,[24]p of plates : ill(some col.),maps,2plans ; 29cm
Bibliography: p153-158. — Includes index
ISBN 0-19-580434-1 : Unpriced B82-24076

709'.6 — African visual arts *— Collectors' guides*

Gillon, Werner. Collecting African art / Werner Gillon ; with an introduction by William Fagg ; and photographs by Werner Forman, Jo Furman and the late Eliot Elisofor. — London : Studio Vista, 1979. — x,183p,[24]p of plates : ill(some col.),maps(some col.) ; 29cm
Maps on lining papers. — Includes bibliographies and index
ISBN 0-289-70897-4 : £25.00 B82-19350

709'.71'07402132 — London. Westminster *(London Borough).* **Art galleries: Canada House Cultural Centre Gallery. Exhibits: Canadian visual arts,** *ca 1940-1981 — Catalogues*

Canadian art in Britain : contemporary works from collections in Britain : Canada House Cultural Centre Gallery, Trafalgar Square, London SW1Y 5BJ, 3 February-9 March 1982. — London ([Canada House, Trafalgar Sq., SW1Y 5BJ]) : [Canadian High Commission], [1982]. — [56]p : col.ill ; 25cm
Unpriced (pbk) B82-17640

709'.8 — Pre-Columbian Latin American visual arts *— Critical studies*

Parsons, Lee A.. Pre-Columbian art / by Lee A. Parsons ; photography by Jack Savage ; charts and drawings by Ryntha Johnson. — New York ; London : Harper & Row, c1980. — xiv,320p,[40]p of plates : ill(some col.),col.maps ; 29cm. — (Icon editions)
Bibliography: p307-308. — Includes index
ISBN 0-06-437000-3 : Unpriced B82-23044

709'.94 — Australian visual arts, *1930-1950 — Critical studies*

Haese, Richard. Rebels and precursors : the revolutionary years of Australian art / Richard Haese. — London : Allen Lane, [1982], c1981. — ix,324p : ill(some col.),ports(some col.) ; 25cm
Originally published: Sydney : Penguin Books Australia, 1981. — Bibliography: p309-312. — Includes index
ISBN 0-7139-1362-2 : £25.00 B82-22283

709'.94'074 — Australian visual arts *— Catalogues*

Eureka! : artists from Australia. — London : Arts Council of Great Britain, 1982. — 67p : ill ; 30cm
Published to accompany an exhibition at the Serpentine Gallery, 13 March-25 April 1982 and the Institute of Contemporary Arts, 24 March-24 April 1982
ISBN 0-7287-0316-5 (pbk) : £2.50
ISBN 0-905263-17-0 (ICA) B82-29336

711 — ENVIRONMENT PLANNING

711 — Environment planning

An **Annotated** reader in environmental planning and management. — Oxford : Pergamon, Sept.1982. — [352]p. — (Urban and regional planning series ; v.29) (Pergamon international library)
ISBN 0-08-024669-9 (cased) : £22.50 : CIP entry
ISBN 0-08-024668-0 (pbk) : £10.25
B82-19090

711'.07'1142753 — Merseyside *(Metropolitan County).* **Liverpool. Universities: University of Liverpool.** *Department of Civic Design, to 1948*

Wright, Myles. The Lever Chair. — London : Hutchinson, Oct.1982. — [224]p
ISBN 0-09-150340-x : £14.95 : CIP entry
B82-24975

711'.092'2 — Great Britain. Environment planning, *1870-1980 - Biographies*

Pioneers in British planning. — London : Architectural Press, May 1981. — [240]p
ISBN 0-85139-563-5 (pbk) : £8.95 : CIP entry
B81-12369

711'.0941 — Great Britain. Environment planning

Cullingworth, J. B.. Town and country planning in Britain / J.B. Cullingworth. — 8th ed. — London : Allen & Unwin, 1982. — 369p ; 23cm. — (The New local government series ; no.8)
Previous ed.: 1979. — Bibliography: p349-360. — Includes index
ISBN 0-04-711010-4 (cased) : Unpriced : CIP rev.
ISBN 0-04-711011-2 (pbk) : Unpriced
B82-10584

Ratcliffe, John. An introduction to town and country planning / John Ratcliffe. — 2nd ed. — London : Hutchinson, 1981. — 506p : ill,maps,plans ; 22cm. — (The Built environment series)
Previous ed.: 1974. — Bibliography: p483-487. — Includes index
ISBN 0-09-144020-3 (cased) : £15.00
ISBN 0-09-144021-1 (pbk) : £6.95 B82-02152

711'.0941 — Great Britain. Environment planning. Policies of government, *1939-1969*

Cullingworth, J. B.. Environmental planning, 1939-1969. — London : H.M.S.O.. — (Peacetime history)
Includes index
Vol.4: Land values, compensation and betterment / by J.B. Cullingworth. — 1980. — xv,582p,[1]folded leaf of plates : 1col.map ; 25cm
ISBN 0-11-630185-6 : £35.00 B82-05569

711'.0941 — Great Britain. Environment planning. Political aspects

Cherry, Gordon E.. The politics of town planning. — London : Longman, Sept.1982. — [192]p. — (Politics today)
ISBN 0-582-29540-8 (pbk) : £3.95 : CIP entry
B82-20256

711'.09411 — Scotland. Environment planning — *For surveying*

The **Development** plan system / prepared by the Planning and Development Division of the Scottish Branch of the Royal Institution of Chartered Surveyors. — Edinburgh : [The Institution], [1981?]. — 32p ; 30cm. — (Planning practice note (Scotland) ; no.3)
Bibliography: p31
£1.75 (pbk) B82-05168

711'.0942 — England. Environment planning — *Council for the Protection of Rural England viewpoints*

Planning : friend or foe? : a countryside concern discussion paper / by Council for the Protection of Rural England. — London : 4 Hobart Place, SW1W 0HY : The Council, c1981. — 31p : ill ; 21cm
Unpriced (unbound) B82-11622

711'.0942 — England. Green belts. Environment planning

Cherrett, Trevor. The implementation of Green Belt policy : three case studies / Trevor Cherrett. — Gloucester (Oxstalls Lane, Gloucester, GL2 1HW) : Dept. of Town and Country Planning, Gloucestershire College of Arts and Technology, 1982. — iii,53p : maps ; 30cm. — (Gloucestershire papers in local and rural planning, ISSN 0144-4875 ; no.15)
Bibliography: p50-51
Unpriced (pbk) B82-39729

711'.0973 — United States. Environment planning. Policies

The **Land** use policy debate in the United States / edited by Judith I. de Neufville. — New York ; London : Plenum, c1981. — xiii,269p : maps ; 24cm. — (Environment, development, and public policy. Environmental policy and planning)
Includes bibliographies and index
ISBN 0-306-40718-3 : Unpriced B82-13998

711'.1 — England. Environment planning. Decisions of local authorities. Appeals *— Manuals*

Blundell, Lionel A.. Blundell and Dobry's planning appeals and inquiries. — 3rd ed. / by Robert Carnwath ; consulting editor George Dobry. — London : Sweet & Maxwell, 1982. — xxi,146p ; 25cm
Spine title: Planning appeals and inquiries. — Previous ed.: / by Paul L. Rose and Michael Barnes. 1970. — Includes index
ISBN 0-421-25350-9 (pbk) : £9.75 : CIP rev.
B81-34393

711'.1 — England. Planning permission *— Manuals*

The **Making** of a planning application : a guide for practitioners / [prepared by the Planning & Development Division, The Royal Institution of Chartered Surveyors]. — London : Published on behalf of the Royal Institution of Chartered Surveyors by Surveyors Publications, c1981. — 7p ; 30cm. — (A Practice note, ISSN 0141-1462)
ISBN 0-85406-164-9 (unbound) : £2.50 (£2.25 to members of the Institution) B82-09381

711'.2'0722 — Structure planning. Analysis *— Case studies*

Bracken, Ian. Classification and analysis of strategic land-use policies / by Ian Bracken. — Cardiff (King Edward VII Ave., Cardiff CF1 3NU) : Dept. of Town Planning, University of Wales Institute of Science and Technology, 1981. — ii,26p : ill ; 30cm. — (Papers in planning research ; 32)
Bibliography: p23-24
Unpriced (pbk) B82-26829

711′.3′0941 — Great Britain. Structure planning — *Conference proceedings*

Progress in structure planning : integration of local government services : papers from the CES/RTPI Conference held in Birmingham, 26-28 March 1973. — London : Centre for Environmental Studies, 1974. — 100p : ill ; 30cm. — (Conference paper ; 8)
Includes bibliographies
£1.00 (pbk) B82-08893

711′.3′094115 — Scotland. Highland Region. Structure planning — *Proposals*

Highland Region. *Council.* Structure plan : report of survey (update), changes likely to occur 1978-88, written statement, state of publicity, representations and consultation / Highland Regional Council. — [Inverness] (Glenurquhart Rd., Inverness IV3 5NY]) : [The Council], 1979. — 112p : col.ill,col.maps ; 30cm
Unpriced (pbk) B82-09744

711′.3′0941223 — Scotland. Grampian Region. Moray *(District).* **Speyside. Environment planning** — *Proposals*

Moray. *Department of Physical Planning & Development.* Speyside local plan. — Elgin ([District Headquarters, Elgin, Morayshire, IV30 1BX]) : Department of Physical Planning & Development, Moray District Council, 1981. — 34leaves : maps ; 30cm
In plastic wallet. — Speyside local plan proposals map (folded sheet) as insert
Unpriced (spiral) B82-26489

711′.3′094124 — Scotland. Grampian Region. Kincardine and Deeside *(District).* **Environment planning** — *Proposals*

Kincardine & Deeside. *District Council.* Kincardine suburban area local plan : to be adopted. — [Stonehaven] ([Carlton House, Arduthie Rd., Stonehaven, AB3 2DP]) : Kincardine and Deeside District Council, [1982?]. — 131p : ill,col.maps + 4 proposals maps(63x81cm folded to 16x21cm)
Cover title. — Proposals maps in plastic folders
£2.00 (spiral) B82-21477

711′.3′094124 — Scotland. Grampian Region. Kincardine and Deeside *(District).* **Environment planning. Publicity & consultation**

Publicity and consultation : Kincardine suburban area local plan. — [Stonehaven] ([Carlton House, Arduthie Rd, Stonehaven, AB3 2DP]) : Kincardine and Deeside Council, [1982?]. — 114p : ill,maps,facsims,ports ; 30cm
£0.50 (spiral) B82-21468

711′.3′094126 — Scotland. Tayside Region. Angus *(District).* **Rural regions. Environment planning** — *Proposals*

Angus. *District Planning Department.* Angus District : settlement and development in the countryside / Angus District Planning Department. — [Forfar] ([County Buildings, Market St., Forfar DD8 3LG]) : [The Department], 1981. — 21p ; 30cm
Unpriced (spiral) B82-12640

711′.3′094126 — Scotland. Tayside Region. Forfar Loch region. Environment planning — *Proposals*

Angus. *District Planning Department.* Forfar Loch : a development policy / [produced by the Planning Service of Angus District Council]. — Forfar ([County Buildings, Forfar DD8 3LG]) : Angus District Planning Department, 1976. — 21p,[1]folded leaf of plates : 1map,1col.plan ; 30cm
Cover title
Unpriced (pbk) B82-13314

711′.3′0941295 — Scotland. Fife Region. Kirkcaldy *(District).* **Structure planning** — *Proposals*

Fife. *Regional Council.* Structure plan for Dunfermline & Kirkcaldy Districts : final written statement. — [Glenrothes] ([Fife House, North St., Glenrothes, Fife]) : [Fife Regional Council], [1982]. — 111p,[8]leaves of plates(1 folded) : maps,(some col.) ; 29cm
Author: Fife Regional Council
Unpriced (pbk)
Also classified at 711′.3′0941298 B82-37927

711′.3′0941298 — Scotland. Fife Region. Dunfermline *(District).* **Coastal regions. Environment planning** — *Proposals*

Dunfermline district (coastal settlements) local plan. — [Dunfermline] ([3 New Row, Dunfermline]) : Dunfermline District Council, [Planning Dept.]
Appendix. — 1981. — [72]p : 1ill,1map ; 30cm
Cover title
Unpriced (pbk) B82-37398

Dunfermline district (coastal settlements) local plan. — [Dunfermline] ([3 New Row, Dunfermline]) : Dunfermline District Council, [Planning Dept.]
Report of survey. — 1981. — [94]p,[23]folded leaves of plates : maps ; 30cm
Cover title
Unpriced (pbk) B82-37396

Dunfermline district (coastal settlements) local plan. — [Dunfermline] ([3 New Row, Dunfermline]) : Dunfermline District Council, [Planning Dept.]
Statement of publicity and consultation. — 1982. — [49]p : ill,maps ; 30cm
Cover title
Unpriced (pbk) B82-37397

Dunfermline district (coastal settlements) local plan. — [Dunfermline] ([3 New Row, Dunfermline]) : Dunfermline District Council, [Planning Dept.]
Written statement. — 1982. — [56]p,[6]folded leaves of plates : maps ; 30cm
Cover title
Unpriced (pbk) B82-37395

711′.3′0941298 — Scotland. Fife Region. Dunfermline *(District).* **Structure planning** — *Proposals*

Fife. *Regional Council.* Structure plan for Dunfermline & Kirkcaldy Districts : final written statement. — [Glenrothes] ([Fife House, North St., Glenrothes, Fife]) : [Fife Regional Council], [1982]. — 111p,[8]leaves of plates(1 folded) : maps,(some col.) ; 29cm
Author: Fife Regional Council
Unpriced (pbk)
Primary classification 711′.3′0941295 B82-37927

711′.3′0941298 — Scotland. Fife Region. North-eastern Dunfermline *(District).* **Environment planning** — *Proposals*

Dunfermline. *District Council.* North East Sector local plan : written statement / Dunfermline District Council. — Dunfermline (Planning Dept., 3 New Row, Dunfermline) : Dunfermline District Council, 1981. — 50p,[14]folded p of plates : maps ; 30cm
Unpriced (spiral) B82-11033

711′.3′0941312 — Scotland. Central Region. Stirling region. Structure planning. Participation of public

Central Region. *Regional Council.* Stirling-Alloa structure plan, publicity and consultations report / Central Regional Council. — [Stirling] (Viewforth, Stirling FK8 2ET) : Central Regional Council Planning Department, 1980. — 12p : 1facsim ; 30cm
Unpriced (pbk)
Also classified at 711′.3′0941315 B82-15454

711′.3′0941312 — Scotland. Central Region. Stirling region. Structure planning — *Proposals*

Central Region. *Regional Council.* Stirling-Alloa structure plan, draft written statement / Central Regional Council. — [Stirling] ([Viewforth, Stirling FK8 2ET]) : [Central Regional Council], 1979. — 78p,[8]leaves of plates (1 folded) : col.maps ; 30cm
Unpriced (unbound)
Also classified at 711′.3′0941315 B82-15452

Central Region. *Regional Council.* Stirling-Alloa structure plan, written statement / Central Regional Council. — [Stirling] ([Viewforth, Stirling FK8 2ET]) : [Central Regional Council], 1980. — 79p,[8]leaves of plates (1folded) : col.maps ; 30cm
Cover title
Unpriced (pbk)
Also classified at 711′.3′0941315 B82-15451

711′.3′0941312 — Scotland. Central Region. Western Stirling *(District).* **Structure planning. Participation of public**

Central Regional Council : western rural area structure plan : publicity and consultations report. — [Stirling] ([Viewforth, Stirling FK8 2ET]) : Central Regional Council, Planning Department, 1981. — 13p ; 30cm
Unpriced (pbk) B82-15459

711′.3′0941312 — Scotland. Central Region. Western Stirling *(District).* **Structure planning** — *Proposals*

Central Region. *Department of Planning.* Central Regional Council : western rural area structure plan : [written statement] / prepared on behalf of the Central Regional Council by the Department of Planning. — [Stirling] ([Viewforth, Stirling FK8 2ET]) : [Central Regional Council], 1981. — 63p,[1]folded leaf of plates : maps(some col.) ; 30cm
Unpriced (pbk) B82-15458

711′.3′0941315 — Scotland. Central Region. Clackmannan *(District).* **Structure planning. Participation of public**

Central Region. *Regional Council.* Stirling-Alloa structure plan, publicity and consultations report / Central Regional Council. — [Stirling] (Viewforth, Stirling FK8 2ET) : Central Regional Council Planning Department, 1980. — 12p : 1facsim ; 30cm
Unpriced (pbk)
Primary classification 711′.3′0941312
B82-15454

711′.3′0941315 — Scotland. Central Region. Clackmannan *(District).* **Structure planning** — *Proposals*

Central Region. *Regional Council.* Stirling-Alloa structure plan, draft written statement / Central Regional Council. — [Stirling] ([Viewforth, Stirling FK8 2ET]) : [Central Regional Council], 1979. — 78p,[8]leaves of plates (1 folded) : col.maps ; 30cm
Unpriced (unbound)
Primary classification 711′.3′0941312
B82-15452

Central Region. *Regional Council.* Stirling-Alloa structure plan, written statement / Central Regional Council. — [Stirling] ([Viewforth, Stirling FK8 2ET]) : [Central Regional Council], 1980. — 79p,[8]leaves of plates (1folded) : col.maps ; 30cm
Cover title
Unpriced (pbk)
Primary classification 711′.3′0941312
B82-15451

711′.3′094133 — Scotland. Lothian Region. West Lothian *(District).* **Environment planning**

West Lothian District Council planning information handbook. — London : Pyramid Press, [1980]. — 48p : ill,1map ; 21cm
Unpriced (pbk) B82-14591

711′.3′094136 — Scotland. Lothian Region. Western East Lothian *(District).* **Environment planning** — *Proposals*

East Lothian. *Department of Physical Planning.* West Sector local plan : written statement — policies and proposals. — [Haddington] : East Lothian District Council, Department of Physical Planning, 1981. — 51p,[8]leaves of plates(some folded) : maps ; 31cm
Cover title
£3.00 (pbk) B82-27732

711′.3′094141 — Scotland. Strathclyde Region. Structure planning. Participation of public

Strathclyde structure plan 1981 : consultation report / Strathclyde Regional Council. — Glasgow : The council, [1981]. — 93p : 2maps ; 30cm
Unpriced (pbk) B82-17867

711′.3′094141 — Scotland. Strathclyde Region. Structure planning — *Proposals*

Strathclyde. *Regional Council.* Strathclyde structure plan 1979. — [Glasgow] ([Strathclyde House, India St, Glasgow]) : Strathclyde Regional Council, [1980]. — 3v. : maps(some col.) ; 31-45cm
Unpriced (pbk) B82-23640

711′.3′094141 — Scotland. Strathclyde Region. Structure planning — *Proposals*
continuation

Strathclyde. *Regional Council*. Strathclyde structure plan 1981 : written statement / Strathclyde Regional Council. — Glasgow : The council, [1981]. — 87p : 3col.maps ; 30cm
Three maps on 3 folded sheets as inserts
Unpriced (pbk) B82-17866

711′.3′0941425 — Scotland. Loch Lomond region. Environment planning — *Proposals*

Loch Lomond Planning Group. Loch Lomond local (subject) plan for recreation, tourism and landscape conservation, consultative draft / Loch Lomond Planning Group. — [Dumbarton] ([c/o Dumbarton District Council, Crosslet House, Argyll Ave., Dumbarton G82 3NS]) : Loch Lomond Planning Group, 1980. — 78p : ill,col.maps ; 30cm + 1 sheet(84x58cm folded to 21x29cm : col.map)
Unpriced (pbk) B82-15455

711′.3′0941449 — Scotland. Strathclyde Region. Northern Motherwell *(District)*. **Environment planning** — *Proposals*

Motherwell. *District Council*. Northern Area local plan written statement / [Motherwell District Council]. — [Motherwell] : The Council, 1981. — [102]p,[4]folded leaves of plates : maps ; 30cm + 1sheet(Map; 98x120cm folded to 25x19cm)
Map in pocket
ISBN 0-903207-11-7 (spiral) : Unpriced
B82-16793

711′.3′094223 — Kent. Structure planning — *Proposals*

Kent structure plan : proposed alterations to the written statement, consultative draft / Kent County Council. — Maidstone (Springfield, Maidstone, Kent ME14 2LX) : The Council, 1980. — 150p,[3]leaves of plates(some col.) : maps(some col.) ; 30cm
£4.00 (pbk) B82-21651

711′.3′09422323 — Kent. Rochester upon Medway *(District)*. **Environment planning**

Planning handbook / Rochester upon Medway City Council. — [London] ([Publicity House, Streatham Hill, SW2 4TR]) : [Pyramid Press], [1982?]. — 40p : ill,maps ; 21cm
Unpriced (pbk) B82-37408

711′.3′094226 — West Sussex. Structure planning — *Proposals*

West Sussex county structure plan : written statement. — Chichester : [West Sussex County Council], 1980. — 186p,[2]leaves of plates(1 folded) : ill(some col.),maps(some col.) ; 30cm
ISBN 0-86260-000-6 (spiral) : £4.00
B82-35060

711′.3′094227 — Hampshire. Environment planning — *Proposals*

Hampshire. *County Council*. Development plan scheme / [Hampshire County Council]. — [Winchester] : [The Council], 1982. — 35,xiiip ; 30cm
Unpriced (pbk) B82-21835

711′.3′094227 — South Hampshire. Structure planning — *Serials*

[Monitoring report *(Hampshire. County Planning Department)*]. Monitoring report / Hampshire County Planning Department. — Aug. 1977-. — Winchester (The Castle, Winchester) : The Department, 1977-. — v. : maps ; 30cm. — (South Hampshire strategic planning paper)
ISSN 0263-9009 = Monitoring report - Hampshire County Planning Department : £0.60 B82-36725

711′.3′0942275 — South-west Hampshire. Environment planning. Policies of Hampshire. *County Council*

Hampshire. *County Council*. South West Hampshire strategic planning policies. — [Winchester] ([The Castle, Winchester]) : Hampshire County Council, 1978. — 8,iip,leaf of plate : map ; 30cm. — (Hampshire strategic planning paper ; no.2)
Unpriced (unbound) B82-38211

711′.3′0942315 — Western Wiltshire. Structure planning — *Proposals*

Wiltshire. *County Council*. Western Wiltshire structure plan : operative plan / Wiltshire County Council. — [Trowbridge] : [The Council], 1981. — xvi,6p,[3]leaves of plates : 3col.maps ; 30cm
ISBN 0-86080-089-x (pbk) : Unpriced
B82-21900

Wiltshire. *County Council*. Western Wiltshire structure plan : explanatory memorandum / Wiltshire County Council. — [Trowbridge] : [The Council], 1981. — 97p : ill,col.maps ; 30cm
Includes index
ISBN 0-86080-090-3 (pbk) : Unpriced
B82-21901

711′.3′094233 — Dorset. Structure planning. Participation of public

Statement of public involvement : Dorset (excluding south-east) Structure Plan / prepared by Dorset County Council .... — [Dorchester] : The Council, 1981. — ii,54p : ill,facsims ; 30cm. — (DSP ; 23)
ISBN 0-85216-287-1 (pbk) : £1.00 B82-02513

711′.3′094233 — Dorset. Structure planning — *Proposals*

Dorset. *County Council*. Explanatory memorandum : Dorset (excluding south-east) Sturcture Plan / prepared by Dorset County Council .... — [Dorchester] : The Council, 1981. — iv,183p : maps(some col.) ; 30cm. — (DSP ; 22)
ISBN 0-85216-286-3 (pbk) : £2.00 (£1.50 without key diagram) B82-02514

Dorset. *County Council*. Written statement : Dorset (excluding south-east) Stucture Plan / prepared by Dorset County Council .... — [Dorchester] : The Council, 1981. — v,31p : maps(some col.) ; 30cm. — (DSP ; 21)
Key diagram (map, 1folded sheet) in pocket
ISBN 0-85216-285-5 (pbk) : £1.00(£0.50 without key diagram) B82-02512

711′.3′094233 — South-east Dorset. Structure planning. Dorset. *County Council*. **South east Dorset structure plan. Implementation**

Monitoring report, 1981 : South east Dorset structure plan. — [Dorchester] : Structure Plan Team, Dorset County Council, 1981. — iv,34p : ill,2col.maps,1plan ; 30cm. — (SP ; 27)
ISBN 0-85216-291-x (pbk) : £0.75 B82-08052

711′.3′094235 — Devon. Environment planning. Procedure

Derounian, James. Planning : a guide for Devon people / by James Derounian. — [Devon] : Community Council of Devon, [1982]. — 42p : ill ; 21cm
Cover title. — Text on inside covers. — Includes index
ISBN 0-86114-357-4 (pbk) : Unpriced
B82-40530

711′.3′094235 — Devon. Structure planning. Policies of Devon. *County Council*. **Implementation** — *Serials*

Devon. *Planning Department*. Devon county structure plan progress report / County Planning Department. — 1981-. — Exeter (County Hall, Topsham Rd, Exeter EX2 4QH) : Devon County Council. Planning Department, 1981-. — v. ; 30cm
Annual
ISSN 0261-2488 = County structure plan progress report (Devon County Council. Planning Department) : Unpriced B82-11154

711′.3′094235 — Devon. Structure planning — *Proposals*

Devon. *Planning Department*. Devon County structure plan : first alteration project. — Exeter : Devon County Council, 1982. — 7p : ill ; 30cm
ISBN 0-86114-363-9 (pbk) : £0.40 B82-25035

Devon county structure plan : policies and proposals. — Exeter : Devon County Planning Department, 1981. — 40p : col.maps ; 30cm
Seven maps on 6 leaves and 1 folded sheet in pocket. — Includes index
ISBN 0-86114-342-6 (pbk) : £1.00 B82-07465

711′.3′094237 — Cornwall. Environment planning

Development plan scheme : second review, 1982-83 / Cornwall County Council. — [Truro] ([County Hall, Truro TR1 3AY]) : County Planning Officer, Cornwall County Council, 1982. — 19,[20]p : maps ; 30cm
Unpriced (pbk) B82-34036

711′.3′094237 — Cornwall. Structure planning — *Proposals*

Cornwall. *County Council*. Countryside subject plan : draft written statement. — [Truro] : Cornwall County Council, 1982. — 90p,[34]p of plates(some folded) : ill,maps ; 30cm
ISBN 0-902319-40-x (pbk) : Unpriced
B82-36005

Cornwall County structure plan : written statement, key diagram. — [Truro] : Cornwall County Council, 1981. — 36p : 1col.map ; 30cm
"Cornwall County structure plan key diagram" (1 folded sheet) in pocket
ISBN 0-902319-38-8 (pbk) : Unpriced
B82-19125

Cornwall County structure plan : explanatory memorandum. — [Truro] : Cornwall County Council, 1981. — 235p : ill,maps(some col.) ; 30cm
"Cornwall County structure plan key diagram" (1 folded sheet) in pocket
ISBN 0-902319-39-6 (pbk) : Unpriced
B82-19124

711′.3′094239 — Avon. Structure planning. Participation of public

County of Avon structure plan : report on public consultation / Avon County Planning Department. — Bristol : [The Department], 1980. — ii,114p : ill,maps,facsims ; 30cm
ISBN 0-86063-103-6 (pbk) : £2.50 B82-21641

711′.3′094239 — Avon. Structure planning — *Proposals*

County of Avon structure plan : written statement / Avon County Planning Department. — Bristol : [The Department], 1980. — 146p,3leaves of plates : col.maps ; 30cm
ISBN 0-86063-106-0 (pbk) : £7.50 B82-21642

Digest of policies : consultation draft : Avon county structure plan. — [Bristol] : [Avon County Planning Department], [1981]. — 31p,[1]folded leaf of plate : 1col.map ; 30cm
ISBN 0-86063-132-x (spiral) : Unpriced
B82-12217

Structure plan written statement incorporating explanatory memorandum. — Bristol : Avon County Planning Department, 1981. — 150p,[3]leaves of plates (1 folded) : 3col.maps ; 30cm
ISBN 0-86063-130-3 (pbk) : £5.00 B82-12218

711′.3′0942397 — Avon. Wansdyke *(District)*. **Environment planning**

Wansdyke District Council planning handbook. — [London] : Pyramid Press, [1980]. — 44p : ill ; 21cm
Unpriced (pbk) B82-14592

711′.3′094241 — Gloucestershire. Rural regions. Structure planning. Influence of analysis of economic activity of women

West, Christopher. Rural female economic activity : an empirical study of the determinants of female economic activity rates in rural Gloucestershire / Christopher West. — Gloucester : Department of Town and Country Planning, Gloucestershire College of Arts and Technology, 1981. — 17p : ill,1map ; 30cm. — (Gloucestershire papers in local planning, ISSN 0144-4875 ; Issue no.13)
Bibliography: p13
Unpriced (pbk) B82-16001

711′.3′094244 — Hereford and Worcester. Environment planning

Hereford & Worcester through the 80′s. — [Worcester] ([County Hall, Spetchley Rd., Worcester, WR5 2NP]) : [County Planning Department], 1982. — [4]p : ill,1map ; 30cm
Unpriced (unbound) B82-32049

711'.3'094244 — Hereford and Worcester. Structure planning — *Proposals*

Hereford & Worcester. *County Council.* Review of structure plans : Hereford and Worcester County : draft written statement. — [Worcester] (c/o County Planner, County Hall, Spetchley Rd., Worcester WR5 2NP) : Hereford and Worcester County Council, 1982. — i,60p : 3maps(some col.) ; 30cm
Unpriced (pbk) B82-32090

Hereford & Worcester. *County Council.* Review of structure plans : Hereford and Worcester County : draft explanatory memorandum. — [Worcester] (c/o County Planner, County Hall, Spetchley Rd., Worcester) : Hereford and Worcester County Council, 1982. — i,166p : maps(some col.) ; 29cm
Unpriced (pbk) B82-32091

711'.3'094245 — Shropshire. Structure planning — *Proposals*

Development plan scheme for Shropshire / prepared by Shropshire County Council in consultation with the district councils. — [Shrewsbury] ([c/o County Planning Officer, Shirehall, Abbey Foregate, Shrewsbury]) : [Shropshire County Council], [1982]. — 22,5,1p ; 30cm
Cover title
Unpriced (spiral) B82-33070

711'.3'0942511 — Derbyshire. High Peak *(District).* **Environment planning** — *Practical information*

Morris, Michael W.. Planning information handbook. — 1981 ed. / designed and written by Michael W. Morris for High Peak Borough Council. — [Wallington, Surrey] : Home Publishing, [1981]. — 43p : ill,1map ; 21cm
Previous ed.: 1977
Unpriced (pbk) B82-13303

711'.3'094252 — Nottinghamshire. Structure planning

Payne, V. S.. Nottinghamshire structure plan : first monitoring report / V.S. Payne. — [Nottingham] ([Trent Bridge House, Fox Rd., West Bridgford, Nottingham, NG2 6BJ]) : Nottinghamshire County Council [Planning and Transportation Dept.], 1982. — 44p : 1map ; 30cm
Unpriced (spiral) B82-32922

711'.3'094253 — Lincolnshire. Coastal regions. Environment planning — *Proposals*

Development on the Lincolnshire coast : subject plan. — [Lincoln] ([County Offices, Lincoln]) : Lincolnshire County Council, 1982. — 88p,A1-A10,[36]p of plates : maps(some col.) ; 21x30cm
Unpriced (spiral) B82-40195

711'.3'0942579 — Oxfordshire. South Oxfordshire *(District).* **Environment planning** — *Proposals*

South Oxfordshire. *District Council.* Planning policy statements / South Oxfordshire District Council. — [Didcot] ([Churchill House, Didcot, Oxon. OX11 8RH]) : South Oxfordshire District Council, Planning Department, 1980. — 23,A-Cp ; 30cm
Cover title
Unpriced (pbk) B82-27272

711'.3'0942581 — Hertfordshire. North Hertfordshire *(District).* **Environment planning**

Project report / [North Hertfordshire District Council]. — [Letchworth] ([Council Offices, Gernon Rd., Letchworth, Herts. SG6 3JF]) : [The Council], 1978. — 17p ; 30cm
£0.35 (pbk) B82-11582

711'.3'0942581 — Hertfordshire. North Hertfordshire *(District).* **Environment planning. Participation of public**

North Hertfordshire. *District Council.* Report on public participation activities stages I to III : North Hertfordshire district plan. — [Letchworth] : North Hertfordshire District Council, 1981. — 36p : ill,maps,facsims,forms ; 30cm
£2.00 (pbk) B82-25366

711'.3'0942581 — Hertfordshire. North Hertfordshire *(District).* **Environment planning** — *Proposals*

North Hertfordshire. *District Council.* Written statement : North Hertfordshire district plan. — [Letchworth] : North Hertfordshire District Council, 1981. — iii,103p : ill,maps(some col.) ; 30cm + proposals maps(60cmx85cm)
£3.00 (pbk) B82-25365

711'.3'0942584 — Hertfordshire. Dacorum *(District).* **Environment planning. Policies of Dacorum.** *District Council*

Planning information handbook / Dacorum District Council. — Wallington (20 Belmont Rd., Wallington, Surrey, SM6 8TA) : Home Publishing, 1982. — 44p : ill,1map ; 21cm
Unpriced (pbk) B82-37094

711'.3'0942587 — Hertfordshire. Broxbourne *(District).* **Environment planning** — *Practical information*

Broxbourne planning handbook / [Broxbourne Borough Council]. — London (Publicity House, Streatham Hill, SW2 4TR) : Pyramid Press, [1982]. — 40p : ill,1map ; 21cm
Unpriced (pbk) B82-37384

711'.3'094259 — Buckinghamshire. Structure planning. Participation of public

Buckinghamshire county structure plan : proposed alterations 1981 : report on public consultation. — [Aylesbury] : [Buckinghamshire County Council, Planning Department], 1981. — 30p ; 30cm
Cover title
ISBN 0-86059-206-5 (pbk) : £0.50 B82-12631

711'.3'094259 — Buckinghamshire. Structure planning — *Proposals*

Buckinghamshire county structure plan : proposed alterations 1981 : written statement and explanatory memorandum. — [Aylesbury] : [Buckinghamshire County Council, Planning Department], 1981. — 56p : ill,maps ; 21x30cm
Cover title
ISBN 0-86059-201-4 (pbk) : £1.00 B82-12630

711'.3'094261 — Norfolk. Structure planning

Norfolk structure plan : fifth monitoring report : the county strategy / Norfolk County Council Planning and Transportation Committee. — Norwich ([c/o] County Planning Officer, County Hall, Martineau Lane, Norwich, Norfolk NR1 1DH) : Norfolk County Council, 1982. — 87p : ill,maps ; 30cm
£1.20 (spiral) B82-32057

711'.3'094264 — Suffolk. Environment planning

Development plan scheme : second amendment / Suffolk County Council. — Ipswich : The Council, 1982. — [9]p ; 30cm
ISBN 0-86055-084-2 (pbk) : Unpriced B82-31371

711'.3'0942641 — Suffolk. Lowestoft region. Environment planning — *Proposals*

The **Lowestoft** and North Waveney district plan : consultation draft / Waveney District Council, Broads Authority. — [Lowestoft] ([District Planning Officer, Rectory Rd, Lowestoft]) : [Waveney District Council], [1981?]. — 98p : ill,maps ; 30cm
Map on folded sheet in pocket
£1.50 (pbk) B82-08591

711'.3'0942651 — Cambridgeshire. Peterborough *(District).* **Environment planning**

Planning handbook / Peterborough City Council. — London (Publicity House, Streatham Hill, SW2 4TR) : Pyramid Press, [1982?]. — 60p : ill ; 21cm
Unpriced (pbk) B82-37409

711'.3'094267 — Essex. Environment planning. Structure plans

Essex. *County Council.* Written statement : approved by the Secretary of State for the Environment on 30th March, 1982 / Essex County Council. — [Chelmsford] ([County Hall, Chelmsford CM1 1LF]) : Essex County Council Planning Department, 1982. — ii,104p : maps(some col.) ; 30cm
Cover title: Essex structure plan : approved written statement. — Map on sheet as insert
£3.50 (spiral) B82-36040

711'.3'09426712 — Essex. Uttlesford *(District).* **Environment planning**

Uttlesford planning information handbook. — London (Publicity House, Streatham Hill, SW2 4TR) : Pyramid Press, [1982]. — 40p : ill ; 21cm
Unpriced (pbk) B82-37407

711'.3'09426712 — Essex. Uttlesford *(District).* **Rural regions. Environment planning** — *Proposals*

Uttlesford. *District Council.* Rural areas district plan. — [Saffron Walden] ([Debden Rd, Saffron Walden]) : Uttlesford District Council
Cover title
Pt.2: Birchanger. — [1982]. — 7p,1folded leaf of plates : 1map ; 30cm
Unpriced (spiral) B82-32744

711'.3'09427 — Northern England. Environment planning

Clarke, Chris. Planning in the North / written by Chris Clarke on behalf of the Northern Branch of the Royal Town Planning Institute. — Newcastle Upon Tyne : Royal Town Planning Institute, Northern Branch, 1981. — 48p : ill ; 21cm
ISBN 0-901151-55-6 (pbk) : Unpriced B82-09821

711'.3'0942716 — Cheshire. Macclesfield Forest region. Environment planning — *Proposals*

Macclesfield Forest and Wildboarclough : joint management plan. — [Bakewell] : [Peak Park Joint Planning Board], [1982]. — v,94p : maps,plans ; 30cm
Cover title
ISBN 0-901428-97-3 (spiral) : Unpriced B82-35635

711'.3'094273 — Greater Manchester *(Metropolitan County).* **Tame Valley. Environment planning** — *Proposals*

Tame Valley : summary of survey and issues / prepared by Greater Manchester Council ... [et al.]. — [Manchester] ([County Hall, Piccadilly Gardens, Manchester M60 3HS]) : The Council, 1981. — 16p : ill ; 15x21cm
Unpriced (pbk) B82-11018

711'.3'094276 — North-east Lancashire. Structure planning — *Proposals*

Lancashire. *County Council.* Written statement : North East Lancashire structure plan / Lancashire County Council. — [Preston] : County Planning Department, 1980. — v,106p : ill(some col.),col.maps ; 30cm
1 folded map attached inside back cover
Unpriced (pbk) B82-19745

711'.3'094278 — Cumbria. Environment planning — *Proposals*

Cumbria. *County Council.* Development plan scheme 1980-85 : approved June 1980. — 79p in various pagings : maps,1plan ; 30cm
Unpriced (spiral) B82-27383

711'.3'094278 — Cumbria. Structure planning. Participation of public

Whitfield, T. J. R.. Cumbria & Lake District joint structure plan : public participation statement / T.J.R. Whitfield, M.J.L. Taylor. — [Kendal] : Cumbria County Council, 1980. — 45p : ill,1facsim ; 30cm
ISBN 0-905404-16-5 (pbk) : £1.50 B82-21300

711'.3'0942825 — South Yorkshire *(Metropolitan County).* **Barnsley** *(District).* **Environment planning**

Planning in Barnsley / issued by authority of Barnsley Metropolitan Borough Council. — Wallington : Home Publishing, [1981]. — 68p : ill,maps ; 21cm
Unpriced (pbk) B82-01663

711'.3'094283 — Humberside. Structure planning — *Proposals*

Humberside. *County Council.* Humberside structure plan / Humberside County Council. — [Beverley] ([Manor Rd., Beverley, N. Humberside, HU17 7BX]) : [The Council], [1979]. — x,98p,[5]folded leaves of plates : maps ; 30cm
Cover title
Unpriced (pbk) B82-15228

711'.3'094286 — Durham (County). Structure planning — *Proposals*

Durham *(England : County).* Durham County structure plan and Darlington urban structure plan / Durham County Council. — Durham (County Hall, Durham, DH1 5UF) : The Council, [1981?]. — 138,30p,[2]folded leaves of plates : maps,plans ; 30cm
£3.00 (pbk) B82-03890

711'.3'094287 — Tyne and Wear *(Metropolitan County).* **Structure planning** — *Proposals*

Tyne and Wear. *County Council.* Tyne and Wear County Council structure plan / [Tyne and Wear County Council]. — Newcastle upon Tyne (Planning Dept., Sandyford House, Newcastle upon Tyne NE2 1ED) : The Council [Policies]. — 1982. — 52p ; 27cm + folded sheet(col.map) + label
Unpriced (pbk) B82-35288

711'.3'0942951 — Powys. Machynlleth region. Environment planning

Project brief : Machynlleth district plan. — [Welshpool] ([Council Offices, Welshpool, Montgomeryshire, SY21 7AS]) : Montgomery District Council, [1981]. — 9p ; 30cm
Unpriced (unbound) B82-01475

711'.3'0974 — New England. Environment planning

New England prospects : critical choices in a time of change / Carl H. Reidel, editor. — Hanover ; London : University Press of New England, 1982. — xii,206p : ill,maps ; 22cm. — (Futures of New England)
ISBN 0-87451-213-1 (cased) : Unpriced
ISBN 0-87451-220-4 (pbk) : Unpriced
B82-39735

711'.4 — Cities. Environment planning. Social aspects

Wiedenhoeft, Ronald. Cities for people : practical measures for improving urban environments / Ronald Wiedenhoeft. — New York ; London : Van Nostrand Reinhold, c1981. — 224p : ill ; 29cm
Includes index
ISBN 0-442-29429-8 : £19.50 B82-09764

711'.4 — Environment planning. Role of local authorities — *Conference proceedings*

Local government and environmental planning and control / edited by Frank Joyce. — London : Gower, c1981. — xiii, 301p : ill,maps,plans ; 23cm
Includes two chapters in French. — Includes bibliographies
ISBN 0-566-00440-2 : Unpriced : CIP rev.
B81-34282

711'.4 — Town planning

Barnett, Jonathan. An introduction to urban design / by Jonathan Barnett. — New York ; London : Harper & Row, c1982. — vii,260p : ill,maps,plans ; 24cm. — (Icon editions)
Includes index
ISBN 0-06-430376-4 (cased) : Unpriced
ISBN 0-06-430114-1 (pbk) : Unpriced
B82-38725

Bracken, Ian. Urban planning methods. — London : Methuen, Oct.1981. — [400]p
ISBN 0-416-74860-0 (cased) : £12.00 : CIP entry
ISBN 0-416-74870-8 (pbk) : £6.00 B81-25297

Houghton-Evans, W.. Planning cities : legacy and portent / William Houghton-Evans. — London : Lawrence and Wishart, 1975 (1978 [printing]). — 203p : ill,maps,plans ; 21x30cm
Includes index
ISBN 0-85315-473-2 (pbk) : £3.95 B82-35047

Rodwin, Lloyd. Cities and city planning / Lloyd Rodwin with Hugh Evans ... [et al.]. — New York ; London : Plenum, c1981. — viii,309p,8p of plates : ill ; 22cm. — (Environment, development, and public policy. Cities and development)
Includes index
ISBN 0-306-40666-7 : Unpriced B82-14000

711'.4 — Town planning. Architectural design

Rossi, Aldo. The architecture of the city / Aldo Rossi ; introduction by Peter Eisenman ; translation by Diane Ghirardo and Joan Ockman. — American ed. / revised ... by Aldo Rossi and Peter Eisenman. — Cambridge, Mass. ; London : Published by [i.e. for] the Graham Foundation for Advanced Studies in the Fine Arts and the Institute for Architecture and Urban Studies by MIT, 1982. — 201p : ill,maps,plans ; 26cm. — (Oppositions books)
Translation of: L'Architettura della città. — Includes index
ISBN 0-262-18101-0 : £21.00 B82-35667

711'.4 — Town planning - *Conference proceedings*

Traffic, transportation and urban planning. — London : Godwin, Apr.1981. — (International forum series)
Conference papers
Vol.1. — [256]p
ISBN 0-7114-5713-1 (pbk) : £12.00 : CIP entry
B81-05156

Traffic, transportation and urban planning. — London : Godwin, Apr.1981. — (International forum series)
Conference papers
Vol.2. — [256]p
ISBN 0-7114-5714-x (pbk) : £12.00 : CIP entry
B81-05157

711'.4 — Urban regions. Environment planning — *Conference proceedings*

City landscape. — London : Butterworth, Nov.1982. — [176]p
Conference papers
ISBN 0-408-01165-3 : £20.00 : CIP entry
B82-28278

711'.4 — Urban renewal

Gibson, M.. An introduction to urban renewal. — London : Hutchinson Education, Sept.1982. — [368]p
ISBN 0-09-147501-5 (pbk) : £6.95 : CIP entry
B82-19104

711'.4'071141 — Great Britain. Higher education institutions. Curriculum subjects: Town planning. Practical work

Reade, Eric. Practical work in planning education / Eric Reade. — Oxford ([Oxford Polytechnic, Headington, Oxford]) : Department of Town Planning Oxford Polytechnic, 1981. — iii,105p ; 30cm. — (Working paper ; no.54)
Bibliography: p77-105
£3.15 (pbk) B82-01645

711'.4'071141 — Great Britain. Town planners. Professional education, *1960-1979*

Thomas, A. H. (Alun Huw). Town planning education in the 1970's / A.H. Thomas and W.K. Thomas. — Oxford ([Oxford Polytechic, Headington, Oxford]) : Department of Town Planning Oxford Polytechnic, 1981. — iii,36p ; 30cm. — (Working paper ; no.55)
£1.50 (pbk) B82-01644

711'.4'0722 — United States. Urban regions. Environment planning — *Case studies*

Roeseler, W. G.. Successful American urban plans / W.G. Roeseler. — [Lexington, Mass.] : Lexington Books ; [Aldershot] : Gower [distributor], c1982. — 200p : ill,maps ; 24cm
Includes index
ISBN 0-669-04540-3 : £19.50 B82-25103

711'.4'0904 — Urban renewal, *1945-1981*

Sim, Duncan. Change in the city centre. — Aldershot : Gower, July 1982. — [132]p
ISBN 0-566-00405-4 : £10.50 : CIP entry
B82-12972

711'.4'0924 — United States. Cities. Environment planning, *1860-1890* — *Personal observations*

Olmsted, Frederick Law. Civilizing American cities : a selection of Frederick Law Olmsted's writings on city landscapes / edited by S.B. Sutton. — Cambridge, Mass. ; London : MIT Press, 1971 (1979 [printing]). — 310p : ill,maps,plans ; 23cm
Includes index
ISBN 0-262-65012-6 (pbk) : Unpriced
B82-26459

711'.4'0937 — Ancient Rome. Town planning, *B.C.300-A.D.150* — *For children*

Macaulay, David. City : a story of Roman planning and construction / David Macaulay. — London : Collins, 1975, c1974 (1982 [printing]). — 112p : ill,plans ; 31cm
Originally published: Boston, Mass. : Houghton Mifflin, 1974
ISBN 0-00-192143-6 (pbk) : £3.50
Also classified at 624 B82-15441

711'.4'094 — Western Europe. Cities. Inner areas. Urban renewal. Role of local authorities

Punter, Lesley. The inner city and local government in Western Europe : a review of some of the administrative structures and systems adopted for the renewal of inner urban areas in West Germany, Italy, France and England / research undertaken by Lesley Punter. — [Reading] ([Whiteknights, Reading, RG6 2AW]) : [College of Estate Management], [1981]. — 123p ; 30cm. — (CALUS research report)
Bibliography: p121-123p
Unpriced (pbk) B82-01680

711'.4'094 — Western Europe. Town planning. Idealism, *to 1981*

Rosenau, Helen. The ideal city in European history. — 3rd ed. — London : Methuen, Dec.1982. — [196]p
Previous ed. published as: The ideal city: its architectural evolution, London : Studio Vista, 1974
ISBN 0-416-32850-4 : £15.00 : CIP entry
B82-29759

711'.4'0941 — Great Britain. Cities. Inner areas. Redevelopment

Home, Robert K.. Inner city regeneration. — London : Spon, Sept.1982. — [180]p
ISBN 0-419-12150-1 (cased) : £15.00 : CIP entry
ISBN 0-419-12160-9 (pbk) : £8.00 B82-19663

711'.4'0941 — Great Britain. Town planning

Self, Peter. Planning the urban region. — London : Allen and Unwin, May 1982. — [176]p
ISBN 0-04-352098-7 (cased) : £12.95 : CIP entry
ISBN 0-04-352099-5 (pbk) : £5.95 B82-07230

711'.4'0941 — Great Britain. Town planning. Geographical aspects

Conzen, M. R. G.. The urban landscape : historical development and management : papers / by M.R.G. Conzen ; edited by J.W.R. Whitehand. — London : Academic Press, 1981. — viii,166p : ill,maps,plans ; 26cm. — (Institute of British Geographers special publication, ISSN 0073-9006 ; no.13) (Special publication / Institute of British Geographers, ISSN 0073-9006 ; 13)
Includes index
ISBN 0-12-747020-4 : £16.00 : CIP rev.
B81-35913

711'.4'0941 — Great Britain. Town planning. Structure planning. Forecasting. Methodology

Bracken, Ian. Key activity forecasting in structure plans : a critique / by Ian Bracken and David Hume. — Cardiff (King Edward VII Av, Cardiff, CF1 3NU, Wales) : Dept. of Town Planning, University of Wales Institute of Science and Technology, 1981. — iileaves,72p : ill ; 30cm. — (Papers in planning research ; 26)
Bibliography: p66-72
Unpriced (pbk) B82-31898

711'.4'0941 — Great Britain. Town planning — *Technical data*

Some useful numbers / [compiled by] R.C. Fordham. — Oxford (43 Rectory Rd., Oxford OX4 1BU) : Aunt Sally, 1982. — 166p : ill,chiefly facsims ; 21cm
Cover title
£2.00 (pbk) B82-32955

711'.4'0941 — Great Britain. Urban regions. Environment. Aesthetic aspects. Projects: Art and the Built Environment Working Parties Project — *Serials*

Art and the Built Environment Working Parties Project. Bulletin / Schools Council Project/Art and the Built Environment Working Parties Project. — 1-. — [London] ([c/o E. Adams, Design Education Unit, Royal College of Art, Kensington Gore, SW7 2EU]) : The Project, [1981]-. — v. ; 31cm
ISSN 0262-754X = Bulletin - Schools Council Project, Art and the Built Environment. Working Parties Project : Unpriced
B82-19860

711'.4'0941 — Great Britain. Urban regions. Environment planning. Policies of government, *1945-1980*

Sylvester-Evans, Alun. Urban renaissance : a better life in towns : report on United Kingdom urban policies / prepared for the Department of the Environment by Alun Sylvester-Evans. — London : Council of Europe, European Compaign for Urban Renaissance : The Department, 1980 : H.M.S.O. [[distributor]]. — 103p : ill(some col.),maps ; 24cm
Ill on inside covers. — Bibliography: p101-103
ISBN 0-11-751489-6 (pbk) : £5.00 B82-35007

711'.4'09411 — Scotland. Environment planning. Local plans — *Conference proceedings*

Future policy for local planning in Scotland : proceedings of a one day seminar / Keith Hayton (editor). — Glasgow (Bourdon Building, 177 Renfrew St, Glasgow G3) : Glasgow School of Art, Dept. of Planning, 1982. — 45leaves ; 30cm. — (Occasional papers / Glasgow School of Art, Department of Planning ; no.7)
Unpriced (spiral) B82-25862

711'.4'0941235 — Scotland. Grampian Region. Aberdeen. Lower Deeside. Environment planning — *Proposals*

Lower Deeside draft local plan / Department of Planning and Building Control, City of Aberdeen District Council. — Aberdeen (St. Nicholas House, Broad St., Aberdeen AB9 1BW) : [The Department], 1982. — 51p,[6] leaves of plates (some folded) : ill,maps(some col.) ; 30cm
Unpriced (spiral) B82-30648

711'.4'0941235 — Scotland. Grampian Region. Northern Aberdeen *(District).* **Environment planning** — *Proposals*

Aberdeen *(Grampian). Department of Planning and Building Control.* City North draft local plan / Department of Planning and Building Control, City of Aberdeen District Council. — Aberdeen : The Department, 1982. — 69p,[1] fold leaf of plates : maps(some col.) ; 30cm
Unpriced (spiral) B82-38916

711'.4'094126 — Scotland. Tayside Region. Arbroath. Environment planning — *Proposals*

Angus. *District Planning Department.* Arbroath inner area study / [produced by the Planning Service of Angus District Council]. — [Forfar] ([County Buildings, Market St., Forfar DD8 3LG]) : [Angus District Planning Department]
Pt.1: A planning review and future policy statement. — 1977. — 40p : 1map ; 30cm
Cover title
Unpriced (pbk) B82-12644

Angus. *District Planning Department.* Arbroath local plan : draft written statement / Angus District Planning Department. — [Forfar] ([County Buildings, Market St., Forfar DD8 3LG]) : [The Department], 1981. — 131p : maps,plans ; 30cm
Map (1 folded sheet) as insert
£1.00 (spiral) B82-12642

711'.4'094126 — Scotland. Tayside Region. Carnoustie. Environment planning — *Proposals*

Angus. *District Council.* Carnoustie local plan : draft written statement. — [Forfar] ([County Buildings, Market St., Forfar DD8 3LG]) : Angus District Council, 1980. — 88p ; 30cm + 1map : 59x80cm folded to 30x21cm
Cover title
Unpriced (spiral) B82-12650

Angus. *District Council.* Carnoustie local plan : written statement / Angus District Council. — [Forfar] ([County Buildings, Market St., Forfar DD8 3LG]) : [The Council], 1981. — 89p : col.maps,plans(some col.) ; 30cm
"Carnoustie local plan proposals maps" (1folded sheet) as insert
Unpriced (spiral) B82-12649

711'.4'094126 — Scotland. Tayside Region. Forfar. Environment planning — *Proposals*

Forfar. *District Council.* Draft written statement : Forfar local plan. — [Forfar] : Angus District Council, 1982. — 109p : col.plans ; 30cm + 1col.plan(60x85cm folded to 30x21cm)
£1.50 (spiral) B82-28808

711'.4'094126 — Scotland. Tayside Region. Friockheim. Environment planning — *Proposals*

Angus. *District Planning Department.* Friockheim interim village plan, September 1977 / [produced by the Planning Service of Angus District Council]. — [Forfar] ([County Buildings, Forfar DD8 3LG]) : Angus District Planning Department, 1977. — 15p : 1plan ; 30cm
Cover title
Unpriced (pbk) B82-13315

711'.4'094126 — Scotland. Tayside Region. Lethan. Enviroment planning — *Proposals*

Angus. *District Planning Department.* Letham interim village plan / [produced by the Planning Service of Angus District Council]. — [Forfar] ([County Buildings, Market St., Forfar DD8 3LG]) : [Angus District Planning Department], 1977. — 13p,[1]folded leaf of plates : 1map ; 30cm
Cover title
Unpriced (spiral) B82-12645

711'.4'094126 — Scotland. Tayside Region. Monikie. Environment planning — *Proposals*

Angus. *District Planning Department.* Monikie interim village plan, March 1978 / [produced by the Planning Service of Angus District Council]. — [Forfar] ([County Buildings, Forfar DD8 3LG]) : Angus District Planning Department, 1978. — 11p : 1plan ; 30cm
Cover title
Unpriced (pbk) B82-13316

711'.4'094126 — Scotland. Tayside Region. Montrose. Environment planning — *Proposals*

Angus. *District Council.* Montrose local plan : written statement / Angus District Council. — Forfar ([County Buildings, Forfar DD8 3LG]) : Angus District Council, 1980. — 116p : 1ill,maps,plans ; 30cm + 1map ; 83x59cm folded to 30x21cm
Unpriced (spiral) B82-13313

711'.4'094126 — Scotland. Tayside Region. Newtyle. Environment planning — *Proposals*

Newtyle interim village plan. — [Forfar] ([County Buildings, Forfar]) : [Planning Services of Angus District Council], 1980. — 16p,[1]folded leaf of plates : 1map ; 30cm
Cover title
Unpriced (pbk) B82-23433

711'.4'094128 — Scotland. Tayside Region. Perth. Central areas. Environment planning — *Proposals*

Local plan, Perth Central Area. — Perth (16 Tay St., Perth, PH1 5LQ) : Planning Department Perth & Kinross District Council, 1979. — 29p,[10]leaves of plates : ill,col.maps ; 30cm
Cover title
Unpriced (pbk) B82-40582

711'.4'0941295 — Scotland. Fife Region. Levenmouth. Environment planning — *Proposals*

Kirkcaldy. *District Council.* Levenmouth local plan : written statement / Kirkcaldy District Council. — Kirkcaldy (Town House, Kirkcaldy, KY1 1XW) : Director of Planning, 1982. — 35p : maps ; 30cm
Proposals maps (2 folded sheets) as insert
Unpriced (pbk) B82-27485

Levenmouth local plan written statement / Douglas M. Nelson. — Kirkcaldy (Town House, Kirkcaldy) : Kirkcaldy District Council, 1981. — 35p ; 30cm + 2 sheets(maps ; 64x60cm folded to 21x17cm)
Unpriced (spiral) B82-11081

711'.4'0941298 — Scotland. Fife Region. Dunfermline. Town centre. Environment planning — *Proposals*

Dunfermline. *District Council.* Dunfermline town centre local plan : written statement / [Dunfermline District Council]. — [Dunfermline] (Planning Dept., 3 New Row, Dunfermline) : [Dunfermline District Council], 1980. — 52p,[1]folded leaf of plate : 2maps ; 30cm
Unpriced (spiral) B82-11034

711'.4'0941312 — Scotland. Central Region. Callander. Environment planning — *Proposals*

Stirling. *District Council.* Local plans : Callander / local plan adopted by Stirling District Council and operative from 5 November 1981. — Stirling (Planning & Building Control Dept., Municipal Buildings, Stirling, FK8 2HU) : Stirling District Council, [1981]. — 21p : ill,1plan ; 22x30cm
Plan (60x56cm folded to 16x23cm) in pocket
Unpriced (spiral) B82-26382

711'.4'094133 — Scotland. Lothian Region. Broxburn region. Environment planning — *Proposals*

Broxburn area local plan : draft policies and proposals. — [Linlithgow] ([Old County Buildings, High Street, Linlithgow, West Lothian, EH49 7EZ]) : West Lothian District Council, 1981. — 33,10leaves of plates(some folded) : ill,plans ; 30cm
Plan on folded sheet attached to inside cover
£3.00 (pbk) B82-03794

711'.4'094134 — Edinburgh. Environment planning. Policies of Edinburgh. *District Council*

Edinburgh. *District Council.* Planning policies at October 1981 / the City of Edinburgh District Council. — Edinburgh (18 Market St., Edinburgh EH1 1BJ) : City of Edinburgh District Council, Planning Department, [1981?]. — [44]p : ill ; 30cm
£2.50 (spiral) B82-10321

Edinburgh. *Planning Department.* Planning policies for the first new town. — Edinburgh (18 Market St., Edinburgh EH1 1BJ) : City of Edinburgh Planning Department, 1982. — 24leaves : ill,plans ; 21x30cm
£2.50 (spiral) B82-17635

711'.4'094135 — Scotland. Lothian Region. Gorebridge region. Environment planning — *Proposals*

Gorebridge local plan / [Midlothian District Council]. — [Dalkeith] ([1 White Hart St., Dalkeith, Midlothian]) : [The Council]
Vol.3: Policies & proposals. — 1980. — p81-123,[4]leaves of plates : col.maps ; 30cm + 2sheets(col.maps 54x60 folded to 28x15)
Cover title
Unpriced (pbk) B82-23434

711'.4'094135 — Scotland. Lothian Region. Penicuik. Environment planning — *Proposals*

Penicuik local plan : issues and options / [prepared by Midlothian District Council, Department of Planning & Building Control]. — Roslin (7 Station Rd., Roslin, Midlothian) : The Department, 1982. — 25,viip,[8]p of plates : ill,col.maps ; 30cm
Col. map on folded sheet in pocket
Unpriced (spiral) B82-40181

Penicuik local plan technical appendix : survey / [prepared by Midlothian District Council, Department of Planning & Building Control]. — Roslin (7 Station Rd., Roslin, Midlothian) : The Depatment, 1982. — 87p,19leaves of plates : ill,col.maps ; 30cm
Unpriced (spiral) B82-40182

711'.4'0941395 — Scotland. Borders Region. Eyemouth region. Environment planning — *Proposals*

Borders Region. *Department of Physical Planning and Development.* Eyemouth local plan : written statement. — St. Boswells (Regional Headquarters, Newton, St. Boswells) : Borders Regional Council Department of Physical Planning and Development, 1980. — 40p,[1] folded leaf of plates : maps ; 30cm
Eyemouth local plan proposals map (1folded sheet) in pocket
Unpriced (pbk) B82-23441

711'.4'094141 — Scotland. Strathclyde Region. Environment planning. Local plans, *to 1980*

Coon, Anthony. A comparison of rates of development plan progress under the old and new planning systems / Anthony Coon. — Glasgow (Bourdon Building, 177 Renfrew St, Glasgow G3) : Glasgow School of Art, Dept. of Planning, 1981. — 12,[7]leaves ; 30cm. — (Occasional papers / Glasgow School of Art, Department of Planning ; no.5)
Unpriced (spiral) B82-25856

711'.4'0941434 — Scotland. Strathclyde Region. Bearsden and Milngavie *(District).* **Rural regions. Environment planning** — *Proposals*

Bearsden and Milngavie. *District Council.* Landward area comprehensive local plan : written statement : modified in terms of Regulation 38 of the Town and Country Planning (Structure and local plans) (Scotland) Regulations, 1976, following a public local enquiry. — Milngavie (2 Grange Ave., Milngavie, Glasgow, G62 8AQ) : The Council, 1979. — 36leaves : 2coats of arms,maps ; 30cm
"Bearsden urban area local-plan land use survey" and "Landward area local plan land use survey" maps (2 folded sheets) as inserts
Unpriced (spiral) B82-35137

711'.4'0941443 — Scotland. Strathclyde Region. Drumchapel. Environment planning — *Proposals*

Drumchapel local plan. — [Glasgow] ([84, Queen Street, Glasgow G1 3DP]) : City of Glasgow District Council, [1981?]. — 127p : maps ; 30cm
Unpriced (spiral) B82-03888

711'.4'0941443 — Scotland. Strathclyde Region. Glasgow. Carmyle. Environment planning — *Proposals*

Carmyle local plan : written statement. — Glasgow (84 Queen St., Glasgow G1 3Dp) : Glasgow Department of Planning, 1982. — 30p : plans ; 30cm
At head of title: City of Glasgow District Council
Unpriced (spiral) B82-40279

711'.4'0941443 — Scotland. Strathclyde Region. Glasgow. Parkhead. Environment planning — *Proposals*

Glasgow. *Planning Department.* Written statement : Parkhead local plan. — Glasgow (84 Queen St, Glasgow, G1 3DP) : Glasgow District Council Planning Department, 1979. — 72p : maps,plans ; 30cm
Cover title
Unpriced (spiral) B82-28849

Parkhead local plan : written statement. — Glasgow (84 Queen St., Glasgow G1 3DP) : Glasgow District Council Planning Department, 1979. — 72p,[6]leaves of plates : maps ; 30cm
Unpriced (spiral) B82-23277

711'.4'0941443 — Scotland. Strathclyde Region. Glasgow. Shettleston & Tollcross. Environment planning

Glasgow. *Planning Department.* Written statement : Shettleston-Tollcross local plan. — Glasgow (84 Queen St, Glasgow, G1 3DP) : [Glasgow District Council Planning Dept.], 1979. — 59p,13leaves of plates : maps,plans ; 30cm
Cover title
Unpriced (spiral) B82-28850

711'.4'0941454 — Scotland. Strathclyde Region. East Kilbride. East Mains. Environment planning. Participation of public

East Kilbride District (East Mains and Village) local plan, statement of public participation. — East Kilbride : East Kilbride District Council, 1981. — 8,[16]p : maps,facsims ; 30cm
Unpriced (pbk) B82-09644

711'.4'0941454 — Scotland. Strathclyde Region. East Kilbride. East Mains. Environment planning — *Proposals*

East Kilbride District (East Mains and Village) local plan, written statement. — East Kilbride : East Kilbride District Council, 1981. — iii,46p,1folded leaf of plates : ill,maps,plans ; 30cm
Unpriced (pbk) B82-09645

711'.4'0941461 — Scotland. Strathclyde Region. Ardrossan, Saltcoats & Stevenston. Environment planning. Participation of public

Report on public participation : Ardrossan, Saltcoats, Stevenston local plan. — Irvine (Cunninghame House, Irvine) : Cunninghame District Council, 1980. — [36]leaves ; 30cm
Unpriced (spiral) B82-11351

711'.4'0941461 — Scotland. Strathclyde Region. Ardrossan, Saltcoats & Stevenston. Environment planning — *Proposals*

Cunninghame. *District Council.* Local plan : Ardrossan, Saltcoats, Stevenston : adopted on 30th Sept. 1980. — Irvine (Cunninghame House, Irvine) : Cunninghame District Council, 1980. — 56p ; 30cm + 2 plans(100x240cm folded to 31x27cm and 84x288cm folded to 37x22cm)
Cover title
Unpriced (spiral) B82-11350

Survey report : Ardrossan, Saltcoats, Stevenston local plan. — [Irvine] ([Cunninghame House, Irvine]) : Cunninghame District Council, [1980?]. — [85]p,[36]leaves ; 30cm
Cover title. — Contents: Report on public participation. Originally published: 1980 — Local plan. Originally published: 1980
Unpriced (sprial) B82-20902

711'.4'0941464 — Scotland. Strathclyde Region. Ayr region. Environment planning. Participation of public

Ayr/Prestwick local plan : newspaper summary. — Special ed. — Ayr (Burns House, Ayr) : Kyle and Carrick District Council, Planning Department, 1982. — [6]p : ill,1map ; 42cm
Unpriced (unbound) B82-29921

711'.4'09421 — London. Environment planning

Field, Brian. Local planning in London : some preliminary findings / Brian Field and David Frith. — London : Dept. of Town Planning at the Polytechnic of the South Bank, 1977 (1981 [printing]). — iii,18leaves ; 30cm. — (Occasional paper / Polytechnic of the South Bank. Department of Town Planning, ISSN 0143-4888)
ISBN 0-905267-28-1 (spiral) : £2.00
B82-40789

Smith, Brian, *1947-*. An enquiry into the manageability of town planning / Brian Smith. — London : Dept. of Town Planning at the Polytechnic of the South Bank, c1977 (1981 [printing]). — iv,95leaves : ill ; 30cm. — (Occasional paper / Polytechnic of the South Bank. Department of Town Planning, ISSN 0143-4888)
Bibliography: leaves 94-95
ISBN 0-905267-25-7 (spiral) : £2.00
B82-40790

711'.4'09421 — London. Town planning, *1700-1900*

Olsen, Donald J.. Town planning in London. — 2nd ed. — London : Yale University Press, Oct.1982. — [320]p
Previous ed.: 1964
ISBN 0-300-02914-4 (cased) : £25.00 : CIP entry
ISBN 0-300-02915-2 (pbk) : £8.95 B82-35195

711'.4'09421 — London. Town planning. Rejected proposals, *1600-1981*

Barker, Felix. London : as it might have been / Felix Barker, Ralph Hyde. — London : Murray, 1982. — 223p : ill,maps,plans,ports ; 27cm
Bibliography: p217-220. — Includes index
ISBN 0-7195-3857-2 : £12.50 : CIP rev.
B82-07591

711'.4'0942142 — London. Camden *(London Borough).* **Conservation areas. Environment planning** — *Proposals*

Camden. *Borough Council.* A plan for Camden : conservation area policy : Camden's central area. — [London] ([Town Hall, Euston Rd., NW1 1RU]) : [Camden Borough Council, 1976. — 22p : ill,maps,plans ; 30cm
Unpriced (unbound) B82-21474

711'.4'0942165 — London. Lambeth *(London Borough).* **Environment planning** — *Proposals*

Lambeth. Lambeth development plan : district plan for the borough except Waterloo. — [London] : London Borough of Lambeth, 1981. — 324p : ill,maps(some col.),plans ; 30cm + 1 pamphlet(Unpriced ; 30cm)
1 proposals map (118x62cm folded to 30x21cm) as insert
Unpriced (pbk) B82-00987

711'.4'0942175 — London. Barking and Dagenham *(London Borough).* **Environment planning**

Barking and Dagenham planning information handbook. — London : Pyramid Press, [1980]. — 32p : ill ; 21cm
Unpriced (pbk) B82-14588

711'.4'0942189 — London. Enfield *(London Borough).* **Environment planning** — *Practical information*

Planning handbook / London Borough of Enfield. — London (Publicity House, Streatham Hill, SW2 4TR) : Pyramid Press, [1982]. — 60p : ill,1map ; 21cm
Unpriced (pbk) B82-37383

711'.4'0942191 — London. Croydon *(London Borough).* **Environment planning** — *Proposals*

Croydon. *Department of Development.* London Borough of Croydon district plan : written statement. — [Croydon] : Department of Development, London Borough of Croydon, 1982. — 78p ; 30cm
Unpriced (pbk) B82-38972

Croydon. *Department of Development.* London Borough of Croydon district plan proposed modifications. — [Croydon] ([Taberner House, Park La., Croydon CR9 3JS]) : Department of Development, London Borough of Croydon, 1981. — [40]p : plans ; 30cm
Unpriced (spiral) B82-12658

711'.4'0942234 — Kent. Canterbury. Environment planning — *Proposals*

Canterbury City district plan / summary report of survey. — [Canterbury] ([14 Dane John, Canterbury, Kent, CT1 2QP]) : Canterbury City Council, 1979. — 122p,16leaves of plates (some folded) : maps(some col.) ; 30cm
Unpriced (pbk) B82-40584

711'.4'0942332 — Dorset. Shaftesbury. Conservation areas: Shaftesbury conservation area. Environment planning — *Proposals*

Shaftesbury : conservation policy and proposals / [Dorset County Council, North Dorset District Council]. — [Dorchester] (County Planning Dept., County Hall, Dorchester, Dorset) : Dorset County Council : North Dorset District Council, [1981?]. — 21p,[12]p of plates(some folded) : ill,maps(some col.),plans ; 30cm
ISBN 0-85216-294-4 (pbk) : £0.50 B82-11035

711'.4'0942336 — Dorset. Lytchett Matravers. Environment planning — *Proposals*

Lytchett Matravers. — Wareham : [The Department], 1980. — 38p : 1ill,maps(some col.) ; 30cm + 1 col.map(on sheet 59x65 folded to 30x17cm)
ISBN 0-907458-00-9 (pbk) : £0.50 B82-22458

Purbeck. *Planning Department.* Lytchett Matravers district plan 1980-1996 : modified draft / [Purbeck District Council Planning Department]. — [Wareham] (District Planning Officer, Bridge House, South St., Wareham) : Purbeck District Council, [1981]. — 9p ; 30cm
Col. map(folded sheet) as insert
ISBN 0-907458-01-7 (unbound) B82-08715

711'.4'0942336 — Dorset. Sandford & northern Wareham. Environment planning — *Proposals*

Sandford and Northern Wareham district plan : consultative draft / Purbeck District Council. — [Wareham] : [The Council], 1982. — 45p : 1ill,maps(some col.) ; 30cm + 2maps(64x46cm folded to 23x16cm)
Cover title
ISBN 0-907458-02-5 (pbk) : £1.00 B82-35414

711'.4'0942356 — Devon. Exeter. Conservation areas

Conservation areas in Exeter. — Exeter : Exeter City Council Planning Department, [197-?]. — [4]p,[3]folded leaves of plates : ill,col.maps ; 30cm
ISBN 0-86114-184-9 (unbound) : Unpriced B82-40957

711'.4'0942393 — Avon. Bristol. Environment planning. Amenity societies

The **Fight** for Bristol : planning and the growth of public protest / editors Gordon Priest, Pamela Cobb ; contributors Dorothy Brown ... [et al.]. — Bristol : Bristol Civic Society, 1980. — 124p : ill,maps ; 21cm
Includes index
ISBN 0-905459-25-3 (pbk) : £2.95 B82-21827

711'.4'0942396 — Avon. Nailsea. Town planning — *Proposals*

Nailsea town centre plan. — Bristol (P.O. Box 46, Avon House North, St. James Barton, Bristol BS99 7EU) : Avon County Planning Department, 1982. — 45p,17leaves of plates (some folded) : ill,plans ; 30cm
ISBN 0-86063-139-7 (sprial) : £1.00 B82-29245

711'.4'0942534 — Lincolnshire. Lincoln. Bailgate. Environment planning — *Proposals*

Bailgate planning brief. — Lincoln (City Hall, Beaumont Fee, Lincoln LN1 1DF) : [Department of Planning and Architecture], 1982. — 6p : 1map ; 30cm
Unpriced (pbk) B82-40457

Bailgate planning brief draft. — Lincoln (c/o J.S. Anderson, Director of Planning and Architecture, City Hall, Beaumont Fee, Lincoln LN1 1DF) : [City of Lincoln Council], [1982?]. — 5p,[1]leaf of plates : 1map ; 30cm
Unpriced (unbound) B82-17843

711'.4'0942534 — Lincolnshire. Lincoln. Marjorie Avenue area. Environment planning — *Proposals*

Land at Marjorie Avenue : developers design guide. — Lincoln (City Hall, Beaumont Fee, Lincoln LN1 1DF) : Lincoln City Council, 1981. — [40]p : ill,1map ; 30cm
Cover title
£0.40 (pbk) B82-08217

711'.4'0942539 — Lincolnshire. Spalding & Pinchbeck. Environment planning — *Proposals*

South Holland. *District Council*. The Spalding and Pinchbeck district plan / South Holland District Council. — [Spalding] : The District Council
Transportation. — 1981. — [65]p,[11]leaves of plates(some col.) : ill,maps ; 30cm
Unpriced (spiral) B82-15262

711'.4'0942542 — Leicestershire. Leicester. Hamilton. Environment planning — *Proposals*

Leicestershire. *County Council*. Hamilton District Plan : draft written statement / Leicestershire County Council. — [Leicester] ([County Hall, Glenfield, Leicester LE3 8RI]) : The Council, 1981. — 47p,[1]folded leaf of plates : ill,2maps ; 30cm
Map on folded sheet in pocket
Unpriced (spiral) B82-02857

711'.4'0942549 — Leicestershire. Desford. Environment planning — *Proposals*

Hinckley and Bosworth. *Development Department*. Desford interim policy statement / [Hinckley and Bosworth Borough Council, Development Department]. — Hinckley (Council Offices, Argents Mead, Hinkley, LE10 1BZ) : The Department, 1980. — 11,2p : maps (some folded) ; 30cm
Folded map in pocket
£1.10 (pbk) B82-23435

711'.4'0942554 — Northamptonshire. Irthlingborough. Environment planning — *Proposals*

Irthlingborough district plan : written statement. — Thrapston (Council Offices, Midland Rd., Thrapston NN14 4LZ) : East Northamptonshire District Council, 1981. — [66]p,[1]folded leaf of plates : 1map,plans ; 30cm
Unpriced (spiral) B82-11885

711'.4'0942561 — Bedfordshire. Bedford. Central areas. Environment planning — *Proposals*

Bedford Town centre plan : consultation 2 draft proposals. — [Bedford] (37/45 Goldington Rd., Bedford MK40 3LQ]) : [North Bedfordshire Borough Council, Planning Division], [1982]. — 44p,[7]folded leaves of plates : maps ; 30cm
Cover title
Unpriced (pbk) B82-38553

711'.4'0942561 — Bedfordshire. Bedford. Conservation areas: Bedford conservation area

Bedford conservation area / [Department of Planning and Development, North Bedfordshire Borough Council]. — [Bedford] ([37-45 Goldington Rd, Bedford MK40 3LQ]) : The Department, 1975. — [4]p,[1]folded leaf of plate : 1col.map ; 30cm
Cover title
Unpriced (pbk) B82-41051

711'.4'0942561 — Bedfordshire. Bedford. Great Ouse River region. Environment planning — *Proposals*

River Great Ouse informal local plan : consultation draft / North Bedfordshire Borough Council. — [Bedford] ([37-45 Goldington Rd, Bedford MK40 3LQ]) : [The Council], 1979. — 11,12,iiip,xileaves ; 30cm
Unpriced (unbound) B82-41056

711'.4'0942561 — Bedfordshire. Bedford. Queen's Park. Environment planning — *Proposals*

Queen's Park district plan : consultation draft. — [Bedford] ([37-45 Goldington Rd., Bedford MK40 3LQ]) : North Bedfordshire Borough Council, [1982]. — 26p : 1form,1map,1plan ; 30cm
Cover title. — Plan and form in pocket
Unpriced (pbk) B82-32760

711'.4'0942561 — Bedfordshire. Bedford. South Bedford. Environment planning — *Proposals*

South Bedford district plan : consultation draft. — [Bedford] ([37-45 Goldington Road, Bedford, MK40 3LQ]) : North Bedfordshire Borough Council, 1982. — 62,xvip : 1map ; 30cm
One map on folded sheet in pocket
Unpriced (pbk) B82-29506

711'.4'0942561 — Bedfordshire. Bedford. Town planning, *1945-1974*

Jones, Arthur. For the record — Bedford 1945-74 : land use and financial planning. — Bedford (6 Mill St., Bedford) : Roberts Publishing, Nov.1981. — 1v.
ISBN 0-9507778-0-3 (pbk) : £7.25 : CIP entry B81-33646

711'.4'0942561 — Bedfordshire. Kempston. Conservation areas: Kempston conservation area

Kempston conservation area / [Department of Planning and Development, North Bedfordshire Borough Council]. — [Bedford] ([37-45 Goldington Rd, Bedford MK40 3LQ]) : [The Department], 1975. — [3]p : 1col.map ; 30cm
Cover title
Unpriced (pbk) B82-41050

711'.4'0942561 — Bedfordshire. Kempston. Environment planning

Kempston district plan : project report / [North Bedfordshire Borough Council]. — [Bedford] ([37-45 Goldington Rd, Bedford MK40 3LQ]) : The Council, 1977. — 13p : 1ill,1map ; 30cm
Cover title
Unpriced (pbk) B82-41054

711'.4'0942561 — Bedfordshire. Kempston. Environment planning. Participation of public

Kempston district plan : community involvement / North Bedfordshire Borough Council. — [Bedford] ([37-45 Goldington Rd, Bedford MK40 3LQ]) : [The Council]
Stage 1. — 1977. — 15,viiip : facsims ; 30cm
Unpriced (pbk) B82-41055

711'.4'0942561 — Bedfordshire. Kempston. Environment planning — *Proposals*

Kempston district plan : consultation draft / North Bedfordshire Borough Council. — [Bedford] ([37-45 Goldington Rd, Bedford MK40 3LQ]) : [The Council], 1978. — 46p : 1col.map ; 30cm
Map and comments sheet in pocket
Unpriced (pbk) B82-41053

Kempston district plan brief / North Bedfordshire Borough Council. — [Bedford] : Bedfordshire County Council, 1977. — 13p ; 30cm
Unpriced (pbk) B82-41058

711'.4'0942561 — Bedfordshire. Sharnbrook. Environment planning — *Proposals*

Sharnbrook village plan / North Bedfordshire Borough Council. — Bedford (37 Goldington Rd., Bedford MK40 3LQ) : North Bedfordshire Borough Council, 1981. — 18p,1leaf of plates,ii leaves : 1map ; 30cm + 1sheet(map ; folded to 15x21cm in pocket)
Unpriced (pbk) B82-03049

Sharnbrook village plan. — [Bedford] ([37-45 Goldington Road, Bedford, MK40 3LQ]) : North Bedfordshire Borough Council, 1982. — 25,iip : 3ill,2maps ; 30cm
One map on folded sheet in pocket
£0.75 (pbk) B82-29507

711'.4'0942561 — Bedfordshire. Wilshamstead. Environment planning — *Proposals*

Wilshamstead village plan : draft proposals / [North Bedfordshire Borough Council]. — [Bedford] ([37-45 Goldington Rd, Bedford MK40 3LQ]) : [The Council], 1979. — 29p : maps ; 30cm
Maps in pocket
Unpriced (pbk) B82-41057

711'.4'0942574 — Oxfordshire. Oxford. Environment planning — *Proposals*

District plan for Oxford : matters proposed to be included in the plan / City of Oxford. — Oxford ([109 St. Aldate's, Oxford OX1 1DX]) : City Architect and Planning Officer, 1981. — 214p,5 folded leaves of plates : ill,maps ; 30cm
Unpriced (pbk) B82-05014

District plan for Oxford : appendices / City of Oxford. — [Oxford] ([109 St. Aldate's, Oxford OX1 1DX]) : [City Architect and Planning Officer], [1981?]. — 106p : ill,maps ; 30cm
Unpriced (pbk) B82-05015

711'.4'0942586 — Hertfordshire. Welwyn Garden City. Central areas. Environment planning — *Proposals*

Welwyn Garden City 1976-1981 : town centre map / Welwyn Hatfield District Council. — [East Hatfield] ([16 St. Albans Rd., East Hatfield, Herts.]) : [Welwyn Hatfield District Council], [1981?]. — 21,[15]p,[1]folded leaf of plates : ill,1col.map,1plan ; 30cm
Cover title
Unpriced (spiral) B82-02885

711'.4'09425892 — Hertfordshire. Watford. Environment planning — *Proposals*

Information report : Watford district plan. — [Watford] ([Town Hall, Watford, Herts.]) : Watford Borough Council, 1982. — 15p ; 30cm
Cover title
Unpriced (pbk) B82-40848

Report of studies : Watford district plan. — [Watford] ([Town Hall, Watford, Herts.]) : Watford Borough Council, 1978. — 259p,12leaves of plates(some folded) : maps ; 30cm
Bibliography: p256-259
£2.00 (pbk) B82-40847

Town centre review : Watford district plan : report of studies. — [Watford] ([Town Hall, Watford, Herts.]) : Watford Borough Council, 1981. — 85p,6leaves of plates(some folded) : maps ; 30cm
Cover title
Unpriced (pbk) B82-40849

Watford. *Borough Council*. Written statement : Watford district plan. — [Watford] ([Town Hall, Watford, Herts.]) : Watford Borough Council, 1981. — 116p ; 30cm + 1col.map (94x86cm folded to 27x17cm)
£5.00 (pbk) B82-40850

711'.4'0942654 — Cambridgeshire. Earith. Environment planning — *Proposals*

Earith village study 1981 : Earith village plan approved by Huntingdon District Planning Committee on 23rd January, 1978, and Earith conservation study approved on 2nd March, 1981. — Huntingdon (Pathfinder House, St. Mary's St., Huntingdon PE18 6TN) : Huntingdon District Council, 1981. — 28p : ill,maps,plans ; 30cm
£1.50 (pbk) B82-16734

711'.4'0942654 — Cambridgeshire. Great Gransden. Environment planning — *Proposals*

Huntingdon. *District Planning Committee*. Great Gransden village study : approved by the Huntingdon District Council Planning Committee 19th January, 1981. — Huntingdon (Pathfinder House, St. Mary's St., Huntingdon, Cambs.) : Huntingdon District Council [Planning Department], 1981. — 42p,[6]folded leaves of plates : ill,maps ; 30cm
Unpriced (pbk) B82-33163

711'.4'0942657 — Cambridgeshire. Babraham, Pampisford & Sawston. Environment planning — *Proposals*

Sawston, Pampisford & Babraham, report of survey and draft district plan / South Cambridgeshire District Council. — [Cambridge] ([South Cambridgeshire Hall, Hills Rd., Cambridge CB2 1PB]) : [the Council], 1981. — i,52p,[5] folded leaves of plates : maps ; 30cm
Cover title
Unpriced (spiral) B82-01499

711'.4'0942657 — Cambridgeshire. Landbeach & Waterbeach. Environment planning — *Proposals*

South Cambridgeshire. *District Council*. Waterbeach & Landbeach district plan. — Cambridge (South Cambridgeshire Hall, Hills Rd, Cambridge CB2 1PB) : South Cambridgeshire District Council, 1982. — 20,iiip,[3]folded leaves of plates : maps ; 30cm
Unpriced (spiral) B82-32905

711'.4'0942657 — Cambridgeshire. Waterbeach & Landbeach. Environment planning. Participation of public

Waterbeach & Landbeach district plan : statement on public participation and consultation procedure. — Cambridge (South Cambridgeshire Hall, Hills Rd, Cambridge, CB2 1PB) : South Cambridgeshire District Council, 1982. — 68p(in various pagings) : forms,maps ; 30cm
Unpriced (spiral) B82-32904

711'.4'094267 — Essex. Environment planning. Local plans. Plan making — *Proposals*

Essex. *County Council*. Development plan scheme / Essex County Council. — Chelmsford (County Hall, Chelmsford CM1 1LF) : The Council, 1980. — [38]p : maps ; 30cm
Unpriced (unbound) B82-22457

Essex. *County Council*. Development plan scheme / Essex County Council
[Pt.4]: [Schedule of plans and programmes]. — [Chelmsford] ([County Hall, Chelmsford, CM1 1LF]) : [Planning Department], 1982. — [40]p : maps ; 21x30cm
£0.50 (unbound) B82-37327

711'.4'09426712 — Essex. Newport. Environment planning — *Proposals*

Uttlesford. *District Council*. Newport district plan : written statement of policies. — [Saffron Walden] ([Debden Rd, Saffron Walden]) : Uttlesford District Council, 1982. — 29p,2folded leaves of plates : 2maps ; 30cm
Cover title
Unpriced (spiral) B82-32742

Uttlesford. *District Council*. Uttlesford district council, Newport district plan, written statement of policies : consultation report and the recommended amendments to the draft plan. — [Saffron Walden] ([Debden Rd, Saffron Walden]) : [The Council], 1982. — 13p ; 30cm
Cover title
Unpriced (pbk) B82-32741

711'.4'09426715 — Essex. Great Saling. Environment planning — *Proposals*

Great Saling / [prepared by the Planning Department, Braintree District Council]. — [Braintree] ([Hay La., Braintree, Essex, CM7 6DY]) : Braintree District Council, [1978?]. — 7p : 1col.map ; 21x30cm + 1map(40x54cm folded to 20x27cm). — (Rural planning settlement policy. Village guideline)
Map in pocket
£0.50 (pbk) B82-40581

711'.4'09426752 — Essex. Chelmsford. Environment planning — *Proposals*

Consultation plan 1981 : Chelmsford town centre district plan. — Chelmsford : Chelmsford Borough Council, 1981. — 72p ; 30cm + 1sheet(1col.map ; 56x66cm folded to 28x17cm)
Unpriced (pbk) B82-08730

711'.4'0942734 — Greater Manchester *(Metropolitan county)*. **North Reddish. Environment planning** — *Proposals*

Stockport. *Development and Town Planning Division*. North Reddish District plan : draft written statement parts 1 & 2. — Stockport ([Greenhale, Piccadilly, Stockport]) : Metropolitan Borough of Stockport [Development & Town Planning Division], 1981. — 62p : ill,col.maps,col.plans ; 30cm
Cover title. — Plan (84x60cm folded to 21x30cm) as insert
Unpriced (spiral) B82-08216

711'.4'0942865 — Durham *(County)*. **Durham. Environment planning** — *Proposals*

City of Durham district plan : draft for consultation. — [Durham] ([City Planning Office, Byland Lodge, Hawthorn Terrace, Durham DH1 4TD]) : [City of Durham], 1981. — 224,15p,[15]p of plates(some folded) : maps ; 30cm
City of Durham district plan proposals map (1 folded sheet) as insert
Unpriced (spiral) B82-35028

Planning the new city of Durham : introduction. — Durham (City Planning Office, Byland Lodge, Hawthorn Terrace, Durham DH1 4TD) : City of Durham, 1975 (1976 [printing]). — [4]p : ill,1plan ; 30cm
Unpriced (unbound) B82-35027

711'.4'095125 — Hong Kong. Urban regions. Environment planning

Keung, John. Urban planning in Hong Kong — a political/administrative perspective / by John Keung. — Cardiff (King Edward VII Ave., Cardiff CF1 3NU) : Dept. of Town Planning, University of Wales Institute of Science and Technology, 1981. — ii,36p ; 30cm. — (Papers in planning research ; 39)
Unpriced (pbk)
Also classified at 388.4'0951'25 B82-26831

711'.4'0954552 — India *(Republic)*. **Chandigarh. Town planning**

Sarin, Madhu. Urban planning in the Third World : the Chandigarh experience. — London : Mansell, Sept.1982. — [256]p
ISBN 0-7201-1637-6 : £20.00 : CIP entry B82-22433

711'.4'097 — North America. Cities. Environment planning, *to 1850*

Crouch, Dora P.. Spanish city planning in North America / Dora P. Crouch, Daniel J. Garr, and Axel I. Mundigo. — Cambridge, Mass. ; London : MIT Press, c1982. — xxii,298p : ill,maps,plans ; 24cm
Bibliography: p284-292. — Includes index
ISBN 0-262-03081-0 : Unpriced B82-35069

711'.4'0973 — United States. Urban regions. Environment planning — *Manuals*

De Chiara, Joseph. Urban planning and design criteria / Joseph De Chiara, Lee Koppelman. — 3rd ed. — New York ; London : Van Nostrand Reinhold, c1982. — x,723p : ill,maps,plans ; 24x31cm
Previous ed.: 1975. — Includes index
ISBN 0-442-21946-6 : £57.40 B82-34333

711'.4'0973 — United States. Urban renewal

Butler, Stuart M.. Enterprise zones. — London : Heinemann Educational, Oct.1982. — [192]p
Originally published: New York : Universe Books, 1981
ISBN 0-435-84531-4 (pbk) : £4.95 : CIP entry B82-24000

711'.4'097471 — New York *(City)*. **Environment planning,** *1857-1890 — Correspondence, diaries, etc.*

Olmsted, Frederick Law. Landscape into cityscape : Frederick Law Olmsted's plans for a greater New York City / edited with an introductory essay and notes by Albert Fein. — New York ; London : Van Nostrand Reinhold, 1981. — 490p,[30]p of plates : ill,maps,facsims,ports ; 23cm
Originally published: Ithaca, N.Y. : Cornell University Press, 1968. — Includes index
ISBN 0-442-22539-3 (pbk) : £10.15 B82-09762

711'.5'0941 — Great Britain. Buildings. Rehabilitation

Rehabilitation and associated economic factors : a study / by the Practice and Techniques Committee of RICS Building Surveyors Division ; [prepared by a working party of the Building Surveyors Division, The Royal Institution of Chartered Surveyors]. — London : Published on behalf of the Royal Institution of Chartered Surveyors by Surveyors Publications, c1981. — 25p : ill ; 30cm
Text on inside cover. — Bibliography: p20
ISBN 0-85406-165-7 (pbk) : £3.00(£2.60 to members of RICS) B82-25802

711'.552 — Shopping centres. Planning

Beddington, Nadine. Design for shopping centres. — London : Butterworths, Mar.1982. — [160]p
ISBN 0-408-00357-x : £15.00 : CIP entry B82-00921

711'.5522 — Scotland. Strathclyde Region. Eastern Glasgow. Hypermarkets. Planning

Glasgow eastern area renewal hypermarket study : report of a working group [set up by] Strathclyde Regional Council ... [et al.]. — Glasgow ([20 India St., Glasgow G2 4PF]) : [The Council], 1979. — 86leaves : maps,plans ; 30cm
Bibliography: leaf 84-86
Unpriced (pbk) B82-35010

711'.5522'0942 — England. Shopping centres. Development. Joint ventures

Shopping centre partnerships : a guide to current practice / [prepared by a working party of the Institution]. — London : Published on behalf of the Royal Institution of Chartered Surveyors by Surveyors Publication, c1981. — 31p ; 15x22cm
ISBN 0-85406-160-6 (pbk) : Unpriced B82-07762

711'.5522'0942579 — Oxfordshire. Littlemore. Heyford Hill. Shopping centres. Planning — *Proposals*

Consultation on possible development : Heyford Hill / Oxford City Council. — [Oxford] ([109 At. Aldate's, Oxford OX1 1DX]) : [City Architect and Planning Officer], [1981?]. — [9]p : 2maps ; 30cm
Unpriced (unbound) B82-05021

711'.557 — England. Peak District. Camping & caravanning. Sites. Environment planning — *Proposals*

Peak Park Joint Planning Board. *Joint Study Officer Working Party*. Policy and recommendations report of the Joint Study Officer Working Party. — Bakewell : Peak Park Joint Planning Board on behalf of the Officer Working Party, 1980. — iv,89p,[1] folded leaf of plates : ill,maps,plans ; 30cm
Cover title: Camping and caravanning in and around the Peak District
ISBN 0-901428-61-2 (pbk) : Unpriced B82-35115

711′.557 — Hampshire. Camping & caravanning. Sites. Environment planning. Policies of Hampshire. *County Council*

Camping and caravanning in Hampshire. — [Winchester] ([The Castle, Winchester]) : Hampshire County Council, 1978. — 24p,folded leaf of plate : 1map ; 30cm. — (Strategic planning paper ; no.3)
£1.00 plus postage (pbk) B82-38212

711′.557 — Humberside. Coastal regions. Camping & caravanning. Sites. Environment planning — *Proposals*

Coastal caravans and camping plan / Humberside County Council. — [Beverley] ([c/o Director of Planning, Manor Rd, Beverley HU17 7BX]) : [Humberside County Council], 1981. — 34p,[9]leaves of plate(some folded) : col.maps ; 30cm
£3.00 (spiral) B82-09963

Coastal caravans and camping plan / Humberside County Council. — [Beverley] ([Manor Rd., Beverley, N. Humberside, HU17 7BX]) : [The Council], 1981. — 34p,[10]leaves of plates(some col.) : ill,col.maps ; 30cm
Unpriced (spiral) B82-15230

711′.557 — Scotland. Tayside Region. Angus *(District).* **Caravanning. Sites. Environment planning** — *Proposals*

Angus. *District Planning Department.* Angus District : caravan site location policy / [Angus District Planning Department]. — [Forfar] ([County Buildings, Market St., Forfar DD8 3LG]) : [The Department], 1981. — 17p,[1] folded leaf of plates : 1map ; 30cm
Cover title
Unpriced (spiral) B82-12643

711′.558 — Recreation facilities. Planning

Recreation planning and management issues. — London : Spon, Jan.1983. — [350]p
ISBN 0-419-12930-8 (pbk) : £14.00 : CIP entry B82-34575

711′.558′072042 — England. Local authorities. Leisure facilities. Planning. Research — *Conference proceedings*

Recreation research in local authorities : proceedings of a seminar held at Birmingham University on 30th June 1976 / edited by A.J. Veal. — [Brimingham] : Centre for Urban and Regional Studies, University of Birmingham, 1977. — 52p : ill ; 30cm. — (Conference and seminar papers / Centre for Urban and Regional Studies, University of Birmingham ; no.4)
ISBN 0-7044-0260-2 (pbk) : £1.00 B82-22001

711′.558′09413 — Scotland. Central Lowlands. Canals: Union Canal. Recreational use. Planning — *Proposals*

The Union canal : development of recreation and amenity : summary and recommendations / [prepared by officers from Lothian Regional Council ... et al.]. — London (Melbury House, Melbury Terrace, London NW1 6JZ) : British Waterways Board, [1977?]. — viip : 2maps ; 22x30cm
Unpriced (unbound) B82-15460

711′.558′094131 — Scotland. Central Region. Recreation facilities. Planning — *Proposals*

Central Region. *Department of Planning.* Revised STARPS strategy for Central Region / prepared by the Planning Department, Central Regional Council, in consultation with Clackmannan, Falkirk and Stirling District Councils. — [Stirling] ([Viewforth, Stirling FK8 2ET]) : [Central Regional Council], [1981?]. — 35p ; 30cm
Unpriced (unbound)
Also classified at 338.4′7914131 B82-15462

711′.558′09425892 — Hertfordshire. Watford. Colne Valley. Recreation facilities. Planning — *Proposals*

Survey & issues report : the Colne Valley in Watford : a linear park plan. — [Watford] : Watford Borough Council, 1980. — 81[ie 123] p,[18]p of plates(some folded) : ill,maps ; 30cm
Unpriced (spiral) B82-37591

Watford. *Borough Council.* Proposals and policies : the Colne Valley in Watford : a linear park plan. — [Watford] : Watford Borough Council, 1981. — iii,30p,[14]p of plates(some folded) : ill,maps(some col.) ; 30cm
Cover title
Unpriced (spiral) B82-37590

711′.558′094283 — England. Humber River region. Inland waterways. Recreation facilities. Planning — *Proposals*

Yorkshire and Humberside Council for Sport and Recreation. Development of an inland waterways network : regional recreation strategy subject report / Yorkshire and Humberside Council for Sport and Recreation. — [Leeds] ([Coronet House, Queen St., Leeds LS1 4PW]) : [The Council], 1981. — iileaves,22p : 1map ; 30cm
Cover title
Unpriced (pbk) B82-03271

711′.58′0941441 — Scotland. Difficult-to-let local authority housing estates. Improvement — *Study regions: Strathclyde Region. Paisley. Ferguslie Park*

Gilbert, J. (John). Housing investment strategies for difficult-to-let public sector housing estates / J. Gilbert and L. Rosenburg. — Edinburgh (New St Andrews House, Edinburgh EH1 3SZ) : Central Research Unit, 1980. — iv,77p : ill,plans ; 30cm. — (Central Research Unit papers)
Unpriced (spiral) B82-02091

711′.58′0941443 — Scotland. Strathclyde Region. Glasgow. Housing. Environment planning — *Proposals*

Widening the choice : peripheral areas initiatives. — [Glasgow] ([9, George Sq., Glasgow G2 1TG]) : City of Glasgow District Council, [1981]. — 5pamphlets : maps(some col.),plans ; 31cm
Unpriced B82-28691

711′.59′0941 — Great Britain. Residences. Rehabilitation — *Standards*

Specification clauses for rehabilitation and conversion work / Levitt Bernstein Associates and Anthony Richardson and Partners. — London : Architectural, 1981, c1982. — 138p : ill,forms ; 30cm
ISBN 0-85139-582-1 (pbk) : £9.95 B82-25045

711′.7 — Transport. Planning

Bayliss, B. T.. Planning and control in the transport sector / Brian Bayliss. — Aldershot : Gower, c1981. — xiv,202p : ill ; 23cm
Includes index
ISBN 0-566-00407-0 : Unpriced : CIP rev. B81-16363

711′.7′0941 — Great Britain. Transport. Planning

Transport, location and spatial policy. — Aldershot : Gower, Feb.1983. — [272]p
ISBN 0-566-00527-1 : £12.50 : CIP entry B82-38720

711′.7′09411 — Scotland. Transport. Planning — *Proposals*

Scottish Association for Public Transport. Scottish transport in the 1980′s : policy options / Scottish Association for Public Transport. — Edinburgh (11 St. Colne St., Edinburgh EH3 6AG) : The Association, [1980]. — 11leaves ; 30cm
£0.60 (unbound) B82-23429

711′.7′094132 — Scotland. Lothian Region. Transport. Planning — *Proposals*

Lothian. *Regional Council.* Transport policies and programme. — [Edinburgh] ([19 Market St., Edinburgh, EH1 1BL]) : Lothian Regional Council
No.7: 1982-87. — 1982. — 65p,[1]folded leaf of plates : ill,1col.map ; 30cm
Cover title
Unpriced (pbk) B82-41132

Lothian. *Regional Council.* Transport policies and programme 1977/82 / Lothian Regional Council. — [Edinburgh] ([Regional Chambers, Parliament Sq, Edinburgh 1]) : The Council, 1976. — 102leaves : maps(some col.) ; 30cm
Unpriced (spiral) B82-25858

Lothian. *Regional Council.* Transport policies and programme 1979-84. — [Edinburgh] ([Regional Chambers, Parliament Sq, Edinburgh 1]) : Lothian Regional Council, 1978. — 33,3,[11] leaves : ill ; 30cm
Unpriced (pbk) B82-25859

Lothian. *Regional Council.* Transport policies and programme 1980-1985 / Lothian Regional Council. — [Edinburgh] ([Regional Chambers, Parliament Sq, Edinburgh 1]) : The Council, 1980. — 20,[4]leaves ; 30cm
Unpriced (pbk) B82-25860

Lothian. *Regional Council.* Transport policies and programme 1981-86 / Lothian Regional Council. — [Edinburgh] ([Regional Chambers, Parliament Sq, Edinburgh 1]) : The Council], 1981. — 15leaves ; 30cm
Unpriced (pbk) B82-25861

711′.72 — Cycling facilities. Planning

Hudson, Mike. Bicycle planning : policy and practice / Mike Hudson in association with Caren Levy ... [et al.]. — London : Architectural, 1982. — viii,135p : ill,facsims,forms ; 31cm
Bibliography: p130-132. — Includes index
ISBN 0-85139-058-7 : £39.50 B82-25044

711′.72′0941 — Great Britain. Cycling facilities. Planning by local authorities

Levy, Caren. On our bikes? : a survey of local authority cycle planning in Britain / by Caren Levy. — London : Friends of the Earth, c1982. — iii,59p ; 30cm
ISBN 0-905966-28-7 (spiral) : £2.95 B82-28938

711′.73′094115 — Scotland. Highland Region. Roads. Planning — *Proposals*

Road needs in Highland Region / British Road Federation/Transport Action Scotland. — London (388 Oxford St., WIN 9HF) : British Road Federation, [1982?]. — 8p : 2maps(some col.) ; 30cm
Unpriced (unbound) B82-31372

711′.73′094233 — Dorset. Roads. Planning — *Proposals*

Draft major road improvement proposals : Dorset structure plan (excluding South East Dorset) / Structure Plan Team, Dorset County Council. — [Dorchester] : Dorset County Council, 1980. — 11,14p : maps ; 30cm. — (DSP.17)
ISBN 0-85216-277-4 (pbk) : Unpriced B82-23443

711′.73′09426752 — Essex. Chelmsford. Roads. Planning — *Proposals*

Chelmsford town centre : Parkway stage 3 / Essex County Council, Chelmsford Borough Council. — [Essex] : [Essex County Council and Chelmsford Borough Council Planning Departments], 1981. — 36p : 2maps(some col.) ; 30cm
Cover title. — Map on folded sheet in pocket
£1.00 (spiral) B82-01294

Chelmsford town centre : Parkway Stage 3 : design briefs / Essex County Council, Chelmsford Borough Council. — [Essex] : [Essex County Council and Chelmsford Borough Council Planning Departments], 1981. — 15 leaves,[14]leaves of plates(some folded) : plans ; 30cm
Cover title
Unpriced (spiral) B82-01295

711′.76 — Scotland. Central Lowlands. Canals: Forth and Clyde Canal. Environment planning — *Proposals*

Draft written statement : Forth and Clyde Canal Local (Subject) Plan. — [Glasgow] ([Strathclyde House, 20 India St., Glasgow G2 4PF]) : Forth and Clyde Canal Working Party, 1981. — i,37p,[31]p of plates(some folded) : ill,maps ; 21x30cm
′Forth & Clyde Canal Local (Subject) Plan′ (1 folded sheet) as insert
Unpriced (pbk) B82-12028

712 — LANDSCAPE DESIGN

712 — Great Britain. Large gardens. Planning & management

Wright, Tom, *1928-*. Large gardens and parks : maintenance, management and design. — London : Granada, July 1982. — [208]p
ISBN 0-246-11402-9 : £15.00 : CIP entry
B82-12576

712'.023'41 — Great Britain. Landscape contracting — *Career guides*

Working in landscape contracting. — [Beckenham] ([32 Beckenham Rd, Beckenham, Kent BR3 4PB]) : Agricultural Training Board on behalf of the Joint Working Party on Careers Literature, 1980. — [4]p : 2ill ; 21cm. — (Careers in horticulture) (Job leaflet)
Unpriced (unbound) B82-19440

712'.092'4 — Gardens. Planning. Jekyll, Gertrude — *Biographies*

Edwards, Joan. Gertrude Jekyll : embroiderer, gardener and craftsman : the fourth of Joan Edwards' small books on the history of embroidery. — Dorking : Bayford, c1981. — 24p : ill ; 21cm. — (Joan Edwards' small books on the history of embroidery ; 4)
Cover title
ISBN 0-907287-03-4 (pbk) : £1.60 : CIP rev.
B81-30477

Jekyll, Gertrude. Miss Gertrude Jekyll 1843-1932 : gardener. — London : Architectural Association, 1981. — 49p : ill,plans,1port ; 18cm
Published in conjunction with the exhibition of work by Miss Gertrude Jekyll at the Architectural Association, London during November-December 1981. — Text on inside covers
ISBN 0-904503-12-7 (pbk) : Unpriced
B82-08556

712'.092'4 — United States. Landscape design. Olmsted, Frederick Law — *Correspondence, diaries, etc*

Olmsted, Frederick Law. The papers of Frederick Law Olmsted / Charles Capen McLaughlin, editor-in-Chief. — Baltimore ; London : Johns Hopkins University Press
Vol.2: Slavery and the South 1852-1957 / Charles E. Beveridge, Charles Capen McLaughlin, editors ; David Schuyler, assistant editor. — c1981. — xxi,503p : ill,maps,ports ; 24cm
Includes index
ISBN 0-8018-2242-4 : £19.50 B82-02237

712'.0941 — Great Britain. Landscape design

Brown, Jane. The everywhere landscape / Jane Brown. — London : Wildwood House, 1982. — 154p,[16]p of plates : ill,maps ; 22cm
Bibliography: p138-140. — Includes index
ISBN 0-7045-3058-9 (pbk) : £4.95 : CIP rev.
B82-04624

712'.6 — Gardens — *For children*

Jekyll, Gertrude. Children and gardens. — Woodbridge : Antique Collectors' Club, Oct.1982. — [212]p
Originally published: London : Country Life, 1908
ISBN 0-907462-27-8 : £12.50 : CIP entry
B82-24619

712'.6 — Gardens. Landscape design

Crowe, Sylvia. Garden design / Sylvia Crowe. — Chichester : Packard in association with Thomas Gibson, 1981. — 224p : ill,plans ; 26cm
Bibliography: p220. — Includes index
ISBN 0-906527-05-8 : £20.00 B82-08138

712'.6 — Gardens. Planning — *Amateurs' manuals*

The **Garden** planner / [editor Piers Dudgeon] ; consultant editor Ashley Stephenson. — [London] : Fontana, 1981. — 247p : ill(some col.),col.ports ; 30cm
Includes index
ISBN 0-00-636206-0 (pbk) : Unpriced
B82-02218

712'.6 — Gardens. Planning. Use of colour

Jekyll, Gertrude. Colour schemes for the flower garden. — 8th ed. — Woodbridge : Antique Collectors' Club, Feb.1982. — [300]p
Originally published: London : Country Life, 1936
ISBN 0-907462-17-0 : £12.50 : CIP entry
B82-03135

712'.6 — Japanese Zen Buddhist gardens. Design & construction

Davidson, A. K.. Zen gardening / A.K. Davidson. — London : Rider, 1982. — 156p,[8]p of plates : ill,plans ; 24cm
Includes index
ISBN 0-09-146301-7 (pbk) : £5.95 : CIP rev.
B82-10690

712'.6 — Rock gardens, water gardens & woodland gardens. Planning — *Manuals*

Jekyll, Gertrude. Wall, water and woodland gardens. — 8th ed. — Woodbridge : Antique Collectors' Club, Sept.1982. — [480]p
Reprint of 8th ed.: London : Country Life, 1933
ISBN 0-907462-26-x : £12.50 : CIP entry
B82-18780

712'.6 — Small gardens. Planning — *Amateurs' manuals*

Farthing, Donald. Designs for the smaller garden / by Donald Farthing and Guy Farthing. — London : Foulsham, c1982. — 120p : ill(some col.),plans ; 23cm
ISBN 0-572-01049-4 : £5.95 B82-17785

712'.6 — Town gardens. Planning — *Amateurs' manuals*

Dale, John C.. Town gardening / John C. Dale. — London : Ebury, c1980. — 132p : ill(some col.),plans ; 28cm
Includes index
ISBN 0-85223-173-3 : £6.50 B82-19315

712'.6'0222 — Gardens — *Illustrations*

Midda, Sara. In and out of the garden / Sara Midda. — London : Sidgwick & Jackson, 1981. — [127]p : col.ill ; 21cm
Bibliography: p127
ISBN 0-283-98822-3 : £5.95 B82-02773

712'.6'0917671 — Islamic countries. Gardens

Brookes, John. Gardens of Islam. — London : Quartet, Oct.1982. — [160]p
ISBN 0-7043-2243-9 : £15.00 : CIP entry
B82-23211

712'.6'0922 — Great Britain. Gardens. Planning. Jekyll, Gertrude & Lutyens, *Sir* Edwin

Brown, Jane. Gardens of a golden afternoon : the story of a partnership : Edwin Lutyens & Gertrude Jekyll / Jane Brown. — London : Allen Lane, 1982. — 208p,[16]p of plates : ill (some col.),facsims,plans,ports ; 26cm
Ill on lining papers. — Bibliography: p204. — Includes index
ISBN 0-7139-1440-8 : £12.95 B82-32567

712'.6'0924 — Gardens. Planning. Jekyll, Gertrude — *Correspondence, diaries, etc.*

Jekyll, Gertrude. Gertrude Jekyll, gardener : letters to the artist William Nicholson following the completion of her portrait, January 1921 / edited by J.R. Gretton. — Dereham (5 Quebec Rd., Dereham, Norfolk) : Dereham Books, 1981. — 9p,[4]p of plates : facsims,1col.port ; 26cm
Limited ed. of 200 numbered copies. — Port on inside cover
Unpriced (pbk) B82-32692

712'.6'094 — Western Europe. Gardens, *ca 500-1548*

Harvey, John, *1911-*. Mediaeval gardens / John Harvey. — London : Batsford, 1981. — xvi,199p,viiip of plates : ill(some col.),maps,facsims,plans ; 26cm
Bibliography: p144-147. — Includes index
ISBN 0-7134-2395-1 : £17.50 B82-03476

712'.6'0941 — Great Britain. Gardens, *1850-1980*

Massingham, Betty. A century of gardeners. — London : Faber, Oct.1982. — 1v.
ISBN 0-571-11811-9 : £12.50 : CIP entry
B82-28469

712'.6'0941 — Great Britain. Small gardens. Planning — *Amateurs' manuals*

Seddon, George. Planning a family garden / George Seddon. — London : Macdonald, 1982. — 191p : ill ; 26cm
Includes index
ISBN 0-356-08539-2 : £7.95 B82-16946

712'.6'09411 — Scotland. Gardens

Scotland's gardens / edited by G. Allan Little. — Edinburgh : Spurbooks in association with the Scotland's Gardens Scheme, 1981. — 280p : ill (some col.),maps,plans ; 26cm
Includes index
ISBN 0-7157-2091-0 : £12.95 B82-12799

712'.6'0942 — England. Cottages. Gardens, *to 1980*

Scott-James, Anne. The cottage garden / Anne Scott-James. — Harmondsworth : Penguin, 1982, c1981. — 159p,[16]p of plates : ill(some col.) ; 24cm
Originally published: London : Allen Lane, 1981. — Includes index
ISBN 0-14-046397-6 (pbk) : £4.95 B82-22491

712'.6'0942 — England. Country houses. Gardens. Design

Jekyll, Gertrude. Gardens for small country houses / by Gertrude Jekyll & Lawrence Weaver. — [Woodbridge] : Antique Collectors' Club, c1981. — xvi,260p : ill,plans ; 29cm
Originally published: London : Country Life, 1912. — Ill on lining papers. — Includes index
ISBN 0-907462-10-3 : £17.50 B82-13943

712'.6'0942 — England. Gardens. Landscape design — *Early works — Facsimiles*

Repton, Humphry. Observations on the theory and practice of landscape gardening. — Oxford : Phaidon, 1980. — 222p[30]leaves of plates : ill(some col.),maps(some col.),plans,1port ; 35cm
Written by Humphry Repton. — Facsim. of: 1st ed. London : J. Taylor, 1803. — Limited ed. of 445 numbered copies. — Includes index
ISBN 0-7148-2182-9 : Unpriced B82-05821

712'.6'0942 — England. Landscape gardens, *1620-1820 — Readings from contemporary sources*

The **Genius** of the place : the English landscape garden 1620-1820 / edited by John Dixon Hunt and Peter Willis. — London : Elek, 1975 (1979 [printing]). — xx,390p : ill,plans,ports ; 25cm
Bibliography: p380-382. — Includes index
ISBN 0-236-40166-1 (pbk) : £6.95 B82-24067

712'.6'0942236 — Kent. Sevenoaks. Country houses: Great Comp. Gardens, *1957-1980*

Cameron, R.. Great Comp and its garden : one couple's achievement in seven acres / by R. Cameron. — Maidstone : Bachman & Turner, 1981. — 184p : ill(some col.),maps,ports ; 31cm
Maps on lining papers. — Includes index
ISBN 0-85974-100-1 : £10.75 B82-01032

712'.6'0942319 — Wiltshire. Stourton. Country houses: Stourhead House. Gardens. Landscaping, *1743-1969*

Woodbridge, Kenneth. The Stourhead landscape : Wiltshire / Kenneth Woodbridge. — New ed. — [London] : National Trust, c1982. — 72p : ill,maps,plans ; 25cm
Previous ed.: 1971. — Bibliography: p71-72
Unpriced (pbk) B82-38003

712'.6'0942440924 — Hereford and Worcester. Worcestershire. Farmhouses: Clack's Farm. Gardens — *Personal observations*

Billitt, Arthur. The story of Clack's Farm. — London : Ward Lock, Sept.1981. — [176]p
ISBN 0-7063-5995-x (cased) : £6.95 : CIP entry
ISBN 0-7063-6134-2 (pbk) : £3.95 B81-23837

712'.6'094257 — Oxfordshire. Gardens, *to 1981*

Of Oxfordshire gardens. — Oxford : Oxford Polytechnic Press, Mar.1982. — [120]p
ISBN 0-902692-24-0 : £9.95 : CIP entry
B82-01153

712′.7 — England. Electricity generation & transmission industries: Central Electricity Generating Board. Sites. Landscape design

Landscape in the making. — Gloucester : Central Electricity Generating Board, 1982. — [32]p : ill(some col.) ; 21x30cm
Cover title. — Text on inside covers
ISBN 0-902543-67-9 (pbk) : £2.00 B82-31234

712′.7 — Great Britain. Royal residences. Gardens

Plumptre, George. Royal gardens / George Plumptre ; with photographs by Derry Moore. — London : Collins, 1981. — 224p : ill(some col.),1plan ; 28cm
Includes index
ISBN 0-00-211871-8 : £9.95 : CIP rev.
B81-24585

712′.7′0942574 — Oxfordshire. Oxford. Universities: University of Oxford. Gardens, ***to 1981***

Batey, Mavis. Oxford gardens : the university′s influence on garden history. — Amersham : Avebury Publishing, June 1982. — [252]p
ISBN 0-86127-002-9 (cased) : £11.95 : CIP entry
ISBN 0-86127-005-3 (pbk) : £6.95 B82-16216

714 — Garden features: Concrete ponds. Construction — *Manuals*

Carson, S. McB.. How to build a pond using concrete / by Seán Carson. — [Hitchin] ([c/o Hon. Sec., Offley Place, Great Offley, Hitchin, Herts. SG5 3DS]) : Hertfordshire & Middlesex Trust for Nature Conservation, [1981]. — 15p : ill ; 21cm
Cover title
£0.25 (pbk) B82-09514

715 — Garden features. Trees & shrubs

Foster, Raymond. Trees & shrubs in garden design / Raymond Foster. — Newton Abbot : David & Charles, c1982. — 231p : ill(some col.) ; 24cm
Includes index
ISBN 0-7153-8271-3 : £10.95 : CIP rev.
B82-04873

715 — North America. Gardens. Landscaping. Use of wild flowers — *Manuals*

Diekelmann, John. Natural landscaping : designing with native plant communities / John Diekelmann, Robert Schuster ; illustrations by Renee Graef. — New York ; London : McGraw-Hill, c1982. — ix,276p,[8]p of plates : ill(some col.),maps,plans ; 25cm
Includes bibliographies and index
ISBN 0-07-016813-x : £18.95 B82-31693

715′.2 — Great Britain. Landscape design. Policies of Great Britain. ***Forestry Commission***

Great Britain. *Forestry Commission*. The Forestry Commission & landscape design. — Edinburgh : The Commission, [1980]. — 8p : col.ill ; 21cm. — (Policy and procedure paper ; no.3)
ISBN 0-85538-076-4 (pbk) : Unpriced
B82-15523

715′.2 — Landscape design. Use of trees

Thomas, Graham Stuart. Planting the landscape. — London : Cape, Feb.1983. — 1v.
ISBN 0-224-02051-x : £8.95 : CIP entry
B82-37834

716 — Garden features: Coloured foliage plants

Grounds, Roger. The multi-coloured garden : a new approach to gardening with coloured foliage / Roger Grounds. — London : Pelham, 1982. — 160p,[12]p of plates : ill(some col.),plans ; 23cm
Includes index
ISBN 0-7207-1388-9 : £9.95 : CIP rev.
B82-04886

716 — Landscape design. Use of plants

Hackett, Brian. Planting design / Brian Hackett. — London : Spon, 1979 (1982 [printing]). — x,174p,[8]p of plates : ill(some col.) ; 24cm
Bibliography: p169-170. — Includes index
ISBN 0-419-11090-9 (cased) : Unpriced
ISBN 0-419-12730-5 (pbk) : Unpriced
B82-38090

717 — Europe. Mazes

Trojaburgen : the works of Aspelin, Hamkens, Sieber & Mössinger / Caerdroia/I.G.R. ; [translated by Michael Behrend and Debbie Saward]. — Benfleet (53 Thundersley Grove, Thundersley, Benfleet, Essex) : Caerdroia Project, 1982. — 12p : ill ; 21cm
Translated from the German
Unpriced (unbound) B82-14665

717 — Garden features: Ornaments

Jekyll, Gertrude. Garden ornament. — Woodbridge : Antique Collectors′ Club, Apr.1982. — [460]p
Originally published: London : Country Life and George Newnes, 1918
ISBN 0-907462-16-2 : £19.50 : CIP entry
B82-12806

717 — Gardens. Grottoes, ***to 1981***

Miller, Naomi. Heavenly caves. — London : Allen & Unwin, June 1982. — [200]p
ISBN 0-04-725001-1 : £15.00 : CIP entry
B82-10585

717 — New Zealand. Gardens. Pavements. Design & construction — *Manuals*

Bennett, Earl H.. Paths and paving for New Zealand : what to use and how to use it / Earl H. Bennett. — Christchurch [N.Z.] ; London : Whitcoulls, 1981. — 88p : ill ; 24cm
ISBN 0-7233-0661-3 (pbk) : Unpriced
B82-09795

719 — NATURAL LANDSCAPES

719′.06′0411 — Scotland. Landscape conservation. Organisations: National Trust for Scotland — *Serials*

National Trust for Scotland. News / the National Trust for Scotland. — Mar. 1981-. — Edinburgh (5 Charlotte Sq., Edinburgh EH2 4DU) : The Trust, 1981-. — v. : ill,ports ; 30cm
Three issues yearly. — Continues: National Trust for Scotland. News letter. — Description based on: June 1982
ISSN 0263-8452 = News - National Trust for Scotland : Unpriced
Also classified at 363.6′9′060411 B82-32368

719′.0941 — Great Britain. Landscape. Effects of industrial development

Landscape and industry : essays in memory of Geoffrey Gullett / edited by Eric Grant and Peter Newby. — [Barnet] : Middlesex Polytechnic, 1982. — 157p : ill,maps,1port ; 29cm
Includes bibliographies
ISBN 0-904804-17-8 (pbk) : Unpriced : CIP rev. B82-20788

Trinder, Barrie. The making of the industrial landscape. — London : Dent, Nov.1982. — [288]p
ISBN 0-460-04427-3 : £10.95 : CIP entry
B82-27531

719′.0941 — Great Britain. Rural regions. Landscape conservation. Agreements between landowners & local authorities

Cowap, Charles. Management agreements in rural planning : a review of the literature / Charles Cowap. — [Cheltenham] ([Pittville, Gloucester GL52 3JG]) : Dept. of Town and Country Planning, Gloucestershire College of Arts and Technology, 1982. — 17p ; 30cm. — (Gloucestershire papers in local and rural planning, ISSN 0144-4875 ; no.14)
Bibliography: p15-16
Unpriced (pbk) B82-23833

719′.09411 — Scotland. Landscape conservation. Agreements between landowners & local authorities

Management agreements. — Redgorton : Countryside Commission for Scotland, 1982. — 9p ; 20cm
ISBN 0-902226-60-6 (pbk) : Unpriced
B82-33045

719′.09411′5 — Scotland. Highland Region. Landscape — *For environment planning*

Moira, Betty L. C.. Highland landscape : a report on a landscape appraisal and building in the countryside / prepared for the Highland Regional Council by Betty L.C. Moira. — [Inverness] ([Glenurquhart Rd., Inverness IV3 5NY]) : [Highland Regional Council], 1979. — 39p : ill ; 30cm
Cover title
Unpriced (pbk) B82-09742

719′.09413′12 — Scotland. Loch Lomond region. Landscape. Effects of proposed widening of roads

Rees, Joan, *1936-*. Vegetation structure and landscape appearance : a methodology / Joan Rees and Joy Tivy. — [Glasgow] : University of Glasgow, Department of Geography, 1981. — 14p : ill,maps ; 30cm. — (Occasional papers / Geography Department Glasgow University ; no.5)
Bibliography: p12-13
Unpriced (spiral) B82-27870

719′.09423′31 — Dorset. West Dorset ***(District).*** **Coastal regions. Heritage coasts: West Dorset Heritage Coast. Environment planning** — *Proposals*

West Dorset Heritage Coast : consultation document / Dorset County Council, West Dorset District. — Dorchester : Dorset County Council, 1982. — 53p,10folded leaves of plates : ill,maps(some col.) ; 30cm
ISBN 0-85216-310-x (pbk) : £1.75 B82-35553

719′.32′09411 — Scotland. Country parks. Development — *Proposals*

A Policy for country parks in Scotland. — Rev. — Redgorton : Countryside Commission for Scotland, 1982. — 5p ; 20cm
Previous ed.: 1973
ISBN 0-902226-53-3 (pbk) : Unpriced
B82-33044

719′.32′09411 — Scotland. Regional parks. Development — *Proposals*

A Policy for regional parks in Scotland. — Redgorton : Countryside Commission for Scotland, 1982. — 5p ; 20cm
ISBN 0-902226-58-4 (pbk) : Unpriced
B82-33049

719′.32′0942 — England. National parks — *Conference proceedings*

The National parks : conference / YHA . SELG. — [St. Albans] : [YHA], [1976?]. — 36p ; 30cm
Cover title
Unpriced (pbk) B82-14993

719′.32′0942511 — England. Peak District. National parks: Peak District National Park

A Guide to policies affecting the Peak District National Park. — 2nd ed. — [Bakewell] : [Peak Park Joint Planning Board], 1982. — 40p : ill,maps ; 30cm. — (A Peak National Park planning publication)
Previous ed.: 197-?
ISBN 0-907543-00-6 (pbk) : Unpriced
B82-35117

719′.32′0942511 — England. Peak District. National parks: Peak District National Park. Structure planning — *Proposals*

Peak Park Joint Planning Board. Peak District National Park approved structure plan / The Peak Park Joint Planning Board. — Bakewell : [Peak Park Joint Planning Board], 1982. — 98p,[1]folded leaf of plates : maps(some col.) ; 30cm
ISBN 0-901428-95-7 (pbk) : Unpriced
B82-35116

719′.32′0942956 — South Wales. National parks: Brecon Beacons National Park

Group visits : general information for group leaders. — [Brecon] ([Glamorgan St., Brecon, Powys LD3 7DP]) : Brecon Beacons National Park, [1982?]. — 1portfolio : ill,3forms,1map ; 16x24cm
Unpriced B82-30919

National park : study resources (general). — Brecon (7 Glamorgan St., Brecon, Powys LD3 7DP) : Brecon Beacons National Park, [1982]. — 1portfolio : ill,1map ; 23x32cm
Includes bibliographies
Unpriced B82-30918

719'.32'0942956 — South Wales. National parks: Brecon Beacons National Park *continuation*

720 — ARCHITECTURE

720'.1 — Architecture. Criticism. Theories

Teymur, Necdet. Environmental discourse. — London (P.O. Box 162, N2 9LZ) : ?uestion Press, Oct.1982. — [234]p
ISBN 0-946160-00-7 (cased) : £11.95 : CIP entry
ISBN 0-946160-01-5 (pbk) : £4.95 B82-26093

720'.22'2 — American architectural drawings — *Collections*

Architectural drawing : the art and the process / [compiled] by Gerald Allen and Richard Oliver. — New York : Whitney Library of Design ; London : Architectural Press, 1981. — 199p : ill(some col.),plans(some col.) ; 29cm
ISBN 0-85139-734-4 : £19.50 B82-17727

720'.22'2 — Architectural drawings, *1900-1980 — Illustrations*

Jacoby, Helmut. New techniques of architectural rendering / Helmut Jacoby ; translated by John W. Gabriel. — 2nd ed. — New York ; London : Van Nostrand Reinhold, 1981. — 167p : chiefly ill(some col.),plans ; 23x29cm
Translated from the German. — Previous ed.: New York : Praeger ; London : Thames and Hudson, 1971. — Also available in pbk: £12.70
ISBN 0-442-21210-0 : £21.20 B82-02858

720'.22'2 — Architectural drawings. Entourage — *Illustrations*

Burden, Ernest. Entourage : a tracing file : for architecture and interior design drawing / Ernest Burden. — New York ; London : McGraw-Hill, c1981. — 248p : chiefly ill ; 28cm. — (McGraw-Hill paperbacks)
Includes index
ISBN 0-07-008930-2 (pbk) : £10.95
B82-01007

Evans, Larry. Illustration guide : for architects, designers and students / Larry Evans. — New York ; London : Van Nostrand Reinhold, c1982. — [300]p : chiefly ill ; 31cm
ISBN 0-442-22199-1 (pbk) : £16.10
B82-38595

720'.22'2 — French architectural drawings. Corbusier, Le — *Illustrations*

Corbusier, Le. Le Corbusier selected drawings / introduction by Michael Graves. — London : Academy, 1981. — 143p : all ill(some col.),plans(some col.) ; 25cm
ISBN 0-85670-740-6 (pbk) : £10.50
B82-06183

720'.22'2 — German architectural drawings. Schinkel, Karl Friedrich — *Illustrations*

Schinkel, Karl Friedrich. [Sammlung architectonischer Entwürfe]. Collected architectural designs / Karl Friedrich Schinkel. — London : Academy Editions, 1982. — viii,174p of plates : all ill,plans ; 31cm
Foreword and list of plates in English. — Originally published: with commentary. Berlin? : s.n., 1819-1840
ISBN 0-312-44952-6 (cased) : £15.95
ISBN 0-312-44953-4 (pbk) : £9.95 B82-23032

720'.23 — Architecture — *Career guides*

Burston, Oliver. Careers in architecture. — London : Kogan Page, Jan.1983. — [100]p. — (Kogan Page careers series)
ISBN 0-85038-611-x (cased) : £6.95 : CIP entry
ISBN 0-85038-647-0 (pbk) : £2.50 B82-35186

720'.28'4 — Architectural drawings. Linear perspective. Techniques

Bärtschi, Willy A.. Linear perspective : its history, directions for construction, and aspects in the environment and in the fine arts / by Willy A. Bärtschi ; translated by Fred Bradley. — New York ; London : Van Nostrand Reinhold, 1981. — 252p : ill,plans ; 31cm
Translation of: Perspektive. — Bibliography: p252. — Includes index
ISBN 0-442-24344-8 : £21.20 B82-22578

Burden, Ernest. Architectural delineation : a photographic approach to presentation / Ernest Burden. — 2nd ed. — New York ; London : McGraw Hill, c1982. — viii,280p : ill(some col.),plans ; 29cm
Previous ed.: New York : McGraw Hill, 1971. — Includes index
ISBN 0-07-008925-6 : Unpriced B82-37618

720'.28'4 — Architectural drawings. Metric sizes — *Technical data*

Frishman, Bernard Lyon. Metric architectural drawing : a manual for designers and draftsmen / Bernard Lyon Frishman, Lionel Loshak and Charles S. Strelka. — New York ; Chichester : Wiley, c1981. — x,191p : ill,plans ; 29cm
Includes index
ISBN 0-471-07724-0 : £22.25 B82-08718

720'.28'4 — Architectural drawings. Techniques — *Manuals*

Weidhaas, Ernest R.. Architectural drafting and construction / Ernest R. Weidhaas. — 2nd ed. — Boston, Mass. ; London : Allyn and Bacon, c1981. — xii,564,[46]p : ill,plans ; 29cm
Previous ed.: 1974. — Includes index
ISBN 0-205-07102-3 : £17.50 B82-34139

720'.28'4 — Architectural drawings. Techniques — *Manuals — For teaching*

Weidhaas, Ernest R.. A guidebook for teaching architectural drafting / Ernest R. Weidhaas. — Boston, Mass. ; London : Allyn and Bacon, c1982. — x,194p : ill,forms,plans ; 28cm. — (A Guidebook for teaching)
Includes bibliographies
ISBN 0-205-07808-7 (pbk) : Unpriced
B82-28487

720'.28'4 — Architectural working drawings

McHugh, Robert C.. Working drawing handbook : a guide for architects and builders / Robert C. McHugh. — New York ; London : Van Nostrand Reinhold, c1982. — ix,165p : ill,forms,plans ; 22x28cm
Previous ed.: 1977. — Bibliography. — Includes index
ISBN 0-442-25648-5 (cased) : Unpriced
ISBN 0-442-26326-0 (pbk) : £11.00
B82-36644

720'.28'4 — Architectural working drawings. Techniques — *Manuals — For construction industries*

Styles, Keith. Working drawings handbook / Keith Styles. — London : Architectural Press, 1982. — vii,131p : ill,forms,plans ; 21x30cm
Includes index
ISBN 0-85139-712-3 (pbk) : £9.75 : CIP rev.
B82-07018

720'.28'6 — United States. Buildings. Renovation & remodelling. Design

Lion, Edgar. Building renovation and recycling / Edgar Lion. — New York ; Chichester : Wiley, c1982. — ix,132p : ill ; 23cm. — (A Wiley-Interscience publication)
Includes index
ISBN 0-471-86444-7 : £19.50 B82-28697

720'.28'8 — Great Britain. Buildings. Architectural features. Conservation — *Serials*

Architectural preservation and new design in conservation. — Vol.1, no.1 (Apr. 1982)-. — London (38 Mount Pleasant, WC1X 0AP) : Architectural Preservation, 1982-. — v. : ill,plans ; 30cm
Monthly. — Also entitled: AP
ISSN 0262-219X = Architectural preservation and new design in conservation : £20.00 per year B82-33857

720'.47 — Architecture. Applications of solar energy

Knowles, Ralph L.. Sun rhythm form / Ralph L. Knowles. — Cambridge, Mass. ; London : MIT Press, 1981. — xiv,289p : ill,plans ; 27cm
Includes index
ISBN 0-262-11078-4 : Unpriced B82-29452

720'.47 — Buildings. Daylight. Provision. Architectural design

Evans, Benjamin H.. Daylight in architecture / Benjamin H. Evans. — New York ; London : Architectural Record, c1981. — x,204p : ill,plans ; 29cm
Includes index
ISBN 0-07-019768-7 : £22.95 B82-23886

720'.6'01 — Commonwealth countries. Architecture. Organisations: Commonwealth Association of Architects — *Serials*

Commonwealth Association of Architects. CAA handbook / Commonwealth Association of Architects. — 1976-. — London (26 Store St., WC1E 7BT) : CAA, 1976-. — v. : maps ; 29cm
Irregular. — Continues: Commonwealth Association of Architects. Handbook of Commonwealth architects. — Description based on: 1979 issue
ISSN 0263-0087 = CAA handbook : £3.00
B82-12470

720'.68 — Great Britain. Architectural design. Practices. Management

Bennett, Philip H. P.. Architectural practice and procedure : from appointment to final account for architects, surveyors and the building industry / Philip H.P. Bennett. — London : Batsford Academic and Educational, 1981. — 186p : ill,forms ; 25cm
Spine title: Mitchell's architectural practice and procedure. — Includes index
ISBN 0-7134-1315-8 : £12.50 B82-06275

720'.7 — Architecture. Information sources

Information sources in architecture. — London : Butterworths, Feb.1983. — [382]p. — (Butterworths guides to information sources)
ISBN 0-408-10763-4 : £28.00 : CIP entry
B82-38290

720'.7'041 — Great Britain. Architecture, *to 1980.* **Information sources —** *Lists*

Kamen, Ruth H.. British and Irish architectural history : a bibliography and guide to sources of information / Ruth H. Kamen. — London : Architectural, 1981. — vi,249p ; 26cm
Includes index
ISBN 0-85139-077-3 : £30.00 : CIP rev.
B81-30416

720'.7'114436 — France. Paris. Art schools: École des Beaux-Arts. Curriculum subjects: Architecture

The **Beaux-arts** : and nineteenth-century French architecture / edited by Robin Middleton. — London : Thames and Hudson, c1982. — 280p : ill(some col.),maps,plans,facsims ; 26cm
Includes index
ISBN 0-500-34086-2 : £18.00 B82-16127

720'.7'1173 — United States. Higher education institutions. Curriculum subjects: Architectural design — *For teaching*

Weidhaas, Ernest R.. Instructor's manual to accompany Architectural drafting and design, fourth edition, and, Architectural drafting and construction, second edition / Ernest R. Weidhaas. — Boston, Mass. ; London : Allyn and Bacon, c1981. — 217p : ill,forms ; 28cm
£4.50 (pbk) B82-35051

720.9 — ARCHITECTURE. HISTORICAL AND GEOGRAPHICAL TREATMENT

720'.9 — Architecture, *to ca 1965*

World architecture : an illustrated history from earliest times / edited by Trewin Copplestone ... — London : Hamlyn, c1963 (1981 [printing]). — 348p : ill(some col.),plans ; 34cm
Includes index
ISBN 0-600-34260-3 (pbk) : £6.95 B82-04443

720'.92'2 — Great Britain. Architectural design. Deane, *Sir* **Thomas & Woodward, Benjamin —** *Critical studies*

Blau, Eve. Ruskinian gothic : the architecture of Deane and Woodland 1845-1861 / Eve Blau. — Princeton ; Guildford : Princeton University Press, c1982. — xix,219p,[72]p of plates : ill,facsims,plans,ports ; 27cm
Bibliography: p201-209. — Includes index
ISBN 0-691-03984-4 (cased) : £28.10
ISBN 0-691-10127-2 (pbk) B82-31742

720'.92'2 — United States. Architects, *ca 1750-1981* **—** *Biographies*

Three centuries of notable American architects / edited by Joseph J. Thorndike, Jr.. — London : Orbis, 1982, c1981. — 348p : ill(some col.),facsim,plans,ports(some col.) ; 29cm
Originally published: New York : American Heritage, 1981. — Includes index
ISBN 0-85613-398-1 : £20.00 B82-16628

720'.92'4 — Architechtural design. Lutyens, *Sir* **Edwin —** *Critical studies*

Gradidge, Roderick. Edwin Lutyens : architect laureate / Roderick Gradidge. — London : Allen & Unwin, 1981. — xxi,167p : ill,plans,1port ; 26cm
Includes index
ISBN 0-04-720023-5 : Unpriced : CIP rev. B81-22567

720'.92'4 — Architectural design. Andrews, John, *1933-* **—** *Critical studies*

Andrews, John, *1933-*. Architecture : a performing art / John Andrews & Jennifer Taylor. — Guildford : Lutterworth, 1982. — 176p : ill(some col.),plans(some col.) ; 24x26cm
ISBN 0-7188-2532-2 : £15.00 B82-22202

720'.92'4 — Architectural design. Burges, William — *Catalogues*

The **Strange** genius of William Burges, 'art-architect', 1827-1881 : a catalogue to a centenary exhibition organised jointly by the National Museum of Wales, Cardiff, and the Victoria and Albert Musuem, London in 1981 / edited by J. Mordaunt Crook ; catalogue entries by Mary Axon and Virginia Glenn. — Cardiff : National Museum of Wales, 1981 (1982 [printing]). — 155p : ill ; 25cm
Bibliography: p154
ISBN 0-7200-0259-1 (cased) : £6.00
ISBN 0-7200-0234-6 (pbk) : Unpriced B82-37433

720'.92'4 — Architectural design. Erskine, Ralph — *Biographies*

Collymore, Peter. The architecture of Ralph Erskine. — London : Granada, Sept.1982. — [192]p
ISBN 0-246-11250-6 : £20.00 : CIP entry B82-18848

720'.92'4 — Architectural design. Roca, Miguel Angel — *Critical studies*

Glusberg, Jorge. Miguel Angel Roca / texts by Jorge Glusberg & Oriol Bohigas. — London : Academy Editions, 1981. — 160p : ill(some col.),plans(some col.) ; 25cm
Parallel English and Spanish text. — Bibliography: p160
Unpriced (pbk) B82-03780

720'.92'4 — Architectural design. Rossi, Aldo — *Biographies*

Rossi, Aldo. A scientific autobiography / Aldo Rossi ; postscript by Vincent Scully ; translation by Lawrence Venuti. — Cambridge, Mass. ; London : Published for the Graham Foundation for Advanced Studies in the Fine Arts, Chicago, Illinois, and the Institute for Architecture and Urban Studies, New York by the MIT Press, 1981. — 119p : ill ; 26cm. — (Oppositions books)
Translation from the Italian
ISBN 0-262-18104-5 : Unpriced B82-29451

720'.92'4 — Architectural design. Schultz, Robert Weir — *Biographies*

Stamp, Gavin. Robert Weir Schultz, architect, and his work for the Marquesses of Bute : an essay / by Gavin Stamp. — Mount Stuart : [Marguess of Bute], 1981. — 79p,[20]p of plates : ill,plans,ports ; 24cm
£8.50 (pbk) B82-05864

720'.92'4 — Architectural design. Stuart, James — *Biographies*

Watkin, David. Athenian Stuart. — London : Allen & Unwin, Aug.1982. — [128]p
ISBN 0-04-720026-x (cased) : £9.95 : CIP entry
ISBN 0-04-720027-8 (pbk) : £4.95 B82-20743

720'.92'4 — Architectural design. Talman, William — *Biographies*

Harris, John. William Talman. — London : Allen & Unwin, Aug.1982. — [104]p
ISBN 0-04-720024-3 (cased) : £9.95 : CIP entry
ISBN 0-04-720025-1 (pbk) : £4.95 B82-17938

720'.92'4 — Architectural design. Tschumi, Bernard — *Illustrations*

Tschumi, Bernard. The Manhattan transcripts / Bernard Tschumi. — [London] : Academy Editions, c1981. — 63p : chiefly ill ; 28cm
Accompanies the exhibition Manhattan transcripts Part 4 at the Max Protetch Gallery, New York, December 3, 1981-January 2, 1982. — Bibliography: p62
ISBN 0-85670-771-6 (pbk) : £4.95 B82-14291

720'.92'4 — Architectural design. Wright, Frank Lloyd — *Biographies*

Wright, Frank Lloyd. An autobiography / Frank Lloyd Wright. — [New ed.]. — London : Quartet, c1977. — 620p,[40]p of plates : ill,1facsim,ports ; 25cm
Previous ed.: London : Longmans, Green and Co., 1932. — Facsim. on lining papers
ISBN 0-7043-2196-3 : £10.00 B82-05707

720'.92'4 — England. Architectural design. Lubetkin, Berthold — *Critical studies*

Coe, Peter, *1942-*. Lubetkin and Tecton : architecture and social commitment : a critical study / Peter Coe, Malcolm Reading. — London : Arts Council of Great Britain and the University of Bristol, 1981. — 202p : ill,plans,ports ; 20x21cm
Bibliography: p200-201
ISBN 0-7287-0273-8 (corrected : pbk) : £6.30
ISBN 0-906515-86-6 (University of Bristol) B82-06153

720'.92'4 — England. Architectural design. Wren, *Sir* **Christopher —** *Critical studies*

Downes, Kerry. The architecture of Wren. — London : Granada, Sept.1982. — 1v.
ISBN 0-246-11582-3 : £15.00 : CIP entry B82-18852

720'.92'4 — England. Buildings designed by Wren, *Sir* **Christopher. Architectural features**

Beard, Geoffrey. The work of Christopher Wren. — Edinburgh : Bartholomew, July 1982. — [256]p
ISBN 0-7028-8071-x : £14.00 : CIP entry B82-13001

720'.92'4 — Finland. Architectural design. Aalto, Alvar

Porphyrios, Demetri. Sources of modern eclecticism : studies on Alvar Aalto / Demetri Porphyrios. — London : Academy Editions, 1982. — xvii,138p : ill,plans ; 24cm
Includes index
ISBN 0-312-74673-3 (cased) : £15.95
ISBN 0-312-74674-1 (pbk) : £12.50 B82-34396

720'.92'4 — Finland. Architectural design. Aalto, Alvar — *Critical studies*

Quantrill, Malcolm. Alvar Aalto. — London : Secker & Warburg, Nov.1982. — [256]p
ISBN 0-436-39400-6 : £25.00 : CIP entry B82-29440

720'.92'4 — Germany. Architectural design. Taut, Bruno — *Critical studies*

Whyte, Iain Boyd. Bruno Taut and the architecture of activism / Iain Boyd Whyte. — Cambridge : Cambridge University Press, 1982. — xiii,280p : ill,ports ; 26cm. — (Cambridge urban and architectural studies ; 6)
Bibliography: p264-272. — Includes index
ISBN 0-521-23655-x : £35.00 : CIP rev. B82-15823

720'.92'4 — Germany. Architectural design. Weinbrenner, Friedrich — *Catalogues*

Friedrich Weinbrenner, 1766-1826 : an exhibition arranged by the Architectural Association, London / Architectural Association, London, 7 June-26 June 1982, Fitzwilliam Museum, Cambridge, 13 July-30 August 1982, Mackintosh School of Art, Glasgow, 1 October-25 October 1982. — London : Architectural Association, c1982. — 48p : ill,plans ; 18cm
Catalogue entries and one essay translated from the German. — Bibliography: p48. — Includes three essays and the catalogue of exhibits
ISBN 0-904503-18-6 (pbk) : Unpriced B82-36901

720'.92'4 — Italy. Architectural design. Brunelleschi, Filippo — *Illustrations*

Brunelleschi, Filippo. Brunelleschi : the complete work / [edited by] Eugenio Battisti. — London : Thames and Hudson, 1981. — 400p : ill,facsims,plans ; 29cm
Translation of: Filippo Brunelleschi. — Bibliography: p385-394. — Includes index
ISBN 0-500-34072-2 : £32.00 B82-03995

720'.92'4 — Japan. Architectural design. Isozaki, Arata — *Critical studies*

Drew, Philip. The architecture of Arata Isozaki. — London : Granada, June 1982. — [216]p
ISBN 0-246-11254-9 : £17.50 : CIP entry B82-09984

720'.92'4 — London. Lambeth *(London Borough).* **Art galleries: Hayward Gallery. Exhibits: Architectural design. Lutyens,** *Sir* **Edwin —** *Catalogues*

Lutyens, *Sir* **Edwin**. Lutyens : the work of the English architect Sir Edwin Lutyens (1869-1944) : Hayward Gallery London SE1 18 November 1981-31 January 1982. — London : Arts Council of Great Britain, c1981. — 200p : ill(some col.),1map,plans,ports ; 25cm
"Sponsors of the Lutyens exhibition" and 1 folded sheet (information leaflet) as inserts. — Bibliography: p199-200
ISBN 0-7287-0304-1 (cased) : Unpriced
ISBN 0-7287-0303-3 (pbk) : Unpriced B82-13041

720'.92'4 — United States. Architectural design. Burnham, Daniel — *Biographies*

Hines, Thomas S.. Burnham of Chicago : architect and planner / Thomas S. Hines. — Phoenix ed. — Chicago ; London : University of Chicago Press, 1979. — xxiii,445p : ill,2maps,plans,ports ; 23cm
Previous ed.: New York : Oxford University Press, 1974. — Bibliography: p387-400. — Includes index
ISBN 0-226-34171-2 (pbk) : £4.55 B82-21516

720'.92'4 — United States. Architectural design. Wright, Frank Lloyd — *Critical studies*

Writings on Wright : selected comment on Frank Lloyd Wright / edited with an introduction and commentary by H. Allen Brooks. — Cambridge, Mass. ; London : MIT, 1981. — xvi,229p : ill,plans ; 24cm
Includes index
ISBN 0-262-02161-7 : £12.25 B82-13665

720'.92'4 — West Germany. Architectural design. Behrens, Peter — *Biographies*

Windsor, Alan. Peter Behrens : architect and designer / Alan Windsor. — London : Architectural Press, 1981. — 186p : ill,plans,ports ; 24cm
Bibliography: p177-180. — Includes index
ISBN 0-85139-072-2 : £12.95 B82-00411

720'.941 — Great Britain. Architecture, *1900-1910* **—** *Biographies* **—** *Encyclopaedias*

Gray, A. Stuart. Edwardian architecture. — London : Duckworth, Oct.1981. — [384]p
ISBN 0-7156-1012-0 : £45.00 : CIP entry B81-30494

720'.941 — Great Britain. Buildings, *1790-1840.* **Architectural features**

Watkin, David. Regency : a guide and gazetteer / David Watkin. — London : Barrie & Jenkins, 1982. — 192p : ill,maps,plans ; 22cm. — (The Buildings of Britain)
Bibliography: p188. — Includes index
ISBN 0-09-147990-8 (cased) : Unpriced : CIP rev.
ISBN 0-09-147991-6 (pbk) : £4.95 B82-07259

720'.941 — Great Britain. Suburbs. Architectural features

The Anglo American suburb / guest edited by Robert A.M. Stern with John Montague Massengale. — London : Architectural Design, c1981. — 96p : ill(some col.),maps,plans ; 28cm. — (Architectural Design profile)
Ill on inside covers. — Bibliography: p95-96
ISBN 0-85670-690-6 (pbk) : £4.95
Primary classification 720'.973 B82-14287

720'.9412 — North-eastern Scotland. Buildings. Architectural design — *Illustrations*

Local modern architecture / compiled by the Dundee Institute of Architects & Junior Chambers, Dundee. — [Dundee] : [The Institute], 1981. — 15p : ill ; 30cm
Unpriced (unbound) B82-20670

720'.9412'95 — Scotland. Fife Region. West Wemyss. Buildings. Architectural features. Walkers' guides — *For teaching*

Look at architecture in West Wemyss. — [West Wemyss] : West Wemyss Environmental Education Centre, [1982]. — 44p,[2]leaves of plates : ill,1map,forms ; 21cm
Cover title. — Text on inside cover
Unpriced (pbk) B82-19480

720'.9412'98 — Scotland. Fife Region. Dunfermline. Buildings. Architectural features — *For teaching*

Brown, Edmund. Buildings in Dunfermline : walkabout : teachers guide. — [Dunfermline] : [Dunfermline Environmental Education Research Group], 1980. — 36p,[2]leaves of plates : ill,3maps ; 22cm
Cover title. — Author: Edmund Brown. — Text on inside cover
Unpriced (pbk) B82-19631

720'.9414'43 — Scotland. Strathclyde Region. Glasgow. Architecture, *1837-1901*

Worsdall, Frank. Victorian city : a selection of Glasgow's architecture. — Glasgow : Drew, Oct.1982. — [160]p
ISBN 0-904002-91-8 : £9.95 : CIP entry B82-24602

720'.9418'35 — Dublin. Buildings. Architectural features, *1700-1969* — *Illustrations*

O'Dwyer, Frederick. Lost Dublin / Frederick O'Dwyer. — Dublin : Gill and Macmillan, 1981. — viii,152p : ill,facsims ; 29cm
Includes index
ISBN 0-7171-1047-8 : Unpriced B82-08999

720'.942 — England. Architectural design. Partnerships: Foster Associates. Projects

Foster Associates / introduction by Reyner Banham. — London : RIBA Publications, c1979. — 72p : ill ; 20cm
ISBN 0-900630-74-4 (pbk) : £3.75 B82-37918

720'.942 — England. Buildings of historical importance, *1900-1939.* **Architectural features** — *Illustrations*

Forsyth, Alastair. Buildings for the age : new building types 1900-1939 / Alastair Forsyth. — [London] : Royal Commission on Historical Monuments, 1982. — [84]p : ill ; 25cm. — (National Monuments Record photographic archives)
Ill on inside covers. — Includes index
ISBN 0-11-700998-9 (pbk) : £4.95 B82-26963

720'.942 — England. Towns. Buildings of historical importance. Architectural features

Clifton-Taylor, Alec. Six more English towns / Alec Clifton-Taylor. — London : British Broadcasting Corporation, 1981. — 207p : ill,maps,1coat of arms,ports ; 27cm
Includes index
ISBN 0-563-17908-2 : £10.95 B82-04446

720'.9421 — Inner London. Buildings. Architectural features

Survey of London / general editor F.H.W. Sheppard. — London : Athlone for the Greater London Council
Vol.30: The Grosvenor estate in Mayfair
Pt.2: The buildings. — 1980. — xix,429p,[96]p of plates(1folded) : ill,1col.map,plans ; 30cm
Map on folded sheet in pocket. — Includes index
ISBN 0-485-48240-1 : £55.00 : CIP rev. B80-25959

720'.9421'83 — London. Hillingdon *(London Borough).* **Harefield. Buildings. Architectural features**

Evans, M. (Margaret). Harefield's old buildings / written & illustrated by M. Evans. — Uxbridge : Hillingdon Borough Libraries, c1982. — 24p : ill,1map ; 21cm
ISBN 0-907869-00-9 (pbk) : £0.70 B82-22083

720'.9421'89 — London. Enfield *(London Borough).* **Buildings of historical importance. Architectural features** — *Illustrations*

Enfield's architectural heritage / [edited by Valerie Carter, Peter Perryman, Alan Skilton]. — [Enfield] : Enfield Preservation Society, c1977. — 57p,106p of plates : ill,maps ; 19x25cm
Bibliography: p56
Unpriced B82-40009

720'.9423 — South-west England. Buildings, *1550-1750.* **Architectural features**

Brown, Patrick. South west England / Patrick Brown. — Ashbourne : Moorland Publishing, c1981. — 159p : ill,1map,1plan ; 26cm. — (Buildings of Britain 1550-1750)
Bibliography: p153-154. — Includes index
ISBN 0-86190-030-8 : £8.95 : CIP rev. B81-28024

720'.9423'93 — Avon. Bristol. Buildings, *1831-1906.* **Architectural features**

Crick, Clare. Victorian buildings in Bristol / by Clare Crick. — [Bristol] : Bristol & West Building Society in conjunction with the City Art Gallery, Bristol, 1975, c1978 [printing]. — 73p : ill ; 18x21cm
Bibliography: p73. — Includes index
ISBN 0-905459-09-1 (pbk) : £1.40 B82-21819

720'.9425'91 — Buckinghamshire. Milton Keynes. Buildings. Architectural features

Walker, Derek, *1932-.* The architecture and planning of Milton Keynes / Derek Walker. — London : Architectural Press, 1982. — iii,140p : ill(some col.),maps,plans ; 26cm
ISBN 0-85139-735-2 (pbk) : £7.95 B82-17696

720'.9426 — East Anglia. Buildings, *1920-1980.* **Architectural features**

McKean, Charles. Architectural guide to Cambridge and East Anglia since 1920 / Charles McKean. — England : ERA Publications Board, RIBA Eastern Region ; London : RIBA Publications [[distributor]], c1982. — 192p : ill,maps ; 22cm
Includes index
ISBN 0-907598-01-3 (pbk) : £5.25 B82-21839

720'.9428'36 — Humberside. Beverley. Buildings. Architectural features

Beverley : an archaelogical and architectural study / Keith Miller ... [et al.]. — London : H.M.S.O., 1982. — vii,96p : ill,maps(col.) ; 28cm. — (Royal Commission on Historical Monuments supplementary series ; 4)
2 maps in pocket on folded leaves. — Bibliography: p85-86. — Includes index
ISBN 0-11-701129-0 (pbk) : £7.50 B82-36205

720'.9428'43 — North Yorkshire. York. Buildings of historical importance. Architectural features — *Illustrations*

York : historic buildings in the central area : a photographic record / Royal Commission on Historical Monuments England. — London : H.M.S.O., 1981. — vii,24,200p,[8]p of plates : chiefly ill(some col.),col.maps,1plan ; 27cm
ISBN 0-11-700912-1 (pbk) : £7.50 B82-14338

720'.9428'65 — Durham *(County).* **Durham. Buildings of historical importance. Architectural features**

Durham *(Durham, England). Council.* City of Durham : our heritage : an exhibition November-December 1980. — [Durham] ([City Planning Office, Byland Lodge, Hawthorn Terrace, Durham DH1 4TD]) : [City of Durham], [1982?]. — [20]p : ill,1port ; 21cm
Cover title
Unpriced (pbk) B82-35032

720'.943 — Germany. Architecture, *1510-1618*

Hitchcock, Henry-Russell. German Renaissance architecture / Henry-Russell Hitchcock. — Princeton ; Guildford : Princeton University Press, c1981. — xxxiv,379p,[262]p of plates : ill,plans ; 29cm
Bibliography: pxxiii-xxvii. — Includes index
ISBN 0-691-03959-3 : £47.30 B82-23394

720'.945'31 — Italy. Venice. Buildings. Architectural features, *ca 1460-ca 1525*

McAndrew, John. Venetian architecture of the early Renaissance / John McAndrew. — Cambridge, Mass. ; London : MIT, c1980. — xiii,599p : ill,plans ; 29cm
Plan on lining papers. — Bibliography: p564-593. — Includes index
ISBN 0-262-13157-9 : £24.80 B82-15053

720'.945'632 — Italy. Rome. Architecture. Baroque style

Blunt, Anthony. Guide to Baroque Rome. — London : Granada, July 1982. — [256]p
ISBN 0-246-11762-1 : £15.00 : CIP entry B82-12233

720'.953'32 — Yemen *(Arab Republic).* **Buildings. Architectural features**

Varanda, Fernando. Art of building in Yemen / Fernando Varanda. — London : Aarp, 1981. — 292p : ill(some col.),maps,plans ; 31cm
Map on lining papers
ISBN 0-906468-06-x : Unpriced B82-14594

720'.955'35 — Iran. Plateau region. Buildings. Architectural features

Beazley, Elizabeth. Living with the desert. — Warminster : Aris & Phillips, Nov.1982. — [132]p
ISBN 0-85668-192-x (pbk) : £18.00 : CIP entry B82-32864

720'.973 — United States. Architectural design, *1920-1980*

Wolfe, Tom. From Bauhaus to our house / Tom Wolfe. — London : Cape, 1982, c1981. — 143p : ill,ports ; 22cm
Originally published: New York : Farrar Straus Giroux, 1981
ISBN 0-224-02030-7 : £6.95 : CIP rev. B82-14042

720'.973 — United States. Architectural design. Gwathmey Siegel Architects — *Critical studies*

Abercrombie, Stanley. Gwathmey Siegel / by Stanley Abercrombie. — New York : Whitney Library of Design ; London : Granada, 1982. — 120p : ill(some col.),plans ; 24cm. — (Monographs on contemporary architecture)
Originally published: New York : Whitney Library of Design, 1981
ISBN 0-246-11737-0 : £10.95 B82-24515

720'.973 — United States. Architecture. Classical style, *1960-1981*

Free-style classicism / guest-edited by Charles Jencks. — London : Architectural Design, c1982. — 120p : ill(some col.),plans ; 28cm. — (Architectural design profile)
Ill on inside covers
ISBN 0-85670-769-4 (pbk) : £7.50 B82-17404

720'.973 — United States. Architecture, *to 1978*

Roth, Leland M.. A concise history of American architecture / Leland M. Roth. — New York ; London : Harper & Row, c1979 (1980 [printing]). — xxvi,400p : ill,plans ; 24cm. — (Icon editions)
Bibliography: p374-381. — Includes index
ISBN 0-06-438490-x (cased) : Unpriced
ISBN 0-06-430086-2 (pbk) : £5.95 B82-14324

720'.973 — United States. Buildings, *1970-1980.* **Architectural features**

Architecture 1970-1980 : a decade of change / edited by Jeanne M. Davern ; designed by Jan V. White. — New York ; London : McGraw-Hill, c1980. — xxi,265p : ill(some col.),plans ; 31cm. — (Architectural record books)
Includes index
ISBN 0-07-002352-2 : £19.95 B82-01063

720′.973 — United States. Buildings of historical importance. Architectural features — *Illustrations*

Historic American buildings / [edited with introductions by David G. De Long]. — New York ; London : Garland
New York
Vol.2. — 1979. — 391p : ill,chiefly plans ; 24x31cm
ISBN 0-8240-3187-3 : Unpriced B82-05991

Historic American buildings / [edited with introductions by David G. De Long]. — New York ; London : Garland
New York
Vol.4. — 1979. — 335p : ill,chiefly plans ; 24x31cm
ISBN 0-8240-3189-x : Unpriced B82-05992

Historic American buildings / [edited with introductions by David G. De Long]. — New York ; London : Garland
New York
Vol.5. — 1979. — 311p : ill,chiefly plans ; 24x31cm
ISBN 0-8240-3190-3 : Unpriced B82-14152

Historic American buildings / [edited with introductions by David G. De Long]. — New York ; London : Garland
New York
Vol.6. — 1979. — 403p : all ill,plans ; 24x32cm
ISBN 0-8240-3191-1 : Unpriced B82-23521

720′.973 — United States. Experimental structures. Architectural features — *Illustrations*

SITE : architecture as art / with contributions by Pierre Restany, Bruno Zevi and SITE. — London : Academy Editions, 1980. — 112p : chiefly ill(some col.) ; 24cm
Bibliography: p20-21
£6.95 (pbk) B82-35014

720′.973 — United States. Suburbs. Architectural features

The **Anglo** American suburb / guest edited by Robert A.M. Stern with John Montague Massengale. — London : Architectural Design, c1981. — 96p : ill(some col.),maps,plans ; 28cm. — (Architectural Design profile)
Ill on inside covers. — Bibliography: p95-96
ISBN 0-85670-690-6 (pbk) : £4.95
Also classified at 720′.941 B82-14287

720′.9747′1 — New York *(City)*. Manhattan. Buildings. Architectural features

Goldberger, Paul. New York : a guide to the architecture of Manhattan / Paul Goldberger ; photography by David W. Dunlap. — Harmondsworth : Penguin, 1982, c1979. — xix,347p : ill,maps ; 24cm. — (The City observed) (Penguin handbooks)
Originally published: New York : Vintage, 1979. — Includes index
ISBN 0-14-046495-6 (pbk) : £5.95 B82-15308

720′.9945′1 — Australia. Victoria. Melbourne. Buildings, *1837-1954*. Architectural features

Wilson, Granville, *1922-*. Building a city : 100 years of Melbourne architecture / Granville Wilson and Peter Sands. — Melbourne ; Oxford : London University Press, 1981. — vii,201p : ill ; 23x26cm
Bibliography: p175-176. — Includes index
ISBN 0-19-554292-4 : £23.50 B82-36553

721 — ARCHITECTURAL DESIGN

721 — Architectural design

Rykwert, Joseph. The necessity of artifice : ideas in architecture / Joseph Rykwert. — London : Academy Editions, 1982. — 143p : ill,plans,ports ; 30cm
Includes index
ISBN 0-85670-761-9 (cased) : £15.95
ISBN 0-85670-593-4 (pbk) : £9.95 B82-32697

Smithies, K. W.. Principles of design architecture / K.W. Smithies ; with drawings by Steve Tompkins. — New York ; London : Van Nostrand Reinhold, c1981. — vi,88p : ill,plans ; 22x30cm
Bibliography: p86. — Includes index
ISBN 0-442-30441-2 (cased) : Unpriced
ISBN 0-442-30442-0 (pbk) : £4.50 B82-00857

721 — Architectural design. Decision making

Mackinder, Margaret. Design decision making in architectural practice : a report on a research project supported by the Building Research Establishment, Department of the Environment, examining the roles of information, experience and other influences during the design process / Margaret Mackinder, Heather Marvin. — [York] ([The King′s Manor, York YO1 2EP]) : Institute of Advanced Architectural Studies, University of York, 1982. — 114p : ill,maps,plans ; 30cm. — (Research paper / Institute of Advanced Architectural Studies, University of York ; 19)
Bibliography: p108-112
Unpriced (pbk) B82-33696

721 — Architectural design. Environmental aspects

Environmental physics in construction : its application in architectural design / Erich Schild ... [et al.] ; edited by M. Finbow. — London : Granada, 1981. — 213p : ill,plans ; 31cm
Translation of: Bauphysik. — Bibliography: p203-209. — Includes index
ISBN 0-246-11224-7 : Unpriced : CIP rev.
B81-35796

721 — Architectural design. Role of colour & light

Birren, Faber. Light, colour and environment : a discussion of the biological and psychological effects of color, with historical data and detailed recommendations for the use of color in the environment / Faber Birren. — Rev. ed. — New York ; London : Van Nostrand Reinhold, c1982. — 128p : ill(some col.) ; 28cm
Previous ed.: 1969. — Bibliography: p124-126. — Includes index
ISBN 0-442-21270-4 (pbk) : £12.70
B82-36642

721 — Buildings. Design & construction

Building design and construction handbook / [edited by] Frederick S. Merritt. — 4th ed. — New York ; London : McGraw-Hill, c1982. — 883p in various pagings : ill ; 24cm
Previous ed. published as: Building construction handbook. 1975. — Includes bibliographies and index
ISBN 0-07-041521-8 : £49.95 B82-29455

721 — Buildings. Design & construction. Implications of climate

Givoni, B.. Man, climate and architecture. — 2nd ed. — London : Applied Science Publishers, Jan.1982. — [483]p. — (Architectural science series)
Previous ed.: Amsterdam ; Barking : Elsevier, 1969
ISBN 0-85334-108-7 : £15.00 : CIP entry
B81-33787

Sealey, Antony. Introduction to building climatology / by Antony Sealey. — London : Commonwealth Association of Architects, 1979. — 44p : ill,maps ; 30cm
Bibliography: p43. — Publisher′s no.: T7901
ISBN 0-906633-00-1 (pbk) : £3.00 B82-04539

721 — Buildings. Special features. Design & construction — *Manuals*

Handbook of specialty elements in architecture / Andrew Alpern, editor in chief. — New York ; London : McGraw-Hill, c1982. — xix,484p : ill ; 29cm
Includes bibliographies and index
ISBN 0-07-001360-8 : £26.50 B82-07087

721′.01′03 — Architectural design, *to 1975*. Social aspects

Pevsner, Nikolaus. A history of building types / Nikolaus Pevsner. — London : Thames and Hudson, 1976 (1979 [printing]). — 352p : ill,plans,ports ; 29cm
Bibliography: p295-326. — Includes index
ISBN 0-500-27174-7 (pbk) : £8.95 B82-25283

721′.021′2 — Architectural design — *Standards*

Rich, Peter. Principles of element design. — 2nd ed. — London : George Godwin, Jan.1982. — [150]p
Previous ed.: 1977
ISBN 0-7114-5627-5 (pbk) : £8.50 : CIP entry
B81-33982

721′.0228 — Architectural models. Construction — *Manuals*

Pattinson, Graham Day. A guide to professional architectural and industrial scale model building / Graham Day Pattinson. — Englewood Cliffs ; London : Prentice-Hall, c1982. — xiv,369p : ill ; 29cm
Bibliography: p360. — Includes index
ISBN 0-13-370601-x : £27.70 B82-31910

721′.0246 — Architectural design — *For technicians*

Barritt, C. M. H.. Architectural design procedures / C.M.H. Barritt ; illustrated by the author. — London : Longman, 1982. — xii,194p : ill,forms,1map,plans ; 22cm. — (Longman technician series. Construction and civil engineering)
Bibliography: p191. — Includes index
ISBN 0-582-41250-1 (pbk) : £4.95 : CIP rev.
B82-20263

721′.0246 — Buildings. Design & construction — *For technicians*

Hill, David A.. Design procedures : level II / David A. Hill. — New York ; London : Van Nostrand Reinhold, 1982. — xi,191p : ill ; 25cm
Bibliography: p191
ISBN 0-442-30484-6 (cased) : Unpriced
ISBN 0-442-30485-4 (pbk) : £5.95 B82-23246

Zunde, J. M.. Design procedures, level 4 / J.M. Zunde. — London : Longman, 1982. — vii,227p : ill ; 22cm
Includes index
ISBN 0-582-41106-8 (pbk) : £4.95 : CIP rev.
B82-12919

Zunde, J. M.. Design technology / J.M. Zunde ; illustrated by Peter Zunde. — London : Longman. — (Longman technician series. Construction and civil engineering)
Includes index
Level 5. — 1982. — viii,203p : ill,plans ; 22cm
ISBN 0-582-41262-5 (pbk) : £5.95 : CIP rev.
B82-20269

721′.028′54 — Architectural design. Applications of digital computer systems

Evans, Nigel. The architect and the computer : a guide through the jungle / Nigel Evans. — London : RIBA, c1981. — 40p : ill,2plans ; 30cm
ISBN 0-900630-77-9 (pbk) : £2.75 B82-13209

721′.042 — United States. Skyscrapers, *to 1980*

Goldberger, Paul. The skyscraper / Paul Goldberger. — London : Allen Lane, 1982, c1981. — x,180p,[8]p of plates : ill(some col.),ports ; 29cm
Originally published: New York : Knopf, 1981. — Includes index
ISBN 0-7139-1475-0 : £14.95 B82-15309

721′.044522 — Precast concrete buildings

Design philosophy for precast buildings of two or more storeys / [FIP Commission on Prefabrication]. — Slough : Fédération Internationale de la Précontrainte, 1982. — 66p : ill,1form,plans ; 30cm. — (Technical report / Fédération Internationale de la Précontrainte)
Cover title
ISBN 0-907862-08-x (pbk) : Unpriced
B82-37104

721′.04471 — New York *(City)*. Buildings with cast iron structural components. Architectural features, *ca 1865* — *Illustrations*

Badger, Daniel D.. Badger′s illustrated catalogue of cast-iron architecture / by Daniel D. Badger ; with a new introduction by Margot Gayle. — New York : Dover ; London : Constable, 1981. — xvii,35p,cii p of plates : ill ; 32cm. — (Dover books on architecture)
Facsim of: ed. published as Illustrations of iron architecture made by the Architectural Iron Works of the City of New York. New York : Baker & Godwin, 1865
ISBN 0-486-24223-4 (pbk) : £6.75 B82-39653

721′.0448 — England. Cruck buildings. Architectural features

Alcock, N. W.. Cruck construction : an introduction and catalogue / by N.W. Alcock ; with sections by P.V. Addyman ... [et al.]. — London : Council for British Archaeology, 1981. — vii,177p : ill,maps ; 30cm. — (Research report, ISSN 0589-9036 ; no.42)
Bibliography: p172-174. — Includes index
ISBN 0-906780-11-x (pbk) : Unpriced : CIP rev. B81-26691

721′.04496 — Buildings. Architectural features: Mirrors

Heyne, Pamela. Today's architectural mirror : interiors, buildings, and solar designs / Pamela Heyne. — New York ; London : Van Nostrand Reinhold, c1982. — xi,175p,[16]p of plates : ill (some col.),plans ; 22x29cm
Bibliography: p169-170. — Includes index
ISBN 0-442-23424-4 : £27.65 B82-22584

721′.04497 — Prefabricated buildings

Russell, Barry. Building systems, industrialization and architecture / Barry Russell. — London : Wiley, 1981. — xii,758p : ill,1map,plans,2forms,1port ; 26cm
Bibliography: p713-734. — Includes index
ISBN 0-471-27952-8 : £28.50 : CIP rev. B81-32592

721′.0462′09485 — Sweden. Architectural design for physically handicapped persons

Rathbone, Philip. A wheelchair for all seasons / Philip Rathbone. — London : Royal Institution of Chartered Surveyors, c1981. — 64p : ill,2maps,ports ; 30cm
ISBN 0-85406-161-4 (pbk) : £2.00
Also classified at 721′.0462′09489 B82-25800

721′.0462′09489 — Denmark. Architectural design for physically handicapped persons

Rathbone, Philip. A wheelchair for all seasons / Philip Rathbone. — London : Royal Institution of Chartered Surveyors, c1981. — 64p : ill,2maps,ports ; 30cm
ISBN 0-85406-161-4 (pbk) : £2.00
Primary classification 721′.0462′09485 B82-25800

721′.0467 — Buildings. Design & construction. Implications of alternative energy sources

Davis, A. J.. Alternative natural energy sources : in building design / A.J. Davis and R.P. Schubert. — 2nd ed. — New York ; London : Van Nostrand Reinhold, 1981. — 287p : ill,maps,plans ; 22x28cm
Previous ed.: Blacksbourg, Va. : Davis, 1974 ; New York : London : Van Nostrand Reinhold, 1976. — Includes bibliographies and index
ISBN 0-442-23143-1 (cased) : £15.25
ISBN 0-442-23142-3 (pbk) : £8.45 B82-11742

721′.0467 — European Community countries. Buildings. Passive solar energy heating systems. Architectural design

Passive solar architecture in Europe : the results of the first European Passive Solar Competition, 1980 / editor Ralph M. Lebens. — London : Architectural Press, [1981]. — 218p,[20]p : ill(some col.),maps,plans,forms ; 21cm
At head of title: Commission of the European Communities
ISBN 0-85139-961-4 (pbk) : £9.95 B82-02251

721′.05 — Architectural design — *Serials*

AA files. — Vol.1, no.1 (Winter 1981-82)-. — London (36 Bedford Sq., WC1B 3ES) : Architectural Association, 1981-. — v. : ill,plans,ports ; 30cm
Annual
ISSN 0261-6823 = AA files : Unpriced B82-15761

[Contact *(Manchester)*]. Contact : the TAC magazine for designers. — Issue 1-. — Manchester (P.O. Box 22, Trafford Park, Manchester M17 1RV) : TAC Construction Materials, 1982-. — v.ill(some col.) : ports ; 30cm
Quarterly
ISSN 0263-7588 = Contact (Manchester) : Unpriced B82-32152

721′.5 — Cable-suspended roofs

. Structural design of cable-suspended roofs. — Chichester : Ellis Horwood, Oct.1982. — [288] p. — (Ellis Horwood series in engineering science)
Translation of: Függótetók Számítása
ISBN 0-85312-222-9 : £25.00 : CIP entry B82-24264

721′.823′094134 — Edinburgh. Buildings. Windows. Design. Environmental factors

Window alteration : a design guide / the City of Edinburgh District Council. — Edinburgh : City of Edinburgh Planning Department, 1982. — 1folded sheet([6]p) : ill ; 22x10cm
Unpriced B82-29917

722 — ARCHITECTURE. ANCIENT AND ORIENTAL

722′.12 — Ancient Japanese structures. Architectural features

Tamburello, Adolfo. Japan / text by Adolfo Tamburello ; foreword by Yasunari Kawabata. — London : Reader's Digest, 1980, c1973. — 192p : ill(some col.),maps,plans ; 34cm. — (Monuments of civilization)
Translation of: Giappone. — Originally published: New York : Madison Square, 1973 ; London : Cassell, 1975. — Bibliography: p190. — Includes index
£7.95 B82-30898

722′.2 — Ancient Egyptian structures. Architectural features

Barocas, Claudio. Egypt / text by Claudio Barocas ; foreword by Oscar Niemayer. — London : Reader's Digest Association, 1974 (1979 [printing]). — 188p : col.ill,1map,plans ; 34cm. — (Monuments of civilization)
Translation of: Egitto. — Includes index
£7.95 B82-30896

722′.4 — Ancient Cambodian structures. Architectural features

Mazzeo, Donatello. Ancient Cambodia / text by Donatello Mazzeo and Chiara Silvi Antonini ; foreword by Han Suyin. — London : Reader's Digest Association, 1978 (1980 [printing]). — 191p : col.ill,2maps,plates ; 34cm. — (Monuments of civilization)
Translation of: Civiltà Khmer. — Bibliography: p188-189. — Includes index
£7.95 B82-30893

722′.44 — Ancient Indian structures. Architectural features

Taddei, Maurizio. India / text by Maurizio Taddei ; foreword by Clement Greenberg. — London : Reader's Digest Association, 1977 (1980 [printing]). — 191p : ill(some col.),1map,plans ; 34cm. — (Monuments of civilization)
Translation of: India antica. — Bibliography: p185. — Includes index
£7.95 B82-30894

722′.44′79 — India. Deccan. Islamic buildings, *1347-1686*. Architectural features

Merklinger, Elizabeth Schotten. Indian Islamic architecture : the Deccan 1347-1686 / Elizabeth Schotten Merklinger. — Warminster : Aris & Phillips, c1981. — xiv,146p : ill,1map,plans ; 30cm
Bibliography: pxi-xiii
ISBN 0-85668-193-8 : Unpriced : CIP rev. B81-13746

722′.5 — Ancient Middle Eastern structures. Architectural features

Laroche, Lucienne. The Middle East / text by Lucienne Laroche ; foreword by Henry Moore. — London : Reader's Digest Association, 1974 (1980 [printing]). — 190p : col.ill,1map,plans ; 34cm. — (Monuments of civilization)
Translation of: Dai Sumeri ai Sassanidi. — Bibliography: p186. — Includes index
£7.95 B82-30892

722′.7 — Italy. Ancient Roman structures. Architectural features

Coarelli, Filippo. Rome / text by Filippo Coarelli ; foreword by Pier Luigi Nervi. — London : Reader's Digest, 1979, c1972. — 191p : ill (some col.),1map,plans ; 34cm. — (Monuments of civilization)
Translation of: Roma. — Originally published: New York : Madison Square, 1972 ; London : Cassell, 1973. — Bibliography: p187. — Includes index
£7.95 B82-30901

722′.8 — Ancient Greek structures. Architectural features

D'Agostino, Bruno. Greece / text by Bruno D'Agostino ; foreword by Giorgio Seferis. — London : Cassell, 1974 (1978 [printing]). — 191p : ill(some col.),1map,plans ; 34cm. — (Monuments of civilization)
Translation of: Grecia. — Bibliography: p186. — Includes index
ISBN 0-304-29437-3 : £11.95 B82-34382

722′.91 — Central America. Maya structures. Architectural features

Ivanoff, Pierre. Maya / text by Pierre Ivanoff ; foreword Miguel Angel Asturias. — London : Cassell, 1975, c1973 (1978 [printing]). — 190p : ill(some col.),maps,plans ; 34cm. — (Monuments of civilization)
Translation of: Città Maya. — Originally published: New York : Madison Square, 1973. — Bibliography: p189. — Includes index
ISBN 0-304-29434-9 : £9.95 B82-34383

722′.91 — Peru. Inca structures. Architectural features

Guidoni, Enrico. The Andes / text by Enrico Guidoni and Roberto Magni ; foreword by Pablo Neruda. — London : Reader's Digest Association, 1977 (1980 [printing]). — 189p : ill(some col.),1map,plans ; 34cm. — (Monuments of civilization)
Translation of: Civiltà Andine. — Bibliography: p185-186. — Includes index
£7.95 B82-30895

723 — ARCHITECTURE. MEDIAEVAL PERIOD, CA 300-1400

723 — Europe. Architecture, *900-1500*

Focillon, Henri. The art of the West in the Middle Ages / Henri Focillon ; edited and introduced by Jean Bony. — 3rd ed. — Oxford : Phaidon, 1980. — 2v. : ill ; 21cm. — (Landmarks in art history)
Translation of: Art d'Occident. — Previous ed.: 1969. — Includes bibliographies
ISBN 0-7148-2099-7 (pbk) : Unpriced : CIP rev.
ISBN 0-7148-2100-4 (v.2) : £5.95 B80-06006

723′.3 — Islamic structures, *to 1857*. Architectural features

Scerrato, Umberto. Islam / text by Umberto Scerrato ; foreword by Richard Ettinghausen. — London : Reader's Digest, 1980, c1976. — 192p : ill(some col.),1map,plans ; 34cm. — (Monuments of civilization)
Translation of: Islam. — Originally published: London : Cassell, 1976. — Bibliography: p188. — Includes index
£7.95 B82-30900

723′.5 — Europe. Architecture. Gothic style

Mark, Robert, *19---*. Experiments in gothic structure / Robert Mark. — Cambridge, Mass. ; London : MIT Press, c1982. — x,135p,[8]p of plates : ill(some col.) ; 27cm
Includes index
ISBN 0-262-13170-6 : £10.50 B82-37724

724 — ARCHITECTURE. MODERN PERIOD, 1400-

724 — Architectural design, *1400-1981*

Lesnikowski, Wojciech G.. Rationalism and romanticism in architecture / Wojciech G. Lesnikowski. — New York ; London : McGraw-Hill, c1982. — x,326p : ill,plans ; 23x29cm
Bibliography: p319-321. — Includes index
ISBN 0-07-037416-3 (cased) : Unpriced
ISBN 0-07-037417-1 (pbk) : £14.50 B82-37578

724 — Architectural design, *ca 1800-1981*

Risebero, Bill. Modern architecture and design. — London : Herbert Press, Nov.1982. — [256]p
ISBN 0-906969-18-2 : £9.95 : CIP entry B82-28764

724'.19 — Europe. Architecture. Baroque style

Baroque and Rococo : architecture and decoration. — London : Granada, July 1982. — [352]p
Originally published: London : Paul Elek, 1978
ISBN 0-246-11846-6 (pbk) : £15.00 : CIP entry
Also classified at 729'.094 B82-12234

724.9'1 — Architecture, *1900-1980*

Colquhoun, Alan. Essays in architectural criticism : modern architecture and historical change / Alan Colquhoun ; preface by Kenneth Frampton. — Cambridge, Mass. ; London : Published for the Graham Foundation for Advanced Studies in the Fine Arts, Chicago, Illinois, and the Institute for Architecture and Urban Studies, New York by MIT Press, 1981. — 215p : ill,plans ; 26cm. — (Oppositions books)
Bibliography: p208-210. — Includes index
ISBN 0-262-03076-4 : Unpriced B82-29450

International handbook of contemporary developments in architecture / edited by Warren Sanderson. — Westport, Conn. ; London : Greenwood Press, 1981. — xiv,623p : ill,1map,plans ; 29cm
Includes bibliographies and index
ISBN 0-313-21439-5 : Unpriced B82-30524

724.9'1 — Architecture, *1900-1981*

Curtis, William J. R.. Modern architecture since 1900. — Oxford : Phaidon, Oct.1982. — [416]p
ISBN 0-7148-2199-3 : £20.00 : CIP entry B82-23000

725 — ARCHITECTURE. PUBLIC BUILDINGS

725'.0954'56 — India *(Republic).* **Delhi. Public buildings. Architectural features,** *1900-1939*

Irving, Robert Grant. Indian summer : Lutyens, Baker and Imperial Delhi. — London : Yale University Press, Nov.1981. — [352]p
ISBN 0-300-02422-3 : £20.00 : CIP entry B81-35022

725.2 — ARCHITECTURE. COMMERCIAL BUILDINGS

725'.2 — England. Commercial buildings. Floorspace — *Statistics*

Commercial and industrial floorspace statistics, England : general information. — [London] : Department of the Environment, [1981]. — 3,ivp : 1form ; 30cm
Unpriced (unbound) B82-34001

Commercial and industrial floorspace statistics England 1977-1980 / Department of the Environment. — London : H.M.S.O.
No.9: Changes April 1977 to March 1980, estimated stock as at 1 April 1980. — 1981. — xxiv,40p : ill,maps ; 30cm
ISBN 0-11-751581-7 (pbk) : £5.60 B82-05167

725'.21 — Shops. Design

Mun, David. Shops : a manual of planning and design / David Mun. — London : Architectural, 1981. — 154p : ill,plans ; 31cm
Bibliography: p151. — Includes index
ISBN 0-85139-610-0 : £40.00 : CIP rev. B81-30414

725'.23 — Great Britain. Doctors. Trade unions. Buildings: British Medical Association House. Architectural features, *to 1981*

British Medical Association. BMA House : a guide and history / [British Medical Association]. — London : British Medical Association, c1982. — 9p,[4]p of plates : ill (some col.),1facsim,plans ; 30cm
ISBN 0-7279-0095-1 (pbk) : Unpriced B82-38752

725'.23'097 — North America. Offices. Multi-storey steel-framed buildings. Design & construction

Design and construction methods for multi-storey office building in North America. — Croydon : Constrado, c1981. — 36p : ill ; 30cm
Cover title
ISBN 0-86200-028-9 (pbk) : Unpriced B82-25546

725.3 — ARCHITECTURE. TRANSPORTATION AND STORAGE BUILDINGS

725'.31 — London. Underground railways. Stations. Architectural features, *to 1981*

Green, Oliver. London transport architecture / [text by Oliver Green]. — [London] ([39 Wellington St., WC2E 7BB]) : London Transport Museum, c1981. — [4]p : ill ; 30cm
£0.10 (unbound) B82-35693

725'.31'0942492 — West Midlands *(Metropolitan County).* **Walsall. Railways. Stations: Walsall Station. Architectural features,** *to 1980*

Fink, D. P. J.. Walsall stations : a study on historical lines / [D.P.J. Fink (text)] ; [J.N. Barratt, M.E. Tongue (illustrations)]. — [Walsall] : Walsall Local History Society, 1981. — 20p : ill,2maps,coats of arms,1plan ; 21cm. — (Walsall local history paper, ISSN 0144-445x ; no.3)
Cover title. — Text, ill on inside covers. — Bibliography: p12
ISBN 0-906895-02-2 (pbk) : Unpriced B82-15215

725.4 — ARCHITECTURE. INDUSTRIAL BUILDINGS

725'.4 — England. Pennines. Textile manufacturing mills. Preservation

Powell, Ken. Pennine mill trail / [compiled by Ken Powell]. — [London] : Save Britain's Heritage, [1982?]. — 40p : ill(some col.),1map,1plan ; 21cm
Cover title. — Bibliography: p40
Unpriced (pbk) B82-21439

725'.4 — Industrial buildings. Design & construction

Bates, William. Introduction to the design of industrial buildings / W. Bates. — Croydon : Constrado, c1978. — 23p : ill ; 30cm
Bibliography: p23
Unpriced (pbk) B82-17745

725'.4'0941 — Great Britain. Industrial buildings. Architectural design

Factories : planning and design. — London : Architectural Press, Nov.1981. — [320]p
ISBN 0-85139-302-0 : £29.95 : CIP entry B81-30415

725'.4'0941 — Great Britain. Rural regions. Industrial buildings. Design

Industrial buildings : a design guide. — Exeter : Devon Conservation Forum, 1981. — 35p : ill (some col.),1plan ; 30cm
ISBN 0-86114-324-8 (pbk) : £3.00 B82-03308

725.5 — ARCHITECTURE. HEALTH AND WELFARE BUILDINGS

725'.5'0973 — United States. Health services. Buildings. Design

Malkin, Jain. The design of medical and dental facilities / Jain Malkin. — New York ; London : Van Nostrand Reinhold, 1982. — xii,320p,16p of plates : ill(some col.),plans,forms ; 22x28cm
Includes index
ISBN 0-442-24493-2 : £31.05 B82-16312

725'.51'0942 — England. Hospitals. Design. Standard methods: Nucleus

Nucleus hospitals : whole hospital policies. — [London] : Department of Health & Social Security, 1980. — ii,25leaves ; 30cm
Unpriced (spiral) B82-17765

Users guide to Nucleus : a handbook for Nucleus project teams. — [London] : Department of Health & Social Security, 1980. — 8leaves ; 30cm
Unpriced (spiral) B82-17764

725'.54 — England. Day care centres for handicapped persons. Design

Symons, Jean. Day care centres : a study of some developments in England 1970-1980 especially of centres of mixed handicaps and in adapted buildings / Jean Symons ; illustrations by Louis Hellman. — London : Centre on Environment for the Handicapped, 1981. — 105p : ill,plans ; 30cm
ISBN 0-903976-05-6 (pbk) : £2.00 B82-12091

725.6 — ARCHITECTURE. PRISON AND REFORMATORY BUILDINGS

725'.6'0942 — England. Prisons. Architectural features, *1750-1840*

Evans, Robin. The fabrication of virtue : English prison architecture, 1750-1840. — Cambridge : Cambridge University Press, July 1982. — [496]p
ISBN 0-521-23955-9 : £37.50 : CIP entry B82-29348

725.7 — ARCHITECTURE. REFRESHMENT AND PARK STRUCTURES

725'.71'0942 — England. Restaurants. Architectural features, *1830-1980* — *Illustrations*

Hotels & restaurants : 1830 to the present day / [compiled by] Priscilla Boniface. — London : H.M.S.O., 1981. — [82]p : chiefly ill ; 25cm. — (National Monuments Record photographic archives)
Photographs taken from the collection of the Royal Commission on Historical Monuments (England). — Bibliography: p4
ISBN 0-11-700993-8 (pbk) : £4.95
Primary classification 728'.5'0942 B82-14339

725.8 — ARCHITECTURE. RECREATION BUILDINGS

725'.8043 — Sports facilities. Design & planning

Perrin, Gerald A.. Design for sport / Gerald A. Perrin. — London : Butterworths, 1981. — 163p : ill,maps,plans ; 29cm. — (Butterworths design series for architects and planners)
Includes index
ISBN 0-408-00365-0 : £20.00 : CIP rev. B81-31721

725'.822'0941 — Great Britain. Cinemas. Architectural features — *Serials*

Picture house : the magazine of the Cinema Theatre Association. — 1st issue (Spring 1982)-. — Swindon (c/o 211 Whitworth Rd., Swindon, Wilts. SN2 3BX) : The Association, 1982-. — v. : ill,plans ; 30cm
ISSN 0263-7553 = Picture house : £1.00 (free to members) B82-31735

725'.822'0941 — Great Britain. Cinemas. Architectural features, *to 1979*

Atwell, David. Cathedrals of the movies : a history of British cinemas and their audiences / David Atwell. — London : Architectural Press, 1980 (1981 [printing]). — xiv,194p : ill,plans,ports ; 25cm
Bibliography: p189-190. — Includes index
ISBN 0-85139-773-5 (pbk) : £5.95 B82-00017

725'.822'0973 — United States. Cinemas, *to 1980.* **Architectural features**

Naylor, David, *1955-*. American picture palaces : the architecture of fantasy / David Naylor. — New York ; London : Van Nostrand Reinhold, c1981. — 224p : chiefly ill(some col.),1col.facsim,1plan,1port ; 29cm
Bibliography: p221. — Includes index
ISBN 0-442-23861-4 : £21.20 B82-13201

725'.84 — Great Britain. Indoor sports centres. Design

Sports centre design with management in mind. — Bedford (28 Bromham Rd., Bedford MK40 2QP) : Eastern Council for Sport and Recreation, 1979. — 20p : ill ; 21cm
£0.50 (pbk) B82-05427

725.9 — ARCHITECTURE. EXHIBITION BUILDINGS, MEMORIAL BUILDINGS, ETC

725′.94′0942132 — London. Westminster *(London Borough)*. Memorials: Albert Memorial. Architectural design
Bayley, Stephen, *1951-*. The Albert Memorial : the monument in its social and architectural context / Stephen Bayley. — London : Scolar, 1981. — 160p : ill,facsims,plans,1port ; 26cm
Includes index
ISBN 0-85967-594-7 : £18.50 B82-01490

726 — ARCHITECTURE. RELIGIOUS BUILDINGS

726 — Great Britain. Religious buildings. Acoustics — *For architectural design*
Allen, William, *1914-*. Acoustic treatment for places of worship / William Allen. — [Newcastle upon Tyne] : Ecclesiastical Architects' and Surveyors' Associaton, c1981. — 22p : ill ; 30cm. — (EASA papers ; 2)
Cover title
ISBN 0-907866-01-8 (pbk) : £1.00 B82-10825

726 — Religious buildings. Architectural features
Davies, J. G.. Temples, churches and mosques. — Oxford : Blackwell, Apr.1982. — [256]p
ISBN 0-631-12887-5 : £9.50 : CIP entry B82-04589

726′.5 — Churches. Architectural features — *For children*
Storr, Dorothy M.. Churches. — London : Black, Jan.1983. — [32]p. — (History explorers)
ISBN 0-7136-2273-3 (cased) : £2.95 : CIP entry
ISBN 0-7136-2274-1 (pbk) : £1.45 B82-32597

726′.5′0321 — Churches. Architectural features — *Dictionaries*
Recording a church. — London : Council for British Archaeology, June 1982. — [48]p
ISBN 0-906780-21-7 (pbk) : £1.75 : CIP entry B82-19291

726′.5′0942 — England. Parish churches. Architectural features
Addison, *Sir* William. Local styles of the English parish church / Sir William Addison. — London : Batsford, 1982. — 192p : ill,plans ; 26cm
Bibliography: p183. — Includes index
ISBN 0-7134-2564-4 : £12.50 B82-17649

726′.5′0942 — England. Parish churches. Architectural features, *to 1975*
Randall, Gerald. The English parish church / Gerald Randall. — London : Batsford, 1982. — 192p : ill,plans ; 26cm
Bibliography: p183-184. — Includes index
ISBN 0-7134-3404-x : £15.00 B82-33824

726′.5′0942234 — Kent. Canterbury. Churches. Architectural features, *1000-1220 — Conference proceedings*
Medieval art and architecture at Canterbury before 1220. — [Leeds] : British Archaeological Association published Jointly with the Kent Archaeological Society, 1982. — 128p,[39]p of plates (3 folded) : ill,plans ; 25cm. — (Conference transactions ; 5, 1979)
Conference papers
ISBN 0-907307-05-1 (cased) : Unpriced
ISBN 0-907307-04-3 (pbk) : Unpriced B82-30634

726′.5′094241 — Gloucestershire. Churches. Architectural features
Gloucestershire churches / edited by David Verey ; foreword by Bishop of Gloucester. — Gloucester : Sutton, 1981. — 64p : ill(some col.),1map ; 25cm
ISBN 0-904387-80-1 (pbk) : £2.95 : CIP rev. B81-08835

726′.5′0942417 — England. Cotswolds. Parish churches. Architectural features
Verey, David. Cotswold churches / David Verey. — New ed. — Gloucester : Sutton, 1982. — 189p : ill,2plans ; 22cm
Previous ed.: London : Batsford, 1976. — Includes index
ISBN 0-904387-78-x (pbk) : £3.95 : CIP rev. B81-24650

726′.5′094264 — Suffolk. Churches. Architectural features
Cautley, H. Munro. Suffolk churches and their treasures. — 5th ed. with supplement. — Woodbridge : Boydell & Brewer, July 1982. — [448]p
Previous ed.: 1976
ISBN 0-85115-143-4 : £19.50 : CIP entry B82-13521

726′.5′094264 — Suffolk. Churches. Architectural features, *1837-1901*
Riches, Anne. Victorian church building and restoration in Suffolk. — Woodbridge : Boydell Press, June 1982. — [80]p
ISBN 0-85115-176-0 : £12.50 : CIP entry B82-17905

726′.5′09427 — Northern England. Nonconformist churches. Buildings. Architectural features
Powell, Ken. The fall of Zion : northern chapel architecture and its future / by Ken Powell ; special photography by Keith Parkinson. — London : SAVE Britain's Heritage, 1980. — [48]p : ill ; 31cm
Text on inside cover
ISBN 0-905978-06-4 (pbk) : Unpriced B82-34704

726′.5′0947 — Eastern Europe. Wooden churches. Architectural features
Buxton, David, *1910-*. The wooden churches of Eastern Europe : an introductory survey / David Buxton. — Cambridge : Cambridge University Press, 1981. — 405p : ill,maps,plans ; 29cm
Maps on lining papers. — Bibliography: p395-397. — Includes index
ISBN 0-521-23786-6 : £42.50 : CIP rev. B81-37001

726′.5′09563 — Turkey. Istanbul. Churches: Myrelaion *(Istanbul)*. Architectural features
Striker, Cecil L.. The Myrelaion (Bodrum Camii) in Istanbul / by Cecil L. Striker ; with an appendix on the excavated pottery by J.W. Hayes. — Princeton, N.J. ; Guildford : Princeton University Press, c1981. — xii,50p,[14]leaves and [37]p of plates : ill,plans ; 32cm
Bibliography: p46-47. — Includes index
ISBN 0-691-03546-6 : £26.50 B82-29219

726′.5′09566 — Eastern Turkey. Tur 'Abdin. Churches. Architectural features
Bell, Gertrude. The churches and monasteries of Tur 'Abdin. — London (66 Lyncroft Gardens, NW6 1JY) : Pindar Press, Mar.1982. — [208]p
ISBN 0-907132-08-1 : £58.00 : CIP entry B82-01160

726′.6′0942234 — Kent. Canterbury. Cathedrals: Canterbury Cathedral. Architectural features, *to 1980*
Woodman, Francis. The architectural history of Canterbury Cathedral / Francis Woodman. — London : Routledge & Kegan Paul, c1981. — xviii,282p : ill,plans ; 25cm
Plans on lining papers. — Bibliography: p269-276. — Includes index
ISBN 0-7100-0752-3 : £35.00 B82-09130

726′.6′0942448 — Hereford and Worcester. Worcester. Cathedrals: Worcester Cathedral. Architectural features, *to 1900*
Medieval art and architecture at Worcester Cathedral. — [London] ([61 Old Park Ridings, N21 2ET]) : British Archaeological Association], 1978. — vii,189p xxviiip of plates : ill,plans ; 26cm. — (Conference transactions / British Archaeological Association ; 1975, 1)
Editor: Glenys Popper. — Bibliography: p196-189
Unpriced
Also classified at 709′.424′48 B82-16313

726′.6′0942585 — Hertfordshire. St Albans. Cathedrals: St Albans Cathedral. Architectural features
A **Guide** to Saint Albans Cathedral / Royal Commission on Historical Monuments (England). — 2nd ed. — London : H.M.S.O., 1982. — 32p,[16]p of plates : plans ; 21cm
Previous ed.: 1952. — Bibliography: p4
ISBN 0-11-701128-2 (pbk) : £1.25 B82-28898

726′.6′0942962 — Dyfed. St David's. Cathedrals: St. Davids Cathedral. Archicectural features, *to 1981*
Evans, Wyn. Eglwys Gadeiriol Tyddewi 1181-1981 = 1181-1981 St. Davids Cathedral = [1181-1981] La Cathédrale de St. David = [1181-1981] St. Davids Kathedrale / Wyn Evans, Roger Worsley ; cyfieithwyd gan Huw I. James. — St. Davids, [Dyfed] : Gwasg yr Oriel Fach, 1981. — 162p : ill(some col.),1plan ; 31cm
Parallel English text and Welsh, French and German translations. — Map on lining papers. — Bibliography: p162
ISBN 0-905421-02-7 : £12.50 : CIP rev. B81-21599

726′.6′094451 — France. Chartres. Cathedrals: Cathédrale de Chartres. Architectural features
Adams, Henry. Mont-Saint-Michel and Chartres / by Henry Adams ; with an introduction by Ralph Adams Cram. — Princeton ; Guildford : Princeton University Press, 1981, c1933. — xiv,401p,[12]leaves of plates : ill,1port,3geneal.tables ; 24cm
Originally published: Boston : Houghton Mifflin, 1913. — Includes index
ISBN 0-691-03971-2 (cased) : Unpriced
ISBN 0-691-00335-1 (pbk) : £6.30
Also classified at 726′.7 B82-14554

James, John, *1931-*. Chartres : the masons who built a legend / John James. — London : Routledge & Kegan Paul, 1982. — 200p : ill,plans ; 25cm
Bibliography: p196. — Includes index
ISBN 0-7100-0886-4 : £17.50 B82-30117

726′.7 — France. Mont-Saint-Michel. Abbeys: Abbaye de Mont-Saint-Michel. Architectural features
Adams, Henry. Mont-Saint-Michel and Chartres / by Henry Adams ; with an introduction by Ralph Adams Cram. — Princeton ; Guildford : Princeton University Press, 1981, c1933. — xiv,401p,[12]leaves of plates : ill,1port,3geneal.tables ; 24cm
Originally published: Boston : Houghton Mifflin, 1913. — Includes index
ISBN 0-691-03971-2 (cased) : Unpriced
ISBN 0-691-00335-1 (pbk) : £6.30
Primary classification 726′.6′094451 B82-14554

727 — ARCHITECTURE. EDUCATIONAL AND RESEARCH BUILDINGS

727 — England. Schools. Architectural design. Briefing
The **Briefing** process in school design : the report of a research project by the University of Bristol School of Advanced Urban Studies. — London : Architects & Building Branch, Department of Education and Science, [1979]. — iileaves,51p ; 30cm. — (A & b paper ; no.5 (1979))
Unpriced (pbk) B82-13342

727′.0973 — United States. Schools. Buildings. Architectural design
Castaldi, Basil. Educational facilities : planning, modernization, and management / Basil Castaldi. — 2nd ed. — Boston, [Mass.] ; London : Allyn and Bacon, c1982. — x,420p : ill,forms ; 25cm
Previous ed.: 1977. — Includes index
ISBN 0-205-07745-5 : Unpriced B82-27104

727′.1′0941443 — Scotland. Strathclyde Region. Glasgow. Primary schools: (Glasgow) Scotland Street School *(Glasgow)* Architectural features — *Illustrations*
Charles Rennie Mackintosh : Scotland Street School : a new survey : a Glasgow Print Studio Gallery exhibition. — Glasgow (128 Ingram St., G1 1EJ) : The Gallery, [1982?]. — 62p : ill,plans ; 20x21cm
Unpriced (pbk) B82-25238

727′.8 — Libraries. Buildings. Planning & architectural design
Library design. — Hertford (County Hall, Hertford, Herts. SG13 8EJ) : Hertfordshire Library Service, Sept.1982. — [32]p
ISBN 0-901354-22-8 (pbk) : £2.00 : CIP entry B82-28607

727′.8 — Libraries. Lighting

CIBS lighting guide libraries. — London : Chartered Institution of Building Services (Lighting Division), 1982. — 42p : ill ; 30cm
Bibliography: p37-38
ISBN 0-900953-25-x (pbk) : Unpriced
B82-36235

727′.82441 — Great Britain. Medium-sized public libraries. Design

Designing a medium-sized public library / a joint publication by Architects and Building Branch and the Office of Arts and Libraries, Department of Education and Science. — London : H.M.S.O., 1981. — iii,83p : ill(some col.),plans ; 30cm. — (Building bulletin ; no.60) (Library information series ; no.11)
Bibliography: p83
ISBN 0-11-270524-3 (pbk) : £6.75 B82-07777

728 — ARCHITECTURE. RESIDENCES

728 — Earth sheltered residences. Architectural design

Earth sheltered community design : energy-efficient residential development / Underground Space Center, University of Minnesota ; [written by] Raymond Sterling, John Carmody, Gail Elnicky. — New York ; London : Van Nostrand Reinhold, c1981. — 270p : ill,maps,plans ; 22x28cm
Bibliography: p261-262. — Includes index
ISBN 0-442-28557-4 (cased) : Unpriced
ISBN 0-442-28558-2 (pbk) : £12.70
B82-13198

728 — Residences. Architectural design — *Manuals*

Hepler, Donald E.. Architecture : drafting and design / Donald E. Hepler, Paul I. Wallach. — 3rd ed. — New York ; London : McGraw-Hill, c1977. — viii,568p : ill(some col.),plans(some col.),1form ; 26cm
Previous ed.: 1971. — Includes index
ISBN 0-07-028291-9 : £12.00 B82-02288

728′.0941 — Great Britain. Residences. Interiors, *1900-1914*

Service, Alaistair. Edwardian interiors. — London : Barrie & Jenkins, Aug.1982. — [160]p
ISBN 0-09-147000-5 : £12.95 : CIP entry
B82-15658

728′.0973 — United States. Residences. Architectural design, *1842 — Early works*

Downing, Andrew Jackson. Victorian cottage residences / by Andrew Jackson Downing ; with a new preface by Adolf K. Placzek. — New York : Dover ; London : Constable, 1981. — xvi,261p,[40]leaves of plates : ill,plans ; 22cm. — (Dover architectural series)
Facsim of: new (i.e. 5th) ed., New York : Wiley, 1873
ISBN 0-486-24078-9 (pbk) : £3.75 B82-13555

728.3 — United States. Houses. Design & construction. Implications of climate

Conklin, Groff. The weather-conditioned house / Groff Conklin. — Rev. and updated / by S. Blackwell Duncan. — New York ; London : Van Nostrand Reinhold, 1982, c1958. — 287p : ill,maps,plans ; 29cm
Bibliography: p272-274. — Includes index
ISBN 0-442-22655-1 : £16.10 B82-16596

728.3′094 — Western Europe. Houses designed by architects, *ca 1960-ca 1980 — Illustrations*

Einzig, Richard. Classic modern houses in Europe / Richard Einzig. — London : Architectural Press, 1981. — 176p : ill,plans ; 29cm
ISBN 0-85139-479-5 : £16.95 : CIP rev.
B81-30437

728.3′0942 — England. Vernacular houses. Architectural features, *1300-1900*

Brunskill, R. W.. Houses / R.W. Brunskill. — London : Collins, 1982. — 224p,[16]p of plates : ill,maps,plans ; 24cm. — (Collins archaeology)
Bibliography: p216-220. — Includes index
ISBN 0-00-216243-1 : £13.95 : CIP rev.
B81-20151

728.3′09423′83 — Somerset. Frome. Trinity. Houses. Architectural features, *to ca 1800*

Leech, Roger. Early industrial housing : the Trinity Area of Frome / Roger Leech. — London : H.M.S.O., 1981. — viii,44p,20p of plates : ill,maps,plans ; 28cm. — (Supplementary series / Royal Commission on Historical Monuments (England) ; 3)
At head of title: Royal Commission on Historical Monuments England
ISBN 0-11-700907-5 (pbk) : £6.95 B82-34242

728.3′095 — East & South-east Asia. Houses. Architectural features, *to 1981 — Conference proceedings*

The **House** in East and Southeast Asia. — London : Curzon Press, Mar.1982. — [204]p. — (Scandinavian Institute of Asian Studies monograph series, ISSN 0069-1712 ; 30)
Conference papers
ISBN 0-7007-0104-4 (pbk) : £6.50 : CIP entry
B82-08416

728.3′0973 — United States. Custom-built houses. Architectural features — *Illustrations*

More houses architects design for themselves / edited by Walter F. Wagner. — New York ; London : McGraw-Hill, c1982. — viii,160p : ill (some col.),maps,plans ; 32cm. — (An Architectural record book)
Includes index
ISBN 0-07-002365-4 : £22.95 B82-41110

728.3′12 — Great Britain. Terraced houses. Exteriors. Maintenance, repair & improvement. Aesthetic aspects — *Amateurs′ manuals*

Pyke, Beverley. The good looking house / Beverley Pyke. — Bristol : Redcliffe, 1980. — 64p : ill ; 25cm
ISBN 0-905459-23-7 (pbk) : £2.25 B82-21833

728.3′12′0942 — England. Terraced houses, *to 1981*

Muthesius, Stefan. The English terraced house. — London : Yale University Press, Oct.1982. — [288]p
ISBN 0-300-02871-7 : £12.50 : CIP entry
B82-34086

728.3′14 — Flats. Architectural design — *Manuals*

Housing / John Macsai ... [et al.] ; illustrator Alfred J. Hidvegi. — 2nd ed. — New York ; Chichester : Wiley, c1982. — xv,590p : ill,plan ; 29cm
Previous ed.: 1976. — Bibliography: p563-567. — Includes index
ISBN 0-471-08126-4 : £37.00 B82-28144

728.3′73 — California. Stanford. Houses designed by Wright, Frank Lloyd: Hanna-Honeycomb House, *1935-1980*

Hanna, Paul R.. Frank Lloyd Wright′s Hanna House : the clients′ report / Paul R. and Jean S. Hanna. — New York : Architectural History Foundation ; Cambridge, Mass. ; London : MIT, c1981. — 148p : ill(some col.),facsims,plans ; 27cm. — (The Architectural History Foundation/MIT Press series ; 5)
Bibliography: p147
ISBN 0-262-08109-1 : Unpriced B82-21011

728′.5′0942 — England. Large hotels. Architectural features, *1830-1980 — Illustrations*

Hotels & restaurants : 1830 to the present day / [compiled by] Priscilla Boniface. — London : H.M.S.O., 1981. — [82]p : cheifly ill ; 25cm. — (National Monuments Record photographic archives)
Photographs taken from the collection of the Royal Commission on Historical Monuments (England). — Bibliography: p4
ISBN 0-11-700993-8 (pbk) : £4.95
Also classified at 725′.71′0942 B82-14339

728′.67′0942 — England. Cottages & farmhouses. Architectural features, *1450-1900*

Cook, Olive. English cottages and farmhouses / Olive Cook ; with 177 photographs, 14 in colour, by Edwin Smith. — London : Thames and Hudson, c1982. — 208p : ill(some col.) ; 26cm
Bibliography: p206. — Includes index
ISBN 0-500-24114-7 : £9.95 B82-31750

728.8′2094641 — Spain. Escorial. Palaces: Escorial. Design & construction

Kubler, George. Building the Escorial / George Kubler. — Princeton, N.J. ; Guildford : Princeton University Press, c1982. — xvi,185p,[93]p of plates : ill,1map,plans,1port ; 29cm
Bibliography: p173-179. — Includes index
ISBN 0-691-03975-5 : £28.10 B82-28231

728.8′3′0941486 — Scotland. Dumfries and Galloway Region. New Abbey. Country houses: Shambellie House. Design & construction

Rowan, Alistair. The creation of Shambellie : the story of a Victorian building contract / Alistair Rowan. — [Edinburgh] : Royal Scottish Museum, 1982. — 64p : ill,facsims,plans,ports ; 21cm
ISBN 0-900733-24-1 (pbk) : Unpriced
B82-35778

728.8′3′0944 — France. Country houses, *1700-1800*. Architectural features

Zerbe, Jerome. Les pavillons : French pavilions of the eighteenth century / Jerome Zerbe & Cyril Connolly. — New York ; London : Norton, c1979. — 233p : ill ; 27cm
Originally published: London : Hamilton, 1962
ISBN 0-393-01279-4 (pbk) : £6.95 B82-32834

728′.9 — Ornamental greenhouses, *1800-1900*. Architectural features

Koppelkamm, Stefan. Glasshouses and wintergardens of the nineteenth century / Stefan Koppelkamm ; translated by Kathrine Talbot. — London : Granada, 1981. — 111p : ill(some col.),plans ; 29cm
Translation of: Gewächshäuser und Wintergärten im 19. Jahrhundert
ISBN 0-246-11630-7 : Unpriced : CIP rev.
B81-25785

728′.92 — Great Britain. Agricultural industries. Farms. Buildings. Conservation

Kamm, Jonathan. Saving old farm buildings / [text by Jonathan Kamm]. — Winchester : Hampshire County Planning Dept. in association with the District Councils of Hampshire, 1982. — 20p : ill ; 30cm. — (Hampshire′s heritage)
Bibliography: p20
ISBN 0-900908-71-8 (pbk) : Unpriced
B82-28937

728′.92′0942576 — Oxfordshire. Coleshill. Agricultural industries. Farms. Buildings. Architectural features

Coleshill Model Farm Oxfordshire : past present future : architect George Lamb : perspective from the builder 1854 / report of working seminar April 1980 ; editor John Weller. — [Birmingham] ([Margaret St., Birmingham 3]) : [Architects in Agriculture Group, [1981]. — 30p : ill,maps,plans,ports ; 30cm. — (Architects in Agriculture Group occasional paper ; no.1)
£3.00 (pbk) B82-39542

729 — ARCHITECTURAL DETAIL AND DECORATION

729 — Architectural design. Space. Social aspects

Greenbie, Barrie B.. Spaces : dimensions of the human landscape / text and photographs by Barrie B. Greenbie. — New Haven, Conn. ; London : Yale University Press, c1981. — xiii,321p : ill ; 29cm
Bibliography: p297-300. — Includes index
ISBN 0-300-02549-1 (cased) : £32.25 : CIP rev.
ISBN 0-300-02560-2 (pbk) : Unpriced
B82-02445

729′.092′4 — Great Britain. Buildings. Architectural features. Decorations. Lewis, Max B.

Lewis, Marjorie. Inheritance and heritage / Marjorie Lewis. — Bognor Regis : New Horizon, c1982. — 39p,[18]p of plates : ill ; 21cm
ISBN 0-86116-692-2 : £3.25 B82-14556

729′.094 — Europe. Buildings. Architectural features. Decorations. Rococo style

Baroque and Rococo : architecture and decoration. — London : Granada, July 1982. — [352]p
Originally published: London : Paul Elek, 1978
ISBN 0-246-11846-6 (pbk) : £15.00 : CIP entry
Primary classification 724′.19 B82-12234

729′.1 — Ireland. Buildings. Façades. Precast concrete structural components. Open drained joints. Design

O'Dea, Chris. Aspects of design and performance of a precast concrete facade with open drained joints / Chris O'Dea and Nicholas M. Ryan. — Dublin : An Foras Forbartha, 1981. — v,24p : ill ; 30cm
ISBN 0-906120-53-5 (spiral) : £2.50
B82-15376

729′.19 — Buildings. Signs. Design

McLendon, Charles B.. Signage : graphic communications in the built world / Charles B. McLendon and Mick Blackistone. — New York ; London : McGraw-Hill, c1982. — xiii,146p : ill ; 29cm
Bibliography: p142-143. — Includes index
ISBN 0-07-005740-0 : £20.95 B82-27407

729′.25′042 — Buildings. Access by physically handicapped persons — *Conference proceedings*

Into the eighties — access to the built environment : symposium papers given at the Polytechnic of the South Bank Thursday June 5th 1980 / Greater London Association for the Disabled ; photographs Maria Bartha ; editor John Keet ; assistant editor Virginia Armstrong ; symposium organiser Margaret Lorek. — London (1 Thorpe Close, W10 5XL) : The Association, [1982?]. — 24p : ill,ports ; 30cm
Unpriced (pbk) B82-23266

729′.25′042 — Public places. Access by physically handicapped persons — *Technical data — For architectural design*

Kamm, Jonathan. Designing for disabled people : the external environment / [text by Jonathan Kamm] ; [prepared by the Hampshire County Planning Department] ; [designed and illustrated by Paul Jones]. — [Winchester] ([The Castle, Winchester, Hants.]) : The Department in association with the District Councils of Hampshire, 1981. — 13p : ill ; 30cm
Unpriced (pbk) B82-17403

729′.28 — Buildings. Interiors. Electric lighting. Design

Traister, John E.. Practical lighting applications for building construction / John E. Traister. — New York ; London : Van Nostrand Reinhold, c1982. — vii,215p : ill,plans ; 24cm
Includes index
ISBN 0-442-24727-3 : £16.10 B82-23247

729′.29 — Buildings. Acoustics — *For architectural design*

Smith, B. J.. Acoustics and noise control. — London : Longman, Nov.1981. — [300]p
ISBN 0-582-41125-4 (pbk) : £7.95 : CIP entry
B81-30152

729′.29 — Buildings. Interiors. Acoustics

Creamer, Lothar. Principles and applications of room acoustics. — Lonodn : Applied Science, Aug.1982
Translation of 2nd ed. of : Die wissenschaftlichen Grundlagen der Raumakustik
Vol.1. — [640]p
ISBN 0-85334-113-3 : £55.00 : CIP entry
B82-16657

Cremer, Lothar. Principles and applications of room acoustics. — London : Applied Science, Aug.1982
Translation of 2nd ed. of : Die wissenschaftlichen Grundlagen der Raumakustik
Vol.2. — [416]p
ISBN 0-85334-114-1 : £40.00 : CIP entry
B82-16658

729′.38 — China. Lattice-work. Designs — *Illustrations*

Dye, Daniel Sheets. The new book of Chinese lattice designs / by Daniel Sheets Dye ; edited and with an introduction by Nancy Balderston Conrad. — New York : Dover ; London : Constable, 1981. — 119p : ill,2ports ; 29cm. — (Dover pictorial archive series)
ISBN 0-486-24128-9 (pbk) : £3.40 B82-08401

729′.4 — Buildings. Architectural features. Painting

Porter, Tom. Colour outside. — London : Architectural Press, June 1982. — [128]p
ISBN 0-85139-772-7 : £10.95 : CIP entry
B82-09866

729′7′0941 — Great Britain. Ancient Roman mosaics

Neal, David S.. Roman mosaics in Britain. — Gloucester (17a Brunswick Rd., Gloucester GL1 1HG) : Alan Sutton, June 1981. — [208]p
ISBN 0-904387-64-x (pbk) : £9.95 : CIP entry
B81-09466

729′.93 — Gloucestershire. Gloucester. Cathedrals: Gloucester Cathedral. Choir stalls. Misericords. Wood carvings — *Illustrations*

Farley, Jack. The misericords of Gloucester Cathedral / Jack Farley. — Gloucester : J. Farley, c1981. — [126]p : chiefly ill ; 21x14cm
ISBN 0-9507396-0-x (pbk) : Unpriced
B82-11180

730 — SCULPTURES AND OTHER PLASTIC ARTS

730′.09182′3074 — Pacific region tribal plastic arts — *Catalogues*

Royal Scottish Museum. Pacific art in the Royal Scottish Museum / by Dale Idiens ; [photography by A. Hunter]. — [Edinburgh] : [Royal Scottish Museum], 1982. — 80p : ill (some col.) ; 25cm. — (Royal Scottish Museum studies)
Bibliography: p79
ISBN 0-900733-28-4 (pbk) : Unpriced
B82-39114

730′.74 — Sculptures, *to 1978* — *Catalogues*

Said with feeling : tactile sculpture for the blind and sighted to share : Castle Museum, Nottingham, March 10th to April 29th. — [Nottingham] ([Nottingham, NG1 6EL]) : [Castle Museum], [1979]. — [23]p : ill ; 21cm
Published to accompany an exhibition. — Cover title
Unpriced (pbk) B82-40683

730′.74′02142 — London. Camden *(London Borough).* **Museums: British Museum. Exhibits: Sculptures** — *Illustrations*

Moore, Henry, *1898-*. Henry Moore at the British Museum. — London : British Museum Publications, Oct.1981. — [128]p
ISBN 0-7141-2010-3 : £7.95 : CIP entry
B81-30319

730′.9 — Sculptures, *to 1981*

Bazin, Germain. A concise history of world sculpture / Germain Bazin. — Newton Abbot : David & Charles, c1981. — 317p : col.ill,col.ports ; 30cm
Includes index
ISBN 0-7153-8225-x : £14.95 B82-06207

730′.92′2 — Cumbria. Carlisle *(District).* **Brampton. Art galleries: LYC Museum and Art Gallery. Exhibits: English sculptures. Langdown, Claire & Gaputyle, Elena** — *Catalogues*

Clarie [i.e. Claire] Langdown, Elena Gaputyte, Geoffrey Shesrd [i.e. Sheard] : 81 October 3. — Brampton : LYC Museum & Art Gallery, 1981. — [36]p : ill ; 14cm
ISBN 0-9504571-1-6 (pbk) : £0.35
Also classified at 779′.092′4 B82-01267

730′.92′4 — American sculptures. Blumenfeld, Helaine — *Illustrations*

Blumenfeld, Helaine. The sculptures of Helaine Blumenfeld. — London (10 Archway Close, N19 3TD) : Sinclair Browne, Sept.1982. — [64]p
ISBN 0-86300-024-x (pbk) : £12.50 : CIP entry
B82-27190

730′.92′4 — American sculptures. Smithson, Robert — *Critical studies*

Hobbs, Robert Carleton. Robert Smithson : sculpture / Robert Hobbs with contributions by Lawrence Alloway, John Coplans, Lucy R. Lippard. — Ithaca ; London : Cornell University Press, 1981. — 261p,[12]p of plates : ill(some col.),facsims,ports ; 29cm
Bibliography: p245-255. — Includes index
ISBN 0-8014-1324-9 : Unpriced B82-13714

730′.92′4 — Cumbria. Carlisle *(District).* **Brampton. Art galleries: LYC Museum and Art Gallery. Exhibits: Australian sculptures. Shields, Harvey** — *Catalogues*

81 November 7 / Kate Nicholson, Harvey Shields, Lawrence Upton. — Brampton (Banks, Brampton, Cumbria CA8 2JH) : LYC Museum & Art Gallery, c1981. — [45]p : ill,2ports ; 14cm
ISBN 0-9504571-1-6 (unbound) : Unpriced
Primary classification 759.2 B82-08952

730′.92′4 — English sculpture. Shepherd, David, *1944-* — *Critical studies*

David Shepherd : cerfluniau, sculpture / [text by Eric Rowan] ; [Welsh translation by Siân Edwards]. — Cardiff : Welsh Arts Council, 1981. — 1folded sheet : ill ; 21cm
Accompanies an exhibition held at Oriel, Cardiff, 8 October-21 November 1981. — Parallel English text and Welsh translation
ISBN 0-905171-79-9 : Unpriced B82-05872

730′.92′4 — English sculptures. Berlin, Sven — *Critical studies*

Sven Berlin : an artist and his work. — Wimborne (26 West St., Wimborne, Dorset) : Wimborne Bookshop, 1981. — 36p,[16]p of plates : ill ; 24cm
Limited ed. of 750 numbered copies. — Bibliography: p21-30
ISBN 0-9507844-0-0 (pbk) : £2.00 B82-09237

730′.924 — English sculptures. Caro, Anthony — *Catalogues*

Caro, Anthony. Caro : five sculptures by Anthony Caro : an Arts Council Collection exhibition. — [London] : Arts Council of Great Britain, c1982. — 32p : ill(some col.),ports ; 21x22cm
Bibliography: p31
ISBN 0-7287-0309-2 (pbk) : Unpriced
B82-29331

730′.92′4 — English sculptures. Caro, Anthony — *Critical studies*

Waldman, Diane. Anthony Caro. — Oxford : Phaidon, Apr.1982. — [232]p
ISBN 0-7148-2246-9 : £50.00 : CIP entry
B82-04510

730′.92′4 — English sculptures. Chantrey, *Sir* **Francis**

Sir Francis Chantrey : sculptor to an age 1781-1841 / edited by Clyde Binfield. — [Sheffield] : University of Sheffield, c1981. — 103p : ill,1facsim,ports ; 21cm
Bibliography: p98-100. — Includes index
ISBN 0-900660-77-5 (pbk) : £3.50 B82-02878

730′.92′4 — English sculptures. Flanagan, Barry — *Catalogues*

Flanagan, Barry. Barry Flanagan : sculpture : British Pavilion, Venice Biennale, 13 June-12 September 1982, Museum Haus Ester, Krefeld, 10 October-12 December 1982, Whitechapel Art Gallery, London, 7 January-20 February 1983. — London : British Council, Fine Arts Department, 1982. — 94p : ill(some col.) ; 27cm
Catalogue to accompany the exhibitions. — Bibliography: p94
ISBN 0-901618-78-0 (pbk) : Unpriced
B82-39935

730′.92′4 — English sculptures. Hepworth, Barbara — *Catalogues*

Hepworth, Barbara. Barbara Hepworth carvings. — London (6 Albermarle St., W1X 3HF) : Marlborough Fine Art, 1982. — 43p : chiefly ill(some col.),1port ; 30cm
Catalogue of an exhibition held at Marlborough Fine Art, July-August 1982
Unpriced (pbk) B82-38748

730′.92′4 — English sculptures. Moore, Henry, *1898- — Catalogues*

Moore, Henry, *1898-*. Important sculptures by Henry Moore. — New York : Marlborough Gallery ; London (6 Albemarle St., W1X 3HF) : Marlborough Fine Art, 1982. — 23p : chiefly col.ill ; 21x30cm
Unpriced (pbk) B82-36823

730′.92′4 — English sculptures. Moore, Henry, *1898— — Illustrations*

Moore, Henry, *1898-*. Henry Moore sculpture : with comments by the artist / edited by David Mitchinson ; introduction by Franco Russoli. — London : Macmillan, 1981. — 316p : chiefly ill(some col.),ports ; 30cm
ISBN 0-333-27804-6 : £35.00 : CIP rev.
B81-23942

730′.92′4 — English sculptures. Rysbrack, Michael *— Catalogues*

Eustace, Katharine. Michael Rysbrack : sculptor 1694-1770 / Katharine Eustace. — [Bristol] : City of Bristol Museum and Art Gallery, 1982. — 204p ; 26cm
Catalogue of the exhibition held 6 March-1 May 1982. — Bibliography: p198-202
ISBN 0-900199-16-4 (pbk) : Unpriced
B82-32264

730′.924 — French sculptures. Degas, Edgar — *Catalogues*

Degas, Edgar. The sculptures of Degas : an Arts Council exhibition. — London : Arts Council of Great Britain, c1982. — 40p : ill ; 20cm
Published to accompany an exhibition visiting Canterbury, Plymouth, Norwich and Glasgow between March and September 1982
ISBN 0-7287-0312-2 (pbk) : £2.25 B82-29330

730′.92′4 — Great Britain. Arts. Patronage. Organisations: Arts Council of Great Britain. Exhibits: English sculptures. King, Phillip — *Catalogues*

Phillip King. — London : Arts Council of Great Britain, c1981. — 84p : ill(some col.),1port ; 24cm
Accompanies an exhibition held at the Hayward Gallery, London, 24 April-14 June 1981. — Bibliography: p84
ISBN 0-7287-0276-2 (pbk) : £5.25 B82-06147

730′.92′4 — Irish sculptures. Kelly, Oisín — *Catalogues*

Kelly, Oisín. The work of Oisín Kelly, sculptor : a retrospective exhibition, 1978. — [Belfast] ([181a Stranmillis Rd., Belfast BT9 5DU]) : Arts Councils of Ireland, [1982?]. — 40p : ill (some col.) ; 30x14cm
Published to accompany an exhibition at the Ulster Museum, Belfast ; the Douglas Hyde Gallery, Dublin ; the Crawford Municipal Art Gallery, Cork. 1978
Unpriced (pbk) B82-29309

730′.92′4 — Irish sculptures. McWilliam, F. E. — *Critical studies*

Marle, Judy. F.E. McWilliam / Judy Marle and T.P. Flanagan. — [Belfast] ([181a Stranmillis Rd., Belfast BT9 5DU]) : Arts Council of Northern Ireland, [1981]. — x,110p : ill,ports ; 26cm
Bibliography: p105
Unpriced (pbk) B82-29310

730′.92′4 — Italian sculptures. Bernini, Gian Lorenzo — *Critical studies*

Wittkower, Rudolf. Gian Lorenzo Bernini : the sculptor of the Roman Baroque / Rudolf Wittkower. — 3rd ed. / revised by Howard Hibbard, Thomas Martin and Margot Wittkower. — Oxford : Phaidon, 1981. — xii,290p : ill ; 32cm
Previous ed.: 1966. — Bibliography: p167-171. — Includes index
ISBN 0-7148-2193-4 : £27.50 : CIP rev.
B81-27969

730′.92′4 — Italian sculptures. Donatello. Influence of classical sculptures — *Critical studies*

Greenhalgh, Michael. Donatello and his sources. — London : Duckworth, Oct.1981. — [212]p
ISBN 0-7156-1562-9 : £18.00 : CIP entry
B81-31176

730′.92′4 — Japanese sculptures. Enkū — *Critical studies*

Tanahashi, Kazuaki. Monk Enku. — London : Wildwood House, Nov.1981. — [192]p
ISBN 0-7045-0382-4 (pbk) : £5.95 : CIP entry
B81-30350

730′.92′4 — Romanian sculptures. Brancusi, Constantin — *Critical studies*

Brancusi, Constantin. Brancusi′s photographs : published to accompany the exhibition Brancusi′s photographs / organised by the Centre Georges Pompidou, Musée national d′art moderne, Paris and presented by the Arts Council of Great Britain. — London : Arts Council of Great Britain, c1981. — [32]p : ill,2ports ; 15cm
Text on inside cover
ISBN 0-7287-0299-1 (pbk) : Unpriced
B82-13037

730′.92′4 — Scotland. Strathclyde Region. Glasgow. Art galleries: Third Eye Centre. Exhibits: Scottish sculptures. Boyle, Jimmy — *Catalogues*

Boyle, Jimmy. Jimmy Boyle sculpture 1974-76 : Third Eye Centre, Glasgow, 7-28 February 1976. — Glasgow (350 Sauchiehall St., Glasgow G2 3JD) : Third Eye Centre, c1976. — 9p : ill,1facsim,1port ; 22cm
Text and ill on inside cover
£0.75 (pbk) B82-12800

730′.92′4 — Scottish sculptures. Schotz, Benno — *Biographies*

Schotz, Benno. Bronze in my blood : the memoirs of Benno Schotz. — Edinburgh : Gordon Wright, c1981. — 243p,xxxiip of plates : ill,1facsim,ports ; 24cm
Includes index
ISBN 0-903065-37-1 : £12.50 B82-08015

730′.941 — British sculptures, *1830-1914 — Critical studies*

Read, Benedict. Victorian sculpture / Benedict Read. — New Haven ; London : Published for the Paul Mellon Centre for Studies in British Art by Yale University Press, 1982. — x,414p : ill,ports ; 29cm. — (Studies in British art)
Bibliography: p397-403. — Includes index
ISBN 0-300-02506-8 : Unpriced : CIP rev.
B82-21082

730′.941 — British sculptures, *1900-1981 — Critical studies*

British sculpture in the twentieth century / edited by Sandy Nairne and Nicholas Serota. — [London] : Whitechapel Art Gallery, 1981. — 263p : ill,ports ; 28cm
′Image and form 1901-1950′ and ′Symbol and imagination 1951-1980′ (1 booklet and 1 folded sheet) as insert. — Bibliography: p236-247
ISBN 0-85488-054-2 (pbk) : Unpriced
B82-16078

730′.941 — British sculptures, *1905-1976 — Critical studies*

Wilson, Simon. [British art]. Holbein to Hockney. — London : Bodley Head, Sept.1982. — [208]p
Originally published as: British art. 1979
ISBN 0-370-30946-4 (pbk) : £5.95 : CIP entry
Primary classification 759.2 B82-19208

730′.942 — England. Anglo-Saxon stone sculptures — *Catalogues*

Corpus of Anglo-Saxon stone sculpture. — Oxford : Oxford University Press for the British Academy, Dec.1982
Vol.1: Durham and Northumberland. — 2v.([528]p)
ISBN 0-19-726012-8 : £60.00 : CIP entry
B82-30304

730′.943 — German limewood sculptures, *ca 1475-1525 — Critical studies*

Baxandall, Michael. The limewood sculptors of Renaissance Germany. — London : Yale University Press, Feb.1982. — [420]p
Originally published: 1980
ISBN 0-300-02829-6 (pbk) : £8.95 : CIP entry
B82-07095

730′.973′074 — American clay sculptures — *Catalogues*

Marshall, Richard, *1947-*. Ceramic sculpture: six artists : Peter Voulkos, John Mason, Kenneth Price, Robert Arneson, David Gilhooly, Richard Shaw / Richard Marshall and Suzanne Foley. — New York ; London : Whitney Museum of American Art in association with the University of Washington Press, c1981. — 144p : ill(some col.),ports ; 29cm
Published to accompany an exhibition at the Whitney Museum of American Art and the San Francisco Museum of Modern Art, 1982. — Includes bibliographies
ISBN 0-295-95889-8 : Unpriced B82-40112

730′.9773′11 — Illinois. Chicago. Buildings. Sculptures

Riedy, James L.. Chicago sculpture / text and photographs by James L. Riedy. — Urbana ; London : University of Illinois Press, c1981. — xii,339p : ill,maps ; 26cm
Includes index
ISBN 0-252-00819-7 : £17.50 B82-13106

731 — SCULPTURES. MATERIALS, EQUIPMENT, TECHNIQUES, FORMS

731.4′62 — Wood carvings. Techniques — *Manuals*

Upton, John, *1897-*. A woodcarver′s primer / by John Upton. — New York : Sterling ; London : Oak Tree, 1981, c1976. — 160p : ill ; 26cm
Originally published: New York : Drake, 1973. — Includes index
ISBN 0-8069-8788-x (pbk) : £4.95 B82-35071

731.4′62 — Wood sculptures. Techniques — *Manuals*

Carstenson, Cecil C.. The craft and creation of wood sculpture / Cecil C. Carstenson ; edited by William S. Brown. — New York : Dover ; London : Constable, 1981, c1971. — ix,179p : ill ; 24cm
Originally published: New York : Scribner, 1971 ; London : Dent, 1973. — Bibliography: p172. — Includes index
ISBN 0-486-24094-0 (pbk) : £3.40 B82-08231

731′.74 — Clay sculptures. Special subjects: Man. Head. Techniques — *Illustrations*

Lucchesi, Bruno. Modeling the head in clay / sculpture by Bruno Lucchesi ; text and photographs by Margit Malmstrom. — New York ; Watson-Guptill ; London : Pitman, 1979. — 159p : ill,1port ; 29cm
Includes index
ISBN 0-273-01351-3 : £9.95 B82-05701

731′.75 — Masks. Making — *Amateurs′ manuals*

Boekholt, Albert. Puppets & masks / Albert Boekholt ; translated and adapted by Louisa Bumagin Hellegers]. — New York : Sterling ; Poole : Blandford [distributor], c1981. — 96p,[4]p of plates : ill(some col.) ; 26cm
Translation of: Masques et marottes. — Includes index
ISBN 0-8069-7042-1 : £5.95
Also classified at 745.592′24 B82-21869

731′.76 — Northern Lincolnshire. Churchyards. Headstones. Sculptures — *Illustrations*

Russell, Rex C.. Headstones in Lincolnshire : as works of art and as evidence of craftsmanship / Rex C. Russell. — [Barton-Upon-Humber] ([11 Priestgate, Barton-Upon-Humber, DN18 5ET]) : Barton on Humber branch of the Workers′ Educational Association, 1981. — [48]p : ill ; 30cm
Ill on inside covers. — Bibliography: p6
Unpriced (pbk)
Also classified at 731′.76 B82-05975

Russell, Rex C.. Headstones in Lincolnshire / Rex C. Russell. — [Barton-Upon-Humber] ([11 Priestgate, Barton-Upon-Humber, DN18 5ET]) : Barton Branch Workers Educational Association
Pt.2. — 1982. — [50]p : ill ; 30cm
Ill on inside covers. — Bibliography: p13
Unpriced (pbk) B82-19576

731′.76 — South Humberside. Churchyards. Headstones. Sculptures — *Illustrations*

Russell, Rex C.. Headstones in Lincolnshire : as works of art and as evidence of craftsmanship / Rex C. Russell. — [Barton-Upon-Humber] ([11 Priestgate, Barton-Upon-Humber, DN18 5ET]) : Barton on Humber branch of the Workers' Educational Association, 1981. — [48]p : ill ; 30cm
Ill on inside covers. — Bibliography: p6
Unpriced (pbk)
Primary classification 731′.76 B82-05975

731′.76′09422735 — Hampshire. Winchester. Cathedrals: Winchester Cathedral. Monuments

Blore, G. H.. The monuments of Winchester Cathedral. — 3rd ed. — Farnborough, Hants. : St. Michael's Abbey Press, Oct.1982. — [48]p
Previous ed. published as: Notes on the monuments of Winchester Cathedral. Winchester : Winchester Cathedral, 1949
ISBN 0-907077-18-8 (pbk) : £1.00 : CIP entry
B82-25948

731′.76′0942845 — North Yorkshire. Ryther. Parish churches: All Saints *(Church : Ryther).* **Monuments**

Routh, Pauline E.. A Ryther legacy : the monuments assessed / Pauline Routh, Richard Knowles. — Wakefield : Bedesman, 1981. — 36p : ill,facsims ; 21cm
ISBN 0-907887-00-7 (pbk) : Unpriced
B82-20665

731′.76′0942849 — North Yorkshire. Coxwold. Parish churches: Parish Church of St. Michael, Coxwold. Belasyse *(Family)* **monuments**

Routh, Pauline E.. Coxwold and the Belasyse monuments / Pauline E. Sheppard Routh. — Leeds (2 Tinshill La., Leeds LS16 7AP) : P.E.S. Routh, c1981. — 14p : ill,ports ; 21cm
Unpriced (pbk) B82-00583

731′.82 — Wood carvings. Special subjects: Human figures. Techniques — *Manuals*

Higginbotham, Bill. Carving country characters : step-by-step instructions for 18 projects / Bill Higginbotham. — New York : Dover ; London : Constable, 1981. — 60p : ill(some col.) ; 28cm
Ill on inside covers
ISBN 0-486-24135-1 (pbk) : £1.90 B82-08402

731′.8856 — New York *(City).* **Art galleries: Metropolitan Museum of Art. Exhibits: Italian nativity crèches: Neapolitan nativity crèches** — *Critical studies*

Svensson, Borje. The nativity / watercolours by Borje Svensson adapted from an eighteenth-century Neapolitan Christmas crèche ; [notes by Joanna Hecht]. — Harmondsworth : Kestrel, 1981. — [6]p : col.ill ; 31cm
"The Neapolitan crèche figures are in the collection of the Metropolitan Museum of Art" — cover. — Cover title
ISBN 0-7226-5764-1 : Unpriced B82-01259

732 — PRIMITIVE, ANCIENT, ORIENTAL SCULPTURES

732′.2′0966 — Yoruba sculptures

Fagg, William. Yoruba : sculpture of West Africa / text by William Fagg ; descriptive catalog by John Pemberton 3rd ; edited by Bryce Holcombe. — London : Collins, 1982. — xiii,208p : ill(some col.),1map ; 32cm
Bibliography: p201-208
ISBN 0-00-216637-2 : £18.00 B82-26929

732′.2′09669 — Ancient Nigerian sculptures — *Critical studies*

Eyo, Ekpo. Treasures of ancient Nigeria. — London : Collins, Oct.1982. — [162]p
Originally published: New York : Knopf, 1980
ISBN 0-00-217086-8 (pbk) : £9.95 : CIP entry
B82-23073

732′.4 — South Indian Hindu bronze sculptures, *1800-1900*

Mitchell, A. G.. Hindu gods and goddesses / A.G. Mitchell. — London : H.M.S.O., 1982. — xv,120p : ill ; 22cm
At head of title: Victoria and Albert Museum. — Bibliography: pxv. — Includes index
ISBN 0-11-290372-x (pbk) : £3.95 B82-40013

732′.8 — Ancient Egyptian relief sculptures & stelae. Collections — *Catalogues*

Egyptian stelae, reliefs and paintings from the Petrie collection. — Warminster : Aris and Phillips
Part 3: The Late period. — Jan.1983. — [120]p
ISBN 0-85668-171-7 (pbk) : £18.00 : CIP entry
B82-33115

732′.8 — Egypt. Abydos. Ancient Egyptian temples: Temple of Seti I *(Abydos).* **Relief sculptures. Special subjects: Ancient Egyptian religion. Rituals**

David, Rosalie. A guide to religious ritual at Abydos / Rosalie David. — Warminster : Aris & Philips, c1981. — xiv,182p,[6]p of plates : ill,plans ; 17x25cm. — (Modern Egyptology)
Bibliography: pvii-xiii
ISBN 0-85668-060-5 (pbk) : Unpriced : CIP rev. B81-08832

732′.8 — London. Camden *(London Borough).* **Museums: British Museum.** *Department of Egyptian Antiquities.* **Stock: Ancient Egyptian royal statues. Identification**

Davies, W. V.. A royal statue reattributed / W.V. Davies. — London : British Museum, 1981. — 56p ; 30cm. — (Occasional paper ; no.28)
ISBN 0-86159-029-5 (corrected : pbk) : Unpriced B82-16811

733 — CLASSICAL SCULPTURES

733 — Classical sculptures — *Catalogues*

Vermeule, Cornelius C.. Greek and Roman sculpture in America : masterpieces in public collections in the United States and Canada / Cornelius C. Vermeule. — Malibu : J. Paul Getty Museum ; Berkeley ; London : University of California Press, c1981. — ix,406p,[30]p of plates : chiefly ill(some col.),ports(some col.) ; 29cm
Bibliography: p391-393. — Includes index
ISBN 0-520-04324-3 : £37.50 B82-34361

733′.3 — Ancient Athenian sculptures

Stewart, Andrew, *1948-*. Attika : studies in Athenian sculpture of the Hellenistic age / by Andrew Stewart. — London : Society for the Promotion of Hellenic Studies, 1979. — xv,192p,[29]p of plates : ill,ports ; 22cm. — (Supplementary paper ; no.14)
Includes index
ISBN 0-902984-10-1 (pbk) : Unpriced
B82-39643

733′.3 — Ancient Greek sculptures, *B.C.500-B.C.400*

Ridgway, Brunilde Sismondo. Fifth century styles in Greek sculpture / by Brunilde Sismondo Ridgway. — Princeton ; Guildford : Princeton University Press, c1981. — xxiv,256p,[74]p of plates : ill ; 29cm
Includes bibliographies and index
ISBN 0-691-03965-8 (cased) : £31.60
ISBN 0-691-10116-7 (pbk) : £10.50
B82-02833

733′.3 — Ancient Greek sculptures, *ca B.C.660-ca B.C.150*

Barron, John, *1934-*. An introduction to Greek sculpture / John Barron. — Extended, rev. and up-dated version. — London : Athlone, 1981. — 176p : ill ; 24cm
Previous ed.: published as Greek sculpture. London : Studio Vista, 1965. — Includes index
ISBN 0-485-11196-9 (cased) : £15.00
ISBN 0-485-12033-x (pbk) : £5.95 B82-10287

733′.5′0216 — Ancient Roman sculptures — *Lists*

Corpus signorum imperii Romani = Corpus of sculpture of the Roman world. — Oxford : Published for the British Academy by the Oxford University Press
Great Britain
Vol.1. Fasc.2: Bath and the rest of Wessex / by B.W. Cunliffe, M.G. Fulford. — 1982. — xvi,59p,[48]p of plates : ill ; 28cm
Bibliography: pix-x. — Includes index
ISBN 0-19-726004-7 : £42.00 : CIP rev.
B82-12900

735 — SCULPTURES. MODERN PERIOD, 1400-

735′.21′074 — Art galleries. Exhibits: European sculptures, *1400-1500* — *Catalogues*

Reynolds, Catherine, *1952-*. Paintings and sculpture of the fifteenth century / [compiled by] Catherine Reynolds. — London : Warne, 1981. — 112p ; 22cm. — (An Observer's guide. Where is it?)
ISBN 0-7232-2759-4 (pbk) : £2.95
Primary classification 759.03′074 B82-06904

735′.21′074 — Art galleries. Exhibits: European sculptures, *1500-1600* — *Catalogues*

Beresford, Richard. Paintings and sculpture of the Sixteenth Century / Richard Beresford. — London : Warne, 1982. — 117p ; 22cm. — (An Observer's guide. Where is it?)
ISBN 0-7232-2887-6 (pbk) : £2.95
Primary classification 759.03′074 B82-22826

736 — CARVING AND CARVINGS

736′.2′028 — Lapidary — *Manuals*

Perry, Nance. Practical gemcutting : a guide to shaping and polishing / Nance and Ron Perry. — Newton Abbot : David & Charles, 1982, c1980. — 95p : ill ; 27cm
Originally published: 1980. — Includes index
ISBN 0-7153-8301-9 : £6.95 : CIP rev.
B82-07581

736′.4 — United States. Houses. Exteriors. Wood carvings, *1800-1900* — *Illustrations*

Karp, Ben. Ornamental carpentry on nineteenth-century American houses / Ben Karp. — rev. ed. — New York : Dover ; London : Constable, 1981. — 130p : ill ; 28cm
Previous ed.: published as Wood motifs in American domestic architecture. South Brunswick : Barnes, 1966
ISBN 0-486-24144-0 (pbk) : £5.25 B82-18051

736′.4 — Wood carvings. Designs — *Illustrations*

Bridgewater, Alan. A treasury of woodcarving designs / Alan and Gill Bridgewater. — New York ; London : Van Nostrand Reinhold, c1981. — 192p : chiefly ill,ports ; 29cm
Includes index
ISBN 0-442-20084-6 : £16.95 B82-21855

736′.4 — Wood carvings. Special subjects: Legendary characters & plants. Techniques — *Manuals*

Tangerman, E. J.. Carving flora & fables in wood / E.J. Tangerman. — New York : Sterling ; London : Oak Tree, c1981. — 128p : ill ; 21cm
Includes index
ISBN 0-8069-8982-3 (corrected : pbk) : £3.50
B82-24896

736′.4 — Wood carvings, *to 1900* — *Collectors' guides*

Curtis, Tony, *1939-*. Carved wood / compiled by Tony Curtis. — Galashiels : Lyle, c1982. — 126p : ill ; 17cm. — (Antiques and their values)
Includes index
ISBN 0-86248-018-3 : £2.50 B82-28535

736′.5′09423 — South-west England. Churches. Stone carvings, *ca 1050-1530*

Betley, J. H.. Sacred & satiric : medieval stone carving in the West country / J.H. Betley and C.W.G. Taylor. — Bristol : Redcliffe, 1982. — 64p : ill ; 25cm
Bibliography: p64
ISBN 0-905459-32-6 (pbk) : £2.25 B82-40977

736′.5′094233 — Dorset. Parish churches. Stone carvings, *1856-1880*

Brocklebank, Joan. Victorian stone carvers in Dorset churches 1856-1880 / Joan Brocklebank ; with excerpts from the reports of the consecration ceremonies in the Dorset County Chronicle and other sources. — Wimborne : Dovecote, 1979. — 72p,[16]p of plates : ill,1map ; 26cm
Map on lining papers. — Bibliography: p69. — Includes index
ISBN 0-9503518-3-0 : £8.50 B82-25346

736′.5′094238 — Somerset. Parish churches. Stone carvings, *1450-1550*

Wright, Peter Poyntz. Hunky punks : a study in Somerset stone carving / by Peter Poyntz Wright. — Amersham : Avebury, 1982. — x,159p : ill ; 22cm
ISBN 0-86127-014-2 (pbk) : £7.95 : CIP rev. B82-11122

736′.5′09447 — France. Aquitaine. Churches. Façades. Stone carvings, *1000-1200*

Seidel, Linda. Songs of glory : the Romanesque façades of Aquitaine / Linda Seidel. — Chicago ; London : University of Chicago Press, 1981. — ix,220p : ill,map ; 25cm
Bibliography: p129-153. — Includes index
ISBN 0-226-74513-9 : £10.20 B82-09670

736′.6 — Horn arterfacts — *Collectors′ guides*

Hardwick, Paula. Discovering horn / Paula Hardwick. — Guildford : Lutterworth, 1981. — 192p : ill(some col.),1coat of arms,ports ; 26cm
Bibliography: p185-187. — Includes index
ISBN 0-7188-2520-9 : £18.00 B82-04532

736′.62 — New York *(City)*. **Museums: Metropolitan Museum of Art. Exhibits: English carved ivory crosses: Bury St Edmunds cross. Acquisition** — *Personal observations*

Hoving, Thomas. King of the Confessors / Thomas Hoving. — London : Hamilton, 1981. — 365p : ill(some col.) ; 25cm
Bibliography: p353-354. — Includes index
ISBN 0-241-10674-5 : £9.95 : CIP rev. B81-30219

736′.62′09 — Ivory carvings, *to 1975* — *Collectors′ guides*

Curtis, Tony, *1939-*. Ivory / compiled by Tony Curtis. — Galashiels : Lyle, c1982. — 126p : chiefly ill ; 17cm. — (Antiques and their values)
Includes index
ISBN 0-86248-021-3 : £2.50 B82-28516

736′.62′094 — European ivory carvings, *500-1050*

Williamson, Paul, *1954-*. An introduction to medieval ivory carvings / Paul Williamson. — London : H.M.S.O., 1982. — 47p : ill(some col.) ; 26cm
At head of cover title: Victoria & Albert Museum. — Bibliography: p47
ISBN 0-11-290377-0 : £3.50 B82-14855

736′.68 — Japanese miniature carvings: Netsuke

Davey, Neil K.. Netsuke : a comprehensive study based on the M.T. Hindson Collection / Neil K. Davey ; foreword by W.W. Winkworth. — Rev. ed. — [London] : Sotheby, c1982. — 566p,[28]p of plates : ill(some col.) ; 31cm
Previous ed.: London : Faber, 1974. — Bibliography: p448. — Includes index
ISBN 0-85667-116-9 : Unpriced B82-38335

736′.68′07402393 — Avon. Bristol. Museums: City of Bristol Museum and Art Gallery. Stock: Netsuke — *Catalogues*

City of Bristol Museum and Art Gallery. A descriptive catalogue of the permanent collection of netsuke and related carvings from Japan / Peter Hardie. — [Bristol] : City of Bristol Museum & Art Gallery, 1981. — 64p : ill ; 19x21cm
Bibliography: p11
ISBN 0-900199-15-6 (pbk) : Unpriced B82-15291

736′.93′0922 — Wax modelling — *Biographies*

Pyke, E. J.. A biographical dictionary of wax modellers (supplement) / E.J. Pyke. — London : E.J. Pyke, c1981. — lix,57p,[26]p of plates : ill,ports ; 24cm
Bibliography: p45-48. — Includes index
ISBN 0-9507518-0-4 : £16.50 B82-02886

736′.98 — Paper chains. Making — *Manuals*

Leeson, Bill. Paper chains / [text and diagrams by Bill Leeson]. — London : Search Press, 1979. — 31p : ill(some col.) ; 17cm. — (Leisure crafts ; 71)
ISBN 0-85532-482-1 (pbk) : Unpriced B82-08501

736′.98′028 — Paper sculptures. Techniques — *Manuals*

Angrave, Bruce. Paper into sculpture / Bruce Angrave. — London : Warne, 1981. — 94p,[21]p of plates : ill(some col.) ; 25cm. — (Warne′s art and craft series)
ISBN 0-7232-2710-1 : £6.95 B82-00861

737 — NUMISMATICS

737′.03′21 — Numismatics — *Encyclopaedias*

Mackay, James. Key definitions in numismatics / James Mackay. — London : Muller, 1982. — 148p ; 20cm. — (A Language of its own)
ISBN 0-584-11017-0 (pbk) : £3.95 : CIP rev. B82-04581

737′.05 — Numismatics — *Serials*

Spink numismatic circular. — Vol.90, no.1 (Feb. 1982)-. — London (5 King St., St. James′s SW1Y 6QR) : Spink & Son, 1982-. — v. : ill ; 28cm
Ten issues yearly. — Continues: Numismatic circular
ISSN 0263-7677 = Spink numismatic circular : £8.00 per year B82-33861

737′.075 — Coins & medals. Collecting — *Serials*

[Coin news *(London)*]. Coin news : incorporating Coins and medals. — Vol.19, no.1 (Dec. 1981)-. — London (P.O. Box 3DE, W1A 3DE) : Epic Pub. Ltd. (U.K.), 1981-. — v. : ill,facsims ; 28cm
Monthly. — Cover title: Coin & medal news. — Continues: Coins and medals (1974). — With: Medal news
ISSN 0261-7072 = Coin news (London) : £10.00 per year B82-18501

Medal news : incorporating Medals international. — Vol.6, no.1 (Dec. 1981)-. — London (P.O. Box 3DE, W1A 3DE) : Epic Pub. Ltd. (U.K.), 1981-. — v. : ill,facsims ; 28cm
Monthly. — Cover title: Coin & medal news. — Continues: Medals international. — With: Coin news (London)
ISSN 0262-3625 = Medal news : £10.00 per year B82-18502

737′.2 — Great Britain. Schools. Silver badges & medals, *to ca 1850*

Grimshaw, M. E.. Silver medals, badges and trophies from schools in the British Isles 1550-1850 / M.E. Grimshaw. — Cambridge (Newnham College, Cambridge) : M.E. Grimshaw, [1981?]. — 64p : ill ; 27cm
Bibliography: p61-62. — Includes index
Unpriced (pbk) B82-03939

737′.22′07402142 — London. Camden *(London Borough)*. **Museums: British Museum.** *Department of Coins and Medals.* **Stock: French medals** — *Catalogues*

British Museum. *Department of Coins and Medals.* A catalogue of the French medals in the British Museum. — London : British Museum Publications, July 1982
Vol.1: 1402-1610. — [288]p
ISBN 0-7141-0855-3 : £35.00 : CIP entry B82-14074

737′.222′0941 — British commemorative medals, *1760-1960*

Brown, Laurence. A catalogue of British historical medals 1760-1960 / Laurence Brown. — London : Seaby
Vol.1: The accession of George III to the death of William IV. — 1980. — xxvi,469p : ill,ports ; 31cm
Includes index
ISBN 0-900652-56-x : £45.00 : CIP rev. B80-22309

737′.222′09438 — Expatriate Polish commemorative medals & badges, *1939-1977* — *Lists* — *Polish texts*

Brzezicki, Marian J.. Medale i odznaki : polskie i Polski dotycz ace : bite poza Polsk a w latach 1939-1977 / Marian J. Brzezicki. — Londyn : Instytut Polski i Muzeum im. gen. Sikorskiego, 1979. — 375p : ill,port ; 25cm
Polish text, introduction and conclusion in Polish and English. — Title on added t.p.: Polish and Polish related commemorative medals and badges. — Includes index
Unpriced (pbk) B82-02718

737′.223′0941 — Great Britain. *Army.* **Medals,** *1815-1972* — *Illustrations*

Gould, Robert W.. Campaign medals of the British Army 1815-1972 / by Robert W. Gould. — 2nd ed. with price guide supplement. — London : Arms and Armour, 1982. — 71p : ill ; 23cm
Previous ed.: 1972. — Bibliography: p15
ISBN 0-85368-515-0 : £4.95 B82-28413

737′.3′094 — Europe. Jettons, *to ca 1700*

Barnard, Francis Pierrepont. The casting-, counter and the counting-board : a chapter in the history of numismatics and early arithmetic / by Francis Pierrepont Barnard. — Castle Cary : Fox, 1981. — 357p,lxiii leaves of plates : ill ; 30cm
Originally published: Oxford : Clarendon, 1916. — Bibliography: p11-24. — Includes index
ISBN 0-907498-00-0 : £30.00 B82-03328

737′.3′0941 — British tradesmen′s tokens, *ca 1700-1830*

Newmark, Jim. Trade tokens of the industrial revolution / Jim Newmark. — Princes Risborough : Shire, 1981. — 32p : ill ; 21cm. — (Shire album ; 79)
Bibliography: p32
ISBN 0-85263-582-6 (pbk) : £0.95 B82-31142

737.4′075 — Coins. Collecting — *Manuals*

Freeman, Michael. Buying and selling coins. — London : Barrie & Jenkins, Nov.1982. — [112]p
ISBN 0-09-150401-5 : £3.95 : CIP entry B82-26903

737.4′09 — Coins, *to 1979*

Coins : an illustrated survey : 650BC to the present day / general editor Martin Jessop Price. — London : Hamlyn published in association with British Museum Publications, c1980. — 320p : ill(some col.) ; 35cm
In slip case. — Bibliography: p318. — Includes index
ISBN 0-600-32023-5 : £25.00 B82-24887

737.4′09 — Coins, *to 1980* — *For children*

Briers, Audrey. True stories about money / written and designed by Audrey Briers. — Oxford : Ashmolean Museum, 1981. — 46p : ill(some col.),1map ; 15x21cm
ISBN 0-900090-81-2 (pbk) : £1.20
ISBN 0-7093-0061-1 (Birmingham Museums and Art Gallery) B82-02891

737.4′09 — Coins, *to ca 1910.* **Cultural aspects**

Hoberman, Gerald. The art of coins and their photography : an illustrated photographic treatise with an introduction to numismatics / by Gerald Hoberman. — London : Spink in association with Lund Humphries Publishers, [1981]. — 397p : ill(some col.) ; 27cm
Bibliography: p355-362. — Includes index
ISBN 0-85331-450-0 : £40.00 B82-15282

737.4′0904 — Coins, *1900-1982* — *Catalogues*

Schön, Günter. World coin catalogue : twentieth century / by Günter Schön. — 4th ed. — London : Barrie & Jenkins, c1982. — 1424p : ill,coats of arms ; 19cm
Translation of: Weltmünzkatalog, XX. Jahrhundert. — Previous ed.: 197-
ISBN 0-09-150571-2 (pbk) : £7.95 B82-40715

737.4937 — Ancient Roman bronze coins, *ca 300-400*

Kent, J. P. C.. The pattern of bronze coinage under Constantine 1 / by J.P.C. Kent. — [Manchester] ([c/o Dept. of Coins & Medals, Manchester Museum, Oxford Rd, Manchester]) : [British Association of Numismatic Societies], [1982?]. — p17-77,[6]leaves of plates : ill ; 24cm. — (Doris Stockwell memorial papers ; no.3)
Reprinted from the Numismatic chronicle. Sixth series, vol.17. 1957
Unpriced (pbk) B82-24282

737.4937 — Ancient Roman coins

Carson, R. A. G.. Principal coins of the Romans / R.A.G. Carson. — London : Published for the Trustees of the British Museum by British Museum Publications
Vol.2: The principate : 31BC-AD296. — c1980. — 167p : ill ; 26cm
Includes index
ISBN 0-7141-0852-9 : £25.00 : CIP rev.
ISBN 0-7141-0839-1 (set) : Unpriced
B79-05222

737.4937 — Ancient Roman silver coins — *Collectors' guides*

Seaby, H. A.. Roman silver coins. — London : Seaby
Vol.3: Pertinax to Balbinus and Pupienus. — 2nd rev. ed. — June 1982. — [168]p
Previous ed.: 1969
ISBN 0-900652-61-6 : £10.00 : CIP entry
B82-14396

Seaby, H. A.. Roman silver coins. — London : Seaby
Previous ed.: 1971
Vol.4: Gordian III to Postumus. — 2nd rev. ed. — June 1982. — [148]p
ISBN 0-900652-62-4 : £10.00 : CIP entry
B82-25722

737.4937 — Great Britain. Ancient Roman coins, *to 420.* **Hoards**

Coin hoards from Roman Britain. — London : British Museum. — (Occasional paper, ISSN 0142-4815 ; no.31)
Vol.2 / edited by A.M. Burnett. — 1981. — iv,121p : ill ; 30cm
ISBN 0-86159-031-7 (pbk) : Unpriced
B82-05184

Coin hoards from Roman Britain. — London : British Museum. — (Occasional paper / British Museum, ISSN 0142-4815 ; no.33)
Vol.3: The Blackmoor hoard / [edited by] Roger Bland. — 1982. — v,115p : ill ; 30cm
ISBN 0-86159-033-3 (pbk) : Unpriced
B82-18704

737.4937 — Greek Imperial coins

Sear, David R.. Greek imperial coins : and their values : the local coinage of the Roman Empire / David R. Sear. — London : Seaby, c1982. — xxxiii,636p : ill,10maps ; 23cm
Includes index
ISBN 0-900652-59-4 : £27.50 : CIP rev.
B82-10889

737.4937 — Gwent. Usk. Ancient Roman coins

Boon, George C.. The coins / George C. Boon. Inscriptions and graffiti / Mark Hassall with other contributions by R.P. Wright and George C. Boon. — Cardiff : Published on behalf of the Board of Celtic Studies of the University of Wales [by] University of Wales Press, 1982. — 72p,[2]p of plates : ill ; 30cm. — (Report on the excavations at Usk 1965-1976)
ISBN 0-7083-0789-2 : Unpriced
ISBN 0-7083-0741-8 (set)
Also classified at 089'.71 B82-36889

737.4937'03'21 — Ancient Roman coins — *Dictionaries*

Stevenson, Seth W.. A dictionary of Roman coins Republican and Imperial. — London : Seaby, Apr.1982. — [929]p
Originally published: London : Bell, 1899
ISBN 0-900652-60-8 : £16.00 : CIP entry
B82-08105

737.4937'074'0291443 — Scotland. Strathclyde Region. Glasgow. Museums: University of Glasgow. *Hunterian Museum.* **Stock: Ancient Roman coins. Collections: Hunter Coin Cabinet** *— Catalogues*

University of Glasgow. *Hunterian Museum.* Roman imperial coins in the Hunter Coin Cabinet : University of Glasgow / by Anne S. Robertson. — London : Published for the University of Glasgow by the Oxford University Press
5: Diocletian (Reform) to Zeno. — 1982. — 529p,96leaves of plates : ill ; 26cm
Bibliography: pxxxii-xli. — Includes index
ISBN 0-19-713310-x : £50.00 : CIP rev.
B82-01111

737.4939'4 — Turkey. Sardis. Ancient Middle Eastern coins

Greek, Roman, and Islamic coins from Sardis / T.V. Buttrey ... [et al.] with a contribution by J.A. Charles. — Cambridge, Mass. ; London : Harvard University Press, 1981. — xxix,274p,10p of plates : ill,1map,1plan ; 29cm. — (Archaeological exploration of Sardis. Monograph ; 7)
Bibliography: pxxv-xxix
ISBN 0-674-36305-1 : Unpriced B82-35390

737.4941 — Coins: British gold sovereigns, *to 1980*

Marsh, Michael A.. The gold sovereign / Michael A. Marsh. — Cambridge : M.A. Marsh, 1980. — x,72p : ill ; 22cm
Bibliography: p72
ISBN 0-9506929-0-5 : £4.85 B82-25962

737.4941'0216 — British coins *— Catalogues*

Sylloge of coins of the British Isles. — 30. — London : Oxford University Press for the British Academy, Mar.1982. — [100]p
ISBN 0-19-726011-x : £27.00 : CIP entry
B82-01536

Warhurst, Margaret. Sylloge of coins of the British Isles. — Oxford : Oxford University Press, Feb.1983
Vol.29: Merseyside. — [156]p
ISBN 0-19-726007-1 : £23.50 : CIP entry
B82-36595

737'.49415 — Irish coins, *995- — Collectors' guides*

Collectors coins : Ireland. — 5th ed., special revision. — [Torquay] : [Retrographic], [1980?]. — 50p : ill ; 16cm
Previous ed.: 1978
ISBN 0-901170-89-5 (pbk) : Unpriced
B82-26659

737.4942'074 — English silver coins, *1816-1980 — Catalogues*

Davies, Peter J.. British silver coins since 1816 : with engravers' patterns and proofs and unofficial pieces / by Peter J. Davies. — [Birmingham] : [P.J. Davies], 1982. — 128p : ill ; 22cm
ISBN 0-9507913-0-x : Unpriced B82-33689

737.49495 — Byzantine coins, *491-1453*

Grierson, Philip. Byzantine coins. — London : Methuen, Sept.1982. — [470]p. — (The Library of numismatics)
ISBN 0-416-71360-2 : £70.00 : CIP entry
B82-20178

737.4973 — American coins, *to 1979*

Schwarz, Ted. A history of United States coinage / Ted Schwarz. — San Diego : Barnes ; London : Tantivy, c1980. — 392p : ill ; 25cm
Bibliography: p388-392. — Includes index
ISBN 0-498-02164-5 : £8.95 B82-36376

737'.6'07402132 — Great Britain. *Public Record Office.* **Stock: Seals** *— Catalogues*

Great Britain. *Public Record Office.* Catalogue of seals in the Public Record Office. — London : H.M.S.O.
Personal seals / compiled by Roger H. Ellis ; with plates from photographs by J.D. Millen
Vol.2. — 1981. — vi,129p,34p of plates : ill ; 25cm
ISBN 0-11-440111-x (pbk) : £15.00
B82-00432

737.6'074'02142 — London. Camden *(London Borough).* **Museums: British Museum. Stock: Western Asiatic seals** *— Catalogues*

British Museum. Catalogue of Western Asiatic seals in the British Museum. — London : British Museum
Cylinder seals 2. — June 1982. — [186]p
ISBN 0-7141-1104-x : £30.00 : CIP entry
B82-09610

738 — CERAMICS

738'.092'4 — London. Westminster *(London Borough).* **Art galleries: Crafts Council.** *Gallery.* **Exhibits: English pottery. Poncelet, Jacqui —** *Catalogues*

Deacon, Richard, *1949-*. Jacqui Poncelet, new ceramics / [text by Richard Deacon]. — London : Crafts Council, c1981. — 16p : ill (some col.),1port ; 30cm
Accompanies a Crafts Council touring exhibition, held at 6 different venues, from 30 May 1981 to 31 January 1982. — Bibliography: p16
ISBN 0-903798-54-9 (pbk) : Unpriced
B82-06305

738'.0951 — Chinese ceramics, *960-1278*

Tregear, Mary. Song ceramics / Mary Tregear. — London : Thames and Hudson, 1982. — 262p : ill(some col.),maps ; 33cm
Bibliography: p239-242. — Includes index
ISBN 0-500-23346-2 : £42.00 B82-25010

738.1 — CERAMICS. MATERIALS, EQUIPMENT, TECHNIQUES

738.1 — Japanese pottery. Making

Simpson, Penny. The Japanese pottery handbook = Tōgei handobukku / written by Penny Simpson, Kanji Sodeoka ; drawings and layout Lucy Kitto. — Tokyo : Kodansha ; Oxford : Phaidon [[distributor]], 1979 (1980 printing). — 118p : ill,4maps,plans ; 19x27cm
Includes some parallel English text and Japanese translation. — Bibliography: p114-118
ISBN 0-87011-373-9 (pbk) : Unpriced
B82-35127

738.1 — Pottery. Making *— Manuals*

Baker, Denys Val. Let's make pottery / Denys Val Baker. — London : Warne, 1981. — 87p : ill ; 22cm. — (An Observer's guide. Art and craft)
Bibliography: p77-78. — Includes index
ISBN 0-7232-2709-8 (pbk) : £1.95 B82-00871

Birks, Tony. The new potter's companion / Tony Birks. — Rev. ed. — Glasgow : Collins, 1982. — 168p : ill(some col.) ; 27cm
Previous ed.: published as The potter's companion. 1974. — Includes index
ISBN 0-00-411856-1 : £7.95 B82-15304

Holden, Andrew. The self-reliant potter. — London : A. & C. Black, Sept.1982. — [144]p
ISBN 0-7136-2244-x : £7.95 : CIP entry
B82-20363

Thomas, Gwilym. Step-by-step guide to pottery / Gwilym Thomas. — Rev. ed. — London : Hamlyn, 1982. — 64p : ill ; 26cm
Previous ed.: 1973. — Includes index
ISBN 0-600-34297-2 : £2.99 B82-32758

738.1 — Slab pottery. Making

Marshall, West. Slab building / West Marshall. — London : A. and C. Black, 1982. — 96p : ill ; 22cm. — (Ceramic skillbooks)
Bibliography: p93. — Includes index
ISBN 0-7136-2207-5 (cased) : £3.95
ISBN 0-7136-2208-3 (pbk) : £2.95 B82-33540

738.1'3 — Pottery. Making. Electric pottery kilns. Use *— Manuals*

Cooper, Emmanuel. Electric kiln pottery : the complete guide / Emmanuel Cooper. — London : Batsford, 1982. — 144p,[4]p of plates : ill(some col.) ; 26cm
Ill on lining papers. — Bibliography: p139-140. — Includes index
ISBN 0-7134-4037-6 : £9.95 B82-41041

738.1'8 — Pottery & porcelain. Restoration & repair *— Manuals*

Grayson, Joan. The repair & restoration of pottery & porcelain / Joan Grayson. — London : Evans, 1982. — 151p : ill ; 18x21cm
ISBN 0-237-45582-x : £6.95 : CIP rev.
B82-01866

White, Muriel. Restoring fine china / Muriel White. — London : Batsford, 1981. — 167p,[4]p of plates : ill(some col.) ; 26cm
Bibliography: p159. — Includes index
ISBN 0-7134-1837-0 : £12.50 B82-06213

738.1'8 — Pottery & porcelain. Restoration & repair — *Manuals* *continuation*

738.2 — PORCELAIN

738.2 — Crested porcelain. Collecting — *Serials*

The **Crested** circle : a bi-monthy magazine for collectors of the products of the crested china manufacturers. — Vol.1, no.1 (Jan./Feb. 1980)-. — Dagenham (c/o F. Owen, 21 Urswick Rd, Dagenham, Essex RM9 6EA) : The Crested Circle, 1980-. — v. : ill ; 20cm
Six issues yearly. — Description based on: Vol.1, no.10 (July/Aug. 1981)
ISSN 0262-7140 = Crested circle : £3.00 per year B82-09068

738.2'0278 — Pottery & porcelain. Marks, *to 1900* — *Lists*

Kybalová, Jana. Ceramic marks of the world / Jana Kybalová. — London : Hamlyn, c1981. — 255p : ill ; 20cm
Bibliography: p248. — Includes index
ISBN 0-600-34229-8 : £2.99 B82-19424

738.2'03'21 — Pottery & porcelain — *Encyclopaedias*

Savage, George. An illustrated dictionary of ceramics : defining 3,054 terms relating to wares, materials, processes, styles, patterns and shapes from antiquity to the present day / George Savage, Harold Newman ; with an introductory list of the principal European factories and their marks, compiled by John Cushion. — 2nd rev. ed. — London : Thames and Hudson, 1976. — 320p,[16]p of plates : ill (some col.) ; 26cm
Previous ed.: 1974
ISBN 0-500-23151-6 : £12.50 B82-16030

Savage, George. An illustrated dictionary of ceramics : defining 3,054 terms relating to wares, materials, processes, styles, patterns and shapes from antiquity to the present day / George Savage, Harold Newman ; with an introductory list of principal European factories and their marks compiled by John Cushion. — 2nd rev. ed. — London : Thames and Hudson, 1976. — 319p : ill ; 26cm
Previous ed.: 1974
£12.50 B82-22527

738.2'09 — Porcelain, *to 1981*

The **History** of porcelain / general editor Paul Atterbury. — London : Orbis, 1982. — 256p : ill(some col.),facsims,1port ; 31cm
In a slip case. — Bibliography: p244-247. — Includes index
ISBN 0-85613-344-2 : £17.50 B82-39036

738.2'09 — Pottery & porcelain, *to ca 1970*

World ceramics : an illustrated history from earliest times / edited by Robert J. Charleston ... — London : Hamlyn, c1968 (1981 [printing]). — 352p : ill(some col.),maps ; 34cm
Includes index
ISBN 0-600-34261-1 (pbk) : £6.95 B82-04442

738.2'094 — European porcelain, *1400-1970* — *Collectors' guides*

European china / compiled by Tony Curtis. — Galashiels : Lyle, c1981. — 126p : chiefly ill ; 17cm. — (Antiques and their values)
Includes index
ISBN 0-86248-008-6 : £2.50 B82-08195

738.2'094 — European porcelain, *1700-1900* — *Collectors' guides*

Miller, Judith H.. Continental porcelain / by Judith H. Miller ; consultant editor Gordon Lang. — Tenterden : MJM, c1982. — 120p : ill ; 22cm. — (Buyer's price guides)
Includes index
ISBN 0-905879-19-8 : £3.95 B82-33576

738.2'0941 — British miniature pottery & porcelain, *1750-1982*

Milbourn, Maurice. Miniature British pottery and porcelain 1750- present. — Woodbridge : Antique Collectors' Club, Jan.1983. — [200]p
ISBN 0-907462-30-8 : £12.50 : CIP entry B82-36165

738.2'0942 — English porcelain, *ca 1700-ca 1900* — *Buyers' guides*

English porcelain : buyer's price guide / compiled and edited by Judith H. Miller ; consultant editor Gordon Lang. — Tenterden : MJM, 1981?. — 100p : ill ; 11cm
Includes index
ISBN 0-905879-05-8 : £2.95 B82-12796

738.2'095 — Oriental porcelain, *1368-1911* — *Collectors' guides*

Oriental china / compiled by Tony Curtis. — Galashiels : Lyle, c1981. — 125p : chiefly ill ; 17cm. — (Antiques and their values)
Includes index
ISBN 0-86248-015-9 : £2.50 B82-08196

738.2'0951 — Chinese porcelain, *ca 1300-ca 1900* — *Collectors' guides*

Lang, Gordon. Chinese porcelain / by Gordon Lang. — Tenterden : MJM, c1982. — 95p : ill ; 22cm. — (Buyer's price guides)
Includes index
ISBN 0-905879-20-1 : £2.95 B82-33581

738.2'0952'2 — East Germany. Dresden. Art galleries: Dresdener Portzellansammlung. Exhibits: Japanese porcelain: Arita porcelain

Reichel, Friedrich. Early Japanese porcelain : Arita porcelain in the Dresden Collection / by Friedrich Reichel ; photographs by Jürgen Karpinski ; [translated from the German by Barbara Beedham]. — London : Orbis, 1981, c1980. — 156p : ill(some col.),2maps ; 23cm
In slip case. — Bibliography: p154-156
ISBN 0-85613-392-2 : £10.00 B82-16584

738.2'3 — Mason porcelain & ironstone ware, *1796-1853*

Mason : a family of potters / [edited Deborah S. Skinner]. — Stoke-on-Trent : City Museum & Art Gallery, [1982]. — 36p : ill,coats of arms,facsims,1port ; 20x22cm
Published to accompany an exhibition at the City Museum and Art Gallery, 1982. — Bibliography: p35
ISBN 0-905080-17-3 (pbk) : Unpriced
Primary classification 929'.2'0942 B82-33686

738.2'3 — Mason porcelain & ironstone ware, *1796-1853* — *Collectors' guides*

Godden, Geoffrey A.. Godden's guide to Mason's china and the ironstone wares / Geoffrey A. Godden. — Rev. and enlgd. ed. — Woodbridge : Antique Collectors' Club, c1980. — 316p : ill (some col.) ; 29cm
Previous ed.: published as The illustrated guide to Mason's patent ironstone china. London : Barrie & Jenkins, 1971. — Ill on lining papers. — Bibliography: p311-312. — Includes index
ISBN 0-902028-86-3 : £17.50 : CIP rev. B80-03752

738.2'7 — Bow porcelain, *to 1770* — *Catalogues*

Freeman, Geoffrey. Bow porcelain : the collection formed by Geoffrey Freeman / written and compiled by Anton Gabszewicz in collaboration with Geoffrey Freeman. — London : Lund Humphries, 1982. — 164p,[8]p of plates : ill(some col.) ; 25cm
Bibliography: p159-161. — Includes index
ISBN 0-85331-452-7 : £30.00 B82-37404

738.2'7 — Bow porcelain, *to ca 1780*

Adams, Elizabeth, *1929-*. Bow porcelain / by Elizabeth Adams and David Redstone. — London : Faber and Faber, 1981. — 251p,[16]p of plates : ill(some col.),2maps,2facsims,1port ; 25cm. — (The Faber monographs on pottery and porcelain)
Maps on lining papers. — Bibliography: p239-242. — Includes index
ISBN 0-571-11696-5 : £27.50 : CIP rev. B81-31177

738.2'7 — Chamberlain Worcester porcelain, *1788-1852*

Godden, Geoffrey A.. Chamberlain-Worcester porcelain 1788-1852 / Geoffrey A. Godden. — London : Barrie & Jenkins, 1982. — 375p,[16]p of plates : ill(some col.),coats of arms(some col.),facsims,1port ; 29cm
Bibliography: p367-370. — Includes index
ISBN 0-09-145860-9 : £55.00 : CIP rev. B82-07251

738.2'7 — Derby porcelain, *1750-1770*

Rice, Dennis G.. Derby porcelain. — Newton Abbot : David & Charles, Jan.1983. — [192]p
ISBN 0-7153-8249-7 : £18.00 : CIP entry B82-32609

738.2'7 — Sèvres porcelain. Dinner services: Service Egyptien

Victoria and Albert Museum. The Sèvres Egyptian service 1810-12 / Charles Truman. — [London] : Victoria and Albert Museum, c1982. — 72p : ill(some col.),2facsims,1port ; 20cm
Bibliography: p30
ISBN 0-905209-24-9 (pbk) : Unpriced B82-39786

738.2'7 — Staffordshire. Stoke on Trent. Museums: City Museum and Art Gallery *(Stoke-on-Trent).* **Stock: London porcelain: Tower Hamlets** *(London Borough)* **porcelain: Bow porcelain** — *Catalogues*

Bow porcelain : 14 Sept-31 Oct 1981 / [written by David Redstone ; edited by Pat Halfpenny]. — Hanley : Stoke-on-Trent City Museum Art Gallery, [1981]. — 40p : ill ; 21cm
Accompanies an exhibition held at Stoke-on-Trent City Museum & Art Gallery. — Bibliography: p39
ISBN 0-905080-13-0 (pbk) : Unpriced B82-00105

738.3 — POTTERY

738.3'012 — Classification. Cultural aspects — *Study examples: Pottery*

Kempton, Willett. The folk classification of ceramics : a study of cognitive prototypes / Willett Kempton. — New York ; London : Academic Press, 1981. — xvi,237p : ill ; 24cm. — (Language, thought, and culture)
Bibliography: p220-233. — Includes index
ISBN 0-12-404080-2 : £16.20 B82-21245

738.3'0932'07402659 — Cambridgeshire. Cambridge. Museums: Fitzwilliam Museum. Exhibits: Ancient Egyptian pottery — *Catalogues*

Bourriau, Janine. Umm el-Ga'ab : pottery from the Nile valley before the Arab conquest : exhibition organised by the Fitzwilliam Museum, Cambridge, 6 October to 11 December 1981 / cataloque by Janine Bourriau. — Cambridge : Cambridge University Press, 1981. — 141p : ill,1map ; 29cm
Spine title: Pottery from the Nile valley
ISBN 0-521-24065-4 : £20.00 : CIP rev. B81-32522

738.3'09361 — Great Britain. Imported pottery, *ca 300-ca 600* — *Lists*

Thomas, Charles, *1928-*. A provisional list of imported pottery in post-Roman Western Britain & Ireland / Charles Thomas ; (with an appendix on Tintagel by O.J. Padel). — Redruth : Institute of Cornish Studies, 1981. — 32p ; 30cm. — (Special report ; no.7)
Bibliography: p30-32
ISBN 0-903686-33-3 (Corrected : pbk) : Unpriced B82-16294

738.3'09362'8104 — North Yorkshire. York. Ancient Roman pottery. Archaeological investigations

Perrin, J. R.. Roman pottery from the Colonia. — London : Council for British Archaeology, Aug.1981. — [68]p. — (The Archaeology of York ; v.16)
ISBN 0-900312-71-8 (pbk) : £6.00 : CIP entry B81-25127

738.3'09385 — Ancient Athenian pottery — *For schools*

Harrison, J. A. (James Alexander). Athenian painted pottery / J.A. Harrison. — London : Bell & Hyman, 1979. — 32p : ill ; 21cm. — (The Ancient world in action)
ISBN 0-7135-0237-1 (pbk) : Unpriced B82-27070

738.3'0941 — British pottery, *1960-1976*

Birks, Tony. Art of the modern potter / Tony Birks. — Rev. and enlarged ed. — London : Country Life Books, 1976 (1982 [printing]). — 206p : ill(some col.),ports ; 28cm
£6.95 (pbk) B82-33959

738.3'0942 — English brown stoneware, ***1670-1900***

Oswald, Adrian. English brown stoneware : 1670-1900. — London : Faber, Oct.1982. — [288]p
ISBN 0-571-11905-0 : CIP entry B82-29075

738.3'09422'76 — Hampshire. Southampton. Pottery, ***700-1100.*** **Excavation of remains**

Hodges, Richard, *1952-*. The Hamwih Pottery : the local and imported wares from 30 years' excavations at Middle Saxon Southampton and their European context / by Richard Hodges ; with a contribution by J.F. Cherry. — London : Published for the Southampton Archaeological Research Committee by the Council for British Archaeology, 1981. — vii,108p : ill,maps ; 30cm. — (Southampton Archaeological Research Committee report ; 2) (Research report, ISSN 0589-9036 ; no.37)
Bibliography: p100-103. — Includes index
ISBN 0-900312-99-8 (pbk) : Unpriced : CIP rev. B81-20575

738.3'0952'074014461 — Massachusetts. Boston. Art galleries: Museum of Fine Arts, Boston. Stock: Japanese pottery. Collections: Morse collection — *Catalogues*

Morse, Edward S.. Catalogue of the Morse collection of Japanese pottery / by Edward S. Morse ; with an introduction to the new edition by Terence Barrow. — Rutland, Vermont : Tuttle ; London : Prentice-Hall [[disributor]], 1979. — xix,396p,[109]p of plates : ill ; 27cm
Originally published: Cambridge, Mass. : Riverside Press for the Museum of Fine Arts, Boston, 1901. — Includes index
ISBN 0-8048-1299-3 : £22.55 B82-02054

738.3'09593 — Northern Thai pottery, ***1000-1620***

Shaw, J. C. (John Christopher). Northern Thai ceramics / J.C. Shaw. — Kuala Lumpur ; Oxford : Oxford University Press, 1981. — ix,270p : ill(some col.),maps ; 26cm. — (Oxford in Asia studies in ceramics)
Map on lining paper. — Bibliography: p94-97. — Includes index
ISBN 0-19-580475-9 : £38.00 B82-31498

738.3'7 — Blue & white transfer printed pottery, ***1780-1880 — Encyclopaedias***

Coysh, A. W.. The dictionary of blue and white printed pottery, 1780-1880. — Woodbridge : Antique Collectors' Club, Nov.1981. — 1v.
ISBN 0-907462-06-5 : £19.50 : CIP entry B81-30621

738.3'7 — Italian majolica, ***1460-1570 — Critical studies — Facsimiles***

Fortnum, Charles Drury Edward. Maiolica : a historical treatise on the glazed and enamelled earthenwares of Italy, with marks and monograms. Also some notice of the Persian, Damascus, Rhodian and Hispano-Moresque wares / Charles Drury Edward Fortnum. — New York ; London : Garland, 1979. — xv,357,189p,21leaves of plates : ill ; 24cm. — (A Dealers' and collectors' bookshelf. Ceramics and glass)
Facsim. of: ed. published Oxford : Clarendon, 1896. — Bibliography: p155-167. — Includes index
ISBN 0-8240-3393-0 : Unpriced B82-14683

738.3'7 — Lincolnshire, Humberside & South Yorkshire ***(Metropolitan County).*** **Ancient Roman Parisian stamped pottery**

Elsdon, S. M.. Parisian ware : a study of stamped wares of the Roman period in Lincolnshire, Humberside and South Yorkshire / by S.M. Elsdon. — Highworth : Vorda, 1982. — 56p : ill,maps ; 30cm. — (Vorda research series ; 4)
Bibliography: p53-55
ISBN 0-907246-03-6 (pbk) : Unpriced B82-37765

738.3'7 — Norfolk. Norwich. Museums: Norwich Castle Museum. Stock: Norfolk pottery: Norwich pottery, ***ca 200-ca 1780 — Catalogues***

Jennings, Sarah. Eighteen centuries of pottery from Norwich / by Sarah Jennings with M.M. Karshner, W.F. Milligan and S.V. Williams ; principal illustrator Martin Creasey. — Norwich (Centre of East Anglian Studies, Earlham Hall, University of East Anglia, Norwich NR4 7TJ) : The Norwich Survey in conjunction with The Scole Archaeological Cttee Ltd, [1981]. — xii,281p : ill,maps ; 30cm. — (East Anglian archaeology report ; no.13)
Bibliography: p274-280
Unpriced B82-13108

738.3'7 — Samian pottery

Bulmer, Margaret. An introduction to Roman samian ware : with special reference to collections in Chester and the North West / by Margaret Bulmer. — [Chester] ([c/o Bookland, 12 Bridge St., Chester]) : Chester Archaeological Society, 1980. — 72p : ill(some col.),2maps ; 25cm
Reprinted from the Journal of the Chester Archaeological Society, v.62, for 1979. — Bibliography: p60-72
Unpriced (pbk) B82-26661

738.3'7 — Staffordshire pottery — *Collectors' guides*

Oliver, Anthony. Staffordshire pottery : the tribal art of England / Anthony Oliver. — London : Heinemann, 1981. — xii,177p : ill ; 25cm
Bibliography: p173. — Includes index
ISBN 0-434-54392-6 : £25.00 B82-02605

738.3'7 — Staffordshire. Stoke-on-Trent. Museums: City Museum and Art Gallery ***(Stoke-on-Trent).*** **Exhibits: Hand-painted pottery. Gray's Pottery** — *Catalogues*

Hand-painted Gray's pottery : 1 February-13 March 1982 Stoke-on-Trent City Museum & Art Gallery / [edited Kathy Niblett]. — Stoke-on-Trent : City Museum and Art Gallery, c1982. — 57p : ill(some col.),facsims,ports ; 20x21cm
ISBN 0-905080-12-2 (pbk) : Unpriced B82-16390

738.3'82'0938 — Classical pottery vases — *Catalogues*

Corpus vasorum antiquorum. — (Toronto ; fasc.1) (Canada ; fasc.1)
At head of title: Union académique internationale
Canada
Royal Ontario Museum Toronto
Attic black figure and related wares / by J.W. Hayes. — Oxford : Published for the British Academy and the Royal Ontario Museum by Oxford University Press, 1981. — Portfolio : ill ; 35cm
Includes index
ISBN 0-19-726000-4 : Unpriced B82-30564

738.3'82'09385 — Ancient Athenian pottery. Black figure vases & red figure vases. Paintings — *Lists*

Burn, Lucilla. Beazley addenda. — Oxford : Oxford University Press for the British Academy, Oct.1982. — [300]p
ISBN 0-19-726018-7 : £18.00 : CIP entry B82-27024

738.3'82'09385 — Ancient Athenian pottery: Vases. Decorations, ***ca 505 B.C.-460 B.C. — Illustrations***

Beazley, *Sir* **John**. The Berlin painter. — Oxford : Clarendon, May 1982. — [100]p. — (Oxford monographs on classical archaeology)
ISBN 0-19-813220-4 : £25.00 : CIP entry B82-07509

738.3'82'09388 — Mycenaean pottery vases. Paintings

Vermeule, Emily. Mycenaean pictorial vase painting / Emily Vermeule, Vassos Karageorghis. — Cambridge, Mass. ; London : Harvard University Press, 1982. — xii,417p : ill,maps ; 31cm
Bibliography: p189-191. — Includes index
ISBN 0-674-59650-1 : £42.00 B82-38444

738.4 — ENAMELS

738.4 — Handicrafts: Enamelling — *Manuals*

Strosahl, J. Patrick. A manual of cloisonné & champlevé enamelling / J. Patrick Strosahl, Judith Lull Strosahl, Coral L. Barnhart ; illustrations by Barbara Becker. — London : Thames and Hudson, 1982. — ix,197p,[8]p of plates : ill(some col.),1plan,1port ; 28cm
Bibliography: p193-194. — Includes index
ISBN 0-500-23349-7 : £16.00 B82-19967

738.4'0944'66 — London. Camden ***(London Borough).*** **Museums: British Museum. Exhibits: Limoges painted enamels. Collections: Keir Collection** — *Catalogues*

Gauthier, Marie-Madeleine. Medieval enamels masterpieces from the Keir Collection. — London : British Museum for the Abbas Establishment, Vaduz, Liechtenstein, Oct.1981. — 1v.
ISBN 0-7141-1358-1 : £8.95 : CIP entry B81-30190

738.5 — MOSAICS

738.5'2'09362 — England. Ancient Roman mosaics

Neal, David S.. Roman mosaics in Britain : an introduction to their schemes and a catalogue of paintings / by David S. Neal. — London (31 Gordon Sq., WC1H 0PP) : Society for the Promotion of Roman Studies, 1981. — 127p,[82]p of plates : ill(some col.) ; 30cm. — (Britannia monograph series ; no.1)
Two micro-fiche in pockets. — Bibliography: p9-15. — Includes index
Unpriced (pbk) B82-22364

738.6 — ORNAMENTAL BRICKS AND TILES

738.6'09'02 — London. Camden ***(London Borough).*** **Museums: British Museum.** ***Department of Medieval and Later Antiquities.*** **Stock: Lead-glazed pottery tiles,** ***500-1500 — Catalogues***

British Museum. *Department of Medieval and Later Antiquities*. Catalogue of medieval lead-glazed earthenware tiles in the Department of Medieval and Later Antiquities, British Museum / Elizabeth S. Eames. — London : Published for the Trustees of the British Museum by British Museum Publications, c1980. — 2v. : ill(some col.),1map ; 29cm
Bibliography: p766-781. — Includes index
ISBN 0-7141-1338-7 : £135.00 : CIP rev.
ISBN 0-7141-1339-5 (v.1) : Unpriced
ISBN 0-7141-1340-9 (v.2) : Unpriced B78-33916

738.6'0942 — English decorated tiles, ***ca 1300-ca 1550***

Eames, E. S.. Medieval tiles / E.S. Eames. — London : Published for the Trustees of the British Museum by British Museum Publications, 1968 (1976 [printing]). — x,34p,[20]p of plates : ill(some col.) ; 23cm
Bibliography: p32-34
ISBN 0-7141-1337-9 (cased) : £2.50
ISBN 0-7141-1326-3 (pbk) : Unpriced B82-09085

738.8 — LIGHTING FIXTURES, STOVES, FIGURINES, ETC

738.8 — Art objects: English pottery fairings, ***1837-1901 — Collectors' guides***

Anderson, Margaret, *1926-*. Victorian fairings / compiled & edited by Margaret Anderson. — Galashiels : Lyle, c1982. — 126p : ill ; 17cm. — (Antiques and their values)
Includes index
ISBN 0-86248-037-x : £2.50 B82-28673

738.8 — London. Westminster ***(London Borough).*** **Museums: Museum of Mankind. Exhibits: African terracottas,** ***to 1969 — Catalogues***

Fagg, William. The potter's art in Africa / William Fagg, John Picton. — 2nd ed. — London : Published for the Trustees of the British Museum by British Museum Publications, 1978. — 47p : ill ; 24cm
Exhibits selected from the African pottery held in the Museum of Mankind. — Previous ed.: 1970
ISBN 0-7141-1545-2 (pbk) : Unpriced B82-08866

738.8 — Northamptonshire. Northampton. Museums: Northampton Museum. Stock: English mugs, *to ca 1980* **—** *Illustrations*

Northampton Museum. Mugs in Northampton Museum / by Jo Draper. — [Northampton] ([Central Museum, Guildhall Rd., Northampton, NN1 1DP]) : Published for Northampton Museums and Art Gallery by Northampton Borough Council, 1977. — 33p : ill ; 21x30cm
Bibliography: p33
Unpriced (pbk) B82-09755

738.8 — Oxfordshire. Oxford. Museums: Ashmolean Museum. *Department of Antiquities.* **Stock: Ancient Greek terracottas —** *Catalogues*

Ashmolean Museum. Greek terracottas / by C.E. Vafopoulou-Richardson. — Oxford : The Museum, 1981. — ix,45p,[46]p of plates : ill ; 21cm. — (Ashmolean Museum publications. Archaeology, history & classical studies)
At head of title: University of Oxford, Ashmolean Museum
ISBN 0-900090-80-4 (pbk) : £3.65 B82-21440

738.8′2′0942 — English porcelain figurines, *1745-1795* **—** *Collectors′ guides*

Bradshaw, Peter. 18th century English porcelain figures 1745-1795 / Peter Bradshaw. — [Woodbridge] : Antique Collectors′ Club, c1981. — 327p : ill(some col.) ; 29cm
Ill on lining papers. — Bibliography: p319. — Includes index
ISBN 0-902028-83-9 : £25.00 B82-13939

739 — ART METALWORK

739 — Corkscrews, *to 1980* **—** *Collectors′ guides*

Watney, Bernard M.. Corkscrews : for collectors / Bernard M. Watney and Homer D. Babbidge. — London : Sotheby Parke Bernet, 1981. — 160p,[16]p of plates : ill(some col.) ; 26cm
Bibliography: p158. — Includes index
ISBN 0-85667-113-4 : £12.95 B82-08516

739′.0917′671074 — Islamic metalwork, *1100-1600* **—** *Catalogues*

Allan, James W.. Islamic metalwork : the Nuhad Es-Said Collection / James W. Allan. — [London] : Sotheby, 1982. — 128p : ill(some col.),1map ; 34cm
Bibliography: p125-128
ISBN 0-85667-164-9 : Unpriced B82-27671

739′.0955′074 — Iranian base metal metalwork, *700-1800* **—** *Catalogues*

Victoria and Albert Museum. Islamic metalwork from the Iranian world : 8-18th centuries / [written by] Asadullah Souren Melikian-Chirvani. — London : H.M.S.O., 1982. — 445p : ill(some col.),1map ; 29cm. — (Victoria and Albert Museum catalogue)
Based on the collection in the Victoria and Albert Museum. — Bibliography: p369-380. — Includes index
ISBN 0-11-290252-9 : £60.00 B82-39402

739.2 — WORK IN PRECIOUS METALS

739.2′02′78 — London goldware & silverware. Makers′ marks, 1697-1837 — *Lists*

Grimwade, Arthur G.. London goldsmiths, 1697-1837. — 2nd ed. — London : Faber, Nov.1982. — [735]p
Previous ed.: 1976
ISBN 0-571-18065-5 : CIP entry
Primary classification 739′.2′0922 B82-29074

739′.2′0922 — London. Goldsmiths & silversmiths, *1697-1837* **—** *Biographies*

Grimwade, Arthur G.. London goldsmiths, 1697-1837. — 2nd ed. — London : Faber, Nov.1982. — [735]p
Previous ed.: 1976
ISBN 0-571-18065-5 : CIP entry
Also classified at 739.2′02′78 B82-29074

739.2′094′074 — European goldware & silverware, *300-1700* **—** *Catalogues*

Schroder, Timothy. The Schroder collection : virtuoso goldsmiths′ work from the age of Humanism : an exhibition held at Goldsmiths′ Hall, Foster Lane, London, EC2 9th-26th October, 1979 / catalogue compiled by Timothy Schroder. — [London] ([Goldsmiths′ Hall, Foster Lane, EC2]) : [Worshipful Company of Goldsmiths], [1979?]. — [88]p : ill (some col.) ; 30cm
Bibliography: p87. — Ill on inside cover
Unpriced (pbk) B82-27925

739.2′2722 — Scotland. Grampian Region. Aberdeen. Goldsmiths, *1450-1850*

James, I. E.. The goldsmiths of Aberdeen / I.E. James. — Aberdeen ([85 North Deeside Rd., Bieldside, Aberdeen]) : Bieldside Books, c1981. — 156p : ill,facsims ; 26cm
Limited ed. of 500 copies. — Bibliography: p151. — Inlcudes index
Unpriced B82-22470

739.2′274′07403 — Germany. Museums. Exhibits: European goldware, *500-1500* **—** *Catalogues* **—** *German texts*

Braun, Joseph. Meisterwerke der deutschen Goldschmiedekunst der vorgotischen Zeit / Joseph Braun. — New York ; London : Garland, 1979. — 255p in various pagings : chiefly ill ; 26cm. — (A Dealers′ and collectors′ bookshelf. Metalwork)
Text in German. — Facsim of: 1st ed. Munich : Riehn & Reusch, 1922. — Two vols. bound in one
ISBN 0-8240-3354-x : Unpriced B82-18909

739.2′3 — Scotland. Strathclyde Region. Glasgow. Museums: Glasgow Art Gallery and Museum. Exhibits: Silver trophies of Lipton, *Sir* **Thomas —** *Catalogues*

Watt, Rosemary. Sir Thomas J. Lipton : Sir Thomas Lipton′s silver. — [Glasgow] : [Glasgow Museums and Art Galleries], c1981. — [8]p : ill ; 30cm
Catalogue prepared by Rosemary Watt
£0.25 (unbound) B82-12207

739.2′3′0278 — English silverware. Hallmarks, *to 1978*

Bly, John. Discovering halls marks on English silver / John Bly. — 5th ed. — Princes Risborough : Shire, 1981. — 64p : ill ; 18cm
Previous ed.: 1979
ISBN 0-85263-578-8 (pbk) : £1.25 B82-31009

739.2′37′032 — Silverware, *1650-1800* **—** *Collectors′ guides*

Silver 1650-1800 / compiled by Tony Curtis. — Galashiels : Lyle, c1981. — 126p : chiefly ill ; 17cm. — (Antiques and their values)
Includes index
ISBN 0-86248-016-7 : £2.50 B82-08186

739.2′37′034 — Silverware, *1800-1950* **—** *Collectors′ guides*

Silver 1800-1950 / compiled by Tony Curtis. — Galashiels : Lyle, c1981. — 126p : chiefly ill ; 17cm. — (Antiques and their values)
Includes index
ISBN 0-86248-005-1 : £2.50 B82-08187

739.2′3724 — England. Silversmithing. Jones, A. Edward — *Critical studies*

Wild, Glennys. A. Edward Jones metalcraftsman : Birmingham Museum and Art Gallery 16 February-23 March 1980 / [text by Glennys Wild]. — Birmingham : Publications Unit, City Museum and Art Gallery, [1980?]. — [30]p : ill,ports ; 20x21cm
ISBN 0-7093-0055-7 (pbk) : Unpriced B82-37022

739.2′3724 — English silverware. Durbin, Leslie — *Catalogues*

Durbin, Leslie. Leslie Durbin : fifty years of silversmithing : a retrospective exhibition 6th to 22nd July 1982. — London (Goldsmiths′ Hall, Foster La., EC2V 6BN) : [Worshipful Company of Goldsmiths], [1982]. — 37p : ill,1port ; 30cm
£2.00 (pbk) B82-37768

739.2′3737′074094 — Europe. Museums. Exhibits: Ancient Roman silver products: Esquiline treasure

Shelton, Kathleen J.. The Esquiline Treasure. — London : British Museum Publications, Apr.1981. — [192]p
ISBN 0-7141-1356-5 : £30.00 : CIP entry B81-02122

739.2′3742 — English silverware, *1400-1981* **—** *Collectors′ guides*

Banister, Judith. The Country life collector′s pocket book of silver / Judith Banister. — [Richmond upon Thames] : Country Life Books, 1982. — 288p : ill ; 16cm
Bibliography: p275-277. — Includes index
ISBN 0-600-38271-0 : £4.50 B82-23616

739.2′3742843′074042843 — North Yorkshire. York. Cathedrals: York Minster. Stock: York silverware, *1475-1858.* **Collections: William Lee Collection —** *Catalogues*

York silver 1475-1858 : a short history of York Silver, together with an illustrated catalogue of the William Lee Collection now on permanent loan in the Treasury, York Minster Undercroft. — Rev. ed. — [York] : The Dean & Chapter of York, 1981. — 24p,[16]p of plates ; 24cm
Previous ed.: 1972
ISBN 0-900657-59-6 (pbk) : £2.00 B82-15098

739.2′38 — Silver products — *Collectors′ guides*

Hughes, Eleanor. Silver for collectors / Eleanor Hughes ; illustrated by Peter Henville. — London : Hamlyn, 1974 (1982 [printing]). — 159p : col.ill,coats of arms ; 19cm
Bibliography: p156. — Includes index
ISBN 0-600-33790-1 (cased) : £2.99
ISBN 0-600-38060-2 (pbk) : £1.75 B82-37048

739.2′38 — Silverware — *Buyers′ guides*

Waldron, Peter. The price guide to antique silver. — 2nd ed. — Woodbridge : Antique Collectors′ Club, Mar. 1982. — [325]p
Previous ed.: 1969
ISBN 0-907462-08-1 : CIP entry B82-03390

739.27 — JEWELLERY

739.27 — Jewellery. Making — *Manuals*

Wiener, Louis. Handmade jewelry : a manual of techniques / Louis Wiener. — 3rd ed. — New York ; London : Van Nostrand Reinhold, 1981. — 192p : ill ; 29cm
Previous ed.: 1960. — Bibliography: p185. — Includes index
ISBN 0-442-29308-9 : £16.10 B82-21856

739.27 — Jewellery. Making. Projects

Pelissier, Jaime. The jeweler′s craft : mastering traditional techniques / Jaime Pelissier ; [translated by Serena Pelinier]. — New York ; London : Van Nostrand Reinhold, c1981. — 112p : ill ; 24cm
Translated from the Spanish. — Bibliography: p109. — Includes index
ISBN 0-442-24336-7 : £11.00 B82-21852

739.27′03′21 — Jewellery — *Encyclopaedias*

Newman, Harold, *1899-*. An illustrated dictionary of jewelry : 2,530 entries, including definitions of jewels, gemstones, materials, processes, and styles and entries on principal designers and makers, from antiquity to the present day / Harold Newman. — London : Thames and Hudson, c1981. — 334p,xvip of plates : ill (some col.) ; 26cm
ISBN 0-500-23309-8 : £12.95 B82-05698

739.27′074′0212 — London *(City).* **Gold & silver industries & trades. Guilds: Worshipful Company of Goldsmiths. Exhibits: Jewellery —** *Catalogues*

Loot VII : Goldsmith′s Hall, London, November 2nd-21st, 1981 / [exhibition organized by Brian Beaumont-Nesbitt with the assistance of Isobel Solon and Anne Williams]. — [London] ([Foster La., EC2V 6BN]) : [Worshipful Company of Goldsmiths], c1981. — 55p : ill,1plan ; 21cm
Text on inside cover
£0.70 (pbk) B82-08844

739.27′075 — Jewellery — *Collectors′ guides*

Blakemore, Kenneth, *1918-*. Buying jewellery : a practical guide / Kenneth Blakemore. — London : Barker, c1982. — 158p : ill ; 23cm
Bibliography: p153. — Includes index
ISBN 0-213-16821-9 : £5.95 B82-13969

739.27′09 — Jewellery, *B.C.3000-A.D.1950 — Collectors′ guides*

Poynder, Michael. The price guide to jewellery 3000B.C.-1950A.D. / by Michael Poynder. — [Woodbridge] : Antique Collectors′ Club, c1976 (1981 [printing]). — 385p : ill(some col.) ; 29cm
Bibliography: p385
ISBN 0-902028-50-2 : £19.50 B82-16028

739.27′09 — Jewellery, *to ca 1900 — Illustrations*

Jewelry : a pictorial archive of woodcuts and engravings : over 1000 copyright-free illustrations for artists and designers / edited by Harold H. Hart. — New York : Dover Publications ; London : Constable, 1981, c1978. — 144p : chiefly ill ; 32cm
Facsim of: Rev. ed. / prepared by Robert Sietsema, with text by Nancy Goldberg. New York : Hart, 1978. — Bibliography: p142. — Includes index
ISBN 0-486-24161-0 (pbk) : £3.75 B82-13724

739.27′09′02 — Jewellery, *ca 1100-1450*

Hinton, David A.. Medieval jewellery : from the eleventh to the fifteenth century / David A. Hinton. — Princes Risborough : Shire, 1982. — 48p : ill ; 21cm. — (Shire archaeology)
Bibliography: p24. — Includes index
ISBN 0-85263-576-1 (pbk) : £1.95 B82-31003

739.27′0938′8 — London. Camden *(London Borough).* **Museums: British Museum. Stock: Mycenaean gold jewellery. Collections: Aegina Treasure**

Higgins, R. A.. The Aegina Treasure : an archaeological mystery / Reynold Higgins. — London : British Museum Publications, c1979. — 71p : ill,maps,ports ; 24cm. — (A Colonnade book)
Includes index
ISBN 0-7141-8006-8 (pbk) : Unpriced B82-12225

739.27′2 — Metal jewellery, *500-600*

Aspects of production and style in Dark Age metalwork : selected papers given to the British Museum seminar on jewellery AD500-600 / edited by L. Webster. — London : British Museum, 1982. — vi,50p : ill ; 30cm. — (Occasional paper / British Museum, ISSN 0142-4815 ; no.34)
Bibliography: p49-50
ISBN 0-86159-034-1 (pbk) : Unpriced B82-25625

739.27′8 — Celtic animal penannular brooches

Kilbride-Jones, H. E.. Zoomorphic penannular brooches / by H.E. Kilbride-Jones. — [London] : Society of Antiquaries of London, 1980. — viii,153p : ill,maps ; 28cm
Includes index
ISBN 0-500-99030-1 : £20.00 B82-17993

739.3 — CLOCKS AND WATCHES

739′.37′03 — Clocks & watches, *1650-1930 — Collectors′ guides*

Clocks & watches / compiled by Tony Curtis. — Galashiels : Lyle, c1981. — 126p : chiefly ill ; 17cm. — (Antiques and their values)
Includes index
ISBN 0-86248-010-8 : £2.50 B82-08194

739′.3773 — American clocks *— Collectors′ guides*

Tyler, E. J.. American clocks for the collector / by E.J. Tyler. — London : Hale, 1981. — xii,209p,[12]p of plates : ill(some col.),1map ; 24cm
Includes index
ISBN 0-7091-8870-6 : £12.50 B82-04184

739.4 — IRONWORK

739′.47′034 — Buildings. Decorative ironwork. Art nouveau style *— Illustrations*

Art nouveau decorative ironwork : 137 photographic illustrations / selected by Theodore Menten. — New York : Dover ; London : Constable, 1981. — 119p : of ill ; 29cm
Selection of photographs from Ferronnerie de style moderne (1st and 2nd series) and Ferronnerie moderne & de style modernisé (3rd series)
ISBN 0-486-23986-1 (pbk) : £4.50 B82-13561

739.5 — WORK IN COPPER, BRASS, TIN, ETC

739′.511′094 — European copperware, *to ca 1900 — Collectors′ gudies*

Curtis, Tony, *1939-.* Copper & brass / compiled by Tony Curtis. — Galashiels : Lyle, c1982. — 126p : ill ; 16cm. — (Antiques and their values)
Includes index
ISBN 0-86248-020-5 : £2.50
Also classified at 739′.52′094 B82-29161

739′.512′09 — Bronzeware, *to ca 1950 — Collectors′ guides*

Bronzes / compiled by Tony Curtis. — Galashiels : Lyle, c1981. — 126p : chiefly ill ; 17cm. — (Antiques and their values)
Includes index
ISBN 0-86248-012-4 : £2.50 B82-08192

739′.52′094 — European brassware, *ca 1100-1920*

Turner, Eric. An introduction to brass / Eric Turner. — London : H.M.S.O., 1982. — 48p : col.ill ; 26cm
At head of cover title: Victoria & Albert Museum. — Bibliography: p48
ISBN 0-11-290376-2 : £3.50 B82-14857

739′.52′094 — European brassware, *to ca 1900 — Collectors′ guides*

Curtis, Tony, *1939-.* Copper & brass / compiled by Tony Curtis. — Galashiels : Lyle, c1982. — 126p : ill ; 16cm. — (Antiques and their values)
Includes index
ISBN 0-86248-020-5 : £2.50
Primary classification 739′.511′094 B82-29161

739′.522′094258 — Hertfordshire. Monumental brasses *— Lists*

Rensten, Mary. Hertfordshire brasses : a guide to the figure brasses in the churches of Hertfordshire / by Mary Rensten. — Stevenage (c/o East Divisional Library Headquarters, 38 High St, Stevenage Old Town, Herts.) : Hertfordshire Publications, 1982. — vii,103p : ill,1map ; 21cm pbk
Bibliography: p95-97. — Includes index
ISBN 0-901354-20-1 : Unpriced : CIP rev. B82-14398

739′.53 — Sheffield Britannia metalware, *to 1920*

Bambery, Anneke. Sheffield Britannia metal / [written by Anneke Bambery]. — Sheffield : Sheffield City Museums, c1981. — [20]p : ill ; 12cm
Cover title. — Bibliography: on inside cover
ISBN 0-900660-74-0 (pbk) : Unpriced B82-30869

739′.533′094 — European pewterware, *to ca 1850 — Collectors′ guides*

Curtis, Tony, *1939-.* Pewter / compiled by Tony Curtis. — Galashiels : Lyle, c1982. — 125p : ill ; 17cm. — (Antiques and their values)
Includes index
ISBN 0-86248-023-x : £2.50 B82-28676

739.7 — ARMS AND ARMOUR

739.7′094′074 — European weapons & armour, *1350-1800 — Catalogues*

Norman, A. V. B.. Treasures from the Tower of London / arms and armour ; A.V.B. Norman and G.M. Wilson. — London : Arms and Armour, 1982. — 131p : ill(some col.) ; 28cm
Bibliography: p121-123
ISBN 0-85368-541-x : £11.95 B82-36222

739.7′2 — Edged weapons *— Collectors′ guides*

Southwick, Leslie. The price guide to antique edged weapons. — Woodbridge : Antique Collectors′ Club, Sept.1981. — 1v.
ISBN 0-902028-94-4 : CIP entry B81-25657

739.7′22′0952074094945 — Switzerland. Geneva. Art galleries: Collections Baur. Stock: Japanese swords. Fittings *— Catalogues*

Collections Baur. The Baur collection, Geneva. Japanese sword-fittings and associated metalwork / by B.W. Robinson. — Genève : Collections Baur ; London : [Distributed by] Kegan Paul, Trench, Trubner, c1980. — 444p : ill(some col.) ; 30cm
English text, French and English prefaces. — Includes index
ISBN 2-88031-003-2 : £85.00 B82-21528

741 — DRAWINGS

741 — Colouring books *— Texts*

Striker, Susan. The third anti-colouring book / Susan Striker ; illustrated by Susan Striker and Edward Kimmel with Brent Brolin, Evelyn Osborne, Linda Gen. — London : Scholastic, 1981, c1980. — [8],[46]leaves of plates(some col.) : ill ; 28cm. — (Hippo books)
Originally published: New York : Holt, Rinehart & Winston, 1980
ISBN 0-590-70096-0 (pbk) : £1.65 B82-03223

741 — Colouring books *— Texts — For pre-school children*

Cowell, Norma C.. Read, write and colour : with Voirrey and Juan in the Isle of Man / [written and compiled by Norma C. Cowell] ; [illustrated by Mavis Kelly]. — Onchan : Shearwater
Cover title
Book 1: For infants. — 1979. — 20p : chiefly ill ; 21cm
ISBN 0-904980-36-7 (pbk) : £0.75
Primary classification 428.6 B82-02241

741 — Picture books *— Texts*

Corbett, Grahame. What number now? / Grahame Corbett. — London : Methuen Children′s Books, c1982. — [16]p : all col.ill ; 15cm
ISBN 0-416-06200-8 (unbound) : Unpriced B82-40706

Corbett, Grahame. Who am I? / Grahame Corbett. — London : Methuen Children′s Books, c1982. — [16]p : all col.ill ; 15cm
ISBN 0-416-06170-2 (unbound) : Unpriced B82-40708

Corbett, Grahame. Who are you? / Grahame Corbett. — London : Methuen Children′s Books, c1982. — [16]p : all col.ill ; 15cm
ISBN 0-416-06210-5 (unbound) : Unpriced B82-40707

Corbett, Grahame. Who is hiding / Grahame Corbett. — London : Methuen Children′s Books, c1982. — [16]p : all col.ill ; 15cm
ISBN 0-416-06190-7 (unbound) : Unpriced B82-40705

Corbett, Grahame. Who is next? / Grahame Corbett. — London : Methuen Children′s Books, c1982. — [16]p : all col.ill ; 15cm
ISBN 0-416-06180-x (unbound) : Unpriced B82-40709

Goodall, John S.. Paddy finds a job / John S. Goodall. — London : Macmillan Children′s, 1981. — [16]p : all col.ill ; 15x19cm. — (A Pop-up story)
ISBN 0-333-31578-2 : £2.95 B82-05999

Goodall, John S.. Shrewbettina goes to work / John S. Goodall. — London : Macmillan Children′s, 1981. — [14]p : all col.ill ; 15x19cm. — (A Pop-up story)
ISBN 0-333-31579-0 : £2.95 B82-05998

Spanner, Helmut. Mouse′s train ride / illustrations Helmut Spanner. — London : Methuen Children′s, 1982. — 1folded sheet ([12]p) : all col.ill ; 13cm
ISBN 0-416-25110-2 : Unpriced B82-34231

Spanner, Helmut. Where is mouse? / illustrations Helmut Spanner. — London : Methuen Children′s, 1982. — 1folded sheet([12]p) : all col.ill ; 13cm
ISBN 0-416-25100-5 : Unpriced B82-34230

741'.074'02574 — Oxfordshire. Oxford. Museums : Ashmolean Museum. Exhibits : Drawings — *Catalogues*

Ashmolean Museum. Catalogue of the collection of drawings in the Ashmolean Museum. — Oxford : Clarendon Press, May 1982
Vol.4: The earlier British drawings. — [672]p
ISBN 0-19-817375-x : £50.00 : CIP entry
B82-07512

741'.074'02574 — Oxfordshire. Oxford. Museums: Ashmolean Museum. Stock: Drawings — *Catalogues*

Ashmolean Museum. Catalogue of the collection of drawings in the Ashmolean Museum. — Oxford : Clarendon
Vol.3: Italian schools : supplement : by Hugh Macandrew. — 1980. — xvi,368p,[1],Cp of plates : ill,1port ; 23cm
Vol.3 has title: Catalogue of the collection of drawings. — Bibliography: pxi-xii. — Includes index
ISBN 0-19-817347-4 : £26.50 : CIP rev.
B79-30234

741'.088054 — Children's drawings — *Critical studies*

Six children draw / edited by Sheila Paine. — London : Academic Press, c1981. — 99p : ill ; 21cm
Published to accompany an exhibition of children's drawings presented by the University of London Institute of Education Arts Centre, in association with Suffolk Education Committee
ISBN 0-12-543950-4 (pbk) : £3.85 B82-13054

741'.092'4 — English cartoons. Moyse, Arthur — *Biographies*

Moyse, Arthur. Fragments of notes for an autobiography. — Telford (84 Wolverley Court, Woodside, Telford, Shropshire) : Woody Books, Apr.1982. — [32]p
ISBN 0-907751-10-5 (pbk) : £1.25 : CIP entry
B82-12891

741'.092'4 — English drawings. Farington, Joseph — *Correspondence, diaries, etc.*

Farington, Joseph. The diary of Joseph Farington / edited by Kenneth Garlick and Angus Macintyre. — New Haven ; London : Yale University Press for the Paul Mellon Centre for Studies in British Art. — (Studies in British art)
Vol.7: January 1805-June 1806 ; Vol.8 : July 1806-December 1807 / edited by Kathryn Cave. — 1982. — 2v.(p.2486-3185) : ill ; 23cm
ISBN 0-300-02768-0 : £35.00 : CIP rev.
B82-07099

Farington, Joseph. The diary of Joseph Farington. — London : Yale University Press. — (Studies in British art)
Vol.9 ; Vol.10 : January 1808-December 1810. — Sept.1982. — 2v.([664]p)
ISBN 0-300-02859-8 : £45.00 : CIP entry
B82-29126

741'.092'4 — English drawings. Turner, J. M. W.. Special subjects: Edinburgh. Visits by George IV, *King of Great Britain, 1822 — Critical studies*

Finley, Gerald. Turner and George the Fourth in Edinburgh 1822 / Gerald Finley. — London : Tate Gallery in association with Edinburgh University Press, 1981. — viii,86,[172]p : ill,ports ; 16x26cm
Accompanies an exhibition held at the Tate Gallery 3 Nov.-13 Dec. 1981 and at the National Gallery of Scotland, Edinburgh, 3-31 Jan. 1982. — Bibliography: p71-72. — Includes index
ISBN 0-85224-432-0 : £15.00 B82-16149

741'.092'4 — English illustrations. Blake, William, *1757-1827.* **Illustrations for Grave,** *The* **by Blair, Robert,** *1699-1746 — Critical studies*

Essick, Robert N.. Robert Blair's The grave illustrated by William Blake : a study with facsimile / by Robert N. Essick and Morton D. Paley. — London : Scolar, 1982. — x,243p : ill ; 36cm
Bibliography: p191-200. — Includes index
ISBN 0-85967-529-7 : £45.00 : CIP rev.
B81-04285

741'.092'4 — English illustrations. Pout, Dudley — *Biographies*

Pout, Dudley. The life and art of one man of Kent / Dudley Pout. — Rainham : Meresborough, c1982. — 48p : ill,ports ; 32cm
Cover title. — Text on inside cover
ISBN 0-905270-52-5 (pbk) : £2.95 B82-36927

741'.0945 — Italian drawings, *1400-1500 — Critical studies*

Ames-Lewis, Francis. Drawing in early Renaissance Italy / Francis Ames-Lewis. — New Haven ; London : Yale University Press, 1981. — xi,196p : ill(some col.) ; 27cm
Bibliography: p185-188. — Includes index
ISBN 0-300-02551-3 : Unpriced : CIP rev.
B81-30243

741.2 — DRAWINGS. MATERIALS, EQUIPMENT, TECHNIQUES

741.2 — Drawing — *Manuals*

Ashwin, Clive. Encyclopaedia of drawing. — London : Batsford, Sept.1982. — [288]p
ISBN 0-7134-0133-8 : £10.00 : CIP entry
B82-20043

741.2 — Drawings. Techniques — *Comparative studies*

Malins, Frederick. Drawing ideas of the masters : artists' techniques compared abd contrasted / Frederick Malins. — Oxford : Phaidon, 1981. — 128p : ill(some col.),ports(some col.) ; 29cm
Bibliography: p126. — Includes index
ISBN 0-7148-2123-3 : £9.95 : CIP rev.
B81-30480

741.2 — Drawings. Techniques — *For children*

Murfy, Albert. Anyone can draw / Albert Murfy & Sara Silcock ; introduced by Tony Hart. — London : Fontana Paperbacks, 1981. — 96p : ill ; 20cm. — (An Armada original)
ISBN 0-00-691743-7 (pbk) : £0.90 B82-08304

741.2 — Drawings. Techniques — *Manuals*

Andrewes, Elizabeth. A manual for drawing & painting / Elizabeth Andrewes. — Sevenoaks : Hodder and Stoughton, 1978 (1979 [printing]). — 208p : ill(some col.) ; 19cm. — (Teach yourself books)
Bibliography: p208. — Includes index
ISBN 0-340-22243-3 (pbk) : £2.95
Also classified at 751.4 B82-32817

Art school : an instructional guide based on the teaching of leading art colleges / consultant editor Colin Saxton. — London : Macmillan, 1981. — 224p : ill,ports ; 26cm
Includes index
ISBN 0-333-32306-8 : £9.95
Also classified at 751.4 B82-06957

Blake, Wendon. The drawing book / by Wendon Blake ; drawings by Ferdinand Petrie, John Laun and Uldis Klavins. — New York : Watson-Guptill ; London : Pitman House, 1980. — 336p : ill ; 32cm
ISBN 0-273-01611-3 : Unpriced B82-01389

Camp, Jeffery. Draw : how to master the art / Jeffery Camp ; foreword by David Hockney. — London : Deutsch, 1981. — 255p : ill(some col.) ; 29cm
Includes index
ISBN 0-233-97387-7 (corrected) : £10.95
B82-01525

Jaxtheimer, Bodo W.. How to paint and draw / Bodo W. Jaxtheimer ; with 300 illustrations in colour and 150 in black-and-white. — London : Thames and Hudson, c1962 (1982 [printing]). — 408p : ill(some col.),ports(some col.) ; 22cm
Translation of: Knaurs Mal-und Zeichenbuch. — Includes index
ISBN 0-500-27252-2 (pbk) : £3.50
Primary classification 751.4 B82-20415

Mendelowitz, Daniel M.. Mendelowitz's guide to drawing. — 3rd ed. / revised by Duane A. Wakenham. — New York ; London : Holt, Rinehart and Winston, c1982. — viii,288p : ill (some col.) ; 28cm
Previous ed.: published as A guide to drawing. 1976. — Includes index
ISBN 0-03-057294-0 (pbk) : £16.95
B82-28664

Raynes, John. Step-by-step guide to drawing / John Raynes. — London : Hamlyn, c1982. — 64p : ill,1port ; 26cm
Includes index
ISBN 0-600-34270-0 : £2.99 B82-32755

Smith, Stan, *1929-*. Drawing & sketching / Stan Smith. — London : Ebury, 1982. — 176p : ill (some col.) ; 25cm. — (The Artist's handbook series) (A Quarto book)
Includes index
ISBN 0-85223-217-9 : £8.95 B82-32934

Thiel, Philip. Freehand drawing / Philip Thiel. — New York ; London : Van Nostrand Reinhold, 1981, c1965. — 127p : ill ; 28cm
Originally published: Seattle : University of Washington Press, 1965
ISBN 0-442-28296-6 (pbk) : £7.60 B82-26168

741.2'4 — Colour pencil drawings. Techniques — *Manuals*

Doyle, Michael E.. Color drawing : a marker/colored-pencil approach for architects, landscape architects, interior and graphic designers and artists / Michael E. Doyle. — New York ; London : Van Nostrand Reinhold, [1979]. — 320p : ill(some col.),col.plans ; 23x28cm
Bibliography: p309-311. — Includes index
ISBN 0-442-22184-3 : £29.75 B82-00746

741.2'6 — Drawings using felt-tip pens. Techniques — *Manuals*

Wang, Thomas C.. Sketching with markers / Thomas C. Wang. — New York ; London : Van Nostrand Reinhold, c1981. — 104p : ill (some col.) ; 22x28cm
Bibliography: p102. — Includes index
ISBN 0-442-26340-6 (cased) : £14.40
ISBN 0-442-26341-4 (pbk) : £8.45 B82-09814

741.5 — CARTOONS, CARICATURES

741.5 — Chalk cartoons. Drawing — *Manuals*

Findler, Gerry. How to draw chalk cartoons / Gerry Findler. — [Bideford] ([64 High St., Bideford, Devon]) : Supreme Magic, c1982. — 43p : ill ; 18cm
Unpriced (pbk) B82-29912

741.5 — Humorous cartoons. Drawing — *Manuals*

Caket, Colin. Drawing cartoons / Colin Caket. — Poole, Blandford, 1982. — 96p : ill ; 25cm
ISBN 0-7137-1181-7 (pbk) : £2.95 : CIP rev.
B82-03119

Maddocks, Peter. So you want to be a cartoonist? / written & illustrated by Peter Maddocks. — London : Elm Tree, 1982. — 96p : ill ; 25cm
ISBN 0-241-10734-2 : £4.95 : CIP rev.
B82-09975

741.5 — Humorous cartoons. Drawing. Techniques — *Manuals*

ffolkes, Michael. Draw cartoons / ffolkes. — London : Adam & Charles Black, 1982. — 48p : ill ; 28cm
ISBN 0-7136-2197-4 (pbk) : £1.75 B82-17829

741.5'09 — Caricatures, *to 1980 — Critical studies*

Lucie-Smith, Edward. The art of caricature / Edward Lucie-Smith. — London : Orbis, 1981. — 128p : ill ; 29cm
Bibliography: p126. — Includes index
ISBN 0-85613-070-2 : £8.95
ISBN 0-85613-393-0 (pbk) : £5.95 B82-05837

741.5'9 — Satirical cartoons — *Collections*

Man bites man : two decades of drawings and cartoons by 22 comic and satiric artists 1960 to 1980 / R.O. Blechman ... [et al.] ; edited by Steven Heller ; foreword by Tom Wolfe ; design assistance by Tony Ho. — London : Hutchinson, 1981. — 224p : ill(some col.) ; 31cm
Bibliography: p222-224
ISBN 0-09-145130-2 (pbk) : £6.95 : CIP rev.
B81-20490

741.5'941 — British comics — *Texts*
Blockbuster. — No.1 (June 1981)-. — London (205 Kentish Town Rd, NW5) : Marvel Comics, 1981-. — v. : chiefly ill ; 28cm
Monthly. — Description based on: No.5 (Oct. 1981)
ISSN 0262-2424 = Blockbuster : £0.45 per issue B82-11141

[Buttons *(London : 1981)*]. Buttons : for play school children. — No.1 (3rd to 9th Oct. 1981)-. — [London] : [Polystyle Publications], 1981-. — v. : ill(some col.) ; 30cm
Weekly
ISSN 0262-5326 = Buttons (London. 1981) : £0.20 per issue B82-25482

[Eagle *(London : 1982)*]. Eagle. — No.1 (27th Mar. 1982)-. — London : IPC Magazines, 1982-. — v. : mainly ill(some col.),ports ; 30cm
Weekly
£0.20 per issue B82-25485

Play box : the lots to do weekly. — No.1 (3rd Apr. 1982)-. — London : IPC Magazines, 1982-. — v. : ill(some col.) ; 30cm
£0.20 per issue B82-25487

Walt Disney Productions. The black hole / Walt Disney Productions. — London : IPC Magazines Ltd, c1980. — [44]p : ill(some col.),ports(some col.) ; 28cm
£0.65 (pbk) B82-39244

741.5'9416 — English humorous cartoons. Special subjects: Northern Ireland — *Collections from individual artists*
Friers, Rowel. On the borderline with Rowel Friers. — Belfast : Blackstaff Press, Nov.1982. — [88]p
ISBN 0-85640-266-4 (pbk) : £2.95 : CIP entry B82-31310

741.5'942 — English cartoons. Bateman, H. M. — *Biographies*
Anderson, Anthony. H.M. Bateman : the story of a cartoonist. — Exeter : Webb & Bower, Oct.1982. — [224]p
ISBN 0-906671-57-4 : £9.95 : CIP entry B82-24597

741.5'942 — English cartoons: Cartoons for 'Vanity fair' — *Critical studies*
Matthews, Roy T.. In Vanity fair. — London : Scolar Press, Sept.1981. — [300]p
ISBN 0-85967-597-1 : £20.00 : CIP entry B81-22545

741.5'942 — English comics — *Texts*
The **Super** heroes annual. — 1982-. — London (70 Old Compton St., W1V 5PA) : London Editions, 1981-. — v. : chiefly ill ; 28cm
ISSN 0262-3501 = Super heroes annual : £1.95 B82-02380

Superman annual. — 1979-. — London (70 Old Compton St., W1V 5PA) : London Editions, 1978-. — v. : chiefly ill ; 28cm
Description based on: 1982
ISSN 0262-351x = Superman annual : £2.50 B82-02379

Whacko : all British comix. — Ballachulish (McReady & Yates Bldgs, Ballachulish, Invernesshire, Scotland) : McReady & Yates Fund for Radical Artists, c1982. — 23p : ill ; 30cm
Cover title
£0.45 (pbk) B82-28183

Wonder Woman annual. — 1980-1982. — London (70 Old Compton St., W1V 5PA) : London Editions, 1979-1981. — 3v. : chiefly ill ; 28cm
Only three issues published. — Description based on: 1982
£2.50 B82-02382

741.5'942 — English comics — *Texts — For children*
Anderson, Gerry. Gerry Anderson's thunderbirds special. — London : Polystyle, c1982. — [48]p : ill(some col.) ; 29cm
£0.50 (unbound) B82-33279

Bugs Bunny : a TV comic holiday special. — London : Polystyle, 1982. — [48]p : ill(some col.) ; 29cm
£0.50 (unbound) B82-36102

[Dreamer *(London)*]. Dreamer. — No.1 (19th Sept. 1981)-May 1982. — London : IPC Magazines, 1981-1982. — ?v. : chiefly ill(some col.),ports(some col.) ; 30cm
Weekly. — Merged with: Girl (London : 1981), to become: Girl & dreamer
ISSN 0262-1185 = Dreamer (London) : £0.20 per issue B82-07648

Jack and Jill and Teddy Bear's playtime. — 31st Oct. 1981-. — London : IPC Magazines, 1981-. — v. : chiefly ill(chiefly col.) ; 30cm
Weekly. — Merger of: Teddy bear's playtime; and, Jack and Jill (London : 1954)
ISSN 0262-3528 = Jack and Jill and Teddy Bear's playtime : £0.18 per issue B82-36735

Pink Panther. — London : Polystyle, c1982. — [48]p : chiefly ill(some col.) ; 29cm. — (A TV Comic holiday special)
£0.50 (unbound) B82-35452

A **Pippin** Doctor Snuggles holiday special. — London : Polystyle, c1982. — [48]p : ill(some col.) ; 30cm
£0.50 (unbound) B82-33278

Popeye. — London : Polystyle, c1982. — [48]p : chiefly ill(some col.) ; 29cm. — (A TV Comic holiday special)
£0.50 (unbound) B82-35450

Tom and Jerry. — London : Polystyle, c1982. — [48]p : chiefly ill(some col.) ; 29cm. — (A TV Comic holiday special)
£0.50 (unbound) B82-35451

Victor and Scoop. — No.1078 (Oct. 17th 1981)-. — London : D.C. Thomson, 1981-. — v. : chiefly ill(some col.),ports ; 31cm
Weekly. — Merger of: Victor ; and, Scoop (London : 1978)
ISSN 0262-2823 = Victor and Scoop : £0.12 per issue B82-07647

741.5'942 — English humorous cartoons, *1841-1901 — Collections*
Great drawings and illustrations from Punch 1841-1901 : 192 works by Leech, Keene, du Maurier, May and 21 others / edited by Stanley Appelbaum & Richard Kelly. — New York : Dover Publications ; London : Constable, 1981. — xix,133p : all ill ; 31cm
ISBN 0-486-24110-6 (pbk) : £4.50 B82-13729

741.5'942 — English humorous cartoons — *Collections*
Laughter : Daily Mirror cartoons. — London : Mirror, 1982. — [64]p : ill ; 24cm
ISBN 0-85939-308-9 (pbk) : £0.50 B82-29320

741.5'942 — English humorous cartoons — *Collections from individual artists*
Baxter, Glen. Atlas. — London : Cape, Sept.1982. — [96]p
ISBN 0-224-02941-x : £5.50 : CIP entry B82-25156

Baxter, Glen. The impending gleam / Glen Baxter. — London : Cape, 1981. — [96]p : chiefly ill ; 26cm
ISBN 0-224-01992-9 : £4.95 : CIP rev. B81-28075

Calman, Mel. Help! and other ruminations / Mel Calman. — London : Methuen, 1982. — [128]p : ill ; 21cm
ISBN 0-413-50690-8 (pbk) : £2.50 B82-39200

Calman, Mel. How about a little quarrel before bed? : and other diversions / Mel Calman. — London : Eyre Methuen, 1981. — [128]p : chiefly ill ; 21cm
ISBN 0-413-48830-6 (pbk) : £2.50 B82-31573

ffolkes, Michael. Ruder, if you please. — London : Allen & Unwin, Nov.1982. — [96]p
ISBN 0-04-827070-9 (pbk) : £1.50 : CIP entry B82-27825

Laughter. — London : Mirror Books, 1982. — [64]p : chiefly ill ; 24cm
ISBN 0-85939-322-4 (pbk) : £0.50 B82-41011

Mahood, Kenneth. The secret sketchbook of a Bloomsbury lady. — London : Bodley Head, Sept.1982. — [64]p
ISBN 0-370-30475-6 (pbk) : £3.95 : CIP entry B82-19206

Morrow, Skip. The official I hate cats book / by Skip Morrow. — London : Heinemann, 1981. — [64]p : all ill ; 21x13cm
ISBN 0-434-47956-x (pbk) : £1.50 B82-03661

Robinson, W. Heath. Absurdities / W. Heath Robinson. — London : Duckworth, 1975 (1981 [printing]). — 95p : all ill ; 29cm
ISBN 0-7156-1583-1 (pbk) : Unpriced
ISBN 0-7156-0920-3 B82-01625

Roger. It's kidstuff / by Roger. — London : ITV Books, 1981. — [94]p : chiefly ill ; 18cm
ISBN 0-09-927200-8 (pbk) : £1.00 B82-03666

Roger. Kidstuff with Willie / by Roger. — London : ITV Books, 1982. — [37]p : col.ill ; 22cm
ISBN 0-900727-90-x : £2.50 B82-38964

Smythe, Reg. Laugh at life with Andy Capp / by Reg Smythe. — London : Mirror Books, 1982. — [64]p : chiefly ill ; 29cm. — (Andy Capp ; no.46)
£0.65 (pbk) B82-27077

Thelwell. Thelwell's gymkhana. — London : Magnum, 1981, c1979. — 96p : chiefly ill ; 20cm
Originally published: London : Eyre Methuen, 1979
ISBN 0-417-01130-x (pbk) : £1.10 B82-15542

Tolley, Cheree. Straight from the horse's mouth : a hard day's work / narrated by Twinks ; Cheree Tolley. — Braunton : Merlin, 1982. — [21]p : ill ; 15cm
ISBN 0-86303-016-5 (pbk) : £0.60 B82-26583

Waite, Keith. The worlds of Waite : Cartoons from Daily mirror and Sunday mirror. — London : Mirror, 1981. — 96p : chiefly ill ; 20cm
ISBN 0-85939-277-5 (pbk) : £1.00 B82-01897

Youens, Paula. Lone thoughts from a broad : cartoons / Paula Youens. — London : Women's Press, 1981. — 76p : ill ; 21cm
ISBN 0-7043-3881-5 (pbk) : £2.50 : CIP rev. B81-32092

741.5'942 — English humorous cartoons — *Collections from individual artists — For children*
Robinson, W. Heath. Bill the minder. — London : Hodder & Stoughton Children's Books, Apr.1982. — [256]p
ISBN 0-340-27732-7 : £12.95 : CIP entry
ISBN 0-340-27965-6 (limited ed.) : £30.00 B82-03818

741.5'942 — English humorous cartoons. Special subjects: Feminism — *Collections*
Sourcream 2 / Cathy Porter ... [et al.]. — London : Sheba Feminist, 1981. — 95p : chiefly ill ; 15x23cm
ISBN 0-907179-10-x (pbk) : £1.75 B82-10308

741.5'942 — English humorous cartoons. Special subjects: Livestock: Horses. Riding — *Collections from individual artists*
Thelwell. Thelwell's horse sense. — London : Methuen, 1980. — [32]p : chiefly col.ill ; 23cm
These illustrations originally published in Thelwell's riding frieze. London : Methuen's Children's Books, 1977
ISBN 0-416-88050-9 : £2.95 B82-22725

741.5'942 — English humorous cartoons. Special subjects: Livestock: Horses. Riding — *Collections from individual artists*

continuation

Thelwell. Thelwell's pony cavalcade. — London : Eyre Methuen, 1981. — 350p : chiefly ill ; 22cm
Contents: Angels on horseback. Originally published: London : Methuen, 1957 — A leg at each corner. Originally published: London : Methuen, 1962 — Riding academy. Originally published: London : Methuen, 1965
ISBN 0-413-49150-1 : £6.95 B82-15591

741.5'942 — English humorous cartoons. Special subjects: Love — *Collections from individual artists*

Heath, Michael. Love all. — London : Blond & Briggs, Sept.1982. — [96]p
ISBN 0-85634-133-9 (pbk) : £1.95 : CIP entry B82-21989

741.5'942 — English humorous cartoons. Special subjects: Pets: Cats — *Collections from individual artists*

Bond, Simon. A hundred and one more uses of a dead cat / Simon Bond. — London : Methuen, 1982. — [101]p : all ill ; 14x18cm
ISBN 0-413-51470-6 (cased) : Unpriced
ISBN 0-413-50900-1 (pbk) : £2.50 B82-34808

Grant, Don. Kit bag / Don Grant. — London : Arthur Barker, c1982. — [64]p : chiefly ill ; 22cm
ISBN 0-213-16834-0 : £3.50 B82-38605

741.5'942 — English humorous cartoons. Special subjects: Politics — *Collections from individual artists*

Evans, Phil. The joke works : the political cartoons of Phil Evans / by Phil Evans and Steve Irons ; with a foreword by Dave Widgery. — London : Socialist Worker, c1981. — 109p : ill ; 30cm
Bibliography: p109
ISBN 0-905998-27-8 (pbk) : £2.95 B82-26852

741.5'942 — English humorous cartoons. Special subjects: Sailing — *Collections from individual artists*

Peyton, Mike. They call it sailing / Mike Peyton. — London (4 Little Essex St., WC2R 3LF) : Nautical Books, 1981. — 95p : chiefly ill ; 22cm
ISBN 0-333-32215-0 : £3.95 B82-06636

741.5'942 — English humorous cartoons. Special subjects: Stately homes — *Collections from individual artists*

Thelwell. Some damn fool's signed the Rubens again. — London : Methuen, Apr.1982. — [96]p
ISBN 0-413-50190-6 : £3.95 : CIP entry B82-04045

741.5'942 — English humorous strip cartoons — *Collections from individual artists*

Appleby, Dobs. The gambols / by Dobs and Barry Appleby. — London : Express Newspapers
Book no.30. — c1981. — 96p : ill(some col.) ; 15x22cm
ISBN 0-85079-116-2 (pbk) : Unpriced B82-15298

Bell, Steve. Maggie's farm / Steve Bell. — Harmondsworth : Penguin, 1981. — 90p : chiefly ill ; 19x27cm
ISBN 0-14-006078-2 (pbk) : £2.50 B82-08035

Dodd, Maurice. The Perishers book / written by Maurice Dodd & drawn by Dennis Collins. — London : Mirror
Book 25. — 1980. — [96]p : chiefly ill ; 14x22cm
ISBN 0-85939-235-x (pbk) : £0.80 B82-39250

Hendry, Gordon. Everyday adventures / by Gordon Hendry, Alan Hendry and David Cormack. — Wick (17 Breadalbane Terrace, Wick, Caithness KW1 5AT) : [G. Hendry], 1981. — [18]p : chiefly ill ; 21cm
Limited ed. of 300 copies
£0.25 (pbk) B82-10074

Kettle, Roger. The adventures of Legionnaire Beau Peep / by Roger Kettle & Andrew Christine. — London : Express Newspapers [Bk. no.3]. — c1982. — [128]p : ill ; 15x22cm
Book 3 has title Beau Peep
ISBN 0-85079-125-1 (pbk) : £1.00 B82-39205

McKenna, Terry. The fox and the circus bear / Terry McKenna. — London : Gollancz, 1982. — [32]p : chiefly col.ill ; 25cm
ISBN 0-575-02918-8 : £3.95 B82-09784

Simmonds, Posy. Pick of Posy. — London : Cape, Oct.1982. — [96]p
ISBN 0-224-02007-2 : £5.50 : CIP entry B82-24364

Simmonds, Posy. True love / Posy Simmonds. — London : Cape, 1981. — [45]p : ill(some col.) ; 23x27cm
ISBN 0-224-01895-7 : £4.95 : CIP rev. B81-27338

Smythe, Reg. Curtain up, Andy Capp! : cartoons / by Reg Smythe. — London : Mirror Books, 1982. — [62]p : ill ; 29cm. — (Andy Capp ; 47)
ISBN 0-85939-317-8 (pbk) : £0.75 B82-34206

Smythe, Reg. The world of Andy Capp : bumper issue / cartoons by Reg Smythe. — London : Mirror Books, 1981. — [192]p : chiefly ill ; 14x22cm
ISBN 0-85939-282-1 (pbk) : £1.00 B82-05995

Tidy, Bill. Fosdyke saga : from the famous Daily Mirror strip / by Bill Tidy. — London : Mirror
9. — 1980. — [159]p : ill ; 14x22cm
ISBN 0-85939-217-1 (pbk) : £1.10 B82-21930

741.5'942 — English humorous strip cartoons — *Collections from individual artists — For children*

Bananaman, football fever. — London : D.C. Thomson, c1982. — 66p : col.ill ; 18cm. — (Beano comic library ; no.8)
Cover title
£0.20 (pbk) B82-40871

Exam time with the Bash Street kids. — London (185 Fleet St.) : D.C. Thomson, 1982. — 66p : col.ill ; 18cm. — (Beano comic library ; no.2)
Cover title
£0.20 (pbk) B82-29621

King Dennis the Menace. — London (185 Fleet St., EC4A 2HS) : D.C. Thomson, 1982. — (Beano comic library ; no.1)
Cover title
£0.20 B82-29614

Minnie the Minx in Follow that star. — London : D.C. Thomson, c1982. — 66p : col.ill ; 18cm. — (Beano comic library ; no.7)
Cover title
£0.20 (pbk) B82-40872

741.5'942 — English humorous strip cartoons — *Collections — Serials*

National inverted. — [No.1]-. — [Poole] ([5 Grand Parade, High St., Poole, Dorset BH15 1AD]) : [Con Luz], [1981]-. — v. : chiefly ill ; 21cm
Description based on: [No.2]
ISSN 0262-8368 = National inverted : £0.40 per issue B82-11830

741.5'942 — English humorous strip cartoons. Special subjects: Pets: Mice — *Collections from individual artists — For children*

Waddell, Martin. The great green mouse disaster / idea by Martin Waddell ; pictures by Philippe Dupasquier. — London : Andersen Press, c1981. — [24]p : all col.ill ; 32cm
ISBN 0-86264-006-7 : £3.95 : CIP rev. B81-27414

741.5'942 — English strip cartoons — *Collections from individual artists*

Briggs, Raymond. When the wind blows / Raymond Briggs. — London : Hamish Hamilton, 1982. — [40]p : col.ill ; 31cm
ISBN 0-241-10721-0 : £3.95 : CIP rev. B82-01830

Murdoch, Graham. The mystery of Achnaghoulash / [written and drawn by Graham Murdoch and Dave Smith]. — Aberdeen : Aberdeen People's Press, 1979. — [28]p : chiefly ill(some col.) ; 28cm. — (Keltik komix)
Cover title
ISBN 0-906074-09-6 (pbk) : £0.65 B82-02401

Root, Betty. 20,000 leagues under the sea / by Jules Verne ; adapted Betty Root. — London : Watts, c1980. — 23p : ill ; 30cm. — (Picture classics)
ISBN 0-85166-808-9 (cased) : Unpriced
ISBN 0-85166-827-5 (pbk) : £1.50 B82-40824

Root, Betty. King Solomon's mines / by H. Rider Haggard ; adapted by Betty Root. — London : Watts, c1980. — 31p : all ill ; 30cm
ISBN 0-85166-806-2 (cased) : £2.50
ISBN 0-85166-825-9 (pbk) : £1.50 B82-39247

Root, Betty. Oliver Twist / by Charles Dickens ; adapted by Betty Root. — London : Watts, c1980. — 31p : all ill ; 30cm
ISBN 0-85166-805-4 (cased) : £2.50
ISBN 0-85166-824-0 (pbk) : £1.50 B82-39246

Root, Betty. The prince and the pauper / by Mark Twain ; adapted by Betty Root. — London : Watts, c1980. — 23p : all ill ; 30cm
ISBN 0-85166-807-0 (cased) : £2.50
ISBN 0-85166-826-7 (pbk) : £1.50 B82-39245

Werewolf : a chilling excursion into the twilight domain of the man-wolves!. — [London] ([205 Kentish Town Rd., London N.W.5]) : [Marvel Comics], [1981]. — 50p : all ill ; 28cm. — (A Marvel super special)
£0.45 (pbk) B82-08842

741.5'942 — English strip cartoons — *Collections from individual artists — For children*

Osband, Gillian. Double cross!. — London : Hodder & Stoughton Children's Books, Sept.1982. — [24]p. — (The Swampees)
ISBN 0-340-28450-1 : £1.50 : CIP entry B82-18816

Osband, Gillian. Freeze-up!. — London : Hodder & Stoughton Children's Books, Sept.1982. — [24]p. — (The Swampees)
ISBN 0-340-28452-8 : £1.50 : CIP entry B82-18817

Osband, Gillian. In trouble. — London : Hodder & Stoughton Children's Books, Sept.1982. — [24]p. — (The Swampees)
ISBN 0-340-28454-4 : £1.50 : CIP entry B82-18818

Osband, Gillian. The rarest egg. — London : Hodder & Stoughton Children's Books, Sept.1982. — [24]p
ISBN 0-340-28449-8 : £1.50 : CIP entry B82-18815

Stern, Simon. Neptune's treasure / by Simon Stern. — London : Methuen Children's Books, 1972 (1981 [printing]). — [30]p : col.ill ; 30cm. — (The Astonishing adventures of Captain Ketchup)
ISBN 0-416-21290-5 (pbk) : £1.50 B82-15603

741.5'942 — English strip cartoons — *Collections from individual artists — Serials*

Western gunfighters. — [No.1]-. — London (205 Kentish Town Rd, NW5) : Marvel Comics, [1980?]-. — v. : chiefly ill ; 29cm
Irregular. — Description based on: [No. 3]
ISSN 0262-5660 = Western gunfighters : £0.45 B82-05214

741.5′942′05 — English cartoons — *Collections — Serials*

Pssst! : [the cartoon and strip monthly for mature reader]. — Vol.1 (Jan. 1982)-. — London (3rd Floor, 38 Mount Pleasant, WC1X 0AP) : Never Ltd, 1982-. — v. : all ill(some col.) ; 29cm
ISSN 0262-9143 = Pssst! : £0.95 per issue B82-14270

741.5′943 — German humorous cartoons — *Collections from individual artists*

Busch, Wilhelm. The genius of Wilhelm Busch : comedy of frustration : an English anthology / edited and translated by Walter Arndt. — Berkeley, [Calif.] ; London : University of California Press, c1982. — 253p : ill,1col.port ; 27cm
Bibliography: p251-252. — Includes index
ISBN 0-520-03897-5 : Unpriced
Primary classification 831′.8 B82-28299

741.5′9438 — Polish homorous cartoons. Special subjects: Poland. Political events, *1977-1981* — *Collections from individual artists*

Krauze, Andrzej. Andrzej Krauze′s Poland / with a preface by George Mikes. — London (28 Lanacre Ave., NW9 5FN) : Nina Karsov, 1981. — 95p : chiefly ill ; 19cm
English, Polish and Russian text
ISBN 0-907652-01-8 (pbk) : Unpriced : CIP rev. B81-30636

741.5′9438 — Polish humorous cartoons. Special subjects: Political events, *1980-1981* — *Collections*

Rok odnowy : karykatury i rysunki z prazy zachodniej / [zebral i opracowal Andrzej J. Chilecki]. — Londyn : Polonia Book Fund, 1981. — 40p : chiefly ill ; 21cm
Polish text
Unpriced (pbk) B82-11312

741.5′944 — French caricatures, *1800-1900* — *Critical studies*

Wechsler, Judith. A human comedy : physiognomy and caricature in 19th century Paris / Judith Wechsler ; foreword by Richard Sennett. — London : Thames and Hudson, c1982. — 208p : ill,facsims,ports ; 27cm
Bibliography: p201-206. — Includes index
ISBN 0-500-01268-7 : £18.50
Also classified at 842′.8′09353 B82-31749

741.5′944 — French humorous cartoons — *Collections from individual artists*

Sempé. Displays of affection / by Jean-Jacques Sempé ; translation and introduction by Edward Koren. — London : Methuen, 1982. — [96]p : chiefly ill ; 14x18cm
Translation from the French
ISBN 0-413-50540-5 (pbk) : £2.50 B82-37149

741.5′944 — French humorous cartoons — *Collections from individual artists — For children — English texts*

Goscinny. Asterix in Belgium / text by Goscinny ; drawings by Uderzo ; translated by Anthea Bell and Derek Hockridge. — London : Hodder Dargaud, 1980 (1981 [printing]). — 48p : col.ill ; 30cm
Translation of: Astérix chez les Belges
ISBN 0-340-25735-0 : £2.50 B82-00534

741.5′944 — French humorous strip cartoons — *Collections from individual artists*

Goscinny. L′Odyssee d′Asterix. — London : Hodder and Stoughton Children′s Books, Mar.1982. — [48]p
ISBN 0-340-27477-8 : £3.95 : CIP entry B82-02652

741.5′944 — French humorous strip cartoons — *Collections from individual artists — English texts*

Delporte. The astrosmurf / written by Delporte and Peyo ; translated by Anthea Bell and Derek Hockridge. — London : Hodder and Stoughton, 1979. — [42]p : col.ill ; 30cm. — (Stories of the Smurfs)
Translated from the French
ISBN 0-340-24095-4 (cased) : £1.80 : CIP rev.
ISBN 0-340-24131-4 (pbk) : £0.95 B79-05227

Delporte. Romeo and Smurfette / Delporte and Peyo ; translated by Anthea Bell and Derek Hockridge. — London : Hodder and Stoughton, 1979. — [45]p : col.ill ; 30cm. — (Stories of the Smurfs)
Translated from the French. — Includes Smurfery and Travelling Smurf
ISBN 0-340-24096-2 (cased) : £1.80 : CIP rev.
ISBN 0-340-24132-2 (pbk) : £0.95 B79-05228

Goscinny. Asterix and Caesar′s gift / text by Goscinny ; drawings by Uderzo ; translated by Anthea Bell and Derek Hockridge. — [Sevenoaks] : Knight, 1982, c1977. — 48p : of col.ill ; 20cm
Translation of: Le cadeau de César. — Originally published: London : Hodder and Stoughton, 1977
ISBN 0-340-27755-6 (pbk) : £0.95 : CIP rev. B82-00248

Goscinny. Asterix and the Normans / text by Goscinny ; drawings by Uderzo ; translated by Anthea Bell and Derek Hockridge. — [Sevenoaks] : Knight, 1982, c1978. — 48p : of col.ill ; 20cm
Translation of: Astérix et les Normands. — Originally published: London : Hodder and Stoughton, 1978
ISBN 0-340-27748-3 (pbk) : £0.95 : CIP rev. B82-00247

Goscinny. Asterix in Belgium / text by Goscinny ; drawings by Uderzo ; translated by Anthea Bell and Derek Hockridge. — London : Hodder Dargaud, 1980. — 48p : col.ill ; 30cm
Translation of Astérix chez les Belges
ISBN 0-340-25735-0 : £2.25 : CIP rev. B80-13481

Goscinny. Asterix in Corsica / text by Goscinny ; drawings by Uderzo ; translated by Anthea Bell and Derek Hockridge. — London : Hodder Dargaud, 1980 (1982 [printing]). — 48p : col.ill,1col.map ; 29cm
Translation from the French
ISBN 0-340-27754-8 (pbk) : £1.35 : CIP rev. B82-10015

Goscinny. Ma Dalton / text by Goscinny ; drawings by Morris ; translated by Frederick W. Nolan. — London : Hodder Dargaud, 1980. — 46p : col.ill ; 29cm. — (Lucky Luke)
Translated from the French
ISBN 0-340-25342-8 (pbk) : £1.50 : CIP rev. B80-20014

Goscinny. [Obelix et compagnie. English]. Obelix and Co. / text by Goscinny ; drawings by Uderzo ; translated by Anthea Bell and Derek Hockridge. — London : Hodder Dargaud, 1978 (1980 [printing]). — 48p : col.ill,1col.map ; 29cm
Translation of: Obelix et compagnie
ISBN 0-340-25307-x (pbk) : £1.25 : CIP rev. B80-13918

Goscinny. Three adventures of Asterix / [text by Goscinny] ; [drawings by Uderzo] ; [translated by Anthea Bell and Derek Hockridge]. — [London] : Hodder & Stoughton, [1979?]. — 3v. : col.ill,col.maps ; 30cm
Cover title. — Contents: Asterix in Britain. Originally published: Leicester : Brockhampton, 1970. Translation of: Astérix chez les Bretons. — Asterix in Switzerland. Originally published: Leicester : Brockhampton, 1973. Translation of: Astérix chez les Helvtes. — Asterix the Gaul. Originally published: Leicester : Brockhampton, 1969. Translation of: Astérix le Gaulois
ISBN 0-340-10388-4 (cased) : Unpriced
ISBN 0-340-17221-5 (Asterix in Britain (pbk))
ISBN 0-340-17062-x (Asterix in Switzerland (cased))
ISBN 0-340-19270-4 (Asterix in Switzerland (pbk))
ISBN 0-340-04240-0 (Asterix in Gaul (cased))
ISBN 0-340-17210-x (Asterix in Gaul (pbk)) B82-18298

Petit, Pierre. Euclid rules OK?. — London : Murray, Sept.1982. — [72]p. — (The Adventures of Archibald Higgins)
Translation of: Le geometricon
ISBN 0-7195-3983-8 : £4.95 : CIP entry B82-21987

Petit, Pierre. Flight of fancy. — London : Murray, Sept.1982. — [64]p. — (The Adventures of Archibald Higgins)
Translation of: Si on volait
ISBN 0-7195-3982-x : £4.95 : CIP entry B82-21986

Petit, Pierre. Informagic. — London : Murray, Sept.1982. — [72]p. — (The Adventures of Archibald Higgins)
Translation of: L′informagique
ISBN 0-7195-3981-1 : £4.95 : CIP entry B82-21985

Peyo. The Smurfs and the howlibird / Peyo ; translated by Anthea Bell and Derek Hockridge. — London : Hodder and Stoughton, c1980. — 42p : col.ill ; 30cm. — (Stories of the Smurfs)
Translated from the French
ISBN 0-340-24239-6 (cased) : £2.50 : CIP rev.
ISBN 0-340-24240-x (pbk) : £1.50 B80-12999

Uderzo. Asterix and the black gold / written and illustrated by Uderzo ; translated by Anthea Bell and Derek Hockridge. — London : Hodder and Stoughton, 1982. — 48p : col.ill ; 30cm
Translation from the French. — At head of title: Goscinny and Uderzo present an Asterix adventure
ISBN 0-340-27476-x : £2.50 : CIP rev. B82-02651

741.5′944 — French humorous strip cartoons — *Collections from individual artists — Welsh texts*

Goscinny. Asterix ac anrheg Cesar / testun gan Goscinny ; lluniau gan Uderzo ; troswyd o′r Ffrangeg gan Alun Jones. — Caerdydd : Gwasg y Dref Wen, c1981. — 48p : col.ill,1col.map ; 30cm
Translation of: Le Cadeau de César
£2.95 B82-10641

741.5′973 — American comics — *Texts*

The **Disney** magazine. — No.0 ; [Nov. 1981-Dec. 1981] ; No.1 (Feb. 1982)-. — London (70 Old Compton St., W1V 5PA) : London Editions Magazines, 1981-. — v. : chiefly col.ill ; 30cm
Monthly. — Description based on: [Nov. 1981] issue
ISSN 0262-3463 = Disney magazine : £0.25 per issue B82-27636

Hanna Barbera′s Scooby-Doo and his t.v. friends. — No.1 (1982)-. — London (205 Kentish Town Rd, NW5) : Marvel Comics, 1982-. — v. : chiefly ill(some col.) ; 30cm
Weekly. — Description based on: No.7 (7th Apr. 1982)
£0.25 per issue B82-32158

The **Incredible** Hulk. — No.1 (Mar. 31 1982)-. — London (205 Kentish Town Rd, NW5) : Marvel Comics, 1982-. — v. : chiefly ill(some col.) ; 30cm
Weekly
£0.25 per issue B82-32163

Marvel madhouse. — No.1 (June ′81)-. — London (205 Kentish Town Rd, NW5) : Marvel Comics Ltd., 1981-. — v. : chiefly ill ; 29cm
Monthly. — Absorbed: Frantic (London), 1981. — Description based on: No.6 (Nov. ′81)
ISSN 0262-544x = Marvel madhouse : £4.80 per year B82-05739

Super Spider-man TV comic. — No.450 (Oct. 21st)-. — London (205 Kentish Town Rd, NW5) : Marvel Comics, 1981-. — v. : mainly ill(some col.) ; 30cm
Weekly. — Continues: Spider-man and Hulk team-up. — Description based on: No.451 (Oct. 28th)
£0.20 B82-25483

The **X-men** pocket book. — No.1-. — London (205 Kentish Town Rd, NW5) : Marvel Comics, 1980-. — v. : chiefly ill ; 21cm. — (Marvel digest series)
Monthly. — Description based on: No.15
ISSN 0263-144x = X-men pocket book : £0.25 per issue B82-18511

741.5′973 — American humorous cartons. Techniques — *Case studies*

Meglin, Nick. The art of humorous illustration / by Nick Meglin. — New York : Watson-Guptill ; London : Pitman, 1973 (1981 printing). — 160p : ill ; 28cm
Includes index
ISBN 0-8230-0269-1 (pbk) : Unpriced B82-22980

741.5′973 — American humorous cartoons — *Collections from individual artists*

Addams, Charles. Creature comforts / Chas Addams. — London : Heinemann, 1981. — [112]p : all ill ; 29cm
Originally published: New York : Simon and Schuster, 1981
ISBN 0-434-00703-x : £7.95 B82-11360

Hodge. Cat′s revenge II : more uses for dead people / by Hodge ; illustrated by Jeff Danziger ; produced by Philip Lief. — Sevenoaks : New English Library, 1982. — [92]p : chiefly ill ; 14x21cm
ISBN 0-450-05524-8 (pbk) : £1.95 B82-37705

Kliban, B.. Never eat anything bigger than your head and other drawings / B. Kliban. — London : Methuen, 1982, c1976. — [160]p : chiefly ill ; 13x21cm
Originally published: New York : Workman Publishing Co., 1976 ; London : Eyre Methuen, 1978
ISBN 0-413-39110-8 (pbk) : £2.50 B82-38095

Kliban, B.. Tiny footprints : and other drawings / by B. Kliban. — London : Methuen, 1982, c1978. — [158]p : col.ill ; 13x21cm
Originally published: New York : Workman Publishing Co., 1978
ISBN 0-413-49700-3 (pbk) : £2.50 B82-33889

Kliban, B.. Two guys fooling around with the moon : and other drawings / B. Kliban. — London : Methuen, 1982, c1978. — [140]p : ill ; 13x21cm
Originally published: [U.S.] : Workman, 1978
ISBN 0-413-51180-4 (pbk) : £2.50 B82-36609

Koren, Edward. Well, there′s your problem : cartoons / by Edward Koren. — Harmondsworth : Penguin, 1981, c1980. — [112]p : all ill ; 17x22cm
Originally published: New York : Pantheon, 1980
ISBN 0-14-005967-9 (pbk) : £1.95 B82-16757

Lief, Philip. Cat′s revenge. — London : New English Library, Apr.1982. — [96]p
ISBN 0-450-05459-4 (pbk) : £1.95 : CIP entry B82-03599

741.5′973 — American humorous cartoons — *Collections from individual artists — For children*

Davis, Jim. The Garfield treasury. — London : Hodder and Stoughton Children′s Books, Oct.1982. — [128]p
ISBN 0-340-28785-3 (pbk) : £3.95 : CIP entry B82-24837

741.5′973 — American humorous cartoons. Special subjects: Women & pet cats — *Collections from individual artists*

Gorey, Edward. Dancing cats ; and Neglected murderesses / Edward Gorey. — London : Dent, 1980. — [79]p : chiefly ill ; 17cm
Originally published: New York : Workman Publishing, 1980
ISBN 0-460-06068-6 (pbk) : £1.50 : CIP rev. B80-12445

741.5′973 — American humorous strip cartoons — *Collections from individual artists*

Browne, Dik. Hägar the horrible / Dik Browne. — London : London Editions, 1981. — [96]p : ill ; 16x23cm
Originally published: New York : King Features Syndicate, 1981
ISBN 0-86173-040-2 (pbk) : £1.50 B82-02299

Hart, Johnny. Ala ka zot! / Johnny Hart and Brant Parker. — [Sevenoaks] : Hodder and Stoughton, 1981, c1979. — [127]p : of ill ; 18cm. — (Coronet books)
Originally published: Greenwich, Conn., Fawcett, 1979
ISBN 0-340-26802-6 (pbk) : £0.85 : CIP rev. B81-31158

Hart, Johnny. B.C. the sun comes up the sun goes down / Johnny Hart. — London : Coronet, 1981, c1979. — [126]p : chiefly ill ; 18cm
Originally published: New York : Fawcett, 1979
ISBN 0-340-26679-1 (pbk) : £0.75 : CIP rev. B81-18121

Hart, Johnny. I, B.C. / Johnny Hart. — London : Coronet, 1982, c1974. — [125]p : ill ; 18cm
Originally published: New York : Fawcett, 1974
ISBN 0-340-26803-4 (pbk) : £0.85 : CIP rev. B82-01844

Parker, Brant. The wizard of Id - well, this is another fine how do you do. — London : Hodder & Stoughton, Nov.1982. — [128]p
ISBN 0-340-32049-4 : £0.85 : CIP entry B82-27334

Plant, Peter. Flash Filstrup : the fastest overcoat in town / by Peter Plant. — London : Arrow, 1982, c1981. — [92]p : ill ; 11x18cm
ISBN 0-09-929080-4 (pbk) : £1.00 B82-35594

Rechin, Bill. Crock, you′re all heart / Bill Rechin & Don Wilder. — London : Hodder and Stoughton, 1982, c1981. — [127]p : ill ; 18cm. — (Coronet books)
ISBN 0-340-28784-5 (pbk) : £0.85 : CIP rev. B82-15755

Schulz, Charles M.. Blaze the trail, Snoopy. — London : Hodder and Stoughton, Sept.1982. — [128]p
ISBN 0-340-28436-6 (pbk) : £0.85 : CIP entry B82-18746

Schulz, Charles M.. Happiness is — a warm puppy / by Charles M. Schulz. — London : Collins, 1982, c1979. — [130]p : col.ill ; 18cm
Originally published: San Francisco : Determined Productions, 1979
ISBN 0-00-195320-6 (pbk) : Unpriced B82-23951

Schulz, Charles M.. Love is — walking hand-in-hand / by Charles M. Schulz. — London : Collins, 1982, c1979. — [130]p : col.ill ; 18cm
Originally published: San Francisco : Determined Productions, 1979
ISBN 0-00-195319-2 (pbk) : Unpriced B82-23952

Schulz, Charles M.. Snoopy top dog : selected cartoons from The Beagle has landed, volume 2 / Charles M. Schulz. — London : Coronet, 1982, c1977. — [124]p : ill ; 18cm
Originally published: New York : Fawcett, 1981
ISBN 0-340-27861-7 (pbk) : £0.85 : CIP rev. B82-00242

Schulz, Charles M.. Snoopy treasury. — London : Hodder and Stoughton Children′s Books, Nov.1981. — [160]p
ISBN 0-340-25341-x : £4.95 : CIP entry B81-31288

Schulz, Charles M.. [Summers fly, winters walk. Selections]. Love and kisses, Snoopy : selected cartoons from Summers fly, winters walk volume 2 / Charles M. Schulz. — London : Coronet, 1981, c1976. — [124]p : chiefly ill ; 18cm. — (Coronet books)
Originally published: New York : Fawcett, 1976?
ISBN 0-340-26801-8 (pbk) : £0.75 : CIP rev. B81-25756

Schulz, Charles M.. [Summers fly, winters walk. Selections]. Stay with it, Snoopy : selected cartoons from Summers fly, winters walk Vol.3 / Charles M. Schulz. — London : Coronet, 1981, c1977. — [127]p : chiefly ill ; 18cm
Originally published: New York : Fawcett, 1981
ISBN 0-340-27265-1 (pbk) : £0.75 : CIP rev. B81-31445

Schulz, Charles M.. This is the best time of year, Charlie Brown. — London : Hodder & Stoughton, Jan.1983. — [128]p
ISBN 0-340-32091-5 (pbk) : £0.85 : CIP entry B82-34082

Schulz, Charles M.. You′re our kind of dog, Snoopy. — London : Hodder and Stoughton, June 1982. — [128]p. — (Coronet books)
ISBN 0-340-28253-3 (pbk) : £0.85 : CIP entry B82-10472

Schwarz, Haller. Pac-mania!. — London : Hodder & Stoughton, Dec.1982. — [96]p
ISBN 0-340-32805-3 (pbk) : £0.95 : CIP entry B82-33334

Trudeau, G. B.. Ask for May, settle for June. — London : Hodder and Stoughton, Nov.1982. — [128]p. — (Doonesbury ; 2)
ISBN 0-450-05521-3 (pbk) : £1.50 : CIP entry B82-27534

Trudeau, G. B.. In search of Ragan′s brain. — London : Hodder and Stoughton, Nov.1982. — [128]p. — (Doonesbury ; 1)
ISBN 0-450-05520-5 (pbk) : £1.50 : CIP entry B82-27533

Young, Dean. Blondie & Dagwood / Dean Young & Rick Marschall. — London : Arthur Barker, 1982. — 144p : ill(some col.),ports ; 28cm
Bibliography: p144
ISBN 0-213-16830-8 (pbk) : £4.50 B82-19567

741.5′973 — American humorous strip cartoons — *Collections from individual artists — For children*

Feininger, Lyonel. The Kin-der-Kids / Lyonel Feininger. — New York : Dover ; London : Constable, 1980. — 32p : chiefly col.ill ; 37cm
ISBN 0-486-23918-7 (pbk) : £4.50 B82-16695

Schulz, Charles M.. Peanuts classics. — London : Hodder and Stoughton Children′s Books, Aug.1982. — [224]p
ISBN 0-340-27976-1 : £5.95 : CIP entry B82-15731

Walt Disney Productions. The fox and the hound / Walt Disney Productions. — Cheshire (Regent House, Heaton La., Stockport, Cheshire, SK4 1DG) : London Editions Magazines, c1981. — [64]p : chiefly col.ill ; 29cm
£0.95 (pbk) B82-06155

741.5′973 — American strip cartoons — *Collections from individual artists*

Gray, Harold. Little orphan Annie in the great depression / Harold Gray. — New York : Dover ; London : Constable, 1979. — 58p : ill ; 28cm
ISBN 0-486-23737-0 (pbk) : £1.75 B82-40826

O′Neil, Denis. Dragonslayer / [Denis O′Neil script]. — London : Marvel Comics, [1982]. — 50p : chiefly col.ill ; 28cm
£0.75 (pbk) B82-22104

Schulz, Charles M.. Think thinner, Snoopy : selected cartoons from Don′t hassle me with your sighs, Chuck, Vol.2 / Charles M. Schulz. — London : Hodder Fawcett, 1980. — [127]p : chiefly ill ; 18cm
ISBN 0-340-25478-5 (pbk) : £0.65 : CIP rev. B80-11105

741.5'973 — American strip cartoons — *Collections from individual artists — Serials*

Superman spectacular. — No.1-. — London (70 Old Compton St., 8 W1V 5PA) : London Editions Magazines, 1982-. — v. : chiefly col.ill ; 29cm
Irregular
ISSN 0263-1423 = Superman spectacular : £0.75 per issue B82-18513

741.5'973 — American strip cartoons — *Collections — Serials*

Classics : Marvel Comics. — No.1 (Oct. 81)-no.12 (1982)-. — [London] ([205 Kentish Town Rd, NW5]) : [Marvel Comics], [1981]-[1982]. — 12v. : chiefly ill ; 20cm
Fortnightly
ISSN 0263-2357 = Classics : £0.25
B82-22667

741.5'982 — Argentinian humorous cartoons — *Collections from individual artists*

Mordillo, Guillermo. Mordillo : cartoons/opus 2 : where words fail, pictures speak clearly — and vice versa / [with a foreword by Marcel Marceaux]. — London : Hutchinson, 1982, c1978. — [79]p : ill(some col.) ; 32cm
Ill on lining papers
ISBN 0-09-146940-6 : £6.95 : CIP rev.
B82-06220

741.5'982 — Argentinian humorous cartoons. Special subjects: Association football — *Collections from individual artists*

Mordillo, Guillermo. Mordillo football. — London : Hutchinson, 1981. — [69]p : all ill (some col.),1port ; 32cm
Ill on lining papers
ISBN 0-09-146460-9 : £5.95 : CIP rev.
B81-26798

741.5'994 — Australian humorous cartoons — *Collections from individual artists*

Leunig, Michael. The bedtime Leunig / Michael Leunig. — London : Angus & Robertson, 1981. — [124]p : chiefly ill
ISBN 0-207-14505-9 (pbk) : £3.95 B82-08987

741.6 — COMMERCIAL ART

741.6 — Graphics. Design — *Manuals*

Porter, Tom. Manual of graphic techniques 2 : for architects, graphic designers, & artists / Tom Porter and Sue Goodman. — London : Astragal, 1982. — 128p : ill,plans ; 21x28cm
Includes index
ISBN 0-906525-24-1 (pbk) : £6.95 B82-25043

741.6 — Graphics. Design. Purchase — *For business enterprise*

Murray, Ray. How to brief designers and buy print. — London : Business Books, Feb.1983. — [176]p
ISBN 0-09-150190-3 : £20.00 : CIP entry
B82-36607

741.6'0148 — Graphic design. Symbols — *Encyclopaedias*

Thompson, Philip. The dictionary of visual language / Philip Thompson/Peter Davenport. — Harmondsworth : Penguin, 1982, c1980. — vii,258p : ill ; 23cm
Originally published: Bergstrom and Boyle, 1980
ISBN 0-14-051117-2 (pbk) : £4.95 B82-30518

741.6'03'21 — Graphic design — *Encyclopaedias*

Mintz, Patricia Barnes. Dictionary of graphic arts terms : a communication tool for people who buy type and printing / Patric[i]a Barnes Mintz. — New York ; London : Van Nostrand Reinhold, c1981. — vii,318p : ill ; 24cm
Bibliography: p315-318
ISBN 0-442-26711-8 : £15.25 B82-00854

741.64'092'4 — Swedish illustrations. Larsson, Carl. Illustrations for books — *Illustrations*

Rudström, Lennart. Our family / Lennart Rudstrom ; English version by Olive Jones ; pictures by Carl Larsson. — London : Methuen, 1980. — [32]p : ill(some col.),ports (some col.) ; 24x32cm
Translation of: Carl Larsson och bilder av familjen. — Translation and revision of: 'Carl Larsson och hans bilder av familjen'. Stockholm : Bonniers, 1979. — Based on the life of Carl Larsson
ISBN 0-416-88560-8 : £4.50 : CIP rev.
Primary classification 839.7'374[F] B79-37407

741.64'0941 — British illustrations: Illustrations for books, *1800-1914*

Houfe, Simon. The dictionary of British book illustrators and caricaturists 1800-1914 : with introductory chapters on the rise and progress of the art / Simon Houfe. — Rev. — [Woodbridge] : Antique Collectors' Club, 1981. — 520p : ill(some col.),facsims(some col.) ; 29cm
Previous ed.: 1978. — Ill on lining papers. — Bibliography: p511. — Includes index
ISBN 0-902028-73-1 : £25.00 B82-09822

741.64'0942 — English illustrations. Illustrations for English literature, *1558-1900 — Critical studies*

Hodnett, Edward. Image and text : studies in the illustration of English literature / Edward Hodnett. — London : Scolar, 1982. — vii,271p : ill ; 27cm
Bibliography: p259-265. — Includes index
ISBN 0-85967-603-x : £17.50 : CIP rev.
B81-04194

741.64'0942 — English illustrations. Illustrations for fiction in English by Hardy, Thomas, *1840-1928 — Critical studies*

Jackson, Arlene M.. Illustration and the novels of Thomas Hardy / Arlene M. Jackson. — London : Macmillan, 1982, c1981. — xiii,151p,[64]p of plates : ill ; 25cm
Originally published: Totowa : Rowman & Littlefield, 1981. — Bibliography: p145-149. — Includes index
ISBN 0-333-32303-3 : £15.00 B82-06896

741.64'0954 — Indian illustrated books. Illustrations, *to ca 1850 — Critical studies*

Losty, Jeremiah P.. The art of the book in India / by Jeremiah P. Losty. — London : British Library, c1982. — 160p,[20]p of plates : ill (some col.),facsims ; 28cm
'Catalogue of an exhibition mounted at the British Library, Reference Division, 16 April-1 August 1982'. — Bibliography: p156-160
ISBN 0-904654-78-8 : £17.95 : CIP rev.
B82-05775

741.64'2'0922 — European illustrations. Illustrations for children's books — *Biographies*

Modern European children's book illustrators. — London : Hutchinson, July 1982. — [120]p
ISBN 0-09-149350-1 : £20.00 : CIP entry
B82-16476

741.64'2'0924 — English illustrations. Shaw, Byam. Illustrations for nursery rhymes in English — *Illustrations*

Shaw, Byam. Old King Cole's book of nursery rhymes / illustrated by Byam Shaw. — Facsim. ed. — London : Macmillan, 1980. — 99p : col.ill ; 29cm. — (Facsimile classics series)
ISBN 0-333-30784-4 : £3.95 B82-23043

741.64'2'0924 — English illustrations. Tarrant, Margaret. Illustrations for children's books — *Critical studies*

Gurney, John. Margaret Tarrant & her pictures / by John Gurney. — London : Medici Society, 1982. — 24p : ill(some col.),2ports ; 19x22cm. — (Medici art books)
Text and ill on inside covers
ISBN 0-85503-063-1 (pbk) : Unpriced
B82-25690

741.65'2 — British illustrations. Illustrations for Radio Times, *to 1980 — Illustrations*

The **Art** of Radio times : the first sixty years / compiled by David Driver ; introduction by Asa Briggs. — London : BBC, 1981. — 252p : chiefly ill(some col.),ports ; 32cm
Includes index
ISBN 0-563-17906-6 : £15.95
ISBN 0-904866-19-x (European Illustration)
B82-10091

741.67'2 — Fashion design. Drawings. Techniques — *Manuals*

Ireland, Patrick John. Fashion design drawing and presentation / Patrick John Ireland. — London : Batsford Academic and Educational, 1982. — 120p : ill ; 25cm
ISBN 0-7134-3518-6 (cased) : Unpriced
ISBN 0-7134-3519-4 (pbk) : £5.95 B82-36936

741.67'2 — Women's clothing. Fashion design. Drawings. Techniques — *Manuals*

Ireland, Patrick John. Fashion drawing / Patrick John Ireland. — Cambridge : Cambridge University Press, 1980 (1982 [printing]). — 32p : ill(some col.) ; 30cm
Bibliography: p32
ISBN 0-521-21994-9 (pbk) : £1.85 B82-37894

741.9 — DRAWINGS. COLLECTIONS

741.94 — European drawings, *1933-1957.* **Special subjects: German prisons. Prisoners**, *1933-1945 — Illustrations*

Blatter, Janet. Art of the holocaust / by Janet Blatter and Sybil Milton ; historical introduction by Henry Friecdlander ; preface by Irving Howe. — London : Pan, 1982, c1981. — 272p : ill(some col.) ; 31cm
Originally published: New York : Rutledge, 1981. — Bibliography: p270-272
ISBN 0-330-26634-9 (pbk) : £7.50
Also classified at 757 B82-20436

Blatter, Janet. Art of the holocaust / project editor Lori Stein ; by Janet Blatter and Sybil Milton ; historical introduction by Henry Friedlander ; preface by Irving Howe. — London : Orbis, 1982, c1981. — 272p : ill(some col.),1map,facsims(some col.),ports(some col.) ; 32cm
Originally published: New York : Rutledge, 1981. — Maps on lining papers. — Bibliography: p270-272
ISBN 0-85613-386-8 : £12.50
Also classified at 757 B82-20437

741.94'074 — European drawings, *1500-1800 — Catalogues*

National Gallery of Scotland. Drawings from the bequest of W.F. Watson, 1881-1981. — Edinburgh : National Gallery of Scotland, 1981. — [50]p : ill(1col.) ; 21cm
ISBN 0-903148-36-6 (pbk) : Unpriced
B82-31366

741.941 — British landscape drawings, *1630-1950 — Catalogues*

Town, country, shore and sea : British drawings and watercolours from Anthony Van Dyck to Paul Nash : an exhibition from the Fitzwilliam Museum, Cambridge. — Cambridge : Cambridge University Press, 1982. — xix,135p : ill(some col.) ; 26cm
Bibliography: pxix. — Includes index
ISBN 0-521-24491-9 (cased) : £22.50 : CIP rev.
ISBN 0-521-28722-7 (pbk) : £5.95
Also classified at 758'.1'0941 B82-11512

741.941 — Connecticut. New Haven. Art galleries: Yale Center for British Art. Stock: British drawings, *1500-1850.* **Special subjects: Equestrian sports & field sports. Collections: Paul Mellon collection** — *Catalogues*

Egerton, Judy. British sporting and animal drawings c.1500-1850 / a catalogue compiled by Judy Egerton & Dudley Snelgrove. — London : Tate Gallery for the Yale Center for British Art, 1978. — vi,126p,[144]p of plates : ill(some col.),ports ; 30cm. — (The Paul Mellon collection) (Sport in art and books)
Bibliography: pxv. — Includes index
ISBN 0-905005-52-x : Unpriced B82-22079

741.9415 — Irish drawings. Clarke, Harry — *Critical studies*

Bowe, Nicola Gordon. Harry Clarke. — Portlaoise : Dolmen Press, Sept.1982. — [120]p
ISBN 0-85105-359-9 : £20.00 : CIP entry
ISBN 0-85105-387-7 (limited) : £75.00
B82-20210

741.942 — Cambridgeshire. Cambridge. Art galleries: Kettle's Yard Gallery. Exhibits: English drawings. Vellacott, Elisabeth — *Catalogues*

Vellacott, Elisabeth. Elisabeth Vellacott : paintings and drawings, 1942-81 : Kettle's Yard, Cambridge 19 September-18 October 1981 : Warwick Arts Trust, 33 Warwick Square, London SW1 29 October-5 December 1981. — Cambridge ([Northampton St.], Cambridge [CB3 OAQ]) : Kettle's Yard, [1981]. — [48]p : chiefly ill(some col.) ; 23cm
Unpriced (pbk)
Primary classification 759.2 B82-00685

741.942 — English drawings. Auerbach, Frank — *Catalogues*

Auerbach, Frank. Frank Auerbach : recent paintings and drawings. — New York : Marlborough Gallery ; London (6 Albemarle St., W1X 3HF) : Marlborough Fine Art, 1982. — 44p : ill(some col.),ports(some col.) ; 30cm
Includes bibliographies
Unpriced (pbk)
Also classified at 759.2 B82-36824

741.942 — English drawings. Barton, David — *Illustrations*

Barton, David. Empty embrace / David Barton. — London : D. Barton, c1982. — [216]p : all ill ; 21cm
ISBN 0-907559-04-2 (pbk) : £4.50 B82-38021

741.942 — English drawings. Burne-Jones, Edward — *Illustrations*

Burne-Jones, Edward. Pre-Raphaelite drawings by Burne-Jones : 46 illustrations / by Sir Edward Coley Burne-Jones. — New York : Dover ; London : Constable, 1981. — 43p : all ill ; 29cm. — (Dover art library)
ISBN 0-486-24113-0 (pbk) : £1.50 B82-05280

741.942 — English drawings. Constable, John, *1776-1837* **—** *Catalogues*

Constable, John, *1776-1837*. Constable : paintings, watercolours & drawings / Leslie Parris, Ian Fleming-Williams, Conal Shields. — 2nd ed., rev. — London : The Tate Gallery, 1976. — 208p,[12]p of plates : ill(some col.) ; 30cm
Published to accompany the bicentenary exhibition at the Tate Gallery. — Previous ed.: 1976
ISBN 0-905005-05-8 (cased) : £4.00
ISBN 0-905005-20-1 (pbk) : £2.75
Primary classification 759.2 B82-29171

741.942 — English drawings. Craighead, Meinrad. Special subjects: Trees — *Illustrations*

Craighead, Meinrad. The sign of the tree : meditations in images & words / Meinrad Craighead. — London : Artists House, 1979. — 192p : ill ; 30cm
Bibliography: p192
ISBN 0-86134-013-2 : £12.00 B82-12944

741.942 — English drawings. Dubsky, Mario. Special subjects: Men: Nudes — *Illustrations*

Dubsky, Mario. Tom Pilgrim's progress among the consequences of Christianity and other drawings / Mario Dubsky ; introduction by Edward Lucie-Smith. — London : Gay Men's Press, 1981. — 83p : chiefly ill ; 25cm
Text on inside covers. — Bibliography: p82
ISBN 0-907040-09-8 (pbk) : £4.95 : CIP rev.
B81-27417

741.942 — English drawings. Gill, Eric — *Catalogues*

Gill, Eric. Eric Gill 1882-1940 : drawings & carvings : a centenary exhibition. — London : Anthony d'Offay, [1982]. — 62p : ill,ports ; 22cm
£3.00 (pbk) B82-35239

741.942 — English drawings. Graham, Rigby. Special subjects: Ireland — *Illustrations*

Graham, Rigby. Some Irish drawings / Rigby Graham. — Leicester : Toni Savage, c1980. — [38]p : chiefly ill ; 21cm
Limited ed. of 80 copies signed by the artist
ISBN 0-901870-39-0 : £10.00 B82-02850

741.942 — English drawings. Moore, George, *d.1914*. **Special subjects: Bicycles —** *Illustrations*

Moore, George, *d.1914*. The George Moore collection. — London (152 Ilderton Rd., SE15 1NT) : Beekay
Facsim reprints from 'Bicycling news'
Vol.4: 1888-1889. — 1981. — 103p : ill,ports ; 31cm
Limited ed. of 1,000 copies
Unpriced B82-15472

741.942 — English drawings. Tremlett, David — *Illustrations*

Peter Joseph, Richard Long, David Tremlett in Newlyn. — [Penzance] : Newlyn Orion Galleries, 1978. — 1portfolio : ill ; 23x27cm
Produced to accompany an exhibition at the Newlyn Art Gallery in 1978
Unpriced
Primary classification 709'.42 B82-05968

741.942 — English illustrations. Shepard, Ernest H. Illustrations for Winnie-the-Pooh stories by Milne, A. A. — *Illustrations*

Shepard, Ernest H.. The Pooh sketchbook. — London : Methuen, June 1982. — [96]p
ISBN 0-416-24420-3 : £6.95 : CIP entry
B82-14498

741.942 — English portrait drawing. Pre-Raphaelitism. Special subjects: Pre-Raphaelite Brotherhood — *Critical studies*

Rose, Andrea. Pre-Raphaelite portraits / Andrea Rose. — Yeovil : Oxford Illustrated Press, c1981. — 144p : ill,ports ; 31cm
Bibliography: p140. — Includes index
ISBN 0-902280-74-0 (cased) : £9.95
ISBN 0-902280-82-1 (pbk) : Unpriced
Primary classification 757'.0942 B82-11024

741.942 — English portrait drawings. Special subjects: Blake, William, *1757-1827* **—** *Illustrations*

The **Complete** portraiture of William and Catherine Blake / with an essay and an iconography by Geoffrey Keynes Kt.. — London : Published by the Trianon Press for the William Blake Trust, 1977. — 155p : facsims,ports ; 30cm
In slip case. — Limited ed. of 562 copies
Unpriced B82-25781

741.942 — Great Britain. Arts. Patronage. Organisations: Arts Council of Great Britain. Exhibits: English drawings. Spencer, Stanley. Special subjects: Dockyards, *1940-1945* **—** *Catalogues*

Spencer, Stanley. Spencer in the shipyard : paintings and drawings by Stanley Spencer and photographs by Cecil Beaton from the Imperial War Museum. — London : Arts Council of Great Britain, c1981. — [28]p(4fold.) : chiefly ill(some col.),ports ; 27cm
Accompanies an Arts Council travelling exhibition held at 10 different venues from 2 May 1981 to 18 April 1982
ISBN 0-7287-0277-0 (pbk) : £3.75
Also classified at 759.2 ; 779'.962383'0924
B82-06146

741.942 — Merseyside *(Metropolitan County)*. **Liverpool. Art galleries: Bluecoat Gallery. Exhibits: English drawings. Farthing, Stephen —** *Catalogues*

Farthing, Stephen. The construction of a monument : paintings and drawings / by Stephen Farthing. — Liverpool (School La., Liverpool L1 3BX) : Bluecoat Gallery, 1981. — 1sheet : ill ; 21x45cm
Published to accompany an exhibition at the Bluecoat Gallery October 31st-November 21st 1981
Unpriced (unbound)
Primary classification 759.2 B82-09033

741.942'074'023 — South-west England. Art galleries. Exhibits: English drawingss — *Illustrations*

A **Sense** of place : Lizzie Cox, John Danvers, Paul Hempton, Peter Lloyd-Jones, Michael Upton : a book of drawings produced in conjunction with the exhibition 'A sense of place' / ... organised jointly by Arnolfini, Bristol and South West Arts. — [Bristol] : [Arnolfini], 1981. — [16]p : ill ; 21cm
Bibliography: p[16]
ISBN 0-907738-02-8 (pbk) : Unpriced
B82-17639

741.942'074'02753 — Merseyside *(Metropolitan County)*. **Liverpool. Art galleries: Bluecoat Gallery. Exhibits: English drawings,** *1907-1945* **—** *Catalogues*

An **Honest** patron : a tribute to Sir Edward Marsh / sponsored by Liverpool daily post. — Liverpool : Bluecoat Gallery, 1976. — 52p : ill,facsims ; 21cm
Published to accompany an exhibition at the Bluecoat Gallery May 5th-June 5th 1976. — Bibliography: p51-52
£0.50 (pbk)
Primary classification 759.2'074'02753
B82-09030

741.943 — German drawings. Dürer, Albrecht — *Illustrations*

White, Christopher, *1930-*. Dürer : the artist and his drawings / Christopher White. — Oxford : Phaidon, 1971 (1981 [printing]). — 231p : ill (some col.) ; 29cm
Bibliography: p225. — Includes index
ISBN 0-7148-1436-9 : £15.00 B82-03965

741.943 — Great Britain. Art galleries. Exhibits: German drawings. Kollwitz, Käthe — *Catalogues*

Käthe Kollwitz 1867-1945 : the graphic works : an exhibition / organised by Kettle's Yard in association with the Scottish National Gallery of Modern Art and the Institute of Contemporary Arts. — Cambridge : Kettle's Yard, c1981. — 79p : ill,1port ; 21cm
ISBN 0-907074-11-1 (pbk) : Unpriced
Also classified at 769.92'4 B82-06092

741.9'437 — Czechoslovak drawings. Hollar, Wenceslaus — *Catalogues*

Griffiths, Antony. Wenceslaus Hollar : prints and drawings. — London : British Museum Publications, Feb.1983. — [96]p
Published to accompany an exhibition at the British Museum, London, and at the National Gallery, Prague
ISBN 0-7141-0787-5 : CIP entry
Also classified at 769.92'4 B82-39440

741.9437 — Czechoslovak drawings. Mucha, Alphonse — *Illustrations*

Mucha, Alphonse. Mucha's figures décoratives / 40 plates by Alphonse Mucha ; with a new introduction by Anna Dvořák. — New York : Dover ; London : Constable, 1981. — 39p : chiefly ill ; 31cm
Originally published: Paris : Librairie Centrale des Beaux Arts, 1905
ISBN 0-486-24234-x (pbk) : £3.40 B82-35423

741.944 — French drawings. Grandville, J. J. — *Illustrations*

Grandville, J. J.. Grandville's animals : the world's vaudeville / with an introduction by Bryan Holme. — New York ; London : Thames and Hudson, 1981. — 63p : chiefly ill (some col.) ; 20x23cm
ISBN 0-500-23340-3 : £4.95 B82-04231

741.944 — French ink drawings. Bonnard, Pierre, *1867-1947*. **Illustrations for La 628-E8 —** *Illustrations*

Bonnard, Pierre, *1867-1947*. Pierre Bonnard : 1867-1947 : the complete collection of one hundred and four brush and Chinese ink drawings for Octave Mirbeau's 1908 travelogue La 628-E8 / presented by the Royal Scottish Academy on the occasion of the 33rd Edinburgh International Festival, 18 August-15 September 1979 ... ; loaned and arranged by Richard Nathanson. — [London] ([7 Broadbent St., W1X 9HJ]) : [R. Nathanson Publications], c1978. — [56]p : ill,1port ; 19x25cm
Bibliography: p54
Unpriced (pbk) B82-24180

741.944 — London. Kensington and Chelsea *(London Borough).* **Art galleries: Taranman. Exhibits: French drawings. Staël, Nicolas de** — *Catalogues*

Staël, Nicolas de. Nicolas de Staël : drawings and engraved work / with a preface by Denys Sutton ; and an essay by Nicolas Barker. — London : Taranman, 1981. — 56p,[1]leaf of plates : ill ; 26cm
Published to accompany an exhibition at Taranman, 12 October-28 November 1981. — Limited ed. of 400 copies
ISBN 0-906499-12-7 (pbk) : Unpriced
B82-04455

741.945 — London. Camden *(London Borough).* **Museums: British Museum.** *Department of Prints and Drawings.* **Exhibits: Italian drawings** — *Catalogues*

British Museum. *Department of Prints and Drawings.* Italian drawings in the Department of Prints and Drawings in the British Museum. — London : British Museum Publications, Apr.1982
Artists working in Rome c.1550-c.1640. — 2v.
ISBN 0-7141-0783-2 : £40.00 : CIP entry
ISBN 0-7141-0781-6 (catalogue)
ISBN 0-7141-0782-4 (plates) B82-04503

741.945 — New Jersey. Princeton. Art galleries: Princeton University. *Art Museum.* **Exhibits: Italian drawings of Bernini, Gian Lozenzo from Museum der Bildenden Künste** — *Catalogues*

Lavin, Irving. Drawings by Gianlorenzo Bernini : from the Museum der Bildenden Künste Leipzig, German Democratic Republic / exhibition and catalogue prepared in a graduate seminar, Department of Art and Archaeology, Princeton University by Irving Lavin and Pamela Gordon ... [et al.]. — Princeton ; Guildford : Published by the Art Museum, Princeton University in association with Princeton University Press, c1981. — xviii,365p : ill,facsims,1plan,ports ; 29cm
Bibliography: p349-356. — Includes index
ISBN 0-691-03976-3 : £35.30 B82-12043

741.945′074′02134 — London. Kensington and Chelsea *(London Borough).* **Museums: Victoria and Albert Museum. Stock: Italian drawings,** *1300-1800* — *Catalogues*

Victoria and Albert Museum. Italian drawings / [Victoria and Albert Museum] ; [compiled by] Peter Ward-Jackson. — London : H.M.S.O.. — (Victoria and Albert Museum catalogues)
Vol.2: 17th-18th century. — 1980. — 229p : ill ; 29cm
Bibliography: p211-214. — Includes index
ISBN 0-11-290258-8 : £45.00 B82-24799

741.946 — Spanish drawings. Picasso, Pablo — *Illustrations*

Picasso, Pablo. Picasso line drawings and prints / 44 works by Pablo Picasso. — New York : Dover ; London : Constable, 1981. — 43p : of ill ; 28cm. — (Dover art library)
ISBN 0-486-24196-3 (pbk) : £1.50
Also classified at 769.92′4 B82-37393

741.9492 — Dutch drawings. Velde, Willem Van de, *1611-1693* **& Velde, Willem Van de,** *1633-1707* — *Catalogues*

Art of the Van de Veldes *(Exhibition) (1982 : National Maritime Museum).* The art of the Van de Veldes : paintings and drawings by the great Dutch marine artists and their English followers / [catalogue of the exhibition 'The art of the Van de Veldes' held at the National Maritime Museum, London from 23 June to 5 December 1982]. — London : National Maritime Museum, 1982. — 143p : ill(some col.),1map,ports ; 21x25cm
Bibliography: p143
ISBN 0-905555-62-7 (pbk) : Unpriced
Primary classification 759.9492 B82-35827

741.9492 — Dutch language drawings. Rembrandt — *Illustrations*

Rembrandt. Rembrandt landscape drawings : 60 works / by Rembrandt van Rijn. — New York : Dover ; London : Constable, 1981. — 59p : ill ; 29cm. — (Dover art library)
ISBN 0-486-24160-2 (pbk) : £1.70 B82-13377

741.9492′074 — Art galleries. Exhibits: Dutch drawings from Pierpont Morgan Library, *1600-1700:* **Exhibitions at art galleries** — *Catalogues*

Pierpont Morgan Library. Rubens and Rembrandt in their century : Flemish & Dutch drawings of the 17th century from the Pierpont Morgan Library / Felice Stampfle ; [in memoriam Frits Lugt 1884-1970, Jacoba Lugt-Klever 1888-1969]. — New York : Pierpont Morgan Library ; Oxford : Oxford University Press, 1979. — 298p : ill,ports ; 29cm
Published to accompany a series of exhibitions in Paris, Antwerp, London and New York, 1979-1980. — Includes index
£25.00
Also classified at 741.9493′074 B82-05888

741.9493′074 — Art galleries. Exhibits: Flemish drawings from Pierpont Morgan Library, *1600-1700* — *Catalogues*

Pierpont Morgan Library. Rubens and Rembrandt in their century : Flemish & Dutch drawings of the 17th century from the Pierpont Morgan Library / Felice Stampfle ; [in memoriam Frits Lugt 1884-1970, Jacoba Lugt-Klever 1888-1969]. — New York : Pierpont Morgan Library ; Oxford : Oxford University Press, 1979. — 298p : ill,ports ; 29cm
Published to accompany a series of exhibitions in Paris, Antwerp, London and New York, 1979-1980. — Includes index
£25.00
Primary classification 741.9492′074
B82-05888

741.973 — American drawings, *1900-1981* — *Illustrations*

Twentieth-century drawings : selections from the Whitney Museum of American Art / selected and with commentary by Paul Cummings. — New York : Dover ; London : Constable, 1981. — 136p : ill,ports ; 31cm
ISBN 0-486-24143-2 (pbk) : £4.50 B82-29990

741.9′73 — American illustrations. Kent, Rockwell — *Illustrations*

Kent, Rockwell. Rockwell Kent. — London : Collins, Nov.1982. — [384]p
ISBN 0-00-216659-3 : £30.00 : CIP entry
B82-35201

741.973 — Merseyside (Metropolitan County). Liverpool. Art galleries: Bluecoat Gallery. Exhibits: American illustrations. Mousdale, Peter — *Catalogues*

Mousdale, Peter. Songs and journeys : recent works / by Peter Mousdale. — Liverpool (School La., Liverpool L1 3BX) : Bluecoat Gallery, [1981?]. — [4]p : ill ; 21cm
Published to accompany an exhibition at the Bluecoat Gallery, November 28th-December 19th 1981
Unpriced (unbound) B82-09040

742 — DRAWINGS. PERSPECTIVE

742 — Drawings. Perspective. Techniques — *Manuals*

Brown, David, *1926-*. Draw perspective / David Brown. — London : Adam & Charles Black, 1982. — 48p : ill ; 28cm
ISBN 0-7136-2194-x (pbk) : £1.75 B82-17827

Coulin, Claudius. Step by step perspective drawing : for architects, draftsmen, and designers / Claudius Coulin ; translated by John H. Yarbrough. — New York ; London : Van Nostrand Reinhold, 1971 (1982 [printing]). — 112p : ill ; 28cm
Translation of: Zeichenlehre für Architekten, Bauzeichner, und Designer. — Bibliography: p3. — Includes index
ISBN 0-442-22522-9 (pbk) : £7.60 B82-34332

743 — DRAWINGS. SPECIAL SUBJECTS

743′.4 — Drawings. Special subjects: Human figures. Techniques — *Manuals*

Raynes, John. Figure drawing : a practical manual for all students of art / John Raynes. — London : Hamlyn, 1981. — 159p : ill,ports ; 31cm
Ill on lining papers. — Bibliography: p159
ISBN 0-600-34206-9 (cased) : £6.95
ISBN 0-600-34258-1 (pbk) : Unpriced
B82-02769

743′.42 — Portrait drawings. Techniques — *Manuals*

Fletcher, Geoffrey. Figure and portrait drawing / Geoffrey Fletcher ; with drawings by the author. — London : Daily Telegraph, 1978. — 43p : ill ; 26cm
£1.15 (pbk) B82-09493

743′.49 — Drawings. Special subjects: Man. Face. Techniques — *Manuals*

Raynes, John. Draw faces and expressions / John Raynes. — London : Adam & Charles Black, 1982. — 48p : ill ; 28cm
ISBN 0-7136-2196-6 (pbk) : Unpriced
B82-17828

743′.49 — Man. Anatomy — *For life drawing*

Peck, Stephen Rogers. Atlas of human anatomy for the artist / Stephen Rogers Peck. — Oxford : Oxford University Press, 1951, c1979 (1982 [printing]). — xv,272p : ill ; 26cm
Includes index
ISBN 0-19-503095-8 (pbk) : £6.95 B82-34908

743′.6 — Drawings. Special subjects: Animals. Techniques — *Manuals*

Brown, David, *1926-*. Draw wild animals / David Brown. — London : Pitman House, 1980. — 48p : chiefly ill ; 28cm
Originally published: New York : Taplinger, 1980 (book)
ISBN 0-273-01553-2 (pbk) : £1.50 B82-39126

Spencer, Roy. Draw zoo animals / Roy Spencer. — London : Pitman House, 1980. — 47p : chiefly ill ; 28cm
Originally published: New York : Taplinger, 1980 (book)
ISBN 0-273-01564-8 (pbk) : £1.50 B82-39125

743′.68 — Drawings. Special subjects: Birds. Techniques — *Manuals*

Brown, David, *1926-*. Draw birds / David Brown. — London : Pitman House, 1980. — 48p : chiefly ill ; 28cm
Originally published: New York : Taplinger, 1980 (book)
ISBN 0-273-01566-4 (pbk) : £1.50 B82-39122

743′.69725 — Livestock: Ponies. Drawing — *Manuals*

Thelwell. How to draw ponies. — London : Methuen Children's Books, Mar.1982. — [64]p
Based on: Ponies. London : Studio Vista, 1966
ISBN 0-416-24530-7 : £3.50 : CIP entry
B82-01716

743′.6974428 — Drawings. Special subjects: Pets: Cats. Techniques — *Manuals*

Brown, David, *1926-*. Draw cats / David Brown. — London : Pitman House, 1980. — 48p : chiefly ill ; 28cm
Originally published: New York : Taplinger, 1980 (book)
ISBN 0-273-01551-6 (pbk) : £1.50 B82-39127

743′.7 — Drawings. Special subjects: Plants. Techniques — *Manuals*

Seymour, Mary. Draw flowers and plants / Mary Seymour. — London : Pitman House, 1980. — 46p : chiefly ill ; 28cm
Originally published: New York : Taplinger, 1980 (book)
ISBN 0-273-01555-9 (pbk) : £1.50 B82-39123

743′.7 — Drawings. Special subjects: Trees. Techniques — *Manuals*

Battershill, Norman. Draw trees / Norman Battershill. — London : Pitman House, 1980. — 48p : chiefly ill ; 28cm
Originally published: New York : Taplinger, 1980 (book)
ISBN 0-273-01559-1 (pbk) : £1.50 B82-39124

743′.837 — Drawings. Special subjects: Seashore. Techniques — *Manuals*

Ursell, Martin. Draw the seashore / Martin Ursell. — London : Adam & Charles Black, 1982. — 48p : ill ; 28cm
ISBN 0-7136-2195-8 (pbk) : £1.75 B82-17825

743′.89629046 — Drawings. Special subjects: Vehicles. Techniques — *Manuals*

Gibbs, Victor. Draw transport / Victor Gibbs. — London : Adam & Charles Black, 1982. — 48p : ill ; 28cm
ISBN 0-7136-2192-3 (pbk) : £1.75 B82-17824

743′.897126 — Drawings. Special subjects: Gardens. Techniques — *Manuals*

Vincer, Carole. Draw your garden / Carole Vincer. — London : Adam & Charles Black, 1982. — 48p : ill ; 28cm
ISBN 0-7136-2193-1 (pbk) : £1.75 B82-17826

743′.924′09034 — Illustrations, *1837-1945.* **Special subjects: Women** — *Illustrations*

Barker, Ronnie. Sugar and spice / by Ronnie Barker. — London : Hodder & Stoughton, 1981. — 120p : ill(some col.) ; 28cm
ISBN 0-340-27817-x (cased) : Unpriced : CIP rev.
ISBN 0-340-27000-4 (pbk) : £4.50
Also classified at 828′.91409 B81-23932

745 — DECORATIVE AND MINOR ARTS

745′.092′2 — Decorative arts. Women artists, *to ca 1920* — *Biographies*

Prather-Moses, Alice Irma. The international dictionary of women workers in the decorative arts : a historical survey from the distant past to the early decades of the twentieth century / compiled by Alice Irma Prather-Moses. — Metuchen ; London : Scarecrow, 1981. — xvii,200p ; 23cm
Bibliography: pxi-xvii. — Includes index
ISBN 0-8108-1450-1 B82-10849

745′.092′2 — English decorative arts. Bloomsbury Group

Anscombe, Isabelle. Omega and after : Bloomsbury and the decorative arts / Isabelle Anscombe ; photographs by Howard Grey ; foreword by John Lehmann. — London : Thames and Hudson, c1981. — 176p : ill(some col.),ports ; 26cm
Bibliography: p170-171. — Includes index
ISBN 0-500-23337-3 : £10.50 B82-05697

745′.092′4 — French decorative arts. Gallé, Emile — *Critical studies*

Garner, Philippe. Emile Gallé / Philippe Garner. — London : Academy Editions, 1976 (1979 [printing]). — 167p,[24]p of plates : ill(some col.) ; 31cm
Includes 1 chapter in French. — Bibliography: p163. — Includes index
ISBN 0-85670-416-4 (cased) : Unpriced B82-10743

745′.0952 — Japanese decorative arts, *1600-1900*

Smith, Lawrence. Japanese decorative arts from the 17th to the 19th centuries. — London : British Museum, Nov.1982. — [136]p
ISBN 0-7141-1421-9 : £6.95 : CIP entry B82-28571

745′.0956 — Ottoman decorative arts

Tulips, arabesques & turbans : decorative arts from the Ottoman Empire / edited by Yanni Petsopoulos. — London : Alexandria Press, 1982. — 200p,[98p of plates] : ill(some col.),1map ; 29cm
Ill on lining papers. — Includes index
ISBN 0-85667-151-7 : Unpriced B82-37687

745′.0971 — Canada. German decorative arts — *Critical studies*

Bird, Michael, *1941-*. A splendid harvest : Germanic folk and decorative arts in Canada / Michael Bird & Terry Kobayashi. — New York ; London : Van Nostrand Reinhold, c1981. — 240p : ill(some col.),maps,facsims (some col.),ports ; 25cm
Bibliography: p232-235. — Includes index
ISBN 0-442-29620-7 : £25.45 B82-21854

745.1 — ANTIQUES

745.1 — Antiques

The **Best** of Antique collecting. — [Woodbridge] : Antique Collectors′ Club, c1981. — 199p : ill (some col.) ; 29cm
The articles in this book first appeared in Antique collecting, the journal of the Antique Collectors′ Club, between September 1979 and September 1981
ISBN 0-907462-09-x : £8.95 B82-13942

Bygones 5 / edited by Dick Joice. — Woodbridge : Boydell Press, c1980. — 144p : ill,facsims,ports ; 21cm
Bygones presented by Anglia Television
ISBN 0-85115-134-5 (pbk) : £3.95 B82-39144

745.1 — Antiques — *Collectors′ guides*

Hillier, Bevis. Bevis Hillier′s pocket guide to antiques. — London : Mitchell Beazley, c1981. — 192p : ill(some col.) ; 20x10cm
Includes index
ISBN 0-85533-317-0 : £3.95 B82-00853

Ketchum, William C.. The catalog of world antiques : a fully illustrated collector′s guide to styles and prices / by William C. Ketchum, Jr. ; photography by Chun Y. Lai. — [Leicester] : Windward, 1981. — 320p : chiefly ill(some col.) ; 32cm
Bibliography: p312-313. — Includes index
ISBN 0-7112-0212-5 : Unpriced B82-02868

Price, Bernard. Antiques you can afford / Bernard Price. — London (36 Park St., W1Y 4DE) : Park Lane Press, 1981. — 80p : col.ill ; 28cm
Includes index
£1.10 (pbk) B82-17370

745.1 — Antiques — *Collectors′ guides* — *Illustrations*

The **Antique** dealers pocketbook / [compiled and edited by Tony Curtis]. — Galashiels : Lyle, c1981. — 160p : chiefly ill ; 17cm
Includes index
ISBN 0-86248-025-6 : £2.50 B82-08176

The **Gentle** art of collecting. — [Overseas ed.]. — Beaconsfield (26 London End, Beaconsfield, Bucks. HP9 2JH) : David Messum ... in association with K. Chappell Antiques and Fine Art, [1982?]. — 22leaves : col.ill ; 22cm
Published to accompany an exhibition at David Messum Fine Paintings, Beaconsfield
Unpriced (pbk) B82-39958

745.1 — Antiques. Purchase & sale — *Amateurs′ manuals*

Rowland, Tom. Selling antiques from home / Tom Rowland. — London : Pelham, 1982. — 110p : ill ; 21cm. — (Business from home)
Bibliography: p103. — Includes index
ISBN 0-7207-1401-x : £5.95 : CIP rev. B82-07598

745.1 — Boxes, *to ca 1930* — *Collectors′ guides*

Curtis, Tony, *1939-*. Caddies & boxes / compiled by Tony Curtis. — Galashiels : Lyle, c1982. — 126p : ill ; 17cm. — (Antiques and their values)
Includes index
ISBN 0-86248-017-5 : £2.50 B82-28534

745.1 — Bryant & May matchboxes, *1861-1961* — *Catalogues*

Hardware Bryant & May : 1861-1961 : matchbox-slides, grips, covers, Vesta, Vesuvian, Fuzee containers, match stands & containers, wax taper tubes / [compiled] by J.H. Luker. — Camberley : Vesta, 1982. — 128p : ill,facsims ; 21x32cm. — (World matchbox label series)
ISBN 0-905040-13-9 (unbound) : Unpriced B82-31032

745.1 — European spoons, *to 1900* — *Collectors′ guides*

Houart, Victor. Antique spoons : a collector′s guide / Victor Houart. — London : Souvenir, 1982. — 144p,[8]p of plates : ill(some col.) ; 23cm. — (Collectors guides series)
Bibliography: p143-144
ISBN 0-285-62499-7 : £8.95 B82-27117

745.1′028′8 — Antiques. Restoration — *Amateurs′ manuals*

Curtis, Tony, *1939-*. Tricks of the antique trade / Tony Curtis and Stuart Barton. — Galashiels : Lyle, 1975 (1979 [printing]). — 123p : ill ; 22cm
Includes index
ISBN 0-902921-25-8 (pbk) : £1.50 B82-08175

Mills, John FitzMaurice. Collecting & looking after antiques / John FitzMaurice Mills. — London : Hamlyn, 1979, c1973. — 158p : col.ill ; 19cm
Originally published: 1973. — Bibliography: p157. — Includes index
ISBN 0-600-30484-1 : £2.50 B82-20728

Mills, John Fitzmaurice. Look after your antiques / John Fitzmaurice Mills. — London : Ebury Press, 1980. — 160p ; 23cm
ISBN 0-85223-179-2 : £6.50 B82-24162

Rowland, Tom. A-Z guide to cleaning and renovating antiques / Tom Rowland. — London : Constable, 1981. — 215p : ill ; 18cm
ISBN 0-09-463630-3 : £5.95 B82-06392

745.1′0942 — English antiques, *1837-1901* — *Buyers′ guides*

Victoriana : buyer′s price guide / compiled and researched by Stuart Brunger ; edited by Judith and Martin Miller. — Tenterden : MJM, 1981?. — 93p : ill ; 12cm
Includes index
ISBN 0-905879-06-6 : £2.95 B82-12795

745.1′095 — Oriental antiques, *to ca 1950* — *Collectors′ guides*

Curtis, Tony, *1939-*. Oriental antiques / compiled by Tony Curtis. — Galashiels : Lyle, c1982. — 126p : ill ; 17cm. — (Antiques and their values)
Includes index
ISBN 0-86248-022-1 : £2.50 B82-28674

745.1′0971 — Canadian antiques — *Collectors′ guides*

Hearn, John. Collector′s items : a guide to antique hunting across Canada / John Hearn. — Toronto ; London : Van Nostrand Reinhold, c1981. — vii,136p : ill,1map ; 28cm
Bibliography: p132-134. — Includes index
ISBN 0-442-29701-7 (pbk) : £10.15 B82-22586

745.2 — INDUSTRIAL DESIGN

745.2 — Design. Aesthetics

Pye, David. The nature & aesthetics of design. — London : Herbert Press, Dec.1982. — [160]p
ISBN 0-906969-27-1 (pbk) : £6.95 : CIP entry B82-30747

745.2 — Industrial design — *Conference proceedings*

Design ′82. — Oxford : Pergamon, Nov.1982. — [425]p. — (Institution of Chemical Engineers symposium series ; 76)
Conference papers
ISBN 0-08-028773-5 : £31.50 : CIP entry B82-31281

745.2′07′1141 — Great Britain. Higher education institutions. Curriculum subjects: Industrial design. Courses — *Directories*

Design courses in Britain 1981-82. — London : Design Council, 1981. — 110p ; 21cm
ISBN 0-85072-122-9 (pbk) : £2.50 : CIP rev. B81-31956

745.4 — DESIGN AND DECORATION

745.4 — Design

Changing design / edited by Barrie Evans, James A. Powell, Reg Talbot. — Chichester : Wiley, 1982. — viii,379p : ill,plans ; 26cm
Includes bibliographies and index
ISBN 0-471-28045-3 : Unpriced : CIP rev. B82-10766

745.4 — Design. Patterns

Justema, William. The pleasures of pattern / William Justema. — New York ; London : Van Nostrand Reinhold, 1982, c1968. — 240p : ill ; 28cm
Originally published: New York : Reinhold, 1968. — Bibliography 227-233. — Includes index
ISBN 0-442-24531-9 (pbk) : £10.15
B82-28153

745.4 — Geometrical patterns — *Collections*

Wade, David. Geometric patterns and borders / David Wade. — London : Wildwood House, 1982. — [190]p : chiefly ill(some col.) ; 24cm
ISBN 0-7045-0460-x (pbk) : £6.95 : CIP rev.
B82-08446

745.4 — Isometric perspective designs — *Illustrations*

Locke, John, *1955-*. Isometric perspective designs : and how to create them / original designs and text by John Locke. — New York : Dover ; London : Constable, 1981. — 16p,32p of plates : ill(some col.) ; 28cm. — (Dover pictorial archive series)
Ill on inside covers
ISBN 0-486-24123-8 (pbk) : £2.35 B82-13562

745.4'0246864 — Graphics. Designs — *Illustrations — For photoreproduction*

Bigg, Barry. The copy catalogue / by Barry Bigg. — Harmondsworth : Penguin, 1981. — [112] leaves : chiefly ill,maps ; 28cm
ISBN 0-14-005992-x (pbk) : £3.95 B82-08037

745.4'025 — Design — *Directories — Serials*

World design sources directory = Répertoire des sources d'information en design / edited by the Centre de création industrielle for ICOGRADA, International Council of Graphic Design Associations [and] ICSID, International Council of Societies of Industrial Design. — 1980-. — Oxford : Pergamon, 1980-. — v. ; 22cm
Text in English, foreword and introduction also in French
£11.50 B82-19865

745.4'028'54 — Design. Applications of digital computer systems — *Serials*

CAD/CAM digest. — Vol.1, no.1 (Sept. 1977)-. — Peterborough ([170a Park Rd, Peterborough, Cambs]) : [CAD/CAM Publications], 1977-. — v. : ill ; 30cm
Description based on: Vol.2, no.7 (Nov.-Dec 1979)
ISSN 0263-6190 = CAD CAM digest : £20.00 per year B82-40036

CadCam international. — Sept. 1981-. — London (43 St John St., EC1M 4AN) : Woodpecker Publications, 1981-. — v. : ill,ports ; 30cm
Monthly
ISSN 0261-6920 = CadCam international : £18.00 per year
Primary classification 338.4'567'05 B82-05221

745.4'07'1141 — Great Britain. Higher education institutions. Curriculum subjects: Design

Casson, *Sir* **Hugh**. The arts and the academies : the Romanes lecture for 1979-80 : delivered in Oxford on 13 November 1979 / Sir Hugh Casson. — Oxford : Clarendon, 1980. — 25p ; 22cm
ISBN 0-19-951525-5 (pbk) : £1.50 : CIP rev.
B80-11106

Council for National Academic Awards. *Committee for Art and Design*. Report on the review of BA Honours Degree courses in art and design, 1975-76 / Committee for Art and Design. — London (344 Gray's Inn Rd., WC1X 8BP) : CNAA, 1979. — 30p ; 21cm
Unpriced (pbk) B82-40159

745.4'07'1241 — Great Britain. Secondary schools. Curriculum subjects: Design

Kimbell, Richard. Design education : the foundation years / Richard Kimbell. — London : Routledge and Kegan Paul, 1982. — vii,177p : ill ; 22cm. — (Routledge education books)
Bibliography: p173-174. — Includes index
ISBN 0-7100-9018-8 (pbk) : £6.95 B82-39525

745.4'07'12411 — Scotland. Secondary schools. Curriculum subjects: Design — *Inquiry reports*

Design Council. *Scottish Committee*. Design education at secondary level in Scotland. — Glasgow : Design Council Scottish Committee, 1981. — 16p ; 30cm. — (A Design Council report)
Cover title
ISBN 0-85072-120-2 (pbk) : £1.00 B82-40177

745.4'442 — Design, *1970-1979*

Potter, Norman. Designing a present : a pamphlet / by Norman Potter and invited contributors to accompany the book What is a designer. — Reading : Hyphen, 1980. — 39p : ill ; 21cm
Cover title
ISBN 0-907259-02-2 (pbk) : £1.50 B82-13317

745.4'4924 — Design. Sottsass, Ettore — *Critical studies*

Sparke, Penny. Ettore Sottsass Jnr / Penny Sparke. — London : Design Council, 1982. — 87p : ill,ports ; 21cm
ISBN 0-85072-126-1 (pbk) : £6.50 : CIP rev.
B82-11780

745.4'494 — Celtic design — *Illustrations*

Rigan, Alice. Celtic renaissance : prints from Findhorn / by Alice Rigan. — Forres : New Findorn Directions, c1980. — [96]p : ill ; 30cm
ISBN 0-906191-48-3 (pbk) : £3.50 B82-03960

745.4'4941 — British design, *1880-1981*

MacCarthy, Fiona. British design since 1880 : a visual history / Fiona MacCarthy. — London : Lund Humphries, 1982. — 229p : ill(some col.) ; 24cm
Bibliography: p191-202. — Includes index
ISBN 0-85331-461-6 (cased) : £17.50
ISBN 0-85331-447-0 (pbk) : £11.95
B82-23655

745.4'4941 — Great Britain. Design, *1850-1940*

Pevsner, Nikolaus. Studies in art, architecture and design, Victorian and after / Nikolaus Pevsner ; with 518 illustrations. — London : Thames and Hudson, 1982, c1968. — 288p : ill,facsims,plans ; 29cm
Originally published: as Vol.2 of Studies in art, architecture and design. 1968. — Includes index
ISBN 0-500-27256-5 (pbk) : £7.50 B82-20418

745.4'49485 — Swedish design, *to 1980 — Conference proceedings*

Svensk Form : a conference about Swedish design / [edited by Nicola Hamilton]. — London : Design Council, 1981. — 48p : ill ; 28cm
ISBN 0-85072-118-0 (pbk) : Unpriced : CIP rev. B81-12382

745.5 — HANDICRAFTS

745.5 — Handicrafts — *For children*

Brown, Rosalie. More things to make. — Wendover : John Goodchild, Jan.1983. — [96]p
ISBN 0-903445-60-3 : £3.50 : CIP entry
B82-37628

745.5 — Handicrafts — *Manuals*

Homecraft mirror : 150 gifts to make for Christmas / in association with Womancraft. — London : Mirror Books, 1981. — 26p : ill (some col.),1port ; 37cm. — (Daily Mirror homecraft special)
ISBN 0-85939-284-8 (unbound) : £0.50
B82-06350

Presents. — Newton Abbot : David & Charles, Sept.1982. — [140]p
ISBN 0-7153-8213-6 : £7.95 : CIP entry
B82-20372

745.5 — Handicrafts — *Manuals — For children*

Brown, Arthur. How to make and play indoor games. — Wendover : John Goodchild No.1. — Feb.1983. — [96]p
ISBN 0-903445-62-x : £3.50 : CIP entry
Also classified at 790 B82-39289

Brown, Arthur. How to make and play indoor games. — Wendover : John Goodchild No.2. — Feb.1983. — [96]p
ISBN 0-903445-63-8 : £3.50 : CIP entry
Also classified at 790 B82-39290

Brown, Rosalie. Things to make. — 2nd ed. — Wendover : Goodchild, Jan.1983. — [96]p
Previous ed.: 1977
ISBN 0-903445-59-x : £3.50 : CIP entry
B82-37629

Caket, Colin. The present book / by Colin Caket. — London : Macmillan Childrens, 1981. — 96p : ill ; 24cm
Includes index
ISBN 0-333-31542-1 : £2.95 B82-06694

Cartlidge, Michelle. The bear's bazaar : a story/craft book / Michelle Cartlidge. — [London] : Fontana, 1982, c1979. — [32]p : col.ill ; 22cm. — (Picture lions)
Originally published: London : Heinemann, 1979
ISBN 0-00-661792-1 (pbk) : £0.90 B82-09319

Craft, Ruth. Play School play ideas. — Sevenoaks : Hodder & Stoughton, Feb.1983. — [96]p
ISBN 0-340-33299-9 (pbk) : £1.10 : CIP entry
B82-37675

Daitz, Myrna. Crafty ideas / Myrna Daitz & Shirley Williams ; with illustrations by Annie Tomlin. — London : Severn House, c1981. — 124p : col.ill ; 25cm
ISBN 0-7278-2009-5 : £6.95 : CIP rev.
B81-24678

Lister, Sally. Simple crafts for fun / Sally Lister. — London : WI Books, 1981. — 24p : ill(some col.) ; 21cm
Cover title
ISBN 0-900556-70-6 (pbk) : Unpriced : CIP rev. B81-33629

745.5 — Handicrafts — *Manuals — For schools*

Hampson, B. L.. Make it today : Brian Hampson & Sheila Howkins. — Edinburgh : Oliver & Boyd
2
Teacher's guide. — 1981. — 64p : ill ; 25cm
ISBN 0-05-003428-6 (pbk) : £2.50 B82-11471

Hampson, B. L.. Make it today / Brian Hampson & Sheila Howkins. — Edinburgh : Oliver & Boyd
3 / [illustrations by Beverly Curl]. — 1982. — 63p : col.ill ; 26cm
Cover title. — Text on inside cover
ISBN 0-05-003429-4 (pbk) : £1.85 B82-33142

745.5 — Handicrafts. Special subjects: Fiction in English. Milne, A. A. Winnie-the-Pooh stories — *Manuals — For children*

Friedrichsen, Carol S.. The Pooh craft book. — London : Methuen Children's Books, Oct.1982. — [64]p
Originally published: New York : Dutton, 1976
ISBN 0-416-23200-0 : £4.95 : CIP entry
B82-24484

745.5'0240816 — Handicrafts — *Manuals — For physically handicapped persons*

Anderson, Enid. Crafts and the disabled / Enid Anderson. — London : Batsford, 1982. — 144p : ill ; 26cm
Bibliography: p138. — Includes index
ISBN 0-7134-2181-9 : £8.50 B82-31187

745.5'028 — Great Britain. Handicrafts materials — *Buyers' guides — Serials*

The **Craft** buyer's guide. — 1982. — London : Kogan Page, Feb.1982. — [90]p
ISBN 0-85038-502-4 (pbk) : £5.95 : CIP entry
B82-00149

745.5'05 — Handicrafts — *Serials*

Craft quarterly. — Issue 1 (Summer 1981)-. — Sunderland (c/o Ms S. Jones, 17 Shakespeare Terrace, Sunderland SR2 7JG,) : Craft Quarterly, 1981-. — v. : ill ; 30cm
ISSN 0261-5126 = Craft quarterly : £4.00 per year B82-03399

745.5′068′8 — Handicrafts. Marketing
Janitch, Valerie. Crafts on the counter : advice, ideas and designs to help you sell your work / Valerie Janitch. — London : Frederick Muller, 1982. — 131p,[8]p of plates : ill ; 21cm
ISBN 0-584-10374-3 : £6.95 : CIP rev. B82-01211

745.5′0880544 — Handicrafts for children, 6-12 years — *Manuals*
Stewart, Imogen. Six things to make / Imogen Stewart. — London : H.M.S.O., 1981. — 23p : ill(some col.) ; 20cm
At head of title: Bethnal Green Museum of Childhood. — Ill on inside cover
ISBN 0-11-290370-3 (pbk) : £1.25 B82-09892

745.51 — Handicrafts using weathered wood — *Manuals*
Turk, John. Weathered wood / [text by John Turk]. — London : Search Press, 1979. — 31p : ill(some col.) ; 17cm. — (Leisure crafts ; 53)
ISBN 0-85532-351-5 (pbk) : Unpriced B82-08500

745.53′1 — Handicrafts using leather — *Manuals*
Willcox, Donald J.. Modern leather design / Donald Willcox. — New York : Watson-Guptill ; London : Pitman, 1981, c1969. — 159p : ill ; 28cm
Originally published: New York : Watson-Guptill, 1969. — Bibliography: p154. — Includes index
ISBN 0-8230-3101-2 (pbk) : Unpriced B82-22981

745.53′1 — Leatherware. Conservation
Leather conservation. — London (Leather Trade House, 9 St Thomas St., SE1 9SA) : Leather Conservation Centre, June 1982. — [30]p
ISBN 0-946072-02-7 (pbk) : £5.00 : CIP entry B82-17946

745.54 — Handicrafts using paper — *Manuals*
Grater, Michael. [Paper play]. Creative paper toys and crafts / Michael Grater ; illustrated by the author ; photographs by John Hunnex. — New York : Dover ; London : Constable, 1981. — 217p : ill ; 23cm. — (Dover craft books)
Originally published: London : Mills & Boon ; New York : Taplinger, 1972
ISBN 0-486-24184-x (pbk) : £3.75 B82-29995

745.58′4 — Handicrafts using stones
Epple, Doris. Stone on stone / [text and models by Doris Epple] ; [translated by John Griffiths]. — London : Search, 1977. — 32p : ill(some col.) ; 17cm. — (Leisure crafts ; 66)
Translated from the German. — Ill on inside covers
ISBN 0-85532-487-2 (pbk) : Unpriced B82-26500

745.592 — Wooden toys. Making — *Manuals*
Blizzard, Richard E.. Making wooden toys / Richard E. Blizzard. — London : Murray, 1982. — 63p : ill,plans ; 31cm
ISBN 0-7195-3942-0 : £5.95 : CIP rev. B82-09306

745.592′2 — Hessian model human figures. Making — *Manuals*
Hutchings, Margaret. Modelling in hessian. — London : Bell & Hyman, May 1982. — [110]p
Originally published: London : Mills & Boon, 1975
ISBN 0-7135-2029-9 (pbk) : £3.95 : CIP entry B82-11102

745.592′21 — Character dolls. Making — *Manuals*
Luckin, Joyce. Character handmade dolls / Joyce Luckin. — London : Hale, 1982. — 213p,[8]p of plates : ill(some col.) ; 26cm
ISBN 0-7091-8865-x : £12.50 B82-24786

745.592′21 — Paper dolls, *1850-1920* — *Collectors′ guides*
Howard, Marian B.. Those fascinating paper dolls : an illustrated handbook for collectors / Marian B. Howard ; with a new introduction by Barbara Whitton Jendrick. — New York : Dover ; London : Constable, 1981. — 307p : ill,facsims ; 29cm
Originally published: Miami : M.B. Howard, 1965. — Includes index
ISBN 0-486-24055-x (pbk) : £7.50 B82-13559

745.592′21 — Paper dolls — *Collectors′ guides*
Wallach, Anne Tolstoi. Paper dolls : how to find, recognize, buy, collect and sell the cutouts of two centuries / Anne Tolstoi Wallach ; with photographs by Peter Bosch. — New York ; London : Van Nostrand Reinhold, c1982. — 164p,[32]p of plates : ill(some col.),facsims ; 29cm
Bibliography: p161. — Includes index
ISBN 0-442-20046-3 : £25.45 B82-34331

745.592′24 — Glove puppets. Crocheting — *Patterns*
Verkest, Susan. Crocheting storybook hand puppets : complete instructions for 21 easy-to-make projects / Susan Verkest. — New York : Dover ; London : Constable, 1981. — 48p : ill(some col.) ; 28cm. — (Dover needlework series)
Ill on inside covers
ISBN 0-486-23887-3 (pbk) : £1.70 B82-35420

745.592′24 — Puppets. Making — *Amateurs′ manuals*
Boekholt, Albert. Puppets & masks / Albert Boekholt ; translated and adapted by Louisa Bumagin Hellegers]. — New York : Sterling ; Poole : Blandford [distributor], c1981. — 96p,[4]p of plates : ill(some col.) ; 26cm
Translation of: Masques et marottes. — Includes index
ISBN 0-8069-7042-1 : £5.95
Primary classification 731′.75 B82-21869

745.592′24 — Puppets. Making — *Manuals* — *For children*
Connell, Stephanie. Puppets / Stephanie Connell, Diana Stoker ; illustrated by Joan Hickson. — London : Methuen Children′s in association with Thames Television International, 1981. — [32]p : col.ill ; 19cm. — (Rainbow things to do) (A Thames/Magnet book)
Also published in one volume with ′Dressing-up′ and ′Messy things′
ISBN 0-423-00110-8 (pbk) : £0.85 B82-17595

745.592′3 — Dolls′ houses. Making — *Manuals*
Dodge, Venus. The dolls′ house D.I.Y. book / Venus and Martin Dodge. — Newton Abbot : David & Charles, [1982?]. — 224p : ill(some col.),plans ; 26cm
Bibliography: p220. — Includes index
ISBN 0-7153-8289-6 : £8.95 : CIP rev. B82-13068

745.592′3 — Dolls′ houses. Soft furnishings. Crocheting & knitting. Techniques — *Manuals*
Drysdale, Rosemary. Miniature crocheting and knitting for dollhouses / Rosemary Drysdale. — New York : Dover ; London : Constable, 1981. — 47p : ill(some col.) ; 28cm. — (Dover needlework series)
Ill on inside covers
ISBN 0-486-23964-0 (pbk) : £1.70 B82-37391

745.592′3′05 — Dolls′ houses. Making — *Serials*
The **Home** miniaturist. — Vol.1, no.1-. — Dorking (18 Calvert Rd, Dorking, Surrey, RH4 1LS) : [s.n.], [1979]-. — v. : ill ; 25cm
Quarterly. — Description based on: Vol.2, no.3
ISSN 0143-554x = Home miniaturist : £5.00 per year B82-09073

745.592′4 — Soft toys based on characters from Potter, Beatrix. Making — *Manuals*
Hutchings, Margaret. Toys from the tales of Beatrix Potter. — London : Bell & Hyman, July 1982. — [316]p
Originally published: London : Mills and Boon, 1973
ISBN 0-7135-2027-2 (cased) : £9.95 : CIP entry
ISBN 0-7135-1344-6 (pbk) : £5.95 B82-17915

745.592′4 — Soft toys. Making — *Manuals*
Jaffke, Freya. Making soft toys / Freya Jaffke ; translated by Rosemary Gebert ; illustrations by E. von Bekum ... [et al.]. — Millbrae, Cal. : Celestial Arts ; Edinburgh : Floris, 1981. — 59p : ill ; 17x19cm. — (A Dawne-Leigh book)
Translation of: Spielzeug von Eltern selbstgemacht
ISBN 0-903540-46-0 (pbk) : £2.75 : CIP rev. B81-20493

745.592′4 — Soft toys. Making — *Manuals* — *For children*
Morton, Brenda. Toys from knitted squares / by Brenda Morton. — [London] ([17-19 Buckingham Palace Rd., SW1N 0PT]) : [Girl Guides Association], 1982. — 20p : ill ; 19x21cm
£0.60 (pbk) B82-33300

745.592′4 — Toys. Knitting — *Manuals*
Burnham, Nellie. Knitted toys and dolls : complete instructions for 17 easy-to-do projects / Nellie Burnham. — New York : Dover ; London : Constable, 1981. — 32p : ill(some col.) ; 28cm. — (Dover needlework series)
Ill on inside covers
ISBN 0-486-24148-3 (pbk) : £1.50 B82-37389

745.592′8 — Model ships in bottles. Construction — *Manuals*
Schouten, Joop van. Sailing in glass / Joop van Schouten. — London : Nautical Books, 1981. — 96p : ill(some col.) ; 19cm
ISBN 0-333-32216-9 : £5.95 B82-10631

745.592′8 — Wooden birds. Carving — *Amateurs′ manuals*
Green, H. D.. Patterns and instructions for carving authentic birds / H.D. Green. — New York : Dover ; London : Constable, 1982. — 57p : ill ; 28cm. — (Dover books on woodworking and carving)
ISBN 0-486-24222-6 (pbk) : £2.05 B82-39655

745.592′82 — Toy soldiers
Johnson, Peter, *19---*. Toy armies / Peter Johnson ; photography by Norman Potter. — London : Batsford, 1981. — 144p,[48]p of plates : ill(some col.),ports ; 31cm
Bibliography: p140-141. — Includes index
ISBN 0-7134-3901-7 : £9.95 B82-05159

745.592′82′0954 — Indian toy soldiers, *1795-1825*
Digby, Simon. Toy soldiers and ceremonial in post Mughal India / by Simon Digby and J.C. Harle. — Oxford : Ashmolean Museum, 1982. — 12p,14p of plates : ill,1map ; 19cm
ISBN 0-900090-91-x (pbk) : £0.95 B82-40532

745.593 — Wooden sundials. Making. Projects
Stoneman, Milton. Easy-to-make wooden sundials : instructions and plans for five projects with suggestions for designing your own pocket sundial / Milton Stoneman. — New York : Dover ; London : Constable, 1982. — 38p,vi leaves of plates : ill ; 28cm. — (Dover books on woodworking and carving)
Bibliography: p38
ISBN 0-486-24141-6 (pbk) : £2.25 B82-39654

745.593′2 — Lampshades. Making — *Manuals*
Cox, Dorothy. Making lampshades. — London : WI Books, July 1982. — [40]p
ISBN 0-900556-75-7 (pbk) : £1.25 : CIP entry B82-19271

745.593′2 — Mission style lampshades. Making — *Amateurs′ manuals*
Adams, John D.. [Lamps and shades in metal and art glass]. How to make mission style lamps and shades / Popular Mechanics Company. — New York : Dover ; London : Constable, 1982. — 114p : ill ; 21cm
Written by John D. Adams. — Originally published: Chicago : Popular Mechanics Company, 1911
ISBN 0-486-24244-7 (pbk) : £2.25
Also classified at 749′.63 B82-40185

745.593′32 — Decorative candles. Making — *Manuals*
Bass, Margaret. Candlemaking / Margaret Bass. — Leicester : Dryad, 1979. — 15p : col.ill ; 15x21cm. — (Dryad leaflet ; 531)
ISBN 0-85219-136-7 (pbk) : Unpriced B82-09891

745.594 — Greetings cards. Making — *Manuals*
Bristow, Martin. Greetings cards / [text and models by Martin Bristow] ; [photographs by Search Press Studios]. — London : Search, 1979. — 32p : ill(some col.) ; 17cm. — (Leisure crafts ; 74)
ISBN 0-85532-481-3 (pbk) : Unpriced B82-08531

745.594'4 — Eggs. Decoration — *Manuals*
Stacey, Allan. The art of egg decorating / Allan Stacey. — London : Routledge & Kegan Paul, 1982. — x,102p,[4]p of plates : ill,music ; 25cm
Includes index
ISBN 0-7100-9026-9 (cased) : £7.95
ISBN 0-7100-9027-7 (pbk) : £4.95 B82-23816

745.6 — LETTERING, ILLUMINATION, HERALDIC DESIGN

745.6'1 — Calligraphy — *Manuals*
Butterworth, Emma Macalik. The complete book of calligraphy / Emma Macalik Butterworth. — Wellingborough : Thorsons, 1981, c1980. — 160p : ill(some col.),facsims ; 24cm
Bibliography: p157
ISBN 0-7225-0704-6 (pbk) : £3.95 : CIP rev. B81-16871

Droge, Dennis. [Woman's day book of calligraphy]. An introduction to calligraphy / Dennis Droge, Janice Glander-Bandyk. — Newton Abbot : David & Charles, 1982. — 95p : ill ; 29cm
Originally published: New York : CBS Publications, 1980
ISBN 0-7153-8300-0 : £6.95 : CIP rev. B82-13069

Gomme, Eileen. An introduction to hand lettering. — London : WI Books, Oct.1982. — [12]p
ISBN 0-900556-77-3 (unbound) : £0.85 : CIP entry B82-24615

Pearce, Charles. The little manual of calligraphy / Charles Pearce. — London : Collins, 1982, c1981. — [32]p : ill ; 21x26cm
Cover title. — Originally published: New York : Taplinger, 1981. — Bibliography: p32
ISBN 0-00-411811-1 : £1.95 B82-22888

Sassoon, Rosemary. The practical guide to calligraphy / Rosemary Sassoon. — London : Thames and Hudson, c1982. — 96p : ill(some col.),facsims ; 26cm
Bibliography: p95
ISBN 0-500-27251-4 (pbk) : £3.95 B82-23253

Shepherd, Margaret. Capitals for calligraphy : a sourcebook of decorative letters / Margaret Shepherd. — Wellingborough : Thorsons, 1982, c1981. — viii,118p : ill ; 28cm
Originally published: New York : Macmillan, 1981. — Bibliography: p109-114. — Includes index
ISBN 0-7225-0761-5 (spiral) : £5.95 : CIP rev. B82-09838

745.6'1 — Lettering — *Illustrations*
Decorative alphabets for needleworkers, craftsmen & artists / edited by Carol Belanger Grafton. — New York ; Dover ; London : Constable, 1981. — 121p ; 29cm. — (Dover pictorial archive series)
ISBN 0-486-24175-0 (pbk) : £3.00 B82-37392

745.6'1 — Ornamental alphabets — *Illustrations*
Bizarre and ornamental alphabets / edited by Carol Belanger Grafton. — New York : Dover ; London : Constable, 1981. — 121p : all ill ; 29cm. — (Dover pictorial archive series)
ISBN 0-486-24105-x (pbk) : £3.00 B82-08400

745.6'1'07 — Children. Curriculum subjects: Handwriting. Teaching. Activities — *For parents & teaching*
Gourdie, Tom. Fun and games / Tom Gourdie. — Edinburgh : Macdonald Publishers, c1981. — 32p : ill ; 21x30cm. — (Teaching children to write ; bk.1)
Cover title
ISBN 0-904265-63-3 : Unpriced B82-05321

745.6'1'07 — Children. Curriculum subjects: Handwriting. Teaching — *Manuals* — *For parents & teaching*
Fagg, Ruth. Handwriting / Ruth Fagg. — Sevenoaks : Produced exclusively for W.H. Smith by Hodder and Stoughton
Bk.1: Learning to write — pencil. — 1982. — 32p ; 25cm
ISBN 0-340-28051-4 (pbk) : £0.75 B82-27675

Fagg, Ruth. Handwriting / Ruth Fagg. — Sevenoaks : Produced exclusively for W.H. Smith by Hodder and Stoughton
Bk.2: Learning to join and write in ink. — 1982. — 48p : col.ill ; 25cm
ISBN 0-340-28050-6 (pbk) : £0.75 B82-27676

Gourdie, Tom. Learning to write / Tom Gourdie. — Edinburgh : Macdonald Publishers, c1981. — 32p : ill ; 21x30cm. — (Teaching children to write ; bk.2)
Cover title
ISBN 0-904265-64-1 (pbk) : Unpriced B82-05322

Michael, Bill. Write first time / Bill Michael. — London : Evans Brothers, 1980. — 48p : ill (some col.) ; 21cm
ISBN 0-237-29244-0 (pbk) : Unpriced B82-17992

745.6'1'076 — Handwriting — *Questions & answers* — *For children*
Jarman, Christopher. Handwriting skills / Christopher Jarman. — [Oxford] : Blackwell
For use in conjunction with Christopher Jarman's The development of handwriting skills
Copybook 1. — 1982. — 32p : ill ; 25cm
Cover title. — Text on inside covers
ISBN 0-631-91600-8 (pbk) : Unpriced B82-37568

Jarman, Christopher. Handwriting skills / Christopher Jarman. — [Oxford] : Blackwell
For use in conjunction with Christopher Jarman's The development of handwriting skills
Copybook 2. — 1982. — 32p : ill ; 25cm
Cover title. — Text on inside covers
ISBN 0-631-91610-5 (pbk) : Unpriced B82-37573

Jarman, Christopher. Handwriting skills / Christopher Jarman. — [Oxford] : Blackwell
For use in conjunction with Christopher Jarman's The development of handwriting skills
Copybook 2. — 1982. — 32p : ill ; 25cm
Cover title. — Text on inside covers
ISBN 0-631-91640-7 (pbk) : Unpriced B82-37570

Jarman, Christopher. Handwriting skills / Christopher Jarman. — [Oxford] : Blackwell
For use in conjunction with Christopher Jarman's The development of handwriting skills
Copybook 3. — 1982. — 32p : ill ; 25cm
Cover title. — Text on inside covers
ISBN 0-631-91620-2 (pbk) : Unpriced B82-37572

Jarman, Christopher. Handwriting skills / Christopher Jarman. — [Oxford] : Blackwell
For use in conjunction with Christopher Jarman's The development of handwriting skills
Copybook 4. — 1982. — 32p : ill ; 25cm
Cover title. — Text on inside covers
ISBN 0-631-91630-x (pbk) : Unpriced B82-37571

Jarman, Christopher. Handwriting skills / Christopher Jarman. — [Oxford] : Blackwell
For use in conjunction with Christopher Jarman's The development of handwriting skills
Activity book. — 1982. — 32p : ill ; 25cm
Cover title. — Text on inside covers
ISBN 0-631-91650-4 (pbk) : Unpriced B82-37569

745.6'1'09 — Lettering, *to 1973*
Gardner, William, *1914-*. Alphabet at work / William Gardner. — London : A. & C. Black, 1982. — xvi,112p : ill,facsims ; 26cm
Bibliography: p101-103. — Includes index
ISBN 0-7136-2206-7 : £9.95 B82-34642

745.6'1'0903 — Calligraphy, *1500-1800* — *Illustrations*
Masterpieces of calligraphy : 261 examples, 1500-1800 / edited by Peter Jessen. — New York : Dover ; London : Constable, 1981. — xi,[200]p ; 29cm
Translation of: Meister der Schreibkunst aus drei Jahrhunderten
ISBN 0-486-24100-9 (pbk) : £4.50 B82-08230

745.6'1'0924 — English lettering. Jones, David, *1895-1974* — *Catalogues*
Gray, Nicolete. The painted inscriptions of David Jones / Nicolete Gray. — London : Gordon Fraser, c1981. — 113p : ill,facsims(some col.) ; 32cm
Bibliography: p111. — Includes index
ISBN 0-86092-058-5 : £29.50 : CIP rev. B81-04289

745.6'197 — Latin alphabet. Calligraphy
Goines, David Lance. A constructed Roman alphabet including the Greek characters and the Arabic numerals. — London (45 Blackfriars Rd., SE1 8NZ) : Kudos & Godine, May 1982. — [128]p
ISBN 0-906293-30-8 : £25.00 : CIP entry B82-09207

745.6'197 — Latin alphabet. Handwriting — *For Arab students*
Hartley, Bernard. Basic handwriting in English / by Bernard Hartley and Peter Viney. — Walton-on-Thames : Nelson, 1982. — 63p ; 25cm
Text on inside covers
ISBN 0-17-555326-2 (pbk) : £1.05 B82-22931

745.6'1977 — Mercator's italic writing — *Illustrations*
Baker, Arthur, *19---*. Arthur Baker's copybook of renaissance calligraphy : (Mercator's Italic hand) / with an introduction by William Hogarth. — New York : Dover ; London : Constable, 1981. — 25p ; 29cm. — (Dover pictorial archive series)
ISBN 0-486-24162-9 (pbk) : £1.30 B82-13376

745.6'19916 — Celtic manuscripts. Lettering — *Illustrations*
Bain, George. Celtic art : the methods of construction / by George Bain. — Glasgow : MacLellan. — (Embryo book)
Book 5: Lettering. — Rev. mini book ed. — 1981. — [32]p : ill ; 11x17cm
Previous ed.: 1944. — Text and ill on inside covers
ISBN 0-85335-170-8 (pbk) : Unpriced : CIP rev. B82-16507

745.6'19927 — Arabic alphabet. Calligraphy — *Manuals*
Ḥakim, Salīm. al-Ḫaṭṭ al'arabī / Salim Ḥakim, Fāruq Imām, Ḥusayn Ḥaydar. — [Oxford] : Oxford University Press
1. — [1981?]. — 1v. : ill ; 24cm
Set of 10 identical books in plastic envelope
ISBN 0-19-917012-6 : Unpriced B82-14025

Ḥakim, Salīm. al-Ḫaṭṭ al'arabī / Salim Ḥakim, Fāruq Imām, Ḥusayn Ḥaydar. — [Oxford] : Oxford University Press
3. — [1981?]. — 1v. : ill ; 24cm
Set of 10 identical books in plastic envelope
ISBN 0-19-917014-2 : Unpriced B82-14023

Ḥakim, Salīm. al-Ḫaṭṭ al'arabī / Salim Ḥakim, Fāruq Imām, Ḥusayn Ḥaydar. — [Oxford] : Oxford University Press
4. — [1981?]. — 1v. : ill ; 24cm
Set of 10 identical books in plastic envelope
ISBN 0-19-917015-0 : Unpriced B82-14024

745.6'19927 — London. Camden *(London Borough)*. **Art galleries: Iraqi Cultural Centre.** *Gallery.* **Exhibits: Islamic calligraphy** — *Catalogues*
The **Influence** of calligraphy on contemporary Arab art : 20 Feb-14 March 1980. — London (177-178 Tottenham Court Rd, W1) : The Iraqi Cultural Centre, 1980. — [20]p : ill(some col.) ; 30cm
Published to accompany an exhibition at the Centre. — Cover title
Unpriced (pbk) B82-20669

745.6'1995 — Oriental sacred calligraphy
Stevens, John, *1947-*. Sacred calligraphy of the East / John Stevens. — Boulder ; London : Shambhala, 1981 ; London : Distributed by Routledge & Kegan Paul. — xii,206p : ill,facsims ; 28cm
Bibliography: p201-203. — Include index
ISBN 0-87773-198-5 (pbk) : £6.95 B82-03279

745.6′19951 — Chinese calligraphy. Brushwork, *to 1980*

Kwo, Da-Wei. Chinese brushwork : its history, aesthetics, and techniques / Kwo Da-Wei. — Montclair : Allanheld & Schram ; London : Prior, c1981. — xvii,204p : ill,1map ; 28cm
Bibliography: p193-199. — Includes index
ISBN 0-86043-661-6 : Unpriced B82-25811

745.6′19951 — Chinese calligraphy, *to 1980*

Chinese calligraphy : its history and aesthetic motivation : the record of an exhibition of Chinese calligraphic art held in the University of Malaya from 17 October to 10 November 1977 / descriptive and appreciatory comments by William Willetts. — Hong Kong ; Oxford : Oxford University Press, 1981. — xii,264p,[8]p of plates : ill(some col.) ; 26cm
Includes Chinese description of exhibits. — Half title page in Chinese. — Bibliography: p263-264. — Includes index
ISBN 0-19-580478-3 : £23.00 B82-38458

745.6′7 — Illuminated manuscripts. Illuminations, *to 1500.* **Special subjects: Birds**

Yapp, Brunsdon. Birds in medieval manuscripts. — London : British Library Reference Division, Oct.1981. — [192]p
ISBN 0-904654-54-0 : £9.50 : CIP entry B81-27939

745.6′7′0942 — English illuminated manuscripts, *1100-1300:* **Bible. N.T. Epistles of Paul.** *Latin.* **Characters: Paul,** *the Apostle, Saint.* **Illustrations** — *Critical studies*

Eleen, Luba. The illustration of the Pauline Epistles in French and English Bibles of the twelfth and thirteenth centuries. — Oxford : Oxford University Press, Nov.1982. — [212]p
ISBN 0-19-817344-x : £40.00 : CIP entry
Also classified at 745.6′7′0944 B82-26886

745.6′7′0944 — French illuminated manuscripts, *1100-1300:* **Bible. N.T. Epistles of Paul.** *Latin.* **Characters: Paul,** *the Apostle, Saint.* **Illustrations** — *Critical studies*

Eleen, Luba. The illustration of the Pauline Epistles in French and English Bibles of the twelfth and thirteenth centuries. — Oxford : Oxford University Press, Nov.1982. — [212]p
ISBN 0-19-817344-x : £40.00 : CIP entry
Primary classification 745.6′7′0942 B82-26886

745.6′7′094531 — Venetian illuminated manuscripts. Miniature paintings, *ca 1470-1490.* **Special subjects: Classical antiquity** — *Critical studies*

Armstrong, Lilian. Renaissance miniature painters & classical imagery : the Master of the Putti and his Venetian workshop / Lilian Armstrong ; with 152 illustrations. — London : Harvey Miller, c1981. — viii,223p,[3]leaves of plates : ill,facsims(some col.) ; 28cm
Bibliography: p139-148. — Includes index
ISBN 0-905203-24-0 : £28.00 B82-20447

745.6′7′0956107402142 — Great Britain. National libraries: British Library. *Department of Oriental Manuscripts and Printed Books.* **Stock: Turkish illuminated manuscripts. Miniature paintings** — *Catalogues*

British Library. Miniatures from Turkish manuscripts : a catalogue and subject index of paintings in the British Library and British Museum / by Norah M. Titley. — London : British Library, c1981. — 144p,[48]p of plates : ill,1map ; 29cm
Limited ed. of 500 copies. — Bibliography: p140-144
ISBN 0-904654-71-0 : £45.00 : CIP rev.
Primary classification 745.6′7′0956107402142 B81-34011

745.6′7′0956107402142 — London. Camden *(London Borough).* **Museums: British Museum. Stock: Turkish illuminated manuscript. Miniature paintings** — *Catalogues*

British Library. Miniatures from Turkish manuscripts : a catalogue and subject index of paintings in the British Library and British Museum / by Norah M. Titley. — London : British Library, c1981. — 144p,[48]p of plates : ill,1map ; 29cm
Limited ed. of 500 copies. — Bibliography: p140-144
ISBN 0-904654-71-0 : £45.00 : CIP rev.
Also classified at 745.6′7′0956107402142 B81-34011

745.92 — FLOWER ARRANGEMENT

745.92 — Flower arrangement

Brack, Edith. Modern flower arranging / Edith Brack. — London : Batsford, 1982. — vii,135p,[8]p of plates : ill(some col.) ; 26cm
Bibliography: p132. — Includes index
ISBN 0-7134-3893-2 : £7.95 B82-17655

Derbyshire, Jane. The flower arranger′s year / Jane Derbyshire. — London : Collins, 1981. — 157p : ill(some col.) ; 26cm
Includes index
ISBN 0-00-411655-0 : £7.95 B82-01761

745.92 — Flower arrangement — *Manuals*

Jekyll, Gertrude. Flower decoration in the house. — Woodbridge : Antique Collectors′ Club, Dec.1982. — [171]p
ISBN 0-907462-31-6 : £12.50 : CIP entry B82-35233

Stevenson, Violet. Creative flower arranging / Violet Stevenson ; Violet Stevenson ; photography by Leslie Johns. — London : Hamlyn, 1982. — 156p : ill(some col.) ; 26cm
Ill on lining papers. — Includes index
ISBN 0-600-30525-2 : £5.95 B82-36861

Stratmann, Lyn. Modern flower arranging / Lyn Stratmann ; photographs by C.J. Stratmann. — Brighton : Angus & Robertson, 1979. — xiii,79p : ill(some col.) ; 25cm
Includes index
ISBN 0-207-95794-0 : £5.95 B82-30158

Wright, Bernadette. Flower fingers : step-by-step flower arranging / by Bernadette Wright ; photography by Paul C. Wright ; consultant editor Jim Mather. — London : Foulsham, c1982. — 120p : ill(some col.) ; 23cm. — ([Know-how books])
Includes index
ISBN 0-572-01144-x : £4.95 B82-24413

745.92 — Flowering plants. Preservation — *Manuals*

Gordon, Lesley. The complete guide to drying and preserving flowers. — Exeter : Webb & Bower, Aug.1982. — [224]p
ISBN 0-906671-58-2 : £9.95 : CIP entry B82-17232

745.92′252 — Ikebana

Sawano, Takashi. Ikebana : basic principles / Takashi Sawano. — London : Ward Lock, 1981. — 127p : ill(some col.) ; 25cm
Includes index
ISBN 0-7063-6029-x : Unpriced B82-11628

745.92′252 — Ikebana — *Manuals*

Komoda, Shusui. Ikebana : spirit and technique / Shusui Komoda and Horst Pointer. — Poole : Blandford Press, 1980. — 184p,32p of plates : ill(some col.) ; 21cm
Translation of: Ikebanapraxis. — Bibliography: p184
ISBN 0-7137-1040-3 : £6.95 : CIP rev. B80-19347

745.92′6 — Churches. Flower arrangement — *Manuals*

Maurice, Grizelda. Flower arranging & flower festivals in church / Grizelda Maurice. — London : Batsford, 1982. — 111p,[20]p of plates : ill(some col.) ; 23cm
Bibliography: p107. — Includes index
ISBN 0-7134-4033-3 : £6.95 B82-27495

Taylor, Jean, *1921-*. Flowers in Church / Jean Taylor. — London : Mowbray, 1976 (1981 [printing]). — 161p,[8]p of plates : ill(some col.) ; 22cm
Includes index
ISBN 0-264-66220-2 (pbk) : £3.50 B82-18624

745.92′6 — Churches. Flower arrangements — *Manuals*

Macqueen, Sheila. Church flower arranging. — London : Ward Lock, Mar.1982. — [104]p. — (A Hyperion book)
ISBN 0-7063-6068-0 : £8.95 : CIP entry B82-02631

745.92′8 — Pressed flower pictures. Making — *Manuals*

Scott, Margaret Kennedy. Making pressed flower pictures / Margaret Kennedy Scott and Mary Beazley. — London : Batsford, 1979 (1981 [printing]). — 120p,[4]p of plates : ill(some col.) ; 25cm. — (A Batsford craft paperback)
Includes index
ISBN 0-7134-1971-7 (pbk) : £3.95 B82-01605

746 — TEXTILE HANDICRAFTS

746 — London. Camden *(London Borough).* **Crafts. Organisations: British Crafts Centre. Exhibits: Miniature textiles** — *Catalogues*

International Exhibition of Miniature Textiles *(2nd : 1976 : London).* 2nd International Exhibition of Miniature Textiles 1976. — London (43 Earlham St., WC2H 9LD) : British Crafts Centre, [1976?]. — [86]p : chiefly ill ; 21cm
Catalogue of the exhibition held in London
Unpriced (pbk) B82-21520

International Exhibition of Miniature Textiles *(1974 : London).* International Exhibition of Miniature Textiles 1974 : held at the British Crafts Centre, London, 5-29 November 1974. — [London] ([43 Earlham St., WC2H 9LD]) : [British Crafts Centre], [1974]. — [45]p : ill ; 21cm
Catalogue of the exhibition
Unpriced (pbk) B82-22743

746′.0431 — Handicrafts using wool

Dixon, Margaret. The wool book / Margaret Dixon. — London : Hamlyn, 1979. — 140p : ill(some col.) ; 26cm
Bibliography: p137. — Includes index
ISBN 0-600-39426-3 : £5.00 B82-12387

746′.092′4 — Scottish patterned textiles. Designs. Mackintosh, Charles Rennie — *Illustrations*

Billcliffe, Roger. Mackintosh textile designs / Roger Billcliffe. — London : Murray, 1982. — 80p : ill(some col.),1port ; 28cm
Bibliography: p79. — Includes index
ISBN 0-7195-3965-x : £12.50 : CIP rev. B82-20385

746′.0956′07402132 — London. Westminster *(London Borough).* **Art galleries: P. and D. Colnaghi and Co.. Exhibits: Ottoman textiles** — *Catalogues*

King, Donald. Imperial Ottoman textiles : catalogue / by Donald King ; introduction by Michael Goedhuis. — London (14 Old Bond St., W1X 4JL) : Colnaghi, [1980]. — 61p : ill (some col.),1map ; 30cm
Bibliography: p11
Unpriced (pbk) B82-07270

746′.0958 — Turkoman textile arts — *Critical studies*

Turkoman studies. — London : Oguz
1: Aspects of the weaving and decorative arts of Central Asia / edited by Robert Pinner and Michael Franses. — 1980. — 288p : ill(some col.) ; 28cm
Bibliography: p277. — Includes index
ISBN 0-905820-05-3 : Unpriced : CIP rev. B79-36901

746′.09595′4 — Iban textiles — *Catalogues*

Haddon, Alfred C.. Iban or sea Dayak fabrics and their patterns : a descriptive catalogue of the Iban fabrics in the Museum of Archaeology and Ethnology Cambridge / Alfred C. Haddon and Laura E. Start ; with new preface and extended bibliography by D.A. Swallow. — [2nd ed.]. — Carlton : Ruth Bean, 1982. — xvii,160p : ill ; 23cm
Previous ed.: Cambridge : Cambridge University Press, 1936. — Bibliography: p156-160
ISBN 0-903585-11-1 (pbk) : £6.00 B82-29996

746′.09598 — Indonesian textiles, *to 1980*

Warming, Wanda. The world of Indonesian textiles. — London (10 Parkfields, SW15 6NH) : Serindia, May 1981. — [200]p
ISBN 0-906026-08-3 : £25.00 : CIP entry B81-08883

746'.097281 — Guatemalan Central American Indian textiles. Designs, *1880-1980*

Rowe, Ann Pollard. A century of change in Guatemalan textiles / Ann Pollard Rowe. — New York : The Center for Inter-American Relations ; Seattle ; London : Distributed by the University of Washington Press, c1981. — 151p : ill,1map ; 28cm
Ill on inside covers. — Bibliography: p149-151
ISBN 0-295-95908-8 (pbk) : Unpriced B82-37805

746'.0984 — Bolivian textiles

Wasserman, Tamara E.. Bolivian Indian textiles : traditional designs and costumes / text & photography by Tamara E. Wasserman & Jonathan S. Hill. — New York : Dover ; London : Constable, 1981. — 28p,32p of plates : ill(some col.),1map ; 29cm. — (Dover pictorial archive series)
Bibliography: p18
ISBN 0-486-24118-1 (pbk) : £6.00 B82-05281

746.1 — HANDICRAFTS. SPINNING, WEAVING, ETC

746.1 — Yarns. Dyeing, spinning & weaving — *Amateurs' manuals*

Sutton, Ann, *1935-*. The craft of the weaver / Ann Sutton, Peter Collingwood, Geraldine St Aubyn Hubbard ; edited by Anna Jackson. — London : British Broadcasting Corporation, 1982. — 152p : ill(some col.) ; 31cm
'This book accompanies the BBC Television series "The craft of the weaver" ... '. — Bibliography: p151-152
ISBN 0-563-16507-3 (cased) : £9.75
ISBN 0-563-16363-1 (pbk) : £7.50 B82-12853

746.1'2 — Handicrafts: Spinning — *Manuals*

Chadwick, Eileen, *19---*. The craft of hand spinning / Eileen Chadwick. — London : Batsford, 1980 (1981 [printing]). — 167p,[4]p of plates : ill(some col.) ; 25cm. — (A Batsford craft paperback)
Bibliography: p163. — Includes index
ISBN 0-7134-1012-4 (pbk) : £3.95 B82-01602

Fannin, Allen. Handspinning : art & technique / Allen Fannin. — New York ; London : Van Nostrand Reinhold, 1970 (1981 [printing]). — 208p : ill ; 25cm
Includes index
ISBN 0-442-22541-5 (pbk) : £8.45 B82-08352

Kroll, Carol. The whole craft of spinning : from the raw material to the finished yarn / Carol Kroll. — New York : Dover ; London : Constable, 1981. — 48p : ill ; 28cm
Bibliography: p46
ISBN 0-486-23968-3 (pbk) : £1.90 B82-13556

Mercer, John, *1934-*. The spinner's workshop / John Mercer. — Dorchester : Prism, 1978 (1979 [printing]). — 150p : ill ; 23cm
Bibliography: p145-146. — Includes index
ISBN 0-904727-97-1 (cased) : Unpriced
ISBN 0-904727-77-7 B82-13211

Wickens, Hetty M.. Beginner's guide to spinning / Hetty M. Wickens. — London : Newnes Technical Books, 1982. — 183p,[2]p of plates : ill(some col.) ; 19cm
Bibliography: p179-180. — Includes index
ISBN 0-408-00573-4 (pbk) : £3.95 : CIP rev. B82-04026

746.1'4 — Hand loom weaving — *Amateurs' manuals*

Sutton, Ann. The structure of weaving. — London : Hutchinson, Sept.1982. — 1v.
ISBN 0-09-149500-8 : £12.95 : CIP entry B82-22415

746.1'4 — Handicrafts: Card weaving — *Manuals*

Collingwood, Peter. The techniques of tablet weaving. — London : Faber, Nov.1982. — [408]p
ISBN 0-571-10829-6 : CIP entry B82-29072

746.1'4 — Handicrafts: Weaving

Regensteiner, Else. The art of weaving / Else Regensteiner. — 2nd ed. — New York ; London : Van Nostrand, 1981, c1970. — 192p,[12]p of plates : ill(some col.) ; 27cm
Previous ed.: New York ; London : Van Nostrand, 1970. — Bibliography: p189-190. — Includes index
ISBN 0-442-27571-4 : £16.10 B82-16329

746.1'4 — Handicrafts: Weaving - *Manuals*

Murray, Rosemary. The essential handbook of weaving. — London : Bell & Hyman, July 1981. — [160]p
ISBN 0-7135-1282-2 : £8.95 : CIP entry B81-18108

746.1'4 — Handicrafts: Weaving — *Manuals*

Ponting, Ken. Beginner's guide to weaving. — London : Newnes Technical Books, Feb.1982. — [160]p
ISBN 0-408-00574-2 (pbk) : £3.60 : CIP entry B81-36374

746.1'4 — Handicrafts: Weaving using inkle looms — *Manuals*

Bradley, Lavinia. Inkle weaving : a comprehensive manual / Lavinia Bradley. — London : Routledge & Kegan Paul, 1982. — ix,83p : ill ; 24cm
Bibliography: p79. — Includes index
ISBN 0-7100-9086-2 (pbk) : £3.95 B82-39944

746.1'4041 — Handicrafts: Weaving — *Patterns*

Meltzer, Marilyn. Weave it! : 28 projects for your home / Marilyn Meltzer. — New York ; London : Van Nostrand Reinhold, c1981. — 96p : ill ; 29cm
Includes index
ISBN 0-442-25326-5 : £12.70 B82-07882

Plath, Iona. [The craft of handweaving]. The handweaver's pattern book : over 120 designs for upholstery, curtains, place mats, etc. / Iona Plath. — New York : Dover ; London : Constable, 1981. — 127p : ill ; 28cm
Originally published: New York : Scribners, 1972. — Includes index
ISBN 0-486-24166-1 (pbk) : £3.75 B82-23893

746.1'4'096711 — Cameroon. Handicrafts: Weaving. Traditional techniques, *to 1980*

Lamb, Venice. Au Cameroun : weaving : tissage / Venice and Alastair Lamb. — Hertingfordbury : for Elf Serepca Cameroun ... by Roxford Books, 1981. — 192p : ill(some col.),2maps,ports(some col.) ; 29cm
Parallel English and French text. — Bibliography: p192
ISBN 0-907129-01-3 : Unpriced B82-13796

746.2 — LACE MAKING AND RELATED HANDICRAFTS

746.2'2 — Lace. Making — *Manuals*

Kinmond, Jean. The Coats book of lacecrafts / Jean Kinmond. — London : Batsford, 1978 (1981 [printing]). — 96p,[4]p of plates : ill (some col.) ; 25cm. — (A Batsford craft paperback)
ISBN 0-7134-0784-0 (pbk) : £3.95 B82-01607

746.2'2041 — Lace. Knitting. Shetland designs — *Patterns*

Don, Sarah. The art of Shetland lace. — London : Bell & Hyman, May 1982. — [118]p
Originally published: London : Mills & Boon, 1980
ISBN 0-7135-2021-3 : £7.95 : CIP entry B82-14493

746.2'2'07402354 — Devon. Tiverton. Craft schools: English Lace School. Exhibits: Lace. Collections: Dr. A. I. Spriggs' Collection — *Catalogues*

Dr. A.I. Sprigg's collection of antique lace. — Tiverton (42 St. Peters St, Tiverton) : English Lace School, c1980. — 95p : ill,ports ; 21cm
Cover title: Catalogue of antique lace. — Includes index
£3.50 (pbk) B82-26600

746.2'2'09 — Lace, *to 1980*

Bullock, Alice-May. Lace and lace making / Alice-May Bullock. — London : Batsford, 1981. — 160p : ill,facsims,port ; 26cm
Ill on lining papers. — Bibliography: p157. — Includes index
ISBN 0-7134-2231-9 : £9.95 B82-01685

746.2'22 — Bobbin lace. Making — *Manuals*

Collier, Ann. Creative design in bobbin lace / Ann Collier. — London : Batsford, 1982. — 144p : ill ; 26cm
Bibliography: p141. — Includes index
ISBN 0-7134-2393-5 : £7.95 B82-22241

Mincoff, Elizabeth. Pillow lace : a practical hand-book / by Elizabeth Mincoff and Margaret S. Marriage ; with illustrations by Ernest Marriage and fifty patterns. — Carlton (Victoria Farmhouse, Carlton, Bedford MK43 7LP) : Ruth Bean, 1981. — xii,231p,[48]p of plates : ill ; 23cm
Originally published: London : John Murray, 1907. — Ill on 2 folded leaves in pocket. — Bibliography: p223-226. — Includes index
ISBN 0-903585-10-3 : Unpriced B82-02105

746.2'22 — Bucks point lace. Techniques

Nottingham, Pamela. The techniques of Bucks Point lace / Pamela Nottingham. — London : Batsford, 1981. — 168p : ill(some col.) ; 26cm
Bibliography: p166. — Includes index
ISBN 0-7134-2175-4 : £9.95 B82-06217

746.3 — TAPESTRIES

746.3 — Wall hangings. Making — *Manuals*

Babington, Audrey. Creative wall-hangings & panels / Audrey Babington. — Newton Abbot : David & Charles, c1982. — 183p : ill(some col.) ; 26cm
Bibliography: p178. — Includes index
ISBN 0-7153-8168-7 : £7.95 : CIP rev. B82-04866

746.394'074'02134 — London. Kensington and Chelsea *(London Borough).* **Museums: Victoria and Albert Museum. Stock: European tapesteries,** *1200-1499 — Catalogues*

Victoria and Albert Museum. The tapestry collection : medieval and renaissance / Victoria and Albert Museum ; George Wingfield Digby assisted by Wendy Hefford. — London : H.M.S.O., 1980. — 83p,108p of plates : ill ; 23x28cm
ISBN 0-11-290246-4 : Unpriced B82-17175

746.3944 — French tapestries: Bayeux Tapestry. Military aspects

Jewell, Brian, *1925-*. Conquest & Overlord. — Speldhurst : Midas, June 1981. — 1v.
ISBN 0-85936-247-7 (pbk) : £4.95 : CIP entry
Also classified at 746.44 B81-14462

746.4 — BASKETRY, KNITTING, EMBROIDERY, ETC

746.4 — Needlework — *Manuals*

Allen, Helen. Beginner's guide to sewing & knitting / Helen Allen ; illustrated by Diana McLean ; edited by Lisa Watts. — London : Usborne, 1979. — 64p : ill(some col.) ; 19cm. — (Usborne pocketbooks)
Includes index
ISBN 0-86020-312-3 : £1.85 B82-07755

The **Harmony** guide to decorative needlecraft / [edited by Kit Pyman and Carole Edwards] ; [text and samples by Frances Healey ... et al.] ; [drawings and diagrams by Judith Milne]. — London : Lyric, 1982. — 78p : ill(some col.) ; 30cm
Bibliography: p78. — Includes index
ISBN 0-7111-0012-8 (pbk) : Unpriced B82-23519

746.4'094 — Europe. Needlework, *600-1980*

Synge, Lanto. Antique needlework / Lanto Synge. — Poole : Blandford, 1982. — xxii,202p : ill(some col.) ; 26cm
Ill on lining papers. — Bibliography: p193-195. — Includes index
ISBN 0-7137-1007-1 : £12.95 : CIP rev. B81-22534

746.41′2 — Willow basketry

Heseltine, Alastair. Baskets and basketmaking / Alastair Heseltine. — Princes Risborough : Shire, 1982. — 32p : ill ; 21cm. — (Shire album ; 92)
ISBN 0-85263-611-3 (pbk) : £0.95 B82-39392

746.42 — Ropework — *Manuals*

Fry, Eric C.. The Shell combined book of knots and ropework : (practical and decorative) / Eric C. Fry ; photographs by Peter Wilson. — Newton Abbot : David & Charles, c1981. — [174]p : ill ; 26cm
Originally published: in 2 bks. as The Shell book of knots and ropework, 1977 and The Shell book of practical and decorative ropework, 1978. — Includes index
ISBN 0-7153-8197-0 : £7.50 : CIP rev.
Primary classification 623.88′82 B81-22507

746.42′22 — Macramé — *Amateurs′ manuals*

Pesch, Imelda Manalo. Macramé : creative knotting / Imelda Manalo Pesch and Grethe la Croix. — New York : Sterling ; London : Oak Tree, c1981. — 95p : ill(some col.) ; 19cm
Originally published: in two books as Macramé. New York : Sterling, 1970 and Macramé plus beads. New York : Sterling, 1971
ISBN 0-7061-2819-2 (pbk) : £3.50
Also classified at 746.5 B82-21871

Pyman, Kit. Macrame : bags and belts / [text and designs by Kit Pyman]. — London : Search Press, 1979. — 31p : ill(some col.) ; 17cm. — (Leisure crafts ; 76)
ISBN 0-85532-479-1 (pbk) : Unpriced B82-08502

746.42′22 — Macramé — *Manuals*

Schmid-Burleson, Bonny. The technique of macramé / Bonny Schmid-Burleson. — London : Batsford, 1974 (1981 [printing]). — 128p,[4]p of plates : ill(some col.) ; 25cm. — (A Batsford craft paperback)
Bibliography: p127. — Includes index
ISBN 0-7134-2522-9 (pbk) : £4.95 B82-01604

746.42′24 — Nets. Making — *Manuals*

Winch, Quinton. Nets and knots : for fishermen and others / Quinton Winch. — 2nd ed. — Leicester : Dryad, 1979. — 71p : ill ; 21cm
Previous ed.: 1972. — Includes index
ISBN 0-85219-137-5 (pbk) : Unpriced B82-13580

746.43 — Knitting & crocheting — *Manuals*

Stitch by stitch : the illustrated encyclopedia of sewing, knitting & crochet. — London : Marshall Cavendish, Feb.1982. — 20v.
ISBN 0-85685-768-8 : CIP entry
Primary classification 646.2 B82-02469

746.43′2 — Knitting — *For children*

Dine, Judith. [My first knitting book]. My first 'show me how' knitting book / written by Judith Dine ; illustrated by Jan Howarth ; photographs by Reg Morrison. — London : Dean, 1981, c1973. — 45p : col.ill ; 26cm
Originally published: 1975
ISBN 0-603-00259-5 : Unpriced B82-26755

746.43′2 — Knitting — *Manuals*

Zimmermann, Elizabeth. Elizabeth Zimmerman′s knitter′s almanac : projects for each month of the year / photographs by Tom Zimmerman, drawings by the author. — New York : Dover Publications ; London : Constable, c1981. — 150p : ill ; 21cm
Originally published: New York : Scribner, 1974. — Includes index
ISBN 0-486-24178-5 (pbk) : £1.90 B82-26167

746.43′2041 — Knitting — *Patterns*

Good Housekeeping knitting / [chief contributor/project editor Dorothea Hall]. — London : Ebury, 1981. — 96p : ill(some col.) ; 23cm
Includes index
ISBN 0-85223-200-4 : £3.95 B82-02307

Morgan, Gwyn. Traditional knitting of the British Isles. — London : Ward Lock, Apr.1981. — [104]p
ISBN 0-7063-5787-6 : £6.95 : CIP entry B81-01041

Roberts, Patricia, *1945 Jan.2-*. Patricia Roberts knitting book. — London : W.H. Allen, 1981. — 120p : ill(some col.) ; 30cm
ISBN 0-491-02635-8 : £6.95 B82-00115

746.43′2041′0941 — Knitting. British designs — *Patterns*

The **30s** family knitting book / introduced & edited by Jane Waller. — London : Duckworth, 1981. — 96p : all facsims ; 29cm. — (Paperduck)
ISBN 0-7156-1601-3 (pbk) : £5.95 : CIP rev. B81-20604

746.43′2041′0948 — Knitting. Traditional Scandinavian designs — *Patterns*

Starmore, Alice. Scandinavian knitwear. — London : Bell & Hyman, Feb.1982. — [128]p
ISBN 0-7135-1308-x : £8.50 : CIP entry B81-35833

746.43′4 — Broomstick crocheting — *Patterns*

Wilkes, Margaret Helen. Broomstick crochet / Margaret Helen Wilkes. — Rev. & enl. ed. — London : WI Books, 1981. — 32p : ill ; 21cm
Cover title. — Previous ed.: 197-?
ISBN 0-900556-68-4 (pbk) : Unpriced : CIP rev. B81-20651

746.43′4 — Crocheting — *Manuals*

Svinicki, Eunice. Old-fashioned crochet / Eunice Svinicki & Karla Thompson. — New York ; London : Van Nostrand Reinhold, c1981. — 128p : ill ; 25cm
Bibliography: p125. — Includes index
ISBN 0-442-23120-2 : £11.85 B82-08349

746.43′4 — Crocheting. Patchwork — *Manuals*

Lep, Annette. Crocheting patchwork patterns : 23 granny squares for afghans, sweaters & other projects / Annette Lep. — New York : Dover ; London : Constable, 1981. — xii,50p : ill(some col.) ; 28cm. — (Dover needlework series)
Ill on inside covers
ISBN 0-486-23967-5 (pbk) : £1.90 B82-05282

746.43′4041 — Crocheting — *Patterns*

Good Housekeeping crochet / [chief contributor/project editor Dorothea Hall]. — London : Ebury, 1981. — 96p : ill(some col.) ; 23cm
Includes index
ISBN 0-85223-204-7 : £3.95 B82-02310

746.43′6 — Tatting — *Manuals*

Auld, Rhoda L.. Tatting : the contemporary art of knotting with a shuttle / Rhoda L. Auld ; drawings by James Wood ; photographs by Lawrence Auld. — New York ; London : Van Nostrand Reinhold, c1974, (1981 [printing]). — 128p : ill(some col.),1port ; 24cm
Bibliography: p126. — Includes index
ISBN 0-442-20416-7 (pbk) : £7.60 B82-00849

746.44 — Danish embroidery. Cross-stitch — *Patterns*

Contemporary Danish cross-stitch designs. — London : Bell & Hyman, Sept.1982. — [96]p
Translation of: Vor tids korssting
ISBN 0-7135-1342-x (pbk) : £9.95 : CIP entry B82-20353

746.44 — Danish embroidery. Cross-stitch. Special subjects: Christmas — *Patterns*

Counted cross-stitch designs for Christmas / designs created by the Danish Handcraft Guild. — London : Bell & Hyman in association with Scribner, New York, [1981], c1977. — 79p : ill(some col.) ; 21cm
Translation of: Sy julekorssting. — Originally published: New York : Scribner, 1978
ISBN 0-684-15975-9 (pbk) : £4.50 B82-04106

746.44 — Embroidery. Cross-stitch — *Patterns*

Gostelow, Mary. The cross stitch book / Mary Gostelow. — London : Batsford, 1982. — 144p,[4]p of plates : ill(some col.),1facsim ; 26cm
Includes index
ISBN 0-7134-4123-2 : £8.95 B82-17654

746.44 — Embroidery. Lettering

Williams, Janice. Lettering in embroidery / Janice Williams. — London : Batsford, 1982. — 120p : ill ; 26cm
Bibliography: p118. — Includes index
ISBN 0-7134-3956-4 : £7.95 B82-36537

746.44 — Embroidery — *Manuals*

Good Housekeeping embroidery / [chief contributor Dorothea Hall]. — London : Ebury, 1981. — 96p : ill(some col.) ; 23cm
Includes index
ISBN 0-85223-201-2 : £3.95 B82-02306

746.44 — Embroidery. Smocking — *Manuals*

Dean, Audrey Vincente. Smocking. — London : Paul, Oct.1982. — [144]p
ISBN 0-09-150201-2 : £5.95 : CIP entry B82-24972

Durand, Dianne. Dianne Durand′s complete book of smocking / Dianne Durand. — New York ; London : Van Nostrand Reinhold, c1982. — 136p,[4]p of plates : ill(some col.) ; 28cm
Includes index
ISBN 0-442-24510-6 : £15.25 B82-36643

Picton-Turberville, Jean. Simple smocking. — London : WI Books, June 1982. — [16]p
ISBN 0-900556-74-9 (pbk) : £0.65 : CIP entry B82-22396

746.44 — Embroidery. White work, *to 1930*

Swain, Margaret. Ayrshire and other whitework / Margaret Swain. — Princes Risborough : Shire, 1982. — 32p : ill ; 21cm. — (Shire album ; 88)
Bibliography: p32
ISBN 0-85263-589-3 (pbk) : £0.95 B82-31140

746.44 — English embroidery: Overlord Embroidery. Military aspects

Jewell, Brian, *1925-*. Conquest & Overlord. — Speldhurst : Midas, June 1981. — 1v.
ISBN 0-85936-247-7 (pbk) : £4.95 : CIP entry
Primary classification 746.3944 B81-14462

746.44 — Shisha mirror embroidery — *Manuals*

Gross, Nancy D.. Shisha embroidery : traditional Indian mirror work with instructions and transfer patterns / Nancy D. Gross & Frank Fontana. — New York : Dover Publications ; London : Constable, 1981. — 21p,24leaves of plates : ill(some col.),1map ; 28cm
Ill on inside covers
ISBN 0-486-24043-6 (pbk) : £2.45 B82-08960

746.44 — Stumpwork

Baker, Muriel. Stumpwork : the art of raised embroidery / Muriel Baker. — London : Bell & Hyman in association with Scribner, New York, c1978. — 116p,[8]p of plates : ill(some col.) ; 28cm
Bibliography: p113. — Includes index
ISBN 0-684-15360-2 : £8.50 B82-04105

746.44′028 — Machine embroidery — *Manuals*

Coleman, Anne. The creative sewing machine / Anne Coleman. — London : Batsford, 1979 (1981 [printing]). — 120p,[4]p of plates : ill (some col.) ; 25cm. — (A Batsford craft paperback)
Includes index
£3.95 (pbk) B82-01603

746.44′041 — Swedish embroidery. Cross-stitch - *Patterns*

Counted cross-stitch patterns and designs. — London : Bell & Hyman, July 1981. — [72]p
Translation of: Korsstygns boken
ISBN 0-7135-1276-8 (pbk) : £4.50 : CIP entry B81-14397

746.44′042 — Embroidery. Stitches — *Manuals*

Millington, Ruth. Simple and creative stitchery / [Ruth Millington]. — Leicester : Dryad, c1979. — 15p : col.ill ; 15x21cm. — (Dryad leaflet ; 528)
ISBN 0-85219-132-4 (unbound) : Unpriced B82-14576

746.44'042 — Embroidery. Stitches — *Manuals continuation*

Snook, Barbara. Embroidery stitches / Barbara Snook. — London : Batsford, 1963 (1981 [printing]). — 127p : ill ; 22cm
Bibliography: p8. — Includes index
ISBN 0-7134-2611-x (pbk) : £4.50 B82-07323

746.44'09 — Embroidery, *to 1981*

Parker, Rozsika. The subversive stitch. — London : Women's Press, Feb.1983. — 1v.
ISBN 0-7043-3883-1 (pbk) : CIP entry B82-38873

746.44'0941 — British embroidery, *1900-1939*

Howard, Constance. Twentieth-century embroidery in Great Britain to 1939 / Constance Howard. — London : Batsford, 1981. — 192p,[8]p of plates : ill(some col.) ; 26cm
Bibliography: p188-189. — Includes index
ISBN 0-7134-3942-4 : £17.50 B82-06209

746.44'2 — Canvas embroidery — *Manuals*

Adler, Richard, *1936-*. Needlepoint : a new look / Richard & Elizabeth Adler. — London : Sidgwick & Jackson, 1981. — 176p : ill(some col.),1col.port ; 26cm
Includes index
ISBN 0-283-98797-9 : £9.95 B82-35181

Close, Eunice. An introduction to needlepoint / [by Eunice Close]. — [Wolverhampton] ([23 Marnel Court, Gail Park, Trysull Rd., Wolverhampton]) : [E. Close], [1981?]. — 11p : ill ; 22cm
Unpriced (pbk) B82-12484

Good Housekeeping needlepoint / [chief contributor Dorothea Hall]. — London : Ebury, 1981. — 96p : ill(some col.) ; 23cm
Includes index
ISBN 0-85223-202-0 : £3.95 B82-02308

746.44'2041 — Textured canvas embroidery — *Patterns*

Projansky, Ella. Sculptured needlepoint stitchery / Ella Projansky. — London : Bell & Hyman in association with Charles Scribner's Sons, c1978. — vii,132p,[4]p of plates : ill(some col.) ; 28cm
Includes index
ISBN 0-684-15371-8 : £8.50 B82-05702

746.46 — Clothing. Quilting — *Manuals*

Avery, Virginia. Quilts to wear. — London : Bell & Hyman, Oct.1982. — [224]p
ISBN 0-7135-1350-0 : £10.95 : CIP entry B82-22989

746.46 — Patchwork — *Manuals*

Colby, Averil. Patchwork / Averil Colby. — London : Batsford, 1958 (1981 [printing]). — 201p : ill ; 25cm. — (A Batsford craft paperback)
Includes index
ISBN 0-7134-0392-6 (pbk) : £4.95 B82-03480

746.46 — Patchwork quilts. Making — *Manuals*

Weeks, Linda S.. Quilting : patchwork & trapunto / by Linda S. Weeks and Jo Ippolito Christensen. — New York : Sterling, 1980 ; [London] : Oak Tree [distributor], 1981. — 96p : ill(some col.) ; 19cm
Originally published: in 2 books as Patchwork & other quilting. New York : Sterling, 1973 and Trapunto : decorative quilting. New York : Sterling, 1972. — Includes index
ISBN 0-8069-8930-0 (pbk) : £3.50 B82-21875

746.46 — Patchwork. Use of sewing machines — *Manuals*

Murwin, Susan Aylsworth. Quick and easy patchwork on the sewing machine : step-by-step instructions and full-size templates for 12 quilt blocks / Susan Aylsworth Murwin and Suzzy Chalfant Payne. — New York ; Dover ; London : Constable, 1979. — 37p,16leaves of plates : ill ; 28cm. — (Dover needlework series)
Ill on inside covers
ISBN 0-486-23770-2 (pbk) : £2.30 B82-35927

746.46'041 — Patchwork — *Patterns*

Good Housekeeping patchwork and appliqué / [chief contributor/art editor Michele Walker]. — London : Ebury, 1981. — 96p : ill(some col.) ; 23cm
Includes index
ISBN 0-85223-203-9 : £3.95 B82-02309

746.46'041 — Patchwork. Patterns. Design — *Manuals*

Beyer, Jinny. Patchwork patterns. — London : Bell & Hyman, Sept.1982. — [216]p
ISBN 0-7135-1346-2 (pbk) : £7.95 : CIP entry B82-18770

746.46'041 — Quilts. Geometrical designs — *Patterns*

Beyer, Jinny. The quilter's album of blocks and borders. — London : Bell & Hyman, Sept.1982. — [208]p
ISBN 0-7135-1345-4 (pbk) : £6.95 : CIP entry B82-20354

746.46'09716 — Nova Scotian patchwork quilts. Making — *Manuals*

Houck, Carter. Nova Scotia patchwork patterns : instructions and full-size templates for 12 quilts / Carter Houck. — New York : Dover : London : Constable, 1981. — 64p : ill(some col.) ; 28cm. — (Dover needlework series)
Ill on inside covers
ISBN 0-486-24145-9 (pbk) : £3.00 B82-37390

746.5 — BEADWORK

746.5 — Beadwork — *Amateurs' manuals*

Pesch, Imelda Manalo. Macramé : creative knotting / Imelda Manalo Pesch and Grethe la Croix. — New York : Sterling ; London : Oak Tree, c1981. — 95p : ill(some col.) ; 19cm
Originally published: in two books as Macramé. New York : Sterling, 1970 and Macramé plus beads. New York : Sterling, 1971
ISBN 0-7061-2819-2 (pbk) : £3.50
Primary classification 746.42'22 B82-21871

746.6 — TEXTILE HANDICRAFTS. PRINTING AND DYEING

746.6 — Fabrics. Dyeing & printing — *Amateurs' manuals*

Robinson, Stuart. Beginner's guide to fabric dyeing and printing / Stuart and Patricia Robinson. — London : Newnes Technical, 1982. — 183p,[4]p of plates : ill(some col.) ; 19cm
Includes index
ISBN 0-408-00575-0 (pbk) : Unpriced : CIP rev. B81-36375

746.6 — Japan. Textiles. Ikat — *Amateurs' manuals*

Tomita, Jun. Japanese ikat weaving. — London : Routledge & Kegan Paul, Oct.1982. — [128]p
ISBN 0-7100-9234-2 (pbk) : £5.95 : CIP entry B82-25069

746.6 — Textiles. Dyeing — *Amateurs' manuals*

Goodwin, Jill. A dyer's manual / Jill Goodwin. — London : Pelham, c1982. — 128p : ill(some col.) ; 25cm
Bibliography: p120-122. — Includes index
ISBN 0-7207-1327-7 : £9.95 : CIP rev. B81-35849

746.6'0966 — Textiles. Dyeing. West African techniques

Polakoff, Claire. [Into indigo]. African textiles and dyeing techniques / Claire Polakoff. — London : Routledge & Kegan Paul, 1982, c1980. — xiii,265p,[4]p of plates : ill(some col.),1map,ports ; 21cm
Originally published: Garden City, N.Y. : Anchor, 1980. — Bibliography: p243-250. — Includes index
ISBN 0-7100-0908-9 (pbk) : £6.95 B82-13468

746.6'64 — Fabrics. Tie-dying

Itō, Toshiko. Tsujigahana : the flower of Japanese textile art. — London (10 Parkfields, SW15 6NH) : Serindia Publications, Sept.1981. — [202]p
Translation of: Tsujigahanazome
ISBN 0-906026-09-1 : £115.00 (£95.00 pre-publication) : CIP entry B81-23897

746.7 — TEXTILE HANDICRAFTS. RUGS AND CARPETS

746.7'2'0922 — English woven fabrics. Collingwood, Peter & Harris, Ruth

Peter Collingwood : 6 February-14 March 1981 : Crafts Council Gallery. — [London] : [Crafts Council], c1981. — [24]p : ill ; 21cm
Exhibition catalogue. — Bound tête-bêche with: Ruth Harris : 6 February-14 March 1981 : British Crafts Centre
ISBN 0-903798-53-0 (pbk) : Unpriced B82-35526

746.7'2'09561 — Turkish flat woven fabrics

Ziemba, W. T.. Turkish flat weaves : an introduction to the weaving and culture of Anatolia / William T. Ziemba, Abdulkadir Akatay and Sandra L. Schwartz. — London : Scorpion, 1979. — 143p : ill(some col.),1map ; 21x22cm
Bibliography: p43-46. — Includes index
ISBN 0-905906-25-x : £8.95 B82-05673

746.7'5 — Oriental rugs

Herbert, Janice Summers. Affordable oriental rugs : the buyer's guide to rugs from China, India, Pakistan, and Romania / by Janice Summers Herbert. — London : Studio Vista, 1980. — 160p : ill(some col.),maps ; 26cm
Bibliography: p156-157. — Includes index
ISBN 0-289-70980-6 : £9.95 B82-13453

Walker, Daniel S.. Oriental rugs of the Hajji Babas / Daniel S. Walker. — London : Published in association with the Asia Society, New York and Sotheby's [by] Thames and Hudson, 1982. — 32p,50[i.e. 100]p of plates : ill(some col.),ports ; 29cm
Published to accompany an exhibition at the Asia Society, New York, 1982 and at the Textile Museum, Washington D.C., the Seattle Art Museum and the Cincinnati Art Museum. — Bibliography: p29-32
ISBN 0-500-23356-x : £18.00 B82-29494

746.7'5 — Oriental rugs & carpets. Designs

Ford, P. R. J.. Oriental carpet design : a guide to traditional motifs, patterns and symbols / P.R.J. Ford. — London : Thames and Hudson, c1981. — 352p : ill(some col.),maps ; 33cm
Bibliography: p342. — Includes index
ISBN 0-500-23328-4 : £30.00 B82-01309

746.7'5 — Oriental rugs — *Collectors' guides*

Aschenbrenner, Erich. Oriental rugs. — Woodbridge (5 Church St., Woodbridge, Suffolk) : Oriental Textile Press
Translation of: Orientteppiche
Vol.2: Persian. — Feb.1982. — [272]p
ISBN 0-907462-12-x : £19.50 : CIP entry B82-03391

746.7'5'0288 — Oriental rugs. Maintenance & repair — *Manuals*

Amini, Majid. Oriental rugs : care and repair / Majid Amini. — London : Orbis, 1981. — 128p : ill(some col.),1map ; 30cm
Includes index
£10.00 B82-01483

746.7'59 — Caucasian rugs, *1780-1930*

Oriental rugs. — [S.l.] : Oriental Textile Press ; Woodbridge : Antique Collectors' Club [distributor]
Vol.1: Caucasian / Ian Bennett. — c1981. — 376p : ill(some col.),1map ; 26cm
Map on lining papers. — Bibliography: p374-376
ISBN 0-902028-58-8 (corrected) : Unpriced : CIP rev. B81-25662

746.7951 — Chinese carpets

Gans-Ruedin, E.. Chinese carpets. — London : Allen & Unwin, Jan.1982. — [198]p
ISBN 0-04-746015-6 : £30.00 : CIP entry B81-33906

746.9 — TEXTILE HANDICRAFTS. COSTUME, FURNISHINGS, ETC

746.9'2 — British shawls, *to 1880*

Clabburn, Pamela. Shawls : in imitation of the Indian / Pamela Clabburn. — Princes Risborough : Shire, 1981. — 32p : ill,1facsim ; 21cm. — (Shire album ; 77)
ISBN 0-85263-579-6 (pbk) : £0.95 B82-31135

746.9′2 — Clothing. Design
Davis, Marian L.. Visual design in dress / Marian L. Davis. — Englewood Cliffs ; London : Prentice-Hall, c1980. — xii,339p,[8]p of plates : ill(some col.) ; 25cm
Bibliography: p329-332. — Includes index
ISBN 0-13-942409-1 : £14.20 B82-26461

746.9′2 — English fashion — *Serials*
[I-D *(London)*]. I-D : fashion magazine. — No.1-. — [London] ([71 Sherriff Rd, NW6 2AS]) : T.J. Informat Design, [1980]-. — v. : chiefly ill,ports ; 21x30cm
ISSN 0262-3579 = i-D (London) : £5.00 per year B82-09689

746.9′2 — Lingerie. Fashion design. Reger, Janet — *Illustrations*
Chastity in focus / lingerie Janet Reger ; design Brian Clarke ; foreword Francesca Thyssen. — London : Quartet, 1980. — [148]p : chiefly ill (some col.) ; 31cm
ISBN 0-7043-3390-2 (pbk) : £7.50 B82-14292

746.9′2 — Magazines for women: Vogue. Illustrations: Lingerie, *1910-1980* — *Critical studies*
Probert, Christina. Lingerie in Vogue since 1910 / Christina Probert. — London : Thames and Hudson, c1981. — 95p : ill(some col.) ; 24cm
ISBN 0-500-27255-7 (pbk) : £4.95 B82-21922

746.9′2 — Magazines for women: Vogue. Illustrations: Women's hats, *1910-1981* — *Critical studies*
Probert, Christina. Hats in Vogue since 1910 / Christina Probert. — London : Thames and Hudson, c1981. — 90p : ill(some col.),ports ; 24cm
ISBN 0-500-27254-9 (pbk) : £4.95 B82-21923

746.9′2 — Women's clothing. Fashion design. Erté, *1918-1932* — *Illustrations*
Erté. Erté's fashion designs : 218 illustrations from 'Harper's bazar' 1918-1932 / Erté. — New York : Dover ; London : Constable, 1981. — 71p : chiefly ill(some col.) ; 31cm
ISBN 0-486-24235-8 (cased) : Unpriced
ISBN 0-486-24203-x (pbk) : Unpriced B82-18044

746.9′2 — Women's clothing. Fashion design. Fortuny, Mariano — *Biographies*
Osma, Guillermo de. Fortuny : Mariano Fortuny, his life and work / Guillermo de Osma. — London : Aurum, c1980. — 223p : ill(some col.),ports(some col.) ; 31cm
Bibliography: p221-223. — Includes index
ISBN 0-906053-11-0 : £14.95 B82-25204

746.9′2 — Womn's clothing. Fashion design. Lopez, Antonio — *Illustrations*
Lopez, Antonio. Antonio's girls / Antonio Lopez ; text by Christopher Hemphill ; designed by Juan Ramos ; devised and edited by Karen Amiel. — London : Thames and Hudson, 1982. — 128p : ill(some col.),ports(some col.) ; 29cm
ISBN 0-500-27265-4 (pbk) : £8.95
Also classified at 659.1′52 B82-24935

746.9′2′0924 — Haute couture. Chanel, Gabrielle — *Biographies*
Charles-Roux, Edmonde. Chanel and her world / by Edmonde Charles-Roux. — London : Weidenfeld & Nicolson, 1981. — 354p : ill,music,facsims,ports ; 30cm
Translated from the French. — Includes index
ISBN 0-297-78024-7 : £25.00 B82-02497

746.9′2′0924 — Haute couture. Dior, Christian. Illustrations for Vogue — *Critical studies*
Keenan, Brigid. Dior in Vogue / Brigid Keenan ; foreword by Margot Fonteyn. — London : Octopus, 1981. — 192p : ill(some col.) ; 31cm
Includes index
ISBN 0-7064-1634-1 : £9.95 B82-03923

746.9′7 — Coverlets: Afghans. Crocheting — *Patterns*
Feldman, Annette. The big book of afghans / Annette Feldman ; designed by Allan Mogel ; photography by Ernest Silva. — New York ; Van Nostrand Reinhold, c1981. — 160p : ill (some col.) ; 29cm. — (A Genie book)
Includes index
ISBN 0-442-22528-8 : £13.55 B82-14307

747 — INTERIOR DESIGN

747 — Residences for old persons & residences for physically handicapped persons. Interior design — *Manuals*
Raschko, Bettyann Boetticher. Housing for the disabled and elderly / Bettyann Boetticher Raschko. — New York ; London : Van Nostrand Reinhold, c1982. — xvii,360p : ill,plans ; 22x28cm
Bibliography: p303-312. — Includes index
ISBN 0-442-22001-4 : £29.35 B82-36639

747 — Residences. Interior design
Douglas, Peter, *1936-*. The Ideal home book of interiors / Peter Douglas and Clive Helm. — Poole : Blandford, 1982. — 128p : col.ill ; 29cm
Includes index
ISBN 0-7137-1093-4 : £10.95 : CIP rev. B81-23851

747 — Residences. Interior design — *Amateurs' manuals*
Dickson, Elizabeth. The Laura Ashley book of home decorating / Elizabeth Dickson and Margaret Colvin ; foreword by Laura Ashley. — London : Octupus, 1982. — 160p : ill(some col.) ; 29cm
Includes index
ISBN 0-7064-1478-0 : £7.95
Also classified at 643′.7 B82-24563

Gilliatt, Mary. The decorating book / Mary Gilliatt ; special photography by Michael Dunne. — London : Joseph, 1981. — 368p,[32]p of plates : ill(some col.) ; 27cm
Bibliography: p362. — Includes index
ISBN 0-7181-2019-1 : £16.95 B82-01470

747′.05 — Interior design — *Serials*
What's new in interiors. — Sept. 1981-. — London (30 Calderwood St., SE18 6QH) : Morgan-Grampian, 1981-. — v. : ill ; 30cm
Six issues yearly. — Description based on: Nov./Dec. 1981
ISSN 0262-2742 = What's new in interiors : £12.00 per year B82-11837

747′.05 — Residences. Interior design — *Serials*
[Interiors *(London)*]. Interiors. — Nov.1981-. — London (228 Fulham Rd, SW10 9NB) : Pharos Publications, 1981-. — v. : col.ill,ports ; 28cm
Monthly
ISSN 0263-1520 = Interiors (London) : £24.00 per year B82-19854

747.213 — United States. Residences. Interior design — *Amateurs' manuals*
The **Apartment** book / by the editors of Apartment Life magazine ; text by Rick Mitz. — London : Mitchell Beazley, 1980, c1979. — 317p : col.ill ; 30cm
Originally published: New York : Harmony, 1979. — Includes index
ISBN 0-86134-021-3 : £13.95 B82-08376

747.22 — England. Buildings. Interior design, *1660-1820*
Beard, Geoffrey. Craftsmen and interior decoration in England 1660-1820 / Geoffrey Beard. — Edinburgh : Bartholomew, 1981. — xxiv,311,[16]p of plates : ill(some col.),plans,ports ; 31cm
In slip case. — Bibliography: p297-302. — Includes index
ISBN 0-7028-8430-8 : £35.00 B82-03440

747.22 — Great Britain. Residences. Interior design, *1930-1951*
A **New** design for living. — London (21 Southbank House, Black Prince Rd.) : Lane Publications, Dec.1982. — [48]p
ISBN 0-946375-00-3 (pbk) : £4.50 : CIP entry B82-39268

747.22 — Houses. English interior design. Lutyens, *Sir* **Edwin** — *Illustrations*
Lutyens, *Sir* **Edwin**. Lutyens and the sea captain / introduction by Margaret Richardson. — London : Scolar Press, 1981. — [44]p : ill(some col.),1facsim,ports ; 22cm
ISBN 0-85967-646-3 : £5.95 : CIP rev. B81-32011

747′.3 — Wallpaper, *to 1979* — *Catalogues*
Victoria and Albert Museum. Wallpapers : a history and illustrated catalogue of the collection of the Victoria and Albert Museum / Charles C. Oman and Jean Hamilton ; bibliography by E.A. Entwisle. — [London] : Sotheby in association with the Victoria and Albert Museum, 1982. — 486p : ill(some col.) ; 29cm
Bibliography: p457-466. — Includes index
ISBN 0-85667-096-0 : Unpriced B82-27670

747.7′8 — Residences. Bathrooms. Interior design
Manser, José. The kitchen and bathroom book : planning & decorating your two most functional rooms / José Manser. — London : Pan, 1982. — 160p : ill(some col.) ; 30cm
Includes index
ISBN 0-330-26579-2 (pbk) : £5.95
Primary classification 747.7′97 B82-20442

Manser, José. The kitchen and bathroom book : planning & decorating your two most functional rooms / José Manser. — London : Orbis, 1982. — 160p : ill(some col.),plans ; 30cm
Includes index
ISBN 0-85613-403-1 : £8.95
Primary classification 747.7′97 B82-20443

747.7′97 — Residences. Kitchens. Interior design
Manser, José. The kitchen and bathroom book : planning & decorating your two most functional rooms / José Manser. — London : Pan, 1982. — 160p : ill(some col.) ; 30cm
Includes index
ISBN 0-330-26579-2 (pbk) : £5.95
Also classified at 747.7′8 B82-20442

Manser, José. The kitchen and bathroom book : planning & decorating your two most functional rooms / José Manser. — London : Orbis, 1982. — 160p : ill(some col.),plans ; 30cm
Includes index
ISBN 0-85613-403-1 : £8.95
Also classified at 747.7′8 B82-20443

747′.8521 — United States. Bookshops. Interior design
White, Ken, *1923-*. Bookstore planning and design / Ken White. — New York ; London : McGraw-Hill, c1982. — xiii,181p : ill,plans ; 28cm
Includes index
ISBN 0-07-069851-1 : £30.95 B82-25264

747′.88′094 — Western Europe. Residences. Interior decoration, *1600-1700*
Thornton, Peter. Seventeenth century interior decoration in England, France and Holland. — London : Yale University Press, Sept.1981. — [439]p. — (Studies in British art)
Originally published: 1978
ISBN 0-300-02776-1 (pbk) : £9.95 : CIP entry B81-28157

747′.98 — Residences. Interior design. Use of plants
Muller-Idzerda, A. C.. Decorating with plants : living colour in the home / A.C. Muller-Idzerda & Elisabeth de Lestrieux in collaboration with Jonneke Krans. — Newton Abbot : David & Charles, c1981. — 144p : ill (some col.) ; 30cm
Translation of: Groener wonen. — Includes index
ISBN 0-7153-8175-x : £6.95 : CIP rev. B81-28051

748 — HANDICRAFTS. GLASS

748.2 — Glassware — *Collectors' guides*
Mehlman, Felice. Phaidon guide to glass. — Oxford : Phaidon Press, July 1982. — [256]p
ISBN 0-7148-2202-7 : £9.95 : CIP entry B82-13062

748.29′037 — Glassware, *1700-1950* — *Collectors' guides*
Glass / compiled by Tony Curtis. — Galashiels : Lyle, c1981. — 126p : chiefly ill ; 17cm. — (Antiques and their values)
Includes index
ISBN 0-86248-006-x : £2.50 B82-08190

748.2913 — American decorative glassware. M'Kee and Brothers, *1859-1871* — *Catalogues*

M'Kee and Brothers. M'Kee Victorian glass : five complete glass catalogs from 1859-60 to 1871 / by M'Kee and Brothers ; with introduction and text by Lowell Innes and Jane Shadel Spillman. — Corning : The Corning Museum of Glass in Association with Dover ; London : Constable, c1981. — vi,186p : ill,facsims ; 24cm
Bibliography: pvi
ISBN 0-486-24121-1 (pbk) : £3.75 B82-23972

748.292 — British glassware, *1837-1901*

Manley, Cyril. Decorative Victorian glass. — London : Ward Lock, June 1981. — [128]p
ISBN 0-7063-5966-6 : £17.95 : CIP entry
B81-12841

Wakefield, Hugh. Nineteenth century British glass / Hugh Wakefield. — 2nd ed. — London : Faber, 1982. — 168p,[8]p of plates : ill(some col.) ; 26cm. — (Faber monographs on glass)
Previous ed.: 1961. — Bibliography: p162-163. — Includes index
ISBN 0-571-18054-x : £25.00 : CIP rev.
B82-12979

748.294 — French decorative glassware. René Lalique et Cie, *1932* — *Illustrations*

René Lalique et Cie. Lalique glass : the complete illustrated catalogue for 1932 / René Lalique et Cie. — New York : Corning Museum of Glass in association with Dover ; London : Constable, 1981. — iii,27,[119]p of plates : ill ; 28cm
French text, English introduction. — Facsim of ed.: published as Catalogue des verreries de René Lalique. Paris : René Lalique & Cie, 1932
ISBN 0-486-24122-x (pbk) : £6.75 B82-18045

748.299562 — Turkey. Sardis. Byzantine decorated glassware. Excavation of remains, *1958-1978*

Saldern, Axel von. Ancient and Byzantine glass from Sardis / Axel von Saldern. — Cambridge, Mass. ; London : Harvard University Press, 1980. — xv,118,[33]p of plates : ill,maps,plans ; 29cm. — (Archaeological exploration of Sardis. Monograph ; 6)
Bibliography: pxii-xi. — Includes index
ISBN 0-674-03303-5 : £21.00 B82-20136

748.5'028'2 — Glass. Painting — *Manuals*

Elskus, Albinas. The art of painting on glass : techniques and designs for stained glass / Albinas Elskus. — London : Routledge & Kegan Paul, 1981. — 147p,8p of plates : ill (some col.) ; 28cm
Bibliography: p140. — Includes index
ISBN 0-7100-0906-2 : £12.50 : CIP rev.
B81-13722

748.5'028'2 — Handicrafts using stained glass — *Manuals*

Wood, Paul W.. Working with stained glass / Paul W. Wood. — New York : Sterling ; London : Oak Tree, c1981. — 96p : ill ; 20cm
Includes index
ISBN 0-8069-5440-x : £5.95 B82-21873

748.592 — England. Churches. Stained glass windows, *1150-1550*

Coe, Brian, *1930-*. Stained glass in England : 1150-1550 / Brian Coe. — London : W.H. Allen, 1981, c1980. — 143p,[18]p of plates : ill (some col.) ; 32cm
Bibliography: p132-134. — Includes index
ISBN 0-491-02794-x : £25.00 B82-22836

748.592 — Great Britain. Churches. Stained glass windows

Crown in glory : a celebration of craftmanship : studies in stained glass / edited by Peter Moore. — Norwich : Jarrold, [1982]. — 80p : ill,1facsims,1map ; 25cm
ISBN 0-7117-0029-x (pbk) : Unpriced
B82-32422

748.594'4 — France. Burgundy. Churches. Stained glass windows, *ca 1200-ca 1300*

Raguin, Virginia Chieffo. Stained glass in thirteenth-century Burgundy / Virginia Chieffo Raguin. — Princeton ; Guildford : Princeton University Press, c1982. — xviii,182p,[81]p of plates : ill(some col.),1map ; 29cm
Bibliography: p175-178. — Includes index
ISBN 0-691-03987-9 : £30.00 B82-41121

748.5994 — Europe. Religious buildings. Stained glass windows. Special subjects: Jesus Christ. Passion, death & resurrection — *Illustrations*

Halliday, Sonia. The Easter story in stained glass / photographs by Sonia Halliday and Laura Lushington. — Tring : Lion, 1982. — 32p : col.ill ; 22cm
ISBN 0-85648-350-8 : £1.95 B82-17135

748.6 — Glass. Decoration

Duthie, Arthur Louis. Decorative glass processes : cutting, etching, staining and other traditional techniques / Arthur Louis Duthie ; with a new preface by William A. Prindle. — Corning : Corning Museum of Glass in association with Dover ; London : Constable, 1982. — xii,267p : ill ; 21cm
Originally published: London : Constable, 1908. — Includes index
ISBN 0-486-24270-6 (pbk) : £3.40 B82-40186

748.6 — Handicrafts: Glass engraving — *Manuals*

Graham, Boyd. Engraving glass : a beginner's guide / Boyd Graham. — New York ; London : Van Nostrand Reinhold, c1982. — 127p,[4]p of plates : ill(some col.) ; 24cm
Includes index
ISBN 0-442-23852-5 : £14.00 B82-36638

Matcham, Jonathan. The techniques of glass engraving / Jonathan Matcham and Peter Dreiser. — London : Batsford, 1982. — 168p,[4]p of plates : ill(some col.) ; 26cm
Bibliography: p160. — Includes index
ISBN 0-7134-2536-9 : £12.50 B82-14091

748.8 — British drinking glasses & decanters, *to 1900* — *Collectors' guides*

Hughes, Therle. Decanters and glasses / Therle Hughes. — [London] : Country Life Books ; London : Hamlyn [distributor], 1982. — 128p : ill(some col.),1facsim ; 23cm. — (The Country life library of antiques)
Includes index
ISBN 0-600-30458-2 : £6.95 B82-19928

748.8'2 — Decanters. Collecting — *Manuals*

Hollingworth, Jane. Collecting decanters / Jane Hollingworth. — London : Studio Vista, 1980. — 127p : ill(some col.) ; 26cm. — (Christie's South Kensinton collectors series)
ISBN 0-289-70920-2 : £6.95 B82-22513

748.8'2 — Ink bottles — *Collectors' guides*

Tansley, June. The collectors book of ink bottles / by June Tansley ; edited by Andy Payne. — Southampton : Southern Collectors
Vol.1. — 3rd ed. — 1980. — 58p : ill ; 21cm
Previous ed.: 1976
ISBN 0-905438-19-1 (pbk) : £1.65 B82-17058

748.8'2'075 — Antique glass bottles. Collecting, *to 1982* — *Collectors' guides*

Dumbrell, Roger. Collecting antique wine bottles. — Woodbridge : Antique Collectors' Club, June 1982. — [200]p
ISBN 0-907462-14-6 : £12.50 : CIP entry
B82-16503

749 — FURNITURE AND ACCESSORIES

749'.0288 — Furniture. Restoration — *Amateurs' manuals*

Mason, David, *19---*. Which? way to repair and restore furniture / [compiled by David Mason]. — London : Consumers' Association, 1980. — 180p : ill ; 19x21cm
ISBN 0-85202-193-3 (pbk) : Unpriced
ISBN 0-85202-193-3 (Hodder & Stoughton) : Unpriced
Primary classification 684.1'044 B82-40548

749'.1'0288 — Antique furniture. Restoration — *Amateurs' manuals*

Meyers, L. Donald. The furniture lover's book : finding, fixing, finishing / L. Donald Meyers. — New York ; London : Van Nostrand Reinhold, 1982, c1977. — 234p : ill ; 28cm
Originally published: New York : Dutton, 1977. — Includes index
ISBN 0-442-26314-7 (pbk) : £7.20 B82-08235

749.2'036 — Furniture, *1650-1800* — *Collectors' guides*

Furniture 1650-1800 / compiled by Tony Curtis. — Galashiels : Lyle, c1981. — 125p : chiefly ill ; 17cm. — (Antiques and their values)
Includes index
ISBN 0-86248-014-0 : £2.50 B82-08189

749.2'04 — Furniture, *1800-1950* — *Collectors' guides*

Furniture 1800-1950 / compiled by Tony Curtis. — Galashiels : Lyle, c1981. — 125p : chiefly ill ; 17cm. — (Antiques and their values)
Includes index
ISBN 0-86248-007-8 : £2.50 B82-08188

749.2'049 — Furniture, *1950-1981*

Contemporary furniture. — London : Design Council, Aug.1982. — [308]p
ISBN 0-85072-129-6 : £17.50 : CIP entry
B82-22792

749.213 — American furniture, *1620-1980*

Bates, Elizabeth Bidwell. American furniture : 1620 to the present / Elizabeth Bidwell Bates, Jonathan L. Fairbanks. — London : Orbis, 1981. — xii,561p : ill(some col.) ; 26cm
Bibliography: p537-552. — Includes index
ISBN 0-85613-394-9 : £25.00 B82-20150

749.213 — American furniture. Breuer, Marcel — *Critical studies*

Wilk, Christopher. Marcel Breuer : furniture and interiors / by Christopher Wilk ; introduction by J. Stewart Johnson. — London : Architectural Press, 1981. — 192p : ill,plans,ports ; 26cm
Accompanies the Marcel Breuer exhibition held at the Museum of Modern Art. — Originally published: New York : Museum of Modern Art, 1981. — Bibliography: p191-192
ISBN 0-85139-393-4 (pbk) : £8.95 B82-00016

749.213 — American oak furniture, *to 1974* — *Illustrations*

Weiss, Jeffrey. Made with oak / by Jeffrey Weiss and Herbert H. Wise with Andrea Alberts. — New York ; London : Quick Fox, c1975. — [95]p : all col.ill ; 24cm
ISBN 0-8256-3052-5 (pbk) : £3.95 B82-10033

749.22 — English furniture, *1860-1930* — *Collectors' guides*

Andrews, John, *1936-*. The price guide to Victorian, Edwardian and 1920s furniture (1860-1930) / John Andrews. — [Woodbridge] : Antique Collectors' Club, c1980 (1981 [printing]). — 217p : ill ; 28cm
Ill on lining papers. — Bibliography: p217
ISBN 0-902028-89-8 : £14.50 B82-13940

749.22 — English furniture. Race, Ernest — *Critical studies*

Conway, Hazel. Ernest Race / Hazel Conway. — London : Design Council, 1982. — 80p : ill,1port ; 21cm
Bibliography: p78-79
ISBN 0-85072-128-8 (pbk) : £6.50 : CIP rev.
B82-11781

749.22 — English furniture. Russell, Gordon — *Critical studies*

Baynes, Ken. Gordon Russell / Ken & Kate Baynes. — London : Design Council, 1981, c1980. — 71p : ill,facsims,ports ; 21cm
Bibliography: p71
ISBN 0-85072-119-9 (pbk) : £5.00 : CIP rev.
B81-10003

749.22'911 — Scottish furniture. Mackintosh, Charles Rennie — *Critical studies*

Billcliffe, Roger. Charles Rennie Mackintosh : the complete furniture, furniture drawings & interior designs / Roger Billcliffe. — 2nd ed. — Guildford : Lutterworth, 1980. — 264p,[16]p of plates : ill(some col.),plans ; 35cm
Previous ed.: 1979. — Includes index
ISBN 0-7188-2513-6 : £36.00 B82-14294

749.294 — European furniture, *1800-1900 — Collectors' guides*

Payne, Christopher, *1948-*. The price guide to 19th century European furniture (excluding British) / Christopher Payne. — [Woodbridge] : Antique Collectors' Club, c1981. — 503p : chiefly ill(some col.) ; 29cm
Ill on lining papers. — Bibliography: p506
ISBN 0-902028-91-x : £25.00 : CIP rev.
B81-28013

749.294'029'4 — European oak furniture — *Buyers' guides*

Oak furniture : buyer's price guide / compiled and researched by Richard Davidson. — Tenterden : MJM, 1981?. — 96p : ill ; 11cm
ISBN 0-905879-10-4 : £2.95 B82-12794

749'.3 — Chairs & couches, *1650-1950 — Collectors' guides*

Chairs & couches / compiled by Tony Curtis. — Galashiels : Lyle, c1981. — 126p : chiefly ill ; 17cm. — (Antiques and their values)
Includes index
ISBN 0-86248-013-2 : £2.50 B82-08197

749'.3 — English domestic bookcases & desks, *to 1900*

Bernasconi, John R.. The English desk and bookcase / John R. Bernasconi. — Reading : College of Estate Management, c1981. — 32p : ill ; 15x21cm
Text on inside cover
ISBN 0-902132-64-4 (pbk) : Unpriced
B82-11562

749'.3 — Tables — *Collectors' guides*

Curtis, Tony, *1939-*. Tables / compiled by Tony Curtis. — Galashiels : Lyle, c1982. — 126p : chiefly ill ; 17cm. — (Antiques and their values)
Includes index
ISBN 0-86248-024-8 : £2.50 B82-28515

749'.32'0973 — American painted chairs, *ca 1800-ca 1900.* **Restoration** — *Manuals*

Blanchard, Roberta Ray. How to restore and decorate chairs : in Early American styles / by Roberta Ray Blanchard. — New York : Dover ; London : Constable, 1981, c1980. — 128p : ill ; 28cm
Originally published: New York : M. Barrows, 1952. — Includes index
ISBN 0-486-24177-7 (pbk) : £3.00 B82-13560

749'.63 — Decorated Jewish oil lamps, *70-135 — Lists*

Sussman, Varda. Ornamental Jewish oil lamps. — Warminster : Aris & Phillips, Oct.1982. — [144]p
Translated from the Hebrew
ISBN 0-85668-164-4 (pbk) : CIP entry
B82-27216

749'.63 — London. Camden *(London Borough).* **Museums: British Museum. Exhibits: Classical oil lamps,** *to ca 650 — Catalogues*

British Museum. A catalogue of the lamps in the British Museum. — London : Published for the Trustees of the British Museum by British Museum Publications
2: Roman lamps made in Italy / D.M. Bailey. — c1980. — xvii,458p,104p of plates : ill ; 29cm
Bibliography: pxiv-xvii. — Includes index
ISBN 0-7141-1259-3 : £1.00 : CIP rev.
B78-23578

749'.63 — Mission style lamps. Making — *Amateurs' manuals*

Adams, John D.. [Lamps and shades in metal and art glass]. How to make mission style lamps and shades / Popular Mechanics Company. — New York : Dover ; London : Constable, 1982. — 114p : ill ; 21cm
Written by John D. Adams. — Originally published: Chicago : Popular Mechanics Company, 1911
ISBN 0-486-24244-7 (pbk) : £2.25
Primary classification 745.593'2 B82-40185

749'.7 — Picture frames. Making — *Amateurs' manuals*

Banister, Manly. Making picture frames in wood / Manly Banister. — New York : Sterling ; Poole : Distributed by Blandford, c1982. — 127p : ill ; 21cm. — (Home craftsman series)
Previous ed.: Published as Making picture frames. New York : Sterling ; London : distributed by Ward Lock, 1973. — Includes index
ISBN 0-8069-5450-7 (cased) : Unpriced
ISBN 0-8069-7542-3 (pbk) : Unpriced
ISBN 0-8069-5451-5 (lib.bdg.) : Unpriced
B82-28203

749'.7 — Pictures. Framing — *Manuals*

Picture framing & mounting. — London : WI, 1982. — 12p : ill ; 21cm
ISBN 0-900556-71-4 (unbound) : Unpriced : CIP rev. B81-33628

Purchase, Nigel. Picture framing / Nigel Purchase. — London : Warne, 1982. — 64p : ill ; 22cm. — (An Observer's guide. Art and craft)
Bibliography: p64
ISBN 0-7232-2760-8 (pbk) : £1.95 B82-22823

Woods, Michael, *1933-*. Mounting & framing pictures / Michael Woods. — London : Batsford, 1978 (1981 [printing]). — 96p : ill ; 25cm. — (A Batsford craft paperback)
Includes index
ISBN 0-7134-0744-1 (pbk) : £3.95 B82-01609

750 — PAINTINGS

750'.74'02132 — London. Westminster *(London Borough).* **Art galleries: Tate Gallery. Stock: Acquisitions** — *Catalogues*

Tate Gallery. The Tate Gallery 1978-80 : illustrated catalogue of acquisitions. — London : The Gallery Publications Department, 1981. — 175p : ill,ports ; 25cm
ISBN 0-905005-82-1 (pbk) : £3.00 B82-21364

750'.74'029128 — Scotland. Tayside Region. Perth. Art galleries: Perth Museum and Art Gallery. Exhibits — *Catalogues*

Perth Museum and Art Gallery. Catalogue of the permanent collection of paintings and drawings. — Perth : Perth Museum and Art Gallery, 1981. — [96]p : ill,ports ; 25cm
ISBN 0-907495-00-1 (pbk) : Unpriced
B82-08485

750'.74'0291835 — Dublin. Art galleries: National Gallery of Ireland. Exhibits: Paintings — *Catalogues*

National Gallery of Ireland. Illustrated summary catalogue of paintings / National Gallery of Ireland ; introduction by Homan Potterton. — Dublin : Gill and Macmillan, 1981. — xxxxii,363p : ill,ports ; 25cm
ISBN 0-7171-1144-x (cased) : Unpriced : CIP rev.
ISBN 0-7171-1145-8 (pbk) : £12.00
B81-31235

751 — PAINTINGS. MATERIALS, EQUIPMENT, TECHNIQUES, FORMS

751 — Paintings. Materials & techniques — *Amateurs' manuals*

Mills, John Fitzmaurice. Paint! / by John FitzMaurice Mills. — London : British Broadcasting Corporation, 1981. — 64p : ill (some col.) ; 22cm
ISBN 0-563-16458-1 (pbk) : £2.75 B82-01679

Parramón, J. M.. Painting with pastels : — plus wax, gouache, collage, knife and monotype techniques / J. M. Parramon. — Watford : Fountain, 1981. — 123p : ill(some col.) ; 26cm. — (Improve your painting and drawing)
Translation of: Asi se pinta al pastel. — 1 sheet (48x33cm folded to 24x17cm) as insert
£3.95 (pbk) B82-31347

751 — Paintings. Materials & techniques — *Manuals*

Mayer, Ralph. The artist's handbook of materials and techniques / by Ralph Mayer ; edited by Edwin Smith. — 4th ed., rev. and expanded. — [London] : Faber, 1982, c1981. — xv,756p : ill ; 25cm
Previous ed.: 1973. — Bibliography: p695-728. — Includes index
ISBN 0-571-18033-7 (cased) : £18.50
ISBN 0-571-11693-0 (pbk) : Unpriced
B82-39366

751.4 — Paintings. Special subjects: Boats. Techniques — *Manuals*

Crawshaw, Alwyn. Learn to paint boats and harbours / Alwyn Crawshaw. — Glasgow : Collins, 1982. — 64p : ill(some col.),col.ports ; 28cm
ISBN 0-00-411877-4 (pbk) : £3.95 B82-15440

751.4 — Paintings. Special subjects: Flowers. Techniques — *Manuals*

Jameson, Kenneth. Flower painting for beginners / Kenneth Jameson. — London : Studio Vista, 1979. — 102p : ill(some col.) ; 20cm. — (A pocket how to do it)
Includes index
ISBN 0-289-70902-4 (pbk) : £1.95 B82-03942

751.4 — Paintings. Techniques — *Manuals*

Andrewes, Elizabeth. A manual for drawing & painting / Elizabeth Andrewes. — Sevenoaks : Hodder and Stoughton, 1978 (1979 [printing]). — 208p : ill(some col.) ; 19cm. — (Teach yourself books)
Bibliography: p208. — Includes index
ISBN 0-340-22243-3 (pbk) : £2.95
Primary classification 741.2 B82-32817

Art school : an instructional guide based on the teaching of leading art colleges / consultant editor Colin Saxton. — London : Macmillan, 1981. — 224p : ill,ports ; 26cm
Includes index
ISBN 0-333-32306-8 : £9.95
Primary classification 741.2 B82-06957

Jaxtheimer, Bodo W.. How to paint and draw / Bodo W. Jaxtheimer ; with 300 illustrations in colour and 150 in black-and-white. — London : Thames and Hudson, c1962 (1982 [printing]). — 408p : ill(some col.),ports(some col.) ; 22cm
Translation of: Knaurs Mal-und Zeichenbuch. — Includes index
ISBN 0-500-27252-2 (pbk) : £3.50
Also classified at 741.2 B82-20415

751.4 — Paintings. Techniques — *Manuals — For children*

Layfield, Kathie. Painting / written and illustrated by Kathie Layfield with contributions by Jenny Cook & Frank Humphris ; photographs by Tim Clark. — Loughborough : Ladybird, c1980. — 51p : col.ill ; 18cm. — (Learnabout—)
Text and col. ill on lining papers. — Includes index
ISBN 0-7214-0496-0 : £0.40 B82-16033

751.4 — Still-life paintings. Techniques — *Manuals*

Huntly, Moira. Imaginative still life. — London : A. & C. Black, Jan.1983. — [160]p
ISBN 0-7136-2259-8 : £12.00 : CIP entry
B82-32595

751.42'2 — Watercolour paintings. Techniques — *Manuals*

Cooper, Mario. Painting with watercolor / Mario Cooper. — New York ; London : Van Nostrand Reinhold, 1971 (1981 [printing]). — 143p : ill(some col.),ports ; 28cm
Includes index
ISBN 0-442-21509-6 (pbk) : £9.30 B82-14308

Du Moulin, Yvonne. Creative watercolor techniques / Yvonne du Moulin. — New York ; London : Van Nostrand Reinhold, c1981. — 80p : ill(some col.) ; 24cm
Bibliography: p77. — Includes index
ISBN 0-442-21876-1 (pbk) : £6.75 B82-30348

751.42'2 — Watercolour paintings. Techniques — *Manuals* *continuation*

Gwynn, Kate. Painting in watercolour / Kate Gwynn. — London : Ebury, 1982. — 176p : ill (some col.) ; 25cm. — (The Artist's handbook series) (A Quarto book)
Includes index
ISBN 0-85223-221-7 : £8.95 B82-32933

Hilder, Rowland. Starting with watercolour / Rowland Hilder. — London : Studio Vista, 1979. — 104p : ill(some col.) ; 20cm. — (A pocket how to do it)
Includes index
ISBN 0-289-70909-1 (pbk) : £1.95 B82-03943

Mills, John FitzMaurice. Materials & techniques of watercolour / John FitzMaurice Mills. — London : Warne, 1981. — 63p : ill(some col.) ; 22cm. — (An Observer's guide. Art and craft)
ISBN 0-7232-2474-9 (pbk) : £2.50 B82-00867

Partner, Jason. Guide to sketching and water-colour painting / by Jason Partner ; with illustrations by the author. — Ely, Cambs. : Providence Press, 1982. — 58p : ill(some col.) ; 21cm
ISBN 0-903803-07-0 (pbk) : £3.90 B82-31253

751.42'2436 — Watercolour landscape paintings. Techniques — *Manuals*

Fletcher-Watson, James. Water-colour painting : landscapes & townscapes / James Fletcher-Watson. — London : Batsford, 1982. — 142p,[4]p of plates : ill(some col.) ; 26cm
Includes index
ISBN 0-7134-3978-5 : £8.95 B82-17663

751.42'6 — Acrylic paintings. Techniques — *Manuals*

Mills, John FitzMaurice. Materials & techniques of acrylic painting / John FitzMaurice Mills. — London : Warne, 1981. — 48p : ill(some col.) ; 22cm. — (An Observer's guide. Art and craft)
ISBN 0-7232-2476-5 (pbk) : £2.50 B82-00869

751.45 — Oil paintings. Techniques

Paint & painting : an exhibition and working studio sponsored by Winsor & Newton to celebrate their 150th anniversary. — London : Tate Gallery, 1982. — 118p : ill(some col.),facsims,ports(some col.) ; 21cm
Published in connection with an exhibition at the Tate Gallery. London, 1982. — Bibliography: p116-117
ISBN 0-905005-68-6 (pbk) : £2.95 B82-33697

751.45 — Oil paintings. Techniques — *Amateurs' manuals*

Brooks, Leonard, *1911-*. Oil painting : traditional and new / Leonard Brooks. — New York ; London : Van Nostrand Reinhold, 1981 (1981 [printing]). — 160p : ill(some col.) ; 28cm
Includes index
ISBN 0-442-26427-5 (pbk) : £10.15 B82-09753

Kominsky, Nancy. Oil painting for the beginner : including a unique colour mixing guide / Nancy Kominsky. — London : Collins, 1982. — 64p : ill(some col.) ; 29cm
ISBN 0-00-411866-9 : £5.95 B82-34849

751.45 — Oil paintings. Techniques — *Case studies*

Tate Gallery. Completing the picture : materials and techniques of twenty-six paintings in the Tate Gallery. — London : The Gallery, 1982. — 120p : ill(some col.) ; 21cm
Bibliography: p118-119
ISBN 0-905005-63-5 (pbk) : £5.95 B82-33694

751.45 — Oil paintings. Techniques — *Manuals*

Chieffo, Clifford T.. The contemporary oil painter's handbook : a complete guide to oil painting : materials, tools, techniques, and auxiliary services for the beginning and professional artist / Clifford T. Chieffo. — New York ; London : Van Nostrand Reinhold, 1982, c1976. — xiii,130p : ill ; 23cm
Originally published: Englewood Cliffs ; London : Prentice-Hall, 1976. — Bibliography: p117. — Includes index
ISBN 0-442-21492-8 (pbk) : £5.95 B82-24922

Mills, John FitzMaurice. Materials & techniques of oil painting / John FitzMaurice Mills. — London : Warne, 1981. — 63p : ill(some col.),1col.port ; 22cm. — (An Observer's guide. Art and craft)
ISBN 0-7232-2472-2 (pbk) : £2.50 B82-00866

751.45'42 — Oil portrait paintings. Techniques — *Manuals*

Burns, Paul C.. The portrait painter's problem book / by Paul C. Burns and Joe Singer. — New York : Watson-Guptill ; London : Pitman, 1979. — 144p : ports(some col.) ; 31cm
Bibliography: p142. — Includes index
ISBN 0-273-01349-1 : Unpriced B82-01390

751.7'3'09361 — Great Britain. Ancient Roman wall paintings. Preservation & restoration

Davey, Norman. Wall-painting in Roman Britain. — Gloucester : Alan Sutton, Mar.1982. — [232]p
ISBN 0-904387-96-8 (pbk) : £11.95 : CIP entry B82-08410

751.7'7'07402134 — London. Kensington and Chelsea *(London Borough)*. **Museums: Victoria and Albert Museum. Stock: Miniature paintings —** *Catalogues*

Hall, Garth. Summary catalogue of miniatures in the Victoria and Albert Museum. — Haslemere (Thursley Hall, Haslemere, Surrey GU27 1HA) : Emmett Microform, Sept.1981. — [136]p
ISBN 0-907696-01-5 (pbk) : £3.95 : CIP entry B81-28701

751.7'7'095407402164 — Great Britain. *Foreign and Commonwealth Office*. **Libraries: India Office Library. Stock: Indian miniature paintings,** *ca 1560-1970 — Catalogues*

India Office Library. Indian miniatures in the India Office Library / Toby Falk, Mildred Archer. — London : Sotheby Parke Bernet, 1981. — 559p,16p of plates : ill(some col.),ports ; 30cm
Bibliography: p333-338. — Includes index
ISBN 0-85667-100-2 : £57.50 B82-08514

753/758 — PAINTINGS. SPECIAL SUBJECTS

753'.7 — Great Britain. National libraries: British Library. *Department of Oriental Manuscripts and Printed Books*. **Stock: Islamic illuminated manuscripts. Miniature paintings. Special subjects: Dragons**

Titley, Norah M.. Dragons in Persian, Mughal and Turkish art / Norah M. Titley. — London : British Library, c1981. — 36p : ill(some col.) ; 24cm
Text, ill on inside covers. — Bibliography: on inside back cover
ISBN 0-904654-70-2 (pbk) : Unpriced : CIP rev. B81-25862

754'.0941 — British genre paintings, *1837-1901*

Lambourne, Lionel. An introduction to 'Victorian' genre painting : from Wilkie to Firth / Lionel Lambourne. — London : H.M.S.O., 1982. — 48p : ill(some col.) ; 26cm
At head of cover title: Victoria & Albert Museum. — Bibliography: p48
ISBN 0-11-290379-7 : £3.50 B82-14856

755'.2 — Painted icons, *to ca 1700*

The **Icon** / Kurt Weitzmann ... [et al.]. — London : Evans, 1982. — 419p : ill(some col.) ; 32cm
Translation of: Le icone. — Bibliography: p413-415
ISBN 0-237-45645-1 : £45.00 B82-39659

755.943 — Tibetan tangkas

Fischle, Willy H.. The way to the centre. — Dulverton : Watkins, Sept.1982. — [80]p
Translation of: Der Weg zur Mitte
ISBN 0-7224-0209-0 : £9.95 : CIP entry B82-23862

756 — Paintings. Special subjects: Historical events. Theories of Diderot, Denis

Mortier, Roland. Diderot and the 'Grand Goût'. — Oxford : Clarendon Press, Sept.1982. — [18]p. — (The Zaharoff lecture ; 1981-2)
ISBN 0-19-951536-0 (pbk) : £1.95 : CIP entry B82-30303

757 — Avon. Weston-super-Mare. Museums: Woodspring Museum. Exhibits: English oil portrait paintings. Special subjects: Smyth-Pigott *(Family) — Catalogues*

Woodspring Museum. Portraits of the Smyth-Pigott family : a catalogue of the oil paintings and busts in Woodspring Museum, Weston-super-Mare. — [Weston-super-Mare] : Woodspring District Council, Leisure Services Department, [1980?]. — [20]p : ports,1geneal.table ; 21cm
£0.50 (pbk) B82-23974

757 — European paintings, *1933-1957*. **Special subjects: German prisons. Prisoners,** *1933-1945 — Illustrations*

Blatter, Janet. Art of the holocaust / by Janet Blatter and Sybil Milton ; historical introduction by Henry Friecdlander ; preface by Irving Howe. — London : Pan, 1982, c1981. — 272p : ill(some col.) ; 31cm
Originally published: New York : Rutledge, 1981. — Bibliography: p270-272
ISBN 0-330-26634-9 (pbk) : £7.50
Primary classification 741.94 B82-20436

Blatter, Janet. Art of the holocaust / project editor Lori Stein ; by Janet Blatter and Sybil Milton ; historical introduction by Henry Friedlander ; preface by Irving Howe. — London : Orbis, 1982, c1981. — 272p : ill(some col.),1map,facsims(some col.),ports(some col.) ; 32cm
Originally published: New York : Rutledge, 1981. — Maps on lining papers. — Bibliography: p270-272
ISBN 0-85613-386-8 : £12.50
Primary classification 741.94 B82-20437

757'.0942 — English portrait paintings. Pre-Raphaelitism. Special subjects: Pre-Raphaelite Brotherhood — *Critical studies*

Rose, Andrea. Pre-Raphaelite portraits / Andrea Rose. — Yeovil : Oxford Illustrated Press, c1981. — 144p : ill,ports ; 31cm
Bibliography: p140. — Includes index
ISBN 0-902280-74-0 (cased) : £9.95
ISBN 0-902280-82-1 (pbk) : Unpriced
Also classified at 741.942 B82-11024

757'.7'0941 — British miniature portrait paintings, *to ca 1975 — Collectors' guides*

Foskett, Daphne. Collecting miniatures / Daphne Foskett. — [Woodbridge] : Antique Collectors' Club, c1979. — 498p : ill,ports(some col.) ; 29cm
Ill on lining papers. — Bibliography: p476-481. — Includes index
ISBN 0-902028-79-0 : £25.00 : CIP rev. B79-09691

757'.7'0942 — English miniature portrait paintings, *ca 1500-1900*

The **English** miniature / John Murdoch ... [et al.]. — New Haven ; London : Yale University Press, 1981. — vi,230p : ill(some col.),ports (some col.) ; 27cm
Includes index
ISBN 0-300-02769-9 (cased) : Unpriced : CIP rev.
ISBN 0-300-02778-8 (pbk) : Unpriced B82-03101

758'.1'090407402 — Great Britain. Arts. Patronage. Organisations: Arts Council of Great Britain. Exhibits: Landscape paintings, *1911-1978 — Catalogues*

Romanticism continued : an Arts Council exhibition ... — London : Arts Council of Great Britain, c1981. — [4]p : ill ; 30cm. — (Approaches to modern art)
Catalogue of an exhibition
ISBN 0-7287-0289-4 (unbound) : Unpriced B82-13038

758'.1'0941 — British watercolour landscape paintings, *1630-1950 — Catalogues*

Town, country, shore and sea : British drawings and watercolours from Anthony Van Dyck to Paul Nash : an exhibition from the Fitzwilliam Museum, Cambridge. — Cambridge : Cambridge University Press, 1982. — xix,135p : ill(some col.) ; 26cm
Bibliography: pxix. — Includes index
ISBN 0-521-24491-9 (cased) : £22.50 : CIP rev.
ISBN 0-521-28722-7 (pbk) : £5.95
Primary classification 741.941 B82-11512

758′.1′0942 — English landscape paintings, *1500-1980 — Critical studies*

Rosenthal, Michael. British landscape painting. — Oxford : Phaidon, Apr.1982. — [192]p
ISBN 0-7148-2198-5 : £14.95 : CIP entry
B82-04508

758′.1′0942 — English landscape paintings, *1780-1830 — Critical studies*

Hawes, Louis. Presences of nature. — London : Yale University Press, Oct.1982. — [224]p
ISBN 0-300-02930-6 (cased) : £20.00 : CIP entry
ISBN 0-300-02931-4 (pbk) : £8.95 B82-35194

758′.1′0942 — English landscape paintings. Constable, John, *1776-1837 — Critical studies*

Paulson, Ronald. Literary landscape : Turner and Constable. — London : Yale University Press, Sept.1982. — [288]p
ISBN 0-300-02804-0 : £15.00 : CIP entry
B82-29122

758′.1′09492 — Dutch landscape paintings, *1600-1700 — Critical studies*

Stechow, Wolfgang. Dutch landscape painting of the seventeenth century / by Wolfgang Stechow. — 3rd ed. (photographically reprinted). — Oxford : Phaidon, 1981. — x,494p : ill ; 21cm. — (Landmarks in art history)
Previous ed.: 1968. — Originally issued in series: National Gallery of Art : Kress Foundation studies in the history of European art. — Bibliography: p223-233. — Includes index
ISBN 0-7148-2185-3 (pbk) : £7.50 : CIP rev.
B81-16941

758′.3 — English paintings, *1625-1980.* **Special subjects: Livestock: Dogs** *— Catalogues*

Just dogs : an exhibition of animal painting over two centuries. — Beaconsfield (26 London End, Beaconsfield, Bucks. HP9 2JH) : David Messum Fine Paintings, [1977?]. — [16]p : ill (some col.) ; 28cm
Published to accompany an exhibition held at David Messum Fine Paintings, London. — Ill on inside covers
Unpriced (pbk) B82-39949

758′.4′094 — European still-life paintings, *to 1980*

Sterling, Charles. Still life painting : from antiquity to the twentieth century / Charles Sterling ; [translation by James Emmons]. — 2nd rev. ed. — New York ; London : Harper & Row, c1981. — 325p : ill ; 26cm. — (Icon editions)
Translation of: La nature morte de l'antiquité à nos jours. — Previous ed.: Paris : Editions Pierre Tisne, 1959. — Bibliography: p305-315. — Includes index
ISBN 0-06-438530-2 (cased) : Unpriced
ISBN 0-06-430096-x (pbk) : £6.95 B82-34909

758′.42′0942 — English paintings. Special subjects: Flowering plants *— Illustrations*

Thornton, Robert. The temple of flora / by Robert Thornton ; introduction by Ronald King. — London : Weidenfeld & Nicolson, c1981. — 110p : ill(some col.),facsims, ports ; 38cm
ISBN 0-297-77984-2 : £18.50 B82-04008

758′.5 — European paintings, *to 1900.* **Special subjects: Gardens** *— Critical studies*

Holme, Bryan. The enchanted garden : images of delight / Bryan Holme. — London : Thames and Hudson, c1982. — 96p : ill(some col.) ; 25cm
ISBN 0-500-01265-2 : £5.95 B82-24927

758′.7 — English watercolour paintings. Special subjects: England. Churches *— Catalogues*

British Museum. English cathedrals and churches : twelve watercolours from the British Museum / notes on the plates by Ann Wilson ; notes on the artists by Paul Goldman. — London : British Museum, c1982. — [24]p : col.ill ; 25x35cm
ISBN 0-7141-0790-5 (pbk) : £2.95 B82-35090

758′.9798′094107401468 — Connecticut. New Haven. Art galleries: Yale Center for British Art. Stock: British paintings, *1655-1867.* **Special subjects: Equestrian sports. Collections: Paul Mellon Collection** *— Catalogues*

Egerton, Judy. British sporting and animal paintings 1655-1867 / a catalogue compiled by Judy Egerton. — London : Tate Gallery For the Yale Center For British Art, 1978. — xxiv,382p,163p of plates : ill(some col.),ports (some col.) ; 30cm. — (The Paul Mellon collection) (Sport in art and books)
Bibliography: p349-353. — Includes index
ISBN 0-905005-51-1 : Unpriced
Also classified at 758′.9799′094107401468
B82-26641

758′.9799′094107401468 — Connecticut. New Haven. Art galleries: Yale Center for British Art. Stock: British paintings, *1655-1867.* **Special subjects: Field sports. Collections: Paul Mellon Collection** *— Catalogues*

Egerton, Judy. British sporting and animal paintings 1655-1867 / a catalogue compiled by Judy Egerton. — London : Tate Gallery For the Yale Center For British Art, 1978. — xxiv,382p,163p of plates : ill(some col.),ports (some col.) ; 30cm. — (The Paul Mellon collection) (Sport in art and books)
Bibliography: p349-353. — Includes index
ISBN 0-905005-51-1 : Unpriced
Primary classification 758′.9798′094107401468
B82-26641

758′.994229107 — Berkshire. Newbury. Museums: Newbury District Museum. Exhibits: English paintings. Special subjects: Berkshire. Newbury, *ca 1790-1979 — Catalogues*

Newbury in the past : an exhibition held at Newbury District Museum as a contribution to the Newbury Spring Festival 8th May to 7th June 1980. — [Newbury] : Newbury District Museum, [1980]. — [8]p ; 21cm
Unpriced (pbk)
Also classified at 769′.4994229107 B82-05164

758′.994239307 — Avon. Bristol. Art galleries: City of Bristol Museum and Art Gallery. Stock: English paintings, *1789-1836.* **Special subjects: Avon. Bristol** *— Illustrations*

City of Bristol Museum and Art Gallery. The Bristol scene : views of Bristol by Bristol artists from the collection of the City Art Gallery / [text] by Jennifer Gill. — Bristol (PO Box 27, Broad Quay, Bristol BS99 7AX) : Bristol & West Building Society, 1973 (1978 [printing]). — 32p : ill(some col.),ports ; 21x26cm
ISBN 0-905459-10-5 (pbk) : £0.85 B82-21831

758′.9942807 — English watercolour paintings, *ca 1720-1830.* **Special subjects: North-east England** *— Catalogues*

The **Picturesque** tour : in Northumberland and Durham, c.1720-1830 : a catalogue to accompany the exhibition held in the Laing Art Gallery, Newcastle upon Tyne, 17 April-31 May 1982 / sponsored by Christie's and Northern Rock Building Society. — [Newcastle upon Tyne] : Tyne and Wear County Council Museums, [1982?]. — 103p : ill ; 20x26cm
Maps on inside covers. — Bibliography: p101-103
ISBN 0-905974-06-9 (pbk) : Unpriced
B82-31701

759 — PAINTINGS. HISTORICAL AND GEOGRAPHICAL TREATMENT

759 — Paintings, *ca 1300-ca 1950 — Critical studies*

Great paintings / edited by Edwin Mullins ; contributors Anita Brookner ... [et al.]. — London : British Broadcasting Corporation, 1981. — 344p : ill(some col.),ports(some col.) ; 29cm
Published in conjunction with the BBC2 series 100 great paintings. — Includes index
ISBN 0-563-17709-8 : £22.95 B82-08873

759 — Paintings, *to 1960 — Critical studies*

Janson, H. W.. [The picture history of painting]. The story of painting : from cave painting to modern times / H.W. and Dora Jane Janson. — London : Thames and Hudson, 1968, c1961 (1982 [printing]). — 259p : ill(some col.),ports (some col.) ; 21cm. — (The World of art library)
Originally published: New York : H.N. Abrams, 1957. — Includes index
ISBN 0-500-20189-7 (pbk) : £3.95 B82-34979

759 — Paintings. Women artists, *1550-1970 — Catalogues*

The **Women's** art show 1550-1970. — [Nottingham] : Nottingham Castle Museum, 1982. — 95p,viiip of plates : ill(some col.),ports (some col.) ; 21cm
Published to accompany an exhibition at Nottingham Castle Museum. — Bibliography: p95
ISBN 0-905634-03-9 (pbk) : Unpriced
B82-37938

759 — Western paintings. Painters, *to 1980 — Biographies*

Larousse dictionary of painters. — London : Hamlyn, 1981. — ix,467p : ill(some col.),ports (some col.) ; 30cm
Translation of: Le Larousse des grands peintres. — Bibliography: p449-456. — Includes index
ISBN 0-600-34035-x : £15.00 B82-02723

759.01′13′0944 — France. Palaeolithic rock paintings

Leroi-Gourhan, André. The dawn of European art : an introduction to palaeolithic cave painting / André Leroi-Gourhan ; translation by Sara Champion. — Cambridge : Cambridge University Press, 1982. — 77p,[62]p of plates : ill(some col.) ; 25cm. — (The Imprint of man)
Translation of: I più antichi artisti d'Europa. — Ill on lining papers. — Bibliography: p77
ISBN 0-521-24459-5 : £9.95 : CIP rev.
B82-21724

759.01′13′09467 — Eastern Spain. Prehistoric rock paintings

Beltrán, Antonio. Rock art of the Spanish Levant / Antonio Beltrán ; translated by Margaret Brown. — Cambridge : Cambridge University Press, 1982. — 91p,[62]p of plates : ill(some col.),2maps ; 25cm. — (The Imprint of man)
Translation of: Da cacciatori ad allevatori. — Ill on lining papers. — Bibliography: p83-91
ISBN 0-521-24568-0 : £9.95 : CIP rev.
B82-21725

759.01′13′096811 — San rock paintings. Symbolism

Lewis-Williams, J. David. Believing and seeing : symbolic meanings in southern San rock paintings / J. David Lewis-Williams. — London : Academic Press, 1981. — xiii,151p : ill,2maps,1facsim ; 23x31cm. — (Studies in anthropology)
Bibliography: p137-144. — Includes index
ISBN 0-12-447060-2 : £18.00 : CIP rev.
B81-06622

759.03′074 — Art galleries. Exhibits: European paintings, *1400-1500 — Catalogues*

Reynolds, Catherine, *1952-*. Paintings and sculpture of the fifteenth century / [compiled by] Catherine Reynolds. — London : Warne, 1981. — 112p ; 22cm. — (An Observer's guide. Where is it?)
ISBN 0-7232-2759-4 (pbk) : £2.95
Also classified at 735′.21′074 B82-06904

759.03′074 — Art galleries. Exhibits: European paintings, *1500-1600 — Catalogues*

Beresford, Richard. Paintings and sculpture of the Sixteenth Century / Richard Beresford. — London : Warne, 1982. — 117p ; 22cm. — (An Observer's guide. Where is it?)
ISBN 0-7232-2887-6 (pbk) : £2.95
Also classified at 735′.21′074 B82-22826

759.05′074 — Art galleries. Exhibits: European paintings, *1800-1900 — Catalogues*

Bugler, Caroline. European paintings of the nineteenth century / [compiled by] Caroline Bugler. — London : Warne, 1981. — 122p ; 22cm. — (An Observer's guide. Where is it?)
ISBN 0-7232-2421-8 (pbk) : £2.95 B82-06906

759.05′2 — European paintings. Romanticism, *1760-1870 — Critical studies*

Clay, Jean. Romanticism / by Jean Clay ; with a foreword by Robert Rosenblum. — Oxford : Phaidon, 1981. — 320p : ill(some col.),ports (some col.) ; 32cm
Translation of: Le Romantisme. — Includes index
ISBN 0-7148-2223-x : £25.00 B82-01916

759.05'3 — Naive paintings, *to 1978* **—** *Critical studies*
Kallir, Jane. The folk art tradition : naïve painting in Europe and the United States / Jane Kallir ; foreword by Robert Bishop. — London : Allen Lane, 1982, c1981. — 100p : ill (some col.),ports(some col.) ; 28cm
Originally published: New York : Viking, 1982
ISBN 0-7139-1483-1 : £12.95 B82-30994

759.05'6'07402132 — London. Westminster *(London Borough).* **Art galleries: Royal Academy of Arts. Exhibits: European paintings. Post-impressionism —** *Catalogues*
Post-impressionism : cross-currents in European painting : Royal Academy of Arts London 1979-80. — London : [Royal Academy of Arts] in association with Weidenfeld and Nicolson, c1979 (1981 [printing]). — 303p : ill(some col.),ports(some col.) ; 28cm
Bibliography: p298-299. — Includes index
ISBN 0-297-78034-4 (pbk) : Unpriced B82-01370

759.06 — Paintings, *1900-1980* **—** *Critical studies*
Farthing, Joni. Modern British painting / Joni Farthing. — St. Albans : Hart-Davis Educational, 1981. — 48p : ill ; 18cm. — (Insights into English)
ISBN 0-247-13095-8 (pbk) : Unpriced B82-09830

759.06'63 — European paintings. Surrealism — *Illustrations*
Surrealist painting. — New enlarged ed. — Oxford : Phaidon, Aug.1982. — [128]p. — (Phaidon colour library)
Previous ed.: 1976
ISBN 0-7148-2234-5 (cased) : £10.50 : CIP entry
ISBN 0-7148-2244-2 (pbk) : £7.50 B82-15834

759.11 — Canadian paintings. Bateman, Robert, *1930-.* **Special subjects: Animals —** *Illustrations*
Bateman, Robert, *1930-.* The art of Robert Bateman / introduction by Roger Tory Peterson ; text by Ramsay Derry. — London : Allen Lane, 1981. — 178p : ill(some col.),ports ; 29x31cm
Bibliography: p178. — Includes index
ISBN 0-670-13497-x : £20.00 B82-05907

759.13 — American erotic watercolour paintings. Vargas, Alberto — *Illustrations*
Vargas, Alberto. Vargas. — London (30 Craven St., WC2N 5NT) : Plexus, Apr.1981. — [128]p
Originally published: New York : Harmony Books, 1978
ISBN 0-85965-027-8 (cased) : £10.95 : CIP entry
ISBN 0-85965-043-x (pbk) : £5.95 B81-02389

759.13 — American paintings. Abstract expressionism, *to 1950* **—** *Critical studies*
Hobbs, Robert Carleton. Abstract expressionism : the formative years / by Robert Carleton Hobbs and Gail Levin. — Ithaca, N.Y. ; London : Cornell University Press, 1981, c1978. — 140p : ill(some col.),ports ; 29cm
Originally published: Ithaca, N.Y. : Herbert F. Johnson Museum of Art, Cornell University, 1978
ISBN 0-8014-1365-6 : £17.50 B82-11848

759.13 — American paintings. Chicago, Judy — *Biographies*
Chicago, Judy. Through the flower. — London : Women's Press, Oct.1982. — [256]p
ISBN 0-7043-3893-9 (pbk) : £4.95 : CIP entry B82-23214

759.13 — American paintings. Gorky, Arshile — *Catalogues*
Jordan, Jim M.. The paintings of Arshile Gorky : a critical catalogue / by Jim M. Jordan and Robert Goldwater. — New York ; London : New York University Press, c1982. — xxix,576p : ill(some col.),ports ; 29cm
Bibliography: p561-576
ISBN 0-8147-4160-6 : £55.70 B82-35941

759.13 — American paintings. Hofmekler, Uri — *Illustrations*
Hofmekler, Uri. Hofmekler's VIP's. — London : New English Library, Nov.1982. — [96]p
ISBN 0-450-05529-9 (pbk) : £4.95 : CIP entry B82-27515

759.13 — American paintings. Hopper, Edward — *Critical studies*
Levin, Gail. Edward Hopper : the art and the artist / Gail Levin. — New York ; London : Norton in association with the Whitney Museum of American Art, 1980. — xv,299p : ill(some col.),ports(some col.) ; 29cm
Published to accompany a travelling exhibition held 1981-1982. — Bibliography: p72-74. — Includes index
ISBN 0-393-01374-x : £19.95 B82-36967

759.13 — American paintings. Modernism, *1910-1935* **—** *Critical studies*
Davidson, Abraham A.. Early American modernist painting 1910-1935 / Abraham A. Davidson. — New York ; London : Harper & Rowe, c1981. — viii,324p,8p of plates : ill (some col.) ; 25cm. — (Icon editions)
Bibliography: p295-304. — Includes index
ISBN 0-06-430975-4 : £15.00 B82-08948

759.13 — American paintings. Schnabel, Julian — *Catalogues*
Schnabel, Julian. Julian Schnabel : the Tate Gallery 1982. — London : Tate Gallery Publications Department, 1982. — 16p : ill (some col.),1port ; 25cm
ISBN 0-905005-73-2 (pbk) : £2.50 B82-37738

759.13 — American paintings. Tobey, Mark. Special subjects: Washington *(State).* **Seattle. Markets: Seattle Public Market —** *Illustrations*
Tobey, Mark. The world of a market / Mark Tobey. — Seattle ; London : University of Washington Press, 1981, c1964. — 64p : all ill (some col.) ; 28cm
Originally published: Seattle : University of Washington Press, 1964
ISBN 0-295-95843-x : £7.00 B82-19572

759.2 — British naive paintings, *ca1900-1981* **—** *Critical studies*
Melly, George. A tribe of one : great naïve painters of the British Isles / George Melly. — Yeovil : Haynes, c1981. — 77p : ill(some col.),ports ; 26cm
ISBN 0-902280-80-5 : £6.95 B82-06187

759.2 — British paintings, *1533-1975* **—** *Critical studies*
Wilson, Simon. [British art]. Holbein to Hockney. — London : Bodley Head, Sept.1982. — [208]p
Originally published as: British art. 1979
ISBN 0-370-30946-4 (pbk) : £5.95 : CIP entry
Also classified at 730'.941 B82-19208

759.2 — British watercolour paintings, *1850-1920* **—** *Critical studies*
Vassall-Adams, Rory. The Victorian watercolour : an appreciation / by Rory Vassall-Adams. — London : Castletown, c1981. — 75p : col.ill,1port ; 29cm
ISBN 0-9507800-0-6 : Unpriced B82-19899

759.2 — British watercolour paintings — *Collectors' guides*
Brunger, Stuart M.. British watercolours / by Stuart M. Brunger. — Tenterden : MJM, c1982. — 100p : ill ; 22cm. — (Buyer's price guides)
ISBN 0-905879-22-8 : £2.95 B82-33577

759.2 — British watercolour paintings, *to 1920* **—** *Biographies*
Mallalieu, H. L.. Dictionary of British water colour artists up to 1920 / H.L. Mallalieu. — Woodbridge : Antique Collectors' Club
Vol.2: The plates. — c1979. — p289-557 : ill ; 29cm
Ill on lining paper
ISBN 0-902028-63-4 : £17.50 : CIP rev. B79-28890

759.2 — Cambridgeshire. Cambridge. Art galleries: Kettle's Yard Gallery. Exhibits: English paintings. Vellacott, Elizabeth — *Catalogues*
Vellacott, Elisabeth. Elisabeth Vellacott : paintings and drawings, 1942-81 : Kettle's Yard, Cambridge 19 September-18 October 1981 : Warwick Arts Trust, 33 Warwick Square, London SW1 29 October-5 December 1981. — Cambridge ([Northampton St.], Cambridge [CB3 OAQ]) : Kettle's Yard, [1981]. — [48]p : chiefly ill(some col.) ; 23cm
Unpriced (pbk)
Also classified at 741.942 B82-00685

759.2 — Cambridgeshire. Cambridge. Museums: Fitzwilliam Museum. Exhibits: English landscape paintings. Linnell, John — *Catalogues*
Crouan, Katharine. John Linnell : a centennial exhibition. — Cambridge : Cambridge University Press, Oct.1982. — [70]p
ISBN 0-521-24737-3 (cased) : £18.50 : CIP entry
ISBN 0-521-28923-8 (pbk) : £5.95
Also classified at 759.2 B82-23333

759.2 — Connecticut. New Haven. Art galleries: Yale Center for British Art. Exhibits: English landscape paintings. Linnell, John — *Catalogues*
Crouan, Katharine. John Linnell : a centennial exhibition. — Cambridge : Cambridge University Press, Oct.1982. — [70]p
ISBN 0-521-24737-3 (cased) : £18.50 : CIP entry
ISBN 0-521-28923-8 (pbk) : £5.95
Primary classification 759.2 B82-23333

759.2 — Cornwall. Newlyn. Art galleries: Newlyn Art Gallery. Exhibits: English paintings. Haughton, David — *Catalogues*
Haughton, David. David Haughton : paintings, drawings, prints 1948-1979. — [Penzance] : Newlyn Orion, c1979. — 8p : chiefly ill ; 29x21cm
Produced to accompany an exhibition at Newlyn Art Gallery Sept./Oct. 1979
Unpriced (pbk) B82-05967

759.2 — Cornwall. Penzance. Art galleries: Orion Gallery. Exhibits: English paintings: Wells, John, *1907-* **Mackenzie, Alexander,** *1923-* **& Dannatt, George —** *Catalogues*
Wells, John, *1907-*. John Wells, Alex Mackenzie, George Dannatt. — Penzance (Orion Gallery, Morrab Rd., Penzance, Cornwall) : Newlyn Orion Galleries, [1975]. — [12]p : ill ; 16x21cm
Catalogue of an exhibition held at the Orion Gallery, Penzance, Cornwall, 24 April-13 May 1975
Unpriced (unbound) B82-05471

759.2 — Cumbria. Carlisle *(District).* **Brampton. Art galleries: LYC Museum and Art Gallery. Exhibits: English paintings. Nicholson, Kate —** *Catalogues*
81 November 7 / Kate Nicholson, Harvey Shields, Lawrence Upton. — Brampton (Banks, Brampton, Cumbria CA8 2JH) : LYC Museum & Art Gallery, c1981. — [45]p : ill,2ports ; 14cm
ISBN 0-9504571-1-6 (unbound) : Unpriced
Also classified at 709'.2'4 ; 730'.92'4 B82-08952

759.2 — England. Art galleries. Exhibits: English paintings. Gilman, Harold — *Catalogues*
Gilman, Harold. Harold Gilman 1876-1919. — London : Arts Council of Great Britain, c1981. — 95p : ill(some col.),ports ; 21cm
Published to accompany an exhibition at the City Museum and Art Gallery Stoke-on-Trent, 10 October-14 November 1981, York City Art Gallery 25 November 1981-3 January 1982, Birmingham Museum and Art Gallery 14 January-14 February 1982, Royal Academy of Arts London 25 February-4 April 1982. — Bibliography: p94-95
ISBN 0-7287-0296-7 (pbk) : Unpriced B82-13035

759.2 — English landscape paintings. Miller, John, *19---* **—** *Catalogues*
Miller, John, *19---*. John Miller : new horizons : a major exhibition of his work on view 19th June-3rd July 1982. — Beaconsfield (26 London End, Beaconsfield, Bucks. HP9 2JH) : David Messum, [1982]. — [62]p : ill(some col.),1port ; 30cm
Published to accompany an exhibition held at David Messum Fine Paintings, 1982
Unpriced (pbk) B82-39954

759.2 — English marine paintings. Wyllie, W. L. — *Critical studies*
Quarm, Roger. W.L. Wyllie : marine artist, 1851-1931 / Roger Quarm & John Wyllie ; foreword by Sir Hugh Casson. — London : Barrie & Jenkins, 1981. — 142p : ill(some col.) ; 29cm
Bibliography: p139. — Includes index
ISBN 0-09-146220-7 : £25.00 : CIP rev. B81-28795

759.2 — English oil paintings. Auerbach, Frank — *Catalogues*

Auerbach, Frank. Frank Auerbach : recent paintings and drawings. — New York : Marlborough Gallery ; London (6 Albemarle St., W1X 3HF) : Marlborough Fine Art, 1982. — 44p : ill(some col.),ports(some col.) ; 30cm
Includes bibliographies
Unpriced (pbk)
Primary classification 741.942 B82-36824

759.2 — English oil paintings. Mason, George Heming — *Catalogues*

Mason, George Heming. George Heming Mason / this exhibition was organised by Stoke-on-Trent City Museum and Art Gallery, with financial assistance for the catalogue from the Paul Mellon Centre for Studies in British Art, London. — [Hanley] : [Stoke-on-Trent City Museum and Art Gallery], [1982]. — [52]p : ill,1port ; 15x21cm
ISBN 0-905080-15-7 (pbk) : Unpriced
B82-28533

759.2 — English oil paintings. Shayer *(Family)* **—** *Critical studies*

Stewart, Brian. The Shayer family of painters / Brian Stewart and Mervyn Cutten. — London : F. Lewis, 1981. — xiv,143p,[4]p of plates : ill (some col.),1coat of arms,facsims,ports,1geneal.table ; 29cm
Bibliography: p87-88. — Includes index
ISBN 0-85317-092-4 : £25.00 : CIP rev.
B81-30421

759.2 — English paintings. Bacon, Francis — *Interviews*

Sylvester, David, *1924-*. Interviews with Francis Bacon : 1962-1979 / David Sylvester. — New and enl. ed. — London : Thames and Hudson, 1980. — 176p : ill ; 24cm
Previous ed.: 1975
ISBN 0-500-27196-8 (pbk) : £4.95 B82-40813

759.2 — English paintings. Breckon, Don. Special subjects: Great Britain. Railways — *Illustrations*

Breckon, Don. The railway paintings of Don Breckon. — Newton Abbot : David & Charles, c1982. — 76p,[4]p of plates : ill(some col.) ; 29x37cm
ISBN 0-7153-8206-3 : £17.50 : CIP rev.
B81-36396

759.2 — English paintings. Brown, C. W. — *Critical studies*

C.W. Brown : the Potteries' primitive : an introduction to the collection of paintings and drawings bequeathed to the City Museum and Art Gallery, Stoke-on-Trent. — [Stoke-on-Trent] ([Broad St., Hanley, Stoke-on-Trent]) : [Stoke-on-Trent City Museum and Art Gallery], [1981?]. — [24]p : ill(some col.),2 ports(some col.) ; 22cm
Unpriced (pbk) B82-08289

759.2 — English paintings. Brown, Ford Maddox — *Correspondence, diaries, etc.*

Brown, Ford Madox. The diary of Ford Madox Brown / edited by Virginia Surtees. — New Haven ; London : Published for the Paul Mellon Centre for Studies in British Art by Yale University Press, 1981. — xv,237p : ill,1facsim,2ports ; 25cm. — (Studies in British art)
Includes index
ISBN 0-300-02743-5 : Unpriced : CIP rev.
B81-32082

759.2 — English paintings. Burne-Jones, Edward, *1895-1898 — Interviews*

Burne-Jones, Edward. Burne-Jones talking : his conversations 1895-1898 preserved by his studio assistant Thomas Rooke / edited by Mary Lago. — London : Murray, 1982, c1981. — xi,211p,[8]p of plates : ill,ports ; 22cm
Bibliography: p200-205. — Includes index
ISBN 0-7195-3891-2 : £12.50 : CIP rev.
B82-16487

759.2 — English paintings. Burne-Jones, Edward — *Illustrations*

Burne-Jones, Edward. Burne-Jones : all-colour paperback / introduction by Mary Johnson. — London : Academy, 1979. — 48[i.e.96]p of plates : chiefly col.ill ; 24cm
Unpriced (pbk) B82-23160

759.2 — English paintings. Burra, Edward — *Personal observations — Collections*

Edward Burra : a painter remembered by his friends / John Aiken ... [et al.] ; edited by William Chappell ; foreword by George Melly. — London : Deutsch in association with the Lefevre Gallery, 1982. — 120p : ill(some col.),ports ; 25cm
ISBN 0-233-97450-4 : £8.95 B82-21125

759.2 — English paintings, *ca 1530-1964 — Illustrations*

David Messum Fine Paintings. David Messum : spring preview : on view from 28 April 1979 for two weeks ... — Beaconsfield (26 London End, Beaconsfield, Bucks. HP9 2JH) : David Messum, [1979?]. — [95]p : ill(some col.),ports ; 27cm
Unpriced (pbk) B82-39953

David Messum Fine Paintings. David Messum 1981 : an autumn exhibition on view from 7th-22nd November. — Beaconsfield (26 London End, Beaconsfield, Bucks. HP9 2JH) : David Messum, [1981?]. — [64]p : ill(some col.) ; 30cm
Unpriced (pbk) B82-39951

David Messum Fine Paintings. Exhibition of oil paintings from October 27th 1979 for two weeks ; Exhibition of water colours from November 3rd 1979 for two weeks. — Beaconsfield (26 London End, Beaconsfield, Bucks. HP9 2JH) : David Messum, [1979?]. — [114]p : ill(some col.),ports ; 27cm
Unpriced (pbk) B82-39952

759.2 — English paintings. Colman, Samuel. Belshazzar's feast — *Critical studies*

Whidden, Margaret. Samuel Colman, Belshazzar's Feast : a painting in its context / by Margaret Whidden. — [Oldham] ([Central Library, Union St., Oldham OL1 1DN]) : Oldham Libraries, Art Galleries and Museums, 1981. — 24p : ill ; 22x30cm
Bibliography: p24
£2.20 (pbk) B82-27672

759.2 — English paintings. Constable, John, *1776-1837 — Catalogues*

Constable, John, *1776-1837*. Constable : paintings, watercolours & drawings / Leslie Parris, Ian Fleming-Williams, Conal Shields. — 2nd ed., rev. — London : The Tate Gallery, 1976. — 208p,[12]p of plates : ill(some col.) ; 30cm
Published to accompany the bicentenary exhibition at the Tate Gallery. — Previous ed.: 1976
ISBN 0-905005-05-8 (cased) : £4.00
ISBN 0-905005-20-1 (pbk) : £2.75
Also classified at 741.942 B82-29171

759.2 — English paintings. Cook, Beryl — *Illustrations*

Cook, Beryl. Private view / Beryl Cook. — Harmondsworth : Penguin, 1981, c1980. — [64]p : col.ill ; 25cm
Originally published: London : J. Murray, 1980
ISBN 0-14-005654-8 (pbk) : £2.50 B82-03031

Cook, Beryl. The works / Beryl Cook. — Harmondsworth : Penguin, 1979, c1978 (1981 [printing]). — [64]p : col.ill ; 25cm
Originally published: London: J. Murray, 1978
ISBN 0-14-005343-3 (pbk) : £2.50 B82-05693

759.2 — English paintings. DeWint, Peter — *Biographies*

Smith, Hammond. Peter DeWint 1784-1849. — London : F. Lewis, Jan.1983. — [208]p
ISBN 0-85317-057-6 : £35.00 : CIP entry
B82-33109

759.2 — English paintings. Ennion, Eric. Special subjects: Birds — *Illustrations*

Ennion, Eric. The living birds of Eric Ennion. — London : Gollancz, Oct.1982. — [128]p
ISBN 0-575-03157-3 : £10.95 : CIP entry
B82-23343

759.2 — English paintings. Gilman, Harold — *Critical studies*

Causey, Andrew. Harold Gilman 1876-1919 : his life and work / [Andrew Causey]. — [London] : Arts Council of Great Britain, [1981?]. — [4]p : ill,ports ; 27cm
Accompanies an Arts Council of Great Britain exhibition
Unpriced (unbound) B82-13034

759.2 — English paintings. Hodgkins, Frances — *Biographies*

McCormick, E. H.. Portrait of Frances Hodgkins / E.H. McCormick. — Auckland : Auckland University Press ; [Oxford] : Oxford University Press, 1981. — 159p : ill(some col.),facsims,ports ; 24cm
Includes index
ISBN 0-19-647991-6 (corrected) : £15.00
B82-05064

759.2 — English paintings. Hogarth, William. Marriage à-la-mode — *Critical studies*

Cowley, Robert L. S.. Marriage a-la-mode : a re-view of Hogarth's narrative art. — Manchester : Manchester University Press, Nov.1982. — [240]p
ISBN 0-7190-0884-0 : £30.00 : CIP entry
B82-29108

759.2 — English paintings. John, Gwen — *Biographies*

Chitty, Susan. Gwen John : 1876-1939 / Susan Chitty. — London : Hodder and Stoughton, 1981. — 223p,[16]p of plates : ill(some col.),2facsims,ports ; 24cm
Bibliography: p204-205. — Includes index
ISBN 0-340-24480-1 : £9.95 : CIP rev.
B81-23953

759.2 — English paintings. Joicey, Richard — *Biographies*

Joicey, Richard. Joicey Minor : sketches from life / by Richard Joicey. — Havant : Pallant, 1981. — 191p : ill,ports ; 23cm
ISBN 0-9507141-1-9 : £5.95 B82-07360

759.2 — English paintings. Joseph, Peter — *Illustrations*

Peter Joseph, Richard Long, David Tremlett in Newlyn. — [Penzance] : Newlyn Orion Galleries, 1978. — 1portfolio : ill ; 23x27cm
Produced to accompany an exhibition at the Newlyn Art Gallery in 1978
Unpriced
Primary classification 709'.42 B82-05968

759.2 — English paintings. Landseer, *Sir* **Edwin —** *Critical studies*

Ormond, Richard. Sir Edwin Landseer / Richard Ormond with contributions by Joseph Rishel and Robin Hamlyn. — London : Thames and Hudson in association with the Philadelphia Museum of Art and the Tate Gallery, London, 1981. — 223p : ill(some col.),1map,ports ; 30cm
Bibliography: p220-221. — Includes index
ISBN 0-500-09152-8 : £16.00 B82-03997

759.2 — English paintings. Newlyn school, *1880-1900 — Critical studies*

Artists of the Newlyn school (1880-1900) : shortened catalogue / [text by] Caroline Fox, Francis Greenacre. — [Penzance] : [Newlyn Art Gallery], [1979?]. — 16p ; 30cm
Produced to accompany an exhibition at Newlyn Art Gallery 6 May-9 June, Plymouth City Museum and Art Gallery 16 June-21 July, City of Bristol Museum and Art Gallery 28 July-15 September. — Cover title
Unpriced (pbk) B82-05970

759.2 — English paintings. Pledger, Maurice. Special subjects: Game birds — *Illustrations*

Pledger, Maurice. Game birds / illustrated by Maurice Pledger ; written by Charles Coles. — London : Collins, c1981. — 117p : ill(some col.) ; 43cm
In slip case. — Bibliography: p117
ISBN 0-00-219538-0 : £50.00 B82-06463

759.2 — English paintings. Pre-Raphaelitism — *Critical studies*
Wood, Christopher, *1941-*. The Pre-Raphaelites / Christopher Wood. — London : Weidenfeld and Nicolson, 1981. — 160p : ill(some col.),ports(some col.) ; 32cm
Ill on lining papers. — Bibliography: p156. — Includes index
ISBN 0-297-78007-7 : £18.00 B82-03484

759.2 — English paintings. Pre-Raphaelitism — *Illustrations*
Rose, Andrea. The Pre-Raphaelites / Andrea Rose. — Rev. and enl. [ed.]. — Oxford : Phaidon, 1981. — 31,[96]p : ill(some col.),ports (some col.) ; 31cm
Previous ed.: 1977. — Bibliography: p28
ISBN 0-7148-2180-2 (cased) : £9.95 : CIP rev.
ISBN 0-7148-2166-7 (pbk) : £6.95 B81-16940

759.2 — English paintings. Reuss, Albert — *Illustrations*
Reuss, Albert. Albert Reuss 1889-1976 : an introduction. — [Penzance] ([Orion Gallery, Morrab Rd., Penzance, Cornwall]) : Newlyn Orion, 1980. — [12]p : ill(some col.) ; 23cm
Unpriced (pbk) B82-05472

759.2 — English paintings. Sutherland, Graham — *Critical studies*
Ormond, John. Graham Sutherland, O.M. : a memorial address : anerchiad coffa : discorso commemorativo : eloge funèbre / by John Ormond. — [Cardiff] : National Museum of Wales, 1981. — [36]p : 1port ; 20cm
English, Welsh, Italian and French text
ISBN 0-7200-0244-3 (pbk) : Unpriced B82-05365

759.2 — English paintings. Symonds, Ken — *Critical studies*
Rosenthal, T. G.. Ken Symonds / [written by T.G. Rosenthal]. — Newlyn ([Newlyn, Cornwall]) : Newlyn Orion Galleries, 1977. — [7]p : ill(some col.),1port ; 16x21cm
Accompanies an exhibition held at the Newlyn Art Gallery, 3-29 September 1977
£0.15 (unbound) B82-05468

759.2 — English paintings. Turner, J. M. W. — *Catalogues*
Turner and Dr. Whitaker / Towneley Hall Art Gallery & Museums ; [compiled by Stanley Warburton] ; [edited by Susan Bourne]. — [Burnley] ([Towneley Hall, Burnley]) : Burnley Borough Council, 1982. — 53p,[1]leaf of plates : ill(some col.),1map,ports ; 20x21cm
Catalogue of an exhibition held at Towneley Hall Art Gallery & Museums, July 4th-Sept. 5th, 1982. — Bibliography: p53
£2.00 (pbk) B82-40179

759.2 — English paintings. Turner, J. M. W. — *Illustrations*
Turner, J. M. W.. Turner at the Tate : ninety-two oil paintings by J.M.W. Turner in the Tate Gallery / reproduced in colour and with an introduction by Martin Butlin. — London : Tate Gallery, 1980. — 20p,92p of plates : col.ill ; 21x30cm
ISBN 0-905005-66-x (pbk) : £4.95 B82-21933

759.2 — English portrait paintings. Richmond, George, *1809-1896 — Critical studies*
Lister, Raymond. George Richmond : a critical biography / Raymond Lister. — London : Garton, 1981. — 181p : ill(some col.),ports (some col.) ; 29cm
Includes index
ISBN 0-906030-13-7 : Unpriced B82-03784

759.2 — English watercolour paintings, *1600-1800 — Critical studies*
Clarke, Michael, *1952-*. The tempting prospect. — London : British Museum Publications, Sept.1981. — [160]p
ISBN 0-7141-8016-5 : £13.95 : CIP entry B81-22652

759.2 — English watercolour paintings. Bewick, Thomas. Special subjects: Birds — *Illustrations*
Bewick, Thomas. Thomas Bewick's birds : watercolours and engravings. — London : Gordon Fraser, 1981. — 52p : ill(some col.) ; 18cm
Ill on lining papers
ISBN 0-86092-059-3 : £4.95 : CIP rev.
Also classified at 769.92'4 B81-27439

759.2 — English watercolour paintings. Boys, Thomas Shotter — *Critical studies*
Boys, Thomas Shotter. Pupil and painter : as study of Thomas Shotter Boys (1803-1874) at Crewe Hall / with an introduction and notes by James Roundell ... — Beaconsfield (26 London End, Beaconsfield, Bucks. HP9 2JH) : David Messum, [1980?]. — [16]p : ill,1port ; 21cm
Published to accompany an exhibition at David Messum, Beaconsfield, 1980. — Text, port on inside covers
Unpriced (pbk) B82-39950

759.2 — English watercolour paintings. Cameron, Elizabeth. Special subjects: White flowers — *Illustrations*
Cameron, Elizabeth, *1915-*. A book of white flowers : twenty four paintings / by Elizabeth Cameron ; with a foreword by Christopher Lloyd. — Foss ([Frenich, Foss, Pitlochry, Perthshire PH16 5NG]) : K.D. Duval, 1980. — [61]p : all col.ill ; 43cm
Limited ed. of 250 signed copies. — In slip case
Unpriced B82-40544

759.2 — English watercolour paintings. Cotman, John Sell — *Critical studies*
Cotman, John Sell. John Sell Cotman : 1782-1842 / edited by Miklos Rajnai. — London : Herbert, 1982. — 172 : ill(some col.),2ports ; 25cm
Bibliography: p35-37
ISBN 0-906969-19-0 : Unpriced : CIP rev. B82-11118

759.2 — English watercolour paintings. Hunt, William Henry — *Biographies*
Witt, John. William Henry Hunt. — London : Barrie & Jenkins, Apr.1982. — [208]p
ISBN 0-09-146690-3 : £35.00 : CIP entry B82-03747

759.2 — English watercolour paintings. Jackson, Ashley — *Biographies*
Jackson, Ashley. My brush with fortune. — London : Secker & Warburg, Sept.1982. — [128]p
ISBN 0-436-22035-0 : £9.95 : CIP entry B82-25516

759.2 — English watercolour paintings. Thorburn, Archibald. Special subjects: Great Britain. Animals — *Illustrations*
Southern, John. Thorburn's landscape : the major natural history paintings / John Southern. — London : Elm Tree Books, 1981. — 120p : ill (some col.),1port ; 24x32cm
Ill on lining papers. — List of works: p115-120
ISBN 0-241-10679-6 : £12.50 : CIP rev. B81-26754

759.2 — English watercolour paintings. Turner, J. M. W.. Special subjects: Scotland. Borders Region — *Illustrations*
Turner in Scotland. — Aberdeen : Aberdeen Art Gallery and Museum, Oct.1982. — [64]p
ISBN 0-900017-09-0 (pbk) : £2.00 : CIP entry B82-31315

759.2 — English watercolour paintings. Turner, J. M. W. Special subjects: Western Europe — *Illustrations*
Turner, J. M. W.. Turner abroad. — London : British Museum Publications, Sept.1982. — [208]p. — (A Colonnade book)
ISBN 0-7141-8047-5 : £16.95 : CIP entry B82-20367

759.2 — English watercolour paintings. Whistler, Rex — *Illustrations*
An anthology of mine 1923 / [compiled and illustrated by Rex Whistler]. — London : Hamish Hamilton, 1981. — [72]p : col.ill ; 17cm
ISBN 0-241-10667-2 : £3.95 : CIP rev.
Also classified at 821'.008 B81-22676

759.2 — Great Britain. Art galleries. Exhibits: English paintings. Andrews, Michael, *1927 or 8- — Catalogues*
Andrews, Michael, *1927 or 8-*. Michael Andrews : Hayward Gallery, London 31 October 1980-11 January 1981, Fruit Market Gallery, Edinburgh, 24 January-21 February 1981, Whitworth Art Gallery, University of Manchester, 6 March-20 April 1981. — London : Arts Council of Great Britain, [1981]. — 94p : ill(some col.),ports(some col.) ; 26cm
Catalogue to accompany the exhibitions. — Bibliography: p52
ISBN 0-7287-0260-6 (pbk) : Unpriced
ISBN 0-7287-0254-1 (pbk) : Unpriced B82-21712

759.2 — Great Britain. Art galleries. Exhibits: English paintings. Scully, Sean — *Catalogues*
Scully, Sean. Sean Scully paintings 1971-1981 : Ikon Gallery, Birmingham, September 5th-September 30th 1981 ... — [Birmingham] : [Ikon Gallery], 1981. — 39p : ill(some col.) ; 30cm
ISBN 0-907594-02-6 (pbk) : Unpriced B82-11358

759.2 — Great Britain. Art galleries. Exhibits: English paintings. Sickert, Walter Richard — *Catalogues*
Sickert, Walter Richard. Late Sickert : paintings 1927 to 1942 : Hayward Gallery, South Bank, London 18 November 1981 to 31 January 1982, Sainsbury Centre for the Visual Arts, University of East Anglia, Norwich 2 March to 4 April 1982, Wolverhampton Art Gallery 12 April to 22 May 1982. — London : Arts Council of Great Britain, c1981. — 112p : ill (some col.),ports(some col.) ; 26cm
Bibliography: p32
ISBN 0-7287-0302-5 (cased) : Unpriced
ISBN 0-7287-0301-7 (pbk) : Unpriced B82-13036

759.2 — Great Britain. Arts. Patronage. Organisations: Arts Coucnil of Great Britain. Exhibits: English paintings. Potter, Mary — *Catalogues*
Potter, Mary. Mary Potter : paintings 1922-80. — London : Arts Council of Great Britain, c1981. — [46]p : chiefly ill(some col.),ports ; 21cm
Accompanies an Arts Council travelling exhibition, held at the Serpentine Gallery, London, 23 May-28 June 1981; Fermoy Art Gallery, King's Lynn, 13 July-2 August 1981 ; Mappin Art Gallery, Sheffield, 8 August-6 September 1981; Pallant House Gallery, Chichester, 12 September-10 October 1981
ISBN 0-7287-0284-3 (pbk) : £3.00 B82-06148

759.2 — Great Britain. Arts. Patronage. Organisations: Arts Council of Great Britain. Exhibits: English paintings. Spencer, Stanley. Special subjects: Dockyards, *1940-1945 — Catalogues*
Spencer, Stanley. Spencer in the shipyard : paintings and drawings by Stanley Spencer and photographs by Cecil Beaton from the Imperial War Museum. — London : Arts Council of Great Britain, c1981. — [28]p(4fold.) : chiefly ill(some col.),ports ; 27cm
Accompanies an Arts Council travelling exhibition held at 10 different venues from 2 May 1981 to 18 April 1982
ISBN 0-7287-0277-0 (pbk) : £3.75
Primary classification 741.942 B82-06146

759.2 — Humberside. Hull. Art galleries: Ferens Art Gallery. Exhibits: English paintings. Frampton, Meredith — *Catalogues*
Morphet, Richard. Meredith Frampton / Richard Morphet. — London : Tate Gallery, 1982. — 79p : ill(some col.),ports(some col.) ; 21cm
Published to accompany exhibitions at the Tate Gallery and at the Ferens Art Gallery, Hull, 1982
ISBN 0-905005-33-3 (pbk) : £4.50
Primary classification 759.2 B82-20348

759.2 — London. Kensington and Chelsea *(London Borough).* **Museums: Victoria and Albert Museum. Exhibits: Sketches for English landscape paintings. Constable, John,** *1776-1837* — *Catalogues*

Victoria and Albert Museum. Sketches by John Constable in the Victoria and Albert Museum / C.M. Kauffmann. — London : H.M.S.O., 1981. — 48p : ill(some col.),1port ; 20x21cm
Port on inside cover. — Bibliography: p47-48
ISBN 0-11-290343-6 (pbk) : £2.95 B82-00775

759.2 — London. Westminster *(London Borough).* **Art galleries: Tate Gallery. Exhibits: English paintings. Constable, Lionel** — *Catalogues*

Parris, Leslie, *1941-*. Lionel Constable / Leslie Parris & Ian Fleming-Williams. — London : Tate Gallery, 1982. — 111p : ill(some col.),ports ; 21cm
Published to accompany an exhibition in 1982
ISBN 0-905005-38-4 (pbk) : £5.95 B82-20347

759.2 — London. Westminster *(London Borough).* **Art galleries: Tate Gallery. Exhibits: English paintings. Frampton, Meredith** — *Catalogues*

Morphet, Richard. Meredith Frampton / Richard Morphet. — London : Tate Gallery, 1982. — 79p : ill(some col.),ports(some col.) ; 21cm
Published to accompany exhibitions at the Tate Gallery and at the Ferens Art Gallery, Hull, 1982
ISBN 0-905005-33-3 (pbk) : £4.50
Also classified at 759.2 B82-20348

759.2 — Merseyside *(Metropolitan County).* **Liverpool. Art galleries: Bluecoat Gallery. Exhibits: English acrylic paintings. Farthing, Stephen** — *Catalogues*

Farthing, Stephen. The construction of a monument : paintings and drawings / by Stephen Farthing. — Liverpool (School La., Liverpool L1 3BX) : Bluecoat Gallery, 1981. — 1sheet : ill ; 21x45cm
Published to accompany an exhibition at the Bluecoat Gallery October 31st-November 21st 1981
Unpriced (unbound)
Also classified at 741.942 B82-09033

759.2 — Merseyside *(Metropolitan County).* **Liverpool. Art galleries: Bluecoat Gallery. Exhibits: English paintings. Kelly, Mick & Prewett, Christopher** — *Catalogues*

Kelly, Mick. Paintings : 30 April-21 May / Mick Kelly & Christopher Prewett. — Liverpool (School La., Liverpool L1 3BX) : Bluecoat Gallery, [1981?]. — [4]p : 2ill ; 21cm
Unpriced (unbound) B82-09036

759.2 — Merseyside *(Metropolitan County).* **Liverpool. Art galleries: Bluecoat Gallery. Exhibits: English paintings. McKinlay, Don** — *Catalogues*

Going Backwards *(Exhibition) (1980 : Liverpool).* 'Going Backwards' : December 3-24 1980 : an exhibition / by Don McKinlay and Sam Walsh. — Liverpool (School La., Liverpool L1 3BX) : Bluecoat Gallery, [1980?]. — [4]p : 2ill ; 15x21cm
Unpriced (unbound)
Also classified at 759.2'915 ; 769.92'4
B82-09032

759.2 — Merseyside *(Metropolitan County).* **Liverpool. Art galleries: Bluecoat Gallery. Exhibits: English paintings. Taborn, David** — *Catalogues*

Taborn, David. David Taborn : paintings and drawings, 1979-1981. — Nottingham ([Portland Building, University Park, Nottingham NG7 2RD]) : Nottingham University Art Gallery, Department of Fine Art, [1981?]. — [20]p : ill (some col.) ; 21cm
Published to accompany an exhibition at Nottingham University Art Gallery May 9th-June 13th 1981 and the Bluecoat Gallery July 11th-August 1st 1981
£0.50 (pbk)
Primary classification 759.2 B82-09029

759.2 — Nottinghamshire. Nottingham. Art galleries: Nottingham University Art Gallery. Exhibits: English paintings. Taborn, David — *Catalogues*

Taborn, David. David Taborn : paintings and drawings, 1979-1981. — Nottingham ([Portland Building, University Park, Nottingham NG7 2RD]) : Nottingham University Art Gallery, Department of Fine Art, [1981?]. — [20]p : ill (some col.) ; 21cm
Published to accompany an exhibition at Nottingham University Art Gallery May 9th-June 13th 1981 and the Bluecoat Gallery July 11th-August 1st 1981
£0.50 (pbk)
Also classified at 759.2 B82-09029

759.2 — Surrey. Guildford. Art galleries: Guildford House Gallery. Exhibits: English watercolour paintings. Hyde, William — *Catalogues*

Rogers, Kate. Two Victorian artists from Shere : Kate Rogers 1861-1942, William Hyde 1859-1925 : 2-30 January 1982 : Monday to Saturday 10.30-5.00. — [Guildford] (155 High St., Guildford, Surrey, GU1 3AJ) : Guildford House Gallery, [1982]. — [16]p : ill,ports ; 20cm
Published to accompany an exhibition at the Guildford House Gallery, 1982. — Cover title
Unpriced (pbk)
Primary classification 759.2 B82-15292

759.2 — Surrey. Guildford. Art galleries: Guildford House Gallery. Exhibits: English watercolour paintings. Rogers, Kate — *Catalogues*

Rogers, Kate. Two Victorian artists from Shere : Kate Rogers 1861-1942, William Hyde 1859-1925 : 2-30 January 1982 : Monday to Saturday 10.30-5.00. — [Guildford] (155 High St., Guildford, Surrey, GU1 3AJ) : Guildford House Gallery, [1982]. — [16]p : ill,ports ; 20cm
Published to accompany an exhibition at the Guildford House Gallery, 1982. — Cover title
Unpriced (pbk)
Also classified at 759.2 ; 769.92'4 B82-15292

759.2 — Tyne and Wear *(Metropolitan County).* **Sunderland. Art galleries: Sunderland Museum and Art Gallery. Exhibits: English paintings. Stanfield, Clarkson** — *Catalogues*

The **Spectacular** career of Clarkson Stanfield 1793-1867 : seaman, scene-painter, Royal Academician. — [Newcastle Upon Tyne] : Tyne and Wear County Council Museums, 1979. — 184p,[12]p of plates : ill(some col.),facsims,ports ; 26cm
Catalogue of an exhibition held at Sunderland Museum and Art Gallery, 1979. — Bibliography: p183-184
ISBN 0-905974-03-4 (pbk) : £3.20 B82-24185

759.2 — West Yorkshire *(Metropolitan County).* **Bradford. Art galleries: Cartwright Hall. Exhibits: European paintings,** *1433-1863.* **Reproductions. Bramley, Barrington** — *Catalogues*

Bramley, Barrington. New life for old masters / paintings by Barrington Bramley. — Bradford : Bradford Art Galleries and Museums, c1981. — 24p : ill,ports ; 30cm
Unpriced (pbk) B82-13528

759.2'07 — English paintings, *ca 1600-1835.* **Pigments. Information sources**

Harley, R-D.. Artists' pigments c.1600-1835. — 2nd ed. — London : Butterworth Scientific, June 1982. — [312]p. — (Studies in museology and conservation)
Previous ed.: 1970
ISBN 0-408-70945-6 : £16.00 : CIP entry
B82-14066

759.2'074 — Art galleries. Exhibits: British paintings, *1800-1900* — *Catalogues*

Gordon, Catherine. British paintings of the nineteenth century / [compiled by] Catherine Gordon. — London : Warne, 1981. — 90p ; 22cm. — (An Observer's guide. Where is it?)
ISBN 0-7232-2420-x (pbk) : £2.95 B82-06905

759.2'074 — English paintings, *1700-1970* — *Catalogues*
David Messum Fine Paintings. Recent acquisitions : having a particular focus on marine paintings : on view from May 17th to May 31st 1980. — Beaconsfield (26 London End, Beaconsfield, Bucks. HP9 2JH) : David Messum, [1980]. — [60]p : ill(some col.) ; 21cm
Unpriced (pbk) B82-39957

759.2'074 — English paintings, *ca 1650-1965* — *Catalogues*
David Messum Fine Paintings. David Messum : spring 1978. — Beaconsfield (26 London End, Beaconsfield, Bucks. HP9 2JH) : David Messum, [1978?]. — [28]p : ill(some col.),1port ; 21x30cm
Published to accompany exhibitions of recent acquisitions at David Messum Fine Paintings, 1978. — Text on inside covers
Unpriced (pbk) B82-39956

759.2'074 — English paintings — *Catalogues*
St Martin's painters : an exhibition of work by the current staff of the Painting Department of St Martin's School of Art : 28 April to 15 May 1982, 10am to 6pm Seven Dials Gallery, Earlham Street, Covent Garden, London WC2. — London (107 Charing Cross Rd., WC2H 0DU) : St Martin's School of Art, [1982]. — [35]p : ports ; 21cm
Cover title
£1.00 (pbk) B82-36344

759.2'074'02132 — London. Westminster *(London Borough).* **Art galleries: Fischer Fine Art. Exhibits: British paintings. Realism** — *Catalogues*
The **Real** British : an anthology of the new realism of British painting, October-November 1981 / edited by Edward Lucie-Smith. — London (30 King St., St James's, SW1) : Fischer Fine Art, [1981]. — 28p : ill,ports ; 26cm
Exhibition catalogue. — Bibliography: p5
Unpriced (pbk) B82-03306

759.2'074'02496 — West Midlands *(Metropolitan County).* **Birmingham. Art galleries: Birmingham Museums & Art Gallery. Exhibits: English watercolour painting,** *1760-1930* — *Catalogues*
Birmingham Museums & Art Gallery. British watercolours 1760-1930 : from the Birmingham Museum and Art Gallery : a touring exhibition arranged by the Arts Council in collaboration with Birmingham City Museum and Art Gallery. — [London] : Arts Council of Great Britain, [1980]. — 48p : ill(some col.),1ports ; 24cm
Catalogue to accompany the exhibition
ISBN 0-7287-0255-x (pbk) : Unpriced
B82-21702

759.2'074'02753 — Merseyside *(Metropolitan County).* **Liverpool. Art galleries: Bluecoat Gallery. Exhibits: English paintings,** *1907-1945* — *Catalogues*
An **Honest** patron : a tribute to Sir Edward Marsh / sponsored by Liverpool daily post. — Liverpool : Bluecoat Gallery, 1976. — 52p : ill,facsims ; 21cm
Published to accompany an exhibition at the Bluecoat Gallery May 5th-June 5th 1976. — Bibliography: p51-52
£0.50 (pbk)
Also classified at 741.942'074'02753
B82-09030

759.2'074'0291298 — Scotland. Fife Region. Dunfermline. Public buildings. Stock: British paintings — *Lists*
Cameron, Neil, *1962-*. Catalogue of art works in Dunfermline. — [Dunfermline] ([Central Library, Abbot St., Dunfermline]) : [Director of Libraries, Museum and Art Galleries], [1981?]. — 59p,4p of plates : ill,ports ; 21cm
Cover title. — Compiled by Neil Cameron
Unpriced (pbk) B82-08891

759.2'911 — England. Art galleries. Exhibits: Scottish paintings. Blackadder, Elizabeth — *Catalogues*
Blackadder, Elizabeth. Elizabeth Blackadder. — [Edinburgh] : [Scottish Arts Council], [1981]. — 64p : chiefly ill(some col.),2ports ; 23cm
Published to accompany an exhibition tour, 1981-82
ISBN 0-902989-73-1 (pbk) : Unpriced
B82-23036

759.2'911 — Great Britain. Art galleries. Exhibits: Scottish paintings. Aitchison, Craigie — *Catalogues*
Aitchison, Craigie. Craigie Aitchison paintings 1953-1981 : Serpentine Gallery, London, 1 December 1981-24 January 1982, Midland Group, Nottingham 6 February-7 March 1982, City Museum and Art Gallery, Old Portsmouth 7 April-16 May 1982, Central Library Exhibition Gallery, Milton Keynes 26 May-26 June 1982, Museum and Art Gallery, Bolton 3 July-7 August 1982. — [London] : Arts Council of Great Britain, c1981. — [17] p,[16]leaves of plates : col.ill,col.ports ; 22cm
ISBN 0-7287-0298-3 (pbk) : Unpriced
B82-13028

759.2'911 — Great Britain. Art galleries. Exhibits: Scottish paintings. Pringle, John Quinton — *Catalogues*
Pringle, John Quinton. John Quinton Pringle. — [Edinburgh] : Scottish Arts Council, [c1981]. — 48p : ill(some col.),ports ; 20x22cm
Published to accompany an exhibition tour, 1981-82. — Bibliography: p47
ISBN 0-902989-74-x (pbk) : Unpriced
B82-23034

759.2'911 — Great Britain. Art galleries. Exhibits: Scottish paintings. Roberts, David, ***1796-1864*** **—** *Catalogues*
Roberts, David, *1796-1864*. Artist adventurer David Roberts, 1796-1864. — [Edinburgh] : [Scottish Arts Council], [1981]. — 55p : ill (some col.),1facsim,1port ; 23cm
Published to accompany an exhibition tour, 1981-82. — Bibliography: p54
ISBN 0-902989-72-3 (pbk) : Unpriced
B82-23035

759.2'911 — Scottish oil paintings. Fergusson, J. D. (John Duncan) — *Catalogues*
Fergusson, J. D. (John Duncan). J D Fergusson : 1905-1915 / a work-in-progress exhibition researched by Diana Sykes ; presented by the Crawford Centre for the Arts. — [St Andrews] : [Crawford Centre for the Arts], [1982]. — 52p : ill ; 15x22cm
Bibliography: p50-52
ISBN 0-906272-07-6 (pbk) : Unpriced
B82-29844

759.2'911 — Scottish paintings. Faed ***(Family)*** **—** *Biographies*
McKerrow, Mary. The Faeds : a biography / Mary McKerrow. — Edinburgh : Canongate, 1982. — xviii,158p : ill,1geneal.table,ports ; 27cm
Bibliography: p142-143
ISBN 0-903937-31-x : £20.00 B82-29557

759.2'915 — Irish paintings. Collins, Patrick, ***1911-*** **—** *Critical studies*
Ruane, Frances. Patrick Collins / by Frances Ruane. — Dublin : An Chomhairle Ealaion, c1982. — 119p : ill(some col.) ; 21cm
Unpriced B82-37935

759.2'915 — Irish paintings. Le Brocquy, Louis — *Critical studies*
Walker, Dorothy. Louis le Brocquy. — Dublin (Knocksedan House, Forrest Great, Swords, Co. Dublin) : Ward River Press, Oct.1981. — [164]p
ISBN 0-907085-13-x : £20.00 : CIP entry
B81-30474

759.2'915 — Irish paintings. Orpen, ***Sir*** **William —** *Catalogues*
Orpen, ***Sir*** **William**. William Orpen 1878-1931 : a centenary exhibition. — Dublin : National Gallery of Ireland, c1978. — 90p,32p of plates : ill,ports ; 25cm
Catalogue of the exhibition held at the National Gallery of Ireland 1 Nov.-15 Dec., 1978
Unpriced (pbk) B82-31225

759.2'915 — Merseyside ***(Metropolitan County).*** **Liverpool. Art galleries: Bluecoat Gallery. Exhibits: Irish paintings. McAleer, Clement —** *Catalogues*
McAleer, Clement. Viewpoints : recent paintings / by Clement McAleer. — Liverpool (School La., Liverpool L1 3BX) : Bluecoat Gallery, [1981]. — [4]p : ill ; 21cm
Published to accompany an exhibition at the Bluecoat Gallery October 3rd-24th 1981
Unpriced (unbound) B82-09035

759.2'915 — Merseyside ***(Metropolitan County).*** **Liverpool. Art galleries: Bluecoat Gallery. Exhibits. Irish paintings: Walsh, Sam —** *Catalogues*
Going Backwards ***(Exhibition) (1980 : Liverpool).*** 'Going Backwards' : December 3-24 1980 : an exhibition / by Don McKinlay and Sam Walsh. — Liverpool (School La., Liverpool L1 3BX) : Bluecoat Gallery, [1980?]. — [4]p : 2ill ; 15x21cm
Unpriced (unbound)
Primary classification 759.2 B82-09032

759.3 — German paintings. Dürer, Albrecht — *Biographies*
Anzelewsky, Fedja. Durer. — London : Gordon Fraser, Oct.1982. — [276]p
ISBN 0-86092-068-2 : £49.50 : CIP entry
B82-24606

759.3 — German paintings. Grosz, George — *Biographies*
Grosz, George. A small yes, a big no. — London : Allison & Busby, June 1982. — [289]p
Translation of: Ein kleines Ja und ein grosses Nein
ISBN 0-85031-455-0 : £9.95 : CIP entry
B82-13502

759.3 — German paintings. Lüpertz, Markus — *Catalogues*
Lüpertz, Markus. Markus Lüpertz : 'stil' paintings 1977-79 : 21 September-28 October, Whitechapel Art Gallery, London. — [London] : Trustees of the Whitechapel Art Gallery, [1979?]. — [24]p : ill(some col.) ; 27cm
ISBN 0-85488-046-1 (pbk) : Unpriced
B82-35923

759.3 — German paintings. Modersohn-Becker, Paula — *Critical studies*
Perry, Gillian. Paula Modersohn-Becker : her life and work. — London : Women's Press, Sept.1981. — [160]p
Originally published: 1979
ISBN 0-7043-3843-2 (pbk) : £4.95 : CIP entry
B81-23801

759.3 — London. Tower Hamlets ***(London Borough).*** **Art galleries: Whitechapel Art Gallery. Exhibits: German paintings. Beckmann, Max —** *Catalogues*
Max Beckmann : the triptychs : an exhibition organised by the Whitechapel Art Gallery in association with the Arts Council of Great Britain, 13 November 1980-11 January 1981 / [edited by Nicholas Serota]. — London : Whitechapel Art Gallery, 1980. — 59p : ill (some col.),1port ; 21x27cm
Catalogue of an exhibition. — Bibliography: p58-59
ISBN 0-85488-050-x (pbk) : Unpriced
B82-21522

759.38 — London. Camden ***(London Borough).*** **Arts centres: Camden Arts Centre. Exhibits: Polish paintings. Herman, Josef —** *Catalogues*
Josef Herman : retrospective exhibition, the Camden Arts Centre, Arkwright Road, London N.W.3. 17 January-2 March 1980. — London : The Centre, c1980. — 23p : ill(some col.),ports ; 27cm
Catalogue of the exhibition
ISBN 0-901389-35-8 (pbk) : Unpriced
B82-08814

759.38 — Polish paintings. Ruszkowski, Zdzislaw — *Illustrations*
Ruszkowski, Zdzislaw. The paintings of Ruszkowski / with an introduction by Michael Simonow. — London : Mechanick Exercises, 1982. — 128p : col.ill,col.ports ; 26cm
ISBN 0-9508003-0-9 : Unpriced B82-37525

759.4 — Edinburgh. Art galleries: National Gallery of Scotland. Exhibits: French paintings. Poussin, Nicolas — *Catalogues*
Poussin, Nicolas. Poussin : sacraments and bacchanals : paintings and drawings on sacred and profane themes by Nicolas Poussin 1594-1665 : [catalogue of an exhibition at] National Gallery of Scotland, Edinburgh, 16 October-13 December 1981. — Edinburgh : Trustees of the National Galleries of Scotland, 1981. — 124p : ill(some col.),1port ; 24cm
Bibliography: p122
ISBN 0-903148-38-2 (pbk) : Unpriced
B82-11603

759.4 — France. Paris. Art galleries: Galeries Nationales du Grand Palais. Exhibits: French paintings. Staël, Nicolas de — *Catalogues*
Staël, Nicolas de. Nicolas de Staël : Paris, Galeries Nationales du Grand Palais, 22 May-24 August 1981, London, The Tate Gallery, 7 October-29 November 1981 : an exhibition arranged by the Musée National d'Art Moderne, Centre Georges Pompidou, Paris. — London : Tate Gallery, c1981. — 176p : chiefly ill(some col.) ; 30cm
Bibliography: p174-175
ISBN 0-905005-28-7 (pbk) : £7.00
Primary classification 759.4 B82-02877

759.4 — French paintings, ***1800-1900*** **—** *Biographies*
Hardouin-Fugier, Elisabeth. The pupils of Redouté / by Elisabeth Hardouin-Fugier. — Leigh-on-Sea : F. Lewis, 1981. — 64p : ill ; 30cm
ISBN 0-85317-069-x : £18.50 B82-37537

759.4 — French paintings, ***1845-1862*** **—** *Reviews*
Baudelaire, Charles. Art in Paris 1845-1862 : salons and other exhibitions / reviewed by Charles Baudelaire ; translated and edited by Jonathan Mayne. — 2nd ed. (photographically reprinted). — Oxford : Phaidon, 1981. — xiv,241p,[70]p of plates : ill,1facsim,ports ; 21cm. — (Landmarks in art history)
Previous ed.: London : Phaidon, 1965. — Includes index
ISBN 0-7148-2138-1 (pbk) : £5.95 : CIP rev.
B81-18117

759.4 — French paintings, ***ca 1700-ca 1800*** **—** *Critical studies*
Bryson, Norman. Word and image : French painting of the ancien régime / Norman Bryson. — Cambridge : Cambridge University Press, 1981. — xviii,281p : ill,ports ; 26cm
Bibliography: p272-276. — Includes index
ISBN 0-521-23776-9 : £27.50 : CIP rev.
B81-36242

Conisbee, Philip. Painting in eighteenth-century France / Philip Conisbee. — Oxford : Phaidon, 1981. — 223p : ill(some col.),ports(some col.) ; 29cm
Bibliography: p215-216. — Includes index
ISBN 0-7148-2147-0 : £20.00 : CIP rev.
B81-09987

759.4 — French paintings. Claude, ***1600-1682.*** **Enchanted castle —** *Critical studies*
National Gallery. Claude — The enchanted castle / exhibition organised and text written by Michael Wilson : The National Gallery, London 13 July-19 September 1982. — London : The Publications Department, The National Gallery, London, c1982. — 19p : ill(some col.),ports ; 23cm. — (Acquisition in focus)
ISBN 0-901791-83-0 (pbk) : Unpriced
B82-40422

759.4 — French paintings. Courbet, Gustave. Influence of political events in France, ***1848-1851***
Clark, T. J.. Image of the people : Gustave Courbet and the 1848 Revolution / T.J. Clark ; with 50 illustrations. — London : Thames and Hudson, 1973 (1982 [printing]). — 208p : ill,ports ; 24cm
Includes appendices in French. — Bibliography: p193-202. — Includes index
ISBN 0-500-27245-x (pbk) : £4.95 B82-20413

759.4 — French paintings. Degas, Edgar — *Critical studies*
Lefébure, Amaury. Degas / Amaury Lefébure. — London : Methuen, 1982. — 32p,[72]p of plates : ill(some col.) ; 17cm. — (Master painters series)
Translated from the French
ISBN 0-413-50980-x : Unpriced B82-39573

759.4 — French paintings. Degas, Edgar — *Illustrations*
Roberts, Keith. Degas. — Rev. and enl. ed. — Oxford : Phaidon, Mar.1982. — [128]p. — (Phaidon colour library)
Previous ed.: 1976
ISBN 0-7148-2226-4 (cased) : £10.50 : CIP entry
ISBN 0-7148-2240-x (pbk) : £7.50 B82-01217

759.4 — French paintings. Delacroix, Eugène — *Correspondence, diaries, etc.*

Delacroix, Eugène. The journal of Eugène Delacroix : a selection / edited with an introduction by Hubert Wellington ; translated from the French by Lucy Norton. — 2nd ed. — Oxford : Phaidon, 1980. — xxxv,504p,xvip of plates : ill,1facsim,ports ; 22cm. — (Landmarks in art history)
Previous ed.: 1951. — Bibliography: pxxxv. — Includes index
ISBN 0-7148-2105-5 (pbk) : £6.50 : CIP rev.
B80-11999

Delacroix, Eugène. The Journal of Eugene Delacroix / translated from the French by Walter Pach. — New York : Hacker Art Books, 1980 ; London : Distributed by Art Books. — 731p,[56]p of plates : ill,ports ; 24cm
Translation of: Journal de Eugène Delacroix
ISBN 0-87817-275-0 : £30.00 B82-22737

759.4 — French paintings. Delacroix, Eugène. Influence of Raphael

Lichtenstein, Sara. Delacroix and Raphael / Sara Lichtenstein. — New York ; London : Garland, 1979. — xiv,389p,[102]p of plates : ill ; 24cm. — (Outstanding dissertations in the fine arts)
ISBN 0-8240-3972-6 : Unpriced B82-18912

759.4 — French paintings. Impressionism, *ca 1860-ca 1920*

Blunden, Maria. Impressionists and impressionism / main text Maria and Godfrey Blunden ; documentary notices, synoptic sequence of witness accounts by the painters, their friends and the writers and critics of the Impressionist period Jean-Luc Daval. — Geneva : Skira ; London : Macmillan, 1980. — 231p : ill(some col.),facsims,ports(some col.) ; 29cm
Translation of: Journal de L'impressionnisme. — Originally published: New York : World Publishing Co., 1970. — Includes index
ISBN 0-333-30777-1 : £12.95 B82-07789

The **Impressionists** / [compiled by] Howard Pickersgill. — London (36 Park St., W1Y 4DE) : Albany, 1979. — 93p : col.ill,2col.ports ; 29cm
Ill on lining paper
£2.50 B82-34668

759.4 — French paintings. Impressionism — *Critical studies*

Wilson, Michael. The Impressionist circle. — Oxford : Phaidon, July 1982. — [192]p
ISBN 0-7148-2230-2 : £15.00 : CIP entry
B82-13063

759.4 — French paintings. Manet, Edouard — *Illustrations*

Manet, Edouard. Manet. — New enlarged ed. — Oxford : Phaidon, Aug.1982. — [128]p. — (Phaidon colour library)
Previous ed.: 1976
ISBN 0-7148-2233-7 (cased) : £10.50 : CIP entry
ISBN 0-7148-2243-4 (pbk) : £7.50 B82-15833

759.4 — French paintings. Monet, Claude. Special subjects: France. Argenteuil — *Critical studies*

Tucker, Paul Hayes. Monet at Argenteuil. — London : Yale University Press, Apr.1982. — [211]p
ISBN 0-300-02577-7 : £15.00 : CIP entry
B82-13490

759.4 — French paintings. Pissarro, Camille — *Critical studies*

Lloyd, Christopher, *1945-*. Camille Pissarro / Christopher Lloyd. — Geneva : Skira ; London : Macmillan, 1981. — 151p : ill(some col.),1port ; 35cm
Includes index
ISBN 0-333-31908-7 : Unpriced B82-01531

Pissarro, Camille. Pissarro : Camille Pissarro 1830-1903. — [London] : Arts Council of Great Britain, c1980. — 264p : ill(some col.),maps,facsims,ports ; 25cm
Published to accompany exhibitions at the Hayward Gallery, London, Grand Palais, Paris and Museum of Fine Arts, Boston, 1981. — Bibliography: p250-261
ISBN 0-7287-0261-4 (cased) : Unpriced
ISBN 0-7287-0253-3 (pbk) : Unpriced
B82-15087

759.4 — French paintings. Pissarro, Lucien. Local associations: Essex. Epping

Pratt, Barbara. Lucien Pissarro in Epping / by Barbara Pratt. — Loughton : Barbara Pratt Publications, c1982. — 36p : ill,1geneal.table ; 21cm
Bibliography: p36
ISBN 0-9507871-1-6 (pbk) : £1.50 B82-32896

759.4 — French paintings. Renoir, Pierre Auguste — *Critical studies*

Gaunt, William. Renoir. — 3rd ed., New enlarged ed. — Oxford : Phaidon, June 1982. — [128]p. — (Phaidon colour library)
Previous ed.: 1976
ISBN 0-7148-2229-9 (cased) : £10.50 : CIP entry
ISBN 0-7148-2242-6 (pbk) : £7.50 B82-09616

759.4 — French paintings. Rousseau, Henri — *Biographies*

Le Pichon, Yann. Henri Rousseau. — Oxford : Phaidon, Oct.1982. — [286]p
Translation of: Le monde du Douanier Rousseau
ISBN 0-7148-2256-6 : £30.00 : CIP entry
B82-23004

759.4 — French paintings. Rousseau, Henri — *Illustrations*

Rousseau, Henri. Rousseau / Frank Elgar ; [translation by Jane Brenton]. — London : Eyre Methuen, 1981. — 39p,[76]p of plates : ill (some col.),music,1ports ; 17cm
Translation from the French
ISBN 0-413-48230-8 (pbk) : Unpriced
B82-17555

759.4 — French paintings. Tissot, James — *Critical studies*

Warner, Malcolm, *1953-*. Tissot / by Malcolm Warner. — London : Medici Society, 1982. — 25p : ill(some col.),ports(some col.) ; 19x22cm
Text, ill on inside covers. — Bibliography: p25
ISBN 0-85503-065-8 (pbk) : £0.75 B82-41118

759.4 — French paintings. Utrillo, Maurice — *Critical studies*

Werner, Alfred. Maurice Utrillo / text by Alfred Werner ; commentaries by Alfred Werner and Sabine Reweld. — London : Thames and Hudson, 1981. — 158p : ill(some col.),ports ; 34cm. — (The Library of great painters)
Bibliography: p153-154. — Includes index
ISBN 0-500-09151-x : £16.00 B82-07071

759.4 — French paintings. Utrillo, Maurice — *Illustrations*

Utrillo, Maurice. Maurice Utrillo 1883-1955. — London (147 New Bond St., W1Y 0NX) : Wildenstein, 1980. — 32p : ill(some col.) ; 28cm
Unpriced (pbk) B82-21349

759.4 — London. Westminster *(London Borough)*. **Art galleries: Tate Gallery. Exhibits: French paintings. Staël, Nicolas de —** *Catalogues*

Staël, Nicolas de. Nicolas de Staël : Paris, Galeries Nationales du Grand Palais, 22 May-24 August 1981, London, The Tate Gallery, 7 October-29 November 1981 : an exhibition arranged by the Musée National d'Art Moderne, Centre Georges Pompidou, Paris. — London : Tate Gallery, c1981. — 176p : chiefly ill(some col.) ; 30cm
Bibliography: p174-175
ISBN 0-905005-28-7 (pbk) : £7.00
Also classified at 759.4 B82-02877

759.4'074 — French paintings, *1830-1960 — Catalogues*

National Museum of Wales. French art from the Davies bequest / by Peter Hughes. — Cardiff : National Museum of Wales, 1982. — 82p : chiefly ill(some col.),ports ; 21cm
Also available in Welsh, French and German
ISBN 0-7200-0255-9 (cased) : £6.50
ISBN 0-7200-0235-4 (pbk) : £3.25 B82-38311

759.4'074 — French paintings, *1830-1960 — Catalogues — French texts*

National Musuem of Wales. L'art français du legs Davies / par Peter Hughes ; traduit et adapté en français par Lise F. Perreault Jones. — Cardiff : Musée national du Pays de Galles, 1982. — 82p : chiefly ill(some col.),ports ; 21cm
Translated from the English. — Also available in Welsh, English and German
ISBN 0-7200-0256-7 (cased) : £6.50
ISBN 0-7200-0236-2 (pbk) : £3.25 B82-38313

759.4'074 — French paintings, *1830-1960 — Catalogues — Welsh texts*

National Museum of Wales. Celf Ffrengig o gymynrodd Davies / gan Peter Hughes ; cyfieithwyd i'r Gymraeg gan Hywel Gealy Rees. — Caerdydd : Amgueddfa Genedlaethol Cymru, 1982. — 82p : chiefly ill(some col.),ports ; 21cm
Translated from the English. — Also available in English, French and German
ISBN 0-7200-0258-3 (cased) : £6.50
ISBN 0-7200-0238-9 (pbk) : £3.25 B82-38314

759.4'074 — French paintings — *Catalogues — German texts*

National Museum of Wales. Französische Kunst aus dem Davies Vermächtnis / von Peter Hughes ; ins Deutsche übertragen von Penny Stempel. — Cardiff : Nationalmuseum von Wales, 1982. — 82p : chiefly ill(some col.),ports ; 21cm
Translated from the English. — Also available in English, Welsh and French
ISBN 0-7200-0257-5 (cased) : £6.50
ISBN 0-7200-0237-0 (pbk) : 3.25 B82-38312

759.4'074'04361 — France. Paris. Art galleries: Académie Royale de Peinture et de Sculpture. Exhibits: French paintings, *1759-1781 — Critical studies — French texts*

Diderot, Denis. Salons. — 2nd ed. — Oxford : Clarendon, July 1982
Previous ed.: 1963
Vol.3: 1767. — [388]p
ISBN 0-19-817372-5 : £60.00 : CIP entry
B82-12545

759.5 — Italian frescoes. Castagno, Andrea del — *Critical studies*

Horster, Marita. Andrea Del Castagno : complete edition with a critical catalogue / Marita Horster. — Oxford : Phaidon, 1980. — 224p,viiip of plates : ill(some col.),ports ; 29cm
In slip case. — Bibliography: p215-219. — Includes index
ISBN 0-7148-1426-1 : £35.00 : CIP rev.
B80-04341

759.5 — Italian painting. Piero, *della Francesca — Critical studies*

Clark, Kenneth. Piero della Francesca : complete edition / Kenneth Clark. — 2nd ed. — Oxford : Phaidon, 1969 (1981 [printing]). — 239p : chiefly ill(some col.),ports(some col.) ; 32cm
Previous ed.: 1951. — Includes index
ISBN 0-7148-1380-x : £29.50 B82-03962

759.5 — Italian paintings, *1420-1535 — Critical studies*

Beck, James. Italian Renaissance painting / James Beck. — New York ; London : Harper & Row, c1981. — 484p : ill,1map,ports ; 25cm. — (Icon editions)
Bibliography: p453-460. — Includes index
ISBN 0-06-430382-9 (cased) : Unpriced
ISBN 0-06-430082-x (pbk) : £7.50 B82-10917

759.5 — Italian paintings. Botticelli, Sandro — *Critical studies*

Lightbown, R. W.. Sandro Botticelli / Ronald Lightbown. — London : Elek, 1978. — 2v. : ill (some col.),ports ; 29cm
In slip case. — Includes bibliographies and index
ISBN 0-236-30930-7 : £65.00 B82-02230

759.5 — Italian paintings, *ca 1250-1770 — Critical studies*

Berenson, Bernard. The Italian painters of the Renaissance / Bernard Berenson. — 3rd ed. — Oxford : Phaidon, 1980. — xiii,488p : ill ; 21cm. — (Landmarks in art history)
Previous ed.: 1952. — Includes index
ISBN 0-7148-2103-9 (pbk) : £7.95 : CIP rev. B80-12000

759.5 — Italian paintings. Canaletto, *1697-1768 — Critical studies*

Links, J. G.. Canaletto. — Oxford : Phaidon Press, Aug.1982. — [240]p
ISBN 0-7148-2232-9 : £25.00 : CIP entry B82-15832

759.5 — Italian paintings. Chia, Sandro *— Critical studies*

Seymour, Anne. The draught of Dr Jekyll : an essay on the work of Sandro Chia / [Anne Seymour]. — London ([9 and 23 Dering Street, New Bond St., W1]) : Anthony d'Offay, 1981. — [8]p,8p of plates : ill ; 18cm
Unpriced (pbk) B82-14882

759.5 — Italian paintings. Gentile, *da Fabriano — Critical studies*

Christiansen, Keith. Gentile da Fabriano / Keith Christiansen. — London : Chatto & Windus, 1982. — ix,193p,[98]p of plates : ill(some col.) ; 26cm
Bibliography: p177-181. — Includes index
ISBN 0-7011-2468-7 : £35.00 B82-32674

759.5 — Italian paintings. Mantegna, Andrea *— Critical studies*

Lightbown, Ronald. Mantegna. — Oxford : Phaidon, June 1982. — [304]p
ISBN 0-7148-2023-7 : £60.00 : CIP entry B82-09614

759.5 — Italian paintings. Piero, *della Francesca.* **Baptism of Christ** *— Critical studies*

Lavin, Marilyn Aronberg. Piero Della Francesca's Baptism of Christ / Marilyn Aronberg Lavin ; with an appendix by B.A.R. Carter. — New Haven, Conn. ; London : Yale University Press, c1981. — xx,182p : ill(some col.) ; 22cm. — (Yale publications in the history of art ; 29)
Bibliography: p173-177. — Includes index
ISBN 0-300-02619-6 : £19.50 : CIP rev. B82-01320

759.5 — Italian paintings. Reni, Guido *— Illustrations*

Reni, Guido. Guido Reni. — Oxford : Phaidon, Sept.1982. — [312]p
ISBN 0-7148-2047-4 : £50.00 : CIP entry B82-20369

759.5 — Italian paintings. Tiziano Vecellio *— Critical studies*

Titian : his world and his legacy / edited by David Rosand. — New York ; Guildford : Columbia University Press, 1982. — xviii,349p : ill(some col.),1facsim,geneal.tables,maps,music,plans,ports ; 28cm. — (Bampton lectures in America ; no. 21)
Includes index
ISBN 0-231-05300-2 : £32.50 B82-32693

759.5 — Italian paintings. Vivarini, Alvise *— Critical studies*

Steer, John. Alvise Vivarini : his art and influence / John Steer. — Cambridge : Cambridge University Press, 1982. — xiii,311p : ill,ports ; 26cm
Bibliography: p285-292. — Includes index
ISBN 0-521-23363-1 : £49.50 : CIP rev. B81-40271

759.5 — Italian paintings. Volterra, Daniele da *— Catalogues*

Barolsky, Paul. Daniele da Volterra : a catalogue raisonné / Paul Barolsky. — New York ; London : Garland, 1979. — xv,162p,124p of plates : ill,1port ; 23cm. — (Garland reference library of the humanities ; v.130)
Bibliography: p153-162
ISBN 0-8240-9811-0 : Unpriced B82-08716

759.5 — London. Westminster *(London Borough).* **Art galleries: P. and D. Colnaghi and Co.. Exhibits: Italian oil paintings. Ricci, Sebastiano** *— Catalogues*

Works by Sebastiano Ricci : from British collections : a loan exhibition in aid of the Udine Art Restoration Fund, 1st February to 8th March 1978. — London (14 Old Bond St., W1X 4JL) : Colnaghi, [1978]. — [40]p,xxp of plates : ill ; 25cm
Unpriced (pbk) B82-07271

759.6 — London. Lambeth *(London Borough).* **Art galleries: Hayward Gallery. Exhibits: Spanish paintings. Picasso, Pablo** *— Catalogues*

Green, Christopher, *1943-.* Picasso's Picassos : an exhibition from the Musée Picasso, Paris : a guide to the exhibition, Hayward Gallery, 17 July-11 October 1981 / written by Christopher Green. — [London] : Arts Council of Great Britain, c1981. — [16]p : ill,2plans ; 21cm
£0.30 (unbound) B82-06151

759.6 — Spanish paintings. Picasso, Pablo, *1881-1907 — Critical studies*

Palau i Fabre, Josep. [Picasso vivent 1881-1907. English]. Picasso : life and work of the early years 1881-1907 / Josep Palau i Fabre. — Oxford : Phaidon, c1981. — 559p : chiefly ill (some col.) ; 32cm
Translation of: Picasso vivent 1881-1907. — Bibliography: p558-559
ISBN 0-7148-2219-1 : £95.00 : CIP rev. B81-24679

759.6 — Spanish paintings. Picasso, Pablo *— Catalogues*

Picasso, Pablo. Picasso's Picassos : an exhibition from the Musée Picasso, Paris, Hayward Gallery, London 17 July-11 October 1981 / selected by Sir Roland Penrose, John Golding, Dominique Bozo ; [catalogue edited by Michael Raeburn]. — London : Arts Council, c1981. — 240p : ill(some col.),ports(some col.) ; 26cm
ISBN 0-7287-0282-7 (cased) : Unpriced
ISBN 0-7287-0281-9 (pbk) : Unpriced B82-35858

759.6 — Spanish paintings. Picasso, Pablo *— Critical studies*

A Picasso anthology : documents, criticism, reminiscences / edited by Marilyn McCully. — London : Arts Council of Great Britain in association with Thames and Hudson, 1981. — 288p : ill,1facsim,ports ; 21cm
Published on the occasion of the Arts Council exhibition Picasso's Picassos, an exhibition from the Musée Picasso, Paris at the Hayward Gallery, London. — Includes index
ISBN 0-500-27244-1 (pbk) : £4.95 B82-08701

759.6 — Spanish paintings. Velazquez, Diego Rodriguez de Silva y *— Critical studies*

Harris, Enriqueta. Velazquez. — Oxford : Phaidon, Oct.1982. — [240]p
ISBN 0-7148-2231-0 : £25.00 : CIP entry B82-23003

759.6'074 — Spanish paintings, *1650-1700 — Catalogues*

Painting in Spain 1650-1700 *(Exhibition) (1982 : Art Museum, Princeton University, and the Detroit Institute of Arts).* Painting in Spain 1650-1700 : from North American collections / Edward J. Sullivan and Nina A. Mallory ; with an historical essay by J.H. Elliott. — Princeton ; Guildford : Published by the Art Museum, Princeton University in association with Princeton University Press, c1982. — xvi,182p : ill(some col.),ports ; 29cm
Bibliography: p175-182
ISBN 0-691-03992-5 : £23.00 B82-32662

759.6'074 — Spanish paintings *— Catalogues*

New Spanish figuration : paintings by Chema Cobo, Costus, Luis Gordillo, Guillermo Pérez-Villalta : an exhibition organised by Kettle's Yard Gallery ... / edited by Jeremy Lewison. — Cambridge : Kettle's Yard Gallery, c1982. — [52]p : ill(some col.) ; 20x21cm
Bibliography: on final page
ISBN 0-907074-13-8 (pbk) : Unpriced B82-34633

759.7 — Russian paintings. Aĭvazovskiĭ, Ivan Konstantinovich *— Illustrations*

Aĭvazovskiĭ, Ivan Konstantinovich. Aivazovsky / [compiled and introduced by Nikolai Novouspensky] ; [translated from the Russian by Richard Ware]. — London : Pan, 1980. — 17p,[70]p of plates : chiefly ill(some col.),2ports ; 29cm
ISBN 0-330-26304-8 (pbk) : Unpriced B82-03983

759.7 — Russian paintings. Pasternak, Leonid *— Biographies*

Pasternak, Leonid. The memoirs of Leonid Pasternak. — London : Quartet, Sept.1982. — [224]p
Translated from the Russian
ISBN 0-7043-2343-5 : £11.95 : CIP entry B82-29085

759.917'671 — Islamic paintings, *1200-1600 — Critical studies*

Ipşiroğlu, Mazhar Ş. Masterpieces from the Topkapi Museum : paintings and miniatures / Mazhar Ş. Ipşiroğlu ; [translated from the Turkish by Adair Mill]. — London : Thames and Hudson, 1980. — 150p : col.ill ; 26x28cm
In slip case. — Bibliography: p145-146. — Includes index
ISBN 0-500-23323-3 : £24.00 B82-25206

759.94 — European paintings, *1300-1900.* **Perspective** *— Critical studies*

Tyndall, Audrey. Watch this space : an exhibition about perspective in painting / the National Gallery ; booklet by Audrey Tyndall. — London : Publications Department, National Gallery, 1982. — 12p : ill,ports ; 25cm
Published to accompany an exhibition held at the National Gallery, 1982. — Cover title
ISBN 0-901791-82-2 (pbk) : Unpriced B82-35122

759.94 — European paintings, *1300-1937.* **Masterpieces** *— Critical studies*

Great paintings / [compiled by] Howard Pickersgill. — London (36 Park St., W1Y 4DE) : Albany, 1979. — 125p : col.ill,col.ports ; 29cm
Ill on lining papers
Unpriced B82-34669

759.94'074 — European paintings, *1500-1900 — Catalogues*

Miller, James, *1951-.* The catalogue of paintings at Bowood House / compiled and written by James Miller. — London : Curwen, 1982. — 51p ; 25cm
Unpriced (pbk) B82-27736

Wellington Museum. Catalogue of paintings in the Wellington Museum / [compiled by] C.M. Kauffmann. — London : H.M.S.O., 1982. — 176p : ill,ports ; 25cm
At head of title: Victoria and Albert Museum. — Includes index
ISBN 0-11-290380-0 (cased) : £15.00
ISBN 0-11-290373-8 (pbk) : £6.95 B82-36834

759.94'074'02132 — London. Westminster *(London Borough).* **Art galleries: National Gallery. Stock: European paintings,** *1300-1975 — Catalogues*

National Gallery. 100 great paintings : Duccio to Picasso : European painting from the 14th to the 20th century illustrated in colour / The National Gallery, London ; [text by] Dillian Gordon. — London : Sponsored by Coutts & Co. and published by order of the Trustees, Publications Department, National Gallery, 1981. — 223p : ill(some col.) ; 27cm
Includes index
ISBN 0-901791-75-x (pbk) : Unpriced
ISBN 0-00-217066-3 (Collins) B82-05447

759.94′074′02527 — Nottinghamshire. Nottingham. Art galleries: Nottingham University Art Gallery. Exhibits: European paintings, *1300-1850* **from private collections in stately homes in East Midlands** — *Catalogues*

Nottingham University Centenary Exhibition. Masterpieces from great houses in the East Midlands : Nottingham University Centenary Exhibition. — Nottingham (Department of Fine Art, Portland Building, University Park, Nottingham) : Nottingham University Art Gallery, 1981. — 61p,[8]p of plates : ill,ports ; 25cm
Accompanies the exhibition held at Nottingham University Art Gallery, 1st-28th October, 1981. — Includes index
Unpriced (pbk) B82-07567

759.9492 — Dutch paintings, *1400-1500* — *Critical studies*

Châtelet, Albert. Early Dutch painting : painting in the northern Netherlands in the fifteenth century / Albert Châtelet ; translated by Christopher Brown and Anthony Turner. — Oxford : Phaidon, 1981. — 264p : ill(some col.),1map,ports ; 31cm
Translation of: Les primitifs hollandais. — Bibliography: p247-257. — Includes index
ISBN 0-7148-2095-4 : £48.00 : CIP rev. B81-17539

759.9492 — Dutch paintings. Bosch, Hieronymus — *Critical studies*

Beagle, Peter S.. The garden of earthly delights / by Peter S. Beagle. — London : Pan, 1982. — 127p : ill(some col.) ; 29cm. — (Picador)
Bibliography: p124-125. — Includes index
ISBN 0-330-26716-7 (pbk) : £5.95 B82-36883

Beagle, Peter S.. The garden of earthly delights / by Peter S. Beagle. — London : Secker & Warburg, 1982. — 127p : ill(some col.) ; 30cm
Bibliography: p124-125
ISBN 0-436-03695-9 : £13.50 B82-36882

759.9492 — Dutch paintings. Hals, Frans — *Critical studies*

Baard, H. P.. Frans Hals / text by H.P. Baard ; translated from the Dutch by George Stuyck. — London : Thames and Hudson, 1981. — 167p : ill(some col.),ports(some col.) ; 34cm. — (The Library of great painters)
Bibliography: p164. — Includes index
ISBN 0-500-09150-1 : £16.00 B82-07070

759.9492 — Dutch paintings. Rembrandt — *Critical studies*

Kitson, Michael. Rembrandt. — 3rd ed. rev. and enl. — Oxford : Phaidon, June 1982. — [128]p. — (Phaidon colour library)
Previous ed.: 197-?
ISBN 0-7148-2228-0 (cased) : £10.50 : CIP entry
ISBN 0-7148-2241-8 (pbk) : £7.50 B82-09615

Rosenberg, Jakob. Rembrandt : life and work / Jakob Rosenberg. — 4th ed. — Oxford : Phaidon, 1980. — viii,386p : ill,ports ; 21cm. — (Landmarks in art history)
Previous ed.: 1968. — Bibliography: p367-381. — Includes index
ISBN 0-7148-2129-2 (pbk) : £6.95 : CIP rev. B80-12002

759.9492 — Dutch paintings. Velde, Willem Van de, *1611-1693* **& Velde, Willem Van de,** *1633-1707* — *Catalogues*

Art of the Van de Veldes *(Exhibition) (1982 : National Maritime Museum)*. The art of the Van de Veldes : paintings and drawings by the great Dutch marine artists and their English followers / [catalogue of the exhibition 'The art of the Van de Veldes' held at the National Maritime Museum, London from 23 June to 5 December 1982]. — London : National Maritime Museum, 1982. — 143p : ill(some col.),1map,ports ; 21x25cm
Bibliography: p143
ISBN 0-905555-62-7 (pbk) : Unpriced
Also classified at 741.9492 B82-35827

759.9492 — Dutch paintings. Vermeer, Jan — *Critical studies*

Wheelock, Arthur K.. Jan Vermeer / text by Arthur K. Wheelock, Jr.. — London : Thames and Hudson, 1981. — 167p : ill(some col.),1map,ports ; 34cm. — (The Library of great painters)
Bibliography: p163-164. — Includes index
ISBN 0-500-09149-8 : £16.00 B82-07072

759.9492 — Dutch self-portrait paintings. Rembrandt — *Illustrations*

Rembrandt. Rembrandt : self-portraits. — London : Gordon Fraser, Sept.1982. — [160]p
ISBN 0-86092-054-2 : £11.95 : CIP entry B82-21544

759.9492′074 — Art galleries. Exhibits: Dutch paintings, *1600-1700* — *Catalogues*

Wright, Christopher, *1945-*. Dutch and Flemish paintings of the seventeenth century / [compiled by] Christopher Wright. — [London] : Warne, 1981. — 121p ; 22cm. — (An Observer's guide. Where is it?)
ISBN 0-7232-2458-7 (pbk) : £2.95
Also classified at 759.9493′074 B82-06903

759.9492′074 — Dutch paintings, *1600-1700* — *Catalogues*

Netherlandish paintings and drawings from the collection of F.C. Butôt : by little-known and rare masters of the seventeenth century / Laurens J. Bol and George S. Keyes ; catalogue by F.C. Butôt. — London : Sotheby Parke Bernet, 1981. — 263p : chiefly ill(some col.) ; 26cm
Bibliography: p262-263 — Includes index
ISBN 0-85667-103-7 : Unpriced B82-33962

759.9492′07402132 — London. Westminster *(London Borough)*. **Art galleries: Alan Jacobs Gallery. Exhibits: Dutch paintings from Shipley Art Gallery,** *1600-1800* — *Catalogues*

Dutch and Flemish 16th and 17th century paintings from the Shipley Collection : London, Alan Jacobs Gallery, 20th March-13th May ... : catalogue / compiled by Christopher Wright. — London : The Gallery, c1979. — xiii,[65]p : ill,ports ; 25cm
Includes foreword in Dutch. — Bibliography: [p1]
ISBN 0-9503121-4-2 (pbk) : Unpriced
Also classified at 759.9493′07402132 B82-22622

759.9493 — Flemish landscape paintings. Rubens, Peter Paul — *Critical studies*

Vergara, Lisa. Rubens and the poetics of landscape. — London : Yale University Press, Nov.1982. — [228]p
ISBN 0-300-02508-4 : £27.00 : CIP entry B82-40339

759.9493 — Flemish paintings. Bruegel, Pieter — *Illustrations*

Roberts, Keith. Bruegel. — 3rd ed. — Oxford : Phaidon, Mar.1982. — [128]p
Previous ed.: 1971
ISBN 0-7148-2225-6 (cased) : £10.50 : CIP entry
ISBN 0-7148-2239-6 (pbk) : £7.50 B82-01218

759.9493 — Flemish paintings, *ca 1500-1650* — *Critical studies*

Held, Julius S.. Rubens and his circle / studies by Julius S. Held ; edited by Anne W. Lowenthal, David Rosand, John Walsh. — Princeton ; Guildford : Princeton University Press, c1982. — xxiv,207p,[74]p of plates : ill (some col.),ports ; 29cm
Includes index
ISBN 0-691-03968-2 : £24.70
ISBN 0-691-00332-7 (pbk) : Unpriced B82-40615

759.9493 — Flemish paintings. Dyck, *Sir* **Anthony van** — *Biographies*

Brown, Christopher. Van Dyck. — Oxford : Phaidon, Nov.1982. — [240]p
ISBN 0-7148-2211-6 : £25.00 : CIP entry B82-26392

759.9493 — Flemish paintings. Eyck, Jan van — *Critical studies*

Purtle, Carol J.. The Marian paintings of Jan van Eyck / Carol J. Purtle. — Princeton ; Guildford : Princeton University Press, c1982. — xviii,221p,[48]p of plates : ill,ports ; 29cm
Bibliography: p203-218. — Includes index
ISBN 0-691-03989-5 : £31.80 B82-34455

759.9493′074 — Art galleries. Exhibits: Flemish paintings, *1600-1700* — *Catalogues*

Wright, Christopher, *1945-*. Dutch and Flemish paintings of the seventeenth century / [compiled by] Christopher Wright. — [London] : Warne, 1981. — 121p ; 22cm. — (An Observer's guide. Where is it?)
ISBN 0-7232-2458-7 (pbk) : £2.95
Primary classification 759.9492′074 B82-06903

759.9493′07402132 — London. Westminster *(London Borough)*. **Art galleries: Alan Jacobs Gallery. Exhibits: Flemish paintings from Shipley Art Gallery,** *1600-1800* — *Catalogues*

Dutch and Flemish 16th and 17th century paintings from the Shipley Collection : London, Alan Jacobs Gallery, 20th March-13th May ... : catalogue / compiled by Christopher Wright. — London : The Gallery, c1979. — xiii,[65]p : ill,ports ; 25cm
Includes foreword in Dutch. — Bibliography: [p1]
ISBN 0-9503121-4-2 (pbk) : Unpriced
Primary classification 759.9492′07402132 B82-22622

759.9494 — Swiss oil paintings. Hodler, Ferdinand — *Critical studies*

Hirsh, Sharon L.. Ferdinand Hodler / Sharon L. Hirsh. — London : Thames and Hudson, 1982. — 144p : ill(some col.),ports(some col.) ; 30cm
Bibliography: p143-144
ISBN 0-500-09157-9 : £24.00 B82-38917

759.951 — Chinese paintings, *1600-1700* — *Critical studies*

Cahill, James. The compelling image : nature and style in seventeenth-century Chinese painting / James Cahill. — Cambridge, Mass. ; London : Harvard University Press, 1982. — 250p : ill (some col.),2maps ; 29cm. — (The Charles Eliot Norton lectures ; 1979)
Includes index
ISBN 0-674-15280-8 : £24.50 B82-32840

759.951 — Chinese paintings. Wu, Zuoren & Xiao, Shufang — *Illustrations*

Wu, Zuoren. Selected paintings of Wu Zuoren and Xiao Shufang. — Oxford : Pergamon, June 1982. — 1v.
ISBN 0-08-027950-3 : £25.00 : CIP entry B82-20746

759.951′074 — Chinese ink paintings, *1886-1966* — *Catalogues*

Whitfield, Roderick. Chinese traditional painting 1886-1966 : five modern masters : Zhong Guo Jin dai wu wei jie chu hua jia : Royal Academy of Arts 1982 / this exhibition is presented under the auspices of the People's Republic of China and of Her Britannic Majesty's Government ... ; organised with the assistance of the Visiting Arts Unit of Great Britain and the British Council ... ; [catalogue by Roderick Whitfield]. — [London] ([Burlington House, Piccadilly, S.W.1]) : The Academy, c1982. — 50p : col.ill,ports ; 27cm
Transliterated Chinese subtitle. — Bibliography: p44-45
Unpriced (pbk) B82-38952

759.953′67 — Kuwaiti paintings. Alkazzi, Basil — *Illustrations*

Alkazzi, Basil. My heart has opened unto every form : the art of Basil Alkazzi / Max Wykes-Joyce. — London ([Porchester Pl. W2]) : Drian Galleries, 1982. — [34]p,[87]p of plates : ill(some col.) ; 24cm
Unpriced B82-18386

759.954'074 — Indian paintings, *1525-1825* **—** *Catalogues*
McInerney, Terence. Indian painting : 1525-1825 / an exhibition arranged and catalogued by Terence McInerney. — London (15 Duke St, St. James's SW1Y 6DB) : David Carritt Ltd., [1982]. — 83p : ill(some col.),2facsims,1port ; 25cm
At head of title: Artemis Group. — Includes bibliographies
Unpriced (pbk) B82-27711

759.972 — Mexican paintings, *1940-1970* **—** *Critical studies*
Goldman, Shifra M.. Contemporary Mexican painting in a time of change / by Shifra M. Goldman. — Austin ; London : University of Texas Press, c1981. — xxvi,229p : ill(some col.),ports ; 29cm. — (The Texas Pan American series)
Bibliography: p209-217. — Includes index
ISBN 0-292-71061-5 : £21.00 B82-15444

759.994 — Australian paintings. Campbell, Sophia Palmer & Campbell, Marrianne Collinson — *Critical studies*
Kerr, Joan. From Sydney Cove to Duntroon. — London : Gollancz, Oct.1982. — [128]p
ISBN 0-575-03039-9 : £9.95 : CIP entry B82-23339

759.994'074 — Australian paintings, *to 1979* **—** *Catalogues*
Thomas, Daniel, *19---*. Outlines of Australian art : the Joseph Brown Collection / Daniel Thomas. — Expanded ed. — South Melbourne ; London : Macmillan, 1980. — 90p,205p of plates : chiefly ill(some col.),ports(some col.) ; 30cm
Previous ed.: 1973
ISBN 0-333-29942-6 : Unpriced B82-28530

760 — GRAPHIC ARTS, PRINTS

760'.0442 — European graphic arts, *ca 1400-1980.* **Special subjects: Painters —** *Critical studies*
Levey, Michael. The painter depicted : painters as a subject in painting / Michael Levey. — [London] : Thames and Hudson, c1981. — 72p : ill,ports ; 22cm
ISBN 0-500-55013-1 : £4.50 B82-10279

760'.0444 — London. Croydon *(London Borough).* **Arts centres: Fairfield Halls. Exhibits: Graphic arts. Special subjects: London. Bromley** *(London Borough).* **Recreation centres: Crystal Palace —** *Catalogues*
The **Crystal** Palace Museum and Park restoration project. — [London] ([84, Anerley Rd., Crystal Palace S.E.19]) : Crystal Palace Foundation, [1981]. — 1portfolio : ill,1facsim,plans ; 31cm
£2.00
Primary classification 333.78'3'0942178 B82-05576

760'.0447 — Graphic arts. Special subjects: Unicorns — *Illustrations*
Unicorns / edited by Jeanne Griffiths. — London : W.H. Allen, 1981. — 53p : ill(some col.) ; 15cm
ISBN 0-491-02785-0 : £2.50
Primary classification 808.8'0375 B82-05025

760'.04499421081 — English graphic arts, *1837-1900.* **Special subjects: London —** *Critical studies*
Victorian artists and the city : a collection of critical essays / edited by Ira Bruce Nadel, F.S. Schwarzbach. — New York ; Oxford : Pergamon, 1980. — xvi,170p,ivp of plates : ill (some col.),facsims,1plan,ports ; 29cm
Includes index
ISBN 0-08-023381-3 : £19.75 B82-08047

760'.044995498 — English graphic arts. Special subjects: Bhutan, *1783* **—** *Illustrations*
Davis, Samuel, *1760-1819*. Views of medieval Bhutan : the diary and drawings of Samuel Davis 1783 / [selected and edited by] Michael Aris. — London : Serindia, 1982. — 124p : ill (some col.),maps,1facsim,1plan,ports(some col.) ; 20x29cm
Bibliography: p122. — Includes index
ISBN 0-906026-10-5 : £18.00 : CIP rev.
Primary classification 954.9'8'00994 B81-34642

760'.092'2 — English graphic arts. Horton, Brian & Horton, Sheila — *Catalogues*
Horton, Brian. The Hortons of Taplow : an exhibition of their collected works : June 21st-July 5th 1980. — Beaconsfield (26 London End, Beaconsfield, Bucks. HP9 2JH) : David Messum, [1980?]. — [16]p : ill(some col.) ; 17cm
Published to accompany an exhibition held at David Messum Fine Paintings, Beaconsfield. — Artists: Brian and Sheila Horton. — Text on inside covers
Unpriced (pbk) B82-39955

760'.092'2 — Graphic arts. Artists. Monograms, signatures & symbols, *to 1975* **—** *Encyclopaedias*
Caplan, H. H.. The classified directory of artists' signatures, symbols & monograms / [compiled by] H.H. Caplan. — Enlarged and rev. ed. — London : Prior, 1982. — viii,873p : chiefly facsims ; 31cm
English text, English, French, German, Spanish and Italian introduction. — Previous ed.: 1976
ISBN 0-86043-658-6 : £55.00 : CIP rev. B82-08413

760'.092'4 — American graphic arts. Mugnaini, Joseph — *Illustrations*
Mugnaini, Joseph. Joseph Mugnaini : drawings and graphics / with a foreword by Ray Bradbury. — Metuchen, N.J. ; London : Scarecrow, 1982. — [164]p : chiefly ill,ports ; 29cm
ISBN 0-8108-1521-4 : £16.00 B82-38100

760'.092'4 — Art galleries. Exhibits: American graphic arts. Rivers, Larry — *Catalogues*
Rivers, Larry. Larry Rivers : the continuing interest in abstract art : Oct.16-25, 1981 F.I.A.C. ... November, 1981 Marlborough Fine Art (London) Ltd. ... Feb. 3-27, 1982 Marlborough Gallery Inc. ... — New York : Marlborough Gallery Inc. ; London (6 Albemarle St., W1X 3HF) : Marlborough Fine Art (London) Ltd., [1981?]. — 28p : col.ill ; 22x28cm
Unpriced (pbk) B82-07780

760'.092'4 — Cornwall. Newlyn. Art galleries: Newlyn Art Gallery. Exhibits: English graphic arts. MacKenzie, Alexander, *1923-* **—** *Catalogues*
Mackenzie, Alexander, *1923-*. Alexander Mackenzie : paintings, collages, drawings, 7 June-12 July 1980, Newlyn Art Gallery. — [Penzance] ([Newlyn Art Gallery, Newlyn, Cornwall]) : Newlyn Orion, 1980. — [12]p : chiefly ill ; 20x21cm
Accompanies an exhibition
Unpriced (pbk) B82-05470

760'.092'4 — English graphic arts. Collins, Cecil. Special subjects: Fools — *Illustrations*
Collins, Cecil. The vision of the fool / Cecil Collins. — New ed., with additional illustrations. — Chipping Norton : Kedros, 1981. — vii,40p,4p of plates : ill(some col.) ; 25cm
Previous ed.: 1947
ISBN 0-907454-03-8 (cased) : Unpriced
ISBN 0-907454-02-x (pbk) : £3.30 B82-05903

760'.092'4 — English graphic arts. Constable, John, *1776-1837.* **Special subjects: Suffolk. East Bergholt region,** *1797-1830* **—** *Catalogues*
Constable's country : a loan exhibition at Gainsborough's House, Sudbury, Suffolk 5-27th June 1976 / Robert McPherson, Michael Rosenthal. — [Sudbury] ([Sudbury, Suffolk]) : [Gainsborough's House], [1976]. — [16]p : ill ; 21cm
Unpriced (pbk) B82-30877

760'.092'4 — English graphic arts. Crumplin, Colin — *Illustrations*
Crumplin, Colin. Colin Crumplin / [text, photos and layout by Colin Crumplin]. — Bristol ([Narrow Quay, Britol BS1 4QA]) : Arnolfini Gallery, 1981. — 16p : ill ; 21cm
To accompany the exhibition Substance and accident, held at the Arnolfini Gallery, 12 September-17 October 1981. — Cover title. — Limited ed. of 1000 copies
ISBN 0-9503885-8-0 (pbk) : Unpriced B82-02323

760'.092'4 — English graphic arts. Fisher, Joel — *Illustrations*
Fisher, Joel. Joel Fisher / [text, photos and layout by Joel Fisher]. — Bristol ([Narrow Quay, Bristol BS1 4QA]) : Arnolfini Gallery, 1981. — 15p : ill ; 21cm
To accompany the exhibition Substance and accident, held at the Arnolfini Gallery, 12 September-17 October 1981. — Cover title. — Limited ed. of 1000 copies
ISBN 0-9503885-9-9 (pbk) : Unpriced B82-02322

760'.092'4 — English graphic arts. Herkomer, *Sir* **Hubert von —** *Critical studies*
A **Passion** for work : Sir Hubert von Herkomer 1849-1914 / Watford Museum. — Watford : Watford Borough Council, 1982. — 56p,16p of plates : ill,ports ; 21cm
Published to accompany an exhibition at Watford Museum 15.2.82-10.3.82. — Cover title
ISBN 0-907958-00-1 (pbk) : Unpriced B82-23159

760'.092'4 — English graphic arts. Houghton, Arthur Boyd — *Critical studies*
Hogarth, Paul. Arthur Boyd Houghton / Paul Hogarth. — London : Gordon Fraser, 1981. — 143p : ill,ports ; 24x26cm
Bibliography: p139-140. — Includes index
ISBN 0-900406-75-5 : £19.50 B82-25892

760'.092'4 — English graphic arts. Orr, Chris. Special subjects: Ruskin, John — *Illustrations*
Orr, Chris. Chris Orr's John Ruskin : 'history is a dead liberty' / images and story by Chris Orr ; with notes and an essay by Robert Hewison. — London : Signford, 1976. — 32p : ill ; 21x30cm
£3.00 (pbk) B82-01290

760'.092'4 — English graphic arts. Stern, Bernard — *Illustrations*
Antoine, Jean. Bernard Stern / texts by — textes de — Texte von Jean Antoine & Bernard Stern. — London : Academy Editions, 1981. — 96p : ill(some col.) ; 25cm
Parallel English, French and German text. — Bibliography: p96
Unpriced B82-03205

760'.092'4 — English graphic arts. Sutherland, Graham — *Biographies*
Berthoud, Roger. Graham Sutherland : a biography / by Roger Berthoud. — London : Faber, 1982. — 328p,[56]p of plates : ill(some col.),facsims,ports(some col.) ; 25cm
Includes index
ISBN 0-571-11882-8 : £12.50 : CIP rev. B82-06859

760'.092'4 — English graphic arts. Sutherland, Graham — *Catalogues*
Alley, Ronald. Graham Sutherland / Ronald Alley. — London : Tate Gallery, 1982. — 184p : ill(some col.),maps,ports(some col.) ; 30cm
Published to accompany an exhibition at the Tate Gallery, London, 1982
ISBN 0-905005-48-1 (pbk) : £7.95 B82-31344

760'.092'4 — German graphic arts. Huetz-Davisson, Christine von — *Catalogues*
Huetz-Davisson, Christine von. Christine von Huetz-Davisson : water colours, drawings, etchings, tinprints, : 14th May-19th June 1982. — London (9 Hereford Rd, W2) : Leinster Fine Art, [1982]. — [16]p : ill,1port ; 21cm
Published to accompany an exhibition at Leinster Fine Art, London, 1982
Unpriced (unbound) B82-36208

760'.092'4 — Great Britain. Art galleries. Exhibits: English graphic arts. Kokoschka, Oskar — *Catalogues*
Kokoschka, Oskar. Oskar Kokoschka : memorial exhibition of drawings, watercolours, graphics from British collections : an exhibition presented by the Goethe Institute, London in association with the Goethe Institute, Dublin, the Goethe Institute, Manchester, the Goethe Institute, Glasgow. — [London] ([50, Princes Gate, Exhibition Rd, SW7 2PH]) : [Goethe Institute], [1981]. — 48p : ill,ports ; 21cm
Unpriced (pbk) B82-11691

760'.092'4 — London. Hackney *(London Borough).* **Museums: Geffrye Museum. Exhibits: English graphic arts. Bird, Edward** — *Catalogues*

Bird, Edward. Edward Bird 1772-1819 : Wolverhampton Art Gallery February 27th-April 3rd 1982 : Geffrye Museum, London April 16th-May 30th 1982 / catalogue by Sarah Richardson. — [Wolverhampton] : [Wolverhampton Art Gallery], [1982]. — 44p,[28]p of plates : ill,ports ; 22cm
Unpriced (pbk)
Primary classification 760'.092'4 B82-22463

760'.092'4 — London. Westminster *(London Borough).* **Art galleries: Anthony d'Offay** *(Firm).* **Exhibits: English graphic arts. Grant, Duncan** — *Catalogues*

Grant, Duncan. Duncan Grant (1885-1978) : works on paper. — London (9 Dering St., New Bond St., W.1) : Anthony d'Offay, [1981]. — [22]p,[16]p of plates : ill,ports ; 22cm
Catalogue of an exhibition, 25 November to 18 December 1981
Unpriced (pbk) B82-09471

760'.092'4 — London. Westminster *(London Borough).* **Art galleries: Serpentine Gallery. Exhibits: German graphic arts. Dörflinger, Johannes** — *Catalogues*

Dörflinger, Johannes. Johannes Dörflinger : life cycle, paintings and drawings : 17 October-22 November 1981, Serpentine Gallery London / organised by the Arts Council of Great Britain with the support of the Federal Republic of Germany. — London : Arts Council of Great Britain, c1981. — 36p : ill(some col.) ; 16x21cm
ISBN 0-7287-0305-x (pbk) : Unpriced
Also classified at 831'.914 B82-13040

760'.092'4 — London. Westminster *(London Borough).* **Cultural institutions: Goethe Institute** *(London).* **Exhibits: English graphic arts. Kokoschka, Oskar** — *Catalogues*

Kokoschka, Oskar. Oskar Kokoschka : memorial exhibition of drawings, watercolours, graphics from British collections : an exhibition presented by the Goethe Institute, London in association with Goethe Institute, Dublin, the Goethe Institute, Manchester, the Goethe Institute, Glasgow. — [London] ([9 Hereford Rd., W2 4AB]) : [Leinster Fine Art Limited], [1981?]. — 48p : ill,ports ; 21cm
Catalogue of the travelling exhibition held at the Goethe Institutes in London, Dublin, Sheffield and Glasgow, from 20th November 1981 to 30th June 1982
Unpriced (pbk) B82-08795

760'.092'4 — Scotland. Art galleries. Exhibits: Scottish graphic arts. Wilson, Helen F. — *Catalogues*

Wilson, Helen F.. Helen F. Wilson : paintings, drawings, surprises : touring exhibition 1981-1982, Collins Exhibition Hall, Glasgow, 3 October-30 October 1981, the MacRobert Centre, Stirling, 17 November-5 December 1981, Artspace Gallery, Aberdeen, 10 April-8 May 1982 / [edited by Fiona Wilson]. — [Glasgow] : [Collins Exhibition Hall], c1981. — [12]p,[12]p of plates : ill,ports ; 20x21cm. — (A Collins Exhibition Hall touring exhibition)
ISBN 0-907114-04-0 (pbk) : Unpriced
B82-01460

760'.092'4 — Welsh graphic arts. Richards, Ceri — *Critical studies*

Burns, Richard, *1943-.* Keys to transformation : Ceri Richards and Dylan Thomas / a monograph by Richard Burns. — London : Enitharmon, 1981. — 137p : ill ; 25cm
Bibliography: p135-137
ISBN 0-905289-13-7 (cased) : £8.95
ISBN 0-905289-08-0 (pbk) : £4.95 B82-22461

760'.092'4 — West Midlands *(Metropolitan County).* **Wolverhampton. Art galleries: Wolverhampton Art Gallery and Museums. Exhibits: English graphic arts. Bird, Edward** — *Catalogues*

Bird, Edward. Edward Bird 1772-1819 : Wolverhampton Art Gallery February 27th-April 3rd 1982 : Geffrye Museum, London April 16th-May 30th 1982 / catalogue by Sarah Richardson. — [Wolverhampton] : [Wolverhampton Art Gallery], [1982]. — 44p,[28]p of plates : ill,ports ; 22cm
Unpriced (pbk)
Also classified at 760'.092'4 B82-22463

760'.094'074 — European graphic arts, *ca 1450-1920* — *Catalogues*

Master prints and drawings : 15th to 19th centuries : an exhibition at David Caritt Limited. — London (6a Masons Yard, St James, SW1Y 6BH) : Artemis, 1982. — 108p,1p of plates : ill(some col.) ; 25cm
Unpriced (pbk) B82-36854

760'.0941'074 — British graphic arts, *ca 1750-1950* — *Catalogues*

Ying Guo su miao ji shui cai hua zhan : zhong hua ren min gong he guo yi jiv ba er nian san yue / Ying Guo wen hua wei yuan hui zhu ban = British drawings and watercolours : the People's Republic of China, 1982 / an exhibition organised by the British Council. — [London] ([10 Spring Gardens, SW1A 2BN]) : [British Council], [1982]. — 174p : ill(some col),1map ; 22x24cm
Text in Chinese and English
Unpriced (pbk) B82-27733

760'.0973'0740182254 — Nebraska. Omaha. Art galleries: Center for Western Studies. Exhibits: American graphic arts. Collections: InterNorth Art Foundation Collection — *Catalogues*

Goetzmann, William H.. The West as romantic horizon / by William H. Goetzmann & Joseph C. Porter ; with artists' biographies by David C. Hunt. — Omaha : Center for Western Studies, Joslyn Art Museum ; Lincoln, Neb. ; London : University of Nebraska Press [distributor], c1981. — 128p : ill(some col.),col.ports ; 29cm
Selections from the collections of the InterNorth Art Foundation housed at the Joslyn Art Museum. — Includes index
ISBN 0-936364-04-1 (cased) : Unpriced
ISBN 0-936364-05-x (pbk) : £13.30
B82-13565

760'.28 — Prints. Techniques

The **Complete** guide to prints and printmaking : techniques and materials / edited by John Dawson. — Oxford : Phaidon, 1981. — 192p : ill(some col.) ; 31cm
Includes index
ISBN 0-7148-2184-5 : £13.95 : CIP rev.
B81-14424

Goldman, Paul. Looking at prints : a guide to technical terms / Paul Goldman. — London : British Museum Publications, c1981. — 16p : ill ; 24cm
Cover title. — Text, ill on inside covers
ISBN 0-7141-0788-3 (pbk) : £0.95 B82-37260

760'.75 — Prints. Collecting — *Manuals*

Warner, Glen. Building a print collection : a guide to buying original prints and photographs / Glen Warner. — Toronto ; London : Van Nostrand Reinhold, c1981. — 192p : ill ; 22cm
Bibliography: p185-186. — Includes index
ISBN 0-442-29662-2 (pbk) : £7.60 B82-07883

761 — RELIEF PRINTS

761 — Relief prints. Making. Use of wood — *Manuals*

Bridgewater, Alan. Printing with wood blocks, stencils and engravings. — Newton Abbot : David & Charles, Jan.1983. — [160]p
ISBN 0-7153-8309-4 : £9.50 : CIP entry
B82-32611

761 — Stamp pad prints. Techniques — *Amateurs' manuals*

Gleason, Kay. Stamp it! : a project book of stamp pad prints and patterns / Kay Gleason. — New York ; London : Van Nostrand Reinhold, c1981. — 128p : ill ; 25cm
Includes index
ISBN 0-442-26161-6 : £10.15 B82-14305

767 — ETCHING AND DRYPOINT

767'.2 — Etchings. Techniques — *Manuals*

Lalanne, Maxime. The technique of etching / Maxime Lalanne ; translated by S.R. Koehler ; edited and with an introduction by Jay M. Fisher. — New York : Dover ; London : Constable, 1981. — 67p : ill ; 22cm
Translation of: Traité de la gravure à l'eauforte. — Originally published: as A treatise on etching. Boston, Mass. : Estes & Lauriat ; London : Samson Low, 1880. — Bibliography: p63-67
ISBN 0-486-24182-3 (pbk) : £2.60 B82-34630

769 — PRINTS, BOOK PLATES, POSTCARDS, POSTERS, PAPER MONEY, POSTAGE STAMPS, ETC

769 — Prints — *Collectors' guides*

Gohm, D. C.. Maps and prints : for pleasure and investment / by D.C. Gohm. — 2nd rev. ed. — London : Gifford, 1978. — 196p,[16]p of plates : ill(some col.),maps(some col.),ports ; 24cm
Previous ed.: 1969. — Bibliography: p196. — Includes index
ISBN 0-7071-0567-6 : £7.50
Also classified at 912 B82-23656

Russell, Ronald. Discovering antique prints / Ronald Russell. — Princes Risborough : Shire, 1982. — 88p : ill ; 18cm. — (The Discovering series ; 266)
Bibliography: p84-85. — Includes index
ISBN 0-85263-587-7 (pbk) : £1.25 B82-39401

769'.12 — Prints. Collecting — *Manuals*

Simmons, Rosemary. Collecting original prints / Rosemary Simmons. — London : Studio Vista in association with Christie's Contemporary Art, 1980. — 128p : ill(some col.),ports ; 26cm
Bibliography: p116-117
ISBN 0-289-70900-8 : £7.95 B82-22512

769.4'2 — Athletics. Track & field events — *Manuals* — *For children*

Jarver, Jess. Athletics : for young beginners : track and field athletics - fundamental techniques and training procedures / Jess Jarver. — London : Batsford, 1982. — 80p : ill ; 22cm. — (Competitive sports series)
Includes index
ISBN 0-7134-3547-x (pbk) : £3.95 B82-17653

769'.432 — British postcards, *to 1980.* **Special subjects: Cats**

Mobbs, A.. The cat-fancier : a guide to cat-land postcards. — London : Longman, Sept.1982. — [128]p
ISBN 0-582-50312-4 (pbk) : £4.95 : CIP entry
B82-20264

769'.436'09492 — Dutch landscape prints, *1600-1700* — *Critical studies*

Freedberg, David. Dutch landscape prints : of the seventeenth century / David Freedberg. — London : British Museum, c1980. — 79p,[48]p of plates : ill ; 26cm. — (British Museum prints and drawings series) (A Colonnade book)
Bibliography: p73-74. — Includes index
ISBN 0-7141-8032-7 : £9.95 B82-08787

769'.493805'094223 — Picture postcards, *1900-1930.* **Special subjects: Kent. Transport** — *Illustrations*

Kent transport in old postcards / [compiled] by Eric Baldock. — Rainham : Meresborough, c1981. — 48p : chiefly ill,1map ; 32cm
Cover title. — Text on inside cover
ISBN 0-905270-32-0 (pbk) : £2.50 B82-36919

769'.49629133 — Picture postcards. Special subjects: Aircraft — *Lists* — *Serials*

Aviation postcard collector. — Issue no.1 (Aug. 1980)-. — Hounslow (74 St. Leonards Gardens, Heston, Hounslow, Middx TW5 9DH) : A.P.C. Publications, 1980-. — v. : ill ; 22cm
Quarterly. — Description based on: Issue no.3 (Feb. 1981)
ISSN 0144-3976 = Aviation postcard collector : £5.00 per year B82-09690

769′.4979143′0942 — Advertising posters. Special subjects: Cinema films produced by Ealing Studios — *Illustrations*

Projecting Britain : Ealing Studios film posters. — London : BFI Publishing, Oct.1982. — [96]p
ISBN 0-85170-122-1 : £9.95 : CIP entry
B82-25068

769′.49798′094107401468 — Connecticut. New Haven. Art galleries: Yale Center for British Art. Stock: British prints, *1658-1874*. Special subjects: Equestrian sports. Collections: Paul Mellon collection — *Catalogues*

Snelgrove, Dudley. British sporting and animal prints 1658-1974 / a catalogue compiled by Dudley Snelgrove. — London : Tate Gallery for the Yale Center for British Art, 1981. — xxii,257p [139]p of plates : ill(some col.),ports ; 30cm. — (The Paul Mellon Collection) (Sport in art and books)
Bibliography: pxix-xx. — Includes index
ISBN 0-905005-54-6 : Unpriced
Also classified at 769′.49799′094107401468
B82-22081

769′.49799′094107401468 — Connecticut. New Haven. Art galleries: Yale Center for British Art. Stock: British prints, *1658-1874*. Special subjects: Field sports. Collections: Paul Mellon collection — *Catalogues*

Snelgrove, Dudley. British sporting and animal prints 1658-1974 / a catalogue compiled by Dudley Snelgrove. — London : Tate Gallery for the Yale Center for British Art, 1981. — xxii,257p [139]p of plates : ill(some col.),ports ; 30cm. — (The Paul Mellon Collection) (Sport in art and books)
Bibliography: pxix-xx. — Includes index
ISBN 0-905005-54-6 : Unpriced
Primary classification 769′.49798′094107401468
B82-22081

769′.49941 — British picture postcards, *1900-1979*. Special subjects: Great Britain. Exhibitions, *1900-1979* — *Collectors′ guides*

Fletcher, F. A.. British and foreign exhibitions and their postcards / by F.A. Fletcher & A.D. Brooks. — [London] (3-9 Dane St, WC1) : Fleetway Press
Pt 2: 1915-1979. — [1980]. — 68p : ill(some col.),facsims,maps,plans ; 30cm
£3.25 (pbk)
Also classified at 060 B82-40964

769′.49942195 — English prints, *1705-1901*. Special subjects: London. Richmond upon Thames *(London Borough)*. Twickenham region — *Critical studies*

Gascoigne, Bamber. Images of Twickenham : with Hampton and Teddington : narrative Bamber Gascoigne / catalogue Jonathan Ditchburn ; gallery of prints Harriet and Peter George. — Richmond-upon-Thames : Saint Helena Press, 1981. — 303p : ill,1map ; 31cm. — (Images of London ; v.2)
Limited ed. of 1000 numbered cloth bound copies. — Bibliography: p274-283. — Includes index
ISBN 0-906964-04-0 : £7.00
ISBN 0-906964-05-9 (limited leather ed.) : Unpriced B82-19302

769′.499422372 — Picture postcards, *ca 1900-ca 1930*. Special subjects: Kent. Tonbridge. Social life — *Illustrations*

Old Tonbridge : a selection of postcards first published between 1900 and 1930 / [compiled] by Don Skinner. — Rainham : Meresborough, c1981. — 48p : chiefly ill,ports ; 32cm
Cover title. — Text on inside cover
ISBN 0-905270-39-8 (pbk) : £2.50 B82-36929

769′.499422375 — Picture postcards, *ca 1900-ca 1930*. Special subjects: Kent. Maidstone — *Illustrations*

Old Maidstone. — Rainham : Meresborough
Vol.1: A selection of postcards from the early years of this century / [compiled] by Kay Baldock and Irene Hales. — Revised. — 1982, c1980. — 48p : chiefly ill,ports ; 30cm
Cover title. — Previous ed.: 1980. — Text on inside cover
ISBN 0-905270-09-6 (pbk) : £2.50 B82-36930

Old Maidstone. — Rainham : Meresborough
Vol.2: A second selection of postcards from the early years of this century / [compiled] by Irene Hales. — c1981. — 48p : chiefly ill,ports ; 32cm
Cover title. — Text on inside cover
ISBN 0-905270-38-x (pbk) : £2.50 B82-36931

769′.499422375 — Picture postcards, *ca 1900-ca 1930*. Special subjects: Kent. Maidstone region. Villages — *Illustrations*

Villages around old Maidstone : a selection of postcards from the early years of this century / [compiled] by Irene Hales. — Rainham : Meresborough, c1980. — 48p : chiefly ill,1map,1port ; 32cm
Cover title. — Text and map on inside cover
ISBN 0-905270-23-1 (pbk) : £2.50 B82-36928

769′.49942254 — European print, *1765-1883*. Special subjects: East Sussex. Hove — *Critical studies*

Ford, John, *1936-*. Images of Brighton / John and Jill Ford ; gallery of prints Harriet and Peter George. — Richmond-upon-Thames : Saint Helena Press, 1981. — 383p,[9]p of plates : ill(some col.),1map ; 31cm
Bibliography: p359-364. — Includes index
ISBN 0-906964-02-4 : £90.00
ISBN 0-906964-03-2 (limited leather ed.) : Unpriced B82-19303

769′.4994229107 — Berkshire. Newbury. Museums: Newbury District Museum. Exhibits: English prints. Special subjects: Berkshire. Newbury, *1700-1862* — *Catalogues*

Newbury in the past : an exhibition held at Newbury District Museum as a contribution to the Newbury Spring Festival 8th May to 7th June 1980. — [Newbury] : Newbury District Museum, [1980]. — [8]p ; 21cm
Unpriced (pbk)
Primary classification 758′.994229107
B82-05164

769′.49942398 — English prints, *1650-1860*. Special subjects: Avon. Bath — *Critical studies*

Lees-Milne, James. Images of Bath / narrative James Lees-Milne ; gallery and catalogue David Ford. — Richmond-upon-Thames : Saint Helena, 1982. — 398p,[9]p of plates : ill (some col.),2maps,1plan ; 31cm
Bibliography: p362-373. — Includes index
ISBN 0-906964-08-3 : £95.00
ISBN 0-906964-09-1 (limited ed.) : Unpriced
B82-39108

769′.49959 — Great Britain. National libraries: India Office Library. Stock: English prints, *1786-1824*. Special subjects: South-east Asia — *Critical studies*

India Office Library. Prints of Southeast Asia in the India Office Library : the East India Company in Malaysia and Indonesia 1786-1824 / John Bastin and Pauline Rohatgi. — London : H.M.S.O., 1979. — xxiii,228p : ill(some col.) ; 20x25cm
Bibliography: p221-224. — Includes index
ISBN 0-11-580189-8 : £25.00 B82-17174

769.5 — British cigarette cards, *to 1940* — *Collectors′ guides*

Bennett, Tessa. Cigarette cards / compiled and edited by Tessa Bennett. — Galashiels : Lyle, c1982. — 126p : ill ; 16cm. — (Antiques and their values)
Includes index
ISBN 0-86248-019-1 : £2.50 B82-29162

769.5 — British cigarette cards, *to 1980* — *Collectors′ guides*

The **Complete** catalogue of British cigarette cards / compiled by the London Cigarette Card Company. — Exeter : Webb & Bower, 1981. — 224p : ill(some col.),facsims,ports(some col.) ; 30cm
Bibliography: p224
ISBN 0-906671-48-5 : £12.50 : CIP rev.
B81-27437

769.5 — British cigarette cards, *to 1982* — *Collectors′ guides*

The **Complete** catalogue of British cigarette cards. — Exeter : Webb & Bower, Nov.1982. — [256]p
ISBN 0-906671-85-x : £9.95 : CIP entry
B82-26721

769.5 — British postcards, *1894-1939* — *Catalogues* — *Serials*

Picton′s priced postcard catalogue and handbook. — 1983. — London : Longman, Sept.1982. — [160]p
ISBN 0-582-50320-5 (pbk) : £4.95 : CIP entry
B82-20265

769.5 — British railway postcards

Silvester, Reginald. Official railway postcards of the British Isles / by Reginald Silvester. — [Chippenham] : Picton Publishing
Pt.2: Great Western for America, Great Central for Paris. — 1981. — 100p : ill,facsims ; 21cm
ISBN 0-902633-75-9 (pbk) : Unpriced
B82-00936

769.5 — Christmas cards *to 1900* — *Illustrations*

Holder, Judith. Christmas fare. — Exeter : Webb & Bower, Nov.1981. — [64]p
ISBN 0-906671-34-5 : £3.95 : CIP entry
Also classified at 641.5′66 B81-30976

769.5 — Cigarette cards, *to 1982* — *Collectors′ guides*

The **Catalogue** of international cigarette cards. — Exeter : Webb & Bower, Nov.1982. — [96]p
ISBN 0-906671-86-8 : £7.95 : CIP entry
B82-26717

769.5 — European picture postcards, *to ca 1930*

What the postman saw / [compiled by] Andy Brooks, Fred Fletcher and Brian Lund. — Nottingham (Keyworth, Nottingham) : Reflections of a Bygone Age, c1982. — 100p : ill,facsims ; 22cm
£2.25 (pbk) B82-25617

769.5 — Great Britain. Railway services. Luggage labels, *to 1923* — *Collectors′ guides*

David, Trefor. Pre-Grouping luggage labels / by Trefor David. — Cheltenham (53 Shaw Green La., Prestbury, Cheltenham) : Railway Print Society, 1981. — 72p,19p of plates : facsims ; 30cm
Unpriced (pbk) B82-05588

769.5 — Greater Manchester *(Metropolitan County)*. Stockport. Art galleries: Stockport Art Gallery. Exhibits: British Christmas cards, *1840-1900* — *Catalogues*

Victorian Christmas cards : from the Seddon collection. — [Stockport] : Recreation & Culture Division, Metropolitan Borough of Stockport, [1981]. — [46]p ; 22cm
Catalogue of an exhibition at Stockport Art Gallery, 29 November 1980 to 3 January 1981. — Bibliography: p[46]
ISBN 0-905164-30-x (pbk) : £0.70 B82-19937

769.5 — Investments: Bonds & shares — *Collectors′ guides*

Hollender, Keith. Scripophily : collecting bond and share certificates. — London : Ward Lock, Sept.1982. — [144]p
ISBN 0-7063-6155-5 : £8.95 : CIP entry
B82-20012

769.5 — Matchboxes. Labels. Abbreviations, *to 1979* — *Lists*

Gwyn-Smith, Sid. AZ : a beginning to label identification : an alphabetical glossary comprising several hundred clues to identification / compiled by Sid Gwyn-Smith. — 3rd expanded ed. — [Oxford?] : British Matchbox Label Society Bookshop, 1980. — 36p ; 15cm
Previous ed.: 1978
ISBN 0-906937-01-9 (pbk) : Unpriced
B82-28790

769.5 — Matchboxes. Labels — *Catalogues*

Gladwish, Victor E. R.. The Gladwish encyclopedia of matchbox labels / compiled by Victor Gladwish. — Huntingdon (58 The Trundle, Somersham, Huntingdon, Cambs.) : U.P.E.C.
[Letter L]
[Pt.1]: [L-Lin] issue 156. — 3rd ed. — 1980. — 69p : facsims ; 30cm
Previous ed.: 1977. — Includes index
£5.60 (pbk) B82-18641

769.5 — Merseyside *(Metropolitan County).* **Liverpool. Art galleries: Bluecoat Gallery. Exhibits: Czechoslovakian posters,** *1962-1980 — Catalogues*

Recent posters from Czechoslovakia : April 3-25. — Liverpool (School La., Liverpool L1 3BX) : Bluecoat Gallery, [1981?]. — [18]p : ill ; 21cm
Published to accompany an exhibition at the Bluecoat Gallery, April 3rd-25th 1981. — Bibliography: p18
£0.50 (unbound) B82-09038

769.5 — Merseyside *(Metropolitan County).* **Liverpool. Art galleries: Bluecoat Gallery. Exhibits: English illustrations. Illustrations for sleeves of sound discs of rock music —** *Catalogues*

Cover versions : April 30-May 21 1981. — Liverpool (School La., Liverpool L1 3BX) : Bluecoat Gallery, [1981?]. — 1sheet : ill ; 21x51cm folded to 21x15cm
Published to accompany an exhibition of record covers at the Bluecoat Gallery
Unpriced (unbound) B82-09039

769.5 — Sri Lanka matchboxes. Labels — *Collectors' guides*

Luker, J. H.. Ceylon : get on the right track / [compiled] by J.H. Luker. — [Cambridge] ([c/o Pine Ridge County School, Esher Rd., Old Dean Estate, Camberley, Surrey]) : Vesta, 1981. — 57p : facsims ; 29cm. — (World matchbox label series)
Cover title
£3.00 (pbk) B82-04947

769.56 — Jamaica. Military postal services. Mail. Censorship devices, *1900-1960*

Sutcliffe, A. P. D.. The military mail of Jamaica / by A.P.D. Sutcliffe. — Harrogate : Roses Caribbean Philatelic Society, c1982. — 148p : 1map,facsims ; 30cm. — (Roses Caribbean philatelic handbook ; no.5)
Limited ed. of 400 numbered copies
Unpriced (pbk) B82-27867

769.56'03'21 — Postage stamps — *Encyclopaedias*

Rennie, David. The language of stamp collecting / David Rennie. — [London] : Star, 1982. — 112p ; 20cm
ISBN 0-352-31088-x (pbk) : £1.50 B82-22769

769.56'05 — Postage stamps — *Serials*

Stamp & postal history news : incorporating Philately, the official journal of the British Philatelic Federation Ltd. — June 24-July 7, 1981-. — London (P.O. Box 3DE, WIA 3DE) : Epic Pub. for the Federation, 1981-. — v. : ill,col.facsims,maps ; 40cm
Fortnightly. — Absorbed: Philately (London), 1981. — Description based on: Feb. 17-Mar. 2, 1982 issue
ISSN 0261-1899 = Stamp & postal history news : £0.25 per issue B82-22680

769.56'075 — Postage stamps. Collecting — *Serials*

The Philatelist and PJGB. — [Vol.1, no.1] Feb. 1981-. — London (50 Pall Mall, SW1Y 5JZ) : [Pall Mall Stamp Co. for Robson Lowe], 1981-. — v. : ill(some col.) ; 25cm
Six issues yearly. — Merger of: the Philatelist ; and, the Philatelic Journal of Great Britain
ISSN 0260-6739 = Philatelist and PJGB : £8.00 per year B82-01076

769.56'3 — Postage stamps. Cancellations, *1900-1981.* **Special subjects: Visits to Commonwealth countries by British royal families**

Scott, F. H.. Royal tour : cancellations, cachets and adhesives / by F.H. Scott. — Batley : H. Hayes, c1981. — 46p : facsims ; 21cm
ISBN 0-9507924-0-3 (pbk) : Unpriced B82-12488

769.56'3 — Postage stamps. Special subjects: Scottish celebrities, *1550-1980*

James, Alwyn. Other men's heroes : Scots honoured on the world's stamps / Alwyn James. — Edinburgh : Macdonald, c1982. — 173p,[32]p of plates : ill(some col.),ports ; 24cm
ISBN 0-904265-54-4 : £9.95 B82-18950

769.56'5'0941 — British first day covers, *1840- — Catalogues — Serials*

Collect first day covers, Great Britain including Channel Islands and Isle of Man. — 1982 ed.-. — [Hythe] ([24 High St., Hythe, Kent CT21 5AT]) : [BB Publications], [c1981]-. — v. : ill (chiefly col.),facsims ; 21cm
Annual. — Caption title: Collectors guide to Great Britain first day covers. — Continues: Great Britain, including Channel Islands and Isle of Man, first day covers
ISSN 0140-9417 = Collectors guide to Great Britain first day covers : £1.75 B82-03406

769.56'5'0941 — British first day covers, *1971-1981 — Catalogues*

Porter, N. C.. Collecting modern first day covers of Great Britain 1971-81 / by N.C. Porter ; edited by A.G. Bradbury. — Leicester ([Leicester First Day Covers, 35 Northdene Rd, Leicester LE2 6FJ]) : A.G. Bradbury, 1982. — 64p : ill ; 22cm
£2.95 (pbk) B82-27121

769.56'6 — Great Britain. *Post Office.* **Postcards —** *Catalogues — Serials*

Collect Post Office cards : also includes air letters, P.O. commemorative covers & presentation packs. — 1st ed. (1982)-. — [Hythe] ([24 High St., Hythe, Kent CT21 5AT]) : B.B. Publications, 1981-. — v. : ill ; 21cm
Annual
ISSN 0262-1142 = Collect Post Office cards : £1.50 B82-01064

769.56'7'0941 — British postmarks, *1924-1969*

Mackay, James A.. British post office numbers, 1924-1969 / by James A. Mackay. — Dumfries (11 Newall Terrace, Dumfries, DG1 1LN) : J.A. Mackay, c1981. — 50p : facsims ; 30cm
£3.36 (pbk) B82-03184

769.56'7'0941 — British telegraphic postmarks. Identity codes, *1870-1924 — Lists*

Mackay, James A.. Telegraphic codes of the British Isles, 1870-1924 / by James A. Mackay. — Dumfries (11 Newall Terrace, Dumfries, DG1N 1LN) : J.A. Mackay, c1981. — 90p : ill,facsims ; 30cm
£5.00 (pbk) B82-03185

769.56'7'09415 — Irish postmarks, *1840-1980*

Mackay, James A.. Irish postmarks since 1840 / by James A. Mackay. — Dumfries (11, Newall Terr., Dumfries DG1 1LN) : J. Mackay, c1982. — 222p : ill ; 30cm
Bibliography: p221-222
£8.70 (pbk) B82-38400

769.56'7'0956944 — Jerusalem postmarks, *1917-1948 — Catalogues*

Glassman, Emanuel. The postmarks and other markings of Mandate Jerusalem (1917-1948) / by E. Glassman and M. Sacher. — London : Ze'ev Galibov, [1982]. — 179p : ill,facsims,maps ; 30cm. — (Handbooks for Holyland collectors ; 4)
"The postmarks of Mandate Jerusalem" (3 sheets) in pocket. — Bibliography: p175-176
ISBN 0-905234-03-0 (spiral) : Unpriced B82-38942

769.56'7'0972981 — Barbados postmarks, *to 1981 — Lists*

Clarke, George L. W.. Barbados Post Office markings to 1981 / by George L.W. Clarke, Reynold Radford and Stephen Cave. — [Great Britain?] : The British West Indies Study Circle, 1982. — 71p : ill,1 map ; 26cm
Limited ed. of 500 copies
ISBN 0-9506535-1-9 : Unpriced B82-28806

769.56'7'099711 — Falkland Islands postage stamps. Cancellations, *to 1980*

Barnes, Robert, *1924-*. The postal cancellations of the Falkland Islands / by Robert Barnes. — [Baldock] ([35, The Sycamores, Baldock, Herts SG7 5BJ]) : [R. Barnes], [1982]. — vii,144p : ill ; 26cm
Bibliography: p143-144
Unpriced B82-39407

769.569 — Postage stamps, *to 1981*

Mackay, James. The Guinness book of stamps facts and feats. — Enfield : Guinness Superlatives, Oct.1982. — [224]p
ISBN 0-85112-241-8 : £8.95 : CIP entry B82-24255

769.569171'241'0216 — Commonwealth postage stamps, *1957-1981.* **Miniature sheets —** *Catalogues*

Commonwealth catalogue of miniature sheets : including post-independence countries / compiled by Minisheets (Regd.). — 3rd ed. / edited by R.J. Marles. — Torquay : Rotographic, 1982. — 80p : ill(some col.) ; 22cm
Previous ed.: 1981
ISBN 0-901170-93-3 (pbk) : £1.80 B82-20935

769.56941'0216 — British postage stamps, *1953- — Catalogues — Serials*

G.B. stamps + varieties : Queen Elizabeth II — £.s.d. and decimal. — 3rd ed. (1982)-. — Torquay : Rotographic Publications, 1982-. — v. : ill ; 16cm
Annual. — Continues: Collectors stamps of Great Britain
ISSN 0262-5687 = G.B. stamps + varieties : £1.20 B82-05742

769.569415'0216 — Irish postage stamps, *to 1978 — Catalogues*

Stamps of Ireland specialised catalogue. — 8th ed. / edited by David Mac Donnell. — Dublin : D. Macdonell and David Feldman, 1979. — 123p : ill ; 22cm
Previous ed.: 197-
ISBN 0-9502619-2-0 (pbk) : Unpriced B82-17624

769.5696'0216 — African postage stamps — *Catalogues — Serials*

Stanley Gibbons stamp catalogue. Part 14, Africa since independence, N-Z. — 1st ed. (1981)-. — London : Stanley Gibbons, 1981-. — v. : ill ; 22cm
Irregular. — Continues in part: Stanley Gibbons foriegn stamp catalogue. Overseas
ISSN 0261-7145 = Stanley Gibbons stamp catalogue. Part 14. Africa since independence. N-Z (corrected) : £10.50 B82-09680

769.569685 — South African postage stamps: Orange Free State postage stamps, *to 1915*

Buckley, G. D.. The stamps of the Orange Free State / [G.D. Buckley and W.B. Marriott]. — London (141 St Julians Farm Rd., West Norwood SE27 0RP) : Orange Free State Study Circle
[3]. — [1976?]. — 247p : ill,facsims ; 21cm
Unpriced B82-18606

769.56969'82 — Mauritian postage stamps, *1847-1859*

Kanai, Hiroyuki. Classic Mauritius : the locally printed postage stamps 1847-59 / Hiroyuki Kanai. — London : Gibbons, 1981. — xi,132p : ill,2maps,facsims(some col.) ; 29cm
Based on a preliminary study published in Japanese in 1976. — In slip case. — Includes index
ISBN 0-85259-251-5 : £50.00 B82-02776

769.56997'11 — Falkland Islands overprinted postage stamps, *1918-1920*

Bunt, John P.. The war stamp overprints of the Falkland Islands : 1918-1920 / John P. Bunt. — Truro : J.P. Blunt, c1981. — 40p,[12]p of plates : ill,1port ; 25cm
Bibliography: p40
ISBN 0-9507833-0-7 (cased) : Unpriced
ISBN 0-9507833-1-5 (pbk) : Unpriced B82-07866

769.56997'3 — Ascension Island postage stamps & postmarks, *to 1980*

Attwood, J. H.. Ascension : the stamps and postal history / J.H. Attwood. — London : Published by Pall Mall Stamp Co. for Robson Lowe, 1981. — viii,71p : ill,facsims ; 25cm
ISBN 0-85397-197-8 : £8.00 B82-00624

769.5′7 — British newspaper duty stamps, *to 1870*

Chandler, John H. (John Harris). The newspaper & almanac stamps of Great Britain & Ireland / John H. Chandler and H. Dagnall. — Saffron Walden : Published for the Great Britain Philatelic Society by G.B. Philatelic Publications Ltd, 1981. — 302p : ill,facsims ; 26cm
Includes index
ISBN 0-907630-00-6 : Unpriced B82-06144

769.9 — Western prints, *1400-1980 — Critical studies*

Print / Michel Melot ... [et al.]. — Geneva : Skira ; London : Macmillan, 1981. — 278p : ill (some col.),ports ; 35cm. — (History of an art)
Bibliography: p259-266. — Includes index
ISBN 0-333-31909-5 : Unpriced B82-01530

769.92′2 — Great Britain. Arts. Patronage. Organisations: Arts Council of Great Britain. Exibits: English screen prints. Greaves, Derrick; Medley, Robert & Middleditch, Edward — *Catalogues*

Books and folios : screenprints by Derrick Greaves, Robert Medley and Edward Middleditch. — London : Arts Council of Great Britain, c1981. — 16p : ill ; 22cm + 3cards in pocket(ill ; 20cm)
Accompanies an Arts Council travelling exhibition held at 10 different venues between 30 May 1981 and 25 July 1982
ISBN 0-7287-0287-8 (pbk) : £1.15 B82-06150

769.92′4 — Children's picture postcards. Illustrations. James, Ivy Millicent — *Biographies*

Ivy Millicent James 1879-1965 : a children's postcard artist : the story of her life and work / [with a contribution from Dawn and Peter Cope]. — Weston-super-Mare ([Burlington St., Weston-super-Mare, Avon BS23 1PR]) : Woodspring Museum, 1980. — 19p : ill(some col.),ports ; 15x21cm
£0.85 (pbk) B82-16524

769.92′4 — Czechoslovak etchings. Hollar, Wenceslaus — *Catalogues*

Pennington, Richard. A descriptive catalogue of the etched work of Wenceslaus Hollar 1607-1677 / Richard Pennington. — Cambridge : Cambridge University Press, 1982. — lxiv,452p : 1port ; 26cm
Bibliography: p408-424. — Includes index
ISBN 0-521-22408-x : £80.00 : CIP rev. B82-25494

769.92′4 — Czechoslovak prints. Hollar, Wenceslaus — *Catalogues*

Griffiths, Antony. Wenceslaus Hollar : prints and drawings. — London : British Museum Publications, Feb.1983. — [96]p
Published to accompany an exhibition at the British Museum, London, and at the National Gallery, Prague
ISBN 0-7141-0787-5 : CIP entry
Primary classification 741.9′437 B82-39440

769.92′4 — Dutch prints. Escher, M. C. — *Critical studies*

Escher : with a complete catalogue of the graphic works / F.H. Bool ... [et al.] ; general editor J.L. Locher ; with 606 illustrations, including 36 in colour. — London : Thames and Hudson, c1982. — 349p : ill(some col.),facsims,ports ; 31cm
Translation of: Leven en werk van M.C. Escher. — Bibliography: p345. — Includes index. — Includes essays by M.C. Escher
ISBN 0-500-09153-6 : £35.00 B82-26518

769.92′4 — English colour prints. Cox, Morris — *Illustrations*

Cox, Morris. Studio book : 50 original colourprints / Morris Cox. — London : Gogmagog ; London : Distributed by Bertram Rota, c1980. — [64]p : col.ill ; 29cm
Limited ed. of 35 numbered and signed copies in slip case
£105.00 B82-06893

769.92′4 — English engravings. Blake, William, *1757-1827.* **Illustrations for Bible. O.T. Job —** *Critical studies*

Raine, Kathleen. The human face of God : William Blake and the Book of Job / Kathleen Raine ; with 130 illustrations. — [London] : Thames and Hudson, c1982. — 320p : ill,facsims ; 25cm
Bibliography: p313-314. — Includes index
ISBN 0-500-23334-9 : £20.00 B82-19966

769.92′4 — English engravings. Gill, Eric — *Biographies*

Allen, George, *19---*. Eric Gill / by George Allen. — Hove (9 Brunswick Sq., Hove, E. Sussex BN3 1EN) : Chichester Diocesan Fund and Board of Finance, [1981]. — 13p : 1port ; 22cm
Bibliography: p13
Unpriced (unbound) B82-05242

Yorke, Malcolm. Eric Gill : man of flesh and spirit / Malcolm Yorke. — London : Constable, 1981. — 304p : ill,ports ; 24cm
Bibliography: p289. — Includes index
ISBN 0-09-463740-7 : £12.50 B82-06882

769.92′4 — English engravings. Gill, Eric — *Personal observations*

Kindersley, David. Eric Gill : further thoughts by an apprentice / David Kindersley. — [New ed.]. — London : Wynkyn de Worde Society, 1982. — xii,24p,[24]p of plates : ill,facsims,ports ; 18cm
Previous ed.: New York : The Typhophiles, 1967
ISBN 0-85331-459-4 (pbk) : Unpriced B82-24530

769.92′4 — English engravings. Milton, Thomas. Special subjects: Ireland. Country houses, *1783-1794 — Illustrations*

Milton, Thomas. The seats and demesnes of the nobility and gentry of Ireland. — Clifden : Boethius Press, Nov.1982. — [80]p. — (Boethius Press series four ; 2)
ISBN 0-86314-067-x : £24.00 : CIP entry B82-33206

769.92′4 — English etchings. Palmer, Samuel, *1805-1881 — Catalogues*

Strudwick, R. F.. A catalogue of Samuel Palmer's etchings. — [London] ([2, Castle Close, Sandgate, Kent CT20 3AG]) : [R.F. Strudwick], [1982]. — [25]leaves ; 23cm
Compiled by R.F. Strudwick. — Limited ed. of 50 copies. — Bibliography: leaf 25
Unpriced (pbk) B82-31411

769.92′4 — English etchings. Tilson, Joe. Oak Mantra. Making

Tilson, Joe.. The making of Oak Mantra / Joe Tilson. — Cape Town : Joseph Wolpe Gallery ; London : David Krut Fine Art, 1981. — 32p : ill(some col.),ports ; 21cm
Published to accompany an exhibition held in South Africa and London, 1981
ISBN 0-9507891-0-0 (pbk) : £2.00 B82-11928

769.92′4 — English lithographs. Harte, Glynn Boyd — *Illustrations*

Betjeman, John. Metro-land / verses by Sir John Betjeman ; lithographs by Glynn Boyd Harte. — [London] : Warren, 1977. — [31]leaves : col.ill ; 19x25cm
Limited ed. of 220 signed copies
ISBN 0-9505969-0-6 : Unpriced
Primary classification 821′.912 B82-32651

769.92′4 — English lithographs. O'Connor, John, *1913-.* **Illustrations for Diary of Francis Kilvert —** *Illustrations*

Kilvert, Francis. A view of Kilvert : passages from the diary of Francis Kilvert / selected and illustrated in colour by John O'Connor ; and introduced by John Ryder. — Glasgow (c/o Glasgow School of Art, 167 Renfrew St., Glasgow G3 6RQ) : Foulis Archive Press, 1979. — 1portfolio : col.ill ; 35cm
Limited ed. of 50 copies signed by the artist
Unpriced (unbound) B82-12802

769.92′4 — English prints. Dighton, Robert. Special subjects: London. Social life, *1775-1814 — Critical studies*

Rose, Dennis. Life, times and recorded works of Robert Dighton (1752-1814) actor, artist and printseller and three of his artist sons : portrayers of Georgian pageantry and wit / by Dennis Rose. — Great Britain : D. Rose ; Tisbury : Distributed by Element, c1981. — 95p : ill(some col.),1facsim,ports ; 25cm
Bibliography: p95
ISBN 0-9507579-0-x : £8.95 B82-20727

769.92′4 — English wood engravings. Bewick, Thomas — *Biographies*

Bewick, Thomas. My life / Thomas Bewick ; edited and with an introduction by Iain Bain ; with numerous wood-engravings and watercolours by the author. — London : Folio Society, 1981. — 192p,[16]p of plates : ill(some col.),1port ; 24cm
Unpriced B82-00621

769.92′4 — English wood engravings. Bewick, Thomas. Special subjects: Birds — *Illustrations*

Bewick, Thomas. Thomas Bewick's birds : watercolours and engravings. — London : Gordon Fraser, 1981. — 52p : ill(some col.) ; 18cm
Ill on lining papers
ISBN 0-86092-059-3 : £4.95 : CIP rev.
Primary classification 759.2 B81-27439

769.92′4 — English wood engravings. Hermes, Gertrude. Special subjects: Medicinal plants — *Illustrations*

A Florilege / chosen from the old herbals by Irene Gosse ; and illustrated with twenty wood engravings by Gertrude Hermes. — Old Woking : Gresham, c1981. — [40]leaves of plates : ill ; 31cm
Limited ed. of 250 numbered copies
ISBN 0-905418-94-8 : Unpriced B82-40643

769.92′4 — English wood engravings. Mackley, George E. — *Critical studies*

Mackley, George E.. Confessions of a woodpecker / by George Mackley. — Old Woking : Gresham, 1981. — 48p : ill ; 31cm
Limited ed. of 250 numbered copies
ISBN 0-905418-92-1 : Unpriced B82-03979

769.92′4 — English wood engravings. Stone, Reynolds — *Biographies*

Reynolds Stone : 1909-1979. — Dorchester : Dorset Natural History and Archaeological Society, 1981. — 41p : ill ; 22cm
ISBN 0-900341-09-2 (pbk) : Unpriced B82-26604

769.92′4 — English wood engravings. Stone, Reynolds — *Catalogues*

Reynolds Stone 1909-1979 : an exhibition held in the library of the Victoria and Albert Museum from 21 July to 31 October 1982. — [London] : Victoria and Albert Museum, c1982. — 84p : ill ; 22cm
Bibliography: p82-84
ISBN 0-905209-22-2 (pbk) : Unpriced B82-40222

769.92′4 — English wood engravings. Stone, Reynolds — *Critical studies*

Murdoch, Iris. Reynolds Stone : an address given by Iris Murdoch in St James's Church, Piccadilly, London, on 20 July 1979. — London : Warren Editions, 1981. — [10]p : 1port ; 22cm
Limited ed. of 750 copies
ISBN 0-9505969-3-0 (pbk) : Unpriced B82-32687

769.92′4 — English wood engravings. Stone, Reynolds — *Illustrations*

The **Turn** of the years / with an introduction by Paul Theroux. — Salisbury : Michael Russell, 1982. — 48p : ill ; 19cm
Contents: The seasons' course / selected engravings by Reynolds Stone — As old as the century / V.S. Pritchett
ISBN 0-85955-085-0 : £3.95
Primary classification 305.2′6′0924 B82-31960

769.92′4 — French lithographs. Delacroix, Eugène. Illustrations for 'Faust' — *Illustrations*

The **Complete** illustrations from Delacroix's 'Faust' and Manet's 'The raven' / edited and with an introduction by Breon Mitchell. — Bloomington : Lilly Library of Indiana University in association with Dover, 1981. — x,4,[50]p : ill ; 31cm
English and French text
ISBN 0-486-24127-0 (pbk) : £3.00
Also classified at 769.92′4 B82-18050

769.92′4 — French lithographs. Manet, Edouard. Illustrations for The Raven — *Illustrations*

The **Complete** illustrations from Delacroix's 'Faust' and Manet's 'The raven' / edited and with an introduction by Breon Mitchell. — Bloomington : Lilly Library of Indiana University in association with Dover, 1981. — x,4,[50]p : ill ; 31cm
English and French text
ISBN 0-486-24127-0 (pbk) : £3.00
Primary classification 769.92′4 B82-18050

769.92′4 — French prints. Bonnard, Pierre, *1867-1947* — *Illustrations*

Bonnard, Pierre, *1867-1947*. Bonnard : the complete graphic work / Francis Bouvet ; introduction by Antoine Terrasse. — London : Thames and Hudson, 1981. — 351p : chiefly ill (some col.),facsims ; 34cm
Translation from the French. — Bibliography: p339-340
ISBN 0-500-09148-x : £35.00 B82-03994

769.92′4 — French prints. Jacoulet, Paul — *Catalogues*

Miles, Richard, *19---*. The prints of Paul Jacoulet : a complete illustrated catalog / by Richard Miles. — London : Sawers in association with the Pacific Asia Museum, 1982. — 140p : ill (some col.),ports(some col.) ; 30cm
Published in conjunction with an exhibition at the Pacific Asia Museum, Pasadena, 1982. — Bibliography: p133. — Includes index
ISBN 0-903697-14-9 (cased) : Unpriced
ISBN 0-903697-13-0 (pbk) : Unpriced
B82-27701

769.92′4 — Great Britain. Art galleries. Exhibits: American portrait screen prints. Warhol, Andy — *Catalogues*

Warhol, Andy. Andy Warhol : portrait screen prints 1965-80. — [London] : Arts Council of Great Britain, c1981. — [22]p(some folded) : ill,ports(some col.) ; 15cm
Published to accompany a touring exhibition of Andy Warhol's portrait screenprints
ISBN 0-7287-0297-5 (unbound) : Unpriced
B82-13033

769.92′4 — Great Britain. Art galleries. Exhibits: German prints. Kollwitz, Käthe — *Catalogues*

Käthe Kollwitz 1867-1945 : the graphic works : an exhibition / organised by Kettle's Yard in association with the Scottish National Gallery of Modern Art and the Institute of Contemporary Arts. — Cambridge : Kettle's Yard, c1981. — 79p : ill,1port ; 21cm
ISBN 0-907074-11-1 (pbk) : Unpriced
Primary classification 741.943 B82-06092

769.92′4 — Japanese woodcuts. Kitagawa, Utamaro. Special subjects: Birds — *Illustrations*

Kitagawa, Utamaro. A chorus of birds / Utamaro ; with an introduction by Julia Meech-Pekarik ; and a note on kyōka and translations by James T. Kenney. — London : Secker & Warburg, 1982, c1981. — 1folded sheet([48]p) : chiefly ill (some col.) ; 26cm
Translation of: Momo-chidori kyōka awase. — In slip case
ISBN 0-436-54940-9 : £12.50 B82-18084

769.92′4 — Jersaise etchings. Bois, G. J. C.. Special subjects: Jersiaise superstitions — *Illustrations*

Bois, G. J. C.. Jersey superstitions in etching & poetry / G.J.C. Bois. — [St. Saviour] ([Alphington House, Grands Vaux, St. Saviour, Jersey]) : G.J.C. Bois, c1981. — 53p : ill ; 23cm
Bibliography: p53
ISBN 0-9507966-0-3 : £9.95
Primary classification 821′.914 B82-20215

769.92′4 — London. Kensington and Chelsea *(London Borough)*. **Museums: Victoria and Albert Museum. Exhibits: French Lithographs. Matisse, Henri** — *Catalogues*

Lambert, Susan. Matisse : lithographs / Susan Lambert. — London : H.M.S.O., 1972 (1981 [printing]). — 71p : ill ; 20x21cm
At head of title: Victoria & Albert Museum. — Bibliography: p20
ISBN 0-11-290356-8 (pbk) : £2.95 B82-00774

769.92′4 — Merseyside *(Metropolitan County)*. **Liverpool. Art galleries: Bluecoat Gallery. Exhibits: English prints. McKinlay, Don** — *Catalogues*

Going Backwards *(Exhibition) (1980 : Liverpool)*. 'Going Backwards' : December 3-24 1980 : an exhibition / by Don McKinlay and Sam Walsh. — Liverpool (School La., Liverpool L1 3BX) : Bluecoat Gallery, [1980?]. — [4]p : 2ill ; 15x21cm
Unpriced (unbound)
Primary classification 759.2 B82-09032

769.92′4 — Nigerian prints. Onobrakpeya, Bruce — *Biographies*

Jacob, Paul. Reconstruction of Bruce Onobrakpeya / Paul Jacob. — Bognor Regis : New Horizon, c1982. — 40p,[17]p of plates : ill,1port ; 21cm
ISBN 0-86116-566-7 : £4.50 B82-11255

769.92′4 — Northern Irish etchings. McDonnell, Hector — *Illustrations*

McDonnell, Hector. The ballad of William Bloat. — Belfast : Blackstaff, Nov.1982. — [40]p
ISBN 0-85640-273-7 (pbk) : £1.95 : CIP entry
B82-29422

769.92′4 — Spanish prints. Goya, Francisco de — *Critical studies*

Bareau, Juliet Wilson. Goya's prints. — London : British Museum Publications, Oct.1981. — [144]p
ISBN 0-7141-0789-1 (pbk) : £7.95 : CIP entry
B81-30266

769.92′4 — Spanish prints. Picasso, Pablo — *Illustrations*

Picasso, Pablo. Picasso line drawings and prints / 44 works by Pablo Picasso. — New York : Dover ; London : Constable, 1981. — 43p : of ill ; 28cm. — (Dover art library)
ISBN 0-486-24196-3 (pbk) : £1.50
Primary classification 741.946 B82-37393

769.92′4 — Surrey. Guildford. Art galleries: Guildford House Gallery. Exhibits: English prints. Hyde, William — *Catalogues*

Rogers, Kate. Two Victorian artists from Shere : Kate Rogers 1861-1942, William Hyde 1859-1925 : 2-30 January 1982 : Monday to Saturday 10.30-5.00. — [Guildford] (155 High St., Guildford, Surrey, GU1 3AJ) : Guildford House Gallery, [1982]. — [16]p : ill,ports ; 20cm
Published to accompany an exhibition at the Guildford House Gallery, 1982. — Cover title
Unpriced (pbk)
Primary classification 759.2 B82-15292

769.92′4 — Swiss prints. Vallotton, Felix — *Illustrations*

St. James, Ashley. Vallotton graphics / Ashley St James. — London : Ash & Grant, 1978. — 31p,xxxii leaves of plates : ill,ports ; 30cm
Bibliography: p26
ISBN 0-904069-18-4 (cased) : Unpriced : CIP rev. B78-27512

769.94′074′02132 — London. Westminster *(London Borough)*. **Art galleries: P. and D. Colnaghi and Co.. Exhibits: European prints,** *1496-1956* — *Catalogues*

A Catalogue of fine prints 1496-1956. — London (14 Old Bond St., W1X 4JL) : Colnaghi, [1979]. — [170]p : chiefly ill(some col.),ports ; 27cm
Includes index
Unpriced (pbk) B82-07272

769.941 — British wood engravings. Illustrations for books & illustrations for serials, *1770-1900* — *Critical studies*

De Maré, Eric. The Victorian woodblock illustrators / Eric de Maré. — London : Fraser, 1980. — 200p : ill(some col.),1port ; 23x25cm
Bibliography: p195-196. — Includes index
ISBN 0-900406-58-5 : £29.50 : CIP rev.
B79-27770

769.941 — English wood engravings, *1900-1976*

British wood engraving of the 20th century : a personal view / [compiled by] Albert Garrett ; preface by Dorothea Braby. — London : Scolar, 1980. — 223p : ill,ports ; 28cm
Includes index
ISBN 0-85967-604-8 (cased) : Unpriced : CIP rev.
ISBN 0-85967-608-0 (pbk) : £6.95 B80-04896

769.945′074′02132 — London. Westminster *(London Borough)*. **Art galleries: Christopher Mendez** *(Firm)*. **Stock: Italian prints,** *ca 1450-1780* — *Catalogues*

Italian prints. — London (51 Lexington St., W1R 4HL) : Christopher Mendez, 1981. — 31p : chiefly ill,1port ; 24cm. — (Catalogue ; 48)
Includes index
Unpriced (pbk) B82-07861

769.952 — Japanese colour prints, *1660-1800* — *Illustrations*

Hillier, J.. Japanese colour prints / J. Hillier. — Rev. and enl. [ed.]. — Oxford : Phaidon, 1981. — 31,[97]p : ill(some col.),ports (some col.) ; 31cm
Previous ed.: London : Phaidon, 1966. — Bibliography: p[97]
ISBN 0-7148-2167-5 (cased) : £9.95 : CIP rev.
ISBN 0-7148-2165-9 (pbk) : £6.95 B81-22654

769.952 — Japanese pillar prints, *1740-1840* — *Illustrations*

Pins, Jacob. The Japanese pillar print : Hashira-e / Jacob Pins ; foreword by Roger Keyes. — London : Sawers, c1982. — 389p : ili(some col.) ; 35cm
In slipcase. — Limited ed. of 1000 numbered copies
ISBN 0-903697-12-2 : Unpriced B82-28302

769.952 — Japanese prints. Ukiyo-e style. Utagawa, Kuniyoshi. Special subjects: Warriors

Robinson, B. W.. Kuniyoshi. — Oxford : Phaidon, May 1982. — [240]p
ISBN 0-7148-2227-2 : £25.00 : CIP entry
B82-14388

769.973 — Printed ephemera with American imprints, *to 1980* — *Collectors' guides*

McCulloch, Lou W.. Paper Americana : a collector's guide / Lou W. McCulloch ; photographs Thomas R. McCulloch. — San Diego : Barnes ; London : Tantivy, c1980. — 183p,[16]p of plates : ill(some col.),facsims (some col.) ; 29cm
Bibliography: p175-176. — Includes index
ISBN 0-498-02392-3 : £7.95 B82-37911

770 — PHOTOGRAPHY

770 — Photography

Craven, George M.. Object and image : introduction to photography / George M. Craven. — 2nd ed. — Englewood Cliffs ; London : Prentice-Hall, c1982. — ix,273p,[8]p of plates : ill(some col.) ; 28cm
Previous ed.: 1975. — Bibliography: p253-257. — Includes index
ISBN 0-13-628974-6 (pbk) : £13.45
B82-27559

Hill, Paul, *1941-*. Approaching photography / Paul Hill ; with a foreword by Aaron Scharf. — London : Focal, 1982. — 130p : ill,ports ; 26cm
Includes index
ISBN 0-240-51145-x : Unpriced : CIP rev.
B82-01539

770 — Photography — *Early works*

Doyle, *Sir* Arthur Conan. Essays on photography. — London : Secker & Warburg, May 1982. — [224]p
Originally published in British journal of photography, 1882
ISBN 0-436-13302-4 : £6.95 : CIP entry B82-07664

770′.1 — Photography. Theories

Thinking photography / edited by Victor Burgin. — London : Macmillan, 1982. — 239p : ill,ports ; 23cm. — (Communications and culture)
Bibliography: p217-219. — Includes index
ISBN 0-333-27194-7 (cased) : £18.00
ISBN 0-333-27195-5 (pbk) : Unpriced B82-21619

770′.23′2 — Photography as a profession

Bluffield, Bob. Making and managing a photographic studio / Bob Bluffield. — Newton Abbot : David & Charles, c1982. — 142p : ill,forms ; 22cm
Bibliography: p133-134. — Includes index
ISBN 0-7153-8245-4 : £6.95 : CIP rev. B82-13067

770′.28 — Freelance photography — *Manuals*

The **Freelance** book / edited by John Tracy & Steward Gibson. — London : BFP Books, 1980. — 194p : ill,ports ; 25cm
Includes index
ISBN 0-907297-00-5 : £9.95 B82-14971

770′.28 — Monochrome photography — *Amateurs′ manuals*

Wasley, John. Black-and-white photography. — London : Focal Press, Jan.1983. — [168]p
ISBN 0-240-51117-4 (pbk) : £6.95 : CIP entry B82-33500

770′.28 — Monochrome photography. Processing — *Amateurs′ manuals*

Casagrande, Bob. Better black and white darkroom techniques. — Poole : Blandford Press, Dec.1982. — 1v.. — (Master photography series)
ISBN 0-7137-1285-6 : £6.95 : CIP entry B82-30215

770′.28 — Photography — *Amateurs′ manuals*

Berner, Jeff. The foolproof guide to taking pictures / Jeff Berner ; with photographs by the author ; drawings by Liisa Rahkonen. — Toronto ; London : Bantam, 1981. — 101p : ill ; 18cm
ISBN 0-553-20298-7 (pbk) : £1.00 B82-21598

Bowskill, Derek. Photography : made simple / Derek Bowskill. — London : Heinemann, 1975 (1982 [printing]). — xiii,253p : ill ; 23cm. — (Made simple books)
Bibliography: p249-250. — Includes index
ISBN 0-434-98529-5 (cased) : Unpriced
ISBN 0-434-98530-9 (pbk) : £2.95 B82-21599

Brück, Axel. Creative camera techniques. — London : Focal Press, Apr.1981. — [180]p
Translation and adaptation of: Fotografische technik und gestaltung
ISBN 0-240-51106-9 : CIP entry B81-00212

Busselle, Michael. Basic photography : how to take and make great pictures / Michael Busselle. — London : Octopus, 1982. — 80p : ill(some col.) ; 33cm
Ill on lining papers. — Includes index
ISBN 0-7064-1731-3 : £3.95 B82-34476

Busselle, Michael. Photography pocket guide / Michael Busselle. — London : Octopus, 1981. — 128p : ill(some col.),2ports(some col.) ; 19cm
Includes index
ISBN 0-7064-1520-5 : £2.95 B82-08368

Darker, Roger. Make the most of your pictures. — London : Focal Press, Jan.1982. — [168]p
ISBN 0-240-51112-3 (pbk) : £5.00 : CIP entry B81-34404

Frair, John. Effective photography / John Frair and Birthney Ardoin. — Englewood Cliffs ; London : Prentice-Hall, c1982. — xii,354p : ill ; 24cm
Bibliography: p340-342. — Includes index
ISBN 0-13-244459-3 (cased) : £15.70
ISBN 0-13-244442-9 (pbk) : Unpriced B82-16715

How to take good pictures : a photo guide by Kodak. — London : Collins, 1982. — 192p : col.ill ; 22cm
Includes index
ISBN 0-00-411897-9 (cased) : Unpriced
ISBN 0-00-411898-7 (pbk) : Unpriced B82-32940

Lynch, David, *1939-*. The Focalguide to better pictures / David Lynch. — London : Focal, 1981. — 136p : ill(some col.) ; 19cm
Includes index
ISBN 0-240-51053-4 (pbk) : Unpriced B82-06377

Newnes book of photography. — London : Newnes Technical, Oct.1982. — [144]p
ISBN 0-408-01162-9 (pbk) : £7.00 : CIP entry B82-24467

Partridge, Joe. Me and my camera. — London : Ash & Grant, July 1981. — [128]p
ISBN 0-904069-46-x : £4.95 : CIP entry B81-14905

Strickland, David. Book of photography : picture taking & making / David Strickland. — Poole : Blandford, [1981]. — 95p : ill(some col.),1port ; 15cm. — ('How to')
Includes index
ISBN 0-7137-1056-x (pbk) : £1.95 B82-20223

Wakefield, George L.. Beginner′s guide to photography / George L. Wakefield. — London : Newnes Technical Books, 1981. — 186p,[8]p of plates : ill(some col.) ; 19cm
Includes index
ISBN 0-408-00400-2 (pbk) : Unpriced B82-05666

Wooller, Maurice. Taking up photography / Maurice Wooller ; illustrated throughout with photographs by the author and line drawings by Ray Martin. — London : Warne, 1981. — 119p : ill(some col.),ports ; 25cm. — (Warne′s art and craft series)
ISBN 0-7232-2763-2 : £6.95 B82-00860

770′.28 — Photography — *Manuals*

Bailey, David, *1938-*. David Bailey′s book of photography : how to take better pictures / photographs by David Bailey ; text by George Hughes. — London : Dent, 1981. — 212p,[16]p of plates : ill(some col.),ports ; 30cm
Includes index
ISBN 0-460-04531-8 : £14.95 : CIP rev. B81-28825

Darker, R. W.. Photographic know-how / R.W. Darker. — Watford : Argus, 1980. — 240p : ill ; 26cm
ISBN 0-85242-504-x (pbk) : £6.95 B82-01383

Kodak handbook for the professional photographer. — [Hemel Hempstead] : Kodak
Vol.4: Indices, publications, quick-reference tables and formulary. — c1982. — 80p in various pagings : 1ill ; 30cm
ISBN 0-901023-20-5 (pbk) : Unpriced B82-40524

Lichfield, Patrick. Lichfield on photography / Patrick Lichfield. — London : Collins, 1981. — 192p : ill(some col.),ports ; 28cm
ISBN 0-00-216469-8 : £9.95 : CIP rev. B81-28154

770′.28 — Photography — *Manuals — For children*

De Vaux-Balbirnie, T. R.. Fun with photography / T.R. de Vaux-Balbirnie. — London : Kaye & Ward, c1981. — 64p : ill ; 22cm
ISBN 0-7182-1324-6 : £4.25 B82-00840

Haines, George. The young photographer′s handbook / George Haines. — London : Hamlyn, 1982. — 223p : ill(some col.),1facsim,ports(some col.) ; 19cm
Includes index
ISBN 0-600-37237-5 : £3.50 B82-28828

Wright, Christopher, *1937-*. [The Puffin book of photography]. Snap! : a handbook of photography for beginners / Christopher Wright ; illustrated by Graham Round ; photographs by Christopher Wright. — Harmondsworth : Puffin, 1979 (1981 [printing]). — 182p : ill ; 20cm
Includes index
ISBN 0-14-031449-0 (pbk) : £1.50 B82-07305

770′.28 — Photography. Techniques, *to 1980 — Case studies*

Techniques of the world′s great photographers / [contributors Brian Coe ... et al.]. — Oxford : Phaidon, 1981. — 192p : ill(some col.),ports ; 31cm
Includes index
ISBN 0-7148-2187-x : £14.50 B82-01925

770′.28′2 — Cameras — *Amateurs′ manuals*

Barratt, Mike. Cameras / Mike Barratt. — London : Newnes Technical, 1981. — 117p : ill ; 17cm. — (Questions and answers)
Includes index
ISBN 0-408-01138-6 (pbk) : Unpriced : CIP rev. B81-31183

Watkins, Derek. Beginner′s guide to cameras / Derek Watkins. — London : Newnes Technical Books, 1981. — 165p,[8]p of plates : ill(some col.) ; 19cm
Includes index
ISBN 0-408-00510-6 (pbk) : Unpriced : CIP rev. B81-00215

770′.28′22 — 35mm single lens reflex cameras — *Amateurs′ manuals*

Grill, Tom. [Taking better pictures with 35mm SLR]. Taking better pictures with your 35mm SLR : a practical guide with special emphasis on 35mm automatic cameras / Tom Grill and Mark Scanlon. — London : Hale, 1982, c1981. — ix,142p : ill(some col.) ; 29cm
Originally published: New York : Harper & Row, c1981. — Includes index
ISBN 0-7091-9626-1 : £9.75 B82-19788

770′.28′3 — Monochrome photography. Processing — *Manuals*

Coote, Jack H.. Monochrome darkroom practice : a manual of black-and-white processing and printing / Jack H. Coote. — London : Focal, 1982. — 320p : ill,ports ; 25cm
Includes index
ISBN 0-240-51061-5 : Unpriced : CIP rev. B82-04727

770′.28′3 — Photography. Processing — *Amateurs′ manuals*

Foster, Stuart. Film and paper processing. — Sevenoaks : Newnes Technical Books, June 1981. — [160]p
ISBN 0-408-00512-2 (pbk) : £3.00 : CIP entry B81-13561

770′.28′4 — Photography. Printing — *Amateurs′ manuals*

Reynolds, Clyde. Beginner′s guide to processing and printing / Clyde Reynolds. — London : Newnes Technical Books, 1981. — 203p,[8]p of plates : ill(some col.) ; 19cm
Includes index
ISBN 0-408-00550-5 (pbk) : Unpriced : CIP rev. B81-13859

770′.28′6 — Photographs. Conservation

Swan, Alice. The care and conservation of photographic material : five articles / by Alice Swan. — London : Crafts Council, 1981. — 48p : ill ; 30cm
ISBN 0-903798-55-7 (pbk) : Unpriced B82-06123

770′.5 — Photography — *Serials*

Creative photography. — Nov. 1981-. — [London] : [Carlton Communications], 1981-. — v. : ill(some col.),ports ; 27cm
Monthly
ISSN 0261-412X = Creative photography : £15.00 per year B82-22701

770'.9 — Photography, *to 1980*

Jeffrey, Ian. Photography : a concise history / Ian Jeffrey. — London : Thames and Hudson, 1981. — 248p : ill(some col.),ports ; 22cm. — ([The World of art library])
Includes index
ISBN 0-500-18187-x : £7.95 B82-04660

770'.92'4 — English documentary photography. Special subjects: Expeditions — *Personal observations*

Dickinson, Leo. Filming the impossible / Leo Dickinson. — London : Cape, 1982. — 255p : col.ill ; 26cm
ISBN 0-224-02015-3 : £12.50 : CIP rev.
B82-08439

770'.92'4 — English photography. Baker, Deborah — *Critical studies*

Deborah Baker : photographs. — Cardiff (53 Charles St., Cardiff) : Oriel, [1981]. — 1sheet ; 30x21cm
Accompanies an exhibition held from Oct. 8 to Oct. 29 at Oriel, the Welsh Arts Council's Gallery. — English and Welsh text
Unpriced B82-05478

770'.92'4 — English photography. Beaton, Cecil, *1926-1974 — Correspondence, diaries, etc.*

Beaton, Cecil. Self-portrait with friends : the selected diaries of Cecil Beaton 1926-1974 / edited by Richard Buckle. — Harmondsworth : Penguin, 1982, c1979. — x,435p,[24]p of plates : ill,ports ; 21cm
Originally published: London : Weidenfeld and Nicolson, 1979. — Includes index
ISBN 0-14-005100-7 (pbk) : £4.95 B82-33965

770'.92'4 — English photography. Fincher, Terry — *Biographies*

Fincher, Terry. The Fincher file / Terry Fincher and Tony Lynch. — London : Quartet, 1981. — 197p : ill,facsims,ports ; 29cm
ISBN 0-7043-2293-5 : £11.95 : CIP rev.
B81-21494

770'.92'4 — French photography. Lartigue, J. H. - *Biographies*

Lartigue, J. H.. The autochromes of J.H. Lartigue. — London : Ash and Grant, Sept.1981. — [80]p
Translation of: Les autochromes de J.H. Lartigue
ISBN 0-904069-45-1 : £15.00 : CIP entry
B81-20492

770'.92'4 — Photography — *Personal observations*

Barthes, Roland. Camera Lucida : reflections on photography / Roland Barthes ; translated by Richard Howard. — London : Cape, 1982, c1981. — 119p,[1]leaf of plates : ill(some col.),ports ; 22cm
Translation of: La chambre claire
ISBN 0-224-02929-0 : £7.50 : CIP rev.
B81-40242

770'.92'4 — Scottish photography. Wilson, George Washington — *Critical studies*

Taylor, Roger, *19---*. George Washington Wilson. — Aberdeen : Aberdeen University Press, Nov.1981. — [224]p
ISBN 0-08-025760-7 : £20.00 : CIP entry
B81-28790

770'.941 — Great Britain. Photography — *Serials*

[British and overseas members' reference book and buyers' guide *(Institute of Incorporated Photographers)*]. British and overseas members' reference book and buyers' guide / Institute of Incorporated Photographers. — 1981-. — London (86 Edgware Rd, W2) : Sterling Publications for the Institute, 1981-. — v. : ill ; 30cm
Annual. — Continues: Institute of Incorporated Photographers. IIP register
ISSN 0260-3764 = British and overseas members' reference book and buyers' guide - Institute of Incorporated Photographers :
Unpriced B82-13402

771 — PHOTOGRAPHY. EQUIPMENT AND MATERIALS

771 — Photographic equipment — *Manuals*

Holloway, Adrian. The handbook of photographic equipment and techniques. — London (9 Henrietta St., W.C.2) : Ash and Grant, June 1981. — [216]p
ISBN 0-904069-44-3 : £7.95 : CIP entry
B81-12861

771'.05 — Photographic equipment — *Serials* — *For retail photographic trades*

Camera counter : [the magazine for the retailer of popular photographic equipment]. — Vol.1, no.1 (Nov. 1981)-. — London (202 Kensington Church St., W8 4DP) : Joint Marketing & Publishing Services Ltd, 1981-. — v. : ill,ports ; 30cm
Quarterly
ISSN 0262-5008 = Camera counter : £5.00 per year B82-14275

771.3'029'4 — Cameras — *Buyers' guides* — *Serials*

Camera choice. — No.1 (Apr. 1982)-. — Sutton : IPC Specialist and Professional Press, 1982-. — v. : ill(some col.),maps,ports ; 29cm
Monthly
ISSN 0263-0834 = Camera choice : Unpriced
B82-40055

Which camera?. — No.1 (Nov. 1981)-. — Teddington : Haymarket Pub., 1981-. — v. : ill ; 21cm
Monthly
ISSN 0263-9106 = Which camera? : £0.80 per issue B82-32374

771.3'074'02134 — London. Kensington and Chelsea *(London Borough).* **Museums: Science Museum. Stock: Cameras,** *to ca 1980* — *Catalogues*

Science Museum. The Science Museum camera collection : incorporating the Arthur Frank Collection. — [London] ([Exhibition Rd., Kensington, S.W.7]) : The Museum, [1981?]. — 133p : ill,facsims ; 30cm
Bibliography: p133. — Includes index
Unpriced (pbk) B82-04783

771.3'1 — Canon A series cameras

Gaunt, Leonard. Canon A series. — London : Focal, Oct.1982. — [128]p
ISBN 0-240-51183-2 (pbk) : £4.95 : CIP entry
B82-23489

771.3'1 — Canon single lens reflex cameras — *Manuals*

Gaunt, Leonard. The Canon SLR book for AE-1, AT-1, FTb & TX users / Leonard Gaunt. — London : Focal Press, 1978 (1981 [printing]). — 136p : ill(some col.) ; 22cm. — (Focal camera books)
ISBN 0-240-50987-0 (pbk) : Unpriced
B82-08853

771.3'1 — Hasselblad cameras — *Manuals*

Wildi, Ernst. The Hasselblad manual : a comprehensive guide to the system / Ernst Wildi. — 2nd ed. — London : Focal Press, 1982. — 302p,[64]p of plates : ill(some col.) ; 24cm
Previous ed.: 1980. — Includes index
ISBN 0-240-51186-7 : Unpriced : CIP rev.
B82-07659

771.3'1 — Mamiya M645 cameras

Borell, Alexander. Mamiya M645. — London : Focal, Oct.1982. — [128]p
Translation of: Die Mamiya M645
ISBN 0-240-51197-2 (pbk) : £4.95 : CIP entry
B82-23490

771.3'1 — Nikon cameras & Nikkormat cameras — *Manuals*

Keppler, H.. The Nikon way. — 3rd ed. — London : Focal Press, Oct.1982. — [450]p
Previous ed.: 1978
ISBN 0-240-51185-9 : £13.00 : CIP entry
B82-23488

771.3'1 — Nikon F3 cameras

Crawley, Geoffrey. Camera test : Nikon F3 / Geoffrey Crawley. — London : H. Greenwood, [c1981]. — 75p : ill ; 21cm
Originally published: as a series of reviews in the British journal of photography, 1980. — Includes index
ISBN 0-900414-20-0 (pbk) : £2.50 B82-38582

771.3'1 — Pentax K series & M series cameras — *Manuals*

Reynolds, Clyde. The Asahi Pentax book : for ME, MX, K2, KX, KM and K1000 users / Clyde Reynolds. — London : Focal Press, 1978 (1981 [printing]). — 136p : ill(some col.) ; 22cm. — (Focal camera books)
ISBN 0-240-51125-5 (pbk) : Unpriced
B82-09796

771.3'1 — Pentax Spotmatic cameras — *Manuals*

Reynolds, Clyde. Asahi Pentax S models : for Spotmatic F, SP 1000 and ESII users / Clyde Reynolds. — London : Focal Press, 1975 (1981 [printing]). — 136p : ill(some col.) ; 21cm. — (Focal camera books)
ISBN 0-240-50899-8 (pbk) : Unpriced
B82-12524

774 — HOLOGRAPHY

774 — Holography

Abramson, Nils. The making and evaluation of holograms / Nils Abramson. — London : Academic, 1981. — xv,326p : ill ; 24cm
Includes index
ISBN 0-12-042820-2 : £23.40 : CIP rev.
B81-30187

778.5 — FILM AND TELEVISION PHOTOGRAPHY

778.5'3 — Cinematographic equipment: Cameras

Raimondo Souto, H. Mario. The technique of the motion picture camera / by H. Mario Raimondo Souto. — 4th ed. — London : Focal, 1982. — 396p : ill ; 23cm. — (The Library of communication techniques)
Previous ed.: 1977. — Includes index
ISBN 0-240-51123-9 : £14.00 : CIP rev.
B82-10803

778.5'3 — Independent cinematography

Harvey, Sylvia. Independent cinema? / Sylvia Harvey. — Stafford : West Midlands Arts, c1978. — 20p ; 20cm
ISBN 0-9504364-3-7 (pbk) : Unpriced
B82-16254

778.5'3'09 — Cinematography, *to 1980*

Coe, Brian, *1930-*. The history of movie photography / Brian Coe. — London : Ash & Grant, 1981. — 176p : ill(some col.),ports ; 29cm
Bibliography: p173. — Includes index
ISBN 0-904069-38-9 : £10.00 B82-40509

778.5'343 — Cinematography. Lighting

Millerson, Gerald. The technique of lighting for television and motion pictures / by Gerald Millerson. — 2nd ed. — London : Focal, 1982. — 391p : ill ; 22cm. — (The Library of communication techniques)
Bibliography: p385-386. — Includes index
ISBN 0-240-51128-x : £16.00 : CIP rev.
Primary classification 778.59 B81-13798

778.5'345 — Cinema films. Cinematography. Special effects. Development. Role of conjurers, *to 1910*

Barnouw, Erik. The magician and the cinema / Erik Barnouw. — New York ; Oxford : Oxford University Press, 1981. — 128p : ill,facsims,ports ; 24cm
Bibliography: p117-122. — Includes index
ISBN 0-19-502918-6 : £9.95 B82-01000

778.5'3491 — Super 8mm cinematography — *Amateurs' manuals*

Arrowsmith, Frank. Beginner's guide to Super 8 film making / Frank Arrowsmith. — London : Newnes Technical Books, 1981. — 162p,[8]p of plates : ill(some col.) ; 19cm
Includes index
ISBN 0-408-00509-2 (pbk) : Unpriced
B82-05667

778.5′35 — Cinema films. Editing — *Manuals*
Crittenden, Roger. The Thames and Hudson manual of film editing / Roger Crittenden. — London : Thames and Hudson, c1981. — 160p : ill,facsims,ports ; 25cm. — (The Thames and Hudson manuals)
Bibliography: p157. — Includes index
ISBN 0-500-67023-4 : £7.95 B82-03490

Walter, Ernest. The technique of the film cutting room / by Ernest Walter. — 2nd ed. rev., with revisions. — London : Focal, 1982. — 330p : ill ; 23cm. — (The Library of communication techniques)
Previous ed.: 1973. — Includes index
ISBN 0-240-50657-x : Unpriced B82-22216

778.59 — Television programmes. Lighting
Millerson, Gerald. The technique of lighting for television and motion pictures / by Gerald Millerson. — 2nd ed. — London : Focal, 1982. — 391p : ill ; 22cm. — (The Library of communication techniques)
Bibliography: p385-386. — Includes index
ISBN 0-240-51128-x : £16.00 : CIP rev.
Also classified at 778.5′343 B81-13798

778.59′9 — Videorecording
Owen, David, *1939-*. The complete handbook of video : everything you need to know about video — from home entertainment to everyday office use / David Owen, Mark Dunton. — Harmondsworth : Penguin, 1982. — 224p : ill (some col.) ; 26cm
Bibliography: p216-217. — Includes index
ISBN 0-14-046545-6 (pbk) : £4.95 B82-37536

Owen, David, *1939-*. The complete handbook of video : everything you need to know about video — from home entertainment to everyday office use / David Owen, Mark Dunton. — London : Allen Lane, 1982. — 224p : ill(some col.) ; 26cm
Bibliography: p216-217. — Includes index
ISBN 0-7139-1493-9 : £8.95 B82-37535

778.59′9 — Videotape equipment — *Amateurs′ manuals*
Matthewson, D. K.. An introduction to video. — London : Babani, May 1982. — [96]p
ISBN 0-85934-075-9 (pbk) : £1.95 : CIP entry B82-07037

778.59′9′0288 — Videotape equipment. Maintenance & repair
Beeching, Steve. Domestic videorecorder techniques. — London : Newnes Technical, Feb.1983. — [144]p
ISBN 0-408-01103-3 (pbk) : £14.50 : CIP entry B82-38297

778.59′92′028 — Videorecording. Techniques — *Manuals*
Foss, Hannen. How to make your own video programmes : for family, educational and business use / Hannen Foss. — London : Elm Tree, 1982. — 124p : ill(some col.) ; 27cm
Includes index
ISBN 0-241-10572-2 : £7.95 : CIP rev. B81-36382

778.59′93 — Sony AU 3400 Portapack videotape recorders — *Manuals*
Leissner, Dan. How to use video / by Dan Leissner with assistance from West Midlands Arts. — Stoke-on-Trent : West Midlands Arts, 1981. — 15p : ill ; 21cm
Cover title
ISBN 0-9504364-4-5 (pbk) : Unpriced B82-16393

778.59′93′0294 — Videocassette tape recorders — *Buyers′ guides* — *For schools*
Hughes, J. (John), *1934 Nov.7-*. Video recording in schools : a guide to currently available video-recording and playback machines. — [Rev. and updated ed.]. — [Sheffield] : [Sheffield Media Resources Organising Committee], 1981. — [20]p ; 21cm. — (Occasional paper, ISSN 0144-7513 ; 2)
Cover title. — Prepared on behalf of the Sheffield Media Resources Organising Committee by J. Hughes, J. Reeves and G. Bennett. — Previous ed.: 1979
ISBN 0-907802-00-1 (pbk) : Unpriced B82-06967

778.6 — COLOUR PHOTOGRAPHY

778.6 — Colour photography — *Amateurs′ manuals*
Gilhuis, Wout. Creative colour transparencies / Wout Gilhuis. — [Watford] : Fountain, 1980. — 160p : col.ill ; 25cm
ISBN 0-85242-711-5 : £8.50 B82-08286

Wakefield, George L.. Colour films. — Sevenoaks : Focal Press, Jan.1982. — [160]p
ISBN 0-240-51109-3 : £5.00 : CIP entry B81-34323

778.6 — Colour photography — *Manuals*
Making the most of colour / consultant editor Christopher Angeloglou. — London : Collins, 1982, c1981. — 96p : chiefly col.ill ; 28cm. — (You and your camera photography series)
Includes index
ISBN 0-00-411640-2 (pbk) : £3.95 B82-23922

Marvullo, Joe. Improving your colour photography. — Poole : Blandford Press, Sept.1982. — [176]p. — (Master class photography series)
ISBN 0-7137-1284-8 : £6.95 : CIP entry B82-21098

778.6′6 — Colour photography. Printing — *Amateurs′ manuals*
Trapmore, Alison. Colour printing. — London : Focal Press, Feb.1983. — [168]p
ISBN 0-240-51113-1 (pbk) : £6.95 : CIP entry B82-37822

778.6′6 — Colour photography. Processing — *Amateurs′ manuals*
Watkins, Derek. The focalguide to colour film processing. — 2nd ed. — London : Focal Press, July 1982. — [200]p
Previous ed.: 1978
ISBN 0-240-51126-3 (pbk) : £3.25 : CIP entry B82-25177

778.7 — PHOTOGRAPHY UNDER SPECIAL CONDITIONS

778.7′2 — Electronic flashlight photography
Edgerton, Harold E.. Electronic flash, strobe / Harold E. Edgerton. — 2nd ed. — Cambridge, Mass. ; London : MIT, 1979. — xxiv,366p : ill ; 23cm
Previous ed.: New York : London : McGraw-Hill, 1970. — Includes index
ISBN 0-262-55008-3 (pbk) : £7.00 B82-03521

778.7′2 — Electronic flashlight photography — *Manuals*
Herwig, Ellis. [Amphoto guide to flash photography]. PSL guide to flash photography / Ellis Herwig. — Cambridge : Stephens, 1981. — 168p : ill(some col.),ports ; 22cm
Originally published: New York : Amphoto, 1981. — Bibliography: p162-163. — Includes index
ISBN 0-85059-583-5 (cased) : Unpriced
ISBN 0-85059-584-3 (pbk) : £3.50 B82-18330

778.7′2 — Flashlight photography — *Amateurs′ manuals*
Watkins, Derek. Flash. — London : Focal Press, Dec.1982. — [168]p
ISBN 0-240-51119-0 (pbk) : £5.95 : CIP entry B82-14958

778.7′2 — Indoor photography — *Amateurs′ manuals*
Lynch, David. Indoor photography. — London : Focal, Nov.1982. — [168]p
ISBN 0-240-51115-8 (pbk) : £6.95 : CIP entry B82-27381

778.7′3 — Underwater photography — *Manuals*
Turner, John, *1952-*. Underwater photography / John Turner. — London : Focal Press, 1982. — 125p,[8]p of plates : ill(some col.) ; 26cm
Includes index
ISBN 0-240-51122-0 : £12.95 : CIP rev. B81-33928

778.8 — TRICK PHOTOGRAPHY

778.8 — Photography. Special effects — *Amateurs′ manuals*
Langford, Michael. The book of special effects photography / Michael Langford. — London : Ebury, 1981. — 168p : ill(some col.) ; 25cm
Includes index
ISBN 0-85223-209-8 : £7.95 B82-02914

Wade, John. Special effects in the camera. — London : Focal Press, Feb.1983. — [168]p
ISBN 0-240-51184-0 (pbk) : £5.95 : CIP entry B82-37823

778.9 — PHOTOGRAPHY OF SPECIAL SUBJECTS

778.9′2 — Photography. Special subjects: Human figures — *Manuals*
Busselle, Michael. The handbook of photographing people / Michael Busselle. — London : Mitchell Beazley, 1980. — 224p : ill (some col.) ; 29cm
Bibliography: p220. — Includes index
ISBN 0-86134-023-x : £12.50 B82-08377

Photographing people : how to take successful pictures of those around you / consulting editor Jack Schofield. — London : Hamlyn, 1982. — 240p : col.ill ; 29cm
ISBN 0-600-38473-x : £9.95 B82-36216

Photographing people / Clive Corless consultant editor. — London : Ebury, 1982. — 64p : ill (some col.) ; 28cm
ISBN 0-85223-246-2 (cased) : Unpriced
ISBN 0-85223-251-9 (pbk) : £3.95 B82-37160

778.9′2 — Portrait photography — *Amateurs′ manuals*
Gnade, Michael. People in my camera : portraiture, figure studies, photographic approach, composition, processing, experiments / Michael Gnade. — [Watford] : Fountain Press, 1979. — 198p : ill(some col.),ports ; 25cm
Translation of: Fotos von Menschen
ISBN 0-85242-632-1 : £7.50 B82-05175

Lewinski, Jorge. The book of portrait photography / Jorge Lewinski and Mayotte Magnus. — London : Ebury, 1982. — 168p : ill(some col.),ports(some col.) ; 25cm
Includes index
ISBN 0-85223-226-8 : £8.50 B82-32328

Wade, John. Portrait photography. — London : Newnes Technical Books, June 1981. — [160]p
ISBN 0-408-00513-0 (Pbk) : £3.00 : CIP entry B81-13540

778.9′21 — Photography. Special subjects: Nudes — *Manuals*
Busselle, Michael. Nude & glamour photography / Michael Busselle. — London : Macdonald, 1981. — 224p : ill(some col.) ; 29cm
Bibliography: p220. — Includes index
ISBN 0-354-04784-1 : £12.95 B82-01062

778.9′24 — Glamour photography — *Manuals*
Nude and glamour photography / consultant editor Jack Schofield. — London : Collins, 1982, c1981. — 96p : chiefly col.ill ; 28cm. — (You and your camera photography series)
Includes index
ISBN 0-00-411639-9 (pbk) : £3.95 B82-23923

778.9′24 — Photography. Special subjects: Pin-ups — *Manuals*
Lichfield, Patrick. Lichfield′s calendar book. — London : Collins, Sept.1982. — [196]p
ISBN 0-00-216470-1 : £7.95 : CIP entry
ISBN 0-00-216473-6 (pbk) : Unpriced B82-19062

778.9′24 — Photography. Special subjects: Women: Nudes — *Amateurs′ manuals*
Boys, Michael. The book of nude photography / text and photographs by Michael Boys. — London : Ebury Press, 1981. — 168p : ill(some col.) ; 25cm
Includes index
ISBN 0-85223-208-x : £7.95 B82-02915

778.9'24 — Photography. Special subjects: Women: Nudes — *Amateurs' manuals* *continuation*

Successful glamour photography. — London : Hamlyn, c1981. — 173p : col.ill ; 31cm. — (A Quarto book)
Includes index
ISBN 0-600-38472-1 : £7.95 B82-17610

778.9'3 — Photography. Special subjects: Nature — *Manuals*

Angel, Heather. The book of nature photography / text and photographs by Heather Angel. — London : Ebury, 1982. — 168p : ill(chiefly col.) ; 25cm
Includes index
ISBN 0-85223-227-6 : £8.50 B82-32329

Freeman, Michael, *1945-*. Wildlife & nature photography / Michael Freeman ; consultant Nigel Sitwell. — London : Croom Helm, 1981. — 224p : ill(some col.) ; 29cm
Bibliography: p219. — Includes index
ISBN 0-7099-1008-8 : £13.95 B82-07325

Successful nature photography : how to take beautiful pictures of the living world / edited by Christopher Angeloglou and Jack Schofield ; with an introduction by Heather Angel. — London : Collins, 1982. — 240p : ill(some col.) ; 29cm
Includes index
ISBN 0-00-411899-5 : £12.95 B82-33510

778.9'32 — Photography. Special subjects: Birds — *Manuals*

Warham, John. The technique of bird photography. — 4th ed. — London : Focal Press, July 1981. — [328]p
Previous ed.: 1973
ISBN 0-240-51084-4 : CIP entry B81-15822

778.9'35 — Photography. Special subjects: Still life — *Manuals*

Pendleton, Bruce. Creative still life photography. — Poole : Blandford Press, Sept.1982. — [176] p. — (Master class photography series)
ISBN 0-7137-1286-4 : £6.95 : CIP entry B82-21099

778.9'36 — Landscape photography — *Manuals*

Brück, Axel. Practical landscape photography. — London : Focal Press, Nov.1981. — [192]p
ISBN 0-240-51080-1 : £9.95 : CIP entry B81-30444

778.9'37 — Marine photography

Kampa, Theo. This is photography afloat / Theo Kampa and Wulf Barow ; translated by Susanne Platt. — London : Nautical, 1981. — 152p : ill(some col.) ; 21cm
Translation of: Fotografieren an bord
ISBN 0-333-31811-0 (corrected pbk) : £7.95 B82-10179

778.9'4 — Photography. Special subjects: Great Britain — *Manuals*

Lewinski, Jorge. The Shell guide to photographing Britain. — London : Hutchinson, June 1982. — [240]p
ISBN 0-09-147060-9 : £9.95 : CIP entry B82-11289

778.9'4 — Photography. Special subjects: Places — *Manuals*

Corless, Clive. Travel photography / Clive Corless, consultant editor. — London : Ebury, 1982. — 64p : col.ill ; 28cm
ISBN 0-85223-247-0 (cased) : Unpriced
ISBN 0-85223-252-7 (pbk) : £3.95 B82-36944

778.9'4 — Photography. Special subjects. Southern California — *Manuals*

Moldvay, Albert. Photographing Los Angeles and Southern California / Albert Moldvay, Erika Fabian. — New York ; Amphoto ; Cambridge : Stephens, 1981. — 125p : ill(some col.),col.maps ; 24cm. — (PSL travel guide)
Includes index
ISBN 0-85059-535-5 (pbk) : £2.95 B82-08775

778.9'4 — Photography. Special subjects: Washington, D.C. — *Manuals*

Moldvay, Albert. Photographing Washington D.C. / Albert Moldvay, Erika Fabian. — New York : Amphoto ; Cambridge : Stephens, 1981. — 125p : ill(some col.),col.maps ; 24cm. — (PSL travel guide)
Includes index
ISBN 0-85059-537-1 (pbk) : £2.95 B82-08774

778.9'96251 — Photography. Special subjects: Railways

Treacy, Eric. Eric Treacy — railway photographer. — Newton Abbot : David & Charles, Oct.1982. — [216]p
ISBN 0-7153-8367-1 : £12.50 : CIP entry B82-23014

779 — PHOTOGRAPHY. COLLECTIONS

779 — Micrographs & non-visible light photographs — *Collections*

The **Invisible** world : sights too fast, too slow, too far, too small for the naked eye to see. — London : Secker & Warburg, 1981. — 160p : chiefly ill(some col.) ; 29cm
ISBN 0-436-37680-6 : £12.50 B82-15525

779 — Photography — *Collections*

The **Camera** never lies. — Exeter : Webb & Bower, Nov.1982. — [128]p
ISBN 0-906671-43-4 : £4.95 : CIP entry B82-32866

779'.074'01471 — New York *(City)*. **Public libraries: New York Public Library. Stock: Photographs,** *1840-1910* — *Illustrations*

New York Public Library. From Talbot to Stieglitz : masterpieces of early photography from the New York Public Library / [compiled by] Julia Van Haaften. — London : Thames and Hudson, 1982. — 125p : chiefly ill,ports ; 29cm
Includes index
ISBN 0-500-54077-2 : £15.00 B82-20417

779'.074'02 — Great Britain. Art galleries. Exhibits: Photography, *1830-1980* — *Catalogues*

Photographer as printmaker : 140 years of photographic printmaking. — [London] : Arts Council of Great Britain, c1981. — 47p : ill,2ports ; 30cm + Brief technical guide([8]p : ill ; 21cm)
Catalogue of an Arts Council of Great Britain touring exhibition. — Catalogue written by Gerry Badger
ISBN 0-7287-0294-0 (pbk) : Unpriced B82-13032

779'.074'0275 — Merseyside *(Metropolitan County)*. **Photography. Collections** — *Lists*

Merseyside directory of photographic sources. — Liverpool : Open Eye, Jan.1982. — [104]p
ISBN 0-9507818-0-0 (pbk) : £3.95 : CIP entry B81-38821

779'.092'2 — Edinburgh. Art galleries: Scottish National Portrait Gallery. Exhibits: Scottish calotypes. Hill, David Octavius & Adamson, Robert — *Catalogues*

Scottish National Portrait Gallery. David Octavius Hill and Robert Adamson : catalogue of their calotypes taken between 1843 and 1847 in the collection of the Scottish National Portrait Gallery / Sara Stevenson. — Edinburgh : National Galleries of Scotland, 1981. — 220p : ill,ports ; 30cm
ISBN 0-903148-37-4 : Unpriced B82-01879

779'.092'4 — American photography, *1900-1950* — *Collections from individual artists*

Orkin, Ruth. A photo journal / Ruth Orkin. — London : Secker & Warburg, 1981. — 152p : all ill(some col.),ports(some col.) ; 28cm
Originally published: New York : Viking Press, 1981
ISBN 0-436-34050-x : £15.00 B82-08700

Outerbridge, Paul. Paul Outerbridge Jr : photographs 1921-1939 / edited by Graham Howe and G. Ray Hawkins ; text by Graham Howe and Jacqueline Markham. — London : Thames and Hudson, 1980. — 158p : ill(some col.),ports ; 29cm
ISBN 0-500-54066-7 : £14.00 B82-25205

Ray, Man. Man Ray : photographs / introduction by Jean-Hubert Martin ; with three texts by Man Ray. — London : Thames and Hudson, 1982. — 255p : chiefly ill,ports ; 31cm
Based on an exhibition held at the Centre d'Art et de Culture Georges Pompidou, Paris, December 1981 — April 1982. — Translation of: Man Ray photographe. — Ill on lining papers. — Includes index
ISBN 0-500-54079-9 : £18.00 B82-34980

Siskind, Aaron. Aaron Siskind : photographs 1932-1978. — Oxford : Museum of Modern Art, 1979. — [64]p : all ill ; 21x25cm
Accompanies an exhibition of Siskind's work held at the Museum of Modern Art, Oxford. — Bibliography: p[63]
ISBN 0-905836-16-2 (pbk) : £3.95 B82-09969

Smith, W. Eugene. W. Eugene Smith : master of the photographic essay / edited with commentary by William S. Johnson ; foreword by James Enyeart. — [New York] : Aperture ; Oxford : Phaidon [distributor], c1981. — 223p : chiefly ill,ports ; 30cm
Bibliography: p223
ISBN 0-89381-070-3 (cased) : Unpriced
ISBN 0-89381-071-1 (pbk) : Unpriced B82-24532

779'.092'4 — American photography, *1950-* — *Collections from individual artists*

McCartney, Linda. Linda's pictures : a collection of photographs / photographs and words by Linda McCartney ; reviewed by Paul McCartney. — London : Pavilion, 1982, c1976. — xiv,148p of plates : all ill(some col.),chiefly ports(some col.) ; 32cm
Originally published: London : Cape, 1976
ISBN 0-907516-09-2 (pbk) : £5.95 B82-17723

McCartney, Linda. Photographs. — London (196 Shaftesbury Ave., WC2H 8JL) : Pavilion Books, Sept.1982. — [128]p
ISBN 0-907516-15-7 : £15.00 : CIP entry B82-21581

779'.092'4 — Canadian photography, *1850-1900* — *Collections from individual artists*

Gilmour, *Lady* **Henrietta**. Beauty, beasts & ballgowns : photographs from the camera of Lady Henrietta Gilmour 1890-1910 : an exhibition selected from negatives deposited at the University of St. Andrews by her grandson, Sir John Gilmour, and first shown at the Crawford Centre for the Arts. — [St. Andrews] : Crawford Centre for the Arts, [1982?]. — [12]p : ill,ports ; 21cm
Unpriced (unbound) B82-27468

779'.092'4 — Cornwall. Newlyn. Art galleries: Newlyn Art Gallery. Exhibits: English photography. Mayne, Roger — *Catalogues*

Mayne, Roger, *1929-*. Roger Mayne : landscape photographs 18 October-22 November 80. — Penzance : Newlyn Art Gallery, [1980?]. — 1sheet : ill ; 42x60cm folded to 30x21cm
Unpriced B82-05969

779'.092'4 — Cumbria. Carlisle *(District)*. **Brampton. Art galleries: LYC Museum and Art Gallery. Exhibits: English photography. Sheard, Geoffrey** — *Catalogues*

Clarie [i.e. Claire] Langdown, Elena Gaputyte, Geoffrey Shesrd [i.e. Sheard] : 81 October 3. — Brampton : LYC Museum & Art Gallery, 1981. — [36]p : ill ; 14cm
ISBN 0-9504571-1-6 (pbk) : £0.35
Primary classification 730'.92'2 B82-01267

779'.092'4 — English photography, *1950-* — *Collections from individual artists*

Carlos Clarke, Bob. Obsession / Bob Carlos Clarke ; foreword by Patrick Lichfield ; introduction by Philippe Garner. — London : Quartet, 1981. — 15p,[i.e. 151]p : chiefly ill (some col.) ; 40cm
ISBN 0-7043-2298-6 : £15.00 B82-02591

Godwin, Fay. Bison at Chalk Farm and other snaps. — London : Routledge & K. Paul, Nov.1982. — [38]p
ISBN 0-7100-9345-4 (pbk) : £4.95 : CIP entry B82-27972

779'.092'4 — English photography, *1950- — Collections from individual artists*

continuation

McBean, Angus. Angus McBean. — London : Quartet, Oct.1982. — [128]p
ISBN 0-7043-2352-4 : £25.00 : CIP entry
B82-29133

Peter Joseph, Richard Long, David Tremlett in Newlyn. — [Penzance] : Newlyn Orion Galleries, 1978. — 1portfolio : ill ; 23x27cm
Produced to accompany an exhibition at the Newlyn Art Gallery in 1978
Unpriced
Primary classification 709'.42 B82-05968

779'.092'4 — New Zealand photography, *1950- — Collections from individual artists*

Hunter, Alexis. Photographic narrative sequences : approaches to fear 1976-78, romantic love and sexual hatred 1978-1979, on politics 1978-1980, new work 1981 / Alexis Hunter ; critical essays by Lucy R. Lippard and Margaret Richards. — London : Edward Totah Gallery, [1981?]. — [48]p : ill ; 21x27cm
ISBN 0-907773-00-1 (pbk) : Unpriced
B82-10320

779'.092'4 — Russian photography, *1950- — Collections from individual artists*

Evtushenko, Evgeniĭ. Invisible threads / Yevgeny Yevtushenko. — London : Secker & Warburg, 1981. — 64,157p : chiefly ill(some col.) ; 29cm
ISBN 0-436-59220-7 : £12.50 (£9.95 until 31.12.81) : CIP rev. B81-30354

779'.094 — European photography, *1950 — Collections — Serials*

European photography. — 81-. — Basel : Polygon Editions ; London (12 Carlton House Terrace, SW1 5AH) : D & AD/European Illustration [distributor], 1981-. — v. : chiefly ill(chiefly col.),ports(chiefly col.) ; 32cm
Annual. — Text in English, French and German
ISBN 0-904866-06-8 : Unpriced B82-36715

779'.0952'074094 — Europe. Art galleries. Exhibits: Japanese photography, *to 1978 — Catalogues*

Japanese photography today and its origin : Comune di Bologna Galleria d'Arte Moderna, January-February 1979, Comune di Milano Ripartizione Cultura e Spettacolo Palazzo Reale, March-April 1979, Palais des Beaux-Arts, Paleis voor Schone Kunsten, Brussels, June-July 1979, I.C.A. London, August-September 1979 / [text Attilio Colombo] ; [text on Japanese culture Isabella Doniselli] ; [translations Kanjiro Azuma et al.]. — Bologna : Grafis Edizioni d'Arte ; London : Distributed by Travelling Light, c1979. — 185p : ill ; 20cm
Bibliography: p185
ISBN 0-906333-06-7 (pbk) : £3.95 B82-00142

779'.2'0924 — American photography, *1950-*. **Special subjects: Persons, 90 years-** *— Collections from individual artists*

Mathan, Gerda Straus. Valentina's uncle : portrait of an old man / by Gerda Straus Mathan in collaboration with Valentina Zavarin. — New York : Collier ; London : Collier Macmillan, c1981. — 175p : ill,ports ; 26cm
ISBN 0-02-095990-7 (pbk) : £7.95 B82-05152

779'.2'0924 — American portrait photography, *1900-1950 — Collections from individual artists*

Eisenstaedt, Alfred. People / Alfred Eisenstaedt. — Harmondsworth : Penguin, 1979, c1973. — 259p : chiefly ill ; 28cm
Originally published: New York : Viking Press, 1973. — Includes index
ISBN 0-14-005073-6 (pbk) : £3.95 B82-07997

779'.2'0924 — English portrait photography, *1900-1950 — Collections from individual artists*

Brandt, Bill. Portraits : photographs by Bill Brandt / introduction by Alan Ross. — London : Fraser, 1982. — 104p : chiefly ports ; 29cm
ISBN 0-86092-062-3 : £19.50 : CIP rev.
B82-04831

779'.2092'4 — English portrait photography, *1900-1950 — Collections from individual artists*

Vanessa Bell's family album. — London : Jill Norman, Oct.1981. — [160]p
ISBN 0-906908-36-1 : £8.95 : CIP entry
B81-27436

779'.24'0924 — American photography, *1900-1950.* **Special subjects: Women: Nudes** *— Collections from individual artists*

Dunas, Jeff. Captured women / Jeff Dunas. — Cambridge : Patrick Stevens, 1981. — 112p : all col.ill ; 32cm
ISBN 0-85059-570-3 : £12.95 B82-08943

779'.24'0924 — English photography, *1950-*. **Special subjects: Adolescent girls** *— Collections from individual artists*

Hamilton, David, *1933-*. The best of David Hamilton / text by Denise Couttès. — London : Collins, 1977, c1976 (1981 [printing]). — 143p : chiefly ill(some col.) ; 29cm
ISBN 0-00-216078-1 (pbk) : £6.95 B82-14989

779'.24'0924 — English photography, *1950-*. **Special subjects: Large breasted women** *— Collections from individual artists*

Xavier, John. Fling presents every inch a lady / Arv Miller editor & designer ; John Xavier photographer & writer. — [Emsworth] : Axe Books, [1981]. — 69p : ill(some col.),ports (some col.) ; 28cm. — (Fling bonus edition ; no.2)
ISBN 0-9507713-0-9 : Unpriced B82-12881

779'.24'0924 — English photography, *1950-*. **Special subjects: Women** *— Collections from individual artists*

Hamilton, David. A summer in St Tropez. — London : Collins, Oct.1982. — [120]p
ISBN 0-00-216666-6 : £12.00 : CIP entry
B82-23071

Lichfield, Patrick. The most beautiful women / Lichfield ; designed by Craig Dodd. — London : Elm Tree, 1981. — 156p : ill,ports(some col.) ; 31cm
ISBN 0-241-10555-2 : £10.00 : CIP rev.
B81-25866

779'.24'0924 — English photography, *1950- .* **Special subjects: Women: Nudes** *Collections from individual artists*

Swannell, John. Fine lines. — London : Quartet, Apr.1982. — [128]p
ISBN 0-7043-2323-0 : £15.00 : CIP entry
B82-06236

779'.24'0924 — German photography, *1950-*. **Special subjects: Women: Nudes** *— Collections from individual artists*

Newton, Helmut. Helmut Newton : 47 nudes / introduction by Karl Lagerfeld. — London : Thames and Hudson, 1982, c1981. — 80p : chiefly ill,ports ; 32cm
Bibliography: p79
ISBN 0-500-54082-9 : £12.50 B82-30167

779'.24'0924 — Swiss photography, *1950-*. **Special subjects: Women: Nudes** *— Collections from individual artists*

Nazarieff, Serge. Naked elements. — London : Quartet, Aug.1982. — [96]p
ISBN 0-7043-2351-6 : £12.50 : CIP entry
B82-21966

779'.28 — Erotic photography, *1950- - Collections*

Leidmann, Cheyco. Foxy lady. — London : Plexus, June 1981. — [120]p
ISBN 0-85965-042-1 : £15.95 : CIP entry
B81-09480

779'.32'0924 — English photography, *1950-*. **Special subjects: Animals** *— Collections from individual artists*

Doidge, John. So who says we're not human?. — Watford : Exley, Nov.1982. — [128]p
ISBN 0-905521-65-x : £4.95 : CIP entry
B82-27032

779'.36'097307402 — England. Art galleries. Exhibits. American landscape photography, *1950- — Catalogues*

New topographics : photographs / by Robert Adams, Lewis Baltz, Joe Deal. — Bristol : Arnolfini, 1981. — 23p : ill ; 22x28cm
Published on the occasion of an exhibition held at the Arnolfini Gallery, Bristol and elsewhere
ISBN 0-907738-00-1 (pbk) : Unpriced
B82-02019

779'.37 — English photography, *1950-*. **Special subjects: Yachts** *— Collections from individual artists*

Greenway, Ambrose. All at sea. — Havant : Kenneth Mason, Oct.1982. — [64]p
ISBN 0-85937-289-8 : £2.95 : CIP entry
B82-24123

779'.4 — French photography, *1850-1900.* **Special subjects: France. Paris** *— Collections from individual artists*

Atget, Eugène. The work of Atget : old Paris. — London : Gordon Fraser, Oct.1982. — [192]p
ISBN 0-86092-067-4 : £25.00 : CIP entry
B82-24605

779'.4'0924 — Monochrome photography. Special subjects: Urban landscapes *— Collections from individual artists*

Bailey, David. Bailey NW1. — London : Dent, Nov.1982. — [96]p
ISBN 0-460-04588-1 : £17.50 : CIP entry
B82-32870

779'.9305562'0942074 — English photography, *1860-1940.* **Special subjects: Working classes. Social life** *— Catalogues*

Linkman, Audrey. Family albums : [an exhibition of photographs dating from the earlier decades of the century from the family albums of working people] / exhibition selected, designed and mounted by Caroline Warhurst ; photographic reproduction by Christine Stephens ; text by Audrey Linkman and Caroline Warhurst ; catalogue design by Caroline Warhurst. — [Manchester] : [Manchester Studies Unit], c1982. — 43p : ill,ports ; 30cm
Cover title
ISBN 0-9506905-1-1 (pbk) : Unpriced
B82-39691

779'.9613'0924 — English photography, *1950-. Special subjects: Man. Health. Sexual aspects — Collections from individual artists*

Thorpe, David, *1944-*. Rude health / photographed by David Thorpe ; written by Pierre Le Poste ; disigned by Martin Reavley. — London : Macmillan, 1981. — [48]p : chiefly col.ill ; 29cm
ISBN 0-333-32570-2 (pbk) : £3.95 : CIP rev.
B81-27366

779'.962383'0924 — Great Britain. Arts. Patronage. Organisations: Arts Council of Great Britain. Exhibits: English photography. Beaton, Cecil. Special subjects: Dockyards, *1940-1945 — Catalogues*

Spencer, Stanley. Spencer in the shipyard : paintings and drawings by Stanley Spencer and photographs by Cecil Beaton from the Imperial War Museum. — London : Arts Council of Great Britain, c1981. — [28]p(4fold.) : chiefly ill(some col.),ports ; 27cm
Accompanies an Arts Council travelling exhibition held at 10 different venues from 2 May 1981 to 18 April 1982
ISBN 0-7287-0277-0 (pbk) : £3.75
Primary classification 741.942 B82-06146

779'.964121'0924 — English photography, *1950-*. **Special subjects: Alcoholic drinks. Sexual aspects** *— Collections from individual artists*

Thorpe, David, *1944 Apr.6-*. Vin rude / photographed by David Thorpe ; written by Pierre Le Poste. — London : Macmillan, 1980. — [48]p : col.ill ; 29cm
ISBN 0-333-30977-4 (pbk) : £3.50 : CIP rev.
B80-24600

779'.96413'00924 — English photography, ***1950-*****. Special subjects: Food. Sexual aspects —** *Collections from individual artists*

Thorpe, David, *1944-*. Rude food / photographed by David Thorpe ; written by Pierre Le Poste ; designed by Martin Reavley. — London : Macmillan, 1981. — [47]p : chiefly col.ill ; 29cm
ISBN 0-333-32769-1 (pbk) : £3.95 B82-07083

779'.99394'007402876 — Tyne and Wear *(Metropolitan County).* **Newcastle upon Tyne. Universities. Libraries: University of Newcastle upon Tyne.** *Library.* **Stock: Photographs,** *1899-1926.* **Special subjects: Ancient Middle Eastern antiquities. Collections: Gertrude Bell Photographic Archive —** *Catalogues*

Hill, Stephen. Catalogue of the Gertrude Bell Photographic Archive. — Newcastle upon Tyne (University of Newcastle upon Tyne, Newcastle upon Tyne NE1 7RU) : Dept. of Archaeology, Aug.1982. — [158]p
ISBN 0-905423-01-1 (pbk) : CIP entry
B82-28609

779'.9941081 — Great Britain. Arts. Patronage. Organisations: Arts Council of Great Britain. Exhibits: British photography. Special subjects: Working life, *1839-1939 — Catalogues*

The **British** worker : photographs of working life, 1839-1939. — London : Arts Council of Great Britain, c1981. — [35]p : ill,ports ; 30cm
An Arts Council travelling exhibition held at 10 different venues, 16 May 1981-10 August 1982
ISBN 0-7287-0280-0 (unbound) : £2.10
B82-06145

779'.99411081'0924 — Scottish photography, *1850-1900.* **Special subjects: Scotland —** *Collections from individual artists*

Keith, Thomas. Thomas Keith's Scotland : the work of a Victorian amateur photographer 1852-57 / [edited by] John Hannavy. — Edinburgh : Cannongate, 1981. — x,86p : chiefly ill,ports ; 29cm
Ill on lining papers. — Bibliography: p85. — Includes index
ISBN 0-903937-73-5 (cased) : £7.95
ISBN 0-86241-006-1 (pbk) : £3.95 B82-28567

779'.9941292 — Scotland. Fife Region. St. Andrews. Art galleries: Crawford Centre for the Arts. Exhibits: Scottish photography, *1950-***. Special subjects: Scotland. Fife Region. East Neuk —** *Catalogues*

A **Fresh** approach : an exhibition about the East Neuk devised by the Crawford Centre for the Arts, University of St Andrews, with commissioned photographs of the East Neuk by Fay Godwin who selected the exhibits from submissions by many photographers. — St Andrews : Crawford Centre for the Arts, 1980. — 16p : chiefly ill(some col.) ; 15x21cm
ISBN 0-906272-02-5 (pbk) : Unpriced
B82-21526

779'.99415081 — Irish photography, *1850-1900.* **Special subjects: Ireland,** *1893 — Collections*

Ireland from old photographs 1893. — Belfast : Appletree Press, June 1982. — [28]p
ISBN 0-86281-005-1 (unbound) : £2.50 : CIP entry B82-20783

779'.9944081'0924 — French photography, *1850-1900.* **Special subjects: France —** *Collections from individual artists*

Atget, Eugène. The work of Atget / John Szarkowski, Maria Morris Hambourg. — London : Gordon Fraser. — (Spring Mills series on the art of photography)
Vol.1: Old France. — c1981. — 177p : ill ; 31cm
Originally published: New York : The Museum of Modern Art, 1981
ISBN 0-86092-060-7 : £25.00 : CIP rev.
B81-25329

780 — MUSIC

780 — Music

Bush, Alan. In my eighth decade & other essays / by Alan Bush. — London : Kahn & Averill, 1980. — 92p : music ; 22cm
Music on inside covers. — List of works: p81-91
ISBN 0-900707-61-5 (pbk) : £2.75 B82-37368

Dimond, Peter. Music made simple / Peter Dimond. — London : Heinemann, c1982. — xii,276p ; 23cm. — (Made simple books)
Includes index
ISBN 0-434-98509-0 (cased) : Unpriced
ISBN 0-434-98512-0 (pbk) : £2.95 B82-32243

Lovelock, William. The rudiments of music. — London : Bell & Hyman, Nov.1981. — [128]p
Originally published: 1966
ISBN 0-7135-0744-6 (pbk) : £2.95 : CIP entry
B81-34713

Newbould, Brian. Music to an unpurged ear / Brian Newbould. — Hull : University of Hull, 1981. — 24p : music ; 21cm
An inaugural lecture delivered in the University of Hull, 10 March 1981
ISBN 0-85958-436-4 (pbk) : £0.75 B82-13802

780 — Music — *For children*

Headington, Christopher. The performing world of the musician. — London : H. Hamilton, May 1981. — [128]p
ISBN 0-241-10587-0 : £5.95 : CIP entry
B81-12815

McLeish, Kenneth. A first companion to music. — London : Oxford University Press, Apr.1982. — [192]p
ISBN 0-19-314303-8 : £7.50 : CIP entry
B82-04281

780 — Music — *For Irish students*

Lally, Maureen. Listen sing and play / Maureen Lally. — Dublin : Educational Company
4: Fifth class: lessons 46-52, sixth class: lessons 53-60
Workbook. — c1978. — 32p : ill,music ; 19x25cm
Cover title
Unpriced (pbk) B82-23737

Mackenzie, Colin C.. Complete course in intermediate musicianship / Colin C. Mackenzie ; [illustrations Terry Myler (musical instruments)]. — Dublin : Educational Company, 1981. — 152p : ill,music,ports ; 21cm
Bibliography: p148. — Includes index
Unpriced (pbk) B82-02548

780 — Music — *Plot outlines — For schools*

Ensor, Wendy-Ann. Heroes and heroines in music / Wendy-Ann Ensor. — London : Oxford University Press, 1981. — 48p : ill(some col.),1map,music ; 28cm
ISBN 0-19-314925-7 (cased) : Unpriced
ISBN 0-19-321105-x (pbk) : Unpriced
B82-23033

780 — Music — *Stories, anecdotes*

Borge, Victor. [My favorite comedies in music]. Borge's musical briefs / Victor Borge [& Robert Sherman]. — London : Methuen London, 1982, c1981. — 150p ; 20cm
Originally published: London : Robson, 1981
ISBN 0-417-07500-6 (pbk) : £1.95 B82-39018

780 — Musical activities for children. Special subjects: Elizabeth I, *Queen of England — For schools*

Bagenal, Alison. A box of delights for Queen Elizabeth I / compiled by Alison and Michael Bagenal. — [Huntingdon] ([45 West St., Godmanchester, Huntingdon, Cambs.]) : [A. & M. Bagenal], [1981?]. — 1v.(loose leaf) : ill,music ; 30cm. — (Box of delights packs)
£1.75 B82-03931

780 — Musical activities for children. Special subjects: Pepys, Samuel — *For schools*

Bagenal, Alison. A box of delights for Samuel Pepys ... / compiled by Alison & Michael Bagenal. — [Huntingdon] ([45 West St., Godmanchester, Huntingdon, Cambs.]) : [A. & M. Bagenal], [1981?]. — 1v.(loose-leaf) : ill,music ; 30cm. — (Box of delights packs)
£1.75 B82-03932

780'.01 — Music, *800-1979.* **Research. Use of source materials —** *Case studies*

Source materials and the interpretation of music : a memorial volume to Thurston Dart / edited by Ian Bent. — London : Stainer & Bell, c1981. — 473p,[1]folded leaf of plates : ill,music,1port ; 25cm
Includes index
ISBN 0-85249-511-0 : £35.00 : CIP rev.
B80-05532

780'.01'0924 — Austria. Musicology. Adler, Guido. Interpersonal relationships with Mahler, Gustav

Reilly, Edward R.. Gustav Mahler and Guido Adler : records of a friendship / Edward R. Reilly. — Cambridge : Cambridge University Press, 1982. — viii,163p : music ; 22cm
Translation of: Gustav Mahler. — Bibliography: p144-155. — Includes index
ISBN 0-521-23592-8 : £12.50 : CIP rev.
Primary classification 780'.92'4 B82-03614

780'.01'0944 — Music. Research by Académie des sciences, *to ca 1790*

Cohen, Albert. Music in the French Royal Academy of Sciences : a study in the evolution of musical thought / by Albert Cohen. — Princeton ; Guildford : Princeton University Press, c1981. — xvii,150p,[8]p of plates : ill,facsims ; 25cm
Bibliography: p123-139. — Includes index
ISBN 0-691-09127-7 : £10.50 B82-13947

780'.08 — Western music *related to* **poetry,** *to 1980*

Winn, James Anderson. Unsuspected eloquence : a history of the relations between poetry and music / James Anderson Winn. — New Haven ; London : Yale University Press, c1981. — xiv,381p : ill,music ; 25cm
Bibliography: p347-365. — Includes index
ISBN 0-300-02615-3 : £13.25 : CIP rev.
B81-22673

780'.1 — Music. Aesthetics

Dahlhaus, Carl. Esthetics of music / Carl Dahlhaus ; translated by William W. Austin. — Cambridge : Cambridge University Press, 1982. — xii,115p ; 23cm
Translation of: Musikästhetik. — Bibliography: p101-112. — Includes index
ISBN 0-521-23508-1 (cased) : £9.95 : CIP rev.
ISBN 0-521-28007-9 (pbk) : £3.95 B81-37537

780'.1 — Music — *Philosophical perspectives — German texts*

Humanität Musik Erziehung / Karl Heinrich Ehrenforth (Hrsg.) ; mit Beiträgen von Rudolf Affeman ... [et al.]. — Mainz ; London : Schott, c1981. — 269p ; 24cm
German text
ISBN 3-7957-0064-7 (pbk) : £10.80
B82-12503

780'.1'5 — Music. Analysis. Theories of Schenker, Heinrich

Jonas, Oswald. Introduction to the theory of Heinrich Schenker : the nature of the musical work of art / Oswald Jonas ; translated and edited by John Rothgeb. — New York ; London : Longman, 1982. — xvi,175p : 1facsim,1port ; 25cm
Translation of: Einführung in die Lehre Heinrich Schenker
ISBN 0-582-28227-6 : £17.50 B82-34355

780'.1'5 — Music. Appreciation

Harrison, Sidney. How to appreciate music / Sidney Harrison. — London : Elm Tree, 1981. — 86p : ill,music ; 24cm
ISBN 0-241-10681-8 (pbk) : £6.95 : CIP rev.
ISBN 0-241-10682-6 (pbk) : £3.50 B81-32007

Schwartz, Elliott. Music : ways of listening / Elliott Schwartz. — New York ; London : Holt, Rinehart and Winston, c1982. — xvi,534p : ill,music,facsims,ports ; 25cm
Includes index
ISBN 0-03-044676-7 : £15.95 B82-25374

Short, Michael. Your book of music. — London : Faber, Oct.1982. — 1v.
ISBN 0-571-18031-0 : CIP entry B82-29077

780'.1'5 — Music. Criticism

On criticizing music : five philosophical perspectives / edited by Kingsley Price. — Baltimore, Md. ; London : Johns Hopkins University Press, c1981. — ix,117p : ill,music ; 27cm. — (The Alvin and Fanny Blaustein Thalheimer lectures ; 1978-79)
ISBN 0-8018-2613-6 : Unpriced B82-28090

780'.1'5 — Music — *For music appreciation*

Baker, Richard, *1925-*. Richard Baker's music guide. — London : Unwin, 1982, c1979. — 144p ; 18cm
Originally published: Newton Abbot : David and Charles, 1979. — Includes index
ISBN 0-04-780025-9 (pbk) : £1.50 : CIP rev. B82-03709

Hopkins, Antony. Understanding music / Antony Hopkins. — London : Dent, 1979 (1982 [printing]). — 255p : ill,music ; 24cm
Bibliography: p249. — Includes index
ISBN 0-460-02234-2 (pbk) : £4.95 B82-21594

780'.1'5 — Music — *For music appreciation — For schools*

Bennett, Roy, *1938-*. Enjoying music / Roy Bennett. — Harlow : Longman
Text on inside covers
Workbook 1. — 1981. — 32p : ill,music ; 19x25cm
ISBN 0-582-22067-x (pbk) : £0.75 B82-02035

Bennett, Roy, *1938-*. Enjoying music / Roy Bennett. — Harlow : Longman
Text on inside covers
Workbook 2. — 1981. — 32p : ill,music ; 19x25cm
ISBN 0-582-22068-8 (pbk) : £0.75 B82-02036

Bennett, Roy, *1938-*. Enjoying music / Roy Bennett. — Harlow : Longman
Text on inside covers
Workbook 3. — 1981. — 32p : ill,1map, music ; 19x25cm
ISBN 0-582-22069-6 (pbk) : £0.75 B82-02037

780'.1'5 — Music — *Formal analyses*

Tovey, Donald Francis. Essays in musical analysis / by Donald Francis Tovey. — New ed. — London : Oxford University Press
Previous ed.: published in 6v. 1935-1939
Concertos and choral works. — 1981. — viii,440p : music ; 23cm
ISBN 0-19-315148-0 (cased) : £9.50 : CIP rev.
ISBN 0-19-315149-9 (pbk) : Unpriced B81-25832

Tovey, Donald Francis. Essays in musical analysis / by Donald Francis Tovey. — New ed. — London : Oxford University Press
Previous ed.: published in 6v. 1935-1939
Symphonies and other orchestral works. — 1981. — xi,561p : music ; 23cm
ISBN 0-19-315146-4 (cased) : £9.50 : CIP rev.
ISBN 0-19-315147-2 (pbk) : £4.50 B81-25783

780'.23'41 — Great Britain. Music — *Career guides*

Parker, Julia M.. Working in the world of music / Julia M. Parker and Anna Alston. — London : Batsford Academic and Educational, 1982. — 132p,[8]p of plates : ill ; 23cm. — (Careers series)
Includes index
ISBN 0-7134-3959-9 : £5.95 B82-32785

780'.25'427 — Northern England. Music — *Directories*

Directory of northern music / compiled by Margaret Cowell. — 2nd ed. — Ashington : Mid-Northumberland Arts Group, 1981. — 53p ; 30cm
Previous ed.: 1981
ISBN 0-904790-14-2 (pbk) : £4.50 B82-39638

780'.3'21 — Music — *Encyclopaedias*

Dictionary of music / edited by Alan Isaacs, Elizabeth Martin. — London : Hamlyn, 1982. — 425p : ill,music ; 22cm
ISBN 0-600-33211-x : £6.95 B82-28404

780'.42 — Pop music

Baker, Glenn A.. The new music / Glenn A. Baker & Stuart Coupe. — London : Ring, 1980. — 128p : ill(some col.),ports ; 28cm
ISBN 0-85835-493-4 (pbk) : £2.95 B82-40536

780'.42 — Pop music — *Career guides*

Hayward, Hilary. Careers in the music business. — London : Kogan Page, Jan.1983. — [100]p. — (Kogan Page careers series)
ISBN 0-85038-609-8 (cased) : £6.95 : CIP entry
ISBN 0-85038-610-1 (pbk) : £2.50 B82-37465

780'.42 — Pop music — *For children*

Pirrie, Alastair. Razzmatazz : the all-action pop book / Alastair Pirrie ; additional research by Chris Cowey. — [London] : Sparrow, 1982. — 80p,[8]p of plates : ill,ports ; 18cm
ISBN 0-09-927890-1 (pbk) : £0.95 B82-16536

780'.42 — Pop music — *For schools*

Farmer, Paul, *1950-*. The story of pop / Paul Farmer. — Harlow : Longman, 1982. — 24p : ill,ports ; 23cm. — (Longman music topics)
ISBN 0-582-20017-2 (pbk) : £0.95 B82-35559

780'.42 — Pop music. Hit parade — *Serials*

Chart watch : Britain's densest music quarterly. — Vol.1, no.1 (1981)-. — Ilminster (17 Springfield, Ilminster, Somerset) : [s.n.], 1981-. — v. : ill,ports ; 30cm
ISSN 0262-9577 = Chart watch : £2.20 per year B82-12451

780'.42'05 — Pop music — *Serials*

New sounds, new styles. — No.1 (1981)-. — Market Harborough (New Sounds New Styles Subscriptions Department, Competition House, Market Harborough, Leics.) : EMAP National Publications Ltd, 1981-. — v. : ill(some col.),ports(some col.) ; 28cm
Monthly. — Description based on: No.6 (Dec. 1981)
ISSN 0262-5598 = New sounds, new styles : £7.80 per year B82-17254

780'.42'05 — Popular music — *Serials*

Popular music. — 1-. — Cambridge : Cambridge University Press, 1981-. — v. : ill,music,ports ; 24cm
Annual
ISSN 0261-1430 = Popular music : Unpriced B82-31721

780'.42'07041 — Great Britain. Educational institutions. Curriculum subjects: Popular music. Teaching

Pop, rock and ethnic music in school / edited by Graham Vulliamy and Ed Lee. — Cambridge : Cambridge University Press, 1982. — ix,244p : ill,1map,music ; 24cm. — (Resources of music)
Includes bibliographies and index
ISBN 0-521-23341-0 (cased) : Unpriced : CIP rev.
ISBN 0-521-29927-6 (pbk) : Unpriced B82-01718

Vulliamy, Graham. Popular music : a teacher's guide / Graham Vulliamy, Edward Lee. — London : Routledge & Kegan Paul, 1982. — viii,127p : ill,music ; 22cm. — (Routledge popular music)
Includes bibliographies and lists of sound discs
ISBN 0-7100-0895-3 (pbk) : £4.95 B82-29259

780'.42'076 — Pop music — *Questions & answers*

Sinclair, Jill. Pop quiz : from the BBC televison programme / questions compiled by Jill Sinclair and Frances Whitaker. — London : British Broadcasting Corporation, 1982. — 64p : maps,ports ; 20cm
ISBN 0-563-20085-5 (pbk) : £1.25 B82-31349

780'.42'09 — Popular music, *to 1981 — For children*

McLeish, Kenneth. The Oxford first companion to music round the world / Kenneth and Valerie McLeish. — London : Oxford University Press Music Department, 1982. — 32p : ill(some col.),1map,music,ports(some col.) ; 32cm
Also published as section B of the Oxford first companion to music. — Cover title. — Text on inside cover
ISBN 0-19-321434-2 (pbk) : Unpriced B82-39417

780'.42'0904 — Popular music, *1900-1968*

Shepherd, John. Tin Pan Alley / John Shepherd. — London : Routledge & Kegan Paul, 1982. — vi,154p : ill,facsims,ports ; 23cm. — (Routledge popular music)
Bibliography: p150-151. — List of sound discs: p151. — Includes index
ISBN 0-7100-0904-6 : £5.95 B82-29260

780'.42'0904 — Popular music, *ca 1950-1981*

Norman, Philip. The road goes on for ever. — London : Hamilton, Sept.1982. — [192]p
ISBN 0-241-10862-4 (pbk) : £5.95 : CIP entry B82-20166

780'.42'09046 — Popular music, *1963-1978*

Jewell, Derek. The popular voice : a musical record of the 60s and 70s / Derek Jewell. — London : Sphere, 1981, c1980. — 256p,[8]p of plates : ports ; 20cm
Originally published: London : Deutsch, 1980. — Includes index
ISBN 0-7221-5099-7 (pbk) : £2.25 B82-07078

780'.42'0941 — British popular music, *to 1914*

Lee, Ed. Folksong & music hall / Edward Lee. — London : Routledge & Kegan Paul, 1982. — x,148p : ill,facsims,ports ; 23cm. — (Routledge popular music)
Bibliography: p145-146. — List of sound discs: p146. — Includes index
ISBN 0-7100-0902-x : £5.95 : CIP rev. B82-09597

780'.42'0941 — Great Britain. Pop music — *For non-English speaking students*

Rees-Parnall, Hilary. Tune in : pop music in Britain today / Hilary Rees-Parnall. — London : Harrap, 1981. — 48p : ill,ports ; 22cm. — (Britain today. Intermediate)
ISBN 0-245-53716-3 (pbk) : £1.10 B82-00743

780'.42'0973 — American pop music, *1975-1980*

Giddins, Gary. Riding on a blue note : jazz and American pop / Gary Giddins. — New York ; Oxford : Oxford University Press, 1981. — xv,313p ; 22cm
Includes index
ISBN 0-19-502835-x : £12.95
Primary classification 785.42'0973 B82-25968

780'.5 — Music — *For children — Serials*

Concert magazine. — Vol.1, no.1 (24 Oct. 1981)-. — London (143 King Henry's Rd, NW3 3RD) : Ernest Read Music Association, 1981-. — v. : ill,music ; 21cm
Six issues yearly. — Description based on: Vol.1, no.5 (27 Mar. 1982)
ISSN 0263-3841 = Concert magazine : £0.20 per issue B82-24761

780'.5 — Music — *Serials*

Classical sounds. — No.1 (June 1982)-. — Stamford (1 Wothorpe Rd., Stamford, Lincs. PE9 2JR) : Key Pub., 1982-. — v. : ill(some col.),ports ; 30cm
Monthly
ISSN 0262-8961 = Classical sounds : £12.00 per year B82-33854

Collusion. — Issue 1 (Aug. 1981)-. — London (114 Philip La., N15) : Music/Context, 1981-. — v. : ill,ports ; 30cm
Three issues yearly
ISSN 0262-7078 = Collusion : £3.50 per issue B82-06790

780'.6 — Music. Clubs. Organisation — *Manuals*

Dutton, Phyl. Music clubs, festivals & concerts : and how to organise them / by Phyl Dutton. — Old Woking : Gresham, 1981. — 113p : ill,1port ; 21cm
Bibliography: p113. — Includes index
ISBN 0-905418-86-7 (pbk) : £5.50 B82-37737

780'.6'041 — Great Britain. Music. Organisations: Incorporated Society of Musicians, *to 1982*

Incorporated Society of Musicians. The ISM — the first hundred years : a short history of the Society / compiled and written by Edmund Bohan ; in honour of the centenary in October 1982 of Incorporated Society of Musicians. — London (10 Stratford Place, W1N 9AE) : The Society, [1982]. — 80p : ill,facsims,ports ; 30cm
Bibliography: p80. — Includes index
Unpriced (pbk) B82-26905

780′.7 — Education. Curriculum subjects: Music — *Conference proceedings — German texts*
Bundesschulmusikwoche *(13th : 1980 : Braunschweig).* Musikerziehung als Herausforderung der Gegenwart : didaktische Interpretation von Musik, Beurteilungskriterien im Musikunterricht, Methodenrepertoire : Kongressbericht 13. Bundesschulmusikwoche, Braunschweig 1980 / herausgegeben im Auftrag des Verbandes Deutscher Schulmusikerzieher von Karl Heinrich Ehrenforth. — Mainz ; London : Schott, c1981. — 391p : ill,music ; 21cm
ISBN 3-7957-2643-3 (pbk) : £10.20
B82-37967

780′.7′043 — Germany. Education. Curriculum subjects: Music. Teaching, *1918-1933 — German texts*
Martin, Wolfgang. Studien zur Musikpädagogik der Weimarer Republik : Ansätze einer Theorie des Musiklernens bei W. Kühn, F. Reuter, G. Schünemann und R. Wicke / Wolfgang Martin. — Mainz ; London : Schott, c1982. — 285p ; 21cm. — (Musikpädagogik, ISSN 0172-8202 ; bd.19)
Bibliography: p275-285. — Includes index
ISBN 3-7957-1718-3 (pbk) : £9.60 B82-37968

780′.7′2 — Secondary schools. Curriculum subjects: Music. Teaching
Swanwick, Keith. Discovering music : developing the music curriculum in secondary schools / Keith Swanwick, Dorothy Taylor. — London : Batsford, c1982. — 144p : music ; 23cm
Bibliography: p140-141. — Includes index
ISBN 0-7134-4065-1 : £6.95 : CIP rev.
B82-15921

780′.7′2941 — Great Britain. Middle schools. Activities: Creative music. Projects
Sturman, Paul. Creating music / Paul Sturman. — Harlow : Longman, 1982. — 64p : ill,maps,music,ports ; 22x28cm
ISBN 0-582-20001-6 (pbk) : £1.75 B82-17770

780′.7′2941 — Great Britain. Schools. Curriculum subjects: Music
Issues in music education / Charles Plummeridge ... [et al.]. — London : University of London Institute of Education, c1981. — 45p ; 21cm. — (Bedford Way papers, ISSN 0261-0078 ; 3)
ISBN 0-85473-105-9 (pbk) : £1.50 B82-08683

780′.7′2942 — England. Comprehensive schools. Curriculum subjects: Music
Farmer, Paul, *1950-.* Music in the comprehensive school / Paul Farmer. — London : Oxford University Press, 1979. — 74p : ill,music ; 22cm
Bibliography: p68-74
ISBN 0-19-317415-4 (pbk) : £3.95 B82-14605

780′.7′2942 — England. Secondary schools. Curriculum subjects: Music. Teaching
Paynter, John. Music in the secondary school curriculum. — Cambridge : Cambridge University Press, Aug.1982. — [256]p
ISBN 0-521-24627-x (cased) : £10.50 : CIP entry
ISBN 0-521-28860-6 (pbk) : £5.75 B82-28455

780′.7′2973 — United States. Education. Curriculum subjects: Music, *to 1981*
Keene, James A.. A history of music education in the United States / James A. Keene. — Hanover ; London : University Press of New England, 1982. — ix,396p,[4]p of plates : music,ports ; 25cm
Includes index
ISBN 0-87451-212-3 : £22.50 B82-39736

780′.7′3 — Gospel music. Concerts. Organisation — *Manuals*
Concert presentations : a handbook for gospel concert organisers / editor Eric A. Thorn. — Maidstone : Third Day Enterprises, 1981. — 15p : ill ; 21cm
ISBN 0-9505912-4-6 (pbk) : £0.75 : CIP rev.
B81-13467

780′.7′3 — Music. Performance — *Stories, anecdotes*
Lebrecht, Norman. Discord. — London : Deutsch, Sept.1982. — [240]p
ISBN 0-233-97442-3 : £8.95 : CIP entry
B82-18842

780′.75′094385 — Poland. Grüssau. Monasteries: Grüssau *(Monastery).* **Musical scores. Disappearance,** *1946*
Lewis, Nigel. Paperchase : Mozart, Beethoven, Bach — the search for their lost music / by Nigel Lewis. — London : Hamilton, 1981. — x,246p : 2maps ; 23cm
Includes index
ISBN 0-241-10235-9 : £9.95 : CIP rev.
B81-25703

780′.7′924 — Music festivals, *1980 — Personal observations*
Levin, Bernard. Conducted tour / Bernard Levin. — London : Cape, 1981. — viii,240p ; 22cm
Includes index
ISBN 0-224-01896-5 : £7.50 : CIP rev.
B81-27343

Levin, Bernard. Conducted tour. — London : Coronet, Feb.1983. — [256]p
Originally published: London : Cape, 1981
ISBN 0-340-32359-0 (pbk) : £2.50 : CIP entry
B82-38069

780.9 — MUSIC. HISTORICAL AND GEOGRAPHICAL TREATMENT

780′.9 — Music, *to 1700 — Serials*
Early music history. — 1-. — Cambridge : Cambridge University Press, 1981-. — v. : ill,music,facsims ; 24cm
Annual
ISSN 0261-1279 = Early music history : Unpriced B82-27655

780′.9 — Music, *to 1960*
The **New** Oxford history of music. — Oxford : Oxford University Press, Oct.1982
Vol.8: The age of Beethoven 1790-1830. — [752]p
ISBN 0-19-316308-x : £20.00 : CIP entry
B82-23678

780′.9 — Music, *to 1981 — For children*
McLeish, Kenneth. The Oxford first companion to the story of music / Kenneth and Valerie McLeish. — London : Oxford University Press Music Department, 1982. — 32p : ill(some col.),music,ports ; 32cm
Also published as section E of the Oxford first companion to music. — Cover title. — Text on inside covers
ISBN 0-19-321437-7 (pbk) : Unpriced
B82-39415

780′.9 — Western music, *to 1980*
Grout, Donald Jay. A history of western music. — London : Dent, Dec.1981. — [864]p
ISBN 0-460-04546-6 : £12.95 : CIP entry
B81-31723

780′.902 — Western music, *1000-1650 — Encyclopaedias*
Roche, Jerome. A dictionary of early music : from the Troubadours to Monteverdi / by Jerome & Elizabeth Roche. — London : Faber Music in association with Faber & Faber, 1981. — 208p : ill,music ; 19cm
ISBN 0-571-10035-x (cased) : £6.95 : CIP rev.
ISBN 0-571-10036-8 (pbk) : Unpriced
B81-21533

780′.903′4 — Music, *ca 1780-ca 1970 — Critical studies*
Cooke, Deryck. Vindications : essays on romantic music / by Deryck Cooke ; with a memoir of the author by Bryan Magee. — London : Faber, 1982. — 226p : music ; 23cm
ISBN 0-571-11795-3 : £12.50 : CIP rev.
B82-11308

780′.904 — Music, *ca 1950-1980 — Critical studies — German texts*
Reflexionen über Musik heute : Text und Analysen / herausgegeben von Wilfried Gruhn ; mit Beiträgen von Wilfried Gruhn ... [et al.]. — Mainz ; London ([48 Great Marlborough St., W1V 2BN]) : Schott, c1981. — 348p : ill,music ; 24cm
Bibliography: p318-338. — Includes index
ISBN 3-7957-2648-4 (pbk) : £20.40
B82-25659

780′.92′2 — American music. Composers — *Interviews*
Soundpieces : interviews with American composers / [compiled] by Cole Gagne and Tracy Caras ; with introductory essays by Nicolas Slonimsky and Gilbert Chase ; photographs by Gene Bagnato. — Metuchen ; London : Scarecrow, 1982. — xviii,418p : ports ; 23cm
Includes lists of works and index
ISBN 0-8108-1474-9 : £18.00 B82-17416

780′.92′2 — English music. Britten, Benjamin & Tippett, Michael — *Critical studies*
Whittall, Arnold. The music of Britten and Tippett : studies in themes and techniques / Arnold Whittall. — Cambridge : Cambridge University Press, 1982. — vii,314p : music,1port ; 24cm
Bibliography: p308. — Includes index
ISBN 0-521-23523-5 : £24.00 : CIP rev.
B82-13258

780′.92′2 — Instrumentalists, *1900-1950*
Hamilton, David, *1935 Jan.18-.* Great instrumentalists / by David Hamilton. — Poole : Blandford, 1982. — 136p : ports ; 23cm. — (The Listener′s guide) (A Quarto book)
Includes index
ISBN 0-7137-1253-8 : £4.95 : CIP rev.
B82-01199

780′.92′2 — Irish music. Composers — *Biographies*
Irish composers. — Dublin (70 Merrion Sq., Dublin 2) : Arts Council, [1980]. — 1portfolio : ports ; 30cm
Unpriced B82-23432

780′.92′2 — Music. Composers, *1567-1981 — Biographies — For children*
McLeish, Kenneth. The Oxford first companion to composers and their music / Kenneth and Valerie McLeish. — London : Oxford University Press Music Department, 1982. — 32p : ill(some col.),1col.map,music,ports(some col.) ; 32cm
Also published as section F of the Oxford first companion to music. — Cover title. — Text on inside covers
ISBN 0-19-321438-5 (pbk) : Unpriced
B82-39418

780′.92′2 — Music. Composers, *1860-1960 — Illustrations*
Great composers in historic photographs : 244 portraits from the 1860s to the 1960s / edited by James Camner. — New York : Dover ; London : Constable, 1981. — 125p : of ports ; 29cm
ISBN 0-486-24132-7 (pbk) : £6.00 B82-13378

780′.92′2 — Norwegian music. Composers, *1920-1980*
Grinde, Nils. Contemporary Norwegian music 1920-1980 / Nils Grinde ; translated by Sandra Hamilton. — Oslo : Universitetsforlaget ; London : Global Book Research [[distributor]], c1981. — 117p : ill,ports ; 25cm
Translation from the Norwegian. — Bibliography: p115-117. — Includes index
ISBN 82-00-05693-7 (pbk) : £11.00
B82-01787

780′.92′2 — Western music. Composers, *1730-1980 — Critical studies*
Granville Barker, Frank. Music / Frank Granville Barker ; introduction by Riccardo Muti. — [London] : Windward, c1981. — 288p : ill(some col.),music,3facsims,ports(some col.] ; 25cm
Includes index
ISBN 0-7112-0099-8 : £9.95 B82-03946

780′.92′2 — Western music. Women composers, *ca 1940-1980 — Biographies*
Contemporary concert music by women : a directory of the composers and their works / compiled and edited by Judith Lang Zaimont and Karen Famera ; a project of the International League of Women Composers. — Westport, Conn. ; London : Greenwood Press, 1981. — x,355p : music,ports ; 25cm
Includes index
ISBN 0-313-22921-x : £18.95 B82-18370

780'.92'2 — Western music. Women composers, *to 1980 — Biographies*
Cohen, Aaron I.. International encyclopedia of women composers / Aaron I. Cohen. — New York ; London : Bowker, 1981. — xviii,597p : 1ill,ports ; 29cm
Bibliography: p587-597
ISBN 0-8352-1288-2 : Unpriced B82-06194

780'.92'4 — American music. Cage, John, *1912- — Critical studies*
Griffiths, Paul. Cage / Paul Griffiths. — London : Oxford University Press, 1981. — 50p : ill,music ; 22cm. — (Oxford studies of composers ; 18)
Bibliography: p50
ISBN 0-19-315450-1 (pbk) : £4.95 B82-01262

780'.92'4 — American music. Grainger, Percy Aldridge *— Biographies*
Bird, John, *1941-*. Percy Grainger / John Bird. — London : Faber and Faber, 1982. — xv,319p,[24]p of plates : ill,ports ; 24cm
Originally published: London : Elek, 1976. — Bibliography: p258-260. — Includes index
ISBN 0-571-11717-1 (pbk) : £5.95 : CIP rev. B81-38320

780'.92'4 — American music. Grainger, Percy Aldridge *— Critical studies*
The **Percy** Grainger companion / edited by Lewis Foreman. — London : Thames, 1981. — 268p : ill,music,facsims,ports ; 25cm
Ill, ports on lining papers. — Bibliography: p251-257. — List of sound discs: p237-240. — Includes index
ISBN 0-905210-12-3 : £14.95 : CIP rev. B81-14786

780'.92'4 — American music. Grainger, Percy Aldridge *— Lists*
Percy Grainger. — London : Schott in association with the Percy Grainger Society, 1982. — 44p ; 21cm
ISBN 0-901938-79-3 (pbk) : Unpriced B82-33995

780'.92'4 — American music. Stravinsky, Igor *— Biographies*
Druskin, Mikhail Semyonovich. Igor Stravinsky : his life, works and views. — Cambridge : Cambridge University Press, Sept.1982. — [194]p
Translation of: Igor Stravinsky — lichnost', tvorchestvo, vzglîady
ISBN 0-521-24590-7 : £13.50 : CIP entry B82-25500

780'.92'4 — American music. Stravinsky, Igor *— Correspondence, diaries, etc.*
Stravinskiĭ, Igor'. Selected correspondence. — London : Faber
Vol.1. — Apr.1982. — [416]p
ISBN 0-571-11724-4 : £25.00 : CIP entry B82-04859

780'.92'4 — American music. Stravinsky, Igor *— Critical studies*
Keller, Hans. Stravinsky seen and heard. — London (40 Floral St., W.C.2) : Toccata Press, Mar.1982. — [128]p
ISBN 0-907689-01-9 (cased) : £5.95 : CIP entry
ISBN 0-907689-02-7 (pbk) : £2.95 B82-06535

780'.92'4 — American music. Stravinsky, Igor *— Illustrations*
Igor and Vera Stravinsky : a photograph album 1921 to 1971 / text from Stravinsky's interviews 1912-1963 ; 258 photographs selected by Vera Stravinsky and Rita McCaffrey ; captions by Robert Craft. — [London] : Thames and Hudson, c1982. — 144p : ill,ports ; 30cm
ISBN 0-500-01283-0 : £10.00 B82-32914

780'.92'4 — American music. Stravinsky, Igor *— Interviews*
Stravinsky, Igor. Dialogues / Igor Stravinsky and Robert Craft. — London : Faber Music, 1982. — 152p : ill,ports ; 21cm
Originally published with extracts from Robert Craft's diary as : Dialogues and a diary, 1968. — Includes index
ISBN 0-571-10043-0 (pbk) : £3.95 : CIP rev. B81-30966

Stravinsky, Igor. Expositions and developments / Igor Stravinsky and Robert Craft. — London : Faber Music in association with Faber, 1962 (1981 [printing]). — 168p : ill,1map,music,1facsim,1plan,ports ; 21cm
Includes index
ISBN 0-571-10034-1 (pbk) : £3.50 B82-01774

Stravinsky, Igor. Memories and commentaries / Igor Stravinsky and Robert Craft. — London : Faber Music in association with Faber, 1960, c1959 (1981 [printing]). — 183p : ill,music,facsims,ports,1geneal.table ; 21cm
Includes index
ISBN 0-571-10033-3 (pbk) : £3.50 B82-01773

780'.92'4 — Austrian music. Mahler, Gustav. Interpersonal relationships with Adler, Guido
Reilly, Edward R.. Gustav Mahler and Guido Adler : records of a friendship / Edward R. Reilly. — Cambridge : Cambridge University Press, 1982. — viii,163p : music ; 22cm
Translation of: Gustav Mahler. — Bibliography: p144-155. — Includes index
ISBN 0-521-23592-8 : £12.50 : CIP rev.
Also classified at 780'.01'0924 B82-03614

780'.92'4 — Austrian music. Mozart, Wolfgang Amadeus *— Biographies*
Baker, Richard, *1925-*. Mozart / Richard Baker. — [London] : Thames and Hudson, c1982. — 144p : ill,1map,music,facsims,ports ; 24cm
Bibliography: p137. — Includes index
ISBN 0-500-01269-5 : £6.95 B82-22447

Hildesheimer, Wolfgang. Mozart. — London : Dent, Jan.1982. — [415]p
ISBN 0-460-04347-1 : £15.00 : CIP entry B81-34496

780'.92'4 — Austrian music. Schubert, Franz *— Biographies*
Gammond, Peter. Schubert / Peter Gammond. — London : Methuen, 1982. — xi,182p : 1port ; 20cm. — (The Composer as contemporary)
Bibliography: p174-175. — Includes index
ISBN 0-413-46990-5 : £8.95 : CIP rev. B82-19230

780'.92'4 — Belgian music. Lassus, Orlande de *— Critical studies*
Roche, Jerome. Lassus / Jerome Roche. — London : Oxford University Press, 1982. — vi,58p : music ; 22cm. — (Oxford studies of composers ; 19)
Bibliography: p58
ISBN 0-19-315237-1 (pbk) : £4.95 : CIP rev. B82-04840

780'.92'4 — Czechoslovak music. Janáček, Leoš *— Biographies*
Horsbrugh, Ian. Leoš Janáček : the field that prospered / Ian Horsbrugh. — Newton Abbot : David & Charles, c1981. — 327p : ill,1map,music,facsims,ports ; 24cm
Bibliography: p317-318. — Includes index
ISBN 0-7153-8060-5 : £12.50 : CIP rev. B81-30578

Vogel, Jaroslav. Leoš Janáček : a biography / by Jaroslav Vogel ; with a foreword by Sir Charles Mackerras. — Rev. ed. / prepared by Karel Janovický. — London : Orbis, 1981. — 439p,[16]p of plates : ill,2maps,music,facsims,ports ; 25cm
Translation from the Czech. — Previous ed.: London : Hamlyn, 1962
ISBN 0-85613-045-1 : Unpriced B82-01484

780'.92'4 — English music. Bax, Arnold *— Biographies*
Foreman, Lewis. Bax. — London : Scolar Press, May 1982. — [464]p
ISBN 0-85967-643-9 : £25.00 : CIP entry B82-07679

780'.92'4 — English music. Britten, Benjamin *— Biographies*
Headington, Christopher. Britten. — London : Eyre Methuen, July 1981. — [200]p. — (The composer as contemporary)
ISBN 0-413-46510-1 : £7.00 : CIP entry
ISBN 0-413-48280-4 (pbk) : Unpriced B81-15846

Kennedy, Michael, *1926-*. Britten. — London : Dent, Jan.1983. — [368]p. — (The Master musicians series)
Originally published: 1981
ISBN 0-460-02201-6 (pbk) : £5.95 : CIP entry B82-34609

White, Eric Walter. Benjamin Britten. — New ed. — London : Faber, Feb.1983. — [32]p
Previous ed.: 1970
ISBN 0-571-18066-3 (cased) : CIP entry
ISBN 0-571-11946-8 (pbk) B82-38700

780'.92'4 — English music. Davies, Peter Maxwell *— Critical studies*
Griffiths, Paul. Peter Maxwell Davies / Paul Griffiths. — London : Robson, 1982, c1981. — 196p,[8]p of plates : ill,music,1port ; 23cm. — (The Contemporary composers)
Bibliography: p191-192. — Includes index
ISBN 0-86051-138-3 : £7.95 : CIP rev. B81-27443

780'.92'4 — English music. Delius, Frederick *— Personal observations*
Fenby, Eric. Delius : as I knew him / Eric Fenby. — New and rev. ed. — London : Faber, 1981 300 262p,[8]p of plates : ill (music,1facsim), 20cm [pbk]. — [288]p
Previous ed.: i.e. New ed.: London : Icon, 1966. — Includes index
ISBN 0-571-11836-4 (pbk) : £3.95 : CIP rev. B81-27411

780'.92'4 — English music. Dowland, John *— Critical studies*
Poulton, Diana. John Dowland / Diana Poulton. — New and rev. ed. — London : Faber, 1982. — 528p,[16]p of plates : ill,facsims,music,ports ; 26cm
Previous ed.: 1972. — Bibliography: p1972. — Includes index
ISBN 0-571-18022-1 (cased) : £15.00 : CIP rev. B81-21468

780'.92'4 — English music. Elgar, Edward *— Biographies*
Kennedy, Michael, *1926-*. Portrait of Elgar / Michael Kennedy. — 2nd ed. — London : Oxford University Press, 1982. — 391p,[12]p of plates : ill,facsims,ports ; 22cm
Previous ed.: 1968. — Bibliography: p360-363. — Includes index
ISBN 0-19-315414-5 (cased) : Unpriced : CIP rev.
ISBN 0-19-315432-3 (pbk) : £6.95 B82-01580

780'.92'4 — English music. Gurney, Ivor, *1915-1918 — Correspondence, diaries, etc.*
Gurney, Ivor. War letters. — Manchester : Carcanet Press, Oct.1982. — [224]p
ISBN 0-85635-408-2 : £6.95 : CIP entry B82-24118

780'.92'4 — English music. Head, Michael *— Biographies*
Bush, Nancy. Michael Head. — London : Kahn & Averill, Apr.1982. — [96]p
ISBN 0-900707-73-9 (pbk) : £2.95 : CIP entry B82-10678

780'.92'4 — English music. Holst, Gustav *— Biographies*
Holst, Imogen. Holst / Imogen Holst. — 2nd ed. — London : Faber & Faber, 1981. — 93p : ill,music,facsims,ports ; 23cm. — (The Great composers)
Previous ed.: 1974. — Bibliography: p88. — Includes index
ISBN 0-571-18032-9 : £4.95 : CIP rev. B81-31105

780'.92'4 — English music. Hopkins, Antony *— Biographies*
Hopkins, Antony. Beating time / by Antony Hopkins. — London : Joseph, 1982. — 224p,[24]p of plates : ill,ports ; 25cm
Includes index
ISBN 0-7181-2131-7 : £8.95 B82-28500

780'.92'4 — English music. Le Fleming, Christopher — *Biographies*

Le Fleming, Christopher. Journey into music : (by the slow train) : an autobiography / Christopher le Fleming. — Bristol (Redcliffe), 1982. — viii,200p,[12]p of plates : ill,ports ; 25cm
Includes index
ISBN 0-905459-42-3 : £8.50 B82-26918

780'.92'4 — English music. Purcell, Henry — *Critical studies*

Hutchings, Arthur. Purcell / Arthur Hutchings. — London : British Broadcasting Corporation, 1982. — 87p : music ; 20cm. — (BBC music guides)
Includes index
ISBN 0-563-17184-7 (pbk) : £3.00 B82-37179

780'.92'4 — English music. Tippett, Michael — *Critical studies*

Bowen, Meirion. Michael Tippett / Meirion Bowen. — London : Robson, 1982, c1981. — 196p,[8]p of plates : ill,music,1facsim,ports ; 23cm. — (The Contemporary composers)
Bibliography: p175-177. — Includes index
ISBN 0-86051-137-5 : £7.95 : CIP rev. B81-27450

780'.92'4 — French music. Berlioz, Hector — *Biographies*

Berlioz, Hector. The memoirs of Hector Berlioz, member of The French Institute : including his travels in Italy, Germany, Russia and England, 1803-1865 / translated and edited by David Cairns. — London : Granada, 1970, c1969 (1981 [printing]). — 792p,[8]p of plates : ill,1facsim,ports ; 18cm. — (A Panther book)
Translation of: Mémoires de Hector Berlioz. — Originally published: London : Gollancz, 1969. — Bibliography: p769-772. — Includes index
ISBN 0-586-03408-0 (pbk) : £3.95 B82-06357

Macdonald, Hugh. Berlioz. — London : Dent, Oct.1982. — [288]p. — (The Master musicians series)
ISBN 0-460-03156-2 : £8.95 : CIP entry B82-23989

780'.92'4 — French music. Chabrier, Emmanuel — *Biographies*

Poulenc, Francis. Emmanuel Chabrier / Francis Poulenc ; translated by Cynthia Jolly. — London : Dobson, 1981. — 104p,[8]p of plates : ill,music,2facsims,ports ; 22cm
Translation of: Emmanuel Chabrier
ISBN 0-234-77252-2 : £6.95 B82-14706

780'.92'4 — French music. Chausson, Ernest — *Critical studies*

Grover, Ralph Scott. Ernest Chausson : the man and his music / Ralph Scott Grover. — London : Athlone, 1980. — 245p : music,1port ; 22cm
Originally published: Lewisburg : Bucknell University Press, 1980. — Lists of sound discs: p228-229. — Bibliography: p230-236. — Includes index
ISBN 0-485-11217-5 : £9.50 : CIP rev. B80-30119

780'.92'4 — French music. Couperin, François — *Critical studies*

Tunley, David. Couperin / David Tunley. — London : British Broadcasting Corporation, 1982. — 104p : music ; 20cm. — (BBC music guides)
Includes index
ISBN 0-563-17851-5 (pbk) : £3.00 B82-38955

780'.92'4 — French music. Dufay, Guillaume — *Critical studies*

Fallows, David, *1945-*. Dufay / David Fallows. — London : Dent, 1982. — viii,321p,[12]p of plates : ill,facsims,3maps,music,ports ; 23cm. — (The Master musicians series)
Bibliography: p259-273. — Includes index
ISBN 0-460-03180-5 : £9.95 : CIP rev. B82-06844

780'.92'4 — German music, *1940-1980* — *Personal observations*

Henze, Hans Werner. Music and politics : collected writings 1953-81 / Hans Werner Henze ; translated by Peter Labanyi. — London : Faber, 1982. — 286p,[8]p of plates : ill,ports ; 23cm
Based on Musik und Politik: Schriften und Gespräche 1955-1975 edited by Jens Brockmeier. — Translations from the German
ISBN 0-571-11719-8 : £15.00 : CIP rev. B82-11301

780'.92'4 — German music. Beethoven, Ludwig van — *Critical studies*

Beethoven studies. — Cambridge : Cambridge University Press, July 1982
Vols. 1 & 2 published by Oxford University Press
3. — [292]p
ISBN 0-521-24131-6 : £25.00 : CIP entry B82-13263

780'.92'4 — German music. Eisler, Hanns — *Critical studies*

Betz, Albrecht. Hanns Eisler political musician / Albrecht Betz ; translated by Bill Hopkins. — Cambridge : Cambridge University Press, 1982. — ix,326p : facsims,music,ports ; 23cm
Translation of: Hanns Eisler. — Bibliography: p270-275. — Includes index
ISBN 0-521-24022-0 : £25.00 : CIP rev. B82-13262

780'.92'4 — German music. Mendelssohn Bartholdy, Felix — *Biographies*

Moshansky, Mozelle. Mendelssohn : his life and times / Mozelle Moshansky. — Speldhurst : Midas, 1982. — 144p : ill,facsims,music,ports ; 26cm
Bibliography: p7. — Includes index
ISBN 0-85936-083-0 : £7.50 B82-24082

780'.92'4 — German music. Schumann, Robert — *Biographies*

Dawley, Tim. Schumann : his life and times / Tim Dawley. — Speldhurst : Midas, 1982. — 144p : ill,facsims,music,ports ; 26cm
Bibliography: p142. — Includes index
ISBN 0-85936-150-0 : £7.50 B82-24083

Taylor, Ronald, *1924-*. Robert Schumann : his life and work. — London : Granada, Aug.1982. — [352]p
ISBN 0-246-11361-8 : £12.50 : CIP entry B82-15703

780'.92'4 — German music. Strauss, Richard — *Biographies*

Schuh, Willi. Richard Strauss : a chronicle of the early years 1864-1898 / Willi Schuh ; translated by Mary Whittall. — Cambridge : Cambridge University Press, 1982. — xvii,555p : ill,facsims,ports ; 24cm
Translation of: Richard Strauss. — Bibliography : p534-535. — Includes index
ISBN 0-521-24104-9 : £35.00 : CIP rev. B82-09738

780'.92'4 — German music. Wagner, Cosima — *Biographies*

Marek, George. Cosima Wagner. — London : Julia Macrae, Feb.1983. — [292]p
ISBN 0-86203-120-6 : £12.95 : CIP entry B82-39824

780'.92'4 — German music. Wagner, Cosima. Marriage to Wagner, Richard

Skelton, Geoffrey. Richard and Cosima Wagner : biography of a marriage / by Geoffrey Skelton. — London : Gollancz, 1982. — 319p,[12]p of plates : ill,ports ; 24cm
Bibliography: p307-310. — Includes index
ISBN 0-575-03017-8 : £17.50 : CIP rev.
Primary classification 782.1'092'4 B81-38324

780'.92'4 — Irish music. O'Riada, Sean — *Critical studies*

Integrating tradition : the achievement of Sean O'Riada. — Dublin : Irish Humanities Centre, Oct.1981. — [170]p
ISBN 0-906462-04-5 : £10.00 : CIP entry B81-28012

780'.92'4 — Italian music. Monteverdi, Claudio — *Critical studies*

Arnold, Denis. Monteverdi church music / Denis Arnold. — London : British Broadcasting Corporation, 1982. — 64p ; 20cm. — (BBC music guides)
Includes index
ISBN 0-563-12884-4 (pbk) : £2.25 B82-36847

780'.92'4 — Italian music. Paganini, Nicolò — *Biographies*

Kendall, Alan, *1939-*. Paganini. — London : Hamilton, Oct.1982. — [160]p
ISBN 0-241-10845-4 : £9.95 : CIP entry B82-23463

780'.92'4 — Music. Legge, Walter — *Biographies*

Schwarzkopf, Elisabeth. On and off the record : a memoir of Walter Legge. — London : Faber, Sept.1982. — [250]p
ISBN 0-571-11928-x : £9.50 : CIP entry
Also classified at 780'.92'4 B82-19549

780'.92'4 — Music — *Personal observations*

Burgess, Anthony. This man and music / Anthony Burgess. — London : Hutchinson, 1982. — 192p : music ; 23cm
ISBN 0-09-149610-1 : £7.95 : CIP rev. B82-17191

Schwarzkopf, Elisabeth. On and off the record : a memoir of Walter Legge. — London : Faber, Sept.1982. — [250]p
ISBN 0-571-11928-x : £9.50 : CIP entry
Primary classification 780'.92'4 B82-19549

780'.92'4 — Poland. Óswięcim. Concentration camps: Auschwitz *(Concentration camp).* **Women prisoners,** *1944-1945:* **Musicians** — *Personal observations*

Fénelon, Fania. Playing for time / Fania Fénelon with Marcelle Routier ; translated from the French by Judith Landry. — London : Sphere, 1980, c1979 (1981 [printing]). — 253p ; 18cm
Translation of: Sursis pour l'orchestre. — Originally published: as The musicians of Auschwitz. — London : Joseph, 1977
ISBN 0-7221-3468-1 (pbk) : £1.25 B82-00075

780'.92'4 — Polish music. Gliński, Mateusz — *Correspondence, diaries, etc. — Polish texts*

Gliński, Mateusz. Testament Mateusza Glińskiego / spisany przez Zofi e Glińsk a. — Londyn : Oficyna Poetów i Malarzy, 1982. — 112p,[12]p of plates : ill,facsims,ports ; 22cm
Includes index
Unpriced (pbk) B82-24154

780'.92'4 — Russian music. Chaĭkovskiĭ, Petr Il'ich — *Biographies*

Brown, David, *1929-*. Tchaikovsky : a biographical and critical study. — London : Gollancz
Vol.2: The crisis years (1874-1878). — Nov.1982. — [320]p
ISBN 0-575-03132-8 : £17.50 : CIP entry B82-26565

780'.92'4 — Russian music. Shostakovich, Dmitriĭ Dmitrievich — *Biographies*

Roseberry, Eric. Shostakovich : his life and times / Eric Roseberry. — Speldhurst : Midas, 1982, c1981. — 191p : ill,facsims,1map,music,ports ; 26cm
Bibliography: p187-188. — Includes index
ISBN 0-85936-144-6 : £8.50 B82-24084

Shostakovich, D.. Dmitry Shostakovich : about himself and his times / [compiled by L. Grigoryev, Ya. Platek] ; [translated from the Russian by Angus and Neilian Roxburgh]. — Moscow : Progress ; [London] : distributed by Central, c1981. — 343p : ill(some col.),ports ; 27cm
Translation of: Dmitriĭ Shostakovich : sbornik
ISBN 0-7147-1690-1 : £6.95 B82-29286

780'.92'4 — Russian music. Shostakovich, Dmitriĭ Dmitrievich — *Critical studies*

Shostakovich : the man and his music / edited by Christopher Norris. — London : Lawrence and Wishart, 1982. — 233p : music ; 23cm
Includes index
ISBN 0-85315-502-x : £12.50 B82-27730

780′.92′4 — Spanish music. Falla, Manuel de — *Critical studies*

Crichton, Ronald. Falla / Ronald Crichton. — London : British Broadcasting Corporation, 1982. — 104p : music ; 20cm. — (BBC music guides)
Includes index
ISBN 0-563-17820-5 (pbk) : £3.00 B82-38954

780′.92′4 — Welsh music. Davies, Evan Thomas — *Biographies — Welsh texts*

Williams, A. Tudno. E.T. Davies : arloeswr cerdd / A. Tudno Williams. — Dinbych [Denbigh] ([Chapel St., Denbigh, Clwyd]) : Gwasg Gee, c1981. — 103p : music ; 23cm
Bibliography: p101-103
£2.50 B82-12196

780′.941 — Great Britain. Music — *Serials*

British music yearbook. — 1982. — London : A. & C. Black, Nov.1981. — [500]p
ISBN 0-7136-2179-6 (pbk) : £12.50 : CIP entry B81-30361

780′.9415 — Ireland. Music, *1798-1916*

The **Voice** of the people : songs and history of Ireland. — Dublin : O'Brien, May 1982. — [200]p
ISBN 0-905140-91-5 : £12.00 : CIP entry B82-16210

780′.9423′38 — Dorset. Bournemouth. Music. Performance, *1900-1978*

George, Eric A.. Music in Bournemouth : a brief survey of professional music / by Eric A. George. — Bournemouth : Bournemouth Local Studies Publications, 1979. — 13p ; 21cm
ISBN 0-906287-19-7 (pbk) : £0.20 B82-40682

781 — MUSIC. PRINCIPLES AND TECHNIQUES

781 — Music. Theories

Cooper, Paul. Perspectives in music theory : an historical-analytical approach / Paul Cooper. — 2nd ed. — New York ; London : Harper & Row, c1981. — xii,564p : music ; 25cm
Previous ed.: New York : Dodd, Mead, 1973. — Includes index
ISBN 0-06-041373-5 : £10.25 B82-14987

Music theory : special topics / edited by Richmond Browne. — New York ; London : Academic Press, c1981. — xii,179p : music ; 24cm
Includes index
ISBN 0-12-138080-7 : £14.60 B82-07714

781′.07′1173 — United States. Higher education institutions. Curriculum subjects: Theory of music — *For teaching*

White, John D.. Guidelines for college teaching of music theory / John D. White. — Metuchen ; London : Scarecrow, 1981. — vii,182p : music ; 23cm
Bibliography: p163-177. — Includes index
ISBN 0-8108-1456-0 : £10.00 B82-04115

781′.1 — Music. Neuropsychological aspects

Music, mind and brain : the neuropsychology of music / edited by Manfred Clynes. — New York ; London : Plenum, c1982. — xiii,430p : ill,music ; 26cm
Sound disc (ca.6min. : 33 1/3 rpm : stereo ; 6in.) in pocket. — Includes bibliographies and index. — Includes papers presented at the Third Workshop on the Physical and Neuropsychological Foundation of Music, Aug. 8-12, 1980, Ossiach, Austria
ISBN 0-306-40908-9 : Unpriced B82-38674

781′.22 — Music. Intonation

Podnos, Theodor. Intonation for strings, winds, and singers : a six-month course / Theodor Podnos. — Metuchen ; London : Scarecrow, 1981. — ix,195p : ill,music,ports ; 29cm
Bibliography: p184-186. — Includes index
ISBN 0-8108-1465-x : £14.00 B82-08580

781′.22 — Twelve note music

Perle, George. Serial composition and atonality : an introduction to the music of Schoenberg, Berg and Webern / by George Perle. — 5th ed., rev. — Berkeley ; London : University of California Press, 1981. — xiv,164p ; 26cm
Previous ed.: 1977. — Includes index
ISBN 0-520-04365-0 : £11.50 B82-28098

781′.24 — Music. Notation

Stewart, Dave. Introducing the dots : reading & writing music for rock musicians / by Dave Stewart. — Poole : Blandford, 1982. — 127p : ill,music ; 25cm
ISBN 0-7137-1125-6 (pbk) : £4.95 : CIP rev. B82-09607

781′.24 — Music. Notation — *Early works — Facsimiles*

English psalmody prefaces : popular methods of teaching, 1562-1835 / Bernarr Rainbow and various authors. — Kilkenny : Reproduced under the direction of Leslie Hewitt for Boethius Press, c1982. — 158p : music,facsims ; 26cm. — (Classic texts in music education ; 2)
Facsim reprint of 11 texts
ISBN 0-86314-021-1 : £14.60 B82-31582

Rousseau, Jean-Jacques. Project concerning new symbols for music, 1742 / Jean-Jacques Rousseau ; translated and introduced by Bernarr Rainbow. — Kilkenny : Reproduced under the direction of Leslie Hewitt for Boethius Press, c1982. — [48]p : music ; 24cm. — (Classic texts in music education ; 1)
Parallel English and French text of: Project concernant de nouveaux signes pour la musique ; introduction in English. — Facsimile of the 1742 text
ISBN 0-86314-020-3 : £7.80 B82-31583

781′.24 — Music. Notation: Horizontal method

Davies-Walker, Muriel. The horizontal method / [by Muriel Davies-Walker]. — Manchester (541, Royal Exchange, Manchester M2 7EN) : Cresswell, c1982. — [20]p : ill,music ; 30cm
Unpriced (spiral) B82-23240

781′.24 — Western music. Notation, *to 1981*

Rastall, Richard. The notation of Western music. — London : Dent, Sept.1982. — [320]p
ISBN 0-460-04205-x : £15.00 : CIP entry B82-19696

781′.24′071 — Music. Sol-fa notation. Teaching — *Manuals — Early works — Facsimiles*

Glover, Sarah. Scheme for rendering psalmody congregational, 1835 ; together with The sol-fa tune book, 1839 / Sarah Glover ; introduced by Bernarr Rainbow. — Kilkenny : Reproduced under the direction of Leslie Hewitt for Boethius Press, c1982. — 124p,1folded leaf : music,1port ; 20cm
Facsims respectively of 1st ed. Norwich : Jarrold, 1835 and 3rd ed. Norwich : Jarrold, 1839
ISBN 0-86314-032-7 : £11.60 B82-31580

781.3 — MUSIC. HARMONY

781.3 — Music. Harmony

Schoenberg, Arnold. Theory of harmony. — London : Faber, Feb.1983. — [464]p
Translation from the German. — Originally published: 1978
ISBN 0-571-13078-x (pbk) : CIP entry B82-38699

781.3′2 — Music. Figured bass

Williams, Peter, *1937 May 14*. Figured bass accompaniment. — Edinburgh : Edinburgh University Press, Oct.1982. — 2v.
Originally published: 1970
ISBN 0-85224-452-5 (pbk) : £15.00 : CIP entry B82-29029

781.5 — MUSICAL FORMS

781.5 — Music. Form

Wade, Graham, *1940-*. The shape of music : an introduction to form in classical music / Graham Wade. — London : Allison & Busby, 1981. — 89p ; 23cm
Bibliography: p85-86. — Includes index
ISBN 0-85031-427-5 (cased) : £5.95 : CIP rev.
ISBN 0-85031-428-3 (pbk) : Unpriced B81-16415

781′.57 — Jazz. Harmony — *German texts*

Jungbluth, Axel. Jazz Harmonielehre : Funktionsharmonik und Modalität / Axel Jungbluth. — Mainz ; London : Schott, c1981. — 311p : music ; 24cm
ISBN 3-7957-2412-0 (pbk) : £6.00 B82-37969

781.6 — MUSIC. COMPOSITION AND PERFORMANCE

781.6′1 — Music. Composition — *Early works*

Kirnberger, Johann Philipp. The art of strict musical composition / Johann Philipp Kirnberger ; translated by David Beach and Jurgen Thym ; introduction and explanatory notes by David Beach. — New Haven ; London : Yale University Press, c1982. — xix,423p : music ; 25cm. — (Music theory translation series ; 4)
Translation of: selections from Die Kunst des reinen Satzes in der Musik. — Includes index
ISBN 0-300-02483-5 : £28.00 : CIP rev. B82-02443

781.6′1 — Music. Composition — *Manuals — German texts*

Treibmann, Karl Ottomar. Strukturen in neuer Musik : anregungen zum zeitgenössischen Tonsatz / Karl Ottomar Treibmann. — [Leipzig] : VEB Deutscher Verlag für Musik Leipzig ; [London] : [Fentone Music], c1981. — 199p : music ; 30cm
Bibliography: p198. — Includes index
£10.00 (pbk) B82-37806

781.6′1′09411 — Scotland. Music. Composition — *Serials*

Stretto / the Scottish Society of Composers. — No.3 (Summer 1981)-no.5 (Winter 1981) ; Vol.2, no.1 (Spring 1982)-. — Glasgow (c/o Scottish Music Archive, University of Glasgow, 7 Lilybank Gardens, Glasgow G12 8RZ) : The Society, 1981-. — v. ; 21cm
Quarterly. — Continues: Newsletter (Scottish Society of Composers)
ISSN 0263-5763 = Stretto : Free to Society members B82-28133

781.6′3 — European music. Baroque style. Performance. Interpretation

Donington, Robert. Baroque music : style and performance : a handbook / by Robert Donington. — London : Faber Music in association with Faber, 1982. — 206p : music ; 24cm
Bibliography: p184-193. — Includes index
ISBN 0-571-10041-4 (pbk) : £4.95 : CIP rev. B82-00374

781.6′3 — Music, *1700-1800*. **Performance. Interpretation —** *Manuals*

Rangel-Ribeiro, Victor. Baroque music : a practical guide for the performer / Victor Rangel-Ribeiro. — New York ; Schirmer ; London : Collier Macmillan, c1981. — xiii,306p : music ; 24cm
Includes index
ISBN 0-02-871980-8 : £20.95 B82-20407

781.6′3 — Music. Interpretation — *For conducting*

Leinsdorf, Erich. The composer's advocate. — London : Yale University Press, July 1982. — [226]p
ISBN 0-300-02887-3 (pbk) : £5.95 : CIP entry B82-22777

781.6′35 — Music. Conducting

Matheopoulos, Helena. Maestro. — London : Hutchinson, Sept.1982. — [560]p
ISBN 0-09-149010-3 : £12.95 : CIP entry B82-24351

781.6′35 — Music. Conducting — *Stories, anecdotes*

Gattey, Charles Neilson. Peacocks on the podium. — London : Hutchinson, Nov.1982. — [160]p
ISBN 0-09-150870-3 : £5.95 : CIP entry
B82-28725

781.7 — MUSIC OF ETHNIC AND NATIONAL ORIENTATION

781.7 — Folk music — *Conference proceedings*

International Folk Music Council. *United Kingdom National Committee. Conference (1980 : Cambridge)*. Studies in traditional music & dance : proceedings of the 1980 conference of the United Kingdom National Committee of the International Folk Music Council / edited by Peter Cooke. — [Edinburgh] (c/o P. Cooke, 27 George Sq., Edinburgh EH8 9LD) : [The Committee], c1981. — 84p ; 21cm
Unpriced (pbk)
Also classified at 793.3′1 B82-01254

781.7′09182′1 — Caribbean music — *For schools*

Sealey, John, *1932-*. Music in the Caribbean / John Sealey and Krister Malm ; introduction by The Mighty Chalkdust (Hollis Liverpool). — London : Hodder and Stoughton, 1982. — iv,44p : ill,ports ; 25cm
Bibliography: p44
ISBN 0-340-26291-5 (pbk) : Unpriced : CIP rev. B82-01846

781.7′2′00973 — United States. Ethnic minority music

Tawa, Nicholas. A sound of strangers : musical culture, acculturation, and the post-Civil War ethnic American / Nicholas Tawa. — Metuchen ; London : Scarecrow, 1982. — xiii,304p : music ; 22cm
Bibliography: p237-259. — Includes index
ISBN 0-8108-1504-4 : £14.00 B82-31805

781.7′2927′0321 — Arab music — *Encyclopaedias*

Al Faruqi, Lois Ibsen. An annotated glossary of Arabic musical terms / compiled by Lois Ibsen al Faruqi ; forewords by Ali Jihad Racy and Don Michael Randel. — Westport ; London : Greenwood Press, 1981. — xxii,511p : music ; 25cm
Bibliography: p498-511
ISBN 0-313-20554-x : Unpriced B82-18024

781.738 — Ancient Greek music

Jenkins, Ian. Greek music : illustrated notes for teachers / [by Ian Jenkins and Sue Bird]. — [London] : British Museum Education Service, [1982?]. — 14p : ill ; 30cm. — (Greek & Roman daily life studies ; 4)
Bibliography: p14
Unpriced (unbound) B82-27926

781.741 — British music, *1800-1914*

The **Romantic** Age 1800-1914 / edited by Nicholas Temperley. — London : Athlone, 1981. — xii,548p : music ; 24cm. — (The Athlone history of music in Britain)
Bibliography: p516-536. — Includes index
ISBN 0-485-13005-x : £45.00 : CIP rev.
B81-30556

781.7415 — Irish folk music

Ó Riada, Seán. Our musical heritage / Seán Ó Riada ; edited by Thomas Kinsella ; music editor Tomás Ó Canainn. — Portlaoise : Fundúireacht an Riadaigh i gcomhar Le Dolmen Press, 1982. — 83p : ill,music,1port ; 22cm
Bibliography: p83. — List of sound discs: p81-83
ISBN 0-85105-389-0 (pbk) : £4.90 B82-13577

781.742 — English music, *ca 1700-ca 1800* — *Festschriften*

Music in eighteenth-century England : essays in memory of Charles Cudworth. — Cambridge : Cambridge University Press, Sept.1982. — [262]p
ISBN 0-521-23525-1 : £22.50 : CIP entry
B82-19538

781.7429 — Welsh folk music — *Welsh texts*

Cerdd a chân : golwg ar gerddoriaeth draddodiadol yng Nghymru / golygwyd gan Wyn Thomas. — [Denbigh] : Gwasg Gee, 1982. — 167p ; 22cm
£4.00 (pbk) B82-39559

781.743 — German music, *1800-1826* — *Critical studies* — *Early works*

Weber, Carl Maria von. Writings on music / Carl Maria von Weber ; translated by Martin Cooper ; edited and introduced by John Warrack. — Cambridge : Cambridge University Press, 1981. — xi,402p : music ; 24cm
Includes index
ISBN 0-521-22892-1 : £35.00 : CIP rev.
B81-25815

781.75 — Asian music — *Critical studies* — *German texts*

Kuckertz, Joseph. Musik in Asien. — Basel ; London : Bärenreiter Kassel. — (Musik aktuell)
1: Indien und der Vordere Orient / Josef Kuckerz. — 1982. — 80p : 1map,music ; 25cm + Beispielheft(24p : ill ; 19x25cm)
Includes index
ISBN 3-7618-0653-1 (pbk) : Unpriced
B82-31782

781.754 — Northern Indian music. Performance

Sorrell, Neil. Indian music in performance : a practical introduction / Neil Sorrell and Ram Narayan ; with accompanying recording by Ram Narayan ; foreword by Yehudi Menuhin. — Manchester : Manchester University Press, 1980. — xvi,190p : ill,music,1port ; 21cm
In slip case with cassette. — Bibliography: p175-177. — Includes index
ISBN 0-7190-0756-9 (pbk) : £14.95 : CIP rev.
B80-00841

781.766′09 — West African music, *to 1980*

Charters, Samuel. The roots of the blues. — London : Quartet, Nov.1982. — [160]p
ISBN 0-7043-3416-x (pbk) : £3.95 : CIP entry
B82-29084

781.91 — MUSICAL INSTRUMENTS

781.91 — Musical instruments

Donington, Robert. Music and its instruments. — London : Methuen, Oct.1982. — [320]p
ISBN 0-416-72270-9 (cased) : £10.95 : CIP entry
ISBN 0-416-72280-6 (pbk) : £5.95 B82-23982

781.91 — Musical instruments — *For children*

McLeish, Kenneth. The Oxford first companion to instruments and orchestras / Kenneth and Valerie McLeish. — London : Oxford University Press Music Department, 1982. — 32p : ill(some col.),music,ports(some col.) ; 32cm
Also published as section C of the Oxford first companion to music. — Cover title. — Text on inside covers
ISBN 0-19-321435-0 (pbk) : Unpriced
B82-39419

781.91 — Musical instruments — *For schools*

Bennett, Roy, *1938-*. Instruments of the orchestra / Roy Bennett. — Cambridge : Cambridge University Press, 1982. — 72p : ill,music ; 25cm. — (Cambridge assignments in music)
ISBN 0-521-29814-8 (pbk) : £1.60 B82-35653

781.91 — Musical instruments. Making — *Manuals* — *For children*

McLean, Margaret. Making musical instruments / Margaret McLean ; illustrated by Ken Stott. — [London] : Macmillan Children's, 1982. — 32p : ill(some col.),music ; 29cm. — (Help yourself books)
ISBN 0-333-30857-3 : £2.95 : CIP rev.
B81-35785

781.91 — Musical instruments. Tuning — *Amateurs' manuals*

Meffen, John. A guide to tuning musical instruments / John Meffen. — Newton Abbot : David & Charles, c1982. — 160p : ill,music,2ports ; 23cm
Bibliography: p156-158. — Includes index
ISBN 0-7153-8169-5 : £7.95 : CIP rev.
B82-13065

781.91 — Orchestras. Musical instruments

Hopkins, Antony. Sounds of music : a study of orchestral texture / Antony Hopkins. — London : Dent, 1982. — 170p : ill,music ; 24cm
Bibliography: p164-165. — Includes index
ISBN 0-460-04447-8 : £7.95 : CIP rev.
B82-01988

781.91 — Orchestras. Musical instruments — *For schools*

Farmer, Paul, *1950-*. Instruments of the orchestra / Paul Farmer. — [Harlow] : Longman, [1982]. — 24p : ill,music ; 23cm. — (Longman music topics)
ISBN 0-582-20018-0 (pbk) : £0.95 B82-35560

781.91′05 — Musical instruments — *Serials*

[Music world *(London)*]. Music world : the definitive music trade magazine : incorporating Music trades international. — Vol.1, no.1 (Mar. 1979)-. — London (886 High Rd., N12 9SB) : Turret Press, 1979-. — v. : ill,ports ; 30cm
Monthly. — Absorbed: Music trades international. 1981. — Description based on: Vol.3, no.11 (Apr. 1982)
ISSN 0263-6956 = Music world (London) : £15.50 per year B82-30477

782.1 — OPERA

782.1 — Opera

Gattey, Charles Neilson. The elephant that swallowed a nightingale. — London : Hutchinson, Oct.1981. — [160]p
ISBN 0-09-146060-3 : £4.95 : CIP entry
B81-27407

Osborne, Charles. How to enjoy opera. — Loughton : Judy Piatkus, May 1982. — [192]p. — (Melvyn Bragg's arts series)
ISBN 0-86188-144-3 : £5.95 : CIP entry
B82-07056

782.1 — Opera — *Critical studies*

English National Opera guides. — London : John Calder, July 1982. — (The Opera library)
Vol.2: La traviata, Tristan and Isolde, Otello, Der Rosenkavalier. — [392]p
ISBN 0-7145-3916-3 : £15.00 : CIP entry
Also classified at 782.1′2 B82-17212

782.1′06′042132 — London. Westminster *(London Borough)*. **Opera. Companies: Royal Opera**

Royal Opera. The Royal Opera 1980/81 / editor Noël Goodwin. — London : Royal Opera House Covent Garden, c1980. — 48p : ill(some col.),ports(some col.) ; 30cm
ISBN 0-9502123-8-5 (pbk) : Unpriced
B82-29936

782.1′06′07471 — New York *(City)*. **Opera. Companies: New York City Opera**, *to 1981*

Sokol, Martin L.. The New York City Opera : an American adventure / Martin L. Sokol. — New York : Macmillan ; London : Collier Macmillan, c1981. — xiv,532p,[64]p of plates : ports ; 25cm
Bibliography: p507-510. — Includes index
ISBN 0-02-612280-4 : £14.95 B82-26200

782.1′07′1 — Opera. Performance — *Stories, anecdotes*

Vickers, Hugh. Even greater operatic disasters. — London : Jill Norman & Hobhouse, Oct.1981. — [80]p
ISBN 0-906908-62-0 : £3.95 : CIP entry
B81-27419

782.1′076 — Opera — *Questions & answers*

Camner, James. The operatic quiz book / James Camner. — London : Robson, 1982. — 125p : ill,music,ports ; 22cm
Originally published: New York : St. Martin's Press, 1982
ISBN 0-86051-174-x : £5.95 : CIP rev.
B82-01565

782.1′09′031 — Opera, *to ca 1700*

Donington, Robert. The rise of opera / Robert Donington. — London : Faber, 1981. — 399p,[16]p of plates : ill,music ; 26cm
Bibliography: p345-361. — Includes index
ISBN 0-571-11674-4 : £15.00 : CIP rev.
B81-12845

782.1'09'034 — Opera, *1758-ca 1850*
Dent, Edward J.. The rise of romantic opera / Edward J. Dent ; edited by Winton Dean. — Cambridge : Cambridge University Press, 1976 (1979 [printing]). — x,198p ; 22cm
Includes index
ISBN 0-521-29659-5 (pbk) : Unpriced B82-21659

782.1'092'2 — Opera. Composers, *to 1900 — Humour*
Borge, Victor. My favorite intermissions / by Victor Borge and Robert Sherman ; drawings by Thomas Winding. — London : Robson, 1982, c1971. — 189p : ill ; 23cm
Originally published: Garden City, N.Y. : Doubleday, 1971
ISBN 0-86051-204-5 : £5.95 : CIP rev. B82-17931

782.1'092'4 — England. Opera. Rosenthal, Harold, *1917- — Biographies*
Rosenthal, Harold, *1917-*. My mad world of opera / Harold Rosenthal. — London : Weidenfeld and Nicolson, c1982. — xiv,234p ; 25cm
Includes index
ISBN 0-297-78016-6 : £10.95 B82-40226

782.1'092'4 — Opera in Czech. Janáček, Leoš. Káťa Kabanová *— Critical studies*
Leoš Janáček : Káta Kabanová / compiled by John Tyrrell. — Cambridge : Cambridge University Press, 1982. — xv,234p : ill,facsims,music ; 23cm. — (Cambridge opera handbooks)
Bibliography: p226-227. — Includes list of sound recordings and index
ISBN 0-521-23180-9 (cased) : £15.00 : CIP rev.
ISBN 0-521-29853-9 (pbk) : £4.95 B82-15933

782.1'092'4 — Opera in English. Stravinsky, Igor. Rake's Progress *— Critical studies*
Griffiths, Paul. Igor Stravinsky: The rake's progress. — Cambridge : Cambridge University Press, July 1982. — [110]p. — (Cambridge opera handbooks)
ISBN 0-521-23746-7 (cased) : £9.95 : CIP entry
ISBN 0-521-28199-7 (pbk) : £3.95 B82-13261

782.1'092'4 — Opera in French. Bizet, Georges. Carmen *— Critical studies*
Bizet, Georges. Carmen. — London : Calder, Aug.1982. — [96]p. — (Opera guide ; 13)
ISBN 0-7145-3937-6 (pbk) : £2.00 : CIP entry
Also classified at 782.1'2 B82-21749

782.1'092'4 — Opera in French. Debussy, Claude. Pelléas et Mélisande *— Critical studies*
Debussy, Claude. Pelléas & Mélisande / Claude Debussy. — London : Calder, 1982. — 96p : ill,music,ports ; 22cm. — (Opera guide ; 9)
Essays in English, parallel French libretto and English translation. — Libretto by Maurice Maeterlinck, translation by Hugh Macdonald. — Bibliography: p95. — List of sound recordings: p96
ISBN 0-7145-3906-6 (pbk) : £2.00 : CIP rev.
Also classified at 782.1'2 B82-09174

782.1'092'4 — Opera in German & opera in Italian. Mozart, Wolfgang Amadeus *— Critical studies*
Gianturco, Carolyn. Mozart's early operas / Carolyn Gianturco. — London : Batsford, 1981. — 216p,[8]p of plates : ill,music,ports ; 24cm
Includes index
ISBN 0-7134-2240-8 : £15.00 B82-14093

782.1'092'4 — Opera in German. Berg, Alban *— Critical studies*
Perle, George. The operas of Alban Berg / George Perle. — Berkeley, Calif. ; London : University of California Press
Vol.1: Wozzeck. — 1980. — xvii,231p,[16]p of plates : ill,music,facsims,ports ; 27cm
Includes German libretto. — Bibliography: p223-226. — Includes index
ISBN 0-520-03440-6 : £10.50 B82-17995

782.1'092'4 — Opera in German. Berg, Alban. Lulu *- Critical studies*
Calder, John Mackenzie. The Lulu opera guide. — London : Calder, Apr.1981. — [224]p
ISBN 0-7145-3847-7 (pbk) : £2.00 : CIP entry
Also classified at 782.1'2 B81-05174

782.1'092'4 — Opera in German. Mozart, Wolfgang Amadeus. Zauberflöte, *Die — Critical studies*
Mozart, Wolfgang Amadeus. The magic flute / Wolfgang Amadeus Mozart. — London : Calder, 1980. — 128p : ill,music,1port ; 22cm. — (English National Opera guides ; 3)
Parallel German text and English translation / lyrics by Michael Geliot and dialogue by Anthony Besch. — Includes the libretto by Emanuel Schikaneder and Carl Ludwig Giesecke. — Bibliography: p128. — List of sound discs: p124-127
ISBN 0-7145-3768-3 (pbk) : £2.00 : CIP rev.
Also classified at 782.1'2 B80-04353

782.1'092'4 — Opera in German. Strauss, Richard. Ariadne auf Naxos *— Critical studies*
Forsyth, Karen. Ariadne auf Naxos by Hugo von Hofmannsthal and Richard Strauss : its genesis and meaning / Karen Forsyth. — Oxford : Oxford University Press, 1982. — viii,291p : music ; 22cm. — (Oxford modern languages and literature monographs)
Bibliography: p282-287. — Includes index
ISBN 0-19-815536-0 : 20.00 : CIP rev. B82-01112

782.1'092'4 — Opera in German. Strauss, Richard. Productions, *to 1979*
Hartmann, Rudolf. Richard Strauss : the staging of his operas and ballets. — Oxford : Phaidon, Mar.1982. — [280]p
Translation of: Richard Strauss : die Bühnenwerke von Uraufführung bis heute
ISBN 0-7148-2254-x : £25.00 : CIP entry
Also classified at 792.8'4 B82-01556

782.1'092'4 — Opera in German. Wagner, Richard *— Biographies*
Gregor-Dellin, Martin. Richard Wagner. — London : Collins, Jan.1983. — [900]p
Translated from the German
ISBN 0-00-216669-0 : £14.95 : CIP entry B82-33582

782.1'092'4 — Opera in German. Wagner, Richard *— Critical studies*
Williamson, Audrey, *1913-*. Wagner opera / Audrey Williamson. — 2nd rev. ed. — London : Calder, 1982. — 191p : ill,music,plans ; 21cm
Previous ed.: 1962. — Bibliography: p181-182
ISBN 0-7145-0603-6 (pbk) : £3.95 B82-13302

782.1'092'4 — Opera in German. Wagner, Richard. Fliegende Holländer *— Critical studies*
Wagner, Richard. Der fliegende Holländer = The flying Dutchman / Richard Wagner. — London : Calder, 1982. — 80p : ill,music,ports ; 22cm. — (Opera guide ; 12)
Essays in English, parallel German libretto and English translation. — Translation of libretto by David Pountney. — Bibliography: p80. — List of sound recordings: p78-79
ISBN 0-7145-3920-1 (pbk) : £2.00 : CIP rev.
Also classified at 782.1'2 B82-09175

782.1'092'4 — Opera in German. Wagner, Richard. Marriage to Wagner, Cosima
Skelton, Geoffrey. Richard and Cosima Wagner : biography of a marriage / by Geoffrey Skelton. — London : Gollancz, 1982. — 319p,[12]p of plates : ill,ports ; 24cm
Bibliography: p307-310. — Includes index
ISBN 0-575-03017-8 : £17.50 : CIP rev.
Also classified at 780'.92'4 B81-38324

782.1'092'4 — Opera in German. Wagner, Richard. Productions, *to 1981*
Osborne, Charles, *1927-*. The world theatre of Wagner. — Oxford : Phaidon, Sept.1982. — [224]p
ISBN 0-7148-2258-2 : £25.00 : CIP entry B82-20371

782.1'092'4 — Opera in German. Wagner, Richard. Ring des Nibelungen. Composition. Influence of Oresteia by Aeschylus
Ewans, Michael. Wagner and Aeschylus : the Ring and the Oresteia / Michael Ewans. — London : Faber, 1982. — 271p : music ; 23cm
Bibliography: p261-265. — Includes index
ISBN 0-571-11808-9 : £12.50 : CIP rev. B82-12978

782.1'092'4 — Opera in Italian. Donizetti, Gaetano *— Critical studies*
Ashbrook, William. Donizetti and his operas / William Ashbrook. — Cambridge : Cambridge University Press, 1982. — viii,744p : music ; 24cm
Bibliography: p701-707. — Includes index
ISBN 0-521-23526-x : £25.00 : CIP rev. B82-11478

782.1'092'4 — Opera in Italian. Mozart, Wolfgang Amadeus. Don Giovanni *— Critical studies*
Rushton, Julian. W.A. Mozart : Don Giovanni / Julian Rushton. — Cambridge : Cambridge University Press, 1981. — ix,165p : ill,music ; 22cm. — (Cambridge opera handbooks)
Bibliography: p153-158. — List of sound discs: p159-161. — Includes index
ISBN 0-521-22826-3 (cased) : £9.95
ISBN 0-521-29663-3 (pbk) : £3.95 B82-02679

782.1'092'4 — Opera in Italian. Mozart, Wolfgang Amadeus. Nozze di Figaro *- Critical studies*
Calder, John Mackenzie. The marriage of Figaro. — London : Calder, Apr.1981. — [128]p. — (Royal Opera House guide ; 5)
ISBN 0-7145-3771-3 (pbk) : £2.00 : CIP entry
Also classified at 782.1'2 B81-05172

782.1'092'4 — Opera in Italian. Puccini, Giacomo *— Biographies*
Greenfeld, Howard. Puccini : a biography / by Howard Greenfeld. — London : Hale, 1981, c1980. — 299p,[8]p of plates : ill,ports ; 24cm
Bibliography: p278-281. — Includes index
ISBN 0-7091-9368-8 : £11.50 B82-14627

782.1'092'4 — Opera in Italian. Puccini, Giacomo. Bohème *— Critical studies*
Puccini, Giacomo. La Bohème. — London : Calder, Aug.1982. — [96]p. — (Opera guide ; 14)
ISBN 0-7145-3938-4 (pbk) : £2.00 : CIP entry
Also classified at 782.1'2 B82-22409

782.1'092'4 — Opera in Italian. Puccini, Giacomo. Tosca *— Critical studies*
Puccini, Giacomo. Tosca. — London : Calder, Aug.1982. — [96]p. — (Opera guide ; 16)
ISBN 0-7145-3772-1 (pbk) : £2.00 : CIP entry
Also classified at 782.1'2 B82-21748

782.1'092'4 — Opera in Italian. Rossini, Gioacchino. Cenerentola, *La — Critical studies*
Rossini, Gioacchino. La Cenerentola = (Cinderella) / Gioacchino Rossini. — London : Calder, 1980. — 96p : ill,music,1facsim,ports ; 22cm. — (English National Opera guides ; 1)
Includes the libretto by Giacomo Ferretti ; Parallel Italian text and English translation by Arthur Jacobs. — Bibliography: p95. — List of Sound discs: p96
ISBN 0-7145-3819-1 (pbk) : £2.00 : CIP rev.
Also classified at 782.1'2 B80-04354

782.1'092'4 — Opera in Italian. Verdi, Giuseppe *— Critical studies*
Budden, Julian. The operas of Verdi / Julian Budden. — London : Cassell
3: From Don Carlos to Falstaff. — 1981. — x,546p : music ; 24cm
Bibliography: p533-538. — Includes index
ISBN 0-304-30740-8 : £21.00 B82-32042

782.1'092'4 — Opera in Italian. Verdi, Giuseppe. Falstaff *— Critical studies*
Verdi, Giuseppe. Falstaff / Giuseppe Verdi. — London : Calder, 1982. — 128p : ill,music,ports ; 22cm. — (Opera guide ; 10)
Essays in English, parallel Italian libretto and English translation. — Libretto by Arrigo Boito, translation by Andrew Porter. — Bibliography: p128. — List of sound recordings: p126
ISBN 0-7145-3921-x (pbk) : £2.00 : CIP rev.
Also classified at 782.1'2 B82-09176

782.1'092'4 — Opera in Italian. Verdi, Giuseppe. Rigoletto *— Critical studies*
Verdi, Giuseppe. Rigoletto. — London : Calder, Aug.1982. — [96]p. — (Opera guide ; 15)
ISBN 0-7145-3939-2 (pbk) : £2.00 : CIP entry
Also classified at 782.1'2 B82-21750

782.1′092′4 — Opera in Russian. Musorgskiĭ, M. P.. Boris Godunov — *Critical studies*

Musorgskiĭ, M. P.. Boris Godunov / Modest Mussorgsky. — London : Calder in association with English National Opera and The Royal Opera, 1982. — 112p : ill,music,ports ; 22cm. — (Opera guide ; 11)
Parallel transliterated Russian text and English translation by David Lloyd-Jones. — Text on inside covers. — Bibliography: p112. — List of sound discs: p111
ISBN 0-7145-3922-8 (pbk) : £2.00 : CIP rev.
Also classified at 782.1′2 B82-09177

782.1′092′4 — Opera. Singing. Angeles, Victoria de los — *Biographies*

Roberts, Peter, *19---*. Victoria de los Angeles / Peter Roberts. — London : Weidenfeld & Nicolson, c1982. — vii,184p,[32]p of plates : ill,ports ; 24cm
Discography: 169-177. — Includes index
ISBN 0-297-78099-9 : £8.95 B82-40163

782.1′092′4 — Opera. Singing. Baker, Janet — Biographies

Baker, Janet. Full circle. — London : MacRae, Oct.1982. — [256]p
ISBN 0-86203-107-9 : £9.95 : CIP entry B82-24587

782.1′092′4 — Opera. Singing. Callas, Maria, *1947-1959 — Personal observations*

Meneghini, Giovanni Battista. My wife Maria Callas. — London : Bodley Head, Jan.1983. — [320]p
Translation of: Maria Callas mia moglie
ISBN 0-370-30502-7 : £8.95 : CIP entry B82-34422

782.1′092′4 — Opera. Singing. Callas, Maria — *Biographies*

Stassinopoulos, Arianna. Maria Callas : the woman behind the legend / Arianna Stassinopoulos. — London : Hamlyn, 1981, c1980. — 429p : ports ; 18cm
Originally published: London : Weidenfeld and Nicolson, 1980. — Includes index
ISBN 0-600-20404-9 (pbk) : £1.75 B82-00083

782.1′092′4 — Opera. Singing. Kelly, Michael, *1762-1826 — Stories, anecdotes*

Jacob, Naomi. The Irish boy : a romantic biography / Naomi Jacob. — London : Remploy, 1980. — 288p ; 20cm
Originally published: London : Hutchinson, 1955
ISBN 0-7066-0859-3 : £4.70 B82-10624

782.1′092′4 — Opera. Singing. Langdon, Michael — *Biographies*

Langdon, Michael. Notes from a low singer. — London : MacRae, Sept.1982. — [224]p
ISBN 0-86203-106-0 : £9.95 : CIP entry B82-21555

782.1′092′4 — Opera. Singing. Te Kanawa, Kiri — *Biographies*

Fingleton, David. Kiri Te Kanawa. — London : Collins, Oct.1982. — [224]p
ISBN 0-00-216365-9 : £8.95 : CIP entry B82-25533

782.1′092′4 — Opera. Singing. Te Wiata, Inia — *Biographies*

Te Wiata, Beryl. Most happy fella. — London : Hutchinson, Jan.1983. — [308]p
ISBN 0-09-150880-0 : £9.95 : CIP entry B82-33327

782.1′092′4 — Opera. Singing. Wallace, Ian, *1919- — Biographies*

Wallace, Ian, *1919-*. Promise me you'll sing Mud! : the autobiography of Ian Wallace. — Rev. 2nd ed. — London : Calder, 1981, c1982. — 240p,[12]p of plates : ill,ports ; 22cm
Previous ed.: 1975. — Includes index
ISBN 0-7145-3594-x (pbk) : £3.95 B82-11593

782.1′0924 — Opera. Singing. Wallace, Ian, *b.1919 — Biographies*

Wallace, Ian. Nothing quite like it. — London : Hamilton, Sept.1982. — [176]p
ISBN 0-241-10853-5 : £12.50 : CIP entry B82-18839

782.1′092′4 — Operas in Italian. Librettos: Da Ponte, Lorenzo — *Biographies*

Fitzlyon, April. Lorenzo da Ponte. — London : Calder, Aug.1982. — [288]p
Originally published: as The libertine librettist. 1955
ISBN 0-7145-3783-7 (pbk) : £3.95 : CIP entry B82-21376

782.1′09421′32 — London. Westminster *(London Borough)*. **Opera houses: Royal Opera House,** *1732-1982*

A History of the Royal Opera House : Covent Garden 1732-1982. — London : Royal Opera House, Dec.1982. — [144]p
ISBN 0-946338-00-0 (cased) : £9.95 : CIP entry
ISBN 0-946338-01-9 (pbk) : £5.95 B82-36168

782.1′09421′32 — London. Westminster *(London Borough)*. **Opera houses: Royal Opera House,** *to 1980 — Illustrations*

Drogheda, Charles Garrett Ponsonby Moore, *Earl of*. The Covent garden album : 250 years of theatre, opera and ballet / Lord Drogheda, Ken Davison, Andrew Wheatcroft. — London : Routledge & Kegan Paul, 1981. — 207p : ill,facsims,ports ; 31cm
ISBN 0-7100-0880-5 : £15.95 : CIP rev. B81-27983

Drogheda, Charles Garrett Ponsonby Moore, *Earl of*. The Covent Garden album : 250 years of theatre, opera and ballet / Lord Drogheda, Ken Davison, Andrew Wheatcroft. — London : Routledge & Kegan Paul, 1981. — 207p : ill,facsims,ports ; 30cm
ISBN 0-7100-9336-5 (pbk) : £5.95 B82-40499

782.1′0942132 — London. Westminster *(London Borough)*. **Opera houses: Royal Opera House,** *to 1982*

Boursnell, Clive. The Royal Opera House. — London : Hamilton, Sept.1982. — [256]p
ISBN 0-241-10891-8 : £20.00 : CIP entry B82-21760

782.1′2 — Opera in Finnish. Sallinen, Aulis — *Librettos — English texts*

Sallinen, Aulis. The red line = Punainen viiva : an opera in two acts / libretto and music by Aulis Sallinen ; English translation for singing by Stephen Oliver. — Sevenoaks : Novello, c1982. — v,24p ; 21cm
Ten men, 6 women. — Parallel Finnish text and English translation
ISBN 0-85360-115-1 (pbk) : £1.00 B82-33978

782.1′2 — Opera in French. Bizet, Georges — *Librettos — French-English parallel texts*

Bizet, Georges. Carmen. — London : Calder, Aug.1982. — [96]p. — (Opera guide ; 13)
ISBN 0-7145-3937-6 (pbk) : £2.00 : CIP entry
Primary classification 782.1′092′4 B82-21749

782.1′2 — Opera in French. Debussy, Claude — *Librettos — French-English parallel texts*

Debussy, Claude. Pelléas & Mélisande / Claude Debussy. — London : Calder, 1982. — 96p : ill,music,ports ; 22cm. — (Opera guide ; 9)
Essays in English, parallel French libretto and English translation. — Libretto by Maurice Maeterlinck, translation by Hugh Macdonald. — Bibliography: p95. — List of sound recordings: p96
ISBN 0-7145-3906-6 (pbk) : £2.00 : CIP rev.
Primary classification 782.1′092′4 B82-09174

782.1′2 — Opera in German. Berg, Alban - *Librettos - German-English parallel texts*

Calder, John Mackenzie. The Lulu opera guide. — London : Calder, Apr.1981. — [224]p
ISBN 0-7145-3847-7 (pbk) : £2.00 : CIP entry
Primary classification 782.1′092′4 B81-05174

782.1′2 — Opera in German. Mozart, Wolfgang Amadeus — *Librettos — German-English parallel texts*

Mozart, Wolfgang Amadeus. The magic flute / Wolfgang Amadeus Mozart. — London : Calder, 1980. — 128p : ill,music,1port ; 22cm. — (English National Opera guides ; 3)
Parallel German text and English translation / lyrics by Michael Geliot and dialogue by Anthony Besch. — Includes the libretto by Emanuel Schikaneder and Carl Ludwig Giesecke. — Bibliography: p128. — List of sound discs: p124-127
ISBN 0-7145-3768-3 (pbk) : £2.00 : CIP rev.
Primary classification 782.1′092′4 B80-04353

782.1′2 — Opera in German. Wagner, Richard — *Librettos — German-English parallel texts*

Wagner, Richard. Der fliegende Holländer = The flying Dutchman / Richard Wagner. — London : Calder, 1982. — 80p : ill,music,ports ; 22cm. — (Opera guide ; 12)
Essays in English, parallel German libretto and English translation. — Translation of libretto by David Pountney. — Bibliography: p80. — List of sound recordings: p78-79
ISBN 0-7145-3920-1 (pbk) : £2.00 : CIP rev.
Primary classification 782.1′092′4 B82-09175

782.1′2 — Opera in Italian. Mozart, Wolfgang Amadeus - *Librettos - Italian-English parallel texts*

Calder, John Mackenzie. The marriage of Figaro. — London : Calder, Apr.1981. — [128]p. — (Royal Opera House guide ; 5)
ISBN 0-7145-3771-3 (pbk) : £2.00 : CIP entry
Primary classification 782.1′092′4 B81-05172

782.1′2 — Opera in Italian. Puccini, Giacomo — *Librettos — Italian-English parallel texts*

Puccini, Giacomo. La Bohème. — London : Calder, Aug.1982. — [96]p. — (Opera guide ; 14)
ISBN 0-7145-3938-4 (pbk) : £2.00 : CIP entry
Primary classification 782.1′092′4 B82-22409

Puccini, Giacomo. Tosca. — London : Calder, Aug.1982. — [96]p. — (Opera guide ; 16)
ISBN 0-7145-3772-1 (pbk) : £2.00 : CIP entry
Primary classification 782.1′092′4 B82-21748

782.1′2 — Opera in Italian. Rossini, Gioacchino — *Librettos — Italian-English parallel texts*

Rossini, Gioacchino. La Cenerentola = (Cinderella) / Gioacchino Rossini. — London : Calder, 1980. — 96p : ill,music,1facsim,ports ; 22cm. — (English National Opera guides ; 1)
Includes the libretto by Giacomo Ferretti ; Parallel Italian text and English translation by Arthur Jacobs. — Bibliography: p95. — List of Sound discs: p96
ISBN 0-7145-3819-1 (pbk) : £2.00 : CIP rev.
Primary classification 782.1′092′4 B80-04354

782.1′2 — Opera in Italian. Verdi, Giuseppe — *Librettos — Italian-English parallel texts*

Verdi, Giuseppe. Falstaff / Giuseppe Verdi. — London : Calder, 1982. — 128p : ill,music,ports ; 22cm. — (Opera guide ; 10)
Essays in English, parallel Italian libretto and English translation. — Libretto by Arrigo Boito, translation by Andrew Porter. — Bibliography: p128. — List of sound recordings: p126
ISBN 0-7145-3921-x (pbk) : £2.00 : CIP rev.
Primary classification 782.1′092′4 B82-09176

Verdi, Giuseppe. Rigoletto. — London : Calder, Aug.1982. — [96]p. — (Opera guide ; 15)
ISBN 0-7145-3939-2 (pbk) : £2.00 : CIP entry
Primary classification 782.1′092′4 B82-21750

782.1′2 — Opera in Russian. Musorgskiĭ, M. P. — *Librettos — Russian-English parallel texts*

Musorgskiĭ, M. P.. Boris Godunov / Modest Mussorgsky. — London : Calder in association with English National Opera and The Royal Opera, 1982. — 112p : ill,music,ports ; 22cm. — (Opera guide ; 11)
Parallel transliterated Russian text and English translation by David Lloyd-Jones. — Text on inside covers. — Bibliography: p112. — List of sound discs: p111
ISBN 0-7145-3922-8 (pbk) : £2.00 : CIP rev.
Primary classification 782.1′092′4 B82-09177

782.1′2 — Opera — *Librettos*

English National Opera guides. — London : John Calder, July 1982. — (The Opera library)
Vol.2: La traviata, Tristan and Isolde, Otello, Der Rosenkavalier. — [392]p
ISBN 0-7145-3916-3 : £15.00 : CIP entry
Primary classification 782.1 B82-17212

782.1′3 — Opera in German. Wagner, Richard — *Plot outlines*

De Rico, Ul. The ring of the Nibelung : Wagner's epic drama / illustrated [and retold] by Ul de Rico ; foreword by Sir Georg Solti. — London : Thames and Hudson, 1980. — 204p : col.ill,1geneal.table ; 35cm
Unpriced B82-21345

782.1′3 — Opera in German. Wagner, Richard — *Plot outlines — For children*

Blyth, Alan, *1929-*. Lohengrin : the story of Wagner's opera / retold by Alan Blyth ; with pictures by Maria Antonietta Gambaro. — London : MacRae, 1981. — [28]p : col.ill ; 29cm
Text on inside cover
ISBN 0-86203-068-4 : £4.50 : CIP rev. B81-17529

782.1′3 — Opera in Italian. Rossini, Gioacchino — *Plot outlines — For children*

Blyth, Alan, *1929-*. Cinderella : [La Cenerentola] : the story of Rossini's opera / retold by Alan Blyth ; with pictures by Emanuele Luzzati. — London : MacRae, 1981. — [24]p : ill(some col.),music ; 29cm
Music on lining papers
ISBN 0-86203-073-0 : £4.50 : CIP rev. B81-17530

782.1′3 — Opera — *Plot outlines — For children*

Spence, Keith. Tales from the opera. — London : Methuen/Walker, Sept.1981. — [112]p
ISBN 0-416-05810-8 : £5.95 : CIP entry B81-21628

782.8 — THEATRE MUSIC

782.8′0945 — Italy. Theatre. Music, *1400-1700*

Pirrotta, Nino. Music and theatre from Poliziano to Monteverdi / Nino Pirrotta and Elena Povoledo ; translated by Karen Eales. — Cambridge : Cambridge University Press, 1982. — xi,392p,[24]p of plates : ill,music ; 26cm. — (Cambridge studies in music)
Translation of: Li due Orfei. — Includes index
ISBN 0-521-23259-7 : £30.00 : CIP rev. B81-37553

782.81′092′2 — American musical shows. Actors & actresses, *1860-1950 — Illustrations*

Stars of the American musical theater in historic photographs : 361 portraits from the 1860s to 1950 / edited by Stanley Appelbaum and James Camner. — New York ; Dover ; London : Constable, 1981. — 168p : chiefly ports ; 29cm
Includes index
ISBN 0-486-24209-9 (pbk) : £7.50 B82-37394

782.81′092′2 — Operettas in English. Gilbert, W. S. & Sullivan, *Sir* Arthur — *Critical studies*

Williamson, Audrey, *1913-*. Gilbert and Sullivan opera : an assessment / by Audrey Williamson. — Rev. [ed.]. — London : Boyars, 1982. — xii,292p,[32]p of plates : ill,1facsim,music,ports ; 23cm
Previous ed.: London : Rockcliff, 1953. — Includes index
ISBN 0-7145-2766-1 : £9.95 : CIP rev. B82-07112

782.81′0973 — American cinema films: Musicals — *Critical studies*

Genre : the musical : a reader / edited by Rick Altman. — London : Routledge & Kegan Paul in association with the British Film Institute, 1981. — vii,228p,[8]pof plates : ill ; 23cm. — (British Film Institute readers in film studies)
Bibliography: p208-215. — Includes index
ISBN 0-7100-0816-3 (pbk) : £9.95
ISBN 0-7100-0817-1 (pbk) : £4.95 B82-04456

782.81′0973 — American cinema films: Musicals, *to 1980 — Critical studies*

Hirschhorn, Clive. The Holywood musical / Clive Hirschhorn. — London : Octopus, 1981. — 456p : ill(some col.) ; 33cm
Includes index
ISBN 0-7064-1280-x : £10.95 B82-00988

782.81′0973 — American cinema films: Musicals, *to 1980 — Encyclopaedias*

Green, Stanley, *1923-*. Encyclopaedia of the musical film / Stanley Green. — New York : Oxford University Press, 1981. — 344p ; 24cm
Bibliography: p335-336. — List of sound discs
ISBN 0-19-502958-5 : £12.50 B82-05663

782.81′09794′94 — California. Los Angeles. Hollywood. Cinema films: Musicals, *1927-1977*

Mordden, Ethan. The Hollywood musical / by Ethan Mordden. — Newton Abbot : David & Charles, 1982, c1981. — xii,261p,[18]p of plates : ill ; 24cm
Originally published: New York : St. Martin's Press, 1981. — Bibliography: p239-242. — Includes index
ISBN 0-7153-8319-1 : £7.95 : CIP rev. B82-07585

782.81′2 — Children's musical plays in English. Adams, Chris & Sullivan, Michael — *Librettos*

Adams, Chris. The evacuees : a musical play for schools : the script / book and music by Chris Adams ; lyrics by Chris Adams & Michael Sullivan. — Kingston upon Thames (43 Clifton Rd., Kingston upon Thames, Surrey KT2 6PJ) : Youngsong Music, c1981. — 41p ; 21cm
Text on inside covers. — Bibliography: p41
Unpriced (pbk) B82-32924

782.81′2 — Children's musical plays in English. Canwell, Peter — *Librettos*

Canwell, Peter. Jack Frost : a Christmas fairy tale / by Peter Canwell. — London (50 New Bond St., W1A 2BR) : Chappell Music, 1981. — 15p ; 26cm
Unpriced (pbk) B82-07347

782.81′2 — Children's musical plays in English. Chapple, Reginald — *Librettos*

Chapple, Reginald. The man from Galilee : the Easter story in words and music / Reginald Chapple. — Exeter : Wheaton, 1982. — 44p : music,1plan ; 30cm + children's words(10v. ; 21cm)
ISBN 0-08-027886-8 (pbk) : £4.50
ISBN 0-08-027887-6 (Children's words) B82-06378

782.81′2 — Children's musical plays in English. Lloyd Webber, Andrew — *Librettos*

Lloyd Webber, Andrew. Joseph and the amazing technicolor dreamcoat / Tim Rice & Andrew Lloyd Webber ; with pictures by Quentin Blake. — London : Pavilion, 1982. — [40]p : col.ill ; 29cm
ISBN 0-907516-02-5 : £4.95 : CIP rev. B82-01157

782.81′2 — Children's musical plays in English. Wood, David, *1944-* — *Librettos*

Wood, David, *1944 Feb.21-*. Aladdin : a family musical : book, music and lyrics / by David Wood. — London : French, c1981. — 57p ; 22cm
ISBN 0-573-16403-7 (pbk) : £2.25 B82-13903

Wood, David, *1944-*. Nutcracker sweet : a family musical / book, music and lyrics by David Wood. — London : French, c1981. — 58p : ill ; 22cm
Four men, 3 women
ISBN 0-573-15002-8 (pbk) : £2.25 B82-02904

782.81′2 — Musical plays in English. Cole, Keith R & Pickering, Kenneth — *Librettos*

Pickering, Kenneth. Beowulf : a rock musical / Ken Pickering and Keith Cole. — London : French, c1982. — vii,27p : music ; 22cm
ISBN 0-573-08052-6 (pbk) : Unpriced B82-13908

782.81′2 — Musical plays in English. Coleman, Cy — *Librettos*

Coleman, Cy. I love my wife / book and lyrics by Michael Stewart ; music composed and arranged by Cy Coleman. — New York ; London : French, c1980. — 78p : plans ; 22cm
Six men, 2 women
ISBN 0-573-68110-4 (pbk) : £2.10 B82-39111

782.81′2 — Musical plays in English. Gilder, Eric — *Librettos*

Crocker, John, *1925-*. Sinbad the sailor : a pantomime / by John Crocker ; with words and music by Eric Gilder. — London : Evans Plays, c1980. — [112]p ; 21cm
ISBN 0-237-75058-9 (pbk) : £1.40 B82-16320

782.81′2 — Musical plays in English. Hamilton, Kelly — *Librettos*

Hamilton, Kelly. Trixie True : teen detective : a musical / book, music and lyrics by Kelly Hamilton. — New York ; London : Samuel French, c1981. — 76p : 1plan ; 21cm
Five men, 5 women
ISBN 0-573-68165-1 (pbk) : £3.00 B82-12739

782.81′2 — Musical plays in English. Lloyd Webber, Andrew — *Librettos*

Lloyd Webber, Andrew. Cats : the book of the musical / music by Andrew Lloyd Webber ; based on Old Possum's Book of Practical Cats by T.S. Eliot. — [London] : Faber and Faber, 1981. — 110p : ill(some col.),ports ; 28cm
ISBN 0-571-11862-3 (cased) : £8.95
ISBN 0-571-11863-1 (pbk) : Unpriced B82-04257

782.81′2 — Musical plays in English. Reiser, Dave & Sharkey, Jack — *Librettos*

Sharkey, Jack. The saloonkeeper's daughter : a musical melodrama / by Jack Sharkey & Dave Reiser. — New York ; London : French, c1982. — 103p : 1plan ; 19cm
Six men, six women
ISBN 0-573-61868-2 (pbk) : £3.00 B82-23566

Sharkey, Jack. Slow down, sweet chariot : a musical comedy / by Jack Sharkey and Dave Reiser. — New York ; London : French, c1982. — 82p : 1 plan ; 21cm
Four men, 7 women
ISBN 0-573-61630-2 (pbk) : £3.00 B82-31575

782.81′2 — Musical plays in English. Savage, Tom — *Librettos*

Savage, Tom. Musical chairs : a musical play in two acts / book by Barry Berg, Ken Donnelly and Tom Savage ; music and lyrics by Tom Savage ; based on an original story concept by Larry J. Pontillo. — New York ; London : French, c1982. — 80p : 1plan ; 21cm
Eight men, 8 women. — Plan on inside cover
ISBN 0-573-68145-7 (pbk) : £3.00 B82-28496

782.81′2 — Musical plays in English. Sharkey, Jack & Reiser, Dave — *Librettos*

Sharkey, Jack. The picture of Dorian Gray : a musical drama : (based on the novel by Oscar Wilde) / book, music and lyrics by Jack Sharkey & Dave Reiser. — New York ; London : French, c1982. — 109p ; 18cm
Six men, 4 women. — Text on inside cover
ISBN 0-573-61450-4 (pbk) : £2.75 B82-28340

Sharkey, Jack. Woman overboard : a musical comedy / by Jack Sharkey & Dave Reiser. — New York ; London : French, c1982. — 98p ; 18cm
Six men, 5 women
ISBN 0-573-61822-4 (pbk) : £2.75 B82-28339

782.81′2 — Musical plays in English. Sharkey, Jack — *Librettos*

Sharkey, Jack. "My son the astronaut" / by Jack Sharkey. — Rev. and re-written. — New York ; London : French, c1982. — 98p ; 18cm
Eight men, 4 women, supers. — Previous ed.: published as Pie in the sky. 1963
ISBN 0-573-61861-5 (pbk) : £2.75 B82-34121

782.81′2 — Musical shows in English. Durrent, Peter — *Librettos*

Macalpine, Joan. Liberty beat : a musical / book and lyrics by Joan Macalpine ; music by Peter Durrent. — London : French, c1980. — x,41p : 1plan ; 22cm
ISBN 0-573-08051-8 (pbk) : £2.00 B82-15102

782.81′2 — Operettas in German. Lehár, Franz — *Librettos — English texts*

Lehár, Franz. Gipsy love : operetta in three acts / English book and lyrics by Adam Carstairs ; original book and lyrics by A.M. Willner and Robert Bodanzky ; music by Franz Lehár. — London : Glocken Verlag, c1976. — 64p ; 20cm
Translation of: Zigeunerliebe
Unpriced (pbk) B82-16256

782.95 — BALLET MUSIC

782.9′5′0924 — American ballet music. Stravinsky, Igor. Performances, *to 1981*

Schouvaloff, Alexander. Stravinsky on stage / Alexander Schouvaloff, Victor Borovsky. — London : Stainer & Bell, c1982. — 226p : ill (some col.),1facsim,ports ; 29cm
Bibliography: p211-213. — Includes index
ISBN 0-85249-604-4 : £9.95 B82-37092

783 — RELIGIOUS MUSIC

783′.02′6 — East & West Sussex. Church music, *to 1900*

Allen, Gillian. A short history of music in Sussex churches / by Gillian Allen. — Hove (9 Brunswick Sq., Hove, E. Sussex BN3 1EN) : Chichester Diocesan Fund and Board of Finance, [1981?]. — 8p ; 22cm
Unpriced (unbound) B82-05244

783′.02′6 — English church music, *1545-1650*

The **Treasury** of English church music 1545-1650. — Cambridge : Cambridge University Press, June 1982. — [254]p
Originally published: London : Blandford Press, 1965
ISBN 0-521-24889-2 : £21.00 : CIP entry
ISBN 0-521-28405-8 (pbk) : £7.95 B82-14376

783′.02′63 — Church of England. Parish churches. Music *— Manuals*

Dakers, Lionel. A handbook of parish music : a working guide for clergy and organists / by Lionel Dakers. — Rev. ed. — London : Mowbray, 1982. — xvii,135p : music ; 19cm
Previous ed.: 1976. — Includes index
ISBN 0-264-66836-7 (pbk) : £3.75 B82-40403

783′.092′4 — German religious music. Beethoven, Ludwig van *— Critical studies*

Mellers, Wilfrid. Beethoven and the voice of God. — London : Faber, Oct.1982. — [300]p
ISBN 0-571-11718-x : CIP entry B82-28468

783.2′1 — European religious music. Masses, *to 1980*

Georgiades, Thrasybulos. Music and language. — Cambridge : Cambridge University Press, Oct.1982. — [151]p
Translation of: 2nd ed. of Musik und Sprache
ISBN 0-521-23309-7 (cased) : £15.00 : CIP entry
ISBN 0-521-29902-0 (pbk) : £4.95 B82-26228

783.3′092′4 — Oratorios in English. Handel, George Frideric. Messiah *— Critical studies*

Shaw, Watkins. A textual and historical companion to Handel's Messiah / Watkins Shaw. — Sevenoaks : Novello, 1982, c1965. — 217,15p,[4]p of plates,[2]leaves of plates : ill,facsims ; 22cm
Originally published: 1966. — Bibliography: p211-212. — Includes index
ISBN 0-85360-033-3 (pbk) : £7.00 B82-37371

783.6′2′0942 — Carols in English. Words — *Anthologies*

Jasper, Tony. Rejoice — hymns and carols for great Christian festivals. — London : Miller, Oct.1982. — [160]p
ISBN 0-584-11024-3 : £5.95 : CIP entry B82-23363

783.6′52 — Christmas carols in English. Words — *Texts — For children*

The **Friendly** beasts. — London : Methuen Children's Books, Aug.1982. — [48]p
ISBN 0-416-22200-5 : £3.95 : CIP entry B82-15788

783.6′552 — Christmas carols in English — *Collections*

The **Wexford** carols. — Portlaoise : Dolmen Press, Nov.1981. — [96]p : music
ISBN 0-85105-376-9 (pbk) : £6.00 : CIP entry B81-33649

783.9′5 — Christian church. Public worship. Hymns *— Collections*

Favourite hymns and carols. — London : Methuen, Oct.1982. — [128]p
ISBN 0-413-80210-8 : £5.95 : CIP entry B82-23976

783.9′52 — Christian church. Public worship. Hymns *— Collections*

Hymns for today's church. — London : Hodder & Stoughton, Nov.1982. — [1216]p
ISBN 0-340-27045-4 : £7.95 : CIP entry B82-27339

784 — VOCAL MUSIC

784 — Singing *— For children*

Blackwood, Alan, *1932-*. The performing world of the singer. — London : H. Hamilton, May 1981. — [128]p
ISBN 0-241-10588-9 : £4.95 : CIP entry B81-12819

784 — Songs in English, *to 1980.* **Words** *— Critical studies*

Booth, Mark W.. The experience of songs / Mark W. Booth. — New Haven ; London : Yale University Press, c1981. — ix,226p : 1ill,music,1facsim ; 22cm
Includes index
ISBN 0-300-02622-6 : £12.25 : CIP rev. B81-30241

784′.09 — Vocal music, *to 1981 — For children*

McLeish, Kenneth. The Oxford first companion to singing and dancing / Kenneth and Valerie McLeish. — London : Oxford University Press Music Department, 1982. — 32p : ill(some col.),ports(some col.) ; 32cm
Also published as section D of the Oxford first companion to music. — Cover title. — Text on inside covers
ISBN 0-19-321436-9 (pbk) : Unpriced B82-39416

784′.0924 — Reggae music. Marley, Bob — *Biographies*

Goldman, Vivian. Bob Marley. — London : Hutchinson, July 1981. — [96]p
ISBN 0-09-146481-1 (pbk) : £2.95 : CIP entry B81-22592

784′.092′4 — Singing. Baillie, Isobel *— Biographies*

Baillie, Isobel. Never sing louder than lovely. — London : Hutchinson, Oct.1982. — [176]p
ISBN 0-09-150460-0 : £8.95 : CIP entry B82-24977

784′.092′4 — Songs in English. French, Percy — *Biographies*

French, Percy. The world of Percy French / by Brendan O'Dowda ; music copyist Elizabeth Bicker. — Dundonald : Blackstaff, 1981. — viii,192p : ill,music,facsims,ports ; 24cm
Bibliography: p191. — Includes index
ISBN 0-85640-255-9 (pbk) : £5.95 : CIP rev.
Primary classification 784.3′06 B81-31205

784′.0942 — Songs in English. Words *— Texts*

Jones, Roger, *1948-*. Apostle / Roger Jones. — Maidstone : Third Day Enterprises
Audience participation leaflet. — [1982?]. — [4]p ; 22cm
£0.04 (unbound) B82-31110

Jones, Roger, *1948-*. Apostle / Roger Jones. — Maidstone : Third Day Enterprises
Words ed. — 1982. — 10p ; 22cm
ISBN 0-9505912-8-9 (unbound) : £0.40 B82-31109

784′.0973 — Songs in English: American songs, *1880-1980 — Critical studies*

Friedberg, Ruth C.. American art song and American poetry / Ruth C. Friedberg. — Metuchen, N.J. ; London : Scarecrow
Vol.1: America comes of age. — 1981. — viii,167p : music ; 23cm
Bibliography: p145-152. — Includes index
ISBN 0-8108-1460-9 : £12.00 B82-05358

784′.09931 — Songs in English. New Zealand writers. Words *— Texts*

Charles, Joe. Black billy tea : New Zealand ballads / by Joe Charles ; drawings by Jean Oates. — Christchurch, N.Z. ; London : Whitcoulls, 1981. — 96p : ill ; 25cm
ISBN 0-7233-0656-7 : Unpriced B82-06579

784.3′0092′4 — Lieder. Singing. Fischer-Dieskau, Dietrich

Whitton, Kenneth S.. Dietrich Fischer-Dieskau. — London : Wolff, Oct.1981. — [320]p
ISBN 0-85496-405-3 : £15.00 : CIP entry B81-25737

784.3′0092′4 — Lieder. Wolf, Hugo *— Critical studies*

Carner, Mosco. Hugo Wolf songs / Mosco Carner. — London : British Broadcasting Corporation, 1982. — 72p : music ; 20cm. — (BBC music guides)
Includes index
ISBN 0-563-17877-9 (pbk) : £2.25 B82-33169

784.3′05 — Songs in English. Words — *Anthologies — For cub scouts*

Cub scout songs : a collection of folk songs and others complete with guitar chords / compiled by Brian J. Sims. — Glasgow : Brown, Son & Ferguson, 1972, c1981 (1981 [printing]). — vii,66p : ill ; 15cm
Includes index
ISBN 0-85174-202-5 (pbk) : £1.80 B82-12286

784.3′06 — Songs in English *— Collections*

French, Percy. The world of Percy French / by Brendan O'Dowda ; music copyist Elizabeth Bicker. — Dundonald : Blackstaff, 1981. — viii,192p : ill,music,facsims,ports ; 24cm
Bibliography: p191. — Includes index
ISBN 0-85640-255-9 (pbk) : £5.95 : CIP rev.
Also classified at 784′.092′4 B81-31205

784.3′06 — Songs in Old French, *1150-1300 — Collections*

Chanter m'estuet = Songs of the trouvères / edited by Samuel N. Rosenberg ; music edited by Hans Tischler. — London : Faber Music, 1981. — xlvii,560p : music ; 25cm
Old French text, English introduction and notes. — Bibliography: pxxxii-xlvii. — Includes index
ISBN 0-571-10042-2 : £25.00 B82-09970

784.4′9411 — Folk songs in English: Scottish folk songs *— Collections*

Macgregor, Jimmie. Jimmie Macgregor's folk songs of Scotland : words, music, pictures. — Norwich : Jarrold
Bk.1. — 1981. — 31p : ill(some col.),music ; 25cm
Cover title. — Text, ill on inside covers
ISBN 0-85306-933-6 (pbk) : Unpriced B82-01361

Macgregor, Jimmie. Jimmie Macgregor's folk songs of Scotland : words, music, pictures. — Norwich : Jarrold
Bk.2. — 1981. — 32p : ill(some col.),music,2ports ; 25cm
Cover title. — Text, ill, music on inside covers
ISBN 0-85306-957-3 (pbk) : Unpriced B82-01362

784.4′9411 — Folk songs in Gaelic. Anthologies. Carmichael, Alexander. Carmina Gadelica — *Critical studies*

Campbell, J. L.. Notes on Alexander Carmichael's Carmina Gadelica / by J.L. Campbell. — [Isle of Canna] : [J.L. Campbell], 1982. — [68]p ; 21cm
'Privately reprinted from Scottish Gaelic Studies'. — Includes text in Gaelic. — Limited ed. of 45 copies
Unpriced B82-29345

784.4′942 — Folk songs in English — *Collections*

Deacon, George. John Clare, folk collector. — London (10 Archway Close, N19 3TD) : Sinclair Browne, May 1982. — [288]p
ISBN 0-86300-008-8 : £15.00 : CIP entry
B82-07694

784.5′0028 — Popular songs. Composition — *Manuals*

Neal, Roy. Compose your own tunes : the Roy Neal tune-tutor. — Peterborough (P.O. Box 118, Peterborough PE3 6UY) : Sceptre Publishers, c1981. — 32p : ill,music ; 31cm
Cover title
Unpriced (pbk) B82-07136

784.5′006 — Pop music. Groups. Organisation — *Manuals — For schools — German texts*

Pop-Musik mit Schülern : Arbeitshilfe zur Leitung und Beratung von Popgruppen / herausgegeben von Josef Brock und Jürgen Moser ; mit Beiträgen von Paul Bumbalek ... [et al.]. — Mainz ; London : Schott, c1981. — 108p : ill,music ; 21cm. — (Bausteine für Musikerziehung, ISSN 0172-7222)
ISBN 3-7957-1036-7 (pbk) : £4.50 B82-37966

784.5′006 — Popular music. Groups. Organisation — *Humour*

Barlow, David, *1943-*. The Instant Sunshine book : with hints for struggling supergroups / David Barlow ... [et al.] ; songs by Peter Christie ; drawings by Heath. — London : Robson, 1980. — 96p : ill ; 24cm
ISBN 0-86051-119-7 : £3.95
Primary classification 784.5′06 B82-28905

784.5′0092′2 — English pop music. Beatles, *1967-1981*

Woffinden, Bob. The Beatles apart / Bob Woffinden. — London : Proteus, 1981. — [145]p : ill,ports(some col.) ; 28cm. — (Proteus rocks)
Bibliography: p[145]. — List of sound recordings : p[143]-[144]
ISBN 0-906071-89-5 (pbk) : £4.95 B82-05631

784.5′0092′2 — English pop music. Police, *to 1980*

Sutcliffe, Phil. The Police : l'historia bandido / by Phil Sutcliffe and Hugh Fielder. — London : Proteus, 1981. — 96p : ill,ports(some col.) ; 28cm. — (Proteus rocks)
ISBN 0-906071-77-1 (cased) : Unpriced
B82-06671

784.5′0092′2 — English pop music. Shadows, *to 1980*

Geddes, George T.. The Shadows : a history and discography / by George Geddes. — Glasgow (102 Dorchester Ave., Glasgow, G12 0EB) : G. and M. Geddes, 1981. — 178p ; 30cm
Bibliography: p173-175
£5.00 (spiral)
Also classified at 016.7899′1245′00922
B82-03930

784.5′0092′2 — English pop music. Shadows, *to 1982*

The **Story** of the Shadows. — London : Hamilton, Sept.1982. — [192]p
ISBN 0-241-10861-6 (cased) : £9.95 : CIP entry
ISBN 0-241-10887-x (pbk) : £5.95 B82-20622

784.5′0092′2 — Pop music. Beatles. Long-playing sound discs — *Critical studies*

Russell, Jeff. The Beatles album file and complete discography 1961-1982. — Poole : Blandford, Dec.1982. — 1v.
ISBN 0-7137-1277-5 (cased) : £7.95 : CIP entry
ISBN 0-7137-1294-5 (pbk) : £4.95 B82-30214

784.5′0092′2 — Pop music. Beatles, *to 1964 — Personal observations*

Epstein, Brian. A cellarful of noise / Brian Epstein. — London : New English Library, 1965, c1964 (1981 [printing]). — 119p ; 18cm
Originally published: London : Souvenir, 1964
ISBN 0-450-05388-1 (pbk) : £1.25 B82-08675

784.5′0092′2 — Pop music. Beatles, *to 1970*

Norman, Philip. Shout! : the true story of the Beatles / Philip Norman. — [London] : Corgi, 1982, c1981. — 426p,[16]p of plates : ill,ports ; 20cm
Originally published: London : Elm Tree, 1981
ISBN 0-552-11961-x (pbk) : £2.50 B82-36740

Ranson, Arthur. The Beatles : their story in pictures / drawn by Arthur Ranson ; written by Angus P. Allan. — London : ITV Books ; London : Distributed by TV Times, c1982. — 49p : all ill,ports ; 30cm. — (A TV times/Look-in special)
ISBN 0-907965-04-0 (pbk) : £0.50 B82-35294

784.5′0092′2 — Pop music. Beatles, *to 1978*

Davies, Hunter. The Beatles : the authorized biography / Hunter Davies. — [New ed.]. — London : Mayflower, 1978 (1979 [printing]). — 400p,[40]p of plates : ill,facsims,ports ; 18cm
Previous ed.: London : Heinemann, 1968. — List of discs: p387-396
ISBN 0-586-05014-0 (pbk) : £1.95 B82-38666

784.5′0092′2 — Pop music. Beatles, *to 1981*

Blake, John, *1948-*. All you needed was love : the Beatles after the Beatles / John Blake. — Feltham : Hamlyn Paperbacks, 1981. — 227p,[8]p of plates : ports ; 18cm. — (A Hamlyn original)
ISBN 0-600-20466-9 (pbk) : £1.50 B82-02837

784.5′0092′2 — Pop music. Lennon, John & McCartney, Paul — *Biographies*

Doney, Malcolm. Lennon and McCartney / Malcolm Doney. — Tunbridge Wells : Midas, 1981. — 128p,[8]p of plates : ports ; 23cm
List of sound recordings: p121-128
ISBN 0-85936-236-1 : £4.95 B82-00121

784.5′0092′2 — Pop music. Lennon, John & Ono, Yoko — *Interviews*

Lennon, John. The Playboy interviews with John Lennon and Yoko Ono / conducted by David Sheff ; edited by G. Barry Golson. — Sevenoaks : New English Library, 1982, c1981. — xiv,193p : ports ; 20cm
Originally published: New York : Playboy Press, c1981
ISBN 0-450-05489-6 (pbk) : £2.50 : CIP rev.
B82-12577

784.5′0092′2 — Pop music. Queen — *Illustrations*

Queen's greatest pix / compiled, edited & designed by Jacques Lowe ; text by Ray Bonici ... [et al.] ; cover photo by Snowdon ; interior photos by Neal Preston and others. — London : Quartet, 1981. — 95p : chiefly ill(some col.),ports(some col.) ; 28cm
List of sound discs : p94
ISBN 0-7043-3389-9 (pbk) : £3.95 B82-04782

784.5′0092′2 — Pop music. Rolling Stones, *to 1973*

Stoned / photographs, Gered Mankowitz ; editor and designer, Pearce Marchbank ; music selection, Peter Evans. — London : Wise, c1982. — 63p : ill,music,ports ; 31cm
ISBN 0-86001-914-4 (pbk) : Unpriced
B82-37750

784.5′0092′2 — Pop music. Who, *to 1980*

Swenson, John. The Who / John Swenson. — London : W.H. Allen, 1981. — 167p,[8]p of plates : ill,ports ; 18cm. — (A Star book)
Originally published: New York : Tempo, 1979. — List of sound discs: p163-167
ISBN 0-352-30943-1 (pbk) : £1.50 B82-03036

784.5′0092′2 — Pop music. Wings *(Group)* — *Serials*

Club sandwich / Wings Fun Club. — No.1 (Feb./Mar. 1977)-. — London (P.O. Box 4UP, W1A 4UP) : The Club, 1977-. — v. : ill,ports ; 59cm
Irregular. — Description based on: No.24 (1981)
ISSN 0262-9054 = Club sandwich : Unpriced
B82-12473

784.5′0092′4 — American pop music. Dylan, Bob — *Critical studies*

Herdman, John. Voice without restraint : a study of Bob Dylan's lyrics and their background / John Herdman. — Edinburgh : Harris, [1982]. — 164p ; 23cm
Bibliography: p155-6. — Includes index
ISBN 0-86228-019-2 (cased) : £8.95
ISBN 0-86228-037-0 (pbk) : £4.95 B82-17545

784.5′0092′4 — American pop music. Springsteen, Bruce — *Biographies*

Marsh, Dave. [Born to run]. Springsteen : born to run : the story of Bruce Springsteen / by Dave Marsh. — London : Omnibus Press, 1981, c1979. — 191p : ill,ports ; 27cm
Originally published: Garden City : Dolphin, 1979
ISBN 0-86001-807-5 (pbk) : Unpriced
B82-05987

784.5′0092′4 — American popular music. Singing. Jolson, Al — *Biographies*

Oberfirst, Robert. Al Jolson : you ain't heard nothin yet / Robert Oberfirst. — San Diego : Barnes ; London : Tantivy, 1982, c1980. — 341p : ill,ports ; 23cm
ISBN 0-498-02589-6 (pbk) : £5.75 B82-35430

784.5′0092′4 — English pop music. Bowie, David, *to 1980*

Charlesworth, Chris. David Bowie : profile / by Chris Charlesworth. — [London] : Proteus, 1981. — 95p : ill,ports(some col.) ; 28cm. — (Proteus rocks)
List of sound recordings: p93-95
ISBN 0-906071-82-8 (cased) : Unpriced
B82-06672

784.5′0092′4 — English pop music. McCartney, Mike — *Biographies*

McCartney, Mike. Thank U very much : Mike McCartney's family album. — London : Barker, 1981. — [188]p : ill,facsims,ports ; 29cm
ISBN 0-213-16816-2 : £5.95 B82-04366

784.5′0092′4 — Pop music. Lennon, John — *Biographies*

Ryan, David Stuart. John Lennon's secret. — London (48a Astonville St., SW18 5AL) : Kozmik Press Centre, Oct.1982. — [320]p
ISBN 0-905116-07-0 (cased) : £9.85 : CIP entry
ISBN 0-905116-08-9 (pbk) : £6.50 B82-24613

784.5′0092′4 — Pop music. O'Connor, Hazel — *Biographies*

O'Connor, Hazel. Hazel O'Connor-uncovered plus / by Hazel O'Connor. — London : Proteus, 1981. — 127p : col.ill,facsims,ports (some col.) ; 26cm
List of sound discs: p125
ISBN 0-86276-008-9 : £7.95
ISBN 0-906071-81-x (pbk) : Unpriced
B82-09084

784.5′0092′4 — Pop music. Singing. Jones, Grace — *Illustrations*

Gonde, Jean Paul. Jungle fever. — London : Quartet, Oct.1982. — [144]p
ISBN 0-7043-2339-7 : £15.00 : CIP entry
B82-20049

784.5′0092′4 — Pop music. Singing. Lewis, Jerry Lee — *Biographies*

Tosches, Nick. Hellfire : the Jerry Lee Lewis story. — London : Plexus, June 1982. — [288]p
ISBN 0-85965-053-7 (cased) : £8.95 : CIP entry
ISBN 0-85965-052-9 (pbk) : £4.95 B82-17904

784.5′0092′4 — Pop music. Singing. Presley, Elvis

The **Complete** Elvis / edited by Martin Torgoff ; art direction by Ed Caraeff. — London : Sidgwick & Jackson, 1982. — 253p : ill,ports (some col.) ; 29cm
Originally published: United States : Delilah, 1982. — Bibliography: p252-253
ISBN 0-283-98855-x : £8.95 B82-23527

784.5′0092′4 — Pop music. Singing. Presley, Elvis — *Biographies*

Crumbaker, Marge. Up and down with Elvis Presley / Marge Crumbaker with Gabe Tucker. — London : New English Library, 1982, c1981. — 209p,[16]p of plates : ill,ports ; 18cm
Originally published: New York : Putnam, 1981
ISBN 0-450-05492-6 (pbk) : £1.75 : CIP rev. B82-15808

784.5′0092′4 — Pop music. Singing. Presley, Elvis — *Biographies — For children*

Wooton, Richard. Elvis Presley : king of rock and roll / [Richard Wooton]. — London : Hodder and Stoughton, 1982. — 128p : ill,ports ; 24cm. — (Twentieth century people)
Includes index
ISBN 0-340-26954-5 : £5.95 : CIP rev. B82-01090

784.5′0092′4 — Pop music. Singing. Presley, Elvis — *Encyclopaedias*

Worth, Fred L.. All about Elvis / Fred L. Worth and Steve D. Tamerius. — Toronto ; London : Bantam, 1981. — xxx,414p ; 18cm
Bibliography: p411-414
ISBN 0-553-14129-5 (pbk) : £1.95 B82-08040

784.5′0092′4 — Pop music. Singing. Presley, Elvis — *Illustrations*

Naphray, A. R.. Goodbye / [A.R. Naphray] ; [1975 photographs by J. Rock Caile, 1976 and 1977 photographs by John Herman]. — [Wednesbury] ([2 Engine La., Wednesbury, West Midlands]) : [Bavie], [1977]. — 5v. : ill,ports ; 30cm
Cover title
Unpriced (pbk)
Also classified at 821′.914 B82-21277

Naphray, A. R.. Pyromania / [A.R. Naphray]. — Wednesbury (2 Engine La., Wednesbury, West Midlands) : Bavie, 1976, c1975. — 5v. : ill,ports ; 30cm
Unpriced (pbk)
Also classified at 821′.914 B82-21276

784.5′0092′4 — Pop music. Singing. Presley, Elvis — *Interviews*

Presley, Elvis. Elvis in his own words : compiled by Mick Farren / designed and edited by Pearce Marchbank. — London : W.H. Allen, 1981, c1977. — 123p : ill,chiefly ports ; 27cm
Originally published: London : Omnibus, 1977
ISBN 0-491-02776-1 : £4.95 B82-04932

784.5′0092′4 — Pop music. Singing. Richard, Cliff — *Biographies*

Doncaster, Patrick. Cliff / Patrick Doncaster & Tony Jasper, written in co-operation with Cliff Richard. — London : Sidgwick & Jackson, 1981. — 240p : ports ; 24cm
List of sound recordings: p209-223. — List of films: p223-225. — Includes index
ISBN 0-283-98783-9 : £7.50 B82-00585

Richard, Cliff. Cliff in his own words / compiled by Kevin St. John. — London : W.H. Allen, 1981. — 127p : ill,ports ; 27cm
ISBN 0-491-02786-9 : £4.95 B82-13188

784.5′0092′4 — Pop music. Singing. Richard, Cliff - *Biographies*

Richard, Cliff. Which one′s Cliff?. — Sevenoaks : Hodder & Stoughton, Aug.1981. — [256]p. — (Coronet books)
Originally published: London : Hodder & Stoughton, 1977
ISBN 0-340-27159-0 (pbk) : £1.25 : CIP entry B81-15906

784.5′0092′4 — Popular music. Singing. Chevalier, Maurice — *Biographies*

Harding, James, *1929-*. Maurice Chevalier. — London : Secker and Warburg, Oct.1982. — [224]p
ISBN 0-436-19107-5 : £7.95 : CIP entry B82-24009

784.5′0092′4 — Popular music. Singing. Cole, Nat King — *Biographies*

Cole, Maria. Nat King Cole / Maria Cole. — London : W.H. Allen, 1972 (1982 [printing]). — 184p,[8]p of plates : ports ; 18cm. — (A Star book)
Originally published: New York : Morrow, 1971. — Includes list of sound recordings
ISBN 0-352-31037-5 (pbk) : £1.50 B82-11714

784.5′0092′4 — Popular music. Singing. Fields, Gracie — *Biographies*

Fields, Gracie. Sing as we go : the autobiography of Gracie Fields. — Large print ed. — Bath : Chivers, 1981, c1960. — 290p ; 23cm. — (A New Portway large print book)
Originally published: London : Muller, 1960
ISBN 0-85119-136-3 : Unpriced : CIP rev. B81-25798

784.5′0092′4 — Popular music. Singing. Manilow, Barry — *Biographies*

Jasper, Tony. Barry Manilow / Tony Jasper. — London : W.H. Allen, 1981. — 159p,[8]p of plates : 1facsim,ports ; 18cm. — (A star book)
List of sound discs: p129-159
ISBN 0-352-31002-2 (pbk) : £1.50 B82-09517

784.5′0092′4 — Popular music. Singing. Manilow, Barry, *to 1980*

Clarke, Alan. The magic of Barry Manilow / Alan Clarke. — [London] : Prize Books, 1981. — 48p : ports ; 28cm
List of sound recordings: p44-48
ISBN 0-86276-009-7 (pbk) : £1.95 B82-05629

784.5′0092′4 — Popular music. Singing. O′Hara, Mary, *19---* — *Biographies*

O′Hara, Mary, *1935-*. The scent of the roses / by Mary O′Hara. — Large print ed. — Long Preston : Magna Print, 1981, c1980. — 528p ; 23cm
Originally published: London : Joseph, 1980. — Published in large print
ISBN 0-86009-359-x : Unpriced : CIP rev. B81-22501

784.5′0092′4 — Popular music. Singing. Sinatra, Frank — *Biographies*

Howlett, John, *1940-*. Frank Sinatra / John Howlett. — London : Plexus, c1980. — 176p : facsims,ports ; 30cm
List of films: p158-167. — List of sound discs: p168-175. — Bibliography: p176
ISBN 0-85965-022-7 (cased) : £7.95 : CIP rev.
ISBN 0-85965-021-9 (pbk) : £4.95 B79-30254

784.5′0092′4 — Popular music. Singing. Streisand, Barbra — *Biographies*

Zec, Donald. Barbra. — London : New English Library, Sept.1982. — [416]p
ISBN 0-450-05398-9 (pbk) : £1.95 : CIP entry B82-19689

784.5′0092′4 — Scottish pop music. Stewart, Rod — *Biographies*

Nelson, Paul. Rod Stewart / Paul Nelson & Lester Bangs. — London : Sidgwick & Jackson, 1982, c1981. — 159p : ports(some col.) ; 28cm
Originally published: New York : Delilah Communications, 1981
ISBN 0-283-98836-3 (pbk) : £4.95 B82-14156

784.5′05 — Pop songs in English. Words — *Texts*

Ant, Adam. Adam and the Ants ″Kings″ : the official Adam and the Ants song book / [words & music by Adam Ant and Marco Pirroni] ; [text Stephen Lavers]. — London : Mirror Books, 1981. — [44]p : ill(some col.),music,ports(some col.) ; 31cm
ISBN 0-85939-301-1 (unbound) : £1.25 B82-09027

Landesman, Miles Davis. In real life : the rock lyrics of Miles Davis Landesman. — London : Golden Handshake, 1981. — 32p ; 21cm
ISBN 0-905150-33-3 (pbk) : £1.25 B82-01592

784.5′05 — Popular songs in English, *1850-1969*. **Words** — *Anthologies*

Stanley Holloway, more monologues and songs / edited and with an introduction by Michael Marshall ; illustrated by Bill Tidy. — London : Elm Tree Books, 1980. — xvii,77p : ill ; 20cm
List of sound discs: p75-77
ISBN 0-241-10478-5 (pbk) : £2.25
Also classified at 821′.07′08 B82-09137

784.5′05 — Popular songs in English. Words — *Texts*

Tate, Carole. When father papered the parlour / illustrated by Carole Tate ; words and music R.P. Weston & F.J. Barnes. — London : Macmillan Children′s, 1981. — [24]p : col.ill,music ; 26cm
Music on lining papers
ISBN 0-333-32167-7 : £3.95 B82-06899

784.5′06 — Humorous popular songs in English — *Collections*

Barlow, David, *1943-*. The Instant Sunshine book : with hints for struggling supergroups / David Barlow ... [et al.] ; songs by Peter Christie ; drawings by Heath. — London : Robson, 1980. — 96p : ill ; 24cm
ISBN 0-86051-119-7 : £3.95
Also classified at 784.5′006 B82-28905

784.5′092′4 — Popular music. Singing. Piaf, Edith — *Biographies*

Lange, Monique. Piaf. — London : Plexus, Oct.1981. — [240]p
Translation of: Histoire de Piaf
ISBN 0-85965-046-4 (pbk) : £5.95 : CIP entry B81-27468

784.5′2′005 — Bluegrass music — *Serials*

′Grass seen. — Issue 1-. — London (130 Baring Rd, SE12) : ′Grass Seen, [1982]-. — v. : ports ; 30cm
Irregular
ISSN 0263-3833 = ′Grass seen : £0.80 B82-24758

784.5′2′00924 — American country music. Riley, Jeannie C. — *Biographies*

Riley, Jeannie C.. From Harper Valley to the mountain top / Jeannie C. Riley with Jamie Buckingham. — Eastbourne : Kingsway, 1981. — 211p ; 18cm
Originally published: Lincoln, Va. : Chosen Books, 1981
ISBN 0-86065-155-x (pbk) : £1.60 B82-00716

784.5′2′00924 — American country music. Williams, Hank — *Biographies*

Williams, Roger M.. Sing a sad song : the life of Hank Williams / Roger M. Williams. — 2nd ed. / with a discography by Bob Pinson. — Urbana ; London : University of Illinois Press, c1981. — ix,318p ; 23cm. — (Music in American life)
Previous ed.: New York : Ballantine Books, 1973. — List of sound discs: p263-303. — Includes index
ISBN 0-252-00844-8 (cased) : Unpriced
ISBN 0-252-00861-8 (pbk) : £5.60 B82-12775

784.5′2′00973 — Scotland. American country music — *Serials*

Scottish country music express. — May-. — [South Queensferry] ([17 Echline Green, South Queensferry, West Lothian]) : [Scottish Country Music Express], [1981]-. — v. : ports ; 30cm
Monthly. — Description based on: March [1982] issue
ISSN 0263-2527 = Scottish country music express : £0.20 per issue B82-20894

784.5′3′00922 — United States. Blues. Musicians — *Biographies*

McKee, Margaret. Beale black & blue : life and music on black America′s main street / Margaret McKee, Fred Chisenhall. — Baton Rouge ; London : Louisiana State Uiversity Press, c1981. — xii,265p : ill,1map,ports ; 24cm
Bibliography: p257-258. — Includes index
ISBN 0-8071-0863-4 : £12.50
Also classified at 976.8′19 B82-15449

784.5'3'00924 — United States. Blues. King, B. B. — *Biographies*

Sawyer, Charles. B.B. King. — London : Quartet, Aug.1982. — [288]p
Originally published: Poole : Blandford, 1980
ISBN 0-7043-3415-1 (pbk) : £4.95 : CIP entry
B82-21967

784.5'3'00973 — United States. Blues, *to 1975*

Vulliamy, Graham. Jazz & blues / Graham Vulliamy. — London : Routledge & Kegan Paul, 1982. — ix,158p : ill,facsims,ports ; 23cm. — (Routledge popular music)
Bibliography: p153-154. — List of sound discs: p154. — Includes index
ISBN 0-7100-0894-5 : £5.95 : CIP rev.
Also classified at 785.42'0973 B82-11770

784.5'3'00973 — United States. Blues, *to 1980*

Bane, Michael. White boy singin' the blues / by Michael Bane. — Harmondsworth : Penguin, 1982. — 269p ; 20cm
Includes index
ISBN 0-14-006045-6 (pbk) : £2.50 B82-41155

Evans, David, *1944-*. Big road blues : tradition and creativity in the folk blues / David Evans. — Berkeley ; London : University of California Press, c1982. — xiii,379p : ill,music,ports,27cm
Bibliography: p351-364. — Includes index
ISBN 0-520-03484-8 : £19.50 B82-31181

Guralnick, Peter. The blues / Peter Guralnick. — Poole : Blandford, 1982. — 134p : ports ; 23cm. — (The Listener's guide) (A Quarto book)
Includes index
ISBN 0-7137-1251-1 : £4.95 : CIP rev.
B82-01202

784.5'4 — Heavy metal rock music — *Serials*

Kerrang!. — No.1 (June 1981)-. — [London] ([40 Longacre, WC2]) : [Spotlight Publications], 1981-. — v. : ill(some col.),ports ; 28cm
Monthly (1981-Jan. 1982), Fortnightly (Feb. 11 1982-). — Description based on: No.7 (Jan. 1982)
ISSN 0262-6624 = Kerrang! : £0.50 per issue
B82-20889

784.5'4'005 — Rock music — *Serials*

The **Rock** yearbook. — 1981-. — New York : Delilah/Grove Press ; [London] ([95 Ladbroke Grove, W11 1PG]) : [Virgin Books], [1980]-. — v. : ill(some col.),ports(some col.) ; 28cm
ISSN 0275-9187 = The Rock year book : £12.50 for 1982 issue B82-03405

784.5'4'009 — Rock & roll music, *to 1960*

Colman, Stuart. They kept on rockin' : the giants of rock'n'roll / Stuart Colman. — Poole : Blandford, 1982. — 160p : ill,facsims,ports ; 25cm
Includes index
ISBN 0-7137-1217-1 (pbk) : £4.95 : CIP rev.
B82-06250

Rogers, Dave. Rock 'n' roll / Dave Rogers. — London : Routledge & Kegan Paul, 1982. — ix,148p : ill,facsims,ports ; 23cm. — (Routledge popular music)
Bibliography: p144-145. — List of sound discs: p145. — Includes index
ISBN 0-7100-0938-0 : £5.95 : CIP rev.
B82-11771

784.5'4'009 — Rock music, *to 1980*

Marsh, Dave. The book of rock lists / by Dave Marsh and Kevin Stein. — London : Sidgwick & Jackson, 1981. — xxvii,643p : ill,ports ; 21cm. — (A Rolling Stone Press book)
Originally published: New York : Dell Publishing, 1981. — Bibliography: p641-643
ISBN 0-283-98837-1 (pbk) : £4.95 B82-08061

784.5'4'009 — Rock music, *to 1981* — *Statistics*

Tobler, John. The rock lists album. — London : Plexus, Oct.1982. — [144]p
ISBN 0-85965-049-9 (cased) : £9.95 : CIP entry
ISBN 0-85965-048-0 (pbk) : £4.95 B82-29145

784.5'4'009047 — Rock music, *1967-1980* — *Interviews*

The **Rolling** Stone interviews 1967-1980 : talking with the legends of rock & roll 1967-1980 / by the editors of Rolling Stone ; introduction by Ben Fong-Torres ; edited by Peter Herbst. — London : Rolling Stone Press, 1981. — 426p : ports ; 28cm
Originally published: New York : St Martin's Press, 1981
ISBN 0-213-16818-9 (pbk) : £6.50 B82-04009

784.5'4'00922 — Pop music. Blondie — *Biographies*

Harry, Debbie. Making tracks : the rise of Blondie / by Debbie Harry, Chris Stein and Victor Bockris. — London : Elm Tree, 1982. — 192p : ill(some col.),ports(some col.) ; 28cm
ISBN 0-241-10838-1 (pbk) : £5.95 : CIP rev.
B82-09204

784.5'4'00922 — Punk rock music. Sex Pistols — *Interviews*

The **Sex** Pistols : the inside story / [compiled by] Fred and Judy Vermovel. — Revised ed. — London : W.H. Allen, 1981. — 287p,[16]p of plates : ill,2facsims,ports ; 18cm. — (A star book)
Previous ed.: 1978
ISBN 0-352-31058-8 (pbk) : £2.50 B82-08479

784.5'4'00922 — Rock music — *Biographies*

York, William. Who's who in rock music / William York. — Rev. ed. — London : Arthur Barker, 1982. — 413p ; 28cm
Previous ed.: Seattle : Atomic Press, c1978
ISBN 0-213-16820-0 (pbk) : £8.95 B82-31054

784.5'4'00922 — Rock music. Jam *(Group), to 1982*

Honeyford, Paul. The Jam : the modern world by numbers / Paul Honeyford. — London : W.H. Allen, 1982, c1980. — 125p,[4]p of plates : ill,ports ; 18cm. — (A Star book)
Originally published: London : Eel Pie, 1980. — List of sound recordings: p9
ISBN 0-352-31138-x (pbk) : £1.60 B82-34871

784.5'4'00922 — Rock music. Led Zeppelin, *to 1980*

Bunton, Richard. Led Zeppelin : in the light 1968-1980 / Richard Bunton & Howard Mylett. — London : Proteus, c1981. — 96p : ill,ports(some col.) ; 28cm. — (Proteus rocks)
List of sound recordings: p95
ISBN 0-906071-65-8 (pbk) : £4.50 B82-05630

784.5'4'00922 — Rock music. Roxy Music, *to 1981*

Rogan, Johnny. Roxy music : style with substance - Roxy's first ten years / Johnny Rogan. — [London] : Star, 1982. — 219p,[12]p of plates : ports ; 18cm
List of sound discs: p217-219
ISBN 0-352-31076-6 (pbk) : £1.75 B82-22768

784.5'4'00922 — Rock music. Stars

Gambaccini, Paul. Masters of rock / Paul Gambaccini. — London : British Broadcasting Corporation, 1982. — 223p : ports ; 23cm
ISBN 0-563-20068-5 (pbk) : £4.95
ISBN 0-7119-0081-7 (Omnibus Press)
B82-35357

784.5'4'00922 — Rock music. Stars — *Serials*

[The face *(London)*]. The face. — Issue no.1 (May 1980)-. — London ([4th Floor, 5 Mortimer St., W1]) : [s.n.], 1980-. — v. : ill (some col.),ports ; 31cm
Monthly
ISSN 0263-1210 = Face (London) : £0.65
B82-18484

784.5'4'00922 — Rock music, *to 1980* — *Biographies*

Bane, Michael. Who's who in rock / by Michael Bane ; researcher Kenny Kertok. — Oxford : Clio Press, c1981. — x,259p : ports ; 29cm
Originally published: New York : Facts on File, c1981. — Includes index
ISBN 0-87196-465-1 : £12.50 B82-09000

784.5'4'00924 — Rock music. Hendrix, Jimi — *Biographies*

Henderson, David, *1942-*. 'Scuse me while I kiss the sky : the life of Jimi Hendrix / David Henderson. — Rev. ed. — Toronto ; London : Bantam, 1981. — x,384p : ill,ports ; 23cm
Previous ed.: published as Jimi Hendrix. Garden City, N.Y. : Doubleday, 1978
ISBN 0-553-01334-3 (pbk) : £3.95 B82-10206

784.5'4'00924 — Rock music. Richards, Keith — *Biographies*

Charone, Barbara. Keith Richards / Barbara Charone. — London : Futura, 1979. — 192p : ill,ports ; 25cm
List of sound discs: p191-192
ISBN 0-7088-1658-4 (pbk) : £3.50 B82-36920

784.5'4'00941 — Great Britain. Rock music, *1970-1979*

Van der Kiste, John. Roxeventies : popular music in Britain, 1970-79 / John Van der Kiste. — Torpoint : Kawabata, 1982. — 41p : ill ; 21cm
ISBN 0-906110-34-3 (pbk) : £1.00 B82-21420

784.5'4'009429 — Welsh rock music

Gwreiddiau canu roc Cymraeg / Geraint Jarman ... [et al.]. — Penygroes, Gwynedd (40 Stryd y Wyddfa, Penygroes, Gwynedd) : Cyhoeddwyd gyda chydweithrediad BBC Radio Cymru gan Gyhoeddiadau Mei, 1981. — 58p : ill,ports ; 16x18cm
£1.00 (pbk) B82-27460

784.5'4'0922 — Rock music. Stars

Herman, Gary. Rock'n'roll Babylon. — London : Plexus, Sept.1981. — [192]p
ISBN 0-85965-040-5 (cased) : £8.95 : CIP entry
ISBN 0-85965-041-3 (pbk) : £4.95 B81-23797

784.6'24 — Children's songs in English — *Texts*

Kennedy, Jimmy. Teddy bears' picnic / from the lyric by Jimmy Kennedy ; illustrated by Barbara Sampson. — Cambridge : Dinosaur, c1981. — [25]p : col.ill ; 16x19cm. — (Dinosaur's Althea books)
ISBN 0-85122-312-5 (cased) : Unpriced
ISBN 0-85122-328-1 (pbk) : Unpriced
B82-31059

784.6'24'0091821 — Children's action songs in English: Caribbean songs. Words — *Anthologies*

Benjamin, Joe. A musical journey for littleys : with songs and song games / by Joe Benjamin. — [London] ([142 Kennington Park Rd, SE11 4DJ]) : Thomas Joseph, c1982. — 31p : ill,ports ; 30cm
Cover title
Unpriced (pbk) B82-27243

784.6'2405 — Children's songs in English. Words — *Anthologies*

Tinder-box : 66 songs for children / chosen by Sylvia Barratt and Sheena Hodge. — Words ed. / with drawings by Lisa Kopper. — London : Black, 1982. — [60]p : ill ; 15x21cm
Text and ill on inside covers. — Includes index
ISBN 0-7136-2218-0 (pbk) : £1.35 B82-27910

784.6'2406 — Children's songs in English — *Collections* — *For non-English speaking students*

Ward, Sheila Aristotelous. Dippitydoo : songs and activities for children / Sheila Aristotelous Ward. — Harlow : Longman
Teacher's guide. — 1980. — 48p : ill,music ; 22cm
ISBN 0-582-51004-x (pbk) : £1.00 B82-13909

784.6'833583 — English songs. Special subjects: Anarchism. Words — *Anthologies*

Anarchist songbook : (to tunes you know) / compiled by South London Anarchist Group. — London (121 Railton Rd., Herne Hill, S.E.24) : The Group, [1981?]. — v,58p : ill ; 20cm
£0.80 (pbk) B82-02852

784.6'8574192 — Songs in English. Special subjects: Biochemistry — *Collections*

Baum, Harold. The biochemists' songbook / by Harold Baum. — Oxford : Pergamon, 1982. — xii,62p : ill,music ; 23cm
ISBN 0-08-027370-x (pbk) : Unpriced : CIP rev. B81-24598

784.6′86238 — Sea songs in English — *Collections*
Everyman's book of sea songs. — London : Dent, Oct.1982. — [288]p
ISBN 0-460-04470-2 : £12.00 : CIP entry
B82-23991

784.6′8796352 — Songs in English. Special subjects: Golf. Words — *Texts*
Hopkins, Antony. Songs for swinging golfers / Antony Hopkins ; illustrated by Alex Hay. — London : Michael Joseph, 1981. — 59p : ill ; 15x18cm
ISBN 0-7181-2070-1 : £2.95 B82-05179

784.7′196726 — Patriotic songs in Kikuyu. Words — *Anthologies* — *English texts*
Thunder from the mountains : Mau Mau patriotic songs / edited by Maina wa Kinyatti. — London : Zed, 1980. — x,116p ; 23cm. — (Africa series)
ISBN 0-905762-83-5 : £7.50 : CIP rev.
B80-13492

784.9 — MUSIC. VOICE TRAINING AND PERFORMANCE

784.9 — Counter tenors
Giles, Peter. The counter tenor / Peter Giles ; with additional material by David Mallinder. — London : Frederick Muller, 1982. — xiii,221p,[8]p of plates : ill,music,ports ; 24cm
Bibliography: p209-212. — Includes index
ISBN 0-584-10474-x : £12.95 : CIP rev.
B81-26688

784.9 — Singing — *Manuals*
Butenschøn, Sine. Voice and song / Sine Butenschøn and Hans M. Borchgrevink. — Cambridge : Cambridge University Press, 1982. — ix,62p : ill,music ; 26cm
Translation of: Stemme og sang. — Bibliography: p56-57. — Includes index
ISBN 0-521-28011-7 : £9.95 : CIP rev.
B82-12723

Hines, Jerome. Great singers on great singing. — London : Gollancz, Feb.1983. — [352]p
ISBN 0-575-03246-4 : £9.95 : CIP entry
B82-38692

784.9′3 — Singing — *Amateurs' manuals*
Barr, Claudio. The Claudio Barr method of voice production : a foundation course in singing. — East Barnet (76 Windsor Drive, Cat Hill, East Barnet, Herts.) : Gianclaudio, [1982]. — 56p : ill ; 21cm + 1 sound cassette
Unpriced (pbk) B82-15419

784.9′32 — French language, German language & Italian language. Singing. Diction — *Manuals*
Phonetic readings of songs and arias / Berton Coffin ... [et al.]. — 2nd ed., with rev. German transcriptions. — Metuchen ; London : Scarecrow, 1982. — xvi,384p ; 25cm
Songs in Italian, German and French. — Bibliography: pxiii-xvi. — Includes index
ISBN 0-8108-1533-8 (pbk) : £12.80
B82-31804

784.9′32 — German language. Singing. Diction — *Manuals*
Odom, William. German for singers : a textbook of diction and phonetics / William Odom. — New York : Schirmer ; London : Collier Macmillan, c1981. — xviii,169p : ill,music ; 24cm
English and German text
ISBN 0-02-871750-3 (pbk) : £6.50 B82-05147

784.9′32 — Voice production. Exercises — *For singers*
Rose, Arnold. Contemporary exercises for classical and popular singers. — London : Scolar Press, Mar.1982. — [40]p
ISBN 0-85967-544-0 (pbk) : £3.95 : CIP entry
B82-07117

784.9′34 — Songs. Performance — *Manuals*
Moore, Gerald, *1899-*. Singer and accompanist : the performance of fifty songs / by Gerald Moore. — London : Hamilton, 1982. — x,235p : music ; 23cm
Originally published: London : Methuen, 1953. — Includes index
ISBN 0-241-10741-5 : £9.95 : CIP rev.
B81-34657

784.9′4 — Music. Sight-singing — *Manuals* — *Early works* — *Facsimiles*
Bathe, William. A briefe introduction to the skill of song, c.1587 / William Bathe ; introduced by Bernarr Rainbow. — Kilkenny : Reproduced under the direction of Leslie Hewitt for Boethius Press, c1982. — 18,[50] p,1folded leaf : music ; 22cm. — (Classic texts in music education ; 3)
Facsim of: 1st ed. London : Thomas Este, [1596?]. — Bibliography: p18
ISBN 0-86314-022-x : £8.60 B82-31581

785 — MUSIC. INSTRUMENTAL ENSEMBLES

785′.028′4 — Orchestration — *Manuals*
Jacob, Gordon. Orchestral technique : a manual for students / by Gordon Jacob. — 3rd ed. — London : Oxford University Press, 1982. — 100p : music ; 22cm
Previous ed.: 1940. — Includes index
ISBN 0-19-318204-1 (pbk) : £4.95 : CIP rev.
B82-01709

785′.06′2421 — England. Chamber orchestras: Academy of St Martin in the Fields, *to 1980*
Harries, Meirion. The Academy of St. Martin in the Fields / Meirion and Susie Harries. — London : Joseph, 1981. — ix,278p : ill,music,facsims,ports ; 25cm
List of sound recordings: p241-264. — Includes index
ISBN 0-7181-2049-3 : £12.50 B82-03048

785′.06′242733 — Greater Manchester *(Metropolitan County).* **Manchester. Symphony orchestras: Hallé Orchestra** — *Serials*
Hallé yearbook. — 81/82-. — Manchester (30 Cross St., Manchester M2 7BA) : Hallé Concerts Society, [1981]-. — v. : ill,ports ; 25cm
Merger of: Hallé; and, Hallé prospectus
ISSN 0262-7272 = Hallé yearbook : £1.50
B82-11804

785′.06′24733 — Greater Manchester *(Metropolitan County).* **Manchester. Symphony orchestras: Hallé Orchestra,** *1858-1983*
Kennedy, Michael, *1926-*. The Hallé 1858-1983. — Manchester : Manchester University Press, Dec.1982. — [144]p
ISBN 0-7190-0921-9 (cased) : £12.95 : CIP entry
ISBN 0-7190-0932-4 (pbk) : £4.95 B82-30220

785′.06′6 — Orchestras — *For children*
Bruxner, Mervyn. The orchestra / by Mervyn Bruxner ; illustrated by Thomas B. Pitfield. — London : Oxford University Press, 1960 (1980 [printing]). — 56p : ill,music ; 21cm. — (The Young reader's guides to music ; 4)
ISBN 0-19-314923-0 (pbk) : £2.50 B82-25967

785′.06′607 — Orchestral music. Performance. Interpretation
Del Mar, Norman. Anatomy of the orchestra / Norman Del Mar. — London : Faber & Faber, 1981. — 528p : music ; 25cm
Includes index
ISBN 0-571-11552-7 : £25.00 : CIP rev.
B81-23779

785′.06′660973 — United States. Popular music. Big bands, *1935-1981*
Simon, George T.. The big bands / George T. Simon ; with a foreword by Frank Sinatra. — 4th ed. — New York : Schirmer ; London : Collier Macmillan, c1981. — xvii,614p : ill,facsims,ports ; 25cm
Previous ed.: New York : Macmillan : London : Collier Macmillan, 1974. — Ill on lining papers. — List of sound discs: p567-581. — Includes index
ISBN 0-02-872420-8 (cased) : £13.95
ISBN 0-02-872430-5 (pbk) : £6.95 B82-20409

785′.06′71 — American military forces. Military bands, *1861—1865*
Olson, Kenneth E.. Music and musket : bands and bandsmen of the American Civil War / Kenneth E. Olson. — Westport, Conn. ; London : Greenwood Press, 1981. — xx,299p ; 24cm. — (Contributions to the study of music and dance, ISSN 0193-9041 ; no.1)
Bibliography: p267-286. — Includes index
ISBN 0-313-22112-x : Unpriced B82-02146

785′.092′2 — Music. Conductors — *Biographies*
Holmes, John L.. Conductors on record / by John L. Holmes. — London : Gollancz, 1982. — xv,734p ; 24cm
Bibliography: p734
ISBN 0-575-02781-9 : £25.00 : CIP rev.
B82-00200

785′.092′4 — Brass band music. Mortimer, Harry — *Biographies*
Mortimer, Harry. Harry Mortimer on brass : an autobiography / written with Alan Lynton. — Sherborne : Alphabooks, 1981. — 224p,[4]p of plates : ill(some col.),music,facsims,ports ; 26cm
Includes index
ISBN 0-906670-04-7 : £8.95 B82-00033

785′.092′4 — Music. Conducting. Previn, André — *Biographies*
Bookspan, Martin. André Previn : a biography / Martin Bookspan & Ross Yockey. — London : Hamilton, 1981. — 398p,[24]p of plates : ports ; 23cm
Includes index
ISBN 0-241-10676-1 : £8.95 : CIP rev.
B81-26780

785′.092′4 — Music. Conducting. Stokowski, Leopold — *Biographies*
Opperby, Preben. Leopold Stokowski / Preben Opperby. — Tunbridge Wells : Midas, 1982. — 288p : ill,music,facsims,plans,ports ; 24cm
Bibliography: p185-186. — List of sound recordings: p187-269. — Includes index
ISBN 0-85936-253-1 : £12.50 B82-23242

785′.092′4 — Music. Conducting. Toscanini, Arturo — *Biographies*
Matthews, Denis. Arturo Toscanini / Denis Matthews ; with selected discography by Ray Burford. — Tunbridge Wells : Midas, 1982. — 176p : ill,ports ; 24cm
Includes index. — List of sound discs : p125-170
ISBN 0-85936-172-1 : £9.50 B82-40406

785.1′1′0924 — German symphonies. Beethoven, Ludwig van — *Critical studies*
Hopkins, Antony. The nine symphonies of Beethoven / Antony Hopkins. — London : Pan in association with Heinemann Educational, 1982, c1981. — 290p : music ; 20cm
Originally published: London : Heinemann, 1981. — Bibliography: p286. — Includes index
ISBN 0-330-26670-5 (pbk) : £3.95 B82-37693

785.1′3′05 — Military band music — *Serials*
Band international : the journal of the International Military Music Society. — [Vol.1, no.1 (1979)?]-. — [London] ([c/o R.H.P. von Motz, 15 Oakdale Ave., Kenton, Harrow, Middx HA3 0UJ]) : The Society, [1979?]-. — v. : ill,ports ; 21cm
Quarterly. — Description based on: Vol.4, no.1 (Mar. 1982)
ISSN 0263-5240 = Band international : Free to Society members B82-26140

785.3′1′0924 — Austrian divertimenti & Austrian serenades. Mozart, Wolfgang Amadeus — *Critical studies*
Smith, Erik. Mozart serenades, divertimenti and dances / Erik Smith. — London : British Broadcasting Corporation, 1982. — 68p : music ; 20cm. — (BBC music guides)
Includes index
ISBN 0-563-12862-3 (pbk) : £2.25
Also classified at 785.4′1′0924 B82-37162

785.3′2′0924 — Russian orchestral programme music. Prokof′ev, S. S. — *Librettos*
Prokof′ev, S. S.. Peter and the wolf / Serge Prokofieff ; [illustrated by Warren Chappell] ; with a foreword by Serge Koussevitsky. — London : Kaye & Ward, 1980, c1940. — [32]p : ill(some col.),music ; 20x26cm
Originally published: London : Edmund Ward, 1961. — Ill on lining papers
ISBN 0-7182-0653-3 : £3.95 B82-25276

785.4′1′0924 — Austrian dance music. Mozart, Wolfgang Amadeus — *Critical studies*

Smith, Erik. Mozart serenades, divertimenti and dances / Erik Smith. — London : British Broadcasting Corporation, 1982. — 68p : music ; 20cm. — (BBC music guides)
Includes index
ISBN 0-563-12862-3 (pbk) : £2.25
Primary classification 785.3′1′0924 B82-37162

785.42 — Jazz

McCalla, James. Jazz : a listener′s guide / James McCalla. — Englewood Cliffs ; London : Prentice-Hall, c1982. — viii,152p : 2ill,ports ; 23cm
Bibliography: p141-142. — Includes index
ISBN 0-13-510172-7 (pbk) : £7.15 B82-34728

785.42′092′2 — Jazz. Musicians, *1931-1944* — *Biographies*

Lyttelton, Humphrey. The best of jazz / Humphrey Lyttelton. — London : Robson
2: Enter the giants. — 1981. — 239p,[8]p of plates : ill,ports ; 23cm
Bibliography: p226-227. — List of sound recordings: p228-230. — Includes index
ISBN 0-86051-107-3 : £6.95 : CIP rev. B81-27457

785.42′092′2 — Jazz musicians — *Interviews*

Taylor, Arthur. Notes and tones. — London : Quartet, Jan.1983. — [304]p
ISBN 0-7043-2365-6 : CIP entry B82-40307

785.42′092′4 — Great Brtain. Jazz. Performance, *1970-1981* — *Personal observations*

Melly, George. Mellymobile : 1970-1981 / George Melly ; illustrated by Trog. — London : Robson Books, 1982. — 167p : ill ; 23cm
ISBN 0-86051-162-6 : £6.50 : CIP rev. B82-04829

785.42′092′4 — Jazz. Ellington, Duke — *Biographies*

George, Don. The real Duke Ellington / Don George. — London : Robson, 1982, c1981. — 272p,[8]p of plates : music,ports ; 25cm
Includes index
ISBN 0-86051-166-9 : £7.95 : CIP rev. B82-00345

785.42′092′4 — Jazz. Mingus, Charles — *Biographies*

Priestley, Brian. Charles Mingus. — London : Quartet Books, Dec.1982. — 1v.
ISBN 0-7043-2275-7 : £11.95 : CIP entry B82-30042

785.42′092′4 — Jazz. Trumpet playing. Gillespie, Dizzy — *Biographies*

Gillespie, Dizzy. Dizzy. — London : Quartet, Sept.1981. — [576]p
ISBN 0-7043-3381-3 (pbk) : £6.95 : CIP entry B81-23855

785.42′092′4 — Nigerian jazz. Kuti, Fela Anikulapo — *Biographies*

Moore, Carlos. Fela. — London : Allison & Busby, Oct.1982. — [288]p
ISBN 0-85031-464-x (pbk) : £4.95 : CIP entry B82-24740

785.42′0973 — United States. Jazz, *1975-1980*

Giddins, Gary. Riding on a blue note : jazz and American pop / Gary Giddins. — New York ; Oxford : Oxford University Press, 1981. — xv,313p ; 22cm
Includes index
ISBN 0-19-502835-x : £12.95
Also classified at 780′.42′0973 B82-25968

785.42′0973 — United States. Jazz, *to 1978*

Vulliamy, Graham. Jazz & blues / Graham Vulliamy. — London : Routledge & Kegan Paul, 1982. — ix,158p : ill,facsims,ports ; 23cm. — (Routledge popular music)
Bibliography: p153-154. — List of sound discs: p154. — Includes index
ISBN 0-7100-0894-5 : £5.95 : CIP rev.
Primary classification 784.5′3′00973 B82-11770

785.42′09794′6 — California. San Francisco Bay area. Jazz, *to 1940*

Stoddard, Tom. Jazz on the Barbary Coast / by Tom Stoddard. — Chigwell : Storyville, c1982. — 192p : ill,music,facsims,ports ; 21cm
Bibliography: 186-187. — Includes index
ISBN 0-902391-02-x : Unpriced B82-27386

785.42′0994 — Australian jazz, *to 1980* — *Interviews*

Williams, Mike, *19---*. The Australian jazz explosion / Mike Williams ; photographs by Jane March. — London : Angus & Robertson, 1981. — 171p : ports ; 29cm
Includes index
ISBN 0-207-14381-1 : £8.95 B82-10035

785.7′009 — Chamber music, *to 1980*

Headington, Christopher. Chamber music / Christopher Headington. — Poole : Blandford, 1982. — 138p : ports ; 23cm. — (The Listener′s guide) (A Quarto book)
Includes index
ISBN 0-7137-1252-x : £4.95 : CIP rev. B82-01200

785.7′00942 — English chamber music

Meyer, Ernst Hermann. Early English chamber music : from the Middle Ages to Purcell / Ernst H. Meyer. — 2nd rev. ed. / edited by the author and Diana Poulton. — London : Lawrence and Wishart, 1982. — xvi,363p : music ; 23cm
Previous ed.: published as English chamber music. 1946. — Bibliography: p288-291. — Includes index
ISBN 0-85315-411-2 : £15.00 B82-27731

785.7′0471′0924 — Hungarian string quartets. Bartók, Béla — *Critical studies*

Walsh, Stephen. Bartók chamber music / Stephen Walsh. — London : British Broadcasting Corporation, 1982. — 88p ; 20cm. — (BBC music guides)
ISBN 0-563-12465-2 (pbk) : £3.00 B82-36848

786 — MUSIC. KEYBOARD INSTRUMENTS

786 — Keyboard instrument playing. Harmony. Improvisation — *Manuals*

Campbell, Laura, *1918-*. Sketching at the keyboard : harmonisation by ear for students of all ages / by Laura Campbell. — London : Stainer & Bell, c1982. — 258p : music,1port ; 25cm
ISBN 0-85249-605-2 (pbk) : £5.95 : CIP rev. B82-09871

786.1′09 — Pianos & piano music, *to 1980*

Kentner, Louis. Piano / Louis Kentner. — London : MacDonald, 1976 (1980 [printing]). — xi,204p : ill,music ; 22cm. — (Yehudi Menuhin music guides)
Bibliography: p190. — List of sound discs: p191-198. — Includes index
ISBN 0-356-04713-x (cased) : £8.50
ISBN 0-356-04714-8 (pbk) : £5.50
Also classified at 786.3′041 B82-13917

786.1′092′2 — Piano playing — *Biographies*

Kehler, George. The piano in concert / compiled and annotated by George Kehler. — Metuchen, N.J. ; London : Scarecrow, 1982. — 2v.(xxxiv,1431p) ; 29cm
ISBN 0-8108-1469-2 : £70.00 B82-38101

786.1′092′4 — Music. Accompaniment: Piano playing. Moore, Gerald, *1899-* — *Biographies*

Moore, Gerald, *1899-*. Furthermoore. — London : Hamilton, Jan.1983. — [160]p
ISBN 0-241-10909-4 : £8.95 : CIP entry B82-33503

786.1′092′4 — Piano playing. Arrau, Claudio — *Biographies*

Horowitz, Joseph. Conversations with Arrau. — London : Collins, Oct.1982. — [250]p
ISBN 0-00-216290-3 : £8.95 : CIP entry B82-23067

786.1′092′4 — Piano playing. Paderewski, Ignacy Jan — *Biographies*

Zamoyski, Adam. Paderewski / Adam Zamoyski. — London : Collins, 1982. — xii,289p : ill,2maps,ports ; 24cm
Bibliography: p267-275. — Includes index
ISBN 0-00-216642-9 : £12.95 : CIP rev. B82-07217

786.2′074′029134 — Edinburgh. Museums: Edinburgh University Collection of Historic Musical Instruments. Stock: Struck string instruments — *Catalogues*

University of Edinburgh. A check-list of the plucked and hammered stringed instruments in the Edinburgh University collection of historic musical instruments / Anne Macaulay. — Edinburgh : University of Edinburgh, 1982. — iv,18p ; 30cm
ISBN 0-907635-03-2 (unbound) : £1.00
Also classified at 787′.05′074029134 B82-17373

786.2′3 — Harpsichords. Interiors. Decorations: Paper — *Manuals*

Mactaggart, Peter. Laying & decorating harpsichord papers / Peter & Ann Mactaggart. — Welwyn : Mac & Me, c1981. — 19p,9p of plates : ill ; 21cm
Bibliography: p19
ISBN 0-9507782-0-6 (pbk) : Unpriced B82-01821

786.3 — Keyboard instrument playing — *Manuals* — *Early works* — *Collections*

Anthology of early keyboard methods / edited and translated by Barbara Sachs and Barry Ife. — Cambridge : Gamut, 1981. — 71p : music,facsims ; 30cm
Bibliography: p70-71
ISBN 0-907761-00-3 (pbk) : Unpriced B82-14164

786.3′041 — Christmas carols in English. Accompaniment: Piano playing. Techniques — *Manuals* — *For children*

Varnum, Brooke Minarik. Play & sing - It′s Christmas! : a piano book of easy-to-play carols / Brooke Minarik Varnum ; illustrated by Emily Arnold McCully. — New York : Macmillan ; London : Collier Macmillan, 1980. — 48p : col.ill ; 26cm
ISBN 0-02-045420-1 (spiral) : £1.95 B82-00982

786.3′041 — Piano music. Performance. Interpretation

Siki, Béla. Piano repertoire : a guide to interpretation and performance / Béla Siki. — New York : Schirmer ; London : Collier Macmillan, c1981. — xi,331p : music ; 24cm
Bibliography: p329-330
ISBN 0-02-872390-2 : £13.95 B82-18897

786.3′041 — Piano playing

Taylor, Harold. The pianist′s talent. — London : Kahn and Averill, Mar.1982. — [96]p
Originally published: 1979
ISBN 0-900707-74-7 (pbk) : £2.95 : CIP entry B82-03130

786.3′041 — Piano playing — *Manuals*

Harrison, Sidney. The young person′s guide to playing the piano / Sidney Harrison. — 2nd ed., repr. with corrections. — London : Faber, 1976 (1982 [printing]). — 100p : ill,music ; 21cm
Includes index
ISBN 0-571-11864-x (pbk) : £2.75 : CIP rev. B82-09432

Kentner, Louis. Piano / Louis Kentner. — London : MacDonald, 1976 (1980 [printing]). — xi,204p : ill,music ; 22cm. — (Yehudi Menuhin music guides)
Bibliography: p190. — List of sound discs: p191-198. — Includes index
ISBN 0-356-04713-x (cased) : £8.50
ISBN 0-356-04714-8 (pbk) : £5.50
Primary classification 786.1′09 B82-13917

786.3'041 — Piano playing. Teaching methods: Group methods

Lee, Julia. Group piano lessons : a practical guide / by Julia Lee. — Manchester (126 Deansgate, Manchester) : Forsyth, c1981. — 31p : music,1form ; 30cm
Bibliography: p30-31
Unpriced (pbk) B82-10326

786.3'041 — Piano playing. Techniques — *Manuals*

Bernstein, Seymour. With your own two hands : self-discovery through music / by Seymour Bernstein. — New York : Schirmer ; London : Collier Macmillan, c1981. — xvi,296p : ill,music ; 25cm
Includes index
ISBN 0-02-870310-3 : £8.95 B82-20404

Grindea, Carola. We make our own music. — 2nd ed. — London : Kahn & Averill, Nov.1981. — [64]p
Previous ed.: 1972
ISBN 0-900707-66-6 (pbk) : £1.50 : CIP entry B81-30222

Palmer, King. The piano / King Palmer. — 2nd ed. — Sevenoaks : Hodder and Stoughton, 1981. — 133p : ill ; 20cm
Previous ed.: 1957. — Includes index
ISBN 0-340-26833-6 (pbk) : £2.95 : CIP rev. B81-31724

Philipp, Lillie H.. Piano technique : tone, touch, phrasing and dynamics / by Lillie H. Philipp. — New York : Dover ; London : Constable, 1982. — 90p : ill,music ; 29cm
Originally published: New York : MCA Music, 1969
ISBN 0-486-24272-2 (pbk) : £3.40 B82-39656

Sandor, Gyorgy. On piano playing : motion, sound and expression / Gyorgy Sandor. — New York ; Schirmer ; London : Collier Macmillan, c1981. — xii,240p : ill,music ; 25cm
Includes index
ISBN 0-02-872280-9 : £8.95 B82-20403

786.3'041'09 — Piano playing, *to 1980* — *For schools*

Isherwood, Millicent. The piano / Millicent Isherwood. — London : Oxford University Press, 1981. — 48p : ill,1map,music,ports ; 19x25cm. — (Oxford topics in music)
ISBN 0-19-321331-1 (pbk) : Unpriced B82-13572

786.5'092'4 — Durham *(County)*. Durham. Cathedrals: Durham Cathedral. Pipe organ playing, *1871-1875* — *Correspondence, diaries, etc.*

Collinson, Thomas Henry. The diary of an organist's apprentice at Durham Cathedral 1871-1875. — Aberdeen : Aberdeen University Press, Aug.1982. — [80]p
ISBN 0-08-028461-2 : £6.00 : CIP entry B82-16636

786.5'092'4 — German pipe organ music. Bach, Johann Sebastian — *Critical studies*

Williams, Peter, *1937 May 14-*. The organ music of J.S. Bach / by Peter Williams. — Cambridge : Cambridge University Press. — (Cambridge studies in music)
Vol.1: Preludes, toccatas, fantasias, fugues, sonatas, concertos and miscellaneous pieces (BWV 525-598, 802-805 etc.). — 1980. — 365p : music ; 26cm
List of musical sources: p346-350. — Bibliography: p351-356. — Includes index
ISBN 0-521-21723-7 : £30.00 B82-17994

786.6'241 — Musical instruments: British pipe organs, *to 1980*

Clutton, Cecil. The British organ. — Rev. and enl. — London : Eyre Methuen, Oct.1981. — [336]p
Previous ed.: London : Batsford, 1963
ISBN 0-413-48630-3 : £20.00 : CIP entry B81-25114

786.6'241235 — Scotland. Grampian Region. Aberdeen. Cathedrals: St. Andrew's Cathedral *(Aberdeen)*. Musical instruments: Pipe organs, *to 1981*

Morrisson, A. R.. The organ and organists of St. Andrew's Cathedral, Aberdeen / A.R. Morrisson, R.B. Turbet ; foreword by Donald Howard. — Aberdeen : Armusic, 1981. — 16p : facsims ; 21cm
Includes list of sound recordings
ISBN 0-9507337-0-9 (unbound) : Unpriced B82-11077

786.6'242 — Musical instruments: English pipe organs, *1820-1873* — *Early works* — *Facsimiles*

Sutton, *Sir* John, *1820-1873*. A short account of organs built in England from the reign of King Charles II to the present time / by Sir John Sutton ; with an introduction by Canon Hilary Davidson. — Oxford : Positif, 1979. — 17,xxiii,113p : ill,1port ; 19cm
Facsim. of: ed. published London : Masters, 1847
ISBN 0-9503892-9-3 (pbk) : £5.50 B82-28509

786.6'242264 — West Sussex. Horsham. Boys' public schools: Christ's Hospital *(Horsham)*. Musical instruments: Pipe organs, *to 1980*

Christ's Hospital *(Horsham)*. The organs and music masters of Christ's Hospital / by N.M. Plumley. — [London] : Christ's Hospital, 1981. — 94p : ill,facsims ; 25cm. — (The Christ's Hospital papers ; 1)
Includes index
ISBN 0-9507843-0-3 (pbk) : Unpriced B82-26295

786.6'242457 — Shropshire. Ludlow. Parish churches: St. Laurence's Parish Church *(Ludlow)*. Musical instruments. Pipe organs, *to 1982*

Francis, Richard, *1946-*. The organ and organists of Ludlow Parish Church / by Richard Francis and Peter Klein ; with a foreword by David Lloyd. — [Ludlow] ([32 Corve St., Ludlow, Shropshire SY8 1DA]) : St. Laurence's Parish Church Organ Appeal Committee, 1982. — 90p,[5]p of plates : ill,facsims,ports ; 21cm
£1.50 (pbk) B82-31264

786.6'242982 — West Glamorgan. Swansea. Concert halls: Brangwyn Hall. Musical instruments: Pipe organs, *to 1979*

Alban, J. R.. The Brangwyn Hall organ / J.R. Alban and J.M. Fussell. — Swansea (Chief Executive and Town Clerk's Department, Guildhall, Swansea SA1 4PE) : Swansea City Council, 1980. — 32p : ill,ports ; 21cm. — (City archives publication ; B.9)
Unpriced (pbk) B82-18074

786.7 — Organ playing. Harmony

Ratcliffe, T.. Root note linked organ chords : a simple memory aid enabling any chord to be found in seconds / by T. Ratcliffe. — Preston (20 Cockersand Ave, Hutton, Preston, Lancs. PR2 5FN) : T. Ratcliffe, [1982?]. — 14p : ill ; 21cm
Cover title. — Text on covers
Unpriced (pbk) B82-38239

786.7 — Organ playing — *Manuals*

Neal, Roy. The Roy Neal survey of organ registrations and techniques. — Peterborough (P.O. Box 118, Peterborough, PE3 6UY) : Scepte, c1982. — vi,148p,[2]p of plates : ill,music,2ports ; 23cm
Includes index
£6.50 B82-23399

786.9'2'05 — Musical instruments: Electronic organs — *Serials*

Keyboards and music player. — Vol.1, no.1 (Sept. 1981)-. — Watford (60A Market St., Watford WD1 7AX) : Fenchurch Design Ltd., 1981-. — v. : ill,music,ports ; 30cm
Monthly
ISSN 0263-6212 = Keyboards and music player : £12.50 per year B82-28112

787 — MUSIC. STRING INSTRUMENTS

787'.01'0714 — Bowed string instrument playing. Intonation — *German texts*

Heman, Christine. Intonation auf Streichinstrumenten : melodisches und harmonisches hören / Christine Heman. — Kassel ; London : Bärenreiter, 1981, c1964. — 64p : music ; 29cm
Bibliography: p5
Unpriced (pbk) B82-33998

787'.012'074 — Bowed string instruments — *Catalogues*

Emery, Bernard. A check list of the bowed string musical instruments in the Edinburgh University Collection of Historic Musical Instruments / Bernard Emery. — Edinburgh : Reid School of Music, 1982. — 9p ; 30cm
ISBN 0-907635-05-9 (unbound) : £1.00 B82-37400

787'.05'074029134 — Edinburgh. Museums: Edinburgh University Collection of Historic Musical Instruments. Stock: Plucked string instruments — *Catalogues*

University of Edinburgh. A check-list of the plucked and hammered stringed instruments in the Edinburgh University collection of historic musical instruments / Anne Macaulay. — Edinburgh : University of Edinburgh, 1982. — iv,18p ; 30cm
ISBN 0-907635-03-2 (unbound) : £1.00
Primary classification 786.2'074'029134 B82-17373

787.1'07 — Violin playing. Teaching — *Manuals*

Chipper, Barbara. Fundamentals of fiddle teaching / Barbara Chipper. — Waltham Abbey : Wardley, [1981?]. — 19p : music ; 22cm
ISBN 0-9507523-0-4 (pbk) : Unpriced B82-09094

787.1'07'14 — Pennsylvania. Buffalo Valley. Fiddle playing, *to 1980*

Gunthorp, Matthew G.. Learning the fiddler's ways / Matthew G. Gunthorp ; foreword by Samuel P. Bayard ; introduction by Robert C. Doyle. — University Park, Pa. ; London : Pennsylvania State University Press, c1980. — 159p : ill,1map,music,ports,1geneal.table ; 21cm. — (Keystone books)
ISBN 0-271-00237-9 (cased) : £9.65
ISBN 0-271-02248-4 (pbk) : Unpriced B82-09483

787.1'09411 — Scottish fiddle music, *to 1982*

Alburger, Mary Anne. Scottish fiddlers and their music. — London : Gollancz, Jan.1983. — [240]p
ISBN 0-575-03174-3 : £15.00 : CIP entry B82-32453

787'.3'0712 — Cello playing — *Manuals*

Bunting, Christopher. Essay on the craft of cello-playing. — Cambridge : Cambridge University Press, Oct.1982
Vol.1: Prelude, bowing, coordination. — [112]p
ISBN 0-521-24142-1 : £19.50 : CIP entry B82-29380

Bunting, Christopher. Essay on the craft of cello-playing. — Cambridge : Cambridge University Press, Oct.1982
Vol.2: The left hand. — [176]p
ISBN 0-521-24184-7 : £19.50 : CIP entry B82-29379

Pleeth, William. Cello / William Pleeth ; compiled and edited by Nona Pyron. — London : Macdonald, 1982. — xiv,290p : ill,facsims,music ; 23cm. — (Yehudi Menuhin music guides)
Includes bibliographies and index
ISBN 0-356-07864-7 (cased) : £9.95
ISBN 0-356-07865-5 (pbk) : £6.50 B82-37382

787'.4 — Bowed psaltery playing — *Manuals*

Greenham, Maurice. The Bill Lucy & Roy Woolgrove introduction to the bowed psaltery / written by Maurice Greenham. — Newcastle-under-Lyme (29 Gallowstree La., Westland, Newcastle-under-Lyme) : R. Woolgrove, c1981. — 32p : ill,music ; 28cm
Unpriced (pbk) B82-07741

787′.42′0924 — English bass viol music. Jenkins, John, *1592-1678 — Critical studies*

Urquhart, Margaret. Musical research in Durham Cathedral library : 'Mr John Jenkins in particular' / Margaret Urquhart. — [Durham] (Durham Cathedral, Durham) : Dean and Chapter of Durham, c1979. — 15p : music ; 21cm. — (Durham Cathedral lecture ; 1979)
Unpriced (pbk) B82-40579

787.6′1′0712 — Guitar playing. Folk techniques — *Manuals*

Abbs, Malcom. Finger & thumb keep moving : second stage folk guitar / written by Malcom Abbs ; edited by Iris Sprankling. — London : British Broadcasting Corporation, 1982. — 48p : ill,music(some col.) ; 25cm
Music on inside cover
ISBN 0-563-16532-4 (pbk) : £2.95 B82-35346

Pearse, John. Hold down a chord : a guitar course for beginners / by John Pearse. — Rev. ed. — London : B.B.C., 1981. — 35p : ill(some col.) ; 30cm + 1 sound disc(33-1/3 rpm; stereo)
Previous ed.: 1967
ISBN 0-563-16496-4 (pbk) : £2.50 B82-01871

787.6′1′0712 — Guitar playing — *Manuals*

Artzt, Alice. The art of practising / Alice Artzt. — [Shaftesbury] : [Musical New Services], c1978. — 28p : ill,music ; 30cm. — (A Guitar magazine project)
ISBN 0-86175-229-5 (pbk) : Unpriced B82-14652

Denyer, Ralph. The guitar handbook. — London (9 Henrietta St., WC2E 8PS) : Dorling Kindersley, Oct.1982. — [256]p
ISBN 0-86318-004-3 : £9.95 : CIP entry B82-21586

Welch, Reg. Guitar work shop / Reg Welch. — [Preston] ([20 Guildhall St., Preston, Lancs. PR1 3NU]) : [Greenwoods], c1981. — 236p : ill,music ; 22cm
Cover title
£5.75 (spiral) B82-21849

787.6′1′0712 — Spanish guitar playing — *Manuals*

Morgan, Dan. Spanish guitar : with special selections on finger-picking jazz and folk and blues styles / Dan Morgan ; includes line drawings by Mike Miller. — London : Corgi, 1982. — 187p : ill,music ; 18cm
ISBN 0-552-11973-3 (pbk) : £1.50 B82-36958

787.6′1′0714 — Guitar playing. Techniques, *to ca 1800*

Tyler, James. The early guitar : a history and handbook / by James Tyler. — London : Music Department, Oxford University Press, 1980. — 176p : ill,music,facsims ; 25cm. — (Early music series ; 4)
Bibliography: p163-176
ISBN 0-19-323182-4 (pbk) : £7.95
Primary classification 787.6′12 B82-23792

787.6′1′0924 — Guitar playing. Segovia, Andrés — *Biographies*

Wade, Graham, *1940-*. Andres Segovia : a celebration of the man and his music. — London : Allison & Busby, Feb.1983. — [192]p
ISBN 0-85031-491-7 (cased) : £7.95 : CIP entry
ISBN 0-85031-492-5 (pbk) : £3.50 B82-39435

787.6′12 — Electric guitars. Customising — *Amateurs′ manuals*

Legg, Adrian. Customising your electric guitar / Adrian Legg. — London : Kaye & Ward, c1981. — 64p : ill ; 27cm
ISBN 0-7182-3730-7 (pbk) : £3.95 B82-11598

787.6′12 — Guitars, *to ca 1800*

Tyler, James. The early guitar : a history and handbook / by James Tyler. — London : Music Department, Oxford University Press, 1980. — 176p : ill,music,facsims ; 25cm. — (Early music series ; 4)
Bibliography: p163-176
ISBN 0-19-323182-4 (pbk) : £7.95
Also classified at 787.6′1′0714 B82-23792

787.6′12 — Spanish guitars. Making — *Amateurs′ manuals*

Doubtfire, Stanley. Make your own classical guitar / Stanley Doubtfire. — London : Gollancz, 1981. — 120p : ill,ports ; 28cm
Includes index
ISBN 0-575-02980-3 : £15.00 B82-07751

788 — MUSIC. WIND INSTRUMENTS

788′.05′0712 — Woodwind instrument playing

Bartolozzi, Bruno. New sounds for woodwind / Bruno Bartolozzi ; translated and edited by Reginald Smith Brindle. — 2nd ed. — London : Oxford University Press, 1982. — 113p : ill,music ; 23cm + 1sound disc : 45rpm,mono ; 7in
Previous ed.: 1967
ISBN 0-19-318611-x : £12.50 B82-26670

788′.056′074029134 — Edinburgh. Museums: Edinburgh University Collection of Historic Musical Instruments. Stock: Double reed instruments — *Catalogues*

University of Edinburgh. A check-list of the double-reed musical instruments in the Edinburgh University collection of historic musical instruments / Lyndesay Langwill. — Edinburgh : University of Edinburgh, 1981. — 8p ; 30cm
ISBN 0-907635-02-4 (unbound) : £1.00 B82-17374

788′.1′0924 — Jazz. Trumpet playing. Davis, Miles *- Biographies*

Carr, Ian. Miles Davis. — London : Quartet, June 1981. — [352]p
ISBN 0-7043-2273-0 : £9.50 : CIP entry B81-14422

788′.5 — Cornetts — *German texts*

Overton, Friend Robert. Der Zink : Geschichte, Bauweise und Spieltechnik eines historischen Musikinstruments / Friend Robert Overton. — Mainz ; London : Schott, c1981. — 260p : ill,music,facsims ; 24cm
German text. — Bibliography: p208-214. — Includes index
ISBN 3-7957-1781-7 (pbk) : £14.40 B82-12504

788′.5′094074 — European flute family instruments *— Catalogues*

Dick, John, *1939-*. A checklist of the flutes and whistles in the Edinburgh University Collection of Historic Musical Instruments / John Dick and Arnold Myers. — Edinburgh : Reid School of Music, 1982. — 25p ; 30cm
ISBN 0-907635-04-0 (unbound) : £1.00 B82-37401

788′.51′0712 — Flute playing — *Manuals*

Harrison, Howard. How to play the flute. — London : Hamilton, Nov.1982. — [96]p
ISBN 0-241-10875-6 (cased) : £6.95 : CIP entry
ISBN 0-241-10876-4 (pbk) : £3.50 B82-32289

788′.51′0712 — Flute playing — *Manuals — Early works*

Quantz, Johann Joachim. On playing the flute. — 3rd ed. — London : Faber, Sept.1981. — [400]p
Translation of: Versuch einer Anweisung, die Flöte traversiere zu spielen. Berlin : Voss, 1752. — Previous ed.: 1976
ISBN 0-571-18046-9 (pbk) : £5.95 : CIP entry B81-21470

788′.512 — Flutes. Making. Techniques

Cooper, Albert. The flute / by Albert Cooper. — [London] ([2 Cromwell House, Vauxhall Walk SE11 5EP]) : [A. Cooper], c1980. — 47p : ill,ports ; 26cm
Unpriced (pbk) B82-25236

788′.53′0712 — Recorder playing — *Manuals*

Wollitz, Kenneth. The recorder book / Kenneth Wollitz. — London : Gollancz, 1982, c1981. — xxv,259p : ill,music ; 23cm
Originally published: New York : Knopf, 1982. — Bibliography: p252-255. — Includes index
ISBN 0-575-03144-1 (cased) : £9.95 : CIP rev.
ISBN 0-575-03182-4 (pbk) : £5.95 B82-19553

788′.53′0712 — Recorder playing — *Manuals — For schools*

Gregory, David, *1948-*. The Chappell recorder book / David Gregory. — London : Hamilton, 1982. — 48p : ill,music ; 28cm
ISBN 0-241-10658-3 : Unpriced : CIP rev. B82-01833

788′.66′0924 — Saxophones. Sax, Adolphe — *Biographies*

Horwood, Wally. Adolphe Sax, 1814-1894 : his life and legacy / Wally Horwood. — Bramley : Bramley Books, 1980, c1979. — 191p : ill,1facsim,ports ; 21cm
Bibliography: p181-183. — Includes index
ISBN 0-9507389-0-5 (pbk) : Unpriced B82-18709

788′.92′0924 — Northumbrian pipe playing. Allan, James, *1734-1810 — Biographies — Early works*

The **History** of James Allan : the celebrated Northumberland piper. — [Ilford] ([67 Middleton Gardens, Gants Hill, Ilford, Essex]) : [Alan Brignull], c1981. — [26]p : ill,music,1port ; 14cm
Originally published: Newcastle-upon-Tyne : John Gilbert, 181?-
Unpriced (unbound) B82-05466

788′.92′094115 — Scottish Highland bagpipe music: Piobaireachd, *to 1900*

Haddow, A. J.. The history and structure of Ceol Mor : a collection of critical and historical essays : a guide to piobaireachd, the classical music of the great Highland bagpipe / by A.J. Haddow. — [Glasgow?] : [s.n.], c1982. — 222p : col.ill,1map,music,geneal.tables ; 21cm
Text on inside covers. — Bibliography: p217-222
Unpriced (pbk) B82-28053

789.01 — MUSIC. PERCUSSION INSTRUMENTS

789′.5′0714 — Cambridgeshire. Cambridge. Parish churches: St. Mary the Great *(Church : Cambridge).* **Bells. Change ringing,** *to 1980*

Ockelton, C. M. G.. The tower, bells & ringers of Great S. Mary′s Church, Cambridge / by C.M.G. Ockelton. — Cambridge ([c/o C.Y. Barlow, 16 Victoria St., Cambridge CB1 1JP]) : Society of Cambridge Youths, 1981. — 19p ; 22cm
Unpriced (pbk) B82-14860

789.7 — MUSIC. MECHANICAL INSTRUMENTS

789′.71′0924 — Austrian barrel organ music. Haydn, Joseph — *Critical studies*

Ord-Hume, Arthur W. J. G.. Joseph Haydn and the mechanical organ. — Cardiff : University College Cardiff Press, Oct.1982. — [180]p
ISBN 0-906449-37-5 : £17.00 : CIP entry B82-27218

789.9 — ELECTRONIC MUSICAL INSTRUMENTS, MUSIC RECORDING

789.9 — Electro-acoustic music

Schrader, Barry. Introduction to electro-acoustic music / Barry Schrader. — Englewood Cliffs, N.J. ; London : Prentice-Hall, c1982. — xvi,223p : ill,ports ; 24cm
Bibliography: p211-218. — Lists of sound discs. — Includes index
ISBN 0-13-481515-7 (pbk) : Unpriced B82-28400

789.9′1 — Popular music. Sound discs. Production *— Interviews*

Tobler, John. The record producers / John Tobler & Stuart Grundy. — London : British Broadcasting Corporation, 1982. — 248p : ports ; 30cm
Includes index
ISBN 0-563-17958-9 (pbk) : £6.95 B82-28975

789.9′1245 — Pop music. Sound discs. Top twenty singles, *1955-1982*

Savile, Jimmy. The nostalgia book of hit singles. — London : Muller, Nov.1982. — [320]p
ISBN 0-584-11037-5 (pbk) : £4.95 : CIP entry B82-26566

789.9′13621′0924 — Opera. Singing. Callas, Maria. Sound recordings — *Critical studies*

Ardoin, John. The Callas legacy / John Ardoin. — London : Duckworth, 1977 (1981 [printing]). — xi,224p,[1]leaf of plates : 1port ; 22cm
Bibliography: p212-213. — Includes index
ISBN 0-7156-1617-x (pbk) : £5.95 B82-02491

789.9′136453′00924 — United States. Blues. Singing. Smith, Bessie. Sound recordings — *Critical studies*

Brooks, Edward. The Bessie Smith companion. — Wheathampstead (1 Ash Grove, Wheathampstead, St. Albans, Herts. AL4 8DF) : Cavendish Publishing, Oct.1982. — [224]p
ISBN 0-9508246-0-7 : £6.95 : CIP entry B82-24366

789.9′9 — Musical instruments: Synthesisers

Devarahi. The complete guide to synthesizers / by Devarahi. — Englewood Cliffs ; London : Prentice-Hall, c1982. — x,214p : ill ; 28cm
Bibliography: p206-209. — Includes index. — List of sound recordings: p201-205
ISBN 0-13-160630-1 (pbk) : Unpriced B82-28423

789.9′9′071 — Schools. Curriculum subjects: Electronic music. Composition. Techniques — *For teaching*

Electronic music for schools / edited by Richard Orton. — Cambridge : Cambridge University Press, 1981. — viii,196p : ill ; 24cm
Bibliography: p181-183. — List of sound discs: p.184-187. — Includes index
ISBN 0-521-22994-4 (cased) : £9.50
ISBN 0-521-28026-5 (pbk) : £4.95 B82-08318

790 — RECREATIONS

790 — Games — *Manuals*

Barry, Sheila Anne. Super-colossal book of puzzles tricks and games / Sheila Anne Barry ; illustrated by Doug Anderson. — New York : Sterling ; London : Oak Tree, c1978 (1979 [printing]). — 640p : ill ; 25cm
ISBN 0-7061-2590-8 : £10.95
ISBN 0-8069-4581-8 (U.S.)
Also classified at 793.8 B82-25232

Zigo, Hereward. Summer games : for adults and children / Hereward Zigo. — Cambridge : Oleander Press, c1982. — 64p : ill ; 20cm
Includes index
ISBN 0-906672-05-8 (cased) : £4.20 : CIP rev.
ISBN 0-906672-06-6 (pbk) : £1.95 B81-36056

790 — Games — *Manuals — For children*

Brown, Arthur. How to make and play indoor games. — Wendover : John Goodchild No.1. — Feb.1983. — [96]p
ISBN 0-903445-62-x : £3.50 : CIP entry
Primary classification 745.5 B82-39289

Brown, Arthur. How to make and play indoor games. — Wendover : John Goodchild No.2. — Feb.1983. — [96]p
ISBN 0-903445-63-8 : £3.50 : CIP entry
Primary classification 745.5 B82-39290

Jobin, André. Games : for indoors and out / André Jobin, Monique Félix. — London : Evans, c1982. — 32p : chiefly col.ill ; 22cm. — (Busy books)
ISBN 0-237-45599-4 : £2.25 B82-26259

Smith, R. A. (Robert Alan). Blue Bell Hill games / compiled by R.A. Smith ; illustrated by David McKee. — Harmondsworth : Penguin, c1982. — 93p : ill,music ; 20x24cm. — (Kestrel books)
ISBN 0-7226-5726-9 : £4.95 B82-26120

790 — Recreation services. Programmes. Planning

Russell, Ruth V.. Planning programs in recreation / Ruth V. Russell. — St. Louis, Mo. ; London : Mosby, 1982. — xvi,352p : ill,facsims,forms ; 24cm
Bibliography: p333-339. — Includes index
ISBN 0-8016-4231-0 (pbk) : £10.75 B82-31861

790 — Recreations — *For children*

Toddlers 1st pop-up book. — London : Dean, 1978, c1974 (1982 [printing]). — [8]p : col.ill ; 24cm. — (A Dean's playtime pop-up book)
Cover title. — Text and ill on lining papers
Unpriced B82-30500

790 — Tournaments. Order of play — *Manuals*

Searl. The order of play book / by Searl and Dale. — Welwyn Garden City (6, Waterfield, Welwyn Garden City, Herts.) : Searl and Dale, c1981. — 18leaves : ill ; 21cm
Unpriced (spiral) B82-05659

790′.025′41 — Great Britain. Conference centres. Reception facilities — *Directories — Serials*

The **Conference** green book. — 1981/82-. — [London] ([183 Askew Rd, W12 9AX]) : [Spectrum Pub.], [1981]-. — v. : ill,maps,plans ; 30cm
Annual
ISSN 0260-2199 = Conference green book : £10.00 B82-04913

790′.06′8 — Adventure playgrounds for children, to 8 years. Organisation — *Manuals*

Berrington Walk, Highgate, Birmingham : a sculptured playarea / compiled by Dave Swingle. — [Birmingham] ([723, Coventry Rd., Birmingham B10 0JL]) : [East Birmingham Family Service Unit], [1978?]. — 22p : ill ; 22x31cm. — (A West Midlands Arts 'self-help' publication ; no.1)
Unpriced (unbound) B82-14649

790′.06′8 — Great Britain. Adventure playgrounds. Safety measures — *Standards*

Towards a safer adventure playground. — London (25 Ovington Sq., SW3 1LQ) : National Playing Fields Association, c1980. — 50p ; 30cm
Cover title. — Bibliography: p48-50
Unpriced (spiral) B82-19339

790′.06′8411 — Scotland. Sports centres — *Conference proceedings*

National seminars on sports centres and swimming pools : summary report. — Edinburgh : Scottish Sports Council, 1981. — 242p : ill,plans ; 30cm
ISBN 0-906599-27-x (spiral) : £5.00
Also classified at 797.2′1′09411 B82-02781

790′.06′8931 — New Zealand. Outdoor recreation centres: Outdoor Pursuits Centre, *to 1980*

Dingle, Graeme. Seven year adventure. — London : Hodder & Stoughton, Feb.1982. — 1v.
ISBN 0-340-25692-3 : £7.95 : CIP entry B81-35690

790′.0941 — Great Britain. Leisure activities — *Practical information — For children*

Brownlee, Geoff. Madabout / Geoff Brownlee ; illustrations by Helen Cammack. — London : Sparrow, 1981. — 94p : ill ; 18cm
ISBN 0-09-927670-4 (pbk) : £0.95 B82-08362

790′.0942 — England. Recreations, *1700-1850*

Malcolmson, Robert W.. Popular recreations in English society 1700-1850 / Robert W. Malcolmson. — Cambridge : Cambridge University Press, 1973 (1981 [printing]). — x,188p,[9]p of plates : ill ; 23cm
Bibliography: p174-184. — Includes index
ISBN 0-521-29595-5 (pbk) : Unpriced B82-01766

790′.0973 — United States. Recreation services

Weiskopf, Donald C.. Recreation and leisure : improving the quality of life / Donald C. Weiskopf. — 2nd ed. — Boston, Mass. ; London : Allyn and Bacon, c1982. — xii,449p : ill ; 24cm
Previous ed.: published as A guide to recreation and leisure. 1975. — Includes index
ISBN 0-205-07712-9 : Unpriced B82-28486

790.1 — Activities for children — *For children*

The **Tiswas** phantom flan flinger's fun book / compiled by Helen Piddock ; illustrated by Mike Miller. — London : Carousel, 1981. — 136p : ill ; 20cm
ISBN 0-552-54167-2 (pbk) : £0.85 B82-14558

790.1′3 — Practical jokes — *Manuals*

Boston, Richard. The C.O. Jones compendium of practical jokes. — London : Severn House, Sept.1982. — [192]p
ISBN 0-7278-3003-1 : £6.95 : CIP entry B82-20777

790.1′34 — Competitions. Winners — *Lists*

The **Guinness** book of winners and champions / Chris Cook, Anne Marshall ; sports editor Peter Matthews. — 2nd ed. — Enfield : Guinness Superlatives, 1981. — 255p,[8]p of plates : ill(some col.),ports(some col.) ; 26cm
Previous ed.: 1979. — Includes index
ISBN 0-85112-218-3 : £6.95 : CIP rev. B81-28089

790.1′922 — Activities for children — *For children*

Brandreth, Gyles. Challenge / Gyles Brandreth ; illustrated by Peter Stevenson. — London : Transworld, 1981. — 159p : ill ; 18cm. — (A Carousel book)
ISBN 0-552-54194-x (pbk) : £0.85 B82-10208

Gill, Rosemary. Swap shop : book four / written by Rosemary Gill and Crispin Evans. — London : British Broadcasting Corporation, c1981. — 128p : ill(some col.),1col.map,ports (some col.) ; 24cm
ISBN 0-563-17989-9 (pbk) : £2.50 B82-07747

The **KnowHow** omnibus. — London : Usborne, 1979. — 192p : col.ill ; 29cm
Contents: Paper fun / Annabelle Curtis and Judy Hindley — Jokes and tricks / Heather Amery and Ian Adair — Flying models / Mary Jean McNeil — Action toys / Heather Amery — Spycraft / Falcon Travis and Judy Hindley — Detection / Judy Hindley and Donald Rumbelow
ISBN 0-86020-357-3 : £4.95 B82-13393

Rosen, Michael. Everybody here. — London : Bodley Head, Nov.1982. — [64]p
ISBN 0-370-30944-8 : £3.95 : CIP entry B82-26710

Why don't you — ? / compiled by Hilary Murphy. — London : British Broadcasting Corporation, 1982. — 95p : ill ; 20cm
Includes index
ISBN 0-563-20051-0 (pbk) : £0.95 : CIP rev.
ISBN 0-340-28083-2 (pbk) : Knight B82-12930

790.1′922 — Games for children — *Collections — For children*

Colgan, Brendan. Let's play / Brendan Colgan. — Belfast : Blackstaff, 1980. — 29p : ill ; 15x21cm
ISBN 0-85640-083-1 (pbk) : £1.75 : CIP rev. B80-23607

790.1′922 — Items of interest to children: Items available by post — *For children*

Gundrey, Elizabeth. Send off for it / Elizabeth Gundrey. — Rev. ed. — London : Beaver, 1979. — 142p : ill ; 18cm
Previous ed.: 1978. — Includes index
ISBN 0-600-20038-8 (pbk) : £0.65 B82-12389

790.1′922 — Practical jokes — *Manuals — For children*

Brandreth, Gyles. The big book of practical jokes : 100 ways to fool your friends / Gyles Brandreth ; illustrated by Jacqui Sinclair. — London : Carousel, 1979. — 128p : ill ; 20cm
ISBN 0-552-54141-9 (pbk) : £0.65 B82-04018

790.1′922′024372 — Activities for pre-school children — *Manuals — For teaching — Serials*

[Activity booklets *(Scottish Pre-School Playgroups Association)***]**. Activity booklets / Scottish Pre-school Playgroups Association. — No.1 (Oct. 1980)-. — Glasgow (7 Royal Terrace, Glasgow G3 7NT) : The Association, 1980-. — v. : ill ; 21cm
£0.25 B82-29055

790.1′922′02491 — Games for children on car journeys — *Collections*

Barnard, D. St. P.. The Puffin book of car games / D.St.P. Barnard ; illustrated by Nigel Paige. — Harmondsworth : Puffin, 1977 (1982 [printing]). — 199p : ill ; 19cm
ISBN 0-14-030845-8 (pbk) : £1.00 B82-34378

790.1′922′0942 — England. Activities for children — *Practical information*
James, Betty. The Young Observer action guide. — London : Unwin Paperbacks, Mar.1982. — [192]p
ISBN 0-04-790004-0 (pbk) : £1.95 : CIP entry
B82-00281

790.1′922′0942 — England. Activities for children — *Practical information — For children*
James, Betty. The Young Observer action guide : things to do, places to visit, sports and holidays in England and Wales / compiled by Betty James and Pat Salmon. — London : Allen & Unwin in association with the Observer, 1982. — 168p ; 21cm
Includes index
ISBN 0-04-790005-9 (cased) : Unpriced : CIP rev.
ISBN 0-04-790004-0 (pbk) : £1.95 B82-04722

790.1′94 — Games for scouts — *Collections*
McKay, Colin, *1936-*. Games galore : a collection of games for scout troops and youth groups / by Colin McKay ; illustrations by Peter Harrison and Colin Watson. — Glasgow : Brown, Son & Ferguson, 1975, c1981 (1981 [printing]). — 104p : ill ; 19cm
Includes index
ISBN 0-85174-420-6 (pbk) : £2.50 B82-12287

790.1′96 — Physical activities for mentally handicapped persons. Teaching — *Manuals*
Latto, Kay. Give us the chance : sport and physical recreation with mentally handicapped people / Kay Latto ; illustrations by Elaine Batt. — London : Disabled Living Foundation, 1981. — x,198p : ill ; 30cm
Includes bibliographies and index
ISBN 0-901908-38-x (pbk) : Unpriced
B82-40979

790.2′023′41 — Great Britain. Performing arts — *Career guides*
Rowley, Lillian. So you want to go on the stage / Lillian Rowley. — 2nd ed. — Eastbourne : Offord, 1981. — 64p ; 21cm
Previous ed.: Havant : Mason, 1970
ISBN 0-903931-39-7 (pbk) : £1.90 B82-21155

790.2′06′0411 — Scotland. Performing arts. Organisations — *Directories*
Music, dance and drama promoters in Scotland. — [Edinburgh] : Scottish Arts Council, 1981. — iii,56p : 1map ; 21cm
Cover title. — Includes index
ISBN 0-902989-69-3 (pbk) : Unpriced
B82-05860

790.2′079 — Great Britain. Performing arts. Patronage by royal families, *to 1980*
Pertwee, Bill. By royal command / Bill Pertwee. — Newton Abbot : David & Charles, c1981. — 175p : ill,facsims,ports ; 24cm
Ill on lining papers. — Includes index
ISBN 0-7153-8200-4 : £8.95 : CIP rev.
B81-24663

790.2′09747′1 — New York *(City)*. **Performing arts centres: Lincoln Center for the Performing Arts,** *to 1980*
Young, Edgar B.. Lincoln Center : the building of an institution / Edgar B. Young ; with a foreword by Frank Stanton. — New York ; London : New York University Press, c1980. — xvi,334p : ill,ports ; 27cm
Includes index
ISBN 0-8147-9656-7 : £18.50 B82-38741

791 — PUBLIC ENTERTAINMENT

791′.092′2 — Comedy. Morecambe, Eric & Wise, Ernie — *Biographies*
Morecambe, Eric. There's no answer to that!!. — London : Hodder and Stoughton, Oct.1982. — [144]p
Originally published: London : Barker, 1981
ISBN 0-340-28442-0 (pbk) : £1.25 : CIP entry
B82-24829

791′.092′2 — Northern English comedians, *ca 1950-1981*
Welland, Colin. Colin Welland's anthology of northern humour / cartoons by 'Albert'. — Feltham : Hamlyn Paperbacks, 1982. — 142p : ill ; 18cm
ISBN 0-600-20202-x (pbk) : £1.25 B82-40191

791′.092′4 — Comedy. Allen, Woody — *Biographies*
Jacobs, Diane. The magic of Woody Allen. — London : Robson, Sept.1982. — [192]p
ISBN 0-86051-196-0 : £6.95 : CIP entry
B82-20870

791′.092′4 — Comedy. Allen, Woody — *Critical studies*
Hirsch, Foster. Love, sex, death, and the meaning of life : Woody Allen's comedy / Foster Hirsch. — New York ; London : McGraw-Hill, c1981. — 231p ; 21cm. — (McGraw-Hill paperbacks)
Bibliography: p215-218. — Includes index
ISBN 0-07-029054-7 (pbk) : £3.25 B82-02333

791′.092′4 — Comedy. Brooks, Mel — *Critical studies*
Yacowar, Maurice. [Method in madness, the art of Mel Brooks]. The comic art of Mel Brooks / Maurice Yacowar. — London : W.H. Allen, 1982, c1981. — 224p,[8]p of plates : ill ; 23cm
Originally published: New York : St Martin's, 1981. — Bibliography: p211-214. — Includes index
ISBN 0-491-02917-9 : £7.95 B82-34873

791′.092′4 — Comedy. Burns, George — *Biographies*
Burns, George. The third time around / George Burns. — London : W.H. Allen, c1980 (1981 [printing]). — 219p,[8]p of plates : ill,1facsim,ports ; 18cm. — (A Star book)
ISBN 0-352-30962-8 (pbk) : £1.60 B82-03040

791′.092′4 — Comedy. Chapman, Graham, *1941-* — *Biographies*
Chapman, Graham, *1941-*. A liar's autobiography : volume VII / by Graham Chapman and David Sherlock and also Alex Martin Oh, and David Yallop and also too by Douglas Adams (whose autobiography it isn't) ; with drawings by Jonathan Hills. — London : Magnum, 1981, c1980. — 239p : ill ; 20cm
Originally published: London : Eyre Methuen, 1980
ISBN 0-417-07200-7 (pbk) : £1.50 B82-17664

791′.092′4 — Comedy. Holliday, Judy — *Biographies*
Carey, Gary. Judy Holliday. — London : Robson Books, Feb.1983. — [288]p
ISBN 0-86051-169-3 : £7.95 : CIP entry
B82-39618

791′.092′4 — Comedy. Hope, Bob, *1903-* — *Biographies*
Faith, William Robert. Bob Hope. — London : Granada, Feb.1983. — [416]p
ISBN 0-246-11926-8 : £8.95 : CIP entry
B82-37826

Thompson, Charles. Bob Hope : the road from Eltham / Charles Thompson. — London : Thames Methuen, 1981. — 250p,[16]p of plates : ports ; 22cm
Includes index
ISBN 0-423-00040-3 : £7.50 : CIP rev.
B81-22641

Thompson, Charles. Bob Hope : portrait of a superstar / Charles Thompson. — [London] : Fontana, 1982, c1981. — 250p,[8]p of plates : ports ; 18cm
Originally published: London : Thames Methuen, 1981. — Includes index
ISBN 0-00-636431-4 (pbk) : £1.75 B82-32976

791′.092′4 — Comedy. Jewel, Jimmy — *Biographies*
Jewel, Jimmy. Three times lucky. — London : Severn House, Oct.1982. — [192]p
ISBN 0-7278-3005-8 : £7.95 : CIP entry
B82-24250

791′.092′4 — Comedy. Lewis, Jerry — *Biographies*
Lewis, Jerry. Jerry Lewis in person. — London : Robson Books, Feb.1983. — [320]p
ISBN 0-86051-176-6 : £7.95 : CIP entry
B82-39619

791′.092′4 — Entertainments. Grenfell, Joyce — *Correspondence, diaries, etc.*
Grenfell, Joyce. An invisible friendship : an exchange of letters 1957-1979 / Joyce Grenfell, Katharine Moore. — London : Macmillan in association with Allison & Busby, 1981. — 267p ; 23cm
ISBN 0-333-32236-3 : £8.95
Also classified at 823′.914 B82-06637

791′.092′4 — Great Britain. Animal imitation. Edwards, Percy — *Biographies*
Edwards, Percy. The road I travelled / by Percy Edwards. — Long Preston : Magna, 1982, c1979. — 378p ; 23cm
Originally published: London : A. Barker, 1979. — Published in large print
ISBN 0-86009-386-7 : Unpriced : CIP rev.
B82-00359

791′.092′4 — Great Britain. Entertainments. Everett, Kenny — *Biographies*
Everett, Kenny. The custard stops at Hatfield. — London : Collins, Sept.1982. — [128]p
ISBN 0-00-218040-5 : £6.95 : CIP entry
B82-21380

791′.092′4 — Great Britain. Entertainments. Grossmith, George — *Biographies*
Joseph, Tony. George Grossmith : biography of a Savoyard / by Tony Joseph. — Bristol : [T. Joseph], 1982. — x,212p : ill,ports ; 24cm
Bibliography: p199-200. — Includes index
ISBN 0-9507992-0-3 (pbk) : £5.50 B82-37696

791′.092′4 — Great Britain. Entertainments. Secombe, Harry — *Biographies*
Secombe, Harry. Goon abroad / Harry Secombe ; illustrations by the author. — London : Robson, 1982. — 160p : ill ; 23cm
ISBN 0-86051-193-6 : £5.95 : CIP rev.
B82-24143

791′.092′4 — Great Britain. Entertainments. Sherry, Peter — *Biographies*
Sherry, Joan. Dance for your Uncle Sam / presented by Joan Sherry. — [Sandown] ([4a Wilkes Rd., Sandown, I.O.W PO36 8EZ]) : J. Sherry, c1981. — iv,80p : facsims,ports ; 21cm
£2.50 (pbk) B82-13281

791′.092′4 — Wales. Entertainments. Davies, Thomas Ryan — *Biographies — Welsh texts*
Jones, Rhydderch T.. Cofiant Ryan / Rhydderch T. Jones. — 3 argraffiad. — [Swansea] ([P.O. Box 207, Mumbles, Swansea]) : Gwasg y Mynydd Du, 1980. — 100p,[12]p of plates : ill,music,ports ; 22cm
Previous ed.: 1979
ISBN 0-85088-871-9 : £2.95 B82-02412

791′.0941 — British comedy, *1960-1980*
Wilmut, Roger. From fringe to flying circus : celebrating a unique generation of comedy 1960-1980 / Roger Wilmut ; preface by Bamber Gascoigne. — London : Methuen, 1982, c1980. — xxii,264p : ill,facsims,ports ; 25cm
Originally published: London : Eyre Methuen, 1980. — Includes index
ISBN 0-413-50770-x (pbk) : £4.95 B82-33881

791′.0941 — Great Britain. Entertainments — *Serials*
[Blitz *(London)*]. Blitz. — Issue no.1 (Nov. 1980)-. — [London] ([1 Lower James St., W1]) : [Blitz], 1980-. — v. : ill,ports ; 43cm
Quarterly. — Description based on: Issue no.3 (Summer 1981)
ISSN 0263-2543 = Blitz (London) : £0.70 per issue B82-22683

791′.09422′5 — East & West Sussex. Entertainments — *Serials*
P.S.S.T! : performance and social (Southern) times : the 'what's on' paper in the South!. — Vol.1, no.1-. — Brighton (87 Gloucester Rd., Brighton, [Sussex]) : [S.n.], [1981]-. — v. : ill,ports ; 37cm
Monthly
ISSN 0262-7686 = P.S.S.T!. Performance and social, Southern, times : £0.20 per issue
B82-09674

791.1 — PUBLIC ENTERTAINMENT. TRAVELLING SHOWS

791′.1 — Norfolk. Thursford. Steam powered fairground equipment. Preservation. Cushing, George — *Biographies*
Cushing, George. Steam at Thursford / George Cushing with Ian Starsmore. — Newton Abbot : David & Charles, c1982. — 174p : ill(some col.),ports ; 22cm
ISBN 0-7153-8154-7 : £7.95 : CIP rev.
B81-35822

791′.1′0924 — Great Britain. Entertainments: Fairs. Blondini, Michael — *Biographies*
Blondini, Michael. Bed of nails : the story of the amazing Blondini with experiences : an autobiographical introduction / [as told to] Gordon Thomas. — Dublin : O'Brien Press, 1981. — 338p : ports
Originally published: London : Wingate, 1955
ISBN 0-86278-006-3 (cased) : Unpriced : CIP rev.
ISBN 0-86278-007-1 (pbk) : Unpriced
B81-22586

791′.1′0924 — United States. Travelling shows: Buffalo Bill's Wild West. Entertaining. Oakley, Annie — *Biographies*
Sayers, Isabelle S.. Annie Oakley and Buffalo Bill's Wild West / Isabelle S. Sayers. — New York : Dover ; London : Constable, 1981. — 89p : ill,ports ; 28cm
ISBN 0-486-24120-3 (pbk) : £3.75 B82-13375

791.3 — CIRCUSES

791.3 — Circuses — *For children*
Alfaenger, Peter K.. Make your own circus / written and illustrated by Peter K. Alfaenger. — London : Blackie, 1982. — 55p : ill(some col.) ; 27x28cm
Translation of: Le cirque
ISBN 0-216-91184-2 : £5.95 : CIP rev.
B82-01080

791.3′09 — Circuses, *to 1979*
Speaight, George. A history of the circus / by George Speaight. — London : Tantivy, c1980. — 216p,[8]p of plates : ill(some col.),facsims,ports ; 29cm
Bibliography: p199-202. — Includes index
ISBN 0-498-02470-9 : £9.95 B82-19405

791.3′092′4 — Great Britain. Circuses. Whiteley, Henry Allen Alexander — *Biographies* — *Manuscripts* — *Facsimiles*
Whiteley, Henry Allen Alexander. Memories of circus, variety etc. as I knew it / Henry Allen Alexander Whiteley ; edited by George Speaight. — London : Society for Theatre Research, 1981. — 332p,[16]p of plates : ill (some col.),ports,2geneal.tables ; 25cm
Facsim of the original manuscript. — Limited ed. of 250 numbered copies
ISBN 0-85430-035-x (spiral) : Unpriced
B82-14688

791.3′092′4 — Soviet Union. Circuses, *ca 1920-ca 1950* — *Personal observations*
Durova, Natalia. "Your turn!" : stories / Natalia Durova ; translated from the Russian by Jan Butler ; designed by A. Markevich and K. Syunnerberg. — Moscow : Progress, c1980 ; [London] : Distributed by Central Books. — 220p : ill,ports ; 23cm
Translation of: Vash nomer
ISBN 0-7147-1638-3 : £2.95 B82-02760

791.3′092′4 — United States. Circuses. Barnum, P. T. — *Biographies*
Barnum, P. T.. Struggles and triumphs, or, Forty years' recollections of P.T. Barnum / edited and abridged with an introduction by Carl Bode. — Abridged ed. — Harmondsworth : Penguin, 1981. — 394p : 1port ; 19cm. — (The Penguin American library)
Previous ed.: Hartford : Burr, 1869. — Port on inside cover
ISBN 0-14-039004-9 (pbk) : £2.50 B82-22087

791.3′3 — Clowns. Techniques — *Manuals*
Stolzenberg, Mark. Clown : for circus & stage / Mark Stolzenberg ; photographs by Neil Sapienza. — New York : Sterling ; London : Oak Tree, c1981. — 159p : ill ; 27cm
Includes index
ISBN 0-7061-2796-x : £7.95 B82-21872

791.3′3′0924 — Circuses. Clowns: Campbell, William — *Biographies*
Campbell, William. Villi the clown / William Campbell. — London : Faber, 1981. — 256p ; 23cm
Includes index
ISBN 0-571-11794-5 : £7.50 : CIP rev.
B81-23776

791.43 — CINEMA

791.43 — Cinema films
Giannetti, Louis D.. Understanding movies / Louis Giannetti. — 3rd ed. — Englewood Cliffs ; London : Prentice-Hall, c1982. — xi,500p : ill,ports ; 24cm
Previous ed.: 1976. — Includes bibliographies and index
ISBN 0-13-936310-6 (pbk) : £10.45
B82-31824

791.43 — Cinema films — *Feminist viewpoints*
Kuhn, Annette. Women's pictures : feminism and cinema / Annette Kuhn. — London : Routledge & Kegan Paul, 1982. — xiv,226p : ill ; 21cm
Text on inside covers. — Bibliography: p211-217. — Includes index
ISBN 0-7100-9044-7 (pbk) : £4.95 B82-28979

791.43 — Cinema films - *For children*
Hill, Gordon. Secrets of film and television. — Sevenoaks : Hodder & Stoughton, May 1981. — [128]p
ISBN 0-340-25496-3 (pbk) : £0.95 : CIP entry
Also classified at 791.45 B81-05158

791.43 — Cinema films. Influence of political events in France, *1968*
Harvey, Sylvia. May '68 and film culture / Sylvia Harvey. — London : British Film Institute, 1978 (1980 [printing]). — 169p ; 21cm
Bibliography: p167-169
ISBN 0-85170-104-3 (pbk) : £3.25 B82-13181

791.43 — Great Britain. Cinema films. Censorship. Organisations: British Board of Film Censors
British Board of Film Censors. Memorandum on the work of the British Board of Film Censors. — [London] : [British Board of Film Censors], [1981?]. — 5p ; 30cm
Unpriced (unbound) B82-05112

791.43 — Great Britain. Cinema films. Censorship — *Serials*
British Board of Film Censors. Monthly report for ... / British Board of Film Censors. — Jan. 1976- Dec. 1978. — [London] ([3 Soho Sq., W1]) : The Board, 1976-1978. — 36v. ; 30cm
Continued by: British Board of Film Censors. Report
ISSN 0142-5781 = Monthly report - British Board of Film Censors : Unpriced B82-05219

British Board of Film Censors. Report / British Board of Film Censors. — No.1 (1979)- no.3 (1979). — [London] ([3 Soho Sq. W1]) : The Board, 1979-1979. — 3v. ; 30cm
Irregular. — Continues: British Board of Film Censors. Monthly report for ...
Unpriced B82-05220

791.43 — Oscar winning cinema films, *to 1981*
Pickard, Roy. The Oscar movies from A-Z. — Rev. ed. — London : Muller, Oct.1982. — [368]p
Previous ed.: Feltham : Hamlyn, 1978
ISBN 0-584-11041-3 : £10.95 : CIP entry
B82-23365

791.43′01 — Cinema films. Aesthetics
Cavell, Stanley. The world viewed : reflections on the ontology of film : Stanley Cavell. — Enl. ed. — Cambridge, Mass. ; London : Harvard University Press, 1979. — xxv,253p ; 22cm. — (Harvard film studies)
Previous ed.: New York : Viking, 1974. — Includes index
ISBN 0-674-96197-8 (cased) : Unpriced
B82-25669

791.43′01′9 — Cinema films — *Psychoanalytical perspectives*
Metz, Christian. Psychoanalysis and cinema : the imaginary signifier / Christian Metz ; translated by Celia Britton ... [et al.]. — London : Macmillan, 1982. — vii,327p ; 23cm. — (Language, discourse, society series)
Translation of: Le signifiant imaginaire. — Includes index
ISBN 0-333-27805-4 : £15.00 B82-20912

791.43′0232′0924 — American animated cinema films. Production. Disney, Walt — *Biographies*
Thomas, Bob. Walt Disney / Bob Thomas. — London : W.H. Allen, 1981. — xvii,392p ; 18cm. — (A Star book)
Originally published: New York : Simon and Schuster, 1976
ISBN 0-352-30972-5 (pbk) : £2.50 B82-11709

791.43′0232′0924 — American cinema films. Production. Mayer, Louis B. — *Biographies*
Carey, Gary. All the stars in heaven : Louis B. Mayer's M-G-M / Gary Carey. — London : Robson, 1982, c1981. — xiv,320p,[18]p of plates : ill,ports ; 24cm
Originally published: New York : Dutton, 1981. — Bibliography: p307-309. — Includes index
ISBN 0-86051-164-2 : £7.95 : CIP rev.
B82-00344

791.43′0233′0924 — American cinema films. Directing. Polanski, Roman — *Biographies*
Kiernan, Thomas. [The Roman Polanski story]. Repulsion : the life and times of Roman Polanski / Thomas Kiernan. — Sevenoaks : New English Library, 1981, c1980 (1982 [printing]). — 288p,[24]p of plates : ill,ports ; 18cm
Originally published: New York : Grove Press, 1980
ISBN 0-450-05264-8 (pbk) : £1.75 : CIP rev.
B82-12350

Leaming, Barbara. Palanski : his life and films / by Barbara Leaming. — London : Hamilton, 1982. — xii,153p,[16]p of plates : ill,ports ; 24cm
Includes index
ISBN 0-241-10752-0 (cased) : £9.95 : CIP rev.
ISBN 0-241-10766-0 (pbk) : £5.95 B82-01825

791.43′0233′0924 — British documentary films. Directing. Jennings, Humphrey — *Biographies*
Humphrey Jennings : film-maker, painter, poet / edited by Mary-Lou Jennings. — London : British Film Institute in association with Riverside Studios, 1982. — 75p : ill,facsims,ports ; 21cm
Published to accompany an exhibition at the Riverside Studios, 1982. — Bibliography: p75. — List of films: p73-74
ISBN 0-85170-118-3 (pbk) : £3.75 : CIP rev.
B81-38854

791.43′0233′0924 — Cinema films directed by Buñuel, Luis — *Critical studies*
Edwards, Gwynne. The discreet art of Luis Buñuel. — London : Marian Boyars, June 1982. — [288]p
ISBN 0-7145-2754-8 : £15.00 : CIP entry
B82-09611

791.43′0233′0924 — Cinema films directed by Kubrick, Stanley
Ciment, Michel. Kubrick. — London : Collins, Nov.1982. — [242]p
Translation of: Kubrick
ISBN 0-00-216353-5 : £12.50 : CIP entry
B82-27791

791.43′0233′0924 — Cinema films. Directing. Edwards, Blake — *Critical studies*
Lehman, Peter. Blake Edwards / by Peter Lehman & William Luhr. — Athens [Ohio] ; London : Ohio University Press, c1981. — xiv,288p : ill,ports ; 24cm
Bibliography: p263-265. — List of films: p267-283. — Includes index
ISBN 0-8214-0605-1 (cased) : Unpriced
ISBN 0-8214-0616-7 (pbk) : £6.30 B82-19653

791.43'0233'0924 — Cinema films. Directing. Godard, Jean-Luc — *Critical studies*
MacCabe, Colin. Godard : images, sounds, politics / text Colin MacCabe with Mick Eaton and Laura Mulvey ; interviews Jean-Luc Godard. — [London] : BFI, 1980. — 175p : ill ; 23cm. — (British Film Institute cinema series)
Bibliography: p174-175. — List of films: p169-173
ISBN 0-333-29073-9 (cased) : £12.00 : CIP rev.
ISBN 0-333-29074-7 (pbk) : £4.95 B80-18453

791.43'0233'0924 — Cinema films. Directing. Hitchcock, Alfred — *Biographies*
Spoto, Donald. The life of Alfred Hitchcock. — London : Collins, Jan.1983. — [576]p
ISBN 0-00-216352-7 : £10.95 : CIP entry B82-33200

Taylor, John Russell. Hitch : the life and work of Alfred Hitchcock / John Russell Taylor. — London : Abacus, 1981, c1978. — xvi,304p,[8]p of plates : ill,ports ; 20cm
Originally published: London : Faber, 1978. — Includes index
ISBN 0-349-13385-9 (pbk) : £2.75 B82-02180

791.43'0233'0924 — Cinema films. Directing. Hitchcock, Alfred — *Critical studies*
Rothman, William. Hitchcock : the murderous gaze / William Rothman. — Cambridge, Mass. ; London : Harvard University Press, 1982. — 371p : ill,ports ; 26cm. — (Harvard film studies)
Includes index
ISBN 0-674-40410-6 : £19.25 B82-27091

791.43'0233'0924 — Cinema films. Directing. Ivory, James, *1962-1983* — *Critical studies*
Pym, John. The wandering company : twenty one years of Merchant Ivory films. — London : BFI Publishing, Jan.1983. — [96]p
ISBN 0-85170-127-2 : £3.95 : CIP entry B82-40302

791.43'0233'0924 — Cinema films. Directing. Visconti, Luchino — *Biographies*
Servadio, Gaia. Luchino Visconti : a biography / Gaia Servadio. — London : Weidenfeld & Nicolson, 1981, c1982. — x,262p,[16]p of plates : ill,ports ; 25cm
Bibliography: p225—226. — Includes index
ISBN 0-297-77812-9 : £12.95 B82-27778

791.43'0233'0924 — French cinema films. Directing. Rouch, Jean — *Critical studies*
Anthropology, reality, cinema : the films of Jean Rouch / edited by Mick Eaton. — London : British Film Institute, 1979. — 77p ; 20cm
ISBN 0-85170-090-x (pbk) : £1.75 B82-28246

791.43'0233'0924 — Swedish cinema films. Directing. Bergman, Ingmar — *Critical studies*
Livingston, Paisley. Ingmar Bergman and the rituals of art / Paisley Livingston. — Ithaca ; London : Cornell University Press, 1982. — 291p : ill ; 24cm
List of films: p271-275. — Bibliography: p276-287. — Includes index
ISBN 0-8014-1452-0 : £15.00 B82-36989

Mosley, Philip. Ingmar Bergman : the cinema as mistress / Philip Mosley. — London : Boyars, 1981. — 192p : ill,1port ; 23cm
List of films: p13-14. — Bibliography: p188-189. — Includes index
ISBN 0-7145-2644-4 : £8.95 : CIP rev. B81-09486

791.43'028 — American cinema films. Acting — *Manuals*
Barr, Tony. Acting for the camera / Tony Barr. — Boston [Mass.] ; London : Allyn and Bacon, c1982. — ix,310p : ill ; 22cm
Includes index
ISBN 0-205-07368-9 (pbk) : Unpriced B82-06669

791.43'028 — Cinema films. Performers: Mammals
Rothel, David. The great show business animals / by David Rothel. — San Diego : Barnes ; London : Tantivy, c1980. — 292p : ill,ports ; 29cm
Bibliography: p285-286. — Includes index
ISBN 0-498-02519-5 : £11.50 B82-31488

791.43'028'0922 — American cinema films. Acting. Stars, *to 1980* — *Filmographies*
Quinlan, David, *1941-*. The illustrated directory of film stars / David Quinlan. — London : Batsford, 1981. — 499p : ports ; 26cm
Bibliography: p498-499
ISBN 0-7134-3891-6 : £14.95 B82-01601

791.43'028'0922 — American cinema films. Actors & actresses — *Biographies*
Shipman, David. The great movie stars : the golden years / David Shipman. — New rev. ed. — London : Angus & Robertson, 1979. — 592p : ill,ports ; 26cm
Previous ed.: Feltham : Hamlyn, 1970. — Bibliography: p586-588. — Includes index
ISBN 0-207-95829-7 : £15.00 B82-03261

791.43'028'0922 — Cinema films. British character actors — *Biographies*
Pettigrew, Terence. British film character actors : great names and memorable moments / Terence Pettigrew. — Newton Abbot : David & Charles, 1982. — 208p : ports ; 26cm
Includes lists of films and index
ISBN 0-7153-8270-5 : £12.95 : CIP rev. B82-09623

791.43'028'0924 — America cinema films. Acting. Poitier, Sydney — *Biographies*
Poitier, Sydney. This life. — London : Coronet, Apr.1981. — [448]p
Originally published
ISBN 0-340-26673-2 (pbk) : £1.50 : CIP entry B81-02651

791.43'028'0924 — American cinema films. Acting. Ball, Lucille — *Biographies*
Andrews, Bart. Loving Lucy : an illustrated tribute to Lucille Ball / Bart Andrews and Thomas J. Watson ; foreword by Gale Gordon. — London : Robson, 1980. — 226p : ill,ports ; 28cm
Includes index
ISBN 0-86051-127-8 : £7.95 B82-05906

791.43'028'0924 — American cinema films. Acting. Brooks, Louise — *Biographies*
Brooks, Louise. Lulu in Hollywood / by Louise Brooks ; introduction by William Shawn. — London : Hamilton, 1982. — viii,109p,[40]p of plates : ill,ports ; 24cm
ISBN 0-241-10761-x : £8.95 : CIP rev. B82-04309

791.43'028'0924 — American cinema films. Acting. Chaplin, Charles, *1889-1977* — *Biographies*
Chaplin, Charles, *1889-1977*. My early years. — Large print ed. — Bath : Chivers, Sept.1982. — [312]p. — (A Lythway book)
Originally published: in My autobiography. London : Bodley Head, 1964
ISBN 0-85119-843-0 : £6.90 : CIP entry B82-20503

791.43'028'0924 — American cinema films. Acting. Cody, Iron Eyes — *Biographies*
Cody, Iron Eyes. Iron Eyes : my life as a Hollywood Indian. — London : Muller, Nov.1982. — [384]p
ISBN 0-584-11050-2 : £7.95 : CIP entry B82-26567

791.43'028'0924 — American cinema films. Acting. Davis, Bette, *1908-* — *Biographies*
Higham, Charles, *1931-*. Bette : a biography of Bette Davis / Charles Higham. — London : New English Library, 1981. — vi,250p : ill,ports ; 25cm
Ports on lining papers. — Includes index
ISBN 0-450-04875-6 : £7.95 : CIP rev. B81-31954

Higham, Charles, *1931-*. Bette Davis. — London : New English Library, Dec.1982. — [400]p
Originally published: 1981
ISBN 0-450-05509-4 (pbk) : £1.95 : CIP entry B82-30088

Stine, Whitney. Mother Goddam : the story of the career of Bette Davis / by Whitney Stine with a running commentary by Bette Davis. — London : W.H. Allen, 1982, c1974. — 308p,[4]p of plates : ill,ports ; 18cm. — (A Star book)
Originally published: 1974
ISBN 0-352-31142-8 (pbk) : £1.95 B82-33973

791.43'028'0924 — American cinema films. Acting. Dean, James, *1931-1955* — *Illustrations*
Schatt, Roy. James Dean : a portrait / Roy Schatt. — London : Sidgwick & Jackson, 1982. — 146p : ill,ports ; 28cm
ISBN 0-283-98877-0 (pbk) : £4.95 B82-31978

791.43'028'0924 — American cinema films. Acting. Farmer, Frances — *Biographies*
Farmer, Frances. Will there really be a morning? : an autobiography / by Frances Farmer. — London : Allison & Busby, 1974 (1982 [printing]). — 318p,[4]p of plates : ports ; 23cm
ISBN 0-85031-109-8 : £7.95 B82-26839

791.43'028'0924 — American cinema films. Acting. Granger, Stewart — *Biographies*
Granger, Stewart. Sparks fly upwards / Stewart Granger. — London : Granada, 1981 (1982 [printing]). — 416p,[32]p of plates : ill,ports ; 18cm. — (A Panther book)
Includes index
ISBN 0-586-05599-1 (pbk) : £1.95 B82-40719

791.43'028'0924 — American cinema films. Acting. Lamour, Dorothy — *Biographies*
Lamour, Dorothy. My side of the road / Dorothy Lamour as told to Dick McInnes. — London : Robson : 1981, c1980. — 244p,[24]p of plates : ill,ports ; 24cm
List of films: p227-235. — Includes index
ISBN 0-86051-126-x : £7.50 B82-37224

791.43'028'0924 — American cinema films. Acting. McQueen, Steve — *Biographies*
Satchell, Tim. McQueen / Tim Satchell ; picture editor Harvey Mann. — London : Sidgwick & Jackson, 1981. — 137p : ill,4facsims,ports ; 28cm
List of films: p129-135. — Includes index
ISBN 0-283-98778-2 (cased) : £8.95
ISBN 0-283-98779-0 (pbk) : £6.95 B82-00029

791.43'028'0924 — American cinema films. Acting. Peck, Gregory - *Biographies*
Freedland, Michael. Gregory Peck. — London : Hodder and Stoughton, Aug.1981. — [296]p
Originally published: London : W.H. Allen, 1980
ISBN 0-340-26681-3 (pbk) : £1.75 : CIP entry B81-18145

791.43'028'0924 — American cinema films. Acting. Sedgwick, Edie — *Biographies*
Stein, Jean. Edie. — London : Cape, Nov.1982. — [360]p
ISBN 0-224-02068-4 : £9.95 : CIP entry B82-26868

791.43'028'0924 — American cinema films. Acting. Smith, C. Aubrey — *Biographies*
Allen, David Rayvern. Sir Aubrey : a biography of C. Aubrey Smith, England cricketer, West End actor, Hollywood film star / by David Rayvern Allen. — London : Elm Tree, 1982. — xiii,172p,[8]p of plates : ill,ports ; 23cm
Bibliography: p167-168. — Includes index
ISBN 0-241-10590-0 : £12.50 : CIP rev. B82-07396

791.43'028'0924 — American cinema films. Acting. Swanson, Gloria — *Biographies*
Swanson, Gloria. Swanson on Swanson / Gloria Swanson. — Feltham : Hamlyn, 1981, c1980. — vi,519p,[32]p of plates : ill,ports ; 20cm
Originally published: London : Joseph, 1981. — Includes index
ISBN 0-600-20496-0 (pbk) : £2.50 B82-18957

791.43'028'0924 — American cinema films. Acting. Wayne, John, *1907-1979* — *Biographies*
Goldstein, Norm. John Wayne : a tribute / foreword by James Stewart ; by Norm Goldstein. — [New York] : Associated Press ; [London] : Windward, c1979. — 159p : ill,ports ; 29cm
List of films: p135-159
ISBN 0-7112-0018-1 : £3.95 B82-01683

791.43′028′0924 — British cinema films. Acting. Caine, Michael — *Biographies*

Hall, William, *1935-*. Raising Caine : the authorized biography / William Hall. — London : Sidgwick & Jackson, 1981. — 260p,[16]p of plates : ports ; 24cm
List of films: p231-256. — Includes index
ISBN 0-283-98777-4 : £7.50 B82-01021

791.43′028′0924 — Cinema films. Acting. Bergman, Ingrid, *1915-* — *Biographies*

Bergman, Ingrid, *1915-*. Ingrid Bergman : my story / Ingrid Bergman and Alan Burgess. — London : Sphere, 1981, c1980. — xvii,556p,[16]p of plates : ill,ports ; 18cm
Originally published: New York : Delacorte Press ; London : Joseph, 1980. — List of films: p534-545. — Includes index
ISBN 0-7221-1631-4 (pbk) : £1.95 B82-07075

791.43′028′0924 — Cinema films. Acting. Chevalier, Maurice — *Biographies*

Freedland, Michael. Maurice Chevalier / Michael Freedland. — London : Arthur Barker, c1981. — 287p : ill,ports ; 24cm
ISBN 0-213-16789-1 : £8.95 B82-14629

791.43′028′0924 — Cinema films. Acting. Dors, Diana — *Biographies*

Dors, Diana. Dors by Diana. — London : Macdonald Futura, 1981. — 317p,[16]p of plates : ill,ports ; 21cm
ISBN 0-362-00549-4 (cased) : £7.95
ISBN 0-7088-2025-5 (pbk) : £1.60 B82-00845

791.43′028′0924 — Cinema films. Acting. Finch, Peter — *Biographies*

Dundy, Elaine. Finch, bloody Finch : a biography of Peter Finch / Elaine Dundy. — [London] : Magnum, 1981, c1980. — 354p,[16]p of plates : ports ; 19cm
Originally published: London : Joseph, 1980. — Includes index
ISBN 0-417-06600-7 (pbk) : £1.95 B82-17572

791.43′028′0924 — Cinema films. Acting. Fonda, Jane — *Biographies*

Guiles, Fred Lawrence. Jane Fonda : the actress in her time / Fred Lawrence Guiles. — London : Michael Joseph, 1981. — 278p,[32]p of plates : ill,ports ; 24cm
Bibliography: p277-278. — Includes index
ISBN 0-7181-2071-x : £8.95 B82-01291

Guiles, Fred Lawrence. Jane Fonda : the actress in her time. — London : Coronet, Dec.1982. — [336]p
Originally published: London : Michael Joseph, 1981
ISBN 0-340-32061-3 (pbk) : £1.95 : CIP entry B82-29650

Kiernan, Thomas. Jane Fonda. — London : Granada, Oct.1982. — [320]p
ISBN 0-246-11921-7 : £7.95 : CIP entry B82-23470

791.43′028′0924 — Cinema films. Acting. Grable, Betty — *Biographies*

Warren, Doug. Betty Grable : the reluctant movie queen / Doug Warren. — London : Robson, 1982, c1981. — 237p,[24]p of plates : ill,ports ; 22cm
Originally published: New York : St. Martin's Press, 1981. — List of films: p219-232. — Includes index
ISBN 0-86051-165-0 : £7.50 : CIP rev. B82-00343

791.43′028′0924 — Cinema films. Acting. Sellers, Peter — *Biographies*

Sellers, Michael, *1954-*. P.S. I love you : Peter Sellers 1925-1980 / Michael Sellers with Sarah and Victoria Sellers. — [London] : Fontana/Collins, 1982, c1981. — 238p,[8]p of plates : ill,facsims,ports ; 18cm
Originally published: London : Collins, 1981
ISBN 0-00-636515-9 (pbk) : £1.75 B82-38007

Walker, Alexander. Peter Sellers. — London : Hodder and Stoughton, Apr.1982. — [320]p. — (Coronet books)
Originally published: London : Weidenfeld & Nicolson, 1981
ISBN 0-340-28103-0 (pbk) : £1.75 : CIP entry B82-06500

791.43′028′0924 — Cinema films. Acting. Taylor, Elizabeth, *1932-* — *Biographies*

Kelley, Kitty. Elizabeth Taylor : the last star / Kitty Kelley. — London : Joseph, c1981. — ix,346p : ill,ports ; 25cm
Bibliography: p309-310. — List of films: p311-336. — Includes index
ISBN 0-7181-2075-2 : £8.95 B82-04235

Kelley, Kitty. Elizabeth Taylor : the last star. — London : Hodder and Stoughton, Aug.1982. — [432]p. — (Coronet books)
Originally published: London : Joseph, 1981
ISBN 0-340-28345-9 (pbk) : £1.95 : CIP entry B82-15744

Waterbury, Ruth. Elizabeth Taylor : her life, her loves, her future / by Ruth Waterbury with Gene Arcerci. — Toronto ; London : Bantam, 1982. — 293p,[14]p of plates : ill,ports ; 18cm
Originally published: New York : Appleton-Century ; London : Hale, 1964
ISBN 0-553-22613-4 (pbk) : £1.50 B82-38959

Zec, Donald. Liz : the men, the myths, and the miracle — an intimate portrait of Elizabeth Taylor / by Donald Zec. — London : Mirror Books, 1982. — 48p : ill(some col.),ports(some col.) ; 30cm
ISBN 0-85939-316-x (pbk) : £1.25 B82-34550

791.43′028′0924 — Cinema films. Acting. Wilding, Michael, *1912-1979* — *Biographies*

Wilding, Michael, *1912-1979*. Apple sauce : the story of my life as told to Pamela Wilcox / Michael Wilding. — London : Allen & Unwin, 1982. — xiii,190p,[32]p of plates : ill,ports ; 23cm
List of films: p182-187. — Includes index
ISBN 0-04-920064-x : Unpriced : CIP rev. B82-07984

791.43′03′21 — Cinema films — *Encyclopaedias*

Halliwell, Leslie. Halliwell's film guide / Leslie Halliwell. — 3rd ed. — London : Granada, 1981. — xiii,1153p : facsims ; 26cm
Previous ed.: 1979. — Includes index
ISBN 0-246-11533-5 : £17.50 B82-09232

791.43′05 — Cinema films — *Serials*

[Cinema *(London : 1982)***]**. Cinema : the magazine of motion pictures. — No.1 (May)-. — London (205 Kentish Town Rd, NW5 2JU) : Marvel Comics, [1982]-. — v. : ill(some col.),ports ; 30cm
Monthly. — Description based on: No.2 (June)
ISSN 0263-8487 = Cinema (London. 1982) : £0.75 per issue B82-32367

791.43′068′8 — Great Britain. Cinema films. Distribution — *Inquiry reports*

Great Britain. *Interim Action Committee on the Film Industry*. The distribution of films for exhibition in cinemas and by other means : fifth report of the Interim Action Committee on the Film Industry. — London : H.M.S.O., [1982]. — iii,29p ; 25cm. — (Cmnd. ; 8530)
ISBN 0-10-185300-9 (unbound) : £3.05 B82-24639

791.43′076 — Cinema films — *Questions & answers* — *For children*

Pickard, Roy. The children's movie quiz book / Roy Pickard. — London : Muller, 1979. — 62p : ill,ports ; 26cm
ISBN 0-584-62057-8 : £2.95 : CIP rev. B79-02993

791.43′09 — Cinema films, *to 1978*

The **Book** of the cinema / foreword by Francois Truffaut. — London : Artists House, 1979. — 240p : ill,ports ; 32cm
Bibliography: p235. — Includes index
ISBN 0-86134-010-8 : £13.95 B82-00589

791.43′09 — Cinema films, *to 1980*

Brooker, John. Movie memories / John Brooker ; foreword by Roy Hudd. — Cambridge : Stephens, 1982. — 152p : ill,ports ; 25cm
Ill on lining papers. — Bibliography: p152. — List of sound recordings: p152. — Lists of films
ISBN 0-85059-556-8 : £6.95 : CIP rev. B82-04987

Robinson, David, *1930-*. World cinema : a short history / David Robinson. — [2nd ed., rev. and expanded]. — London : Eyre Methuen, 1981. — xv,494p : ill,facsims,ports ; 24cm
Previous ed.: 1973. — Filmography: p401-471. — Includes index
ISBN 0-413-48030-5 (cased) : £14.95
ISBN 0-413-34890-3 (pbk) : Unpriced B82-38832

791.43′09 — Cinema films, *to 1981*

Halliwell, Leslie. Halliwell's hundred. — London : Granada, July 1982. — [256]p
ISBN 0-246-11330-8 : £8.95 : CIP entry B82-12575

791.43′09 — Cinema films, *to 1981* — *Critical studies*

Peary, Danny. Cult movies. — London : Vermilion, Oct.1982. — [416]p
ISBN 0-09-150601-8 (pbk) : £5.95 : CIP entry B82-24984

791.43′09 — Cinema films, *to 1981* — *Illustrations*

A **pictorial** history of the talkies. — Rev. ed / by Daniel Blum and John Kobal. — Feltham : Optimum, 1982. — 411p : chiefly ill,ports ; 31cm
Previous ed.: 1974. — Includes index
ISBN 0-600-34296-4 (pbk) : Unpriced B82-40537

791.43′09′04 — Cinema films, *1920-1974* — *Critical studies*

Truffaut, François. The films in my life / François Truffaut ; translated by Leonard Mayhew. — Harmondsworth : Penguin, 1982. — x,358p,[8]p of plates : ill,ports ; 20cm
Translation of: Les films de ma vie. — Originally published: New York : Simon & Schuster, 1978 ; London : Allen Lane, 1980
ISBN 0-14-005409-x (pbk) : £3.50 B82-30514

791.43′09′04 — Cinema films, *1940—1980* — *Critical studies*

Champlin, Charles. The movies grow up : 1940-1980 / by Charles Champlin. — Chicago ; London : Swallow, c1981. — 284p : ill,ports ; 26cm
Bibliography: p270-271. — Includes index
ISBN 0-8040-0363-7 (cased) : Unpriced
ISBN 0-8040-0364-5 (pbk) : £9.10 B82-19566

791.43′09′091 — Surrealist cinema films, *to 1980* — *Critical studies*

Williams, Linda, *1946-*. Figures of desire : a theory and analysis of surrealist film / Linda Williams. — Urbana ; London : University of Illinois Press, c1981. — xv,229p : ill ; 24cm
Bibliography: p219-225. — Includes index
ISBN 0-252-00878-2 : £15.00 B82-19646

791.43′09′0915 — American cinema films: Science fiction films, *1950-1960* — *Critical studies*

Warren, Bill, *1943-*. Keep watching the skies! : American science fiction movies of the fifties / by Bill Warren ; research associate, Bill Thomas. — Jefferson ; London : McFarland ; Folkestone : distributed by Bailey Bros. & Swinfen
Vol.1: 1950-1957. — 1982. — xvi,467p : ill ; 24cm
Includes index
ISBN 0-89950-032-3 : Unpriced B82-36662

791.43′09′0916 — Cinema films: Horror films, *to 1981* — *Encyclopaedias*

Frank, Alan, *1937-*. The horror film handbook / Alan Frank. — London : Batsford, 1982. — 194p : ill,ports ; 26cm
Includes index
ISBN 0-7134-2724-8 : £9.95 B82-18942

791.43′09′0932411 — Cinema films. Special subjects: Scotland — *Critical studies*

McArthur, Colin. Scotch reels : Scotland in cinema and television. — London : BF1 Publishing, Aug.1982. — [96]p
ISBN 0-85170-121-3 (pbk) : £2.95 : CIP entry
Also classified at 791.45′09′0932411
B82-21964

791.43'09'09355 — American cinema films, *1920-1980.* **Special subjects: Juvenile delinquency** — *Critical studies*

McGee, Mark Thomas. The J.D. films : juvenile delinquency in the movies / by Mark Thomas McGee and R.J. Robertson. — Jefferson, N.C. ; London : McFarland, c1982. — x,197p : ill ; 23cm
Bibliography: p177-178. — Includes index
ISBN 0-89950-038-2 (pbk) : £11.15 B82-37986

791.43'09'09357 — Cinema films, *1950-1980.* **Special themes: Rock music** — *Encyclopaedias*

Dellar, Fred. The NME guide to rock cinema / Fred Dellar ; with a foreword by Monty Smith. — Feltham : Hamlyn Paperbacks, 1981. — 191p,[16]p of plates : ill ; 18cm
ISBN 0-600-20367-0 (pbk) : £1.50 B82-02836

791.43'09'09375 — Cinema films: Horror films. Special subjects: Monsters — *Serials*

Monster monthly. — No.1-. — London (205 Kentish Town Rd, NW5) : Marvel Comics, 1982-. — v. : ill,ports ; 28cm
Description based on: No.4 (July [1982])
£0.50 per issue B82-32353

791.43'09426'725 — Essex. Harwich. Cinemas: Electric Palace *(Harwich),* *to 1979*

Strachan, Chris. The Harwich Electric Palace / by Chris Strachan. — [Harwich] : C. Strachan, 1979. — [32]p : ill(some col.),facsims,plans (some col.) ; 21x30cm
Ill on inside covers
ISBN 0-9506681-0-9 (pbk) : Unpriced B82-11930

791.43'0943 — German cinema films, *1950-1980* — *Critical studies*

Sandford, John. The new German cinema / John Sandford. — London : Eyre Methuen, 1981, c1980. — 180p : ill,ports ; 23cm
Originally published: London : Wolff, 1980. — Bibliography: p169-170. — Includes index
ISBN 0-413-48890-x (pbk) : £4.95 B82-17575

791.43'0943 — German silent cinema films, *1920-1929* — *Illustrations*

Great film stills of the German silent era : 125 stills from the Stiftung Deutsche Kinemathek / compiled and edited by John Kobal ; with an introduction by Lotte H. Eisner. — New York : Dover ; London : Constable, 1981. — 111p : chiefly ill ; 28cm
ISBN 0-486-24195-5 (pbk) : £6.00 B82-35422

791.43'0945 — Italian cinema films, *1960-1980*

Witcombe, R. T.. The new Italian cinema : studies in dance and despair / R.T. Witcombe. — London : Secker & Warburg, 1982. — x,294p : ill,ports ; 22cm
Includes index
ISBN 0-436-57810-7 (cased) : Unpriced
ISBN 0-436-57811-5 (pbk) : £6.95 B82-25627

791.43'09566'2 — Armenian cinema films

Pilikian, Hovhanness I.. Armenian cinema : a source book / Hovhanness I. Pilikian. — London : Counter-Point Publications, c1981. — 104p : ill ; 24cm
Includes index
ISBN 0-906192-07-2 (pbk) : Unpriced : CIP rev. B82-05781

791.43'0972 — Mexican cinema films, *to 1980*

Mora, Carl J.. Mexican cinema : reflections of a society 1896-1980 / Carl J. Mora. — Berkeley ; London : University of California Press, c1982. — xv,287p : ports ; 25cm
Bibliography: p261-277. — Includes index
ISBN 0-520-04287-5 : £22.25 B82-40218

791.43'0973 — American avant garde cinema films, *1950-1975* — *Critical studies*

Films by American artists : one medium among many : a touring collection of films / chosen by Regina Cornwell. — [London] : Arts Council of Great Britain, c1981. — 64p : ill ; 15x18cm
List of films: p59-64
ISBN 0-7287-0269-x (pbk) : Unpriced B82-13029

791.43'0973 — American B cinema films, *to 1980*

Cross, Robin. The big book of B movies, or, How low was my budget / Robin Cross. — London : Muller, 1981. — 208p : ill,ports ; 28cm. — (A Charles Herridge Book)
Bibliography: p204. — Includes index
ISBN 0-584-97074-9 (pbk) : £4.95 B82-00809

791.43'0973 — American cinema films, *to 1980*

Anatomy of the movies / editor, David Pirie. — London : Windward, 1981. — 320p : ill,ports ; 26cm
Includes index
ISBN 0-7112-0064-5 : £7.95 B82-05866

791.43'3 — Puppet cinema films, *to 1970*

Wilson, S. S.. Puppets and people : dimensional animation combined with live action in the cinema / S.S. Wilson. — San Diego : Barnes ; London : Tantivy, c1980. — 170p : ill ; 25cm
Bibliography: p165-170. — List of films: p156-164
ISBN 0-498-02312-5 : £5.95 B82-32566

791.43'72 — American cinema films — *Scripts*

Allen, Woody. Four films of Woody Allen : Annie Hall ; Interiors ; Manhattan ; Stardust memories. — London : Faber, Nov.1982. — [448]p
ISBN 0-571-11824-0 (pbk) : CIP entry B82-29073

791.43'72 — British cinema films: Gandhi. Production

Attenborough, *Sir* **Richard.** In search of Gandhi. — London : Bodley Head, Dec.1982. — [160]p
ISBN 0-370-30943-x : £8.95 : CIP entry B82-29669

791.43'72 — British cinema films: Gandhi. Production. Role of Kothari, Motilal

Kothari, Raj. To tell the world. — Dulverton : Robinson & Watkins, Nov.1982. — [200]p
ISBN 0-7224-0220-1 (pbk) : £4.00 : CIP entry B82-26050

791.43'72 — British cinema films — *Scripts*

Palin, Michael. The missionary. — London : Methuen, Oct.1982. — [128]p
ISBN 0-413-51010-7 (cased) : £6.50 : CIP entry
ISBN 0-413-51390-4 (pbk) B82-25185

791.43'72 → British cinema films - *Scripts*

Palin, Michael. Time bandits. — London : Hutchinson, June 1981. — [160]p
ISBN 0-09-145461-1 : £4.95 : CIP entry B81-19132

791.43'72 — British cinema films — *Scripts*

Pinter, Harold. The screenplay of The French lieutenant's woman : based on the novel by John Fowles / Harold Pinter ; with a foreword by John Fowles. — London : Cape in association with Eyre Methuen, 1981. — xvi,104p ; 23cm
ISBN 0-224-01983-x : £5.50 : CIP rev. B81-22450

791.43'72 — German cinema films: Hitler

Syberberg, Hans-Jurgen. Hitler : a film from Germany. — Manchester : Carcanet Press, Dec.1982. — [186]p
ISBN 0-85635-405-8 : £9.95 : CIP entry B82-39264

791.43'72 — Russian cinema films: Ivan Groznyi — *Critical studies*

Thompson, Kristin. Eisenstein's Ivan the Terrible : a neoformalist analysis / by Kristin Thompson. — Princeton ; Guildford : Princeton University Press, c1981. — x,321p,[34]p of plates : ill(some col.) ; 25cm
Bibliography: p307-315. — Includes index
ISBN 0-691-06472-5 (cased) : £22.40
ISBN 0-691-10120-5 (pbk) : Unpriced B82-22168

791.43'75 — American cinema films, *1927-1982.* **Dialogues** — *Collections*

Marlowe, Derek. Soundtracks : the best of Hollywood movie dialogue. — London : Elm Tree Books, Feb.1983. — [256]p
ISBN 0-241-10945-0 : £9.95 : CIP entry B82-39273

791.43'75 — American cinema films: Comedies, *1930-1950.* **Special subjects: Remarriage** — *Critical studies*

Cavell, Stanley. Pursuits of happiness : the Hollywood comedy of remarriage / Stanley Cavell. — Cambridge, Mass. ; London : Harvard University Press, 1981. — 283p : ill ; 25cm. — (Harvard film studies)
Includes index
ISBN 0-674-73905-1 : £12.25 B82-13737

791.43'75 — Cinema films based on plays, *to 1980* — *Encyclopaedias*

Leonard, William Torbert. Theatre : stage to screen to television / by William Torbert Leonard. — Metuchen ; London : Scarecrow, 1981. — 2v.(vii,1804p) ; 23cm
Includes index
ISBN 0-8108-1374-2 : £59.60
Primary classification 792.9'5 B82-08579

791.43'75 — Cinema films — *Reviews*

Selected film criticism / edited by Anthony Slide. — Metuchen, N.J. ; London : Scarecrow
1912-1920. — 1982. — xiii,309p ; 23cm
ISBN 0-8108-1525-7 : £14.80 B82-38103

791.43'75 — Cinema films, *to 1982* — *Critical studies*

Sight and Sound : a fiftieth anniversary selection. — London : Faber, Aug.1982. — [352]p
ISBN 0-571-11943-3 : CIP entry B82-16646

791.44 — BROADCASTING

791.44'092'4 — Great Britain. Radio & television programmes. Broadcasting. Barnett, Isobel — *Biographies*

Gallagher, Jock. Isobel Barnett. — London : Methuen, Nov.1982. — [202]p
ISBN 0-413-51320-3 : £7.50 : CIP entry B82-28283

791.44'092'4 — Great Britain. Radio & television programmes. Broadcasting. Johnston, Brian — *Biographies*

Johnston, Brian. It's been a lot of fun : an autobiography / Brian Johnston. — London : W.H. Allen, 1982, c1974. — 208p ; 18cm
Originally published: 1974
ISBN 0-352-39810-8 (pbk) : £1.75 B82-33969

791.44'092'4 — Great Britain. Radio programmes. Broadcasting. Berryman, Gwen — *Biographies*

Berryman, Gwen. The life and death of Doris Archer / Gwen Berryman. — London : Eyre Methuen, 1981. — 203p,[20]p of plates : ill,ports ; 23cm
Includes index
ISBN 0-413-48640-0 : £6.95 : CIP rev. B81-25307

Berryman, Gwen. The life and death of Doris Archer / Gwen Berryman. — Large print ed. — Bath : Chivers, 1982, c1981. — 259p ; 23cm
Originally published: London : Eyre Methuen, 1981
ISBN 0-85119-821-x : Unpriced : CIP rev. B82-05011

791.44'0941 — Great Britain. Broadcasting

Hughes, Patrick, *1947-.* British broadcasting : programmes and power / Patrick Hughes. — Bromley : Chartwell-Bratt, c1981. — 223p : ill ; 23cm
Includes index
ISBN 0-86238-023-5 (pbk) : Unpriced B82-35646

791.44'5 — Great Britain. Educational radio programmes — *Forecasts*

Murray, J. F.. The future of educational broadcasting : a discussion paper / by J.F. Murray. — Glasgow : S.C.E.T., 1981. — 46p ; 22cm. — (Occasional working paper ; 9)
ISBN 0-86011-044-3 (pbk) : £1.00
Also classified at 791.45'5 B82-20731

791.44′5 — Great Britain. Radio programmes. Comedies, *to 1980*

Took, Barry. Laughter in the air : an informal history of British radio comedy / Barry Took. — Rev. and enl. ed. — London : Robson, 1981. — ix,182p,[20]p of plates : ill,ports ; 24cm
Previous ed.: 1976
ISBN 0-86051-149-9 (pbk) : £3.95
ISBN 0-563-17197-9 (British Broadcasting Corporation) B82-01381

791.44′72 — Great Britain. Radio programmes: Any questions?, *to 1977 — Personal observations*

Bowen, Michael. Any questions? / Michael Bowen with David Jacobs. — London : Robson, 1981. — 302p,[12]p of plates : ill,ports ; 23cm
ISBN 0-86051-156-1 : £6.95 : CIP rev. B81-27453

791.44′72 — Radio programmes: Sports programmes: 'Test Match Special', *to 1980*

Test match special / edited by Peter Baxter ; illustrated by Griffin. — London : Unwin Paperbacks, 1982, c1981. — 202p : ill,ports ; 18cm
Originally published: London : Queen Anne, 1981
ISBN 0-04-796064-7 (pbk) : £1.75 : CIP rev. B82-11280

791.44′75 — London. Local radio programmes, *1981*

Local Radio Workshop. Local radio in London. — London (12 Praed St., W2 1QY) : Local Radio Workshop, May 1982. — [80]p
ISBN 0-9508114-0-8 (pbk) : £2.00 : CIP entry B82-14923

791.45 — Television programmes *- For children*

Hill, Gordon. Secrets of film and television. — Sevenoaks : Hodder & Stoughton, May 1981. — [128]p
ISBN 0-340-25496-3 (pbk) : £0.95 : CIP entry
Primary classification 791.43 B81-05158

791.45′0232 — Television programmes. Production *— Manuals*

Watts, Harris. The programme-maker's handbook : or goodbye totter TV / by Harris Watts. — London : Starstream, 1982. — 230p : ill ; 21cm
Includes index
ISBN 0-9507582-1-3 (cased) : £9.95 : CIP rev.
ISBN 0-9507582-0-5 (pbk) : £5.95 B81-31953

791.45′025 — Television. Lighting *— Manuals*

Millerson, Gerald. TV lighting methods / Gerald Millerson. — 2nd ed. — London : Focal, 1982. — 152p : ill ; 22cm. — (Media manuals)
Previous ed.: 1975. — Bibliography: p138
ISBN 0-240-51181-6 (pbk) : Unpriced : CIP rev. B82-04305

791.45′025 — Television programmes. Sets. Design

Millerson, Gerald. Basic TV staging. — 2nd ed. — London : Focal Press, July 1982. — [176]p. — (Media manuals)
Previous ed.: 1974
ISBN 0-240-51191-3 (pbk) : £6.95 : CIP entry B82-16239

791.45′09 — Television programmes, *to 1981*

Passingham, Ken. The Guinness book of television facts and feats. — Enfield : Guinness Superlatives, Dec.1982. — [256]p
ISBN 0-85112-228-0 : £8.95 : CIP entry B82-30223

791.45′09′0932411 — Television programmes. Special subjects: Scotland *— Critical studies*

McArthur, Colin. Scotch reels : Scotland in cinema and television. — London : BF1 Publishing, Aug.1982. — [96]p
ISBN 0-85170-121-3 (pbk) : £2.95 : CIP entry
Primary classification 791.43′09′0932411 B82-21964

791.45′09′09357 — Television programmes. Special subjects: Visual arts

Hearst, Stephen. Artistic heritage and its treatment by television / by Stephen Hearst. — London : British Broadcasting Corporation, [1981?]. — 22p ; 21cm
" ... an edited version of a paper presented for a study meeting of art historians, curators and television producers organised by the Prix Italia (RAI Televisione Italiana) in Siena, Italy, on 17 September 1981"
Unpriced (pbk) B82-19786

791.45′092′4 — Great Britain. Broadcasting services: British Broadcasting Corporation. Television programmes. Making *— Personal observations*

Wilcox, Desmond. 'Kill the chocolate biscuit' : or Behind the screen / by Desmond Wilcox and Esther Rantzen ; cartoons by Rod Jordan. — London : Severn House, 1982, c1981. — 221p : ill ; 21cm
Includes index
ISBN 0-7278-0772-2 : £6.95 B82-17870

Wilcox, Desmond. Kill the chocolate biscuit, or, Behind the screen / by Desmond Wilcox and Esther Rantzen ; cartoons by Rod Jordon. — London : Pan, 1981. — 221p : ill ; 18cm. — (Pan original)
Includes index
ISBN 0-330-26532-6 (pbk) : £1.50 B82-04259

791.45′092′4 — Great Britain. Television programmes. Broadcasting. Boyle, Katie *— Biographies*

Boyle, Katie. What this Katie did : an autobiography / Katie Boyle. — London : Sphere, 1982, c1980. — 212p,[8]p of plates : ill,ports ; 18cm
Originally published: London : Weidenfeld & Nicolson, 1980. — Includes bibliographies and index
ISBN 0-7221-1787-6 (pbk) : £1.75 B82-21275

791.45′092′4 — Great Britain. Television programmes. Broadcasting. Whicker, Alan *— Biographies*

Whicker, Alan. Within Whicker's world : an autobiography / by Alan Whicker. — London : Elm Tree, 1982. — ix,390p : ill,ports ; 25cm
Includes index
ISBN 0-241-10747-4 : £8.95 : CIP rev. B82-01824

791.45′0941 — Great Britain. Television programmes *— Encyclopaedias*

Halliwell, Leslie. Halliwell's television companion. — 2nd ed. — London : Granada, Sept.1982. — [600]p
Previous ed. published as: Halliwell's teleguide. 1979
ISBN 0-246-11714-1 : £12.50 : CIP entry
Also classified at 791.45′0973 B82-18857

791.45′09411 — Scotland. Commercial television services. Television programmes *— Calendars — Serials*

TV times magazine. STV. — Vol.104, no.41 (3-9 Oct. [1981])-. — London : Independent Television Publications, 1981-. — v. : ill,ports ; 30cm
Weekly. — Continues: TV times. STV
ISSN 0262-1258 = TV times magazine. STV : £0.20 B82-04090

791.45′09412′1 — Scotland. Grampian Region. Commercial television services. Television programmes *— Calendars — Serials*

TV times magazine. Grampian. — Vol.104, no.41 (3-9 Oct. [1981])-. — London : Independent Television Publications, 1981-. — v. : ill,ports ; 30cm
Weekly. — Continues: TV times. Grampian
ISSN 0262-1363 = TV times magazine. Grampian : £0.20 B82-04082

791.45′09413′7 — Scotland. Border country. Commercial television services. Television programmes *— Calendars — Serials*

TV times magazine. Border. — Vol.104, no.41 (3-9 Oct. [1981])-. — London : Independent Television Publications, 1981-. — v. : ill,ports ; 30cm
Weekly. — Continues: TV times. Border
ISSN 0262-1320 = TV times magazine. Border : £0.20
Also classified at 791.45′09428′8 B82-04093

791.45′09416 — Northern Ireland. Commercial television services. Television programmes *— Calendars — Serials*

TV times magazine. Ulster. — Vol.104, no.41 (3-9 Oct. [1981])-. — London : Independent Television Publications, 1981-. — v. : ill,ports ; 30cm
Weekly. — Continues: TV times. Ulster
ISSN 0262-1304 = TV times magazine. Ulster : £0.20 B82-04083

791.45′09421 — London region. Commercial television services. Television programmes *— Calendars — Serials*

TV times magazine. Thames/LWT. — Vol.104, no.41 (3-9 Oct. [1981])-. — London : Independent Television Publications, 1981-. — v. : ill,ports ; 30cm
Weekly. — Continues: TV times. Thames/LWT
ISSN 0262-222x = TV times magazine. Thames, LWT : £0.20 B82-04092

791.45′09422 — Southern England. Commercial television services. Television programmes *— Calendars — Serials*

TV times magazine. Southern. — Vol.104, no.41 (3-9 Oct. [1981])-Vol.105, no.52 (19 Dec. 1981-1 Jan. 1982). — London : Independent Television Publications, 1981-1981. — 2v. : ill,ports ; 30cm
Weekly. — Continues: TV times. Southern. — Continued by: TV times magazines. TVS
ISSN 0262-1347 = TV times magazine. Southern : £0.20 B82-04087

TV times magazine. TVS. — Vol.106, no.1 (2-8 Jan. 1982)-. — London : Independent Television Publications, 1982-. — v. : ill,ports ; 30cm
Weekly. — Continues: TV times magazine. Southern
ISSN 0263-0117 = TV times magazine. TVS : £0.25 per issue B82-14256

791.45′09423 — South-west England. Commercial television services. Television programmes *— Calendars — Serials*

TV times magazine. TSW. — Vol.106, no.1 (2-8 Jan. 1982)-. — London : Independant Television Publications, 1982-. — v. : ill,ports ; 30cm
Weekly. — Continues: TV times magazine. Westward
ISSN 0263-0141 = TV times magazine. TSW : £0.25 per issue B82-14255

TV times magazine. Westward. — Vol.104, no.41 (3-9 Oct. [1981])-Vol.105, no.52 (19 Dec. 1981-1 Jan. 1982). — London : Independent Television Publications, 1981-1981. — 2v. : ill,ports ; 30cm
Weekly. — Continues: TV times. Westward. — Continued by: TV times magazine. TSW
ISSN 0262-1290 = TV times magazine. Westward : £0.20 B82-04084

791.45′09424 — England. Midlands. Commercial television services. Television programmes *— Calendars — Serials*

TV times magazine. ATV. — Vol.104, no.41 (3-9 Oct. [1981])-Vol.105, no.52 (19 Dec. 1981-1 Jan. 1982). — London : Independent Television Publications, 1981-1981. — 2v. : ill,ports ; 30cm
Weekly. — Continues: TV times. ATV. — Continued by: TV times magazine. Central
ISSN 0262-1274 = TV times magazine. ATV : £0.20 B82-04094

TV times magazine. Central. — Vol.106, no.1 (2-8 Jan. 1982)-. — London : Independent Television Publications, 1982-. — v. : ill,ports ; 30cm
Weekly. — Continues: TV times magazine. ATV
ISSN 0263-0109 = TV times magazine. Central : £0.25 per issue B82-14254

791.45′09426 — East Anglia. Commercial television services. Television programmes *— Calendars — Serials*

TV times magazine. Anglia. — Vol.104, no.41 (3-9 Oct. [1981])-. — London : Independent Television Publications, 1981-. — v. : ill,ports ; 30cm
Weekly. — Continues: TV times. Anglia
ISSN 0262-1312 = TV times magazine. Anglia : £0.20 B82-04091

791.45'09427 — North-west England. Commercial television services. Television programmes — *Calendars — Serials*

TV times magazine. Granada. — Vol.104, no.41 (3-9 Oct. [1981])-. — London : Independent Television Publications, 1981-. — v. : ill,ports ; 30cm
Weekly. — Continues: TV times. Granada
ISSN 0262-1339 = TV times magazine. Granada : £0.20 B82-04086

791.45'09428 — North-east England. Commercial television services. Television programmes — *Calendars — Serials*

TV times magazine. Tyne Tees. — Vol.104, no.41 (3-9 Oct. [1981])-. — London : Independent Television Publications, 1981-. — v. : ill,ports ; 30cm
Weekly. — Continues: TV times. Tyne Tees
ISSN 0262-1266 = TV times magazine. Tyne Tees : £0.20 B82-04088

791.45'09428'1 — Yorkshire. Commercial television services. Television programmes — *Calendars — Serials*

TV times magazine. Yorkshire. — Vol.104, no.41 (3-9 Oct. [1981])-. — London : Independent Television Publications, 1981-. — v. : ill,ports ; 30cm
Weekly. — Continues: TV times. Yorkshire
ISSN 0262-1355 = TV times magazine. Yorkshire : £0.20 B82-04089

791.45'09428'8 — England. Border country. Commercial television services. Television programmes — *Calendars — Serials*

TV times magazine. Border. — Vol.104, no.41 (3-9 Oct. [1981])-. — London : Independent Television Publications, 1981-. — v. : ill,ports ; 30cm
Weekly. — Continues: TV times. Border
ISSN 0262-1320 = TV times magazine. Border : £0.20
Primary classification 791.45'09413'7
B82-04093

791.45'09429 — Wales. Commercial television services. Television programmes — *Calendars — Serials*

TV times magazine. HTV. — Vol.104, no.41 (3-9 Oct. [1981])-. — London : Independent Television Publications, 1981-. — v. : ill,ports ; 30cm
Weekly. — Continues: TV times. HTV/Wales and West
ISSN 0262-1282 = TV times magazine. HTV : £0.20 B82-04085

791.45'0973 — United States. Television programmes

Sklar, Robert. Prime-time America : life on and behind the television screen / Robert Sklar. — New York ; Oxford : Oxford University Press, 1980. — xi,200p,[8]p of plates : ill,ports ; 22cm
ISBN 0-19-502765-5 : £11.00 B82-00507

791.45'0973 — United States. Television programmes — *Encyclopaedias*

Halliwell, Leslie. Halliwell's television companion. — 2nd ed. — London : Granada, Sept.1982. — [600]p
Previous ed. published as: Halliwell's teleguide. 1979
ISBN 0-246-11714-1 : £12.50 : CIP entry
Primary classification 791.45'0941 B82-18857

791.45'5 — Great Britain. Educational television programmes — *Forecasts*

Murray, J. F.. The future of educational broadcasting : a discussion paper / by J.F. Murray. — Glasgow : S.C.E.T., 1981. — 46p ; 22cm. — (Occasional working paper ; 9)
ISBN 0-86011-044-3 (pbk) : £1.00
Primary classification 791.44'5 B82-20731

791.45'72 — Children's television drama series in English: Doctor Who

Road, Alan. Doctor Who : the making of a television series / introduction by Peter Davison ; by Alan Road ; photographed by Richard Farley. — London : Deutsch, 1982. — 56p : ill(some col.),ports(some col.) ; 28cm
Ill on lining papers
ISBN 0-233-97444-x : £4.95 : CIP rev.
B82-07531

791.45'72 — Children's television drama series in English: Doctor Who — *Questions & answers*

The **Doctor** Who quiz book / compiled by Nigel Robinson. — London : W.H. Allen, 1981. — 128p ; 18cm. — (A target book)
ISBN 0-426-20143-4 (pbk) : £1.25 B82-07895

791.45'72 — Children's television drama series in English: Grange Hill — *Serials — For children*

The **Grange** Hill annual. — 1981-. — London : IPC Magazines, 1980-. — v. : ill(some col.),ports ; 28cm
Annual. — Description based on: 1982 issue
ISSN 0262-9089 = Grange Hill annual : £2.50
B82-11155

791.45'72 — Children's television programmes: Tiswas

Astley, Gordon. The Tiswas file / by Gordon Astley ; illustrated by Tony Baldwin. — Feltham : Beaver, 1982. — 62p : ill,music,ports ; 25cm
ISBN 0-600-20666-1 (pbk) : £1.25 B82-29842

791.45'72 — Great Britain. Television programmes: Parkinson, *to 1982 — Personal observations*

Parkinson, Michael, *1935-*. The best of Parkinson. — London : Pavilion, Nov.1982. — [192]p
ISBN 0-907516-14-9 : £7.95 : CIP entry
B82-26706

791.45'72 — Television drama series in English: Blake's seven — *Serials*

Blakes 7 : a Marvel monthly. — No.1 (Oct. 1981)-. — London (205 Kentish Town Rd, NW5) : Marvel Comics, 1981-. — v. : chiefly ill,ports ; 28cm
Cover title: Terry Nation's Blakes 7
ISSN 0262-7728 = Blakes 7 : £5.40 per year
B82-08465

791.45'72 — Television drama series in English: Coronation Street

Kershaw, H. V.. The street where I live / H.V. Kershaw. — London : Granada, 1981. — 192p,[16]p of plates : ill,1facsim,ports ; 23cm
ISBN 0-246-11734-6 : £6.95 B82-09246

Kershaw, H. V.. The street where I live / H.V. Kershaw. — Large print ed. — Bath : Chivers, 1982, c1981. — 266p ; 23cm. — (A Lythway book)
Originally published: London : Granada, 1981
ISBN 0-85119-822-8 : Unpriced : CIP rev.
B82-07017

791.45'72 — Television drama series in English: Crossroads — *Personal observations*

Hobson, Dorothy. Crossroads : the drama of a soap opera / Dorothy Hobson. — London : Methuen, 1982. — 176p : 1ill ; 23cm
Includes index
ISBN 0-413-50140-x (cased) : £8.95 : CIP rev.
ISBN 0-413-50150-7 (pbk) : Unpriced
B82-11295

791.45'72 — Television drama series in English: Poldark — *Personal observations*

Clarke, David, *1937 May 10-*. Poldark country / by David Clarke. — Bodmin : Bossiney Books, 1977 (1981 [printing]). — 72p : ill,ports ; 21cm
ISBN 0-906456-49-5 (pbk) : £1.20 B82-41117

791.45'72 — Television programmes. Comedies: M*A*S*H, *to 1980*

Reiss, David S.. M*A*S*H : the exclusive inside story of TV's most popular show / David S. Reiss ; foreword by Alan Alda. — London : Arthur Barker, 1981, c1980. — 159p : ill,ports ; 28cm
Originally published: Indianapolis : Bobbs-Merrill, 1980
ISBN 0-213-16813-8 (pbk) : £3.95 B82-00587

791.45'72 — Television programmes. Comedies: Melting pot — *Scripts*

Milligan, Spike. Spike Milligan's The melting pot. — London : Robson, Oct.1982. — [128]p
ISBN 0-86051-195-2 : £4.95 : CIP entry
B82-24144

791.45'72 — Television programmes. Comedies: Monty Python's Flying Circus. Censorship

Hewison, Robert. Monty Python : the case against : irreverence, scurrility, profanity, vilification and licentious abuse / Robert Hewison. — London : Methuen, 1981. — 96p : ill,music,facsims,ports ; 28cm
ISBN 0-413-48650-8 (cased) : Unpriced : CIP rev.
ISBN 0-413-48660-5 (pbk) : £3.95 B81-23949

791.45'72 — Television programmes. Comedies: Muppet Show. Production

Finch, Christopher, *19---*. Of muppets & men : the making of The Muppet show / by Christopher Finch. — London : Muppet Press/Joseph, 1982. — 178p : ill(some col.),ports(some col.) ; 32cm
ISBN 0-7181-2112-0 : £12.50 B82-22746

791.45'75 — Drama in English, *1900-1980*. **Television productions,** *to 1980 — Encyclopaedias*

Leonard, William Torbert. Theatre : stage to screen to television / by William Torbert Leonard. — Metuchen ; London : Scarecrow, 1981. — 2v.(vii,1804p) ; 23cm
Includes index
ISBN 0-8108-1374-2 : £59.60
Primary classification 792.9'5 B82-08579

791.45'75 — Great Britain. Television programmes, *1976-1979 — Reviews*

James, Clive. The crystal bucket : television criticism from the Observer 1976-79 / Clive James. — London : Picador, 1982, c1981. — 237p ; 20cm
Originally published: London : Cape, 1981
ISBN 0-330-26745-0 (pbk) : £1.95 B82-37692

791.45'75 — Great Britain. Television programmes, *1979-1982 — Reviews*

James, Clive. Glued to the box. — London : Cape, Jan.1983. — [224]p
ISBN 0-224-02066-8 : £7.95 : CIP entry
B82-33498

791.45'75 — Television drama in English. Production by British Broadcasting Corporation. *Pebble Mill Studios, 1970-1980*

Films and plays from Pebble Mill : ten years of regional drama. — Stafford : West Midlands Arts, c1980. — 35p : ill ; 22cm
ISBN 0-9504364-5-3 (pbk) : Unpriced
B82-37988

791.45'75 — Television drama series in English, *1971-1981*

Cooke, Alistair. Masterpieces : a decade of classics on British television / by Alistair Cooke. — London : Bodley Head, 1982, c1981. — 236p : ill(some col.),ports ; 29cm
ISBN 0-370-30476-4 : £14.95 : CIP rev.
B82-06736

791.45'75 — Television programmes — *Critical studies*

Conrad, Peter, *1948-*. Television : the medium and its manners / Peter Conrad. — Boston ; London : Routledge & Kegan Paul, 1982. — 170p ; 22cm
ISBN 0-7100-9040-4 (cased) : £6.95
ISBN 0-7100-9041-2 (pbk) : £2.95 B82-27454

791.45'75 — United States. Television drama series, *1975-1980 — Chronologies*

Gianakos, Larry James. Television drama series programming : a comprehensive chronicle, 1975-1980 / by Larry James Gianakos. — Metuchen, N.J. ; London : Scarecrow, 1981. — xiii,457p ; 23cm
Includes index
ISBN 0-8108-1438-2 : £20.00 B82-05361

791.45'75 — United States. Television programmes — *Critical studies*

Williams, Martin. TV : the casual art / Martin Williams. — New York ; Oxford : Oxford University Press, 1982. — xiii,161p ; 22cm
Includes index
ISBN 0-19-502992-5 : £12.00 B82-37008

791.5 — MINIATURE, TOY, SHADOW THEATRES

791.5′3′0924 — Great Britain. Puppet theatre. Barnard, Richard — *Biographies*
Barnard, Richard, *b.1854*. The life and travels of Richard Barnard marionette proprietor / edited by George Speaight. — London : Society for Theatre Research, 1981. — 97p,[8]p of plates : ill,ports ; 22cm
Includes index
ISBN 0-85430-034-1 (pbk) : £6.00 B82-14689

791.5′3′0924 — Great Britain. Puppet theatre: Potten, I. A. — *Biographies*
Potten, I. A.. A woman with Punch : a true story / I.A. Potten. — Ilfracombe : Stockwell, 1981. — 122p ; 19cm
ISBN 0-7223-1489-2 : £4.35 B82-06303

791.6 — PAGEANTS, PROCESSIONS, ILLUMINATIONS, ETC

791′.64 — Cheerleading & songleading — *Manuals*
Egbert, Barbara. Cheerleading and songleading / by Barbara Egbert ; photos by Scott Smith and others. — New York : Sterling ; London : Oak Tree, c1980. — 128p : ill ; 27cm
Includes index
ISBN 0-7061-2727-7 (cased) : £7.95
ISBN 0-8069-8950-5 (pbk) : £4.95 B82-21870

791.8 — ANIMAL PERFORMANCES

791′.8 — Cockfighting, *to ca 1930*
Atkinson, Herbert. Cock-fighting and game fowl : from the note-book of Herbert Atkinson of Ewelme ; together with, The life and letters of John Harris, the Cornis cocker / edited and with an introductory memoir by Game Cock. — Hindhead : Saiga, c1977 (1981 [printing]). — viii,253p,[17]leaves of plates : ill(some col.),1facsim,1col.port ; 26cm
Facsim of: 1st ed., Bath : Bayntun, 1938. — The life and letters of John Harris originally published: Great Britain : H. Atkinson?, 1910. — Includes index
ISBN 0-904558-23-1 : £12.00 B82-11613

792 — THEATRE

792 — Theatre
Cook, Philip. How to enjoy theatre. — Loughton : Judy Piatkus, Mar.1982. — [192]p. — (Melvyn Bragg′s arts series)
ISBN 0-86188-142-7 : £5.95 : CIP entry B82-00348

Radford, C. B.. A dramatist in search of his public : an inaugural lecture delivered before the Queen′s University of Belfast on 29th October 1975. — Belfast : The University, 1977. — 20p ; 21cm. — (New lecture series ; no.99)
ISBN 0-85389-117-6 (pbk) : £0.40 B82-24397

Stuart, Pauline. Theatre procedures and practice. — Banbury (P.O. Box 441, Banbury, Oxon. OX15 4EQ) : Kemble Press, Oct.1982. — [128]p
ISBN 0-906835-11-9 (spiral) : £3.00 : CIP entry B82-27026

792 — Theatre — *For children*
May, Robin. Looking at theatre / consultant J.C. Trewin ; author Robin May ; editor Jo Jones. — London : Marshall Cavendish Childrens Books, 1979. — 44p : ill(some col.),ports(some col.) ; 28cm. — (Woodpecker books)
Text and ill on lining papers
ISBN 0-85685-685-1 : Unpriced B82-11165

792′.02 — Stagecraft — *For schools*
Ramsden, Timothy. Stagecraft / Timothy Ramsden & Pauline Courtice. — London : Harrap, 1982. — 48p : ill,facsims ; 25cm
ISBN 0-245-53655-8 (pbk) : £1.95 B82-32424

792′.02 — Theatre. Stage management — *Manuals*
Stern, Lawrence. Stage management : a guidebook of practical techniques / Lawrence Stern. — 2nd ed. — Boston [Mass.] ; London : Allyn and Bacon, c1982. — xv,285p : ill,plans,forms ; 24cm
Previous ed.: 1974
ISBN 0-205-07384-0 (pbk) : £8.95 B82-08540

792′.022 — United States. Alternative theatre, *ca 1960-1980*
Shank, Theodore. American alternative theatre / Theodore Shank. — London : Macmillan, 1982. — xi,202p : ill ; 25cm. — (Macmillan modern dramatists)
Bibliography: p194-198. — Includes index
ISBN 0-333-28883-1 (cased) : Unpriced
ISBN 0-333-28885-8 (pbk) B82-23366

792′.0222′0941 — Great Britain. Amateur theatre — *Statistics*
Husbands, Peter G. Amateur theatre in Great Britain / Central Council for Amateur Theatre. — Banbury : Kemble, c1979. — 28leaves : 2maps ; 30cm
Map, text on inside covers
ISBN 0-906835-01-1 (pbk) : Unpriced : CIP rev. B79-28903

792′.0226 — Children. Amateur theatre — *Manuals*
Olfson, Lewy. Beginners on stage please! : based on You can act and You can put on a show / by Lewy Olfson ; edited by Margaret Crush ; illustrated by Anni Axworthy. — London : Picolo, 1982. — 144p : ill ; 18cm
Includes index
ISBN 0-330-26547-4 (pbk) : £1.25 B82-15119

792′.0226 — Children′s plays. Production — *For children*
Chambers, Aidan. Plays for young people to read and perform. — Stroud (Lockwood, Station Rd., South Woodchester, Stroud, Glos. GL5 5EQ) : Thimble Press, Nov.1982. — [72]p. — (Signal bookguides)
ISBN 0-903355-10-8 (pbk) : £2.75 : CIP entry B82-34101

792′.0233 — Theatre. Directing
Hodge, Francis. Play directing : analysis, communication, and style / Francis Hodge. — 2nd ed. — Englewood Cliffs ; London : Prentice-Hall, c1982. — xiv,385p : ill,plans ; 24cm
Previous ed.: 1971. — Bibliography: p369-375. — Includes index
ISBN 0-13-682823-x : £14.20 B82-23233

792′.0233′0904 — Theatre. Directing, *1870-1981*
Braun, Edward. The director and the stage : from naturalism to Grotowski / Edward Braun. — London : Methuen, 1982. — 218,[8]p of plates : ill ; 23cm
Includes index
ISBN 0-413-46290-0 (cased) : £8.95
ISBN 0-413-46300-1 (pbk) : £4.50 B82-33778

792′.0233′0924 — Germany. Theatre. Directing. Reinhardt, Max — *Critical studies*
Styan, J. L.. Max Reinhardt / J.L. Styan. — Cambridge : Cambridge University Press, 1982. — xvi,171p : ill,ports ; 24cm. — (Directors in perspective)
Bibliography: p164-165. — Includes index
ISBN 0-521-22444-6 (cased) : £17.50
ISBN 0-521-29504-1 (pbk) : £5.95 B82-41112

792′.0233′0924 — Italy. Theatre. Directing. Pirandello, Luigi — *Critical studies*
Sogliuzzo, A. Richard. Luigi Pirandello, director : the playwright in the theatre / by A. Richard Sogliuzzo. — Metuchen ; London : Scarecrow, 1982. — xxix,274p : ill,ports ; 23cm
Bibliography: p254-265. — Includes index
ISBN 0-8108-1488-9 : £14.00 B82-29263

792′.0233′0924 — Sweden. Theatre. Directing. Bergman, Ingmar — *Critical studies*
Marker, Lise-Lone. Ingmar Bergman : four decades in the theater / Lise-Lone Marker, Frederick J. Marker. — Cambridge : Cambridge University Press, 1982. — xvii,262p : ill,plans,ports ; 24cm. — (Directors in perspective)
Bibliography: p256-257. — Includes index
ISBN 0-521-22441-1 (cased) : £19.50
ISBN 0-521-29501-7 (pbk) : Unpriced B82-21616

792′.0233′0924 — West Germany. Theatre. Directing. Stein, Peter, *1937-* — *Critical studies*
Patterson, Michael. Peter Stein : Germany′s leading theatre director / Michael Patterson. — Cambridge : Cambridge University Press, 1981. — xv,186p : ill,2plans,ports ; 24cm. — (Directors in perspective)
Bibliography: p178-180. — Includes index
ISBN 0-521-22442-x (cased) : £17.50 : CIP rev.
ISBN 0-521-29502-5 (pbk) : Unpriced B81-37550

792′.025 — Drama in English. Shakespeare, William. Productions. Sets
Williams, John T. (John Tynerman). Costumes and settings for Shakespeare′s plays / John T. Williams ; drawings by Jack Cassin-Scott. — London : Batsford Academic and Educational, 1982. — 120p : ill,plans ; 26cm
Bibliography: p113-114. — Includes index
ISBN 0-7134-2572-5 : £6.95 : CIP rev.
Also classified at 792′.026 B82-01203

792′.025 — Theatre. Stage lighting — *Manuals*
Reid, Francis, *1931-*. The stage lighting handbook / Francis Reid. — 2nd ed. — London : A. and C. Black, 1982. — 145p : ill ; 24cm
Previous ed.: 1976. — Includes index
ISBN 0-7136-2225-3 : £5.95 : CIP rev. B82-04497

Sellman, Hunton D.. Essentials of stage lighting / Hunton D. Sellman, Merrill Lessley. — Englewood Cliffs ; London : Prentice-Hall, c1982. — xvii,198p,[4]p of plates : ill(some col.),plans ; 25cm
Previous ed.: New York : Appleton-Century-Croft, 1972. — Bibliography: p191-193. — Includes index
ISBN 0-13-289249-9 : £14.95 B82-27562

792′.025 — Theatre. Stage lighting. Use of colour
Warfel, William B.. Color science for lighting the stage / William B. Warfel and Walter R. Klappert. — New Haven ; London : Yale University Press, c1981. — xiv,158p : ill ; 29cm
Ill on 2folded sheets in pocket
ISBN 0-300-02554-8 (spiral) : £17.50 : CIP rev. B82-01319

792′.025′0924 — Stage design. Appia, Adolphe — *Catalogues*
Appia, Adolphe. Adolphe Appia 1862-1928 : actor-space-light / exhibition produced by Pro Helvetia-Arts Council of Switzerland ; designed by Denis Bablet and Marie-Louise Bablet ; [translation ... Burton Melnick]. — Rev. ed. — London : Calder, c1982. — 94p,24p of plates : ill,facsims,1port ; 18x21cm
Translation from the French. — Previous ed.: 197-?
ISBN 0-7145-3964-3 (pbk) : £4.50 B82-36985

792′.025′0941 — Great Britain. Theatre. Scenery. Design, *1700-1830*
Rosenfeld, Sybil. Georgian scene painters and scene painting / Sybil Rosenfeld. — Cambridge : Cambridge University Press, 1981. — xiv,206p,[41]p of plates : ill ; 26cm
Includes index
ISBN 0-521-23339-9 : £29.50 : CIP rev. B81-25881

792′.026 — Drama in English. Shakespeare, William. Productions. Costumes
Williams, John T. (John Tynerman). Costumes and settings for Shakespeare′s plays / John T. Williams ; drawings by Jack Cassin-Scott. — London : Batsford Academic and Educational, 1982. — 120p : ill,plans ; 26cm
Bibliography: p113-114. — Includes index
ISBN 0-7134-2572-5 : £6.95 : CIP rev.
Primary classification 792′.025 B82-01203

792′.026 — Theatre. Costumes. Design & making — *Manuals*
Thomas, Beverly Jane. A practical approach to costume design and construction / Beverly Jane Thomas. — Boston, Mass. ; London : Allyn and Bacon
Vol.1: Fundamentals and design. — c1982. — xv,236p,[4]p of plates : ill(some col.),geneal.tables ; 25cm
Bibliography: p227-229. — Includes index
ISBN 0-205-07273-9 : £21.95 B82-22027

792'.026 — Theatre. Costumes. Design & making — *Manuals* *continuation*

Thomas, Beverly Jane. A practical approach to costume design and construction / Beverly Jane Thomas. — Boston ; London : Allyn and Bacon
Vol.2: Construction. — c1982. — x,322p ; 28cm
Bibliography: p315-316. — Includes index
ISBN 0-205-07367-0 (spiral) : Unpriced
B82-19601

792'.026'0903 — Theatre. Costume, *1600-1940*

De Marly, Diana. Costume on the stage 1600-1940 / Diana de Marly. — London : Batsford, 1982. — 167p : ill ; 26cm
Bibliography: p160-162. — Includes index
ISBN 0-7134-3770-7 : £12.50 B82-41040

792'.026'0924 — Theatre. Costumes. Design — *Collections from individual artists*

Erté. Erte's theatrical costumes : in full color. — New York : Dover ; London : Constable, c1979. — 49p : of col.ill ; 31cm
ISBN 0-486-23813-x (pbk) : £4.50 B82-28174

792'.027 — Theatre. Make-up. Techniques — *Manuals*

Blore, Richard. Stage make-up / by Richard Blore. — Bromley (1 Hawthorndene Rd., Hayes, Bromley, Kent) : Stacey, [1981?]. — 51p : ill ; 22cm. — (Amateur stage handbooks)
Cover title
£1.30 (pbk) B82-03445

792'.028 — Acting — *For children*

Swift, Clive. The performing world of the actor. — London : H. Hamilton, May 1981. — [128]p
ISBN 0-241-10585-4 : £4.95 : CIP entry
B81-12822

792'.028 — Secondary schools. Activities: Drama. Improvisation — *For schools*

Nash, S. G.. Outlines : improvised group drama for 14-year-olds and over / S.G. Nash. — Huddersfield : Schofield & Sims, 1981. — 48p ; 24cm
ISBN 0-7217-0428-x (pbk) : £0.75 B82-09467

792'.028'0922 — Acting — *Personal observations — Collections*

A **Night** at the theatre. — London : Methuen, Sept.1982. — [160]p
ISBN 0-413-49950-2 : £6.95 : CIP entry
B82-22421

792'.028'0922 — England. Theatre. Acting, *to 1980 — Personal observations — Collections*

Miles, Bernard. Curtain calls / Bernard Miles and J.C. Trewin. — Guildford : Lutterworth, 1981. — 191p : ill,1map,facsims,ports ; 24cm
Facsims on lining papers. — Includes index
ISBN 0-7188-2476-8 : £8.95 B82-03182

792'.028'0924 — Acting. Berlioz, Harriet Smithson — *Biographies*

Raby, Peter. 'Fair Ophelia' : a life of Harriet Smithson Berlioz. — Cambridge : Cambridge University Press, Sept.1982. — [214]p
ISBN 0-521-24421-8 : £12.95 : CIP entry
B82-29361

792'.028'0924 — Acting. Howard, Leslie — *Biographies*

Howard, Leslie. Trivial fond records / by Leslie Howard ; edited by Ronald Howard. — London : Kimber, 1982. — 187p,[16]p of plates : ill,ports ; 25cm
Includes index
ISBN 0-7183-0418-7 : £9.50 B82-35348

792'.028'0924 — Acting. West, Mae — *Biographies*

Cashin, Fergus. Mae West : a biography / Fergus Cashin. — London : W.H. Allen, 1982, c1981. — 197p : ill ; 18cm. — (A Star book)
Originally published: 1981. — Ill on inside covers
ISBN 0-352-31094-4 (pbk) : £1.75 B82-33974

792'.028'0924 — Austria. Theatre. Acting. Schratt, Katharina. Interpersonal relationships with Franz Joseph, *Emperor of Austria*

Haslip, Joan. The Emperor & the actress : the love story of Emperor Franz Josef & Katharina Schratt / Joan Haslip. — London : Weidenfeld and Nicolson, 1982. — x,284p,[8]p of plates : ill,1geneal.table,ports ; 23cm
Bibliography: p273-274. — Includes index
ISBN 0-297-78102-2 : £9.95
Primary classification 943.6'04'0924
B82-38941

792'.028'0924 — Great Britain. Acting. Adams, Shirley. Interpersonal relationships with Adams, Peter — *Personal observations*

Adams, Peter. Knockback. — London : Duckworth, Oct.1982. — [200]p
ISBN 0-7156-1677-3 : £6.95 : CIP entry
Primary classification 364.1'523'0924
B82-28574

792'.028'0924 — Great Britain. Acting. Casson, *Sir* **Lewis** — *Biographies*

Devlin, Diana. A speaking part. — London : Hodder and Stoughton, Sept.1982. — [256]p
ISBN 0-340-28090-5 : £9.95 : CIP entry
B82-18799

792'.028'0924 — Great Britain. Acting. Ellis, Mary — *Biographies*

Ellis, Mary. Those dancing years. — London : Murray, Oct.1982. — [224]p
ISBN 0-7195-3984-6 : £9.50 : CIP entry
B82-23023

792'.028'0924 — Great Britain. Acting. Hampshire, Susan — *Biographies*

Hampshire, Susan. Susan's story : an autobiographical account of my struggle with words / Susan Hamphire. — London : Sidgwick & Jackson, 1981. — 167p,[24]p of plates : ill,1form,ports ; 23cm
Bibliography: p166-167
ISBN 0-283-98735-9 : £6.95 B82-02432

Hampshire, Susan. Susan's story. — Large print ed. — Bath : Chivers, Dec.1982. — [232]p. — (A Lythway book)
Originally published: London : Sidgwick & Jackson, 1981
ISBN 0-85119-876-7 : £6.90 : CIP entry
B82-30231

792'.028'0924 — Great Britain. Acting. Sinden, Donald — *Biographies*

Sinden, Donald. A touch of the memoirs / Donald Sinden. — London : Hodder and Stoughton, 1982. — 256p,[16]p of plates : ill,1map,facsims,ports ; 24cm
Includes index
ISBN 0-340-26235-4 : £7.95 : CIP rev.
B82-01847

792'.028'0924 — Great Britain. Acting. White, Carol — *Biographies*

White, Carol. Carol comes home. — London : New English Library, Nov.1982. — [192]p
ISBN 0-450-05528-0 (pbk) : £1.60 : CIP entry
B82-27514

792'.028'0924 — Great Britain. Theatre. Acting. Garrick, David, *1717-1779 — Biographies*

Smith, Helen R.. David Garrick, 1717-1779 : a brief account / by Helen R. Smith. — London : British Library, c1979. — 80p : ill,facsims, ports ; 21cm. — (British Library monograph ; no.1)
Written to accompany the British Library's exhibition held in the King's Library from 30 November 1979-11 May 1980 to commemorate the bicentenary of the death of Garrick. — Bibliography: p76-77
ISBN 0-904654-40-0 (pbk) : £3.00 : CIP rev.
B79-32723

792'.028'0924 — Great Britain. Theatre. Acting. Terry, Ellen — *Biographies*

Terry, Ellen. The story of my life / Ellen Terry. — Woodbridge : Boydell, 1982. — viii,240p ; 22cm. — (Bookmarks)
ISBN 0-85115-204-x (pbk) : £4.95 : CIP rev.
B82-12887

792'.028'0924 — Great Britain. Theatre. Olivier, Laurence Olivier, *Baron — Biographies*

Kiernan, Thomas. Olivier : the life of Lawrence Olivier / Thomas Kiernan. — London : Sidgwick & Jackson, 1981. — x,302p,[8]p of plates : ill,ports ; 25cm
Includes index
ISBN 0-283-98671-9 : £8.95 B82-06137

792'.028'0924 — Great Britain. Theatre. Richardson, *Sir* **Ralph** — *Biographies*

O'Connor, Garry. Ralph Richardson. — London : Hodder and Stoughton, Oct.1982. — [288]p
ISBN 0-340-27041-1 : £9.95 : CIP entry
B82-24816

792'.028'0924 — South America. Theatre. Tours by Duse, Eleonora, *1906-1907 — Correspondence, diaries, etc.*

Noccioli, Guido. Duse on tour : Guido Noccioli's diaries, 1906-07 / translated and edited with an introduction and notes by Giovanni Pontiero. — Manchester : Manchester University Press, c1982. — x,178p : ill,1facsim,ports ; 24cm
Bibliography: p174-178
ISBN 0-7190-0847-6 : £25.00 : CIP rev.
B82-13268

792'.028'0924 — Theatre. Acting. Bloom, Claire — *Biographies*

Bloom, Claire. Limelight and after : the education of an actress / Claire Bloom. — London : Weidenfeld & Nicolson, 1982. — 187p,[40]p of plates : ill,ports ; 22cm
ISBN 0-297-78051-4 : £8.95 B82-19489

792'.028'0924 — Theatre. Coward, Noël — *Correspondence, diaries, etc.*

Coward, Noël. The Noel Coward diaries / edited by Graham Payn and Sheridan Morley. — London : Weidenfeld and Nicolson, 1982. — 698p ; 25cm
Includes index
ISBN 0-297-78142-1 : £15.00 B82-38926

792'.02'907 — Theatre. Performance — *Stories, anecdotes*

Brandreth, Gyles. Great theatrical disasters. — London : Granada, Oct.1982. — [192]p
ISBN 0-246-11770-2 : £5.95 : CIP entry
B82-23468

792'.02'9341 — Great Britain. Theatre — *Career guides*

Chudley, Philippa. Careers in the theatre / Philippa Chudley. — Totnes : Hamilton House, 1981. — 23p ; 21cm. — (Careerscope ; 3)
ISBN 0-906888-20-4 (pbk) : Unpriced
B82-03067

792'.07 — Education. Curriculum subjects: Drama. Teaching

Heathcote, Dorothy. Heathcote at the National : drama teacher — facilitator or manipulator? / NATD's first annual lecture given with financial assistance from Heinemann Educational Ltd. ; edited by Tony Goode. — Banbury : Published in association with the National Association for the Teaching of Drama by Kemble, c1982. — 46p : ill,2ports ; 22cm
ISBN 0-906835-09-7 (pbk) : Unpriced
B82-40395

792'.07 — Education. Role of drama

Children and drama / edited by Nellie McCaslin. — 2nd ed. — New York ; London : Longman, c1981. — xxx,249p : ill ; 23cm
Previous ed.: New York : McKay, 1975. — Includes index
ISBN 0-582-28250-0 (pbk) : £9.95 B82-02901

792'.07'041 — Great Britain. Education. Curriculum subjects: Drama — *Serials*

2D : drama, dance. — Vol.1, no.1 (Autumn 1981)-. — Leicester (Advisory Centre (Drama/Dance), Education Dept., County Hall, Glenfield, Leicester LE3 8RF) : [s.n.], 1981-. — v. : ill ; 21cm
Three issues yearly
ISSN 0261-6939 = 2D : £3.50 per year
Also classified at 793.3'2'07041 B82-13408

792'.07'1 — Schools. Activities: Drama

Adland, David. Group approach to drama 1 / David Adland. — 2nd ed. — Harlow : Longman, 1981. — 92p ; 21cm
Previous ed.: 1964
ISBN 0-582-21960-4 (pbk) : £1.30 B82-07455

Adland, David. Group approach to drama 2 / David Adland. — 2nd ed. — Harlow : Longman, 1981. — 92p : plans ; 21cm
Previous ed.: 1964
ISBN 0-582-21961-2 (pbk) : £1.30 B82-07456

Adland, David. Group approach to drama 3 / David Adland. — 2nd ed. — Harlow : Longman, 1981. — 108p : ill ; 21cm
Previous ed.: 1965
ISBN 0-582-21962-0 (pbk) : £1.30 B82-07457

792'.07'1 — Schools. Curriculum subjects: Drama. Teaching

Linnell, Rosemary. Approaching classroom drama. — London : Edward Arnold, July 1982. — [96]p. — (Teaching matters)
ISBN 0-7131-0724-3 (pbk) : £3.50 : CIP entry B82-17918

792'.07'1041 — Great Britain. Schools. Curriculum subjects: Drama

Drama in education : a curriculum for change : the report of the 1981 annual conference / edited by John Norman. — Banbury : Published in association with the National Association for the Teaching of Drama by Kemble, 1982. — 123p : ill ; 22cm
Bibliography: p118
ISBN 0-906835-08-9 (pbk) : Unpriced : CIP rev. B82-14196

792'.07'1042 — England. Schools. Activities: Drama. Teaching

New directions in drama teaching. — London : Heinemann Educational, Oct.1982. — [208]p
ISBN 0-435-18927-1 (pbk) : £5.95 : CIP entry B82-28739

792'.07'12 — Secondary schools. Curriculum subjects: Drama. Teaching

O'Neill, Cecily. Structures for drama lessons. — London : Hutchinson Education, May 1982. — [216]p
ISBN 0-09-147811-1 (pbk) : £4.95 : CIP entry B82-07250

792'.088042 — Great Britain. Theatre. Role of women, *1900-1980 — Feminist viewpoints*

Wandor, Michelene. Understudies : theatre and sexual politics / by Michelene Wandor. — London : Eyre Methuen, 1981. — 88p ; 21cm
ISBN 0-413-40060-3 (pbk) : £2.95 B82-27490

792.09 — THEATRE. HISTORICAL AND GEOGRAPHICAL TREATMENT

792'.09 — Theatre, *to 1980*

Brockett, Oscar G.. History of the theatre / Oscar G. Brockett. — 4th ed. — Boston ; London : Allyn and Bacon, c1982. — x,768p : ill,maps,plans ; 24cm
Previous ed.: 1977. — Bibliography: p725-742. — Includes index
ISBN 0-205-07661-0 : £11.95 B82-17781

792'.09 — Theatre, *to 1981*

Billington, Michael. The Guinness book of theatre facts and feats. — Enfield : Guinness Superlatives, Dec.1982. — [256]p
ISBN 0-85112-239-6 : £8.95 : CIP entry B82-30225

Mitchley, Jack. Five thousand years of theatre / Jack Mitchley, Peter Spalding ; drawings by Anthony Kinsey. — London : Batsford, 1982. — 138p : ill ; 23cm
Includes bibliographies and index
ISBN 0-7134-3423-6 : £5.50 : CIP rev. B82-01204

792'.09'04 — Theatre, *1873-1979*

Brockett, Oscar G.. Modern theatre : realism and naturalism to the present / Oscar G. Brockett. — Boston, Mass. ; London : Allyn and Bacon, c1982. — vi,201p : ill,maps,plans,ports ; 24cm
Bibliography: p183-189. — Includes index
ISBN 0-205-07760-9 (pbk) : Unpriced B82-28489

792'.092'2 — Theatre, *to 1980 — Biogaphies*

The **Entertainers** / foreword by Sir John Gielgud ; [general editor Clive Unger-Hamilton]. — [London] : Pitman House, [1980]. — 320p : ill (some col.),ports(some col.) ; 31cm
Includes index
ISBN 0-273-01542-7 : £9.95 B82-08919

792'.092'4 — Great Britain. Theatre, *1910-1935 — Personal observations*

Mac Liammóir, Michéal. Enter a goldfish : memoirs of an Irish actor, young and old / Michéal Mac Liammóir. — London : Granada, 1981, c1977. — 224p : music ; 18cm. — (A Panther book)
Originally published: London : Thames and Hudson, 1977
ISBN 0-586-05388-3 (pbk) : £1.25 B82-11158

792'.092'4 — Great Britain. Theatre, *1928-1974.* **Management** *— Personal observations*

Cartlidge, W. "Bill". Golden Hill to golden square / W. "Bill" Cartlidge. — Bognor Regis : New Horizon, c1982. — 505p,[36]p of plates : ill,facsims,ports ; 22cm
ISBN 0-86116-912-3 : Unpriced B82-26927

792'.092'4 — New York *(City).* **Theatre,** *1938-1960 — Personal observations*

Hanff, Helene. Underfoot in show business / Helene Hanff. — London : Futura, 1981, c1980. — 174p ; 18cm
Originally published: New York : Harper & Row, 1962 ; London : Deutsch, 1980
ISBN 0-7088-2125-1 (pbk) : £1.25 B82-10626

792'.092'4 — Popular theatre *— Personal observations*

McGrath, John. A good night out : popular theatre : audience, class and form / John McGrath ; with a foreword by Raymond Williams. — London : Eyre Methuen, 1981. — xiv,126p ; 21cm. — (An Eyre Methuen dramabook)
ISBN 0-413-49330-x (cased) : Unpriced
ISBN 0-413-48700-8 (pbk) : £3.95 B82-17557

792'.0938 — Ancient Greece. Theatre

Simon, Erika. The ancient theatre / Erika Simon ; translated by C.E. Vafopoulou-Richardson. — London : Methuen, 1982. — ix,50p,16p of plates : ill,1plan ; 23cm
Translation of: Das antike Theater. — Includes index
ISBN 0-416-32520-3 (cased) : Unpriced : CIP rev.
ISBN 0-416-32530-0 (pbk) : Unpriced B82-10503

792'.09415 — Ireland. Theatre *— History*

Hogan, Robert. The modern Irish drama. — Dublin : Dolman Press, Sept.1982. — (The Irish theatre series ; 12)
Vol.5: The art of the amateur 1916-1920. — [512]p
ISBN 0-85105-372-6 : £20.00 : CIP entry B82-18774

792'.09417 — Ireland *(Republic).* **Theatre** *— Serials*

Prompts : bulletin of the Irish Theatre Archive. — No.1 (June 1981)-. — Dubluin (Archives Division, City Hall, Dublin 2) : The Archive, 1981-. — v. : ill ; 21cm
Unpriced B82-10131

792'.09418'35 — Dublin. Theatres: Abbey Theatre, *to 1909 — Correspondence, diaries, etc.*

Yeats, W. B.. Theatre business / the correspondence of the first Abbey Theatre directors: William Butler Yeats, Lady Gregory and J.M. Synge ; selected and edited by Ann Saddlemyer. — Gerrards Cross : Smythe, 1982. — 330p,[8]p of plates : ill,ports ; 23cm
Bibliography: p301-307. — Includes index
ISBN 0-86140-042-9 : Unpriced : CIP rev. B80-22375

792'.0942 — England. Theatre, *ca 1575-1620 — For children*

Brown, John Russell. Shakespeare and his theatre / John Russell Brown ; illustrated by David Gentleman. — Harmondsworth : Kestrel, 1982. — 64p : col.ill,col.ports ; 25cm
ISBN 0-7226-5558-4 : £5.50 B82-20809

792'.0942 — England. Theatre, *to ca 1975*

The **Revels** history of drama in English / [general editors Clifford Leech and T.W. Craik]. — London : Methuen
Vol.4: 1613-1660 / Philip Edwards ... [et al.]. — 1981. — lvii,337p,[24]p of plates : ill,facsims,ports ; 24cm
General editor: Lois Potter. — Ill on lining papers. — Bibliography: p307-328. — Includes index
ISBN 0-416-13050-x : £25.00 : CIP rev.
Primary classification 822'.009 B81-30321

792'.09421 — London. Theatre, *1700-1800*

The **Stage** and the page : London's 'whole show' in the eighteenth-century theatre / edited by Geo. Winchester Stone, Jr. — Berkeley ; London : University of California Press, 1981. — x,251p : music,facsims ; 24cm. — (Publications from the Clark Library professorship, UCLA ; 6)
Bibliography: p231-237. — Includes index
ISBN 0-520-04201-8 : £11.50 B82-22623

792'.09421 — London. Theatre. Audiences, *1576-1642*

Cook, Ann Jennalie. The privileged playgoers of Shakespeare's London 1576-1642 / Ann Jennalie Cook. — Princeton ; Guildford : Princeton University Press, c1981. — x,316p : ill,1map ; 23cm
Bibliography: p283-305. — Includes index
ISBN 0-691-06454-7 : £13.40 B82-05269

792'.09421 — London. Theatre. Productions *— Indexes — Serials*

London theatre index. — 1981-. — Twickenham (4 Cross Deep Gardens, Twickenham, Middx. TW1 4QU) : London Theatre Record, 1982-. — v. ; 30cm
Annual. — Also acts as index to: London theatre record
ISSN 0263-2322 = London theatre index : £5.00 B82-20892

792'.09421'2 — London. Theatre. Companies: Children of Paul's, *1553-1608*

Gair, Reavley. The Children of Paul's : the story of a theatre company, 1553-1608. — Cambridge : Cambridge University Press, Oct.1982. — [213]p
ISBN 0-521-24360-2 : £19.50 : CIP entry B82-25505

792'.09421'76 — London. Newham *(London Borough).* **Theatre. Companies: Theatre Workshop,** *to 1980*

Goorney, Howard. The Theatre Workshop story / Howard Goorney. — London : Eyre Methuen, 1981. — xii,226p,[16]p of plates : ill,ports ; 24cm
Includes index
ISBN 0-413-47610-3 (cased) : £8.95
ISBN 0-413-48760-1 (pbk) : Unpriced B82-25868

792'.09423'93 — Avon. British. Theatres: Theatre Royal *(Bristol), to 1980*

The **Story** of the Theatre Royal Bristol. — [Bristol] : Trustees of the Theatre Royal, c1981. — 19p : ill,2coats of arms,2facsims,1plan ; 19x26cm
Cover title. — Bibliography: p19
ISBN 0-9502155-1-1 (pbk) : £0.75 B82-28497

792'.09424'89 — Warwickshire. Stratford-upon-Avon. Theatres. Companies: Royal Shakespeare Company, *to 1981*

Beauman, Sally. The Royal Shakespeare Company : a history of ten decades / Sally Beauman. — Oxford : Oxford University Press, 1982. — xii,388p,[32]p of plates : ill,ports ; 24cm
Includes index
ISBN 0-19-212209-6 : £12.95 : CIP rev. B82-07498

792′.09424′96 — West Midlands *(Metropolitan County).* **Birmingham. Theatres: Crescent Theatre,** *to 1982*
Golden jubilee 1932-1982 : a souvenir brochure to commemorate fifty years of theatre at the Crescent Theatre, Birmingham and one year of Radio Lollipop at the Childrens Hospital, Birmingham / [compiled by Brian Butler. — Birmingham : Crescent Theatre Ltd., c1982. — [20]p : ill(some col.),ports ; 30cm
Col. ill on inside covers
ISBN 0-9508102-0-7 (pbk) : £1.50 B82-38547

792′.09424′98 — West Midlands *(Metropolitan County).* **Coventry. Theatre,** *to 1642 — Readings from contemporary sources*
Coventry / edited by R.W. Ingram. — [Manchester] : Manchester University Press, c1981. — lxxii,712p : maps ; 26cm. — (Records of early English drama)
Bibliography: plxx-lxxiii. — Includes index
ISBN 0-7190-0837-9 : £55.00 : CIP rev. B81-08876

792′.09428′37 — Humberside. Hull. Theatres. Companies: Hull Truck Theatre Company, *to 1981*
Hull Truck Theatre Company. Hull Truck Theatre Company 1971-81 : the first ten years / by Anthony Meech. — Hull (35 High St., Hull HU1 1NQ) : Hull Truck Theatre Company, [1982?]. — ill,ports ; 21cm
Cover title
Unpriced (pbk) B82-23371

792′.0945 — Italy. Theatre, *ca 1730-ca 1920*
Carlson, Marvin. The Italian stage : from Goldoni to D′Annunzio / by Marvin Carlson. — Jefferson, N.C. ; London : McFarland, 1981. — viii,228p ; 24cm
Bibliography: p203-214. — Includes index
ISBN 0-89950-000-5 : £15.35 B82-18949

792′.0973 — United States. Theatre
Cassady, Marshall. Theatre : a view of life / Marshall Cassady, Pat Cassady. — New York ; London : Holt, Rinehart and Winston, c1982. — xi,291p,[8]p of plates : ill(some col.),facsims,plans,ports ; 24cm
Bibliography: p260-263. — Includes index
ISBN 0-03-050551-8 (pbk) : £11.95 B82-17014

792.3 — PANTOMIME

792.3′0941 — Great Britain. Pantomime, *to 1980*
Salberg, Derek. Once upon a pantomime / by Derek Salberg ; foreword by Arthur Askey. — Luton : Cortney, 1981. — ix,198p : ill,facsim, ports ; 25cm
Includes index
ISBN 0-904378-13-6 (pbk) : £3.95 B82-05684

792.7 — MUSIC HALL, REVUE, NIGHT CLUBS, ETC

792.7′0944′36 — France. Paris. Music halls: Folies Bergère, *to 1981*
Castle, Charles, *1939-*. The Folies Bergère. — London : Methuen, Nov.1982. — [256]p
ISBN 0-413-49470-5 : £8.95 : CIP entry B82-27207

792.8 — BALLET

792.8 — Ballet
Crisp, Clement. How to enjoy ballet. — Loughton : Judy Piatkus, Mar.1982. — [192]p. — (Melvyn Bragg′s arts series)
ISBN 0-86188-147-8 : £6.95 : CIP entry B82-00349

792.8 — Ballet *— For children*
May, Robin. Discovering ballet / [author Robin May]. — London : Marshall Cavendish Children′s, 1979. — 77p : ill(some col.),ports (some col.) ; 30cm. — (Woodpecker books)
In association with the Royal Ballet. — Ill on lining papers. — Includes index
ISBN 0-85685-680-0 : Unpriced B82-05452

Willson, Robina Beckles. Ballet / Robina Beckles Willson. — London : Hamlyn, 1982. — 128p : ill(some col.),ports(some col.) ; 18cm. — (Hamlyn junior pocket books)
Bibliography: p120-123. — Includes index
ISBN 0-600-31600-9 : £1.99 B82-23623

792.8′026 — Ballet. Costume. Design, *to 1980*
Strong, Roy. Designing for the dancer. — London (20 Garrick St., WC2E 8BJ) : Elron, Apr.1981. — [140]p
ISBN 0-904499-11-1 (pbk) : £4.95 : CIP entry B81-07478

792.8′03′21 — Ballet *— Encyclopaedias*
Koegler, Horst. Concise Oxford dictionary of ballet. — 2nd ed. — Oxford : Oxford University Press, Oct.1982. — [592]p
Previous ed.: 1977
ISBN 0-19-311325-2 (cased) : £15.00 : CIP entry
ISBN 0-19-311330-9 (pbk) : £5.95 B82-23677

792.8′07′10421 — London. Ballet schools: Royal Ballet School. School life *— Personal observations*
Glasstone, Richard. I really want to dance. — London : Thames/Methuen, July 1982. — [64]p
ISBN 0-423-00370-4 : £4.95 : CIP entry B82-14366

792.8′09 — Ballet, *to 1981*
Kerensky, Oleg. The Guinness guide to ballet / Oleg Kerensky. — Enfield : Guinness Superlatives, c1981. — 224p : ill(some col.),ports(some col.) ; 30cm
Includes index
ISBN 0-85112-226-4 : £11.95 : CIP rev. B81-31198

Steeh, Judith A.. History of ballet and modern dance / Judith Steeh. — London : Hamlyn, 1982. — 256p : ill(some col.),ports(some col.) ; 32cm
Includes index
ISBN 0-600-34164-x : £7.95 B82-30762

792.8′09′034 — Ballet, *1820-1870 — Illustrations*
Great ballet prints of the Romantic era / Parmenia Migel. — New York : Dover ; London : Constable, 1981. — xiv,109p : chiefly ill(some col.),ports ; 31cm
Bibliography: p104-106. — Includes index
ISBN 0-486-24050-9 (pbk) : £6.00 B82-18047

792.8′092′4 — Ballet. Criticism. Buckle, Richard *— Biographies*
Buckle, Richard. In the wake of Diaghilev. — London : Collins, Sept.1982. — [256]p
ISBN 0-00-216544-9 : £9.00 : CIP entry B82-19067

792.8′092′4 — Ballet. Fonteyn, *Dame* **Margot** *— Biographies — For children*
Sebba, Anne. Margot Fonteyn. — London : MacRae Books, Feb.1983. — [48]p. — (Blackbird series)
ISBN 0-86203-118-4 : £2.95 : CIP entry B82-39820

792.8′0942 — England. Ballet. Companies: Ballet Rambert, *to 1981*
Ballet Rambert : 50 years and on / edited by Clement Crisp, Anya Sainsbury, Peter Williams. — Rev. and enl. ed. — London : Ballet Rambert, 1981. — 111p : ill,1facsim,ports ; 24cm
Previous ed.: published as 50 years of Ballet Rambert, 1926-1976, 1976. — Text and ill on inside covers. — List of works performed: p99-103. — Includes index
ISBN 0-9505478-1-6 (pbk) : £3.00 B82-08295

792.8′0942 — England. Ballet. Companies: Royal Ballet *(Covent Garden)* **& Sadler′s Wells Royal Ballet**
Royal Ballet *(Covent Garden).* The Royal Ballet & Sadler′s Wells Royal Ballet 1980/81 / edited by Noël Goodwin. — London : Royal Opera House Covent Garden, c1980. — 56p : ill(some col.),ports(some col.) ; 30cm
ISBN 0-9502123-7-7 (pbk) : Unpriced B82-29935

792.8′0942 — England. Ballet. Companies: Royal Ballet *(Covent Garden) — Illustrations*
Eagling, Wayne. The company we keep / by Wayne Eagling, Robert Jude and Ross MacGibbon. — London : Angus & Robertson, 1981. — 94p : ill,ports ; 29cm
Ill on lining papers
ISBN 0-207-95950-1 : £6.95 B82-10036

792.8′0944′949 — Monarco. Monte Carlo. Ballet. Companies: Ballet Russe de Monte Carlo, *to 1952*
Walker, Katherine Sorley. De Basil′s Ballets Russes / Katherine Sorley Walker. — London : Hutchinson, 1982. — xvii,317p,[16]p of plates : ill,ports ; 25cm
Bibliography: p304-306. — Includes index
ISBN 0-09-147510-4 : £12.95 : CIP rev. B82-07963

792.8′0973 — United States. Ballet. Companies: Ballet Russe de Monte Carlo, *to 1962*
Anderson, Jack. The one and only : the Ballet Russe de Monte Carlo / Jack Anderson. — London : Dance Books, 1981. — xxiv,355p,[32]p of plates : ill,ports ; 24cm
Bibliography: p307-309. — Includes index
ISBN 0-903102-65-x : Unpriced B82-31127

792.8′2 — Ballet. Dancing *— For children*
Isadora, Rachel. My ballet class / Rachel Isadora. — London : Angus & Robertson, 1981, c1980. — [32]p : ill(some col.) ; 26cm
Originally published: New York : Greenwillow Books, 1980
ISBN 0-207-14223-8 : Unpriced B82-08988

792.8′2 — Ballet. Dancing *— Interviews*
Newman, Barbara, *1944-*. Striking a balance : dancers talk about dancing / Barbara Newman. — London : Elm Tree, 1982. — 402p : ports ; 24cm
Ports on lining papers. — Includes index
ISBN 0-241-10684-2 : £12.50 B82-30680

792.8′2 — Ballet. Techniques
Robbins, Jane, *1948-*. Classical dance : the balletgoer′s guide to technique and performance / Jane Robbins. — Newton Abbot : David & Charles, 1982, c1981. — xvi,190p : ill ; 22cm
Originally published: New York : Holt, Rinehart and Winston, 1981. — Includes index
ISBN 0-7153-8274-8 : £6.95 : CIP rev. B81-35823

792.8′2′0922 — Ballet dancers, *1960-1980 — Illustrations*
Crickmay, Anthony. Dancers / Anthony Crickmay ; introduction by Andrew Porter. — London : Collins, 1982. — [135]p : all ill ; 37cm
Includes index
ISBN 0-00-216291-1 : £30.00 B82-34281

792.8′2′0924 — Ballet. Choreography. Saint-Léon, Arthur *— Correspondence, diaries, etc.*
Saint-Léon, Arthur. Letters from a ballet-master : the correspondence of Arthur Saint-Léon / edited by Ivor Guest. — London : Dance, 1981. — 158p,[20]p of plates : ill,music,1facsim,ports ; 25cm
Includes index
ISBN 0-903102-58-7 : £6.95 B82-00523

792.8′2′0924 — Ballet. Dancing. Baryshnikov, Mikhail *— Biographies*
Smakov, Gennady. Baryshnikov : from Russia to the west / Gennady Smakov. — London : Orbis, 1981. — x,244p : ill,ports ; 24cm
Includes index
ISBN 0-85613-395-7 : £7.95 B82-05838

792.8′2′0924 — Ballet. Dancing. Dolin, *Sir* **Anton** *— Biographies*
Dolin, *Sir* **Anton**. Dolin : friends and memories / compiled by Andrew Wheatcroft ; foreword by Dame Ninette de Valois. — London : Routledge & Kegan Paul, 1982. — [190]p : ill,facsims,ports ; 31cm
ISBN 0-7100-9199-0 : £15.95 : CIP rev. B82-14217

792.8′2′0924 — Ballet. Dancing. Flett, Una *— Biographies*
Flett, Una. Falling from grace : my early years in ballet / Una Flett. — Edinburgh : Canongate, 1981. — 194p ; 23cm
ISBN 0-86241-011-8 : £5.95 B82-09056

792.8′2′0924 — Ballet. Dancing. Gilpin, John — *Biographies*

Gilpin, John. A dance with life / by John Gilpin ; foreword by Sir Anton Dolin. — London : Kimber, 1982. — 176p,[24]p of plates : ill,ports ; 24cm
Includes index
ISBN 0-7183-0408-x : £9.50 B82-31051

792.8′2′0924 — Ballet. Dancing. Karsavina, Tamara — *Biographies*

Karsavina, Tamara. Theatre Street : the reminiscences of Tamara Karsavina. — [New ed.]. — London : Dance Books, 1981. — 362p : ill,ports ; 26cm
Previous ed.: London : Constable, 1948. — Includes index
ISBN 0-903102-47-1 : £8.95 B82-09240

792.8′2′0924 — Ballet. Dancing. McDonald, Elaine — *Illustrations*

Elaine McDonald / edited by John S. Dixon ; editorial assistant David Proud. — Leeds (31 The Towers, Leeds LS12 3SQ) : Arno, [1982?]. — [110]p : chiefly ill,ports ; 28cm
£3.95 (pbk) B82-27491

792.8′2′0924 — Ballet. Dancing. Nijinsky, Vaslav — *Biographies*

Nijinska, Bronislava. Bronislava Nijinska : early memories / translated and edited by Irina Nijinska and Jean Rawlinson ; with an introduction by and in consultation with Anna Kisselgoff. — London : Faber, 1982, c1981. — xxv,546p,[64]p of plates : ill,facsims, ports ; 25cm
Originally published: New York : Holt, Rinehart and Winston, 1981. — Includes index
ISBN 0-571-11892-5 : £15.00 : CIP rev.
B81-33790

792.8′2′0924 — Ballet. Dancing. Nureyev, Rudolf — *Biographies*

Dodd, Craig. Rudolf Nureyev. — London : Hamilton, Oct.1982. — [64]p
ISBN 0-241-10849-7 : £3.25 : CIP entry
B82-23454

792.8′2′0924 — Ballet. Dancing. Seymour, Lynn — *Biographies*

Austin, Richard. Lynn Seymour : an authorised biography / Richard Austin. — London : Angus and Robertson, 1980. — 224p : ill,ports ; 25cm
Includes index
ISBN 0-207-95900-5 : Unpriced B82-05916

792.8′4 — Ballet. Strauss, Richard. Productions, *to 1979*

Hartmann, Rudolf. Richard Strauss : the staging of his operas and ballets. — Oxford : Phaidon, Mar.1982. — [280]p
Translation of: Richard Strauss : die Bühnenwerke von Uraufführung bis heute
ISBN 0-7148-2254-x : £25.00 : CIP entry
Primary classification 782.1′092′4 B82-01556

792.8′42 — Ballet. Adam, Adolphe. Giselle. Performance by Pavlova, Nadezhda & Solov'ev, Iuriĭ — *Illustrations*

Gregory, John, *1914-*. Giselle immortal / by John Gregory ; with photographs by Alexander Ukladnikov. — London : Robson, 1982. — 58p : ill,ports ; 24cm
Bibliography: p58
ISBN 0-86051-177-4 (pbk) : £4.95 : CIP rev.
B82-15923

792.8′42 — Ballet. Chaĭkovskiĭ, Petr Il'ich. Shchelkunchik. Productions, *to 1978*

Anderson, Jack. The nutcracker ballet / Jack Anderson. — London : Bison, c1979. — 223p : ill(some col.),ports ; 29cm
Bibliography: p218-219. — Includes index
ISBN 0-86124-010-3 : £6.95 B82-01888

792.8′42 — Ballet. MacMillan, Kenneth. 'Isadora'. Production

Thorpe, Edward. Creating a ballet : MacMillan's Isadora / Edward Thorpe ; with photographs by Robert Jude and Ross MacGibbon. — London : Evans, 1981. — 79p,[64]p of plates : ill ; 26cm
ISBN 0-237-45554-4 : £7.95: CIP rev.
B81-25730

792.8′45 — Ballet — *Plot outlines — For children*

Farjeon, Annabel. The book of ballet stories / Annabel Farjeon. — Tadworth : Kaye & Ward, 1981. — 124p : ill ; 23cm
ISBN 0-7182-1273-8 : £5.50 B82-06267

792.8′45 — Russian ballet, *1877-1910 — Plot outlines — Collections — For children*

Hughes, Roger. The nutcracker. — London : Hodder and Stoughton's Children's Books, Oct.1982. — [32]p
ISBN 0-340-28353-x : £3.95 : CIP entry
B82-24825

792.9 — THEATRE. SPECIFIC PRODUCTIONS

792.9′2 — Drama in English. Nunn, Trevor. Nicholas Nickleby. Production by Royal Shakespeare Company, *1980*

Rubin, Leon. The Nicholas Nickleby story : the making of the historic Royal Shakespeare Company production / Leon Rubin. — London : Heinemann, 1981. — 192p : ill,ports ; 25cm
ISBN 0-434-65530-9 (cased) : Unpriced
ISBN 0-434-65531-7 (pbk) : £4.95 B82-03896

792.9′2 — Drama in English. Shakespeare, William. Midsummer night's dream. Production by Brook, Peter, *1925-, 1970*

Selbourne, David. The making of a Midsummer night's dream : an eye-witness account of Peter Brook's production from first rehearsal to first night / David Selbourne ; with an introductory essay by Simon Trussler. — London : Methuen, 1982. — xxxvii,327p : ill,ports ; 23cm
Includes extracts from the play
ISBN 0-413-49720-8 : £15.00 B82-37379

792.9′2 — Drama in English. Shakespeare, William. Winter's tale. Performance in Great Britain & United States, *1611-1976*

Bartholomeusz, Dennis. The Winter's tale in performance in England and America 1611-1976. — Cambridge : Cambridge University Press, Sept.1982. — [278]p
ISBN 0-521-24529-x : £27.50 : CIP entry
B82-25502

792.9′5 — Drama in English, *1900-1980.* **Productions,** *to 1980 — Encyclopaedias*

Leonard, William Torbert. Theatre : stage to screen to television / by William Torbert Leonard. — Metuchen ; London : Scarecrow, 1981. — 2v.(vii,1804p) ; 23cm
Includes index
ISBN 0-8108-1374-2 : £59.60
Also classified at 791.45′75 ; 791.43′75
B82-08579

792.9′5 — Drama in English. Shakespeare, William. Performance, *to 1981 — Illustrations*

A **Pictorial** companion to Shakespeare's plays / devised and designed by Robert Tanitch. — London : Muller, 1982. — 128p : ill ; 29cm
Ill on lining papers. — Includes index
ISBN 0-584-11027-8 : £10.25 : CIP rev.
B82-11766

792.9′5 — Drama in English. Shakespeare, William. Productions by Harrow School, *1941-1981*

The **Harrow** achievement : 1941-1981 / edited by Huon Mallalieu ; with contributions by Herbert Harris ... [et al.] ; illustrations Maurice Percival. — [London] ([64 Speed House, Barbican EC2]) : The Old Harrovian Players, c1982. — 221p : ill,1port ; 22cm
Limited ed. of 300 copies
Unpriced (pbk) B82-34565

792.9′5 — Theatre. Performances, *to 1981 — Reviews — Collections*

Rigg, Diana. No turn unstoned. — London : Hamilton, Sept.1982. — [192]p
ISBN 0-241-10855-1 : £6.95 : CIP entry
B82-20165

792.9′5′09421 — London. Theatre. Performances — *Illustrations — Serials*

Cooper, Donald, *1946-*. Theatre year : a selection of photographs by Donald Cooper of productions in London and Stratford. — Oct. 1979 to Nov. 1980-. — London (21 Wellington St., WC2) : In (Parenthesis) Ltd., 1980-. — v. : chiefly ill ; 23cm
Annual
ISSN 0261-2348 = Theatre year : Unpriced
B82-05215

793 — INDOOR GAMES AND AMUSEMENTS

793 — English pub games

Finn, Timothy. Pub games of England. — 2nd ed. — Cambridge : Oleander, June 1981. — [196]p. — (Oleander games & pastimes ; v.5)
Previous ed.: London : Queen Anne Press, 1975
ISBN 0-900891-66-1 (cased) : £7.50 : CIP entry
ISBN 0-900891-67-x (pbk) : £4.95 B81-14806

793 — Games using coins & games using matches — *Collections*

Eldin, Peter. Match play : safe puzzles, games and tricks with matchsticks / Peter Eldin ; illustrated by Pinpoint Design Company. — London : Granada, 1982. — 128p : ill ; 18cm. — (A Dragon book)
ISBN 0-583-30510-5 (pbk) : £0.85 B82-33989

793 — Indoor activities — *Manuals — For children*

Brandreth, Gyles. The great games gazette : parlour fun for home entertainers / Gyles Brandreth ; illustrated by David Farris and Rowan Barnes-Murphy. — [Sevenoaks] : Knight Books, 1978 (1982 [printing]). — 128p : ill ; 18cm
ISBN 0-340-23192-0 (pbk) : £0.95 B82-38990

793 — Indoor games. Design — *Manuals*

Ellington, Henry. A handbook of game design / Henry Ellington, Eric Addinall & Fred Percival. — London : Kagan Page, 1982. — 156p : ill ; 23cm
Bibliography: p145-147. — Includes index
ISBN 0-85038-568-7 : £11.95 : CIP rev.
B82-14920

793 — Indoor games — *Manuals*

Asquith, Eric L.. Armchair sport / Eric L. Asquith. — Braunton : Merlin, 1982. — 39p ; 22cm
ISBN 0-86303-009-2 : £2.50 B82-27719

The **Complete** book of indoor games / editor, Peter Arnold. — London : Hamlyn, 1981. — 320p : col.ill ; 27cm
Includes index
ISBN 0-600-34132-1 : £4.95 B82-04356

Pritchard, David, *1919-*. Brain games : the world's best games for two / David Pritchard. — Harmondsworth : Penguin, 1982. — 202p : ill ; 18cm
Bibliography: p200-202
ISBN 0-14-005682-3 (pbk) : £1.75 B82-22092

793 — Indoor games — *Manuals — For children*

Kebby, Stella. 101 ideas for a rainy day / compiled by Stella Kebby. — London : Hamlyn, 1982. — 157p : col.ill ; 22cm
ISBN 0-600-36648-0 : £2.95 B82-35844

McToots, Rudi. The kids' book of games / text and illustrations by Rudi McToots ; design by Dreadnaught. — [London] : Beaver, 1982, c1980. — [141]p : ill ; 13x21cm
ISBN 0-600-20477-4 (pbk) : £1.50 B82-23274

793 — Musical games for children — *Collections*

Nelson, Esther L.. Musical games : for children of all ages / by Esther L. Nelson ; illustrations by Shizu Matsuda. — New York : Sterling ; London : Oak Tree Press, c1976 (1981 printing). — 72p : ill,music ; 22x26cm
Includes index
ISBN 0-8069-7520-2 (spiral) : £3.95
B82-39687

793 — Musical games for children — *Collections continuation*

Nelson, Esther L.. Singing and dancing games for the very young / by Esther L. Nelson ; illustrations by Minn Matsuda ; photographs by Shirley Zeiberg. — New York : Sterling ; Poole : Distributed by Blandford Press, c1977 (1982 printing). — 72p : ill,music ; 22x26cm
Includes index
ISBN 0-8069-7572-5 (spiral) : £3.95
B82-39686

Storms, G.. Handbook of music games / G. Storms ; translated by Anne Griffiths. — London : Hutchinson, 1981. — 145p : ill,music ; 22cm
Translation of: Muzikaal Spelenboek
ISBN 0-09-144531-0 (pbk) : £4.95 : CIP rev.
B81-20179

793'.024372 — Indoor games — *Manuals* — *For teaching*

Parratt, Alison L.. Indoor games and activities. — London : Hodder and Stoughton, Jan.1983. — [144]p
ISBN 0-340-32400-7 (pbk) : £3.75 : CIP entry
B82-34405

793'.05 — Indoor games — *Serials*

The **Gamer** : Britain's premier magazine for games players. — Issue 1 (July/Aug. 1981)-. — Luton (23a George St., Luton, Beds.) : AHC Publications, 1981-. — v. : ill ; 28cm
Six issues yearly. — Continues in part: Games & puzzles
ISSN 0262-804x = Gamer : £0.60 per issue
B82-09066

793.2 — Party games for adults — *Manuals*

Melsom, Andrew. Are you there, Moriarty? : Debrett's house party games and amusements / Andrew Melsom ; illustrations by Charlotte Christian. — London : Debrett's Peerage, 1981. — xiii,111p : ill ; 21cm
ISBN 0-905649-52-4 : £4.95 B82-05301

Treat, Lawrence. Crime and puzzlement. — London (9 Henrietta St., WC2E 8PS) : Dorling Kindersley, Sept.1982. — [78]p
ISBN 0-86318-005-1 (pbk) : £1.95 : CIP entry
B82-21565

793.2 — Party games — *Manuals*

DeFoyer, Crispin. Christmas games : for adults and children / Crispin DeFoyer. — Cambridge : Oleander Press, c1982. — 64p : ill ; 20cm
Includes index
ISBN 0-906672-08-2 (cased) : £4.20 : CIP rev.
ISBN 0-906672-09-0 (pbk) : £1.95 B82-01406

Dickinson, Philippa. Go! : a book of games / compiled by Philippa Dickinson ; illustrated by Robin Lawrie. — Harmondsworth : Puffin, 1982. — 124p : ill ; 18cm
ISBN 0-14-031440-7 (pbk) : £0.90 B82-30551

Have fun, have a party : games, magic, tricks. — London (124 Auckland Rd., S.E.19) : G. Richardson, [1980]. — 38p : ill ; 20cm. — (An Adamant book)
Unpriced (pbk) B82-16114

793.2'1 — Party games for children. Special subjects: Shadows — *Manuals* — *For children*

Brandreth, Gyles. Shadow shows / Gyles Brandreth ; illustrated by David Farris. — London : Carousel, 1981. — 127p : ill ; 20cm
ISBN 0-552-54192-3 (pbk) : £0.85 B82-04342

793.3 — Italian court dancing, *1945* — *Early works*

Cornazano, Antonio. The book on the art of dancing / Antonio Cornazano ; translated by Madeleine Inglehearn and Peggy Forsyth ; introduction and notes by Madeleine Inglehearn. — London : Dance Books, 1981. — 46p : ill,music ; 24cm
Translated from the Italian
ISBN 0-903102-63-3 : £4.95 B82-40084

793.3 — Pavans & minuets. Dancing — *For theatre*

Guthrie, John. Historical dances for the theatre : the pavan and the minuet / by John Guthrie. — London : Dance Books, 1982. — 79p : ill,music ; 25cm
Originally published: Worthing : Aldridge, 1950. — Bibliography: p79
ISBN 0-903102-68-4 (pbk) : £4.95 B82-31123

793.3'194115 — Scottish Highland dancing — *Manuals*

The **Official** textbook of the Scottish Official Board of Highland Dancing. — 3rd ed. — Edinburgh : Holmes McDougall, [1981?]. — x,71p : ill,1form ; 26cm
Originally published: 1975
ISBN 0-7157-1321-3 : £6.75 B82-09642

793.3'07'041 — Great Britain. Education. Curriculum subjects: Dancing — *Inquiry reports*

Dance education and training in Britain. — London : Calouste Gulbenkian Foundation, UK and Commonwealth Branch, 1980. — xiv,238p : ill,2maps ; 23cm
Ill on inside covers. — Includes index
ISBN 0-903319-18-7 (pbk) : £5.50 B82-14420

793.3'092'2 — Dancers, *ca 1930-ca 1960* — *Illustrations*

Van Vechten, Carl. The dance photography of Carl van Vechten / selected and with an introduction by Paul Padgette. — New York : Schirmer ; London : Collier Macmillan, c1981. — ix,212p : chiefly ill,ports ; 32cm. — (A Dance horizons book)
Bibliography: pix. — Includes index
ISBN 0-02-872680-4 : £14.95 B82-20401

793.3'1 — Folk dancing — *Conference proceedings*

International Folk Music Council. *United Kingdom National Committee. Conference (1980 : Cambridge)*. Studies in traditional music & dance : proceedings of the 1980 conference of the United Kingdom National Committee of the International Folk Music Council / edited by Peter Cooke. — [Edinburgh] (c/o P. Cooke, 27 George Sq., Edinburgh EH8 9LD) : [The Committee], c1981. — 84p ; 21cm
Unpriced (pbk)
Primary classification 781.7 B82-01254

793.3'1'024372 — Folk dancing — *Manuals* — *For teaching*

Notes for the professional examinations, grade examinations and dancers' medal tests / compiled by the Committee of the National Dance Branch. — 4th ed. (rev.). — London (Euston Hall, Birkenhead St., WC1H 8BE) : Imperial Society of Teachers of Dancing, National Dance Branch, 1979. — 126p ; 21cm
Previous ed.: 1971
£3.00 (pbk) B82-30036

793.3'1938 — Ancient Greek dancing. Techniqus — *Manuals*

Ginner, Ruby. The technique of the revived Greek dance : technical handbook for teachers and students / by Ruby Ginner. — London : Imperial Society of Teachers of Dancing, 1981. — 103p : ill,1port ; 19cm
Originally published: 1963. — Port on inside back cover
£3.00 (pbk) B82-02510

793.3'1941 — British folk dancing — *Serials*

Traditional dance. — Vol.1-. — Crewe (c/o T. Buckland, 10 Addison Close, Wistaston, Crewe, Cheshire CW2 8BY) : Crewe and Alsager College of Higher Education, 1982-. — v. : music ; 21cm
ISSN 0263-9033 = Traditional dance : Unpriced B82-36719

793.3'1942 — English country dancing — *Collections*

English country dances : Fallibroome collection. — London : English Folk Dance and Song Society
4: Seventeen country dances from various sources 1713-1799 / selected and edited by Bernard J. Bentley. — 1971 (1980 [printing]). — [24]p : music ; 14x21cm
ISBN 0-85418-134-2 (pbk) : Unpriced
B82-23823

English country dances : Fallibroome collection. — London : English Folk Dance and Song Society
5: Eighteen country dances from various sources 1713-1799 / selected and edited by Bernard J. Bentley. — 1971 (1980 [printing]). — [24]p : music ; 14x21cm
ISBN 0-85418-135-0 (pbk) : Unpriced
B82-23824

793.3'1942417'014 — Cotswold morris dancing. Terminology

Glossary : Cotswold. — [Boston] ([40 Allington Garden, Boston, Lincs. PE21 9DW]) : Women's Morris Federation, 1981. — ii,14leaves : ill ; 30cm. — (Cotswold glossary ; issue A) (Workshop series / Women's Morris Federation)
Cover title
£2.00 (spiral) B82-23603

793.3'19492 — Dutch folk dancing — *Serials*

Jaffé, Nigel. The Netherlands. — Skipton (5 Mill Bridge, Skipton, North Yorkshire) : Folk Dance Enterprises, Oct.1982. — [128]p. — (European folk dance series ; v.1)
ISBN 0-946247-00-5 : £10.50 : CIP entry
B82-30609

793.3'2 — Bellydancing

Buonaventura, Wendy. Belly dancing. — London : Virago, Feb.1983. — [192]p
ISBN 0-86068-279-x (pbk) : £5.95 : CIP entry
B82-39620

793.3'2 — Bellydancing — *Manuals*

Hobin, Tina. Belly dancing / Tina Hobin ; with photographs by Kristyna K'ashvili. — London : Duckworth, 1982. — 96p : ill ; 22cm
ISBN 0-7156-1605-6 (pbk) : £2.50 : CIP rev.
B82-02642

793.3'2'07 — Educational institutions. Curriculum subjects: Dancing

Redfern, Betty. Concepts in modern educational dance / by Betty Redfern. — London : Dance Books, 1982. — 153p ; 21cm
Originally published: London : Kimpton, 1973. — Bibliography: p143-146. — Includes index
ISBN 0-903102-67-6 (pbk) : £4.95 B82-31124

793.3'2'07041 — Great Britain. Education. Curriculum subjects: Dancing

Adshead, Janet. The study of dance / Janet Adshead. — London : Dance Books, 1981. — xv,127p : ill ; 23cm
Includes bibliographies and index
ISBN 0-903102-66-8 : £7.50 B82-12627

793.3'2'07041 — Great Britain. Education. Curriculum subjects: Dancing — *Serials*

2D : drama, dance. — Vol.1, no.1 (Autumn 1981)-. — Leicester (Advisory Centre (Drama/Dance), Education Dept., County Hall, Glenfield, Leicester LE3 8RF) : [s.n.], 1981-. — v. : ill ; 21cm
Three issues yearly
ISSN 0261-6939 = 2D : £3.50 per year
Primary classification 792'.07'041 B82-13408

793.3'2'0924 — Dancing. Baker, Josephine - *Biographies*

Haney, Lynn. Naked at the feast : a biography of Josephine Baker. — London : Robson, May 1981. — [352]p
ISBN 0-86051-140-5 : £7.50 : CIP entry
B81-10006

793.3'3 — Ballroom dancing. Techniques — *Manuals*

Monte, John. The Fred Astaire dance book / compiled by John Monte, with Bobbie Laurence ; photos by Chip Casanave. — Rev. 2nd. updated ed. — London : Pelham, 1979, c1978. — 190p : ill ; 24cm
Previous ed.: London : Souvenir, 1962
ISBN 0-7207-1202-5 : £5.50 B82-08781

Silvester, Victor. Modern ballroom dancing. — Rev. ed. — London : Paul, May 1982. — [256]p
Previous ed.: London : Barrie and Jenkins, 1974
ISBN 0-09-149800-7 (pbk) : £2.95 : CIP entry
B82-16495

793.3′3 — Ballroom dancing. Techniques — *Manuals* *continuation*

Silvester, Victor. Modern ballroom dancing : history and practice / Victor Silvester. — London : Stanley Paul, 1982. — 249p : ill ; 19cm
Originally published: London : Barrie & Jenkins, 1977
ISBN 0-09-149801-5 (pbk) : £2.95 B82-32084

793.73 — General knowledge — *Questions & answers*

Ardley, Bridget. 1001 questions and answers. — London (Elsley Court, 20 Great Titchfield St., W1P 7AD) : Kingfisher, Sept.1981. — [160]p
ISBN 0-86272-000-1 : £3.95 : CIP entry B81-20166

Batey, Derek. The new Mr & Mrs quiz book / Derek Batey ; cartoons by Artie Jackson. — London : ITV books, 1982. — 128p : ill ; 17cm
ISBN 0-09-928080-9 (pbk) : £1.00 B82-16521

Calveley, Christina. The second family quiz book / Christina Calveley. — Harmondsworth : Penguin, 1982. — 143p ; 19cm
ISBN 0-14-006077-4 (pbk) : £0.95 B82-30253

Hickman, Norman G.. Quintessential quizzes : a collection of curious words, derivations, literary allusions, and little-known oddities of fact and fiction / Norman G. Hickman ; adapted by Ian Gillies ; foreword by Irene Thomas. — London : Unwin, 1982. — 142p ; 18cm
Originally published: New York : St Martin′s Press, 1979
ISBN 0-04-793050-0 (pbk) : £1.95 : CIP rev. B81-33907

Jace. The standard quiz book / by Jace. — Kingswood : Elliot Right Way, c1982. — 127p : ill ; 18cm. — (Paperfronts)
Includes index
ISBN 0-7160-0672-3 (pbk) : £0.75 B82-23915

The **King** William′s College tests. — London : Hutchinson, Oct.1982. — [288]p
ISBN 0-09-149871-6 (pbk) : £4.95 : CIP entry B82-24969

Lane, Roger, *1946-*. The jubilee quiz book : 2500 questions and answers for an interesting and varied quiz / devised by Roger Lane. — Kenilworth : National Federation of Young Farmers Clubs, [1982?]. — iv,125p : 1ill,1form,1port ; 21cm
Text on inside cover
ISBN 0-906863-02-3 (pbk) : Unpriced B82-36421

May, Robin. The Beaver holiday quiz / by Robin May ; illustrated by Alan Rogers. — London : Beaver, 1981. — 95p : ill ; 18cm
ISBN 0-600-20166-x (pbk) : £0.85 B82-02840

Messiter, Ian. The impossible quiz book / Ian Messiter ; impossibly illustrated by William Rushton. — London : W.H. Allen, 1980. — 160p : ill ; 18cm. — (A Star book)
ISBN 0-352-30555-x (pbk) : £1.25 B82-11708

Messiter, Ian. The incredible quiz book. — London : Unwin Paperbooks, Dec.1982. — [112]p
ISBN 0-04-793053-5 : £6.75 : CIP entry B82-29865

The **New** Ask the family quiz book. — London : BBC/Knight, Oct.1982. — [96]p
ISBN 0-563-20118-5 (pbk) : £0.95 : CIP entry
ISBN 0-340-32360-4 (Hodder & Stoughton) B82-24023

793.73 — General knowledge — *Questions & answers — For children*

Hollyer, Bellinda. Why, how, when, where?. — London : Ward Lock, Sept.1982. — [240]p
ISBN 0-7063-6212-8 : £5.95 : CIP entry B82-20016

Kilroy, Sally. The young Puffin quiz book / by Sally Kilroy. — Harmondsworth : Puffin, 1982. — 78p : ill ; 20cm. — (A young Puffin original)
ISBN 0-14-031443-1 (pbk) : £0.85 B82-35542

Reed, Simon. Quick quiz / Simon Reed ; illustrations by Harry Hargreaves. — London : Armada, 1981. — 105p : ill ; 18cm
ISBN 0-00-691956-1 (pbk) : £0.85 B82-07929

Taylor, Boswell. Test your child′s general knowledge / Boswell Taylor. — Sevenoaks : Produced exclusively for W.H. Smith by Hodder and Stoughton, 1982. — [32]p ; 25cm
ISBN 0-340-28053-0 (pbk) : £0.60 B82-27677

Whizz kids quiz book / illustrated by Sara Silcock. — London : Macdonald, 1982. — 93p : ill ; 18cm
ISBN 0-356-07838-8 (pbk) : £0.85 B82-37074

Yuile, Pauline. The little red quiz book / compiled by Pauline Yuile. — [Motherwell] : Motherwell District Libraries, [1981?]. — 29p ; 21cm
ISBN 0-903207-10-9 (pbk) : Unpriced B82-12038

793.73 — Jigsaw puzzles, *to 1980*

Hannas, Linda. The jigsaw book. — London : Hutchinson, Oct.1981. — [96]p
ISBN 0-09-145541-3 (pbk) : £7.95 : CIP entry B81-26766

793.73 — Logical puzzles — *Collections*

Bragdon. Diabolical diversions / by Bragdon, Fellows. — London : Muller, 1981. — 128p : ill ; 24cm
Originally published: Garden City : Doubleday, 1980. — Includes index
ISBN 0-584-97070-6 (pbk) : £2.50 : CIP rev. B81-03160

Bryant, Victor, *19---*. The Sunday times book of brain teasers. — London : Unwin Paperbacks
Bk.1: 50 master problems / selected, compiled and edited by Victor Bryant, Ronald Postill. — 1980. — [155]p : ill ; 18cm
ISBN 0-04-793045-4 (pbk) : £1.95 : CIP rev. B80-18455

Francis, Darryl. Puzzles and teasers for everyone / compiled by Darryl Francis ; edited with an introduction by David Pritchard. — Kingswood : Paperfronts, 1974 (1981 [printing]). — 160p : ill ; 19cm
Includes index
ISBN 0-7160-0669-3 (pbk) : £0.75 B82-01801

Pritchard, David, *1919-*. Puzzles and teasers for the easy chair / selected and edited with an introduction by David Pritchard. — Kingswood : Paperfronts, 1975 (1981 [printing]). — 160p : ill ; 19cm
Includes index
ISBN 0-7160-0670-7 (pbk) : £0.75 B82-01800

Serebriakoff, Victor. A Mensa puzzle book : or problems, posers, puzzles and pastimes for the superintelligent / by Victor Serebriakoff. — London : Muller, 1982. — 131p : ill ; 22cm
ISBN 0-584-11020-0 (pbk) : £2.95 : CIP rev. B82-04582

Summers, George J.. Mind teasers : logic puzzles & games of deduction / by George J. Summers ; illustrated by Arthur Friedman. — New York : Stirling ; London : Oak Tree, 1977 (1980 [printing]). — 128p : ill ; 21cm
Includes index
£3.95 B82-25223

793.73 — Palindromes

Pool, Jonathan. Lid off a daffodil. — London : Hutchinson, Oct.1982. — [64]p
ISBN 0-09-146040-9 : £3.95 : CIP entry B82-24962

793.73 — Pictorial puzzles — *Collections*

Myers, Bernard. Mystery pictures. — London : Muller, Feb.1983. — [96]p
ISBN 0-584-11059-6 (pbk) : £1.95 : CIP entry B82-37481

793.73 — Pictorial puzzles — *Collections — For children*

Flash Gordon versus Bloody Brazor and the Metal Men : an action-packed picture puzzle book from the planet Mongo!. — [London] : Beaver Books, 1979. — 80p : all ill ; 18cm. — (Puzzle book ; 2)
ISBN 0-600-37234-0 (pbk) : £0.50 B82-40691

Flash Gordon versus Ming the Merciless : an action-packed picture puzzle book from the planet Mongo!. — [London] : Beaver, 1979. — 80p : all ill ; 18cm. — (Puzzle book ; 1)
ISBN 0-600-37233-2 (pbk) : £0.50 B82-40690

Sagesser, Walter. Puzzles : word games and mazes / Walter Sagesser. — London : Evans, c1982. — 32p : chiefly col.ill ; 22cm. — (Busy books)
ISBN 0-237-45600-1 : £2.25 B82-26260

793.73 — Pictorial puzzles. Special subjects: Ancient Roman armies — *Collections — For children*

Sutton, Harry T.. Museum puzzle-picture book of the Roman Army / [text Harry T. Sutton] ; [illustrations John Green] ; sponsored by the Museums Association. — London : Heritage, 1982. — 16p : col.ill ; 17x22cm
ISBN 0-582-39187-3 (pbk) : £0.65 B82-24057

793.73 — Pictorial puzzles. Special subjects: Ancient Roman civilization — *Collections — For children*

Sutton, Harry T.. Museum puzzle-picture book of life in Roman times / [text Harry T. Sutton] ; [illustrations John Green] ; sponsored by the Museums Association. — London : Heritage, 1982. — 16p : col.ill ; 17x22cm
ISBN 0-582-39188-1 (pbk) : £0.65 B82-24056

793.73 — Pictorial puzzles. Special subjects: Birds. Observation — *Collections — For children*

Sutton, Harry T.. Museum puzzle-picture book of bird spotting : in parks and gardens / [text Harry T. Sutton] ; [illustrations John Green] ; sponsored by the Museums Association. — London : Heritage, 1982. — 16p : ill(some col.) ; 17x22cm
ISBN 0-582-39192-x (pbk) : £0.65 B82-24055

793.73 — Pictorial puzzles. Special subjects: Great Britain. Steam locomotives — *Collections — For children*

Sutton, Harry T.. Museum puzzle-picture book of steam trains / [text Harry T. Sutton] ; [illustrations Peter Gregory] ; sponsored by the Museums Association. — London : Heritage, 1982. — 16p : ill(some col.) ; 17x22cm
ISBN 0-582-39191-1 (pbk) : £0.65 B82-24052

793.73 — Pictorial puzzles. Special subjects: Motoring, *to ca 1930 — Collections — For children*

Sutton, Harry T.. Museum puzzle-picture book of motoring / [text Harry T. Sutton] ; [illustrations Peter Gregory] ; sponsored by the Museums Association. — London : Heritage, 1982. — 16p : col.ill ; 17x22cm
ISBN 0-582-39190-3 (pbk) : £0.65 B82-24053

793.73 — Pictorial puzzles. Special subjects: Seafaring — *Collections — For children*

Sutton, Harry T.. Museum puzzle-picture book of life at sea / [text Harry T. Sutton] ; [illustrations Joseph McEwan] ; sponsored by the Museums Association. — London : Heritage, 1982. — 16p : col.ill ; 17x22cm
ISBN 0-582-39189-x (pbk) : £0.65 B82-24054

793.73 — Puzzles — *Collections*

Brandreth, Gyles. The complete puzzler / Gyles Brandreth. — London : Hale, 1982. — 190p : ill ; 23cm
ISBN 0-7091-9629-6 : £7.50 B82-26983

Brandreth, Gyles. The puzzle mountain / Gyles Brandreth. — Harmondsworth : Penguin, 1981. — 256p : ill ; 26cm
ISBN 0-14-005949-0 (pbk) : £4.95 B82-07298

Bruce, Loretta. A plentitude [i.e. plenitude] of puzzles / Loretta Bruce. — Bognor Regis : New Horizon, c1982. — 243p : ill ; 21cm
ISBN 0-86116-558-6 : £6.25 B82-14555

793.73 — Puzzles — *Collections*
continuation

Eastaway, Robert. Enigmas. — London : Arlington Books, Oct.1982. — [128]p
ISBN 0-85140-594-0 (pbk) : £5.95 : CIP entry B82-23877

Messiter, Ian. Ian Messiter says pick up a pencil : pencil puzzles for everyone / [compiled by David Wells]. — London : Foulsham, c1981. — 64p : ill ; 18cm
ISBN 0-572-00968-2 (pbk) : £0.95 B82-11862

Oddities : in words, pictures and figures. — Reprinted with amendments. — London : Readers Digest Association, 1981. — 48p : ill ; 15cm
Previous ed.: 1975
Unpriced (pbk) B82-05141

Raudsepp, Eugene. Brain stretchers / Eugene Raudsepp. — London : Frederick Muller, 1982, c1980. — 201p : ill ; 20cm
Originally published: New York: Putnams Sons, 1980
ISBN 0-584-11019-7 (pbk) : £2.95 B82-20321

Shaw, Ern. The pocket puzzle pie : a compendium of puzzles, problems, quizzes and brain teasers with solutions / by Ern Shaw. — Hull (39 High St., Hull, N. Humberside) : Bradley, c1977. — 48p : ill ; 19cm
£0.30 (pbk) B82-09376

793.73 — Puzzles — *Collections — For children*

Barnes-Murphy, Rowan. Ghosts, ghouls and bones / Rowan Barnes-Murphy. — [London] : Piccolo, 1982. — 54p : ill ; 20cm. — (The Cryptic library)
ISBN 0-330-26812-0 (pbk) : £0.95 B82-37045

Barnes-Murphy, Rowan. Monstrous mysteries / Rowan Barnes-Murphy. — [London] : Piccolo, 1982. — 54p : ill ; 20cm
ISBN 0-330-26838-4 (pbk) : £0.95 B82-37043

Barnes-Murphy, Rowan. Muddled mummies / Rowan Barnes-Murphy. — [London] : Piccolo, 1982. — 54p : ill ; 20cm. — (The Cryptic library)
ISBN 0-330-26839-2 (pbk) : £0.95 B82-37042

Barnes-Murphy, Rowan. Vexed vampires / Rowan Barnes-Murphy. — [London] : Piccolo, 1982. — 54p : ill ; 20cm. — (The Cryptic library)
ISBN 0-330-26813-9 (pbk) : £0.95 B82-37044

Play school holiday special. — London : Polystyle, c1982. — [48]p : ill(some col.) ; 29cm
£0.50 (unbound) B82-33277

Whizz kids crazy puzzle book / illustrated by Sara Silcock. — London : Macdonald, 1982. — 95p : ill ; 18cm
ISBN 0-356-07837-x (pbk) : £0.85 B82-37075

793.73 — Puzzles: Mazes — *Collections*

Farris, David. Amazing!. — London : Allen & Unwin, Oct.1982. — [96]p
ISBN 0-04-793054-3 (pbk) : £1.50 : CIP entry B82-24368

Wood, Les. Mazes and mandalas / Les Wood. — London : Muller, 1981. — 80p : ill(some col.) ; 22x28cm
ISBN 0-584-10419-7 (pbk) : £3.95 : CIP rev. B81-14458

793.73 — Puzzles: Mazes — *Collections — For children*

Koziakin, Vladimir. Superworld mazes / Vladimir Koziakin. — [London] : Piccolo, 1982. — [96]p : ill ; 18cm. — (A Piccolo original)
ISBN 0-330-26546-6 (pbk) : £0.95 B82-10172

793.73 — Puzzles. Special subjects: Criminal investigation — *Collections — For children*

Butler, William Vivian. The Sherlock Holmes challenge book : 50 opportunities to pit your wits against the greatest detective in the history of the world : based on characters created by Sir Arthur Conan Doyle / W.V. Butler ; illustrated by Marilyn O'Neons. — London : Granada, 1981. — 126p : ill ; 18cm. — (A Dragon book)
ISBN 0-583-30460-5 (pbk) : £0.85 B82-00792

Travis, Falcon. Super sleuth. — London : Hodder & Stoughton, Mar.1982. — [96]p. — (Knight books)
ISBN 0-340-26816-6 (pbk) : £0.85 : CIP entry B82-01095

793.73 — Puzzles. Special subjects: Humberside. Bridlington — *Collections*

The **First** Bridlington holiday fun and quiz book. — [Bridlington] ([28 Auburn Close, Bridlington, East Yorkshire]) : [M. Wilson], c1982. — [24]p : ill,maps ; 22cm
£0.60 (pbk) B82-26481

793.73 — Puzzles. Special subjects: Television programmes — *Serials*

TV puzzletime : incorporating Puzzletime monthly. — Vol.1, no.1 (June 1981) - v.1, no.8 (Jan. 1982). — London (30 Langham St., W1N 5LB) : Atlantic Publishing, 1981-1982. — 8v. : chiefly ill,ports ; 28cm
Monthly. — Continues: Puzzletime monthly. — Continued by: TV puzzletime wordfind. — Description based on: Vol.1, no.4 (Sept. 1981)
£0.40 B82-05233

793.73 — Scrabble — *Manuals*

Brandreth, Gyles. The complete book of scrabble / Gyles Brandreth. — London : Sphere, 1981, c1980. — x,178p : ill ; 18cm
Originally published: London : Hale, 1980
ISBN 0-7221-1860-0 (pbk) : £1.50 B82-02176

793.73 — Word games — *Collections*

Brandreth, Gyles. Wordplay / Gyles Brandreth. — London : Severn House, 1982. — 320p : ill ; 21cm
ISBN 0-7278-2017-6 : £7.95 : CIP rev. B81-24664

Espy, Willard R.. Another almanac of words at play / [compiled by] Willard R. Espy. — London : Deutsch, 1981, c1980. — viii,362p : ill,facsims,music ; 25cm
Originally published: New York : C.N. Potter : distributed by Crown Publishers, 1980. — Includes index
ISBN 0-233-97288-9 (pbk) : £4.95 B82-39075

Parlett, David. The Penguin book of ... word games ... / David Parlett. — Harmondsworth : Penguin, 1982, c1981. — 235p ; 18cm
Bibliography: p230-231. — Includes index
ISBN 0-14-005686-6 (pbk) : £1.50 B82-22091

793.73 — Word puzzles — *Collections*

Doig, Clive. The third book of jigsaw puzzles / Clive Doig ; illustrated by Malcolm Bird. — [London] : Knight, 1981. — 94p : ill,1map,music ; 18cm
ISBN 0-340-27746-7 (pbk) : £0.85 : CIP rev.
ISBN 0-563-20016-2 (BBC) B81-30129

Parsons, Colin. Sunday telegraph puzzle book / compiled by Colin Parsons. — [London] : Sunday Telegraph, 1981. — 128p ; 18cm
ISBN 0-901684-65-1 (pbk) : £1.25 B82-08783

The **wordfinder** puzzlebook 3. — London : Sphere, 1981. — 80,[48]p : ill ; 18cm
ISBN 0-7221-9252-5 (pbk) : £1.00 B82-07077

793.73 — Word puzzles — *Collections — For children*

Doig, Clive. The second book of jigsaw puzzles / Clive Doig ; illustrated by Malcolm Bird. — [London] : Knight, 1981. — 93p : ill ; 18cm
ISBN 0-340-27745-9 (pbk) : £0.85 : CIP rev.
ISBN 0-563-20016-2 (B.B.C.) B81-24617

793.73 — Word puzzles — *Collections — Serials*

Fitword. — Issue 1 (Aug. 1982)-. — London : IPC Magazines, 1982-. — v. : ill ; 25cm
£0.45 B82-32151

793.73'05 — Puzzles — *Collections — For children — Serials*

Oor Wullie Summer fun special. — [No.1]-. — London : D.C. Thomson, c1981-. — v. : chiefly ill ; 25cm
Issued every two years
ISSN 0262-9127 = Oor Wullie Summer fun special : £0.30 B82-12466

Walt Disney's funtime annual. — 1981-1982. — London (70 Old Compton St., W1V 5PA) : London Editions, 1980-1981. — 2v. : chiefly ill ; 28cm
Only two issues published. — Description based on: 1982
£1.95 B82-02381

Walt Disney's puzzle magazine. — No.1-. — [Stockport] ([Regent House, Heaton La., Stockport SK4 1DG]) : [London Editions Magazines], [c1981]-. — v. : chiefly ill ; 30cm
ISSN 0262-2432 = Walt Disney's puzzle magazine : £0.50 per issue B82-06164

793.73'05 — Puzzles — *Collections — Serials*

Popular puzzles. — Vol.4, no.9-. — Horsham (Faygate, Horsham, W. Sussex) : Micron Publications, 1982-. — v. : ill,ports ; 24cm
Monthly. — Continues: Pop puzzles
£0.45 B82-31715

793.73'2 — Crossword puzzles — *Collections*

The **15th** Penguin book of Daily Telegraph crosswords. — Harmondsworth : Penguin, 1979 (1982 [printing]). — 186p ; 18cm. — (Penguin crossword puzzles)
ISBN 0-14-005088-4 (pbk) : £1.35 B82-38096

The **40th** Pan book of crosswords / edited by Mike Grimshaw. — London : Pan, 1981. — 126p ; 18cm
ISBN 0-330-26558-x (pbk) : £0.90 B82-08255

Coronet quick crosswords. — London : Hodder and Stoughton, Mar.1982. — (Coronet books)
Book 5. — [128]p
ISBN 0-340-27903-6 (pbk) : £1.10 : CIP entry B82-00249

Coronet quick crosswords. — London : Hodder and Stoughton, Mar.1982. — (Coronet books)
Book 6. — [128]p
ISBN 0-340-27904-4 (pbk) : £1.10 : CIP entry B82-00250

Daily mail book of crossword puzzles. — London (Carmelite House, Carmelite St., EC4Y 0JA) : Harmsworth Publications for Associated Newspaper Group
Originally published: in the Daily mail
No.14 : Containing 72 quick and 72 cryptic puzzles. — 1981. — [125]p : ill ; 18cm
£0.60 (pbk) B82-01872

Daily mirror crossword book. — London : Mirror Books
66. — 1982. — [128]p ; 18cm
ISBN 0-85939-296-1 (pbk) : £0.95 B82-28015

The **Daily** Telegraph 11th crossword puzzle book. — Harmondsworth : Penguin, 1972 (1982 [printing]). — 222p ; 18cm. — (Penguin crossword puzzles)
ISBN 0-14-003538-9 (pbk) : £1.25 B82-33966

The **Daily** telegraph 14th crossword puzzle book. — Harmondsworth : Penguin, 1978 (1982 [printing]). — 187p ; 18cm. — (Penguin crossword puzzles)
ISBN 0-14-004756-5 (pbk) : £1.10 B82-33529

The **Daily** telegraph 16th crossword puzzle book. — Harmondsworth : Penguin, 1981. — 142p ; 18cm
ISBN 0-14-005873-7 (pbk) : £1.25 B82-08144

793.73′2 — Crossword puzzles — *Collections continuation*

The **Fifth** Penguin book of Sun crosswords. — Harmondsworth : Penguin, 1981. — 142p ; 18cm. — (Penguin crossword puzzles)
ISBN 0-14-006120-7 (pbk) : £0.85 B82-30355

The **Fourth** Penguin book of Sun crosswords. — Harmondsworth : Penguin, 1978 (1982 [printing]). — 187p ; 18cm. — (Penguin crossword puzzles)
ISBN 0-14-004594-5 (pbk) : £0.95 B82-33531

Hall, Barbara, *19---*. The twentieth Fontana book of crosswords / Barbara Hall. — [London] : Fontana, 1981. — 190p ; 18cm
ISBN 0-00-616090-5 (pbk) : £0.95 B82-22562

Henchard, Frank. The twelfth Arrow book of crosswords / compiled by Frank Henchard. — London : Arrow, 1982. — 70,[25]p : ill ; 18cm
ISBN 0-09-927300-4 (pbk) : £1.00 B82-16535

Jewell, Elizabeth. The fifth Penguin book of Sunday Times crosswords / compiled by Elizabeth and Derek Jewell with solvers′ guide by the authors. — Harmondsworth : Penguin, 1980 (1982 [printing]). — 201p ; 18cm
ISBN 0-14-005029-9 (pbk) : £1.25 B82-39085

Jewell, Elizabeth. The fourth Penguin book of Sunday times crosswords / compiled by Elizabeth and Derek Jewell ; with solver′s guide by the authors. — Harmondsworth : Penguin, 1979 (1982 [printing]). — 223p ; 19cm. — (Penguin crossword puzzles)
ISBN 0-14-005013-2 (pbk) : £1.25 B82-37246

Jewell, Elizabeth. The second Penguin book of Sunday Times crosswords / compiled by Elizabeth and Derek Jewell, with solver′s guide by the authors. — Harmondsworth : Penguin, 1976 (1982 [printing]). — 223p : ill ; 18cm. — (Penguin crossword puzzles)
ISBN 0-14-004160-5 (pbk) : £1.25 B82-29670

Jewell, Elizabeth. The sixth Penguin book of Sunday Times crosswords / compiled by Elizabeth and Derek Jewell, and ′Set-square′, with solver′s guide by Elizabeth and Derek Jewell. — Harmondsworth : Penguin, 1981. — 176p ; 18cm. — (Penguin crossword puzzles)
ISBN 0-14-005556-8 (pbk) : £1.25 B82-08034

Jewell, Elizabeth. The third Penguin book of Sunday Times crosswords / compiled by Elizabeth and Derek Jewell, with solver′s guide by the authors. — Harmondsworth : Penguin, 1978 (1982 [printing]). — 223p : ill ; 18cm. — (Penguin crossword puzzles)
ISBN 0-14-004755-7 (pbk) : £1.25 B82-29671

Murphy, Peter. Peter Murphy′s international quizbook. — Dublin : Able Press, 1981. — 112p : ill,ports ; 21cm
ISBN 0-906281-02-4 (pbk) : £1.72 B82-09897

The **Penguin** book of Sun crosswords. — Harmondsworth : Penguin, 1974 (1982 [printing]). — 187p ; 18cm
ISBN 0-14-003772-1 (pbk) : £0.95 B82-30352

The **second** Penguin book of Sun crosswords. — Harmondsworth : Penguin, 1975 (1982 [printing]). — 186p ; 18cm. — (Penguin crossword puzzles)
ISBN 0-14-004050-1 (pbk) : £0.95 B82-33530

The **Sixth** Penguin book of Sun crosswords. — Harmondsworth : Penguin, 1982. — 142p ; 19cm. — (Penguin crossword puzzles)
ISBN 0-14-006121-5 (pbk) : £0.80 B82-36225

The **Sunday** express book of prize crosswords. — London : Sphere
3. — 1982. — 92p : ill ; 18cm
ISBN 0-7221-8265-1 (pbk) : £1.25 B82-29499

The **Sunday** express book of prize crosswords 4. — London : Sphere, 1982. — 92p ; 18cm
ISBN 0-7221-8264-3 (pbk) : £1.25 B82-36966

The **Sunday** mirror ′quickie′ crossword book. — London : Mirror
4. — 1981. — [116p] ; 18cm
ISBN 0-85939-272-4 (pbk) : £0.95 B82-01896

The **Third** Penguin book of Sun crosswords. — Harmondsworth : Penguin, 1977 (1981 [printing]). — 187p ; 18cm
With answers
ISBN 0-14-004226-1 (pbk) : £0.85 B82-20320

793.73′2 — Crossword puzzles — *Collections — For children*

Brown, David, *1950-*. A first book of easy English crosswords / by David and Rosemary Brown ; illustrated by Che Kamsiah Mohamood. — London : Macmillan, 1981. — 23p : ill ; 21cm
ISBN 0-333-32265-7 (pbk) : Unpriced B82-40527

Curl, Michael. The seventeenth Armada crossword book / compiled by Michael Curl. — London : Armada, 1981. — [125]p : ill ; 18cm
ISBN 0-00-691985-5 (pbk) : £0.85 B82-07930

Whizz kids crazy crossword book / illustrated by David Knight. — London : Macdonald, 1982. — 95p : ill ; 18cm
ISBN 0-356-07835-3 (pbk) : £0.85 B82-35470

793.73′2 — Crossword puzzles. Composition & solution — *Manuals*

Kurzban, Stanley A.. The compleat cruciverbalist : how to solve, compose and sell crossword puzzles / Stan Kurzban and Mel Rosen. — New York ; London : Barnes & Noble, c1981. — xvi,167p : ill ; 21cm
Originally published: New York : Van Nostrand Reinhold, 1980
ISBN 0-06-463544-9 (corrected : pbk) : Unpriced B82-17801

793.73′2 — Crossword puzzles. Solution — *Manuals*

Abbott, May. How to do crosswords / May Abbott. — New ed. — Glasgow : Collins, 1982. — 167p : ill ; 20cm
Previous ed.: published as The crossword solver′s guide. 1975
ISBN 0-00-434163-5 (pbk) : £1.95 B82-18886

Robins, Alec. [Crosswords]. The ABC of crosswords / Alec Robins. — Harmondsworth : Penguin, 1981, c1975. — 318p ; 18cm
Originally published: London : Teach Yourself Books, 1975. — Includes index
ISBN 0-552-11843-5 (pbk) : £1.75 B82-08148

793.73′2 — Crossword puzzles. Special subjects: Bible — *Collections — For children*

Crewe, E. G.. Junior Bible crosswords / E.G. Crewe. — Ilkeston : Moorley′s Bible & Bookshop, [1981]. — 51p : ill ; 21cm
ISBN 0-86071-105-6 (pbk) : £0.65 B82-05568

793.73′2 — Crossword puzzles. Special subjects: Cinema films — *Collections*

Smith, Ted. Movie crosswords / Ted Smith. — [London] : T. Smith
[Book 1]. — 1982. — 120p ; 21cm
ISBN 0-906726-01-8 (pbk) : £2.00 B82-26672

793.73′2 — Crossword puzzles. Special subjects: Fiction in English. Christie, Agatha — *Collections*

Toye, Randall. The Agatha Christie crossword puzzle book / compiled by Randall Toye and Judith Hawkins Gaffney. — London : Angus & Robertson, 1981. — 131p ; 22cm
ISBN 0-207-14529-6 (pbk) : £2.95 B82-18290

793.73′2 — Crossword puzzles. Special subjects: Islam — *Collections — For children*

Gamiet, Arshad. Muslim cross word puzzles / author Arshad Gamiet. — Leicester : Islamic Foundation, 1981. — [24]p ; 21cm. — (Muslim children′s library)
Cover title
ISBN 0-86037-102-6 (pbk) : Unpriced B82-11929

793.73′2 — Crossword puzzles. Special subjects: Television programmes — *Collections*

Smith, Ted. TV crosswords / Ted Smith. — [London] : T. Smith
[Book 1]. — 1982. — 44p ; 21cm
ISBN 0-906726-02-6 (pbk) : £2.00 B82-26671

793.73′2 — English language. Anagrams — *Lists — For crossword puzzles*

Curl, Michael. The anagram dictionary / by Michael Curl. — London : Hale, 1982. — 248p ; 21cm
ISBN 0-7091-9674-1 : £7.95 B82-24785

Hunter, Samuel C.. Dictionary of anagrams / Samuel C. Hunter. — London : Routledge & Kegan Paul, 1982. — viii,267p ; 23cm
ISBN 0-7100-9006-4 : £6.95 B82-23813

793.73′2 — English language. Words — *Lists — For crossword puzzles*

Pocket crossword decoder. — Harlow : Longman, 1982. — 270p ; 12cm. — (Longman top pocket series)
ISBN 0-582-55547-7 (pbk) : £0.75 B82-29197

793.73′2 — English language. Words — *Lists — For word games*

Dunn, John. John Dunn′s curious collection. — London : Muller, Sept.1982. — [96]p
ISBN 0-584-95030-6 : £6.50 : CIP entry B82-19811

793.73′2′05 — Crossword puzzles — *Collections — Serials*

Daily Mirror crosswords. — Vol.1, no.1 (1982)-. — London : Mirror Books, 1982-. — v. : ill ; 20cm
Monthly
ISSN 0262-2912 = Daily Mirror crosswords : £3.50 B82-29046

Weekend crossword puzzles book. — No.1-. — London : Published by Harmsworth Publications for Associated Newspapers Group, 1981-. — v. : ill ; 18cm
£0.60 B82-32175

793.73′5 — Children′s riddles in English. American writers, *1945-*. Special subjects: Pets — *Anthologies*

Rosenbloom, Joseph. Ridiculous Nicholas pet riddles / by Joseph Rosenbloom ; drawings by Joyce Behr. — New York : Sterling ; London : Oak Tree, c1981. — [68]p : col.ill ; 22cm
ISBN 0-7061-2815-x : £3.95 B82-22248

793.73′5 — Children′s riddles in English — *Texts*

Crossley-Holland, Kevin. The riddle book. — London : Macmillan′s Children′s Books, Oct.1982. — [128]p
ISBN 0-333-33008-0 : £3.95 : CIP entry B82-24806

Rosenbloom, Joseph. Ridiculous Nicholas riddle book / by Joseph Rosenbloom ; drawings by Joyce Behr. — New York ; Sterling ; London : Oak Tree, c1981. — 64p : col.ill ; 22cm
ISBN 0-7061-2816-8 : £3.95 B82-20230

793.73′5 — Riddles in English — *Anthologies — For children*

Cole, William, *1919-*. Do you give up? / William Cole and Mike Thaler. — London : Granada, 1981, c1979. — [64]p : ill ; 20cm. — (A Dragon book)
Originally published: London : Watts, 1979
ISBN 0-583-30492-3 (pbk) : £0.75 B82-11160

Thaler, Mike. Never tickle a turtle : cartoons, riddles and funny stories / Mike Thaler. — London : Granada, 1981, c1979. — [64]p : ill ; 20cm
Originally published: London : Watts, 1979
ISBN 0-583-30493-1 (pbk) : £0.75 B82-11161

793.7′4 — Games for children: Number games — *Collections*

Hussey, Mike. Counting games for kids / Mike Hussey. — London : Ward Lock, 1982. — 64p : ill ; 32x13cm
ISBN 0-7063-6186-5 (pbk) : £0.99 : CIP rev. B82-13008

793.7′4 — Magic squares
Subhedar, V. L.. Metamagix, or, The algebra, geometry and optics of magic squares / V.L. Subhedar. — Ipswich ([43 Radcliffe Drive, Ipswich, IP2 9QZ]) : Vatsayana, 1981. — 21p : ill ; 21cm
Cover title. — Text on inside covers. — Bibliography: on inside cover
Unpriced (pbk) B82-02544

793.7′4 — Mathematical puzzles — *Collections*
Berlekamp, E. R.. Winning ways. — London : Academic Press, Sept.1981
Vol.1. — [400]p
ISBN 0-12-091101-9 (pbk) : CIP entry B81-21635

Berlekamp, Elwyn R.. Winning ways : for your mathematical plays / Elwyn R. Berlekamp, John H. Conway, Richard K. Guy. — London : Academic Press, 1982. — 2v.(xxxi,850,xip) : ill(some col.) ; 26cm
Includes bibliographies and index
ISBN 0-12-091150-7 : Unpriced : CIP rev.
ISBN 0-12-091152-3 (v.2) : £31.40 B81-21636

Gardner, Martin. Mathematical circus : more games, puzzles, paradoxes, and other mathematical entertainments from Scientific American ... / Martin Gardner. — Harmondsworth : Penguin, 1981, c1979. — xiii,272p : ill ; 20cm
Originally published: New York : Knopf, 1979 ; London : Allen Lane, 1981. — Bibliography: p263-272
ISBN 0-14-022355-x (pbk) : £1.95 B82-08147

Wells, D. G.. Can you solve these? : mathematical problems to test your thinking powers / [David Wells]. — Stadbroke : Tarquin, c1982. — 78p : ill ; 18cm. — (David Wells series ; no.1)
ISBN 0-906212-22-7 (pbk) : £1.60 B82-40402

793.7′4 — Mathematical puzzles — *Collections — For schools*
Bolt, Brian. Mathematical activities : a resource book for teachers / Brian Bolt. — Cambridge : Cambridge University Press, 1982. — xii,207p : ill ; 25cm
Bibliography: p205-206
ISBN 0-521-28518-6 (pbk) : Unpriced : CIP rev. B82-03617

793.7′4 — Mathematical puzzles using pocket electronic calculators — *Collections*
Rothery, Andrew. Calculator puzzles / Andrew Rothery ; [illustrated by Nigel Paige]. — London : Harrap, 1981. — 47p : ill ; 18cm
ISBN 0-245-53722-8 (pbk) : £1.50 B82-01890

793.7′4 — Number puzzles — *Collections*
Chester, Joyce. Make it count puzzles : linked to the Yorkshire Television series Make it count / by Joyce Chester and Peter Avis. — Cambridge : National Extension College, 1977 (1981 [printing]). — 65p : ill ; 21cm
ISBN 0-86082-102-1 (pbk) : Unpriced B82-70275

Smith, Frank, *1913-*. Ian Messiter says what's the number? / [compiled by Frank Smith]. — London : Foulsham, c1982. — 63p : ill ; 18cm
ISBN 0-572-01149-0 (pbk) : £0.95 B82-37188

793.7′4 — Pyraminx. Solution
Werneck, Tom. Mastering the magic pyramid : the secrets of the Pyraminx unlocked / Tom Werneck. — London : Evans Brothers, 1981. — 112p : ill(some col.) ; 18cm
Translation from the German
ISBN 0-237-45591-9 (pbk) : £1.50 B82-10719

793.7′4 — Rubik's cube. Games — *Collections*
Taylor, Don, *1945-*. Cube games : 92 classic games, puzzles and solutions / Don Taylor and Leanne Rylands. — Harmondsworth : Penguin, 1981. — 49p : ill(some col.) ; 22cm
ISBN 0-14-006207-6 (pbk) : £1.75 B82-10135

793.7′4 — Rubik's cube — *Humour*
Bindweed, W. C.. Not another cube book! / W.C. Bindweed, David Godwin and Mahood. — London : Pan, 1981. — 93p : ill ; 12cm
ISBN 0-330-26778-7 (pbk) : £0.95 B82-08250

793.7′4 — Rubik's cube — *Serials*
Cubic circular : a quarterly newsletter for Rubik cube addicts. — Issue 1 (Autumn 1981)-. — London (66 Mount View Rd, N4 4JR) : David Singmaster Ltd., 1981-. — v. : ill ; 20cm
ISSN 0261-8362 = Cubic circular : Unpriced B82-15156

793.7′4 — Rubik's cube. Solution
Edd, *Mr.*. The simple way to cube / Mr. Edd. — Coldstream (Commercial Inn, Coldstream, Berwickshire, Scotland) : Edward Park, c1981. — 28p : ill,1port ; 21cm
Cover title
Unpriced (pbk) B82-19584

793.7′4 — Rubik's cube. Solution. Mathematical techniques
Frey, Alexander H.. Handbook of cubik math / by Alexander H. Frey and David Singmaster. — Hillside, N.J. : Enslow ; Guildford : Lutterworth, c1982. — viii,193p : ill ; 24cm
Includes index
ISBN 0-89490-060-9 (cased) : Unpriced
ISBN 0-89490-058-7 (pbk) : £5.95 B82-36393

Singmaster, David. Notes on Rubik's magic cube / David Singmaster. — 5th ed. — Harmondsworth : Penguin, 1981, c1980. — iv,60,[8]p : ill ; 21cm
Previous ed.: London : D. Singmaster, 1980?. — Bibliography: pB1-2. — Includes index
ISBN 0-14-006149-5 (pbk) : £1.95 B82-00088

793.7′4 — Rubik's snake — *Manuals*
Fiore, Albie. Shaping Rubik's snake / Albie Fiore. — Harmondsworth : Penguin, 1981. — 127p : ill ; 12cm
ISBN 0-14-006181-9 (pbk) : £0.95 B82-04691

793.8 — Conjuring — *Amateurs' manuals*
Barry, Sheila Anne. Super-colossal book of puzzles tricks and games / Sheila Anne Barry ; illustrated by Doug Anderson. — New York : Sterling ; London : Oak Tree, c1978 (1979 [printing]). — 640p : ill ; 25cm
ISBN 0-7061-2590-8 : £10.95
ISBN 0-8069-4581-8 (U.S.)
Primary classification 790 B82-25232

Fulves, Karl. Self-working table magic : 97 foolproof tricks with everyday objects / Karl Fulves ; with illustrations by Joseph K. Schmidt. — New York : Dover ; London : Constable, 1981. — vi,122p : ill ; 22cm
ISBN 0-486-24116-5 (pbk) : £1.90 B82-05277

Sellers, Tom. Supreme present — Three for magicians only / by Tom Sellers. — Bideford (64 High St., Bideford, Devon) : Supreme Magic, c1982. — 6p : ill ; 25cm
Contents: Five ace Alex — The Magician's count — A baffling ring off string
Unpriced (unbound) B82-29906

793.8 — Conjuring — *Amateurs' manuals — For children*
Bongo, Ali. Ali Bongo's book of magic / illustrated by Geoffrey Campion. — London : Macdonald, 1981. — 92p : ill(some col.) ; 27cm. — (A Whizz kids special)
Includes index
ISBN 0-356-06400-x : £3.50 B82-00113

Daniels, Paul. More magic / Paul Daniels ; illustrated by Roger Walker. — London : Piccolo, 1981. — 75p : ill ; 18cm. — (A Piccolo original)
Includes index
ISBN 0-330-26627-6 (pbk) : £0.85 B82-04256

793.8 — Conjuring. Use of human body
Fisher, John. Body magic. — London : Hodder & Stoughton, Nov.1981. — [192]p
Originally published: 1979
ISBN 0-340-27109-4 (pbk) : £1.50 : CIP entry B81-30143

793.8 — Floating ball tricks — *Manuals*
Supreme Magic present Orb of the orient : Okito — Fu Manchu — Mohammed Bey, the perfect no-assistant one-man floating ball : a Supreme Exclusive routine by arrangement with Harry Stanley's Magic Studio. — [Bideford] ([64 High St., Bideford, Devon]) : [Supreme Magic], c1982. — [6]p : ill ; 26cm
Unpriced (unbound) B82-29910

793.8 — Rope tricks — *Manuals*
Panama plus : a trilogy of rope mysteries. — Bideford (64 High St., Bideford, Devon) : Supreme Magic, c1982. — 7p : ill ; 26cm
Unpriced (unbound) B82-29903

Supreme magic present — Stretching a rope plus. — Bideford (64 High St., Bideford, Devon) : Supreme Magic, c1982. — 7p : ill ; 26cm
Unpriced (unbound) B82-29905

793.8 — Tricks using paper — *Manuals*
Fogel, Maurice. Fogel's headline hunter. — [Bideford] ([64 High St., Bideford, Devon]) : [Supreme Magic], c1982. — [6]p : ill ; 26cm
Unpriced (unbound) B82-29911

Supreme magic present — Tearing them up. — Bideford (64 High St., Bideford, Devon) : Supreme Magic, c1982. — 8p : ill ; 26cm
Unpriced (unbound) B82-29907

793.8 — Tricks using tumblers — *Manuals*
Sterling, Harold. No bottoms : (50 tricks with a bottomless tumbler) / Harold Sterling. — Bideford (64 High St., Bideford, Devon) : Supreme Magic, c1982. — 8p ; 26cm
Unpriced (unbound) B82-29904

793.8 — Ventriloquism, *to 1980*
Vox, Valentine. I can see your lips moving : the history and art of ventriloquism / by Valentine Vox. — Tadworth : Kaye & Ward, 1981. — 171p : ill(some col.),facsims,ports(some col.) ; 26cm
Facsims on lining papers. — Bibliography: p170-171. — Includes index
ISBN 0-7182-5870-3 : £12.50 B82-10166

793′.9 — Fantasy role-playing games
Galloway, Bruce. Fantasy wargaming. — Cambridge : Stephens, Nov.1981. — [200]p
ISBN 0-85059-465-0 : £9.95 : CIP entry B81-30581

Holmes, John Eric. Fantasy role playing games : dungeons, dragons, and adventures in fantasy gaming / John Eric Holmes. — London : Arms and Armour, c1981. — 224p : ill,plans ; 24cm
ISBN 0-85368-158-9 : £7.50 B82-02826

Livingstone, Ian. Dicing with dragons. — London : Routledge & Kegan Paul, Sept.1982. — 1v.
ISBN 0-7100-9466-3 (pbk) : £2.95 : CIP entry B82-27193

793′.9 — Proprietary board war games — *Manuals*
Palmer, Nicholas. The comprehensive guide to board wargaming / Nicholas Palmer. — London : Sphere, 1980, c1977. — 223p : ill,maps ; 24cm
Originally published: London : Arthur Barker, 1977
ISBN 0-7221-6667-2 (pbk) : £3.95 B82-20555

793′.9 — War games based on Napoleonic Wars — *Manuals*
Quarrie, Bruce. Napoleon's campaigns on miniature. — 2nd ed. — Cambridge : Patrick Stephens, Sept.1982. — [192]p
Previous ed.: 1977
ISBN 0-85059-606-8 : £8.95 : CIP entry B82-20492

793′.9 — War games — *Rules*
War games rules 3000 BC to 1485 AD. — [6th ed.]. — [Goring by Sea] ([75, Ardingly Drive, Goring by Sea, Sussex]) : Wargames Research Group, 1980. — 56p ; 24cm
One quick reference sheet as insert. — Previous ed: 197-?
Unpriced (pbk) B82-21307

793′.9 — War games. Simulations. Applications of digital computer systems — *Serials*
The **War** machine. — Issue 1 (July/Aug 1981)-. — Nottingham (17 Langbank Ave., Rise Park, Nottingham NG5 5BU) : The War Machine, 1981-. — v. : ill ; 30cm
Monthly
ISSN 0263-905X = War machine : £13.00 per year B82-38538

794 — INDOOR GAMES OF SKILL

794 — Board games — *Collections*
Bell, R. C.. The boardgame book / R.C. Bell. — London : Marshall Cavendish, 1979. — 160p : ill(some col.),ports ; 34cm
In slip case. — Eight map games and pieces (5 folded sheets) as insert. — Bibliography: p156. — Includes index
ISBN 0-85685-447-6 : £14.95 B82-00787

794 — Board games — *Collections* — *For children*
Campbell, Rod. Rod Campbell's book of board games. — London : Abelard-Schuman, Sept.1982. — [12]p
ISBN 0-200-72794-x : £2.95 : CIP entry B82-28444

794 — Computer games & video games
Blumenthal, Howard J.. The complete guide to electronic games / Howard J. Blumenthal with Sharon Blumenthal. — London : Sphere, 1982, c1981. — 214p ; 18cm
Originally published: New York : New American Library, 1981
ISBN 0-7221-1762-0 (pbk) : £1.75 B82-29176

Kubey, Craig. The winners' book of video games / Craig Kubey. — London : W.H. Allen, 1982. — xviii,270p : ill ; 20cm. — (A Star book)
ISBN 0-352-31205-x (pbk) : £2.50 B82-39019

794 — Computer games. Applications of Apple microcomputer systems. Programming languages: Pascal language
Hergert, Douglas. Apple Pascal games / Douglas Hergert and Joseph T. Kalash. — Berkeley, Calif. : Sybex ; Birmingham : the Computer Bookshop [distributor], 1981. — xiii,371p : ill ; 22cm
ISBN 0-89588-074-1 (pbk) : Unpriced B82-27393

794 — Computer games. Applications of digital computer systems. Programming languages: Basic language
Mateosian, Richard. Inside BASIC games / Richard Mateosian. — [Berkeley, Calif.] : Sybex ; Birmingham : Computer Bookshop [[distributor]], 1981. — xx,325p : ill ; 23cm
Includes index
ISBN 0-89588-055-5 (pbk) : Unpriced B82-27624

794 — Computer games. Applications of Rockwell 6502 microcomputer systems. Programming
Zaks, Rodnay. 6502 games / Rodnay Zaks. — Berkeley, Calif. : Sybex ; Birmingham : the Computer Bookshop [distributor], c1980. — x,292p : ill,facsims ; 22cm. — (6502 series ; v.4)
Includes index
ISBN 0-89588-022-9 (pbk) : Unpriced B82-27392

794 — Pac-Man — *Manuals*
How to win at Pac-Man / by the editors of Consumer Guide. — Harmondsworth : Penguin, 1982. — 32p : col.ill ; 18cm
ISBN 0-14-006542-3 (pbk) : £0.95 B82-35805

Uston, Ken. Mastering Pac-Man / Ken Uston. — London : Futura, 1982, c1981. — 127p : ill ; 18cm
ISBN 0-7088-2216-9 (pbk) : £1.10 B82-35806

794′.05 — Computer games & video games — *Serials*
Computer & video games. — No.1 (Nov. 1981)-. — Peterborough (Bretton Court, Bretton, Peterborough PE3 8D2) : EMAP National Publications, 1981-. — v. : ill(some col.) ; 30cm
Monthly
ISSN 0261-3697 = Computer & video games : £10.00 per year B82-09080

794.1 — CHESS

794.1 — Chess
Bronstein, D.. Chess in the eighties. — Oxford : Pergamon, May 1982. — [112]p. — (Pergamon Russian chess series)
Translation of: Prekrasnyi i yarostnyi mir
ISBN 0-08-024126-3 : £6.50 : CIP entry B82-07240

Evans, Larry. The chess beat / by Larry Evans. — Oxford : Pergamon, 1982. — x,105p : ill ; 30cm. — (Pergamon chess series)
Includes index
ISBN 0-08-026926-5 (cased) : Unpriced : CIP rev.
ISBN 0-08-026925-7 (pbk) : £5.95 B82-05372

794.1 — Chess. Problems — *Collections*
Larsen, Bent. Bent Larsen's good move guide / translated from the original Danish by Lene Knudsen and Ken Whyld. — Oxford : Oxford University Press, 1982. — 136p : ill ; 21cm. — (Oxford chess books)
Translation of: Shak skole
ISBN 0-19-217593-9 (pbk) : £4.95 : CIP rev. B81-25796

Russ, Colin. Miniature chess problems from many countries : 400 compositions with solutions and comments / Colin Russ. — London : Heinemann, c1981. — x,262p : ill ; 22cm
Bibliography: p254-255. — Includes index
ISBN 0-434-65850-2 : £8.50 B82-12876

794.1′06′04259 — Buckinghamshire. Chess. Organisations: Buckinghamshire County Chess Association, *to 1982*
Buckinghamshire County Chess Association. A history of the Buckinghamshire County Chess Association, 1932-1982 / compiled by A.J. Cox. — [High Wycombe?] : The Association, [1982]. — 20p ; 30cm
Cover title
Unpriced (pbk) B82-38943

794.1′076 — Chess — *Questions & answers*
Livshitz, A.. Test your chess IQ / by A. Livshitz ; translated and edited by Kenneth P. Neat. — Oxford : Pergamon. — (Pergamon Russian chess series)
Book 2. — 1981. — v,233p : ill ; 26cm
Translation from the Russian. — Includes index
ISBN 0-08-026881-1 (cased) : Unpriced : CIP rev.
ISBN 0-08-026880-3 (pbk) : £6.50 B81-30971

794.1′09 — Chess, *to 1978*
A **Picture** history of chess / edited by Fred Wilson. — New York : Dover Publications ; London : Constable, 1981. — 182p : ill,facsims,ports ; 29cm. — (Dover books on chess)
Includes index
ISBN 0-486-23856-3 (pbk) : £6.75 B82-08958

794.1′092′2 — Chess. Championships: World Chess Championship. Winners, *to 1979*
World chess champions / edited by E.G. Winter. — Oxford : Pergamon, 1981. — xiv,185p,[8] of plates : ill,ports ; 26cm. — (Pergamon chess series)
Bibliography: p170-174. — Includes index
ISBN 0-08-024094-1 (cased) : Unpriced : CIP rev.
ISBN 0-08-024117-4 (pbk) : £5.50 B80-27435

794.1′2 — Chess. Combinations — *Manuals*
Neishtadt, ÎÂkov. Test your tactical ability / Yakov Neishtadt ; translated by Mark Sawko. — London : Batsford, 1981. — 210p : ill ; 22cm. — (A Batsford chess book)
Translation from the Russian
ISBN 0-7134-4013-9 (pbk) : £5.95 B82-22269

794.1′2 — Chess — *Manuals*
Abrahams, Gerald. The Pan book of chess / Gerald Abrahams. — London : Pan, 1966 (1981 [printing]). — 287p : ill ; 17cm
Previous ed.: 1965
ISBN 0-330-23073-5 (pbk) : £1.50 B82-00394

Harding, T. D.. Why you lose at chess / Tim Harding with contributions by Cenek Kottnauer, George Botterill, Bob Wade. — London : Batsford, 1982. — vi,120p : ill ; 22cm. — (A Batsford chess book)
Bibliography: pvi
ISBN 0-7134-2760-4 (pbk) : £4.95 B82-22267

Harston, William. Play chess. — London : Hodder & Stoughton. — (Knight books)
2. — Dec.1981. — [96]p
ISBN 0-340-27822-6 (pbk) : £0.95 : CIP entry B81-31372

Keene, Raymond. Ray Keene's good move guide / Raymond Keene and Andrew Whiteley. — Oxford : Oxford University Press, 1982. — 141p : ill ; 21cm. — (Oxford chess books)
ISBN 0-19-217582-3 (pbk) : £4.95 : CIP rev. B82-07499

Pandolfini, Bruce. Let's play chess : a step-by-step guide for beginners / Bruce Pandolfini. — London : Hamlyn, c1982. — 193p : ill ; 22cm
Includes index
ISBN 0-600-36666-9 : £2.50 B82-34852

Sokol′skiĭ, A. P.. Your first move : chess for beginners / Alexei Sokolsky. — Moscow : Progress ; [London] : Distributed by Central, c1981. — 296p : ill ; 19cm
Translation of: Vash pervyĭ khod
ISBN 0-7147-1736-3 : £2.50 B82-29283

Suetin, A. S.. Three steps to chess mastery / by A.S. Suetin ; translated by Kenneth P. Neat. — Oxford : Pergamon, 1982. — ix,192p : ill ; 25cm. — (Pergamon Russian chess series)
Translation from the Russian. — Includes index
ISBN 0-08-024139-5 (cased) : Unpriced : CIP rev.
ISBN 0-08-024138-7 (pbk) : £5.95 B81-34508

Taulbut, Shaun. Positional chess. — London : Allen & Unwin, Jan.1983. — [176]p
ISBN 0-04-794017-4 : £8.95 : CIP entry B82-33600

794.1′2 — Chess — *Manuals* — *For children*
Hartston, William R.. Play chess 2 / William Hartston & Jeremy James. — London : British Broadcasting Corporation, c1981. — 94p : ill ; 20cm
ISBN 0-563-20031-6 : £4.95 B82-08639

794.1′2 — Chess. Sacrifices — *Manuals*
Shamkovich, Leonid. The modern chess sacrifice / Leonid Shamkovich. — London : Batsford, 1980. — xi,225p : ill ; 22cm. — (Batsford chess books)
Originally published: New York : McKay, 1978. — Includes index
ISBN 0-7134-2498-2 (cased) : Unpriced
ISBN 0-7134-2499-0 (pbk) : £4.50 B82-08647

794.1′22 — Chess. Openings: Alekh′in′s Defence — *Manuals*
Hort, Vlastimil. Alekhine's defence / Vlastimil Hort ; with additional material on Owen's defence and Nimzovich defence by Raymond Keene. — London : A. & C. Black, 1981. — 256p : ill ; 22cm
ISBN 0-7136-2205-9 (pbk) : £6.95 : CIP rev. B81-35830

794.1′22 — Chess. Openings: Caro-Kahn Defence — *Manuals*
Varnusz, Egon. Play the Caro-Kann. — Oxford : Pergamon, June 1982. — [175]p. — (Pergamon chess openings)
ISBN 0-08-024130-1 : £6.95 : CIP entry B82-10591

794.1'22 — Chess. Openings — *Collections*

Enciklopedija šahovskih otvaranja = Entsiklopediia shakhmatnykh debiutov = Encyclopaedia of chess openings = Enzyklopädie der Schach-Eröffnungen = Encyclopedie des ouvertures d'echecs = Enciklopedia de aperturas de ajedrez = Enciclopedia delle aperture negli scacchi = Encyklopedi över spelöppningar i schack / [editor-in-chief Aleksandar Matanović]. — London : Batsford
C: 1.e4 e6, 1.e4 e5. — New ed. — 1981. — 487p : ill ; 25cm
Previous ed.: 1974
ISBN 0-7134-2697-7 : £19.95

794.1'22 — Chess. Openings: English Opening — *Manuals*

Levy, D. N. L.. The English Opening : a quantitative analysis of the opening / [from the program conceived by David Levy, Kevin O'Connell and David Watt]. — London : Imprint Capablanca, c1981. — xv,114p : ill ; 29cm
Includes index
ISBN 0-907352-01-4 : Unpriced B82-38774

794.1'22 — Chess. Openings: Four Knights — *Manuals*

Povah, Nigel. English: Four Knights : I c4 e5 2 [N]c3 [N]f6 3 [N]f3 [N]c6 / Nigel Povah. — London : Batsford, 1982. — vii,184p : ill ; 22cm. — (Batsford library of tournament openings) (A Batsford chess book)
ISBN 0-7134-0669-0 (pbk) : £7.95 B82-22268

794.1'22 — Chess. Openings: Grünfeld Defence. Exchange Variation — *Manuals*

Pein, Malcolm. Grünfeld defence : exchange variation ... / Malcolm Pein. — London : Batsford, 1981. — 140p : ill ; 22cm. — (A Batsford chess book) (The Batsford library of tournament openings)
Includes index
ISBN 0-7134-3594-1 (pbk) : £6.95 B82-03558

794.1'22 — Chess. Openings: Grünfeld Defence — *Manuals*

Botvinnik, M. M.. The Gruenfeld defence / Mikhail Botvinnik, Yakov Estrin. — New York : R.H.M. ; London : Pitman House, c1980. — xvii,371p : ill ; 21cm
ISBN 0-273-01490-0 (pbk) : £5.25 B82-28811

794.1'22 — Chess. Openings: King's Gambit — *Manuals*

Estrin, Y. B.. Play the King's Gambit. — Oxford : Pergamon, July 1982. — (Pergamon chess openings)
Translation of: Korolevskiĭ gambit
Vol.1: King's Gambit accepted. — [200]p
ISBN 0-08-026873-0 (cased) : £12.00 : CIP entry
ISBN 0-08-026872-2 (pbk) : £6.00 B82-12413

Estrin, Y. B.. Play the King's Gambit. — Oxford : Pergamon, July 1982. — (Pergamon chess openings)
Translation of: Korolevskiĭ gambit
Vol.2: King's Gambit declined. — [130]p
ISBN 0-08-026875-7 (cased) : £9.00 : CIP entry
ISBN 0-08-026874-9 (pbk) : £5.90 B82-12414

794.1'22 — Chess. Openings: King's Indian Defence — *Manuals*

Levy, D. N. L.. The King's Indian : a quantitative analysis of the opening / [from the program conceived by David Levy, Kevin O'Connell, and David Watt]. — London : Imprint Capablanca, c1981. — xv,95p : ill ; 29cm
Includes index
ISBN 0-907352-02-2 : Unpriced B82-38775

794.1'22 — Chess. Openings — *Manuals*

Assiac. Opening preparation / by Assiac and O'Connell. — Oxford : Pergamon, 1982. — v,161p : ill ; 21cm
Includes index
ISBN 0-08-024095-x (cased) : Unpriced : CIP rev.
ISBN 0-08-024096-8 (pbk) : £4.50 B81-28844

Estrin, ĨA. Comprehensive chess openings / by Y. Estrin and V.N. Panov ; translated by Kenneth P. Neat and Heri-Bert Steimel. — Oxford : Pergamon, 1980. — 3v. : ill ; 21cm. — (Pergamon-Russian chess series)
Translation of: Kurs debiutov. 5e. perera b. l dop. izd. — Includes index
ISBN 0-08-024114-x (cased) : £25.00 : the set : CIP rev.
ISBN 0-08-024113-1 (set : pbk) : £15.00
ISBN 0-08-023103-9 (v.1) : £9.00
ISBN 0-08-023102-0 (v.1 : pbk) : £5.95
ISBN 0-08-024110-7 (v.2) : £8.00
ISBN 0-08-024109-3 (v.2 : pbk) : £4.95
ISBN 0-08-024112-3 (v.3) : £9.00
ISBN 0-08-024111-5 (v.3 : pbk) : £5.95
B79-31944

Keene, Raymond. Dynamic chess openings / Raymond Keene. — London : Batsford, 1982. — 88p : ill ; 22cm. — (A Batsford chess book) (The Tournament player's collection)
Bibliography: p88. — Includes index
ISBN 0-7134-4003-1 (pbk) : £4.95 B82-34730

Korn, Walter. Modern chess openings / Walter Korn. — 12th ed. — London : A. & C. Black, 1982. — xiv,457p : ill ; 23cm
Originally published: New York : D. McKay, 1980. — Bibliography: px-xii. — Includes index
ISBN 0-7136-2199-0 (pbk) : £8.95 : CIP rev.
B81-35831

Mednis, Edmar. From the opening into the endgame. — Oxford : Pergamon, Feb.1983. — [176]p. — (Pergamon chess series)
ISBN 0-08-026917-6 (cased) : £8.95 : CIP entry
ISBN 0-08-026916-8 (pbk) : £5.50
Also classified at 794.1'24 B82-36471

Pachman, Ludek. The opening game in chess / Ludek Pachman ; translated by John Littlewood. — London : Routledge & Kegan Paul, 1982. — x,197p : ill ; 22cm
Translation of: Eröffnungs-praxis im Schach. — Includes index
ISBN 0-7100-9222-9 (pbk) : £4.25 B82-39523

794.1'22 — Chess. Openings: Nimzo-Indian Defence — *Manuals*

Keene, Raymond. How to play the Nimzo-Indian defence / Raymond Keene, Shaun Taulbut. — London : Batsford, 1982. — 133p : ill ; 22cm. — (A Batsford chess book)
Bibliography: p[vi]. — Includes index
ISBN 0-7134-4007-4 (pbk) : £5.95 B82-17650

794.1'22 — Chess. Openings: Queen's Gambit Declined. Chigorin Defence — *Manuals*

Watson, John L.. Queen's gambit : Chigorin defence / John L. Watson. — London : Batsford, 1981. — 102p : ill ; 22cm. — (Tournament player's repertoire of openings) (A Batsford chess book)
Bibliography: p[7]. — Includes index
ISBN 0-7134-3996-3 (pbk) : £5.95 B82-17652

794.1'22 — Chess. Openings: Queen's Indian Defence — *Manuals*

Geller, Efim. Queen's Indian Defence / Efim Geller ; translated by K.P. Neat ; updated from the Russian edition by R.G. Wade. — London : Batsford, 1982. — viii,247p : ill ; 22cm. — (The Batsford library of tournament openings)
Includes index
ISBN 0-7134-2546-6 (pbk) : £9.95 B82-28770

794.1'22 — Chess. Openings: Sicilian Defence. Boleslavsky Variation, La Bourdonnais Variation & Lasker Variation — *Manuals*

Harding, T. D.. Sicilian : lines with — e5 / T.D. Harding, P.R. Markland. — Rev. ed. — London : Batsford, 1982. — xiv,105p : ill ; 22cm. — (A Batsford chess book) (Tournament player's repertoire of openings)
Previous ed.: 1976. — Includes index
ISBN 0-7134-4020-1 (corrected : pbk) : £6.95
B82-08750

794.1'22 — Chess. Openings: Sicilian Defence. Keres attack — *Manuals*

Kinlay, Jon. Sicilian : Keres attack / Jon Kinlay. — London : Batsford, 1981. — 102p : ill ; 22cm. — (The Tournament player's repertoire of openings) (A Batsford chess book)
ISBN 0-7134-2139-8 (pbk) : Unpriced
B82-03559

794.1'22 — Chess. Openings: Sicilian Defence — *Manuals*

Levy, D. N. L.. The Sicilian Defence : a quantitative analysis of the opening / [from the program conceived by David Levy, Kevin O'Connell, and David Watt]. — London : Imprint Capablanca, c1981. — xvii,221p : ill ; 29cm
Includes index
ISBN 0-907352-00-6 : Unpriced B82-38773

794.1'22 — Chess. Openings: Sicilian Defence. Najdorf Variation — *Manuals*

Nunn, John. Sicilian defence: Najdorf variation / John Nunn, Michael Stean. — London : Batsford, 1982. — vi,186p : ill ; 22cm. — (The Tournament player's repertoire of openings) (A Batsford chess book)
Includes index
ISBN 0-7134-4016-3 (pbk) : £7.95 B82-36094

794.1'22 — Chess. Openings: St. George Opening — *Manuals*

Basman, Michael. Play the St. George. — Oxford : Pergamon, Oct.1982. — [96]p. — (Pergamon chess openings)
ISBN 0-08-029718-8 (cased) : £7.95 : CIP entry
ISBN 0-08-029717-x (pbk) : £4.50 B82-24960

794.1'23 — Chess. Middle games — *Manuals*

Pachman, Ludek. The middle game in chess. — London : Routledge & K. Paul, Oct.1982. — [176]p
Translation of: Mittelspielpraxis im Schach
ISBN 0-7100-9071-4 (pbk) : £3.95 : CIP entry
B82-23205

794.1'24 — Chess. Endgame studies — *Collections*

Roycroft, A. J.. The chess endgame study : a comprehensive introduction / by A.J. Roycroft. — 2nd rev. ed. — New York : Dover ; London : Constable, 1981. — 370p : ill ; 22cm
Previous ed.: published as Test tube chess. London : Faber, 1972. — Includes index
ISBN 0-486-24186-6 (pbk) : £4.50 B82-34628

794.1'24 — Chess. Endgames — *Manuals*

Averbakh, Y.. Comprehensive chess endings. — Oxford : Pergamon, Oct.1982
Translation of: Shakhmatnye okontchaniia
Vol.1: Bishop endings ; Knight endings. — [250]p
ISBN 0-08-026900-1 : £9.90 : CIP entry
B82-24954

Mednis, Edmar. From the opening into the endgame. — Oxford : Pergamon, Feb.1983. — [176]p. — (Pergamon chess series)
ISBN 0-08-026917-6 (cased) : £8.95 : CIP entry
ISBN 0-08-026916-8 (pbk) : £5.50
Primary classification 794.1'22 B82-36471

Portisch, Lajos. Six hundred endings. — Oxford : Pergamon, Sept.1981. — [328]p. — (Pergamon chess series)
Translation of: 600 vegjatek
ISBN 0-08-024137-9 : £6.95 : CIP entry
B81-22546

Speelman, Jon. Endgame preparation / Jon Speelman. — London : Batsford, c1981. — 177p : ill ; 22cm. — (Tournament player's collection) (A Batsford chess book)
Includes index
ISBN 0-7134-3999-8 (cased) : Unpriced
ISBN 0-7134-4000-7 (pbk) : £6.95 B82-14092

794.1'5 — Chess. Games, *ca 1200-1981* — *Collections*

Dickins, Anthony. 100 classics of the chess board. — Oxford : Pergamon, Feb.1983. — [208]p. — (Pergamon chess series)
ISBN 0-08-026921-4 (cased) : £8.50 : CIP entry
ISBN 0-08-026920-6 (pbk) : £4.95 B82-36472

794.1'5 — Chess. Games — *Collections*

Karpov, Anatoliĭ. Chess kaleidoscope / by A. Karpov and Y. Gik ; translated by Kenneth P. Neat. — Oxford : Pergamon, 1981. — viii,168p : ill ; 24cm. — (Pergamon Russian chess series)
Translation of: Shakhmaty kaleidoscope
ISBN 0-08-026897-8 : £9.95 : CIP rev.
ISBN 0-08-026896-x (pbk) : £4.95 B81-20568

Smyslov, Vasiliĭ. Selected games. — Oxford : Pergamon, Nov.1982. — [250]p. — (Pergamon Russian chess series)
Translation of: Izbrannye partii
ISBN 0-08-026912-5 : £7.95 : CIP entry B82-27832

794.1'5 — Chess. Games ending in draws — *Collections*

Heidenfeld, Wolfgang. Draw!. — London : Allen & Unwin, Nov.1982. — [256]p
ISBN 0-04-794014-x : £8.95 : CIP entry B82-27824

794.1'52 — Chess. Master matches. Games, *1970-1980 — Collections*

Speelman, Jon. Best chess games 1970-1980. — London : Allen & Unwin, Sept.1982. — [336]p
ISBN 0-04-794015-8 (cased) : £9.95 : CIP entry
ISBN 0-04-794016-6 (pbk) : £4.95 B82-19084

794.1'57 — Chess. Championships: World Chess Championship *(1981 : Merano)*. **Matches** — *Collections*

Keene, Raymond. Karpov-Korchnoi : massacre in Merano / Raymond Keene. — London : Batsford, 1981. — 122p : ill ; 22cm. — (A Batsford chess book)
ISBN 0-7134-4254-9 (pbk) : £3.95 B82-14595

794.1'57 — Chess. Tournaments: Carlsbad International Chess Tournament *(1929)*. **Games** — *Collections*

Nimzowitsch, Aron. Carlsbad International Chess Tournament 1929 / annotated by Aron Nimzovich ; translated from the Russian by Jim Marfia. — New York : Dover ; London : Constable, 1981. — xiii,146p : ill ; 22cm
Translation of: Izbrannye partii mezhdunarodnogo turnira v Karlsbade 1929
ISBN 0-486-24115-7 (pbk) : £2.60 B82-17677

794.1'57 — Chess. Tournaments: Tournament of Stars (1979 : Montreal). Games — *Collections*

Tal', Mikhail. Montreal 1979 : tournament of stars / by M. Tal, V. Chepizhny, A. Roshal ; translated by Kenneth P. Neat. — Oxford : Pergamon, 1980. — xxxi,204p : ill,ports ; 26cm. — (Pergamon Russian chess series)
Translation of: Turnir Zvëzd. — Includes index
ISBN 0-08-024132-8 (cased) : £7.95 : CIP rev.
ISBN 0-08-024131-x (pbk) : £4.95 B80-12016

794.1'57 — Switzerland. Zürich. Chess. Tournaments: Zürich International Chess Tournament *(1953)*. **Games** — *Collections*

Bronshteĭn, David. The chess struggle in practice : Candidates Tournament, Zurich 1953 / David Bronstein ; translated by Oscar D. Freedman ; edited by Burt Hochberg ; introduction by Max Ewe. — London : Batsford, 1980. — xxvii,499p : ill ; 23cm. — (Batsford chess books)
Translation of: Mezhdunarodnyĭ turnir grossmeĭsterov. 2nd ed. — Originally published: New York : McKay, 1978. — Includes index
ISBN 0-7134-2496-6 : £9.95 B82-08649

794.1'57'05 — Chess. Tournaments. Games — *Collections — Serials*

Tournament chess. — Vol.1-. — Oxford : Pergamon, 1981-. — v. ; 25cm
Quarterly
ISSN 0276-7090 = Tournament chess : Unpriced B82-12450

794.1'57'0924 — Chess. Championships — *Personal observations — Russian texts*

Korchnoĭ, Viktor. Antishakhmaty / Viktor Korchnoĭ ; predislovie Vladimira Bukovskogo. — London : Overseas Publications Interchange, 1981. — 121p,[4]p of plates : ill,ports ; 18cm
Russian text. — Added t.p. in English: Anti-chess
ISBN 0-903868-34-2 (pbk) : Unpriced B82-03287

794.1'57'0924 — Chess. Championships: World Chess Championship *(1981 : Merano) — Personal observations*

Hartston, William R.. Karpov v Korchnoi : the World Chess Championship 1981 / W.R. Hartston. — [London] : Fontana, 1981. — 124p : ill ; 20cm
ISBN 0-00-636511-6 (pbk) : £2.50 B82-15112

794.1'59 — Chess. Capablanca, José Raúl. Games — *Collections*

Chernev, Irving. Capablanca's best chess endings : 60 complete games / by Irving Chernev. — New York : Dover ; London : Constable, 1982, c1978. — x,288p : ill ; 22cm
Originally published: Oxford : Oxford University Press, 1978. — Bibliography: p286-288
ISBN 0-486-24249-8 (pbk) : Unpriced B82-34629

794.1'59 — Chess. Denker, Arnold S.. Games — *Collections*

Denker, Arnold S.. My best chess games 1929-1976 / Arnold S. Denker. — Enl. [ed.]. — New York : Dover ; London : Constable, 1981. — xvi,208p : ill ; 21cm. — (Dover books on chess)
Previous ed.: / published as If you must play chess. Philadelphia : McKay, 1947
ISBN 0-486-24035-5 (pbk) : £3.40 B82-08957

794.1'59 — Chess. Korchnoĭ, Viktor. Games — *Collections*

Korchnoĭ, Viktor. Viktor Korchnoi's best games / annotated by Viktor Korchnoi. — London : Philidor, 1978. — lx,294p : ill ; 22cm
Originally published: 1977. — Includes index
ISBN 0-08-023028-8 : £5.00 : CIP rev. B78-06279

794.1'59 — Chess. Short, Nigel. Games — *Collections*

Short, David, *1938-*. Nigel Short : chess prodigy : his career and best games / David Short ; edited by Leonard Barden ; discussion and analysis of games by George Botterill and comments by Nigel Short. — London : Faber, 1981. — 258p ; 21cm
Includes index
ISBN 0-571-11786-4 (cased) : £7.95 : CIP rev.
ISBN 0-571-11860-7 (pbk) : Unpriced B81-25325

794.1'59 — Chess. Tal', Mikhail. Games, *1967-1973 — Collections*

Thomas, Hilary. Complete games of Mikhail Tal 1967-73 / Hilary Thomas. — London : Batsford, 1979. — 188p : ill ; 22cm. — (Batsford chess books)
Includes index
ISBN 0-7134-2138-x (cased) : Unpriced
ISBN 0-7134-2137-1 (pbk) : £5.95 B82-08648

794.1'7 — Chess. Playing. Applications of digital computer systems

Advances in computer chess 3. — Oxford : Pergamon, Oct.1982. — [170]p. — (Pergamon chess series)
ISBN 0-08-026898-6 : £12.50 : CIP entry B82-24953

794.1'7 — Chess. Playing. Applications of microcomputer systems

Harding, T. D.. The chess computer book / by T.D. Harding. — Oxford : Pergamon, 1982, c1981. — 215p : ill ; 23cm. — (Pergamon chess series)
Bibliography: p213. — Includes index
ISBN 0-08-026885-4 (cased) : Unpriced : CIP rev.
ISBN 0-08-026884-6 (pbk) : £4.95 B81-28767

794.2 — DRAUGHTS AND SIMILAR GAMES

794.2'2 — Draughts — *Manuals*

Chernev, Irving. The compleat draughts player / Irving Chernev. — Oxford : Oxford University Press, 1981. — 314p : ill ; 21cm
Includes index
ISBN 0-19-217587-4 : £8.95 : CIP rev.
ISBN 0-19-217586-6 (pbk) : Unpriced B81-02357

794.3 — DARTS

794.3 — Darts — *Manuals*

Young, John. Winning darts / by John Young ; edited by Geoff Martin. — London : Foulsham, c1981. — 64p : ill ; 19cm
ISBN 0-572-01147-4 (pbk) : £0.95 B82-11863

794.3'09 — Darts, *to 1980*

Brown, Derek. Guinness book of darts / Derek Brown. — Enfield : Guinness Superlatives, c1981. — 157p,[8]p of plates : ill,ports ; 27cm
Includes index
ISBN 0-85112-229-9 : £7.50 : CIP rev. B81-20133

Brown, Derek. The Guinness book of darts. — Rev. and updated. — Enfield : Guinness Superlatives, Sept.1982. — [179]p
Previous ed.: 1981
ISBN 0-85112-254-x (pbk) : £5.95 : CIP entry B82-20495

794.73 — POOL AND SNOOKER

794.7'3 — Pool — *Manuals*

Pool / [contributions from Barrie Denton ... et al.] ; [editor George Muncaster]. — Wakefield : Produced in collaboration with British Association of Pool Table Operators [by] EP Publishing, 1980 (1982 [printing]). — 32p : ill ; 14x21cm. — (Know the game)
ISBN 0-7158-0675-0 (pbk) : £0.85 B82-20093

794.7'35 — Snooker

Pot black / compiled by Reg Perrin. — New rev. ed. — London : British Broadcasting Corporation, 1982. — 176p : ill,ports ; 20cm
Previous ed.: 1975
ISBN 0-563-17994-5 (pbk) : £2.00 B82-18885

794.7'35 — Snooker — *Manuals*

Clifford, W. G.. Winning snooker / by W.G. Clifford ; edited by Geoff Martin. — London : Foulsham, c1981. — 64p : ill ; 19cm
ISBN 0-572-01148-2 (pbk) : £0.95 B82-11861

Davis, Steve. Successful snooker / Steve Davis. — London : Published in collaboration with World of Sport by Letts, 1982. — 95p : ill (some col.) ; 22cm. — (Letts guide)
Includes index
ISBN 0-85097-437-2 (pbk) : £2.95 B82-31659

794.7'35'05 — Snooker — *Serials*

World snooker. — [No.1]-. — London : Pelham Books, 1981-. — v. : ill(some col.),ports ; 30cm
ISSN 0263-239x = World snooker : £5.95 B82-23598

794.7'35'09 — Snooker, *to 1980*

Everton, Clive. Guinness book of snooker / Clive Everton. — Enfield : Guinness Superlatives, c1981. — 162p : ill(some col.),ports ; 27cm
Includes index
ISBN 0-85112-230-2 : £7.50 : CIP rev. B81-25828

794.7'35'09 — Snooker, *to 1981*

Everton, Clive. The Guinness book of snooker. — Rev. ed. — Enfield : Guinness Superlatives, Aug.1982. — [162]p
Previous ed.: 1981
ISBN 0-85112-256-6 : £5.95 : CIP entry B82-20779

794.7'35'0924 — Snooker. Davis, Steve — *Biographies*

Davis, Steve. Steve Davis : snooker champion / his own story as told to Brian Radford. — London : Barker, 1981. — xii,137p,[16]p of plates : ports ; 24cm
ISBN 0-213-16817-0 : £5.95 B82-04357

794.7'35'0924 — Snooker. Reardon, Ray — *Biographies*

Reardon, Ray. Ray Reardon / Ray Reardon with Peter Buxton. — Newton Abbot : David & Charles, c1982. — 159p : ill,ports ; 23cm
ISBN 0-7153-8262-4 : £6.95 : CIP rev. B82-04872

795.4 — CARD GAMES

795.4 — Card games & tricks — *Manuals — For children*

Page, Patrick. Card games & tricks / by Patrick Page ; illustrated by Ron Hayward. — London : Macdonald, 1982. — 63p : col.ill ; 21cm. — (Whizz kids ; 24)
Bibliography: p61. — Includes index
ISBN 0-356-06384-4 (cased) : £2.95
ISBN 0-356-06344-5 (pbk) : £1.25 B82-22965

795.4 — Card games — *Manuals*

Parlett, David. Card games for everyone. — London : Hodder & Stoughton, Feb.1983. — [576]p
ISBN 0-340-32007-9 : £7.95 : CIP entry B82-38037

Pennycook, Andrew. The book of card games / Andrew Pennycook. — London : Granada, 1982. — 656p ; 19cm
Includes index
ISBN 0-246-11756-7 (cased) : £8.95
ISBN 0-583-12910-2 (pbk) : Unpriced B82-24203

795.4 — Card games: Tarot, *to 1979*

Dummett, Michael. The game of tarot : from Ferrara to Salt Lake City / Michael Dummett with the assistance of Sylvia Mann. — London : Duckworth, 1980. — xxxii,600p,32p of plates : ill(some col.),1col.port ; 29cm
Text on lining papers. — Includes index
ISBN 0-7156-1014-7 : £45.00 : CIP rev. B79-35977

795.41′5 — Contract bridge

Fox, G. C. H.. The second Daily telegraph book of bridge / G.C.H. Fox. — London : Hale, 1982. — 176p ; 23cm
ISBN 0-7091-9727-6 : £6.50 B82-39338

Markus, Rixi. Aces and places. — London : Allen & Unwin, Oct.1982. — [144]p
Originally published: London : Secker & Warburg, 1972
ISBN 0-04-793052-7 (pbk) : £2.50 : CIP entry B82-23097

Reese, Terence. Miracles of card play / Terence Reese and David Bird. — London : Gollancz in association with Peter Crawley, 1982. — 160p ; 23cm
ISBN 0-575-03079-8 : £6.95 : CIP rev. B82-09437

795.41′5 — Contract bridge — *Manuals*

Goren, Charles H.. Goren's bridge complete / Charles H. Goren. — Rev. ed. — London : Stanley Paul, 1982. — xiii,689p : ill ; 24cm
Originally published: London : Barrie & Jenkins, 1977. — Includes index
ISBN 0-09-149200-9 : £9.95 B82-36077

Goren, Charles H.. Play as you learn bridge / Chas H. Goren. — London : Hale, 1982, c1979. — 116p : ill ; 21cm
Originally published: New York : Doubleday, c1979
ISBN 0-7091-9975-9 : £4.95 B82-28636

Lederer, Tony. Learn bridge with the Lederers. — London : Allen & Unwin, Oct.1982. — [208]p
Originally published: London : Cassell, 1977
ISBN 0-04-793051-9 (pbk) : £2.50 : CIP entry B82-24367

Markus, Rixi. Bid boldly, play safe / Rixi Markus. — London : Unwin Paperbacks, 1980, c1977. — 284p ; 20cm
Previous ed.: London : Blond, 1966
ISBN 0-04-793044-6 (pbk) : £2.50 : CIP rev. B80-09802

Reese, Terence. Bridge / Terence Reese. — Harmondsworth : Penguin, 1961, c1971 (1982 [printing]). — 207p : ill ; 20cm. — (Penguin handbooks)
Bibliography: p203. — Includes index
ISBN 0-14-046065-9 (pbk) : £1.95 B82-35263

795.41′5 — Contract bridge. Pairs games — *Manuals*

Greenwood, David, *19---*. The pairs game / David Greenwood ; introduction by Terence Reese. — London : Faber, 1982. — x,150p : ill ; 22cm
Originally published: London : Cassell, 1978
ISBN 0-571-11906-9 (pbk) : £2.75 : CIP rev. B82-10782

Hoffman, Martin. Hoffman on pairs play / Martin Hoffman. — London : Faber, 1982. — 184p : ill ; 21cm
ISBN 0-571-11750-3 : £6.95 : CIP rev. B81-23778

795.41′5′076 — Contract bridge — *Questions & answers*

Jannersten, Eric. Find the mistakes. — London : Gollancz, Sept.1982. — [160]p. — (Master bridge series)
Translation of: Finn felet
ISBN 0-575-03172-7 : £6.95 : CIP entry B82-18760

Sontag, Alan. Improve your bridge — fast / by Alan Sontag and Peter Steinberg. — London : Hale, 1982. — 159p : ill ; 23cm. — (Hale bridge books)
ISBN 0-7091-9892-2 : £6.50 B82-32749

795.41′52 — Contract bridge. Acol bidding — *Manuals*

Cohen, Ben. Basic Acol. — 4th ed. — London : Unwin Paperbacks, Oct.1981. — [122]p
Previous ed.: 1979
ISBN 0-04-793049-7 (pbk) : £1.75 : CIP entry B81-25145

795.4′152 — Contract bridge. Acol bidding — *Questions & answers*

Lederer, Rhoda. Acol-ites quiz. — London : Unwin Paperbacks, Nov.1982. — [224]p
Originally published: 1978
ISBN 0-04-793058-6 : £2.50 : CIP entry B82-27829

795.41′52 — Contract bridge. Bidding. Conventions — *Manuals*

Keech, Ray. The conventional way / Ray Keech, John Beard. — Plymouth : J & R Bridge Enterprises, 1981. — 64p : ill ; 21cm
£1.50 (pbk) B82-05116

795.41′52′0285 — Contract bridge. Bidding. Applications of digital computer systems

Lindelöf, E. T.. COBRA : the computer-designed bidding system. — London : Gollancz, Mar.1982. — [320]p
ISBN 0-575-02987-0 : £9.95 : CIP entry B82-00201

795.41′53 — Contract bridge. Card play — *Manuals*

Darvas, Robert. Spotlight on card play : a new approach to the practical analysis of bridge hands / by Robert Darvas and Paul Lukacs ; foreword by Hugh Kelsey. — London : Gollancz in association with Peter Crawley, 1982, c1960. — 160p ; 20cm. — (Master bridge series)
Originally published: London : Kaye, 1960
ISBN 0-575-03078-x (pbk) : £3.95 : CIP rev. B81-38322

Lawrence, Mike. The complete book on overcalls. — London : Pelham, Sept.1982. — [216]p
ISBN 0-7207-1411-7 : £8.95 : CIP entry B82-20388

795.41′53 — Contract bridge. Card play. Problems — *Collections*

Jannersten, Eric. The only chance / Eric Jannersten ; adapted and translated from the Swedish by Hugh Kelsey. — London : Bodley Head, 1980. — 171p : ill ; 21cm
ISBN 0-370-30266-4 : £4.95 : CIP rev. B80-13940

Kelsey, H. W.. The needle match / H.W. Kelsey. — London : Faber, 1982. — 189p : ill ; 23cm
ISBN 0-571-11872-0 : £7.50 : CIP rev. B82-10779

Kelsey, H. W.. Test your card-reading / by Hugh Kelsey. — London : Gollancz in association with Peter Crawley, 1982. — 80p : ill ; 20cm. — (Master bridge series)
ISBN 0-575-03170-0 (pbk) : £2.95 : CIP rev. B82-19555

Kelsey, H. W.. Test your communications / by Hugh Kelsey. — London : Gollancz in association with Peter Crawley, 1982. — 80p : ill ; 20cm. — (Master bridge series)
ISBN 0-575-03171-9 (pbk) : £2.95 : CIP rev. B82-19556

795.41′53 — Contract bridge. Deceptive play — *Manuals*

Kelsey, H. W.. Deceptive plays in bridge / Hugh Kelsey. — London : Hale, 1982. — 187p : ill ; 23cm. — (Hale bridge books)
ISBN 0-7091-9992-9 : £7.25 B82-39714

795.41′53 — Contract bridge. Endplay — *Manuals*

Coffin, George. [Endplays]. Endplays in bridge : eliminations, squeezes & coups. — New York : Dover ; London : Constable, 1981. — 211p ; 22cm
Originally published: London : Duckworth, 1975. — Bibliography: p211
ISBN 0-486-24230-7 (pbk) : £3.00 B82-34625

795.41′53 — Contract bridge. Safety play — *Manuals*

Jannersten, Eric. Play safe - and win / Eric Jannersten and Jan Wohlin ; translated by Hugh Kelsey. — London : Gollancz in association with Peter Crawley, 1981. — 160p : ill ; 22cm
Translation of: Med all säkerhet
ISBN 0-575-03006-2 : £5.95 B82-01477

795.41′58 — Contract bridge. Card play. Games — *Collections*

Mollo, Victor. Bridge à la carte / Victor Mollo. — London : Pelham, 1982. — 158p : ill ; 23cm
Includes index
ISBN 0-7207-1385-4 : £8.95 : CIP rev. B81-35848

795.41′58 — Contract bridge. International tournaments: Grand Slam *(Bridge tournament) (1981).* **Games** — *Collections*

James, Jeremy. Grand slam : an international television bridge tournament / Jeremy James. — London : British Broadcasting Corporation, 1981. — 140p ; 20cm
ISBN 0-563-20047-2 (pbk) : £2.95 B82-12481

795.4′3 — Card games: Patience — *Manuals*

Botterill, Ruth D.. The new book of patience games : mystery, mustery & mastery and some jiggery pokery / Ruth D. Botterill. — London : Foulsham, c1982. — 64p : ill ; 19cm
Includes index
ISBN 0-572-01169-5 (pbk) : £0.95 B82-37189

795.4′38 — Card tricks — *Manuals*

Adair, Ian. The complete guide to card conjuring / Ian Adair ; illustrations by the author ; photographs by A.C. Littlejohns. — San Diego : A.S. Barnes ; London : Tantivy, 1980. — 108p : ill ; 25cm
Bibliography: p106-108
ISBN 0-498-02238-2 : £3.95 B82-32245

De Courcy, Ken. Pasteboard prowler / Ken de Courcy. — Bideford (64 High St., Bideford, Devon) : Supreme Magic, c1982. — 4p : ill ; 26cm
Cover title
Unpriced (pbk) B82-29908

De Courcy, Ken. Supreme easy everywhere and nowhere / by Ken de Courcy. — Bideford (64 High St., Bideford, Devon) : Supreme Magic, c1982. — 6p : ill ; 25cm
Unpriced (pbk) B82-29909

795.4′38 — Tricks using credit cards — *Manuals*

De Courcy, Ken. Creditable conjuring : magic with credit cards / Ken de Courcy ; (illustrated by the author). — [Bideford] ([64 High St., Bideford, Devon]) : Supreme Magic, c1982. — 12p : ill ; 25cm
Unpriced (pbk) B82-29913

796 — SPORTS AND GAMES

796 — Cooperative sports & games for children — *Collections*
Orlick, Terry. The cooperative sports & games book : challenge without competition / Terry Orlick. — London : Writers and Readers Publishing Cooperative, 1979, c1978. — x,129p : ill ; 26cm
Originally published: New York : Pantheon, 1978. — Bibliography: p121-123. — Includes index
ISBN 0-906495-01-6 (corrected) : £4.95
B82-03477

796 — Outdoor games — *Manuals*
Fluegelman, Andrew. More new games! : and playful ideas from the New Games Foundation / text and photographs by Andrew Fluegelman. — Garden City, N.Y. : Dolphin Books, 1981 ; [London] : [Sidgwick & Jackson] [[distributor]], [1982]. — 190p : ill ; 23cm. — (A Headlands Press book)
ISBN 0-283-98840-1 (pbk) : £5.95 B82-14155

796 — Sports
Chu, Donald. Dimensions of sport studies / Donald Chu. — New York ; Chichester : Wiley, c1982. — xii,299p : ill ; 24cm
Includes bibliographies and index
ISBN 0-471-08576-6 : £13.30 B82-26263

796 — Sports & games — *Manuals* — *For teaching*
Armbruster, David A.. Sports and recreational activities for men and women / David A. Armbruster, Frank F. Musker, Dale Mood ; with 723 illustrations. — 7th ed. — St Louis ; London : Mosby, 1979. — ix,402p : ill,plans ; 28cm
Previous ed.: published as Basic skills in sports for men and women. 1975. — Includes bibliographies
ISBN 0-8016-0286-6 (pbk) : Unpriced
B82-38376

796 — Sports — *Stories, anecdotes*
Winkworth, Stephen. Famous sporting fiascos. — London : Bodley Head, Oct.1982. — [160]p
ISBN 0-370-30450-0 : £5.95 : CIP entry
B82-24448

796 — Winter outdoor leisure activities — *Practical information*
Hunter, Rob. Winter skills / Rob Hunter. — London : Constable, 1982. — 246p : ill ; 18cm
Bibliography: p223-225. — Includes index
ISBN 0-09-463900-0 : £5.95 B82-13351

796′.01 — Athletes. Competitiveness. Improvement. Psychological aspects
Rushall, Brent S.. Psyching in sport : the psychological preparation for serious competition in sport / Brent S. Rushall. — London : Pelham, 1979. — 190p : ill ; 23cm
Bibliography: p149-156. — Includes index
ISBN 0-7207-1193-2 : £6.50 B82-14001

796′.01 — Sports. Psychological aspects
Sport psychology : an analysis of athlete behavior / edited by William F. Straub. — 2nd ed. — Ithaca : Mouvement ; Gayton (19 Oaksway, Gayton, Wirral L60 3SP) : M.E. Brodie [[distributor]], c1980. — 464p : ill ; 23cm
Previous ed.: 1978. — Includes bibliographies and index
ISBN 0-932392-03-2 (pbk) : Unpriced
B82-03517

796′.01′5 — Sports & games. Scientific aspects. Experiments — *For schools*
Kincaid, Doug. Sports and games / Doug Kincaid, Peter S. Coles ; designed & illustrated by John Hill. — [Amersham] : Hulton, 1981. — 64p : ill(some col.),ports ; 25cm. — (Science in a topic)
Text and ill. on inside covers. — Bibliography: on inside cover
ISBN 0-7175-0885-4 (pbk) : Unpriced
B82-08389

796′.019c19 — Sports. Geographical aspects
Bale, John R.. Geographical perspectives on sport. — London : Lepus, Apr.1981. — [192]p
ISBN 0-86019-044-7 (pbk) : £9.50 : CIP entry
B81-10500

796′.01′94 — Sports. Role of women — *Conference proceedings*

International Congress on Women and Sport *(1980 : Rome)*. Women and sport : an historical, biological, physiological and sportsmedical approach : selected papers of the International Congress on Women and Sport, Rome, Italy, July 4-8, 1980 / volume editors J. Borms, M. Hebbelinck and A. Venerando. — Basel ; London : Karger, c1981. — xiii,229p : ill ; 24cm. — (Medicine and sport ; v.14)
Includes bibliographies and index
ISBN 3-8055-2725-x : £35.95 B82-18201

796′.01′960941 — Great Britain. Handicapped persons. Sports — *Conference proceedings*

Sport for the disabled : at Bulmershe College of Higher Education, Reading, on Saturday 10th October 1981 / arranged in conjunction with the British Sports Association for the Disabled, Southern Region and sponsored by the Sports Council ... [et al.] ; chairmen M. O'Flynn, L.J. Bridgeman. — Reading (Watlington House, Watlington St., Reading RG1 4RJ) : Sports Council (Southern Region), [1981?]. — 32p ; 31cm. — (Conference report)
Bibliography: p31-32
£2.00 (pbk) B82-15123

796′.01′960942 — Southern England. Physically handicapped persons. Sports — *Serials*

[Sportsnews *(Southern Region edition)*].
Sportsnews : newspaper of the Sports Council (Southern Region). — [Southern Region ed.]. — 1981-. — Reading (Watlington House, Watlington St., Reading, Berks. RG1 4RJ) : Sports Council (Southern Region) in conjunction with Coles & Sons, 1981-. — v. : ill,ports ; 42cm
Two issues yearly. — Continues: Sport south
ISSN 0262-382X = Sportsnews. Newspaper of the Sports Council, Southern Region : Unpriced B82-36711

796′.023′41 — Great Britain. Sports — *Career guides*

Professional sport. — [London] : Careers & Occupational Information Centre, [197-?]. — 16p : col.ill ; 21x30cm. — (Working in ; 19)
ISBN 0-86110-087-5 (unbound) : £0.55
B82-40963

796′.025′41 — Great Britain. Sports facilities — *Directories*

Pelham sports guide. — London : Pelham, c1982. — 528p : ill,maps ; 21cm
ISBN 0-7207-1386-2 (pbk) : £5.95 : CIP rev.
B81-33843

796′.05 — Sports — *For children* — *Serials*

Scoop sports annual. — 1982-. — London : D.C. Thomson, 1981-. — v. : ill ; 28cm
Continues: Scoop (Annual)
ISSN 0262-4206 = Scoop sports annual : £1.65 B82-03424

796′.05 — Sports — *Serials*

Adventure sports. — No.1-no.10. — London : Interlink, 1979-1981. — 10v. : ill ; 30cm
Continued by: Adventure sports & travel
£0.75 B82-07645

Adventure sports & travel. — No.11-. — London (17 South Molton St., W1) : Danpalm, [1981]-. — v. : ill ; 30cm
Six issues yearly. — Continues: Adventure sports
ISSN 0262-5768 = Adventure sports & travel : £6.50 per year
Also classified at 910′.5 B82-07646

The **Guardian** book of sport. — 1981/2-. — London : Secker & Warburg, 1981-. — v. : ill,ports ; 26cm
Annual
ISSN 0263-1245 = Guardian book of sport : £12.50 B82-18485

Sports international : the journal and newsletter of the Centre for International Sports Exchange. — No.1 (Spring 1980)-. — London (44 Baker St., W1M 2HJ) : Central Bureau for Educational Visits and Exchanges for the Centre, 1980-. — v. : ill,ports ; 30cm
Quarterly (1980), annual (1981-). — Continues: Sports exchange world. — Description based on: No.5 (Spring 1981)
ISSN 0144-3844 = Sports international : £1.50
B82-04907

796′.06′9 — Great Britain. Sports. Management — *Serials*
Sports industry. — No.1 (Sept./Oct. 1981)-. — Sutton : IPC Industrial Press, 1981-. — v. : ill ; 30cm
Six issues yearly
ISSN 0261-5665 = Sports industry : £9.50 per year B82-11835

796′.06′9 — Southern England. Educational institutions. Sports facilities. Use by public. Management aspects — *Conference proceedings*
Community use of education facilities : management considerations, Tuesday, December 16th 1980 / Chairman L.J. Bridgeman. — Reading (Watlington House, Watlington St., Reading RG1 4RJ) : Southern Council for Sports and Recreation, [1981?]. — 18leaves ; 31cm. — (Seminar report)
Unpriced (pbk) B82-15124

796′.076 — Sports — *Questions & answers*
Rhys, Chris. Brain of sport. — London : BBC/Knight, Sept.1982
2. — 1v.
ISBN 0-340-28655-5 (pbk) : £0.95 : CIP entry
ISBN 0-563-20086-3 (BBC) B82-18749

World of Sport quiz book. — London : Stanley Paul, Oct.1982. — [160]p
ISBN 0-09-149901-1 (pbk) : £3.95 : CIP entry
B82-23104

796′.07′7 — Sportsmen. Coaching
Matveev, L.. Fundamentals of sports training / L. Matveyev ; [translated from the Russian by Albert P. Zdornykh]. — Moscow : Progress ; [London] : distributed by Central, c1981. — 309p : ill ; 21cm
Translation of: Osnovy sportivnoĭ trenirovki. — Includes index
ISBN 0-7147-1700-2 : £4.95 B82-29290

796′.07′7 — United States. Sports & games. Coaching. Psychological aspects
Fuoss, Donald E. Effective coaching : a psychological approach / Donald E. Fuoss, Robert J. Troppmann. — New York ; Chichester : Wiley, c1981. — xvii,348p : ill ; 24cm
Includes bibliographies and index
ISBN 0-471-03233-6 : Unpriced B82-01521

796′.079 — Great Britain. Sports. Sponsorship by business firms
A report on the allocation of monies by companies towards sponsorship of sport in the U.K. / [prepared for the Information Centre by General Marketing Services]. — London : Sports Council, c1981. — xiv,89p : forms ; 30cm. — (Information series ; no.6)
At head of title: The Sports Council
ISBN 0-906577-18-7 (pbk) : £50.00
B82-04642

796′.079 — Great Britain. Sports. Sponsorship by business firms — *Serials*
Sponsorship news : a monthly update of sponsorship news in sport and the arts. — Vol.1, issue 1 (Feb. 1982)-. — [Wokingham] ([31A Rose St., Wokingham, Berks. RG11 1XS]) : [Charterhouse Business Publications], 1982-. — v. : ill,ports ; 30cm
ISSN 0263-3809 = Sponsorship news : £24.00 per year
Primary classification 700′.7′9 B82-24751

796′.08997 — Mississippi. Choctaw Indians. Sports & games
Blanchard, Kendall. The Mississippi Choctaws at play : the serious side of leisure / Kendall Blanchard. — Urbana ; London : University of Illinois Press, c1981. — xv,196p,[20]p of plates : ill ; 24cm
Bibliography: p183-191. — Includes index
ISBN 0-252-00866-9 : £11.20 B82-13569

796'.09'04 — Sporting events, *1900-1981*

Barrett, Norman. Great moments in sport / Norman Barrett ; editor Deborah Brammer. — Bristol : Purnell, 1982. — 115p : ill(some col.),ports(some col.) ; 30cm
Ill on lining papers. — Includes index
ISBN 0-361-05307-x : £6.99 B82-35490

796'.092'2 — Great Britain. Sports. Participation of royal families. *1837-1981*

Lemoine, Serge. The sporting Royal Family / with photographs by Serge Lemoine ; and text by Grania Forbes. — London : Queen Anne Press, 1982. — 128p : ports(some col.) ; 30cm
ISBN 0-356-08603-8 : £7.95 B82-24542

796'.092'4 — Sports — *Personal observations*

Modern sports writers : a collection of prose / edited by John Byrne. — London : Batsford Academic and Educational, 1982. — 173p ; 23cm
Includes index
ISBN 0-7134-4303-0 : £5.95 B82-30754

796'.0941 — Great Britain. Sports & games — *For non-English speaking students*

Bowen, Nick. Play the game : sport in Britain today / Nick Bowen. — London : Harrap, 1981. — 48p : ill,ports ; 22cm. — (Britain today. Intermediate)
ISBN 0-245-53638-8 (pbk) : £1.10 B82-00744

796'.0941 — Great Britain. Sports. Geographical aspects

Bale, John. Sport and place. — London : C. Hurst, Sept.1982. — [200]p
ISBN 0-905838-65-3 : £9.50 : CIP entry B82-21738

796'.0942 — England. Sports & games, *to 1900.* **Cultural aspects**

Goulstone, J.. The midsummer games : elements of cult and custom in traditional English sport / by J. Goulstone. — Bexleyheath ([10 Haslemere Rd, Bexleyheath, Kent DA7 4NQ]) : J. Goulstone, c1982. — 68p ; 26cm
£2.50 (pbk) B82-34560

796'.09425 — England. East Midlands. Schools. Sports facilities. Joint provision & multiple use

Sport and recreation on school facilities : joint provision and dual use in the East Midlands / [The Regional Council for Sport and Recreation, East Midlands]. — Nottingham (26 Musters Rd., West Bridgford, Nottingham NG2 7PL) : The Sports Council, East Midland Region, 1980. — 34,xp ; 30cm
£1.50 (pbk) B82-39910

796'.09426 — East Anglia. Sports, *to 1980*

Johnson, Derek E.. East Anglian sporting days / by Derek Johnson. — Ipswich : East Anglian Magazine, c1981. — 120p : ill,ports ; 22cm
ISBN 0-900227-52-4 (pbk) : £3.50 B82-01676

796'.09428'1 — Yorkshire. Sports facilities & recreation facilities. Provision — *Proposals*

Yorkshire and Humberside Council for Sport and Recreation. 1/3 of our time : a strategy for sport and recreation / Yorkshire and Humberside Council for Sport and Recreation. — Leeds (Coronet House, Queen St., Leeds LS1 9PW) : The Council, 1982?. — 16p : ill,1port ; 30cm
Recommendations from subject reports ([18]p : unbound) in pocket on back cover
£4.00 (pbk) B82-40282

796'.0973 — United States. Sports & games

Curtis, Joseph E.. Recreation : theory and practice / Joseph E. Curtis. — St Louis ; London : Mosby, 1979. — xiv,312p : ill ; 24cm
Includes bibliographies and index
ISBN 0-8016-1183-0 (pbk) : £12.75 B82-38656

796.3 — BALL GAMES

796.31 — Ball games: Bowls — *Serials*

Bowls international. — 1981-. — Stamfoard (1 Wothorpe Rd, Stamford, Lincs. PE9 2JR) : Key Pub. Ltd., 1981-. — v. : ill,ports ; 30cm
Monthly. — Description based on: Jan. 1982
ISSN 0262-6942 = Bowls international : £11.30 per year B82-18545

796.32 — Netball — *Manuals*

Miles, Anne, *1942-*. Success in netball / Anne Miles. — London : Murray, 1981. — 94p : ill ; 23cm
ISBN 0-7195-3840-8 : £3.95 : CIP rev. B81-30316

796.323 — BASKETBALL

796.32'3'02022 — Basketball — *Rules*

Official basketball rules, 1980-84 : as adopted by the International Amateur Basketball Federation (F.I.B.A.) / English Basket Ball Association. — [Leeds] ([Calomax House, Lupton Ave., Leeds 9]) : The Association, c1980. — 68p : ill,plans ; 19cm
Includes index
Unpriced (pbk) B82-10952

796.32'3'0604281 — Yorkshire. Basketball. Organisations: Yorkshire and North Humberside Basketball Association. Development — *Proposals*

Yorkshire and North Humberside Basketball Association. Development plan / Yorkshire & North Humberside Basketball Association. — Leeds (Coronet House, Queen St., Leeds LS1 4PW) : Sports Council, Yorkshire and Humberside, 1981. — 15p : ill,1map ; 30cm
Cover title
Unpriced (pbk) B82-03272

796.32'3'077 — England. Basketball. Coaching. Award schemes

Basketball award schemes : coaching awards, refereeing awards, national award for table officials, proficiency awards. — Leeds (Calomax House, Lupton Ave., Leeds LS9 7EE) : English Basket Ball Association, 1981. — 24p : forms ; 21cm
Unpriced (pbk)
Also classified at 796.32'33'079 B82-10953

796.32'3'0942 — England. Basketball

Basketball. — [Leeds] ([Calomax House, Lupton Ave., Leeds LS9 7EE]) : [English Basket Ball Association], 1981. — [15]p : ill ; 21cm
Unpriced (unbound) B82-10954

796.32'32 — Basketball — *Manuals* — *For coaching*

Coleman, Brian E.. Coaching basketball : a guide for the potential basketball coach / Brian E. Coleman. — Leeds (Calomax House, Lupton Ave., Leeds 9) : English Basket Ball Association, c1972 (1980 [printing]). — 72p : ill ; 19cm
Unpriced (pbk) B82-10948

796.32'32 — Basketball. Tactics

Smith, Dean. Basketball : multiple offense and defense / by Dean Smith ; with a special section on the shuffle offense by Bob Spear ; foreword by Bob Knight ; coordinated and edited by Bob Savod. — Englewood Cliffs ; London : Prentice-Hall, c1982. — xvi,304p : ill,ports ; 25cm
Includes index
ISBN 0-13-072090-9 : £11.20 B82-16717

796.32'33 — Basketball. Refereeing — *Manuals*

Basketball officiating manual : a guide to the techniques of basketball refereeing : as adopted by the English Basket Ball Association. — Leeds (Calomax House, Lupton Ave., Leeds 9) : English Basket Ball Association, c1979. — 55p : ill(some col.) ; 19cm
Unpriced (pbk) B82-10947

796.32'33'079 — England. Basketball. Refereeing. Award schemes

Basketball award schemes : coaching awards, refereeing awards, national award for table officials, proficiency awards. — Leeds (Calomax House, Lupton Ave., Leeds LS9 7EE) : English Basket Ball Association, 1981. — 24p : forms ; 21cm
Unpriced (pbk)
Primary classification 796.32'3'077 B82-10953

796.32'38 — Mini-basketball — *Manuals* — *For children*

Mini-basketball : a ball game for the 8 to 12 years old. So easy to learn and play!. — Royston (c/o K.G. Charles, Greneway School, Garden Walk, Royston, Herts. SG8 7JF) : [English Mini Basket Ball Association?], [1981?]. — [14]p : ill,1plan ; 22cm
Unpriced (unbound) B82-10951

796.32'38 — Mini-basketball — *Manuals* — *For coaching*

Mini-basketball : guidelines for the teacher, leader and coach : a ball game for the 8 to 12 years old. So easy to learn and play!. — Royston (c/o K.G. Charles, Greneway School, Garden Walk, Royston, Herts. SG8 7JF) : [English Mini Basket Ball Association?], [1981?]. — [27]p : ill ; 21cm
Unpriced (unbound) B82-10950

796.32'38 — Women's basketball — *Manuals*

Basketball for women and schoolgirls. — [Leeds] ([Calomax House, Lupton Ave., Leeds LS9 7EE]) : English Basket Ball Association, [1981?]. — [12]p : ill ; 21cm
Bibliography: p[11]
Unpriced (unbound) B82-10949

796.33 — FOOTBALL

796.33 — Belfast. Gaelic football. Teams: Queen's University of Belfast. *Gaelic Football Club, to 1982*

Queen's University of Belfast. *Gaelic Football Club*. Cumann Peile Ollscoil na Riona : stair chuimhneacháin. — [Belfast] ([c/o F. MacCormaic, 28 Elmwood Ave., Belfast 9]) : [Queen's G.F.C.], 1982. — 53p : ill,facsims,ports ; 20cm
Cover title: Queen's G.F.C.
Unpriced (pbk) B82-37950

796.33 — Wexford *(County)*. **Piercestown. Gaelic football. Clubs: St Martins GAA Club,** *to 1982*

St Martins GAA Club. St Martins GAA Club 1932-1982 / editor: Edward Culleton. — Wexford : The Club, 1982. — viii,162p : ill,1map,ports ; 23cm
Includes one chapter in Irish
Unpriced (pbk)
Also classified at 796.35 B82-21508

796.332 — AMERICAN FOOTBALL

796.332'07'7 — American football. Coaching — *Manuals*

Lombardi, Vince. Vince Lombardi on football / edited by George L. Flynn ; introduction by Red Smith. — New York ; London : Van Nostrand Reinhold, 1981, c1973. — 352p : ill,ports ; 29cm
Originally published: in 2v. Greenwich, Conn. : New York Graphic Society, 1973. — Includes index
ISBN 0-442-22540-7 : £16.95 B82-13199

796.333 — RUGBY FOOTBALL

796.33'3 — Rugby Union football

Irvine, David. The joy of rugby / David Irvine. — Rev. ed. — London : Luscombe, 1979. — 143p : ill,ports ; 24cm
Previous ed.: 1978. — Includes index
ISBN 0-86002-125-4 (pbk) : £1.95 B82-02192

John, Barry. Barry John's world of rugby. — London : Muller, Sept.1982. — [152]p
ISBN 0-584-11036-7 : £5.95 : CIP entry B82-21978

796.33'3'0207 — Rugby Union football — *Humour*

Burton, Mike. Have balls — will travel. — London : Collins, Oct.1982. — [96]p
ISBN 0-00-218005-7 : £5.95 : CIP entry B82-23076

Hollands, Eileen. Never marry a rugger player! / by Eileen Hollands ; illustrated by Christine Townsend. — Sidmouth : Quill, 1979. — 146p : ill ; 22cm
ISBN 0-904596-01-x : Unpriced B82-15297

796.33'3'06842819 — West Yorkshire *(Metropolitan County).* **Leeds. Headingley. Rugby league football grounds: Headingley Rugby Ground,** *to 1979*

Dalby, Ken. The Headingley story / by Ken Dalby. — Leeds (12 Talbot Mount, Leeds LS4 2PF) : K. Dalby
Vol.3: White is the rose : a record of County Cricket at Headingley 1891-1980. — [1981?]. — 146p : ill,ports ; 25cm
£3.00 (pbk)
Also classified at 796.35'8'06842819
B82-00766

796.33'3'077 — Rugby League football. Coaching — *Manuals*

French, Ray. Coaching Rugby League. — London : Faber, Aug.1982. — 1v.
ISBN 0-571-11954-9 (cased) : CIP entry
ISBN 0-571-11955-7 (pbk) : Unpriced
B82-16648

796.33'3'077 — Rugby Union football. Coaching — *Manuals — Conference proceedings*

Dawes, John. The principles of rugby football. — London : Allen and Unwin, Feb.1983. — [208]p
Conference papers
ISBN 0-04-796067-1 : £9.95 : CIP entry
B82-36450

796.33'3'09 — Rugby League football, *to 1980*

Hodgkinson, David. The world of Rugby League / David Hodgkinson and Paul Harrison ; with a contribution by Mick Stephenson. — London : Allen & Unwin, 1981. — 110p : ill,facsims,ports ; 26cm
Includes index
ISBN 0-04-796059-0 : Unpriced : CIP rev.
B81-22568

796.33'3'09 — Rugby League football, *to 1981*

Waring, Eddie. Eddie Waring on Rugby League. — London : Muller, 1981. — 160p : ill,ports ; 24cm
Includes index
ISBN 0-584-10358-1 : £4.95 : CIP rev.
B81-18110

796.33'3'09 — Rugby Union football, *to 1980*

Hopkins, John, *1945-*. Rugby / John Hopkins. — London : Cassell, 1979. — 192p : ill(some col.),ports(some col.) ; 26cm. — (The Schweppes leisure library. Sport)
Includes index
ISBN 0-304-30299-6 : £7.95 B82-13473

796.33'3'09 — Rugby Union football, *to 1981*

Godwin, Terry. The Guinness book of rugby facts & feats / Terry Godwin and Chris Rhys. — Enfield : Guinness Superlatives, c1981. — 258p : ill(some col.),ports(some col.) ; 24cm
Bibliography: p258. — Includes index
ISBN 0-85112-214-0 (cased) : £7.95 : CIP rev.
ISBN 0-85112-248-5 (pbk) : Unpriced
B81-31200

796.33'3'0924 — England. Rugby Union football. Beaumont, Bill — *Biographies*

Beaumont, Bill. Thanks to rugby. — London : Stanley Paul, Oct.1982. — [208]p
ISBN 0-09-150750-2 : £6.95 : CIP entry
B82-28443

796.33'3'0924 — England. Rugby Union football. Burton, Mike — *Biographies*

Burton, Mike. Never stay down : an autobiography / Mike Burton and Steve Jones. — London : Queen Anne Press, 1982. — 186p,[8]p of plates : ill,1facsim,ports ; 24cm
ISBN 0-356-08565-1 : £7.95 B82-21123

796.33'3'0924 — England. Rugby Union football. Cotton, Fran — *Biographies*

Cotton, Fran. Fran : an autobiography / Fran Cotton. — London : Queen Anne Press, c1981. — 192p : ill,facsims,ports ; 25cm
Includes index
ISBN 0-362-00582-6 : £7.95 B82-04764

796.33'3'0924 — England. Rugby Union football. Uttley, Roger — *Biographies*

Uttley, Roger. Pride in England : a rugby autobiography / Roger Uttley with David Norrie. — London : Stanley Paul, 1981. — 189p,[16]p of plates : ports ; 23cm
ISBN 0-09-146320-3 : £6.95 : CIP rev.
B81-30263

796.33'3'0924 — Great Britain. Rugby League football & Rugby Union football. Watkins, David, *1942-* — *Biographies*

Watkins, David, *1942-*. David Watkins : an autobiography / David Watkins : edited by David Parry-Jones. — London : Cassell, 1980. — 234p,[8]p of plates : ports ; 23cm
Includes index
ISBN 0-304-30692-4 : £6.95 B82-25235

796.33'3'0924 — Wales. Rugby union football. Bennett Phil — *Biographies*

Bennett, Phil. Everywhere for Wales / Phil Bennett and Martyn Williams. — London : Stanley Paul, 1981. — 175p,[16]p of plates : ill,ports ; 23cm
ISBN 0-09-146310-6 : £5.95 : CIP rev.
B81-26803

796.33'3'0941 — Great Britain. Rugby League football — *Serials*

Rothmans rugby league yearbook. — 1981-82-. — Aylesbury (Oxford Rd, Aylesbury, Bucks.) : Rothmans Publications, 1981-. — v. : ill,ports ; 21cm
ISSN 0262-4745 = Rothmans rugby league yearbook : £4.50 B82-04075

796.33'3'09424 — England. Midlands. Rugby Union football — *Serials*

Rugby Football Union. *Midland Group*. Bass, Mitchells & Butlers Midland counties rugby football handbook : official handbook for the Midland Group. — 1977-78-. — [Birmingham] ([c/o A. Appleton, 70 Hawthorne Rd, Birmingham B30 1EG]) : The Midland Group Committee, [1977]-. — v. : ill,facsims ; 23cm
Annual. — Continues: Rugby Football Union. Midland Group. Midland counties rugby football handbook. — Description based on: 1979-80 issue
ISSN 0263-2551 = Bass, Mitchells & Butlers Midland counties rugby football handbook : £1.00 per issue B82-22677

796.33'362'0942837 — Humberside. Hull. Rugby League football. Clubs: Hull Football Club & Hull Kingston Rovers, *to 1981*

Elton, Christopher. Hull & Rovers : through 88 seasons / by Christopher Elton. — Hull (195 Park Ave., Hull HU5 4DE) : C. Elton, c1981. — 98p ; 21cm
£3.00 (pbk) B82-12959

796.33'375 — Rugby Union football. International matches played by English teams, *to 1982*

Griffiths, John. The book of English international rugby 1871-1982. — London : Collins, Sept.1982. — [480]p
ISBN 0-00-218006-5 : £14.50 : CIP entry
B82-19070

796.334 — ASSOCIATION FOOTBALL

796.334 — Association football

Barrett, Norman. Young footballer's pocket book / Norman Barrett ; illustrated by Paul Buckle. — Bristol : Purnell, 1982. — 128p : ill ; 19cm
Bibliography: p128
ISBN 0-361-05070-4 (pbk) : £1.95 B82-35837

Rollin, Jack. The Guinness book of soccer facts and feats / by Jack Rollin. — 4th ed. — Enfield : Guinness Superlatives, 1981. — 256p : ill(some col.),facsims,ports ; 25cm
Previous ed.: 1980. — Includes index
ISBN 0-85112-227-2 : £6.95 : CIP rev.
B81-25827

796.334 — Association football — *For African students*

Football and great footballers : star portraits, facts & figures, training tips, games & quizzes, great match reports. — Harlow : Longman, 1981. — 48p : ill,1plan,ports ; 25cm
Cover title
ISBN 0-582-78522-7 (pbk) : £1.10 B82-07572

796.334 — Association football — *For children*

Baker, John P. (John Peter). Football / written by John P. Baker ; illustrations by Peter Robinson. — Loughborough : Ladybird, 1982. — 51p : ill(some col.),ports(some col.) ; 18cm. — (Learnabout)
Text on lining papers. — Includes index
ISBN 0-7214-0697-1 : £0.50 B82-09750

796.334 — Association football — *Stories, anecdotes*

Kevin Keegan's international football book / [compiled by B. Apsley]. — Manchester : World International, c1981. — 59p : ill(some col.),ports(some col.) ; 28cm
Ill on lining papers
ISBN 0-7235-6634-8 : £2.25 B82-39530

Parkinson, Michael, *1935-*. Parkinsons lore / Michael Parkinson ; with drawings by Michael Lewis. — London : Pavilion, 1981. — 156p : ill ; 23cm
ISBN 0-907516-05-x : £5.95 : CIP rev.
Primary classification 796.35'8 B81-25740

796.334 — Great Britain. Association football. Betting. Pools — *Manuals*

Jones, Dennis, *19---*. The pools punter's guide to a fortune / Dennis Jones. — New ed. — London : Foulsham, 1980. — 96p : forms ; 18cm
Previous ed.: 1980
ISBN 0-572-01159-8 (pbk) : £1.25 B82-04016

796.334'03'61 — Association football — *Spanish-English dictionaries*

Sierra, Jose Antonio. English-Spanish sports dictionary for soccer. — Dublin : Wolfhound Press, Apr.1982. — [96]p
ISBN 0-905473-84-1 (cased) : £4.95 : CIP entry
ISBN 0-905473-85-x (pbk) : £2.00 B82-11976

796.334'05 — Association football — *Serials — For children*

Top soccer annual. — 1981-. — London : IPC Magazines, 1980-. — v. : ill(some col.),ports ; 28cm
Supplement to: Top soccer. — Only one issue published
£2.00 B82-18529

796.334'07 — Association football. Teaching

Gibbon, Alan. Teaching soccer. — London : Bell & Hyman, Oct.1981. — [128]p
ISBN 0-7135-1257-1 (pbk) : £3.95 : CIP entry
B81-25833

796.334'07'7 — Association football. Coaching — *Manuals*

Ford, George. Basic soccer : strategies for successful player and program development / George Ford. — Boston [Mass.] ; London : Allyn and Bacon, c1982. — xii,259p : ill ; 24cm
Includes index
ISBN 0-205-07157-0 : £19.95 B82-08628

796.334'092'2 — Association football. Players, *to 1981 — Biographies*

Glanville, Brian. Brian Glanville's Book of footballers. — Harmondsworth : Puffin, 1978 (1982 [printing]). — 167p,[16]p of plates : ports ; 19cm. — (Puffin plus)
ISBN 0-14-031508-x (pbk) : £1.25 B82-22486

796.334'092'2 — Great Britain. Association footballers, *to 1979*

Butler, Bryon. Soccer choice / Bryon Butler and Ron Greenwood. — London : Pelham, 1979. — 176p,[16]p of plates : ports ; 23cm
ISBN 0-7207-1184-3 : £5.95 B82-09243

796.334'092'4 — England. Association football. Brooking, Trevor — *Biographies*

Brooking, Trevor. Trevor Brooking / with the assistance of Brian Scovell. — London : Pelham, 1981. — 189p[16]p of plates : ill,ports ; 23cm
ISBN 0-7207-1374-9 : £6.95 : CIP rev.
B81-28054

796.334'092'4 — England. Association football. Hoddle, Glenn — *Biographies*

Hoddle, Glenn. Glenn Hoddle. — London : Pelham, Nov.1982. — [176]p
ISBN 0-7207-1433-8 : £5.95 : CIP entry B82-26409

796.334'092'4 — England. Association football. Hughes, Emlyn — *Biographies*

Hughes, Emlyn. Crazy Horse / Emlyn Hughes. — London : Macdonald Futura, 1981, c1980. — 171p,[8]p of plates : ill,ports ; 18cm. — (A Futura book)
Originally published: London : A Barker, 1980
ISBN 0-7088-2091-3 (pbk) : £1.35 B82-00525

796.334'092'4 — England. Association football. Matthews, Stanley, *1965-1979* — *Biographies*

Matthews, Stanley. Back in touch / Stanley and Mila Matthews with a helping hand from Don Taylor. — London : Arthur Barker, [1981?]. — viii,262p : ports ; 24cm
ISBN 0-213-16806-5 : £7.50 B82-00586

796.334'092'4 — England. Association football. Shilton, Peter — *Biographies*

Tomas, Jason. Peter Shilton : the magnificent obsession / Jason Tomas with Peter Shilton. — Tadworth : World's Work, c1982. — 137p : ill,facsims,ports ; 26cm
Ill on lining papers
ISBN 0-437-17430-1 : £7.95 B82-19396

796.334'092'4 — England. Association football. Stock, Alec — *Biographies*

Stock, Alec. A little thing called pride : an autobiography / Alec Stock. — London : Pelham, c1982. — 172p,[8]p of plates : ill,ports ; 23cm
ISBN 0-7207-1395-1 : £7.95 : CIP rev. B82-04966

796.334'092'4 — England. Association football. Watson, Dave — *Personal observations*

Watson, Penny. My dear Watson : the story of a football marriage / Penny Watson. — London : Arthur Barker, c1981. — 134p,[8]p of plates : ill,ports ; 23cm
ISBN 0-213-16814-6 : £5.95 B82-04116

796.334'092'4 — Northern Ireland. Association football. Best, George — *Biographies*

Best, George. Where do I go from here? / George Best and Graeme Wright. — London : Futura, 1982, c1981. — 256p : ill,ports ; 18cm
Originally published: London : Queen Anne Press, 1981
ISBN 0-7088-2203-7 (pbk) : £1.60 B82-37790

796.334'092'4 — Scotland. Association football. Dalglish, Kenny — *Biographies*

Dalglish, Kenny. King Kenny : an autobiography / Kenny Dalglish ; with Ken Gallacher. — London : Stanley Paul, 1982. — 134p,[12]p of plates : ill,ports ; 23cm
ISBN 0-09-147730-1 : £6.95 : CIP rev. B82-09206

796.334'092'4 — Scotland. Association football. Lennox, Bobby — *Biographies*

Lennox, Bobby. A million miles for Celtic. — London : Stanley Paul, Oct.1982. — 1v.
ISBN 0-09-150240-3 : £6.95 : CIP entry B82-24974

796.334'0941 — Great Britain. Association football

Football champions / edited by Norman Barrett. — Bristol : Purnell, 1981. — 69p : ill (some.col.),ports(some col.) ; 27cm
Text, ill on lining papers
ISBN 0-361-05091-7 : £2.25 B82-03654

796.334'0941 — Great Britain. Association football, *1870-1910*

Hutchinson, John. The football industry. — Glasgow (20 Park Circus, Glasgow G3 6BE) : Richard Drew, Nov.1981. — [96]p
ISBN 0-904002-81-0 (pbk) : £4.95 : CIP entry B81-30894

796.334'0941 — Great Britain. Association football. Matches, *1870-1980* — *Records of achievement*

The **Hamlyn** A-Z of British football records / [compiled by] Phil Soar. — London : Hamlyn, 1981. — 192p : ill(some col.),facsims(some col.),ports(some col.) ; 29cm
Bibliography: p192. — Includes index
ISBN 0-600-34662-5 : £6.95 B82-00071

796.334'0941 — Great Britain. Association football — *Serials*

The **Football** Association year book. — 1981-1982. — London : Pelham, Aug.1981. — [192]p
ISBN 0-7207-1352-8 (pbk) : £2.25 : CIP entry B81-23805

[Report *(Association of Football Statisticians)*]. Report / the Association of Football Statisticians. — No.1 (Dec. 1978)-. — Basildon (c/o R. Spiller, 5 Hempstalls, Basildon, Essex SS15 5AA) : The Association, 1978-. — v. : facsims,ports ; 21cm
Six issues yearly. — Description based on: No.21 (Nov. 1981)
ISSN 0263-1342 = Report - Association of Football Statisticians : Unpriced B82-17243

796.334'0941 — Great Britain. Association football — *Statistics* — *Serials*

[Annual *(Association of Football Statisticians)*]. Annual / the Association of Football Statisticians. — 1888-89-. — Basildon (c/o R.J. Spiller, 5 Hempstalls, Basildon, Essex SS15 5AA) : The Association, 1981-. — v. : facsims,ports ; 21cm
Three issues yearly. — Results and statistics from the English and Scottish football season. — Description based on: 1890-91 issue
ISSN 0263-0354 = Annual - Association of Football Statisticians : Unpriced B82-14779

796.334'09411 — Scotland. Association football — *Serials*

The **Scottish** football book. — No.27. — London : Paul, Sept.1981. — [96]p
ISBN 0-09-146091-3 (pbk) : £3.95 : CIP entry B81-20586

796.334'2 — Association football — *Manuals*

Smith, Mike, *1936-*. Success in football / Mike Smith ; with a foreword by Allen Wade. — 3rd ed. — London : Murray, 1982. — 96p : ill,ports ; 23cm. — (Success sportsbooks)
Previous ed.: 1978
ISBN 0-7195-3900-5 : £3.95 B82-32751

Tindall, Ron. Soccer fundamentals / Ron Tindall. — Newton Abbot : David & Charles, c1982. — 64p : ill ; 26cm
Includes index
ISBN 0-7153-8361-2 : £3.95 B82-39633

Tully, Tom. [The Beaver book of football]. Football : a complete guide to better soccer / Tom Tully ; illustrated by Mike Jackson ; cartoons by David Mostyn. — London : Severn House, 1980, c1979. — 126p : ill ; 21cm
Originally published: London : Beaver, 1979
ISBN 0-7278-0685-8 : £3.95 : CIP rev. B80-17907

Yaxley, Mike. Soccer / Mike Yaxley. — London : Batsford Academic and Educational, 1982. — 63p : ill ; 26cm. — (Competitive sports series)
Includes index
ISBN 0-7134-3980-7 : £4.50 : CIP rev. B81-37576

796.334'2 — Association football — *Manuals* — *For children*

Banks, Gordon, *1937-*. You can play football / Gordon Banks ; illustrated by Mike Miller. — [London] : Carousel, [1982]. — 119p : ill ; 20cm
ISBN 0-552-54200-8 (pbk) : £0.95 B82-18697

Banks, Gordon, *1937-*. [You can play football]. You can play soccer / Gordon Banks ; illustrated by Mike Miller. — London : Severn House, 1982. — 119p : ill ; 21cm
Originally published: London : Carousel, 1982
ISBN 0-7278-0806-0 : £5.95 B82-36253

Freeman, Simon, *19---*. Football / by Simon Freeman ; illustrated by George Fryer. — London : Macdonald, 1982. — 64p : ill(some col.) ; 21cm. — (Whizz kids ; 23)
Includes index
ISBN 0-356-06383-6 (cased) : £2.95
ISBN 0-356-06343-7 (pbk) : £1.25 B82-25712

796.334'2 — Association football. Techniques

Widdows, Richard. The Hamlyn book of football techniques and tactics / Richard Widdows ; illustrated by Paul Buckle. — Feltham : Hamlyn, 1982. — 192p : ill(some col.) ; 31cm
Includes index
ISBN 0-600-34641-2 : £6.95 B82-37016

796.334'62'0941 — Great Britain. Association football. Non-league clubs — *Serials*

Rothmans F.A. non-league football yearbook. — 1981-82-. — Aylesbury (Oxford Rd, Aylesbury, Bucks.) : Rothmans Publications, 1981-. — v. : ill,maps,ports ; 21cm
Continues: The F.A. non-league football annual
ISSN 0262-4850 = Rothmans F.A. non-league football yearbook : £3.95 B82-04074

796.334'62'0941467 — Scotland. Strathclyde Region. Glenbuck. Amateur association football. Clubs: Glenbuck Cherrypickers, *to 1935*

Faulds, M. H.. The Cherrypickers : Glenbuck, nursery of footballers / M.H. Faulds and Wm. Tweedie, Jnr. — Cumnock : Cumnock and Doon Valley District Council, 1981, c1951. — 20p : ill,ports ; 15x22cm
Originally published: Muirkirk : Muirkirk Advertiser and Douglasdale Gazette, 1951
ISBN 0-9506568-1-x (pbk) : £0.50 B82-05149

796.334'63'0941 — Great Britain. Football League football, *1914-1918* — *Statistics*

War report / The Association of Football Statisticians. — Basildon (5 Hempstalls, Basildon, Essex SS15 5AA) : The Association
No.1: Season 1915/16. — [1982?]. — 46p : ports ; 22cm
Unpriced (unbound) B82-27241

War report / The Association of Football Statisticians. — Basildon (5 Hemptalls, Basildon, Essex SS15 5AA) : The Association
No.3: Season 1917/18. — [1982?]. — 42p : facsims,ports ; 21cm
Cover title
Unpriced (pbk) B82-39869

796.334'63'0941 — Great Britain. Football League football. Matches, *to 1981* — *Statistics*

Lovett, Norman. The draw experts / by Norman Lovett. — Hull : British Programme Collectors Club, c1981. — (Facts and figures on the Football League Clubs ; no.33)
Subtitle: With special pools guide including details of the top 2,100 matches which the home clubs failed to win from 1888-1981
Vol.1. — 104p ; 21cm
ISBN 0-907263-02-x (pbk) : Unpriced B82-08512

796.334'63'0941 — Great Britain. Football League footballers, *1946-1981* — *Records of achievement*

Hugman, Barry J.. Rothmans football league players records : the complete A-Z 1946-1981 / compiled by Barry J. Hugman ; foreword by B.B.C.'s John Motson. — Aylesbury : Rothmans Publications, 1981. — x,500p : ports ; 31cm
ISBN 0-907574-08-4 : £9.95 B82-09893

796.334'63'0941318 — Scotland. Association football. Clubs: East Stirlingshire Football Club, *to 1981*

McMillan, Alan. Showing in black & white only / by Alan McMillan. — Kilsyth (Market Sq., Kilsyth) : Garrell, [1981?]. — 45p : ill,ports ; 30cm
'Published to mark the centenary of East Stirlingshire FC'
£1.00 (pbk) B82-29918

796.334'63'0941443 — Scotland. Association football. Clubs: Glasgow Celtic Football Club — *Serials*

Playing for Celtic. — No.13. — London : Paul, Sept.1981. — [96]p
ISBN 0-09-146081-6 (pbk) : £3.95 : CIP entry B81-20584

796.334'63'0941443 — Scotland. Association football. Clubs: Glasgow Celtic Football Club — *Serials* *continuation*
Playing for Celtic. — No.14. — London : Paul, Sept.1982. — [96]p
ISBN 0-09-149921-6 (pbk) : £3.95 : CIP entry
B82-19815

796.334'63'0941443 — Scotland. Association football. Clubs: Rangers Football Club — *Serials*
Playing for Rangers. — No.13. — London : Paul, Sept.1981. — [96]p
ISBN 0-09-146071-9 (pbk) : £3.95 : CIP entry
B81-20585

796.334'63'0942 — England. Football League football. Clubs — *Statistics*
Lovett, Norman. Facts and figures — on the football league clubs / by Norman Lovett. — Hull : British Programme Club
No.4-27: The ex-League clubs (1888-1981). — c1981. — 102p ; 21cm
ISBN 0-9504273-6-5 (pbk) : £3.50 B82-16344

796.334'63'0942134 — England. Association football. Clubs: Chelsea Football Club, *to 1982*
Moynihan, John. The Chelsea story / John Moynihan ; foreword by Sebastian Coe. — London : Barker, c1982. — x,173p : ill,facsims,ports ; 26cm
Ill on lining papers
ISBN 0-213-16823-5 : £5.95 B82-36627

796.334'63'0942143 — England. Association football. Clubs: Arsenal Football Club, *to 1981*
Rippon, Anton. The story of Arsenal / Anton Rippon. — Ashbourne : Moorland Publishing, c1981. — 95p : ill,ports ; 26cm
ISBN 0-86190-023-5 : £4.95 : CIP rev.
B81-28134

796.334'63'0942188 — England. Association football. Clubs: Tottenham Hotspur Football Club, *to 1982*
Soar, Phil. And the Spurs go marching on ... / by Phil Soar with Danny Blanchflower ... [et al.]. — London : Hamlyn, 1982. — 256p : ill (some col.),ports(some col.) ; 31cm
Ill on lining papers. — Includes index
ISBN 0-600-34664-1 : £9.95 B82-40749

796.334'63'0942496 — England. Association football. Clubs: Aston Villa Football Club, *to 1981*
Saunders, Ron. Ron Saunders' Aston Villa scrapbook / by Ron Saunders. — [London] : Pictorial Presentations, c1981. — 143p : ill,ports ; 24cm
ISBN 0-285-62512-8 (cased) : £6.95
ISBN 0-285-62513-6 (pbk) : £4.95 B82-01776

796.334'63'0942733 — England. Football League football. Clubs: Manchester City Football Club, *to 1980 — Statistics*
Lovett, Norman. Manchester City : (including Ardwick) 1892-1980 : results, league tables, would you believe it items, facts & figures / by Norman Lovett. — Hull : British Programme Collectors Club, c1981. — 101p ; 21cm. — (Facts and figures on the Football League clubs ; no.32)
ISBN 0-907263-01-1 (pbk) : £2.50 B82-00786

796.334'63'09428 — North-east England. Football League football. Clubs, *to 1981*
Rippon, Anton. Great soccer clubs of the North East / Anton Rippon. — Ashborne : Moorlan Publishing, c1981. — 126p : ill,ports ; 26cm
ISBN 0-86190-022-7 (pbk) : £5.50 : CIP rev.
B81-28135

796.334'63'0942831 — England. Association football. Clubs: Scunthorpe United Football Club, *to 1980*
Staff, John. The history of Scunthorpe United Football Club / by John Staff. — [Scunthorpe] ([36 Goodwood, Bottesford, Scunthorpe, S. Humberside DN17 2TP]) : [John Staff Enterprises], [1980]. — 250p,[6]p of plates : ill,ports ; 21cm
Cover title
Unpriced (pbk) B82-15075

796.334'63'0942982 — Wales. Association football. Clubs: Swansea City Association Football Club, *to 1982*
Farmer, David. Swansea City 1912-1982. — London : Pelham, Nov.1982. — [208]p
ISBN 0-7207-1413-3 : £8.50 : CIP entry
B82-26407

796.334'64 — England. Association football. Competitions: F.A. Cup. Giant killers, *1879-1981*
Butler, Bryon. The giant killers / Bryon Butler. — London : Pelham, 1982. — 184p,[12]p of plates : ill,ports ; 23cm
ISBN 0-7207-1371-4 : £6.95 : CIP rev.
B82-00340

796.334'64 — England. Association football. Competitions: F.A. Cup. Matches, *1939-1946 — Statistics*
War time report. — [Basildon] ([5, Hemstalls, Basildon, Essex SS15 5AA]) : Association of Football Statisticians, [1981?]. — 8v. ; 21cm
£7.00 (unbound) B82-16004

796.334'64 — Great Britain. Association football. Competitions: F.A. Cup. Matches, *1915-1919 — Statistics*
War report / Association of Football Statisticians. — Basildon (5 Hemptalls, Basildon, Essex) : The Association
No.2: Season 1916/17. — [1982?]. — 47p ; 21cm
Unpriced (unbound) B82-32420

796.334'66 — Association football. Competitions: World Cup *(Football championship), to 1978*
Glanville, Brian. The history of the world cup / Brian Glanville. — Rev. ed. — London : Faber, 1980. — 255p,[16]p of plates : ill,ports ; 24cm
Previous ed.: published as The Sunday times history of the World Cup. London : Times Newspapers, 1973. — Includes index
ISBN 0-571-11498-9 : £8.50 : CIP rev.
B80-12472

796.334'66 — Association football. Competitions: World Cup *(Football championship), to 1982*
Barnes, David. The game of the century : World Cup Spain 1982 / David Barnes. — London : Sidgwick & Jackson, 1982. — 187p,[8]p of plates : ill(some col.),ports(some col.) ; 24cm
Includes index
ISBN 0-283-98846-0 : £6.95 B82-22264

Croker, Peter. Disney's family guide to the World Cup 82 / Peter Croker & Alex Martin ; foreword by Ron Greenwood. — [London] : Target, 1982. — 127p : ill,2maps,forms,ports ; 18cm
ISBN 0-426-20137-x (pbk) : £1.35 B82-22767

Greaves, Jimmy. The World Cup : 1930-1982 / Jimmy Greaves ; edited by Norman Giller. — London : Harrap, 1982. — 139p : ill,forms,1map,ports ; 24cm
ISBN 0-245-53884-4 : £4.95 B82-30543

796.334'66 — Association football. Competitions: World Cup, *to 1978*
Glanville, Brian. The history of the World Cup / Brian Glanville. — Rev. ed. — London : Faber, 1980 (1982 [printing]). — 255p,16p of plates : ill,ports ; 24cm
Previous ed.: published as The Sunday Times history of the World Cup. London : Times Newspapers, 1973. — Includes index
ISBN 0-571-11919-0 (pbk) : £2.95 B82-12854

796.334'66 — Association football. English teams, *to 1981*
Rippon, Anton. Eng-land! : the story of the national soccer team / Anton Rippon. — Ashbourne : Moorland Publishing, c1981. — 144p : ill,ports ; 26cm
ISBN 0-86190-032-4 : £5.95 : CIP rev.
B81-28010

796.334'66 — Spain. Association football. Competitions: World Cup *(Football championship) (1982 : Spain)*
Chippindale, Peter. The unofficial World Cup book / Peter Chippindale. — [London] : Corgi, 1982. — 960p : ill,forms,ports ; 29cm
Ill on folded sheet as insert
ISBN 0-552-99003-5 (pbk) : £2.99 B82-28822

Daily Mail World Cup souvenir / edited by Ian Chimes. — [Great Britain] : Published by Breystand for Harmsworth, c1982. — 48p : ill (some col.),ports(some col.) ; 30cm + chart (59x41cm)
Ill on inside covers. — Chart stapled in centre
ISBN 0-86333-000-2 (pbk) : £1.25 B82-35810

Evans, Philip, *1943 Apr.4-*. World Cup 82 / Philip Evans. — New ed. — Sevenoaks : Knight Books, 1982. — 143p,[16]p of plates : 1map,ports ; 18cm
Previous ed.: i.e. rev. ed., published as World Cup '78. 1978
ISBN 0-340-27747-5 (pbk) : £1.25 : CIP rev.
B82-01714

Keith, Nicholas. World Cup '82 : a complete guide / Nicholas Keith and Norman Fox ; with photographs by Peter Robinson. — London : Park Lane Press, c1982. — 128p : ill (some col.),forms,1col.map,ports(some col.) ; 28cm
ISBN 0-902935-26-7 (pbk) : £1.95 B82-35777

796.334'66 — Spain. Association football. Competitions: World Cup *(Football championship : 1982 : Spain)*
Morgan, John, *1943-*. Rothmans presents World Cup '82 / John Morgan & David Emery. — Aylesbury (PO Box 100, Oxford Rd, Aylesbury, Bucks. HP21 8SZ) : Rothmans, c1982. — 128p : ill ; 19x9cm
Unpriced (pbk) B82-17605

Morgan, John, *1943-*. Rothmans presents World Cup '82 / John Morgan & David Emery. — Aylesbury : Rothmans Publications, c1982. — 128p : ill,1map,ports ; 19x9cm
Unpriced (pbk) B82-26365

796.334'66 — Spain. Association football. Competitions: World Cup *(Football championship) (1982 : Spain)*
Morgan, John, *1943-*. Rothmans presents World Cup 1982 / John Morgan & David Emery. — Aylesbury : Rothmans, c1982. — 256p : ill,1map,ports ; 20cm
ISBN 0-907574-12-2 (pbk) : £2.95 B82-28513

Soar, Phil. Spain '82 : the winning of the World Cup / Phil Soar & Richard Widdows ; photographers Erich Baumann ... [et al.]. — London : Hamlyn, 1982. — 240p : col.ill,1col.map,col.ports ; 31cm
ISBN 0-600-34676-5 : £12.95 B82-40751

World Cup '82 : a souvenir guide to football's premier competition / [written and edited by Daily Mirror Sports Department]. — London : Mirror Books, 1982. — 26p : ill,ports(some col.) ; 36cm. — (A Daily Mirror soccer special)
ISBN 0-85939-314-3 (unbound) : £0.50
B82-33672

796.334'66 — Spain. Association football. Competitions: World Cup *(Football championship) (1982 : Spain).* **English teams**
Davies, Hunter. England! : the 1982 World Cup squad / Hunter Davies. — London : Futura, 1982. — 144p,4p of plates : ill,ports(some col.) ; 20cm
ISBN 0-356-07910-4 (cased) : £5.95
ISBN 0-7088-2200-2 (pbk) : £1.95 B82-24098

796.334'66 — Spain. Association football. Competitions: World Cup *(Football championship) (1982 : Spain) — For children*
Baker, John P. (John Peter). World Cup 82 / written by John P. Baker ; designed by Chris Reed. — Loughborough : Ladybird, c1982. — 51p : col.ill,col.maps,col.ports ; 18cm
Ill on lining papers
ISBN 0-7214-0739-0 : £0.50 B82-25889

796.342 — TENNIS

796.342'05 — Lawn tennis — *Serials*
[Tennis *(London : 1981)*]. Tennis. — No.21 (Winter 1981)-. — London : Thelmill ; London (168 Victoria St., SW1) : Distributed by Ocean Publications, 1981-. — v. : ill ; 30cm
Eight issues yearly. — Continues: Top tennis
ISSN 0262-9224 = Tennis (London. 1981) : £7.00 per year B82-11815

796.342'074'02193 — London. Merton *(London Borough).* **Museums: Wimbledon Lawn Tennis Museum** — *Visitors' guides*

Wimbledon Lawn Tennis Museum. The Wimbledon Lawn Tennis Museum / Valerie Warren. — Wimbledon : The Museum, c1982. — 24p : ill(some col.),ports ; 21cm
Cover title. — Text, ill on inside covers
ISBN 0-906741-09-2 (pbk) : Unpriced
B82-38740

796.342'092'2 — Lawn tennis. Borg, Björn. Interpersonal relationships with Borg, Mariana — *Personal observations*

Borg, Mariana. Love match : my life with Björn / Mariana Borg. — London : Sidgwick & Jackson, 1981 (1982 [printing]). — 125p : ports ; 17cm
ISBN 0-283-98878-9 (pbk) : £1.75 B82-30171

796.342'092'4 — Lawn tennis. Ashe, Arthur — *Biographies*

Ashe, Arthur. Off the court. — London : Eyre Methuen, Feb.1982. — [240]p
ISBN 0-413-49680-5 : £7.50 : CIP entry
B81-36381

796.342'092'4 — Lawn tennis. King, Billie Jean — *Biographies*

King, Billie Jean. The autobiography of Billie Jean King. — London : Granada, May 1982. — [224]p
ISBN 0-246-11792-3 : £6.95 : CIP entry
B82-07410

796.342'092'4 — Lawn tennis. Lloyd, Chris Evert — *Biographies*

Lloyd, Chris Evert. Chrissie / Chris Evert Lloyd with Neil Amdur. — London : Methuen, 1982. — 239p,[24]p of plates : ill,ports ; 24cm
ISBN 0-413-49560-4 : £6.95 : CIP rev.
B82-10499

796.342'092'4 — Lawn tennis. McEnroe, John — *Biographies*

Adams, Ian. John McEnroe : rebel without applause / Ian Adams. — [London] : Corgi, 1982. — 186p : ports ; 18cm
ISBN 0-552-11978-4 (pbk) : £1.50 B82-29731

Cross, Tania. McEnroe : the man with the rage to win / Tania Cross. — London : Arrow, 1982. — 155p,[16]p of plates : ports ; 18cm
ISBN 0-09-928780-3 (pbk) : £1.50 B82-23928

Evans, Richard, *1939-*. McEnroe : a rage for perfection : a biography / by Richard Evans ; written in co-operation with John McEnroe. — London : Sidgwick & Jackson, 1982. — 192p : ill,ports ; 24cm
Includes index
ISBN 0-283-98854-1 : £7.50 B82-32979

Pryor, Sean. McEnroe : superman or superbrat? / Sean Pryor. — London : Star, 1982. — 153p,8p of plates : ports ; 18cm
ISBN 0-352-31093-6 (corrected : pbk) : £1.60
B82-33009

796.342'0941 — Great Britain. Lawn tennis — *Serials*

Tennis club : the tennis club management magazine. — No.1 (Dec. 1981)-. — Berkhamsted (Media House, Boxwell Rd., Berkhamsted, Herts. HP4 3ET) : Dennis Fairey Publishing, 1981-. — v. : ill,ports ; 30cm
Six issues yearly. — Description based on: No.2 (Feb./Mar. 1982)
ISSN 0263-7642 = Tennis club : £3.00 per year B82-32169

796.342'09415 — Ireland. Lawn tennis — *Serials*

Irish Lawn Tennis Association. Tennis : the official handbook of the Irish Lawn Tennis Association. — 1980-. — [Dublin] ([22 Upper Fitzwilliam St., Dublin 2]) : [The Association], 1980-. — v. ; 30cm
Annual. — Continues: Irish Lawn Tennis Association. Irish tennis yearbook. — Description based on: 1981
Unpriced B82-04888

796.342'09421'93 — London. Merton *(London Borough).* **Lawn tennis. Competitions: Lawn Tennis Championships**

Little, Alan, *1928-*. Wimbledon : the official guide to the Championships / by Alan Little. — Wimbledon : All England Lawn Tennis & Croquet Club, 1982. — 37p : ill,ports ; 21cm
Plans on inside covers. — Includes index
ISBN 0-9507105-2-0 (pbk) : Unpriced
B82-38734

796.342'09421'93 — London. Merton *(London Borough).* **Lawn tennis. Competitions: Lawn Tennis Championships** — *Serials*

[Media guide *(London : 1977)*]. Media guide : the lawn tennis championships. — 1977-. — London (52 Vicarage Cres., SW11 3UL) : Programme Publications, 1977-. — v. : plans ; 22cm
Annual. — Description based on: 1982 issue
ISSN 0263-9025 = Media guide (London. 1977) : Unpriced B82-36720

796.342'09421'93 — London. Merton *(London Borough).* **Lawn tennis. Competitions: Lawn Tennis Championships,** *to 1980*

Cole, Arthur. Rothmans Wimbledon on camera : Arthur Cole's pictorial history of the world's greatest tennis tournament / researched and designed by Robert Duncan ; story by Lance Tingay ; foreword by Dan Maskell ; Arthur Cole's biography by Jack Prosser ; edited by Geoff Peters. — Aylesbury : Rothmans, c1981. — 256p : chiefly ill,ports(some col.) ; 30cm
Includes index
ISBN 0-907574-04-1 : £7.50 B82-31489

796.342'09421'93 — London. Merton *(London Borough).* **Lawn tennis. Competitions: Lawn Tennis Championships,** *to 1981*

Atkin, Ronald. The book of Wimbledon / by Ronald Atkin ; photographed by Eamon McCabe. — London : Heinemann, 1981. — 93p : ill(some col.),ports ; 29cm
Ill on lining papers
ISBN 0-434-98011-0 (cased) : £7.95 (pbk) : £4.95 B82-25634

Landon, Charles. Classic moments of Wimbledon / Charles Landon. — Ashbourne : Moorland, [1982?]. — 143p : ill,ports ; 26cm
ISBN 0-86190-052-9 : £6.95 B82-37197

796.342'2 — Lawn tennis — *Manuals*

Douglas, Paul. The handbook of tennis / Paul Douglas ; foreword by John McEnroe ; preface by Dan Maskell ; colour photographs by Gerry Cranham. — London : Pelham, 1982. — 288p : ill(some col.),ports(some col.) ; 25cm
Includes index
ISBN 0-7207-1383-8 : £10.95 B82-22606

Gensemer, Robert. Tennis / Robert Gensemer. — 3rd ed. — Philadelphia ; London : Saunders College Publishing, c1982. — x,102p : ill ; 24cm. — (Saunders physical activities series)
Previous ed.: 1975. — Bibliography: p100-102
ISBN 0-03-060106-1 (pbk) : £4.95 B82-20710

Georgeson, Dudley. Tennis : the Georgeson way / by Dudley Georgeson ; cooperation in production and publishing by Andrew Greenow. — Wheathampstead (44 The Hill, Wheathampstead, Herts.) : Georgeson/Greenow, c1982. — 189p : ill,ports ; 20cm
Unpriced (pbk) B82-26186

Jones, Clarence. Successful tennis / Clarence Medlycott Jones. — London : Published in collaboration with World of Sport by Letts, 1982. — 95p : ill(some col.),ports(some col.) ; 22cm
Includes index
ISBN 0-85097-452-6 (pbk) : £2.95 B82-31660

Tennis / produced in collaboration with the Lawn Tennis Association. — 7th rev. ed. — Wakefield : EP Publishing, 1982. — 40p : ill ; 14x21cm. — (Know the game)
Ill on inside front cover
ISBN 0-7158-0812-5 (pbk) : £0.85 B82-34903

796.343 — SQUASH RACKETS

796.34'3 — Squash rackets — *Manuals*

Barrington, Jonah, *1941-*. Murder in the squash court : the only way to win / Jonah Barrington with Angela Patmore. — London : Stanley Paul, 1982. — 158p,[8]p of plates : ports ; 23cm
ISBN 0-09-147560-0 : £5.95 : CIP rev.
B82-01142

796.34'3'05 — Squash rackets — *Serials*

Squash news : the official newspaper of the Squash Rackets Association. — No.1 (197-)-. — London (Francis House, Francis St., SW1P 1DE) : The Association, [197-]-. — v. : ill,ports ; 38cm
Irregular. — Description based on: No.9 (Oct. 1981)
ISSN 0263-2640 = Squash news : Unpriced
B82-22665

796.34'3'09411 — Eastern Scotland. Squash rackets — *Serials*

East of Scotland Squash Rackets Association. Handbook / East of Scotland Squash Rackets Association. — 1980-81-. — [Edinburgh] ([c/o M. Fitchett, Sports Centre, Heriot-Watt University, Riccarton, Edinburgh EH14 4AS]) : [The Association], [1980]-. — v. : ill,ports ; 21cm
Annual
ISSN 0263-2586 = Handbook - East of Scotland Squash Rackets Association : £0.50 per issue B82-23599

796.345 — BADMINTON

796.34'5 — Badminton — *Manuals*

Davis, Pat. Badminton : the complete practical guide / Pat Davis. — Newton Abbot : David & Charles, c1982. — 192p : ill,plans,ports ; 26cm
Includes index
ISBN 0-7153-8163-6 : £8.95 : CIP rev.
B82-15836

Wright, Les. Successful badminton / Les Wright. — London : Published in collaboration with World of Sport by Letts, 1982. — 95p : ill (some col.),ports(some col.) ; 22cm
Includes index
ISBN 0-85097-432-1 (corrected : pbk) : £2.95
B82-34648

796.34'5 — Badminton — *Rules*

International Badminton Federation. Statute book : addendum to 1981-82 edition : 1982-83 / the International Badminton Federation. — Cheltenham (24 Winchcombe House, Winchcombe St., Cheltenham, Gloucestershire) : The Federation, [1982]. — 27p : ill ; 19cm
Unpriced (unbound) B82-41136

796.34'5'06042 — England. Badminton. Organisations: Badminton Association of England — *Serials*

Badminton Association of England. Annual handbook / the Badminton Association of England. — 1981-82 ed.-. — Milton Keynes (National Badminton Centre, Bradwell Rd, Loughton Lodge, Milton Keynes MK8 9LA) : The Association, [1981]-. — v. : ill ; 21cm
Continues: Badminton Association of England. Badminton Association of England's annual handbook
ISSN 0262-1940 = Annual handbook - Badminton Association of England (1981) : £1.50 B82-02390

796.34'5'0924 — Badminton. Gilks, Gillian - *Biographies*

Hunn, David. Gillian Gilks. — London : Ward Lock, June 1981. — [160]p
ISBN 0-7063-6114-8 : £6.95 : CIP entry
B81-12889

796.35 — SPORTS USING BALL DRIVEN BY CLUB, MALLET, BAT

796.35 — Ireland *(Republic).* **Hurling. Keher, Eddie** — *Biographies*

Macken, Ultan. Eddie Keher's hurling life : a biography of the famous Kilkenny hurler / by Ultan Macken. — Dublin : Mercier, c1978. — 146p,[16]p of plates : ports ; 19cm
ISBN 0-85342-574-4 : £5.00 B82-17686

796.35 — Wexford *(County)*. **Piercestown. Hurling. Clubs: St Martins GAA Club,** *to 1982*
St Martins GAA Club. St Martins GAA Club 1932-1982 / editor: Edward Culleton. — Wexford : The Club, 1982. — viii,162p : ill,1map,ports ; 23cm
Includes one chapter in Irish
Unpriced (pbk)
Primary classification 796.33 B82-21508

796.352 — GOLF

796.352 — Golf
Dobereiner, Peter. For the love of golf : the best of Dobereiner / Peter Dobereiner. — London : Stanley Paul, 1981. — 256p : ill ; 24cm
ISBN 0-09-145150-7 : £7.95 : CIP rev. B81-11958

Down the nineteenth fairway. — London : Deutsch, Sept.1982. — [224]p
ISBN 0-233-97495-4 : £8.95 : CIP entry B82-20621

796.352 — Golf — *Stories, anecdotes*
In celebration of golf. — St Albans : Granada, Aug.1982. — [256]p
ISBN 0-246-11142-9 : £9.95 : CIP entry B82-15701

796.352′01′9 — Golf. Psychological aspects
Gallwey, W. Timothy. The inner game of golf / [W. Timothy Gallwey]. — London : Cape, 1981, c1979. — 207p ; 24cm
ISBN 0-224-02922-3 : £5.95 : CIP rev. B81-28074

796.352′0207 — Golf — *Humour*
Alliss, Peter. More bedside golf / Peter Alliss ; illustrations by Colin Whittock. — London : Collins, 1982. — 88p : ill(some col.) ; 26cm
Ill on lining papers
ISBN 0-00-216496-5 : £5.95 : CIP rev. B82-19065

Hepburn, Tom. Great golf holes of New Zealand / Tom Hepburn, Selwyn Jacobson. — Auckland ; London : Collins, 1981 (1982 [printing]). — [40]p : col.ill ; 29cm
ISBN 0-00-216996-7 (pbk) : £2.95 B82-26114

Tresidder, Phil. The golfer who laughed / Phil Tresidder ; illustrated by Mike Watkins. — London : Stanley Paul, c1982. — 127p : ill ; 21cm
ISBN 0-09-137630-0 : £4.95 : CIP rev. B82-06218

796.352′03′21 — Golf — *Encyclopaedias*
Scott, Tom, *1906-*. The observer's book of golf / Tom Scott. — New ed. — London : Warne, 1982. — 191p,8p of plates : ill(some col.),ports (some col.) ; 15cm. — (The Observer's pocket series ; 58)
Previous ed.: 1975
ISBN 0-7232-1621-5 : Unpriced B82-30672

796.352′06′805 — Golf courses — *Serials*
Golf holidays. — Issue 1 (Autumn '81)-. — Norwich (130 Ber St., Norwich NR1 3AQ) : Printel Ltd, 1981-. — v. : ill(some col.),ports ; 30cm
Quarterly
ISSN 0263-4821 = Golf holidays : £0.80 per issue B82-27637

796.352′06′809 — Golf courses, *to 1981*
Cornish, Geoffrey S.. The golf course / Geoffrey S. Cornish and Ronald E. Whitten ; special photography by Brian D. Morgan ; foreword by Robert Trent Jones. — [Leicester] : Windward, c1981. — 320p : ill(some col.),facsims ; 29cm
Bibliography: p314-315. — Includes index
ISBN 0-7112-0223-0 : £15.00 B82-08380

796.352′06′841 — Great Britain. Golf courses — *Directories*
Steel, Donald. The golf course guide to the British Isles / by Donald Steel. — 6th rev. ed. — [London] : Collins with Daily Telegraph, 1982. — 176p : maps ; 26cm
Previous ed.: 1980. — Includes index
ISBN 0-00-434179-1 (pbk) : £3.95 B82-22877

796.352′06′841 — Great Britain. Golf courses — *Directories* — *Serials*
Golf — where to play and where to stay : a golfers guide to hotels and courses in the United Kingdom and Ireland. — 4th. ed.-. — [Macclesfield] ([Charles Roe House, Chestergate, Macclesfield, Cheshire]) : [McMillan Martin Ltd], 1980-. — v. : ill,maps ; 21cm
Annual. — Continues: Where to stay and where to play
ISSN 0263-4066 = Golf, where to play and where to stay : £1.95
Also classified at 647′.944101 B82-19862

796.352′06′84115 — Scotland. Highland Region. Golf courses — *Directories*
Golf in the Highland Region / Highland Region. — Inverness (Glenurquhart Rd, Inverness N3 5NX) : Highland Regional Council, [1982?]. — [16]p : 1map ; 21cm
£0.30 (pbk) B82-29246

Golfing : a guide to the golf courses in the Highland Region. — Inverness : Highland Regional Council, [1981?]. — [16]p : 2maps ; 21cm
Cover title
£0.30 (pbk) B82-07345

796.352′06′84136 — Scotland. Lothian Region. Musselburgh. Golf courses, *to 1980*
Colville, George M.. Five Open Champions and the Musselburgh golf story / by George M. Colville. — Musselburgh : Colville, 1980. — 115p : ill,facsims,ports ; 25cm
ISBN 0-9507179-0-8 : £6.95 B82-00825

796.352′06′84137 — Scotland. Borders Region. Golf courses — *Directories*
Golf. — Newtown St. Boswells (Newtown St. Boswells, Roxburghshire) : Borders Regional Council, 1982. — 1folded sheet([6]p) : map ; 21cm. — (The Scottish Borders)
Unpriced B82-32908

796.352′09 — Golf — *Records of achievement*
Steel, Donald. The Guinness book of golf facts and feats. — 2nd ed. — Enfield : Guinness Superlatives, Oct.1982. — [256]p
Previous ed.: 1980
ISBN 0-85112-242-6 (cased) : £8.95 : CIP entry
ISBN 0-85112-257-4 (pbk) : £7.50 B82-24256

796.352′09 — Golf, *to 1914*
Henderson, Ian T.. The Compleat golfer. — London : Gollancz, Oct.1982. — [96]p
ISBN 0-575-03218-9 : £6.95 : CIP entry B82-23351

796.352′09 — Golf, *to 1980* — *Records of achievement*
Steel, Donald. The Guinness book of golf facts & feats / Donald Steel. — Enfield : Guinness Superlatives, c1980. — 256p : ill(some col.),1col.map,facsims,ports(some col.) ; 24cm
Map, text on lining papers. — Includes index
ISBN 0-85112-215-9 : £7.95 : CIP rev. B80-22402

796.352′09 — Golf, *to 1981*
The **World** of golf / edited by Gordon Menzies. — London : British Broadcasting Corporation, 1982. — 224p : ill(some col.),ports(some col.) ; 26cm
ISBN 0-563-20018-9 : £9.95 B82-32984

796.352′092′2 — Golf — *Biographies*
The **Golfers** : the inside story / by members of the Association of Golf Writers ; edited by Peter Dobereiner ; foreword by Henry Cotton. — London : Collins, 1982. — 190p ; 22cm
ISBN 0-00-216385-3 : £6.95 : CIP rev. B82-07216

796.352′092′4 — Golf. Alliss, Peter — *Biographies*
Alliss, Peter. Peter Alliss : an autobiography. — [London] : Fontana, 1982, c1981. — 253p,[8]p of plates : ill,ports ; 18cm
Originally published: London : Collins, 1981. — Includes index
ISBN 0-00-636516-7 (pbk) : £1.95 B82-32977

796.352′092′4 — Golf. Ballesteros, Severiano — *Biographies*
Ballesteros, Severiano. Seve : the young champion / Severiano Ballesteros and Dudley Doust ; illustrations by Jim McQueen ; foreword by Lee Trevino. — London : Hodder & Stoughton, c1982. — 156p,[8]p of plates : ill (some col.),1map,ports ; 26cm
Includes index
ISBN 0-340-25272-3 : £8.95 : CIP rev. B82-14085

796.352′092′4 — Golf. Dexter, Ted — *Biographies*
Dexter, Ted. My golf / Ted Dexter. — London : Arthur Baker, c1982. — 113p,[16]p of plates : ill,1facsim,ports ; 23cm
ISBN 0-213-16824-3 : £5.95 B82-35686

796.352′092′4 — Golf — *Personal observations*
Alliss, Peter. The Shell book of golf / Peter Alliss. — Newton Abbot : David & Charles, c1981. — 231p : ill(some col.),ports ; 24cm
Includes index
ISBN 0-7153-7988-7 : £9.50 : CIP rev. B81-30331

796.352′3 — Golf — *Manuals*
Nicklaus, Jack. Play better golf. — London : Hodder and Stoughton, Mar.1982. — (Coronet books)
Vol.2: The short game and scoring. — [208]p
ISBN 0-340-27860-9 (pbk) : £1.10 : CIP entry B82-00243

Peper, George. Golf's supershots : how the pros played them — how you can play them / George Peper ; illustrated by Ron Ramsey. — London : Stanley Paul, 1982. — xii,146p : ill (some col.),ports ; 27cm
ISBN 0-09-147770-0 : £9.95 : CIP rev. B82-14210

Player, Gary. Gary Player's golf class / instruction by Gary Player ; script by Iain Reid ; drawings by Gary Keane from photographs by Sidney Harris. — London : Express Newspapers, c1980. — [96]p : chiefly ill,ports ; 17x23cm. — (A Sunday Express publication)
ISBN 0-85079-107-3 (pbk) : £1.25 B82-41033

Trevino, Lee. I can help your game / Lee Trevino with Oscar Fraley. — London : Star, 1982, c1971. — 159p : ill,1port ; 18cm
Originally published: Greenwich, Conn. : Fawcett, 1971 ; London : W.H. Allen, 1972
ISBN 0-352-31052-9 (pbk) : £1.60 B82-30904

796.352′3 — Golf — *Manuals* — *Welsh texts*
Griffith, William Lloyd. Cerdd daro : sef celfyddyd chwarae golff / gan William Lloyd Griffith. — [Nant Peris] ([Old School, Nant Peris, Caernarfon, Gwynedd]) : Gwasg Gwynedd, 1980. — 55p : ill ; 16x22cm
£1.00 (pbk) B82-26743

796.352′7′0941292 — Scotland. Fife Region. St Andrews. Golf. Clubs: Royal and Ancient Golf Club of St Andrews. Competitions, *to 1980* — *Records of achievement*
Royal and Ancient Championship records 1860-1980 / edited by Peter Ryde. — St. Andrews : Royal and Ancient Golf Club, 1981. — xxxi,535p : ill(some col.),facsims,ports(some col.) ; 27cm
Ill on lining papers
ISBN 0-907583-01-6 (cased) : Unpriced
ISBN 0-907583-02-4 (pbk) : Unpriced
ISBN 0-907583-00-8 (limited ed.) : Unpriced B82-25547

796.355 — HOCKEY

796.35′5 — Women's hockey
Women's hockey in the 80's / edited by Paul McNaught-Davis. — [Eastbourne] ([Trevin Towers, Gaudick Rd., Eastbourne BN20 7SP]) : Brighton Polytechnic, Chelsea School of Human Movement, c1982. — 51leaves : ill ; 30cm. — (Occasional papers on sports performance ; no.1)
Includes bibliographies
Unpriced (spiral) B82-35984

796.35'5 — Women's hockey — *Manuals*

Do's and don'ts for hockey players / written by international players and by a captain, umpire, selector and match secretary. — 4th ed. — Lechlade (Whitemilnes, Kencot, Lechlade, Glos.) : Marjorie Pollard, 1980. — 31p ; 15cm
Previous ed.: 1955?
£0.60 (pbk) B82-18613

796.357 — BASEBALL

796.357'8 — Softball — *Manuals*

Drysdale, Sharon J.. Complete handbook of winning softball / Sharon J. Drysdale, Karen S. Harris. — Boston [Mass.] ; London : Allyn and Bacon, c1982. — xvi,347p : ill ; 24cm
Includes index
ISBN 0-205-07597-5 : Unpriced B82-26764

796.358 — CRICKET

796.35'8 — Cricket

Benson and Hedges cricket year. — London : Pelham Books, Nov.1982. — [480]p
ISBN 0-7207-1429-x : £8.95 : CIP entry B82-33351

Eagar, Patrick. Summer of the all-rounder. — London : Collins, Nov.1982. — [128]p
ISBN 0-00-216631-3 : £6.95 : CIP entry B82-40881

796.35'8 — Cricket — *For children*

Bradshaw, Tony. Cricket / written by Tony Bradshaw ; illustrations by Chris Reed ; photographs by Tim Clark. — Loughborough : Ladybird, 1982. — 51p : col.ill,col.ports ; 18cm. — (Learnabout)
Text, ill on lining papers. — Includes index
ISBN 0-7214-0696-3 : £0.50 B82-09749

796.35'8 — Cricket — *Stories, anecdotes*

Botham, Ian. Botham's choice. — London : Collins, Sept.1982. — [160]p
ISBN 0-00-216490-6 : £5.95 : CIP entry B82-19063

Mell, George. This curious game of cricket / by George Mell ; illustrated by Bill Tidy. — London : Allen & Unwin, 1982. — ix,127p : ill ; 21cm
ISBN 0-04-796063-9 : Unpriced : CIP rev. B82-07238

Parkinson, Michael, *1935-*. Parkinsons lore / Michael Parkinson ; with drawings by Michael Lewis. — London : Pavilion, 1981. — 156p : ill ; 23cm
ISBN 0-907516-05-x : £5.95 : CIP rev.
Also classified at 796.334 B81-25740

796.35'8 — Limited-over cricket, *1943-1981*

Lemmon, David. Great one-day cricket matches. — London : Pelham, Aug.1982. — [192]p
ISBN 0-7207-1409-5 : £6.95 : CIP entry B82-15847

796.35'8'0207 — Cricket — *Humour*

Brayshaw, Ian. The wit of cricket / Ian Brayshaw. — London : Deutsch, 1982, c1981. — 111p : ill,ports ; 21cm
Originally published: Milson's Point : Currawong, 1981
ISBN 0-233-97476-8 : £4.50 B82-32986

Tyson, Frank. The cricketer who laughed / Frank Tyson ; illustrated by Vane Lindesay. — London : Stanley Paul, c1982. — 147p : ill ; 21cm
ISBN 0-09-137790-0 : £4.95 : CIP rev. B82-07105

796.35'8'05 — Cricket — *Serials*

Pelham cricket year. — 3rd ed. — London : Pelham, Nov.1981. — [688]p
Previous ed.: 1980
ISBN 0-7207-1363-3 : £6.95 : CIP entry B81-30584

Wisden cricket monthly. — Vol.1, no.1 (June 1979)-. — London (56 Moorgate, EC2R 6EL) : Wisden Cricket Magazines, 1979-. — v. : ill (some col.),ports(some col.) ; 30cm
ISSN 0263-9041 = Wisden cricket monthly : £7.25 per year B82-36722

796.35'8'06842819 — West Yorkshire *(Metropolitan County)*. **Leeds. Headingley. Cricket grounds: Headingley Cricket Ground,** *to 1980*

Dalby, Ken. The Headingley story / by Ken Dalby. — Leeds (12 Talbot Mount, Leeds LS4 2PF) : K. Dalby
Vol.3: White is the rose : a record of County Cricket at Headingley 1891-1980. — [1981?]. — 146p : ill,ports ; 25cm
£3.00 (pbk)
Primary classification 796.33'3'06842819 B82-00766

796.35'8'075 — Cricket. Items associated with cricket, *to 1981*. **Collecting**

Green, Stephen, *1943-*. Cricketing bygones / Stephen Green. — Princes Risborough : Shire, 1982. — 32p : ill,facsims,ports ; 22cm. — (Shire album ; 90)
Bibliography: p32
ISBN 0-85263-605-9 (pbk) : £0.95 B82-39398

796.35'8'09 — Cricket, *1954-1977 — Records of achievement*

Barker, Ralph. Innings of a lifetime. — London : Collins, Oct.1982. — [249]p
ISBN 0-00-211866-1 : £7.95 : CIP entry B82-35200

796.35'8'09 — Cricket, *to 1979*

Lodge, Derek. Figures on the green / Derek Lodge. — London : Allen & Unwin, 1982. — xii,188p ; 23cm
Includes index
ISBN 0-04-796061-2 : £8.95 : CIP rev. B82-10587

796.35'8'09 — Cricket, *to 1982*

Rippon, Anton. Cricket around the world. — Ashbourne : Moorland, Oct.1982. — [192]p
ISBN 0-86190-055-3 : £7.50 : CIP entry B82-30319

796.35'8'0904 — Cricket, *1940-1963 — Readings from contemporary sources*

Wisden anthology 1940-1963 / edited by Benny Green. — London : Queen Anne Press, 1982. — vi,1009p ; 24cm
Includes index
ISBN 0-356-08547-3 : £25.00 B82-35991

796.35'8'0922 — Cricket — *Biographies*

Compton, Denis. Compton on cricketers past and present / Denis Compton. — London : Cassell, 1980. — xi,204p,[8]p of plates : ports ; 23cm
Includes index
ISBN 0-304-30685-1 : £6.95 B82-19352

796.35'8'0922 — Cricket — *Personal observations — Collections*

The **Best** of cricket : an anthology of stories reports and quotes / selected by Roy Peskett. — London : Hamlyn, c1982. — 239p : 1facsim ; 23cm
ISBN 0-600-34674-9 : £5.95 B82-27144

796.35'8'0922 — Cricketers, *1857-1917 — Illustrations*

The **Cricketers** of Vanity fair / [compiled by] Russell March ; introduction by John Arlott. — Exeter : Webb & Bower, 1982. — 112p : col.ports ; 32cm
ISBN 0-906671-52-3 : £9.95 : CIP rev. B82-05783

796.35'8'0922 — Cricketers, *1905-1978*

Arlott, John. John Arlott's book of cricketers / John Arlott. — London : Sphere, 1982, c1979. — x,149p ; 18cm
Originally published: Guildford : Lutterworth, 1979. — Includes index
ISBN 0-7221-1277-7 (pbk) : £1.75 B82-33812

796.35'8'0924 — Cricket. Abel, Bobby — *Biographies*

Kynaston, David. Bobby Abel. — London : Secker & Warburg, Nov.1982. — [176]p
ISBN 0-436-23951-5 : £8.50 : CIP entry B82-33337

796.35'8'0924 — Cricket. Barrington, Ken — *Biographies*

Scovell, Brian. Ken Barrington : a tribute / by Brian Scovell. — London : Harrap, 1982. — 176p,[16]p of plates : ill,facsims,ports ; 23cm
Includes index
ISBN 0-245-53867-4 : £7.95 B82-32671

796.35'8'0924 — Cricket. Boycott, Geoff — *Biographies*

Callaghan, John. Boycott : a cricketing legend. — London : Pelham, Sept.1982. — [192]p
ISBN 0-7207-1421-4 : £7.95 : CIP entry B82-20389

796.35'8'0924 — Cricket. Boycott, Geoff — *Biographies — For children*

Callaghan, John, *1938-*. Geoffrey Boycott / John Callaghan ; illustrated by Karen Heywood. — London : Hamilton, 1982. — 62p : ill,ports ; 22cm. — (Profiles (Hamilton))
ISBN 0-241-10712-1 : £3.25 B82-20815

796.35'8'0924 — Cricket. Boycott, Geoff. Matches. Scores — *Statistics*

Sheen, Steven. The Geoffrey Boycott file / Steven Sheen. — London : Hamlyn, c1982. — 191p : 1port ; 19cm
ISBN 0-600-34675-7 (pbk) : £2.25 B82-28401

796.35'8'0924 — Cricket. D'Oliveira, Basil — *Biographies*

D'Oliveira, Basil. Time to declare : an autobiography / Basil d'Oliveira with Patrick Murphy. — London : W.H. Allen, 1982, c1980. — x,180p,[8]p of plates : ill,1facsim,ports ; 18cm. — (A Star book)
Originally published: London : Dent, 1980. — Includes index
ISBN 0-352-31078-2 (pbk) : £1.60 B82-30645

796.35'8'0924 — Cricket. Freeman, A. P. — *Biographies*

Lemmon, David. 'Tich Freeman : and the decline of the leg-break bowler / by David Lemmon. — London : Allen & Unwin, 1982. — 144p,[8]p of plates : ill,ports ; 22cm
Includes index
ISBN 0-04-796055-8 : Unpriced : CIP rev. B82-03719

796.35'8'0924 — Cricket. Harris, George Robert Canning, *Baron* — *Biographies*

Coldham, James D.. Lord Harris. — London : Allen and Unwin, Feb.1983. — [176]p
ISBN 0-04-796068-x : £10.95 : CIP entry B82-36451

796.35'8'0924 — Cricket. Hobbs, Jack, *1882-1963 — Biographies*

Arlott, John. Jack Hobbs : profile of the master / John Arlott. — London : Murray, 1981. — 144p,[16]p of plates : 1ill,facsims,ports ; 23cm
Bibliography: p137. — Includes index
ISBN 0-7195-3886-6 : £6.95
ISBN 0-7067-0214-x (Davis-Poynter) B82-11531

796.35'8'0924 — Cricket. Hobbs, *Sir* **Jack** - *Biographies*

Hobbs, *Sir* **Jack**. My life story. — London (35 Gloucester Ave., NW1 7AX) : Hambledon Press, July 1981. — [352]p
Originally published: 1935
ISBN 0-907628-00-1 : £6.95 : CIP entry B81-20529

796.35'8'0924 — Cricket. Lillee, Dennis — *Biographies*

Lillee, Dennis. My life in cricket. — London : Methuen, Nov.1982. — [256]p
ISBN 0-413-51410-2 : £7.50 : CIP entry B82-28284

796.35'8'0924 — Cricket. Marsh, Rodney — *Biographies*

Marsh, Rodney. Gloves of irony. — London : Pelham, Nov.1982. — [128]p
ISBN 0-7207-1443-5 : £5.95 : CIP entry B82-30326

796.35'8'0924 — Cricket — *Personal observations*
Boycott, Geoff. Opening up / Geoff Boycott. — London : Sphere, 1982, c1980. — 217p,[8]p of plates : ill,ports ; 18cm
Originally published: London : Barker, 1980
ISBN 0-7221-1759-0 (pbk) : £1.75 B82-29177

Raven, Simon. Shadows on the grass / Simon Raven. — London : Blond & Briggs, 1982. — 227p ; 23cm
ISBN 0-85634-125-8 : £7.95 : CIP rev. B82-11096

Roebuck, Peter. Slices of cricket / Peter Roebuck. — London : Allen & Unwin, 1982. — xiv,140p,[12]p of plates : ill,ports ; 23cm
ISBN 0-04-796062-0 : Unpriced : CIP rev. B82-12423

Wellings, E. M.. Vintage cricketers. — London : Allen and Unwin, Feb.1983. — [208]p
ISBN 0-04-796066-3 : £9.95 : CIP entry B82-36449

796.35'8'0924 — Cricket. Richards, Viv — *Biographies*
Richards, Viv. Viv Richards / Viv Richards with David Foot. — London : W.H. Allen, 1982. — 169p,[8]p of plates : ports ; 18cm. — (A Star book)
Originally published: Tadworth : World's Work, 1979
ISBN 0-352-31208-4 (pbk) : £1.60 B82-39012

796.35'8'0924 — Cricket. Trueman, Fred
Trueman, Fred. My most memorable matches / Fred Trueman with Don Mosey ; cartoons by Roy Ulyett. — London : Stanley Paul, 1982. — 140p,[8]p of plates : ill,ports ; 23cm
ISBN 0-09-147760-3 : £5.95 : CIP rev. B82-08433

796.35'8'09422735 — Hampshire. Hambledon. Cricket, *to ca 1800*
Knight, Ronald D.. Hambledon's cricket glory / [Ronald D. Knight]. — Weymouth : R.D. Knight
Vol.7: 1772. — c1981. — 48p,[8]p of plates : ill,ports ; 21cm
Bibliography: p48
ISBN 0-903769-07-7 (pbk) : £1.35 B82-11016

796.35'82 — Cricket — *Manuals*
Bailey, Trevor, *1923-*. Cricketers in the making / Trevor Bailey. — London : Queen Anne Press, c1982. — 119p : ill ; 24cm
ISBN 0-356-08597-x : £7.95 B82-29446

Cricket. — 9th ed., incorporating the 1980 code of the laws of cricket. — Wakefield : EP Publishing in collaboration with the Marylebone Cricket Club, 1976 (1982 [printing]). — 48p : ill(some col.),1form ; 14x21cm. — (Know the game)
Includes index
ISBN 0-7158-0432-4 (pbk) : £0.85 B82-39320

Philpott, Peter. Cricket fundamentals / Peter Philpott. — London : Batsford, 1982, c1978. — 111p : ill,ports ; 25cm. — (Competitive sports series)
Originally published: Sydney : Reed, 1978
ISBN 0-7134-4456-8 (pbk) : £4.95 : CIP rev. B82-01206

796.35'82 — Cricket — *Manuals — For children*
Dexter, Ted. You can play cricket / Ted Dexter ; illustrated by Mike Miller. — [London] : Carousel, [1982]. — 128p : ill ; 20cm
ISBN 0-552-54199-0 (pbk) : £0.95 B82-18698

Dexter, Ted. You can play cricket / Ted Dexter ; illustrated by Mike Miller. — London : Severn House, 1982. — 122p : ill,1facsim ; 21cm
Originally published: London : Carousel, 1982
ISBN 0-7278-0805-2 : £5.95 B82-36252

796.35'822 — Cricket. Spin bowling
Murphy, Patrick, *1947-*. The spinner's turn / Patrick Murphy ; foreword by G.O. Allen. — London : Dent, 1982. — 208p : ill,ports ; 24cm
Includes index
ISBN 0-460-04552-0 : £7.95 : CIP rev. B82-06847

796.35'822'0922 — Cricket. Fast bowlers, *ca 1775-1982*
Frith, David, *1937-*. The fast men : a 200-year cavalcade of speed bowlers / David Frith. — Rev. and updated ed. — London : Allen & Unwin, 1982. — 177p,[36]p of plates : ill,ports ; 22cm
Previous ed.: Wokingham : Van Nostrand Rheinhold, 1975. — Includes index
ISBN 0-04-796060-4 : Unpriced : CIP rev. B82-03720

796.35'826'0222 — Cricket. Batting. Techniques — *Illustrations*
Boycott, Geoff. Master class / Geoffrey Boycott ; drawings by George Stokes. — London : Arthur Barker, c1982. — [154]p : chiefly ill ; 15cm
ISBN 0-213-16832-4 : £3.95 B82-19500

796.35'862'0941 — Great Britain. Club cricket — *Serials*
Rothmans club cricket yearbook. — 1982-. — Aylesbury : Rothmans, 1982-. — v. : ill,ports ; 21cm
ISSN 0263-7502 = Rothmans club cricket yearbook : £5.50 B82-31728

796.35'862'0941232 — Scotland. Grampian Region. Inverurie. Cricket. Clubs: Inverurie Cricket Club, *to 1981*
Inverurie Cricket Club. Inverurie Cricket Club 1931-1981. — [Inverurie] ([c/o N.R. Brownlee, 9, Meilde Gardens, Westhill, Inverurie]) : [Inverurie Cricket Club], [1982?]. — 92p : ports ; 21cm
(pbk) B82-34708

796.35'862'0942 — England. Cricket. Clubs: Zingari, *to 1981*
Arrowsmith, R. L.. The history of I Zingari. — London : Paul, Oct.1982. — [160]p
ISBN 0-09-150550-x : £12.95 : CIP entry B82-24982

796.35'863'0942 — England. County cricket, *to 1980*
County champions. — London : Heinemann, c1982. — 198p : ill ; 25cm
ISBN 0-434-98024-2 : £7.95 B82-32247

796.35'863'094218 — Middlesex. County cricket. Clubs: Middlesex County Cricket Club, *to 1981*
Rippon, Anton. The story of Middlesex County Cricket Club. — Ashbourne : Moorland, Mar.1982. — [141]p
ISBN 0-86190-036-7 : £6.95 : CIP entry B82-09173

796.35'865 — Australia. Cricket. Tours by English cricket team, *1932-1933*
Mason, Ronald. Ashes in the mouth : the story of the bodyline tour 1932-3. — London : Hambledon Press, Nov.1982. — [258]p
ISBN 0-907628-31-1 : £7.50 : CIP entry B82-33371

796.35'865 — Cricket. English teams. Test matches with Australian teams, *to 1980*
Ibbotson, Doug. A hundred years of the Ashes / by Doug Ibbotson and Ralph Dellor ; foreword by Richie Benaud ; edited by David Frith. — Aylesbury : Rothmans, c1982. — 228p : ill,ports ; 26cm
Includes index
ISBN 0-907574-03-3 : £12.95 B82-30637

796.35'865 — Cricket. English teams. Test matches with Australian teams, *to 1981*
Rippon, Anton. Classic moments of the Ashes / Anton Rippon. — Ashbourne : Moorland, c1982. — 160p : ill,ports ; 26cm
Ill on lining papers
ISBN 0-86190-051-0 : £6.95 : CIP rev. B82-09172

796.35'865 — England. Cricket. Australian teams. Test matches with English teams, *1981 — Illustrations*
Eager, Patrick. A summer to remember : England v Australia 1981 / Patrick Eager ; with commentary by Alan Ross. — London : Collins, 1981. — 128p : chiefly ill,ports ; 26cm
ISBN 0-00-216388-8 (pbk) : £4.95 B82-09231

796.35'865 — England. Cricket. Australian teams. Test matches with English teams, *1981 — Personal observations*
Brearley, Mike. Phoenix from the Ashes : the story of the England-Australia series 1981 / Mike Brearley ; foreword by Ian Botham ; postscript by Dennis Lillee. — London : Hodder and Stoughton, c1982. — 160p,[8]p of plates : ill(some col.),ports(some col.) ; 25cm
Includes index
ISBN 0-340-28088-3 : £7.95 : CIP rev. B82-07949

796.35'865 — England. Cricket. Competitions: Prudential Cup *(1979)*
Prudential Cup : official guide '79 : England, Australia, West Indies, New Zealand, India, Pakistan, Associates A&B. — London (142 Holborn Bars, EC1N 2NH) : Prudential Assurance Co., [1979?]. — 19p : ill,ports ; 23cm
Unpriced (unbound) B82-20672

796.35'865 — England. Cricket. English teams. Test matches, *1981.* **Australian teams** — *Personal observations*
Botham, Ian. The incredible tests 1981 / Ian Botham. — London : Pelham, 1981. — 160p : ill,facsims,ports ; 25cm
ISBN 0-7207-1394-3 : £6.95 B82-06627

796.35'865 — England. Cricket. English teams. Test matches with Australian teams, *1882-1981*
Illingworth, Ray. The Ashes : a centenary / Ray Illingworth and Kenneth Gregory. — London : Collins, 1982. — 272p : ill,ports ; 22cm
Includes index
ISBN 0-00-216542-2 : £7.95 : CIP rev. B82-03699

796.35'865 — England. Cricket. English teams. Test matches with Australian teams, *1981*
Melford, Michael. Botham rekindles the ashes : the Daily telegraph story of the 81 Test Series / Michael Melford. — 2nd rev. ed. — London : Daily Telegraph, 1981. — vi,161p,[16]p of plates : ports ; 23cm
Previous ed.: 1981
ISBN 0-901684-72-4 (cased) : £4.95
ISBN 0-901684-71-6 (pbk) : £1.95 B82-08779

796.35'865 — India *(Republic).* **Cricket. English teams. Test matches with Indian teams,** *1981-1982*
Berry, Scyld. Cricket wallah : with England in India 1981-2 / Scyld Berry ; with photographs by Adrian Murrell ; foreword by Raman Subba Row. — London : Hodder and Stoughton, c1982. — 192p : ill,1map,ports ; 25cm
Bibliography: p158-159. — Includes index
ISBN 0-340-28087-5 : £8.95 : CIP rev. B82-18567

796.35'865 — Kent. Cricket. Kent teams. Matches with Australian teams, *1882-1977*
Porter, Clive W.. The white horse and the kangaroo : Kent v the Australians 1882-1977 / Clive W. Porter. — Rainham : Meresborough, 1981. — 128p : ports ; 22cm
ISBN 0-905270-31-2 : £5.50 B82-36409

796.35'865 — West Indies. Cricket. Tours by English cricket team, *1981 — Personal observations*
Keating, Frank. Another bloody day in paradise! / Frank Keating. — London : Deutsch, 1981. — 177p,[13]p of plates : 1map,ports ; 24cm
Facsims on lining papers
ISBN 0-233-97400-8 : £6.95 B82-02596

796.35'865'0924 — Cricket. English teams. Test matches, *1981 — Personal observations*
Gooch, Graham. My cricket diary '81 : the West Indies, Australia, India / Graham Gooch with Alan Lee. — London : Stanley Paul, 1982. — 176p,[12]p of plates : ill,ports ; 23cm
ISBN 0-09-147750-6 : £6.95 : CIP rev. B82-07106

796.4 — ATHLETICS

796.4 — Athletics, *to 1981*
London, Charles. Classic moments of athletics. — Ashbourne : Moorland, Oct.1982. — [144]p
ISBN 0-86190-053-7 : £7.50 : CIP entry B82-30599

796.4′06′041 — Great Britain. Athletics. Organisations: Amateur Athletic Association, *to 1979*

Lovesey, Peter. The official centenary history of the Amateur Athletic Association / Peter Lovesey. — Enfield : Guinness Superlatives, c1979 (1980 [printing]). — 223p : ill(some col.),ports(some col.) ; 30cm
Bibliography: p207. — Includes index
ISBN 0-900424-95-8 : £8.95 B82-14425

796.4′06′041443 — Scotland. Strathclyde Region. Glasgow. Universities: University of Glasgow. Athletics. Organisations: Glasgow University Athletic Club, *to 1981*

Glasgow University Athletic Club. Glasgow University Athletic Club : the story of the first hundred years / by R.O. MacKenna. — [Glasgow] : G.U.A.C., 1981. — 128p,[5]p of plates : ill,1map ; 21cm
ISBN 0-85261-170-6 (pbk) : £4.00 B82-05146

796.4′1 — Gymnastics — *Manuals — For children*

Lennox, Avril. You can be a gymnast / Avril Lennox ; illustrated by Mike Miller. — [London] : Carousel, [1982]. — 143p : ill ; 20cm
ISBN 0-552-54198-2 (corrected : pbk) : £0.95 B82-21064

796.4′1 — Gymnastics — *Serials — For children*

Bella′s book of gymnastics. — 1981-. — London : IPC Magazines, 1980. — v. : chiefly ill ; 28cm
Only one issue published
£1.80 B82-18528

796.4′1 — Gymnastics, *to 1981*

Goodbody, John. The illustrated history of gymnastics. — London : Stanley Paul, Sept.1982. — [144]p
ISBN 0-09-143350-9 : £8.95 : CIP entry B82-19101

796.4′1 — Schools. Curriculum subjects: Gymnastics. Teaching

Mace, Roger, *1940-*. Gymnastic skills : the theory and practice of teaching and coaching / Roger Mace, Barry Benn. — London : Batsford, 1982. — 134p : ill ; 26cm
Bibliography: p131. — Includes index
ISBN 0-7134-4307-3 : £6.95 B82-39884

796.4′1 — Schools. Curriculum subjects: Gymnastics. Teaching — *Manuals*

Long, Bruce. Educational gymnastics : step by step / Bruce Long. — London : Edward Arnold, 1982. — 127p : ill ; 25cm
ISBN 0-7131-0623-9 (pbk) : £4.25 : CIP rev. B81-37560

796.4′1 — Sports: Bodybuilding — *Manuals*

Muscle building for beginners / edited by Oscar Heidenstam ; cover photographs of Robert Mitchell and half-tone plates from photographs by Edward Hankey ; line drawings by Jak (for Part 1) and Ben (for Part 2). — London : Foulsham, c1981. — 96p,[8]p of plates : ill,ports ; 22cm
ISBN 0-572-01137-7 (pbk) : £2.75 B82-04241

Schwarzenegger, Arnold. Arnold′s bodybuilding for men / by Arnold Schwarzenegger with Bill Dobbins. — London : Pelham, 1981. — 240 : ill,ports ; 29cm
Includes index
ISBN 0-7207-1379-x : £8.95 : CIP rev. B81-30390

796.4′1 — Weight training — *Manuals*

Westcott, Wayne L.. Strength fitness : physiological principles and training techniques / Wayne L. Westcott. — Boston ; London : Allyn and Bacon, c1982. — xi,192,[25]p : ill ; 24cm
Bibliography: p[18-21]. — Includes index
ISBN 0-205-07746-3 (pbk) : Unpriced B82-29326

796.4′1 — Weight training — *Manuals — For sports*

The **Manual** of weight training. — London : Stanley Paul, Mar.1982. — [208]p
ISBN 0-09-147821-9 (pbk) : £4.95 : CIP entry B82-01706

796.4′2 — Athletics. Track & field events — *Manuals*

Jarver, Jess. Athletics fundamentals / Jess Jarver. — Newton Abbot : David & Charles, c1981. — 88p : ill ; 26cm
Originally published: Sydney : Reed, 1980
ISBN 0-7153-8189-x : £3.95 B82-23625

796.4′2 — Athletics. Track & field events, *to 1981*

Matthews, Peter. The Guinness book of athletic facts and feats. — Enfield : Guinness Superlatives, Dec.1982. — [288]p
ISBN 0-85112-238-8 : £8.95 : CIP entry B82-30224

796.4′2′077 — Athletics. Coaching

Dick, Frank W.. But first — : basic work for coaches and teachers of beginner athletes / prepared by Frank W. Dick. — [London] : British Amateur Athletic Board, [1982]. — 88p : ill ; 30cm
Cover title
ISBN 0-85134-066-0 (pbk) : £3.50 B82-41074

796.4′26 — Athletics. Marathon running

Temple, Cliff. Challenge of the marathon : a runner′s guide / Cliff Temple ; photography by Mark Shearman. — London : Stanley Paul, 1981. — 174p,[8]p of plates : ill,ports ; 22cm
ISBN 0-09-146431-5 (pbk) : £4.95 : CIP rev. B81-30974

796.4′26 — Athletics. Marathon running — *Manuals*

Brasher, Christopher. The marathon. — London : Hodder & Stoughton, Dec.1981. — [128]p
ISBN 0-340-27900-1 (pbk) : £2.95 : CIP entry B81-31437

796.4′26 — Athletics. Middle-distance running — *Manuals*

Watts, Denis. The complete middle distance runner. — London : Paul, July 1982. — [128]p
Originally published: 1978
ISBN 0-09-150171-7 (pbk) : £2.95 : CIP entry B82-15927

796.4′26 — Athletics. Track events — *Manuals*

McNab, Tom. Successful track athletics / Tom McNab. — London : Published in collaboration with World of Sport by Letts, 1982. — 95p : ill(some col.),ports(some col.) ; 22cm. — (Letts guide)
Includes bibliographies and index
ISBN 0-85097-417-8 (pbk) : £2.95 B82-34649

796.4′26′05 — Athletics. Running — *Serials*

Stride out. — No.1-. — Stoke-on-Trent (16 The Square, Oakamoor, Stoke-on-Trent ST10 3AB, Staffs.) : Nemadis Press, 1979-. — v. : ill,ports ; 21cm
ISSN 0143-876X = Stride out : £1.25 per issue B82-19875

796.4′26′0922 — Athletics. Four-minute mile runners, *to 1981 — Biographies*

Giller, Norman. The golden milers. — London : Pelham, Aug.1982. — [96]p
ISBN 0-7207-1402-8 : £6.50 : CIP entry B82-15846

796.4′26′0924 — Athletics. Long-distance running. Hill, Ron, *1938- — Biographies*

Hill, Ron, *1938-*. The long hard road : an autobiography / by Ron Hill. — Hyde : Ron Hill Sports
Pt.1: Nearly to the top. — 1981. — 405p : ill,ports ; 22cm
ISBN 0-9507882-0-1 (cased) : £7.95
ISBN 0-9507882-1-x (pbk) : £4.95 B82-13579

796.4′26′0924 — Athletics. Marathon running. Alder, Jim — *Biographies*

McKenzie, Arthur T.. Marathon and chips : biography of Jim Alder, world record holder / by Arthur T. McKenzie. — Morpeth : Alder Sports, 1981. — 136p : ill,1facsim,ports ; 21cm
ISBN 0-9507604-1-2 (cased) : Unpriced
ISBN 0-9507604-0-4 (pbk) : £1.95 B82-01677

796.4′26′0924 — Athletics. Middle-distance running. Coe, Sebastian — *Biographies*

Coe, Sebastian. Running free / Sebastian Coe with David Miller. — Rev. and updated. — London : Sidgwick & Jackson, 1982. — 191p,[16]p of plates : ill,ports ; 18cm
Previous ed.: 1981. — Includes index
ISBN 0-283-98857-6 (pbk) : £1.50 : CIP rev. B82-07421

Wilson, Neil. Sebastian Coe. — London : Hamilton, Oct.1982. — [64]p
ISBN 0-241-10848-9 : £3.25 : CIP entry B82-23453

796.4′26′0924 — Athletics. Middle distance running. Ovett, Steve — *Biographies*

Wilson, Harry. Steve Ovett. — London : Paul, May 1982. — [200]p
ISBN 0-09-147740-9 : £6.95 : CIP entry B82-09205

796.4′3 — Athletics. Field events — *Manuals*

Anthony, Don. Field athletics / Don Anthony. — London : Batsford Academic and Educational, 1982. — 64p : ill ; 26cm. — (Competitive sports series)
Bibliography: p62-63. — Includes index
ISBN 0-7134-4281-6 : £4.50 : CIP rev. B81-35834

796.4′3 — Athletics. Field events. Techniques

Le Masurier, John. Athletics — field events / John Le Masurier and Denis Watts. — London : Black, 1982. — 96p : ill,ports ; 21cm. — (Black′s picture sports)
Includes index
ISBN 0-7136-2147-8 : £3.50 : CIP rev. B81-22528

796.4′32′071 — Schools. Curriculum subjects: Athletics. Jumping. Teaching

Adams, Gordon. How to teach the jumps : a guide for class teachers / Gordon Adams. — London : British Amateur Athletic Board, [1981?]. — 38p : ill ; 22cm
Cover title. — Text on inside cover
£0.80 (pbk) B82-12025

796.4′35′0924 — Athletics. Shot putting. Capes, Geoff - *Biographies*

Capes, Geoff. Big shot. — London : Paul, Apr.1981. — [160]p
ISBN 0-09-144970-7 : £5.95 : CIP entry B81-01080

796.5 — OUTDOOR LIFE

796.5 — England. Youth hostelling — *Personal observations*

Parr, Edwin. A holiday with a difference / Edwin Parr. — [Great Britain] : E. Parr, 1981. — 23p : ill ; 21cm
Cover title
Unpriced (pbk) B82-21417

796.5 — Ireland *(Republic)*. **Youth hostelling. Organisations: Irish Youth Hostel Association,** *to 1980*

Trench, Terry. Fifty years young : the story of An Oige / Terry Trench. — Dublin : Irish Youth Hostel Association, 1981. — 136p : ill,ports ; 21cm
Includes index
ISBN 0-9500292-9-7 (pbk) : £3.00 (Irish) B82-38988

796.5 — Orienteering — *Manuals*

Disley, John I.. Tackle orienteering / John I. Disley. — London : Stanley Paul, 1982. — 96p : ill,maps ; 24cm
ISBN 0-09-145030-6 (cased) : Unpriced : CIP rev.
ISBN 0-09-145031-4 (pbk) : £3.95 B82-14355

Smith, Roger, *1938-*. The Penguin book of orienteering / Roger Smith ; illustrated by Raymond Turvey. — Harmondsworth : Penguin, 1982. — 310p : ill,maps ; 19cm. — (Penguin handbooks)
Bibliography: p294-295. — Includes index
ISBN 0-14-046438-7 (pbk) : £1.95 B82-33154

796.5′05 — Orienteering — *Serials*

Compass sport/The orienteer. — No.2 (1982)-. — Twickenham (c/o Ned Paul, 22 Sherland Rd, Twickenham, Middx TWA 4HD) : Compass Sport/The Orienteer, 1982-. — v. : ill(some col.),maps,ports(some col.) ; 30cm
Six issues yearly. — Merger of: Compass sport; and, The orienteer
ISSN 0263-6697 = Compass sport/The orienteer : £4.75 per year B82-28873

796.5′1 — Backpacking — *Manuals*

Adshead, Robin. The Spur master guide to backpacking / Robin Adshead. — Edinburgh : Spurbooks, c1982. — 96p : ill ; 21cm. — (A Spurbooks master guide)
Bibliography: p95
ISBN 0-7157-2090-2 (pbk) : £3.50 B82-22944

796.5′1 — England. West Midlands. Rural regions. Guided walks, *1982* — *Lists*

Explore your local countryside : programme of walks for the family. — [Cheltenham] : Countryside Commission, [1982]. — 28p : ill,1map ; 21cm
Cover title. — Map on inside cover
ISBN 0-86170-036-8 (pbk) : Unpriced B82-25963

796.5′1 — Scotland. Borders Region. Rural regions. Guided walks, *1982* — *Lists*

Ranger led walks. — Newtown St. Boswells (Newtown St. Boswells, Roxburghshire) : Borders Regional Council, 1982. — 1folded sheet([6]p) : map ; 21cm. — (The Scottish Borders)
Unpriced B82-32911

796.5′1′0922 — Recreations. Walking — *Personal observations* — *Collections*

The **Winding** trail / edited by Roger Smith ; with cartoons by Sheridan Anderson. — London : Diadem, 1981. — 477p,[32]p of plates : ill (some col.),maps,ports ; 23cm
Includes index
ISBN 0-906371-75-9 : £10.50 B82-01778

796.5′1′0941 — Great Britain. Backpacking — *Manuals*

Merrill, John N.. Striding with Merrill : John Merrill′s personal guide to walking and backpacking / sketches by Paul Boyes. — Winster, Derbyshire : Walking Boots, c1981. — 52p : ill ; 21cm. — (A Walking Boot publication)
Bibliography: p51
ISBN 0-907496-01-6 (pbk) : Unpriced B82-08199

796.5′1′0941 — Great Britain. Recreations: Long-distance walking — *Visitors′ guides*

Nicolson, Adam. The National Trust book of long walks / Adam Nicolson ; photographs by Charlie Waite. — London : National Trust, c1981. — 287p : ill(some col.),maps ; 29cm
Ill on lining papers. — Includes bibliographies and index
ISBN 0-297-77928-1 : £10.95 B82-00428

796.5′1′094213 — West London. Inland waterways. Recreations: Walking — *Guidebooks*

Stott, Peter. Waterside walks in West London / Peter & Carolyn Stott. — Edinburgh : Spurbooks, c1981. — 64p : 2maps ; 19cm
ISBN 0-7157-2096-1 (pbk) : Unpriced B82-14597

796.5′1′094216 — South London. Recreations: Walking — *Visitors′ guides*

Owen, Susan. Discovering country walks in South London / Susan Owen and Angela Haine. — Princes Risborough : Shire, 1982. — 63p : maps ; 18cm. — (The Discovering series ; 271)
Includes index
ISBN 0-85263-610-5 (pbk) : £1.25 B82-39396

796.5′1′09422 — Southern England. Long-distance footpaths: Ridgeway. Recreations: Walking — *Visitors′ guides*

Charles, Alan. The Ridgeway Path / Alan Charles. — Edinburgh : Spurbooks, c1981. — 91p : ill,maps ; 19cm. — (A Spurbooks long-distance footpath guide)
Bibliography: p91
ISBN 0-7157-2106-2 (pbk) : £2.50 B82-22948

796.5′1′094221 — Surrey. Recreations: Walking — *Visitors′ guides*

Bagley, William A.. Surrey : walks for motorists / Wm. A. Bagley ; 30 circular walks with sketch maps by the author. — 2nd ed. — London : Warne, 1982. — 99p : maps ; 21cm. — (Warne Gerrard guides for walkers. Walks for motorists series)
Previous ed.: published as London countryside walks for motorists, south western area. Harrow : Gerard, 1976
ISBN 0-7232-2808-6 (pbk) : £1.75 B82-33952

Youle, Joan. Surrey rambles / Joan Youle. — Edinburgh : Spurbooks, c1981. — 64p : maps ; 19cm. — (A Spurbooks footpath guide)
Bibliography: p64
ISBN 0-7157-2100-3 (pbk) : £1.25 B82-12506

796.5′1′094223 — North Kent. Recreations: Walking — *Visitors′ guides*

Bagley, William A.. Kent : walks for motorists : northern area / Wm. A. Bagley ; 30 circular walks with sketch maps by the author. — 2nd ed. — London : Warne, 1982. — 101p : maps ; 21cm. — (Warne Gerrard guides for walkers. Walks for motorists series)
Previous ed.: published as London countryside walks for motorists, south eastern area. Gerrard, 1976
ISBN 0-7232-2806-x (pbk) : £1.75 B82-33953

796.5′1′0942236 — Kent. Sevenoaks *(District)*. **Recreations: Walking** — *Visitors′ guides*

Spayne, Janet. Walks in the hills of Kent / Janet Spayne & Audrey Krynski. — 2nd ed. — Edinburgh : Spurbooks, 1981. — 64p : maps ; 19cm. — (Spur footpath guides)
Previous ed.: 1976
ISBN 0-7157-2066-x (pbk) : £1.25 B82-31064

796.5′1′094226 — East & West Sussex. South Downs. Recreations: Walking — *Visitors′ guides*

Ulph, Colin. Southdown walks / by Colin Ulph ; illustrated with sketch. — Shoreham by Sea (281 Upper Shoreham Rd., Shoreham by Sea, W. Sussex BN4 6BB) : C.Ulph, c1981. — 80p : ill,maps ; 18cm
Text, ill on inside covers
£1.00 (pbk) B82-14344

796.5′1′094227 — Hampshire. Recreations: Walking — *Visitors′ guides*

MacLaren, Roberta. Hampshire and the New Forest : walks for motorists / Roberta MacLaren. — London : Warne, c1982. — 105p : maps ; 21cm. — (Warne Gerrard guides for walkers. Walks for motorists)
ISBN 0-7232-2169-3 (pbk) : £1.75 B82-22829

796.5′1′094228 — Isle of Wight. Recreations: Walking — *Visitors′ guides*

McInnes, R. G.. Isle of Wight : walks for motorists / R.G. McInnes ; 30 circular walks with sketch maps by F. Rodney Fraser. — London : Warne, c1982. — 103p : maps ; 21cm. — (Warne Gerrard guides for walkers. Walks for motorists)
ISBN 0-7232-2805-1 (pbk) : £1.75 B82-22827

796.5′1′0942298 — Berkshire. Binfield. Recreations: Walking — *Visitors′ guides*

Walks and rides around Binfield. — 2nd ed. — [Bracknell] ([Easthampstead House, Town Sq., Bracknell, Berks.]) : Binfield Parish Council, [1982?]. — 31p : ill,maps ; 21cm
Previous ed.: 197-?
£0.30 (pbk) B82-23127

796.5′1′09424 — England. Midlands. Recreations: Walking — *Visitors′ guides*

Shurey, Richard. Family walks in Midland counties / Richard Shurey. — London : Warne, 1982. — 101p : maps ; 21cm. — (Warne Gerrard guides for walkers. Walks for motorists)
ISBN 0-7232-2170-7 (pbk) : £1.75 B82-22822

796.5′1′0942485 — Warwickshire. Rugby region. Recreations: Walking — *Visitors′ guides*

25 walks near Rugby. — [Rugby] : [Rugby Group, Ramblers′ Association], c1982. — 68p : ill,maps ; 21cm
ISBN 0-900613-47-5 (pbk) : £1.20 B82-27463

796.5′1′0942489 — Warwickshire. Stratford-upon-Avon region. Recreations: Walking — Visitors′ guides

Stratford walks : detailed guidance for nine excursions on foot from Stratford-upon-Avon into the surrounding countryside. — Stratford-upon-Avon : The Ramblers Association Stratford-upon-Avon Group, 1982. — 32p : ill,maps ; 22cm
ISBN 0-900613-46-7 (pbk) : £0.75 B82-22582

796.5′1′09425 — England. Chilterns. Recreations: Walking — *Visitors′ guides*

Burden, Vera. Walks in the Chiltern Hills / by Vera Burden. — Edinburgh : Spurbooks, c1982. — 64p : maps ; 19cm. — (A Spurbooks footpath guide)
ISBN 0-7157-2111-9 (pbk) : £1.25 B82-22941

Pigram, Ron. Discovering walks in the Chilterns / Ron Pigram. — 2nd ed. — Princes Risborough : Shire, 1982. — 63p : maps ; 18cm. — (The Discovering series ; 136)
Previous ed.: 1972. — Includes index
ISBN 0-85263-615-6 (pbk) : £1.25 B82-39394

796.5′1′094251 — Southern Derbyshire. Recreations: Walking — *Visitors′ guides*

Thompson, Clifford. Derbyshire : walks for motorists : Southern area / Clifford Thompson. — London : Warne, c1982. — 70p : maps ; 21cm. — (Warne Gerrard guides for walkers. Walks for motorists)
ISBN 0-7232-2804-3 (pbk) : £1.75 B82-22828

796.5′1′0942511 — Derbyshire. White Peak region. Recreations: Walking — *Visitors′ guides*

Merrill, John N.. Walks in the White Peak / by John N. Merrill ; maps by Geoff Arnold. — Clapham, N. Yorkshire : Dalesman, c1981. — 56p : maps ; 21cm
ISBN 0-85206-647-3 (pbk) : £1.25 B82-03629

796.5′1′094257 — Oxfordshire. Recreations: Walking — *Visitors′ guides*

Rambles in Oxfordshire / illustrations by D.J.R. Kimber ; front cover design by Margherita M. Davidson. — [Oxford] ([c/o R.A. Brown, 45 Bainton Rd., Oxford OX2 7AG]) : Oxford Fieldpaths Society, 1979. — ill,maps ; 21cm
Unpriced (pbk) B82-26793

796.5′1′0942576 — Oxfordshire. Vale of White Horse *(District)*. **Recreations: Walking** — *Visitors′ guides*

Hammond, Nigel. Walks in the White Horse country : fifteen country rambles near Oxford, Swindon and Newbury : with historical notes / Nigel Hammond. — Newbury : Countryside Books, 1982. — 80p : maps ; 22cm
ISBN 0-905392-14-0 (pbk) : £2.50 B82-32895

796.5′1′094258 — Hertfordshire. Recreations: Walking — *Visitors′ guides*

Bagley, William A.. Hertfordshire : walks for motorists / Wm. A. Bagley ; 30 circular walks with sketch maps by the author. — London : Warne, 1982. — 99p : maps ; 21cm. — (Warne Gerrard guides for walkers. Walks for motorists series)
"Walks 1-23 first published in London countryside walks for motorists: north western area, 1975; walks 25-29 first published in London countryside walks for motorists: north eastern area. 1977"
ISBN 0-7232-2809-4 (pbk) : £1.75 B82-33951

796.5′1′094267 — West Essex. Recreations: Walking — *Visitors′ guides*

Bagley, William A.. Essex : walks for motorists / Wm. A. Bagley with the collaboration of Fred Matthews. — 2nd ed. — London : Warne, 1982. — 110p : maps ; 21cm. — (Warne Gerrard guides for walkers. Walks for motorists series)
Previous ed.: published as London countryside walks for motorists, north eastern area. Harrow : Gerrard, 1977
ISBN 0-7232-2807-8 (pbk) : £1.75 B82-33950

796.5'1'09426723 — Essex. Colchester region. Recreations: Walking — *Visitors' guides*

Keeble, Derek. The Camuplodunum : a pedestrians' route around Britain's oldest recorded town — Colchester / by Derek Keeble. — 2nd ed. — Colchester (9, Shelley Rd., Colchester CO3 4MN) : Roy Tover Ventures, 1982. — 16p : ill ; 22cm
Previous ed.: 1974
£0.84 (unbound) B82-31227

796.5'1'09427 — Northern England. Recreations: Long-distance walking — *Practical information*

Wimbush, Tony. Long distance walks. — Clapham : Dalesman
Vol.2: The Yorkshire Dales / by Tony Wimbush and Alan Gott. — 1982. — 72p : ill,maps ; 21cm
ISBN 0-85206-676-7 (pbk) : £1.95 B82-31382

796.5'1'094276 — Lancashire. Recreations: Walking — *Visitors' guides*

The **Lancashire** trail : a series of short walks which link together to form a long distance route connecting St. Helens, Wigan, Bolton, Blackburn & Burnley with the Pennine Way at Thornton-in-Craven. — [Wigan] ([The Rambles Secretary, 40 St. Mary's Ave, Birchley, Billinge, Nr. Wigan]) : St. Helens & District CHA & HF Rambling Club, [1982?]. — 28p : col.maps ; 21cm
£1.50 (pbk) B82-19429

796.5'1'0942769 — Lancashire. Lune Valley. Recreations: Walking — *Visitors' guides*

Walks in the Lune Valley / by the Ramblers Association (Lancaster Group). — Clapham (N. Yorks) : Dalesman, 1982. — 56p : maps ; 20cm
ISBN 0-85206-675-9 (pbk) : £1.40 B82-31957

796.5'1'094278 — Cumbria. Lake District. Recreations: Walking — *Visitors' guides*

Poucher, W. A.. The Lakeland peaks : a pictorial guide to walking in the district and to the safe ascent of its principal mountain groups / W.A. Poucher. — 7th ed. [i.e. 8th ed.]. — London : Constable, 1981. — 441p : ill,maps ; 18cm
Previous ed.: 1979. — Includes index
ISBN 0-09-464390-3 : £5.95 B82-12507

796.5'1'0942786 — Cumbria. Eden Valley. Recreations: Walking — *Visitors' guides*

Sowerby, Harold. Walking in the Eden Valley / by Harold and Brenda Sowerby on behalf of the Lake District Area of the Ramblers' Association. — Clapham, N. Yorkshire : Dalesman, 1979. — 72p : ill,maps ; 19cm. — (A Dalesman mini-book)
Map on inside cover
ISBN 0-85206-497-7 (pbk) : £1.10 B82-03627

796.5'1'094281 — West Yorkshire *(Metropolitan County)*. **Brighouse region. Recreations: Walking** — *Visitors' guides*

Nortcliffe, David. Country walks around Brighouse / by David Nortcliffe & George Howe. — 2nd (enl.) ed. — [Halifax] ([3 Cobden Terrace, Hipperholme, Halifax, HX3 8JH]) : Brighouse Civic Trust, 1982. — 52p : ill,maps ; 22cm
Previous ed.: 1978?. — Text on inside cover
Unpriced (pbk) B82-21684

796.5'1'0942817 — West Yorkshire *(Metropolitan County)*. **Bradford region. Recreations: Walking** — *Visitors' guides*

Countryside walks around Bradford / compiled by The Senior Wayfarers. — Clapham, [North Yorkshire] : Dalesman, 1981. — 56p : maps ; 21cm
ISBN 0-85206-660-0 (pbk) : £1.25 B82-14851

796.5'1'0942817 — West Yorkshire *(Metropolitan County)*. **Ilkley region. Recreations: Walking** — *Visitors' guides*

Wade, Roland, *1906-*. "Evergreen" walks : from Ilkley. — Ilkley (11, St. Helens Way, Ilkley, W. Yorks. LS29 8NP) : Clive Dougherty, c1982. — 24p : ill,maps ; 19cm
Authors: Roland Wade, Alfred Wood, Fred Wilson and Clive Dougherty. — Ill on covers
£1.00 (pbk) B82-32039

796.5'1'0942819 — West Yorkshire *(Metropolitan County)*. **Leeds region. Long-distance footpaths: Leeds Country Way. Recreations: Walking** — *Visitors' guides*

Leeds country way. — [Wakefield] ([County Hall, Wakefield WF1 2QW]) : West Yorkshire Metropolitan County Council, Recreation and Arts Division, Countryside Unit
Part 1: Golden Acre Park to Barwick-in-Elmet. — [1981?]. — 1sheet ; 42x31cm folded to 22x16cm : 3col.maps ; 22cm
Unpriced (unbound) B82-08587

Leeds country way. — [Wakefield] ([County Hall, Wakefield WF1 2QW]) : West Yorkshire Metropolitan County Council, Recreation and Arts Division, Countryside Unit
Part 4: Cockersdale to Golden Acre Park. — [1981?]. — 1sheet ; 43x30cm folded to 22x15cm : 3col.maps ; 22cm
Unpriced (unbound) B82-08588

796.5'1'094284 — North Yorkshire. Dales. Recreations: Walking — *Visitors' guides*

Wade, H. O.. Afoot in the Yorkshire Dales / H.O. Wade. — Edinburgh : Spurbooks, c1981. — 64p : maps ; 19cm. — (A Spurbooks footpath guide)
ISBN 0-7157-2097-x (pbk) : £1.25 B82-22947

796.5'1'094284 — North Yorkshire. National parks: Yorkshire Dales National Park. Recreations. Walking — *Visitors' guides*

Duerden, Frank. Great walks of the Yorkshire Dales. — London : Ward Lock, Mar.1982. — [192]p
ISBN 0-7063-6164-4 (pbk) : £3.50 : CIP entry B82-01725

796.5'1'0942843 — North Yorkshire. York region. Recreations: Walking — *Visitors' guides*

Piggin, Ken. Countryside walks around York / by Ken Piggin. — Clapham (via Lancaster) : Dalesman, 1982. — 56p : maps ; 21cm
ISBN 0-85206-670-8 (pbk) : £1.40 B82-23612

796.5'1'0942846 — North Yorkshire. North York Moors. Recreations: Walking: Lyke Wake Walk, *to 1978*

Cowley, Bill. Lyke Wake Walk : forty miles across the north York moors / by Bill Cowley. — 9th ed. — Clapham (via Lancaster) : Dalesman, 1980. — 88p : ill,maps,ports ; 21cm
Previous ed.: 1979
ISBN 0-85206-501-9 (pbk) : £1.75 B82-23611

796.5'1'0942846 — North Yorkshire. North York Moors. Recreations: Walking — *Visitors' guides*

Walking on the North York moors / compiled by The Ramblers' Association (North Yorkshire and South Durham Area). — New ed. — Clapham, N. Yorkshire : Dalesman, 1981. — 56p : maps ; 21cm
Previous ed.: 1973
ISBN 0-85206-649-x (pbk) : £1.25 B82-03628

796.5'1'0942846 -- North Yorkshire. Ryedale *(District)*. **Recreations: Walking** — *Visitors' guides*

Boyes, Malcolm. Rosedale and Farndale / by Malcolm Boyes. — Clapham, North Yorkshire : Dalesman, 1979. — 47p : maps ; 19cm. — (Walks from your car)
ISBN 0-85206-530-2 (pbk) : £0.75 B82-14853

796.5'1'0954 — Asia. Himalayas. Backpacking — *Manuals*

Swift, Hugh. Trekker's guide to the Himalaya and the Karakoram. — London : Hodder and Stoughton, Nov.1982. — [288]p
ISBN 0-340-32350-7 : £5.95 : CIP entry B82-27341

796.5'22 — Cumbria. Lake District. Hill walking & rock climbing. Organisations: Fell and Rock Climbing Club of the English Lake District, *to 1981*. **Exhibits** — *Catalogues*

Fell & Rock *(Exhibition)*. Fell & Rock : an exhibition held to celebrate the first seventy-five years of the Fell & Rock Climbing Club of the English Lake District : 1906-1981 : Keswick, October 31-November 1, Kendal, November 7-28 / edited by June Tarrington. — [Lancaster] : F.R.C.C., 1981. — 52p : ill ; 22cm
Limited ed. of 1000 copies
ISBN 0-85028-028-1 (pbk) : Unpriced B82-21457

796.5'22 — Mountaineering

Ascent : the mountaineering experience in word and image / edited by Allen Steck and Steve Roper. — San Francisco : Sierra Club ; Leicester : Diadem, c1980. — 272p : ill(some col.),1map,ports(some col.) ; 28cm
Bibliography: p196
ISBN 0-906371-70-8 (pbk) : £8.95 B82-18643

796.5'22 — Mountaineering — *Manuals*

Mountaineering : the freedom of the hills. — 4th ed. / editor, Ed Peters ; Revision Committee Roger Anderson ... [et al.] ; illustrations Robert Cram and Ramona Hammerly. — Seattle, Washington : The Mountaineers ; Leicester : Distributed by Cordee, 1982. — xii,550p : ill ; 24cm
Previous ed.: 1975. — Includes bibliographies and index
ISBN 0-904405-71-0 : £9.95 B82-20213

796.5'22 — Mountains. Ice pitches & snow pitches. Mountaineering — *Manuals*

Chouinard, Yvon. Climbing ice / Yvon Chouinard. — London : Hodder and Stoughton, 1978 (1981 [printing]). — 192p : ill (some col.),ports ; 28cm
Originally published: San Francisco : Sierra Club Books, 1978. — Includes index
ISBN 0-340-27147-7 (pbk) : £5.95 : CIP rev. B81-18112

796.5'22 — Scotland. Mountains. Recreations: Walking — *Visitors' guides*

Poucher, W. A.. The Scottish peaks : a pictorial guide to walking in this region and to the safe ascent of its most spectacular mountains / W.A. Poucher. — 6th ed. — London : Constable, 1982, c1965. — 511p : ill,1form,maps ; 18cm
Previous ed.: 1979. — Includes index
ISBN 0-09-464680-5 : £5.95 B82-39754

796.5'22'09 — Mountaineering, *to 1976*

Hindley, Geoffrey, *1935-*. The roof of the world / by Geoffrey Hindley. — London : Reader's Digest Association, 1981, c1971. — 191p : ill (some col.),facsims(some col.),col.maps,ports (some col.) ; 27cm. — (Discovery and exploration)
Originally published: London : Aldus, 1971. — Includes index
£6.97 B82-31542

796.5'22'0924 — Asia. Himalayas. Mountaineering, *1979* — *Personal observations*

Hillary, Peter. A sunny day in the Himalayas. — London : Hodder and Stoughton, May 1981. — [166]p
ISBN 0-340-25685-0 : £7.50 : CIP entry B81-04242

796.5'22'0924 — Europe. Alps. Mountaineering — *Personal observations*

Desmaison, René. Total alpinism. — London : Granada, Sept.1982. — [256]p
Translation of: La montagne à mains nues and 342 heures dans les Grandes Jorasses
ISBN 0-246-11112-7 : £10.00 : CIP entry B82-18846

796.5'22'0924 — Mountaineering, *1952-1978* — *Personal observations*

MacInnes, Hamish. Look behind the ranges : a mountaineer's selection of adventures / Hamish MacInnes. — Harmondsworth : Penguin, 1981, c1979. — 256p,[8]p of plates : ill,ports ; 19cm
Originally published: Sevenoaks : Hodder and Stoughton, 1979. — Includes index
ISBN 0-14-005630-0 (pbk) : £1.95 B82-08027

796.5'22'0924 — Mountaineering. Messner, Reinhold — *Biographies*

Faux, Ronald. High ambition : a biography of Reinhold Messner / by Ronald Faux. — London : Gollancz, 1982. — 180p,[24]p of plates : ill,maps,ports ; 24cm
Maps on lining papers. — Bibliography: p175. — Includes index
ISBN 0-575-03069-0 : £9.95 : CIP rev. B81-35884

796.5′22′0924 — Mountaineering — *Personal observations*

Boardman, Peter. Sacred summits : a climber′s year / Peter Boardman. — London : Hodder and Stoughton, 1982. — 264p,[24]p of plates : ill(some col.),maps,col.ports ; 24cm
Includes index
ISBN 0-340-24659-6 : £9.95 : CIP rev.
B82-12247

Cassin, Riccardo. 50 years of Alpinism / by Riccardo Cassin ; translated by Renato Sottile. — London : Diadem, c1981. — 207p,[80]p of plates : ill,ports ; 23cm
Translation of: Cinquant′anni di alpinismo. — Bibliography: p203. — Includes index
ISBN 0-906371-65-1 : £8.95 : CIP rev.
B80-27452

796.5′22′0924 — Mountaineering. Tasker, Joe — *Biographies*

Tasker, Joe. Savage arena. — London : Methuen, Sept.1982. — [256]p
ISBN 0-413-50630-4 : £7.95 : CIP entry
B82-19232

796.5′22′0924 — Scotland. National libraries: National Library of Scotland. Exhibits: Items associated with Graham Brown, Thomas — *Catalogues*

Thomas Graham Brown 1882-1965. — Edinburgh : National Library of Scotland, 1982. — 19p : ill,facsims,ports ; 25cm. — (Exhibition catalogue / National Library of Scotland ; no.20)
Catalogue of an exhibition to mark the centenary of the birth of Thomas Graham Brown in 1882
ISBN 0-902220-49-7 (pbk) : Unpriced
B82-20910

796.5′22′0943642 — Austria. Stubai Alps. Mountaineering — *Visitors′ guides*

Roberts, Eric, *1945-1979*. Stubai Alps : a survey of popular walking and climbing routes / compiled by Eric Roberts. — Repr. with supplement. — Reading : West Col, 1981. — 167p : ill ; 17cm. — (West Col alpine guides)
Previous ed.: 1972. — Includes index
ISBN 0-906227-18-6 : £7.50 B82-16573

796.5′22′0944945 — France. Corsica. Mountaineering — *Visitors′ guides*

Collomb, Robin G.. Corsica mountains / Robin G. Collomb. — Reading : West Col, 1982. — 93p : ill,maps ; 18cm. — (Guide Collomb ; 2)
Includes index
ISBN 0-906227-19-4 (pbk) : £5.25 B82-16574

796.5′22′094947 — Switzerland. Eiger. North Face. Mountaineering, *to 1980*

Roth, Arthur. Eiger : wall of death / Arthur Roth. — London : Gollancz, 1982. — 350p : ill,ports ; 24cm
Includes index
ISBN 0-575-03087-9 : £9.50 : CIP rev.
B82-01551

796.5′223 — Rock climbing — *Manuals*

Nock, Peter. Rock climbing / by Peter Nock ; edited and revised by Donald Law. — New, rev. ed. — London] : Foyles Handbooks, 1975. — 80p : ill ; 19cm
Previous ed.: 1963
ISBN 0-7071-0512-9 : Unpriced B82-32978

796.5′223′09411 — Scotland. Winter rock climbing — *Manuals*

MacInnes, Hamish. Scottish winter climbs / Hamish MacInnes. — London : Constable, 1982. — 480p : ill,maps ; 18cm. — (A Constable guide)
Bibliography: p472. — Includes index
ISBN 0-09-463620-6 : £5.95 B82-31266

796.5′223′09422 — South-east England. Sandstone regions. Rock climbing — *Manuals*

Daniells, Tim. Southern sandstone. — 4th ed. / by Tim Daniells ; chalk sea cliffs section by Mike Fowler ; diagrams and maps by Don Sargeant ; cover photographs and photograph compilation by Chris Griffiths. — [London] : Climbers′ Club, with financial assistance from the British Mountaineering Council, 1981. — 128p,[16]p of plates : maps,ports ; 18cm. — (Climbers′ Club guides)
Previous ed.: i.e. 1st ed., 2nd revision published as South east England / by Edward C. Pyatt. 1969. — Maps on inside covers
ISBN 0-901601-17-9 (pbk) : £4.50 B82-35086

796.5′223′0942925 — Gwynedd. Snowdonia. Rock climbing — *Manuals*

James, Ron. Rock climbing in Wales / Ron James. — 3rd ed. rev. — London : Constable, 1982. — 265p : ill ; 18cm. — (A Constable guide)
Previous ed.: 1975
ISBN 0-09-464530-2 : £5.95 B82-34623

796.5′25 — Northern England. Underground sumps — *Lists* — *For cave diving*

Griffith, Julian. Northern sump index : in memory of Bear and Ian / [compiled by Julian Griffiths]. — [Bristol] ([Withey House, Withey Close West, Bristol, BS9 3SZ]) : [Cave Diving Group], [1981]. — 111p : ill,maps ; 30cm
Cover title. — Includes index
£3.50 (pbk) B82-23940

796.5′25′05 — Caves. Exploration — *Serials*

[Cave science *(1982)*]. Cave science : the transactions of the British Cave Research Association. — Vol.9, no.1 (Feb. 1982)-. — Bridgwater : The Association, 1982-. — v. : ill,maps ; 30cm
Quarterly. — Also entitled: Transactions of the British Cave Research Association (1982). — Continues: Transations of the British Cave Research Association (1974)
ISSN 0263-760X = Cave science (1982) : Unpriced B82-32150

[Newsletter *(Unit Two Cave Research and Exploration Group)*]. Newsletter / Unit Two : cave research and exploration. — 1979-. — Redhill (c/o P. Burgess, 5 Oakwood Close, Redhill, Surrey) : The Group, 1979-. — v. : ill ; 30cm
Three issues yearly. — Description based on: No.1 (1982)
ISSN 0263-4953 = Newsletter (Unit Two Cave Research and Exploration Group) : Unpriced
B82-32181

796.5′25′0924 — Caves. Exploration — *Personal observations*

Eyre, Jim. The cave explorers / by Jim Eyre. — Calgary : Stalactite ; [Leicester] : Cordee, 1981. — viii,264p : ill ; 22cm
ISBN 0-904405-31-1 : £8.50 B82-08859

796.54 — Camping — *Manuals*

McGee, Eddie. Go camping with Eddie McGee : the first time camper′s guide to safer, better camping / illustrated by Mike Miller. — London : Corgi, 1982. — 144p : ill ; 18cm
ISBN 0-552-11953-9 (pbk) : £1.25 B82-21601

796.54 — Camping — *Manuals* — *For children*

Jeffries, Ron. Camping / by Ron Jeffries and Paul Moynihan ; illustrated by Ed Carr. — London : Macdonald, 1982. — 64p : ill(some col.) ; 21cm. — (Whizz kids ; 21)
Bibliography: p62. — Includes index
ISBN 0-356-06381-x (cased) : £2.95
ISBN 0-356-06341-1 (pbk) : £1.25 B82-22964

796.54 — Camping — *Manuals* — *For families*

Pond, Philip. Family camping / Philip Pond. — Edinburgh : Spurbooks, c1982. — 96p : ill,2maps ; 22cm. — (Spur family guides) (A Spurbooks master guide)
Cover title: The Spur book of family camping. — Bibliography: p94-95
ISBN 0-7157-2095-3 (pbk) : £3.50 B82-22946

796.54 — Lightweight camping equipment. Making — *Amateurs′ manuals*

Constance, Hazel. Gear for outdoors : and how to make : a comprehensive manual / by Hazel Constance. — London : Hale, 1982. — 240p,[12]p of plates : ill ; 23cm
Includes index
ISBN 0-7091-9630-x : £8.95 B82-39544

796.6 — CYCLING

796.6 — Cycling

Osman, Tony. The new cyclist / Tony Osman. — London : Collins, 1982. — 96p : ill(some col.),facsims,1port ; 25cm
Text on back cover. — Bibliography: p94. — Includes index
ISBN 0-00-216880-4 (cased) : £9.95 : CIP rev.
ISBN 0-00-316881-2 (pbk) : £4.95 B81-04360

796.6′09413′7 — Scotland. Borders Region. Cycling — *Practical information*

Cycling. — Newtown St. Boswells (Newtown St. Boswells, Roxburghshire) : Borders Regional Council, 1982. — 1folded sheet([6]p) ; 21cm. — (The Scottish Borders)
Unpriced B82-32909

796.6′09421′4 — North-east London. Cycling — *Practical information*

Bike it! : a guide to cycling in North and East London. — Ilford (20 Talbot Gardens, Ilford, Essex) : Redbridge Friends of the Earth Cycling Campaign, 1981. — 27,22p : ill,maps (some col.) ; 21cm
Cover title. — Text on inside cover. — Bibliography: p26
£0.50 (pbk) B82-19126

796.6′2′060426 — Eastern England. Bicycles. Racing. Clubs: North Road Cycling Club, *to 1980*

Smith, A. B.. Along the Great North and other roads : the North Road cycling club 1885-1980 / A.B. Smith. — Gloucester : Sutton, 1981. — 190p : ill,facsims,ports ; 23cm
ISBN 0-904387-73-9 : Unpriced : CIP rev.
B81-07489

796.6′2′0924 — Bicycles. Racing. Coppi, Fausto — *Biographies*

Duker, Peter. ″Coppi″ / Peter Duker. — Bognor Regis : New Horizon, c1982. — 92p,[20]p of plates : 1facsim,ports ; 23cm
ISBN 0-86116-945-x : £4.75 B82-35407

796.7 — MOTORING

796.7 — Great Britain. Motorcycling, *1917-1960*

Vintage motor cycle album / compiled & edited by Dennis Howard. — London : Warne, 1982. — 96p : ill,ports ; 31cm. — (An MHB book)
Ill on lining papers. — Includes index
ISBN 0-7232-2874-4 : £7.95 B82-35431

796.7 — Motorcycle touring

Thoeming, Peter. Motorcycle touring / Peter ″the Bear″ Thoeming and Peter Rae. — London : Osprey, 1982. — 191p,[8]p of plates : ill(some col.),3maps,ports ; 26cm
Includes index
ISBN 0-85045-436-0 : £9.95 : CIP rev.
B82-04977

796.7 — Motorcycling

Carless, Geoff. Advanced motorcycling / Geoff Carless. — Wakefield : EP, 1982, c1981. — 128p : ill,1port ; 21cm
ISBN 0-7158-0776-5 (pbk) : £2.95 B82-34789

The **Motorcyclist′s** handbook : the complete guide to biking / [edited and designed by Marshall Editions Ltd.] ; [editor Graeme Ewens]. — London : Pan, 1981. — 239p : ill (some col.),ports(some col.) ; 22cm
Includes index
ISBN 0-330-26566-0 (cased) : £5.95
ISBN 0-330-26526-1 (pbk) : Unpriced
B82-01591

796.7 — Motorcycling, *to 1978 — Records of achievement*
Setright, L. J. K.. The Guinness book of motorcycling facts and feats. — Rev. ed. — Enfield : Guinness Superlatives, July 1982. — [258]p
Previous ed.: 1979
ISBN 0-85112-255-8 : £7.95 : CIP entry B82-15930

796.7′06′041 — Great Britain. Motoring. Organisations: Automobile Association, *to 1980*
Automobile Association. The AA : a history of the first 75 years of the Automobile Association 1905-1980 / by Hugh Barty-King. — Basingstoke : AA, c1980. — 319p : ill(some col.),col.coat of arms,facsims(some col.),ports (some col.) ; 27x30cm
Ill on lining papers. — Bibliography: p312-313. — Includes index
ISBN 0-86145-024-8 : £14.50 B82-32202

796.7′0941 — Great Britain. Motoring. Policies of government. Formulation. Role of Royal Automobile Club
Royal Automobile Club. A report of the RAC′s public policy activities during 1980 / RAC. — Croydon : RAC, [1981?]. — 32p : ill ; 25cm
Unpriced (pbk) B82-10196

796.72 — MOTOR RACING

796.7′2 — Alfa Romeo racing cars. Racing, *1929-1939*
Orsini, Luigi. The Scuderia Ferrari : 1929 to 1939 : Enzo Ferrari racing with Alfa Romeo / by Luigi Orsini and Franco Zagari ; translated by Aldo Piombini ; edited by Doug Nye. — London : Osprey, 1981. — 429p : ill,facsims,plans,ports ; 28cm
Translation from the Italian
ISBN 0-85045-378-x : £39.95 : CIP rev. B81-18095

796.7′2 — British Leyland Mini cars. Rallying, *1959-1970*
Browning, Peter, *1936-*. The works Minis : an illustrated history of the works entered Minis in international rallies and races / by Peter Browning. — [Yeovil] : Foulis, 1971 (1979 [printing]). — x,206p : ill,ports ; 22cm. — (A Foulis motoring book)
Includes index
ISBN 0-85429-278-0 (pbk) : £2.95 B82-36688

796.7′2 — Cars. Rallying *— Serials*
Rothmans world rallying. — 4. — London : Osprey, Mar.1982. — [176]p
ISBN 0-85045-424-7 : £7.95 : CIP entry
ISSN 0144-6711 B82-00375

796.7′2 — Cars. Rallying, *to 1980*
Robson, Graham. An illustrated history of rallying / Graham Robson. — London : Osprey, 1981. — 208p,[8]p of plates : ill(some col.),ports ; 26cm
Includes index
ISBN 0-85045-407-7 : £9.95 : CIP rev. B81-14908

796.7′2 — Ferrari boxer racing cars. Racing, *to 1980*
Thompson, Jonathan. Boxer : the Ferrari flat-12 racing and GT cars / Jonathan Thompson. — Costa Mesa, Calif. : Newport Press ; London : Osprey, c1981. — 184p : ill(some col.),ports ; 31cm
ISBN 0-85045-409-3 : £14.95 B82-05210

796.7′2 — Ferrari Turbo racing cars. Racing, *to 1981*
Thompson, Jonathan. Ferrari Turbo. — London : Osprey, July 1982. — [116]p
ISBN 0-85045-465-4 : £9.95 : CIP entry B82-21956

796.7′2 — Formula 1 racing cars. Racing, *1953-1978 — Illustrations*
Photo formula 1 : the best of Automobile year 1953-1978 / translated by Tim Chivers ; foreword by Ami Guichard and Yves Debraine. — Cambridge : Stephens, 1979. — 155p : chiefly ill(some col.),ports(some col. ; 33cm
Translation of: Photo formule 1
ISBN 0-85059-411-1 : £17.50 : CIP rev. B79-23983

796.7′2 — Formula 1 racing cars. Racing *— For children*
Little, Peter. Motor racing : start here if you want to be a world-champion racing driver / Peter Little and David English ; with expert advice from Vic Waterhouse. — Harmondsworth : Puffin, 1981. — [64]p : ill (some col.),col.ports ; 20cm. — (Puffin adventure sports)
ISBN 0-14-031150-5 (pbk) : £0.95 B82-07309

796.7′2 — Jaguar cars. Racing, *to 1953*
Whyte, Andrew. Jaguar : sports racing & works competition cars to 1953 / Andrew Whyte ; foreword by F.R.W. England. — [Yeovil] : Foulis : Haynes, 1982. — 415p : ill,facsims,ports ; 28cm. — (A Foulis motoring book)
Includes index
ISBN 0-85429-277-2 : £19.95 B82-17868

796.7′2 — Racing cars. Racing. Races: Grands Prix, *to 1979*
Dymock, Eric. The Guinness guide to grand prix motor racing / Eric Dymock. — Enfield : Guinness Superlatives, c1980. — 264p : ill (some col.),ports(some col.) ; 30cm
Ill on lining papers. — Includes index
ISBN 0-85112-206-x : £11.95 : CIP rev. B80-02533

796.7′2 — Racing cars. Racing. Races: Grands Prix, *to 1980*
Lang, Mike. Grand Prix! / by Mike Lang. — [Sparkford] : Foulis. — (A Foulis motoring book)
[Vol.2]: [1966-1973]. — 1982. — 259p : ill,ports ; 28cm
ISBN 0-85429-321-3 : Unpriced B82-38378

796.7′2′0922 — Racing cars. Racing. Championships. Winners, *to 1980*
Winners : a who′s who of motor racing champions / edited by Brian Laban. — London : Orbis, 1981. — 190p,[16]p of plates : ports ; 24cm
ISBN 0-85613-042-7 : £7.95 B82-01485

796.7′2′0941 — Great Britain. Racing cars. Drag racing
Hardcastle, David. Drive it! : the complete book of British drag racing / David Hardcastle & Peter Jones. — Yoevil : Foulis, 1981. — 182p : ill,ports ; 28cm
ISBN 0-85429-290-x : Unpriced B82-01233

796.7′2′0941 — Great Britain. Racing cars. Racing *— Serials*
Motor racing directory : Mike Kettlewell′s guide to British motor racing. — [1979]. — Boston, Lincs. (The Mill House, Station Rd., Eastville, Boston, Lincs. PE22 8LS) : Kettlewell Transport Information Trade Services, 1979. — ill,ports ; 21cm
Continued by: The Pace motor racing directory. — Only one issue published under this title
£7.95 B82-04073

The **Pace** motor racing directory : Mike Kettlewell′s guide to British motor racing. — 1981-. — Boston, Lincs. (The Mill House, Station Rd., Eastville, Boston, Lincs. PE22 8LS) : Kettlewell Transport Information Trade Services, 1981-. — v. : ill,ports ; 21cm
Annual. — Continues: Motor racing directory
ISSN 0262-4710 = Pace motor racing directory : £7.95 B82-04071

796.75 — MOTORCYCLE RACING

796.7′5 — Racing motorcycles. Grass-track racing
The **Gemini** book of grasstrack / compiled & edited by John Simcock. — Bristol : Gemini Graphics & Print, 1981. — 144p : ill(some col.),ports(some col.) ; 21cm
ISBN 0-9507974-0-5 (pbk) : Unpriced B82-20929

796.7′5 — Racing motorcycles. Junior moto-cross
Venables, Ralph. Schoolboy scrambling : and other motorcycle sports / Ralph Venables. — 2nd ed. — Yeovil : Oxford Illustrated Press, 1977 (1981 [printing]). — 92p : ill,ports ; 26cm
Previous ed.: 1975
ISBN 0-902280-28-7 : £4.50 B82-13212

796.7′5 — Racing motorcycles. Moto-cross *— Serials*
Dirt bike rider : a motor cycle news magazine. — No.1 (1981)-. — Peterborough (Bretton Court, Bretton, Peterborough PE3 8DZ) : EMAP National Publications, 1981-. — v. : ill(some col.),ports ; 30cm
Six issues yearly. — Description based on: No.3 (Nov./Dec. 1981)
ISSN 0262-5628 = Dirt bike rider : £0.85 per issue B82-15159

796.7′5 — Racing motorcycles. Speedway racing
The **Lada** international book of speedway. — London : Paul, May 1982. — [96]p
ISBN 0-09-149581-4 (pbk) : £3.95 : CIP entry B82-16494

796.7′5 — Racing motorcycles. Speedway racing. Championships: World Speedway Championship. Finals, *to 1978*
Chaplin, John. Speedway : the story of the World Championship / by John Chaplin. — Ipswich : Studio Publications, c1979. — 128p : ill,ports ; 28cm
ISBN 0-904584-80-1 : £4.50 B82-30450

796.7′5 — Suzuki racing motorcycles. Racing. Teams: Team Suzuki, *to 1981*
Battersby, Ray. Team Suzuki. — London : Osprey, Oct.1982. — [272]p
ISBN 0-85045-416-6 : £11.95 : CIP entry B82-29408

796.7′5′0321 — Racing motorcycles. Racing *— Encyclopaedias*
Carrick, Peter. Encyclopaedia of motor-cycle sport / compiled by Peter Carrick. — 2nd ed. — London : Hale, 1982. — 240p,[16]p of plates : ill,ports ; 25cm
Previous ed.: 1977. — Includes index
ISBN 0-7091-8874-9 : £8.50 B82-34872

796.7′5′09 — Racing motorcycles. Racing, *to 1979*
Hailwood, Mike. Bikes : thirty years and more of the motor-cycle world championships / by Mike Hailwood with Peter Carrick ; technical review by Vic Willoughby. — Sevenoaks : New English Library, 1982. — ix,148p,[16]p of plates : ports ; 23cm
Includes index
ISBN 0-450-04878-0 : £7.95 : CIP rev. B82-10657

796.7′5′09045 — Racing motorcycles. Racing, *1950-1959*
McKinnon, Andrew. Motorcycle road racing of the fifties. — London : Osprey, Apr.1982. — [184]p
ISBN 0-85045-405-0 : £7.95 : CIP entry B82-06521

796.7′5′0924 — Great Britain. Racing motorcycles. Sprinting. Brown, George, *1912-1979 — Biographies*
Brown, Cliff. George Brown : sprint superstar / Cliff Brown. — Yeovil : Foulis : Haynes, 1981. — 141p : ill,1facsim,ports ; 24cm. — (A Foulis motorcycling book)
Includes index
ISBN 0-85429-295-0 : Unpriced B82-03208

796.7′5′0924 — Racing motorcycles. Racing. Gleave, Syd *— Biographies*
Maybury, Paul. Syd Gleave and his Specials : the story of a T.T. rider / Paul Maybury. — Macclesfield : Upton, c1981. — 60p : ill,facsims,ports ; 16x21cm
ISBN 0-9507599-0-2 (pbk) : £1.50 B82-22579

796.7′5′0924 — Racing motorcycles. Racing. Roberts, Kenny *— Biographies*
Coleman, Barry. Kenny Roberts : okie, racer, philosopher, king / Barry Coleman. — London : Barker, c1982. — 197p,[16]p of plates : ill,ports ; 23cm
ISBN 0-213-16825-1 : £6.95 B82-21674

796.7′5′0924 — Racing motorcycles. Racing. Sheene, Barry *— Biographies*
Harris, Nick. Barry Sheene. — London : Hamilton, Oct.1982. — [64]p
ISBN 0-241-10851-9 : £3.25 : CIP entry B82-23455

796.7′5′09411 — Scotland. Motorcycles. Racing. Races: Scottish Six Days Trial, *to 1981*

Sandham, Tommy. The Castrol book of the Scottish Six Days Trial / Tommy Sandham. — [Yeovil] : Foulis, 1982. — 186p : ill,facsims,ports ; 28cm. — (A Foulis motorcycling book)
Includes index
ISBN 0-85429-296-9 : £4.95 B82-27568

796.7′5′09422145 — Surrey. Weybridge. Racetracks: Brooklands. Racing motorcycles. Racing, *1920-1929*

Hartley, Peter, *1933-*. Brooklands bikes in the twenties / by Peter Hartley. — Watford : Argus, 1980. — vii,244p,[22]p of plates : ill,ports ; 22cm
Includes index
ISBN 0-85242-620-8 (pbk) : £6.95 B82-07372

796.79 — CARAVANNING

796.7′9 — Caravanning — *Practical information*

Fagg, Christine. The caravan book. — Watford : Exley, June 1982. — [224]p
ISBN 0-905521-45-5 (cased) : £7.95 : CIP entry
ISBN 0-905521-46-3 (pbk) : £4.95 B82-18593

796.7′9′05 — Caravanning — *Serials*

Popular caravan. — Apr. 1982-. — Brentwood (Sovereign House, Brentwood, Essex CM14 4SE) : Sovereign Publications for Popular Caravan Ltd, 1982-. — v. : ill ; 29cm
Monthly
ISSN 0262-4001 = Popular caravan : £0.70 per issue B82-20888

796.8 — COMBAT SPORTS

796.8 — Martial arts

Payne, Peter. Martial arts : the spiritual dimension / Peter Payne. — London : Thames and Hudson, c1981. — 96p : ill(some col.),ports ; 28cm. — (Art and imagination)
Bibliography: p96
ISBN 0-500-81025-7 (pbk) : £3.95 B82-01784

796.8 — Martial arts — *Encyclopaedias*

Shapiro, Amy. [Running Press glossary of martial arts language]. The language of martial arts / Amy Shapiro. — London : W.H. Allen, 1981, c1978. — 112p ; 20cm. — (A Star book)
Originally published: Running Press, 1978
ISBN 0-352-30956-3 (pbk) : £1.50 B82-03035

796.8′092′4 — England. Conjuring. Fawkes, Isaac

Dawes, Edwin A.. Isaac Fawkes : fame and fable / Edwin A. Dawes. — [Hull] ([c/o E.A. Dawes, Department of Biochemistry, The University, Hull HU6 7RX]) : Anlaby, 1979. — 8p : ill,ports ; 25cm
Limited ed. of 200 numbered copies. — Bibliography: p8
Unpriced (pbk) B82-31429

796.812 — WRESTLING

796.8′123′0924 — Soviet Union. Free-style wrestling — *Personal observations*

Preobrazhenskiĭ, Sergeĭ. Wrestling is a man's game / Sergei Preobrazhensky ; [translated from the Russian by Albert Zdornykh]. — Moscow : Progress ; [London] : Distributed by Central, c1981. — 108p,[28]p of plates : ports ; 21cm
Translation of: Bor'ba — Zanīatie muzhskoe. Rev. ed
ISBN 0-7147-1703-7 : £2.50 B82-29276

796.815 — JUJITSUS

796.8′152 — Judo — *Manuals*

Fromm, Alan. Judo : the gentle way / Alan Fromm and Nicolas Soames. — London : Routledge & Kegan Paul, 1982. — x,117p,16p of plates : ill,ports ; 22cm
ISBN 0-7100-9025-0 (pbk) : £5.95 B82-23815

Murphy, Kevin. Judo : sports illustrated. — Authorised British ed. / revised by Kevin Murphy. — London : Black, 1980. — 92p : ill ; 22cm
Previous ed.: published as Sports illustrated judo / by Paul Stewart. Philadelphia : Lippincott, c1976. — Includes index
ISBN 0-7136-2002-1 : £2.95 : CIP rev. B79-35985

Reay, Tony. The judo manual / Tony Reay & Geoffrey Hobbs. — London : Stanley Paul, 1982. — 176p : ill(some col.),ports ; 30cm
Originally published: London : Barrrie and Jenkins, 1979. — Includes index
ISBN 0-09-150421-x (pbk) : £6.95 B82-34843

796.8′153 — Karate — *Manuals*

Kanazawa, Hirokazu. Kanazawa's karate / by Hirokazu Kanazawa, Nick Adamou. — [Isleworth] : Dragon Books, [1981]. — 167p : ill,ports ; 30cm
ISBN 0-86568-026-4 (pbk) : Unpriced B82-14850

Kozuki, Russell. Karate for young people / by Russell Kozuki ; with photographs by the author. — New York : Sterling ; London : Oak Tree Press, c1974 (1981 printing). — 128p : ill ; 20cm
Includes index
ISBN 0-8069-7560-1 (pbk) : £2.50 B82-39880

Morris, P. M. V.. The karate-dō manual / P.M.V. Morris. — London : Stanley Paul, 1982. — 176p : ill(some col.),ports ; 30cm
Originally published: London : Barrie and Jenkins, 1979
ISBN 0-09-150411-2 (pbk) : £6.95 B82-34844

Oyama, Mas. Mas Oyama's essential karate / by Mas Oyama ; [translated by Tomoko Murakami and Jeffrey Cousminer]. — New York : Sterling ; London : Oak Tree Press, 1981, c1978. — 256p : ill ; 26cm
Translated from the Japanese. — Originally published: New York : Sterling ; London : Ward Lock, 1978. — Includes index
ISBN 0-7061-2557-6 (pbk) : £4.95 B82-21066

796.8′153 — Karate — *Manuals* — *For children*

Little, Peter. Karate : start her if you want to be a black belt in karate / Peter Little and David English ; with expert advice from the Martial Arts Commission. — Harmondsworth : Puffin, 1981. — [64]p : ill(some col.) ; 20cm. — (Puffin adventure sports)
ISBN 0-14-031149-1 (pbk) : £0.95 B82-07306

796.8′154 — Aikido — *Manuals*

Loi, Lee Ah. Tomiki aikido / Lee Ah Loi. — London : Crompton
Bk.2. — 1979. — 74p : ill ; 22cm
ISBN 0-901764-46-9 (pbk) : Unpriced B82-16590

796.83 — BOXING

796.8′3 — Boxing

Carpenter, Harry. The hardest game / Harry Carpenter ; photographs by Chris Moyse. — London : British Broadcasting Corporation, 1981. — 123p : ill,ports ; 26cm
Ill on lining papers
ISBN 0-563-17945-7 : £5.50 B82-01804

Cooper, Henry, *1934-*. Henry Cooper's book of boxing. — London : Barker, c1982. — viii,168p,[32]p of plates : ill,facsims,ports ; 23cm
ISBN 0-213-16842-1 : £6.50 B82-39886

McIlvanney, Hugh. McIlvanney on boxing. — London : Stanley Paul, Nov.1982. — 1v.
ISBN 0-09-149940-2 : £7.95 : CIP entry B82-37642

796.8′3′09 — Boxing, *to 1980*

Carpenter, Harry. Boxing : an illustrated history / Harry Carpenter. — Rev. ed. — London : Collins, 1982. — 192p : ill,ports ; 26cm
Previous ed.: 1975. — Includes index
ISBN 0-00-411767-0 (pbk) : £4.95 B82-37316

796.8′3′0904 — Boxing. Matches, *1889-1980*

Sugar, Bert Randolph. The great fights : a pictorial history of boxings greatest bouts / by Bert Randolph Sug ar and the editors of the Ring magazine. — [London] : Windward, c1981. — 255p : ill,ports ; 29cm
ISBN 0-7112-0211-7 : £6.95 B82-07062

796.8′3′0924 — Boxing. Dempsey, Jack — *Biographies*

Dempsey, Jack. Dempsey / Jack Dempsey with Barbara Piatelli Dempsey. — South Yarmouth : John Curley ; [Skipton] : Magna Print [distributor], 1978, c1977. — 2v.(xvii,666p) ; 22cm
Originally published: New York : Harper & Row, 1977 ; London : W.H. Allen, 1977. — Published in large print
ISBN 0-89340-125-0 : Unpriced B82-15099

796.8′3′0924 — Boxing. Holland, John, *19--* — *Biographies*

Holland, John, *1904-1981*. Sixty years in boxing 1911-1974 / John Holland. — Bognor Regis : New Horizon, c1982. — 164p,[8]p of plates : ports ; 21cm
ISBN 0-86116-567-5 : £5.25 B82-11252

796.86 — FENCING

796.8′6 — Sports: Sabre fencing — *Manuals*

Evered, D. F.. Sabre fencing / D.F. Evered. — London : Duckworth, 1982. — 92p : ill ; 22cm
ISBN 0-7156-1647-1 (pbk) : £5.95 B82-38308

796.91 — ICE SKATING

796.91 — Ice skating

Bass, Howard. Skating : elegance on ice / Howard Bass. — Secaucus : Chartwell ; London : Marshall Cavendish, c1980. — 96p : ill(some col.),ports(some col.) ; 30cm
Ill on lining papers. — Includes index
ISBN 0-85685-858-7 : £4.95 B82-21290

796.91′092′4 — Ice skating: Figure skating. Cousins, Robin — *Biographies*

Cousins, Robin. Skating for gold / Robin Cousins with Howard Bass. — London : Sphere, 1981, c1980. — xv,142p,[16]p of plates : ill(some col.),ports(some col.) ; 18cm
Originally published: London : Stanley Paul, 1980
ISBN 0-7221-2636-0 (pbk) : £1.50 B82-07079

796.93 — SKIING

796.93 — Alpine skiing — *Manuals*

Evans, Harold, *1928-*. We learned to ski. — 4th ed. — London : Collins, Sept.1982. — [256]p
Previous ed.: 1978
ISBN 0-00-217096-5 (pbk) : £7.95 : CIP entry B82-25909

Evans, Harold, *1928-*. We learned to ski / Harold Evans, Brian Jackman and Mark Ottaway of the Sunday Times. — Rev. pbk. ed. — London, Collins, 1978 (1981 [printing]). — 255p : ill(some col.),facsims,ports ; 24cm
Previous ed.: 1976. — Includes index
ISBN 0-00-216868-5 (pbk) : £7.95
ISBN 0-00-216746-8 (hbk) : Unpriced B82-08504

796.93 — Free-style skiing — *Manuals*

Wieman, Randy. Freestyle skiing : a complete guide to the fundamentals of hot dogging / Randy Wieman ; photography Robbi Newman. — London : Angus & Robertson, 1979 (1980 [printing]). — 156p,[16]p of plates : ill(some col.) ; 25cm
Originally published: 1979. — Includes index
ISBN 0-207-13856-7 : £7.95
ISBN 0-207-14321-8 (pbk) : Unpriced B82-04101

796.93 — Ski racing. Championships: World Cup *(Ski racing championship), 1967-1981*

Samuel, John. Ski Sunday / John Samuel. — London : British Broadcasting Corporation, 1982. — 160p : ill(some col.),maps,ports(some col.) ; 24cm
Text and ill on inside cover
ISBN 0-563-17992-9 (pbk) : £4.95 B82-13696

796.93 — Skiing - *Manuals*

The **Complete** skiing handbook. — 2nd rev. ed. — London : Martin Dunitz, Aug.1981. — [240]p
Translation of: Das Grosse DSV Skihandbuch
ISBN 0-906348-30-7 : £9.95 : CIP entry
B81-19134

796.93 — Skiing — *Manuals*

Gamma, Karl. The handbook of skiing / Karl Gamma. — London : Pelham, 1981. — 320p : ill(some col.),maps ; 24cm
Includes index
ISBN 0-7207-1367-6 : £12.50 B82-01292

Learning to ski / edited by Duncan Prowse ; contributors and consultants David Vine ... [et al.] ; illustrations by Gerard Pestarque ; cartoons David Lock. — Haywards Heath : Schools Abroad, c1981. — 96p : chiefly col.ill ; 27cm
Includes index
ISBN 0-905703-60-x (pbk) : Unpriced
B82-11476

Nelson, Dennis. Let's go skiing / text by Dennis Nelson and Sally Gordon ; illustrations by Gerard Pestarque. — London : Octopus, 1981. — 77p : col.ill,1map ; 31cm
Ill on lining papers. — Includes index
ISBN 0-7064-1553-1 : £2.95 B82-03925

796.93'05 — Skiing — *Serials*

[Ski magazine *(London)***]**. Ski magazine. — Vol.3, no.1 (Sept. 1978)-. — London (34 Buckingham Palace Rd., SW1W 0RE) : Ocean Publications, 1978-. — v. : ill(some col.),ports ; 30cm
Six issues yearly (Monthly from Sept. to Feb.). — Continues: British ski magazine. — Description based on: Vol.6, no.1 (Sept. 1981/82)
ISSN 0262-7353 = Ski magazine (London) : £7.50 per year B82-12476

796.96 — ICE GAMES

796.9'6 — Curling, *to 1980*

Smith, David B. (David Buchanan). Curling : an illustrated history / David B. Smith. — Edinburgh : Donald, c1981. — vii,232p,[8]p of plates : ill(some col.),facsims,ports ; 29cm
Includes index
ISBN 0-85976-074-x : £9.50 B82-01500

797.1 — BOATING

797.1 — England. Punting

Rivington, R. T.. Punts and punting : some extract from Punting: its history and techniques / R.T. Rivington. — Oxford (36 Park End St, Oxford) : R.T. Rivington,, 1982. — 32p : ill,maps,ports ; 28cm
Text on inside covers
ISBN 0-9508045-0-9 (pbk) : £1.50 B82-31584

797.1 — France. Inland waterways. Cruising

Bristow, Philip. Through the French canals. — 5th ed. — London : Macmillan, July 1982. — [208]p
Previous ed.: Lymington : Nautical Publishing Co., 1979
ISBN 0-333-32927-9 : £6.95 : CIP entry
B82-12275

797.1'0243694 — Boating — *Manuals — For scouting*

Scout boating / edited & designed by T.A. Stringer ; illustrated by Mike Peyton. — 3rd ed. — London : Scout Association, 1981. — 68p : ill(some col.),1chart,maps ; 15x21cm
Previous ed. [i.e. 1st]: 1976
ISBN 0-85165-167-4 (pbk) : £2.95 B82-03438

797.1'22 — Canoeing — *Manuals*

Canoeing handbook / edited by Geoff Good assisted by Bob Gray. — Weybridge : British Canoe Union, 1981. — ix,349p : ill,1form,plans,ports ; 21cm
Ill on inside covers. — Bibliography: p340-344. — Includes index
ISBN 0-900082-03-8 (pbk) : Unpriced
B82-29705

797.1'22 — Canoeing — *Manuals — For children*

Little, Peter. Canoeing : start here if you want to paddle your own canoe / Peter Little and David English ; with expert advice from Geoff Good of the British Canoe Union. — Harmondsworth : Puffin, 1981. — [64]p : ill (some col.) ; 20cm. — (Puffin adventure sports)
ISBN 0-14-031153-x (pbk) : £0.95 B82-07307

797.1'23'06042351 — Devon. Bideford. Rowing. Clubs: Bideford Amateur Rowing Club, *to 1982*

Hold, Chris. 100 years of Bideford Amateur Rowing Club / Chris Hold. — Yelland : C. Hold, 1982. — 104p : ill,facsims,ports ; 22cm
ISBN 0-7223-1612-7 (pbk) : Unpriced
B82-31755

797.1'24 — Free-style wind surfing — *Manuals*

Hofmann, Sigi. 101 freestyle windsurfing tricks. — London : Stanford Maritime, Oct.1982. — [120]p
Translation of: Tricksurfen
ISBN 0-540-07412-8 (pbk) : £4.95 : CIP entry
B82-25184

797.1'24 — Great Britain. National twelve class yachts. Yachting

National twelves : handbook of the National Twelve Owners' Association. — 3rd ed. — Woking (Royal Yachting Association, Victoria Way, Woking, Surrey, GU21 1EQ) : National Twelve Owners' Association, 1981. — 136p : ill,1map,ports ; 21cm
Previous ed.: 1977
Unpriced (pbk) B82-04107

797.1'24 — Great Britain. National twelve class yachts. Yachting, *to 1977*

National Twelve Owners' Association. National twelves : handbook of the National Twelve Owners Association. — 2nd ed. — Woking (c/o Royal Yacht Association, Victoria Way, Woking, Surrey GU21 1EQ) : The Association, 1977. — 119p : ill,1map,ports ; 21cm
Previous ed.: 1972
£3.00 (free to members of the Association) (pbk) B82-17309

797.1'24 — Great Britain. Sailing dinghies. Cruising — *Manuals*

Dye, Frank. Open-boat cruising : coastal and inland waters / Frank and Margaret Dye ; preface by Ian Proctor. — Newton Abbot : David & Charles, c1982. — 152p : ill,maps ; 23cm
Includes index
ISBN 0-7153-8247-0 : £6.95 : CIP rev.
B82-07586

797.1'24 — Great Britain. Wind surfing. Organisations — *Directories*

Daily Mail Peter Stuyvesant Travel windsurfing guide / editor Stephen Turner ; major contributors Will Sutherland, Cliff Webb, Steve Turner ; other contributors Carole Munn ... [et al.] ; photographers Cliff Webb ... [et al.]. — [London?] : Published by Windsurf and Boardsailing magazine in co-operation with the UK Boardsailing Association, c1982. — 336p : ill(some col.),maps ; 20x22cm
ISBN 0-9507836-1-7 (pbk) : Unpriced
B82-37773

797.1'24 — Sailing

Johnson, Peter, *1930 Mar.26-*. The Guinness guide to sailing / Peter Johnson. — Enfield : Guinness Superlatives, c1981. — 240p : ill (some col.),maps,plans ; 30cm
Includes index
ISBN 0-85112-216-7 : £11.95 : CIP rev.
B81-31199

Ulian, Richard. Sailing : an informal primer / Richard Ulian. — New York ; London : Van Nostrand Reinhold, c1982. — 149p : ill,charts ; 24cm
Includes index
ISBN 0-442-28665-1 (cased) : £11.00
ISBN 0-442-28789-5 (pbk) : Unpriced
B82-28150

797.1'24 — Sailing boats. Cruising — *Manuals*

Sleightholme, J. D.. [This is sailboat cruising]. This is cruising / J.D. Sleightholme ; illustrated by Peter A.G. Milne. — [London] : Fontana, 1982. — 168p : col.ill ; 20cm
Originally published: Lymington : Nautical Publishing, 1976. — Includes index
£5.95 (pbk) B82-10710

797.1'24 — Sailing catamarans. Sailing — *Manuals*

Berman, Phil. Catamaran sailing : from start to finish / Phil Berman ; illustrations by Bradford Scott. — New York ; London : Norton, c1982. — 209p : ill ; 26cm
Bibliography: p209
ISBN 0-393-00084-2 (pbk) : £8.50 B82-35675

797.1'24 — Sailing dinghies. Sailing — *Manuals*

Caig, John. Topper sailing / John Caig ; photographs by Tim Hore. — London : Fernhurst, 1982. — 64p : ill ; 25cm
ISBN 0-906754-04-6 (pbk) : £4.95 B82-36969

Fitzgerald, Gerald, *1928-*. The Spur book of dinghy sailing / Gerald Fitzgerald. — Edinburgh : Spurbooks, c1981. — 63p : ill ; 19cm. — (A Spurbooks venture guide)
ISBN 0-7157-2061-9 (pbk) : £1.25 B82-22942

797.1'24 — Sailing - *Manuals*

The **Complete** sailing handbook. — 2nd rev. ed. — London : Dunitz, July 1981. — [344]p
Translation of: Das Grosse Handbuch des Segelns. — Previous ed.: 1979
ISBN 0-906348-29-3 : £9.95 : CIP entry
B81-14977

797.1'24 — Trailed sailing boats. Sailing — *Practical information*

Winters, Jacey. Trail and sail / Jacey Winters. — London : Macmillan, c1981. — 176p : ill ; 22cm
Includes index
ISBN 0-333-32218-5 : £7.95 B82-06873

797.1'24 — Wind surfing — *Manuals*

Steverink, Wilma. Wind surfing / by Wilma Steverink and Wim Thijs. — Wakefield : EP Publishing, 1982, c1981. — 36p : ill ; 14x21cm. — (Know the game)
Translated from the Dutch
ISBN 0-7158-0810-9 (pbk) : £0.85 B82-34902

Stickl, Niko. Windsurfing technique / Niko Stickl, Michael Garff. — London : Stanford Maritime, 1981. — 176p : ill(some col.) ; 25cm
Translation of: Windsurfing Technik
ISBN 0-540-07407-1 : £9.95 : CIP rev.
B81-14374

Taylor, Glenn. [Wherever there's water and wind]. Tackle windsurfing / Glenn Taylor ; adapted by Graham Fuller. — London : Stanley Paul, 1982. — 120p : ill,ports ; 23cm. — (The Tackle series)
Originally published: Menlo Park, Calif. : Bay Windsurfing, 1979
ISBN 0-09-145041-1 (pbk) : £4.95 : CIP rev.
B81-13718

Wagensveld, Peter van. This is freestyle windsurfing. — London : Macmillan, June 1982. — [128]p
Translation of: Daf ist freestyle Surfen
ISBN 0-333-32531-1 : £6.95 : CIP entry
B82-09999

Winkler, Reinhart[This is surfboard sailing]. This is windsurfing / Reinhart Winkler. — [London] : Fontana, 1982. — viii,208p : col.ill ; 20cm
Originally published: Lymington : Nautical Publishing, 1979
ISBN 0-00-636504-3 (pbk) : £5.95 B82-22564

797.1'24 — Yachts. Cruising — *Manuals*

Sleightholme, J. D.. Better boat handling. — London : Stanford Maritime, Oct.1982. — [192]p
ISBN 0-540-07148-x : £8.50 : CIP entry
B82-29128

797.1′24 — Yachts. Cruising — *Manuals — For parents*

Andrews, Judy. Family boating. — London : Hollis & Carter, Apr.1982. — [192]p
ISBN 0-370-30407-1 (cased) : £5.95 : CIP entry
ISBN 0-370-30473-x (pbk) : £4.50 B82-03839

797.1′24′0207 — Sailing — *Humour*

Beard, Henry. Sailing : a sailor's dictionary / by Henry Beard & Roy McKie. — London : Macmillan, 1982, c1981. — 93p : ill ; 21cm
Originally published: New York : Workman, 1981
ISBN 0-333-32845-0 (pbk) : £2.95 B82-19397

797.1′24′0321 — Sailing — *Encyclopaedias*

Schult, Joachim. The sailing dictionary / Joachim Schult ; translated and extensively revised by Barbara Webb. — London : Adlard Coles : Granada, 1981. — vii,331p : ill(some col.),maps ; 24cm
Translation of: Segler-lexicon. — Ill on lining papers
ISBN 0-229-11619-1 : £9.95 B82-00677

797.1′24′06042 — England. Yachting. Organisations: Royal Engineer Yacht Club, *1865-1982*

Duke, *Sir* Gerald. The history of the Royal Engineer Yacht Club. — Twineham (Bob Lane Cottage, Bob La., West Sussex) : Geoffrey Tulett, Jan.1983. — [120]p
ISBN 0-946403-00-7 : £13.00 : CIP entry
B82-40298

797.1′24′0924 — Scotland. Strathclyde Region. Glasgow. Museums: Glasgow Art Gallery and Museum. Exhibits: Items associated with Lipton, *Sir* **Thomas** — *Catalogues*

Sir **Thomas** J. Lipton : Sir Thomas Lipton 1850-1931 : a handlist of exhibition material. — [Glasgow] : [Glasgow Museums and Art Galleries], [1981?]. — 1sheet ; 30x42cm folded to 30x11cm
Unpriced B82-12208

797.1′4 — Sailing boats. Racing — *Manuals*

Twiname, Eric. Sail, race and win. — London : Macmillan, June 1982. — [192]p
ISBN 0-333-33174-5 : £8.95 : CIP entry
B82-10002

797.1′4 — Sailing dinghies. Racing — *Manuals*

Baird, Ed. Laser racing / Ed Baird ; photographs by Tim Hore and Wilson Barnes. — London : Fernhurst, 1982. — 64p : ill ; 25cm
ISBN 0-906754-05-4 (pbk) : £4.95 B82-36970

Copley, Peter. Dingy racing / Peter Copley ; illustrated by Heather Sherratt. — Sevenoaks : Hodder and Stoughton, 1981. — 165p : ill ; 19cm. — (Teach yourself books)
Includes index
ISBN 0-340-25978-7 (pbk) : £1.75 B82-29713

797.1′4 — Wildwater canoeing. Racing — *Manuals*

Evans, Eric, *1950-*. Whitewater racing : a comprehensive guide to whitewater slalom and wildwater racing in canoes and kayaks / by Eric Evans and John Burton. — New York ; London : Van Nostrand Reinhold, c1980. — 166p : ill,ports ; 22cm
ISBN 0-442-22282-3 (pbk) : £1.60 B82-00750

797.1′4 — Wind surfboards. Racing — *Manuals*

Gutjahr, Rainer. Sailboard racing / Rainer Gutjahr. — London : Nautical, 1981. — 119p : ill ; 21cm
Translation of: Das ist Regatta-Surfen. — Ill on lining papers
ISBN 0-333-32213-4 : £7.95 : CIP rev.
B81-27359

797.1′4 — Yachts. Racing, *1893-1937*

Leather, John. The big class racing yachts. — London : Stanford Maritime, Nov.1982. — [192]p
ISBN 0-540-07417-9 : £10.95 : CIP entry
B82-32871

797.1′4 — Yachts. Racing. Cutters: Jolie Brise *(Ship), to 1981*

Bryer, Robin. Jolie Brise : a tall ship's tale / Robin Bryer. — London : Secker & Warburg, 1982. — xiii,254p,[16]p of plates : ill,maps,ports ; 25cm
ISBN 0-436-07181-9 : £10.00 : CIP rev.
B82-09721

797.1′4 — Yachts. Racing. Rules

Sambrooke-Sturgess, Gerald. The rules in action. — London : Granada, Aug.1982. — [140]p
ISBN 0-229-11664-7 : £8.95 : CIP entry
B82-15687

797.1′4′09 — Racing sailing boats. Racing. Races, *to 1978*

Burton, Robin. Sailing the great races / Robin Burton ; foreword by Chay Blyth. — London : Lyric, 1979. — 160p : col.ill,col.maps,col.ports ; 31cm
Ill on lining papers. — Includes index
ISBN 0-7111-0002-0 : £5.95 B82-04102

797.1′4′0924 — North Atlantic Ocean. Sailing ships. Racing. Races: Tall Ships Race, *1980 — Personal observations*

Hollins, Holly. The tall ships are sailing : the Cutty Sark Tall Ships Races / Holly Hollins ; foreword by Greville Howard. — Newton Abbot : David & Charles, c1982. — 192p : ill,1map,ports ; 25cm
Bibliography: p183-187. — Includes index
ISBN 0-7153-8028-1 : £9.50 : CIP rev.
B81-33852

797.1′4′0924 — North Atlantic Ocean. Yachts. Racing. Races: Observer Singlehanded Transatlantic Race, *1980.* **Trimarans: Moxie** *(Ship) — Personal observations*

Weld, Philip S.. Moxie : the American challenge. — London : Bodley Head, Sept.1982. — [256]p
ISBN 0-370-30492-6 : £8.95 : CIP entry
B82-19207

797.1′4′0924 — Yachts. Racing. Competitions: America's Cup. Challenges by Lipton, *Sir* **Thomas,** *1899-1930*

Olding, Simon. Sir Thomas J. Lipton : the race for the America's Cup. — [Glasgow] : [Glasgow Museums and Art Galleries], c1981. — [4]p : ill,2ports ; 30cm
Author: Simon Olding
Unpriced (unbound) B82-12206

797.1′4′0924 — Yachts. Racing. Races: Whitbread Round-the-World Race *(1977-1978).* **Yachts: ADC Accutrac** *(Ship) — Personal observations*

Francis, Clare. Come wind or weather / Clare Francis. — London : Sphere, 1979, c1978 (1981 [printing]). — 253p : ill,charts,ports ; 18cm
Originally published: London : Pelham, 1978
ISBN 0-7221-3639-0 (pbk) : £1.50 B82-00077

797.1′4′0924 — Yachts. Racing. Races: Whitbread Round-the-World Race *(1981-1982).* **Yachts: Ceramco New Zealand** *(Ship) — Personal observations*

Blake, Peter. Blake's odyssey. — London : Hodder & Stoughton, Jan.1983. — [224]p
ISBN 0-340-27994-x : £12.95 : CIP entry
B82-33332

797.2 — SWIMMING AND DIVING

797.2 — Swimming & diving — *Manuals*

Midtlyng, Joanna. Swimming / Joanna Midtlyng. — 2nd ed. — Philadelphia ; London : Saunders College, c1982. — viii,119p : ill ; 24cm. — (Saunders physical activities series)
Previous ed.: 1974. — Bibliography: p118-119
ISBN 0-03-058371-3 (pbk) : £5.50 B82-25414

797.2′007 — Swimming & diving. Teaching — *Manuals*

Palmer, Mervyn L.. The science of teaching swimming / Mervyn L. Palmer. — London : Pelham, 1979. — 525p : ill ; 23cm
Includes index
ISBN 0-7207-1117-7 : £10.50 B82-24660

797.2′1 — Swimming — *Manuals*

Eady, Roger. Successful swimming / Roger Eady. — London : Published in collaboration with World of Sport by Letts, 1982. — 95p : ill (some col.),ports(some col.) ; 22cm. — (Letts guide)
Includes index
ISBN 0-85097-407-0 (pbk) : £2.95 B82-31658

Gorton, Eddie. Swimming / Eddie Gorton. — London : Batsford Academic and Educational, 1982. — 64p : ill ; 26cm. — (Competitive sports series)
Includes index
ISBN 0-7134-4079-1 : £4.50 : CIP rev.
B81-37575

Wilkie, David. Splash!. — London : Paul, Nov.1982. — [128]p
ISBN 0-09-150280-2 (cased) : £7.95 : CIP entry
ISBN 0-09-140281-0 (pbk) : £4.95 B82-26902

797.2′1 — Swimming — *Manuals — For children*

Haller, David. You can swim / David Haller ; illustrated by Mike Miller. — [London] : Carousel, [1982]. — 134p : ill ; 20cm
ISBN 0-552-54183-4 (pbk) : £0.95 B82-18696

797.2′1′07 — Swimming. Teaching — *Manuals*

The **teaching** of swimming. — 11th ed. — Loughborough : Amateur Swimming Association in liaison with Swimming Times, [198-?]. — 104p : ill ; 30cm
Previous ed.: 1974
Unpriced (pbk) B82-32942

797.2′1′09411 — Scotland. Swimming pools — *Conference proceedings*

National seminars on sports centres and swimming pools : summary report. — Edinburgh : Scottish Sports Council, 1981. — 242p : ill,plans ; 30cm
ISBN 0-906599-27-x (spiral) : £5.00
Primary classification 790′.06′8411 B82-02781

797.2′3 — Recreations: Underwater diving — *Manuals*

The **British** Sub-Aqua Club diving manual : a comprehensive guide to the techniques of under-water swimming. — 10th ed., 4th revise. — London : The Club, 1982. — x,572p : ill,1map ; 21cm
Previous ed.: i.e. 10th ed., 3rd revise : 1980. — Includes bibliographies and index
ISBN 0-9506786-1-9 (pbk) : Unpriced
B82-40473

797.2′3 — Skin diving & snorkelling — *Manuals — For children*

Little, Peter. Skin-diving : start here if you want to go skin-diving / Peter Little and David English ; with expert advice from the British Sub-Aqua Club. — Harmondsworth : Puffin, 1981. — [64]p : ill(some col.) ; 20cm. — (Puffin adventure sports)
ISBN 0-14-031151-3 (pbk) : £0.95 B82-07308

797.2′3 — Underwater swimming & diving — *Manuals*

Hazzard, Jerry. Discover underwater diving / Jerry Hazzard. — London : Ward Lock, 1979. — 120p : ill ; 24cm
ISBN 0-7063-4227-5 (pbk) : Unpriced
ISBN 0-7063-5809-0 B82-25333

797.2′5 — Water polo — *Manuals*

Bland, Hamilton. Waterpolo / by Hamilton Bland in conjunction with the A.S.A. Education Committee. — 2nd ed. / revised by David Reeves. — Wakefield : EP Publishing, 1978. — 36p : ill(some col.),form ; 14x21cm. — (Know the game)
Previous ed.: 1972
ISBN 0-7158-0622-x (pbk) : £0.85 B82-24863

797.5 — AIR SPORTS

797.5′2 — Seaplanes. Competitions: Coupe d'aviation maritime Jacques Schneider *(Contest), to 1931*

Barker, Ralph. The Schneider Trophy races / Ralph Barker. — Shrewsbury : Airlife, 1981. — 272p : ill,maps,ports ; 23cm
Originally published: London : Chatto and Windus, 1971. — Bibliography: p260-264. — Includes index
ISBN 0-906393-15-9 : £8.95 B82-00757

797.5′5 — Recreations: Gliding — *Manuals*

Delafield, John. Gliding competitively / John Delafield. — London : Black, 1982. — x,134p : ill,maps ; 22cm
Includes index
ISBN 0-7136-2224-5 : £8.95 : CIP rev. B82-07578

797.5′5 — Recreations: Hang gliding — *Manuals*

Mackay, Bob, *19---*. An introduction to hang gliding / by Bob Mackay. — Cheltenham : Thornhill Press, [1981]. — 100p : ill,ports ; 18cm
ISBN 0-904110-92-3 (pbk) : £2.00 B82-00733

Welch, Ann. The Spur book of hang-gliding / Ann Welch. — Edinburgh : Spurbooks, c1982. — 64p : ill ; 19cm. — (A Spurbooks venture guide)
ISBN 0-7157-2109-7 (pbk) : £1.25 B82-22943

798 — EQUESTRIAN SPORTS AND ANIMAL RACING

798 — Equestrian sports — *Manuals*

The **Illustrated** encyclopedia of equestrian sports / contributing editors Sally Gordon, Peter Roberts, Elwyn Hartley Edwards. — London : Pelham, 1982. — 208p : ill(some col.),ports 31cm
Includes index
ISBN 0-7207-1373-0 : £9.95 : CIP rev. B81-30393

798.2 — HORSEMANSHIP

798.2 — Horsemanship

Brander, Michael. The complete guide to horsemanship. — 2nd. — London : Black, Sept.1982. — [448]p
Previous ed.: 1971
ISBN 0-7136-2227-x : £7.95 : CIP entry B82-20356

798.2 — Horsemanship — *Amateurs' manuals*

Gordon, Sally. The horse and pony book / Sally Gordon. — London : Published by Octopus for W.H. Smith & Son, 1980. — 157p : ill(some col.) ; 29cm
Ill on lining papers. — Includes index
ISBN 0-7064-1149-8 : £3.45 B82-40575

798.2 — Horsemanship — *Manuals*

Equitation : training of rider and horse to advanced levels / British Horse Society. — [London] : Country Life in association with the British Horse Society, 1982. — 144p : ill ; 22cm
Includes index
ISBN 0-600-36827-0 : £3.95 B82-24065

Twelveponies, Mary. Everyday training : backyard dressage / Mary Twelveponies. — San Diego : Barnes ; London : Tantivy, c1980. — 173p : ill,1form,ports ; 25cm
Includes index
ISBN 0-498-02526-8 : £5.95 B82-38427

798.2 — Livestock: Ponies. Horsemanship — *Manuals*

Woodhouse, Barbara. Barbara Woodhouse's book of ponies. — [Rev. ed.]. — [Harmondsworth] : Kestrel, 1981, c1954. — 93p,[12]p of plates : ill ; 21cm
Previous ed. i.e. New ed.: published as The book of ponies. Rickmansworth : B. Woodhouse, 1970
ISBN 0-7226-5766-8 : £3.95 B82-01252

798.2′3 — Livestock: Horses. Riding. Dressage — *Manuals*

Marshall, Leonie. Novice to advanced dressage. — London : J.A. Allen, Nov.1981. — [140]p
ISBN 0-85131-373-6 (pbk) : £3.00 : CIP entry B81-34964

798.2′3 — Livestock: Horses. Riding — *Manuals*

Best, Heidi. Book of riding and horse care / Heidi Best. — Poole : Blandford, [1981]. — 95p : ill(some col.),1port ; 15cm. — ('How to')
Includes index
ISBN 0-7137-1057-8 (pbk) : £1.95 B82-20224

Saar, Yvonne. Preparing to ride : a new approach to riding technique / Yvonne Saar. — London : Pelham, 1979. — 173p : ill ; 21cm. — (Pelham horsemaster series)
Includes index
ISBN 0-7207-1166-5 : £6.50 B82-13999

798.2′3 — Livestock: Horses. Riding — *Manuals — For children*

Chitly, Susan. The young rider / Susan Chitly ; illustrated with photographs and with drawings by Christine Bousfield. — London : Angus & Robertson, c1979. — 95p : ill ; 26cm
ISBN 0-207-95782-7 : £4.25 B82-00108

798.2′3 — Livestock: Ponies. Riding — *Manuals — For children*

Allen, Jane, *1942-*. Hello to riding / Jane Allen and Mary Danby ; illustrated by Alison Prince. — London : Armada, 1982, c1980. — 127p : ill ; 20cm
Originally published: London : Heinemann, 1980. — Includes index
£0.90 (pbk) B82-15114

Murphy, Genevieve. Young rider's pocket book / Genevieve Murphy. — Bristol : Purnell, 1982. — 128p : ill ; 19cm
Includes index
ISBN 0-361-05333-9 (pbk) : £1.99 B82-40489

798.2′3′088055 — Livestock: Horses. Riding by young women — *Illustrations*

Vavra, Robert. All those girls in love with horses / Robert Vavra. — London : Collins, 1981. — 240p : col.ill,col.ports ; 29cm
ISBN 0-00-216382-9 : £18.00 B82-04251

798.2′3′0924 — Livestock: Horses. Riding — *Personal observations*

Akrill, Caroline. Not quite a horsewoman. — London : Arlington Books, Oct.1982. — [224]p
ISBN 0-85140-593-2 : £7.95 : CIP entry B82-24745

798.2′4 — Horse shows — *Manuals*

Streeter, Carol. My kingdom for a horse : an owner's manual / Carol Streeter. — San Diego : Barnes ; London : Tantivy, c1980. — 125p : ill ; 25cm
Bibliography: p124-125. — Includes index
ISBN 0-498-02226-9 : £3.95 B82-37018

798.2′4 — Riding competitions: Dressage — *Manuals*

Kidd, Jane. A festival of dressage / Jane Kidd. — London : Stanley Paul, 1981. — 143p : ill (some col.),1form,ports(some col.) ; 30cm
ISBN 0-09-146190-1 : £6.50 : CIP rev. B81-26801

798.2′4′05 — Riding competitions — *Serials*

Pelham horse year. — 2. — London : Pelham, Mar.1982. — [272]p
ISBN 0-7207-1392-7 : £6.95 : CIP entry B82-01557

798.2′4′0924 — Eventing. Prior-Palmer, Lucinda — *Biographies — For children*

Hartley Edwards, Elwyn. Lucinda Prior-Palmer / E. Hartley Edwards ; illustrated by Frederick St. Ward. — London : Hamilton, 1982. — 62p : ill,ports ; 22cm. — (Profiles (Hamilton))
ISBN 0-241-10710-5 : £3.25 B82-20915

798.2′5 — Show jumping — *Manuals*

Churchill, Peter, *1933-*. The beginner's guide to show jumping / Peter Churchill. — Poole : Blandford, 1982. — 120p : ill,ports ; 22cm
Includes index
ISBN 0-7137-1096-9 : £4.95 : CIP rev. B82-12157

798.4 — HORSE RACING

798.4 — Racehorses. Racing — *Stories, anecdotes*

Wogan, Terry. To horse! To horse!. — London : Collins, Sept.1982. — [128]p
ISBN 0-00-218085-5 : £6.95 : CIP entry B82-21381

798.4′003′41 — Racehorses. Racing — *French & English dictionaries*

Kearney, Mary-Louise. A glossary of French bloodstock terminology / Mary-Louise Kearney. — London : J.A. Allen, 1981. — 48p : ill ; 18cm
ISBN 0-85131-354-x (pbk) : £2.00 : CIP rev.
Primary classification 636.1′2 B81-13553

798.4′00941 — Great Britain. Racehorses. Racing

Rodney, Bob. Daily Mirror companion to racing / Bob Rodney. — London : Mirror Books, 1981. — 168p ; 18cm
ISBN 0-85939-239-2 (pbk) : £1.25 B82-37529

798.4′01 — Racehorses. Racing. Form. Analysis — *Manuals*

Midgley, M. L.. Form book analysis. — London : Longman, Jan.1983. — [96]p
ISBN 0-582-50317-5 : £8.50 : CIP entry B82-32469

798.4′3′0207 — Flat racing — *Humour*

Carson, Willie. Bedside racing. — London : Dent, Sept.1982. — [96]p
ISBN 0-460-04559-8 : £5.95 : CIP entry B82-19700

798.4′3′09 — Flat racing. Classic races. Racehorses, *to 1980*

Willett, Peter. The classic racehorse / Peter Willett. — London : Stanley Paul, 1981. — 271p,[8]p of plates : ill ; 24cm
Includes index
ISBN 0-09-146110-3 : £10.95 : CIP rev. B81-20582

798′.4′30924 — Flat racing. Jockeys: Piggott, Lester - *Biographies*

Lawton, James. Lester Piggott. — Sevenoaks : Hodder & Stoughton, June 1981. — [176]p
Originally published: London : Barker, 1980
ISBN 0-340-26669-4 (pbk) : £1.25 : CIP entry B81-09990

798.4′3′0941 — Great Britain. Flat racing, *1982*

They're off! : A complete guide to the 1982 flat racing season. — London : Mirror Books, 1982. — 26p : ill(some col.),ports ; 36cm. — (A Daily Mirror racing special)
ISBN 0-85939-303-8 (unbound) : £0.50 B82-21288

798.4′3′0942 — England. Flat racing, *to 1981*

Craig, Dennis, *1906-*. Horse-racing : the breeding of thoroughbreds and a short history of the English turf / by Dennis Craig. — 4th ed. / revised by Miles Napier. — London : J.A. Allen, 1982, c1963. — ix,286p,[12]p of plates : ill ; 23cm
Previous ed.: 1963. — Bibliography: p214. — Includes index
ISBN 0-85131-357-4 : £9.95 : CIP rev. B81-31509

798.4′3′0942585 — Hertfordshire. Harpenden. Racehorses. Flat racing. Races: Harpenden Races, *to 1915*

Brandreth, Eric. The Harpenden races / by Eric Brandreth. — Harpenden : Harpenden & District Local History Society, c1981. — 19p : ill,1map,1facsim,ports ; 21cm. — (Harpenden and district local history series ; no.4)
Cover title. — Text on inside cover
ISBN 0-9505941-3-x (pbk) : Unpriced B82-19349

798.4′3′0944361 — France. Longchamp. Racecourses: Longchamp. Flat racing. Races: Prix de l'Arc de Triomphe, *1949-1964*

Fitzgerald, Arthur. Prix de l'Arc de Triomphe, 1949-1964. — London : J.A. Allen, Sept.1982
Vol.2. — [287]p
ISBN 0-85131-371-x : £14.00 : CIP entry
B82-20650

798.4′5 — Great Britain. National Hunt racehorses: Spanish Steps

Tanner, Michael. My friend Spanish Steps / by Michael Tanner. — [Sleaford] ([Fenland House, Church St., Great Hale, Sleaford, Lincs.]) : [M. Tanner], [1982?]. — 104p : ill,ports ; 21cm
£3.25 (pbk) B82-39888

798.4′5 — Steeplechasing — *Manuals*

Hislop, John. Steeplechasing. — 2nd ed. — London : J.A. Allen, July 1982. — [280]p
Previous ed.: 1970
ISBN 0-85131-375-2 : £12.50 : CIP entry
B82-13522

798.4′5′0924 — Great Britain. National Hunt racing. Champion, Bob — *Biographies*

Champion, Bob. Champion's story : a great human triumph / Bob Champion and Jonathan Powell. — [London] : Fontana, 1982, c1981. — 211p,[8]p of plates : ill,ports ; 18cm
Originally published: London : Gollancz, 1981. — Ill. on inside covers. — Includes index
ISBN 0-00-636485-3 (pbk) : £1.50 B82-20333

Champion, Bob. A champion's story. — Large print ed. — Anstey : Ulverscroft, Feb.1983. — 1v.. — (Ulverscroft large print series)
Originally published: London : Gollancz, 1981
ISBN 0-7089-0913-2 : CIP entry B82-38875

798.4′5′0924 — Great Britain. National Hunt racing. Jockeys: Biddlecombe, Terry — *Biographies*

Biddlecombe, Terry. Winner's disclosure : an autobiography / Terry Biddlecombe with Pat Lucas. — London : Stanley Paul, 1982. — 229p,[16]p of plates : ill,ports ; 24cm
Includes index
ISBN 0-09-147550-3 : £7.95 : CIP rev.
B82-01143

798.4′5′0924 — National Hunt racing. Jockeys: Francis, Dick — *Biographies*

Francis, Dick. The sport of queens : the autobiography of Dick Francis. — Rev. — London : Pan, 1982, c1974. — 224p,[8]p of plates : ill,ports ; 18cm
Previous ed.: i.e. Rev. ed. 1974. — Includes index
ISBN 0-330-26685-3 (pbk) : £1.50 B82-15117

798.4′5′0924 — National hunt racing. Jockeys: Francis, Dick — *Biographies*

Francis, Dick. The sport of queens. — Large print ed. — Anstey : Ulverscroft, Dec.1982. — 1v.. — (Ulverscroft large print series)
Originally published: London : Joseph, 1957
ISBN 0-7089-0896-9 : £5.00 : CIP entry
B82-30790

798.4′5′0924 — National Hunt racing. Jockeys: Francis, Dick — *Biographies*

Francis, Dick. The sport of Queens : the autobiography of Dick Francis. — 3rd rev. ed. — London : Joseph, 1982. — 254p,[16]p of plates : ill,ports ; 23cm
Previous ed.: 1974. — Includes index
ISBN 0-7181-2113-9 : £8.95 B82-19972

798.4′5′0941 — Great Britain. Racehorses. Racing. National Hunt races. Winners: Horses — *Lists — Serials*

Turf racehorse annual. National hunt. — 1981-82. — Rugeley ([Market Sq.], Rugeley, Staffs.) : Turf Publications, 1981-. — v. ; 16cm
ISSN 0262-4494 = Turf racehorse annual. National hunt : Unpriced B82-04918

798.6 — DRIVING AND COACHING

798′.6 — Horse-drawn carriages. Show driving

Philip, *Prince, consort of Elizabeth II, Queen of Great Britain*. Competition carriage driving / the Duke of Edinburgh. — Macclesfield : Horse Drawn Carriages, c1982. — 112p : ill (some col.),ports (some col.) ; 26cm
Bibliography: p112. — Includes index
ISBN 0-9500804-8-9 : £15.00 : CIP rev.
B82-09214

798′.6 — Livestock: Horses. Driving — *Manuals*

British Driving Society. The British Driving Society book of driving / edited by B.M.I. Watney. — New Milton (10, Marley Ave., New Milton, Hants.) : British Driving Society, 1981. — 63p : ill ; 22cm
Bibliography: p63
Unpriced (pbk) B82-09045

Pape, Max. The art of driving. — London : J.A. Allen, Sept.1981. — [192]p
Translation of: Die Kunst des Fahrens
ISBN 0-85131-339-6 : £15.00 : CIP entry
B81-23787

798.8 — RACING ANIMALS OTHER THAN HORSES

798′.8 — Great Britain. Greyhounds. Racing, *to 1980 — Encyclopaedias*

Genders, Roy. The encyclopaedia of greyhound racing : a complete history of the sport / Roy Genders. — London : Pelham, 1981. — 400p : ill,ports ; 25cm
Bibliography: p387-388. — Includes index
ISBN 0-7207-1106-1 : £9.95 B82-02913

799.1 — RECREATIONS. FISHING

799.1′025′41 — Great Britain. Angling — *Directories*

Where to fish. — 1982-1983. — London : Harmsworth, Sept.1981. — [476]p
ISBN 0-7136-2180-x : £7.95 : CIP entry
B81-22532

799.1′092′4 — Great Britain. Angling — *Personal observations*

Heaps, Ian. Ian Heaps on fishing / Ian Heaps & Colin Mitchell. — London : Buchan & Enright, 1982. — 112p : ill,ports ; 23cm
ISBN 0-907675-02-6 : £5.95 B82-22054

799.1′1 — Freshwater angling — *Manuals*

Prichard, Michael. Michael Prichard's pocket guide to freshwater fishing. — London : Collins, 1982. — 160p : col.ill,col.maps ; 17cm
Includes index
ISBN 0-00-411645-3 (pbk) : £2.95 B82-20212

799.1′1′0924 — Freshwater angling — *Personal observations*

Gunn, Iain. With a rod in four continents / Iain Gunn. — Golspie : Method, 1981. — 100p,[4]p of plates : ill,ports ; 23cm
Unpriced B82-24504

Taylor, Fred J.. Reflections on the water : the best of Fred J. Taylor / compiled by Fred Rashbrook ; illustrated by Ted Andrews. — London : Buchan & Enright, 1982. — 195p : ill ; 23cm
ISBN 0-907675-05-0 : £7.95 B82-39932

799.1′1′094295 — England. Wye River. Freshwater angling

Baverstock, L.. The Angling times book of the Wye / Leslie Baverstock. — Newton Abbot : David & Charles in association with Angling Times, c1981. — 192p : ill,maps ; 23cm
ISBN 0-7153-8254-3 : £8.50 : CIP rev.
B81-30582

799.1′2 — Angling

Holden, John. Long distance casting. — Marlborough (Crowood House, Ramsbury, Marlborough, Wiltshire SN8 2HE) : Crowood Press, Nov.1982. — [96]p
ISBN 0-946284-00-8 : £6.95 : CIP entry
B82-31327

799.1′2 — Angling — *Early works*

Walton, Izaak. The compleat angler / Izaak Walton and Charles Cotton ; edited by John Buxton ; with an introduction by John Buchan. — Oxford : Oxford University Press, 1935 (1982 [printing]). — xxxiv,379p : ill,facsims ; 19cm. — (The World's classics)
ISBN 0-19-281511-3 (pbk) : £1.95 : CIP rev.
B81-35769

799.1′2 — Angling — *Manuals*

Wrangles, Alan. The Daily express guide to fishing / Alan Wrangles ; illustrated by Brian Robertshaw. — London : Star, 1982. — 211p : ill,1map ; 18cm
ISBN 0-352-30814-1 (pbk) : £1.95 B82-30905

799.1′2 — Angling — *Manuals — For children*

Morland, Brian. Fishing / Brian Morland. — London : Hamlyn, 1982. — 128p : ill(some col.) ; 18cm. — (Hamlyn junior pocket books)
Includes index
ISBN 0-600-36491-7 : £1.99 B82-23621

799.1′2 — Coarse fish. Angling

Prichard, Michael. The Guinness guide to coarse fishing / Michael Prichard and Michael Shepley. — London : Guinness Superlatives, c1982. — 240p : ill(some col.) ; 30cm
Includes index
ISBN 0-85112-244-2 : £10.95 : CIP rev.
B82-01448

799.1′2 — Coarse fish. Angling. Matches — *Manuals*

The **Match** fisherman / compiled and edited by David Hall. — London : Pelham, 1982. — 175p,[8]p of plates : ill,ports ; 23cm
Includes index
ISBN 0-7207-1340-4 : £7.95 : CIP rev.
B82-00380

799.1′2 — England. Freshwater angling: Match fishing, *1968-1981*

Smith, Clive. Championships match fishing : ten of the best / Clive Smith. — Newton Abbot : David & Charles, c1982. — 158p : ill,ports ; 23cm
ISBN 0-7153-8252-7 : £6.95 : CIP rev.
B82-08102

799.1′2 — Fly fishing — *Manuals*

Pawson, Tony. Competitive fly-fishing. — London : Pelham, Sept.1982. — [256]p
ISBN 0-7207-1414-1 : £7.95 : CIP entry
B82-20482

799.1′2 — Game fish. Angling — *Manuals*

Currie, William B.. The Guinness guide to game fishing / William B. Currie. — Enfield : Guinness Superlatives, c1980. — 238p : ill (some col.),1map ; 30cm
Includes index
ISBN 0-85112-208-6 : £9.95 : CIP rev.
B80-07472

799.1′2 — Great Britain. Still waters. Coarse fish. Angling — *Manuals*

Marsden, Graham. Coarse fishing on stillwaters. — London : Ward Lock, May 1982. — [88]p
ISBN 0-7063-6172-5 (pbk) : £2.95 : CIP entry
B82-06945

799.1′2 — Pole fishing — *Manuals*

Carr, Dickie. Success with the pole / Dickie Carr. — Enfield : Beekay, 1982. — 96p : ill,ports ; 20cm
ISBN 0-9507598-2-1 (pbk) : £4.50 B82-31029

799.1′2 — Sea angling — *Manuals*

Mitchell, John, *1928-*. Better fishing : saltwater / by John Mitchell. — rev. ed. — London : Kaye & Ward, 1981. — 96p : ill ; 23cm. — (The Key to improved sport)
Previous ed. 1971. — Includes index
ISBN 0-7182-1474-9 : £3.95 B82-16550

799.1′2′09 — Angling, *to 1980*

The **Sportsmans** companion / compiled by Eric Begbie ; artwork by Pamela Hardwick ... [et al.]. — Hindhead : Saiga, c1981. — x,256p : ill,ports ; 24cm
ISBN 0-86230-038-x : £8.50
Also classified at 799.2′13′09 B82-10837

799.1′2′0924 — Angling — *Personal observations*

Taylor, Fred J.. My fishing years / Fred J. Taylor. — Newton Abbot : David & Charles, c1981. — 208p : ill,ports ; 23cm
ISBN 0-7153-8105-9 : £7.95 : CIP rev. B81-30334

799.1′2′0941 — Great Britain. Angling

Collins encyclopedia of fishing in Britain and Ireland / edited by Michael Prichard. — Rev. ed. — Glasgow : Collins, 1982, c1977. — 256p : ill (some col.),col.maps,ports(some col.) ; 31cm
Previous ed.: published as Encylopedia of fishing in the British Isles. 1977. — Ill on lining papers. — Includes index
ISBN 0-00-411694-1 : £8.95 B82-39413

799.1′2′094137 — Scotland. Borders Region. Angling — *Practical information*

Fishing. — Newtown St. Boswells (Newtown St. Boswells, Roxburghshire) : Borders Regional Council, 1982. — 1folded sheet([6]p) : map ; 21cm. — (The Scottish Borders)
Unpriced B82-32913

799.1′2′0942 — England. Lakes. Angling — *Practical information*

Du Broff, Sidney. Fishing the English lakes. — London : Longman, Feb.1983. — [176]p
ISBN 0-582-50307-8 (pbk) : £4.95 : CIP entry B82-38858

799.1′6 — Coastal waters. Shore angling — *Manuals*

Darling, John. Shore fishing. — London : Ward Lock, Mar.1982. — [128]p
ISBN 0-7063-6088-5 : £6.95 : CIP entry B82-00220

Forsberg, Ray. Sea angling from the shore / Ray Forsberg ; line illustrations by Baz East. — Newton Abbot : David & Charles, c1982. — 191p : ill ; 23cm
Includes index
ISBN 0-7153-8147-4 : £7.95 : CIP rev. B82-13064

799.1′6 — Sea angling

The **Sea** fisherman′s bedside book / edited by Bill Nathan ; with drawings by Roz Nathan. — London : Duckworth, 1982. — ix,155p : ill ; 25cm
ISBN 0-7156-1537-8 : £7.95 : CIP rev. B82-01427

799.1′6′0941 — Great Britain. Coastal waters. Sea angling — *Manuals*

The **Angler′s** mail guide to basic sea fishing / consultant editors John Ingham & Roy Westwood. — London : Hamlyn, c1981. — 124p : ill(some col.),2col.ports 28cm
Includes index
ISBN 0-600-35385-0 : £3.99 B82-04325

Prichard, Michael. Michael Prichard′s pocket guide to saltwater fishing. — London : Collins, 1982. — 160p : ill(some col.),ports(some col.) ; 17cm
Includes index
ISBN 0-00-411646-1 (pbk) : £2.95 B82-22887

799.1′6′0941 — Great Britain. Coastal waters. Sea angling — *Practical information*

Darling, John. The sea angler′s guide to Britain and Ireland / John Darling. — Guildford : Lutterworth, 1982. — 160p : ill(some col.),col.maps ; 24cm
Includes index
ISBN 0-7188-2509-8 (cased) : £8.50
ISBN 0-7188-2510-1 (pbk) : £5.95 B82-31062

799.1′6′0941 — Great Britain. Sea angling — *Manuals*

Catching seafish. — 3rd ed. — Wokingham (Ditchfield La., Wokingham, Berks.) : Jogger, c1982. — [24]p : ill ; 16cm. — (Waterproof field guide)
Previous ed.: 197-?. — Notebook format (unbound) B82-40113

799.1′6′094121 — Scotland. Grampian Region. Coastal waters. Sea angling — *Practical information*

Sea angling and pleasure trips / Grampian Region. — Aberdeen (Woodhill House, Ashgrove Rd. West, Aberdeen AB9 2LU) : Department of Leisure, Recreation and Tourism, Grampian Regional Council, [1982]. — 1sheet : ill ; 21x40cm folded to 21x10cm
Unpriced B82-30034

799.1′752 — Carp. Angling — *Manuals*

Maddocks, Kevin. Carp fever / Kevin Maddocks. — Enfield : Beekay, 1981. — 267p : ill,ports ; 23cm
Includes index
ISBN 0-9507598-0-5 (cased) : £9.00
ISBN 0-9507598-1-3 (pbk) : £6.50 B82-21657

799.1′753 — Pike. Angling

Buller, Fred. Pike and the pike angler. — London : Paul, Nov.1981. — [288]p
ISBN 0-09-146260-6 : £15.95 : CIP entry B81-28148

799.1′755 — Great Britain. Grayling. Angling — *Manuals*

Roberts, John, *1953-*. The grayling angler / by John Roberts. — London : Witherby, 1982. — 208p,6p of plates : ill(some col.),ports(some col.) ; 23cm
Bibliography: p203. — Includes index
ISBN 0-85493-141-4 : £8.50 B82-37610

799.1′755 — Great Britain. Still waters. Trout. Fly fishing — *Manuals*

Lapsley, Peter. Trout from stillwaters / Peter Lapsley. — London : A. & C. Black, 1981. — xiv,207p,[4]p of plates : ill(some col.) ; 24cm
Bibliography: p199. — Includes index
ISBN 0-7136-2171-0 : £9.95 : CIP rev. B81-24673

799.1′755 — Salmon. Angling

Sutherland, Douglas, *1919-*. The salmon book / Douglas Sutherland ; foreword by Lord Home. — London : Collins, 1982. — 160p : ill,ports ; 25cm
ISBN 0-00-216664-x : £7.95 : CIP rev. B82-10564

799.1′755 — Salmon. Fly fishing — *Manuals*

Graesser, Neil. Fly fishing for salmon. — Woodbridge : Boydell & Brewer, Sept.1982. — [144]p
ISBN 0-85115-172-8 : £9.95 : CIP entry B82-20497

799.1′755 — Still waters. Trout. Fly fishing

Lapsley, Peter. Successful small-stillwater trouting / by Peter Lapsley ; (photographs by Malcolm J. Kelly). — [Sandleheath] ([Allens Farm, Sandleheath, Nr. Fordingbridge, Hants. SP6 1QG]) : Allens Farm Trout Lakes, c1981. — 32p : ill,1port ; 21cm. — (An Allens Farm Trout Lakes publication)
Unpriced (pbk) B82-10529

799.1′755 — Still waters. Trout. Fly fishing. Flies

Price, Taff. Taff Price′s stillwater flies : a modern account of natural history, flydressing and fishing technique. — London : Benn
Book 3. — 1981. — p193-260,[4]p of plates : ill(some col.) ; 25cm
ISBN 0-510-22543-8 (pbk) : £5.95
Also classified at 592.092′9 B82-05909

799.1′755 — Trout. Angling

Walker, Richard, *1918-*. Dick Walker′s trout fishing / Richard Walker. — Newton Abbot : David & Charles, c1982. — 180p : ill,ports ; 23cm
ISBN 0-7153-8255-1 : £7.95 : CIP rev. B82-09622

799.1′755 — Trout. Fly fishing — *Manuals*

Sceats, David. Trout fishing / David Sceats. — London : Adam and Charles Black, 1982. — 96p : ill ; 21cm. — (Black′s picture sports)
Bibliography: p95. — Includes index
ISBN 0-7136-2111-7 : £3.50 : CIP rev. B81-22525

799.1′755 — Wiltshire. East Avon River. Angling waters: Trout fisheries. Management — *Personal observations*

Pease, Richard. The river keeper : caring for an angler′s trout stream / Richard Pease. — Newton Abbot : David & Charles, c1982. — 136p : ill,1map ; 23cm
ISBN 0-7153-8248-9 : £6.95 : CIP rev. B81-33820

799.2 — RECREATIONS. HUNTING

799.2 — Hunting

Hunting / [editor-in-chief Turlough Johnston] ; [editor Kerstin M. Stålbrand] ; [assistant editor Jeremy Franks]. — London : Marshall Cavendish, 1980. — 320p : ill(some col.) ; 31cm
Ill on lining papers. — Bibliography: p316. — Includes index
ISBN 0-85685-833-1 : £20.00 B82-11704

799.2′13′09 — Sports: Shooting, *to 1980*

The **Sportsmans** companion / compiled by Eric Begbie ; artwork by Pamela Hardwick ... [et al.]. — Hindhead : Saiga, c1981. — x,256p : ill,ports ; 24cm
ISBN 0-86230-038-x : £8.50
Primary classification 799.1′2′09 B82-10837

799.2′13′0941 — Great Britain. Game animals. Shooting — *Amateurs′ manuals*

Jackson, Tony, *1945 Nov.1-*. Shotguns and shooting / Tony Jackson. — London : Ward Lock, 1982. — 92p : ill ; 23cm
Includes index
ISBN 0-7063-6173-3 : £5.95 : CIP rev. B82-04616

Marchington, John. The complete shot / John Marchington. — London : A. & C. Black, 1981. — 198p : ill ; 24cm
Text on lining papers. — Includes index
ISBN 0-7136-2145-1 : £8.95 : CIP rev. B81-22527

Marchington, John. Shooting. — London : Faber, Sept.1982. — [180]p
Originally published: 1972
ISBN 0-571-11932-8 (pbk) : CIP entry B82-28464

Smith, Guy N.. Gamekeeping and shooting for amateurs / by Guy N. Smith ; drawings by Bob Sanders. — 2nd ed. — Hindhead : Saiga, c1981. — vii,209p : ill ; 23cm. — (Field sports library)
Previous ed.: Liss : Spur, 1976
ISBN 0-904558-93-2 : £6.00
Also classified at 639.9′5′0941 B82-08705

799.2′13′09426 — East Anglia. Game animals. Shooting, *1810-1910*

Johnson, Derek E.. Victorian shooting days : East Anglia 1810-1910 / Derek E. Johnson. — Woodbridge : Boydell, 1981. — 111p : ill,ports ; 26cm
Ports. on lining papers
ISBN 0-85115-156-6 : £8.95 : CIP rev. B81-24668

799.2′3 — Great Britain. Ferreting — *Manuals*

Smith, Guy N.. Ferreting and trapping for amateur gamekeepers / by Guy N. Smith ; photographs by Lance Smith ; drawings by Pat Larkin. — 2nd ed. — Hindhead : Spur, 1979. — 159p : ill,1plan ; 23cm
Previous ed.: 1978. — Includes index
ISBN 0-904558-73-8 : £5.50
Also classified at 639.9′6 B82-08776

799.2′32 — Falconry

Oswald, C. A.. The history and practice of falconry / Allan Oswald. — Jersey : Spearman, 1982. — 119p : ill,ports ; 22cm
ISBN 0-85978-045-7 (cased) : Unpriced
ISBN 0-85978-050-3 (pbk) : £2.50 B82-29547

799.2′32 — Falconry — *Manuals*

Ford, Emma. Birds of prey / Emma Ford. — London : Batsford, 1982. — 64p : col.ill,col.ports ; 20cm. — (A Batsford paperback)
Includes index
ISBN 0-7134-4164-x (pbk) : £2.25 B82-33826

799.2′32 — Falconry — *Manuals — Early works*

Harting, James Edmund. Hints on the management of hawks and practical falconry / by James Edmund Harting. — 2nd ed. — Hindhead : Saiga, c1981. — x,276p,[11]leaves of plates : ill(some col.) ; 23cm
Facsim. of: 2nd ed. London : Cox, 1898. — Includes index
ISBN 0-86230-031-2 : £9.50 B82-08709

799.2′34 — Great Britain. Hunting with hounds. Hunts, *to 1981*

Watson, J. N. P.. British & Irish hunts & huntsmen / J.N.P. Watson. — London : Batsford
Vol.1. — 1982. — 264p : ill,maps,ports ; 26cm
Includes index
ISBN 0-7134-2169-x : £20.00 B82-39657

Watson, J. N. P.. British & Irish hunts & huntsmen / J.N.P. Watson. — London : Batsford
Vol.2. — 1982. — 240p : ill,maps,ports ; 26cm
Includes index
ISBN 0-7134-2093-6 : £20.00 B82-39658

799.2′34 — Hunting with hounds. Hunts — *Directories — Serials*

Baily′s hunting directory. — 1982/83. — London : J.A. Allen, Nov.1982. — [425]p
ISBN 0-85131-377-9 : £11.95 : CIP entry B82-30583

799.2′4′0941 — Great Britain. Game birds. Shooting, *1700-1978 — Readings from contemporary sources*

A Portait of shooting / compiled by John Marchington. — Rugby : Atha, c1979. — 252p : ill(some col.) ; 30x31cm
In a slip case
ISBN 0-904475-25-5 : Unpriced B82-18383

799.2′597357 — Deer. Stalking

Whitehead, G. Kenneth. Hunting & stalking deer throughout the world / G. Kenneth Whitehead. — London : Batsford, 1982. — 336p,[32]p of plates : ill,maps ; 24cm
Bibliographpy: p323-326. — Inlcludes index
ISBN 0-7134-2490-7 : £15.00 B82-33961

799.2′597357 — New Zealand. Deer. Hunting — *Personal observations*

Tinsley, Ray. Call of the wapiti / by Ray Tinsley. — Wellington ; London : A.H. & A.W. Reed, 1979. — xiii,145p,[24]p of plates : ill ; 22cm
Maps on lining papers
ISBN 0-589-01216-9 : £5.95 B82-02062

799.2′5974442 — England. Foxes. Hunting. Barker, Stanley — *Biographies*

Newsham, Stuart. The hunting diaries of Stanley Barker / Stuart Newsham ; pencil drawings by Michael Lyne. — Tetbury : Standfast, 1981. — 237p : ill,maps,1facsim,ports ; 25cm
Maps on lining papers
ISBN 0-904602-18-4 : £10.00 B82-12628

799.2′5974442 — Foxes. Hunting

Fox-hunting. — Oxford : Oxford University Press, Nov.1982. — [120]p. — (Small Oxford books)
ISBN 0-19-214140-6 : £3.95 : CIP entry B82-26889

799.2′5974442 — Galway *(County)*. **Foxes. Hunting. Hunts: County Galway Hunt,** *to 1979*

Mahony, Edmund. The Galway Blazers : memoirs / by Edmund Mahony. — Galway : Kenny′s Bookshops and Art Galleries, 1979. — 125p : ill,maps,ports ; 26cm
ISBN 0-906312-15-9 : £8.80
ISBN 0-906312-16-7 (1/4 morocco) : Unpriced
ISBN 0-906312-17-5 (fine binding) : Unpriced B82-21238

799.2′5974442 — Gibraltar. Foxes. Hunting. Hunts: Royal Calpe Hunt, *to 1939*

Fergusson, Gordon. Hounds are home : the history of the Royal Calpe Hunt / Gordon Fergusson ; with illustrations by Lionel Edwards, Gerald Hare, Madeline Selfe. — London : Springwood, 1979. — xviii,364p,[8]p of plates : ill(some col.),1coat of arms,facsims,1col.map,ports ; 26cm
Ill. on lining papers. — 'Hunting map of the country near Gibraltar' (1 folded sheet) attached to end papers. — Bibliography: p348-354. — Includes index
ISBN 0-905947-23-1 : £10.50 B82-40410

799.2′6′0924 — Africa. Big game. Hunting — *Personal observations*

Morkel, Bill. Hunting in Africa / Bill Morkel. — Aylesbury : Howard Timmins, 1980. — 252p,[12]p of plates : ill ; 25cm
ISBN 0-86978-177-4 : £8.95 B82-03288

799′.2′6′09798 — Alaska. Big game. Hunting, *to ca 1945*

Sherwood, Morgan B.. Big game in Alaska : a history of wildlife and people / Morgan Sherwood. — New Haven, Conn. ; London : Yale University Press, c1981. — xii,200p,[6]p of plates : ports ; 25cm. — (Yale Western Americana series ; 33)
Bibliography: p180-192. — Includes index
ISBN 0-300-02625-0 : £19.25 : CIP rev. B82-01321

799.2′92′4 — New Zealand. Hunting, *ca 1945-1980 — Personal observations*

Holden, Philip. On target. — London : Hodder & Stoughton, July 1981. — [192]p
ISBN 0-340-26506-x : £7.95 : CIP entry B81-20645

799.292′4 — Scotland. Highlands. Game animals. Hunting, *1845-1856 — Personal observations*

St. John, Charles. The wild sports & natural history of the Highlands / Charles St John ; introduction by Sir John Moncreiffe of that Ilk. — London : Macdonald Futura, 1981. — xxvii,346p ; 18cm. — (Heritage) (A Futura book)
Originally published: London : Murray, 1863
ISBN 0-7088-2108-1 (pbk) : £2.25 B82-00838

799.292′4 — Staffordshire. Hunting — *Personal observations — Correspondence, diaries, etc.*

Plummer, David Brian. Diary of a hunter / D. Brian Plummer. — Woodbridge : Boydell Press, 1981. — 187p : ill,1facsims,ports ; 29cm
ISBN 0-85115-153-1 : £9.95 : CIP rev. B81-22588

799.2941 — Great Britain. Hunting, *to 1982*

Windeatt, Phil. The hunt and the anti-hunt. — London : Pluto, Oct.1982. — [64]p
ISBN 0-86104-387-1 (pbk) : £1.95 : CIP entry B82-27202

799.3 — TARGET SHOOTING

799.3′12 — Target air gun shooting

Churchill, Bob. Modern airweapon shooting / Bob Churchill & Granville Davies ; drawings by Ann Churchill. — Newton Abbot : David & Charles, c1981. — 196p : ill ; 23cm
Bibliography: p189. — Includes index
ISBN 0-7153-8123-7 : £7.50 : CIP rev. B81-22506

799.32 — ARCHERY

799.3′2′028 — Sports equipment: Archery equipment

Elliott, Cheri. Archer′s digest / edited by Jack Lewis. — 3rd ed. / by Cheri Elliott. — London : Arms and Armour Press, c1982. — 288p : ill ; 28cm
Previous ed.: Northfield, Ill. : DBI, 1977
ISBN 0-910676-40-2 (pbk) : Unpriced B82-39688

800 — LITERATURE

801 — Literature. Interpretation by readers. Semiotic aspects

Eco, Umberto. The role of the reader : explorations in the semiotics of texts / Umberto Eco. — London : Hutchinson, 1981. — viii,273p : ill ; 24cm. — (Hutchinson university library)
Bibliography: p267-273. — Includes index
ISBN 0-09-146391-2 (pbk) : £5.50 : CIP rev. B81-26800

801 — Literature. Semiotic aspects

Scholes, Robert. Semiotics and interpretation / Robert Scholes. — New Haven ; London : Yale University Press, c1982. — xiv,161p ; 22cm
Bibliography: p151-155. — Includes index
ISBN 0-300-02798-2 : £9.00 : CIP rev. B82-13487

801 — Literature. Theories

Blanchot, Maurice. The siren′s song / selected essays by Maurice Blanchot ; edited with an introduction by Gabriel Josipovici ; translated by Sacha Rabinovitch. — Brighton : Harvester, 1982. — vi,255p ; 23cm
Translated from the French
ISBN 0-85527-738-6 : £20.00 : CIP rev. B81-40263

Di Girolamo, Costanzo. A critical theory of literature / Costanzo Di Girolamo. — Madison, Wis. ; London : University of Wisconsin Press, 1981. — vii,113p : ill ; 22cm
Translation of: Critica della letterarietà. — Bibliography: p97-110. — Includes index
ISBN 0-299-08120-6 : £10.50 B82-15526

Modern literary theory : a comparative introduction / edited by Ann Jefferson and David Robey ; with contributions from David Forgacs ... [et al.]. — London : Batsford Academic and Educational, 1982. — 186p : ill ; 22cm
Bibliography: p170-179. — Includes index
ISBN 0-7134-3454-6 (pbk) : £4.95 : CIP rev. B82-01205

801 — Literature. Theories, *ca 1300-ca 1450*

Mimms, Alistair J.. Medieval theory of authorship. — London : Scolar Press, Dec.1982. — [376]p
ISBN 0-85967-641-2 : £19.50 : CIP entry B82-30591

801 — Literature. Theories of French writers

French literary theory today. — Cambridge : Cambridge University Press, Oct.1982. — [239]p
Translated from the French
ISBN 0-521-23036-5 (cased) : £19.50 : CIP entry
ISBN 0-521-29777-x (pbk) : £5.95 B82-26227

801 — Literature, *to 1981 — Philosophical perspectives*

Phillips, D. Z.. Through a darkening glass. — Oxford : Blackwell, Jan.1982. — [224]p
ISBN 0-631-12995-2 : £9.95 : CIP entry B81-34290

801′.3 — Literature - *Sociological perspectives*

Goldmann, Lucien. Essays on method in the sociology of literature. — Oxford : Blackwell, Apr.1981. — [160]p
ISBN 0-631-12769-0 (cased) : £4.95 : CIP entry
ISBN 0-631-12809-3 (pbk) : Unpriced B81-04323

801′.3 — Literature — *Sociological perspectives*

Lerner, Laurence. The literary imagination : essays on literature and society / Laurence Lerner. — Brighton : Harvester, 1982. — xi,204p ; 23cm
Includes index
ISBN 0-7108-0097-5 : £18.95 : CIP rev. B81-21497

801'.4 — Literature. Linguistic aspects

Fowler, Roger. Literature as social discourse : the practice of linguistic criticism / Roger Fowler. — London : Batsford Academic and Educational, 1981. — 215p ; 22cm
Bibliography: p201-211. — Includes index
ISBN 0-7134-3699-9 (cased) : Unpriced
ISBN 0-7134-3700-6 (pbk) : £4.95 B82-03562

801'.9 — Literature. Genres

Dubrow, Heather. Genre. — London : Methuen, June 1982. — [120]p. — (The Critical idiom ; 42)
ISBN 0-416-74680-2 (cased) : £5.95 : CIP entry
ISBN 0-416-74690-x (pbk) : £2.25 B82-10506

Fowler, Alistair. Kinds of literature. — Oxford : Clarendon Press, Oct.1982. — [368]p
ISBN 0-19-812812-6 : £15.00 : CIP entry B82-23682

801'.95 — Literature. Criticism

Daiches, David. Critical approaches to literature / David Daiches. — 2nd ed. — London : Longman, 1981. — vii,408p ; 22cm
Previous ed.: 1956. — Includes index
ISBN 0-582-49180-0 (pbk) : £5.95 : CIP rev. B81-31823

Hartman, Geoffrey H.. Criticism in the wilderness. — London : Yale University Press, Feb.1982. — [336]p
Originally published: 1980
ISBN 0-300-02839-3 (pbk) : £3.95 : CIP entry B82-07094

Juhl, P. D.. Interpretation : an essay in the philosophy of literary criticism / P.D. Juhl. — Princeton ; Guildford : Princeton University Press, c1980. — x,332p ; 23cm
Bibliography: p301-322. — Includes index
ISBN 0-691-07242-6 : £11.20 B82-14134

McGilchrist, Iain. Against criticism / Iain McGilchrist. — London : Faber, 1982. — 271p ; 23cm
Includes index
ISBN 0-571-11922-0 : £12.50 B82-28499

Robson, W. W.. The definition of literature and other essays. — Cambridge : Cambridge University Press, Oct.1982. — [288]p
ISBN 0-521-24495-1 : £19.50 : CIP entry B82-23332

Wellek, René. A history of modern criticism 1750-1950 / by René Wellek. — Cambridge : Cambridge University Press
1: The later eighteenth century. — 1981. — vii,358p ; 23cm
Originally published: London : Cape, 1955. — Includes bibliographies and index
ISBN 0-521-28295-0 (pbk) : £8.95 : CIP rev. B81-20538

Wellek, René. A history of modern criticism 1750-1950 / by René Wellek. — Cambridge : Cambridge University Press
2: The Romantic age. — 1981. — 459p ; 23cm
Originally published: London : Cape, 1955. — Includes bibliographies and index
ISBN 0-521-28296-9 (pbk) : £9.95 : CIP rev. B81-20539

801'.95 — Literature. Criticism. Linguistic aspects

Donoghue, Denis. Ferocious alphabets / Denis Donoghue. — London : Faber, 1981. — 211p ; 23cm
ISBN 0-571-11809-7 : £8.95 : CIP rev. B81-27412

801'.95 — Literature. Criticism. Semiotic aspects

Norris, Christopher. Deconstruction. — London : Methuen, May 1982. — [200]p. — (New accents)
ISBN 0-416-32060-0 (cased) : £6.50 : CIP entry
ISBN 0-416-32070-8 (pbk) : £2.95 B82-06756

801'.95 — Literature. Criticism. Social aspects

Frye, Northrop. The stubborn structure : essays on criticism and society / Northrop Frye. — London : Methuen, 1970 (1980 [printing]). — xii,316p ; 23cm
Originally published: Ithaca, N.Y. : Cornell University Press ; London : Methuen, 1970
ISBN 0-416-74400-1 : £17.50 : CIP rev. B80-08907

801'.95 — Literature. Criticism. Structuralism

Leitch, Vincent B.. Deconstructive criticism. — London : Hutchinson, Nov.1982. — [400]p
ISBN 0-09-150690-5 (cased) : £15.00 : CIP entry
ISBN 0-09-150691-3 (pbk) : £5.95 B82-26856

Todorov, Tzvetan. Introduction to poetics / Tzvetan Todorov ; translated from the French by Richard Howard. — Brighton : Harvester, 1981. — xxxii,83p ; 24cm
Translation of: Poétíque. — Bibliography: p75-79. — Includes index
ISBN 0-7108-0328-1 (cased) : £13.95 : CIP rev.
ISBN 0-7108-0333-8 (pbk) : Unpriced B81-20559

Untying the text : a post-structuralist reader / edited and introduced by Robert Young. — Boston ; London : Routledge & Kegan Paul, 1981. — x,326p ; 23cm
Includes bibliographies and index
ISBN 0-7100-0804-x (cased) : £12.50 : CIP rev.
ISBN 0-7100-0805-8 (pbk) : £4.95 B81-13725

801'.95 — Literature. Criticism. Theories

Sharratt, Bernard. Reading relations : structures of literary production : a dialectical text-book / Bernard Sharratt. — Brighton : Harvester, 1982. — 341p ; 25cm
ISBN 0-7108-0059-2 : £18.95 : CIP rev. B81-31641

801'.95 — Literature. Criticism. Theories — *Conference proceedings*

Interpretation of narrative / edited by Mario J. Valdés and Owen J. Miller. — Toronto ; London : University of Toronto Press, c1978. — xi,202p : ill ; 24cm
Conference proceedings. — Bibliography: p191-197. — Includes index
ISBN 0-8020-5443-9 : £10.50 B82-16401

801'.95 — Literature. Hermeneutic criticism

Bruns, Gerald L.. Inventions : writing, textuality and understanding in literary history. — London : Yale University Press, Sept.1982. — [202]p
ISBN 0-300-02786-9 : £14.50 : CIP entry B82-29123

801'.95'05 — Literature. Comparative criticism — *Serials*

Comparative criticism. — 3. — Cambridge : Cambridge University Press, Nov.1981. — [352]p
ISBN 0-521-23276-7 : £20.00 : CIP entry
ISSN 0144-7564 B81-31192

Comparative criticism. — 4. — Cambridge : Cambridge University Press, Nov.1982. — [372]p
ISBN 0-521-24578-8 : £25.00 : CIP entry B82-29391

801'.95'0924 — Literature. Criticism. Qu, Qiubai — *Critical studies*

Pickowicz, Paul G.. Marxist literary thought in China : the influence of Ch'ü Ch'iu-pai / Paul G. Pickowicz. — Berkeley ; London : University of California Press, c1981. — xvii,259p : 1port ; 24cm
Bibliography: p243-248. — Includes index
ISBN 0-520-04030-9 : Unpriced B82-17786

801'.95'0924 — Literature. Marxist criticism. Benjamin, Walter — *Critical studies*

Wolin, Richard. Walter Benjamin : an aesthetic of redemption / Richard Wolin. — New York ; Guildford : Columbia University Press, 1982. — xvi,316p : ill,1port ; 24cm
Bibliography: p305-312. — Includes index
ISBN 0-231-05422-x : £14.80 B82-39488

801'.95'0924 — Literature. Marxist criticism. Benjamin, Walter. Interpersonal relationships with Scholem, Gershom — *Personal observations*

Scholem, Gershom. Walter Benjamin : the story of a friendship. — London : Faber, Aug.1982. — [242]p
Translation of: Walter Benjamin : die Geschichte einer Freundschaft
ISBN 0-571-11970-0 : £10.00 : CIP entry
Also classified at 296.7'1'0924 B82-18577

801'.95'0943 — Literature. German criticism, *1800-1981*

Hohendahl, Peter Owe. The institution of criticism / Peter Owe Hohendahl. — Ithaca ; London : Cornell University Press, 1982. — 287p ; 23cm
Includes index
ISBN 0-8014-1325-7 : £14.75 B82-35759

801'.95'0973 — Literature. American criticism, *ca 1920-1970 — Critical studies*

Daiches, David. The new criticism / by David Daiches. — Portree : Aquila, 1982. — [22]p ; 21cm. — (Aquila essays ; no.5)
ISBN 0-7275-0221-2 (pbk) : Unpriced B82-25607

801'.951 — Poetry in European languages. Criticism. Theories, *1200-1500*

Allen, Judson Boyce. The ethical poetic of the later Middle Ages : a decorum of convenient distinction / Judson Boyce Allen. — Toronto ; London : University of Toronto Press, c1982. — xix,327p ; 23cm
Includes index
ISBN 0-8020-2370-3 : Unpriced B82-27903

803'.21 — Literature — *Encyclopaedias*

Cuddon, J. A.. A dictionary of literary terms / J.A. Cuddon. — Rev. ed. — Harmondsworth : Penguin, 1982. — 759p ; 20cm
Originally published: London : Deutsch, 1979
ISBN 0-14-051112-1 (pbk) : £4.95 B82-22490

807.9 — Great Britain. Literature. Prizes — *Lists*

Guide to literary prizes, grants and awards. — 2nd ed. — London : National Book League, May 1982. — [32]p
Previous ed.: 1979
ISBN 0-85353-368-7 (pbk) : £1.20 : CIP entry B82-12828

808 — English language. Style

Language and literature : an introductory reader in stylistics. — London : Allen & Unwin, Aug.1982. — [256]p. — (Aspects of English)
ISBN 0-04-407018-7 (cased) : £12.50 : CIP entry
ISBN 0-04-407017-9 (pbk) : £5.50 B82-15643

808 — Metaphor

Metaphor : problems and perspectives / edited by David S. Miall. — Brighton : Harvester, 1982. — xix,172p : ill ; 23cm
Bibliography: p159-167. — Includes index
ISBN 0-7108-0033-9 : £18.95 : CIP rev. B82-09599

808 — Rhetoric

Smith, Adam, *1723-1790*. Lectures on rhetoric and belles lettres. — Oxford : Clarendon Press, Nov.1982. — [416]p. — (The Glasgow edition of the works and correspondence of Adam Smith ; 4)
ISBN 0-19-828186-2 : £20.00 : CIP entry B82-26873

808 — Writers in English. Pseudonyms, *1900-1980 — Lists*

Atkinson, Frank, *1922-*. Dictionary of literary pseudonyms : a selection of popular modern writers in English / Frank Atkinson. — 3rd ed. — London : Bingley, 1982. — 305p ; 23cm
Previous ed.: 1977
ISBN 0-85157-323-1 : Unpriced : CIP rev. B81-31528

808 — Writers in English: South-east English writers — *Directories*

Directory of writers : in the south east of England. — Tunbridge Wells (9-10 Crescent Rd., Tunbridge Wells, Kent TN1 2LU) : South East Arts, [1982?]. — [16]p : ill ; 30cm
Unpriced (unbound) B82-28817

808′.001 — Rhetoric — *Philosophical perspectives*
A General rhetoric / by Group [mu] J. Dubois ... [et al.] ; translated by Paul B. Burrell and Edgar M. Slotkin. — Baltimore ; London : Johns Hopkins University Press, c1981. — xix,254p : ill ; 24cm
Translation of: Rhétorique générale. — Includes index
ISBN 0-8018-2326-9 : £13.25 B82-02233

808′.009′034 — European literatures, *ca 1850-ca 1930.* **Rhetoric. Semiotic aspects** — *Case studies*
De Man, Paul. Allegories of reading. — London : Yale University Press, Mar.1982. — [320]p
Originally published: 1979
ISBN 0-300-02845-8 (pbk) : £4.95 : CIP entry
Primary classification 848′.508 B82-12136

808′.02 — Authorship
Josipovici, Gabriel. Writing and the body. — Brighton : Harvester, Apr.1982. — [128]p
ISBN 0-7108-0495-4 : £15.95 : CIP entry B82-05405

808′.02 — Authorship. Style — *Manuals*
MHRA style book : notes for authors, editors and writers of dissertations / edited by A.S. Maney and R.L. Smallwood in consultation with the Committee of the Association. — 3rd ed. — London : Modern Humanities Research Association, 1981. — vi,73p : ill ; 21cm
Previous ed.: 1978. — Bibliography: p58. — Includes index
ISBN 0-900547-79-0 (pbk) : Unpriced B82-34993

808′.02 — Literature. Style. Analysis. Statistical methods
Kenny, Anthony. The computation of style : an introduction to statistics for students of literature and humanities / by Anthony Kenny. — Oxford : Pergamon, 1982. — vii,176p : ill ; 21cm
Includes index
ISBN 0-08-024282-0 (cased) : Unpriced : CIP rev.
ISBN 0-08-024281-2 (pbk) : Unpriced B82-07241

808′.02 — Literature. Style. Linguistic aspects. Analysis
Cummings, Michael. The language of literature. — Oxford : Pergamon, Nov.1982. — [192]p. — (Materials for language practice)
ISBN 0-08-028629-1 (pbk) : £6.95 : CIP entry B82-27835

808′.02 — Typescripts. Copy-editing — *Manuals*
Butcher, Judith. Copy-editing : the Cambridge handbook / Judith Butcher. — 2nd ed. — Cambridge : Cambridge University Press, 1981. — xi,332p ; 24cm
Previous ed.: 1975. — Bibliography: p312-313. — Includes index
ISBN 0-521-23868-4 : £25.00 : CIP rev. B81-31061

Notes for readers, typesetters and copywriters. — Rev. ed. — Cirencester : Brann, 1980. — 48p : ill ; 21cm
Previous ed.: 1975. — Includes index
ISBN 0-9504923-4-5 (pbk) : £1.95 B82-35957

Stainton, Elsie Myers. Author and editor at work : making a better book / Elsie Myers Stainton. — Toronto ; London : University of Toronto Press, c1982. — x,85p ; 23cm
Includes index
ISBN 0-8020-6449-3 (pbk) : £4.00 B82-35661

808′.02 — Typescripts. Preparation
Butcher, Judith. Typescripts, proofs and indexes / Judith Butcher. — Cambridge : Cambridge University Press, 1980. — 32p ; 22cm. — (Cambridge authors′ and publishers′ guides)
ISBN 0-521-29739-7 (pbk) : £1.25 B82-26372

808′.02′05 — Authorship — *Serials*
Wordsmith : a monthly report on the art of writing, publishing & being published. — Vol.1, no.1 (Oct. 1981)-. — [Oxford] ([P.O. Box 125, Oxford]) : [Research Associates], 1981-. — v. ; 30cm
Description based on: Vol.1, no.4 (Jan. 1982)
ISSN 0262-6748 = Wordsmith : Unpriced
Also classified at 070.5′05 B82-22696

Writers′ and artists′ yearbook. — 1982. — London : A. & C. Black, Nov.1981. — [500]p
ISBN 0-7136-2178-8 : £3.50 : CIP entry B81-30362

Writers′ and artists′ yearbook. — 1983. — London : A. & C. Black, Nov.1982. — [514]p
ISBN 0-7136-2245-8 (pbk) : £3.95 : CIP entry B82-28570

808′.042 — Creative writing — *Manuals*
Doubtfire, Dianne. Creative writing. — London : Teach Yourself Books Feb.1983. — [192]p. — (Teach yourself books)
ISBN 0-340-28765-9 (pbk) : £2.50 : CIP entry B82-38073

Fairfax, John, *1930-*. The way to write / John Fairfax and John Moat ; foreword by Ted Hughes. — London : Elm Tree Books, 1981. — xix,87p ; 23cm
ISBN 0-241-10556-0 (cased) : Unpriced
ISBN 0-241-10557-9 (pbk) : £3.95 B82-40390

808′.042 — English language. Composition — *For non-English speaking students*
Jupp, T. C.. Basic writing skills in English. — London : Heinemann Educational
Students′ book / T.C. Japp & John Milne. — 1980. — 74p : ill,maps,forms ; 24cm
ISBN 0-435-28495-9 (pbk) : £1.20 B82-21445

Kindler, Don. Picture prompts / Don Kindler. — Walton-on-Thames : Nelson, 1981. — [64]p : ill ; 16x22cm + Teacher′s notes(33p ; 22cm)
ISBN 0-17-555355-6 (pbk) : £0.95
ISBN 0-17-555356-4 (Teacher′s notes) : £0.95 B82-00823

808′.042 — English language. Composition — *For non-English speaking undergraduates*
Campbell, Ann F.. Organise your English. — London : Hodder and Stoughton, May 1982. — [96]p
ISBN 0-340-26202-8 : £2.95 : CIP entry B82-07432

808′.042 — English language. Composition — *For schools*
Proud, Alan. Upgrade your English : basic skills in composition / Alan Proud. — London : Edward Arnold, 1980. — 93p : 2ill,facsims ; 25cm
ISBN 0-7131-0463-5 (pbk) : £2.25 B82-16885

808′.042 — English language. Composition — *For undergraduates*
Hartwell, Patrick. Open to language : a new college rhetoric / Patrick Hartwell with Robert H. Bentley. — New York ; Oxford : Oxford University Press, 1982. — xxv,642p : ill ; 25cm
Text on lining papers. — Includes bibliographies and index
ISBN 0-19-503080-x : £12.50 B82-37010

808′.042 — English language. Composition — *Manuals*
Leggett, Glenn. Prentice-Hall handbook for writers / Glenn Leggett, C. David Mead, William Charvat. — 8th ed. / with the editorial supervision of Richard S. Beal. — Englewood Cliffs ; London : Prentice-Hall, c1982. — xvi,544p ; 22cm
Previous ed.: 1978. — Includes index
ISBN 0-13-695734-x : £8.20 B82-21019

808′.042 — English language. Writing skills — *Conference proceedings*
Learning to write : first language/second language. — London : Longman, Oct.1982. — [304]p. — (Applied linguistics and language study)
Conference papers
ISBN 0-582-55371-7 (pbk) : £3.80 : CIP entry B82-25928

808′.042 — English language. Writing skills — *For African students*
Tetlow, J. G.. Developing writing skills / J.G. Tetlow. — Harlow : Longman, 1981. — vi,72p : ill ; 25cm
ISBN 0-582-65055-0 (pbk) : £1.40 B82-12361

808′.042 — English language. Writing skills — *For American students*
Adams, Judith-Anne. English for academic uses : a writing workbook / Judith-Anne Adams and Margaret A. Dwyer. — Englewood Cliffs ; London : Prentice-Hall, c1982. — xii,228p : ill ; 24cm
ISBN 0-13-279653-8 (pbk) : £7.45 B82-16839

808′.042 — English language. Writing skills — *For non-English speaking students*
Carrier, Michael. Intermediate language skills, writing / Michael Carrier. — London : Hodder and Stoughton, 1981. — 95p : ill,1map,facsims,1plan,forms ; 25cm
ISBN 0-340-24408-9 (pbk) : Unpriced: CIP rev. B81-10437

Case, Doug. Developing writing skills in English. — London : Heinemann Educational
Student′s book. — July 1982. — [80]p
ISBN 0-435-28021-x (pbk) : £1.50 : CIP entry B82-14081

Case, Doug. Developing writing skills in English. — London : Heinemann Educational
Teachers′ handbook. — Aug.1982. — [56]p
ISBN 0-435-28022-8 (pbk) : £2.25 : CIP entry B82-20756

Case, Doug. Developing writing skills in English. — London : Heinemann Educational, Aug.1982
Workbook. — [48]p
ISBN 0-435-28023-6 (unbound) : £0.75 : CIP entry B82-21089

Pincas, Anita. Writing in English / Anita Pincas with the assistance of Kate Allen. — London : Macmillan
Bk.1. — 1982. — xiii,62p : ill,forms,maps ; 25cm
ISBN 0-333-31761-0 (pbk) : £1.50 B82-37418

Stephens, Rory D.. Sequence : a basic writing course / Rory D. Stephens. — New York ; London : Holt, Rinehart and Winston, c1982. — xi,253p : ill,forms ; 24cm
Includes index
ISBN 0-03-055256-7 (pbk) : £8.50 B82-23309

808′.042 — English language. Writing skills — *For schools*
Barrass, Robert. Students must write. — London : Methuen, Oct.1982. — [120]p
ISBN 0-416-33620-5 (pbk) : £2.50 : CIP entry B82-23979

808′.042 — Great Britain. Secondary schools. Students. Writing skills. Research projects: Writing Across the Curriculum, 11-16 Years *(Project)* — *Critical studies*
Writing and learning across the curriculum 11-16 / Nancy Martin ... [et al. of the] Schools Council Writing Across the Curriculum Project. — [London] : Ward Lock Educational for the Schools Council, 1976 (1981 [printing]). — 176p : ill ; 22cm
Includes bibliographies and index
ISBN 0-7062-3499-5 (cased) : Unpriced
ISBN 0-7062-3498-7 (pbk) : Unpriced B82-11932

808′.042 — Writing. Sexism. Avoidance — *Manuals*
Miller, Casey. The handbook of non-sexist writing : for writers, editors and speakers / Casey Miller & Kate Swift. — British ed. / revised by Stephanie Dowrick. — London : Women′s Press, 1981. — 119p ; 20cm
Previous ed.: New York : Lippincott & Crowell, 1980. — Includes index
ISBN 0-7043-3878-5 (pbk) : £3.25 : CIP rev. B81-31647

808′.042 — Writing. Techniques — *Manuals*
Cox, Sidney. Indirections : for those who want to write / by Sidney Cox. — London : Kudos & Godine, 1982. — xi,139p ; 19cm
Originally published: David R. Godine, 1981
ISBN 0-87923-389-3 (pbk) : £2.95 : CIP rev. B82-03385

808′.042 — Writing. Techniques — *Manuals continuation*

Elbow, Peter. Writing with power : techniques for mastering the writing process / Peter Elbow. — Oxford : Oxford University Press, 1981. — xi,384p ; 22cm
Bibliography: p375-377. — Includes index
ISBN 0-19-502912-7 (cased) : £12.00
ISBN 0-19-502913-5 (pbk) : £4.95 B82-00509

Hull, Raymond. How to write how-to books and articles. — London (13 Burlington Lodge Studios, Rigault Rd, SW6 4JJ) : Poplar Press, Jan.1982. — [256]p
ISBN 0-907657-01-x : £8.95 : CIP entry B81-33756

808′.042′024372 — English language. Composition — *For teaching*

A **Programme** for written English development in primary schools / Strathclyde Regional Council, Department of Education, Glasgow Division. — [Glasgow] : Strathclyde Regional Council, Department of Education, Glasgow Division, [1982?]. — 3v. : ill,facsims ; 30cm
£1.50 (pbk) B82-31104

808′.042′024638 — Writing. Techniques — *Manuals — For bee-keeping*

Writing about apiculture : guide-lines for authors. — Gerrards Cross : International Bee Research Association, Apr.1982. — [6]p. — (Source materials for apiculture ; no.10)
ISBN 0-86098-120-7 (pbk) : £1.00 : CIP entry B82-16200

808′.042′02465 — English language. Composition — *For typewriting — For schools*

Wells, Rosemary. Type or write. — London : Edward Arnold, Sept.1982. — [96]p
ISBN 0-7131-0360-4 (pbk) : £2.50 : CIP entry B82-20027

808′.042′076 — English language. American usage. Composition — *Questions & answers*

Kinsella, Paul. The techniques of writing / Paul Kinsella. — 3rd ed. — New York ; London : Harcourt Brace Jovanovich, c1981. — xii,364p ; 24cm
Previous ed.: 1975
ISBN 0-15-589728-4 (pbk) : Unpriced B82-39572

808′.042′076 — English language. Composition — *Questions & answers*

Adams, W. Royce. Think, read, react, plan, write, rewrite / W. Royce Adams. — 3rd ed. — New York ; London : Holt, Rinehart and Winston, c1982. — xiii,346p : 1ill ; 24cm
Previous ed.: 1979. — Includes index
ISBN 0-03-059116-3 (pbk) : £8.95 B82-15364

Brereton, John C.. A plan for writing / John C. Brereton. — 2nd ed. — New York ; London : Holt, Rinehart and Winston, c1982. — x,256p : ill ; 24cm
Previous ed.: 1978. — Includes index
ISBN 0-03-058943-6 (pbk) : £8.95 B82-15349

Herman, William. Troubleshooting : basic writing skills / by William Herman, Jeffrey M. Young. — 2nd ed. — New York ; London : Holt, Rinehart and Winston, c1982. — ix,291p : forms ; 24cm
Previous ed.: 1978
ISBN 0-03-059118-x (pbk) : £8.50 B82-23310

808′.042′076 — English language. Composition — *Questions & answers — For schools*

Finn, F. E. S.. In your own words : practice in summary, comprehension and composition / F.E.S. Finn. — [London] : J. Murray, c1981. — xi,84p : ill ; 22cm
ISBN 0-7195-3878-5 (pbk) : £1.10 : CIP rev.
Primary classification 428.2 B81-27405

Finn, F. E. S.. In your own words : practice in summary, comprehension and composition / F.E.S. Finn. — [London] : J. Murray [Teachers' book]. — c1981. — xi,84p : ill ; 22cm
ISBN 0-7195-3879-3 (pbk) : £1.50 : CIP rev.
Primary classification 428.2 B81-27408

McCarthy, Ursula. Let's write / Ursula McCarthy ; [illustrations Jan Mitchell]. — [Tallaght] : Folens
1. — c1981. — 40p : ill ; 18x25cm
Cover title. — Text on inside cover
ISBN 0-86141-118-8 (pbk) : Unpriced B82-13285

McCarthy, Ursula. Let's write / Ursula McCarthy ; [illustrations Jan Mitchell]. — [Tallaght] : Folens
2. — c1981. — 40p : ill ; 18x25cm
Cover title. — Text on inside cover
Unpriced (pbk) B82-15400

McCarthy, Ursula. Let's write / Ursula McCarthy ; [illustrations Jan Mitchell]. — [Tallaght] : Folens
3. — c1981. — 40p : ill,1map ; 18x25cm
Cover title. — Text on inside cover
Unpriced (pbk) B82-13550

Woodhead, Chris. Writing and responding : a course for English language examinations / Chris Woodhead with Anne Miller and Pat O'Shea. — Oxford : Oxford University Press, 1981. — 190p : ill,facsims,1plan,ports ; 24cm
Includes index
ISBN 0-19-831246-6 (pbk) : £2.50 B82-10927

808′.042′076 — English language. Writing skills — *Questions & answers*

Glazier, Teresa Ferster. The least you should know about English : basic writing skills / Teresa Ferster Glazier. — New York ; London : Holt, Rinehart and Winston
Form A. — 2nd ed. — c1982. — viii,283p ; 24cm
Previous ed.: 1977. — Text on inside cover
ISBN 0-03-059781-1 (pbk) : £8.50 B82-15358

Sullivan, Tony. Writing / by Tony Sullivan. — Cambridge : National Extension College, c1979. — 45p ; 21cm. — (Studying skills series) (National Extension College course ; no.ED19)
ISBN 0-86082-168-4 (pbk) : Unpriced B82-40820

808′.042′076 — English language. Writing skills — *Questions & answers — For schools*

Collinson, D. J.. Writing English : a workbook for students / D.J. Collinson. — London : Pan, 1982. — 226p : ill ; 18cm
Bibliography: p164-166. — Includes index
ISBN 0-330-26584-9 (pbk) : £1.50 B82-11639

808′.042′076 — English languages. Composition — *Questions & answers — For African students*

Sheal, Peter. Advanced level writing skills / Peter Sheal. — Harlow : Longman, 1981. — viii,135p : ill ; 22cm
ISBN 0-582-64307-4 (pbk) : Unpriced B82-36507

808′.0431 — German language. Composition — *For schools*

Phillips, David. So was!. — London : Hodder and Stoughton, Nov.1982. — 1v.
ISBN 0-340-26916-2 (pbk) : £1.95 : CIP entry B82-27345

Richardson, G.. Kleine Geschichten. — London : Edward Arnold, Aug.1982. — [32]p
ISBN 0-7131-0727-8 (pbk) : £1.60 : CIP entry B82-15915

808′.0441′0712 — Secondary schools. Curriculum subjects: French language. Essays. Writing

Hares, R. J.. Compo! : French language essay writing. — London : Hodder and Stoughton, Aug.1982. — [96]p
ISBN 0-340-28255-x (pbk) : £1.95 : CIP entry B82-18568

808′.0441′076 — French language. Composition — *Questions & answers — For schools*

Dolan, Conleath. Rédactions choisies : intermediate certificate compositions / Conleath Dolan. — Dublin (Ballymount Rd., Walkinstown, Dublin 12) : Helicon, 1981. — 48p : ill ; 21cm
Text on inside cover
Unpriced (pbk) B82-08204

Dolan, Conleath. Rédactions choisies : leaving certificate compositions / Conleath Dolan. — Dublin (Ballymount Rd., Walkinstown, Dublin 12) : Helicon, 1981. — 64p ; 21cm
Unpriced (pbk) B82-08205

808′.066 — Note-taking — *Questions & answers — For non-English speaking students*

Adkins, Alex. Text to note : study skills for advanced learners. — London : E. Arnold, Nov.1982. — [128]p
ISBN 0-7131-8077-3 (pbk) : £3.00 : CIP entry B82-29433

Adkins, Alex. Text to note : key. — London : E. Arnold, Nov.1982. — [32]p
ISBN 0-7131-8093-5 (pbk) : £1.00 : CIP entry B82-29432

808′.066 — Official documents. Writing — *Manuals*

Cutts, Martin. Writing plain English : why it should be done? how it's been done? how you can do it? / Martin Cutts, Chrissie Maher. — Salford : Plain English Campaign, 1980. — 42p : ill,facsims,forms,2ports ; 21x30cm
ISBN 0-907424-00-7 (pbk) : £2.95 B82-17511

808′.066 — Reports. Writing — *Manuals*

Sussams, John E.. Effective report writing. — Aldershot : Gower, Jan.1983. — [100]p
ISBN 0-566-02323-7 : £9.50 : CIP entry B82-32443

808′.066 — Research reports. Writing — *Manuals*

Turabian, Kate L.. A manual for writers : of research papers, theses and dissertations / Kate L. Turabian. — British ed. / prepared by John E. Spink. — London : Heinemann, 1982. — 227p : ill ; 22cm
Previous ed. (i.e. 4th ed.): Chicago : University of Chicago Press, 1973. — Includes index
ISBN 0-434-79970-x (pbk) : £3.95 B82-15431

808′.066336021 — Great Britain. Taxation. Forms. Filling — *Manuals — Serials*

Official tax forms manual. — 1982-. — London : Oyez Longman, 1982-. — v. : forms ; 25cm
Annual. — Continues: Tax forms manual
ISSN 0263-8045 = Official tax forms manual : Unpriced B82-36717

808′.0665021 — Science. Serial articles. Writing — *Manuals*

Booth, Vernon. Writing a scientific paper and speaking at scientific meetings / Vernon Booth. — 5th ed. — London : The Biochemical Society, 1981. — 48p : ill
Previous ed.: 1977. — Includes index
£2.50 (pbk) B82-06880

The **Manuscript** : guidelines for the preparation of manuscripts and bibliographies of scientific papers : with a list of title abbreviations for selected medical and related journals. — 7th rev. and expanded ed. — Basel ; London : Karger, 1981. — iv,52p : ill,facsims ; 28cm
ISBN 3-8055-2563-x (pbk) : £4.00 B82-01522

808′.0665021 — Scientific writing — *Manuals*

Turk, Christopher. Effective writing : improving scientific, technical and business communication / Christopher Turk, John Kirkman. — London : Spon, 1982. — 257p : ill ; 22cm
Includes index
ISBN 0-419-11670-2 (cased) : Unpriced : CIP rev.
ISBN 0-419-11680-x (pbk) : Unpriced B81-31165

808′.0666021 — Technical writing — *For data processing*

Van Duyn, J.. The D P professional's guide to writing effective technical communications / J. Van Duyn. — New York ; Chichester : Wiley, c1982. — ix,218p : ill ; 24cm
Includes index
ISBN 0-471-05843-2 : £18.00 B82-32738

808'.0666021 — Technical writing — *For students in American higher education institutions*

Lay, Mary M.. Strategies for technical writing : a rhetoric with readings / Mary M. Lay. — New York ; London : Holt, Rinehart and Winston, c1982. — xv,308p : ill ; 24cm
Includes index
ISBN 0-03-053636-7 (pbk) : £11.25
B82-19432

808'.0666021 — Technical writing — *Manuals*

Eisenberg, Anne. Effective technical communication / Anne Eisenberg. — New York ; London : McGraw-Hill, c1982. — xii,355p : ill,facsims,1form,1port ; 25cm
Includes index
ISBN 0-07-019096-8 (cased) : £13.75 (pbk) : Unpriced
B82-27227

808'.06661021 — Written communication — *Manuals — For medicine*

Sheen, Anitra Peebles. Breathing life into medical writing : a handbook / Anitra Peebles Sheen. — St. Louis ; London : Mosby, 1982. — xi,108p : ill ; 24cm
Bibliography: p103. — Includes index
ISBN 0-8016-4589-1 (pbk) : £8.75 B82-22920

808'.066615021 — Drugs. Labels. Comprehensibility

Understanding labels : problems for poor readers. — London : Adult Literacy Support Services Fund, c1980. — 18,[56]p : ill,forms ; 30cm
Cover title. — Bibliography: p18
ISBN 0-906965-04-7 (spiral) : £2.00
B82-35058

808'.066616021 — Medicine. Psychiatry. Diagnosis. Reports. Writing

Kellerman, Henry. Handbook of psychodiagnostic testing : personality analysis and report writing / Henry Kellerman, Anthony Burry. — New York ; London : Grune & Stratton, c1981. — xv,222p ; 24cm
Bibliography: p212-215. — Includes index
ISBN 0-8089-1403-0 : £16.20
Primary classification 616.89'075 B82-18351

808'.066651021 — Business correspondence in English — *For non-English speaking students*

McKellen, J. S.. Business matters : practice materials for business communication in English / J.S. McKellen and M.D. Spooner. — Oxford : Pergamon, 1982. — ix,101p : facsims,forms ; 25cm. — (Materials for language practice)
ISBN 0-08-025356-3 (pbk) : £2.95 : CIP rev.
B81-13453

808'.066651021 — Business correspondence — *Manuals*

Pearsall, Thomas E.. How to write for the world of work / Thomas E. Pearsall, Donald H. Cunningham. — 2nd ed. — New York ; London : Holt, Rinehart and Winston, c1982. — xiii,397p : ill,forms ; 24cm
Previous ed.: 1978. — Text on inside cover. — Includes index
ISBN 0-03-059486-3 (pbk) : Unpriced
Primary classification 808'.066658 B82-20713

808'.066651021 — Business correspondence — *Manuals — For non-English speaking students*

Farthing, Joni. Out of the in-tray / Joni Farthing. — St. Albans : Hart-Davis Educational, 1982. — 80p ; 30cm
ISBN 0-247-13149-0 (pbk) : Unpriced
B82-24512

808'.066651021 — English language. Business English — *For non-English speaking students*

Blundell, J. A.. Career : developments / J.A. Blundell, N.M.G. Middlemiss. — Oxford : Oxford University Press, 1982. — 175p : ill,forms ; 25cm. — (English for the business and commercial world)
ISBN 0-19-451324-6 (pbk) : £3.25 B82-39759

Smith, Pamela, *1938-*. Career English / Pamela Smith, John Gibbons, Kenneth Westcott. — Walton-on-Thames : Nelson, 1982. — 224p : ill ; 22cm + Teachers' book(65p : 22cm)
ISBN 0-17-580007-3 (pbk) : £2.45
ISBN 0-17-580021-9 (Teachers' book) : £1.25
B82-21335

808'.066651021 — English language. Business English — *For non-English speaking students — Serials*

Business express : the magazine for students of business English. — Vol.1, no.1 (Sept. 1980)-. — London : Modern English Publications in collaboration with the Regent School of Languages, 1980-. — v. : ill,maps,ports ; 25cm + sound cassette
Quarterly. — Cassette available with every issue. — Description based on: Vol.2, no.2 (Dec. 1981) [lacking the cassette]
ISSN 0262-7019 = Business express : £19.00 per year (5.60 for magazine only) B82-22682

808'.066651021 — English language. Business English — *Manuals*

Keenan, John. Feel free to write : a guide for business and professional people / John Keenan. — New York ; Chichester : Wiley, c1982. — xii,190p : ill ; 22cm
Bibliography: p185-186. — Includes index
ISBN 0-471-09696-2 : £7.35 B82-27723

808'.066651021 — English language. Business English — *Questions & answers*

Davies, Susan. Pitman business English / Susan Davies and Richard West. — London : Pitman, 1982
Includes index
1: Clerical. — viii,195p : ill,1map ; 30cm
ISBN 0-273-01617-2 (pbk) : Unpriced
B82-30557

Gillibrand, Patrick. The manager and his words / Patrick Gillibrand and Vivienne Maddock. — Oxford : Pergamon, 1982. — ix,128p : ill ; 25cm. — (Materials for language practice)
ISBN 0-08-028637-2 (pbk) : £4.50 : CIP rev.
B82-10599

808'.066651021 — English language. Business English — *Questions & answers — For non-English speaking students*

Methold, Ken. Office to office : practical business communication / K. Methold and J. Tadman. — Harlow : Longman, 1982. — 158p : ill,facsims ; 24cm
Includes index
ISBN 0-582-55324-5 (pbk) : £2.25 B82-21790

Moore, Brendan. English for business studies / Brendan Moore, Chris Parsons. — London : Macmillan, 1981. — viii,183p : ill,facsims ; 25cm
Includes index
ISBN 0-333-31735-1 (pbk) : Unpriced
B82-08379

Norman, Susan. We mean business : an elementary course in business English / Susan Norman. — Harlow : Longman
Teacher's book. — 1982. — xxix,185p : ill,facsims,forms,1geneal.table,1map ; 22cm
ISBN 0-582-51545-9 (pbk) : £2.50 B82-30194

Norman, Susan. We mean business : an elementary course in business English / Susan Norman. — Harlow : Longman
Workbook. — 1982. — 46p : ill ; 25cm
ISBN 0-582-74852-6 (pbk) : £0.80 B82-15197

Rowlands, K. E.. Management English / K.E. Rowlands. — London : Hodder and Stoughton
Project book. — 1980. — 80p : ill,plans,1form,facsim ; 25cm
ISBN 0-340-24417-8 (pbk) : £2.50 : CIP rev.
B80-03731

We mean business : an elementary course in business English. — Harlow : Longman
Students' bk. / Susan Norman and Eleanor Melville. — 1982. — iv,140p : ill,maps,facsims,forms ; 25cm
ISBN 0-582-51543-2 (pbk) : £2.25 B82-21796

808'.066651021 — English language. Business English. Writing skills

Londo, Richard J.. Common sense in business writing / Richard J. Londo. — New York : Macmillan ; London : Collier Macmillan, c1982. — x,470p : ill ; 26cm
Includes index
ISBN 0-02-371740-8 (pbk) : £9.75 B82-26384

808'.066658 — Reports. Writing — *Manuals — For management*

Pearsall, Thomas E.. How to write for the world of work / Thomas E. Pearsall, Donald H. Cunningham. — 2nd ed. — New York ; London : Holt, Rinehart and Winston, c1982. — xiii,397p : ill,forms ; 24cm
Previous ed.: 1978. — Text on inside cover. — Includes index
ISBN 0-03-059486-3 (pbk) : Unpriced
Also classified at 808'.066651021 B82-20713

808'.066658021 — United States. Business firms. Reports. Writing — *Manuals*

Poe, Roy W.. The McGraw-Hill guide to effective business reports / Roy W. Poe. — New York ; London : McGraw-Hill, c1982. — viii,208p : ill,1plan,forms ; 25cm
Bibliography: p170-171. — Includes index
ISBN 0-07-050341-9 : £15.50 B82-16884

Treece, Malra. Effective reports / Malra Treece. — Boston ; London : Allyn and Bacon, c1982. — ix,470p : ill ; 25cm
Bibliography: p464-468. — Includes index
ISBN 0-205-07703-x : Unpriced B82-26935

808'.06669021 — Buildings. Management. Manuals. Writing — *Manuals*

Building management manuals : a guide for practitioners / prepared by the Building Surveying Division, the Royal Institution of Chartered Surveyors. — London : Published on behalf of The Institution by Surveyors Publications, c1981. — 12p ; 30cm. — (A Practice note, ISSN 0143-3342)
Bibliography: p12
ISBN 0-85406-156-8 (unbound) : £2.60
B82-08053

808'.066791021 — Audiovisual materials. Scripts. Writing — *Manuals*

Swain, Dwight V.. Scripting for video and audiovisual media / Dwight V. Swain. — London : Focal, 1981. — 256p : ill,1map ; 24cm
Bibliography: p249. — Includes index
ISBN 0-240-51075-5 : Unpriced : CIP rev.
B81-02363

808'.066791021 — United States. Radio & television. Advertisements. Writing

Orlik, Peter B.. Broadcast copywriting / Peter B. Orlik. — 2nd ed. — Boston, Mass. ; London : Allyn and Bacon, c1982. — xiii,511p : ill,facsims,music ; 25cm
Previous ed.: Boston, Mass. : Holbrook Press, 1978. — Includes index
ISBN 0-205-07691-2 : Unpriced B82-28774

808'.0669021 — England. Secondary schools. Students, 15-16 years. Curriculum subjects: History. Essays. Writing — *Case studies*

D'Arcy, Pat. The examination years : writing in geography history and social studies / Pat D'Arcy. — London : Ward Lock Educational for the Schools Council, 1978. — 52p ; 21cm. — (Writing Across the Curriculum 11-16 Project publications)
Bibliography: p52
ISBN 0-7062-3652-1 (pbk) : £1.25
Primary classification 808'.06691021
B82-18669

808'.06691021 — England. Secondary schools. Students, 15-16 years. Curriculum subjects: Geography. Essays. Writing — *Case studies*

D'Arcy, Pat. The examination years : writing in geography history and social studies / Pat D'Arcy. — London : Ward Lock Educational for the Schools Council, 1978. — 52p ; 21cm. — (Writing Across the Curriculum 11-16 Project publications)
Bibliography: p52
ISBN 0-7062-3652-1 (pbk) : £1.25
Also classified at 808'.0669021 B82-18669

808'.06692021 — Living persons. Biographies. Writing & publishing — *Manuals*

Henderson-Luff, R. J.. Biography pioneering : a new and exciting business opportunity / by R.J. Henderson-Luff. — [Bath] ([50 Clevedon Rd., Midsomer Norton, Bath, Avon BA3 2ED]) : [Heritage Publications], [1981]. — 24leaves ; 30cm
Unpriced (pbk) B82-09741

808.06'8 — Children's literature in English. Composition — *Manuals*

Aiken, Joan. The way to write for children / Joan Aiken. — London : Elm Tree, 1982. — 97p ; 22cm. — (The way to write series)
ISBN 0-241-10745-8 (cased) : £7.95 : CIP rev.
ISBN 0-241-10746-6 (pbk) : £4.95 B82-09420

808.06'8 — Children's picture books. Writing. Techniques — *Manuals*

Roberts, Ellen E. M.. The children's picture book. — London : Poplar Press, Mar.1982. — [224]p
ISBN 0-907657-02-8 : £10.95 : CIP entry
B82-01409

808.1 — Great Britain. Schools. Curriculum subjects: Poetry in English. Composition. Teaching

Brownjohn, Sandy. What rhymes with 'secret'? : teaching children to write poetry / Sandy Brownjohn ; with a foreword by Ted Hughes. — London : Hodder and Stoughton, 1982. — 104p ; 22cm
Bibliography: p102-104
ISBN 0-340-28271-1 (pbk) : Unpriced : CIP rev. B82-10796

808.1 — Poetry

Raine, Kathleen. The inner journey of the poet : and other papers / by Kathleen Raine ; edited by Brian Keeble. — London : Allen & Unwin, 1982. — 208p,[8]p of plates : ill ; 23cm
ISBN 0-04-821054-4 : Unpriced : CIP rev.
B81-25869

Scannell, Vernon. How to enjoy poetry. — Loughton : Judy Piatkus, May 1982. — [192]p. — (Melvyn Bragg's arts series)
ISBN 0-86188-143-5 : £5.95 : CIP entry
B82-07055

808.1 — Poetry. Appreciation — *For schools*

Sadler, R. K.. Enjoying poetry. — London : Macmillan Education, Feb.1983. — [232]p
Originally published: Melbourne : Macmillan, 1981
ISBN 0-333-34028-0 (pbk) B82-38059

808.1 — Poetry. Composition

Baldwin, Michael. The way to write poetry / Michael Baldwin. — London : Elm Tree, 1982. — 111p ; 22cm. — ('The Way to write' series)
Includes index
ISBN 0-241-10748-2 (cased) : Unpriced : CIP rev.
ISBN 0-241-10749-0 (pbk) : £4.95 B82-11293

808.1 — Poetry in English. Composition — *For schools*

Rosen, Michael. I see a voice / Michael Rosen. — London : Thames, 1981. — 96p : ill,music,1port ; 21cm
ISBN 0-09-146861-2 (pbk) : Unpriced
B82-01920

808.1 — Poetry in English. Composition — *Personal observations*

Berryman, John. One answer to a question / by John Berryman. — Portree : Aquila, 1981. — [12]p ; 21cm. — (Aquila essays ; no.2)
ISBN 0-7275-0218-2 (pbk) : Unpriced
B82-25606

808.1 — Poetry — *Questions & answers — For schools*

Into verse. — London : Edward Arnold, Dec.1982. — [64]p
ISBN 0-7131-0800-2 (pbk) : £1.60 : CIP entry
B82-30200

808.1 — Poets

Corso, Gregory. Some of my beginnings and what I feel right now / by Gregory Corso. — Portree : Aquila, 1982. — [14]p ; 21cm. — (Aquila essays ; no.7)
ISBN 0-7275-0221-2 (pbk) : Unpriced
B82-25610

808.1'092'4 — Poetry. Theories of Horace

Brink, C. O.. Horace on poetry. — Cambridge : Cambridge University Press, Sept.1982. — [672]p
ISBN 0-521-20069-5 : £47.50 : CIP entry
B82-29366

808.1'092'4 — Poetry. Theories of Wordsworth, William, *1770-1850 related to* **philosophy of Whitehead, Alfred North**

Cappon, Alexander P.. About Wordsworth and Whitehead : a prelude to philosophy / by Alexander P. Cappon. — New York : Philosophical Library ; London : George Prior [distributor], c1982. — xi,190p ; 22cm
Includes index
ISBN 0-8022-2386-9 : £9.50
Primary classification 192 B82-24278

808.2 — Drama. Composition

Griffiths, Stuart. How plays are made. — London : Heinemann Educational, Oct.1982. — [128]p
ISBN 0-435-18380-x (pbk) : £3.95 : CIP entry
B82-23994

808.2 — Drama — *For schools*

Adland, David. Group approach to drama / David Adland. — 2nd ed. — Harlow : Longman
Teacher's book. — 1982. — 96p ; 21cm
Previous ed.: 1964. — Bibliography: p93-96
ISBN 0-582-21964-7 (pbk) : £1.95 B82-03297

808.2 — Drama. Theories — *Quotations — Collections*

Analytical sourcebook of concepts in dramatic theory / Oscar Lee Brownstein and Darlene M. Daubert. — Westport ; London : Greenwood Press, 1981. — xxi,560p ; 24cm
Includes index
ISBN 0-313-21309-7 : Unpriced B82-17884

808.2'2 — Television drama in English. Scripts. Writing

Ah! mischief : the writer and television / David Edgar ... [et al.]. — London : Faber, 1982. — 110p ; 22cm
ISBN 0-571-11881-x (pbk) : £2.95 : CIP rev.
B82-10763

808.3 — Fiction. Bestsellers. Composition — *Manuals*

Koontz, Dean R.. How to write best-selling fiction. — London (13 Burlington Lodge Studios, Rigault Rd., S.W.6.) : Poplar Press, Oct.1981. — [304]p
ISBN 0-907657-00-1 : £8.95 : CIP entry
B81-25742

808.3 — Fiction. Narrative — *Critical studies*

Elsbree, Langdon. The rituals of life : patterns in narratives / Langdon Elsbree. — Port Washington ; London : Kennikat, 1982. — viii,145p ; 22cm. — (Series in modern literary criticism) (National university publications)
Bibliography: p135-140. — Includes index
ISBN 0-8046-9295-5 : £12.75 B82-37697

808.3 — Fiction. Narrative. Linguistic aspects

Banfield, Ann. Unspeakable sentences : narration and representation in the language of fiction / Ann Banfield. — London : Routledge & Kegan Paul, 1982. — x,340p ; 22cm
Bibliography: p320-331. — Includes index
ISBN 0-7100-0905-4 : £15.95 B82-30998

808.3 — Fiction. Narrative. Spatial structure

Spatial form in narrative / edited by Jeffrey R. Smitten and Ann Daghistany ; with a foreword by Joseph Frank. — Ithaca ; London : Cornell University Press, 1981. — 275p ; 23cm
Bibliography: p248-263. — Includes index
ISBN 0-8014-1375-3 : £13.75 B82-12187

808.3 — Fiction. Narrative. Viewpoints

Lanser, Susan Sniader. The narrative act : point of view in prose fiction / Susan Sniader Lanser. — Princeton ; Guildford : Princeton University Press, c1981. — x,308p : ill ; 23cm
Bibliography: p295-300. — Includes index
ISBN 0-691-06486-5 : £14.80 B82-21005

808.4 — Essays. Composition — *Manuals*

Jenkins, John P.. Approaches to essay writing / John P. Jenkins and Vivian Summers. — Exeter : Wheaton, 1982. — 43p : ill ; 21cm
ISBN 0-08-025624-4 (pbk) : £0.85 B82-32262

808.4 — Essays in English. Composition — *Manuals*

Horton, Susan R.. Thinking through writing / Susan R. Horton. — Baltimore ; London : Johns Hopkins University Press, c1982. — x,217p : ill ; 24cm
Bibliography: p206-212. — Includes index
ISBN 0-8018-2716-7 (cased) : £18.00
ISBN 0-8018-2717-5 (pbk) : Unpriced
B82-34985

808.5 — Voice production — *Manuals*

Marafioti, P. Mario. Caruso's method of voice production : the scientific culture of the voice / by P. Mario Marafioti ; preface by Victor Maurel. — New York : Dover ; London : Constable, 1981, c1949. — xix,308p,2leaves of plates : ill,music,facsims,ports ; 22cm
Facsim of: 1st ed., New York : Appleton, 1922
ISBN 0-486-24180-7 (pbk) : £3.75 B82-13557

808.5'1 — Public speaking — *Manuals*

Atkins, Margaret Walsh. Meeting points : 'how to say a few words' / Margaret Walsh Atkins. — London (Murray House, Vandon St., SW1H 0AG) : Women's Corona Society, c1978. — 17p ; 21cm
Unpriced (unbound) B82-26363

Bower, Sharon. Painless public speaking. — Wellingborough : Thorsons, Oct.1982. — [240]p
ISBN 0-7225-0765-8 (pbk) : £3.50 : CIP entry
B82-24242

Castle, Dennis. Public speaking. — London : Hodder and Stoughton, Feb.1983. — [160]p
Originally published: Sevenoaks : Teach Yourself Books, 1980
ISBN 0-340-32160-1 (pbk) : £2.50 : CIP entry
B82-38025

Kenny, Peter. A handbook of public speaking for scientists and engineers. — Bristol : Hilger, Oct.1982. — [192]p
ISBN 0-85274-553-2 (pbk) : £6.00 : CIP entry
B82-24240

Speaking : back to fundamentals / Cal M. Logue ... [et al.]. — 3rd ed. — Boston, Mass. ; London : Allyn and Bacon, c1982. — ix,326p ; ill ; 24cm
Previous ed.: 1979. — Includes index
ISBN 0-205-07692-0 (pbk) : Unpriced
B82-27063

808.5'1 — Public speaking — *Manuals — For businessmen*

Janner, Greville. [The businessman's guide to speech-making and to the laws and conduct of meetings]. Janner's complete speechmaker : including compendium of draft speeches and retellable tales / Greville Janner ; cartoons by Calman and Tobi. — London : Business Books, 1981. — xii,324p : ill ; 23cm
Originally published: 1968. — Includes index
ISBN 0-09-142980-3 : Unpriced : CIP rev.
B81-27372

808.5'1 — Rhetorical communication

McCroskey, James C.. An introduction to rhetorical communication / James C. McCroskey. — 4th ed. — Englewood Cliffs ; London : Prentice-Hall, c1982. — xi,323p : ill ; 23cm
Previous ed.: 1978. — Includes index
ISBN 0-13-495457-2 (pbk) : £11.95
B82-20088

808.5'1'0240901 — Public speaking — *Manuals — For research workers*

Dixon, Diana, *19---*. Talking about your research / Diana Dixon and Philip Hills. — Leicester : Primary Communications Research Centre, c1981. — 36p : ill,2maps ; 21cm. — (Aids to scholarly communication, ISSN 0142-7288) (BL (R & D) report ; no.5640)
ISBN 0-906083-19-2 (pbk) : Unpriced : CIP rev. B81-21541

808.5'1'024657 — Public speaking — *Manuals — For accountancy*
Holgate, John, *1911-*. Effective speaking for accountants / John Holgate. — London : Institute of Chartered Accountants in England and Wales, 1981. — viii,88p : 2ill ; 21cm
ISBN 0-85291-308-7 (pbk) : Unpriced B82-11624

808.5'1'088329 — Newfoundland. Politicians. Public speaking, *1977-1979*
Paine, Robert. Ayatollahs & turkey trots : political rhetoric in the new Newfoundland : Crosbie, Jamieson and Peckford / by Robert Paine with Cynthia Lamson ; foreword by Dalton Camp. — St. John's ; London : Breakwater, c1981. — ix,147p,[16]p of plates : ill,ports ; 24cm
ISBN 0-919948-70-7 : Unpriced B82-37946

808.5'43 — Story-telling
Jackson, Gordon, *1938-*. The promised end : a century of observations on the philosophy & pattern of story, & the parables of Jesus / Gordon Jackson. — Lincoln (1 Stonefield Ave., Lincoln) : Asgill, 1981. — 38p ; 22cm
Limited ed. of 400 numbered copies
£0.90 (pbk) B82-08954

808.5'43 — Story-telling — *For children*
Allington, Richard. Stories. — Oxford : Blackwell Raintree, Nov.1982. — [32]p. — (Beginning to learn about)
ISBN 0-86256-057-8 : £2.95 : CIP entry B82-26069

808.56 — Conversation — *Manuals*
Carroll, Donald. Why didn't I say that?. — London : New English Library, Nov.1982. — [128]p
ISBN 0-450-05292-3 (pbk) : £1.25 : CIP entry B82-27524

808.56 — Conversation. Questioning — *Manuals*
Kaiser, Artur. Questioning techniques / Artur Kaiser ; [authorised translation by Norbert M. Lechelt and Ullah Marten]. — Farnham : Momenta, 1979. — 117p : forms ; 21cm
Translation of: Fragetechnik. — Bibliography: p117
ISBN 0-86164-103-5 (pbk) : £2.45 B82-01382

808.56 — Conversation. Structure
Goodwin, Charles. Conversational organization : interaction between speakers and hearers / Charles Goodwin. — New York ; London : Academic Press, 1981. — xii,195p : ill ; 24cm. — (Language, thought, and culture)
Bibliography: p179-189. — Includes index
ISBN 0-12-289780-3 : £17.20 B82-15535

808.6 — Correspondence in English — *Manuals*
Groves, Paul. Smudge and chewpen letters / Paul Groves, Nigel Grimshaw. — London : Edward Arnold, 1982. — 71p ; 22cm
ISBN 0-7131-0677-8 (pbk) : £1.50 : CIP rev. B82-06912

808.6 — Correspondence in French — *For schools*
Fowler, Ena. Amitiés / CSE and 'O' level letter-writing course ; Ena Fowler ; [illustrated by David Farris]. — London : Harrap, c1980. — 64p : ill ; 24cm
English and French text
ISBN 0-245-53544-6 (pbk) : £1.95 B82-18644

808.6 — Correspondence in Spanish — *Manuals — Spanish texts*
Jackson, Mary H.. Guide to correspondence in Spanish : a practical guide to social and commercial correspondence = Guía de correspondencía española / Mary H. Jackson. — Cheltenham : Thornes, 1981, c1978. — v,53p ; 23cm
Spanish text, English preface and vocabulario. — Originally published: Skokie : National Textbook, 1978
ISBN 0-85950-335-6 (pbk) : £2.75 : CIP rev. B81-23802

808.7 — Humour
Schaeffer, Neil. The art of laughter / Neil Schaeffer. — New York ; Guildford : Columbia University Press, 1981. — 166p ; 24cm
Includes index
ISBN 0-231-05224-3 : £13.30 B82-05628

808.8 — LITERATURE. GENERAL ANTHOLOGIES

808.8 — Scotland. Literature — *Critical studies*
Literature of the north. — Aberdeen : Aberdeen University Press, Jan.1983. — [224]p
ISBN 0-08-028453-1 (cased) : £9.00 : CIP entry
ISBN 0-08-028468-x (pbk) : £4.90 B82-36124

808.8'0024 — Literature, *ca 1500 — Anthologies — Manuscripts — Facsimiles*
The **Winchester** anthology. — Woodbridge : D.S. Brewer, Oct.1981. — [480]p
ISBN 0-85991-083-0 : £80.00 : CIP entry B81-27430

808.8'033256944 — Literature, *to 1980*. **Special subjects: Jerusalem** — *Anthologies*
Jerusalem : the Holy City in literature. — 2nd ed. — London : Kahn & Averill, Oct.1981. — [244]p
Previous ed.: London : Adam Books, 1968
ISBN 0-900707-65-8 (pbk) : £7.50 : CIP entry B81-30270

808.8'0353 — Literature, *to 1900*. **Special subjects: Sex relations** — *Anthologies*
The **Dirty** bits / collected and introduced by Lesley Cunliffe, Craig Brown and Jon Connell. — London : Deutsch, 1981. — vii,143p : ill ; 23cm
Text on lining papers. — Includes index
ISBN 0-233-97395-8 : £4.95 : CIP rev. B81-26739

808.8'0354 — Literature, *to 1981*. **Special sujects: Love** — *Anthologies — English texts*
A **World** of love. — London : Hamish Hamilton, Jan.1982. — [96]p
ISBN 0-241-10714-8 : £4.95 : CIP entry B81-34666

808.8'036 — Literature, *to 1980*. **Special subjects: Frogs** — *Anthologies — English texts*
Frogs / edited by Lynn Hughes. — London : W.H. Allen, 1982. — 56p : ill(some col.) ; 15cm
ISBN 0-491-02836-9 : £3.50 B82-13373

808.8'0375 — Literature, *to 1980*. **Special subjects: Unicorns** — *Anthologies — English texts*
Unicorns / edited by Jeanne Griffiths. — London : W.H. Allen, 1981. — 53p : ill(some col.) ; 15cm
ISBN 0-491-02785-0 : £2.50
Also classified at 760'.0447 B82-05025

808.81 — Poetry, *to 1981 — Anthologies — English texts*
Hall, Donald, *1928-*. To read poetry / Donald Hall. — New York ; London : Holt, Rinehart and Winston, c1982. — xxi,401p ; 24cm
Bibliography: p378-384. — Includes index
ISBN 0-03-060549-0 (pbk) : £9.95 B82-15348

La **Fontaine** fables and other poems. — Gerrards Cross : Colin Smythe, June 1982. — [144]p
Enlarged version of: By a lovely sea. Hong Kong : Hong Kong University Press, 1959
ISBN 0-86140-122-0 (pbk) : £5.00 : CIP entry B82-10699

808.81'9351 — Poetry in European languages, *ca 1570-1980*. **Special subjects: Mary**, *Queen of Scots — Anthologies — English texts*
Mary Queen of Scots : an anthology of poetry / chosen and with an introduction by Antonia Fraser ; illustrated by Rebecca Fraser. — London : Eyre Methuen, 1981. — 80p : ill ; 21cm
Includes index
ISBN 0-413-48550-1 : £4.50 : CIP rev. B81-23912

808.83'1 — Children's short stories in European languages, *to 1980 — Anthologies — English texts*
366 dreamtime stories. — London : Hodder & Stoughton Children's Books, Sept.1982. — [128]p
ISBN 0-340-28575-3 : £1.50 : CIP entry B82-18814

808.83'1 — Short stories, *1830-1980 — Anthologies*
Elements of fiction : an anthology / [compiled by] Robert Scholes. — New York ; Oxford : Oxford University Press, 1981. — x,998p ; 24cm
ISBN 0-19-502881-3 (pbk) : £7.95 B82-00501

808.83'1 — Short stories. Women writers, *1945-*. **Special subjects: Women** — *Anthologies — English texts*
Sex & sensibility / stories by contemporary women writers from nine countries. — London : Sidgwick & Jackson, 1981. — viii,248p : ports ; 23cm
'Translated and published simultaneously in America, Sweden, Germany, Italy, Holland, Spain, France, England and Israel'
ISBN 0-283-98670-0 : £6.95 B82-01626

808.86'9354 — Love letters, *ca 900-1947 — Anthologies — English texts*
Written with love : passionate love-letters / selected by Barbara Cartland. — London : Hutchinson, 1981. — 110p ; 21cm
ISBN 0-09-146620-2 : £2.95 : CIP rev. B81-30207

808.88'2 — Quotations — *For Christianity*
The **Hodder** book of Christian quotations. — London : Hodder & Stoughton, Oct.1982. — [320]p
ISBN 0-340-32339-6 (cased) : £8.95 : CIP entry
ISBN 0-340-32338-8 (pbk) : £5.95 B82-24844

808.88'7 — Insults, *to 1980 — Anthologies — English texts*
The **Encyclopaedia** of insulting behaviour. — London : Futura, 1981. — 191p : ill ; 18cm
ISBN 0-7088-2085-9 (pbk) : £1.25 B82-06628

McPhee, Nancy. The second book of insults. — London : New English Library, Nov.1982. — [144]p
Originally published: London : Deutsch, 1981
ISBN 0-450-05518-3 (pbk) : £1.25 : CIP entry B82-27527

809 — LITERATURE. HISTORY AND CRITICAL STUDIES

809 — European literatures, *ca 1600-1960 — Philosophical perspectives — Conference proceedings*
The **Philosophical** reflection of man in literature : selected papers from several conferences held by the International Society for Phenomenology and Literature in Cambridge, Massachusetts / edited by Anna-Teresa Tymieniecka. — Dordrecht ; London : Reidel, c1982. — xi,485p ; 23cm. — (Analecta husserliana ; v.12)
Includes index
ISBN 90-277-1312-x : Unpriced B82-23505

809 — Literature — *Critical studies*
Auden, W. H.. A certain world. — London : Faber, Sept.1982. — [464]p
Originally published: 1971
ISBN 0-571-11940-9 (pbk) : £5.95 : CIP entry B82-25171

Burroughs, William S.. The third mind / William S. Burroughs and Brion Gysin. — London : Calder, 1979. — 194p : ill ; 21cm
Originally published: New York : Viking, 1978
ISBN 0-7145-3862-0 (cased) : Unpriced
ISBN 0-7145-3737-3 B82-12523

Lukács, Georg. Reviews and articles from Die rote Fahne. — London : Merlin Press, Mar.1982. — [80]p
Translation from the German
ISBN 0-85036-281-4 (pbk) : £2.50 : CIP entry B82-06253

Oates, Joyce Carol. Contraries : essays / Joyce Carol Oates. — New York : Oxford University Press [1981]. — xi,187p ; 22cm
ISBN 0-19-502884-8 : £10.00 B82-05420

809 — Literature — *Critical studies*
continuation

Weiss, Theodore. The man from Porlock : engagements, 1944-1981 / Theodore Weiss. — Princeton ; Guildford : Princeton University Press, c1982. — 320p ; 25cm. — (Princeton series of collected essays)
ISBN 0-691-06518-7 (cased) : £24.70
ISBN 0-691-01396-9 (pbk) : £7.05 B82-37431

809 — Literature — *Critical studies* — *Serials*

Strathclyde modern language studies : occasional papers presented in the Department of Modern Languages of the University of Strathclyde. — Vol.1-. — Glasgow (Livingstone Tower, 26 Richmond St., Glasgow G1 1XH) : Department of Modern Languages, University of Strathclyde, 1981-. — v. ; 21cm
Irregular
ISSN 0261-099x = Strathclyde modern language studies : £1.00 per issue
Also classified at 410′.5 B82-04890

809′.02 — European literatures. Courtly literature — *Critical studies* — *Conference proceedings*

International Courtly Literature Society Congress *(3rd : 1980 : Liverpool)*. Court and poet : selected proceedings of the Third Congress of the International Courtly Literature Society (Liverpool 1980) / edited by Glyn S. Burgess ; assistant editors A.D. Deyermond ... [et al.]. — Liverpool : Francis Cairns, c1981. — xii,364p ; 23cm. — (Arca, ISSN 0309-5541 ; 5)
ISBN 0-905205-06-5 : £15.00 B82-02820

809′.02 — Literature, *ca 500-1500* — *Critical studies* — *Serials*

Assays : critical approaches to Medieval and Renaissance texts. — Vol.1-. — Pittsburgh : University of Pittsburgh Press ; London : Feffer and Simons, 1981-. — v. ; 24cm
Annual
Unpriced B82-23584

809′.03 — Literature *1558-1982* — *Critical studies*

Bradbrook, M. C.. The collected papers of Muriel Bradbrook. — Brighton : Harvester Press
Vol.2: Women and literature, 1779-1982. — Oct.1982. — [192]p
ISBN 0-7108-0401-6 : £18.95 : CIP entry B82-23181

809′.03 — Literature, *1837-1968* — *Critical studies*

Trilling, Lionel. Speaking of literature and society. — Oxford : Oxford University Press, Jan.1982. — [445]p. — (The works of Lionel Trilling)
ISBN 0-19-212221-5 : £9.95 : CIP entry B81-34373

809′.033 — European literatures, *1789-1800* **Influence of political events in France** *1789* — *Sociological perspectives* — *conference proceedings*

1789: reading writing revolution. — Colchester : University of Essex, Department of Literature, July 1982. — [300]p
Conference papers
ISBN 0-901726-19-2 (pbk) : £5.95 : CIP entry B82-21763

809′.04 — European literatures. Writers, *1900-* — *Interviews*

Writers at work : the Paris review interviews. — Harmondsworth : Penguin
Originally published: New York : Viking, 1967 ; London : Secker & Warburg, 1968
3rd ser. / edited by George Plimpton ; introduced by Alfred Kazin. — 1977, c1967 (1982 [printing]). — xv,368p : facsims,ports ; 20cm
ISBN 0-14-004542-2 (pbk) : £2.95 B82-37817

809′.04 — Western European literatures. Influence of Wagner, Richard, *ca 1880-1980*

Furness, Raymond. Wagner and literature / Raymond Furness. — Manchester : Manchester University Press, c1982. — xiii,159p : ill ; 24cm
Bibliography: p149-154. — Includes index
ISBN 0-7190-0844-1 : £14.50 : CIP rev. B81-31242

809.1 — Poetry — *Critical studies*

Bloom, Harold. The breaking of the vessels / Harold Bloom. — Chicago ; London : University of Chicago Press, 1982. — xiii,107p ; 21cm. — (The Wellek Library lectures at the University of California, Irvine)
ISBN 0-226-06043-8 : Unpriced B82-35073

Grigson, Geoffrey. The private art. — London : Allison & Busby, Feb.1982. — [160]p
ISBN 0-85031-420-8 : £7.95 : CIP entry B82-02461

Lipking, Lawrence. The life of the poet : beginning and ending poetic careers / Lawrence Lipking. — Chicago ; London : University of Chicago Press, 1981. — xvi,243p : ill ; 24cm
Includes index
ISBN 0-226-48450-5 : £14.00 B82-17772

809.1 — Poetry, *to ca 1980* — *Critical studies* — *For African students*

Finnegan, Eddie. Essential poetry : for Ordinary Level and School Certificate : a guided course / Eddie Finnegan & Brian O′Mahony. — London : Heinemann, 1981. — viii,116p : ill ; 22cm
ISBN 0-435-92256-4 (pbk) : Unpriced B82-05072

809.1′024 — Poetry in European languages, *1500-1600* — *Critical studies*

Greene, Thomas M.. The light in Troy. — London : Yale University Press, Aug.1982. — [368]p. — (Elizabethan Club series ; 7)
ISBN 0-300-02765-6 : £21.00 : CIP entry B82-27189

809.1′034 — Poetry, *1850-1967* — *Critical studies*

Hamburger, Michael. The truth of poetry. — London : Methuen, Nov.1982. — [352]p
Originally published: London : Weidenfeld & Nicolson, 1969
ISBN 0-416-34240-x (pbk) : £4.95 : CIP entry B82-28292

809.1′034 — Poetry in European languages, *1850-ca 1970* — *Critical studies*

Hamburger, Michael. The truth of poetry. — New ed. — Manchester : Carcanet Press, Nov.1982. — [360]p
Previous ed.: London : Weidenfeld & Nicolson, 1969
ISBN 0-85635-438-4 : £9.95 : CIP entry B82-26327

809.1′034 — Poetry in European languages, *1900-* — *Critical studies*

Pilling, John. A reader′s guide to fifty modern European poets. — London : Heinemann Educational, Sept.1982. — [468]p
ISBN 0-435-18724-4 : £9.50 : CIP entry B82-20630

809.1′04 — Poetry in European languages, *1908-1918.* **Modernism** — *Critical studies*

Hermans, Theo. The structure of modernist poetry / Theo Hermans. — London : Croom Helm, c1982. — 264p ; 23cm
Bibliography: p249-260. — Includes index
ISBN 0-7099-0002-3 : £14.95 : CIP rev. B81-34303

809.1′3 — Epic poetry — *Critical studies*

DuBois, Page. History, rhetorical description and the epic : from Homer to Spenser / Page DuBois. — Cambridge : Brewer, 1982. — 130p ; 25cm
Includes index
ISBN 0-85991-093-8 : £15.00 : CIP rev. B82-10886

809.1′3 — Epic poetry in European languages, *1450-1600* — *Critical studies*

Fichter, Andrew. Poets historical. — London : Yale University Press, Sept.1982. — [238]p
ISBN 0-300-02721-4 : £14.00 : CIP entry B82-29119

809′.1′3 — Epic poetry in European languages, *to 1200.* **Characters: Heroes & kings** — *Critical studies*

Jackson, W. T. H.. The hero and the king : an epic theme / W.T.H. Jackson. — New York ; Guildford : Columbia University Press, 1982. — viii,141p ; 22cm
Bibliography: p139-141
ISBN 0-231-05354-1 : £14.45 B82-21494

809.1′9354 — Love poetry in European languages, *ca 1200-ca 1600* — *Critical studies*

Regan, Mariann Sanders. Love words : the self and the text in medieval and renaissance poetry / Mariann Sanders Regan. — Ithaca ; London : Cornell University Press, 1982. — 284p ; 23cm
Includes index
ISBN 0-8014-1415-6 : £14.75 B82-35758

809.1′9382 — Islamic poetry, *to 1980* — *Critical studies*

Schimmel, Annemarie. As through a veil : mystical poetry in Islam / Annemarie Schimmel. — New York ; Guildford : Columbia University Press, 1982. — x,359p,8p of plates : ill,1facsim ; 22cm. — (Lectures on the history of religions. New series ; no. 12)
Bibliography: p293-326. — Includes index
ISBN 0-231-05246-4 : £19.90 B82-32691

809.2 — Drama — *Critical studies* — *For African students*

Crow, Brian. Studying drama. — London : Longman, Nov.1982. — [192]p
ISBN 0-582-64425-9 (pbk) : £3.95 : CIP entry B82-26542

809.2 — Drama. Dialogue — *Critical studies*

Kennedy, Andrew K.. Dramatic dialogue. — Cambridge : Cambridge University Press, Nov.1982. — [283]p
ISBN 0-521-24620-2 (cased) : £25.00 : CIP entry
ISBN 0-521-28845-2 (pbk) : £7.50 B82-29389

809.2 — Drama, *to 1980.* **Mimesis**

Drama and mimesis. — Cambridge : Cambridge University Press, 1980. — xix,265p : ill ; 24cm. — (Themes in drama ; 2)
Includes index
ISBN 0-521-22179-x : £17.50 B82-26370

809.2′0096 — Drama. African writers — *Critical studies*

Etherton, Michael. The development of African drama / Michael Etherton. — London : Hutchinson, 1982. — 368p : ill ; 22cm. — (Hutchinson university library for Africa)
Bibliography: p358-363. — Includes index
ISBN 0-09-146420-x (cased) : Unpriced : CIP rev.
ISBN 0-09-146421-8 (pbk) : £5.95 B82-00266

809.2′512 — Drama in European languages. Tragedies, *1870-1980* — *Sociological perspectives*

Orr, John. Tragic drama and modern society : studies in the social and literary theory of drama from 1870 to the present / John Orr. — London : Macmillan, 1981. — xix,280p ; 23cm
Bibliography: p270-275. — Includes index
ISBN 0-333-24083-9 : £15.00 B82-10833

809.2′915 — Drama in European languages, *ca 1600-1980.* **Symbolism** — *Critical studies*

Drama and symbolism / [edited by James Redmond]. — Cambridge : Cambridge University Press, 1982. — x,264p : ill ; 24cm. — (Themes in drama ; 4)
Includes index
ISBN 0-521-22181-1 : £19.50 : CIP rev. B82-00235

809.3 — Fiction. Forms: Novels, *to 1979* — *Critical studies*

Knight, Everett W.. The novel as structure and praxis : from Cervantes to Malraux / Everett W. Knight. — Atlantic Highlands : Humanities ; Gloucester : distributed by Sutton, c1980. — 214p ; 23cm
ISBN 0-391-00938-9 : Unpriced B82-38117

Miller, J. Hillis. Fiction and repetition. — Oxford : Basil Blackwell, Apr.1982. — [256]p
ISBN 0-631-13032-2 : £12.50 : CIP entry B82-04586

809.3 — Fiction in European languages, *to 1981.* **Forms: Novels** — *Sociological perspectives*
Jones, Gwyn, *1907-*. Y nofel a chymdeithas = The novel and society / Gwyn Jones. — [Bangor, Gwynedd] ([10 Wellfield House, Bangor, Gwyneed LL57 1ER]) : North Wales Arts Association, 1981, c1980. — [28]p ; 22cm. — (Darlith Ben Bowen Thomas = Ben Bowen Thomas lecture)
Parallel Welsh and English text
ISBN 0-901833-99-1 (pbk) : Unpriced
B82-00708

809.3′876 — Science fiction, *to 1969* — *Critical studies*
Rose, Mark. Alien encounters : anatomy of science fiction / Mark Rose. — Cambridge, Mass. ; London : Harvard University Press, 1981. — 216p ; 22cm
Includes index
ISBN 0-674-01565-7 : £9.10 B82-03757

809.3′034 — Fiction. Forms: Novels, *1800-1900* — *Critical studies*
The **Nineteenth-century** novel : critical essays and documents / edited by Arnold Kettle. — Revised ed. — London : Heinemann Educational in association with the Open University Press, 1981. — 351p ; 20cm
Previous ed.: 1972. — Includes index
ISBN 0-435-18515-2 (pbk) : £3.95 B82-09828

809.3′04 — Fiction in European languages, *1900-1945.* **Influence of Nietzsche, Friedrich**
Foster, John Burt. Heirs to Dionysus : a Nietzchean current in literary modernism / John Burt Foster, Jr.. — Princeton, N.J. ; Guildford : Princeton University Press, c1981. — xiv,474p ; 23cm
Includes index
ISBN 0-691-06480-6 : £19.30 B82-19599

809.3′04 — Fiction in European languages, *1900-1950* — *Critical studies*
Savater, Fernando. Childhood regained : the art of the storyteller / Fernando Savater ; translated by Frances M. López-Morillas. — New York ; Guildford : Columbia University Press, 1982. — xv,208p : ill ; 24cm. — (European perspectives)
Translation of: La infancia recuperada
ISBN 0-231-05320-7 : £12.30 B82-21495

809.3′876 — Science fiction, *to 1900.* **Special subjects: Moon. Manned space flight** — *Critical studies*
Ridley, F. A.. Three lunar vogages / by F.A. Ridley. — [London] (Limehouse Town Hall, E14) : Museum of Labour History, 1980. — [14]p ; 21cm. — (Hyde Park pamphlet ; no.1)
Originally published: in ′New World antiquity′, vol.24, nos.11 and 12, Nov.-Dec. 1977, as Early speculations about Selene
Unpriced (unbound) B82-15126

809.3′912 — Fiction in European languages, *1840-1962.* **Realism** *related to* **myth**
Lucente, Gregory L.. The narrative of realism and myth : Verga, Lawrence, Faulkner, Pavese / Gregory L. Lucente. — Baltimore ; London : Johns Hopkins University Press, c1981. — xi,189p : 3ill ; 24cm
Includes index
ISBN 0-8018-2609-8 : Unpriced
Primary classification 809.3′915 B82-16987

809.3′915 — Fiction in European languages, *1840-1962.* **Myth** *related to* **realism**
Lucente, Gregory L.. The narrative of realism and myth : Verga, Lawrence, Faulkner, Pavese / Gregory L. Lucente. — Baltimore ; London : Johns Hopkins University Press, c1981. — xi,189p : 3ill ; 24cm
Includes index
ISBN 0-8018-2609-8 : Unpriced
Also classified at 809.3′912 B82-16987

809.3′915 — Fiction in European languages, *1860-1980.* **Fantasy** — *Critical studies*
Brooke-Rose, Christine. A rhetoric of the unreal : studies in narrative and structure, especially of the fantastic / Christine Brooke-Rose. — Cambridge : Cambridge University Press, 1981. — vii,446p ; 23cm
Bibliography: p417-431. — Includes index
ISBN 0-521-22561-2 : £25.00 B82-00976

809.3′916 — Horror stories, *to 1980* — *Critical studies*
King, Stephen, *1947-*. Stephen King′s Danse macabre. — [London] : Futura, 1982, c1981. — 479p ; 18cm. — (A Futura book)
Originally published: New York : Everest House, 1980 ; London : Macdonald, 1981. — Bibliography: p466-468. — List of films: p463-465. — Includes index
ISBN 0-7088-2181-2 (pbk) : £2.50 B82-34731

809.3′923 — Fiction. Forms: Novels, *to 1980.* **First-person narrative** — *Critical studies*
Kawin, Bruce F.. The mind of the novel : reflexive fiction and the ineffable / Bruce F. Kawin. — Princeton ; Guildford : Princeton University Press, c1982. — xiv,376p ; 23cm
Bibliography: p357-369. — Includes index
ISBN 0-691-06509-8 : £17.70 B82-41122

809.3′9353 — Fiction in European languages, *1800-1900.* **Special subjects: Physiognomy** — *Critical studies*
Tytler, Graeme. Physiognomy in the European novel : faces and fortunes / by Graeme Tytler. — Princeton ; Guilford : Princeton University Press, c1982. — xix,436p : ill,1facsim,ports ; 23cm
Bibliography: p393-419. — Includes index
ISBN 0-691-06491-1 : £19.10 B82-23391

809.3′937 — Fiction in European languages, *ca 1600-ca 1954.* **Special themes: Magic** — *Critical studies*
Wilson, Anne. Magical thought in creative writing. — South Woodchester (Lockwood, Station Rd, South Woodchester, Stroud, Glos. GL5 5EQ) : Thimble Press, Nov.1982. — [176]p
ISBN 0-903355-09-4 : £9.50 : CIP entry
B82-26719

809′.889′24 — Jewish literature, *1900-1981* — *Critical studies*
Baumgarten, Murray. City scriptures : modern Jewish writing / Murray Baumgarten. — Cambridge, Mass. ; London : Harvard University Press, 1982. — viii,185p ; 24cm
Includes index
ISBN 0-674-13278-5 : £12.95 B82-36049

809′.88924 — Jewish literature, *1900-1981* — *Critical studies*
Yudkin, Leon I.. Jewish writing and identity in the twentieth century / Leon Israel Yudkin. — London : Croom Helm, c1982. — 166p ; 23cm
Bibliography: p159-164. — Includes index
ISBN 0-7099-2900-5 : £11.95 : CIP rev.
B81-33889

809′.891821 — Western European literature. Caribbean writers. Influence of resistance movements of Caribbean region, *to 1980*
Cudjoe, Selwyn R.. Resistance and Caribbean literature / Selwyn R. Cudjoe. — Chicago ; London : Ohio University Press, c1980. — xii,319p ; 23cm
Bibliography: p301-307. — Includes index
ISBN 0-8214-0353-2 (cased) : £14.00
ISBN 0-8214-0573-x (pbk) : Unpriced
B82-15530

809′.891821 — Western European literatures. Caribbean negro writers — *Critical studies*
Dathorne, O. R.. Dark ancestor : the literature of the Black man in the Caribbean / O.R. Dathorne. — Baton Rouge ; London : Louisiana State University Press, c1981. — x,288p ; 24cm
Bibliography: p267-278. — Includes index
ISBN 0-8071-0757-3 : £14.00 B82-03478

809′.891823 — Literatures. Pacific region writers. Cultural aspects
Writers in East-West encounter : new cultural bearings / edited by Guy Amirthanayagam. — London : Macmillan, 1982. — xii,218p ; 23cm
Includes index
ISBN 0-333-27342-7 : £15.00 B82-20944

809′.89282 — Children′s literature
Marshall, Margaret R.. An introduction to the world of children′s books. — Aldershot : Gower, Apr.1982. — [192]p. — (A Grafton book)
ISBN 0-566-03437-9 : £9.50 : CIP entry
B82-09215

809′.89282 — Children′s literature — *Critical studies* — *Conference proceedings*
Loughborough International Conference on Children′s Literature *(14th : 1981 : Dublin)*. Loughborough ′81 : conference proceedings. — Dublin (c/o Dublin Public Libraries, Central Department, Cumberland House, Fenian St., Dublin 2) : Committee of 14th Loughborough International Conference on Children′s Literature, 1982. — 94p ; 30cm
ISBN 0-9508134-0-0 (pbk) : Unpriced
B82-35123

809′.89282 — Children′s literature — *Critical studies* — *Serials*
[Children′s literature *(New Haven)***]Children′s** literature. — Vol.10. — London : Yale University Press, Mar.1982. — [240]p
ISBN 0-300-02805-9 (cased) : £14.00 : CIP entry
ISBN 0-300-02806-7 (pbk) : £6.25 B82-12679

809′.89287 — African literatures. Women writers, *1964-1979* — *Critical studies*
Brown, Lloyd W.. Women writers in Black Africa / Lloyd W. Brown. — Westport, Conn. ; London : Greenwood Press, 1981. — 204p ; 22cm. — (Contributions in women′s studies, ISSN 0147-104x ; no.21)
Bibliography: p191-196. — Includes index
ISBN 0-313-22540-0 : Unpriced B82-01943

809′.89287 — Literature. Women writers — *Feminist viewpoints* — *Serials*
Women and writing newsletter. — 1-. — Middlesbrough (c/o Ms R. O′Rourke, Adult Education Centre, 37 Harrow Rd, Middlesbrough, [Cleveland]) : [s.n.], [198-?]-. — v. ; 30cm
Irregular. — Description based on: 5
Unpriced B82-26153

809′.896 — African literatures, *to 1980* — *Critical studies*
Nkosi, Lewis. Tasks and masks : themes and styles of African literature / Lewis Nkosi. — Harlow : Longman, 1981. — 202p ; 23cm. — (Longman studies in African literature)
Includes index
ISBN 0-582-64145-4 (cased) : Unpriced : CIP rev.
ISBN 0-582-64146-2 (pbk) : £4.50 B82-01125

809′.896′0222 — Literatures. African writers — *Illustrations*
Hallett, George. African writers portfolio / George Hallett. — London : Heinemann Educational, [1981?]. — 1portfolio : ports ; 43cm. — (African writers series)
ISBN 0-435-90502-3 : Unpriced B82-05100

809′.8966 — Literatures. West African writers, *1930-1970* — *Critical studies*
Taiwo, Oladele. An introduction to West African literature / by Oladele Taiwo. — Walton-on-Thames : Nelson, 1967 (1981 [printing]). — 191p ; 22cm
Bibliography: p183-185. — Includes index
ISBN 0-17-511277-0 (pbk) : Unpriced
B82-05979

809′.91 — Literature. Irony
Muecke, D. C.. Irony and the ironic / D.C. Muecke. — 2nd ed. — London : Methuen, 1982. — 110p ; 20cm. — (The Critical idiom ; 13)
Previous ed.: published as Irony. 1970. — Bibliography: p102-106. — Includes index
ISBN 0-416-32940-3 (cased) : Unpriced : CIP rev.
ISBN 0-416-32860-1 (pbk) : Unpriced
B82-06758

809′.912 — Literature. Realism
Bell, Michael. The sentiment of reality. — London : Allen and Unwin, Feb.1983. — [224]p
ISBN 0-04-801023-5 : £12.50 : CIP entry
B82-36452

809′.9145 — European literatures, *1700-1800.* **Romanticism** — *Critical studies*
Thacker, Christopher. The wildness pleases : the origins of romanticism. — London : Croom Helm, Feb.1983. — [288]p
ISBN 0-7099-2409-7 : £20.00 : CIP entry
B82-38897

809′.9145 — European literatures, *1740-1830.* **Romanticism** — *Critical studies*

Morse, David, *1938-*. Romanticism : a structural analysis / David Morse. — London : Macmillan, 1982. — ix,306p ; 23cm
Includes index
ISBN 0-333-28297-3 : £15.00 B82-32409

809′.9145 — European literatures, *1797-1850.* **Romanticism** — *Critical studies*

Macpherson, Jay. The spirit of solitude. — London : Yale University Press, July 1982. — [364]p
ISBN 0-300-02632-3 : £18.50 : CIP entry B82-22785

809′.915 — European literatures, *300-1920.* **Allegory, myth & symbolism**

Allegory, myth and symbol / edited by Morton W. Bloomfield. — Cambridge, Mass. ; London : Harvard University Press, 1981. — x,390p ; 22cm. — (Harvard English studies ; 9)
ISBN 0-674-01640-8 (cased) : £21.00
ISBN 0-674-01641-6 (pbk) : Unpriced B82-27090

809′.915 — Western European literatures, *1900-*. **Myth. Criticism** — *Structuralist perspectives*

Gould, Eric. Mythical intentions in modern literature / Eric Gould. — Pinceton ; Guildford : Pinceton University Press, c1981. — ix,279p ; 23cm
Bibliography: p273-276. — Includes index
ISBN 0-691-06482-2 : £15.40 B82-11654

809′.915 — Western European literatures. Allegory. Theories, *B.C.400-1400*

Rollinson, Philip. Classical theories of allegory and Christian culture / by Philip Rollinson ; with an appendix on primary Greek sources by Patricia Matsen. — Pittsburgh : Duquesne University Press ; Brighton : Harvester, c1981. — xx,175p ; 24cm. — (Duquesne studies. Language and literature series ; v.3)
Includes index
ISBN 0-7108-0386-9 : £18.95 B82-07356

809′.916 — Literature. Tragedy *compared with* **Passion of Christ**

Anderson, David, *1919-*. The passion of man in gospel and literature / David Anderson. — [London] : BRF, 1980. — 104p ; 20cm. — (BRF book club ; no.8)
Includes index
ISBN 0-900164-53-0 (pbk) : £1.75
Primary classification 232.9′6 B82-15085

809′.923 — Narrative literature. Characters: Women — *Critical studies*

May, Keith M.. Characters of women in narrative literature / Keith M. May. — London : Macmillan, 1981. — 182p ; 23cm
Bibliography: p176-178. — Includes index
ISBN 0-333-30054-8 : £15.00 B82-06650

809′.927 — European literatures, *to ca 1970.* **Comic characters** — *Critical studies*

McFadden, George. Discovering the comic / George McFadden. — Princeton ; Guildford : Princeton University Press, c1982. — 268p : ill ; 23cm
Bibliography: p255-262. — Includes index
ISBN 0-691-06496-2 : Unpriced B82-20335

809′.927 — Literature. Eponymous characters — *Encyclopaedias*

Forrest, A. J.. Forrest′s dictionary of eponymous fictions. — Brandon : A.J. Forrest, 1982. — 30p ; 16cm
Cover title
ISBN 0-9508054-0-8 (pbk) : £1.00 B82-23653

809′.9332 — Literature, *to 1981.* **Special subjects: Travel** — *Critical studies*

The **Art** of travel. — London : Cass, Oct.1982. — [176]p
ISBN 0-7146-3205-8 : £9.95 : CIP entry B82-30325

809′.93321732 — European literatuares, *1800-1980.* **Special themes: Cities** — *Critical studies*

Pike, Burton. The image of the city in modern literature / by Burton Pike. — Princeton ; Guildford : Princeton University Press, c1981. — xv,168p ; 23cm. — (Princeton essays in literature)
Bibliography: p153-162. — Includes index
ISBN 0-691-06488-1 : £10.50 B82-05880

809′.9335 — Western literatures, *to ca 1967.* **Special subjects: Adventure** — *Critical studies*

Zweig, Paul. The adventurer / Paul Zweig. — Princeton ; Guildford : Princeton University Press, 1981, c1974. — x,275p : ill ; 22cm
Originally published: New York : Basic books ; London : Dent, 1974. — Includes index
ISBN 0-691-06451-2 (cased) : Unpriced
ISBN 0-691-01387-x (pbk) : £4.20 B82-17161

809′.933520625 — Literature. Special subjects: Peasants. Social life — *Conference proceedings*

Peasants and countrymen in literature : a symposium organised by the English Department of the Roehampton Institute in February 1981 / edited by Kathleen Parkinson and Martin Priestman. — [London] : English Dept. of the Roehampton Institute of Higher Education, c1982. — 210p : ill ; 21cm
ISBN 0-9507975-0-2 (pbk) : £2.00 B82-21841

809′.93353 — European literatures, *1000-1500.* **Special subjects: Knighthood** — *Critical studies*

Knighthood in medieval literature / edited by W.H. Jackson. — Woodbridge : Brewer, c1981. — 105p ; 25cm
ISBN 0-85991-094-6 : £9.50 : CIP rev. B82-08424

809′.933′53 — Literature. Special subjects: Prostitution — *Critical studies*

Kishtaing, Khalid. The prostitute in progressive literature. — London : Allison & Busby, July 1982. — [144]p
ISBN 0-85031-439-9 : CIP entry B82-16231

809′.93353 — Literature. Special subjects: Sex relations — *Critical studies*

Atkins, John, *1916-*. Sex in literature. — London : John Calder
Vol.4: High noon. — Jan.1982. — [320]p
ISBN 0-7145-3756-x : £9.95 : CIP entry B81-33834

809′.93354 — Literature, *to ca 1350.* **Special themes: Courtly love** — *Critical studies*

O′Donoghue, Bernard. The courtly love tradition. — Manchester : Manchester University Press, Nov.1982. — [192]p. — (Literature in context ; 5)
ISBN 0-7190-0887-5 (cased) : £12.50 : CIP entry
ISBN 0-7190-0910-3 (pbk) : £4.50 B82-29017

809′.93358 — Literature. Special themes: Political events, *1965-1975*

Cantor, Jay. The space between : literature and politics / Jay Cantor. — Baltimore ; London : Johns Hopkins University Press, c1981. — xviii,163p : ill ; 24cm
Bibliography: p159-163
ISBN 0-8018-2672-1 : £8.25 B82-39775

809′.9337 — European literatures. Grail legends

Matthews, John. The grail : quest for the eternal / John Matthews. — London : Thames and Hudson, c1981. — 96p : ill(some col.) ; 28cm. — (Art and imagination)
Bibliography: p96
ISBN 0-500-81027-3 (pbk) : £3.95 B82-01786

809′.9337 — European literatures. Special themes: Metamorphoses — *Critical studies*

Skulsky, Harold. Metamorphosis : the mind in exile / Harold Skulsky. — Cambridge, Mass. ; London : Harvard University Press, 1981. — 244p ; 24cm
Includes index
ISBN 0-674-57085-5 : £11.55 B82-03870

809′.93384 — European literature, *1558-*. **Special themes: Man** — *Philosophical perspectives*

Kolenda, Konstantin. Philosophy in literature : metaphysical darkness and ethical light / Konstantin Kolenda. — London : Macmillan, 1982. — xii,237p ; 23cm
Includes index
ISBN 0-333-31282-1 : £15.00 B82-28395

809′.93384 — Literature, *1745-1900.* **Special subjects: Self** — *Critical studies*

Garber, Frederick. The autonomy of the self from Richardson to Huysmans / Frederick Garber. — Princeton ; Guildford : Princeton University Press, c1982. — xi,326p ; 23cm
Includes index
ISBN 0-691-06481-4 : £17.60 B82-21061

809′.93522 — Bible. Literary aspects

Frye, Northrop. The great code : the Bible and literature / Northrop Frye. — London : Routledge & Kegan Paul, 1982. — xxiii,261p : ill ; 25cm
ISBN 0-7100-9038-2 : £9.95 : CIP rev. B82-12013

809′.935′92 — European literatures. Autobiographical works, *400-1850* — *Critical studies*

Spengemann, William C.. The forms of autobiography. — London : Yale University Press, Aug.1982. — [254]p
ISBN 0-300-02886-5 (pbk) : £6.00 : CIP entry B82-26698

810 — AMERICAN LITERATURE

810.8′09287 — English literature. New England women writers, *1607-1900* — *Anthologies*

The **Writing** women of New England, 1630-1900 : an anthology / edited by Arlen Gilman Runzler Westbrook and Perry D. Westbrook. — Metuchen, N.J. ; London : Scarecrow, 1982. — vii,273p ; 23cm
ISBN 0-8108-1544-3 : £13.20 B82-38244

810.8′09729 — English literature. Caribbean writers, *1945-* — *Anthologies*

An **Anthology** of African and Caribbean writing in English. — London : Heinemann Educational in association with the Open University, Dec.1982. — [320]p. — (Open University Third World readers ; 2)
ISBN 0-435-91297-6 (pbk) : £5.95 : CIP entry
Primary classification 820.8′096 B82-29773

810.9 — AMERICAN LITERATURE. HISTORY AND CRITICAL STUDIES

810.9 — English literature. American writers, *1600-1974* — *Stories, anecdotes*

The **Oxford** book of American literary anecdotes / edited by Donald Hall. — New York ; Oxford : Oxford University Press, 1981. — xxiv,360p : ill ; 23cm
Includes index
ISBN 0-19-502938-0 : Unpriced B82-02147

810.9 — English literature. American writers, *1720-1861* — *Critical studies*

Lawrence, D. H.. Studies in classic American literature / D.H. Lawrence. — Harmondsworth : Penguin in association with William Heinemann, 1971, c1961 (1977 [printing]). — 187p ; 18cm
Originally published: New York : Thomas Seltzer, 1923 ; London : Martin Secker, 1924
ISBN 0-14-003300-9 (pbk) : £1.75 B82-10515

810.9 — English literature. American writers, *1776-1861* — *Critical studies*

Lease, Benjamin. Anglo-American encounters : England and the rise of American literature / Benjamin Lease. — Cambridge : Cambridge University Press, 1981. — xv,299p ; 23cm
Includes index
ISBN 0-521-23666-5 : £22.50 : CIP rev. B81-34417

810.9 — English literature. American writers, *ca 1750-1980* — *Critical studies*

Harding, Brian. American literature in context. — London : Methuen
2: 1830-1865. — May 1982. — [260]p
ISBN 0-416-73900-8 (cased) : £8.95 : CIP entry
ISBN 0-416-73910-5 (pbk) : £3.95 B82-06761

810.9 — English literature. American writers — *Critical studies*

Massa, Ann. American literature in context. — London : Methuen
4: 1900-1930. — Apr.1982. — [220]p
ISBN 0-416-73920-2 (cased) : £8.50 : CIP entry
ISBN 0-416-73930-x (pbk) : £3.95 B82-04054

810.9 — English literature. American writers, *to 1980* **—** *Critical studies*

Spiller, Robert E.. Late harvest : essays and addresses in American literature and culture / Robert E. Spiller. — Westport ; London : Greenwood, 1981. — xi,280p ; 22cm. — (Contributions in American studies ; no.49)
Bibliography: p251-262. — Includes index
ISBN 0-313-22023-9 : Unpriced B82-01527

810.9′001 — English literature. American writers, *1607-1830* **—** *Critical studies*

Elliott, Emory. Revolutionary writers : literature and authority in the new republic 1725-1810 / Emory Elliott. — New York ; Oxford : Oxford University Press, 1982. — x,324p ; 22cm
Bibliography: p303-315. — Includes index
ISBN 0-19-502999-2 : £14.00 B82-41064

810.9′002 — English literature. American writers, *1776-1831.* **Influence of British writers**

Peach, Linden. British influence on the birth of American literature / Linden Peach. — London : Macmillan, 1982. — xi,218p ; 23cm
Bibliography: p208-212. — Includes index
ISBN 0-333-31510-3 : £17.50 B82-38788

810.9′0052 — English literature. American writers, *1900-1945* **—** *Critical studies*

Klein, Marcus. Foreigners : the making of American literature 1900-1940 / Marcus Klein. — Chicago ; London : University of Chicago Press, 1981. — xi,332p ; 24cm
Includes index
ISBN 0-226-43956-9 : £15.00 B82-09583

810.9′0054 — English literature. American writers: Beat writers, *1945-* **—** *Critical studies*

The **Beats** : essays in criticism / edited by Lee Bartlett. — Jefferson, N.C. ; London : McFarland, 1981. — 237p ; 24cm
Bibliography: p195-230. — Includes index
ISBN 0-89950-026-9 : £13.95 B82-11475

810.9′145 — English literature. American writers. Romanticism, *to 1980*

Literary romanticism in America / edited by William L. Andrews. — Baton Rouge ; London : Louisiana State University Press, c1981. — xiv,136p ; 23cm
ISBN 0-8071-0760-3 : £10.45 B82-01305

810.9′321732 — English literature. American writers. Special subjects: Urban regions — *Conference proceedings*

Literature & the American urban experience : essays on the city and literature / edited by Michael C. Jaye and Ann Chalmers Watts. — Manchester : Manchester University Press, c1981. — xv,256p ; 23cm
Conference papers
ISBN 0-7190-0848-4 (pbk) : £7.50 : CIP rev. B81-31275

810.9′355 — English literature. American writers, *1830-1861.* **Special subjects: California. Gold mining communities. Social life,** *1849-1850* **—** *Critical studies*

Fender, Stephen. Plotting the golden west : American literature and the rhetoric of the California Trail / Stephen Fender. — Cambridge : Cambridge University Press, 1981. — ix,240p : ill,1map ; 24cm
Bibliography: p212-230. — Includes index
ISBN 0-521-23924-9 : £15.00 : CIP rev. B81-34327

810.9′358 — English literature. American writers, *1900-1977.* **Special subjects: War —** *Critical studies*

Walsh, Jeffrey. American war literature, 1914 to Vietnam / Jeffrey Walsh. — London : Macmillan, 1982. — xii,218p ; 23cm
Includes index
ISBN 0-333-26149-6 : £15.00 B82-32220

810.9′897 — English literature. North American Indian writers — *Biographies*

Littlefield, Daniel F.. A biobibliography of native American writers, 1772-1924 / by Daniel F. Littlefield, Jr. and James W. Parins. — Metuchen ; London : Scarecrow, 1981. — xvii,343p ; 23cm. — (Native American bibliography series ; no.2)
Includes index
ISBN 0-8108-1463-3 : £15.60
Primary classification 016.8108′0897 B82-08577

810.9′9729 — English literature. West Indian writers, *to 1979* **—** *Biographies*

Hughes, Michael, *19---.* A companion to West Indian literature / Michael Hughes. — [London] : Collins, 1979. — 135p ; 21cm
Includes bibliographies
ISBN 0-00-325280-9 (pbk) : Unpriced B82-25870

810.9′978 — English literature. American writers: Great Plains writers, *to 1980* **—** *Critical studies*

Vision and refuge : essays on the literature of the Great Plains / edited by Virginia Faulkner with Frederick C. Luebke. — Lincoln, [Neb.] ; London : University of Nebraska Press for the Center for Great Plains Studies, c1982. — xiv,146p ; 23cm
Includes index
ISBN 0-8032-1960-1 : Unpriced B82-38419

811 — AMERICAN POETRY

811 — Poetry in English. Barbadian writers, *1945-* **—** *Texts*

Brathwaite, Edward. Sun poem / Edward Kamau Brathwaite. — Oxford : Oxford University Press, 1982. — viii,104p ; 22cm
ISBN 0-19-211945-1 (pbk) : £4.95 : CIP rev. B82-00888

811 — Poetry in English. Guyanese writers, *1945-* **—** *Texts*

Agard, John. I din do nuttin. — London : Bodley Head, Oct.1982. — [48]p
ISBN 0-370-30459-4 : £3.75 : CIP entry B82-24848

811 — Poetry in English. Jamaican writers, *1945-* **—** *Texts*

Shakka Gyata Dedi. Afrikan hartbeet 1 : songs of unity, love & struggle / Shakka Gyata Dedi. — London : Nubia, 1982. — 54p : ill(some col.),maps,ports ; 21cm
ISBN 0-907752-00-4 (pbk) : £2.50 B82-26019

811 — Poetry in English. Trinidadian writers, *1945-* **—** *Texts*

De Lima, Arthur. A mixed grill / Arthur De Lima. — Ilfracombe : Stockwell, 1982. — 54p ; 19cm
ISBN 0-7223-1558-9 : Unpriced B82-36654

Johnson, Amryl. Long road to nowhere / Amryl Johnson. — [Oxford] : [Sable], [c1982]. — [27]p : ill ; 21cm
Cover title
ISBN 0-9507902-0-6 (pbk) : £1.00 B82-09958

Walcott, Derek. The fortunate traveller / Derek Walcott. — London : Faber and Faber, 1982. — 99p ; 19cm
ISBN 0-571-11893-3 (pbk) : £3.95 : CIP rev. B82-10784

811 — Poetry in English. Trinidadian writers, *1945-. - Texts*

Walcott, Derek. Selected poetry. — London : Heinemann Educational, Apr.1981. — [160]p. — (Caribbean writers series)
ISBN 0-435-98747-x (pbk) : £2.50 : CIP entry B81-06886

811′.07′089282 — Children's humorous poetry in English. American writers, *1945-* **—** *Anthologies*

Oh, such foolishness! / poems selected by William Cole ; pictures by Tomie de Paola. — London : Methuen Children's, 1982, c1978. — 96p : ill ; 20cm. — (A Magnet book)
Originally published: 1980
ISBN 0-416-24830-6 (pbk) : £0.95 B82-33922

811′.07′09 — Humorous poetry in English. American writers — *Critical studies*

Bishop, Morris. Light verse in America / by Morris Bishop. — Portree : Aquila, 1982. — [20]p ; 21cm. — (Aquila essays ; no.8)
ISBN 0-7275-0224-7 (pbk) : Unpriced B82-27845

811.4 — AMERICAN POETRY, 1861-1900

811′.4 — Poetry in English. American writers. Dickinson, Emily — *Critical studies*

Diehl, Joanne Feit. Dickinson and the romantic imagination / Joanne Feit Diehl. — Princeton ; Guildford : Princeton University Press, c1981. — ix,205p ; 23cm
Bibliography: p187-195. — Includes index
ISBN 0-691-06478-4 : £11.70 B82-12505

811.52 — AMERICAN POETRY, 1900-1945

811′.52 — Poetry in English. American writers, *1900-1945* **—** *Texts*

Bode, Carl. Practical magic : poems / by Carl Bode. — Chicago ; London : Swallow, c1981. — 54p ; 23cm
ISBN 0-8040-0362-9 (cased) : Unpriced
ISBN 0-8040-0373-4 (pbk) : £3.50 B82-13959

. Collected poems / E.L. Mayo ; edited and with an introduction by David Ray. — Chicago ; London : Swallow, c1981. — 268p : 1port ; 23cm. — (A New letters book)
ISBN 0-8040-0385-8 (cased) : £5.50 B82-19497

Eaton, Seymour. The Roosevelt Bears go to Washington / by Seymour Eaton (Paul Piper) ; illustrations by R.K. Culver. — New York : Dover ; London : Constable, 1981. — 186p : ill ; 24cm
ISBN 0-486-24163-7 (pbk) : £3.00 B82-22711

Hunter, Rex. And tomorrow comes / by Rex Hunter. — Norfolk : Warren House, 1982. — 41p ; 22cm
Limited ed. of 150 numbered copies, of which 100 are for sale. — Originally published: Copenhagen: s.n., 1924
£7.50 B82-29951

Lewis, Janet, *1899-.* Poems old and new : 1918-1978 / by Janet Lewis. — Chicago ; London : Swallow, c1981. — 112p ; 22cm
ISBN 0-8040-0371-8 (cased) : Unpriced
ISBN 0-8040-0372-6 (pbk) : £5.60 B82-13961

Nash, Ogden. A penny saved is impossible / by Ogden Nash ; with drawings by Ken Maryanski. — London : Deutsch, 1982, c1981. — ix,120p : ill ; 21cm
Originally published: Boston, Mass.: Little, Brown, 1981
ISBN 0-233-97454-7 : £5.95 B82-18234

811′.52 — Poetry in English. American writers. Crane, Hart — *Critical studies*

Hart Crane : a collection of critical essays / edited by Alan Trachtenberg. — Englewood Cliffs ; London : Prentice-Hall, c1982. — iv,224p ; 22cm. — ([Twentieth century views]) (A Spectrum book)
Bibliography: p218-220. — Includes index
ISBN 0-13-383935-4 (cased) : Unpriced
ISBN 0-13-383927-3 (pbk) : £4.45 B82-28512

811′.52 — Poetry in English. American writers. Frost, Robert, *1874-1963* **—** *Critical studies*

Poirier, Richard. Robert Frost : the work of knowing / Richard Poirier. — Oxford : Oxford University Press, 1977 (1979 [printing]). — xvii,322p ; 21cm
Bibliography: p314-315. — Includes index
ISBN 0-19-502615-2 (pbk) : £3.95 B82-05148

Potter, James L.. Robert Frost handbook / James L. Potter. — University Park ; London : The Pennsylvania State University Press, c1980. — xvi,205p ; 24cm
Bibliography: p177-198. — Includes index
ISBN 0-271-00230-1 : £12.00 B82-35657

811'.52 — Poetry in English. American writers. H. D. — ***Biographies***
Robinson, Janice S.. H.D., the life and work of an American poet. — London : Scolar, Sept.1982. — [502]p
ISBN 0-85967-669-2 : £12.50 : CIP entry
B82-26056

811'.52 — Poetry in English. American writers. Moore, Marianne, ***1887-1972 — Critical studies***
Costello, Bonnie. Marianne Moore : imaginary possessions / Bonnie Costello. — Cambridge, Mass. ; London : Harvard University Press, 1981. — 281p ; 24cm
Includes index
ISBN 0-674-54848-5 : £12.95 B82-03871

811'.52 — Poetry in English. American writers. Moore, Marianne, ***1887-1972 — Interviews***
Moore, Marianne. Answers to some questions posed by Howard Nemerov / by Marianne Moore. — Isle of Skye : Aquila, c1982. — [14]p ; 21cm. — (Aquila essays ; no.12)
ISBN 0-7275-0254-9 (pbk) : £0.60 B82-35576

811'.52 — Poetry in English. American writers. Pound, Ezra. Correspondence with Ford, Ford Madox
Pound, Ezra. Pound/Ford : the story of a literary friendship. — London : Faber, Sept.1982. — [384]p
ISBN 0-571-11968-9 : £20.00 : CIP entry
Also classified at 823'.912 B82-19552

811'.52 — Poetry in English. American writers. Pound, Ezra — ***Critical studies***
Pearson, Norman Holmes. The escape from time : poetry, language and symbol : Stein, Pound, Eliot / by Norman H. Pearson. — Portree : Aquila, 1982. — [12]p ; 21cm. — (Aquila essays ; no.11)
ISBN 0-7275-0242-5 (pbk) : £0.60
Primary classification 818'.5209 B82-27844

Smith, Paul. Pound revised. — London : Croom Helm, May 1982. — [176]p
ISBN 0-7099-2346-5 : £12.00 : CIP entry
B82-06949

811'.52 — Poetry in English. American writers. Pound, Ezra. Influence of right-wing political movements, ***1920-1940***
Craig, Cairns. Yeats, Eliot, Pound and the politics of poetry : richest to richest / Cairns Craig. — London : Croom Helm, c1982. — 323p ; 22cm
Bibliography: p313-317. — Includes index
ISBN 0-85664-997-x : £11.95 : CIP rev.
Primary classification 821'.912'09 B81-15905

811'.52 — Poetry in English. American writers. Winters, Yvor — ***Critical studies***
Isaacs, Elizabeth. An introduction to the poetry of Yvor Winters / Elizabeth Isaacs. — Chicago ; London : Swallow, c1981. — 216p ; 24cm
Bibliography: p211-216
ISBN 0-8040-0353-x : £11.90 B82-15531

811'.52 — Poetry in English. Canadian writers, ***1900-1945 — Texts***
Service, Robert, ***1874-1958***. Later collected verse / by Robert Service. — London : Ernest Benn, 1979, c1965. — xvi,477p ; 21cm
Originally published: New York : Dodd, Mead, 1965
ISBN 0-510-32404-5 : £6.95 : CIP rev.
B79-23427

811'.52'08 — Poetry in English. American writers, ***1900- — Anthologies***
From A to Z : 200 contemporary American poets : 200 poets from New letters magazine / edited by David Ray. — Chicago ; London : Swallow, c1981. — xi,259p : ill ; 23cm. — (An New letters book)
ISBN 0-8040-0369-6 (cased) : Unpriced
ISBN 0-8040-0370-x (pbk) : £6.30 B82-13960

811'.52'09 — Poetry in English. American writers, ***1900-ca 1970 — Critical studies***
Aitken, Conrad. Poetry and the mind of modern man / by Conrad Aitken. — Portree : Aquila, 1981. — [10]p ; 21cm. — (Aquila essays ; no.4)
ISBN 0-7275-0219-0 (pbk) : Unpriced
B82-25608

811'.52'09 — Poetry in English. American writers, ***1900- — Critical studies***
Revell, Peter. Quest in modern American poetry / by Peter Revell. — London : Vision, 1981. — 245p ; 23cm. — (Critical studies series)
Includes index
ISBN 0-85478-454-3 : £13.95 B82-06876

811'.52'09 — Poetry in English. American writers. Cummings, E.E. ; Stevens, Wallace & Williams, William Carlos — ***Critical studies***
Whicher, Stephen E.. The art of poetry : Cummings, Williams, Stevens / by Stephen E. Whicher. — Portree : Aquila, 1982. — [16]p ; 21cm. — (Aquila essays ; no.9)
ISBN 0-7275-0223-9 (pbk) : Unpriced
B82-31224

811.54 — AMERICAN POETRY, 1945-

811'.54 — Poetry in English. American writers, ***1945- — Personal observations***
Simpson, Eileen. Poets in their youth. — London : Faber, Sept.1982. — [288]p
ISBN 0-571-11925-5 : £10.50 : CIP entry
B82-25170

811'.54 — Poetry in English. American writers, ***1945- — Texts***
Ashbery, John. Shadow train / poems by John Ashbery. — Manchester : Carcanet, 1982, c1981. — 50p ; 21cm
Originally published: New York : Viking, 1981
ISBN 0-85635-424-4 : Unpriced : CIP rev.
B81-38831

Barnes, Jim. The American book of the dead / poems by Jim Barnes. — Urbana, Ill. ; London : University of Illinois Press, c1982. — 107p ; 21cm
ISBN 0-252-00937-1 (cased) : Unpriced
ISBN 0-252-00938-x (pbk) : Unpriced
B82-36526

Benedikt, Michael. The badminton at Great Barrington : or, Gustave Mahler & the Chattanooga choo choo / by Michael Benedikt. — Pittsburgh : University of Pittsburgh Press ; London : Feffer and Simons, c1980. — 79p ; 22cm. — (Pitt poetry series)
ISBN 0-8229-3423-x (cased) : Unpriced
ISBN 0-8229-5322-6 (pbk) : Unpriced
B82-22722

Berg, Stephen. With Akhmatova at the black gates : variations / Stephen Berg ; foreword by Hayden Carruth. — Urbana ; London : University of Illinois Press, c1981. — xi,67p ; 21cm
ISBN 0-252-00833-2 (cased) : £7.00
ISBN 0-252-00834-0 (pbk) : Unpriced
B82-06553

Bly, Robert. Finding an old ant mansion / Robert Bly. — Bedford : Booth, 1981. — [6]p ; 20cm
Limited ed. of 130 numbered copies, with nos.1-30 signed by the poet
Unpriced (pbk) B82-35456

Cook, Albert, ***1925-***. Adapt the living / Albert Cook. — Chicago ; London : Swallow, c1981. — 83p ; 23cm
ISBN 0-8040-0350-5 (cased) : Unpriced
ISBN 0-8040-0359-9 (pbk) : £3.50 B82-19504

Disch, Thomas M.. Burn this / Tom Disch. — London : Hutchinson, 1982. — 63p ; 23cm
ISBN 0-09-146960-0 : £7.50 : CIP rev.
B82-00154

Frumkin, Gene. Clouds and red earth / Gene Frumkin. — Chicago ; London : Swallow Press, c1981. — 67p ; 24cm
ISBN 0-8040-0418-8 (cased) : Unpriced
ISBN 0-8040-0375-0 (pbk) : Unpriced
B82-29184

Goodman, Linda. Linda Goodman's love poems : levels of love awareness. — London : Pan, 1981, c1980. — 148p : ill,1port ; 18cm
Originally published: New York : Harper & Row, 1980
ISBN 0-330-26425-7 (pbk) : £1.25 B82-06409

Hathaway, William. The gymnast of inertia : poems / by William Hathaway. — Baton Rouge ; London : Louisiana State University Press, 1982. — 71p ; 22cm
ISBN 0-8071-0981-9 (cased) : Unpriced
ISBN 0-8071-0982-7 (pbk) : Unpriced
B82-35877

Hugo, Richard. The right madness on Skye : poems / Richard Hugo. — New York ; London : Norton, c1980. — 63p ; 21cm
ISBN 0-393-01353-7 (cased) : £7.95
ISBN 0-393-00982-3 (pbk) : £2.95 B82-41088

Hummer, T. R.. The angelic orders : poems / by T.R. Hummer. — Baton Rouge ; London : Louisiana State University Press, 1982. — 61p ; 24cm
ISBN 0-8071-0999-1 (cased) : Unpriced
ISBN 0-8071-1000-0 (pbk) : Unpriced
B82-35874

Jakubowski, Janet J.. Green lady house : poetry / by Janet J. Jakubowski. — Edinburgh (14a Albany St., Edinburgh) : Exiles Press, c1980. — [20]p : ill ; 25cm
£0.30 (pbk) B82-20983

Jeffers, Susan. Three jovial huntsmen / adapted and illustrated by Susan Jeffers. — London : Hamilton, 1982, c1973. — [24]p : ill(chiefly col.) ; 28cm
Originally published: Scarsdale, N.Y. : Bradbury, 1973 ; London : Hamilton, 1974. — Ill on lining papers
ISBN 0-241-02490-0 : £4.25 B82-31068

Jong, Erica. At the edge of the body / Erica Jong. — London : Granada, 1981, c1979. — 99p ; 19cm
Originally published: New York : Holt, Rinehart and Winston, 1979
ISBN 0-246-11518-1 (cased) : £4.95
ISBN 0-586-05395-6 (pbk) : Unpriced
B82-08916

Jong, Erica. Selected poems / Erica Jong. — London : Granada. — (A Panther book)
2. — 1980. — 138p ; 18cm
Includes selections from: Fruit and vegetables — Half-lives — Loveroot
ISBN 0-586-05229-1 (pbk) : £1.25 B82-09546

Kaplan, Edward. Mechos / by Edward Kaplan. — Paisley : Gleniffer, 1982. — [17]leaves ; 30x11cm
Limited ed. of 150 numbered copies
ISBN 0-906005-04-3 : Unpriced B82-20229

Kinzie, Mary. The threshold of the year / poems by Mary Kinzie. — Columbia ; London : University of Missouri Press, 1982. — 55p ; 21cm. — (A Breakthrough book ; 36)
ISBN 0-8262-0361-2 (pbk) : Unpriced
B82-36528

Landesman, Fran. Is it overcrowded in heaven? / Fran Landesman. — London : Golden Handshake, 1981. — 61p ; 22cm
ISBN 0-905150-38-4 (pbk) : £2.50 : CIP rev.
B81-30271

Levinson, Alfred. Travelogs : selections from a celebrated journey - / by Alfred Levinson. — London : Signford, 1981. — 76p : maps ; 20x21cm
ISBN 0-9507687-0-7 (pbk) : Unpriced
B82-00603

Ludvigson, Susan. Northern lights : poems / by Susan Ludvigson. — Baton Rouge ; London : Louisiana State University Press, 1981. — 71p ; 23cm
ISBN 0-8071-0879-0 (cased) : Unpriced
ISBN 0-8071-0880-4 (pbk) : £4.20 B82-13956

Miller, Calvin. The finale / Calvin Miller. — Eastbourne : Falcon, 1981, c1979. — 174p : ill ; 22cm
Originally published: Downers Grove, Ill. : InterVarsity, c1979
ISBN 0-86239-001-x (pbk) : £2.75 B82-16866

811′.54 — Poetry in English. American writers, 1945- — Texts *continuation*

Morgan, Frederick. Northbook / poems by Frederick Morgan. — Urbana, Ill. ; London : University of Illinois Press, c1982. — 78p ; 21cm
ISBN 0-252-00947-9 (cased) : Unpriced
ISBN 0-252-00948-7 (pbk) : Unpriced
B82-36527

Ostriker, Alicia. A woman under the surface : poems and prose poems / by Alicia Ostriker. — Princeton ; Guildford : Princeton University Press, c1982. — ix,77p ; 25cm. — (Princeton series of contemporary poets)
ISBN 0-691-06512-8 (cased) : £7.80
ISBN 0-691-01390-x (pbk) : Unpriced
B82-31217

Pinsky, Robert. An explanation of America / Robert Pinsky. — Manchester : Carcanet, c1979. — 65p ; 22cm
ISBN 0-85635-304-3 (pbk) : £2.95 B82-00413

Prunty, Wyatt. The times between / Wyatt Prunty. — Baltimore ; London : Johns Hopkins University Press, c1982. — 65p ; 24cm. — (Johns Hopkins poetry and fiction)
ISBN 0-8018-2403-6 (cased) : Unpriced
ISBN 0-8018-2407-9 (pbk) : Unpriced
B82-32971

Rakosi, Carl. History. — London (12 Stevenage Rd, SW6 6ES) : Oasis Books, July 1981. — [36]p
ISBN 0-903375-53-2 (pbk) : £1.20 : CIP entry
B81-14391

Ratner, Rochelle. Practicing to be a woman : new and selected poems / by Rochelle Ratner. — Metuchen, N.J. ; London : Scarecrow, 1982. — viii,141p ; 23cm. — (Poets now ; 2)
ISBN 0-8108-1510-9 : £10.80 B82-35887

Rice, Helen Steiner. Somebody loves you / Helen Steiner Rice. — London : Hutchinson, 1978, c1976 (1981 [printing]). — 127p : ill ; 21cm
Originally published: Old Tappan : Revell, 1976
ISBN 0-09-145970-2 : £2.95 B82-02031

Rogers, Pattiann. The expectations of light / Pattiann Rogers. — Princeton ; Guildford : Princeton University Press, c1981. — ix,97p ; 23cm. — (Princeton series of contemporary poets)
ISBN 0-691-06494-6 (cased) : £7.80
ISBN 0-691-01386-1 (pbk) : £4.20 B82-12382

Silverstein, Shel. A light in the attic. — London : Cape, Oct.1982. — [176]p
ISBN 0-224-02063-3 : CIP entry B82-26220

Slavitt, David R.. Dozens : a poem / by David R. Slavitt. — Baton Rouge ; London : Louisiana State University Press, 1981. — 72p ; 19cm
ISBN 0-8071-0787-5 (cased) : Unpriced
ISBN 0-8071-0788-3 (pbk) : £3.45 B82-00489

Smith, Dave. Dream flights : poems / by Dave Smith. — Urbana ; London : University of Illinois Press, 1981. — 76p : 1ill ; 21cm
ISBN 0-252-00862-6 (cased) : Unpriced
ISBN 0-252-00863-4 (pbk) : £3.50 B82-04687

Smith, Dave. Homage to Edgar Allan Poe : poems / by Dave Smith. — Baton Rouge ; London : Louisiana State University Press, 1981. — 83p ; 24cm
ISBN 0-8071-0873-1 (cased) : £9.05
ISBN 0-8071-0874-x (pbk) : £4.20 B82-06550

Smith, William Jay. The traveler's tree : new and selected poems / by William Jay Smith ; woodcuts by Jacques Hnizdovsky. — Manchester : Carcanet New Press, 1981. — 167p : 3ill ; 25cm
Originally published: New York : Persea Books, 1980
ISBN 0-85635-333-7 (corrected) : £4.95
B82-18208

Sobin, Gustaf. Caesurae : midsummer. — Plymouth : Blue Guitar Books ; London (12 Stevenage Rd., SW6 6ES) : Independent Press Distribution [distributor], Sept.1981. — [20]p
ISBN 0-907562-00-0 (pbk) : £0.80 : CIP entry
B81-20500

Spicer, Jack. Admonitions / by Jack Spicer. — Portree : Aquila, 1981. — [16]p ; 21cm
Originally published: New York : Adventures in Poetry, 1974
ISBN 0-7275-0225-5 (pbk) : Unpriced
B82-23958

Squires, Radcliffe. Gardens of the world : poems / by Radcliffe Squires. — Baton Rouge ; London : Louisiana State University Press, 1981. — 60p ; 23cm
ISBN 0-8071-0754-9 (cased) : Unpriced
ISBN 0-8071-0755-7 (pbk) : £3.45 B82-00490

Steel, Danielle. Love poems / Danielle Steel. — London : Sphere Books, 1982. — 251p ; 18cm
ISBN 0-7221-8240-6 (pbk) : £1.50 B82-33894

Twichell, Chase. Northern spy : poems / by Chase Twichell. — Pittsburgh : University of Pittsburgh Press ; London : Feffer and Simons, c1981. — 64p ; 22cm. — (Pitt poetry series)
ISBN 0-8229-3437-x (cased) : Unpriced
ISBN 0-8229-5328-5 (pbk) : Unpriced
B82-22721

Van Walleghen, Michael. More trouble with the obvious : poems / by Michael Van Walleghen. — Urbana ; London : University of Illinois Press, 1981. — 60p ; 21cm
ISBN 0-252-00864-2 (cased) : Unpriced
ISBN 0-252-00865-0 (pbk) : £3.50 B82-04686

Walsh, Chad. Hang me up my begging bowl / Chad Walsh. — Chicago ; London : Swallow, c1981. — viii,98p ; 23cm. — (An Associated writing programs award book)
ISBN 0-8040-0358-0 (pbk) : £4.90 B82-19494

Williams, Jonathan. Get hot or get out : a selection of poems, 1957-1981 / by Jonathan Williams. — Metuchen ; London : Scarecrow, 1982. — xi,175p ; 23cm. — (Poets now ; 1)
ISBN 0-8108-1495-1 : £10.80 B82-36810

Williams, Miller. Distractions : poems / by Miller Williams. — Baton Rouge ; London : Louisiana State University Press, 1981. — 67p ; 24cm
Includes poems in French, German, Italian and Spanish with parallel English translations by the author
ISBN 0-8071-0796-4 (cased) : £8.40
ISBN 0-8071-0797-2 (pbk) : Unpriced
B82-00491

Wojahn, David. Icehouse lights / David Wojahn ; foreword by Richard Hugo. — New Haven, CT ; London : Yale University Press, c1982. — xiii,69p ; 21cm. — (Yale series of younger poets ; 77)
ISBN 0-300-02816-4 (cased) : Unpriced : CIP rev.
ISBN 0-300-02817-2 (pbk) : Unpriced
B82-17894

811′.54 — Poetry in English. American writers. Antin, David — *Critical studies*

Paul, Sherman. So to speak : rereading David Antin / Sherman Paul. — London : Binnacle, c1982. — 53p : ill ; 21cm
Ill on inside cover. — Bibliography: p52-53
ISBN 0-907826-01-6 (pbk) : Unpriced
B82-28977

811′.54 — Poetry in English. American writers. Corso, Gregory — *Interviews*

Corso, Gregory. Gregory Corso / edited by Gavin Selerie ; with essays by Jim Burns and Michael Horovitz. — London : Binnacle, 1982. — 74p : ill,ports ; 21cm. — (The Riverside interviews, ISSN 0261-3042 ; 3)
Limited ed. of 500 copies. — Ports on inside cover. — Bibliography: p71-74
ISBN 0-907826-00-8 (pbk) : Unpriced
B82-21488

811′.54 — Poetry in English. American writers. Levertov, Denise — *Critical studies*

Middleton, Peter, *1950-*. Revelation and revolution in the poetry of Denise Levertov / Peter Middleton. — London ([106, Ladbroke Grove, W11 1EH]) : Binnacle, 1981. — 17p ; 30cm
Unpriced (pbk) B82-08788

811′.54 — Poetry in English. American writers. Levertov, Denise. O taste and see — *Critical studies*

Slaughter, William. The imagination's tongue : Denise Levertov's poetic / by William Slaughter. — Portree : Aquila, 1981. — [16]p ; 21cm. — (Aquila essays ; no.1)
ISBN 0-7275-0214-x (pbk) : Unpriced
B82-25604

811′.54 — Poetry in English. American writers. Olson, Charles — *Critical studies*

Corman, Cid. Projectile, percussive, prospective : the making of a voice / by Cid Corman. — Portree : Aquila, 1982. — [21]p ; 21cm. — (Aquila essays ; no.4)
ISBN 0-7275-0223-9 (pbk) : Unpriced
B82-25609

811′.54 — Poetry in English. Canadian writers, 1945- — *Texts*

Atwood, Margaret. True stories. — London : Cape, Oct.1982. — [104]p
ISBN 0-224-02071-4 : £3.95 : CIP entry
B82-25523

Eden, Laura. Summer magic. — London : Hodder & Stoughton, Feb.1983. — [256]p. — (Silhouette special edition)
ISBN 0-340-32943-2 (pbk) : £0.95 : CIP entry
B82-38269

White, Roger, *1929-*. The witness of pebbles / poems and portrayals ; by Roger White ; with an introduction by Geoffrey Nash. — Oxford : Ronald, c1981. — xv,217p ; 22cm
ISBN 0-85398-108-6 (cased) : £4.60
ISBN 0-85398-109-4 (pbk) : Unpriced
B82-10292

811′.54′080375 — Children's poetry in English. American writers, *1945-*. Special subjects: Ghosts — *Anthologies*

Ghost poems / edited by Daisy Wallace ; illustrated by Tomie de Paola. — Leeds : Pepper, 1981, c1979. — 30p : ill ; 24cm
Originally published: New York : Holiday House, 1979
ISBN 0-560-74518-4 : £3.50 B82-06459

811′.54′09 — Poetry in English. American writers, *1945-* — *Critical studies*

Gefin, Laszlo K.. Ideogram. — Milton Keynes : Open University Press, Oct.1982. — [256]p
ISBN 0-335-10113-5 : £11.95 : CIP entry
B82-25194

Nelson, Cary. Our last first poets : vision and history in contemporary American poetry / Cary Nelson. — Urbana ; London : University of Illinois Press, c1981. — xvi,220p ; 24cm
Includes index
ISBN 0-252-00885-5 : £12.30 B82-20087

Paul, Sherman. The lost America of love : rereading Robert Creeley, Edward Dorn, and Robert Duncan / Sherman Paul. — Baton Rouge ; London : Louisiana State University Press, c1981. — xvi,276p : 3ports ; 23cm
ISBN 0-8071-0865-0 : £12.25 B82-09917

Peters, Robert, *1924-*. The great American poetry bake-off : second series / by Robert Peters. — Metuchen ; London : Scarecrow Press, 1982. — xv,391p ; 23cm
Bibliography: p375-379. — Includes index
ISBN 0-8108-1502-8 : £18.00 B82-38908

Thorp, Willard. Poetry raw or cooked? / by Willard Thorp. — Portree : Aquila, c1982. — [15]p ; 21cm. — (Aquila essays ; no.13)
ISBN 0-7275-0257-3 (pbk) : £0.60 B82-39870

812 — AMERICAN DRAMA

812 — Drama in English. Trinidadian writers, *1945- — Texts*

Matura, Mustapha. Play mas ; Independence ; and Meetings : three plays / by Mustapha Matura. — London : Methuen, 1982. — 107p ; 21cm. — (A Methuen new theatrescript ; no.7)
Play mas: nine men, 3 women. — Independence: Four men, 2 women. — Meetings: one man, 2 women
ISBN 0-413-50760-2 (pbk) : £2.95 B82-33929

812.52 — AMERICAN DRAMA, 1900-1945

812'.52 — Drama in English. American writers, *1900-1945 — Texts*

Hellman, Lillian. The little foxes ; Another part of the forest / Lillian Hellman. — Harmondsworth : Penguin, 1982. — 290p ; 20cm
Originally published: New York : Viking, 1973
ISBN 0-14-048132-x (pbk) : £2.25 B82-28803

Miller, Arthur. The price / Arthur Miller. — Harmondsworth : Penguin, 1970, c1968 (1979 printing). — 95p ; 18cm
Originally published: London : Secker & Warburg, 1968
ISBN 0-14-048098-6 (pbk) : £0.95 B82-00136

Wilder, Thornton. Our town ; The skin of our teeth ; The matchmaker / Thornton Wilder. — Harmondsworth : Penguin, 1962, c1957 (1982 [printing]). — 280p ; 18cm. — (Penguin plays)
This collection originally published: London : Longmans, Green, 1958
ISBN 0-14-048027-7 (pbk) : £1.50 B82-22314

812'.52 — Drama in English. American writers. McCutcheon, George Barr — *Critical studies*

Lazarus, A. L.. Beyond Graustark : George Barr McCutcheon, playwright, discovered / A.L. Lazarus and Victor H. Jones. — Port Washington ; London : Kennikat Press, 1981. — xvi,187p : 1port ; 23cm
Bibliography: p178-180. — Includes index
ISBN 0-8046-9280-7 : £12.75 B82-29215

812'.52 — Drama in English. American writers. Miller, Arthur — *Critical studies*

Arthur Miller : new perspectives / edited and with introduction by Robert A. Martin. — Englewood Cliffs ; London : Prentice-Hall, c1982. — x,223p ; 21cm. — (Twentieth century views) (A Spectrum book)
Bibliography: p205-219. — Includes index
ISBN 0-13-048801-1 (cased) : Unpriced
ISBN 0-13-048793-7 (pbk) : £3.70 B82-19946

Carson, Neil. Arthur Miller / Neil Carson. — London : Macmillan, 1982. — 168p,8p of plates : ill ; 20cm. — (Macmillan modern dramatists)
Bibliography: p160-163. — Includes index
ISBN 0-333-28923-4 (cased) : Unpriced
ISBN 0-333-28924-2 (pbk) : Unpriced
B82-24537

812'.52 — Drama in English. American writers. O'Neill, Eugene — *Correspondence, diaries, etc.*

O'Neill, Eugene. 'The theatre we worked for' : the letters of Eugene O'Neill to Kenneth Macgowan / edited by Jackson R. Bryer, with the assistance of Ruth M. Alvarez ; with introductory essays by Travis Bogard. — New Haven ; London : Yale University Press, c1982. — xiii,274p : ill,ports ; 25cm
Includes index
ISBN 0-300-02583-1 : £17.50 : CIP rev.
B82-07089

812'.52 — Drama in English. American writers. O'Neill, Eugene. Style. Linguistic aspects

Chothia, Jean. Forging a language : a study of the plays of Eugene O'Neill / Jean Chothia. — Cambridge : Cambridge University Press, 1981, c1979. — xii,242p ; 22cm
Bibliography: p226-237. — Includes index
ISBN 0-521-28523-2 (pbk) : £6.50 : CIP rev.
B81-32523

812'.52 — Scripts. Writing. Koch, Howard — *Biographies*

Koch, Howard. As time goes by : memoirs of a writer / by Howard Koch. — New York ; London : Harcourt Brace Jovanovich, c1979. — xvii,220p,[8]p of plates : ports ; 22cm
ISBN 0-15-109769-0 : Unpriced B82-13548

812'.52'09 — Drama in English. American writers, *1900- — Critical studies*

Bigsby, C. W. E.. A critical introduction to twentieth-century American drama / C.W.E. Bigsby. — Cambridge : Cambridge University Press
1: 1900-1940. — 1982. — ix,342p : ill ; 24cm
Bibliography: p330-334. — Includes index
ISBN 0-521-24227-4 (cased) : £24.00
ISBN 0-521-27116-9 (pbk) : £7.95 B82-40506

812.54 — AMERICAN DRAMA, 1945-

812'.54 — Drama in English. American writers, *1945- — Texts*

Abbot, Rick. 'But why bump off Barnaby' : a mystery-farce / by Rick Abbot. — New York ; London : French, 1981. — 103p : 1plan ; 19cm
Four men, 6 women
ISBN 0-573-60657-9 (pbk) : £2.50 B82-06158

Abbot, Rick. Dracula : the musical? : book, music, lyrics / by Rick Abbot. — New York ; London : French, c1982. — 57p : 1plan ; 21cm
Five men, 3 women
ISBN 0-573-60841-5 (pbk) : £3.00 B82-37877

Carmichael, Fred. The three million dollar lunch : a farce in one act / by Fred Carmichael. — New York ; London : French, c1981. — 32p ; 18cm
Five women
ISBN 0-573-63365-7 (pbk) : £1.00 B82-22387

Davis, Marty. Welcome home : a comedy / by Marty Davis. — New York ; London : French, c1981. — 73p : 1plan ; 18cm
Four men, 3 women
ISBN 0-573-61857-7 (pbk) : £2.75 B82-17381

Fuller, Charles. Zooman and the sign / by Charles Fuller. — New York ; London : French, c1979 (1982 [printing]). — 71p : 1plan ; 18cm
Six men, 3 women
ISBN 0-573-61845-3 (pbk) : £2.75 B82-33323

Gentile, Vito A.. Amidst the gladiolas / by Vito A. Gentile, Jr. — New York ; London : French, c1982. — 71p : 1plan ; 18cm
Two men, 6 women
ISBN 0-573-60571-8 (pbk) : £2.75 B82-34210

Granger, Percy. Vivien : a drama in one act / by Percy Granger. — London : French, c1982. — 34p ; 18cm
Two men, 1 woman
ISBN 0-573-62571-9 (pbk) : £1.00 B82-30446

Grass, Alan. The man in 605 : a drama / by Alan Grass. — London : French, 1981, c1979. — 73p : plans ; 19cm
'Conceived as a project for Earplay'. — Three men. — Text, plan on inside covers
ISBN 0-573-64028-9 (pbk) : £3.00 B82-02905

Hailey, Oliver. I won't dance / by Oliver Hailey. — New York ; London : French, c1982. — 78p : 1plan ; 18cm
One man, 2 women
ISBN 0-573-61090-8 (pbk) : £2.75 B82-33322

Harris, Richard, *1934-*. Is it something I said? : a play / Richard Harris. — London : French, c1982. — 22p : 1plan ; 19cm
Two men, 1 woman
ISBN 0-573-12119-2 (pbk) : £0.75 B82-22183

Heelan, Kevin. Heartland : a drama in two acts / by Kevin Heelan. — New York ; London : French, c1982. — 62p : 1plan ; 18cm
ISBN 0-573-61051-7 (pbk) : £2.75 B82-30949

Ingham, Robert E.. Custer : a play in two acts / by Robert E. Ingham. — Rev. and re-written. — New York ; London : French, c1982. — 76p : 1plan ; 18cm
Seven men, 3 women. — Previous ed.: published as Whoever heard of Fred Benteen? 1977
£2.75 (pbk) B82-37936

Jacobs, Michael. Cheaters : a comedy in two acts / by Michael Jacobs. — New York ; London : French, c1982. — 73p : 1plan ; 18cm
Three men, 3 women
ISBN 0-573-60753-2 (pbk) : £2.75 B82-34379

Kadison, Luba. The Chekhov sketchbook : three short stories by Anton Chekhov / dramatized by Luba Kadison and Joseph Buloff. — New York ; London : French, c1982. — 66p : plans,1port ; 18cm
Contents: The vagabond — The witch — In a music shop
£2.75 (corrected : pbk) B82-34377

Karshner, Roger. The dream crust : a drama / by Roger Karshner. — New York ; London : French, c1982. — 77p ; 19cm
Four men, 3 women
ISBN 0-573-60840-7 (pbk) : £2.75 B82-37879

Karshner, Roger. The man with the plastic sandwich : a comedy / by Roger Karshner. — London : French, c1982. — 75p : 2plans ; 18cm
Two men, 2 women
ISBN 0-573-61859-3 (pbk) : £2.75 B82-30445

Kelly, Tim. Dark deeds at Swan's place, or, Never trust a tattooed sailor : (for a flexible cast of fourteen, seven female, seven male. Extras, if desired) / by Tim Kelly. — New York ; London : French, c1981. — 103p ; 18cm
ISBN 0-573-60838-5 (pbk) : £2.75 B82-27263

Kerr, Jean. Lunch hour : a comedy / by Jean Kerr. — New York ; London : French, c1981. — 101p : 1facsim,1plan ; 18cm
Three men, 2 women
ISBN 0-573-61862-3 (pbk) : £2.75 B82-22385

King, Ramona. Steal away : a folktale / by Ramona King. — New York ; London : French, c1982. — 67p : 1plan ; 19cm
Six women
ISBN 0-573-63019-4 (pbk) : £2.75 B82-37875

Lauro, Shirley. I don't know where you're coming from at all! : a one act play / by Shirley Lauro. — London : French, c1982. — 19p : 1plan ; 18cm
One man, 2 women
ISBN 0-573-62228-0 (pbk) : £1.00 B82-30444

Marowitz, Charles. Sex wars : free adaptations of Ibsen and Strindberg. — London : Marion Boyars, Feb.1982. — [192]p
ISBN 0-7145-2721-1 (cased) : £6.95 : CIP entry
ISBN 0-7145-2722-x (pbk) : £3.95 B81-39247

Metcalfe, Steve. Vikings : a drama / by Steve Metcalfe. — New York ; London : French, c1982. — 70p : 1facsim,1plan ; 19cm
Three men, 1 woman
ISBN 0-573-61756-2 (pbk) : £2.75 B82-22388

Parnell, Peter. Sorrows of Stephen : a comedy / by Peter Parnell. — New York ; London : French, c1980. — 102p : 1plan ; 19cm
Four men, 5 women
ISBN 0-573-61629-9 (pbk) : £2.50 B82-07330

Ribalow, Meir Z.. Sundance : a comedy in one act / by M.Z. Ribalow. — New York ; London : French, c1982. — 30p : 1plan ; 19cm
Five men
ISBN 0-573-64230-3 (pbk) : £1.00 B82-37878

812′.54 — Drama in English. American writers, *1945- — Texts* *continuation*

Rustan, John. The tangled snarl : a one-act comedy / by John Rustan & Frank Semerano. — New York ; London : French, c1982. — 34p : 1plan ; 19cm
Three men, 2 women
ISBN 0-573-62557-3 (pbk) : £1.00 B82-37876

Sharkey, Jack. Your flake or mine? : a comedy / by Jack Sharkey. — New York ; London : French, c1982. — 101p : music,1plan ; 18cm
Three men, 3 women
ISBN 0-573-61829-1 (pbk) : £2.75 B82-33321

Shepard, Sam. Chicago ; Icarus′s mother ; Red cross ; Fourteen hundred thousand ; Melodrama play / Sam Shepard. — London : Faber, 1969 (1982 [printing]). — 170p ; 21cm
Originally published: 1969
ISBN 0-571-18043-4 (pbk) : £6.25 B82-16901

Shepard, Sam. True West / Sam Shepard. — London : Faber, 1981. — 63p ; 20cm
ISBN 0-571-11833-x (pbk) : £2.95 : CIP rev. B81-21613

Shepard, Sam. True west / by Sam Shepard. — New York ; London : French, c1981. — 71p ; 18cm
Three men, 1 woman
ISBN 0-573-61728-7 (pbk) : £2.75 B82-34209

Sherman, Martin. Bent / by Martin Sherman. — New York ; London : French, c1979. — 116 : ill,plans ; 18cm
ISBN 0-573-64031-9 (pbk) : £2.75 B82-30948

Sweet, Jeffrey. After the fact / by Jeffrey Sweet. — New York ; London : French, c1981. — 20p ; 18cm
One man, 1 woman
ISBN 0-573-62028-8 (pbk) : £1.00 B82-17380

Tally, Ted. Coming attractions / by Ted Tally ; music by Jack Feldman ; lyrics by Bruce Sussman & Jack Feldman. — New York ; London : French, c1982. — 89p : 1plan ; 19cm
Five men, 2 women
ISBN 0-573-60763-x (pbk) : £3.00 B82-37874

Taylor, Renée. It had to be you : a comedy / by Renée Taylor & Joseph Bologna. — New York ; London : French, c1982. — 66p : 1facsim,2plans ; 19cm
One man, 1 woman
ISBN 0-573-61866-6 (pbk) : £2.75 B82-22386

Tesich, Steve. Division Street : a comedy / by Steve Tesich. — New York ; London : French, c1981. — 96p ; 18cm
Five men, 3 women
ISBN 0-573-60839-3 (pbk) : £2.75 B82-27262

Tobias, John. My husband′s wild desires almost drove me mad : a comedy in two acts / by John Tobias. — New York ; London : French, c1980. — 99p : 1plan ; 18cm
Three men, 2 women
ISBN 0-573-61852-6 (pbk) : £1.90 B82-41087

Van Zandt, William. Suitehearts : a comedy / by William Van Zandt & Jane Milmore. — London : French, 1981, c1979. — 89p : 1plan ; 19cm
Three men, 2 women. — Originally published: as ′Honeymoon quartet′, 1980
ISBN 0-573-61049-5 (pbk) : £2.55 B82-02911

White, Edgar. Lament for Rastafari ; and, Like them that dream. — London : Marion Boyars, Jan.1982. — [160]p
ISBN 0-7145-2753-x (cased) : £6.95 : CIP entry
ISBN 0-7145-2756-4 (pbk) : £4.50 B81-37534

Williams, Tennessee. Sweet bird of youth ; A streetcar named desire ; The glass menagerie / Tennessee Williams ; edited by E. Martin Browne. — Harmondsworth : Penguin in association with Secker & Warburg, 1962 (1982 [printing]). — 313p ; 19cm. — (Penguin plays)
Sweet bird of youth originally published: New York : New Directions, 1959. — A streetcar named desire originally published: New York : New Directions, 1947. — The glass menagerie originally published: New York : Random House, 1945
ISBN 0-14-048015-3 (pbk) : £1.25 B82-16768

812′.54′08 — Drama in English. American writers, *1945- — Anthologies*

[New American drama]. Four American plays / with an introduction by Charles Marowitz. — Harmondsworth : Penguin in association with Cape and Secker & Warburg, 1966 (1982 [printing]). — 203p ; 18cm. — (Penguin plays)
Contents: The American dream / Edward Albee — Gallous humour / Jack Richardson — The typists / Murray Schisgal — Incident at Vichy / Arthur Miller
ISBN 0-14-048129-x (pbk) : £1.95 B82-29577

812′.54′09 — Drama in English. American writers, *1945- — Critical studies*

Cohn, Ruby. New American dramatists 1960-1980 / Ruby Cohn. — London : Macmillan, 1982. — ix,186p,[16]p of plates : ill,ports ; 20cm. — (Macmillan modern dramatists)
ISBN 0-333-28913-7 (cased) : Unpriced
ISBN 0-333-28914-5 (pbk) B82-23367

813 — AMERICAN FICTION

813 — Fiction in English. Barbadian writers. Lamming, George *— Critical studies*

Paquet, Sandra Pouchet. The novels of George Lamming. — London : Heinemann Educational, July 1982. — [144]p. — (Studies in Caribbean literature)
ISBN 0-435-91831-1 (pbk) : £4.95 : CIP entry B82-18463

813 — Fiction in English. Trinidadian writers. Naipaul, V. S.. House for Mr. Biswas *— Study outlines*

Pitt, Rosemary. A house for Mr Biswas : notes / by Rosemary Pitt. — Harlow : Longman, 1982. — 64p ; 21cm. — (York notes ; 180)
Bibliography: p57-58
ISBN 0-582-78293-7 (pbk) : £0.90 B82-36752

813[F] — Fiction in English. Belizean writers, *1945- — Texts*

Edgell, Zee. Beka Lamb / Zee Edgell. — London : Heinemann, 1982. — 171p ; 19cm. — (Caribbean writers series ; 26)
ISBN 0-435-98400-4 (pbk) : £1.50 B82-17878

813[F] — Fiction in English. Dominican writers, *1900-1945 — Texts*

Rhys, Jean. After leaving Mr Mackenzie / Jean Rhys. — Harmondsworth : Penguin, 1971, c1930 (1981 [printing]). — 137p ; 19cm
ISBN 0-14-003256-8 (pbk) : £1.25 B82-08662

Rhys, Jean. Good morning, midnight / Jean Rhys. — Harmondsworth : Penguin, 1969 (1981 [printing]). — 158p ; 19cm
ISBN 0-14-002961-3 (pbk) : £1.10 B82-08666

Rhys, Jean. [Postures]. Quartet / Jean Rhys. — Harmondsworth : Penguin, 1973 (1982 [printing]). — 143p ; 19cm
ISBN 0-14-003610-5 (pbk) : £1.25 B82-08663

Rhys, Jean. Voyage in the dark / Jean Rhys. — Harmondsworth : Penguin, 1969 (1981 [printing]). — 158p ; 19cm
ISBN 0-14-002960-5 (pbk) : £1.25 B82-08664

Rhys, Jean. Wide Sargasso Sea / Jean Rhys ; introduction by Frances Wyndham. — Harmondsworth : Penguin, 1968, c1966 (1981 [printing]). — 155p ; 19cm
Originally published: London : Deutsch, 1966
ISBN 0-14-002878-1 (pbk) : £1.25 B82-11610

813[F] — Fiction in English. Dominican writers, *1945- — Texts*

Allfrey, P. Shand. The orchid house / P. Shand Allfrey ; with a new introduction by Elaine Campbell. — London : Virago, 1982, c1953. — xvi,234p ; 20cm
Originally published: London : Constable, 1953
ISBN 0-86068-242-0 (pbk) : £2.95 : CIP rev. B81-36023

813[F] — Fiction in English. Guyanese writers, *1900-1945 — Texts*

Mittelholzer, Edgar. My bones and my flute / Edgar Mittelholzer. — Harlow : Longman, 1982, c1955. — 174p ; 18cm. — (Drumbeat ; 55)
Originally published: London : Secker & Warburg, 1955
ISBN 0-582-78552-9 (pbk) : £1.50 B82-34833

813[F] — Fiction in English. Guyanese writers, *1945- — Texts*

Bradner, James. Danny boy / James Bradner. — Harlow : Longman, 1981. — 138p ; 19cm. — (Drumbeat ; 36)
ISBN 0-582-78536-7 (pbk) : £1.35 B82-11710

Heath, Roy A. K.. Genetha : a novel / by Roy A.K. Heath. — London : Allison & Busby, 1981. — 185p ; 23cm
ISBN 0-85031-410-0 (cased) : £6.95 : CIP rev.
ISBN 0-85031-411-9 (pbk) : Unpriced B81-27981

Heath, Roy A. K.. Kwaku, or, The man who could not keep his mouth shut. — London : Allison & Busby, Sept.1982. — [288]p
ISBN 0-85031-470-4 : £6.95 : CIP entry B82-21988

813[F] — Fiction in English. St Christopher-Nevis writers, *1945- — Texts*

Gilchrist, Rupert. The house at 3 o′clock / by Rupert Gilchrist. — London : Souvenir, 1982. — 232p ; 21cm. — (Slaves without masters ; v.1)
ISBN 0-285-62516-0 : £6.95 B82-22112

813[F] — Fiction in English. Trinidadian writers, *1900-1945 — Texts*

Mendes, Alfred Hubert. Pitch Lake : a story from Trinidad / by Alfred Hubert Mendes ; with an introduction by Kenneth Ramchand ; original 1934 introduction by Aldous Huxley. — London : New Beacon, 1981. — xiii,352p ; 19cm
ISBN 0-901241-38-5 (pbk) : Unpriced B82-00675

813[F] — Fiction in English. Trinidadian writers, *1945- — Texts*

De Lima, Arthur. The great quake / Arthur De Lima. — Ilfracombe : Stockwell, 1982. — 192p ; 22cm
ISBN 0-7223-1564-3 (pbk) : £3.00 B82-36655

De Lima, Arthur. The house of Jacob : the saga of the De Alvas / Arthur De Lima. — Ilfracombe : Stockwell, 1981. — 244p ; 22cm
ISBN 0-7223-1474-4 : £6.00 B82-05540

De Lima, Arthur. Oritumbe / Arthur De Lima. — Ilfracombe : Stockwell, 1982. — 194p ; 23cm
ISBN 0-7223-1539-2 : £7.00 B82-19025

Lovelace, Earl. The wine of astonishment / Earl Lovelace. — London : Deutsch, 1982. — 146p ; 22cm
ISBN 0-233-97218-8 : £6.50 : CIP rev. B82-10759

Naipaul, Shiva. Fireflies / Shiva Naipaul. — Harlow : Longman, 1981, c1970. — 416p ; 18cm. — (Drumbeat ; 39)
Originally published: London : Deutsch, 1970
ISBN 0-582-78538-3 (pbk) : £1.95 B82-06161

813[F] — Short stories in English. Dominican writers, *1900-1945 — Texts*

Rhys, Jean. Sleep it off lady / stories by Jean Rhys. — Harmondsworth : Penguin, 1979, c1976 (1981 [printing]). — 175p ; 19cm
Originally published: London : Deutsch, 1976
ISBN 0-14-004733-6 (pbk) : £1.50 B82-08584

813[F] — Short stories in English. Dominican writers, *1900-1945 — Texts* *continuation*

Rhys, Jean. Tigers are better-looking ; with a selection from The Left Bank / Jean Rhys. — Harmondsworth : Penguin, 1972 (1981 [printing]). — 220p ; 19cm
Originally published: London : Deutsch, 1968
ISBN 0-14-003512-5 (pbk) : £1.35 B82-08583

813'.009 — Fiction in English. American writers, *1830-1977 — Critical studies*

Kirby, David. The sun rises in the evening : monism and quietism in Western culture / by David Kirby. — Metuchen ; London : Scarecrow, 1982. — xi,172p ; 23cm
Includes index
ISBN 0-8108-1536-2 : £10.00 B82-37702

Smith, Henry Nash. Democracy and the novel : popular resistance to classic American writers / Henry Nash Smith. — Oxford : Oxford University Press, 1981, c1978. — viii,204p ; 21cm. — (A Galaxy book)
Originally published: New York : Oxford University Press, 1978. — Includes index
ISBN 0-19-502896-1 (pbk) : £3.95 B82-00510

813'.009'3273 — Fiction in English. American writers, *to 1980.* **Special themes: American civilization** *— Critical studies*

Fossum, Robert H.. The American dream / Robert H. Fossum and John K. Roth. — Durham : British Association for American Studies, 1981. — 44p : ill,facsims ; 22cm. — (BAAS pamphlets in American studies ; 6)
Bibliography: p38-41
Unpriced (pbk) B82-14327

813'.009'327471 — Fiction in English. American writers, *to 1975.* **Special subjects: New York** *(City) — Critical studies*

Zlotnick, Joan. Portrait of an American city : the novelists' New York / Joan Zlotnick. — Port Washington ; London : Kennikat, 1982. — 250p ; 22cm. — (Interdisciplinary urban studies series) (National university publications)
Bibliography: p263-241. — Includes index
ISBN 0-8046-9310-2 : £19.10 B82-37698

813'.009'35203893 — Fiction in English. American writers, *1830-1977.* **Characters: Greek persons** *— Critical studies*

Karanikas, Alexander. Hellenes & hellions : modern Greek characters in American literature / Alexander Karanikas. — Urbana ; London : University of Illinois Press, c1981. — xvi,551p ; 24cm
Bibliography: p526-537. — Includes index
ISBN 0-252-00792-1 : £17.50 B82-19647

813'.009'355 — Fiction in English. American writers, *1825-1960.* **Special themes: Sports** *— Critical studies*

Messenger, Christian K.. Sport and the spirit of play in American fiction : Hawthorne to Faulkner / Christian K. Messenger. — New York ; Guildford : Columbia University Press, 1981. — xv,369p ; 24cm
Includes index
ISBN 0-231-05168-9 : £17.30 B82-05615

813'.009'9287 — Fiction in English. American women writers, *1795-1980 — Critical studies*

McNall, Sally Allen. Who is in the house? : a psychological study of two centuries of women's fiction in America, 1795 to the present / Sally Allen McNall. — New York ; Oxford : Elsevier, c1981. — xii,153p ; 24cm
Includes bibliographies and index
ISBN 0-444-99081-x : Unpriced B82-02249

813'.01'08[FS] — Short stories in English. American writers, *1819-1973 — Anthologies*

The **Penguin** book of American short stories / edited by James Cochrane. — Harmondsworth : Penguin, 1969 (1982 [printing]). — 422p ; 18cm
ISBN 0-14-002919-2 (pbk) : £1.75 B82-30520

813'.01'08[FS] — Short stories in English. American writers, *1900- — Anthologies*

American / chosen by Christopher Parry. — London : Murray, c1982. — 120p ; 20cm. — (The Short story series)
ISBN 0-7195-3870-x (pbk) : £1.10 : CIP rev. B81-30958

813'.01'08[FS] — Short stories in English. American writers, *1945- — Anthologies*

Alive and screaming / [edited by] Alfred Hitchcock. — London : Severn House, 1981, c1980. — 236p ; 21cm
ISBN 0-7278-0745-5 : £6.95 : CIP rev. B81-31625

813'.01'0816[FS] — Horror short stories in English. American writers, *1900- — Anthologies*

Alfred Hitchcock's tales to scare you stiff. — London : Reinhardt, Aug.1981. — [352]p
Originally published: New York : Davis Publications, 1978
ISBN 0-370-30298-2 : £5.95 : CIP entry B81-18028

Alfred Hitchcock's Tales to take your breath away / edited by Eleanor Sullivan. — London : Max Reinhardt, 1982, c1977. — 380p ; 21cm
Originally published: New York : Dial Press, 1977
ISBN 0-370-30297-4 : £6.95 : CIP rev. B82-15758

Mysterious menacing & macabre : an anthology chosen by Helen Hoke. — London : Dent, 1981. — 148p ; 24cm
Originally published: New York : Elsevier-Nelson, 1981
ISBN 0-460-06086-4 : £4.95 : CIP rev. B81-25818

813'.01'0816[FS] — Horror short stories in English. American writers, *1945- — Anthologies*

Dark forces : new stories of suspense and supernatural horror / edited by Kirby McCauley. — London : Macdonald Futura, 1980 (1981 [printing]). — xiv,551p ; 18cm
Originally published: New York : Viking, 1980
ISBN 0-7088-1979-6 (pbk) : £1.95 B82-00049

Killers at large / Alfred Hitchcock, editor. — London : Severn House, 1982, c1978. — 223p ; 21cm
Originally published: New York : Davis, 1978
ISBN 0-7278-0811-7 : £6.95 B82-35464

813'.01'08975[FS] — Short stories in English. American writers: Southern states writers, *1900- — Anthologies*

Stories of the modern South / edited by Ben Forkner and Patrick Samway. — Harmondsworth : Penguin, 1981. — xxii,439p ; 20cm
Originally published: New York : Bantam, 1977
ISBN 0-14-005848-6 (pbk) : £2.75 B82-16787

813'.0872[FS] — Detective short stories in English. American writers, *1900- — Anthologies*

The **Great** American detective / edited and with an introduction by William Kittredge and Steven M. Krauzer. — New York : New American Library ; London : New English Library, c1978. — xxxiv,414p ; 18cm. — (A Mentor book)
Bibliography: p396-414
ISBN 0-451-61689-8 (pbk) : Unpriced B82-04670

813'.0872[J] — Detective fiction in English: Children's stories. American writers, *1945- — Anthologies*

Three great Alfred Hitchcock mysteries. — London : Fontana, 1981. — 480p : ill ; 19cm. — (An Armada three-in-one)
Contents: The mystery of the flaming footprints / text by M.V. Carey ; based on characters created by Robert Arthur. Originally published: London : Collins, 1972. — The mystery of the coughing dragon / text by Nick West ; based on characters created by Robert Arthur. Originally published: London : Collins, 1971. — The mystery of the singing serpent / text by M.V. Carey ; characters created by Robert Arthur. Originally published: London : Collins, 1973
ISBN 0-00-691991-x (pbk) : £1.75 B82-03166

813'.0876'08[FS] — Science fiction in English. American writers, *1945- — Anthologies*

Carr, Jayge. Leviathan's deep / Jayge Carr. How the gods wove in Kyrannon / Ardath Mayhar. The ravens of the moon / Charles L. Grant. — London : Sidgwick & Jackson, 1981. — 578p in various pagings ; 21cm. — (Science fiction special ; 39)
Leviathan's deep originally published: Garden City, NY : Doubleday, 1979 ; London : Sidgwick and Jackson, 1980 — How the gods wove in Kyrannon originally published: Garden City, NY : Doubleday, 1979 ; London : Sidgwick and Jackson, 1980 — The ravens of the moon originally published : New York : Doubleday, 1978 ; London : Sidgwick and Jackson, 1979
ISBN 0-283-98810-x : £8.95 B82-02264

Lampton, Chris. Gateway to limbo / Chris Lampton. Wheels within wheels / F. Paul Wilson. The planet masters / Allen Wold. — London : Sidgwick & Jackson, 1981. — 590p in various pagings ; 21cm. — (Science fiction special ; 38)
Gateway to limbo originally published: Garden City, NY : Doubleday, 1979 ; London : Sidgwick and Jackson, 1980 — Wheels within wheels originally published: Garden City, NY : Doubleday, 1978 ; London : Sidgwick and Jackson, 1980 — The planet masters originally published: New York : St.Martin's Press, 1979 ; London : Sidgwick and Jackson, 1980
ISBN 0-283-98809-6 : £8.95 B82-02265

813'.0876'08[FS] — Science fiction short stories in English. American writers, *1945- — Anthologies*

Nebula winners / edited by Frederik Pohl. — London : Star
14. — 1982, c1980. — xi,259p ; 18cm
Originally published: New York : Harper & Row, 1980 ; London : W.H. Allen, 1981
ISBN 0-352-31047-2 (pbk) : £1.75 B82-16099

813.2 — AMERICAN FICTION, 1776-1830

813'.2[F] — Fiction in English. American writers, *1776-1830 — Texts*

Cooper, James Fenimore. The last of the Mohicans / by J. Fenimore Cooper. — Abridged ed. — London : Dean, 198-?. — 184p ; 19cm. — (Dean's classics)
ISBN 0-603-03025-4 : Unpriced B82-26096

813.3 — AMERICAN FICTION, 1830-1861

813'.3 — Fiction in English. American writers. Hawthorne, Nathaniel, *1856-1864 — Biographies*

Hull, Raymona E.. Nathaniel Hawthorne : the English experience, 1853-1864 / Raymona E. Hull. — Pittsburgh : University of Pittsburgh Press ; London : Feffer and Simons, c1980. — xvi,307p : ill,ports ; 24cm
Includes index
ISBN 0-8229-3418-3 : Unpriced B82-23747

813'.3 — Fiction in English. American writers. Hawthorne, Nathaniel *— Critical studies*

Nathaniel Hawthorne : new critical essays / edited by A. Robert Lee. — London : Vision, 1982. — 254p ; 22cm
Includes index
ISBN 0-85478-464-0 : £13.95 B82-32095

813'.3 — Fiction in English. American writers. Melville, Herman. Moby Dick. Special themes: Man. Identity *— Critical studies*

Cameron, Sharon. The corporeal self : allegories of the body in Melville and Hawthorne / Sharon Cameron. — Baltimore ; London : Johns Hopkins University Press, c1981. — ix,166p ; 24cm
ISBN 0-8018-2643-8 : Unpriced
Primary classification 813'.3 B82-22604

813'.3 — Short stories in English. American writers. Hawthorne, Nathaniel. Special themes: Man. Identity *— Critical studies*

Cameron, Sharon. The corporeal self : allegories of the body in Melville and Hawthorne / Sharon Cameron. — Baltimore ; London : Johns Hopkins University Press, c1981. — ix,166p ; 24cm
ISBN 0-8018-2643-8 : Unpriced
Also classified at 813'.3 B82-22604

813′.3[F] — Fiction in English. American writers, *1830-1861 — Texts*

Melville, Herman. Moby-Dick, or, The whale / Herman Melville. — Berkeley ; London : University of California Press, 1981, c1979. — xv,576p : ill,maps ; 27cm
Originally published: San Francisco : Arion, 1979
ISBN 0-520-04354-5 : £14.00 B82-15556

813′.3[F] — Short stories in English. American writers, *1830-1861 — Texts*

Poe, Edgar Allan. The complete tales of mystery and imagination ; The narrative of Arthur Gordon Pym ; The Raven and other poems / Edgar Allan Poe. — London : Octopus, 1981. — 782p : ill ; 25cm. — (Treasury of world masterpieces)
ISBN 0-7064-1552-3 : £6.95 B82-00440

813.4 — AMERICAN FICTION, 1861-1900

813′.4 — Fiction in English. American works. Crawford, F. Marion — *Critical studies*

Moran, John C.. An F. Marion Crawford companion / John C. Moran ; with introductory essays by Edward Wagenknecht, Russell Kirk and Donald Sidney-Fryer. — Westport, Conn. ; London : Greenwood Press, 1981. — xxxviii,548p : ill,facsims,ports,1geneal.table ; 25cm
Includes index
ISBN 0-313-20926-x : £33.75 B82-18368

813′.4 — Fiction in English. American writers, *1861-1900 — Texts — Facsimiles*

Hazelton, *Lieut.-Col.*. The Seminole chief, or, The captives of the Kissimmee / Lieut.-Col. Hazelton. Old Rube the hunter, or, The crow captive / Hamilton Holmes. — [New York] ; [London] : [Garland], [1979]. — 47p ; 23cm. — (The Garland library of narratives of North American Indian captivities ; v.80)
Half title page title. — Facsims of: The Seminole chief published New York : Beadle, 1865. — Old Rube the hunter published New York : American News Co., 1866
ISBN 0-8240-1704-8 : Unpriced B82-08743

813′.4 — Fiction in English. American writers, *1861-1900 — Texts with commentaries*

Twain, Mark. A Connecticut Yankee in King Arthur′s court an authoritative text, backgrounds and sources, composition and publication, criticism / Samuel Langhorne Clemens ; edited by Allison R. Ensor. — New York ; London : Norton, c1982. — xi,455p : ill ; 22cm. — (A Norton critical edition)
Bibliography: p453-455
ISBN 0-393-01378-2 (cased) : Unpriced
ISBN 0-393-95137-5 (pbk) : Unpriced
B82-37954

Twain, Mark. Pudd′nhead Wilson ; and, Those extraordinary twins / Samuel Langhorne Clemens ; authoritative texts, textual introduction and tables of variants, criticism edited by Sidney E. Berger. — New York ; London : Norton, c1980. — xii,384p : ill ; 22cm. — (A Norton critical edition)
Bibliography: p382-384
ISBN 0-393-01337-5 (cased) : Unpriced
ISBN 0-393-95027-1 (pbk) : Unpriced
B82-33034

813′.4 — Fiction in English. American writers. Bonner, Sherwood — *Biographies*

McAlexander, Hubert Horton. The prodigal daughter : a biography of Sherwood Bonner / Hubert Horton McAlexander. — Baton Rouge ; London : Louisiana State University Press, c1981. — xvi,247p : ill,ports ; 24cm
Bibliography: p231-237. — Includes index
ISBN 0-8071-0862-6 : £15.75 B82-22552

813′.4 — Fiction in English. American writers. Crane, Stephen. Red badge of courage — *Critical studies*

Berryman, John. Stephen Crane : The Red Badge of Courage / by John Berryman. — Portree : Aquila, 1981. — [13]p ; 21cm. — (Aquila essays ; no.3)
ISBN 0-7275-0217-4 (pbk) : Unpriced B82-25605

813′.4 — Fiction in English. American writers. Howells, William Dean. Rise of Silas Lapham — *Study outlines*

Michaux, Armand. The rise of Silas Lapham : notes / by Armand Michaux. — Harlow : Longman, 1982. — 80p ; 21cm. — (York notes ; 175)
Bibliography: p77-78
ISBN 0-582-78233-3 (pbk) : £0.90 B82-36753

813′.4 — Fiction in English. American writers. James, Henry, *1843-1916 — Critical studies*

Holland, Laurence B.. The expense of vision : essays on the craft of Henry James / Laurence B. Holland. — Baltimore ; London : Johns Hopkins University Press, 1982. — xiv,440p ; 22cm
Originally published: Princeton : Princeton University Press, 1964. — Includes index
ISBN 0-8018-2755-8 (pbk) : £6.00 B82-34345

813′.4 — Fiction in English. American writers. James, Henry, *1843-1916.* **Style** — *Critical studies*

Norrman, Ralf. The insecure world of Henry James′s fiction : intensity and ambiguity / Ralf Norrman. — London : Macmillan, 1982. — 216p ; 23cm
Bibliography: p207-210. — Includes index
ISBN 0-333-32196-0 : £17.50 B82-39742

813′.4 — Fiction in English. American writers. James, Henry. Daisy Miller — *Study outlines*

McEwan, Neil. Daisy Miller : notes / by Neil McEwan. — Harlow : Longman, 1981. — 72p ; 21cm. — (York notes ; 147)
Bibliography: p68-69
ISBN 0-582-78265-1 (pbk) : £0.90 B82-16460

813′.4 — Fiction in English. American writers. Twain, Mark. Huckleberry Finn — *Study outlines*

Cannon, Michael, *19---*. Huckleberry Finn / Michael Cannon. — Dublin (Ballymount Rd., Walkinstown, Dublin 12) : Helicon, 1981. — 72p ; 22cm. — (Helicon notes)
Unpriced (pbk) B82-07374

Currie, W. T.. Brodie′s notes on Mark Twain′s Huckleberry Finn / W.T. Currie. — London : Pan, 1977. — vii,37p ; 20cm. — (Pan study aids)
ISBN 0-330-50058-9 (pbk) : £0.90 B82-24650

813′.4[F] — Fiction in English. American writers, *1861-1900 — Texts*

Chopin, Kate. The awakening / Kate Chopin ; introduced by Helen Taylor. — London : Women′s Press, 1978 (1981 [printing]). — xxi,190p ; 18cm
ISBN 0-7043-3822-x (pbk) : £1.95 B82-06416

Green, Anna Katharine. The Leavenworth case : a lawyer′s story / by Anna Katharine Green ; with a new introduction by Michele Slung. — New York : Dover ; London : Constable, 1981. — xii,331p ; 22cm
ISBN 0-486-23865-2 (pbk) : £3.75 B82-33787

Hough, Emerson. Heart′s desire : the story of a contented town, certain peculiar citizens and two fortunate lovers : a novel / by Emerson Hough ; introduction by Peter White. — Lincoln, Neb. ; London : Unversity of Nebraska Press, 1981. — xi,367p,[7]leaves of plates : ill ; 21cm
ISBN 0-8032-2315-3 (cased) : Unpriced
ISBN 0-8032-7209-x (pbk) : £4.90 B82-17359

James, Henry. The American / by Henry James ; edited with an introduction by William Spengemann. — Harmondsworth : Penguin, 1981. — 471p : 1port ; 19cm. — (The Penguin American library)
Port on inside cover. — Bibliography: p27-28
ISBN 0-14-039009-x (pbk) : £1.75 B82-19905

James, Henry, *1843-1916.* The Europeans / Henry James ; introduction by Gilbert Phelps ; lithographs by Robin Jacques. — London : Folio Society, 1982. — 188p,[9]leaves of plates : col.ill ; 23cm
In slip case
Unpriced B82-39223

James, Henry, *1843-1916.* The portrait of a lady / Henry James ; with an introduction by Graham Greene. — Oxford : Oxford University Press, 1947 (1981 [printing]). — xli,645p ; 19cm. — (The World′s classics)
Bibliography: pxix-xxi
ISBN 0-19-281514-8 (pbk) : Unpriced : CIP rev. B81-28856

James, Henry, *1843-1916.* The spoils of Poynton. — Oxford : Oxford University Press, Nov.1982. — [224]p. — (The World′s classics)
ISBN 0-19-281605-5 (pbk) : £1.75 : CIP entry
B82-26896

James, Henry, *1843-1916.* Washington Square. — Oxford : Oxford University Press, Nov.1982. — [224]p. — (The World′s classics)
ISBN 0-19-281611-x (pbk) : £1.25 : CIP entry
B82-26897

Twain, Mark. The adventures of Huckleberry Finn. — London : Macmillan Education, Feb.1983. — [320]p
ISBN 0-333-32130-8 (pbk) : £0.95 : CIP entry
B82-37857

Twain, Mark. The adventures of Tom Sawyer ; The adventures of Huckleberry Finn ; The prince and the pauper ; Pudd′nhead Wilson ; Short stories ; A Connecticut Yankee at King Arthur′s court / Mark Twain. — London : Octopus, 1981. — 799p : ill,facsims,1port ; 25cm. — (Treasury of world masterpieces)
ISBN 0-7064-1565-5 : £6.95 B82-00437

Twain, Mark. The Mark Twain reader. — Leicester : Windward, c1981. — 951p ; 22cm
ISBN 0-7112-0214-1 : £4.95 B82-06000

Twain, Mark. Roughing it / by Mark Twain ; edited with an introduction by Hamlin Hill. — Harmondsworth : Penguin, 1981. — 590p : 1port ; 19cm. — (The Penguin American library)
Port on inside cover. — Bibliography: p25-26
ISBN 0-14-039010-3 (pbk) : £2.95 B82-19910

813′.4[F] — Short stories in English. American writers, *1861-1900 — Texts*

Chopin, Kate. Portraits. — London : Women′s Press, Aug.1982. — [240]p
Originally published: 1979
ISBN 0-7043-3844-0 (pbk) : £3.25 : CIP entry
B82-15902

Crane, Stephen. The Western writings of Stephen Crane / edited and with an introduction by Frank Bergon. — New York : New American Library ; London : New English Library, 1979. — vi,230p ; 18cm. — (A Signet classic)
Bibliography: p229-230
ISBN 0-451-51189-1 (pbk) : £1.25 B82-16612

James, Henry, *1843-1916.* Henry James : selected tales / selected by Peter Messent and Tom Paulin ; introduction by Peter Messent. — London : Dent, 1982. — xli ; 18cm
Bibliography: pxxxix-xli
ISBN 0-460-01245-2 (pbk) : £2.75 : CIP rev.
B82-06843

813′.4[J] — Children′s stories in English. American writers, *1861-1900 — Texts*

Alcott, Louisa M.. Little women / by Louisa M. Alcott. — Abridged ed. — London : Dean, [198-?]. — 186p ; 19cm. — (Dean′s classics)
ISBN 0-603-03006-8 : Unpriced B82-26102

Burnett, Frances Hodgson. The secret garden / Frances Hodgson Burnett. — Harmondsworth : Puffin, 1951 (1982 [printing]). — 253p ; 19cm. — (Puffin classics)
ISBN 0-14-035004-7 (pbk) : £0.95 B82-40373

Coolidge, Susan. What Katy did / Susan Coolidge. — Harmondsworth : Puffin, 1982. — 184p ; 19cm. — (Puffin classics)
ISBN 0-14-035011-x (pbk) : £0.85 B82-40368

813'.4[J] — Children's stories in English. American writers, *1861-1900 — Texts* *continuation*
Twain, Mark. The adventures of Tom Sawyer / Mark Twain. — Harmondsworth : Puffin, 1950 (1982 [printing]). — 221p ; 18cm. — (Puffin classics)
ISBN 0-14-035003-9 (pbk) : £0.90 B82-40670

Twain, Mark. The adventures of Tom Sawyer / Mark Twain. — Abridged ed. — London : Dean, [198-?]. — 183p ; 19cm. — (Dean's classics)
ISBN 0-603-03038-6 : Unpriced B82-26103

813'.4'099287 — Fiction in English. American women writers. Southern states writers, *1861-1936 — Critical studies*
Jones, Anne Goodwyn. Tomorrow is another day : the woman writer in the South, 1859-1936 / Anne Goodwyn Jones. — Baton Rouge ; London : Louisiana State University Press, c1981. — xvii,413p : ports ; 23cm
Bibliography: p383-401. — Includes index
ISBN 0-8071-0776-x (cased) : Unpriced
ISBN 0-8071-0866-9 (pbk) : £9.10 B82-22551

813.52 — AMERICAN FICTION, 1900-1945

813'.52 — Children's stories in English. American writers. Stratemeyer, Edward *— Critical studies*
Dizer, John T.. Tom Swift & Company : "boys' books" by Stratemeyer and others / by John T. Dizer, Jr. — Jefferson ; London : McFarland, c1982. — viii,183p : ill,1port ; 24cm
Bibliography: p131-177. — Includes index
ISBN 0-89950-024-2 : £12.55 B82-17412

813'.52 — Fiction in English. American writers. Bellow, Saul *— Critical studies*
Bradbury, Malcolm. Saul Bellow / Malcolm Bradbury. — London : Methuen, 1982. — 110p ; 20cm. — (Contemporary writers)
Bibliography: p107-110
ISBN 0-416-31650-6 (pbk) : Unpriced : CIP rev. B82-06747

813'.52 — Fiction in English. American writers. Bellow, Saul. Henderson the rain king *— Study outlines*
Schraepen, Edmond. Henderson the rain king : notes / by Edmond Schraepen and Pierre Michel. — Harlow : Longman, 1981. — 64p ; 21cm. — (York notes ; 146)
Bibliography: p63-64
ISBN 0-582-78168-x (pbk) : £0.90 B82-16365

813'.52 — Fiction in English. American writers. Burroughs, Edgar Rice. Characters: Tarzan *— Critical studies*
Holtsmark, Erling B.. Tarzan and tradition : classical myth in popular literature / Erling B. Holtsmark. — Westport, Conn. ; London : Greenwood Press, 1981. — xv,196p : 1geneal.table ; 22cm. — (Contributions to the study of popular culture, ISSN 0198-9871 ; no.1)
Bibliography: p179-181. — Includes index
ISBN 0-313-22530-3 : Unpriced B82-01951

813'.52 — Fiction in English. American writers. Chandler, Raymond *— Correspondence, diaries, etc.*
Chandler, Raymond. Selected letters of Raymond Chandler / edited by Frank MacShane. — London : Cape, 1981. — xx,501p : 1port ; 24cm
Includes index
ISBN 0-224-01962-7 : £12.50 : CIP rev. B81-27341

813'.52 — Fiction in English. American writers. Dos Passos, John *— Critical studies*
Donald, Miles. John Dos Passos' 'U.S.A.' : the politics of ambivalence / Miles Donald and Geoffrey Jones. — Winchester (Winchester S022 4NR) : King Alfred's College, 1980. — 31p ; 21cm. — (Contexts and connections)
Unpriced (pbk) B82-13900

Rosen, Robert C.. John Dos Passos : politics and the writer / by Robert C. Rosen. — Lincoln [Neb.] ; London : University of Nebraska Press, c1981. — xv,191p ; 23cm
Bibliography: p176-184. — Includes index
ISBN 0-8032-3860-6 : £11.20 B82-22548

813'.52 — Fiction in English. American writers. Dreiser, Theodore. Sister Carrie *— Study outliens*
Michel, Pierre. Sister Carrie : notes / by Pierre Michel. — Harlow : Longman, 1982. — 63p ; 21cm. — (York notes ; 179)
Bibliography: p62-63
ISBN 0-582-78273-2 (pbk) : £0.90 B82-36756

813'.52 — Fiction in English. American writers. Faulkner, William *— Critical studies*
Matthews, John T.. The play of Faulkner's language / John T. Matthews. — Ithaca ; London : Cornell University Press, 1982. — 278p ; 23cm
Includes index
ISBN 0-8014-1413-x : £14.75 B82-35757

Pikoulis, John. The art of William Faulkner / John Pikoulis. — London : Macmillan, 1982. — xii,242p ; 23cm
List of works: p263-238. — Includes index
ISBN 0-333-30094-7 : £17.50 B82-38811

Strandberg, Victor. A Faulkner overview : six perspectives / Victor Strandberg. — Port Washington ; London : National University Publications : Kennikat, 1981. — 122p ; 23cm. — (Literary criticism series)
Includes index
ISBN 0-8046-9289-0 : £11.45 B82-12276

813'.52 — Fiction in English. American writers. Faulkner, William. Go down, Moses *— Study outlines*
Ross, Mary. Go down, Moses! : notes / by Mary Ross. — Harlow : Longman, 1982. — 80p ; 21cm. — (York notes ; 163)
Bibliography: p77
ISBN 0-582-78266-x (pbk) : £0.90 B82-36758

813'.52 — Fiction in English. American writers. Faulkner, William. Sound and the fury *— Critical studies*
Collins, Carvel. William Faulkner : the sound and the fury / by Carvel Collins. — Isle of Skye : Aquila, c1982. — [15]p ; 21cm. — (Aquila essays ; no.14)
ISBN 0-7275-0256-5 (pbk) : £0.60 B82-35575

813'.52 — Fiction in English. American writers. Faulkner, William. Sound and the fury *— Study outlines*
Nicholson, C. E.. The sound and the fury : notes / by C.E. Nicholson and R.W. Stevenson. — Harlow : Longman, 1981. — 87p ; 21cm. — (York notes ; 136)
Bibliography: p84-87
ISBN 0-582-78195-7 (pbk) : £0.90 B82-16363

813'.52 — Fiction in English. American writers. Fitzgerald, F. Scott *— Biographies*
Bruccoli, Matthew J. (Matthew Joseph), *1931-*. Some sort of epic grandeur : the life of F. Scott Fitzgerald / by Matthew J. Bruccoli ; with a genealogical afterword by Scottie Fitzgerald Smith. — London : Hodder and Stoughton, 1981. — xxxi,624p : ill,facsims,ports,1geneal.table ; 25cm
Bibliography: p545-569. — Includes index
ISBN 0-340-27579-0 : £14.95 : CIP rev. B81-26735

813'.52 — Fiction in English. American writers. Fitzgerald, F. Scott *— Correspondence, diaries, etc.*
Fitzgerald, F. Scott. The letters of F. Scott Fitzgerald / edited by Andrew Turnbull. — Harmondsworth : Penguin, 1968, c1963 (1982 [printing]). — 636p ; 20cm
Originally published: New York : Scribner, 1963 ; London : Bodley Head, 1964. — Includes index
ISBN 0-14-002612-6 (pbk) : £3.95 B82-41149

813'.52 — Fiction in English. American writers. Hemingway, Ernest *— Critical studies*
Hemingway : the critical heritage / edited by Jeffrey Meyers. — London : Routledge & Kegan Paul, 1982. — xvi,611p ; 23cm. — (The Critical heritage series)
Bibliography: p592-594. — Includes index
ISBN 0-7100-0929-1 : £16.50 B82-14743

813'.52 — Fiction in English. American writers. Hemingway, Ernest. Farewell to arms *— Study outlines*
King, Adele. A farewell to arms : notes / by Adele King. — Harlow : Longman, 1981. — 64p : 2maps ; 21cm. — (York notes ; 145)
Bibliography: p59-60
ISBN 0-582-78162-0 (pbk) : £0.90 B82-16366

813'.52 — Fiction in English. American writers. London, Jack *— Biographies*
Barltrop, Robert. Jack London : the man, the writer, the rebel / Robert Barltrop. — London : Pluto, 1978, c1976. — 206p : ill,ports ; 22cm
Originally published: 1976. — Includes index
ISBN 0-904383-18-0 (pbk) : £2.95 B82-26589

813'.52 — Fiction in English. American writers. Nin, Anaïs *— Critical studies*
Paine, Sylvia. Beckett, Nabokov, Nin : motives and modernism / Sylvia Paine. — Port Washington ; London : National University Publications : Kennikat, 1981. — x,102p ; 23cm. — (Literary criticism series)
Bibliography: p79-100. — Includes index
ISBN 0-8046-9288-2 : £12.75
Primary classification 828'.91209 B82-12285

813'.52 — Fiction in English. Canadian writers. Salverson, Laura Goodman *— Biographies*
Salverson, Laura Goodman. Confessions of an immigrant's daughter / Laura Goodman Salverson ; with an introduction by K.P. Stich. — Toronto ; London : University of Toronto Press, c1981. — xvi,415p ; 23cm. — (Social history of Canada ; 34)
Originally published: London : Faber, 1939
ISBN 0-8020-2424-6 : £21.00
ISBN 0-8020-6434-5 (pbk) : Unpriced B82-13934

813'.52 — Short stories in English. American writers. Faulkner, William *— Critical studies*
Skei, Hans H.. William Faulkner : the short story career : an outline of Faulkner's short story writing from 1919 to 1962 / Hans H. Skei. — Oslo : Universitetsforlaget ; London : Global Book Resources [distributor], c1981. — 164p ; 22cm
Bibliography: p137-157. — Includes index
ISBN 82-00-05826-3 (pbk) : £9.50 B82-29828

813'.52[F] — Fiction in English. American writers, *1900-1945 — Texts*
Armstrong, Charlotte. The dream walker / Charlotte Armstrong. — London : Keyhole Crime, 1982, c1955. — 141p ; 18cm
Originally published: London : Peter Davies, 1955
ISBN 0-263-73960-0 (pbk) : £0.95 B82-36071

Arthur, Burt. Brothers of the range / Burt and Budd Arthur. — London : Hale, 1982. — 176p ; 20cm
ISBN 0-7091-9527-3 : £4.95 B82-11065

Baker, Dorothy. Cassandra at the wedding. — London : Virago, Jan.1982. — [238]p. — (Virago modern classics)
Originally published: Boston, Mass. : Houghton Mifflin ; London : Gollancz, 1962
ISBN 0-86068-244-7 (pbk) : £2.95 : CIP entry B81-38301

Barnes, Djuna. Ryder. — London : Faber, Apr.1982. — [352]p
ISBN 0-571-11807-0 : £6.95 : CIP entry B82-04620

Beagle, Peter S.. [The fantasy worlds of Peter Beagle]. A fine and private place. — London : Unwin Paperbacks, Nov.1982. — [224]p
Originally published: New York : Viking Press, 1978 ; London : Souvenir Press, 1980
ISBN 0-04-823219-x (pbk) : £2.75 : CIP entry B82-27828

Bellow, Saul. The dean's December : a novel / by Saul Bellow. — London : Secker & Warburg, 1982. — 312p ; 23cm. — (An Alison press book)
ISBN 0-436-03952-4 : £7.95 : CIP rev. B82-00162

813'.52[F] — Fiction in English. American writers, *1900-1945 — Texts* *continuation*

Bragg, W. F.. Bullet proof / W.F. Bragg. — Bath : Chivers, 1982, c1981. — 234p ; 23cm. — (Atlantic large print) (A Gunsmoke large print western)
ISBN 0-85119-480-x : Unpriced : CIP rev. B82-13092

Bragg, W. F.. Rawhide roundup / W.F. Bragg. — Large print ed. — Bath : Chivers, 1982, c1957. — 216p ; 23cm. — (Atlantic large print) (A Gunsmoke large print Western)
Originally published: New York : Arcadia House, 1957
ISBN 0-85119-468-0 : Unpriced : CIP rev. B82-07621

Brand, Max. The Blue Jay / Max Brand. — London : Prior, 1981, c1926. — 378p ; 25cm
Published in large print
ISBN 0-86043-628-4 : £6.95 B82-02930

Brand, Max. Bull hunter / Max Brand. — London : Hale, 1981. — 176p ; 21cm
ISBN 0-7091-9301-7 : £4.95 B82-00539

Brand, Max. Clung / Max Brand. — Hornchurch : Ian Henry, 1982, c1948. — 217p ; 21cm
ISBN 0-86025-205-1 : £5.65 B82-18231

Brand, Max. Destry rides again / Max Brand. — Hornchurch : Ian Henry, 1981, c1931. — 191p ; 21cm
ISBN 0-86025-192-6 : £5.45 B82-03257

Brand, Max. Galloping danger / Max Brand. — London : Hale, 1980, c1951. — 200p ; 20cm
ISBN 0-7091-8662-2 : £4.95 B82-16800

Brand, Max. The Jackson trail / Max Brand. — South Yarmouth, Mass. : Curley, 1979, c1960 ; [Long Preston] : Distributed by Magna. — 488p ; 22cm. — (A Hildegarde Dolson western)
Published in large print
ISBN 0-89340-199-4 (pbk) : Unpriced B82-13663

Brand, Max. The man from the wilderness / Max Brand. — London : Hale, 1982, c1953. — 219p ; 20cm
ISBN 0-7091-9350-5 : £4.95 B82-12613

Brand, Max. Seven trails / by Max Brand. — Hornchurch : Ian Henry, 1982, c1952. — 191p ; 21cm
Originally published: London : Hodder & Stoughton, 1952
ISBN 0-86025-208-6 : £5.45 B82-27440

Brand, Max. Wild freedom / by Max Brand. — London : Hale, 1982, c1981. — 231p ; 20cm
Originally published: New York : Dodd, Mead, 1981
ISBN 0-7091-9864-7 : Unpriced B82-34170

Burnett, W. R.. Good-bye, Chicago / by W.R. Burnett. — London : Hale, 1982, c1981. — 175p ; 20cm
ISBN 0-7091-9698-9 : £6.75 B82-18308

Cain, James M.. The butterfly / James M. Cain. — London : Pan, 1981, c1946. — 125p ; 18cm
Originally published: New York : Knopf, 1947 ; London : Hale, 1949
ISBN 0-330-26563-6 (pbk) : £1.25 B82-06410

Cain, James M.. Mildred Pierce / James M. Cain. — Feltham : Hamlyn, 1982. — 237p ; 18cm
ISBN 0-600-20439-1 (pbk) : £1.35 B82-08772

Cain, James M.. Serenade / James M. Cain. — London : Severn House, 1982, c1938. — 173p ; 21cm
ISBN 0-7278-0790-0 : £5.95 B82-30470

Caldwell, Taylor. Answer as a man / Taylor Caldwell. — London : Fontana, 1982, c1980. — 509p ; 18cm
Originally published: London : Collins, 1981
ISBN 0-00-616506-0 (pbk) : £1.95 B82-19738

Caldwell, Taylor. Captains and the kings. — Large print ed. — Anstey : Ulverscroft, Feb.1983. — 1v.. — (Charnwood library series)
Originally published: New York : Doubleday, 1972
ISBN 0-7089-8096-1 : £7.95 : CIP entry B82-38891

Carr, John Dickson. The four false weapons / John Dickson Carr. — Feltham : Hamlyn, 1982, c1937. — 190p ; 18cm. — (A Hamlyn whodunnit)
ISBN 0-600-20382-4 (pbk) : £1.25 B82-11325

Cather, Willa. My mortal enemy / Willa Cather ; with a new introduction by A.S. Byatt. — London : Virago, 1982. — xiii,122p : ill ; 20cm. — (Virago modern classics)
ISBN 0-86068-246-3 (pbk) : £2.50 : CIP rev. B82-07053

Cather, Willa. The song of the lark / Willa Cather ; with a new introduction by A.S. Byatt. — London : Virago, 1982. — xix,580p ; 20cm. — (Virago modern classics)
ISBN 0-86068-245-5 (pbk) : £3.95 : CIP rev. B82-07052

Chandler, Raymond. Farewell, my lovely / Raymond Chandler. — Harmondsworth : Penguin in association with Hamilton, 1949, c1940 (1982 [printing]). — 252p ; 19cm. — (Penguin crime fiction)
ISBN 0-14-000701-6 (pbk) : £1.75 B82-16770

Cheever, John. Oh what a paradise it seems / John Cheever. — London : Cape, 1982. — 99p ; 23cm
ISBN 0-224-02930-4 : £5.50 : CIP rev. B82-12564

Cheever, John. The Wapshot scandal / John Cheever. — London : Abacus, 1982, c1964. — 251p ; 20cm
Originally published: New York : Harper and Row ; London : Gollancz, 1964
ISBN 0-349-10504-9 (pbk) : £2.50 B82-14899

Cole, Jackson. Shootout trail ; and, The land pirates / Jackson Cole. — Large print ed. — Leicester : Ulverscroft, 1981. — 381p ; 23cm
ISBN 0-7089-0729-6 : £5.00 : CIP rev. B81-32608

Cole, Jackson. Vaquero guns, ; and, Gun fight at Deep River / Jackson Cole. — Large print ed. — Leicester : Ulverscroft, 1982, c1966. — 406p ; 23cm. — (Ulverscroft large print)
ISBN 0-7089-0813-6 : Unpriced : CIP rev. B82-18553

Cooper, Louise Field. Breakaway / Louise Field Cooper. — South Yarmouth, Mass. : Curley, 1978, c1977 ; [Long Preston] : Distributed by Magna. — 391p ; 23cm
Originally published: New York : Knopf, 1977. — Published in large print
ISBN 0-89340-122-6 : Unpriced B82-13659

Cooper, Louise Field. One dragon too many / Louise Field Cooper. — South Yarmouth, Mass. : Curley, 1978, c1970 ; [Long Preston] : Distributed by Magna. — 428p ; 23cm
Originally published: New York : Knopf, 1970. — Published in large print
ISBN 0-89340-123-4 : Unpriced B82-13658

Cummings, E. E.. The enormous room / E.E. Cummings ; with an introduction by the author. — Harmondsworth : Penguin, 1971, c1968 (1982 [printing]). — 268p ; 20cm. — (Penguin modern classics)
ISBN 0-14-003257-6 (pbk) : £2.95 B82-25228

Cunningham, E. V.. The case of the one-penny orange / E.V. Cunningham. — Large print ed. — Bath : Chivers, 1981, c1978. — 184p ; 23cm. — (A New Portway large print book)
Originally published: London : Deutsch, 1978
ISBN 0-85119-140-1 : Unpriced : CIP rev. B81-30570

Cunningham, E. V.. The case of the poisoned eclairs / E.V. Cunningham. — Large print ed. — Bath : Chivers, 1981, c1979. — 218p ; 23cm. — (A New Portway large print book)
Originally published: London : Deutsch, 1980
ISBN 0-85119-144-4 : Unpriced : CIP rev. B81-31835

Cunningham, E. V.. The case of the sliding pool / E.V. Cunningham. — London : Gollancz, 1982, c1981. — 178p ; 21cm
Originally published: New York : Delacorte, 1981
ISBN 0-575-03099-2 : £6.95 B82-09779

De Camp, L. Sprague. Conan the barbarian / L. Sprague De Camp and Lin Carter ; based on a screenplay by John Milius and Oliver Stone. — London : Sphere, 1982. — ix,181p ; 18cm
ISBN 0-7221-4750-3 (pbk) : £1.25 B82-37345

De Vries, Peter. Madder music / Peter De Vries. — Harmondsworth : Penguin, 1982, c1977. — 221p ; 20cm
Originally published: Boston, Mass. : Little, Brown : 1977
ISBN 0-14-006133-9 (pbk) : £1.95 B82-40990

De Vries, Peter. Sauce for the goose / Peter De Vries. — London : Gollancz, 1982, c1981. — 232p ; 23cm
Originally published: Boston : Little, Brown, 1981
ISBN 0-575-03076-3 : £6.95 B82-09781

De Vries, Peter. The tunnel of love / by Peter De Vries. — Harmondsworth : Penguin, 1964, c1954 (1982 [printing]). — 246p ; 20cm
Originally published: Boston : Little, Brown, 1954 ; London : Gollancz, 1955
ISBN 0-14-002200-7 (pbk) : £1.95 B82-29583

Eberhart, Mignon G.. The Bayou Road / Mignon G. Eberhart. — South Yarmouth, Mass. : John Curley, c1979 ; [Long Preston] : Magna [distributor]. — 440p ; 23cm
Originally published: New York : Random House ; London : Collins, 1979. — Published in large print
ISBN 0-89340-216-8 : £5.25 B82-01041

Eberhart, Mignon G.. Family affair / M.G. Eberhart. — London : Collins : , 1981. — 233p ; 21cm. — (The Crime Club)
Originally published: Boston, Mass. : G.K. Hall, 1981
ISBN 0-00-231292-1 : £6.50 : CIP rev. B81-28773

Eberhart, Mignon G.. Never look back / Mignon G. Eberhart. — Sth. Yarmouth, Mass. : Curley, 1978, c1951 ; [Skipton] : distributed by Magna. — 452p ; 22cm
Originally published: New York : Random House ; London : Collins, 1951. — Published in large print
ISBN 0-89340-102-1 (pbk) : Unpriced B82-14123

Eberhart, Mignon G.. Next of kin. — London : Collins, Jan.1983. — [224]p
Originally published: New York : Random House, 1982
ISBN 0-00-231495-9 : £6.75 : CIP entry B82-33589

Fast, Howard. The legacy / Howard Fast. — London : Hodder and Stoughton, 1981. — 359p : 2geneal.tables ; 23cm
ISBN 0-340-25750-4 : £6.95 : CIP rev. B81-30138

813'.52[F] — Fiction in English. American writers, *1900-1945* — *Texts* *continuation*

Fast, Howard. The legacy. — London : Hodder & Stoughton, July 1982. — [368]p. — (Coronet books)
Originally published: Boston, Mass. : G.K. Hall ; London : Hodder & Stoughton, 1981
ISBN 0-340-28312-2 (pbk) : £1.75 : CIP entry
B82-12308

Fast, Howard. Max. — London : Hodder & Stoughton, Jan.1983. — [400]p
ISBN 0-340-32956-4 : £7.95 : CIP entry
B82-34084

Faulkner, William. Absalom, Absalom! / William Faulkner. — Harmondsworth : Penguin, 1971, c1964 (1982 [printing]). — 316p : 1map ; 20cm. — (Penguin modern classics)
ISBN 0-14-003254-1 (pbk) : £2.95 B82-33532

Faulkner, William. Intruder in the dust / William Faulkner. — Harmondsworth : Penguin in association with Chatto & Windus, 1960, c1948 (1982 [printing]). — 237p ; 20cm. — (Penguin modern classics)
Originally published: New York : Random House, 1948 ; London : Chatto & Windus, 1949
ISBN 0-14-001432-2 (pbk) : £2.50 B82-25225

Faulkner, William. The reivers : a reminiscence / William Faulkner. — Harmondsworth : Penguin in association with Chatto & Windus, 1970, c1962 (1982 [printing]). — 253p ; 20cm. — (Penguin modern classics)
Originally published: New York : Random House ; London : Chatto & Windus, 1962
ISBN 0-14-002993-1 (pbk) : £2.75 B82-29817

Faulkner, William. The unvanquished / William Faulkner. — Harmondsworth : Penguin in association with Chatto & Windus, 1955, c1934 (1982 [printing]). — 174p ; 20cm. — (Penguin modern classics)
ISBN 0-14-001058-0 (pbk) : £1.95 B82-25224

Fergusson, Harvey. Wolf song / Harvey Fergusson. — Lincoln [Neb.] ; London : University of Nebraska Press, 1981, c1955. — 206p ; 21cm. — (A Bison book)
ISBN 0-8032-6855-6 (pbk) : £3.85 B82-06551

Fitzgerald, F. Scott. The beautiful and damned / F. Scott Fitzgerald. — Harmondsworth : Penguin, 1966 (1982 [printing]). — 363p : ill ; 18cm
ISBN 0-14-002414-x (pbk) : £1.95 B82-39086

Fitzgerald, F. Scott. The great Gatsby / F. Scott Fitzgerald. — Harmondsworth : Penguin, 1950, c1926 (1982 [printing]). — 187p ; 18cm
ISBN 0-14-000746-6 (pbk) : £1.25 B82-25423

Fitzgerald, F. Scott. This side of paradise / F. Scott Fitzgerald. — Harmondsworth : Penguin in association with Bodley Head, 1963, c1920 (1982 [printing]). — 254p ; 18cm
ISBN 0-14-001867-0 (pbk) : £1.50 B82-32487

Floren, Lee. Frontier lawman / Lee Floren. — London : Prior, 1981, c1971. — 277p ; 25cm
ISBN 0-86043-680-2 : Unpriced B82-28213

Franken, Rose. Another Claudia / Rose Franken. — Large print ed. — Leicester : Ulverscroft, 1982, c1948. — 325p ; 23cm. — (Ulverscroft large print series)
ISBN 0-7089-0761-x : Unpriced : CIP rev.
B82-18438

Franken, Rose. Claudia / Rose Franken. — Large print ed. — Leicester : Ulverscroft, 1982, c1946. — 387p ; 23cm
ISBN 0-7089-0734-2 : £5.00 : CIP rev.
B81-33964

Franken, Rose. Claudia and David / Rose Franken. — Large print ed. — Leicester : Ulverscroft, 1982. — 369p ; 23cm. — (Ulverscroft large print series)
Originally published: London : W.H. Allen, 1946
ISBN 0-7089-0789-x : Unpriced : CIP rev.
B82-01736

Franken, Rose. From Claudia to David. — Large print ed. — Anstey : Ulverscroft, Feb.1983. — 1v.. — (Ulverscroft large print series)
Originally published: London : W.H. Allen, 1949
ISBN 0-7089-0918-3 : CIP entry B82-38880

Franken, Rose. The marriage of Claudia. — Large print ed. — Anstey : Ulverscroft, Oct.1982. — [352]p. — (Ulverscroft large print series)
Originally published: W.H. Allen, 1948
ISBN 0-7089-0860-8 : £5.00 : CIP entry
B82-26681

Franken, Rose. Young Claudia / Rose Franken. — Large print ed. — Leicester : Ulverscroft, 1982, c1946. — 427p ; 23cm. — (Ulverscroft large print series)
Originally published: New York : Rinehart, 1946 ; London : W.H. Allen, 1947
ISBN 0-7089-0819-5 : Unpriced : CIP rev.
B82-18465

Freedman, Nancy. Prima donna : a novel / by Nancy Freedman. — London : Prior, 1981. — 560p ; 25cm
Published in large print
ISBN 0-86043-682-9 : Unpriced B82-28220

Gallico, Paul. Beyond the Poseidon adventure / Paul Gallico. — Large print ed. — Bath : Chivers, 1981, c1978. — 276p ; 23cm. — (A New Portway large print book)
Originally published: London : Heinemann, 1978
ISBN 0-85119-141-x : Unpriced : CIP rev.
B81-30571

Gallico, Paul. Coronation / Paul Gallico. — Large print ed. — Bath : Chivers, 1981, c1962. — 140p ; 23cm. — (A New Portway large print book)
Originally published: London : Heinemann, 1962
ISBN 0-85119-142-8 : Unpriced : CIP rev.
B81-30572

Gallico, Paul. Mrs Harris goes to Moscow / Paul Gallico. — Large print ed. — Bath : Chivers, 1981, c1974. — 214p ; 23cm. — (A New Portway large print book)
Originally published: London : Heinemann, 1974
ISBN 0-85119-145-2 : Unpriced : CIP rev.
B81-31836

Gallico, Paul. Mrs Harris, M.P. / Paul Gallico. — Large print ed. — Bath : Chivers, 1981, c1965. — 166p ; 23cm. — (A New Portway large print book)
Originally published: London : Heinemann, 1965
ISBN 0-85119-146-0 : Unpriced : CIP rev.
B81-31837

Gallico, Paul. Scruffy / Paul Gallico. — Harmondsworth : Penguin, 1977, c1962 (1982 [printing]). — 287p ; 19cm
Originally published: London : Joseph, 1962
ISBN 0-14-002628-2 (pbk) : £1.50 B82-18629

Gann, Ernest K.. The aviator / Ernest K. Gann. — London : Prior, 1981. — 265p ; 25cm
Originally published: London : Hodder, c1981. — Published in large print
ISBN 0-86043-669-1 : £6.50 B82-16176

Gann, Ernest K.. The aviator. — London : Hodder and Stoughton, Aug.1982. — [192]p. — (Coronet books)
Originally published: 1981
ISBN 0-340-27917-6 (pbk) : £1.25 : CIP entry
B82-15726

Gardner, Erle Stanley. The case of the baited hook / Erle Stanley Gardner. — Sth. Yarmouth, Mass. : Curley, 1978, c1940 ; [Skipton] : distributed by Magna. — 415p ; 22cm. — (A Perry Mason mystery)
Published in large print
ISBN 0-89340-141-2 (pbk) : Unpriced
B82-14130

Gardner, Erle Stanley. The case of the drowning duck / Erle Stanley Gardner. — London : Severn House, 1982. — 244p ; 21cm
ISBN 0-7278-0760-9 : £5.95 B82-12076

Gardner, Erle Stanley. The case of the green-eyed sister / Erle Stanley Gardner. — Sth. Yarmouth, Mass. : Curley, 1978, c1953 ; [Skipton] : distributed by Magna. — 426p ; 22cm. — (A Perry Mason mystery)
Originally published: New York : Morrow, 1953. — Published in large print
ISBN 0-89340-140-4 (pbk) : Unpriced
B82-14124

Gardner, Erle Stanley. The case of the lame canary / Erle Stanley Gardner. — Sth. Yarmouth, Mass. : Curley, 1978, c1937 ; [Skipton] : distributed by Magna. — 381p ; 22cm. — (A Perry Mason mystery)
Published in large print
ISBN 0-89340-139-0 (pbk) : Unpriced
B82-14125

Gregory, Jackson. The man from painted rock / Jackson Gregory. — London : Collins, 1949 (1979 [printing]). — 192p ; 19cm. — (Collins western)
ISBN 0-00-247517-0 : £3.50 B82-10303

Grey, Romer Zane. King of the outlaw horde. — Large print ed. — Anstey : Ulverscroft Large Print Books, Dec.1982. — 1v.. — (Ulverscroft large print series)
ISBN 0-7089-0897-7 : £5.00 : CIP entry
B82-30796

Grey, Romer Zane. The lawless land. — Large print ed. — Anstey : Ulverscroft, Aug.1982. — [432]p
ISBN 0-7089-0841-1 : £5.00 : CIP entry
B82-27019

Grey, Zane. Captives of the desert / Zane Grey. — London : Prior, 1981, c1954. — 480p ; 25cm
'This story was published serially under the title Desert Bound' — t.p. verso. — Originally published: New York : Harper, 1952 ; London : Hodder & Stoughton, 1953. — Published in large print
ISBN 0-86043-673-x (corrected) : Unpriced
B82-31111

Grey, Zane. Fighting caravans / Zane Grey. — Large print ed. — Leicester : Ulverscroft, 1981, c1957. — 462p ; 23cm. — (Ulverscroft large print)
ISBN 0-7089-0701-6 : £5.00 : CIP rev.
B81-28095

Grey, Zane. The fugitive trail / Zane Grey. — Sth. Yarmouth, Mass. : Curley, 1978, c1957 ; [Skipton] : distributed by Magna. — 393p ; 22cm
Published in large print
ISBN 0-89340-134-x (pbk) : Unpriced
B82-14122

Grey, Zane. The last of the plainsmen / Zane Grey. — South Yarmouth, Mass. : Curley ; [Long Preston] : distributed by Magna, c1976. — 423p ; 23cm
Published in large print
ISBN 0-89340-359-8 : Unpriced B82-13680

Grey, Zane. The rainbow trail / Zane Grey. — Abridged ed. — Hornchurch : Henry, 1981, c1943. — 172p ; 21cm
Originally published: London : World Distributors, 1965
ISBN 0-86025-195-0 : £5.25 B82-10151

813'.52[F] — Fiction in English. American writers, *1900-1945* — *Texts* *continuation*

Grey, Zane. Shadow on the trail / by Zane Grey. — Hornchurch : Henry, 1982. — 190p ; 21cm
Originally published: London : Hodder & Stoughton, 1946
ISBN 0-86025-206-x : £5.45 B82-16874

Grey, Zane. Thieves' canyon / Zane Grey. — Hornchurch : Ian Henry, 1981, c1930. — 155p ; 21cm
This abridged version of Robbers' roost originally published: London : Sphere, 1967
ISBN 0-86025-194-2 : £5.25 B82-07352

Grey, Zane. West of the Pecos / Zane Grey. — Sth. Yarmouth, Mass. : Curley, 1978, c1965 ; [Skipton] : distributed by Magna. — 481p ; 22cm
Published in large print
ISBN 0-89340-135-8 (pbk) : Unpriced B82-14121

Grey, Zane. Wild Horse mesa / Zane Grey. — London : Prior, 1981, c1929. — 438p ; 25cm
Published in large print
ISBN 0-86043-622-5 : £6.95 B82-02935

Haines, William Wister. Command decision / William Wister Haines. — South Yarmouth, Mass. : Curley, c1974 ; [Long Preston] : Magna [distributor]. — 413p ; 23cm
Originally published: Boston, Mass. : Little, Brown, 1947 ; London : Cassell, 1948. — Published in large print
ISBN 0-89340-357-1 : Unpriced B82-09486

Hammett, Dashiell. The Maltese falcon / Dashiell Hammett. — Large print ed. — South Yarmouth, Mass. : Curley ; Skipton : Magna Print [distributor], [1982?], c1957. — 413p ; 22cm
ISBN 0-89340-330-x : Unpriced B82-27418

Haycox, Ernest. Trouble shooter / Ernest Haycox. — London : Prior, 1981, c1964. — 471p ; 25cm
Published in large print
ISBN 0-86043-636-5 : £7.50 B82-16191

Hayes, Joseph. No escape : by Joseph Hayes. — London : Deutsch, 1982. — 313p ; 25cm
ISBN 0-233-97428-8 : £7.95 B82-22382

Hemingway, Ernest. Fiesta. — Large print ed. — Anstey : Ulverscroft, Feb.1983. — 1v.. — (Charnwood library series)
ISBN 0-7089-8098-8 : £5.95 : CIP entry B82-38889

Hemingway, Ernest. For whom the bell tolls / Ernest Hemingway. — Leicester : Charnwood, 1982. — 715p ; 23cm. — (Charnwood large type)
Published in large print
ISBN 0-7089-8057-0 : Unpriced : CIP rev. B82-15969

Hill, Grace Livingston. Beauty for ashes / Grace Livingston Hill. — Sth. Yarmouth, Mass. : Curley, 1979, c1935 ; [Skipton] : distributed by Magna. — 486p ; 22cm
Published in large print
ISBN 0-89340-160-9 : £4.75 B82-14118

Hill, Grace Livingston. Crimson roses / Grace Livingston Hill. — Sth. Yarmouth, Mass. : Curley, 1979, c1928 ; [Skipton] : distributed by Magna. — 416p ; 22cm
Published in large print
ISBN 0-89340-162-5 : £4.75 B82-14117

Hill, Grace Livingston. Where two ways met / Grace Livingston Hill. — Sth. Yarmouth, Mass. : Curley, 1979, c1946 ; [Skipton] : distributed by Magna. — 474p ; 22cm
Originally published: Philadelphia : Lippincott, 1947. — Published in large print
ISBN 0-89340-161-7 : £4.75 B82-14119

Horgan, Paul. Mexico Bay. — Henley on Thames : Aidan Ellis, Sept.1982. — [256]p
ISBN 0-85628-117-4 : £6.95 : CIP entry B82-20780

Hum-ishu-ma. Cogewea : the half-blood : a depiction of the Great Montana cattle range / by Hum-ishu-ma "Mourning Dove" ; given through Sho-pow-tan ; with notes and biographical sketch by Lucullus Virgil McWhorter ; introduction by Dexter Fisher. — Lincoln [Nb.] ; London : University of Nebraska Press, 1981. — xxix,302p : facsims,1port ; 21cm
Facsim. of: ed. originally published Boston : Four Seas, 1927
ISBN 0-8032-3069-9 (cased) : Unpriced
ISBN 0-8032-8110-2 (pbk) : Unpriced B82-02104

L'Amour, Louis. Borden Chantry / Louis L'Amour. — London : Corgi, 1978, c1977 (1982 [printing]). — 170p ; 18cm
Originally published: United States : s.n., 1977
ISBN 0-552-10639-9 (pbk) : £0.95 B82-26842

L'Amour, Louis. The Buckskin Run / Louis L'Amour. — [London] : Corgi, 1982, c1981. — xi,175p ; 18cm
ISBN 0-552-11910-5 (pbk) : £0.95 B82-19463

L'Amour, Louis. Callaghen / Louis L'Amour. — London : Corgi, 1972 (1982 [printing]). — 183p ; 18cm
Originally published: New York : Bantam, 1972
ISBN 0-552-09006-9 (pbk) : £0.95 B82-18422

L'Amour, Louis. Catlow / Louis L'Amour. — Large print ed. — Leicester : Ulverscroft, 1982, c1963. — 262p ; 22cm. — (Ulverscroft Large print series)
Originally published: New York : Bantam, 1963
ISBN 0-7089-0757-1 : £5.00 : CIP rev. B81-36935

L'Amour, Louis. Chancy / Louis L'Amour. — London : Corgi, 1968 (1982 [printing]). — 138p ; 18cm
ISBN 0-552-08007-1 (pbk) : £0.95 B82-23950

L'Amour, Louis. Comstock code / Louis L'Amour. — London : Corgi, 1982, c1981. — 406p ; 18cm
Originally published: London : Bantam, 1981
ISBN 0-552-11983-0 (pbk) : £1.75 : CIP rev. B82-35254

L'Amour, Louis. Conagher / Louis L'Amour. — London : Hale, 1981. — 175p ; 19cm
Originally published: London : Corgi, 1969
ISBN 0-7091-4358-3 : £4.95 B82-07209

L'Amour, Louis. The Ferguson rifle / Louis L'Amour. — London : Corgi, 1973 (1982 [printing]). — 180p ; 18cm
Originally published: Totonto : Bantam, 1973
ISBN 0-552-09264-9 (pbk) : £0.95 B82-18421

L'Amour, Louis. Flint / Louis L'Amour. — [London] : Corgi, 1961, c1960 (1982 [printing]). — 151p ; 17cm
ISBN 0-552-08574-x (pbk) : £0.95 B82-24173

L'Amour, Louis. Galloway ; and Sackett's land / Louis L'Amour. — Large print ed. — Leicester : Ulverscroft, 1981, c1970. — 516p ; 23cm. — (Ulverscroft large print series)
Galloway originally published: New York : Bantam ; London : Corgi, 1970. — Sackett's land originally published: New York : Saturday Review Press, 1974 ; London : Corgi, 1975
ISBN 0-7089-0715-6 : £5.00 : CIP rev. B81-30508

L'Amour, Louis. High lonesome / Louis L'Amour. — London : Corgi, 1963, c1962 (1982 [printing]). — 119p ; 18cm
Originally published: Toronto : Bantam, 1962
ISBN 0-552-08341-0 (pbk) : £0.95 B82-18425

L'Amour, Louis. Kid Rodelo / Louis L'Amour. — [London] : Corgi, 1966 (1982 [printing]). — 120p ; 17cm
ISBN 0-552-08388-7 (pbk) : £0.95 B82-24174

L'Amour, Louis. Killoe / Louis L'Amour. — London : Corgi, 1962 (1982 [printing]). — 120p ; 18cm
ISBN 0-552-08386-0 (pbk) : £0.95 B82-18420

L'Amour, Louis. Lonely on the mountain / Louis L'Amour. — London : Prior, 1981, c1980. — 341p ; 25cm
Originally published: New York : Bantam, 1980 ; London : Corgi, 1981. — Published in large print
ISBN 0-86043-635-7 : £6.50 B82-16184

L'Amour, Louis. The man called Noon / Louis L'Amour. — London : Corgi, 1970, c1970, c1969 (1982 [printing]). — 150p ; 18cm
Originally published: New York : Bantam, 1969
ISBN 0-552-09317-3 (pbk) : £0.95 B82-30507

L'Amour, Louis. The man from Skibbereen / Louis L'Amour. — London : Corgi, 1973 (1982 [printing]). — 184p ; 18cm
ISBN 0-552-09387-4 (pbk) : £0.95 B82-26844

L'Amour, Louis. Milo Talon / Louis L'Amour. — London : Corgi, 1981. — 212p ; 18cm
ISBN 0-552-11838-9 (pbk) : £0.95 B82-06469

L'Amour, Louis. Shalako / by Louis L'Amour. — London : Hale, 1982, c1962. — 173p ; 19cm
Originally published: London : Corgi, 1962
ISBN 0-7091-4384-2 : £5.50 B82-39183

L'Amour, Louis. Tucker / Louis L'Amour. — London : Corgi, 1972, c1971 (1982 [printing]). — 185p ; 18cm
Originally published: Toronto : Bantam, 1971
ISBN 0-552-08939-7 (pbk) : £0.95 B82-18423

L'Amour, Louis. Tucker / by Louis L'Amour. — London : Hale, 1982, c1971. — 174p ; 20cm
Originally published: New York : Bantam, 1971 ; London : Corgi, 1972
ISBN 0-7091-4360-5 : £5.50 B82-31620

L'Amour, Louis. Under the sweetwater rim / Louis L'Amour. — London : Hale, 1982, c1971. — 182p ; 20cm
Originally published: New York : Bantam ; London : Corgi, 1971
ISBN 0-7091-4359-1 : £5.25 B82-18312

L'Amour, Louis. Where the long grass blows / Louis L'Amour. — London : Corgi, 1977, c1976 (1982 [printing]). — 185p ; 18cm
Originally published: 1976
ISBN 0-552-10357-8 (pbk) : £0.95 B82-18424

Le Sueur, Meridel. The girl. — London : Women's Press, Jan.1982. — [156]p
Originally published: Cambridge, Mass. : West End Press, 1978
ISBN 0-7043-3880-7 (pbk) : £2.50 : CIP entry B81-37539

Lee, Ranger. Big horse / Ranger Lee. — London : Collins, 1953 (1979 [printing]). — 192p ; 19cm
ISBN 0-00-247048-9 : £3.50 B82-06317

Lockridge, Richard. The old die young / Richard Lockridge. — London : Hale, 1981, c1980. — 178p ; 20cm
ISBN 0-7091-9506-0 : £6.50 B82-03154

Lockridge, Richard. The old die young / Richard Lockridge. — South Yarmouth : Curley ; [Skipton] : Magna Print, [1981], c1980. — 331p ; 22cm
Originally published: New York : Lippincott & Crowell, 1980. — Published in large print
ISBN 0-89340-343-1 : Unpriced B82-05036

Lockridge, Richard. Or was he pushed / Richard Lockridge. — South Yarmouth, Mass. : Curley, c1975 ; [Long Preston] : Magna [distributor]. — 357p ; 23cm
Originally published: Philadelphia : Lippincott, 1975 ; London : Long, 1976. — Published in large print
ISBN 0-89340-345-8 : Unpriced B82-09488

813'.52[F] — Fiction in English. American writers, *1900-1945 — Texts* *continuation*

Longstreet, Stephen. The Pedlocks / Stephen Longstreet. — London : Star, 1974, c1951 (1982 [printing]). — 400p ; 18cm
Originally published: New York : Simon & Schuster, 1951 ; London : W.H. Allen, 1971
ISBN 0-352-30031-0 (pbk) : £1.75 B82-17816

Longstreet, Stephen. The Pembroke colours / Stephen Longstreet. — London : W.H. Allen, 1982, c1981. — 320p ; 23cm
Originally published: New York : Putnam's, 1981
ISBN 0-491-02816-4 : £7.95 B82-11376

Loos, Anita. Gentlemen prefer blondes ; But gentlemen marry brunettes / Anita Loos. — [London] : Picador, [1982]. — 156,96p : ports ; 20cm
Spine title. — Text and ports. on inside covers
ISBN 0-330-26777-9 (pbk) : £2.95 B82-22143

Loring, Emilie. A key to many doors / Emilie Loring. — London : Prior, 1981, c1967. — 384p ; 25cm
Originally published: Boston, Mass. : Little, Brown, 1967 ; London : Hale, 1969. — Published in large print
ISBN 0-86043-625-x : £6.95 B82-02933

McCarthy, Mary, *1912-*. Cannibals and missionaries / Mary McCarthy. — Harmondsworth : Penguin, 1982, c1979. — 369p : 1ill ; 19cm
Originally published: New York : Harcourt, Brace Jovanovich ; London : Weidenfeld and Nicolson, 1979
ISBN 0-14-005693-9 (pbk) : £1.95 B82-32574

McCarthy, Mary, *1912-*. The company she keeps / Mary McCarthy. — London : Weidenfeld and Nicolson, 1982, c1942. — vii,246p ; 23cm
ISBN 0-297-78038-7 : £6.95 B82-12602

McCloy, Helen. The sleepwalker. — Large print ed. — Anstey : Ulverscroft, Oct.1982. — [320] p. — (Ulverscroft large print series)
Originally published: London : Gollancz, 1974
ISBN 0-7089-0857-8 : £5.00 : CIP entry B82-26678

McCullers, Carson. The heart is a lonely hunter / Carson McCullers. — Harmondsworth : Penguin, 1981, c1943. — 311p ; 20cm. — (King penguin)
ISBN 0-14-006012-x (pbk) : £2.50 B82-06438

Macdonald, Ross, *1915-*. Blue city : a famous first / Ross Macdonald. — London : Collins, 1981, 1947. — 220p ; 21cm. — (The Crime Club)
Originally published: / by Ross Macdonald writing as Kenneth Millar. New York : Knopf, 1947 ; London : Cassell, 1949
ISBN 0-00-231027-9 : £6.50 B82-03077

MacDonald, William Colt. Action at Arcanum : a Gregory Quist story / by William Colt MacDonald. — London : Remploy, 1980, c1958. — 192p ; 20cm
Originally published: Philadelphia : Lippincott, 1958 ; London : Hodder & Stoughton, 1961
ISBN 0-7066-0836-4 : £4.00 B82-09338

MacDonald, William Colt. Destination, danger / by William Colt MacDonald. — London : Remploy, 1979. — 191p ; 20cm
Originally published: London : Hodder & Stoughton, 1957
ISBN 0-7066-0834-8 : £3.90 B82-16895

MacInnes, Helen. The hidden target / Helen MacInnes. — [London] : Fontana, 1982, c1980. — 352p ; 18cm
Originally published: London : Collins, 1980
ISBN 0-00-616329-7 (pbk) : £1.75 B82-09317

MacInnes, Helen. The hidden target / Helen MacInnes. — Large print ed. — Leicester : Charnwood, 1982, c1980. — 551p ; 23cm. — (Charnwood library series)
Originally published: London : Collins, 1980. — Published in large print
ISBN 0-7089-8022-8 : £6.50 : CIP rev. B81-33990

Marshall, Gary. Bandits of the brush country / Gary Marshall. — London : Collins, 1955 (1979 [printing]). — 192p ; 19cm. — (Collins western)
ISBN 0-00-247046-2 : £3.50 B82-10306

Marshall, Gary. Line fence / Gary Marshall. — London : Collins, 1954 (1979 [printing]). — 192p ; 19cm. — (Collins western)
ISBN 0-00-247458-1 : £3.50 B82-10307

Marshall, Gary. Lost loot / Gary Marshall. — London : Collins, 1955 (1979 [printing]). — 192p ; 19cm. — (Collins western)
ISBN 0-00-247449-2 : £3.50 B82-10305

Marshall, Gary. Mountain gold / Gary Marshall. — London : Collins, 1952 (1979 [printing]). — 188p ; 19cm. — (Collins western)
ISBN 0-00-247519-7 : £3.50 B82-10304

Mulford, Clarence E.. Black buttes / [Clarence E. Mulford]. — London : Remploy, 1979. — 319p ; 20cm
ISBN 0-7066-0815-1 : £4.50 B82-16875

Nin, Anaïs. A spy in the house of love / Anaïs Nin. — Harmondsworth : Penguin, 1973, c1954 (1982 [printing]). — 123p ; 20cm. — (A King Penguin)
Originally published: New York : British Book Centre, 1954 ; London : Spearman, 1956
ISBN 0-14-006021-9 (pbk) : £1.95 B82-32236

Pentecost, Hugh. Murder in luxury / Hugh Pentecost. — London : Hale, 1981. — 182p ; 21cm
ISBN 0-7091-9302-5 : £6.50 B82-07190

Pentecost, Hugh. Sow death, reap death / Hugh Pentecost. — London : Hale, 1982, c1981. — 187p ; 20cm
Originally published: New York : Dodd, Mead, 1981
ISBN 0-7091-9695-4 (corrected) : £6.75 B82-20997

Queen, Ellery. The house of brass / Ellery Queen. — South Yarmouth, Mass. : Curley, 1978, c1968 ; [Long Preston] : Distributed by Magna. — 397p ; 22cm
Originally published: New York : New American Library ; London : Gollancz, 1968. — Published in large print
ISBN 0-89340-109-9 (pbk) : Unpriced B82-17026

Queen, Ellery. Inspector Queen's own case / Ellery Queen. — South Yarmouth, Mass. : Curley, 1978, c1956 ; [Long Preston] : Distributed by Magna. — 408p ; 22cm. — (An Ellery Queen mystery)
Originally published: New York : Simon and Schuster ; London : Gollancz, 1956. — Published in large print
ISBN 0-89340-104-8 (pbk) : Unpriced B82-17030

Queen, Ellery. The player on the other side / Ellery Queen. — South Yarmouth, Mass. : Curley, 1978, c1963 ; [Long Preston] : Distributed by Magna. — 471p ; 23cm. — (An Ellery Queen mystery)
Originally published: New York : Random House ; London : Gollancz, 1963. — Published in large print
ISBN 0-89340-107-2 : Unpriced B82-17029

Queen, Ellery. The Roman hat mystery : a problem in deduction / Ellery Queen. — Feltham : Hamlyn Paperbacks, 1981, c1929. — 319p : 1plan ; 18cm. — (A Hamlyn whodunnit)
ISBN 0-600-20074-4 (pbk) : £1.50 B82-34113

Seifert, Elizabeth. Army doctor. — London : Severn House, May 1981. — [272]p
ISBN 0-7278-0705-6 : £6.50 : CIP entry B81-07622

Seifert, Elizabeth. The doctor's promise / Elizabeth Seifert. — South Yarmouth, Mass. : Curley, c1979 ; [Long Preston] : Magna [distributor]. — 377p ; 23cm
Originally published: New York : Dodd, Mead ; London : Collins, 1979. — Published in large print
ISBN 0-89340-294-x : Unpriced B82-09487

Seifert, Elizabeth. The doctor's promise / by Elizabeth Seifert. — London : Collin, 1981, c1979. — 236p ; 21cm
Originally published: New York : Dodd, Mead, 1979
ISBN 0-00-222135-7 : £6.95 : CIP rev. B81-28772

Seifert, Elizabeth. [Healing hands]. The doctor's healing hands / Elizabeth Seifert. — London : Severn House, 1982. — 255p ; 21cm
ISBN 0-7278-0768-4 : £5.95 B82-16178

Seifert, Elizabeth. Legacy for a doctor / Elizabeth Seifert. — London : Severn House, 1981, c1963. — 272p ; 21cm
Originally published: New York : Mead, 1963; London : Collins, 1964
ISBN 0-7278-0726-9 : £5.95 : CIP rev. B81-23816

Seifert, Elizabeth. Rebel doctor / Elizabeth Seifert. — South Yarmouth, Mass. : Curley, 1979, c1978 ; [Long Preston] : Distributed by Magna. — 486p ; 23cm. — (An Elizabeth Seifert romance)
Originally published: New York : Dodd, Mead, 1978. — Published in large print
ISBN 0-89340-202-8 : £5.25 B82-17028

Seifert, Elizabeth. Two doctors and a girl / Elizabeth Seifert. — South Yarmouth, Mass. : Curley, 1978, c1976 ; [Long Preston] : Distributed by Magna. — 370p ; 22cm. — (An Elizabeth Seifert romance)
Originally published: New York : Dodd, Mead, 1976 ; London : Collins, 1978. — Published in large print
ISBN 0-89340-146-3 (pbk) : Unpriced B82-17027

Seton, Anya. Avalon / Anya Seton. — Large print ed. — Leicester : Ulverscroft, 1982, c1965. — 586p ; 23cm. — (Ulverscroft large print)
Originally published: London : Hodder & Stoughton, 1966
ISBN 0-7089-0750-4 : £5.00 : CIP rev. B81-36941

Shaw, Irwin. Bread upon the waters. — London : New English Library, Sept.1982. — [480]p
ISBN 0-450-05451-9 (pbk) : £2.25 : CIP entry B82-19690

Shaw, Irwin. Bread upon the waters / Irwin Shaw. — Leicester : Charnwood, 1982, c1981. — 657p ; 23cm. — (Charnwood library series)
Originally published: London : Weidenfeld and Nicolson, 1981. — Published in large print
ISBN 0-7089-8050-3 : Unpriced : CIP rev. B82-15949

Shaw, Irwin. Voices of a summer day. — London : Severn House, Dec.1982. — [192]p
Originally published: London : New English Library, 1977
ISBN 0-7278-0851-6 : £6.95 : CIP entry B82-34075

Sheldon, Sidney. Bloodline / Sidney Sheldon. — Leicester : Charnwood, 1982, c1978. — 454p ; 23cm. — (Charnwood library series)
Originally published: New York : Morrow ; London : Collins, 1978. — Published in large print
ISBN 0-7089-8051-1 : Unpriced : CIP rev. B82-15950

813'.52[F] — Fiction in English. American writers, *1900-1945 — Texts* *continuation*

Sheldon, Sidney. Rage of angels / Sidney Sheldon. — Leicester : Charnwood, 1981, c1980. — 596p ; 23cm. — (Charnwood library series)
Originally published: London : Collins, 1980. — Published in large print
ISBN 0-7089-8003-1 : £6.50 : CIP rev. B81-22659

Sinclair, Upton. The jungle / Upton Sinclair. — Harmondsworth : Penguin, 1936 (1982 [printing]). — 411p ; 19cm. — (Penguin modern classics)
ISBN 0-14-000049-6 (pbk) : £1.95 B82-28634

Slaughter, Frank G.. Doctor's daughters / Frank G. Slaughter. — London : Hutchinson, 1982. — 305p ; 23cm
ISBN 0-09-147100-1 : £7.50 : CIP rev. B82-07962

Smith, E. E. Doc. Lord Tedric / E.E. 'Doc' Smith. — London : W.H. Allen, 1978. — 159,143p ; 18cm. — (A Star book)
Contents: Lord Tedric. — Originally published: London : Wright, 1978. — Lord Tedric, alien worlds
ISBN 0-352-30980-6 (pbk) : £1.25 B82-02912

Stein, Aaron Marc. A body for a buddy / by Aaron Marc Stein. — London : Hale, 1981. — 189p ; 20cm
ISBN 0-7091-9509-5 : £6.50 B82-03152

Stein, Aaron Marc. Hangman's row / Aaron Marc Stein. — London : Hale, 1982. — 181p ; 20cm
ISBN 0-7091-9912-0 : £6.75 B82-36520

Stone, Irving. Lust for life : the story of Vincent Van Gogh / Irving Stone. — [London] : Magnum, 1980. — 430p ; 18cm
ISBN 0-417-05390-8 (pbk) : £1.50 B82-24820

Stone, Irving. The origin / Irving Stone. — [London] : Corgi, 1982, c1980. — 815p : 1map ; 18cm
Originally published: London : Cassell, 1981
ISBN 0-552-11920-2 (pbk) : £2.95 B82-19460

Stout, Rex. [Fer-de-lance]. Nero Wolfe : fer-de-lance / by Rex Stout. — London : Prior, 1981, c1962. — 462p ; 25cm
Published in large print
ISBN 0-86043-667-5 : £6.95 B82-16188

Stout, Rex. The golden spiders / Rex Stout. — [London] : Fontana, 1964 (1981 [printing]). — 191p ; 18cm
Originally published: London : Collins, 1954
ISBN 0-00-616469-2 (pbk) : £1.35 B82-13649

Stout, Rex. The golden spiders / Rex Stout. — London : Severn House, 1982. — 191p ; 21cm
Originally published: London : Collins, 1954
ISBN 0-7278-0778-1 : £5.95 B82-13854

Stout, Rex. The League of Frightened Men / by Rex Stout. — London : Prior, 1981, c1963. — 495p ; 25cm
At head of title: Nero Wolfe. — Published in large print
ISBN 0-86043-626-8 : £7.95 B82-02937

Stout, Rex. Might as well be dead / Rex Stout. — [London] : Fontana, 1963, c1957 (1981 [printing]). — 192p ; 18cm
Originally published: London : Collins, 1957
ISBN 0-00-616470-6 (pbk) : £1.35 B82-13650

Stout, Rex. [The red box]. Nero Wolfe : the red box / Rex Stout. — London : Prior, 1981, 1965. — 439p ; 25cm
Published in large print
ISBN 0-86043-666-7 : £6.95 B82-16189

Stout, Rex. The rubber band / by Rex Stout. — London : Prior, 1981, c1964. — 417p ; 25cm
At head of title: Nero Wolfe. — Published in large print
ISBN 0-86043-627-6 : £6.95 B82-02936

Van Dine, S. S.. The Greene murder case : a Philo Vance mystery / S.S. Van Dine. — London : Remploy, 1982, c1956. — 288p : 1plan ; 20cm
ISBN 0-7066-0920-4 : £6.90 B82-30001

Viertel, Joseph. Life lines : a novel / by Joseph Viertel. — London : Deutsch, 1982. — 526p ; 24cm
ISBN 0-233-97492-x : £8.95 B82-38629

Welty, Eudora. Delta wedding / Eudora Welty ; with a new introduction by Paul Binding. — London : Virago, 1982. — ix,247p : 1map ; 20cm. — (Virago modern classics)
ISBN 0-86068-289-7 (pbk) : £2.95 : CIP rev. B82-14207

Welty, Eudora. Losing battles / Eudora Welty. — London : Virago, 1982, c1970. — 436p : 1map ; 21cm
Originally published: New York : Random House, 1970
ISBN 0-86068-288-9 : £8.95 : CIP rev. B82-07824

Welty, Eudora. The robber bridegroom / Eudora Welty ; with a new introduction by Paul Binding. — London : Virago, 1982. — xiv,185p ; 20cm. — (Virago modern classics)
ISBN 0-86068-290-0 (pbk) : £2.95 : CIP rev. B82-07680

Wharton, Edith. Ethan Frome ; and, Summer. — Oxford : Oxford University Press, Oct.1982. — [264]p. — (Oxford paperbacks)
ISBN 0-19-281366-8 (pbk) : £2.95 : CIP entry B82-23670

Whitney, Phyllis A.. Blue fire. — Large print ed. — Anstey : Ulverscroft, Aug.1982. — [480]p. — (Ulverscroft large print series)
Originally published: London : Hodder & Stoughton, 1962
ISBN 0-7089-0835-7 : £5.00 : CIP entry B82-26998

Whitney, Phyllis A.. Blue fire. — Loughton : Piatkus, Sept.1982. — [224]p
Originally published: London : Hodder & Stoughton, 1962
ISBN 0-86188-185-0 : £6.50 : CIP entry B82-21549

Whitney, Phyllis A.. Domino. — London : Hodder and Stoughton, Jan.1982. — [320]p. — (Coronet books)
Originally published: Garden City, N.Y. : Doubleday, 1979 ; London : Hutchinson, 1980
ISBN 0-340-27537-5 (pbk) : £1.50 : CIP entry B81-34134

Whitney, Phyllis A.. The glass flame. — London : Hodder and Stoughton, Jan.1982. — [320]p. — (Coronet books)
Originally published: Garden City, N.Y. : Doubleday ; London : Heinemann, 1979
ISBN 0-340-27536-7 (pbk) : £1.50 : CIP entry B81-34130

Whitney, Phyllis A.. Hunter's Green / Phyllis A. Whitney. — London : Prior, 1981, c1968. — 464p ; 25cm
Originally published: New York : Doubleday, 1968 ; London : Heinemann, 1969. — Published in large print
ISBN 0-86043-671-3 (corrected) : £7.50 B82-17806

Whitney, Phyllis A.. The moonflower : a novel / by Phyllis A. Whitney. — Loughton : Piatkus, 1982, c1958. — 224p ; 21cm
Originally published: New York : Appleton Century-Crofts, 1958
ISBN 0-86188-182-6 : £6.50 : CIP rev. B82-10249

Whitney, Phyllis A.. Poinciana. — London : Coronet, Feb.1983. — [352]p
Originally published: London : Heinemann, 1980
ISBN 0-340-32075-3 (pbk) : £1.50 : CIP entry B82-38068

Whitney, Phyllis A.. The Quicksilver pool / Phyllis A. Whitney. — Large print ed. — Leicester : Ulverscroft, 1981, c1955. — 507p ; 23cm
Originally published: New York : Appleton-Century-Crofts, 1955
ISBN 0-7089-0723-7 : £5.00 : CIP rev. B81-32032

Whitney, Phyllis A.. Skye Cameron. — Loughton : Piatkus, Feb.1982. — [224]p
Originally published: London : Hurst & Blackett, 1959
ISBN 0-86188-151-6 : £5.95 : CIP entry B81-36019

Williamson, Jack. The reign of wizardry / Jack Williamson. — London : Sphere, 1981, c1979. — xv,174p ; 18cm
ISBN 0-7221-9185-5 (pbk) : £1.50 B82-06013

Wister, Owen. The Virginian / Owen Wister ; drawings by Val Biro ; introduction by Kenneth Ulyatt. — London : Folio Society, 1981. — 285p : ill ; 23cm
In slip case
Unpriced B82-00622

813'.52[F] — Short stories in English. American writers, *1900-1945 — Texts*

Boyle, Kay. Fifty stories / Kay Boyle. — Harmondsworth : Penguin, 1981, c1980. — 648p ; 20cm
Originally published: Garden City, N.Y. : Doubleday, 1980
ISBN 0-14-005922-9 (pbk) : £2.95 B82-16764

Cheever, John. The stories of John Cheever. — Harmondsworth : Penguin, 1982, c1978. — 693p ; 20cm. — (A King Penguin)
Originally published: New York : Knopf, 1978 ; London : Cape, 1979
ISBN 0-14-005575-4 (pbk) : £4.95 B82-22319

Cole, Jackson. Two guns for Texas ; and, Tin-star target / Jackson Cole. — Large print ed. — Leicester : Ulverscroft, 1982, c1982. — 357p ; 23cm. — (Ulverscroft large print series)
ISBN 0-7089-0785-7 : Unpriced : CIP rev. B82-08096

Dobie, J. Frank. Tongues of the Monte / J. Frank Dobie. — Austin ; London : University of Texas Press, 1980, c1975. — xiv,301p : ill ; 21cm
ISBN 0-292-78035-4 (pbk) : Unpriced B82-36531

Fitzgerald, F. Scott. Bits of paradise / twenty-one uncollected stories by F. Scott and Zelda Fitzgerald ; selected by Scottie Fitzgerald Smith and Matthew J. Bruccoli ; with a foreword by Scottie Fitzgerald Smith. — Harmondsworth : Penguin, 1976, c1973 (1982 [printing]). — 346p ; 18cm
Originally published: London : Bodley Head, 1973
ISBN 0-14-004071-4 (pbk) : £1.75 B82-39084

Fitzgerald, F. Scott. [The Bodley Head Scott Fitzgerald. 5. Short stories]. Bernice bobs her hair : and other stories. — Harmondsworth : Penguin, 1968, c1963 (1982 [printing]). — 175p ; 18cm. — (The Stories of F. Scott Fitzgerald ; v.4)
Originally published: London : Bodley Head, 1963
ISBN 0-14-002736-x (pbk) : £1.25 B82-27555

Fitzgerald, F. Scott. The lost decade : and other stories / F. Scott Fitzgerald. — Harmondsworth : Penguin, 1968, c1963 (1982 [printing]). — 125p ; 18cm. — (The Stories of F. Scott Fitzgerald ; v.5)
Originally published: London : Bodley Head, 1963
ISBN 0-14-002891-9 (pbk) : £1.25 B82-33016

Fitzgerald, F. Scott. The price was high / edited by Matthew J. Bruccoli. — London : Pan. — (The last uncollected stories of F. Scott Fitzgerald) (Picador)
Originally published: New York : Harcourt Brace Jovanovich ; London : Quartet, 1979
Vol.2. — 1981, c1979. — 410p ; 20cm
ISBN 0-330-26366-8 (pbk) : £2.50 B82-03149

813'.52[F] — Short stories in English. American writers, *1900-1945 — Texts continuation*

Gardner, Erle Stanley. The case of the Crimson kiss / Erle Stanley Gardner. — London : Methuen, 1982. — 189p ; 18cm
Originally published: New York : Morrow, 1971 ; London : Heinemann, 1975
ISBN 0-417-06830-1 (pbk) : £1.25 B82-34370

Gardner, Erle Stanley. Whispering sands / Erle Stanley Gardner ; edited by Charles G. Waugh and Martin H. Greenberg. — South Yarmouth, Mass. : Curley ; [Long Preston] : Distributed by Magna, c1981. — 581p ; 23cm
These stories originally published in Argosy magazine between 1930-1934. — Published in large print
ISBN 0-89340-391-1 : Unpriced B82-33164

Henderson, Robert. Into the wind : stories / by Robert Henderson. — Urbana ; London : University of Illinois Press, c1981. — 149p ; 21cm. — (Illinois short fiction)
ISBN 0-252-00899-5 (cased) : Unpriced
ISBN 0-252-00924-x (pbk) : £3.50 B82-17389

Riding, Laura. Progress of stories. — New ed. — Manchester : Carcanet Press, Oct.1982. — [320]p
Previous ed.: London : Constable, 1935
ISBN 0-85635-402-3 : £7.95 : CIP entry B82-24116

Sanford, John, *1904-*. To feed their hopes : a book of American women / John Sanford ; foreword by Annette K. Baxter. — Urbana ; London : University of Illinois Press, c1980. — xxii,198p ; 24cm
ISBN 0-252-00804-9 : £9.70 B82-35067

Welty, Eudora. The collected stories of Eudora Welty. — London : Boyars, 1981, c1980. — xvi,622p ; 25cm
Originally published: New York : Harcourt Brace Jovanovich, 1980
ISBN 0-7145-2728-9 : £15.00 B82-05296

813'.52[J] — Children's short stories in English. American writers, *1900-1945 — Texts*

Brown, Margaret Wise. Once upon a time in a pigpen : and three other stories / Margaret Wise Brown ; pictures by Ann Strugnell. — London : Hutchinson, 1981, c1980. — 63p : ill (some col.) ; 24cm
Originally published: Reading, Mass : Addison-Wesley, 1977
ISBN 0-09-146150-2 : £4.95 : CIP rev. B81-20556

813'.52[J] — Children's stories in English. American writers, *1900-1945 — Texts*

Arthur, Robert, *1899-*. Alfred Hitchcock and the Three Investigators in the mystery of the green ghost / text by Robert Arthur. — London : Armada, 1970, c1968 (1982 [printing]). — 160p ; 18cm
Originally published: New York : Random House, 1965 ; London : Collins, 1968
ISBN 0-00-692013-6 (pbk) : £0.85 B82-16813

Arthur, Robert, *1899-*. Alfred Hitchcock and the three investigators in the mystery of the silver spider / text by Robert Arthur. — London : Armada, 1972, c1967 (1982 [printing]). — 126p : ill ; 18cm
Originally published: New York : Random House, 1967 ; London : Collins, 1969
ISBN 0-00-692058-6 (pbk) : £0.85 B82-25447

Arthur, Robert, *1899-*. Alfred Hitchcock and the Three Investigators in the mystery of the talking skull / text by Robert Arthur. — London : Armada, 1973, c1970 (1981 [printing]). — 127p : ill ; 19cm
Originally published: New York : Random House, 1969 ; London : Collins, 1970
ISBN 0-00-691921-9 (pbk) : £0.85 B82-03190

Baum, L. Frank. The Wizard of Oz / L. Frank Baum ; illustrated by David McKee. — Harmondsworth : Puffin, 1982. — 171p : ill ; 19cm. — (Puffin classics)
ISBN 0-14-035001-2 (pbk) : £0.85 B82-40375

Baum, L. Frank. The wizard of Oz / L. Frank Baum ; illustrated by Michael Hague. — London : Methuen, 1982. — ix,219p : col.ill ; 26cm
ISBN 0-416-26590-1 : £8.95 B82-35639

DeJong, Meindert. The wheel on the school / Meindert DeJong ; pictures by Maurice Sendak. — Harmondsworth : Puffin, 1961, c1954 (1981 [printing]). — 203p : ill ; 19cm
Originally published: New York : Harper, 1954 ; London : Lutterworth Press, 1956
ISBN 0-14-030152-6 (pbk) : £1.25 B82-01393

Disney, Walt. Walt Disney presents Winnie the Pooh. — Bristol : Purnell, 1974 (1981 [printing]). — [12]p : col.ill ; 21cm
Text, ill on lining papers
ISBN 0-361-03845-3 : Unpriced B82-12521

Dixon, Franklin W.. The hooded hawk mystery / Franklin W. Dixon. — London : Armada, 1980, c1954. — 159p : 1ill ; 18cm. — (The Hardy boys mystery stories)
Originally published: New York : Grosset and Dunlap, 1954 ; London : Low, Marston, 1965
ISBN 0-00-691803-4 (pbk) : £0.75 B82-41090

Dixon, Franklin W.. [The missing chums]. The mystery of the missing friends / Franklin W. Dixon. — London : Armada, 1982, c1974. — 156p : ill ; 18cm. — (The Hardy boys mystery stories)
Originally published as The missing chums. London : Collins, 1974
ISBN 0-00-692078-0 (pbk) : £0.85 B82-36066

Dixon, Franklin W.. The mummy case / Franklin W. Dixon ; illustrated by Leslie Morrill. — London : Armada, 1982, c1980. — 180p : ill ; 18cm. — (The Hardy boys mystery stories)
Originally published: New York : Wanderer Books, 1980 ; London : Angus & Robertson, 1981
ISBN 0-00-691822-0 (pbk) : £0.95 B82-25432

Dixon, Franklin W.. Three great Hardy boys mysteries / [Franklin W. Dixon]. — London : Fontana, 1981. — 480p : 1map ; 18
Contents: The Arctic patrol mystery. Originally published: London : Collins, 1971. — The twisted claw. Originally published: London : Collins, 1972. — The Secret of pirates hill. Originally published: London : Collins, 1972
ISBN 0-00-691990-1 (pbk) : £1.75 B82-03163

Dixon, Franklin W.. The tower treasure / Franklin W. Dixon. — [London] : Armada, 1982, c1974. — 159p : ill ; 19cm. — (The Hardy boys mystery stories ; 31)
ISBN 0-00-691912-x (pbk) : £0.85 B82-09780

Duvoisin, Roger. The importance of Crocus / Roger Duvoisin. — London : Bodley Head, 1980. — [30]p : col.ill ; 26cm
ISBN 0-370-30343-1 : £4.25 : CIP rev. B80-19991

Enright, Elizabeth. Spiderweb for two / written and illustrated by Elizabeth Enright. — Harmondsworth : Puffin, 1970, c1951 (1982 [printing]). — 172p : ill ; 19cm
Originally published: New York : Rinehart, 1951 ; London : Heinemann, 1956
ISBN 0-14-030427-4 (pbk) : £0.95 B82-18415

Enright, Elizabeth. Then there were five / written and illustrated by Elizabeth Enright. — Harmondsworth : Puffin, 1969 (1982 [printing]). — 207p : ill ; 18cm
ISBN 0-14-030418-5 (pbk) : £1.10 B82-18628

Farley, Walter. The black stallion mystery / Walter Farley. — London : Severn House, 1982, c1957. — 159p ; 21cm
Originally published: New York : Random House, 1957 ; Leicester : Knight, 1973
ISBN 0-7278-0770-6 : £4.50 B82-18285

Farley, Walter. The black stallion's ghost / Walter Farley. — Sevenoaks : Knight Books, 1982, c1969. — 154p ; 18cm
Originally published: New York : Random House, 1969
ISBN 0-340-26531-0 (pbk) : £0.95 : CIP rev. B82-12255

Keene, Carolyn. The haunted lagoon / Carolyn Keene. — London : Sparrow, 1982, c1973. — 177p ; 18cm. — (Dana girls mystery ; no.8)
Originally published: New York : Grosset & Dunlap, 1973
ISBN 0-09-928470-7 (pbk) : £0.95 B82-35591

Keene, Carolyn. The mystery of the fire dragon / Carolyn Keene. — London : Armada, 1982, c1973. — 160p : 1ill ; 19cm. — (The Nancy Drew mystery stories)
Originally published: New York : Grosset & Dunlap, 1961 ; London : Low, Marston, 1964
ISBN 0-00-691982-0 (pbk) : £0.85 B82-09399

Keene, Carolyn. The mystery of the moss-covered mansion / Carolyn Keene. — London : Armada, 1982, c1973. — 159p : ill ; 18cm. — (The Nancy Drew mystery stories ; no.29)
Originally published: New York : Grosset & Dunlap, 1971 ; London : Collins, 1973
ISBN 0-00-691983-9 (pbk) : £0.85 B82-34106

Keene, Carolyn. Mystery of the stone tiger / Carolyn Keene. — London : Severn House, 1982, c1972. — 170p ; 21cm. — (A Dana Girls mystery)
Originally published: New York : Grosset & Dunlap, 1972
ISBN 0-7278-0762-5 : £4.95 B82-12075

Keene, Carolyn. Nancy's mysterious letter / Carolyn Keene. — London : Armada, 1981, c1973. — 157p ; 18cm. — (The Nancy Drew mystery stories ; no.26)
Originally published: London : Collins, 1973
ISBN 0-00-691916-2 (pbk) : £0.85 B82-03168

Keene, Carolyn. The phantom of Pine Hill / Carolyn Keene. — London : Armada, 1981, c1973. — 156p : ill ; 18cm. — (The Nancy Drew mystery stories ; no.27)
Originally published: New York : Grosset and Dunlap, 1953 ; London : Low, Marston, 1965
ISBN 0-00-691914-6 (pbk) : £0.85 B82-01248

Keene, Carolyn. The phantom surfer / Carolyn Keene. — [London] : Sparrow, 1982, c1972. — 170p ; 18cm. — (Dana girls mystery ; no.6)
Originally published: New York : Grosset & Dunlap, 1968
ISBN 0-09-927690-9 (pbk) : £0.95 B82-19018

Keene, Carolyn. The riddle of the frozen fountain / Carolyn Keene. — London : Severn House, 1982, c1972. — 168p ; 21cm
Originally published: New York : Sparrow, 1964 ; London : Arrow, 1972
ISBN 0-7278-0813-3 : £4.95 B82-35457

Keene, Carolyn. The secret in the old lace / Carolyn Keene ; illustrated by Ruth Sanderson. — London : Armada, 1982, c1980. — 167p : ill ; 18cm
Originally published: S.l. Wanderer, 1980
ISBN 0-00-691840-9 (pbk) : £0.85 B82-19733

Keene, Carolyn. The secret of the minstrel's guitar / Carolyn Keene. — London : Sparrow, 1981, c1972. — 169p ; 18cm. — (Dana girls mystery ; no.5)
Originally published: New York : Grosset & Dunlap, 1967
ISBN 0-09-927480-9 (pbk) : £0.95 B82-06565

Keene, Carolyn. The secret of the Swiss chalet / Carolyn Keene. — London : Sparrow, 1982, c1973. — 174p ; 18cm. — (Dana girls mystery ; no.7)
Originally published: New York : Grosset & Dunlap, 1973
ISBN 0-09-928420-0 (pbk) : £0.95 B82-35592

813'.52[J] — Children's stories in English. American writers, *1900-1945 — Texts*
continuation

Keene, Carolyn. Three great Nancy Drew mysteries / [Carolyn Keene]. — London : Fontana, 1981. — 478p ; 18. — (An Armada three-in-one)
Contents: The Secret of Shadow Ranch. Originally published: London : Collins, 1971. — The Message in the hollow oak. Originally published: London : Collins, 1972. — Mystery at the ski jump. Originally published: London : Collins, 1971
ISBN 0-00-691992-8 (pbk) : £1.75 B82-03162

Price, Willard. Arctic adventure / Willard Price ; illustrated by Pat Marriott. — London : Hodder & Stoughton, 1982, c1980. — 222p ; 18cm
Originally published: 1980
ISBN 0-340-26806-9 (pbk) : £0.95 : CIP rev. B82-07439

813'.52[J] — Children's stories in English. Canadian writers, *1900-1945 — Texts*

Montgomery, L. M.. Anne's house of dreams / L.M. Montgomery. — Harmondsworth : Penguin, 1981. — 297p ; 19cm
ISBN 0-14-031470-9 (pbk) : £1.25 B82-08660

813'.52'09 — Fiction in English. American writers: Paperback books with American imprints, *1900- — Critical studies*

O'Brien, Geoffrey. Hardboiled America : the lurid years of paperbacks / Geoffrey O'Brien. — New York ; London : Van Nostrand Reinhold, c1981. — 144p : facsims(some col.) ; 24cm
Bibliography: p143. — Includes index
ISBN 0-442-23140-7 : £14.40 B82-00856

813'.52'0912 — Fiction in English. American writers. Modernism, *1900-1979 — Critical studies*

Mellard, James M.. The exploded form : the modernist novel in America / James M. Mellard. — Urbana ; London : University of Illinois Press, c1980. — xv,208p ; 24cm
Includes index
ISBN 0-252-00801-4 : Unpriced B82-35901

813'.52'09896073 — Fiction in English. American negro writers, *1900-1945 — Critical studies*

Ikonné, Chidi. From Du Bois to Van Vechten : the early new Negro literature, 1903-1926 / Chidi Ikonné. — Westport ; London : Greenwood, 1981. — xiii,218p ; 22cm. — (Contributions in Afro-American and African studies ; no.60)
Includes index
ISBN 0-313-22496-x : Unpriced B82-17883

813.54 — AMERICAN FICTION, 1945-

813'.54 — Fiction in English. American writers. Barthelme, Donald — *Critical studies*

Couturier, Maurice. Donald Barthelme. — London : Methuen, Oct.1982. — [96]p. — (Contemporary writers)
ISBN 0-416-31870-3 (pbk) : £1.95 : CIP entry B82-24492

Molesworth, Charles. Donald Barthelme's fiction : the ironist saved from drowning / Charles Molesworth. — Columbia ; London : University of Missouri Press, 1982. — 89p ; 21cm. — (A Literary frontiers edition)
ISBN 0-8262-0338-8 (pbk) : Unpriced B82-38422

813'.54 — Fiction in English. American writers. Burroughs, William S. — *Interviews*

Bockris, Victor. With William Burroughs. — London : Vermilion, Oct.1982. — [272]p
ISBN 0-09-150591-7 (pbk) : £4.95 : CIP entry B82-24983

813'.54 — Fiction in English. American writers. Lee, Harper. To kill a mocking bird — *Questions & answers — For schools*

Craigs, Edward. To kill a mockingbird, Harper Lee / by Edward Craigs. — London : Mary Glasgow Publications, c1980. — 15p : ill(some col.),col.maps ; 30cm. — (Guidelines)
ISBN 0-86158-519-4 (unbound) : Unpriced B82-23269

813'.54 — Fiction in English. American writers. Nabokov, Vladimir — *Critical studies*

Nabokov : the critical heritage / edited by Norman Page. — London : Routledge & Kegan Paul, 1982. — xii,252p ; 23cm. — (The Critical heritage series)
Bibliography: p244. — Includes index
ISBN 0-7100-9223-7 : £10.50 B82-30179

Paine, Sylvia. Beckett, Nabokov, Nin : motives and modernism / Sylvia Paine. — Port Washington ; London : National University Publications : Kennikat, 1981. — x,102p ; 23cm. — (Literary criticism series)
Bibliography: p79-100. — Includes index
ISBN 0-8046-9288-2 : £12.75
Primary classification 828'.91209 B82-12285

813'.54 — Fiction in English. American writers. Pynchon, Thomas — *Critical studies*

Tanner, Tony. Thomas Pynchon / Tony Tanner. — London : Methuen, 1982. — 95p ; 20cm. — (Contemporary writers)
Bibliography: p93-95
ISBN 0-416-31670-0 (pbk) : Unpriced : CIP rev. B82-06753

813'.54 — Fiction in English. American writers. Pynchon, Thomas. Crying of lot 49 — *Study outlines*

Nicholson, C. E.. The crying of lot 49 : notes / by C.E. Nicholson and R.W. Stevenson. — Harlow : Longman, 1981. — 88p ; 21cm. — (York notes ; 148)
Bibliography: p84-85
ISBN 0-582-78249-x (pbk) : £0.90 B82-16455

813'.54 — Fiction in English. American writers. Roth, Philip — *Critical studies*

Lee, Hermione. Philip Roth. — London : Methuen, Oct.1982. — [96]p. — (Contemporary writers)
ISBN 0-416-32980-2 (pbk) : £1.95 : CIP entry B82-24494

813'.54 — Fiction in English. American writers. Vonnegut, Kurt — *Critical studies*

Klinkowitz, Jerome. Kurt Vonnegut / Jerome Klinkowitz. — London : Methuen, 1982. — 96p ; 20cm. — (Contemporary writers)
Bibliography: p93-96
ISBN 0-416-33480-6 (pbk) : Unpriced : CIP rev. B82-06760

813'.54 — Fiction in English. Canadian writers. Davies, Robertson — *Critical studies*

Monk, Patricia. The smaller infinity : the Jungian self in the novels of Robertson Davies / Patricia Monk. — Toronto ; London : University of Toronto Press, c1982. — 241p ; 24cm
Includes index
ISBN 0-8020-5544-3 : Unpriced B82-39342

813'.54[F] — Fiction in English. American writers, *1945- — Texts*

Aczél, Tamás. Illuminations : a novel / by Tamas Aczel. — London : Faber and Faber, 1982. — viii,373p ; 24cm
Originally published: New York : Pantheon, 1981
ISBN 0-571-11827-5 : £7.95 : CIP rev. B82-11857

Adams, Tracy. The moth and the flame. — London : Hodder & Stoughton, Jan.1982. — [192]p. — (Silhouette romance)
ISBN 0-340-27666-5 (pbk) : £0.75 : CIP entry B81-33929

Alimo, Guy. Cruise / Guy Alimo. — [London] : Corgi, 1982. — 271p ; 18cm
ISBN 0-552-11943-1 (pbk) : £1.75 B82-28360

Allen, Clay. Cougar Canyon / Clay Allen. — Large print ed. — Bath : Chivers, 1982, c1980. — 161p ; 23cm. — (A Lythway book)
Originally published: London : Hale, 1980
ISBN 0-85119-831-7 : Unpriced : CIP rev. B82-15863

Allen, Clay. Piute Range / by Clay Allen. — London : Hale, 1981. — 156p ; 19cm
ISBN 0-7091-9378-5 : £4.95 B82-07211

Allen, Clay. The wagon road / by Clay Allen. — London : Hale, 1982. — 159p ; 20cm
ISBN 0-7091-9406-4 : £5.25 B82-15475

Alter, Stephen. Neglected lives / Stephen Alter. — Harmondsworth : Penguin, 1982, c1978. — 155p ; 20cm
Originally published: New York : Farrar, Straus and Giroux, 1978 ; London : Deutsch, 1979
ISBN 0-14-005800-1 (pbk) : £1.95 B82-33022

Alther, Lisa. Original sins / Lisa Alther. — Harmondsworth : Penguin, 1982, c1981. — 584p ; 18cm
Originally published: London : Womens Press, 1981
ISBN 0-14-005894-x (pbk) : £2.50 B82-22708

Anderson, Poul. The high crusade / Poul Anderson. — London : Severn House, 1982, c1960. — 143p ; 21cm
Originally published: Garden City, N.Y. : Doubleday, 1960
ISBN 0-7278-0777-3 : £6.50 B82-30473

Anderson, Poul. The merman's children / Poul Anderson. — London : Sphere, 1981, c1979. — x,258p ; 18cm
Originally published: New York : Berkley Publishing, 1979
ISBN 0-7221-1129-0 (pbk) : £1.75 B82-02127

Anderson, Poul. Three worlds to conquer : science fiction / by Poul Anderson. — London : Sidgwick & Jackson, 1982, c1964. — 181p ; 21cm
Originally published: New York : Pyramid, 1964 ; London : Mayflower, 1966
ISBN 0-283-98835-5 : £6.95 B82-19958

Anderson, Poul. Three worlds to conquer / Poul Anderson. — London : Sphere, 1982, c1964. — 181p ; 18cm
Originally published: Moonachie : Pyramid, 1964 ; St. Albans : Mayflower, 1966
ISBN 0-7221-1128-2 (pbk) : £1.50 B82-27889

Andrews, A. A.. The short guns of Texas. — Large print ed. — Bath : Chivers, Sept.1982. — [240]p. — (A Lythway book)
Originally published: London : Hale, 1965
ISBN 0-85119-841-4 : £6.40 : CIP entry B82-20511

Andrews, Virginia. Flowers in the attic. — Large print ed. — Anstey : Ulverscroft, Aug.1982. — [544]p. — (Charnwood library series)
Originally published: Loughton : Judy Piatkus, 1980
ISBN 0-7089-8060-0 : £6.50 : CIP entry B82-26996

Andrews, Virginia. My sweet Audrina. — Loughton : Piatkus, Aug.1982. — [320]p
ISBN 0-86188-197-4 : £7.50 : CIP entry B82-16685

Andrews, Virginia. Petals on the wind. — Large print ed. — Anstey : Ulverscroft, Dec.1982. — 1v.. — (Charnwood library series)
Originally published: New York : Simon and Schuster ; London : Fontana, 1980
ISBN 0-7089-8084-8 : £6.50 : CIP entry B82-30791

Anonymous. Her / by Anonymous. — London : Arrow, 1982, c1970. — 294p ; 18cm
Originally published: New York : L. Stuart, 1970
ISBN 0-09-927400-0 (pbk) : £1.50 B82-11436

Anonymous. Him / by Anonymous. — London : Arrow, 1982, c1972. — 296p ; 18cm
ISBN 0-09-927390-x (pbk) : £1.50 B82-11437

Anonymous. Me / by Anonymous. — London : Arrow, 1982, c1976. — x,273p ; 18cm
Originally published: New York : Bantam, 1976
ISBN 0-09-927380-2 (pbk) : £1.50 B82-19016

813'.54[F] — Fiction in English. American writers, *1945-* — *Texts* *continuation*

Anonymous. Them. — London : Arrow, 1982, c1978. — ix,289p ; 18cm
Originally published: New York : Bantam, 1978
ISBN 0-09-927410-8 (pbk) : £1.50 B82-19014

Anson, Jay. 666 / Jay Anson. — London : Granada, 1982. — 286p ; 23cm
ISBN 0-246-11363-4 : £7.95 : CIP rev. B81-38304

Anson, Jay. 666 / Jay Anson. — London : Granada, 1982, c1981. — 286p ; 18cm. — (A Mayflower book)
Originally published: New York : Simon and Schuster, 1981
ISBN 0-583-13267-7 (pbk) : £1.95 B82-33676

Anthony, Diana. Once a lover / Diana Anthony. — [London] : Fontana, 1982. — 314p ; 18cm
ISBN 0-00-616566-4 (pbk) : £1.75 B82-32107

Arathorn, D. W.. Kamal / D.W. Arathron. — London : Macmillan, 1982. — 351p ; 25cm
ISBN 0-333-33432-9 : £7.95 B82-35914

Armour, John, *1916-*. Carter valley / by John Armour. — London : Hale, 1982. — 157p ; 20cm
ISBN 0-7091-9642-3 : £5.25 B82-17518

Arnett, Caroline. Theodora / Caroline Arnett. — South Yarmouth, Mass. : Curley, 1979, c1977 ; [Long Preston] : Distributed by Magna. — 390p ; 23cm. — (A Regency romance)
ISBN 0-89340-194-3 : £5.25 B82-13664

Arnold, Margot. The Cape Cod caper. — Large print ed. — Bath : Chivers, Oct.1982. — [328] p. — (Atlantic large print)
ISBN 0-85119-500-8 : £5.25 : CIP entry B82-24232

Arnold, Margot. Exit actors, dying / Margot Arnold. — [Bath] : Chivers Press, 1982, c1979. — 305p ; 23cm
ISBN 0-85119-482-6 : Unpriced : CIP rev. B82-13094

Arnold, Margot. The officer's woman / Margot Arnold. — Large print ed. — Leicester : Charnwood, 1982, c1972. — 452p ; 23cm. — (Charnwood library series)
Originally published: London : Allan Wingate, 1972. — Published in large print
ISBN 0-7089-8018-x : £5.25 : CIP rev. B81-33993

Arnold, Margot. Zadok's treasure / Margot Arnold. — Large print ed. — Bath : Chivers, 1982, c1980. — 333p ; 23cm. — (Atlantic large print)
Originally published: New York : Playboy Press, 1980
ISBN 0-85119-470-2 : Unpriced : CIP rev. B82-07623

Asher, Sandy. [Daughters of the law]. Friends and sisters / by Sandy Asher. — London : Gollancz, 1982. — 124p ; 21cm
ISBN 0-575-03124-7 : £5.50 : CIP rev. B82-04612

Ashley, Juliet. One man forever. — London : Hodder and Stoughton, Feb.1983. — [192]p. — (Silhouette romance)
ISBN 0-340-32760-x (pbk) : £0.85 : CIP entry B82-38029

Ashton, Violet. Swan song. — London : Hodder & Stoughton, Sept.1982. — [352]p. — (Coronet books)
Originally published: New York : Fawcett Gold Medal Books, 1979
ISBN 0-340-28437-4 (pbk) : £2.95 : CIP entry B82-18747

Asimov, Isaac. Foundation / Isaac Asimov. — Large print. — South Yarmouth, Mass. : John Curley, [1981], c1951 ; Long Preston : Distributed by Magna Print. — 435p ; 23cm. — (The Foundation trilogy)
Originally published: New York : Gnome Press, 1951 ; London : Weidenfeld & Nicolson, 1953
ISBN 0-89340-209-5 : £5.25 B82-00597

Asimov, Isaac. Foundation's edge. — London : Granada, Feb.1983. — [368]p
ISBN 0-246-12012-6 : £7.95 : CIP entry B82-37829

Auel, Jean M.. The valley of horses. — London : Hodder & Stoughton, Feb.1983. — [576]p. — (Earth's children)
ISBN 0-340-28134-0 (cased) : £8.95 : CIP entry
ISBN 0-340-26840-9 (pbk) : £5.50 B82-38043

Avel, Jean M.. The clan of the Cave Bear. — London : Hodder & Stoughton, May 1981. — [592]p
Originally published: 1980
ISBN 0-340-26883-2 (pbk) : £1.75 : CIP entry B81-03821

Babson, Marian. Bejewelled death / Marian Babson. — London : Keyhole Crime, 1982, c1981. — 192p ; 18cm
Originally published: London : Collins, 1981
ISBN 0-263-73961-9 (pbk) : £0.95 B82-36065

Babson, Marian. Dangerous to know. — Large print ed. — Bath : Chivers, Jan.1983. — [256] p. — (A Lythway book)
Originally published: London : Collins, 1980
ISBN 0-85119-881-3 : £6.90 : CIP entry B82-33095

Babson, Marian. Death beside the seaside / Marian Babson. — London : Collins, 1982. — 177p ; 20cm. — (The Crime Club)
ISBN 0-00-231039-2 : £6.50 : CIP rev. B82-23081

Babson, Marian. Death warmed up. — London : Collins, Mar.1982. — [224]p. — (The Crime Club)
ISBN 0-00-231326-x : £6.50 : CIP entry B82-00898

Babson, Marian. Queue here for murder / Marian Babson. — Large print ed. — Bath : Chivers, 1982, c1980. — 217p ; 23cm. — (A Lythway book)
Originally published: London : Collins, 1980
ISBN 0-85119-781-7 : Unpriced : CIP rev. B81-35865

Bachman, Richard. Rage. — London : New English Library, Jan.1983. — [224]p
ISBN 0-450-05379-2 (pbk) : £1.50 : CIP entry B82-36137

Baehr, Consuelo. [Best friends]. Girlfriends / Consuelo Baehr. — London : Pan, 1982, c1980. — 313p ; 18cm
Originally published: New York : Delacorte, c1980 ; London : Gollancz, 1981
ISBN 0-330-26718-3 (pbk) : £1.75 B82-34260

Baker, Judith. When last we loved. — London : Hodder & Stoughton, Nov.1982. — [192]p. — (Silhouette desire)
ISBN 0-340-32862-2 (pbk) : £0.95 : CIP entry B82-28733

Ball, Donna. Winners. — Loughton : Piatkus, Feb.1983. — [268]p
ISBN 0-86188-226-1 : £7.50 : CIP entry B82-39808

Ball, John, *1911-*. Then came violence / John Ball. — Feltham : Hamlyn, 1982, c1980. — 186p : ill ; 18cm. — (A Hamlyn whodunnit)
Originally published: London : Joseph, 1981
ISBN 0-600-20487-1 (pbk) : £1.50 B82-31944

Ball, John, *1911-*. Then came violence. — Large print ed. — Anstey : Ulverscroft, Nov.1982. — [352]p. — (Ulverscroft large print series)
Originally published: Garden City, N.Y. : Doubleday, 1980 ; London : Joseph, 1981
ISBN 0-7089-0870-5 : £5.00 : CIP entry B82-29086

Ball, John, *1911-*. Trouble for Tallon / John Ball. — London : Hale, 1982, c1981. — 179p ; 20cm
Originally published: Garden City, N.Y. : Doubleday for the Crime Club, 1981
ISBN 0-7091-9752-7 : £6.75 B82-30282

Ballantyne, Sheila. Imaginary crimes. — London : Gollancz, Feb.1983. — [256]p
Originally published: New York : Viking Press, 1982
ISBN 0-575-03241-3 : £8.95 : CIP entry B82-38688

Bambara, Toni Cade. The salt eaters. — London : Women's Press, Mar.1982. — [304]p
Originally published: New York : Random House, 1980
ISBN 0-7043-3882-3 (pbk) : £3.50 : CIP entry B82-01724

Banis, V. J.. The earth and all it holds / V.J. Banis. — London : New English Library, 1980 (1981 [printing]). — 413p ; 18cm
ISBN 0-450-05001-7 (pbk) : £1.95 B82-03696

Banks, Carolyn. The darkroom / Carolyn Banks. — London : Corgi, 1981, c1980. — 286p ; 18cm
Originally published: New York : Viking Press, 1980
ISBN 0-552-11855-9 (pbk) : £1.50 B82-09059

Barnett, James. Marked for destruction. — London : Secker and Warburg, Sept.1982. — [288]p
ISBN 0-436-03299-6 : £7.50 : CIP entry B82-19677

Barth, John. Chimera / John Barth. — London : Granada, 1982, c1972. — 286p ; 18cm
Originally published: New York : Random House, 1972 ; London : Deutsch, 1974
ISBN 0-586-05522-3 (pbk) : £1.95 B82-37212

Barth, John. Letters : a novel / John Barth. — London : Granada, 1981, c1979. — 770p ; 20cm. — (A Panther book)
Originally published: New York : Putnam, 1979 ; London : Secker & Warburg, 1980
ISBN 0-586-05279-8 (pbk) : £3.95 B82-02995

Barth, John. Sabbatical : a romance / John Barth. — London : Secker & Warburg, 1982. — 366p ; 24cm
ISBN 0-436-03675-4 : £7.50 B82-33832

Bartholomew, Cecilia. The dark is mine / Cecilia Bartholomew. — London : Methuen London, 1982, c1981. — 285p ; 18cm
Originally published: London : Hale, 1981
ISBN 0-417-06930-8 (pbk) : £1.50 B82-33933

Barton, Wayne. Ride down the wind / by Wayne Barton. — London : Hale, 1982, c1981. — 184p ; 20cm
Originally published: Garden City, N.Y. : Doubleday, 1981
ISBN 0-7091-9800-0 : £5.50 B82-30279

Batchelor, Reg. The nighthawks / by Reg Batchelor. — London : Hale, 1982. — 154p ; 20cm
ISBN 0-7091-9759-4 : £5.50 B82-25996

Bauer, Steven. Satyrday : a fable / by Steven Bauer ; illustrated by Ron Miller. — London : Souvenir, 1981, c1980. — 213p : ill ; 23cm. — (Nightowl books)
Originally published: New York : Berkley Publishing Corp., 1980
ISBN 0-285-62502-0 : £6.95 B82-03672

813'.54[F] — Fiction in English. American writers, *1945- — Texts* *continuation*

Baxter, Mary Lynn. All our tomorrows. — London : Hodder & Stoughton, Dec.1982. — [256]p. — (Silhouette special edition)
ISBN 0-340-32080-x (pbk) : £0.95 : CIP entry B82-29655

Baxter, Mary Lynn. Tears of yesterday. — London : Hodder and Stoughton, Dec.1982. — [256]p. — (Silhouette special edition)
ISBN 0-340-32678-6 (pbk) : £0.95 : CIP entry B82-29658

Bayer, William. Peregrine / William Bayer. — London : Severn House, 1982, c1981. — 243p ; 21cm
ISBN 0-7278-0792-7 : £6.95 B82-31423

Beagle, Peter S.. The last unicorn / Peter Beagle. — London : Unwin Paperbacks, 1982, c1968. — 169p ; 20cm
Originally published: London : Bodley Head, 1968
ISBN 0-04-823206-8 : £1.95 : CIP rev. B81-38293

Beattie, Ann. Falling in place / Ann Beattie. — Harmondsworth : Penguin, 1982, c1980. — 342p ; 19cm
Originally published: New York : Random House, 1980 ; London : Secker & Warburg, 1981
ISBN 0-14-005865-6 (pbk) : £1.95 B82-35608

Beck, Harry. The blazed trail. — Large print ed. — Bath : Chivers, Oct.1982. — [216]p. — (A Lythway book)
Originally published: London : Gresham, 1966
ISBN 0-85119-850-3 : £6.70 : CIP entry B82-20519

Becker, Stephen. The blue-eyed Shan / Stephen Becker. — London : Collins, 1982. — 270p : 1map,1plan ; 25cm
ISBN 0-00-222138-1 : £7.50 B82-32117

Becker, Stephen. The last mandarin / Stephen Becker. — London : Sphere, 1982, c1979. — 294p ; 18cm
Originally published: London : Chatto & Windus, 1979
ISBN 0-7221-1516-4 (pbk) : £1.75 B82-09394

Beckman, Patti. Angry lover / Patti Beckman. — [Sevenoaks] : Silhouette Books, 1981. — 189p ; 17cm. — (Silhouette romance ; 72)
ISBN 0-340-27260-0 (pbk) : £0.65 : CIP rev. B81-30139

Beckman, Patti. Bitter victory. — London : Hodder & Stoughton, Sept.1982. — [256]p. — (Silhouette special edition)
ISBN 0-340-32082-6 (pbk) : £0.95 : CIP entry B82-20167

Beckman, Patti. Daring encounter. — London : Hodder and Stoughton, Jan.1983. — [192]p. — (Silhouette romance)
ISBN 0-340-32722-7 (pbk) : £0.85 : CIP entry B82-34407

Beckman, Patti. Love's treacherous journey. — London : Hodder and Stoughton, Mar.1982. — [192]p. — (Silhouette romance)
ISBN 0-340-27984-2 (pbk) : £0.75 : CIP entry B82-00261

Beckman, Patti. Spotlight to fame. — London : Hodder & Stoughton, Aug.1982. — [192]p. — (Silhouette romance)
ISBN 0-340-28633-4 (pbk) : £0.75 : CIP entry B82-15748

Belmont, James. The filibusters / James Belmont. — Bognor Regis : New Horizon, c1981. — 298p : 1map ; 19cm. — (A Tornado book)
ISBN 0-86116-581-0 (pbk) : £2.95 B82-00640

Benchley, Peter. The girl of the Sea of Cortez / Peter Benchley. — London : Deutsch, 1982. — 213p ; 24cm
ISBN 0-233-97463-6 (pbk) : £6.95 B82-30010

Benford, Gregory. Jupiter project / Gregory Benford. — Rev. ed. — London : Sphere, 1982, c1980. — 182p ; 18cm
Previous ed.: Nashville : Nelson, 1975
ISBN 0-7221-1572-5 (pbk) : £1.50 B82-37339

Benford, Gregory. Timescape / Gregory Benford. — London : Sphere, 1982, c1980. — 412p ; 18cm
Originally published: New York : Simon and Schuster ; London : Gollancz, 1980
ISBN 0-7221-1630-6 (pbk) : £1.75 B82-09389

Benton, Will. Secret valley / by Will Benton. — London : Hale, 1982. — 160p ; 20cm
ISBN 0-7091-9555-9 : £4.95 B82-12610

Bergen, Fran. Yearning of angels. — London : Hodder and Stoughton, Nov.1982. — [256]p. — (Silhouette special edition)
ISBN 0-340-32615-8 (pbk) : £0.95 : CIP entry B82-28263

Betcherman, Barbara. Suspicions / Barbara Betcherman. — [London] : Futura, 1982, c1980. — 410p ; 18cm
Originally published: London : Macdonald Futura, 1980
ISBN 0-7088-1937-0 (pbk) : £1.95 B82-35718

Bickham, Jack M.. All the days were summer / by Jack M. Bickham. — London : Hale, 1982, c1981. — 208p ; 20cm
ISBN 0-7091-9810-8 : £7.75 B82-30277

Birdwell, Cleo. Amazons / Cleo Birdwell. — London : Granada, 1980 (1982 [printing]). — 379p ; 18cm. — (A Mayflower book)
Originally published: New York : Holt, Rinehart and Winston ; London : Granada, 1980
ISBN 0-583-13539-0 (pbk) : £1.95 B82-19983

Bishop, Michael. No enemy but time : a novel / by Michael Bishop. — London : Gollancz, 1982. — 397p ; 21cm
ISBN 0-575-03121-2 : £8.95 : CIP rev. B82-09441

Bjorgum, Kenneth. The desert sentinels / by Kenneth L. Bjorgum. — London : Hale, 1981, c1980. — 180p ; 20cm
Originally published: Garden City, N.Y. : Doubleday, 1980
ISBN 0-7091-9377-7 : £4.95 B82-02809

Black, Campbell. Brainfire / Campbell Black. — London : Sphere, 1981, c1979. — 295p ; 18cm
Originally published: New York : Morrow, 1979 ; London : Joseph, 1980
ISBN 0-7221-1747-7 (pbk) : £1.75 B82-02126

Black, Campbell. Raiders of the lost Ark : novel / by Campbell Black ; adapted from a screenplay by Lawrence Kasdan ; based on a story by George Lucas and Philip Kaufman. — London : Severn House, 1981. — 181p ; 21cm
ISBN 0-7278-0736-6 : £5.95 : CIP rev. B81-18098

Black, Jonathan, *1927-*. Ride the golden tiger / Jonathan Black. — London : Granada, 1977 (1981 [printing]). — 319p ; 18cm. — (A Mayflower book)
Originally published: London : Hart-Davis, MacGibbon, 1976
ISBN 0-583-12618-9 (pbk) : £1.50 B82-00546

Blagowidow, George. [Border crossing]. Operation parterre / George Blagowidow. — London : Sphere, 1982. — 283p : ill ; 18cm
Originally published: London : Piatkus, 1982
ISBN 0-7221-1751-5 (pbk) : £1.75 B82-37346

Blagowidow, George. Border crossing / George Blagowidow. — Loughton : Piatkus, 1982. — 283p ; 21cm
ISBN 0-86188-159-1 : £6.95 : CIP rev. B82-05761

Blaisdell, Anne. Consequence of crime / Elizabeth Linington as Anne Blaisdell. — [Bath] : Chivers, 1982, c1980. — 373p ; 23cm. — (Atlantic large print) (A Midnight large print mystery)
Originally published: New York : Doubleday, 1980 ; London : Gollancz, 1981
ISBN 0-85119-476-1 : Unpriced : CIP rev. B82-09854

Blaisdell, Anne. Skeletons in the closet. — London : Gollancz, Feb.1983. — [192]p
ISBN 0-575-03238-3 : £6.95 : CIP entry B82-38686

Blake, Stephanie. Unholy desires / Stephanie Blake. — Feltham : Hamlyn Paperbacks, 1982, c1980. — 271p ; 18cm
ISBN 0-600-20546-0 (pbk) : £1.50 B82-22392

Blankenship, William D.. Brotherly love : a novel / by William D. Blankenship. — London : Souvenir, 1982, c1981. — 345p ; 24cm
Originally published: New York : Arbor House, 1981
ISBN 0-285-62526-8 (corrected) : £7.50 B82-22194

Blickle, Katrinka. Days of destiny / Katrinka Blickle. — Loughton : Piatkus, 1982, c1981. — 359p ; 21cm
ISBN 0-86188-192-3 : £7.95 : CIP rev. B82-12928

Block, Lawrence. Ariel / Lawrence Block. — London : Sphere, 1981, c1980. — 248p ; 18cm
Originally published: New York : Arbor House, 1980
ISBN 0-7221-1745-0 (pbk) : £1.50 B82-07178

Block, Lawrence. The burglar who liked to quote Kipling / Lawrence Block. — London : Hale, 1981, c1979. — 196p ; 20cm
Originally published: New York : Random House, 1979
ISBN 0-7091-8746-7 : £6.50 B82-07191

Block, Lawrence. The burglar who studied Spinoza / Lawrence Block. — London : Hale, 1982, c1980. — 213p ; 20cm
ISBN 0-7091-9404-8 : £6.75 B82-22130

Block, Lawrence. A star in the dark / Lawrence Block. — London : Hale, 1982, c1981. — 192p ; 21cm
Originally published: New York : Arbor, 1981
ISBN 0-7091-9885-x : Unpriced B82-36519

Block, Thomas H.. Orbit / Thomas Block. — Sevenoaks : New English Library, 1982. — 297p ; 23cm
ISBN 0-450-04916-7 : £7.95 B82-38798

Blume, Judy. Tiger eyes / Judy Blume. — London : Heinemann, 1982, c1981. — 142p ; 23cm
Originally published: Scarsdale, N.Y. : Bradbury Press, 1981
ISBN 0-434-92885-2 : £4.95 B82-31392

Bobker, Lee R.. The Unicorn group / Lee R. Bobker. — London : Methuen London, 1982, c1979. — 251p ; 18cm. — (A Methuen paperback)
Originally published: New York : Morrow, 1979 ; London : Constable, 1980
ISBN 0-417-06090-4 (pbk) : £1.50 B82-34006

Bogner, Norman. California dreamers / Norman Bogner. — London : Sphere, 1982. — 345p ; 18cm
ISBN 0-7221-1760-4 (pbk) : £1.75 B82-34178

Bonds, Parris Afton. Made for each other / Parris Afton Bonds. — [Sevenoaks] : Silhouette Books, 1981. — 188p ; 2maps ; 17cm. — (Silhouette romance ; 70)
ISBN 0-340-27258-9 (pbk) : £0.65 : CIP rev. B81-30140

813'.54[F] — Fiction in English. American writers, *1945- — Texts* *continuation*

Bonham, Frank. Trago. — Large print ed. — Bath : Chivers, Feb.1983. — [288]p. — (Atlantic large print)
Originally published: New York : Dell, 1962
ISBN 0-85119-524-5 : £5.75 : CIP entry
B82-39576

Boorstin, Paul. Savage / Paul Boorstin. — [London] : Corgi, 1981, c1980. — 299p ; 18cm
Originally published: New York : R. Marek, 1980
ISBN 0-552-11811-7 (pbk) : £1.50 B82-03229

Booth, Edwin, *1906-*. Rebel's return / Edwin Booth. — Large print ed. — [Bath] : Chivers, 1982, c1981. — 288p ; 23cm. — (Atlantic large print) (A Gunsmoke large print western)
ISBN 0-85119-474-5 : Unpriced : CIP rev.
B82-09852

Bordill, Judith. A candle for Lydia / Judith Bordill. — Feltham : Hamlyn, 1982. — 159p ; 18cm. — (A Sapphire romance)
ISBN 0-600-20533-9 (pbk) : £0.75 B82-16297

Bosworth, Frank. Rawhide / by Frank Bosworth. — London : Hale, 1982. — 155p ; 20cm
ISBN 0-7091-9862-0 : £5.50 B82-26027

Boucheron, Rose. The House of Delaney / by Rose Boucheron. — London : Hale, 1981. — 191p ; 20cm
ISBN 0-7091-9459-5 : £5.95 B82-03157

Bowdler, Roger. Hart to Hart : talent for adventure / Roger Bowdler. — London : Severn House, 1982, c1981. — 255p ; 21cm
Originally published: London : Mayflower, 1981
ISBN 0-7278-0793-5 : £6.95 B82-30463

Bowie, Donald. [Cable Harbor]. Beach of passion / Donald Bowie. — London : W.H. Allen, 1981 (1982 [printing]). — 327p ; 18cm. — (A Star book)
ISBN 0-352-31081-2 (pbk) : £1.95 B82-29193

Bowles, Paul. Points in time / Paul Bowles. — London : Owen, 1982. — 92p : 2maps ; 23cm
Maps on lining papers
ISBN 0-7206-0594-6 : £6.95 B82-37598

Box, Edgar. Death before bedtime / Edgar Box. — London : Granada, 1982, c1952. — 205p ; 18cm. — (A Panther book)
Originally published: New York : Dutton, 1953 ; London : Heinemann, 1954
ISBN 0-586-05408-1 (pbk) : £1.25 B82-36061

Box, Edgar. Death in the fifth position / Edgar Box. — London : Granada, 1982, c1978. — 176p ; 18cm. — (A Panther book)
Originally published: London : Heinemann, 1954
ISBN 0-586-05411-1 (pbk) : £1.25 B82-33680

Box, Edgar. Death likes it hot / Edgar Box. — London : Granada, 1982, c1978. — 191p ; 18cm. — (A Panther book)
Originally published: New York : Dutton ; London : Heinemann, 1954
ISBN 0-586-05410-3 (pbk) : £1.25 B82-37217

Boyle, T. Coraghessan. Water music : a novel / T. Coraghessan Boyle. — London : Gollancz, 1982, c1981. — 437p : 1map ; 22cm
Originally published: Boston, Mass. : Little, Brown, 1981
ISBN 0-575-03068-2 : £8.95 : CIP rev.
B82-00165

Bradford, Will. The hangrope posse / by Will Bradford. — London : Hale, 1982. — 158p ; 20cm
ISBN 0-7091-9863-9 : £5.50 B82-34171

Bradley, Concho. Lynch law. — Large print ed. — Bath : Chivers, Dec.1982. — [232]p. — (A Lythway book)
Originally published: London : Hale, 1964
ISBN 0-85119-869-4 : £6.70 : CIP entry
B82-30243

Bradley, Marion Zimmer. Two to conquer : a Darkover novel / Marion Zimmer Bradley. — London : Arrow, 1982, c1980. — 335p ; 18cm
ISBN 0-09-929040-5 (pbk) : £1.75 B82-35586

Bradshaw, Gillian. Hawk of May / Gillian Bradshaw. — London : Magnum, 1981, c1980. — 270p : 1map ; 18cm
Originally published: New York : Simon and Schuster, 1980 ; London : Eyre Methuen, 1981
ISBN 0-417-06760-7 (pbk) : £1.50 B82-15548

Bradshaw, Gillian. In winter's shadow. — London : Eyre Methuen, Mar.1982. — [256]p
ISBN 0-413-48110-7 : £7.50 : CIP entry
B82-01994

Bradshaw, Gillian. Kingdom of summer / Gillian Bradshaw. — London : Methuen London, 1982, c1981. — 255p : 1map ; 18cm. — (A Methuen paperback)
Originally published: New York : Simon & Schuster, 1981 ; London : Eyre Methuen, 1981
ISBN 0-417-06750-x (pbk) : £1.50 B82-33295

Brady, Maureen. Give me your good ear / Maureen Brady ; afterword by Jacqueline St. John. — London : Women's Press rc 1981, c1979. — 141p ; 20cm
Originally published: Argyle, New York : Spinsters, Ink, 1979
ISBN 0-7043-3874-2 (pbk) : £2.95 : CIP rev.
B81-28065

Bragg, W. F.. Maverick showdown. — Large print ed. — Bath : Chivers, Nov.1982. — [248] p. — (Atlantic large print)
Originally published: New York : Nordon, 1981
ISBN 0-85119-504-0 : £5.25 : CIP entry
B82-26433

Bragg, W. F.. Texas fever. — Large print ed. — Bath : Chivers, Jan.1983. — [232]p. — (Atlantic large print)
Originally published: New York : Nordon Publications, 1955
ISBN 0-85119-517-2 : £5.25 : CIP entry
B82-33089

Brandner, Gary. Cat people : a novel / by Gary Brandner ; based on the story by DeWitt Bodeen. — London : Sphere, 1982. — 221p ; 18cm
ISBN 0-7221-1847-3 (pbk) : £1.50 B82-37341

Brandner, Gary. Cat people. — London : Severn House, Oct.1982. — [224]p
ISBN 0-7278-0839-7 : £6.95 : CIP entry
B82-28581

Brandner, Gary. Hellborn / Gary Brandner. — London : Hamlyn, 1982, c1981. — 187p ; 18cm
ISBN 0-600-20465-0 (pbk) : £1.25 B82-12059

Braun, Matt. Hangman's creek / Matt Braun. — London : Sphere, 1982, c1979. — 166p ; 18cm
ISBN 0-7221-1924-0 (pbk) : £1.25 B82-32115

Braun, Matt. Jury of six / Matt Braun. — London : Sphere, 1982, c1980. — 181p ; 18cm
ISBN 0-7221-1923-2 (pbk) : £1.25 B82-32112

Braun, Matt. The spoilers / Matt Braun. — London : Sphere, 1982, c1981. — 180p ; 18cm
ISBN 0-7221-1921-6 (pbk) : £1.25 B82-32113

Braun, Matt. Tombstone / Matt Braun. — London : Sphere, 1982, c1981. — 182p ; 18cm
ISBN 0-7221-1922-4 (pbk) : £1.25 B82-32114

Brautigan, Richard. The Tokyo-Montana express / Richard Brautigan. — [London] : Picador, 1982, c1980. — 190p : 1form ; 20cm
Originally published: New York : Delacorte Press / Seymour Lawrence, 1980 ; London : Cape, 1981
ISBN 0-330-26786-8 (pbk) : £2.50 B82-34255

Brennan, Peter. Razorback / Peter Brennan. — [London] : Fontana, 1982, c1981. — 383p ; 18cm
Originally published: [U.S.] : Jove, 1981
ISBN 0-00-615931-1 (pbk) : £1.75 B82-33558

Brennan, Will. Cowman's vengeance / by Will Brennan. — London : Hale, 1982. — 157p ; 20cm
ISBN 0-7091-9720-9 : £5.25 B82-22911

Brent, Madeleine. The long masquerade / by Madeleine Brent. — London : Souvenir, 1981. — 319p ; 21cm
ISBN 0-285-62493-8 : £6.95 B82-04557

Brent, Madeleine. The long masquerade / Madeleine Brent. — Large print ed. — Leicester : Ulverscroft, 1982, c1981. — 502p ; 23cm. — (Ulverscroft large print series)
Originally published: London : Souvenir, 1981
ISBN 0-7089-0817-9 : Unpriced : CIP rev.
B82-15957

Breslin, Jimmy. Son of Sam / Jimmy Breslin and Dick Schaap. — London : Futura, 1978. — 358p ; 18cm. — (A Futura book)
ISBN 0-7088-1440-9 (pbk) : £1.00 B82-32964

Bright, Freda. Options / Freda Bright. — London : Pan, 1982. — 348p ; 18cm
Originally published: New York : Pocket Books, 1982
ISBN 0-330-26589-x (pbk) : £1.50 B82-13722

Bright, Laurey. Sweet vengeance. — London : Hodder & Stoughton, Aug.1982. — [192]p
ISBN 0-340-28634-2 (pbk) : £0.75 : CIP entry
B82-15749

Bright, Laurey. Tears of morning. — London : Hodder & Stoughton, May 1982. — [192]p. — (Silhouette romance)
Originally published: New York : Silhouette Books, 1981
ISBN 0-340-27933-8 (pbk) : £0.75 : CIP entry
B82-07945

Brinkley, William. Breakpoint : a novel about winning / William Brinkley. — London : Futura, 1979, c1978. — 324p ; 18cm
Originally published: New York : Morrow ; London : Raven, 1978
ISBN 0-7088-1555-3 (pbk) : £0.95 B82-32129

Brinkley, William. Peeper / William Brinkley. — London : New English Library, 1982. — 311p ; 23cm
Originally published: New York : Viking Press, 1981
ISBN 0-450-04849-7 : £7.50 : CIP rev.
B82-01975

Briskin, Jacqueline. [California generation]. Decade / Jacqueline Briskin. — London : Granada, 1981 (1982 [printing]). — 630p ; 18cm
Originally published: London? : Anthony Blond, 1970
ISBN 0-583-13158-1 (pbk) : £2.50 B82-40246

Briskin, Jacqueline. The onyx. — London : Granada, Apr.1982. — [608]p
ISBN 0-246-11791-5 : £7.95 : CIP entry
B82-04321

Brister, Richard. Law killer. — Large print ed. — Bath : Chivers, Oct.1982. — [264]p. — (Atlantic large print)
ISBN 0-85119-498-2 : £5.25 : CIP entry
B82-24230

813'.54[F] — Fiction in English. American writers, 1945- — Texts *continuation*

Brister, Richard. Renegade brand / Richard Brister. — Large print ed. — [Bath] : Chivers, 1982, c1964. — 253p ; 23cm. — (A Gunsmoke large print western) (Atlantic large print)
Originally published: New York : Avon Books, 1964
ISBN 0-85119-462-1 : Unpriced : CIP rev. B82-05000

Brister, Richard. The wolf streak / Richard Brister. — [Bath] : Chivers, 1982, c1958. — 254p ; 23cm. — (Atlantic large print) (A Gunsmoke large print western)
Originally published: London : Hale, 1960
ISBN 0-85119-481-8 : Unpriced : CIP rev. B82-13093

Brookes, Owen. Inheritance / Owen Brookes. — [London] : Fontana, 1981, c1980. — 282p ; 18cm
Originally published: London : Hutchinson, 1980
ISBN 0-00-616166-9 (pbk) : £1.50 B82-06313

Browning, Dixie. East of today. — London : Hodder and Stoughton, Feb.1982. — [192]p. — (Silhouette romance)
ISBN 0-340-27673-8 (pbk) : £0.75 : CIP entry B81-38314

Browning, Dixie. Island on the hill. — London : Hodder and Stoughton, Feb.1983. — [192]p. — (Silhouette romance)
ISBN 0-340-32762-6 (pbk) : £0.85 : CIP entry B82-38031

Browning, Dixie. Renegade player. — London : Hodder and Stoughton, Nov.1982. — [192]p. — (Silhouette romance)
ISBN 0-340-32687-5 (pbk) : £0.75 : CIP entry B82-28265

Browning, Dixie. Winter blossom. — London : Hodder & Stoughton, June 1982. — [192]p. — (Silhouette romance)
Originally published: New York : Silhouette Books, 1981
ISBN 0-340-27939-7 (pbk) : £0.75 : CIP entry B82-10019

Browning, Dixie. Wren of paradise / Dixie Browning. — [Sevenoaks] : Silhouette Books, 1981. — 190p ; 17cm. — (Silhouette romance ; 73)
ISBN 0-340-27261-9 (pbk) : £0.65 : CIP rev. B81-30545

Bryant, Dorothy. Killing Wonder. — London : Women's Press, Nov.1982. — [190]p
Originally published: Berkeley, Calif. : Ata Books, 1981
ISBN 0-7043-2841-0 (cased) : £2.95 : CIP entry
ISBN 0-7043-3896-3 (pbk) B82-30334

Buckley, William F.. Marco Polo, if you can / William F. Buckley, Jr. — London : Allen Lane, 1982. — 233p ; 23cm
Originally published: Garden City, N.Y. : Doubleday, 1982
ISBN 0-7139-1360-6 : £6.95 B82-25991

Bugliosi, Vincent. Shadow of Cain : a novel / by Vincent Bugliosi and Ken Hurwitz. — New York ; London : Norton, c1981. — 309p ; 22cm
ISBN 0-393-01466-5 : Unpriced B82-32100

Bukowski, Charles. Factotum / Charles Bukowski. — London : W.H. Allen, 1981, c1975 (1982 [printing]). — 205p ; 18cm. — (A Star book)
Originally published: Los Angeles : Black Sparrow, 1975
ISBN 0-352-31049-9 (pbk) : £1.50 B82-34184

Burchardt, Bill. Black marshal / by Bill Burchardt. — London : Hale, 1982, c1981. — 183p ; 20cm
Originally published: Garden City, N.Y. : Doubleday, 1981
ISBN 0-7091-9865-5 : £5.50 B82-33196

Burnham, Charles. Blackfeet country / by Charles Burnham. — London : Hale, 1982. — 156p ; 20cm
ISBN 0-7091-9927-9 : £5.50 B82-35890

Burroughs, William S.. The naked lunch. — London : John Calder, Aug.1982. — [320]p
Originally published: Paris : Olympia Press, 1959 ; London, Calder, 1965
ISBN 0-7145-3967-8 (cased) : £6.95 : CIP entry
ISBN 0-7145-3969-4 (pbk) : £3.95 B82-21968

Butler, Albert. Lockhart's trail / Albert Butler. — Hornchurch : Henry, 1981, c1980. — 176p ; 21cm
ISBN 0-86025-197-7 : £5.25 B82-16873

Byrne, Robert. The dam. — London : Hodder & Stoughton, Sept.1982. — [320]p. — (Coronet books)
Originally published: New York : Atheneum, 1981
ISBN 0-340-28438-2 (pbk) : £1.25 : CIP entry B82-18748

Cade, Steven. Barrington's women / by Steven Cade. — London : Souvenir, 1982. — 253p ; 21cm
ISBN 0-285-62471-7 : £6.95 B82-30876

Cain, James M.. Galatea / James M. Cain. — [London] : Magnum, 1981. — 158p ; 18cm
Originally published: London : Hale, 1954
ISBN 0-417-05840-3 (pbk) : £1.10 B82-15108

Camp, Elaine. To have, to hold. — London : Hodder and Stoughton, Mar.1982. — [192]p. — (Silhouette romance)
For adolescents
ISBN 0-340-27925-7 (pbk) : £0.75 : CIP entry B82-00259

Campbell, Jeffrey. The homing / Jeffrey Campbell. — London : Sphere, 1982, c1980. — 216p ; 18cm
Originally published: New York : Putnam ; London : Joseph, 1980
ISBN 0-7221-2230-6 (pbk) : £1.50 B82-27885

Campbell, Joanna. The thoroughbred / Joanna Campbell. — Toronto ; London : Bantam, 1981. — 163p ; 18cm
ISBN 0-553-20601-x (pbk) : £0.65 B82-23913

Caplan, Thomas. Line of chance / Thomas Caplan. — London : Arrow, 1982, c1979. — 468p ; 18cm
Originally published: New York : Morrow, 1979 ; London : Severn House, 1980
ISBN 0-09-927290-3 (pbk) : £1.75 B82-11444

Capote, Truman. The grass harp / Truman Capote. — Harmondsworth : Penguin, 1966, c1951 (1981 [printing]). — 124p ; 19cm
Originally published: New York : Random House, 1951 ; London : Heinemann, 1952
ISBN 0-14-002563-4 (pbk) : £1.25 B82-01397

Caputo, Philip. Horn of Africa / Philip Caputo. — London : Macdonald Futura, 1981, c1980. — viii,486p ; 18cm. — (A Futura book)
Originally published: New York : Holt, Rinehart and Winston, c1980
ISBN 0-7088-2020-4 (pbk) : £1.95 B82-06603

Carey, Suzanne. Kiss and tell. — London : Hodder & Stoughton, Nov.1982. — [192]p. — (Silhouette desire)
ISBN 0-340-32861-4 (pbk) : £0.95 : CIP entry B82-29067

Carlile, Clancy. Honkytonk man / Clancy Carlile. — London : Sphere, 1982, c1980. — 345p ; 18cm
Originally published: New York : Simon & Schuster, 1980
ISBN 0-7221-2359-0 (pbk) : £1.95 B82-27900

Carlson, Ron. Truants : a novel / Ron Carlson. — London : Murray, 1982, c1981. — 255p ; 23cm
Originally published: New York : Norton, 1981
ISBN 0-7195-3917-x : £7.50 : CIP rev. B82-00354

Carr, Eleni. Mayan moon. — London : Hodder & Stoughton, Sept.1982. — [256]p. — (Silhouette special edition)
ISBN 0-340-32085-0 (pbk) : £0.95 : CIP entry B82-20170

Carroll, James. Mortal friends : a novel / James Carroll. — London : Futura, 1979, c1978. — 731p ; 18cm
Originally published: Boston, Mass. : Little, Brown, 1978
ISBN 0-7088-1564-2 (pbk) : £1.50 B82-32965

Carroll, Jonathan. The land of laughs / Jonathan Carroll. — [Feltham] : Hamlyn Paperbacks, 1982, c1980. — 241p ; 18cm
Originally published: New York : Viking, 1980
ISBN 0-600-20597-5 (pbk) : £1.75 B82-28800

Carroll, Mary. Divide the wind / Mary Carroll. — [Sevenoaks] : Silhouette Books, 1981. — 190p : 1map ; 17cm. — (Silhouette romance ; 75)
ISBN 0-340-27263-5 (pbk) : £0.65 : CIP rev. B81-30540

Carroll, Mary. Take this love. — London : Hodder & Stoughton, July 1982. — [192]p. — (Silhouette romance)
Originally published: New York : Silhouette Books, 1981
ISBN 0-340-28466-8 (pbk) : £0.75 : CIP entry B82-12312

Carter, Ashley. Heritage of Blackoaks / Ashley Carter. — London : W.H. Allen, 1982, c1981. — 444p ; 21cm
Originally published: New York : Fawcett Gold Medal, 1981
ISBN 0-491-02685-4 : £8.95 B82-11441

Carter, Forrest. Watch for me on the mountain / Forrest Carter. — Large print ed. — Leicester : Ulverscroft, 1982, c1978. — 483p ; 23cm. — (Ulverscroft large print series)
Originally published: New York : Delacorte, 1978 ; London : Hamilton, 1979
ISBN 0-7089-0771-7 : Unpriced : CIP rev. B82-01745

Carter, Nick. Hawaii. — London : W.H. Allen, 1982, c1979. — 206p ; 18cm. — (A Star book)
Originally published: United States : Charter Books, 1979
ISBN 0-352-31115-0 (pbk) : £1.35 B82-29196

Carter, Nick. The nowhere weapon / Nick Carter. — London : W.H. Allen, 1982, c1979. — 238p ; 18cm. — (A Star book)
ISBN 0-352-31117-7 (pbk) : £1.35 B82-22061

Carter, Nick. Tropical deathpact / Nick Carter. — London : W.H. Allen, 1982, c1979. — 242p : ill ; 18cm. — (A Star book)
ISBN 0-352-31140-1 (pbk) : £1.35 B82-34117

Carter, Nick. Under the wall / Nick Carter. — London : Star, 1982, c1978. — 186p ; 18cm
Originally published: New York : Charter Communications, 1978?
ISBN 0-352-31146-0 (pbk) : £1.35 B82-38404

Chais, Pamela. Final cut / Pamela Chais. — London : New English Library, 1982, c1981. — 304p ; 23cm
Originally published: New York : Simon and Schuster, 1981
ISBN 0-450-04841-1 : £6.95 : CIP rev. B82-11277

Chalker, Jack L.. Exiles at the well of souls / Jack L. Chalker. — Harmondsworth : Penguin, 1982, c1978. — xi,335p ; 18cm. — (The Wars of the Well ; part 1)
Originally published: New York : Ballantine Books, c1978
ISBN 0-14-005525-8 (pbk) : £1.95 B82-25562

813'.54[F] — Fiction in English. American writers, *1945- — Texts* *continuation*

Chalker, Jack L.. Midnight at the well of souls / Jack L. Chalker. — Harmondsworth : Penguin, 1981, c1977. — 360p ; 19cm
Originally published: New York : Ballantine, 1977
ISBN 0-14-005524-x (pbk) : £1.75 B82-35866

Chalker, Jack L.. Quest for the Well of Souls / Jack L. Chalker. — Harmondsworth : Penguin, 1982, c1978. — 302p ; 18cm. — (The Wars of the Well ; pt.2)
Originally published: New York : Ballantine, 1978
ISBN 0-14-005526-6 (pbk) : £1.75 B82-35387

Chapple, Steve. Don't mind dying. — London : New English Library, Mar.1982. — [256]p
Originally published: 1981
ISBN 0-450-05366-0 (pbk) : £1.50 : CIP entry B82-01983

Charles, Maggi. Love's golden shadow. — London : Hodder and Stoughton, Oct.1982. — [256]p. — (Silhouette special edition)
ISBN 0-340-32609-3 (pbk) : £0.95 : CIP entry B82-24718

Charles, Maggi. Love's tender trial. — London : Hodder and Stoughton, Feb.1983. — [256]p. — (Silhouette special edition)
ISBN 0-340-32944-0 (pbk) : £0.95 : CIP entry B82-38264

Charles, Maggi. Magic crescendo. — London : Hodder & Stoughton, Sept.1982. — [192]p. — (Silhouette romance)
ISBN 0-340-32067-2 (pbk) : £0.75 : CIP entry B82-18786

Charnas, Suzy McKee. Motherlines. — London : Hodder & Stoughton, Oct.1981. — [256]p. — (Coronet books)
Originally published: 1980
ISBN 0-340-26789-5 (pbk) : £1.50 : CIP entry B81-26727

Charnas, Suzy McKee. Walk to the end of the world. — London : Hodder & Stoughton, Oct.1981. — [256]p. — (Coronet books)
Originally published: 1979
ISBN 0-340-26788-7 (pbk) : £1.50 : CIP entry B81-26734

Charters, Samuel. Mr. Jabi and Mr. Smythe. — London : Boyars, Oct.1982. — [160]p
ISBN 0-7145-2779-3 : £7.95 : CIP entry B82-24735

Chastain, Thomas. The diamond exchange / Thomas Chastain. — London : Hale, 1981. — 230p ; 21cm
ISBN 0-7091-9486-2 (corrected : pbk) : £6.95 B82-08751

Cheever, Susan. Looking for work / Susan Cheever. — [London] : Corgi, 1981, c1979. — 175p ; 18cm
Originally published: New York : Simon and Schuster, 1979 ; London : Weidenfeld and Nicolson, 1980
ISBN 0-552-11783-8 (pbk) : £1.25 B82-03236

Cherryh, C. J.. Fires of Azeroth / C.J. Cherryh. — London : Methuen, 1982, c1979. — 236p ; 18cm
Originally published: New York? : Daw, 1979
ISBN 0-417-07440-9 (pbk) : £1.50 B82-34180

Cherryh, C. J.. Serpent's reach / C.J. Cherryh. — London : Macdonald, 1981, c1980. — 331p ; 21cm
Originally published: Garden City, N.Y. : Nelson Doubleday, 1980
ISBN 0-356-08515-5 : £6.50 B82-08651

Cherryh, C. J.. Serpent's reach / C.J. Cherryh. — London : Futura, 1982, c1980. — 334p ; 18cm. — (An Orbit book)
Originally published: London : Macdonald, 1981
ISBN 0-7088-8085-1 (pbk) : £2.25 B82-15314

Chesbro, George C.. City of whispering stone / George C. Chesbro. — London : Severn House, 1981, c1978. — 217p ; 21cm. — ([A Mongo mystery])
Originally published: New York : Simon and Schuster, 1978
ISBN 0-7278-0733-1 : £6.95 : CIP rev. B81-21615

Chesbro, George C.. Turn loose the dragons. — London : Severn House, Sept.1982. — [352]p
ISBN 0-7278-0797-8 : £7.95 : CIP entry B82-23863

Chiu, Tony. [Port Arthur chicken]. Onyxx / Tony Chiu. — [London] : Fontana, 1982, c1979. — 395p ; 18cm
Originally published : New York : Morrow, 1979 ; London : Collins, 1980
ISBN 0-00-616552-4 (pbk) : £1.75 B82-13640

Clancy, Ambrose. Blind pilot / Ambrose Clancy. — Harmondsworth : Penguin, 1982, c1980. — 414p : 1map ; 19cm
Originally published: New York : Morrow, 1980
ISBN 0-14-005988-1 (pbk) : £1.75 B82-40989

Clark, Mary Higgins. The cradle will fall. — Large print ed. — Anstey : Ulverscroft, Oct.1982. — [352]p. — (Charnwood library series)
Originally published: London : Fontana, 1980
ISBN 0-7089-8073-2 : £5.25 : CIP entry B82-26689

Clavell, James. King rat / James Clavell. — London : Hodder and Stoughton, 1982, c1962. — 397p ; 23cm
Originally published: London : Joseph, 1963
ISBN 0-340-28257-6 : £7.95 : CIP rev. B82-12238

Clavell, James. Tai-Pan : a novel of Hong Kong / James Clavell. — London : Hodder and Stoughton, 1982, c1966. — 725p ; 24cm
Originally published: London : Joseph, 1966
ISBN 0-340-28258-4 : £8.95 : CIP rev. B82-12239

Clay, Randall. The Oceola Kid. — Large print ed. — Bath : Chivers, Sept.1982. — [272]p. — (Atlantic large print)
ISBN 0-85119-492-3 : £5.25 : CIP entry B82-20499

Clay, Rita. Wanderer's dreams. — London : Hodder and Stoughton, Mar.1982. — [192]p. — (Silhouette romance)
ISBN 0-340-27922-2 (pbk) : £0.75 : CIP entry B82-00258

Clay, Rita. Wise folly. — London : Hodder & Stoughton, Nov.1982. — [192]p. — (Silhouette desire)
ISBN 0-340-32860-6 (pbk) : £0.95 : CIP entry B82-29066

Clemeau, Carol. The Ariadne clue. — London : Collins, Jan.1983. — [196]p. — (The Crime Club)
ISBN 0-00-231034-1 : £6.50 : CIP entry B82-33587

Clinton, Jeff. Killer's choice. — Large print ed. — Bath : Chivers, Jan.1983. — [280]p. — (Atlantic large print)
Originally published: New York : Medallion Books, 1964
ISBN 0-85119-518-0 : £5.25 : CIP entry B82-33090

Coburn, Andrew. Company secrets / Andrew Coburn. — London : Secker & Warburg, 1982. — 276p ; 23cm
ISBN 0-436-10292-7 : £7.50 : CIP rev. B82-06865

Coburn, Andrew. Off duty / Andrew Coburn. — London : Sphere, 1981, c1980 (1982 [printing]). — 245p ; 18cm
Originally published: London : Norton, 1980
ISBN 0-7221-2473-2 (pbk) : £1.50 B82-33912

Coen, Franklin. The plunderers / Franklin Coen. — London : Sphere, 1982, c1980. — 310p ; 18cm
Originally published: New York : Coward, McCann and Geoghegan, 1980 ; London : Severn House, 1981
ISBN 0-7221-2485-6 (pbk) : £1.75 B82-34177

Coffman, Virginia. The alpine coach / Virginia Coffman. — Large print ed. — Leicester : Ulverscroft, 1981, c1976. — 330p ; 23cm. — (Ulverscroft large print series)
Originally published: New York : Dell, 1976 ; London : Souvenir, 1980
ISBN 0-7089-0709-1 : £5.00 : CIP rev. B81-30502

Coffman, Virginia. The beach house / by Virginia Coffman. — Loughton : Piatkus, 1982, c1970. — 206p ; 21cm
ISBN 0-86188-135-4 : £6.50 : CIP rev. B81-36020

Coffman, Virginia. Dinah Faire : a novel / by Virginia Coffman. — London : Souvenir, 1982, c1979. — 311p ; 23cm
Originally published: New York : Arbor House, 1979
ISBN 0-285-62511-x : £6.95 B82-10075

Coffman, Virginia. From Satan with love. — Loughton : Piatkus, Jan.1983. — [224]p
ISBN 0-86188-223-7 : £6.95 : CIP entry B82-33226

Coffman, Virginia. Hyde Place : a novel / by Virginia Coffman. — London : Prior, 1981, c1974. — 473p ; 25cm
Originally published: New York : Arbor, 1974. — Published in large print
ISBN 0-86043-675-6 : Unpriced B82-28211

Coffman, Virginia. Night at Sea Abbey / Virginia Coffman. — Feltham : Hamlyn, 1981, c1972. — 156p ; 18cm
Originally published: Loughton : Piatkus, 1981
ISBN 0-600-20485-5 (pbk) : £1.00 B82-25312

Coffman, Virginia. Priestess of the damned / Virginia Coffman. — Loughton : Piatkus, 1982, c1970. — 216p ; 21cm
ISBN 0-86188-191-5 : £6.50 : CIP rev. B82-12926

Cole, Gerald. Any which way you can / novelisation by Gerald Cole ; from the screenplay by Stanford Sherman ; and based on characters created by Jeremy Joe Kronsberg. — London : Star, 1982. — 160p ; 18cm
ISBN 0-352-31040-5 (pbk) : £1.25 B82-16094

Cole, Gerald. Britannia hospital / Gerald Cole ; based on the screenplay by David Sherwin. — London : W.H. Allen, 1982. — 156p ; 18cm. — (A Star book)
ISBN 0-352-31079-0 (pbk) : £1.50 B82-29954

Cole, Gerald. Britannia Hospital / Gerald Cole ; based on the screenplay by David Sherwin. — London : Severn House, 1982. — 156p ; 21cm
ISBN 0-7278-0824-9 : £6.95 : CIP rev. B82-21375

Cole, Jackson. Red runs the Rio ; Bugles on the bighorn. — Large print ed. — Anstey : Ulverscroft Large Print Books, Nov.1982. — [416]p. — (Ulverscroft large print series)
ISBN 0-7089-0883-7 : £5.00 : CIP entry B82-29099

Coleman, Lonnie. Beulah Land / Lonnie Coleman. — London : Arrow, 1981, c1973. — 541p ; 18cm
Originally published: Garden City, N.Y. : Doubleday, 1973 ; London : Pan, 1974
ISBN 0-09-927260-1 (pbk) : £1.95 B82-03686

Collins, Larry. The fifth horseman / Larry Collins and Dominique Lapierre. — London : Granada, 1980 (1981 [printing]). — 573p : 2maps ; 18cm. — (A Panther book)
ISBN 0-586-04803-0 (pbk) : £1.95 B82-00543

813′.54[F] — Fiction in English. American writers, *1945- — Texts* *continuation*

Collins, Michael, *1924-*. The blood-red dream / Michael Collins. — Sth. Yarmouth, [Mass.] : Curley ; [Long Preston] : Distributed in the U.K. by Magna Print, c1976. — 339p ; 22cm
Originally published: New York : Dodd, 1976 ; London : Hale, 1977. — Published in large print
ISBN 0-89340-396-2 : Unpriced B82-36275

Collins, Randall. The case of the philosophers′ ring / by Dr John H. Watson ; [written by] Randall Collins. — Brighton : Harvester, 1980, c1978. — vii,152p,[4]p of plates : ports ; 24cm
Originally published: New York : Crown, c1978
ISBN 0-85527-458-1 : £6.95 : CIP rev. B80-09390

Condé, Nicholas. The religion / Nicholas Condé. — London : Hutchinson, 1982. — 375p ; 25cm
ISBN 0-09-149740-x : £7.95 : CIP rev. B82-16478

Condon, Richard. The entwining / Richard Condon. — London : Arrow, 1982, c1980. — 287p ; 18cm
Originally published: New York : R. Marek, 1980
ISBN 0-09-928700-5 (pbk) : £1.95 B82-31608

Condon, Richard. The Manchurian candidate / Richard Condon. — Leicester : Charnwood, 1981, c1959. — 407p ; 23cm. — (Charnwood library series)
Originally published: New York : McGraw-Hill ; London : Joseph, 1960. — Published in large print
ISBN 0-7089-8011-2 : £5.25 : CIP rev. B81-22653

Condon, Richard. The Manchurian candidate / Richard Condon. — London : Arrow, 1982, c1959. — 284p ; 18cm
Originally published: New York : McGraw-Hill, 1959
ISBN 0-09-928400-6 (pbk) : £1.75 B82-31607

Condon, Richard. Prizzi′s honour / Richard Condon. — London : Joseph, 1982. — 293p : 1geneal.table ; 23cm
ISBN 0-7181-2120-1 : £7.95 B82-28799

Condon, Richard. Winter kills / Richard Condon. — Leicester : Charnwood, 1982, c1974. — 418p ; 22cm
Originally published: New York : Dial Press ; London : Weidenfeld and Nicolson, 1974. — Published in large print
ISBN 0-7089-8030-9 : Unpriced : CIP rev. B82-08108

Conroy, Pat, *19---*. The lords of discipline / Pat Conroy. — London : Corgi, 1982, c1980. — 498p ; 18cm
Originally published: London : Secker & Warburg, 1981
ISBN 0-552-12054-5 (pbk) : £1.95 B82-37554

Constantine, K. C.. The man who liked slow tomatoes. — London (45 Blackfriars Rd, SE1 8NZ) : David Godine, Mar.1982. — [176]p
ISBN 0-906293-05-7 : £6.95 : CIP entry B82-01733

Constantine, K. C.. The Rocksburg railroad murders ; The blank page. — London (45 Blackfriars Rd, SE1 8NZ) : David Godine, Mar.1982. — [256]p. — (A Godine double detective)
ISBN 0-906293-10-3 : £4.50 : CIP entry B82-01734

Converse, Jane. Heartstorm. — London : Hodder & Stoughton, Jan.1983. — [256]p. — (Silhouette special edition)
ISBN 0-340-32939-4 (pbk) : £0.95 : CIP entry B82-34418

Converse, Jane. Moonlit path. — London : Hodder & Stoughton, Aug.1982. — [192]p. — (Silhouette romance)
ISBN 0-340-28638-5 (pbk) : £0.75 : CIP entry B82-15753

Converse, Jane. Paradise postponed. — London : Hodder & Stoughton, June 1982. — [256]p. — (Silhouette special edition)
ISBN 0-340-28583-4 (pbk) : £0.95 : CIP entry B82-10791

Conway, Theresa. Crimson glory / Theresa Conway. — London : Futura, 1979. — 446p ; 18cm. — (A Troubadour spectacular)
ISBN 0-7088-1586-3 (pbk) : £1.25 B82-32962

Cook, Robin, *1940-*. Fever / Robin Cook. — London : Macmillan, 1982. — 365p ; 23cm
Originally published: New York : Putnam, 1982
ISBN 0-333-33433-7 : £6.95 B82-31418

Cooney, Caroline B.. Rear-view mirror / Caroline B. Cooney. — [London] : Magnum, 1981, c1980. — 196p : ill ; 18cm
Originally published: New York : Random House, 1980
ISBN 0-417-06490-x (pbk) : £1.40 B82-15612

Coppel, Alfred. The apocalypse brigade / Alfred Coppel. — London : Macmillan, 1981. — 310p ; 24cm
Originally published: New York : Holt, Rinehart and Winston, 1981
ISBN 0-333-32329-7 : £6.95 B82-05734

Corman, Avery. The old neighbourhood / Avery Corman. — [London] : Fontana, 1981, c1980. — 188p ; 18cm
Originally published: London : Collins, 1980
ISBN 0-00-616330-0 (pbk) : £1.25 B82-06310

Coxhead, Nona. Big-time baby / Nona Coxhead. — London : Magnum, 1981. — 343p : music ; 18cm
ISBN 0-417-06610-4 (pbk) : £1.75 B82-15545

Crane, Caroline. The girls are missing / by Caroline Crane. — London : Hale, 1981, c1980. — 219p ; 20cm
Originally published: New York : Dodd, Mead, 1980
ISBN 0-7091-9453-6 : £6.50 B82-02787

Crane, Caroline. Wife found slain / Caroline Crane. — Sth. Yarmouth, [Mass.] : Curley ; [Long Preston] : Distributed in the U.K. by Magna Print, c1981. — 389p ; 22cm
Published in large print
ISBN 0-89340-395-4 : Unpriced B82-36273

Crane, Caroline. Wife found slain / Caroline Crane. — London : Hale, 1982, c1981. — 202p ; 20cm
ISBN 0-7091-9826-4 : £6.75 B82-33903

Cravens, Gwyneth. Love and work / Gwyneth Cravens. — London : Hamish Hamilton, 1982. — 341p ; 23cm
ISBN 0-241-10866-7 : £7.95 : CIP rev. B82-15700

Crichton, Michael. Congo / Michael Crichton. — Harmondsworth : Penguin, 1981, c1980. — xiv,348p ; 18cm
Originally published: New York : Knopf, 1980. — Bibliography: 345-348
ISBN 0-14-005863-x (pbk) : £1.75 B82-16765

Crosby, John, *1912-*. Dear judgement. — London : Hodder & Stoughton, Mar.1982. — [288]p. — (Coronet books)
Originally published: London : Cape, 1979
ISBN 0-340-26796-8 (pbk) : £1.25 : CIP entry B82-01842

Crowley, John. Engine summer / John Crowley. — London : Methuen London, 1982, c1979. — 182p ; 18cm
Originally published: Garden City, N.Y. : Doubleday, 1979 ; London : Gollancz, 1980
ISBN 0-417-05880-2 (pbk) : £1.50 B82-33932

Crowley, John. Little, big / John Crowley. — London : Gollancz, 1982. — 538p : ill,1geneal.table ; 23cm
ISBN 0-575-03065-8 (cased) : £8.95 : CIP rev. B82-04604

Crumley, James. The last good kiss / James Crumley. — London : Granada, 1981, c1978. — 254p ; 18cm. — (A Panther book)
Originally published: New York : Random House, 1978 ; London : Granada, 1979
ISBN 0-586-04958-4 (pbk) : £1.50 B82-03000

Cussler, Clive. Night probe!. — Large print ed. — Anstey : Ulverscroft, Aug.1982. — [592]p. — (Charnwood library series)
Originally published: London : Hodder and Stoughton, 1981
ISBN 0-7089-8061-9 : £6.50 : CIP entry B82-26995

Cussler, Clive. Night probe / Clive Cussler. — London : Sphere, 1982, c1981. — 372p ; 17cm
Originally published: London : Hodder and Stoughton, 1981
ISBN 0-7221-2746-4 (pbk) : £1.95 B82-36545

Dailey, Janet. Night way / Janet Dailey. — London : Macdonald, 1982, c1981. — 320p ; 21cm
Originally published: London : Futura, 1981
ISBN 0-356-08642-9 : £5.95 B82-33909

Dailey, Janet. This Calder sky / Janet Dailey. — London : Macdonald, 1982, c1981. — 432p ; 21cm
ISBN 0-356-08641-0 : £7.50 B82-33905

Daley, Brian. Han Solo and the lost legacy : from the Adventures of Luke Skywalker / by Brian Daley ; based on the characters and situations created by George Lucas. — London : Sphere, 1981, c1980. — 184p ; 18cm
Originally published: New York : Ballantine, 1980
ISBN 0-7221-2826-6 (pbk) : £1.00 B82-07184

Daley, Robert. Year of the dragon : a novel / by Robert Daley. — London : Hodder and Stoughton, 1982, c1981. — 507p ; 23cm
ISBN 0-340-27644-4 : £7.95 : CIP rev. B81-36366

Damore, Leo. The "crime" of Dorothy Sheridan / Leo Damore. — Large print ed. — South Yarmouth, Mass. : Curley ; Skipton : Magna Print [distributor], [1980?], c1978. — 613p ; 22cm
Originally published: New York : Arbor House, 1978
ISBN 0-89340-223-0 : Unpriced B82-27417

Daniels, Dorothy. Saratoga / Dorothy Daniels. — London : W.H. Allen, 1981. — 320p ; 18cm. — (A Star book)
Originally published: New York : Nordon, 1981
ISBN 0-352-31009-x (pbk) : £1.25 B82-10101

Daniels, Les. The silver skull / Les Daniels. — London : Sphere, 1981, c1979. — 222p ; 18cm
Originally published: New York : Scribner, 1979
ISBN 0-7221-2833-9 (pbk) : £1.35 B82-02130

Danielson, Peter. The shepherd kings / Peter Danielson. — Toronto ; London : Bantam, 1981. — 595p : ill,2maps ; 18cm. — ([The Children of the Lion ; Bk.2])
ISBN 0-553-14653-x (pbk) : £1.75 B82-03233

Darcy, Clare. Caroline and Julia / Clare Darcy. — London : Macdonald, 1982. — 185p ; 23cm
ISBN 0-356-07895-7 : £5.95 B82-35279

Darcy, Clare. Eugenia / Clare Darcy. — London : Macdonald Futura, 1979, c1977 (1980 [printing]). — 251p ; 18cm. — (A Troubadour regency romance)
Originally published: New York : Walker, 1977 ; London : Raven Books, 1978
ISBN 0-7088-1502-2 (pbk) : £1.00 B82-32963

Davis, Gordon. The Sergeant #2 Hell harbor / by Gordon Davis. — [London] : Corgi, 1982, c1980. — 270p ; 17cm
ISBN 0-552-11864-8 (pbk) : £0.95 B82-12593

813'.54[F] — Fiction in English. American writers, 1945- — Texts *continuation*

Davis, Gordon. The Sergeant #3 Bloody bush / by Gordon Davis. — [London] : Corgi, 1982, c1980. — 288p ; 17cm
ISBN 0-552-11865-6 (pbk) : £0.95 B82-12592

Davis, Gordon. The Sergeant #4 : The liberation of Paris / Gordon Davis. — London : Corgi, 1982, c1981. — 199p ; 18cm
Originally published: U.S. : Kensington, 1981
ISBN 0-552-11955-5 (pbk) : £0.95 B82-32944

Davis, Gordon. The Sergeant #5 : Doom river / Gordon Davis. — London : Corgi, 1982, c1981. — 185p ; 18cm
Originally published: U.S. : Kensington, 1981
ISBN 0-552-11956-3 (pbk) : £0.95 B82-32943

Davis, Gordon. The sergeant # 6 : slaughter city / Gordon Davis. — London : Corgi, 1982, c1981. — 196p ; 18cm
ISBN 0-552-12075-8 (pbk) : £0.95 B82-35252

Davis, Gordon. The Sergeant # 7 : bullet bridge / Gordon Davis. — London : Corgi, 1982. — 183p ; 18cm
ISBN 0-552-12076-6 (pbk) : £0.95 B82-35251

Davis, Gordon. The Sgt. #1 Death train / by Gordon Davis. — [London] : Corgi, 1982, c1980. — 268p ; 17cm
ISBN 0-552-11863-x (pbk) : £0.95 B82-12594

Davis, Maggie. Eagles / Maggie Davis. — London : Corgi, 1982, c1980. — 400p ; 18cm
Originally published: New York : Morrow, 1980
ISBN 0-552-11888-5 (pbk) : £1.95 B82-16738

Davis, Robert P. (Robert Prunier). The divorce / Robert P. Davis. — London : Corgi, 1982, c1980. — 300p ; 18cm
Originally published: New York : Morrow, 1980 ; London : Hale, 1981
ISBN 0-552-12004-9 (pbk) : £1.50 B82-37550

De Blasis, Celeste. The Tiger's woman / Celeste De Blasis. — London : Granada, 1982. — 656p ; 18cm. — (A Mayflower book)
ISBN 0-583-13561-7 (pbk) : £2.50 B82-33674

De Felitta, Frank. For love of Audrey Rose. — London : New English Library, Nov.1982. — [480]p
ISBN 0-450-05533-7 (pbk) : £1.95 : CIP entry B82-27517

De Mille, Nelson. By the rivers of Babylon. — Large print ed. — Anstey : Ulverscroft, Jan.1983. — [624]p. — (Charnwood library series)
Originally published: New York : Harcourt Brace Jovanovich, 1978
ISBN 0-7089-8091-0 : £7.95 : CIP entry B82-32541

De Mille, Nelson. Cathedral / Nelson De Mille. — London : Granada, 1981 (1982 [printing]). — 556p ; 18cm. — (A Panther book)
ISBN 0-586-05160-0 (pbk) : £1.95 B82-30954

De Mille, Nelson. Cathedral. — Large print ed. — Anstey : Ulverscroft, Nov.1982. — [720]p. — (Charnwood library series)
ISBN 0-7089-8079-1 : £7.50 : CIP entry B82-29101

De Silva, Colin. The winds of Sinhala. — London : Granada, June 1982. — [576]p
Originally published: New York : Doubleday, 1980
ISBN 0-246-11839-3 : £7.95 : CIP entry B82-14219

De Winter, Michelle. Janine / Michelle de Winter. — London : Hodder Fawcett, 1980, c1979. — 316p ; 18cm
Originally published: New York : Fawcett, 1979 (book)
ISBN 0-340-25680-x (pbk) : £1.40 : CIP rev. B80-12054

Dean, S. F. X.. By frequent anguish : a love story interrupted by a murder and introducing Professor Neil Kelly / S.F.X. Dean. — London : Collins, 1982. — 253p ; 21cm. — (The Crime Club)
ISBN 0-00-231031-7 : £6.95 : CIP rev. B82-12429

Dee, Sherry. Make no promises. — London : Hodder & Stoughton, Feb.1983. — [192]p. — (Silhouette desire)
ISBN 0-340-32919-x (pbk) : £0.95 : CIP entry B82-38034

Delaney, Laurence. Blood red wine / Laurence Delaney. — London : Sphere, 1982, c1981. — 506p ; 18cm
ISBN 0-7221-2994-7 (pbk) : £2.25 B82-18176

Denker, Henry. The Warfield syndrome / Henry Denker. — London : Macdonald & Co., 1982, c1981. — 264p ; 23cm
Originally published: New York : Putnam, c1981
ISBN 0-356-08536-8 : £6.95 B82-15329

Dennis, Ralph. MacTaggart's war / Ralph Dennis. — London : Coronet, 1981, c1979. — 384p ; 18cm
Originally published: London : Hodder and Stoughton, 1979
ISBN 0-340-26670-8 (pbk) : £1.50 : CIP rev. B81-22544

Dew, Robb Forman. Dale loves Sophie to death / Robb Forman Dew. — Harmondsworth : Penguin, 1982, c1981. — 217p ; 20cm. — (The Penguin contemporary American fiction series)
Originally published: New York : Farrar, Straus, Giroux, 1981
ISBN 0-14-006183-5 (pbk) : £1.95 B82-40366

Dial, Joan. Lovers and warriors / Joan Dial. — London : Hodder Fawcett, 1981, c1978. — 347p ; 18cm. — (Coronet books)
Originally published: Greenwich, Conn. : Fawcett Gold Medal Books, 1978
ISBN 0-340-27267-8 (pbk) : £1.75 : CIP rev. B81-31466

Dick, Philip K.. The divine invasion / Philip K. Dick. — London : Corgi, 1982, c1981. — 242p ; 18cm
ISBN 0-552-11893-1 (pbk) : £1.50 B82-16939

Dick, Philip K.. The transmigration of Timothy Archer. — London : Gollancz, Oct.1982. — [256]p
ISBN 0-575-03220-0 : £6.95 : CIP entry B82-23352

Dick, Philip K.. Valis / Philip K. Dick. — London : Corgi, 1981. — 227p ; 18cm
ISBN 0-552-11841-9 (pbk) : £1.25 B82-06419

Dixon, Diana. Gamble of desire. — London : Hodder and Stoughton, Oct.1982. — [256]p. — (Silhouette special edition)
ISBN 0-340-32610-7 (pbk) : £0.95 : CIP entry B82-24719

Dixon, Diana, *1940-*. Mexican rhapsody. — London : Hodder & Stoughton, June 1982. — [256]p. — (Silhouette special edition)
ISBN 0-340-28581-8 (pbk) : £0.95 : CIP entry B82-10793

Doctorow, E. L.. Loon lake / E.L. Doctorow. — London : Pan in association with Macmillan, 1981, c1980 (1982 [printing]). — 251p ; 17cm
ISBN 0-330-26426-5 (pbk) : £1.50 B82-18099

Doctorow, E. L.. Ragtime / E.L. Doctorow. — London : Pan in association with Macmillan, 1976, c1975 (1982 printing). — 235p ; 18cm
Originally published: New York : Random House ; London : Macmillan, 1975
ISBN 0-330-24648-8 (pbk) : £1.50 B82-20310

Dolson, Hildegarde. Beauty sleep / Hildegarde Dolson. — South Yarmouth, Mass. : Curley, 1979, c1977 ; [Long Preston] : Distributed by Magna. — 380p ; 23cm. — (A Hildegarde Dolson mystery)
Originally published: Philadelphia : Lippincott, 1977 ; London : Hale, 1979. — Published in large print
ISBN 0-89340-180-3 : £4.75 B82-13661

Dolson, Hildegarde. A dying fall / Hildegarde Dolson. — South Yarmouth, Mass. : Curley, 1979, c1973 ; [Long Preston] : Distributed by Magna. — 391p ; 23cm. — (A Hildegarde Dolson mystery)
Originally published: Philadelphia : Lippincott, 1973. — Published in large print
ISBN 0-89340-181-1 : £4.75 B82-13662

Dolson, Hildegarde. To spite her face / Hildegarde Dolson. — South Yarmouth, Mass. : Curley, 1979, c1971 ; [Long Preston] : Distributed by Magna. — 462p ; 23cm. — (A Hildegarde Dolson mystery)
Originally published: Philadelphia : Lippincott, 1971. — Published in large print
ISBN 0-89340-182-x : £4.75 B82-13660

Donaldson, Stephen. The one tree / Stephen Donaldson. — London : Fontana, 1982. — 479p : ill ; 18cm. — (The Second chronicles of Thomas Covenant)
ISBN 0-00-616383-1 (pbk) : £1.95 B82-22901

Douglas, Billie. Time to love. — London : Hodder and Stoughton, Dec.1982. — [256]p. — (Silhouette special edition)
ISBN 0-340-32679-4 (pbk) : £0.95 : CIP entry B82-29659

Douglas, Gregory A.. The nest / Gregory A. Douglas. — Sevenoaks : New English Library, 1982, c1980. — 448p ; 18cm
Originally published: New York : Kensington, 1980
ISBN 0-450-05372-5 (pbk) : £1.75 : CIP rev. B82-03593

Douglass, Billie. Search of a new dawn. — London : Hodder & Stoughton, June 1982. — [256]p. — (Silhouette special edition)
ISBN 0-340-28584-2 (pbk) : £0.95 : CIP entry B82-10790

Downey, Bill. Black Viking / Bill Downey. — London : Sphere, 1982, c1981. — 316p ; 18cm
ISBN 0-7221-3014-7 (pbk) : £1.75 B82-37343

Drew, Wayland. Dragonslayer / Wayland Drew ; based on the screenplay written by Hal Darwood & Matthew Robbins. — London : Fontana, 1982, c1981. — 218p ; 18cm
Originally published: New York : Ballantine, 1981
ISBN 0-00-616432-3 (pbk) : £1.25 B82-17070

Drucker, Peter F.. The last of all possible worlds : a novel / Peter F. Drucker. — London : Heinemann, 1982. — vi,218p ; 25cm
ISBN 0-434-20955-4 : £7.50 B82-36808

Drummond, Brenna. Proud vintage. — London : Hodder & Stoughton, Jan.1983. — [256]p. — (Silhouette special edition)
ISBN 0-340-32941-6 (pbk) : £0.95 : CIP entry B82-34420

Drury, Allen. The hill of summer : a novel of the Soviet conquest / Allen Drury. — London : Joseph, 1982, c1981. — 484p ; 23cm
Originally published: Garden City, N.Y. : Doubleday, 1981
ISBN 0-7181-2117-1 : £8.95 B82-22049

Du Pont, Diane. The emerald embrace / Diane du Pont. — London : Sphere, 1982, c1980. — 319p ; 18cm
Originally published: New York : Fawcett, 1980
ISBN 0-7221-3107-0 (pbk) : £1.75 B82-09395

813'.54[F] — Fiction in English. American writers, *1945- — Texts* *continuation*

DuBarry, Michele. Toward love's horizon / Michele DuBarry. — London : W.H. Allen, 1981. — 320p ; 18cm. — (The Loves of Angela Carlyle ; v.3) (A Star book)
Originally published: New York : Nordon, 1981
ISBN 0-352-31028-6 (pbk) : £1.25 B82-10102

Duncan, Lois. I know what you did last summer / by Lois Duncan. — London : Hamilton, 1982, c1973. — 199p ; 23cm
Originally published: Boston : Little, Brown, 1973
ISBN 0-241-10723-7 : £4.95 : CIP rev. B81-36222

Duncan, Lois. Stranger with my face. — London : Hamilton, Feb.1983. — [256]p
ISBN 0-241-10913-2 : £5.50 : CIP entry B82-37852

Duncan, Robert L.. Brimstone / Robert L. Duncan. — London : Sphere, 1982, c1980. — 280p ; 18cm
Originally published: New York ; London : Joseph, 1980
ISBN 0-7221-3109-7 (pbk) : £1.75 B82-22597

Duncan, Robert L.. The day the sun fell / Robert L. Duncan. — London : Sphere, 1981, c1970. — 378p ; 18cm
Originally published: New York : Morrow ; Harmondsworth : Penguin, 1970
ISBN 0-7221-3110-0 (pbk) : £1.75 B82-07182

Duncan, W. R.. The queen's messenger : a novel / by W.R. Duncan. — London : Joseph, 1982. — 373p ; 23cm
ISBN 0-7181-2116-3 : £7.95 B82-22577

Dunne, John Gregory. Dutch Shea, Jr. / John Gregory Dunne. — London : Weidenfeld and Nicolson, 1982. — 352p ; 23cm
ISBN 0-297-78164-2 : £7.50 B82-38610

Dunne, John Gregory. True confessions / John Gregory Dunne. — London : Futura, 1981, c1979. — 371p ; 18cm
Originally published: New York : Dutton, 1977 ; London : Weidenfeld and Nicolson, 1978
ISBN 0-7088-1565-0 (pbk) : £1.50 B82-09351

Dunning, John. Deadline / by John Dunning. — London : Gollancz, 1982, c1981. — 222p ; 21cm
ISBN 0-575-03107-7 : £6.95 : CIP rev. B82-06930

Durham, John. Guns along the border. — Large print ed. — Bath : Chivers, Nov.1982. — [208] p. — (A Lythway book)
Originally published: London : Hale, 1966
ISBN 0-85119-861-9 : £6.70 : CIP entry B82-26439

Durham, John, *1916-*. The Tennyson rifle / by John Durham. — London : Hale, 1982. — 158p ; 20cm
ISBN 0-7091-9866-3 : £5.50 B82-31618

Dwyer, K. R.. Dragonfly / K.R. Dwyer. — London : Sphere, 1979, c1975. — 244p ; 18cm
Originally published: New York : Random House, 1975 ; London : P. Davies, 1977
ISBN 0-7221-3149-6 (pbk) : £0.95 B82-08986

Ebert, Alan. Traditions. — London : Granada, May 1982. — [600]p
Originally published: New York : Crown, 1981
ISBN 0-246-11841-5 : £7.95 : CIP entry B82-07412

Edmondson, G. C.. The aluminum man / G.C. Edmondson. — London : Hale, 1982, c1975. — 172p ; 19cm
ISBN 0-7091-9298-3 : £6.75 B82-22121

Egan, Lesley. Look back on death / Lesley Egan. — Large print ed. — Leicester : Ulverscroft, 1981, c1978. — 318p ; 23cm
Originally published: London : Gollancz, 1979
ISBN 0-7089-0716-4 : £5.00 : CIP rev. B81-30409

Egan, Lesley. The miser / Lesley Egan. — London : Gollancz, 1982. — 182p ; 21cm
ISBN 0-575-03044-5 : £5.95 B82-10543

Egan, Lesley. Random death. — London : Gollancz, Sept.1982. — [192]p
ISBN 0-575-03195-6 : £6.95 : CIP entry B82-18764

Ehrlich, Max. Shaitan. — London : Severn House, Nov.1982. — [352]p
ISBN 0-7278-0841-9 : £7.95 : CIP entry B82-34066

Elder, Mark. The Prometheus operation / Mark Elder. — London : Hale, 1981, c1980. — 281p ; 24cm
Originally published: New York : McGraw-Hill, 1980
ISBN 0-7091-9382-3 : £7.50 B82-22125

Elegant, Robert S.. A kind of treason / Robert Elegant. — Harmondsworth : Penguin, 1982, c1966. — 248p ; 18cm
Originally published: New York : Holt, Rinehart and Winston, 1966 ; Loughton : Piatkus, 1980
ISBN 0-14-005303-4 (pbk) : £1.50 B82-34165

Elegant, Robert S.. Manchu / Robert Elegant. — Harmondsworth : Penguin, 1981, c1980. — 634p ; 19cm
Originally published: London : Allen Lane, 1980
ISBN 0-14-005748-x (pbk) : £1.95 B82-00776

Elegant, Robert S.. The seeking / Robert Elegant. — Harmondsworth : Penguin, 1982, c1969. — 397p ; 18cm
Originally published: New York : Funk & Wagnalls, 1969
ISBN 0-14-005306-9 (pbk) : £1.75 B82-22320

Ellin, Stanley. Star light, star bright / Stanley Ellin. — London : Keyhole Crime, 1982, c1979. — 189p ; 18cm
Originally published: London : Cape, 1979
ISBN 0-263-73959-7 (pbk) : £0.95 B82-36070

Elliot, Elisabeth. No graven image : a novel / by Elisabeth Elliot. — London : Hodder and Stoughton, 1966 (1981 [printing]). — 244p ; 18cm. — (Hodder Christian paperbacks)
Originally published: New York : Harper and Row ; London : Hodder & Stoughton, 1966
ISBN 0-340-26355-5 (pbk) : £1.95 : CIP rev. B81-25750

Ellison, Harlan. Phoenix without ashes : a novel of the starlost / Harlan Ellison, Ed Bryant. — Manchester : Savory, 1978, c1975. — 128p ; 21cm
Originally published: / by Edward Bryant and Harlan Ellison. Greenwich, Conn. : Fawcett, 1975
ISBN 0-86130-003-3 (pbk) : £1.25 B82-27326

Ellison, Harlan. Shatterday / Harlan Ellison. — London : Hutchinson, 1982, c1980. — 312p ; 23cm
Originally published: Boston : Houghton Mifflin, 1980
ISBN 0-09-147640-2 : £7.95 : CIP rev. B82-04125

Ellman, Claire. North of evil / Claire Ellman. — London : Methuen Paperbacks, 1981. — 253p ; 18cm. — (Magnum books)
ISBN 0-417-06710-0 (pbk) : £1.50 B82-15500

Engel, Peter. [A controlling interest]. High risk / Peter Engel. — London : Fontana, 1982, c1980. — 318p ; 18cm
Originally published: New York : St. Martins Press, 1981
ISBN 0-00-616340-8 (pbk) : £1.75 B82-19740

Erdman, Paul. The crash of '79 / Paul E. Erdman. — Leicester : Charnwood, 1981, c1976. — 480p ; 23cm. — (Charnwood library series) (Charnwood large type)
Originally published: New York : Simon and Schuster, 1976 ; London : Secker and Warburg, 1977
ISBN 0-7089-8017-1 : £6.50 : CIP rev. B81-22651

Erikson, Paul. The dynast / Paul Erikson. — Feltham : Hamlyn, 1982, c1979. — 222p ; 18cm
Originally published: New York : Morrow, 1979
ISBN 0-600-20115-5 (pbk) : £1.25 B82-09006

Erskine, Helen. Fortunes of love. — London : Hodder & Stoughton, Oct.1982. — [192]p. — (Silhouette romance)
ISBN 0-340-32073-7 (pbk) : £0.75 : CIP entry B82-24842

Esler, Anthony. Bastion / Anthony Esler. — London : Macdonald, 1982, c1980. — 335p ; 21cm
Originally published: London : Futura, 1980
ISBN 0-354-04742-6 : £5.95 B82-36291

Estleman, Loren D.. Motor city blue / Loren D. Estleman. — London : Hale, 1982, c1980. — 219p ; 20cm
Originally published: Boston : Houghton Mifflin, 1980
ISBN 0-7091-9701-2 : £6.75 B82-22122

Eulo, Ken. The bloodstone. — London : Hodder and Stoughton, June 1982. — [330]p. — (Coronet books)
Originally published: New York : Pocket Books, 1981
ISBN 0-340-28069-7 (pbk) : £1.50 : CIP entry B82-10470

Eustis, Helen. The horizontal man / by Helen Eustis. — Harmondsworth : Penguin, 1949, c1946 (1982 [printing]). — 255p ; 19cm
Originally published: New York : Harper & Row, 1946 ; London : Hamilton, 1947
ISBN 0-14-000718-0 (pbk) : £1.50 B82-35609

Evans, Tabor. Longarm and the hatchet men / Tabor Evans. — London : Methuen Paperbacks, 1981, c1979. — 241p ; 18cm. — (Magnum books)
Originally published: New York : Jove, 1979
ISBN 0-417-06660-0 (pbk) : £1.25 B82-15504

Evans, Tabor. Longarm and the Wendigo / Tabor Evans. — London : Magnum, 1979, c1978. — 256p ; 18cm
ISBN 0-417-04510-7 (pbk) : £0.95 B82-25319

Fahy, Christopher. Nightflier / Christopher Fahy. — [London] : Corgi, 1982. — 250p ; 18cm
ISBN 0-552-11914-8 (pbk) : £1.50 B82-19465

Farber, James. Blood island / James Farber. — Feltham : Hamlyn, 1982, c1981. — 240p ; 18cm
ISBN 0-600-20493-6 (pbk) : £1.35 B82-08773

Farmer, Philip José. Dark is the sun / Philip José Farmer. — London : Granada, 1981, c1979 (1982 [printing]). — 400p ; 18cm. — (A Panther book) (Panther science fiction)
Originally published: New York : Ballantine, 1979
ISBN 0-586-05177-5 (pbk) : £1.95 B82-19981

Farmer, Philip José. Inside-outside / Philip José Farmer. — London : Corgi, 1982, c1964. — 134p ; 18cm
ISBN 0-552-11931-8 (pbk) : £1.25 B82-23906

Farmer, Philip José. Jesus on Mars / Philip José Farmer. — London : Granada, 1982, c1979. — 237p ; 18cm. — (A Panther book)
ISBN 0-586-05308-5 (pbk) : £1.50 B82-28801

813'.54[F] — Fiction in English. American writers, *1945- — Texts* *continuation*

Farmer, Philip José. The lovers / Philip José Farmer. — [London] : Corgi, 1982, c1979. — 200p ; 18cm
Originally published: New York : Ballantine, 1961
ISBN 0-552-11911-3 (pbk) : £1.50 B82-19461

Farmer, Philip José. Night of light / Philip José Farmer. — Harmondsworth : Penguin, 1972, c1966 (1982 [printing]). — 175p ; 19cm. — (Penguin science fiction)
Originally published: United States, 1966
ISBN 0-14-003392-0 (pbk) : £1.25 B82-18417

Farmer, Philip José. Tongues of the moon / Philip José Farmer. — [London] : Corgi, 1981, c1964. — 160p ; 18cm
Originally published: New York : Pyramid Books, 1964
ISBN 0-552-11821-4 (pbk) : £1.00 B82-03230

Farrington, Gene. The breath of kings. — London : Muller, Oct.1982. — [542]p
ISBN 0-584-31161-3 : £7.95 : CIP entry B82-25735

Farris, John. Catacombs / John Farris. — London : Hodder and Stoughton, 1982, c1981. — 439p ; 23cm
ISBN 0-340-27827-7 : £6.95 : CIP rev. B81-34148

Farris, John. The uninvited. — London : Hodder & Stoughton, Jan.1983. — [256]p
ISBN 0-340-32351-5 : £7.95 : CIP entry B82-33333

Fast, Jonathan, *1948-*. The beast / Jonathan Fast. — London : Methuen London, 1982, c1981. — 290p ; 18cm. — (A Methuen paperback)
Originally published: New York : Random House, 1981
ISBN 0-417-07060-8 (pbk) : £1.75 B82-33291

Federman, Raymond. The twofold vibration / Raymond Federman. — Bloomington : Indiana University Press ; Brighton : Harvester, 1982. — 175p ; 24cm
ISBN 0-7108-0460-1 : £7.50 B82-32973

Ferrell, Olivia. Love has its reasons. — London : Hodder and Stoughton, Feb.1983. — [256]p. — (Silhouette special edition)
ISBN 0-340-32947-5 (pbk) : £0.95 : CIP entry B82-38263

Ficks, R. Snowden. Deep space processional / by R. Snowden Ficks and Roger Beaumont. — London : Hale, 1982. — 190p ; 19cm
ISBN 0-7091-9635-0 : £6.25 B82-22119

Fielding, Joy. Kiss mummy goodbye. — Loughton : Piatkus, Aug.1981. — [288]p
ISBN 0-86188-112-5 : £6.50 : CIP entry B81-15864

Fish, Robert L.. Rough diamond / Robert L. Fish. — London : Heinemann, 1982, c1981. — 348p ; 22cm
Originally published: Garden City, N.Y. : Doubleday, 1981
ISBN 0-434-26345-1 : £6.95 B82-22096

Fleck, Betty. The love that never was / by Betty Fleck. — London : Remploy, 1981, c1969. — 191p ; 19cm
Originally published: London : Hale, 1969
ISBN 0-7066-0913-1 : £5.40 B82-18251

Fleischer, Leonore. Annie. — London : Severn House, Oct.1982. — [172]p
ISBN 0-7278-0833-8 : £6.95 : CIP entry B82-28578

Fleischer, Leonore. Ice castles / Leonore Fleischer. — London : Futura, 1979, c1978. — 220p ; 18cm. — (A Troubadour book)
ISBN 0-7088-1518-9 (pbk) : £0.80 B82-34233

Ford, Robert Curry. Hex / Robert Curry Ford. — London : Sphere, 1982, c1980. — 288p ; 18cm
Originally published: New York : Playboy Press, 1980
ISBN 0-7221-3602-1 (pbk) : £1.50 B82-09396

Foster, Alan Dean. Dark star / Alan Dean Foster ; adapted from a script by Dan O'Bannon and John Carpenter. — London : Futura in association with Ballantine, 1979, c1974. — 183p ; 18cm. — (An Orbit book)
Originally published: New York : Ballantine, 1974
ISBN 0-7088-8048-7 (pbk) : £0.90 B82-34237

Foster, Alan Dean. The thing : a novel / by Alan Dean Foster ; based on a screenplay by Bill Lancaster. — London : Corgi, 1982, c1981. — 196p ; 18cm
ISBN 0-552-12055-3 (pbk) : £1.25 B82-37548

Frankel, Sandor. The Aleph solution. — London : New English Library, Mar.1982. — [224]p
Originally published: New York : Stein and Day, 1979
ISBN 0-450-05272-9 (pbk) : £1.50 : CIP entry B82-01981

Freeman, Cynthia. Come pour the wine / a novel ; by Cynthia Freeman. — London : Prior, 1981, c1980. — 613p ; 25cm
Originally published: New York : Arbor House, 1980 ; Loughton : Piatkus, 1981. — Published in large print
ISBN 0-86043-633-0 : £8.50 B82-02938

Freeman, Cynthia. Come pour the wine. — Loughton (17 Brook Rd, Loughton, Essex) : Piatkus, Apr.1981. — [400]p
ISBN 0-86188-095-1 : £6.95 : CIP entry B81-07606

Freeman, Cynthia. Come pour the wine / Cynthia Freeman. — [London] : Corgi, 1982, c1980. — 352p ; 18cm
Originally published: New York : Arbor House, 1980 ; Loughton : Piatkus, 1981
ISBN 0-552-11925-3 (pbk) : £1.75 B82-19374

Freeman, Cynthia. The days of winter / by Cynthia Freeman. — [London] : Corgi, 1979, c1978 (1981 [printing]). — 406p ; 18cm
Originally published: New York : Arbor House, 1978
ISBN 0-552-11852-4 (pbk) : £1.95 B82-09002

Freeman, Cynthia. Fairytales / Cynthia Freeman. — [London] : Corgi, 1981, c1977. — 402p ; 18cm
Originally published: New York : Arbor House, 1977 ; London : Bantam, 1978
ISBN 0-552-11776-5 (pbk) : £1.95 B82-03234

Freeman, Cynthia. No time for tears. — Large print ed. — Anstey : Ulverscroft, Nov.1982. — [688]p. — (Charnwood library series)
ISBN 0-7089-8080-5 : £7.50 : CIP entry B82-29102

Freeman, Cynthia. No time for tears : a novel / by Cynthia Freeman. — Loughton : Piatkus, 1982, c1981. — 411p ; 21cm
ISBN 0-86188-187-7 : £8.50 : CIP rev. B82-05765

Freeman, Cynthia. A world full of strangers. — Loughton : Piatkus, Feb.1983. — [640]p
ISBN 0-86188-239-3 : £8.95 : CIP entry B82-39811

Freeman, Judy. Matinee / Judy Freeman & Donna Schuman. — London : Sphere, 1982, c1980. — 252p ; 18cm
ISBN 0-7221-3670-6 (pbk) : £1.75 B82-37344

Friedman, Philip. Termination order. — London : Hodder & Stoughton, Jan.1982. — [256]p. — (Coronet books)
Originally published: New York : Dial Press, 1979 ; London : Hodder & Stoughton, 1980
ISBN 0-340-27545-6 (pbk) : £1.25 : CIP entry B81-34133

Furst, Alan. The Paris drop. — London : Quartet, July 1982. — [240]p
ISBN 0-7043-2336-2 : £6.50 : CIP entry B82-13003

Gardner, John, *1933-*. Freddy's book / John Gardner. — London : Secker & Warburg, 1981, c1980. — 185p ; 23cm
Originally published: New York : Knopf, 1980
ISBN 0-436-17250-x : £6.95 : CIP rev. B81-27421

Gardner, John, *1933-*. Mickelsson's ghosts. — London : Secker and Warburg, Oct.1982. — [544]p
ISBN 0-436-17251-8 : £7.95 : CIP entry B82-24006

Garnet, A. H.. The Santa Claus killer. — London : Gollancz, Aug.1982. — [320]p
Originally published: New Haven : Tickner & Fields, 1981
ISBN 0-575-03140-9 : £7.95 : CIP entry B82-19554

Gilman, Dorothy. The tightrope walker / Dorothy Gilman. — London : Methuen, 1982, c1979. — 186p ; 18cm
Originally published: Garden City, N.Y. : Doubleday, 1979; London : Hale, 1980
ISBN 0-417-05450-5 (pbk) : £1.50 B82-36611

Glass, Isabel. Bedside manners / Isabel Glass. — London : Star, 1982, c1979. — 380p ; 18cm
Originally published: Greenwich, Conn. : Fawcett, 1979 ; London : W.H. Allen, 1981
ISBN 0-352-30934-2 (pbk) : £1.95 B82-16103

Glendinning, Ralph. The ultimate game / Ralph Glendinning. — London : New English Library, 1981. — 383p ; 23cm
ISBN 0-450-04885-3 : £6.95 B82-06487

Glut, Donald F.. The Empire strikes back : from the adventures of Luke Skywalker : a novel / by Donald F. Glut ; based on the story by George Lucas. — London : Severn House, 1980. — 215p ; 21cm
ISBN 0-7278-0629-7 : £5.95 : CIP rev. B80-18892

Gluyas, Constance. The passionate savage / Constance Gluyas. — London : Sphere, 1982, c1980. — 393p ; 18cm
Originally published: New York : New American Library, 1980
ISBN 0-7221-3901-2 (pbk) : £2.25 B82-37342

Godey, John. Nella / John Godey. — London : Sphere, 1982, c1981. — 372p ; 18cm
Originally published: New York : Delacorte, 1981
ISBN 0-7221-3971-3 (pbk) : £1.75 B82-34225

Godey, John. Nella / John Godey. — London : Severn House, 1982, c1981. — 341p ; 25cm
Originally published: New York : Delacorte, 1981
ISBN 0-7278-0803-6 : £7.95 B82-35465

Godwin, Gail. A mother and two daughters / Gail Godwin. — London : Heinemann, 1982. — 564p ; 23cm
ISBN 0-434-29750-x : £7.95 B82-11361

Godwin, Gail. Violet Clay / Gail Godwin. — [London] : Pavanne, 1982, c1978. — 298p ; 18cm
Originally published: London : Gollancz, 1978
ISBN 0-330-26844-9 (pbk) : £1.75 B82-35741

Goforth, Ellen. A new dawn. — London : Hodder and Stoughton, Nov.1982. — [192]p. — (Silhouette romance)
ISBN 0-340-32689-1 (pbk) : £0.75 : CIP entry B82-28267

Gold, Herbert. He — She : a novel / by Herbert Gold. — London : Severn House, 1982, c1980. — 213p ; 21cm
Originally published: New York : Arbor House, 1980
ISBN 0-7278-0798-6 : £6.95 B82-30466

813'.54[F] — Fiction in English. American writers, *1945- — Texts* *continuation*

Goldman, Laurel. Sounding the territory. — London : Faber, Aug.1982. — [320]p
ISBN 0-571-11962-x : CIP entry B82-16649

Goldman, William, *1931-*. Control / William Goldman. — London : Hodder and Stoughton, 1982. — 305p ; 23cm
ISBN 0-340-28360-2 : £7.95 : CIP rev. B82-15745

Goodrum, Charles A.. Dewey decimated / Charles A. Goodrum. — Sth. Yarmouth, Mass. : Curley, 1978, c1977 ; [Skipton] : distributed by Magna. — 431p ; 23cm
Published in large print
ISBN 0-89340-128-5 : Unpriced B82-14120

Gordon, Mary, *1949-*. The company of women / Mary Gordon. — London : Corgi, 1982, c1980. — 332p ; 18cm
Originally published: London : Cape, 1981
ISBN 0-552-12001-4 (pbk) : £1.75 B82-37549

Gosling, Paula. Loser's blues / Paula Gosling. — London : Pan, 1981, c1980. — 255p ; 18cm
Originally published: London : Macmillan, 1980
ISBN 0-330-26502-4 (pbk) : £1.25 B82-00780

Gosling, Paula. The zero trap / Paula Gosling. — Large print ed. — Leicester : Ulverscroft, 1981, c1979. — 411p ; 23cm. — (Ulverscroft large print series)
Originally published: London : Macmillan, 1979
ISBN 0-7089-0724-5 : £5.00 : CIP rev. B81-32605

Gosling, Paula. [Zero trap]. Loser's blues / Paula Gosling. — Large print ed. — Leicester, Ulverscroft, 1982, c1980. — 418p ; 23cm. — (Ulverscroft large print)
Originally published: London : Macmillan, 1980
ISBN 0-7089-0815-2 : Unpriced : CIP rev. B82-18464

Goth, Louis A.. Red — 12 / Louis A. Goth. — [London] : Corgi, 1982, c1979. — 279p ; 17cm
ISBN 0-552-11871-0 (pbk) : £1.75 B82-12595

Gould, Lois. La presidenta / Lois Gould. — [Feltham] : Hamlyn Paperbacks, 1982, c1981. — 318p ; 18cm
Originally published: New York : Linden, 1981
ISBN 0-600-20653-x (pbk) : £1.75 B82-33683

Grady, James, *1949-*. The great pebble affair / James Grady. — [Sevenoaks] : Hodder and Stoughton, 1979, c1976. — 192p ; 18cm. — (Coronet books)
Originally published: under the name Brit Shelby. New York : Putnam, c1976
ISBN 0-340-24492-5 (pbk) : £0.95 : CIP rev. B79-26636

Granger, Bill. Public murders / Bill Granger. — London : New English Library, 1981, c1980 (1982 [printing]). — 268p ; 18cm
Originally published: United States : Jove, 1980
ISBN 0-450-05370-9 (pbk) : £1.75 : CIP rev. B81-36200

Granger, Bill. Schism / Bill Granger. — Sevenoaks : New English Library, 1982, c1981. — 319p ; 23cm
Originally published: New York : Crown, 1981
ISBN 0-450-04902-7 : £7.95 B82-33513

Gray, Vanessa. The dutiful daughter / Vanessa Gray. — South Yarmouth, Mass. : John Curley, c1979 ; [Long Preston] : Magna [distributor]. — 529p ; 23cm
Originally published: New York : New American Library, 1979. — Published in large print
ISBN 0-89340-327-x : Unpriced B82-01042

Greeley, Andrew M.. The cardinal sins / Andrew M. Greeley. — London : W.H. Allen, 1981. — 350p ; 24cm
Originally published: New York : Warner Books, 1981
ISBN 0-491-02995-0 : £7.95 B82-00053

Greeley, Andrew M.. The cardinal sins / Andrew M. Greeley. — Leicester : Charnwood, 1982, c1981. — 486p ; 23cm. — (Charnwood large type)
Originally published: New York : Warner ; London : W.H. Allen, 1981. — Published in large print
ISBN 0-7089-8056-2 : Unpriced : CIP rev. B82-15955

Green, Bette. Get on out of here, Philip Hall. — London : Hamilton, Oct.1982. — [150]p
For adolescents
ISBN 0-241-10881-0 : £5.25 : CIP entry B82-23111

Green, Gerald. The chains / Gerald Green. — London : Macdonald Futura, 1981, c1980. — 576p ; 18cm
Originally published: New York : Seaview Book, c1980
ISBN 0-7088-1975-3 (pbk) : £2.50 B82-35715

Green, Gerald. Murfy's men / Gerald Green. — London : Severn House, 1982. — 332p ; 21cm
ISBN 0-7278-0769-2 : £6.95 B82-17493

Greenburg, Dan. What do women want? / Dan Greenburg. — London : Enigma, 1982. — 414p ; 25cm
ISBN 0-7278-3001-5 : £7.95 : CIP rev. B82-20399

Greene, Yvonne. Cover girl / Yvonne Greene. — Toronto ; London : Bantam, 1982. — 132p ; 18cm. — (Sweet dreams)
ISBN 0-553-20744-x (pbk) : £0.65 B82-28551

Greenleaf, Stephen. Death bed. — London : New English Library, Sept.1982. — [256]p
Originally published: New York : Dial Press, 1980
ISBN 0-450-04913-2 : £6.95 : CIP entry B82-18754

Greenlee, Sam. The spook who sat by the door. — London : Allison & Busby, Aug.1982. — [128]p
ISBN 0-85031-474-7 (pbk) : £1.95 : CIP entry B82-18579

Grey, Romer Zane. King of the range / by Romer Zane Grey. — Large print ed. — Leicester : Ulverscroft, 1982. — 442p ; 23cm. — (Ulverscroft large print)
ISBN 0-7089-0743-1 : £5.00 : CIP rev. B81-33952

Grey, Romer Zane. King of the range and Rustlers of the cattle range / Romer Zane Grey. — Hornchurch : Henry, 1981. — [134]p ; 21cm
ISBN 0-86025-198-5 : £5.25 B82-06576

Grey, Romer Zane. Siege at Forlorn River : based on characters created by Zane Grey / by Romer Zane Grey. — Large print ed. — Leicester : Ulverscroft, 1982, c1972. — 404p ; 23cm. — (Ulverscroft large print series)
At head of title: Zane Grey's Yaqui. — Contents: Siege at Forlorn River — Riders of the Kiowa trail — Heritage of the Legion
ISBN 0-7089-0799-7 : Unpriced : CIP rev. B82-18561

Grey, Romer Zane. Three deaths for Buck Duane and Track the man down / Romer Zane Grey. — Hornchurch : Henry, 1981. — [159]p ; 21cm
ISBN 0-86025-200-0 : £5.25 B82-06577

Gross, Joel. Maura's dream / Joel Gross. — London : New English Library, 1982, c1981. — 434p ; 23cm
Originally published: New York : Seaview Books, 1981
ISBN 0-450-04893-4 : £7.95 : CIP rev. B82-01978

Grossbach, Robert. — And justice for all : a novel / written by Robert Grossbach ; based on a motion picture written by Valerie Curtin & Barry Levinson. — London : Severn House, 1980. — 175p ; 21cm
Originally published: New York : Ballantine, 1979
ISBN 0-7278-0609-2 : £5.25 : CIP rev. B80-10274

Guest, Judith. Ordinary people / Judith Guest. — London : Prior, 1981, c1976. — 416p ; 25cm
Originally published: New York : Viking Press, 1976 ; London : Collins, 1977. — Published in large print
ISBN 0-86043-634-9 : £6.95 B82-02932

Gutcheon, Beth. The new girls / Beth Gutcheon. — London : Sphere, 1982, c1979. — 326p ; 18cm
ISBN 0-7221-4130-0 (pbk) : £1.75 B82-18174

Guy, Rosa. Ruby : a novel / by Rosa Guy. — London : Gollancz, 1981, c1976. — 217p ; 21cm
Originally published: New York : Viking, c1976
ISBN 0-575-03052-6 : £5.50 B82-03552

Hailey, Elizabeth Forsyth. Life sentences. — London : Hodder & Stoughton, Nov.1982. — [256]p
ISBN 0-340-28741-1 : £7.95 : CIP entry B82-28730

Haldeman, Joe. Worlds / Joe Haldeman. — London : Macdonald, 1982, c1981. — 262p ; 21cm
Originally published: New York : Viking Press, 1981
ISBN 0-356-08521-x : £5.95 B82-26018

Haldeman, Joe. Worlds : a novel of the near future / Joe Haldeman. — London : Futura, 1982, c1981. — 262p ; 18cm. — (An Orbit book)
Originally published: London : Macdonald, 1982
ISBN 0-7088-8090-8 (pbk) : £1.75 B82-22615

Haldeman, Linda. The lastborn of Elvinwood / by Linda Haldeman. — London : Souvenir Press, 1981, c1978. — 237p ; 23cm. — (Nightowl books)
Originally published: Garden City : Doubleday, 1978
ISBN 0-285-62503-9 : £6.95 B82-03664

Hale, Arlene. Legacy of love / Arlene Hale. — Sth. Yarmouth, Mass. : Curley, 1979, c1977 ; [Skipton] : distributed by Magna. — 352p ; 22cm
Published in large print
ISBN 0-89340-165-x : £4.75 B82-14114

Hale, Arlene. Lovers' reunion / Arlene Hale. — Sth. Yarmouth, Mass. : Curley, 1979, c1977 ; [Skipton] : distributed by Magna. — 329p ; 21cm
Published in large print
ISBN 0-89340-163-3 (pbk) : Unpriced B82-14112

Hale, Arlene. Love's destiny / Arlene Hale. — Sth. Yarmouth, Mass. : Curley, 1979, c1976 ; [Skipton] : distributed by Magna. — 352p ; 22cm
Published in large print
ISBN 0-89340-164-1 : £4.75 B82-14113

813'.54[F] — Fiction in English. American writers, *1945- — Texts* *continuation*

Hale, Arlene. A vote for love / Arlene Hale. — South Yarmouth : Curley ; [Skipton] : Magna Print, [1981], c1977. — 319p ; 22cm
Originally published: New York : New American Library, 1977. — Published in large print
ISBN 0-89340-340-7 : Unpriced B82-05035

Halldorson, Phyllis. To start again. — London : Hodder & Stoughton, Dec.1981. — [192]p. — (Silhouette romance)
ISBN 0-340-27659-2 (pbk) : £0.65 : CIP entry B81-31472

Halston, Carole. Collision course. — London : Hodder & Stoughton, Jan.1983. — [256]p. — (Silhouette special edition)
ISBN 0-340-32940-8 (pbk) : £0.95 : CIP entry B82-34419

Halston, Carole. Keys to Daniel's house. — London : Hodder & Stoughton, Dec.1982. — [256]p. — (Silhouette special edition)
ISBN 0-340-32079-6 (pbk) : £0.95 : CIP entry B82-29654

Halston, Carole. Love legacy. — London : Hodder & Stoughton, Jan.1982. — [192]p. — (Silhouette romance)
ISBN 0-340-27663-0 (pbk) : £0.75 : CIP entry B81-34481

Halston, Carole. Undercover girl. — London : Hodder and Stoughton, Dec.1982. — [192]p. — (Silhouette romance)
ISBN 0-340-32697-2 (pbk) : £0.75 : CIP entry B82-29667

Hamilton, Lucy. A woman's place. — London : Hodder & Stoughton, Sept.1982. — [256]p. — (Silhouette special edition)
ISBN 0-340-32087-7 (pbk) : £0.95 : CIP entry B82-20172

Hampson, Anne. Chateau in the palms / Anne Hampson. — Large print ed. — Bath : Chivers Press, 1982, c1979. — 214p ; 23cm. — (A Seymour book)
Originally published: London : Mills & Boon, 1979
ISBN 0-85119-449-4 : Unpriced : CIP rev. B81-33807

Hampson, Anne. Desire. — London : Hodder & Stoughton, July 1982. — [192]p. — (Silhouette romance)
Originally published: New York : Silhouette Books, 1981
ISBN 0-340-28465-x (pbk) : £0.75 : CIP entry B82-12311

Hampson, Anne. Enchantment. — London : Hodder and Stoughton, Mar.1982. — [192]p. — (Silhouette romance)
ISBN 0-340-27920-6 (pbk) : £0.75 : CIP entry B82-00256

Hampson, Anne. Fascination. — London : Hodder & Stoughton, May 1982. — [192]p. — (Silhouette romance)
Originally published: New York : Silhouette Books, 1981
ISBN 0-340-27934-6 (pbk) : £0.75 : CIP entry B82-07946

Hampson, Anne. Follow a shadow / by Anne Hampson. — London : Mills & Boon, c1981 (1982 [printing]). — 191p ; 18cm
ISBN 0-263-73920-1 (pbk) : £0.85 B82-36106

Hampson, Anne. Hunter of the East / Anne Hampson. — Large print ed. — Bath : Chivers, 1982, c1973. — 274p ; 23cm. — (Atlantic large print)
Originally published: London : Mills & Boon, 1973
ISBN 0-85119-466-4 : Unpriced : CIP rev. B82-07619

Hampson, Anne. A kiss from Satan. — Large print ed. — Long Preston : Magna Print, Dec.1982. — [336]p
Originally published: London : Mills and Boon, 1973
ISBN 0-86009-448-0 : £5.50 : CIP entry B82-30728

Hampson, Anne. The laird of Locharrun / Anne Hampson. — Large print ed. — [Bath] : Chivers Press, 1982, c1980. — 258p ; 23cm. — (Atlantic large print) (A Seymour large print romance)
Originally published: London : Mills & Boon, 1980
ISBN 0-85119-484-2 : Unpriced : CIP rev. B82-15857

Hampson, Anne. A man to be feared / by Anne Hampson. — Long Preston : Magna Print, 1982, c1976. — 321p ; 22cm
Originally published: London : Mills & Boon, 1976. — Published in large print
ISBN 0-86009-413-8 : Unpriced : CIP rev. B82-13157

Hampson, Anne. Realm of the pagans. — London : Hodder & Stoughton, Aug.1982. — [192]p. — (Silhouette romance)
ISBN 0-340-28637-7 (pbk) : £0.75 : CIP entry B82-15752

Hampson, Anne. Reap the whirlwind / by Anne Hampson. — Long Preston : Magna Print, 1981, c1975. — 300p ; 23cm
Originally published: London : Mills & Boon, 1975. — Published in large print
ISBN 0-86009-360-3 (corrected) : Unpriced : CIP rev. B81-14435

Hampson, Anne. Shadow of Apollo / Anne Hampson. — London : Silhouette, 1981. — 188p ; 18cm. — (Silhouette romance ; 64)
ISBN 0-340-27119-1 (pbk) : £0.65 : CIP rev. B81-26706

Hampson, Anne. Wife for a penny. — Large print ed. — Bath : Chivers, Oct.1982. — [280] p. — (Atlantic large print)
Originally published: London : Mills and Boon, 1972
ISBN 0-85119-497-4 : £5.25 : CIP entry B82-24229

Hannah, Barry[Dr. Ray]. Ray / Barry Hannah. — Harmondsworth : Penguin, 1981, c1980. — 113p ; 20cm. — (Penguin contemporary American fiction series)
Originally published: as Dr. Ray. New York : Knopf, 1980
ISBN 0-14-005945-8 (pbk) : £1.95 B82-16756

Hansen, Joseph. Gravedigger : a Dave Brandstetter mystery / Joseph Hansen. — London : Peter Owen, 1982. — 183p : ill ; 21cm
ISBN 0-7206-0591-1 : £7.50 B82-27257

Hansen, Ron. Desperadoes / Ron Hansen. — London : Corgi, 1981, c1979. — 271p ; 18cm
Originally published: New York : Knopf, 1979 ; London : Souvenir, 1980
ISBN 0-552-11835-4 (pbk) : £1.25 B82-06421

Hanson, Joseph. A smile in his lifetime / Joseph Hansen. — London : Peter Owen, 1982, c1981. — 292p ; 23cm
Originally published: New York : Holt, Rinehart and Winston, c1981
ISBN 0-7206-0596-2 : £8.50 B82-25467

Hardy, David A.. Galactic tours : Thomas Cook out of this world vacations / interstellar images : David Hardy ; extraterrestrial travelogue : Bob Shaw. — New York ; London : Proteus, 1981. — 95p : col.ill ; 31cm
ISBN 0-86276-005-4 (cased) : Unpriced
ISBN 0-906071-97-6 (pbk) : £4.95 B82-03214

Hardy, Laura. Burning memories. — London : Hodder and Stoughton, Dec.1981. — [192]p. — (Silhouette romance)
ISBN 0-340-27656-8 (pbk) : £0.65 : CIP entry B81-31434

Harrington, R. E.. The doomsday game / R.E. Harrington. — London : Corgi, 1982, c1981. — 221p ; 18cm
Originally published: London : Secker & Warburg, 1981
ISBN 0-552-12006-5 (pbk) : £1.50 B82-37133

Harrington, R. E.. Proud man / R.E. Harrington. — London : Secker & Warburg, 1982. — 404p ; 23cm
ISBN 0-436-19113-x (corrected) : £7.50 : CIP rev. B82-01973

Harris, Brian. World War III. — London : New English Library, Mar.1982. — [240]p
ISBN 0-450-05488-8 (pbk) : £1.25 : CIP entry B82-05397

Harris, Charlaine. [Sweet and deadly]. Dead dog / by Charlaine Harris. — London : Hale, 1982, c1981. — 179p ; 20cm
Originally published: Boston, Mass. : Houghton Mifflin, 1981
ISBN 0-7091-9700-4 : £6.75 B82-22867

Harris, MacDonald. Herma / Macdonald Harris. — London : Gollancz, 1982. — 431p ; 25cm
ISBN 0-575-03072-0 : £8.95 B82-12804

Harris, Marilyn. This other Eden / Marilyn Harris. — London : Macdonald Futura, 1980, c1977 (1981 [printing]). — 561p ; 18cm. — (A Troubadour spectacular)
Originally published: New York : Putnam, 1977
ISBN 0-7088-1746-7 (pbk) : £2.25 B82-05485

Harris, Marilyn. The women of Eden / Marilyn Harris. — London : Futura, 1981, c1980. — 602p ; 18cm. — (A Troubadour book)
Originally published: New York : Putnam, 1980
ISBN 0-7107-3021-7 (pbk) : £2.25 B82-05488

Harris, Thomas. Red dragon. — London : Bodley Head, Apr.1982. — [384]p
ISBN 0-370-30448-9 : £6.95 : CIP entry B82-03841

Harrison, Fred, *1916-*. The long rope / by Fred Harrison. — London : Hale, 1982. — 156p ; 20cm
ISBN 0-7091-9547-8 : £4.95 B82-12619

Harrison, Harry. Make room! Make room! / Harry Harrison. — Harmondsworth : Penguin, 1967, c1966 (1982 [printing]). — 224p ; 19cm. — (Penguin science fiction)
Originally published: Garden City, N.Y. : Doubleday, 1966. — Bibliography: p223-224
ISBN 0-14-002664-9 (pbk) : £1.50 B82-18416

Harrison, Harry. Rebel in time. — London : Granada, Feb.1983. — [304]p
ISBN 0-246-11766-4 : £7.95 : CIP entry B82-37825

Harrison, Harry. Starworld / Harry Harrison. — London : Granada, 1981. — 208p ; 18cm. — (A Panther book)
"Volume 3 in the To the stars trilogy"
ISBN 0-586-05053-1 (pbk) : £1.25 B82-00549

Harrison, Jim. Warlock / Jim Harrison. — London : Collins, 1981. — 262p ; 22cm
Originally published: New York : Delacorte Press, 1981
ISBN 0-00-222625-1 : £6.95 B82-07338

Harrison, William, *1933-*. Savannah blue / William Harrison. — London : Severn House, 1982. — 287p ; 21cm
ISBN 0-7278-0779-x : £6.95 B82-17497

Hart, Johnny. BC but theriously folkth. — London : Coronet Books, Feb.1983. — [128]p
Originally published: New York : Ballantine, 1982
ISBN 0-340-32054-0 (pbk) : £0.85 : CIP entry B82-38064

813'.54[F] — Fiction in English. American writers, *1945- — Texts* *continuation*

Hartman, Dane. Death on the docks / Dane Hartman. — Sevenoaks : New English Library, 1982, c1981. — 189p ; 18cm. — (Dirty Harry ; no.2)
Originally published: New York : Warner, 1981
ISBN 0-450-05420-9 (pbk) : Unpriced : CIP rev. B82-09424

Hartman, Dane. Duel for cannons / Dane Hartman. — Sevenoaks : New English Library, 1982, c1981. — 173p ; 18cm. — (Dirty Harry ; no.1)
Originally published: New York : Warner, 1981
ISBN 0-450-05419-5 (pbk) : £1.25 : CIP rev. B82-09423

Hartman, Dane. The Mexico kill. — London : New English Library, Jan.1983. — [192]p. — (Dirty Harry ; 4)
ISBN 0-450-05511-6 (pbk) : £1.25 : CIP entry B82-34600

Hassler, Jon. The love hunter : a novel / by Jon Hassler. — London : Weidenfeld and Nicolson, 1982, c1981. — 311p ; 22cm
Originally published: New York : Morrow, 1981
ISBN 0-297-78041-7 : £6.95 B82-11716

Hastings, Brooke. Intimate strangers. — London : Hodder & Stoughton, June 1982. — [256]p. — (Silhouette special edition)
ISBN 0-340-28580-x (pbk) : £0.95 : CIP entry B82-10794

Hastings, Brooke. Island conquest / Brooke Hastings. — London : Silhouette, 1981. — 189p ; 18cm. — (Silhouette romance ; 67)
ISBN 0-340-27122-1 (pbk) : £0.65 : CIP rev. B81-26776

Hastings, Brooke. Winner takes all. — London : Hodder and Stoughton, Apr.1982. — [192]p. — (Silhouette romance)
ISBN 0-340-27928-1 (pbk) : £0.75 : CIP entry B82-03826

Hautzig, Deborah. Hey, dollface / Deborah Hautzig. — London : Fontana, 1982, c1978. — 151p ; 18cm. — (Lions)
Originally published: London : Hamilton, 1979. — For adolescents
ISBN 0-00-671964-3 (pbk) : £1.00 B82-19736

Haviland, Diana. Defy the storm. — London : Coronet, Nov.1982. — [352]p
Originally published: New York : Fawcett, 1981
ISBN 0-340-28644-x (pbk) : £2.25 : CIP entry B82-27369

Hawkes, John. Virginie, her two lives. — London : Chatto & Windus, Jan.1983. — [208]p
ISBN 0-7011-3908-0 : £6.95 : CIP entry B82-32522

Hayden, Jay. The Canada kid / by Jay Hayden. — London : Hale, 1981, c1964. — 160p ; 20cm
Originally published: London : Gresham, 1964
ISBN 0-7091-9467-6 : £3.25 B82-00516

Heinlein, Robert A.. Friday. — London : New English Library, Nov.1982. — [432]p
ISBN 0-450-05549-3 (pbk) : £1.95 : CIP entry B82-27521

Hellerstein, Harry. Wired. — London : Severn House, Nov.1982. — [256]p
Originally published: New York : St. Martin's Press, 1982
ISBN 0-7278-0848-6 : £6.95 : CIP entry B82-34072

Henege, Thomas. A cargo of tin / Thomas Henege. — London : Deutsch, 1982, c1981. — 201p ; 23cm
ISBN 0-233-97449-0 : £6.95 B82-15320

Henissart, Paul. Margin of error / Paul Henissart. — London : Arrow, 1981, c1980. — 334p ; 18cm
Originally published: London : Hutchinson, 1980
ISBN 0-09-926460-9 (pbk) : £1.60 B82-06572

Herbert, Frank. Direct descent / Frank Herbert. — Sevenoaks : New English Library, 1982,c1980. — 186p : ill ; 21cm
Originally published: New York : Ace, 1980
ISBN 0-450-05406-3 (pbk) : £2.25 : CIP rev. B82-09694

Herbert, Frank. The Dosadi experiment / Frank Herbert. — London : Futura, 1978, c1977 (1981 [printing]). — 336p ; 18cm. — (An Orbit book)
Originally published: New York : Putnam, 1977 ; London : Gollancz, 1978
ISBN 0-7088-8035-5 (pbk) : £1.60 B82-34232

Herbert, Frank. God emperor of Dune / Frank Herbert. — London : New English Library, 1981 (1982 [printing]). — 454p ; 18cm
Originally published: London : Gollancz, 1981
ISBN 0-450-05262-1 (pbk) : £2.50 : CIP rev. B82-03591

Herbert, Frank. The white plague. — London : Gollancz, Feb.1983. — [448]p
ISBN 0-575-03240-5 : £7.95 : CIP entry B82-38687

Higgins, George V.. The patriot game / George V. Higgins. — London : Secker & Warburg, 1982. — 237p ; 22cm
ISBN 0-436-19589-5 : £7.50 B82-30290

Highsmith, Patricia. Edith's diary / Patricia Highsmith. — Harmondsworth : Penguin, 1980, c1977 (1982 [printing]). — 317p ; 19cm
Originally published: London : Heinemann, 1977
ISBN 0-14-004802-2 (pbk) : £1.75 B82-33534

Highsmith, Patricia. Ripley under ground / Patricia Highsmith. — Harmondsworth, Penguin, 1973, c1970 (1982 [printing]). — 263p ; 17cm
ISBN 0-14-003602-4 (pbk) : £1.50 B82-25123

Highsmith, Patricia. Ripley's game / Patricia Highsmith. — Harmondsworth : Penguin, 1976, c1974 (1982 [printing]). — 255p ; 18cm
Originally published: London : Heinemann, 1974
ISBN 0-14-003778-0 (pbk) : £1.50 B82-32489

Highsmith, Patricia. Slowly, slowly in the wind. — Large print ed. — Bath : Chivers, Oct.1982. — [320]p. — (Atlantic large print)
Originally published: London : Heinemann, 1979
ISBN 0-85119-501-6 : £5.25 : CIP entry B82-24233

Hill, Roger, *1916-*. Redstone / by Roger Hill. — London : Hale, 1981. — 160p ; 20cm
ISBN 0-7091-9417-x : £4.95 B82-03153

Hillerman, Tony. The dark wind. — London : Gollancz, Feb.1983. — [224]p
ISBN 0-575-03188-3 : £6.95 : CIP entry B82-38681

Hillerman, Tony. People of darkness / Tony Hillerman. — London : Gollancz, 1982, c1980. — 202p ; 21cm. — (Gollancz thriller)
ISBN 0-575-03133-6 : £6.95 : CIP rev. B82-12983

Hinkemeyer, Michael T.. Dark angel pass by / Michael T. Hinkemeyer. — London : Futura, 1979. — 301p ; 18cm
ISBN 0-7088-1510-3 (pbk) : £0.95 B82-34236

Hirschfeld, Burt. The men of Dallas / Burt Hirschfeld. — [London] : Corgi, 1981. — 267p ; 18cm
ISBN 0-552-11844-3 (pbk) : £1.35 B82-09008

Hirschfeld, Burt. The men of Dallas / a novel by Burt Hirschfeld ; based on the series created by David Jacobs and on the teleplays by Rena Down ... [et al.]. — London : Severn House, 1982, c1981. — 267p ; 21cm
ISBN 0-7278-0776-5 : £6.95 B82-12074

Hoban, Russell. Riddley Walker / Russell Hoban. — London : Pan, 1982, c1980. — 213p : 1map ; 20cm. — (Picador)
Originally published: New York : Summit Books, 1980 ; London : Cape, 1980
ISBN 0-330-26645-4 (pbk) : £1.95 B82-09946

Hobhouse, Janet. Nellie without Hugo / Janet Hobhouse. — London : Cape, 1982. — 192p ; 23cm
ISBN 0-224-01969-4 : £6.95 : CIP rev. B82-01154

Hodge, Jane Aiken. Wide is the water. — Large print ed. — Anstey : Ulverscroft, Jan.1983. — [528]p. — (Ulverscroft large print series)
Originally published: London : Hodder and Stoughton, 1981
ISBN 0-7089-0903-5 : £6.25 : CIP entry B82-32531

Hoffman, Alice. Angel Landing / Alice Hoffman. — [London] : Pavanne, 1982, c1980. — 236p ; 18cm
Originally published: New York : Putnam, 1980 ; London : Severn House, 1982
ISBN 0-330-26808-2 (pbk) : £1.50 B82-35742

Hoffman, Alice. Angel Landing / Alice Hoffman. — London : Severn House, 1982, c1980. — 220p ; 21cm
Originally published: New York : Putnam, c1980
ISBN 0-7278-0766-8 : £6.50 B82-16170

Hoffman, Lee. Fox / Lee Hoffman. — London : Hale, 1980, c1976. — 186p ; 20cm
Originally published: Garden City, N.Y. : Doubleday, 1976
ISBN 0-7091-7540-x : £4.95 B82-15580

Hoffman, Lee. Gunfight at Laramie / by Lee Hoffman. — London : Hale, 1982, 1966. — 159p ; 19cm
Originally published: New York : Ace Books, 1966
ISBN 0-7091-7785-2 : £5.50 B82-39188

Hoffman, Lee. Return to Broken Crossing / Lee Hoffman. — London : Hale, 1982, c1969. — 159p ; 20cm
Originally published: New York : Ace, 1969
ISBN 0-7091-7784-4 : £5.25 B82-22912

Hoffman, Lee. Trouble valley / by Lee Hoffman. — London : Hale, 1982, c1976. — 192p ; 20cm
Originally published: New York : Ballantine Books, 1976
ISBN 0-7091-7783-6 : £4.95 B82-19132

Hogan, Ray. The doomsday bullet / by Ray Hogan. — London : Hale, 1982, c1981. — 182p ; 20cm
Originally published: Garden City, N.Y. : Doubleday, 1981
ISBN 0-7091-9867-1 : £5.50 B82-34173

Holland, Cecelia. The sea beggars / Cecelia Holland. — London : Gollancz, 1982. — 305p ; 23cm
ISBN 0-575-03042-9 : £8.95 : CIP rev. B82-19561

Holland, Isabelle. The lost madonna / Isabelle Holland. — London : Collins, 1982, c1981. — 279p ; 22cm
Originally published: New York : Rawson, Wade, 1981
ISBN 0-00-222608-1 : £7.50 B82-09041

Holmes, Nancy. [The big girls]. The power girls / Nancy Holmes. — London : Star, 1982. — 399p ; 18cm. — (A Star book)
Originally published: Garden City, N.Y. : Doubleday ; London : W.H. Allen, 1982
ISBN 0-352-31134-7 (pbk) : £1.95 B82-33020

813′.54[F] — Fiction in English. American writers, *1945- — Texts* *continuation*

Holmes, Nancy. The power girls / Nancy Holmes. — London : W.H. Allen, 1982. — 399p ; 21cm
Originally published: New York : Doubleday, 1982
ISBN 0-491-02817-2 : £8.95 B82-34181

Hope, Jacqueline. Love captive. — London : Hodder and Stoughton, Nov.1982. — [192]p. — (Silhouette romance)
ISBN 0-340-32690-5 (pbk) : £0.75 : CIP entry B82-28268

Horn, Richard. Designs / Richard Horn. — Feltham : Hamlyn, 1982, c1980. — 284p ; 18cm
Originally published: New York : M. Evans, 1980
ISBN 0-600-20497-9 (pbk) : £1.75 B82-30986

Hornung, Patricia. Favours / Patricia Hornung. — London : Arrow, 1981. — 327p ; 18cm
ISBN 0-09-922170-5 (pbk) : £1.75 B82-06574

Horvitz, Leslie A.. The compton effect / Leslie A. Horvitz and H. Harris Gerhard. — London : Sphere, 1981, c1980. — 299p ; 18cm
ISBN 0-7221-4743-0 (pbk) : £1.50 B82-06010

Hotchner, A. E.. The man who lived at the Ritz / a novel by A.E. Hotchner. — London : Weidenfeld and Nicolson, 1982. — 286p ; 22cm
ISBN 0-297-78112-x : £6.95 B82-18270

Houston, Robert. Bisbee ′17 : a novel / by Robert Houston. — London : Writers and Readers Publishing Cooperative, 1979. — 287p ; 23cm
ISBN 0-906495-17-2 : £5.95 B82-00810

Houston, Will. Death of a gambler / by Will Houston. — London : Hale, 1982. — 158p ; 20cm
ISBN 0-7091-9928-7 : £5.50 B82-35893

Howard, Linda. All that glitters. — London : Hodder and Stoughton, Oct.1982. — [256]p. — (Silhouette special edition)
ISBN 0-340-32608-5 (pbk) : £0.95 : CIP entry B82-24717

Howard, Linda. An independent wife. — London : Hodder & Stoughton, Feb.1983. — [256]p. — (Silhouette special edition)
ISBN 0-340-32945-9 (pbk) : £0.95 : CIP entry B82-37656

Howard, Linda U.. Expecting miracles / Linda U. Howard. — London : Sphere, 1981, c1980. — 343p ; 18cm
Originally published: New York : Putnam, 1980
ISBN 0-7221-4746-5 (pbk) : £1.50 B82-02124

Hoyt, Richard. Decoys / by Richard Hoyt. — London : Hale, 1982, c1980. — 203p ; 20cm
Originally published: New York : M. Evans, 1980
ISBN 0-7091-9828-0 : £6.75 B82-33195

Hufford, Susan. Reflections / Susan Hufford. — London : Methuen London, 1982, c1981. — 325p ; 21cm
Originally published: New York : Seaview, 1981
ISBN 0-413-50340-2 (cased) : £6.95
ISBN 0-417-07510-3 (pbk) : £1.75 B82-33931

Hughes, Robert. Strange behaviour. — London : New English Library, May 1982. — [160]p
ISBN 0-450-05321-0 (pbk) : £1.25 : CIP entry B82-06749

Hugo, Richard. Death and the good life / Richard Hugo. — London : Hale, 1982, c1981. — 215p ; 20cm
Originally published: New York : St. Martin′s Press, 1981
ISBN 0-7091-9829-9 : £6.75 B82-31634

Hunter, Elizabeth. Written in the stars. — London : Hodder and Stoughton, Feb.1982. — [192]p. — (Silhouette romance)
ISBN 0-340-27671-1 (pbk) : £0.75 : CIP entry B81-38313

Hunter, Elizabeth, *1934-*. One more time. — London : Hodder & Stoughton, Oct.1982. — [192]p. — (Silhouette romance)
ISBN 0-340-32070-2 (pbk) : £0.75 : CIP entry B82-24839

Hunter, Evan. Love, dad / Evan Hunter. — London : Corgi, 1982, c1981. — 413p ; 18cm
Originally published: London : Joseph, 1981
ISBN 0-552-11980-6 (pbk) : £1.95 B82-35476

Hunter, Stephen. The master sniper / Stephen Hunter. — London : Pan, 1982, c1980. — 269p ; 18cm
Originally published: New York : Morrow ; London : Heinemann, 1980
ISBN 0-330-26590-3 (pbk) : £1.50 B82-13721

Hurling, Joan. Influence / Joan Hurling. — London : Arrow, 1982, c1981. — 284p ; 18cm
ISBN 0-09-929110-x (pbk) : £1.75 B82-35589

Huson, Paul. The keepsake / Paul Huson. — London : Severn House, 1982, c1981. — 320p : ill ; 21cm
ISBN 0-7278-0821-4 : £7.95 B82-35462

Husted, Darrell. Chastity′s prize / Darrell Husted. — South Yarmouth, Ma. : John Curley ; Long Preston : Distributed by Magna Print, c1980. — 353p ; 22cm
Published in large print
ISBN 0-89340-371-7 : Unpriced B82-15321

Husted, Darrell. Courting / Darrell Husted. — South Yarmouth, Mass. : Curley, c1980 ; [Long Preston] : distributed by Magna. — 365p ; 23cm
Originally published: New York : Collier, 1980. — Published in large print
ISBN 0-89340-377-6 : Unpriced B82-19718

Hyde, Christopher. The Icarus seal. — London : Hodder and Stoughton, Jan.1983. — 1v.
ISBN 0-340-25563-3 : £6.95 : CIP entry B82-37647

Hyman, Vernon Tom. Giant killer / Vernon Tom Hyman. — Feltham : Hamlyn Paperbacks, 1982, c1981. — 331p ; 18cm
ISBN 0-600-20634-3 (pbk) : £1.75 B82-37141

Ingalls, Rachel. Mrs Caliban / Rachel Ingalls. — London : Faber, 1982. — 125p ; 21cm
ISBN 0-571-11826-7 : £6.50 : CIP rev. B81-33791

Ipcar, Dahlov. A dark horn blowing / Dahlov Ipcar. — London : Fontana, 1981, c1978. — 222p ; 18cm. — (Lions)
Originally published: New York : Viking, 1978 ; London : Macdonald, 1980
ISBN 0-00-671896-5 (pbk) : £1.00 B82-03006

Irving, John, *1942-*. The Hotel New Hampshire / John Irving. — London : Cape, 1981. — 401p ; 23cm
ISBN 0-224-01961-9 : £6.95 : CIP rev. B81-28104

Isaacs, Susan, *1943-*. Close relations / Susan Isaacs. — London : Futura, 1981. — 351p ; 18cm
Originally published: London : Macdonald, 1981
ISBN 0-7088-1981-8 (pbk) : £1.60 B82-05480

Jackson, Guida. Passing through / Guida Jackson. — London : Hamlyn Paperbacks, 1981, c1979. — 234p ; 18cm
Originally published: New York : Simon & Schuster, 1979
ISBN 0-600-20194-5 (pbk) : £1.25 B82-00652

Jaffe, Rona. Away from home. — London : Hodder & Stoughton, Aug.1982. — [336]p
Originally published: London : Cape, 1960
ISBN 0-340-28110-3 (pbk) : £1.95 : CIP entry B82-15737

Jaffe, Rona. Family secrets. — London : Hodder and Stoughton, Mar.1982. — [512]p. — (Coronet books)
Originally published: 1975
ISBN 0-340-27906-0 (pbk) : £2.50 : CIP entry B82-00252

Jaffe, Rona. Mazes and monsters / Rona Jaffe. — London : Hodder and Stoughton, 1982, c1981. — 329p ; 23cm
Originally published: New York : Delacorte, 1981
ISBN 0-340-27820-x : £6.95 : CIP rev. B81-35685

Jaffe, Rona. The other woman. — London : Hodder and Stoughton, Mar.1982. — [192]p. — (Coronet books)
Originally published: 1973
ISBN 0-340-27905-2 (pbk) : £1.50 : CIP entry B82-00251

Jaffee, Annette Williams. Adult education / Annette Williams Jaffee. — London : Allen Lane, 1982, c1981. — 230p ; 22cm
Originally published: Princeton, N.J. : Ontario Review, 1981
ISBN 0-7139-1465-3 : £6.95 B82-13591

Jakes, John. North and South / John Jakes. — London : Collins, 1982. — 740p ; 25cm
ISBN 0-00-222672-3 : £8.95 B82-32132

James, Arlene. City girl. — London : Hodder & Stoughton, Oct.1982. — [192]p. — (Silhouette romance)
ISBN 0-340-32074-5 (pbk) : £0.75 : CIP entry B82-24843

James, Stephanie. Corporate affair. — London : Hodder & Stoughton, Nov.1982. — [192]p. — (Silhouette desire)
ISBN 0-340-32858-4 (pbk) : £0.95 : CIP entry B82-28732

James, Stephanie. Dangerous magic. — London : Hodder & Stoughton, Sept.1982. — [256]p. — (Silhouette special edition)
ISBN 0-340-32084-2 (pbk) : £0.95 : CIP entry B82-20169

James, Stephanie. A passionate business. — London : Hodder and Stoughton, Feb.1982. — [192]p. — (Silhouette romance)
ISBN 0-340-27669-x (pbk) : £0.75 : CIP entry B81-38311

James, Stephanie. Stormy challenge. — London : Hodder and Stoughton, Dec.1982. — [256]p. — (Silhouette special edition)
ISBN 0-340-32682-4 (pbk) : £0.95 : CIP entry B82-31290

James, Stephanie. Velvet touch. — London : Hodder & Stoughton, Feb.1983. — [192]p. — (Silhouette desire)
ISBN 0-340-32922-x (pbk) : £0.95 : CIP entry B82-38266

Jeffers, H. Paul. The adventure of the stalwart companions / H. Paul Jeffers. — London : Magnum, 1981, c1978. — 190p ; 18cm
Originally published: New York : Harper and Row, 1978 ; London : Cassell, 1979
ISBN 0-417-04740-1 (pbk) : £1.50 B82-15552

Jennings, Gary. Aztec / Gary Jennings. — London : Futura, 1981 (1982 [printing]). — 754p ; 18cm
ISBN 0-7088-2064-6 (pbk) : £3.50 B82-18269

Jessup, Richard. Threat. — Large print ed. — Anstey : Ulverscroft, Dec.1982. — 1v.. — (Ulverscroft large print series)
Originally published: London : Gollancz, 1981
ISBN 0-7089-8085-6 : £5.25 : CIP entry B82-30792

813′.54[F] — Fiction in English. American writers, *1945- — Texts* *continuation*

John, Nancy. A man for always. — London : Hodder & Stoughton, June 1982. — [192]p. — (Silhouette romance)
Originally published: New York : Silhouette Books, 1981
ISBN 0-340-27941-9 (pbk) : £0.75 : CIP entry B82-10463

John, Nancy. Outback summer. — London : Hodder & Stoughton, Jan.1982. — [192]p. — (Silhouette romance)
ISBN 0-340-27665-7 (pbk) : £0.75 : CIP entry B81-34484

John, Nancy. So many tomorrows. — London : Hodder & Stoughton, Sept.1982. — [256]p. — (Silhouette special edition)
ISBN 0-340-32086-9 (pbk) : £0.95 : CIP entry B82-20171

John, Nancy. Web of passion. — London : Hodder & Stoughton, Jan.1983. — [256]p. — (Silhouette special edition)
ISBN 0-340-32937-8 (pbk) : £0.95 : CIP entry B82-34416

Johnson, Barbara Ferry. The heirs of love / Barbara Ferry Johnson. — London : Sphere, 1981, c1980. — 633p ; 18cm
Originally published: New York : Avon, 1980
ISBN 0-7221-5074-1 (pbk) : £1.95 B82-02128

Johnson, Diane. Burning / Diane Johnson. — London : Granada, 1981, c1971. — 250p ; 18cm. — (A Panther book)
Originally published: London : Heinemann, 1971
ISBN 0-586-05336-0 (pbk) : £1.95 B82-00550

Johnson, Diane. Loving hands at home / Diane Johnson. — London : Granada, 1981, c1968. — 256p ; 18cm. — (A Panther book)
Originally published: New York : Harcourt, Brace & World, 1968 ; London : Heinemann, 1969
ISBN 0-586-05337-9 (pbk) : £1.95 B82-09544

Johnson, Sandy. The CUPPI. — London : Hodder and Stoughton, Oct.1982. — [256]p. — (Coronet books)
Originally published: 1980
ISBN 0-340-28445-5 (pbk) : £1.95 : CIP entry B82-24832

Johnston, Velda. A presence in an empty room / Velda Johnston. — London : W.H. Allen, 1982, c1980. — 160p ; 21cm
Originally published: New York : Dodd, Mead, 1980
ISBN 0-491-02926-8 : £6.95 B82-11440

Jones, John G.. The Amityville horror 2 : based on the story of George and Kathleen Lutz / John G. Jones. — [Sevenoaks] : New English Library, 1982. — 396p ; 18cm
ISBN 0-450-05468-3 (pbk) : £1.75 : CIP rev. B82-09425

Jong, Erica. Fanny : being the true history of the adventures of Fanny Hackabout-Jones / a novel ; by Erica Jong. — London : Granada, 1980 (1981 [printing]). — xx,559p : 1col.port ; 18cm
ISBN 0-586-05327-1 (pbk) : £1.95 B82-09535

Jordan, Lee. Cat′s eyes. — London : Coronet, Jan.1983. — [176]p
Originally published: London : Hodder and Stoughton, 1981
ISBN 0-340-26871-9 (pbk) : £1.40 : CIP entry B82-33728

Jupp, Kenneth, *1938-*. Echo / Kenneth Jupp. — London : W.H. Allen, 1981, c1980. — 231p ; 18cm. — (A Star book)
Originally published: London : Deutsch, 1980
ISBN 0-352-30966-0 (pbk) : £1.60 B82-06478

Kahn, Evelyn. The wayward winds / Evelyn Kahn. — [London] : Corgi, 1982, c1981. — 442p ; 18cm
Originally published: United States : s.n., 1981
ISBN 0-552-11944-x (pbk) : £1.75 B82-28366

Kallen, Lucille. C.B. Greenfield : no lady in the house / Lucille Kallen. — London : Collins, 1982. — 230p ; 21cm. — (The Crime Club)
ISBN 0-00-231690-0 : £6.75 : CIP rev. B82-19073

Kaminsky, Stuart M.. High midnight. — London : Severn House, Nov.1982. — [200]p
ISBN 0-7278-0845-1 : £6.95 : CIP entry B82-34069

Kaminsky, Stuart M.. Murder on the yellow brick road / Stuart Kaminsky. — Sth. Yarmouth, Mass. : Curley, 1979, c1977 ; [Skipton] : distributed by Magna. — 280p ; 22cm
Originally published: New York : St Martins Press, 1977. — Published in large print
ISBN 0-89340-167-6 (corrected) : £4.75 B82-15398

Kaminsky, Stuart M.. Murder on the Yellow Brick Road / Stuart Kaminsky. — London : Severn House, 1981, c1977. — 197p ; 21cm. — ([A Toby Peters mystery])
Originally published: New York : St. Martin′s Press, 1977
ISBN 0-7278-0732-3 : £6.95 : CIP rev. B81-23819

Kaminsky, Stuart M.. Rostnikov′s corpse / Stuart M. Kaminsky. — London : Macmillan, 1981. — 239p ; 21cm
ISBN 0-333-31846-3 : £5.95 B82-05737

Kantor, Hal. Blown away / Hal Kantor. — London : Sphere, 1981, c1980. — 341p ; 18cm
Originally published: New York : Morrow, 1980
ISBN 0-7221-5145-4 (pbk) : £1.75 B82-02133

Kastle, Herbert. Sunset people / Herbert Kastle. — London : Granada, 1982, c1980. — 368p ; 18cm. — (A Mayflower book)
Originally published: London : W.H. Allen, 1980
ISBN 0-583-13418-1 (pbk) : £1.95 B82-17352

Katz, William. Copperhead / William Katz. — London : Deutsch, 1982. — 268p ; 23cm
ISBN 0-233-97278-1 : £6.95 B82-25705

Katz, William. Ghost flight / William Katz. — London : Arrow, 1981, c1980. — 362p ; 18cm
ISBN 0-09-927250-4 (pbk) : £1.75 B82-06571

Kay, Mara. Lolo / Mara Kay. — London : Macmillan, 1981. — 125p ; 21cm
For adolescents
ISBN 0-333-31732-7 : £4.95 : CIP rev. B81-23947

Kaye, Marvin. The Laurel & Hardy murders / Marvin Kaye. — Sth. Yarmouth, Mass. : Curley, 1979, c1977 ; [Skipton] : distributed by Magna. — 350 ; 22cm
Originally published: New York : Dutton, 1977. — Published in large print
ISBN 0-89340-168-4 : £4.75 B82-14115

Keene, Sarah. Eye of the hurricane. — London : Hodder & Stoughton, Sept.1982. — [256]p. — (Silhouette special edition)
ISBN 0-340-32083-4 (pbk) : £0.95 : CIP entry B82-20168

Kennedy, Adam. Debt of honour / Adam Kennedy. — London : W.H. Allen, 1981. — 374p ; 23cm
ISBN 0-491-02606-4 : £7.95 B82-03663

Kerouac, Jack. Big Sur / Jack Kerouac. — London : Granada, 1980, c1962 (1982 [printing]). — 204p ; 18cm. — (A Panther book)
Originally published: New York : Farrar, Straus and Cudahy, 1962 ; London : Deutsch, 1963
ISBN 0-586-04884-7 (pbk) : £1.50 B82-31942

Kerouac, Jack. Maggie Cassidy / Jack Kerouac. — London : Granada, 1982, c1959. — 171p ; 18cm. — (A Panther book)
Originally published: New York : Avon Book Division, 1959
ISBN 0-586-05544-4 (pbk) : £1.50 B82-40247

Kerouac, Jack. The subterraneans / with a preface by Henry Miller ; Pic / two novels by Jack Kerouac. — London : Granada, 1981. — 192p ; 18cm. — (A Panther book)
Originally published: London : Deutsch, 1973. — The subterraneans originally published: New York : Grove Press, 1958 ; London : Deutsch, 1960. — Pic originally published: New York : Grove Press, 1971
ISBN 0-586-04885-5 (pbk) : £1.50 B82-00548

Kerouac, Jan. Baby driver. — London : Deutsch, Aug.1982. — [208]p
Originally published: New York : St Martin′s Press, 1981
ISBN 0-233-97487-3 : £6.95 : CIP entry B82-15689

Ketchum, Frank. Idaho trail / Frank Ketchum. — Large print ed. — Bath : Chivers, 1982, c1978. — 173p ; 23cm. — (A Lythway book)
Originally published: London : Hale, 1978
ISBN 0-85119-794-9 : Unpriced : CIP rev. B82-01432

Kidwell, Catherine. The woman I am. — Bath : Firecrest, Jan.1983. — [192]p
Originally published: London : Sphere, 1981
ISBN 0-85997-508-8 : £5.95 : CIP entry B82-33125

Kienzle, William. Death wears a red hat. — Sevenoaks : Hodder & Stoughton, June 1981. — [288]p
ISBN 0-340-26742-9 (pbk) : £1.50 : CIP entry B81-12347

Kilgore, John. Topar Rim / John Kilgore. — Large print ed. — Bath : Chivers, 1982, c1979. — 151p ; 23cm. — (A Lythway book)
Originally published: London : Hale, 1979
ISBN 0-85119-785-x : Unpriced : CIP rev. B81-35861

King, Frank. Raya / Frank King. — London : Sphere, 1981, c1980. — viii,183p ; 18cm
Originally published: New York : Marek, 1980
ISBN 0-7221-5255-8 (pbk) : £1.25 B82-06017

King, Stephen, *1947-*. Carrie / Stephen King. — Sevenoaks : New English Library, 1974 (1982 [printing]). — 222p : ill ; 18cm
ISBN 0-450-05475-6 (pbk) : £1.50 B82-36790

King, Stephen, *1947-*. Cujo / Stephen King. — London : Macdonald, 1982, c1981. — 345p ; 24cm
Originally published: New York : Viking, 1981
ISBN 0-354-04759-0 : £6.95 B82-09531

King, Stephen, *1947-*. Cujo / Stephen King. — [London] : Futura, 1982, c1981. — 345p ; 18cm
Originally published: New York : Viking, 1981 ; London Macdonald, 1982
ISBN 0-7088-2171-5 (pbk) : £1.95 B82-35719

King, Stephen, *1947-*. The dead zone / Stephen King. — London : Macdonald Futura, 1980, c1979 (1981 [printing]). — 467p ; 18cm
Originally published: London: Macdonald & Jane′s, 1979
ISBN 0-7088-1874-9 (pbk) : £1.75 B82-02044

813'.54[F] — Fiction in English. American writers, *1945-* — Texts *continuation*

King, Stephen, *1947-*. Firestarter. — Large print ed. — Anstey : Ulverscroft, Dec.1982. — 1v.. — (Ulverscroft large print series)
Originally published: London : Futura, 1980
ISBN 0-7089-8086-4 : £7.50 : CIP entry B82-30793

King, Stephen, *1947-*. Night shift / Stephen King. — London : New English Library, 1978 (1982 [printing]). — 316p ; 18cm
ISBN 0-450-05479-9 (pbk) : £1.75 B82-36791

King, Stephen, *1947-*. 'Salem's lot / Stephen King. — London : New English Library, 1976, c1975 (1981 [printing]). — xix,427p ; 18cm
Originally published: New York : Doubleday, 1975
ISBN 0-450-05476-4 (pbk) : £1.95 B82-36787

King, Stephen, *1947-*. The shining / Stephen King. — London : New English Library, 1977 (1981 [printing]). — 416p ; 18cm
ISBN 0-450-05478-0 (pbk) : £1.95 B82-36786

King, Stephen, *1947-*. The stand / Stephen King. — London : New English Library, 1979, c1978 (1980 [printing]). — 734p ; 18cm
Originally published: New York : Doubleday, 1978
ISBN 0-450-05480-2 (pbk) : £1.95 B82-36788

King, Tabitha. Small world / Tabitha King. — London : New English Library, 1982, c1981. — 281p ; 18cm
Originally published: New York : Macmillan, 1981
ISBN 0-450-05368-7 (pbk) : £1.75 : CIP rev. B81-36201

Kistler, Mary. Night of the tiger / Mary Kistler. — Loughton : Piatkus, 1982, c1972. — 253p ; 21cm
Originally published: United States : s.n., 1972
ISBN 0-86188-172-9 : £6.95 : CIP rev. B82-07057

Klein, Norma. Domestic arrangements / Norma Klein. — London : Futura, 1982, c1981. — 285p ; 18cm
Originally published: New York : M. Evans, c1981
ISBN 0-7088-2152-9 (pbk) : £1.50 B82-06609

Klem, Kaye Wilson. East of Jamaica. — London : Hodder and Stoughton, Aug.1982. — [320]p. — (Coronet books)
Originally published: New York : Fawcett Publications, 1979
ISBN 0-340-28109-x (pbk) : £1.95 : CIP entry B82-15736

Knebel, Fletcher. Crossing in Berlin / Fletcher Knebel. — London : Deutsch, 1982, c1981. — 392p ; 23cm
Originally published: Garden City, N.Y. : Doubleday, 1981
ISBN 0-233-97455-5 : £6.95 B82-18233

Knight, Spencer. Frank Bear / Spencer Knight. — London : Hale, 1981, c1979. — 207p ; 20cm
Originally published: New York : Manor, 1979
ISBN 0-7091-9396-3 : £4.95 B82-03173

Koeing, Laird. Rockabye. — Loughton : Piatkus, Dec.1982. — [256]p
ISBN 0-86188-209-1 : £6.95 : CIP entry B82-30597

Kohan, Rhea. Hand-me-downs / Rhea Kohan. — London : Sphere, 1982, c1980. — 344p ; 18cm
Originally published: New York : Random, 1980
ISBN 0-7221-5246-9 (pbk) : £1.75 B82-33911

Kominsky, Stuart M.. Bullet for a star / Stuart Kominsky. — Sth. Yarmouth, Mass. : Curley, 1978, c1977 ; [Skipton] : distributed by Magna. — 273p ; 22cm
Originally published: New York : St Martins Press, 1977. — Published in large print
ISBN 0-89340-131-5 : Unpriced B82-14116

Konvitz, Jeffrey. The beast. — London : New English Library, Jan.1983. — [448]p
ISBN 0-450-05532-9 (pbk) : £1.95 : CIP entry B82-34602

Koontz, Dean R.. Whispers / Dean R. Koontz. — London : W.H. Allen, 1981, c1980 (1982 [printing]). — 502p ; 18cm. — (A Star book)
Originally published: New York : Putnam, 1980
ISBN 0-352-30935-0 (pbk) : £1.95 B82-29195

Korman, Keith. Swan dive / by Keith Korman. — London : Hale, 1982, c1980. — 279p ; 23cm
Originally published: New York : Random House, 1980
ISBN 0-7091-9249-5 : £6.95 B82-25994

Kosinski, Jerzy. Cockpit / Jerzy Kosinski. — London : Arrow, 1982, c1975. — 273p : ill ; 18cm
Originally published: London : Hutchinson, 1975
ISBN 0-09-927960-6 (pbk) : £1.60 B82-22074

Kosinski, Jerzy. The devil tree / Jerzy Kosinski. — Rev. and expanded ed. — London : Arrow, 1982. — 211p ; 18cm
Previous ed.: St Albans : Hart-Davis McGibbon, 1973
ISBN 0-09-927520-1 (pbk) : £1.50 B82-14913

Kosinski, Jerzy. The painted bird / Jerzy Kosinski. — London : Arrow, 1982, c1966. — 251p ; 18cm
Originally published: London : W.H. Allen, 1966
ISBN 0-09-927950-9 (pbk) : £1.60 B82-22076

Kosinski, Jerzy. Passion play / Jerzy Kosinski. — London : Arrow, 1982, c1979. — 305p ; 18cm
Originally published: New York : St Martin's Press, 1979 ; London : Joseph, 1980
ISBN 0-09-927510-4 (pbk) : £1.50 B82-14914

Kosinski, Jerzy. Pinball / Jerzy Kosinski. — London : Joseph, 1952. — 287p ; 23cm
ISBN 0-7181-2133-3 (cased) : £7.95
ISBN 0-7181-2135-x (pbk) : Unpriced B82-26034

Kotzwinkle, William. Jack in the box / William Kotzwinkle. — [London] : Abacus, 1981, c1980. — 218p ; 20cm
Originally published: New York : Putnam, 1980
ISBN 0-349-12119-2 (pbk) : £1.95 B82-02129

Kozloff, Charles. The Ondine / Charles Kozloff. — London : Star, 1980. — 322p ; 18cm. — (A Star book)
Originally published: New York : St. Martin's Press ; London : W.H. Allen, 1980
ISBN 0-352-30673-4 (pbk) : £1.50 B82-33014

Kunstler, James Howard. A clown in the moonlight / James Howard Kunstler. — London : Sphere, 1982, c1981. — 218p ; 18cm
ISBN 0-7221-5248-5 (pbk) : £1.75 B82-34226

Kurtz, Irma. Sob, sister / Irma Kurtz. — London : Michael Joseph, 1981. — 207p ; 23cm
ISBN 0-7181-2053-1 : £6.95 B82-00003

L'Amour, Louis. Silver canyon. — Large print ed. — Anstey : Ulverscroft, Jan.1983. — [288] p. — (Ulverscroft large print series)
Originally published: New York : Avalon Books, 1956 ; London : Transworld, 1958
ISBN 0-7089-0907-8 : £6.25 : CIP entry B82-32535

Langan, Ruth. Just like yesterday. — London : Hodder & Stoughton, July 1982. — [192]p. — (Silhouette romance)
ISBN 0-340-28467-6 (pbk) : £0.75 : CIP entry B82-12313

Larkin, Rochelle. Glitterball. — London : New English Library, Dec.1982. — [288]p
ISBN 0-450-05539-6 (pbk) : £1.75 : CIP entry B82-30089

Larkin, Rochelle. Golden days, silver nights / Rochelle Larkin. — London : New English Library, 1982. — 313p ; 18cm
ISBN 0-450-05373-3 (pbk) : £1.75 : CIP rev. B82-03594

LaRosa, Linda J.. The random factor / Linda J. LaRosa, Barry Tanenbaum. — London : Futura 1980, c1978. — 318p ; 18cm
Originally published: Garden City, N.Y. : Doubleday, 1978 ; London : Gollancz, 1979
ISBN 0-7088-1859-5 (pbk) : £1.25 B82-13628

Lathen, Emma. Accounting for murder / Emma Lathen. — Bath : Chivers, 1982, c1964. — 269p ; 23cm. — (A New Portway large print book)
Originally published: New York : Macmillan, 1964 ; London : Gollancz, 1965. — Published in large print
ISBN 0-85119-180-0 : Unpriced : CIP rev. B82-15855

Lathen, Emma. Banking on death / Emma Lathen. — Bath : Chivers Press, 1982, c1961. — 278p ; 23cm. — (A New Portway large print book)
Originally published: New York : Macmillan, 1961 ; London : Gollancz, 1962. — Published in large print
ISBN 0-85119-178-9 : Unpriced : CIP rev. B82-15853

Lathen, Emma. Going for gold. — Large print ed. — Anstey : Ulverscroft, Feb.1983. — 1v.. — (Ulverscroft large print series)
Originally published: London : Gollancz, 1981
ISBN 0-7089-0920-5 : CIP entry B82-38882

Lathen, Emma. Green grow the dollars / by Emma Lathen. — London : Gollancz, 1982. — 222p ; 21cm
ISBN 0-575-03067-4 : £6.95 : CIP rev. B82-01550

Lathen, Emma. Murder makes the wheels go round / Emma Lathen. — Bath : Chivers Press, 1982, c1966. — 301p ; 23cm. — (A New Portway large print book)
Originally published: New York : Macmillan, 1965 ; London : Gollancz, 1966. — Published in large print
ISBN 0-85119-181-9 : Unpriced : CIP rev. B82-15856

Lathen, Emma. A place for murder / Emma Lathen. — Bath : Chivers Press, 1982, c1963. — 293p ; 23cm. — (A New Portway large print book)
Originally published: New York : Macmillan, 1963 ; London : Gollancz, 1964. — Published in large print
ISBN 0-85119-179-7 : Unpriced : CIP rev. B82-15854

Laumer, Keith. Earthblood / Keith Laumer and Rosel George Brown. — Sevenoaks : Hodder and Stoughton, 1979, c1966. — 228p ; 18cm. — (Coronet books)
Originally published: Garden City, N.Y. : Doubleday, 1966
ISBN 0-340-24516-6 (pbk) : £0.95 : CIP rev. B79-29680

Lavender, William. The fields above the sea / William Lavender. — London : Sphere, 1981, c1980. — 437p ; 18cm
Originally published: United States : s.n., 1980
ISBN 0-7221-5463-1 (pbk) : £1.75 B82-07181

Layman, Richard. Out are the lights. — London : New English Library, Aug.1982. — [192]p
ISBN 0-450-05496-9 (pbk) : £1.75 : CIP entry B82-15807

Le Guin, Ursula K.. The eye of the heron. — London : Gollancz, Sept.1982. — [144]p
ISBN 0-575-03211-1 : £6.95 : CIP entry B82-18766

813'.54[F] — Fiction in English. American writers, *1945- — Texts* *continuation*

Leamer, Laurence. Assignment / by Laurence Leamer. — London : Hodder and Stoughton, 1981. — 211p : 1map ; 23cm
ISBN 0-340-27038-1 : £6.95 : CIP rev. B81-21645

Leason, Barney. Scandals / Barney Leason. — London : Arrow, 1982, c1981. — 439p ; 18cm
ISBN 0-09-928680-7 (pbk) : £1.95 B82-31612

Leavitt, Caroline. Meeting Rozzy halfway / Caroline Leavitt. — London : Weidenfeld and Nicolson, 1982, c1980. — 294p ; 23cm
Originally published: New Yok : Seaview, 1980
ISBN 0-297-78044-1 : £6.95 B82-12803

Lee, Patrick. Gundown at Golden Gate / Patrick Lee. — London : W.H. Allen, 1982, 1981. — 176p ; 18cm. — (Six-gun samurai)
Originally published: S.l. : Pinnacle, 1981
ISBN 0-352-31077-4 (pbk) : £1.25 B82-22069

Lee, Susan. Dear John / Susan Lee and Sondra Till Robinson. — London : Sphere, 1982, c1980. — 232p ; 18cm
Originally published: New York : R. Marek, 1980
ISBN 0-7221-7424-1 (pbk) : £1.50 B82-33917

Lee, Wayne C.. Guns at Genesis / Wayne C. Lee. — Large print ed. — [Bath] : Chivers, 1982, c1981. — 277p ; 23cm. — (Atlantic large print) (A Gunsmoke large print Western)
ISBN 0-85119-475-3 : Unpriced : CIP rev. B82-09853

Leimas, Brooke. The intruder / Brooke Leimas. — [London] : Fontana, 1982, c1980. — 256p ; 18cm
Originally published: New York : New American Library, 1980
ISBN 0-00-616445-5 (pbk) : £1.35 B82-09323

Leonard, Elmore. City primeval / Elmore Leonard. — London : Star, 1982, c1980. — xii,275p ; 18cm. — (A Star book)
Originally published: New York : Arbor House, 1980 ; London : W.H. Allen, 1981
ISBN 0-352-31082-0 (pbk) : £1.75 B82-33024

Leonard, Elmore. The switch / Elmore Leonard. — London : Hamlyn Paperbacks, 1981, c1978. — 186p ; 18cm
Originally published: New York : Bantam, 1978 ; London : Secker and Warburg, 1979
ISBN 0-600-20342-5 (pbk) : £1.25 B82-00650

Lester, Julius. Basketball game / Julius Lester. — [Harmondsworth] : Puffin, 1982. — 91p ; 19cm. — (Puffin plus)
Originally published: Harmondsworth : Penguin, 1977
ISBN 0-14-031421-0 (pbk) : £0.85 B82-35859

Levine, Robert. Rising sons / Robert Levine. — [London] : Fontana, 1982. — 407p ; 18cm
ISBN 0-00-616188-x (pbk) : £1.95 B82-30769

Levy, Edward. The beast within / Edward Levy. — Feltham : Hamlyn Paperbacks, 1982, c1981. — 219p ; 18cm
Originally published: New York : Arbor House, 1981
ISBN 0-600-20616-5 (pbk) : £1.25 B82-18347

Lewerth, Margaret. Lilith / Margaret Lewerth. — [London] : Fontana, 1981. — 316p ; 18cm. — (The Roundtree women ; bk.IV)
Originally published: New York : Dell, 1981
ISBN 0-00-616401-3 (pbk) : £1.50 B82-03009

Lewin, Michael Z.. Missing woman / Michael Z. Lewin. — London : Hale, 1982, c1981. — 213p ; 20cm
ISBN 0-7091-9699-7 : £6.75 B82-26023

Lewin, Michael Z.. Night cover / Michael Z. Lewin. — Sevenoaks : Hodder and Stoughton, 1979, c1976. — 222p : ill ; 18cm. — (Coronet books)
Originally published: New York : Knopf ; London : Hamilton, 1976
ISBN 0-340-23843-7 (pbk) : £0.95 : CIP rev. B79-18683

Lewis, Stephen. Natural victims. — London : Coronet, Jan.1983. — [352]p
Originally published: New York : Fawcett Books, 1978
ISBN 0-340-32055-9 (pbk) : £1.95 : CIP entry B82-34403

Lieberman, Herbert. Brilliant kids / Herbert Lieberman. — London : Arrow, 1982, c1975. — 298p ; 18cm
Originally published: New York : Macmillan, 1975
ISBN 0-09-924020-3 (pbk) : £1.50 B82-11367

Lindley, Meredith. Against the wind. — London : Hodder & Stoughton, June 1982. — [192]p. — (Silhouette romance)
Originally published: New York : Silhouette Books, 1981
ISBN 0-340-27942-7 (pbk) : £0.75 : CIP entry B82-10464

Linzee, David. Belgravia / by David Linzee. — London : Hale, 1982, c1979. — 192p ; 20cm
Originally published: New York : Seaview, 1979
ISBN 0-7091-9505-2 : £6.75 B82-13843

Linzee, David. Discretion / by David Linzee. — London : Hale, 1981, c1977. — 189p ; 20cm
ISBN 0-7091-9542-7 : £6.50 B82-03160

Lipez, Richard. Grand scam / Richard Lipez & Peter Stein. — London : Methuen Paperbacks, 1981, c1979. — 233p ; 18cm. — (Magnum books)
Originally published: New York : Dial, c1979
ISBN 0-417-06140-4 (pbk) : £1.50 B82-15606

Lippincott, David. Black prism / David Lippincott. — London : Corgi, 1981, c1980. — 255p ; 18cm
Originally published: London : W.H. Allen, 1980
ISBN 0-552-11833-8 (pbk) : £1.25 B82-06420

Littell, Robert, *1935-*. The amateur. — London : Hodder and Stoughton, Sept.1982. — [272]p. — (Coronet books)
Originally published: London : Cape, 1981
ISBN 0-340-28549-4 (pbk) : £1.25 : CIP entry B82-18793

Littell, Robert, *1935-*. The debriefing / Robert Littell. — London : Arrow, 1982, c1979. — 202p ; 18cm
Originally published: London : Hutchinson, 1979
ISBN 0-09-924840-9 (pbk) : £1.25 B82-22075

Llywelyn, Morgan. Lion of Ireland / Morgan Llywelyn. — London : Futura, 1982, c1979. — 559p : 1map ; 18cm
Originally published: London : Bodley Head, 1980
ISBN 0-7088-1846-3 (pbk) : £1.95 B82-22612

Logan, Sara. Games of hearts. — London : Hodder & Stoughton, Sept.1982. — [192]p. — (Silhouette romance)
ISBN 0-340-32068-0 (pbk) : £0.75 : CIP entry B82-18787

Longyear, Barry B.. Circus world / Barry B. Longyear. — London : Macdonald, 1982, c1981. — 219p ; 21cm
ISBN 0-356-08629-1 : £5.95 B82-28928

Longyear, Barry B.. Circus world / Barry B. Longyear. — London : Futura, 1982, c1981. — 219p ; 18cm
ISBN 0-7088-8091-6 (pbk) : £1.60 B82-27080

Longyear, Barry B.. Manifest destiny / Barry B. Longyear. — London : Macdonald, 1982, c1980. — 284p ; 21cm
ISBN 0-356-08628-3 : £5.95 B82-28929

Longyear, Barry B.. Manifest destiny / Barry B. Longyear. — London : Futura, 1982, c1980. — 284p ; 18cm
ISBN 0-7088-8092-4 (pbk) : £1.75 B82-27079

Lord, Bette Bao. Spring moon : a novel of China / Bette Bao Lord. — London : Gollancz, 1982, c1981. — 464p : ill ; 22cm
Originally published: New York : Harper & Row, 1981. — Ill on lining papers
ISBN 0-575-03066-6 : £7.95 : CIP rev. B82-01722

Lorin, Amii. Morning rose : (morning rose, evening savage) / Amii Lorin. — London : Mills & Boon, 1982, c1980. — 187p ; 19cm
ISBN 0-263-10018-9 : £5.25 B82-18134

Lucas, Jeremy. The longest flight. — London : Cape, Sept.1982. — [152]p
ISBN 0-224-01960-0 : £6.50 : CIP entry B82-25158

Ludlum, Robert. The Chancellor manuscript. — Large print ed. — Anstey : Ulverscroft, Sept.1982. — [704]p. — (Charnwood library series)
Originally published: London : Hart-Davis MacGibbon, 1977
ISBN 0-7089-8069-4 : £7.50 : CIP entry B82-27010

Ludlum, Robert. The Matlock paper / Robert Ludlum. — Large print ed. — Leicester : Charnwood, 1982, c1973. — 430p ; 22cm. — (Charnwood library series)
Originally published: St. Albans : Hart-Davis McGibbon, 1973. — Published in large print
ISBN 0-7089-8034-1 : Unpriced : CIP rev. B82-08112

Ludlum, Robert. The Osterman weekend / Robert Ludlum. — Leicester : Charnwood, 1982, c1972. — 339p ; 23cm. — (Charnwood library series)
Originally published: London : Hart-Davis, 1972. — Published in large print
ISBN 0-7089-8043-0 : Unpriced : CIP rev. B82-15942

Ludlum, Robert. The Parsifal mosaic / Robert Ludlum. — London : Granada, 1982. — 637p ; 22cm
ISBN 0-246-11417-7 : £7.95 : CIP rev. B82-01865

Ludlum, Robert. The Rhinemann exchange. — Large print ed. — Anstey : Ulverscroft, Feb.1983. — 1v.. — (Charnwood library series)
Originally published: New York : Dial Press, 1974
ISBN 0-7089-8100-3 : £7.95 : CIP entry B82-38892

Ludlum, Robert. The road to Gandolfo / Robert Ludlum. — London : Granada, 1982, c1975. — 315p ; 18cm
Originally published: New York : Dial, 1975 ; and under the name Michael Shepherd: London : Hart-Davis, MacGibbon, 1976
ISBN 0-586-04375-6 (pbk) : £1.95 B82-31786

Ludlum, Robert. The Scarlatti inheritance / Robert Ludlum. — Leicester : Charnwood, 1981, c1971. — 510p ; 23cm. — (Charnwood library series)
Originally published: London : Hart-Davis, 1971. — Published in large print
ISBN 0-7089-8009-0 : £6.50 : CIP rev. B81-22668

Lutz, Giles A.. Blood feud. — Large print ed. — Bath : Chivers, Dec.1982. — [352]p. — (Atlantic large print)
Originally published: New York : Fawcett Publications, 1974
ISBN 0-85119-510-5 : £5.25 : CIP entry B82-30238

813'.54[F] — Fiction in English. American writers, *1945- — Texts* *continuation*

Lutz, Giles A.. Outcast gun. — Large print ed. — Bath : Chivers, Oct.1982. — [296]p. — (Atlantic large print)
ISBN 0-85119-499-0 : £5.25 : CIP entry B82-24231

Lutz, Giles A.. Relentless gun / Giles A. Lutz. — Large print ed. — [Bath] : Chivers Press, 1982, c1958. — 260p ; 23cm. — (Atlantic large print) (A Gunsmoke large print western)
Originally published: London : Jenkins, 1967
ISBN 0-85119-486-9 : Unpriced : CIP rev. B82-15859

Lynn, Elizabeth A.. The dancers of Arun / Elizabeth A. Lynn. — Feltham : Hamlyn, 1982, c1979. — 256p : 1map,1geneal.table. — (Hamlyn science fantasy)
Originally published: New York : Berkley Publishing, 1979
ISBN 0-600-20223-2 (pbk) : £1.50 B82-08771

Lynn, Jack. The factory. — London : Robson, Oct.1982. — [320]p
ISBN 0-86051-183-9 : £5.95 : CIP entry B82-24138

Lynn, Jack. The professor : a novel / by Jack Lynn. — London : Robson, 1982, c1971. — x,277p ; 23cm
Originally published: London : Allison and Busby, 1971
ISBN 0-86051-182-0 : £7.50 : CIP rev. B82-24137

Lyon, Buck. Sundown / Buck Lyon. — Large print ed. — Bath : Chivers, 1982, c1978. — 173p ; 23cm. — (A Lythway book)
Originally published: London : Hale, 1978
ISBN 0-85119-820-1 : Unpriced : CIP rev. B82-09864

Lyons, Nan. Champagne blues. — London : Hodder & Stoughton, Aug.1982. — [256]p. — (Coronet books)
Originally published: London : Cape, 1979
ISBN 0-340-25071-2 (pbk) : £1.50 : CIP entry B82-15718

McBain, Ed. Beauty and the beast / by Ed McBain. — London : Hamish Hamilton, 1982. — 199p ; 23cm
ISBN 0-241-10769-5 : £7.50 : CIP rev. B82-05385

McBain, Ed. Ghosts : an 87th Precinct novel / Ed McBain. — London : Prior, 1981, c1980. — 379p ; 25cm
Originally published: New York : Viking Press, 1979 ; London : Hamilton, 1980. — Published in large print
ISBN 0-86043-606-3 : £6.95 B82-02931

McBain, Ed. Ghosts : an 87th precinct mystery / Ed McBain. — London : Pan, 1982, c1980. — 190p ; 18cm
Originally published: London : Hamilton, 1980
ISBN 0-330-26370-6 (pbk) : £1.25 B82-18119

McBain, Ed. Heat : an 87th Precinct novel / Ed McBain. — London : Hamilton, 1981. — 227p ; 23cm
ISBN 0-241-10693-1 : £6.95 : CIP rev. B81-31460

McBain, Ed. Killer's wedge / Ed McBain. — London : Severn House, 1981, c1959. — 141p ; 21cm
Originally published: New York : Simon and Schuster, 1959 ; London : Boardman, 1961
ISBN 0-7278-0749-8 : £5.95 B82-05437

McBain, Ed. King's ransom / Ed McBain. — London : Severn House, 1982, c1959. — 171p ; 21cm
Originally published: New York : Simon & Schuster, 1959 ; London : Boardman, 1961
ISBN 0-7278-0783-8 : £6.50 B82-28919

McBain, Ed. Rumpelstiltskin / Ed McBain. — London : Corgi, 1982, c1981. — 266p ; 18cm
Originally published: London : Hamilton, 1981
ISBN 0-552-12021-9 (pbk) : £1.50 B82-37547

McBain, Ed. Shotgun : an 87th precinct mystery / Ed McBain. — London : Pan, 1971, c1969 (1982 printing). — 157p : ill ; 18cm
Originally published: London : Macmillan, 1969
ISBN 0-330-02702-6 (pbk) : £1.25 B82-20305

McBain, Ed. Ten plus one. — London : Severn House, Nov.1982. — [192]p
Originally published: London : Pan Books, 1979
ISBN 0-7278-0840-0 : £6.95 : CIP entry B82-34065

McBain, Ed. Vanishing ladies / Ed McBain ; originally published under the pseudonym Richard Marsten. — Harmondsworth : Penguin, 1982, c1957. — 143p ; 18cm
Originally published: New York : Permabooks, 1957
ISBN 0-14-005516-9 (pbk) : £1.25 B82-29811

McCaffrey, Anne. The crystal singer / Anne McCaffrey. — London : Severn House, 1982. — 302p ; 25cm
ISBN 0-7278-2022-2 : £6.95 B82-22730

McCaffrey, Anne. Decision at Doona / Anne McCaffrey. — [London] : Corgi, 1971, c1969 (1981 [printing]). — 221p ; 18cm
Originally published: New York : Ballantine Books, 1969 ; London : Rapp & Whiting, 1970
ISBN 0-552-11789-7 (pbk) : £1.50 B82-09003

McCaffrey, Anne. Dragondrums / Anne McCaffrey. — London : Corgi, 1981. — 223p : 1map ; 18cm
Originally published: London : Sidgwick & Jackson, 1979
ISBN 0-552-11804-4 (pbk) : £1.25 B82-06471

McCaffrey, Anne. Dragonquest / Anne McCaffrey. — London : Corgi, 1982, c1971. — 325p : 1map ; 18cm
Originally published: New York : Ballantine, 1971 ; London : Rapp and Whiting : Deutsch, 1973
ISBN 0-552-11635-1 (pbk) : £1.75 B82-16745

McCaffrey, Anne. The ship who sang / Anne McCaffrey. — London : Corgi, 1972, c1969 (1982 [printing]). — 206p ; 18cm
Originally published: New York : Walker, 1969 ; London : Rapp and Whiting, 1971
ISBN 0-552-11936-9 (pbk) : £1.50 B82-23903

McCammon, Robert R.. They thirst / Robert R. McCammon. — London : Sphere, 1981. — 531p ; 18cm
ISBN 0-7221-5876-9 (pbk) : £1.75 B82-07180

McClary, Jane McIlvaine. Maggie Royal. — Loughton : Piatkus, Oct.1982. — [416]p
ISBN 0-86188-208-3 : £7.95 : CIP entry B82-24577

McCormmach, Russell. Night thoughts of a classical physicist / Russell McCormmach. — Cambridge, Mass. ; London : Harvard University Press, 1982. — 217p : ill ; 25cm
ISBN 0-674-62460-2 : Unpriced B82-26795

McCoy, Ron. Thieves' Road / by Ron McCoy. — London : Hale, 1981, c1980. — 176p ; 20cm
ISBN 0-7091-9407-2 : £4.95 B82-03156

McDonald, Frank, *1941-*. Provenance / Frank McDonald. — London : Macdonald, 1980, c1979 (1981 [printing]). — 495p ; 18cm. — (A Futura book)
Originally published: Boston, Mass. : Little, Brown, 1979 ; London : Raven, 1980
ISBN 0-7088-1877-3 (pbk) : £1.75 B82-03141

McDonald, Gregory. The buck passes Flynn / by Gregory McDonald. — London : Gollancz, 1982, c1981. — 216p ; 21cm
ISBN 0-575-03092-5 : £6.95 : CIP rev. B82-04607

Mcdonald, Gregory. Fletch's Moxie. — London : Gollancz, Feb.1983. — [192]p
ISBN 0-575-03243-x : £6.95 : CIP entry B82-38689

MacDonald, John D.. Cinnamon skin : the twentieth adventure of Travis McGee / John D. MacDonald. — London : Collins, 1982. — 275p ; 22cm
ISBN 0-00-222651-0 : £7.50 B82-40988

MacDonald, John D.. Free fall in crimson / John D. MacDonald. — London : Collins, 1981. — 246p ; 22cm
ISBN 0-00-222607-3 : £6.95 B82-05541

MacDonald, John D.. The green ripper / John D. MacDonald. — London : Hale, 1980, c1979. — 221p ; 23cm. — (The Travis McGee series)
Originally published: New York : Lippincott, 1979
ISBN 0-7091-8330-5 : £6.25 B82-13363

MacDonald, John D.. A Travis McGee omnibus / John D. MacDonald. — London : Hale, 1982. — 191,206,192p ; 21cm
Contents: The quick red fox. Originally published: Greenwich, Conn. : Fawcett, 1964 ; London : Hale, 1966 — A deadly shade of gold. Originally published: Greenwich, Conn. : Fawcett, 1965 ; London : Hale, 1967 — Bright orange for the shroud. Originally published: Greenwich, Conn. : Fawcett, 1965 ; London : Hale, 1967
ISBN 0-7091-9808-6 : £7.95 B82-27422

Macdonald, Ross, *1915-*. The drowning pool / Ross Macdonald. — South Yarmouth, Mass. : Curley, 1979, c1950 ; [Long Preston] : Distributed by Magna. — 414p ; 22cm
Originally published: New York : Knopf, 1950 ; London : Cassell, 1952. — Published in large print
ISBN 0-89340-170-6 (pbk) : Unpriced B82-17025

MacDougall, Ruth Doan. Aunt Pleasantine / Ruth Doan MacDougall. — South Yarmouth, Mass. : Curley, 1979, c1978 ; [Long Preston] : Distributed by Magna. — 422p ; 23cm
Originally published: New York : Harper & Row, 1978. — Published in large print
ISBN 0-89340-173-0 : Unpriced B82-17023

McDowell, Michael. The amulet / Michael McDowell. — London : Collins, 1982, c1979. — 316p ; 18cm
Originally published: S.l. : Avon, 1979
ISBN 0-00-616269-x (pbk) : £1.50 B82-19728

McGivern, William. Summitt. — London : Collins, Feb.1983. — [350]p
ISBN 0-00-222284-1 : £8.95 : CIP entry B82-36464

McInerny, Ralph. Her death of cold / Ralph McInerny. — South Yarmouth, Mass. : Curley, 1979, c1977 ; [Long Preston] : Distributed by Magna. — 367p ; 23cm. — (A Father Dowling mystery)
Originally published: New York : Vanguard, 1977 ; London : Hale, 1979. — Published in large print
ISBN 0-89340-196-x : £5.25 B82-17033

McIntyre, Vonda N.. The entropy effect / Vonda N. McIntyre. — London : Macdonald, 1981. — 224p ; 18cm. — (A Star trek novel) (An Orbit book)
ISBN 0-7088-8083-5 (pbk) : £1.25 B82-00455

McIntyre, Vonda N.. Star trek : the wrath of Khan / by Vonda N. McIntyre ; screenplay by Jack B. Sowards ; based on a story by Harve Bennet and Jack B. Sowards. — London : Macdonald, 1982. — 223p ; 21cm
ISBN 0-356-08687-9 : £5.95 B82-36292

813′.54[F] — Fiction in English. American writers, 1945- — Texts *continuation*

McIntyre, Vonda N.. Star trek : the wrath of Khan : a novel by Vonda N. McIntyre / screenplay by Jack B. Sowards based on a story by Harve Bennett and Jack B. Sowards. — [London] : Futura, 1982. — 223p ; 18cm
ISBN 0-7088-8095-9 (pbk) : £1.25 B82-33793

Mackay, Amanda. [Death on the Eno]. A death on the river. — London : Gollancz, Jan.1983. — [240]p
Originally published: Boston : Little, Brown, 1981
ISBN 0-575-03242-1 : £6.95 : CIP entry
B82-32462

McKay, Rena. Desert devil. — London : Hodder and Stoughton, Feb.1982. — [192]p. — (Silhouette romance)
ISBN 0-340-27672-x (pbk) : £0.75 : CIP entry
B81-38319

McLaglen, John J.. Bloodline / John J. McLaglen. — London : Corgi, 1982. — 124p ; 18cm. — (Herne the hunter ; 19)
ISBN 0-552-11990-3 (pbk) : £0.95 B82-35249

McLaglen, John J.. Dying ways / John J. McLaglen. — London : Corgi, 1982. — 130p ; 18cm. — (Herne the hunter ; 18)
ISBN 0-552-11892-3 (pbk) : £0.95 B82-16744

MacLeod, Charlotte. The luck runs out / Charlotte MacLeod. — Sth. Yarmouth : Curley ; [Long Preston] : Distributed by Magna Print, c1979. — 421p ; 22cm
Published in large print
ISBN 0-89340-381-4 : Unpriced B82-27419

MacLeod, Charlotte. The palace guard / Charlotte MacLeod. — London : Collins, 1982, c1981. — 205p ; 21cm
Originally published: Garden City, N.Y. : Doubleday, 1981
ISBN 0-00-231923-3 : £6.50 : CIP rev.
B82-07983

MacLeod, Charlotte. The withdrawing room / Charlotte MacLeod. — Sth. Yarmouth, Mass. : Curley ; [Long Preston] : Distributed by Magna Print, c1980. — 414p ; 22cm
Published in large print
ISBN 0-89340-380-6 : Unpriced B82-27420

MacLeod, Charlotte. Wrack and rune. — London : Collins, Nov.1982. — [230]p. — (The Crime Club)
ISBN 0-00-231727-3 : £6.75 : CIP entry
B82-27799

McMullen, Mary. But Nellie was so nice / Mary McMullen. — Large print ed. — Bath : Chivers, 1982, c1979. — 264p ; 23cm. — (A Lythway mystery)
Originally published: Garden City, N.Y. : Doubleday, 1979 ; London : Collins, 1981
ISBN 0-85119-802-3 : Unpriced : CIP rev.
B82-05009

McMullen, Mary. My cousin death. — Large print ed. — Bath : Chivers, Feb.1983. — [312] p. — (Atlantic large print)
Originally published: New York : Doubleday, 1980 ; London : Collins, 1981
ISBN 0-85119-527-x : £5.75 : CIP entry
B82-39578

McMullen, Mary. The other shoe / Mary McMullen. — London : Collins, 1982, c1981. — 176p ; 20cm. — (The Crime club)
ISBN 0-00-231691-9 : £6.50 : CIP rev.
B82-12432

McMullen, Mary. Something of the night / Mary McMullen. — London : Collins, c1982, c1980. — 190p ; 20cm. — (The Crime Club)
Originally published: Garden City, N.Y. : Doubleday, 1980
ISBN 0-00-231719-2 : £6.50 : CIP rev.
B81-33927

McMullen, Mary. Welcome to the grave / Mary McMullen. — Large print ed. — Bath : Chivers, 1981, c1979. — 291p ; 23cm. — (A Lythway book)
Originally published: Garden City, N.Y. : Doubleday, 1979 ; London : Collins, 1980
ISBN 0-85119-754-x : Unpriced : CIP rev.
B81-25813

McNaughton, Brian. Satan′s mistress / Brian McNaughton. — London : Star, 1981, c1978. — 252p ; 18cm. — (A Star book)
Originally published: New York : Carlyle, 1978
ISBN 0-352-30693-9 (pbk) : £1.25 B82-33018

MacPherson, Malcolm. The Lucifer key / Malcolm MacPherson. — London : Hamlyn, 1982, c1981. — 336p ; 18cm
ISBN 0-600-20476-6 (pbk) : £1.50 B82-12060

Mahan, Colleen. The Lodge / Colleen Mahan. — Sevenoaks : New English Library, 1981, c1980 (1982 [printing]). — 280p ; 18cm
Originally published: Garden City, N.Y. : Doubleday, 1979
ISBN 0-450-05404-7 (pbk) : £1.75 : CIP rev.
B82-09692

Majerus, Janet. Grandpa and Frank / Janet Majerus. — South Yarmouth, Mass. : Curley, 1978, c1976 ; [Long Preston] : Distributed by Magna. — 344p ; 23cm
Originally published: Philadelphia : Lippincott, 1976. — Published in large print
ISBN 0-89340-129-3 : Unpriced B82-17031

Major, Ann. A touch of fire. — London : Hodder & Stoughton, Dec.1982. — [192]p. — (Silhouette romance)
ISBN 0-340-32695-6 (pbk) : £0.75 : CIP entry
B82-29665

Major, Ann. Wild lady. — London : Hodder and Stoughton, Feb.1982. — [192]p. — (Silhouette romance)
For adolescents
ISBN 0-340-27670-3 (pbk) : £0.75 : CIP entry
B81-38318

Malamud, Bernard. God′s grace. — London : Chatto & Windus, Oct.1982. — [240]p
ISBN 0-7011-2647-7 : £6.95 : CIP entry
B82-26044

Malamud, Bernard. A new life / Bernard Malamud. — Harmondsworth : Penguin in association with Chatto & Windus, 1981, c1961. — 315p ; 18cm
Originally published: New York : Farrar, Straus & Cudahy, 1961 ; London : Eyre & Spottiswoode, 1962
ISBN 0-14-002666-5 (pbk) : £1.95 B82-06435

Malamud, Bernard. Pictures of Fidelman : an exhibition. — London : Chatto & Windus, Sept.1982. — [208]p. — (The Collected works of Bernard Malamud)
ISBN 0-7011-2452-0 : £7.50 : CIP entry
B82-20295

Malamud, Bernard. The tenants / Bernard Malamud. — Harmondsworth : Penguin, in association with Chatto & Windus, 1972, c1971 (1982 [printing]). — 173p ; 19cm
Originally published: New York : Farrar, Straus and Giroux, 1971 ; London : Eyre Methuen, 1972
ISBN 0-14-003508-7 (pbk) : £1.75 B82-33021

Malamud, Bernard. The tenants. — London : Chatto & Windus, Oct.1981. — [240]p
ISBN 0-7011-2451-2 : £7.50 : CIP entry
B81-27999

Mallory, Kathryn. A Frenchman′s kiss. — London : Hodder & Stoughton, Nov.1982. — [192]p. — (Silhouette desire)
ISBN 0-340-32863-0 (pbk) : £0.95 : CIP entry
B82-29068

Malone, Michael. Dingley falls / Michael Malone. — London : Hamlyn Paperbacks, 1981, c1980. — 496p ; 18cm
Originally published: New York : Harcourt Brace Jovanovich, 1980
ISBN 0-600-20503-7 (pbk) : £1.95 B82-00651

Mandel, Sally. Quinn / Sally Mandel. — London : Futura, 1982, c1979. — 272p ; 18cm
Originally published: United States : S.E.M. Productions, 1979
ISBN 0-7088-2145-6 (pbk) : £1.60 B82-15318

Mann, Patrick. Steal big. — Large print ed. — Bath : Chivers, Nov.1982. — [296]p. — (Atlantic large print)
Originally published: London : Hart-Davis, MacGibbon, 1978
ISBN 0-85119-506-7 : £5.25 : CIP entry
B82-26435

Manning, Jason. Killer gray / by Jason Manning. — London : Hale, 1981, c1979. — 188p ; 20cm
Originally published: New York : Manor, 1979
ISBN 0-7091-9416-1 : £4.95 B82-03177

Marasco, Robert. Parlour games. — London : Hodder & Stoughton, Oct.1981. — [304]p. — (Coronet books)
Originally published: 1979
ISBN 0-340-27264-3 (pbk) : £1.50 : CIP entry
B81-25754

Margolin, Phillip M.. The last innocent man / Phillip M. Margolin. — London : Macmillan, 1982. — 247p ; 21cm
ISBN 0-333-33434-5 : £6.95 B82-35915

Marlowe, Delphine. Bonnaire / Delphine Marlowe. — London : Sphere, 1982. — 343p ; 18cm
″First published in America in a longer version by Jove Books 1980″ — t.p. verso
ISBN 0-7221-5833-5 (pbk) : £1.75 B82-27899

Marshall, Paule. Brown girl, brownstones / Paule Marshall ; with an afterword by Mary Helen Washington. — London : Virago, 1980, c1959. — 324p ; 20cm. — (Virago modern classics)
Originally published: New York : Random House, 1959
ISBN 0-86068-265-x (pbk) : £3.50 : CIP rev.
B82-16677

Martin, Dwight. The Triad imperative : a novel / by Dwight Martin. — Feltham : Hamlyn, 1982, c1980. — 282p ; 18cm
Originally published: New York : Congdon & Lattes, 1980
ISBN 0-600-20469-3 (pbk) : £1.50 B82-16299

Martin, George R. R.. Windhaven / George R.R. Martin and Lisa Tuttle. — London : New English Library, 1982, c1981. — 315p : 1map ; 18cm
Originally published: New York : Timescape, 1981
ISBN 0-450-04666-4 (pbk) : £1.50 : CIP rev.
B81-36207

Martini, Thérèse. The other side of love / Thérès Matini. — London : Sphere, 1982, c1980. — 320p ; 18cm
ISBN 0-7221-5739-8 (pbk) : £1.75 B82-18175

Marton, George. Alarum / by George Marton. — Long Preston : Magna Print, 1982, c1977. — 420p ; 22cm
Originally published: London : W.H. Allen, 1977. — Published in large print
ISBN 0-86009-391-3 : Unpriced : CIP rev.
B82-04826

Marvin, James W.. Crow 6 : the sisters / James W. Marvin. — [London] : Corgi, 1981. — 124p ; 18cm
ISBN 0-552-11858-3 (pbk) : £0.95 B82-09116

Marvin, James W.. Crow 7: one-eyed death / James W. Marvin. — [London] : Corgi, 1982. — 128p ; 18cm
ISBN 0-552-11949-0 (pbk) : £1.00 B82-28367

813'.54[F] — Fiction in English. American writers, *1945- — Texts* *continuation*

Marvin, James W.. A good day / James W. Marvin. — London : Corgi, 1982. — 125p ; 18cm. — (Crow ; 8)
ISBN 0-552-12011-1 (pbk) : £1.00 B82-37131

Masters, John. The Himalayan concerto. — Large print ed. — Anstey : Ulverscroft, Aug.1982. — [496]p. — (Ulverscroft large print series)
Originally published: London : Joseph, 1976
ISBN 0-7089-0839-x : £5.00 : CIP entry B82-27001

Masterton, Graham. The devils of D-Day. — Bath : Firecrest, Jan.1983. — [192]p
Originally published: London : Sphere, 1979
ISBN 0-85997-511-8 : £5.95 : CIP entry B82-33128

Masterton, Graham. Famine / Graham Masterton. — London : Severn House, 1981. — 376p ; 21cm
ISBN 0-7278-0729-3 : £6.95 : CIP rev. B81-18101

Masterton, Graham. The heirloom / Graham Masterton. — London : Sphere, 1981. — 217p ; 18cm
ISBN 0-7221-6005-4 (pbk) : £1.25 B82-06016

Masterton, Graham. Railroad / Graham Masterton. — London : Sphere, 1981 (1982 [printing]). — 631p ; 18cm
Originally published: London : Hamilton, 1981
ISBN 0-7221-5990-0 (pbk) : £2.75 B82-33258

Masterton, Graham. Solitaire / by Graham Masterton. — London : Hamilton, 1982. — 567p ; 23cm
ISBN 0-241-10785-7 : £8.50 : CIP rev. B82-18831

Masur, Harold Q.. The mourning after. — London : Gollancz, Jan.1983. — [224]p
ISBN 0-575-03224-3 : £6.95 : CIP entry B82-32459

Matthews, Patricia. Embers of dawn / by Patricia Matthews. — Toronto ; London : Bantam, 1982. — 326p ; 21cm
ISBN 0-553-01368-8 (pbk) : £3.95 B82-39212

Matthews, Patricia. Love's bold journey / Patricia Matthews. — [London] : Corgi, 1981, c1980. — 440p ; 18cm
ISBN 0-552-11813-3 (pbk) : £1.95 B82-03239

Matthews, Patricia. Midnight whispers / Patricia Matthews and Clayton Matthews. — London : Corgi, 1982, c1981. — 308p ; 18cm
ISBN 0-552-11924-5 (pbk) : £1.50 B82-23899

Matthews, Patricia. Tides of love / Patricia Matthews. — [London] : Corgi, 1982, c1981. — 298p ; 17cm
Originally published: Toronto : London : Bantam, 1981
ISBN 0-552-11868-0 (pbk) : £1.75 B82-12591

Matthews, Patricia. Tides of love / by Patricia Matthews. — London : Severn House, 1982, c1981. — 326p ; 21cm
Originally published: Toronto ; London : Bantam, 1981
ISBN 0-7278-0788-9 : £6.95 B82-30467

May, Julian. The golden torc / Julian May. — London : Pan, 1982, c1981. — 377p : 3maps ; 18cm. — (The Saga of the exiles ; bk.2)
ISBN 0-330-26719-1 (pbk) : £1.75 B82-34256

May, Julian. The many-colored land / Julian May. — London : Pan, 1982, c1981. — 411p : 1map,music ; 18cm. — (The Saga of Pliocene exile ; v.1)
Originally published: Boston, Mass. : Houghton Mifflin, 1981
ISBN 0-330-26656-x (pbk) : £1.75 B82-10169

Mazer, Harry. I love you, stupid! / Harry Mazer. — London : Bodley Head, 1982, c1981. — 158p ; 20cm. — (A Book for new adults)
Originally published: New York : Crowell, 1981
ISBN 0-370-30913-8 (pbk) : £3.50 : CIP rev. B82-00906

Meggs, Brown. The war train : a novel of 1916 / Brown Meggs. — London : Hamilton, 1981. — 339p : 1map,1plan ; 24cm
Originally published: New York : Atheneum, 1981
ISBN 0-241-10393-2 : £7.95 : CIP rev. B81-20176

Melchior, Ib. The watchdogs of Abaddon / Ib Melchior. — London : Sphere, 1980, c1979 (1981 [printing]). — 444p : ill ; 18cm
Originally published: New York : Harper and Row ; London : Souvenir, 1979. — Bibliography: p443-444
ISBN 0-7221-6023-2 (pbk) : £1.75 B82-02132

Mensing, Steve. Gold in the Black Hills / by Steve Mensing. — Hornchurch : Henry, 1982, c1981. — 175p ; 21cm
Originally published: New York : Tower, 1981?
ISBN 0-86025-203-5 : £5.25 B82-36360

Meschery, Joanne. In a high place. — London : Bodley Head, Feb.1982. — [368]p
ISBN 0-370-30444-6 : £6.50 : CIP entry B81-36370

Meyer, Lawrence. A capitol crime / Lawrence Meyer. — Large print ed.. — [Bath] : Chivers Press, 1982, c1977. — 406p ; 23cm. — (Atlantic large print) (A Seymour large print thriller)
Originally published: New York : Viking Press, 1976 ; London : Collins, 1977
ISBN 0-85119-488-5 : Unpriced : CIP rev. B82-15861

Meyer, Lawrence. False front / Lawrence Meyer. — Large print ed. — [Bath] : Chivers, 1982, c1979. — 427p ; 23cm. — (Atlantic large print) (A Midnight large print thriller)
Originally published: New York : Viking ; London : Collins, 1979
ISBN 0-85119-477-x : Unpriced : CIP rev. B82-09855

Meyer, Nicholas. Confessions of a homing pigeon : a novel / by Nicholas Meyer. — London : Hodder and Stoughton, 1982, c1981. — 378p ; 23cm
ISBN 0-340-27829-3 : £7.95 : CIP rev. B81-36368

Michaels, Barbara. Wait for what will come : Barbara Michaels. — Large print ed. — Leicester : Ulverscroft, 1981, c1978. — 395p ; 23cm. — (Ulverscroft large print series)
Originally published: New York : Dodd, Mead, 1978 ; London : Souvenir Press, 1980
ISBN 0-7089-0695-8 : £5.00 : CIP rev. B81-28091

Michaels, Barbara. Wings of the falcon. — Large print ed. — Anstey : Ulverscroft, Feb.1983. — 1v.. — (Ulverscroft large print series)
Originally published: New York : Dodd, Mead, 1977 ; London : Souvenir, 1979
ISBN 0-7089-0921-3 : CIP entry B82-38883

Michaels, Barbara. The wizard's daughter / Barbara Michaels. — London : Souvenir, 1982, c1980. — 279p ; 23cm
Originally published: New York : Dodd, Mead, 1980
ISBN 0-285-62505-5 : £6.95 B82-09110

Michaels, Fern. Beyond tomorrow. — London : Hodder & Stoughton, Jan.1982. — [192]p. — (Silhouette romance)
ISBN 0-340-27667-3 (pbk) : £0.75 : CIP entry B81-34482

Michaels, Fern. The delta ladies / Fern Michaels. — Sevenoaks : Coronet, 1981, c1980. — 330p : col.ill ; 18cm
Originally published: New York : Pocket Books, 1980. — Ill on inside covers
ISBN 0-340-27106-x (pbk) : £1.75 : CIP rev. B81-26730

Michaels, Fern. Nightstar. — London : Hodder and Stoughton, Nov.1982. — [192]p. — (Silhouette romance)
ISBN 0-340-32691-3 (pbk) : £0.75 : CIP entry B82-28269

Michaels, Fern. Paint me rainbows. — London : Hodder & Stoughton, June 1982. — [192]p. — (Silhouette romance)
Originally published: New York : Silhouette Books, 1981
ISBN 0-340-27940-0 (pbk) : £0.75 : CIP entry B82-10020

Michener, James A.. The bridges at Toko-Ri / James A. Michener. — London : Prior, 1981, c1953. — 168p : ill ; 25cm
Originally published: New York : Random ; London : Secker & Warburg, 1953. — Published in large print
ISBN 0-86043-674-8 : Unpriced B82-28217

Michener, James A.. Caravans : a novel / by James A. Michener. — London : Prior, 1981, c1963. — 525p ; 25cm
Originally published: New York : Random, 1963 ; London : Secker & Warburg, 1964. — Published in large print
ISBN 0-86043-678-0 : Unpriced B82-28215

Michener, James A.. The covenant / James A. Michener. — London : Corgi, 1981, c1980 (1982 [printing]). — 1079p : geneal.tables ; 18cm
Originally published: London : Secker & Warburg, 1980
ISBN 0-552-11755-2 (pbk) : £2.95 B82-16740

Michener, James A.. Space. — London : Secker & Warburg, Nov.1982. — [640]p
ISBN 0-436-27967-3 : £8.95 : CIP entry B82-29129

Michener, James A.. Tales of the South Pacific / by James A. Michener. — London : Prior, 1981, c1947. — 635p ; 25cm
Originally published: New York : Macmillan, 1947 ; London : Collins, 1951
ISBN 0-86043-684-5 : Unpriced B82-28388

Milan, Angel. Autumn harvest. — London : Hodder & Stoughton, Jan.1983. — [256]p. — (Silhouette special edition)
ISBN 0-340-32938-6 (pbk) : £0.95 : CIP entry B82-34417

Millar, Jeff. Private sector / Jeff Millar. — London : Pan in association with Macmillan London, 1981, c1979. — 251p ; 18cm
Originally published: New York : Dial Press, 1979 ; London : Macmillan, 1980
ISBN 0-330-26576-8 (pbk) : £1.75 B82-10170

Millar, Margaret. Mermaid / by Margaret Millar. — London : Gollancz, 1982. — 215p ; 21cm
ISBN 0-575-03093-3 : £6.95 : CIP rev. B82-01552

Miller, Walter M.. A canticle for Leibowitz / Walter M. Miller, Jr. — [London] : Corgi, 1963, c1959 (1979 [printing]). — 278p ; 18cm
Originally published: Philadelphia : Lippincott ; London : Weidenfeld & Nicolson, 1960
ISBN 0-552-11178-3 (pbk) : £1.25 B82-41092

Minahan, John. The janitor / John Minahan ; based on a screenplay written by Steve Tesich. — London : Macdonald, c1981. — 171p ; 18cm. — (A Futura book)
ISBN 0-7088-2119-7 (pbk) : £1.10 B82-00456

813'.54[F] — Fiction in English. American writers, *1945- — Texts* *continuation*

Miner, Valerie. Murder in the English department. — London : Women's Press, July 1982. — [244]p
ISBN 0-7043-3890-4 (pbk) : £3.95 : CIP entry B82-13006

Minot, Stephen. Surviving the flood. — London : Gollancz, Feb.1983. — [304]p
Originally published: New York : Atheneum, 1981
ISBN 0-575-03237-5 : £7.95 : CIP entry B82-38685

Mitgang, Herbert. The Montauk fault / Herbert Mitgang. — South Yarmouth, Ma. : Curley ; [Skipton] : distributed by Magna, c1981. — 446p ; 23cm
Published in large print
ISBN 0-89340-393-8 : Unpriced B82-32474

Monet, Nicole. Love's silver web. — London : Hodder & Stoughton, Nov.1982. — [192]p. — (Silhouette desire)
ISBN 0-340-32859-2 (pbk) : £0.95 : CIP entry B82-29065

Mooney, Ted, *19---*. Easy travel to other planets / Ted Mooney. — London : Cape, 1982, c1981. — 278p ; 21cm
Originally published: New York : Farrar, Straus, Giroux, 1981
ISBN 0-224-02931-2 : £6.95 : CIP rev. B82-04303

Moore, Robin. The Black Sea connection / Robin Moore & Hugh McDonald. — London : Severn House, 1981, c1978. — 246p ; 21cm
ISBN 0-7278-0713-7 : £6.95 : CIP rev. B81-23814

Moore, Robin. The establishment. — London : Severn House, Nov.1982. — [256]p
ISBN 0-7278-0846-x : £6.95 : CIP entry B82-34070

Morgan, Frank, *1916-*. San Saba trail / by Frank Morgan. — London : Hale, 1982. — 156p ; 20cm
ISBN 0-7091-9649-0 : £5.25 B82-17477

Morgan, John, *1916-*. Bluegrass Range / by John Morgan. — London : Hale, 1982. — 152p ; 20cm
ISBN 0-7091-9721-7 : £5.25 B82-22914

Morris, Janet E.. Cruiser dreams / Janet E. Morris. — [London] : Fontana, 1981. — 316p ; 18cm. — (The Kerrion saga)
ISBN 0-00-616288-6 (pbk) : £1.75 B82-13644

Morrison, Toni. Tar baby / Toni Morrison. — London : Chatto & Windus, 1981. — 309p ; 21cm
ISBN 0-7011-2596-9 : £6.95 : CIP rev. B81-16857

Muir, James A.. Bad habits / James A. Muir. — London : Sphere, 1981. — 119p ; 18cm. — (Breed ; no.16) (A Sphere adult western)
ISBN 0-7221-8999-0 (pbk) : £1.00 B82-06014

Muir, James A.. Breed : day of the gun / James A. Muir. — London : Sphere, 1982. — 121p ; 18cm. — (A Sphere adult western)
ISBN 0-7221-9018-2 (pbk) : £1.00 B82-27884

Murphy, Brian, *1939-*. The enigma variations / Brian Murphy. — London : Blond & Briggs, 1982, c1981. — 265p ; 22cm
Originally published: New York : Scribner, 1981
ISBN 0-85634-118-5 : £6.50 B82-09777

Murphy, Warren. Destroyer 38 : Bay City blast / Warren Murphy. — [London] : Corgi, 1981, c1979. — 179p ; 18cm
Originally published: New York : Pinnacle?, 1979?
ISBN 0-552-11818-4 (pbk) : £0.95 B82-09009

Musgrave, Jacqueline. Northern lights. — London : New English Library, Oct.1982. — [256]p
ISBN 0-340-32606-9 (pbk) : £0.95 : CIP entry B82-24715

Mykel, A. W.. The Windchime legacy / A.W. Mykel. — London : Corgi, 1981, c1980. — 489p ; 18cm
Originally published: New York : St Martin's Press, 1980 ; London : Severn House, 1981
ISBN 0-552-11850-8 (pbk) : £1.75 B82-09058

Myrer, Anton. A green desire : a novel / by Anton Myrer. — London : Hamilton, 1982, c1981. — 511p ; 24cm
Originally published: New York : Putnam, 1981
ISBN 0-241-10794-6 : £8.95 : CIP rev. B82-07981

Nabokov, Vladimir. Despair / Vladimir Nabokov. — Harmondsworth : Penguin, 1981, c1965. — 176p ; 20cm
Originally published: New York : Putnam, 1965 ; London : Weidenfeld & Nicolson, 1966
ISBN 0-14-005474-x (pbk) : £2.50 B82-06436

Nash, N. Richard. Aphrodite's cave / N. Richard Nash. — London : Star, 1982. — x,466p ; 18cm
Originally published: Garden City, N.Y. : Doubleday, 1980 ; London : W.H. Allen, 1981
ISBN 0-352-31068-5 (pbk) : £1.95 B82-22052

Niven, Larry. The magic goes away / Larry Niven. — London : Futura, 1982, c1978. — 139p ; 18cm. — (An Orbit book)
Originally published: New York : Ace Books, 1978
ISBN 0-7088-8093-2 (pbk) : £1.25 B82-38623

Niven, Larry. The mote in God's eye / Larry Niven and Jerry Pournelle. — London : Macdonald, 1982, c1974. — x,560p ; 21cm
Originally published: New York : Simon and Schuster, 1974 ; London : Weidenfeld and Nicolson, 1975
ISBN 0-356-08529-5 : £7.95 B82-22573

Niven, Larry. Oath of fealty / Larry Niven and Jerry Pournelle. — London : Macdonald, 1982, c1981. — 328p ; 21cm
ISBN 0-356-08526-0 : £6.95 B82-22574

Niven, Larry. Oath of fealty / Larry Niven and Jerry Pournelle. — London : Futura, 1982, c1981. — 328p ; 18cm
ISBN 0-7088-8089-4 (pbk) : £1.95 B82-18265

Niven, Larry. The patchwork girl / Larry Niven. — [London] : Futura, 1982, c1980. — 144p ; 18cm
Originally published: New York : Ace Books, c1980
ISBN 0-7088-8094-0 (pbk) : £1.25 B82-35721

Nolan, Frederick. White nights, red dawn / Frederick Nolan. — London : Arrow, 1982, c1980. — 471p ; 18cm
Originally published: New York : Macmillan, 1980
ISBN 0-09-928130-9 (pbk) : £1.95 B82-33315

Nolan, Madeena S.. The gift / Madeena S. Nolan. — London : Corgi, 1982, c1981. — 284p ; 18cm
ISBN 0-552-12005-7 (pbk) : £1.50 B82-37140

Norman, John, *19---*. Ghost dance / John Norman. — London : Star, 1981, c1970. — 342p ; 18cm
Originally published: New York : Ballantine Book, 1970
ISBN 0-352-30974-1 (pbk) : £1.95 B82-16101

Norman, John, *19---*. Guardsman of Gor / John Norman. — London : Star, 1982, c1981. — 304p ; 18cm. — (Chronicles of Counter Earth)
Originally published: New York : Daw, 1981
ISBN 0-352-31189-4 (pbk) : £1.95 B82-38405

North, Sam. Ramapo! / Sam North. — London : Arlington, 1981. — 271p ; 23cm
ISBN 0-85140-533-9 : £6.95 : CIP rev. B81-20098

Nova, Craig. The good son. — London : Bodley Head, Sept.1982. — [304]p
ISBN 0-370-30488-8 : £7.50 : CIP entry B82-19199

Nye, Nelson C.. Gunfight at the O.K. Corral. — Large print ed. — Bath : Chivers, Feb.1983. — [256]p. — (Atlantic large print)
Originally published: New York : Norden, 1956
ISBN 0-85119-525-3 : £5.75 : CIP entry B82-39577

Oates, Joyce Carol. Angel of light / Joyce Carol Oates. — London : Cape, 1981. — 434p ; 24cm
Originally published: New York : Dutton, 1981
ISBN 0-224-02927-4 : £7.50 : CIP rev. B81-30965

O'Brien, Saliee. Black ivory / Saliee O'Brien. — London : Sphere, 1982, c1980. — 354p ; 18cm
Originally published: New York : Bantam, 1980
ISBN 0-7221-6488-2 (pbk) : £1.75 B82-09393

O'Brien, Tim, *1955 Mar.3-*. Northern lights / Tim O'Brien. — London : Granada, 1981, c1975. — 363p ; 18cm. — (A Panther book)
Originally published: New York : Delacorte, 1975 ; London : Marion Boyars, 1976
ISBN 0-586-05288-7 (pbk) : £1.50 B82-02999

O'Conner, Clint. Broken bow range / by Clint O'Conner. — London : Hale, 1982. — 158p ; 19cm
ISBN 0-7091-9947-3 : £5.50 B82-39189

O'Conner, Clint. Mule-train / Clint O'Conner. — Large print ed. — Bath : Chivers, 1982, c1978. — 154p ; 23cm. — (A Lythway western)
Originally published: London : Hale, 1978
ISBN 0-85119-804-x : Unpriced B82-20127

O'Grady, Leslie. Lady Jade / Leslie O'Grady. — Loughton : Piatkus, 1982, c1981. — 325p ; 21cm
ISBN 0-86188-160-5 : £6.95 : CIP rev. B81-36047

Olcott, Anthony. Murder at the Red October / Anthony Olcott. — London : Hodder and Stoughton, 1982, c1981. — 223p ; 22cm
Originally published: Chicago : Academy Chicago, 1981
ISBN 0-340-28264-9 : £6.95 : CIP rev. B82-06729

Oliver, Tess. Double or nothing. — London : Hodder & Stoughton, Dec.1981. — [192]p. — (Silhouette romance)
ISBN 0-340-27658-4 (pbk) : £0.65 : CIP entry B81-31447

Olsen, T. V.. Bonner's stallion / T.V. Olsen. — London : Coronet, 1981, c1977. — 254p ; 18cm
Originally published: Greenwich, Conn. : Fawcett Goldmedal, 1977
ISBN 0-340-27557-x (pbk) : £1.25 : CIP rev. B81-31464

Olsen, T. V.. Bonner's stallion. — Large print ed. — Anstey : Ulverscroft, Oct.1982. — [352]p. — (Ulverscroft large print series)
Originally published: New York : Fawcett, 1977
ISBN 0-7089-0869-1 : £5.00 : CIP entry B82-27018

Osborn, David. Love and treason. — London : Granada, Sept.1982. — [256]p
ISBN 0-246-11597-1 : £7.95 : CIP entry B82-18853

813'.54[F] — Fiction in English. American writers, *1945- — Texts* *continuation*

Osborn, John Jay. The man who owned New York / by John Jay Osborn, Jr. — London : Hale, 1982, c1981. — 191p ; 23cm
Originally published: Boston : Houghton Mifflin, 1981
ISBN 0-7091-9820-5 : £7.25 B82-34503

Ottum, Bob. See the kid run : a novel / by Bob Ottum. — London : Arrow, 1981, c1978. — 288p ; 18cm
Originally published: London : Allen, 1978
ISBN 0-09-926250-9 (pbk) : £1.50 B82-03534

Page, Jake. Shoot the moon / Jake Page. — London : Hale, 1980, c1979. — 218p ; 20cm
Originally published: Indianapolis : Bobbs-Merrill, 1979
ISBN 0-7091-8679-7 : £5.75 B82-15575

Page, Thomas, *1942-*. [Sigmet active]. Skyfire / Thomas Page. — [Feltham] : Hamlyn Paperbacks, 1980, c1978 (1982 [printing]). — 218p ; 18cm
Originally published: New York : Times Books, 1978 ; Feltham : Hamlyn Paperbacks, 1980
ISBN 0-600-20614-9 : £1.50 B82-17473

Paine, Lauran. Adobe wells / by Lauran Paine. — London : Hale, 1982. — 157p ; 20cm
ISBN 0-7091-9117-0 : £5.25 B82-15491

Paine, Lauran. The lord of Lost Valley / by Lauran Paine. — London : Hale, 1982. — 156p ; 20cm
ISBN 0-7091-9306-8 : £5.50 B82-31619

Paine, Lauran. Scarface / by Lauran Paine. — London : Hale, 1981. — 157p ; 20cm
ISBN 0-7091-9083-2 : £4.95 B82-11061

Palmer, Diana. The cowboy and the lady. — London : Hodder & Stoughton, Feb.1983. — [192]p. — (Silhouette desire)
ISBN 0-340-32923-8 (pbk) : £0.95 : CIP entry B82-38267

Palmer, Dianna. Heather's song. — London : Hodder and Stoughton, Dec.1982. — [256]p. — (Silhouette special edition)
ISBN 0-340-32680-8 (pbk) : £0.95 : CIP entry B82-29660

Palmer, Linda. Starstruck / by Linda Palmer. — London : Macmillan, 1982, c1981. — 299p ; 23cm
Originally published: New York : Putnam, 1981
ISBN 0-333-32982-1 : £6.95 B82-13593

Palmer, Michael, *1942-*. The sisterhood / Michael Palmer. — London : Hodder and Stoughton, 1982. — 270p ; 23cm
ISBN 0-340-28365-3 : £7.95 : CIP rev. B82-16474

Palmer, Thomas. The transfer. — London : Collins, Feb.1983. — [400]p
ISBN 0-00-222721-5 : £8.95 : CIP entry B82-36460

Paretsky, Sara. Indemnity only : a novel / by Sara Paretsky. — London : Gollancz, 1982. — 244p ; 21cm
ISBN 0-575-03109-3 : £6.95 : CIP rev. B82-06931

Parker, Chauncey G.. The visitor. — London : New English Library, Oct.1982. — [256]p
ISBN 0-450-05514-0 (pbk) : £1.60 : CIP entry B82-24724

Parker, Robert B.. The Godwulf manuscript / Robert B. Parker. — South Yarmouth : Curley ; [Skipton] : Magna Print, [1979], c1973. — 343p ; 23cm
Originally published: Boston, Mass. : Houghton Mifflin, 1974. — Published in large print
ISBN 0-89340-218-4 : £5.25 B82-05033

Parker, Robert B.. The Judas goat / Robert B. Parker. — London : Deutsch, 1982, c1978. — 175p ; 23cm
Originally published: Boston, Mass. : Houghton Mifflin, 1978
ISBN 0-233-97046-0 : £6.95 B82-22383

Parker, Robert B.. Looking for Rachel Wallace : a Spenser novel / Robert B. Parker. — Loughton : Piatkus, 1982, c1980. — 219p ; 21cm
Originally published: New York : Delacorte / S. Lawrence, c1980
ISBN 0-86188-174-5 : £6.50 : CIP rev. B82-05764

Parker, Robert B.. A savage place. — Loughton : Piatkus, Sept.1982. — [224]p
ISBN 0-86188-196-6 : £6.50 : CIP entry B82-21550

Patrick, Ronald. Beyond the threshold / Ronald Patrick. — London : Sphere, 1982, c1980. — 246p ; 18cm
Originally published: Hollywood : Ermine, 1978
ISBN 0-7221-6731-8 (pbk) : £1.50 B82-33910

Patten, Lewis B.. The ordeal of Jason Ord / Lewis B. Patten. — South Yarmouth, Mass. : Curley, 1979, c1973 ; [Long Preston] : Distributed by Magna. — 286p ; 23cm. — (A Lewis B. Patten western)
Originally published: Garden City, N.Y. : Doubleday, 1973. — Published in large print
ISBN 0-89340-186-2 : £4.75 B82-17035

Patten, Lewis B.. Ride a tall horse / Lewis B. Patten. — London : Hale, 1981. — 181p ; 19cm
Originally published: New York : Doubleday, 1980
ISBN 0-7091-9064-6 : £4.95 B82-07212

Patten, Lewis B.. Ride a tall horse / Lewis B. Patten. — London : Prior, 1981, c1980. — 291p ; 25cm
Originally published: New York : Doubleday, 1980 ; London : Hale, 1981. — Published in large print
ISBN 0-86043-676-4 (corrected) : Unpriced B82-31903

Paul, Charlotte. The image / Charlotte Paul. — [Sevenoaks] : Hodder and Stoughton, 1981, c1980. — 302p ; 18cm. — (Coronet books)
Originally published: New York : Warner Books, 1980
ISBN 0-340-27271-6 (pbk) : £1.50 : CIP rev. B81-30142

Pendleton, Don. Detroit deathwatch / Don Pendleton. — London : Corgi, 1976, c1974 (1982 [printing]). — 182p ; 18cm. — (Executioner ; 19)
Originally published: New York : Pinnacle, 1974
ISBN 0-552-12000-6 (pbk) : £1.25 B82-37136

Pendleton, Don. Jersey guns / Don Pendleton. — London : Corgi, 1975, c1974 (1982 [printing]). — 169p ; 18cm. — (Executioner ; 17)
Originally published: New York : Pinnacle, 1974
ISBN 0-552-11998-9 (pbk) : £1.25 B82-37134

Pendleton, Don. Panic in Philly / Don Pendleton. — London : Corgi, 1975, c1973 (1982 [printing]). — 190p : ill ; 18cm. — (Executioner ; 15)
Originally published: New York : Pinnacle, 1973
ISBN 0-552-11997-0 (pbk) : £1.25 B82-37135

Pendleton, Don. Texas storm / Don Pendleton. — London : Corgi, 1975, c1974 (1982 [printing]). — 188p ; 18cm. — (Executioner ; 18)
Originally published: New York : Pinnacle, 1974
ISBN 0-552-11999-7 (pbk) : £1.25 B82-37137

Peters, Elizabeth. The curse of the Pharaohs / by Elizabeth Peters. — London : Souvenir, 1982, c1981. — 357p ; 23cm
Originally published: New York : Dodd, Mead, 1981
ISBN 0-285-62517-9 : £6.95 B82-17532

Peters, Elizabeth. Devil-may-care. — London : Coronet, Apr.1981. — [240]p
Originally published: London : Cassell, 1978
ISBN 0-340-25081-x (pbk) : £1.25 : CIP entry B81-01144

Peters, Elizabeth. The love talker / Elizabeth Peters. — Large print ed. — Leicester : Ulverscroft, 1982, c1980. — 396p ; 22cm. — (Ulverscroft Large print series)
Originally published: New York : Dodd, Mead, 1980
ISBN 0-7089-0751-2 : £5.00 : CIP rev. B81-36940

Peters, Maureen. Song for a strolling player / Maureen Peters. — London : Hale, 1981. — 176p ; 21cm
ISBN 0-7091-9052-2 : £6.50 B82-00540

Peters, Stephen. The park is mine / Stephen Peters. — London : Blond & Briggs, 1982, c1981. — 305p : map ; 23cm
Originally published: New York : Doubleday, 1981. — Map on lining papers
ISBN 0-85634-122-3 : £6.95 B82-09484

Peters, Sue. One special rose / Sue Peters. — Large print ed. — [Bath] : Chivers Press, 1982, c1976. — 297p ; 23cm. — (Atlantic large print) (A Seymour large print romance)
Originally published: London : Mills & Boon, 1976
ISBN 0-85119-485-0 : Unpriced : CIP rev. B82-15858

Pettit, Mike. The Axmann agenda / Mike Pettit. — London : Sphere, 1982, c1980. — 284p ; 18cm
ISBN 0-7221-6814-4 (pbk) : £1.75 B82-33916

Picano, Felice. Late in the season / Felice Picano. — London : New English Library, 1982, c1981. — 219p ; 18cm
Originally published: New York : Delacorte, 1981
ISBN 0-450-05410-1 (pbk) : £1.75 : CIP rev. B82-12352

Picano, Felice. The lure / Felice Picano. — London : New English Library, 1981, c1979. — 415p ; 18cm
Originally published: New York : Delacorte Press, 1979
ISBN 0-450-05198-6 (pbk) : £1.75 B82-08654

Piercy, Marge. Braided lives / Marge Piercy. — London : Allen Lane, 1982. — 444p ; 23cm
ISBN 0-7139-1478-5 : £7.95 B82-30475

Piercy, Marge. Vida. — London : Women's Press, May 1982. — [416]p
Originally published: 1980
ISBN 0-7043-3851-3 (pbk) : £4.95 : CIP entry B82-09303

Pike, Charles R.. Double cross. — Large print ed. — Bath : Chivers, Sept.1982. — [200]p. — (Jubal Cade ; 2) (A Lythway book)
Originally published: London : Granada Publishing, 1974
ISBN 0-85119-849-x : £6.40 : CIP entry B82-20518

Pike, Charles R.. The golden dead. — Large print ed. — Bath : Chivers, Feb.1983. — [200] p. — (Jubal Cade ; 7) (A Lythway book)
Originally published: London : Granada/Panther, 1976
ISBN 0-85119-900-3 : £6.40 : CIP entry B82-39588

813′.54[F] — Fiction in English. American writers, *1945- — Texts* *continuation*

Pike, Charles R.. The hungry gun. — Large print ed. — Bath : Chivers, Oct.1982. — [200]p. — (Jubal Cade ; 3) (A Lythway book)
Originally published: London : Granada, 1975
ISBN 0-85119-857-0 : £6.70 : CIP entry
B82-20523

Pike, Charles R.. Jubal Cade : the burning man. — Large print ed. — Bath : Chivers, Jan.1983. — [200]p. — (A Lythway book)
Originally published: London ; St Albans : Mayflower, 1976
ISBN 0-85119-887-2 : £6.40 : CIP entry
B82-33101

Pike, Charles R.. Killer silver. — Large print ed. — Bath : Chivers, Nov.1982. — [200]p. — (Jubal Cade ; 4) (A Lythway book)
Originally published: London : Granada, 1975
ISBN 0-85119-863-5 : £6.70 : CIP entry
B82-26306

Pike, Charles R.. Vengeance hunt. — Large print ed. — Bath : Chivers Press, Dec.1982. — [200] p. — (Jubal Cade ; 5) (A Lythway book)
Originally published: London : Granada, 1976
ISBN 0-85119-873-2 : £6.70 : CIP entry
B82-30228

Pilcer, Sonia. Maiden rites : a romance / Sonia Pilcer. — London : Weidenfeld and Nicolson, 1982. — 278p ; 23cm
ISBN 0-297-78165-0 : £7.95 B82-40251

Pilpel, Robert H.. To the honour of the fleet / Robert H. Pilpel. — London : Futura, 1980, c1979 (1982 [printing]). — 579p : 1map,2plans ; 18cm
Originally published: London : Weidenfeld and Nicolson, 1979
ISBN 0-7088-1796-3 (pbk) : £2.50 B82-22613

Pinchot, Ann. Doctors and wives. — Loughton : Piatkus, Aug.1982. — [408]p
Originally published: New York : Arbor, 1980
ISBN 0-86188-194-x : £7.95 : CIP entry
B82-16684

Plain, Belva. Eden burning / Belva Plain. — London : Collins, 1982. — 448p ; 23cm
ISBN 0-00-222658-8 : £7.95 B82-34029

Plante, David. The woods : a novel / by David Plante. — London : Gollancz, 1982. — 123p : 1ill ; 21cm
ISBN 0-575-02776-2 : £7.95 B82-10545

Pohl, Frederick. Survival kit / Frederick Pohl. — London : Granada, 1979. — 192p ; 18cm. — (Panther)
ISBN 0-586-04963-0 (pbk) : £1.25 B82-34375

Pohl, Frederik. The age of the pussyfoot / Frederik Pohl. — London : Granada, 1979, c1969. — 187p ; 18cm. — (Panther)
Originally published: New York : Ballantine, 1969 ; London : Gollancz, 1970
ISBN 0-586-04830-8 (pbk) : £1.25 B82-31785

Pohl, Frederik. Beyond the blue event horizon / Frederik Pohl. — London : Futura, 1982, c1980. — 327p ; 18cm
Originally published: London : Gollancz, 1980
ISBN 0-7088-8088-6 (pbk) : £1.95 B82-15313

Pohl, Frederik. Man plus / Frederik Pohl. — London : Granada, 1978, c1976 (1982 [printing]). — 228p ; 18cm. — (A Panther book)
Originally published: London : Gollancz, 1976
ISBN 0-586-04709-3 (pbk) : £1.25 B82-40504

Pohl, Frederik. Starburst / Frederik Pohl. — London : Gollancz, 1982. — 219p ; 21cm
ISBN 0-575-03134-4 : £6.95 : CIP rev.
B82-15890

Pohl, Frederik. Syzygy / Frederik Pohl. — Toronto ; London : Bantam, 1982. — 248p ; 17cm
ISBN 0-553-20527-7 (pbk) : £1.25 B82-24172

Pollachek, Ellin Ronee. Seasons / Ellin Ronee Pollachek. — London : W.H. Allen, 1982, c1980. — 352p ; 18cm. — (A Star book)
Originally published: United States : Zebra Books, 1980
ISBN 0-352-31026-x (pbk) : £1.60 B82-29192

Pollock, J. C.. Mission M.I.A.. — London : New English Library, July 1982. — [256]p
ISBN 0-450-04911-6 : £6.95 : CIP entry
B82-18575

Potok, Chaim. The book of lights / Chaim Potok. — London : Heinemann, 1982, c1981. — 369p ; 21cm
Originally published: New York : Knopf, 1981
ISBN 0-434-59604-3 : £7.95 B82-22095

Pournelle, Jerry. Janissaries / Jerry Pournelle. — London : Macdonald, 1981. — 255p ; 21cm
ISBN 0-354-04762-0 : £5.50 B82-00538

Pournelle, Jerry. Janissaries / Jerry Pournelle. — London : Futura, 1981. — 255p ; 18cm
ISBN 0-7088-8084-3 (pbk) : £1.65 B82-05484

Pournelle, Jerry. King David′s spaceship / Jerry Pournelle. — London : Futura, 1981, c1980. — 332p : 2maps ; 18cm. — (An Orbit book)
ISBN 0-7088-8087-8 (pbk) : £1.95 B82-10542

Poyer, Joe. Vengeance 10 / Joe Poyer. — London : Sphere, 1982, c1980. — 339p : ill,1map ; 18cm
Originally published: New York : Atheneum, 1980 ; London : Joseph, 1981
ISBN 0-7221-7012-2 (pbk) : £1.75 B82-27888

Pronzini, Bill. Labyrinth / Bill Pronzini. — London : Hale, 1981, c1980. — 186p ; 19cm
Originally published: New York : St. Martin′s Press, 1980
ISBN 0-7091-9269-x : £6.25 B82-07213

Quin-Harkin, Janet. Love match / Janet Quin-Harkin. — Toronto ; London : Bantam, 1982. — 168p ; 18cm
ISBN 0-553-20745-8 (pbk) : £0.65 B82-28552

Quinnell, A. J.. The Mahdi. — Large print ed. — Anstey : Ulverscroft, Nov.1982. — [416]p. — (Charnwood library series)
ISBN 0-7089-8081-3 : £5.25 : CIP entry
B82-29103

Rainer, Iris. The boys in the mailroom / Iris Rainer. — London : Pan in association with Collins, 1982, c1980. — 410p ; 17cm
Originally published: London : Collins, 1980
ISBN 0-330-26606-3 (pbk) : £1.50 B82-18100

Rand, Suzanne. Green eyes / Suzanne Rand. — Toronto ; London : Bantam, c1981. — 140p ; 18cm
ISBN 0-553-20604-4 (pbk) : £0.65 B82-23912

Randall, Bob. The calling : a novel / by Bob Randall. — London : Severn House, 1982, c1981. — 205p ; 21cm
Originally published: New York : Simon and Schuster, 1981
ISBN 0-7278-0801-x : £6.95 B82-31426

Randall, Bob. The calling. — London : New English Library, Jan.1983. — [192]p
ISBN 0-450-05545-0 (pbk) : £1.60 : CIP entry
B82-36140

Randall, Clay. Amos Flagg rides out. — Large print ed. — Bath : Chivers, Dec.1982. — [256] p. — (Atlantic large print)
Originally published: New York : Fawcett Publications, 1966
ISBN 0-85119-511-3 : £5.25 : CIP entry
B82-30239

Randall, Clay. Bushwhacked. — Large print ed. — Bath : Chivers, Nov.1982. — [232]p. — (Atlantic large print)
Originally published: New York : Fawcett Publications, 1967
ISBN 0-85119-505-9 : £5.25 : CIP entry
B82-26434

Redenius, Ken. McMasters′ horses / Ken Redenius. — Hornchurch : Henry, 1981, c1980. — 176p : ill ; 21cm
Originally published: New York : Nordon, 1980
ISBN 0-86025-201-9 : £4.95 B82-10150

Reed, Barry. The verdict. — London : Granada, Sept.1982. — [285]p
ISBN 0-246-11538-6 : £7.95 : CIP entry
B82-18850

Reese, John. Maximum range / by John Reese. — London : Hale, 1982, c1981. — 177p ; 20cm
Originally published: Garden City, N.Y. : Doubleday, 1981
ISBN 0-7091-9872-8 : £5.50 B82-30434

Reiss, Bob. Summer fires / Bob Reiss. — London : Pan in association with Secker and Warburg, 1981, c1980. — 239p ; 18cm
Originally published: New York : Simon and Schuster ; London : Secker and Warburg, 1980
ISBN 0-330-26555-5 (pbk) : £1.50 B82-08753

Reno, Marie R.. When the music changed / Marie R. Reno. — London : Methuen Paperbacks, 1981, c1980. — x,530p ; 18cm. — (Magnum books)
Originally published: New York : New American Library, 1980 ; London : Eyre Methuen, 1981
ISBN 0-417-06950-2 (pbk) : £1.95 B82-15502

Reynolds, Elizabeth. An ocean of love. — London : Hodder and Stoughton, Jan.1983. — [192]p. — (Silhouette romance)
ISBN 0-340-32726-x (pbk) : £0.85 : CIP entry
B82-34411

Rhinehart, Luke. The long voyage back. — London : Granada, Aug.1982. — [608]p
ISBN 0-246-11795-8 : £7.95 : CIP entry
B82-25153

Rhodes, Richard, *1937-*. The last safari / Richard Rhodes. — London : Corgi, 1981, c1980. — 293p ; 18cm
Originally published: London : Deutsch, 1980
ISBN 0-552-11836-2 (pbk) : £1.50 B82-09060

Richmond, Donald. The Dunkirk directive / Donald Richmond. — [London] : Corgi, 1982, c1980. — 394p ; 18cm
Originally published: New York : Stein and Day, 1980
ISBN 0-552-11887-7 (pbk) : £1.85 B82-22576

Richmond, Roe. Rio Grande riptide / Roe Richmond. — [Bath] : Chivers Press, 1982, c1980. — 289p ; 23cm. — (Atlantic large print) (A Gunsmoke large print western)
ISBN 0-85119-487-7 : Unpriced : CIP rev.
ISBN 0-89340-415-2 (U.S.) B82-15860

Richmond, Roe. Wyoming Way / Roe Richmond. — Large print ed. — [Bath] : Chivers, 1982, c1958. — 316p ; 23cm. — (A Gunsmoke large print western) (Atlantic large print)
Originally published: New York : Nordon, 1958
ISBN 0-85119-463-x : Unpriced : CIP rev.
B82-05001

Riefe, Barbara. So wicked the heart / Barbara Riefe. — London : Sphere, 1982, c1980. — 368p ; 18cm
ISBN 0-7221-7363-6 (pbk) : £1.95 B82-33914

Riefe, Barbara. Tempt not this flesh / Barbara Riefe. — London : Sphere, 1981, c1979. — 398p ; 18cm
ISBN 0-7221-7353-9 (pbk) : £1.75 B82-07177

813'.54[F] — Fiction in English. American writers, *1945- — Texts* *continuation*

Ripy, Margaret. The flaming tree. — London : Hodder and Stoughton, Nov.1982. — [256]p. — (Silhouette special edition)
ISBN 0-340-32614-x (pbk) : £0.95 : CIP entry B82-28262

Ripy, Margaret. A second chance of love / Margaret Ripy. — [Sevenoaks] : Silhouette Books, 1981. — 188p : 1map ; 17cm. — (Silhouette romance ; 71)
ISBN 0-340-27259-7 (pbk) : £0.65 : CIP rev. B81-30546

Robbins, Harold. 79 Park Avenue / Harold Robbins. — Leicester : Charnwood, 1981, c1955. — 434p ; 23cm. — (Charnwood library series)
Originally published: New York : Knopf, 1955 ; London : Hale, 1961. — Published in large print
ISBN 0-7089-8010-4 : £5.25 : CIP rev. B81-21474

Robbins, Harold. The carpetbaggers / Harold Robbins. — Sevenoaks : New English Library, 1982, c1962. — 548p ; 23cm
Originally published: New York : Simon & Schuster, 1961 ; London : Blond, 1963
ISBN 0-450-04899-3 : £8.50 B82-29194

Robbins, Harold. Goodbye, Janette. — London : New English Library, Mar.1982. — [384]p
Originally published: 1981
ISBN 0-450-05315-6 (pbk) : £2.50 : CIP entry B82-01982

Robbins, Harold. Never leave me / Harold Robbins. — Large print ed. — Leicester : Charnwood, 1982, c1956. — 255p ; 23cm. — (Charnwood library series)
Originally published: London : Hale, 1956. — Published in large print
ISBN 0-7089-8023-6 : £4.50 : CIP rev. B81-33989

Robbins, Harold. Never love a stranger / Harold Robbins. — Leicester : Charnwood, 1982, c1958. — 65p ; 23cm. — (Charnwood library series)
Originally published: New York : Knopf, 1948 ; London : Hale, 1958. — Published in large print
ISBN 0-7089-8039-2 : Unpriced : CIP rev. B82-08099

Robbins, Harold. Spellbinder. — London : New English Library, Oct.1982. — [320]p
ISBN 0-450-04921-3 : £7.95 : CIP entry B82-23319

Robbins, Harold. Stiletto. — Large print ed. — Anstey : Ulverscroft, Feb.1983. — 1v.. — (Charnwood library series)
Originally published: United States, 1960 ; London : Mayflower, 1963
ISBN 0-7089-8101-1 : £5.95 : CIP entry B82-38893

Robbins, Harold. A stone for Danny Fisher / Harold Robbins. — Leicester : Charnwood, 1982, c1955. — 550p ; 22cm
Originally published: New York : Knopf, 1952 ; London : Hale, 1955. — Published in large print
ISBN 0-7089-8035-x : Unpriced : CIP rev. B82-08113

Robbins, Tom. Even cowgirls get the blues / Tom Robbins. — [London] : Corgi, 1977, c1976 (1981 [printing]). — 416p ; 18cm
Originally published: Boston, Mass. : Houghton Mifflin, 1976
ISBN 0-552-11827-3 (pbk) : £1.75 B82-03231

Robbins, Tom. Still life with woodpecker / Tom Robbins. — London : Corgi, 1981, c1980. — 264p ; 18cm
Originally published: New York : Bantam ; London : Sidgwick & Jackson, 1980
ISBN 0-552-11781-1 (pbk) : £1.50 B82-04340

Roberts, Nora. Blithe images. — London : Hodder & Stoughton, Aug.1982. — [192]p. — (Silhouette romance)
ISBN 0-340-28636-9 (pbk) : £0.75 : CIP entry B82-15751

Roberts, Nora. Irish thoroughbred. — London : Hodder and Stoughton, Dec.1981. — [192]p. — (Silhouette romance)
ISBN 0-340-27661-4 (pbk) : £0.65 : CIP entry B81-31435

Roberts, Nora. Search for love, — London : Hodder and Stoughton, Feb.1983. — [192]p. — (Silhouette romance)
ISBN 0-340-32761-8 (pbk) : £0.85 : CIP entry B82-38030

Roberts, Nora. Song of the west. — London : Hodder and Stoughton, Nov.1982. — [192]p. — (Silhouette romance)
ISBN 0-340-32688-3 (pbk) : £0.75 : CIP entry B82-28266

Robinson, Marilynne. Housekeeping / Marilynne Robinson. — Harmondsworth : Penguin, 1982, c1981. — 186p ; 20cm. — (A King Penguin)
Originally published: New York : Farrar, Strauss & Giroux, 1980 ; London : Faber, 1981
ISBN 0-14-006062-6 (pbk) : £2.25 B82-32234

Rock, Phillip. Circles of time / Phillip Rock. — London : Hodder and Stoughton, 1982, c1981. — 309p ; 23cm
ISBN 0-340-24658-8 : £7.95 : CIP rev. B82-01839

Roderus, Frank. Cowboy / by Frank Roderus. — London : Hale, 1982. — 184p ; 20cm
ISBN 0-7091-9573-7 : £5.25 B82-15490

Roderus, Frank. Old Kyle's boy / Frank Roderus. — London : Hale, 1981. — 185p ; 20cm
ISBN 0-7091-9364-5 : £4.95 B82-00520

Rodgers, Shirlaw Johnston. Old Baldy's map / by Shirlaw Johnston Rodgers. — London : Hale, 1982. — 155p ; 20cm
ISBN 0-7091-9807-8 : £5.50 B82-35870

Rogers, Rosemary. Dark fires / Rosemary Rogers. — London : Macdonald, 1982, c1975. — 604p ; 21cm
Originally published: New York : Avon, 1975 ; London : Futura, 1977
ISBN 0-356-08644-5 : £7.95 B82-33908

Rogers, Rosemary. Love play / Rosemary Rogers. — London : Sphere, 1982, c1981. — 307p ; 18cm
Originally published: New York : Avon, 1981
ISBN 0-7221-7436-5 (pbk) : £1.75 B82-22599

Rogers, Rosemary. Love play / Rosemary Rogers. — London : Severn House, 1982, c1981. — 307p ; 24cm
Originally published: New York : Aron 1981
ISBN 0-7278-0782-x : £5.95 B82-25982

Rogers, Rosemary. Sweet savage love / Rosemary Rogers. — London : Macdonald, 1982, c1974. — 636p ; 21cm
Originally published: United States : s.n., 1974? ; London : Futura, 1977
ISBN 0-356-08643-7 : £7.95 B82-33906

Rogers, Rosemary. The wildest heart / Rosemary Rogers. — London : Macdonald, 1982, c1976. — 608p ; 21cm
Originally published: United States : s.n., 1976 ; London : Futura, 1977
ISBN 0-356-08645-3 : £7.95 B82-33907

Roosevelt, James. A family matter / James Roosevelt with Sam Toperoff. — London : Severn House, 1982, c1980. — 316p ; 21cm
Originally published: New York : Simon & Schuster, 1980
ISBN 0-7278-0725-0 : £6.95 : CIP rev. B81-18102

Rosenberger, Joseph. The Albanian connection / by Joseph R. Rosenberger. — London : Corgi, 1982, c1973. — 191p ; 18cm. — (Death merchant ; 6)
Originally published: Los Angeles : Pinnacle, 1973
ISBN 0-552-11890-7 (pbk) : £0.95 B82-16741

Rosenberger, Joseph. The Castro file / Joseph Rosenberger. — London : Corgi, 1982, c1974. — 218p ; 18cm
Originally published: S.l. : Pinnacle, 1974
ISBN 0-552-11947-4 (pbk) : £0.95 B82-35250

Rosenberger, Joseph. Satan strike / Joseph Rosenberger. — London : Corgi, 1981. — 188p ; 18cm. — (Death merchant ; 5)
ISBN 0-552-11839-7 (pbk) : £0.95 B82-06472

Ross, Susan. Heart. — London : Severn House, Oct.1982. — [320]p
ISBN 0-7278-0832-x : £6.95 : CIP entry B82-28577

Rossner, Judith. Emmeline. — London : Coronet, July 1981. — [352]p
Originally published: London : Cape, 1980
ISBN 0-340-26785-2 (pbk) : £1.95 : CIP entry B81-13890

Roszak, Theodore. Bugs / by Theodore Roszak. — Wimbledon : Blond & Briggs, 1982. — 352p ; 23cm
ISBN 0-85634-126-6 : £7.50 : CIP rev. B82-06052

Rotsler, William. Grease 2 / a novel by William Rotsler based on the screenplay by Ken Finkleman. — London : Sphere Books, 1982. — 152p,[8]p of plates : ill,ports ; 18cm
ISBN 0-7221-7505-1 (pbk) : £1.25 B82-33896

Rowe, Melanie. Sands of Xanadu. — London : Hodder & Stoughton, Sept.1982. — [192]p. — (Silhouette romance)
ISBN 0-340-32066-4 (pbk) : £0.75 : CIP entry B82-18785

Rubin, Louis D.. Surfaces of a diamond : a novel / by Louis D. Rubin, Jr. — Baton Rouge ; London : Louisiana State University Press, 1981. — 209p ; 24cm
ISBN 0-8071-0897-9 : Unpriced B82-34131

Rucker, Rudolf V. B.. White light / Rudy Rucker. — London : Virgin, c1980. — 128p : 1ill ; 21cm
ISBN 0-907080-01-4 (pbk) : £1.95 B82-22907

Sadler, Geoffrey. Justus: bloodwater / Geoffrey Sadler. — Sevenoaks : New English Library, 1982. — 204p ; 18cm
ISBN 0-450-05440-3 (pbk) : £1.25 : CIP rev. B82-12355

Sadler, Geoffrey. Justus: the lash / Geoffrey Sadler. — London : New English Library, 1982. — 206p ; 18cm
ISBN 0-450-05369-5 (pbk) : £1.25 : CIP rev. B82-03592

Sanders, Lawrence. The tenth commandment : a novel / by Lawrence Sanders. — London : Prior, 1981, c1980. — 678p ; 25cm
Originally published: New York : Putnam, 1980 ; London : Granada, 1981. — Published in large print
ISBN 0-86043-624-1 : £8.95 B82-02939

Sanders, Lawrence. The tenth commandment / Lawrence Sanders. — London : Granada, 1981, c1980 (1982 [printing]). — 443p ; 18cm. — (A Panther book)
Originally published: New York : Putnam, 1980
ISBN 0-586-05030-2 (pbk) : £1.95 B82-36057

Sargent, Lynda. Judith Duchesne / Lynda Sargent. — South Yarmouth, Mass. : Curley ; Long Preston : Magna [distributor], c1979. — 402p ; 23cm
Published in large print
ISBN 0-89340-353-9 : Unpriced B82-08756

813′.54[F] — Fiction in English. American writers, 1945- — Texts *continuation*

Saul, John. Cry for the strangers / John Saul. — [Sevenoaks] : Hodder and Stoughton, 1980, c1979. — 320p ; 18cm. — (Coronet books)
Originally published: New York : Dell, 1979
ISBN 0-340-25548-x (pbk) : £1.50 : CIP rev.
B80-11194

Saul, John. When the wind blows. — London : Hodder and Stoughton, Aug.1982. — [300]p. — (Coronet books)
Originally published: New York : Dell, 1981
ISBN 0-340-28107-3 (pbk) : £1.50 : CIP entry
B82-15734

Sawyer, Lee. Time remembered. — London : Hodder and Stoughton, Jan.1983. — [192]p. — (Silhouette romance)
ISBN 0-340-32724-3 (pbk) : £0.85 : CIP entry
B82-34409

Scarborough, Chuck. The Myrmidon project / Chuck Scarborough and William Murray. — Loughton : Piatkus, c1981. — 311p ; 21cm
ISBN 0-86188-131-1 : £6.95 : CIP rev.
B81-30382

Schiff, Barry. The Vatican target / Barry Schiff and Hal Fishman. — London : Severn House, 1982 c1978. — 273p ; 21cm
Originally published: New York : St Martin′s Press, 1979 ; London : Arrow, 1981
ISBN 0-7278-0608-4 : £6.95 : CIP rev.
B80-12111

Schwartz, Lynne Sharon. Balancing acts / Lynne Sharon Schwartz. — London : Gollancz, 1982. — 155p ; 22cm
ISBN 0-575-03086-0 : £7.95 : CIP rev.
B82-00203

Schwartz, Lynne Sharon. Rough strife / Lynne Sharon Schwartz. — Sth. Yarmouth, [Mass.] : Curley ; [Long Preston] : Distributed in the U.K. by Magna Print, c1980. — 382p ; 22cm
Originally published: New York : Harper & Row, 1980 ; London : Gollancz, 1981. — Published in large print
ISBN 0-89340-389-x : Unpriced B82-36274

Schwartz, Marian. Realities / Marian Schwartz. — Loughton : Piatkus, 1982, c1981. — 337p ; 21cm
Originally published: New York : St Martin′s Press, 1981
ISBN 0-86188-156-7 : £6.95 : CIP rev.
B82-05763

Scofield, Carin. Winterfire. — London : Hodder & Stoughton, July 1982. — [192]p. — (Silhouette romance)
Originally published: New York : Silhouette Books, 1981
ISBN 0-340-28468-4 (pbk) : £0.75 : CIP entry
B82-12314

Scott, Joanna. A flight of swallows. — London : Hodder & Stoughton, Nov.1982. — [256]p. — (Silhouette special edition)
ISBN 0-340-32612-3 (pbk) : £0.95 : CIP entry
B82-28260

Scott, Joanna. Manhattan masquerade. — London : Hodder & Stoughton, June 1982. — [192]p. — (Silhouette romance)
Originally published: New York : Silhouette Books, 1981
ISBN 0-340-27943-5 (pbk) : £0.75 : CIP entry
B82-10465

Scott, Joanna. The marriage bargain / Joanna Scott. — London : Silhouette, 1981. — 189p ; 18cm. — (Silhouette romance ; 68)
ISBN 0-340-27123-x (pbk) : £0.65 : CIP rev.
B81-26775

Scott, Justin. The man who loved the Normandie. — London : Granada, July 1982. — [480]p
ISBN 0-246-11759-1 : £6.95 : CIP entry
B82-12232

Scott, Michael William. The Rakehell dynasty / Michael William Scott. — New York : Warner, 1980 ; [London] : Star [distributor]. — 542p : 1map ; 18cm
ISBN 0-446-95201-x (pbk) : £1.95 B82-02675

Searls, Hank. Firewind / Hank Searls. — London : Sphere, 1982, c1981. — 337p : 1map ; 18cm
ISBN 0-7221-7685-6 (pbk) : £1.75 B82-14910

Sellers, Con. Last flower / Con Sellers. — London : Sphere, 1982, c1980. — 346p ; 18cm
ISBN 0-7221-7701-1 (pbk) : £1.75 B82-27898

Sennett, Richard. The frog who dared to croak. — London : Faber, Oct.1982. — [158]p
ISBN 0-571-11989-1 : £7.95 : CIP entry
B82-28478

Setlowe, Richard. The experiment / Richard Setlowe. — London : Arrow, 1982, c1980. — 299p ; 18cm
Originally published: New York : Holt, Rinehart and Winston, 1980
ISBN 0-09-928690-4 (pbk) : £1.75 B82-33319

Seton, Anya. The turquoise. — Large print ed. — Anstey : Ulverscroft Large Print Books, Dec.1982. — 1v.. — (Ulverscroft large print series)
Originally published: Boston : Houghton Mifflin ; London : Hodder and Stoughton, 1946
ISBN 0-7089-0890-x : £5.00 : CIP entry
B82-30801

Shambaugh, William. Cameron / William Shambaugh. — London : Hale, 1982, c1981. — 186p ; 20cm
Originally published: Garden City, N.Y. : Doubleday, 1981
ISBN 0-7091-9722-5 : £5.25 B82-22124

Shannon, Dell. The motive on record / by Dell Shannon. — London : Gollancz, 1982. — 227p ; 21cm
ISBN 0-575-03080-1 : £6.95 : CIP rev.
B82-09438

Sharp, Helen. Love and Heather / by Helen Sharp. — London : Remploy, 1981, c1969. — 190p ; 20cm
Originally published: London : Hale, 1969
ISBN 0-7066-0914-x : £5.40 B82-22845

Sharp, Marilyn. Masterstroke / Marilyn Sharp. — Feltham : Hamlyn, 1982, c1981. — 283p ; 18cm
Originally published: New York : R. Marek, 1981
ISBN 0-600-20583-5 (pbk) : £1.75 B82-30984

Sharp, Marilyn. Masterstroke / Marilyn Sharp. — London : Severn House, 1982, c1981. — 360p ; 21cm
Originally published: New York : R. Marek, 1981
ISBN 0-7278-0765-x : £6.95 B82-11427

Shaw, Linda. All she ever wanted. — London : Hodder & Stoughton, Feb.1983. — [256]p. — (Silhouette special edition)
ISBN 0-340-32942-4 (pbk) : £0.95 : CIP entry
B82-38268

Shaw, Linda. December′s wine. — London : Hodder and Stoughton, Oct.1982. — [256]p. — (Silhouette special edition)
ISBN 0-340-32605-0 (pbk) : £0.95 : CIP entry
B82-24714

Shea, Robert. Shiké : time of the dragons / Robert Shea. — [London] : Fontana, 1981. — 444p : 2maps ; 18cm
Originally published: New York : Jove, 1981
ISBN 0-00-616447-1 (pbk) : 1.75 B82-03667

Shea, Robert. Shiké : last of the Zinja / Robert Shea. — [London] : Fontana, 1982, c1981. — 448p : 2maps ; 18cm
Originally published: New York : Jove, 1981
ISBN 0-00-616448-x (pbk) : £1.75 B82-13868

Shea, Robert. Shiké : time of the dragons / Robert Shea. — Loughton : Piatkus, 1982, c1981. — 444p : 2maps ; 21cm
Originally published: New York : Jove, 1981 ; London : Fontana, 1981
ISBN 0-86188-130-3 : £7.95 : CIP rev.
B81-30378

Shea, Robert. Shike. — Loughton : Piatkus, June 1982. — [448]p
ISBN 0-86188-164-8 : £7.95 : CIP entry
B82-12924

Sheldon, Mary. Perhaps I′ll dream of darkness / Mary Sheldon. — [London] : Fontana, 1982, c1981. — 178p ; 18cm
Originally published: New York : Random House, 1981
ISBN 0-00-616681-4 (pbk) : £1.35 B82-33557

Sheldon, Sidney. Masters of the game. — London : Collins, Jan.1983. — [496]p
ISBN 0-00-222614-6 : £8.95 : CIP entry
B82-35203

Sheldon, Sidney. The naked face. — Large print ed. — Anstey : Ulverscroft, Nov.1982. — [272] p. — (Charnwood library series)
Originally published: London : Hodder and Stoughton, 1971
ISBN 0-7089-8082-1 : £4.50 : CIP entry
B82-29104

Sheldon, Sidney. The other side of midnight. — Large print ed. — Anstey : Ulverscroft, Jan.1983. — [624]p. — (Charnwood library series)
Originally published: London : Hodder and Stoughton, 1974
ISBN 0-7089-8093-7 : £7.95 : CIP entry
B82-32543

Sheldon, Sidney. A stranger in the mirror. — London : Hodder & Stoughton, Nov.1982. — [288]p
Originally published: 1976
ISBN 0-340-32039-7 : £7.95 : CIP entry
B82-27335

Sherlock, John. J.B.′s daughter / John Sherlock. — London : Star, 1982, c1981. — 350p ; 18cm
Originally published: London : W.H. Allen, 1981
ISBN 0-352-30971-7 (pbk) : £1.95 B82-16098

Sherlock, John, *1932-*. The most dangerous gamble. — London : Granada, Aug.1982. — [256]p
ISBN 0-246-11561-0 : £7.95 : CIP entry
B82-15707

Sherman, Dan. Dynasty of spies / by Dan Sherman. — London : Gollancz, 1982. — 301p ; 21cm
ISBN 0-575-03055-0 : £7.50 : CIP rev.
B82-01147

Sherman, Jory. The bamboo demons / Jory Sherman. — London : New English Library, 1981, c1979. — 182p ; 18cm
Originally published: Los Angeles : Pinnacle, 1979
ISBN 0-450-05270-2 (pbk) : £1.25
ISBN 0-450-04560-9 B82-01511

Sherman, Jory. The fugitive gun / Jory Sherman. — London : Hale, 1982, c1980. — 175p ; 20cm
ISBN 0-7091-9528-1 : £4.95 B82-11072

Sherman, Jory. [Vegas vampire]. Vampire / Jory Sherman. — London : New English Library, 1981, c1980. — 176p ; 18cm
Originally published: as ′Vegas vampire′, Los Angeles : Pinnacle Books, 1980
ISBN 0-450-05284-2 (pbk) : £1.25 B82-08652

Shobin, David. The unborn / David Shobin. — London : Pan in association with Heinemann, 1981, c1980. — 238p ; 18cm
Originally published: London : Heinemann, 1981
ISBN 0-330-26571-7 (pbk) : £1.50 B82-09947

813'.54[F] — Fiction in English. American writers, *1945- — Texts* *continuation*

Shyer, Marlene Fanta. Welcome home, Jellybean / Marlene Fanta Shyer. — London : Granada, 1981, c1978 (1982 [printing]). — 128p ; 18cm. — (A Dragon book)
Originally published: New York : Scribner, 1978
ISBN 0-583-30485-0 (pbk) : £0.85 B82-36056

Silverberg, Robert. [The anvil of time]. Hawksbill station / Robert Silverberg. — London : W.H. Allen, 1982, c1968. — 192p ; 18cm. — (A Star book)
Originally published: London : Sidgwick and Jackson, 1969
ISBN 0-352-31090-1 (pbk) : £1.50 B82-22068

Silverberg, Robert. Lord Valentine's castle / Robert Silverberg. — London : Pan, 1981, c1980. — 505p : ill,maps ; 18cm
Originally published: London : Gollancz, 1980
ISBN 0-330-26462-1 (pbk) : £1.95 B82-00783

Silverberg, Robert. Majipoor chronicles : a novel / by Robert Silverberg. — London : Gollancz, 1982. — 314p : maps ; 23cm
ISBN 0-575-03153-0 : £8.95 : CIP rev.
B82-19564

Silverberg, Robert. The man in the maze / Robert Silverberg. — London : Star, 1971, c1969 (1982 [printing]). — 192p ; 18cm
Originally published: London : Sidgwick & Jackson, 1969
ISBN 0-352-31089-8 (pbk) : £1.50 B82-16100

Silverberg, Robert. [Vornan-19]. The masks of time / Robert Silverberg. — London : W.H. Allen, 1982, c1968. — 252p ; 18cm
Originally published: London : Sidgwick & Jackson, 1968
ISBN 0-352-31091-x (pbk) : £1.50 B82-22067

Simms, Suzanne. Moment in time. — London : Hodder & Stoughton, Feb.1983. — [192]p. — (Silhouette desire)
ISBN 0-340-32920-3 (pbk) : £0.95 : CIP entry
B82-38035

Simon, Roger L.. Peking duck / Roger L. Simon. — London : Methuen, 1982, c1979. — 255p ; 18cm
Originally published: London : Deutsch, 1979
ISBN 0-417-05670-2 (pbk) : £1.50 B82-34367

Simpson, Dorothy. The night she died. — Large print ed. — Anstey : Ulverscroft, Jan.1983. — [352]p. — (Ulverscroft large print series)
Originally published: London : Joseph, 1980
ISBN 0-7089-0909-4 : £6.25 : CIP entry
B82-32537

Sinclair, Tracy. Holiday in Jamaica. — London : Hodder & Stoughton, July 1982. — [192]p. — (Silhouette romance)
Originally published: New York : Silhouette Books, 1981
ISBN 0-340-28469-2 (pbk) : £0.75 : CIP entry
B82-12315

Sinclair, Tracy. Mixed blessings. — London : Hodder and Stoughton, Dec.1982. — [192]p. — (Silhouette special edition)
ISBN 0-340-32681-6 (pbk) : £0.95 : CIP entry
B82-29661

Sinclair, Tracy. Never give your heart. — London : Hodder & Stoughton, Dec.1982. — [256]p. — (Silhouette special edition)
ISBN 0-340-32078-8 (pbk) : £0.95 : CIP entry
B82-31289

Slade, E. R.. Jornado / E.R. Slade. — London : Hale, 1981, c1979. — 174p ; 20cm
Originally published: New York : Manor, 1979
ISBN 0-7091-9395-5 : £4.95 B82-03171

Sladek, John. Roderick, or, The education of a young machine / John Sladek. — London : Granada, 1980 (1982 [printing]). — 347p ; 18cm. — (A Panther book)
ISBN 0-586-04539-2 (pbk) : £1.95 B82-17355

Slaughter, Frank G.. Plague ship. — Large print ed. — Anstey : Ulverscroft, Dec.1982. — 1v.. — (Ulverscroft large print series)
Originally published: Garden City, N.Y. : Doubleday, 1976 ; London : Arrow, 1979
ISBN 0-7089-0895-0 : £5.00 : CIP entry
B82-30784

Smith, Alana. Whenever I love you. — London : Hodder & Stoughton, Feb.1983. — [192]p. — (Silhouette desire)
ISBN 0-340-32921-1 (pbk) : £0.95 : CIP entry
B82-38265

Smith, Dave. Onliness : a novel / by Dave Smith. — Baton Rouge ; London : Louisiana State University Press, 1981. — 262p : 1map ; 24cm
ISBN 0-8071-0871-5 : £9.05 B82-06556

Smith, David, *1936 Sept.19-*. The Leo conversion / David Smith. — South Yarmouth, Mass. : John Curley, c1980 ; [Long Preston] : Magna [distributor]. — 575p ; 23cm
Originally published: New York : Dodd, Mead, c1980. — Published in large print
ISBN 0-89340-337-7 : Unpriced B82-01043

Smith, David, *1936 Sept.19-*. The Leo conversion / by David Smith. — London : Hale, 1982, c1980. — 280p : 1map ; 23cm
Originally published: New York : Dodd, Mead, 1980
ISBN 0-7091-9748-9 : £7.25 B82-25998

Smith, Joan, *1938-*. An affair of the heart / Joan Smith. — South Yarmouth, Mass. : Curley ; [Skipton] : Magna Print [distributor], 1978, c1977. — 456p ; 22cm. — (A Regency romance)
Originally published: Greenwich, Conn. : Fawcett Books, 1977. — Published in large print
ISBN 0-89340-155-2 : Unpriced B82-17044

Smith, Joan, *1938-*. Aunt Sophie's diamonds / Joan Smith. — South Yarmouth, Mass. : Curley ; [Skipton] : Magna Print [distributor], 1978, c1977. — 485p ; 22cm. — (A Regency romance)
Originally published: Greenwich, Conn. : Fawcett Books, 1977. — Published in large print
ISBN 0-89340-156-0 : Unpriced B82-17046

Smith, Joan, *1938-*. Escapade / Joan Smith. — South Yarmouth, Mass. : Curley ; [Skipton] : Magna Print [distributor], 1978, c1977. — 466p ; 22cm. — (A Regency romance)
Originally published: Greenwich, Conn. : Fawcett Books, 1977. — Published in large print
ISBN 0-89340-154-4 : Unpriced B82-17045

Smith, Joan, *1938-*. Imprudent lady / Joan Smith. — South Yarmouth, Mass. : Curley ; [Long Preston] : Magna [distributor], c1978. — 450p ; 23cm. — (A Regency romance)
Published in large print
ISBN 0-89340-205-2 : £5.25 B82-04556

Smith, Joan, *1938-*. Lace for milady / Joan Smith. — London : Prior, 1981, c1979. — 364p ; 25cm
Originally published: New York : Walker, 1980. — Published in large print
ISBN 0-86043-605-5 : £6.95 B82-02940

Smith, Martin Cruz-. The analog bullet / Martin Cruz-Smith. — London : Severn House, 1982, c1977
ISBN 0-7278-0789-7 : £6.95 B82-30468

Smith, Martin Cruz. Canto for a gypsy. — London : Collins, Sept.1982. — [190]p
ISBN 0-00-231693-5 : £6.50 : CIP entry
B82-20352

Smith, Martin Cruz. Gorky Park / Martin Cruz Smith. — London : Prior, 1981. — 639p ; 25cm
Originally published: New York : Random House ; London : Collins, 1981. — Published in large print
ISBN 0-86043-677-2 : Unpriced B82-28387

Smith, Martin Cruz. Gypsy in amber. — London : Collins, Sept.1982. — [190]p
ISBN 0-00-231692-7 : £6.50 : CIP entry
B82-19074

Smith, Martin Cruz. The Indians won. — London : Severn House, Aug.1982. — [224]p
ISBN 0-7278-0809-5 : £6.95 : CIP entry
B82-21104

Smith, Mason McCann. When the emperor dies / Mason McCann Smith. — London : Hamilton, 1982, c1981. — 393p : maps ; 24cm
Originally published: New York : Random House, 1981
ISBN 0-241-10697-4 : £7.95 : CIP rev.
B81-34319

Smith, Robert Kimmel. Jane's house. — London : Collins, Nov.1982. — [352]p
ISBN 0-00-222671-5 : £7.95 : CIP entry
B82-28716

Sorrentino, Gilbert. Crystal vision : a novel / Gilbert Sorrentino. — London : Boyars, 1982. — 289p ; 23cm
ISBN 0-7145-2759-9 : £7.95 : CIP rev.
B82-05409

South, Barbara. Wayward lover. — London : Hodder & Stoughton, May 1982. — [192]p. — (Silhouette romance)
Originally published: New York : Silhouette Books, 1981
ISBN 0-340-27937-0 (pbk) : £0.75 : CIP entry
B82-07948

Sparkia, Roy. Amazon / Roy Sparkia. — Toronto ; London : Bantam, 1981. — 362p ; 18cm
ISBN 0-553-13808-1 (pbk) : £1.50 B82-19384

Spence, Michele. Shadow play / Michele Spence. — London : Sphere, 1982, c1981. — 320p ; 18cm
ISBN 0-7221-8065-9 (pbk) : £1.75 B82-22593

Spike, Paul. Last rites. — St Albans : Granada, Mar.1982. — [288]p
Originally published: New York : American Library, 1981
ISBN 0-246-11771-0 : £7.95 : CIP entry
B82-01150

Spillane, Mickey. Kiss me deadly. — London : New English Library, Nov.1982. — [160]p
Originally published: New York : Dutton, 1952 ; London : Barker, 1953
ISBN 0-450-05544-2 (pbk) : £1.50 : CIP entry
B82-27519

Spillane, Mickey. My gun is quick. — London : New English Library, Jan.1983. — [176]p
ISBN 0-450-05553-1 (pbk) : £1.50 : CIP entry
B82-36144

Spillane, Mickey. Vengeance is mine. — London : New English Library, Nov.1982. — [160]p
Originally published: New York : Dutten, 1950
ISBN 0-450-05527-2 (pbk) : £1.50 : CIP entry
B82-27513

Spinrad, Norman. Songs from the stars / Norman Spinrad. — London : Arrow, 1982, 1980. — 275p ; 18cm
Originally published: New York : Simon and Schuster, 1980
ISBN 0-09-928070-1 (pbk) : £1.60 B82-30458

St Clair, Leonard. Obsessions / Leonard St Clair. — London : Pan, 1981, c1980. — 285p ; 18cm
ISBN 0-330-26531-8 (pbk) : £1.50 B82-00782

St. Claire, Erin. Not even for love. — London : Hodder and Stoughton, Feb.1983. — [192]p. — (Silhouette desire)
ISBN 0-340-32918-1 (pbk) : £0.95 : CIP entry
B82-38023

813'.54[F] — Fiction in English. American writers, *1945- — Texts* *continuation*

St. George, Edith. Dream once more. — London : Hodder & Stoughton, Aug.1982. — [192]p. — (Silhouette romance)
ISBN 0-340-28635-0 (pbk) : £0.75 : CIP entry B82-15750

St. George, Edith. Midnight wine. — London : Hodder and Stoughton, Mar.1982. — [192]p. — (Silhouette romance)
ISBN 0-340-27983-4 (pbk) : £0.75 : CIP entry B82-00260

Stallman, Robert. The orphan : the first book of the Beast / Robert Stallman. — London : Granada, 1981, c1980. — 251p ; 18cm. — (A Mayflower book)
Originally published: New York : Pocket Books, 1980
ISBN 0-583-13475-0 (pbk) : £1.50 B82-03001

Standish, Buck. The line riders / by Buck Standish. — London : Hale, 1982. — 160p ; 20cm
ISBN 0-7091-9930-9 : £5.50 B82-35873

Stanford, Sandra. And then came dawn. — London : Hodder and Stoughton, Feb.1982. — [192]p. — (Silhouette romance)
ISBN 0-340-27668-1 (pbk) : £0.75 : CIP entry B81-38312

Stanford, Sandra. Yesterday's shadow. — London : Hodder and Stoughton, Apr.1982. — [192]p. — (Silhouette romance)
ISBN 0-340-27926-5 (pbk) : £0.75 : CIP entry B82-03824

Stanford, Sondra. Magnolia moon. — London : Hodder & Stoughton, Jan.1983. — [256]p. — (Silhouette special edition)
ISBN 0-340-32936-x (pbk) : £0.95 : CIP entry B82-34415

Stanford, Sondra. Silver mist. — London : Hodder & Stoughton, Dec.1982. — [256]p. — (Silhouette special edition)
ISBN 0-340-32076-1 (pbk) : £0.95 : CIP entry B82-29652

Stanford, Sondra. Tarnished vows. — London : Hodder & Stoughton, Sept.1982. — [192]p. — (Silhouette romance)
ISBN 0-340-32064-8 (pbk) : £0.75 : CIP entry B82-18783

Stanford, Sondra. Whisper wind. — London : Hodder & Stoughton, June 1982. — [192]p. — (Silhouette romance)
Originally published: New York : Silhouette Books, 1981
ISBN 0-340-27938-9 (pbk) : £0.75 : CIP entry B82-10018

Stanwood, Brooks. The seventh child / Brooks Stanwood. — London : Macdonald, 1982. — 316p ; 23cm
ISBN 0-356-07907-4 : £7.95 B82-35436

Stashelf, Christopher. A wizard in bedlam / Christopher Stashelf. — London : Granada, 1982, c1979. — 224p ; 18cm. — (A Mayflower book)
Originally published: Garden City, N.Y. : Doubleday, 1979
ISBN 0-583-13425-4 (pbk) : £1.25 B82-17360

Steel, Danielle. Crossings. — London : Hodder & Stoughton, Feb.1983. — [400]p
ISBN 0-340-33246-8 : £7.95 : CIP entry B82-38271

Steel, Danielle. Golden moments / Danielle Steel. — Loughton : Judy Piatkus, 1981. — 380p ; 21cm
ISBN 0-86188-085-4 : £6.95 : CIP rev. B81-31636

Steel, Danielle. Loving / Danielle Steel. — Leicester : Charnwood, 1982, c1980. — 415p ; 23cm. — (Charnwood library series)
Originally published: London : Sphere, 1980. — Published in large print
ISBN 0-7089-8053-8 : Unpriced : CIP rev. B82-15952

Steel, Danielle. Palomino / Danielle Steel. — London : Prior, 1981. — 518p ; 25cm
Originally published: New York : Dell, 1981. — Published in large print
ISBN 0-86043-670-5 : £8.50 B82-16190

Steel, Danielle. Palomino / Danielle Steel. — London : Sphere Books, 1982, c1981. — 323p ; 18cm
Originally published: Boston, Mass. : G.K. Hall, 1981
ISBN 0-7221-8177-9 (pbk) : £1.75 B82-33895

Steel, Danielle. Palomino / Danielle Steel. — Loughton : Piatkus, 1982. — 323p ; 21cm
ISBN 0-86188-180-x : £7.50 : CIP rev. B82-10248

Steel, Danielle. A perfect stranger / Danielle Steel. — London : Sphere Books, 1982, c1981. — 278p ; 20cm
ISBN 0-7221-8178-7 (pbk) : £3.50 B82-33897

Steel, Danielle. A perfect stranger. — Loughton : Piatkus, July 1982. — [288]p
ISBN 0-86188-184-2 : £6.95 : CIP entry B82-13167

Steel, Danielle. The promise / Danielle Steel ; based on a screenplay by Garry Michael White. — Leicester : Ulverscroft, 1982, c1978. — 364p ; 23cm. — (Ulverscroft large print series)
Originally published: London : Sphere, 1978
ISBN 0-7089-0762-8 : Unpriced : CIP rev. B82-01746

Steel, Danielle. Remembrance / Danielle Steel. — London : Hodder and Stoughton, 1982, c1981. — 469p ; 23cm
Originally published: New York : Delacorte Press, 1981
ISBN 0-340-27837-4 : £6.95 : CIP rev. B82-03816

Steel, Danielle. Remembrance. — Large print ed. — Anstey : Ulverscroft, Jan.1983. — [720]p. — (Charnwood library series)
ISBN 0-7089-8094-5 : £7.95 : CIP entry B82-32544

Steel, Danielle. The ring / Danielle Steel. — London : Sphere, 1981, c1980. — 344p ; 18cm
Originally published: London : Hodder & Stoughton, 1981
ISBN 0-7221-8179-5 (pbk) : £1.75 B82-09392

Steel, Danielle. The ring. — Large print ed. — Anstey : Ulverscroft, Oct.1982. — [512]p. — (Charnwood library series)
Originally published: London : Hodder and Stoughton, 1981
ISBN 0-7089-8077-5 : £5.25 : CIP entry B82-26693

Steel, Danielle. Season of passion / Danielle Steel. — Leicester : Charnwood, 1982, c1979. — 492p ; 22cm. — (Charnwood library series)
Originally published: London : Sphere, 1979. — Published in large print
ISBN 0-7089-8041-4 : Unpriced : CIP rev. B82-08101

Steel, Danielle. To love again. — Large print ed. — Anstey : Ulverscroft, Sept.1982. — [352]p. — (Charnwood library series)
Originally published: Loughton : Piatkus, 1980
ISBN 0-7089-8071-6 : £5.25 : CIP entry B82-27008

Steinberg, S.. A fairy tale : a novel / by S. Steinberg. — London : W.H. Allen, 1980 (1981 [printing]). — 184p ; 18cm. — (A Star book)
ISBN 0-352-30973-3 (pbk) : £1.60 B82-06479

Stephan, Leslie. Murder R.F.D. / Leslie Stephan. — South Yarmouth, Mass. : Curley ; [Skipton] : Magna Print [distributor], 1979, c1978. — 408p ; 22cm
Originally published: New York : Scribner, 1978. — Published in large print
ISBN 0-89340-183-8 : Unpriced B82-17037

Stephens, Jeanne. Bride in Barbados. — London : Hodder and Stoughton, Nov.1982. — [256]p. — (Silhouette special edition)
ISBN 0-340-32616-6 (pbk) : £0.95 : CIP entry B82-28264

Stephens, Jeanne. Pride's possession. — London : Hodder & Stoughton, Feb.1983. — [256]p. — (Silhouette special edition)
ISBN 0-340-32946-7 (pbk) : £0.95 : CIP entry B82-38270

Stephens, Jeanne. Wonder and desire. — London : Hodder and Stoughton, Dec.1981. — [192]p. — (Silhouette romance)
ISBN 0-340-27660-6 (pbk) : £0.65 : CIP entry B81-31439

Stephens, Reed. The man who killed his brother / Reed Stephens. — [London] : Fontana, 1982, c1980. — 192p ; 18cm
Originally published: New York : Ballantine, 1980
ISBN 0-00-616355-6 (pbk) : £1.50 B82-33556

Stewart, Edward. For richer, for poorer / Edward Stewart. — London : Gollancz, 1982, c1981. — 492p ; 22cm
Originally published: New York : Doubleday, 1981
ISBN 0-575-03115-8 : £7.95 : CIP rev. B82-06936

Stockwell, John, *1937-*. Red sunset / John Stockwell. — London : Gollancz, 1982. — 360p ; 23cm
ISBN 0-575-03126-3 : £8.50 : CIP rev. B82-07670

Stone, Robert, *19---*. A flag for sunrise / Robert Stone. — London : Secker & Warburg, 1981. — 403p ; 23cm
ISBN 0-436-49681-x : £6.95 : CIP rev. B81-28003

Stovall, Walter. Presidential emergency. — London : Coronet, Dec.1982. — [272]p
Originally published: 1978
ISBN 0-340-28649-0 (pbk) : £1.25 : CIP entry B82-29645

Straub, Peter. Shadowland / Peter Straub. — London : Fontana, 1982, c1980. — 445p ; 18cm
Originally published: New York : Coward, McCann & Geoghegan, 1980 ; London : Collins, 1981
ISBN 0-00-616546-x (pbk) : £1.95 B82-25444

Strieber, Whitley. The wolfen / Whitley Strieber. — [Sevenoaks] : Hodder and Stoughton, 1978 (1979 [printing]). — 252p ; 18cm. — (Coronet books)
Originally published: New York : Morrow ; London : Hodder and Stoughton, 1978
ISBN 0-340-24167-5 (pbk) : £0.85 : CIP rev. B79-08266

Susans, Wendy. Duet / Wendy Susans. — London : W.H. Allen, 1981. — 381p ; 18cm. — (A Star book)
ISBN 0-352-30939-3 (pbk) : £1.75 B82-34176

Sutton, Stack. End of the tracks / by Stack Sutton. — London : Hale, 1982, c1981. — 183p ; 20cm
Originally published: Garden City, N.Y. : Doubleday, 1981
ISBN 0-7091-9723-3 : £5.25 B82-22126

Swerdlow, Joel. Code Z / Joel Swerdlow. — London : Sphere, 1981, c1979. — 244p ; 18cm
Originally published: New York : Putnam, 1978 ; London : Secker and Warburg, 1979
ISBN 0-7221-8312-7 (pbk) : £1.50 B82-07183

813'.54[F] — Fiction in English. American writers, *1945- — Texts* *continuation*

Szulc, Tad. Diplomatic immunity : a novel / by Tad Szulc. — London : Heinemann, 1982, c1981. — 405p ; 22cm
Originally published: New York : Simon and Schuster, 1981
ISBN 0-434-75350-5 : £7.50 B82-22097

Tanous, Peter. The Earthart mission / Peter Tanous. — London : Arrow, 1982, c1978. — 223p ; 18cm
Originally published: New York : Simon and Schuster, 1979 ; London : Deutsch, 1980
ISBN 0-09-921470-9 (pbk) : £1.50 B82-14915

Taylor, Day. The black swan / Day Taylor. — London : Macdonald Futura, 1979, c1978 (1981 [printing]). — 765p ; 18cm. — (A Troubadour spectacular)
ISBN 0-7088-1534-0 (pbk) : £1.95 B82-10550

Taylor, Joan, *1945-*. Asking for it / Joan Taylor. — London : Sphere, 1981, c1980. — 212p ; 18cm
Originally published: New York : Congdon & Lattes, 1980
ISBN 0-7221-8391-7 (pbk) : £1.25 B82-07185

Taylor, Joan, *1945-*. Asking for it / by Joan Taylor. — London : Severn House, 1982, c1980. — 212p ; 21cm
Originally published: New York : Congdon & Lattes, 1980
ISBN 0-7278-0756-0 : £5.95 B82-12073

Taylor, Mildred D.. Let the circle be unbroken / Mildred D. Taylor. — London : Gollancz, 1982, c1981. — 394p ; 22cm
Originally published: New York : Dial, 1981
ISBN 0-575-03084-4 : £6.50 B82-10544

Taylor, Peter, *19---*. Vengeance in his guns / by Peter Taylor. — London : Hale, 1982. — 140p ; 20cm
ISBN 0-7091-9643-1 : £5.25 B82-17471

Taylor, Sheila Ortiz. Fault line. — London : Women's Press, Oct.1982. — [144]p
ISBN 0-7043-3900-5 (pbk) : £2.50 : CIP entry B82-23215

Teed, Jack Hamilton. Fire-force / Jack Hamilton Teed. — London : Star, 1982. — 192p ; 18cm
ISBN 0-352-31154-1 (pbk) : £1.75 B82-38406

Tennenbaum, Silvia. Yesterday's streets / Silvia Tennenbaum. — London : Gollancz, 1981. — 528p : 1geneal.table ; 25cm
ISBN 0-575-03056-9 : £8.95 B82-16896

Terman, Douglas. Free flight / Douglas Terman. — London : Futura, 1981, c1980 (1982 [printing]). — 352p ; 18cm
Originally published: New York : Scribner, 1980 ; London : Macdonald, 1981
ISBN 0-7088-2061-1 (pbk) : £1.75 B82-30778

Tesich, Steve. Summer crossing. — London : Chatto & Windus, Feb.1983. — [368]p
ISBN 0-7011-2689-2 : £7.95 : CIP entry B82-38869

Tessier, Thomas. Shock waves / Thomas Tessier. — [London] : Fontana, 1982. — 222p ; 18cm. — (Nightshades)
ISBN 0-00-616211-8 (pbk) : £1.00 B82-18091

Thayer, James Stewart. The Earhart betrayal / James Stewart Thayer. — Feltham : Hamlyn, 1981, c1980. — 324p ; 18cm
Originally published: New York : Putnam, 1980
ISBN 0-600-20452-9 (pbk) : £1.50 B82-16818

Thayer, Nancy. Three women at the waters' edge / Nancy Thayer. — London : Hodder and Stoughton, 1982, c1981. — 370p ; 23cm
Originally published: New York : Doubleday, 1981
ISBN 0-340-27819-6 : £6.95 : CIP rev. B82-00245

Theroux, Paul. Jungle lovers / Paul Theroux. — Harmondsworth : Penguin, 1982, c1971. — 281p ; 19cm
Originally published: London : Bodley Head, 1971
ISBN 0-14-005496-0 (pbk) : £1.75 B82-32579

Theroux, Paul. The mosquito coast. — Large print ed. — Anstey : Ulverscroft, Aug.1982. — [592]p. — (Charnwood library series)
Originally published: London : Hamilton, 1981
ISBN 0-7089-8064-3 : £6.50 : CIP entry B82-26993

Theroux, Paul. World's end : and other stories / Paul Theroux. — Harmondsworth : Penguin, 1982, c1980. — 211p ; 18cm
Originally published: London : Hamilton, 1980
ISBN 0-14-005793-5 (pbk) : £1.50 B82-32578

Thiels, Kathryn. Texas rose. — London : Hodder & Stoughton, Dec.1982. — [256]p. — (Silhouette special edition)
ISBN 0-340-32077-x (pbk) : £0.95 : CIP entry B82-29653

Thomas, Bruce, *1916-*. Blue sage country / by Bruce Thomas. — London : Hale, 1982. — 160p ; 20cm
ISBN 0-7091-9960-0 : £5.50 B82-39203

Thomas, Michael M.. Someone else's money / Michael M. Thomas. — London : Hutchinson, 1982. — 501p ; 24cm
Originally published: New York : Wyndham Books, 1982
ISBN 0-09-147620-8 : £8.95 : CIP rev. B82-10608

Thomas, Ross. Cast a yellow shadow / Ross Thomas. — London : Methuen London, 1982, c1967. — 256p ; 18cm. — (A Methuen paperback)
Originally published: New York : Morrow, 1967 ; London : Hodder & Stoughton, 1968
ISBN 0-417-05260-x (pbk) : £1.50 B82-34013

Thompson, Buck. The warbonnet / by Buck Thompson. — London : Hale, 1982. — 156p ; 19cm
ISBN 0-7091-9724-1 : £5.25 B82-27315

Thompson, Raymond, *1949-*. The number to call is — / Raymond Thompson and Treve Daly. — [London] : Corgi, 1980, c1979. — 319p ; 18cm
Originally published: London : Souvenir, 1979
ISBN 0-552-11524-x (pbk) : £1.50 B82-15578

Thompson, Russ. The night-riders. — Large print ed. — Long Preston : Magna, Feb.1983. — [288]p
Originally published: London : Hale, 1964
ISBN 0-86009-504-5 : £5.75 : CIP entry B82-39617

Thompson, Russ. Range law / Russ Thompson. — Large print ed. — Bath : Chivers, 1982. — 176p ; 23cm. — (A Lythway book)
Originally published: London : Hale, 1976
ISBN 0-85119-828-7 : Unpriced : CIP rev. B82-13101

Thompson, Steven L.. Countdown to China. — London : New English Library, Jan.1983. — [304]p
ISBN 0-450-05547-7 (pbk) : £1.75 : CIP entry B82-36143

Thompson, Thomas, *1933-*. Celebrity / Thomas Thompson. — London : Lane, 1982. — 561p ; 24cm
ISBN 0-7139-1485-8 : £7.95 B82-32972

Thorne, Sabina. Reruns / Sabina Thorne. — Feltham : Hamlyn, 1982, c1981. — 203p ; 18cm
Originally published: New York : Viking, 1981
ISBN 0-600-20581-9 (pbk) : £1.35 B82-27052

Thornton, Carolyn. Love is surrender. — London : Hodder & Stougton, Dec.1982. — [256]p. — (Silhouette special edition)
ISBN 0-340-32081-8 (pbk) : £0.95 : CIP entry B82-29656

Tilford, Van W.. Treasure trail / Van W. Tilford. — Large print ed. — Bath : Chivers, 1982, c1981. — 227p ; 23cm. — (Atlantic large print) (A Gunsmoke large print Western)
ISBN 0-85119-469-9 : Unpriced : CIP rev. B82-07622

Tilley, Patrick. Mission / Patrick Tilley. — London : Joseph, 1981. — 398p ; 22cm
Originally published: Boston, Mass. : Little, Brown, 1981
ISBN 0-7181-1997-5 (cased) : £7.95
ISBN 0-7181-2094-9 (pbk) : £4.95 B82-03026

Tine, Robert. State of grace. — London : Collins, Dec.1982. — [250]p. — (The Crime Club)
Originally published: New York : Viking Press, 1980
ISBN 0-00-231926-8 : £6.75 : CIP entry B82-29859

Tourney, Leonard. The player's boy is dead / Leonard Tourney. — London : Hale, 1982, c1980. — 192p ; 19cm
ISBN 0-7091-9696-2 : £6.75 B82-22123

Tracy, Susan. Yesterday's bride. — London : Hodder and Stoughton, Jan.1983. — [192]p. — (Silhouette romance)
ISBN 0-340-32727-8 (pbk) : £0.85 : CIP entry B82-34412

Travis, Tristan. Lamia. — London : Deutsch, Feb.1983. — [448]p
Originally published: New York : Dutton, 1981
ISBN 0-233-97508-x : £7.95 : CIP entry B82-37848

Trent, Brenda. Run from heartache. — London : Hodder and Stoughton, Feb.1983. — [192]p. — (Silhouette romance)
ISBN 0-340-32759-6 (pbk) : £0.85 : CIP entry B82-38028

Trent, Brenda. A stranger's wife. — London : Hodder & Stoughton, May 1982. — [192]p. — (Silhouette romance)
Originally published: New York : Silhouette Books, 1981
ISBN 0-340-27936-2 (pbk) : £0.75 : CIP entry B82-07947

Trent, Brenda. Winter dreams / Brenda Trent. — [Sevenoaks] : Silhouette Books, 1981. — 189p ; 17cm. — (Silhouette romance ; 74)
ISBN 0-340-27262-7 (pbk) : £0.65 : CIP rev. B81-30141

Trevanian. Shibumi / Trevanian. — Leicester : Charnwood, 1981, c1979. — 618p ; 23cm. — (Charnwood library series)
Originally published: London : Granada, 1979. — Published in large print
ISBN 0-7089-8004-x : £6.50 : CIP rev. B81-22656

Trevanian. The loo sanction. — Large print ed. — Anstey : Ulverscroft, Jan.1983. — [400]p. — (Charnwood library series)
Originally published: London : Heinemann, 1974
ISBN 0-7089-8095-3 : £6.25 : CIP entry B82-32545

Trott, Susan. When your lover leaves — / Susan Trott. — Feltham : Hamlyn, 1982, c1980. — 215p ; 18cm
Originally published: New York : St. Martin's Press, 1980 ; London : Gollancz, 1981
ISBN 0-600-20577-0 (pbk) : £1.50 B82-28553

Truman, Margaret. Murder in the White House / Margaret Truman. — London : Sphere, 1982, c1980. — 252p ; 18cm
Originally published: Boston, Mass. : G.K. Hall, 1980
ISBN 0-7221-8617-7 (pbk) : £1.50 B82-27890

813′.54[F] — Fiction in English. American writers, *1945- — Texts* *continuation*

Truman, Margaret. Murder on Capitol Hill / Margaret Truman. — London : Sphere, 1982, c1981. — 244p ; 18cm
Originally published: New York : Arbor House, 1981
ISBN 0-7221-8627-4 (pbk) : £1.75 B82-37340

Tyler, Anne. Dinner at the Homesick Restaurant. — London : Chatto & Windus, Sept.1982. — [320]p
ISBN 0-7011-2648-5 : £7.50 : CIP entry
B82-20304

Tyler, W. T.. The ants of god / W.T. Tyler. — London : Collins, 1982, c1981. — 320p ; 22cm
Originally published: New York : Dial, 1981
ISBN 0-00-222074-1 : £7.95 B82-12665

Tyler, W. T.. The man who lost the war / W.T. Tyler. — London : Fontana, 1981, c1980. — 347p ; 18cm
Originally published: Collins, 1980
ISBN 0-00-616085-9 (corrected : pbk) : £1.50
B82-04271

Uhnak, Dorothy. False witness / Dorothy Uhnak. — London : Hutchinson, 1982, c1981. — 314p ; 22cm
Originally published: New York : Simon & Schuster, 1981
ISBN 0-09-147120-6 : £6.95 : CIP rev.
B82-00271

Uhnak, Dorothy. The ledger / Dorothy Uhnak. — South Yarmouth : Curley ; Long Preston : Distributed by Magna, [1981?], c1970. — 469p ; 23cm
Originally published: New York : Simon & Schuster, 1970 ; London : Hodder & Stoughton, 1971. — Published in large print
ISBN 0-89340-338-5 : Unpriced B82-04659

Updike, John. Rabbit is rich / John Updike. — London : Deutsch, 1982, c1981. — 467p ; 24cm
Originally published: New York : Knopf, 1981
ISBN 0-233-97424-5 : £7.95 B82-09944

Valin, Jonathan. Dead letter : a Harry Stoner novel / Jonathan Valin. — London : Collins, 1982, c1981. — 224p ; 21cm. — (The Crime Club)
Originally published: New York : Dodd, Mead, 1981
ISBN 0-00-231328-6 : £6.75 : CIP rev.
B82-15620

Valin, Jonathan. Final notice / Jonathan Valin. — South Yarmouth, Mass. : Curley ; [Long Preston] : Magna [distributor], c1980. — 415p ; 23cm
Published in large print
ISBN 0-89340-354-7 : Unpriced B82-08755

Valin, Jonathan. Final notice / Jonathan Valin. — London : Collins, 1981, c1980. — 212p ; 21cm. — (The Crime Club)
Originally published: New York : Dodd, Mead, 1980
ISBN 0-00-231293-x : £6.25 : CIP rev.
B81-25139

Van Hazinga, Cynthia. White columns / Cynthia van Hazinga. — London : Sphere, 1982, c1980. — 302p ; 18cm
ISBN 0-7221-4490-3 (pbk) : £1.95 B82-18172

Van Lustbader, Eric. Sirens / Eric van Lustbader. — London : Granada, 1982, c1981. — 592p ; 18cm. — (A Panther book)
Originally published: New York : M. Evans, 1981
ISBN 0-586-05536-3 (pbk) : £1.95 B82-37208

Van Slyke, Helen. Best place to be. — London : New English Library, June 1982. — [360]p
ISBN 0-450-04909-4 : £7.95 : CIP entry
B82-20758

Van Slyke, Helen. No love lost / Helen Van Slyke. — Leicester : Charnwood, 1982, c1980. — 676p ; 23cm. — (Charnwood library series)
Originally published: London : Heinemann, 1980. — Published in large print
ISBN 0-7089-8046-5 : Unpriced : CIP rev.
B82-15945

Van Slyke, Helen. The Santa Ana wind. — London : Severn House, Sept.1982. — [224]p
ISBN 0-7278-0819-2 : £6.95 : CIP entry
B82-23866

Van Vogt, A. E.. Cosmic encounter / A.E. van Vogt. — London : New English Library, 1981, c1980. — 212p ; 18cm
Originally published: New York : Doubleday, 1980
ISBN 0-450-05354-7 (pbk) : £1.50 B82-08653

Vance, Jack. The book of dreams. — London : Hodder and Stoughton, June 1982. — [240]p. — (Coronet books)
ISBN 0-340-28102-2 (pbk) : £1.25 : CIP entry
B82-10471

Vance, Jack. Galactic effectuator. — London : Coronet Books, Feb.1983. — [224]p
Originally published: New York : Ace Books, 1981
ISBN 0-340-32112-1 (pbk) : £1.50 : CIP entry
B82-38066

Vandergriff, Aola. Daughters of the misty isles / Aola Vandergriff. — New York : Warner ; [London] : Star [distributor], 1981. — 443p ; 18cm
ISBN 0-352-31031-6 (pbk) : £1.75 B82-02670

Varley, John, *1947-*. Titan / John Varley ; illustrated by Freff. — London : Futura, 1979. — 302p : ill,1map,1plan ; 18cm. — (An Orbit book)
ISBN 0-7088-8044-4 (pbk) : £1.25 B82-10551

Veley, Charles. Night whispers / Charles Veley. — London : Granada, 1981, c1980. — 334p ; 18cm. — (A Mayflower book)
Originally published: New York : Doubleday, 1980
ISBN 0-583-13344-4 (pbk) : £1.50 B82-09542

Vernon, Dorothy. Fire under snow. — London : Hodder & Stoughton, May 1982. — [192]p. — (Silhouette romance)
Originally published: New York : Silhouette Books, 1981
ISBN 0-340-27935-4 (pbk) : £0.75 : CIP entry
B82-09287

Vidal, Gore. Creation / Gore Vidal. — London : Granada, 1982, c1981. — 702p ; 18cm. — (A Panther book)
Originally published: London : Heinemann, 1981
ISBN 0-586-05458-8 (pbk) : £2.50 B82-33677

Villars, Elizabeth. One night in Newport / Elizabeth Villars. — London : Prior, 1981. — 465p ; 25cm
Published in large print
ISBN 0-86043-679-9 : Unpriced B82-28216

Vitacolonna, Giovanni. A sweet and sour romance. — London (P.O. Box 247, N15 6RW) : Gay Men's Press, Nov.1982. — [160]p
ISBN 0-907040-15-2 (pbk) : £3.50 : CIP entry
B82-29041

Vitek, Donna. Game of chance. — London : Hodder and Stoughton, Jan.1983. — [192]p. — (Silhouette romance)
ISBN 0-340-32725-1 (pbk) : £0.85 : CIP entry
B82-34410

Vitek, Donna. Garden of the moongate. — London : Hodder & Stoughton, Oct.1982. — [192]p. — (Silhouette romance)
ISBN 0-340-32072-9 (pbk) : £0.75 : CIP entry
B82-24841

Vitek, Donna. Promises from the past / Donna Vitek. — London : Silhouette, 1981. — 188p ; 18cm. — (Silhouette romance ; 66)
ISBN 0-340-27121-3 (pbk) : £0.65 : CIP rev.
B81-27355

Vitek, Donna. Valaquez bride. — London : Hodder & Stoughton, June 1982. — [256]p. — (Silhouette special edition)
ISBN 0-340-28582-6 (pbk) : £0.95 : CIP entry
B82-10792

Vitek, Donna. Veil of gold. — London : Hodder & Stoughton, Jan.1982. — [192]p. — (Silhouette romance)
ISBN 0-340-27664-9 (pbk) : £0.75 : CIP entry
B81-34483

Vitek, Donna. Where the heart is. — London : Hodder and Stoughton, Apr.1982. — [192]p. — (Silhouette romance)
ISBN 0-340-27930-3 (pbk) : £0.75 : CIP entry
B82-03828

Vonnegut, Kurt. Deadeye Dick. — London : Cape, Feb.1983. — [272]p
ISBN 0-224-02945-2 : £7.50 : CIP entry
B82-40311

Wager, Walter. Blue leader / Walter Wager. — South Yarmouth, Mass. : Curley ; [Long Preston] : Magna [distributor], c1979. — 673p ; 23cm
Published in large print
ISBN 0-89340-225-7 : £5.50 B82-22568

Wagner, Karl Edward. Dark crusade. — London : Coronet, July 1981. — [224]p
Originally published: New York : Warner Books, 1976
ISBN 0-340-25077-1 (pbk) : £1.40 : CIP entry
B81-13897

Walker, Alice. Meridian. — London : Women's Press, Feb.1982. — [240]p
Originally published: New York : Harcourt Brace Jovanovich, 1976
ISBN 0-7043-3885-8 (pbk) : £2.95 : CIP entry
B82-02456

Wallach, Anne Tolstoi. Women's work : a novel / Anne Tolstoi Wallach. — London : New English Library, 1981. — 419p ; 24cm
ISBN 0-450-04884-5 : £6.95 B82-06486

Wallach, Anne Tolstoi. Women's work. — London : New English Library, Jan.1983. — [384]p
Originally published: 1981
ISBN 0-450-05460-8 (pbk) : £1.95 : CIP entry
B82-36141

Waller, L.. The 'K' assignment. — Large print ed. — Bath : Chivers, Nov.1982. — [240]p. — (Atlantic large print)
Originally published: New York : Fawcett Publications, 1963
ISBN 0-85119-507-5 : £5.25 : CIP entry
B82-26436

Waller, Leslie. Blood and dreams / Leslie Waller. — London : Granada, 1981, c1980. — 415p ; 23cm
ISBN 0-246-11365-0 : £6.95 B82-14722

Waller, Leslie. Gameplan. — London : Granada, Feb.1983. — [352]p
ISBN 0-246-11366-9 : £7.95 : CIP entry
B82-37824

Waller, Leslie. Hide in plain sight / Leslie Waller. — Large print ed.. — [Bath] : Chivers Press, 1982, c1976. — x,383p ; 23cm. — (Atlantic large print) (A Midnight large print thriller)
Originally published: New York : Delacorte, 1976 ; London : Panther, 1978
ISBN 0-85119-489-3 : Unpriced : CIP rev.
B82-15862

813'.54[F] — Fiction in English. American writers, *1945- — Texts* *continuation*

Walsh, Sheila. A highly respectable marriage. — London : Hutchinson, Feb.1983. — [272]p
ISBN 0-09-151050-3 : £6.95 : CIP entry B82-36567

Walsh, Sheila. The incomparable Miss Brady / Sheila Walsh. — London : Arrow, 1982. — 317p ; 18cm
Originally published: London : Hutchinson, 1980
ISBN 0-09-928340-9 (pbk) : £1.50 B82-31611

Walsh, Sheila. The incomparable Miss Brady. — Large print ed. — Long Preston : Magna Print, Nov.1982. — [550]p
Originally published: London : Hutchinson, 1980
ISBN 0-86009-443-x : £5.50 : CIP entry B82-26343

Walsh, Sheila. The rose domino. — London : Hutchinson, Jan.1982. — 1v.
ISBN 0-09-146730-6 : £6.50 : CIP entry B81-33988

Walsh, Thomas, *1908-*. The dark window / Thomas B. Walsh. — London : Remploy, 1979. — 192p ; 20cm
Originally published: London : Hamilton, 1956
ISBN 0-7066-0861-5 : £4.30 B82-09341

Walton, Todd. Forgotten impulses / Todd Walton. — London : Granada, 1982, c1980. — 219p ; 18cm. — (A Panther book)
Originally published: New York : Simon and Schuster, 1980
ISBN 0-586-05150-3 (pbk) : £1.25 B82-17361

Wambaugh, Joseph. The black marble / Joseph Wambaugh. — London : Futura, 1978, c1977. — 354p ; 18cm
Originally published: New York : Delacorte, 1977 ; London : Weidenfeld & Nicolson, 1978
ISBN 0-7088-1390-9 (pbk) : £1.75 B82-10552

Wambaugh, Joseph. The Glitter Dome / Joseph Wambaugh. — South Yarmouth, Mass. : Curley ; [Long Preston] : Distributed by Magna, c1981. — 646p ; 23cm
Originally published: New York : Morrow ; London : Weidenfeld and Nicolson, 1981. — Published in large print
ISBN 0-89340-376-8 : Unpriced B82-19717

Wambaugh, Joseph. The glitter dome / Joseph Wambaugh. — London : Futura, 1982, c1981. — 317p ; 18cm
Originally published: London : Weidenfeld & Nicolson, 1981
ISBN 0-7088-2161-8 (pbk) : £1.75 B82-38608

Ward, Jonas. Buchanan's stolen railway. — London : Coronet, Jan.1983. — [224]p
Originally published: New York : Fawcett Books, 1978
ISBN 0-340-27911-7 (pbk) : £1.25 : CIP entry B82-33731

Ward, Jonas. Buchanan's Texas treasure. — London : Hodder and Stoughton, Apr.1982. — [160]p. — (Coronet books)
ISBN 0-340-26099-8 (pbk) : £0.95 : CIP entry B82-04701

Watson, Clarissa. The bishop in the back seat / Clarissa Watson. — London : Hale, 1981. — 241p ; 22cm
ISBN 0-7091-9450-1 : £6.95 B82-00541

Waugh, Hillary. The Billy Cantrel case / Hillary Waugh. — London : Gollancz, 1982, c1981. — 221p ; 21cm
ISBN 0-575-03145-x : £6.95 : CIP rev. B82-15891

Waugh, Hillary. The Doria Rafe case / by Hillary Waugh. — London : Gollancz, 1982, c1980. — 188p ; 21cm
ISBN 0-575-03047-x : £6.50 : CIP rev. B81-37572

Wayne, Les. West of Omaha. — Large print ed. — Bath : Chivers, Sept.1982. — [296]p. — (Atlantic large print)
ISBN 0-85119-493-1 : £5.25 : CIP entry B82-20500

Webb, Charles, *19---*. The wilderness effect : a novel / by Charles Webb. — London : Chatto & Windus, 1982, c1981. — 238p ; 21cm
ISBN 0-7011-2595-0 : £6.95 : CIP rev. B81-23811

Webb, James, *1946-*. A sense of honour / James Webb. — London : Granada, 1982, c1981. — 308p : ill,1map ; 24cm
Originally published: Englewood Cliffs : Prentice Hall, 1981
ISBN 0-246-11761-3 : £8.95 B82-25707

Westheimer, David. Von Ryan's return / David Westheimer. — London : Sphere, 1982, c1980. — 270p ; 18cm
Originally published: London : Joseph, 1980
ISBN 0-7221-9013-1 : £1.50 B82-18170

Westlake, Donald E.. Nobody's perfect. — London : Coronet, July 1981. — [288]p
Originally published: New York : M. Evans, 1977 ; London : Hodder & Stoughton, 1978
ISBN 0-340-26677-5 (pbk) : £1.50 : CIP entry B81-13779

Whalen, Steve. It takes a man to cry / Steve Whalen. — London : Arlington, 1980. — 400p ; 25cm
ISBN 0-85140-493-6 : £6.50 : CIP rev. B80-18025

Whalen, Steve. It takes a man to cry / Steve Whalen. — London : Corgi, 1982, c1980. — 378p ; 18cm
Originally published: London : Arlington, 1980
ISBN 0-552-11905-9 (pbk) : £1.95 B82-23898

Wharton, William. A midnight clear. — London : Cape, Oct.1982. — [237]p
ISBN 0-224-02050-1 : £6.95 : CIP entry B82-23493

White, Stuart. Death game / Stuart White. — London : Methuen, 1982. — 255p ; 18cm
ISBN 0-417-07430-1 (pbk) : £1.50 B82-39195

Wiegand, William. At last, Mr. Tolliver / William Wiegand. — London : Remploy, 1981, c1950. — 255p ; 20cm
Originally published: New York : Rinehart, 1950 ; London : Hodder & Stoughton, 1951
ISBN 0-7066-0812-7 : £4.60 B82-09340

Wilcox, Collin. Power plays / Collin Wilcox. — London : Hale, 1982, c1979. — 212p ; 20cm
Originally published: New York : Random House, 1979
ISBN 0-7091-9375-0 : £6.75 B82-22127

Wilder, Robert. Flamingo Road / Robert Wilder. — [London] : Corgi, 1961, c1942 (1981 [printing]). — 283p ; 18cm
ISBN 0-552-11848-6 (pbk) : £1.50 B82-09005

Will, Ed. Red blood at white river / Ed Will. — London : Hale, 1981, c1980. — 184p ; 20cm
Originally published: New York : Manor, 1980
ISBN 0-7091-9415-3 : £4.95 B82-03159

Williams, Neal. Blow out / Neal Williams. — London : Corgi, 1981. — 152p ; 18cm
ISBN 0-552-11845-1 (pbk) : £1.00 B82-06468

Wilson, Carter. Treasures on earth / Carter Wilson. — London : Joseph, 1982, c1981. — 244p ; 23cm
Originally published: New York : Knopf, 1981
ISBN 0-7181-2105-8 : £7.95 B82-13656

Wilson, F. Paul. The Keep. — London : New English Library, Feb.1982. — [384]p
ISBN 0-450-04889-6 : £6.95 : CIP entry B81-37583

Wilson, Fran. Amber wine. — London : Hodder & Stoughton, Oct.1982. — [192]p. — (Silhouette romance)
ISBN 0-340-32071-0 (pbk) : £0.75 : CIP entry B82-24840

Wilson, Robert Anton. Schrödinger's cat / Robert Anton Wilson. — London : Sphere
2: The trick top hat. — 1981. — 254p ; 18cm
ISBN 0-7221-9227-4 (pbk) : £1.95 B82-07179

Wilson, Robert Anton. Schrodinger's cat / Robert Anton Wilson. — London : Sphere
3: The homing pigeons. — 1982, c1981. — 207p ; 18cm
ISBN 0-7221-9228-2 (pbk) : £1.95 B82-33915

Winston, Daoma. Family of strangers. — Loughton : Piatkus, Feb.1983. — [192]p
ISBN 0-86188-227-x : £6.95 : CIP entry B82-39809

Winston, Daoma. Flight of a fallen angel. — Loughton : Piatkus, Mar.1982. — [192]p
ISBN 0-86188-141-9 : £6.50 : CIP entry B82-00350

Winston, Daoma. The hands of death / Daoma Winston. — Loughton : Piatkus, 1982, c1972. — 219p ; 21cm
ISBN 0-86188-193-1 : £6.50 : CIP rev. B82-13523

Winston, Daoma. House of mirror images / Daoma Winston. — Loughton : Piatkus, 1981, c1970. — 189p ; 21cm
ISBN 0-86188-088-9 : £6.50 : CIP rev. B81-15850

Winston, Daoma. House of mirror images / Daoma Winston. — Feltham : Hamlyn Paperbacks, [1982], c1970. — 155p ; 18cm
Originally published: London : Piatkus, 1981
ISBN 0-600-20531-2 (pbk) : £1.25 B82-34110

Winston, Daoma. House of mirror images. — Large print ed. — Bath : Chivers, Jan.1983. — [256]p. — (A Lythway book)
Originally published: Loughton : Piatkus, 1981
ISBN 0-85119-891-0 : £6.90 : CIP entry B82-33104

Winston, Daoma. Kingdom's castle / Daoma Winston. — Feltham : Hamlyn, 1982, c1972. — 158p ; 18cm
Originally published: s.l. : s.n., 1972 ; Loughton : Piatkus, 1981
ISBN 0-600-20431-6 (pbk) : £1.00 B82-09108

Winston, Daoma. Mira / Daoma Winston. — London : Macdonald, 1982, c1981. — 284p ; 21cm
Originally published: New Yoprk : Arbor House, 1981
ISBN 0-356-08511-2 : £6.95 B82-26014

Wisdom, Linda. Bright tomorrow. — London : Hodder & Stoughton, Sept.1982. — [192]p. — (Silhouette romance)
ISBN 0-340-32065-6 (pbk) : £0.75 : CIP entry B82-18784

Wisdom, Linda. Fourteen karat beauty. — London : Hodder and Stoughton, Mar.1982. — [192]p. — (Silhouette romance)
ISBN 0-340-27921-4 (pbk) : £0.75 : CIP entry B82-00257

Wisdom, Linda. A man with doubts. — London : Hodder and Stoughton, Nov.1982. — [256]p. — (Silhouette special edition)
ISBN 0-340-32613-1 (pbk) : £0.95 : CIP entry B82-28261

Wolf, Joan. The counterfeit marriage / Joan Wolf. — South Yarmouth, Mass. : Curley ; [Long Preston] : Distributed by Magna, c1980. — 408p ; 23cm
Published in large print
ISBN 0-89340-387-3 : Unpriced B82-33165

813'.54[F] — Fiction in English. American writers, *1945- — Texts* *continuation*

Wolf, Joan. A kind of honor / Joan Wolf. — Sth. Yarmouth, Mass. : Curley ; [Long Preston] : Distributed by Magna Print, c1980. — 351p ; 22cm
Published in large print
ISBN 0-89340-386-5 : Unpriced B82-27421

Wolf, Joan. A London season / Joan Wolf. — Large print ed. — South Yarmouth, Mass. : Curley ; Skipton : Magna Print [distributor], c1980. — 321p ; 22cm. — (Regency romance)
ISBN 0-89340-385-7 : Unpriced B82-27416

Wolfe, Gene. The claw of the conciliator / Gene Wolfe. — London : Arrow, 1982, c1981. — 303p ; 18cm. — (The Book of the new sun ; v.2)
Originally published: New York : Simon & Schuster ; London : Sidgwick & Jackson, 1981
ISBN 0-09-927470-1 (pbk) : £1.60 B82-19008

Wolfe, Gene. The sword of the Lictor : science fiction / by Gene Wolfe. — London : Sidgwick & Jackson, 1982, c1981. — 302p ; 21cm. — (The Book of the new sun ; v.3)
ISBN 0-283-98860-6 : £7.95 B82-25561

Wolfe, Winifred. Josie's way : a novel / by Winifred Wolfe. — Loughton : Piatkus, 1981, c1980. — 313p : ill ; 21cm
Originally published: New York : Arbor House, 1980
ISBN 0-86188-092-7 : £6.95 : CIP rev. B81-30402

Wolfe, Winifred. Occupant penthouse 4. — Loughton : Piatkus, Oct.1982. — [256]p
ISBN 0-86188-176-1 : £7.50 : CIP entry B82-24576

Wolff, Sonia. What they did to Miss Lily. — London : New English Library, Nov.1982. — [304]p
ISBN 0-450-05535-3 (pbk) : £1.95 : CIP entry B82-27518

Wolff, Tobias. Hunters in the snow : a collection of short stories / by Tobias Wolff. — London : Cape, 1982. — 175p ; 21cm
ISBN 0-224-01986-4 : £6.95 : CIP rev. B82-01115

Wood, Barbara. The watch gods / Barbara Wood. — London : New English Library, 1981 (1982 [printing]). — 347p ; 18cm
ISBN 0-450-05382-2 (pbk) : £1.95 : CIP rev. B82-06822

Wood, Barbara, *1947-*. Childsong. — Loughton : Piatkus, July 1982. — [256]p
ISBN 0-86188-202-4 : £6.95 : CIP entry B82-12929

Wood, Barbara, *1947-*. Yesterday's child / Barbara Wood. — Feltham : Hamlyn Paperbacks, 1981, c1979. — 254p ; 18cm. — (A Moonshadow romance)
Originally published: Garden City, N.Y. : Doubleday, 1979
ISBN 0-600-20263-1 (pbk) : £1.25 B82-03017

Woodiwiss, Kathleen E.. The flame and the flower / Kathleen E. Woodiwiss. — London : Macdonald Futura, 1975, c1972 (1981 [printing]). — 430p ; 18cm. — (A Futura book)
Originally published: New York : Avon, 1972
ISBN 0-86007-182-0 (pbk) : £1.75 B82-03479

Woodiwiss, Kathleen E.. Shanna / Kathleen Woodiwiss. — London : Macdonald Futura, 1977 (1981 [printing]). — 661p ; 18cm. — (A Troubadour spectacular)
ISBN 0-7088-1352-6 (pbk) : £2.50 B82-01515

Woods, Stuart. Chiefs / by Stuart Woods. — New York ; London : Norton, c1981. — 427p ; 24cm
ISBN 0-393-01461-4 : £10.50 B82-32586

Woolfolk, William. The Sendai / William Woolfolk. — London : Macdonald Futura, c1980. — 288p ; 18cm
ISBN 0-7088-2094-8 (pbk) : £1.50 B82-03293

Wouk, Herman. Don't stop the carnival / Herman Wouk. — London : Fontana, 1966, c1965 (1981 [printing]). — 384p ; 18cm
Originally published: London : Collins, 1965
ISBN 0-00-616453-6 (pbk) : £1.95 B82-03165

Wyllie, John. The long dark night of Baron Samedi / by John Wyllie. — London : Hale, 1982. — 180p ; 20cm
ISBN 0-7091-9780-2 : £6.75 B82-31627

Wynne, John. Crime wave. — London : John Calder, Feb.1982. — [256]p
ISBN 0-7145-3870-1 : £6.95 : CIP entry B81-35827

Yablonsky, Yabo. Escape to victory / Yabo Yablonsky ; based on a screenplay by Evan Jones and Yabo Yablonsky ; from a story by Yabo Yablonsky and Djordje Milicevic & Jeff Maguire. — London : Severn House, 1981. — 164p ; 21cm
ISBN 0-7278-0742-0 : £5.95 B82-00591

Yerby, Frank. The foxes of Harrow / Frank Yerby. — Leicester : Charnwood, 1982. — 757p ; 23cm. — (Charnwood library series)
Originally published: New York : Dial, 1946 ; London : Heinemann, 1947. — Published in large print
ISBN 0-7089-8047-3 : Unpriced : CIP rev. B82-15946

Yerby, Frank. The golden hawk / Frank Yerby. — London : Granada, 1971 (1981 [printing]). — 288p ; 18cm. — (A Mayflower book)
Originally published: London : Heinemann, 1949
ISBN 0-583-11837-2 (pbk) : £1.25 B82-02799

Yglesias, Helen. Sweetsir. — London : Coronet Books, Oct.1982. — [309]p
ISBN 0-340-28435-8 (pbk) : £1.95 : CIP entry B82-24827

York, Georgia. Savage Key. — London : Coronet Books, Feb.1983. — 1v.
Originally published: New York : Fawcett, 1979
ISBN 0-340-32053-2 (pbk) : CIP entry B82-38063

Young, Brittany. Arranged marriage. — London : Hodder and Stoughton, Feb.1983. — [192]p. — (Silhouette romance)
ISBN 0-340-32763-4 (pbk) : £0.85 : CIP entry B82-38032

Yurick, Sol. Richard A.. — London : Methuen London, Nov.1982. — [446]p
ISBN 0-413-51100-6 : £7.95 : CIP entry B82-28295

Zacharia, Don. The match trick. — London : Hutchinson, Sept.1982. — [224]p
ISBN 0-09-149750-7 : £7.50 : CIP entry B82-19814

Zacharias, Lee. Lessons : a novel / by Lee Zacharias. — London : Faber, 1982, c1981. — 342p ; 23cm
Originally published: Boston, Mass. : Houghton Mifflin, 1981
ISBN 0-571-11910-7 : £7.95 : CIP rev. B82-10762

Zeidner, Lisa. Customs / Lisa Zeidner. — London : Cape, 1981. — 271p ; 23cm
ISBN 0-224-02923-1 : £6.95 : CIP rev. B81-28194

Zelazny, Roger. The courts of Chaos / Roger Zelazny. — London : Sphere, 1982, c1978. — 142p ; 18cm. — (Sphere science fiction)
Originally published: Garden City, N.Y. : Doubleday, 1978
ISBN 0-7221-9441-2 (pbk) : £1.50 B82-34115

Zelazny, Roger. The guns of Avalon / Roger Zelazny. — London : Sphere, 1982, c1973. — 203p ; 18cm. — (Sphere science fiction)
Originally published: Garden City, N.Y. : Doubleday, 1973 ; London : Faber, 1974
ISBN 0-7221-9440-4 (pbk) : £1.50 B82-14907

813'.54[F] — Fiction in English. Canadian writers, *1945- — Texts*

Allen, Charlotte Vale. Acts of kindness. — London : New English Library, Oct.1982. — [240]p
ISBN 0-450-05513-2 (pbk) : £1.50 : CIP entry B82-23321

Allen, Charlotte Vale. Daddy's girl. — London : New English Library, Jan.1983. — [272]p
ISBN 0-450-05555-8 (pbk) : £1.75 : CIP entry B82-36145

Allen, Charlotte Vale. Intimate friends. — London : Hutchinson, Feb.1983. — [288]p
ISBN 0-09-151390-1 : £7.95 : CIP entry B82-37661

Allen, Charlotte Vale. The marmalade man / Charlotte Vale Allen. — London : Hutchinson, 1981. — 412p ; 23cm
ISBN 0-09-146140-5 : £7.95 : CIP rev. B81-16848

Allen, Charlotte Vale. Moments of meaning / Charlotte Vale Allen. — Sevenoaks : New English Library, 1982, c1979. — 217p ; 19cm. — (The Crime Club)
ISBN 0-450-05454-3 (pbk) : £1.50 : CIP rev. B82-06827

Allen, Charlotte Vale. Perfect fools / Charlotte Vale Allen. — London : New English Library, 1981. — 253p ; 18cm
ISBN 0-450-05273-7 (pbk) : £1.50 B82-08656

Allen, Charlotte Vale. Promises / Charlotte Vale Allen. — London : Arrow, 1982, c1980. — 505p ; 18cm
Originally published: London : Hutchinson, 1980
ISBN 0-09-927930-4 (pbk) : £1.95 B82-22077

Atwood, Margaret. Bodily harm / Margaret Atwood. — London : Cape, 1982, c1981. — 301p ; 23cm
ISBN 0-224-02016-1 : £7.50 : CIP rev. B82-14957

Atwood, Margaret. Lady oracle / Margaret Atwood. — London : Virago, 1982, c1976. — 345p ; 20cm. — (Virago modern classics)
Originally published: Toronto : McClelland and Stewart, 1976 ; London : Deutsch, 1977
ISBN 0-86068-303-6 (pbk) : £3.50 : CIP rev. B82-10240

Atwood, Margaret. Life before man. — London : Virago, Jan.1982. — [320]p
Originally published: Toronto : McClelland and Stewart, 1979
ISBN 0-86068-192-0 (pbk) : £2.95 : CIP entry B81-33762

Beresford-Howe, Constance. The marriage bed. — London : New English Library, Nov.1982. — [240]p
ISBN 0-450-04920-5 : £7.95 : CIP entry B82-34087

Cooper, Bryan. The wildcatters / Bryan Cooper. — London : Futura, 1979, c1976. — 214p ; 18cm
Originally published: London : Macdonald and Jane's 1976
ISBN 0-7088-1579-0 (pbk) : £0.95 B82-32966

Davies, Robertson. The rebel angels / Robertson Davies. — London : Allen Lane, 1982, c1981. — 326p ; 22cm
Originally published: New York : Viking, 1982
ISBN 0-7139-1473-4 : £6.95 B82-16865

Dennis, Charles. Talent / Charles Dennis. — London : Arrow, 1982. — 427p ; 18cm
ISBN 0-09-927230-x (pbk) : £1.75 B82-30459

813'.54[F] — Fiction in English. Canadian writers, *1945- — Texts* *continuation*

Dunmore, Spencer. Ace / Spencer Dunmore. — London : Pan in association with Heinemann/Peter Davies, 1982, c1981. — 270p ; 18cm
Originally published: London : Heinemann, 1981
ISBN 0-330-26741-8 (pbk) : £1.50 B82-35748

Eden, Laura. Mistaken identity. — London : Hodder & Stoughton, Apr.1982. — [192]p. — (Silhouette romance)
ISBN 0-340-27931-1 (pbk) : £0.75 : CIP entry B82-05392

Engel, Howard. The ransom game : a Benny Cooperman mystery / Howard Engel. — London : Gollancz, 1982, c1981. — 218p ; 21cm
ISBN 0-575-03141-7 : £6.95 : CIP rev. B82-19562

Hailey, Arthur. Wheels. — Large print ed. — Anstey : Ulverscroft, Oct.1982. — [624]p. — (Charnwood library series)
Originally published: London : Souvenir Press, 1971
ISBN 0-7089-8076-7 : £6.50 : CIP entry B82-26692

Hastings, Brooke. Rough diamond. — London : New English Library, Oct.1982. — [256]p. — (Silhouette special edition)
ISBN 0-340-32607-7 (pbk) : £0.95 : CIP entry B82-24716

Hill, Douglas. The huntsman / Douglas Hill. — London : Heinemann, 1982. — 135p ; 23cm
ISBN 0-434-94284-7 : £4.95 B82-31391

Houston, James. Spirit wrestler / James Houston. — Large print ed. — Leicester : Ulverscroft, 1982, c1980. — 479p : 1map ; 23cm. — (Ulverscroft large print series)
Originally published: London : Collins, 1980
ISBN 0-7089-0768-7 : Unpriced : CIP rev. B82-01743

Hyde, Christopher. Styx. — London : Severn House, Oct.1982. — [256]p
ISBN 0-7278-0837-0 : £6.95 : CIP entry B82-28580

Mackenzie, Donald, *1908-*. Raven feathers his nest / Donald Mackenzie. — Large print ed. — Leicester : Ulverscroft, 1982, c1979. — 316p ; 23cm. — (Ulverscroft large print series : mystery)
Originally published: London : London : Macmillan, 1979
ISBN 0-7089-0787-3 : Unpriced : CIP rev. B82-18440

MacKenzie, Donald, *1908-*. Raven's revenge / Donald MacKenzie. — London : Macmillan, 1982. — 191p ; 21cm
ISBN 0-333-32880-9 : £5.95 B82-27442

Moore, Brian, *1921-*. The Mangan inheritance / Brian Moore. — London : Corgi, 1981, c1979. — 283p ; 18cm
Originally published: London : Cape, 1979
ISBN 0-552-11762-5 (pbk) : £1.95 B82-37130

Munro, Alice. Lives of girls and women / Alice Munro. — Harmondsworth : Penguin, 1982, c1971. — 250p ; 20cm. — (King Penguin)
Originally published: New York : McGraw-Hill, 1971 ; London : Allen Lane, 1973
ISBN 0-14-005996-2 (pbk) : £2.25 B82-40367

Richler, Mordecai. Joshua then and now / Mordecai Richler. — London : Granada, 1982, c1980. — 464p ; 18cm. — (A Panther book)
Originally published: New York : Knopf ; London : Macmillan, 1980
ISBN 0-586-05456-1 (pbk) : £2.50 B82-36055

Slater, Ian. Air glow red / by Ian Slater. — London : Severn House, 1982, c1981. — 346p ; 21cm
Originally published: Garden City, N.Y. : Doubleday, 1981
ISBN 0-7278-0796-x : £7.50 B82-31425

813'.54[F] — Short stories in English. American writers, *1945- — Texts*

Anderson, Poul. [Seven conquests]. Conquests / Poul Anderson. — London : Granada, 1981, c1969. — 250p ; 18cm. — (A Panther book)
Originally published: New York : Macmillan, 1969
ISBN 0-586-05041-8 (pbk) : £1.50 B82-09541

Breen, Jon L.. Hair of the sleuthhound : parodies of mystery fiction / by Jon L. Breen. — Metuchen ; London : Scarecrow, 1982. — x,208p ; 23cm
ISBN 0-8108-1505-2 : £10.00 B82-22976

Brown, Fredric. The best short stories of Fredric Brown. — London : New English Library, Sept.1982. — [448]p
ISBN 0-450-05501-9 (pbk) : £1.50 : CIP entry B82-19691

Camoin, François. The end of the world is Los Angeles / stories by François Camoin. — Columbia ; London : University of Missouri Press, 1982. — 94p ; 21cm
ISBN 0-8262-0365-5 (pbk) : Unpriced B82-36529

Carver, Raymond. What we talk about when we talk about love. — London : Collins, 1982. — 159p ; 22cm
ISBN 0-00-222624-3 : £6.50 B82-03075

Corrington, John William. The Southern reporter : stories / by John William Corrington. — Baton Rouge ; London : Louisiana State University Press, 1981. — 191p ; 23cm
ISBN 0-8071-0869-3 : £6.95 B82-00494

Disch, Thomas M.. The man who had no idea : a collection of stories / by Thomas M. Disch. — London : Gollancz, 1982. — 186p ; 20cm
ISBN 0-575-03057-7 : £7.95 : CIP rev. B82-04603

Ellison, Harlan. All the sounds of fear / Harlan Ellison. — London : Granada, 1973 (1981 [printing]). — 158p ; 18cm. — (A Panther book)
ISBN 0-586-03899-x (pbk) : £1.25 B82-02788

Ellison, Harlan. The time of the eye / Harlan Ellison. — London : Granada, 1974, c1971 (1981 [printing]). — 156p ; 18cm. — (A Panther book)
ISBN 0-586-03935-x (pbk) : £1.25 B82-02801

Foster, Alan Dean. Star trek / Alan Dean Foster ; based on the popular animated series created by Gene Roddenberry. — London : Severn House
Log 2. — 1982, c1974. — 176p ; 21cm
ISBN 0-7278-0820-6 : £6.95 B82-35463

Gilchrist, Ellen. In the land of dreamy dreams. — London : Faber, Oct.1982. — [176]p
Originally published: Fayetteville : University of Arkansas Press, 1981
ISBN 0-571-11965-4 : £6.95 : CIP entry B82-25176

Highsmith, Patricia. Slowly, slowly in the wind / Patricia Highsmith. — Harmondsworth : Penguin, 1981, c1979. — 204p ; 18cm. — (Penguin crime fiction)
Originally published: London : Heinemann, 1979
ISBN 0-14-005413-8 (pbk) : £1.25 B82-22317

Kornblatt, Joyce Reiser. Nothing to do with love. — London : Women's Press, July 1982. — [208]p
ISBN 0-7043-3891-2 (pbk) : £2.50 : CIP entry B82-13007

McBain, Ed. The McBain brief. — London : Hamilton, Nov.1982. — [272]p
ISBN 0-241-10884-5 : £7.95 : CIP entry B82-27374

Makuck, Peter. Breaking and entering : stories / by Peter Makuck. — Urbana ; London : University of Illinois Press, c1981. — 172p ; 21cm. — (Illinois short fiction)
ISBN 0-252-00898-7 (cased) : Unpriced
ISBN 0-252-00925-8 (pbk) : £3.50 B82-17390

Malamud, Bernard. Rembrandt's hat / Bernard Malamud. — London : Chatto & Windus, 1982. — 204p ; 22cm. — (The Collected works of Bernard Malamud)
Originally published: New York : Farrar-Straus-Giroux ; London : Eyre Methuen, 1973
ISBN 0-7011-2450-4 : £7.50 : CIP rev. B82-01193

Matthews, Jack. Dubious persuasions : short stories / by Jack Matthews. — Baltimore ; London : Johns Hopkins University Press, c1981. — 155p ; 24cm. — (Johns Hopkins: Poetry and fiction)
ISBN 0-8018-2692-6 : Unpriced B82-15330

Miller, Walter M.. Conditionally human and other stories / Walter M. Miller Jr. — London : Corgi, 1982, c1980. — 228p ; 18cm
ISBN 0-552-11991-1 (pbk) : £1.50 B82-35246

Miller, Walter M.. The Darfsteller and other stories / Walter M. Miller Jr. — [London] : Corgi, 1982. — 223p ; 18cm
ISBN 0-552-11950-4 (pbk) : £1.75 B82-28361

Ozick, Cynthia. Levitation : five fictions / Cynthia Ozick. — London : Secker & Warburg, 1982. — 157p ; 22cm
ISBN 0-436-25482-4 : £6.95 B82-19794

Pesetsky, Bette. Stories up to a point / Bette Pesetsky. — London : Bodley Head, 1982. — 113p ; 23cm
ISBN 0-370-30483-7 : £5.95 : CIP rev. B82-15759

Rothberg, Abraham. The four corners of the house : stories / by Abraham Rothberg. — Urbana ; London : University of Illinois Press, c1981. — 157p ; 21cm. — (Illinois short fiction) (An Illini book)
ISBN 0-252-00922-3 (cased) : Unpriced
ISBN 0-252-00926-6 (pbk) : £3.45 B82-17538

Skiles, Don. Miss America / stories by Don Skiles. — Boston ; London : Boyars, 1982. — 159p ; 22cm
ISBN 0-7145-2755-6 : £6.95 : CIP rev. B81-35828

Sladek, John. Alien accounts / John Sladek. — London : Granada, 1982. — 202p ; 18cm. — (A Panther book)
ISBN 0-586-04758-1 (pbk) : £1.95 B82-33681

Stockanes, Anthony E.. Ladies who knit for a living : stories / by Anthony E. Stockanes. — Urbana ; London : University of Illinois Press, c1981. — 131p ; 21cm. — (Illinois short fiction) (An Illini book)
ISBN 0-252-00904-5 (cased) : Unpriced
ISBN 0-252-00927-4 (pbk) : £3.45 B82-17539

Theroux, Paul. The London embassy. — London : Hamilton, Oct.1982. — [224]p
ISBN 0-241-10872-1 : £7.95 : CIP entry B82-23457

Van Vogt, A. E.. Pendulum / A.E. van Vogt. — Sevenoaks : New English Library, 1982, c1978. — 223p ; 18cm
Originally published: New York : Daw, 1978
ISBN 0-450-05477-2 (pbk) : £1.25 : CIP rev. B82-12356

813′.54[F] — Short stories in English. American writers, *1945- — Texts* *continuation*

Walker, Alice. You can′t keep a good woman down. — London : Women′s Press, Feb.1982. — [176]p
ISBN 0-7043-3884-x (pbk) : £2.50 : CIP entry B82-02455

Wolfe, Gene. The island of Doctor Death : and other stories / Gene Wolfe. — London : Arrow, 1981, c1980. — 410p ; 18cm
ISBN 0-09-926580-x (pbk) : £1.95 B82-03536

813′.54[F] — Short stories in English. Canadian writers, *1945- — Texts*

Atwood, Margaret. Dancing girls. — London : Cape, Oct.1982. — [256]p
ISBN 0-224-01835-3 : CIP entry B82-26703

Creal, Margaret. The man who sold prayers. — London : Dent, Jan.1983. — [208]p
ISBN 0-460-04592-x : £7.95 : CIP entry B82-34612

McCaffrey, Anne. Get off the unicorn. — London : Severn House, Oct.1982. — [320]p
Originally published: New York : Ballantine, 1977 ; London : Corgi, 1979
ISBN 0-7278-0817-6 : £7.95 : CIP entry B82-28576

Munro, Alice. The beggar maid : stories of Flo and Rose / Alice Munro. — Harmondsworth : Penguin, 1980, c1979 (1981 [printing]). — 210p ; 20cm. — (A King Penguin)
Originally published: New York : Knopf, 1979 ; London : Allen Lane, 1980
ISBN 0-14-006011-1 (pbk) : £2.25 B82-05943

Palmer, C. Everard. Beppo Tate and Roy Penner ; The runaway marriage brokers : two stories / by C. Everard Palmer. — London : Deutsch, 1980. — 118p ; 21cm
ISBN 0-233-97258-7 : £3.95 : CIP rev. B80-12585

813′.54[J] — Children′s short stories in English. American writers, *1945- — Texts*

Cameron, Ann. [The stories Julian tells]. The Julian stories / Ann Cameron ; illustrated by Ann Strugnell. — London : Gollancz, 1982, c1981. — 72p : ill ; 22cm
Originally published: New York : Pantheon, 1981
ISBN 0-575-03143-3 : £4.95 : CIP rev. B82-16482

Disney′s classic favourites. — Bristol : Purnell, 1982. — 117p : col.ill ; 29cm
ISBN 0-361-05344-4 : £3.99 B82-30912

Lobel, Arnold. Fables / written and illustrated by Arnold Lobel. — London : Cape, 1980. — 40p : col.ill ; 30cm
ISBN 0-224-01866-3 : £3.95 : CIP rev. B80-11220

Lurie, Alison. The heavenly zoo : legends and tales of the stars / retold by Alison Lurie with pictures by Monika Beisner. — London : Eel Pie, 1979. — 61p : ill(some col.) ; 25cm
ISBN 0-906008-11-5 : £1.95 B82-10072

813′.54[J] — Children′s stories in English. American writers, *1945- — Texts*

Adler, C. S.. Footsteps on the stairs / C.S. Adler. — London : Hamilton, 1982. — 151p ; 23cm
ISBN 0-241-10725-3 : £4.95 : CIP rev. B81-36384

Allard, Harry. I will not go to market today / by Harry Allard ; pictures by James Marshall. — London : Transworld, 1981, c1979. — [32]p : col.ill ; 19cm. — (A Carousel book)
Originally published: New York : Dial Press, 1979
ISBN 0-552-52149-3 (pbk) : £0.90 B82-09111

Arden, William. Alfred Hitchcock and the Three Investigators in the mystery of the dead man′s riddle / text by William Arden ; based on characters created by Robert Arthur. — London : Armada, 1979, c1967 (1982 [printing]). — 159p : ill ; 19cm
Originally published: New York : Random House, 1964 ; London : Collins, 1967
ISBN 0-00-692012-8 (pbk) : £0.85 B82-09404

Arden, William. Alfred Hitchcock and the Three Investigators in the mystery of the deadly double / text by William Arden ; based on characters created by Robert Arthur ; illustrated by Roger Hall. — London : Armada, 1982, c1979. — 158p : ill ; 18cm
Originally published: New York : Random House, 1978 ; London : Collins, 1979
ISBN 0-00-691984-7 (pbk) : £0.85 B82-16814

Arden, William. Alfred Hitchcock and the three investigators in the secret of the crooked cat / text by William Arden ; based on characters created by Robert Arthur. — London : Armada, 1973, c1970 (1982 [printing]). — 124p : ill ; 19cm
Originally published: New York : Random House, 1970
ISBN 0-00-691922-7 (pbk) : £0.85 B82-33833

Asch, Frank. The last puppy / Frank Asch. — London : Transworld, 1982, c1980. — [30]p : col.ill ; 19cm. — (A Carousel book)
Originally published: New York : Prentice-Hall, 1980 ; London : Evans, 1981
ISBN 0-552-52204-x (pbk) : £0.95 B82-35546

Asher, Sandy. Just like Jenny. — London : Gollancz, Oct.1982. — [160]p
ISBN 0-575-03199-9 : £5.95 : CIP entry B82-23348

Barrett, Judi. Animals should definitely not act like people / written by Judi Barrett ; and drawn by Ron Barrett. — Kingswood : Kaye & Ward, 1981, c1980. — [32]p : col.ill ; 24cm
Originally published: New York : Atheneum, 1980
ISBN 0-7182-1720-9 B82-00959

Bellairs, John. The treasure of Alpheus Winterborn / John Bellairs ; illustrated by Judith Gwyn Brown. — London : Hutchinson, 1982, c1978. — 180p : ill ; 21cm
Originally published: New York : Harcourt Brace Jovanovich, 1978
ISBN 0-09-145740-8 : £5.50 : CIP rev. B82-00291

Blume, Judy. It′s not the end of the world / Judy Blume. — London : Heinemann Educational, 1982, c1972. — 111p ; 20cm. — (The New windmill series ; 261)
Originally published: Scarsdale Bradbury, 1972
ISBN 0-435-12261-4 : £1.35 B82-33454

Blume, Judy. Superfudge / Judy Blume. — [London] : Piccolo, 1982, c1980. — 139p ; 18cm
Originally published: London : Bodley Head, 1980
ISBN 0-330-26602-0 (pbk) : £1.25 B82-13638

Bosse, Malcolm J.. Ganesh / Malcolm J. Bosse. — London : Chatto and Windus, 1982. — 185p ; 21cm
ISBN 0-7011-2621-3 : £5.50 : CIP rev. B82-01197

Bridgman, Elizabeth. New dog next door / by Elizabeth Bridgman. — London : Scholastic, 1982, c1978. — 30p : ill ; 18cm. — (Hippo books)
Originally published: New York : Harper & Row, 1978
ISBN 0-590-70082-0 (pbk) : £0.90 B82-09333

Brown, Marc. The true Francine / Marc Brown. — London : Pepper Press, 1982. — [30]p : col.ill ; 26cm
Originally published: Boston, Mass.: Little, Brown, 1981
ISBN 0-237-45635-4 : £3.95 B82-26584

Buckingham, Jamie. Jesus world / Jamie Buckingham. — Eastbourne : Kingsway, 1982, c1981. — 132p ; 18cm
Originally published: Lincoln, Va. : Chosen, 1981
ISBN 0-86065-182-7 (pbk) : £1.25 B82-33452

Byars, Betsy. The animal, the vegetable, and John D. Jones / Betsy Byars. — London : Bodley Head, 1982. — 123p ; 22cm
ISBN 0-370-30914-6 : £3.95 : CIP rev. B82-04022

Byars, Betsy. Good-bye, Chicken Little / Betsy Byars. — Harmondsworth : Puffin, 1982, c1979. — 95p ; 18cm
Originally published: New York : Harper & Row ; London : Bodley Head, 1979
ISBN 0-14-031329-x (pbk) : £0.90 B82-34163

Byars, Betsy. The two-thousand-pound goldfish. — London : Bodley Head, Oct.1982. — [128]p
ISBN 0-370-30945-6 : £3.95 : CIP entry B82-24459

Calvert, Patricia. The snowbird. — London : Macmillan Children′s Books, Feb.1983. — [160]p
ISBN 0-333-34249-6 : £5.95 : CIP entry B82-36309

Campbell, Julie. Trixie Belden and the gatehouse mystery / by Julie Campbell ; cover by Jack Wacker. — London : Dean, 1982, c1977. — 185p ; 20cm. — (A Trixie Belden mystery ; no.3)
Cover title: The gatehouse mystery. — Originally published: Racine, Wis. : Whitman, 1951
ISBN 0-603-00298-6 : Unpriced B82-25587

Campbell, Julie. Trixie Belden and the mysterious visitor / by Julie Campbell ; cover by Jack Wacker. — London : Dean, 1982, c1977. — 188p ; 20cm. — (A Trixie Belden mystery ; no.4)
Cover title: The mysterious visitor. — Originally published: Racine, Wis. : Whitman, 1954
ISBN 0-603-00299-4 : Unpriced B82-25588

Campbell, Julie. Trixie Belden and the mystery in Arizona / by Julie Campbell ; cover by Jack Wacker. — London : Dean, 1982, c1977. — 186p ; 20cm. — (A Trixie Belden mystery ; no.6)
Cover title: The mystery in Arizona. — Originally published: Racine, Wis. : Whitman, 1954
ISBN 0-603-00301-x : Unpriced B82-25590

Campbell, Julie. Trixie Belden and the mystery off Glen Road / by Julie Campbell ; cover by Jack Wacker. — London : Dean, 1982, c1977. — 188p ; 20cm. — (A Trixie Belden mystery ; no.5)
Cover title: The mystery off Glen Road. — Originally published: Racine, Wis. : Whitman, 1956
ISBN 0-603-00300-1 : Unpriced B82-25589

Campbell, Julie. Trixie Belden and the red trailer mystery / by Julie Campbell ; cover by Jack Wacker. — London : Dean, 1982, c1977. — 187p ; 20cm. — (A Trixie Belden mystery ; no.2)
Cover title: The red trailer mystery. — Originally published: Racine, Wis. : Whitman, 1950
ISBN 0-603-00297-8 : Unpriced B82-25586

Campbell, Julie. Trixie Belden and the secret of the mansion / by Julie Campbell ; cover by Jack Wacker. — London : Dean, 1982, c1977. — 186p ; 20cm. — (A Trixie Belden mystery ; no.1)
Cover title: The secret of the mansion. — Originally published: Racine, Wis. : Whitman, 1948
ISBN 0-603-00296-x : Unpriced B82-25585

813'.54[J] — Children's stories in English. American writers, *1945-* — *Texts*
continuation

Carey, M. V.. Alfred Hitchcock and the Three Investigators in The mystery of Death Trap Mine / text by M.V. Carey ; based on characters created by Robert Arthur. — London : Armada, 1980, c1977. — 158p ; 18cm. — (Alfred Hitchcock mystery series ; 24)
Originally published: New York : Random House, 1976 ; London : Collins, 1977
ISBN 0-00-691574-4 (pbk) : £0.75 B82-39228

Carey, M. V.. Alfred Hitchcock and the Three Investigators in the mystery of the invisible dog / text by M.V. Carey ; based on characters created by Robert Arthur. — London : Armada, 1979 (1981 [printing]). — 160p ; 18cm
Originally published: New York : Random House, 1975 ; London : Collins, 1976
ISBN 0-00-692011-x (pbk) : £0.85 B82-06443

Cate, Rikki. A cat's tale. — London : Methuen Children's Books, Aug.1982. — [48]p
ISBN 0-416-26330-5 : £3.50 : CIP entry B82-15789

Cauley, Lorinda Bryan. Goldilocks and the three bears. — London : Ward Lock, Sept.1981. — [32]p
ISBN 0-7063-6154-7 : £3.50 : CIP entry B81-23809

Clavell, James. The children's story / James Clavell in association with Michaela Clavell Crisman. — London : Hodder and Stoughton, 1982, c1981. — [89]p : ill ; 23cm
Originally published: New York : Delacorte-Eleanor Friede, 1981
ISBN 0-340-28167-7 : £4.95 : CIP rev. B82-04699

Cleary, Beverly. Henry and Beezus / Beverly Cleary ; illustrated by Thelma Lambert. — London : Fontana, 1981, c1980. — 125p : ill ; 20cm. — (Lions)
Originally published: New York : Morrow, 1952 ; London : Hamilton, 1980
ISBN 0-00-671875-2 (pbk) : £0.95 B82-01046

Cleary, Beverly. Ramona and her father / Beverly Cleary ; illustrated by Alan Tiegreen. — Harmondsworth : Puffin, 1981, c1978. — 144p : ill ; 19cm
Originally published: New York : Morrow, 1977 ; London : Hamilton, 1978
ISBN 0-14-031303-6 (pbk) : £0.90 B82-06425

Cleary, Beverly. Ramona and her mother / Beverly Cleary ; illustrated by Alan Tiegreen. — Harmondsworth : Puffin, 1982, c1979. — 171p : ill ; 19cm. — (A Puffin book)
Originally published: New York : Morrow ; London : Hamish Hamilton Children's Books, 1979
ISBN 0-14-031328-1 (pbk) : £0.95 B82-29594

Cooney, Barbara. Miss Rumphius. — London : MacRae, Oct.1982. — [32]p
ISBN 0-86203-100-1 : £5.25 : CIP entry B82-24586

Copper and Tod grow up / Walt Disney Productions. — Bristol : Purnell, 1982. — [40]p : col.ill ; 15cm. — (A Disney playmate)
ISBN 0-361-05341-x (pbk) : £0.50 B82-28901

Copper and Tod play together / Walt Disney Productions. — Bristol : Purnell, 1982. — [40]p : col.ill ; 15cm. — (A Disney Playmate)
ISBN 0-361-05341-x (pbk) : £0.50 B82-28902

Copper the puppy. — Bristol : Purnell, c1981. — [8]p : chiefly col.ill ; 27cm. — (The Fox and the hound)
Cover title
ISBN 0-361-05295-2 : £0.99 B82-17530

De Paola, Tomie. The hunter and the animals. — London : Andersen Press, Feb.1982. — [32]p
ISBN 0-86264-014-8 : £3.95 : CIP entry B81-36963

De Paola, Tomie. Now one foot, now the other / story and pictures by Tomie de Paola. — London : Methuen Children's, 1982, c1981. — [46]p : col.ill ; 20cm
ISBN 0-416-22210-2 : £2.95 : CIP rev. B82-02000

Demarest, Chris L.. Benedict finds a home. — London : Hamilton, Aug.1982. — [40]p
ISBN 0-241-10839-x : £4.50 : CIP entry B82-15697

Deyneka, Anita. Alexi and the mountain treasure / Anita Deyneka. — London (130 City Rd., EC1V 2NJ) : Kingfisher Books, 1981, c1979. — 111p ; 18cm. — (Leopard books)
Originally published: Elgin, Ill. : Cook, 1979
ISBN 0-85421-953-6 (pbk) : Unpriced B82-09398

Dixon, Franklin W.. The Apeman's secret / Franklin W. Dixon ; illustrated by Leslie Morrill. — London : Armada, 1981, c1980. — 184p : ill ; 19cm. — (The Hardy boys mystery stories)
Originally published: New York : Wanderer, 1980
ISBN 0-00-691821-2 (pbk) : £0.85 B82-03013

Dixon, Franklin W.. The mystery of smugglers cove / Franklin W. Dixon ; illustrated by Leslie Morrill. — London : Armada, 1982, c1980. — 181p : ill ; 19cm. — (The Hardy boys mystery stories ; 62)
Originally published: New York : Wanderer, 1980
ISBN 0-00-691823-9 (pbk) : £0.85 B82-33835

Dubleman, Richard. The adventures of Holly Hobbie / Richard Dubleman ; illustrated by Doreen McGuiness. — London : Granada, 1981, c1979. — 222p : ill,2maps ; 20cm
Originally published: New York : Delacorte, 1980
ISBN 0-583-30437-0 (pbk) : £1.25 B82-09547

Ehrlich, Amy. Thumbelina / Hans Christian Andersen ; pictures by Susan Jeffers ; retold by Amy Ehrlich. — London : Hamilton Children's, 1980, c1979. — [32]p : col.ill ; 31cm
Originally published: New York : Dial, 1979
ISBN 0-241-10451-3 : £4.25 : CIP rev. B80-24892

Ehrlich, Amy. The wild swans / Hans Christian Andersen ; pictures by Susan Jeffers ; retold by Amy Ehrlich. — London : Macmillan Children's Books, 1982, c1981. — 40p : col.ill ; 32cm
Originally published: New York : Dial, 1981
ISBN 0-333-32659-8 : £4.95 : CIP rev. B82-01857

Erickson, Russell E.. Warton and the castaways / by Russell E. Erickson ; pictures by Lawrence Di Fiori. — London : Hodder and Stoughton, 1982. — 112p : ill ; 22cm
ISBN 0-340-28147-2 : £3.95 : CIP rev. B82-12269

Erickson, Russell E.. Warton and the King of the Skies. — London : Knight, Oct.1982. — [96]p
Originally published: 1980
ISBN 0-340-28639-3 (pbk) : £0.95 : CIP entry B82-24836

Erickson, Russell E.. Warton's Christmas Eve adventure. — London : Knight, Oct.1982. — [96]p
Originally published: 1979
ISBN 0-340-28047-6 (pbk) : £0.95 : CIP entry B82-24820

Farrar, Susan Clement. Samantha on stage / Susan Clement Farrar. — [Sevenoaks] : Knight, 1981, c1979. — 125p ; 18cm
Originally published: New York : Dial Press, 1979 ; London : Julia MacRae, 1980
ISBN 0-340-26542-6 (pbk) : £0.95 : CIP rev. B81-31446

Fleischer, Leonore. Annie : a novel / by Leonore Fleischer ; based on a screenplay by Carol Sobieski. — London : Sparrow, 1982. — 190p ; 18cm
ISBN 0-09-929440-0 (pbk) : £1.00 B82-33320

Flory, Jane. The bear on the doorstep / Jane Flory ; illustrated by Carolyn Croll. — London : Chatto & Windus, 1982. — 32p : col.ill ; 19cm
Originally published: Boston, Mass. : Houghton Mifflin, 1980
ISBN 0-7011-2620-5 : £3.50 : CIP rev. B82-04578

The fox and the hound. — [London] : Collins, 1981. — [10]p : col.ill ; 28cm
A pop-up book
ISBN 0-00-183765-6 : £3.50 B82-08918

The Fox and the hound : based upon the Walt Disney Productions film of the same name. — London : Scholastic, 1982, c1981. — 30p : col.ill ; 23cm. — (Hippo books)
Originally published: New York : Golden Press, 1981
ISBN 0-590-70131-2 (pbk) : £1.25 B82-09337

Freschet, Berniece. Black bear baby / by Berniece Freschet ; pictures by Jim Arnosky. — Tadworth : World's Work, 1982, c1981. — 47p : ill(some col.) ; 23cm
ISBN 0-437-41304-7 : £3.95 B82-30435

Fujikawa, Gyo. The flyaway kite. — London : Hodder & Stoughton Children's Books, Aug.1981. — [32]p
ISBN 0-340-27080-2 : £1.75 : CIP entry B81-18029

Fujikawa, Gyo. Fraidy cat. — London : Hodder & Stoughton Children's Books, Oct.1982. — [32]p
ISBN 0-340-28603-2 (pbk) : £1.95 : CIP entry B82-27353

Fujikawa, Gyo. Jenny and Jupie / Gyo Fujikawa. — London : Hodder and Stoughton, 1982, c1981. — [26]p : ill(some col.) ; 24cm. — (Our stories)
Originally published: New York : Grosset & Dunlap, 1981
ISBN 0-340-27811-0 : £1.75 : CIP rev. B82-00264

Fujikawa, Gyo. The magic show / Gyo Fujikawa. — London : Hodder and Stoughton, 1982, c1981. — [26]p : ill(some col.) ; 24cm. — (Our stories)
Originally published: New York : Grosset & Dunlap, 1981
ISBN 0-340-27812-9 : £1.75 : CIP rev. B82-00265

Fujikawa, Gyo. Me too!. — London : Hodder & Stoughton Children's Books, Oct.1982. — [32]p
ISBN 0-340-28604-0 (pbk) : £1.95 : CIP entry B82-27354

Fujikawa, Gyo. Shag has a dream. — London : Hodder & Stoughton Children's Books, Aug.1981. — [32]p
ISBN 0-340-27079-9 : £1.75 : CIP entry B81-18030

Fujikawa, Gyo. Welcome is a wonderful word / Gyo Fujikawa. — London : Hodder and Stoughton, 1981, c1980. — [28]p : ill(some col.) ; 25cm
Originally published: New York : Grosset & Dunlap, 1980
ISBN 0-340-26768-2 : £1.75 B82-41008

Galdone, Paul. Hans in luck : retold from the Brothers Grimm / by Paul Galdone. — Tadworth : World's Work, 1981, c1979. — [40]p : col.ill ; 24cm. — (A World's Work children's book)
Originally published: New York : Parents' Magazine Press, 1979
ISBN 0-437-42530-4 : £3.95 B82-02792

813'.54[J] — Children's stories in English. American writers, *1945- — Texts*
continuation

Galdone, Paul. King of the cats : a ghost story / by Joseph Jacobs ; retold and illustrated by Paul Galdone. — Tadworth : World's Work, 1982, c1980. — [29]p : col.ill ; 20x25cm. — (A World's Work children's book)
Originally published: New York : Houghton Mifflin/Clarion, 1980
ISBN 0-437-42531-2 : £4.50 B82-22047

Galdone, Paul. The three sillies / by Joseph Jacobs ; retold and illustrated by Paul Galdone. — Kingswood : Worlds Work, 1982. — [40]p : col.ill ; 26cm
ISBN 0-437-42533-9 : £4.50 B82-36101

Ginsberg, Mirra. Good morning, chick / adapted from a story by Korney Chukovsky by Mirra Ginsberg ; pictures by Byron Barton. — London : Transworld, 1982, c1980. — [32]p : col.ill ; 21x25cm. — (A carousel book)
Originally published: New York : Greenwillow ; London : McRae, 1980
ISBN 0-552-52171-x (corrected : pbk) : £0.95 B82-37934

Ginsburg, Mirra. Across the stream. — London : MacRae, Feb.1983. — [32]p
ISBN 0-86203-113-3 : £4.95 : CIP entry B82-39816

Gipson, Fred. Hound-dog man / by Fred Gipson. — Lincoln, [Neb.] ; London : University of Nebraska Press, 1980, c1949. — 247p ; 20cm. — (A Bison book)
Originally published: New York : Harper, 1949
ISBN 0-8032-7005-4 (pbk) : £3.75 B82-34697

Goble, Paul. The gift of the sacred dog / story and illustrations by Paul Goble. — London : Macmillan, 1981, c1980. — [32]p : col.ill ; 26cm
Originally published: Scarsdale, NY : Bradbury Press, 1980
ISBN 0-333-31845-5 : £3.95 B82-11674

Grant, Myrna. Ivan and the informer / Myrna Grant. — Eastbourne : Kingsway, 1978, c1977. — 78p : ill ; 18cm
ISBN 0-86065-028-6 (pbk) : £0.70 B82-38624

Greene, Bette. Summer of my German soldier / Bette Greene. — Harmondsworth : Puffin, in association with Hamilton Children's Books, 1977, c1973 (1982 [printing]). — 205p ; 19cm. — (Puffin plus)
Originally published: New York : Dial, 1973 ; London : Hamilton : 1974
ISBN 0-14-030985-3 (pbk) : £1.25 B82-28631

Guy, Rosa. The friends / Rosa Guy. — London : Macmillan Education, 1982. — 196p ; 21cm. — (M books)
Originally published: London : Gollancz, 1974
ISBN 0-333-29514-5 : Unpriced : CIP rev. B82-01849

Hahn, Mary Downing. The Sara summer / Mary Downing Hahn. — London : Fontana, 1982, c1979. — 128p ; 18cm. — (Lions)
Originally published: New York : Houghton Mifflin, 1979
ISBN 0-00-672028-5 (pbk) : £1.00 B82-33553

Harrison, David L. (David Lee). Detective Bob and the great ape escape / by David L. Harrison ; pictures by Ned Delaney. — London : Hamilton, 1982, c1980. — [44]p : col.ill ; 24cm
Originally published: New York : Parents Magazine, 1980
ISBN 0-241-10770-9 : £4.25 : CIP rev. B82-12569

Hoban, Russell. The battle of Zormla / Russell Hoban ; pictures by Colin McNaughton. — London : Methuen/Walker, 1982. — [26]p : col.ill ; 16x19cm
ISBN 0-416-05960-0 : Unpriced : CIP rev. B82-04846

Hoban, Russell. Bread and jam for Frances / by Russell Hoban ; pictures by Lillian Hoban. — Harmondsworth : Puffin in associaton with Faber, 1977, c1964 (1982 [printing]). — 31p : col.ill ; 23cm. — (Picture Puffins)
Originally published: New York : Harper & Row, 1964 ; London : Faber, 1966
ISBN 0-14-050176-2 (pbk) : £1.10 B82-29592

Hoban, Russell. Flat cat / written by Russell Hoban ; illustrated by Clive Scruton. — London : Methuen/Walker Books, 1980. — [26]p : col.ill ; 22cm
ISBN 0-416-89960-9 : £3.50 : CIP rev. B80-18916

Hoban, Russell. The flight of Bembel Rudzuk / Russell Hoban ; pictures by Colin McNaughton. — London : Methuen/Walker, 1982. — [26]p : col.ill ; 16x19cm
ISBN 0-416-05950-3 : Unpriced : CIP rev. B82-04845

Hoban, Russell. The great fruit gum robbery / Russell Hoban ; pictures by Colin McNaughton. — London : Methuen, 1981. — [26]p : col.ill ; 16cm
ISBN 0-416-05790-x : £2.95 : CIP rev. B81-23743

Hoban, Russell. They came from Aargh! / Russell Hoban ; pictures by Colin McNaughton. — London : Methuen/Walker, 1981. — [28]p : col.ill ; 12x19cm
ISBN 0-416-05840-x : £2.95 : CIP rev. B81-23744

Hogan, Paula. Mum, will dad ever come back? / by Paula Hogan ; illustrated by Dora Leder. — Oxford : Blackwell Raintree, c1981. — 31p : col.ill ; 24cm
Originally published: Milwaukee : Raintree, 1980
ISBN 0-86256-002-0 : £2.50 : CIP rev. B81-20172

Hogan, Paula. Sometimes I don't like school. — Oxford : Blackwell Raintree, May 1982. — [32]p
ISBN 0-86256-005-5 : £2.50 : CIP entry B82-07685

Hogan, Paula Z.. Sometimes I get so angry. — Oxford : Blackwell Raintree, May 1982. — [32]p
ISBN 0-86256-006-3 : £2.50 : CIP entry B82-07686

Hope, Laura Lee. The Rose Parade mystery / Laura Lee Hope ; illustrated by Ruth Sanderson. — London : Transworld, 1982. — 91p : ill ; 18cm. — (The Bobbsey twins ; 5) (A Carousel book)
ISBN 0-552-52164-7 (pbk) : £0.85 B82-19370

Isadora, Rachel. Max / story & pictures by Rachel Isadora. — London : Carousel, 1982, c1976. — [32]p : ill ; 18x22cm
Originally published: New York : Macmillan, 1976
ISBN 0-552-52166-3 (pbk) : £0.95 B82-29321

Kahn, Joan. Hi, Jock, run around the block / by Joan Kahn ; pictures by Whitney Darrow, Jr. — New York ; London : Harper & Row, c1978. — 24p : col.ill ; 21cm
ISBN 0-06-023079-7 : £2.95
ISBN 0-06-023078-9 (pbk) : Unpriced B82-16801

Kalan, Robert. Jump, frog, jump! / by Robert Kalan ; pictures by Byron Barton. — London : MacRae, 1982, c1981. — [32]p : col.ill ; 21x26cm
Originally published: New York : Greenwillow, 1981
ISBN 0-86203-078-1 : £4.95 : CIP rev. B82-04714

Kellogg, Steven. The mystery of the magic green ball / story and pictures by Steven Kellogg. — [London] : Carousel, 1982, c1978. — [32]p : col.ill ; 19cm
Originally published: New York : Dial, 1978 ; London : Bodley Head, 1980
ISBN 0-552-52206-6 (pbk) : £0.95 B82-37872

Kellogg, Steven. The mystery of the missing red mitten / story and pictures by Steven Kellogg. — [London] : Carousel, 1982, c1974. — [32]p : col.ill ; 19cm
Originally published: New York : Dial, 1974 ; London : Bodley Head, 1980
ISBN 0-552-52205-8 (pbk) : £0.95 B82-37873

Kellogg, Steven. A rose for Pinkerton / story and pictures by Steven Kellogg. — London : Warne, 1982, c1981. — [32]p : col.ill ; 27cm
Originally published: New York : Dial, 1981
ISBN 0-7232-2901-5 : £3.95 B82-22135

Kenny, Kathryn. Trixie Belden and the black jacket mystery / by Kathryn Kenny ; cover by Jack Wacker. — London : Dean, 1982, c1977. — 187p ; 20cm. — (A Trixie Belden mystery ; no.8)
Cover title: The black jacket mystery. — Originally published: Racine, Wis. : Whitman, 1961
ISBN 0-603-00303-6 : Unpriced B82-25595

Kenny, Kathryn. Trixie Belden and the Happy Valley mystery / by Kathryn Kenny ; cover by Jack Wacker. — London : Dean, 1982, c1977. — 186p ; 20cm. — (A Trixie Belden mystery ; no.9)
Cover title: The Happy Valley mystery. — Originally published: Racine, Wis. : Whitman, 1962
ISBN 0-603-00304-4 : Unpriced B82-25592

Kenny, Kathryn. Trixie Belden and the marshland mystery / by Kathryn Kenny ; cover by Jack Wacker. — London : Dean, 1982, c1977. — 186p ; 20cm. — (A Trixie Belden mystery ; no.10)
Cover title: The marshland mystery. — Originally published: New York : Golden Press, 1967
ISBN 0-603-00305-2 : Unpriced B82-25596

Kenny, Kathryn. Trixie Belden and the mysterious code / by Kathryn Kenny ; cover by Jack Wacker. — London : Dean, 1982, c1977. — 186p ; 20cm. — (A Trixie Belden mystery ; no.7)
Cover title: The mysterious code. — Originally published: Racine, Wis. : Whitman, 1966
ISBN 0-603-00302-8 : Unpriced B82-25591

Kenny, Kathryn. Trixie Belden and the mystery at Bob-White Cave / by Kathryn Kenny ; cover by Jack Wacker. — London : Dean, 1982, c1977. — 187p ; 20cm. — (A Trixie Belden mystery ; no.11)
Cover title: The mystery at Bob-White Cave. — Originally published: Racine, Wis. : Whitman, 1963
ISBN 0-603-00306-0 : Unpriced B82-25593

Kenny, Kathryn. Trixie Belden and the mystery of the blinking eye / by Kathryn Kenny ; cover by Jack Wacker. — London : Dean, 1982, c1977. — 186p ; 20cm. — (A Trixie Belden mystery ; no.12)
Cover title: The mystery of the blinking eye. — Originally published: Racine, Wis. : Whitman, 1963
ISBN 0-603-00307-9 : Unpriced B82-25594

Kenny, Kevin. Sometimes my mum drinks too much / by Kevin Kenny and Helen Krull ; illustrated by Helen Coganchery. — Oxford : Blackwell Raintree, c1981. — 31p : col.ill ; 24cm
Originally published: Milwaukee : Raintree, 1980
ISBN 0-86256-004-7 : £2.50 : CIP rev. B81-20167

813'.54[J] — Children's stories in English. American writers, *1945-* — *Texts*
continuation

Kjelgaard, Jim. Lion hound / by Jim Kjelgaard ; illustrated by Jacob Landau. — London : Transworld, 1982, c1955. — 131p : ill ; 20cm. — (A Carousel book)
Originally published: New York : Holiday House, 1955
ISBN 0-552-52161-2 (pbk) : £0.95 B82-12583

Levy, Elizabeth. The case of the counterfeit race horse / Elizabeth Levy. — [London] : Knight Books, 1982, c1980. — 123p ; 18cm. — (A Jody and Jake mystery)
Originally published: New York : Pocket, 1980
ISBN 0-340-28333-5 (pbk) : £0.95 : CIP rev. B82-16472

Levy, Elizabeth. The case of the fire raising gang / Elizabeth Levy. — London : Knight Books, 1982, c1981. — 123p ; 18cm. — (A Jody and Jake mystery)
Originally published: New York : Pocket, 1980
ISBN 0-340-28585-0 (pbk) : £0.95 : CIP rev. B82-15757

Levy, Elizabeth. The case of the frightened rock star / Elizabeth Levy. — [London] : Knight Books, 1982, c1980. — 128p ; 18cm. — (A Jody and Jake mystery)
Originally published: New York : Pocket, 1980
ISBN 0-340-28332-7 (pbk) : £0.95 : CIP rev. B82-16473

Levy, Elizabeth. The case of the wild river ride. — London : Knight Books Feb.1983. — [128]p
Originally published: New York : Pocket Books, 1981
ISBN 0-340-32793-6 (pbk) : £0.95 : CIP entry B82-38071

Lionni, Leo. Cornelius. — London : Andersen Press, Feb.1983. — [36]p
ISBN 0-86264-038-5 : £4.50 : CIP entry B82-39826

Lionni, Leo. Let's make rabbits. — London : Andersen Press, Sept.1982. — [32]p
ISBN 0-86264-023-7 : £4.50 : CIP entry B82-21559

Lobel, Arnold. Frog and toad tales / Arnold Lobel. — Tadworth : World's Work, 1981, c1976. — 190p : col.ill ; 22cm
ISBN 0-437-55717-0 : £3.95 B82-06159

Lobel, Arnold. Ming Lo moves the mountain. — London : MacRae, Oct.1982. — [32]p
ISBN 0-86203-110-9 : £4.95 : CIP entry B82-24588

Lorenz, Lee. The feathered ogre / Lee Lorenz. — London : Dent, 1982, c1981. — [32]p : chiefly col.ill ; 29cm
Originally published: Englewood Cliffs : Prentice-Hall, 1981
ISBN 0-460-06098-8 : £3.95 : CIP rev. B81-38309

McKinley, Robin. The blue sword. — London : Julia MacRae, Feb.1983. — [272]p
Originally published: New York : Greenwillow, 1982
ISBN 0-86203-123-0 : £6.95 : CIP entry B82-39288

Madler, Trudy. Why did gramdma die? by Trudy Madler / illustrated by Gwen Connelly. — Oxford : Blackwell Raintree, c1981. — 31p : col.ill ; 24cm
Originally published: Milwaukee : Raintree, 1980
ISBN 0-86256-001-2 : £2.50 : CIP rev. B81-20170

Marshall, Edward. Fox and his friends. — London : Bodley Head, Sept.1982. — [64]p. — (Bodley beginners)
ISBN 0-370-30935-9 : £3.50 : CIP entry B82-19203

Marshall, James, *1942-*. Portley McSwine / James Marshall. — London : Transworld, 1981, c1979. — [39]p : col.ill ; 19cm. — (A Carousel book)
Originally published: Boston : Houghton Mifflin, 1979
ISBN 0-552-52150-7 (pbk) : £0.90 B82-09112

Marshall, James, *1942-*. Taking care of Carruthers. — London : Bodley Head, Oct.1982. — [128]p
Originally published: Boston : Houghton Mifflin, 1981
ISBN 0-370-30939-1 : £3.95 : CIP entry B82-24456

Mayer, Marianna. The unicorn and the lake. — London : Methuen Children's Books, Feb.1983. — [32]p
ISBN 0-416-27100-6 : £5.95 : CIP entry B82-38262

Meehan, Thomas. Annie : an old-fashioned story / by Thomas Meehan. — London : Granada, 1982, c1980. — 188p ; 23cm
Originally published: New York : Macmillan, 1980
ISBN 0-246-11735-4 : £4.95 B82-22626

Montgomery, R. A.. Journey under the sea / R.A. Montgomery ; illustrated by Paul Granger. — Toronto ; London : Bantam, 1979 (1981 printing). — 117p : ill ; 18cm
Originally published: Waitsfield : Vermont Crossroads, 1977
ISBN 0-553-20979-5 (pbk) : £0.75 B82-19381

Montgomery, R. A.. Space and beyond / R.A. Montgomery ; illustrated by Paul Granger. — Toronto ; London : Bantam, 1980, c1979 (1982 printing). — 116p : ill ; 18cm. — (Choose your own adventure ; 4)
ISBN 0-553-20891-8 (pbk) : £0.75 B82-19376

Moxley, Susan. Gardener George goes to town. — London : Hodder & Stoughton Children's Books, Oct.1982. — [24]p
ISBN 0-340-28622-9 : £4.95 : CIP entry B82-24835

Myers, Walter Dean. The golden serpent / by Walter Dean Myers ; illustrated by Alice and Martin Provensen. — London : MacRae, 1981, c1980. — [40]p : col.ill ; 19x23cm
Originally published: New York : Viking, 1980
ISBN 0-86203-087-0 : £4.25 B82-18166

Newman, Robert, *1909-*. The case of the vanishing corpse / Robert Newman. — London : Hutchinson, 1981. — 174p ; 21cm
Originally published: New York : Atheneum, 1980
ISBN 0-09-145750-5 : £4.95 : CIP rev. B81-20183

Nygren, Bill. Teeny tiny gnome tomes / illustrated by Rien ; [adapted by Bill Nygren]. — [London] : Methuen, 1981. — 1case : col.ill ; 11cm
Adaptation of: Leven en werken de Kabouter. — Title from case. — Contents: A gnome counting book — Gnomes to the rescue — Little gnome facts
ISBN 0-416-24400-9 : £2.75 B82-15553

Packard, Edward. The cave of time / Edward Packard ; illustrated by Paul Granger. — Toronto ; London : Bantam, 1979 (1981 printing). — 115p : ill ; 18cm. — (Choose your own adventure ; 1)
ISBN 0-553-20892-6 (pbk) : £0.75 B82-19379

Packard, Edward. The mystery of Chimney Rock / Edward Packard ; illustrated by Paul Granger. — Toronto ; London : Bantam, 1980 (1981 printing). — 121p : ill ; 18cm. — (Choose your own adventure ; 5)
ISBN 0-553-20961-2 (pbk) : £0.75 B82-19377

Packard, Edward. [The Third planet from Altair]. Exploration infinity / Edward Packard ; illustrated by Barbara Carter. — London : Magnet, 1982, c1979. — 96p : ill ; 18cm
Originally published: Philadelphia : Lippincott, 1979 ; London : Evans Brothers, 1980
ISBN 0-416-24450-5 (pbk) : £0.95 B82-33296

Packard, Edward. Your code name is Jonah / Edward Packard ; illustrated by Paul Granger. — Toronto ; London : Bantam, 1980, c1979 (1981 printing). — 114p : ill ; 18cm. — (Choose your own adventure ; 6)
ISBN 0-553-20913-2 (pbk) : £0.75 B82-19378

Parish, Peggy. Amelia Bedelia and the baby / Peggy Parish ; pictures by Lynn Sweat. — Tadworth : World's Work, 1982. — 63p : col.ill ; 22cm
Originally published: New York : Greenwillow, 1981
ISBN 0-437-66109-1 : £3.95 B82-26950

Peet, Bill. Encore for Eleanor. — London : Deutsch, Oct.1982. — [32]p
Originally published: Boston : Houghton Mifflin, 1981
ISBN 0-233-97491-1 : £4.50 : CIP entry B82-24712

Perl, Lila. That crazy April / Lila Perl. — London : Fontana, c1974 (1982 [printing]). — 160p ; 18cm. — (Lions)
Originally published: New York : Seabury, 1974 ; London : Collins, 1975
ISBN 0-00-671228-2 (pbk) : £1.00 B82-36230

Philips, Barbara. Don't call me fatty / by Barbara Philips ; illustrated by Helen Cogancherry. — Oxford : Blackwell Raintree, c1981. — 31p : col.ill ; 24cm
Originally published: Milwaukee : Raintree, 1980
ISBN 0-86256-003-9 : £2.50 : CIP rev. B81-20169

Quigley, Stacey. Do I have to? / by Stacy Quigley ; illustrated by Susan Lexa. — Oxford : Blackwell Raintree, c1981. — 31p : col.ill ; 24cm
Originally published: Milwaukee : Raintree, 1980
ISBN 0-86256-000-4 : £2.50 : CIP rev. B81-20168

Quin-Harkin, Janet. Magic growing powder / by Janet Quin-Harkin ; pictures by Art Cumings. — London : Hamilton, 1982, c1980. — [44]p : col.ill ; 24cm
Originally published: New York : Parents Magazine, 1980
ISBN 0-241-10771-7 : £4.25 : CIP rev. B82-12570

Rice, Eve. Benny bakes a cake / story and pictures by Eve Rice. — London : Bodley Head, 1982, c1981. — [32]p : col.ill ; 21x26cm
Originally published: New York : Greenwillow Books, 1981
ISBN 0-370-30921-9 : £3.95 : CIP rev. B82-00294

Rose, Anne. The talking turnip / Anne Rose ; Paul Galdone drew the pictures. — Tadworth : World's Work, 1981, c1979. — [40]p : col.ill ; 24cm. — (A World's Work children's book)
Originally published: New York : Parents' Magazine Press, 1979
ISBN 0-437-71680-5 : £3.95 B82-02791

Rotsler, William. Mr Merlin 1 / by William Rotsler ; based on characters created by Larry Rosen and Larry Tucker in association with Columbia Pictures Television. — [London] : Beaver, 1982, c1981. — 94p ; 18cm
Originally published: New York : Wanderer, 1981
ISBN 0-600-20637-8 (pbk) : £0.85 B82-13043

813'.54[J] — Children's stories in English. American writers, *1945-* — Texts
continuation

Rotsler, William. Mr Merlin 2 / by William Rotsler ; based on characters created by Larry Rosen and Larry Tucker in association with Columbia Pictures Television. — [London] : Beaver, 1982, c1981. — 93p ; 18cm
Originally published: New York : Wanderer, 1981
ISBN 0-600-20638-6 (pbk) : £0.85 B82-13042

Scarry, Richard. Richard Scarry's Best Christmas book ever!. — Glasgow : Collins, 1981. — [44]p : col.ill,music ; 28cm
Ill on lining papers
ISBN 0-00-138087-7 : £3.50 B82-03497

Selden, George. The cricket in Times Square / George Selden ; illustrated by Garth Williams. — Harmondsworth : Kestrel, 1982, c1960. — 140p : ill ; 23cm
Originally published: Ariel, 1960
ISBN 0-7226-5799-4 : £4.95 B82-36114

Selden, George. The cricket in Times Square / George Selden ; illustrated by Garth Williams. — Harmondsworth, Penguin, 1982, c1960. — 140p : ill ; 18cm
Originally published: New York : Ariel, 1960 ; London : Dent, 1961
ISBN 0-14-030183-6 (pbk) : £0.95 B82-39317

Shannon, George. Dance away. — London : MacRae, Jan.1983. — [32]p
ISBN 0-86203-114-1 : £4.95 : CIP entry B82-33229

Shannon, George. Lizard's song / George Shannon ; illustrated by Jose Aruego and Ariane Dewey. — London : MacRae, 1982, c1981. — [32]p : col.ill,music ; 21x26cm
Originally published: New York : Greenwillow, 1981
ISBN 0-86203-057-9 : £4.95 : CIP rev. B81-34663

Shannon, George. The Piney Woods peddler / told by George Shannon ; pictures by Nancy Tafuri. — London : Julia MacRae, 1982, c1981. — 32p : col.ill ; 21x26cm
Originally published: New York : Greenwillow Books, 1981
ISBN 0-86203-061-7 : £4.95 : CIP rev. B81-37584

Sheldon, Ann. [Linda Craig and the clue on the desert trail]. The clue on the desert trail / Ann Sheldon ; illustrated by St Ward. — London : Armada, 1982, c1962. — 187p : ill ; 18cm. — (Linda Craig ; 2)
Originally published: Garden City, N.Y. : Doubleday, 1962
ISBN 0-00-692023-3 (pbk) : £0.90 B82-25431

Sheldon, Ann. [Linda Craig and the palomino mystery]. The palomino mystery / Ann Sheldon ; illustrated by St Ward. — London : Armada, 1982, c1962. — 187p : ill ; 18cm. — (Linda Craig ; 1)
Originally published: Garden City, N.Y. : Doubleday, 1962
ISBN 0-00-692022-5 (pbk) : £0.90 B82-25430

Shire, Ellen. The chicken scandal at Number 7 Rue Petite / by Ellen Shire. — London : Hamilton, 1980, c1978. — [32]p : col.ill ; 21cm
Originally published: New York : Random House, c1978
ISBN 0-241-10454-8 : £3.95 : CIP rev. B80-11225

Shyer, Marlene Fanta. My brother, the thief / Marlene Fanta Shyer. — London : Granada, 1982, c1980. — 125p : ill ; 23cm
Originally published: New York : Scribner, 1980
ISBN 0-246-11635-8 : £4.95 B82-22902

Simon, Seymour. Einstein Anderson shocks his friends / Seymour Simon ; illustrated by John Millington. — London : Scholastic, 1981, c1980. — 95p : ill ; 18cm. — (Hippo books)
Originally published: New York : Viking, 1980
ISBN 0-590-70081-2 (pbk) : £0.70 B82-02268

Smath, Jerry. But no elephants / by Jerry Smath. — London : Hamilton, 1980. — [41]p : col.ill ; 24cm
Originally published: New York : Parent Magazine Press, c1979
ISBN 0-241-10449-1 : £3.95 : CIP rev. B80-18526

Stevenson, James. The night after Christmas. — London : Gollancz, Oct.1982. — [32]p
ISBN 0-575-03129-8 : £4.95 : CIP entry B82-23341

Stevenson, Jocelyn. The muppets go camping : starring Jim Henson's muppets / by Jocelyn Stevenson ; illustrated by Bruce McNally. — London : Sphere, 1982, c19881. — [32]p : col.ill ; 18cm
ISBN 0-7221-8245-7 (pbk) : £0.95 B82-22596

Stevenson, Jocelyn. Robin Hood : a high-spirited tale of adventure starring Jim Henson's Muppets ... / [written by Jocelyn Stevenson] ; [designed and illustrated by Bruce McNally]. — London : Joseph, 1981. — [20]p : col.ill ; 29cm
Ill on lining papers
ISBN 0-7181-2069-8 : £3.95 B82-03294

Stevenson, John, *1959-*. The whale tale : starring Jim Henson's muppets / written and illustrated by John Stevenson. — London : Sphere, 1982, c1981. — [32]p : col.ill ; 18cm
Originally published: New York : Random House, 1981
ISBN 0-7221-8244-9 (pbk) : £0.95 B82-22595

Terman, Douglas. By balloon to the Sahara / D. Terman ; illustrated by Paul Granger. — Toronto ; London : Bantam, 1979 (1982 printing). — 117p : ill ; 18cm. — (Choose your own adventure ; 3)
ISBN 0-553-20949-3 (pbk) : £0.75 B82-19380

The **Three** little pigs / with illustrations by Erik Blegvad. — London : MacRae, 1980. — 31p : col.ill ; 19cm
ISBN 0-86203-090-0 : £3.75 : CIP rev. B80-22612

Tod the fox cub. — Bristol : Purnell, c1981. — [8p] : chiefly col.ill ; 28cm. — (The Fox and the hound)
Cover title
ISBN 0-361-05295-2 : £0.99 B82-17529

Wahl, Jan. Sylvester Bear overslept / Jan Wahl ; pictures by Lee Lorenz. — Tadworth : World's Work, 1981, c1979. — [40]p : col.ill ; 24cm. — (A World's Work children's book)
Originally published: New York : Parents' Magazine Press, 1979
ISBN 0-437-84186-3 : £3.95 B82-02790

Walt Disney presents Sleeping Beauty. — Bristol : Purnell, 1982. — [40]p : col.ill ; 15cm. — (A Disney Playmate)
ISBN 0-361-05341-x (pbk) : £0.50 B82-27622

Walt Disney presents Snow White and the seven dwarfs. — Bristol : Purnell, 1982. — [40p] : col.ill ; 15cm. — (A Disney playmate)
ISBN 0-361-05341-x (pbk) : £0.50 B82-28903

Walt Disney Productions presents Bambi grows up. — [London] : [Collins], c1979. — [48]p : col.ill ; 15cm. — (Collins colour cubs)
ISBN 0-00-123745-4 (pbk) : £0.50 B82-25581

Walt Disney Productions presents Lady and the tramp. — [London] : [Collins], c1981. — [48]p : col.ill ; 15cm. — (Collins colour cubs)
ISBN 0-00-123743-8 (pbk) : £0.50 B82-25580

Walt Disney Productions' The fox and the hound . — Bristol : Purnell, 1981. — [34]p : col.ill ; 29cm
ISBN 0-361-05367-3 : Unpriced B82-15302

Walt Disney's if I met Mickey. — Bristol : Purnell, 1982. — 1folded sheet(16p) : col.ill ; 80x90mm
Cover title
ISBN 0-361-05430-0 : £1.50 B82-22341

Wells, Rosemary, *19---*. Good night, Fred / Rosemary Wells. — London : Macmillan Children's Books, 1982, c1982. — [28]p : col.ill ; 20cm
Originally published: New York : Dial, 1981
ISBN 0-333-32660-1 : £2.95 : CIP rev. B82-01858

Westcott, Nadine Bernard. The giant vegetable garden / by Nadine Bernard Westcott. — London : Hutchinson, 1981. — 32p : chiefly col.ill ; 26cm
ISBN 0-09-146630-x : £3.95 : CIP rev. B81-30267

Wilkes, Marilyn Z.. C.L.U.T.Z.. — London : Gollancz, Oct.1982. — [128]p
ISBN 0-575-03200-6 : £4.95 : CIP entry B82-23349

Williams, Gregory. Kermit and Cleopigtra : starring Jim Henson's Muppets / written by Gregory Williams ; illustrated by Sue Venning. — London : Joseph, 1982, c1981. — [38]p : col.ill ; 29cm
Originally published: New York : Random House, 1981
ISBN 0-7181-2109-0 : £3.95 B82-17350

Wittman, Sally. [A special trade]. A special swap / by Sally Wittman ; pictures by Karen Gundersheimer. — London : Scholastic, 1980, c1978. — [32]p : col.ill ; 18cm. — (A Hippo book)
Originally published: New York : Harper & Row, 1978
ISBN 0-590-70040-5 (pbk) : £0.85 B82-16803

Wolkoff, Judie. Wally / Judie Wolkoff. — London : Scholastic, 1981, c1977. — 141p ; 18cm. — (A Hippo book)
Originally published: Scarsdale, N.Y. : Bradbury, 1977
ISBN 0-590-72154-2 (pbk) : £0.70 B82-14127

Worth, Valerie. Imp and Biscuit : the fortunes of two pugs / Valerie Worth ; with pictures by Natalie Babbitt. — London : Chatto & Windus, 1981, c1980. — 51p : ill ; 21cm
Originally published: New York : Farrar, Straus and Giroux, 1980
ISBN 0-7011-2606-x : £3.95 : CIP rev. B81-28062

Wright, Betty Ren. My new mum and me. — Oxford : Blackwell Raintree, May 1982. — [32]p
ISBN 0-86256-008-x : £2.50 : CIP entry B82-07688

Wright, Betty Ren. My sister is different. — Oxford : Blackwell Raintree, May 1982. — [32]p
ISBN 0-86256-007-1 : £2.50 : CIP entry B82-07687

Zalben, Jane Breskin. Norton's night-time / story and pictures by Jane Breskin Zalben. — [London] : Fontana, 1981, c1979. — [28]p : col.ill ; 21cm. — (Picture Lions)
Originally published: London : Collins, 1979
ISBN 0-00-661771-9 (pbk) : £0.90 B82-09325

Zelonky, Joy. I can't always hear you. — Oxford : Blackwell Raintree, May 1982. — [32]p
ISBN 0-86256-009-8 : £2.50 : CIP entry B82-07689

813'.54[J] — Children's stories in English. Canadian writers, *1945-* — Texts

Hill, Douglas. Day of the starwind / Douglas Hill. — London : Piccolo, 1982, c1980. — 123p ; 18cm
Originally published: London : Gollancz, 1980
ISBN 0-330-26652-7 (pbk) : £1.10 B82-22152

813′.54[J] — Children's stories in English. Canadian writers, *1945-* **—** *Texts*
continuation

Houston, James. River runners : a tale of hardship and bravery / by James Houston ; drawings by the author. — Hardmondsworth : Penguin, 1981, c1979. — 142p : ill ; 19cm
Originally published: New York : Atheneum, 1979
ISBN 0-14-031430-x (pbk) : £0.95 B82-08659

Munsch, Robert N.. The paper bag princess / by Robert N. Munsch ; illustrated by Michael Martchenko. — London : Scholastic, 1982, c1980. — 26p : col.ill ; 20cm. — (A Hippo book)
ISBN 0-590-71126-1 (pbk) : £0.85 B82-14128

813′.54′0803520396073 — Fiction in English. Negro American writers, *1945-.* **Special subjects: United States. Negroes —** *Anthologies — For schools*

Black lives, white worlds / [edited by] Keith Ajegbo. — Cambridge : Cambridge University Press, 1982. — 139p : ill ; 21cm
ISBN 0-521-28463-5 (pbk) : £1.75 : CIP rev.
B82-17204

813′.54′09 — Fiction in English. American writers, *1945-* **—** *Critical studies*

Hendin, Josephine. Vulnerable people : a view of American fiction since 1945 / Josephine Hendin. — Oxford : Oxford University Press, 1979, c1978. — 237p ; 22cm. — (A Galaxy book)
Originally published: New York : Oxford University Press, 1978. — Includes index
ISBN 0-19-502319-6 (cased) : Unpriced
ISBN 0-19-502620-9 (pbk) : £3.50 B82-25896

Kernan, Alvin B.. The imaginary library : an essay on literature and society / Alvin B. Kernan. — Princeton ; Guildford : Princeton University Press, c1982. — 186p ; 23cm
Bibliography: p176-179. — Includes index
ISBN 0-691-06504-7 : £10.60 B82-21059

Stevick, Philip. Alternative pleasures : postrealistic fiction and the tradition / Philip Stevick. — Urbana ; London : University of Illinois Press, c1981. — xii,156p ; 24cm
Includes index
ISBN 0-252-00877-4 : £9.80 B82-05726

814.52 — AMERICAN ESSAYS, 1900-1945

814′.52 — Essays in English. American writers, *1900-1945* **—** *Texts*

Trilling, Lionel. The last decade. — Oxford : Oxford University Press, Jan.1982. — [250]p. — (The works of Lionel Trilling)
ISBN 0-19-212220-7 : £8.95 : CIP entry
B81-34372

817.54 — AMERICAN SATIRE AND HUMOUR, 1945-

817′.54′0809282 — Children's humour in English. American writers, *1945-* **—** *Anthologies*

Gomez, Victoria. Wags to witches : jokes, riddles and puns / by Victoria Gomez ; illustrated by Joel Schick. — London : Scholastic, 1982, c1981. — 64p : ill ; 18cm
Originally published: New York : Lothrop, Lee & Shepherd, 1981
ISBN 0-590-70112-6 (pbk) : £0.70 B82-31945

818.2 — AMERICAN MISCELLANY, 1776-1830

818′.209 — English literature. American writers. Darby, William, *1775-1854* **—** *Biographies*

Kennedy, J. Gerald. The astonished traveler : William Darby, frontier geographer and man of letters / J. Gerald Kennedy. — Baton Rouge ; London : Louisiana State University Press, c1981. — xiii,238p : 2maps,2facsims ; 24cm
Bibliography: p231-234. — Includes index
ISBN 0-8071-0886-3 : £15.75 B82-22550

818.3 — AMERICAN MISCELLANY, 1830-1861

818′.308 — Prose in English. American writers, *1830-1861* **—** *Texts*

Whitman, Walt. Thoughts under an oak : a dream / Walt Whitman. — Great Crosby (51 York Ave., Great Crosby, Liverpool L23 5RN) : Cracked Bell Press, 1979. — [12]p ; 13cm
Unpriced (pbk) B82-27267

818′.309 — English literature. American writers, *1830-1861* **—** *Texts*

Emerson, Ralph Waldo. The portable Emerson / edited by Carl Bode in collaboration with Malcolm Cowley. — Rev. ed. — Harmondsworth : Penguin, 1981. — xxxix,670p ; 18cm
Previous ed.: 1946. — Bibliography: p669-670
ISBN 0-14-015094-3 (pbk) : £2.95 B82-26444

Poe, Edgar Allan. [Works]. The complete tales and poems of Edgar Allan Poe. — Harmondsworth : Penguin, 1982, c1965. — 1026p ; 21cm
ISBN 0-14-009001-0 (pbk) : £3.95 B82-30265

818′.309 — English literature. American writers. Thoreau, Henry David — *Correspondence, diaries, etc.*

Thoreau, Henry David. Journal / Henry D. Thoreau. — Priceton, N.J. ; Guildford : Princeton University Press. — (The writings of Henry D. Thoreau)
Vol.1: 1837-1844 / John C. Broderick general editor ; edited by Elizabeth Hall Witherell ... [et al.]. — 1981. — 702p,[4]p of plates : ill,facsims ; 21cm
Bibliography: p534-541. — Includes index
ISBN 0-691-06361-3 : £16.10 B82-02429

818.4 — AMERICAN MISCELLANY, 1861-1900

818′.408 — Prose in English. American writers, *1861-1900* **—** *Texts*

Babbitt, Irving. Irving Babbitt : representative writings / edited with an introduction by George A. Panichas. — Lincoln, [Neb.] ; London : University of Nebraska Press, c1981. — xxxix,315p : 1port ; 23cm
Bibliography: p293-297. — Includes index
ISBN 0-8032-3655-7 : £14.55 B82-37679

Twain, Mark. Early tales and sketches. — Berkeley ; London : Published for the Iowa Center for Textual Studies by the University of California Press. — (The Works of Mark Twain ; v.15)
Vol.2: 1864-1865 / edited by Edgar Marquess Branch and Robert H. Hirst with the a ssistance of Harriet Elinor Smith. — 1981. — xx,763p : ill,facsims,ports ; 24cm
Includes index
ISBN 0-520-04382-0 : £26.25 B82-02227

818′.409 — English literature. American writers. Chesnut, Mary Boykin — *Biographies*

Muhlenfeld, Elisabeth. Mary Boykin Chesnut : a biography / Elisabeth Muhlenfeld. — Baton Rouge ; London : Louisiana State University Press, c1981. — xv,271p : ill,facsims,ports ; 24cm. — (Southern biography series)
Bibliography: p253-261. — Includes index
ISBN 0-8071-0852-9 : £14.00 B82-01301

818′.409 — English literature. American writers. Twain, Mark — *Correspondence, diaries, etc.*

Twain, Mark. The selected letters of Mark Twain / edited with an introduction and commentary by Charles Neider. — New York ; London : Harper & Row, c1982. — xxi,328p : facsims,1port ; 25cm
Includes index
ISBN 0-06-014946-9 : £8-95 B82-30679

818.52 — AMERICAN MISCELLANY, 1900-1945

818′.5207 — Humorous prose in English. American writers, *1900-1945* **—** *Texts*

Perelman, S. J.. The last laugh / S.J. Perelman ; introduction by Paul Theroux. — London : Methuen London : 1982, c1981. — 192p ; 20cm
Originally published: London : Eyre Methuen, 1981
ISBN 0-413-50680-0 (pbk) : £3.95 B82-36075

Perelman, S. J.. The last laugh / S.J. Perelman ; introduction by Paul Theroux. — London : Eyre Methuen, 1981. — 192p ; 23cm
ISBN 0-413-48820-9 : £6.50 B82-17560

Sale, Charles. [I'll tell you why]. The master builder. — London : Putnam, Sept.1982. — [48]p
Originally published as: I'll tell you why. St. Louis : Specialist Publishing Co., 1930
ISBN 0-370-30927-8 : £1.95 : CIP entry
B82-19209

818′.5208 — Prose in English. American writers, *1900-1945* **—** *Texts*

Nin, Anaïs. A woman speaks / the lectures, seminars and interviews of Anaïs Nin ; edited with an introduction by Evelyn J. Hinz. — [London] : Star, 1982, c1975. — xviii,270p ; 18cm
Originally published: Chicago : Swallow, 1975. — Includes index
ISBN 0-352-30444-8 (corrected : pbk) : £1.60
B82-33632

818′.5209 — English literature. American writers, *1900-1945* **—** *Texts*

White, E. B.. Poems and sketches of E.B. White. — New York ; London : Harper & Row, c1981. — xvi,217p : ill ; 24cm
ISBN 0-06-014900-0 : Unpriced B82-08882

818′.5209 — English literature. American writers. Agee, James — *Biographies*

Doty, Mark A.. Tell me who I am : James Agee's search for selfhood / Mark A. Doty. — Baton Rouge ; London : Louisiana State University Press, c1981. — xiii,144p ; 24cm
Bibliography: p135-140. — Includes index
ISBN 0-8071-0758-1 : £11.20 B82-01299

818′.5209 — English literature. American writers. Stein, Gertrude — *Critical studies*

Pearson, Norman Holmes. The escape from time : poetry, language and symbol : Stein, Pound, Eliot / by Norman H. Pearson. — Portree : Aquila, 1982. — [12]p ; 21cm. — (Aquila essays ; no.11)
ISBN 0-7275-0242-5 (pbk) : £0.60
Also classified at 811′.52 ; 821′.912
B82-27844

818′.5209 — English literature. American writers. Warren, Robert Penn — *Critical studies*

Justus, James H.. The achievement of Robert Penn Warren / James H. Justus. — Baton Rouge ; London : Louisiana State University Press, c1981. — xiv,362p ; 24cm. — (Southern literary studies)
Includes index
ISBN 0-8071-0875-8 (cased) : Unpriced
ISBN 0-8071-0899-5 B82-22554

818′.5209 — Humour in English. American writers. Thurber, James — *Correspondence, diaries, etc*

Thurber, James. The collected letters of James Thurber. — London : Hamish Hamilton, Jan.1982. — [256]p
ISBN 0-241-10706-7 : £8.95 : CIP entry
B81-34317

818.54 — AMERICAN MISCELLANY, 1945-

818′.5407 — Documentary novels in English. American writers, *1945-* **—** *Critical studies*

Hellmann, John. Fables of fact : the new journalism as new fiction / John Hellmann. — Urbana ; London : University of Illinois Press, c1981. — xii,164p ; 24cm
Bibliography: p152-160. — Includes index
ISBN 0-252-00847-2 : £9.10 B82-05913

818′.5407 — Humorous prose in English. American writers, *1945-* **—** *Texts*

Lebowitz, Fran. Social studies / Fran Lebowitz. — London : Sidgwick & Jackson, 1982. — 147p ; 23cm
ISBN 0-283-98829-0 : £6.50 B82-14691

818'.5407'08 — Humorous prose in English. American writers, *1945-* **—** *Anthologies*

The **Official** explanations / [compiled by] Paul Dickson. — London : Arrow Books, 1981, c1980. — 252p : 1ill ; 18cm
Originally published: New York : Delacorte Press, 1980
ISBN 0-09-926650-4 (pbk) : £1.60 B82-04629

818'.5408 — Prose in English. American writers, *1945-* **—** *Texts*

Bach, Richard. A gift of wings / Richard Bach. — London : Granada, 1982, c1974. — 299p : ill ; 18cm. — (A Panther book)
Originally published: London : Heinemann, 1974
ISBN 0-586-05627-0 (pbk) : £1.50 B82-37068

Capote, Truman. Music for chameleons : new writing / by Truman Capote. — London : Sphere, 1982, c1980 (1982 [printing]). — 240p ; 18cm
Originally published: New York : Random House, 1980
ISBN 0-7221-2243-8 (pbk) : £1.50 B82-14909

Mailer, Norman. The essential Mailer / Norman Mailer. — Sevenoaks : New English Library, 1982. — 586p ; 23cm
ISBN 0-450-04897-7 : £9.95 B82-41078

Vidal, Gore. Pink triangle and yellow star : and other essays (1976-1981) / Gore Vidal. — London : Heinemann, 1982. — 278p ; 24cm
ISBN 0-434-83075-5 : £10.00 B82-37286

818'.5409 — English literature. American writers, *1945-* **—** *Texts*

Griffin, Susan. Made from the earth. — London : Women's Press, Nov.1982. — [288]p
ISBN 0-7043-3894-7 (pbk) : £4.95 : CIP entry B82-27961

820 — ENGLISH LITERATURE

820'.7'042753 — Merseyside *(Metropolitan County)*. **Liverpool. Community & youth work. Activities: English literature. Projects: Windows Project,** *to 1978*

Windows Project. City of poems : a guidebook to the work of the Windows Project 1974-8 / [compiled by Dave Calder and Dave Ward]. — [Liverpool] (23a Brent Way, Halewood, Liverpool L26 9XH)) : [The project], 1979. — [58]p : ill,maps ; 19x26cm
Unpriced (pbk) B82-14766

820'.7'1041 — Great Britain. Educational institutions. Curriculum subjects: English literature. Teaching. Political aspects — *Serials*

LTP : journal of literature, teaching, politics. — No.1 (1982)-. — Cardiff (c/o A. Belsey, Department of Philosophy, University College, Cardiff CF1 1XL) : LTP, 1982-. — v. : ill ; 21cm
Annual
ISSN 0262-575X = LTP. Journal of literature teaching politics : £3.00 B82-28129

820'.7'10941 — Great Britain. Schools. Curriculum subjects: English literature. Teaching

Abbs, Peter. English within the arts. — London : Hodder & Stoughton, Aug.1982. — [160]p
ISBN 0-340-28377-7 (pbk) : £3.95 : CIP entry B82-20753

820'.7'1141 — Great Britain. Universities. Curriculum subjects: English literature. Courses — *Directories*

A **Guide** to degree courses in English 1981-82 : a comparative guide to first degree courses in English at the Universities of the United Kingdom and the Republic of Ireland and at some polytechnics and colleges. — 5th ed. / compiled for the English Association by Ann Becher. — London : The English Association, 1980. — 256p ; 21cm
Previous ed.: 1978
ISBN 0-900232-08-0 (pbk) : £5.50 B82-40010

820'.7'1142 — Great Britain. Higher education institutions. Curriculum subjects: English literature — *Critical studies*

Re-reading English. — London : Methuen, May 1982. — [250]p. — (New accents)
ISBN 0-416-74700-0 (cased) : £6.50 : CIP entry
ISBN 0-416-31150-4 (pbk) : £3.25 B82-06762

820'.7'1242 — England. Secondary schools & sixth form colleges. Students, 16-19 years. Curriculum. Development — *Study examples: Curriculum subjects: English literature*

Adams, Anthony. Sixth sense : alternatives in education at 16-19 : English : a case study / Anthony Adams and Ted Hopkin. — Glasgow : Balckie, 1981. — ix,209p : ill ; 22cm
Bibliography: p207-209
ISBN 0-216-91074-9 (pbk) : £5.25
Primary classification 420'.7'1242 B82-05313

820.72 — English literature. Research

Altick, Richard D.. The art of literary research / Richard D. Altick. — 3rd ed. / revised by John J. Fenstermaker. — New York ; London : Norton, c1981. — xii,318p ; 22cm
Previous ed.: 1975. — Bibliography: p241-254. — Includes index
ISBN 0-393-95176-6 : £10.50 B82-34639

820'.76 — English literature — *Questions & answers — For schools*

Gordon, Elizabeth. Answering English literature questions. — London : Macmillan Education, Feb.1983. — [112]p
ISBN 0-333-30877-8 (pbk) : £1.50 : CIP entry B82-37856

820.8 — English literature, *800-1914 — Anthologies — Manuscripts — Facsimiles*

Klinkenborg, Verlyn. British literary manuscripts / catalogue by Verlyn Klinkenborg ; checklist by Herbert Cahoon ; introduction by Charles Ryskamp. — New York : Pierpont Morgan Library in association with Dover ; London : Constable, 1981. — 2v. : facsims ; 31cm
Includes index
ISBN 0-486-24124-6 (pbk) : Unpriced
ISBN 0-486-24125-4 (series 2) : £9.40 B82-05276

820.8 — English literature — *Anthologies*

Hard lines. — London : Faber, Jan.1983. — [64]p
ISBN 0-571-13073-9 (pbk) : CIP entry B82-32450

A **Way** with words. — London (10 Archway Close, N19 3TD) : Sinclair Browne, Oct.1982. — [192]p
ISBN 0-86300-021-5 : £5.95 : CIP entry B82-27191

820.8 — English literature — *Anthologies — For schools*

Doyle, B.. Poetry, prose and short stories 1981 : lower course / B. Doyle. — Dublin : Folens, c1979. — 48p ; 22cm. — (Folens' student aids. Intermediate certificate)
ISBN 0-86121-093-x (pbk) : Unpriced B82-28071

Doyle, B.. Poetry, prose and short stories 1981 : additional pieces for higher level / B. Doyle. — Dublin : Folens, c1979. — 80p ; 22cm. — (Folens' student aids. Intermediate certificate)
ISBN 0-86121-098-0 (pbk) : Unpriced B82-28072

Knott, Peter, *1934-*. Outlook : themes for writing / Peter Knott. — London : Murray, 1982. — vi,106p : ill ; 24cm
ISBN 0-7195-3876-9 (pbk) : £1.60 : CIP rev. B81-31533

820.8'001 — English literature, *1066-1400 — Anthologies*

Early Middle English verse and prose / edited by J.A.W. Bennett and G.V. Smithers ; with a glossary by Norman Davis. — 2nd ed. — Oxford : Clarendon, 1968 (1982 [printing]). — lxi,620p ; 19cm
Text in Middle English, introduction and notes in English. — Previous ed.: 1966
ISBN 0-19-871101-8 (pbk) : £9.50 : CIP rev. B82-03357

820.8'003 — English literature, *1558-1625 — Anthologies*

The **Portable** Elizabethan reader / edited and with an introduction by Hiram Haydn. — Harmondsworth : Penguin, 1980, c1946. — xvi,688p ; 18cm. — (The Viking portable library)
Originally published: New York : Viking, 1946
ISBN 0-14-015027-7 (pbk) : £1.95 B82-16355

820.8'008 — English literature, *1837-1900 — Anthologies*

The **Yellow** book. — Woodbridge : Boydell Press, Sept.1982. — [320]p
ISBN 0-85115-207-4 (pbk) : £4.95 : CIP entry
Also classified at 709'.42 B82-18775

820.8'00912 — English literature, *1900- — Anthologies — Serials*

New writing and writers. — 19. — London : J. Calder, Jan.1982. — [248]p
ISBN 0-7145-3815-9 (cased) : £5.95 : CIP entry
ISBN 0-7145-3811-6 (pbk) : £3.50 B81-34644

New writing and writers. — 20. — London : Calder, June 1982. — [256]p
ISBN 0-7145-3868-x (cased) : £6.95 : CIP entry
ISBN 0-7145-3869-8 (pbk) : £3.90 B82-17954

820.8'00914 — English literature, *1945- — Anthologies*

Arts magazine. — [Glossop?] (c/o Mrs. G. Reeve, Glossop Festival Committee, Glossop) : Glossop Festival, 1981. — [40]p : ill ; 30cm (pbk) B82-08658

Corrugated ironworks : poems and stories / by the Hut Writers. — [Bristol] : [Bristol Broadsides], [c1980]. — 35p : ports ; 21cm
Cover title
ISBN 0-906944-07-4 (pbk) : £0.50 B82-19903

Write here : a second anthology of poetry and short stories from writers in Milton Keynes. — Milton Keynes : People's Press of Milton Keynes, c1980. — 48p : ill ; 21cm
ISBN 0-904847-09-8 (pbk) : £1.00 B82-39206

820.8'00914 — English literature, *1945- — Anthologies — For schools*

Big dipper : stories, poems, songs and activities for young children / edited by June Epstein ... [et al.] ; music by June Epstein ; designed by Dorothy Rickards ; illustrated by Alison Lester. — Melbourne ; Oxford : Oxford University Press, 1980. — 12p : ill(some col.),music ; 28cm
Includes index
ISBN 0-19-554289-4 (pbk) : £4.95 B82-34026

820.8'00914 — English literature, *1945- — Anthologies — Serials*

Bristol writes. — No.1-. — Bristol (110 Cheltenham Rd, Bristol BS6 5RW) : Bristol Broadsides, 1982-. — v. ; 21cm
ISSN 0263-9211 = Bristol writes : Unpriced B82-38496

Chocolate news. — 1-. — London (49 Danbury St., N1) : [s.n.], 1981-. — v. : ill ; 21cm
Quarterly
ISSN 0261-3085 = Chocolate news : £0.65 per issue B82-06781

Firebird. — 1-. — Harmondsworth : Penguin Books, 1982-. — v. ; 24cm
Annual
ISSN 0263-3078 = Firebird : £3.95 B82-22697

[Fusion *(London : 1979)*]. Fusion : Poetry, fiction. — 1-. — London (c/o K. Mann, 22 Pennethorne Rd., Peckham, SE15 5TQ) : [s.n.], 1979-. — v. ; 21cm
Description based on: 2
ISSN 0260-2172 = Fusion (London. 1979) : £1.00 per issues B82-11818

820.8'00914 — English literature, *1945- — Anthologies — Serials* *continuation*
LAMB : standing for literature, art, music, & baa. — No.1 (June 1981)-. — London : The Literary Supplement, Nothing Doing (Formally in London) ; London (11 Lamb's Conduit Passage, WC1) : Nick Kimberley's Book Shop [distributor], 1981-. — v. ; 15cm
Irregular
ISSN 0261-0957 = LAMB : £0.22 per issue
B82-10114

[Poet *(Kettlesing)***]**. Poet. — 12 (June 1976)-. — Kettlesing (Harecott, Kettlesing, Harrogate, [West Yorkshire]) : Curlew Press, 1976-. — v. : ill ; 22cm
Continues: Poet quarterly (Kettlesing)
£2.00 per year B82-08467

[Poet quarterly *(Kettlesing)***]**. Poet quarterly. — No.11 (Spring 1976). — Kettlesing (Harecott, Kettlesing, Harrogate, [West Yorkshire]) : Curlew Press, 1976-. — 1v. ; 22cm
Continues: Curlew (Kettlesing). — Continued by: Poet (Kettlesing). — Only one issue published
Unpriced B82-08468

The **Polluted** pocket. — [No.?]1-. — Hull (c/o T. Zunder, 109 Victoria Ave, Hull, N. Humberside HU5 3DP) : Jean-Tom, 1982-. — v. : ill ; 30cm
Issued every one or two months. — Description based on: No.2
ISSN 0262-9011 = Polluted pocket : £1.20 for 6 issues B82-20878

[Write on *(Manchester)***]**. Write on : some writing from the Commonword Writers' Workshop. — No.1-. — [Manchester] ([61 Bloom St., Manchester 1]) : Commonword, [1977]-. — v. : ill ; 30cm
Quarterly. — Subtitle varies. — Description based on: No.4
ISSN 0261-7250 = Write on (Manchester) : £1.65 per year B82-04912

820.8'00914 — English literature. Compositions by members of Home Truths, *1945- — Anthologies*
Home truths : writing by North West women. — Manchester : Commonword, [1982]. — 71p : ill ; 21cm
ISBN 0-9505997-5-1 (pbk) : £0.50 B82-40214

820.8'00914 — English literature. Compositions by members of Tollcross Writers Workshop, *1945- — Anthologies*
Clock work : stories and poems from Tollcross Writers' Workshop. — Edinburgh : Workers Educational Association, [1981?]. — 33p ; 21cm
Text on inside cover
ISBN 0-902303-02-3 (pbk) : £1.00 B82-09637

820.8'0321734 — English literature, *ca 1500-ca 1950.* **Special subjects: Countryside** — *Anthologies*
A **Country** book : poems and prose / selected and illustrated by Diane Elson. — Kingswood : World's Work, 1981. — 106p : ill(some col.) ; 26cm
Includes index
ISBN 0-437-37704-0 : £4.95 B82-05467

820.8'032411 — English literature, *to 1980.* **Special subjects: Scotland** — *Anthologies*
A **Book** of Scotland / edited by G.F. Maine. — [Glasgow] : Molendinar Press, 1981. — 384p ; 18cm
Originally published: London : Collins, 1950. — Includes index
ISBN 0-904002-67-5 (pbk) : £1.95 B82-39010

820.8'03242445 — English literature, *1945-.* **Special subjects: Hereford and Worcester. Kilpeck** — *Anthologies*
The **Kilpeck** anthology / edited by Glenn Storhaug. — [Madley] : Five Seasons Press, 1981. — 53p : ill,1facsim ; 30cm
ISBN 0-9504606-3-x (pbk) : £3.75 B82-10620

820.8'032426 — English literature, *to 1981.* **Special subjects: East Anglia** — *Anthologies*
East Anglia in verse and prose. — London : Secker & Warburg, Oct.1982. — [112]p
ISBN 0-436-57607-4 : £5.50 : CIP entry
B82-29130

820.8'032429 — English literature, *to 1981.* **Special subjects: Wales** — *Anthologies*
Wales / compiled by Jan Morris. — Oxford : Oxford University Press, 1982. — v,114p : ill,ports ; 21cm. — (Small Oxford books)
Includes index
ISBN 0-19-214118-x : £3.95 : CIP rev.
B82-04151

820.8'033 — English literature, *to 1978.* **Special subjects: Seasons** — *Anthologies*
Words for all seasons / chosen by Malcolm Saville. — Tring : Lion, 1981, c1979. — 192p : ill ; 18cm. — (A Lion paperback)
Originally published: Guildford : Lutterworth, 1979. — Includes index
ISBN 0-85648-475-x (pbk) : £1.50 B82-08023

820.8'0352054 — Children's literature in English, *1837-1900.* **Special subjects: Children. Moral development** — *Anthologies*
What I cannot tell my mother is not fit for me to know : stories, lessons, poems, and songs our great-great-grandmothers and our great-great-grandfathers heard, read, and sang in school and at home : taken mainly from school textbooks, readers, reciters, and songbooks of the nineteenth century / chosen by Gwladys and Brian Rees-Williams. — Oxford : Oxford University Press, 1981. — x,198p,[8]leaves of plates : ill(some col.),1facsim ; 23cm
Bibliography: p192-193. — Includes index
ISBN 0-19-212223-1 : £7.95 : CIP rev.
B81-25854

820.8'0352054 — English literature, *to 1980.* **Special subjects: Children** — *Anthologies*
Muir, Frank. Frank Muir on children / Frank Muir and Simon Brett ; research by Virginia Bell ; illustrated by Joseph Wright. — London : Sphere, 1982, c1980. — 120p : ill ; 20cm
Originally published: London : Heinemann, 1980
ISBN 0-7221-6296-0 (pbk) : £1.75 B82-34737

820.8'0353 — English literature, *to 1981.* **Special subjects: Snobbery** — *Anthologies*
Snobs / compiled by Jasper Griffin. — Oxford : Oxford University Press, 1982. — viii,112p : ill ; 21cm. — (Small Oxford books)
Includes index
ISBN 0-19-214128-7 : £3.95 : CIP rev.
B82-04153

820.8'0354 — English literature, *ca 1558-1981.* **Special subjects: Marriage** — *Anthologies*
Marriage, a keepsake. — Watford : Exley, Oct.1982. — [80]p
ISBN 0-905521-66-8 : £4.95 : CIP entry
B82-24620

820.8'0355 — English literature, *to 1981.* **Special subjects: Racehorses. Racing** — *Anthologies*
The **Turf** / compiled by Alan Ross. — Oxford : Oxford University Press, 1982. — vi,112p : ill ; 21cm. — (Small Oxford books)
Includes index
ISBN 0-19-214114-7 : £3.95 : CIP rev.
B82-04150

820.8'0356 — English literature, *to 1981.* **Special subjects: Railways** — *Anthologies*
My favourite railway stories / edited by Paul Jennings. — Guildford : Lutterworth Press, c1982. — 128p : ill ; 23cm
ISBN 0-7188-2529-2 : £5.95 B82-39747

The **Train** / compiled by Roger Green. — Oxford : Oxford University Press, 1982. — viii,112p : ill,facsims ; 21cm. — (Small Oxford books)
Includes index
ISBN 0-19-214127-9 : £3.95 : CIP rev.
B82-04152

820.8'037 — Children's literature in English, *1500-1970.* **Special subjects: Supernatural** — *Anthologies*
Ghosts and shadows / chosen and edited by Dorothy Edwards ; illustrated by Jane Walmsley. — [London] : Fontana, 1982, c1980. — 160p : ill ; 20cm. — (Lions)
Originally published: Guildford : Lutterworth Press, 1980
ISBN 0-00-671950-3 (pbk) : £1.00 B82-10713

820.8'0375 — Children's literature in English, *1945-.* **Special subjects: Dragons** — *Anthologies*
The **Ladybird** book of dragons. — [Loughborough] : Ladybird, c1982. — 56p : col.ill ; 31cm
Ill on lining papers
ISBN 0-7214-7520-5 : £2.50 B82-35636

820.8'0382 — English literature, *to 1980.* **Special themes: Christian life** — *Anthologies*
Urch, Elizabeth. Ladders up to heaven / by Elizabeth Urch. — Evesham : James
Pt.1: Christmas. — 1980. — 46p : music ; 20cm
ISBN 0-85305-226-3 (pbk) : £1.50 B82-21002

Urch, Elizabeth. Ladders up to heaven / by Elizabeth Urch. — Evesham : James
Pt.2: Friendship. — 1980. — 56p ; 20cm
Includes index
ISBN 0-85305-229-8 (pbk) : £1.75 B82-21003

820.8'09282 — Children's literature in English, *1300-1979 — Anthologies*
Marshall, Sybil. So big, so small. — Cambridge : Cambridge University Press, Apr.1981. — [48] p. — (Lanterns)
ISBN 0-521-28157-1 (sd) : £1.50 : CIP entry
B81-02573

820.8'09282 — Children's literature in English, *1837-1980 — Anthologies*
The **Armada** funny story book / compiled by Mary Danby ; with drawings by Bryan Reading. — [London] : Armada, 1980. — 124p : ill ; 18cm
ISBN 0-00-691512-4 (pbk) : £0.75 B82-13116

Boswell, Hilda. A Hilda Boswell little treasury : stories, poems, rhymes. — [London] : Collins Colour Cubs
Green treasury. — c1980. — [48]p : col.ill ; 15cm
ISBN 0-00-123583-4 (pbk) : £0.40 B82-39237

Boswell, Hilda. A Hilda Boswell little treasury : stories, poems, rhymes. — [London] : Collins Colour Cubs
Orange treasury. — c1980. — [48]p : col.ill ; 15cm
ISBN 0-00-123580-x (pbk) : £0.40 B82-39238

Boswell, Hilda. A Hilda Boswell little treasury : stories, poems, rhymes. — [London] : Collins Colour Cubs
Yellow treasury. — c1980. — [48]p : col.ill ; 16cm
ISBN 0-00-123581-8 (pbk) : £0.40 B82-39236

820.8'09282 — Children's literature in English, *1945- — Anthologies*
Something to think about : an anthology of stories, poems and songs from the BBC radio series / edited by Paddy Bechely ; illustrated by Alan Burton. — London : British Broadcasting Corporation, 1982. — 111p : ill ; 21cm
ISBN 0-563-31975-5 (pbk) : Unpriced
B82-39192

820.8'09282 — Children's literature in English. New Zealand writers, *1945- — Anthologies*
The **Magpies** said : stories and poems from New Zealand / collected by Dorothy Butler ; illustrated by Lyn Kriegler. — Harmondsworth : Puffin, 1982, c1980. — 192p : ill ; 18cm. — (A Puffin book)
Originally published: Harmondsworth : Kestrel, 1980
ISBN 0-14-031480-6 (pbk) : £0.95 B82-30247

820.8'09282 — English literature. Child writers, *1945- — Anthologies*
Young writers : 23rd year : award-winning entries for the W.H. Smith Young Writers' Competition. — London : Heinemann, 1982. — 190p : ill ; 22cm
Includes index
ISBN 0-435-13412-4 (pbk) : £2.95 B82-28504

820.8'09282 — English literature. Compositions by children, *1945- — Anthologies*
Young thougths / six children. — Bognor Regis : New Horizon, c1981. — 68p ; 21cm
ISBN 0-86116-803-8 : £3.25 B82-10134

820.8′09282 — English literature. New Zealand writers, *1945- — Anthologies — For children*

Marty and the dragon : and other stories plays and poems / selected by Stephen Barnett. — London : Pelham, 1981. — 112p : ill(some col.) ; 25cm
ISBN 0-7207-1286-6 : £4.95 B82-02256

820.8′09287 — English literature. Women writers, *1558-1628 — Anthologies*

The **Paradise** of women : writings by Englishwomen of the Renaissance / compiled and edited by Betty Travitsky. — Westport, Conn. ; London : Greenwood Press, 1981. — xiv,283p ; 25cm. — (Contributions in women′s studies, ISSN 0147-104x ; no.22)
Bibliography: p265-273. — Includes index
ISBN 0-313-22177-4 : £22.95 B82-18367

820.8′09287 — English literature. Women writers, *1945- — Anthologies*

Girls are powerful : young women′s writings from Spare rib. — London : Sheba Feminist Publishers, 1982. — 157p : ill,ports ; 20cm
ISBN 0-907179-12-6 (pbk) : £3.75 B82-24319

820.8′09415 — English literature. Irish writers, *1900- — Anthologies*

Soft day : a miscellany of contemporary Irish writing / edited by Peter Fallon & Seán Golden. — Dublin : Wolfhound Press, 1980. — xviii,224p ; 24cm
ISBN 0-905473-21-3 (cased) : Unpriced
ISBN 0-905473-24-8 (pbk) : Unpriced
B82-33756

820′.8′0942256 — English literature. Hanover Community Centre writers, *1945- — Anthologies*

Writers at Hanover / [by James Berry ... et al.]. — Brighton (Hanover Community Centre, 33 Southover St., Brighton, E. Sussex) : Hanover Writers Press, c1981. — 39p ; 21cm
£0.50 (pbk) B82-16610

820.8′0942932 — English literature. Clwyd writers: Prestatyn writers, *1945- — Anthologies*

Pen to paper / Prestatyn Writers Circle. — [Prestatyn] ([15 Derwent Close, Prestatyn, Clwyd LL19 7TT]) : [Prestatyn Writers Circle], [c1981]. — 36p : ill ; 21cm
Cover title
£0.70 (pbk) B82-12939

820.8′096 — English literature. African writers, *1945- — Anthologies*

An **Anthology** of African and Caribbean writing in English. — London : Heinemann Educational in association with the Open University, Dec.1982. — [320]p. — (Open University Third World readers ; 2)
ISBN 0-435-91297-6 (pbk) : £5.95 : CIP entry
Also classified at 810.8′09729 B82-29773

820.9 — ENGLISH LITERATURE. HISTORY AND CRITICAL STUDIES

820.9 — English literature, *1500-1980.* **Language** — *Critical studies*

Chapman, Raymond. The language of English literature / Raymond Chapman. — London : Edward Arnold, 1982. — x,148p ; 22cm
Bibliography: p141-143. — Includes index
ISBN 0-7131-6371-2 (pbk) : £3.95 : CIP rev.
B82-13058

820.9 — English literature, *1558-1961 — Critical studies*

Van Doren, Mark. The essays of Mark van Doren (1924-1972) / selected with an introduction by William Claire. — Westport ; London : Greenwood, 1980. — xxv,270p : 1port ; 22cm. — (Contributions in American studies ; no.47)
Bibliography: p261-265. — Includes index
ISBN 0-313-22098-0 : Unpriced B82-14978

820′.9 — English literature, *1642 - Critical studies - Conference proceedings*

1642 : literature and power in the seventeenth century. — Colchester (Department of Literature, University of Essex, Colchester) : Essex Sociology of Literature Conference Committee, May 1981. — [340]p
Conference papers
ISBN 0-901726-18-4 (pbk) : £4.85 : CIP entry
B81-14965

820.9 — English literature, *1750-1914 — Critical studies*

Lucas, John. Romantic to modern : essays on literature and ideas, 1750-1914. — London : Harvester Press, Aug.1982. — [256]p
ISBN 0-7108-0405-9 : £18.95 : CIP entry
B82-15911

820′.9 — English literature, *1926-1980. Imagery — Critical studies*

Grabes, Herbert. The mutable glass. — Cambridge : Cambridge University Press, Dec.1982. — [432]p
Translation of: Speculum, mirror und looking-glass
ISBN 0-521-22203-6 : £39.50 : CIP entry
B82-30300

820.9 — English literature — *Critical studies*

Chapman, Raymond. English literature in a changing world : an inaugural lecture / Raymond Chapman. — London : London School of Economics and Political Science, 1982. — 18p ; 21cm
ISBN 0-85328-077-0 (pbk) : Unpriced
B82-28493

820′.9 — English literature — *Critical studies*

Grigson, Geoffrey. Blessings, kicks and curses. — London : Allison & Busby, Feb.1982. — [288]p
ISBN 0-85031-437-2 : £9.95 : CIP entry
B82-02462

820.9 — English literature — *Critical studies*

Taylor, Richard, *1935-*. Understanding the elements of literature : its forms, techniques and cultural conventions / Richard Taylor. — London : Macmillan, 1981. — xiii,234p,[8]p of plates : ill ; 23cm
Bibliography: p216-219. — Includes index
ISBN 0-333-26320-0 (cased) : Unpriced
ISBN 0-333-26321-9 (pbk) : Unpriced
B82-34916

820.9 — English literature — *Critical studies — Serials*

Essays and studies. — 1982. — London : Murray, May 1982. — [128]p
ISBN 0-7195-3939-0 : £8.50 : CIP entry
B82-07594

820′.9 — English literature — *Critical studies — Serials*

Essays by divers hands. — Vol.42. — Woodbridge : Boydell, Dec.1982. — [208]p
ISBN 0-85115-173-6 : £8.95 : CIP entry
B82-30226

820.9 — English literature — *Critical studies — Serials*

[The Gadfly *(Retford)***]**. The Gadfly : a quarterly review of English letters : in succession to the Human world. — Vol.5, no.1 (Feb. 1982)-. — Retford (15 Cobwell Rd, Retford, Notts. DN22 7BN) : Brynmill Press Ltd, 1982-. — v. ; 19cm
Continues: Human world
ISSN 0263-1644 = Gadfly (Retford) (corrected) : £8.00 per year B82-22654

The **Year′s** work in English studies. — Vol.60. — London : Murray, Mar.1982. — [552]p
ISBN 0-7195-3940-4 : £17.50 : CIP entry
B82-00355

820.9 — English literature. Criticism. Applications of stylistics

Essays in modern stylistics / edited by Donald C. Freeman. — London : Methuen, 1981. — viii,416p : ill ; 24cm
Bibliography: p412-416. — Includes index
ISBN 0-416-74420-6 (cased) : Unpriced
ISBN 0-416-74430-3 (pbk) : £6.95 B82-17585

820.9 — English literature. Criticism. Davie, Donald — *Biographies*

Davie, Donald. These the companions : recollections / Donald Davie. — Cambridge : Cambridge University Press, 1982. — xiii,176p : ill,ports ; 24cm
ISBN 0-521-24511-7 : £12.50 : CIP rev.
B82-14500

820.9 — English literature. Criticism. Eliot, T. S. — *Critical studies*

Edwards, Michael. Eliot/language. — 2nd ed. — Portree : Aquila, Jan.1983. — [48]p. — (Prospice, ISSN 0308-2776 ; v.4)
Previous ed.: 1975
ISBN 0-7275-0101-1 (pbk) : £1.50 : CIP entry
B82-32631

820.9 — English literature. Criticism. Garnett, Edward — *Biographies*

Jefferson, George. Edward Garnett : a life in literature / George Jefferson. — London : Cape, 1982. — x,350p ; 22cm
Includes index
ISBN 0-224-01488-9 : £12.50 : CIP rev.
B82-01133

820.9 — English literature. Criticism. Gladstone, W. E. (William Ewart) — *Critical studies*

Ramm, Agatha. Gladstone as man of letters : a James Bryce memorial lecture delivered in the hall of Somerville College on 28 May 1981 / by Agatha Ramm. — [Oxford] ([60, Hurst St., Oxford]) : [Ziprint Parchment], [1982?]. — 16p ; 21cm
ISBN 0-9504486-2-1 (pbk) : Unpriced
B82-26293

820.9 — English literature. Criticism. Leavis, F. R. — *Critical studies*

Walsh, William, *1916-*. F.R. Leavis / William Walsh. — London : Chatto & Windus, 1980. — 189p ; 23cm
Includes index
ISBN 0-7011-2503-9 : £8.95 : CIP rev.
B80-13958

820.9 — English literature. Criticism. Leavis, Q. D. — *Critical studies*

Kinch, M. B.. Q.D. Leavis 1906-1981 : an appreciation / M.B. Kinch. — Retford : Brynmill, 1982. — 24p ; 19cm
Bibliography: p22-24
ISBN 0-907839-01-0 (unbound) : £1.05
B82-19351

820.9 — English literature. Criticism. Serials: ′Scrutiny′ — *Critical studies*

Mulhern, Francis. The moment of ′Scrutiny′ / Francis Mulhern. — London : Verso, 1981. — x,354p ; 21cm
Originally published: London : NLB, 1979. — Bibliography: p333-345. — Includes index
ISBN 0-86091-745-2 (pbk) : £3.95 : CIP rev.
B81-30150

820.9 — English literature. Criticism. Theories

Gardner, Helen, *1908-*. In defence of the imagination : the Charles Eliot Norton Lectures 1979-1980 / Helen Gardner. — Oxford : Clarendon, 1982. — vii,197p ; 22cm
Includes index
ISBN 0-19-812639-5 : £12.50 : CIP rev.
B81-25855

820.9 — English literature. Criticism. Yeats, W. B. — *Critical studies*

Sena, Vinod. [The Poet as critic]. W.B. Yeats : the poet as critic / Vinod Sena. — London : Macmillan, 1981, c1980. — xii,232p ; 23cm
Originally published: New Delhi : Macmillan India, 1980. — Bibliography: p212-220. — Includes index
ISBN 0-333-32666-0 : Unpriced B82-28683

820.9 — English literature. Language. Cultural aspects

English literature : opening up the canon / edited by Leslie A. Fiedler and Houston A. Baker. — Baltimore ; London : Johns Hopkins University Press, c1981. — xiii,161p ; 21cm. — (Selected papers from the English Institute, 1979. New series ; no.4)
ISBN 0-8018-2591-1 : £6.00 B82-02221

820.9 — English literature, *to 1815 — Critical studies*
Wordsworth, William, *1770-1850.* Wordsworth's literary criticism / reprint of the edition by Nowell C. Smith ; with new preface, introduction, bibliography & notes by Howard Mills and two additional letters. — Bristol : Bristol Classical Press, 1980. — xix,269p ; 21cm
Facsim. of: 1st ed. London : Henry Frowde, 1905. — Bibliography: pxix
ISBN 0-906515-66-1 (pbk) : Unpriced B82-05339

820'.9 — English literature, *to 1976 — Critical studies*
Tolkien, J. R. R.. The monsters and the critics and other essays. — London : Allen and Unwin, Feb.1983. — [256]p
ISBN 0-04-809019-0 : £9.95 : CIP entry B82-39269

820.9 — English literature, *to 1978 — Critical studies*
Leavis, F. R.. The critic as anti-philosopher. — London : Chatto and Windus, Nov.1982. — [240]p
ISBN 0-7011-2644-2 : £9.95 : CIP entry B82-27964

820.9 — English literature, *to 1979 — Chronologies*
Rogal, Samuel J.. A chronological outline of British literature / Sammel J. Rogal. — Westport ; London : Greenwood Press, 1980. — xv,341p ; 25cm
Bibliography: pxiii-xv. — Includes index
ISBN 0-313-21477-8 : Unpriced B82-14982

820'.9 — English literature, *to 1980.* **Linguistic aspects**
Blake, N. F.. Language variety in English literature. — London : Deutsch, Nov.1981. — [224]p. — (Language library)
ISBN 0-233-97311-7 (cased) : £8.95 : CIP entry
ISBN 0-233-97422-9 (pbk) : £5.50 B81-28800

820.9 — English literature, *to ca 1950 — Critical studies*
Lewis, C. S.. Selected literary essays / by C.S. Lewis ; edited by Walter Hooper. — Cambridge : Cambridge University Press, 1969 (1980 [printing]). — xx,329p ; 22cm
Includes index
ISBN 0-521-07441-x (cased) : Unpriced
ISBN 0-521-29680-3 (pbk) : £6.95 B82-00423

820.9 — English literature. Writers. Local associations: West Cornwall
Baker, Denys Val. A view from Land's End : writers against a Cornish background / Denys Val Baker. — London : Kimber, 1982. — 188p ; 23cm
Includes index
ISBN 0-7183-0438-1 : £5.95 B82-28244

820.9 — Great Britain. Secondary schools. Curriculum subjects: English literature. Style. Linguistics aspects — *For teaching*
Literary text and language study / edited by Ronald Carter, Deirdre Burton. — London : Edward Arnold, 1982. — 115p : ill ; 22cm. — (Explorations in language study)
Includes bibliographies
ISBN 0-7131-6263-5 (pbk) : £3.95 : CIP rev. B81-33840

820.9'001 — English literature, *1066-1400 — Critical studies*
Burrow, J. A.. Medieval writers and their work : Middle English literature and its background 1100-1500 / J.A. Burrow. — Oxford : Oxford University Press, 1982. — 148p ; 21cm
Bibliography: p140-143. — Includes index
ISBN 0-19-219135-7 (cased) : Unpriced : CIP rev.
ISBN 0-19-289122-7 (pbk) : £3.95 B82-04158

Medieval literature : Chaucer and the alliterative tradition : with an anthology of Medieval poems and drama / edited by Boris Ford. — Rev. and expanded ed. — Harmondsworth : Penguin, 1982. — 646p ; 19cm. — (The New Pelican guide to English literature ; v.1 ; pt.1)
Previous ed.: 1954. — Bibliography: p609-635. — Includes index
ISBN 0-14-022264-2 (pbk) : £2.95 B82-30182

820.9'001 — English literature, *1066-1558 — Festschriften*
Medieval studies : for J.A.W. Bennett : aetatis suae LXX / edited by P.L. Heyworth. — Oxford : Clarendon Press, 1981. — xi,425p,[8]p of plates : ill,music,facsims,1port ; 23cm
Bibliography: p395-412. — Includes index
ISBN 0-19-812628-x : £27.50 B82-08382

820.9'001 — Great Britain. Society *expounded by* **English literature,** *1066-1558*
The **Later** middle ages / edited by Stephen Medcalf. — London : Methuen, 1981. — viii,312,[8]p : ill,ports ; 21cm. — (The Context of English literature)
Includes index
ISBN 0-416-85990-9 (cased) : Unpriced : CIP rev.
ISBN 0-416-86000-1 (pbk) : £5.95 B81-32535

820.9'002 — English literature, *1400-1625 — Critical studies*
Roston, Murray. Sixteenth-century English literature / Murray Roston. — [London] : Macmillan, 1982. — vi,235p,[12]p of plates : ill,facsims,ports ; 23cm. — (Macmillan history of literature)
Bibliography: p223-226. — Includes index
ISBN 0-333-27143-2 (cased) : Unpriced
ISBN 0-333-27144-0 (pbk) : Unpriced B82-39715

820.9'003 — English literature, *1558-1625 — Critical studies*
The **Age** of Shakespeare / edited by Boris Ford. — Rev. and expanded ed. — Harmondsworth : Penguin, 1982. — 576p : music ; 19cm. — (The New Pelican guide to English literature ; v.2)
Previous ed.: 1955. — Bibliography: p501-564. — Includes index
ISBN 0-14-022265-0 (pbk) : £2.95 B82-30183

Bradbrook, M. C.. The artist and society in Shakespeare's England / M.C. Bradbrook. — Brighton : Harvester, 1982. — x,176p ; 23cm. — (The Collected papers of Muriel Bradbrook ; v.1)
ISBN 0-7108-0391-5 : £18.95 : CIP rev. B82-12153

Sinfield, Alan. Literature in Protestant England 1560-1660. — London : Croom Helm, Nov.1982. — [176]p
ISBN 0-7099-2367-8 : £11.95 : CIP entry B82-26708

820.9'003 — English literature, *1558-1702 — Critical studies*
Aers, David. Literature, language and society in England 1580-1680 / David Aers, Bob Hodge, Gunther Kress. — Dublin : Gill and Macmillan, 1981. — xi,217p ; 22cm
Includes index
ISBN 0-7171-0978-x : £16.00 B82-13472

From Donne to Marvell / edited by Boris Ford. — Rev. and expanded ed. — Harmondsworth : Penguin, 1982. — 410p ; 19cm. — (The New Pelican guide to English literature ; v.3)
Previous ed.: 1956. — Bibliography: p369-398. — Includes index
ISBN 0-14-022266-9 (pbk) : £1.95 B82-30184

820.9'003 — English literature, *1558-1702.* **Influence of French culture**
Richmond, Hugh M.. Puritans and libertines : Anglo-French literary relations in the Reformation / Hugh M. Richmond. — Berkeley ; London : University of California Press, c1981. — xii,401p,[8]p of plates : ports ; 24cm
Bibliography: p377-394. — Includes index
ISBN 0-520-04179-8 : £19.25 B82-11909

820.9'004 — English literature, *1625-1702 — Critical studies*
King, Bruce, *1933-*. Seventeenth-century English literature / Bruce King. — London : Macmillan, 1982. — x,295p,[16]p of plates : ill,ports ; 23cm. — (Macmillan history of literature)
Bibliography: p266-268. — Includes index
ISBN 0-333-26917-9 (cased) : Unpriced
ISBN 0-333-26918-7 (pbk) : Unpriced B82-39716

820.9'005 — English literature, *1702-1745 — Critical studies*
Rogers, P.. Eighteenth century encounters : essays on literature and society in the age of Walpole. — London : Prior, Sept.1982. — [220]p
ISBN 0-86043-485-0 : £8.50 : CIP entry B82-20862

820.9'005 — English literature, *1702-1800 — Critical studies*
Barrell, John. English literature in history 1730-80. — London : Hutchinson Education, Feb.1983. — [240]p
ISBN 0-09-149820-1 (cased) : £12.00 : CIP entry
ISBN 0-09-149821-x (pbk) : £5.50 B82-36455

From Dryden to Johnson / edited by Boris Ford. — Rev. and expanded ed. — Harmondsworth : Penguin, 1982. — 527p ; 19cm. — (The New Pelican guide to English literature ; v.4)
Previous ed.: 1957. — Bibliography: p455-507. — Includes index
ISBN 0-14-022267-7 (pbk) : £2.50 B82-30185

820.9'006 — English literature, *1745-1837 — Critical studies*
Sales, Roger. English literature in history 1780-1830. — London : Hutchinson Education, Feb.1983. — [256]p
ISBN 0-09-149830-9 (cased) : £12.00 : CIP entry
ISBN 0-09-149831-7 (pbk) : £5.50 B82-36456

820.9'006 — Great Britian. Society *expounded by* **English literature,** *1745-1837*
The **Romantics** / edited by Stephen Prickett. — London : Methuen, 1981. — 267p,[8]p of plates : ill ; 21cm. — (The Context of English literature)
Includes bibliographies and index
ISBN 0-416-72010-2 (cased) : Unpriced : CIP rev.
ISBN 0-416-72020-x (pbk) : £4.95 B81-25295

820.9'007 — English literature, *1800-1900 — Critical studies*
Mill, John Stuart. Autobiography and literary essays / by John Stuart Mill ; edited by John M. Robson and Jack Stillinger. — Toronto : University of Toronto Press ; London : Routledge & Kegan Paul, c1981. — liv,766p : facsims ; 25cm. — (Collected works of John Stuart Mill ; v.1)
Includes index
ISBN 0-7100-0718-3 : £32.50
Primary classification 192 B82-17794

820.9'008 — English literature, *1837-1900.* **Decadence** — *Critical studies*
Thornton, R. K. R.. The decadent dilemma. — London : Arnold, Dec.1982. — [160]p
ISBN 0-7131-6372-0 : £16.50 : CIP entry B82-30208

820.9'008 — English literature, *1837-1980 — Structuralist perspectives*
Lodge, David. Working with structuralism : essays and reviews on nineteenth and twentieth-century literature / David Lodge. — London : Routledge & Kegan Paul, 1981 (1982 [printing]). — xii,207p ; 22cm
Includes index
ISBN 0-7100-9330-6 (pbk) : £3.95 B82-39522

820.9'008 — English literature, *1837- — Critical studies*
Hussey, Maurice. Explorations in English : a correspondence course to study for your pleasure / [authors: Maurice Hussey and Rudy Wood]. — Cambridge : National Extension College, 1971 (1978 [printing]). — 102p : ill,ports ; 30cm. — (National Extension College correspondence texts ; course no.E6)
Includes bibliographies
ISBN 0-902404-06-7 (pbk) : Unpriced B82-38351

820.9'008 — English literature. Influence of Wagner, Richard, *1837-1945*
Martin, Stoddard. Wagner to The waste land : a study of the relationship of Wagner to English literature / Stoddard Martin. — London : Macmillan, 1982. — xi,277p : music ; 23cm
Includes index
ISBN 0-333-28998-6 : £20.00 B82-39150

820.9′00912 — English arts. Bloomsbury Group. English writers, *ca 1920-ca 1930 — Personal observations*

Anand, Mulk Raj. Conversations in Bloomsbury / Mulk Raj Anand. — London : Wildwood House, 1981. — 159p ; 22cm
ISBN 0-7045-3061-9 : £5.95 B82-02413

820.9′00912 — English literature, *1900- — Critical studies*

Blamires, Harry. Twentieth-century English literature / Harry Blamires. — [London] : Macmillan, 1982. — vii,304p,[16]p of plates : ill,1facsim,ports ; 23cm. — (Macmillan history of literature)
Bibliography: p275-278. — Includes index
ISBN 0-333-27020-7 (cased) : Unpriced
ISBN 0-333-27021-5 (pbk) : Unpriced B82-39717

Hooker, Jeremy. Poetry of place : essays and reviews 1970-1981 / Jeremy Hooker. — Manchester : Carcanet, 1982. — 197p ; 23cm
Bibliography: p191-193. — Includes index
ISBN 0-85635-409-0 : Unpriced : CIP rev. B82-12908

Symons, Julian. Critical observations / Julian Symons. — London : Faber, 1981. — 213p ; 23cm
ISBN 0-571-11688-4 : £9.75 : CIP rev. B81-31277

820.9′00912 — English literature, *1900- — Interviews*

Writers at work : The Paris review interviews. — Harmondsworth : Penguin
1st ser. / edited and with an introduction by Malcolm Cowley. — 1977, c1958 (1981 [printing]). — 309p ; 20cm
Originally published: New York : Viking ; London : Secker & Warburg, 1958
ISBN 0-14-004540-6 (pbk) : £2.95 B82-22494

Writers at work : the Paris review interviews. — Harmondsworth : Penguin, 1977, c1963 (1982 [printing])
2nd series / edited by George Plimpton ; introduced by Van Wyck Brooks. — 368p : facsims,ports ; 20cm
Originally published: New York : Viking ; London : Secker & Warburg, 1963
ISBN 0-14-004541-4 (pbk) : £2.95 B82-30246

820.9′00912 — English literature. Belloc, H. & Chesterton, G. K.. Political beliefs

Corrin, Jay P.. G.K. Chesterton & Hilaire Belloc : the battle against modernity / by Jay P. Corrin. — Athens [Ohio] ; London : Ohio University Press, c1981. — xv,262p ; 24cm
Bibliography: p240-250. — Includes index
ISBN 0-8214-0604-3 : £14.70
Primary classification 828′.91209 B82-19571

820.9′00912 — English literature. Powys family — *Biographies*

Hopkins, Kenneth. The Powys brothers. — 2nd ed. — London (10 Archway Close, N19 3TD) : Sinclair Browne, Mar.1982. — [288]p
Previous ed.: Southrepps : Warren House Press, 1972
ISBN 0-86300-006-1 (pbk) : £4.95 : CIP entry B82-01577

820.9′00912 — English literature. Writers, *1900-1980 — Personal observations*

Brinnin, John Malcolm. Sextet : T.S. Eliot & Truman Capote & others / John Malcolm Brinnin. — London : Deutsch, 1982, c1981. — vi,278p : ill,ports ; 24cm
Originally published: New York: Delacorte Press/Seymour Lawrence, 1981
ISBN 0-233-97451-2 : £7.95 B82-16076

820.908′0355 — English literature. Special subjects: Cricket — *Anthologies*

Summer days. — London : Eyre Methuen, Sept.1981. — [224]p
ISBN 0-413-49060-2 : £6.95 : CIP entry B81-23913

820.9′145 — English literature. Irish writers, *1789-1850.* **Romanticism** *— Critical studies*

Rafroidi, Patrick. Irish literature in English : the Romantic Period / Patrick Rafroidi. — Gerrards Cross : Smythe, 1980. — 2v. : ill,ports ; 23cm
Translation of: L'Irlande et le Romantisme. — Bibliography: Vol.2. — Includes index
ISBN 0-901072-40-0 : £32.50 : CIP rev. B79-13087

820.9′15 — Fanzines in English — *Reviews — Serials*

Fanzine frantique. — 1-. — Lancaster (6 Vine St., Greaves, Lancaster, Lancs. LA1 4UF) : K. and R. Walker, [1981]-. — v. ; 30cm
Continues: Fanzine fanatique
ISSN 0263-0796 = Fanzine frantique : Unpriced B82-15142

820.9′32 — English literature, *1900-1945.* **Special subjects: Travel** *— Critical studies*

Fussell, Paul. Abroad : British literary traveling between the wars / Paul Fussell. — Oxford : Oxford University Press, 1982, c1980. — viii,246p : ill,maps,ports ; 21cm
Originally published: New York : Oxford University Press, 1980. — Bibliography: p229-239. — Includes index
ISBN 0-19-281360-9 (pbk) : £2.95 B82-39635

820.9′32 — English literature, *1918-1939.* **Special subjects: Travel** *— Critical studies*

Fussell, Paul. Abroad : British literary traveling between the wars / Paul Fussell. — New York ; Oxford : Oxford University Press, 1980. — viii,246p : ill,maps,ports ; 24cm
Facsims on lining papers. — Bibliography: p229-239. — Includes index
ISBN 0-19-502767-1 : Unpriced B82-10202

820.9′351 — English literature, *to 1945.* **Special subjects: Arthur,** *King — Critical studies*

Arthurian literature. — Cambridge : D. S. Brewer
1 / edited by Richard Barber. — c1981. — vii,173p : ill ; 24cm
ISBN 0-85991-081-4 : £15.00 B82-07998

Arthurian literature. — Woodbridge : D.S. Brewer
2. — Nov.1982. — [224]p
ISBN 0-85991-095-4 : £17.50 : CIP entry B82-26331

820.9′352042 — English literature. Irish writers. Special subjects: Women *— Critical studies*

Gallagher, S. F.. Woman in Irish legend, life and literature. — Gerrards Cross : Smythe, Jan.1983. — [160]p. — (Irish literary studies, ISSN 0140-895x ; 14)
ISBN 0-86140-159-x : £9.50 : CIP entry B82-37463

820.9′356 — English literature, *1837-1900.* **Special subjects: Science** *— Critical studies*

Coslett, Tess. Science and literature in Victorian England. — Brighton : Harvester Press, Oct.1982. — [192]p
ISBN 0-7108-0302-8 : £18.95 : CIP entry B82-23179

820.9′382 — English literature, *1066-1400.* **Special subjects: Christian life. Mysticism** *— Critical studies*

The **Medieval** mystical tradition in England : papers read at Dartington Hall, July 1982 / edited by Marion Glasscoe. — Exeter : University of Exeter, 1982. — 261p ; 21cm. — (Exeter medieval English texts and studies)
ISBN 0-85989-183-6 (pbk) : Unpriced B82-40176

820.9′382 — English literature, *1600-1800.* **Special themes: Theology** *— Critical studies*

Stock, R. D.. The holy and the daemonic from Sir Thomas Browne to William Blake / R.D. Stock. — Princeton, N.J. ; Guildford : Princeton University Press, c1982. — 395p : ill,1facsim ; 23cm
Includes index
ISBN 0-691-06495-4 : £19.40 B82-24507

820.9′9282 — Children's literature in English, *1900- — Critical studies*

Egoff, Sheila A.. Thursday's child : trends and patterns in contemporary children's literature / Sheila A. Egoff. — Chicago : American Library Association ; London : distributed by Eurospan, 1981. — 323p ; 24cm
Includes bibliographies and index
ISBN 0-8389-0327-4 : £11.50 B82-39800

820.9′9287 — English literature. Women writers, *1800-1900 — Critical studies*

Rogers, Katharine M.. Feminism in eighteenth-century England / Katharine M. Rogers. — Brighton : Harvester, 1982. — 291p ; 24cm
Includes index
ISBN 0-7108-0427-x : £25.00 : CIP rev. B82-23182

820.9′9411 — English literature. Scottish writers, *1500-1934 — Critical studies*

Muir, Edwin. Edwin Muir : uncollected Scottish criticism / edited and introduced by Andrew Noble. — London : Vision, c1982. — 269p ; 23cm. — (Critical studies series)
Includes index
ISBN 0-85478-324-5 : £14.95 B82-15418

820.9′9411 — English literature. Scottish writers, *1603-1980.* **Cultural aspects**

Daiches, David. Literature and gentility in Scotland : the Alexander Lectures at the University of Toronto, 1980 / David Daiches. — Edinburgh : Edinburgh University Press, 1982. — 114p ; 21cm
Includes index
ISBN 0-85224-438-x : £6.00 : CIP rev. B82-10857

820.9′9411 — English literature. Scottish writers, *1900- — Directories*

Writers' register : a directory of writers in Scotland. — Edinburgh (19 Charlotte Sq., Edinburgh EN2 4DF) : The Scottish Arts Council, [c1979]. — [16]p ; 22cm
Cover title. — List of films: p[15]. — List of sound recordings: p[16]
Unpriced (pbk) B82-08219

820.9′9415 — English literature. Irish writers, *1800-1981 — Critical studies*

Literature and the changing Ireland / edited by Peter Connolly. — Gerrards Cross : Smythe, 1982. — viii,230p ; 23cm. — (Irish literary studies, ISSN 0140-895x ; 9)
Conference papers. — Includes index
ISBN 0-86140-043-7 : Unpriced : CIP rev. B81-09478

820.9′9415 — English literature. Irish writers, *1837-1900 — Critical studies*

Hall, Wayne E.. Shadowy heroes. — Brighton : Harvester Press, Apr.1981. — lv.p
ISBN 0-7108-0053-3 : Unpriced : CIP entry B81-01855

820.9′9415 — English literature. Irish writers, *to 1980 — Critical studies*

Warner, Alan. A guide to Anglo-Irish literature / Alan Warner. — Dublin : Gill and Macmillan, 1981. — 295p ; 23cm
Bibliography: p281-291. — Includes index
ISBN 0-7171-1003-6 : £15.00 B82-10280

820.9′94245 — English literature. Shropshire writers, *ca 1300-1980 — Lists*

Dickins, Gordon. A literary guide to Shropshire / by Gordon Dickins. — Shrewsbury : Shropshire Libraries, 1980. — [4],34p : ill,1map ; 21cm
Bibliography: p[4]. — Includes index
ISBN 0-903802-13-9 (pbk) : £0.80 B82-16523

820.9′9429 — English literatute. Welsh writers, *1900- — Personal observations*

Jones, Glyn, *1905-*. Setting out : a memoir of literary life in Wales / by Glyn Jones. — Cardiff ([38 Park Place, Cardiff CF1 3BB]) : Department of Extra Mural Studies, University College, Cardiff, 1982. — iv,16p ; 21cm. — (Park Place paper ; 13)
'A lecture given at a weekend school at Dyffryn House'
Unpriced (pbk) B82-31810

820.9'96 — English literature. African writers, *1945- — Critical studies*
Irele, Abiola. The African experience in literature and ideology. — London : Heinemann Educational, Sept.1981. — [224]p. — (Studies in African literature)
ISBN 0-435-91631-9 (pbk) : £5.95 : CIP entry
Also classified at 840.9'96 B81-22601

820.9'96 — English literature. African writers, *1945- — Critical studies — Serials*
African literature today. — London : Heinemann Educational
No.12: New writing, new approaches. — Oct.1981. — [224]p
ISBN 0-435-91648-3 (cased) : £9.95 : CIP entry
ISBN 0-435-91649-1 (pbk) : £4.95
Also classified at 840.9'96 B81-28035

820.9'968 — English literature. South African negro writers, *1914-1980 — Critical studies*
Barnett, Ursula A.. A vision of order. — London (10 Archway Close, N19 3TD) : Sinclair Browne, Nov.1982. — [320]p
ISBN 0-86300-007-x : £15.00 : CIP entry
B82-27192

820.9'994 — English literature. Australian writers, *to 1980 — Critical studies*
Wilkes, G. A.. The stockyard and the croquet lawn : literary evidence for Australian cultural development / G.A. Wilkes. — London : Edward Arnold, 1981. — 153p ; 23cm. — (Studies in Australian culture)
Bibliography: p151-153
ISBN 0-7131-8042-0 : £9.95 B82-13570

821 — ENGLISH POETRY

821 — Poetry in English. African writers, *1945-*. **Practical criticism**
Burton, S. H.. African poetry in English : an introduction to practical criticism / S.H. Burton, C.J.H. Chacksfield ; advised by Wingrove Dwamina. — London : Macmillan, 1979. — xiv,154p : ill ; 20cm
Bibliography: p153-154
ISBN 0-333-27050-9 (cased) : £5.95 : CIP rev.
ISBN 0-333-25812-6 (pbk) : £1.95 B79-17790

821 — Poetry in English. Australian writers, *1945- — Texts*
Cherjo. Sap, wake up! / Cherjo. — Edwardstown : Cherjo, c1981 (Ilfracombe : Stockwell). — 8p ; 18cm
ISBN 0-7223-1429-9 (pbk) : Unpriced
B82-19022

Day, Peter A.. A crippled phoenix : a collection / Peter A. Day. — [Old Harlow] ([57, High St., Old Harlow, Essex, CM17 0DN]) : [P.A. Day], c1981. — [20]p : ill,1map ; 23cm
Unpriced (pbk) B82-02297

Fatchen, Max. Songs for my dog and other people / Max Fatchen ; illustrated by Michael Atchison. — Harmondsworth : Puffin, 1982, c1980. — 63p : ill ; 20cm
Originally published: Harmondsworth : Kestrel, 1980
ISBN 0-14-031398-2 (pbk) : £0.80 B82-22304

Isacké, Peter P.. Australian poems / by Peter Isacké. — Walton-on-Thames : Outposts Publications, 1982. — 26p ; 21cm
£1.20 (pbk) B82-35570

MacLeod, Doug. In the garden of badthings : poems / by Doug MacLeod ; pictures by Peter Thomson. — [Ringwood, Vic.] ; [Harmondsworth] : Kestrel, 1981. — [36]p : ill (some col.) ; 24cm
ISBN 0-7226-5680-7 : £3.95 B82-17517

Murray, Les A.. The vernacular republic : poems 1961-1981 / Les A. Murray. — Edinburgh : Canongate, c1982. — x,219p ; 19cm
ISBN 0-86241-022-3 (pbk) : £3.95 B82-27611

Niland, Kilmeny. My world / Kilmeny Niland. — Sydney ; London : Hodder and Stoughton, 1981. — [32]p : col.ill ; 26cm
ISBN 0-340-26626-0 : £4.95 B82-18103

821 — Poetry in English. Greek writers, *1945- — Texts*
Constantinides, Erricos. Poems and chapter verse / by Erricos Constantinides. — London (24 Conway St. W.1.) : E. Constantinides, 1982. — 101 leaves : ill ; 23cm
Text in English and Greek
Unpriced (unbound)
Also classified at 889'.134 B82-20142

821 — Poetry in English. Indian writers, *1947- — Texts*
Naik, Balwant. Petals of roses / Balwant Naik. — Southall : B. Naik, 1982. — 64p ; 19cm
ISBN 0-7223-1560-0 (pbk) : Unpriced
B82-19023

821 — Poetry in English. New Zealand writers, *1907- — Texts*
Edmond, Lauris. Salt from the north : poems / by Lauris Edmond. — Wellington ; Oxford : Oxford University Press, c1980. — 48p ; 21cm
ISBN 0-19-558064-8 (pbk) : £5.95 B82-00409

Laizer, S. J.. Maelström : poems & photographs / S.J. Laizer. — London : Samurai, 1981. — 32p,[8]leaves of plates : ill(some col.) ; 21cm
ISBN 0-9507816-0-6 (pbk) : £3.50 B82-10346

O'Sullivan, Vincent, *1937-*. Brother Jonathan, brother Kafka / poems by Vincent O'Sullivan ; with prints by John Drawbridge. — Wellington [N.Z.] ; Oxford : Oxford University Press, c1980. — [55]p : ill ; 22cm
ISBN 0-19-558047-8 (pbk) : £7.25 B82-32646

Shaw, Helen, *1913-*. Circles and stones / by Helen Shaw. — Stevenage (7 The Towers, Stevenage, Herts) : Ore Publications, 1982. — 8p ; 21cm. — (The Chariot poets ; no.10)
£0.40 (pbk) B82-33941

Smither, Elizabeth. Casanova's ankle / Elizabeth Smither ; drawings by Jürgen Waibel. — Auckland : Oxford University Press, c1981. — 46p : ill ; 22cm
ISBN 0-19-558078-8 (pbk) : Unpriced
B82-34228

Veronique. Potpourri / Veronique. — Mission Bay : Veronique, c1982 (Ilfracombe : Stockwell). — 24p ; 18cm
ISBN 0-7223-1554-6 (pbk) : Unpriced
B82-19021

821 — Poetry in English. Nigerian writers, *1960- — Texts*
Chandler, Keith. Kett's Rebellion and other poems / Keith Chandler. — Manchester : Carcanet, 1982. — 59p ; 20cm
ISBN 0-85635-277-2 (pbk) : £3.25 : CIP rev.
B82-19835

821 — Poetry in English. South African writers, *1909-1961 — Texts*
Campbell, Roy. The selected poems of Roy Campbell / chosen by Peter Alexander. — Oxford : Oxford University Press, 1982. — xxi,131p ; 22cm
List of works: pxvii-xviii. — Includes index
ISBN 0-19-211946-x : £7.50 : CIP rev.
B82-10424

Cope, Jack. Jack Cope / C J Driver. — Cape Town ; London : Philip, 1979. — 58p ; 22cm. — (Mantis poets)
ISBN 0-908396-11-2 (cased) : £7.15
ISBN 0-908396-12-0 (pbk) : Unpriced
B82-33985

821 — Poetry in English. South African writers, *1961- — Anthologies*
Macnab, Roy. Roy Macnab/Douglas Reid Skinner. — Cape Town ; London : David Philip, 1981. — 58p ; 22cm. — (Mantis poets)
ISBN 0-908396-42-2 (cased) : £8.60
ISBN 0-908396-43-0 (pbk) : Unpriced
B82-03665

821 — Poetry in English. South African writers. Campbell, Roy *— Biographies*
Alexander, Peter, *1917-*. Roy Campbell : a critical biography / Peter Alexander. — Oxford : Oxford University Press, 1982. — x,277p,[12]p of plates : ill,1facsim,ports ; 24cm
Bibliography: p243-247. — Includes index
ISBN 0-19-211750-5 : £12.50 : CIP rev.
B82-04148

821 — Poetry in English. Sri Lanka writers, *1947- — Texts*
Norman, Praema De F. A.. Hearts and flowers : selected poems / of Praema De F.Z. Norman. — London : Regency Press, 1981. — 48p ; 22cm
£1.75 (pbk) B82-07299

821 — Poetry in English. Zimbabwean writers, *1960- — Texts*
Alannah. Reflections in plastic / Alannah. — Bognor Regis : New Horizon, c1982. — 71p ; 21cm
ISBN 0-86116-721-x : £3.95 B82-17411

Zimunya, Musaemura Bonas. Thought-tracks / Musaemura Bonas Zimunya. — Harlow : Longman, 1982. — xii,131p ; 19cm. — (Drumbeat)
ISBN 0-582-78560-x (pbk) : £1.75 B82-27567

821'.008 — Poetry in English, *1550-1830 - Anthologies - For non-English speaking students*
Introducing English verse. — London : Longman, May 1981. — [672]p
ISBN 0-582-49014-6 (pbk) : £7.95 : CIP entry
B81-07909

821'.008 — Poetry in English, *1558-1945 — Anthologies*
Other men's flowers : an anthology of poetry / compiled by A.P. Wavell ; with an introduction by his son. — Rev. ed. — Harmondsworth : Penguin, 1960 (1981 [printing]). — 448p ; 20cm
Originally published: London : Cape, 1948. — Includes index
ISBN 0-14-042052-5 (pbk) : £2.95 B82-08025

821'.008 — Poetry in English, *1670-1760 — Anthologies*
English verse, 1670-1760. — London : Longman, Dec.1982. — [480]p. — (Longman annotated anthologies of English verse ; v.4)
ISBN 0-582-48380-8 (pbk) : £5.95 : CIP entry
B82-30065

821'.008 — Poetry in English *— Anthologies — For schools*
Poetry plus. — Huddersfield : Schofield & Sims
Bk 1: A diary of poems / written and compiled by B.R. Marney ... [et al] ; illustrated by Margaret Sherry. — 1982. — 80p : ill ; 21cm
ISBN 0-7217-0431-x (pbk) : £1.15 B82-33274

821'.008 — Poetry in English, *to 1923 — Anthologies*
An **anthology** of mine 1923 / [compiled and illustrated by Rex Whistler]. — London : Hamish Hamilton, 1981. — [72]p : col.ill ; 17cm
ISBN 0-241-10667-2 : £3.95 : CIP rev.
Primary classification 759.2 B81-22676

821'.008 — Poetry in English, *to 1980 — Anthologies*
Everyman's book of evergreen verse / edited by David Herbert. — London : Dent, 1981. — vi,387p ; 19cm
Includes index
ISBN 0-460-01246-0 (pbk) : £3.95 : CIP rev.
B81-25820

Poems I like. — London : Hutchinson, Feb.1983. — [160]p
ISBN 0-09-150650-6 : £5.95 : CIP entry
B82-36563

The **Wild** wave : an anthology of poetry / [compiled by] H.S. Houghton-Hawksley and A.B.S. Eaton. — London : Murray, 1982. — xv,280p ; 22cm
Includes index
ISBN 0-7195-3964-1 (pbk) : Unpriced : CIP rev. B82-06520

821'.008 — Poetry in English, *to ca 1970 — Anthologies*

A book of faith. — London : Hodder & Stoughton, Jan.1982. — [352]p
ISBN 0-340-27470-0 (pbk) : £2.50 : CIP entry
B81-34139

821'.008'03241443 — Poetry in English, *1745-1900.* **Special subjects: Scotland. Strathclyde Region. Glasgow** *— Anthologies*

Four Glasgow poems. — [Glasgow] : Glasgow District Libraries, 1981. — 23p : ill ; 21cm
ISBN 0-906169-04-6 (pbk) : Unpriced
B82-18690

821'.008'032421 — Poetry in English, *ca 1600-1981.* **Special subjects: London** *— Anthologies*

London lines. — London : Methuen, Apr.1982. — [160]p
ISBN 0-413-49460-8 : £6.95 : CIP entry
B82-04710

821'.008'032421 — Poetry in English. Special themes: London *— Anthologies*

London in verse. — London : Secker & Warburg, Nov.1982. — [112]p
ISBN 0-436-25675-4 : £5.50 : CIP entry
B82-32869

821'.008'0324257 — Poetry in English, *1600-1981.* **Special subjects: Oxfordshire** *— Anthologies*

Oxford and Oxfordshire : in verse / edited and with an introduction by Antonia Fraser with the collaboration of Flora Powell-Jones ; illustrations by Rebecca Fraser. — London : Secker & Warburg, 1982. — xix,85p : ill ; 23cm
ISBN 0-436-16260-1 : £5.50 : CIP rev.
B82-11991

821'.008'0351 — Poetry in English, *1300-1980.* **Special subjects: Mary,** *Mother of Jesus Christ — Anthologies*

In praise of Our Lady / edited by Elizabeth Jennings ; with a foreword by Cardinal Hume. — London : Batsford, 1982. — 124p : ill(some col.) ; 23cm
Ill on lining papers. — Includes index
ISBN 0-7134-4087-2 : £4.95 B82-31186

821'.008'0354 — Poetry in English, *1564-1965.* **Special subjects: Childhood** *— Anthologies*

A Mother's posy / edited by Celia Haddon. — London : Joseph, 1982. — 48p : col.ill ; 16cm
ISBN 0-7181-2143-0 : £2.50 B82-27607

821'.008'0355 — Poetry in English, *1300-1980.* **Special subjects: Chess** *— Anthologies*

The Poetry of chess / edited and introduced by Andrew Waterman. — London : Anvil Press Poetry, 1981. — 159p ; 22cm
Bibliography: p155-158. — Includes index
ISBN 0-85646-067-2 (pbk) : £4.95 B82-11935

821'.008'0355 — Poetry in English, *1800-1979.* **Special subjects: London. East End. Labour movements** *— Anthologies*

Bricklight : poems from the labour movement in East London / edited and introduced by Chris Searle. — London : Pluto in association with the National Museum of Labour History, 1980. — 247p ; 22cm
ISBN 0-86104-332-4 (pbk) : £1.95 B82-17563

821'.008'0355 — Poetry in English. Special themes: Food *— Anthologies*

A Packet of poems. — Oxford : Oxford University Press, Sept.1982. — [112]p
ISBN 0-19-276049-1 : £5.50 : CIP entry
B82-19185

821'.008'036 — Children's poetry in English. Special subjects: Animals *— Anthologies*

Birds, beasts and fishes : animal verse for children / edited by Samuel Carr. — London : Batsford, 1982. — 72p : ill(some col.) ; 23cm
Includes index
ISBN 0-7134-4151-8 : £5.95 B82-35182

821'.008'036 — Poetry in English, *1558-1960.* **Special subjects: Animals** *— Anthologies*

Fellow mortals : an anthology of animal verse / chosen by Roy Fuller ; with original illustrations by David Koster. — Plymouth : Macdonald & Evans, 1981. — xxviii,274p : ill ; 23cm
"Published in support of the World Wildlife Fund". — Includes index
ISBN 0-7121-0635-9 : £9.95 B82-05028

821'.008'036 — Poetry in English, *1700-1900.* **Special subjects: Geology** *— Anthologies*

The Poetry of geology / edited by Robert M. Hazen. — London : Allen & Unwin, 1982. — 98p : ill ; 21cm
ISBN 0-04-808032-2 : Unpriced : CIP rev.
B82-10586

821'.008'036 — Poetry in English, *ca 1560-ca 1920.* **Special subjects: Nightingales** *— Anthologies*

A Watch of nightingales / edited by Geoffrey Keynes and Peter Davidson. — [London] ([219a Victoria Park Rd, ED9]) : Stourton, 1981. — [61]p ; 23cm
Limited ed. of 400 numbered copies
Unpriced B82-32660

821'.008'036 — Poetry in English, *ca 1800-ca 1980.* **Special subjects: Scotland. Mountains — Anthologies**

Poems of the Scottish hills. — Aberdeen : Aberdeen University Press, Oct.1982. — [216]p
ISBN 0-08-028476-0 (cased) : £11.00 : CIP entry
ISBN 0-08-028477-9 (pbk) : £6.00 B82-25195

821'.008'036 — Poetry in English. Special subjects: Birds *— Anthologies*

Mockler, Mike. Flights of imagination. — Poole : Blandford Press, Apr.1982. — [128]p
ISBN 0-7137-1164-7 : £6.95 : CIP entry
B82-04501

821'.008'036 — Poetry in English. Special subjects: Farmyards *- Anthologies*

A Farmyard companion. — London : Jill Norman, Sept.1981. — [160]p
ISBN 0-906908-51-5 : £7.95 : CIP entry
B81-20525

821'.008'036 — Poetry in English, *to 1980.* **Special subjects: Weather** *— Anthologies*

Out of the blue : an anthology of weather poems / chosen by Fiona Waters ; with drawings and etchings by Veroni. — London : Fontana, c1982. — 96p : ill ; 20cm. — (Lions original)
Includes index
ISBN 0-00-671960-0 (pbk) : £1.00 B82-32808

821'.008'036 — Poetry in English, *to 1981.* **Special subjects: Animals** *— Anthologies — For children*

The Beaver book of animal verse / compiled by Raymond Wilson ; illustrated by Tessa Barwick. — London : Hamlyn, 1982. — 159p : ill ; 18cm. — (Beaver books)
Includes index
ISBN 0-600-20324-7 (pbk) : £1.10 B82-10281

821'.008'0382 — Christian poetry in English, *ca 650-1979 — Anthologies*

The Lion book of Christian poetry / compiled by Pat Alexander with biographies by Veronica Zurdel. — Tring : Lion Publishing, 1981. — 125p : ill,1facsim ; 25cm. — (A Lion book)
Ill on lining papers. — Includes index
ISBN 0-85648-313-3 : £4.95 B82-02165

821'.008'0382 — Christian poetry in English, *ca 650-1981 — Anthologies*

The Sun, dancing : Christian verse / compiled and introduced by Charles Causley. — [Harmondsworth] : Kestrel, 1982. — 248p ; 23cm
Includes index
ISBN 0-7226-5593-2 : £6.95 B82-25136

821'.008'09282 — Children's poetry in English, *1550-1978 — Anthologies*

I like this poem : a collection of best-loved poems chosen by children for other children / embellished Antony Maitland ; edited Kaye Webb. — Harmondworth : Penguin, 1979 (1981 printing). — 191p : ill ; 20cm. — (A Puffin original)
Includes index
ISBN 0-14-031295-1 (pbk) : £1.25 B82-07779

821'.008'09282 — Children's poetry in English, *to 1968 — Anthologies*

This way delight : a book of poetry for the young / selected by Herbert Read ; illustrated by Charles Stewart. — London : Faber Fanfares, 1982. — 192p : ill ; 19cm
Originally published: London : Faber, 1957. — Includes index
ISBN 0-571-18056-6 (pbk) : £1.50 : CIP rev.
B82-04598

821'.008'09282 — Children's poetry in English, *to 1980 — Anthologies*

All the day through / poems collected by Wes Magee ; illustrated by David Sim. — London : Evans, 1982. — 128p : ill ; 22cm
Includes index
ISBN 0-237-45597-8 : £4.95 B82-33936

Have you heard the sun singing? : poems / collected by Adrian Rumble. — London : Evans, 1981. — 240p ; 22cm
Includes index
ISBN 0-237-45552-8 : £6.25 : CIP rev.
B81-00330

821'.008'09282 — Children's poetry in English, *to 1981 — Anthologies*

Once upon a rhyme. — London : Faber, Aug.1982. — [160]p
ISBN 0-571-11913-1 : CIP entry B82-16645

821'.008'09282 — Poetry in English, *1800-1978 — Anthologies — For children*

Watchwords one / [compiled by] Michael & Peter Benton. — London : Hodder and Stoughton, c1979. — 95p : ill,maps,music ; 18x26cm
Includes index
ISBN 0-340-24698-7 : £1.95
ISBN 0-340-21229-2 (pbk) : £1.45 B82-40572

821'.008'09282 — Poetry in English, *1800-1980 — Anthologies — For schools*

Interactions : a poetry teaching anthology / compiled and edited by Geoffrey Halson. — Harlow : Longman, 1982. — 184p ; 24cm
Includes index
ISBN 0-582-33127-7 (pbk) : £2.50 B82-39923

821'.008'09282 — Poetry in English, *to 1980 — Anthologies — For schools*

Watchwords three. — London : Hodder and Stoughton, May 1982. — [96]p
ISBN 0-340-21231-4 (pbk) : £1.85 : CIP entry
B82-12703

821'.008'09287 — Poetry in English. Women writers, *1820-1980 — Anthologies*

Bread and roses : an anthology of nineteenth and twentieth-century poetry by women writers. — London : Virago, Nov.1982. — [208]p
ISBN 0-86068-235-8 (pbk) : £4.50 : CIP entry
B82-26346

821'.00809411 — Poetry in English. Scottish writers, *to 1982 — Anthologies — For children*

A Scottish poetry book. — Oxford : Oxford University Press, Feb.1983. — [128]p
ISBN 0-19-916029-5 (cased) : £3.95 : CIP entry
ISBN 0-19-916030-9 (pbk) : £2.25 B82-37866

821'.009 — Poetry in English, *1300-1900 — Critical studies*

Doyle, B.. English poetry 1981 : additional pieces for higher level / B. Doyle. — Dublin : Folens, c1979. — 100p ; 22cm. — (Folens' student aids. Leaving certificate)
ISBN 0-86121-091-3 (pbk) : Unpriced
B82-28069

821'.009 — Poetry in English, *1500-1700 — Critical studies*

Poetic traditions of the English Renaissance. — London : Yale University Press, Sept.1982. — [320]p
ISBN 0-300-02785-0 : £17.50 : CIP entry
B82-32877

821'.009 — Poetry in English, *1558-1900 — Study outlines*

Doyle, B.. English poetry 1982 : additional pieces for higher level / B. Doyle. — Dublin : Folens, c1980. — 116p ; 22cm. — (Folens' student aids leaving certificate)
ISBN 0-86121-135-9 (pbk) : Unpriced B82-36377

821'.009 — Poetry in English, *1625-1945 — Critical studies*

Harding, D. W. (Denys Wyatt). Experience into words / D.W. Harding. — Cambridge : Cambridge University Press, 1982, c1963. — 199p ; 22cm
Originally published: London : Chatto & Windus, 1963. — Includes index
ISBN 0-521-28543-7 (pbk) : £5.95 : CIP rev. B82-01333

821'.009 — Poetry in English, *1800-1900 — Critical studies*

Armstrong, Isobel. Language as living form in 19th century poetry. — Brighton : Harvester Press, Sept.1982. — [224]p
ISBN 0-7108-0350-8 : £18.95 : CIP entry B82-20023

821'.009 — Poetry in English, *ca 1500-1969 — Critical studies*

Doyle, B.. English poetry 1981 : ordinary level / B. Doyle. — Dublin : Folens, c1979. — 78p ; 22cm. — (Folens' student aids. Leaving certificate)
ISBN 0-86121-090-5 (pbk) : Unpriced B82-28070

821'.009 — Poetry in English, *ca 1558-ca 1980.* **Practical criticism** *— Manuals*

Rodway, Allan. The craft of criticism. — Cambridge : Cambridge University Press, Dec.1982. — [192]p
ISBN 0-521-23320-8 (cased) : CIP entry
ISBN 0-521-29909-8 (pbk) : £4.50 B82-30074

821'.009 — Poetry in English, *ca 1600-1978 — Critical studies*

Gunn, Thom. The occasions of poetry : essays in criticism and autobiography / by Thom Gunn ; edited and with an introduction by Clive Wilmer. — London : Faber, 1982. — 188p ; 23cm
ISBN 0-571-11733-3 : £6.95 : CIP rev.
Also classified at 821'.914 B81-38308

821'.009 — Poetry in English. English criticism, *1765-1970 — Critical studies*

Needham, John. The completest mode : I.A. Richards and the continuity of English literary criticism / John Needham. — Edinburgh : Edinburgh University Press, c1982. — 210p ; 22cm
Bibliography: p191-193. — Includes index
ISBN 0-85224-387-1 : £12.00 : CIP rev. B81-37528

821'.009 — Poetry in English. Metre

Attridge, Derek. The rhythms of English poetry. — London : Longman, Feb.1982. — [approx.352]p. — (English language series ; 14)
ISBN 0-582-55106-4 (cased) : £13.00 : CIP entry
ISBN 0-582-55105-6 (pbk) : £6.50 B81-38336

821'.009 — Poetry in English, *to 1981.* **Structure**

Boulton, Marjorie. The anatomy of poetry / by Marjorie Boulton ; with a foreword by L.A.G. Strong. — Rev. ed. — London : Routledge & Kegan Paul, 1982. — xvi,255p ; 19cm
Previous ed.: 1953. — Bibliography: p217-239. — Includes index
ISBN 0-7100-9087-0 (pbk) : £3.95 B82-38567

821'.009 — Poetry in English. Versification

Hollander, John. Rhyme's reason : a guide to English verse / John Hollander. — New Haven ; London : Yale University Press, c1981. — viii,54p ; 22cm
Bibliography: p53-54
ISBN 0-300-02735-4 (cased) : Unpriced : CIP rev.
ISBN 0-300-02740-0 (pbk) : Unpriced B81-34717

821'.009'15 — Poetry in English, *ca 1590-1970.* **Allusion** *— Critical studies*

Hollander, John. The figure of echo : a mode of allusion in Milton and after / John Hollander. — Berkeley ; London : University of California Press, c1981. — x,155p ; 21cm
Includes index
ISBN 0-520-04187-9 : Unpriced B82-16918

821'.009'324134 — Poetry in English. Scottish writers, *1510-1965.* **Special subjects: Edinburgh** *— Critical studies*

Daiches, David. The butterfly and the Cross / David Daiches. — [Edinburgh] ([Regional Headquarters, George IV Bridge, Edinburgh EH 1UQ]) : [Recreation and Leisure Department of the Lothian Regional Council], [1980]. — 17p : ports ; 21cm
Lecture given in the Hume Tower of the University of Edinburgh on 15 Feb., 1978
Unpriced (pbk) B82-41028

821'.009'382 — Poetry in English, *to ca 1950.* **Special subjects: Jesus Christ. Passion** *— Critical studies*

Bennett, J. A. W.. Poetry of the Passion : studies in twelve centuries of English verse / J.A.W. Bennett. — Oxford : Clarendon, 1982. — viii,240p ; 23cm
Includes index
ISBN 0-19-812804-5 : £17.50 : CIP rev. B82-04283

821'.03'09 — Epic poetry in English, *1558-1625 — Critical studies*

Hulse, Clark. Metamorphic verse : the Elizabethan minor epic / Clark Hulse. — Princeton, N.J. ; Guildford : Princeton University Press, c1981. — xiv,296p : ill ; 23cm
Includes index
ISBN 0-691-06483-0 : £15.80 B82-13692

821'.03'09 — Narrative poetry in English, *1066-1400 — Critical studies*

Boitani, Piero. English medieval narrative in the thirteenth and fourteenth centuries / Piero Boitani ; translated by Joan Krakover Hall. — Cambridge : Cambridge University Press, 1982. — ix,309p ; 23cm
Translation of: La narrativa del medioevo Inglese. — Bibliography: p292-300. — Includes index
ISBN 0-521-23562-6 : £25.00 : CIP rev. B82-13259

821'.07 — Limericks in English, *to 1981 — Anthologies*

Illuminated limericks / compiled and introduced by Roger Kilroy ; illustrated by McLachlan. — [London] : Corgi, 1982. — 96p : ill ; 20cm
ISBN 0-552-11913-x (pbk) : £1.25 B82-21658

821'.07'08 — Humorous poetry in English, *1900-1945.* **Monologues** *— Anthologies*

Stanley Holloway, more monologues and songs / edited and with an introduction by Michael Marshall ; illustrated by Bill Tidy. — London : Elm Tree Books, 1980. — xvii,77p : ill ; 20cm
List of sound discs: p75-77
ISBN 0-241-10478-5 (pbk) : £2.25
Primary classification 784.5'05 B82-09137

821'.07'08 — Humorous poetry in English, *1900-:* **Monologues** *— Anthologies*

The **Book** of comic and dramatic monologues / compiled and introduced by Michael Marshall. — London : Elm Tree Books/EMI Music, 1981. — xi,206p : 1facsim ; 27cm
ISBN 0-241-10738-5 (cased) : Unpriced : CIP rev.
ISBN 0-241-10670-2 (pbk) : £6.50 B81-28796

821'.07'08 — Humorous poetry in English, *ca 1480-ca 1960 — Anthologies*

A **Choice** of comic and curious verse / edited by J.M. Cohen. — London : Allen Lane, 1982, c1975. — 469p ; 23cm
Originally published: Harmondsworth : Penguin, 1975. — Includes index
ISBN 0-7139-1471-8 : £8.95 B82-17057

821'.07'08 — Humorous poetry in English, *ca 1750-ca 1982 — Anthologies*

Fletcher, Cyril. Terse verse : a collection of the world's shortest and sharpest poems. — London : Century Publishing, Oct.1982. — [160]p
ISBN 0-7126-0011-6 : £4.95 : CIP entry B82-23882

821'.07'08 — Poetry in English. Nonsense rhymes, *to 1978 — Anthologies*

The **Faber** book of nonsense verse : with a sprinkling of nonsense prose / chosen, with an introduction, by Geoffrey Grigson. — London : Faber, 1979 (1982 [printing]). — 352p ; 20cm
Includes index
ISBN 0-571-11787-2 (pbk) : £3.25 : CIP rev. B82-04599

821'.07'08 — Satirical poetry in English, *1660-1980 — Anthologies*

I have no gun but I can spit / [edited by] Kenneth Baker. — London : Methuen, 1980 (1982 [printing]). — 204p ; 20cm
Includes index
ISBN 0-413-50830-7 (pbk) : £2.95 B82-39202

821'.07'089282 — Children's humorous poetry in English, *1945- — Anthologies*

The **Land** of utter nonsense. — London : Hutchinson Junior, Feb.1983. — [96]p
ISBN 0-09-151240-9 : £4.95 : CIP entry B82-36570

Never wear your wellies in the house : and other poems to make you laugh / collected by Tom Baker ; illustrated by children from special schools ; organized through MENCAP. — London : Sparrow, 1981. — 63p : ill ; 18cm
Includes index
ISBN 0-09-927340-3 (pbk) : £0.85 B82-05446

821'.07'089282 — Children's humorous poetry in English, *to 1978 — Anthologies*

Funny poems / edited by Deborah Manley ; illustrated by Gillian Chapman. — London : Granada, 1982. — 96p : ill ; 18cm. — (A Dragon book)
Includes index
ISBN 0-583-30503-2 (pbk) : £0.80 B82-28368

821'.07'089282 — Humorous poetry in English, *to 1980 — Anthologies — For children*

The **Lion** book of humorous verse / chosen by Ruth Petrie. — London : Collins, 1972 (1979 [printing]). — 127p : ill ; 18cm
ISBN 0-00-670943-5 (pbk) : £0.60 B82-08947

821.1 — ENGLISH POETRY, 1066-1400

821'.1 — Poetry in English, *1066-1400 — Texts*

Barbour, John. Barbour's Bruce : a fredome is a noble thing! / edited by Matthew P. McDiarmid, James A.C. Stevenson. — Edinburgh (c/o School of Scottish Studies, 27 George Sq., Edinburgh EH8 9LD) : Scottish Text Society
Vol.2. — 1980. — xvi,270p ; 23cm
Scots text, Introduction in English
Unpriced B82-23575

Barbour, John. Barbour's Bruce : a fredome is a noble thing!. — Edinburgh (27 George Sq., Edinburgh EH8 9LD) : Scottish Text Society
Vol.3 / edited by Matthew P. McDiarmid, James A.C. Stevenson. — 1981. — 264p ; 23cm
Unpriced B82-32108

Chaucer, Geoffrey. The Canterbury tales / by Geoffrey Chaucer ; edited from the Hengwrt manuscript by N.F. Blake. — London : Edward Arnold, 1980. — 707p ; 24cm. — (York medieval text. Second series)
Bibliography: p19-26
ISBN 0-7131-6271-6 : £11.80 : CIP rev. B79-36455

821′.1 — Poetry in English, *1066-1400 — Texts continuation*

Chaucer, Geoffrey. [Canterbury tales. Selections]. The Canterbury tales / by Geoffrey Chaucer ; edited by A. Kent Hieatt and Constance Hieatt ; selected, with translations, a critical introduction, and notes by the editors. — Toronto ; London : Bantam, 1964 (1982 [printing]). — xxiv,423p ; 18cm. — (A Bantam classic)
Bibliography: p422-423
ISBN 0-553-21082-3 (pbk) : £1.50 B82-37132

Chaucer, Geoffrey. The Franklin′s tale : from the Canterbury tales / Geoffrey Chaucer ; edited by Gerald Morgan. — London : Hodder and Stoughton, 1980. — viii,116p ; 21cm. — (The London Medieval and Renaissance series)
Bibliography: p115-116
ISBN 0-340-25168-9 (pbk) : £3.15 : CIP rev. B80-02538

Chaucer, Geoffrey. Sir Thopas. — Sevenoaks (88 West End, Kensing, Sevenoaks, Kent TN15 6PZ) : Peter Danckwerts, May 1982. — [16]p
ISBN 0-907553-02-8 (pbk) : £1.00 : CIP entry B82-21115

Chaucer, Geoffrey. Troilus and Criseyde. — London : Longman, Dec.1982. — [608]p
ISBN 0-582-49072-3 : £35.00 : CIP entry B82-30066

Gower, John. Selected poetry. — Manchester : Carcanet Press, Aug.1982. — [192]p. — (Fyfield books)
ISBN 0-85635-415-5 (pbk) : £3.95 : CIP entry B82-19262

Sir Gawain and the Green Knight / edited by J.A. Burrow. — Harmondsworth : Penguin, 1972 (1982 [printing]). — 176p ; 20cm
ISBN 0-14-042295-1 (pbk) : £2.50 B82-35607

Sir Gawain and the Green Knight. — London : Yale University Press, Aug.1982. — [176]p. — (The English poets ; 13)
Originally published: Harmondsworth : Penguin, 1972
ISBN 0-300-02906-3 : £7.50 : CIP entry B82-28447

821′.1 — Poetry in English. Chaucer, Geoffrey. Canterbury tales. Nun′s priest′s tale & Pardoner′s tale — *Critical studies*

Elliott, Ralph W. V.. The nun′s priest′s tale ; The pardoner′s tale / Ralph W.V. Elliott. — Oxford : Basil Blackwell, 1965 (1982 [printing]). — iv,80p ; 22cm. — (Notes on English literature)
Bibliography: p80
ISBN 0-631-97670-1 (pbk) : Unpriced B82-35848

821′.1 — Poetry in English. Chaucer, Geoffrey. Canterbury tales. Prologue — *Critical studies*

Elliott, Ralph W. V.. The prologue to the Canterbury tales / Ralph W.V. Elliott. — Oxford : Basil Blackwell, 1960 (1982 [printing]). — 73p ; 22cm. — (Notes on English literature)
Bibliography: p72-73
ISBN 0-631-97530-6 (pbk) : Unpriced B82-35847

821′.1 — Poetry in English. Chaucer, Geoffrey — *Critical studies*

Clemen, Wolfgang. Chaucer′s early poetry / Wolfgang Clemen ; translated by C.A.M. Sym. — London : Methuen, 1963 ([1980] printing). — x,214p ; 23cm
Translated from the German. — Bibliography: pix-x. — Includes index
ISBN 0-416-74370-6 : £13.50 : CIP rev. B80-08918

Companion to Chaucer studies / edited by Beryl Rowland. — Rev. ed. — New York ; Oxford : Oxford University Press, 1979. — x,516p ; 21cm
Previous ed.: 1968. — Includes bibliographies and index
ISBN 0-19-502489-3 (pbk) : £3.75 B82-15224

Hussey, S. S.. Chaucer : an introduction / S.S. Hussey. — 2nd ed. — London : Methuen, 1981. — 245p ; 22cm
Previous ed.: 1971. — Bibliography: p235-241. — Includes index
ISBN 0-416-72130-3 (cased) : Unpriced : CIP rev.
ISBN 0-416-72140-0 (pbk) : £4.95 B81-25668

Roscow, G. H.. Syntax and style in Chaucer′s poetry / G.H. Roscow. — Cambridge : Brewer, 1981. — x,158p ; 24cm. — (Chaucer studies ; 6)
Bibliography: p142-146. — Includes index
ISBN 0-85991-080-6 : £19.50 : CIP rev. B81-32022

821′.1 — Poetry in English. Chaucer, Geoffrey. Special themes: Paganism — *Critical studies*

Minnis, A. J.. Chaucer and pagan antiquity. — Woodbridge : Boydell & Brewer, Sept.1982. — [192]p. — (Chaucer studies ; 8)
ISBN 0-85991-098-9 : £19.50 : CIP entry B82-20850

821′.1 — Poetry in English. Langland, William. Piers Plowman. Characters: Piers Plowman — *Critical studies*

Goldsmith, Margaret E.. The figure of Piers Plowman : the image on the coin / Margaret E. Goldsmith. — Cambridge : D. S. Brewer, c1981. — viii,128p ; 24cm. — (Piers Plowman studies ; 2)
Bibliography: p120-122. — Includes index
ISBN 0-85991-077-6 : £12.00 : CIP rev. B81-30448

821′.1 — Poetry in English. Sir Gawain and the Green Knight — *Critical studies*

Barron, W. R. J.. Trawthe and treason : the sin of Gawain reconsidered : a thematic study of Sir Gawain and the green knight / W.R.J. Barron. — Manchester : Manchester University Press, c1980. — x,150p ; 23cm
Bibliography: p147-150
ISBN 0-7190-1294-5 : £12.00 : CIP rev. B80-10204

821′.1′08 — Poetry in English, *1066-1400 — Anthologies*

The Harley lyrics : the Middle English lyrics of Ms. Harley 2253 / edited by G.L. Brook. — 4th ed. — Manchester : Manchester University Press, 1968, c1956 (1978 [printing]). — xii,131p : 1facsim ; 22cm. — (Old and Middle English texts)
Bibliography: p127-131. — Includes index
ISBN 0-7190-0749-6 (pbk) : £4.25 B82-29545

821′.109 — Alliterative poetry in English, *1066-1400 — Critical studies*

Middle English alliterative poetry and its literary background. — Woodbridge : Brewer, Nov.1982. — 1v.
ISBN 0-85991-097-0 : £19.50 : CIP entry B82-27219

821′.109 — Poetry in English, *1066-1400 — Critical studies*

Stevens, John, *1921-*. The old sound and the new : an inaugural lecture / John Stevens. — Cambridge : Cambridge University Press, 1982. — 24p : music ; 22cm
Cover title
£1.50 (pbk) B82-32686

821′.109 — Poetry in English. Prick of conscience. Manuscripts — *Critical studies*

Lewis, Robert E.. A descriptive guide to the manuscripts of the Prick of conscience. — Oxford : Society for the Study of Mediaeval Languages and Literature, Oct.1982. — [172]p. — (Medium aevum monographs. New series ; 12)
ISBN 0-907570-02-x (pbk) : £6.00 : CIP entry B82-25755

821′.1′09382 — Christian poetry in English, *1066-1400.* **John,** *of Grimestone.* **Preaching notes** — *Indexes*

Wilson, Edward. A descriptive index of the English lyrics in John of Grimestone′s preaching book / by Edward Wilson. — [Oxford?] : [Society for the Study of Mediaeval Languages and Literature], 1977, c1973. — xxiii,73p ; 21cm. — (Medium Aevum monographs. New series ; 2)
Originally published: Oxford : Blackwell for the Society for the Study of Mediaeval Languages and Literature. 1973
ISBN 0-631-15400-0 (pbk) : Unpriced B82-24179

821.2 — ENGLISH POETRY, 1400-1558

821′.2 — Poetry in English, *1400-1558 — Texts*

Hoccleve, Thomas. Selected poems / Thomas Hoccleve ; edited with an introduction by Bernard O′Donoghue. — Manchester : Fyfield, 1982. — 104p ; 18cm
Middle English text, English introduction and notes
ISBN 0-85635-321-3 (pbk) : £3.25 : CIP rev. B81-27397

821.3 — ENGLISH POETRY, 1558-1625

821′.3 — Poetry in English, *1558-1625 — Texts*

Donne, John. The divine poems / John Donne ; edited with introduction and commentary by Helen Gardner. — 2nd ed. — Oxford : Clarendon, 1978 (1982 [printing]). — xcviii,158p,[1]leaf of plates : 1port ; 22cm
ISBN 0-19-871100-x (pbk) : £5.50 : CIP rev. B82-03096

Herbert, George. The country parson ; The temple / George Herbert ; edited, with an introduction by John N. Wall, Jr. ; preface by A.M. Allchin. — London : SPCK, 1981. — xxii,354p ; 23cm. — (The Classics of Western spirituality)
Originally published: New York : Paulist Press, c1981. — Bibliography: p335-339. — Includes index
ISBN 0-281-03821-x (pbk) : £8.50
Primary classification 253′.2 B82-08474

Jonson, Ben. The complete poems. — London : Yale University Press, May 1982. — [640]p. — (The English poets)
ISBN 0-300-02825-3 : £17.50 : CIP entry B82-17895

Spenser, Edmund. The faerie queene / Edmund Spenser ; edited by A.C. Hamilton. — London : Longman, 1977 (1980 [printing]). — xiii,753p ; 25cm. — (Longman annotated English poets)
Bibliography: p745-753
ISBN 0-582-49705-1 (pbk) : £8.50 : CIP rev. B80-10205

Spenser, Edmund. Prothalamion : or a spousall verse / by Edmund Spenser. — Hexham (Low Shield, Sparty Lea, Hexham, Northumberland) : Septentrio, 1981. — [16]p ; 22cm
Subtitle: in honour of the double mariage of the two honorable & vertuous ladies, the Ladie Elizabeth, and the Ladie Katherine Somerset, daughters to the Right Honourable the Earle of Worcester, and espoused to the two worthie gentlemen M. Henry Gilford and M. William Peter Esquyers. — Limited ed. of c.140 numbered copies
Private circulation (pbk) B82-26033

821′.3 — Poetry in English. Donne, John — *Critical studies*

Winny, James. A preface to Donne / James Winny. — Rev. ed. — London : Longman, 1981. — ix,196p : ill,maps,facsims,ports ; 21cm. — (Preface books)
Previous ed.: 1970. — Bibliography: p191-192. — Includes index
ISBN 0-582-35246-0 (pbk) : £3.25 : CIP rev. B81-28060

Zunder, William. The poetry of John Donne. — Brighton : Harvester Press, Sept.1982. — [192]p
ISBN 0-7108-0457-1 : £16.95 : CIP entry B82-21390

821'.3 — Poetry in English. Herbert, George, *1593-1633 — Critical studies*
Asals, Heather A. R.. Equivocal predication : George Herbert's way to God / Heather A.R. Asals. — Toronto ; London : University of Toronto Press, c1981. — xii,145p ; 24cm
Bibliography: p131-139. — Includes index
ISBN 0-8020-5536-2 : £17.50 B82-06985

821'.3 — Poetry in English. Shakespeare, William. Sonnets — *Critical studies*
Fairhead, P. J.. Bombyx Mora : a study of Shakespeare's sonnets and Hamlet throwing light into the poet's origin / P.J. Fairhead. — [Cambridge] : Roperian Research, c1980. — 227p,[4]folded leaves of plates : ill,facsims,ports (some col.) ; 25cm
Limited ed. of 100 numbered copies. — 'Skeleton outline of events contemporary to Lady Margaret Roper (Alexander Alesius)' (1 folded leaf) in pocket. — Includes index
ISBN 0-9507395-0-2 : Unpriced
Also classified at 822.3'3 B82-21590

Giroux, Robert. The book known as Q : a consideration of Shakespeare's sonnets / Robert Giroux. — London : Weidenfeld and Nicolson, 1982. — xv,334p : ill,facsims,ports ; 23cm
Includes index. — Includes facsimile reprint : Shake-speares sonnets. London : G. Eld, 1609
ISBN 0-297-78152-9 : £10.95 B82-39071

Muir, Kenneth. Shakespeare's sonnets / Kenneth Muir. — London : Allen & Unwin, 1982. — 179p ; 22cm. — (Unwin critical library)
Originally published: 1979. — Bibliography: p175-176. — Includes index
ISBN 0-04-821055-2 (pbk) : Unpriced : CIP rev. B82-00278

821'.3 — Poetry in English. Spenser, Edmund. Faerie queene. Narrative — *Structuralist perspectives*
Goldberg, Jonathan. Endlesse worke : Spenser and the structures of discourse / Jonathan Goldberg. — Baltimore ; London : Johns Hopkins University Press, c1981. — xv,177p : 1ill,1map,1facsim,ports ; 24cm
Includes index
ISBN 0-8018-2608-x : £10.25 B82-12186

821'.3 — Poetry in English. Spenser, Edmund. Faerie queene. Special themes: Elizabeth I, *Queen of England*
Wells, Robin Headlam. Spenser's Faerie queene and the cult of Elizabeth. — London : Croom Helm, Dec.1982. — [176]p
ISBN 0-7099-2761-4 : £12.50 : CIP entry B82-30809

821'.3 — West Yorkshire *(Metropolitan County).* **Leeds. Universities. Libraries: Brotherton Library. Stock: Poetry in English. Daniel, Samuel. Manuscripts**
Pitcher, John. Samuel Daniel — the Brotherton manuscript : a study in authorship / John Pitcher. — [Leeds] : University of Leeds, School of English, 1981. — xii,214p : ill,facsims ; 32cm. — (Leeds texts and monographs. Newseries ; no.7)
Includes index
Unpriced (pbk) B82-21172

821'.3'08 — Poetry in English, *1558-1702 — Anthologies*
Poetry 1600 to 1660 / selected and edited by Maurice Hussey. — Harlow : Longman, 1981. — x,190p ; 20cm. — (Longman English series)
Bibliography: p188-189
ISBN 0-582-35319-x (pbk) : £1.95 B82-12364

821'.3'08 — Poetry in English, *1600-1660 — Anthologies*
Jacobean and Caroline poetry. — London : Methuen, Sept.1981. — [352]p
ISBN 0-416-31060-5 (cased) : £9.50 : CIP entry
ISBN 0-416-31070-2 (pbk) : £4.95 B81-21571

821'.3'09 — Metaphysical poetry in English, *1558-1702 — Critical studies*
Sloane, Mary Cole. The visual in metaphysical poetry / by Mary Cole Sloane. — Atlantic Highlands : Humanities ; Gloucester : distributed by Sutton, c1981. — 110p,[3]p of plates : ill ; 23cm
Includes index
ISBN 0-391-02299-7 : Unpriced B82-38120

821'.3'09357 — Poetry in English, *1558-1625.* **Special subjects: Visual arts** — *Critical studies*
Gent, Lucy. Picture and poetry 1560-1620 : relations between literature and the visual arts in the English Renaissance / Lucy Gent. — Leamington Spa : Hall, 1981. — 100p : ill,ports ; 22cm
Bibliography: p78-86. — Includes index
ISBN 0-907471-00-5 (pbk) : £5.95 B82-03844

821.4 — ENGLISH POETRY, 1625-1702

821'.4 — Poetry in English, *1625-1702 — Texts*
Cotton, Charles. Selected poems. — Manchester : Carcanet Press, Dec.1982. — [128]p. — (Fyfield books)
ISBN 0-85635-413-9 (pbk) : £2.95 : CIP entry B82-30713

Marvell, Andrew. Andrew Marvell : the complete poems / edited by Elizabeth Story Donno. — Harmondsworth : Penguin, 1972 (1981 [printing]). — 314p ; 20cm. — (Penguin English poets)
Includes index
ISBN 0-14-042213-7 (pbk) : £2.95 B82-09146

821'.4 — Poetry in English. Crashaw, Richard — *Critical studies*
Young, R. V.. Richard Crashaw and the Spanish golden age. — London : Yale University Press, Nov.1982. — [240]p. — (Yale studies in English ; 191)
ISBN 0-300-02766-4 : £15.50 : CIP entry B82-40335

821'.4 — Poetry in English. King, Henry, *1592-1669 — Biographies*
Hobbs, Mary. Henry King 1592-1669 : bishop, poet and refugee / by Mary Hobbs. — Hove (9 Brunswick Sq., Hove, E. Sussex BN3 1EN) : Chichester Diocesan Fund and Board of Finance, [1981]. — 7p : 1port ; 21cm
Unpriced (unbound) B82-06278

821'.4 — Poetry in English. Marvell, Andrew — *Critical studies*
Wallace, John M.. Destiny his choice : the loyalism of Andrew Marvell / by John M. Wallace. — Cambridge : Cambridge University Press, 1968 (1980 [printing]). — x,265p ; 22cm
Includes index
ISBN 0-521-06725-1 (cased) : Unpriced : CIP rev.
ISBN 0-521-28042-7 (pbk) : £6.50 B80-28674

821'.4 — Poetry in English. Milton, John, *1608-1674 — Biographies*
Wilson, A. N.. The life of John Milton. — Oxford : Oxford University Press, Jan.1983. — [320]p
ISBN 0-19-211776-9 : £9.50 : CIP entry B82-33473

821'.4 — Poetry in English. Milton, John, *1608-1674.* **Inspiration** — *Critical studies*
Williams, Meg Harris. Inspiration in Milton and Keats / Meg Harris Williams. — London : Macmillan, 1982. — xi,212p ; 23cm
Bibliography: p202-206. — Includes index
ISBN 0-333-29479-3 : Unpriced
Also classified at 821'.7 B82-33844

821'.4 — Poetry in English. Milton, John, *1608-1674.* **Paradise lost** — *Critical studies*
Danielson, Dennis Richard. Milton's good God : a study in literary theodicy / Dennis Richard Danielson. — Cambridge : Cambridge University Press, 1982. — xi,292p,[1]leaf of plates : 1ill ; 23cm
Bibliography: p271-287. — Includes index
ISBN 0-521-23744-0 : £20.00 B82-29929

Hamilton, K. G.. Paradise lost : a humanist approach / K.G. Hamilton. — St. Lucia ; London : University of Queensland Press, c1981. — xiii,122p ; 22cm. — (The University of Queensland Press scholars' library)
Bibliography: p11-117. — Includes index
ISBN 0-7022-1626-7 : £19.50 B82-39737

Hunter, G. K.. Paradise lost / G.K. Hunter. — London : Allen & Unwin, 1982. — 213p ; 22cm. — (Unwin critical library)
Originally published: 1980. — Bibliography: p208-211. — Includes index
ISBN 0-04-800007-8 (pbk) : Unpriced : CIP rev. B82-00277

Ruddick, William, *1938-*. Paradise lost I & II / William Ruddick. — Oxford : Blackwell, 1969 (1982 [printing]). — iii,91p ; 22cm. — (Notes on English literature)
Bibliography: p91
ISBN 0-631-97820-8 (pbk) : Unpriced B82-40507

821'.4 — Poetry in English. Milton, John, *1608-1674 — Study outlines*
Bayley, Peter, *1921-*. Selected poems : notes / by Peter Bayley. — Harlow : Longman, 1982. — 104p ; 21cm. — (York notes ; 177)
At head of title: John Milton. — Bibliography: p97-98
ISBN 0-582-78289-9 (pbk) : £0.90 B82-36747

821'.4 — Poetry in English. Milton, John, *1608-1674.* **Style** — *Critical studies*
Burnett, Archie. Milton's style : the shorter poems, Paradise regained, and Samson agonistes / Archie Burnett. — London : Longman, 1981. — 187p ; 23cm
Includes index
ISBN 0-582-49128-2 (cased) : £8.50
ISBN 0-582-49129-0 (pbk) : £3.95 B82-14436

821'.4 — Poetry in English. Rochester, John Wilmot, *Earl of — Critical studies*
Spirit of wit. — Oxford : Basil Blackwell, Nov.1981. — [256]p
ISBN 0-631-12897-2 : £12.00 : CIP entry B81-30169

821'.4 — Poetry in English. Vaughan, Henry — *Critical studies*
Rudrum, Alan. Henry Vaughan / Alan Rudrum. — [Cardiff] : University of Wales Press on behalf of the Welsh Arts Council, 1981. — 135p : 1facsim ; 25cm. — (Writers of Wales)
Limited ed. of 1000 numbered copies. — Bibliography: p125-131
ISBN 0-7083-0787-6 (pbk) : £2.50 : CIP rev. B81-02375

821.5 — ENGLISH POETRY, 1702-1745

821'.5 — Poetry in English, *1702-1745 — Texts*
Pope, Alexander. An essay on man / Alexander Pope ; edited by Maynard Mack. — London : Methuen, 1950 (1982 [printing]). — xc,186p : 2ill ; 23cm. — (The Twickenham edition of the poems of Alexander Pope ; v.3,i)
Includes index
ISBN 0-416-34010-5 : Unpriced : CIP rev. B82-07660

821'.5 — Poetry in English. Pope, Alexander — *Critical studies*
Pope : recent essays / by several hands ; edited by Maynard Mack and James A. Winn. — Brighton : Harvester, 1980. — xi,872p ; 23cm
ISBN 0-85527-408-5 : £24.00 : CIP rev. B80-04390

821.6 — ENGLISH POETRY, 1745-1800

821'.6 — Poetry in English, *1745-1800 — Texts*
Burns, Robert, *1759-1796*. Robert Burns / selected and introduced by Karl Miller ; photographs by John Hedgecoe. — London : Weidenfeld and Nicolson, c1981. — 127p : ill ; 24cm. — (Landscape poets)
ISBN 0-297-77991-5 : £5.95 B82-31571

Cowper, William. The poems of William Cowper / edited by John D. Baird and Charles Ryskamp. — Oxford : Clarendon
Vol.1: 1748-1782. — 1980. — 597p ; 23cm
Includes index
ISBN 0-19-811875-9 : £25.00 : CIP rev. B79-22707

821′.6 — Poetry in English, *1745-1800* **—** *Texts continuation*

Johnson, Samuel. The complete English poems. — London : Yale University Press, July 1982. — [256]p. — (The English poets ; 11)
Originally published: Harmondsworth : Penguin, 1971
ISBN 0-300-02824-5 : £11.00 : CIP entry B82-22782

Smart, Christopher. The poetical works of Christopher Smart. — Oxford : Clarendon
Vol.1: Jubilate Agno / edited with an introduction by Karina Williamson. — 1980. — xxxi,143p,[3]leaves of plates : 2facsims,1port ; 23cm
Bibliography: pxi-xiv. — Includes index
ISBN 0-19-811869-4 : £13.50 : CIP rev. B80-23658

Smart, Christopher. The poetical works of Christopher Smart. — Oxford : Clarendon Press. — (Oxford English texts)
Vol.2: Religious poetry 1763-1771. — Jan.1983. — [200]p
ISBN 0-19-812767-7 : £17.50 : CIP entry B82-33491

821′.6 — Poetry in English, *1745-1800* **—** *Texts — Facsimiles*

Hayley, William. A poetical epistle to an eminent painter ... / William Hayley ; with an introduction for the Garland edition by Donald H. Reiman. — New York ; London : Garland, 1978. — xvi,159p ; 24cm. — (Romantic context)
Contents: A poetical epistle to an eminent painter. Facsim of: London : Payne, 1778 — An elegy on the ancient Greek model. Facsim of: Cambridge : Hodson, 1779 — Epistle to Admiral Keppel. Facism of: London : Fielding and Walker, 1779 — Epistle to a friend on the death of John Thornton. Facsim of: London : Dodsley, 1780 — An essay on history. Facsim of: London : Dodsley, 1780
ISBN 0-8240-2156-8 : Unpriced B82-19605

821′.6 — Poetry in English, *1745-1800* **—** *Texts with commentaries*

Johnson, Samuel, *1709-1784*. Johnson's Juvenal / edited with introduction, notes, Latin texts and translations by Niall Rudd. — Bristol : Bristol Classical Press, 1981. — xvi,106p ; 21cm
English text with some chapters in Latin with English translations. — Bibliography: pxv-xvi. — Contents: London — The vanity of human wishes
ISBN 0-906515-64-5 (pbk) : Unpriced
Also classified at 871′.01 B82-05338

821′.6 — Poetry in English. Burns, Robert, *1759-1796* **—** *Biographies*

Bailey, Kenneth. Robert Burns / Kenneth Bailey ; drawings by Richard Hook. — Edinburgh : Spurbooks, c1982. — 64p : ill,ports ; 19cm. — (Introducing Scotland)
Bibliography: p63. — Includes index
ISBN 0-7157-2076-7 (pbk) : £1.25 B82-20588

821′.6 — Poetry in English. Burns, Robert, *1759-1796* **—** *Critical studies*

The **Art** of Robert Burns / edited with an introduction by R.D.S. Jack and Andrew Noble. — London : Vision, 1982. — 240p : music ; 23cm. — (Critical studies series)
Includes index
ISBN 0-85478-274-5 : £13.95 B82-37584

Daiches, David. Robert Burns / David Daiches. — Edinburgh : Spurbooks, c1981. — 334p ; 22cm
Originally published: London : Deutsch, 1966. — Includes index
ISBN 0-7157-2093-7 (pbk) : £6.95 B82-12216

821′.6 — Poetry in English. Cowper, William — *Correspondence, diaries, etc.*

Cowper, William. The letters and prose writings of William Cowper. — Oxford : Clarendon Press
Vol.3: Letters 1787-1791. — Oct.1982. — [628]p
ISBN 0-19-812608-5 : £35.00 : CIP entry
Primary classification 828′.608 B82-23681

821′.6 — Poetry in English. Cowper, William — *Critical studies*

Hutchings, Bill. The poetry of William Cowper. — London : Croom Helm, Nov.1982. — [256]p
ISBN 0-7099-1249-8 : £12.95 : CIP entry B82-27205

Newey, Vincent. Cowper's poetry. — Liverpool : Liverpool University Press, Sept.1982. — [384] p. — (Liverpool English texts and studies ; 20)
ISBN 0-85323-344-6 : £14.50 : CIP entry B82-20826

821′.6′09145 — Poetry in English, *1745-1837*. **Romanticism —** *Critical studies*

Purkis, John. The world of the English poets : a visual approach / by John Purkis. — London : Heinemann, 1982. — 190p : ill,facsims,maps,2plans ; 25cm
Ill on lining papers. — Bibliography: p186. — Includes index
ISBN 0-435-18735-x : £12.50 : CIP rev. B82-07975

821.7 — ENGLISH POETRY, 1800-1837

821′.7 — Poetry in English, *1800-1837* **—** *Texts*

Blake, William, *1757-1827*. William Blake : the complete poems / edited by Alicia Ostriker. — Harmondsworth : Penguin, 1977 (1981 [printing]). — 1071p ; 20cm. — (Penguin English poets)
Includes index
ISBN 0-14-042215-3 (pbk) : £5.95 B82-09145

Blake, William, *1757-1827*. William Blake : selected poems. — London : Dent, Oct.1982. — [288]p
ISBN 0-460-01125-1 (pbk) : £3.50 : CIP entry B82-23988

Byron, George Gordon Byron, *Baron*. The complete poetical works / Lord Byron ; edited by Jerome J. McGann. — Oxford : Clarendon
Vol.1. — 1980. — xlvii,464p : 1facsim ; 23cm
Includes index
ISBN 0-19-811890-2 : £35.00 : CIP rev. B80-11149

Byron, George Gordon Byron, *Baron*. Don Juan / Lord Byron ; edited by T.G. Steffan, E. Steffan and W.W. Pratt. — Repr. with revisions and additions. — Harmondsworth : Penguin, 1982. — 759p ; 20cm
Originally published: 1973. — Bibliography: p27-31
ISBN 0-14-042216-1 (pbk) : £5.95 B82-40476

Byron, George Gordon Byron, *Baron*. Don Juan. — London : Yale University Press, Aug.1982. — [768]p
Originally published: Harmondsworth : Penguin, 1977
ISBN 0-300-02678-1 : £12.50 : CIP entry B82-27188

Clare, John, *1793-1864*. The rural muse : poems / by John Clare ; a second edition of Clare's volume of 1835 edited by R.K.R. Thornton from the original manuscript ; with an essay by Barbara M.H. Strang. — Ashington : Mid Northumberland Arts Group, 1982. — 184p : 2facsims ; 23cm
Includes index
ISBN 0-904790-18-5 : £5.95 B82-38628

Fulcher, G. W.. The village paupers : an anti-Poor Law poem of the 1840's / by G.W. Fulcher of Sudbury ; [edited by E.A. Goodwyn]. — Beccles ([Cherry Hill, Ashmans Rd, Beccles, Suffolk]) : [E.A. Goodwyn], 1981. — 30p ; 20cm
£1.30 (pbk) B82-30775

Hogg, James, *1770-1835*. The king's anthem ; and Mary Gray : two poems / by James Hogg. — Stirling : University of Stirling Bibliographical Society, 1981. — [12]p ; 22cm. — (Occasional publication / University of Stirling Bibliographical Society ; no.2)
ISBN 0-907250-01-7 (pbk) : Unpriced B82-11375

Hood, Thomas. Hood winked. — London : Chatto & Windus, Sept.1982. — [48]p
ISBN 0-7011-2626-4 : £3.95 : CIP entry B82-20298

Keats, John, *1795-1821*. John Keats : an approach to his poetry / commentary by K.R. Roberts ; illustrations by Brian Halton. — Huddersfield : Schofield & Sims, 1982. — 72p : ill,1facsim ; 23cm
ISBN 0-7217-0436-0 (pbk) : £0.95 B82-19922

Shoel, Thomas. On Allington Hill, near Bridport / by Thomas Shoel, 1819. — Guernsey : Toucan Press, 1982. — [4]p ; 22cm
Limited ed. of 25 copies
ISBN 0-85694-258-8 (pbk) : Unpriced B82-08990

Wordsworth, William, *1770-1850*. Daffodils / William Wordsworth. — [Liverpool] ([51 York Ave., Great Crosby, Liverpool L23 5RN]) : Cracked Bell, 1980. — [8]p ; 12cm
Unpriced (pbk) B82-26042

Wordsworth, William, *1770-1850*. [Poems]. William Wordsworth : the poems / edited by John O. Hayden. — New Haven ; London : Yale University Press, 1981. — 2v. ; 21cm. — (The English poets)
Originally published: Harmondsworth : Penguin, 1977. — Includes bibliographies and index
ISBN 0-300-02751-6 (cased) : Unpriced : CIP rev.
ISBN 0-300-02754-0 (v.1 : pbk) : Unpriced
ISBN 0-300-02755-9 (v.2 : pbk) : Unpriced B82-01325

Wordsworth, William, *1770-1850*. Poems / William Wordsworth ; edited by John O. Hayden. — Harmondsworth : Penguin, 1977 (1982 [printing])
Vol.1. — 1066p ; 19cm
Includes index
ISBN 0-14-042211-0 (pbk) : £8.95 B82-22100

Wordsworth, William, *1770-1850*. William Wordsworth : The prelude : a parallel text / edited by J.C. Maxwell. — New Haven ; London : Yale University Press, 1981, c1971. — 573p : 1 map ; 21cm. — (The English poets)
Parallel text of 1805 and 1850 eds.. — Originally published: Harmondsworth : Penguin, 1971. — Bibliography: p31-32
ISBN 0-300-02753-2 (cased) : £15.00 : CIP rev.
ISBN 0-300-02756-7 (pbk) : Unpriced B82-01326

821′.7 — Poetry in English, *1800-1837* **—** *Texts — Facsimiles*

Barrett, Eaton Stannard. Woman / Eaton Stannard Barrett. Henry Schultze / with an introduction for the Garland edition by Donald H. Reiman. — New York ; London : Garland, 1979. — 1v.(various pagings) : ill ; 19cm
Woman: facsim of: edition published, London : J. Murray, 1810 ; Henry Schultze: facsim of: edition published, London : C & J Ollier, 1821
ISBN 0-8240-2105-3 : Unpriced B82-09328

821′.7 — Poetry in English. Blake, William, *1757-1827*. **Influence of Bible**

Tannenbaum, Leslie. Biblical tradition in Blake's early prophecies : the great code of art / Leslie Tannenbaum. — Princeton ; Guildford : Princeton University Press, c1982. — xiii,373p ; 23cm
Bibliography: p337-362. — Includes index
ISBN 0-691-06490-3 : £17.60 B82-25706

821′.7 — Poetry in English. Blake, William, *1757-1827*. **Songs of innocence & Songs of experience —** *Study outlines*

Hyland, Dominic. Songs of innocence, and Songs of experience : notes / by Dominic Hyland. — Harlow : Longman, 1982. — 88p ; 21cm. — (York notes ; 173)
Bibliography: p81
ISBN 0-582-78284-8 (pbk) : £0.90 B82-36757

821′.7 — Poetry in English. Blake, William, *1757-1827 — Study outlines*

Chatwin, Deryn. Notes on Blake′s poetry / compiled by Deryn Chatwin. — London : Methuen Paperbacks, 1979. — 75p ; 20cm. — (Methuen notes. Study-aid series)
Bibliography: p75
ISBN 0-417-21610-6 (pbk) : £0.75 B82-25815

821′.7 — Poetry in English. Byron, George Gordon Byron, *Baron — Biographies*

Raphael, Frederic. Byron / Frederic Raphael. — [London] : Thames and Hudson, c1982. — 224p : ill,1facsim,ports ; 24cm
Bibliography: p216-217. — Includes index
ISBN 0-500-01278-4 : £8.95 B82-34978

821′.7 — Poetry in English. Byron, George Gordon Byron, *Baron — Correspondence, diaries, etc.*

Byron, George Gordon Byron, *Baron*. Byron′s letters and journals / edited by Leslie A. Marchand. — London : Murray
Vol.12: The trouble of an index : anthology of memorable passages and index to the eleven volumes. — 1982. — vii,166p ; 23cm
ISBN 0-7195-3885-8 : £15.00 B82-00353

Byron, George Gordon Byron, *Baron*. [Byron′s letters and journals. Selections]. Lord Byron : selected letters and journals. — London : Murray, Oct.1982. — [416]p
ISBN 0-7195-3974-9 : £12.50 : CIP entry B82-23020

821′.7 — Poetry in English. Byron, George Gordon Byron, *Baron — Critical studies*

Martin, Philip W.. Byron : a poet before his public / Philip W. Martin. — Cambridge : Cambridge University Press, 1982. — x,253p : ill ; 23cm
Bibliography: p238-247. — Includes index
ISBN 0-521-24186-3 (cased) : £18.50 : CIP rev.
ISBN 0-521-28766-9 (pbk) : £6.95 B82-22794

821′.7 — Poetry in English. Byron, George Gordon Byron, *Baron*. **Don Juan** *— Critical studies*

De Almeida, Hermione. Byron and Joyce through Homer : Don Juan and Ulysses / Hermione de Almeida. — London : Macmillan, 1981. — x,233p ; 23cm
Includes index
ISBN 0-333-30072-6 : £15.00
Also classified at 823′.912 B82-06643

821′.7 — Poetry in English. Clare, John, *1793-1864 — Biographies*

Storey, Edward. A right to song. — London : Methuen, Sept.1982. — [368]p
ISBN 0-413-39940-0 : £10.00 : CIP entry B82-18752

821′.7 — Poetry in English. Clare, John, *1793-1864 — Correspondence, diaries, etc*

Clare, John, *1793-1864*. The journal, essays, the journey from Essex / John Clare ; edited and with an introduction by Anne Tibble. — Manchester : Carcanet New Press, 1980. — 139p : ill,2facsims,1port ; 23cm
Bibliography: p137-139
ISBN 0-85635-344-2 : £6.95 B82-13740

821′.7 — Poetry in English. Coleridge, Samuel Taylor *— Critical studies*

Holmes, Richard, *1945-*. Coleridge / Richard Holmes. — Oxford : Oxford University Press, 1982. — vi,102p ; 19cm. — (Past masters)
Bibliography: p98-100. — Includes index
ISBN 0-19-287592-2 (cased) : Unpriced : CIP rev.
ISBN 0-19-287591-4 (pbk) : £1.25 B82-00886

Mileur, Jean-Pierre. Vision and revision : Coleridge′s art of immanence / Jean-Pierre Mileur. — Berkeley ; London : University of California Press, c1982. — xi,184p ; 23cm
Includes index
ISBN 0-520-04447-9 : £14.25 B82-35753

821′.7 — Poetry in English. Coleridge, Samuel Taylor. Marginal notes *— Collections*

Coleridge, Samuel Taylor. Marginalia / [Samuel Taylor Coleridge] ; edited by George Whalley. — London : Routledge & Kegan Paul. — (The Collected works of Samuel Taylor Coleridge ; 12) (Bollingen series ; LXXV)
1: Abbt to Byfield. — c1980. — clxxiv,879p,3leaves of plates : 1ill,2facsims ; 23cm
£32.00 B82-09258

821′.7 — Poetry in English. Coleridge, Samuel Taylor. Special themes: Science *— Critical studies*

Levere, Trevor H.. Poetry realized in nature : Samuel Taylor Coleridge and early nineteenth-century science / Trevor H. Levere. — Cambridge : Cambridge University Press, 1981. — xiii,271p : ill ; 24cm
Includes index
ISBN 0-521-23920-6 : £22.50 B82-02676

821′.7 — Poetry in English. Coleridge, Samuel Taylor *— Study outlines*

Gravil, Richard. Selected poems : notes / by Richard Gravil. — Harlow : Longman, 1982. — 88p ; 21cm. — (York notes ; 165)
Bibliography: p85-86
ISBN 0-582-78259-7 (pbk) : £0.90 B82-16464

821′.7 — Poetry in English. Hogg, James, *1770-1835 — Critical studies — Serials*

Newsletter of the James Hogg Society. — Issue no.1 (May 1982)-. — Stirling (The Haldane Room, Stirling University Library, Stirling FK9 4LA) : The Society, 1981-. — v. ; 21cm
Annual
ISSN 0263-7022 = Newsletter of the James Hogg Society : Unpriced B82-31731

821′.7 — Poetry in English. Keats, John, *1795-1821*. **Inspiration** *— Critical studies*

Williams, Meg Harris. Inspiration in Milton and Keats / Meg Harris Williams. — London : Macmillan, 1982. — xi,212p ; 23cm
Bibliography: p202-206. — Includes index
ISBN 0-333-29479-3 : Unpriced
Primary classification 821′.4 B82-33844

821′.7 — Poetry in English. Shelley, Percy Bysshe *— Critical studies*

Essays on Shelley / edited by Miriam Allott. — Liverpool : Liverpool University Press, 1982. — xviii,286p ; 23cm. — (Liverpool English texts and studies)
Bibliography: p279-281. — Includes index
ISBN 0-85323-294-6 : £12.50 : CIP rev. B81-30420

821′.7 — Poetry in English. Shelley, Percy Bysshe. Influence of Italy

Folliot, Katherine. Shelley′s Italian sunset / by Katherine Folliot. — Richmond : H & B Publications, 1979. — 128p ; 21cm
Bibliography: p125-128
ISBN 0-9506371-1-4 (pbk) : £1.50 B82-03574

821′.7 — Poetry in English. Wordsworth, William, *1770-1850 — Biographies*

Davies, Hunter. William Wordsworth / Hunter Davies. — London : Hamlyn, 1981, c1980. — xvi,367p : ill,1map,ports,1geneal.table ; 20cm
Originally published: London : Weidenfeld and Nicolson, 1980. — Bibliography: p349-352. — Includes index
ISBN 0-600-20376-x (pbk) : £1.95 B82-00076

821′.7 — Poetry in English. Wordsworth, William, *1770-1850 — Correspondence, diaries, etc.*

Wordsworth, William, *1770-1850*The letters of William and Dorothy Wordsworth / edited by the late Ernest De Selincourt. — 2nd ed. — Oxford : Clarendon
6: The later years
Previous ed.: 1939
Pt.2: 1835-1839 / revised, arranged and edited by Alan G. Hill. — 1982. — xxv,794p,[3]leaves of plates : 3ports ; 23cm
Bibliography: pvii-ix. — Includes index
ISBN 0-19-812483-x : £35.00 : CIP rev.
Also classified at 828′.709 B82-23680

821′.7 — Poetry in English. Wordsworth, William, *1770-1850 — Critical studies*

Heaney, Seamus. The making of a music : reflections on the poetry of Wordsworth and Yeats / by Seamus Heaney. — Liverpool : University of Liverpool Press, c1978. — 18p ; 21cm. — (The Kenneth Allott lectures ; no.1)
ISBN 0-906370-05-1 (pbk) : Unpriced
Also classified at 821′.8 B82-16115

Pirie, David B.. William Wordsworth : the poetry of grandeur and tenderness. — London : Methuen, Mar.1982. — [300]p
ISBN 0-416-31300-0 : £14.00 : CIP entry B82-01992

Simpson, David, *1951-*. Wordsworth and the figurings of the real / David Simpson. — London : Macmillan, 1982. — xxvii,183p ; 23cm
Bibliography: p176-179. — Includes index
ISBN 0-333-30631-7 : £20.00 B82-28525

Wordsworth, Jonathan. William Wordsworth : the borders of vision. — Oxford : Clarendon Press, Nov.1982. — [300]p
ISBN 0-19-812097-4 : £17.50 : CIP entry B82-26880

821′.7′09 — Poetry in English. Wordsworth, Mary & Wordsworth, William *— Correspondence, diaries, etc.*

Wordsworth, William, *1770-1850*. The love letters of William and Mary Wordsworth / edited by Beth Darlington. — London : Chatto & Windus, 1982, c1981. — 265p : ill,2maps,facsims,ports,1geneal.table ; 23cm
Originally published: Ithaca, N.Y. : Cornell University Press, 1981. — Includes index
ISBN 0-7011-2570-5 : £10.95 : CIP rev. B81-27960

Wordsworth, William, *1770-1850*. My dearest love / letters of William and Mary Wordsworth 1810 ; edited in facsimile by Beth Darlington ; with a foreword by Jonathan Wordsworth. — Ambleside ([Grasmere, Ambleside, Cumbria LA22 9SG]) : Trustees of Dove Cottage, 1981. — 81p : facsims ; 35cm
Limited ed. of 300 numbered copies, of which 35 are signed. — In slipcase
Unpriced B82-34863

821′.7′09145 — Poetry in English, *1800-1837*. **Romanticism** *— Critical studies*

Frye, Northrop. A study of English romanticism. — Brighton : Harvester, Nov.1982. — [182]p
Originally published: New York : Random House, 1968
ISBN 0-7108-0414-8 (pbk) : £4.95 : CIP entry B82-31299

821.8 — ENGLISH POETRY, 1837-1900

821′.8 — Poetry in English, *1837-1900 — Texts*

Browning, Elizabeth Barrett. Aurora Leigh : her novel in verse : with other poems / Elizabeth Barrett Browning ; introduced by Cora Kaplan. — London : Women′s Press, 1978 (1981 [printing]). — 416p ; 20cm
Bibliography: p416
ISBN 0-7043-3820-3 (pbk) : £4.95 B82-10026

Browning, Robert, *1812-1889*. The Pied Piper of Hamelin / Robert Browning ; illustrated by John Spencer. — Kingswood : World′s Work, c1981. — [32]p : col.ill ; 24cm. — (A World′s Work children′s book)
ISBN 0-437-29650-4 : £3.95 B82-03969

Browning, Robert, *1812-1889*. [Poems]. Robert Browning : the poems / edited by John Pettigrew ; supplemented and compiled by Thomas J. Collins. — New Haven ; London : Yale University Press, 1981. — 2v. ; 21cm. — (The English poets)
Includes bibliographies and index
ISBN 0-300-02675-7 (cased) : Unpriced : CIP rev.
ISBN 0-300-02683-8 (v.1 : pbk) : Unpriced
ISBN 0-300-02676-5 (v.2) : £22.50
ISBN 0-300-02684-6 (v.2 : pbk) : Unpriced B82-01322

821'.8 — Poetry in English, *1837-1900* **—** *Texts continuation*

Browning, Robert, *1812-1889.* The poetical works of Robert Browning. — Oxford : Oxford University Press, Aug.1982. — (Oxford English texts)
Vol.1. — [964]p
ISBN 0-19-811893-7 : £40.00 : CIP entry
B82-15680

Burgess, J. J. Haldane. Rasmie's büddie : poems in the Shetlandic / by J.J. Haldane Burgess ; illustrations by Frank Walterson. — Lerwick : Shetland Publishing Company, 1979. — xxii,104p : ill,1port ; 23cm
ISBN 0-906736-00-5 : £3.95 B82-08595

Carroll, Lewis. [Alice's adventures in Wonderland. Selections]. Jabberwocky : and other poems : from Alice's adventures in Wonderland and Through the looking-glass / by Lewis Carroll. — London : Macmillan Children's Books, 1981. — 47p : ill ; 20cm
ISBN 0-333-32410-2 : £1.95 B82-06321

Clough, Arthur Hugh. [The bothie of Toper-na-fuosich]. The bothie / Arthur Hugh Clough ; the text of 1848 edited by Patrick Scott. — [St. Lucia, Queensland] : University of Queensland Press ; Hemel Hempstead : Prentice-Hall [distributor], c1976. — 55,82p ; 22cm. — (Victorian texts ; 4)
Facsim of: 1st ed. Oxford : Macpherson, 1848. — Bibliography: p20-21
ISBN 0-7022-1153-2 (cased) : £7.50
ISBN 0-7022-1163-x (pbk) : Unpriced
B82-00972

Dolben, Digby Mackworth. The poems and letters of Digby Mackworth Dolben 1848-1867 / edited, with an introduction and commentary, by Martin Cohen. — [Amersham] : Avebury, 1981. — x,174p : 1port ; 23cm
Includes index
ISBN 0-86127-219-6 : Unpriced : CIP rev.
B81-31811

Gissing, George. Six sonnets on Shakespearean heroines / George Gissing ; with an introductory note by Pierre Coustillas. — London (74 Fortune Green Rd NW6) : Eric & Joan Stevens, 1982. — [16]p ; 26cm
Limited ed. of 250 copies
Unpriced (pbk) B82-22184

Hardy, Thomas, *1840-1928.* The complete poetical works of Thomas Hardy. — Oxford : Clarendon Press, Nov.1982. — (Oxford English texts)
Vol.1: Wessex poems; Poems of the past and the present; Time's laughingstocks. — [400]p
ISBN 0-19-812708-1 : £35.00 : CIP entry
B82-26881

Hardy, Thomas, *1840-1928.* Thomas Hardy / selected and introduced by Peter Porter ; photographs by John Hedgecoe. — London : Weidenfeld and Nicolson, c1981. — 128p : ill ; 24cm. — (Landscape poets)
ISBN 0-297-77992-3 : £5.95 B82-38613

Hardy, Thomas, *1840-1928.* Thomas Hardy : selected poems. — London : Dent, Sept.1982. — [320]p
ISBN 0-460-10783-6 (cased) : £6.95 : CIP entry
ISBN 0-460-11783-1 (pbk) : £3.95 B82-23318

Herbison, David. Webs of fancy : poems of David Herbison, the bard of Dunclug / a selection edited with an introduction by Ivan Herbison. — Oxford : Dunclug Press, 1980. — 59p : 1port ; 21cm
Bibliography: p58-59
ISBN 0-9507296-0-4 (pbk) : £1.50 B82-31570

Lear, Edward. The Courtship of the Yonghy-Bonghy-Bo ; & the new vestments / Edward Lear ; illustrated by Kevin Maddison. — London : Ash & Grant, 1980. — [30]p : col.ill,music ; 24cm
ISBN 0-904069-22-2 : £2.95 : CIP rev.
B79-16134

Lear, Edward. The Jumblies ; and, The Dong with a luminous nose / Edward Lear ; illustrated by Edward Gorey. — London : Methuen, 1982. — [85]p : ill ; 16x23cm
ISBN 0-413-50530-8 : £4.95 B82-36612

Lear, Edward. The pelican chorus; and, The Quangle Wangle's hat. — London : Ash & Grant, Sept.1981. — [32]p
ISBN 0-904069-40-0 : £3.50 : CIP entry
B81-25871

McGonagall, William. Further poetic gems / William McGonagall. — London : Duckworth, 1980. — 80p ; 19cm
ISBN 0-7156-1510-6 (pbk) : £1.00 B82-41094

Swinburne, Algernon Charles. Swinburne : selected poems / edited by L.M. Findlay. — Manchester : Fyfield Books, 1982. — vi,274p ; 23cm
ISBN 0-85635-137-7 : Unpriced : CIP rev.
B81-27946

Tennyson, Alfred Tennyson, *Baron.* The Lady of Shalott / Alfred Lord Tennyson. — Sevenoaks : Danckwerts, 1982. — [10]p ; 6cm
Limited ed. of 250 numbered copies
ISBN 0-907553-00-1 (pbk) : £0.75 : CIP rev.
B82-07833

Tennyson : in memoriam / edited by Susan Shatto and Marion Shaw. — Oxford : Clarendon, 1982. — xvi,397p,[4]p of plates : facsims ; 23cm
Includes index
ISBN 0-19-812747-2 : £25.00 : CIP rev.
B81-35803

Wilde, Oscar. The sphinx. — London : Century, Sept.1981. — 2v.
Facsim. of: 1st ed. London : Elkin Mathews & John Lane, 1894
ISBN 0-907492-00-2 : £250.00 : CIP entry
B81-20501

Wordsworth. — Brighton : Harvester Press, Oct.1981. — [224]p. — (Cornell Wordsworth)
ISBN 0-7108-0315-x : £30.00 : CIP entry
B81-30329

821'8 — Poetry in English, *1837-1900* **—** *Texts — Manuscripts — Facsimiles*

Morris, William, *1834-1896.* A book of verse : a facsimile of the manuscript written in 1870 / by William Morris. — London : Scolar, 1981, c1980. — [14],51p : col.ill,facsims,ports ; 25cm
Originally published.: 1980. — Facsim. of manuscript held in Victoria and Albert Museum. — Bibliography: 14th Prelim. page
ISBN 0-85967-605-6 : £7.95 : CIP rev.
B81-04284

821'.8 — Poetry in English. Arnold, Matthew — *Biographies*

Trilling, Lionel. Matthew Arnold. — Oxford : Oxford University Press, Jan.1982. — [504]p. — (The works of Lionel Trilling)
Originally published: London : Allen & Unwin, 1975
ISBN 0-19-212222-3 : £9.95 : CIP entry
B81-34374

821'.8 — Poetry in English. Blunt, Wilfred Scawen. Interpersonal relationships with Morris, Jane, *b.1840*

Faulkner, Peter. Wilfrid Scawen Blunt and the Morrises : the first annual Kelmscott Lecture of the William Morris Society given at the Society of Antiquaries on Tuesday 30th September 1980 / by Peter Faulkner. — London : William Morris Society, 1981. — 45p ; 22cm
ISBN 0-903283-01-8 (pbk) : £2.50
Also classified at 942.081'092'4 B82-06596

821'.8 — Poetry in English. Blunt, Wilfrid Scawen — *Biographies*

Longford, Elizabeth. A pilgrimage of passion : the life of Wilfrid Scawen Blunt / Elizabeth Longford. — London : Granada, 1982, c1979. — xv,473p,[8]p of plates : ill,ports,geneal.table ; 20cm. — (A Panther book)
Originally published: London : Weidenfeld and Nicolson, 1979. — Bibliography: p435-438. — Includes index
ISBN 0-586-05307-7 (pbk) : £3.95 B82-19602

821'.8 — Poetry in English. Browning, Robert, *1812-1889 — Biographies*

Thomas, Donald. Robert Browning : a life within life / Donald Thomas. — London : Weidenfeld and Nicolson, c1982. — xiv,334p ; 25cm
Bibliography: p317-319. — Includes index
ISBN 0-297-78092-1 : £12.95 B82-39483

821'.8 — Poetry in English. Browning, Robert, *1812-1889 — Critical studies*

Slinn, E. Warwick. Browning and the fictions of identity / E. Warwick Slinn. — London : Macmillan, 1982. — xi,173p ; 23cm
Includes index
ISBN 0-333-30056-4 : £15.00 B82-38795

821'.8 — Poetry in English. Browning, Robert, *1812-1889 — Study outlines*

Barnish, Valerie L.. Notes on Browning's poetry / compiled by Valerie L. Barnish. — London : Methuen Paperbacks, 1979. — 90p ; 20cm. — (Methuen notes. Study-aid series)
Bibliography: p88. — Includes index
ISBN 0-417-21620-3 (pbk) : £0.75 B82-25814

821'.8 — Poetry in English. Field, Michael — *Correspondence, diaries, etc*

Ricketts, Charles. Letters from Charles Ricketts to 'Michael Field' (1903-1913) / edited sby J.G. Paul Delaney. — Edinburgh : Tragara, c1981. — 30p ; 24cm
Limited ed. of 145 numbered copies
ISBN 0-902616-72-2 (pbk) : £9.50
Primary classification 709'.2'4 B82-01388

821'.8 — Poetry in English. Hardy, Thomas, *1840-1928 — Study outlines*

Elliott, Roger. Selected poems : notes / by Roger Elliott. — Harlow : Longman, 1982. — 80p ; 21cm. — (York notes ; 169)
At head of title: Thomas Hardy. — Bibliography: p72-73
ISBN 0-582-78294-5 (pbk) : £0.90 B82-36754

821'.8 — Poetry in English. Hopkins, Gerard Manley. Special themes: Christian life. Religious experiences

Walhout, Donald. Send my roots rain : a study of religious experience in the poetry of Gerard Manley Hopkins / Donald Walhout. — Athens [Ohio] ; London : Ohio University Press, c1981. — 203p ; 24cm
Bibliography: p198-200. — Includes index
ISBN 0-8214-0565-9 : £11.20 B82-15529

821'.8 — Poetry in English. Tennyson, Alfred Tennyson, *Baron — Correspondence, diaries, etc.*

Tennyson, Alfred Tennyson, *Baron.* The letters of Alfred Lord Tennyson / edited by Cecil Y. Lang and Edgar F. Shannon, Jr.. — Oxford : Clarendon
Vol.1: 1921-1850. — 1982. — xxxviii,366p ; 24cm
Includes index
ISBN 0-19-812569-0 : £17.50 : CIP rev.
B81-02089

821'.8 — Poetry in English. Tennyson, Alfred Tennyson, *Baron — Critical studies*

Studies in Tennyson / edited by Hallam Tennyson. — London : Macmillan, 1981. — xiv,229p ; 23cm
Includes index
ISBN 0-333-27884-4 : £15.00 : CIP rev.
B79-36943

821'.8 — Poetry in English. Watson, *Sir* **William,** *1858-1936 — Biographies*

Wilson, Jean Moorcroft. I was an English poet : a critical biography of Sir William Watson (1858-1936) / by Jean Moorcroft Wilson. — London : Woolf, c1981. — xi,243p,[24]p of plates : ill,1facsim,ports ; 25cm
Includes index
ISBN 0-900821-20-5 : £12.50 B82-30105

821′.8 — Poetry in English. Yeats, W. B. — *Biographies*

O'Connor, Frank. W.B. Yeats : a reminiscence / by Frank O'Connor. — Edinburgh : Tragara, 1982. — 17p ; 21cm
Limited ed. of 125 numbered copies
ISBN 0-902616-80-3 (pbk) : £8.00 B82-38991

821′.8 — Poetry in English. Yeats, W. B.. Crazy Jane on the Day of Judgment. Manuscripts — *Critical studies*

Clark, David R.. That black day : the manuscripts of Crazy Jane on the day of judgement / David R. Clark. — Portlaoise : Dolmen Press in association with Humanities Press, 1980. — 55p : ill,facsims ; 25cm. — (New Yeats papers ; 18)
ISBN 0-85105-355-6 (pbk) : Unpriced : CIP rev. B80-10744

821′.8 — Poetry in English. Yeats, W. B. — *Critical studies*

Heaney, Seamus. The making of a music : reflections on the poetry of Wordsworth and Yeats / by Seamus Heaney. — Liverpool : University of Liverpool Press, c1978. — 18p ; 21cm. — (The Kenneth Allott lectures ; no.1)
ISBN 0-906370-05-1 (pbk) : Unpriced
Primary classification 821′.7 B82-16115

Yeats : a collection of critical essays / edited by John Unterecker. — Englewood Cliffs ; London : Prentice-Hall, c1982. — ix,180p ; 21cm. — (Twentieth century views) (A Spectrum book)
Bibliography: p179-180
ISBN 0-13-971911-3 (pbk) : £2.50 B82-29460

821′.8 — Poetry in English. Yeats, W. B.. Influence of Nietzsche, Friedrich

Bohlmann, Otto. Yeats and Nietzsche : an exploration of major Nietzschean echoes in the writings of William Butler Yeats / Otto Bohlmann. — London : Macmillan, 1982. — xviii,222p,[4]p of plates : facsims,ports ; 23cm
Bibliography: p198-202. — Includes index
ISBN 0-333-27601-9 : £17.50 B82-32375

821′.8 — Poetry in English. Yeats, W. B.. Influence of right-wing political movements, *1920-1940*

Craig, Cairns. Yeats, Eliot, Pound and the politics of poetry : richest to richest / Cairns Craig. — London : Croom Helm, c1982. — 323p ; 22cm
Bibliography: p313-317. — Includes index
ISBN 0-85664-997-x : £11.95 : CIP rev.
Primary classification 821′.912′09 B81-15905

821′.8 — Poetry in English. Yeats, W. B. Manuscripts — *Critical studies*

Clark, David R.. Yeats at songs and choruses. — Gerrards Cross : Colin Smythe, Aug.1982. — [286]p
ISBN 0-86140-125-5 : £15.00 : CIP entry B82-19281

821′.8 — Poetry in English. Yeats, W. B.. Symbolism — *Critical studies*

Dyson, A. E.. Yeats, Eliot and R.S. Thomas : riding the echo / A.E. Dyson. — London : Macmillan, 1981. — x,339p ; 23cm
Bibliography: p327-329. — Includes index
ISBN 0-333-13027-8 : £15.00
Primary classification 821′.8′0915 B82-10829

821′.8′08 — Poetry in English, *1837-1900 — Anthologies*

Everyman's book of Victorian verse / edited by J.R. Watson. — London : Dent, 1982. — xxiii,373p ; 24cm
Includes index
ISBN 0-460-04453-2 : £9.50 : CIP rev. B82-02001

821′.8′08 — Poetry in English, *1837-1936 — Anthologies*

Michael Roberts' The Faber book of modern verse. — London : Faber, May 1982. — [416]p
Facsim of: 1st ed.: 1936
ISBN 0-571-11817-8 : £12.50 : CIP entry B82-10765

821′.8′080324237 — Poetry in English, *1840-1980.* **Special subjects: Cornwall —** *Anthologies*

Cornwall : in verse / edited and with an introduction by Peter Redgrove. — London : Secker & Warburg, 1982. — xii,68p : ill ; 23cm
ISBN 0-436-40987-9 : £5.50 : CIP rev. B82-11275

821′.8′0809282 — Children's poetry in English, *1837-1980 — Anthologies*

Amazing monsters : verses to thrill and chill / edited by Robert Fisher ; illustrated by Rowena Allen. — London : Faber and Faber, 1982. — 96p : ill ; 21cm
Includes index
ISBN 0-571-11850-x : £3.95 : CIP rev. B82-00209

Drumming in the sky : poems from Stories and rhymes / edited by Paddy Bechely ; illustrated by Priscilla Lamont. — London : British Broadcasting Corporation, 1981. — 160p : ill ; 22cm
Includes index
ISBN 0-563-17900-7 : £5.95 B82-05993

821′.8′09 — Poetry in English, *1837-1945 — Critical studies*

Perkins, David, *1928-*. A history of modern poetry : from the 1890s to the high Modernist mode / David Perkins. — Cambridge, Mass. ; London : Belknap, 1976 (1979 printing). — xv,623p : ill ; 22cm
Includes index
ISBN 0-674-39945-5 (cased) : Unpriced B82-28624

Sisson, C. H.. English poetry 1900 : an assessment / C.H. Sisson. — Reissued with new matter. — Manchester : Carcanet, 1981. — 271p ; 22cm
Originally published: London : Hart Davies, 1971. — Includes index
ISBN 0-85635-393-0 : £9.95 : CIP rev. B81-31202

821′.8′09 — Poetry in English, *1837-1945 — Critical studies — For schools*

Walsh, James. The modern poets : E. Dickinson, G.M. Hopkins, T. Hardy, T.S. Eliot, D. Thomas / James Walsh. — Tallaght : Folens, c1981. — 74p ; 22cm. — (Succeed in English ; 3)
ISBN 0-86121-147-2 (pbk) : Unpriced B82-10178

821′.8′09 — Poetry in English. Browning, Elizabeth Barrett & Browning, Robert, *1812-1889.* **Influence of French culture**

Gridley, Roy E.. The Brownings and France. — London : Athlone Press, Sept.1982. — [320]p
ISBN 0-485-11231-0 : £15.00 : CIP entry B82-19533

821′.8′0915 — Poetry in English, *1837-1978.* **Symbolism —** *Critical studies*

Dyson, A. E.. Yeats, Eliot and R.S. Thomas : riding the echo / A.E. Dyson. — London : Macmillan, 1981. — x,339p ; 23cm
Bibliography: p327-329. — Includes index
ISBN 0-333-13027-8 : £15.00
Also classified at 821′.8 ; 821′.912 ; 821′.914 B82-10829

821′.8′0994281 — Poetry in English: Poetry in West Yorkshire dialects, *1837-1980 — Critical studies*

Smith, Ken Edward. West Yorkshire dialect poets / by Ken Edward Smith. — Wilsden : Dialect, c1982. — 54p ; 21cm
Bibliography: p52-54
ISBN 0-9508048-0-0 (pbk) : £1.50 B82-35804

821.912 — ENGLISH POETRY, 1900-1945

821′.912 — Poetry in English, *1900-1945 — Texts*

Allen, Jonathan. A pocket book of painful puns and poems. — London : Dent, Sept.1982. — [64]p
ISBN 0-460-06094-5 : £3.50 : CIP entry B82-19705

Auden, W. H.. Norse poems / W.H. Auden, Paul B. Taylor. — London : Athlone Press, 1981. — xiv,256p ; 25cm
Translation from the Icelandic
ISBN 0-485-11226-4 : £7.95 : CIP rev. B81-22649

Bentley, E. Clerihew. The complete clerihews of E. Clerihew Bentley / illustrated by Nicolas Bentley ... [et al.] ; with an introduction by Gavin Ewart. — Oxford : Oxford University Press, 1981, c1951. — xix,145p : ill ; 19cm
Includes index
ISBN 0-19-212978-3 : £5.95 : CIP rev. B81-25795

Betjeman, John. Metro-land / verses by Sir John Betjeman ; lithographs by Glynn Boyd Harte. — [London] : Warren, 1977. — [31]leaves : col.ill ; 19x25cm
Limited ed. of 220 signed copies
ISBN 0-9505969-0-6 : Unpriced
Also classified at 769.92′4 B82-32651

Betjeman, John. Uncollected poems. — London : Murray, Sept.1982. — [96]p
ISBN 0-7195-3969-2 : £6.50 : CIP entry B82-20386

Blunden, Edmund. Edmund Blunden : selected poems / edited by Robyn Marsack. — Manchester : Carcanet, 1982. — viii,107p ; 22cm
ISBN 0-85635-425-2 (pbk) : Unpriced : CIP rev. B82-04809

Buchanan, Frank. Selected poems 1935-1975 / Frank Buchanan. — [Godalming] ([Greenwood, Oakdene Rd., Godalming, Surrey, GU7 1QF]) : [F. Buchanan], c1981. — 3v. ; 21cm
Unpriced (pbk) B82-02903

Cheney, Angela Upton. Garden days and other poems / Angela Upton Cheney. — Bognor Regis : New Horizon, c1982. — 56p : ill ; 21cm
ISBN 0-86116-720-1 : £3.95 B82-08978

Clark, Leonard. The way it was : poems / by Leonard Clark. — London : Enitharmon, 1980. — 77p ; 23cm
ISBN 0-905289-17-x (pbk) : Unpriced
ISBN 0-905288-12-9 (pbk) : £3.00 B82-20245

Clark, Leonard, *1905-*. The corn growing : poems and verses for children / by Leonard Clark ; illustrated by Lisa Kopper. — London : Hodder and Stoughton, 1982. — 56p : ill ; 23cm
ISBN 0-340-27731-9 : £3.50 : CIP rev. B82-12266

Colum, Pádraic. The poet's circuits : collected poems of Ireland / Pádraic Colum. — Centenary ed. / with a preface by Benedict Kiely. — Portlaoise : Dolmen Press, 1981. — xiii,150p ; 22cm
Previous ed.: Oxford : Oxford University Press, 1960
ISBN 0-85105-390-4 (pbk) : £6.00 : CIP rev.
ISBN 0-85105-391-2 (limited ed.) : £40.00 B81-33650

Cooke, Greville. An Easter offering / Greville Cooke. — Bognor Regis : New Horizon, c1982. — 95p ; 21cm
ISBN 0-86116-891-7 : £3.95 B82-30499

Cronin, Anthony. New & selected poems / Anthony Cronin. — Manchester : Carcanet, 1982. — 139p ; 20cm
ISBN 0-85635-367-1 (pbk) : £3.95 : CIP rev.
ISBN 0-906897-49-1 (Raven Arts) B82-19836

Dahl, Roald. Roald Dahl's revolting rhymes / with illustrations by Quentin Blake. — London : Cape, 1982. — [32p] : col.ill ; 29cm
ISBN 0-224-02932-0 : £3.95 : CIP rev. B82-14065

821′.912 — Poetry in English, ***1900-1945*** **— *Texts continuation***

Duncan, Ronald. Ronald Duncan : collected poems : collected and edited by Miranda Weston-Smith. — London : Heinemann, 1981. — xxiii,360p : ill ; 23cm
Includes index
ISBN 0-434-98022-6 : £10.00 B82-15303

Edwards, S. Hylton. Aulder Mill / by S. Hylton Edwards. — Walton-on-Thames : Outposts, 1982. — 40p ; 21cm
£1.70 (pbk) B82-38625

Edwards, S. Hylton. Lyntonwood / by S. Hylton Edwards. — London : Murray, 1982. — viii,46p ; 22cm
Unpriced (pbk) B82-29188

Eliot, T. S.. Old Possum′s book of practical cats. — London : Faber, Nov.1982. — [64]p
ISBN 0-571-11971-9 : £4.95 : CIP entry B82-26574

Ewart, Gavin. The new Ewart : poems 1980-1982 / by Gavin Ewart. — London : Hutchinson, 1982. — 115p ; 22cm
ISBN 0-09-146980-5 (pbk) : £4.95 : CIP rev. B82-01148

Fallon, Padraic. Poems and versions. — Manchester : Carcanet Press, Dec.1982. — [96]p
ISBN 0-85635-431-7 (pbk) : £3.95 : CIP entry B82-30714

Fuller, Roy. House and shop / Roy Fuller. — Edinburgh : Tragara Press, 1982. — 16p ; 24cm
ISBN 0-902616-79-x (pbk) : Unpriced B82-33891

Fuller, Roy. The individual and his times : a selection of the poetry of Roy Fuller / edited by V.J. Lee. — London : Athlone, 1982. — xxiv,99p ; 19cm
ISBN 0-485-61008-6 (pbk) : £2.25 : CIP rev. B82-07669

Gascoyne, David, *1916-*. Early poems / David Gascoyne. — Warwick (Emscote Lawn, Warwick) : Greville Press, c1980. — 29p : ill ; 23cm
Limited ed. of 400 numbered copies signed by the poet
Unpriced B82-22650

Grigson, Geoffrey. Collected poems 1963-1980. — London : Allison & Busby, Feb.1982. — [288]p
ISBN 0-85031-419-4 : £9.95 : CIP entry B82-05414

Gurney, Ivor. Collected poems of Ivor Gurney. — Oxford : Oxford University Press, May 1982. — [320]p
ISBN 0-19-211940-0 : £12.00 : CIP entry B82-07497

Hewitt, John, *1907-*. Mosaic / John Hewitt. — Dundonald : Blackstaff with the assistance of the Arts Council of Northern Ireland, c1981. — 48p ; 21cm
ISBN 0-85640-253-2 (pbk) : £3.50 : CIP rev. B81-30490

Jodjana, Raden Ayou. The art of life / by Raden Ayou Jodjana. — Romford : Fowler, [1982]. — [24]p ; 21cm
Limited ed. of 500 copies
ISBN 0-85243-367-0 (pbk) : £2.50 B82-19420

Kavanagh, Patrick. Lough Derg / Patrick Kavanagh ; with a foreword by Paul Durcan. — London : Martin Brian & O′Keeffe, 1978. — ix,24p ; 25cm
ISBN 0-85616-161-6 (cased) : £7.50 B82-26116

Lawrence, D. H.. Birds, beasts and the third thing / poems by D.H. Lawrence ; selected and illustrated by Alice and Martin Provensen ; introduction by Donald Hall. — London : MacRae, 1982. — [40]p : col.ill ; 27cm
ISBN 0-86203-071-4 : £6.25 : CIP rev. B82-10252

Lindsay, Maurice. A net to catch the winds, and other poems / by Maurice Lindsay. — London : Hale, 1981. — 64p ; 21cm
ISBN 0-7091-9482-x : £4.95 B82-02138

Millward, Joseph. Poems for Dorothy / Joseph Millward. — Lowestoft (6 Dene Rd., Lowestoft, Suffolk NR32 4QE) : Lindley, c1980. — 67p ; 21cm
Includes index
£0.75 (pbk) B82-13361

Nicholson, Norman. Selected poems, 1940-1982. — London : Faber, Oct.1982. — [76]p
ISBN 0-571-11949-2 (cased) : £5.95 : CIP entry
ISBN 0-571-11950-6 (pbk) : £2.95 B82-25174

Sitwell, Sacheverell. Allotment or assignment? / [Sacheverell Sitwell]. — [Daventry] ([Pennywick, Badby, Daventry, Northants.]) : [M. Battison], [1980]. — [9]p : ill ; 22cm
Unpriced (pbk) B82-13366

Sitwell, Sacheverell. Nocturnae Silvani Potenti : leading into an age of amber / [Sacheverell Sitwell]. — [Daventry] ([Pennywick, Badby, Daventry, Northants.]) : [M. Battison], [1980]. — vip ; 22cm
Unpriced (pbk) B82-13365

Sparrow, John. Grave Epigrams and other verses / John Sparrow. — Burford : Cygnet Press, c1981. — 47p ; 23cm
ISBN 0-907435-00-9 : £6.95 B82-07337

Strong, Patience. Poems for the fighting forties. — London : Muller, Nov.1982. — [80]p
ISBN 0-584-11052-9 : £3.95 : CIP entry B82-30582

Thomas, Dylan. Drawings to poems by Dylan Thomas / Ceri Richards ; with an introduction by Richard Burns. — London : Enitharmon, 1980. — xv,169p : ill,1port ; 23cm
ISBN 0-905289-47-1 (cased) : Unpriced
ISBN 0-905289-42-0 (pbk) : Unpriced B82-20248

Thomas, Edward, *1878-1917*. The collected poems of Edward Thomas / edited by R. George Thomas. — Oxford : Oxford University Press, 1981. — xxvi,198p ; 20cm
Includes index
ISBN 0-19-281288-2 (pbk) : £2.95 B82-38470

Thomas, Joan Gale. If I′d been born in Bethlehem / By Joan Gale Thomas. — London : Mowbrays, 1953 (1979 [printing]). — [19]p : ill(some col.) ; 21cm
ISBN 0-264-66704-2 (pbk) : £0.95 B82-23425

Venables, Roger. The Cornish hundreds / by Roger Venables. — Redruth : Printed for St. Just and Pendeen Old Cornwall Society by Redborne Printing Works, c1982. — [12]p ; 20cm
Unpriced (pbk) B82-25321

Venables, Roger. New bread : North Cornish verses / by Roger Venables. — Redruth : Redborne Printing Works, c1981. — [12]p ; 20cm
Unpriced (pbk) B82-25320

Venables, Roger. The stone frigate : verses from West Penwith / by Roger Venables. — Redruth : Printed for St. Just and Pendeen Old Cornwall Society by Redborne Printing Works, c1982. — [12]p ; 21cm
Unpriced (pbk) B82-25322

Warner, Sylvia Townsend. Collected poems / Sylvia Townsend Warner ; edited with an introduction by Claire Harman. — Manchester : Carcanet New Press, c1982. — xxv,290p ; 23cm
Includes index
ISBN 0-85635-339-6 : Unpriced : CIP rev. B82-18467

White, T. H.. A joy proposed. — London : Secker & Warburg, July 1982. — [96]p
ISBN 0-436-56630-3 : £5.50 : CIP entry B82-14229

Williams, Charles, *1886-1945*. The Arthurian poems of Charles Williams. — Woodbridge : Boydell & Brewer, Apr.1982. — [288]p
Contents: The region of the summer stars — Taliessin through Logres
ISBN 0-85991-089-x (pbk) : £6.95 : CIP entry B82-11097

821′.912 — Poetry in English. Allott, Kenneth — *Critical studies*

Davie, Donald. Kenneth Allott and the thirties / by Donald Davie. — [Liverpool] : University of Liverpool, c1980. — 16p ; 21cm. — (The Kenneth Allott lectures ; no.2)
′Delivered on 17 January 1980′
ISBN 0-906370-06-x (pbk) : Unpriced B82-18710

821′.912 — Poetry in English. Auden, W. H. — *Biographies*

Carpenter, Humphrey. W.H. Auden. — London : Unwin Paperbacks, Dec.1982. — [512]p
Originally published: London : Allen & Unwin, 1981
ISBN 0-04-928047-3 (pbk) : £4.50 : CIP entry B82-29866

Osborne, Charles. W.H. Auden : the life of a poet / Charles Osborne. — London : Macmillan, 1982, c1979. — 336p : ill,facsims,ports ; 23cm
Originally published: New York : Harcourt Brace Jovanovich, 1979 ; London : Eyre Methuen, 1980. — Includes index
ISBN 0-333-32954-6 (pbk) : £4.95 B82-32380

821′.912 — Poetry in English. Blunden, Edmund — *Biographies*

Blunden, Edmund. Undertones of war / Edmund Blunden. — Harmondsworth : Penguin, 1937 (1982 [printing]). — 280p ; 18cm. — (Penguin modern classics)
Originally published: London : Cobden-Sanderson, 1928
ISBN 0-14-000082-8 (pbk) : £1.95 B82-22495

821′.912 — Poetry in English. Day Lewis, C. — *Biographies*

Day-Lewis, Sean. C. Day-Lewis : an English literary life / Sean Day-Lewis. — London : Unwin, 1982. — 333p,[8]p of plates : 1facsim,ports ; 20cm
Originally published: London : Weidenfeld & Nicolson, 1980. — List of sound recordings: p312-313. — Includes index
ISBN 0-04-928046-5 (pbk) : £4.50 : CIP rev. B82-15650

821′.912 — Poetry in English. Eliot, T. S., *1909-1922 — Critical studies*

Gray, Piers. T.S. Eliot′s intellectual and poetic development 1909-1922 / Piers Gray. — Brighton : Harvester, 1982. — xii,273p ; 23cm
Bibliography: p255-269. — Includes index
ISBN 0-7108-0046-0 : £22.50 : CIP rev. B81-34018

821′.912 — Poetry in English. Eliot, T. S. — *Critical studies*

Pearson, Norman Holmes. The escape from time : poetry, language and symbol : Stein, Pound, Eliot / by Norman H. Pearson. — Portree : Aquila, 1982. — [12]p ; 21cm. — (Aquila essays ; no.11)
ISBN 0-7275-0242-5 (pbk) : £0.60
Primary classification 818′.5209 B82-27844

821'.912 — Poetry in English. Eliot, T. S. — *Critical studies* *continuation*
T.S. Eliot : the critical heritage / edited by Michael Grant. — London : Routledge & Kegan Paul, 1982. — 2v.(xx,769p) ; 23cm. — (The Critical heritage series)
Bibliography: p746-749. — Includes index
ISBN 0-7100-9226-1 : £25.00
ISBN 0-7100-9224-5 (v.1) : £15.00
ISBN 0-7100-9225-3 (v.2) : £15.00 B82-36073

821'.912 — Poetry in English. Eliot, T. S. — *Critical studies — Welsh texts*
Jones, R. Gerallt. Eliot / R. Gerallt Jones. — [Denbigh] : Gwasg Gee, 1982. — 96p ; 19cm. — (Y Meddwl modern)
Bibliography: p96
£1.90 (pbk) B82-40000

821'.912 — Poetry in English. Eliot, T. S.. Four quartets — *Study outlines*
Quinn, Maire A.. Four quartets : notes / by Maire A. Quinn. — Harlow : Longman, 1982. — 64p ; 21cm. — (York notes ; 167)
Bibliography: p63-64
ISBN 0-582-78252-x (pbk) : £0.90 B82-16458

821'.912 — Poetry in English. Eliot, T. S.. Influence of right-wing political movements, *1920-1940*
Craig, Cairns. Yeats, Eliot, Pound and the politics of poetry : richest to richest / Cairns Craig. — London : Croom Helm, c1982. — 323p ; 22cm
Bibliography: p313-317. — Includes index
ISBN 0-85664-997-x : £11.95 : CIP rev.
Primary classification 821'.912'09 B81-15905

821'.912 — Poetry in English. Eliot, T. S. — *Study outlines*
Herbert, Michael, *1949-*. Selected poems : notes / by Michael Herbert. — Harlow : Longman, 1982. — 88p ; 21cm. — (York notes ; 155)
Bibliography: p84-85
ISBN 0-582-78295-3 (pbk) : £0.90 B82-16453

821'.912 — Poetry in English. Eliot, T. S.. Symbolism — *Critical studies*
Dyson, A. E.. Yeats, Eliot and R.S. Thomas : riding the echo / A.E. Dyson. — London : Macmillan, 1981. — x,339p ; 23cm
Bibliography: p327-329. — Includes index
ISBN 0-333-13027-8 : £15.00
Primary classification 821'.8'0915 B82-10829

821'.912 — Poetry in English. Fuller, Roy — *Biographies*
Fuller, Roy. Vamp till ready : further memoirs / Roy Fuller. — London : London Magazine Editions, 1982. — 185p ; 23cm
ISBN 0-904388-45-x : £8.50 B82-30688

821'.912 — Poetry in English. Gibbon, Monk — *Biographies*
Gibbon, Monk. The pupil. — Dublin : Wolfhound Press, Sept.1981. — [128]p
ISBN 0-905473-68-x : £5.40 : CIP entry B81-24652

821'.912 — Poetry in English. Graves, Robert — *Biographies*
Graves, Robert. Goodbye to all that / Robert Graves. — Rev. ed. — Harmondsworth : Penguin, 1960, c1957 (1982 [printing]). — 281p,[8]p of plates : ill,1map,2ports ; 19cm. — (Penguin modern classics)
Originally published: London : Cassell, 1957
ISBN 0-14-001443-8 (pbk) : £1.95 B82-40382

Seymour-Smith, Martin. Robert Graves : his life and work / Martin Seymour-Smith. — London : Hutchinson, 1982. — xiv,607p,[8]p of plates : ill,ports ; 24cm
Includes index
ISBN 0-09-139350-7 : £14.95 : CIP rev. B82-03741

821'.912 — Poetry in English. Graves, Robert — *Correspondence, diaries, etc.*
Graves, Robert. In broken images : selected letters of Robert Graves, 1914-1946 / edited, with a commentary, by Paul O'Prey. — London : Hutchinson, 1982. — 371p,[8]p of plates : 1ill,facsims,ports ; 24cm
Includes index
ISBN 0-09-147720-4 : £12.95 : CIP rev. B82-07248

821'.912 — Poetry in English. Jones, David, *1895-1974*. **Anathemata** — *Critical studies*
Corcoran, Neil. The song of deeds. — Cardiff : University of Wales Press, July 1982. — [160]p
ISBN 0-7083-0806-6 : £9.95 : CIP entry B82-13010

821'.912 — Poetry in English. MacNeice, Louis, *1941-1963 — Biographies*
MacNeice, Louis. The strings are false : an unfinished autobiography / by Louis MacNeice. — London : Faber and Faber, 1965 (1982 [printing]). — 288p ; 20cm
Includes index
ISBN 0-571-11832-1 (pbk) : £3.25 : CIP rev. B82-04860

821'.912 — Poetry in English. MacNeice, Louis — *Critical studies*
Marsack, Robyn. The cave of making. — Oxford : Clarendon Press, Oct.1982. — [140]p. — (Oxford English manographs)
ISBN 0-19-811718-3 : £13.50 : CIP entry B82-23679

821'.912 — Poetry in English. Muir, Edwin — *Critical studies*
Keeble, Brian. Yourself the finder found : a preface to the poetry of Edwin Muir / Brian Keeble. — Ispwich (3 Cambridge Drive, Ipswich, Suffolk) : Golgonooza, c1981. — 22p ; 23cm
£1.50 (pbk) B82-17797

821'.912 — Poetry in English. Sassoon, Siegfried, *1916-1920 — Biographies*
Sassoon, Siegfried. Siegfried's journey : 1916-1920 / by Siegfried Sassoon. — London : Faber, 1945 (1982 [printing]). — 224p ; 20cm
ISBN 0-571-11917-4 (pbk) : £1.95 : CIP rev. B82-09434

821'.912 — Poetry in English. Sassoon, Siegfried — *Correspondence, diaries, etc.*
Sassoon, Siegfried. Siegfried Sassoon diaries 1920-1922 / edited and introduced by Rupert Hart-Davis. — London : Faber, 1981. — 304p,1leaf of plates : 1port ; 23cm
Includes index
ISBN 0-571-11685-x : £9.95 : CIP rev. B81-28027

821'.912 — Poetry in English. Sitwell, Edith — *Biographies*
Elborn, Geoffrey. Edith Sitwell : a biography / Geoffrey Elborn. — London : Sheldon, 1981. — xii,322p,[8]p of plates : ill,ports ; 24cm
Bibliography: p295-310. — Includes index
ISBN 0-85969-323-6 : £10.00 B82-08182

821'.912 — Poetry in English. Smith, Stevie — *Personal observations*
Dick, Kay. Ivy and Stevie. — London : Allison & Busby, Sept.1982. — [96]p
ISBN 0-85031-483-6 (pbk) : £1.95 : CIP entry
Primary classification 823'.912 B82-18773

821'.912 — Poetry in English. Strong, Patience — *Biographies*
Strong, Patience. With a poem in my pocket. — Large print ed. — Long Preston : Magna Print, Oct.1982. — [700]p
Originally published: London : Muller, 1981
ISBN 0-86009-415-4 : £6.75 : CIP entry B82-20851

821'.912'08 — Poetry in English, *1900-1945 — Anthologies*
Fraser, Arthur. Amoris laus : poems / by Arthur Fraser and Sibyl Crowe. — Oxford : Mouette, 1981. — 157p : 2ports ; 22cm
Includes: Arthur Fraser, a memoir / by Sibyl Crowe
ISBN 0-902672-48-7 (pbk) : Unpriced B82-10362

821'.912'08 — Poetry in English, *1900-1979 — Anthologies*
The **Faber** book of modern verse / edited by Michael Roberts. — 4th ed. / revised by Peter Porter. — London : Faber, 1982. — 432p ; 21cm
Previous ed.: 1965
ISBN 0-571-18055-8 (cased) : £6.95 : CIP rev.
ISBN 0-571-18017-5 (pbk) : Unpriced B82-06861

821'.912'08 — Poetry in English, *1900- — Anthologies*
Topics in modern poetry / edited by E.L. Black. — London : Murray, 1982. — x,134p ; 22cm
Includes index
ISBN 0-7195-3932-3 (pbk) : Unpriced : CIP rev. B81-35850

821'.912'08 — Poetry in English, *1900- — Anthologies — Festschriften*
For David Gascoyne on his sixty-fifth birthday : 10 October 1981 / Anthony Rudolf ... [et al]. — [London] : Enitharmon in association with Ampersand, 1981. — 34p ; 21cm
Limited ed. of 350 copies
ISBN 0-905289-18-8 (pbk) : £3.00 B82-20253

A **Garland** for the Laureate : poems presented to Sir John Betjeman on his 75th birthday. — Stratford-upon-Avon (51 Banbury Rd., Stratford-upon-Avon) : Celandine, c1981. — [45]p ; 28cm
Limited ed. of 350 numbered copies
£8.50 B82-13857

821'.912'080356 — Poetry in English, *1900-1945* **Special subjects: Aeroplanes. Flying —** *Anthologies*
Echoes in the sky. — Poole : Blandford Press, Oct.1982. — [96]p
ISBN 0-7137-1271-6 : £3.95 : CIP entry B82-22996

821'.912'080358 — Poetry in English. Women writers, *1900-1945*. **Special subjects: World War 1** — *Anthologies*
Scars upon my heart : women's poetry and verse of the First World War / edited and introduced by Catherine W. Reilly ; with a preface by Judith Kazantzis. — London : Virago, 1981. — 144p ; 21cm
Includes index
ISBN 0-86068-226-9 (pbk) : £3.75 : CIP rev. B81-30398

821'.912'0809282 — Children's poetry in English, *1900-1976 — Anthologies*
Roger was a razor fish : and other poems / compiled by Jill Bennett ; illustrated by Maureen Roffey. — London : Bodley Head, 1980. — 43p : col.ill ; 22cm
ISBN 0-370-30352-0 : £3.50 : CIP rev. B80-23673

821'.912'0809282 — Children's poetry in English, *1900-1980 — Anthologies*
Hillman, Priscilla. A merry-mouse book of favourite poems / [selected and illustrated by] Priscilla Hillman. — Tadworth : World's Work, 1982, c1981. — [32]p : col.ill ; 26cm. — (A World's Work children's book)
ISBN 0-437-45906-3 (pbk) : £1.95 B82-35440

Tiny Tim : verses for children / [illustrated by] Helen Oxenbury ; chosen by Jill Bennett. — London : Heinemann, c1981. — [32]p : col.ill ; 26cm
ISBN 0-434-95601-5 : £3.95 B82-08884

821'.912'0809282 — Children's poetry in English. Scottish writers, *1900- — Anthologies*
Ram tam toosh : an anthology of Scottish verse for children / edited by Alan Macdonald and Ian Brison ; illustrated by John Harrold. — Edinburgh : Oliver & Boyd in conjunction with the Association for Scottish Literary Studies, 1982. — 48p : ill ; 22cm
Bibliography: p47. — List of sound recordings: p48
ISBN 0-05-003408-1 : Unpriced B82-35701

821'.912'089282 — Children's poetry in English, *1900-1980 — Anthologies*
When a goose meets a moose. — London : Evans Bross, Apr.1981. — [160]p
Originally published: Sydney : Methuen, 1980
ISBN 0-237-45561-7 : £5.95 : CIP entry B81-02091

821′.912′09 — Poetry in English, *1900-1945* — *Critical studies*
Sisson, C. H.. English poetry 1900-1950 : an assessment / C.H. Sisson. — London : Methuen, 1981. — 274p ; 22cm
Originally published: London : Hart-Davies, 1971. — Includes index
ISBN 0-416-32100-3 (pbk) : £3.50 : CIP rev. B81-30518

821′.912′09 — Poetry in English, *1900-1945*. Influence of right-wing political movements
Craig, Cairns. Yeats, Eliot, Pound and the politics of poetry : richest to richest / Cairns Craig. — London : Croom Helm, c1982. — 323p ; 22cm
Bibliography: p313-317. — Includes index
ISBN 0-85664-997-x : £11.95 : CIP rev.
Also classified at 821′.912 ; 811′.52 ; 821′.8
B81-15905

821′.912′09 — Poetry in English, *1900-* — *Critical studies*
Smith, Stan, *1943-*. Inviolable voice : history and twentieth-century poetry / Stan Smith. — Dublin : Gill and Macmillan, 1982. — 243p ; 23cm
Bibliography: p235-238. — Includes index
ISBN 0-7171-1200-4 : £17.00 B82-31557

821′.912′0915 — Poetry in English. Imagism, *1900-1945* — *Critical studies*
Gage, John T.. In the arresting eye : the rhetoric of imagism / John T. Gage. — Baton Rouge ; London : Louisiana State University Press, c1981. — xv,188p : ill ; 24cm
Bibliography: p177-183. — Includes index
ISBN 0-8071-0790-5 : £12.55 B82-01298

821′.912′09358 — Poetry in English, *1900-1945*. Special subjects: World War 1 — *Critical studies*
Lehmann, John. The English poets of the First World War / John Lehmann. — London : Thames and Hudson, c1981 (1982 [printing]). — 144p : ill,facsims,ports ; 24cm
Bibliography: p139-140. — Includes index
ISBN 0-500-27267-0 (pbk) : £3.95 B82-24407

821.914 — ENGLISH POETRY, 1945-

821′.914 — Poetry in English, *1945-* — *Texts*
Aaron, Joseph F.. The swan : poems / by Joseph F. Aaron. — London : Regency Press, c1981. — 32p ; 19cm
£1.75 (pbk) B82-10155

Abrahams, John. Parochial gods / by John Abrahams. — Walton-on-Thames ([72 Burwood Rd., Walton-on-Thames, Surrey KT12 4AL]) : Outposts, 1982. — 28p ; 21cm
£1.10 (pbk) B82-22348

Abrey, Colin. No dark tomorrow / Colin Abrey. — Ilfracombe : Stockwell, 1981. — 48p ; 15cm
ISBN 0-7223-1548-1 (pbk) : Unpriced
B82-10401

Adair, Gilbert. Signs of — [sic] : book 1 : a documentary / Gilbert Adair. — Newcastle upon Tyne : Galloping Dog, 1982, c1981. — 28leaves : ill ; 29cm
Limited ed. of 150 copies, 10 of which are signed by the author
ISBN 0-904837-62-9 (pbk) : £1.50
ISBN 0-904837-63-7 (signed copy) : £4.00
B82-39226

Ahlberg, Janet. Peepo! / by Janet & Allan Ahlberg. — Harmondsworth : Kestrel Books, 1981. — [32]p : chiefly col.ill ; 21x24cm
ISBN 0-7226-5707-2 : £4.50 B82-00968

Aireton, Bridget. Flowers of spirit / Bridget Aireton. — Bognor Regis : New Horizon, c1982. — 34p,[33]p of plates : ill ; 21cm
ISBN 0-86116-180-7 : £3.95 B82-19993

Aldridge, Alan, *1938-*. The lion′s cavalcade / by Alan Aldridge ; illustrated in collaboration with Harry Willock ; poems by Ted Walker. — London : Cape [for] Aurelia Enterprises Ltd, 1980. — [30]p : col.ill ; 29cm
Based on the Lion′s masquerade and Elephant′s champêtre by a Lady (1808)
ISBN 0-224-01701-2 : £3.95 : CIP rev.
B80-13587

Allwood, Arthur. Our beautiful Shropshire / by Arthur Allwood. — Shrewsbury (4 Cross Hill Court, Shrewsbury SY1 1JH) : [A. Allwood], 1982. — 9p ; 22cm
Originally published: 1968
Unpriced (unbound) B82-23959

Allwood, Arthur. Two rolling stones / by Arthur Allwood. — Shrewsbury (4 Cross Hill Court, Shrewsbury SY1 1JH) : [A. Allwood], 1982. — 10p ; 21cm
Unpriced (unbound) B82-23960

Allwood, Martin. New English poems / by Martin Allwood ; with an introduction by G. Singh. — Mullsjö : Anglo-American Center ; Addingham-Ilkley (Casita, Springfield Mount, Addingham-Ilkley) : K. Laycock [distributor], 1981. — 303p ; 22cm
ISBN 91-85412-20-1 (pbk) : Unpriced
B82-19410

Ally, James. Voices of my heart / James Ally ; illustrated by Geoff Evans. — Crawley : Wren, c1981. — 32p : ill ; 21cm
ISBN 0-907820-02-6 (pbk) : £0.50 B82-36501

Anderson, Alex. Hobgoblins also dream / by Alex Anderson. — Liverpool (80 Lark La., Liverpool) : [A. Anderson], 1982. — [55]p ; 22cm
Unpriced (pbk) B82-25572

Anderson, Martin. The kneeling room. — Plymouth : Blue Guitar Books ; London (12 Stevenage Rd., SW6 6ES) : Independent Press Distribution [distributor], Sept.1981. — [20]p
ISBN 0-907562-03-5 (pbk) : £0.80 : CIP entry
B81-20497

Angus, William Stephenson. Christmas cards and other verses. — Aberdeen : Aberdeen University Press, Nov.1981. — [74]p
ISBN 0-08-028462-0 (pbk) : £1.15 : CIP entry
B81-34715

Annand, J. K.. Thrice to show ye / by J.K. Annand ; with illustrations by Dennis Carabine. — Loanhead (Edgefield Rd, Loanhead, Midlothian EH20 9SY) : MacDonald, c1979. — 47p : ill ; 21cm
ISBN 0-904265-29-3 : £1.95 B82-05537

Anticipations / [compiled by] Ian Hamilton Finlay. — [Lanark] ([Stonypath, Little Sparta, Dunsyre, Lanark, Scotland]) : Wild Hawthorn Press, [1982?]. — [4]leaves ; 12cm
Unpriced (unbound) B82-34968

Armstrong, Paul, *1913-*. Echoes of echoes : a book of poems / by Paul Armstrong. — Walton-on-Thames (70 Holly Ave., Walton-on-Thames, Surrey KT12 3AU) : P. Newlin, c1982. — 28p ; 22cm
Unpriced (pbk) B82-30006

Ash, John. The bed. — London : Oasis, Aug.1981. — [56]p
ISBN 0-903375-58-3 (pbk) : £1.50 : CIP entry
B81-22603

Ash, John, *1948-*. The goodbyes / John Ash. — Manchester : Carcanet, 1982. — 63p ; 21cm
ISBN 0-85635-452-x (cased) : £4.00 : CIP rev.
B82-07036

Ashbrook, John. In the footsteps of the opium eater / John Ashbrook. — Liskeard : Harry Chambers/Peterloo Poets, 1980. — 62p ; 22cm
ISBN 0-905291-31-x (pbk) : £3.00 B82-07385

Astra. Battle cries / Astra. — London : A. Blaug, c1981. — [27]p ; 21cm
Cover title
ISBN 0-9507870-0-0 (pbk) : £1.00 B82-39220

Ayres, Pam. The ballad of Bill Spinks′ bedstead : & other poems / Pam Ayres ; illustrations by Don Roberts. — London : Severn House, 1981. — 64p : ill,1port ; 20cm
ISBN 0-7278-2018-4 (pbk) : £1.75 : CIP rev.
B81-31096

Bailey, Gordon. Can a man change / Gordon Bailey ; foreword by Larry Grayson ; illustrations by June Forman. — Bromley : STL Books, 1979. — 96p : ill ; 18cm
ISBN 0-903843-21-8 (pbk) : Unpriced
B82-00638

Bailey, R. J.. Just rumour / by R.J. Bailey. — [Kelso] ([3 Roxburgh Mill, Kelso, Roxburghshire, Scotland]) : [R.J. Bailey], c1981. — 38p ; 15cm
Unpriced (pbk) B82-12673

Baker, Margaret, *1941-*. Love unveiled / by Margaret Baker. — Norwich ('Irashai', 78 Plumstead East Rd., Norwich NR7 9NF) : M. Baker, c1981. — [32]p ; 21cm
£1.10 (pbk) B82-03976

Baker, Martin. One two number zoo / Gabrielle Stoddart and Martin Baker. — London : Hodder and Stoughton, 1982. — [25]p : col.ill ; 29cm
ISBN 0-340-26435-7 : £4.95 : CIP rev.
B82-03805

Ballantyne, G. A.. Sequestered in the cradle : poems / by G.A. Ballantyne. — Canterbury (c/o Albion Bookshop, Mercury La., Canterbury, Kent) : Mapletree Private Press, 1982. — [14]p ; 21cm
Limited ed. of 250 numbered copies
£1.50 (pbk) B82-33190

Barnett, Snowdon. Last entry : a poem : being a romance of Antarctica and Captain R.F. Scott, R.N., C.V.O. / by Snowdon Barnett. — Stocksfield : Oriel Press, 1982. — xv,56p : ill ; 22cm
Also available in a limited ed. bound in full leather
ISBN 0-85362-194-2 (pbk) : £4.00
ISBN 0-85362-198-5 (limited ed) : Unpriced
B82-32101

Barton, Joan. A house under Old Sarum : new and selected poems / Joan Barton. — Liskeard : Harry Chambers/Peterloo Poets, 1981. — 80p ; 22cm
ISBN 0-905291-32-8 (pbk) : £3.00 B82-07382

Batchelor, Joan M.. On the wild side : poems / by Joan M. Batchelor. — Manchester : Commonword, c1979. — 63p : ill ; 21cm
ISBN 0-9505997-2-7 (pbk) : £0.25 B82-25469

Bate, John, *1919-*. Damaged beauty needs a new design : twenty poems / by John Bate. — Kenilworth (2 Rosemary Hill, Kenilworth CV8 1BN) : Walter Ritchie, c1981. — 20p : ill,1port ; 21cm
Limited ed. of 310 numbered copies
Unpriced B82-10539

Bazley, Rosemary. Seedtime and harvest / by Rosemary Bazley. — Walton-on-Thames ([72 Burwood Rd., Walton-on-Thames, Surrey KT12 4AL]) : Outposts, 1982. — 36p ; 21cm
£1.50 (pbk) B82-22346

Beale, Kathleen. Heartfelt and fancy free / Kathleen Beale. — Harleston : K. Beale, 1981. — 32p ; 15cm
ISBN 0-7223-1433-7 (pbk) : Private circulation
B82-15583

Beer, Patricia. The lie of the land. — London : Hutchinson, Feb.1983. — [48]p
ISBN 0-09-150701-4 : £3.95 : CIP entry
B82-36564

Bell, Rebecca. Evening music : poems / by Rebecca Bell. — Braunton : Merlin, 1982. — 24p ; 21cm
ISBN 0-86303-026-2 (pbk) : £0.60 B82-35875

Bendon, Chris. In praise of low music / [Chris Bendon]. — Lampeter : Outcrop, 1981 (1982 [printing]). — 56p ; 21cm
Cover title. — Text on inside covers. — Limited ed. of 300 copies
ISBN 0-907600-03-4 (pbk) : £1.00 B82-38615

821'.914 — Poetry in English, *1945-* — Texts *continuation*

Bensley, Connie. Progress report / Connie Bensley. — Liskeard : Harry Chambers/Peterloo Poets, 1981. — 63p ; 22cm
ISBN 0-905291-29-8 (pbk) : £3.00 B82-07380

Blackburn, Thomas. Bread for the winter birds : the last poems of Thomas Blackburn. — London : Hutchinson, 1980. — 70p ; 23cm
ISBN 0-09-143080-1 : £6.95 : CIP rev. B80-13520

Boadella, Eilidh. I won't paint any tears / by Eilidh Boadella ; with an introduction by Jack Clemo. — Walton-on-Thames ([72 Burwood Rd., Walton-on-Thames, Surrey KT12 4AL]) : Outposts, 1981. — 43p,[1]leaf of plates : 1port ; 21cm
Unpriced (pbk) B82-08876

Bois, G. J. C.. Jersey superstitions in etching & poetry / G.J.C. Bois. — [St. Saviour] ([Alphington House, Grands Vaux, St. Saviour, Jersey]) : G.J.C. Bois, c1981. — 53p : ill ; 23cm
Bibliography: p53
ISBN 0-9507966-0-3 : £9.95
Also classified at 769.92'4 B82-20215

Bonner, Ann. Summerwords / Ann and Roger Bonner. — [London] : Abelard, 1982. — [26]p : col.ill ; 28cm
ISBN 0-200-72607-2 : £5.95 : CIP rev. B82-04290

Booker, Mary. Quartet and other poems / Mary Booker. — Ilfracombe : Stockwell, 1982. — 24p ; 19cm
ISBN 0-7223-1566-x : Unpriced B82-10405

Boothroyd, Christine. The snow island / by Christine Boothroyd. — Portree : Aquila/Isle of Skye, c1982. — [21]p ; 21cm
ISBN 0-7275-0229-8 (pbk) : £0.60
ISBN 0-7275-0230-1 (signed limited ed.) : £1.50 B82-20000

Borland, E. Naden. Peter Moffat and other poems / by E. Naden Borland. — [Leicester] ([15 Evington Rd., Leicester, LE2 1QG]) : [E. Borland], [1982]. — 32p ; 16cm
Cover title
Unpriced (pbk) B82-33829

Bourne-Jones, Derek. Floating reefs / by Derek Bourne-Jones. — Eastbourne : Downlander, 1981. — 47p : 1ill ; 21cm
ISBN 0-906369-15-0 (pbk) : £3.00 B82-37142

Boyle, Charles. House of cards / Charles Boyle. — Manchester : Carcanet, 1982. — 64p ; 20cm
ISBN 0-85635-426-0 (pbk) : £3.25 : CIP rev. B82-19263

Brain, John. Urned income : and other verse / John Brain ; illustrated by Malcolm Lawson-Paul. — Sutherland : Method, 1980. — 64p : ill(some col.) ; 23cm
ISBN 0-903664-01-1 : £3.90 B82-22719

Brennan, Joseph Francis. The sound of — poetry / by Joseph Francis Brennan. — New ed. — London : Regency, 1982. — 32p ; 19cm
Previous ed.: 1975
£0.85 (pbk) B82-36497

Brill, Barbara. Remembering in rhyme / by Barbara Brill. — [Stockport] : Stockport Historical Society, c1979. — [27]p : ill,coat of arms,ports ; 30cm
Seven men, 4 women. — Cover title
£0.40 (pbk) B82-39241

Brisland, Rex. Lap larch : poems / by Rex Brisland ; Irish drawings by Rigby Graham. — [Leicester] : New Broom, 1982. — [10]p : ill ; 21cm
Limited ed. of 100 signed copies
ISBN 0-901870-62-5 (pbk) : £3.00 B82-29952

Brooks, Mary, *1906-*. Landscape of life / Mary Brooks ; edited by Margaret George. — Kingston upon Thames : Court Poetry, 1982. — 20p ; 21cm
ISBN 0-906010-29-2 (pbk) : £0.60 B82-26579

Brown, Christy. The collected poems. — London : Secker & Warburg, July 1982. — [224]p
ISBN 0-436-07089-8 : £7.50 : CIP entry B82-17201

Brown, John, *1912-1981*. War poems / John Brown. — Ilfracombe : Stockwell, 1982. — 16p ; 15cm
ISBN 0-7223-1610-0 (pbk) : £0.55 B82-36660

Brown, Paul, *1949-*. Masker / Paul Brown. — Newcastle upon Tyne : Galloping Dog, 1982. — [82]p ; 20cm
Limited ed. of 250 copies, 10 of which are signed by the author
ISBN 0-904837-56-4 (pbk) : £2.50
ISBN 0-904837-57-2 (signed copy) : £6.00 B82-39227

Buck, Heather. At the window / Heather Buck. — London : Anvil Press Poetry, 1982. — 52p ; 22cm
ISBN 0-85646-071-0 (pbk) : £3.25 B82-33187

Burford, Ted. Imaginary absences : poems / by Ted Burford. — Stafford : Strange Lime Fruit Stone, c1981. — 27p ; 22cm
ISBN 0-905354-02-8 (pbk) : Unpriced B82-30002

Burgis, Allan. Other regions / by Allan Burgis. — Liverpool ([14 Buckingham Ave., Liverpool L17 3BB]) : Glasshouse Press, c1978. — 16p ; 21cm
£0.40 (pbk) B82-16831

Burgon, Noreen. Some poems / Noreen Burgon. — Ilfracombe : Stockwell, 1982. — 8p ; 15cm
ISBN 0-7223-1603-8 (pbk) : Unpriced B82-19031

Burner, W. E. S.. Green pastures / W.E.S. Burner. — [Salcombe] ([Victoria Inn, Salcombe, S. Devon]) : W. Burner, c1979. — 32p : ill,1coat of arms,music ; 21cm
Cover title. — Ill on lining papers
Unpriced (pbk) B82-12675

Burner, W. E. S.. Green pastures : and other poems / [W.E.S. Burner] ; [illustrated by Wacey Hart]. — Repr. with additions and amendments. — [Salcombe] ([Victoria Inn, Salcombe, S. Devon]) : W.E.S. Burner, 1980, [c1979]. — 34p : ill,1coat of arms,music ; 21cm
Previous ed.: 1979. — Includes 1 poem by Julia Murch
Unpriced (pbk) B82-12674

Burns, Richard. Learning to talk : poems / Richard Burns. — London : Enitharmon, 1980. — 79p : ill ; 23cm
1 sheet 27x40cm folded to 13x20 as insert
ISBN 0-905289-76-5 (cased) : £4.20
ISBN 0-905289-71-4 (pbk) : £2.55 B82-20243

Buss, Peter. Enigma / by Peter Buss. — London : Regency Press, c1981. — 32p ; 19cm
Unpriced (pbk) B82-10157

Butler, Tanis. The silvered crown / Tanis Butler. — [Gillingham] : Newlands Prints, 1981. — 60leaves, 7leaves of plates : ports ; 21cm
ISBN 0-9507698-0-0 (pbk) : £3.50 B82-00005

Bye, Jonathan. Delayed shock / Jonathan Bye ; edited by Margaret George. — Kingston upon Thames : Court Poetry, [c1981]. — 27p ; 21cm
ISBN 0-906010-27-6 (pbk) : £0.90 B82-06575

Caddel, Richard. Baby days and moon diaries : being: the second book of aires / by Richard Caddel. — Newcastle upon Tyne : Galloping Dog Press, 1979. — [13]leaves ; 26cm
ISBN 0-904837-21-1 (pbk) : Unpriced
ISBN 0-904837-22-x (signed ed.) B82-39240

Caddick, Arthur. Comfort, the cat / Arthur Caddick ; drawings by Kathie Layfield. — [Leicester] : New Broom, 1982. — [10]p : ill ; 21cm
Limited ed. of 90 copies
ISBN 0-901870-58-7 (pbk) : £2.00 B82-15331

Camp, Rose M.. Varied verses / Rose M. Camp. — Ilfracombe : Stockwell, 1981. — 32p ; 15cm
ISBN 0-7223-1527-9 (pbk) : Unpriced B82-10399

Campbell, John. Saturday night in York Street. — Belfast : Blackstaff Press, May 1982. — [80]p
ISBN 0-85640-267-2 (pbk) : £3.50 : CIP entry B82-14492

Carruthers, Tony. Room for thought / by Tony Carruthers. — London (71 St. Augustines Rd., NW1 9RR) : Street Talk Press, c1982. — 25p ; 21cm
Limited ed. of 100 copies signed and numbered by the author
£0.85 (pbk) B82-19994

Cartwright, Steve. Warbling / Steve Cartwright ; drawings by Rod Felton. — [Leicester] : New Broom, 1982. — [12]p : ill(some col.) ; 21cm
Limited ed. of 100 copies signed and numbered by the printer
ISBN 0-901870-60-9 (pbk) : £3.00 B82-17535

Casey, Gerard. Between the Symplegades : re-visions from a Mythological story by George Seferis / Gerard Casey. — London : Enitharmon, 1980. — 37p ; 23cm
Limited ed. of 400 copies
ISBN 0-905289-86-2 (cased) : £3.75
ISBN 0-905289-81-1 (pbk) : £2.40 B82-20250

Casey, Mary. Christophoros : poems / by Mary Casey ; with a foreword by Charles Lock. — London : Enitharmon, 1981. — 103p ; 22cm
ISBN 0-905289-03-x (cased) : £4.50 : £3.00 B82-20249

Casey, Mary. Full circle : poems / by Mary Casey ; with a foreword by Charles Lock. — London : Enitharmon, 1981. — 70p ; 23cm
ISBN 0-905289-82-x (cased) : £4.50
ISBN 0-905289-62-5 : £3.00 B82-20244

Cassidy, John. Night cries / John Cassidy. — Newcastle upon Tyne : Bloodaxe, 1982. — 102p ; 22cm
ISBN 0-906427-45-2 (pbk) : £3.95 B82-39160

Chamberlain, James Royce. Asthenia or the Hawkesbury look-out / James Royce Chamberlain. — Ilfracombe : Stockwell, 1981. — 252p ; 23cm
ISBN 0-7223-1478-7 : £4.50 B82-10365

Chandler, Alan. Poems from Shropshire / Alan Chandler. — Bishops Castle : Zeus, 1982. — 40p ; 22cm
ISBN 0-900835-06-0 (pbk) : £2.00 B82-28795

Chiari, Joseph. Slanting lights : poems / by Joseph Chiari. — London : Enitharmon, 1981. — 42p ; 23cm
Limited ed. of 350 copies
ISBN 0-905289-27-7 (cased) : £3.75
ISBN 0-905289-22-6 (pbk) : £2.55 B82-20247

Childish, Billy. Big cunt : poeting from 1981-1982 / Billy Childish. — Chatham (181 Walderslade Rd., Chatham, Kent) : Phyroid Press, c1982. — [36]p : ill ; 22cm
Text and ill on inside cover
Unpriced (pbk) B82-36806

Childish, Billy. Bizzar oxen : Billey Childizh [i.e. Childish], Sexton Ming. — Chatham (181 Walderslade Rd., Chatham, Kent) : Phyroid, 1980. — 8p ; 26cm
Unpriced (unbound) B82-29585

821'.914 — Poetry in English, *1945-* — *Texts continuation*

Childish, Billy. Black things hidden in dust : poetry from 1981 / Billy Childish. — Chatham (181 Walderslade Rd., Chatham, Kent) : Phyroid Press, c1982. — 29p : 1port ; 22cm
Unpriced (pbk) B82-17020

Childish, Billy. Bo-pug : the six tails / Billy Childish. — Chatham (181 Walderslade Rd., Chatham, Kent) : Phyroid Press, c1981. — 9p : ill ; 15cm
Cover title
Unpriced (pbk) B82-17021

Childish, Billy. Book of nursry rhims / Billy Childish. — Chatham (181 Walderslade Rd., Chatham, Kent) : Phyroid Press, c1981. — 14p : 1ill,1port ; 22cm
Cover title
Unpriced (pbk) B82-17022

Childish, Billy. The book of prophersy / Billy Childish & Sexton Ming. — Chatham (181 Walderslade Rd., Chatham, Kent) : Phyroid, c1980. — [16]p : ill ; 16cm
Unpriced (unbound) B82-16607

Childish, Billy. Fan Club book / Billy Childish & Sexton Ming. — Chatham (181 Walderslade Rd., Chatham, Kent) : Phyroid Press, 1982. — 12p : ill ; 21cm
Cover title. — Text, ill on inside covers
Unpriced (pbk) B82-19961

Childish, Billy. The first creatcher is jellosey / Billy Childish. — Chatham (181 Walderslade Rd., Chatham, Kent) : Phyroid, 1981. — 52p : ill ; 22cm
Unpriced (pbk) B82-20001

Childish, Billy. Goat gruff / Billy Childish. — Chatham (181 Walderslade Rd, Chatham, Kent) : B. Childish, c1979. — [17]leaves : ill ; 30cm
Unpriced (unbound) B82-39239

Childish, Billy. Mussel horse in Holland / Billy Childish & Sexton Ming. — Chatham (181 Walderslade Rd., Chatham, Kent) : Phyroid, c1980. — [16]p : ill ; 16cm
Unpriced (unbound) B82-16606

Childish, Billy. You me blood n knukle / Billy Childish. — Chatham (181 Walderslade Rd., Chatham, Kent) : Phyroid Press, c1982. — 23p ; 21cm
Cover title. — Text on inside covers
Unpriced (pbk) B82-19960

Claringbowl, Jane Alice. Thoughts put down / Jane Alice Claringbowl. — Leek : Moorlands, 1982. — 24p ; 21cm
ISBN 0-86301-001-6 (pbk) : £0.75 B82-37869

Clark, John, *1910-*. The dodderin's o'an auld foggie : a Culter anthology / by John Clark. — Culter : Culter Community Council, [1982?]. — [38]p ; 22cm
Cover title
Unpriced (pbk) B82-27329

Clark, Lois. Another dimension / by Lois Clark. — Walton-on-Thames : Outposts, 1982. — 28p ; 21cm
£1.20 (pbk) B82-33261

Clarke, Frances R.. Inspirational thoughts - prose - verse / by Frances R. Clarke. — London : Regency Press, 1981. — 32p ; 19cm
Unpriced (pbk) B82-09336

Clarke, Gillian. Letter from a far country. — Manchester : Manchester Carcanet Press, Sept.1982. — [64]p
ISBN 0-85635-427-9 (pbk) : £3.25 : CIP entry B82-19837

Clarke, Leonar. Whispers from eternity / Leonard Clarke. — Ilfracombe : Stockwell, 1981. — 29p ; 15cm
ISBN 0-7223-1541-4 (pbk) : £0.70 B82-05503

Clitheroe, Frederic. Harecastle mint / Frederic Clitheroe. — Newcastle [Staffs.] ([6 St. Edmunds Ave, Newcastle, Staffs.]) : Lymes, [1982]. — 23p ; 21cm
£1.00 (pbk) B82-17536

Clitheroe, Frederic. Harecastle mint / Frederic Clitheroe. — Newcastle [Staffs.] ([6 St. Edmunds Ave., Newcastle, Staffs. ST5 0AB]) : Lymes Press, 1982. — 23p ; 21cm
£1.00 (pbk) B82-19989

Cloudsley, Tim. Poems through love and blood / Tim Cloudsley. — London : Perdode Printers, 1980. — 175p ; 21cm
ISBN 0-9507471-0-6 (pbk) : Unpriced B82-32109

Clough, S. D. P.. Homage to Pushkin : scenes from Eugene Onegin : versions of short poems and prose passages / [S.D.P. Clough]. — Enl. — [Malvern Wells] ([16 Eaton Rd., Malvern Wells, Worcs.]) : S.D.P. Clough, c1982. — 136p : ill ; 21cm
Previous ed.: 1978
£2.00 (pbk) B82-25976

Clucas, Humphrey. Gods & mortals / Humphrey Clucas. — Liskeard : Harry Chambers-Peterloo Poets, 1982. — 48p ; 22cm
ISBN 0-905291-30-1 (pbk) : £3.00 B82-26017

Coker, Christine Camille. Return to the womb / poems by Christine Camille Coker ; illustrated by the author. — Biggleswade : Great Ouse Press, 1981. — 25p : ill ; 21cm
ISBN 0-907351-01-8 (pbk) : £1.50 B82-02305

Colby, F. T.. Litton Cheney 1877 / a poem by F.T. Colby ; with a Latin translation by E.D. Stone ; with an introduction by Reynolds Stone. — [London] (28 Ifield Rd, SW10) : Warren, 1976. — [13]p ; 14cm
Limited ed. of 500 copies of which 150 are signed and numbered by Reynolds Stone
Unpriced (pbk) B82-31937

Compton, Henry. Overtones : poems on musical themes / by Henry Compton. — Walton-on-Thames ([72 Burwood Rd., Walton-on-Thames, Surrey KT12 4AL]) : Outposts, 1982. — 20p ; 21cm
£0.80 (pbk) B82-22345

Compton Miller, John. Poems '81 / John Compton Miller. — [London] ([Sylvia's, 25 Beauchamp Place, S.W.1]) : [J.C. Miller], c1981. — 30leaves ; 21cm
Limited ed. of 200 numbered copies
£1.95 (pbk) B82-11429

Conover, Terence. Poems of the heart / Terence Conover. — Walnut Creek, Calif. : T. Conover (Ilfracombe : Stockwell), c1981. — 16p ; 19cm
ISBN 0-7223-1572-4 : Unpriced B82-10410

Constable, G. D.. A sequence of prose poems from 'The island of storms' / G.D. Constable. — Lampeter : Outcrop, 1981. — 43p ; 21cm
Text on inside covers
Unpriced (pbk) B82-15002

Corbluth, Elsa. I looked for you : poem and photographs / by Elsa Corbluth. — [Crewe] ([c/o Crewe and Alsager College of Higher Education, Crewe, Cheshire]) : [E. Corbluth], [1982]. — [68]p : ill ; 21cm
Unpriced (pbk) B82-18088

Couldery, Austin A.. December 25th and other poems / Austin A. Couldery ; illustrated by Nigel A. Chapman. — Ilfracombe : Stockwell, 1981. — 16p : ill ; 18cm
ISBN 0-7223-1547-3 (pbk) : £0.75 B82-10403

Courtney, N.. The modern forest / by N. Courtney ; illustrations by J.E. Courtney. — [Leicester] ([4 Latimer Close, Blaby, Leicester LE8 3AP]) : [N. Courtney], [1982?]. — 28p : ill ; 21cm
£0.60 (pbk) B82-16928

Cree, Lilian. "They're made for sharing" : children's recitations / by Lilian Cree. — Ilkeston : Moorley's, [1982]. — 29p ; 21cm
ISBN 0-86071-147-1 (pbk) : £0.50 B82-31376

Crick, Philip. Episodes. — Plymouth : Blue Guitar Books ; London (12 Stevenage Rd., SW6 6ES) : Independent Press Distribution [distributor], Sept.1981. — [16]p
ISBN 0-907562-02-7 (pbk) : £0.80 : CIP entry B81-20498

Crossman, Alfred V.. Rhymes and ramblings / Alfred V. Crossman. — Bognor Regis : New Horizon, c1982. — 32p : ill ; 21cm
ISBN 0-86116-758-9 : £3.25 B82-26962

Crozier, Andrew. Duets / Andrew Crozier. — Guildford (22 Sydney Rd., Guildford, Surrey) : Circle Press, c1976. — [24]p ; 22cm
Limited ed. of 150 copies
Unpriced (pbk) B82-22379

Cuddling, Ripyard. More muddling / by Cuddling ; with drawings by Peter Burns. — Whitley Bay : Strong Words in association with Wallsend Arts Centre, c1980. — ill ; 21cm
ISBN 0-905274-10-5 (pbk) : £0.35 B82-30908

Cuddling, Ripyard. Shipyard muddling / by Ripyard Cuddling ; with drawings by Crawford Crowquill. — Whitley Bay (10, Greenhaugh Rd., Whitley Bay, Tyne and Wear NE25 9HF) : Erdesdun in association with Wallsend Arts Centre, 1977. — 27p : ill ; 22cm
£0.30 (pbk) B82-30909

Cullup, Michael. Geographies. — Manchester : Carcanet, Dec.1982. — [64]p
ISBN 0-85635-429-5 (pbk) : £3.25 : CIP entry B82-26326

Curry, Neil. Between root & sky / Neil Curry. — Hitchin : Mandeville, c1982. — [16]p ; 23cm
Limited ed. of 235 copies, of which 35 have been signed by the author
ISBN 0-904533-60-3 (pbk) : Unpriced B82-32951

Dacombe, R. F.. Lakeland dreams / R.F. Dacombe. — Yeovil : R.F. Dacombe, 1981. — 80p ; 15cm
ISBN 0-7223-1565-1 (pbk) : Unpriced B82-19030

Dalton, Ann R.. Reflections / Ann R. Dalton. — Ilfracombe : Stockwell, 1981. — 14p ; 15cm
ISBN 0-7223-1533-3 (pbk) : £0.50 B82-05506

Darlington, Chris. Abstract worlds : short poems / by Chris Darlington. — Runcorn (c/o C. Darlington, 23 Kingsley Rd., Runcorn, Cheshire) : Maggot, [1982?]. — [16]p ; 16cm
Unpriced (pbk) B82-39358

Darlington, Chris. Fisherman's dreams : poems / by Chris Darlington. — Runcorn (23 Kingsley Rd., Runcorn [Cheshire]) : Maggot Press, c1982. — [9]p ; 15cm
Unpriced (pbk) B82-32998

Dash, Tony. From the debris / Tony Dash. — Malvern (61 Belmont Rd, Malvern, Worcs.) : Migrant Press, 1981. — [36]p ; 21cm
Unpriced (pbk) B82-05293

David, Adele. Becoming / Adele David. — Malvern (61 Belmont Rd, Malvern, Worcs.) : Migrant Press, c1980. — 35p : 1ill ; 21cm
Unpriced (pbk) B82-05289

Davidson, Alice Joyce. Because I love you / Alice Joyce Davidson. — London : Hutchinson, 1982. — 95p : ill ; 21cm
ISBN 0-09-149841-4 : £2.95 : CIP rev. B82-22416

821'.914 — Poetry in English, ***1945-*** **—** ***Texts continuation***

Davis, Geoff. Behind the mask / by Geoff Davis. — Walton-on-Thames ([72, Burwood Rd., Walton-on-Thames, Surrey KT12 4AL]) : Outposts, 1981. — 12p ; 21cm
£0.60 (pbk) B82-04667

Davis, Owen. The reflective arrangement / Owen Davis. — Newcastle upon Tyne : Galloping Dog, 1982. — 30leaves ; 28cm
Limited ed. of 200, 10 of which are signed by the author
ISBN 0-904837-50-5 (pbk) : £1.50
ISBN 0-904837-51-3 (signed copy) : £4.00 B82-39224

Davis, Tom. Hilarity of nuclearity. — Telford (84 Wolverley Court, Woodside, Telford, Shropshire) : Woody Books, May 1982. — [64]p
ISBN 0-907751-11-3 (pbk) : £1.25 : CIP entry B82-13501

Day, John Ernest. Scripsit : poems / John Ernest Day. — Lowestoft (48 Dell Rd. East, Lowestoft, Suffolk NR33 9LB) : J.E. Day, [1982?]. — 32p ; 21cm
Unpriced (pbk) B82-22185

De Rous, Peter. Dartmoor allowed / Peter de Rous. — Torpoint : Kowabata, c1982. — [11]p ; 22cm
ISBN 0-906110-28-9 (pbk) : £0.60 B82-19137

Deane, John F.. High sacrifice / John F. Deane. — Portlaoise : Dolmen Press, 1981. — 61p ; 22cm
ISBN 0-85105-382-3 (pbk) : £3.00 : CIP rev.
ISBN 0-85105-383-1 (special ed.) : £10.00 B81-18071

Dickinson, Patric. A rift in time. — London : Chatto & Windus, Oct.1982. — [48]p
ISBN 0-7011-2653-1 : £3.95 : CIP entry B82-23202

Didsbury, Peter. The butchers of Hull / Peter Didsbury. — Newcastle upon Tyne : Bloodaxe, 1982. — 62p ; 22cm
ISBN 0-906427-42-8 (pbk) : £3.25 B82-39159

Digance, Richard. Animal alphabet / Richard Digance ; illustrated by Diana Gold. — London : Beaver, 1982, c1980. — 78p : ill ; 18cm
Originally published: London : Michael Joseph, 1980
ISBN 0-600-20553-3 (pbk) : £0.95 B82-24316

Dixon, Donna. The autumn's gold / Donna & Marie Dixon. — Ilfracombe : Stockwell, 1981. — 152p ; 19cm
ISBN 0-7223-1530-9 : Unpriced B82-05538

Donatelli, J. A.. Tender thoughts / J.A. Donatelli. — Ilfracombe : Stockwell, 1981. — 29p ; 14cm
ISBN 0-7223-1513-9 (pbk) : £0.97 B82-19029

Dosset Maid. Zunshine een the 'vale / by a Dosset maid. — Hedon (Station Lane, Hedon, Nr. Hull [Humberside HU12 8JY]) : I. Thomas, c1982. — 75p : ill ; 19cm
Cover title
£0.99 (pbk) B82-38614

Dougan, Alan. The desolation of solitude / by Alan Dougan. — Portree : Aquila, 1982. — [16]p ; 21cm
ISBN 0-7275-0231-x (pbk) : £0.60
ISBN 0-7275-0232-8 (signed limited ed) : £1.50 B82-23961

Downie, Freda. Plainsong. — London : Secker & Warburg, June 1981. — [64]p
ISBN 0-436-13251-6 : £4.50 : CIP entry B81-09467

Dryden, Alan. The descending dark / Alan Dryden. — Bognor Regis : New Horizon, c1981. — 40p ; 21cm
ISBN 0-86116-625-6 : £3.25 B82-03503

Duffy, E. A. J.. The kiss / by E.A.J. Duffy. — London : Regency Press, c1980. — 48p : ill ; 23cm
ISBN 0-7212-0670-0 : £3.00 B82-15110

Duncan, Anthony D.. The lover within / Anthony Duncan. — Warkworth : A.D. Duncan, c1981. — 31p ; 21cm
ISBN 0-9507864-0-3 (pbk) : £1.00 B82-11717

Dundrow, Michael. Below the hill : a collection of poems / by Michael Dundrow. — Bognor Regis : New Horizon, c1982. — 36p ; 21cm
ISBN 0-86116-785-6 : Unpriced B82-25308

Dunn, Una. River to heaven / by Una M. Dunn. — [Blandford] ([Little Pasture, Stubhampton, Blandford, Dorset]) : [U.M. Dunn], 1982. — [14]p ; 21cm
Unpriced (unbound) B82-22629

Dunn, Una. Tall grasses / by Una Dunn. — [Blandford] (Little Pasture, Stubhampto, Blandford DT11 8JU) : [U. Dunn], [1981]. — [20]p ; 21cm
Cover title
Unpriced (pbk) B82-07353

Durcan, Paul. The selected Paul Durcan. — Belfast : Blackstaff Press, Oct.1982. — [144]p
ISBN 0-85640-269-9 : £4.50 : CIP entry B82-24119

Durrant, Warren. Poems of love and loneliness / Warren Durrant. — Ilfracombe : Stockwell, 1980. — 53p ; 19cm
ISBN 0-7223-1409-4 : £2.60 B82-41089

Dwyer, Winifred. Vengeance on heaven : and other poems / Winifred Dwyer. — Bognor Regis : New Horizon, c1982. — 96p ; 21cm
ISBN 0-86116-576-4 : £3.95 B82-26952

Dyer, Carol. Reflections from the past / Carol Dyer. — Ilfracombe : Stockwell, 1981. — 32p ; 15cm
ISBN 0-7223-1494-9 (pbk) : Unpriced B82-10396

Edwards, Ken. Drumming & poems / Ken Edwards. — Newcastle upon Tyne : Galloping Dog, 1982. — 48p ; 29cm
Limited ed. of 250 copies, 10 of which are signed by the author
ISBN 0-904837-58-0 (pbk) : £2.00
ISBN 0-904837-58-0 (signed copy) : £4.50 B82-69225

Edwards, Mary Stella. The years between : poems / by Mary Stella Edwards. — London : Enitharmon Press, 1982. — 15p ; 22cm
ISBN 0-905289-28-5 (pbk) : £1.95 B82-33181

Edwards, Michael. The magic, unquiet body. — Isle of Skye : Aquila, Dec.1982. — [60]p
ISBN 0-7275-0251-4 (cased) : £4.95 : CIP entry
ISBN 0-7275-0252-2 (pbk) : £2.95 B82-31302

Elliot, Alistair. Talking back. — London : Secker & Warburg, Sept.1982. — [64]p
ISBN 0-436-14260-0 : £4.95 : CIP entry B82-19678

Elliot, Eileen. The glory that excelleth / Eileen Elliot. — Ilfracombe : Stockwell, 1982. — 31p ; 19cm
ISBN 0-7223-1600-3 (pbk) : £0.40 B82-36099

Elliott-Howard. The last of the wine / Elliott-Howard ; drawings by Kathie Layfield. — [Leicester] : [Tony Savage], c1980. — [8]p : ill ; 21cm
Limited ed. of eighty copies
ISBN 0-901870-48-x (unbound) : £2.00 B82-16088

Ellis, Gwen, *1918-*. All my moonshine : poems featuring the Wiltshire dialect, including some poems of local historical interest / by Gwen Ellis ; illustrated by Rosalind Hooper. — Melksham : Venton Educational, c1981. — 160p : ill ; 22cm
ISBN 0-85993-028-9 : £5.95 B82-11391

Ellson, Peter. Halde. — London : Tuba Press, Feb.1983. — [112]p
ISBN 0-907155-05-7 (cased) : £6.60 : CIP entry
ISBN 0-907155-06-5 (pbk) : £2.40 B82-40926

Emberson, Ian M.. Doodles in the margins of my life / Ian M. Emberson ; illustrated by the author. — Heckmondwike : Fighting Cock, c1981. — 32p : ill ; 21cm
ISBN 0-906744-03-2 (pbk) : £1.50 B82-13048

Enderby, Mavis. Enderby's wee bestiary. — Lincoln (1 Stonefield Ave., Lincoln) : Asgill, 1975. — [31]p ; 80x110mm
£0.30 (pbk) B82-08852

Erimus. Poetry for t'peasantry / [Erimus]. — Whitby : William E. Fall, 1981. — 67p ; 19cm
ISBN 0-9504829-4-3 (pbk) : Unpriced B82-26819

Eshleman, Clayton. Grotesca / by Clayton Eshleman. — London (97 Kingsley Flats, Old Kent Rd, SE1 5NL) : New London Pride, 1977. — 38p ; 28cm. — (Exclusive mimeograph masterpieces)
Limited ed. of 280 copies, of which 25 are signed by the author
Unpriced (pbk) B82-32723

Fagan, Patrick. View from Mount Pelier / by Patrick Fagan. — Mullingar (Lynn Industrial Estate, Mullingar) : Topic Group of Newspapers, c1981. — 36p ; 19cm
Text on inside cover
£2.00 (pbk) B82-11676

Fanthorpe, U. A.. Standing to / U.A. Fanthorpe. — Liskeard : Harry Chambers/Peterloo Poets, 1982. — 94p ; 22cm
ISBN 0-905291-35-2 (pbk) : £3.00 B82-33893

Fenech, Victor. Today I waited : four poems / by Victor Fenech ; drawing by Kathie Layfield. — Leicester : New Broom, 1982. — [7]p ; 21cm
Limited ed. of 110 numbered copies signed by the printer
ISBN 0-901870-61-7 (unbound) : £2.00 B82-27989

Fenton, James. Dead soldiers / James Fenton. — [Oxford] (4 Benson Place, Oxford) : Sycamore Press, c1981. — [6]p ; 21cm
Unpriced (pbk) B82-11430

Finch, Peter, *1947-*. Blues & heartbreakers / Peter Finch. — Newcastle upon Tyne : Galloping Dog Press, c1981. — [35]leaves ; 19cm
Limited ed. of 300 copies of which 10 are signed by the author
ISBN 0-904837-46-7 (pbk) : £1.25
ISBN 0-904837-47-5 (Signed ed.) : £3.00 B82-07339

Findlay, Norman E.. Streets of high summer : poems / N.E. Findlay. — Nottingham : Em-Press, c1982. — [19]leaves : ill ; 15x21cm
ISBN 0-9506621-3-5 (unbound) : Unpriced B82-14101

Finlay, Ian Hamilton. 3 developments / [Ian Hamilton Finlay]. — [Lanark] ([Stonypath, Little Sparta, Dunsyre, Lanark, Scotland]) : Wild Hawthorn Press, [1982?]. — [11]leaves ; 10x11cm
Unpriced (unbound) B82-34969

Finlay, Ian Hamilton. Little sermons series / [Ian Hamilton Finlay, Ian Gardner]. — [Lanark] ([Stonypath, Little Sparta, Dunsyre, Lanark, Scotland]) : Wild Hawthorn Press, [1982?]. — [7]p : ill ; 77mmx89mm
Unpriced (pbk) B82-34970

821'.914 — Poetry in English, *1945-* — Texts *continuation*

Finlay, Ian Hamilton. Midway 3 / [Ian Hamilton Finlay, Grahame Jones]. — Lanark (Stonypath, Little Sparta, Dunsyre, Lanark, Scotland) : Wild Hawthorn Press, [1982?]. — [5]p : ill ; 13x26cm
Bibliography: p[5]
Unpriced (pbk) B82-34967

Fisher, Roy. Consolidated comedies / by Roy Fisher. — Durham : Pig Press, 1981. — 16p ; 21cm
Originally published: 1979
ISBN 0-903997-63-0 (pbk) : £1.00 B82-04215

Fisher, Stanley. Scenes from a love life — the greatest : and other poems / Stanley Fisher. — 2nd ed. — Grantham : S. Fisher, 1982. — 54leaves ; 21cm
Previous ed.: 1981
ISBN 0-905143-06-x (pbk) : £2.35 B82-11677

Fisher, W. E.. The young gentleman : & other poems / W.E. Fisher. — Bognor Regis : New Horizon, c1982. — 80p ; 21cm
ISBN 0-86116-683-3 : £3.95 B82-19982

Fitzgerald, Noel. The past and the present / Noel Fitzgerald. — Ilfracombe : Stockwell, 1982. — 16p ; 15cm
ISBN 0-7223-1594-5 (pbk) : £0.55 B82-36661

Flood, Sally. Window on Brick Lane / by Sally Flood. — London (Old Town Hall, Cable St., E.1.) : Basement Writers, c1980. — [33]p : 1ill ; 21cm
Cover title
£0.50 (pbk) B82-15106

Foley, Michael, *1947-*. The GO situation. — Belfast : Blackstaff Press, Mar.1982. — [64]p
ISBN 0-85640-263-x (pbk) : £3.50 : CIP entry B82-05747

Forbes, Peter. The aerial noctiluca : poems 1976-1980 / Peter Forbes. — Hatch End : Poet & Printer, 1981. — 23p ; 22cm
ISBN 0-900597-30-5 (pbk) : £0.90 B82-00619

Ford, Ann. Caterpillar Wood : and other poems in and around Shaftesbury / by Ann Ford. — [Tisbury] (Tisbury Bookshop, Gallery & Tea Room [High St., Tisbury]) : John Danks, [1982?]. — 13p : ill ; 21cm
Cover title. — Text, ill on inside cover
£1.25 (pbk) B82-14901

Fortune, George, *1898-*. Some simple Scots studies : (Scots dialect poems) / by George Fortune. — Edinburgh (137 Captains Rd., Edinburgh EH17 8DT) : G. Fortune, c1981. — 55p ; 21cm
£1.00 (pbk) B82-19995

Fountain, Stephen. Vision for an obscure taste / Stephen Fountain. — [Harrow] : S. Fountain, c1981. — 26p : ill ; 22cm
Limited ed. of 200 copies
Unpriced (pbk) B82-35884

Fowler, Alastair. From the Domain of Arnheim / Alastair Fowler. — London : Secker & Warburg, 1982. — 63p ; 23cm
ISBN 0-436-16180-x : £4.95 : CIP rev. B81-35726

Franklin, James. Rummage / James Franklin. — Bognor Regis : New Horizon, c1981. — 140p ; 21cm
ISBN 0-86116-575-6 : £4.50 B82-03499

Fraser, Douglas, *1910-*. Treasure for eyes to hold : poems / by Douglas Fraser. — Kinnesswood : Lomond, 1981. — 24p ; 21cm
Limited ed. of 350 copies
ISBN 0-907765-00-9 (pbk) : £1.00 B82-12666

Fraser, Olive. The pure accounts. — Aberdeen : Aberdeen University Press, July 1981. — [56]p
ISBN 0-08-025755-0 (pbk) : £3.50 : CIP entry B81-14912

Fuller, John, *1937-*. The ship of sounds / John Fuller ; with a wood engraving by Garrick Palmer. — Sidcot ([Ladram, Sidcot, Winscombe, Somerset]) : Gruffyground Press, 1981. — [16]p : ill ; 25cm
Limited ed. of 130 copies, signed by the author and the illustrator
£20.00 (pbk) B82-17534

Gale, Pamela. Elvis in my words / Pamela Gale. — Braunton : Merlin, 1982. — 36p ; 21cm
ISBN 0-86303-003-3 (pbk) : £0.80 B82-29750

Gant, Roland. Stubble burning / poems by Roland Gant ; with five wood-engravings by Howard Phipps. — Andoversford : Whittington, c1982. — 23p : ill ; 28cm
Limited ed. of 175 copies
ISBN 0-904845-48-6 : £17.50 B82-27608

Garvey, C. F.. The worst of the versed : an humpropatnostic / by C.F. Garvey. — Southgate : C.F. Garvey, c1981. — 51p ; 30cm
Cover title
ISBN 0-946036-00-4 (pbk) : Unpriced B82-19949

Gerrard, Roy. The Favershams / by Roy Gerrard. — London : Gollancz, 1982. — 32p : col.ill ; 29cm
ISBN 0-575-03130-1 : £4.95 : CIP rev. B82-19558

Gilbert, Louis. The Black Lagan Valley / by Louis Gilbert ; illustration by Graham Johnston. — Belfast : Northern Ireland Association for Mental Health, 1980. — 34p : ill ; 21cm
Includes index
ISBN 0-907418-00-7 (pbk) : £0.95 B82-16084

Giles, Eric. Sketch / by Eric Giles. — Walton-on-Thames : Outposts, 1982. — 20p ; 21cm
£0.90 (pbk) B82-35445

Gill, Harold. The collected works of Harold Gill. — London (43 New Oxford St., WC1) : Regency Press, c1981. — 32p ; 19cm
Unpriced B82-24986

Gilliland, Samuel W.. The pen masquerades / Samuel W. Gilliland. — Ilfracombe : Stockwell, 1981. — 58p ; 15cm
ISBN 0-7223-1507-4 : Unpriced B82-05504

Gitin, David. Vacuum tapestries / David Gitin. — Blackburn (1 Spring Bank, Longsight Rd., Salesbury, Blackburn, Lancs. BB1 9EU) : bb, c1981. — 32p : ill,1port ; 21cm
Unpriced (pbk) B82-38616

Glen, Duncan. On midsummer evenin merriest of nichts? / by Duncan Glen. — Nottingham : Akros, 1981. — 62p ; 24cm
Also available in a limited ed. of 50 copies, numbered and signed by the author
£3.50 (pbk) B82-05994

Gohorry, John. The coast of Bohemia / John Gohorry ; illustration George Szirtes. — Hitchin : Mandeville, 1981. — [13]p : ill ; 23cm
Limited ed. of 200 copies, of which 35 have been signed by the author and artist
ISBN 0-904533-54-9 (pbk) : £0.50 B82-05440

Gowans, John. O lord! / by John Gowans ; cover design and graphics by Jim Moss. — London : Salvationist, c1981. — 84p : ill ; 21x10cm
Originally published: in the War Cry
ISBN 0-85412-376-8 (pbk) : Unpriced B82-06482

Graham, Henry. Poker in paradise lost / Henry Graham & Jim Mangnall. — Liverpool ([14 Buckingham Ave., Liverpool L17 3BB]) : [Glasshouse Press], [1977]. — [13]p ; 21cm
£0.30 (unbound) B82-16832

Gray, John, *b.1918*. Memories / John Gray. — Ilfracombe : Stockwell, 1981. — 46p ; 22cm
ISBN 0-7223-1525-2 (pbk) : Unpriced B82-05502

Green, J. C. R.. Sixty haiku / by J.C.R. Green. — Isle of Skye : Aquila, c1982. — [24]p ; 14cm
ISBN 0-7275-0233-6 (pbk) : Unpriced
ISBN 0-7275-0234-4 (signed limited ed.) : Unpriced B82-37602

Green, Paul. The hermaphrodite grimoire / Paul Green. — Bishops Stortford : Great Works, c1981. — [34]leaves ; 30cm
Limited ed. of 200 copies
ISBN 0-905383-15-x (pbk) : £0.75 B82-38618

Green, Roger, *1940-*. Beneath an enormous sky : poems of Wolvercote / Roger Green. — Wolvercote : Atlantis, 1982. — 12p : ill,1map ; 31cm
ISBN 0-907425-02-x (pbk) : Unpriced B82-32110

Greening, John. Westerners. — Sutton (26 Cedar Rd, Sutton, Surrey) : Hippopotamus Press, May 1982. — 1v.
Limited ed. of 525 copies of which 25 are numbered and signed
ISBN 0-904179-27-3 (pbk) : £3.50 : CIP entry
ISBN 0-904179-28-1 (numbered and signed ed.) : £6.50 B82-12831

Griffiths, Vivian L.. Moonscapes, seascrapes / Vivian Griffiths. — London : Tuba Press, 1982. — 32p : 1ill ; 20cm
ISBN 0-907155-04-9 (pbk) : £1.50 : CIP rev. B82-11108

Grigson, Geoffrey. The Cornish dancer and other poems / Geoffrey Grigson. — London : Secker & Warburg, 1982. — 64p ; 23cm
ISBN 0-436-18805-8 : £4.95 : CIP rev. B82-09722

Gunn, Thom. The passages of joy / Thom Gunn. — London : Faber and Faber, 1982. — 93p ; 21cm
ISBN 0-571-11921-2 (cased) : £4.00 : CIP rev.
ISBN 0-571-11867-4 (pbk) : Unpriced B82-11302

Gunson, Douglas. Victim souls / by Douglas Gunson. — Norwich (18A A Cricket Ground Rd., Norwich, NR1 3BQ) : D. Gunson, c1981. — [12]p ; 21cm
Cover title
£0.30 (pbk) B82-02301

Gwen. Everyday thoughts and versatile verses / from the pen of Gwen. — London : Regency Press, c1980. — 64p ; 22cm
£2.25 (pbk) B82-15581

Gwen. Sharing some time with my friends / from the pen of Gwen. — London : Regency Press, c1981. — 64p ; 22cm
ISBN 0-7212-0671-9 (pbk) : £2.75 B82-06445

Gwilym Llaeron. Memories recalled : poems of Gwilym Llaeron. — Pontypridd : Dillwyn Lewis, c1982. — 65p : 3ports ; 21cm
ISBN 0-9500567-4-x (pbk) : Unpriced B82-41099

Haldenby, S. W. W.. Laughter and tears / written and illustrated by S.W.W. Haldenby. — Hull (39 High St., Hull, N. Humberside) : Bradley, c1979. — 49p : ill ; 21cm
£1.80 (pbk) B82-08839

Halsey, Alan. Present state / Alan Halsey. — Peterborough : Spectacular Diseases, 1981. — [20]p ; 16x23cm
Limited ed. of 350 copies, of which 10 are numbered and signed
ISBN 0-9506316-6-3 (pbk) : £2.50 B82-00594

821'.914 — Poetry in English, *1945- — Texts continuation*

Hamilton-Edwards, Gerald. Paris in my youth : and other poems / by Gerald Hamilton-Edwards. — Oxford (32, Bowness Ave. Headington, Oxford OX3 0AL) : G. Hamilton-Edwards, c1982. — 16p : ill ; 21cm
Cover title
£1.20 (pbk) B82-22707

Hampton, Christopher. A cornered freedom / Christopher Hampton. — Liskeard : Harry Chambers/Peterloo Poets, 1980. — 63p ; 22cm
ISBN 0-905291-24-7 (pbk) : £3.00 B82-07386

Hance, Lilian. Sowing and reaping / Lilian Hance. — Ilfracombe : Stockwell, 1980. — 40p ; 15cm
ISBN 0-7223-1418-3 : £2.25 B82-13368

Hanke, Michael. Four : poems / Michael Hanke ; drawing, Rigby Graham. — Leicester : New Broom, 1982. — [7]p : 1ill ; 21cm
ISBN 0-901870-63-3 (unbound) : Unpriced B82-33182

Hannibal : the tale of a local lion / cartoons by Janine Winterburn. — [Weston-super-Mare] : Woodspring Museum, 1980. — [24]p : ill,facsims ; 21cm
Unpriced (pbk) B82-20982

Hardiment, Melville. Doazy bor / Melville Hardiment. — Malvern ([61 Belmont Rd, Malvern, Worcs.]) : Migrant Press, 1978. — [32]p : ill ; 21cm
Cover title. — Limited ed. of 500 copies of which the first 100 are numbered and signed by the author
Unpriced (pbk) B82-05290

Hare, Anne. The mouse whiskers adventure : a four part story in verse / by Anne Hare ; illustrated by Joe Lavery. — Crawley : Wren, c1982. — 44p : ill ; 21cm
ISBN 0-907820-06-9 (pbk) : Unpriced B82-36500

Harmer, Janet. Jesus loves me : poems for very young children / by Janet Harmer. — [Ilkeston] : Moorley's, [1982?]. — 28p ; 21cm
ISBN 0-86071-122-6 (pbk) : £0.40 B82-16342

Harris, David M.. Coventry kid : poems / by David M. Harris. — Coventry (Warwick Rd., Coventry, CV3 6AQ) : Coventry School, King Henry VIII, 1981. — [23]p ; 21cm
Unpriced (pbk) B82-13875

Harris, Joyce N. O.. Shaded views / Joyce N.O. Harris ; illustrated by the author. — Ilfracombe : Stockwell, 1981. — 32p : ill ; 19cm
ISBN 0-7223-1549-x (pbk) : £0.97 B82-05499

Harrison, Tony, *1937-*. Continuous : 50 sonnets from the school of eloquence / Tony Harrison. — London : Collings, 1981. — [62]p ; 24cm
ISBN 0-86036-159-4 (pbk) : £3.95 B82-04512

Harrison, Tony, *1937-*. A kumquat for John Keats / Tony Harrison. — Newcastle upon Tyne : Bloodaxe, 1981. — [12]p : col.ill ; 22cm
ISBN 0-906427-31-2 (pbk) : £0.75
ISBN 0-906427-32-0 (signed ed.) : Unpriced B82-39163

Harrison, Tony, *1937-*. U.S. martial / Tony Harrison. — Newcastle upon Tyne : Bloodaxe, 1981. — [24]p ; 22cm
ISBN 0-906427-29-0 (pbk) : £1.00
ISBN 0-906427-30-4 (signed ed.) : Unpriced B82-39164

Harvey, Andrew. Homage to Toukaram : recreations of an Indian mystic / by Andrew Harvey. — Haye-on-Wye : Other Poetry Editions, [1982]. — [28]p ; 21cm
Cover title
ISBN 0-907149-00-6 (pbk) : £1.95 B82-33184

Harwood, Lee. All the wrong notes / texts by Lee Harwood ; photographs by Judith Walker. — Durham : Pig Press, c1981. — 49p : ill ; 20x20cm
ISBN 0-903997-61-4 (pbk) : £2.90
ISBN 0-903997-62-2 (signed ed.) B82-05572

Havins, Peter J. Neville. Notes from empty churches / Peter J. Neville Havins. — [Millbrook] ([Knill Cross House, Higher Anderton Rd, Millbrook, Cornwall]) : Kawabata, 1981. — [24]p ; 21cm
ISBN 0-906110-32-7 (pbk) : £1.00 B82-06442

Hayes, Priscilla. Poems of simplicity / Priscilla Hayes. — 2nd ed. — Bromley : Taurus, 1982. — 28p ; 21cm
ISBN 0-9506430-7-6 (unbound) : £0.50 B82-17364

Hayton, Hillary. Doris and the mice from Mars / [illustrated] by Hillary Hayton ; verses by Jonathan Langley. — London : Pan, 1981. — [24]p : col.ill ; 25cm. — (Piccolo picture books)
ISBN 0-330-26516-4 (pbk) : £0.95 B82-00969

Heanley, Robert. The streak of gold / by Robert Heanley. — Walton-on-Thames ([72 Burwood Rd., Walton-on-Thames, Surrey KT12 4AL]) : Outposts, 1982. — 28p ; 21cm
£1.10 (pbk) B82-22350

Heath-Stubbs, John. Birds reconvened / John Heath-Stubbs. — London : Enitharmon, 1980. — 37p ; 25cm
ISBN 0-905289-61-7 (cased) : £3.90
ISBN 0-905289-56-0 (pbk) : £2.55 B82-20246

Heath-Stubbs, John. Buzz buzz : ten insect poems / John Heath-Stubbs ; with a wood engraving by Richard Shirley Smith. — Sidcot ([Ladram, Sidcot, Winscombe, Somerset]) : Gruffyground Press, 1981. — [16]p : ill ; 24cm
Limited ed. of 200 copies, signed by the author and the illustrator
£14.00 (pbk) B82-17533

Heath-Stubbs, John. Naming the beasts / John Heath-Stubbs. — Manchester : Carcanet New, 1982. — 61p ; 20cm
ISBN 0-85635-432-5 (pbk) : Unpriced : CIP rev. B82-01730

Heath-Stubbs, John. This is your poem / John Heath-Stubbs. — London : Pisces Press, 1981. — 4p : 1ill ; 20cm
Limited ed. of 100 signed and numbered copies
Unpriced (unbound) B82-02954

Henderson Smith, S. L.. Soundings / by S.L. Henderson Smith. — Huddersfield : [S.L. Henderson Smith], 1982. — 40p ; 21cm
ISBN 0-9507972-0-0 (pbk) : £1.00 B82-25468

Hennessy, Colm. Purgatorial affairs : poems / by Colm Hennessy. — [London] ([33 Colin Cres., NW9 6EU]) : Midsummer, 1982. — [25]p ; 24cm
Unpriced (pbk) B82-27770

Henri, Adrian. Words without a story / Adrian Henri. — Liverpool ([14 Buckingham Ave., Liverpool L17 3BB]) : [Glasshouse Press], c1978. — [24]p : ill ; 21cm
Lines written to accompany woodcuts by Franz Masreel, from Geschichte ohne Worte
£0.40 (pbk) B82-16833

Henry, Robin. Food for thought / Robin Henry. — Ilfracombe : Stockwell, 1982. — 21p ; 15cm
ISBN 0-7223-1593-7 (pbk) : £0.58 B82-36659

Hesketh, Phoebe. The eighth day : selected poems 1948-1978 / Phoebe Hesketh ; with an introduction by John Barron Mays. — London : Enitharmon, 1980. — 89p ; 23cm
ISBN 0-905289-96-x (cased) : £4.95
ISBN 0-905289-91-9 (pbk) : £3.00 B82-20252

Hewitt, John, *1907-*. The selected John Hewitt / edited with an introduction by Alan Warner. — [Belfast] : Blackstaff, c1981. — 119p ; 21cm
ISBN 0-85640-244-3 (pbk) : £3.50 : CIP rev. B81-24646

Hidden, Norman. For my friends / Norman Hidden. — [London] ([2 Culham Court, Granville Rd., N4 4JB]) : [Workshop Press], c1981. — [40]p ; 21cm
Unpriced (pbk) B82-02303

Hill, Richard, *1941-*. Love poems and others / Richard Hill. — Liverpool (5 Bryanston Rd., Liverpool L17 7AL) : Glasshouse Press, c1976. — [32]p : ill ; 21cm
Cover title
£0.35 (pbk) B82-16860

Hill-Pratt, Pamela. Encounters / by Pamela Hill-Pratt. — Eastbourne : Downlander, c1982. — 24p ; 21cm
ISBN 0-906369-17-7 (pbk) : £1.45 B82-37143

Hoadley, J. M.. Rumour of rebellion / by J.M. Hoadley. — London ([J.M. Hoadley, 32 Portland Rd., W.11]) : Druid press, 1982. — [35]p ; 21cm
Limited ed. of 300 copies
£1.00 (pbk) B82-22384

Holland, Emily. Poetic gems through life / Emily Holland. — [Hull] ([39 High St.]) : [Bradley], c1980. — 46p : ill,ports ; 21cm
£1.80 (pbk) B82-09010

Holzapfel, Rudi. A smile dies / by Rudi Holzapfel. — [Blackrock] ([c/o Carraig Books, 25 Newton Ave., Blackrock, Co. Dublin]) : Sunburst Press, 1978. — 77p ; 21cm
Limited ed. of 1000 copies of which 100 have been signed by the author
Unpriced (pbk) B82-09635

Hooker, Jeremy. A view from the source : selected poems / Jeremy Hooker. — Manchester : Carcanet, 1982. — 107p ; 20cm
ISBN 0-85635-379-5 (pbk) : Unpriced : CIP rev. B82-07035

Hope, Ian D.. Glimpses of truth / Ian D. Hope. — Ilfracombe : Stockwell, 1981. — 96p ; 19cm
ISBN 0-7223-1503-1 : Unpriced B82-36658

Horder, John. Meher Baba and the nothingness / John Horder. — London : Menard, 1981, c1980. — 56p ; 22cm
ISBN 0-903400-58-8 (pbk) : £2.40 B82-36069

Howes, Libby. Tea trips / Libby Howes. — Ilfracombe : Stockwell, 1981. — 16p ; 22cm
ISBN 0-7223-1477-9 (pbk) : £0.50 B82-19028

Hoyland, Mary. Poetry for pregnancy / by Mary Hoyland. — London : M. Hoyland, 1982. — 39p : ill ; 22cm. — (Poems for people ; 1)
ISBN 0-9508212-0-9 (pbk) : £1.00 B82-37915

Hugh-Jones, R. J.. Some adventures / poems by R.J. Hugh-Jones ; drawings by Geraldine Morris. — Finstock (Hawthorn Cottage, Ramsden Heath, Finstock, Oxon.) : Stupor Mundi, 1981. — [24]p ; 22cm
Unpriced (pbk) B82-07170

Hughes, Ted. Selected poems 1957-1981 / Ted Hughes. — London : Faber, 1982. — 238p ; 23cm
ISBN 0-571-11877-1 (cased) : £4.95 : CIP rev.
ISBN 0-571-11916-6 (pbk) : Unpriced B82-08080

Hull, Alban. The path of peace and liberty / by Alban Hull. — [Huddersfield] ([c/o Tolson Memorial Museum, Huddersfield]) : [Alban Hull], [1982]. — 30p ; 21cm
Cover title
£1.00 (pbk) B82-32272

821′.914 — Poetry in English, *1945-* — *Texts continuation*

Hulse, Michael. Dole queue / Michael Hulse. — [Great Britain] : The White Friar Press in collaboration with West Midlands Arts, c1981. — [46]p ; 23cm
Unpriced (pbk) B82-13604

Hulse, Michael. Knowing and forgetting. — London : Secker & Warburg, June 1981. — [64]p
ISBN 0-436-20965-9 : £4.50 : CIP entry B81-09454

Hunt, Charles. A surgeon′s dozen : eleven poems / Charles Hunt. — Sevenoaks : Danckwerts, 1982. — [14]p : 1ill ; 17cm
ISBN 0-907553-01-x (pbk) : Unpriced : CIP rev. B82-11100

Huscroft, John. Hummock tales / by John Huscroft. — [Chelmsford] ([Chelmsford, Essex, CM2 9JD]) : John Huscroft Publications, 1982. — 10p,[2]p of plates : 2ports ; 16cm
Limited ed. of 200 copies
£0.60 (pbk) B82-19999

Hussey, Philip. Studley poems / by Philip Hussey. — Port Talbot : Alun, c1980. — 48p ; 19cm
ISBN 0-907117-02-3 : £1.25 B82-02959

Hyland, Paul. Poems of Z / Paul Hyland. — Newcastle upon Tyne : Bloodaxe, 1982. — [52]p ; 22cm
ISBN 0-906427-44-4 (pbk) : £3.25 B82-39165

Hyland, Paul. Riddles for Jack / Paul Hyland. — Newcastle upon Tyne : Northern House, 1978. — [20]p ; 21cm. — (Northern House poets ; 24)
ISBN 0-900570-19-9 (pbk) : £0.65
ISBN 0-900570-20-2 (signed ed.) : Unpriced B82-16605

Imlah, Mick. The zoologist′s bath and other adventures / Mick Imlah. — Oxford (4 Benson Place, Oxford) : Sycamore Press, 1982. — [16]p ; 21cm
Unpriced (pbk) B82-35569

Jackson, David Moreton. Think about it — / by David Moreton Jackson. — [Boston Spa] ([c/o British Library Lending Division, Boston Spa, Wetherby, W. Yorkshire LS23 7BQ]) : [D.M. Jackson], c1981. — [20]p ; 22cm
Unpriced (pbk) B82-02908

Jackson, Gordon, *1938-*. Five Sisters York : a poem / by Gordon Jackson ; illustrated by Paul Jackson. — Lincoln (1 Stonefield Ave., Lincoln) : Asgill, 1980. — 23 : ill ; 25cm
Limited ed. of 400 numbered copies
£1.50 (pbk) B82-08846

Jackson, Gordon, *1938-*. Out of the dunghill : a series of fifty odes / by Gordon Jackson ; with illustrations by Paul Jackson. — Lincoln (1 Stonefield Ave., Lincoln) : Asgill, 1981. — 75p : ill ; 25cm
Limited ed. of 400 numbered copies
£2.10 (pbk) B82-08848

Jackson, Gordon, *1938-*. Scorpions, I might add, do it : some early poems of Gordon Jackson. — Lincoln (1 Stonefield Ave., Lincoln) : Asgill, c1979. — 31p ; 26cm
Limited ed. of 400 numbered copies
£1.20 (pbk) B82-08849

Jaffin, David. The density for color. — Plymouth : Blue Guitar Books ; London (12 Stevenage Rd, SW6 6ES) : Independent Press Distribution, July 1982. — [52]p
Issued to subscribers as issue no.8 of the magazine Shearsman
ISBN 0-907562-05-1 (pbk) : £1.50 : CIP entry B82-14242

Jaffin, David. For the finger′s want of sound. — Plymouth : Blue Guitar Books ; London (12 Stevenage Rd, SW6 6ES) : Independent Press Distribution, July 1982. — [56]p
Issued to subscribers as issue no.8 of the magazine Shearsman
ISBN 0-907562-04-3 (pbk) : £1.50 : CIP entry B82-13173

James, Janice. Life lines / Janice James. — London : Corgi, 1982. — 112p : ill ; 18cm
ISBN 0-552-11881-8 (pbk) : £1.00 B82-16743

Jamieson, Tom. The secret box : poems / by Tom Jamieson. — [Prestwick] ([59 Ayr Rd., Prestwick, Ayrshire KA9 1SY]) : [T. Jamieson], 1980. — 12p ; 21cm
£0.50 (pbk) B82-09948

Jaye, Peter. Twenty new children′s nursery rhymes / Peter Jaye. — Bognor Regis : New Horizon, c1982. — 39p : ill ; 20cm
ISBN 0-86116-820-8 : £3.50 B82-22160

Jefferson, Jean. A peep inside my heart : poetry / by Jean Jefferson. — London : Regency Press, c1981. — 43p ; 21cm
ISBN 0-7212-0661-1 : £2.00 B82-10083

Jefferson, Jean. Poems for pleasure and thought / by Jean Jefferson. — [London] : [Regency Press], c1980. — 32p ; 19cm
£1.00 (pbk) B82-16804

Jennings, Elizabeth. Celebrations and elegies / Elizabeth Jennings. — Manchester : Carcanet, 1982. — 64p ; 20cm
ISBN 0-85635-360-4 (pbk) : Unpriced : CIP rev. B82-04806

John, Roland. The child bride′s diary. — London (12 Stevenage Rd, SW6 6ES) : Oasis Books, July 1981. — [24]p. — (O Books series ; no.2)
ISBN 0-903375-55-9 (pbk) : £0.50 : CIP entry B81-14392

Johnson, Claudius A.. If not / Claudius A. Johnson. — Ilfracombe : Stockwell, 1981. — 23p ; 19cm
ISBN 0-7223-1563-5 (pbk) : £0.97 B82-10408

Johnson, S. (Steven). Andromeda / S. Johnson. — Ilfracombe : Stockwell, 1981. — 16p ; 15cm
ISBN 0-7223-1526-0 (pbk) : £0.55 B82-10400

Johnston, Charles, *1912-*. Choiseul and Talleyrand : a historical novella and other poems / Charles Johnston. with new verse translations of Mozart and Salieri & Count Nulin / by Alexander Pushkin ; and an introduction by Kyril Fitzlyon. — London : Published for C. Johnston by The Bodley Head, c1982. — 88p ; 18cm
Mozart and Salieri and Count Nulin translated from the Russian
ISBN 0-370-30924-3 : £5.25 B82-36359

Jordan, E. D.. Phantasmagoria / E.D. Jordan. — Hexham (Low Shield, Sparty Lea, Hexham, Northumberland) : Septentrio, 1981. — [24]p ; 22cm
Limited ed. of 140 copies
Private circulation (pbk) B82-26043

Joris, Pierre. Tanith flies / Pierre Joris. — London : Ta′wil, 1978. — 28p ; 21cm
Cover title
ISBN 0-85652-044-6 (pbk) : Unpriced B82-32718

Jupp, Marilyn. Words between lines / Marilyn Jupp. — London (21 Earls Court Sq., SW5) : National Poetry Centre, c1981. — [42]p ; 21cm
Unpriced (pbk) B82-02302

Kahlhamer, D. W.. Life seen from a glass-box / D.W. Kahlhamer. — Ilfracombe : Stockwell, 1981. — 16p ; 15cm
ISBN 0-7223-1441-8 (pbk) : Private circulation B82-15582

Kavanagh, P. J.. Selected poems / P.J. Kavanagh. — London : Chatto & Windus, 1982. — 87p ; 22cm
"Consists of poems chosen by P.J. Kavanagh from his five collections published between 1959 and 1979"
ISBN 0-7011-2618-3 : £4.95 : CIP rev. B82-04577

Keats-Rohan, Katharine. Beautiful contortions : and other poems / Katharine Keats-Rohan. — Braunton : Merlin, 1982. — 32p ; 21cm
ISBN 0-86303-010-6 (pbk) : £1.75 B82-26578

Kell, Richard. Heartwood / Richard Kell. — Newcastle upon Tyne : Northern House, 1978. — [18]p ; 21cm. — (Northern House poets ; 25)
ISBN 0-900570-21-0 (pbk) : £0.65
ISBN 0-900570-22-9 (signed ed.) : Unpriced B82-16604

Kelly, Thomas, *1904-*. Take a peep : some poems / by Thomas Kelly. — Laghey P.O. (Innisfad, Laghey P.O. [Co. Donegal]) : T. Kelly, [1981]. — 170p ; 16cm
Unpriced (pbk) B82-02671

Kenedy, R. C.. Sonning : a poem / by R.C. Kenedy ; with wood-engravings by H. Weissenborn. — London : Acorn Press, c1977. — [16]p : ill ; 17cm
Limited ed. of 100 numbered copies signed by the author and artist
Unpriced (pbk) B82-12676

Kenworthy, Nina. Impressions / by Nina Kenworthy. — [Liverpool] ([43, Croxteth Rd., Liverpool L8 3SF]) : [N. Kenworthy], c1981. — 12p ; 21cm
£0.60 (pbk) B82-37321

Keyes, Edward, *1918-*. Intimations / Edward Keyes. — Fordingbridge (Rockbourne, Fordingbridge, Hants.) : E. Keyes (Ilfracombe : Stockwell), 1981. — 32p ; 22cm
ISBN 0-7223-1546-5 (pbk) : Unpriced B82-10389

Killingley, Siew-Yue. Song-pageant from Christmas to Easter / by Siew-Yue Killingley ; with two settings by Percy Lovell. — Newcastle upon Tyne : P. Lovell, 1981. — 13p : music ; 21cm
Text on inside cover
ISBN 0-9507921-0-1 (pbk) : £0.70 B82-10296

King, Pearl S.. Poetryscapes / Pearl S. King. — Ilfracombe : Stockwell, 1981. — 32p ; 19cm
ISBN 0-7223-1483-3 : Unpriced B82-10407

King, Richard Rawcliffe. The front line / Richard Rawcliffe King. — London : Panic Publications, 1981. — 41p ; 22cm
Cover title
ISBN 0-907878-00-8 (pbk) : £1.50 B82-09783

Knight, Kenny. A goddess unrecorded / [Kenny Knight]. — [Plymouth] ([c/o Mr. K. Knight, 6 Hartley Ave., Hartley, Plymouth, Devon]) : See-Saw Press, c1980. — [20]p ; 22cm
£0.60 (pbk) B82-16603

Koppana, Kati. The dragon sleeps / Kati Koppana. — Bognor Regis : New Horizon, c1982. — 34p ; 20cm
ISBN 0-86116-823-2 : £3.95 B82-22157

La Rocca, Filadelfo. After spaghetti : thoughts & verses / Filadelfo la Rocca (Rocco the Sicilian Scouser). — Liverpool ([c/o Anvil Press, 17 Duke St. Liverpool]) : [Grengage], 1981. — 54p : ill ; 22cm
£1.50 (unbound) B82-09634

Langley, Betty. Beverley : prose and cons : a selection of poetry with illustrations as seen and heard by a local lady of the town of Beverley / by Betty Langley. — Hull (39 High St., Hull [N. Humberside]) : Bradley, 1977. — 32p : ill,3ports ; 21cm
£0.75 (pbk) B82-09377

821'.914 — Poetry in English, *1945-* — *Texts continuation*

Laughton, Valerie Joy. Cyril of the striped dunny / poem by Valerie J. Laughton ; pictures by Peter Harrison. — Ilfracombe : Stockwell, 1981. — 12p : ill ; 22cm
ISBN 0-7223-1514-7 (pbk) : Unpriced B82-10398

Leeder, E. E.. Ted's poems : original verse / by E.E. Leeder. — Melton Constable ('The Retreat', St. Giles Rd., Swanton Novers, Melton Constable, Norfolk, NR24 2RB) : E.E. Leeder, 1982. — [15]p ; 21cm
Unpriced (unbound) B82-27988

Leeder, E. E.. Ted's poems : Unknown journey and other poems / by E.E. Leeder. — Melton Constable (The Retreat, St. Giles Rd., Swanton Novers, Melton Constable, Norfolk NR24 2RB) : E.E. Leeder, 1982. — [16]p ; 21cm
Cover title
Unpriced (pbk) B82-33939

Leman, Martin. Ten cats and their tales / Martin Leman. — London : Pelham, 1981. — [24]p : col.ill ; 25x28cm
ISBN 0-7207-1330-7 : £3.95 B82-02253

Lenier, Sue. Swansongs / Sue Lenier. — Cambridge : Oleander, 1982. — 80p : 1port ; 21cm
ISBN 0-906672-04-x (cased) : Unpriced : CIP rev.
ISBN 0-906672-03-1 (pbk) : £4.00 B82-17945

Lenier, Susan Jennifer. Swansongs. — Cambridge : Oleander Press, Sept.1982. — [80]p. — (Oleander modern poets)
ISBN 0-906672-03-1 (pbk) : £4.00 : CIP entry B82-30606

Lerner, Laurence. A.R.T.H.U.R. & M.A.R.T.H.A, or, The loves of the computers / Laurence Lerner. — London : Secker and Warburg, 1980. — 68p ; 13x20cm
ISBN 0-436-24440-3 (pbk) : £2.95 B82-16083

Lester, Paul. Minding the animals / by Paul Lester. — Birmingham (Flat 4, 34 Summerfield Cres., Edgbaston, Birmingham B16 0ER) : Protean Pubs, c1982. — 10p ; 22cm
£0.30 (unbound) B82-33188

Levi, Peter. Private ground / Peter Levi. — London : Anvil Press Poetry, 1981. — 61p ; 22cm
ISBN 0-85646-080-x (pbk) : £3.25 B82-00600

Lindley, John. Cages and fields / John Lindley. — Stockport (82 Bollington Road, Heaton Chapel, Stockport, Cheshire, SK4 5EP) : [J. Lindley], c1982. — [44]p ; 21cm
£0.75 (pbk) B82-19421

Lives, Eric. Diary / Eric Lives. — London : Sea Dream Music, 1982. — 20p ; 21cm
ISBN 0-907888-07-0 (pbk) : £0.20 B82-14100

Lives, Eric. Survival of the fattest / [Eric Lives]. — 3rd ed. — London (28 Earlham Grove, E7 9AW) : Sea Dream Music, [1981]. — 11p ; 21cm
Cover title. — Previous ed.: 1979. — Text on inside cover
£0.15 (pbk) B82-03658

Livingstone, Dinah. Love in time / [Dinah Livingstone]. — London : Katabasis, 1982. — 31p ; 21cm
ISBN 0-904872-08-4 (pbk) : Unpriced B82-35566

Livingstone, Dinah. Prepositions and conjunctions / by Dinah Livingstone. — Manchester : Remploy, 1979, c1977. — 38p ; 22cm
Originally published: S.l. : s.n., 1977
ISBN 0-904872-07-6 (pbk) : £0.70 B82-39316

Lloyd, Jeremy. Captain Beaky / by Jeremy Lloyd ; illustrated by Keith Michell. — London : Sparrow, 1982, c1976. — [60]p : ill ; 20cm
Originally published: London : Chappell, 1976
ISBN 0-09-928110-4 (pbk) : £1.25 B82-31946

Lloyd, Molly. Mythical rhymes / Molly Lloyd. — Ilfracombe : Stockwell, 1982. — 16p ; 15cm
ISBN 0-7223-1608-9 : Unpriced B82-30969

Lopez, Antony. Change : (a prospectus) / by Antony Lopez. — London : New London Pride, 1978. — 23leaves ; 27cm. — (Exclusive mimeograph masterpieces)
Limited ed. of 250 copies, of which 25 are signed by the author
ISBN 0-85652-032-2 (pbk) : Unpriced
ISBN 0-85652-033-0 (signed ed) B82-32721

Lord, Richard. The flick of a serpent's tongue / Richard Lord. — Ilfracombe : Stockwell, 1981. — 32p ; 15cm
ISBN 0-7223-1520-1 (pbk) : Unpriced B82-10397

Loveday, John. The agricultural engineer / John Loveday. — Berkhamsted : Priapus Poets, c1982. — [14]p ; 11x15cm
Limited ed. of 130 copies of which 30 are signed and numbered by the author
Unpriced (pbk) B82-22729

Loveridge, John. God save the Queen : sonnets of Elizabeth 1. — London (34 Middleton Rd, E8 4BS) : Clement Publishers, Oct.1981. — [80]p
ISBN 0-907027-03-2 : £6.50 : CIP entry B81-31101

Loveridge, John. Poems of John Loveridge. — London (6 Stanbrook House, Orchard Grove, Orpington BR6 0SR) : Clement Ltd., Oct.1982. — [208]p
ISBN 0-907027-10-5 : £12.50 : CIP entry B82-32323

Loy, Cliff. Tales of fur, fevvers & fings / written and illustrated by Cliff Loy. — [Sheffield] ([64, The Meadows, Todwick, Sheffield S31 0JG]) : [C. Loy], [1981]. — [32]p : ill ; 21cm
Cover title
Unpriced (pbk) B82-06611

Loydell, Rupert M.. Madness and other voyages : we all verge on sanity sometimes : poetry / by Rupert M. Loydell. — Acton (45 Allan Way, W3 3PW) : R.M. Loydell, 1981. — 32p : ill ; 21cm
£0.60 (pbk) B82-17387

Loydell, Rupert M.. Mistaken identity / Rupert M. Loydell. — [Acton] (45 Allan Way, W3 0PW) : Stride, 1982. — [12]p : ill ; 21cm
£0.20 (unbound) B82-17388

MacBeth, George. Poems from Oby / George MacBeth. — London : Secker & Warburg, 1982. — 67p ; 23cm
ISBN 0-436-27017-x : £4.00 : CIP rev. B82-02648

McCarthy, Thomas, *1954-*. The sorrow garden / Thomas McCarthy. — London : Anvil Press Poetry, 1981. — 64p ; 22cm
ISBN 0-85646-082-6 (pbk) : £3.25 B82-00599

McConnell, Laura. Poems and thrush stories / Laura McConnell. — West Worthing : McConnell, 1981. — 31p ; 15cm
ISBN 0-7223-1574-0 (pbk) : Unpriced B82-19027

McCorrisken, Walter. Cream of the dross : vervy verse / by Walter McCorrisken ; foreword by James Currie ; illustrations by Eric Kennedy. — 2nd ed. — Edinburgh (2-4 Abbeymount, Edinburgh 8) : Albyn, 1980, c1979. — 32p : ill ; 18cm
Previous ed.: 1979
Unpriced (pbk) B82-09941

McDonald, Frank, *1950-*. We call it life / Frank McDonald ; [edited by Matt Simpson]. — Liverpool (23a Brent Way, Halewood, Liverpool 26) : Windows, c1980. — [20]p : ill ; 26cm
Unpriced (unbound) B82-13047

McFadden, Roy. The selected Roy McFadden. — Belfast : Blackstaff, Feb.1983. — [112]p
ISBN 0-85640-282-6 : £4.50 : CIP entry B82-37484

McGough, Roger. Waving at trains. — London : Cape, Sept.1982. — [64]p. — (Cape poetry paperback)
ISBN 0-224-02058-7 (pbk) : £2.50 : CIP entry B82-19005

McGuckian, Medbh. The flower master / Medbh McGuckian. — Oxford : Oxford University Press, 1982. — 51p ; 22cm
ISBN 0-19-211949-4 (pbk) : £4.00 : CIP rev. B82-10425

McKittrick, Ian. With respect / Ian McKittrick. — Chichester : Rose, c1981. — 135p : ill ; 21cm
ISBN 0-85992-230-8 : £5.50 B82-11955

McLean, Icilda. Stop & think / Icilda McLean ; photographs by Colin Thomas. — Liverpool ([23a Brent Way, Halewood, Liverpool L26 9XH]) : Windows Project, 1979. — [40]p : ill ; 21cm
Unpriced (pbk) B82-13049

McNally, J. D.. Moments / J.D. McNally. — Bognor Regis : New Horizon, c1982. — 77p ; 21cm
ISBN 0-86116-725-2 : £3.95 B82-22381

MacSweeney, Barry. Black torch / by Barry MacSweeney. — London : New London Pride, 1978. — 75p ; 28cm. — (Exclusive mimeograph masterpieces)
Limited ed. of 250 copies, of which 25 are signed by the author
ISBN 0-85652-030-6 (pbk) : Unpriced
ISBN 0-85652-031-4 (signed ed) B82-32722

Magee, Wes. A dark age / Wes Magee. — Dundonald : Blackstaff, c1981. — 46p ; 21cm
ISBN 0-85640-256-7 (pbk) : £3.50 : CIP rev. B81-34966

Mahon, Derek. The hunt by night. — Oxford : Oxford University Press, Nov.1982. — [64]p
ISBN 0-19-211953-2 (pbk) : £4.00 : CIP entry B82-26887

Markham, E. A.. Love, politics & food / E.A. Markham. — Cambridge, Mass. : Von Hallett ; London : Walter Rodney Bookshop [distributor], c1982. — 44p ; 21cm. — (A von Hallett book)
ISBN 0-900055-02-2 (pbk) : £1.00 B82-22187

Marsden, Jeanne. Jewels of thought / Jeanne Marsden. — Ilfracombe : Stockwell, 1981. — 19p ; 15cm
ISBN 0-7223-1518-x (pbk) : £0.55 B82-10402

Mason, Gillian. The collected works of Gillian Mason. — London : Regency Press, 1981. — 32p ; 19cm
Unpriced (pbk) B82-10154

Mason, Gordon. Eye to eye / Gordon Mason. — Lincoln : Lincolnshire and Humberside Arts, 1980. — 38p : 1port ; 21cm. — (Paperback poets, ISSN 0140-8550 ; 10)
ISBN 0-906465-04-4 (pbk) : Unpriced B82-13631

Maxton, Hugh. Jubilee for renegades. — Portlaoise : Dolmen Press, July 1982. — [80]p
ISBN 0-85105-392-0 (pbk) : £3.50 : CIP entry B82-21109

821′.914 — Poetry in English, *1945-* **—** *Texts continuation*

Meade, Gordon. Snowballs in hell / by Gordon Meade. — Elie (11A Bank St., Elie, Fife) : G. Meade, [1981]. — 32p ; 18cm
Unpriced (pbk) B82-03500

Mellanby, John. The statues tour of Cambridge / poem John Mellanby ; illustrations David Urwin. — Cambridge : Cambridge Guide Service, 1982. — 8p : ill ; 18cm
ISBN 0-907736-06-8 (unbound) : Unpriced B82-35472

Melsom, M. E.. What′s in a look? / [by M.E. Melsom]. — [Towcester] ([The Chantry, Grafton Regis, Towcester, Northants.]) : M.E. Melsom, c1981. — 26p,[4]p of plates : ill ; 21cm
Unpriced (pbk) B82-10366

Meredith, Lucy. The birds′ wedding : a German folk song / adapted and translated by Lucy Meredith ; pictures by Masako Matsumura. — London : Faber, 1982. — [24]p : col.ill,music ; 29cm
ISBN 0-571-11896-8 : £4.25 : CIP rev. B82-04596

Middleton, Christina Forbes. The dance in the village and other poems. — Aberdeen : Aberdeen University Press, Sept.1981. — [88]p
ISBN 0-08-028438-8 (pbk) : £4.50 : CIP entry B81-21640

Millband, Doug. The mishaps of Millicent Mary / by Doug Millband ; illustrated by Louise Voce. — Leeds : Pepper, 1981. — 32p : ill (some col.) ; 24cm
ISBN 0-560-74526-5 : £3.75 B82-03668

Miller, Elizabeth, *19---*. Echoes of youth / by Elizabeth Miller. — London : Regency Press, c1982. — 31p ; 19cm
ISBN 0-7212-0632-8 (pbk) : Unpriced B82-40704

Millican, John. Rivers in the desert / by John Millican ; drawings by Clarke Hutton. — Esher : Penmiel, 1982. — 31p : ill ; 28cm
Limited ed. of 60 copies
ISBN 0-905542-05-3 : £35.00 B82-41009

Milligan, Spike. The 101 best and only limericks of Spike Milligan / illustrations by Desmond Milligan. — Walton-on-Thames : Hobbs, 1982. — [56]p : ill ; 22cm
ISBN 0-7181-2077-9 : £4.95 B82-18281

Milligan, Spike. If only I were bald / Spike Milligan ; with drawings by Rigby Graham. — Leicester : Savage, 1981. — [16]p : ill ; 20cm
Limited ed. of 100 copies
ISBN 0-901870-57-9 (pbk) : £6.00 B82-02547

Milne, Ewart. The folded leaf. — Isle of Skye : Aquila, Dec.1982. — [60]p
ISBN 0-7275-0248-4 (cased) : £4.95 : CIP entry
ISBN 0-7275-0249-2 (pbk) : £2.95 B82-31301

Mitchell, Adrian. For beauty Douglas / Adrian Mitchell′s collected poems, 1953-79 with pictures by Ralph Steadman. — London : Allison & Busby, 1982. — 263p : ill ; 21cm
ISBN 0-85031-399-6 (cased) : £8.95
ISBN 0-85031-400-3 (pbk) : Unpriced
ISBN 0-85031-468-2 (Limited ed.) : Unpriced B82-27081

Montague, John. Selected poems / John Montague. — Oxford : Oxford University Press, 1982. — 189p : ill ; 23cm
ISBN 0-19-211950-8 (pbk) : £5.95 B82-26945

Moor Jack. Poems o′ No′th Yorkshire / by 'Moor Jack'. — Whitby : Alan Skidmore, 1982. — 36p ; 20cm
ISBN 0-9508006-0-0 (pbk) : Unpriced B82-23957

Morgan, Edwin. Poems of thirty years / Edwin Morgan. — Manchester : Carcanet, 1982. — xiii,442p ; 23cm
ISBN 0-85635-365-5 : Unpriced : CIP rev. B81-30435

Morgan, Pete. One Greek alphabet : a poem sequence / by Pete Morgan ; illustrated by Hella Basu. — Sunderland : Ceolfrith, 1980. — 64p : ill(some col.),2ports ; 21cm
ISBN 0-904461-59-9 (pbk) : £3.60
ISBN 0-904461-60-2 (signed ed.) B82-39168

Morpurgo, Michael. Miss Wirtles revenge / by Michael Morpurgo ; illustrated by Graham Clarke. — Kingswood : Kaye & Ward, 1981. — [32]p : col.ill ; 35cm
ISBN 0-7182-3980-6 : £5.00 B82-06154

Morrice, Kenneth. For all I know. — Aberdeen : Aberdeen University Press, July 1981. — [72]p
ISBN 0-08-025756-9 (pbk) : £3.50 : CIP entry B81-13822

Morrison, Barbara, *1918-*. Forty-one : poems / by Barbara Morrison. — Braunton : Merlin Books, 1982. — 48p ; 21cm
ISBN 0-86303-017-3 (pbk) : £2.00 B82-33511

Mortished, Stuart. Where the puku came / Stuart Mortished. — Ilfracombe : Stockwell, 1981. — 16p ; 15cm
ISBN 0-7223-1524-4 (pbk) : £0.55 B82-05501

Motion, Andrew. Independence / Andrew Motion. — Edinburgh : Salamander Press, 1981. — 28p ; 22cm
ISBN 0-907540-05-8 (cased) : £5.00
ISBN 0-907540-06-6 (pbk) : Unpriced B82-15435

Motion, Andrew. The pleasure steamers / Andrew Motion. — Manchester : Carcanet, c1978 (1979 [printing]). — 58p ; 20cm
ISBN 0-85635-247-0 (pbk) : £3.25 B82-40472

Moules, Sue. Patterns / Sue Moules. — [Lampeter] : Outcrop Publications, c1982. — 31p ; 21cm
Cover title
ISBN 0-907600-06-9 (pbk) : £0.75 B82-22649

Muncaster, Peggy. Woodland tales / Peggy Muncaster ; illustrated by Ann Rees. — Braunton : Merlin, 1981. — 16p : ill ; 20cm
ISBN 0-86303-007-6 (pbk) : £0.50 B82-17382

Murray, Paul. Rites and meditations / Paul Murray. — Portlaoise : Dolmen Press, 1982. — 55p ; 22cm. — (Poetry Ireland choice)
ISBN 0-85105-393-9 (pbk) : £3.00 : CIP rev.
ISBN 0-85105-402-1 (special ed) B82-21110

Mutaleb, Samia Abdul. Arabian songs / Samia Abdul Mutaleb. — London : Ogharit, 1980. — [72]p : ill ; 20cm
Ill on inside cover
Unpriced (pbk) B82-33271

Naphray, A. R.. Goodbye / [A.R. Naphray] ; [1975 photographs by J. Rock Caile, 1976 and 1977 photographs by John Herman]. — [Wednesbury] ([2 Engine La., Wednesbury, West Midlands]) : [Bavie], [1977]. — 5v. : ill,ports ; 30cm
Cover title
Unpriced (pbk)
Primary classification 784.5′0092′4 B82-21277

Naphray, A. R.. Pyromania / [A.R. Naphray]. — Wednesbury (2 Engine La., Wednesbury, West Midlands) : Bavie, 1976, c1975. — 5v. : ill,ports ; 30cm
Unpriced (pbk)
Primary classification 784.5′0092′4 B82-21276

Neish, John. So much alone / by John Neish. — Walton-on-Thames : Outposts, 1981. — 24p ; 21cm
£0.90 (pbk) B82-08738

Nesbitt, Bill. The only place for me. — Dundonald : Blackstaff Press, May 1982. — [64]p
ISBN 0-85640-268-0 (pbk) : £2.95 : CIP entry B82-11788

Noiprox, Max. Around the corner : and other poems / by Max Noiprox. — Colchester (31 Sheepen Rd., Colchester) : Stylus, [1982?]. — [20]p ; 21cm
Unpriced (pbk) B82-38612

Noiprox, Max. Carnival & other poems / Max Noiprox. — Colchester (31 Sheepen Rd., Colchester) : Stylus, c1981. — 18p ; 21cm
Unpriced B82-25979

Noiprox, Max. The magic arrow : and other poems / Max Noiprox. — Colchester (31 Sheepen Place, Colchester) : Stylus, 1980. — 7p ; 22cm
Unpriced (pbk) B82-24523

Noiprox, Max. Maxims / by Max Noiprox. — Corby : Excello & Bollard, 1977. — [24]p ; 15cm. — (An Excello & Bollard minibook)
ISBN 0-904339-60-2 (pbk) : Unpriced B82-29678

Noiprox, Max. Poems / Max Noiprox. — [Colchester] ([31 Sheepen Rd., Colchester, Essex]) : Stylus, [1981?]. — [12]p ; 21cm
Unpriced (pbk) B82-25574

Noiprox, Max. Selected poems / by Max Noiprox. — Colchester (31 Sheepen Rd, Colchester) : Stylus, c1982. — 12p ; 21cm
Cover title
Unpriced (pbk) B82-24524

Noiprox, Max. Seven states of hell / Max Noiprox ; illustrated by W. Lewis. — Leek : Moorlands, 1982. — [20]p : ill ; 21cm
ISBN 0-86301-000-8 (pbk) : £0.75 B82-37871

Oakes, Philip. Selected poems / Philip Oakes. — London : Deutsch, 1982. — 64p ; 23cm
ISBN 0-233-97435-0 : £5.95 B82-37703

O′Donovan, E. C.. A certain slant of light : some poems / by E.C. O′Donovan. — Ilfracombe : Stockwell, 1982. — 94p ; 15cm
ISBN 0-7223-1550-3 : £2.90 B82-19026

O′Driscoll, Dennis. Kist. — Portlaoise : Dolmen, June 1982. — [64]p
ISBN 0-85105-396-3 (pbk) : £3.00 : CIP entry B82-12842

Osborne, Sue. Turnabout : a collection / Sue Osborne ; promoted by the Westminster Group of the National Schizophrenia Fellowship. — Bishops Stortford (111 Canons Close, Bishops Stortford, Herts. CM23 2BJ) : Kennedy Craft, c1982. — 19p : ill ; 22cm
£0.60 (pbk) B82-38084

O′Shea, Joseph. Dedications / Joseph O′Shea. — Bognor Regis : New Horizon, c1982. — 34p ; 21cm
ISBN 0-86116-424-5 : £3.95 B82-11724

Oxley, William. The notebook of Hephaestus and other poems / by William Oxley ; with a foreword by Leonard Clark. — Kinnesswood : The Lomond Press, c1981. — 46p ; 21cm
Limited ed. of 300 copies
ISBN 0-9506424-7-9 (pbk) : £2.70 B82-08875

Palmer, Eileen. Reflections on water / by Eileen Palmer. — Eastbourne : Downlander, 1982. — 24p ; 21cm
ISBN 0-906369-16-9 (pbk) : £1.45 B82-37145

Palmer, Graham. City Slice : Mk. 2 / Graham Palmer. — London (45 Allan Way, Acton, W3 3PW) : Stride, 1982. — [24]p : ill ; 30cm. — (A Stride publication ; step 3)
Unpriced (unbound) B82-23963

821'.914 — Poetry in English, *1945- — Texts continuation*

Parkinson, Olive. Down to earth and up to heaven / Olive Parkinson. — Ilfracombe : Stockwell, 1982. — 47p ; 18cm
ISBN 0-7223-1581-3 (pbk) : £1.75 B82-30971

Parsons, Les. Australia visited / by Les Parsons. — [Darlington] ([11 Kelso Walk, Branksome Estate, Darlington DL3 9UZ]) : [L. Parsons], [1981?]. — [16]leaves ; 30cm
Unpriced (unbound) B82-00765

Parvin, Betty. Prospect poems / Betty Parvin. — Nottingham : Em-press, c1981. — [24]leaves : ill ; 15cm
Cover title
ISBN 0-9506621-2-7 (pbk) : Unpriced B82-04216

Paterson, Alasdair. Alps. — London (12 Stevenage Rd, SW6 6ES) : Oasis Books, July 1981. — [16]p. — (O Books series ; no.1)
ISBN 0-903375-54-0 (pbk) : £0.50 : CIP entry B81-14393

Patten, Brian. Love poems / Brian Patten. — London : Allen & Unwin, 1981. — 96p ; 24cm
ISBN 0-04-821052-8 : Unpriced : CIP rev. B81-22556

Paul, Sebastian. This sloped land / Sebastian Paul. — St Albans : Piccolo, c1981. — 22p ; 17cm. — (First appearance ; 1)
Limited ed. of 100 copies
ISBN 0-906667-03-8 (pbk) : £1.00 B82-04666

Paulin, Tom. The book of juniper / new poems by Tom Paulin ; drawings by Noel Connor. — Newcastle upon Tyne : Bloodaxe, 1981. — [24]p : ill ; 18x25cm
ISBN 0-906427-16-9 (pbk) : £2.25
ISBN 0-906427-17-7 (signed) : Unpriced B82-39157

Pearce, Brian Louis. Leaves for Palinurus / by Brian Louis Pearce. — Eastbourne : Downlander, c1982. — 32p ; 21cm
ISBN 0-906369-18-5 (pbk) : £1.75 B82-37144

Pearce, Brian Louis. Off Cape Oil / Brian Louis Pearce. — London : Stride Publications, 1982. — [16]p ; 21cm
ISBN 0-9508053-2-7 (pbk) : £0.45 B82-33937

Peters, Anne. Rings of green. — Gerrards Cross : Colin Smythe, Mar.1982. — [80]p
ISBN 0-86140-124-7 (cased) : £7.50 : CIP entry
ISBN 0-86140-129-8 (pbk) : £3.00 B82-04731

Pickard, Bill. Loosing my grip : selected poems / by Bill Pickard. — Bristol : Redcliffe, 1982. — 74p ; 21cm
ISBN 0-905459-46-6 (pbk) : £1.75 B82-39204

Pickering, John, *1952-*. Imagine : children's recitations / by John Pickering. — Ilkeston : Moorley's Bible & Bookshop, [1982?]. — 40p ; 21cm
ISBN 0-86071-142-0 (pbk) : £0.55 B82-38086

Pilikian, Hovhanness I.. 1915, an Armemian symphony and other poems / by Hovhanness I. Pilikian ; illustrated by Maggie Cherchian ; with a preface by Christopher Lawrence. — London : Counter-Point, c1980. — 171p : ill ; 22cm
ISBN 0-906192-05-6 (cased) : £8.50 : CIP rev.
ISBN 0-906192-04-8 (pbk) : £5.50 B80-10751

Pitts, Sam. In retrospect / Sam Pitts. — Ilfracombe : Stockwell, 1981. — 72p ; 19cm
ISBN 0-7223-1515-5 : Unpriced B82-10364

Pollock, Samuel. The inner eye / Samuel Pollock. — Bognor Regis : New Horizon
Vol.1. — c1981. — 137p : ill ; 21cm
ISBN 0-86116-748-1 : £5.25 B82-04559

Potten, I. A.. The 'God bless' book of nursery rhymes / I.A. Potten. — Ilfracombe : Stockwell, 1981. — [16]p : ill ; 22cm
ISBN 0-7223-1490-6 (pbk) : £0.55 B82-05505

Pound, Omar S.. By order / [Omar Pound]. — Malvern ([61 Belmont Rd, Malvern, Worcs.]) : Migrant Press, 1979. — [4]p : ill ; 20cm
Unpriced (unbound) B82-05291

Powell, Neil, *1948-*. A season of calm weather / Neil Powell. — Manchester : Carcanet, 1982. — 58p ; 20cm
ISBN 0-85635-353-1 (pbk) : £3.25 : CIP rev. B82-19261

Pratt, Thomas Alan. A whisper of immortality / Thomas Alan Pratt. — Bognor Regis : New Horizon, c1982. — 55p : ill ; 21cm
ISBN 0-86116-711-2 : £3.95 B82-22380

Precious, Jocelynne. Selected short poems / P.J. Precious. — Harrogate (Hare Cottage, Kettlesing, Harrogate, Yorks) : Curlew Press
Vol.1. — c1981. — 22p ; 21cm
Unpriced (pbk) B82-16692

Price, Victor. Two parts water / Victor Price. — Liskeard : Harry Chambers/Peterloo Poets, 1980. — 63p ; 22cm
ISBN 0-905291-27-1 (pbk) : £3.00 B82-07383

Prime, Hilda. Poems by Primo : Norfolk life in verse / Hilda Prime ; illustrated by G. Szego. — Lessingham : Smee Summer Gallery, 1980. — 32p : ill ; 22cm
ISBN 0-9507363-0-9 (pbk) : £0.90 B82-16086

Prynne, J. H.. Poems / J.H. Prynne. — Edinburgh : Agneau 2, 1982. — 319p ; 22cm
ISBN 0-907954-00-6 (cased) : £12.00 : CIP rev.
ISBN 0-907954-01-4 (pbk) : £7.50 B82-07703

Pugh, Sheenagh. Earth studies and other voyages. — Bridgend (56 Parcan Ave., Bridgend, Mid-Glamorgan) : Poetry Wales Press, Dec.1982. — [48]p
ISBN 0-907476-16-3 (pbk) : £2.50 : CIP entry B82-36166

Raikes, Iris M.. Ride on / Iris M. Raikes ; illustrated by the author. — [Ilfracombe?] : Raikes, 1981. — 32p : ill ; 19cm
ISBN 0-7223-1506-6 (pbk) : Unpriced B82-05500

Ramdin, Manon. The collected poetry of Manon Ramdin. — London : Regency Press, c1981. — 32p ; 19cm
ISBN 0-7212-0652-2 (pbk) : Unpriced B82-37912

Ransford, Tessa. Light of the mind : Dulce Lumen, Triste Numen, Suave Lumen, Flecker : selected poems / by Tessa Ransford. — Edinburgh : Ramsey Head, 1980. — 56p ; 23cm
ISBN 0-902859-73-0 : £3.50 B82-24993

Ransom, Peter. Poems / by Peter Ransom. — [Ilfracombe] : [Stockwell], [1981]. — 8p ; 21cm
ISBN 0-7223-1517-1 (pbk) : Unpriced B82-05507

Rattenbury, Arnold. Dull weather dance / Arnold Rattenbury. — Liskeard : Harry Chambers/Peterloo Poets, 1981. — 62p ; 22cm
ISBN 0-905291-26-3 (pbk) : £3.00 B82-07381

Rawling, Tom. Ghosts at my back / Tom Rawling. — Oxford : Oxford University Press, 1982. — 55p ; 22cm
ISBN 0-19-211951-6 (pbk) : £3.95 : CIP rev. B82-10426

Reading, Peter. Tom o' Bedlam's beauties / Peter Reading. — London : Secker & Warburg, 1981. — 57p ; 23cm
ISBN 0-436-40850-3 : £4.50 : CIP rev. B81-30305

Redgrove, Peter. The apple-broadcast : and other new poems / Peter Redgrove. — London : Routledge & Kegan Paul, 1981. — ix,133p ; 22cm
ISBN 0-7100-0884-8 (pbk) : £3.00 B82-02946

Reid, Christopher. Pea soup. — Oxford : Oxford University Press, Sept.1982. — [64]p
ISBN 0-19-211952-4 (pbk) : £4.00 : CIP entry B82-19176

Rice, Helen Steiner. Loving promises / Helen Steiner Rice. — London : Hutchinson, 1978 (1981 [printing]). — 128p : ill ; 21cm
ISBN 0-09-145960-5 : £2.95

Rigley, Sandra. Working for Jesus : children's recitations / by Sandra Rigley. — Ilkeston : Moorley's Bible & Bookshop, [1982?]. — 22p ; 22cm
ISBN 0-86071-141-2 (pbk) : £0.40 B82-31213

Rippier, Jo. Seasons and remembrance : poems / by Jo Rippier. — Gerrards Cross : C. Smythe, 1981. — [21]p ; 20cm
Limited ed. of 100 numbered copies
ISBN 0-86140-113-1 (pbk) : Unpriced : CIP rev. B81-34959

Riviere, Michael V. B.. Late in the day / Michael V.B. Riviere. — Hitchin : Mandeville, 1982. — [12]p ; 22cm
Limited ed. of 250 copies, of which 35 have been signed by the author
ISBN 0-904533-56-5 (pbk) : Unpriced B82-32950

Roberts, Bettrys A.. The ballad of Pilsdon Pen : and other rhymes / by Bettrys A. Roberts. — [Crewkerne] ([West Haven, Church Path, Crewkerne, Somerset TA18 7HX]) : [B.A. Roberts], [1981]. — 41p : ill ; 22cm
Unpriced (pbk) B82-05996

Robins, Anthony. Living and loving / Anthony Robins. — Clondalkin (20, Lindisfarne Drive, Clondalkin, [Co. Dublin]) : A. Robins, c1981. — 33p ; 23cm
Unpriced (pbk) B82-10345

Robins, Anthony. Scattered feelings / Anthony Robins. — Clondalkin (20, Lindisfarne Drive, Clondalkin, Co. Dublin) : A. Robins, c1982. — 27p ; 23cm
£1.50 (pbk) B82-32945

Robinson, Derry. A poem: 'Narrative and list' / (composed from the selected, edited and refined collection of the verse of Derry Robinson). — [Great Britain?] : Alan J. Summers (O.M. Publications), c1977. — 7p ; 22cm
Limited ed. of 50 copies
Unpriced (pbk) B82-23717

Robinson, Peter, *1953 Feb. 18-*. Overdrawn account / Peter Robinson. — London : Many Press, 1980. — 47p ; 21cm
ISBN 0-9504916-9-1 (pbk) : £1.80 : CIP rev. B80-27487

Roche, Paul. New tales from Aesop / by Paul Roche ; illustrations by Pandora Smith. — Notre Dame : University of Notre Dame Press ; London : Honeyglen, 1982. — 103p : ill ; 24cm
ISBN 0-268-00597-4 : Unpriced B82-35883

Rootham, Jasper. Stand fixed in steadfast gaze : XIII poems at seventy / by Jasper Rootham. — Kinnesswood : The Lomond Press, 1981. — 18p ; 21cm
Limited ed. of 225 copies
ISBN 0-9506424-8-7 (pbk) : Unpriced B82-08877

Rose, Emma. Being glass / Emma Rose. — Berkhamsted : Priapus Poets, 1982. — [12]p ; 15cm
Limited ed. of 120 copies of which 30 are signed and numbered by the author
Unpriced (pbk) B82-22728

821′.914 — Poetry in English, ***1945-*** **—** ***Texts continuation***

Rosen, Michael. Wouldn′t you like to know / words by Michael Rosen ; pictures by Quentin Blake. — [New] ed., with new poems. — Harmondsworth : Puffin, 1981. — 95p : ill ; 20cm
Previous ed.: London : Deutsch, 1977
ISBN 0-14-031415-6 (pbk) : £0.90 B82-05956

Ross, M. (Margaret). Just fancy : poems / by M. Ross. — Liverpool (30 Fieldway, Liverpool 15) : Old Swan Writer′s Workshop, [1982?]. — 20leaves ; 30cm
Cover title
Unpriced (pbk) B82-39221

Russell, R. A.. The leaves of life / by R.A. Russell. — London : Regency Press, c1981. — 32p ; 19cm
ISBN 0-7212-0681-6 (pbk) : Unpriced B82-10411

Ryan, David Stuart. Love poems from love worlds. — Revised ed. — London (48A Astonville St., SW18 5AL) : Kozmik Press Centre, Sept.1982. — [100]p
Previous ed.: 1979
ISBN 0-905116-09-7 (pbk) : £7.75 : CIP entry B82-21998

Salisbury, Eric. Astralaqua / [Eric Salisbury]. — Crosby ([51 York Ave., Great Crosby, Liverpool L23 5RN]) : Cracked Bell, 1981. — [18]p : col.ill ; 15cm
Limited ed. of 15 numbered copies
Unpriced (pbk) B82-26035

Salisbury, Eric. Braving the elements / [Eric Salisbury]. — [Great Crosby] ([51 York Ave., Great Crosby, Liverpool L23 5RN]) : Cracked Bell, 1977. — [14]p : 1ill ; 14cm
Unpriced B82-26041

Sampson, W. J.. Image of illusion / W.J. Sampson. — Cardiff : W.J. Sampson, 1980. — 28p ; 15cm
ISBN 0-7223-1385-3 (pbk) : Unpriced B82-30966

Saunders, James H.. Poetry for a changing world and changing moods / James H. Saunders. — Hythe (21 Fisher Close, Hythe, Kent CT21 6AB) : New Creation Enterprises [Vol.1]. — [198-?]. — [75]p : ill ; 21cm
£1.95 (pbk) B82-36891

Saunders, John Whiteside. Clown in the garden / by J.W. Saunders. — Sutton Coldfield (Coles La., Sutton Coldfield, W. Midlands) : MEPS, c1982. — 104p : 1port ; 21cm
Unpriced (pbk) B82-35731

Scammell, William. A second life / William Scammell. — Liskeard : Harry Chambers/Peterloo Poets, 1982. — 60p ; 22cm
ISBN 0-905291-38-7 (pbk) : £3.00 B82-33892

Scannell, Vernon. Winterlude : poems / by Vernon Scannell. — London : Robson, 1982. — 53p ; 22cm
ISBN 0-86051-160-x (cased) : Unpriced : CIP rev.
ISBN 0-86051-161-8 (pbk) : £3.95 B82-06258

Scheurer, Ann. ″Smile — Jesus loves you″ : and other inspirational verses / by Ann Scheurer. — London : Regency Press, c1982. — 32p ; 19cm
ISBN 0-7212-0618-2 (pbk) : Unpriced B82-30426

Scott, Prudence. The fruit bitten / by Prudence Scott. — Walton-on-Thames ([72 Burwood Rd., Walton-on-Thames, Surrey KT12 4AL]) : Outposts, 1982. — 24p ; 21cm
£0.90 (pbk) B82-22349

Scovell, E. J.. The space between / E.J. Scovell. — London : Secker & Warburg, 1982. — 70p ; 23cm
ISBN 0-436-44446-1 : £4.95 : CIP rev. B82-09724

Selerie, Gavin. Hymenaei / Gavin Selerie. — London : Binnacle, c1981. — 16p : ill ; 30cm
Cover title. — Limited ed. of 150 copies
Unpriced (pbk) B82-03968

Sells, Diane E.. Tree of my life / Diane E. Sells. — Ilfracombe : Stockwell, 1980. — 24p ; 15cm
ISBN 0-7223-1407-8 (pbk) : £0.53 B82-13367

Sharpe, Philip. Dog days / Philip Sharpe. — Malvern (61 Belmont Rd, Malvern, Worcs.) : Migrant Press, 1979. — 36p ; 21cm
Unpriced (pbk) B82-05294

Shelly, Elizabeth. A joyful memory : poems / by Elizabeth Shelly. — Ashburton (Ashburton, Devon) : Cock Robin, c1981. — 29p ; 21cm
Limited ed. of 100 numbered copies
Unpriced (pbk) B82-00592

Siddons, Suzy. Good friends : verses / by Suzy Siddons. — [London] : Dean, c1982. — [28]p : col.ill ; 20cm. — (Miss Petticoat)
Ill on lining papers
ISBN 0-603-00326-5 : Unpriced B82-32479

Siddons, Suzy. Happy times : verses / by Suzy Siddons. — [London] : Dean, c1982. — [28]p : col.ill ; 20cm. — (Miss Petticoat)
Ill on lining papers
ISBN 0-603-00325-7 : Unpriced B82-32482

Siddons, Suzy. Let′s play : verses / by Suzy Siddons. — [London] : Dean, c1982. — [28]p : col.ill ; 20cm. — (Miss Petticoat)
Ill on lining papers
ISBN 0-603-00324-9 : Unpriced B82-32481

Siddons, Suzy. Time for play : verses / by Suzy Siddons. — [London] : Dean, c1982. — [28]p : col.ill ; 20cm. — (Miss Petticoat)
Ill on lining papers
ISBN 0-603-00323-0 : Unpriced B82-32480

Silkin, Jon. Flowers poems / Jon Silkin. — 2nd ed. — Newcastle upon Tyne : Northern House, 1978. — 20p ; 21cm. — (Northern House poets ; 27)
Previous ed.: 1964
ISBN 0-900570-25-3 (pbk) : £0.65
ISBN 0-900570-26-1 (signed ed.) : Unpriced B82-16085

Sills-Docherty, Jonathan. Ballads of fantasy and reality / by Jonathan Sills-Docherty. — Manchester (43 Cornbrook Park Rd., Old Trafford, Manchester M15 4EH) : J. Sills-Docherty, c1982. — 40p ; 30cm
Unpriced (pbk) B82-27987

Simms, Colin. A celebration of the stones in a water-course / Colin Simms. — Newcastle upon Tyne : Galloping Dog Press, 1981. — 28leaves ; 26cm
Limited ed. of 300 copies of which 10 are numbered and signed by the author
ISBN 0-904837-43-2 (pbk) : £1.50
ISBN 0-904837-44-0 (signed ed.) : £4.00 B82-07340

Simms, Colin. Time over Tyne : poems / by Colin Simms ; drawings by Steve Herne. — London : Many Press, c1981. — [12]p : ill ; 19cm
Limited ed. of 200 copies
ISBN 0-907326-01-3 (pbk) : Unpriced B82-00593

Simpson, John G.. Poems — / by John G. Simpson. — [Ilkeston] ([366 Nottingham Rd., Ilkeston, Derbyshire DE7 5BN]) : [J.G. Simpson], [1982?]. — 12p ; 21cm
£0.60 (pbk) B82-14898

Simpson, John G.. The unveiling : a poem / by John G. Simpson. — [Ilkeston] ([366 Nottingham Rd., Ilkeston, Derbyshire, DE7 5BN]) : [J.G. Simpson], [1982]. — 19p ; 21cm
Cover title
£0.50 (pbk) B82-30291

Simpson, Matt. Making arrangements / Matt Simpson. — Newcastle upon Tyne : Bloodaxe, 1982. — 55p ; 22cm
ISBN 0-906427-40-1 (pbk) : £2.25 B82-39162

Sirrah, Paul. Dreams of Icarus : (Falling) / Paul Sirrah. — Torpoint : Kawabata, 1982. — [7]p : ill ; 22cm
ISBN 0-906110-30-0 (pbk) : £0.50 B82-19138

Sisson, C. H.. Selected poems / C.H. Sisson. — Manchester : Carcanet, c1981. — 104p ; 20cm
ISBN 0-85635-381-7 (pbk) : Unpriced : CIP rev. B81-30436

Slater, Maureen P.. Before the joy / Maureen P. Slater. — Partington (Moss Lane, Partington, Ches.) : Slater, 1981. — 48p ; 22cm
ISBN 0-7223-1522-8 (pbk) : Unpriced B82-05509

Smith, John, ***1924-***. A landscape of my own : selected poems 1948-1982 / John Smith. — London : Robson, 1982. — 112p ; 23cm
ISBN 0-86051-163-4 : £6.50 : CIP rev. B82-00342

Smith, Ken, ***1938-***. Burned books / Ken Smith. — Newcastle upon Tyne : Bloodaxe, 1981. — 53p ; 22cm
ISBN 0-906427-23-1 (pbk) : £3.00
ISBN 0-906427-24-x (Signed ed.) : Unpriced B82-39161

Smythe, Joe. The peoples road : poems / by Joe Smythe ; with illustrations by Derek Jones. — London (Unity House, Euston Rd., NW1 2BL) : National Union of Railwaymen, 1980. — 64p : ill,ports ; 19cm
′Specially commissioned ... for the Great Railway Exposition, Manchester, 1980′. — Text on inside covers
£0.95 (pbk) B82-25470

Snow, Myke. Conversations on a Friday evening. — Tisbury : M. Snow, 1981. — [24]p : ill ; 21cm
Author: Myke Snow. — Illustrator: Marion Johnson. — Limited ed. of 250 copies
ISBN 0-907470-01-7 (pbk) : Unpriced B82-13688

Splitt, Thomas W.. Harbour of delight / Thomas W. Splitt. — Ilfracombe : Stockwell, 1982. — 56p : ill ; 18cm
ISBN 0-7223-1586-4 (pbk) : £1.00 B82-30968

Stacey, Robb. Don′t you know who I am : (ardent Stacey — 1st) / by Robb Stacey. — Telford (11 Haughmond Ct., Severn Drive, Telford, Shropshire TF1 3JY) : Artzlure, [198-?]. — [12]p ; 21cm
Cover title
ISBN 0-9506964-0-4 (pbk) : £0.35 B82-35885

Starr, Frank. Blades of grass / by Frank Starr ; illustrated by Geoff Evans. — Crawley : Wren, [1982]. — 56p : ill ; 21cm
ISBN 0-907820-08-5 (pbk) : £0.60 B82-38601

Starr, Frank. For all seasons / by Frank Starr ; illustrated by Geoff Evans. — Crawley : Wren, [1982]. — 56p : ill ; 21cm
ISBN 0-907820-07-7 (pbk) : £0.60 B82-36502

Stead, Kathleen. Poems / Kathleen Stead. — Bognor Regis : New Horizon, c1982. — 61p ; 21cm
ISBN 0-86116-674-4 : £3.95 B82-33259

Stevens, E.. The greatest master / E. Stevens. — Telford (111 Wrekin Drive, Donnington, Telford, Salop) : N. Stevens, c1980. — [20]p ; 14cm
Limited ed. of 200 hand set copies
Unpriced (pbk) B82-16598

Stevenson, Anne. Minute by glass minute. — Oxford : Oxford University Press, Sept.1982. — [64]p
ISBN 0-19-211947-8 (pbk) : £4.00 : CIP entry B82-19175

821'.914 — Poetry in English, *1945-* — *Texts continuation*

Studd, Stephen. Fleeting years / Stephen Studd. — Braunton : Merlin, 1981. — 32p ; 21cm
ISBN 0-86303-002-5 (pbk) : £1.50 B82-26577

Sutton, David, *1944-*. Absences and celebrations / by David Sutton. — London : Chatto and Windus, 1982. — 48p ; 22cm. — (The Phoenix living poets)
ISBN 0-7011-2624-8 (pbk) : £3.95 : CIP rev. B82-01198

Swan, Guida. Withymead : a sequence of poems / by Guida Swan. — Oxford : Poetry Titles, [1982]. — [16]p ; 21cm
Limited ed. of 150 copies
ISBN 0-907828-00-0 (pbk) : Unpriced B82-28794

Swinton, Gabrielle. Unexpected wonder : poems / by Gabrielle Swinton. — Nottingham : Em-Press, c1982. — [16]leaves : ill ; 15x22cm
ISBN 0-9506621-4-3 (pbk) : Unpriced B82-38619

Sykala, U.. Illusions / U. Sykala. — Irchester (1 Austin Close, Irchester, Northants.) : Castle Books, 1981. — 24p ; 21cm
£0.50 (pbk) B82-06157

Symons, Eric Edward. Through the years / Eric Edward Symons. — Ilfracombe : Stockwell, 1981. — 47p ; 19cm
ISBN 0-7223-1543-0 (pbk) : £1.95 B82-10406

Szirtes, George. November and May / George Szirtes. — London : Secker & Warburg, 1981. — 64p ; 23cm
ISBN 0-436-50998-9 : £4.50 : CIP rev. B81-30308

Tapner, Vic. The Icarus leaf / by Vic Tapner. — Walton-on-Thames : Outposts, 1982. — 36p ; 21cm
£1.50 (pbk) B82-35447

Tarn, Nathaniel. The land songs. — Plymouth : Blue Guitar Books ; London (12 Stevenage Rd., SW6 6ES) : Independent Press Distribution [distributor], Sept.1981. — [16]p
ISBN 0-907562-01-9 (pbk) : £0.80 : CIP entry B81-20499

Taylor, Brian D.. Strong men cast shadows too / by Brian D. Taylor. — Walton-on-Thames : Outposts, 1982. — 12p ; 21cm
£0.65 (pbk) B82-35446

Taylor, Grace Elliott. Spring has come to town : and other verses / by Grace Elliott Taylor ; illustrations by the author and by J.A. Sharkey. — Chichester (Little Orchard, Ichenor Green, Chichester, W. Sussex PO20 7DA) : [s.n.], 1982. — 16p : ill ; 21cm
Cover title. — Ill on lining papers
£0.85 (pbk) B82-35886

Taylor, I. P.. The hollow places / I.P. Taylor. — Liskeard : Harry Chambers/Peterloo Poets, 1980. — 45p ; 22cm
ISBN 0-905291-23-9 (pbk) : £3.00 B82-07384

Taylor, John. Three familiar birds / by John Taylor. — Chichester (88, Charles Ave., Chichester PO19 4HF) : The Poplar Press, c1982. — 28p : 1port ; 21cm
Port. and text on inside covers
ISBN 0-907429-01-7 (pbk) : £1.00 B82-32647

Taylor, Kathleen F.. Poems / Kathleen F. Taylor. — Ilfracombe : Stockwell, 1982. — 23p ; 15cm
ISBN 0-7223-1569-4 (pbk) : £0.70 B82-30974

Taylor, Lucy Sanderson. The summer sheiling : (and other poems) / Lucy Sanderson Taylor & Dorothy M. Nash. — Bognor Regis : New Horizon, c1982. — 86p ; 20cm
ISBN 0-86116-671-x : £3.95 B82-22159

Taylor, N.. A different drum / N. Taylor. — London : Stride, 1982. — 19p ; 21cm. — (A Stride publication ; step 6)
ISBN 0-9508053-3-5 (pbk) : Unpriced B82-39169

Ten little dogs / illustrated by Janet & Anne Grahame Johnstone. — [Cambridge] : Brimax, 1979. — [20]p : col.ill ; 21x23cm
Cover title
ISBN 0-86112-044-2 : Unpriced B82-07167

Thomas, R. S.. Between here and now / R.S. Thomas. — London : Macmillan, 1981. — 110p,leaf of plate : ill(1col.),ports ; 22cm
ISBN 0-333-32186-3 (cased) : £6.95
ISBN 0-333-32629-6 (pbk) : Unpriced B82-05582

Thomson, Charles, *1953-*. Argh! : 6 poems by / Charles Thomson. — Maidstone (50 Buckland Rd, Maidstone, Kent, ME16 0SH) : Cheapo Publications, [1980?]. — [6]leaves ; 30cm
Published in illustrated and ordinary versions
£0.10 (£0.15 illustrated version) (unbound) B82-39233

Tivey, Rosemary J.. Thank-you for another day : poems and reflections with scriptural verse / by Rosemary J. Tivey. — Wimborne ([60 Lake Road, Verwood, Wimborne, Dorset, BH21 6BX]) : R.J. Tivey, c1981. — 42p ; 21cm
Unpriced (pbk) B82-10409

Towle, John. Take my hand : devotional poetry / John Towle. — Ilkeston : Moorley's Bible & Bookshop, [1982?]. — 25p ; 21cm
ISBN 0-86071-144-7 (pbk) : £0.50 B82-38085

Trinder, Tubby. Feelings / by Tubby Trinder ; illustrated by Geoff Evans. — Crawley : Wren, c1982. — 36p : ill ; 21cm
ISBN 0-907820-03-4 (pbk) : £0.50 B82-36499

Turnbull, Gael. Rain in Wales / Gael Turnbull. — Edinburgh (14 Greenhill Place, Edinburgh 10) : Published for SATIS by Malcolm Rutherford, 1981. — 14p ; 21cm
Limited ed. of 300 numbered copies
Unpriced (pbk) B82-27327

Turnbull, Gael. The small change / Gael Turnbull. — Malvern ([61 Belmont Rd, Malvern, Worcs.]) : Migrant Press, 1980. — [16]p ; 21cm
Limited ed. of 250 copies
Unpriced (pbk) B82-05292

Turner, Joyce. Yorkshire mixtures / by Joyce Turner. — London : Regency, c1982. — 27p ; 19cm
ISBN 0-7212-0627-1 (pbk) : Unpriced B82-36496

Turner, Steve. Up to date. — London : Hodder & Stoughton, Feb.1983. — [128]p
ISBN 0-340-28712-8 (pbk) : £1.75 : CIP entry B82-38040

Upton, Lawrence. Big book : stage one / Lawrence Upton. — London : Good Elf, [1976]. — [20]p : ill ; 30cm
ISBN 0-903710-93-5 (pbk) : £0.20 B82-26946

Vince, Michael. In the new district / Michael Vince. — Manchester : Carcanet New Press, 1982. — 63p ; 20cm
ISBN 0-85635-368-x (pbk) : Unpriced : CIP rev. B82-19264

Vince, Michael. Mountain, epic, & dream / Michael Vince ; illustrated by Jackie Siroto. — Frome (45, Milk St., Frome, Somerset) : Bran's Head, 1981. — 22p : ill ; 15cm. — (Hunting raven chapbooks ; 8)
Limited ed. of 325 copies of which 300 are for sale and the first 20 signed
£0.90 (pbk) B82-11370

Vio, Eric. Airy nothing / by Eric Vio. — Eastbourne : Downlander, 1982. — 32p ; 21cm
ISBN 0-906369-19-3 (pbk) : £2.25 B82-39219

Wadey, Ursula. Diversions ahead! / by Ursula Wadey. — Walton-on-Thames ([72 Burwood Rd., Walton-on-Thames, Surrey KT12 4AL]) : Outposts, 1982. — 36p ; 21cm
£1.35 (pbk) B82-22347

Wain, John. The twofold / John Wain. — Frome (45, Milk St., Frome, Somerset) : Bran's Head, 1981. — 20p ; 15cm
Limited ed. of 325 copies of which 300 are for sale and the first 20 signed
£0.90 (pbk) B82-11373

Wake, Lina. From near and far / Lina Wake. — [Blandford Forum] ([Horwood, 14 Bryanston St., Blandford Forum, Dorset DT11 7AZ]) : L.A.E. Wake, c1982. — 39p : ill ; 21cm
Cover title
£1.20 (pbk) B82-32717

Walker, Hugh Graham. "His glory never fades" / by Hugh Graham Walker. — Newark (Beauna Vista, Chapel La., Farnsfield, Newark, Notts. NG22 8JW) : [H.G. Walker], 1982. — [60]p ; 21cm
Unpriced (pbk) B82-19902

Walker, Hugh Graham. To the glory of God : poetical works / by Hugh Graham Walker. — Newark on Trent (Beauna Vista, Chapel La., Farnsfield, Newark on Trent, Notts.) : H.G. Walker, 1980. — [32]p ; 21cm
Unpriced (pbk) B82-39251

Walker, Hugh Graham. Where the robin sings : children's verses / by Hugh Graham Walker. — Newark on Trent (Buena Vista, Chapel Lane, Farnsfield, Newark on Trent) : H.G. Walker, 1981. — [28p ; 21cm
Cover title
£2.00 (pbk) B82-03071

Ward, Geoffrey. Comeuppance / by Geoffrey Ward ; illustrated by Ian Barraclough. — Liverpool : Délires, c1980. — [80]p : ill ; 21cm
Limited ed. of 1000 copies
ISBN 0-907268-01-3 (pbk) : Unpriced B82-15549

Ward, J. P.. Things / J.P. Ward ; with drawings by Eva Goddard. — Frome (45, Milk St., Frome, Somerset) : Bran's Head, 1981. — 24p : ill ; 15cm. — (Hunting raven chapbooks ; 10)
Limited ed. of 325 copies of which 300 are for sale and the first 20 signed
£0.90 (pbk) B82-11372

Ward, John, *1915-*. A late harvest / John Ward. — Liskeard : Harry Chambers/Peterloo Poets, 1982. — 62p ; 21cm
ISBN 0-905291-34-4 (pbk) : £3.00 B82-25977

Ward, Mary, *1926-*. Perception / Mary Ward. — Ilfracombe : Stockwell, 1981. — 14p ; 15cm
ISBN 0-7223-1537-6 (pbk) : £0.55 B82-05498

Ward, Paul. Serious times / poems Paul Ward ; drawings Kathie Layfield. — [Leicester] : New Broom, c1982. — [8]p : ill ; 21cm
Limited ed. of 100 numbered copies
ISBN 0-901870-59-5 (unbound) : £2.00 B82-15332

Warner, Francis. Spring harvest / Francis Warner. — Drayton, Somerset : Booth, 1981. — [12]p ; 20cm
Limited ed. of 110 copies
Unpriced (pbk) B82-15014

Watson, Catherine. Wat's on : humour and pathos, rhyme and verse. — [Edinburgh] ([17 Mentone Terrace, Edinburgh EH9 2DG]) : [Catherine Watson], [c1982]. — 58p ; 21cm
Author: Catherine Watson
£1.25 (pbk) B82-27771

Weaire, G. C.. Pinkety pig / G.C. Weaire ; illustrated by Bettina Newman and the author. — Braunton : Merlin, 1982. — 32p : ill ; 21cm
ISBN 0-86303-011-4 (pbk) : £1.00 B82-38087

821'.914 — Poetry in English, *1945-* **—** *Texts continuation*

Webb, C. N.. Lyrical lines / C.N. Webb. — Ilfracombe : Stockwell, 1981. — 16p ; 15cm
ISBN 0-7223-1534-1 (pbk) : £0.50 B82-05496

Welch, John, *1942-*. The storms/Lip service / [John Welch]. — London (15 Norcott Rd., N16 7BJ) : Many Press, [1980]. — [14]p ; 21cm
Unpriced (pbk) B82-16806

West, Colin. Not to be taken seriously / poems and pictures : by Colin West. — London : Hutchinson, 1982. — 96p : ill ; 23cm
ISBN 0-09-147180-x : £3.95 : CIP rev.
B82-01146

Weston, Elaine. Vers libre for dolphin / by Elaine Weston. — [Belfast] ([40 Eglantine Ave., Belfast BT9 6DX]) : Ulster Cancer Foundation, [1981]. — 29p ; 20cm
Cover title
£0.75 (pbk) B82-08737

Whateley, Nell. Light and shade : a collection of poems / by Nell Whateley. — London : Regency Press rc 1981. — 32p ; 19cm
Unpriced (pbk) B82-10153

Wheatley, Jeffery. Prince Arthur / by Jeffery Wheatley. — Kingston upon Thames : Court Poetry, [c1981]. — 26p ; 21cm
ISBN 0-906010-28-4 (pbk) : £0.70 B82-13050

Wheatley, Mary. Moments with Mary : a collection of memories, thoughts and experiences / by Mary Wheatley. — [Ilkeston] : [Moorley's Bible], [1980]. — 31p ; 21cm
£0.75 (pbk) B82-16805

Wheeler, V. F.. The collected works of V.F. Wheeler. — London : Regency Press, c1981. — 32p ; 19cm
Unpriced (pbk) B82-10158

Whenary, Roy. Memories we cherish / poems by Roy Whenary. — Staines (1 Bell Weir Close, Wraysbury, Staines, Middx TW19 6HF) : R. Whenary, 1981. — [16]p : ill ; 21cm
£0.75 (pbk) B82-02304

Whittaker, Sue. The verdant tree / Sue Whittaker. — Shoreham-by-Sea : S. Whittaker, 1981. — 64p : ill ; 21cm
ISBN 0-85479-034-9 (pbk) : £1.95 B82-03070

Whitworth, John. Poor butterflies. — London : Secker & Warburg, Sept.1982. — [64]p
ISBN 0-436-57096-3 : £4.95 : CIP entry
B82-19680

Wignall, Colin. Torrents of rain / by Colin Wignall. — Lampeter : C.M. Wignall, [1981?]. — [20]p ; 21cm
Cover title
ISBN 0-9507876-0-4 (pbk) : £0.50 B82-06483

Wijesuriya, Crystal. Jungle prison / Crystal Wijesuriya ; [illustrations by Robert Jaecke]. — London : Regency Press, c1981. — 32p : 2ill ; 19cm
Unpriced (pbk) B82-10156

Wijngaard, Juan. In summer when I go to bed / Juan Wijngaard ; based on a poem by Thomas Hood. — London : Ernest Benn, 1981. — [28]p : col.ill ; 18cm. — (The Little library)
ISBN 0-510-00095-9 : £1.50 B82-00056

Wilkinson, John Lawton. Clinical notes / John Lawton Wilkinson. — Liverpool : Délires, c1980. — 98p ; 28cm
Limited ed. of 1000 copies
ISBN 0-907268-00-5 (pbk) : Unpriced
B82-15550

Williams, John Hartley. Hidden identities / by John Hartley Williams. — London : Chatto & Windus, 1982. — 63p ; 22cm. — (The Phoenix living poets series)
ISBN 0-7011-2623-x (pbk) : £3.95 : CIP rev.
B82-09461

Williams, Rachel M.. Home is where the heart is / Rachel M. Williams. — Ilfracombe : Stockwell, 1980. — 32p ; 15cm
ISBN 0-7223-1414-0 : £2.40 B82-13369

Williams, Terry, *1963-*. Open up and read my mind / Terry Williams. — Ilfracombe : Stockwell, 1982. — 29p ; 15cm
ISBN 0-7223-1532-5 (pbk) : £0.97 B82-05497

Wilmer, Clive. Devotions / Clive Wilmer. — Manchester : Carcanet New Press, 1982. — 63p ; 20cm
ISBN 0-85635-359-0 (pbk) : Unpriced : CIP rev. B82-19265

Wilson, John T. (John Thomas). Heron on the shore / by John T. Wilson. — Goudhurst : Weavers, 1982. — 28p : ill,2ports ; 21cm
ISBN 0-946017-00-x (pbk) : £0.95 B82-35876

Wise, Dorothy A.. Poems for everyone / Dorothy A. Wise ; illustrations by Wendy R. Duffin. — Ilfracombe : Stockwell, 1982. — 48p : ill ; 21cm
ISBN 0-7223-1614-3 (pbk) : £1.50 B82-36656

Wiseman, Christopher. The upper hand / Christopher Wiseman. — London : Enitharmon, 1981. — 52p ; 23cm
ISBN 0-905289-07-2 (cased) : £3.75
ISBN 0-905289-02-1 (pbk) : £2.40 B82-20251

Wolfe, William. Ten scarts on time / William Wolfe. — [Glasgow] : Craigpark, [1982?]. — [16]p ; 18x19cm
Text in Scots and English. — One poem by Douglas Young. — Limited ed. of 500 copies
Unpriced (pbk) B82-30443

Wren, Toby. Sanquhar — another day / Toby Wren ; illustrated by Geoff Evans. — Crawley : Wren, c1982. — 22p : ill ; 21cm
ISBN 0-907820-09-3 (pbk) : £0.35 B82-38602

Wren, Toby. Seasons and interludes / Toby Wren. — Crawley : Wren, c1982. — 38p : 1port ; 21cm
Limited ed. of 50 signed and numbered copies
ISBN 0-907820-04-2 (pbk) : £0.50 B82-36503

Wren, Toby. Silhouettes and shadows / by Toby Wren ; illustrated by Geoff Evans. — Crawley : Wren, c1981. — 56p : ill ; 21cm
ISBN 0-907820-01-8 (pbk) : £0.50 B82-36504

Wren, Toby. The story of Sam Sparrow / by Toby Wren ; with illustrations by Julie Brooks. — Crawley : Wren, c1981. — 27p : ill ; 21cm
ISBN 0-907820-00-x (pbk) : £0.30 B82-36505

Wright, Edmond Leo. The jester hennets / Edmond Leo Wright. — Liskeard : Harry Chambers/Peterloo Poets, 1981. — 63p ; 22cm
ISBN 0-905291-25-5 (pbk) : £3.00 B82-07379

Wright, Kit. Hot dog : and other poems / Kit Wright ; illustrated by Posy Simmonds. — Harmondsworth : Puffin, 1982, c1981. — 72p : ill ; 20cm. — (A Puffin book)
Originally published: Harmondsworth : Kestrel, 1981
ISBN 0-14-031336-2 (pbk) : £0.85 B82-29588

Wroe, Malcolm. Smoke secrets / by Malcolm Wroe. — Walton-on-Thames ([72 Burwood Rd., Walton-on-Thames, Surrey KT12 4AL]) : Outposts, 1982. — 16p ; 21cm
£0.70 (pbk) B82-08985

Wynne, Merle Clare. Variegated verse / Merle Clare Wynne. — Braunton : Merlin Books, 1982. — 32p ; 21cm
ISBN 0-86303-021-1 (pbk) : £0.80 B82-38083

Young, Grahaeme Barrasford. Fractures / Grahaeme Barrasford Young ; with drawings by Robin Grey. — Frome (45, Milk St., Frome, Somerset) : Bran's Head, 1981. — 21p : ill ; 15cm. — (Hunting raven chapbooks ; 9)
Limited ed. of 325 copies of which 300 are for sale and the first 20 signed
£0.90 (pbk) B82-11371

821'.914 — Poetry in English. Abse, Dannie — *Biographies*

Abse, Dannie. Ash on a young man's sleeve / Dannie Abse. — Harmondsworth : Penguin, 1982, c1954. — 167p ; 20cm. — (A King Penguin)
Originally published: London : Hutchinson, 1954
ISBN 0-14-005153-8 (pbk) : £2.25 B82-37459

821'.914 — Poetry in English. Gunn, Thom — *Biographies*

Gunn, Thom. The occasions of poetry : essays in criticism and autobiography / by Thom Gunn ; edited and with an introduction by Clive Wilmer. — London : Faber, 1982. — 188p ; 23cm
ISBN 0-571-11733-3 : £6.95 : CIP rev.
Primary classification 821'.009 B81-38308

821'.914 — Poetry in English. Heaney, Seamus — *Critical studies*

The **Art** of Seamus Heaney. — Bridgend (56 Parcau Ave., Bridgend, Mid Glamorgan) : Poetry Wales Press, Oct.1982. — [140]p
ISBN 0-907476-09-0 : £8.95 : CIP entry
B82-29158

Morrison, Blake. Seamus Heaney / Blake Morrison. — London : Methuen, 1982. — 95p ; 20cm. — (Contemporary writers)
Bibliography: p92-95
ISBN 0-416-31900-9 (pbk) : Unpriced : CIP rev. B82-06755

821'.914 — Poetry in English. Hughes, Ted — *Critical studies*

The **Achievement** of Ted Hughes. — Manchester : Manchester University Press, Dec.1982. — [366]p
ISBN 0-7190-0889-1 : £25.00 : CIP entry
B82-30217

821'.914 — Poetry in English. Jackson, Gordon. Five Sisters York — *Critical studies*

Myers, Peter. Inarticulate fluency : an introduction to Five Sisters York / by Peter Myers. — Lincoln (1 Stonefield Ave., Lincoln) : Asgill, 1980. — 26p ; 21cm
£0.60 (pbk) B82-09649

821'.914 — Poetry in English. Larkin, Philip — *Critical studies*

Larkin at sixty / edited by Anthony Thwaite. — London : Faber, 1982. — 148p,[8]p of plates : ports ; 22cm
ISBN 0-571-11878-x : £7.95 : CIP rev.
B82-06857

Motion, Andrew. Philip Larkin. — London : Methuen, Oct.1982. — [96]p. — (Contemporary writers)
ISBN 0-416-32270-0 (pbk) : £1.95 : CIP entry
B82-24493

821'.914 — Poetry in English. Thomas, R. S.. Symbolism — *Critical studies*

Dyson, A. E.. Yeats, Eliot and R.S. Thomas : riding the echo / A.E. Dyson. — London : Macmillan, 1981. — x,339p ; 23cm
Bibliography: p327-329. — Includes index
ISBN 0-333-13027-8 : £15.00
Primary classification 821'.8'0915 B82-10829

821'.914'08 — Poetry in English, *1945-* **—** *Anthologies*

1980 anthology : Arvon Foundation Poetry Competition / edited and introduced by Ted Hughes and Seamus Heaney. — Todmorden : Kilnhurst, 1982. — 173p ; 24cm
ISBN 0-9508078-0-x (pbk) : Unpriced
B82-27261

The **Badger** poets. — Shaftesbury (30 Melbury Abbas, Shaftesbury, Dorset) : Badger Poets, c1981. — [36]p : ill(some col.) ; 30cm
Unpriced (unbound) B82-11669

821'.914'08 — Poetry in English, ***1945- — Anthologies*** *continuation*

Brown, Hamish M.. Eye to the hills : poems / Hamish Brown & James Macmillan. — Kinghorn : Pettycur, 1982. — 32p ; 21cm
ISBN 0-9508089-0-3 (pbk) : Unpriced B82-26580

Childish, Billy. The wild breed is here / Billy Childish & Sexton Ming. — [Chatham] ([181 Walderslade Rd., Chatham, Kent]) : Phyroid Press, 1982. — 9p ; 26cm
Unpriced (unbound) B82-17018

A **Christmas** anthology. — London : Regency Press, [1981]. — 90p : ill ; 21cm
'With irrelevant engravings from Old England — a museum of popular antiquities, published, c.1850'
ISBN 0-7212-0691-3 : £6.00 B82-10082

Codex bandito V. — Mereworth (3 Pleasant Villas, 189 Kent St., Mereworth, Maidstone, Kent ME18 5QN) : Outcrowd, [1982?]. — [20]p : ill ; 16cm
Unpriced (unbound) B82-17019

A **collage** of poetry. — [Padstow] : [Tabb House] in association with the Camel Art Society, 1982. — [14]p ; 22cm
Cover title
Unpriced (pbk) B82-22051

An **Easter** anthology : with irrelevant engravings from Old England — a museum of popular antiquities c.1850. — London : Regency, [1982?]. — 105p : ill ; 20cm
ISBN 0-7212-0623-9 : £6.00 B82-26961

A **Florilegium** for John Florio / [by Claire Andrews ... et al.]. — Oxford ([4, Benson Place, Oxford]) : Sycamore Press, 1981. — [16]p ; 21cm
Limited ed. of 240 copies
Unpriced (pbk) B82-03296

Folio eleven. — Helston (The Orchard, St Martin, Helston, Cornwall) : Bentley Rimers, [1980]?. — [38]p : ill ; 30cm
Unpriced (spiral) B82-39232

Freebairn, Roger. Thirty by three / by Roger Freebairn, Barry Trapnell, Paul Ward. — Walton-on-Thames : Outposts, 1982. — 28p ; 21cm
Limited ed. of 250 numbered copies
£1.10 (pbk) B82-10611

Gregory Awards anthology 1982. — Manchester : Carcanet Press, Oct.1982. — [96]p
ISBN 0-85635-437-6 (pbk) : £3.95 : CIP entry B82-24117

Harrison, Tony, *1937-*. Looking up / Tony Harrison, Philip Sharpe. — West Malvern ([61 Belmont Rd, Malvern, Worcs.]) : Migrant Press, 1979. — [4]p : 1ill,1facsim ; 21cm
£0.25 (unbound) B82-05295

Hinton, Brian. Poems from an island / Brian Hinton, Val Berry. — Freshwater : [Isle of Wight Poetry Society, 1981. — 32p : ill ; 21cm. — (Isle of Wight Poetry Society pamphlet ; no.1)
Limited ed. of 500 numbered copies
ISBN 0-906328-16-0 (pbk) : £0.90 B82-00601

In praise of Essex / edited by Eric Vanson. — Baldock : Egon, 1980. — 108p ; 16x21cm
ISBN 0-905858-14-x : Unpriced B82-36100

Is there anyone out there? : an anthology of poems by sufferers from schizophrenia / edited by Martha Robinson. — Eastbourne : Downlander, 1981. — 32p ; 21cm
Promoted by the Westminster Group of the National Schizophrenia Fellowship
ISBN 0-906369-11-8 (pbk) : £1.50 B82-13601

McCormick, Eileen. Essence truth and light : poems / by Eileen McCormick, Roger Pawley, Roy Whenary. — Staines ([1, Bell Weir Close, Wraysbury, Staines, Middx]) : R. Whenary, 1981. — [12]p ; 21cm
Cover title. — Text on inside covers
Unpriced (pbk) B82-10412

Mole, John. Christmas past : poems / John Mole, Peter Scupham ; illustrations Mary Norman. — Hitchin : Mandeville, 1981. — [15]p : ill ; 23cm
Limited ed. of 350 copies, of which 60 have been signed by the authors and artist
ISBN 0-904533-58-1 (pbk) : £0.50 B82-05439

New British poetry. — Bognor Regis : New Horizon
Vol.1. — c1982. — 183p ; 22cm
ISBN 0-86116-907-7 : £7.95 B82-30008

New wing / [Isabel Gillard, editor]. — [Stafford] ([c/o I. Gillard, St Lawrence Cottage, Sellman St., Snosall, Stafford]) : Stafford Poetry Group, 1980. — 36p ; 21cm
Unpriced (pbk) B82-16802

Non-hazardous product : poems / by Tarantula. — Stockport : Tarantula, 1981. — 72p ; 21cm
ISBN 0-9507269-0-7 (pbk) : £1.00 B82-00596

Not a bed of roses / [Basic Skills Unit] ; [illustrations by Emlyn Moment]. — Cambridge : The Unit, c1980. — 28p : ill ; 21cm
ISBN 0-86082-200-1 (pbk) : Unpriced B82-14721

Now this won't hurt! / an anthology of poetry by children of the Royal National Orthopaedic Hospital School. — Stanmore : Royal National Orthopaedic Hospital School, c1981. — [107]p : ill ; 20x21cm
ISBN 0-9507570-0-4 (pbk) : £1.50 B82-02906

Pensioners & poets / [edited and published by Keith Murray]. — [Great Britain] : Keith Murray, 1981. — [24]p : ill ; 21cm
Cover title. — Ill on inside covers
£0.25 (pbk) B82-31164

Pieces of eight : an anthology of Driftwood poets / selected by Brian Wake. — [Bootle] : Driftwood, [1981?]. — 75p ; 22cm. — (Driftwood poets series)
ISBN 0-904224-00-7 (pbk) : £0.60 B82-12672

Poems for Charles Causley / [edited by Michael Hanke] ; George Barker ... [et al.]. — London : Enitharmon, 1982. — 39p : ill ; 23cm
Limited ed. of 450 copies
ISBN 0-905289-48-x (cased) : £5.25
ISBN 0-905289-43-9 (pbk) : £3.60 B82-41007

Poems for Roy Fuller on his seventieth birthday. — Oxford (4 Benson Place, Oxford) : Sycamore Press, 1982. — [12]p ; 21cm
Unpriced (pbk) B82-18279

Poetry introduction. — London : Faber
5. — 1982. — 121p ; 21cm
ISBN 0-571-11914-x : £5.25 : CIP rev. B81-34667

Poetry now / edited by Brian Cox. — Manchester : Manchester University Press, [1982?]. — 22p ; 20cm. — (Critical quarterly poetry pamphlet)
Cover title
Unpriced (pbk) B82-28695

A **Rumoured** city : new poets from Hull / edited by Douglas Dunn ; with a foreword by Philip Larkin. — Newcastle upon Tyne : Bloodaxe, 1982. — 110p ; 22cm
ISBN 0-906427-41-x (pbk) : £3.50 B82-39158

Seventeen come Monday : an anthology / selected by Brian Louis Pearce and Hugh Epstein from the December 1981 Festival poetry competition. — Twickenham (Egerton Rd., Twickenham, Middx TW2 7SJ) : Richmond upon Thames College, 1982. — [31]p ; 21cm
£0.50 (pbk) B82-36556

A **Summer** anthology. — London : Regency Press, [1982?]. — 80p ; 21cm
ISBN 0-7212-0642-5 : £6.00 B82-38088

Summer poets : an anthology of contemporary verse. — London : Regency Press, [1981?]. — 149p : ill ; 23cm
ISBN 0-7212-0676-x : £4.50 B82-09366

Telling tales. — London : Murray, Sept.1982. — [96]p
ISBN 0-7195-3993-5 (pbk) : £1.75 : CIP entry B82-19830

Ward, Paul. The meeting of the ways / by Paul Ward, Barry Trapnell, Roger Freebairn. — Walton-on-Thames : Outposts, 1982. — 28p ; 21cm
£1.20 (pbk) B82-33262

Words break through / a collection of poems written by pupils of St. John's School for the Deaf and Partially Hearing, Boston Spa. — Burton Salmon ([Hall Farm, Burton Salmon, Leeds LS25 5JS]) : Old Hall, 1982. — 51p ; 15cm
Unpriced B82-30007

The **Younger** Irish poets / edited by Gerald Dawe. — Belfast : Blackstaff, c1982. — xi,176p ; 21cm
Includes index
ISBN 0-85640-261-3 (pbk) : £4.95 : CIP rev. B82-10219

821'.914'08 — Poetry in English, ***1945- — Anthologies — Serials***

[Divan ***(Liverpool)*****]**. Divan. — 1-. — Liverpool (14 Buckingham Ave., Liverpool L17 3BB) : Glasshouse Press, c1979-. — v. : ill ; 21cm
ISSN 0263-1598 = Divan (Liverpool) : £0.65 per issue B82-18720

New poetry. — 7. — London : Hutchinson, Oct.1981. — [144]p
ISBN 0-09-146450-1 : £6.50 : CIP entry B81-26794

New poetry. — 8. — London : Hutchinson, Nov.1982. — [192]p
ISBN 0-09-150660-3 : £6.95 : CIP entry B82-26857

[Stride ***(London)*****]**. Stride. — 1st-. — London (45 Allan Way, Acton, W3 0PW) : Stride, [1982]-. — v. : ill ; 21cm
Six issues yearly
ISSN 0262-9267 = Stride (London) : £2.50 per year B82-26152

821'.914'08 — Poetry in English. Compositions by students of University of Strathclyde: Compositions for Keith Wright Memorial Poetry Competition, ***1945- — Anthologies***

Keith Wright memorial poetry competition 1981 / University of Strathclyde, Department of English Studies. — [Glasgow] ([George St., Glasgow G1 1XW]) : [The university], [1981?]. — 23p ; 21cm
Unpriced (pbk) B82-20802

821'.914'080324253 — Poetry in English, ***1945-*****. Special subjects: Lincolnshire** — ***Anthologies***

To build a bridge / edited by Douglas Dunn. — Lincoln : Lincolnshire and Humberside Arts, 1982. — x,45p : ill ; 15x21cm
ISBN 0-906465-22-2 (pbk) : Unpriced B82-35698

821'.914'08033 — Poetry in English, ***1945-*****. Special subjects: Christmas** — ***Anthologies***

Poems for Christmas : a Peterloo anthology. — Liskeard : Harry Chambers/Peterloo Poets, 1981. — 34p ; 21cm
ISBN 0-905291-33-6 (pbk) : £1.50 B82-26812

821'.914'080354 — Poetry in English, *1945-.* **Special subjects: Love** — *Anthologies*

Love. — London : Regency Press, [1980]. — 86p ; 23cm
Limited ed. of 200 numbered copies
Unpriced B82-15103

821'.914'080356 — Poetry in English, *1945-.* **Special subjects: Nuclear power** — *Anthologies*

Nuclear fragments : pictures, poetry, prose / edited by Monica Frisch. — Newburn : Earthright, c1982. — 60p : ill,music ; 22cm
Bibliography: p58-59
ISBN 0-907367-01-1 (pbk) : £1.95 B82-25344

821'.914'080382 — Christian poetry in English, *1945-* — *Anthologies — Serials*

Dowry : a quarterly magazine of Catholic poetry. — No.1 (Spring 1982)-. — Liverpool (17 Hadassah Grove, Lark La., Liverpool L17 8XH) : The Gild of St. George, 1982-. — v. ; 30cm
ISSN 0262-8937 = Dowry : £1.50 per year B82-24760

821'.914'0809282 — Children's poetry in English, *1945-* — *Anthologies*

Days are where we live : and other poems / compiled by Jill Bennett ; illustrated by Maureen Roffey. — London : Bodley Head, 1981. — [42]p : col.ill ; 22cm
ISBN 0-370-30432-2 : £3.50 : CIP rev. B81-27395

Fuller, Roy. Upright downfall. — Oxford : Oxford University Press, Feb.1983. — [48]p. — (Three poets ; v.2)
ISBN 0-19-276052-1 : £4.95 : CIP entry B82-36314

Gangsters, ghosts and dragonflies : a book of story poems / chosen by Brian Patten ; illustrated by Terry Oakes. — London : Allen & Unwin, 1981. — 159p : ill ; 24cm
Includes index
ISBN 0-04-821053-6 : Unpriced : CIP rev. B81-25107

Here we go. — London : Evans, Oct.1982. — [128]p. — (Poems and pictures ; 3)
ISBN 0-237-45590-0 (pbk) : £5.95 : CIP entry B82-25074

Lucie Attwell's tiny rhymes pop-up book. — London : Dean, c1982, c1967. — [8]p : col.ill ; 24cm
Cover title. — Text and ill on lining papers
ISBN 0-603-00309-5 : Unpriced B82-25974

Poetry allsorts / compiled by Roger Mansfield ; illustrated by Yvonne Ashby. — London : Edward Arnold, 1981. — 4v. : ill(some col.) ; 19cm
ISBN 0-7131-0634-4 (pbk) : Unpriced
ISBN 0-7131-0635-2 (2) : £1.40
ISBN 0-7131-0636-0 (3) : £1.40
ISBN 0-7131-0637-9 (Teacher's guide) : £1.40 B82-03657

The **Rattle** bag. — London : Faber, Oct.1982. — 1v.
ISBN 0-571-11966-2 (cased) : £10.00 : CIP entry
ISBN 0-571-11976-x (pbk) : £4.95 B82-28475

Scannell, Vernon. Catch the light. — Oxford : Oxford University Press, Sept.1982. — [48]p. — (Three poets)
ISBN 0-19-276050-5 : £4.50 : CIP entry B82-19186

Strictly private : an anthology of poetry / chosen by Roger McGough ; illustrated by Graham Dean. — Harmondsworth : Puffin, 1982, c1981. — 185p : ill ; 20cm
Originally published: Harmondsworth : Kestrel, 1981. — Includes index
ISBN 0-14-031313-3 (pbk) : £1.25 B82-22137

821'.914'0809287 — Poetry in English. Women writers, *1945-* — *Anthologies*

Kazantzis, Judith. Touch papers. — London : Allison & Busby, Sept.1982. — [128]p
ISBN 0-85031-476-3 (cased) : £6.95 : CIP entry
ISBN 0-85031-477-1 (pbk) : £2.95 B82-18771

821'.914'0809416 — Poetry in English. Northern Irish writers, *1945-* — *Anthologies*

Kirkpatrick, Johnston. Trio poetry 3. — Belfast : Blackstaff Press, Nov.1982. — [72]p
ISBN 0-85640-276-1 (pbk) : £3.95 : CIP entry B82-28757

821'.914'080942142 — Poetry in English. London writers: Camden *(London Borough)* **writers,** *1945-* — *Anthologies*

Camden Poetry Group. The voice and its moment : poems from the Camden Poetry Group / edited by Hannah Kelly and Margery Smith. — [London] ([64 Lilyville Rd., S.W.6]) : The Group, 1982. — 48p : ill ; 22cm
Limited ed. of 400 copies
£1.00 (pbk) B82-37301

821'.914'080942142 — Poetry in English. London writers: Highgate writers, *1945-* — *Anthologies*

Kites alive / the Highgate poets ; editor Fleur Bowers ; with an introduction by Alan Brownjohn. — London (10a South Grove, N.6) : Highgate Society, [1981]. — iv,44p ; 21cm
£1.10 (pbk) B82-08905

821'.914'080942464 — Poetry in English. Staffordshire writers: Stafford writers, *1945-* — *Anthologies*

Imago. — [Stafford] ([c/o Mrs. K. Seeton, 41 Wolseley Rd., Kingston Hill, Stafford ST16 3XW]) : Stafford Poetry Group, 1981. — 56p ; 22cm
Unpriced (pbk) B82-11426

821'.914'09 — Poetry in English. Hughes, Ted *compared with* **Larkin, Philip**

Wilson, Jane. Backing horses : a comparison between Larkin's and Hughes' poetry / by Jane Wilson. — Portree : Aquila, c1982. — [13]p ; 21cm. — (Aquila essays ; no.16)
ISBN 0-7275-0259-x (pbk) : £0.60 B82-39866

821'.914'099411 — Poetry in English. Scottish writers, *1945-* — *Interviews*

Seven poets : Hugh MacDiarmid, Norman MacCaig, Ian Chrichton Smith, George Mackay Brown, Robert Garioch, Sorley Maclean, Edwin Morgan / with paintings and drawings by Alexander Moffat ; and photographs by Jessie Ann Matthew ; [edited and designed by Christopher Carrell]. — Glasgow : Third Eye Centre (Glasgow), 1981. — 88p : ill,ports(some col.) ; 21x24cm
Published to accompany an exhibition at the Third Eye Centre, 1981. — Also available in limited ed. of 100 numbered and signed copies
ISBN 0-906474-13-2 (pbk) : £5.00
ISBN 0-906474-14-0 (Limited ed.) : Unpriced B82-20957

822 — ENGLISH DRAMA

822 — Drama in English. Ghanaian writers, *1960-* — *Texts*

Wartemberg, Nanabenyin Kweku. The corpse's comedy / Nanabenyin Kweku Wartemberg. — Ibadan ; Oxford : Oxford University Press, 1977. — 82p ; 19cm. — (A Three Crowns book)
Twelve men, 4 women
ISBN 0-19-575231-7 (corrected : pbk) : £2.25
ISBN 0-19-575231-x B82-03910

822 — Drama in English. New Zealand writers, *1907-* — *Texts*

Fraser, Murray. King for a day. — London : Edward Arnold, 1981. — 24p : ill,1map,1geneal.table ; 22cm
Eleven characters. — Author: Murray Fraser. — Originally published: Adelaide : Rigby, 1979. — Text on inside cover. — Bibliography: p24
ISBN 0-7131-0617-4 (pbk) : £0.95 B82-05084

Hall, Roger, *1939-.* Captain Scrimshaw in space. — London : Edward Arnold, 1981. — 24p : ill,1plan ; 22cm
Fourteen characters. — Author: Roger Hall. — Originally published: Adelaide : Rigby, 1979. — Text on inside cover. — Bibliography: p24
ISBN 0-7131-0619-0 (pbk) : £0.95 B82-05088

Hall, Roger, *1939-.* How the crab got a hard back. — London : Edward Arnold, 1981. — 24p : ill ; 22cm
Eleven characters. — Author: Roger Hall from a West Indian folktale. — Originally published: Adelaide : Rigby, 1979. — Text on inside cover. — Bibliography: p24
ISBN 0-7131-0618-2 (pbk) : £0.95 B82-05089

Holloway, Judith. Jimmy, the ghost-catcher. — London : Edward Arnold, 1981. — 24p : ill,1port ; 22cm
Nine characters. — Author: Judith Holloway. — Originally published: Adelaide : Rigby, 1979. — Text on inside cover. — Bibliography: p24
ISBN 0-7131-0621-2 (pbk) : £0.95 B82-05087

Ross, John, *19---.* Aladdin and his magic lamp. — London : Edward Arnold, 1981. — 24p : ill ; 22cm
Ten characters. — Author: John Ross. — Originally published: Adelaide : Rigby, 1979. — Text on inside cover. — Bibliography: p24
ISBN 0-7131-0620-4 (pbk) : £0.95 B82-05085

Thomson, Jane. Sexton Blake and the missing million. — London : Edward Arnold, 1981. — 24p : ill,1facsim ; 22cm
Seven characters. — Adapted by Jane Thomson. — Originally published: Adelaide : Rigby, 1979. — Text on inside cover. — Bibliography: p24
ISBN 0-7131-0622-0 (pbk) : £0.95 B82-05086

822 — Drama in English. Nigerian writers. Soyinka, Wole. Lion and the jewel — *Study outlines*

Gibbs, James. The lion and the jewel : notes / by James Gibb. — Harlow : Longman, 1982. — 64p ; 21cm. — (York notes ; 158)
Bibliography: p62-64
ISBN 0-582-79207-x (pbk) : £0.90 B82-16450

822 — Drama in English. Nigerian writers. Soyinka, Wole. Swamp dwellers, Strong breed & Trials of Brother Jero — *Study outlines*

Dunton, C. P.. Three short plays : The swamp dwellers, The strong breed, The trials of brother Jero : notes / by C.P. Dunton. — Harlow : Longman, 1982. — 71p ; 21cm. — (York notes ; 172)
At head of title: Wole Soyinka. — Bibliography: p70-71
ISBN 0-582-78260-0 (pbk) : £0.90 B82-36759

822 — Drama in English. Nigerian writers. Soyinka, Wole. Trials of Brother Jero & Jero's metamorphosis — *Study outlines*

Parsons, E. M.. Notes on Wole Soyinka's the Jero Plays / compiled by E.M. Parsons. — London : Methuen paperbacks, 1979. — 42p ; 19cm. — (Methuen notes : study aid series)
Bibliography: p42
ISBN 0-417-20560-0 (pbk) : £0.75 B82-28950

822 — Drama in English. South African writers, *1909-1961* — *Texts*

Fugard, Athol. A lesson from aloes : a play / by Athol Fugard. — Oxford : Oxford University Press, 1981. — xv,79p ; 21cm. — (Oxford paperbacks)
Two men, 1 woman
ISBN 0-19-281307-2 (pbk) : £2.95 : CIP rev. B81-22475

Fugard, Athol. Lesson from aloes : a drama / by Athol Fugard. — New York ; London : French, c1981. — 76p ; 18cm
Two men, 1 woman
ISBN 0-573-61860-7 (pbk) : £2.75 B82-27265

822 — Drama in English. South African writers, *1961-* — *Texts*

Aron, Geraldine. A Galway girl : a play in one act / by Geraldine Aron. — New York ; London : French, c1981. — 21p : 1plan ; 19cm
One man, 1 woman
ISBN 0-573-62204-3 (pbk) : £1.00 B82-11374

822 — Drama in English. South African writers, *1961- — Texts* *continuation*

Benjamin, V. N.. The ants / V.N. Benjamin. — London : New Horizon, c1981. — 85p ; 21cm
ISBN 0-86116-668-x : £3.75 B82-00653

Lan, David. Sergeant Ola and his followers / David Lan. — London : Methuen, 1980. — 45p ; 21cm. — (A Methuen new theatrescript)
ISBN 0-413-47590-5 (pbk) : £1.75 B82-16087

822'.009 — Drama in English, *to 1850 — Critical studies*

Davison, P. H.. Popular appeal in English drama to 1850 / Peter Davison. — London : Macmillan, 1982. — xi,221p,[1]leaf of plates : 1port ; 23cm
Bibliography: p204-210. — Includes index
ISBN 0-333-28084-9 : £17.50 B82-32224

822'.009 — Drama in English, *to ca 1975 — Critical studies*

The **Revels** history of drama in English / [general editors Clifford Leech and T.W. Craik]. — London : Methuen
Vol.4: 1613-1660 / Philip Edwards ... [et al.]. — 1981. — lvii,337p,[24]p of plates : ill,facsims,ports ; 24cm
General editor: Lois Potter. — Ill on lining papers. — Bibliography: p307-328. — Includes index
ISBN 0-416-13050-x : £25.00 : CIP rev.
Also classified at 792'.0942 B81-30321

822'.02'08 — Radio & television plays in English, *1945- — Anthologies — For schools*

School. — London : Hutchinson Education, Jan.1983. — [172]p. — (Studio scripts ; 7)
ISBN 0-09-149271-8 (pbk) : £1.95 : CIP entry B82-33619

822'.02'08 — Radio plays in English, *1945- — Anthologies — For schools*

Cook, Marianne. Winning through : five plays about growing up : based on the BBC School Radio series Exploring society / Marianne Cook. — London : Edward Arnold, 1981. — 72p ; 22cm
ISBN 0-7131-0527-5 (pbk) : £1.40 : CIP rev. B81-31548

822'.02'0817 — Television drama series in English, *1945-*. **Comedies** *— Anthologies*

Situation comedy / edited by David Self. — London : Hutchinson, 1980. — 176p : ill ; 19cm. — (Studio scripts)
ISBN 0-09-142931-5 (pbk) : £1.75 : CIP rev. B80-23676

822'.02'089282 — Television plays in English, *1945- — Anthologies — For schools*

Scene scripts three : a third selection of television plays, from the BBC schools tv series, Scene / by David Hopkins ... [et al.] ; edited by Roy Blatchford. — Harlow : Longman, 1982. — xvi,117p : ill ; 19cm
ISBN 0-582-22309-1 (pbk) : £1.40 B82-24403

822'.02'09 — Radio drama in English, *1920-1965 — Critical studies*

Rodger, Ian. Radio drama / Ian Rodger. — London : Macmillan, 1982. — viii,166p,8p of plates : ill,ports ; 23cm
Bibliography: p161. — Includes index
ISBN 0-333-29428-9 (cased) : £12.00
ISBN 0-333-29429-7 (pbk) : Unpriced B82-14872

822'.041'08 — One-act plays in English, *1945- — Anthologies*

Brandon, Eileen. Panel games / Eileen Brandon. The headmistress and the minister / O.A. Jones. — Basingstoke : Macmillan Education, 1982. — 36p ; 22cm. — (Dramascripts)
ISBN 0-333-30104-8 (pbk) : Unpriced : CIP rev. B80-18474

Morley, Bea. Poor Fred : a comedy sketch for six older women / by Bea Morley. The winning post : a comedy sketch for six older women / by Dorothy M. Payne. — London (129 St John's Hill, SW11 1TO) : Kenyon-Deane, c1978. — 7,6p ; 22cm
Cover title: Two-in-one
£0.60 (pbk) B82-39222

Triad 37. — Macclesfield : New Playwrights' Network, [1981]. — 23,24,37p : 2plans ; 19cm
Contents: Research / by Michael Coyle. — Conscience stricken / by Neil Fitton. — Funny - you don't laugh Jewish! / by Mike Tibbetts
£1.95 (pbk) B82-03249

Triad 38. — Macclesfield : New Playwrights' Network, [1981]. — 23,22,22p : 3plans ; 18cm
Contents: Closing day / by Taylor Lovering. — Murder at midday / by Frances Langhorn. — Looking for rosy / by Leonard Morley
£1.95 (pbk) B82-03248

Triad 39. — Macclesfield : New Playwrights Network, [1982?]. — 36p : 3plans ; 18cm
Contents: Poles apart / by Derek Parkes — The night shelter / by John D. Vose — Little secrets / by Gerry Schilling
£1.95 (pbk) B82-30414

Triad 40. — Macclesfield : New Playwrights Network, [1982?]. — [72]p in various pagings : 3plans ; 18cm
Contents: Tea, set and match / by Sean Street — Turnabout / by Dilys Gater — As short as any dream / by Audrey Evans
£1.95 (pbk) B82-30415

822'.041'08 — One-act plays in English, *1945- — Anthologies — For schools*

Hardwick, Michael. The hound of the Baskervilles and other Sherlock Holmes plays. — London : J. Murray, Sept.1982. — [96]p
ISBN 0-7195-3997-8 (pbk) : £1.50 : CIP entry B82-19829

Wordplays : six short modern plays / edited by Alan Durbnad. — London : Hutchinson
1. — 1982. — 132p : plans ; 19cm
ISBN 0-09-149221-1 (pbk) : Unpriced : CIP rev. B82-04128

Wordplays : six short modern plays / edited by Alan Durband. — London : Hutchinson
2. — 1982. — 119p ; 19cm
ISBN 0-09-149241-6 (pbk) : Unpriced : CIP rev. B82-04129

822'.0512'09 — Drama in English. Tragedies, *1558-1625*. **Speeches** *— Critical studies*

Clemen, Wolfgang. English tragedy before Shakespeare : the development of dramatic speech / by Wolfgang Clemen ; translated by T.S. Dorsch. — London : Methuen, 1961 (1980 [printing]). — 301p ; 23cm
Translation of: Die Tragödie vor Shakespeare. — Bibliography: p293-294. — Includes index
ISBN 0-416-74380-3 : £16.50 : CIP rev. B80-08926

822'.0514'09355 — Historical plays in English, *1558-1625*. **Special subjects: Riots. Social aspects** *— Critical studies*

De Bruyn, Lucy. Mob-rule and riots : the present mirrored in the past / by Lucy de Bruyn. — London : Regency, c1981. — 247p,xxv : ill,1map ; 22cm
Map on lining papers. — Bibliography: pvi-xvi. — Includes index
ISBN 0-7212-0611-5 : £8.50 B82-14762

822'.0516 — Miracle plays in English, *1066-1400 — Anthologies*

Shepherds and kings / [compiled and translated by Ray Barron]. — London : RADIUS, 1981. — 72p : 1plan ; 21cm. — (Plays for the eighties ; no.4)
Translation from the Scots. — Cover title
ISBN 0-907174-04-3 (spiral) : Unpriced B82-10312

822'.0516 — Miracle plays in English. Chester plays *— Critical studies*

Travis, Peter W.. Dramatic design in the Chester cycle / Peter W. Travis. — Chicago ; London : University of Chicago Press, 1982. — xv,310p : 1ill ; 22cm. — (Chicago originals)
Bibliography: p291-304. — Includes index
ISBN 0-226-81164-6 (pbk) : Unpriced B82-35314

822'.0516 — Miracle plays in English. York plays *— Anthologies*

The **York** plays. — London : E. Arnold, Sept.1982. — [604]p. — (York medieval texts. Second series)
ISBN 0-7131-6326-7 : £45.00 : CIP entry B82-20040

822'.0516'08 — Religious drama in English, *1400-1558 — Anthologies*

The **Late** Medieval religious plays of Bodleian MSS Digby 133 and e Museo 160 / edited by Donald C. Baker, John L. Murphy and Louis B. Hall Jr.. — Oxford : Published for the Early English Text Society by the Oxford University Press, 1982. — cviii,284p,[1]p of plates : 2facsims ; 23cm. — (Early English Text Society ; no.283)
Bibliography pci-cviii
ISBN 0-19-722285-4 : Unpriced : CIP rev. B82-16502

822'.0516'09 — Morality plays in English, *1420-1500 — Critical studies*

Davenport, W. A.. Fifteenth-century English drama : the early moral plays and their literary relations / W.A. Davenport. — Cambridge : Brewer, c1982. — 152p ; 25cm
Bibliography: p145-147. — Includes index
ISBN 0-85991-091-1 : £17.50 : CIP rev. B82-07043

822.2 — ENGLISH DRAMA, 1400-1558

822'.2 — Drama in English, *1400-1558 — Texts*

Medwall, Henry. Fulgens a lucres / by mayster Henry Medwall ; edited by Peter Meredith. — [Leeds] ([Leeds, LS2 9JT]) : University of Leeds School of English, c1981. — iv,80p : ill,1facsim ; 21cm. — (Leeds studies in English)
Five men, 2 women
Unpriced (pbk) B82-19133

822'.2'08 — Drama in English, *1400-1558 — Anthologies*

Three late medieval moralities. — London : Benn, Nov.1981. — [208]p. — (The New mermaids)
ISBN 0-510-33505-5 (pbk) : £2.95 : CIP entry B81-30525

Three Tudor classical interludes : Thersites, Jacke Jugeler, Horestes. — Woodbridge : Boydell & Brewer, Oct.1982. — [256]p. — (Tudor interludes, ISSN 0261-9199 ; 3)
ISBN 0-85991-096-2 : £17.50 : CIP entry B82-24126

822.3 — ENGLISH DRAMA, 1558-1625

822'.3 — Drama in English, *1558-1625 — Texts*

Chapman, George, *1559?-1634*. Bussy d'Ambois. — London : Benn, Nov.1981. — [160]p
Originally published: 1965
ISBN 0-510-33306-0 : £2.50 : CIP entry B81-30557

Ford, John, *ca 1586-*. The broken heart / John Ford ; edited by T.J.B. Spencer. — Manchester : Manchester University Press, 1980. — xiv,239p,[1]leaf of plates : 2ill,1facsim,1geneal.table ; 21cm. — (The Revels plays)
Bibliography: pxii-viv. — Includes index
ISBN 0-7190-1527-8 : £16.95 : CIP rev. B80-23677

Jefferay, John. The bugbears : a modernised edition / [edited by] James D. Clark. — New York ; London : Garland, 1979. — ix,271p : music,facsims ; 21cm. — (Renaissance drama)
Attributed to John Jefferay. — Bibliography: p250-253. — Includes index
ISBN 0-8240-9749-1 : Unpriced B82-14677

Jonson, Ben. The complete plays of Ben Jonson / edited by G.A. Wilkes ; based on the edition edited by C.H. Herford and Percy and Evelyn Simpson. — Oxford : Clarendon
Vol.4. — 1982. — 576p ; 23cm
Contents: Bartholomew fair — The devil is an ass — The staple of news — The new inn — The magnetic lady
ISBN 0-19-812603-4 : £45.00 : CIP rev. B79-24649

822′.3 — Drama in English, *1558-1625* — *Texts continuation*

Jonson, Ben. [Selections]. The complete plays of Ben Jonson / edited by G.A. Wilkes ; based on the edition edited by C.H. Herford and Percy and Evelyn Simpson. — Oxford : Clarendon Vol.3. — 1982. — xiv,478p : facsims ; 23cm
Contents: Volpone, or The fox — Epicoene, or The silent woman — The alchemist — Catiline
ISBN 0-19-812602-6 : £45.00 : CIP rev. B79-24648

Jonson, Ben. Volpone. — London : Ernest Benn, May 1981. — [208]p. — (The new mermaids)
ISBN 0-510-34157-8 (pbk) : £2.50 : CIP entry B81-05173

Jonson, Ben. Volpone, or, The fox. — Manchester : Manchester University Press, Apr.1982. — [288]p. — (The Revels plays)
ISBN 0-7190-1529-4 : £16.50 : CIP entry B82-04881

Massinger, Philip. A new way to pay old debts. — London : Benn, Sept.1981. — [128]p. — (The new mermaids)
ISBN 0-510-34021-0 (pbk) : £2.50 : CIP entry B81-20127

Misogonus / edited with an introduction [by] Lester E. Barber. — New York ; London : Garland, 1979. — ii,374p : 2facsims ; 24cm. — (Renaissance drama)
Bibliography: p369-374
ISBN 0-8240-9751-3 : Unpriced B82-15187

Tourneur, Cyril. The revenger′s tragedy. — London : Benn, May 1981. — [144]p. — (The new mermaids)
ISBN 0-510-34206-x (pbk) : £2.25 : CIP entry B81-05160

The **Tragedy** of Master Arden of Faversham. — London : Benn, June 1982. — [160]p. — (The New mermaids)
ISBN 0-510-33508-x (pbk) : £2.95 : CIP entry B82-09734

822′.3 — Drama in English. Jonson, Ben — *Critical studies*

Brock, D. Heyward. A Ben Jonson companion. — Brighton : Harvester, Jan.1983. — 1v.
ISBN 0-7108-0438-5 : £20.00 : CIP entry B82-37674

822′.3 — Drama in English. Marlowe, Christopher, *1564-1593* — *Critical studies*

Marlow : Tamburlaine the Great, Edward the Second and The Jew of Malta : a casebook / edited by John Russell Brown. — London : Macmillan, 1982. — 239p ; 23cm. — (Casebook series)
Bibliography: p230-231. — Includes index
ISBN 0-333-28363-5 (cased) : Unpriced
ISBN 0-333-28364-3 (pbk) : Unpriced B82-25390

822′.3 — Drama in English. Marlowe, Christopher, *1564-1593.* Edward II — *Study outlines*

Murray, Christopher. Edward II : notes / by Christopher Murray. — Harlow : Longman, 1982. — 72p ; 21cm. — (York notes ; 166)
Bibliography: p71-72
ISBN 0-582-78297-x (pbk) : £0.90 B82-16449

822′.3 — Drama in English. Marston, John. Wonder of women — *Critical studies*

Kemp, William, *1942-.* John Marston′s The wonder of women, or, The tragedy of Sophonisba : a critical edition / William Kemp. — New York ; London : Garland, 1979. — 191p ; 24cm. — (Renaissance drama)
Bibliography: p185-191
ISBN 0-8240-9744-0 (corrected) : Unpriced B82-15385

822′.3 — Drama in English. Middleton, Thomas. Political aspects

Heinemann, Margot. Puritanism and theatre : Thomas Middleton and opposition drama under the early Stuarts. — Cambridge : Cambridge University Press, Oct.1982. — [300] p. — (Past and present publications)
Originally published: 1980
ISBN 0-521-27052-9 (pbk) : £6.95 : CIP entry B82-23334

822′.3 — Drama in English. Webster, John, *1580?-1625?* — *Critical studies*

Bliss, Lee. The world′s perspective. — Brighton : Harvester Press, Jan.1983. — [256]p
ISBN 0-7108-0505-5 : £18.95 : CIP entry B82-32556

Webster : the critical heritage / edited by Don D. Moore. — London : Routledge & Kegan Paul, 1981. — viii,161p ; 23cm. — (The Critical heritage series)
Bibliography: p157. — Includes index
ISBN 0-7100-0773-6 : £8.95 B82-06004

822′.3 — Drama in English. Webster, John, *1580?-1625?.* Duchess of Malfi — *Study outlines*

King, Neil. The Duchess of Malfi : notes / by Neil King. — Harlow : Longman, 1982. — 72p ; 21cm. — (York notes ; 171)
Bibliography: p66-67
ISBN 0-582-79200-2 (pbk) : £0.90 B82-36750

822′.3 — Drama in English. Webster, John, *1580?-1625.* White devil — *Study outlines*

Jardine, Michael. The white devil : notes / by Michael Jardine. — Harlow : Longman, 1982. — 72p ; 21cm. — (York notes ; 176)
Bibliography: p66-68
ISBN 0-582-78264-3 (pbk) : £0.90 B82-36751

822′.3 — Masques in English. Jonson, Ben — *Critical studies*

Orgel, Stephen. The Jonsonian masque / Stephen Orgel. — New York ; Guildford : Columbia University Press, 1981. — x,216p,[4]p of plates : ill ; 22cm
Originally published: Cambridge, Mass. : Harvard University Press, 1965. — Includes index
ISBN 0-231-05370-3 (cased) : £16.25
ISBN 0-231-05371-1 (pbk) : £6.10 B82-05625

822′.3′08 — Revels in English, *1558-1625* — *Anthologies*

Three revels from the Inns of Court. — Amersham : Avebury, Nov.1981. — [128]p
ISBN 0-86127-402-4 : £9.00 : CIP entry B81-30429

822′.3′09 — Drama in English, *1558-1625* — *Critical studies*

Putt, S. Gorley. The golden age of English drama : enjoyment of Elizabethan and Jacobean plays / S. Gorley Putt. — Cambridge : published on behalf of the English Association by D.S. Brewer and Rowman and Littlefield, c1981. — vii,231p : ill ; 24cm
Bibliography: p217-221. — Includes index
ISBN 0-85991-076-8 : £15.00 : CIP rev. B81-22540

Scott, Michael, *1949-.* Renaissance drama and a modern audience / Michael Scott. — London : Macmillan, 1982. — xii,127p ; 23cm
Includes index
ISBN 0-333-27599-3 : £17.50 B82-38789

822′.3′09 — Drama in English, *1558-1625.* Dumb show — *Critical studies*

Mehl, Dieter. The Elizabethan dumb show : the history of a dramatic convention / Dieter Mehl. — London : Methuen, 1965 (1982 [printing]). — xiii,207p ; 23cm. — (Methuen library reprints)
Translation of: Die Pantomime im Drama der Shakespearezeit. — Bibliography: p200-201. — Includes index
ISBN 0-416-33980-8 : Unpriced : CIP rev. B82-07968

822′.3′0927 — Drama in English, *1558-1702.* Characters: Women — *Critical studies*

Shepherd, Simon. Amazons and warrior women : varieties of feminism in seventeenth-century drama / Simon Shepherd. — Brighton : Harvester, 1981. — 234p ; 22cm
Bibliography: p225-228. — Includes index
ISBN 0-85527-353-4 : £22.50 B82-10270

822.3′3 — Drama in English. Shakespeare, William. All′s well that ends well. Influence of Decamerone by Boccaccio, Giovanni

Cole, Howard C.. The All′s well story from Boccaccio to Shakespeare / Howard C. Cole. — Urbana ; London : University of Illinois Press, c1981. — xi,145p ; 22cm
Bibliography: p139-145
ISBN 0-252-00883-9 : £9.45 B82-13567

822.3′3 — Drama in English. Shakespeare, William. All′s well that ends well, Measure for measure & Troilus and Cressida — *Critical studies*

Aspects of Shakespeare′s ′problem plays′ : articles reprinted from Shakespeare survey / edited by Kenneth Muir and Stanley Wells. — Cambridge : Cambridge University Press, 1982. — x,153p : ill ; 26cm
ISBN 0-521-23959-1 (cased) : £17.50 : CIP rev.
ISBN 0-521-28371-x (pbk) : £5.50 B81-37536

822.3′3 — Drama in English. Shakespeare, William. Authorship

Lester, Paul. The author in Shakespeare / by Paul Lester. — Birmingham (c/o Centre for Contemporary Cultural Studies, University of Birmingham, Birmingham B15 2TT) : P. Lester, [1981?]. — [8]p ; 30cm
Unpriced (unbound) B82-03771

822.3′3 — Drama in English. Shakespeare, William — *Biographies — For children*

Earle, Geoffrey. William Shakespeare / by Geoffrey Earle ; illustrated by Roger Hall. — Loughborough : Ladybird, c1981. — 50p : col.ill,2facsims,col.ports ; 18cm
Text and facsims on lining papers. — Includes index
ISBN 0-7214-0620-3 : £0.50 B82-18600

822.3′3 — Drama in English. Shakespeare, William. Characters: Women

Dash, Irene G.. Wooing, wedding and power : women in Shakespeare′s plays / Irene G. Dash. — New York ; Guildford : Columbia University Press, 1981. — xiii,295p : ill,facsims,ports ; 24cm
Bibliography: p267-283. — Includes index
ISBN 0-231-05238-3 : £15.80 B82-10946

Jardine, Lisa. Still harping on daughters : women and drama in the age of Shakespeare. — Brighton : Harvester Press, Dec.1982. — [192]p
ISBN 0-7108-0436-9 : CIP entry B82-30078

822.3′3 — Drama in English. Shakespeare, William. Characters: Women — *Critical studies*

The **Woman′s** part : feminist criticism of Shakespeare / edited by Carolyn Ruth Swift Lenz, Gayle Greene and Carol Thomas Neely. — Urbana ; London : University of Illinois Press, 1980. — x,348p : 1ill ; 24cm
Bibliography: p314-335. — Includes index
ISBN 0-252-00751-4 : £13.05 B82-34453

822.3′3 — Drama in English. Shakespeare, William. Comedies — *Critical studies*

Huston, J. Dennis. Shakespeare′s comedies of play / J. Dennis Huston. — London : Macmillan, 1981. — x,169p ; 23cm
Includes index
ISBN 0-333-30923-5 : £15.00 B82-06660

822.3′3 — Drama in English. Shakespeare, William — *Critical studies*

Badawi, M. M.. Background to Shakespeare / M.M. Badawi. — London : Macmillan, 1981. — viii,142p : 1facsim ; 23cm
Includes index
ISBN 0-333-30534-5 (cased) : Unpriced
ISBN 0-333-30535-3 (pbk) : Unpriced B82-06662

Brown, John Russell. Discovering Shakespeare : a new guide to the plays / John Russell Brown. — London : Macmillan, 1981. — viii,168p ; 23cm
Bibliography: p161-163. — Includes index
ISBN 0-333-31633-9 (cased) : Unpriced
ISBN 0-333-31634-7 (pbk) : Unpriced B82-06661

822.3'3 — Drama in English. Shakespeare, William — *Critical studies* *continuation*

Edwards, Philip. Shakespeare and the confines of art / Philip Edwards. — London : Methuen, 1968 (1981 [printing]). — ix,170p ; 23cm. — (Methuen library reprints)
Includes index
ISBN 0-416-32200-x : £11.95 : CIP rev. B81-24644

French, Marilyn. Shakespeare's division of experience / Marilyn French. — London : Cape, 1982, c1981. — 376p ; 24cm
Includes index
ISBN 0-224-02013-7 : £12.50 : CIP rev. B82-04302

Frye, Roland Mushat. Shakespeare. — London : Allen & Unwin, Oct.1981. — [288]p
ISBN 0-04-822043-4 (cased) : £6.95 : CIP entry
ISBN 0-04-822044-2 (pbk) : £2.95 B81-27344

Granville-Barker, Harley. Prefaces to Shakespeare / Harley Granville-Barker. — London : Batsford
Coriolanus. — 1982, c1948. — 156p ; 22cm
Originally published: London : Sidgwick & Jackson, 1930
ISBN 0-7134-4328-6 (pbk) : £3.95 B82-18939

Granville-Barker, Harley. Prefaces to Shakespeare / Harley Granville-Barker. — London : Batsford
Love's labours lost, Romeo and Juliet, The merchant of Venice. — 1982, c1930. — 126p ; 22cm
Originally published: London : Sidgwick & Jackson, 1930
ISBN 0-7134-4330-8 (pbk) : £3.95 B82-18941

Granville-Barker, Harley. Prefaces to Shakespeare / Harley Granville-Barker. — London : Batsford
Othello. — 1982, c1948. — 153p ; 22cm
Originally published: London : Sidgwick & Jackson, 1930
ISBN 0-7134-4326-x (pbk) B82-18940

Honigmann, E. A. J.. Shakespeare's impact on his contemporaries / E.A.J. Honigmann. — London : Macmillan, 1982. — xiv,149p ; 22cm
Includes index
ISBN 0-333-26938-1 : Unpriced B82-32935

International Shakespeare Conference *(18th : 1978 : Stratford-upon-Avon)*. Shakespeare's art of construction / report of the eighteenth International Shakespeare Conference, 1978 : held at the Shakespeare Institute (University of Birmingham) Stratford-on-Avon, 20 to 25 August 1978 / sponsored by the University of Birmingham in association with the Shakespeare Birthplace Trust, the Royal Shakespeare Theatre, the British Council. — Stratford-upon-Avon : Shakespeare Institute, 1978. — vii,24p ; 30cm
ISBN 0-7044-0337-4 (pbk) : Unpriced B82-35114

Lloyd Evans, Gareth. The upstart crow : an introduction to Shakespeare's plays. — London : Dent, Sept.1982. — [384]p
ISBN 0-460-10256-7 (cased) : £12.00 : CIP entry
ISBN 0-460-11256-2 (pbk) : £4.95 B82-19695

822.3'3 — Drama in English. Shakespeare, William — *Critical studies — Serials*

Shakespeare survey. — 34. — Cambridge : Cambridge University Press, Dec.1981. — [214]p
ISBN 0-521-23240-6 : £18.50 : CIP entry B81-34015

Shakespeare survey. — 35. — Cambridge : Cambridge University Press, Dec.1982. — [197]p
ISBN 0-521-24752-7 : £19.50 : CIP entry B82-30077

822.3'3 — Drama in English. Shakespeare, William. Criticism, *1900-1980*

Viswanathan, S.. The Shakespeare play as poem : a critical tradition in perspective / S. Viswanathan. — Cambridge : Cambridge University Press, 1980. — x,236p ; 23cm
Bibliography: p207-226. — Includes index
ISBN 0-521-22547-7 : £12.50 : CIP rev. B80-26098

822.3'3 — Drama in English. Shakespeare, William. Emendations by critics

Craik, T. W.. A fly in Shakespeare's amber : an inaugural lecture / by Thomas Wallace Craik. — Durham : University of Durham, 1981. — 16p ; 22cm
£0.60 (pbk) B82-02507

822.3'3 — Drama in English. Shakespeare, William — *Encyclopaedias*

Wells, Stanley, *1930-*. Shakespeare, an illustrated dictionary / Stanley Wells. — Oxford : Oxford University Press, 1981, c1978. — vii,216p : ill,facsims,ports ; 22cm. — (Oxford paperbacks)
Originally published: London : Kaye and Ward, 1978. — Bibliography: p215-216
ISBN 0-19-871074-7 (pbk) : £4.50 : CIP rev. B81-18178

822.3'3 — Drama in English. Shakespeare, William. Hamlet — *Critical studies*

Fairhead, P. J.. Bombyx Mora : a study of Shakespeare's sonnets and Hamlet throwing light into the poet's origin / P.J. Fairhead. — [Cambridge] : Roperian Research, c1980. — 227p,[4]folded leaves of plates : ill,facsims,ports (some col.) ; 25cm
Limited ed. of 100 numbered copies. — 'Skeleton outline of events contemporary to Lady Margaret Roper (Alexander Alesius)' (1 folded leaf) in pocket. — Includes index
ISBN 0-9507395-0-2 : Unpriced
Primary classification 821'.3 B82-21590

822.3'3 — Drama in English. Shakespeare, William. Hamlet — *Questions & answers*

Sherman, Joseph. William Shakespeare, Hamlet / Joseph Sherman. — London : Edward Arnold, 1980, c1978. — v,72p ; 22cm. — (Close readings)
Originally published: Pietermaritzburg : Shuter & Shooter, c1978
ISBN 0-7131-0425-2 (pbk) : £1.10 : CIP rev. B79-36002

822.3'3 — Drama in English. Shakespeare, William. Henry IV. Part 1 & Henry IV. Part 2. Characters: Falstaff, *Sir* John — *Critical studies*

Wilson, John Dover. The fortunes of Falstaff / by J. Dover Wilson. — Cambridge : Cambridge University Press, 1943 (1979 [printing]). — 143p ; 20cm
ISBN 0-521-09246-9 (pbk) : Unpriced B82-01772

822.3'3 — Drama in English. Shakespeare, William. Henry IV. Part 2 — *Study outlines*

Jardine, Michael. Henry IV, part 2 : notes / by Michael Jardine. — Harlow : Longman, 1981. — 71p : 2ill ; 21cm. — (York notes ; 140)
Bibliography: p68-71
ISBN 0-582-78167-1 (pbk) : £0.90 B82-16364

822.3'3 — Drama in English. Shakespeare, William. Historical plays — *Critical studies*

Smidt, Kristian. Unconformities in Shakespeare's history plays / Kristian Smidt. — London : Macmillan, 1982. — x,207p ; 23cm
Bibliography: p196-201. — Includes index
ISBN 0-333-32389-0 : £17.50 B82-38790

822.3'3 — Drama in English. Shakespeare, William — *Indexes*

Dent, R. W.. Shakespeare's proverbial languages : an index / R.W. Dent. — Berkeley ; London : University of California Press, c1981. — xxviii,289p ; 24cm
Bibliography: p285-289
ISBN 0-520-03894-0 : £20.75 B82-12192

822.3'3 — Drama in English. Shakespeare, William. King Lear — *Critical studies*

Aspects of King Lear. — Cambridge : Cambridge University Press, Oct.1982. — [104]p
ISBN 0-521-24604-0 (cased) : £16.00 : CIP entry
ISBN 0-521-28813-4 (pbk) : £5.50 B82-29372

Morris, Helen, *1909-*. King Lear / Helen Morris. — Oxford : Blackwell, 1965 (1982 [printing]). — 73p ; 22cm. — (Notes on English literature)
ISBN 0-631-97650-7 (pbk) : Unpriced B82-35825

On King Lear / edited by Lawrence Danson. — Princeton ; Guildford : Princeton University Press, c1981. — 185p ; 23cm
ISBN 0-691-06477-6 : Unpriced B82-16625

822.3'3 — Drama in English. Shakespeare, William. King Lear — *Questions & answers*

Johnstone, Mary. William Shakespeare, King Lear / Mary Johnstone and Patrick Collyer. — London : Edward Arnold, 1980, c1978. — vii,61p ; 22cm. — (Close readings)
Originally published: Pietermaritzburg : Shuter & Shooter, 1978
ISBN 0-7131-0427-9 (pbk) : £1.05 : CIP rev. B79-34418

822.3'3 — Drama in English. Shakespeare, William. Language — *Critical studies*

Hussey, S. S.. The literary language of Shakespeare. — London : Longman, Oct.1982. — [208]p
ISBN 0-582-49228-9 (pbk) : £5.50 : CIP entry B82-23357

822.3'3 — Drama in English. Shakespeare, William. Linguistic aspects

Trousdale, Marion. Shakespeare and the rhetoricians / by Marion Trousdale. — London : Scolar, 1982. — xiii,206p ; 23cm
Includes index
ISBN 0-85967-654-4 : £15.00 : CIP rev. B82-07041

822.3'3 — Drama in English. Shakespeare, William. Macbeth — *Critical studies*

Clark, Arthur Melville. Murder under trust, or The topical Macbeth : and other Jacobean matters / Arthur Melville Clark. — Edinburgh : Scottish Academic Press, 1981. — xii,195p,[1] leaf of plates : 1ill ; 26cm
Bibliography: pxi-xii
ISBN 0-7073-0312-5 : £8.50 B82-08861

Focus on Macbeth / edited by John Russell Brown. — London : Routledge & Kegan Paul, 1982. — viii,258p ; 23cm
Includes index
ISBN 0-7100-9015-3 : £9.75 B82-26598

Harvey, W. J.. Macbeth / John Harvey. — Oxford : Basil Blackwell, 1960 (1982 [printing]). — 59p ; 22cm. — (Notes on English literature)
ISBN 0-631-97520-9 (pbk) : Unpriced B82-35846

822.3'3 — Drama in English. Shakespeare, William. Macbeth — *Illustrations*

Shakespeare, William. Macbeth. — London (335 Kennington Rd., SE11 4QE) : Oval Projects, Sept.1982 ; London : Sidgwick & Jackson [distributor]. — [96]p. — (Cartoon Shakespeare)
ISBN 0-283-98888-6 (cased) : £5.95 : CIP entry
ISBN 0-283-98906-8 (pbk) : £3.50 B82-18823

822.3'3 — Drama in English. Shakespeare, William. Macbeth — *Questions & answers*

Rose, Angus. William Shakespeare, Macbeth / Angus Rose. — London : Edward Arnold, 1980, c1978. — v,54p ; 22cm. — (Close readings)
Originally published: Pietermaritzburg : Shuter and Shooter, c1978
ISBN 0-7131-0426-0 (pbk) : £0.95 : CIP rev. B79-34420

822.3'3 — Drama in English. Shakespeare, William. Macbeth — *Study outlines*

Deegan, Anne. Macbeth : a guide to the play in two parts ... / Anne Deegan. — Dublin : Folens, c1981. — 72p ; 22cm. — (Succeed in English ; 2)
ISBN 0-86121-161-8 (pbk) : Unpriced B82-01496

822.3'3 — Drama in English. Shakespeare, William. Macbeth — *Study outlines — For schools*

Sullivan, Theresa. Macbeth - an interpretation for the student at 'O' level / by Theresa Sullivan ; edited by John Griffin. — Huntingdon : Cambridge Learning, c1981. — 122p ; 22cm
ISBN 0-905946-11-1 (pbk) : Unpriced
B82-25881

822.3'3 — Drama in English. Shakespeare, William. Merchant of Venice — *Study outlines*

Corr, Patricia. The Merchant of Venice / Patricia Corr. — Dublin : Gill and Macmillan, 1982. — 26p ; 22cm. — (Study-guide notes)
Bibliography: p26
ISBN 0-7171-0999-2 (pbk) : Unpriced
B82-31162

822.3'3 — Drama in English. Shakespeare, William. Narrative — *Critical studies*

Rees, Joan. Shakespeare and the story. — London : Athlone Press, July 1982. — [240]p
Originally published: 1978
ISBN 0-485-12041-0 (pbk) : £6.95 : CIP entry
B82-13513

822.3'3 — Drama in English. Shakespeare, William — *Psychoanalytical perspectives*

Representing Shakespeare : new psychoanalytic essays / edited by Murray M. Schwartz and Coppélia Kahn. — Baltimore ; London : Johns Hopkins University Press, 1980 (1982 [printing]). — xxi,296p ; 23cm
Bibliography: p264-286. — Includes index
ISBN 0-8018-2825-2 (pbk) : £6.00 B82-34346

822.3'3 — Drama in English. Shakespeare, William. Scenes. Structure

Hirsh, James E.. The structure of Shakespearean scenes / James E. Hirsh. — New Haven ; London : Yale University Press, c1981. — ix,230p ; 22cm
ISBN 0-300-02650-1 : Unpriced : CIP rev.
B81-31943

822.3'3 — Drama in English. Shakespeare, William. Special subjects: Innocent victims — *Critical studies*

White, R. S.. Innocent victims : poetic injustice in Shakespearean tragedy / by R.S. White. — Newcastle Upon Tyne : [School of English Language and Literature, University of Newcastle Upon Tyne], 1982. — 112p ; 21cm
ISBN 0-9507521-1-8 (pbk) : Unpriced
B82-13331

822.3'3 — Drama in English. Shakespeare, William. Special themes: Coming of age — *Critical studies*

Garber, Marjorie. Coming of age in Shakespeare / Marjorie Garber. — London : Methuen, 1981. — viii,248p ; 22cm
Includes index
ISBN 0-416-30350-1 : £12.50 : CIP rev.
B81-14858

822.3'3 — Drama in English. Shakespeare, William. Special themes: Flowering plants — *Critical studies*

De Bray, Lys. Fantastic garlands : an anthology of flowers and plants from Shakespeare / Lys de Bray. — Poole : Blandford, 1982. — 144p : col.ill ; 26cm
Bibliography: p144. — Includes index
ISBN 0-7137-1066-7 : £9.95 : CIP rev.
B81-30326

822.3'3 — Drama in English. Shakespeare, William. Special themes: Flowering plants — *Illustrations*

Crane, Walter. Flowers from Shakespeare's garden : a posy from the plays / pictured by Walter Crane. — London : Studio Vista, 1980. — 40p : chiefly col.ill ; 26cm
Originally published: London : Cassell, 1906. — Ill on lining papers
ISBN 0-289-70910-5 : £4.95 B82-22514

822.3'3 — Drama in English. Shakespeare, William. Special themes: Love

Kirsch, Arthur. Shakespeare and the experience of love / Arthur Kirsch. — Cambridge : Cambridge University Press, 1981. — x,194p ; 22cm
Includes index
ISBN 0-521-23825-0 : £16.00 B82-02402

822.3'3 — Drama in English. Shakespeare, William. Stage directions

Slater, Ann Pasternak. Shakespeare the director. — Brighton : Harvester Press, Aug.1982. — [256]p
ISBN 0-7108-0446-6 : £18.95 : CIP entry
B82-15910

822.3'3 — Drama in English. Shakespeare, William — *Texts*

Shakespeare, William. Hamlet. — London : Methuen, Feb.1982. — [500]p. — (The Arden Shakespeare)
ISBN 0-416-17910-x (cased) : £12.00 : CIP entry
ISBN 0-416-17920-7 (pbk) : £2.95 B81-36391

Shakespeare, William. Henry V. — Oxford : Clarendon Press, June 1982. — [280]p. — (The Oxford Shakespeare) (Oxford English texts)
ISBN 0-19-812912-2 : £10.00 : CIP entry
B82-10445

Shakespeare, William. [Love's labour's lost]. Love's labour's lost / William Shakespeare ; edited by John Kerrigan. — Harmondsworth : Penguin, 1982. — 259p ; 18cm. — (New Penguin Shakespeare)
Bibliography: p37-40
ISBN 0-14-070738-7 (pbk) : £1.50 B82-26635

Shakespeare, William. Macbeth / William Shakespeare ; adapted by Guy Williams and Hugh Black-Hawkins. — Basingstoke : Macmillan Education, 1982. — 58p ; 22cm. — (Dramascript classics)
ISBN 0-333-30105-6 (pbk) : £0.95 : CIP rev.
B80-18475

Shakespeare, William. A midsummer night's dream / edited by Roma Gill. — Oxford : Oxford University Press, 1981. — xxix,90p : ill ; 22cm. — (Oxford school Shakespeare)
Author: William Shakespeare
ISBN 0-19-831938-x (pbk) : £1.25 B82-15557

Shakespeare, William. A midsummer night's dream. — London : Ash & Grant, Oct.1981. — [96]p
ISBN 0-904069-41-9 : £6.95 : CIP entry
B81-27401

Shakespeare, William. A midsummmer night's dream. — London : British Broadcasting Corporation, 1981. — 96p,[4]p of plates : ill (some col.) ; 21cm. — (The BBC TV Shakespeare)
Author: William Shakespeare
ISBN 0-563-20002-2 (pbk) : £2.00 B82-10341

Shakespeare, William. Much ado about nothing / edited by A.R. Humphreys. — London : Methuen, 1981. — xiv,237p ; 21cm. — (The Arden Shakespeare)
ISBN 0-416-17990-8 (cased) : Unpriced : CIP rev.
ISBN 0-416-19430-3 (pbk) : 2.40 B81-30463

Shakespeare, William. Much ado about nothing / edited by Jan McKeith. — Basingstoke : Macmillan Education, 1982. — 223p ; 18cm. — (The Macmillan Shakespeare)
Written by William Shakespeare
ISBN 0-333-28628-6 (pbk) : £0.95 : CIP rev.
B81-35787

Shakespeare, William. Othello. — London : British Broadcasting Corporation, 1981. — 128p,[4]p of plates : ill(some col.) ; 21cm. — (The BBC TV Shakespeare)
Author: William Shakespeare
ISBN 0-563-20003-0 (pbk) : £2.00 B82-10342

Shakespeare, William. [Richard III]. King Richard III / edited by Anthony Hammond. — London : Methuen, 1981. — xvi,382p ; 20cm. — (The Arden Shakespeare)
Bibliography: pxi-xvi
ISBN 0-416-17970-3 (cased) : Unpriced : CIP rev.
ISBN 0-416-17980-0 (pbk) : £2.95 B81-30157

Shakespeare, William. Romeo and Juliet / edited by Roma Gill. — Oxford : Oxford University Press, 1982. — xxxiv,127p : ill ; 22cm. — (Oxford school Shakespeare)
Author: William Shakespeare
ISBN 0-19-831937-1 (pbk) : Unpriced
B82-32266

Shakespeare, William. The taming of the shrew. — London : British Broadcasting Corporation, 1980. — 112p : ill(some col.) ; 21cm. — (The BBC TV Shakespeare)
Author: William Shakespeare
ISBN 0-563-17873-6 (pbk) : £2.00 B82-20981

Shakespeare, William. The taming of the shrew / edited by Brian Morris. — London : Methuen, 1981. — xiv,316p ; 21cm. — (The Arden Shakespeare)
ISBN 0-416-47580-9 (cased) : Unpriced : CIP rev.
ISBN 0-416-17800-6 (pbk) : £2.95 B81-31714

Shakespeare, William. The taming of the shrew. — Oxford : Clarendon Press, Apr.1982. — [256]p. — (The Oxford Shakespeare)
ISBN 0-19-812907-6 : £10.00 : CIP entry
B82-04284

Shakespeare, William. Timon of Athens. — London : British Broadcasting Corporation, 1981. — 111p,[4]p of plates : ill(some col.) ; 21cm. — (The BBC TV Shakespeare)
Author: William Shakespeare
ISBN 0-563-17872-8 (pbk) : £2.00 B82-10340

Shakespeare, William. Troilus and Cressida. — London : British Broadcasting Corporation, 1981. — 128p,[4]p of plates : ill(some col.) ; 21cm. — (The BBC TV Shakespeare)
Author: William Shakespeare
ISBN 0-563-20004-9 (pbk) : £2.00 B82-10339

Shakespeare, William. Troilus and Cressida. — Oxford : Clarendon Press, June 1982. — [260] p. — (The Oxford Shakespeare) (Oxford English texts)
ISBN 0-19-812903-3 : £9.50 : CIP entry
B82-10444

Shakespeare, William. Troilus and Cressida. — London : Methuen, Sept.1982. — [300]p. — (The Arden Shakespeare)
ISBN 0-416-47680-5 (cased) : £11.95 : CIP entry
ISBN 0-416-17790-5 (pbk) : £2.95 B82-20179

Shakespeare, William. Troilus and Cressida / edited by J.H. Walter. — London : Heinemann Educational, 1982. — 304p : ill ; 20cm. — (The Players' Shakespeare)
Author: William Shakespeare. — Text on lining papers
ISBN 0-435-19015-6 : Unpriced : CIP rev.
B81-22600

Shakespeare, William. The winter's tale / edited by Christopher Parry. — Basingstoke : Macmillan Education, 1982. — 274p ; 18cm. — (The Macmillan Shakespeare)
Written by William Shakespeare
ISBN 0-333-28627-8 (pbk) : £0.95 : CIP rev.
B81-35788

Shakespeare, William. [Works]. The complete works of William Shakespeare / edited by Peter Alexander. — London : Collins, 1951 (1981 [printing]). — 647p ; 30cm
Includes index
ISBN 0-00-410515-x (pbk) : £3.95 B82-01019

Shakespeare, William. [Works]. The illustrated Stratford Shakespeare. — London : Chancellor Press, 1982. — 1023p : ill ; 22cm
ISBN 0-907486-15-0 : £6.50 B82-35468

822.3'3 — Drama in English. Shakespeare, William. Tragedies — *Critical studies*

Shakespeare's tragedies : an anthology of modern criticism / edited by Laurence Lerner. — Harmondsworth : Penguin, 1963, c1968 (1982 [printing]). — [317]p ; 19cm. — (Pelican books)
Bibliography: p317
ISBN 0-14-020645-0 (pbk) : £1.95 B82-37606

822.3'3 — Educational institutions. Curriculum subjects: Drama in English. Shakespeare, William. Teaching

O'Brien, Veronica. Teaching Shakespeare. — London : Edward Arnold, July 1982. — [96]p. — (Teaching matters)
ISBN 0-7131-0725-1 (pbk) : £3.50 : CIP entry
B82-17919

822.4 — ENGLISH DRAMA, 1625-1702

822'.4 — Drama in English, *1625-1702* — *Texts*

Congreve, William, *1670-1729*. The comedies of William Congreve. — Cambridge : Cambridge University Press, July 1982. — [407]p. — (Plays by Renaissance and Restoration dramatists)
ISBN 0-521-24747-0 (cased) : £21.00 : CIP entry
ISBN 0-521-28932-7 (pbk) : £7.50 B82-14518

Congreve, William, *1670-1729*. The double dealer. — London : Benn, Nov.1981. — [160]p. — (The New mermaids)
ISBN 0-510-33504-7 (pbk) : £2.95 : CIP entry
B81-30526

Dryden, John, *1631-1700*. Marriage à la mode / John Dryden ; edited by Mark S. Auburn. — London : Edward Arnold, 1981. — xxxi,144p ; 21cm. — (Regents restoration drama series)
ISBN 0-7131-6356-9 (pbk) : £3.95 : CIP rev.
B81-23786

Etherege, *Sir* **George**. The plays of George Etherege. — Cambridge : Cambridge University Press, Sept.1982. — [341]p. — (Plays by Renaissance and Restoration dramatists)
Contents: The comical revenge, or Love in a tub — She would if she could — The man of mode, or, Sir Fopfling Flutter
ISBN 0-521-24654-7 (cased) : £21.00 : CIP entry
ISBN 0-521-28879-7 (pbk) : £7.50 B82-25499

Philips, William. St Stephen's Green, or, The generous lovers / by William Philips ; edited by Christopher Murray. — Portlaoise : Dolmen, 1980. — 155p : 2ill,1facsim ; 23cm. — (Dolmen texts ; 6)
ISBN 0-85105-367-x : £6.00 : CIP rev.
B80-03809

Vanbrugh, *Sir* **John**. The provoked wife / Sir John Vanbrugh ; edited by Antony Coleman. — Manchester : Manchester University Press, 1982. — xii,196p : ill,music ; 21cm. — (The Revels plays)
Six men, 4 women. — Includes index
ISBN 0-7190-1526-x : £27.50 : CIP rev.
B81-35721

822'.4 — Drama in English. Behn, Aphra — *Biographies*

Goreau, Angeline. Reconstructing Aphra : a social biography of Aphra Behn / Angeline Goreau. — Oxford : Oxford University Press, 1980. — x,339p,[16]p of plates : ill,1map,2facsims,ports ; 24cm
Originally published: New York : Dial Press, 1980. — Bibliography: p319-330. — Includes index
ISBN 0-19-822663-2 : £8.95 B82-11572

822'.4 — Drama in English. Congreve, William, *1670-1729 — Critical studies*

Congreve : comedies : The old bachelor, The double-dealer, Love for love, The way of the world : a casebook / edited by Patrick Lyons. — London : Macmillan, 1982. — 244p ; 23cm. — (Casebook series)
Bibliography: p235-236. — Includes index
ISBN 0-333-26456-8 (cased) : Unpriced
ISBN 0-333-26457-6 (pbk) : Unpriced
B82-25392

822'.4'09 — Verse drama in English, *1625-1702 — Critical studies*

Freer, Coburn. The poetics of Jacobean drama / Coburn Freer. — Baltimore, Md. ; London : Johns Hopkins University Press, c1981. — xxi,256p ; 24cm
Includes index
ISBN 0-8018-2545-8 : Unpriced B82-28096

822.5 — ENGLISH DRAMA, 1702-1745

822'.5 — Drama in English, *1702-1745 — Texts*

Gay, John, *1685-1732*. John Gay : dramatic works. — Oxford : Clarendon Press, May 1982. — [868]p. — (Oxford English texts)
ISBN 0-19-812701-4 : £40.00 : CIP entry
B82-07508

822.6 — ENGLISH DRAMA, 1745-1800

822'.6'08 — Drama in English, *1745-1800 — Anthologies*

Plays by David Garrick and George Colman the Elder / edited with an introduction and notes by E.R. Wood. — Cambridge : Cambridge University Press, 1982. — ix,217p : ill,1plan,ports ; 24cm. — (British and American playwrights 1750-1920)
Bibliography: p217. — Contents; The lying valet / by David Garrick — The jealous wife / by George Colman the Elder — The clandenstine marriage / by David Garrick and George Colman the Elder — The Irish widow / by David Garrick — Bon ton / by David Garrick
ISBN 0-521-23590-1 (cased) : £17.50 : CIP rev.
ISBN 0-521-28057-5 (pbk) : £5.95 B82-12697

822.8 — ENGLISH DRAMA, 1837-1900

822'.8 — Drama in English, *1837-1900 — Texts*

Gilbert, W. S.. Plays by W.S. Gilbert / edited with an introduction and notes by George Rowell. — Cambridge : Cambridge University Press, 1982. — ix,189p : ill,facsim,music ; 24cm. — (British and American playwrights 1750-1920)
Bibliography: p188-189. — Contents: The palace of truth — Sweethearts — Princess Toto — Engaged — Rosencrantz and Guildenstern
ISBN 0-521-23589-8 (cased) : £17.50 : CIP rev.
ISBN 0-521-28056-7 (pbk) : £4.95 B82-11479

Jones, Henry Arthur. Plays by Henry Arthur Jones : The silver king, The case of rebellious Susan, The liars. — Cambridge : Cambridge University Press, July 1982. — [228]p. — (British and American playwrights, 1750-1920)
ISBN 0-521-23369-0 (cased) : £17.50 : CIP entry
ISBN 0-521-29936-5 (pbk) : £5.95 B82-13257

Robertson, T.W.. Plays by Tom Robertson / edited with an introduction and notes by William Tydeman. — Cambridge : Cambridge University Press, 1982. — x,237p : ill,1port ; 24cm. — (British and American playwrights 1750-1920)
Bibliography: p236-237. — Contents: Society — Ours — Caste — School
ISBN 0-521-23386-0 (cased) : £19.50
ISBN 0-521-29939-x (pbk) : £5.95 B82-16931

Wilde, Oscar. The importance of being Earnest : a trivial play for serious people / Oscar Wilde ; with an introduction by Adeline Hartcup. — New ed. — London : Eyre Methuen, 1966 (1980 [printing]). — xiii,73p ; 19cm. — (Methuen's theatre classics)
ISBN 0-413-31000-0 (pbk) : £1.95 B82-15562

Wilde, Oscar. Plays / Oscar Wilde. — Harmondsworth : Penguin, 1954 (1982 [printing]). — 347p ; 18cm. — (Penguin plays)
Contents: Lady Windermere's fan — A woman of no importance — An ideal husband — The importance of being Earnest — Salomé
ISBN 0-14-048016-1 (pbk) : £1.10 B82-40803

Wilde, Oscar. Three plays / Oscar Wilde ; introduced by H. Montgomery Hyde. — London : Eyre Methuen, 1981. — 299p ; 18cm. — (The Master playwrights)
Contents: Lady Windermere's fan. Originally published: London : Elkin Mathews & John Lane, 1893 — An ideal husband. Originally published: London : Smithers, 1899 — The importance of being Earnest. Originally published: London : Smithers, 1899
ISBN 0-413-48530-7 (pbk) : £1.50 B82-15609

Wilde, Oscar. Two society comedies. — London : Benn, Jan.1983. — [256]p. — (The new mermaids)
ISBN 0-510-33511-x (pbk) : £4.50 : CIP entry
B82-32429

Yeats, W. B.. The death of Cuchulain : manuscript materials including the author's final text / by W.B. Yeats ; edited by Phillip L. Marcus. — Ithaca ; London : Cornell University Press, 1982. — x,182p : facsims ; 25cm. — (The Cornell Yeats)
ISBN 0-8014-1379-6 : £26.50 B82-36993

822'.8'0809415 — Drama in English. Irish writers, *1837-1945 — Anthologies*

[The Countess Cathleen]. Classic Irish drama / introduced by W.A. Armstrong. — Harmondsworth : Penguin, 1964 (1979 [printing]). — 224p : music ; 19cm. — (Penguin plays)
Contents: The Countess Cathleen / W.B. Yeats — The Playboy of the Western World / J.M. Synge — Cock-a-doodle Dandy / Sean O'Casey
ISBN 0-14-048054-4 (pbk) : £1.25 B82-07277

822.912 — ENGLISH DRAMA, 1900-1945

822'.912 — Drama in English, *1900-1945 — Armenian texts*

Beckett, Samuel. Kal do yertal : Samuel Beckett's Come and go / translated into (Western) Armenian with introduction, notes and commentary by Hovhanness I. Pilikian. — London : Counter-Point, c1982. — 218p ; 21cm
Translation of: Come and go
ISBN 0-906192-03-x (pbk) : £5.00 : CIP rev.
B82-05780

822'.912 — Drama in English, *1900-1945 — Texts*

Burrell, Philippa. The isle, the sea and the crown : an epic drama of Britain / by Philippa Burrell ; music for the song of the Welsh miners composed by William Wordsworth. — Chesterfield : Poets and Patrons, 1981. — 326p : 1ill,music ; 21cm
Limited ed. of 500 numbered and signed copies
ISBN 0-907302-00-9 (pbk) : £3.95 B82-20984

Durbridge, Francis. House guest : a thriller / Francis Durbridge. — London : French, c1982. — 64p : 1plan ; 22cm
Four men, 4 women
ISBN 0-573-11178-2 (pbk) : £2.25 B82-13874

Greene, Graham. The great Jowett / Graham Greene. — London : Bodley Head, 1981. — 43p ; 22cm
Originally written as a BBC radio play and broadcast on May 6th, 1939
ISBN 0-370-30439-x : Unpriced : CIP rev.
B81-27433

Gregory, Isabella Augusta, *Lady*. Selected plays of Lady Gregory. — Gerrards Cross : Smythe, Sept.1982. — [236]p. — (Irish drama selections ; 3)
ISBN 0-86140-099-2 (cased) : £12.50 : CIP entry
ISBN 0-86140-100-x (pbk) : £3.50 B82-25941

Johnston, Denis. Selected plays of Denis Johnston. — Gerrards Cross : Colin Smythe, Sept.1982. — [416]p. — (Irish drama selections, ISSN 0260-7964 ; 2)
Contents: The old lady says 'No!' — The moon in the Yellow River — The golden cuckoo — The dreaming dust — The scythe and the sunset
ISBN 0-86140-123-9 (cased) : £9.00 : CIP entry
ISBN 0-86140-086-0 (pbk) : £3.25 B82-21113

Robinson, Lennox. Selected plays of Lennox Robinson. — Gerrards Cross : Colin Smythe, June 1982. — [400]p. — (Irish drama selections, ISSN 0260-7962 ; 1)
ISBN 0-86140-087-9 (cased) : £9.50 : CIP entry
ISBN 0-86140-088-7 (pbk) : £3.25 B82-10243

Shaw, Bernard. Man and superman : a comedy and a philosophy / Bernard Shaw ; definitive text under the editorial supervision of Dan H. Laurence. — Harmondsworth : Penguin, 1946 (1982 [printing]). — 264p : music ; 18cm. — (Penguin plays)
Six men, 5 women
ISBN 0-14-048006-4 (pbk) : £1.75 B82-40676

822′.912 — Drama in English, *1900-1945 — Texts continuation*

Shaw, Bernard. Plays unpleasant / by Bernard Shaw. — Harmondsworth : Penguin, 1946 (1981 [printing]). — 285p ; 19cm. — (Penguin plays)
Contents: Widowers′ houses — The philanderer — Mrs. Warren′s profession
ISBN 0-14-048012-9 (pbk) : £1.50 B82-05958

Shaw, Bernard. Selected one act plays : definitive text / Bernard Shaw ; with the editorial supervision of Dan H. Laurence. — Harmondsworth : Penguin, 1972 (1982 [printing]). — 357p ; 19cm
This collection orginally published in two volumes. 1965
ISBN 0-14-048123-0 (pbk) : £1.95 B82-25231

Synge, J. M.. The complete plays / J.M. Synge ; with an introduction and notes by T.R. Henn. — London : Eyre Methuen, 1981. — vi,311p ; 18cm. — (The Master playwrights)
ISBN 0-413-48520-x (pbk) : £1.50 B82-15610

Synge J. M.. The well of the saints. — Gerrards Cross : Colin Smyth, Aug.1982. — [96]p. — (Irish dramatic texts)
ISBN 0-86140-127-1 (cased) : £4.95 : CIP entry
ISBN 0-86140-128-x (pbk) : £2.25 B82-16683

822′.912 — Drama in English. Barker, Granville — *Biographies*

Salmon, Eric. Granville Barker : a secret life. — London : Heinemann Educational, Jan.1983. — [352]p
ISBN 0-435-18790-2 : £15.50 : CIP entry B82-34094

822′.912 — Drama in English. Coward, Noël — *Critical studies*

Lahr, John. Coward the playwright / by John Lahr. — London : Methuen, 1982. — x,178p,8p of plates : ill,ports ; 20cm
Bibliography: p175-176. — Includes index
ISBN 0-413-46840-2 (cased) : £7.95
ISBN 0-413-48050-x (pbk) : £3.95 B82-39527

822′.912 — Drama in English. Eliot, T. S.. Murder in the cathedral — *Study outlines*

Bareham, Tony. Murder in the cathedral : notes / by Tony Bareham. — Harlow : Longman, 1981. — 80p ; 21cm. — (York notes ; 149)
Bibliography: p75
ISBN 0-582-78217-1 (pbk) : £0.90 B82-16459

822′.912 — Drama in English. O′Casey, Sean — *Critical studies*

Atkinson, Brooks. Sean O′Casey : from times past / by Brooks Atkinson ; edited by Robert G. Lowery. — London : Macmillan, 1982. — x,175p ; 23cm
Includes index
ISBN 0-333-30010-6 : £17.50 B82-38777

Greaves, C. Desmond. Sean O′Casey : politics and art / by C. Desmond Greaves. — London : Lawrence and Wishart, 1979. — 206p ; 23cm
Bibliography: p197-199. — Includes index
ISBN 0-85315-431-7 : £6.95 B82-27729

The **O′Casey** enigma / edited by Micheál Ó hAodha. — Dublin : Published in collaboration with Radio Telefis Éireann by the Mercier Press, 1980. — 124p : ill ; 18cm. — (The Thomas Davis lecture series)
ISBN 0-85342-637-6 (pbk) : £2.60 (Irish) B82-37053

822′.912 — Drama in English. O′Casey, Sean. Juno and the paycock — *Study outlines*

Hayley, Barbara. Juno and the paycock : notes / by Barbara Hayley. — Harlow : Longman, 1981. — 95p ; 21cm. — (York notes ; 112)
Bibliography: p93-95
ISBN 0-582-78173-6 (pbk) : £0.90 B82-03221

822′.912 — Drama in English. Shaw, Bernard — *Correspondence, diaries, etc.*

Shaw, Bernard. The playwright and the pirate : Bernard Shaw and Frank Harris, a correspondence. — Gerrards Cross : Smythe, Sept.1982. — [276]p
ISBN 0-86140-131-x : £11.00 : CIP entry
Also classified at 828′.91209 B82-26058

822′.912 — Drama in English. Shaw, Bernard. Heartbreak House — *Study outlines*

O′Donnell, Hugh. Heartbreak House / Hugh O′Donnell. — Dublin : Helicon, 1981 : Distributed by Educational Company. — 38p ; 21cm. — (Helicon notes)
Bibliography: p38
Unpriced (pbk) B82-02552

822′.912 — Drama in English. Synge, J. M. — *Critical studies*

Johnson, Toni O′Brien. Synge. — Gerrards Cross : Colin Smythe, June 1982. — [215]p. — (Irish literary studies, ISSN 0140-895X ; 11)
ISBN 0-86140-104-2 : £9.75 : CIP entry B82-14213

822′.912′09 — Drama in English, *1900- — Critical studies*

Nightingale, Benedict. A reader′s guide to fifty modern British plays. — London : Heinemann Educational, Sept.1982. — [464]p
ISBN 0-435-18725-2 : £9.50 : CIP entry B82-20631

822′.912′099415 — Drama in English. Irish writers, *1900-1980 — Critical studies*

Hogan, Robert. 'Since O′Casey' and other essays on Irish drama. — Gerrards Cross : Smythe, Jan.1983. — [200]p. — (Irish literary studies, ISSN 0140-895x ; 15)
ISBN 0-86140-115-8 : £9.75 : CIP entry B82-33225

822.914 — ENGLISH DRAMA, 1945-

822′.914 — Drama in English, *1945- — Texts*

Antrobus, John S.. Hitler in Liverpool and other plays. — London : John Calder, May 1982. — [192]p. — (Playscript ; 100)
ISBN 0-7145-3898-1 (pbk) : £4.95 : CIP entry B82-07674

Ayckbourn, Alan. Season′s greetings : a play / Alan Ayckbourn. — London : French, c1982. — 85p : 1plan ; 22cm
Five men, 4 women
ISBN 0-573-11401-3 (pbk) : £2.50 B82-33183

Barker, Howard. The hang of the goal ; and, Heaven. — London : John Calder, Apr.1982. — [116]p. — (Playscript ; 94)
ISBN 0-7145-3769-1 (pbk) : £5.95 : CIP entry B82-06044

Barker, Howard. Two plays for the right. — London : Calder, Nov.1982. — [120]p. — (Playscript series ; 101)
Contents: The land boy′s life — Birth on a hard shoulder
ISBN 0-7145-3896-5 (pbk) : £4.95 : CIP entry B82-29431

Beckett, Samuel. Three occasional pieces / by Samuel Beckett. — London : Faber, 1982. — 32p ; 20cm
Contents: A piece of monologue — Rockaby — Ohio impromptu
ISBN 0-571-11800-3 (pbk) : £1.25 : CIP rev. B81-36214

Beddow, William. Baboushka offers her gifts : a Christmas play / by William Beddow. — London : Mowbray, 1982. — 15p ; 21cm
Thirteen men, 2 women
ISBN 0-264-66861-8 (pbk) : £0.80 B82-33569

Beddow, William. The coming of the Messiah / by William Beddow. — London : Mowbray, 1982. — 16p ; 21cm
Twenty four characters
ISBN 0-264-66863-4 (pbk) : £0.80 B82-33568

Beddow, William. The first nativity play / by William Beddow. — London : Mowbray, 1982. — 16p ; 21cm
Twenty three characters and supers
ISBN 0-264-66860-x (pbk) : £0.80 B82-33571

Beddow, William. Wenceslas and the Christmas story / by William Beddow. — London : Mowbray, 1982. — 15p ; 22cm
Eighteen characters, and supers
ISBN 0-264-66862-6 : £0.80 B82-33570

Berkoff, Steven. Decadence ; and, Greek. — London : Calder, Nov.1982. — [96]p. — (Playscripts ; 101)
ISBN 0-7145-3954-6 (pbk) : £2.95 : CIP entry B82-29014

Bethell, Andrew. Roots, rules and tribulations / Andrew Bethell. — Cambridge : Cambridge University Press, 1982. — 90p : ill ; 21cm. — (Act now)
Fifteen men and 5 women
ISBN 0-521-28570-4 (pbk) : Unpriced : CIP rev. B82-11483

Betts, Ron. A packet of trouble : a play / by Ron Betts. — Macclesfield : New Playwrights Network, [1982?]. — 92p : 1plan ; 18cm
Eight men, 5 women, supers
£2.20 (pbk) B82-30417

Bogdanov, Michael. Hiawatha / Longfellow′s classic poem adapted by Michael Bogdanov. — London : Heinemann, 1981. — xii,65p ; 19cm
Ten men, 1 woman. — Bibliography: pviii-ix
ISBN 0-435-23080-8 (pbk) : Unpriced B82-08880

Bond, Edward. Restoration ; &, The cat / Edward Bond. — London : Methuen, 1982. — 167p : music ; 20cm. — (Methuen′s modern plays)
Restoration originally published: London : Eyre Methuen, 1981
ISBN 0-413-48840-3 (cased) : £7.50
ISBN 0-413-49920-0 (pbk) : £3.50 B82-34374

Bowyer, E.. The shoemaker′s Christmas surprise / by E. Bowyer. — Ilkeston : Moorley′s Bible & Bookshop, [1981?]. — 15p ; 21cm
ISBN 0-86071-125-0 (pbk) : £0.25 B82-02864

Boyd, John, *1912-*. Collected plays / John Boyd. — Dundonald : Blackstaff
1. — 1981. — xii,260p ; 22cm
Contents: The flats. Rev. ed. Previous ed.: 1973 — The farm — Guests
ISBN 0-85640-250-8 (pbk) : £6.95 : CIP rev. B81-30981

Boyd, John, *1912-*. Collected plays 2 / John Boyd. — Dundonald : Blackstaff, c1982. — viii,165p ; 21cm
Contents: The Street — Facing north
ISBN 0-85640-251-6 (pbk) : £6.95 : CIP rev. B82-06255

Bradbury, Malcolm. The after dinner game : three plays for television / Malcolm Bradbury. — London : Arrow, 1982. — 176p ; 18cm
Partial contents: Love on a gunboat — Standing in for Henry
ISBN 0-09-927910-x (pbk) : £1.75 B82-19009

Brown, John Russell. The complete plays of 'The Wakefield Master′. — London : Heinemann, Sept.1982. — [144]p
ISBN 0-435-23138-3 (pbk) : £2.50 : CIP entry B82-19672

Burton, Brian J.. Drink to me only : a play in one act / Brian J. Burton. — Droitwich : Hanbury, c1982. — 22p ; 21cm
One man, 2 woman
ISBN 0-907926-01-0 (pbk) : £0.75 B82-36534

Burton, Brian J.. Face the Queen : a play in one act / Brian J. Burton. — Droitwich : Hanbury Plays, c1982. — 27p ; 21cm
Seven women
ISBN 0-907926-03-7 (pbk) : £0.75 B82-31212

Burton, Brian J.. From three to four / by Brian J. Burton. — Droitwich : Hanbury Plays, c1982. — 21p ; 21cm
One man, 3 women. — Text on inside cover
ISBN 0-907926-00-2 (pbk) : £0.75 B82-31211

Burton, Brian J.. The last laugh : a play in one act / Brian J. Burton. — Droitwich : Hanbury Plays, c1982. — 23p ; 21cm
Two men, 2 women
ISBN 0-907926-02-9 (pbk) : £0.75 B82-36807

822'.914 — Drama in English, *1945-* — *Texts continuation*

Carew, Jan. Time loop. — London : Hutchinson Education, Jan.1983. — [40]p
ISBN 0-09-149091-x (pbk) : £0.75 : CIP entry B82-33618

Chambers, Aidan. The dream cage. — London : Heinemann Educational, Oct.1982. — [96]p
ISBN 0-435-23168-5 (pbk) : £2.95 : CIP entry B82-28451

Chattaway, Anne C.. Look Easter! : a play for Easter / by Anne C. Chattaway. — [Ilkeston] : Moorley's, [1982?]. — 20p : 1plan ; 21cm
Fourteen men, 8 women, supers
ISBN 0-86071-146-3 (pbk) : £0.30 B82-16341

Corrie, Joe. Robert Burns : a play / by Joe Corrie. — Glasgow : Brown, Son & Ferguson, 1979. — 94p ; 18cm
ISBN 0-85174-342-0 (pbk) : £0.75 B82-37322

Cowper, Trevor. Caught in the act : a comedy / Trevor Cowper. — London : French, c1982. — 58p : 1plan ; 22cm
Four men, 2 women
ISBN 0-573-11139-1 (pbk) : £2.50 B82-19135

Coyle, Michael. Research : a play in one act / by Michael Coyle. — Macclesfield : New Playwrights' Network, [1981]. — 23p : 1plan ; 18cm
Five men, 2 women
£0.65 (pbk) B82-03254

D'Arcy, Margaretta. The little gray home in the west : an Anglo-Irish melodrama / Margaretta D'Arcy and John Arden. — London : Pluto Plays, 1982. — 73p ; 31cm
Eleven men, 2 women
ISBN 0-86104-221-2 (pbk) : £3.50 B82-19412

Davies, Andrew. Going bust : a play / Andrew Davies. — London : French, c1982. — 57p : plan ; 22cm
Five men, 2 women
ISBN 0-573-11162-6 (pbk) : £2.50 B82-33942

Davies, Andrew. Rose : a comedy / by Andrew Davies. — New York ; London : French, c1980. — 70p ; 18cm
Four men, 5 women. — Text on inside covers
ISBN 0-573-61507-1 (pbk) : £2.75 B82-27264

Deiches, I. W.. Bugs Bugsby case / by I.W. Deiches and Jenny Humphrey. — London : Omensheep Show, c1981. — 17leaves : ill ; 30cm. — (Omensheep show ; 2)
Five men, 4 women. — Based on the making of the radio play 'Omensheep show' for Radio Moorfields
ISBN 0-907863-01-9 (spiral) : Unpriced B82-08823

Deiches, I. W.. The curse of Tooting Common / by I.W. Deiches and Jenny Humphrey. — London : Omensheep Show, c1981. — 17leaves : ill ; 30cm. — (Omensheep show ; 4)
Eleven men, 2 women. — Based on the making of the radio play 'Omensheep show' for Radio Moorfields
ISBN 0-907863-03-5 (spiral) : Unpriced B82-08825

Deiches, I. W.. Lost tribe of Backwahtum case / by I.W. Deiches and Jenny Humphrey. — London : Omensheep Show, c1981. — 16leaves : ill ; 30cm. — (Omensheep show ; 3)
Five men, 4 women. — Based on the making of the radio play 'Omensheep show' for Radio Moorfields
ISBN 0-907863-02-7 (spiral) : Unpriced B82-08824

Deiches, I. W.. The Ratso, red-hot sheepdog case / by I.W. Deiches and Jenny Humphrey. — London : Omensheep Show, c1981. — 12leaves : ill ; 30cm. — (Omensheep show ; 1)
Four men, 2 women. — Based on the making of the radio play 'Omensheep show' for Radio Moorfields
ISBN 0-907863-00-0 (spiral) : Unpriced B82-08822

Dewhurst, Keith. Lark Rise to Candleford : 2 plays / by Keith Dewhurst from Flora Thompson's trilogy. — London : Hutchinson, 1980. — 171p : ill ; 19cm
ISBN 0-09-142781-9 (pbk) : £2.50 : CIP rev. B80-13972

Docherty, Gerry. Czechmate / Gerry Docherty and Bill Kinross. — Cambridge : Cambridge University, 1982. — 104p : ill,music ; 21cm. — (Act now plays)
Twenty one men, 7 women, supers
ISBN 0-521-28572-0 (pbk) : £1.00 : CIP rev. B82-25768

Dryden, Ellen. Harvest : a play / Ellen Dryden. — London : French, c1982. — 54p : plans ; 22cm
Two men, 5 women
ISBN 0-573-11171-5 (pbk) : £2.50 B82-19136

Dunn, Sheila. Jesus, friend of — / by Sheila Dunn. — Ilkeston : Moorley's, [1982?]. — 15p ; 21cm
ISBN 0-86071-126-9 (pbk) : £0.25 B82-17753

English, Mike. Closed circuit / Mike English. — Cambridge : Cambridge University Press, 1982. — 60p ; 21cm. — (Act now)
For six men and 7 women
ISBN 0-521-28569-0 (pbk) : £1.00 B82-22647

Evans, Audrey. As short as any dream / by Audrey Evans. — Macclesfield : New Playwrights Network, [1982?]. — 28p : 1plan ; 18cm
Five men, 7 women
£0.70 (pbk) B82-30418

Evans, Audrey. So pitifully slain / by Audrey Evans. — Glasgow : Brown, Son & Ferguson, 1982. — 22p ; 19cm. — (Scottish plays ; no.22)
ISBN 0-85174-430-3 (pbk) : £0.70 B82-26032

Fitton, Neil. Conscience stricken : a play in one act / by Neil Fitton. — Macclesfield : New Playwrights' Network, [1981]. — 24p ; 18cm
Three men, 3 women
£0.65 (pbk) B82-03255

Flannery, Peter. Our friends in the north : a history play / by Peter Flannery. — London : Methuen in association with the Royal Shakespeare Company, 1982. — 72p ; 21cm. — (A Pit playtext)
Fifty-three characters
ISBN 0-413-50090-x (pbk) : £1.95 B82-33924

Flannery, Peter. Savage amusement / Peter Flannery. — London : Collings in association with the Royal Shakespeare Company, 1978. — 64p ; 21cm
Three men, 2 women
ISBN 0-86036-097-0 (pbk) : £2.50 B82-30438

Frayn, Michael. Noises off : a play in three acts / Michael Frayn. — London : Methuen, 1982. — 149p ; 19cm. — (A Methuen paperback)
ISBN 0-413-50670-3 (pbk) : £2.95 B82-33268

Friel, Brian. Volunteers / Brian Friel. — London : Faber, 1979. — 70p ; 20cm
Eight men
ISBN 0-571-10953-5 (pbk) : £2.95 : CIP rev. B79-28961

Gater, Dilys. Turnabout : a play in one act / by Dilys Gater. — Macclesfield : New Playwrights Network, [1982?]. — 24p : 1 plan ; 18cm
£0.70 (pbk) B82-30420

George, Richard R.. James and the giant peach. — London : Allen and Unwin, May 1982. — [96]p
ISBN 0-04-792013-0 : £3.95 : CIP entry B82-07235

Gray, Simon. Stage struck : a play / Simon Gray. — London : French, c1981. — 38p : 1plan ; 22cm
Three men, 1 woman. — Originally published: London : Eyre Methuen, 1979
ISBN 0-573-11414-5 (pbk) : £2.25 B82-02910

Griffiths, Trevor. Country : 'a Tory story' / Trevor Griffiths. — London : Faber, 1981. — 62p ; 20cm
ISBN 0-85111-885-2 (pbk) : £3.95 B82-00876

Griffiths, Trevor. Country : a Tory story. — London : Faber & Faber, Oct.1982. — [72]p
ISBN 0-571-11885-2 (pbk) : £3.95 : CIP entry B82-24730

Griffiths, Trevor. Oi for England / Trevor Griffiths. — London : Faber and Faber, 1982. — 38p ; 20cm
ISBN 0-571-11977-8 (pbk) : £1.95 : CIP rev. B82-14239

Griffiths, Trevor. Sons & lovers. — Nottingham : Spokesman Books, Oct.1982. — [300]p
ISBN 0-85124-333-9 (cased) : £14.50 : CIP entry
ISBN 0-85124-334-7 (pbk) : £4.95 B82-40916

Guinness, Owen. The Mayor of Casterbridge / Thomas Hardy ; adapted for the stage by Owen Guinness. — Basingstoke : Macmillan Education, 1982. — 65p ; 22cm. — (Dramascripts)
ISBN 0-333-30833-6 (pbk) : £0.95 : CIP rev. B81-35801

Hampton, Christopher. Total eclipse. — 2nd ed. — London : Faber, May 1981. — [96]p
Previous ed.: 1969
ISBN 0-571-18048-5 (pbk) : £2.95 : CIP entry B81-12917

Hampton, Christopher, *1946-*. Tales from Hollywood. — London : Faber, Feb.1983. — [96]p
ISBN 0-571-11883-6 (pbk) : CIP entry B82-38701

Harding, Mike. Fur coat and no knickers : a comedy / Mike Harding. — London : French, c1982. — 54p : plans ; 21cm
Thirteen men, 9 women
ISBN 0-573-11145-6 (pbk) : £2.50 B82-17378

Hare, David. A map of the world. — 2nd rev. ed. — London : Faber, Jan.1983. — [84]p
Previous ed.: 1981
ISBN 0-571-11996-4 : £2.00 : CIP entry B82-32448

Harris, Richard, *1934-*. The business of murder : a play / Richard Harris. — London : French, c1981. — 54p : 1plan ; 19cm
Two men, 1 woman
ISBN 0-573-11017-4 (pbk) : £2.25 B82-07332

Haworth, Elizabeth. Family matters. — Nutfield : National Christian Education Council, Mar.1982. — [36]p
ISBN 0-7197-0326-3 (pbk) : £1.00 : CIP entry B82-11084

Haworth, Elizabeth. Three men : a play for all seasons but especially for Passiontide, Easter and Pentecost / by Betty Haworth. — Redhill : National Christian Education Council, 1981. — 36p ; 21cm
Five men, 5 women
ISBN 0-7197-0305-0 (pbk) : £1.10 B82-08768

Hayes, Catherine. Skirmishes / Catherine Hayes. — London : Faber, 1982. — 61p ; 20cm
Three women
ISBN 0-571-11979-4 (pbk) : £2.95 : CIP rev. B82-14941

Hoddinott, Derek. Din dins : a comedy / Derek Hoddinott. — London : French, c1982. — 60p : 1plan ; 22cm
Five men, 3 women
ISBN 0-573-11106-5 (pbk) : £2.50 B82-22186

Hood, Evelyn. I never thought it would be like this : a play / Evelyn Hood. — London : French, c1982. — 19p ; 19cm
Two men, 2 women
ISBN 0-573-12113-3 (pbk) : £0.75 B82-33011

822′.914 — Drama in English, *1945-* **— *Texts continuation***

Horsler, Peter. The intruders : a comedy / Peter Horsler. — London : French, c1981. — 16p : 1plan ; 19cm
Two men, 2 women
ISBN 0-573-12115-x (pbk) : £0.70 B82-02909

Horsler, Peter. On the verge : a farcical comedy / Peter Horsler. — London : French, c1981. — 67p : ill,1plan ; 19cm
Four men, 6 women
ISBN 0-573-11326-2 (pbk) : £2.25 B82-07331

Howard, Roger. The Society of Poets : a grotesquery ; Memorial of the future : a rag : two plays / by Roger Howard. — [Colchester] : [Theatre Action Press] : Distributed by Action Books, c1979. — 20p ; 30cm
Cover title
ISBN 0-900575-08-5 (pbk) : Unpriced B82-07341

Hubbard, C. G.. Love in action : a demonstration / by C.G. Hubbard. — Ilkeston : Moorley's, [1982]. — 12p ; 21cm
Fifteen players
ISBN 0-86071-152-8 (pbk) : £0.30 B82-37263

Idle, Eric. Pass the butler / Eric Idle. — London : Methuen, 1982. — 81p ; 19cm
Six men, 3 women
ISBN 0-413-49990-1 (pbk) : £2.50 B82-27258

Jackson, Gordon, *1938-*. Exodus 17 : a play for voices in the wilderness / by Gordon Jackson. — Lincoln (1 Stonefield Ave., Lincoln) : Asgill, 1980. — 23p ; 22cm
£0.60 (pbk) B82-08851

Johnson, Terry. Insignificance / Terry Johnson. — London : published by Methuen in association with the Royal Court Theatre, 1982. — 30p ; 21cm. — (The Royal Court writers series)
Four men, 1 women
ISBN 0-413-51500-1 (pbk) : Unpriced B82-36116

Kember, Paul. Not quite Jerusalem / Paul Kember. — London : Methuen in association with the Royal Court Theatre, 1982. — 44p ; 21cm. — (The Royal Court writers series)
ISBN 0-413-50280-5 (pbk) : £1.95 B82-36420

Kureishi, Hanif. Outskirts and other plays. — London : John Calder, Jan.1983. — [96]p. — (Playscript series ; 102)
ISBN 0-7145-3971-6 (pbk) : £3.95 : CIP entry B82-39298

Lane, Sheila. Journey to Bethlehem : a nativity play / Sheila Lane and Marion Kemp. — Cambridge : Cambridge University Press, 1982. — 63p : ill,music ; 21cm. — (Playmakers)
ISBN 0-521-28636-0 (pbk) : £0.95 B82-34220

Langhorn, Frances. Murder at midday / by Frances Langhorn. — Macclesfield : New Playwrights' Network, [1981]. — 22p : 1plan ; 18cm
One man, 4 women
£0.65 (pbk) B82-03251

Lee, Anne. Faust and furious / Anne Lee. — Cambridge : Cambridge University Press, 1982. — 66p : ill ; 21cm. — (Act now plays)
Thirty-five characters, supers
ISBN 0-521-28568-2 (pbk) : £1.00 : CIP rev. B82-25769

Leigh, Mike. Goose-pimples : a play / devised by Mike Leigh. — London : French, c1982. — 84p : 1plan ; 22cm
Three men, 2 women
ISBN 0-573-11160-x (pbk) : £2.50 B82-33012

Lives, Eric. Woodwork / [Eric Lives]. — London (28 Earlham Grove, E7 9AW) : Sea Dream Music, 1979. — [4]p : 1ill ; 21cm
£0.05 (unbound) B82-39235

Lovering, Taylor. Closing day : a play in one act / by Taylor Lovering. — Macclesfield : New Playwrights' Network, [1981]. — 23p : 1plan ; 18cm
Three men, 3 women
£0.65 (pbk) B82-03252

Lowcock, Joyce. In case the queen looks in : a comedy / Joyce Lowcock. — London : Evan Plays, [c1980]. — 26p : 1plan ; 21cm
ISBN 0-237-75060-0 (pbk) : £0.60 B82-13630

Lowe, Stephen, *1947-*. Tibetan inroads / by Stephen Lowe. — London : Eyre Methuen in association with the Royal Court Theatre, 1981. — 52p : ill ; 21cm
Eleven men, 9 women, supers
ISBN 0-413-48710-5 (pbk) : £1.95 B82-33923

Lynch, Martin. The interrogation of Ambrose Fogarty : a play in three acts / Martin Lynch. — Dundonald : Blackstaff, c1982. — 81p ; 21cm
Eight men, 1 woman
ISBN 0-85640-270-2 (pbk) : £2.95 : CIP rev. B82-16219

McDonagh, Joe. Opening night / by Joe McDonagh. — Glasgow : Brown, Son & Ferguson, 1982. — 24p : music,1plan ; 19cm. — (Scottish plays ; no.19)
ISBN 0-85174-425-7 (pbk) : £0.70 B82-26031

MacDougall, Carl. Filthy Lucre : an inflationary comedy / by Carl MacDougall. — Crail (Greenbank, West Green, Crail, Fife KY10 3RD) : C. MacDougall, 1982. — 165leaves ; 30cm
Unpriced (pbk) B82-35540

McGillivray, David. The Farndale Avenue Housing Estate Townswomen's Guild Dramatic Society murder mystery : a comedy / David McGillivray and Walter Zerlin Jnr. — London : French, c1981. — vii,42p : 1plan ; 22cm
One man, 5 women
ISBN 0-573-11141-3 (pbk) : £2.25 B82-08739

McGrath, John. The cheviot, the stag and the black, black oil / John McGrath. — Rev., illustrated ed. — London : Eyre Methuen, 1981. — xxix,82p : ill,1port ; 19cm. — (A Methuen modern play)
Previous ed.: Breakish, Isle of Skye : West Highland Publishing, 1974
ISBN 0-413-48880-2 (pbk) : £2.95 B82-15561

Marchant, Tony. Thick as thieves / two plays by Tony Marchant. — London : Methuen, 1982. — 44p ; 21cm. — (A Methuen new theatrescript)
ISBN 0-413-51070-0 (pbk) : £1.95 B82-39193

Martin, Kathleen. One bright star / by Kathleen Martin. — Ilkeston : Moorley's, [1982?]. — 16p ; 21cm
Nine men, 1 woman
ISBN 0-86071-134-x (pbk) : £0.30 B82-33514

Moran, Jane. The Sermon on the mount : eight plays for the classroom / Jane Moran. — London : Edward Arnold, 1980. — 80p ; 22cm
ISBN 0-7131-0474-0 (pbk) : £1.50 : CIP rev. B80-07489

Morgan, Verne. Mother Goose : a pantomime / Verne Morgan. — London : French, c1981. — 52p ; 19cm
Ten men, 6 women, supers
ISBN 0-573-06461-x (pbk) : £2.25 B82-07334

Morley, John, *1924-*. Aladdin : a pantomime / John Morley. — London : French, c1981. — ix,69p ; 22cm
Eight men, 11 women, supers
ISBN 0-573-06462-8 (pbk) : £2.25 B82-08878

Morley, John, *1924-*. Goldilocks and the three bears : a pantomime / John Morley. — London : French, c1981. — 63p ; 19cm
Six men, 4 women, supers
ISBN 0-573-06464-4 (pbk) : £2.25 B82-07329

Morley, John, *1924-*. Jack and the beanstalk : a pantomime / John Morley. — London : French, c1981. — xviii,62p ; 22cm
Nine men, 6 women, supers
ISBN 0-573-06463-6 (pbk) : £2.25 B82-08740

Morley, Leonard. Looking for Rosy / by Leonard Morley. — Macclesfield : New Playwrights' Network, [1981]. — 22p : 1plan ; 18cm
Three men, 2 women
£0.65 (pbk) B82-03253

Mortimer, Colin, *1945-*. Fair weather friends / by Colin Mortimer. — London (21 Kingly St., W1R 5LB) : Dr Jan Van Loewen, [1982]. — 113leaves ; 30cm
Six men, 6 women, 1 dog
Unpriced (unbound) B82-33935

Mortimer, John, *1923-*. A voyage round my father ; The dock brief ; What shall we tell Caroline? / John Mortimer. — Harmondsworth : Penguin, 1982. — 185p ; 20cm. — (Penguin plays)
A voyage round my father originally published: London : Methuen, 1971 ; The dock brief and What shall we tell Caroline? originally published in Three plays. London : Elek, 1958
ISBN 0-14-048169-9 (pbk) : £1.95 B82-22318

Muir, Frank. The Glums : based on the original radio scripts / by Frank Muir & Denis Norden. — London : Robson, 1979. — 144p : ill,facsims,ports ; 25cm
ISBN 0-86051-080-8 : £3.95 : CIP rev. B79-30306

Murch, Edward. The revival : an improbable history in one act with a postscript / by Edward Murch. — Dousland ([Heatherdene, Dousland, Yelverton, Devon, PL20 6LU]) : Yennadon Plays, c1982. — 31p ; 19cm
One man, 2 women
Unpriced (pbk) B82-30774

Nichols, Peter, *1927-*. Poppy / Peter Nichols. — London : Methuen, 1982. — 115p ; 20cm. — (Methuen modern plays)
Seven men, 5 women
ISBN 0-413-49690-2 (cased) : Unpriced
ISBN 0-413-49490-x (pbk) : £2.75 B82-35437

Parker, Jim. The burning bush : a musical for schools in two acts / words by Tom Stanier and Maida Stanier ; lyrics by Tom Stanier ; music by Jim Parker. — London : Heinemann Educational, 1981. — x,61p : ill ; 19cm
Thirty men, 5 women
ISBN 0-435-23820-5 (pbk) : Unpriced B82-08879

Parkes, Derek. Poles apart : a play / by Derek Parkes. — Macclesfield : New Playwrights Network, [1982?]. — 28p : 1plan ; 18cm
£0.65 (pbk) B82-30425

Pearson, Anne. Pinocchio : a new version by Anne Pearson. — Milford Haven (St Peters Rd, Milford Haven, Dyfed) : Torch Theatre, [1980]. — 102leaves ; 30cm
Eight men, 9 women
Unpriced (pbk) B82-39242

Petz, Chris. Heir today - gone tomorrow : a comedy / Chris Petz. — London : French, c1981. — 50p : 1plan ; 19cm
Four men, 4 women
ISBN 0-573-11164-2 (pbk) : Unpriced B82-07333

Pinter, Harold. The birthday party / Harold Pinter ; with a commentary and chronology by Patricia Hern ; and notes by Glenda Leeming. — Rev. 2nd ed. — London : Eyre Methuen, 1965 (1981 [printing]). — xxx,97p : ill ; 19cm
Bibliography: pxxx
ISBN 0-413-39640-1 (pbk) : £1.75 B82-15614

822'.914 — Drama in English, *1945-* — Texts *continuation*

Pinter, Harold. Plays: four / Harold Pinter ; with an introduction by the author. — London : Eyre Methuen, 1981. — xiii,296p ; 18cm. — (The Master playwrights)
Contents: Old times. Originally published: London : Methuen, 1971 — No man's land. Originally published: London : Eyre Methuen, 1975 — Betrayal. Originally published: London : Eyre Methuen, 1978 — Monologue. Originally published: London : Covent Garden Press, 1973 — Family voices. Originally published London : Next Editions in association with Faber, 1981
ISBN 0-413-48490-4 (pbk) : £1.95 B82-15607

Plowman, Gillian. Two summers : a play / Gillian Plowman. — London : French, c1981. — 23p : 1plan ; 19cm
Four men, 2 women
ISBN 0-573-12285-7 (pbk) : £0.70 B82-03659

Poliakoff, Stephen. Favourite nights and Caught on a train : by Stephen Poliakoff. — London : Methuen, 1982. — 106p ; 21cm. — (Methuen's new theatrescripts)
ISBN 0-413-50100-0 (pbk) : £2.95 B82-39194

Reakes, Paul. Act of murder : one act thriller / by Paul Reakes. — Macclesfield (35 Sandringham Rd., Macclesfield, Cheshire SK10 1QB) : New Playwrights' Network, [1980?]. — 39p : 1plan ; 18cm
£0.50 (pbk) B82-20980

Redmond, Peter. Richard Wellington and his cat with no boots : a pantomime / by Peter Redmond. — Macclesfield : New Playwrights Network, [1982?]. — 52p : 1plan ; 18cm
Eight men, 5 women, supers
£1.95 (pbk) B82-30424

Reid, Georgina. Wolfsbane : a play / Georgina Reid. — London : French, c1982. — 49p : 1plan ; 21cm
Two men, 4 women
ISBN 0-573-11503-6 (pbk) : £2.25 B82-17379

Rudkin, David. The sons of light / David Rudkin. — London : Eyre Methuen, 1981. — 78p : music ; 19cm. — (A Methuen modern play)
ISBN 0-413-49120-x (pbk) : £2.95 B82-15560

Rudkin, David. The triumph of death / David Rudkin. — London : Eyre Methuen, 1981. — 54p ; 19cm. — (A Methuen modern play)
ISBN 0-413-49110-2 (pbk) : £2.50 B82-15559

Schilling, Gerry. Little secrets : a comedy in one act / by Gerry Schilling. — Macclesfield : New Playwrights Network, [1982?]. — 36p : 1plan ; 18cm
Two men, 2 women
£0.65 (pbk) B82-30423

Scholey, Arthur. Five plays for Christmas / by Arthur Scholey. — Redhill : NCEC, 1981. — 96p : music ; 19cm
ISBN 0-7197-0310-7 (pbk) : £2.00 B82-08559

Scotland, James. A hundred thousand welcomes : a comedy in three acts / by James Scotland. — Glasgow : Brown, Son & Ferguson, 1982. — 84p ; 18cm
Five men, 8 women
ISBN 0-85174-433-8 (pbk) : £2.00 B82-33512

Sharp, Ian, *1948-*. The Genesis roadshow : a play to be performed, read or taped / Ian Sharp. — London : Edward Arnold, 1981. — 43p ; 22cm
ISBN 0-7131-0615-8 (pbk) : £1.15 : CIP rev. B81-31553

Sotheby, Madeline. Hard times at Batwing Hall. — London : Hutchinson Education, Jan.1983. — [32]p
ISBN 0-09-149081-2 (pbk) : £0.75 : CIP entry B82-33617

Spurling, John. The British Empire, part one : a play / by John Spurling ; with an introductory essay by the author. — London : Boyars, 1982. — xix,130p ; 23cm
ISBN 0-7145-2743-2 (cased) : £7.50 : CIP rev.
ISBN 0-7145-2732-7 (pbk) : £4.50 B81-25135

Stant, David. The Redville wanderer : or holes in our boots : a modern melodrama in prologue, 3 acts & epilogue with song & verse / by David Stant. — Macclesfield : New Playwrights Network, [1982?]. — 93p : 1 plan ; 18cm
Six men, 8 women, supers
£2.20 (pbk) B82-30416

Stoppard, Tom. The real thing. — London : Faber, Nov.1982. — [88]p
ISBN 0-571-11983-2 (pbk) : £2.50 : CIP entry B82-26256

Street, Sean. Tea, set and match : a short play for women / by Sean Street. — Macclesfield : New Playwrights Network, [1982?]. — 20p : 1plan ; 18cm
Three women
£0.70 (pbk) B82-30421

Stygall, Terence. Bones of contention : a comedy in three acts / by Terence Stygall. — Macclesfield : New Playwrights Network, [1982?]. — 68p : 1plan ; 18cm
Six men, 6 women
£1.95 (pbk) B82-30422

Symonds, John. The lunatic asylum is on fire! ; Zilpah / John Symonds. — London : Pindar, 1982. — 253p ; 22cm. — (Plays ; v.2)
Lunatic asylum is on fire!: Two men, 3 women ; Zilpah: Seventeen men, 7 women
ISBN 0-907132-13-8 : £12.00 : CIP rev. B82-02485

Terson, Peter. The pied piper : a play based on Robert Browning's poem / Peter Terson ; music by Jeff Parton. — London : French, c1982. — 78p : music,plan ; 22cm
Twelve men, 3 women
ISBN 0-573-05060-0 (pbk) : £2.50 B82-30952

Terson, Peter. Zigger zagger ; Mooney and his caravans : two plays / by Peter Terson. — Harmondsworth : Penguin, 1970 (1981 [printing]). — 187p : music ; 19cm. — (Penguin plays)
ISBN 0-14-048122-2 (pbk) : £1.25 B82-16773

Tibbetts, Mike. Funny - you don't laugh Jewish! / by Mike Tibbetts. — Macclesfield : New Playwrights' Network, [1981]. — 37p : 1plan ; 18cm
Three men, 2 women
£0.75 (pbk) B82-03250

Tower, Christopher. Victoria the Good / Christopher Tower ; with illustrations by Arthur Barbosa. — London : Weidenfeld and Nicolson, c1981. — 627p,[14]leaves of plates ; 25cm
ISBN 0-297-78020-4 (pbk) : £9.95 B82-18274

Vose, John D.. The night shelter / by John D. Vose. — Macclesfield : New Playwrights Network, [1982?]. — 24p : 1plan ; 18cm
Five men, 2 women
£0.65 (pbk) B82-30419

Walker, David, *1947-*. Dilemmas / David Walker. — London : Edward Arnold 2. — 1982. — 71p ; 22cm
ISBN 0-7131-0646-8 (pbk) : £1.35 : CIP rev. B82-04479

Walker, David, *1947-*. Lorna and John : a play about relationships between the sexes to read, discuss and develop / David Walker. — Harmondsworth : Penguin, 1982. — 78p ; 22cm
ISBN 0-7131-0700-6 (pbk) : Unpriced : CIP rev. B82-20031

Walker, David, *1947-*. That's what friends are for / David Walker. — London : Edward Arnold, 1982. — 72p : ill ; 22cm
ISBN 0-7131-0699-9 (pbk) : Unpriced : CIP rev. B82-15914

Warner, Francis. Requiem : a trilogy comprising Laying figures, Killing time & Meeting ends : together with its Maquettes, Emblems, Troat & Lumen / Francis Warner ; with an introduction by Tim Prentki. — Gerrards Cross : Smythe, 1980. — 248p ; 22cm
Bibliography: p248
ISBN 0-86140-631-1 (pbk) : £3.25 : CIP rev. B80-10756

Way, Brian. Brian Way's Magical faces. — Boston : Baker ; London : French, c1977. — 29p ; 28cm
Two men, 2 women
Unpriced (pbk) B82-40832

Way, Brian. Brian Way's Puss in boots. — Boston : Baker ; London : French, c1977. — 76p ; 28cm
Seven men, 4 women
Unpriced (pbk) B82-40829

Way, Brian. Brian Way's the Island. — Boston : Baker ; London : French, c1977. — 29p ; 28cm
Two men, 2 women
Unpriced (pbk) B82-40831

Way, Brian. Brian Way's the Rainbow box. — Boston : Baker ; London : French, c1977. — 41p ; 28cm
Two men, 2 women
Unpriced (pbk) B82-40830

Wells, John, *1936-*. 'Anyone for Denis?' / John Wells. — London : Faber, 1982. — 72p ; 20cm
Six men, 2 women
ISBN 0-571-11920-4 (pbk) : £2.50 : CIP rev. B81-34654

Wesker, Arnold. Caritas. — London : Cape, Oct.1981. — [64]p
ISBN 0-224-02020-x (pbk) : £2.50 : CIP entry B81-30963

Williams, Guy. Romeo and Juliet / by William Shakespeare ; adapted by Guy Williams. — Basingstoke : Macmillan Education, 1982. — 70p ; 22cm. — (Dramascript classics)
ISBN 0-333-32503-6 (pbk) : Unpriced : CIP rev. B81-35802

Wilson, Pat. Anybody seen my body? / by Pat Wilson. — Middlesborough : Pat Wilson Plays, c1980. — 13p ; 21cm
Five men, 4 women
ISBN 0-906416-15-9 (pbk) : £0.75 B82-22352

Wilson, Pat. Ashes to ashes, crust to crust / by Pat Wilson. — Middlesborough : Pat Wilson Plays, c1976. — 9p ; 21cm
Five women
ISBN 0-906416-11-6 (pbk) : £0.55 B82-22358

Wilson, Pat. Hi Jiminy : a pantomime in three acts / by Pat Wilson. — Middlesborough : Pat Wilson Plays, c1979. — 26p ; 21cm
Ten men, 10 women, supers
ISBN 0-906416-10-8 (pbk) : £1.20 B82-22360

Wilson, Pat. Look both ways / by Pat Wilson. — Middlesborough : Pat Wilson Plays, c1976. — 52p ; 21cm
Three men, 5 women
ISBN 0-906416-24-8 (pbk) : Unpriced B82-22355

Wilson, Pat. Medium rare : a play for five ladies (not too young) / by Pat Wilson. — Middlesborough : Pat Wilson Plays, c1980. — 7p ; 21cm
Five women
ISBN 0-906416-13-2 (pbk) : £0.65 B82-22351

822'.914 — Drama in English, *1945-* — *Texts continuation*

Wilson, Pat. A midsummer nightmare / by Pat Wilson. — Middlesborough : Pat Wilson Plays, c1981. — 38p ; 21cm
Six men, 8 women
ISBN 0-906416-22-1 (pbk) : £1.25 B82-22356

Wilson, Pat. No, my darling daughter / by Pat Wilson. — Middlesborough : Pat Wilson Plays, c1980. — 32p ; 21cm
Three men, 4 women
ISBN 0-906416-21-3 (pbk) : £1.25 B82-22357

Wilson, Pat. Silver wedding / by Pat Wilson. — Middlesborough : Pat Wilson Plays, c1979. — 8p ; 21cm
Two men, 4 women
ISBN 0-906416-07-8 (pbk) : £0.55 B82-22353

Wilson, Pat. There is a fairy upstairs in our attic / by Pat Wilson. — Middlesborough : Pat Wilson Plays, c1979. — 14p ; 21cm
Five men, 5 women, supers
ISBN 0-906416-09-4 (pbk) : £0.75 B82-22359

Wilson, Pat. Things that go bump in the night / by Pat Wilson. — Middlesborough : Pat Wilson Plays, c1979. — 13p ; 21cm
Six men, 5 women
ISBN 0-906416-08-6 (pbk) : £0.75 B82-22354

Wilson, Pat. The wok : a play in one act for six women / by Pat Wilson. — Great Ayton : Pat Wilson's plays, c1982. — 8p ; 21cm
ISBN 0-906416-25-6 (pbk) : £0.65 B82-34965

Wright, Eileen. 'Let's do something different' / by Eileen Wright. — Ilkeston : Moorley's, [1982?]. — 27p : ill ; 21cm
ISBN 0-86071-153-6 (pbk) : £0.40 B82-32041

822'.914 — Drama in English. Arden, John. Serjeant Musgrave's dance — *Study outlines*

Ewart, R. W.. Serjeant Musgrave's dance : notes / R.W. Ewart. — Harlow : Longman, 1982. — 71p ; 21cm. — (York notes ; 159)
Bibliography: p70-71
ISBN 0-582-79206-1 (pbk) : £0.90 B82-16452

822'.914 — Drama in English. Behan, Brendan — *Personal observations*

Arthurs, Peter. With Brendan Behan. — London : Routledge and Kegan Paul, May 1982. — [297]p
ISBN 0-7100-9221-0 (pbk) : £5.95 : CIP entry B82-06950

822'.914 — Drama in English. Mercer, David, *1928-1980* — *Critical studies*

David Mercer : where the difference began / edited by Paul Madden. — [London] : [British Film Institute], c1981. — 40p ; 21cm. — (A BFI TV projects publication)
Unpriced (pbk) B82-34975

822'.914 — Drama in English. Orton, Joe — *Critical studies*

Bigsby, C. W. E.. Joe Orton / C.W.E. Bigsby. — London : Methuen, 1982. — 79p ; 20cm. — (Contemporary writers)
Bibliography: p78-79
ISBN 0-416-31690-5 (pbk) : Unpriced : CIP rev. B82-06754

822'.914 — Drama in English. Osborne, John, *1929-* — *Biographies*

Osborne, John, *1929-*. A better class of person : an autobiography 1929-1956 / John Osborne. — London : Faber, 1981. — 255p,[8]p of plates : ill,facsims,ports ; 25cm
Includes index
ISBN 0-571-11785-6 : £7.95 : CIP rev. B81-28159

822'.914 — Drama in English. Pinter, Harold — *Critical studies*

Dukore, Bernard F.. Harold Pinter / Bernard F. Dukore. — London : Macmillan, 1982. — ix,139p,[8]p of plates : ports ; 20cm. — (Macmillan modern dramatists)
Bibliography: p134-136. — Includes index
ISBN 0-333-28915-3 (cased) : Unpriced
ISBN 0-333-28916-1 (pbk) : Unpriced B82-23276

822'.914 — Drama in English. Shaffer, Peter. Royal hunt of the sun — *Study outlines*

Metcalf, Rosamund. The royal hunt of the sun : notes / by Rosamund Metcalf. — Harlow : Longman, 1982. — 72p ; 21cm. — (York notes ; 170)
Bibliography: p67
ISBN 0-582-78189-2 (pbk) : £0.90 B82-36748

822'.914 — Drama in English. Stoppard, Tom — *Critical studies*

Hunter, Jim. Tom Stoppard's plays / by Jim Hunter. — London : Faber, 1982. — 258p ; 21cm
Bibliography: p215-258
ISBN 0-571-11902-6 : £8.50 : CIP rev. B82-06508

822'.914 — Drama in English. Warner, Francis — *Critical studies*

Pursglove, Glyn. Francis Warner and tradition : an introduction to the plays / Glyn Pursglove. — Gerrards Cross : Colin Smythe, 1981. — viii,232p : ill ; 23cm
Includes index
ISBN 0-86140-083-6 : £11.95 : CIP rev. B81-20159

822'.914'08 — Drama in English, *1945-* — *Anthologies*

A Decade's drama : six Scottish plays. — Todmorden : Woodhouse, 1980. — 330p ; 22cm
ISBN 0-906657-06-7 (pbk) : £6.60 B82-36352

Plays by women. — London : Methuen. — (A Methuen theatrefile)
Vol.1 / edited and introduced by Michelene Wandor. — 1982. — 136p ; 21cm
Contents: Vinegar Tom / by Caryl Churchill. — Dusa, fish, stas and VI / by Pam Gems. — Tissue / by Louise Page. — Aurora Leigh / by Michelene Wandor
ISBN 0-413-50020-9 (pbk) : £3.50 B82-33930

Power / edited by David Self and Andrew Bethell. — London : Hutchinson in association with Thames Television, 1981. — 160p : ill ; 19cm. — (Studio scripts)
ISBN 0-09-146771-3 (pbk) : Unpriced : CIP rev. B81-31234

Russell, Willy. Home truths : three plays / Willy Russell, Alan Ayckbourn, Neville Smith. — Harlow : Longman, 1982. — 96p : ill ; 19cm. — (Knockouts)
ISBN 0-582-20003-2 (pbk) : £0.80 B82-22110

822'.914'08 — Drama in English, *1945-* — *Anthologies — For schools*

Lifetime 1 / edited by Eurfron Gwynne Jones. — Cambridge : Cambridge University Press, 1982. — xiii,60p ; 21cm
ISBN 0-521-28718-9 (pbk) : £1.25 B82-29949

Lifetime 2 / edited by Eurfron Gwynne Jones. — Cambridge : Cambridge University Press, 1982. — xiii,57p ; 21cm
ISBN 0-521-28719-7 (pbk) : £1.25 B82-29948

Take two : duologues for young players / chosen by Anne Harvey. — London : French, c1981. — x,162p ; 21cm
ISBN 0-573-19027-5 (pbk) : Unpriced B82-11368

822'.914'09 — Drama in English, *1945-* — *Critical studies*

Brown, John Russell. A short guide to modern British drama. — London : Heinemann Educational, Oct.1982. — [128]p
ISBN 0-435-18372-9 (pbk) : £2.95 : CIP entry B82-28450

822'.914'09 — Drama in English, *1945-* — *Reviews*

Plays of 1978/9 : a classified guide to play selection / edited by Roy Stacey. — Bromley ([1 Hawthorndene Rd., Hayes, Bromley, Kent]) : Stacey Publications, [1982?]. — 52p ; 21cm. — (Amateur stage handbooks)
Cover title. — Bibliography: p52-51. — Includes index
£1.20 (pbk) B82-25614

823 — ENGLISH FICTION

823 — Fiction in English. African writers, *1945-* — *Critical studies*

Ngara, Emmanuel. Stylistic criticism and the African novel : a study of language, art and content of African fiction / Emmanuel Ngara. — London : Heinemann, 1982. — viii,150p ; 22cm
Bibliography: p143-146. — Includes index
ISBN 0-435-91720-x (pbk) : £3.95 : CIP rev. B81-34504

Recent trends in the novel. — London : Heinemann Educational, Dec.1982. — [288]p. — (African literature today ; 13)
ISBN 0-435-91646-7 (cased) : £12.50 : CIP entry
ISBN 0-435-91647-5 (pbk) : £5.50 B82-29771

823 — Fiction in English. Australian women writers, *1890-1945* — *Critical studies*

Modjeska, Drusilla. Exiles at home : Australian women writers 1925-1945 / Drusilla Modjeska. — London : Sirius, c1981. — 283p : ports ; 23cm
Bibliography: p261-273. — Includes index
ISBN 0-207-14616-0 : Unpriced B82-24433

823 — Fiction in English. Australian writers. Franklin, Miles — *Biographies*

Coleman, Verna. Her unknown (brilliant) career : Miles Franklin in America / Verna Coleman. — London : Angus & Robertson, 1981. — x,219p : ill,ports ; 24cm. — (A Sirius book)
Bibliography: p211-214. — Includes index
ISBN 0-207-14536-9 : Unpriced B82-24432

823 — Fiction in English. Ghanaian writers. Armah, Ayi Kwei. Beautyful ones are not yet born — *Study outlines*

Todd, Jan. The beautyful ones are not yet born : notes / by Jan Todd. — Harlow : Longman, 1982. — 64p ; 21cm. — (York notes ; 154)
Bibliography: p60-61
ISBN 0-582-78245-7 (pbk) : Unpriced B82-16456

823 — Fiction in English. New Zealand writers. Mansfield, Katherine — *Biographies*

Alpers, Antony. The life of Katherine Mansfield / Antony Alpers. — Oxford : Oxford University Press, 1982. — xxvi,467p,[16]p of plates : ill,ports ; 22cm
Originally published: London : Cape, 1980. — Bibliography: p419-429. — Includes index
ISBN 0-19-281332-3 (pbk) : £3.95 : CIP rev. B82-12539

823 — Fiction in English. New Zealand writers. Marsh, Ngaio — *Biographies*

Marsh, Ngaio. Black beech and honeydew : an autobiography / Ngaio Marsh. — Rev. and enl. ed. — Auckland ; London : Collins, 1981, c1965. — 310p,[16]p of plates : ill,ports ; 22cm
Previous ed.: 1966
ISBN 0-00-216367-5 : £8.95 B82-09960

823 — Fiction in English. Nigerian writers. Achebe, Chinua — *Critical studies*

Carroll, David, *1932-*. Chinua Achebe / David Carroll. — London : Macmillan, 1980. — ix,192p ; 20cm. — (Macmillan Commonwealth writers series)
Previous ed.: New York : Twayne, 1970. — Bibliography: p187-190. — Includes index
ISBN 0-333-25574-7 (cased) : £8.50 : CIP rev.
ISBN 0-333-25575-5 (pbk) : £3.50 B79-37459

Wren, Robert M.. Achebe's world : the historical and cultural context of the novels of Chinua Achebe / Robert M. Wren. — Harlow : Longman, 1981, c1980. — xxv,166p ; 24cm. — (Longman studies in African literature)
Originally published: Washington D.C.: Three Continents Press, 1980. — Bibliography: p140-159. — Includes index
ISBN 0-582-64251-5 (cased) : Unpriced
ISBN 0-582-64252-3 B82-07571

823 — Fiction in English. Nigerian writers. Amadi, Elechi. Concubine, *The* — *Study outlines*

Ebbatson, Roger. The concubine : notes / by Roger Ebbatson. — Harlow : Longman, 1981. — 64p ; 21cm. — (York notes ; 139)
Bibliography: p60-61
ISBN 0-582-78248-1 (pbk) : £0.90 B82-16457

823 — Fiction in English. Nigerian writers. Okara, Gabriel. Voice, *The* — *Study outlines*

Probyn, Clive T.. The voice : notes / by Clive T. Probyn. — Harlow : Longman, 1982. — 64p ; 21cm. — (York notes ; 157)
Bibliography: p56-57
ISBN 0-582-78277-5 (pbk) : £0.90 B82-16451

823[F] — Fiction in English. Australian writers, *1890-1945* — *Texts*

Egerton, George. Keynotes and discords. — London : Virago, Feb.1983. — [462]p. — (Virago modern classics)
ISBN 0-86068-293-5 (pbk) : £3.95 : CIP entry B82-39623

Lawson, Henry. Prose works of Henry Lawson. — London : Angus & Robertson, 1948 (1980 [printing]). — vii,688p ; 23cm. — ([Australian literary heritage series])
Includes index
ISBN 0-207-13368-9 : Unpriced B82-29189

Mitchell, Elyne. Brumby racer / Elyne Mitchell ; illustrated by Victor Ambrus. — London : Hutchinson, c1982. — 120p : ill ; 22cm
ISBN 0-09-137560-6 : £4.95 : CIP rev. B81-39213

Prichard, Katharine Susannah. Working bullocks / Katharine Susannah Prichard. — London : Angus & Robertson, 1980, c1926. — 251p ; 19cm. — (Sirius quality paperbacks)
ISBN 0-207-14324-2 (pbk) : £4.50 B82-31494

Richardson, Henry Handel. The adventures of Cuffy Mahony : and other stories / Henry Handel Richardson. — London : Angus & Robertson, c1979. — 196p ; 19cm. — (Sirius quality paperbacks)
Originally published: Sydney : Angus & Robertson, 1979
ISBN 0-207-13771-4 (cased) : Unpriced B82-31495

Richardson, Henry Handel. Australia Felix / Henry Handel Richardson ; with an introduction by Leonie Kramer. — Harmondsworth : Penguin, 1971 (1981 [printing]). — xxvii,376p ; 18cm. — (The Fortunes of Richard Mahony ; v.1) (Penguin modern classics)
ISBN 0-14-003338-6 (pbk) : £1.95 B82-25566

Richardson, Henry Handel. Ultima Thule / Henry Handel Richardson ; with an introduction by Leonie Kramer. — Harmondsworth : Penguin, 1971 (1981 [printing]). — xxvii,279p ; 19cm. — (The Fortunes of Richard Mahony) (Penguin modern classics)
ISBN 0-14-003339-4 (pbk) : £1.95 B82-25543

Stead, Christina. The beauties and furies / Christina Stead ; with a new introduction by Hilary Bailey. — London, Virago, 1982, c1936. — viii,383p ; 20cm. — (Virago modern classics)
ISBN 0-86068-175-0 (pbk) : £3.95 : CIP rev. B82-13161

Stead, Christina. Miss Herbert : (the suburban wife). — London : Virago, Nov.1982. — [320] p. — (Virago modern classics)
Originally published: New York : Random House, 1976 ; London : Virago, 1979
ISBN 0-86068-319-2 (pbk) : £3.50 : CIP entry B82-26348

Tennant, Kylie. Ride on stranger / Kylie Tennant. — London : Angus & Robertson, 1980, c1943. — 301p ; 19cm. — (Sirius quality paperbacks)
ISBN 0-207-14316-1 (pbk) : £4.25 B82-31493

Upfield, Arthur. The battling prophet / Arthur W. Upfield. — London : Angus & Robertson, 1981, c1956. — 225p ; 18cm
Originally published: London : Heinemann, 1956
ISBN 0-207-14094-4 (pbk) : Unpriced B82-22716

Upfield, Arthur. Man of two tribes / Arthur W. Upfield. — London : Angus & Robertson, 1981, c1956. — 214p ; 18cm
Originally published: London : Heinemann, 1956
ISBN 0-207-14102-9 (pbk) : Unpriced B82-22715

Upfield, Arthur. Mr Jelly's business / Arthur W. Upfield. — London : Angus & Robertson, 1981. — 177p ; 18cm
ISBN 0-207-14110-x (pbk) : Unpriced B82-22717

Upfield, Arthur. The widows of Broome / Arthur W. Upfield. — London : Angus & Robertson, 1981, c1951. — 245p ; 18cm
Originally published: London : Heinemann, 1951
ISBN 0-207-14681-0 (pbk) : Unpriced B82-22714

Von Arnim, Elizabeth. Fräulein Schmidt and Mr. Anstrutler. — London : Virago, Feb.1983. — [320]p. — (Virago modern classics)
ISBN 0-86068-317-6 (pbk) : £3.50 : CIP entry B82-39622

Von Arnim, Elizabeth. Vera. — London : Virago, Feb.1983. — [320]p. — (Virago modern classics)
ISBN 0-86068-316-8 (pbk) : £3.50 : CIP entry B82-39621

White, Patrick. The Twyborn affair / Patrick White. — Harmondsworth : Penguin, 1981, c1979. — 378p ; 20cm. — (A King penguin)
Originally published: London : Cape, 1979
ISBN 0-14-006073-1 (pbk) : £2.95 B82-06430

823[F] — Fiction in English. Australian writers, *1945-* — *Texts*

Bail, Murray. Homesickness / Murray Bail. — Ringwood, Vic. ; Harmondsworth : Penguin, 1981, c1980. — 317p ; 18cm
Originally published: South Melbourne ; London : Macmillan, 1980
ISBN 0-14-005895-8 (pbk) : £1.95 B82-16784

Baxter, John, *1939-*. The black yacht. — London : New English Library, Sept.1982. — [352]p
ISBN 0-450-05515-9 : £1.95 : CIP entry B82-19694

Beattie, Tasman. Diamonds. — London : Methuen, June 1982. — [224]p
ISBN 0-413-50180-9 : £7.50 : CIP entry B82-10498

Booth, Angela. Angel in the sky / Angela Booth. — London : Macdonald, 1982. — 218p ; 21cm
ISBN 0-356-08528-7 : £4.95 B82-22570

Booth, Angela. Angel in the sky / Angela Booth. — London : Futura, 1982. — 218p ; 18cm
ISBN 0-7088-2168-5 (pbk) : £1.25 B82-18263

Bowers, Raymond. The spark / Raymond Bowers. — London : Hutchinson, 1982. — 487p ; 23cm
ISBN 0-09-145820-x : £7.95 : CIP rev. B81-35932

Browne, Christabel. The story of Harriet Bland / Christabel Browne. — London : Hutchinson, 1982. — 303p ; 23cm
ISBN 0-09-146740-3 : £7.95 : CIP rev. B81-38335

Carey, Peter. Bliss / Peter Carey. — London : Faber, 1981. — 296p ; 23cm
ISBN 0-571-11769-4 : £6.50 : CIP rev. B81-24591

Cato, Nancy. Brown sugar / Nancy Cato. — London : New English Library, 1982, c1974. — 255p : 1geneal.table ; 18cm
Originally published: London : Heinemann, 1974
ISBN 0-450-05362-8 (pbk) : £1.50 : CIP rev. B81-36204

Cleary, Jon. The golden sabre / Jon Cleary. — [London] : Fontana, 1981. — 288p ; 18cm
Originally published: London : Collins, 1981
ISBN 0-00-616472-2 (pbk) : £1.50 B82-06309

Cleary, Jon. The golden sabre / by Jon Cleary. — Long Preston : Magna Print, 1982, c1981. — 593p ; 22cm
Originally published: London : Collins, 1981. — Published in large print
ISBN 0-86009-442-1 : Unpriced : CIP rev. B82-13160

Cleary, Jon. Spearfield's daughter / Jon Cleary. — Sydney ; London : Collins, 1982. — 567p ; 23cm
ISBN 0-00-222689-8 : £8.50 B82-36276

Cleary, Jon. A very private war / by Jon Cleary. — Long Preston : Magna Print, 1982, c1980. — 520p ; 22cm
Originally published: London : Collins, 1980. — Published in large print
ISBN 0-86009-390-5 : Unpriced : CIP rev. B82-04825

Cork, Dorothy. By honour bound. — London : Hodder and Stoughton, Apr.1982. — [192]p. — (Silhouette romance)
ISBN 0-340-27929-x (pbk) : £0.75 : CIP entry B82-03827

Cork, Dorothy. Reluctant deceiver. — London : Hodder and Stoughton, Dec.1982. — [192]p. — (Silhouette romance)
ISBN 0-340-32693-x (pbk) : £0.75 : CIP entry B82-29663

D'Alpuget, Blanche. Turtle beach / Blanche d'Alpuget. — Ringwood, Vic. ; Harmondsworth : Penguin, 1981. — 286p ; 19cm
ISBN 0-14-005784-6 (pbk) : £1.50 B82-16769

Denton, Kit. The breaker : a novel / by Kit Denton ; with a selection of the verse of Harry (The breaker) Morant. — London : Angus & Robertson, 1973 (1980 [printing]). — 281p ; 18cm
ISBN 0-207-14268-8 (pbk) : £1.50 B82-13632

Drewe, Robert. A cry in the jungle bar / Robert Drewe. — [London] : Fontana, 1981, c1979. — 244p ; 20cm
Originally published: Sydney : Collins, 1979
ISBN 0-00-616018-2 (pbk) : £1.95 B82-33552

Free, Colin. Bay of shadows / Colin Free. — London : Methuen, 1982, c1980. — 379p ; 18cm
Originally published: London : Eyre Methuen, 1980
ISBN 0-417-03950-6 (pbk) : £1.50 B82-34182

Free, Colin. Brannan / Colin Free. — London : Eyre Methuen, 1981. — 348p ; 23cm
ISBN 0-413-47460-7 : £6.95 : CIP rev. B81-25289

Gage, Mary. Praise the egg / Mary Gage ; with illustrations by David Gregson. — London : Angus & Robertson, 1981. — 65p : ill(some col.) ; 23cm
ISBN 0-207-14592-x : £4.95 B82-08989

Gair, Diana. Highlands rapture / by Diana Gair. — London : Mills & Boon, 1982. — 190p ; 20cm
ISBN 0-263-10055-3 : £5.25 B82-27283

Gair, Diana. Jungle antagonist / by Diana Gair. — London : Mills & Boon, 1982. — 192p ; 19cm
ISBN 0-263-10028-6 : £5.25 B82-18135

Garner, Helen. Monkey grip / Helen Garner. — Ringwood, Vic. ; Harmondsworth : Penguin, 1978, c1977 (1981 [printing]). — 245p ; 18cm
Originally published: Melbourne : McPhee Gribble, 1977
ISBN 0-14-004953-3 (pbk) : £1.50 B82-29816

823[F] — Fiction in English. Australian writers, *1945- — Texts* *continuation*

Gibson, Tom. A soldier of India / Tom Gibson. — New York : St. Martin's ; London : Hale, 1982. — 288p ; 23cm
ISBN 0-7091-9686-5 : £7.25 B82-22910

Grant, Maxwell. Inherit the sun. — London : Hodder and Stoughton, Feb.1982. — [448]p. — (Coronet books)
Originally published: 1981
ISBN 0-340-27539-1 (pbk) : £1.95 : CIP entry B81-36362

Halls, Geraldine. Talking to strangers : a novel / by Geraldine Halls. — London : Constable, 1982. — 216p ; 23cm
ISBN 0-09-464560-4 : £6.95 B82-33267

Ireland, *David*. The glass canoe / David Ireland. — Ringwood, Vic. ; Harmondsworth : Penguin, 1982, c1976. — 234p ; 18cm
Originally published: South Melbourne, Vic. : Macmillan, 1976
ISBN 0-14-005911-3 (pbk) : £1.75 B82-29579

Kata, Elizabeth. The death of Ruth. — London : Severn House, Sept.1982. — [128]p
ISBN 0-7278-0830-3 : £6.95 : CIP entry B82-23869

Lord, Gabrielle. Tooth and claw. — London : Bodley Head, Oct.1982. — [192]p
ISBN 0-370-30495-0 : £6.95 : CIP entry B82-24446

McCullough, Colleen. An indecent obsession / Colleen McCullough. — London : Macdonald, 1981. — 314p ; 24cm
ISBN 0-354-04814-7 : £6.95 B82-00435

McCullough, Colleen. An indecent obsession. — Large print ed. — Anstey : Ulverscroft, Aug.1982. — [448]p. — (Charnwood library series)
Originally published: London : Macdonald, 1981
ISBN 0-7089-8063-5 : £5.25 : CIP entry B82-26994

McDonald, Roger. 1915. — London : Faber, Apr.1982. — [426]p
Originally published: New York : Brazillex, 1979
ISBN 0-571-11987-5 (pbk) : £2.50 : CIP entry B82-14047

McDonald, Roger. Slipstream. — London : Faber, Oct.1982. — [328]p
ISBN 0-571-11963-8 : CIP entry B82-29076

Malouf, David. Child's play : with Eustace and The prowler / David Malouf. — London : Chatto & Windus, 1982. — 215p ; 21cm
ISBN 0-7011-3902-1 : £5.50 : CIP rev. B82-06947

Malouf, David. Fly away Peter. — London : Chatto and Windus, Mar.1982. — [128]p
ISBN 0-7011-2625-6 : £4.95 : CIP entry B82-00224

Marshall, William. Thin air / William Marshall. — Harmondsworth : Penguin, 1982, c1977. — 186p ; 19cm. — (A Yellowthread Street mystery) (Penguin crime fiction)
Originally published: London : Hamilton, 1977
ISBN 0-14-006137-1 (pbk) : £1.25 B82-40372

Marshall, William, *1944-*. War machine / William Marshall. — London : H. Hamilton, 1982. — 220p ; 21cm. — (A Yellowthread Street mystery)
ISBN 0-241-10823-3 : £8.95 : CIP rev. B82-15694

Mather, Berkeley. The pagoda tree. — Large print ed. — Anstey : Ulverscroft, Dec.1982. — 1v.. — (Ulverscroft large print series)
Originally published: London : Collins, 1979
ISBN 0-7089-0892-6 : £5.00 : CIP entry B82-30788

Matthews, Chris. Al Jazzar. — London : Allen & Unwin, Sept.1982. — [450]p
ISBN 0-86861-244-8 : £8.50 : CIP entry B82-21566

O'Conner, Elizabeth. The Irishman / Elizabeth O'Conner. — London : Angus & Robertson, 1960 (1978 [printing]). — 318p ; 18cm
ISBN 0-207-13658-0 (pbk) : £1.50 B82-13627

Radley, Paul. Jack Rivers and me. — London : Allen & Unwin, May 1982. — [179]p
ISBN 0-86861-322-3 : £6.95 : CIP entry B82-14491

Radley, Paul. My blue-checker corker and me. — London : Allen & Unwin, Feb.1983. — [180]p
ISBN 0-86861-236-7 : £8.95 : CIP entry B82-39831

Russell, John, *19---*. Threading a dream / John Russell. — Bognor Regis : New Horizon, c1982. — 362p ; 20cm
ISBN 0-86116-590-x : £6.75 B82-15599

Stow, Randolph. The merry-go-round in the sea / Randolph Stow. — Harmondsworth : Penguin, 1968, c1965 (1980 [printing]). — 276p : 1geneal.table ; 18cm
Originally published: London : Macdonald & Co., 1965
ISBN 0-14-002835-8 (pbk) : £1.25 B82-06423

Stow, Randolph. To the islands / Randolph Stow. — Rev. ed. — London : Secker & Warburg, 1982. — ix,126p ; 23cm
Previous ed.: London : MacDonald, 1958
ISBN 0-436-49732-8 : £6.95 B82-15299

Sweeney, Gerald. The plunge / Gerald Sweeney. — London : Angus & Robertson, 1981. — 552p ; 23cm
ISBN 0-207-14488-5 : Unpriced B82-22651

Turner, George. Vaneglory : a science fiction novel / by George Turner. — London : Faber, 1981. — 320p ; 21cm
ISBN 0-571-11664-7 : £6.95 : CIP rev. B81-28028

Turner, George. Yesterday's men. — London : Faber, Jan.1983. — [223]p
ISBN 0-571-11857-7 : £7.95 : CIP entry B82-32445

Walker, Lucy. Monday in summer / Lucy Walker. — Large print ed. — Leicester : Ulverscroft, 1982, c1961. — 380p ; 23cm. — (Ulverscroft large print)
Originally published: under the name Dorothy Lucie Sanders. London : Hodder and Stoughton, 1961
ISBN 0-7089-0805-5 : Unpriced : CIP rev. B82-18449

Walker, Lucy. The runaway girl / Lucy Walker. — [London] : Fontana, 1977, c1976 (1982 [printing]). — 156p ; 18cm
Originally published: London : Collins, 1975
ISBN 0-00-614530-2 (pbk) : £1.25 B82-40490

Weigh, Audrey. A change for Melanie / by Audrey Weigh. — London : Hale, 1982. — 160p ; 20cm
ISBN 0-7091-9859-0 : £6.50 B82-33424

West, Morris. The clowns of God. — London : Hodder & Stoughton, Feb.1982. — [432]p. — (Coronet Books)
ISBN 0-340-27638-x (pbk) : £1.95 : CIP entry B81-36365

West, Morris. The clowns of God / Morris West. — Leicester : Charnwood, 1982, c1981. — 567p ; 23cm. — (Charnwood library series)
Originally published: New York : Morrow ; London : Hodder and Stoughton, 1981. — Published in large print
ISBN 0-7089-8029-5 : £6.50 : CIP rev. B81-36961

West, Morris. McCreary moves in. — London : Coronet, Jan.1983. — [208]p
Originally published: London : Heinemann, 1958
ISBN 0-340-32051-6 (pbk) : £1.25 : CIP entry B82-33753

West, Morris. The naked country. — London : Coronet, Jan.1983. — [208]p
Originally published: London : Heinemann, 1960
ISBN 0-340-32052-4 (pbk) : £1.25 : CIP entry B82-33754

White, Osmar. Silent reach / Osmar White. — London : Futura, 1982, c1978. — 315p ; 18cm
Orginally published: London : Macmillan, 1978
ISBN 0-7088-2133-2 (pbk) : £1.75 B82-18267

Winton, Tim. An open swimmer. — London : Allen & Unwin, Sept.1982. — [182]p
ISBN 0-86861-220-0 : £6.95 : CIP entry B82-23856

823[F] — Fiction in English. Ghanaian writers, *1960 — Texts*

Aidoo, Ama Ata. Our sister killjoy, or, Reflections from a black-eyed squint / Ama Ata Aidoo. — Harlow : Longman, 1977, (1981 [printing]). — 134p ; 18cm. — (Drumbeat ; 35)
ISBN 0-582-64273-6 (pbk) : £1.25 B82-07748

823[F] — Fiction in English. Indian writers, *1947- — Texts*

Markandaya, Kamala. Pleasure city / by Kamala Markandaya. — London : Chatto & Windus, 1982. — 341p ; 21cm
ISBN 0-7011-2617-5 : £7.95 : CIP rev. B82-23199

Olbrich, Freny. Desouza pays the price. — Large print ed. — Anstey : Ulverscroft, Aug.1982. — [352]p. — (Ulverscroft large print series)
Originally published: London : Heinemann, 1978
ISBN 0-7089-0844-6 : £5.00 : CIP entry B82-27175

Olbrich, Freny. Sweet & deadly. — Large print ed. — Long Preston : Magna Print, Aug.1982. — [450]p
Originally published: London : Heinemann, 1979
ISBN 0-86009-421-9 : £5.50 : CIP entry B82-16671

Rushdie, Salman. Midnight's children / Salman Rushdie. — London : Picador, 1982, c1981. — 462p ; 20cm
Originally published: London : Cape, 1981
ISBN 0-330-26714-0 : £2.95 B82-22155

Vashisht, R. P.. A man for the masses / R.P. Vashisht. — Ilfracombe : Stockwell, 1982. — 126p : ill,1map ; 19cm
ISBN 0-7223-1556-2 : £4.40 B82-30973

823[F] — Fiction in English. Israeli writers, *1947- — Texts*

Portugali, Menachem. Khamsin / M. Portugali. — London : Macdonald, 1982. — 272p ; 21cm
Originally published: London : Macdonald Futura, 1981
ISBN 0-354-04617-9 : £5.95 B82-37778

Tammuz, Benjamin. Minotaur. — London : Severn House, Feb.1983. — [210]p
ISBN 0-7278-3006-6 : £7.95 : CIP entry B82-39436

823[F] — Fiction in English. Japanese writers, *1945- — Texts*

Ishiguro, Kazuo. A pale view of hills / Kazuo Ishiguro. — London : Faber, 1982. — 183p ; 21cm
ISBN 0-571-11866-6 : £6.25 : CIP rev. B81-38321

Toda, Katsumi. Shadow on the ninja / Katsumi Toda. — [Isleworth] : Dragon Books, 1982. — 113p : ill,1plan ; 22cm
ISBN 0-946062-00-5 (pbk) : Unpriced B82-39211

823[F] — Fiction in English. New Zealand writers, *1907- — Texts*

Batistich, Amelia. Another mountain, another song / Amelia Batistich. — Auckland ; London : Hodder and Stoughton, 1981. — 243p ; 21cm
ISBN 0-340-26496-9 : £6.95 : CIP rev.
B81-30493

Bream, Freda. Island of fear / by Freda Bream. — London : Hale, 1982. — 159p ; 20cm
ISBN 0-7091-9949-x : £6.75 B82-39175

Eden, Dorothy. The American heiress. — London : Coronet, May 1981. — [256]p
Originally published: 1980
ISBN 0-340-26743-7 (pbk) : £1.25 : CIP entry
B81-04209

Eden, Dorothy. The American heiress / Dorothy Eden. — Large print ed. — Leicester : Ulverscroft, 1982, c1980. — 402p ; 22cm. — (Ulverscroft large print)
Originally published: London : Hodder & Stoughton, 1980
ISBN 0-7089-0733-4 : £5.00 : CIP rev.
B81-33965

Eden, Dorothy. An important family : a novel about New Zealand / Dorothy Eden. — London : Hodder and Stoughton, 1982. — 287p ; 23cm
ISBN 0-340-27836-6 : £6.95 : CIP rev.
B82-07440

Eden, Dorothy. Lamb to the slaughter. — Large print ed. — Anstey : Ulverscroft Large Print Books, Dec.1982. — 1v.. — (Ulverscroft large print series)
Originally published: London : Macdonald, 1953
ISBN 0-7089-0887-x : £5.00 : CIP entry
B82-30798

Eden, Dorothy. Never call it loving / Dorothy Eden. — Large print ed. — Leicester : Ulverscroft, 1981, c1966. — 554p ; 23cm. — (Ulverscroft large print series)
Originally published: London : Hodder & Stoughton, 1966
ISBN 0-7089-0708-3 : £5.00 : CIP rev.
B81-30504

Frame, Janet. Scented gardens for the blind. — London : Women's Press, Sept.1982. — [256]p
ISBN 0-7043-3899-8 (pbk) : £3.75 : CIP entry
B82-25062

Gee, Maurice. Meg / Maurice Gee. — London : Faber, 1981. — 251p ; 21cm
ISBN 0-571-11783-x : £5.95 : CIP rev.
B81-25302

Gee, Maurice. Plumb / Maurice Gee. — London : Faber, 1978 (1982 [printing]). — 272p ; 20cm
ISBN 0-571-11873-9 (pbk) : £3.95 B82-16894

Hall, Sandi. The godmothers. — London : Women's Press, June 1982. — [224]p
ISBN 0-7043-3888-2 (pbk) : £3.50 : CIP entry
B82-09464

Harrison, Craig. The quiet earth. — London : Hodder & Stoughton, Nov.1981. — [242]p
ISBN 0-340-26507-8 : £6.95 : CIP entry
B81-30132

Hughes, Rose. The dangerous goddess / Rose Hughes. — London : Mills & Boon, 1982. — 222p ; 20cm. — (Masquerade)
ISBN 0-263-10061-8 : £5.25 B82-22505

Kalman, Yvonne. Greenstone land / Yvonne Kalman. — [London] : Futura, 1982, c1981. — 475p ; 18cm
Originally published: London : Macdonald, 1981
ISBN 0-7088-2054-9 (pbk) : £1.95 B82-35720

Kidman, Fiona. Mandarin summer : a novel / by Fiona Kidman. — Auckland ; Tadworth : Heinemann, 1981. — 184p ; 23cm
ISBN 0-86863-665-7 : £6.95 B82-11363

Marsh, Ngaio. Clutch of constables / Ngaio Marsh. — London : Fontana, 1970, c1968 (1982 [printing]). — 222p : 1map ; 18cm
Originally published: London : Collins, 1968
ISBN 0-00-616531-1 (pbk) : £1.50 B82-19744

Marsh, Ngaio. Dead water / Ngaio Marsh. — [London] : Fontana, 1966, c1964 (1982 [printing]). — 220p ; 18cm
Originally published: London : Collins, 1964
ISBN 0-00-616465-x (pbk) : £1.35 B82-09403

Marsh, Ngaio. Death at the bar / Ngaio Marsh. — [London] : Fontana, 1954 (1982 [printing]). — 253p ; 18cm
ISBN 0-00-616532-x (pbk) : £1.50 B82-30767

Marsh, Ngaio. Light thickens / Ngaio Marsh. — London : Collins, 1982. — 251p ; 22cm. — (The Crime Club)
ISBN 0-00-231477-0 : £7.50 : CIP rev.
B82-15621

Marsh, Ngaio. A man lay dead : a famous first : the first Roderick Alleyn novel / Ngaio Marsh. — London : Collins, 1981, 1934. — 176p ; 21cm. — (The Crime Club)
ISBN 0-00-231682-x : £6.50 B82-03078

Marsh, Ngaio. Photo-finish / Ngaio Marsh. — [London] : Fontana, 1982, c1980. — 254p ; 18cm
Originally published: London : Collins, 1980
ISBN 0-00-616255-x (pbk) : £1.50 B82-09324

Marsh, Ngaio. Photo-finish / Ngaio Marsh. — Large print ed. — Leicester : Ulverscroft, 1982, c1980. — 415p ; 23cm. — (Ulverscroft large print series)
Originally published: London : Collins for the Crime Club, 1980
ISBN 0-7089-0732-6 : Unpriced : CIP rev.
B82-08083

Marsh, Ngaio. Spinsters in jeopardy / Ngaio Marsh. — [London] : Fontana, 1960, c1954 (1982 [printing]). — 254p ; 18cm
Originally published: London : Collins, 1954
ISBN 0-00-616530-3 (pbk) : £1.50 B82-30781

Morrieson, Ronald Hugh. Predicament / Ronald Hugh Morrieson. — 2nd ed. — London : Hale, 1982. — 248p ; 23cm
Previous ed.: Palmerston North, N.Z. : Dunmore Press, 1974
ISBN 0-7091-9556-7 : £7.25 B82-31626

Noonan, Michael. Magwitch / Michael Noonan. — London : Hodder and Stoughton, 1982. — 222p ; 23cm
ISBN 0-340-28362-9 : £7.50 : CIP rev.
B82-24826

Sandys, Elspeth. Love and war / Elspeth Sandys. — London : Secker & Warburg, 1982. — 374p ; 23cm
ISBN 0-436-44140-3 : £7.95 : CIP rev.
B82-10786

Scrimgeour, G. J.. A woman of her times / G.J. Scrimgeour. — London : Joseph, 1982. — 568p ; 23cm
ISBN 0-7181-2114-7 : £8.95 B82-17349

Shadbolt, Maurice. The Lovelock version. — London : Hodder and Stoughton, June 1982. — [704]p. — (Coronet books)
Originally published: 1980
ISBN 0-340-28594-x (pbk) : CIP entry
B82-14364

Summers, Essie. Heir to Windbush Hill / Essie Summers. — Large print ed. — Leicester : Ulverscroft, 1981, c1966. — 381p ; 23cm. — (Ulverscroft large print series)
Originally published: London : Mills & Boon, 1966
ISBN 0-7089-0707-5 : £5.00 : CIP rev.
B81-30503

Summers, Essie. The house of shining tide / Essie Summers. — Large print ed. — Leicester : Ulverscroft, 1981, c1972. — 346p ; 23cm. — (Ulverscroft large print series)
Originally published: London : Mills & Boon, 1962
ISBN 0-7089-0692-3 : £5.00 : CIP rev.
B81-28103

Summers, Essie. The time and the place. — Large print ed. — Anstey : Ulverscroft Large Print Books, Nov.1982. — [320]p. — (Ulverscroft large print series)
Originally published: London : Mills and Boon, 1958
ISBN 0-7089-0874-8 : £5.00 : CIP entry
B82-29094

Trew, Antony. Sea fever. — Large print ed. — Long Preston : Magna Print, Oct.1982. — [450]p
Originally published: London : Collins, 1980
ISBN 0-86009-431-6 : £5.50 : CIP entry
B82-24128

823[F] — Fiction in English. Nigerian writers, *1960- — Texts*

Aluko, T. M.. Wrong ones in the dock. — London : Heinemann Educational, Feb.1982. — [192]p. — (African writers series ; 242)
ISBN 0-435-90242-3 (pbk) : £1.95 : CIP entry
B81-36226

Ekwuru, Andrew. Songs of Steel / Andrew Ekwuru. — Walton-on-Thames : Nelson, 1980. — 160p ; 19cm. — (Panafrica library)
Originally published: London : Collings, 1979
ISBN 0-17-511617-2 (pbk) : £1.25 : CIP rev.
B80-18485

Emecheta, Buchi. Destination Biafra : a novel / by Buchi Emecheta. — London : Allison & Busby, 1982. — ix,259p ; 23cm
ISBN 0-85031-409-7 : £7.95 : CIP rev.
B81-28087

Emecheta, Buchi. Second-class citizen / Buchi Emecheta. — [London] : Fontana, 1977, c1974 (1982 [printing]). — 192p ; 18cm
Originally published: London : Allison and Busby, 1974
ISBN 0-00-616480-3 (pbk) : £1.25 B82-16827

Fulani, Dan. The fight for life / by Dan Fulani. — London : Hodder and Stoughton, 1982. — 85p ; 20cm
ISBN 0-340-28325-4 (pbk) : Unpriced : CIP rev. B82-06730

Fulani, Dan. God's case : no appeal / by Dan Fulani. — London : Hodder and Stoughton, c1981. — 93p ; 30cm
ISBN 0-340-27578-2 (pbk) : £1.50 : CIP rev.
B81-30144

Fulani, Dan. The price of liberty / by Dan Fulani. — London : Hodder and Stoughton, c1981. — 89p ; 20cm
ISBN 0-340-27771-8 (pbk) : £1.50 : CIP rev.
B81-31468

Fulani, Dan. Sauna, secret agent / by Dan Fulani. — London : Arewa, 1981. — 104p : ill ; 20cm
ISBN 0-340-27051-9 (pbk) : £1.50 : CIP rev.
B81-16862

Iroh, Eddie. The siren in the night. — London : Heinemann Educational, May 1982. — [224]p. — (African writers series ; 255)
ISBN 0-435-90255-5 (pbk) : £1.95 : CIP entry
B82-07663

Iyayi, Festus. The contract / Festus Iyayi. — Harlow : Longman, 1982. — 217p ; 19cm. — (Drumbeat ; 34)
ISBN 0-582-78524-3 (pbk) : £1.50 B82-25573

Okoye, Ifeoma. Behind the clouds / Ifeoma Okoye. — Harlow : Longman, 1982. — 118p ; 19cm. — (Drumbeat ; 58)
ISBN 0-582-78555-3 (pbk) : £1.25 B82-10099

823[F] — Fiction in English. Nigerian writers, *1960- — Texts* *continuation*

Okpewho, Isidore. The last duty / Isidore Okpewho. — Harlow : Longman, 1976 (1981 [printing]). — 243p ; 18cm. — (Drumbeat ; 37)
ISBN 0-582-78535-9 (pbk) : £1.75 B82-06162

Okri, Ben. The landscapes within / Ben Okri. — Harlow : Longman, 1981. — 287p ; 18cm
ISBN 0-582-78539-1 (pbk) : £1.50 B82-18228

Onyeama, Dillibe. Night demon / Dillibe Onyeama. — London : Sphere, 1982. — 153p ; 18cm
ISBN 0-7221-6549-8 (pbk) : £1.50 B82-18171

Thorpe, Victor. The instrument / Victor Thorpe. — London : Macmillan, 1980. — 154p ; 18cm. — (Pacesetters)
ISBN 0-333-29444-0 (pbk) : £0.80 B82-15579

Thorpe, Victor. Stone of vengeance / Victor Thorpe. — London : Macmillan, 1981. — 113p ; 18cm. — (Pacesetters)
ISBN 0-333-32211-8 (pbk) : £0.90 B82-09330

Thorpe, Victor. Stone of vengeance / Victor Thorpe. — London : Macmillan, 1981 (1982 [printing]). — 113p ; 19cm. — (Pacesetters)
ISBN 0-333-34007-8 (cased) : Unpriced
ISBN 0-333-32534-6 (pbk) : Unpriced
B82-32562

823[F] — Fiction in English. Nigerian writers, *to 1960 — Texts*

Soyinka, Wole. The forest of a thousand daemons : a hunter's saga / Wole Soyinka ; illustrated by Bruce Onabrakpeya. — Walton-on-Thames : Nelson, 1982. — 140p : ill ; 19cm. — (Panafrica library)
Adaptation of: Ogboju ode ninu igbo irunmale / by D.O. Fagunwa. — Originally published: 1968
ISBN 0-17-511288-6 (pbk) : £1.30 : CIP rev.
B81-34390

Tutuola, Amos. The witch-herbalist of the remote town / Amos Tutuola. — London : Faber, 1981. — 205p ; 21cm
ISBN 0-571-11703-1 (cased) : £6.50 : CIP rev.
ISBN 0-571-11704-x (pbk) : Unpriced
B81-25304

823[F] — Fiction in English. Norwegian writers, *1945- — Texts*

Sharman, Nick, *1952-*. The surrogate / Nick Sharman. — London : New English Library, 1981, c1980. — 249p ; 18cm
Originally published: New York : New American Library, 1980
ISBN 0-450-05265-6 (pbk) : £1.50 B82-03690

823[F] — Fiction in English. Pakistani writers, *1947- — Texts*

Sidhwa, Bapsi. The bride. — London : Cape, Jan.1983. — [224]p
ISBN 0-224-02047-1 : £7.50 : CIP entry
B82-33497

Sidhwa, Bapsi. The crow eaters / Bapsi Sidhwa. — London : Cape, 1980, c1978. — 283p ; 21cm
ISBN 0-224-01850-7 : £5.95 : CIP rev.
B80-18497

823[F] — Fiction in English. Somali writers, *1960- — Texts*

Farah, Nuruddin. Sardines : a novel / Nuruddin Farah. — London : Allison & Busby, 1981. — 250p ; 23cm
ISBN 0-85031-408-9 : £7.95 : CIP rev.
B81-27940

Farah, Nuruddin. Sardines. — London : Heinemann Educational, July 1982. — [256]p. — (African writers series ; 252)
Originally published: London : Allison and Busby, 1981
ISBN 0-435-90252-0 (pbk) : £2.50 : CIP entry
B82-14938

823[F] — Fiction in English. South African writers, *1909-1961 — Texts*

Abrahams, Peter, *1919-*. Wild conquest / Peter Abrahams. — Walton-on-Thames : Nelson, 1982. — 382p ; 19cm. — (Panafrica library)
Originally published: New York : Harper, 1950 ; London : Faber, 1951
ISBN 0-17-511623-7 (pbk) : £2.50 : CIP rev.
B81-35794

Abrahams, Peter, *1947 June 28-*. The fury of Rachel Monette / Peter Abrahams. — London : Muller, 1981. — 310p ; 23cm
ISBN 0-584-31151-6 : £7.50 B82-01018

Jenkins, Geoffrey. A ravel of waters. — Large print ed. — Anstey : Ulverscroft, Aug.1982. — [448]p. — (Ulverscroft large print series)
Originally published: London : Collins, 1981
ISBN 0-7089-0836-5 : £5.00 : CIP entry
B82-26999

Paton, Alan. Ah, but your land is beautiful / Alan Paton. — London : Cape, 1981. — 271p ; 23cm
ISBN 0-224-01981-3 : £6.95 : CIP rev.
B81-27410

823[F] — Fiction in English. South African writers, *1961- — Texts*

Bennett, Jack, *1934-*. The voyage of the Lucky Dragon / Jack Bennett. — London : Angus & Robertson, 1981. — 149p : ill ; 23cm
ISBN 0-207-14287-4 : Unpriced B82-09042

Brink, André. A chain of voices / André Brink. — London : Faber, 1982. — 525p ; 22cm
ISBN 0-571-11874-7 : £7.95 : CIP rev.
B82-06858

Coetzee, J. M.. Dusklands. — London : Secker & Warburg, Jan.1983. — [144]p
ISBN 0-436-10296-x : £6.50 : CIP entry
B82-34592

Gordimer, Nadine. July's people. — Large print ed. — Bath : Chivers, Jan.1983. — [232]p
Originally published: London : Cape, 1981
ISBN 0-85119-200-9 : £6.30 : CIP entry
B82-33085

Jenkins, Geoffrey. A ravel of waters / Geoffrey Jenkins. — [Glasgow] : Fontana, 1982, c1981. — 252p ; 18cm
Originally published: London : Collins, 1981
ISBN 0-00-616490-0 (pbk) : £1.50 B82-34107

Jenkins, Geoffrey. The unripe gold. — London : Collins, Jan.1983. — [288]p
ISBN 0-00-222619-7 : £7.95 : CIP entry
B82-33583

Jute, André. Reverse negative / André Jute. — London : Sphere, 1981, c1979. — 306p ; 18cm
Originally published: Melbourne : Hyland, 1979 ; London : Secker and Warburg, 1980
ISBN 0-7221-5124-1 (pbk) : £1.50 B82-02125

Jute, André. Sinkhole : a tragedy of the machine age / André Jute. — London : Secker & Warburg, 1982. — 298p ; 23cm
ISBN 0-436-22982-x : £7.50 : CIP rev.
B81-39245

Jute, André. The Zaharoff commission. — London : Secker and Warburg, Oct.1982. — [248]p
ISBN 0-436-22981-1 : £7.50 : CIP entry
B82-24007

McClure, James. The blood of an Englishman : a Kramer and Zondi novel / James McClure. — Large print ed. — Leicester : Ulverscroft, 1982, c1980. — 497p ; 22cm. — (Ulverscroft Large print series)
Originally published: London : Macmillan, 1980
ISBN 0-7089-0744-x : £5.00 : CIP rev.
B81-36945

McClure, James. The gooseberry fool / James McClure. — Harmondsworth : Penguin, 1976, c1974 (1982 [printing]). — 190p ; 19cm
Originally published: London : Gollancz, 1974
ISBN 0-14-004196-6 (pbk) : £1.25 B82-27557

McClure, James. Rogue eagle / James McClure. — Harmondsworth : Penguin, 1978, c1976 (1982 [printing]). — 215p : 1map ; 19cm
Originally published: London : Macmillan, 1976
ISBN 0-14-004617-8 (pbk) : £1.25 B82-40475

McCoy, Andrew. African revenge / Andrew McCoy. — [London] : Corgi, 1981, c1980. — 271p ; 17cm
Originally published: London : Secker & Warburg, 1980
ISBN 0-552-11854-0 (pbk) : £1.75 B82-12585

Mzamane, Mbulelo Vizikhungo. The children of Soweto : a trilogy / by Mbulelo Vizikhungo Mzamane. — Harlow : Longman, 1982. — 246p ; 18cm. — (Drumbeat)
ISBN 0-582-78554-5 (pbk) : £1.60 B82-34695

Rive, Richard. Emergency / Richard Rive. — Walton-on-Thames : Nelson, 1982. — 251p ; 19cm. — (Panafrica library)
Originally published: London : Faber, 1964
ISBN 0-17-511625-3 (pbk) : £2.00 : CIP rev.
B81-35795

Sepamla, Sipho. The root is one / Sipho Sepamla. — Walton-on-Thames : Nelson, 1982. — 131p ; 19cm. — (Panafrica library)
Originally published: London : Collings, 1979
ISBN 0-17-511624-5 (pbk) : £1.30 : CIP rev.
B81-34392

Serote, Mongane W.. To every birth its blood. — London : Heinemann Educational, Jan.1983. — [224]p. — (African writers series ; v.263)
ISBN 0-435-90263-6 (pbk) : £2.90 : CIP entry
B82-34589

Seuffert, Muriel. The passion and the glory / Muriel Seuffert. — London : Macdonald, 1981. — 249p ; 21cm. — (A Minstrel book ; 21)
ISBN 0-354-04819-8 (cased) : £4.95
ISBN 0-7088-2120-0 (pbk) : £0.95 B82-03143

Sharp, Colin Ainsworth. Birthright / Colin Ainsworth Sharp. — London : W.H. Allen, 1982. — 378p : 1map ; 23cm
ISBN 0-491-02907-1 : £7.95 B82-34119

Smith, Wilbur. Hungry as the sea. — Large print ed. — Long Preston : Magna Print, Aug.1982. — [850]p
Originally published: London : Heinemann, 1978
ISBN 0-86009-424-3 : £6.75 : CIP entry
B82-16673

Smith, Wilbur. Wild justice. — Large print ed. — Long Preston : Magna Print, Dec.1982. — [850]p
Originally published: London : Heinemann, 1979
ISBN 0-86009-447-2 : £6.75 : CIP entry
B82-30727

Steiner, Irene Hunter. The year growing ancient. — Large print ed. — Anstey : Ulverscroft Large Print Books, Dec.1982. — 1v.. — (Ulverscroft large print series)
Originally published: New York : St. Martin's Press, 1979 ; Feltham : Hamlyn, 1980
ISBN 0-7089-0891-8 : £5.00 : CIP entry
B82-30802

Van Ees, Erik. The starfish syndrome / Erik van Ees. — London : Macdonald, 1981. — 272p ; 21cm
ISBN 0-356-08518-x : £5.95 B82-17307

Wingate, William. [Hardacre's way]. Hardacre / William Wingate. — London : Pan Books in association with Macmillan London, 1982, c1980. — 236p ; 18cm
Originally published: New York : St Martin's Press ; London : Macmillan, 1980
ISBN 0-330-26638-1 (pbk) : £1.50 B82-22140

823[F] — Fiction in English. South African writers, *to 1909* **— Texts**

Schreiner, Olive. From man to man. — London : Virago, Sept.1982. — [490]p. — (Virago modern classics)
ISBN 0-86068-301-x (pbk) : £3.95 : CIP entry
B82-21542

823[F] — Fiction in English. Zimbabwean writers, *1960-* **— Texts**

Davis, John Gordon. Fear no evil / John Gordon Davis. — London : Collins, 1982. — 359p : 1map ; 25cm
ISBN 0-00-222347-3 : £7.50 B82-33000

Dube, Hope. State secret / Hope Dube. — London : Macmillan, 1981. — 138p ; 18cm. — (Pacesetters)
ISBN 0-333-30424-1 (pbk) : £0.80 B82-13594

Katiyo, Wilson. Going to heaven / Wilson Katiyo. — Harolw : Longman, 1982, c1979. — 139p ; 18cm. — (Drumbeat ; 45)
Originally published: London : Collings, 1979
ISBN 0-582-78547-2 (pbk) : £1.25 B82-16872

Katiyo, Wilson. A son of the soil / Wilson Katiyo. — Harlow : Longman, 1982, c1976. — 147p ; 18cm. — (Drumbeat ; 43)
Originally published: London : Collings, 1976
ISBN 0-582-78548-0 (pbk) : £1.25 B82-16871

Niesewand, Peter. Fallback / Peter Niesewand. — London : Granada, 1982. — 463p ; 24cm
ISBN 0-246-11772-9 : £7.95 : CIP rev.
B81-38323

Page, Nicola. Bride of the sun / Nicola Page. — London : Macdonald, 1981. — 251p ; 18cm. — (A Minstrel book ; 26)
ISBN 0-7088-2129-4 (pbk) : £0.95 B82-09354

Ward, Harvey. The sanctions buster. — Glasgow : William Maclellan, Jan.1982. — [250]p. — (An Embryo book)
ISBN 0-85335-251-8 : £7.95 : CIP entry
B82-01339

823[F] — Short stories in English. Australian writers, *1945-* **— Texts**

Baxter, John, *1939-*. Bidding / John Baxter. — London : Granada, 1980, c1979 (1981 [printing]). — 410p ; 18cm. — (A Panther book)
ISBN 0-586-04693-3 (pbk) : £1.95 B82-09540

Carey, Peter. [The fat man in history]. Exotic pleasures / Peter Carey. — London : Pan, 1981, c1979. — 191p ; 18cm. — (Picador)
Originally published: London : Faber, 1980
ISBN 0-330-26550-4 (pbk) : £1.95 B82-00784

823[F] — Short stories in English. Indian writers, *1947-* **— Texts**

Dhondy, Farrukh. Trip trap. — London : Gollancz, Sept.1982. — [160]p
For adolescents
ISBN 0-575-03193-x : £5.95 : CIP entry
B82-18762

Namjoshi, Suniti. Feminist fables / Suniti Namjoshi ; drawings by Susan Trangmar. — London : Sheba, 1981. — 123p : ill ; 19cm
ISBN 0-907179-04-5 (pbk) : £2.25 B82-09776

823[F] — Short stories in English. New Zealand writers, *1907-* **— Texts**

Mansfield, Katherine. The collected short stories of Katherine Mansfield. — Harmondsworth : Penguin, 1981. — 779p ; 20cm. — (Penguin modern classics)
Originally published: London : Constable, 1945
ISBN 0-14-006146-0 (pbk) : £3.95 B82-06428

823[F] — Short stories in English. Sierra Leone writers, *1960-* **— Texts**

Easmon, R. Sarif. The feud and other stories / R. Sarif Easmon. — Harlow : Longman, 1981. — 298p ; 18cm. — (Drumbeat)
ISBN 0-582-78523-5 (pbk) : £1.75 B82-00496

823[F] — Short stories in English. South African writers, *1909-1961* **— Texts**

Cloete, Stuart. The honey bird : and other African stories / Stuart Cloete. — London : Remploy, 1981, c1964. — 223p ; 22cm
Originally published: London : Collins, 1964
ISBN 0-7066-0909-3 : £5.40 B82-03685

Gordimer, Nadine. A soldier's embrace / stories by Nadine Gordimer. — Harmondsworth : Penguin, 1982, c1980. — 144p ; 20cm
Originally published: New York : Viking, 1980
ISBN 0-14-005925-3 (pbk) : £1.95 B82-29809

823[F] — Short stories in English. South African writers, *1961-* **— Texts**

Hope, Christopher. Private parts and other tales. — London : Routledge & Kegan Paul, Sept.1982. — [180]p
ISBN 0-7100-9346-2 : £6.95 : CIP entry
B82-20647

Matshoba, Mtutuzeli. Call me not a man : and other stories / Mtutuzeli Matshoba. — Harlow : Longman, 1981, c1979. — x,198p ; 19cm. — (Drumbeat ; 42)
Originally published: Johannesburg : Ravan Press ; Birmingham : Third World Publications, 1979
ISBN 0-582-78541-3 (pbk) : Unpriced
B82-06554

Mzamane, Mbulelo Vizikhungo. My cousin comes to Jo'burg and other stories / Mbulelo Mzamane. — Harlow : Longman, 1981, c1980. — 185p ; 19cm. — (Drumbeat)
Originally published: [Johannesburg] : Ravan, 1980
ISBN 0-582-78540-5 (pbk) : £1.50 B82-32475

823[J] — Children's stories in English. Australian writers, *1945-* **— Texts**

Ambrose, Joan. Falcon island / Joan Ambrose. — London : Beaver, 1982. — 159p ; 18cm
ISBN 0-600-20555-x (pbk) : £0.95 B82-02254

Brinsmead, H. F.. Time for Tarquinia / Hesba Brinsmead ; illustrated by Bruce Riddell. — Sydney ; London : Hodder and Stoughton, 1981. — 91p : ill ; 21cm. — (Stoat books)
ISBN 0-340-26617-1 : £3.95 B82-18108

Burke, Susan. The island bike business / Susan Burke ; illustrations by Betty Greenhatch and Graeme Base. — Oxford : Oxford University Press, 1982. — 78p : ill,1map ; 19x26cm
ISBN 0-19-554297-5 : £4.25 B82-26115

Cox, David. Tin Lizzie and Little Nell. — London : Bodley Head, Apr.1982. — [32]p
ISBN 0-370-30922-7 : £4.50 : CIP entry
B82-04023

Edwards, Hazel. Mum on wheels / Hazel Edwards ; illustrated by Joan Saint. — Sydney ; London : Hodder and Stoughton, 1980. — 53p : 53p,ill ; 21cm. — (Stoat books)
ISBN 0-340-25779-2 : £3.95 B82-36914

Favourite fairy tales. — London : Granada, Sept.1982. — [96]p
ISBN 0-246-11881-4 : £5.95 : CIP entry
B82-18864

Greenwood, Ted, *1930-*. A day in the life of curious Eddie / related by Ted Greenwood. — London : Angus & Robertson, 1979. — [32]p : col.ill ; 27cm
ISBN 0-207-13478-2 : £3.50 B82-03662

Greenwood, Ted, *1930-*. The pochetto coat / Ted Greenwood ; illustrated by Ron Brooks. — Ringwood, Vic. ; Harmondsworth : Puffin, 1981, c1978. — 71p : ill ; 20cm
Originally published: Richmond, Vic. : Hutchinson, 1978
ISBN 0-14-031475-x (pbk) : £0.80 B82-16778

Lardner, Kym. The sad little monster & the jelly bean queen / Kym Lardner. — Sydney ; London : Hodder and Stoughton, 1981. — [32]p : col.ill ; 26cm
Ill on lining papers
ISBN 0-340-26628-7 : £5.95 B82-18102

McLean, Andrew. The steam train crew / Andrew and Janet McLean. — Melbourne ; Oxford : Oxford University Press, 1981. — [40]p : col.ill ; 25cm
ISBN 0-19-554320-3 : £4.25 B82-19453

Mattingley, Christobel. Rummage / Christobel Mattingley ; illustrated by Patricia Mullins. — London : Angus & Robertson, 1981. — [32]p : col.ill ; 25cm
ISBN 0-207-95874-2 : Unpriced B82-08984

Moore, Inga. Aktil's bicycle ride / written and illustrated by Inga Moore. — Melbourne ; Oxford : Oxford University Press, 1981. — [36]p : col.ill ; 29cm
ISBN 0-19-554319-x : £4.50 B82-19452

Moore, Inga. Aktil's big swim / written and illustrated by Inga Moore. — Melbourne ; Oxford : Oxford University Press, 1980. — [32]p : chiefly col.ill ; 29cm
ISBN 0-19-554250-9 : £3.95 B82-30437

Park, Ruth. Playing Beatie Bow / Ruth Park. — [Harmondsworth] : Puffin, 1982, c1980. — 196p ; 19cm. — (A Puffin book)
Originally published: West Melbourne : Nelson, 1980 ; Harmondsworth : Kestrel, 1981
ISBN 0-14-031460-1 (pbk) : £1.25 B82-29589

Pavey, Peter. Battles in the bath / Peter Pavey. — London : Hamish Hamilton Children's Books, 1982. — [32]p : chiefly col.ill ; 27cm
ISBN 0-241-10857-8 : £4.50 B82-37080

Pittaway, Margaret. The rainforest children : a story set in tropical Australia / by Margaret Pittaway ; illustrated by Heather Philpott. — Melbourne ; Oxford : Oxford University Press, 1980. — [32]p : col.ill ; 29cm
ISBN 0-19-554238-x : £4.50 B82-38626

Small, Mary. And Alice did the walking / Mary Small ; photographs by Lionel Jensen. — Melbourne ; Oxford : Oxford University Press, 1978 (1981 [printing]). — 25p : ill ; 22cm
ISBN 0-19-554322-x (pbk) : £1.75 B82-34132

Smith, Raymond, *19---*. Dreadful David Dee / Raymond Smith and Henry Schoenheimer. — Melbourne ; London : Hutchinson of Australia, 1980 (1981 [printing]). — [36]p : col.ill ; 30cm
ISBN 0-09-137490-1 : Unpriced B82-16867

Smith, Raymond, *19---*. Greedy glutton Garth / Raymond Smith and Henry Schoenheimer. — Melbourne ; London : Hutchinson of Australia, 1980 (1981 [printing]). — 34p : col.ill ; 30cm
ISBN 0-09-137510-x : Unpriced B82-16868

Smith, Raymond, *19---*. Susan shouted 'shark' / Raymond Smith and Henry Schoenheimer. — Melbourne ; London : Hutchinson of Australia, 1980 (1981 [printing]). — [34]p : col.ill ; 30cm
ISBN 0-09-137500-2 : Unpriced B82-16869

Southall, Ivan. The golden goose / Ivan Southall. — London : Methuen, 1981. — 180p ; 22cm
ISBN 0-416-21360-x : £5.50 B82-15547

Stanton, Susan. Ballet shoes for the goblin. — London : Methuen Children's, Jan.1983. — [128]p. — (A Pied piper book)
ISBN 0-416-26490-5 : £4.95 : CIP entry
B82-34450

White, Osmar. The further adventures of Dr. A.A.A. McGurk, M.D. / Osmar White ; illustrated by Jeff Hook. — Ringwood ; Harmondsworth : Puffin, 1981. — 61p : ill ; 20cm
ISBN 0-14-031408-3 (pbk) : £0.80 B82-22302

White, Osmar. The super-roo of Mungalongaloo / Osmar White ; illustrated by Jeff Hook. — Ringwood, Vic. ; Harmondsworth : Puffin, 1978 (1981 [printing]). — 57p : ill ; 20cm
Originally published: S. Melbourne : Wren, 1973
ISBN 0-14-031110-6 (pbk) : £0.75 B82-16771

823[J] — Children's stories in English. Australian writers, *1945- — Texts* *continuation*

Xhafer, Anita. The powder box lady / written and illustrated by Anita Xhafer. — Melbourne ; Oxford : Oxford University Press, 1980. — [29]p : col.ill ; 26x28cm
ISBN 0-19-554263-0 : Unpriced B82-32190

823[J] — Children's stories in English. New Zealand writers, *1907- — Texts*

Allen, Pamela. Who sank the boat? / Pamela Allen. — London : Hamilton, 1982. — [28]p : col.ill ; 23x26cm
Ill on lining papers
ISBN 0-241-10858-6 : £4.75 B82-37706

Bishop, Gavin. Mrs McGinty and the bizarre plant / story and pictures by Gavin Bishop. — Auckland ; Oxford : Oxford University Press, c1981. — [32]p : chiefly col.ill ; 24x29cm
ISBN 0-19-558074-5 : £3.95 B82-07719

Dallas, Ruth. A dog called Wig / Ruth Dallas ; illustrated by Edward Mortelmans. — [London] : Magnet, 1981, c1970. — 142p : ill ; 18cm
Originally published: London : Methuen, 1970
ISBN 0-416-24360-6 (pbk) : £0.95 B82-15605

Dallas, Ruth. Holiday time in the bush. — London : Methuen Children's, Jan.1983. — [96]p. — (A Read aloud book)
ISBN 0-416-23480-1 : £3.95 : CIP entry B82-34443

Dallas, Ruth. The house on the cliffs / Ruth Dallas ; illustrated by Gavin Rowe. — [London] : Magnet, 1981, c1975. — 156p : ill ; 18cm
Originally published: London : Methuen, 1975
ISBN 0-416-24370-3 (pbk) : £0.95 B82-15613

Gibson, Gloria. Mouse at school. — London : Methuen Children's, Jan.1983. — [126]p. — (A Pied piper book)
ISBN 0-416-23520-4 : £3.95 : CIP entry B82-34444

823[J] — Children's stories in English. Nigerian writers, *1960- — Texts*

Fulani, Dan. Sauna and the bank robbers / by Dan Fulani. — London : Arena, 1981. — 107p : ill ; 20cm
ISBN 0-340-20853-8 (pbk) : Unpriced : CIP rev. B81-08920

Fulani, Dan. Sauna and the drug pedlars. — London : Hodder and Stoughton, Jan.1983. — [96]p
ISBN 0-340-32789-8 (pbk) : £1.50 : CIP entry B82-34413

Fulani, Dan. Sauna to the rescue / by Dan Fulani. — Zaria : Hudahuda ; Sevenoaks : Hodder and Stoughton, 1982. — 91p : ill ; 20cm
ISBN 0-340-28073-5 (pbk) : Unpriced : CIP rev. B82-00262

Meniru, Teresa. Unoma at College / Teresa Meniru. — London : Evans, 1981. — 76p : ill ; 22cm. — (Evans Africa library)
ISBN 0-237-50630-0 (pbk) : Unpriced B82-06634

823[J] — Children's stories in English. South African writers, *1961- — Texts*

Jones, Toeckey. Go well, stay well / Toeckey Jones. — London : Fontana, 1982, c1979. — 201p ; 18cm. — (Lions)
Originally published: London : Bodley Head, 1979
ISBN 0-00-672030-7 (pbk) : £1.25 B82-30782

Moodie, Fiona. The sugar prince. — London : Hutchinson, Oct.1952. — [32]p
ISBN 0-09-150520-8 : £4.95 : CIP entry B82-24980

Seed, Jenny. Gold dust. — London : Hamilton, Aug.1982. — [96]p. — (Antelope books)
ISBN 0-241-10847-0 : £2.75 : CIP entry B82-15699

823[J] — Children's stories in English. Swedish writers, *1945- — Texts*

Lindroos, Marianne. Engine people : a story from Sweden / by Marianne Lindroos ; with pictures by W. Cameron Johnson. — London : Grosvenor, 1980. — [29]p : col.ill ; 21x26cm
ISBN 0-901269-54-9 (cased) : Unpriced
ISBN 0-901269-53-0 (pbk) : £1.20 B82-17566

823[J] — Children's stories in English. Swiss writers, *1945- — Texts*

Brandenberg, Franz. Leo and Emily / by Franz Brandenberg ; illustrated by Aliki. — London : Bodley Head, 1982, c1981. — 55p : col.ill ; 22cm. — (Bodley beginners)
Originally published: New York : Greenwillow Books, 1981
ISBN 0-370-30915-4 : £3.25 : CIP rev. B81-36976

823'.008 — Fiction in English, *1800-1945 — Anthologies*

Best loved books / selected and condensed by the editors of Reader's digest. — London : Reader's Digest Association, c1981. — 575p : chiefly col.ill,1col.map,1facsim,ports(some col.) ; 21cm
ISBN 0-340-27885-4 : £6.95 B82-08125

823'.008'0329451 — Fiction in English. Australian writers, *1854-1977.* **Special subjects: Australia. Victoria. Melbourne** *— Anthologies*

The **Imagined** city : Melbourne in the mind of its writers. — London : Allen & Unwin, Jan.1983. — [112]p
ISBN 0-86861-053-4 : £15.00 : CIP entry B82-33231

823'.008'09287 — Fiction in English. Women writers, *1680-1980 — Anthologies*

Rediscovery : 300 years of stories by and about women / edited by Betzy Dinesen. — London : Women's Press, 1981. — 196p ; 20cm
ISBN 0-7043-3879-3 (pbk) : £3.50 : CIP rev. B81-30351

823'.009 — Fiction in English, *1700-1980.* **Forms: Novels** *compared with* **German novels,** *1700-1980*

Klieneberger, H. R.. The novel in England and Germany. — London : Wolff, Aug.1981. — [254]p
ISBN 0-85496-079-1 (pbk) : £8.00 : CIP entry
Also classified at 833'.009 B81-18114

823'.009 — Fiction in English, *1700-1980.* **Style. Linguistic aspects**

Leech, Geoffrey. Style in fiction : a linguistic introduction to English fictional prose / Geoffrey N. Leech, Michael H. Short. — London : Longman, 1981. — xiii,402p : ill ; 22cm. — (English language series ; no.13)
Bibliography: p382-393. — Includes index
ISBN 0-582-29103-8 (pbk) : £6.95 : CIP rev. B80-26112

823'.009 — Fiction in English, *1800-1981 — Critical studies — Festschriften*

The **Uses** of fiction. — Milton Keynes : Open University Press, Oct.1982. — [320]p
ISBN 0-335-10181-x : £11.95 : CIP entry B82-25515

823'.009 — Fiction in English. Criticism. Leavis, F. R. & Leavis, Q. D. *— Critical studies*

Robertson, P. J. M.. The Leavises on fiction : an historic partnership / P.J.M. Robertson. — London : Macmillan, 1981. — xv,176p ; 23cm
Bibliography: p165-172. — Includes index
ISBN 0-333-27886-0 : £15.00 B82-10810

823'.009'15 — Fantasy fiction in English *— Critical studies — Serials*

Flay, swelter & groan. — [No.1]-. — London (62 Beaufort Mansions, Beaufort St., S.W.3) : P. Palmer, [198-]-. — v. ; 30cm
Irregular
Unpriced B82-31718

823'.009'352055 — Fiction in English, *1700-1970.* **Special subjects: Adolescence** *— Critical studies*

Spacks, Patricia Meyer. The adolescent idea : myths of youth and the adult imagination / Patricia Meyer Spacks. — London : Faber, 1982, c1981. — ix,308p ; 22cm
Originally published: New York : Basic Books, 1981. — Includes index
ISBN 0-571-11915-8 : £15.00 : CIP rev. B82-00208

823'.009'353 — Fiction in English, *1702-1980.* **Special themes: Sex relations**

Charney, Maurice. Sexual fiction / Maurice Charney. — London : Methuen, 1981. — xii,180p ; 20cm. — (New accents)
Bibliography: p170-177. — Includes index
ISBN 0-416-31930-0 (cased) : Unpriced : CIP rev.
ISBN 0-416-31940-8 (pbk) : £2.95 B81-27347

823'.009'355 — Fiction in English, *1750-1850.* **Special themes: England. Social change** *— Critical studies*

Webb, Igor. From custom to capital : the English novel and the industrial revolution / Igor Webb. — Ithaca ; London : Cornell University Press, 1981. — 219p ; 23cm
Includes index
ISBN 0-8014-1392-3 : £12.25 B82-02119

823'.009'37 — Fiction in English, *1700-1980.* **Special subjects: Supernatural** *— Critical studies*

Literature of the occult : a collection of critical essays / edited by Peter B. Messent. — Englewood Cliffs ; London : Prentice-Hall, c1981. — xi,188p ; 21cm. — (Twentieth century views) (A Spectrum book)
Bibliography: p187-188
ISBN 0-13-537712-9 (cased) : Unpriced
ISBN 0-13-537704-8 (pbk) : £3.70 B82-07542

823'.009'9287 — Fiction in English. Women writers, *1745-1900 — Critical studies*

Figes, Eva. Sex and subterfuge : women novelists to 1850 / Eva Figes. — London : Macmillan, 1982. — 178p ; 23cm
Bibliography: p174-175. — Includes index
ISBN 0-333-29208-1 (cased) : Unpriced
ISBN 0-333-29210-3 (pbk) : Unpriced B82-14869

823'.0099287 — Fiction in English. Women writers, *to 1980 — Critical studies*

Pratt, Annis. Archetypal patterns in women's fiction / Annis Pratt with Barbara White, Andrea Loewenstein, Mary Wyer. — Brighton : Harvester, 1982, c1981. — x,211p : 1ill ; 24cm
Originally published: Bloomington, Ind. : Indiana University Press, 1981. —
Bibliography: p190-206. — Includes index
ISBN 0-7108-0381-8 : £18.95 : CIP rev. B81-33851

823'.01'08 — Short stories in English, *1945- — Anthologies — For schools*

Bell & Hyman short stories. — London : Bell & Hyman, Sept.1982
1: Openings. — [128]p
ISBN 0-7135-1336-5 (pbk) : £2.50 : CIP entry B82-20048

823'.01'08[FS] — Short stories in English, *1800-1980 - Anthologies*

The **Oxford** book of short stories. — Oxford : Oxford University Press, June 1981. — [720]p
ISBN 0-19-214116-3 : £12.50 : CIP entry B81-14414

823'.01'08[FS] — Short stories in English, *1900- — Anthologies*

Modern short stories 2 : 1940-1980 / edited by Giles Gordon. — London : Dent, 1982. — xvii,326p ; 18cm
ISBN 0-460-01149-9 (pbk) : £1.95 : CIP rev. B82-13238

The **Quickening** pulse / selected by D.J. Brindley. — London : Hodder and Stoughton
" ... to accompany 'Excellence in English', Books 1-5" — half t.p. verso
Bk.5. — 1982. — 183p ; 22cm
ISBN 0-340-23771-6 (pbk) : Unpriced : CIP rev. B82-08077

823'.01'08[FS] — Short stories in English, *1900- - Anthologies - Serials*
Punch short stories. — 3. — London : Robson, July 1981. — [192]p
ISBN 0-86051-136-7 : £5.95 : CIP entry
B81-14453

823'.01'08[FS] — Short stories in English, *1900- — Anthologies — Serials*
Short stories magazine. — Vol.1, no.1 (1980)-. — Burgess Hill (222 London Rd, Burgess Hill, Sussex RH15 9RD) : Short Stories Magazine Ltd, 1980-. — v. : ill ; 21cm
Monthly. — Description based on: Vol.1, no.8 (July 1981)
ISSN 0260-471x = Short stories magazine : £14.50 per year B82-05228

823'.01'08[FS] — Short stories in English, *1945- — Anthologies*
Anthology of short stories / by the Green Ink Writers Group. — London (84A Marlborough Rd. N22) : Green Ink Writers Group, c1982. — 60p ; 20cm
£1.00 (pbk) B82-26117

Great short stories of the world / edited by Whit and Hallie Burnett. — London : Souvenir, 1965 (1982 [printing]). — 589p ; 23cm
ISBN 0-285-62538-1 : £8.95 B82-17490

New stories 7 / edited by Alan Ross. — London : Hutchinson in association with the Arts Council of Great Britain and PEN, 1982. — 222p ; 23cm
ISBN 0-09-147930-4 : £7.95 : CIP rev.
B82-09276

The **Punch** book of short stories / selected by Alan Coren. — Harmondsworth : Penguin, 1980, c1979 (1982 [printing]). — 191p ; 19cm
Originally published: London : Robson, 1979
ISBN 0-14-005387-5 (pbk) B82-29824

The **Second** Punch book of short stories / selected by Alan Coren. — Harmondsworth : Penguin, 1982, c1981. — 223p ; 18cm
Originally published: London : Robson, 1980
ISBN 0-14-005885-0 (pbk) : £1.50 B82-29823

Short stories from the Second World War. — Oxford : Oxford University Press, Sept.1982. — [296]p
ISBN 0-19-212973-2 : £7.50 : CIP entry
B82-19177

Visitors' book : short stories of their new homeland by famous authors now living in Ireland. — London : Arrow, 1982. — 191p ; 18cm
Originally published: Dublin : Poolbeg Press, 1979
ISBN 0-09-924520-5 (pbk) : £1.25 B82-19015

Winter's tales 27 / edited by Edward Leeson. — London : Macmillan, 1981. — 189p ; 21cm
ISBN 0-333-31072-1 : £5.95 B82-05898

823'.01'08[FS] — Short stories in English, *1945- — Anthologies — Serials*
The **Fiction** magazine. — Vol.1, no.1 (Spring 1982)-. — London (c/o Editorial Office, 5 Jeffreys St., NW1 9PS) : Fiction Magazine, 1982-. — v. : ill,ports ; 30cm
Quarterly
ISSN 0263-6565 = Fiction magazine : £1.25
B82-28862

823'.01'08[FS] — Short stories in English, *ca 1800-1981 — Anthologies*
Short shorts : an anthology of the shortest stories. — London (45 Blackfriars Rd, SE1 8NZ) : Kudos & Godine, Apr.1982. — [368]p
ISBN 0-906293-15-4 : £6.95 : CIP entry
B82-04720

823'.01'08036[J] — Children's animal short stories in English, *to 1981. — Anthologies*
A **Treasury** of animal stories. — London : Kingfisher Books, Sept.1982. — [160]p
ISBN 0-86272-035-4 : £4.95 : CIP entry
B82-21561

823'.01'0809415[FS] — Short stories in English. Irish writers, *1900- — Anthologies*
[The Bodley Head book of Irish short stories]. Irish short stories / selected and introduced by David Marcus. — London : New English Library, 1982, c1980. — 2v. ; 18cm
Originally published in 1 vol. London: Bodley Head, 1980
ISBN 0-450-05378-4 (pbk) : Unpriced : CIP rev.
ISBN 0-450-05421-7 (v.2) : £1.50 B82-03597

Irish stories / chosen by Gerard Wall. — London : Ward Lock Educational, 1982. — 107p ; 20cm. — (WLE short stories ; 21)
ISBN 0-7062-4140-1 (pbk) : Unpriced
ISBN 0-7062-4141-x (schools ed.) : Unpriced
B82-32128

823'.01'0815[FS] — Fantasy short stories in English, *1837- — Anthologies*
Fantasy / chosen by Alyn Shipton. — London : Murray, c1982. — 119p ; 20cm. — (The Short story series)
ISBN 0-7195-3874-2 (pbk) : £1.10 : CIP rev.
B81-30583

823'.01'0815[FS] — Fantasy stories in English, *1837-1980 — Anthologies*
The **Barbarian** swordsmen : great stories of heroic fantasy / edited by Sean Richards. — London : W.H. Allen, 1981. — 172p ; 18cm. — (A Star book)
ISBN 0-352-30831-1 (pbk) : £1.50 B82-03259

823'.01'0815[J] — Children's fantasy short stories in English, *1945- — Anthologies*
Exciting stories of fantasy and the future / illustrated by Oliver Frey. — London : Hamlyn, 1982. — 256p : ill(some col.) ; 22cm. — (Falcon Fiction Club)
ISBN 0-600-36677-4 : £1.75 B82-37511

823'.01'0816[FS] — Horror short stories in English, *1837- — Anthologies*
Great tales of terror and the supernatural. — London : Hutchinson, Sept.1982. — [832]p
ISBN 0-09-149720-5 : £8.95 : CIP entry
B82-20615

823'.01'0816[FS] — Horror short stories in English, *1900- — Anthologies*
Greasepaint and ghosts : an anthology of strange and supernatural stories from the world of the theatre / edited by Peter Haining. — London : Kimber, 1982. — 219p ; 23cm
ISBN 0-7183-0378-4 : £1.50 B82-27260

Horror stories / chosen by Bryan Newton. — London : Ward Lock Educational, 1978 (1980 [printing]). — 127p ; 20cm. — (WLE short stories ; 6)
ISBN 0-7062-3669-6 (pbk) : Unpriced
B82-36234

Stories of terror / chosen by John L. Foster. — London : Ward Lock Educational, 1982. — 122p ; 20cm. — (WLE short stories ; 22)
ISBN 0-7062-4142-8 (pbk) : Unpriced
ISBN 0-7062-4143-6 (schools ed.) : Unpriced
B82-32131

823'.01'0816[FS] — Horror short stories in English, *1945- — Anthologies*
The **22nd** Pan book of horror stories / edited by Herbert van Thal. — London : Pan, 1981. — 188p ; 18cm
ISBN 0-330-26509-1 (pbk) : £1.00 B82-00778

Alfred Hitchcock presents the master's choice. — London : Hodder & Stoughton. — (Coronet books)
Book 2. — Dec.1981. — [336]p
ISBN 0-340-26771-2 (pbk) : £1.25 : CIP entry
B81-31471

Coffin corner / [compiled by] Alfred Hitchcock. — London : Severn House, 1980. — 220p ; 21cm
ISBN 0-7278-0656-4 : £5.50 : CIP rev.
B80-12121

Alfred Hitchcock presents the master's choice. — London : Coronet, July 1981
Originally published: London : Reinhardt, 1979
Book 1. — [192]p
ISBN 0-340-26678-3 (pbk) : £1.23 : CIP entry
B81-13778

Hitchcock, Alfred. Hitchcock's : this one will kill you. — London : Severn House, Nov.1982. — [208]p
ISBN 0-7278-0834-6 : £6.95 : CIP entry
B82-34064

Tales of fear and frightening phenomena. — London : Dent, Sept.1982. — [160]p
ISBN 0-460-06118-6 : £5.95 : CIP entry
B82-19706

Tales to send chills down your spine. — London : Hodder & Stoughton. — (Coronet books)
Book 1. — June 1982. — [192]p
Originally published: London : Max Reinhardt, 1980
ISBN 0-340-26777-1 (pbk) : £1.25 : CIP entry
B82-10007

Tales to send chills down your spine. — London : Coronet
Originally published: New York : Dial Press, 1979 ; London : Reinhardt, 1980
Book 2. — Nov.1982. — [224]p
ISBN 0-340-28647-4 (pbk) : £1.50 : CIP entry
B82-27372

823.01'0816[J] — Children's horror short stories in English, *1945- — Anthologies*
Black eyes : and other spine chillers / by Joan Aiken ... [et al.] ; compiled by Lance Salway ; illustrated by Jill Bennett. — Leeds : Pepper, 1981. — 92p : ill ; 21cm
ISBN 0-560-74523-0 : £3.95 B82-06458

823'.01'0816[J] — Children's horror short stories in English, *1945- — Anthologies*
The **Methuen** book of sinister stories. — London : Methuen, Oct.1982. — [128]p
ISBN 0-416-22240-4 : £4.95 : CIP entry
B82-24486

823'.01'08321734[FS] — Short stories in English, *1837-*. **Special subjects: Countryside —** *Anthologies*
Country / chosen by James Gibson. — London : Murray, c1982. — 120p ; 20cm. — (The Short story series)
ISBN 0-7195-3873-4 (pbk) : £1.10 : CIP rev.
B81-30961

823'.01'083254[FS] — Short stories in English, *1885-1947*. **Special subjects: India. Britons. Social life,** *1785-1947 — Anthologies*
Stories from the Raj : from Kipling to Independence / selected and introduced by Saros Cowasjee ; with a preface by Paul Theroux. — London : Bodley Head, 1982. — 271p ; 23cm
ISBN 0-370-30456-x : £7.50 : CIP rev.
B82-00293

823'.01'08351[FS] — Short stories in English, *1945-*. **Special themes: Drama in English. Shakespeare, William —** *Anthologies*
Shakespeare stories. — London : Hamilton, Oct.1982. — [224]p
ISBN 0-241-10879-9 : £6.95 : CIP entry
B82-23459

823'.01'08355[FS] — Crime short stories in English, *1900-*. **Special subjects: Railways —** *Anthologies*
Beware of the trains / edited by Tony Wilmot. — Hornchurch : Ian Henry, 1981. — ii,176p ; 21cm
ISBN 0-86025-193-4 : £5.95 B82-14329

823'.01'08355[FS] — Short stories in English, *1880-1980*. **Special subjects: Mummies —** *Anthologies*
Mummy! : a chrestomathy of cryptology / [compiled by] Bill Pronzini. — South Yarmouth, Ma. : John Curley ; Long Preston : Magna Print [distributor], 1980. — x,479p ; 22cm
Published in large print
ISBN 0-89340-370-9 (pbk) : Unpriced
B82-17149

823'.01'08358[FS] — Short stories in English, *1837-*. Special subjects: War — *Anthologies*

War / chosen by James Gibson. — London : Murray, c1982. — 121p ; 20cm. — (The Short story series)
ISBN 0-7195-3871-8 (pbk) : £1.10 : CIP rev. B81-30957

823'.01'0836[J] — Children's short stories in English, *1945-*. Special subjects: Animals — *Anthologies*

Animal stories from around the world / illustrated by Terry Gabbey. — London : Hamlyn, 1982. — 256p : ill(some col.) ; 22cm. — (Falcon Fiction Club)
ISBN 0-600-36678-2 : £1.75 B82-37512

823'.01'0836[J] — Children's short stories in English. Compositions by students of Lady Eden's School, *1945-*. Special subjects: Animals — *Anthologies*

Just how stories / by girls of Lady Eden's School, London ; illustrated by Derek Steele. — London : Cape, 1981. — 22p : col.ill ; 27cm
ISBN 0-224-01713-6 : £4.50 : CIP rev. B80-13598

823'.01'08375[FS] — Ghost short stories in English, *1800-1980* — *Anthologies*

The **Twelfth** Fontana book of great ghost stories / selected by R. Chetwynd-Hayes. — [London] : Fontana, 1976 (1981 [printing]). — 190p ; 19cm
ISBN 0-00-616563-x (pbk) : £1.00 B82-07922

823'.01'08375[FS] — Ghost short stories in English, *1837-1980* — *Anthologies*

The **Seventeenth** Fontana book of great ghost stories / selected by R. Chetwynd-Hayes. — [London] : Fontana, 1981. — 189p ; 18cm
ISBN 0-00-616271-1 (pbk) : £1.00 B82-07921

Thirteen famous ghost stories / edited and selected by Peter Underwood. — London : Dent, c1977. — 203p ; 19cm
ISBN 0-460-00749-1 (cased) : Unpriced
ISBN 0-460-01749-7 (pbk) : £0.95 B82-26944

823'.01'08375[FS] — Ghost short stories in English, *1900-1945* — *Anthologies*

The **Supernatural** omnibus. — London : Gollancz, June 1982. — [624]p
ISBN 0-575-03120-4 : £8.95 : CIP entry B82-09440

823'.01'08375[FS] — Ghost short stories in English, *1900-* — *Anthologies*

[The After midnight ghost book]The Fourth bumper book of ghost stories / edited by James Hale. — London : Pan, 1981, c1980. — 316p ; 18cm
Originally published: London : Hamilton, 1980
ISBN 0-330-26536-9 (pbk) : £1.75 B82-03138

Ghosts in country houses / edited by Denys Val Baker. — London : Kimber, 1981. — 192p ; 22cm
ISBN 0-7183-0298-2 : £5.95 B82-04684

823'.01'08375[FS] — Ghost short stories in English, *1945-* — *Anthologies*

The **Twilight** book : a new collection of ghost stories / edited by James Hale. — London : Gollancz, 1981. — 183p ; 22cm
ISBN 0-575-03021-6 : £6.95 B82-02263

West Country tales : stories of mystery and suspense. — Exeter : Webb & Bower in association with BBC TV and Doublejay Films, 1981. — vii,120p : ill ; 23cm
ISBN 0-906671-65-5 : £4.95 : CIP rev. B81-34208

823'.01'08375[J] — Children's ghost short stories in English, *1900-* — *Anthologies*

[Ghostly gallery]. Alfred Hitchcock's ghostly gallery / illustrated by Barry Wilkinson. — Harmondsworth : Penguin in association with Reinhardt, 1982, c1966. — 203p : ill ; 18cm
Originally published: New York : Random House, 1962 ; London : Reinhardt, 1966
ISBN 0-14-031535-7 (pbk) : £1.10 B82-35384

823'.01'08375[J] — Children's ghost short stories in English, *1945-* — *Anthologies*

Chambers, Aidan. Ghost after ghost / compiled by Aidan Chambers ; illustrated by Bert Kitchen. — [Harmondsworth] : Kestrel, 1982. — 172p : ill ; 22cm
ISBN 0-7226-5772-2 : £4.95 B82-40804

Spooky stories / edited by Barbara Ireson. — London : Transworld. — (A Carousel book) No.4 / illustrated by Daniel Woods. — 1982. — 123p : ill ; 18cm
ISBN 0-552-52201-5 (pbk) : £0.95 B82-35547

The **Thirteenth** Armada ghost book / edited by Mary Danby ; illustrated by Peter Archer. — London : Armada, 1981. — 128p : ill ; 18cm
ISBN 0-00-691913-8 (pbk) : £0.85 B82-01249

823'.01'08375[J] — Children's horror short stories in English, *1945-*. Special subjects: Monsters — *Anthologies*

Peter Davison's book of alien monsters. — London : Hutchinson, 1982. — 125p ; 21cm
ISBN 0-09-149210-6 : £4.95 : CIP rev. B82-09200

The **Sixth** Armada monster book / edited by R. Chetwynd-Hayes ; illustrated by Eric Kincaid. — London : Armada, 1981. — 128p : ill ; 18cm
ISBN 0-00-691744-5 (pbk) : £0.85 B82-01251

823'.01'08375[J] — Children's short stories in English, *1900-*. Special subjects: Witches — *Anthologies*

Alfred Hitchcock's witch's brew. — Harmondsworth : Puffin, 1980, c1977 (1982 [printing]). — 140p ; 19cm
Originally published: New York : Random House, 1977 ; London : Reinhardt, 1978
ISBN 0-14-031517-9 (pbk) : £0.95 B82-25535

823'.01'089282[J] — Children's short stories in English, *1800-1900* — *Anthologies*

Book of mystery stories. — Bristol : Purnell, 1982. — 222p : ill ; 21cm
ISBN 0-361-05286-3 : £2.25 B82-36380

823'.01'089282[J] — Children's short stories in English, *1837-* — *Anthologies*

Stories for tens and over / edited by Sara and Stephen Corrin ; illustrated by Victor Ambrus. — Harmondsworth : Puffin in association with Faber, 1982, c1976. — 205p : ill ; 20cm
Originally published: London : Faber, 1976
ISBN 0-14-031364-8 (pbk) : £1.25 B82-16763

A **Time** to laugh : funny stories for children / edited by Sara and Stephen Corrin ; illustrated by Gerald Rose. — [London] : Faber Fanfares, 1980, c1972. — 205p : ill ; 19cm. — (Faber fanfares)
Originally published: London : Faber, 1972
ISBN 0-571-11487-3 (pbk) : £1.25 : CIP rev.
Primary classification 398.2'1 B80-18056

823'.01'089282[J] — Children's short stories in English, *1900-1945* — *Anthologies*

Marshall, Sybil. Wings. — Cambridge : Cambridge University Press, Apr.1981. — [48] p. — (Lanterns)
ISBN 0-521-28155-5 (pbk) : £1.50 : CIP entry B81-01227

823'.01'089282[J] — Children's short stories in English, *1900-* — *Anthologies*

Alfred Hitchcock's sinister spies. — (repr. minus one story). — [Harmondsworth] : Puffin in association with Bodley Head, 1977, c1966 (1982 [printing]). — 186p ; 19cm
Originally published: New York : Random House, 1966 ; London : Reinhardt, 1967
ISBN 0-14-031539-x (pbk) : £1.10 B82-35498

Bedtime stories / compiled by Eileen Colwell ; illustrated by Jennie Schofield, Margaret Gold and David Anstey. — Loughborough : Ladybird, c1982. — 57p : col.ill ; 31cm
Ill on lining papers
ISBN 0-7214-7521-3 : £2.50 B82-35466

The **Faber** book of modern fairy tales / edited by Sara and Stephen Corrin ; illustrated by Ann Strugnell. — London : Faber, 1981. — 312p : ill ; 23cm
ISBN 0-571-11768-6 : £5.95 : CIP rev. B81-21531

823'.01'089282[J] — Children's short stories in English, *1945-* — *Anthologies*

100 nonsense stories / [by Margaret Conroy et al.] ; [illustrations by Linda Birch et al.]. — London : Hamlyn, 1982. — 157p : col.ill ; 22cm
ISBN 0-600-36645-6 : £2.95 B82-33028

100 stories of many lands / [by Margaret Conroy et al.] ; [illustrations by Paul Bonner et al.]. — London : Hamlyn, 1982. — 157p : col.ill ; 22cm
ISBN 0-600-36646-4 : £2.95 B82-33027

All made of fantasy : a book of short stories for children / edited by Marjorie and Jeremy Rowe. — Chipping Norton : The Theatre, 1980. — 204p ; 15x22cm
Unpriced (spiral) B82-22180

Althea. [The big Desmond story book]. Desmond the dinosaur story book / by Althea and some children. — Cambridge : Dinosaur Publications, c1980. — [92]p : col.ill ; 28cm
Originally published: 1979
ISBN 0-85122-224-2 : Unpriced : CIP rev. B80-06678

Book of Brownie stories. — Bristol : Purnell, 1982. — 222p : ill ; 21cm
ISBN 0-361-05318-5 : £2.25 B82-34136

[Daddy, read me a bedtime story]. My second bedtime book of two-minute stories / edited by Mary Parsley ; illustrated by Tony Escott. — London : Peter Lowe, 1982, c1971. — 93p : col.ill ; 28cm
Originally published: London : Eurobook, 1971
ISBN 0-85654-045-5 : £3.50 B82-35449

Listen with mother / illustrated by Priscilla Lamont. — London : Hutchinson in association with the BBC, 1982. — 127p : ill ; 23cm
ISBN 0-09-147160-5 : £2.95 B82-18253

More stories for seven-year-olds : and other young readers / edited by Sara and Stephen Corrin ; illustrated by Shirley Hughes. — Harmondsworth : Puffin in association with Faber, 1982, c1978. — 187p : ill ; 20cm
Originally published: London : Faber, 1978
ISBN 0-14-031347-8 (pbk) : £1.10 B82-16782

My bedtime storybook / illustrated by Peter Skinner. — London : Dean, c1981. — 45p : ill (some col.) ; 20cm. — (New little one's reader series)
ISBN 0-603-00268-4 : Unpriced B82-25599

My favourite storybook / illustrated by Peter Skinner. — London : Dean, c1981. — 45p : ill (some col.) ; 20cm. — (New little one's reader series)
ISBN 0-603-00267-6 : Unpriced B82-25597

My sleepytime storybook / illustrated by Peter Skinner. — London : Dean, c1981. — 45p : ill (some col.) ; 20cm. — (New little one's reader series)
ISBN 0-603-00269-2 : Unpriced B82-25598

My time for bed storybook / illustrated by Peter Skinner. — London : Dean, c1981. — 45p : ill (some col.) ; 20cm. — (New little one's reader series)
ISBN 0-603-00270-6 : Unpriced B82-25600

Pieces of eight : contemporary Anglo-Welsh short stories / editor Robert Nisbet. — Llandysul : Gomer Press, 1982. — 143p ; 22cm
ISBN 0-85088-555-8 (pbk) : £3.95 B82-27247

823'.01'089282[J] — Children's short stories in English, *1945- — Anthologies* *continuation*
. Play School stories. — London : Hodder & Stoughton, Oct.1982. — [128]p
ISBN 0-340-28086-7 (pbk) : £0.95 : CIP entry
B82-24821

School's OK. — London : Evans, Oct.1982. — [128]p
For adolescents
ISBN 0-237-45653-2 : £4.95 : CIP entry
B82-23491

Town and country stories. — Nutfield : National Christian Education Council, Mar.1982. — [128]p
ISBN 0-7197-0306-9 (pbk) : £2.00 : CIP entry
B82-11486

A **Treasury** of bedtime stories. — London (Elsley Court, 20 Great Titchfield St., W1P 7AD) : Kingfisher, Sept.1981. — [160]p
ISBN 0-86272-001-x : £3.95 : CIP entry
B81-20171

The **Whole** world story book. — Oxford : Oxford University Press, Sept.1982. — [160]p
ISBN 0-19-278103-0 (pbk) : £5.95 : CIP entry
B82-19187

823'.01'089287[FS] — Short stories in English. Feminist writers, *1945- — Anthologies*

The **Wall** reader : and other stories. — Dublin : Arlen House — The Women's Press, c1979. — 101p ; 19cm
ISBN 0-905223-10-1 (pbk) : £1.50 B82-16609

823'.01'089411[FS] — Short stories in English. Scottish writers, *1945- — Anthologies*

Modern Scottish short stories. — London : Faber, Sept.1982. — [224]p
Originally published: London : Hamilton, 1978
ISBN 0-571-11953-0 (pbk) : £2.95 : CIP entry
B82-18757

Scottish short stories. — London : Collins 1982. — Aug.1982. — [224]p
ISBN 0-00-222680-4 : £7.50 : CIP entry
B82-15619

823'.01'089429[FS] — Short stories in English. Welsh writers, *1900- — Anthologies*

The **Penguin** book of Welsh short stories / edited by Alun Richards. — Harmondsworth : Penguin, 1976 (1982 [printing]). — 358p ; 20cm
Includes some stories translated from the Welsh
ISBN 0-14-004061-7 (pbk) : £2.50
Also classified at 891.6'6301'08[FS]
B82-30530

823'.01'089729[FS] — Short stories in English. West Indian writers, *1900- — Anthologies — For schools*

Best West Indian stories / [edited by] Kenneth Ramchand. — [Kingston, Jamaica] : Nelson Caribbean ; Walton-on-Thames : Nelson, 1982. — 186p : ports ; 22cm
Bibliography: p5
ISBN 0-17-566251-7 (pbk) : Unpriced
B82-21301

823'.01'09 — Short stories in English, *to 1980 — Critical studies*

Allen, Walter. The short story in English / Walter Allen. — Oxford : Clarendon Press, 1981. — 413p ; 23cm
Bibliography: p395-404. — Includes index
ISBN 0-19-812666-2 : £9.50 : CIP rev.
ISBN 0-19-812667-0 (pbk) : £4.50 B82-04282

Bonheim, Helmut. The narrative modes : techniques of the short story / Helmut Bonheim. — Cambridge : Brewer, c1982. — x,197p : ill ; 24cm
Bibliography: p178-190. — Includes index
ISBN 0-85991-086-5 : £17.50 : CIP rev.
B82-09311

823'.01'099282 — Children's short stories in English. Anthologies. 'So big, so small' *— For teaching*

Marshall, Sybil. 'So big, so small' teaching notes. — Cambridge : Cambridge University Press, Apr.1981. — [29]p. — (Lanterns)
ISBN 0-521-28341-8 (pbk) : £1.20 : CIP entry
B81-12857

823'.087'08[J] — Children's adventure short stories in English, *1945- — Anthologies*

Thrilling stories : of mystery and adventure / illustrated by Kay Wilson ; cover illustration by Ivan Lapper. — London : Hamlyn, 1982. — 256p : ill ; 22cm. — (Falcon fiction club)
ISBN 0-600-36679-0 : £1.75 B82-38758

823'.0872 — Detective fiction in English, *1837-1980 — Critical studies*

Porter, Dennis. The pursuit of crime : art and ideology in detective fiction / Dennis Porter. — New Haven ; London : Yale University Press, c1981. — ix,267p ; 22cm
Includes index
ISBN 0-300-02722-2 : Unpriced : CIP rev.
B81-35029

823'.0872 — Gothic fiction in English, *1745-1966 — Critical studies*

Jarrett, David. The Gothic form in fiction and its relation to history / David Jarrett. — Winchester (Winchester SO22 4NR) : King Alfred's College, 1980. — 35p ; 21cm. — (Contexts and connections ; 5)
Unpriced (pbk) B82-16398

823'.0872[FS] — Crime short stories in English, *1837- — Anthologies*

Crime / chosen by F.E.S. Finn. — London : Murray, c1982. — 119p ; 20cm. — (The Short story series)
ISBN 0-7195-3869-6 (pbk) : £1.10 : CIP rev.
B81-30959

823'.0872[FS] — Detective short stories in English, *1900- — Anthologies*

John Creasey's crime collection 1982. — London : Gollancz, Sept.1982. — [192]p
ISBN 0-575-03148-4 : £6.95 : CIP entry
B82-19559

823'.0872[FS] — Detective short stories in English, *1945- — Anthologies*

Crime wave : world's winning crime stories 1981 / selected by an international jury ; and with an introduction by Desmond Bagley. — London : Collins, 1981. — 287p ; 22cm. — (The Crime Club)
Stories submitted for competition at the 3rd Crime Writers International Congress, held in Stockholm, June 1981
ISBN 0-00-231030-9 : £7.50 : CIP rev.
B81-31524

823'.0872[FS] — Suspense short stories in English, *1837- — Anthologies*

Suspense / chosen by Raymond Wilson. — London : Murray, c1982. — 119p ; 20cm. — (The Short story series)
ISBN 0-7195-3872-6 (pbk) : £1.10 : CIP rev.
B81-30962

823'.0876'05 — Science fiction in English *— Serials*

Best science fiction of the year. — 11. — London : Gollancz, Nov.1982. — [448]p
ISBN 0-575-03156-5 : £8.95 : CIP entry
B82-26559

823'.0876'08[FS] — Science fiction short stories in English, *1900-1945 — Anthologies*

Laughing space. — London : Robson, Sept.1982. — [544]p
ISBN 0-86051-181-2 : £7.95 : CIP entry
B82-20868

823'.0876'08[FS] — Science fiction short stories in English, *1900- — Anthologies*

Weekend book of science fiction / compiled by Stuart Gendall ; illustrated by Reginald Gray. — London : Published by Harmsworth for Associated Newspapers Group, c1981. — 127p : ill ; 22cm
ISBN 0-85144-180-7 (pbk) : £1.00 B82-01016

823'.0876'08[FS] — Science fiction short stories in English, *1945- — Anthologies*

The **Golden** age of science fiction / selected and introduced by Kingsley Amis. — London : Hutchinson, 1981. — 370p ; 22cm
ISBN 0-09-145770-x : £6.95 : CIP rev.
B81-20182

823'.0876'08[FS] — Science fiction short stories, *to 1900 — English texts*

The **Road** to science fiction / edited by James Gunn. — New York : New American Library ; London : New English Library. — (A Mentor book)
1: From Gilgamesh to Wells. — 1977. — 404p : 2maps ; 18cm
Bibliography: p394-404
ISBN 0-451-61850-5 (pbk) : Unpriced
B82-05918

823'.0876'089282[J] — Children's science fiction short stories in English, *1945- — Anthologies*

Peter Davison's book of alien monsters. — London : Sparrow, 1982. — 125p ; 18cm
ISBN 0-09-928300-x (pbk) : £0.95 B82-19013

Pictures at an exhibition : a science fiction anthology / edited by Ian Watson. — [Cardiff] : [Greystoke Mobray], [1981]. — 166p : ill ; 18cm
Cover title
ISBN 0-906901-02-2 (pbk) : £1.25 B82-11671

823'.0876'09 — Science fiction in English *— Reviews — Serials*

Arena S.F.. — [1978]-. — Birchington (6 Rutland Gardens, Birchington, Kent CT7 9SN) : G. Rippington, 1978-. — v. : ill,ports ; 21cm
Continues: Arena (Canterbury). — Description based on: 12
ISSN 0262-5490 = Arena S.F. : £0.60 per issue B82-06786

823.3 — ENGLISH FICTION, 1558-1625

823'.3 — Fiction in English. Sidney, *Sir* **Philip. Arcadia** *— Critical studies*

Rees, Joan. Exploring 'Arcadia' / [an inaugural lecture delivered in the University of Birmingham on 19 May 1981] ; Joan Rees. — [Birmingham] : University of Birmingham, 1981. — 15p ; 21cm
Cover title
ISBN 0-7044-0583-0 (pbk) : Unpriced
B82-09097

823'.3 — Fiction in English. Sidney, *Sir* **Philip. Arcadia. Structure**

Lindheim, Nancy. The structures of Sidney's Arcadia / Nancy Lindheim. — Toronto ; London : University of Toronto Press, c1982. — 224p ; 24cm
Includes index
ISBN 0-8020-2374-6 : Unpriced B82-39346

823.4 — ENGLISH FICTION, 1625-1702

823'.4 — Fiction in English. Bunyan, John *— Biographies*

Bacon, Ernest W.. Pilgrim and dreamer : John Bunyan - his life and work. — Exeter : Paternoster, Oct.1982. — [176]p
ISBN 0-85364-309-1 (pbk) : £4.40 : CIP entry
B82-25087

823'.4[F] — Fiction in English, *1625-1702 — Texts*

Bunyan, John. The pilgrim's progress. — Large print ed. — Anstey : Ulverscroft, Oct.1982. — [416]p. — (Charnwood library series)
ISBN 0-7089-8072-4 : £5.25 : CIP entry
B82-27016

823.5 — ENGLISH FICTION, 1702-1745

823'.5 — Fiction in English, *1702-1745 — Texts — Facsimiles*

Brooke, Henry, *1703?-1783*. The fool of quality / Henry Brooke. — New York ; London : Garland, 1979. — 5v. ; 19cm. — (The Novel, 1720-1805 ; 6)
Facsim
ISBN 0-8240-3655-7 : Unpriced B82-16835

823'.5 — Fiction in English, *1702-1745* **—** *Texts — Facsimiles continuation*

Haywood, Eliza. The history of Miss Betsy Thoughtless / Eliza Haywood. — New York ; London : Garland, 1979. — 4v.(iv,1175p) ; 19cm. — (The Novel, 1720-1805)
Facsims of: ed. published London : T. Gardner, 1751
ISBN 0-8240-3653-0 : Unpriced B82-08744

823'.5 — Fiction in English. Defoe, Daniel — *Critical studies*

Curtis, Laura Ann. The elusive Defoe. — London : Prior, Oct.1982. — [180]p
ISBN 0-86043-448-6 : £6.95 : CIP entry B82-24135

823'.5 — Fiction in English. Defoe, Daniel. Moll Flanders — *Study outlines*

Butler, Lance St. John. Moll Flanders : notes / by Lance St John Butler. — Harlow : Longman, 1982. — 64p ; 21cm. — (York notes ; 153)
Bibliography: p58
ISBN 0-582-78270-8 (pbk) : £0.90 B82-16447

823'.5 — Fiction in English. Fielding, Henry. Shamela — *Concordances*

A **Concordance** and word-lists to Henry Fielding's Shamela. — Swansea (8 Hadland Terrace, West Cross, Swansea SA3 5TT) : Ariel House Publications, July 1982. — [25]p
ISBN 0-906948-02-9 : CIP entry B82-14967

823'.5[F] — Fiction in English, *1702-1745* **—** *Texts*

Defoe, Daniel. [The fortunes and misfortunes of the famous Moll Flanders]. Moll Flanders / Daniel Defoe ; new introduction by Pat Rogers. — London : Dent, 1982. — xxviii,295p ; 18cm. — (Everyman's library)
Bibliography: pxxiv-xxviii
ISBN 0-460-11837-4 (pbk) : £1.50 B82-32970

Defoe, Daniel. The fortunes and misfortunes of the famous Moll Flanders, &c ... / Daniel Defoe ; edited with an introduction by G.A. Starr. — Oxford : Oxford University Press, 1971 (1981 [printing]). — xxxiv,398p ; 19cm. — (The World's classics)
Bibliography: pxxx-xxxii
ISBN 0-19-281570-9 (pbk) : £1.25 : CIP rev. B81-28857

Defoe, Daniel. Robinson Crusoe / by Daniel Defoe. — Toronto ; London : Bantam, 1981. — 278p ; 18cm. — (A Bantam classic)
Bibliography: p276-278
ISBN 0-553-21062-9 (pbk) : £0.85 B82-28548

Fielding, Henry. [Joseph Andrews]. The history of the adventures of Joseph Andrews and of his friend Mr. Abraham Adams / Henry Fielding ; edited with an introduction by Douglas Brooks-Davies. — Oxford : Oxford University Press, 1980. — xxviii,391p ; 19cm. — (The World's classics)
Bibliography: xxiii-xxv. — Contents: Joseph Andrews — Shamela Andrews
ISBN 0-19-281550-4 : £1.95 B82-40487

Swift, Jonathan. Gulliver's travels / Jonathan Swift ; edited by Peter Dixon and John Chalker ; with an introduction by Michael Foot. — Harmondsworth : Penguin, 1967 (1982 [printing]). — 360p : ill,1facsim,maps,1port ; 18cm. — (The Penguin English library)
Port on inside cover. — Bibliography: p29
ISBN 0-14-043022-9 (pbk) : £1.25 B82-29604

Swift, Jonathan. Gulliver's travels / by Jonathan Swift. — Abridged. — London : Dean, [198-?]. — 184p ; 19cm. — (Dean's classics)
ISBN 0-603-03029-7 : Unpriced B82-26104

823.6 — ENGLISH FICTION, 1745-1800

823'.6 — Fiction in English, *1745-1800* **—** *Texts — Facsimiles*

Bage, Robert. Barham Downs / Robert Bage. — London ; New York : Garland, 1979. — 2v. ; 19cm. — (The Novel, 1720-1805)
Facsim. of: edition published : London : G. Wilkie, 1784
ISBN 0-8240-3658-1 : Unpriced B82-09327

Bage, Robert. James Wallace / Robert Bage. — New York ; London : Garland, 1979. — 3v. ; 19cm. — (The Novel, 1720-1805 ; 11)
Facsim
ISBN 0-8240-3660-3 : Unpriced B82-16834

Bage, Robert. Mount Henneth / Robert Bage. — New York ; London : Garland, 1979. — 2v. ; 19cm. — (The Novel, 1720-1805)
Facsim of: ed. published Dublin : printed for Price, 1782
ISBN 0-8240-3657-3 : Unpriced B82-30504

Holcroft, Thomas. Memoirs of Bryan Perdue / Thomas Holcroft. — New York ; London : Garland, 1979. — 3v. ; 19cm. — (The Novel, 1720-1805 ; 15)
Facsim. of ed. published London: Longman, Hurst, Rees and Orme, 1805
ISBN 0-8240-3664-6 : Unpriced B82-30991

823'.6 — Fiction in English. Burney, Fanny — *Correspondence, diaries, etc.*

Burney, Fanny. The journals and letters of Fanny Burney (Madame D'Arblay). — Oxford : Clarendon
Vol.8: 1815 : letter 835-934 / edited by Peter Hughes with Joyce Hemlow, Althea Douglas and Patricia Hawkins. — 1980. — xxii,602p,[2] leaves of plates(1 folded) : 1ill,1plan,1port ; 23cm
Includes some letters in French. — Bibliography: pxx-xxii. — Includes index
ISBN 0-19-812507-0 : £30.00 : CIP rev. B79-09764

Burney, Fanny. The journals and letters of Fanny Burney (Madame D'Arblay). — Oxford : Clarendon Press
Vols. 9 and 10: Bath 1815-1818 : letters 935-1179 / edited by Warren Derry. — 1982. — 2v(xxii,1062p,[6]leaves of plates) : ill,1port ; 22cm
Includes some letters in French. — Includes index
ISBN 0-19-812508-9 : £80.00 B82-20449

823'.6 — Fiction in English. Godwin, William — *Critical studies*

Tysdahl, B. J.. William Godwin as novelist / by B.J. Tysdahl. — London : Athlone, c1981. — 205p ; 23cm
Bibliography: p192-199. — Includes index
ISBN 0-485-11223-x (cased) : £15.00 : CIP rev.
ISBN 0-485-12040-2 (pbk) : Unpriced B81-20459

823'.6 — Fiction in English. Johnson, Samuel, *1709-1784.* **Rasselas —** *Study outlines*

Asfour, Mohammad. Rasselas : notes / by Mohammad Asfour. — Harlow : Longman, 1981. — 71p ; 21cm. — (York notes ; 137)
Bibliography: p69-71
ISBN 0-582-78190-6 (pbk) : £0.90 B82-16368

823'.6 — Fiction in English. Johnson, Samuel, *1709-1784.* **Vanity of human wishes & Rasselas —** *Study outlines*

Cunningham, J. S.. Samuel Johnson : the Vanity of human wishes ; and, Rasselas. — London : E. Arnold, Nov.1982. — [64]p
ISBN 0-7131-6291-0 (pbk) : £1.95 : CIP entry B82-29434

823'.6 — Fiction in English. Richardson, Samuel — *Critical studies*

Eagleton, Terry. The rape of Clarissa : writing, sexuality and class struggle in Samuel Richardson. — Oxford : Blackwell, June 1982. — [128]p
ISBN 0-631-13029-2 (cased) : £12.00 : CIP entry
ISBN 0-631-13031-4 (pbk) : £4.50 B82-09454

Flynn, Carol Houlihan. Samuel Richardson : a man of letters / Carol Houlihan Flynn. — Princeton, N.J. ; Guildford : Princeton University Press, 1982. — xv,342p ; 23cm
Bibliography: p329-336. — Includes index
ISBN 0-691-06506-3 : £17.70 : CIP rev. B82-31402

823'.6 — Fiction in English. Smollett, Tobias — *Critical studies*

Smollett : author of the first distinction / edited by Alan Bold. — London : Vision, 1982. — 233p ; 22cm
Includes index
ISBN 0-85478-434-9 : £13.95 B82-21714

823'.6 — Fiction in English. Sterne, Laurence — *Critical studies*

Loveridge, Mark. Laurence Sterne and the argument about design / Mark Loveridge. — London : Macmillan, 1982. — xi,247p ; 23cm
Bibliography: p228-242. — Includes index
ISBN 0-333-29401-7 : £15.00 B82-28524

823'.6[F] — Fiction in English, *1745-1800* **—** *Texts*

Burney, Fanny. Evelina, or, The history of a young lady's entrance into the world / Fanny Burney ; edited with an introduction by Edward A. Bloom with the assistance of Lillian D. Bloom. — Oxford : Oxford University Press, 1982. — 421p ; 19cm. — (The World's classics)
Originally published: 1968
ISBN 0-19-281596-2 (pbk) : £2.50 : CIP rev. B82-04279

Godwin, William. Caleb Williams / William Godwin ; edited with an introduction by David McCracken. — Oxford : Oxford University Press, 1970 (1982 [printing]). — xxx,351p : 1facsim ; 18cm. — (The World's classics)
Bibliography: pxxvii-xxviii
ISBN 0-19-281621-7 (pbk) : £2.50 : CIP rev. B82-18987

Goldsmith, Oliver. The vicar of Wakefield : a tale supposed to be written by himself ... / Oliver Goldsmith ; edited with an introduction by Arthur Friedman. — Oxford : Oxford University Press, 1974 (1981 [printing]). — xxii,199p ; 19cm. — (The World's classics)
Bibliography: pxxi-xxii
ISBN 0-19-281560-1 (pbk) : Unpriced : CIP rev. B81-28855

Goldsmith, Oliver. The Vicar of Wakefield / Oliver Goldsmith ; edited with an introduction by Stephen Coote. — Harmondsworth : Penguin, 1982. — 213p ; 19cm. — (Penguin English library)
Bibliography: p26-27
ISBN 0-14-043159-4 (pbk) : £1.50 B82-19906

Radcliffe, Ann. The Italian, or, The confessional of the Black Penitents : a romance / Ann Radcliffe ; edited with an introduction by Frederick Garber. — Oxford : Oxford University Press, 1968 (1981 [printing]). — xix,419p ; 19cm. — (The World's classics)
Bibliography: pxix
ISBN 0-19-281572-5 (pbk) : £2.50 : CIP rev. B81-28858

Sterne, Lawrence. The life and opinions of Tristram Shandy, Gentleman. — Oxford : Oxford University Press, Nov.1982. — [640]p. — (The World's classics)
ISBN 0-19-281566-0 (pbk) : £2.25 : CIP entry B82-26895

Walpole, Horace. The castle of Otranto : a Gothic story / Horace Walpole ; edited with an introduction by W.S. Lewis ; with explanatory notes and note on the text by Joseph W. Reed, Jr. — Oxford : Oxford University Press, 1969 (1982 [printing]). — xviii,115p : 1facsim ; 18cm. — (The World's classics)
ISBN 0-19-281606-3 (pbk) : £1.50 : CIP rev. B82-18985

823.7 — ENGLISH FICTION, 1800-1837

823'.7 — Fiction in English. Austen, Jane — *Critical studies*

Scott, P. J. M.. Jane Austen : a reassessment / by P.J.M. Scott. — London : Vision, 1982. — 208p ; 23cm. — (Critical studies series)
Includes index
ISBN 0-85478-494-2 : £11.95 B82-37585

823'.7 — Fiction in English. Austen, Jane. Emma — *Questions & answers*

Meihuizen, Dorothea. Jane Austen, Emma / Dorothea Meihuizen. — London : Edward Arnold, 1980, c1977. — v,41p ; 22cm. — (Close readings)
Originally published: Pietermaritzburg : Shuter & Shooter, 1977
ISBN 0-7131-0422-8 (pbk) : £0.90 : CIP rev. B79-36004

823'.7 — Fiction in English. Austen, Jane. Emma — *Study outlines*

Hayley, Barbara. Emma : notes / by Barbara Hayley. — Harlow : Longman, 1981. — 96p ; 21cm. — (York notes ; 142)
Bibliography: p91-92
ISBN 0-582-78158-2 (pbk) : £0.90 B82-16367

823'.7 — Fiction in English. Austen, Jane. Local associations: Kent

Smithers, David Waldron. Jane Austen in Kent / David Waldron Smithers. — Westerham : Hurtwood, 1981. — 133p : ill,2maps,2plans,2ports,geneal.tables ; 22cm
Bibliography: p125-127. — Includes index
ISBN 0-903696-20-7 : £7.95
ISBN 0-903696-21-5 (signed limited ed.) : £25.00 B82-16306

823'.7 — Fiction in English. Austen, Jane. Northanger Abbey — *Questions & answers*

Meihuizen, Dorothea. Jane Austen, Northanger Abbey / Dorothea Meihuizen ; with an appendix on the Gothic novel containing extracts from The mysteries of Udolpho by Ann Radcliff. — London : Edward Arnold, 1980, c1978. — vi,50p ; 22cm. — (Close readings)
Originally published: Pietermaritzburg : Shuter & Shooter, c1978
ISBN 0-7131-0424-4 (pbk) : £0.95 : CIP rev. B79-36005

823'.7 — Fiction in English. Austen, Jane. Special themes: Feminism — *Critical studies*

Kirkham, Margaret. Jane Austen, feminism and fiction. — Brighton : Harvester Press, Oct.1982. — [224]p
ISBN 0-7108-0468-7 : £18.95 : CIP entry B82-25766

823'.7 — Fiction in English. Scott, *Sir* Walter — *Critical studies*

McMaster, Graham. Scott and society / Graham McMaster. — Cambridge : Cambridge University Press, 1981. — 253p ; 23cm
Includes index
ISBN 0-521-23769-6 : £19.50 : CIP rev. B81-32532

823'.7 — Fiction in English. Scott, *Sir* Walter. Heart of Midlothian — *Study outlines*

Low, Donald A.. The heart of Midlothian : notes / by Donald A. Low. — Harlow : Longman, 1981. — 72p ; 21cm. — (York notes ; 141)
Bibliography: p68
ISBN 0-582-78169-8 (pbk) : £0.90 B82-16448

823'.7 — Short stories in English, *1800-1837* — *Texts — Facsimiles*

Banim, John. The bit o' writin' and other tales / John Banim ; with an introduction by Robert Lee Wolff. — New York ; London : Garland, 1979. — 3v.((lii,304 ; 305 ; 296p)) ; 19cm. — (Ireland. From the Act of Union, 1800 to the death of Parnell, 1891)
Also attributed to the joint authorship of John and Michael Banim writing as the O'Hara Family. — Facsim of: 1st ed., London : Saunders and Otley, 1838
ISBN 0-8240-3473-2 : Unpriced B82-09331

Carleton, William. Traits and stories of the Irish peasantry, second series / William Carleton. — New York ; London : Garland, 1979. — 3v. ; 19cm. — (Ireland ; 35)
Facsim of ed. published: Dublin : Wakeman, 1833
ISBN 0-8240-3484-8 : Unpriced B82-12662

823'.7 — Short stories in English. Carleton, William. Traits and stories of the Irish peasantry. Publication, *1830-1842*

Hayley, Barbara. Carleton's Traits and stories and the 19th century Anglo-Irish tradition. — Gerrards Cross : Smythe, Sept.1982. — [400]p. — (Irish literary studies, ISSN 0140-895x ; 12)
ISBN 0-86140-118-2 : £11.95 : CIP entry B82-21546

823'.7[F] — Fiction in English, *1800-1837* — *Texts*

Austen, Jane. Emma / by Jane Austen. — Toronto ; London : Bantam, 1969 (1981 [printing]). — 446p ; 17cm. — (A Bantam classic)
ISBN 0-553-21019-x (pbk) : £1.00 B82-24177

Austen, Jane. Mansfield Park / Jane Austen ; edited by James Kinsley and John Lucas. — Oxford : Oxford University Press, 1970 (1980 [printing]). — xxvi,438p ; 19cm
Bibliography: pxxiii-xxiv
ISBN 0-19-251021-5 (cased) : £3.50 : CIP rev.
ISBN 0-19-281526-1 (pbk) : £0.95 B80-13525

Austen, Jane. Pride and prejudice / Jane Austen. — London : Cathay, 1981. — 215p ; 22cm
ISBN 0-86178-136-8 : £2.50 B82-15013

Austen, Jane. Pride and prejudice / by Jane Austen ; edited by Raymond Wilson. — London : Macmillan Education, 1982. — xviii,316p : ill,1port ; 18cm. — (Macmillan students' novels)
ISBN 0-333-32132-4 (pbk) : Unpriced : CIP rev. B81-34145

Austen, Jane. The works of Jane Austen. — London : Spring, 1977 (1982 [printing]). — 1098p ; 21cm
ISBN 0-600-00603-4 : £3.95 B82-39156

Austen, Jane, *1775-1817*. Northanger Abbey. — London : Macmillan Education, Feb.1983. — [224]p. — (Macmillan students' novels)
ISBN 0-333-33625-9 B82-38057

Galt, John. The provost. — Oxford : Oxford University Press, Nov.1982. — [192]p. — (The World's classics)
ISBN 0-19-281629-2 (pbk) : £1.95 : CIP entry B82-26899

Marryat, *Captain*. Mr Midshipman Easy / Captain Marryat. — Harmondsworth : Penguin, 1982. — 423p ; 19cm
ISBN 0-14-005295-x (pbk) : £2.25 B82-35867

Maxwell, W. H.. The fortunes of Hector O'Halloran / William Maxwell ; with an introduction by Robert Lee Wolff. — New York ; London : Garland, 1979. — x,412p,[39] leaves of plates : ill ; 23cm. — (Ireland ; 51)
Facsim of: The fortunes of Hector O'Halloran and his man Mark Anthony O'Toole, published: London : Bentley, 1843
ISBN 0-8240-3500-3 : Unpriced B82-05327

Scott, *Sir* Walter. The Heart of Midlothian. — Oxford : Oxford University Press, Sept.1982. — [900]p. — (The World's classics)
ISBN 0-19-281583-0 (pbk) : £3.95 : CIP entry B82-19196

Scott, *Sir* Walter. Kenilworth / Sir Walter Scott. — Leicester : Charnwood, 1982. — 746p ; 23cm. — (Charnwood library series)
Published in large print
ISBN 0-7089-8028-7 : £6.50 : CIP rev. B81-36960

Shelley, Mary Wollstonecraft. Frankenstein / by Mary Shelley ; with an introduction by Diane Johnson. — Toronto ; London : Bantam, 1967 (1981 [printing]). — xxviii, 209p ; 18cm. — (A Bantam classic)
Bibliography: p207-209
ISBN 0-553-21044-0 (pbk) : £0.85 B82-35481

823'.7'08016 — Horror stories in English, *1800-1900 — Anthologies*

Shelley, Mary Wollstonecraft. Frankenstein / by Mary Shelley. Dracula / by Bram Stoker. Dr Jekyll and Mr Hyde / by Robert Louis Stevenson ; with an introduction by Stephen King. — New York : New American Library ; London : New English Library, 1978. — xiv,211,382,70p ; 18cm. — (Signet classic)
ISBN 0-451-51290-1 (pbk) : £1.50 B82-19305

823'.7'09 — Fiction in English, *1800-1900* — *Critical studies*

The **Nineteenth-century** novel and its legacy. — Milton Keynes : Open University Press. — (Arts : a third level course)
At head of title: The Open University
Unit 1: Introduction / prepared for the course team by Arnold Kettle with the help of contributions from P.N. Furbank and Dennis Walder. — 1982. — 33p ; 30cm. — (A312 ; unit 1)
Previous ed.: 1973
ISBN 0-335-11050-9 (pbk) : Unpriced B82-21200

The **Nineteenth-century** novel and its legacy. — Milton Keynes : Open University Press. — (Arts : a third level course)
At head of title: The Open University
Unit 2: A study guide to Mansfield Park / prepared for the course team by Cicely Palser Havely. — 1982. — 28p ; 30cm. — (A312 ; unit 2)
Previous ed.: 1973. — Bibliography: p28
ISBN 0-335-11051-7 (pbk) : Unpriced B82-21202

The **Nineteenth-century** novel and its legacy. — Milton Keynes : Open University Press. — (Arts : a third level course)
At head of title: The Open University
Unit 3: Mansfield Park / prepared for the course team by Cicely Palser Havely. — New rev. ed. — 1982. — 33p : ill ; 30cm. — (A312 ; unit 3)
Previous ed.: 1973. — Bibliography: p33
ISBN 0-335-11052-5 (pbk) : Unpriced B82-21201

The **Nineteenth** century novel and its legacy. — Milton Keynes : Open University Press. — (Arts : a third level course)
At head of title: The Open University
Unit 6: A study guide to Great expections / prepared for the Course Team by Graham Martin. — New rev. ed. — 1982. — 30p : ill,facsims,ports ; 30cm. — (A312 ; unit 6)
Previous ed.: 1973. — Bibliography: p30
ISBN 0-335-11055-x (pbk) : Unpriced B82-32024

The **Nineteenth** century novel and its legacy. — Milton Keynes : Open University Press. — (Arts : a third level course)
At head of title: The Open University
Unit 7: Great expections / prepared for the Course Team by Graham Martin. — New rev. ed. — 1982. — 42p : ill ; 30cm. — (A312 ; unit 7)
Previous ed.: 1973. — Bibliography: p41-42
ISBN 0-335-11056-8 (pbk) : Unpriced B82-32025

The **Nineteenth** century novel and its legacy. — Milton Keynes : Open University Press. — (Arts : a third level course)
At head of title: The Open University
Units 8-9: Cousin Bette / prepared for the Course Team by Arnold Kettle. — New rev. ed. — 1982. — 58p : ill,ports ; 30cm. — (A312 ; units 8-9)
Previous ed.: 1973. — Bibliography: p57-58
ISBN 0-335-11057-6 (pbk) : Unpriced B82-32028

The **Nineteenth** century novel and its legacy. — Milton Keynes : Open University Press. — (Arts : a third level course)
At head of title: The Open University
Unit 10: On the eve / prepared for the Course Team by Arnold Kettle. — New rev. ed. — 1982. — 40p : ill,ports ; 30cm. — (A312 ; unit 10)
Previous ed.: 1973. — Bibliography: p40
ISBN 0-335-11058-4 (pbk) : Unpriced B82-32027

823'.7'09 — Fiction in English, *1800-1900 — Critical studies* *continuation*

The **Nineteenth** century novel and its legacy. — Milton Keynes : Open University Press. — (Arts : a third level course)
At head of title: The Open University
Unit 11: Poor relations and rich publishers / prepared for the Course Team by Arnold Kettle. — New rev. ed. / with the help of contributions from Angus Calder and Beverley Stern. — 1982. — 37p ; 30cm. — (A312 ; unit 11)
Previous ed.: published as The novel in the mid-nineteenth century. 1973. — Bibliography: p37
ISBN 0-335-11059-2 (pbk) : Unpriced
B82-32023

The **Nineteenth** century novel and its legacy. — Milton Keynes : Open University Press. — (Arts : a third level course)
At head of title: The Open University
Units 12-14: Middlemarch / prepared for the Course Team by Graham Martin. — New rev. ed. — 1982. — 72p : ill,ports ; 30cm. — (A312 ; units 12-14)
Previous ed.: 1974. — Bibliography: p70-72
ISBN 0-335-11060-6 (pbk) : Unpriced
B82-32026

The **Nineteenth** century novel and its legacy. — Milton Keynes : Open University Press. — (Arts : a third level course)
At head of title: The Open University
Units 15-16: What Maisie knew / prepared for the Course Team by Cicely Palser Havely. — New rev. ed. — 1982. — 47p : ill,1port ; 30cm. — (A312 ; units 15-16)
Previous ed.: 1973. — Bibliography: p47
ISBN 0-335-11061-4 (pbk) : Unpriced
B82-32022

The **Nineteenth** century novel and its legacy. — Milton Keynes : Open University Press. — (Arts : a third level course)
At head of title: The Open University
Units 17-18: Tess of the d'Urbervilles / prepared for the Course Team by Arnold Kettle. — 1982. — 39p : ill,ports ; 30cm. — (A204 ; units 17-18)
Bibliography: p38-39
ISBN 0-335-11062-2 (pbk) : Unpriced
B82-32021

The **Nineteenth-century** novel and its legacy. — Milton Keynes : Open University Press. — (Arts : a third level course)
At head of title: The Open University
Units 17-32: Legacies / prepared by members of the course team. — 1982. — 186p : ports ; 30cm. — (A312 ; units 27-32)
Includes bibliographies
ISBN 0-335-11067-3 (pbk) : Unpriced
B82-40138

The **Nineteenth-century** novel and its legacy. — Milton Keynes : Open University Press. — (Arts : a third level course)
At head of title: The Open University
Units 19-20: Huckleberry Finn / prepared for the course team by Barry Chambers. — [New ed.]. — 1982. — 29p : ill ; 30cm. — (A312 ; Units 19-20)
Previous ed.: published as A302 Unit 20, 1973
ISBN 0-335-11063-0 (pbk) : Unpriced
B82-34152

The **Nineteenth-century** novel and its legacy. — Milton Keynes : Open University Press. — (Arts : a third level course)
At head of title: The Open University
Units 21-22: Germinal / prepared for the course team by Merryn Williams. — Rev. ed. — 1982. — 31p : ill,1port ; 30cm. — (A312 ; Units 21-22)
Previous ed.: published as A302 Units 21-22, 1973
ISBN 0-335-11064-9 (pbk) : Unpriced
B82-34146

The **Nineteenth-century** novel and its legacy. — Milton Keynes : Open University Press. — (Arts : a third level course)
At head of title: The Open University
Units 23-25: Anna Karenina / prepared for the course team by P.N. Furbank. — Rev. ed. — 1982. — 74p : ill,1port ; 30cm. — (A312 ; Units 23-25)
Previous ed.: published as A302 Units 24-26, 1973
ISBN 0-335-11065-7 (pbk) : Unpriced
B82-34147

The **Nineteenth-century** novel and its legacy. — Milton Keynes : Open University Press. — (Arts : a third level course)
At head of title: The Open University
Unit 26: Points of view / prepared for the course team by Arnold Kettle ... [et al.]. — New rev. ed. — 1982. — 51p ; 30cm. — (A312 ; unit 26)
Previous ed.: published as A302 Unit 23. — Bibliography: p51
ISBN 0-335-11066-5 (pbk) : Unpriced
B82-34148

823.8 — ENGLISH FICTION, 1837-1900

823'.8 — Boys' stories in English. Stables, William Gordon — *Biographies*

Graham, Sarah. An introduction to William Gordon Stables : [Twyford's gentleman gipsy] / Sarah Graham ; illustrations Ron Durant. — [Twyford] ([c/o The Hon. Sec., 20 The Grove, Twyford, Berks.]) : Twyford & Ruscombe Local History Society, c1982. — 40p : ill,1facsim,ports,1geneal.table ; 20cm
Unpriced (pbk) B82-25787

823'.8 — Children's stories in English. Grahame, Kenneth — *Biographies*

Green, Peter. Beyond the wild wood. — Exeter : Webb & Bower, Nov.1982. — [224]p
ISBN 0-906671-44-2 : £9.95 : CIP entry
B82-26716

823'.8 — Fiction in English, *1837-1900 — Manuscripts — Facsimiles*

Dickens, Charles, *1812-1870*. The cricket on the hearth : a fairy tale of home / by Charles Dickens. — Guildford : Genesis, 1981. — [124]p : ill(some col.) ; 28cm
Facsim. of: Pierpont Morgan Library manuscript of The cricket on the hearth. — Limited ed. of 250 signed and numbered copies. — In slipcase
ISBN 0-904351-21-1 : £75.00 B82-08327

823'.8 — Fiction in English, *1837-1900 — Texts — Facsimiles*

Braddon, M. E.. Aurora Floyd / Mary Elizabeth Braddon. — New York ; London : Garland, 1979. — 3v. ; 19cm. — (The Fiction of Mary Elizabeth Braddon ; 1)
Facsim of: ed. published London : Tinsley Brothers, 1863
ISBN 0-8240-4350-2 : Unpriced B82-30503

Braddon, M. E.. Rough justice / Mary Elizabeth Braddon. — New York ; London : Garland, 1979. — viii,392p ; 19cm. — (The Fiction of Mary Elizabeth Braddon ; 12)
Facsim of ed. published London : Simpkin, Marshall, Hamilton, Kent, 1898
ISBN 0-8240-4361-8 : Unpriced B82-30506

Brew, Margaret. The chronicles of Castle Cloyne / Margaret Brew ; with an introduction by Robert Lee Wolff. — New York ; London : Garland, 1981. — 3v. ; 19cm. — (Ireland ; 70)
Facsim of ed. published: London : Chapman and Hall, 1885 ; with a new introduction
ISBN 0-8240-3519-4 : Unpriced B82-12661

Dickens, Charles, *1812-1870*. [Nicholas Nickleby]. The life and adventures of Nicholas Nickleby. — London : Scolar Press, Aug.1982. — [1242]p
Facsim. of original monthly parts: London : Chapman & Hall, 1838-1839
ISBN 0-85967-668-4 (pbk) : £9.95 : CIP entry
B82-16668

Lawless, Emily. Grania : the story of an island / Emily Lawless ; with an introduction by Robert Lee Wolff. — New York ; London : Garland, 1979. — 2v. ; 19cm
Facsim
ISBN 0-8240-3522-4 : Unpriced B82-16836

Lawless, Emily. Hurrish / Emily Lawless ; with an introduction by Robert Lee Wolff. — New York ; London : Garland, 1979. — 2v. ; 19cm. — (Ireland)
Facsim of: ed. published Edinburgh : Blackwood, 1886
ISBN 0-8240-3520-8 : Unpriced B82-30505

Lawless, Emily. With Essex in Ireland / Emily Lawless ; with an introduction by Robert Lee Wolff. — New York ; London : Garland, 1979. — vx,299p ; 19cm. — (Ireland ; 72)
Facsim of ed. published: London : Smith, Elder, 1890
ISBN 0-8240-3521-6 : Unpriced B82-12663

Priests and people, a no-rent romance / with an introduction by Robert Lee Wolff. — New York ; London : Garland, 1979. — 3v. ; 19cm. — (Ireland ; 77)
Facsim
ISBN 0-8240-3526-7 : Unpriced B82-16837

823'.8 — Fiction in English, *1837-1900 — Texts with commentaries*

Dickens, Charles, *1812-1870*. Martin Chuzzlewit. — Oxford : Oxford University Press, May 1982. — [968]p. — (The Clarendon Dickens)
ISBN 0-19-812488-0 : £30.00 : CIP entry
B82-07507

Meredith, George. One of our conquerors / George Meredith ; edited by Margaret Harris. — [St. Lucia, Queensland] : University of Queensland Press ; Hemel Hempstead : Prentice-Hall [distributor], c1975. — 514,52p ; 22cm. — (Victorian texts ; 3)
Facsim of: Memorial ed. London : Constable, 1910. — Bibliography: (1p)
ISBN 0-7022-0966-x (cased) : £12.50
ISBN 0-7022-0967-8 (pbk) : Unpriced
B82-00971

Surtees, R. S.. Mr. Sponge's sporting tour / R.S. Surtees ; edited by Virginia Blain. — London : Batsford Academic and Educational, 1981. — xxiv,483p : ill ; 22cm. — (Victorian texts)
Bibliography: pxvii
ISBN 0-7134-4311-1 : £12.50 B82-00967

823'.8 — Fiction in English. Borrow, George, *1803-1881 — Biographies*

Collie, Michael. George Borrow. — Cambridge : Cambridge University Press, Dec.1982. — [304]p
ISBN 0-521-24615-6 : £19.50 : CIP entry
B82-40895

823'.8 — Fiction in English. Borrow, George — *Biographies*

Williams, David, *1909-*. A world of his own : the double life of George Borrow. — Oxford : Oxford University Press, Sept.1982. — [260]p
ISBN 0-19-211762-9 : £9.50 : CIP entry
B82-19174

823'.8 — Fiction in English. Brontë, Charlotte. Jane Eyre — *Study outlines*

Goad, Kathleen M.. Brodie's notes on Charlotte Brontë's Jane Eyre / Kathleen M. Goad ; revised by Norman T. Carrington. — London : Pan, 1976. — 76p ; 20cm. — (Pan study aids)
ISBN 0-330-50028-7 (pbk) : £0.80 B82-17056

823'.8 — Fiction in English. Butler, Samuel, *1835-1902 — Critical studies*

Jeffers, Thomas L.. Samuel Butler revalued / Thomas L. Jeffers. — University Park ; London : Pennsylvania State University Press, c1981. — 146p ; 23cm
Bibliography: p139-141. — Includes index
ISBN 0-271-00281-6 : Unpriced B82-02183

823'.8 — Fiction in English. Dickens, Charles, *1812-1870 — Critical studies*
Brown, James M.. Dickens : novelist in the market-place / James M. Brown. — London : Macmillan, 1982. — vii,180p ; 23cm
Bibliography: p172-176. — Includes index
ISBN 0-333-30083-1 : £15.00 B82-20955

Butt, John. Dickens at work / John Butt and Kathleen Tillotson. — London : Methuen, 1957 (1982 [printing]). — 238p : 3facsims ; 23cm
Bibliography: p6. — Includes index
ISBN 0-416-34030-x : Unpriced : CIP rev. B82-07661

Gissing, George. Charles Dickens : a critical study. — London : Prior, Oct.1982. — [236]p
Originally published: London : Blackie, 1926
ISBN 0-86043-463-x : £7.50 : CIP entry B82-24136

Hill, Nancy K.. A reformer's art : Dickens' picturesque and grotesque imagery / Nancy K. Hill. — Athens [Ohio] ; London : Ohio University Press, c1981. — xi,169p : ill,1facsim ; 24cm
Bibliography: p161-166. — Includes index
ISBN 0-8214-0586-1 (cased) : Unpriced
ISBN 0-8214-0613-2 (pbk) : £4.90 B82-19658

Hornback, Bert G.. "The hero of my life" : essays on Dickens / Bert G. Hornback. — Athens [Ohio] ; London : Ohio University Press, c1981. — xi,159p : 1facsim ; 24cm
Includes index
ISBN 0-8214-0587-x : £11.90 B82-19650

Perkins, Donald. Charles Dickens : a new perspective / Donald Perkins. — Edinburgh : Floris, 1982. — 125p ; 23cm
Bibliography: p123-125
ISBN 0-903540-53-3 : £6.50 : CIP rev. B82-11793

823'.8 — Fiction in English. Dickens, Charles, *1812-1870.* **Great expectations** *— Questions & answers — For schools*
Fozzard, Peter. Great expectations, Charles Dickens / by Peter Fozzard. — London : Mary Glasgow Publications, c1980. — 15p : ill (some col.),1map ; 30cm. — (Guidelines)
ISBN 0-86158-521-6 (unbound) : Unpriced B82-23267

823'.8 — Fiction in English. Dickens, Charles, *1812-1870.* **Nicholas Nickleby** *— Study outlines*
Niven, Helen. Nicholas Nickleby : notes / by Helen Niven. — Harlow : Longman, 1982. — 80p ; 21cm. — (York notes ; 161)
Bibliography: p73
ISBN 0-582-78271-6 (pbk) : £0.90 B82-16446

823'.8 — Fiction in English. Dickens, Charles, *1812-1870 — Personal observations — Collections*
Dickens : interviews and recollections / edited by Philip Collins. — London : Macmillan, 1981. — 2v.(xxix,368p,16p of plates) : ports ; 23cm
Bibliography: p359-360. — Includes index
ISBN 0-333-26254-9 : Unpriced
ISBN 0-333-26255-7 (v.2) : £15.00 B82-10805

823'.8 — Fiction in English. Dickens, Charles, *1812-1870.* **Special themes: Religion** *— Critical studies*
Walder, Dennis. Dickens and religion / Dennis Walder. — London : Allen & Unwin, 1981. — xiv,232p : ill ; 22cm
Bibliography: p216-224. — Includes index
ISBN 0-04-800006-x : Unpriced : CIP rev. B81-28782

823'.8 — Fiction in English. Eliot, George — *Critical studies*
George Eliot : a centenary tribute / edited by Gordon S. Haight and Rosemary T. VanArsdel. — London : Macmillan, 1982
Conference papers. — Includes index
ISBN 0-333-31475-1 : £17.50 B82-37417

Hardy, Barbara. Particularities : readings in George Eliot / Barbara Hardy. — London : Owen, 1982. — 204p ; 23cm
ISBN 0-7206-0599-7 : £10.50 B82-32927

Pinion, F. B.. A George Eliot companion : literary achievement and modern significance / F.B. Pinion. — London : Macmillan, 1981. — xii,277p,[24]p of plates : ill,maps,ports ; 23cm
Bibliography: p267-269. — Includes index
ISBN 0-333-25594-1 : £20.00 B82-06898

823'.8 — Fiction in English. Eliot, George. Notebooks *— Critical studies*
Waley, Daniel. George Eliot's blotter : a commonplace book / Daniel Waley. — London : British Library, c1980. — 25p : ill,facsims ; 24cm. — (British Library booklets)
Bibliography: p25. — Text on inside cover
ISBN 0-904654-50-8 (pbk) : £1.50 : CIP rev. B80-34094

823'.8 — Fiction in English. Gissing, George — *Biographies*
Halperin, John. Gissing. — Oxford : Oxford University Press, Oct.1981. — [375]p
ISBN 0-19-812677-8 : £17.50 : CIP entry B81-25844

823'.8 — Fiction in English. Gissing, George. Influence of German literature
Bridgwater, Patrick. Gissing and Germany / Patrick Bridgwater. — London : Enitharmon, 1981. — 95p ; 23cm. — (Enitharmon Press Gissing series ; 8)
ISBN 0-905289-52-8 : £6.00 B82-22464

823'.8 — Fiction in English. Gissing, George. Interpersonal relationships with Turgenev, I. S.
Coustillas, Pierre. George Gissing and Ivan Turgenev : including two letters from Turgenev / Pierre Coustillas. — London : Enitharmon, 1981. — 12p ; 22cm. — (Enitharmon Press Gissing series)
Limited ed. of 250 copies
ISBN 0-905289-77-3 (corrected : pbk) : £3.75
Also classified at 891.73'3 B82-26095

823'.8 — Fiction in English. Grand, Sarah — *Biographies*
Kersley, Gillian. Darling madame. — London : Virago, Feb.1983. — [416]p
ISBN 0-86068-307-9 (cased) : £8.95 : CIP entry
ISBN 0-86068-308-7 (pbk) : £4.95 B82-39827

823'.8 — Fiction in English. Hardy, Thomas, *1840-1928 — Biographies*
Millgate, Michael. Thomas Hardy : a biography / Michael Millgate. — Oxford : Oxford University Press, 1982. — xvi,637p,[32]p of plates : ill,coats of arms,facsims,geneal.tables,1map,ports ; 25cm
Includes index
ISBN 0-19-211725-4 : £15.00 : CIP rev. B82-07496

823'.8 — Fiction in English. Hardy, Thomas, *1840-1928 — Correspondence, diaries, etc*
Hardy, Thomas, *1840-1928.* The collected letters of Thomas Hardy / edited by Richard Little Purdy and Michael Millgate. — Oxford : Clarendon
Vol.3: 1902-1908. — 1982. — ix,367p ; 24cm
Includes index
ISBN 0-19-812620-4 : Unpriced : CIP rev. B82-18996

823'.8 — Fiction in English. Hardy, Thomas, *1840-1928 — Critical studies*
Casagrande, Peter J.. Unity in Hardy's novels : 'repetitive symmetries' / Peter J. Casagrande. — London : Macmillan, 1982. — xi,249p ; 22cm
Bibliography: p240-243. — Includes index
ISBN 0-333-28485-2 : £15.00 B82-28654

Gregor, Ian. The great web : the form of Hardy's major fiction / Ian Gregor. — London : Faber and Faber, 1974 (1982 [printing]). — 236p : 1map ; 20cm
Includes index
ISBN 0-571-11852-6 (pbk) : £3.25 : CIP rev. B82-04601

Salter, C. H.. Good little Thomas Hardy / C.H. Salter. — London : Macmillan, 1981. — 200p ; 23cm
Bibliography: p162-166. — Includes index
ISBN 0-333-29387-8 : £15.00 : CIP rev. B81-13788

Taylor, Richard H.. The neglected Hardy : Thomas Hardy's lesser novels / Richard H. Taylor. — London : Macmillan, 1982. — xi,202p ; 22cm
Bibliography: p184-185. — Includes index
ISBN 0-333-31051-9 : Unpriced B82-32936

Thomas Hardy : the writer and his background / edited by Norman Page. — London : Bell & Hyman, 1980. — 275p ; 23cm
Bibliography: p259-272. — Includes index
ISBN 0-7135-1091-9 : £12.50 : CIP rev. B80-05603

823'.8 — Fiction in English. Hardy, Thomas, *1840-1928.* **Far from the madding crowd** *— Study outlines*
Murray, Barbara. Far from the madding crowd : notes / by Barbara Murray. — Harlow : Longman, 1982. — 96p ; 21cm. — (York notes ; 164)
Bibliography: p88-89
ISBN 0-582-78296-1 (pbk) : £0.90 B82-36755

823'.8 — Fiction in English. Hardy, Thomas, *1840-1928.* **Mayor of Casterbridge** *— Study outlines*
Ducke, Joseph. The Mayor of Casterbridge / Joseph Ducke. — Dublin : Educational Company, 1981. — 54p ; 22cm. — (Inscapes ; 20)
Text on inside cover
Unpriced (pbk) B82-02553

823'.8 — Fiction in English. Hardy, Thomas, *1840-1928.* **Special subjects: Women** *— Critical studies*
Boumelha, Perry. Thomas Hardy and women : sexual ideology and narrative form / Perry Boumelha. — Brighton : Harvester Press, 1982. — 178p ; 23cm
Bibliography: p157-173. — Includes index
ISBN 0-7108-0018-5 : £18.95 : CIP rev. B81-31546

823'.8 — Fiction in English. Hardy, Thomas, *1840-1928.* **Woodlanders, The** *— Study outlines*
Luke, Stewart. The woodlanders : notes / by Stewart Luke. — Harlow : Longman, 1982. — 64p ; 21cm. — (York notes ; 160)
Bibliography: p62
ISBN 0-582-78209-0 (pbk) : £0.90 B82-16369

823'.8 — Fiction in English. Jerome, Jerome K. — *Biographies*
Connolly, Joseph, *1950-.* Jerome K Jerome : a critical biography / Joseph Connolly. — London : Orbis, 1982. — 208p ; 24cm
Bibliography: p199-204. — Includes index
ISBN 0-85613-349-3 : £7.95 B82-39473

823'.8 — Fiction in English. Kipling, Rudyard — *Critical studies*
Moss, Robert F.. Rudyard Kipling and the fiction of adolescence / Robert F. Moss. — London : Macmillan, 1982. — xiv,165p ; 23cm
Bibliography: p158-160. — Includes index
ISBN 0-333-30087-4 : £15.00 B82-28521

823'.8 — Fiction in English. Kipling, Rudyard. Special themes: Colonialism *— Critical studies*
McClure, John A.. Kipling and Conrad : the colonial fiction / John A. McClure. — Cambridge, Mass. ; London : Harvard University Press, 1981. — 182p ; 24cm
Includes index
ISBN 0-674-50529-8 : £9.90
Also classified at 823'.912 B82-11846

823'.8 — Fiction in English. Moore, George, *1852-1933 — Critical studies*
The Way back. — Dublin : Wolfhound Press, May 1982. — [176]p. — (Appraisal — Irish and English literature in context ; 1)
ISBN 0-905473-78-7 (cased) : £9.00 : CIP entry
ISBN 0-905473-79-5 (pbk) : £5.00 B82-14962

823'.8 — Fiction in English. Surtees, R. S. — *Biographies*
Welcome, John. The sporting world of R.S. Surtees / John Welcome. — Oxford : Oxford University Press, 1982. — ix,203p,[8]p of plates : ill,1facsim,ports ; 23cm
Bibliography: p191-192. — Includes index
ISBN 0-19-211766-1 : £9.95 : CIP rev. B82-12533

823′.8 — Fiction in English. Thackeray, W. M.. Vanity fair — *Study outlines*

Gilmour, Robin, *1943-*. Thackeray : Vanity fair / by Robin Gilmour. — London : Edward Arnold, 1982. — 64p : ill ; 19cm. — (Studies in English literature ; no.74)
Bibliography: p62. — Includes index
ISBN 0-7131-6321-6 (pbk) : £1.95 : CIP rev.
B82-06043

823′.8 — Fiction in English. Thackeray, William M.. Vanity Fair — *Study outlines*

Cleall, Charles. A guide to Vanity Fair. — Aberdeen : Aberdeen University Press, Sept.1982. — [100]p
ISBN 0-08-028474-4 (pbk) : £4.50 : CIP entry
B82-19100

823′.8 — Fiction in English. Thackeray, William Makepeace — *Biographies*

Monsarrat, Ann. An uneasy Victorian : Thackeray the man 1811-1863 / Ann Monsarrat. — London : Cassell, 1980. — xiii,461p,[16]p of plates : ill,facsims,ports ; 24cm
Includes index
ISBN 0-304-30556-1 : £9.95 B82-31185

823′.8 — Fiction in English. Thackeray, William Makepeace. Vanity fair — *Study outlines*

Brook, Sarah M.. Brodie′s notes on William Makepeace Thackeray′s Vanity fair / Sarah M. Brook. — London : Pan Educational, 1977. — 117p ; 20cm. — (Pan revision aids)
ISBN 0-330-50063-5 (pbk) : Unpriced
B82-24653

823′.8 — Fiction in English. Trollope, Anthony — *Critical studies*

Letwin, Shirley Robin. The gentleman in Trollope : individuality and moral conduct / Shirley Robin Letwin. — London : Macmillan, 1982. — xi,303p ; 23cm
Includes index
ISBN 0-333-31209-0 : £15.00 B82-28397

Overton, Bill. The unofficial Trollope / Bill Overton. — Brighton : Harvester, 1982. — xii,212p ; 23cm
Includes index
ISBN 0-7108-0455-5 : £18.95 : CIP rev.
B82-13012

823′.8 — Short stories in English, *1837-1900* — *Esperanto texts*

Stevenson, Robert Louis. La insulo de vocoj ; La diableto en la botelo / Robert Louis Stevenson ; el la angla tradukis Cynthia C. Vincent. — Glasgow : Eldonejo Kardo, 1982. — 66p : ill ; 21cm
Translations of The island of voices, and The bottled imp
ISBN 0-905149-19-x (pbk) : £2.80 B82-41145

823′.8 — Short stories in English. Dickens, Charles, *1812-1870* — *Critical studies*

Thomas, Deborah A.. Dickens and the short story / Deborah A. Thomas. — London : Batsford Academic and Educational, 1982. — xii,196p ; 24cm
Bibliography: p183-187. — Includes index
ISBN 0-7134-4331-6 : £12.50 B82-34701

823′.8 — Short stories in English. Hardy, Thomas, *1840-1928* — *Critical studies*

Brady, Kristin. The short stories of Thomas Hardy : tales of past and present / Kristin Brady. — London : Macmillan, 1982. — xii,235p ; 23cm
Bibliography: p219-226. — Includes index
ISBN 0-333-31531-6 : £17.50 B82-39743

823′.8 — Women associated with Dickens, Charles, *1812-1870* — *Biographies*

Slater, Michael. Dickens and women. — London : Dent, Jan.1983. — [480]p
ISBN 0-460-04248-3 : £15.00 : CIP entry
B82-34610

823′.8[F] — Fiction in English, *1837-1900* — *Texts*

Bede, Cuthbert. The adventures of Mr. Verdant Green / by Cuthbert Bede ; with illustrations by the author ; introduced by Anthony Powell. — Oxford : Oxford University Press, 1982. — xviii,365p : ill,1port ; 20cm. — (Oxford paperbacks)
ISBN 0-19-281331-5 (pbk) : £3.95 : CIP rev.
B82-04839

Benson, E. F.. Trouble for Lucia / by E.F. Benson ; foreword by Michéal Mac Liammóir. — Bolton-by-Bowland : Magna, 1980. — 478p ; 23cm
Published in large print
ISBN 0-86009-214-3 : £5.50 : CIP rev.
B79-34437

Borrow, George. Lavengro : the scholar — the gypsy — the priest / George Borrow. — Oxford : Oxford University Press, 1982. — 576p ; 20cm. — (Oxford paperbacks)
ISBN 0-19-281357-9 (pbk) : £3.50 : CIP rev.
B82-15675

Brontë, Charlotte. Emma. — London : Hodder and Stoughton, May 1982. — [240]p. — (Coronet books)
ISBN 0-340-26797-6 (pbk) : £1.50 : CIP entry
B82-07438

Brontë, Charlotte. Jane Eyre / Charlotte Brontë. — Leicester : Charnwood, 1981. — 739p ; 23cm. — (Charnwood library series) (Charnwood large type)
ISBN 0-7089-8015-5 : £6.50 : CIP rev.
B81-22664

Brontë, Charlotte. Jane Eyre / by Charlotte Brontë ; edited by F.B. Pinion. — London : Macmillan Education, 1982. — xxvi,470p : ill ; 18cm. — (Macmillan students′ novels)
ISBN 0-333-32131-6 (pbk) : Unpriced : CIP rev. B81-33979

Brontë, Emily. Wuthering Heights / Emily Brontë. — London : Cathay, 1981. — 215p ; 22cm
ISBN 0-86178-135-x : £2.50 B82-15012

Brontë, Emily. Wuthering Heights / by Emily Brontë ; edited by Graham Handley. — London : Macmillan Education, 1982. — xxviii,307p : ill,facsims,1port ; 18cm. — (Macmillan students′ novels)
ISBN 0-333-32128-6 (pbk) : Unpriced : CIP rev. B81-33980

Carroll, Lewis. Alice′s adventures in Wonderland ; and, Through the looking glass : and what Alice found there / Lewis Carroll ; edited with an introduction by Roger Lancelyn Green ; with illustrations by John Tenniel. — Oxford : Oxford University Press, 1971 (1982 [printing]). — xxxiii,278p : ill ; 18cm. — (The World′s classics)
Bibliography: pxxix-xxx
ISBN 0-19-281620-9 (pbk) : £1.75 : CIP rev.
B82-18986

Carroll, Lewis. Alice′s adventures in Wonderland ; & Through the looking glass / by Lewis Carroll ; [text illustrations by John Tenniel] ; with an introduction by Morton N. Cohen. — Toronto ; London : Bantam, 1981. — xxix,223p : ill ; 18cm
ISBN 0-553-21052-1 (pbk) : £0.85 B82-28549

Collins, Wilkie. Hide and seek, or, The mystery of Mary Grice / Wilkie Collins ; with a new introduction by Norman Donaldson. — New York : Dover ; London : Constable, 1981. — xviii,356p ; 22cm
Facsim of: edition published London : Low, 1861
ISBN 0-486-24211-0 (pbk) : £3.75 B82-28923

Collins, Wilkie. The moonstone / William Wilkie Collins ; edited with an introduction by Anthea Trodd. — Oxford : Oxford University Press, 1982. — xxxvi,536p ; 19cm. — (The World′s classics)
Bibliography: pxxiii-xxiv
ISBN 0-19-281579-2 (pbk) : £1.50 : CIP rev.
B82-04278

Collins, Wilkie. The woman in white / edited with an introduction and notes by Julian Symons. — Harmondsworth : Penguin, 1974 (1982 [printing]). — 648p ; 18cm
ISBN 0-14-005980-6 (pbk) : £1.75 B82-19130

Corelli, Marie. Ziska / Marie Corelli. — London : Methuen Paperbacks, 1966 (1979 printing). — 192p ; 18cm. — (Magnum books)
ISBN 0-417-04700-2 (pbk) : £0.95 B82-00875

Dickens, Charles. Dombey and Son / Charles Dickens ; edited with an introduction and notes by Alan Horsman. — Oxford : Oxford University Press, 1982. — xxiv,756p : ill,2facsims ; 19cm. — (The World′s classics)
Originally published: Oxford : Clarendon, 1974. — Bibliography: p756
ISBN 0-19-281565-2 (pbk) : £2.50 : CIP rev.
B81-36955

Dickens, Charles. Great expectations / by Charles Dickens ; edited by James Gibson. — London : Macmillan Education, 1982. — xxiv,452p : ill,1map,1port ; 18cm. — (Macmillan students′ novels)
ISBN 0-333-32127-8 (pbk) : Unpriced : CIP rev. B81-34143

Dickens, Charles. Oliver Twist / Charles Dickens ; edited with an introduction and notes by Kathleen Tillotson. — Oxford : Oxford University Press, 1982. — xxviii,364p : ill,2facsims ; 19cm. — (The World′s classics)
Originally published: Oxford : Clarendon, 1966. — Bibliography: p364
ISBN 0-19-281591-1 (pbk) : £1.25 : CIP rev.
B81-35765

Dickens, Charles. Our mutual friend / Charles Dickens ; edited with an introduction by Stephen Gill. — Harmondsworth : Penguin, 1971 (1981 [printing]). — 910p : 1port ; 19cm. — (Penguin English library)
Port on inside cover
ISBN 0-14-043060-1 (pbk) : £1.95 B82-09140

Dickens, Charles, *1812-1870*. David Copperfield / by Charles Dickens. — Toronto ; London : Bantam, 1981. — xii,814p ; 18cm. — (A Bantam classic)
ISBN 0-553-21051-3 (pbk) : £1.75 B82-37127

Dickens, Charles, *1812-1870*. Great expectations / Charles Dickens ; illustrations by Charles Keeping ; introduction by Christopher Hibbert. — London : Folio Society, 1981. — xv,419p : ill ; 24cm
In slip case
Unpriced B82-00620

Dickens, Charles, *1812-1870*. Great expectations / by Charles Dickens. — Toronto ; London : Bantam, 1981. — 454p ; 18cm. — (Bantam classics)
ISBN 0-553-21015-7 (pbk) : £1.00 B82-16753

Dickens, Charles, *1812-1870*. Great expectations. — Large print ed. — Anstey : Ulverscroft, Aug.1982. — [752]p. — (Charnwood library series)
ISBN 0-7089-8062-7 : £6.50 : CIP entry
B82-27004

Dickens, Charles, *1812-1870*. Hard times / by Charles Dickens ; introduction by Robert Donald Spector. — Toronto ; London : Bantam, 1964 (1981 printing). — 301p ; 18cm. — (A Bantam classic)
ISBN 0-553-21016-5 (pbk) : £0.85 B82-19382

Dickens, Charles, *1812-1870*. Hard times : for these times / Charles Dickens ; edited with an introduction by David Craig. — Harmondsworth : Penguin, 1969 (1982 [printing]). — 328p : 1facsim ; 19cm. — (Penguin English library)
ISBN 0-14-043042-3 (pbk) : £0.90 B82-32105

Dickens, Charles, *1812-1870*. Hard times. — London : Macmillan Education, Feb.1983. — [288]p
ISBN 0-333-33626-7 (pbk) : £0.95 : CIP entry
B82-38058

823'.8[F] — Fiction in English, *1837-1900 — Texts continuation*

Dickens, Charles, *1812-1870.* Little Dorrit / Charles Dickens ; edited with an introduction and notes by Harvey Peter Sucksmith. — Oxford : Oxford University Press, 1982, c1979. — xxv,722p : ill ; 19cm. — (The world's classics)
Bibliography: p722
ISBN 0-19-281592-x (pbk) : £2.50 : CIP rev. B82-10438

Dickens, Charles, *1812-1870.* The mystery of Edwin Drood / Charles Dickens ; edited with an introduction by Margaret Cardwell. — Oxford : Oxford University Press, 1982, c1972. — xxiv,240p : ill ; 19cm. — (The world's classics)
Bibliography: p240
ISBN 0-19-281593-8 (pbk) : £1.25 : CIP rev. B82-10439

Dickens, Charles, *1812-1870.* [Nicholas Nickleby]. The life & adventures of Nicholas Nickleby / by Charles Dickens ; with thirty-nine illustrations by 'Phiz' ; and an introduction by Dame Sybil Thorndike. — Oxford : Oxford University Press, 1950 (1982 [printing]). — xxx,831p : ill ; 19cm. — (The Oxford illustrated Dickens)
ISBN 0-19-281368-4 (pbk) : £1.95 : CIP rev. B82-15676

Dickens, Charles, *1812-1870.* Nicholas Nickleby / Charles Dickens ; edited with an introduction and notes by Michael Slater and original illustrations by Hablot K. Browne ('Phiz'). — Harmondsworth : Penguin, 1978 (1982 [printing]). — 974p : ill ; 19cm
ISBN 0-14-006329-3 (pbk) : £1.95 B82-25425

Dickens, Charles, *1812-1870.* Oliver Twist / by Charles Dickens. — Toronto ; London : Bantam, 1981. — xii,419p ; 18cm. — (A Bantam classic)
ISBN 0-553-21050-5 (pbk) : £1.00 B82-12580

Dickens, Charles, *1812-1870.* Oliver Twist / Charles Dickens. — Large print ed. — Leicester : Charnwood, 1982. — 668p ; 23cm. — (Charnwood library series)
Published in large print
ISBN 0-7089-8019-8 : £6.50 : CIP rev. B81-33992

Dickens, Charles, *1812-1870.* Oliver Twist. — London : Macmillan Education, Feb.1983. — [432]p. — (Macmillan students' novels)
ISBN 0-333-33624-0 (pbk) : £0.95 : CIP entry B82-38056

Dickens, Charles, *1812-1870.* Oliver Twist ; Great expectations ; A tale of two cities / Charles Dickens. — London : Octopus, 1981. — 813p : ill,1port ; 25cm
ISBN 0-7064-1671-6 : £6.95 B82-00438

Dickens, Charles, *1812-1870.* Our mutual friend / Charles Dickens ; introduction by Christopher Hibbert ; drawings by Charles Keeping. — London : Folio Society, 1982. — xvii,779p : ill ; 24cm
In slip case
£16.95 B82-25472

Dickens, Charles, *1812-1870.* [The Pickwick papers]. The posthumous papers of the Pickwick Club / by Charles Dickens with forty-three illustrations by R. Seymour and Phiz. — [London] : [Nottingham Court Press in association with the Dickens Fellowship], [1979]. — xiv,609p,[69]leaves of plates : ill (some col.) ; 23cm
Facsim. of: 1st ed., published : London : Chapman and Hall, 1837
ISBN 0-906691-25-7 : Unpriced B82-00953

Disraeli, Benjamin. Coningsby, or, The new generation / Benjamin Disraeli ; edited by Sheila M. Smith. — Oxford : Oxford University Press, 1982. — xxvi,500p ; 19cm. — (The world's classics)
Bibliography: pxxiv
ISBN 0-19-281580-6 (pbk) : £2.95 : CIP rev. B82-10437

Disraeli, Benjamin. Coningsby, or, The new generation. — Bradenham ed. — London : Prior, Sept.1982. — [480]p. — (The Beaconsfield trilogy)
ISBN 0-86043-464-8 : £9.50 : CIP entry B82-20859

Disraeli, Benjamin. Sybil, or, The two nations. — Bradenham ed. — London : Prior, Sept.1982. — [512]p. — (The Beaconsfield trilogy)
ISBN 0-86043-465-6 : £9.50 : CIP entry B82-20860

Disraeli, Benjamin. Tancred, or, The new crusade. — Bradenham ed. — London : Prior, Sept.1982. — [544]p. — (The Beaconsfield trilogy)
ISBN 0-86043-466-4 : £9.50 : CIP entry B82-20861

Eliot, George. Daniel Deronda / by George Eliot ; with an introduction by Irving Howe. — New York : New American Library ; London : New English Library, 1979. — xxiv,744p ; 18cm. — (A Signet classic)
Bibliography: p743-744
ISBN 0-451-51204-9 (pbk) : £2.25 B82-14897

Eliot, George. Silas Marner / by George Eliot. — Toronto ; London : Bantam, 1981. — 186p ; 18cm. — (Bantam classics)
Bibliography: p185-186
ISBN 0-553-21048-3 (pbk) : £0.85 B82-16754

Fitzpatrick, Thomas, *d.1912.* The King of Claddagh / by Thomas Fitzpatrick. — Abridged ed. / abridged by Una Morrissy. — Dublin : Mercier, c1979. — 101p ; 18cm. — (Mercier Irish classics)
Previous ed.: London : Sands & Co., 1899
ISBN 0-85342-594-9 (pbk) : £2.00 B82-18345

Gaskell, Elizabeth. North and south / Elizabeth Gaskell ; edited with an introduction by Angus Easson. — Oxford : Oxford University Press, 1973, c1982 (1982 [printing]). — xxv,448p ; 19cm. — (The World's classics)
Bibliography: pxxi-xxii
ISBN 0-19-281595-4 (pbk) : £1.95 : CIP rev. B81-35764

Gaskell, Elizabeth. North and South / Elizabeth Cleghorn Gaskell. — Leicester : Charnwood, 1982. — 725p ; 23cm
Published in large print
ISBN 0-7089-8031-7 : Unpriced : CIP rev. B82-08109

Gaskell, Elizabeth. Sylvia's lovers / Elizabeth Gaskell ; edited with an introduction by Andrew Sanders. — Oxford : Oxford University Press, 1982. — xxiv,533p ; 19cm. — (The world's classics)
Bibliography: pxix-xxi
ISBN 0-19-281571-7 (pbk) : £2.95 : CIP rev. B82-10435

Gissing, George. In the year of Jubilee / George Gissing. — New York : Dover ; London : Constable, 1982. — 404p ; 21cm
ISBN 0-486-24251-x (pbk) : £4.50 B82-35638

Gissing, George. Isabel Clarendon / by George Gissing ; edited with a critical introduction by Pierre Coustillas. — Brighton : Harvester Press, 1969, c1982 (1982 [printing]). — 2v in 1 ; 20cm. — (Society & the Victorians)
Facsim of: ed. published. London : Chapman & Hall, 1886. — Bibliography: pxxiii-xxv(vol.2)
ISBN 0-7108-0466-0 : £25.00 B82-33180

Gissing, George. The paying guest. — Brighton : Harvester Press, Nov.1982. — [184]p. — (Harvester critical edition of the novels of George Gissing ; 16)
ISBN 0-85527-892-7 : £9.95 : CIP entry B82-29109

Gissing, George. The private papers of Henry Rycroft. — Brighton : Harvester Press, Apr.1982. — [352]p
ISBN 0-7108-0396-6 (cased) : £9.95 : CIP entry
ISBN 0-7108-3233-0 (pbk) : £4.50 B82-07121

Gissing, George. The town traveller / [by George Gissing] ; edited and with an introduction and notes by Pierre Coustillas. — Brighton : Harvester, 1981. — xxxviii,342p ; 20cm
Bibliography: p321-324
ISBN 0-85527-902-8 : £9.95 : CIP rev. B81-24622

Gissing, George. Will Warburton / George Gissing ; edited and with a new introduction and notes by Colin Partridge. — Brighton : Harvester, 1981. — 337p ; 20cm
Facsim of: ed. published: London : Archibald Constable, 1905. — Bibliography: p335-337
ISBN 0-85527-882-x : £9.95 : CIP rev. B81-30367

Grossmith, George. The diary of a nobody / George and Weedon Grossmith ; with illustrations by Weedon Grossmith. — Harmondsworth : Penguin, 1945 (1979 [printing]). — 233p : ill ; 18cm. — (Penguin modern classics)
£1.25 (pbk)
ISBN 0-14-000510-2 B82-37247

Hardy, Thomas. Jude the obscure. — Large print ed. — Anstey : Ulverscroft, Sept.1982. — [640] p. — (Charnwood library series)
ISBN 0-7089-8067-8 : £6.50 : CIP entry B82-27011

Hardy, Thomas, *1840-1928.* Far from the madding crowd. — Large print ed. — Anstey : Ulverscroft, Jan.1983. — [608]p. — (Charnwood library series)
ISBN 0-7089-8092-9 : £6.95 : CIP entry B82-32542

Hardy, Thomas, *1840-1928.* Jude the Obscure / by Thomas Hardy. — Toronto ; London : Bantam, 1969 (1981 [printing]). — 443p ; 18cm. — (A Bantam classic)
Bibliography: p440-443
ISBN 0-553-21023-8 (pbk) : £1.00 B82-12581

Hardy, Thomas, *1840-1928.* [The Mayor of Casterbridge]. The life and death of the Mayor of Casterbridge : a story of a man of character / by Thomas Hardy. — Large print ed. — Leicester : Charnwood, 1982. — 496p : 1map ; 23cm. — (Charnwood library series)
Published in large print
ISBN 0-7089-8021-x : £5.25 : CIP rev. B81-33991

Hardy, Thomas, *1840-1928.* Tess of the d'Urbervilles / by Thomas Hardy ; introduction by Robert B. Heilman. — Toronto ; London : Bantam, 1971 (1981 printing). — xxxii,414p : 2maps ; 18cm. — (A Bantam classic)
ISBN 0-553-21061-0 (pbk) : £1.00 B82-19383

Hardy, Thomas, *1840-1928.* Tess of the d'Urbervilles. — Oxford : Clarendon Press, Oct.1982. — [600]p
ISBN 0-19-812495-3 : £40.00 : CIP entry B82-23105

Hardy, Thomas, *1840-1928.* Tess of the d'Urbervilles : a pure woman / faithfully presented by Thomas Hardy. — Leicester : Charnwood, 1982. — 649p ; 23cm. — (Charnwood library series)
Published in large print
ISBN 0-7089-8038-4 : Unpriced : CIP rev. B82-08098

Hornung, E. W.. Stingaree / by E.W. Hornung. — Hornchurch : Ian Henry, 1982. — 252p ; 21cm
ISBN 0-86025-202-7 : £5.45 B82-32102

Hume, Fergus. The mystery of a hansom cab / Fergus Hume. — London : Remploy, 1980. — 224p ; 20cm
ISBN 0-7066-0864-x : £4.50 B82-09345

Jefferies, Richard. The dewy morn. — London : Wildwood House, Jan.1982. — [416]p. — (Rediscovery)
Originally published: London : Bentley, 1884
ISBN 0-7045-0461-8 (pbk) : £3.50 : CIP entry B81-37546

823′.8[F] — Fiction in English, *1837-1900 — Texts continuation*

Jerome, Jerome K.. Three men in a boat : to say nothing of the dog! / Jerome K. Jerome. — Harmondsworth : Penguin, 1957 (1982 [printing]). — 184p ; 18cm
ISBN 0-14-001213-3 (pbk) : £1.25 B82-40668

Jerome, Jerome K.. Three men in a boat. — London : Pavilion Books, June 1982. — [192]p
ISBN 0-907516-08-4 : £12.50 : CIP entry B82-10902

Jerome, Jerome K.. Three men on the Bummel / Jerome K. Jerome. — Large print ed. — Bath : Chivers, 1981. — 313p ; 23cm. — (A New Portway large print book)
ISBN 0-85119-138-x : Unpriced : CIP rev. B81-25801

Kipling, Rudyard. Captains courageous : a story of the Grand Banks / Rudyard Kipling. — Leicester : Charnwood, 1982. — 226p ; 22cm
Published in large print
ISBN 0-7089-8032-5 : Unpriced : CIP rev. B82-08110

Lawless, Emily. Maelcho / Emily Lawless ; with an introduction by Robert Lee Wolff. — New York ; London : Garland, 1979. — 2v. ; 19cm. — (Ireland)
Facsim of: ed. published London: Smith & Elder, 1894
ISBN 0-8240-3523-2 : Unpriced B82-22390

MacDonald, George, *1824-1905*. Phantastes / George MacDonald. — Woodbridge : Boydell, 1982. — xi,167p ; 22cm
ISBN 0-85115-201-5 (pbk) : £4.95 : CIP rev. B82-05416

A **Man** with a maid / Anonymous. — London : W.H. Allen, 1981. — xvii,254p ; 18cm. — (A Star book)
ISBN 0-352-31017-0 (pbk) : £1.60 B82-10105

A **man** with a maid / Anonymous. — London : W.H. Allen
V.2. — 1982. — 219p ; 18cm
ISBN 0-352-31092-8 (pbk) : £1.60 B82-22062

Morrison, Arthur. A child of the Jago / Arthur Morrison. — Woodbridge : Boydell, 1982. — 208p ; 22cm
ISBN 0-85115-203-1 (pbk) : £4.95 : CIP rev. B82-08414

Morrison, Arthur. The hole in the wall. — Woodbridge : Boydell & Brewer, Sept.1982. — [192]p
ISBN 0-85115-205-8 (pbk) : £4.95 : CIP entry B82-20498

Sinclair, May. The three sisters / May Sinclair ; with a new introduction by Jean Radford. — London : Virago, 1982, c1946. — x,388p ; 20cm
ISBN 0-86068-243-9 (pbk) : £3.50 : CIP rev. B81-36022

Stevenson, Robert Louis. Catriona. — Large print ed. — Anstey : Ulverscroft, Dec.1982. — 1v.. — (Charnwood Library series)
ISBN 0-7089-8089-9 : £4.50 : CIP entry B82-30795

Stevenson, Robert Louis. Dr. Jekyll and Mr. Hyde / by Robert Louis Stevenson ; with an afterword by Jerome Charyn. — Toronto ; London : Bantam, 1981. — 119p ; 18cm. — (A Bantam classic)
Bibliography: p117-119
ISBN 0-553-21045-9 (pbk) : £0.85 B82-35541

Stevenson, Robert Louis. Kidnapped / Robert Louis Stevenson. — Leicester : Charnwood, 1982. — 318p ; 23cm. — (Charnwood large type)
Published in large print
ISBN 0-7089-8058-9 : Unpriced : CIP rev. B82-15970

Stevenson, Robert Louis. An old song : a newly discovered long story, and ... Edifying letters of the Rutherford family / by Robert Louis Stevenson ; edited and with an introduction by Roger G. Swearingen. — Hamden, Conn. : Archon ; Paisley : Wilfion, 1982. — 102p : 2facsims ; 23cm
ISBN 0-905075-12-9 : Unpriced B82-32949

Stevenson, Robert Louis. Treasure Island / by Robert Louis Stevenson. — Toronto ; London : Bantam, 1982. — 194p : 1map ; 18cm. — (A Bantam classic)
ISBN 0-553-21046-7 (pbk) : £0.85 B82-28547

Stevenson, Robert Louis. Treasure Island. — London : Gollancz, Sept.1982. — [272]p
ISBN 0-575-03149-2 : £9.95 : CIP entry B82-19563

Stoker, Bram. Dracula / by Bram Stoker ; with an introduction by George Stade. — Toronto ; London : Bantam, 1981. — xiv,402p ; 18cm. — (A Bantam classic)
Bibliography: p401-402
ISBN 0-553-21047-5 (pbk) : £1.00 B82-35482

Surtees, R. S.. Mr Facey Romford's hounds. — Craddock (Craddock Cleve, Craddock, Nr Cullompton, Devon EX15 3LW) : R.S. Surtees Society, Sept.1982. — [432]p
Originally published: London : Bradbury & Evans, 1865
ISBN 0-9507697-1-1 : £14.95 : CIP entry B82-21585

Surtees, R. S.. Mr. Sponge's sporting tour / R.S. Surtees ; with an introduction by Joyce Cary and the original illustrations by John Leech. — Oxford : Oxford University Press, 1958 (1982 [printing]). — xxv,500p : ill ; 19cm. — (The World's classics)
ISBN 0-19-281521-0 (pbk) : £2.95 : CIP rev. B82-04276

Surtees, Robert Smith. Mr. Sponge's sporting tour. — Craddock (Craddock Cleve, Craddock, Cullompton, Devon EX15 3LW) : R.S. Surtees Society, Sept.1981. — [432]p
Facsim. of: 1st ed. London : Bradbury and Evans, 1854
ISBN 0-9507697-0-3 : £12.95 : CIP entry B81-28715

Trollope, Anthony. Can you forgive her? / Anthony Trollope ; edited by Andrew Swarbrick ; introduced by Kate Flint ; with a preface by Norman St. John-Stevas. — Oxford : Oxford University Press, 1982. — xliii,449p ; 18cm. — (The Centenary edition of Anthony Trollope's Palliser novels) (The World's classics)
Bibliography: pxxxii-xxxiii
ISBN 0-19-281585-7 (pbk) : £3.50 : CIP rev. B82-19197

Trollope, Anthony. The Eustace diamonds. — Oxford : Oxford University Press, Feb.1983. — [784]p. — (The World's classics)
ISBN 0-19-281588-1 (pbk) : £3.50 : CIP entry B82-36591

Trollope, Anthony. The Kellys and the O'Kellys, or, Landlords and tenants / Anthony Trollope ; edited by W.J. McCormack ; with an introduction by William Trevor. — Oxford : Oxford University Press, 1929 (1982 [printing]). — xix,537p ; 19cm. — (The World's classics)
Bibliography: pxv
ISBN 0-19-281577-6 (pbk) : £2.90 : CIP rev. B82-04277

Trollope, Anthony. Orley Farm / by Anthony Trollope ; with 40 illustrations by John Everett Millais. — New York : Dover ; London : Constable, 1981. — 320,320p,[40]leaves of plates : ill ; 22cm
Facsim of 1st ed. London : Chapman and Hall, 1862
ISBN 0-486-24181-5 (pbk) : £6.75 B82-16694

Trollope, Anthony. Phineas Finn : the Irish member / edited with an introduction by Jacques Berthoud ; with illustrations by T.L.B. Huskinson. — Oxford : Oxford University Press, 1982. — xxxvi,383p : ill ; 18cm. — (The Centenary edition of Anthony Trollope's Palliser novels) (The World's classics)
Bibliography: pxxvi-xxvii
ISBN 0-19-281587-3 (pbk) : £3.50 : CIP rev. B82-19198

Trollope, Anthony. Phineas redux. — Oxford : Oxford University Press, Feb.1983. — [768]p. — (The World's classics)
ISBN 0-19-281589-x (pbk) : £2.50 : CIP entry B82-36592

Trollope, Anthony. The way we live now / Anthony Trollope ; edited by John Sutherland. — Oxford : Oxford University Press, 1941 (1982 [printing]). — xlviii,494p : ill ; 19cm. — (The World's classics)
ISBN 0-19-281576-8 (pbk) : £3.95 : CIP rev. B81-35768

823′.8[F] — Short stories in English, *1837-1900 — Texts*

Gilbert, W. S.. The lost short stories of W.S. Gilbert. — London : Robson, Sept.1982. — [196]p
ISBN 0-86051-200-2 : £6.95 : CIP entry B82-21539

Jacobs, W. W.. Light freights / W.W. Jacobs. — Woodbridge : Boydell, 1982. — 160p ; 22cm
ISBN 0-85115-202-3 (pbk) : £4.95 : CIP rev. B82-05417

Jerome, Jerome K.. Evergreens : and other short stories / Jerome K. Jerome. — Gloucester : Sutton, c1982. — 112p : ill ; 20cm
ISBN 0-86299-011-4 (pbk) : £1.50 B82-35918

Lawless, Emily. Traits and confidences / Emily Lawless ; with an introductioon by Robert Lee Wolff. — New York ; London : Garland, 1979. — xv,272p ; 19cm. — (Ireland)
Facsim of: ed published London : Methuen, 1898
ISBN 0-8240-3524-0 : Unpriced B82-22391

Munro, Neil. Para Handy and other tales / by Hugh Foulis (Neil Munro). — Edinburgh : Blackwood, 1980. — xii,690p ; 19cm
ISBN 0-85158-138-2 : £3.95 B82-20971

Seton, Ernest Thompson. The best of Ernest Thompson Seton / selected and introduced by Richard Adams. — [London] : Fontana, 1982. — 224p : ill ; 18cm
ISBN 0-00-616452-8 (pbk) : £1.75 B82-32106

Yeats, W. B.. The secret rose : and other stories / W.B. Yeats. — London : Papermac, 1982. — vii,261p : 1port ; 20cm
Contents: The celtic twilight — The secret rose — Stories of Red Hanrahan
ISBN 0-333-31637-1 (pbk) : £3.60 B82-13598

823′.8[J] — Children's short stories in English, *1837-1900 — Texts*

Nister, Ernest. Golden tales from long ago / by Ernest Nister. — London : Methuen, 1980, c1979. — 1case : ill(some col.) ; 11cm. — (Methuen's antique library)
ISBN 0-416-89780-0 : £1.95 B82-13633

823′.8[J] — Children's stories in English, *1837-1900 — Texts*

Ballantyne, R. M.. The coral island / R.M. Ballantyne. — Abridged ed. — [Harmondsworth] : Puffin, 1982. — 237p ; 19cm
ISBN 0-14-031547-0 (pbk) : £1.10 B82-35860

Barrie, J. M.. Peter Pan. — London : Hodder & Stoughton, Sept.1981. — [192]p
ISBN 0-340-26430-6 : £7.95 : CIP entry B81-23924

823'.8[J] — Children's stories in English, *1837-1900 — Texts* *continuation*

Blyton, Enid. The seaside family / Enid Blyton ; illustrated by Joyce Smith and David Dowland. — London : Sparrow, 1982. — 88p : ill ; 18cm
Originally published: London : Lutterworth, 1950
ISBN 0-09-927700-x (pbk) : £0.85 B82-33318

Carroll, Lewis. [Alice in Wonderland]. Alice's adventures in Wonderland. — London : Hodder and Stoughton Children's Books, Sept.1982. — [256]p
ISBN 0-340-28395-5 : £12.95 : CIP entry
ISBN 0-340-28394-7 (limited ed.) : £30.00 B82-18810

Carroll, Lewis. Alice in wonderland / Lewis Carroll. — Bristol : Purnell, 1982. — 103p : ill ; 21cm. — (A Purnell children's classic)
ISBN 0-361-05335-5 : £0.99 B82-37780

Carroll, Lewis. Alice's adventures in wonderland ; through the looking glass / [Lewis Carroll] ; [illustrations by Sir John Tenniel]. — New children's ed. — London : Macmillan, 1980. — 1,ill(some col.) ; 22cm
Previous ed.: 1927
ISBN 0-333-29039-9 : £9.95 the set B82-20985

Carroll, Lewis. Through the looking-glass : and what Alice found there / Lewis Carroll ; with the original engravings by John Tenniel. — London : Dent, 1976 (1979 printing). — 140p : ill ; 18cm. — (Everyman's library)
ISBN 0-460-01018-2 (pbk) : £0.95 B82-06156

Grahame, Kenneth. The wind in the willows / Kenneth Grahame. — London : Magnet, 1978 (1982 [printing]). — 190p ; 18cm
ISBN 0-416-25500-0 (pbk) : £0.65
ISBN 0-416-39370-5 (Methuen Children's)
ISBN 0-416-64570-4 (Methuen Children's : pbk) B82-34368

Grahame, Kenneth. The wind in the willows / Kenneth Grahame ; illustrated by Ernest H. Shepard. — Leicester : Charnwood, 1981. — 259p : ill ; 23cm. — (Charnwood library series)
Published in large print
ISBN 0-7089-8007-4 : £4.50 : CIP rev. B81-22662

Grahame, Kenneth. The wind in the willows. — Oxford : Oxford University Press, Jan.1983. — [224]p. — (The World's classics)
ISBN 0-19-281640-3 (pbk) : £1.50 : CIP entry B82-33476

Grahame, Kenneth. The wind in the willows. — London : Hodder and Stoughton, Jan.1983. — [112]p
ISBN 0-340-28573-7 : £3.95 : CIP entry B82-33741

Kingsley, Charles. The water babies. — London : Hodder and Stoughton Children's Books, Oct.1981. — [256]p
ISBN 0-340-27458-1 (cased) : £10.95 : CIP entry
ISBN 0-340-27465-4 (limited ed.) : £30.00 B81-30252

Kingsley, Charles, *1819-1875*. The water-babies / by Charles Kingsley. — London : Dean, [198-?]. — 184p ; 19cm. — (Dean's classics)
ISBN 0-603-03030-0 : Unpriced B82-26100

Kipling, Rudyard. Stalky & Co / Rudyard Kipling. — London : Macmillan, 1982. — ix,272p ; 21cm
ISBN 0-333-32820-5 (cased) : Unpriced
ISBN 0-333-32821-3 (pbk) : £1.95 B82-18239

Molesworth, *Mrs.*. Christmas-tree land / by Mrs. Molesworth ; illustrated by Walter Crane. — London : Macmillan, 1981. — 223p,[7]leaves of plates : ill ; 20cm. — (Facsimile classics series)
Facsim of: ed. published London : Macmillan, 1884
ISBN 0-333-32589-3 : £4.95 B82-05731

Nesbit, E.. Belinda and Bellament / E. Nesbit ; edited by Moira Brady ; illustrated by Stephen Lavis. — London : Macdonald & Co., 1982. — [28]p : col.ill ; 24cm
ISBN 0-354-08125-x : £4.25 B82-15323

Nesbit, E.. Melisande / E. Nesbit ; edited by Moira Brady ; pictures by Peter Firmin. — London : Macdonald & Co., 1982. — [28]p : col.ill ; 24cm
ISBN 0-354-08127-6 : £4.25 B82-15324

Nesbit, E.. New treasure seekers / E. Nesbit. — Harmondsworth : Puffin, 1982. — 218p ; 18cm
ISBN 0-14-031537-3 (pbk) : £0.85 B82-22306

Nesbit, E.. The phœnix and the carpet / by E. Nesbit ; illustrated by H.R. Millar. — London : Ernest Benn, 1978. — 264p : ill ; 20cm
ISBN 0-510-16002-6 : £2.95 B82-01017

Nesbit, E.. The railway children / by E. Nesbit ; with illustrations by C.E. Brock. — Harmondsworth : Puffin, 1960 (1982 [printing]). — 239p : ill ; 19cm. — (Puffin classic)
ISBN 0-14-035005-5 (pbk) : £0.90 B82-40369

Nesbit, E.. The story of the treasure seekers : being the adventures of the Bastable children in search of a fortune / by E. Nesbit ; with illustrations by Gordon Browne. — London : Armada, 1982. — 192p : ill ; 19cm
ISBN 0-00-692014-4 (pbk) : £0.85 B82-09405

Sewell, Anna. Black Beauty / Anna Sewell. — Abridged. — Bristol : Purnell, 1982. — 139p : ill ; 21cm. — (A Purnell children's classic)
ISBN 0-361-05339-8 : £0.99 B82-37786

Stevenson, Robert Louis. Kidnapped : being memoirs of the adventures of David Balfour in the year 1751, written by himself and now set forth by Robert Louis Stevenson. — Abridged ed. — London : Dean, [198-?]. — 183p ; 19cm. — (Dean's classics)
ISBN 0-603-03034-3 : Unpriced B82-26101

Stevenson, Robert Louis. Treasure Island / Robert Louis Stevenson. — Abridged. — Bristol : Purnell, 1982. — 137p : ill ; 21cm. — (A Purnell children's classic)
ISBN 0-361-05340-1 : £0.99 B82-37785

Thackeray, W. M.. The rose and the ring / by W.M. Thackeray. — London : Macmillan Children's, 1981. — vi,128p : ill ; 20cm
Facsim of: New ed. London : Smith, Elder, 1902
ISBN 0-333-32590-7 : £4.95 B82-05894

Wilde, Oscar. The selfish giant / Oscar Wilde ; illustrated by Michael Foreman and Freire Wright. — Harmondsworth : Puffin, 1982, c1978. — [31]p : col.ill ; 18x23cm. — (Picture Puffins)
Originally published: London : Kaye & Ward, 1978
ISBN 0-14-050383-8 (pbk) : £1.10 B82-29590

823'.8'08 — Fiction in English, *1837-1900 — Anthologies*

The **Brontë** sisters : four novels. — London : Spring, 1982. — 1140p ; 21cm
Originally published: London : Hamlyn, 1976. — Contents: Jane Eyre / Charlotte Brontë — Wuthering heights / Emily Brontë — Agnes Grey / Anne Brontë — Villette / Charlotte Brontë
ISBN 0-600-00342-6 : £3.95 B82-36413

823'.8'08 — Fiction in English, *1837-1945 — Anthologies*

Best loved books / selected and condensed by the editors of Reader's Digest. — London : Reader's Digest Association, c1981. — 575p : ill(some col.),ports(some col.) ; 21cm
Contents: A Christmas carol / by Charles Dickens — Florence Nightingale / by Cecil Woodham-Smith — Rogue male / by Geoffrey Household — The red badge of courage / by Stephen Crane — The adventures of Huckleberry Finn / by Mark Twain
ISBN 0-340-27886-2 : £5.95 B82-02540

823'.8'08 — Fiction in English, *1837-1960 — Anthologies*

Best loved books / selected and condensed by the editors of Reader's Digest. — London : Reader's Digest, c1981. — 574p : ill(some col.),ports ; 21cm
Contents: The Nun's story / Kathryn Hulme — Ring of bright water / Gavin Maxwell — Tales of Poe / Edgar Allan Poe — Lorna Doone / R.D. Blackmore
ISBN 0-340-28228-2 : £6.95 B82-14540

823'.8'09 — Fiction in English, *1837-1900 — Critical studies*

Carlisle, Janice. The sense of an audience : Dickens, Thackeray, and George Eliot and mid-century / Janice Carlisle. — Brighton : Harvester Press, 1982, c1981. — xi,242p : ill ; 25cm
Originally published: Athens, Ga. : University of Georgia Press, 1981. — Includes index
ISBN 0-7108-0338-9 : £22.50 : CIP rev. B81-28072

Qualls, Barry V.. The secular pilgrims of Victorian fiction. — Cambridge : Cambridge University Press, Oct.1982. — [236]p
ISBN 0-521-24409-9 : £19.50 : CIP entry
ISBN 0-521-27820-1 (pbk) : £6.95 B82-29376

823'.8'09 — Fiction in English. Brontë *(Family) — Critical studies*

Lloyd Evans, Barbara. Everyman's companion to the Brontës / Barbara and Gareth Lloyd Evans. — London : Dent, 1982. — xviii,400p,[16]p of plates : ill,facsims,map,ports ; 25cm
Bibliography: pxvii-xviii
ISBN 0-460-04455-9 : £10.95 : CIP rev. B82-09709

823'.8'09 — Fiction in English. Socialist writers, *1837-1980 — Critical studies*

The **Socialist** novel in Britain : towards the recovery of a tradition / edited by H. Gustav Klaus. — Brighton : Harvester, 1982. — viii,190p ; 23cm
Includes index
ISBN 0-7108-0340-0 : £18.95 : CIP rev. B81-30603

823'.8'09 — Fiction in English. Women writers, *1837-1975 — Critical studies*

Showalter, Elaine. A literature of their own : British women novelists from Brontë to Lessing. — 2nd ed. — London : Virago, Dec.1982. — [384]p
Previous ed.: Guildford : Princeton University Press, 1977
ISBN 0-86068-285-4 (pbk) : £4.95 : CIP entry B82-30736

823'.8'0915 — Fiction in English, *ca 1860-ca 1970.* **Fantasy** *— Critical studies*

Little, Edmund. The fantasts. — Amersham : Avebury Publishing, Apr.1982. — [160]p
ISBN 0-86127-212-9 (pbk) : £7.95 : CIP entry B82-04732

823'.8'09355 — Fiction in English, *1837-1970.* **Special subjects: School life** *— Critical studies*

Quigly, Isabel. The heirs of Tom Brown : the English school story / by Isabel Quigly. — London : Chatto & Windus, 1982. — 296p : ill ; 23cm
Bibliography: p284-287. — Includes index
ISBN 0-7011-2615-9 : £12.50 : CIP rev. B82-09460

823.912 — ENGLISH FICTION, 1900-1945

823'.912 — Children's stories in English. Blyton, Enid *— Critical studies*

Ray, Sheila G.. The Blyton phenomenon : the controversy surrounding the world's most successful children's writer / Sheila G. Ray. — London : Deutsch, 1982. — viii,246p ; 23cm
Bibliography: p225-234. — Includes index
ISBN 0-233-97441-5 : £10.95 B82-37158

823'.912 — Children's stories in English. Brent-Dyer, Elinor M. *— Biographies*

McClelland, Helen. Behind the Chalet School / Helen McClelland. — Bognor Regis : New Horizon, c1981. — 185p,[25]p of plates : ill,maps,ports ; 22cm
Bibliography: 6p. — Includes index
ISBN 0-86116-548-9 : £6.25 B82-09556

823′.912 — Children′s stories in English. Johns, W. E. (William Earl) — *Biographies*

Ellis, Peter Berresford. By jove, Biggles! : the life of Captain W.E. Johns / Peter Berresford Ellis and Piers Williams. — London : W.H. Allen, 1981. — xii,306p,[4]p of plates : ill,ports ; 23cm
Includes index
ISBN 0-491-02775-3 : £8.95 B82-05151

823′.912 — Children′s stories in English. Lewis, C. S.. Chronicles of Narnia — *Critical studies*

Hooper, Walter. Past watchful dragons / Walter Hooper. — London : Fount Paperbacks, 1980. — 143p ; 18cm
Originally published: New York : Macmillan, 1979. — Bibliography: p139-140. — Includes index
ISBN 0-00-626082-9 (pbk) : £0.95 B82-16322

823′.912 — Children′s stories in English. Milne, A. A. Characters: Winnie the Pooh. Taoism

Hoff, Benjamin. The Tao of Pooh. — London : Methuen, Aug.1982. — [168]p
ISBN 0-416-26250-3 : £4.95 : CIP entry B82-15812

823′.912 — Children′s stories in English. Milne, Christopher — *Biographies*

Milne, Christopher. The hollow on the the hill : the search for a personal philosophy / by Christopher Milne ; with photographs by James Ravilious. — London : Methuen, 1982. — 154p : ill,1port ; 23cm
ISBN 0-413-50200-7 (cased) : £6.95 : CIP rev.
ISBN 0-413-51270-3 (pbk) : Unpriced B82-06746

823′.912 — Children′s stories in English. Potter, Beatrix. Local associations: Scotland. Tayside Region. Dunkeld region

Rolland, Deborah. Beatrix Potter in Scotland / by Deborah Rolland. — London : Frederick Warne, 1981. — 32p : ill(some col.),1facsim,ports ; 21cm
ISBN 0-7232-2911-2 (pbk) : £1.75 B82-06355

823′.912 — Fiction in English, *1900-1945 — Texts — Manuscripts — Facsimiles*

Joyce, James. The James Joyce archive / general editor Michael Groden ; associate editors ... [et al.]. — [New York] ([London]) : Garland
[Notes, criticism, translations & miscellaneous writings] : [a facsimile of manuscripts & typescripts]
[Vol.1] / [preface & arranged by Hans Walter Gabler]. — 1979. — xxiv,703p : music,fasims,1port ; 29cm
English and Italian text. — Includes bibliographies
ISBN 0-8240-2801-5 : Unpriced B82-22214

823′.912 — Fiction in English, *1900-1945 — Texts with commentaries*

Lawrence, D. H.. The lost girl / D.H. Lawrence ; edited by John Worthen. — Cambridge ed. — Cambridge : Cambridge University Press, 1981. — lvii,426p : 1map ; 23cm
ISBN 0-521-22263-x (cased) : £25.00 : CIP rev. B81-23765

Lawrence, D. H.. Sons and lovers. — London : Macmillan Education, Feb.1983. — [448]p
ISBN 0-333-33623-2 (pbk) : £0.95 : CIP entry B82-38055

823′.912 — Fiction in English. Allen, Walter — *Biographies*

Allen, Walter. As I walked down New Grub Street : memories of a writing life / by Walter Allen. — London : Heinemann, 1981. — 276p ; 23cm
Includes index
ISBN 0-434-01829-5 : £8.95 B82-09151

823′.912 — Fiction in English. Bennett, Arnold. Anna of the five towns — *Study outlines*

Last, Brian W.. Anna of the five towns : notes / by Brian W. Last. — Harlow : Longman, 1981. — 64p ; 21cm. — (York notes ; 144)
Bibliography: p57
ISBN 0-582-79205-3 (pbk) : £0.90 B82-16445

823′.912 — Fiction in English. Buchan, John, *1875-1940 — Biographies*

Buchan, William. John Buchan : a memoir / William Buchan. — London : Buchan & Enright, 1982. — 272p,[16]p of plates : ill,ports ; 24cm
ISBN 0-907675-03-4 : £9.95 B82-30979

823′.912 — Fiction in English. Christie, Agatha — *Biographies*

Osborne, Charles, *1927-*. The life and crimes of Agatha Christie / Charles Osborne. — London : Collins, 1982. — 256p,[32]p of plates : ill,facsims,ports ; 24cm
Bibliography: p244-251. — Includes index
ISBN 0-00-216462-0 : £9.95 B82-37759

823′.912 — Fiction in English. Compton-Burnett, I. — *Personal observations*

Dick, Kay. Ivy and Stevie. — London : Allison & Busby, Sept.1982. — [96]p
ISBN 0-85031-483-6 (pbk) : £1.95 : CIP entry
Also classified at 821′.912 B82-18773

823′.912 — Fiction in English. Conrad, Joseph — *Biographies*

Tennant, Roger, *1919-*. Joseph Conrad / Roger Tennant. — London : Sheldon, 1981. — x,276p,[8]p of plates : ill,2facsims,ports ; 24cm
Bibliography: p260-262. — Includes index
ISBN 0-85969-358-9 : £12.50 B82-11253

823′.912 — Fiction in English. Conrad, Joseph — *Critical studies*

Darras, Jacques. Joseph Conrad and the West : signs of empire / Jacques Darras ; translated from the French by Anne Luyat and Jacques Darras. — London : Macmillan, 1982. — vi,158p ; 23cm
Translated from the French. — Bibliography: p151-154. — Includes index
ISBN 0-333-28597-2 : £17.50 B82-32384

Hunter, Allan. Joseph Conrad and the ethics of Darwinism. — London : Croom Helm, Jan.1983. — [224]p
ISBN 0-7099-1265-x : £15.00 : CIP entry B82-33348

Watts, Cedric. A preface to Conrad. — London : Longman, Feb.1982. — [208]p. — (Preface books)
ISBN 0-582-35273-8 (cased) : £5.25 : CIP entry
ISBN 0-582-35274-6 (pbk) : £3.25 B81-36979

823′.912 — Fiction in English. Conrad, Joseph. Heart of darkness — *Study outlines*

Maes-Jelinek, Hena. Heart of darkness : notes / by Hena Maes-Jelinek. — Harlow : Longman, 1982. — 80p ; 21cm. — (York notes ; 152)
Bibliography: p72-74
ISBN 0-582-78170-1 (pbk) : £0.90 B82-16371

823′.912 — Fiction in English. Conrad, Joseph. Lord Jim — *Study outlines*

Steinmann, Theo. Lord Jim : notes / by Theo Steinmann. — Harlow : Longman, 1981. — 80p ; 21cm. — (York notes ; 150)
Bibliography: p72-73
ISBN 0-582-78216-3 (pbk) : £0.90 B82-16461

823′.912 — Fiction in English. Conrad, Joseph. Secret agent — *Study outlines*

Delbaere, Jeanne. The secret agent : notes / by Jeanne Delbaere. — Harlow : Longman, 1981. — 80p ; 21cm. — (York notes ; 138)
Bibliography: p73-74
ISBN 0-582-78193-0 (pbk) : £0.90 B82-16362

823′.912 — Fiction in English. Conrad, Joseph. Special themes: Colonialism — *Critical studies*

McClure, John A.. Kipling and Conrad : the colonial fiction / John A. McClure. — Cambridge, Mass. ; London : Harvard University Press, 1981. — 182p ; 24cm
Includes index
ISBN 0-674-50529-8 : £9.90
Primary classification 823′.8 B82-11846

823′.912 — Fiction in English. Doyle, *Sir* Arthur Conan. Characters: Sherlock Holmes. Higher education

Utechin, Nicholas. Sherlock Holmes at Oxford. — 2nd ed. — Oxford (Corpus Christi College, Oxford OX1 4JF) : Robert Dugdale, July 1981. — [32]p
Previous ed.: 1977
ISBN 0-9503880-8-4 (pbk) : £1.25 : CIP entry B81-23894

823′.912 — Fiction in English. Ford, Ford Madox. Correspondence with Pound, Ezra

Pound, Ezra. Pound/Ford : the story of a literary friendship. — London : Faber, Sept.1982. — [384]p
ISBN 0-571-11968-9 : £20.00 : CIP entry
Primary classification 811′.52 B82-19552

823′.912 — Fiction in English. Forster, E. M. — *Correspondence, diaries, etc.*

Forster, E. M.. The Hill of Devi and other Indian writings. — London : Edward Arnold, Dec.1982. — [400]p
ISBN 0-7131-6374-7 : £25.00 : CIP entry B82-30209

823′.912 — Fiction in English. Forster, E. M. — *Critical studies*

E.M. Forster : centenary revaluations / edited by Judith Scherer Herz and Robert K. Martin. — London : Macmillan, 1982. — xiii,337p ; 23cm
Includes index
ISBN 0-333-29475-0 : £20.00 B82-28688

Gillie, Christopher. A preface to Forster. — London : Longman, Nov.1982. — [208]p. — (Preface books)
ISBN 0-582-35314-9 (cased) : £4.50 : CIP entry
ISBN 0-582-35315-7 (pbk) : £2.75 B82-26531

Trilling, Lionel. E.M. Forster. — Oxford : Oxford University Press, Jan.1982. — [162]p. — (The works of Lionel Trilling)
Originally published: London : Hogarth Press, 1967
ISBN 0-19-212227-4 : £7.95 : CIP entry B81-34375

823′.912 — Fiction in English. Forster, E. M.. Passage to India — *Study outlines*

Shahane, Vasant A.. A passage to India : notes / by Vasant A. Shahane. — Harlow : Longman, 1982. — 88p ; 21cm. — (York notes ; 151)
Bibliography: p80-81
ISBN 0-582-78115-9 (pbk) : £0.90 B82-16370

823′.912 — Fiction in English. Greene, Graham — *Biographies*

Greene, Graham. A sort of life : an autobiography / Graham Greene. — Large print ed. — Bath : Chivers, 1981, c1971. — 234p ; 23cm
Originally published: London : Bodley Head, 1971
ISBN 0-85119-143-6 : Unpriced : CIP rev. B81-31255

Greene, Graham. Ways of escape / Graham Greene. — Harmondsworth : Penguin, 1981, c1980 (1982 [printing]). — 236p ; 19cm
Originally published: London : Bodley Head, 1980
ISBN 0-14-005801-x (pbk) : £1.75 B82-41153

823′.912 — Fiction in English. Gunn, Neil M. — *Biographies*

Hart, Francis Russell. Neil M. Gunn : a Highland life / Francis Russell Hart & J.B. Pick. — London : Murray, 1981. — 314p,[12]p of plates : ill,ports ; 24cm
Bibliography: p302-306. — Includes index
ISBN 0-7195-3856-4 : £15.00 : CIP rev. B81-27382

823′.912 — Fiction in English. Hall, Radclyffe — *Critical studies*

Franks, Claudia Stillman. Radclyffe Hall : beyond The well of loneliness. — Amersham : Avebury Publishing, Dec.1981. — [160]p
ISBN 0-86127-210-2 (cased) : £10.95 : CIP entry
ISBN 0-86127-221-8 (pbk) : £6.95 B81-32600

823'.912 — Fiction in English. Hartley , L. P.. Shrimp and the anemone — *Study outlines*

Milligan, Ian. The shrimp and the anemone : notes / by Ian Milligan. — Harlow : Longman, 1981. — 64p ; 21cm. — (York notes)
Bibliography: p61-62
ISBN 0-582-78196-5 (pbk) : £0.90 B82-02900

823'.912 — Fiction in English. Huxley, Aldous. Brave new world — *Study outlines*

Routh, Michael. Brave new world : notes / by Michael Routh. — Harlow : Longman, 1982. — 80p ; 21cm. — (York notes ; 156)
Bibliography: p74-75
ISBN 0-582-78247-3 (pbk) : £0.90 B82-16462

823'.912 — Fiction in English. Isherwood, Christopher. Interpersonal relationships with Prabhavananda, *Swami*

Isherwood, Christopher. My guru and his disciple / Christopher Isherwood. — [London] : Magnum, 1981, c1980. — 338p ; 17cm
Originally published: London : Eyre Methuen, 1980
ISBN 0-417-05590-0 (pbk) : £1.95
Also classified at 294.5'61 B82-17571

823'.912 — Fiction in English. Jones, Lewis, *1893-1939 — Critical studies*

Smith, David. Lewis Jones. — Cardiff : University of Wales Press, Nov.1982. — [95]p. — (Writers of Wales, ISSN 0141-5050)
ISBN 0-7083-0830-9 (pbk) : £2.50 : CIP entry B82-28744

823'.912 — Fiction in English. Joyce, James, *1882-1941, 1882-1904 — Personal observations*

Joyce, Stanislaus. My brother's keeper / Stanislaus Joyce ; edited and with an introduction by Richard Ellmann ; with a preface by T.S. Eliot. — London : Faber and Faber, 1958 (1982 [printing]). — 257p ; 20cm
Includes index
ISBN 0-571-11803-8 (pbk) : £3.25 : CIP rev. B82-00207

823'.912 — Fiction in English. Joyce, James, *1882-1941 — Biographies*

Davies, Stan Gébler. James Joyce : a portait of the artist / Stan Gébler Davies. — London : Granada, 1982. — 413p,[8]p of plates : 1ill,ports ; 18cm. — (A Panther book)
Originally published: London : Davis-Poynter, 1975. — Bibliography: p393-395. — Includes index
ISBN 0-586-05639-4 (pbk) : £1.95 B82-32054

823'.912 — Fiction in English. Joyce, James, *1882-1941.* **Characters: Women** — *Critical studies*

Women in Joyce. — Brighton : Harvester Press, May 1982. — [216]p
ISBN 0-7108-0389-3 : £18.95 : CIP entry B82-06952

823'.912 — Fiction in English. Joyce, James, *1882-1941.* **Childhood** — *Biographies*

Bradley, Bruce. James Joyce's schooldays / Bruce Bradley ; foreword by Richard Ellman. — Dublin : Gill and Macmillan, 1982. — 179p : ill,facsims,ports ; 24cm
Bibliography: p169-172. — Includes index
ISBN 0-7171-1226-8 : £15.00 B82-32408

823'.912 — Fiction in English. Joyce, James, *1882-1941 — Critical studies*

Burgess, Anthony. Here comes everbody : an introduction to James Joyce for the ordinary reader / Anthony Burgess. — Rev. ed. / with a new foreword by the author. — [London] : Hamlyn Paperbacks, 1982. — 276p ; 18cm
Previous ed.: London : Faber, 1965. — Includes index
ISBN 0-600-20673-4 (pbk) : £1.75 B82-29753

Byrne, Mairéad. Joyce : — a clew / [by Mairead Byrne and Henry J. Sharpe]. — Dublin : Bluett, 1981. — [35]p : ill ; 22cm
ISBN 0-907899-00-5 : £4.95 B82-21688

Gordon, John, *1945-*. James Joyce's metamorphoses / John Gordon. — Dublin : Gill and Macmillan, 1981. — x,207p ; 22cm
Bibliography: p195-202. — Includes index
ISBN 0-7171-1024-9 : £15.00 B82-04771

James Joyce : new perspectives / edited by Colin MacCabe. — Brighton : Harvester, 1982. — xiii,198p ; 23cm
Includes index
ISBN 0-7108-0028-2 : £18.95 : CIP rev. B82-23177

James Joyce : an international perspective : centenary essays in honour of the late Sir Desmond Cochrane / with a message from Samuel Beckett and a foreword by Richard Ellmann ; edited by Suheil Badi Bushrui and Bernard Benstock. — Gerrards Cross : Smythe, 1982. — xiii,301p : 1facsim,1port ; 23cm. — (Irish literary studies, ISSN 0140-895x ; 10)
Includes bibliographies and index
ISBN 0-86140-084-4 : £12.95 : CIP rev. B82-10242

A **starchamber** quiry : a James Joyce centennial volume, 1882-1982. — London : Methuen, Feb.1982. — [200]p
ISBN 0-416-31560-7 : £9.00 : CIP entry B81-35715

823'.912 — Fiction in English. Joyce, James, *1882-1941 — Critical studies — Conference proceedings*

James Joyce and modern literature / edited by W.J. McCormack and Alistair Stead. — London : Routledge & Kegan Paul, 1982. — xiii,222p ; 23cm
Conference papers. — Includes index
ISBN 0-7100-9058-7 : £9.75 B82-26596

The **Seventh** of Joyce. — Brighton : Harvester Press, Nov.1982. — [256]p
ISBN 0-7108-0443-1 : £18.95 : CIP entry B82-27930

823'.912 — Fiction in English. Joyce, James, *1882-1941.* **Dubliners & Portrait of the artist as a young man** — *Critical studies*

Bidwell, Bruce. The Joycean way. — Dublin : Wolfhound Press, Sept.1981. — [160]p
ISBN 0-905473-39-6 : £8.00 : CIP entry B81-23795

823'.912 — Fiction in English. Joyce, James, *1882-1941.* **Dubliners & Portrait of the artist of a young man** — *Commentaries*

Gifford, Don. Joyce annotated : notes for Dubliners and A portrait of the artist as a young man / Don Gifford. — 2nd ed., rev. and enlarged. — Berkeley ; London : University of California Press, 1982. — ix,308p : maps ; 24cm
Previous ed.: published as Notes for Joyce. New York: Dutton, 1967. — Includes index
ISBN 0-520-04189-5 : £20.00 B82-31095

823'.912 — Fiction in English. Joyce, James, *1882-1941.* **Local associations: Dublin**

Delaney, Frank. James Joyce's odyssey. — London : Hodder & Stoughton, Nov.1981. — [256]p
ISBN 0-340-26885-9 : £8.95 : CIP entry B81-31088

823'.912 — Fiction in English. Joyce, James, *1882-1941.* **Ulysses** — *Critical studies*

Cronin, John. Joyce's Ulysses : a capital idea an inaugural lecture delivered before the Queens University of Belfast on 20 October 1981 / J. Cronin. — [Belfast] : Queens University of Belfast, 1981. — 30p ; 21cm. — (New lecture series ; no.128)
ISBN 0-85389-204-0 (pbk) : £0.40 B82-21232

De Almeida, Hermione. Byron and Joyce through Homer : Don Juan and Ulysses / Hermione de Almeida. — London : Macmillan, 1981. — x,233p ; 23cm
Includes index
ISBN 0-333-30072-6 : £15.00
Primary classification 821'.7 B82-06643

Kenner, Hugh. Ulysses / Hugh Kenner. — London : Allen & Unwin, 1982. — 182p ; 22cm. — (Unwin critical library)
Originally published: 1980. — Bibliography: p174-179. — Includes index
ISBN 0-04-800008-6 (pbk) : Unpriced : CIP rev. B82-00279

Lawrence, Karen. The odyssey of style in Ulysses / Karen Lawrence. — Princeton, N.J. : Princeton University Press, c1981. — xi,229p ; 23cm
Bibliography: p211-223. — Includes index
ISBN 0-691-06487-3 : Unpriced B82-32702

823'.912 — Fiction in English. Lawrence, D. H. — *Biographies*

Carswell, Catherine. The savage pilgrimage : a narrative of D.H. Lawrence / by Catherine Carswell ; with a memoir of the author by John Carswell. — Cambridge : Cambridge Univeristy Press, 1981, c1982. — xlv,296p ; 23cm
Originally published: London : Chatto and Windus, 1932. — Includes index
ISBN 0-521-23975-3 (cased) : £17.50 : CIP rev. B81-30446

Neville, G. H.. A memoir of D.H. Lawrence : (The betrayal) / G.H. Neville ; edited by Carl Baron. — Cambridge : Cambridge University Press, 1981. — vii,208p,[4]p of plates : ill,ports ; 23cm
ISBN 0-521-24097-2 : £18.00 : CIP rev. B81-34664

823'.912 — Fiction in English. Lawrence, D. H. — *Correspondence, diaries, etc.*

Lawrence, D. H.. The letters of D.H. Lawrence. — Cambridge : Cambridge University Press, 1982. — (The Cambridge edition of the letters and works of D.H. Lawrence)
V.2: June 1913-October 1916 / edited by George J. Zytaruk and James T. Boulton. — Jan.1982. — xxv,691p : maps ; 23cm
Includes index
ISBN 0-521-23111-6 : £20.00 : CIP rev. B82-01331

823'.912 — Fiction in English. Lawrence, D. H. — *Critical studies*

A **D.H.** Lawrence handbook / Keith Sagar editor. — Manchester : Manchester University Press, c1982. — 454p : ill,maps ; 25cm
ISBN 0-7190-0780-1 : £25.00 : CIP rev. B81-31274

Holderness, Graham. D.H. Lawrence : history, ideology and fiction / Graham Holderness. — Dublin : Gill and Macmillan, 1982. — 248p ; 23cm
Bibliography: p241-246. — Includes index
ISBN 0-7171-1197-0 : £17.00 B82-31558

Salgādo, Gāmini. A preface to Lawrence. — London : Longman, Dec.1982. — [176]p. — (Preface books)
ISBN 0-582-35275-4 (cased) : £5.25 : CIP entry
ISBN 0-582-35276-2 (pbk) : £3.25 B82-30070

823'.912 — Fiction in English. Lawrence, D. H.. Kangaroo — *Critical studies*

Darroch, Robert. D.H. Lawrence in Australia. — Melbourne ; London : Macmillan, 1981. — xiii,130p : ill,facsims,ports ; 24cm
Includes index
ISBN 0-333-33760-3 : £14.95 B82-06693

823'.912 — Fiction in English. Lawrence, D. H. — *Personal observations — Collections*

D.H. Lawrence : interviews and recollections / edited by Norman Page. — London : Macmillan
Vol.1. — 1981. — xv,151p ; 23cm
ISBN 0-333-27081-9 : £15.00 B82-06630

D.H. Lawrence : interviews and recollections / edited by Norman Page. — London : Macmillan
Vol.2. — 1981. — viip,p153-304 ; 23cm
Includes index to vols. 1 and 2
ISBN 0-333-27082-7 : £15.00 B82-06631

823'.912 — Fiction in English. Lawrence, D. H. Special themes: Feminism — *Critical studies*

Simpson, Hilary. D.H. Lawrence and feminism. — London : Croom Helm, Oct.1982. — [160]p
ISBN 0-7099-2336-8 : £11.95 : CIP entry B82-23193

823'.912 — Fiction in English. Lawrence, D. H., *to 1914 — Personal observations*

E. T.. D.H. Lawrence : a personal record / by E.T.. — Cambridge : Cambridge University Press, c1980 (1981 [printing]). — 223p ; 20cm
Originally published: London : Cape, 1935
ISBN 0-521-29919-5 (pbk) : £5.25 : CIP rev.
B80-26245

823'.912 — Fiction in English. Lawrence, D. H.. Women in love — *Study outlines*

McEwan, Neil. Women in love : notes / by Neil McEwan. — Harlow : Longman, 1981. — 72p ; 21cm. — (York notes ; 143)
Bibliography: p66-67
ISBN 0-582-78281-3 (pbk) : £0.90 B82-16443

823'.912 — Fiction in English. Lawrence, Frieda — *Biographies*

Lawrence, Frieda. Not I but the wind. — London : Granada, Oct.1982. — [288]p
Originally published: New York : Viking Press, 1934 ; London : Heinemann, 1935
ISBN 0-246-11817-2 : £6.95 : CIP entry
B82-23469

823'.912 — Fiction in English. Lawrence, Frieda — *Correspondence, diaries, etc.*

Lawrence, Frieda. Frieda Lawrence and her circle : letters from, to and about Frieda Lawrence / edited by Harry T. Moore and Dale B. Montague. — London : Macmillan, 1981. — xiii,145p,[1]leaf of plate : 1port ; 23cm
Includes index
ISBN 0-333-27600-0 : £15.00 : CIP rev.
B80-22635

823'.912 — Fiction in English. Lehmann, Rosamond — *Biographies*

Lehmann, Rosamond. The swan in the evening. — Rev. ed. — London : Virago, Oct.1982. — [168]p
Previous ed.: London : Collins, 1967
ISBN 0-86068-299-4 (pbk) : £2.95 : CIP entry
B82-24148

823'.912 — Fiction in English. Maugham, W. Somerset — *Biographies*

Morgan, Ted. Somerset Maugham / Ted Morgan. — London : Triad, 1981, c1980. — 765p,[16]p of plates : ill,1facsim,ports ; 20cm
Originally published: London : Cape, 1980. — Includes index
ISBN 0-586-05356-5 (pbk) : £3.95 B82-04019

823'.912 — Fiction in English. O'Flaherty, Liam — *Biographies*

O'Flaherty, Liam. Share the devil. — Dublin : Wolfhound Press, July 1981. — [288]p
Originally published: London : Grayson & Grayson, 1934
ISBN 0-905473-64-7 : £8.00 : CIP entry
B81-24651

823'.912 — Fiction in English. Orwell, George — *Biographies*

Crick, Bernard. George Orwell : a life / Bernard Crick. — Rev. ed. — London : Secker & Warburg, 1981. — xxx,473p,[16]p of plates : ill,ports ; 24cm
Previous ed.: 1980. — Includes index
ISBN 0-436-11451-8 : £12.00 : CIP rev.
B81-23792

Crick, Bernard. George Orwell : a life / Bernard Crick. — Harmondsworth : Penguin, 1982, c1980. — 655p,[16]p of plates : ill,ports ; 20cm
Originally published: London : Secker & Warburg, 1980. — Includes index
ISBN 0-14-005856-7 (pbk) : £2.95 B82-30249

Fyvel, T. R.. George Orwell : a personal memoir / T.R. Fyvel. — London : Weidenfeld and Nicolson, 1982. — x,221p,[8]p of plates : ports ; 23cm
Includes index
ISBN 0-297-78012-3 : £9.95 B82-40526

823'.912 — Fiction in English. Orwell, George — *Critical studies*

George Orwell / edited by J.A. Jowitt & R.K.S. Taylor. — Bradford (10 Mornington Villas, Bradford BD8 7HB) : University of Leeds, Department of Adult Education & Extramural Studies, 1981. — 100p ; 21cm. — (Bradford Centre occasional papers, ISSN 0260-8952 ; no.3)
Unpriced (pbk) B82-11738

823'.912 — Fiction in English. Powell, Anthony, *1905- — Biographies*

Powell, Anthony, *1905-*. To keep the ball rolling : the memoirs of Anthony Powell. — London : Heinemann
Vol.1: The strangers are all gone. — 1982. — 208p,[16]p of plates : ill,ports ; 24cm
Includes index
ISBN 0-434-59941-7 : £9.50 B82-30654

823'.912 — Fiction in English. Powys, John Cowper — *Biographies*

Powys, John Cowper. Autobiography / John Cowper Powys ; with an introduction by J.B. Priestley. — London : Pan, 1982, c1967. — xxi,672p ; 20cm. — (Picador)
Reprint of: New ed. London : Macdonald, 1967. — Includes index
ISBN 0-330-25595-9 (pbk) : £3.50 B82-04254

823'.912 — Fiction in English. Richardson, Dorothy M.. Pilgrimage — *Critical studies*

Hanscombe, Gillian E.. The art of life : Dorothy Richardson and the development of feminist consciousness / Gillian E. Hanscombe. — London : Owen, 1982. — 200p ; 23cm
Bibliography: p187-200
ISBN 0-7206-0580-6 : £12.00 B82-40713

823'.912 — Fiction in English. Saki — *Biographies*

Langguth, A. J.. Saki : with six short stories never before collected / A.J. Langguth. — London : Hamilton, 1981. — 366p,[8]p of plates : ill,ports ; 23cm
Includes index
ISBN 0-241-10678-8 : £12.50 : CIP rev.
B81-24612

Langguth, A. J.. Saki : a life of Hector Hugh Munro. — Oxford : Oxford University Press, Oct.1982. — [366]p. — (Oxford paperbacks)
Originally published: London : Hamilton, 1981
ISBN 0-19-281362-5 (pbk) : £3.50 : CIP entry
B82-23668

823'.912 — Fiction in English. Sayers, Dorothy L. — *Biographies*

Hitchman, Janet. 'Such a strange lady' : an introduction to Dorothy L. Sayers (1893-1957) / Janet Hitchman. — London : New English Library, 1975 (1979 [printing]). — 203p : ill ; 18cm
ISBN 0-450-04477-7 (pbk) : £0.95 B82-12857

823'.912 — Fiction in English. Thirkell, Angela — *Critical studies — Serials*

Journal of the Angela Thirkell Society. — No.1 (1981)-. — Bailieborough, Co. Cavan (c/o Mrs. D. McFarlan, Stonewall, Bailieborough, Co. Cavan, Eire) : The Society, 1981-. — v. : maps ; 21cm
Annual
Free to Society members B82-31717

823'.912 — Fiction in English. Tolkien, J. R. R. — *Critical studies*

Shippey, T. A.. The road to middle-earth / by T.A. Shippey. — London : Allen & Unwin, 1982. — xii,252p ; 23cm
Bibliography: px-xii. — Includes index
ISBN 0-04-809018-2 : £9.95 : CIP rev.
B82-15647

823'.912 — Fiction in English. Tolkien, J. R. R.. Lord of the Rings — *Atlases*

Strachey, Barbara. Journeys of Frodo : an atlas of J.R.R. Tolkien's the Lord of the Rings / Barbara Strachey. — London : Allen & Unwin, 1981. — [108]p : maps ; 20x25cm
ISBN 0-04-912016-6 : £6.95 B82-19307

823'.912 — Fiction in English. Uttley, Alison — *Biographies*

Saintsbury, Elizabeth. The world of Alison Uttley : a biography : the life and times of one of the best loved country writers of our century / by Elizabeth Saintsbury. — London : Howard Baker, 1980. — 177p,[8]p of plates : ill,ports ; 22cm
Bibliography: p173. — List of works: p175-177
ISBN 0-7030-0179-5 : £5.95 B82-28505

823'.912 — Fiction in English. Waugh, Evelyn — *Biographies*

Waugh, Evelyn. A little learning. — 2nd ed. — London : Methuen, Jan.1983. — [248]p
Previous ed.: London : Sidgwick and Jackson, 1973
ISBN 0-413-51930-9 : £7.95 : CIP entry
B82-35219

823'.912 — Fiction in English. Waugh, Evelyn — *Critical studies*

Heath, Jeffrey. The picturesque prison : Evelyn Waugh and his writing / Jeffrey Heath. — London : Weidenfeld and Nicolson, c1982. — xviii,334p ; 24cm
Includes index
ISBN 0-297-78018-2 : £15.00 B82-31943

Littlewood, Ian. The writings of Evelyn Waugh. — Oxford : Blackwell, Oct.1982. — [256]p
ISBN 0-631-13211-2 : £12.50 : CIP entry
B82-23173

823'.912 — Fiction in English. Waugh, Evelyn. Decline and fall — *Study outlines*

McEwan, Neil. Decline and fall : notes / by Neil McEwan. — Harlow : Longman, 1982. — 72p ; 21cm. — (York notes ; 178)
Bibliography: p64-65
ISBN 0-582-79201-0 (pbk) : £0.90 B82-36749

823'.912 — Fiction in English. Welch, Denton — *Correspondence, diaries, etc.*

Welch, Denton. The journals of Denton Welch. — London : Allison & Busby, Sept.1982. — [268]p
ISBN 0-85031-480-1 (cased) : £7.95 : CIP entry
ISBN 0-85031-481-x (pbk) : £2.95 B82-18772

823'.912 — Fiction in English. Wells, H. G. — *Critical studies — Serials*

[The Wellsian *(1976)*]. The Wellsian : the journal of the H.G. Wells Society. — New ser. no.1 (1976)-. — [London] ([c/o Hon. General Secretary, H.G. Wells Centre, Dept. of Language & Literature, Polytechnic of North London , Prince of Wales Rd, NW5 3LB]) : The Society, 1976-. — v. ; 21cm
Annual. — Continues: Journal of the H. G. Wells Society. — Description based on: New ser. no.4 (Summer 1981)
ISSN 0263-1776 = Wellsian (1976) : Free to Society members only B82-18499

823'.912 — Fiction in English. Wheatley, Dennis — *Biographies*

Wheatley, Dennis. The time has come : the memoirs of Dennis Wheatley. — London : Arrow, 1981. — 741p,[16]p of plates : ill,ports ; 18cm
Contents: The young man said 1897-1914. Originally published: London : Hutchinson, c1977 — Officer and temporary gentleman 1914-1919. Originally published: London : Hutchinson, c1978 — Drink and ink 1919-1977. Originally published: London : Hutchinson, c1979
ISBN 0-09-926610-5 (pbk) : £2.95 B82-18363

823'.912 — Fiction in English. Wodehouse, P. G. *1939-1945 — Biographies*

Sproat, Iain. Wodehouse at war. — Large print ed. — Bath : Chivers, Nov.1982. — [304]p. — (A Lythway book)
Originally published: London : Milner, 1981
ISBN 0-85119-866-x : £7.20 : CIP entry
B82-26309

823'.912 — Fiction in English. Wodehouse, P. G. — *Critical studies*

P.G. Wodehouse : a centenary celebration, 1881-1981 / James H. Heinemann, Donald R. Bensen editors. — New York : Pierpont Morgan Library ; London : Oxford University Press, c1981. — xxi,197,36p of plates : ill,facsims,ports ; 31cm
Published to accompany an exhibition at the Pierpont Morgan Library, 1981. — Ill on lining papers. — Bibliography: p91-197
ISBN 0-19-520357-7 (cased) : £40.00
ISBN 0-87598-073-2 (pbk) : Unpriced B82-21467

Usborne, Richard. A Wodehouse companion / Richard Usborne. — London : Elm Tree Books, 1981. — 169p : ill,facsims,ports ; 25cm
ISBN 0-241-89955-9 : £12.50 : CIP rev. B81-26748

Wind, Herbert Warren. The world of P.G. Wodehouse / Herbert Warren Wind. — London : Hutchinson, 1981. — 92p,[1]leaf of plates : facsims,1port ; 23cm
Facsims. on lining papers. — Includes index
ISBN 0-09-145670-3 : £5.95 : CIP rev. B81-26769

823'.912 — Fiction in English. Wodehouse, P. G. Local associations

Murphy, N. T. P.. In search of Blandings / by N.T.P. Murphy. — Carshalton (193 Banstead Rd., Carshalton Beeches, Surrey) : N.T.P. Murphy, c1981. — 249p,[14]p of plates : ill,2maps,1port ; 18cm
Limited ed. of 500 numbered copies. — Includes index
£5.20 (pbk) B82-12480

823'.912 — Fiction in English. Woolf, Virginia. Alleged insanity

Poole, Roger. The unknown Virginia Woolf. — Brighton : Harvester Press, July 1981. — [304]p
Originally published: Cambridge : Cambridge University Press, 1978
ISBN 0-7108-0366-4 (pbk) : £5.50 : CIP entry B81-18174

Trombley, Stephen. 'All that summer she was mad' : Virginia Woolf and her doctors. — London : Junction Books, Oct.1981. — [352]p
ISBN 0-86245-039-x : £12.50 : CIP entry B81-30265

823'.912 — Fiction in English. Woolf, Virginia — *Biographies*

Bell, Quentin. Virginia Woolf. — London : Hogarth, Jan.1982. — [560]p
Originally published: 1972
ISBN 0-7012-0461-3 : £12.50 : CIP entry B81-34298

823'.912 — Fiction in English. Woolf, Virginia — *Correspondence, diaries, etc.*

Woolf, Virginia. The diary of Virginia Woolf. — Harmondsworth : Penguin
Vol.3: 1925-30 / edited by Anne Olivier Bell. — 1982, c1980. — xiii,384p : 2maps ; 20cm
Originally published: London : Hogarth, 1980. — Includes index
ISBN 0-14-005284-4 (pbk) : £3.95 B82-41150

Woolf, Virginia. The diary of Virginia Woolf / edited by Anne Olivier Bell ; assisted by Andrew McNeillie. — London : Hogarth
Vol.4: 1931-1935. — 1982. — xiii,402p : maps ; 24cm
Maps on lining papers. — Includes index
ISBN 0-7012-0467-2 : £15.00 : CIP rev. B81-34299

Woolf, Virginia. Leave the letters till we're dead : the letters of Virginia Woolf / editor Nigel Nicolson ; assistant editor Joanne Trautmann. — London : Hogarth, 1980. — xviii,556p : 1facsim,1port ; 24cm. — (The Letters of Virginia Woolf ; v.6, 1936-1941)
Includes index
ISBN 0-7012-0470-2 : £15.00 : CIP rev. B80-18066

Woolf, Virginia. The letters of Virginia Woolf. — London : Chatto & Windus. — (A Chatto & Windus paperback ; CWP63)
Vol.4: 1929-1931. A reflection of the other person. — Oct.1981. — [464]p
Originally published: London : Hogart, 1978
ISBN 0-7011-2597-7 (pbk) : £4.50 : CIP entry B81-27928

Woolf, Virginia. The letters of Virginia Woolf. — London : Chatto & Windus, Sept.1982
Originally published: 1979
Vol.5: 1932-1935. The sickle side of the moon. — [496]p
ISBN 0-7011-2598-5 (pbk) : £5.95 : CIP entry B82-20296

823'.912 — Fiction in English. Woolf, Virginia — *Feminist viewpoints*

New feminist essays on Virginia Woolf / edited by Jane Marcus. — London : Macmillan, 1981. — xx,272p ; 23cm
Includes index
ISBN 0-333-28997-8 : £15.00 B82-10808

823'.912 — Fiction in English. Woolf, Virginia. To the lighthouse — *Study outlines*

Grove-White, Elizabeth. To the lighthouse : notes / by Elizabeth Grove-White. — Harlow : Longman, 1982. — 72p ; 21cm. — (York notes ; 162)
Bibliography: p68-69
ISBN 0-582-79208-8 (pbk) : £0.90 B82-16444

823'.912 — Fiction in English. Yates, Dornford — *Biographies*

Smithers, A. J.. Dornford Yates : a biography / A.J. Smithers. — London : Hodder and Stoughton, 1982. — x,240p,[8p] of plates : ill,facsims,ports,1geneal.table ; 23cm
Includes index
ISBN 0-340-27547-2 : £8.95 : CIP rev. B81-36363

823'.912 — Literature. Criticism — *Study examples: Children's stories in English. Milne, A. A.. Winnie-the-Pooh & House at Pooh Corner — Humour*

Crews, Frederick C.. The Pooh perplex : a student casebook : in which it is discovered that the true meaning of the Pooh stories is not as simple as is usually believed ... / Frederick C. Crews. — Milton Keynes : Robin Clark, 1979, c1963. — x,150p : ill ; 18cm
Originally published: London : Arthur Barker, 1964
ISBN 0-86072-026-8 (pbk) : £1.25 B82-00086

823'.912[F] — Fiction in English, *1900-1945 — Texts*

Allardyce, Paula. Southarn Folly. — Large print ed. — Anstey : Ulverscroft, Aug.1982. — [400] p. — (Ulverscroft large print series)
Originally published: London : Ward Lock, 1957
ISBN 0-7089-0831-4 : £5.00 : CIP entry B82-26675

Ambler, Eric. The care of time. — Large print ed. — Anstey : Ulverscroft, Aug.1982. — [512] p. — (Ulverscroft large print series)
Originally published: London : Weidenfeld and Nicolson, 1981
ISBN 0-7089-0828-4 : £5.00 : CIP entry B82-27172

Ambler, Eric. Dirty story : a further account of the life and adventures of Arthur Abdel Simpson / Eric Ambler. — [London] : Fontana, 1969, c1967 (1982 [printing]). — 191p ; 18cm
Originally published: London : Bodley Head, 1967
ISBN 0-00-616481-1 (pbk) : £1.35 B82-13642

Ashton, Helen. Return to Cheltenham / by Helen Ashton. — London : Remploy, 1979, c1958. — 254p ; 22cm
Originally published: London : Collins, 1958
ISBN 0-7066-0844-5 : £4.70 B82-13690

Audemars, Pierre. The bitter path of death / by Pierre Audemars. — London : Hale, 1982. — 175p ; 20cm
ISBN 0-7091-9909-0 : £6.75 B82-35868

Audemars, Pierre. Now dead is any man / by Pierre Audemars. — Long Preston : Magna, 1982, c1978. — 291p ; 23cm
Originally published: London : Long, 1978. — Published in large print
ISBN 0-86009-404-9 : Unpriced : CIP rev. B82-10231

Ayres, Ruby M.. Dark gentleman / Ruby M. Ayres. — Bath : Chivers, 1982. — 244p ; 23cm. — (A Lythway book)
Originally published: London : Hodder & Stoughton, 1953. — Large print
ISBN 0-85046-347-5 : Unpriced B82-37259

Ayres, Ruby M.. Love's challenge / Ruby M. Ayres. — London : Severn House, 1982, c1973. — 157p ; 21cm
ISBN 0-7278-0794-3 : £5.95 B82-30461

Ayres, Ruby M.. Missing the tide / Ruby M. Ayres. — Large print ed. — Bath : Chivers Press, 1982. — 207p ; 23cm. — (A Seymour book)
Originally published: London : Hodder and Stoughton, 1948
ISBN 0-85119-452-4 : Unpriced : CIP rev. B81-36050

Ayres, Ruby M.. Return journey / Ruby M. Ayres. — Large print ed. — Bath : Chivers, 1982. — 327p ; 23cm. — (A Lythway book)
ISBN 0-85119-832-5 : Unpriced : CIP rev. B82-15864

Ayres, Ruby M.. Wallflower / Ruby M. Ayres. — London : Severn House, 1982, c1966. — 189p ; 21cm
Originally published: London : Hodder & Stoughton, 1966
ISBN 0-7278-0748-x : £5.95 : CIP rev. B81-30589

Ayres, Ruby Mildred. One summer. — Large print ed. — Bath : Chivers, Feb.1983. — [272] p. — (A Lythway book)
ISBN 0-85119-892-9 : £7.20 : CIP entry B82-39580

Bailey, H. C.. Call Mr. Fortune / by H.C. Bailey. — London : Remploy, 1979. — v,279p ; 20cm
ISBN 0-7066-0849-6 : £4.60 B82-00658

Baker, Denys Val. Summer at the Mill / Denys Val Baker. — London : Kimber, 1982. — 207p ; 23cm
ISBN 0-7183-0478-0 : £5.95 B82-25992

Bates, H. E.. The jacaranda tree / H.E. Bates. — Large print ed. — Bath : Chivers Press, 1974, c1961 (1982 [printing]). — 386p ; 23cm. — (A New Portway large print book)
ISBN 0-85997-033-7 : Unpriced B82-12520

Bates, H. E.. Love for Lydia / H.E. Bates. — Bath : Chivers, 1976 (1981 [printing]). — 587p ; 23cm. — (A New Portway large print book)
Originally published: London : Joseph, 1952
ISBN 0-85997-144-9 : Unpriced B82-11615

Bates, H. E.. The purple plain / H.E. Bates. — Bath : Chivers, 1975 (1981 [printing]). — 453p ; 23cm. — (A New Portway large print book)
Originally published: London : Joseph, 1947
ISBN 0-85997-139-2 : Unpriced B82-11614

Beckett, Samuel. Company / Samuel Beckett. — London : Calder, 1980. — 89p ; 21
ISBN 0-7145-3806-x (cased) : £5.50 : CIP rev.
ISBN 0-7145-3857-4 (pbk) : £2.95 B80-06562

Bell, Josephine. The innocent. — London : Hodder and Stoughton, Jan.1983. — [224]p
ISBN 0-340-32014-1 : £6.95 : CIP entry B82-33750

Bennett, Arnold. A great man : a frolic / Arnold Bennett. — London : Remploy, 1979. — viii,240p ; 20cm
ISBN 0-7066-0821-6 : £4.30 B82-00656

823'.912[F] — Fiction in English, *1900-1945* — *Texts* *continuation*

Bennett, Arnold. The grim smile of the five towns / Arnold Bennett. — Harmondsworth : Penguin, 1946 (1982 [printing]). — 191p ; 19cm. — (Penguin modern classics)
ISBN 0-14-000519-6 (pbk) : £1.25 B82-33533

Bennett, Arnold. The pretty lady : a novel / by Arnold Bennett ; with a preface by Frank Swinnerton. — London : Remploy, 1980. — 344p ; 20cm
ISBN 0-7066-0822-4 : £5.00 B82-09347

Blake, Nicholas. The worm of death / Nicholas Blake. — Large print ed. — Leicester : Ulverscroft, 1982, c1961. — 392p ; 23cm. — (Ulverscroft large print series)
Originally published: London : Collins, 1961
ISBN 0-7089-0772-5 : Unpriced : CIP rev. B82-08084

Blake, Nicholas, *1904-1972*. A question of proof : a famous first : the first Nigel Strangeways novel / Nicholas Blake. — London : Collins,, 1981, c1935. — 223p ; 21cm. — (The Crime Club)
ISBN 0-00-231651-x : £6.50 B82-08519

Bloom, Ursula. The abiding city. — Bath : Chivers, Nov.1982. — [192]p. — (Firecrest books)
Originally published: London : Hutchinson, 1958
ISBN 0-85997-500-2 : £5.95 : CIP entry B82-26332

Bloom, Ursula. The beauty surgeon / Ursula Bloom as Sheila Burns. — Bath : Chivers, 1982, c1967. — 230p ; 23cm. — (A Lythway romance)
Originally published: London : Hale, 1967
ISBN 0-85119-805-8 : Unpriced : CIP rev. B82-07009

Bloom, Ursula. The dandelion clock / Ursula Bloom. — Large print ed. — Bath : Chivers Press, 1982, c1966. — 209p ; 23cm. — (A Seymour book)
Originally published: London : Hutchinson, 1966
ISBN 0-85119-453-2 : Unpriced : CIP rev. B81-36049

Bloom, Ursula. Doctor called Harry / Ursula Bloom as Rachel Harvey. — Large print ed. — Bath : Chivers, 1982, c1971. — 232p ; 23cm. — (A Lythway book)
Originally published: London : Hale, 1971
ISBN 0-85119-789-2 : Unpriced : CIP rev. B82-01437

Bloom, Ursula. The doctor who fell in love / Ursula Bloom as Rachel Harvey. — Large print ed. — Bath : Chivers, 1981, c1974. — 204p ; 23cm. — (A Lythway book)
Originally published: London : Hale, 1974
ISBN 0-85119-749-3 : Unpriced : CIP rev. B81-25807

Bloom, Ursula. A doctor's love / Ursula Bloom as Mary Essex. — Large print ed. — Bath : Chivers, 1982, c1974. — 213p ; 23cm. — (A Lythway book) (A Lythway romance)
Originally published: London : Hale, 1974
ISBN 0-85119-774-4 : Unpriced : CIP rev. B81-33809

Bloom, Ursula. Façade / Ursula Bloom. — Bath : Chivers, 1982. — 339p ; 23cm. — (A Lythway book)
Originally published: London : Macdonald, 1948. — Large print
ISBN 0-85046-403-x : Unpriced B82-37258

Bloom, Ursula. The flight of the falcon. — Large print ed. — Bath : Chivers, Oct.1982. — [304] p. — (A Lythway book)
Originally published: London : Hutchinson, 1969
ISBN 0-85119-851-1 : £7.50 : CIP entry B82-20520

Bloom, Ursula. The love story of Nurse Julie / Ursula Bloom as Rachel Harvey. — Large print ed. — Bath : Chivers, 1982, c1975. — 234p ; 23cm. — (A Lythway book)
Originally published: London : Hale, 1975
ISBN 0-85119-813-9 : Unpriced : CIP rev. B82-09856

Bloom, Ursula. Matthew, Mark, Luke and John. — Large print ed. — Bath : Chivers, Feb.1983. — [320]p. — (A Lythway book)
Originally published: London : Hutchinson, 1954
ISBN 0-85119-894-5 : £7.50 : CIP entry B82-39583

Bloom, Ursula. A nurse called Liza / Ursula Bloom as Mary Essex. — Large print ed. — Bath : Chivers, 1982, c1973. — 221p ; 23cm. — (A Lythway romance)
Originally published: London : Hale, 1973
ISBN 0-85119-798-1 : Unpriced : CIP rev. B82-05005

Bloom, Ursula. The old elm tree / Ursula Bloom. — Bath : Chivers, 1982, c1974. — 188p ; 23cm. — (A Lythway book)
Originally published: London : Hutchinson, 1974
ISBN 0-85119-823-6 : Unpriced : CIP rev. B82-13096

Bloom, Ursula. The passionate heart / Ursula Bloom. — Bath : Chivers, 1973 (1982 [printing]). — 464p ; 23cm. — (A Lythway book)
Published in large print
ISBN 0-85046-361-0 : Unpriced B82-40514

Bloom, Ursula. Perchance to dream. — Large print ed. — Bath : Chivers, Dec.1982. — [264] p. — (A Lythway book)
Originally published: London : Hutchinson, 1971
ISBN 0-85119-868-6 : £7.20 : CIP entry B82-30242

Bloom, Ursula. Prelude to yesterday. — Large print ed. — Bath : Chivers, Nov.1982. — [296] p. — (A Lythway book)
Originally published: London : Hutchinson, 1961
ISBN 0-85119-859-7 : £7.20 : CIP entry B82-26437

Bloom, Ursula. Surgeon at sea / Ursula Bloom as Sheila Burns. — Large print ed. — Bath : Chivers, 1981, c1969. — 269p ; 23cm. — (A Lythway book)
Originally published: London : Hale, 1969
ISBN 0-85119-748-5 : Unpriced : CIP rev. B81-25806

Border, Rosemary. Goodbye to Berlin / Christopher Isherwood ; adapted by Rosemary Border. — Oxford : Oxford University Press, c1980. — 94p ; 18cm. — (Alpha general fiction)
ISBN 0-19-424189-0 (pbk) : £0.75 B82-32720

Bowen, Elizabeth. Eva Trout, or, Changing scenes / Elizabeth Bowen. — Harmondsworth : Penguin, 1982, c1968. — 267p ; 20cm
Originally published: London : Cape, 1969
ISBN 0-14-005648-3 (pbk) : £2.50 B82-35613

Bowen, Elizabeth. Friends and relations / Elizabeth Bowen. — Harmondsworth : Penguin, 1943 (1982 [printing]). — 159p ; 20cm. — (Penguin modern classics)
ISBN 0-14-000398-3 (pbk) : £1.95 B82-29609

Bowen, Elizabeth. The heat of the day / Elizabeth Bowen. — London : Cape, 1949 (1982 [printing]). — 284p ; 21cm
ISBN 0-224-60055-9 : £7.50 : CIP rev. B82-08441

Bowen, Elizabeth. The hotel / Elizabeth Bowen. — London : Cape, 1981. — 199p ; 21cm
ISBN 0-224-60057-5 : £6.95 : CIP rev. B81-28840

Bowen, Elizabeth. The house in Paris / Elizabeth Bowen. — London : Cape, 1982. — 212p ; 21cm
ISBN 0-224-60056-7 : £7.50 : CIP rev. B82-08442

Bowen, Elizabeth. The last September / Elizabeth Bowen. — Harmondsworth : Penguin, 1942 (1982 [printing]). — 206p ; 20cm. — (Penguin modern classics)
ISBN 0-14-000372-x (pbk) : £1.95 B82-22311

Bowen, Elizabeth. A world of love / Elizabeth Bowen. — London : Cape, 1981. — 149p ; 21cm
Originally published: 1955
ISBN 0-224-60051-6 : £6.95 : CIP rev. B81-30323

Brand, Christianna. Green for danger / Christianna Brand. — Feltham : Hamlyn, 1982, c1945. — 159p ; 18cm. — (A Hamlyn whodunnit)
Originally published: London : John Lane, 1945
ISBN 0-600-20380-8 (pbk) : £1.10 B82-11328

Brand, Christianna. The rose in darkness / Christianna Brand. — Large print ed. — Bath : Chivers, 1982, c1979. — 416p ; 23cm. — (Atlantic large print)
Originally published: London : Joseph, 1979
ISBN 0-85119-471-0 (pbk) : Unpriced : CIP rev. B82-07624

Bruce, Leo. Case for Sergeant Beef. — Large print ed. — Anstey : Ulverscroft, Sept.1982. — [320]p. — (Ulverscroft large print series)
Originally published: London : Nicolson and Watson, 1947
ISBN 0-7089-0842-x : £5.00 : CIP entry B82-27173

Bruce, Leo. Neck and neck. — Large print ed. — Anstey : Ulverscroft, Jan.1983. — [368]p. — (Ulverscroft large print series)
Originally published: London : Gollancz, 1951
ISBN 0-7089-0898-5 : £6.25 : CIP entry B82-32526

Buchan, John. The free fishers. — London : Severn House, Dec.1982. — [224]p
Originally published: Feltham : Hamlyn, 1982
ISBN 0-7278-0852-4 : £6.95 : CIP entry B82-34074

Buchan, John, *1875-1940*. The courts of the morning / John Buchan. — Bampton : Three Rivers Books, 1982. — 405p : maps ; 23cm
ISBN 0-907951-01-5 : £6.95 B82-37297

Buchan, John, *1875-1940*. The dancing floor / John Buchan. — Bampton : Three Rivers Books, 1982. — 311p : 1map ; 23cm
ISBN 0-907951-02-3 : £6.95 B82-37298

Buchan, John, *1875-1940*. The free fishers / John Buchan. — Feltham : Hamlyn, 1982. — 224p ; 18cm
ISBN 0-600-20566-5 (pbk) : £1.50 B82-16816

Buchan, John, *1875-1940*. Huntingtower / John Buchan. — Feltham : Hamlyn, 1982. — 204p ; 18cm
ISBN 0-600-20562-2 (pbk) : £1.50 B82-16817

Buchan, John, *1875-1940*. Midwinter : certain travellers in old England / John Buchan. — London : Hamlyn Paperbacks, 1981. — 196p ; 18cm
ISBN 0-600-20563-0 (pbk) : £1.50 B82-00647

Burns, Sheila. The dark-eyed sister / Ursula Bloom as Sheila Burns. — Large print ed. — Bath : Chivers, 1982, c1968. — 239p ; 23cm. — (A Lythway book)
Originally published: London : Hale, 1968
ISBN 0-85119-782-5 : Unpriced : CIP rev. B81-35864

823'.912[F] — Fiction in English, *1900-1945 — Texts* *continuation*

Burns, Sheila. Doctor delightful. — Large print ed. — Bath : Chivers, Jan.1983. — [256]p. — (A Lythway book)
Originally published: London : Hale, 1964
ISBN 0-85119-882-1 : £6.90 : CIP entry
B82-33096

Burns, Sheila. A surgeon's sweetheart / Ursula Bloom as Sheila Burns. — Large print ed. — Bath : Chivers, 1981, c1966. — 251p ; 23cm. — (A Lythway book)
Originally published: London : Hale, 1966
ISBN 0-85119-765-5 : Unpriced : CIP rev.
B81-31796

Butler, William Vivian. Gideon's law. — London : Hodder & Stoughton, Mar.1982. — [192]p. — (Coronet books)
Originally published: 1981
ISBN 0-340-25065-8 (pbk) : £1.25 : CIP entry
B82-01836

Cadell, Elizabeth. Canary yellow. — Large print ed. — Anstey : Ulverscroft, Oct.1982. — [368] p. — (Ulverscroft large print series)
Originally published: London : Hodder & Stoughton, 1965
ISBN 0-7089-0859-4 : £5.00 : CIP entry
B82-26680

Cadell, Elizabeth. The fox from his lair / by Elizabeth Cadell. — London : Remploy, 1981, c1965. — 186 : ill ; 19cm
Originally published: London : Hodder & Stoughton, 1965
ISBN 0-7066-0918-2 : £5.20 B82-16859

Cadell, Elizabeth. A lion in the way / Elizabeth Cadell. — London : Hodder and Stoughton, 1982. — 351p ; 21cm
ISBN 0-340-26484-5 : £7.50 : CIP rev.
B82-07435

Cadell, Elizabeth. River Lodge / by Elizabeth Cadell. — London : Hale, 1948, c1978 (1982 [printing]). — 223p ; 21cm
ISBN 0-7091-6677-x : £5.50 B82-01513

Cadell, Elizabeth. River Lodge. — Large print ed. — Anstey : Ulverscroft, Jan.1983. — [384] p. — (Ulverscroft large print series)
Originally published: London : Hale, 1948
ISBN 0-7089-0899-3 : £6.25 : CIP entry
B82-32527

Canning, Victor. Birdcage. — Large print ed. — Anstey : Ulverscroft, Sept.1982. — [416]p. — (Ulverscroft large print series)
Originally published: London : Heinemann, 1978
ISBN 0-7089-0850-0 : £5.00 : CIP entry
B82-27180

Canning, Victor. Fall from grace / Victor Canning. — Large print ed. — Leicester : Ulverscroft, 1982, c1980. — 396p ; 22cm. — (Ulverscroft Large print series)
Originally published: London : Heinemann, 1980
ISBN 0-7089-0754-7 : £5.00 : CIP rev.
B81-36936

Canning, Victor. The Satan sampler / Victor Canning. — Large print ed. — Bath : Chivers, 1982, c1979. — 349p ; 23cm. — (A New Portway large print book)
Originally published: London : Heinemann, 1979
ISBN 0-85119-157-6 : Unpriced : CIP rev.
B82-01445

Carr, Philippa. The adulteress / Philippa Carr. — London : Collins, 1982. — 347p : 1geneal.table ; 22cm. — (Daughters of England ; 9)
ISBN 0-00-222611-1 : £7.50 : CIP rev.
B82-03701

Carr, Philippa. The drop of the dice. — Large print ed. — Anstey : Ulverscroft, Aug.1982. — [512]p. — (Ulverscroft large print series)
Originally published: London : Collins, 1981
ISBN 0-7089-0832-2 : £5.00 : CIP entry
B82-26676

Carr, Philippa. Lament for a lost lover / Philippa Carr. — [London] : Fontana, 1978, c1977 (1982 [printing]). — 318p : 1geneal.table ; 18cm
Originally published: London : Collins, 1977
ISBN 0-00-616479-x (pbk) : £1.50 B82-13652

Carr, Philippa. Saraband for two sisters / Philippa Carr. — London : Fontana, 1977 (1982 [printing]). — 351p : ill ; 18cm
Originally published: London : Collins, 1976
ISBN 0-00-616544-3 (pbk) : £1.65 B82-19741

Cartland, Barbara. [After the night]. Towards the stars / by Barbara Cartland. — Long Preston : Magna, 1981, c1971. — 455p ; 23cm
Originally published: London : Hutchinson, 1945. — Published in large print
ISBN 0-86009-323-9 : Unpriced : CIP rev.
B81-27387

Cartland, Barbara. An angel in hell / Barbara Cartland. — London : Severn House, 1981, c1976. — 170p ; 21cm
Originally published: London : Pan, 1976
ISBN 0-7278-0722-6 : 5.95 : CIP rev.
B81-23815

Cartland, Barbara. The call of the Highlands / Barbara Cartland. — London : Hutchinson, 1982. — 165p ; 21cm
ISBN 0-09-149700-0 : £6.95 : CIP rev.
B82-16477

Cartland, Barbara. Caught by love / Barbara Cartland. — London : Arrow, 1982. — 160p ; 18cm
ISBN 0-09-928480-4 (pbk) : £1.00 B82-33317

Cartland, Barbara. The explosion of love / by Barbara Cartland. — Long Preston : Magna, 1982, c1980. — 297p ; 22cm
Originally published: London : Hutchinson, 1980. — Published in large print
ISBN 0-86009-394-8 : Unpriced : CIP rev.
B82-07044

Cartland, Barbara. For all eternity / Barbara Cartland. — London : Corgi, 1982. — 155p ; 18cm
ISBN 0-552-12009-x (pbk) : £1.00 B82-37555

Cartland, Barbara. The frightened bride / by Barbara Cartland. — Long Preston : Magna Print, 1982, c1975. — 315p ; 22cm
Originally published: London : Pan, 1975. — Published in large print
ISBN 0-86009-368-9 : Unpriced : CIP rev.
B81-33769

Cartland, Barbara. A gamble with hearts / by Barbara Cartland. — Long Preston : Magna, 1981, c1975. — 325p ; 22cm
Originally published: London : Pan, 1975. — Published in large print
ISBN 0-86009-363-8 : Unpriced : CIP rev.
B81-31818

Cartland, Barbara. The golden gondola / by Barbara Cartland. — Bolton-by-Bowland : Magna, 1980, c1958. — 453p ; 23cm
Originally published: London : Hutchinson, 1958. — Published in large print
ISBN 0-86009-231-3 : £5.25 : CIP rev.
B79-36494

Cartland, Barbara. In the arms of love / Barbara Cartland. — London : Hutchinson, 1981. — 153p ; 21cm
ISBN 0-09-146410-2 : £5.95 : CIP rev.
B81-28768

Cartland, Barbara. The incrediable honeymoon. — London : Severn House, Sept.1982. — [176]p
Originally published: London : Pan, 1976
ISBN 0-7278-0799-4 : £6.50 : CIP entry
B82-23864

Cartland, Barbara. The kiss of life. — London : Hutchinson, May 1981. — [160]p
ISBN 0-09-143770-9 : £5.50 : CIP entry
B81-04233

Cartland, Barbara. Kneel for mercy / Barbara Cartland. — Sevenoaks : New English Library, 1982. — 159p ; 23cm
ISBN 0-450-04915-9 : £5.95 B82-36262

Cartland, Barbara. Looking for love. — London : Hutchinson, May 1982. — [208]p
ISBN 0-09-147780-8 : £6.95 : CIP entry
B82-07964

Cartland, Barbara. Love and the marquis / Barbara Cartland. — London : Pan, 1982. — 143p ; 18cm
ISBN 0-330-26840-6 (pbk) : £0.95 B82-34258

Cartland, Barbara. Love leaves at midnight / Barbara Cartland. — London : Arrow, 1980, c1978 (1982 [printing]). — 171p ; 18cm
Originally published: London : Hutchinson, 1978
ISBN 0-09-922710-x (pbk) : £1.00 B82-17436

Cartland, Barbara. Love rules / Barbara Cartland. — London : New English Library, 1982. — 158p ; 23cm
ISBN 0-450-04896-9 : £5.95 : CIP rev.
B82-01979

Cartland, Barbara. Love rules. — London : New English Library, Oct.1982. — [160]p
ISBN 0-450-05500-0 (pbk) : £1.25 : CIP entry
B82-24723

Cartland, Barbara. Love to the rescue. — Large print ed. — Long Preston : Magna, Jan.1983. — [400]p
Originally published: London : Hutchinson, 1967
ISBN 0-86009-484-7 : £5.75 : CIP entry
B82-33217

Cartland, Barbara. Lucifer and the angel / Barbara Cartland. — London : Arrow, 1982, c1980. — 151p ; 18cm
Originally published: London : Hutchinson, 1980
ISBN 0-09-928120-1 (pbk) : £1.00 B82-30453

Cartland, Barbara. Lucky in love / Barbara Cartland. — London : Pan, 1982. — 156p ; 18cm
ISBN 0-330-26735-3 (pbk) : £0.95 B82-18118

Cartland, Barbara. Moments of love / Barbara Cartland. — London : Pan, 1982. — 142p ; 18cm
ISBN 0-330-26724-8 (pbk) : £0.95 B82-18117

Cartland, Barbara. The naked battle / Barbara Cartland. — London : Arrow, 1979, c1978 (1982 [printing]). — 158p ; 18cm
Originally published: London : Hutchinson, 1978
ISBN 0-09-920970-5 (pbk) : £1.00 B82-17437

Cartland, Barbara. The naked battle / by Barbara Cartland. — Long Preston : Magna, 1982, c1978. — 281p ; 23cm
Originally published: London : Hutchinson, 1978. — Published in large print
ISBN 0-86009-380-8 : Unpriced : CIP rev.
B82-00357

Cartland, Barbara. A portrait of love / Barbara Cartland. — [London] : Corgi, 1982. — 154p ; 17cm
ISBN 0-552-11876-1 (pbk) : £0.95 B82-12596

823′.912[F] — Fiction in English, ***1900-1945 — Texts*** *continuation*

Cartland, Barbara. Power and the prince. — London : Severn House, Dec.1982. — [160]p
ISBN 0-7278-0831-1 : £6.50 : CIP entry B82-34080

Cartland, Barbara. Pure and untouched : Barbara Cartland. — London : Arrow, 1981. — 170p ; 18cm
ISBN 0-09-926720-9 (pbk) : £1.00 B82-03538

Cartland, Barbara. The secret fear / by Barbara Cartland. — Long Preston : Magna Print, 1982, c1970. — 421p ; 22cm
Originally published: London : Hutchinson, 1970. — Published in large print
ISBN 0-86009-416-2 : Unpriced : CIP rev. B82-10233

Cartland, Barbara. A shaft of sunlight / Barbara Cartland. — London : Corgi, 1982. — 157p ; 18cm
ISBN 0-552-11930-x (pbk) : £0.95 B82-23904

Cartland, Barbara. The unknown heart. — Large print ed. — Long Preston : Magna Print, Nov.1982. — [400]p
Originally published: London : Hutchinson, 1969
ISBN 0-86009-440-5 : £5.50 : CIP entry B82-26341

Cartland, Barbara. The wild cry of love / Barbara Cartland. — London : Severn House, 1982, c1976. — 173p ; 21cm
Originally published: London : Pan, 1976
ISBN 0-7278-0761-7 : £5.95 B82-31421

Cartland, Barbara. Winged magic / Barbara Cartland. — London : Corgi, 1981. — 150p ; 18cm
ISBN 0-552-11840-0 (pbk) : £0.95 B82-06470

Cartland, Barbara. Winged victory / Barbara Cartland. — London : Pan, 1982. — 143p ; 18cm
ISBN 0-330-26806-6 (pbk) : £0.95 B82-34259

Cartland, Barbara. The wings of love. — Large print ed. — Long Preston : Magna Print, Sept.1982. — [412]p
Originally published: London : Hutchinson, 1962
ISBN 0-86009-425-1 : £5.50 : CIP entry B82-20854

Cary, Joyce. The horse′s mouth / Joyce Cary. — Harmondsworth : Penguin, 1948, c1944 (1982 [printing]). — 374p ; 20cm. — (Penguin modern classics)
ISBN 0-14-000648-6 (pbk) : £2.95 B82-40672

Charteris, Leslie. Count on the Saint. — London : Hodder & Stoughton, Oct.1981. — [176]p. — (Coronet books)
Originally published: 1980
ISBN 0-340-27105-1 (pbk) : £1.25 : CIP entry B81-26725

Charteris, Leslie. The Saint abroad / by Leslie Charteris. — Large print ed. — Long Preston : Magna, 1982, c1969. — 328p ; 23cm
Originally published: New York : Doubleday, 1969 ; London : Hodder & Stoughton, 1970. — Published in large print
ISBN 0-86009-406-5 : Unpriced : CIP rev. B82-10234

Chase, James Hadley. Hand me a fig-leaf / James Hadley Chase. — London : Hale, 1981. — 174p ; 23cm
ISBN 0-7091-8927-3 : £6.50 B82-03175

Chase, James Hadley. Have a nice night / James Hadley Chase. — London : Hale, 1982. — 176p ; 23cm
ISBN 0-7091-9397-1 : £6.95 B82-13849

Chase, James Hadley. More deadly than the male / James Hadley Chase. — [London] : Corgi, 1982, c1981. — 238p ; 18cm
Originally published: London : Hale, 1981
ISBN 0-552-11915-6 (pbk) : £0.95 B82-19462

Chase, James Hadley. Try this one for size / James Hadley Chase. — [London] : Corgi, 1981, c1980. — 168p ; 18cm
Originally published: London : Hale, 1980
ISBN 0-552-11817-6 (pbk) : £0.95 B82-03227

Chesterton, G. K.. The Napoleon of Notting Hill / G.K. Chesterton. — Harmondsworth : Penguin, 1946 (1982 [printing]). — 158p ; 18cm
ISBN 0-14-000550-1 (pbk) : £1.25 B82-25564

Christie, Agatha. Death in the clouds / Agatha Christie. — London : Pan in association with Collins, 1964, c1935 (1981 printing). — 188p ; 18cm
ISBN 0-330-26562-8 (pbk) : £1.00 B82-06412

Christie, Agatha. Death in the clouds / Agatha Christie. — London : Published for the Crime Club by Collins, 1981, c1935. — 256p : 1plan ; 21cm
ISBN 0-00-231187-9 : £6.25 B82-02784

Christie, Agatha. Evil under the sun / Agatha Christie. — London : Collins, 1957, c1941 (1982 [printing]). — 189p ; 18cm
ISBN 0-00-616598-2 (pbk) : £1.25 B82-19729

Christie, Agatha. Five little pigs : a Hercule Poirot mystery / Agatha Christie. — Large print ed. — Leicester : Ulverscroft, 1982, c1970. — 315p ; 23cm. — (Ulverscroft large print)
ISBN 0-7089-0814-4 : Unpriced : CIP rev. B82-15967

Christie, Agatha. The Hollow / Agatha Christie. — [London] : Fontana, 1955, c1946 (1982 [printing]). — 189p ; 18cm
Originally published: London : Collins, 1946
ISBN 0-00-616551-6 (pbk) : £1.25 B82-25436

Christie, Agatha. Lord Edgware dies / Agatha Christie. — [London] : Fontana, 1954, c1933 (1982 [printing]). — 192p ; 18cm
ISBN 0-00-616539-7 (pbk) : £1.25 B82-16826

Christie, Agatha. Murder in Mesopotamia / Agatha Christie. — London : Published for the Crime Club by Collins, 1981. — 284p ; 21cm. — (The Crime Club)
ISBN 0-00-231487-8 : £6.25 B82-11390

Christie, Agatha. A murder is announced / Agatha Christie. — [London] : Fontana, 1953 (1982 [printing]). — 221p ; 18cm
Originally published: London : Collins, 1950
ISBN 0-00-616528-1 (pbk) : £1.25 B82-13651

Christie, Agatha. The pale horse / Agatha Christie. — London : Fontana, 1964, c1961 (1981 [printing]). — 188p ; 18cm
Originally published: London : Collins, 1961
ISBN 0-00-616438-2 (pbk) : £1.00 B82-03164

Christie, Agatha. Passenger to Frankfurt : an extravaganza / Agatha Christie. — [London] : Fontana, 1972, c1970 (1981 [printing]). — 192p ; 18cm
Originally published: London : Collins, 1970
ISBN 0-00-616449-8 (pbk) : £1.25 B82-06312

Christie, Agatha. A pocket full of rye / Agatha Christie. — London : Collins for the Crime Club, 1981. — 191p ; 21cm
ISBN 0-00-231681-1 : £6.25 B82-11389

Christie, Agatha. A Poirot quintet / by Agatha Christie. — London : Collins, 1977 (1981 [printing]). — 1002p ; 23cm
Contents: The murder of Roger Ackroyd — The mystery of the Blue Train — Dumb witness — After the funeral — Death on the Nile
ISBN 0-00-244682-0 : £6.95 B82-03964

Christie, Agatha. Postern of fate / Agatha Christie. — [London] : Fontana, 1976, c1973 (1982 [printing]). — 221p ; 18cm
Originally published: London : Collins, 1973
ISBN 0-00-616527-3 (pbk) : £1.25 B82-36257

Christie, Agatha. The Seven Dials mystery / Agatha Christie. — [London] : Fontana, 1954, c1929 (1982 [printing]). — 188p ; 18cm
ISBN 0-00-616541-9 (pbk) : £1.25 B82-25437

Christie, Agatha. Sleeping murder : Miss Marple′s last case / Agatha Christie. — [London] : Collins, 1977, c1976 (1982 [printing]). — 192p ; 18cm
Originally published: London : Collins, 1976
ISBN 0-00-616533-8 (pbk) : £1.25 B82-09401

Christie, Agatha. Ten little niggers / Agatha Christie. — London : Fontana, 1963 (1982 [printing]). — 190p ; 18cm
ISBN 0-00-616540-0 (pbk) : £1.25 B82-19742

Christie, Agatha. They came to Baghdad / Agatha Christie. — [London] : Fontana, 1954, c1951 (1982 [printing]). — 192p ; 18cm
Originally published: London : Collins, 1951
ISBN 0-00-616605-9 (pbk) : £1.25 B82-33550

Christie, Agatha. They do it with mirrors / Agatha Christie. — [London] : Fontana, 1955, c1952 (1982 [printing]). — 188p ; 18cm
Originally published: London : Collins, 1952
ISBN 0-00-616559-1 (pbk) : £1.25 B82-30779

Christie, Agatha. Third girl / Agatha Christie. — London : Pan in association with Collins, 1982, c1966. — 189p ; 18cm
Originally published: London : Collins, 1966
ISBN 0-330-26742-6 (pbk) : £1.25 B82-35750

Christie, Agatha. Towards zero / Agatha Christie. — [London] : Fontana, 1959, c1944 (1981 [printing]). — 192p : 1map ; 18cm
ISBN 0-00-616385-8 (pbk) : £1.25 B82-06308

Christie, Agatha. Why didn′t they ask Evans? / Agatha Christie. — [London] : Fontana, 1956, c1934 (1982 [printing]). — 191p ; 18cm
ISBN 0-00-616606-7 (pbk) : £1.25 B82-38637

Clarke, T. E. B.. Murder at Buckingham Palace / T.E.B. Clarke. — London : Hale, 1981. — 158p,[4]p of plates : ill,1facsim ; 23cm
ISBN 0-7091-9410-2 : £7.25 B82-01010

Cody, Al. Powder Burns / by Al Cody. — London : Remploy, 1981, c1955. — 160p ; 20cm
Originally published: London : Muller, 1955
ISBN 0-7066-0911-5 : £4.80 B82-03682

Collins, Norman. Little Nelson. — London : Collins, Nov.1981. — [154]p
ISBN 0-00-222610-3 : £5.95 : CIP entry B81-30297

Compton-Burnett, I.. A house and its head / by I. Compton-Burnett. — London : Gollancz, 1972, c1935 (1979 [printing]). — 276p ; 21cm
ISBN 0-575-01579-9 : £5.50 B82-00135

Compton-Burnett, I.. More women than men. — London : Allison & Busby, Oct.1982. — [240]p
Originally published: London : Heinemann, 1933
ISBN 0-85031-484-4 (pbk) : £2.95 : CIP entry B82-28584

Compton-Burnett, I.. Parents and children / by I. Compton-Burnett. — London : Gollancz, 1972, c1941 (1979 [printing]). — 318p ; 21cm
ISBN 0-575-01578-0 : £5.95 B82-00134

Conrad, Joseph. Heart of darkness ; and, The secret sharer / by Joseph Conrad ; introduction by Franklin Walker. — Toronto ; London : Bantam, 1969 (1981 [printing]). — xiv,204p ; 18cm. — (A Bantam classic)
Bibliography: p203-204
ISBN 0-553-21026-2 (pbk) : £1.00 B82-37139

823'.912[F] — Fiction in English, *1900-1945* **—** *Texts continuation*

Conrad, Joseph. Lord Jim / Joseph Conrad. — Leicester : Charnwood, 1981. — 492p ; 23cm. — (Charnwood library series) (Charnwood large type)
ISBN 0-7089-8014-7 : £5.25 : CIP rev. B81-22665

Conrad, Joseph. Lord Jim / by Joseph Conrad ; edited by Peter Hollindale. — London : Macmillan Education, 1982. — xxviii,320p : ill,1facsim,ports ; 18cm. — (Macmillan students' novels)
ISBN 0-333-32129-4 (pbk) : Unpriced : CIP rev. B81-34144

Conway, Laura. The cherished ones. — Large print ed. — Long Preston : Magna, Jan.1983. — [360]p
Originally published: London : Collins, 1974
ISBN 0-86009-469-3 : £5.75 : CIP entry B82-33130

Conway, Laura. Distant landscape. — Large print ed. — Long Preston : Magna Print, Dec.1982. — [320]p
Originally published: London : Collins, 1975
ISBN 0-86009-412-x : £5.50 : CIP entry B82-30724

Cookson, Catherine. The round tower. — Large print ed. — Anstey : Ulverscroft, Feb.1983. — 1v.. — (Charnwood library series)
Originally published: London : Macdonald, 1968
ISBN 0-7089-8097-x : £5.95 : CIP entry B82-38888

Cordell, Alexander. Land of my fathers. — London : Hodder and Stoughton, Jan.1983. — [320]p
ISBN 0-340-26979-0 : £7.95 : CIP entry B82-33729

Cordell, Alexander. Rogue's march. — London : Coronet Books, Nov.1982. — [512]p
Originally published: London : Hodder & Stoughton, 1981
ISBN 0-340-28646-6 (pbk) : £1.95 : CIP entry B82-27371

Cowen, Frances. Sunrise at even / by Frances Cowen. — London : Hale, 1982. — 155p ; 19cm
ISBN 0-7091-9978-3 : £6.50 B82-39190

Creasey, John, *1908-1973*. The baron and the Chinese puzzle / John Creasey as Anthony Morton. — Large print ed. — Bath : Chivers, 1981, c1965. — 311p ; 23cm. — (A Lythway book)
Originally published: Hodder & Stoughton, 1965
ISBN 0-85119-750-7 : Unpriced : CIP rev. B81-25808

Creasey, John, *1908-1973*. A rocket for the Toff. — Large print ed. — Long Preston : Magna Print Books, Apr.1982. — [340]p
Originally published: London : Hodder & Stoughton, 1960
ISBN 0-86009-393-x : £5.50 : CIP entry B82-04828

Creasey, John, *1908-1973*. The Toff and the crooked copper / by John Creasey. — Bolton-by-Bowland : Magna, 1980, c1977. — 286p ; 23cm
Originally published: London : Hodder and Stoughton, 1977. — Published in large print
ISBN 0-86009-283-6 : £5.25 : CIP rev. B80-34104

Crispin, Edmund. The long divorce / Edmund Crispin. — Feltham : Hamlyn Paperbacks, 1982, c1951. — 158p ; 18cm. — (A Hamlyn whodunnit)
Originally published: London : Gollancz, 1951
ISBN 0-600-20513-4 (pbk) : £1.50 B82-34111

Cronin, A. J.. The citadel / A.J. Cronin. — Leicester : Charnwood, 1981. — 591p ; 23cm. — (Charnwood library series)
Published in large print
ISBN 0-7089-8005-8 : £6.50 : CIP rev. B81-22660

Cronin, A. J.. Crusader's tomb / A.J. Cronin. — Leicester : Charnwood, 1982, c1956. — 621p ; 22cm
Originally published: London : Gollancz, 1956. — Published in large print
ISBN 0-7089-8042-2 : Unpriced : CIP rev. B82-15941

Cronin, A. J.. The Judas tree / A.J. Cronin. — Leicester : Charnwood, 1982, c1961. — 437p ; 23cm. — (Charnwood library series)
Originally published: London : Gollancz, 1961. — Published in large print
ISBN 0-7089-8025-2 : £5.25 : CIP rev. B81-36957

Cronin, A. J.. The keys to the kingdom. — Large print ed. — Anstey : Ulverscroft, Nov.1982. — [496]p. — (Charnwood library series)
ISBN 0-7089-8078-3 : £5.25 : CIP entry B82-29100

De la Mare, Walter. Memoirs of a midget / Walter de la Mare ; with a preface by Angela Carter. — Oxford : Oxford University Press, 1982. — xxiii,392p ; 20cm. — (Oxford paperbacks)
ISBN 0-19-281344-7 (pbk) : £3.50 : CIP rev. B82-07505

De Polnay, Peter. A minor giant / Peter de Polnay. — Loughton : Judy Piatkus, 1981. — 234p ; 21cm
ISBN 0-86188-075-7 : £6.50 : CIP rev. B81-15865

De Polnay, Peter. The other self. — Loughton : Piatkus, Jan.1983. — [192]p
ISBN 0-86188-237-7 : £6.95 : CIP entry B82-33227

De Polnay, Peter. Sea mist / Peter de Polnay. — Loughton : Piatkus, 1982. — 239p ; 21cm
ISBN 0-86188-168-0 : £6.95 B82-39555

De Selincourt, Hugh. The games of the season / Hugh de Selincourt ; with an introduction by John Arlott. — Oxford : Oxford University Press, 1982. — xiii,121p ; 20cm. — (Oxford paperbacks)
ISBN 0-19-281352-8 (pbk) : £2.50 : CIP rev. B82-12541

Deane, Sonia. Doctors in shadow / by Sonia Deane. — London : Mills & Boon, 1981. — 188p ; 20cm
ISBN 0-263-09976-8 : £4.55 B82-04657

Delderfield, R. F.. Come home Charlie, and face them. — London : Coronet, Nov.1982. — [288]p
ISBN 0-340-28641-5 (pbk) : £1.50 : CIP entry B82-27367

Delderfield, R. F.. Give us this day. — London : Hodder and Stoughton, Dec.1981. — [768]p
Originally published: 1973
ISBN 0-340-25354-1 (pbk) : £1.75 : CIP entry B81-31444

Delderfield, R. F.. Long summer day 1902-1911 : Book 1 of A horseman riding by / by R.F. Delderfield. — London : Hodder and Stoughton, c1966 (1982 [printing]). — 576p : geneal.tables,1map ; 23cm
ISBN 0-340-28371-8 : £7.95 : CIP rev. B82-07952

Delderfield, R. F.. Post of honour 1911-1940 : Book 2 of A horseman riding by / by R.F. Delderfield. — London : Hodder and Stoughton, c1966 (1982 [printing]). — 575p : geneal.tables,1map ; 23cm
ISBN 0-340-28372-6 : £7.95 : CIP rev. B82-07953

Delderfield, R. F.. The spring madness of Mr Sermon. — London : Coronet, Nov.1982. — [320]p
Originally published: 1963
ISBN 0-340-28642-3 (pbk) : £1.95 : CIP entry B82-27368

Dell, Ethel M.. Charles Rex / Ethel M. Dell ; condensed by Barbara Cartland. — London : Duckworth, 1980, c1978. — 216p ; 23cm. — (Barbara Cartland's library of love ; 18)
ISBN 0-7156-1478-9 : £6.95 : CIP rev. B80-12055

Dickens, Monica. Man overboard / Monica Dickens. — Harmondsworth : Penguin in association with Michael Joseph, 1962, c1958 (1982 [printing]). — 267p ; 18cm
ISBN 0-14-001813-1 (pbk) : £1.75 B82-25122

Doyle, ***Sir*** **Arthur Conan**. The adventures of Sherlock Holmes. — London : Dent, Jan.1983. — [288]p
ISBN 0-460-01279-7 (pbk) : £1.30 : CIP entry B82-34606

Doyle, ***Sir*** **Arthur Conan**. The exploits of Brigadier Gerard / Sir Arthur Conan Doyle. — Large print ed. — Bath : Chivers, 1982. — 292p ; 23cm. — (A New Portway large print book)
ISBN 0-85119-170-3 : Unpriced : CIP rev. B82-09846

Doyle, ***Sir*** **Arthur Conan**. The hound of the Baskervilles / Sir Arthur Conan Doyle. — Harmondsworth : Puffin, 1982. — 174p ; 19cm
ISBN 0-14-031557-8 (pbk) : £0.95 B82-40377

Doyle, ***Sir*** **Arthur Conan**. The hound of the Baskervilles. — London : Dent, Sept.1982. — [160]p. — (Everyman paperbacks)
ISBN 0-460-01253-3 (pbk) : £1.00 : CIP entry B82-18755

Doyle, ***Sir*** **Arthur Conan**. The land of mist / Sir Arthur Conan Doyle. — Large print ed. — Bath : Chivers, 1982. — 334p ; 23cm. — (A New Portway large print book)
ISBN 0-85119-171-1 : Unpriced : CIP rev. B82-09847

Doyle, ***Sir*** **Arthur Conan**. The lost world / Sir Arthur Conan Doyle. — Large print ed. — Bath : Chivers, 1982. — 316p ; 23cm. — (A New Portway large print book)
ISBN 0-85119-172-x : Unpriced : CIP rev. B82-09848

Doyle, ***Sir*** **Arthur Conan**. A study in scarlet / Sir Arthur Conan Doyle. — Harmondsworth : Penguin, 1982. — 135p ; 19cm
ISBN 0-14-005707-2 (pbk) : £0.80 B82-05959

Du Maurier, Daphne. The glass-blowers / Daphne du Maurier. — Harmondsworth : Penguin, 1981, c1963. — 312p ; 18cm
Originally published: London : Gollancz, 1963
ISBN 0-14-002403-4 (pbk) : £1.50 B82-06431

Du Maurier, Daphne. The King's general / Daphne du Maurier. — Large print ed. — Leicester : Charnwood, 1982, c1946. — 539p ; 23cm. — (Charnwood library series)
Originally published: London : Gollancz, 1946. — Published in large print
ISBN 0-7089-8020-1 : £5.25 : CIP rev. B81-33994

Du Maurier, Daphne. Rebecca / Daphne du Maurier. — Leicester : Charnwood, 1981. — 598p ; 23cm. — (Charnwood library series)
Published in large print
ISBN 0-7089-8006-6 : £6.50 : CIP rev. B81-22661

Du Maurier, Daphne. The scapegoat. — Large print ed. — Anstey : Ulverscroft, Oct.1982. — [512]p. — (Charnwood library series)
Originally published: London : Gollancz, 1957
ISBN 0-7089-8074-0 : £5.25 : CIP entry B82-26690

823'.912[F] — Fiction in English, *1900-1945* — *Texts* *continuation*

Du Maurier, Daphne. Three famous Du Maurier novels. — London : Gollancz, Nov.1982. — [704]p
Contents: The King's general — The flight of the falcon — The house on the strand
ISBN 0-575-03215-4 : £8.95 : CIP entry
B82-26564

Dunsany, Edward Plunkett, *Baron*. The king of Elfland's daughter / Lord Dunsany. — London : Unwin Paperbacks, 1982. — 182p ; 20cm
ISBN 0-04-823207-6 (pbk) : £2.50 : CIP rev.
B81-35917

Durbridge, Francis. Breakaway. — London : Coronet, Dec.1982. — [192]p
Originally published: 1981
ISBN 0-340-28660-1 (pbk) : £1.50 : CIP entry
B82-29639

Durbridge, Francis. The doll / Francis Durbridge. — London : Hodder and Stoughton, 1982. — 191p ; 21cm
ISBN 0-340-28526-5 : £6.95 : CIP rev.
B82-15756

Durbridge, Francis. The Tyler mystery. — Large print ed. — Anstey : Ulverscroft, Nov.1982. — [320]p. — (Ulverscroft large print series)
Originally published under the name Paul Temple. London : Hodder & Stoughton, 1957
ISBN 0-7089-0871-3 : £5.00 : CIP entry
B82-29087

Durrell, Lawrence. Constance, or, Solitary practices. — London : Faber, Sept.1982. — [365]p
ISBN 0-571-11757-0 : £7.95 : CIP entry
B82-19547

Edgar, Josephine. Countess / Josephine Edgar ; edited by Lesley Saxby. — London : Futura, 1979, c1978. — 343p ; 18cm. — (A Troubadour book)
Originally published: London : Macdonald & Jane's, 1978
ISBN 0-7088-1494-8 (pbk) : £0.95 B82-05481

Edgar, Josephine. The lady of Wildersley / Josephine Edgar ; edited by Leslie Saxby. — Large print ed. — Bath : Chivers Press, 1981, c1975. — 239p ; 23cm. — (A Lythway book)
Originally published: London : Macdonald and Jane's, 1975
ISBN 0-85119-757-4 : Unpriced : CIP rev.
B81-31249

Edgar, Josephine. Margaret Normanby. — Loughton : Piatkus, Dec.1982. — [512]p
ISBN 0-86188-212-1 : £8.50 : CIP entry
B82-30598

Edgar, Josephine. My sister Sophie / Josephine Edgar. — Large print ed. — Bath : Chivers, 1981, c1964. — 287p ; 23cm. — (A Lythway book)
Originally published: London : Collins, 1964
ISBN 0-85119-751-5 : Unpriced : CIP rev.
B81-25809

Ellis, H. F.. Swan song of A.J. Wentworth / H.F. Ellis. — London : Arrow, 1982. — 115p ; 18cm
ISBN 0-09-929160-6 (pbk) : £1.25 B82-35585

Elsna, Hebe. Heiress presumptive / Hebe Elsna. — London : Hale, 1982. — 172p ; 21cm
ISBN 0-7091-9487-0 : £6.95 B82-12623

Elsna, Hebe. A house called Pleasance / by Hebe Elsna. — Long Preston : Magna Print, 1982, c1977. — 338p ; 22cm
Originally published: London : Collins, 1977. — Published in large print
ISBN 0-86009-420-0 : Unpriced : CIP rev.
B82-13159

Elsna, Hebe. The King's bastard / by Hebe Elsna. — Long Preston : Magna, 1982, c1971. — 325p ; 23cm
Originally published: London : Collins, 1971. — Published in large print
ISBN 0-86009-381-6 : Unpriced : CIP rev.
B82-00314

Elsna, Hebe. The mask of comedy / by Hebe Elsna. — Long Preston : Magna, 1981, c1970. — 313p ; 23cm
Originally published: London : Collins, 1970. — Published in large print
ISBN 0-86009-355-7 : Unpriced : CIP rev.
B81-31815

Elsna, Hebe. My lover — the king / Hebe Elsna. — London : Hale, 1982. — 189p ; 21cm
ISBN 0-7091-9812-4 : £7.25 B82-31617

Elsna, Hebe. Too well beloved. — Large print ed. — Long Preston : Magna Print, Aug.1982. — [336]p
Originally published: London : Hale, 1964
ISBN 0-86009-427-8 : £5.50 : CIP entry
B82-16674

Elsna, Hebe. The undying past. — Large print ed. — Long Preston : Magna Print, Sept.1982. — [320]p
Originally published: London : Hale, 1964
ISBN 0-86009-433-2 : £5.50 : CIP entry
B82-20858

Elsna, Hebe. The wise virgin / by Hebe Elsna. — Long Preston : Magna, 1982, c1967. — 359p ; 23cm
Originally published: London : Collins, 1967. — Published in large print
ISBN 0-86009-403-0 : Unpriced : CIP rev.
B82-10230

Emerson, David, *1900-*. Scrope and the spinster / David Emerson. — London : Remploy, 1979. — 223p ; 20cm
Originally published: London : Hutchinson, 1964
ISBN 0-7066-0832-1 : £3.70 B82-03015

Farnol, Jeffery. The fool beloved / Jeffery Farnol. — London : Remploy, 1981, c1949. — ix,293p ; 19cm
Originally published: London : Sampson Low, Marston, 1949
ISBN 0-7066-0917-4 : £5.80 B82-16858

Fen, Elisaveta. The ebb : a novel / Elisaveta Fen. — Warwick : Stratford Press, 1980. — v,214p ; 23cm
ISBN 0-906643-01-5 : £6.95 B82-06319

Fen, Elisaveta. Tomorrow we die : a novel / by Elisaveta Fen. — Ilfracombe : Stockwell, 1982. — 245p ; 22cm
ISBN 0-7223-1575-9 : £8.50 B82-30988

Ferrars, Elizabeth. Give a corpse a bad name. — Large print ed. — Bath : Chivers, Feb.1983. — [272]p. — (A Lythway book)
ISBN 0-85119-896-1 : £7.20 : CIP entry
B82-39581

Ferrars, Elizabeth. Skeleton in search of a cupboard / Elizabeth Ferrars. — London : Collins, 1982. — 181p ; 20cm. — (The Crime Club)
ISBN 0-00-231925-x : £6.50 : CIP rev.
B82-19075

Ferrars, Elizabeth. Thinner than water / Elizabeth Ferrars. — London : Collins, 1981. — 182p ; 20cm. — (The Crime Club)
ISBN 0-00-231895-4 : £6.25 : CIP rev.
B81-31526

Ferrars, Elizabeth. Witness before the fact / Elizabeth Ferrars. — Large print ed. — Leicester : Ulverscroft, 1981, c1979. — 288p ; 23cm. — (Ulverscroft large print series)
Originally published: London : Collins [for] the Crime Club, 1979
ISBN 0-7089-0688-5 : £5.00 : CIP rev.
B81-28093

The **Floating** admiral / by certain members of the Detection Club. — London : Macmillan, 1981. — 309p : 1map ; 21cm
ISBN 0-333-31955-9 : £5.95 B82-09332

Ford, Ford Madox. The rash act : a novel / by Ford Madox Ford. — Manchester : Carcanet, 1982, c1933. — 348p ; 20cm
ISBN 0-85635-399-x : Unpriced : CIP rev.
B82-04808

Forester, C. S.. The earthly paradise / C.S. Forester. — Harmondsworth : Penguin in association with Michael Joseph, 1981. — 239p ; 19cm
ISBN 0-14-001816-6 (pbk) : £1.50 B82-06434

Forster, *E. M.*. A passage to India / E.M. Forster ; notes by the author. — Leicester : Charnwood, 1981. — 435p ; 23cm. — (Charnwood library series)
Published in large print
ISBN 0-7089-8000-7 : £5.25 : CIP rev.
B81-22657

Gaye, Carol. Love and let love. — Bath : Chivers, Nov.1982. — [160]p. — (Firecrest books)
Originally published: London : Collins, 1970
ISBN 0-85997-501-0 : £5.50 : CIP entry
B82-26333

Gaye, Carol. Love and let love. — Large print ed. — Bath : Chivers, Feb.1983. — [224]p. — (A Lythway book)
Originally published: London : Collins, 1970
ISBN 0-85119-897-x : £6.90 : CIP entry
B82-39585

Gibbs, Philip. Oil lamps and candlelight / Philip Gibbs. — London : Remploy, 1979, c1962. — 253p ; 20cm
Originally published: London : Hutchinson, 1962
ISBN 0-7066-0858-5 : £4.50 B82-04680

Glyn, Elinor. The sequence / by Elinor Glyn ; condensed by Barbara Cartland. — London : Duckworth, 1980, c1978. — 216p ; 23cm. — (Barbara Cartland's library of love ; 17)
Originally published: London : Corgi, 1978
ISBN 0-7156-1477-0 : £6.95 : CIP rev.
B80-12068

Godden, Rumer. The dark horse / Rumer Godden. — London : Macmillan, 1981. — 202p ; 21cm
ISBN 0-333-32183-9 : £4.95 B82-05733

Godden, Rumer. The dark horse. — Large print ed. — Bath : Chivers, Nov.1982. — [264]p. — (A New Portway large print book)
Originally published: London : Macmillan, 1981
ISBN 0-85119-191-6 : £5.90 : CIP entry
B82-26428

Godden, Rumer. The lady and the unicorn / Rumer Godden. — Harmondsworth : Penguin, 1982, c1938. — 187p ; 18cm
ISBN 0-14-005523-1 (pbk) : £1.75 B82-22321

Gogarty, 0liver. Tumbling in the hay / Oliver St. John Gogarty. — London : Sphere, 1982, c1939. — 301p 18cm
ISBN 0-7221-3917-9 (pbk) : £1.75 B82-14904

Goolden, Barbara. The crystal and the dew / Barbara Goolden. — Large print ed. — Bath : Chivers, 1981, c1975. — 247p ; 23cm. — (A Lythway book)
Originally published: London : Heinemann, 1975
ISBN 0-85119-752-3 : Unpriced : CIP rev.
B81-25810

Goudge, Elizabeth. The Dean's watch / Elizabeth Goudge. — Large print ed. — Leicester : Ulverscroft, 1982, c1960. — 472p ; 23cm. — (Ulverscroft large print series)
Originally published: London : Hodder & Stoughton, 1960
ISBN 0-7089-0796-2 : Unpriced : CIP rev.
B82-18558

823'.912[F] — Fiction in English, ***1900-1945 — Texts*** ***continuation***

Graeme, Bruce. The snatch / Bruce Graeme. — Large print ed. — Bath : Chivers, 1981, c1976. — 272p ; 23cm. — (A Lythway book)
Originally published: London : Hutchinson, 1976
ISBN 0-85119-753-1 : Unpriced : CIP rev. B81-25811

Graham, Winston. The merciless ladies / Winston Graham. — [London] : Fontana, 1981, c1979. — 317p ; 18cm
Originally published: London : Bodley Head, 1979
ISBN 0-00-616006-9 (pbk) : £1.75 B82-09407

Graham, Winston. The miller's dance : a novel of Cornwall 1812-1813 / Winston Graham. — London : Collins, 1982. — 415p : geneal.tables ; 22cm
Geneal. tables on lining papers
ISBN 0-00-222674-x : £8.50 : CIP rev. B82-27796

Graham, Winston. The stranger from the sea : a novel of Cornwall 1810-1811 / Winston Graham. — London : Collins, 1981. — 445p ; 22cm
Geneal tables on lining papers
ISBN 0-00-222616-2 : £7.95 : CIP rev. B81-25137

Greene, Graham. The confidential agent / Graham Greene. — Large print ed. — Bath : Chivers, 1982. — 295p ; 23cm. — (A New Portway large print book)
ISBN 0-85119-159-2 : Unpriced : CIP rev. B82-01443

Greene, Graham. Doctor Fischer of Geneva, or, The bomb party / Graham Greene. — Large print ed. — Bath : Chivers, 1982, c1980. — 144p ; 23cm. — (A New Portway large print book)
Originally published: London : Bodley Head, 1980
ISBN 0-85119-168-1 : Unpriced : CIP rev. B82-07618

Greene, Graham. The human factor. — London : Bodley Head, Sept.1982. — [339]p. — (The Collected edition / Graham Greene ; 22)
Originally published: 1978
ISBN 0-370-30929-4 : £6.95 : CIP entry B82-19202

Greene, Graham. The Ministry of fear : an entertainment / Graham Greene. — Harmondsworth : Penguin in association with Heinemann, 1963, c1973 (1982 [printing]). — 220p ; 18cm
ISBN 0-14-001897-2 (pbk) : £1.50 B82-29610

Greene, Graham. Monsignor Quixote. — London : Bodley Head, Sept.1982. — [192]p
ISBN 0-370-30923-5 : £5.50 : CIP entry B82-19200

Greene, Graham. Our man in Havana / Graham Greene. — Large print ed. — Bath : Chivers Press, 1982, c1958. — 292p : ill ; 23cm. — (A New Portway large print book)
Originally published: London : Heinemann, 1958
ISBN 0-85119-151-7 : Unpriced : CIP rev. B81-33811

Greene, Graham. Travels with my aunt / Graham Greene. — London : Heinemann, 1980. — 318p ; 20cm. — (The collected edition ; 20)
Originally published: London : Bodley Head, 1968
ISBN 0-434-30570-7 : £6.95 : CIP rev.
ISBN 0-370-30346-6 (Bodley Head) B80-18893

Hall, Radclyffe. The well of loneliness / Radclyffe Hall ; with a new introduction by Alison Hennegan. — London : Virago, 1982, c1943. — xvii,447p ; 20cm. — (Virago modern classics)
ISBN 0-86068-254-4 (pbk) : £3.50 : CIP rev. B82-04830

Hamilton, Patrick. The slaves of solitude. — Oxford : Oxford University Press, Oct.1982. — [256]p. — (Oxford paperbacks)
Originally published: London : Constable, 1947
ISBN 0-19-281359-5 (pbk) : £2.95 : CIP entry B82-23667

Hanley, James. [The house in the valley]. Against the stream / by James Hanley. — London : Deutsch, 1982, c1981. — 256p : 1ill ; 21cm
Originally published: under the name Patric Shone. London : Cape, 1951
ISBN 0-233-97458-x : £6.95 B82-25466

Hartley, L. P.. The go-between / L.P. Hartley. — Leicester : Charnwood, 1981. — 400p ; 23cm. — (Charnwood library series)
Originally published: London : Hamilton, 1953. — Published in large print
ISBN 0-7089-8001-5 : £5.25 : CIP rev. B81-22658

Harvey, Rachel. Dearest doctor / Ursula Bloom as Rachel Harvey. — Large print ed. — Bath : Chivers, 1981, c1968. — 232p ; 23cm. — (A Lythway book)
Originally published: London : Hurst & Blackett, 1968
ISBN 0-85119-764-7 : Unpriced : CIP rev. B81-31795

Hawkes, Jacquetta. A quest of love / Jacquetta Hawkes. — London : Chatto & Windus, 1980. — 219p ; 21cm
ISBN 0-7011-2536-5 : £6.50 : CIP rev. B80-26150

Heppenstall, Rayner. The pier. — London : Allison & Busby, May 1982. — [192]p
ISBN 0-85031-450-x (cased) : £6.95 : CIP entry
ISBN 0-85031-451-8 (pbk) : £2.95 B82-11779

Herbert, A. P.. The secret battle / A.P. Herbert ; with a preface by Winston S. Churchill and an introduction by John Terraine. — Oxford : Oxford University Press, 1982. — xv,130p ; 20cm. — (Oxford paperbacks)
ISBN 0-19-281328-5 (pbk) : £2.50 : CIP rev. B82-09281

Heyer, Georgette. Arabella. — Large print ed. — Anstey : Ulverscroft Large Print Books, Sept.1982. — [512]p. — (Ulverscroft large print series)
Originally published: London : Pan, 1964
ISBN 0-7089-0848-9 : £5.00 : CIP entry B82-27182

Heyer, Georgette. A blunt instrument / Georgette Heyer. — London : Granada, 1961 (1982 [printing]). — 189p ; 18cm
ISBN 0-586-02669-x (pbk) : £1.25 B82-28375

Heyer, Georgette. The convenient marriage / Georgette Heyer. — London : Pan Books in association with William Heinemann, 1964 (1982 [printing]). — 236p ; 18cm
ISBN 0-330-10304-0 (pbk) : £1.50 B82-22146

Heyer, Georgette. Envious Casca / Georgette Heyer. — London : Granada, 1961 (1982 [printing]). — 216p ; 18cm. — (A Panther book)
ISBN 0-586-01265-6 (pbk) : £1.25 B82-36062

Heyer, Georgette. The masqueraders / Georgette Heyer. — London : Pan in association with Heinemann, 1965 (1981 printing). — 254p ; 18cm
ISBN 0-330-10357-1 (pbk) : £1.50 B82-06413

Heyer, Georgette. Powder and patch : the transformation of Philip Jettan / Georgette Heyer. — London : Pan Books in association with William Heinemann, 1950 (1982 [printing]). — 159p ; 18cm
ISBN 0-330-02063-3 (pbk) : £1.50 B82-22147

Heyer, Georgette. Regency buck / Georgette Heyer. — London : Pan in association with Heinemann, 1959, c1958 (1981 printing). — 318p ; 18cm
ISBN 0-330-20266-9 (pbk) : £1.75 B82-06411

Heyer, Georgette. Regency buck : Georgette Heyer. — Large print ed. — Leicester : Ulverscroft, 1981, c1935. — 503p ; 23cm. — (Ulverscroft large print)
ISBN 0-7089-0694-x : £5.00 : CIP rev. B81-28096

Heyer, Georgette. Why shoot a butler? / Georgette Heyer. — London : Granada, 1963 (1982 [printing]). — 219p ; 18cm. — (A Panther book)
ISBN 0-586-01577-9 (pbk) : £1.25 B82-33678

Holt, Victoria. The curse of the kings / Victoria Holt. — Large print ed. — Leicester : Ulverscroft, 1982, c1973. — 518p ; 23cm. — (Ulverscroft large print)
Originally published: London : Collins, 1973
ISBN 0-7089-0807-1 : Unpriced : CIP rev. B82-18447

Holt, Victoria. The demon lover. — London : Collins, Oct.1982. — [350]p
ISBN 0-00-222692-8 : £7.95 : CIP entry B82-23079

Holt, Victoria. The house of a thousand lanterns. — Large print ed. — Anstey : Ulverscroft, Oct.1982. — [496]p. — (Ulverscroft large print series)
Originally published: London : Collins, 1974
ISBN 0-7089-0861-6 : £5.00 : CIP entry B82-26682

Holt, Victoria. Kirkland revels / Victoria Holt. — [London] : Fontana, 1964, c1962 (1982 [printing]). — 253p ; 18cm
Originally published: London : Collins, 1962
ISBN 0-00-616554-0 (pbk) : £1.50 B82-30771

Holt, Victoria. The mask of the enchantress / Victoria Holt. — [London] : Fontana, 1982, c1980. — 347p ; 18cm
Originally published: London : Collins, 1980
ISBN 0-00-616296-7 (pbk) : £1.75 B82-30770

Holt, Victoria. The pride of the peacock / Victoria Holt. — [London] : Fontana, 1978, c1976 (1982 [printing]). — 285p ; 18cm
Originally published: London : Collins, 1976
ISBN 0-00-616488-9 (pbk) : £1.50 B82-16825

Holt, Victoria. The secret woman / Victoria Holt. — [London] : Fontana, 1972, c1970 (1982 [printing]). — 320p ; 18cm
Originally published: London : Collins, 1971
ISBN 0-00-616577-x (pbk) : £1.75 B82-36260

Holtby, Winifred. Anderby Wold / Winifred Holtby ; with a new introduction by Mary Cadogan. — London : Virago, 1981, c1935. — xix,310p ; 20cm. — (Virago modern classics)
ISBN 0-86068-207-2 (pbk) : £2.95 : CIP rev. B81-30400

Holtby, Winifred. The crowded street / Winifred Holtby ; with a new introduction by Claire Hardisty. — London : Virago, 1981, c1935. — 271p ; 20cm. — (Virago modern classics)
ISBN 0-86068-208-0 (pbk) : £2.95 : CIP rev. B81-30399

Holtby, Winifred. Mandoa, Mandoa! : a comedy of irrelevance / Winifred Holtby ; with a new introduction by Marion Shaw. — London : Virago, 1982, c1935. — xix,382p ; 20cm. — (Virago modern classics)
ISBN 0-86068-251-x (pbk) : £3.50 : CIP rev. B82-16676

Horst, Karl. Caribbean pirate. — London : Severn House, Aug.1982. — [208]p
Originally published: London : Corgi, 1980
ISBN 0-7278-0816-8 : £6.95 : CIP entry B82-21107

823'.912[F] — Fiction in English, ***1900-1945*** **—** *Texts* *continuation*

Household, Geoffrey. Watcher in the shadows / Geoffrey Household. — Hornchurch : Henry, 1981, c1960. — 174p ; 21cm
Originally published: London : Joseph, 1960
ISBN 0-86025-196-9 : £5.25 B82-10152

Hull, E. M.. The lion tamer / by E.M. Hull ; condensed by Barbara Cartland. — London : Duckworth, 1981, c1978. — 181p ; 23cm. — (Barbara Cartland's library of love ; no.24)
ISBN 0-7156-1539-4 : £6.95 : CIP rev. B81-22455

Hutchinson, R. C.. Rising / R.C. Hutchinson. — Harmondsworth : Penguin, 1982, c1976. — 359p ; 20cm. — (King Penguin)
Originally published: London : Joseph, 1976
ISBN 0-14-006151-7 (pbk) : £2.95 B82-16759

Hutchinson, R. C.. Testament / R.C. Hutchinson. — Harmondsworth : Penguin, 1981. — viii,732p ; 20cm. — (A King penguin)
ISBN 0-14-006150-9 (pbk) : £3.95 B82-06424

Huxley, Elspeth. The prince buys the manor. — London : Chatto & Windus, Oct.1982. — [208]p
ISBN 0-7011-2651-5 : £6.95 : CIP entry B82-23201

Innes, Hammond. The angry mountain / Hammond Innes. — London : Fontana, 1957 (1982 [printing]). — 254p ; 18cm
Originally published: London : Collins, 1950
ISBN 0-00-616487-0 (pbk) : £1.50 B82-17069

Innes, Hammond. The black tide / Hammond Innes. — London : Collins, 1982. — 347p ; 22cm
ISBN 0-00-222618-9 : £7.95 B82-37121

Innes, Hammond. Solomons seal / Hammond Innes. — [London] : Fontana, 1982, c1980. — 319p : 2maps ; 18cm
Originally published: London : Collins, 1980
ISBN 0-00-616381-5 (pbk) : £1.75 B82-16823

Innes, Hammond. The strange land / Hammond Innes. — [London] : Fontana, 1964 (1982 [printing]). — 256p ; 18cm
Originally published: London : Collins, 1954
ISBN 0-00-616556-7 (pbk) : £1.50 B82-30780

Innes, Hammond. Wreckers must breathe / Hammond Innes. — [London] : Fontana, 1955 (1982 [printing]). — 191p ; 18cm
ISBN 0-00-616486-2 (pbk) : £1.35 B82-16824

Innes, Michael. Appleby's other story / Michael Innes. — Large print ed. — Bath : Chivers, 1981, c1974. — 287p ; 23cm. — (A New Portway large print book)
Originally published: London : Gollancz, 1974
ISBN 0-85119-137-1 : Unpriced : CIP rev. B81-25800

Innes, Michael. The Gay Phoenix / Michael Innes. — Harmondsworth : Penguin, 1981, c1976. — 192p ; 19cm. — (Penguin crime fiction)
Originally published: London : Gollancz, 1976
ISBN 0-14-004701-8 (pbk) : £1.25 B82-16766

Innes, Michael. Honeybath's haven / Michael Innes. — Harmondsworth : Penguin, 1979, c1977 (1981 [printing]). — 191p ; 18cm. — (Penguin crime fiction)
Originally published: London : Gollancz, 1977
ISBN 0-14-004885-5 (pbk) : £1.25 B82-22315

Innes, Michael. Sheiks and adders : a novel / by Michael Innes. — London : Gollancz, 1982. — 157p ; 21cm
ISBN 0-575-03043-7 : £5.95 : CIP rev. B82-06929

Jacob, Naomi. The beloved physician. — Bath : Chivers, Sept.1982. — [320]p. — (A New Portway book)
ISBN 0-86220-508-5 : £5.95 : CIP entry B82-19838

Jameson, Storm. Company parade / Storm Jameson ; with a new introduction by Elaine Feinstein. — London : Virago, 1982. — xii,345p ; 20cm. — (Virago modern classics)
ISBN 0-86068-297-8 (pbk) : £3.50 : CIP rev. B82-21541

Jameson, Storm. The hidden river / by Storm Jameson. — London : Remploy, 1979. — 265p ; 20cm
Originally published: London : Macmillan, 1955
ISBN 0-7066-0841-0 : £4.50 B82-16899

Jameson, Storm. Women against men / Storm Jameson ; with a new introduction by Elaine Feinstein. — London : Virago, 1982. — xii,293p ; 20cm. — (Virago modern classics)
ISBN 0-86068-298-6 (pbk) : £3.50 : CIP rev. B82-28595

Jenkins, Elizabeth. The tortoise and the hare. — London : Virago, Jan.1983. — [256]p. — (Virago modern classics)
Originally published: London : Gollancz, 1954
ISBN 0-86068-272-2 (pbk) : £2.95 : CIP entry B82-33221

Johnson, Pamela Hansford. The good listener / Pamela Hansford Johnson. — Feltham : Hamlyn Paperbacks, 1982, c1975. — 237p ; 18cm
Originally published: London : Macmillan, 1975
ISBN 0-600-20567-3 (pbk) : £1.50 B82-19455

Johnson, Pamela Hansford. The honours board / Pamela Hansford Johnson. — Feltham : Hamlyn Paperbacks, 1981, c1970. — 250p ; 18cm
Originally published: London : Macmillan, 1970
ISBN 0-600-20584-3 (pbk) : £1.50 B82-03016

Joyce, James, *1882-1941*. [Dubliners. Selections]. The dead : from Dubliners / James Joyce ; with four etchings by Pietro Annigoni. — Pitlochry (Frenich, Foss, Pitlochry, [Perthshire PH16 5NG]) : Dural and Hamilton, 1982, c1967. — 72p,[4]leaves of plates : ill ; 32cm
Limited ed. of 170 signed and numbered copies. — In slip case
Unpriced B82-33934

Kipling, Rudyard. The beginning of the armadilloes. — London : Macmillan, Oct.1982. — [32]p
ISBN 0-333-34138-4 : £2.95 : CIP entry B82-24810

Kyle, Elisabeth. A summer scandal / by Elisabeth Kyle. — Long Preston : Magna Print, 1982, c1979. — 316p ; 22cm
Originally published: London : Peter Davies, 1979. — Published in large print
ISBN 0-86009-389-1 : Unpriced : CIP rev. B82-04824

Lawrence, D. H.. Aaron's rod. — Large print ed. — Anstey : Ulverscroft, Sept.1982. — [480]p. — (Charnwood library series)
ISBN 0-7089-8068-6 : £5.25 : CIP entry B82-27012

Lawrence, D. H.. The escape cock. — Isle of Skye : Aquila, Nov.1982. — [48]p
ISBN 0-7275-0211-5 (pbk) : £1.95 : CIP entry B82-31300

Lawrence, D. H.. Lady Chatterley's lover / D.H. Lawrence. — 2nd ed. / with an introduction by Richard Hoggart. — Harmondsworth : Penguin in association with Heinemann, 1961 (1981 [printing]). — xiv,316p ; 19cm
ISBN 0-14-001484-5 (pbk) : £1.25 B82-01401

Lawrence, D. H.. Lady Chatterley's lover : prefaced by the author's Apropos of Lady Chatterley's lover / D.H. Lawrence. — London : Heinemann, 1963 (1981 [printing]). — 277p ; 23cm
ISBN 0-434-40732-1 : £6.95 B82-02168

Lawrence, D. H.. The lost girl / D.H. Lawrence ; edited by John Worthen ; introduction by Melvyn Bragg. — London : Granada, 1981, c1949. — xii,421p : 1map ; 19cm. — (The Cambridge edition of the works of D.H. Lawrence)
ISBN 0-246-11654-4 (cased) : £6.95
ISBN 0-586-05244-5 (pbk) : £1.95 B82-08821

Lawrence, D. H.. Sons and lovers / D.H. Lawrence. — Leicester : Charnwood, 1981. — 680p ; 23cm. — (Charnwood library series)
Published in large print
ISBN 0-7089-8008-2 : £6.50 : CIP rev. B81-22663

Lawrence, D. H.. The trespasser / D.H. Lawrence ; edited by Elizabeth Mansfield. — Cambridge : Cambridge University Press, 1981. — xv,327p ; 22cm. — (The Cambridge edition of the letters and works of D.H. Lawrence)
ISBN 0-521-22264-8 (cased) : £22.50 : CIP rev.
ISBN 0-521-29424-x (pbk) : £6.95 B82-01330

Lawrence, D. H.. The trespasser. — London : Granada, Sept.1982. — [224]p. — (The Cambridge edition of the works of D.H. Lawrence)
ISBN 0-246-11649-8 (cased) : £7.95 : CIP entry
ISBN 0-586-05240-2 (pbk) : Unpriced B82-18855

Lawrence, D. H.. Women in love / D.H. Lawrence ; introduction by Richard Hoggart ; lithographs by Charles Raymond. — London : Folio Society, 1982. — 447p,[17]leaves of plates : ill ; 26cm
In slip case
£15.95 B82-10297

Lawrence, D. H.. Women in love / D.H. Lawrence ; edited with an introduction and notes by Charles L. Ross. — Harmondsworth : Penguin, 1982, c1950. — 596p ; 19cm. — (Penguin English library)
ISBN 0-14-043156-x (pbk) : £1.50 B82-16760

Lawrence, D. H.. Women in love / D.H. Lawrence. — Leicester : Charnwood, 1982. — 768p ; 23cm. — (Charnwood library series)
Published in large print
ISBN 0-7089-8049-x : Unpriced : CIP rev. B82-15948

Lehmann, Rosamond. The ballad and the source. — London : Virago, Oct.1982. — [328]p. — (Virago modern classics)
ISBN 0-86068-330-3 (pbk) : £3.50 : CIP entry B82-24149

Lehmann, Rosamond. The gypsy's baby and other stories / Rosamond Lehmann ; with a new introduction by Janet Watts. — London : Virago, 1982, c1946. — xiii,192p ; 20cm. — (Virago modern classics)
Originally published: London : Collins, 1946
ISBN 0-86068-247-1 (pbk) : £2.75 : CIP rev. B82-01137

Lehmann, Rosamond. A note in music / Rosamond Lehmann ; with a new introduction by Janet Watts. — London : Virago, 1982, c1930. — xvii,318p ; 20cm. — (Virago modern classics)
ISBN 0-86068-248-x (pbk) : £3.25 : CIP rev. B82-01136

Lehmann, Rosamond. A sea-grape tree. — London : Virago, Oct.1982. — [168]p. — (Virago modern classics)
Originally published: London : Collins, 1976
ISBN 0-86068-335-4 (pbk) : £2.95 : CIP entry B82-24151

Lewis, C. S.. The Screwtape letters / C.S. Lewis ; illustrated by Papas. — London : Collins, 1982, c1942. — 133p : ill ; 20cm
ISBN 0-00-626527-8 (pbk) : £1.95 B82-16807

823'.912[F] — Fiction in English, *1900-1945 — Texts* *continuation*

Lewis, Wyndham, *1882-1957.* The revenge for love / Wyndham Lewis ; with an introduction by Julian Symons. — London : Secker & Warburg in association with the Arts Council of Great Britain, 1982. — xvi,376p ; 23cm
ISBN 0-436-24718-6 : £7.50 B82-30287

Llewellyn, Richard. I stand on a quiet shore / Richard Llewellyn. — London : Joseph, 1982. — 187p ; 23cm
ISBN 0-7181-2098-1 : £7.95 B82-27441

Lofts, Norah. A calf for Venus. — London : Hodder & Stoughton, Feb.1982. — [240]p
ISBN 0-340-25468-8 : £6.95 : CIP entry B81-35686

Lofts, Norah. The claw. — London : Hodder & Stoughton, July 1982. — [224]p. — (Coronet books)
Originally published: 1981
ISBN 0-340-28104-9 (pbk) : £1.60 : CIP entry B82-12240

Lofts, Norah. Lady living alone. — London : Hodder and Stoughton, Nov.1982. — [192]p
ISBN 0-340-32016-8 : £6.95 : CIP entry B82-27342

Lofts, Norah. The old priory / Norah Lofts. — London : Corgi, 1982, c1981. — 213p ; 18cm
Originally published: London : Bodley Head, 1981
ISBN 0-552-11942-3 (pbk) : £1.50 B82-37138

Lofts, Norah. A wayside tavern. — Large print ed. — Anstey : Ulverscroft, Aug.1982. — [592] p. — (Ulverscroft large print series)
Originally published: London : Hodder and Stoughton, 1980
ISBN 0-7089-0838-1 : £5.00 : CIP entry B82-27020

Lymington, John. The terror version / by John Lymington. — London : Hale, 1982. — 158p ; 20cm. — (Hale SF)
ISBN 0-7091-9503-6 : £6.25 B82-25984

Macaulay, Rose. They were defeated / Rose Macaulay ; introduced by Susan Howatch. — Oxford : Oxford University Press, 1981, c1932. — 445p ; 20cm. — (Oxford paperbacks)
ISBN 0-19-281316-1 (pbk) : £2.95 : CIP rev. B81-25793

McCrone, Guy. An independent young man / by Guy McCrone. — London : Remploy, 1979. — 282p : 1geneal.table ; 20cm
Originally published: London : Constable, 1961
ISBN 0-7066-0848-8 : £4.60 B82-16898

McDonald, Eva. The captive lady. — Large print ed. — Bath : Chivers, Oct.1982. — [272]p. — (A Lythway book)
Originally published: London : Hale, 1962
ISBN 0-85119-856-2 : £7.20 : CIP entry B82-20522

McLaughlin, W. R. D.. Sabotage at sea!. — Bath : Chivers, Nov.1982. — [160]p. — (Firecrest books)
Originally published: London : Mayflower, 1978
ISBN 0-85997-504-5 : £5.50 : CIP entry B82-26336

MacLeod, Robert, *1906-*. Ambush at Junction Rock. — Large print ed. — Anstey : Ulverscroft, Sept.1982. — [336]p. — (Ulverscroft large print series)
Originally published: London : Coronet, 1970
ISBN 0-7089-0855-1 : £5.00 : CIP entry B82-27015

Marric, J. J.. Gideon's votes / J.J. Marric. — Large print ed. — Leicester : Ulverscroft, 1982, c1964. — 360p : 1map ; 22cm. — (Ulverscroft Large print series)
Originally published: London : Hodder & Stoughton, 1964
ISBN 0-7089-0745-8 : £5.00 : CIP rev. B81-36942

Marsh, Jean, *1897-*. The rekindled flame / by Jean Marsh. — London : Hale, 1982. — 175p ; 20cm
ISBN 0-7091-9637-7 : £6.25 B82-13871

Marsh, Jean, *1897-*. This foolish love / by Jean Marsh. — London : Hale, 1982. — 189p ; 20cm
ISBN 0-7091-9942-2 : £6.50 B82-39184

Meynell, Laurence. The blue door / Laurence Meynell. — London : Hale, 1982. — 224p ; 21cm
ISBN 0-7091-9667-9 : £6.95 B82-17519

Meynell, Laurence. Hooky gets the wooden spoon / Laurence Meynell. — Large print ed. — Bath : Chivers, 1982, c1977. — 233p ; 23cm. — (A Lythway book) (A Lythway mystery)
Originally published: London : Macmillan, 1977
ISBN 0-85119-778-7 : Unpriced : CIP rev. B81-33795

Meynell, Laurence. The secret of the pit / Laurence Meynell. — London : Macmillan, 1982. — 163p ; 21cm
ISBN 0-333-33331-4 : £6.50 B82-39167

Mitchell, Gladys. The death cap dancers / by Gladys Mitchell. — Long Preston : Magna, 1982, c1981. — 363p ; 23cm
Originally published: London : Joseph, 1981. — Published in large print
ISBN 0-86009-379-4 : Unpriced : CIP rev. B81-36026

Mitchell, Gladys. Here lies Gloria Mundy / Gladys Mitchell. — London : Joseph, 1982. — 181p ; 21cm
ISBN 0-7181-2093-0 : £6.95 B82-11718

Mitchell, Gladys. Mingled with venom / by Gladys Mitchell. — Long Preston : Magna Print, 1981, c1978. — 364p ; 23cm
Originally published: London : Joseph, 1978. — Published in large print
ISBN 0-86009-339-5 : Unpriced : CIP rev. B81-22465

Mitchell, Gladys. My father sleeps / Gladys Mitchell. — London : Severn House, 1981. — 208p : ill ; 21cm
ISBN 0-7278-0724-2 : £5.95 : CIP rev. B81-18103

Mitchell, Gladys. Uncoffin'd clay / by Gladys Mitchell. — Long Preston : Magna, 1982, c1980. — 357p ; 22cm
Originally published: London : Joseph, 1980. — Published in large print
ISBN 0-86009-397-2 : Unpriced : CIP rev. B82-07045

Mitchison, Naomi. Not by bread alone. — London : Marion Boyars, Jan.1983. — [160]p
ISBN 0-7145-2788-2 : £7.95 : CIP entry B82-32605

Mitford, Nancy. Pigeon pie / Nancy Mitford. — [Feltham] : Hamlyn Paperbacks, 1982. — 185p ; 18cm
ISBN 0-600-20625-4 (pbk) : £1.50 B82-28797

Monsarrat, Nicholas. The master mariner / Nicholas Monsarrat. — London : Pan
Originally published: New York : Morrow ; London : Cassell, 1980
Book 2: Darken ship. — 1981, c1980. — 200p : ill,maps ; 18cm
ISBN 0-330-26553-9 (pbk) : £1.50 B82-06407

Muir, Edwin. Poor Tom / by Edwin Muir ; introduction by P.H. Butter. — Edinburgh : Harris, 1982. — 254p ; 23cm. — (The Scottish fiction reprint library)
ISBN 0-86228-023-0 : £6.95 B82-19716

Muskett, Netta. After rain / Netta Muskett. — Large print ed. — Leicester : Ulverscroft, 1982. — 609p ; 22cm. — (Ulverscroft large print)
ISBN 0-7089-0735-0 : £5.00 : CIP rev. B81-33963

Muskett, Netta. Blue haze / Netta Muskett. — Loughton : Piatkus, [1982?]. — 255p ; 21cm
ISBN 0-86188-158-3 : £5.95 : CIP rev. B81-34641

Muskett, Netta. Fire of spring / Netta Muskett. — Loughton : Piatkus, 1982. — 255p ; 21cm
Originally published: London : Hutchinson, 1946
ISBN 0-86188-163-x : £5.95 : CIP rev. B82-10245

Muskett, Netta. The long road. — Large print ed. — Large Print : Magna Print, Aug.1982. — [600]p
Originally published: London : Hale, 1951
ISBN 0-86009-418-9 : £5.50 : CIP entry B82-16670

Muskett, Netta. Love and Deborah / Netta Muskett. — Large print ed. — Leicester : Ulverscroft, 1982, c1963. — 381p ; 23cm. — (Ulverscroft large print series)
Originally published: London : Hutchinson, 1963
ISBN 0-7089-0776-8 : Unpriced : CIP rev. B82-08087

Muskett, Netta. Misadventure. — Loughton : Piatkus, Jan.1983. — [288]p
ISBN 0-86188-238-5 : £6.95 : CIP entry B82-33228

Muskett, Netta. Rock pine. — Large print ed. — Long Preston : Magna Print, Oct.1982. — [580]p
Originally published: London : Hale, 1952
ISBN 0-86009-432-4 : £5.50 : CIP entry B82-24129

Muskett, Netta. Scarlet heels / by Netta Muskett. — Long Preston : Magna, 1981, c1940. — 552p ; 23cm
Published in large print
ISBN 0-86009-364-6 : Unpriced : CIP rev. B81-31819

Muskett, Netta. Tamarisk / Nett Muskett. — Loughton : Piatkus, 1981. — 212p ; 21cm
ISBN 0-86188-113-3 (corrected) : £5.95 : CIP rev. B81-24596

Muskett, Netta. Through many waters. — Loughton : Piatkus, Sept.1982. — [208]p
Originally published: London : Hurst & Blackett, 1968
ISBN 0-86188-162-1 : £6.50 : CIP entry B82-21548

Muskett, Netta. The touchstone / Netta Muskett. — London : Remploy, 1979. — 223p ; 20cm
Originally published: London : Hutchinson, 1962
ISBN 0-7066-0850-x : £4.00 B82-16900

O'Brian, Patrick. Desolation island / Patrick O'Brian. — [London] : Fontana, 1979, c1978 (1982 [printing]). — 276p ; 18cm
Originally published: London : Collins, 1978
ISBN 0-00-616603-2 (pbk) : £1.95 B82-33554

O'Brian, Patrick. The Ionian mission / Patrick O'Brian. — [London] : Fontana, 1982, c1981. — 346p ; 18cm
Originally published: London : Collins, 1981
ISBN 0-00-616583-4 (pbk) : £1.95 B82-33555

O'Brian, Patrick. The Mauritius command / Patrick O'Brian. — London : Fontana, 1978, c1977 (1982 [printing]). — 268p : 3maps ; 18cm
Originally published: London : Collins, 1977
ISBN 0-00-616574-5 (pbk) : £1.65 B82-19743

823'.912[F] — Fiction in English, *1900-1945 — Texts* *continuation*

O'Brien, Kate. The land of spices / Kate O'Brien. — Dublin : Arlen House, c1981. — x,285p ; 18cm. — (Popular classics)
ISBN 0-905223-28-4 (pbk) : £3.95 B82-38634

O'Brien, Kate. The last of summer / Kate O'Brien. — Dublin : Arlen House, c1981. — ix,243p ; 18cm. — (Popular classics)
ISBN 0-905223-29-2 (pbk) : £3.95 B82-38633

O'Donnell, Peadar. The knife / by Peadar O'Donnell. — Dublin : Irish Humanities Centre, 1980. — 287p : 1port ; 23cm
Port on lining paper
ISBN 0-906462-02-9 (cased) : Unpriced
ISBN 0-906462-03-7 (pbk) : Unpriced
B82-38800

O'Flaherty, Liam. The black soul. — Dublin : Wolfhound Press, July 1981. — [200]p
ISBN 0-905473-63-9 : £6.00 : CIP entry
B81-24641

Orwell, George. Nineteen eighty-four / George Orwell. — Leicester : Charnwood, 1982. — 430p ; 23cm. — (Charnwood library series)
Originally published: London : Secker & Warburg, 1949. — Published in large print
ISBN 0-7089-8027-9 : £5.25 : CIP rev.
B81-36959

Parkinson, C. Northcote. The Guernseyman / C. Northcote Parkinson. — London : Murray, 1982. — 175p : maps ; 22cm
ISBN 0-7195-3948-x : £7.50 : CIP rev.
B82-16488

Peake, Mervyn. Gormenghast / Mervyn Peake. — Harmondsworth : Penguin in association with Eyre & Spottiswoode, 1969, c1950 (1982 [printing]). — 511p : ill ; 20cm. — (King Penguin)
Originally published: London : Eyre & Spottiswoode, 1950
ISBN 0-14-006015-4 (pbk) : £2.50 B82-16777

Peters, Ellis. Monk's-hood. — Large print ed. — Anstey : Ulverscroft, Aug.1982. — [384]p. — (Ulverscroft large print series)
Originally published: London : Macmillan, 1980
ISBN 0-7089-0829-2 : £5.00 : CIP entry
B82-26673

Peters, Ellis. One corpse too many : a medieval whodunit / Ellis Peters. — Large print ed. — Leicester : Ulverscroft, 1982, c1979. — 373p : 1map ; 23cm. — (Ulverscroft large print series)
Originally published: London : Macmillan, 1979
ISBN 0-7089-0788-1 : Unpriced : CIP rev.
B82-18441

Peters, Ellis. The virgin in the ice : the sixth chronicle of Brother Cadfael / Ellis Peters. — London : Macmillan, 1982. — 220p : 1map ; 21cm
ISBN 0-333-32914-7 : £5.95 B82-31417

Plaidy, Jean. Edward Longshanks / Jean Plaidy. — London : Pan, 1981, c1979. — 351p : 1geneal.table ; 18cm
Originally published: London : Hale, 1979. — Bibliography: p6
ISBN 0-330-26173-8 (pbk) : £1.75 B82-03139

Plaidy, Jean. Epitaph for three women / Jean Plaidy. — London : Hale, 1981. — 333p ; 23cm. — (Plantagenet saga ; 12)
ISBN 0-7091-8297-x : £6.95 B82-03179

Plaidy, Jean. The Queen's husband / Jean Plaidy. — London : Pan, 1982, c1973. — 365p : 1geneal.table ; 18cm
Originally published: London : Hale, 1973. — Based on the life of Prince Albert, consort of Queen Victoria
ISBN 0-330-26092-8 (pbk) : £1.75 B82-13716

Plaidy, Jean. Red rose of Anjou / Jean Plaidy. — London : Hale, 1982. — 348p : 2coats of arms,3geneal.tables ; 23cm
Bibliography: p7
ISBN 0-7091-8452-2 : £7.25 B82-18314

Plaidy, Jean. The sun in splendour / Jean Plaidy. — London : Hale, 1982. — 365p : ill,geneal.tables ; 23cm
Bibliography: p7
ISBN 0-7091-8837-4 : Unpriced B82-33902

Powys, John Cowper. Weymouth Sands : a novel / John Cowper Powys. — London : Writers and Readers Publishing Cooperative, 1979. — 567p ; 22cm
ISBN 0-906495-20-2 : £5.95 B82-00811

Powys, John Cowper. Wolf Solent / John Cowper Powys. — Harmondsworth : Penguin, 1964, c1929 (1982 [printing]). — 633p ; 20cm. — (Penguin modern classics)
ISBN 0-14-002182-5 (pbk) : £3.50 B82-25227

Prole, Lozania. Albert the beloved. — Large print ed. — Bath : Chivers, Jan.1983. — [256] p. — (A Lythway book)
Originally published: London : Hale, 1974
ISBN 0-85119-883-x : £6.90 : CIP entry
B82-33097

Prole, Lozania. The little Victoria. — Large print ed. — Bath : Chivers, Sept.1982. — [320]p. — (A Lythway book)
Originally published: London : Hale, 1957
ISBN 0-85119-842-2 : £6.90 : CIP entry
B82-20512

Renault, Mary. Funeral games / Mary Renault. — London : Murrray, 1981. — 257p : 1map ; 22cm
ISBN 0-7195-3883-1 : £6.95 : CIP rev.
B81-27409

Richmond, Grace. Guardian of the trees / by Grace Richmond. — London : Hale, 1982. — 160p ; 20cm
ISBN 0-7091-9854-x : £6.50 B82-33421

Richmond, Grace. That villa in Spain / by Grace Richmond. — London : Hale, 1981. — 159p ; 20cm
ISBN 0-7091-9355-6 : £5.95 B82-06315

Robertson, E. Arnot. Four frightened people : a novel / by E. Arnot Robertson ; with a new introduction by Polly Devlin. — London : Virago, 1982, c1931. — xix,349p ; 20cm. — (Virago modern classics)
ISBN 0-86068-280-3 (pbk) : £3.50 : CIP rev.
B82-13164

Robertson, E. Arnot. Ordinary families : a novel / by E. Arnot Robertson ; with a new introduction by Polly Devlin. — London : Virago, 1982, c1933. — xvii,331p ; 20cm. — (Virago modern classics)
ISBN 0-86068-281-1 (pbk) : £3.50 : CIP rev.
B82-13165

Robins, Denise. Climb to the stars / by Denise Robins. — Long Preston : Magna, 1981, c1970. — 316p ; 23cm
Published in large print
ISBN 0-86009-351-4 : Unpriced : CIP rev.
B81-30434

Robins, Denise. Come back yesterday. — Large print ed. — Long Preston : Magna, Feb.1983. — [380]p
Originally published: London : Hodder and Stoughton, 1976
ISBN 0-86009-463-4 : £5.75 : CIP entry
B82-39612

Robins, Denise. Fever of love / Denise Robins. — Bath : Chivers, 1974 (1982 [printing]). — 369p ; 23cm. — (A Lythway book)
Published in large print
ISBN 0-85046-464-1 : Unpriced B82-40513

Robins, Denise. Forbidden. — Large print ed. — Long Preston : Magna Print, Aug.1982. — [336]p
Originally published: London : Hodder & Stoughton, 1971
ISBN 0-86009-417-0 : £5.50 : CIP entry
B82-16669

Robins, Denise. Let me love. — London : Hodder & Stoughton, Oct.1981. — [224]p. — (Coronet books)
Originally published: 1979
ISBN 0-340-27108-6 (pbk) : £1.25 : CIP entry
B81-26729

Robins, Denise. Love and desire and hate / by Denise Robins. — Bolton-by-Bowland : Magna, 1980, c1969. — 372p ; 23cm
Originally published: London : Hodder and Stoughton, 1969. — Published in large print
ISBN 0-86009-281-x : £5.25 : CIP rev.
B80-34131

Robins, Denise. Love's despair. — London : Coronet, Jan.1983. — [192]p
ISBN 0-340-32095-8 (pbk) : £1.25 : CIP entry
B82-34404

Robins, Denise. Murder in Mayfair. — London : Hodder & Stoughton, Aug.1982. — [176]p
ISBN 0-340-28399-8 (pbk) : £1.25 : CIP entry
B82-15747

Robins, Denise. Nightingale's song / by Denise Robins. — Long Preston : Magna Print, 1981, c1963. — 412p ; 23cm
Originally published: London : Hodder & Stoughton, 1963. — Published in large print
ISBN 0-86009-340-9 : Unpriced : CIP rev.
B81-22464

Robins, Denise. The sin was mine / by Denise Robins. — Long Preston : Magna, 1982, c1964. — 393p ; 22cm
Originally published: under the name of Julia Kane. London : Hodder & Stoughton, 1964. — Published in large print
ISBN 0-86009-387-5 : Unpriced : CIP rev.
B82-04822

Robins, Denise. Slave woman / Denise Robins. — Long Preston : Magna Print, 1982, c1961. — 424p ; 22cm
Published in large print
ISBN 0-86009-374-3 : Unpriced : CIP rev.
B81-35702

Robins, Denise. Twice have I loved / by Denise Robins. — Long Preston : Magna, 1982, c1973. — 367p ; 23cm
Originally published: London : Hodder and Stoughton, 1973. — Published in large print
ISBN 0-86009-401-4 : Unpriced : CIP rev.
B82-10228

Robins, Denise. The unlit fire / Denise Robins. — London : Severn House, 1982, c1960. — 191p ; 21cm
Originally published: London : Hodder & Stoughton, 1960
ISBN 0-7278-0829-x : £5.95 B82-35459

Robins, Denise. [War marriage]. Let me love. — Large print ed. — Long Preston : Magna Print, Dec.1982. — [480]p
Originally published as: War marriage: London : Hutchinson, 1942
ISBN 0-86009-445-6 : £5.50 : CIP entry
B82-30730

Robins, Denise. Winged love / Denise Robins. — London : Severn House, 1982. — 206p ; 21cm
ISBN 0-7278-0747-1 : £5.95 B82-09014

Robins, Denise. Women who seek / Denise Robins. — Bath : Chivers, 1982. — 368p ; 23cm. — (A Lythway book)
Large print
ISBN 0-85046-517-6 : Unpriced B82-37257

823'.912[F] — Fiction in English, *1900-1945* — *Texts continuation*

Rolfe, Frederick William. Hadrian the Seventh / Fr. Rolfe (Frederick Baron Corvo). — Harmondsworth : Penguin, 1963 (1982 [printing]). — 359p ; 20cm. — (Penguin modern classics)
ISBN 0-14-002031-4 (pbk) : £1.95 B82-33023

Saki. The unbearable Bassington. — Oxford : Oxford University Press, Oct.1982. — [148]p. — (Oxford paperbacks)
ISBN 0-19-281371-4 (pbk) : £2.50 : CIP entry B82-23672

Sassoon, Siegfried. Sherston's progress. — London : Faber, Feb.1983. — [150]p
ISBN 0-571-13033-x (pbk) : CIP entry B82-38698

Sava, George. Innocence on trial / George Sava. — London : Hale, 1981. — 200p ; 21cm
ISBN 0-7091-9357-2 : £6.95 B82-12622

Sava, George. The price of prejudice / by George Sava. — London : Hale, 1982. — 191p ; 21cm
ISBN 0-7091-9729-2 : £6.95 B82-22908

Sayers, Dorothy L.. Busman's honeymoon : a love story with detective interruptions / Dorothy L. Sayers. — London : Prior, 1981, c1937. — 586p ; 24cm
Published in large print
ISBN 0-86043-638-1 : £8.95 B82-16185

Sayers, Dorothy L.. Clouds of witness / Dorothy L. Sayers. — Sevenoaks : New English Library, 1970 (1982 [printing]). — 248p ; 18cm
ISBN 0-450-05486-1 (pbk) : £1.50 B82-37058

Sayers, Dorothy L.. Five red herrings / Dorothy L. Sayers. — Sevenoaks : New English Library, 1968 (1982 [printing]). — 268p : ill,1map ; 18cm
ISBN 0-450-05485-3 (pbk) : £1.50 B82-37056

Sayers, Dorothy L.. Gaudy night / by Dorothy L. Sayers. — London : Prior, 1981, c1936. — 741p ; 24cm
Published in large print
ISBN 0-86043-639-x : £9.50 B82-16186

Sayers, Dorothy L.. The nine tailors / Dorothy L. Sayers. — Sevenoaks : New English Library, 1968 (1982 [printing]). — 299p : ill,2maps,1plan ; 18cm
ISBN 0-450-05484-5 (pbk) : £1.75 B82-37057

Sayers, Dorothy L.. The nine tailors : changes rung on an old theme in two short touches and two full peals / by Dorothy L. Sayers. — London : Prior, 1981, c1962. — 492p ; 24cm
Published in large print
ISBN 0-86043-640-3 : £8.50 B82-16187

Sayers, Dorothy L.. Whose body? / Dorothy L. Sayers. — Sevenoaks : New English Library, 1968 (1982 [printing]). — 203p ; 18cm
ISBN 0-450-05482-9 (pbk) : £1.50 B82-37059

Scanlan, Nellie M.. Kelly Pencarrow. — Large print ed. — Anstey : Ulverscroft Large Print Books, Dec.1982. — 1v.. — (Ulverscroft large print series)
Originally published: London : Hale, 1958
ISBN 0-7089-0889-6 : £5.00 : CIP entry B82-30800

Shann, Renée. The beauty of embers. — Large print ed. — Bath : Chivers, Jan.1983. — [272] p. — (A Lythway book)
Originally published: London : Collins, 1966
ISBN 0-85119-888-0 : £6.90 : CIP entry B82-33094

Shann, Renée. Bid for happiness / Renée Shann. — Large print ed. — Bath : Lythway, 1980, c1978. — 243p ; 23cm
Originally published: London : Collins, 1978
ISBN 0-85046-916-3 : Unpriced : CIP rev. B80-32460

Shann, Renée. Heart of gold. — Large print ed. — Bath : Chivers, Nov.1982. — [240]p. — (A Lythway book)
Originally published: London : Collins, 1978
ISBN 0-85119-865-1 : £6.90 : CIP entry B82-26308

Shann, Renée. A matter of marriage. — Large print ed. — Bath : Chivers, Feb.1983. — [344] p. — (Atlantic large print)
Originally published: London : Collins, 1949
ISBN 0-85119-523-7 : £5.75 : CIP entry B82-39575

Shann, Renée. Only time will tell / Renée Shann. — Large print ed. — Bath : Chivers Press, 1982, c1977. — 209p ; 23cm
Originally published: London : Collins, 1977
ISBN 0-85119-454-0 : Unpriced : CIP rev. B81-36048

Shann, Renée. Return to happiness / Renée Shann. — Large print ed. — Leicester : Ulverscroft, 1982. — 344p ; 23cm. — (Ulverscroft large print series)
Originally published: London : Collins, 1953
ISBN 0-7089-0821-7 : Unpriced : CIP rev. B82-15960

Shann, Rennée. Flight to happiness / by Renée Shann and Mandy Shann. — London : Hale, 1982. — 188p ; 20cm
ISBN 0-7091-9856-6 : £6.50 B82-35897

Sharp, Margery. The foolish gentlewoman / Margery Sharp. — Large print ed. — Leicester : Ulverscroft, 1982, c1948. — 427p ; 23cm. — (Ulverscroft large print series)
ISBN 0-7089-0777-6 : Unpriced : CIP rev. B82-08088

Shute, Nevil. Most secret / Nevil Shute. — London : Pan in association with Heinemann, 1964 (1982 printing). — 286p ; 18cm
Originally published: London : Heinemann, 1945
ISBN 0-330-20264-2 (pbk) : £1.50 B82-18125

Shute, Nevil. Pastoral / Nevil Shute. — London : Pan in association with Heinemann, 1964 (1982 printing). — 238p ; 18cm
ISBN 0-330-10292-3 (pbk) : £1.50 B82-18124

Shute, Nevil. What happened to the Corbetts. — Large print ed. — Bath : Chivers, Nov.1982. — [384]p. — (A New Portway large print book)
ISBN 0-85119-193-2 : £6.25 : CIP entry B82-26430

Spring, Howard. Fame is the spur / Howard Spring. — [London] : Fontana, 1953 (1982 [printing]). — 640p ; 18cm
ISBN 0-00-616582-6 (pbk) : £1.95 B82-09322

Stephens, James, *1882-1950*. The demi-gods. — Dublin (24 Anglesea St., Dublin 2) : Butler Sims, Oct.1982. — [200]p
ISBN 0-946049-02-5 (pbk) : £2.95 : CIP entry B82-29043

Stevenson, D. E.. Katherine's marriage / D.E. Stevenson. — London : Collins, 1965 (1979 [printing]). — 318p ; 21cm
ISBN 0-00-243404-0 : £5.50 B82-10300

Stevenson, D. E.. Miss Buncle married. — Large print ed. — Anstey : Ulverscroft Large Print Books, Nov.1982. — [515]p. — (Ulverscroft large print series)
Originally published: London : Collins, 1960
ISBN 0-7089-0876-4 : £5.00 : CIP entry B82-29096

Stevenson, D. E.. Miss Buncle's book. — Large print ed. — Anstey : Ulverscroft, Aug.1982. — [464]p. — (Ulverscroft large print series)
ISBN 0-7089-0834-9 : £5.00 : CIP entry B82-27003

Stevenson, D. E.. The two Mrs. Abbotts. — Large print ed. — Anstey : Ulverscroft, Jan.1983. — [416]p. — (Ulverscroft large print series)
ISBN 0-7089-0910-8 : £6.25 : CIP entry B82-32538

Stewart, J. I. M.. The madonna of the astrolabe / J.I.M. Stewart. — London : Methuen, 1982, c1977. — 304p ; 18cm. — (Staircase in Surrey ; v.4)
Originally published: London : Gollancz, 1977
ISBN 0-417-02190-9 (pbk) : £1.75 B82-37243

Stewart, J. I. M.. A villa in France. — London : Gollancz, Oct.1982. — [208]p
ISBN 0-575-03103-4 : £6.95 : CIP entry B82-23340

Stewer, Jan. In chimley corner / Jan Stewer (Albert J. Coles). — Gloucester : Sutton, 1980. — 256p ; 21cm
ISBN 0-904387-56-9 : £4.95 B82-24864

Stewer, Jan. A parcel of ol' crams / Jan Stewer (Albert J. Coles). — Gloucester : Sutton, 1980. — 251p ; 21cm
ISBN 0-904387-57-7 : £4.95 B82-24865

Stuart, Francis, *1902-*. The High Consistory / Francis Stuart. — London : Brian & O'Keeffe, 1981. — 320p ; 21cm
ISBN 0-85616-221-3 : £6.95 B82-36777

Symons, Julian. The Detling murders / Julian Symons. — London : Macmillan, 1982. — 224p ; 21cm
ISBN 0-333-31305-4 : £5.95 B82-31416

Symons, Julian. Sweet Adelaide : a Victorian puzzle solved / Julian Symons. — Large print ed. — Leicester : Ulverscroft, 1982, c1980. — 537p ; 23cm. — (Ulverscroft large print series)
Originally published: London : Collins, 1980
ISBN 0-7089-0759-8 : Unpriced : CIP rev. B82-01747

Tey, Josephine. The daughter of time / Josephine Tey. — Harmondsworth : Penguin, 1954, c1951 (1981 [printing]). — 188p : 2geneal.tables ; 19cm
Originally published: London : P. Davies, 1951
ISBN 0-14-000990-6 (pbk) : £1.25 B82-01396

Tey, Josephine. The Franchise affair / Josephine Tey. — Harmondsworth : Penguin, 1951 (1982 printing). — 252p ; 18cm
Originally published: London : Peter Davies, 1948
ISBN 0-14-000841-1 (pbk) : £1.50 B82-16693

Thomas, Dylan. Adventures in the skin trade / Dylan Thomas ; foreword by Vernon Watkins. — [New] ed. — London : Putnam, 1982. — 115p ; 19cm
Previous ed.: 1955
ISBN 0-370-30928-6 : £5.95 : CIP rev. B82-19210

Thomson, George Malcolm. The ball at Glenkerran / George Malcolm Thomson. — London : Secker & Warburg, 1982. — 228p ; 23cm
ISBN 0-436-52044-3 : £7.50 : CIP rev. B82-12904

Tolkien, J. R. R.. The Lord of the Rings. — London : Unwin Paperbacks, Apr.1981
Originally published: 1954
Part 1: The Fellowship of the Ring. — [536]p
ISBN 0-04-823185-1 (pbk) : £1.50 : CIP entry B81-00399

Tolkien, J. R. R.. The Lord of the Rings. — London : Unwin Paperbacks, Apr.1981
Originally published: 1954
Part 2: The two towers. — [446]p
ISBN 0-04-823186-x (pbk) : £1.50 : CIP entry B81-00400

823'.912[F] — Fiction in English, *1900-1945* **—** *Texts* *continuation*

Tolkien, J. R. R.. The Lord of the Rings. — London : Unwin Paperbacks, Apr.1981
Originally published: 1954
Part 3: The return of the king. — [560]p
ISBN 0-04-823187-8 (pbk) : £1.50 : CIP entry
B81-00401

Tolkien, J. R. R.. The Silmarillion. — Hemel Hempstead : Allen & Unwin, Feb.1983. — [448]p
Originally published: 1977
ISBN 0-04-823230-0 : £2.95 : CIP entry
B82-36477

Tranter, Nigel. David the Prince. — London : Hodder and Stoughton, Apr.1982. — [368]p. — (Coronet books)
Originally published: 1980
ISBN 0-340-27910-9 (pbk) : £1.95 : CIP entry
B82-03821

Tranter, Nigel. Macbeth the king. — London : Coronet, Apr.1981. — [400]p
Originally published: 1978
ISBN 0-340-26544-2 (pbk) : £1.75 : CIP entry
B81-01838

Tranter, Nigel. Margaret the queen. — London : Hodder and Stoughton, Apr.1981. — [432]p
Originally published: London : Hodder and Stoughton, 1979
ISBN 0-340-26545-0 (pbk) : £1.75 : CIP entry
B81-01842

Tranter, Nigel. The master of Gray trilogy / Nigel Tranter. — [Glasgow] : [Molendinar Press], [1981]. — 1177p in various pagings ; 20cm
Cover title. — Contents: The master of Gray. Originally published: London : Hodder and Stoughton, 1961 — The courtesan. Originally published: London : Hodder and Stoughton, 1963 — Past master. Originally published: London : Hodder and Stoughton, 1965
ISBN 0-904002-70-5 (pbk) : £4.95 B82-36789

Tranter, Nigel. The patriot / Nigel Tranter. — London : Hodder and Stoughton, 1982. — 379p ; 23cm
ISBN 0-340-26456-x : £7.95 : CIP rev.
B82-01845

Trevelyan, Percy. Mr Holmes in Cornwall : a critical explanation of the late Dr. Watson's narrative entitled 'the Devil's foot' / by Percy Trevelyan. — Redruth : Penwith, 1980. — 20p : ill,1map,1port ; 21cm
Originally published: Inverness : Printed by Carruthers, 1927
ISBN 0-903686-31-7 (pbk) : Unpriced
B82-18603

Turk, Frances. Salutation / Frances Turk. — Large print ed. — Leicester : Ulverscroft, 1981. — 465p ; 23cm. — (Ulverscroft large print series)
ISBN 0-7089-0693-1 : £5.00 : CIP rev.
B81-28102

Wade, Henry. Gold was our grave / Henry Wade. — London : Remploy, 1980, c1954. — 311p : 1plan ; 20cm
Originally published: London : Constable, 1954
ISBN 0-7066-0871-2 : £4.80 B82-09343

Wade, Henry. Heir presumptive : a murder story / by Henry Wade. — London : Remploy, 1980, c1935. — vi,209p : 1geneal.table ; 22cm
ISBN 0-7066-0872-0 : £4.30 B82-09344

Wallace, Edgar. The four just men / Edgar Wallace. — London : Remploy, 1979. — 157p ; 22cm
ISBN 0-7066-0852-6 : £4.20 B82-16870

Walpole, Hugh, *1884-1941*. Rogue Herries / Hugh Walpole. — London : Pan in association with Macmillan, 1971 (1982 printing). — 445p : 1geneal.table ; 18cm
ISBN 0-330-02557-0 (pbk) : £2.25 B82-20311

Warner, Rex. The aerodrome : a love story / Rex Warner ; with an introduction by Anthony Burgess. — Oxford : Oxford University Press, 1982. — 302p ; 20cm. — (Oxford paperbacks)
ISBN 0-19-281336-6 (pbk) : £2.95 : CIP rev.
B82-07503

Warner, Rex. The aerodrome. — London : Bodley Head, Sept.1982. — [304]p
ISBN 0-370-30926-x : £7.50 : CIP entry
B82-19201

Waugh, Evelyn. The loved one : an Anglo-American tragedy / Evelyn Waugh. — Harmondsworth : Penguin, 1951, c1948 (1981 [printing]). — 126p ; 18cm
Originally published: London : Chapman & Hall, 1948
ISBN 0-14-000823-3 (pbk) : £1.25 B82-01395

Waugh, Evelyn. Scoop : a novel about journalists / Evelyn Waugh ; introduction by James Cameron ; illustrations by Quentin Blake. — London : Folio Society, 1982. — 229p : ill ; 23cm
In slip-case
£8.50 B82-29301

Webb, Mary, *1881-1927*. Gone to earth. — Large print ed. — Anstey : Ulverscroft, Nov.1982. — [432]p. — (Charnwood library series)
ISBN 0-7089-8083-x : £5.25 : CIP entry
B82-29105

Webb, Mary, *1881-1927*. Seven for a secret. — London : Virago, Sept.1982. — [288]p. — (Virago modern classics)
ISBN 0-86068-333-8 (pbk) : £3.50 : CIP entry
B82-21543

Welch, Denton. In youth is pleasure. — Oxford : Oxford University Press, Oct.1982. — [164]p. — (Oxford paperbacks)
ISBN 0-19-281363-3 (pbk) : £2.50 : CIP entry
B82-23669

Wentworth, Patricia. The lonesome road. — London : Coronet, Nov.1982. — [192]p
ISBN 0-340-28645-8 (pbk) : £1.50 : CIP entry
B82-27370

Wentworth, Patricia. Through the wall. — London : Hodder and Stoughton, July 1982. — [272]p. — (Coronet book)
Originally published: 1952
ISBN 0-340-28101-4 (pbk) : £1.25 : CIP entry
B82-12241

West, Rebecca. The harsh voice : four short novels / Rebecca West ; with a new introduction by Alexandra Pringle. — London : Virago, 1982. — xiii,250p ; 20cm. — (Virago modern classics)
Contents: Life sentence — There is no conversation — The salt of the earth — The abiding vision
ISBN 0-86068-249-8 (pbk) : £2.95 : CIP rev.
B81-40236

Wheatley, Dennis. The haunting of Toby Jugg / Dennis Wheatley. — London : Arrow, 1949, c1948 (1979 [printing]). — 351p ; 19cm
Originally published: London : Hutchinson, 1948
ISBN 0-09-907270-x (pbk) : £1.10 B82-00137

Wheatley, Dennis. Herewith the clues / Dennis Wheatley presents a fourth murder mystery ; planned by J.G. Links. — Exeter : Webb & Bower, 1982. — 1v(loose-leaf) : ill,1plan ; 27cm
Cover title
ISBN 0-906671-49-3 : £9.95 : CIP rev.
B81-36038

Wheatley, Dennis. Murder off Miami. — Exeter : Webb & Bower, July 1981. — [328]p
ISBN 0-906671-63-9 (pbk) : £9.95 : CIP entry
B81-20578

Whipple, Dorothy. The priory / Dorothy Whipple. — London : Remploy, 1979. — 528p ; 22cm
ISBN 0-7066-0807-0 : £5.80 B82-16897

White, Antonia. Frost in May / Antonia White. — [London] : Fontana in association with Virago, 1982, c1980
(1). — 506p ; 18cm
Contents: Frost in May. Originally published: London : Harmsworth, 1935 — The lost traveller. Originally published: Andover : Eyre & Spottiswoode, 1950
ISBN 0-00-616421-8 (pbk) : £1.95 B82-27895

White, Antonia. Frost in May / Antonia White. — [London] : Fontana in association with Virago, 1982, c1980
(2). — 506p : ill ; 18cm
Contents: The sugar house. Originally published: Andover : Eyre & Spottiswoode, 1952 — Beyond the glass. Originally published: Andover : Eyre & Spottiswoode, 1954
ISBN 0-00-616422-6 (pbk) : £1.95 B82-27896

Willis, Ted. The most beautiful girl in the world / Ted Willis. — London : Macmillan, 1982. — 256p ; 23cm
ISBN 0-333-32764-0 : £6.95 B82-32564

Wills, Chester. Picture rock / Chester Wills. — London : Collins, 1952 (1979 [printing]). — 188p ; 19cm
ISBN 0-00-247633-9 : £3.50 B82-03074

Wodehouse, P. G.. A damsel in distress / P.G. Wodehouse. — London : Hutchinson, 1982. — 206p ; 20cm
ISBN 0-09-149650-0 : £6.95 B82-30983

Wodehouse, P. G.. Do butlers burgle banks? / P.G. Wodehouse. — London : Hutchinson, 1982, c1968. — 188p ; 20cm
Originally published: London : Jenkins, 1968
ISBN 0-09-149640-3 : £6.95 B82-33270

Wodehouse, P. G.. The little nugget / P.G. Wodehouse. — Harmondsworth : Penguin, 1959, c1913 (1981 [printing]). — 223p ; 18cm
ISBN 0-14-001371-7 (pbk) : £1.25 B82-09139

Wodehouse, P. G.. The old reliable / P.G. Wodehouse. — London : Hutchinson, 1981. — 233p ; 20cm
Originally published: London : Herbert Jenkins, 1951
ISBN 0-257-66125-5 : £6.95 : CIP rev.
B81-13886

Wodehouse, P. G.. Psmith journalist / P.G. Wodehouse. — Harmondsworth : Penguin, 1970, c1915 (1981 [printing]). — 186p ; 18cm
ISBN 0-14-003214-2 (pbk) : £1.25 B82-09138

Wodehouse, P. G.. Sam the Sudden. — Harmondsworth : Penguin, 1974, c1972 (1982 [printing]). — 246p ; 18cm
ISBN 0-14-003836-1 (pbk) : £1.50 B82-25117

Wodehouse, P. G.. Something fresh / P.G. Wodehouse. — London : Hutchinson, 1982. — 191p ; 20cm
ISBN 0-257-66780-6 : £6.95 B82-16933

Wodehouse, P. G.. Thank you, Jeeves / P.G. Wodehouse. — London : Hutchinson, 1980. — 192p ; 20cm
ISBN 0-09-142870-x : £6.50 : CIP rev.
B80-14044

Woodward, Lilian. Give all to love / by Lilian Woodward. — London : Hale, 1982. — 159p ; 20cm
ISBN 0-7091-9785-3 : £6.25 B82-30403

Woodward, Lilian. Out of the past / by Lilian Woodward. — London : Hale, 1982. — 160p ; 19cm
ISBN 0-7091-9987-2 : £6.50 B82-39182

Woolf, Virginia. To the lighthouse. — London : Hogarth Press, June 1982. — [600]p
ISBN 0-7012-0541-5 : £50.00 : CIP entry
B82-09462

823'.912[F] — Fiction in English, *1900-1945* — *Texts* *continuation*

York, Jeremy. Voyage with murder / John Creasey as Jeremy York. — Bath : Chivers, 1982. — 354p ; 23cm. — (A Lythway book)
Originally published: London : Melrose, 1952. — Published in large print
ISBN 0-85046-624-5 : Unpriced B82-39322

823'.912[F] — Short stories in English, *1900-1945* — *Texts*

Acton, Harold. The soul's gymnasium and other stories / by Harold Acton. — London : Hamilton, 1982. — 165p ; 21cm
ISBN 0-241-10740-7 : £7.95 : CIP rev. B81-36386

Baker, Denys Val. Thomasina's island : a novella of Cornwall and other stories / Denys Val Baker. — London : Kimber, 1981. — 190p ; 23cm
ISBN 0-7183-0278-8 : £5.95 B82-02269

Bates, H. E.. The wild cherry tree / H.E. Bates. — Harmondsworth : Penguin, 1971, c1968 (1981 [printing]). — 171p ; 18cm
Originally published: London : Joseph, 1968
ISBN 0-14-003343-2 (pbk) : £1.15 B82-18630

Beckett, Samuel. [Four novellas]. The expelled : and other novellas / Samuel Beckett. — Harmondsworth : Penguin, 1980, c1967 (1982 [printing]). — 92p ; 20cm. — (Penguin modern classics)
Translation from the French. — Originally published: London : Calder, 1977
ISBN 0-14-005202-x (pbk) : £1.75 B82-29818

Betjeman, John. Lord Mount Prospect / by John Betjeman ; illustrations by David Bogie. — Edinburgh ([137 Warrender Park Rd., Edinburgh EH9 1DS]) : Tragara, 1981, c1929. — 29p : ill ; 21cm
Originally published: in London Mercury, 1929. — Limited ed. of 95 numbered copies
ISBN 0-902616-73-0 (pbk) : £15.00 B82-09907

Buchan, John, *1875-1940*. The best short stories of John Buchan / edited by David Daniell. — London : Joseph
Vol.2. — 1982. — 240p ; 23cm
ISBN 0-7181-2121-x : £8.50 B82-28804

Canning, Victor. Delay on turtle : and other stories / Victor Canning. — Large print ed. — Bath : Chivers Press, 1982, c1958. — 277p ; 23cm. — (A New Portway large print book)
Originally published: London : New English Library, 1962
ISBN 0-85119-149-5 : Unpriced : CIP rev. B81-33813

Charteris, Leslie. The fantastic Saint. — London : Hodder & Stoughton, Jan.1983. — [192]p
ISBN 0-340-27194-9 : £6.95 : CIP entry B82-34081

Chesterton, G. K.. The incredulity of Father Brown / G.K. Chesterton. — Harmondsworth : Penguin, 1958, c1926 (1982 [printing]). — 191p ; 19cm
ISBN 0-14-001069-6 (pbk) : £1.50 B82-32572

Chesterton, G. K.. The innocence of Father Brown / G.K. Chesterton. — Harmondsworth : Penguin, 1950 (1982 [printing]). — 248p ; 18cm
ISBN 0-14-000765-2 (pbk) : £1.50 B82-32573

Christie, Agatha. The Agatha Christie hour / Agatha Christie. — London : Collins, 1982. — 190p ; 23cm
ISBN 0-00-231331-6 : £6.50 B82-40418

Christie, Agatha. The labours of Hercules / Agatha Christie. — London : Pan Books in association with Collins, 1971, c1947 (1982 [printing]). — 256p ; 18cm
Originally published: London : Collins, 1947
ISBN 0-330-02780-8 (pbk) : £1.25 B82-24581

Christie, Agatha. Parker Pyne investigates / Agatha Christie. — [London] : Fontana, 1962, c1933 (1982 [printing]). — 158p ; 18cm
ISBN 0-00-616477-3 (pbk) : £1.25 B82-13645

Conrad, Joseph. ['Twixt land & sea tales]. 'Twixt land and sea : three tales / Joseph Conrad. — Harmondsworth : Penguin, 1978 (1982 [printing]). — 207p ; 18cm. — (Penguin modern classics)
Originally published: London : Dent, 1912
ISBN 0-14-004356-x (pbk) : £1.50 B82-39318

Crispin, Edmund. Fen country : twenty-six stories / Edmund Crispin. — Harmondsworth : Penguin, 1981, c1979. — 221p ; 18cm. — (Penguin crime fiction)
Originally published: London : Gollancz, 1979
ISBN 0-14-005946-6 (pbk) : £1.25 B82-19907

Crofts, Freeman Wills. The mystery of the sleeping car express and other stories. — Large print ed. — Bath : Chivers, Nov.1982. — [264] p. — (A Lythway book)
Originally published: London : Hodder and Stoughton, 1956
ISBN 0-85119-860-0 : £7.20 : CIP entry B82-26438

Dahl, Roald. The wonderful story of Henry Sugar : and six more / Roald Dahl. — Harmondsworth : Penguin, 1982, c1977. — 238p ; 19cm
Originally published: London : Cape, 1977
ISBN 0-14-005773-0 (pbk) : £1.50 B82-25424

Detection Club. The scoop ; and, Behind the screen. — London : Gollancz, Jan.1983. — [160]p
ISBN 0-575-03225-1 : £6.95 : CIP entry B82-32460

Doyle, *Sir* **Arthur Conan**. The adventures of Sherlock Holmes ; The memoirs of Sherlock Holmes ; The return of Sherlock Holmes ; A study in scarlet ; The sign of four ; The hound of the Baskervilles / Sir Arthur Conan Doyle. — London : Octopus, 1981. — 799p : ill,1port ; 25cm. — (Treasury of world masterpieces)
Cover title: The celebrated cases of Sherlock Holmes
ISBN 0-7064-1566-3 : £6.95 B82-00439

Doyle, *Sir* **Arthur Conan**. The final adventures of Sherlock Holmes : completing the canon / by Sir Arthur Conan Doyle ; collected and introduced by Peter Haining. — London : W.H. Allen, 1981. — 208p : 1ill ; 18cm. — (A Star book)
ISBN 0-352-31015-4 (pbk) : £1.50 B82-06477

Doyle, *Sir* **Arthur Conan**. The final adventures of Sherlock Holmes : completing the Canon / by Sir Arthur Conan Doyle ; collected and introduced by Peter Haining. — London : W.H. Allen, 1981. — 208p : 1ill ; 22cm
ISBN 0-491-02624-2 : £5.95 B82-15577

Doyle, *Sir* **Arthur Conan**. His last bow : some reminiscences of Sherlock Holmes / Sir Arthur Conan Doyle. — Harmondsworth : Penguin, 1981. — 198p ; 19cm
ISBN 0-14-005709-9 (pbk) : £0.95 B82-05960

Doyle, *Sir* **Arthur Conan**. The poison belt : and other Professor Challenger stories / Sir Arthur Conan Doyle. — Large print ed. — Bath : Chivers, 1982. — 196p ; 23cm. — (A New Portway large print book)
ISBN 0-85119-173-8 : Unpriced : CIP rev. B82-09849

Doyle, *Sir* **Arthur Conan**. Uncollected stories. — London : Secker and Warburg, May 1982. — [320]p
ISBN 0-436-13301-6 : £6.95 : CIP entry B82-07976

Du Maurier, Daphne. The rendezvous : and other stories / Daphne du Maruier. — London : Pan, 1981, c1980. — 234p ; 18cm
Originally published: London : Gollancz, 1980
ISBN 0-330-26554-7 (pbk) : £1.50 B82-03150

Graham, Winston. The Cornish farm : a collection of short stories / Winston Graham. — Bath : Chivers, 1982. — 180p ; 23cm. — (A New Portway large print book)
ISBN 0-85119-176-2 : Unpriced : CIP rev. B82-13089

Graham, Winston. The Japanese girl : a collection of short stories / Winston Graham. — Large print ed. — Bath : Chivers, 1981, c1971. — vii,174p ; 23cm. — (A New Portway large print book)
Originally published: London : Collins, 1971
ISBN 0-85119-147-9 : Unpriced : CIP rev. B81-31838

Jacobs, Violet. The lum hat and other stories. — Aberdeen : Aberdeen University Press, May 1982. — [160]p
ISBN 0-08-028449-3 (cased) : £10.00 : CIP entry
ISBN 0-08-028450-7 (pbk) : £5.50 B82-09269

Lawrence, D. H.. D.H. Lawrence : short stories. — London : Dent, June 1981. — [400]p. — (Everyman's library)
ISBN 0-460-01190-1 (pbk) : £2.50 : CIP entry B81-05165

Lawrence, D. H.. Selected short stories / D.H. Lawrence ; edited with an introduction and notes by Brian Finney. — Harmondsworth : Penguin, 1982. — 540p ; 18cm
Bibliography: p541
ISBN 0-14-043160-8 (pbk) : £1.95 B82-34164

O'Faoláin, Seán. The collected stories of Sean O'Faolain. — London : Constable
Vol.2. — 1981. — 448p ; 23cm
ISBN 0-09-464210-9 : £8.95 B82-04562

O'Flaherty, Liam. Short stories. — Dublin : Wolfhound Press, July 1981. — [224]p
ISBN 0-905473-51-5 (pbk) : £2.50 : CIP entry B81-24643

Pritchett, V.S.. Collected stories / V.S. Pritchett. — London : Chatto & Windus, [1982]. — xi,520p ; 23cm
ISBN 0-7011-3904-8 : £12.50 : CIP rev. B82-11768

Saki. The complete works of Saki / H.H. Munro ; with an introduction by Noël Coward. — Harmondsworth : Penguin, 1982. — xiv,944p ; 21cm
Originally published: Garden City, N.Y. : Doubleday, 1976
ISBN 0-14-009003-7 (pbk) : £4.95 B82-40991

Sayers, Dorothy L.. Hangman's holiday / Dorothy L. Sayers. — Sevenoaks : New English Library, 1974 (1982 [printing]). — 188p ; 18cm
ISBN 0-450-05483-7 (pbk) : £1.25 B82-37054

Sayers, Dorothy L.. Striding folly : including three final Lord Peter Wimsey stories / Dorothy L. Sayers. — Sevenoaks : New English Library, 1973 (1982 [printing]). — 124p : ill ; 18cm
ISBN 0-450-05481-0 (pbk) : £1.25 B82-37055

Stewart, J. I. M.. The bridge at Arta : and other stories / by J.I.M. Stewart. — London : Gollancz, 1981. — 182p ; 22cm
ISBN 0-575-03037-2 : £6.95 B82-04269

Symons, Julian. The great detectives : seven original investigations / Julian Symons ; illustrated by Tom Adams. — London : Orbis, 1981. — 144p : ill(some col.),ports ; 28cm
Bibliography: p136-144
ISBN 0-85613-362-0 : £7.95 B82-00955

Symons, Julian. The tigers of Subtopia : and other stories / Julian Symons. — London : Macmillan, 1982. — 221p ; 21cm
ISBN 0-333-31306-2 : £6.95 B82-31419

823'.912[F] — Short stories in English, *1900-1945 — Texts* *continuation*

Tolkien, J. R. R.. Unfinished tales. — London : Unwin Paperbacks, Oct.1982. — [496]p
Originally published: 1980
ISBN 0-04-823208-4 (pbk) : £2.95 : CIP entry B82-23099

Wodehouse, P. G.. Blandings Castle and elsewhere / P.G. Wodehouse. — London : Hutchinson, 1980. — 206p ; 20cm
ISBN 0-09-142920-x : £6.95 : CIP rev. B80-14052

Wodehouse, P. G.. Carry on, Jeeves / P.G. Wodehouse. — London : Hutchinson, 1982. — 256p ; 20cm
ISBN 0-257-65686-3 : £6.95 B82-16934

Wodehouse, P. G.. The heart of a goof / P.G. Wodehouse. — Harmondsworth : Penguin, 1963, c1951 (1982 [printing]). — 206p ; 18cm
ISBN 0-14-002048-9 (pbk) : £1.25 B82-32495

Wodehouse, P. G.. Tales from the Drones Club / P.G. Wodehouse. — London : Hutchinson, 1982. — 352p ; 23cm
ISBN 0-09-149620-9 : £8.95 : CIP rev. B82-15662

823'.912[J] — Children's short stories in English, *1900-1945 — Texts*

Ashford, Daisy, *d. 1972*. Love and marriage : three stories / by Daisy Ashford and Angela Ashford ; illustrated by Ralph Steadman ; with an introduction by Humphrey Carpenter. — Oxford : Oxford University Press, 1982, c1965. — xii,89p : ill,ports ; 20cm. — (Oxford paperbacks)
Originally published: London : Hart-Davis, 1965
ISBN 0-19-281329-3 : £1.95 : CIP rev. B82-15672

Ballet stories / selected by Ian Woodward ; illustrated by Linda Warrell. — London : Carousel, 1982. — 131p : ill ; 18cm
ISBN 0-552-52169-8 (pbk) : £0.95 B82-28550

Bisset, Donald. The hedgehog who rolled uphill. — London : Methuen Children's Books, Feb.1982. — [96]p
ISBN 0-416-24310-x : £3.50 : CIP entry B81-35710

Blyton, Enid. Adventures of the wishing chair / by Enid Blyton ; illustrated by Georgina Hargreaves. — London : Dean, c1982. — 117p : col.ill ; 28cm
ISBN 0-603-00308-7 : £3.75 B82-34961

Blyton, Enid. Buttercup day and other stories / Enid Blyton ; illustrated by Val Biro. — London : Hamlyn, 1982, c1950. — 189p : ill (some col.) ; 13cm. — (Bumblebee books)
ISBN 0-600-36669-3 : £0.99 B82-36268

Blyton, Enid. The Enid Blyton goodnight story book / illustrated by Maureen Bradley ... [et al.]. — London : Hodder and Stoughton, 1980. — 118p : col.ill ; 32cm
ISBN 0-340-24606-5 : £3.95 : CIP rev. B79-22872

Blyton, Enid. Enid Blyton's Noddy and the magic boots. — Bristol : Purnell, 1979 (1982 [printing]). — [40]p : col.ill ; 15cm. — (A Purnell playmate)
ISBN 0-361-04518-2 (pbk) : £0.50 B82-25845

Blyton, Enid. Enid Blyton's Noddy makes everyone cross. — Bristol : Purnell, 1979 (1982 [printing]). — [40]p : col.ill ; 15cm. — (A Purnell playmate)
ISBN 0-361-04519-0 (pbk) : £0.50 B82-25848

Blyton, Enid. Enid Blyton's Noddy's big balloon. — Bristol : Purnell, 1979 (1982 [printing]). — [40]p : col.ill ; 15cm. — (A Purnell playmate)
ISBN 0-361-04520-4 (pbk) : £0.50 B82-25846

Blyton, Enid. Enid Blyton's Noddy's unlucky day. — Bristol : Purnell, 1979 (1982 [printing]). — [40]p : col.ill ; 15cm. — (A Purnell playmate)
ISBN 0-361-04517-4 (pbk) : £0.50 B82-25847

Blyton, Enid. Enid Blyton's Tell me a story book. — Bristol : Purnell, 1982. — [114]p : col.ill ; 28cm
First published as Enid Blyton's story book and Enid Blyton's good morning book
ISBN 0-361-05321-5 : £3.99 B82-35917

Blyton, Enid. The further adventures of Josie, Click and Bun / Enid Blyton ; illustrated by Dorothy M. Wheeler. — [London] : Beaver, 1982, c1942. — 92p : ill ; 18cm
ISBN 0-600-20536-3 (pbk) : £0.75 B82-19451

Blyton, Enid. Hello Mr Twiddle! / Enid Blyton. — London : Beaver, 1982, c1942. — 94p : ill ; 18cm
ISBN 0-600-20537-1 (pbk) : £0.80 B82-38396

Blyton, Enid. Mike's monkey and other stories / Enid Blyton ; illustrated by Val Biro. — London : Hamlyn, 1982, c1950. — 189p : ill (some col.) ; 13cm. — (Bumblebee books)
ISBN 0-600-36670-7 : £0.99 B82-36269

Blyton, Enid. More goodnight stories. — London : Hodder & Stoughton Children's Books, Oct.1982. — [128]p
ISBN 0-340-28602-4 : £3.95 : CIP entry B82-27352

Blyton, Enid. The runaway cows : and other stories / Enid Blyton ; illustrated by Val Biro. — London : Hamlyn, 1982. — 189p : ill(some col.) ; 13cm. — (Bumblebee books)
Originally published: in Enid Blyton Pennant series
ISBN 0-600-36668-5 : £0.99 B82-37299

Blyton, Enid. Telltale Tommy and other stories / Enid Blyton ; illustrated by Val Biro. — London : Hamlyn, 1982, c1950. — 189p : ill (some col.) ; 13cm. — (Bumblebee books)
ISBN 0-600-36671-5 : £0.99 B82-36264

Blyton, Enid. Welcome, Josie, Click and Bun / Enid Blyton ; illustrated by Dorothy M. Wheeler. — [London] : Beaver, 1982, c1952. — 95p : ill ; 18cm
Originally published: London : Newnes, 1952
ISBN 0-600-20535-5 (pbk) : £0.75 B82-19450

Blyton, Enid. Well, really Mr Twiddle! / Enid Blyton. — London : Beaver, 1982, c1953. — 127p : ill ; 18cm
ISBN 0-600-20538-x (pbk) : £0.80 B82-34109

Clifford, Martin, *1875-1961*. Gay dogs of St. Jim's / by Martin Clifford. — London : Howard Baker, 1980. — [200]p : ill(some col.) ; 28cm. — (Howard Baker Gem ; v.10)
Facsim of: weekly issues of the Gem, 1931
ISBN 0-7030-0187-6 : £7.95 B82-26001

Derwent, Lavinia. The adventures of Tammy Troot / Lavinia Derwent ; illustrated by Virginia Salter. — London : Arrow, 1982. — 96p : ill ; 18cm. — (Sparrow books)
ISBN 0-09-927580-5 (pbk) : £0.95 B82-22071

Hamilton, Charles, *1875-1961*. Tales of Bendover College / by Charles Hamilton (Frank Richards). — London : Howard Baker, c1981. — 95,95p ; 23cm
Contents: Will Hay at Bendover. Originally published: in The Boys' Friend Library, no.647, ca. 1923 — The Barring-out at Bendover. Originally published: in The Boys' Friend Library, no.649, ca. 1923
ISBN 0-7030-0204-x : £5.95 B82-37300

Hunter, Norman. Count Bakwerdz on the carpet : and other incredible stories / Norman Hunter ; illustrated by Babette Cole. — Harmondsworth : Puffin, 1982, c1979. — 144p : ill ; 19cm
Originally published: London : Bodley Head, 1979
ISBN 0-14-031352-4 (pbk) : £0.95 B82-25570

Lamb, G. F.. The Wheaton book of magic stories / G. Lamb ; illustrated by Gwyneth Jones. — Exeter : Wheaton, 1981. — 73p : col.ill ; 22cm
ISBN 0-08-026424-7 : £3.95 B82-08904

Manning-Sanders, Ruth. A book of giants / Ruth Manning-Sanders ; drawings by Robin Jacques. — [London] : Magnet, 1982, c1962. — 124p : ill ; 20cm
Originally published: London : Methuen, 1962
ISBN 0-416-22070-3 (pbk) : £1.00 B82-39201

Manning-Sanders, Ruth. A book of witches / Ruth Manning-Sanders ; drawings by Robin Jacques. — [London] : Magnet, 1981, c1965. — 126p : ill ; 20cm
Originally published: London : Methuen, 1965
ISBN 0-416-21910-1 (pbk) : £0.95 B82-15544

Manning-Sanders, Ruth. Hedgehog and puppy dog / Ruth Manning-Sanders ; illustrated by James Hodgson. — London : Methuen Children's, 1982. — 94p : ill ; 21cm. — ([A Read aloud book])
ISBN 0-416-21810-5 : £3.95 : CIP rev. B82-06750

Manning-Sanders, Ruth. Oh really, Rabbit! / Ruth Manning-Sanders ; illustrated by James Hodgson. — London : Methuen's Children's, 1980. — 92p : ill ; 21cm
ISBN 0-416-87380-4 : £2.95 B82-22389

Richards, Frank, *1875-1961*. The Greyfriars second eleven / by Frank Richards. — London : Howard Baker, 1979. — 204p in various pagings : ill(some col.) ; 28cm. — (Howard Baker Magnet ; v.71)
Facsim reprints of: Magnet issues 918-922, 932-933
ISBN 0-7030-0175-2 : £7.95 B82-15325

Richards, Frank, *1875-1961*. The odd fellows of Greyfriars / by Frank Richards. — London : Howard Baker, 1981. — 1v.(various pagings) : ill(some col.) ; 28cm. — (Howard Baker Magnet ; v.79)
Facsim reprints from Magnet, 1927-1930
ISBN 0-7030-0208-2 : £7.95 B82-33944

Richards, Frank, *1875-1961*. The Shylock of Greyfriars / by Frank Richards. — London : Howard Baker, c1979. — 204p in various pagings : ill(some col.),facsims,1port ; 28cm. — (Howard Baker Magnet ; v.72)
ISBN 0-7030-0178-7 : £8.00 B82-10347

Uttley, Alison. From spring to spring : stories of the four seasons / Alison Uttley ; chosen by Kathleen Lines ; illustrated by Shirley Hughes. — [London] : Faber Fanfares, 1980, c1978. — 131p : ill ; 19cm. — (Faber fanfares)
Originally published: London : Faber, 1978
ISBN 0-571-11491-1 (pbk) : £1.25 : CIP rev. B80-18929

Uttley, Alison. Sam Pig at the circus / Alison Uttley ; illustrated by A.E. Kennedy. — Harmondsworth : Puffin in association with Faber and Faber, 1982. — 201p : ill ; 20cm
ISBN 0-14-031429-6 (pbk) : £1.50 B82-40664

Uttley, Alison. Stories for Christmas / Alison Uttley ; chosen by Kathleen Lines ; illustrated by Gavin Rowe. — Harmondsworth : Puffin in association with Faber, 1981, c1977. — 158p : ill ; 20cm
Originally published: London : Faber, 1977
ISBN 0-14-031349-4 (pbk) : £1.00 B82-05952

Uttley, Alison. Tales of Little Grey Rabbit / Alison Uttley ; illustrated by Faith Jaques. — London : Piccolo Books in association with Heinemann, 1982, c1980. — 110p : ill ; 20cm
Originally published: London : Heinemann, 1980
ISBN 0-330-26601-2 (pbk) : £1.25 B82-22153

823'.912[J] — Children's stories in English, *1900-1945 — Texts*

Ardizzone, Edward. Diana and her rhinoceros / Edward Ardizzone. — London : Bodley Head, 1964 (1979 [printing]). — 32p : ill(some col.) ; 21x26cm
ISBN 0-370-00736-0 : £3.25 B82-15015

823'.912[J] — Children's stories in English, *1900-1945* — Texts *continuation*

Ardizzone, Edward. Tim all alone / by Edward Ardizzone. — London : Oxford University Press, 1956 (1981 [printing]). — [48]p : ill (some col.) ; 26cm
ISBN 0-19-272125-9 (pbk) : £1.75 B82-22631

Ardizzone, Edward. Tim in danger / Edward Ardizzone. — Oxford University Press, 1953 (1979 [printing]). — [48]p : ill(some col.) ; 26cm
ISBN 0-19-272106-2 (pbk) : £1.25 B82-08827

Ardizzone, Edward. Tim to the lighthouse / Edward Ardizzone. — Oxford : Oxford University Press, 1968 (1979 [printing]). — [48]p : ill(some col) ; 26cm
ISBN 0-19-272107-0 (pbk) : £1.25 B82-08828

Baker, Margaret J.. The gift horse / Margaret J. Baker ; illustrated by Mary Russon. — London : Hodder and Stoughton, 1982. — 96p : ill ; 20cm
ISBN 0-340-26434-9 : £3.50 : CIP rev.
B81-36349

'BB'. Brendon chase / 'BB' ; with illustrations by D.J. Watkins-Pitchford. — [London] : Magnet, 1979 (1980 [printing]). — 304p : ill ; 18cm
ISBN 0-416-87600-5 (pbk) : £0.95 B82-17815

'BB'. Lord of the forest / [by] 'BB' ; illustrated by Denys Watkins-Pitchford. — London : Beaver, 1976, c1975 (1982 [printing]). — 127p : ill ; 18cm
Originally published: London : Methuen, 1975
ISBN 0-600-35513-6 (pbk) : £1.00 B82-16160

Blake, Nicholas, *1904-1972*. The widow's cruise / Nicholas Blake. — Feltham : Hamlyn Paperbacks, 1982, c1959. — 192p ; 18cm. — (A Hamlyn whodunnit)
Originally published: London : Collins, 1959
ISBN 0-600-20399-9 (pbk) : £1.25 B82-19457

Blyton, Enid. Adventure stories / Enid Elyton. — London : Armada, 1982. — 188p : ill ; 19cm
Originally published: London : Collins, 1976. — Contents: Mischief at St. Rollo's — The Children of Kidillin
ISBN 0-00-692027-6 (pbk) : £0.85 B82-36258

Blyton, Enid. Amelia Jane again! / Enid Blyton ; illustrated by Rene Cloke. — Rev. ed. — London : Beaver, 1981, c1959. — 111p : ill ; 18cm
Originally published: London : Dean, 1959?
ISBN 0-600-20422-7 (pbk) : £0.70 B82-00641

Blyton, Enid. Billy's bicycle / Enid Blyton ; pictures by Sally Holmes and Ken Stott. — [London] : Collins, c1982. — [32]p : col.ill ; 15cm. — (Collins colour cubs)
ISBN 0-00-123734-9 (pbk) : £0.50 B82-23955

Blyton, Enid. The four cousins / Enid Blyton ; illustrated by Joyce Smith and David Dowland. — [London] : Sparrow, 1981, c1961. — 93p ; 18cm
Originally published: London : Lutterworth, 1962
ISBN 0-09-926640-7 (pbk) : £0.85 B82-03687

Blyton, Enid. The girl who found sixpence / Enid Blyton ; pictures by Sally Holmes and Ken Stott. — London : Collins, c1982. — [32]p : col.ill ; 15cm. — (Collins colour cubs)
ISBN 0-00-123732-2 (pbk) : £0.50 B82-23953

Blyton, Enid. The magic faraway tree / by Enid Blyton. — De luxe ed. / illustrated by Georgina Hargreaves. — London : Dean, c1981. — 115p : col.ill ; 28cm
Previous ed.: i.e. 5th ed. : London : Newnes, 1952
ISBN 0-603-00244-7 : Unpriced B82-26123

Blyton, Enid. Mystery stories : The secret of Cliff Castle and Smuggler Ben / Enid Blyton. — London : Armada, 1982. — 187p : ill ; 18cm
Originally published: London : Collins, 1976. — The secret of Cliff Castle originally published: London : Laurie, 1947. — Smuggler Ben originally published : London : Laurie, 1943
ISBN 0-00-692026-8 (pbk) : £0.85 B82-25448

Blyton, Enid. Naughty Amelia Jane! / Enid Blyton ; illustrated by Rene Cloke. — London : Beaver, 1981, c1959. — 110p : ill ; 18cm
Originally published: London : Dean, 1959?
ISBN 0-600-20421-9 (pbk) : £0.70 B82-00642

Blyton, Enid. Noddy and the Noah's ark adventure picture book / by Enid Blyton. — Bristol : Purnell, 1982, c1967. — [20]p : col.ill ; 27cm
Originally published: London : Low, Marston, 1967. — Ill on lining papers
ISBN 0-361-03157-2 : £0.99 B82-30413

Blyton, Enid. The Saucy Jane family / Enid Blyton ; illustrated by Joyce Smith and David Dowland. — London : Sparrow, 1982. — 94p : ill ; 18cm
Originally published: London : Lutterworth, 1947
ISBN 0-09-927710-7 (pbk) : £0.85 B82-30454

Blyton, Enid. A surprise for Molly / Enid Blyton ; pictures by Sally Holmes and Ken Stott. — [London] : Collins, c1982. — [32]p : col.ill ; 15cm. — (Collins colour cubs)
ISBN 0-00-123735-7 (pbk) : £0.50 B82-23956

Blyton, Enid. Timothy's tadpoles / Enid Blyton ; pictures by Sally Holmes and Ken Stott. — [London] : Collins, c1982. — [32]p : col.ill ; 15cm. — (Collins colour cubs)
ISBN 0-00-123733-0 (pbk) : £0.50 B82-23954

Brent-Dyer, Elinor M.. The coming of age of the Chalet School / Elinor M. Brent-Dyer. — [London] : Armada, 1982. — 160p ; 18cm
Originally published: London : Chambers, 1958
ISBN 0-00-691959-6 (pbk) : £0.90 B82-13639

Briggs, Phyllis. King Arthur and the Knights of the Round Table. — Abridged ed. / retold by Phyllis Briggs. — London : Dean, [198-?]. — 184p ; 19cm. — (Dean's classics)
ISBN 0-603-03012-2 : Unpriced B82-26099

Clive, Mary. Christmas with the Savages / Mary Clive. — Milton Keynes : Robin Clark, 1979, c1955. — vii,177p : ill ; 20cm
Originally published: London : Macmillan, 1955
ISBN 0-86072-027-6 (pbk) : £1.50 B82-00595

Dahl, Roald. James and the giant peach : a children's story / Roald Dahl ; illustrated by Michel Simeon. — London : Allen & Unwin, 1967, c1961 (1981 [printing]). — 110p : ill ; 25cm
Originally published: New York : Knopf, 1961
ISBN 0-04-823078-2 : Unpriced B82-28004

Dahl, Roald. The twits / Roald Dahl ; illustrated by Quentin Blake. — Harmondsworth : Puffin, 1982, c1980. — 95p : ill ; 20cm
Originally published: London : Cape, 1980
ISBN 0-14-031406-7 (pbk) : £0.95 B82-22305

Day Lewis, C.. The Otterbury incident / C. Day Lewis ; illustrated by Edward Ardizzone. — London : Bodley Head, 1966 (1982 [printing]). — 147p : ill ; 21cm
Originally published: London : Putnam, 1948
ISBN 0-370-01002-7 : £3.95 B82-34987

De la Mare, Walter. Molly Whuppie. — London : Faber, Feb.1983. — [32]p
ISBN 0-571-11942-5 : £4.95 : CIP entry
B82-38694

Derwent, Lavinia. Macpherson's mystery adventure / Lavinia Derwent ; illustrated by Lesley Smith. — Glasgow : Blackie, c1982. — 118p : ill ; 21cm
ISBN 0-216-91148-6 : £4.95 : CIP rev.
B81-36034

Gág, Wanda. Millions of cats. — London : Faber, Sept.1982. — [32]p
Originally published: 1976
ISBN 0-571-05361-0 : £3.75 : CIP entry
B82-28460

Godden, Rumer. The dragon of Og / Rumer Godden ; illustrated by Pauline Baynes. — London : Macmillan Children's, 1981. — 60p : ill(some col.) ; 24cm
ISBN 0-333-31731-9 : £3.95 : CIP rev.
B81-23946

Hunter, Norman. Professor Branestawm's building bust-up / Norman Hunter ; illustrated by Gerald Rose. — London : Bodley Head, 1982. — [40]p : ill ; 22cm
ISBN 0-370-30457-8 : £3.25 : CIP rev.
B82-10478

Hunter, Norman. Professor Branestawm's mouse war / Norman Hunter ; illustrated by Gerald Rose. — London : Bodley Head, 1982. — [44]p : ill ; 22cm
ISBN 0-370-30458-6 : £3.25 : CIP rev.
B82-10480

Johns, W. E. (William Earl). Biggles and the noble lord. — London : Hodder and Stoughton, July 1982. — [160]p. — (Knight books)
Originally published: Leicester : Brockhampton Press, 1969
ISBN 0-340-04214-1 (pbk) : £0.85 : CIP entry
B82-12245

Johns, W. E. (William Earl). [The Camels are coming]. Biggles, pioneer air fighter / W.E. Johns. — London : Armada, 1982. — 158p ; 18cm
ISBN 0-00-691957-x (pbk) : £0.90 B82-16812

Kipling, Rudyard. The butterfly that stamped. — London : Macmillan, Oct.1982. — [32]p
ISBN 0-333-34137-6 : £2.95 : CIP entry
B82-24809

Kipling, Rudyard. The cat that walked by himself. — London : Macmillan, Oct.1982. — [32]p
ISBN 0-333-34136-8 : £2.95 : CIP entry
B82-24808

Kipling, Rudyard. The crab that played with the sea. — London : Macmillan, Oct.1982. — [32]p
ISBN 0-333-34134-1 : £2.95 : CIP entry
B82-24807

Lofting, Hugh. Doctor Dolittle and the green canary / written and illustrated by Hugh Lofting. — Harmondsworth : Puffin, 1970, c1951 (1981 [printing]). — 254p : ill ; 18cm
Originally published: London : Cape, 1951
ISBN 0-14-030408-8 (pbk) : £1.25 B82-09161

Lofting, Hugh. Doctor Dolittle in the moon / told and illustrated by Hugh Lofting. — Harmondsworth : Puffin, 1968, c1929 (1981 [printing]). — 168p : ill ; 18cm
ISBN 0-14-030370-7 (pbk) : £1.10 B82-05954

Lofting, Hugh. Doctor Dolittle's return / by Hugh Lofting ; illustrated by the author. — Harmondsworth : Puffin, 1969, c1933 (1981 [printing]). — 165p : ill ; 18cm
ISBN 0-14-030371-5 (pbk) : £1.10 B82-09143

Milne, A. A.. Eeyore has a birthday / A.A. Milne ; illustrated by E.H. Shepard. — London : Magnet, 1981. — [29]p : col.ill ; 19cm
Originally published: London : Methuen, 1975
ISBN 0-416-21720-6 (pbk) : £0.75 B82-15585

823'.912[J] — Children's stories in English, *1900-1945 — Texts* *continuation*

Milne, A. A.. An expotition to the North Pole / A.A. Milne ; illustrated by E.H. Shepard. — London : Magnet, 1981. — [29]p : col.ill ; 19cm
Originally published: London : Methuen, 1975
ISBN 0-416-21690-0 (pbk) : £0.75 B82-15586

Milne, A. A.. Kanga and Baby Roo come to the forest / A.A. Milne ; illustrated by E.H. Shepard. — London : Magnet, 1981. — [29]p : col.ill ; 19cm
Originally published: London : Methuen, 1975
ISBN 0-416-21680-3 (pbk) : £0.75 B82-15590

Milne, A. A.. Piglet meets a Heffalump / A.A. Milne ; illustrated by E.H. Shepard. — London : Magnet, 1981. — [29]p : col.ill ; 19cm
Originally published: London : Methuen, 1975
ISBN 0-416-21710-9 (pbk) : £0.75 B82-15589

Milne, A. A.. Pooh goes visiting and Pooh and Piglet nearly catch a Woozle / A.A. Milne ; illustrated by E.H. Shepard. — London : Magnet, 1981. — [29]p : col.ill ; 19cm
Originally published: London : Methuen, 1975
ISBN 0-416-21700-1 (pbk) : £0.75 B82-15587

Milne, A. A.. Winnie-the-Pooh and some bees / A.A. Milne ; illustrated by E.H. Shepard. — London : Magnet, 1981. — [29]p : col.ill ; 19cm
Originally published: London : Methuen, 1975
ISBN 0-416-21670-6 (pbk) : £0.75 B82-15588

O'Connor, Daniel. The story of Peter Pan. — London : Bell & Hyman, Oct.1982. — [128]p
ISBN 0-7135-1351-9 : £5.95 : CIP entry B82-22990

Ransome, Arthur. The big six / Arthur Ransome. — Rev ed. — London : Cape, 1982. — 367p : ill,maps ; 21cm
Previous ed.: 1940
ISBN 0-224-60639-5 : £5.95 B82-31948

Ransome, Arthur. Coot Club / Arthur Ransome. — Rev. ed. — London : Cape, 1982. — 350p : ill,col.maps ; 21cm
Previous ed.: 1934. — Maps on lining papers
ISBN 0-224-60635-2 : £5.95 B82-32584

Ransome, Arthur. Great Northern? / Arthur Ransome ; illustrated by the author. — Rev. ed. — London : Cape, 1982. — 351p : ill,col.maps ; 21cm
Previous ed.: 1947. — Maps on lining papers
ISBN 0-224-60642-5 : £5.95 B82-32582

Ransome, Arthur. Missee Lee / Arthur Ransome ; illustrated by the author. — Rev. ed. — London : Cape, 1982. — 349p : ill,col.maps ; 21cm
Previous ed.: 1941. — Maps on lining papers
ISBN 0-224-60640-9 : £5.95 B82-32583

Robinson, Joan G.. Charley / Joan G. Robinson ; illustrated by Prudence Seward. — London : Fontana, 1971, c1969 (1981 [printing]). — 189p : ill ; 18cm. — (Lions)
Originally published: London : Collins, 1969
ISBN 0-00-671961-9 (pbk) : £0.95 B82-01247

Robinson, Joan G.. When Marnie was there / Joan G. Robinson ; illustrated by Peggy Fortnum. — London : Fontana, 1971, c1967 (1981 printing). — 223p : ill ; 18cm. — (Lions)
Originally published: London : Collins, 1967
ISBN 0-00-671962-7 (pbk) : £1.00 B82-01246

Todd, Barbara Euphan. The box in the attic / Barbara Euphan Todd ; illustrated by Lynette Hemmant. — London : Transworld, 1982, c1970. — 143p : ill ; 17cm
Originally published: Tadworth : World's Work, 1970
ISBN 0-552-52167-1 (pbk) : £0.95 B82-24175

Todd, Barbara Euphan. The wand from France / Barbara Euphan Todd ; illustrated by Lynette Hemmant. — London : Transworld, 1982, c1972. — 117p : ill ; 18cm. — (A Carousel book)
Originally published: Tadworth : World's Work, 1972
ISBN 0-552-52202-3 (pbk) : £0.95 B82-35545

Todd, Barbara Euphan. Worzel Gummidge and the treasure ship / Barbara Euphan Todd. — London : Sparrow, 1980, c1958 (1981 [printing]). — 187p ; 18cm
Originally published: London : Evans, 1958
ISBN 0-09-924070-x (pbk) : £0.95 B82-09147

Todd, Barbara Euphan. Worzel Gummidge, or, The scarecrow of Scatterbrook / by Barbara Euphan Todd ('Euphan') ; illustrated by Elizabeth Alldridge. — Harmondsworth : Penguin, 1981, c1936. — ix,144p : ill ; 18cm. — (Puffin story books)
Facsim of: 1st ed., 1941
ISBN 0-14-087001-6 (pbk) : £1.00 B82-06464

Tolkein, J. R. R.. Mr Bliss. — London : Allen and Unwin, Aug.1982. — [64]p
ISBN 0-04-823215-7 : £4.95 : CIP entry B82-15648

Tolkien, J. R. R.. The hobbit, or, There and back again. — London : Unwin Paperbacks, Apr.1981. — [288]p
Originally published: 1937
ISBN 0-04-823188-6 (pbk) : £1.25 : CIP entry B81-00409

Tolkien, J. R. R.. The hobbit, or, There and back again. — Large print ed. — Anstey : Ulverscroft, Aug.1982. — [400]p. — (Charnwood library series)
ISBN 0-7089-8065-1 : £5.25 : CIP entry B82-27005

Travers, P. L.. Mary Poppins / by P.L. Travers ; with illustrations by Mary Shepard. — Rev. ed. — London : Collins, 1982. — 221p : ill ; 21cm
Previous ed.: London : P. Davies, 1934
ISBN 0-00-181101-0 : £4.95 B82-32969

Travers, P. L.. Mary Poppins in Cherry Tree Lane / P.L. Travers ; with illustrations by Mary Shepard. — London : Collins, 1982. — 90p : ill ; 22cm
ISBN 0-00-181112-6 : £4.95 B82-18344

Trease, Geoffrey. The running of the deer / by Geoffrey Trease ; illustrated by Maureen Bradley. — London : Hamilton, 1982. — 88p : ill ; 19cm. — (Antelope books)
ISBN 0-241-10789-x : £2.50 : CIP rev. B82-01712

Trease, Geoffrey. Saraband for shadows / Geoffrey Trease. — London : Macmillan Children's, 1982. — 206p ; 21cm
ISBN 0-333-32848-5 : £5.95 : CIP rev. B82-11753

823'.912'09 — Fiction in English, *1900-1945 — Critical studies*

Batchelor, John, *1936-*. The Edwardian novelists / John Batchelor. — London : Duckworth, 1982. — viii,251p,[8]p of plates : ports ; 25cm
Bibliography: p235-247. — Includes index
ISBN 0-7156-1109-7 : £18.00 : CIP rev. B81-14862

Delbanco, Nicholas. Group portrait. — London : Faber, Sept.1982. — [224]p
Originally published: New York : Morrow, 1982
ISBN 0-571-11880-1 : £8.95 : CIP entry B82-25169

Hunter, Jefferson. Edwardian fiction / Jefferson Hunter. — Cambridge, Mass. ; London : Harvard University Press, 1982. — xi,280p ; 25cm
Includes index
ISBN 0-674-24030-8 : £12.25 B82-34323

Johnstone, Richard. The will to believe : novelists of the nineteen-thirties / Richard Johnstone. — Oxford : Oxford University Press, 1982. — viii,141p ; 23cm
Bibliography: p137-138. — Includes index
ISBN 0-19-211779-3 : £9.50 : CIP rev. B82-04837

823'.912'09 — Fiction in English, *1900-1975 — Critical studies*

The **Novel** today : contemporary writers on modern fiction / edited by Malcolm Bradbury. — [Glasgow] : Fontana, 1977 (1982 [printing]). — 256p ; 19cm
Bibliography: p250-253
ISBN 0-00-636500-0 (pbk) : £2.50 B82-18959

823'.912'09 — Fiction in English. Powys, John Cowper & Powys, Llewelyn *— Biographies*

Powys, John Cowper. Confessions of two brothers / John Cowper Powys, Llewelyn Powys ; with an introduction by Malcolm Elwin. — London : Sinclair Browne, c1982. — 265p ; 20cm
Facsim of ed. published: New York : Manas, 1916
ISBN 0-86300-004-5 (cased) : £7.95 : CIP rev.
ISBN 0-86300-005-3 (pbk) : £3.50 B82-01578

823'.912'099283 — Adolescent fiction in English, *to 1900- — Critical studies*

Young adult literature : background and criticism / compiled by Millicent Lenz and Ramona M. Mahood. — Chicago : American Library Association ; London : distributed by Eurospan, 1980. — viii,516p : ill ; 24cm
Includes bibliographies
ISBN 0-8389-0302-9 : £22.95 B82-21148

823.914 — ENGLISH FICTION, 1945-

823'.914 — Children's stories in English, *1945- — Welsh texts*

Hill, Eric. [Spot's first walk. Welsh]. Smot yn gweld y byd / Eric Hill ; addasiad Cymraeg Dilwen M. Evans. — Llandysul : Gwasg Gomer, 1981. — [24]p : col.ill ; 22cm
Translation of: Spot's first walk
ISBN 0-85088-984-7 : Unpriced B82-08977

Hill, Eric. [Where's Spot?. Welsh]. Ble mae Smot? / Eric Hill ; addasiad Cymraeg Dilwen M. Evans. — Llandysul : Gwasg Gomer, 1981. — [24]p : col.ill ; 22cm
Translation of: Where's Spot?
ISBN 0-85088-993-6 : Unpriced B82-08976

823'.914 — Fiction in English. Allan, Mabel Esther *— Biographies*

Allan, Mabel Esther. To be an author : a short autobiography / by Mabel Esther Allan. — [Heswall] ([Glengarth, 11, Oldfield Way, Heswall, Wirral, Merseyside, L60 6RQ]) : M.E. Allan, c1982. — 62p : facsims ; 21cm
Unpriced (pbk) B82-33779

823'.914 — Fiction in English. Cookson, Catherine, *to 1968 — Biographies*

Cookson, Catherine. Our Kate : her personal story / Catherine Cookson. — London : Macdonald, 1969 (1982 printing). — 238p,[8]p of plates : ill,ports ; 24cm
ISBN 0-356-08548-1 (corrected) : £7.95 B82-17804

823'.914 — Fiction in English. Davis, Margaret Thomson *— Biographies*

Davis, Margaret Thomson. The making of a novelist / Margaret Thomson Davis. — London : Allison & Busby, 1982. — 134p ; 22cm
Bibliography: p133. — Includes index
ISBN 0-85031-434-8 (cased) : £6.95 : CIP rev. B81-27964

823'.914 — Fiction in English. Fowles, John *— Critical studies*

Conradi, Peter. John Fowles / Peter Conradi. — London : Methuen, 1982. — 109p ; 20cm. — (Contemporary writers)
Bibliography: p105-109
ISBN 0-416-32250-6 (pbk) : Unpriced : CIP rev. B82-06757

823'.914 — Fiction in English. Golding, William. Lord of the Flies — *Questions & answers — For schools*
Self, David. Lord of the flies, William Golding / by David Self. — London : Mary Glasgow Publications, c1980. — 15p : ill(some col.),1col.map ; 30cm. — (Guidelines)
ISBN 0-86158-523-2 (unbound) : Unpriced B82-23268

823'.914 — Fiction in English. Hines, Barry. Kes — *Study outlines*
Lundy, Damian. Kes : a study guide / Damian Lundy and Edmund Flood. — London (Ealing Abbey, W5 2DY) : A-V for Schools, [1981?]. — 32p ; 22cm
£0.40 (pbk) B82-13611

823'.914 — Fiction in English. Kennaway, James — *Correspondence, diaries, etc.*
Kennaway, James. The Kennaway papers / James and Susan Kennaway. — London : Cape, 1981. — 141p ; 23cm
ISBN 0-224-01865-5 : £5.50 : CIP rev. B80-21146

823'.914 — Fiction in English. Maugham, Robin — *Biographies*
Maugham, Robin. Escape from the shadows / Robin Maugham. — London : Robin Clark, 1981, c1972. — ix,276p,[8]p of plates : ill,ports ; 20cm
Originally published: London : Hodder & Stoughton, 1972. — Includes index
ISBN 0-86072-054-3 (pbk) : £4.25 B82-19790

823'.914 — Fiction in English. Moore, Katharine — *Correspondence, diaries, etc.*
Grenfell, Joyce. An invisible friendship : an exchange of letters 1957-1979 / Joyce Grenfell, Katharine Moore. — London : Macmillan in association with Allison & Busby, 1981. — 267p ; 23cm
ISBN 0-333-32236-3 : £8.95
Primary classification 791'.092'4 B82-06637

823'.914 — Fiction in English. Murdoch, Iris — *Critical studies*
Dipple, Elizabeth. Iris Murdoch : work for the spirit. — London : Methuen, Jan.1982. — [384]p
ISBN 0-416-31290-x : £12.50 : CIP entry B81-34401

823'.914 — Fiction in English. Petty, John — *Biographies*
Petty, John. Five fags a day : the last year of a scrap-picker / John Petty ; Introduction by Angus Wilson. — London : Remploy, 1982. — 233p ; 21cm
Originally published: London : Secker & Warburg, 1956
ISBN 0-7066-0919-0 : £6.50 B82-21942

823'.914 — Fiction in English. Sutcliff, Rosemary — *Biographies*
Sutcliff, Rosemary. Blue remembered hills. — London : Bodley Head, Oct.1982. — [144]p
ISBN 0-370-30940-5 : £5.95 : CIP entry B82-24457

823'.914[F] — Fiction in English, *1945- — Texts*
Aasheim, Ashley. The Artemis sanction / Ashley Aasheim. — London : Muller, 1982. — 318p ; 23cm
ISBN 0-584-31153-2 : £7.95 : CIP rev. B82-12820

Abbot, Francis. Dan Sanda / Francis Abbot. — Bognor Regis : New Horizon, c1982. — 5,312p ; 19cm
ISBN 0-86116-480-6 : £6.25 B82-11672

Ableman, Paul. County Hall : a novel from the BBC-TV series created by Phil Redmond / Paul Ableman. — London : British Broadcasting Corporation, 1982. — 158p ; 22cm
ISBN 0-563-17985-6 : £6.50 B82-19959

Ableman, Paul. County Hall : a novel / Paul Ableman ; from the BBC-TV series created by Phil Redmond. — London : British Broadcasting Corporation, 1982. — 158p ; 18cm
ISBN 0-563-17986-4 (pbk) : £1.50 B82-15594

Ackroyd, Peter, *1949-*. The great fire of London. — London : Hamish Hamilton, Jan.1982. — [192]p
ISBN 0-241-10704-0 : £7.50 : CIP entry B81-34318

Adair, Ruby. Sweet stranger / Ruby Adair. — London : Macdonald & Co., 1982. — 253p ; 21cm
ISBN 0-356-08519-8 : £4.95 B82-15322

Adams, Douglas. Life, the universe and everything / Douglas Adams. — London : Barker, 1982. — 161p ; 23cm
ISBN 0-213-16847-2 : £6.50 B82-39349

Adams, Douglas. Life, the universe, and everything : the Hitch hiker's guide to the galaxy 3 / Douglas Adams. — London : Pan, 1982. — 161p ; 18cm
ISBN 0-330-26738-8 (pbk) : £1.50 B82-35587

Adams, Douglas. The restaurant at the end of the Universe : the hitch hiker's guide to the Galaxy 2 / Douglas Adams. — London : Pan, 1980. — 185p ; 18cm. — (Pan original)
ISBN 0-330-26213-0 (pbk) : £0.95 B82-41093

Adams, Richard, *1920-*. The girl in a swing / Richard Adams. — Leicester : Charnwood, 1982, c1980. — 578p ; 23cm. — (Charnwood large type)
Originally published: London : Allen Lane, 1980. — Published in large print
ISBN 0-7089-8054-6 : Unpriced : CIP rev. B82-15953

Adams, Tessa. Weavers Close / Tessa Adams. — Bognor Regis : New Horizon, c1982. — 111p ; 21cm
ISBN 0-86116-513-6 : £4.25 B82-11723

Agry, Ed. O'Reilly: Blowtorch / Ed Agry. — London : Hale, 1982. — 160p ; 21cm
ISBN 0-7091-9558-3 : £6.75 B82-13847

Aiken, Joan. Foul matter. — London : Gollancz, Jan.1983. — [256]p
ISBN 0-575-03219-7 : £6.95 : CIP entry B82-32456

Aiken, Joan. The young lady from Paris : a novel / by Joan Aiken. — London : Gollancz, 1982. — 288p ; 22cm
ISBN 0-575-03090-9 : £7.50 : CIP rev. B82-04606

Aird, Catherine. Last respects / Catherine Aird. — London : Collins, 1982. — 189p ; 21cm. — (The Crime Club)
ISBN 0-00-231410-x : £6.50 : CIP rev. B82-12431

Aird, Catherine. The religious body : a famous first : the first Inspector Sloan novel / Catherine Aird. — London : Collins, 1981, c1966. — 184p ; 21cm. — (The Crime club)
Originally published: London : Macdonald, 1966
ISBN 0-00-231718-4 : £6.50 B82-03084

Albany, James. Deacon's dagger / James Albany. — London : Pan, 1982. — 191p ; 18cm. — (The Fighting saga of the SAS ; bk.3)
ISBN 0-330-26771-x (pbk) : £1.25 B82-35749

Albany, James. Warrior caste. — London : Severn House, Aug.1982. — [192]p. — (SAS ; bk.1)
ISBN 0-7278-0804-4 : £6.50 : CIP entry B82-21103

Alden, Thea. Flames in the heather / Thea Alden. — London : Macdonald, 1981. — 253p ; 18cm. — (A Minstrel book ; 25)
ISBN 0-7088-2128-6 (pbk) : £0.95 B82-09353

Alden, Thea. Flames in the heather / Thea Alden. — London : Macdonald, c1981 (1982 [printing]). — 253p ; 21cm
ISBN 0-356-08505-8 : £4.95 B82-10295

Alding, Peter. Betrayed by death / by Peter Alding. — London : Hale, 1982. — 191p ; 20cm
ISBN 0-7091-9602-4 : £6.50 B82-22864

Aldiss, Brian W.. The dark light years : a science fiction novel / by Brian W. Aldiss. — London : Remploy, 1979, c1964. — 190p ; 20cm
Originally published: London : Faber, 1964
ISBN 0-7066-0847-x : £4.10 B82-00659

Aldiss, Brian W.. Frankenstein unbound / Brian Aldiss. — [St. Albans] : Triad, 1982, c1973. — 156p ; 18cm
Originally published: London : Cape, 1973
ISBN 0-586-05434-0 (pbk) : £1.25 B82-36059

Aldiss, Brian W.. Greybeard / by Brian W. Aldiss. — London : Remploy, 1979, c1964. — 237p ; 20cm
Originally published: London : Faber, 1964
ISBN 0-7066-0846-1 : £4.30 B82-00657

Aldiss, Brian W.. Helliconia spring / Brian Aldiss. — London : Cape, 1982. — 361p ; 23cm
ISBN 0-224-01843-4 : £6.95 : CIP rev. B81-27364

Aldiss, Brian W.. Hothouse / Brian Aldiss ; with an introduction by Joseph Milicia. — London : Granada, 1979, c1962. — xix,205p ; 18cm. — (Panther)
Originally published: London : Faber & Faber, 1962
ISBN 0-586-04990-8 (pbk) : £1.25 B82-04935

Aldiss, Brian W.. Moreau's other island / Brian Aldiss. — [London] : Triad, 1982, c1980. — 176p ; 18cm
Originally published: London : Cape, 1980
ISBN 0-586-05455-3 (pbk) : £1.25 B82-37214

Alexander, Faith. The seventh child / by Faith Alexander. — London : Hale, 1981, c1980. — 176p ; 20cm
ISBN 0-7091-9408-0 : £5.95 B82-02163

Alexander, Kate. Fields of battle / Kate Alexander. — [London] : Futura, 1982. — 442p ; 18cm. — (A Futura book)
Originally published: London : Macdonald, 1981
ISBN 0-7088-2154-5 (pbk) : £1.95 B82-33789

Alexander, Kate. Friends and enemies / Kate Alexander. — London : Macdonald, 1982. — 350p ; 23cm
ISBN 0-356-08602-x : £7.95 B82-30293

Alexander, Marygold. The long straight / Marygold Alexander. — Bognor Regis : New Horizon, c1982. — 359p ; 20cm
ISBN 0-86116-635-3 : £6.75 B82-14103

Alexander, Robert. Demonstrand / Robert Alexander. — [London] : Corgi, 1982. — 222p ; 17cm
ISBN 0-552-11875-3 (pbk) : £1.50 B82-12590

Alington, Gabriel. The stars are upside down / Gabriel Alington. — [London] : Fontana, 1982, c1980. — 170p ; 18cm. — (Lions)
Originally published: London : Heinemann, 1980
ISBN 0-00-671965-1 (pbk) : £1.00 B82-13646

Allan, Margaret, *1922-*. The kissing gate / by Margaret Allan. — London : Hale, 1982. — 160p ; 20cm
ISBN 0-7091-9534-6 : £5.95 B82-10750

Allan, Margaret, *1922-*. A man called Max / by Margaret Allan. — London : Hale, 1982. — 157p ; 20cm
ISBN 0-7091-9754-3 : £6.25 B82-25988

Allan, Margaret, *1922-*. The summer of love / by Margaret Allan. — London : Hale, 1981. — 174p ; 20cm
ISBN 0-7091-9313-0 : £5.75 B82-00447

823′.914[F] — Fiction in English, *1945-* **—** *Texts continuation*

Allan, Stella. Arrow in the dark. — London : Collins, Nov.1982. — [256]p. — (The Crime Club)
ISBN 0-00-231334-0 : £6.95 : CIP entry B82-27797

Allbeury, Ted. All our tomorrows. — London : Granada, Sept.1982. — [256]p
ISBN 0-246-11855-5 : £7.95 : CIP entry B82-18862

Allbeury, Ted. The lantern network. — Large print ed. — Anstey : Ulverscroft, Oct.1982. — [352]p. — (Ulverscroft large print series)
Originally published: London : P. Davies, 1978
ISBN 0-7089-0864-0 : £5.00 : CIP entry B82-26685

Allbeury, Ted. The lonely margins / Ted Allbeury. — London : Granada, 1982, c1981. — 267p ; 18cm. — (A Mayflower book)
ISBN 0-583-13007-0 (pbk) : £1.50 B82-37216

Allbeury, Ted. The other side of silence / Ted Allbeury. — London : Granada, c1981 (1982 [printing]). — 320p ; 18cm. — (A Mayflower book)
ISBN 0-583-13389-4 (pbk) : £1.50 B82-17357

Allbeury, Ted. The secret whispers. — Large print ed. — Anstey : Ulverscroft, Feb.1983. — 1v.. — (Ulverscroft large print series)
Originally published: London : Granada, 1981
ISBN 0-7089-0912-4 : CIP entry B82-38874

Allbeury, Ted. Shadow of shadows / Ted Allbeury. — London : Granada, 1982. — 236p ; 23cm
ISBN 0-246-11601-3 : £7.95 : CIP rev. B81-36227

Allen, Judy. December flower / Judy Allen. — London : Duckworth, 1982. — 176p ; 23cm
ISBN 0-7156-1644-7 : £7.95 : CIP rev. B82-07827

Allyne, Kerry. Bound for Marando. — Large print ed. — Bath : Chivers, Feb.1983. — [288] p. — (Atlantic large print)
Originally published: London : Mills and Boon, 1977
ISBN 0-85119-521-0 : £5.75 : CIP entry B82-39464

Allyne, Kerry. Valley of lagoons / by Kerry Allyne. — London : Mills & Boon, 1982. — 187p ; 19cm
ISBN 0-263-10037-5 : £5.25 B82-22644

Alverson, Charles. Not sleeping, just dead / Charles Alverson. — [London] : Magnum, 1980, c1977. — 207p ; 18cm
Originally published: Boston, Mass. : Houghton, Mifflin, 1977 ; London : H. Hamilton, 1978
ISBN 0-417-04040-7 (pbk) : £1.25 B82-16600

Amis, Martin. Other people : a mystery story / Martin Amis. — Harmondsworth : Penguin, 1982, c1981. — 206p ; 19cm
Originally published: London : Cape, 1981
ISBN 0-14-006006-5 (pbk) : £1.75 B82-35864

Anand, Valerie. The disputed crown. — London : Chatto & Windus, Oct.1982. — [272]p
ISBN 0-7011-2628-0 : £7.50 : CIP entry B82-23198

Anderson, J. R. L.. Death in the greenhouse / J.R.L. Anderson. — Large print ed. — Leicester : Ulverscroft, 1982, c1978. — 364p ; 22cm. — (Ulverscroft large print)
Originally published: London : Gollancz, 1978
ISBN 0-7089-0730-x : £5.00 : CIP rev. B81-33953

Anderson, J. R. L.. Late delivery / by J.R.L. Anderson. — London (b Gollancz), 1982. — 175p ; 21cm
ISBN 0-575-03085-2 : £6.50 : CIP rev. B82-00164

Anderson, James, *1936-*. Auriol / James Anderson. — London : Muller, 1982. — 351p ; 23cm
ISBN 0-584-31157-5 : £7.95 : CIP rev. B82-12920

Anderson, Rachel. The poacher's son. — Oxford : Oxford University Press, Sept.1982. — [144]p
For adolescents
ISBN 0-19-271468-6 : £5.95 : CIP entry B82-19184

Andrews, Allen. Castle Crespin / Allen Andrews. — London : Hutchinson, 1982. — 238p ; 23cm
ISBN 0-09-147650-x : £7.95 : CIP rev. B82-16479

Andrews, Allen. The pig Plantagenet / Allen Andrews. — London : Arrow, 1982, c1980. — 186p ; 18cm
Originally published: London : Hutchinson, 1980
ISBN 0-09-927870-7 (pbk) : £1.50 B82-11439

Andrews, Lucilla. A weekend in the garden / Lucilla Andrews. — [London] : Corgi, 1982, c1981. — 170p ; 18cm
Originally published: London : Heinemann, 1981
ISBN 0-552-11909-1 (pbk) : £0.95 B82-19464

Andrews, Lucilla. A weekend in the garden / Lucilla Andrews. — Large print ed. — Bath : Chivers, 1982, c1981. — 264p ; 23cm. — (A Lythway book) (A Lythway general novel)
Originally published: London : Heinemann, 1981
ISBN 0-85119-772-8 : Unpriced : CIP rev. B81-37535

Andrews, Virginia. If there be thorns. — Loughton (17 Brook Rd, Loughton, Essex) : Piatkus, Apr.1981. — [288]p
ISBN 0-86188-099-4 : £6.95 : CIP entry B81-04283

Andrews, Virginia. If there be thorns. — Large print ed. — Anstey : Ulverscroft, Jan.1983. — [480]p. — (Charnwood library series)
Originally published: Loughton : Piatkus, 1981
ISBN 0-7089-8090-2 : £6.95 : CIP entry B82-32540

Anthony, Evelyn. Albatross. — London : Hutchinson, Oct.1982. — [288]p
ISBN 0-09-150610-7 : £7.95 : CIP entry B82-24707

Anthony, Evelyn. The avenue of the dead. — London : Hutchinson, Oct.1981. — [224]p
ISBN 0-09-145830-7 : £6.95 : CIP entry B81-24613

Anthony, Evelyn. The defector / Evelyn Anthony. — London : Arrow, 1982, c1980. — 367p ; 18cm
Originally published: London : Hutchinson, 1980
ISBN 0-09-926740-3 (pbk) : £1.75 B82-11442

Anthony, Evelyn. The defector / Evelyn Anthony. — Large print ed. — Leicester : Ulverscroft, 1982, c1980. — 502p ; 22cm. — (Ulverscroft large print)
Originally published: London : Hutchinson, 1980
ISBN 0-7089-0738-5 : £5.00 : CIP rev. B81-33959

Anthony, Evelyn. The occupying power / by Evelyn Anthony. — Long Preston : Magna, 1982, c1973. — 576p ; 23cm
Originally published: London : Hutchinson, 1973. — Published in large print
ISBN 0-86009-383-2 : Unpriced : CIP rev. B82-00300

Anthony, Evelyn. The return. — Large print ed. — Long Preston : Magna Print, Dec.1982. — [550]p
Originally published: London : Hutchinson, 1978
ISBN 0-86009-435-9 : £5.50 : CIP entry B82-30725

Arbor, Jane. Flash of emerald. — Large print ed. — Bath : Chivers, Jan.1983. — [264]p. — (Atlantic large print)
Originally published: London : Mills and Boon, 1977
ISBN 0-85119-514-8 : £5.25 : CIP entry B82-33087

Arbor, Jane. Invisible wife / Jane Arbor. — Large print ed. — [Bath] : Chivers, 1982, c1981. — 230p ; 23cm. — (A Seymour large print romance) (Atlantic large print)
Originally published: London : Mills and Boon, 1981
ISBN 0-85119-460-5 : Unpriced : CIP rev. B82-04998

Arbor, Jane. The price of paradise / by Jane Arbor. — London : Mills & Boon, 1982. — 188p ; 19cm
ISBN 0-263-10029-4 : £5.25 B82-18130

Arbor, Jane. Summer every day. — Large print ed. — Bath : Chivers, Sept.1982. — [240]p. — (Atlantic large print)
Originally published: London : Mills and Boon, 1976
ISBN 0-85119-490-7 : £5.25 : CIP entry B82-20507

Arbor, Jane. Two pins in a fountain / Jane Arbor. — Large print ed. — Bath : Chivers, 1981, c1977. — 228p ; 23cm. — (A Seymour book)
Originally published: London : Mills & Boon, 1977
ISBN 0-85119-436-2 : Unpriced : CIP rev. B81-25802

Archer, Jeffrey. Kane and Abel / Jeffrey Archer. — Leicester : Charnwood, 1982, c1979. — 759p ; 23cm. — (Charnwood large type)
Originally published: London : Hodder & Stoughton, 1979. — Published in large print
ISBN 0-7089-8055-4 : Unpriced : CIP rev. B82-15954

Archer, Jeffrey. The prodigal daughter / Jeffrey Archer. — London : Hodder and Stoughton, 1982. — 447p ; 24cm
ISBN 0-340-27687-8 : £7.95 : CIP rev. B82-12262

Archer, Jeffrey. A quiver full of arrows / Jeffrey Archer. — Large print ed. — Bath : Chivers, 1982, c1980. — 254p ; 23cm. — (A New Portway large print book)
Originally published: London : Hodder & Stoughton, 1980
ISBN 0-85119-166-5 : Unpriced : CIP rev. B82-07616

Archer, Jeffrey. Shall we tell the President? / Jeffrey Archer. — Large print ed. — Bath : Chivers Press, 1982, c1977. — 352p ; 23cm. — (A New Portway large print book)
Originally published: London : Cape, 1977
ISBN 0-85119-174-6 : Unpriced : CIP rev. B82-13087

Armitage, Aileen. Pipistrelle / Aileen Armitage. — Feltham : Hamlyn, 1982. — 219p ; 18cm
ISBN 0-600-20374-3 (pbk) : £1.25 B82-16815

Armstrong, Eve. Flowers of May / by Eve Armstrong. — London : Hale, 1982. — 155p ; 20cm
ISBN 0-7091-9837-x : £6.50 B82-34185

Armstrong, Lindsay. Melt a frozen heart / by Lindsay Armstrong. — London : Mills & Boon, 1982. — 189p ; 20cm
ISBN 0-263-10010-3 : £5.25 B82-13889

Arnold, Bruce. The muted swan / Bruce Arnold. — London : Hamish Hamilton, 1981. — 304p ; 21cm
ISBN 0-241-10687-7 : £7.95 : CIP rev. B81-26785

Ashby, Carter. The timber trail / by Carter Ashby. — London : Hale, 1982. — 160p ; 20cm
ISBN 0-7091-9621-0 : £5.25 B82-15597

823'.914[F] — Fiction in English, *1945-* **— *Texts continuation***

Ashe, Rosalind. Take over / Rosalind Ashe. — [London] : Fontana, 1982. — 224p ; 18cm. — (Nightshades)
ISBN 0-00-616212-6 (pbk) : £1.00 B82-18094

Ashford, Jeffrey. Guilt with honour / Jeffrey Ashford. — London : Collins, 1982. — 159p ; 21cm. — (The Crime Club)
ISBN 0-00-231924-1 : £6.50 : CIP rev. B82-10572

Ashford, Jeffrey. Hostage to death / by Jeffrey Ashford. — Long Preston : Magna, 1982, c1977. — 297p ; 23cm
Originally published: London : Long, 1977. — Published in large print
ISBN 0-86009-377-8 : Unpriced : CIP rev. B81-35701

Ashford, Jeffrey. A recipe for murder / by Jeffrey Ashford. — Long Preston : Magna, 1982, c1980. — 249p ; 23cm
Originally published: London : Long, 1980. — Published in large print
ISBN 0-86009-372-7 : Unpriced : CIP rev. B81-33766

Ashley, Simon. Turnpike road / by Simon Ashley. — London : Hale, 1981. — 173p ; 20cm
ISBN 0-7091-9498-6 : £6.75 B82-07189

Ashton, Elizabeth. White witch / Elizabeth Ashton. — London : Mills & Boon, 1982. — 191p ; 20cm
ISBN 0-263-10001-4 : £5.25 B82-13897

Ashton, Mark. When the sky falls / Mark Ashton. — London : Hale, 1982. — 208p ; 19cm
ISBN 0-7091-9955-4 : £6.75 B82-39187

Atkins, Meg Elizabeth. Palimpsest / Meg Elizabeth Atkins. — London : Quartet, 1981. — 224p ; 23cm
ISBN 0-7043-2310-9 : £6.50 : CIP rev. B81-25710

Austen, M. E.. Love-act / M.E. Austen. — London : Cape, 1982. — 192p ; 23cm
ISBN 0-224-02014-5 : £6.50 : CIP rev. B82-08438

Austin, Geoffrey. The Levant squadron / Geoffrey Austin. — London : Hale, 1982. — 159p ; 20cm
ISBN 0-7091-9802-7 : £7.25 B82-30276

Avery, Gillian. Onlookers. — London : Collins, Feb.1983. — [208]p
ISBN 0-00-222673-1 : £7.50 : CIP entry B82-36463

Avey, Ruby D.. As one small candle / by Ruby D. Avey. — London : Hale, 1982. — 176p ; 20cm
ISBN 0-7091-9650-4 : £6.95 B82-12604

Ayling, Rose. For love of Lise / by Rose Ayling. — London : Hale, 1982. — 160p ; 20cm
ISBN 0-7091-9580-x : £6.25 B82-13846

Ayre, Jessica. Not to be trusted / by Jessica Ayre. — London : Mills & Boon, 1982. — 188p ; 20cm
ISBN 0-263-10013-8 : £5.25 B82-13884

Ayrton, Michael. The maze maker. — London (100 Harbord St., SW6 6PH) : Solitaire Books, Sept.1982. — [288]p
Originally published: London : Longman, 1967
ISBN 0-907387-05-5 (pbk) : £3.50 : CIP entry B82-25064

Bacon, Margaret. The kingdom of the rose / Margaret Bacon. — Loughton : Piatkus, 1982. — 530p ; 21cm
ISBN 0-86188-117-6 : £7.95 : CIP rev. B81-33760

Bagley, Desmond. Bahama crisis / Desmond Bagley. — [London] : Fontana, 1982, c1980. — 250p : 1map ; 18cm
Originally published: London : Collins, 1980
ISBN 0-00-616304-1 (pbk) : £1.50 B82-13655

Bagley, Desmond. Bahama crisis / Desmond Bagley. — Large print ed. — Leicester : Ulverscroft, 1982, c1980. — 412p : maps ; 23cm. — (Ulverscroft large print)
Originally published: London : Collins, 1980. — Map on lining papers
ISBN 0-7089-0752-0 : £5.00 : CIP rev. B81-36939

Bagley, Desmond. Running blind / Desmond Bagley. — [London] : Fontana, 1972, c1970 (1982 [printing]). — 221p ; 18cm
Originally published: London : Collins, 1970
ISBN 0-00-616534-6 (pbk) : £1.35 B82-13654

Bagley, Desmond. Windfall / Desmond Bagley. — London : Collins, 1982. — 320p ; 23cm
ISBN 0-00-222349-x : £7.95 : CIP rev. B82-07219

Bagley, Desmond. Windfall. — London : Collins, Apr.1982. — [320]p
ISBN 0-00-222688-x : £7.95 : CIP entry B82-10666

Bagley, Michael. The plutonium factor. — London : Allison and Busby, Nov.1982. — [272]p
ISBN 0-85031-485-2 : £6.95 : CIP entry B82-31303

Bailey, Jane. Allyssa / by Jane Bailey. — London : Hale, 1982. — 160p ; 20cm
ISBN 0-7091-9513-3 : £6.75 B82-13842

Bailey, Janet. With a little luck / by Janet Bailey. — London : Mills & Boon, 1981. — 188p ; 19cm
ISBN 0-263-09937-7 : £4.55 B82-00045

Bainbridge, Beryl. Sweet William / Beryl Bainbridge. — [London] : Fontana, 1976, c1975 (1982 [printing]). — 160p ; 18cm
Originally published: London : Duckworth, 1975
ISBN 0-00-616576-1 (pbk) : £1.50 B82-16828

Bainbridge, Beryl. A weekend with Claude. — London : Duckworth, Aug.1981. — [160]p
Originally published: London : Hutchinson, 1967
ISBN 0-7156-1596-3 : £6.95 : CIP entry B81-16389

Bainbridge, Beryl. Winter garden / Beryl Bainbridge. — [London] : Fontana, 1981, c1980. — 157p ; 18cm
Originally published: London : Duckworth, 1980
ISBN 0-00-616358-0 (pbk) : £1.50 B82-06311

Ballard, J. G.. The unlimited dream company / J.G. Ballard. — [London] : Triad/Granada, 1981, c1979. — 220p ; 18cm
Originally published: London : Cape, 1979
ISBN 0-586-05205-4 (pbk) : £1.25 B82-09543

Baneham, Sam. The cloud of desolation. — Dublin : Wolfhound Press, Aug.1982. — [272]p
ISBN 0-905473-86-8 (cased) : £7.50 : CIP entry
ISBN 0-905473-87-6 (pbk) : £3.00 B82-17226

Banks, Lynne Reid. An end to running / Lynne Reid Banks. — Harmondsworth : Penguin in association with Chatto & Windus, 1966, c1962 (1982 [printing]). — 283p ; 19cm
Originally published: London : Chatto and Windus, 1962
ISBN 0-14-002442-5 (pbk) : £1.75 B82-35491

Bannister, Don. Burning leaves : a novel / by Don Bannister. — London : Routledge & Kegan Paul, 1982. — 278p ; 21cm
ISBN 0-7100-9209-1 : £6.95 B82-36113

Bannister, Jo. The winter plain / by Jo Bannister. — London : Hale, 1982. — 191p ; 20cm. — (Hale SF)
ISBN 0-7091-9634-2 : £6.25 B82-15493

Banville, John. The Newton letter : an interlude / John Banville. — London : Secker & Warburg, 1982. — 82p ; 24cm
ISBN 0-436-03265-1 : £5.95 : CIP rev. B82-12701

Barber, Frank Douglas. The last white man / Frank Douglas Barber. — London : W.H. Allen, 1982. — 222p ; 18cm. — (A Star book)
Originally published: 1981
ISBN 0-352-31085-5 (pbk) : £1.75 B82-22063

Barber, Noel. Tanamera : a novel of Singapore / Noel Barber. — London : Hodder and Stoughton, 1981. — 640p : 1map ; 23cm
ISBN 0-340-26516-7 : £7.50 : CIP rev. B81-30145

Barber, Noel. Tanamera. — London : Hodder & Stoughton, May 1982. — [768]p. — (Coronet books)
Originally published: 1981
ISBN 0-340-28262-2 (pbk) : £2.50 : CIP entry B82-07951

Barclay, Tessa. A sower went forth / Tessa Barclay. — London : W.H. Allen, 1981, c1980. — 352p ; 21cm
ISBN 0-491-02734-6 : £6.95 B82-38965

Barclay, Tessa. The stony places / Tessa Barclay. — London : W.H. Allen, 1981. — 383p ; 20cm. — (A Star book)
ISBN 0-352-30806-0 (pbk) : £1.75 B82-06476

Bargate, Verity. Tit for tat / Verity Bargate. — [London] : Fontana, 1982, c1981. — 157p ; 18cm
Originally published: London : Cape, 1981
ISBN 0-00-616409-9 (pbk) : £1.50 B82-40488

Barker, Pat. Union Street / Pat Barker. — London : Virago, 1982. — 265p ; 21cm
ISBN 0-86068-282-x (cased) : £6.95 : CIP rev.
ISBN 0-86068-283-8 (pbk) : £2.95 B82-07054

Barlay, Stephen. Crash course. — London : Hodder and Stoughton, July 1981. — [320]p
Originally published: London : Hamilton, 1979
ISBN 0-340-25075-5 (pbk) : £1.25 : CIP entry B81-13889

Barlay, Stephen. The ruling passion / by Stephen Barlay. — London : Hamilton, 1982. — 172p ; 23cm
ISBN 0-241-10695-8 : £7.95 : CIP rev. B81-34151

Barling, Tom. Terminate with prejudice / Tom Barling. — London : Methuen, 1982. — 172p ; 23cm
ISBN 0-413-49360-1 : £7.50 B82-40711

Barnard, Robert. Death and the princess / Robert Barnard. — London : Collins, 1982. — 183p ; 21cm. — (The Crime Club)
ISBN 0-00-231922-5 : £6.50 : CIP rev. B82-10571

Barnard, Robert. Death in a cold climate / Robert Barnard. — London : Prior, 1981, c1980. — 330p ; 25cm
Originally published: London : Collins, 1980. — Published in large print
ISBN 0-86043-683-7 : Unpriced B82-28214

Barnard, Robert. The missing Bronte. — London : Collins, Feb.1983. — [224]p. — (The Crime Club)
ISBN 0-00-231489-4 : £6.75 : CIP entry B82-36461

Barnes, Julian. Before she met me / Julian Barnes. — London : Cape, 1982. — 183p ; 21cm
ISBN 0-224-01985-6 : £6.50 : CIP rev. B82-01126

823′.914[F] — Fiction in English, *1945-* **—** *Texts continuation*

Barnett, James. The firing squad / James Barnett. — [London] : Futura, 1982, c1981. — 266p ; 18cm
Originally published: London : Secker & Warburg, 1981
ISBN 0-7088-2198-7 (pbk) : £1.50 B82-33792

Barnett, James. Palmprint / James Barnett. — London : Methuen Paperbacks, 1981, c1980. — 185p ; 18cm. — (Magnum books)
Originally published: London : Secker & Warburg, 1980
ISBN 0-417-06560-4 (pbk) : £1.50 B82-15499

Barnett, Rebecca. A dancing tree / Rebecca Barnett. — Bognor Regis : New Horizon, c1982. — 240p ; 21cm
ISBN 0-86116-421-0 : £4.75 B82-12946

Barrett, Susan, *1938-*. The beacon / Susan Barrett. — London : Sphere, 1982, c1981. — 250p ; 18cm
Originally published: London : Hamilton, 1981
ISBN 0-7221-1461-3 (pbk) : £1.95 B82-25713

Barstow, Phyllida. Doublecross country / Phyllida Barstow. — London : Futura, 1979. — 224p ; 18cm. — (A Troubadour book)
ISBN 0-7088-1548-0 (pbk) : £0.90 B82-34882

Barstow, Phyllida. Night is for hunting. — London : Century, Nov.1982. — [256]p
ISBN 0-7126-0002-7 : £6.95 : CIP entry B82-27969

Barstow, Stan. A kind of loving / Stan Barstow. — London : Corgi, 1973, c1960 (1982 [printing]). — 272p ; 18cm
Originally published: London : Joseph, 1960
ISBN 0-552-11805-2 (pbk) : £1.50 B82-16735

Barstow, Stan. A kind of loving : the Vic Brown trilogy / Stan Barstow. — London : Joseph, 1981. — 640p ; 23cm
Contents: A kind of loving. Originally published: London : Joseph, 1960 — Watchers on the shore. Originally published: London : Joseph, 1966 — Right true end. Originally published: London : Joseph, 1976
ISBN 0-7181-2089-2 : £7.95 B82-13657

Barstow, Stan. The right true end / Stan Barstow. — London : Corgi, 1978, c1976 (1982 [printing]). — 235p ; 18cm
Originally published: London : Joseph, 1976
ISBN 0-552-11808-7 (pbk) : £1.50 B82-16737

Barstow, Stan. The watchers on the shore / Stan Barstow. — London : Corgi, 1974, c1960 (1982 [printing]). — 205p ; 18cm
Originally published: London : Joseph, 1966
ISBN 0-552-11807-9 (pbk) B82-16736

Bassi, Michael. The kilted parrot / Michael Bassi. — Glasgow : Molendinar, c1981. — 206p ; 23cm
ISBN 0-904002-55-1 : £6.50 B82-38603

Batchelor, David. Children in the dark / David Batchelor. — London : Secker & Warburg, 1982. — 154p ; 22cm
ISBN 0-436-03682-7 : £6.95 : CIP rev. B82-06229

Bauling, Jayne. Valentine′s day / by Jayne Bauling. — London : Mills & Boon, 1982. — 189p ; 19cm
ISBN 0-263-10109-6 : £5.95 B82-37271

Bauling, Jayne. Wait for the storm / by Jayne Bauling. — London : Mills & Boon, 1982. — 188p ; 20cm
ISBN 0-263-10002-2 : £5.25 B82-13883

Bawden, Nina. The grain of truth. — Large print ed. — Bath : Chivers, Feb.1983. — [304]p. — (A New Portway large print book)
Originally published: London : Macmillan, 1968
ISBN 0-85119-204-1 : £6.90 : CIP entry B82-39460

Bawden, Nina. Walking naked / Nina Bawden. — London : Sphere, 1982, c1981. — 221p ; 18cm
Originally published: London : Macmillan, 1981
ISBN 0-7221-1493-1 (pbk) : £1.50 B82-27891

Baxter, Alida. Frankenstein is alive and well and living with Mrs Frankenstein / Alida Baxter. — London : Arrow, 1982, c1980. — 256p ; 18cm
Originally published: London : Arlington, 1980
ISBN 0-09-928460-x (pbk) : £1.50 B82-31610

Baxter, David, *1916-*. The China shop / David Baxter. — Bognor Regis : New Horizon, c1982. — 222p ; 21cm
ISBN 0-86116-613-2 : £5.75 B82-19990

Baxter, Olive. Debbie to the rescue. — Large print ed. — Bath : Chivers, Feb.1983. — [312] p. — (A Lythway book)
Originally published: London : Wright and Brown, 1959
ISBN 0-85119-893-7 : £7.50 : CIP entry B82-39582

Beardwood, Roger. Takeover. — London : Muller, Aug.1982. — [256]p
ISBN 0-584-31152-4 : £7.50 : CIP entry B82-15897

Beaton, Janet. Love charade / by Janet Beaton. — London : Hale, 1982. — 160p ; 20cm
ISBN 0-7091-9704-7 : £6.25 B82-17476

Beattie, Tasman. Judas flight / Tasman Beattie. — London : Magnum, 1980, c1979. — 237p ; 18cm
Originally published: London : Eyre Methuen, 1979
ISBN 0-417-04730-4 (pbk) : £1.00 B82-25318

Beattie, Tasman. Judas flight / by Tasman Beattie. — Long Preston : Magna, 1981, c1979. — 439p ; 23cm
Originally published: London : Eyre Methuen, 1979. — Published in large print
ISBN 0-86009-354-9 : Unpriced : CIP rev. B81-30428

Beaty, David. The white sea-bird / David Beaty. — London : Methuen Paperbacks, 1981, c1979. — 293p ; 18cm. — (Magnum books)
Originally published: London : Secker & Warburg, 1979
ISBN 0-417-06060-2 (pbk) : £1.50 B82-15501

Beaty, David. Wings of the morning / David and Betty Beaty. — London : Macmillan, 1982. — 493p ; 24cm
ISBN 0-333-30068-8 : £7.95 B82-39166

Beckett, Jenifer. Bitterley Edge / Jenifer Beckett. — Feltham : Hamlyn Paperbacks, 1981, c1979. — 245p ; 18cm
Originally published: London : Heinemann, 1979
ISBN 0-600-20426-x (pbk) : £1.25 B82-03020

Bedford, John, *1935-*. The Nemesis concerto / John Bedford. — London : Hale, 1982. — 189p ; 19cm
ISBN 0-7091-9697-0 : £6.75 B82-22116

Bedford, Kenneth. The Piegan Range / by Kenneth Bedford. — London : Hale, 1982. — 159p ; 20cm
ISBN 0-7091-9861-2 : £5.50 B82-30281

Bell, Anne. The Sea Wolf′s lady / Anne Bell. — London : Hale, 1982. — 191p ; 20cm
ISBN 0-7091-9680-6 : £7.50 B82-24899

Bell, Joyce. Draw down the dark moon / by Joyce Bell. — London : Hale, 1982. — 191p ; 20cm
ISBN 0-7091-9916-3 : £6.50 B82-36517

Bellamy, Guy. The sinner′s congregation. — London : Secker & Warburg, Sept.1982. — [192]p
ISBN 0-436-03220-1 : £6.95 : CIP entry B82-20190

Benatar, Stephen. Wish her safe at home. — London : Bodley Head, Aug.1982. — [224]p
ISBN 0-370-30491-8 : £6.95 : CIP entry B82-15777

Benedict, Rachel. Whispers on the wind / Rachel Benedict. — London : Macdonald, 1981. — 254p ; 21cm. — (A Minstrel book ; 24)
ISBN 0-354-04764-7 (cased) : £4.95
ISBN 0-7088-2113-8 (pbk) : £0.95 B82-03142

Benedictus, David. Whose life is it anyway? / David Benedictus. — London : Weidenfeld and Nicolson, 1981. — 151p ; 22cm
ISBN 0-297-78036-0 : £6.50 B82-06555

Bennett, Barbara. A rough music / Barbara Bennett. — Large print ed. — Leicester : Ulverscroft, 1981, c1980. — 427p ; 23cm
Originally published: London : Heinemann, 1980
ISBN 0-7089-0719-9 : £5.00 : CIP rev. B81-32031

Bennett, Barbara. [So wild a love]. There is a season / Barbara Bennet. — Large print ed. — Bath : Chivers, 1982, c1976. — 243p ; 23cm. — (A Lythway book) (A Lythway historical romance)
Originally published: New York : Dell ; London : Heinemann, 1976
ISBN 0-85119-773-6 : Unpriced : CIP rev. B81-33810

Bennett, R. A. (Richard Alan). Silence of guilt / by R.A. Bennett. — London : Hale, 1982. — 175p ; 20cm
ISBN 0-7091-9510-9 : £6.50 B82-12615

Bennetts, Pamela. The Marquis and Miss Jones / Pamela Bennetts. — London : Hale, 1981. — 158p ; 21cm
ISBN 0-7091-9308-4 : £6.75 B82-02816

Bennetts, Pamela. The Michaelmas tree / Pamela Bennetts. — London : Hale, 1982. — 176p ; 20cm
ISBN 0-7091-9740-3 : £7.25 B82-26026

Bennetts, Pamela. Regency rogue / Pamela Bennetts. — London : Hale, 1982. — 175p ; 21cm
ISBN 0-7091-9532-x : £6.95 B82-13872

Benney, H. P.. The Topham tiger hunters / by H.P. Benney. — Eastbourne : Kingsway, 1982, c1971. — 120p ; 18cm
Originally published: London : Victory, 1971
ISBN 0-86065-177-0 (pbk) : £1.00 B82-27747

Benson, Valerie. The impossible dream / by Valerie Benson. — London : Hale, 1982. — 190p ; 20cm
ISBN 0-7091-9925-2 : £6.50 B82-35869

Bentley, Ursula. The natural order / Ursula Bentley. — London : Secker & Warburg, 1982. — 217p ; 23cm
ISBN 0-436-04020-4 : £7.50 : CIP rev. B82-02647

Berg, Rilla. Doctor on safari / by Rilla Berg. — London : Hale, 1982. — 157p ; 20cm
ISBN 0-7091-9519-2 : £5.95 B82-10749

Bermant, Chaim. The patriarch / Chaim Bermant. — Feltham : Hamlyn, 1982, c1981. — 458p ; 18cm
Originally published: London : Weidenfeld and Nicolson, 1981
ISBN 0-600-20585-1 (pbk) : £1.75 B82-28554

Berridge, Elizabeth. People at play : a novel / by Elizabeth Berridge. — London : Heinemann, c1982. — 183p ; 23cm
ISBN 0-434-06804-7 : £6.95 B82-24525

823'.914[F] — Fiction in English, *1945- — Texts continuation*

Berry, Liz. Easy connections. — London : Gollancz, Feb.1983. — [224]p
ISBN 0-575-03245-6 : £5.95 : CIP entry
B82-38691

Best, Nicholas. Where were you at Waterloo? / Nicholas Best. — London : Hale, 1981. — 174p ; 21cm
ISBN 0-7091-9071-9 : £6.95 B82-02134

Betts, David Ian. With interest. — Peterborough (P.O. Box 22, Peterborough, Cambs. PE1 4ST) : Treasure Books, Sept.1982. — [32]p
ISBN 0-946131-00-7 : £4.50 : CIP entry
B82-22820

Bews, Robert. Fort Merinoroo / Robert Bews. — Bognor Regis : New Horizon, c1981. — 227p ; 21cm
ISBN 0-86116-536-5 (corrected) : £5.75
B82-02398

Bianchin, Helen. Wildfire encounter / by Helen Bianchin. — London : Mills & Boon, 1982. — 187p ; 20cm
ISBN 0-263-10063-4 : £5.25 B82-27602

Bianchin, Helen. Wildfire encounter / by Helen Bianchin. — London : Mills & Boon, 1982. — 187p ; 18cm
ISBN 0-263-73863-9 (pbk) : £0.85 B82-36283

Bickers, Richard Townsend. Air strike. — Large print ed. — Long Preston : Magna, Feb.1983. — [400]p
Originally published: London : Hale, 1980
ISBN 0-86009-464-2 : £6.25 : CIP entry
B82-39613

Bickers, Richard Townshend. Bombs gone! / Richard Townshend Bickers. — London : Hale, 1981. — 192p ; 21cm
ISBN 0-7091-9029-8 : £6.95 B82-02135

Bickers, Richard Townshend. The burning blue / by Richard Townshend Bickers. — London : Hale, 1982. — 188p ; 20cm
ISBN 0-7091-9098-0 : £7.25 B82-30275

Bickers, Richard Townshend. Panther Squadron / by Richard Townshend Bickers. — London : Hale, 1982. — 207p ; 20cm
ISBN 0-7091-9050-6 : £7.25 B82-13848

Bickers, Richard Townshend. Sea strike / Richard Townshend Bickers. — Large print ed. — Bath : Chivers, 1982, c1980. — 223p ; 23cm. — (A Lythway general novel)
Originally published: London : Hale, 1980
ISBN 0-85119-797-3 : Unpriced : CIP rev.
B82-05004

Billington, Rachel. Occasion of sin. — London : Hamilton, Oct.1982. — [352]p
ISBN 0-241-10865-9 : £8.50 : CIP entry
B82-23110

Billington, Rachel. A painted devil / Rachel Billington. — Harmondsworth : Penguin, 1981, c1975. — 252p ; 18cm
Originally published: London : Heinemann, 1975
ISBN 0-14-004609-7 (pbk) : £1.50 B82-06427

Bingham, John. Brock. — Large print ed. — Anstey : Ulverscroft Large Print Books, Dec.1982. — 1v.. — (Ulverscroft large print series)
ISBN 0-7089-0884-5 : £5.00 : CIP entry
B82-30797

Bingham, John. Brock and the defector / by John Bingham. — London : Gollancz, 1982. — 221p ; 21cm
ISBN 0-575-03128-x : £6.95 : CIP rev.
B82-09444

Binyon, T. J.. Swan song. — London : Hamilton, Oct.1982. — [240]p
ISBN 0-241-10888-8 : £8.95 : CIP entry
B82-23462

Bird, Veronica. Pressing problems. — Loughton : Piatkus, Aug.1982. — [192]p
ISBN 0-86188-206-7 : £6.50 : CIP entry
B82-17219

Bishop, Martin. Knight's meadow / by Martin Bishop. — London : Hale, 1982. — 160p ; 20cm
ISBN 0-7091-9671-7 : £5.25 B82-17525

Bishop, Sheila. Consequences / Sheila Bishop. — [London] : Corgi, 1981. — 220p ; 18cm
ISBN 0-552-11857-5 (pbk) : £1.25 B82-09109

Bishop, Sheila. The school in Belmont / Sheila Bishop. — London : Corgi, 1982, c1980. — 191p ; 18cm. — (A Georgian romance)
ISBN 0-552-11667-x (pbk) : £1.25 B82-37556

Black, C. H.. Soldier factotum / C.H. Black. — Bognor Regis : New Horizon, c1982. — 224p ; 22cm
ISBN 0-86116-535-7 : £6.95 B82-08979

Black, Gavin. Suddenly, at Singapore : a famous first : the first Paul Harris novel / Gavin Black. — London : Collins, 1961 (1981 [printing]). — 179p ; 21cm. — (The Crime Club)
ISBN 0-00-231797-4 : £6.50 B82-03079

Black, Ian Stuart. In the wake of a stranger / Ian Stuart Black. — London : Remploy, 1979. — 224p ; 20cm
Originally published: London : Dakers, 1953
ISBN 0-7066-0851-8 : £4.30 B82-13691

Black, Ian Stuart. The yellow flag / Ian Stuart Black. — London : Remploy, 1980, c1959. — 231p ; 22cm
Originally published: London : Hutchinson, 1959
ISBN 0-7066-0856-9 : £4.50 B82-09339

Black, Laura. Strathgallant. — London : H. Hamilton, July 1981. — [320]p
ISBN 0-241-10442-4 : £7.50 : CIP entry
B81-14854

Black, Laura. Wild cat / Laura Black. — London : Pan, 1982, c1979. — 287p ; 18cm
Originally published: London : Hamilton, 1979
ISBN 0-330-26250-5 (pbk) : £1.50 B82-10021

Black, Veronica. My pilgrim love / by Veronica Black. — London : Hale, 1982. — 190p ; 21cm
ISBN 0-7091-9893-0 : £7.25 B82-37251

Blackburn, John, *1923-*. Broken boy / by John Blackburn. — Hornchurch : Ian Henry, 1982, c1959. — 159p ; 21cm
Originally published: London : Secker & Warburg, 1959
ISBN 0-86025-207-8 : £5.25 B82-22106

Bladford, Roy. The last ditch / Roy Bradford. — Dundonald : Blackstaff Press, c1981. — 263p ; 22cm
ISBN 0-85640-258-3 (cased) : Unpriced : CIP rev.
ISBN 0-85640-259-1 (pbk) : £3.95 B81-31229

Blair, Emma. Where no man cries / Emma Blair. — London : Arrow, 1982. — 428p ; 18cm
ISBN 0-09-927720-4 (pbk) : £1.75 B82-22073

Blake, Jennifer. Golden fancy / Jennifer Blake. — London : Sphere, 1982, c1980. — 416p ; 18cm
ISBN 0-7221-1765-5 (pbk) : £2.25 B82-34224

Blake, Jennifer. The storm and the splendour / Jennifer Blake. — London : Sphere, 1981, c1979. — 446p ; 18cm
ISBN 0-7221-1744-2 (pbk) : £1.85 B82-06018

Blake, Ken. Foxhole / Ken Blake ; based on the original screenplay by Brian Clemens and Dave Humphries. — London : Sphere, 1982. — 119p ; 18cm. — (The Professionals ; 12)
ISBN 0-7221-1662-4 (pbk) : £1.00 B82-18169

Blake, Ken. Spy probe / Ken Blake ; based on the original screenplays by Tony Barwick and Christopher Wicking. — London : Sphere, 1981. — 121p ; 18cm. — (The Professionals ; 11)
ISBN 0-7221-1661-6 (pbk) : £1.00 B82-06015

Blake, Ken. The untouchables / Ken Blake ; based on the original screenplays by Brian Clemens. — London : Sphere, 1982. — 122p ; 18cm. — (The Professionals ; 13)
ISBN 0-7221-1663-2 (pbk) : £1.00 B82-18173

Blake, L. F.. Heavy metal / novelisation by L.F. Blake ; from a screenplay by Ross Cramer ; from an original idea by Derek Ford. — [London] : Magnum, 1980. — 157p,[8]p of plates : ill ; 18cm
ISBN 0-417-06350-4 (pbk) : £1.00 B82-41091

Blake, Monica. Come in from the dark / by Monica Blake. — London : Hale, 1982. — 154p ; 20cm
ISBN 0-7091-9838-8 : £6.50 B82-31631

Blake, Patrick. Double griffin / Patrick Blake. — London : Macdonald, 1982, c1981. — 320p ; 21cm
ISBN 0-356-08504-x : £5.95 B82-12671

Blake, Sally. The devil's kiss / Sally Blake. — London : Macdonald, 1981. — 255p ; 21cm
ISBN 0-354-04796-5 : £4.95 B82-00615

Blake, Sally. Moonlight mirage / Sally Blake. — London : Macdonald & Co., 1982. — 254p ; 21cm
ISBN 0-356-08522-8 : £4.95 B82-15328

Blumenfeld, Yorick. Jenny Ewing : my diary. — Fontwell : Centaur, c1981. — [90]p : ill ; 22cm
Author: Yorick Blumenfeld
ISBN 0-900001-16-x : £2.95 : CIP rev.
B81-30639

Bogarde, Dirk. A gentle occupation / by Dirk Bogarde. — Long Preston : Magna Print, 1982, c1980. — 735p ; 22cm
Originally published: London : Chatto & Windus, 1980. — Published in large print
ISBN 0-86009-411-1 : Unpriced : CIP rev.
B82-13156

Boggis, David. A time to betray / David Boggis. — London : Macmillan, 1981. — 245p : ill ; 21cm
ISBN 0-333-31984-2 : £5.95 B82-05585

Boland, John. The disposal unit / John Boland. — London : Remploy, 1979, c1966. — 199p ; 22cm
Originally published: London : Harrap, 1966
ISBN 0-7066-0843-7 : £4.40 B82-13687

Boland, John. The Midas touch / John Boland. — Large print ed. — Bath : Chivers, 1981, c1960. — 239pp ; 23cm. — (A Lythway book)
Originally published: London : Boardman, 1960
ISBN 0-85119-766-3 : Unpriced : CIP rev.
B81-31797

Boland, John. Mysterious way / John Boland. — Large print ed. — Bath : Chivers Press, 1981, c1959. — 241p ; 23cm. — (A Lythway book)
Originally published: London : Forest House, 1959
ISBN 0-85119-756-6 : Unpriced : CIP rev.
B81-31250

Bolt, David. Samson / David Bolt. — Loughton : Piatkus, 1982, c1980. — 339p : 1map ; 21cm
Originally published: New York : St. Martin's Press, 1980
ISBN 0-86188-129-x : £7.95 : CIP rev.
B81-34640

823′.914[F] — Fiction in English, *1945-* — *Texts continuation*

Bond, Lewis H.. Black Rock / by Lewis H. Bond. — London : Hale, 1982. — 160p ; 20cm
ISBN 0-7091-9756-x : £5.50 B82-25995

Bonner, Jack. Surprise attack / by Jack Bonner. — London : Hale, 1981. — 159p ; 20cm
ISBN 0-7091-9393-9 : £4.95 B82-06320

Bonner, Jack. The trail rider / by Jack Bonner. — London : Hale, 1982. — 153p ; 19cm
ISBN 0-7091-9719-5 : £5.25 B82-27311

Bovée, Ruth. Angelina / by Ruth Bovée. — London : Remploy, 1981, c1967. — 188p ; 19cm
Originally published: London : Hale, 1967
ISBN 0-7066-0915-8 : £5.40 B82-16864

Bowden, Jean. Wendy Craig′s Nanny / Jean Bowden. — Large print ed. — Bath : Chivers, 1982, c1981. — 225p ; 23cm. — (A Lythway book)
Originally published: London : Granada, 1981
ISBN 0-85119-829-5 : Unpriced : CIP rev. B82-09860

Bowes, Florence. Interlude in Venice / Florence Bowes. — London : Hale, 1982, c1981. — 179p ; 20cm
Originally published: Garden City, N.Y. : Doubleday, 1981
ISBN 0-7091-9552-4 : £5.95 B82-11057

Boyd, William, *1952-*. A good man in Africa / William Boyd. — Harmondsworth : Penguin, 1982, c1981. — 311p ; 18cm
Originally published: London : Hamilton, 1981
ISBN 0-14-005887-7 (pbk) : £1.75 B82-22316

Boyd, William, *1952-*. An ice-cream war. — London : Hamilton, Sept.1982. — [320]p
ISBN 0-241-10868-3 : £8.95 : CIP entry B82-18841

Boylan, Clare. Holy pictures. — London : Hamilton, Feb.1983. — [208]p
ISBN 0-241-10926-4 : £7.95 : CIP entry B82-37853

Brackenbary, Rosalind. The woman in the tower. — Brighton : Harvester Press, Sept.1982. — [128]p
ISBN 0-7108-0432-6 : £7.50 : CIP entry B82-21388

Bradford, Sarah. The Borgias / Sarah Bradford ; based on the televison scripts by John Prebble and Ken Taylor. — London : Macdonald, c1981. — xi,304p : 1map ; 18cm. — (A Futura book)
ISBN 0-7088-2019-0 (pbk) : £1.50 B82-00459

Bradley, Jack. Battle squad : Alamein attack!. — London : Severn House, Oct.1982. — [224]p
ISBN 0-7278-0835-4 : £6.95 : CIP entry B82-28579

Bradley, Muriel. Tanya / Muriel Bradley. — London : Troubadour, 1981, c1980. — 409p ; 18cm
ISBN 0-7107-3019-5 (pbk) : £1.95 B82-06604

Bradshaw, Gillian. Kingdom of summer / Gillian Bradshaw. — London : Eyre Methuen, 1981. — 255p : 1map ; 23cm
Originally published: New York : Simon and Schuster, 1981
ISBN 0-413-47640-5 : £6.95 : CIP rev. B81-25283

Brady, William S.. Blood run / William S. Brady. — [London] : Fontana, 1982. — 127p ; 18cm. — (Peacemaker ; 5)
ISBN 0-00-616522-2 (pbk) : £1.00 B82-30765

Brady, William S.. Death and Jack Shade / William S. Brady. — [London] : Fontana, 1982. — 125p ; 18cm. — (Hawk ; 12)
ISBN 0-00-616362-9 (pbk) : £1.00 B82-25439

Brady, William S.. Lynch law / William S. Brady. — [London] : Fontana, 1981. — 125p ; 18cm. — (Peacemaker ; 4)
ISBN 0-00-615941-9 (pbk) : £1.00 B82-06314

Brady, William S.. Sierra gold / William S. Brady. — [London] : Fontana, 1982. — 124p ; 18cm. — (Hawk ; no.11)
ISBN 0-00-616361-0 (pbk) : £0.95 B82-13643

Bragg, Melvyn. Kingdom come. — London : Hodder & Stoughton, Mar.1982. — [368]p. — (Coronet books)
Originally published: London : Secker and Warburg, 1980
ISBN 0-340-26798-4 (pbk) : £1.50 : CIP entry B82-01843

Bramble, Forbes. Fools. — London : Hamilton, Feb.1983. — [192]p
ISBN 0-241-10895-0 : £7.95 : CIP entry B82-37850

Brandon, Sheila. Nurse in the sun. — Large print ed. — Anstey : Ulverscroft, Sept.1982. — [352]p. — (Ulverscroft large print series)
Originally published: London : Corgi, 1972
ISBN 0-7089-0845-4 : £5.00 : CIP entry B82-27176

Brant, Lewis. Cowboy law / by Lewis Brant. — London : Hale, 1982. — 160p ; 20cm
ISBN 0-7091-9574-5 : £4.95 B82-13841

Brason, John. Kessler / John Brason ; from the BBC TV serial devised by John Brason and Gerald Glaister and directed by Michael Briant and Tristan de Vere Cole. — London : British Broadcasting Corporation, 1981. — 205p ; 18cm
ISBN 0-563-17969-4 (pbk) : £1.50 B82-03021

Brason, John. Kessler / John Brason ; from the BBC-TV serial devised by John Brason and Gerard Glauster and directed by Michael Briant and Tristan de Vere Cole. — London : British Broadcasting Corporation, 1981. — 205p : ill ; 22cm
Bibliography: p6
ISBN 0-563-17970-8 : £6.75 B82-03502

Breese, Andrea. Setting out / by Andrea Breese. — London : John Clare, 1981. — 193p ; 23cm
ISBN 0-906549-21-3 : £6.95 B82-00004

Brett, Simon, *1945-*. Murder in the title. — London : Gollancz, Feb.1983. — [192]p
ISBN 0-575-03266-9 : £6.95 : CIP entry B82-38693

Brett, Simon, *1945-*. Murder unprompted : a crime novel / by Simon Brett. — London : Gollancz, 1982. — 160p ; 21cm
ISBN 0-575-03070-4 : £5.95 B82-12947

Brierley, David. Shooting star. — London : Collins, Jan.1983. — [224]p
ISBN 0-00-222685-5 : £7.95 : CIP entry B82-33586

Briggs, Desmond. The partners / Desmond Briggs. — London : Secker & Warburg, 1982. — 327p ; 23cm
ISBN 0-436-06855-9 : £7.50 : CIP rev. B82-14068

Brindley, Louise. In the shadow of the Brontës / Louise Brindley. — London : Muller, 1982. — 272p ; 23cm
ISBN 0-584-31156-7 : £1.75 : CIP rev. B82-11767

Brinig, Denise. Tears / Denise Brinig. — London : Macdonald, 1981. — 186p ; 21cm
ISBN 0-354-04732-9 : £5.50 B82-08981

Brinig, Denise. Tears / Denise Brinig. — London : Macdonald Futura, 1981. — 186p ; 18cm
ISBN 0-7088-2110-3 (pbk) : £1.10 B82-03140

Britt, Katrina. Conflict of love / by Katrina Britt. — London : Mills & Boon, 1981. — 191p ; 20cm
ISBN 0-263-09958-x : £4.55 B82-04656

Britt, Katrina. The man at Key West / by Katrina Britt. — London : Mills & Boon, 1982. — 189p ; 20cm
ISBN 0-263-09995-4 : £5.25 B82-10383

Brittain, Vera. Account rendered / Vera Brittain. — London : Virago, 1982, c1970. — ix,334p ; 20cm
Originally published: London : Macmillan, 1945
ISBN 0-86068-268-4 (pbk) : £3.50 : CIP rev. B82-16678

Brittain, Vera. Born 1925 : a novel of youth / Vera Brittain. — London : Virago, 1982, c1970. — 378p ; 20cm
Originally published: London : Macdonald, 1948
ISBN 0-86068-270-6 (pbk) : £3.50 : CIP rev. B82-16679

Broderick, John. The trial of Father Dillingham : a novel / by John Broderick. — London : Boyars, 1982. — 221p ; 23cm
ISBN 0-7145-2747-5 : £7.95 : CIP rev. B81-21614

Bromige, Iris. The happy fortress. — London : Hodder and Stoughton, Aug.1982. — [192]p. — (Coronet books)
Originally published: 1978
ISBN 0-340-28106-5 (pbk) : £1.25 : CIP entry B82-15733

Bromige, Iris. A house without love / Iris Bromige. — Large print ed. — Leicester : Ulverscroft, 1981, c1964. — 375p ; 23cm. — (Ulverscroft large print)
Originally published: London : Hodder & Stoughton, 1965
ISBN 0-7089-0705-9 : £5.00 : CIP rev. B81-30499

Bromige, Iris. Laurian Vale. — London : Severn House, Dec.1982. — [192]p
ISBN 0-7278-0842-7 : £6.95 : CIP entry B82-34078

Bromige, Iris. Old love′s domain. — London : Hodder & Stoughton, Nov.1982. — [224]p
ISBN 0-340-32035-4 : £5.95 : CIP entry B82-27336

Bromige, Iris. The paths of summer. — London : Coronet, Apr.1981. — [208]p
Originally published: 1979
ISBN 0-340-26098-x (pbk) : £1.10 : CIP entry B81-01280

Brooke, Jocelyn. The image of a drawn sword. — London : Secker & Warburg, Jan.1983. — [190]p
ISBN 0-436-06951-2 : £7.50 : CIP entry B82-34591

Brookes, Owen. The touch / Owen Brookes. — London : Macdonald, 1981. — 282p ; 18cm. — (A Futura book)
ISBN 0-7088-2132-4 (pbk) : £1.50 B82-09355

Brookner, Anita. Look at me. — London : Cape, Feb.1983. — 1v.
ISBN 0-224-02055-2 B82-37835

Brookner, Anita. Providence / Anita Brookner. — London : Cape, 1982. — 183p ; 21cm
ISBN 0-224-01976-7 : £6.95 : CIP rev. B82-01131

Broome, Susannah. The pearl pagoda / Susannah Broome. — Large print ed. — Leicester : Ulverscroft, 1982, c1980. — 504p ; 23cm. — (Ulverscroft large print series)
Originally published: London : Heinemann, 1980
ISBN 0-7089-0765-2 : Unpriced : CIP rev. B82-01740

823'.914[F] — Fiction in English, *1945-* **— Texts** *continuation*

Brown, Christy. A promising career / Christy Brown. — London : Secker & Warburg, 1982. — 247p ; 23cm
ISBN 0-436-07097-9 : £7.50 : CIP rev. B82-14939

Brown, George Mackay. Andrina and other stories. — London : Hogarth Press, Feb.1983. — [160]p
ISBN 0-7012-0546-6 : £6.95 : CIP entry B82-38870

Browne, Marshall. City of masks / by Marshall Browne. — London : Hale, 1981. — 190p ; 20cm
ISBN 0-7091-9231-2 : £6.25 B82-12608

Browne, Marshall. Dragon strike / by Marshall Browne. — London : Hale, 1981. — 208p ; 20cm
ISBN 0-7091-9336-x : £6.50 B82-22129

Browne, Peter Francis. Land's end. — London : Hodder and Stoughton, May 1982. — [288]p. — (Coronet books)
Originally published: London : Secker & Warburg, 1981
ISBN 0-340-27916-8 (pbk) : £1.25 : CIP entry B82-06725

Brunner, John, *1934-*. Into the slave nebula / John Brunner. — London : Corgi, 1982, c1968. — 156p ; 18cm
Originally published: New York : Lancer, 1968 ; London : Millington, 1980
ISBN 0-552-12012-x (pbk) : £1.50 B82-37129

Brunner, John, *1934-*. The stardroppers / John Brunner. — Feltham : Hamlyn, 1982, c1972. — 144p ; 18cm
Originally published: New York : Daw, 1972
ISBN 0-600-20008-6 (pbk) : £1.10 B82-16819

Brunner, John, *1934-*. While there's hope / John Brunner ; wood engravings by Paul Piech. — Richmond : Keepsake, c1982. — 22p : ill ; 20cm
Translation of: Das Prinzip Hoffnung. — Limited ed. of 230 copies of which 20 copies in hardback have been signed and numbered by the author and the artist
ISBN 0-901924-57-1 (pbk) : £1.50 B82-31941

Bryers, Paul. Hire me a base fellow / Paul Bryers. — London : Macdonald, 1981. — 310p : 1map ; 21cm
ISBN 0-356-08535-x : £7.95 B82-10291

Buckingham, Nancy. The other Cathy / by Nancy Buckingham. — Long Preston : Magna Print, 1981, 1978. — 415p ; 22cm
Originally published: London : Eyre Methuen, 1978. — Published in large print
ISBN 0-86009-345-x : Unpriced : CIP rev. B81-27386

Buckingham, Nancy. Vienna summer / by Nancy Buckingham. — Long Preston : Magna, 1982, c1979. — 428p ; 23cm
Originally published: London : Eyre Methuen, 1979. — Published in large print
ISBN 0-86009-371-9 : Unpriced : CIP rev. B81-33767

Bulmer, Kenneth. Shark raid / Kenneth Bulmer. — London : Severn House, 1982, c1981. — 121p ; 21cm. — (Sea wolf ; 6)
Originally published: London : Sphere, 1982
ISBN 0-7278-0771-4 : £5.50 B82-26094

Burchell, Mary. Masquerade with music / by Mary Burchell. — London : Mills & Boon, 1982. — 188p ; 19cm
ISBN 0-263-10016-2 : £5.25 B82-18131

Burgess, Anthony. Earthly powers / Anthony Burgess. — Harmondsworth : Penguin, 1981, c1980. — 648p ; 20cm
Originally published: London : Hutchinson, 1980
ISBN 0-14-005896-6 (pbk) : £2.50 B82-05942

Burgess, Anthony. The end of the world news. — London : Hutchinson, Oct.1982. — [420]p
ISBN 0-09-150540-2 : £8.95 : CIP entry B82-28442

Burgess, Anthony. Nothing like the sun : a story of Shakespeare's love-life / Anthony Burgess ; with a new foreword by the author. — Feltham : Hamlyn, 1982, c1964. — 233p ; 18cm
Originally published: London : Heinemann, 1964
ISBN 0-600-20598-3 (pbk) : £1.50 B82-25315

Burghley, Rose. The garden of Don José / Rose Burghley. — Large print ed. — Bath : Chivers, 1982, c1977. — 177p ; 23cm. — (A Lythway book) (A Lythway romance)
Originally published: London : Mills & Boon, 1964
ISBN 0-85119-775-2 : Unpriced : CIP rev. B81-33804

Burke, John, *1922-*. The black charade / John Burke. — [Sevenoaks] : Hodder & Stoughton, 1979, c1977. — 220p ; 18cm
Originally published: London : Weidenfeld and Nicolson, 1977
ISBN 0-340-24490-9 (pbk) : £0.95 : CIP rev. B79-25927

Burley, W. J.. Wycliffe's wild-goose chase / by W.J. Burley. — London : Gollancz, 1982. — 176p ; 21cm
ISBN 0-575-03077-1 : £5.95 B82-09782

Burnett, David, *1946-*. The Cranborne chase / David Burnett. — London : Sphere, 1982, c1981. — 339p ; 18cm
Originally published: London : Hamilton, 1981
ISBN 0-7221-2104-0 (pbk) : £1.95 B82-22590

Burnett, June. Helene Bébé. — London : Blond & Briggs, Feb.1983. — [224]p
ISBN 0-85634-129-0 : £6.95 : CIP entry B82-37650

Burnley, Judith. Unrepentant women / Judith Burnley. — London : Heinemann, 1982. — 215p ; 22cm
ISBN 0-434-09856-6 : £6.95 B82-16686

Burns, Alan, *1929-*. The day daddy died : a novel / by Alan Burns ; photo-collages by Ian Breakwell. — London : Allison & Busby, 1981. — 138p : ill ; 22cm
ISBN 0-85031-381-3 (cased) : £6.95
ISBN 0-85031-382-1 (pbk) : Unpriced B82-01013

Burton, Ian J.. All along the skyline / Ian J. Burton. — London : Weidenfeld and Nicolson, c1982. — 163p ; 23cm
ISBN 0-297-78143-x : £6.95 B82-33455

Busby, F. M.. The proud enemy / F.M. Busby. — Feltham : Hamlyn, 1982, c1975. — 215p ; 18cm. — (Hamlyn science fiction)
ISBN 0-600-33183-0 (pbk) : £1.50 B82-27053

Butler, David, *1927-*. Lusitania / David Butler. — London : Futura, 1982, c1981. — 863p ; 18cm
Originally published: London : Macdonald, 1981
ISBN 0-7088-2135-9 (pbk) : £2.50 B82-22608

Butler, Liz, *1948 Dec.10-*. Forewarned / by Liz Butler ; illos by Ann Humphrey. — Strathmartine (c/o Sheila Clark, 6 Craigmill Cottages, Strathmartine, Dundee) : ScoTpress, 1982. — 54p : ill ; 30cm
Unpriced (unbound) B82-34966

Byfield, Sue. To be or not to be / by Sue Byfield. — London : Mills & Boon, 1982. — 189p ; 19cm
ISBN 0-263-10033-2 : £5.25 B82-22641

Callan, Michael Feeney. Diamonds / Michael Feeney Callan ; based on the ATV series by John Brason. — London : Severn House, 1982, c1981. — 204p ; 21cm
ISBN 0-7278-0757-9 : £6.95 B82-30464

Callison, Brian. The Judas ship / by Brian Callison. — Long Preston : Magna, 1981, c1978. — 343p ; 23cm
Originally published: London : Collins, 1978. — Published in large print
ISBN 0-86009-358-1 : Unpriced : CIP rev. B81-31817

Callison, Brian. A ship is dying / by Brian Callison. — Long Preston : Magna, 1981, c1976. — 387p ; 23cm
Originally published: London : Collins, 1976. — Published in large print
ISBN 0-86009-344-1 : Unpriced : CIP rev. B81-22461

Callison, Brian. Trapp's peace / by Brian Callison. — Long Preston : Magna, 1982, c1979. — 344p ; 23cm
Originally published: London : Collins, 1979. — Published in large print
ISBN 0-86009-385-9 : Unpriced : CIP rev. B81-38855

Calvert, Robert. Hype / Robert Calvert. — London : New English Library, 1981. — 221p ; 18cm
ISBN 0-450-05244-3 (pbk) : £1.50 B82-03691

Cameron, Ian, *1924-*. [The lost one]. The island at the top of the world / Ian Cameron. — London : Heinemann Educational, 1982, c1974. — 189p : 1map ; 20cm. — (The New Windmill series ; 262)
Originally published: London : Hutchinson, 1961
ISBN 0-435-12262-2 : £1.70 B82-35732

Candy, F. E.. The word they never said aloud : tract with voices / F.E. Candy. — Bognor Regis : New Horizon, c1982. — 191p ; 22cm
ISBN 0-86116-561-6 : £5.75 B82-05324

Cannon, Elliott. Nobody loves me / by Elliott Cannon. — London : Hale, 1981. — 191p ; 20cm
ISBN 0-7091-9455-2 : £6.50 B82-02815

Carey, Elisabeth. Twist of chance / by Elisabeth Carey. — London : Hale, 1982, c1981. — 224p ; 20cm
ISBN 0-7091-9902-3 : £7.50 B82-36516

Carmichael, Harry. Candles for the dead / Harry Carmichael. — Large print ed. — Leicester : Ulverscroft, 1982, c1973. — 311p ; 23cm. — (Ulverscroft large print series)
Originally published: London : Collins for the Crime Club, 1973
ISBN 0-7089-0774-1 : Unpriced : CIP rev. B82-08085

Carnac, Nicholas. Indigo / Nicholas Carnac. — London : Hamish Hamilton, 1982. — 404p ; 23cm
ISBN 0-241-10146-8 : £8.95 : CIP rev. B81-34150

Carney, Daniel. The square circle / Daniel Carney. — [London] : Corgi, 1982. — 252p : 2maps ; 18cm
ISBN 0-552-11831-1 (pbk) : £1.50 B82-19373

Carney, Daniel. Under a raging sky / Daniel Carney. — London : Corgi, 1980 (1981 [printing]). — 285p ; 18cm
ISBN 0-552-11592-4 (pbk) : £1.50 B82-06418

Carney, Daniel. Under a raging sky. — Bath : Firecrest, Jan.1983. — [288]p
Originally published: London : Corgi, 1980
ISBN 0-85997-506-1 : £7.50 : CIP entry B82-33123

823'.914[F] — Fiction in English, *1945-* **—** *Texts continuation*

Carothers, Annabel. Kilcaraig / Annabel Carothers. — London : Heinemann, 1982. — 537p ; 23cm
ISBN 0-434-10870-7 : £7.95 B82-26003

Carroll, Eden. Bella donna / Eden Carroll. — [Glasgow] : Fontana, 1982. — 191p ; 18cm. — (Nightshades)
ISBN 0-00-616215-0 (pbk) : £1.00 B82-34108

Carsley, Anne. This ravished rose / Anne Carsley. — London : Futura, 1982, c1980. — 372p ; 18cm. — (A Troubadour book)
ISBN 0-7107-3023-3 (pbk) : £1.75 B82-06602

Carter, Angela, *1940-*. The passion of new Eve. — London : Virago, Oct.1982. — [192]p. — (Virago modern classics)
Originally published: London : Gollancz, 1977
ISBN 0-86068-341-9 (pbk) : £2.95 : CIP entry B82-24150

Carter, Brian. A black fox running / Brian Carter. — London : Futura, 1982, c1981. — iv,264p : 2maps ; 18cm
Originally published: London : Dent, 1981
ISBN 0-7088-2190-1 (pbk) : £1.50 B82-30772

Carter, D. Mark. Lion rampant / D. Mark Carter. — Bognor Regis : New Horizon, c1982. — 128p ; 21cm
ISBN 0-86116-927-1 : £4.50 B82-22158

Carter, Rosemary. Adam's bride / Rosemary Carter. — Large print ed. — Bath : Chivers, 1982, c1978. — 214p ; 23cm. — (A Lythway romance)
Originally published: London : Mills and Boon, 1978
ISBN 0-85119-806-6 : Unpriced : CIP rev. B82-07010

Carter, Rosemary. Daredevil / by Rosemary Carter. — London : Mills & Boon, 1982. — 188p ; 20cm
ISBN 0-263-10003-0 : £5.25 B82-13893

Carter, Rosemary. Kelly's man / Rosemary Carter. — Large print ed. — Bath : Chivers Press, 1982, c1980. — 204p ; 23cm. — (A Seymour book)
Originally published: London : Mills & Boon, 1980
ISBN 0-85119-448-6 : Unpriced : CIP rev. B81-33808

Casciani, Patricia. Ice planet / Patricia Casciani. — Bognor Regis : New Horizon, c1982. — 134p ; 21cm
ISBN 0-86116-771-6 : £4.75 B82-19988

Cass, Zoë. Island of the seven hills / Zoë Cass. — Large print ed. — Leicester : Ulverscroft, 1982, c1974. — 385p ; 23cm. — (Ulverscroft large print series)
Originally published: New York : Random House, 1974 ; London : Cassell, 1975
ISBN 0-7089-0793-8 : Unpriced : CIP rev. B82-18555

Cassilis, Robert. Madness of the people / by Robert Cassilis. — London : Hamilton, 1982. — 192p ; 23cm
ISBN 0-241-10258-8 : £8.95 : CIP rev. B82-18471

Castle, Brenda. Man of music / by Brenda Castle. — London : Hale, 1981. — 156p ; 20cm
ISBN 0-7091-9444-7 : £5.95 B82-02161

Cave, Emma. Cousin Henrietta / Emma Cave. — London : Pan in association with Collins, 1982, c1981. — 251p ; 18cm
Originally published: London : Collins, 1981
ISBN 0-330-26740-x (pbk) : £1.50 B82-35745

Cavendish, Clare. A doctor must dream. — Large print ed. — Long Preston : Magna Print, Oct.1982. — [320]p
Originally published: London : Hale, 1974
ISBN 0-86009-451-0 : £5.50 : CIP entry B82-24133

Cavendish, Clare. Village nurse / Clare Cavendish. — London : Hale, 1982. — 172p ; 20cm
ISBN 0-7091-9711-x : £6.25 B82-22859

Cecil, Henry. Unlawful occasions / Henry Cecil. — London : Remploy, 1980, c1962. — 182p ; 22cm
Originally published: London : Joseph, 1962
ISBN 0-7066-0837-2 : £4.50 B82-09342

Challoner, Robert. Jamaica passage / Robert Challoner. — Harmondsworth : Penguin, 1982. — 435p ; 19cm
ISBN 0-14-005317-4 (pbk) : £1.75 B82-40371

Chambers, Aidan. Dance on my grave : a life and a death in four parts, one hundred and seventeen bits, six running reports and two press clippings, with a few jokes, a puzzle or three, some footnotes and a fiasco now and then to help the story along / Aidan Chambers. — London : Bodley Head, 1982. — 251p : ill ; 20cm
ISBN 0-370-30366-0 (pbk) : £4.25 : CIP rev. B82-03834

Chambers, Peter, *1924-*. Female - handle with care / by Peter Chambers. — London : Hale, 1981. — 175p ; 20cm
ISBN 0-7091-9325-4 : £6.50 B82-07197

Chambers, Peter, *1924-*. The highly explosive case / by Peter Chambers. — London : Hale, 1982. — 171p ; 20cm
ISBN 0-7091-9726-8 : £6.75 B82-36525

Chambers, Peter, *1924-*. Murder is its own reward / by Peter Chambers. — London : Hale, 1982. — 160p ; 20cm
ISBN 0-7091-9612-1 : £6.75 B82-22133

Chance, John Newton. The hunting of Mr Exe / by John Newton Chance. — London : Hale, 1982. — 172p ; 20cm
ISBN 0-7091-8017-9 : £6.75 B82-27429

Chance, John Newton. Madman's will / by John Newton Chance. — London : Hale, 1982. — 173p ; 20cm
ISBN 0-7091-7992-8 : £6.50 B82-12600

Chance, John Newton. The mystery of Enda Favell / by John Newton Chance. — London : Hale, 1981. — 172p ; 20cm
ISBN 0-7091-7887-5 : £6.25 B82-00511

Chance, John Newton. The shadow in pursuit / John Newton Chance. — London : Hale, 1982. — 160p ; 20cm
ISBN 0-7091-8223-6 : £6.75 B82-39177

Chandler, A. Bertram. Beyond the galactic rim. — London : Allison & Busby, June 1982. — [128]p
ISBN 0-85031-460-7 : £5.95 : CIP entry B82-12840

Chandler, A. Bertram. Bring back yesterday / A. Bertram Chandler. — London : Allison & Busby, 1981, c1961. — 153p ; 23cm. — (The Rim world series ; v.3)
Originally published: New York : Ace, 1961
ISBN 0-85031-406-2 : £5.95 : CIP rev. B81-30575

Chandler, A. Bertram. Bring back yesterday / A. Bertram Chandler. — London : Sphere, 1982, c1961. — 153p ; 18cm. — (The Rim world series ; v.3) (Sphere science fiction)
Originally published: New York : Ace Books ; London : Allison & Busby, 1981
ISBN 0-7221-2283-7 (pbk) : £1.50 B82-22598

Chandler, A. Bertram. Star loot / A. Bertram Chandler. — London : Hale, 1981, c1980. — 175p ; 19cm. — (Hale SF)
ISBN 0-7091-9502-8 : £6.25 B82-07215

Chappell, Mollie. Cousin Amelia / by Mollie Chappell. — London : Hale, 1982. — 159p ; 20cm
ISBN 0-7091-9901-5 : Unpriced B82-37291

Chard, Judy. Haunted by the past / by Judy Chard. — London : Hale, 1982. — 142p ; 20cm
ISBN 0-7091-9545-1 : £6.25 B82-17469

Chard, Judy. When the journey's over / by Judy Chard. — London : Hale, 1981. — 160p ; 20cm
ISBN 0-7091-9517-6 : £5.95 B82-06322

Chard, Judy. Where the dream begins / by Judy Chard. — London : Hale, 1982. — 160p ; 20cm
ISBN 0-7091-9922-8 : £6.50 B82-35891

Charles, Theresa. Surgeon's sweetheart / by Theresa Charles. — London : Hale, 1981. — 192p ; 20cm
ISBN 0-7091-9285-1 : £5.75 B82-02810

Charles, Wyndham. Hogan's last case / by Wyndham Charles. — London : Hale, 1982. — 188p ; 20cm
ISBN 0-7091-9824-8 : £6.75 B82-34194

Chatham, Andrew. Sea sting / Andrew Chatham. — London : Sphere, 1982. — 251p ; 18cm
ISBN 0-7221-2249-7 (pbk) : £1.75 B82-14911

Chatham, Andrew. Sea sting / Andrew Chatham. — London : Severn House, 1982. — 251p ; 21cm
ISBN 0-7278-0784-6 : £6.50 B82-30465

Chatwin, Bruce. On the Black Hill. — London : Cape, Oct.1982. — [256]p
ISBN 0-224-01980-5 : £7.50 : CIP entry B82-25160

Chatwin, Bruce. The viceroy of Ouidah / Bruce Chatwin. — London : Pan, 1982, c1980. — 125p : 2maps ; 20cm. — (Picador)
Originally published: London : Cape, 1980
ISBN 0-330-26613-6 (pbk) : £1.75 B82-19134

Chesney, Marion. The Marquis takes a bride / Marion Chesney. — London : Macdonald, 1982, c1981. — 173p ; 21cm
ISBN 0-356-08510-4 : £4.95 B82-12670

Chesney, Marion. Quadrille / Marion Chesney. — London : Macdonald, 1982, c1981. — 224p ; 21cm
ISBN 0-356-08527-9 : £4.95 B82-22566

Chester, Deborah. French slippers / Deborah Chester. — London : Joseph, 1982. — 261p ; 23cm
ISBN 0-7181-2110-4 : £7.50 B82-09940

Chester, Deborah. A love so wild / Deborah Chester. — Large print ed. — Leicester : Ulverscroft, 1982, c1980. — 473p ; 23cm. — (Ulverscroft large print series)
Originally published: London : Joseph, 1980
ISBN 0-7089-0764-4 : Unpriced : CIP rev. B82-01739

Chevalier, Paul. The grudge. — London : Hodder and Stoughton, Apr.1982. — [416]p. — (Coronet books)
Originally published: 1980
ISBN 0-340-27912-5 (pbk) : CIP entry B82-03822

Chisholm, Matt. The Arizona climax / Matt Chisholm. — London : Hale, 1982. — 153p ; 20cm
ISBN 0-7091-8974-5 : £5.50 B82-26028

823'.914[F] — Fiction in English, *1945-* — *Texts continuation*

Chisholm, Matt. The Laredo assignment / Matt Chisholm. — London : Hale, 1981, c1979. — 159p ; 20cm
Originally published: London : Hamlyn, 1979
ISBN 0-7091-8703-3 : £4.95 B82-02157

Chisholm, Matt. McAllister and Cheyenne death / Matt Chisholm. — Feltham : Hamlyn, 1982. — 142p ; 18cm
ISBN 0-600-20372-7 (pbk) : £0.95 B82-25311

Chisholm, Matt. McAllister and quarry / Matt Chisholm. — Feltham : Hamlyn Paperbacks, 1982, c1981. — 141p ; 18cm
ISBN 0-600-20516-9 (pbk) : £0.95 B82-34032

Chisholm, Matt. McAllister and the Spanish gold / Matt Chisholm. — Feltham : Hamlyn Paperbacks, 1981. — 156p ; 18cm
ISBN 0-600-20371-9 (pbk) : £0.95 B82-04511

Chisholm, Matt. McAllister never surrenders / Matt Chisholm. — Feltham : Hamlyn, 1982. — 157p ; 18cm. — (McAllister ; 3)
ISBN 0-600-20370-0 (pbk) : £0.95 B82-16300

Chisholm, Matt. McAllister on the Comanche crossing / Matt Chisholm. — Feltham : Hamlyn Paperbacks, 1981. — 158p ; 18cm
ISBN 0-600-20369-7 (pbk) : £0.95 B82-03018

Chisholm, Matt. The Pecos manhunt / Matt Chisholm. — London : Hale, 1982, c1979. — 153p ; 20cm
Originally published: Feltham : Hamlyn, 1979
ISBN 0-7091-8704-1 : £4.95 B82-11056

Christie, Anne. First act. — Loughton : Piatkus, Nov.1982. — [192]p
ISBN 0-86188-216-4 : £6.95 : CIP entry B82-26062

Christie, Anne. My secret gorilla / Anne Christie. — [Feltham] : Hamlyn Paperbacks, 1982, c1981. — 201p ; 18cm
Originally published: Loughton : Piatkus, c1981
ISBN 0-600-20515-0 (pbk) : £1.50 B82-35723

Christie, D. D.. Andy was eight : the story of a small boy at boarding school during the First World War / by Donald D. Christie ; with drawings by the author. — Poole : D.D. Christie, 1980. — 119p : ill,1plan ; 22cm
ISBN 0-9507176-0-6 (pbk) : £3.50 B82-13364

Christie, D. D.. The colleger and the oppidan : a story of two boys at Eton College in 1755, with an appendix of the facts behind the fiction / Donald D. Christie. — Maidstone : Mann, 1981. — 209p ; 23cm
In slip case. — Map on folded sheet as insert. — Bibliography: p190-193
ISBN 0-7041-0200-5 : Unpriced B82-13684

Christopher, Cathy. Either side of the hill / by Cathy Christopher. — London : Hale, 1981. — 156p ; 20cm
ISBN 0-7091-9428-5 : £5.95 B82-00444

Christopher, Eve. The touch / Eve Christopher. — London : W.H. Allen, 1982. — 250p ; 18cm. — (A Star book)
ISBN 0-352-31034-0 (pbk) : £1.60 B82-10103

Cimino, Moyra. Turn down an empty glass / Moyra Cimino. — Bognor Regis : New Horizon, c1981. — 118p,[4]leaves of plates : ill ; 21cm
ISBN 0-86116-454-7 : £4.50 B82-02279

Clair, Daphne. Pacific pretence / by Daphne Clair. — London : Mills & Boon, 1982. — 186p ; 20cm
ISBN 0-263-10064-2 : £5.25 B82-27601

Clair, Daphne. Pacific pretence / by Daphne Clair. — London : Mills & Boon, 1982. — 186p ; 18cm
ISBN 0-263-73871-x (pbk) : £0.85 B82-36280

Clair, Daphne. Promise to pay / by Daphne Clair. — London : Mills & Boon, 1981. — 188p ; 19cm
ISBN 0-263-09960-1 : £4.55 B82-04632

Clare, Ellen. Ripening vine / by Ellen Clare. — London : Mills & Boon, 1981. — 189p ; 20cm
ISBN 0-263-09909-1 : £4.55 B82-09222

Clark, Douglas, *1919-*. Doone walk. — London : Gollancz, Oct.1982. — [176]p
ISBN 0-575-03155-7 : £6.95 : CIP entry B82-23342

Clark, Douglas, *1919-*. The longest pleasure / by Douglas Clark. — London : Gollancz, 1981. — 184p ; 21cm
ISBN 0-575-03058-5 : £5.95 B82-02259

Clark, Douglas, *1919-*. Shelf life / by Douglas Clark. — London : Gollancz, 1982. — 174p ; 21cm
ISBN 0-575-03081-x : £6.95 : CIP rev. B82-04605

Clark, Eric, *1937-*. Send in the lions. — London : Coronet, Nov.1982. — [208]p
Originally published: 1981
ISBN 0-340-28439-0 (pbk) : £1.50 : CIP entry B82-27366

Clark, Sandra. Moonlight enough / by Sandra Clark. — London : Mills and Boon, 1982. — 188p ; 20cm
ISBN 0-263-10089-8 : £5.95 B82-37115

Clark, Sandra. The wolf man / by Sandra Clark. — London : Mills & Boon, 1982. — 191p ; 20cm
ISBN 0-263-09983-0 : £5.25 B82-10377

Clarke, Anna. Poison parsley. — Large print ed. — Long Preston : Magna, Jan.1983. — [380]p
Originally published: London : Collins, 1979
ISBN 0-86009-467-7 : £5.75 : CIP entry B82-33129

Clarke, Anna. The poisoned web / Anna Clarke. — Large print ed. — Bath : Chivers, 1982, c1979. — 221p ; 23cm. — (A Lythway book)
Originally published: London : Collins, 1979
ISBN 0-85119-790-6 : Unpriced : CIP rev. B82-01436

Clarke, Arthur C.. 2010 : Odyssey two. — London : Granada, Nov.1982. — [225]p
ISBN 0-246-11912-8 : £7.95 : CIP entry B82-29064

Clarke, Arthur C.. The lion of Comarre, and Against the fall of night / Arthur C. Clarke. — London : Pan, 1982. — 188p ; 18cm
Originally published: New York : Harcourt, Brace & World, 1968 ; London : Gollancz, 1970
ISBN 0-330-26658-6 (pbk) : £1.50 B82-13717

Clarke, Brenda. The far morning / Brenda Clarke. — Feltham : Hamlyn Paperbacks, 1982. — 382p ; 18cm
ISBN 0-600-20414-6 (pbk) : £1.50 B82-16177

Clavell, James. Noble house. — London : Coronet, June 1981. — [1632]p
ISBN 0-340-26877-8 (pbk) : £2.95 : CIP entry B81-12350

Cleeve, Brian. Hester. — London : Hodder & Stoughton, July 1982. — [400]p
Originally published: London : Cassell, 1979
ISBN 0-340-25084-4 (pbk) : £2.25 : CIP entry B82-12248

Clews, Roy. The drums of war. — Large print ed. — Anstey : Ulverscroft, Oct.1982. — [560] p. — (Ulverscroft large print series)
Originally published: London : Heinemann, 1978
ISBN 0-7089-0866-7 : £5.00 : CIP entry B82-26687

Clews, Roy. The golden city. — Large print ed. — Anstey : Ulverscroft, Feb.1983. — 1v.. — (Ulverscroft large print series)
Originally published: London : Gollancz, 1979
ISBN 0-7089-0914-0 : CIP entry B82-38876

Clews, Roy. The king's bounty / Roy Clews. — Large print ed. — Leicester : Ulverscroft, 1982, c1976. — 685p ; 22cm. — (Ulverscroft large print series)
Originally published: London : Heinemann, 1976
ISBN 0-7089-0782-2 : Unpriced : CIP rev. B82-08093

Clews, Roy. Young Jethro / Roy Clews. — Large print ed. — Leicester : Ulverscroft, 1982, c1975. — 449p ; 23cm
Originally published: London : Heinemann, 1975
ISBN 0-7089-0740-7 : £5.00 : CIP rev. B81-33957

Clifford, Francis. The blind side / Francis Clifford. — Bolton-by-Bowland : Magna, 1980, c1971. — 411p ; 23cm
Originally published: London : Hodder & Stoughton, 1971. — Published in large print
ISBN 0-86009-217-8 : £5.25 : CIP rev. B79-34452

Clifford, Kay. A temporary affair / by Kay Clifford. — London : Mills & Boon, 1982. — 187p ; 19cm
ISBN 0-263-10026-x : £5.25 B82-18129

Climie, David. Sorry! : a novel / by David Climie ; adapted from the TV series by Ian Davidson and Peter Vincent. — London : Star, 1982. — 154p ; 18cm
ISBN 0-352-31050-2 (pbk) : £1.35 B82-16095

Clive, John, *1938-*. Barossa. — London : Granada, June 1982. — [288]p
ISBN 0-246-11773-7 : £6.95 : CIP entry B82-09990

Cody, Liza. Bad company. — London : Collins, Oct.1982. — [224]p. — (The Crime Club)
ISBN 0-00-231037-6 : £6.75 : CIP entry B82-23080

Cody, Liza. Dupe / Liza Cody. — London : Pan in association with Collins, 1982, c1980. — 218p ; 18cm
Originally published: London : Collins, 1980
ISBN 0-330-26591-1 (pbk) : £1.25 B82-13718

Cohen, Anthea. Angel of vengeance. — London : Quartet, Nov.1982. — [192]p
ISBN 0-7043-2356-7 : £6.95 : CIP entry B82-29083

Cohen, Anthea. Angel without mercy. — London : Quartet, July 1982. — [192]p
ISBN 0-7043-2335-4 : £6.50 : CIP entry B82-13002

Coleman, Terry. Thanksgiving / Terry Coleman. — London : Hutchinson, 1982, c1981. — 445p ; 23cm
Originally published: New York : Simon and Schuster, 1981
ISBN 0-09-146530-3 : £7.95 : CIP rev. B81-28168

Colin, Ann. A different class of doctor. — Bath : Firecrest, Jan.1983. — [160]p
Originally published: London : Corgi, 1980
ISBN 0-85997-507-x : £5.50 : CIP entry B82-33124

Collins, Jackie. Chances / Jackie Collins. — London : Pan Books in association with Collins, 1981 (1982 [printing]). — 599p ; 18cm
ISBN 0-330-26663-2 (pbk) : £2.25 B82-22156

Collins, Jackie. Lovehead / Jackie Collins. — London : W.H. Allen, 1974 (1981 [printing]). — 179p ; 21cm
ISBN 0-491-02646-3 : £6.95 B82-06563

823'.914[F] — Fiction in English, ***1945-*** **—** ***Texts continuation***

Collins, Jackie. The stud / Jackie Collins. — London : W.H. Allen, 1981, c1969. — 188p ; 21cm
Originally published: 1969
ISBN 0-491-02945-4 : £5.95 B82-00051

Collins, Jackie. [Sunday Simmons and Charlie Brick]. Sinners / Jackie Collins. — London : W.H. Allen, 1972 (1981 [printing]). — 283p ; 21cm
ISBN 0-491-02656-0 : £7.95 B82-06564

Collins, Lynne. Doctor in pursuit / by Lynne Collins. — London : Mills & Boon, 1982. — 188p ; 18cm. — (Doctor nurse romance)
ISBN 0-263-73925-2 (pbk) : £0.85 B82-36270

Colquhoun, Keith. Filthy rich / Keith Colquhoun. — London : Murray, 1982. — 174p ; 23cm
ISBN 0-7195-3950-1 : £7.50 : CIP rev. B82-04884

Conlon, Kathleen. A forgotten season / Kathleen Conlon. — Large print ed. — Bath : Chivers, 1982, c1980. — 276p ; 23cm. — (A Lythway book)
Originally published: London : Collins, 1980
ISBN 0-85119-814-7 : Unpriced : CIP rev. B82-09857

Conlon, Kathleen. A move in the game / Kathleen Conlon. — Feltham : Hamlyn Paperbacks, 1982, c1979. — 335p ; 18cm
Originally published: London : Collins, 1979
ISBN 0-600-20145-7 (pbk) : £1.50 B82-09057

Conran, Shirley. Lace : a novel / Shirley Conran. — London : Sidgwick & Jackson, 1982. — 604p ; 24cm
Originally published: New York : Simon and Schuster, 1982
ISBN 0-283-98853-3 : £7.95 B82-40419

Conway, Peter, *1929-*. Mirror image / Peter Conway. — London : Hale, 1982. — 175p ; 20cm
ISBN 0-7091-9825-6 : £6.75 B82-31630

Cook, David, *1940-*. Winter doves : a love story / David Cook. — Harmondsworth : Penguin, 1981, c1979. — 212p ; 20cm. — (King Penguin)
Originally published: London : Alison Press, 1979
ISBN 0-14-005541-x (pbk) : £1.95 B82-05964

Cookson, Catherine. The blind miller / Catherine Cookson. — Large print ed. — Leicester : Ulverscroft, 1982, c1963. — 523p ; 22cm. — (Ulverscroft large print)
Originally published: London : Macdonald, 1963
ISBN 0-7089-0741-5 : £5.00 : CIP rev. B81-33956

Cookson, Catherine. The dwelling place / Catherine Cookson. — Large print ed. — Leicester : Ulverscroft, 1982, c1971. — 525p : ill ; 22cm. — (Ulverscroft large print series)
Originally published: London : Macdonald, 1971
ISBN 0-7089-0783-0 : Unpriced : CIP rev. B82-08094

Cookson, Catherine. Fenwick houses / Catherine Cookson. — Large print ed. — Leicester : Ulverscroft, 1981, c1960. — 473p ; 23cm. — (Ulverscroft large print series)
Originally published: London : Macdonald, 1960
ISBN 0-7089-0726-1 : £5.00 : CIP rev. B81-32607

Cookson, Catherine. The glass virgin. — Large print ed. — Anstey : Ulverscroft, Dec.1982. — 1v.. — (Ulverscroft large print series)
Originally published: London : Macdonald, 1970
ISBN 0-7089-0894-2 : £5.00 : CIP entry B82-30786

Cookson, Catherine. Slinky Jane / Catherine Cookson. — London : W.H. Allen, 1979 (1981 [printing]). — 219p ; 18cm. — (A Star book)
Originally published: London : Macdonald and Co., 1959
ISBN 0-426-16360-5 (pbk) : £1.25 B82-06475

Cookson, Catherine. Tilly Trotter / Catherine Cookson. — Large print ed. — Leicester : Ulverscroft, 1981, c1980. — 570p ; 23cm. — (Ulverscroft large print series)
Originally published: London : Heinemann, 1980
ISBN 0-7089-0698-2 : £5.00 : CIP rev. B81-28098

Cookson, Catherine. Tilly Trotter wed / Catherine Cookson. — London : Corgi, 1982, c1981. — 351p : ill,1port ; 18cm
Originally published: London : Heinemann, 1981
ISBN 0-552-11960-1 (pbk) : £1.75 B82-27609

Cookson, Catherine. Tilly Trotter wed / Catherine Cookson. — Large print ed. — Leicester : Ulverscroft, 1982, c1981. — 498p ; 23cm. — (Ulverscroft large print series)
Originally published: London : Heinemann, 1980
ISBN 0-7089-0824-1 : Unpriced : CIP rev. B82-15963

Cookson, Catherine. Tilly Trotter widowed : a novel / by Catherine Cookson. — London : Heinemann, 1982. — 265p ; 23cm
ISBN 0-434-14272-7 : £7.50 B82-11362

Cookson, Catherine. Tilly Trotter widowed. — Large print ed. — Anstey : Ulverscroft, Feb.1983. — 1v.. — (Ulverscroft large print series)
ISBN 0-7089-0915-9 : CIP entry B82-38877

Cooper, Ann. Fool's paradise / Ann Cooper. — Large print ed. — Bath : Chivers, 1982, c1980. — 171p ; 23cm. — (A Seymour book)
Originally published: London : Mills and Boon, 1980
ISBN 0-85119-456-7 : Unpriced : CIP rev. B82-01441

Cooper, Jilly. Bella / Jilly Cooper. — Large print ed. — Bath : Chivers, 1982, c1976. — 245p ; 23cm. — (A Lythway book)
Originally published: London : Arlington, 1976
ISBN 0-85119-834-1 : Unpriced : CIP rev. B82-15866

Cooper, Jilly. Emily / Jilly Cooper. — Large print ed. — Bath : Chivers, 1982, c1975. — 210p ; 23cm. — (A Lythway book)
Originally published: London : Arlington, 1975
ISBN 0-85119-824-4 : Unpriced : CIP rev. B82-13097

Cooper, Jilly. Harriet. — Large print ed. — Bath : Chivers, Sept.1982. — [352]p. — (A Lythway book)
Originally published: London : Arlington Books, 1976
ISBN 0-85119-844-9 : £6.90 : CIP entry B82-20513

Cooper, Jilly. Octavia. — Large print ed. — Bath : Chivers, Oct.1982. — [336]p. — (A Lythway book)
Originally published: London : Arlington, 1977
ISBN 0-85119-852-x : £7.50 : CIP entry B82-24234

Cooper, Jilly. Prudence / Jill Cooper. — South Yarmouth : Curley ; [Skipton] : Magna Print, [1981], c1978. — 379p ; 22cm
Originally published: London : Arlington Books, 1978. — Published in large print
ISBN 0-89340-350-4 : Unpriced B82-05034

Cooper, Lawrence J.. All this and camels too / Lawrence J. Cooper. — Bognor Regis : New Horizon, c1982. — 152p ; 21cm
ISBN 0-86116-271-4 (corrected) : £5.50 B82-08800

Cooper, Lawrence J.. All this and Sherwood too / Lawrence J. Cooper. — Bognor Regis : New Horizon, c1981. — 185p ; 21cm
ISBN 0-86116-266-8 : £5.75 B82-02949

Cooper, Lisa. Over the green mask / by Lisa Cooper. — London : Severn House, 1982, c1981. — 187p ; 21cm
Originally published: London : Mills & Boon, 1981
ISBN 0-7278-0785-4 : £4.95 B82-16171

Cooper, Lisa. A rose for the surgeon. — Large print ed. — Long Preston : Magna, Dec.1982. — [320]p
Originally published: London : Mills and Boon, 1979
ISBN 0-86009-486-3 : £5.50 : CIP entry B82-30731

Cooper, Louise. The blacksmith / Louise Cooper. — Feltham : Hamlyn, 1982. — 220p ; 18cm
ISBN 0-600-20415-4 (pbk) : £1.25 B82-16301

Cooper, Richard, *19---*. Codename Icarus / Richard Cooper. — London : British Broadcasting Corporation, 1981. — 157p ; 22cm
ISBN 0-563-17990-2 (cased) : £5.25 : CIP rev.
ISBN 0-563-20040-5 (pbk) : £0.95
ISBN 0-340-27535-9 (Knight) B81-31438

Copper, Basil. Hang loose / Basil Copper. — London : Hale, 1982. — 160p ; 20cm. — (34.38 special)
ISBN 0-7091-8730-0 : £6.50 B82-15481

Copper, Basil. Shoot-out / Basil Copper. — London : Hale, 1982. — 173p ; 20cm. — (35.38 special)
ISBN 0-7091-8840-4 : £6.75 B82-27423

Coram, Christopher. Prisoner on the dam / Christopher Coram. — London : Hale, 1982. — 191p ; 20cm
ISBN 0-7091-9797-7 : £6.75 B82-31632

Cordell, Alexander. This sweet and bitter earth / Alexander Cordell. — 2nd impression. — Sevenoaks : Hodder & Stoughton, 1977 (1980 [printing]). — 446p ; 18cm. — (Coronet books)
ISBN 0-340-23224-2 (pbk) : £1.50 : CIP rev. B79-19535

Cordell, Alexander. To slay the dreamer. — London : Hodder & Stoughton, Aug.1981. — [320]p. — (Coronet books)
Originally published: London : Hodder & Stoughton, 1980
ISBN 0-340-26675-9 (pbk) : £1.75 : CIP entry B81-18131

Cordell, Alexander. To slay the dreamer / Alexander Cordell. — Large print ed. — Leicester : Ulverscroft, 1982, c1980. — 510p ; 23cm. — (Ulverscroft large print series)
Originally published: London : Hodder and Stoughton, 1980
ISBN 0-7089-0766-0 : Unpriced : CIP rev. B82-01741

Cork, Dorothy. Secret marriage. — London : Hodder & Stoughton, Dec.1981. — [192]p. — (Silhouette romance)
ISBN 0-340-27657-6 (pbk) : £0.65 : CIP entry B81-31433

Corlett, William. The gate of Eden / William Corlett. — London : MacRae, 1982, c1974. — 175p ; 23cm
Originally published: London : H. Hamilton, 1974
ISBN 0-86203-079-x : £5.25 : CIP rev. B82-04715

Cornford, Toni. Beyond the valley / Toni Cornford. — Feltham : Hamlyn Paperbacks, 1981. — 251p ; 18cm
ISBN 0-600-20228-3 (pbk) : £1.35 B82-04516

823'.914[F] — Fiction in English, *1945-* — *Texts continuation*

Cornwell, Bernard. Sharpe's company : Richard Sharpe and the Siege of Badajoz, January to April 1812 / Bernard Cornwell. — London : Collins, 1982. — 280p : 2maps ; 22cm
ISBN 0-00-222131-4 (correced) : £7.50 : CIP rev. B82-10565

Cornwell, Bernard. Sharpe's gold : Richard Sharpe and the destruction of Almeida, August 1810 / Bernard Cornwell. — [London] : Fontana, 1982, c1981. — 256p ; 18cm
Originally published: New York : Viking, 1981
ISBN 0-00-616545-1 (pbk) : £1.50 B82-27886

Corrie, Jane. Ross's girl / by Jane Corrie. — London : Mills & Boon, 1982. — 190p ; 19cm
ISBN 0-263-10032-4 : £5.25 B82-22640

Corrie, Jane. The station boss / Jane Corrie. — Large print ed. — Bath : Chivers, 1981, c1980. — 201p ; 23cm. — (A Seymour book)
Originally published: London : Mills & Boon, 1980
ISBN 0-85119-444-3 : Unpriced : CIP rev. B81-31839

Cost, March. A key to Laurels / March Cost. — Large print ed. — Leicester : Ulverscroft, 1982, c1972. — 363p ; 23cm. — (Ulverscroft large print series)
Originally published: London : Cassell, 1972
ISBN 0-7089-0775-x : Unpriced : CIP rev. B82-08086

Costello, Peter. Leopold Bloom : a biography / Peter Costello. — Dublin : Gill and Macmillan, 1981. — 197p ; 23cm
Includes index
ISBN 0-7171-1100-8 : Unpriced B82-02955

Couper, Elspeth. House of mists / by Elspeth Couper. — London : Hale, 1981. — 189p ; 20cm
ISBN 0-7091-9236-3 : £5.95 B82-11060

Court, Caroline. White rose of rebellion / Caroline Court. — London : Hamlyn, 1982. — 159p ; 18cm
ISBN 0-600-20270-4 (pbk) : £1.25 B82-12062

Courtney, Caroline. Forbidden love. — London : Arlington, Sept.1982. — [208]p
ISBN 0-85140-582-7 : £6.50 : CIP entry B82-20525

Courtney, Caroline. The fortunes of love / Caroline Courtney. — [London] : Corgi, 1981, c1980. — 235p ; 18cm
Originally published: London : Arlington, 1980
ISBN 0-552-11819-2 (pbk) : £1.00 B82-03235

Courtney, Caroline. Heart of honor / Caroline Courtney. — London : Prior, 1981, c1980. — 371p ; 25cm
Published in large print
ISBN 0-86043-637-3 : £6.95 B82-16183

Courtney, Caroline. Heart of honour / Caroline Courtney. — London : Corgi, 1982, c1980. — 219p ; 18cm
Originally published: London : Arlington, 1980
ISBN 0-552-11989-x (pbk) : £1.25 B82-35253

Courtney, Caroline. Heart of honour / Caroline Courtney. — London : Columbia House, 1982. — 222p ; 21cm
ISBN 0-85140-569-x : £6.50 : CIP rev. B81-39223

Courtney, Caroline. Libertine in love. — London : Arlington Books, Apr.1982. — [224]p
ISBN 0-85140-572-x : £6.50 : CIP entry B82-05012

Courtney, Caroline. Love triumphant. — London : Arlington Books, June 1981. — [224]p
ISBN 0-85140-534-7 : £5.95 : CIP entry B81-12793

Courtney, Caroline. Love triumphant / Caroline Courtney. — London : Prior, 1981, c1980. — 352p ; 25cm
Originally published: London : Arlington Books, 1981. — Published in large print
ISBN 0-86043-621-7 : £6.50 B82-02934

Courtney, Caroline. Love triumphant / Caroline Courtney. — London : Corgi, 1982, c1980. — 236p ; 18cm
Originally published: London : Arlington, 1980
ISBN 0-552-11891-5 (pbk) : £1.25 B82-16938

Courtney, Caroline. Love's masquerade. — London : Arlington Books, Sept.1981. — [224]p
ISBN 0-85140-547-9 : £5.95 : CIP entry B81-20185

Courtney, Caroline. Love's masquerade / Caroline Courtney. — London : Prior, 1981, c1980. — 423p ; 25cm
Published in large print
ISBN 0-86043-672-1 : Unpriced B82-31904

Courtney, Caroline. Love's masquerade / Caroline Courtney. — [London] : Corgi, 1982, c1980. — 219p ; 18cm
Originally published: London : Arlington, 1981
ISBN 0-552-11948-2 (pbk) : £1.25 B82-28363

Courtney, Caroline. The tempestuous affair. — London : Arlington Books, Feb.1983. — [208]p
ISBN 0-85140-602-5 : £6.95 : CIP entry B82-39593

Cowie, V. R.. The rich and the mighty / V.R. Cowie. — London : Macdonald Futura, 1981. — 508p ; 18cm
ISBN 0-7088-2122-7 (pbk) : £1.95 B82-05482

Cowper, Richard. A tapestry of time. — London : Gollancz, Oct.1982. — [192]p
ISBN 0-575-03209-x : £6.95 : CIP entry B82-23350

Cox, Richard, *1931-*. The Katanga run / Richard Cox. — London : Arrow, 1981, c1980. — 351p ; 18cm
Originally published: London : Hutchinson, 1980
ISBN 0-09-926530-3 (pbk) : £1.75 B82-03539

Cox, Richard, *1931-*. The KGB directive / Richard Cox. — London : Arrow, 1982, c1981. — 335p ; 18cm
Originally published: London : Hutchinson, 1981
ISBN 0-09-929100-2 (pbk) : £1.75 B82-33316

Cox, Richard, *1931-*. Operation Sealion / edited by Richard Cox. — London : Arrow, 1982, c1974. — 190p : 1map ; 18cm
Originally published: London : Thornton Cox, 1974
ISBN 0-09-928440-5 (pbk) : £1.25 B82-35564

Craddock, Rosemary. Templewood / by Rosemary Craddock. — London : Hale, 1981. — 207p ; 20cm
ISBN 0-7091-9401-3 : £6.95 B82-06331

Cradock, Fanny. Gathering clouds at Castle Rising / Fanny Cradock. — London : W.H. Allen, 1981. — 238p ; 23cm
ISBN 0-491-02835-0 : £6.95 B82-06558

Cradock, Fanny. Uneasy peace at Castle Rising / Fanny Cradock. — London : W.H. Allen, 1979. — 228p : 1geneal.table ; 23cm
ISBN 0-491-02219-0 : £5.95 B82-10073

Cradock, Fanny. Uneasy peace at Castle Rising / Fanny Cradock. — London : W.H. Allen, 1981, c1979. — 228p : 1geneal.table ; 18cm. — (A Star book)
ISBN 0-352-31016-2 (pbk) : £1.60 B82-10104

Crampsey, Robert A.. The manager / Robert A. Crampsey. — London : Hodder and Stoughton, 1982. — 190p ; 23cm
ISBN 0-340-27569-3 : £6.95 : CIP rev. B82-01101

Crane, Teresa. After Louise / Teresa Crane. — [London] : Fontana, 1982. — 219p ; 18cm. — (Nightshades)
ISBN 0-00-616214-2 (pbk) : £1.00 B82-18092

Crane, Teresa. Molly O'Dowd. — London : Gollancz, Sept.1982. — [608]p
ISBN 0-575-02939-0 : £8.95 : CIP entry B82-18758

Cranmer, Kathryn. Passionate enemies / by Kathryn Cranmer. — London : Mills & Boon, 1982. — 190p ; 19cm
ISBN 0-263-10073-1 : £5.25 B82-30933

Craven, Sara. Dark summer dawn / by Sara Craven. — London : Mills & Boon, 1981. — 188p ; 20cm
ISBN 0-263-09961-x : £4.55 B82-04654

Craven, Sara. Unguarded moment / by Sara Craven. — London : Mills & Boon, 1982. — 186p ; 19cm
ISBN 0-263-10111-8 : £5.95 B82-37276

Craven, Sarah. The garden of dreams. — Large print ed. — Long Preston : Magna, Feb.1983. — [320]p
Originally published: London : Mills and Boon, 1975
ISBN 0-86009-490-1 : £5.75 : CIP entry B82-39616

Crawley, Aileen. The shadow of god / Aileen Crawley. — London : Hutchinson, 1982. — 320p ; 23cm
Bibliography: p319-320
ISBN 0-09-147630-5 : £7.95 : CIP rev. B82-15926

Creed, David. Travellers in an antique land / David Creed. — London : Secker and Warburg, 1982. — 214p ; 23cm
ISBN 0-436-11413-5 : £7.95 : CIP rev. B82-15794

Cresswell, Helen. Dear Shrink / Helen Cresswell. — London : Faber, 1982. — 220p ; 21cm
ISBN 0-571-11912-3 : £5.25 : CIP rev. B82-06860

Cresswell, Jasmine. The princess / by Jasmine Cresswell. — London : Hale, 1982. — 207p ; 21cm
ISBN 0-7091-9773-x : £7.25 B82-31621

Crisp, N. J.. The brink / N.J. Crisp. — London : Macdonald, 1982. — 300p ; 23cm
ISBN 0-356-08531-7 : £7.95 B82-17065

Crisp, N. J.. Festival / N.J. Crisp. — London : Macdonald, 1981. — 264p ; 23cm
ISBN 0-354-04517-2 : £7.50 B82-14720

Crisp, N. J.. Festival / N.J. Crisp. — [London] : Futura, 1982, c1981. — 464p ; 18cm. — (A Futura book)
Originally published: London : Macdonald, 1981
ISBN 0-7088-2090-5 (pbk) : £1.50 B82-33790

Cross, Gillian. The dark behind the curtain / Gillian Cross ; illustrated by David Parkins. — Oxford : Oxford University Press, 1982. — 159p : ill ; 22cm
ISBN 0-19-271457-0 : £5.95 : CIP rev. B82-04154

Curtin, Michael. The self-made men / Michael Curtin. — Harmondsworth : Penguin, 1982, c1980. — 288p ; 18cm
Originally published: London : Deutsch, 1980
ISBN 0-14-005718-8 (pbk) : £1.75 B82-29582

823'.914[F] — Fiction in English, *1945- — Texts continuation*

Curtis, Jean. A time to live / by Jean Curtis. — London : Hale, 1982. — 160p ; 19cm
ISBN 0-7091-9839-6 : £6.50 B82-27312

Curtis, Marjorie. Hospital encounter / by Marjorie Curtis. — London : Hale, 1982. — 159p ; 20cm
ISBN 0-7091-9840-x : £6.50 B82-31629

Curzon, Clare. A leaven of malice / Clare Curzon. — Feltham : Hamlyn Paperbacks, 1982, 1979. — 190p ; 18cm
Originally published: London : Collins, 1979
ISBN 0-600-20268-2 (pbk) : £1.50 B82-31947

Dailey, Janet. For the love of God. — London : Hodder & Stoughton, July 1982. — [192]p. — (Silhouette romance)
Originally published: New York : Silhouette Books, 1981
ISBN 0-340-28464-1 (pbk) : £0.75 : CIP entry B82-12310

Dailey, Janet. Foxfire light. — London : Hodder and Stoughton, Dec.1982. — [256]p. — (Silhouette special edition)
ISBN 0-340-32683-2 (pbk) : £0.95 : CIP entry B82-29662

Dailey, Janet. The hostage bride. — London : Hodder & Stoughton, Jan.1982. — [192]p. — (Silhouette romance)
ISBN 0-340-27662-2 (pbk) : £0.75 : CIP entry B81-34480

Dailey, Janet. The ivory cane / Janet Dailey. — Large print ed. — Bath : Chivers, 1982, c1977. — 207p ; 23cm. — (A Lythway book)
Originally published: London : Mills & Boon, 1977
ISBN 0-85119-791-4 : Unpriced : CIP rev. B82-01435

Dailey, Janet. The Lancaster men. — London : Hodder & Stoughton, May 1982. — [192]p. — (Silhouette romance)
Originally published: New York : Silhouette Books, 1981
ISBN 0-340-27932-x (pbk) : £0.75 : CIP entry B82-07944

Dailey, Janet. Night way / by Janet Dailey. — London : Futura, 1981. — 320p ; 18cm
ISBN 0-7088-2134-0 (pbk) : £1.60 B82-09365

Dailey, Janet. Northern magic / by Janet Dailey. — London : Mills & Boon, 1982. — 189p ; 19cm
ISBN 0-263-10015-4 : £5.25 B82-18126

Dailey, Janet. One of the boys. — Large print ed. — Bath, Chivers, Jan.1983. — [224]p. — (Atlantic large print)
Originally published: London : Mills and Boon, 1981
ISBN 0-85119-515-6 : £5.75 : CIP entry B82-36337

Dailey, Janet. Reilly's woman / Janet Dailey. — Large print ed. — Bath : Chivers, 1982, c1977. — 193p ; 23cm. — (A Lythway book) (A Lythway romance)
Originally published: London : Mills & Boon, 1977
ISBN 0-85119-776-0 : Unpriced : CIP rev. B81-33797

Dailey, Janet. Ride the thunder / Janet Dailey. — Loughton : Piatkus, 1981, c1980. — 320p ; 21cm
ISBN 0-86188-132-x : £6.95 : CIP rev. B81-31638

Dailey, Janet. Terms of surrender. — London : Hodder & Stouhgton, June 1982. — [256]p. — (Silhouette special edition)
ISBN 0-340-28579-6 (pbk) : £0.95 : CIP entry B82-10795

Dailey, Janet. That Carolina summer / by Janet Dailey. — London : Mills & Boon, 1981. — 188p ; 20cm
ISBN 0-263-09956-3 : £4.55 B82-04652

Dailey, Janet. This Calder range. — London : Coronet Books, Jan.1983. — [448]p
Originally published: New York : Pocket Books, 1982
ISBN 0-340-28350-5 (pbk) : £2.50 : CIP entry B82-35220

Dailey, Janet. This Calder range. — London : Hodder & Stoughton, Jan.1983. — [352]p
ISBN 0-340-33068-6 : £7.95 : CIP entry B82-34085

Dailey, Janet. This Calder sky / Janet Dailey. — London : Futura, 1982, c1981. — 432p ; 18cm
ISBN 0-7088-2153-7 (pbk) : £1.95 B82-30776

Dailey, Janet. Wildcatter's woman. — London : Hodder & Stoughton, Dec.1982. — [192]p. — (Silhouette romance)
ISBN 0-340-32698-0 (pbk) : £0.75 : CIP entry B82-29668

Daley, John. Making waves / John Daley. — London : Macmillan, 1982. — 172p ; 21cm
ISBN 0-333-32652-0 : £6.95 B82-27330

Dalzell, Helen. In search of Mary Ann / by Helen Dalzell. — London : Mills & Boon, 1982. — 189p ; 19cm
ISBN 0-263-10115-0 : £5.95 B82-37273

Dana, Richard. Mandan Valley / by Richard Dana. — London : Hale, 1981. — 158p ; 20cm
ISBN 0-7091-9365-3 : £4.95 B82-00512

Dana, Richard. Shadow valley / by Richard Dana. — London : Hale, 1982. — 158p ; 20cm
ISBN 0-7091-9560-5 : £5.25 B82-15593

Daneman, Meredith. The groundling / Meredith Daneman. — London : Joseph, 1982. — 185p ; 23cm
ISBN 0-7181-2132-5 : £7.95 B82-28796

Daniel, Jack. Dispatch rider : a novel / by Jack Daniel. — London : Allison & Busby, 1980. — 164p ; 23cm
ISBN 0-85031-267-1 : £6.50 : CIP rev. B80-02550

Daniels, Philip. A genteel little murder / Philip Daniels. — London : Hale, 1982. — 191p ; 20cm
ISBN 0-7091-9551-6 : £6.75 B82-26029

Daniels, Philip. The inconvenient corpse / Philip Daniels. — London : Hale, 1982. — 192p ; 20cm
ISBN 0-7091-9312-2 : £6.50 B82-12609

Daniels, Philip. Nice knight for murder / by Philip Daniels. — London : Hale, 1982. — 176p ; 20cm
ISBN 0-7091-9776-4 : £6.75 B82-39178

Daniels, Philip. Suspicious / by Philip Daniels. — London : Hale, 1981. — 192p ; 20cm
ISBN 0-7091-9104-9 : £6.25 B82-00519

Darby, Catherine. Child of the flesh / by Catherine Darby. — London : Hale, 1981. — 224p ; 22cm
ISBN 0-7091-8104-3 : £7.50 B82-22162

Darby, Catherine. Falcon to the lure / by Catherine Darby. — London : Hale, 1981. — 223p ; 21cm
ISBN 0-7091-6983-3 : £6.95 B82-07186

Darby, Catherine. The Falcon tree. — Large print ed. — Long Preston : Magna Print, Dec.1982. — [380]p
Originally published: London : Hale, 1977
ISBN 0-86009-446-4 : £5.50 : CIP entry B82-30726

Darby, Catherine. Fortune for a falcon / by Catherine Darby. — Bolton-by-Bowland : Magna, 1980, c1976. — 458p : 1geneal.table ; 23cm. — (The Falcon saga ; 3)
Originally published: London : Hale, 1976. — Published in large print
ISBN 0-86009-279-8 : £5.25 : CIP rev. B80-34106

Darby, Catherine. Lass of silver, lad of gold / Catherine Darby. — London : Hale, 1982. — 188p ; 23cm
ISBN 0-7091-8236-8 : £7.25 B82-36518

Darby, Catherine. A pride of Falcons. — Large print ed. — Long Preston : Magna Print, Nov.1982. — [400]p
Originally published: London : Hale, 1977
ISBN 0-86009-441-3 : £5.50 : CIP entry B82-26342

Darby, Catherine. Season of the falcon. — Large print ed. — Long Preston : Magna Print, Oct.1982. — [432]p
Originally published: London : Hale, 1976
ISBN 0-86009-434-0 : £5.50 : CIP entry B82-24130

Darke, Marjorie. A long way to go / Marjorie Darke. — Harmondsworth : Penguin, 1982, c1978. — 189p ; 18cm. — (Puffin plus)
Originally published: Harmondsworth : Kestrel. 1978. — For adolescents
ISBN 0-14-031359-1 (pbk) : £1.25 B82-16767

Darke, Marjorie. Tom Post's private eye. — London : Macmillan Education, Mar.1982. — [112]p. — (Topliner tridents)
ISBN 0-333-31972-9 : £3.95 : CIP entry B82-01855

Darrell, Elizabeth. The jade alliance. — London : Hodder and Stoughton, Mar.1982. — [448]p. — (Coronet books)
Originally published: 1980
ISBN 0-340-27909-5 (pbk) : £1.25 : CIP entry B82-00255

Daveson, Mons. My lord Kasseem / by Mons Daveson. — London : Mills & Boon, 1982. — 189p ; 20cm
ISBN 0-263-10101-0 : £5.95 B82-37434

Daveson, Mons. Sugar country / by Mons Daveson. — London : Mills & Boon, 1981. — 189p ; 19cm
ISBN 0-263-10025-1 : £5.25 B82-18132

Davie-Martin, Hugh. Death's bright angel / by Hugh Davie-Martin. — London : Hale, 1982. — 190p ; 20cm
ISBN 0-7091-9332-7 : £6.25 B82-15003

Davies, Elizabeth. Honey money / Elizabeth Davies. — Bognor Regis : New Horizon, c1982. — 186p ; 21cm
ISBN 0-86116-538-1 : £5.75 B82-12949

Davies, Frederick. Death of a hit-man / Frederick Davies. — London : Hale, 1982. — 219p ; 20cm
ISBN 0-7091-9910-4 : £6.75 B82-35892

Davis, Cliff. The bushwackers / by Clif Davis. — London : Hale, 1981, c1977. — 159p : ill ; 19cm
ISBN 0-7091-8912-5 : £4.95 B82-07210

Davis, Margaret Thomson. A very civilized man. — London : Allison and Busby, June 1982. — [224]p
ISBN 0-85031-449-6 : £6.95 : CIP entry B82-13503

Dawes, Frank V.. A family album / Frank V. Dawes. — London : Hutchinson, 1982. — vii,326p ; 23cm
ISBN 0-09-149520-2 : £7.95 : CIP rev. B82-15661

823'.914[F] — Fiction in English, *1945- — Texts continuation*

Dawson, Les. The Amy Pluckett letters. — London : Robson, Oct.1982. — [196]p
ISBN 0-86051-197-9 : £5.95 : CIP entry
B82-24145

De Montfort, Guiy. All the Queen's men — / Guiy de Montfort. — London : Severn House, 1981, c1980. — 288p ; 21cm
Originally published: London : Hamlyn Paperbacks, 1980
ISBN 0-7278-0727-7 : £6.95 : CIP rev.
B81-23817

De Winters, Danielle. Passionate rebel / Danielle de Winters. — London : Macdonald, 1981. — 256p ; 21cm
ISBN 0-356-08512-0 : £4.95 B82-10084

De Winters, Danielle. Passionate rebel / Danielle de Winters. — London : Macdonald, 1981. — 256p ; 18cm. — (A Minstrel book ; 27)
ISBN 0-7088-2130-8 (pbk) : £0.95 B82-09350

Dearan, Anne. The boat to Rio / Anne Dearan. — London : Granada, 1982. — 200p ; 18cm
ISBN 0-246-11579-3 (cased) : Unpriced
ISBN 0-586-05436-7 (pbk) : £1.25 B82-19976

Deighton, Len. Billion-dollar brain. — Large print ed. — Anstey : Ulverscroft, Jan.1983. — [512]p. — (Ulverscroft large print series)
Originally published: London : Cape, 1966
ISBN 0-7089-0901-9 : £6.25 : CIP entry
B82-32529

Deighton, Len. Goodbye Mickey Mouse. — London : Hutchinson, Sept.1982. — [384]p
ISBN 0-09-149760-4 : £7.95 : CIP entry
B82-21735

Deighton, Len. Horse under water. — Large print ed. — Bath : Chivers, Jan.1983. — [376] p. — (Atlantic large print)
Originally published: London : Cape, 1963
ISBN 0-85119-519-9 : £5.25 : CIP entry
B82-33091

Deighton, Len. The Ipcress file. — Large print ed. — Bath : Chivers, Jan.1983. — [376]p
Originally published: London : Hodder & Stoughton, 1962
ISBN 0-85119-199-1 : £6.90 : CIP entry
B82-33084

Deighton, Len. XPD / Len Deighton. — London : Granada, 1982, c1981. — 431p ; 18cm. — (A Panther book)
Originally published: London : Hutchinson, 1981
ISBN 0-586-05447-2 (pbk) : £1.95 B82-19984

Deighton, Len. XPD / Len Deighton. — Leicester : Charnwood, 1982, c1981. — 562p ; 22cm. — (Charnwood library series)
Originally published: London : Hutchinson, 1981. — Published in large print
ISBN 0-7089-8036-8 : Unpriced : CIP rev.
B82-08097

Delahaye, Michael. The sale of lot 236 / Michael Delahaye. — London : Constable, 1981. — 228p : ill,1facsim ; 23cm. — (Constable crime)
ISBN 0-09-464270-2 : £6.95 B82-02960

Delancey, Diney. Love's dawning / by Diney Delancey. — London : Hale, 1982. — 158p ; 20cm
ISBN 0-7091-9620-2 : £5.95 B82-13836

Delancey, Diney. The secret of Shearwater / by Diney Delancey. — London : Hale, 1982. — 187p ; 20cm
ISBN 0-7091-9972-4 : £6.50 B82-39179

Dempster, Chris. Hit! / Chris Dempster. — London : Corgi, 1982. — 207p ; 18cm
ISBN 0-552-12007-3 (pbk) : £1.50 B82-37551

Denny, Lesley. A taste of treachery / by Lesley Denny. — London : Hale, 1982. — 176p ; 20cm
ISBN 0-7091-9511-7 : £6.50 B82-13845

Derwent, Lavinia. Macpherson's caravan. — London : Hodder and Stoughton, May 1981. — [128]p
Originally published: London : Burke Publishing, 1968
ISBN 0-340-26527-2 (pbk) : £0.85 : CIP entry
B81-04243

Dessau, Joanna. Amazing Grace / Joanna Dessau. — Bath : Chivers, 1982, c1980. — 219p ; 23cm. — (A Lythway historical novel)
Originally published: London : Hale, 1980
ISBN 0-85119-807-4 : Unpriced : CIP rev.
B82-07011

Dessau, Joanna. The constant lover / Joanna Dessau. — London : Hale, 1982. — 175p ; 20cm
ISBN 0-7091-9772-1 : £7.25 B82-27313

Dessau, Joanna. Lord of the ladies / Joanna Dessau. — London : Hale, 1981. — 171p ; 21cm
ISBN 0-7091-9485-4 : £6.75 B82-06332

D'Este, Anne. Before the summer rain. — Loughton : Piatkus, June 1982. — [320]p
ISBN 0-86188-186-9 : £6.95 : CIP entry
B82-10251

Devine, Dominic. My brother's killer : a famous first / Dominic Devine. — London : Collins, 1961 (1981 [printing]). — 234p ; 21cm. — (The Crime Club)
ISBN 0-00-231486-x : £6.50 B82-03083

Devon, Sarah. Bridehaven / Sarah Devon. — Large print ed. — Bath : Chivers, 1982, c1970. — 223p ; 23cm. — (A Lythway book) (A Lythway romantic thriller)
Originally published: London : Hale, 1970
ISBN 0-85119-777-9 : Unpriced : CIP rev.
B81-33796

Devon, Sarah. Darling rebel / by Sarah Devon. — London : Hale, 1982. — 157p ; 20cm
ISBN 0-7091-9553-2 : £5.95 B82-11064

Devon, Sarah. The keeper of the mountain. — Large print ed. — Bath : Chivers, Jan.1983. — [256]p. — (A Lythway book)
Originally published: London : Hale, 1973
ISBN 0-85119-884-8 : £6.90 : CIP entry
B82-33098

Dew, Diana. Angela : the story of a dachshund / Diana Dew. — Bognor Regis : New Horizon, c1981. — 296p ; 21cm
ISBN 0-86116-142-4 : £6.75 B82-03501

Dewar, Margaret. Philippa / by Margaret Dewar. — London : Hale, 1982. — 190p ; 20cm
ISBN 0-7091-9811-6 : £7.25 B82-35872

Dewhurst, Eileen. Whoever I am / Eileen Dewhurst. — London : Collins, 1982. — 237p ; 20cm. — (The Crime club)
ISBN 0-00-231920-9 : £6.75 : CIP rev.
B81-35939

Dewhurst, Keith. Captain of the sands / Keith Dewhurst. — London : Cape, 1982, c1981. — 391p ; 23cm
ISBN 0-224-01619-9 : £7.50 : CIP rev.
B81-28831

Dickinson, Margaret. Carrie / Margaret Dickinson. — London : Hale, 1981. — 191p ; 21cm
ISBN 0-7091-8942-7 : £6.95 B82-00450

Dickinson, Peter, *1927-*. King and joker / Peter Dickinson. — Feltham : Hamlyn Paperbacks, 1982, c1976. — 189p : 1geneal.table ; 18cm. — (A Hamlyn whodunnit)
Originally published: London : Hodder and Stoughton, 1976
ISBN 0-600-20495-2 (pbk) : £1.25 B82-19456

Dickinson, Peter, *1927-*. The last house-party. — London : Bodley Head, May 1982. — [224]p
ISBN 0-370-30477-2 : £5.95 : CIP entry
B82-06737

Dickinson, Peter, *1927-*. A summer in the Twenties. — London : Hodder and Stoughton, Apr.1981. — [256]p
ISBN 0-340-26407-1 : £6.95 : CIP entry
B81-02368

Diffey, Myrna. Precious spring / by Myrna Diffey. — London : Hale, 1982. — 175p ; 20cm
ISBN 0-7091-9763-2 : £6.50 B82-31633

Digance, Richard. Backwater / Richard Digance ; with illustrations by Penny Wurr. — London : Joseph, 1982. — 188p : ill ; 20cm
ISBN 0-7181-2103-1 (cased) : £6.95
ISBN 0-7181-2140-6 (pbk) : £4.95 B82-17354

Digby, Anne, *1935-*. The tennis term at Trebizon / Anne Digby ; illustrated by Gavin Rowe. — London : Granada, 1982, c1981. — 126p : ill ; 19cm
ISBN 0-246-11423-1 (cased) : £3.95
ISBN 0-583-30433-8 (pbk) : Unpriced
B82-22761

Dillon, Eilis. Wild geese. — London : Coronet Books, Feb.1983. — 1v.
Originally published: New York : Simon and Schuster, 1980 ; London : Hodder & Stoughton, 1981
ISBN 0-340-32043-5 (pbk) B82-38061

Dingwell, Joyce. A man like Brady. — Large print ed. — Bath : Chivers, Nov.1982. — [248] p. — (Atlantic large print)
Originally published: London : Mills & Boon, 1981
ISBN 0-85119-502-4 : £5.25 : CIP entry
B82-26431

Dingwell, Joyce. Second chance / Joyce Dingwell. — Large print ed. — Leicester : Ulverscroft, 1981. — 337p ; 23cm
Originally published: London : Mills & Boon, 1956
ISBN 0-7089-0720-2 : £5.00 : CIP rev.
B81-32035

Dix, Isabel. Cast a tender shadow / by Isabel Dix. — London : Mills & Boon, 1981. — 189p ; 19cm
ISBN 0-263-09964-4 : £4.55 B82-04640

Donald, Robyn. The dark abyss / by Robyn Donald. — London : Mills & Boon, 1981. — 188p ; 20cm
ISBN 0-263-09971-7 : £4.55 B82-09364

Donald, Robyn. Dilemma in paradise. — Large print ed. — Long Preston : Magna, Jan.1983. — [320]p
Originally published: London : Mills and Boon, 1978
ISBN 0-86009-491-x : £5.75 : CIP entry
B82-33218

Donald, Robyn. An old passion / by Robyn Donald. — London : Mills & Boon, 1982. — 186p ; 19cm
ISBN 0-263-10042-1 : £5.25 B82-22497

Donald, Vivian. Cathy's choice / by Vivian Donald. — London : Hale, 1982, c1978. — 182p ; 20cm
Originally published: New York : New American Library, 1978
ISBN 0-7091-9781-0 : £6.95 B82-27426

823'.914[F] — Fiction in English, ***1945-*** **— *Texts continuation***

Donnelly, Jane. Behind a closed door / Jane Donnelly. — Large print ed. — Bath : Chivers, 1982, c1979. — 251p ; 23cm. — (A Lythway romance)
Originally published: London : Mills & Boon, 1979
ISBN 0-85119-799-x : Unpriced : CIP rev. B82-05006

Donnelly, Jane. Diamond cut diamond / by Jane Donnelly. — London : Mills & Boon, 1982. — 188p ; 19cm
ISBN 0-263-10035-9 : £5.25 B82-22642

Donnelly, Jane. The frozen jungle / by Jane Donnelly. — London : Mills & Boon, 1981. — 186p ; 20cm
ISBN 0-263-09975-x : £4.55 B82-09230

Donnelly, Jane. A man apart / Jane Donnelly. — Large print ed. — Leicester : Ulverscroft, 1982, c1969. — 328p ; 23cm. — (Ulverscroft large print)
Originally published: London : Mills & Boon, 1968
ISBN 0-7089-0803-9 : Unpriced : CIP rev. B82-18451

Donnelly, Jane. A savage sanctuary / Jane Donnelly. — [Bath] : Chivers, 1982, c1979. — 290p ; 23cm. — (Atlantic large print) (A Seymour large print romance)
Originally published: London : Mills and Boon, 1979
ISBN 0-85119-478-8 : Unpriced : CIP rev. B82-13090

Donson, Cyril. Ghost town marshall / by Cyril Donson. — London : Hale, 1982. — 158p ; 20cm
ISBN 0-7091-9604-0 : £5.25 B82-13840

Dossey, Larry. Space, time and medicine / Larry Dossey ; foreword by Fritjof Capra. — Boulder ; London : Shambhala, c1982. — xv,248p ; 23cm
Includes index
ISBN 0-87773-224-8 (pbk) : £5.95
ISBN 0-394-52465-9 (U.S.)
ISBN 0-394-71091-6 (U.S.) B82-38562

Doubtfire, Dianne. This Jim / Dianne Doubtfire. — Basingstoke : Macmillan, 1980, c1974. — 90p ; 18cm. — (Topliners) (Topliners)
Originally published: London : Heinemann, 1974. — For adolescents
ISBN 0-333-28689-8 (pbk) : £0.70 : CIP rev. B80-12548

Douglas, Colin, *1945-*. Wellies from the Queen / Colin Douglas. — London : Arrow, 1982, c1981. — 251p ; 18cm
Originally published: London : Hutchinson, 1981
ISBN 0-09-927590-2 (pbk) : £1.50 B82-19011

Douglas, Sheila. The uncertain heart / by Sheila Douglas. — London : Mills & Boon, 1982. — 190p ; 19cm
ISBN 0-263-10034-0 : £5.25 B82-22646

Doyle, Amanda. The outback man / Amanda Doyle. — Large print ed. — Bath : Chivers, 1982, c1966. — 234p ; 23cm. — (A Lythway book)
Originally published: London : Mills & Boon, 1966
ISBN 0-85119-815-5 : Unpriced : CIP rev. B82-09858

Doyle, Richard. Havana Special. — London : Arlington Books, May 1982. — [320]p
ISBN 0-85140-575-4 : £6.95 : CIP entry B82-07020

Drabble, Margaret. The Garrick year. — Large print ed. — Bath : Chivers, Oct.1982. — [352] p. — (A New Portway large print book)
Originally published: London : Weidenfeld and Nicolson, 1964
ISBN 0-85119-186-x : £6.25 : CIP entry B82-24224

Drabble, Margaret. The ice age / Margaret Drabble. — Harmondsworth : Penguin, 1978, c1977 (1982 [printing]). — 286p ; 18cm
Originally published: London : Weidenfeld and Nicolson, 1977
ISBN 0-14-004804-9 (pbk) : £1.75 B82-27558

Drabble, Margaret. Jerusalem the golden / Margaret Drabble. — Harmondsworth : Penguin, 1969, c1967 (1982 [printing]). — 205p ; 18cm
Originally published: London : Weidenfeld & Nicolson, 1967
ISBN 0-14-002933-8 (pbk) : £1.50 B82-33015

Drabble, Margaret. Jerusalem the golden. — Large print ed. — Bath : Chivers, Oct.1982. — [384]p. — (A New Portway large print book)
Originally published: London : Weidenfeld and Nicolson, 1967
ISBN 0-85119-187-8 : £6.25 : CIP entry B82-24225

Drabble, Margaret. The millstone / Margaret Drabble. — Harmondsworth : Penguin, 1968, c1965 (1981 [printing]). — 172p ; 18cm
Originally published: London : Weidenfeld and Nicolson, 1965
ISBN 0-14-002842-0 (pbk) : £1.25 B82-25567

Drabble, Margaret. The millstone. — Large print ed. — Bath : Chivers, Oct.1982. — [312]p. — (A New Portway large print book)
Originally published: London : Weidenfeld and Nicolson, 1965
ISBN 0-85119-188-6 : £5.90 : CIP entry B82-24226

Drabble, Margaret. The needle's eye / Margaret Drabble. — Harmondsworth : Penguin, 1973, c1972 (1982 [printing]). — 398p ; 19cm
Originally published: London : Weidenfeld and Nicolson, 1972
ISBN 0-14-003666-0 (pbk) : £1.95 B82-36233

Drabble, Margaret. The realms of gold / Margaret Drabble. — Harmondsworth : Penguin, 1977, c1975 (1982 [printing]). — 357p ; 18cm
Originally published: London : Weidenfeld and Nicolson, 1975
ISBN 0-14-004360-8 (pbk) : £1.95 B82-36232

Drabble, Margaret. A summer bird-cage. — Large print ed. — Bath : Chivers, Oct.1982. — [320]p. — (A New Portway large print book)
Originally published: London : Weidenfeld and Nicolson, 1962
ISBN 0-85119-189-4 : £5.90 : CIP entry B82-24227

Drabble, Margaret. The waterfall / Margaret Drabble. — Harmondsworth : Penguin, 1971, c1969 (1982 [printing]). — 239p ; 18cm
Originally published: London : Weidenfeld & Nicolson, 1969
ISBN 0-14-003317-3 (pbk) : £1.50 B82-27556

Drake, Tony. Half a chance / Tony Drake. — London : Collins, 1982. — 174p ; 22cm
For adolescents
ISBN 0-00-184301-x : £5.50 B82-37124

Dransfield, Evelyn. Night of the leopard / Evelyn Dransfield. — Bognor Regis : New Horizon, c1981. — 124p ; 22cm
ISBN 0-86116-518-7 : £4.50 B82-08819

Draper, Alfred. Grey seal / Alfred Draper. — [London] : Futura, 1982, c1981. — 255p ; 18cm. — (A Futura book)
Originally published: London : Macdonald, 1981
ISBN 0-7088-2192-8 (pbk) : £1.50 B82-33788

Driscoll, Peter. The Barboza credentials / Peter Driscoll. — London : Granada, 1982, c1976. — 320p ; 18cm. — (A Panther book)
Originally published: London : Macdonald, 1976
ISBN 0-586-05347-6 (pbk) : £1.50 B82-28372

Driscoll, Peter. Heritage. — London : Granada, June 1982. — [576]p
ISBN 0-246-11515-7 : £7.95 : CIP entry B82-09986

Driscoll, Peter. The Wilby conspiracy / Peter Driscoll. — London : Granada, 1982, c1972. — 268p ; 18cm. — (A Panther book)
Originally published: Philadelphia : Lippincott, 1972 ; London : Macdonald, 1973
ISBN 0-586-05391-3 (pbk) : £1.50 B82-14106

Driver, Grace. Return to Balandra / by Grace Driver. — London : Hale, 1982. — 188p ; 20cm
ISBN 0-7091-9875-2 : £6.50 B82-39207

Driver, Grace. Shower of gold / by Grace Driver. — London : Hale, 1982. — 176p ; 20cm
ISBN 0-7091-9710-1 : £6.25 B82-27424

Drummond, June. The Trojan mule : a novel / by June Drummond. — London : Gollancz, 1982. — 159p ; 21cm. — (Gollancz thriller)
ISBN 0-575-03135-2 : £6.95 : CIP rev. B82-12984

Drummond, Ursula. Brilliant women : a novel / by Ursula Drummond. — Braunton : Merlin, 1982. — 250p ; 22cm
ISBN 0-86303-012-2 : £7.00 B82-34505

Drysdale, Margaret. Quest for a crown / Margaret Drysdale. — London : Hale, 1982. — 192p ; 21cm
ISBN 0-7091-9795-0 : £7.25 B82-31616

Duff, Moira. The vocation of Pearl Duncan. — London : Women's Press, Oct.1982. — 1v.
ISBN 0-7043-3897-1 : £3.50 : CIP entry B82-27197

Duffy, Maureen. Gor saga / Maureen Duffy. — London : Eyre Metheun, 1981. — 221p ; 23cm
ISBN 0-413-49190-0 : £6.95 : CIP rev. B81-25309

Duffy, Maureen. That's how it was. — London : Virago, Jan.1983. — [224]p. — (Virago modern classics)
Originally published: London : New Authors, 1962
ISBN 0-86068-291-9 (pbk) : £2.95 : CIP entry B82-33222

Duke, Madelaine. Flashpoint / Madelaine Duke. — London : Joseph, 1982. — 286p ; 22cm
ISBN 0-7181-1876-6 : £7.95 B82-18272

Duncan, Alex. God and the doctor / Alex Duncan. — London : Star, 1982, c1981. — 208p ; 18cm
Originally published: London : W.H. Allen, 1981
ISBN 0-352-31051-0 (pbk) : £1.60 B82-16104

Duncan, Jane. My friend Annie. — Large print ed. — Anstey : Ulverscroft, Feb.1983. — 1v.. — (Ulverscroft large print series)
Originally published: London : Macmillan, 1961
ISBN 0-7089-0916-7 : CIP entry B82-38878

Duncan, Jane. My friend Monica. — Large print ed. — Anstey : Ulverscroft, Nov.1982. — [416] p. — (Ulverscroft large print series)
Originally published: London : Macmillan, 1960
ISBN 0-7089-0873-x : £5.00 : CIP entry B82-29089

Duncan, Jane. My friend Muriel. — Large print ed. — Anstey : Ulverscroft, Sept.1982. — [432] p. — (Ulverscroft large print series)
Originally published: London : Macmillan, 1959
ISBN 0-7089-0846-2 : £5.00 : CIP entry B82-27177

823'.914[F] — Fiction in English, *1945- — Texts continuation*

Duncan, Jane. My friends the Miss Boyds / Jane Duncan. — Large print ed. — Leicester : Ulverscroft, 1982, c1959. — 413p ; 23cm. — (Ulverscroft large print series)
Originally published: London : Macmillan, 1959
ISBN 0-7089-0818-7 : Unpriced : CIP rev. B82-15958

Dunnett, Dorothy. King hereafter / Dorothy Dunnett. — London : Joseph, 1982. — 721p : 3maps,3geneal.talbes ; 24cm
Geneal. tables on lining papers
ISBN 0-7181-1661-5 : £9.50 B82-22565

Dupré, Catherine. Gentleman's child / Catherine Dupré. — [London] : Fontana, 1982, c1980. — 382p ; 18cm
Originally published: London : Collins, 1980
ISBN 0-00-616476-5 (pbk) : £1.95 B82-13653

Durbridge, Francis. A man called Harry Brent / Francis Durbridge. — Hornchurch : Ian Henry, 1982, c1970. — 190p ; 21cm
Originally published: London : Hodder & Stoughton, 1970
ISBN 0-86025-199-3 : £5.25 B82-22107

Durman, Hilda. Brad's return / by Hilda Durman. — London : Hale, 1982. — 160p ; 20cm
ISBN 0-7091-9945-7 : £6.50 B82-39176

Durman, Hilda. In love again / by Hilda Durman. — London : Hale, 1981. — 160p ; 20cm
ISBN 0-7091-9327-0 : £5.95 B82-10746

Durman, Hilda. Valley of the sun / by Hilda Durman. — London : Hale, 1982. — 159p ; 20cm
ISBN 0-7091-9603-2 : £6.50 B82-25989

Durrell, Gerald. The Mockery Bird / Gerald Durrell. — London : Collins, 1981. — 224p ; 22cm
ISBN 0-00-222603-0 : £7.50 : CIP rev. B81-28780

Durrell, Gerald. The mockery bird. — Large print ed. — Anstey : Ulverscroft, Jan.1983. — [384]p. — (Ulverscroft large print series)
Originally published: London : Collins, 1981
ISBN 0-7089-0900-0 : £6.25 : CIP entry B82-32528

Dwyer-Joyce, Alice. The Cornelian Strand / Alice Dwyer-Joyce. — London : Hale, 1982. — 189p ; 20cm
ISBN 0-7091-9676-8 : £6.95 B82-17474

Dwyer-Joyce, Alice. The glass heiress / Alice Dwyer-Joyce. — New York : St. Martin's Press ; London : Hale, 1981. — 185p ; 21cm
ISBN 0-7091-9246-0 : £6.95 B82-02808

Dwyer-Joyce, Alice. The glitter-dust / Alice Dwyer-Joyce. — Large print ed. — Leicester : Ulverscroft, 1982, c1978. — 360p ; 22cm. — (Ulverscroft Large print series)
Originally published: New York : St. Martin's Press ; London : Hale, 1978
ISBN 0-7089-0747-4 : £5.00 : CIP rev. B81-36943

Dyke, Carol Hamilton. The last daydream / by Carol Hamilton Dyke. — London : Hale, 1982. — 156p ; 20cm
ISBN 0-7091-9376-9 : £6.25 B82-13838

Dyke, Carol Hamilton. Riverside romance / by Carol Hamilton Dyke. — London : Hale, 1981. — 158p ; 20cm
ISBN 0-7091-9238-x : £5.95 B82-12599

Dyke, Carol Hamilton. That certain look / by Carol Hamilton Dyke. — London : Hale, 1982. — 157p ; 20cm
ISBN 0-7091-9441-2 : £6.50 B82-30433

Ebel, Suzanne. Julia's sister / Suzanne Ebel. — London : Severn House, 1981. — 192p ; 21cm
ISBN 0-7278-0693-9 : £5.95 : CIP rev. B81-07610

Eden, Matthew. The murder of Lawrence of Arabia / Matthew Eden. — London : New English Library, 1980, c1979 (1981 [printing]). — 256p ; 18cm
Originally published: New York : Crowell, 1979
ISBN 0-450-04786-5 (pbk) : £1.75 B82-03695

Edgeworth, Ann. The golden bride / Ann Edgeworth. — London : Mills & Boon, 1982. — 189p ; 20cm. — (Masquerade)
ISBN 0-263-10023-5 : £5.25 B82-13894

Edson, J. T.. The bloody border / by J.T. Edson. — London : Hale, 1982, c1969. — 159p ; 20cm
Originally published: London : Corgi, 1969
ISBN 0-7091-8270-8 : £4.95 B82-18931

Edson, J. T.. Doc Leroy, M.D. / by J.T. Edson. — London : Hale, 1981, c1977. — 190p ; 20cm
Originally published: London : Corgi, 1977
ISBN 0-7091-8247-3 : £4.95 B82-03176

Edson, J. T.. The fastest gun in Texas / by J.T. Edson. — London : Hale, 1982, c1968. — 157p ; 20cm
Originally published: London : Corgi, 1968
ISBN 0-7091-8435-2 : £5.50 B82-39171

Edson, J. T.. The justice of Company 'Z' / J.T. Edson. — [London] : Corgi, 1980. — 172p ; 18cm
ISBN 0-552-11602-5 (pbk) : £0.95 B82-15107

Edson, J. T.. The making of a lawman / by J.T. Edson. — London : Hale, 1981, c1968. — 156p ; 20cm
Originally published: London : Corgi, 1968
ISBN 0-7091-8269-4 : £4.95 B82-11063

Edson, J. T.. Ole Devil at San Jacinto / J.T. Edson. — London : Severn House, 1982, c1977. — 176p ; 21cm
Originally published: London : Corgi, 1978
ISBN 0-7278-0822-2 : £5.95 B82-35461

Edson, J. T.. The quest for Bowie's blade. — London : Severn House, Dec.1982. — [208]p
ISBN 0-7278-0850-8 : £6.95 : CIP entry B82-34076

Edson, J. T.. The sheriff of Rockabye County / J.T. Edson. — [London] : Corgi, 1981. — 192p ; 18cm
ISBN 0-552-11820-6 (pbk) : £0.95 B82-03232

Edson, J. T.. Slaughter's way. — Large print ed. — Anstey : Ulverscroft, Feb.1983. — 1v.. — (Ulverscroft large print series)
Originally published: London : Brown, Watson, 1965
ISBN 0-7089-0917-5 : CIP entry B82-38879

Edson, J. T.. Waco's badge / J.T. Edson. — [London] : Corgi, 1982. — 192p ; 17cm
ISBN 0-552-11877-x (pbk) : £0.95 B82-12588

Edson, J. T.. White stallion, red mare / J.T. Edson. — Large print ed. — Leicester : Ulverscroft, 1982, c1970. — 302p ; 23cm. — (Ulverscroft large print)
Originally published: London : Transworld, 1970
ISBN 0-7089-0827-6 : Unpriced : CIP rev. B82-15968

Edson, J. T.. White stallion, red mare / by J.T. Edson. — London : Hale, 1982,, 1970. — 157p ; 20cm
Originally published: London : Corgi, 1970
ISBN 0-7091-8434-4 : £5.25 B82-30430

Edwards, G. B.. The book of Ebenezer Le Page / G.B. Edwards ; introduction by John Fowles. — Harmondsworth : Penguin, 1982, c1981. — 489p : 1map ; 19cm
Originally published: London : Hamilton, 1981
ISBN 0-14-005898-2 (pbk) : £1.95 B82-32580

Edwards, Rachelle. Fleet wedding / by Rachelle Edwards. — London : Hale, 1981. — 158p ; 20cm
ISBN 0-7091-9352-1 : £6.75 B82-07192

Edwards, Rachelle. Rakehell's daughter / Rachelle Edwards. — London : Hale, 1982. — 173p ; 20cm
ISBN 0-7091-9743-8 : £7.25 B82-34186

Edwards, Rachelle. Runaway bride / by Rachelle Edwards. — London : Hale, 1982. — 160p ; 20cm
ISBN 0-7091-9607-5 : £6.95 B82-18304

Edwards, Rhoda. None but Elizabeth / Rhoda Edwards. — London : Hutchinson, 1982. — 349p ; 23cm
ISBN 0-09-146540-0 : £7.95 : CIP rev. B82-01703

Edwards, Ruth Dudley. Corridors of death / Ruth Dudley Edwards. — London : Quartet Qrime, 1981. — 186p ; 23cm
ISBN 0-7043-2311-7 : £6.50 : CIP rev. B81-28118

Egleton, Clive. Backfire / Clive Egleton. — Large print ed. — Leicester : Ulverscroft, 1982, c1979. — 423p ; 23cm. — (Ulverscroft large print series)
Originally published: London : Hodder and Stoughton, 1979
ISBN 0-7089-0794-6 : Unpriced : CIP rev. B82-18556

Egleton, Clive. A falcon for the hawks / Clive Egleton. — London : Hodder and Stoughton, 1982. — 197p : ill ; 23cm
ISBN 0-340-27087-x : £6.95 : CIP rev. B82-10757

Egleton, Clive. The winter touch. — London : Coronet, Jan.1983. — [240]p
Originally published: London : Hodder and Stoughton, 1981
ISBN 0-340-32044-3 (pbk) : £1.75 : CIP entry B82-33752

Egremont, Max. The ladies man. — London : Secker & Warburg, Feb.1983. — [160]p
ISBN 0-436-14170-1 : £7.50 : CIP entry B82-38295

Eldridge, Roger. The fishers of Darksea. — London : Gollancz, Nov.1982. — [224]p
ISBN 0-575-03208-1 : £7.95 : CIP entry B82-26562

Elliott, Janice. The country of her dreams / Janice Elliott. — London : Hodder and Stoughton, c1982. — 186p ; 23cm
ISBN 0-340-27830-7 : £6.95 : CIP rev. B82-00244

Elliott, Janice. Secret places / Janice Elliott. — Feltham : Hamlyn, 1982, c1981. — 189p ; 18cm
Originally published: London : Hodder and Stoughton, 1981
ISBN 0-600-20582-7 (pbk) : £1.35 B82-25314

Ellis, Alice Thomas. The 27th kingdom / Alice Thomas Ellis. — London : Duckworth, 1982. — 159p ; 23cm
ISBN 0-7156-1645-5 : £7.95 B82-32271

Ellis, Christine. The squirrel year / by Christine Ellis. — London : Hale, 1982. — 159p ; 20cm
ISBN 0-7091-9841-8 : £6.50 B82-34175

Ellis, Christine. Vendetta island / by Christine Ellis. — London : Hale, 1981. — 176p ; 20cm ; corrected
ISBN 0-7091-9458-7 : £5.95 B82-00535

823'.914[F] — Fiction in English, *1945-* **— Texts** *continuation*

Ellis, H. F.. Swansong of A.J. Wentworth. — London : Severn House, Nov.1982. — [128]p
ISBN 0-7278-0847-8 : £6.95 : CIP entry
B82-34071

Ellis, Kathy. Where the wilderness ends / Kathy Ellis. — Feltham : Hamlyn, 1982. — 154p ; 18cm. — (A Sapphire romance)
ISBN 0-600-20288-7 (pbk) : £0.75 B82-16298

Ellis, Peter Berresford. The liberty tree / Peter Berresford Ellis. — London : Joseph, 1982. — 334p ; 23cm
ISBN 0-7181-2009-4 : £8.50 B82-17353

Elsen, Tim. McGovern's horses. — London : Methuen, June 1982. — [224]p
ISBN 0-413-50130-2 : £7.50 : CIP entry
B82-10500

Emery, Denise. Sunrise in Hong Kong / Denise Emery. — Feltham : Hamlyn, 1982, c1980. — 120p ; 18cm. — (A Sapphire romance)
Originally published: London : Severn House, 1980
ISBN 0-600-20266-6 (pbk) : £0.75 B82-16302

. Enderby / Anthony Burgess. — Harmondsworth : Penguin, 1982. — 478p ; 20cm
Contents: Inside Mr. Enderby. Originally published: London : Heinemann, 1963 — Enderby outside. Originally published: London : Heinemann, 1968 — The clockwork testament. Originally published: London : Hart-Davis, MacGibbon, 1974
ISBN 0-14-005957-1 (pbk) : £2.95 B82-16755

Eskapa, Shirley. The secret keeper. — London : Quartet, Oct.1982. — [192]p
ISBN 0-7043-2350-8 : £6.95 : CIP entry
B82-29081

Estey, Dale. Fortress island / Dale Estey. — London : W.H. Allen, 1981. — 223p ; 18cm ; pbk. — (A Star book)
Originally published: 1980
ISBN 0-352-30783-8 : £1.50 B82-02907

Evans, Alan, *1930-*. Dauntless. — London : Hodder and Stoughton, Aug.1982. — [256]p. — (Coronet books)
Originally published: 1980
ISBN 0-340-28113-8 (pbk) : £1.50 : CIP entry
B82-15740

Evans, Alan, *1930-*. Dauntless. — Large print ed. — Anstey : Ulverscroft, Sept.1982. — [464]p. — (Ulverscroft large print series)
Originally published: London : Hodder and Stoughton, 1980
ISBN 0-7089-0851-9 : £5.00 : CIP entry
B82-27007

Evans, Alan, *1930-*. Seek out and destroy! / Alan Evans. — London : Hodder and Stoughton, 1982. — 251p : 1map ; 23cm
ISBN 0-340-27196-5 : £6.95 : CIP rev.
B82-01098

Evans, C. D. (Christopher D.). Capella's golden eyes / Christopher Evans. — London : Granada, 1982, c1980. — 220p ; 18cm. — (A Panther book)
Originally published: London : Faber, 1980
ISBN 0-586-05098-1 (pbk) : £1.50 B82-14105

Evans, C. D. (Christopher D.). The insider / Christopher Evans. — London : Faber, 1981. — 215p 21cm
ISBN 0-571-11774-0 : £6.95 : CIP rev.
B81-31090

Evans, Jean. King's puritan / by Jean Evans. — London : Mills & Boon, 1982. — 188p ; 19cm. — (Masquerade)
ISBN 0-263-09999-7 : £5.25 B82-10373

Evans, Jean. Yukon bride / Jean Evans. — London : Mills & Boon, 1982. — 190p ; 20cm. — (Masquerade)
ISBN 0-263-10105-3 : £5.95 B82-37440

Evans, Jonathan. Chairman of the board / Jonathan Evans. — London : Joseph, 1982. — 341p ; 23cm
ISBN 0-7181-2157-0 : £8.95 B82-34207

Evans, Jonathan. Misfire / Jonathan Evans. — London : Futura, 1982, c1980. — 447p ; 18cm
Originally published: London : Joseph, 1980
ISBN 0-7088-1884-6 (pbk) : £1.95 B82-18268

Evans, Robin. Croak / Robin Evans. — Feltham : Hamlyn Paperbacks, 1981. — 189p ; 18cm
ISBN 0-600-20331-x (pbk) : £1.10 B82-04517

Evans, Stuart. Temporary hearths / Stuart Evans. — London : Hutchinson, 1982. — 418p ; 23cm
ISBN 0-09-146750-0 : £9.95 : CIP rev.
B82-00272

Everton, Ian. Alienation. — London (27 Priory Ave., N8 7RN) : Gay Men's Press, May 1982. — [224]p
ISBN 0-907040-10-1 (pbk) : £2.95 : CIP entry
B82-07696

Fairbairns, Zoë. Stand we at last. — London : Virago, Jan.1983. — [624]p
ISBN 0-86068-259-5 : £7.95 : CIP entry
B82-33220

Faith, Barbara. The moonkissed / Barbara Faith. — London : Macdonald, 1981. — 320p ; 18cm. — (Troubadour)
ISBN 0-7107-3018-7 (pbk) : £1.60 B82-03148

Faith, Barbara. The moonkissed / Barbara Faith. — London : Macdonald, 1981, c1980 (1982 [printing)). — 320p ; 21cm
ISBN 0-354-04755-8 : £7.95 B82-37782

Falcon, Mark. Reluctant outlaw. — Large print ed. — Long Preston : Magna, Jan.1983. — [288]p
Originally published: London : Hale, 1979
ISBN 0-86009-502-9 : £5.75 : CIP entry
B82-33219

Fantoni, Barry. Mike Dime / Barry Fantoni. — Large print ed. — Leicester : Ulverscroft, 1982, c1980. — 332p ; 22cm. — (Ulverscroft large print)
Originally published: London : Hodder & Stoughton, 1980
ISBN 0-7089-0731-8 : £5.00 : CIP rev.
B81-33962

Fantoni, Barry. Mike Dime / Barry Fantoni. — London : Sphere, 1982, c1980. — 198p ; 18cm
Originally published: London : Hodder and Stoughton, 1980
ISBN 0-7221-3433-9 (pbk) : £1.35 B82-14906

Fantoni, Barry. Stickman. — London : Hodder & Stoughton, Oct.1982. — [256]p
ISBN 0-340-27199-x : £6.95 : CIP entry
B82-24818

Farelane, Alexan. The quest of Aah. — Thornton Heath (908 London Rd., Thornton Heath, Surrey CR4 7PE) : Lashbrook & Knight, Nov.1981. — [615]p
ISBN 0-9507559-0-7 : £7.95 : CIP entry
B81-31201

Farely, Alison. Scheming Spanish queen / by Alison Farely. — London : Hale, 1982. — 192p ; 20cm
ISBN 0-7091-9633-4 : £6.95 B82-15494

Farrell, J. G.. The hill station : an unfinished novel ; and, An Indian diary / J.G. Farrell ; edited by John Spurling. — [London] : Fontana, 1982, c1981. — 254p ; 19cm
Originally published: London : Weidenfeld & Nicolson, 1981
ISBN 0-00-616464-1 (pbk) : £1.75 B82-30768

Fassnidge, Virginia. Something else : a novel : by Virginia Fassnidge. — London : Constable, 1981. — 152p ; 23cm
ISBN 0-09-464340-7 : £5.95 B82-02957

Feinstein, Elaine. The survivors / Elaine Feinstein. — London : Hutchinson, 1982. — 316p ; 23cm
ISBN 0-09-145850-1 : £7.95 B82-13856

Feinstein, Elaine. The survivors. — London : Hutchinson, Feb.1982. — [320]p
ISBN 0-09-146970-8 : £7.95 : CIP entry
B82-00155

Ferguson, Janet. Northumbrian nurse / by Janet Ferguson. — London : Hale, 1982. — 159p ; 20cm
ISBN 0-7091-9707-1 : £6.25 B82-18313

Ferguson, Janet. Sister on Musgrave ward / by Janet Ferguson. — London : Mills & Boon, 1979 (1982 [printing]). — 188p ; 20cm
ISBN 0-263-09996-2 : £5.25 B82-10380

Ferrand, Georgina. Assignment in Venice / by Georgina Ferrand. — London : Hale, 1982. — 159p ; 20cm
ISBN 0-7091-9842-6 : £6.50 B82-34190

Field, Sandra. Sight of a stranger / by Sandra Field. — London : Mills & Boon, 1981. — 188p ; 20cm
ISBN 0-263-09965-2 : £4.55 B82-09229

Fielding, Barbara. The toffee-nosed bomb / Barbera [sic] Fielding. — Bognor Regis : New Horizon, 1982. — 131p ; 22cm
ISBN 0-86116-453-9 : £4.50 B82-09938

Finch, Simon. Voyager in bondage / Simon Finch. — London : Pan, 1982, c1981. — 189p : 1map ; 18cm
Originally published: London : Souvenir, 1981
ISBN 0-330-26720-5 (pbk) : £1.50 B82-34253

Fingal, Marc. Memory of tomorrow / Marc Fingal. — Sunderland : J.S. Cairns, c1982. — 142p ; 21cm
ISBN 0-907066-01-1 (pbk) : £1.60 B82-28386

Finn, Timothy. Knapworth at war. — London : Duckworth, Oct.1982. — [160]p
ISBN 0-7156-1676-5 : £6.95 : CIP entry
B82-23880

Firth, Susanna. The overlord / by Susanna Firth. — London : Mills & Boon, 1982. — 188p ; 20cm
ISBN 0-263-10000-6 : £5.25 B82-13888

Fisher, David. Variation on a theme. — London : Quartet, Oct.1982. — [192]p
ISBN 0-7043-2349-4 : £6.50 : CIP entry
B82-29010

Fisher, Graham. The raging torrent. — Large print ed. — Long Preston : Magna Print, Sept.1982. — [500]p
Originally published: London : Hale, 1980
ISBN 0-86009-423-5 : £5.50 : CIP entry
B82-20853

Fisher, Hazel. Prize of gold / by Hazel Fisher. — London : Severn House, 1982, c1980. — 186p ; 21cm
ISBN 0-7278-0780-3 : £4.95 B82-13853

Fisher, Hazel. Prize of gold. — Large print ed. — Long Preston : Magna, Feb.1983. — [320]p
Originally published: London : Severn House, 1982
ISBN 0-86009-488-x : £5.75 : CIP entry
B82-39615

Fitzgerald, Julia. Fallen woman / Julia Fitzgerald. — London : Macdonald, 1982, c1981. — 254p ; 21cm
Originally published: London : Futura, 1981
ISBN 0-356-08650-x : £4.95 B82-26012

823'.914[F] — Fiction in English, ***1945-*** **—** ***Texts continuation***

Fitzgerald, Julia. Royal slave / Julia Fitzgerald. — London : Macdonald, 1981, c1978. — 398p ; 18cm. — (A Troubadour spectacular)
Originally published: London : Futura, 1978
ISBN 0-7088-1405-0 (pbk) : £1.75 B82-03146

Fitzgerald, Julia. Royal slave / Julia Fitzgerald. — London : Macdonald, 1982, c1978. — 398p ; 21cm
Originally published: London : Futura, 1978
ISBN 0-356-08525-2 : £6.95 B82-26011

Fitzgerald, Julia. Scarlet woman / Julia Fitzgerald. — London : Futura, 1979 (1982 [printing]). — 351p ; 18cm. — (A Troubadour spectacular)
ISBN 0-7088-1524-3 (pbk) : £1.75 B82-34235

Fitzgerald, Julia. Slave lady / Julia Fitzgerald. — London : Macdonald, 1981, c1980. — 351p ; 18cm. — (A Troubador spectacular)
Originally published: London : Futura, 1980
ISBN 0-7088-1854-4 (pbk) : £1.75 B82-05696

Fitzgerald, Julia. Venus rising / Julia Fitzgerald. — London : Macdonald, 1982. — 268p ; 21cm
ISBN 0-356-08524-4 : £6.95 B82-26010

Fitzgerald, Julia. Venus rising / Julia Fitzgerald. — London : Futura, 1982. — 368p ; 18cm. — (A Troubadour book)
ISBN 0-7107-3026-8 (pbk) : £1.75 B82-22614

Fitzgerald, Maire. The tender years / Maire Fitzgerald. — Bognor Regis : New Horizon, c1982. — 322p ; 20cm
ISBN 0-86116-589-6 : £5.95 B82-09113

Fitzgerald, Penelope. At Freddie's / Penelope Fitzgerald. — London : Collins, 1982. — 182p ; 22cm
ISBN 0-00-222064-4 : £6.50 : CIP rev.
B82-07218

Fitzgerald, Penelope. Human voices / Penelope Fitzgerald. — Large print ed. — Bath : Chivers, 1982, c1980. — 202p ; 23cm. — (A Lythway book)
Originally published: London : Collins, 1980
ISBN 0-85119-792-2 : Unpriced : CIP rev.
B82-01434

Fitzgerald, Penelope. Offshore / Penelope Fitzgerald. — Large print ed. — Bath : Chivers, 1982, c1979. — 183p ; 23cm. — (A Lythway book)
Originally published: London : Collins, 1979
ISBN 0-85119-783-3 : Unpriced : CIP rev.
B81-35863

Fitzroy, Rosamond. The American duchess / Rosamond Fitzroy. — London : Arlington, 1980. — 260p ; 23cm. — (A Mallamshire novel)
ISBN 0-85140-492-8 : £5.95 : CIP rev.
B80-12065

Fitzroy, Rosamond. The widow's might / Rosamond Fitzroy. — Large print ed. — Leicester : Ulverscroft, 1982, c1980. — 396p ; 22cm. — (Ulverscroft Large print series)
Originally published: London : Arlington, 1980
ISBN 0-7089-0755-5 : £5.00 : CIP rev.
B81-36937

Fleetwood, Hugh. A young fair god. — London : Hamilton, Feb.1982. — [192]p
ISBN 0-241-10715-6 : £7.95 : CIP entry
B81-36387

Fleming, Ian, *1908-1964*. Diamonds are forever / Ian Fleming. — Large print ed. — Bath : Chivers, 1982. — 300p ; 23cm. — (A New Portway large print book)
Originally published: London : Cape, 1956
ISBN 0-85119-158-4 : Unpriced : CIP rev.
B82-01444

Fleming, Ian, *1908-1964*. Dr No / Ian Fleming. — Large print ed. — Bath : Chivers Press, 1982, c1958. — 322p ; 23cm. — (A New Portway large print book)
Originally published: London : Cape, 1958
ISBN 0-85119-150-9 : Unpriced : CIP rev.
B81-33812

Fleming, Ian, *1908-1964*. Goldfinger. — Large print ed. — Bath : Chivers, Feb.1983. — [440] p. — (A New Portway large print book)
Originally published: London : Cape, 1959
ISBN 0-85119-205-x : £6.90 : CIP entry
B82-39461

Fleming, Ian, *1908-1964*. Octopussy and the living daylights. — Large print ed. — Bath : Chivers, Feb.1983. — [104]p. — (A New Portway large print book)
Originally published: London : Cape, 1966
ISBN 0-85119-206-8 : £6.30 : CIP entry
B82-39462

Fleming, Ian, *1908-1964*. On Her Majesty's secret service / Ian Fleming. — Large print ed. — Bath : Chivers, 1982, c1963. — 337p ; 23cm. — (A New Portway large print book)
Originally published: London : Cape, 1963
ISBN 0-85119-162-2 : Unpriced : CIP rev.
B82-04995

Fleming, Ian, *1908-1964*. Thunderball / Ian Fleming. — Large print ed. — Bath : Chivers, 1982, c1961. — 344p ; 23cm. — (A New Portway large print book)
Originally published: London : Cape, 1961
ISBN 0-85119-163-0 : Unpriced : CIP rev.
B82-04996

Fleming, Ian, *1908-1964*. You only live twice / Ian Fleming. — Large print ed. — Bath : Chivers, 1982, c1964. — 282p ; 23cm. — (A New Portway large print book)
Originally published: London : Cape, 1964
ISBN 0-85119-164-9 : Unpriced : CIP rev.
B82-04997

Fleming, Joan. Two lovers too many : a famous first / Joan Fleming. — London : Collins, 1981, c1949. — 272p ; 21cm. — (The Crime Club)
Originally published: London : Heinemann, 1949
ISBN 0-00-231869-5 : £6.50 B82-03076

Fleming, Nicholas. Takeover / Nicholas Fleming. — London : Heinemann, 1982. — 215p ; 22cm
ISBN 0-434-26600-0 : £6.95 B82-18096

Fletcher, Margaret, *1927-*. Unbidden guests / by Margaret Fletcher. — London : Hale, 1982. — 157p ; 20cm
ISBN 0-7091-9389-0 : £5.95 B82-12618

Follett, James. Churchill's gold. — Sevenoaks : Hodder & Stoughton, June 1981. — [224]p
ISBN 0-340-26674-0 (pbk) : £1.50 : CIP entry
B81-12352

Follett, James. The tiptoe boys / James Follett ; based on an original story by George Markstein. — London : Corgi, 1982. — 251p ; 18cm
ISBN 0-552-11975-x (pbk) : £1.50 B82-35248

Follett, Ken. The key to Rebecca / Ken Follett. — Leicester : Charnwood, 1982, c1980. — 509p ; 22cm. — (Charnwood large type series)
Originally published: London : Hamilton, 1980. — Published in large print
ISBN 0-7089-8037-6 : Unpriced : CIP rev.
B82-08082

Follett, Ken. The man from St. Petersburg / Ken Follett. — London : Hamilton, 1982. — 292p ; 23cm
ISBN 0-241-10783-0 : £7.95 : CIP rev.
B82-09978

Follett, Ken. [Storm Island]. Eye of the needle / Ken Follett. — London : Futura, 1978 (1981 [printing]). — 322p ; 18cm
ISBN 0-7088-1355-0 (pbk) : £1.60 B82-09357

Follett, Ken. [Storm island]. Eye of the needle / Ken Follett. — London : Futura, 1978 (1982 [printing]). — 322p ; 18cm
Originally published: London : Raven, 1978
ISBN 0-7088-1388-0 (pbk) : £1.75 B82-38467

Follett, Ken. Triple / Ken Follett. — London : Macdonald Futura, 1980, c1979. — 377p ; 18cm. — (A Futura book)
Originally published: London : Macdonald, 1979
(pbk) B82-00460

Follett, Ken. Triple / Ken Follett. — Leicester : Charnwood, 1981, c1979. — 522p ; 23cm. — (Charnwood library series) (Charnwood large type)
Originally published: London : Raven, 1979
ISBN 0-7089-8013-9 : £6.50 : CIP rev.
B81-21473

Forbes, Colin, *1923-*. Double jeopardy / Colin Forbes. — London : Collins, 1982. — 269p ; 21cm
ISBN 0-00-222657-x : £7.95 B82-36546

Forbes, Colin, *1923-*. The Stockholm syndicate / Colin Forbes. — London : Collins, 1981. — 321p ; 22cm
ISBN 0-00-222299-x : £7.50 : CIP rev.
B81-28769

Forbes, Colin, *1923-*. The Stockholm syndicate / Colin Forbes. — London : Pan in association with Collins, 1982, c1981. — 321p ; 18cm
Originally published: London : Collins, 1981
ISBN 0-330-26769-8 (pbk) : £1.75 B82-35747

Ford, Richard. Quest for the Faradawn. — St. Albans : Granada, Mar.1982. — [320]p
ISBN 0-246-11728-1 : £7.95 : CIP entry
B82-01869

Forest, Antonia. The ready-made family / by Antonia Forest. — [London] : Faber, 1980, c1967. — 194p ; 19cm
Originally published: London : Faber, 1967. — For adolescents
ISBN 0-571-11494-6 (pbk) : £1.25 : CIP rev.
B80-18890

Forest, Paula. Shadow of Penang / Paula Forest. — London : Hale, 1982. — 192p ; 20cm
ISBN 0-7091-9784-5 : £6.50 B82-25987

Forrest, Anthony. Captain justice / Anthony Forrest. — London : Allen Lane, 1981. — 333p ; 23cm
ISBN 0-7139-1442-4 : £6.95 B82-00957

Forrest, Anthony. The Pandora secret. — London : Allen Lane, Oct.1982. — [304]p
ISBN 0-7139-1507-2 : £7.95 : CIP entry
B82-25736

Forster, Margaret. The bride of Lowther Fell : a romance / Margaret Forster. — [Feltham] : Hamlyn Paperbacks, 1982, c1980. — 310p ; 18cm
Originally published: London : Secker & Warburg, 1980
ISBN 0-600-20448-0 (pbk) : £1.75 B82-19454

Forsyth, Frederick. The four novels / Frederick Forsyth. — London : Hutchinson, 1982. — 1096p ; 23cm
Contents: The day of the jackal — The Odessa file — The dogs of war — The Devil's alternative
ISBN 0-09-145720-3 : £9.95 : CIP rev.
B81-20180

Forsyth, Frederick. The Odessa file / Frederick Forsyth. — Large print ed. — Leicester : Ulverscroft, 1981, c1972. — 547p ; 23cm. — (Ulverscroft large print series)
Originally published: London : Hutchinson, 1972
ISBN 0-7089-0710-5 : £5.00 : CIP rev.
B81-30506

823'.914[F] — Fiction in English, *1945- — Texts continuation*

Foster, Delia. William's wife / Delia Foster. — London : Hale, 1982. — 192p ; 19cm
ISBN 0-7091-9706-3 : £6.25 B82-22115

Fowles, Anthony. Mitch. — London : New English Library, Feb.1983. — [224]p
ISBN 0-450-05516-7 (pbk) : £1.50 : CIP entry B82-38300

Fowles, John. Mantissa. — London : Cape, Oct.1982. — [192]p
ISBN 0-224-02938-x : £6.95 : CIP entry B82-25522

Fox, Anthony. Threat warning red / Anthony Fox. — London : Pan, 1982, c1979. — 236p : 2ill,1map ; 18cm
Originally published: London : Joseph, 1979
ISBN 0-330-26721-3 (pbk) : £1.50 B82-34251

Fox, James. White mischief. — London : Cape, Nov.1982. — [288]p
ISBN 0-224-01731-4 : £8.95 : CIP entry B82-26217

Fox, Peter, *1946-*. Mantis / Peter Fox. — London : Pan in association with Macmillan, 1982, c1979. — 236p ; 18cm
Originally published: London : Macmillan, 1979
ISBN 0-330-26170-3 (pbk) : £1.50 B82-18122

Foxall, P. A.. The circle of death / by P.A. Foxall. — London : Hale, 1982. — 159p ; 20cm
ISBN 0-7091-9536-2 : £6.50 B82-10748

Foxall, P. A.. The face of fury / P.A. Foxall. — London : Hale, 1982. — 176p ; 20cm
ISBN 0-7091-9779-9 : £6.75 B82-26021

Foxall, P. A.. On course for murder / P.A. Foxall. — London : Hale, 1982. — 176p ; 20cm
ISBN 0-7091-9954-6 : £6.75 B82-39172

Francis, Dick. Reflex / Dick Francis. — London : Pan, 1982, c1980. — 251p ; 18cm
Originally published: London : Joseph, 1980
ISBN 0-330-26662-4 (pbk) : £1.50 B82-13720

Francis, Dick. Twice shy. — Large print ed. — Anstey : Ulverscroft, Oct.1982. — [496]p. — (Ulverscroft large print series)
Originally published: London : Joseph, 1981
ISBN 0-7089-0865-9 : £5.00 : CIP entry B82-26686

Francis, Richard H.. The enormous dwarf / Richard H. Francis. — London : Granada, 1982. — 282p ; 18cm. — (A Panther book)
ISBN 0-586-05548-7 (pbk) : £1.50 B82-40249

Franklin, Sarah. The iceberg rose. — London : Severn House, Aug.1982. — [192]p
ISBN 0-7278-0814-1 : £5.50 : CIP entry B82-21105

Franks, Alan. Boychester's bugle : a novel / Alan Franks. — London : Heinemann, 1982. — 185p ; 23cm
ISBN 0-434-27060-1 : £6.95 B82-30285

Fraser, Antonia. Cool repentance / Antonia Fraser. — London : Weidenfeld and Nicolson, 1982. — 222p ; 23cm
ISBN 0-297-78127-8 : £6.95 B82-26947

Fraser, Antonia. Quiet as a nun / Antonia Fraser. — Large print ed. — [Bath] : Chivers, 1982, c1977. — 290p ; 23cm. — (A Midnight large print mystery) (Atlantic large print)
Originally published: London : Weidenfeld and Nicolson, 1977
ISBN 0-85119-464-8 : Unpriced : CIP rev. B82-05002

Fraser, Antonia. A splash of red / Antonia Fraser. — London : Methuen, 1982, c1981. — 229p ; 18cm
Originally published: London : Weidenfeld & Nicolson, 1981
ISBN 0-417-07080-2 (pbk) : £1.50 B82-34371

Fraser, Antonia. A splash of red / Antonia Fraser. — [Bath] : Chivers, 1982, c1981. — 405p ; 23cm. — (Atlantic large print) (A Midnight large print mystery)
Originally published: London : Weidenfeld and Nicolson, 1981
ISBN 0-85119-483-4 : Unpriced : CIP rev. B82-13095

Fraser, Christine Marion. Rhanna at war / Christine Marion Fraser. — Rev. ed. — London : Fontana, 1982. — 255p : 1map ; 18cm
Previous ed: London : Blond and Briggs, 1980
ISBN 0-00-616565-6 (pbk) : £1.65 B82-27893

Fraser, George Macdonald. Flashman : from the Flashman papers 1839-1842 / edited and arranged [i.e. written] by George Macdonald Fraser. — Large print ed. — Leicester : Ulverscroft, 1982, c1969. — 476p ; 23cm. — (Ulverscroft large print)
Originally published: London : Jenkins, 1969
ISBN 0-7089-0810-1 : Unpriced : CIP rev. B82-18550

Fraser, George MacDonald. Flashman and the redskins : from The Flashman papers, 1849-50 and 1875-76 / edited and arranged by George MacDonald Fraser. — London : Collins, 1982. — 479p : maps ; 22cm
Maps on lining papers
ISBN 0-00-222661-8 : £7.95 : CIP rev. B82-10566

Fraser, George MacDonald. Mr American / George MacDonald Fraser. — London : Pan in association with Collins, 1982, c1980. — 572p ; 18cm
Originally published: London : Collins, 1980
ISBN 0-330-26580-6 (pbk) : £2.25 B82-34257

Fraser, Guy. The Blackhope legend / by Guy Fraser. — London : Hale, 1982. — 159p ; 20cm
ISBN 0-7091-9426-9 : £6.50 B82-07196

Frayn, Michael. Sweet dreams / Michael Frayn. — [London] : Fontana, 1979, c1973. — 157p ; 18cm
Originally published: London : Collins, 1973
ISBN 0-00-616473-0 (pbk) : £1.25 B82-09406

Fredman, John. The wolf of Masada / John Fredman. — London : W.H. Allen, 1981, c1978. — 407p ; 18cm. — (A Star book)
ISBN 0-352-31054-5 (pbk) : £1.95 B82-10100

Freeling, Nicholas. One damn thing after another. — Large print ed. — Bath : Chivers, Dec.1982. — [408]p. — (Atlantic large print)
Originally published: London : Heinemann, 1981
ISBN 0-85119-512-1 : £5.25 : CIP entry B82-30240

Freeling, Nicolas. Castang's city. — Large print ed. — Bath : Chivers, Feb.1983. — [448]p. — (Atlantic large print)
Originally published: London : Heinemann, 1980
ISBN 0-85119-526-1 : £5.75 : CIP entry B82-39579

Freeling, Nicolas. The widow. — Large print ed. — Bath : Chivers, Sept.1982. — [448]p. — (Atlantic large print)
Originally published: London : Heinemann, 1979
ISBN 0-85119-494-x : £5.25 : CIP entry B82-20509

Freeling, Nicolas. Wolfnight / Nicolas Freeling. — London : Heinemann, 1982. — 200p ; 23cm
ISBN 0-434-27187-x : £6.95 B82-30284

Freeman, Gillian. An Easter egg hunt / Gillian Freeman. — Bath : Chivers, 1982, c1981. — 192p ; 23cm. — (A Lythway mystery)
Originally published: London : Hamilton, 1981
ISBN 0-85119-808-2 : Unpriced : CIP rev. B82-07012

Freemantle, Brian. Charlie Muffin's Uncle Sam / Brian Freemantle. — London : Arrow, 1982, c1980. — 255p ; 18cm
Originally published: London : Cape, 1980
ISBN 0-09-928350-6 (pbk) : £1.60 B82-30455

Freemantle, Brian. Deaken's war. — London : Hutchinson, Sept.1982. — [304]p
ISBN 0-09-149710-8 : £7.95 : CIP entry B82-27023

Freemantle, Brian. Madrigal for Charlie Muffin. — London : Hutchinson, Oct.1981. — 1v.
ISBN 0-09-145260-0 : £6.95 : CIP entry B81-26795

Fremlin, Celia. The parasite person / by Celia Fremlin. — London : Gollancz, 1982. — 176p ; 21cm
ISBN 0-575-03108-5 : £6.95 : CIP rev. B82-06933

Fresson, I. M.. Girl with two faces / I.M. Fresson. — London : Hale, 1982. — 192p ; 20cm
ISBN 0-7091-9734-9 : £6.25 B82-22860

Friedman, Rosemary. Proofs of affection : a novel / by Rosemary Friedman. — London : Gollancz, 1982. — 208p ; 23cm
ISBN 0-575-03127-1 : £7.95 : CIP rev. B82-09443

Frith, Nigel. [The spear of mistletoe]. Asgard. — London : Allen and Unwin, Nov.1982. — [304]p
Originally published: London : Routledge & Kegan Paul, 1977
ISBN 0-04-823209-2 (pbk) : £2.95 : CIP entry B82-29062

Fullbrook, Gladys. And time stood still. — Large print ed. — Bath : Chivers, Oct.1982. — [248] p. — (Atlantic large print)
Originally published: London : Mills and Boon, 1974
ISBN 0-85119-496-6 : £5.25 : CIP entry B82-24228

Fullbrook, Gladys. Egyptian journey / Gladys Fullbrook. — Large print ed. — [Bath] : Chivers, 1982, c1975. — 233p ; 23cm. — (Atlantic large print) (A Seymour large print romance)
Originally published: London : Mills & Boon, 1975
ISBN 0-85119-472-9 : Unpriced : CIP rev. B82-09850

Fullerton, Alexander. All the drowning seas / Alexander Fullerton. — London : Pan, 1982, c1981. — 280p ; 18cm
Originally published: London : Joseph, 1981
ISBN 0-330-26637-3 (pbk) : £1.50 B82-22148

Fullerton, Alexander. Last lift from Crete / Alexander Fullerton. — London : Pan, 1981, c1980. — 253p ; 18cm
Originally published: London : Joseph, 1980
ISBN 0-330-26501-6 (pbk) : £1.50 B82-00785

Fullerton, Alexander. Last lift from Crete / Alexander Fullerton. — Large print ed. — Leicester : Ulverscroft, 1982, c1980. — 479p ; 23cm. — (Ulverscroft large print)
Originally published: London : Joseph, 1980
ISBN 0-7089-0809-8 : Unpriced : CIP rev. B82-18446

Fullerton, Alexander. A share of honour / Alexander Fullerton. — London : Joseph, 1982. — 255p ; 23cm
Maps on lining papers
ISBN 0-7181-2106-6 : £7.95 B82-22572

823'.914[F] — Fiction in English, *1945-* **— Texts** *continuation*

Gale, J. E.. When the zodiac somersaults / J.E. Gale. — Irchester : Castle, 1982. — 223p ; 22cm
ISBN 0-907877-30-3 : £5.50 B82-39350

Gall, Sandy. Chasing the dragon / Sandy Gall. — London : Pan Books in association with Collins, 1982, c1981. — 253p ; 18cm
Originally published: London : Collins, 1981
ISBN 0-330-26639-x (pbk) : £1.50 B82-22151

Gall, Sandy. Gold scoop / Sandy Gall. — Large print ed. — Bath : Chivers, 1982, c1977. — 320p ; 23cm. — (A Lythway book)
Originally published: London : Collins, 1977
ISBN 0-85119-825-2 : Unpriced : CIP rev. B82-13098

Gallagher, Stephen. Chimera / Stephen Gallagher. — London : Sphere, 1982. — 313p ; 18cm
ISBN 0-7221-3757-5 (pbk) : £1.75 B82-37347

Gardam, Jane. God on the rocks / Jane Gardam. — London : Abacus, 1981, c1978. — 153p ; 20cm
Originally published: London : H. Hamilton, 1978
ISBN 0-349-11406-4 (pbk) : £1.95 B82-07176

Garden, Graeme. The seventh man : my part in the defection scandal / by Geoffrey T. Alsop ; as told to Graeme Garden. — London : Eyre Methuen, 1981. — 139p : 1ill,2maps ; 23cm
ISBN 0-413-49080-7 : Unpriced : CIP rev. B81-23773

Gardiner, Judy. My love my land / by Judy Gardiner. — Long Preston : Magna Print, 1982, c1970. — 425p ; 22cm
Published in large print
ISBN 0-86009-410-3 : Unpriced : CIP rev. B82-13155

Gardiner, Judy. Who was Sylvia? / Judy Gardiner. — London : Severn House, 1982. — 207p ; 21cm
ISBN 0-7278-0795-1 : £6.95 B82-31424

Gardner, Jerome. The oldtimers / Jerome Gardner. — Bath : Chivers, 1982, c1979. — 189p ; 23cm. — (A Lythway western)
Originally published: London : Hale, 1979
ISBN 0-85119-809-0 : Unpriced : CIP rev. B82-07013

Gardner, John. Licence renewed. — London : Hodder & Stoughton, Feb.1982. — [272]p
ISBN 0-340-26873-5 (pbk) : £1.75 : CIP entry B81-36351

Gardner, John. Licence renewed. — Large print ed. — Bath : Chivers, Sept.1982. — [408]p. — (A New Portway large print book)
Originally published: London : Cape, 1981
ISBN 0-85119-183-5 : £5.95 : CIP entry B82-20502

Gardner, John, *1919-*. The garden of weapons. — London : Hodder & Stoughton, Oct.1981. — [400]p. — (Coronet books)
Originally published: 1980
ISBN 0-340-27107-8 (pbk) : £1.75 : CIP entry B81-26726

Gardner, John, *1926-*. The corner men / John Gardner. — London : Arrow, 1976, c1974 (1982 [printing]). — 251p ; 18cm
Originally published: London : Joseph, 1974
ISBN 0-09-912860-8 (pbk) : £1.50 B82-22215

Gardner, John, *1926-*. For special services. — London : Cape, Oct.1982. — [256]p
ISBN 0-224-02934-7 : £6.95 : CIP entry B82-24361

Gardner, John, *1926-*. For special services. — London : Hodder & Stoughton, Dec.1982. — [256]p. — (Coronet books)
ISBN 0-340-32111-3 (pbk) : £1.50 : CIP entry B82-40888

Gardner, John, *1926-*. The quiet dogs. — London : Hodder and Stoughton, Sept.1982. — [320]p
ISBN 0-340-24821-1 : £7.95 : CIP entry B82-18801

Gardner, John, *1926-*. Traitor's exit : a Boysie Oakes entertainment / John Gardner. — London : W.H. Allen, 1982, c1970. — 150p ; 18cm. — (A Star book)
Originally published: London : Muller, 1970
ISBN 0-352-31044-8 (pbk) : £1.60 B82-10106

Garfield, Leon. The house of cards. — London : Bodley Head, Oct.1981. — [256]p
ISBN 0-370-30380-6 : £6.50 : CIP entry B81-25771

Garnett, Bill. The unbegotten / Bill Garnett. — Feltham : Hamlyn Paperbacks, 1982. — 160p ; 18cm
ISBN 0-600-20438-3 (pbk) : £1.25 B82-37128

Garrett, Charles C.. The Russian lode / Charles C. Garrett. — London : Sphere, 1980. — 150p ; 18cm. — (Gunslinger)
ISBN 0-7221-5034-2 (pbk) : £0.95 B82-13629

Garrick, Kate. Picture of Julie / Kate Garrick. — Large print ed. — Bath : Chivers, 1981, c1979. — 240p ; 23cm. — (A Seymour book)
Originally published: London : Mills & Boon, 1979
ISBN 0-85119-437-0 : Unpriced : CIP rev. B81-25803

Garve, Andrew. No tears for Hilda : a famous first / Andrew Garve. — London : Collins, 1950 (1981 [printing]). — 228p ; 21cm. — (The Crime Club)
ISBN 0-00-231684-6 : £6.50 B82-03057

Gash, Jonathan. Firefly gadroon : a Lovejoy narrative / Jonathan Gash. — London : Collins, 1982. — 208p ; 20cm. — (The Crime Club)
ISBN 0-00-231296-4 : £6.50 : CIP rev. B82-00897

Gash, Jonathan. The judas pair. — Large print ed. — Anstey : Ulverscroft, Oct.1982. — [368] p. — (Ulverscroft large print series)
Originally published: London : Collins, 1977
ISBN 0-7089-0856-x : £5.00 : CIP entry B82-26677

Gash, Jonathan. The sleepers of Erin. — London : Collins, Jan.1983. — [224]p. — (The Crime Club)
ISBN 0-00-231726-5 : £6.95 : CIP entry B82-33590

Gash, Jonathan. Spend game / Jonathan Gash. — Feltham : Hamlyn Paperbacks, 1982, c1980. — 160p ; 18cm. — (A Hamlyn whodunnit)
Originally published: London : Collins, 1980
ISBN 0-600-20398-0 (pbk) : £1.25 B82-19458

Gaskin, Catherine. Blake's Reach / Catherine Gaskin. — Leicester : Charnwood, 1982, c1958. — 506p ; 23cm. — (Charnwood library series)
Originally published: London : Collins, 1958. — Published in large print
ISBN 0-7089-8026-0 : £5.25 : CIP rev. B81-36958

Gaskin, Catherine. I know my love / Catherine Gaskin. — Leicester : Charnwood, 1982, c1962. — 546p ; 23cm. — (Charnwood library series)
Originally published: London : Collins, 1962. — Published in large print
ISBN 0-7089-8048-1 : Unpriced : CIP rev. B82-15947

Gaskin, Catherine. Promises / Catherine Gaskin. — London : Collins, 1982. — 533p ; 23cm
ISBN 0-00-222613-8 : £7.95 B82-34028

Gaskin, Catherine. Sara Dane. — Large print ed. — Anstey : Ulverscroft, Oct.1982. — [720]p. — (Charnwood library series)
Originally published: London : Collins, 1955
ISBN 0-7089-8075-9 : £7.50 : CIP entry B82-26691

Gaskin, Catherine. The summer of the Spanish woman / Catherine Gaskin. — [London] : Fontana, 1979, c1977 (1982 [printing]). — 444p ; 18cm
Originally published: London : Collins, 1977
ISBN 0-00-616482-x (pbk) : £1.75 B82-13648

Gaskin, Catherine. The Tilsit inheritance / Catherine Gaskin. — [London] : Fontana, 1965, c1963 (1982 [printing]). — 416p ; 18cm
Originally published: London : Collins, 1963
ISBN 0-00-616549-4 (pbk) : £1.75 B82-25438

Gaston, Bill. Winter and the wild rover / Bill Gaston. — London : Hale, 1982. — 206p ; 20cm
ISBN 0-7091-9619-9 : £6.95 B82-13833

Gater, Dilys. Prophecy for a queen / by Dilys Gater. — London : Hale, 1982. — 176p ; 20cm
ISBN 0-7091-9896-5 : £7.25 B82-37254

Gaud, Priscilla. Dear intruder / by Priscilla Gaud. — London : Hale, 1981. — 192p ; 20cm
ISBN 0-7091-9402-1 : £6.95 B82-02814

Gavin, Catherine. How sleep the brave. — London : Hodder & Stoughton, Jan.1982. — [304]p. — (Coronet books)
Originally published: London : Hodder & Stoughton, 1980
ISBN 0-340-27077-2 (pbk) : £1.50 : CIP entry B81-34132

Gavin, Catherine. None dare call it treason. — Large print ed. — Long Preston : Magna, Jan.1983. — [580]p
Originally published: London : Hodder and Stoughton, 1978
ISBN 0-86009-474-x : £6.95 : CIP entry B82-33131

Gavin, Catherine. Traitors' gate. — Large print ed. — Long Preston : Magna Print, Nov.1982. — [580]p
Originally published: London : Hodder & Stoughton, 1976
ISBN 0-86009-453-7 : £6.75 : CIP entry B82-26344

Gayle, Pamela. Vallamont / Pamela Gayle. — London : Granada, c1979 (1982 [printing]). — 333p ; 18cm. — (A Mayflower book)
ISBN 0-583-13463-7 (pbk) : £1.50 B82-36052

Gethin, David. Wyatt. — London : Gollancz, Jan.1983. — [192]p
ISBN 0-575-03226-x : £6.95 : CIP entry B82-32461

Ghose, Zulfikar. A new history of torments / Zulfikar Ghose. — London : Hutchinson, 1982. — 302p ; 23cm
Originally published: New York : Holt, Rinehart and Winston, 1982
ISBN 0-09-147670-4 : £7.95 : CIP rev. B82-09274

Gibbons, June Alison. The Pepsi-cola addict / June Alison Gibbons. — Bognor Regis : New Horizon, c1982. — 129p ; 22cm
ISBN 0-86116-542-x : £4.30 B82-19991

Gibbs, Mary Ann. The Marquess. — Loughton : Piatkus, Nov.1982. — [224]p
ISBN 0-86188-165-6 : £6.95 : CIP entry B82-26354

Gibbs, Mary Ann. The milliner's shop / by Mary Ann Gibbs. — Loughton : Judy Piatkus, 1981. — 220p ; 21cm
ISBN 0-86188-118-4 : £6.50 : CIP rev. B81-30376

823'.914[F] — Fiction in English, *1945- — Texts continuation*

Gibbs, Mary Ann. The tulip tree. — London : Hodder and Stoughton, June 1982. — [192]p. — (Coronet books)
Originally published: London : Hurst and Blackett, 1979
ISBN 0-340-26793-3 (pbk) : £1.25 : CIP entry
B82-10009

Gibbs, Mary Ann. A young lady of fashion. — London : Hodder and Stoughton, June 1982. — [192]p. — (Coronet books)
Originally published: London : Hurst and Blackett, 1978
ISBN 0-340-25101-8 (pbk) : £1.25 : CIP entry
B82-10003

Gidley, Charles. The river running / by Charles Gidley. — London : Fontana, 1982, c1981. — 500p ; 18cm
Originally published: London : Deutsch, 1981
ISBN 0-00-616418-8 (pbk) : £1.95 B82-36261

Gifford, Thomas, *1937-*. The man from Lisbon / Thomas Gifford. — London : Futura, 1978, c1977 (1980 [printing]). — 418p ; 18cm
Originally published: New York : McGraw Hill, 1977 ; London : Hamilton, 1978
ISBN 0-7088-1422-0 (pbk) : £1.50 B82-34239

Gilbert, Anna. Flowers for Lilian. — London : Hodder & Stoughton, Oct.1982. — [192]p. — (Coronet books)
Originally published: 1980
ISBN 0-340-28441-2 (pbk) : £1.25 : CIP entry
B82-24828

Gilbert, Anna. The leavetaking. — London : Coronet, Aug.1981. — [192]p
Originally published: London : Hodder & Stoughton, 1980
ISBN 0-340-26683-x : £1.25 : CIP entry
B81-18033

Gilbert, Anna. Miss Bede is staying / Anna Gilbert. — Loughton : Piatkus, 1982. — 316p : ill ; 21cm
ISBN 0-86188-169-9 : £7.50 : CIP rev.
B82-07681

Gilbert, Jacqueline. The trodden paths / by Jacqueline Gilbert. — London : Mills & Boon, 1982. — 187p ; 19cm
ISBN 0-263-09985-7 : £5.25 B82-10374

Gilbert, Michael. Death in captivity. — Large print ed. — Long Preston : Magna Print, Nov.1982. — [450]p
Originally published: London : Hodder and Stoughton, 1952
ISBN 0-86009-419-7 : £5.50 : CIP entry
B82-26338

Gilbert, Michael. Death of a favourite girl / Michael Gilbert. — Feltham : Hamlyn Paperbacks, 1982, c1980. — 207p ; 18cm. — (A Hamlyn whodunnit)
Originally published: London : Hodder & Stoughton, 1980
ISBN 0-600-20407-3 (pbk) : £1.50 B82-31950

Gilbert, Michael. The empty house / Michael Gilbert. — Large print ed. — Leicester : Ulverscroft, 1981, c1978. — 386p ; 23cm. — (Ulverscroft large print)
Originally published: London : Hodder & Stoughton, 1978
ISBN 0-7089-0702-4 : £5.00 : CIP rev.
B81-30478

Gilbert, Michael. End-game. — London : Hodder and Stoughton, Jan.1983. — [256]p
ISBN 0-340-27895-1 : £7.95 : CIP entry
B82-33730

Gilbert, Michael. The Etruscan net / Michael Gilbert. — Feltham : Hamlyn Paperbacks, 1982, c1969. — 192p ; 18cm. — (A Hamlyn whodunnit)
Originally published: London : Hodder & Stoughton, 1969
ISBN 0-600-20523-1 (pbk) : £1.25 B82-18346

Gilbert, Michael. The Etruscan net. — Large print ed. — Long Preston : Magna Print, Oct.1982. — [480]p
Originally published: London : Hodder & Stoughton, 1969
ISBN 0-86009-450-2 : £5.50 : CIP entry
B82-24132

Gilbert, Michael. Mr Calder and Mr Behrens / Michael Gilbert. — London : Hodder and Stoughton, 1982. — 256p ; 23cm
ISBN 0-340-27195-7 : £6.95 : CIP rev.
B82-03812

Gilbert, Michael. The night of the twelfth / Michael Gilbert. — London : Hamlyn, 1982, c1976. — 189p ; 18cm. — (A Hamlyn whodunnit)
Originally published: London : Hodder and Stoughton, 1976
ISBN 0-600-20522-3 (pbk) : £1.25 B82-12058

Gilbert, Nicholas. Not on the agenda / Nicholas Gilbert. — Bognor Regis : New Horizon, c1982. — 139p ; 21cm
ISBN 0-86116-531-4 : £4.50 B82-15598

Gill, B. M.. Death drop. — London : Hodder and Stoughton, Aug.1982. — [192]p. — (Coronet books)
Originally published: 1981
ISBN 0-340-28111-1 (pbk) : £1.25 : CIP entry
B82-15738

Gill, B. M.. Victims. — London : Hodder and Stoughton, Aug.1982. — [208]p. — (Coronet books)
Originally published: 1979
ISBN 0-340-28112-x (pbk) : £1.25 : CIP entry
B82-15739

Gill, John, *19---*. Kiki / John Gill. — London : Methuen London, 1982, c1979. — 176p ; 18cm
Originally published: London : Cape, 1979
ISBN 0-417-05520-x (pbk) : £1.50 B82-33289

Gill, Rosemary. A glint of gold / by Rosemary Gill. — London : Hale, 1982. — 191p ; 20cm
ISBN 0-7091-9768-3 : £6.50 B82-30278

Gillam, Eric. The scar of inheritance / Eric Gillam. — Bognor Regis : New Horizon, c1982. — 224p ; 22cm
ISBN 0-86116-622-1 : £6.25 B82-26015

Gillespie, Jane. Involvement / by Jane Gillespie. — London : Hale, 1982. — 160p ; 23cm
ISBN 0-7091-9488-9 : £6.95 B82-12616

Gillespie, Jane. Ladysmead / Jane Gillespie. — London : Hale, 1982. — 174p ; 20cm
ISBN 0-7091-9678-4 : £7.25 B82-26022

Gillott, Jacky. Crying out loud / Jacky Gillott. — London : Granada, 1981, c1976. — 256p ; 18cm. — (A Panther book)
Originally published: London : Hodder and Stoughton, 1976
ISBN 0-586-05389-1 (pbk) : £1.50 B82-00551

Gillott, Jacky. A true romance / Jacky Gillot. — London : Granada, 1981, c1975. — 285p ; 18cm. — (A Panther book)
Originally published: London : Hodder and Stoughton, 1975
ISBN 0-586-05390-5 (pbk) : £1.50 B82-02998

Gilman, George G.. Arapaho revenge. — London : New English Library, Jan.1983. — [160]p. — (Edge ; 43)
ISBN 0-450-05543-4 (pbk) : £1.00 : CIP entry
B82-36139

Gilman, George G.. Back from the dead / George G. Gilman. — Sevenoaks : New English Library, 1982. — 160p ; 18cm. — (The Undertaker ; 5)
ISBN 0-450-05491-8 (pbk) : £1.25 : CIP rev.
B82-15806

Gilman, George G.. The big prize / George G. Gilman. — London : New English Library, 1981. — 160p ; 18cm. — (Adam Steele ; 29)
ISBN 0-450-05355-5 (pbk) : £1.00 B82-08655

Gilman, George G.. Bloody sunrise. — London : New English Library, Sept.1982. — [160]p. — (Edge ; 42)
ISBN 0-450-05505-1 (pbk) : £1.25 : CIP entry
B82-19692

Gilman, George G.. The cheaters / George G. Gilman. — Sevenoaks : New English Library, 1982. — 145p ; 18cm. — (Adam Steele ; 3)
ISBN 0-450-05432-2 (pbk) : £1.25 : CIP rev.
B82-12354

Gilman, George G.. Death in the desert. — London : New English Library, Dec.1982. — [160]p. — (Undertaker ; 6)
ISBN 0-450-05541-8 (pbk) : £1.25 : CIP entry
B82-30090

Gilman, George G.. The killer mountains / George G. Gilman. — London : New English Library, 1982. — 157p ; 18cm. — (Adam Steele ; no.30)
ISBN 0-450-05377-6 (pbk) : £1.25 : CIP rev.
B82-03596

Gilman, George G.. The killing claim / George G. Gilman. — London : New English Library, 1982. — 159p ; 18cm. — (Edge ; 41)
ISBN 0-450-05418-7 (pbk) : £1.25 : CIP rev.
B82-09422

Gilman, George G.. Matching pair : Edge meets Steele / George G. Gilman. — Sevenoaks : New English Library, 1982. — 229p ; 18cm. — (Edge-Steele ; 2)
ISBN 0-450-05407-1 (pbk) : £1.50 : CIP rev.
B82-06823

Gilman, George G.. Montana melodrama / George G. Gilman. — London : New English Library, 1982. — 159p ; 18cm. — (Edge ; 40)
ISBN 0-450-05364-4 (pbk) : £1.25 : CIP rev.
B81-36202

Gilman, George G.. The prisoners / George G. Gilman. — London : New English Library, 1981. — 157p ; 19cm. — (Edge ; no.39)
ISBN 0-450-05276-1 (pbk) : £1.00 B82-03697

Gilman, George G.. Slaughter road / George G. Gilman. — London : New English Library, 1977 (1981 [printing]). — 125p ; 18cm. — (Edge ; no.22)
ISBN 0-450-05446-2 (pbk) : £1.00 B82-15595

Gilman, George G.. Steele's war : the preacher / George G. Gilman. — London : New English Library, 1981, c1980. — 160p ; 18cm. — (Adam Steele ; no.26)
ISBN 0-450-04661-3 (pbk) : £1.00 B82-20979

Gilman, George G.. The wrong man. — London : New English Library, Nov.1982. — [160]p
ISBN 0-450-05517-5 (pbk) : £1.00 : CIP entry
B82-27526

Girling, Richard. Ielfstan's place : 15,000 BC-1919 AD / Richard Girling. — London : Heinemann, 1981. — 218p : ill,maps ; 24cm
ISBN 0-434-98019-6 : £7.50 B82-03895

Glendinning, Ralph. The ultimate game. — London : New English Library, Oct.1982. — [384]p
Originally published: 1981
ISBN 0-450-05428-4 (pbk) : £1.75 : CIP entry
B82-24722

Glover, David. The lost village. — London : Robin Clark, Oct.1982. — [177]p
ISBN 0-86072-059-4 : £6.95 : CIP entry
B82-25741

Glover, Judith. The stallion man. — London : Hodder & Stoughton, Nov.1982. — [352]p
ISBN 0-340-27839-0 : £7.95 : CIP entry
B82-27337

823'.914[F] — Fiction in English, *1945-* — *Texts continuation*

Goddard, Anthea. The love murders / Anthea Goddard. — London : Methuen Paperbacks, 1981. — 220p ; 18cm. — (Magnum books)
ISBN 0-417-05980-9 (pbk) : £1.50 B82-15506

Goldin, Stephen. Mindflight / Stephen Goldin. — London : Hamlyn, 1982, c1978. — 185p ; 18cm
ISBN 0-600-36403-8 (pbk) : £1.35 B82-12061

Golding, William. Rites of passage / William Golding. — London : Faber, 1980 (1982 [printing]). — 278p ; 19cm
ISBN 0-571-11788-0 (pbk) : £1.95 : CIP rev. B82-04600

Goodenough, Simon. Sherlock Holmes : A study in scarlet. — Exeter : Webb & Bower, Feb.1983. — [160]p
ISBN 0-906671-59-0 (pbk) : £10.95 : CIP entry B82-39814

Goodwin, Grace. Love is my reason / by Grace Goodwin. — London : Hale, 1982. — 189p ; 20cm
ISBN 0-7091-9764-0 : £6.50 B82-34172

Goodwin, Suzanne. The Winter sisters / Suzanne Goodwin. — London : Methuen Paperbacks, 1982, c1980. — 223p ; 18cm. — (Magnum books)
Originally published: London : Bodley Head, 1980
ISBN 0-417-06170-6 (pbk) : £1.50 B82-34373

Goodwin, Suzanne. The Winter sisters / Suzanne Goodwin. — Large print ed. — Leicester : Ulverscroft, 1982, c1980. — 427p ; 22cm. — (Ulverscroft large print series)
Originally published: London : Bodley Head, 1980
ISBN 0-7089-0778-4 : Unpriced : CIP rev. B82-08089

Goodwin, Suzanne. The winter spring / Suzanne Goodwin. — Large print ed. — Leicester : Ulverscroft, 1982, c1978. — 467p ; 22cm. — (Ulverscroft large print)
Originally published: London : Bodley Head, 1978
ISBN 0-7089-0736-9 : £5.00 : CIP rev. B81-33961

Gordon, Katharine. In the shadow of the peacock / Katharine Gordon. — Large print ed. — Leicester : Ulverscroft, 1982, c1980. — 526p ; 23cm. — (Ulverscroft large print)
Originally published: London : Hodder and Stoughton, 1980
ISBN 0-7089-0806-3 : Unpriced : CIP rev. B82-18448

Gordon, Katharine. Peacock in jeopardy. — London : Hodder and Stoughton, Nov.1982. — [320]p
ISBN 0-340-28230-4 : £7.95 : CIP entry B82-27346

Gordon, Katharine. The peacock ring. — London : Hodder and Stoughton, Apr.1982. — [320]p. — (Coronet books)
Originally published: 1981
ISBN 0-340-27913-3 (pbk) : £1.75 : CIP entry B82-03823

Gordon, Katherine. The peacock ring. — Large print ed. — Anstey : Ulverscroft, Aug.1982. — [560]p. — (Ulverscroft large print series)
Originally published: London : Hodder & Stoughton, 1981
ISBN 0-7089-0833-0 : £5.00 : CIP entry B82-26997

Gordon, Richard, *1921-*. Doctor in the nest / Richard Gordon. — Harmondsworth : Penguin, 1982, c1979. — 214p ; 18cm
Originally published: London : Heinemann, 1979
ISBN 0-14-005403-0 (pbk) : £1.95 B82-35386

Gordon, Richard, *1921-*. Doctor in the nude. — Large print ed. — Bath : Chivers, Dec.1982. — [248]p. — (A New Portway large print book)
Originally published: London : Heinemann, 1973
ISBN 0-85119-195-9 : £6.50 : CIP entry B82-30232

Gordon, Richard, *1921-*. Doctor on the boil. — Large print ed. — Bath : Chivers, Dec.1982. — [296]p. — (A New Portway large print book)
Originally published: London : Heinemann, 1970
ISBN 0-85119-196-7 : £6.50 : CIP entry B82-30233

Gordon, Richard, *1921-*. Doctor on the brain. — Large print ed. — Bath : Chivers, Dec.1982. — [296]p. — (A New Portway large print book)
Originally published: London : Heinemann, 1972
ISBN 0-85119-197-5 : £6.50 : CIP entry B82-30234

Gordon, Richard, *1921-*. Doctor on the job. — Large print ed. — Bath : Chivers, Dec.1982. — [304]p. — (A New Portway large print book)
Originally published: London : Heinemann, 1976
ISBN 0-85119-198-3 : £6.50 : CIP entry B82-30235

Gordon, Richard, *1921-*. Dr Gordon's casebook. — London : Severn House, Oct.1982. — [224]p
ISBN 0-7278-0838-9 : £6.95 : CIP entry B82-29135

Gordon, Stuart. Smile on the void : the mythhistory of Ralph M'Botu Kitaj / Stuart Gordon. — London : Arrow, 1982, c1981. — 294p ; 18cm
Originally published: New York : Berkley, 1980
ISBN 0-09-927310-1 (pbk) : £1.75 B82-11445

Gordon, Victoria. Battle of wills / by Victoria Gordon. — London : Mills & Boon, 1982. — 188p ; 19cm
ISBN 0-263-73974-0 : £5.95 B82-37268

Gordon, Victoria. Blind man's buff / by Victoria Gordon. — London : Mills & Boon, 1982. — 186p ; 20cm
ISBN 0-263-10057-x : £5.25 B82-27278

Gordon, Victoria. Blind man's buff / by Victoria Gordon. — London : Mills & Boon, 1982. — 186p ; 18cm
ISBN 0-263-73856-6 (pbk) : £0.85 B82-36287

Gordon, Victoria. Dinner at Wyatt's / by Victoria Gordon. — London : Mills & Boon, 1982. — 186p ; 19cm
ISBN 0-263-10077-4 : £5.25 B82-30935

Gordon, Victoria. Stag at bay / by Victoria Gordon. — London : Mills & Boon, 1982. — 191p ; 19cm
ISBN 0-263-09987-3 : £5.25 B82-10375

Gordon, Yvonne. Moonlight ecstasy / by Yvonne Gordon. — London : Hale, 1981. — 158p ; 20cm
ISBN 0-7091-9442-0 : £5.95 B82-07205

Gouriet, John. Checkmate Mr President / by John Gouriet. — Glasgow : Maclellan, 1981. — 226p : ill,maps ; 23cm
Maps on lining papers
ISBN 0-85335-250-x : £7.95 : CIP rev. B81-25116

Graham, David, *1919-*. Sidewall / by David Graham. — London : Hale, 1982. — 208p ; 23cm
ISBN 0-7091-9675-x : £7.25 B82-34504

Graham, Elizabeth. Devil on horseback / Elizabeth Graham. — Large print ed. — Bath : Chivers, 1981, c1979. — 228p ; 23cm. — (A Seymour book)
Originally published: London : Mills & Boon, 1979
ISBN 0-85119-440-0 : Unpriced : CIP rev. B81-31254

Graham, Elizabeth. Passionate impostor / by Elizabeth Graham. — London : Mills & Boon, 1981. — 187p ; 19cm
ISBN 0-263-09954-7 : £4.55 B82-04638

Graham, Elizabeth. Stormy vigil / by Elizabeth Graham. — London : Mills & Boon, 1982. — 188p ; 20cm
ISBN 0-263-09981-4 : £5.25 B82-10378

Graham, Harry, *1912-*. Pit prop / Harry Graham. — London : Hale, 1982. — 191p ; 21cm
ISBN 0-7091-9489-7 : £6.95 B82-11392

Gran, Maurice. Holding the fort. — London : Severn House, Dec.1982. — [208]p
ISBN 0-7278-0849-4 : £6.95 : CIP entry B82-34077

Grant, James. The rose medallion. — Large print ed. — Bath : Chivers, Dec.1982. — [312]p. — (A Lythway book)
Originally published: London : Muller, 1977
ISBN 0-85119-875-9 : £7.20 : CIP entry B82-30230

Grant, James, *1933-*. Don't shoot the pianist. — Large print ed. — Bath : Chivers, Oct.1982. — [312]p. — (A Lythway book)
Originally published: Loughton : Piatkus, 1980
ISBN 0-85119-854-6 : £7.20 : CIP entry B82-20521

Gray, Hilary. The white cockcade [i.e. cockade] / by Hilary Gray. — London : Hale, 1982. — 174p ; 20cm
ISBN 0-7091-9803-5 : £7.25 B82-30280

Gray, Juliet. Dawn of desire / by Juliet Gray. — London : Hale, 1982. — 192p ; 20cm
ISBN 0-7091-9541-9 : £5.95 B82-11062

Gray, Juliet. Key to the past / Juliet Gray. — London : Remploy, 1981, c1963. — 176p ; 19cm
Originally published: London : Wright & Brown, 1963
ISBN 0-7066-0916-6 : £5.20 B82-18252

Gray, Juliet. Never say goodbye / by Juliet Gray. — London : Hale, 1982. — 190p ; 20cm
ISBN 0-7091-9741-1 : £6.25 B82-30406

Grayson, Laura. Tomorrow for the roses / by Laura Grayson. — London : Hale, 1981. — 187p ; 20cm
ISBN 0-7091-9514-1 : £5.95 B82-12514

Grayson, Richard. Death stalk / by Richard Grayson. — London : Gollancz, 1982. — 192p ; 21cm
ISBN 0-575-03187-5 : £6.95 : CIP rev. B82-19565

Grayson, Richard. The Montmartre murders : a novel / by Richard Grayson. — London : Gollancz, 1982. — 176p ; 21cm
ISBN 0-575-03091-7 : £6.95 : CIP rev. B82-00204

Greatorex, Wilfred. Airline : take off / Wilfred Greatorex ; based on the TV series by Wilfred Greatorex. — London : Futura, 1982. — 239p ; 18cm
ISBN 0-7088-2141-3 (pbk) : £1.60 B82-10541

Greatorex, Wilfred. Airline 2 : Ruskin's Berlin / Wilfred Greatorex ; based on the television series by Wilfred Greatorex. — London : Macdonald, 1982. — 190p ; 21cm
ISBN 0-356-08523-6 : £4.95 B82-22567

823'.914[F] — Fiction in English, ***1945- — Texts continuation***

Greatorex, Wilfred. Airline: Ruskin's Berlin : based on the Yorkshire Television series by Wilfred Greatorex / Wilfred Greatorex. — London : Futura, 1982. — 190p ; 18cm
ISBN 0-7088-2169-3 (pbk) : £1.25 B82-15311

Greaves, Jimmy. The ball game. — London : Hodder & Stoughton, Nov.1981. — [160]p. — (Coronet books)
Originally published: London : Barker, 1980
ISBN 0-340-26663-5 (pbk) : £1.25 : CIP entry B81-30547

Greaves, Jimmy. The boss. — London : Coronet Books, Oct.1982. — [160]p
Originally published: London : Barker, 1981
ISBN 0-340-26773-9 (pbk) : £1.25 : CIP entry B82-24814

Greaves, Jimmy. The second half / Jimmy Greaves and Norman Giller. — London : Barker, c1981. — 182p ; 23cm
ISBN 0-213-16798-0 : £6.50 B82-03199

Green, Marjorie. A scent of acacias / by Marjorie Green. — London : Hale, 1982. — 172p ; 20cm
ISBN 0-7091-9843-4 : £6.50 B82-34380

Greenaway, Gladys. Trial run / by Gladys Greenaway. — London : Hale, 1982. — 159p ; 20cm
ISBN 0-7091-9647-4 : £6.25 B82-22865

Greene, Julia. Flash back / Julia Greene. — [London] : Fontana, 1982. — 222p ; 18cm. — (Nightshades)
ISBN 0-00-616213-4 (pbk) : £1.00 B82-18093

Greene, Liz. The dreamer of the vine / Liz Greene. — [London] : Corgi, 1982, c1980. — 255p ; 18cm
Originally published: London : Bodley Head, 1980
ISBN 0-552-11904-0 (pbk) : £1.50 B82-19375

Greenwald, Harry J.. Knock twice / by Harry J. Greenwald. — London : Hale, 1981. — 189p ; 20cm
ISBN 0-7091-9334-3 : £6.25 B82-07201

Greenwood, John. Murder, Mr Mosley. — London : Quartet, Jan.1983. — [155]p
ISBN 0-7043-2358-3 : £6.95 : CIP entry B82-32523

Grey, Belinda. Moon of Laughing Flame / Belinda Grey. — London : Mills & Boon, 1980 (1982 [printing]). — 188p ; 19cm. — (Masquerade)
ISBN 0-263-10062-6 : £5.25 B82-22498

Grey, Belinda. Proxy wedding / Belinda Grey. — London : Mills & Boon, 1982. — 190p ; 20cm
ISBN 0-263-10067-7 : £5.25 B82-27600

Grey, Charlotte. Golden butterfly / by Charlotte Grey. — London : Hale, 1981. — 191p 20cm
ISBN 0-7091-9403-x : £6.95 B82-03151

Grey, Charlotte. The spring of the falcon / Charlotte Grey. — London : Hale, 1982. — 174p ; 20cm
ISBN 0-7091-9689-x : £6.95 B82-30429

Griffin, Russell. The makeshift god / Russell Griffin. — London : Granada, 1982, c1979. — 272p ; 18cm. — (A Panther book)
Originally published: United States : s.n., 1979?
ISBN 0-586-05176-7 (pbk) : £1.50 B82-36053

Gross, Robert. Boy and girl / written by Robert Gross ; illustrated by Robert Geers. — [London] : Silvey-Jex, [1982]. — [68]p : ill (some col.) ; 13cm
ISBN 0-907280-09-9 : Unpriced B82-26036

Gulliver, Nicol. Feelings / Nicol Gulliver. — Bognor Regis : New Horizon, c1981. — 88p ; 21cm
ISBN 0-86116-469-5 : £3.50 B82-04560

Gutteridge, Lindsay. Fratricide is a gas / Lindsay Gutteridge. — London : Futura, 1979, c1975. — 191p ; 18cm. — (An Orbit book)
Originally published: London : Cape, 1975
ISBN 0-7088-8047-9 (pbk) : £0.90 B82-34241

Gutteridge, Lindsay. Killer pine / Lindsay Gutteridge. — London : Futura, 1979, c1973. — 156p ; 18cm. — (An Orbit book)
Originally published: London : Cape, 1973
ISBN 0-7088-8046-0 (pbk) : £0.85 B82-34240

Hagar, Judith. Shadow of the eagle / by Judith Hagar. — London : Hale, 1982. — 206p ; 20cm
ISBN 0-7091-9496-x : £6.95 B82-13835

Hagar, Judith. The wind of change / Judith Hagar. — London : Hale, 1982. — 207p ; 20cm
ISBN 0-7091-9813-2 : £7.50 B82-33425

Haggard, William. The heirloom. — London : Hodder and Stoughton, Feb.1983. — 1v.
ISBN 0-340-32665-4 : £7.95 : CIP entry B82-38026

Haggard, William. The median line / William Haggard. — London : Cassell, 1979. — 168p ; 21cm
ISBN 0-304-30464-6 : £4.95 B82-09529

Haggard, William. The mischief-makers / William Haggard. — London : Hodder and Stoughton, 1982. — 173p ; 23cm
ISBN 0-340-27718-1 : £6.50 : CIP rev. B81-36367

Haggard, William. The money men. — Large print ed. — Bath : Chivers, Sept.1982. — [320] p. — (Atlantic large print)
Originally published: London : Hodder and Stoughton, 1981
ISBN 0-85119-495-8 : £5.25 : CIP entry B82-20510

Haines, Pamela. The kissing gate / Pamela Haines. — [London] : Fontana, 1982, c1981. — 704p ; 18cm
Originally published: London : Collins, 1981
ISBN 0-00-616471-4 (pbk) : £2.50 B82-33549

Halam, Ann. The alder tree / by Ann Halam. — London : Allen & Unwin, 1982. — 108p ; 23cm
ISBN 0-04-823205-x : Unpriced : CIP rev. B82-03713

Hale, Julian. Black summer : a novel / by Julian Hale. — London : Hamilton, 1982. — 296p ; 23cm
ISBN 0-241-10767-9 : £7.95 : CIP rev. B82-17924

Halkin, John. Fatal odds / John Halkin. — London : Hale, 1981. — 239p ; 20cm
ISBN 0-7091-9504-4 : £6.50 B82-06325

Hall, Adam. The Pekin target / Adam Hall. — London : Collins, 1981. — 284p ; 22cm
ISBN 0-00-222606-5 : £7.50 : CIP rev. B81-25867

Hall, Unity. But not for long / Unity Hall. — London : Pan, 1982. — 282p ; 18cm
ISBN 0-330-26739-6 (pbk) : £1.50 B82-35746

Hamilton, Tamsin. Paris in the fall / Tamsin Hamilton. — London : Granada, 1981 (1982 [printing]). — 351p ; 18cm. — (A Mayflower book)
ISBN 0-583-13558-7 (pbk) : £1.50 B82-30950

Hammond, Gerald. The game / Gerald Hammond. — London : Macmillan, 1982. — 168p ; 21cm
ISBN 0-333-33113-3 : £5.95 B82-37575

Hammond, Gerald, *1926-*. Fair game / Gerald Hammond. — London : Macmillan, 1982. — 219p ; 21cm
ISBN 0-333-32768-3 : £5.95 B82-18244

Hammond, Gerald, *1926-*. The reward game / Gerald Hammond. — Large print ed. — Leicester : Ulverscroft, 1981, c1980. — 327p : 1map ; 23cm
Originally published: London : Macmillan, 1980
ISBN 0-7089-0717-2 : £5.00 : CIP rev. B81-30408

Hammond, Jane. The secret of Petherick / by Jane Hammond. — London : Hale, 1982. — 188p ; 20cm
ISBN 0-7091-9731-4 : £6.95 B82-25990

Hammond, Marc. Killer mountain / Marc Hammond. — London : Severn House, 1982, c1980. — 320p ; 21cm
Originally published: London : Futura, 1980
ISBN 0-7278-0714-5 : £6.95 : CIP rev. B81-17506

Hammond, Marc. The Spandau wager / Marc Hammond. — London : Severn House, 1981. — 336p ; 21cm
ISBN 0-7278-0752-8 : £6.95 B82-05435

Hammond, Melinda. Fortune's lady / Melinda Hammond. — London : Hale, 1982. — 191p ; 20cm
ISBN 0-7091-9814-0 : £7.25 B82-33191

Hampson, Anne. Coolibah Creek. — Large print ed. — Bath : Chivers, Dec.1982. — [256]p. — (Atlantic large print)
Originally published: London : Mills and Boon, 1979
ISBN 0-85119-508-3 : £5.25 : CIP entry B82-30236

Hampson, Anne. Devotion. — London : Hodder and Stoughton, Jan.1983. — [192]p. — (Silhouette romance)
ISBN 0-340-32723-5 (pbk) : £0.85 : CIP entry B82-34408

Hampson, Anne. A kiss and a promise. — London : Hodder & Stoughton, Dec.1982. — [192]p. — (Silhouette romance)
ISBN 0-340-32696-4 (pbk) : £0.75 : CIP entry B82-29666

Hampson, Anne. Man without honour. — London : Hodder & Stoughton, Oct.1982. — [192]p. — (Silhouette romance)
ISBN 0-340-32069-9 (pbk) : £0.75 : CIP entry B82-24838

Hampson, Anne. Stardust. — London : Hodder and Stoughton, Nov.1982. — [192]p. — (Silhouette romance)
ISBN 0-340-32692-1 (pbk) : £0.75 : CIP entry B82-28270

Hampson, Anne. Strangers may marry. — London : Hodder and Stoughton, Feb.1983. — [192]p. — (Silhouette romance)
ISBN 0-340-32758-8 (pbk) : £0.85 : CIP entry B82-38027

Hanagan, Eva. A knock at the door : a novel / by Eva Hanagan. — London : Constable, 1982. — 189p ; 23cm
ISBN 0-09-464550-7 : £6.50 B82-33786

Handley, Alfred. The vortex assignment / by Alfred Handley. — London : Hale, 1981. — 206p ; 20cm
ISBN 0-7091-9439-0 : £6.50 B82-00518

Haney, Richard. Maelstrom / Richard Haney. — London : Corgi, 1982. — 206p ; 18cm
ISBN 0-552-11986-5 (pbk) : £1.50 B82-35247

823'.914[F] — Fiction in English, *1945- — Texts continuation*

Hankin, Elizabeth R.. Black Prince / by Elizabeth R. Hankin. — London : Hale, 1982. — 192p ; 20cm
ISBN 0-7091-9775-6 : £7.25 B82-27430

Hanley, Gerald. Noble descents. — London : Hamilton, Sept.1982. — [320]p
ISBN 0-241-10869-1 : £8.95 : CIP entry B82-18739

Hann, Elizabeth. Love's traders / Elizbeth Hann. — London : Macdonald, 1982, c1981. — 256p ; 21cm
Originally published: London : Futura, 1981
ISBN 0-356-08653-4 : £4.95 B82-26008

Hanson, Vic J.. Black Heart's bunch / by Vic J. Hanson. — London : Hale, 1982. — 160p ; 20cm
ISBN 0-7091-9583-4 : £5.25 B82-15596

Hanson, Vic J.. Hardneck and Amos / by Vic J. Hanson. — London : Hale, 1982. — 160p ; 20cm
ISBN 0-7091-9760-8 : £5.50 B82-30432

Harcourt, Palma. Agents of influence. — Large print ed. — Anstey : Ulverscroft, Oct.1982. — [368]p. — (Ulverscroft large print series)
Originally published: London : Collins, 1978
ISBN 0-7089-0858-6 : £5.00 : CIP entry B82-26679

Harcourt, Palma. Climate for conspiracy / Palma Harcourt. — Large print ed. — Leicester : Ulverscroft, 1981, c1974. — 341p ; 23cm. — (Ulverscroft large print)
Originally published: London : Collins, 1974
ISBN 0-7089-0703-2 : £5.00 : CIP rev. B81-30479

Harcourt, Palma. Shadows of doubt. — London : Collins, Jan.1983. — [280]p
ISBN 0-00-222681-2 : £7.95 : CIP entry B82-33585

Harcourt, Palma. A turn of traitors / Palma Harcourt. — Large print ed. — Leicester : Ulverscroft, 1982, c1981. — 367p ; 22cm. — (Ulverscroft large print series)
Originally published: London : Collins, 1981
ISBN 0-7089-0781-4 : Unpriced : CIP rev. B82-08092

Harcourt, Palma. The twisted tree. — Large print ed. — Anstey : Ulverscroft, Jan.1983. — [384]p. — (Ulverscroft large print series)
Originally published: London : Collins, 1982
ISBN 0-7089-0902-7 : £6.25 : CIP entry B82-32530

Hardwick, Michael. Bergerac / Michael Hardwick ; based on the BBC-TV series created and produced by Robert Banks Stewart. — London : British Broadcasting Corporation, 1981. — 176p ; 22cm
ISBN 0-563-20028-6 : £6.25 B82-08874

Hardwick, Michael. Bergerac / Michael Hardwick ; based on the BBC-TV series created and produced by Robert Banks Stewart. — London : British Broadcasting Corporation, 1981. — 176p ; 18cm
ISBN 0-563-20029-4 (pbk) : £1.25 B82-04683

Hardwick, Michael. Regency revels / Michael Hardwick. — London : Joseph, 1982. — 236p ; 23cm
ISBN 0-7181-2102-3 : £7.50 B82-11719

Hardwick, Michael. Regency revenge / Michael Hardwick. — London : Sphere, 1981, c1980. — 222p ; 18cm
Originally published: London : Michael Joseph, 1980
ISBN 0-7221-4229-3 (pbk) : £1.35 B82-06012

Hardwick, Mollie. Monday's child / Mollie Hardwick. — London : Macdonald, 1981. — 286p ; 21cm
ISBN 0-354-04768-x : £6.95 B82-03200

Hardwick, Mollie. Willowwood / Mollie Hardwick. — London : Methuen Paperbacks, 1981, c1980. — 316p ; 18cm. — (Magnum books)
Originally published: London : Eyre Methuen, 1980
ISBN 0-417-06410-1 (pbk) : £1.50 B82-15503

Hardwick, Mollie. Willowwood / Mollie Hardwick. — Large print ed. — Leicester : Ulverscroft, 1982, c1980. — 476p ; 23cm. — (Ulverscroft large print series)
Originally published: London : Eyre Methuen, 1980
ISBN 0-7089-0748-2 : Unpriced : CIP rev. B82-18437

Hardy, Laura. Dream master. — London : Hodder & Stoughton, Sept.1982. — [192]p. — (Silhouette romance)
ISBN 0-340-32063-x (pbk) : £0.75 : CIP entry B82-18782

Hardy, Laura. Playing with fire. — London : Hodder and Stoughton, Apr.1982. — [192]p. — (Silhouette romance)
ISBN 0-340-27927-3 (pbk) : £0.75 : CIP entry B82-03825

Hardy, Laura. Tears and red roses. — London : Hodder & Stoughton, Nov.1982. — [256]p. — (Silhouette special edition)
ISBN 0-340-32611-5 (pbk) : £0.95 : CIP entry B82-27332

Hargreaves, Elisabeth. The short weeks of summer / Elisabeth Hargreaves. — Large print ed. — Leicester : Ulverscroft, 1982, c1962. — 415p ; 23cm. — (Ulverscroft large print)
Originally published: London : Hutchinson, 1962
ISBN 0-7089-0804-7 : Unpriced : CIP rev. B82-18450

Hargreaves, Elizabeth. The sound of voices. — Large print ed. — Anstey : Ulverscroft, Sept.1982. — [352]p. — (Ulverscroft large print series)
Originally published: London : Hutchinson, 1968
ISBN 0-7089-0847-0 : £5.00 : CIP entry B82-27178

Harman, Neal. Fall guy / by Neal Harman. — London : Hale, 1981. — 220p ; 20cm
ISBN 0-7091-9508-7 : £6.50 B82-11066

Harper, Lynette. A maid must marry / by Lynette Harper. — London : Hale, 1981. — 207p ; 20cm
ISBN 0-7091-9373-4 : £6.75 B82-07188

Harpwood, Diane. Tea & tranquillisers : the diary of a happy housewife / by Diane Harpwood ; illustrations by Corinne Pearlman. — London : Virago, 1981. — 164p : ill ; 21cm
ISBN 0-86068-123-8 (cased) : £5.95 : CIP rev.
ISBN 0-86068-124-6 (pbk) : Unpriced B81-27471

Harris, Evelyn. From hex to hemlock / Evelyn Harris. — London : Hale, 1982. — 206p ; 20cm
ISBN 0-7091-9827-2 : £6.75 B82-33193

Harris, John, *1916-*. Harkaway's sixth column. — London : Hutchinson, Feb.1983. — [256]p
ISBN 0-09-150960-2 : £7.95 : CIP entry B82-36566

Harris, John, *1916-*. Live free or die! : a novel of the liberation of Paris / John Harris. — London : Hutchinson, 1982. — 253p ; 23cm
ISBN 0-09-147150-8 : £6.95 : CIP rev. B81-38845

Harris, John, *1916-*. North strike / John Harris. — London : Arrow, 1982, c1981. — 271p ; 18cm
Originally published: London : Hutchinson, 1981
ISBN 0-09-928090-6 (pbk) : £1.50 B82-31614

Harris, John, *1916-*. Old trade of killing. — London : Severn House, Dec.1982. — [208]p
ISBN 0-7278-0791-9 : £6.95 : CIP entry B82-34079

Harris, John, *1916-*. Swordpoint. — Large print ed. — Anstey : Ulverscroft, Nov.1982. — [464] p. — (Ulverscroft large print series)
Originally published: London : Hutchinson, 1980
ISBN 0-7089-0878-0 : £5.00 : CIP entry B82-29090

Harris, Wilson. The angel at the gate. — London : Faber, Oct.1982. — [128]p
ISBN 0-571-11929-8 : £7.50 : CIP entry B82-28474

Harrison, Elizabeth. Corridors of healing / Elizabeth Harrison. — Large print ed. — Leicester : Ulverscroft, 1982, c1968. — 389p ; 23cm. — (Ulverscroft large print series)
Originally published: London : Ward Lock, 1968
ISBN 0-7089-0790-3 : Unpriced : CIP rev. B82-18442

Harrison, Elizabeth. The Ravelston affair / Elizabeth Harrison. — Large print ed. — Leicester : Ulverscroft, 1982, c1969. — 303p ; 22cm. — (Ulverscroft Large print series)
Originally published: London : Ward Lock, 1967
ISBN 0-7089-0749-0 : £5.00 : CIP rev. B81-36946

Harrison, Elizabeth. A surgeon called Amanda / by Elizabeth Harrison. — London : Hale, 1982. — 188p ; 20cm
ISBN 0-7091-9762-4 : £6.50 B82-33426

Harrison, Elizabeth. To mend a heart / Elizabeth Harrison. — Large print ed. — Bath : Chivers, 1982, c1977. — 225p ; 23cm. — (A Lythway book)
Originally published: London : Hurst and Blackett, 1977
ISBN 0-85119-835-x : Unpriced : CIP rev. B82-15867

Harrison, Elizabeth. Young Doctor Goddard. — Large print ed. — Bath : Chivers, Sept.1982. — [272]p. — (A Lythway book)
Originally published: London : Hurst and Blackett, 1978
ISBN 0-85119-845-7 : £6.90 : CIP entry B82-20514

Harrison, M. John. In Viriconium. — London : Gollancz, Oct.1982. — [128]p
ISBN 0-575-03212-x : £7.95 : CIP entry B82-25070

Harrison, R. V.. French ordinary murder. — London : Quartet, Jan.1983. — [192]p
ISBN 0-7043-2359-1 : £6.95 : CIP entry B82-33345

Harrod-Eagles, Cynthia. Dead fall / Cynthia Harrod-Eagles. — London : Methuen, 1982. — 174p ; 22cm
ISBN 0-413-50050-0 : £6.95 : CIP rev. B82-01991

Harrod-Eagles, Cynthia. Dynasty I: the founding / Cynthia Harrod-Eagles. — London : Futura, 1980. — 527p : 1geneal.table ; 18cm. — (A Troubadour spectacular)
Cover title: The founding. — Bibliography: p7-8
ISBN 0-7088-1728-9 (pbk) : £1.50 B82-00452

Harrod-Eagles, Cynthia. Hollow night / Cynthia Harrod-Eagles. — [London] : Magnum, 1980. — 176p ; 18cm
ISBN 0-417-05420-3 (pbk) : £1.25 B82-20978

Harrod-Eagles, Cynthia. The Oak apple / Cynthia Harrod-Eagles. — London : Macdonald, 1982. — vi,403p : ill ; 23cm. — (Dynasty ; 4)
ISBN 0-356-08599-6 : £7.95 B82-18248

823'.914[F] — Fiction in English, *1945- — Texts continuation*

Harrod-Eagles, Cynthia. The oak apple / Cynthia Harrod-Eagles. — London : Futura, 1982. — vi,403p : 2plans,1geneal.table ; 18cm. — (Dynasty ; 4)
ISBN 0-7088-2167-7 (pbk) : £1.95 B82-22609

Harrod-Eagles, Cynthia. The princeling / Cynthia Harrod-Eagles. — London : Macdonald, 1981. — 410p : 2plans,1geneal.table ; 18cm. — (Dynasty ; 3) (A Futura book)
Bibliography: p5
ISBN 0-7088-2097-2 (pbk) : £1.95 B82-00453

Hart, David. The colonel. — London : Blond & Briggs, Oct.1982. — [224]p
ISBN 0-85634-136-3 : £7.50 : CIP entry B82-23875

Hart, Tom. Cradle song. — London : Quartet, Feb.1982. — [128]p
ISBN 0-7043-2322-2 : £5.95 : CIP entry B81-35724

Hart-Davis, Duff. The heights of Rimring / Duff Hart-Davis. — London : Macdonald Futura, 1981, c1980. — 332p ; 18cm. — (A Futura-Jade book)
Originally published: London : Cape, 1980
ISBN 0-7088-1964-8 (pbk) : £1.60 B82-09356

Hart-Davis, Duff. The heights of Rimring / Duff Hart-Davis. — Large print ed. — Leicester : Ulverscroft, 1982, c1980. — 447p ; 23cm. — (Ulverscroft large print series)
Originally published: London : Cape, 1980
ISBN 0-7089-0767-9 : Unpriced : CIP rev. B82-01742

Hart-Davis, Duff. Level five / Duff Hart-Davies. — London : Cape, 1982. — 288p ; 21cm
ISBN 0-224-01828-0 : £6.95 : CIP rev. B81-33976

Hartley, Norman. Shadowplay. — London : Collins, Jan.1983. — [288]p
ISBN 0-00-222659-6 : £7.95 : CIP entry B82-33584

Hartman, Dan. The long death. — London : New English Library, Sept.1982. — [192]p. — (Dirty Harry ; 3)
ISBN 0-450-05510-8 (pbk) : £1.50 : CIP entry B82-19693

Hartmann, Michael. Days of thunder / by Michael Hartmann. — Long Preston : Magna, 1982, c1980. — 545p ; 22cm
Originally published: London : Heinemann, 1980. — Published in large print
ISBN 0-86009-399-9 : Unpriced : CIP rev. B82-07046

Hartmann, Michael. Game for vultures / by Michael Hartmann. — Bolton-by-Bowland : Magna, 1980, c1975. — 593p ; 23cm
Originally published: London : Heinemann, 1975. — Published in large print
ISBN 0-86009-285-2 : £5.50 : CIP rev. B80-34117

Hartmann, Michael. Shadow of the leopard / by Michael Hartmann. — Long Preston : Magna, 1981, c1978. — 650p ; 23cm
Originally published: London : Heinemann, 1978. — Published in large print
ISBN 0-86009-350-6 : Unpriced : CIP rev. B81-30431

Harvey, John, *1938-*. Arkansas breakout / John B. Harvey. — London : Pan, 1982. — 124p ; 18cm. — (Hart ; 7)
ISBN 0-330-26640-3 (pbk) : £0.95 B82-22142

Harvey, John, *1938-*. Blood on the border / by John B. Harvey. — London : Hale, 1982, c1981. — 159p ; 20cm
Originally published: London : Pan, 1981
ISBN 0-7091-9432-3 : £4.95 B82-15592

Harvey, John, *1938-*. John Wesley Hardin / John B. Harvey. — London : Pan, 1982. — 143p ; 18cm. — (Hart ; 8)
ISBN 0-330-26641-1 (pbk) : £0.95 B82-22141

Harvey, John, *1938-*. Ride the wide country / by John B. Harvey. — London : Hale, 1982, c1981. — 159p ; 20cm
Originally published: London : Pan, 1981
ISBN 0-7091-9433-1 : £5.50 B82-25997

Harvey, Marianne. The dark horseman / Marianne Harvey. — London : Macdonald, 1982, c1978. — 414p ; 21cm
Originally published: London : Futura, 1978
ISBN 0-356-08625-9 : £6.75 B82-28931

Harvey, Marianne. Foxgate / Marianne Harvey. — London : Macdonald, 1982. — 368p ; 21cm
ISBN 0-356-08627-5 : £6.95 B82-36288

Harvey, Marianne. Foxgate / Marianne Harvey. — London : Futura, 1982. — 368p ; 18cm. — (A Troubadour book)
ISBN 0-7107-3031-4 (pbk) : £1.95 B82-38607

Harvey, Marianne. The proud hunter / Marianne Harvey. — London : Macdonald, 1982, c1980. — 348p ; 21cm
Originally published: London : Futura, 1980
ISBN 0-356-08626-7 : £6.95 B82-28930

Harvey, Marianne. The wild one / Marianne Harvey. — London : Macdonald Futura, 1979 (1980 [printing]). — 348p ; 18cm. — (A Troubadour spectacular)
Originally published: London : Futura, 1979
ISBN 0-7088-1525-1 (pbk) : £1.35 B82-34238

Harvey, Samantha. The distance man / by Samantha Harvey. — London : Mills & Boon, 1982. — 190p ; 19cm
ISBN 0-263-10075-8 : £5.25 B82-30931

Hastings, Phyllis. The overlooker. — London : Hale, 1982. — 192p ; 20cm
ISBN 0-7091-9684-9 : £6.95 B82-18305

Hastings, Phyllis. Tiger's heaven / by Phyllis Hastings. — London : Hale, 1981. — 173p ; 21cm
ISBN 0-7091-9153-7 : £6.75 B82-07195

Hatfield, Michael. Spy fever / Michael Hatfield. — London : Quartet Qrime, 1981. — 186p ; 23cm
ISBN 0-7043-2309-5 : £6.50 : CIP rev. B81-31095

Havill, Steven. The killer / Steven Havill. — London : Hale, 1982. — 178p ; 20cm
ISBN 0-7091-9577-x : £5.25 B82-15484

Hawes, Chris. Blues for Eddie. — London : Macmillan Education, Mar.1982. — [112]p. — (Topliner tridents)
ISBN 0-333-31971-0 : £3.95 : CIP entry B82-01854

Hawkins, Jim. Telford's change / Brian Clark ; adapted by Jim Hawkins. — Large print ed. — Bath : Chivers, 1982. — 278p ; 23cm. — (A New Portway large print book)
Originally published: London : Corgi, 1979
ISBN 0-85119-167-3 : Unpriced : CIP rev. B82-07617

Haydn, Richard, *1931-*. Soldiers of a different war / Richard Haydn. — London : Hale, 1982. — 192p ; 21cm
ISBN 0-7091-9384-x : £6.75 B82-12621

Heal, Anthony. The decimate decision / Anthony Heal. — London : Sphere, 1982, c1979. — 284p ; 18cm
Originally published: London : W.H. Allen, 1979
ISBN 0-7221-4498-9 (pbk) : £1.75 B82-22592

Heal, Anthony. The million cut / Anthony Heal ; drawings by Deborah Penny. — Wymondham : Sycamore Press, c1982. — 216p : ill ; 23cm
ISBN 0-905837-13-4 : £6.90 B82-39364

Heald, Tim. Masterstroke / Tim Heald. — London : Hutchinson, 1982. — 167p ; 23cm
ISBN 0-09-146760-8 : £6.95 : CIP rev. B81-38334

Heath, Sandra. Mally / Sandra Heath. — Feltham : Hamlyn, 1982. — 155p ; 18cm
ISBN 0-600-20153-8 (pbk) : £1.00 B82-08770

Heath, Sandra. The opera dancer / Sandra Heath. — Feltham : Hamlyn, 1982, c1981. — 284p ; 18cm
ISBN 0-600-20239-9 (pbk) : £1.50 B82-25313

Heaven, Constance. The Ravensley touch / Constance Heaven. — London : Heinemann, 1982. — 327p : 1geneal.table ; 23cm
ISBN 0-434-32616-x : £7.50 B82-30286

Hebden, Mark. Death set to music / Mark Hebden. — London : Keyhole Crime, 1982, c1979. — 189p ; 18cm
Originally published: London : Hamilton, 1979
ISBN 0-263-73958-9 (pbk) : £0.95 B82-36064

Hebden, Mark. Pel and the bombers. — London : Hamilton, Jan.1983. — [192]p
ISBN 0-241-10897-7 : £8.50 : CIP entry B82-33502

Hebden, Mark. Pel and the staghound / Mark Hebden. — London : Hamilton, 1982. — 246p ; 21cm
ISBN 0-241-10800-4 : £5.95 : CIP rev. B82-04314

Hederman, John D.. Firedrake / John D. Hederman. — London : F. Muller, 1982. — 250p ; 23cm
ISBN 0-584-31155-9 : £7.50 : CIP rev. B82-06042

Heller, Susan, *19---*. Volcano / Susan Heller and Douglas Wallin. — London : Hamlyn Paperbacks, 1981. — 301p ; 18cm
ISBN 0-600-20491-x (pbk) : £1.50 B82-00643

Hemingway, Amanda. Pzyche / Amanda Hemingway. — London : Faber, 1982. — 235p ; 22cm
ISBN 0-571-11875-5 : £7.95 : CIP rev. B82-10785

Hemstock, Patricia. Lanterns from Bloomsbury Square / by Patricia Hemstock. — London : Hale, 1982. — 175p ; 20cm
ISBN 0-7091-9691-1 : £6.95 B82-25905

Henderson, Anne. Three flowerings before the rain / Anne Henderson. — Bognor Regis : New Horizon, c1982. — 165p,[2]p of plates : 1ill,1facsim ; 21cm
ISBN 0-86116-680-9 : £5.25 B82-30558

Hennessy, Joseph. The challengers' defeat / Joseph Hennessy. — Bognor Regis : New Horizon, c1982. — 163p ; 22cm
ISBN 0-86116-601-9 : £5.25 B82-08980

Hennessy, Max. Back to battle / Max Hennessy. — Large print ed. — Leicester : Ulverscroft, 1982, c1979. — 555p ; 22cm. — (Ulverscroft large print series)
Originally published: London : Hamilton, 1979
ISBN 0-7089-0780-6 : Unpriced : CIP rev. B82-08091

Hennessy, Max. Back to battle / Max Hennessy. — London : Sphere, 1982, c1979. — 297p ; 18cm
Originally published: London : Hamilton, 1979
ISBN 0-7221-0452-9 (pbk) : £1.75 B82-09391

823'.914[F] — Fiction in English, *1945- — Texts continuation*

Hennessy, Max. Blunted lance. — London : H. Hamilton, Sept.1981. — [224]p
ISBN 0-241-10606-0 : £6.95 : CIP entry
B81-25681

Hennessy, Max. The bright blue sky. — London : Hamilton, Oct.1982. — [256]p
ISBN 0-241-10898-5 : £8.95 : CIP entry
B82-23465

Hennessy, Max. The dangerous years / Max Hennessy. — Large print ed. — Leicester : Ulverscroft, 1982, c1978. — 545p ; 22cm. — (Ulverscroft large print)
Originally published: London : Hamilton, 1978
ISBN 0-7089-0739-3 : £5.00 : CIP rev.
B81-33958

Hennessy, Max. The iron stallions / Max Hennessy. — London : Hamilton, 1982. — 247p ; 23cm
ISBN 0-241-10735-0 : £8.50 : CIP rev.
B82-04306

Hennessy, Max. The lion at sea / Max Hennessy. — Large print ed. — Leicester : Ulverscroft, 1981, c1977. — 475p ; 23cm. — (Ulverscroft large print)
Originally published: London : Hamilton, 1977
ISBN 0-7089-0696-6 : £5.00 : CIP rev.
B81-28094

Herbert, Kathleen. The lady of the fountain / Kathleen Herbert. — Frome : Bran's Head, c1982. — 196p ; 21cm
Bibliography: p196
Unpriced (pbk) B82-26009

Herbert, Marie. Winter of the white seal / Marie Herbert. — London : Collins, 1982. — 275p ; 25cm
ISBN 0-00-222132-2 : £6.95 B82-17066

Herries, Anne. Devil's kin / Anne Herries. — London : Mills & Boon, 1981. — 191p ; 19cm. — (Masquerade)
ISBN 0-263-09973-3 : £4.55 B82-04641

Herring, Christine. Regent of Fleuriac / Christine Herring. — London : Hale, 1982. — 192p ; 20cm
ISBN 0-7091-9564-8 : £6.95 B82-13837

Higgins, George V.. Kennedy for the defense. — Large print ed. — Bath : Chivers, Dec.1982. — [328]p. — (Atlantic large print)
Originally published: London : Secker & Warburg, 1980
ISBN 0-85119-513-x : £5.25 : CIP entry
B82-30241

Higgins, Jack. The dark side of the island. — London : Collins, Dec.1982. — [160]p
ISBN 0-00-222730-4 : £7.50 : CIP entry
B82-32275

Higgins, Jack. Dark side of the street. — London : Collins, Dec.1982. — [180]p
ISBN 0-00-222713-4 : £7.50 : CIP entry
B82-29856

Higgins, Jack. East of desolation. — London : Hodder and Stoughton, Jan.1983. — [224]p
Originally published: 1968
ISBN 0-340-32009-5 : £7.50 : CIP entry
B82-33748

Higgins, Jack. Four great thrillers / by Jack Higgins ; introduction by the author. — London : Collins, 1981. — 767p ; 23cm. — (Collins' collectors' choice)
Contents: Day of judgement — The violent enemy — Storm warning — Wrath of the lion
ISBN 0-00-243345-1 : £6.95 : CIP rev.
B81-28770

Higgins, Jack. Hell is always today / Jack Higgins. — Large print ed. — Bath : Chivers, 1982, c1968. — 226p ; 23cm. — (A Lythway book)
Originally published: under the name Harry Patterson. London : Long, 1968
ISBN 0-85119-836-8 : Unpriced : CIP rev.
B82-15868

Higgins, Jack. In the hour before midnight. — London : Collins, Dec.1982. — [190]p
ISBN 0-00-222712-6 : £7.50 : CIP entry
B82-29855

Higgins, Jack. In the hour before midnight. — London : Hodder and Stoughton, Jan.1983. — [192]p
Originally published: 1969
ISBN 0-340-32013-3 : £7.50 : CIP entry
B82-33749

Higgins, Jack. Luciano's luck / Jack Higgins. — Large print ed. — Leicester : Ulverscroft, 1982, c1981. — 367p ; 23cm. — (Ulverscroft large print series)
Originally published: London : Collins, 1981
ISBN 0-7089-0822-5 : Unpriced : CIP rev.
B82-15961

Higgins, Jack. Night judgement at Sinos. — London : Hodder and Stoughton, Jan.1983. — [224]p
Originally published: 1970
ISBN 0-340-32034-6 : £7.50 : CIP entry
B82-33751

Higgins, Jack. A prayer for the dying / Jack Higgins. — London : Pan in association with Collins, 1981, c1973. — 188p ; 18cm
Originally published: London : Collins, 1973
ISBN 0-330-26582-2 (pbk) : £1.50 B82-06408

Higgins, Jack. Toll for the brave / Jack Higgins. — Large print ed. — Bath : Chivers, 1982, c1971. — 231p ; 23cm
Originally published: London : Hutchinson, 1971
ISBN 0-85119-826-0 : Unpriced : CIP rev.
B82-13099

Higgins, Jack. Touch the devil / Jack Higgins. — London : Collins, 1982. — 239p ; 23cm
ISBN 0-00-222693-6 : £7.95 : CIP rev.
B82-20197

Hildick, E. W.. The loop. — London : Hodder and Stoughton, May 1981. — [224]p
Originally published: London : Hamilton, 1977
ISBN 0-340-25089-5 (pbk) : £1.25 : CIP entry
B81-03816

Hill, Pamela. The House of Cray / Pamela Hill. — London : Hale, 1982. — 335p ; 22cm
ISBN 0-7091-9682-2 : £7.50 B82-22163

Hill, Pamela. This rough beginning / Pamela Hill. — London : Hale, 1981. — 188p ; 23cm
ISBN 0-7091-9343-2 : £6.95 B82-06316

Hill, Peter, *1937-*. The washermen. — London : Coronet, Nov.1982. — [192]p
Originally published: London : Peter Davies, 1979
ISBN 0-340-25059-3 (pbk) : £1.25 : CIP entry
B82-27378

Hill, Reginald. Who guards a prince / Reginald Hill. — London : Collins, 1982. — 279p ; 22cm
ISBN 0-00-222612-x : £7.50 : CIP rev.
B82-07220

Hill, Rosa. House of green dragons. — London : Methuen, Oct.1982. — [224]p
ISBN 0-413-50700-9 : £7.50 : CIP entry
B82-24479

Hilliard, Nerina. Dark star / Nerina Hilliard. — Large print ed. — Bath : Chivers, 1982, c1978. — 285p ; 23cm. — (A Lythway book)
Originally published: London : Mills & Boon, 1968
ISBN 0-85119-816-3 : Unpriced : CIP rev.
B82-09859

Hilton, John Buxton. The anathema stone / John Buxton Hilton. — Large print ed. — Leicester : Ulverscroft, 1981, c1980. — 334p ; 23cm. — (Ulverscroft large print)
Originally published: London : Collins, 1980
ISBN 0-7089-0689-3 : £5.00 : CIP rev.
B81-28097

Hilton, John Buxton. The green frontier / John Buxton Hilton. — London : Collins, 1982. — 169p ; 21cm. — (The Crime Club)
ISBN 0-00-231029-5 : £6.50 : CIP rev.
B81-33973

Hilton, John Buxton. Playground of death / John Buxton Hilton. — Large print ed. — Bath : Chivers, 1982, c1981. — 215p ; 23cm. — (A Lythway book)
Originally published: London : Collins, 1981
ISBN 0-85119-793-0 : Unpriced : CIP rev.
B82-01433

Hilton, John Buxton. The sunset law / John Buxton Hilton. — London : Collins, 1982. — 164p ; 21cm. — (Collins crime club)
ISBN 0-00-231723-0 : £6.50 : CIP rev.
B82-12433

Hilton, Margery. Way of a man / by Margery Hilton. — London : Mills & Boon, 1981. — 188p ; 19cm
ISBN 0-263-09953-9 : £4.55 B82-04636

Hines, Barry. The blinder / Barry Hines. — Harmondsworth : Penguin, 1969, c1966 (1982 [printing]). — 239p ; 18cm
Originally published: London : Joseph, 1966
ISBN 0-14-002951-6 (pbk) : £1.50 B82-28633

Hinton, Nigel. Buddy / Nigel Hinton. — London : Dent, 1982. — 133p ; 23cm
ISBN 0-460-06089-9 : £5.95 : CIP rev.
B82-04709

Hinton, Nigel. Getting free / Nigel Hinton. — London : Heinemann Educational, 1981, c1978. — 166p ; 20cm. — (New windmill series ; 256)
Originally published: Oxford : Oxford University Press, 1978. — For adolescents
ISBN 0-435-12256-8 : £1.70 B82-05287

Hinxman, Margaret. The telephone never tells / Margaret Hinxman. — London : Collins, 1982. — 200p ; 21cm. — (The Crime Club)
ISBN 0-00-231896-2 : £6.50 : CIP rev.
B82-03704

Hitchcock, Lydia. The Geneva touch / Lydia Hitchcock. — London : Columbine House, 1982. — 201p ; 23cm
ISBN 0-85140-555-x : £6.95 : CIP rev.
B82-01953

Hitchcock, Raymond. Sea wrack / Raymond Hitchcock. — London : Sphere, 1982, c1980. — 187p ; 18cm
Originally published: London : Joseph, 1980
ISBN 0-7221-4597-7 (pbk) : £1.75 B82-34227

Hobson, Mary. Poor Tom / Mary Hobson. — London : Heinemann, 1982. — 187p ; 22cm
ISBN 0-434-34022-7 : £6.95 B82-18097

Hodge, Jane Aiken. Last act / Jane Aiken Hodge. — Large print ed. — Leicester : Ulverscroft, 1982, c1979. — 451p ; 22cm. — (Ulverscroft large print series)
Originally published: London : Hodder and Stoughton, 1979
ISBN 0-7089-0779-2 : Unpriced : CIP rev.
B82-08090

823'.914[F] — Fiction in English, *1945-* **— Texts** *continuation*

Hodge, Jane Aiken. The lost garden. — London : Hodder and Stoughton, Oct.1982. — [320]p
ISBN 0-340-28089-1 : £7.95 : CIP entry
B82-24822

Hodge, Jane Aiken. Wide is the water. — London : Hodder and Stoughton, Oct.1982. — [336]p
Originally published: 1981
ISBN 0-340-28446-3 : £2.50 : CIP entry
B82-24833

Holden, Frances. Too late! / Frances Holden. — Manchester : Gatehouse Project, c1982. — 14p : ill ; 21cm
ISBN 0-906253-12-8 (pbk) : Unpriced
B82-25427

Holden, Ursula. Penny links / Ursula Holden. — London : Methuen, 1982, c1981. — 155p ; 20cm
Originally published: London : Eyre Methuen, 1981
ISBN 0-417-06570-1 (pbk) : £1.95 B82-36610

Holden, Ursula. Sing about it. — London : Eyre Methuen, Feb.1982. — [160]p
ISBN 0-413-47730-4 : £6.50 : CIP entry
B81-36380

Holland, Jack. The prisoner's wife / Jack Holland. — London : Hale, 1982, c1981. — 177p ; 21cm
Originally published: New York : Dodd, Mead, 1981
ISBN 0-7091-9914-7 : £7.50 B82-37249

Holland, Lillie. The rightful heir / Lillie Holland. — Large print ed. — Bath : Chivers, 1981, c1975. — 242p ; 23cm. — (A Lythway book)
Originally published: London : Hurst & Blackett, 1975
ISBN 0-85119-768-x : Unpriced : CIP rev.
B81-31799

Holland, Margot. The black Marquis / Margot Holland. — London : Mills & Boon, 1981. — 192p ; 19cm. — (Masquerade)
ISBN 0-263-09972-5 : £4.55 B82-04637

Holland, Sarah. Tomorrow began yesterday / by Sarah Holland. — London : Mills & Boon, 1982. — 196p ; 19cm
ISBN 0-263-10081-2 : £5.25 B82-30941

Holland, Sarah. Too hot to handle / by Sarah Holland. — London : Mills & Boon, 1982. — 189p ; 20cm
ISBN 0-263-09991-1 : £5.25 B82-10379

Holles, Robert. Sun blight : a novel / by Robert Holles. — London : Hamilton, 1982. — 257p ; 23cm
ISBN 0-241-10733-4 : £7.95 : CIP rev.
B82-00917

Hollister, Daisy A.. Honour thy father / by Daisy A. Hollister. — Sherborne : Dorset Publishing, c1982. — 134p ; 23cm
ISBN 0-902129-42-2 : £4.95 B82-24934

Holme, Timothy. A funeral of gondolas / Timothy Holme. — London : Macmillan, 1981. — 223p ; 21cm
ISBN 0-333-31838-2 : £5.95 B82-05897

Holmes, B. J.. Bad times at Backwheel / by B.J. Holmes. — London : Hale, 1982. — 160p ; 20cm
ISBN 0-7091-9769-1 : £5.50 B82-30431

Holmes, B. J.. Shard / B.J. Holmes. — London : Hale, 1982. — 160p ; 20cm
ISBN 0-7091-9615-6 : £4.95 B82-12598

Holmes, Clare Frances. The academy of love / by Clare Frances Holmes. — London : Hale, 1982. — 208p ; 20cm
ISBN 0-7091-9490-0 : £6.95 B82-13852

Holt, Kathleen. Miss Moffitt / by Kathleen Holt. — London : Hale, 1982. — 160p ; 20cm
ISBN 0-7091-9844-2 : £6.50 B82-33427

Holt, Maurice. Winged escort : the long voyage / adapted by Maurice Holt from Winged Escort by Douglas Reeman. — London : Hutchinson, 1982. — 128p : 1map ; 19cm. — (The Bulls-eye series)
ISBN 0-09-141011-8 (pbk) : Unpriced : CIP rev. B81-38325

Holt, Richard, *1917-*. The Asian affair / Richard Holt. — Bognor Regis : New Horizon, c1982. — 128p ; 21cm
ISBN 0-86116-504-7 : £4.75 B82-36119

Holt, Victoria. The Judas kiss. — Large print ed. — Anstey : Ulverscroft, Jan.1983. — [512]p. — (Ulverscroft large print series)
Originally published: London : Collins, 1981
ISBN 0-7089-0904-3 : £6.25 : CIP entry
B82-32532

Hone, Joseph. The valley of the fox. — London : Secker and Warburg, Sept.1982. — [256]p
ISBN 0-436-20083-x : £7.50 : CIP entry
B82-25180

Honeycombe, Gordon. The edge of heaven. — London : Hutchinson, May 1981. — [416]p
ISBN 0-09-143030-5 : £6.95 : CIP entry
B81-04256

Hopcraft, Arthur. Mid-century men : by Arthur Hopcraft. — London : Hamilton, 1982. — 254p ; 23cm
ISBN 0-241-10782-2 : £7.95 : CIP rev.
B82-04313

Hopkin, Alannah. A joke goes a long way in the country / by Alannah Hopkin. — London : Hamilton, 1982. — 147p ; 23cm
ISBN 0-241-10798-9 : £7.95 : CIP rev.
B82-12572

Horsley, David. Badlands bonanza / by David Horsley. — London : Hale, 1982. — 160p ; 20cm
ISBN 0-7091-9959-7 : £5.50 B82-39173

Horst, Karl. Sink the Ark Royal / Karl Horst. — London : Severn House, 1981, c1979. — 204p ; 21cm
Originally published: London : Corgi, 1979
ISBN 0-7278-0754-4 : £5.95 B82-03677

Horton, Gordon T.. Big sty / by Gordon T. Horton. — London : Hale, 1981. — 224p ; 20cm
ISBN 0-7091-9369-6 : £7.25 B82-00514

Hosegood, Lewis. The birth of Venus / Lewis Hosegood. — London : Hale, 1982. — 206p ; 21cm
ISBN 0-7091-9788-8 : £7.50 B82-31628

Hough, Richard. Buller's dreadnought / Richard Hough. — London : Weidenfeld and Nicolson, c1982. — 217p ; 23cm
ISBN 0-297-78111-1 : £6.50 B82-22050

Hough, Richard. The fight to the finish / Richard Hough. — London : Cassell, 1979. — 210p ; 21cm
ISBN 0-304-30456-5 : £4.95 B82-09532

Howard, Elizabeth Jane. Getting it right / by Elizabeth Jane Howard. — London : Hamish Hamilton, 1982. — 264p ; 22cm
ISBN 0-241-10805-5 : £7.95 : CIP rev.
B82-09982

Howard, Elizabeth Jane. Something in disguise / Elizabeth Jane Howard. — Harmondsworth : Penguin, 1971, c1969 (1982 [printing]). — 282p ; 18cm
Originally published: London : Cape, 1969
ISBN 0-14-003288-6 (pbk) : £1.75 B82-33013

Howard, Kate. The quest of Caroline Hunt / by Kate Howard. — London : Hale, 1982. — 160p ; 20cm
ISBN 0-7091-9608-3 : £6.75 B82-12617

Howatch, Susan. Sins of the fathers / Susan Howatch. — London : Pan, 1981, c1980. — 718p ; 18cm
Originally published: London : Hamilton, 1980
ISBN 0-330-26423-0 (pbk) : £2.50 B82-00781

Howell, Barbara. A mere formality : a novel / by Barbara Howell. — London : Hodder and Stoughton, 1982. — 267p ; 23cm
ISBN 0-340-28375-0 : £7.95 : CIP rev.
B82-15746

Howlett, Anthony. Pursuit of the owl / by Anthony Howlett. — London : Hale, 1982. — 160p ; 20cm
ISBN 0-7091-9507-9 : £6.50 B82-11055

Howlett, John, *1940-*. Maximum credible accident / John Howlett. — London : Arrow, 1982, 1980. — 333p ; 18cm
Originally published: London : Hutchinson, 1980
ISBN 0-09-928850-8 (pbk) : £1.75 B82-30456

Hoyle, Fred. October the first is too late / Fred Hoyle. — London : Remploy, 1980, c1966. — 199p ; 22cm
Originally published: London : Heinemann, 1966
ISBN 0-7066-0863-1 : £4.50 B82-09346

Hoyle, Trevor. Terry Nation's Blake's Seven : Scorpio attack : a novel / by Trevor Hoyle ; based on the scripts written by Chris Boucher, James Follett, Robert Holmes. — London : British Broadcasting Corporation, c1981. — 156p ; 18cm
ISBN 0-563-17978-3 (cased) : £6.75
ISBN 0-563-20014-6 (pbk) : £1.50 B82-02951

Huddy, Delia. The Humboldt effect / Delia Huddy. — London : MacRae, c1982. — 157p ; 23cm
ISBN 0-86203-043-9 : £5.95 : CIP rev.
B82-07682

Hudson, Christopher. The final act. — London : Hodder & Stoughton, Mar.1982. — [224]p. — (Coronet books)
Originally published: London : Joseph, 1980
ISBN 0-340-26794-1 (pbk) : £1.25 : CIP entry
B82-01841

Hughes, Alison. Appointment with danger / by Alison Hughes. — London : Hale, 1982. — 160p ; 20cm
ISBN 0-7091-9845-0 : £6.50 B82-36521

Hughes, Alison. Melody to remember / by Alison Hughes. — London : Hale, 1981. — 158p ; 20cm
ISBN 0-7091-9515-x : £5.95 B82-07202

Hughes, Glyn. Where I used to play on the green : a novel / by Glyn Hughes. — London : Gollancz, 1982. — 192p ; 23cm
ISBN 0-575-02997-8 : £7.95 : CIP rev.
B81-35886

Hughes, Monica. The guardian of Isis / Monica Hughes. — London : Methuen Children's, 1982, c1981. — 140p ; 18cm. — (A Magnet book)
Originally published: London : Hamilton, 1981
ISBN 0-416-24570-6 (pbk) : £1.25 B82-34005

Hughes, Monica. Ring-rise, ring-set / Monica Hughes. — London : MacRae, 1982. — 129p ; 23cm
ISBN 0-86203-069-2 : £5.95 : CIP rev.
B82-00370

Hughes, Terence J.. Queen's mate. — London : Hodder & Stoughton, Sept.1982. — [325]p
ISBN 0-340-26645-7 : £7.50 : CIP entry
B82-21086

823'.914[F] — Fiction in English, *1945-* — *Texts continuation*

Hulme, Ann. The gamester / Ann Hulme. — London : Mills & Boon, 1982. — 190p ; 19cm. — (Masquerade)
ISBN 0-263-10131-2 : £5.95 B82-37266

Hunt, Alethia. Mystery in Mdina / Alethia Hunt. — London : Hale, 1982. — 192p ; 20cm
ISBN 0-7091-9792-6 : £6.50 B82-30404

Hunt, Donna. Forbidden love / Donna Hunt. — London : Macdonald, 1981. — 250p ; 18cm. — (A Minstrel book ; 28)
ISBN 0-7088-2131-6 (pbk) : £0.95 B82-09352

Hunt, Donna. Forbidden love / Donna Hunt. — London : Macdonald, 1982, c1981. — 250p ; 21cm
ISBN 0-356-08513-9 : £4.95 B82-10081

Hunter, Alan. Fields of heather / Alan Hunter. — London : Constable, 1981. — 158p ; 23cm. — ([A Superintendent Gently suspense novel])
ISBN 0-09-464400-4 : £5.95 B82-00054

Hunter, Alan. Gabrielle's way / Alan Hunter. — Large print ed. — Bath : Chivers, 1982, c1980. — 236p ; 23cm. — (A Lythway book)
Originally published: London : Constable, 1981
ISBN 0-85119-817-1 : Unpriced : CIP rev. B82-09861

Hunter, Elizabeth, *1934-*. A touch of magic / Elizabeth Hunter. — London : Silhouette, 1981. — 188p ; 18cm. — (Silhouette romance ; 65)
ISBN 0-340-27120-5 (pbk) : £0.65 : CIP rev. B81-27356

Hutson, Shaun. Kessler's raid / Shaun Hutson. — London : Hale, 1982. — 191p ; 20cm
ISBN 0-7091-9907-4 : £7.25 B82-35894

Hutson, Shaun. The skull / Shaun Hutson. — Feltham : Hamlyn Paperbacks, 1982. — 188p ; 18cm
ISBN 0-600-20408-1 (pbk) : £1.25 B82-19459

Hutson, Shaun. Sledgehammer / Shaun Hutson. — London : Hale, 1982. — 224p ; 20cm
ISBN 0-7091-9618-0 : £7.50 B82-12597

Hutton, John. Accidental crimes. — London : Bodley Head, Jan.1983. — [256]p
ISBN 0-370-30498-5 : £7.50 : CIP entry B82-34421

Hyde, Christopher. The wave. — London : Hodder & Stoughton, Dec.1981. — [240]p
Originally published: 1980
ISBN 0-340-27270-8 (pbk) : £1.10 : CIP entry B81-31465

Hyde, John, *1943-*. Amen / John Hyde. — London : Futura, c1981. — 218p ; 18cm
ISBN 0-7088-2105-7 (pbk) : £1.25 B82-05483

Hylton, Sara. The Carradice chain / Sara Hylton. — London : Hutchinson, 1981. — 260p ; 23cm
ISBN 0-09-145280-5 : £6.95 : CIP rev. B81-26764

Hylton, Sara. The Carradice chain / Sara Hylton. — London : Arrow, 1982, c1981. — 260p ; 18cm
Originally published: London : Hutchinson, 1981
ISBN 0-09-928450-2 (pbk) : £1.60 B82-33311

Hylton, Sara. The crimson falcon. — London : Hutchinson, Feb.1983. — [272]p
ISBN 0-09-150160-1 : £7.50 : CIP entry B82-36565

Ibbotson, Eva. A countess below stairs / Eva Ibbotson. — London : Macdonald Futura, 1981. — 284p ; 21cm
ISBN 0-354-04714-0 : £5.95 B82-00436

Ibbotson, Eva. Magic flutes. — London : Century, Nov.1982. — [256]p
ISBN 0-7126-0035-3 : £6.95 : CIP entry B82-27970

Ikki. Gaaay time all round / by Ikki ; illustrations by Mizuzumi. — Sodomdon (ex-London) : Rafael Barrett Press, 1999 [i.e. 1982]. — 120p : ill ; 22cm
ISBN 0-907428-00-2 (pbk) : £1.95 B82-30283

Inchbald, Peter. The sweet short grass. — London : Collins, Oct.1982. — [224]p. — (The Crime Club)
ISBN 0-00-231792-3 : £6.75 : CIP entry B82-23083

Innes, Brian. The Red Baron lives. — London : New English Library, Nov.1982. — [288]p
Originally published: 1981
ISBN 0-450-05401-2 (pbk) : £1.60 : CIP entry B82-27525

Ireland, David. City of women : a novel / by David Ireland. — Ringwood, Vic. ; Harmondsworth : Penguin, 1981. — 171p ; 18cm
Originally published: Ringwood, Vic. : Allen Lane, 1981
ISBN 0-14-005821-4 (pbk) : £1.50 B82-32576

Ironside, Virginia. A distant sunset / Virginia Ironside. — London : Arrow, 1982. — 255p ; 18cm
ISBN 0-09-928050-7 (pbk) : £1.50 B82-19020

Irving, Clive. Promise them the earth. — London : Hamilton, Oct.1982. — [448]p
ISBN 0-241-10751-2 : £8.95 : CIP entry B82-23447

Irwin, Frances. Gentleman from Spain / by Frances Irwin. — London : Hale, 1982. — 159p ; 20cm
ISBN 0-7091-9815-9 : £7.25 B82-37292

Jackman, Stuart. The Davidson file : compiled from the personal papers of His Grace the Lord Caiaphas, High Priest of Jewry / by Stuart Jackman. — Guildford : Lutterworth Press, 1982. — [116]p ; 25cm
ISBN 0-7188-2526-8 (pbk) : £5.95 B82-18087

Jackman, Stuart. Sandcatcher. — London : Hodder & Stoughton, June 1982. — [224]p. — (Coronet books)
Originally published: London : Hamilton, 1980
ISBN 0-340-27919-2 (pbk) : £1.25 : CIP entry B82-10017

Jackowska, Nicki. Dr. Marbles and Marianne. — Brighton : Harvester Press, May 1982. — [96]p
ISBN 0-7108-0490-3 : £4.95 : CIP entry B82-10696

Jackson, Eileen. Dance for a lady / Eileen Jackson. — London : Hale, 1982. — 205p ; 20cm
ISBN 0-7091-9492-7 : £6.95 B82-15477

Jackson, Gordon, *1938-*. Purslane : a story / by Gordon Jackson ; illustrated by Paul Jackson. — Lincoln (1 Stonefield Ave., Lincoln) : Asgill, 1980. — [15]p : ill ; 25cm
Limited ed. of 400 numbered copies
£1.00 (pbk) B82-08847

Jackson, Robert, *1941-*. The last battle : Yeoman and the defeat of the Third Reich / Robert Jackson. — London : Barker, c1982. — 151p ; 23cm
ISBN 0-213-16819-7 : £6.50 B82-11715

Jackson, Robert, *1941-*. Malta victory : yeoman on the George Cross Island / Robert Jackson. — [London] : Corgi, 1981, c1980. — 158p : 1map ; 18cm
Originally published: London : Baker, 1980
ISBN 0-552-11856-7 (pbk) : £1.25 B82-09007

Jackson, Robert, *1941-*. Mosquito Squadron : Yeoman in the battle over Germany / Robert Jackson. — London : Corgi, 1982, c1981. — 153p ; 18cm
Originally published: London : Barker, 1981
ISBN 0-552-11987-3 (pbk) : £1.25 B82-35255

Jacobson, Howard. Coming from behind. — London : Chatto & Windus, Feb.1983. — [224]p
ISBN 0-7011-2658-2 : £7.95 : CIP entry B82-38868

Jagger, Brenda. The sleeping sword / Brenda Jagger. — London : Macdonald, 1982. — 448p : 1geneal.table ; 23cm
ISBN 0-356-07896-5 : £7.95 B82-37779

James, Donald, *1931-*. The fall of the Russian Empire. — London : Granada, Jan.1983. — [336]p
ISBN 0-246-11937-3 : £7.95 : CIP entry B82-33709

James, P. D.. The black tower / by P.D. James. — London : Prior, 1981, c1975. — 457p ; 25cm
Originally published: London : Faber, 1975. — Published in large print
ISBN 0-86043-668-3 : £7.95 B82-16175

James, P. D.. P.D. James Omnibus. — London : Faber, 1982. — 748p ; 21cm
Contents: Unnatural causes. Originally published: 1967 — Shroud for a nightingale. Originally published: 1971 — An unsuitable job for a woman. Originally published: 1972
ISBN 0-571-11851-8 : £6.95 : CIP rev. B82-07850

James, P. D.. The skull beneath the skin. — London : Faber, Oct.1982. — [384]p
ISBN 0-571-11961-1 : £7.95 : CIP entry B82-25175

James, Peter, *1948-*. Dead letter drop / Peter James. — London : Star, 1982, c1981. — 203p ; 18cm
Originally published: London : W.H. Allen, 1981
ISBN 0-352-30975-x (pbk) : £1.60 B82-16102

James, Saffron. Patterns of love / Saffron James. — St. Ives : United Writers, c1981. — 463p ; 23cm
ISBN 0-901976-71-7 : £6.95 B82-17496

James, Sally. Lord Fordington's offer / by Sally James. — London : Hale, 1982. — 207p ; 20cm
ISBN 0-7091-9499-4 : £5.95 B82-10747

James, Terry, *1945-*. Waggoners' Walk : the story continues — / Terry James. — London : Robson, 1980. — 224p ; 23cm
ISBN 0-86051-130-8 : £5.95 : CIP rev. B80-28754

James, Terry, *1945-*. waggoners' walk : the story continues — / Terry James. — London : Corgi, 1982, c1980. — 191p ; 18cm
Originally published: London : Robson, 1980
ISBN 0-552-11927-x (pbk) : £1.25 B82-24522

James, Vanessa. The dark one / by Vanessa James. — London : Mills and Boon, 1982. — 190p ; 20cm
ISBN 0-263-10083-9 : £5.95 B82-37114

James, Vincent. The long ride out / by Vincent James. — London : Remploy, 1981. — 192p ; 22cm
Originally published: London : Benn, 1957
ISBN 0-7066-0912-3 : £5.40 B82-03684

Jameson, Claudia. Escape to love / Claudia Jameson. — London : Mills & Boon, 1981. — 191p ; 20cm
ISBN 0-263-09977-6 : £4.55 B82-09223

823′.914[F] — Fiction in English, *1945-* **— *Texts continuation***

Jameson, Claudia. Lesson in love / by Claudia Jameson. — London : Mills & Boon, 1982. — 188p ; 20cm
ISBN 0-263-10058-8 : £5.25 B82-27604

Jameson, Claudia. Lesson in love / by Claudia Jameson. — London : Mills & Boon, 1982. — 188p ; 18cm
ISBN 0-263-73857-4 (pbk) : £0.85 B82-36286

Jeffrey, Elizabeth. Web of destiny / Elizabeth Jeffrey. — Large print ed. — Bath : Chivers Press, 1982, c1979. — 216p ; 23cm. — (A Seymour book)
Originally published: London : Mills & Boon, 1979
ISBN 0-85119-450-8 : Unpriced : CIP rev. B81-33806

Jeffrey, William. Duel at Gold Buttes / by William Jeffrey. — London : Hale, 1982, c1981. — 176p ; 20cm
ISBN 0-7091-9715-2 : £5.25 B82-17521

Jeffries, Roderic. Deadly petard. — London : Collins, Jan.1983. — [224]p. — (The Crime Club)
ISBN 0-00-231362-6 : £6.95 : CIP entry B82-33588

Jeffries, Roderic. Just deserts / Roderic Jeffries. — Large print ed. — Leicester : Ulverscroft, 1982, c1980. — 318p ; 23cm. — (Ulverscroft large print series : mystery)
Originally published: London : Collins for the Crime Club, 1980
ISBN 0-7089-0786-5 : Unpriced : CIP rev. B82-18439

Jenkins, Judith. The dark lord / by Judith Jenkins. — London : Hale, 1982. — 160p ; 20cm
ISBN 0-7091-9712-8 : £6.25 B82-22858

Jenkins, Priscilla. Amaryllis / Priscilla Jenkins. — London : Hutchinson, 1982. — 271p ; 23cm
ISBN 0-09-147110-9 : £6.95 : CIP rev. B82-03088

Jhabvala, Ruth Prawer. Heat and dust / Ruth Prawer Jhabvala. — [London] : Futura, 1976, c1975 (1982 [printing]). — 181p ; 18cm
Originally published: London : J. Murray, 1975
ISBN 0-86007-414-5 (pbk) : £1.50 B82-35716

Jobson, Hamilton. The sleeping tiger / by Hamilton Jobson. — London : Hale, 1982. — 192p ; 20cm
ISBN 0-7091-9613-x : £6.50 B82-12612

Jobson, Hamilton. Waiting for Thursday / Hamilton Jobson. — Large print ed. — Bath : Chivers, 1982, c1977. — 250p ; 23cm. — (A Lythway thriller)
Originally published: London : Collins, 1977
ISBN 0-85119-800-7 : Unpriced : CIP rev. B82-05007

Johns, Larry. A time to die / Larry Johns. — London : Hale, 1981. — 190p ; 21cm
ISBN 0-7091-9330-0 : £6.95 B82-12625

Johnson, Ken. The homunculus / Kenneth Rayner Johnson. — Sevenoaks : New English Library, 1982. — 181p ; 18cm
ISBN 0-450-05416-0 (pbk) : £1.50 : CIP rev. B82-12353

Johnson, Pamela Hansford. The good husband / Pamela Hansford Johnson. — [Feltham] : Hamlyn Paperbacks, 1982, c1978. — 219p ; 18cm
Originally published: London : Macmillan, 1978
ISBN 0-600-20530-4 (pbk) : £1.50 B82-30005

Johnson, Sheila. Of wilful intent / Sheila Johnson. — London : Collins, 1982. — 176p ; 21cm. — (Collins crime club)
ISBN 0-00-231909-8 : £6.50 : CIP rev. B82-10570

Johnson, Stanley, *1940-*. The Marburg virus / Stanley Johnson. — London : Heinemann, 1982. — 262p ; 23cm
ISBN 0-434-37704-x : £6.95 B82-19798

Johnston, Ivan. Sergeant on trial / Ivan Johnston. — London : Hale, 1982. — 175p ; 22cm
ISBN 0-7091-9683-0 : £6.95 B82-27320

Johnston, Jennifer. How many miles to Babylon / Jennifer Johnston. — [London] : Fontana, 1981, c1974. — 156p ; 18cm
Originally published: London : Hamilton, 1974
ISBN 0-00-616306-8 (pbk) : £1.25 B82-13647

Joly, Cyril. Silent night : the defeat of NATO / Cyril Joly. — London : Cassell, 1980. — 240p ; 23cm
ISBN 0-304-30656-8 : £5.95 B82-35286

Jones, Cherry Calvert. The crooked shadow / by Cherry Calvert Jones. — London : Hale, 1982. — 160p ; 20cm
ISBN 0-7091-9497-8 : £6.75 B82-10751

Jones, D. F.. Bound in time / D.F. Jones. — London : Granada, c1981 (1982 [printing]). — 283p ; 18cm. — (A Mayflower book)
ISBN 0-583-13450-5 (pbk) : £1.75 B82-40245

Jones, Eva. Malou. — Loughton : Piatkus, Apr.1982. — [192]p
ISBN 0-86188-161-3 : £6.50 : CIP entry B82-06260

Jones, G. O.. The conjuring show : a story sequence / by G.O. Jones. — Port Talbot : Alun, 1981. — 162p ; 19cm
ISBN 0-907117-08-2 : £5.50 B82-02958

Jones, Gwyn, *1952-*. Up with your hands / Gwyn Jones. — Bognor Regis : New Horizon, c1982. — 151p ; 21cm
ISBN 0-86116-509-8 : £5.25 B82-08816

Jones, Irene Heywood. Sister / Irene Heywood Jones. — London : W.H. Allen, 1982. — 220p ; 18cm. — (A Star book)
ISBN 0-352-31046-4 (pbk) : £1.60 B82-22066

Jones, Irene Heywood. Sister. — Bath : Chivers, Nov.1982. — [192]p. — (Firecrest books)
ISBN 0-85997-503-7 : £5.95 : CIP entry B82-26335

Jones, Jeanne. Ambition's woman. — Loughton : Piatkus, Feb.1983. — [312]p
ISBN 0-86188-228-8 : £7.95 : CIP entry B82-39810

Jones, Mervyn, *1922-*. Two women and their man : a novel / by Mervyn Jones. — London : Deutsch, 1981. — 240p ; 22cm
ISBN 0-233-97423-7 : £6.95 : CIP rev. B82-01859

Jons, Hal. Mustang Valley / by Hal Jons. — London : Hale, 1982. — 159p ; 20cm
ISBN 0-7091-9561-3 : £4.95 B82-12601

Jordan, Lee. Cat's eyes / Lee Jordan. — London : Hodder and Stoughton, 1981. — 170p ; 21cm
ISBN 0-340-27244-9 : £5.95 : CIP rev. B81-31160

Jordan, Neil. The past / Neil Jordan. — London : Abacus, 1982, c1980. — 232p ; 20cm
Originally published: London : Cape, 1980
ISBN 0-349-11857-4 (pbk) : £2.50 B82-27887

Jordan, Penny. Blackmail / by Penny Jordan. — London : Mills & Boon, 1982. — 187p ; 19cm
ISBN 0-263-10022-7 : £5.25 B82-18110

Jordan, Penny. The caged tiger / by Penny Jordan. — London : Mills & Boon, 1982. — 188p ; 20cm
ISBN 0-263-10048-0 : £5.25 B82-22500

Jordan, Penny. Daughter of Hassan / by Penny Jordan. — London : Mills & Boon, 1982. — 187p ; 19cm
ISBN 0-263-10069-3 : £5.25 B82-30932

Jordan, Penny. Island of the dawn / by Penny Jordan. — London : Mills and Boon, 1982. — 188p ; 20cm
ISBN 0-263-10090-1 : £5.95 B82-37113

Jordan, Penny. Long cold winter / by Penny Jordan. — London : Mills & Boon, 1982. — 188p ; 20cm
ISBN 0-263-10007-3 : £5.25 B82-13887

Jordan, Penny. Marriage without love / by Penny Jordan. — London : Mills & Boon, 1981. — 188p ; 20cm
ISBN 0-263-09959-8 : £4.55 B82-04653

Jordan, Penny. An unbroken marriage / by Penny Jordan. — London : Mills & Boon, 1982. — 186p ; 20cm
ISBN 0-263-10102-9 : £5.95 B82-37437

Joseph, Marie. Emma Sparrow / Marie Joseph. — London : Hutchinson, 1981. — 234p ; 23cm
ISBN 0-09-146360-2 : £6.95 : CIP rev. B81-28766

Joseph, Marie. Emma Sparrow / Marie Joseph. — London : Arrow, 1982, c1981. — 234p ; 18cm
Originally published: London : Hutchinson, 1981
ISBN 0-09-928310-7 (pbk) : £1.50 B82-31609

Joseph, Marie. Gemini girls / Marie Joseph. — London : Hutchinson, 1982. — 231p ; 23cm
ISBN 0-09-147660-7 : £6.95 : CIP rev. B82-11290

Joseph, Marie. A leaf in the wind / Marie Joseph. — London : Arrow, 1981, c1980. — 302p ; 18cm
Originally published: London : Hutchinson, 1980
ISBN 0-09-927220-2 (pbk) : £1.50 B82-06566

Joseph, Marie. The listening silence. — London : Hutchinson, Nov.1982. — [256]p
ISBN 0-09-150390-6 : £6.95 : CIP entry B82-26858

Joseph, Marie. Maggie Craig / Marie Joseph. — Large print ed. — Leicester : Ulverscroft, 1982, c1980. — 434p ; 23cm. — (Ulverscroft large print series)
Originally published: London : Hutchinson, 1980
ISBN 0-7089-0769-5 : Unpriced : CIP rev. B82-01744

Josipovici, Gabriel. The air we breathe / Gabriel Josipovici. — Brighton : Harvester Press, 1981. — 114p ; 21cm. — (A Harvester novel)
ISBN 0-7108-0056-8 : £6.95 : CIP rev. B81-30330

Jost, John. Kangaroo court / John Jost. — London : Methuen Paperbacks, 1981, c1979. — 233p : ill ; 18cm. — (Magnum books)
Originally published: London : Angus & Robertson, 1979
ISBN 0-417-05710-5 (pbk) : £1.50 B82-15497

Joyce, Cyril. A bullet for Betty / Cyril Joyce. — London : Hale, 1981. — 159p ; 20cm
ISBN 0-7091-9512-5 : £6.50 B82-07194

Joyce, Cyril. From the grave to the cradle / Cyril Joyce. — London : Hale, 1982. — 159p ; 20cm
ISBN 0-7091-9830-2 : £6.75 B82-30399

Joyce, Jayne. Marriage of revenge / Jayne Joyce. — London : Macdonald Futura, 1981. — 254p ; 18cm. — (A Minstrel book ; 19)
ISBN 0-7088-2103-0 (pbk) : £0.95 B82-01619

823'.914[F] — Fiction in English, *1945-* — *Texts continuation*

Judd, Alan. A breed of heroes / Alan Judd. — London : Hodder and Stoughton, 1981. — 288p ; 24cm
ISBN 0-340-26334-2 : £6.95 : CIP rev. B81-04388

Judge, Sara. They call me Miranda / by Sara Judge. — London : Hale, 1982. — 190p ; 20cm
ISBN 0-7091-9790-x : £7.25 B82-30428

Kapp, Colin. Lost worlds of Chronus. — London : New English Library, Mar.1982. — [176]p. — (Cageworld ; 2)
ISBN 0-450-05409-8 (pbk) : £1.25 : CIP entry B82-01985

Kapp, Colin. Search for the sun. — London : New English Library, Mar.1982. — [176]p. — (Cageworld ; 1)
ISBN 0-450-05131-5 (pbk) : £1.25 : CIP entry B82-01976

Kapp, Colin. Star search. — London : New English Library, Jan.1983. — [176]p. — (Cageworld ; 4)
ISBN 0-450-05531-0 (pbk) : £1.25 : CIP entry B82-34601

Kapp, Colin. The tyrant of Hades / Colin Kapp. — Sevenoaks : New English Library, 1982. — 173p ; 18cm. — (Cageworld ; no.3)
ISBN 0-450-05469-1 (pbk) : £1.25 : CIP rev. B82-15805

Kartun, Derek. I, Norman Harris / Derek Kartun. — London : Sphere, 1982, c1980. — 155p ; 18cm
Originally published: London : Bodley Head, 1980
ISBN 0-7221-5176-4 (pbk) : £1.25 B82-12518

Kavanagh, Dan. Duffy / Dan Kavanagh. — [St. Albans] : Triad, 1982, c1980. — 173p ; 18cm
Originally published: London : Cape, 1980
ISBN 0-586-05398-0 (pbk) : £1.25 B82-17358

Kavanagh, Dan. Fiddle city / Dan Kavanagh. — London : Cape, 1981. — 173p ; 21cm
ISBN 0-224-01977-5 : £5.95 : CIP rev. B81-27335

Kay, D.. The Saturday night soldiers / D. Kay. — Bognor Regis : New Horizon, c1981. — 211p ; 21cm
ISBN 0-86116-751-1 : £5.75 B82-02947

Kaye, Geraldine. Frangipani summer. — London : Macmillan Education, Mar.1982. — [112]p. — (Topliner tridents)
ISBN 0-333-31970-2 : £3.95 : CIP entry B82-01853

Kaye, M. M.. Trade wind / M.M. Kaye. — Rev. ed. — Harmondsworth : Penguin, 1982, c1981. — 630p : 1map ; 19cm
Originally published: London : Allen Lane, 1981
ISBN 0-14-006341-2 (pbk) : £1.95 B82-29819

Keane, Molly. Good behaviour. — Large print ed. — Bath : Chivers, Dec.1982. — [376]p. — (A Lythway book)
Originally published: London : Deutsch, 1981
ISBN 0-85119-870-8 : £7.50 : CIP entry B82-30244

Keating, H. R. F.. Bats fly up for Inspector Ghote. — Large print ed. — Bath : Chivers, Sept.1982. — [304]p. — (A Lythway book)
Originally published: London : Collins, 1974
ISBN 0-85119-846-5 : £6.90 : CIP entry B82-20515

Keating, H. R. F.. Go West, Inspector Ghote. — Large print ed. — Bath : Chivers Press, Dec.1982. — [312]p. — (A Lythway book)
Originally published: London : Collins, 1981
ISBN 0-85119-871-6 : £7.20 : CIP entry B82-30245

Keating, H. R. F.. The lucky Alphonse. — London : Severn House, Oct.1982. — [224]p
ISBN 0-7278-3000-7 : £6.95 : CIP entry B82-24249

Keating, H. R. F.. The perfect murder : a famous first : the first Inspector Ghote novel / H.R.F Keating. — London : Collins, 1964 (1981 [printing]). — 249p ; 21cm. — (The Crime Club)
ISBN 0-00-231683-8 : £6.50 B82-03082

Kebbell, Janet. Hunter's Combe / by Janet Kebbell. — London : Hale, 1981. — 173p ; 20cm
ISBN 0-7091-9445-5 : £5.95 B82-06333

Keene, Tom. Skyshroud / Tom Keene with Brian Haynes. — London : Allen Lane, 1981. — 363p ; 23cm
ISBN 0-7139-1267-7 : £6.95 B82-00958

Keene, Tom. Skyshroud / Tom Keene with Brian Haynes. — Harmondsworth : Penguin, 1982, c1981. — 363p ; 19cm
Originally published: London : Allen Lane, 1981
ISBN 0-14-005217-8 (pbk) : £1.75 B82-35861

Kelaart, Piers. Midas / Piers Kelaart. — London : Severn House, 1982, c1981. — 240p ; 21cm
Originally published: London : Macdonald Futura, 1981
ISBN 0-7278-0763-3 : £6.95 B82-11434

Kelleher, Victor. Master of the grove / Victor Kelleher. — Harmondsworth : Kestrel, 1982. — 182p ; 23cm
For adolescents
ISBN 0-7226-5730-7 : £5.95 B82-19131

Kelley, Leo P.. Luke Sutton : gunfighter / by Leo P. Kelley. — London : Hale, 1982. — 188p ; 20cm
ISBN 0-7091-9868-x : £5.50 B82-33418

Kelley, Leo P.. Luke Sutton: outlaw / Leo P. Kelley. — London : Hale, 1981. — 185p ; 19cm
ISBN 0-7091-9523-0 : £4.95 B82-02159

Kelly, Patrick, *1917-*. Codeword Cromwell / Patrick Kelly. — London : Granada, 1980 (1981 [printing]). — 186p ; 18cm. — (A Mayflower book)
ISBN 0-583-13006-2 (pbk) : £1.25 B82-09533

Kelly, Terence, *1920-*. The Blades of Cordoba / Terence Kelly. — London : Hale, 1981. — 218p ; 21cm
ISBN 0-7091-9400-5 : £7.50 B82-07187

Kemp, Sarah. Goodbye, Pussy / Sarah Kemp. — Large print ed. — Bath : Chivers, 1981, c1979. — 211p ; 23cm. — (A Lythway book)
Originally published: London : Collins, 1979
ISBN 0-85119-769-8 : Unpriced : CIP rev. B81-31800

Kennaway, James. The cost of living like this / James Kennaway ; introduction by Frederic Raphael. — Edinburgh : Mainstream, 1980. — xi,199p ; 23cm
Originally published: London : Longman, 1969
ISBN 0-906391-08-3 : £5.95 B82-30441

Kennaway, James. Tunes of glory / James Kennaway ; introduction by Godfrey Smith. — Edinburgh : Mainstream, 1980. — 200p ; 23cm
Originally published: London : Putnam, 1956
ISBN 0-906391-07-5 : £5.95 B82-30442

Kennedy, Lena. Nelly Kelly / Lena Kennedy. — London : Macdonald Futura, 1981. — 277p ; 18cm
ISBN 0-7088-2053-0 (pbk) : £1.50 B82-27054

Kent, Alexander. The inshore squadron. — Large print ed. — Anstey : Ulverscroft, Jan.1983. — [480]p. — (Ulverscroft large print series)
Originally published: London : Hutchinson, 1978
ISBN 0-7089-0905-1 : £6.25 : CIP entry B82-32533

Kent, Alexander. Stand into danger / Alexander Kent. — Large print ed. — Leicester : Ulverscroft, 1982, c1980. — 480p : maps ; 23cm. — (Ulverscroft large print)
Originally published: London : Hutchinson, 1980. — Map on lining papers
ISBN 0-7089-0753-9 : £5.00 : CIP rev. B81-36938

Kent, Pamela. Flight to the stars / Pamela Kent. — Large print ed. — Bath : Chivers, 1982, c1977. — 189p ; 23cm. — (A Lythway book)
Originally published: London : Mills & Boon, 1977
ISBN 0-85119-784-1 : Unpriced : CIP rev. B81-35862

Kent, Pamela. Sweet Barbary / Pamela Kent. — Large print ed. — Bath : Chivers, 1982, c1976. — 217p ; 23cm. — (A Lythway romance)
Originally published: London : Mills & Boon, 1957
ISBN 0-85119-801-5 : Unpriced : CIP rev. B82-05008

Kent, Sarah, *1924-*. The Darien betrothals / Sarah Kent. — London : Hale, 1982. — 206p ; 20cm
ISBN 0-7091-9539-7 : £6.95 B82-15486

Kenyon, Michael. The God squad bod / Michael Kenyon. — London : Collins, 1982. — 199p ; 20cm. — (The Crime Club)
ISBN 0-00-231488-6 : £6.50 : CIP rev. B82-19072

Kenyon, Michael. May you die in Ireland : a famous first / Michael Kenyon. — London : Collins, 1965 (1981 [printing]). — 224p ; 21cm. — (The Crime Club)
ISBN 0-00-231501-7 : £6.50 B82-03081

Kessler, Leo. Breakthrough / Leo Kessler. — London : Severn, 1981, c1979. — 220p ; 21cm
Originally published: London : Futura, 1979
ISBN 0-7278-0649-1 : £5.25 B82-16799

Kessler, Leo. Death to the Deutschland / Leo Kessler. — London : Macdonald, 1982. — 219p ; 21cm. — (The Sea wolves ; 2)
ISBN 0-356-07911-2 : £5.95 B82-37784

Kessler, Leo. Death to the Deutschland / Leo Kessler. — [London] : Futura, 1982. — 219p ; 18cm. — (The Sea Wolves ; 2)
ISBN 0-7088-2204-5 (pbk) : £1.25 B82-35722

Kessler, Leo. Otto and the Reds / Leo Kessler. — [London] : Futura, 1982. — 219p ; 18cm. — (Otto Stahl ; 3) (A Futura book)
ISBN 0-7088-2196-0 (pbk) : £1.50 B82-33791

Kessler, Leo. Otto's blitzkrieg! / Leo Kessler. — London : Macdonald, 1982. — 254p ; 21cm. — (Otto Stahl ; 2)
ISBN 0-356-08620-8 : £4.95 B82-26016

Kessler, Leo. Otto's blitzkrieg! / Leo Kessler. — London : Futura, 1982. — 254p ; 18cm. — (Otto Stahl ; 2)
ISBN 0-7088-2173-1 (pbk) : £1.50 B82-22610

Kessler, Leo. Sink the Scharnhorst! / Leo Kessler. — London : Macdonald, 1982. — 256p ; 21cm. — (The Sea wolves ; 1)
Originally published: London : Macdonald Futura, 1981
ISBN 0-356-08683-6 : £6.50 B82-37783

Kessler, Leo. Slaughter ground / Leo Kessler. — London : Macdonald, 1982, c1980. — 192p ; 21cm
Originally published: London : Futura, 1980
ISBN 0-356-08517-1 : £4.95 B82-10079

823'.914[F] — Fiction in English, *1945- — Texts continuation*

Kesson, Jessie. Glitter of mica / Jessie Kesson ; introduction by William Donaldson. — Edinburgh : Harris, 1982. — 155p ; 23cm. — (The Scottish fiction reprint library)
Originally published: London : Chatto and Windus, 1963
ISBN 0-86228-021-4 : £6.95 B82-35448

Keyworth, Anne. Spring bride / by Anne Keyworth. — London : Hale, 1982. — 192p ; 20cm
ISBN 0-7091-9644-x : £6.95 B82-18307

Kidd, Flora. Between pride and passion / by Flora Kidd. — London : Mills & Boon, 1982. — 186p ; 20cm
ISBN 0-263-10104-5 : £5.95 B82-37435

Kidd, Flora. Makebelieve marriage / by Flora Kidd. — London : Mills & Boon, 1982. — 186p ; 19cm
ISBN 0-263-10044-8 : £5.25 B82-22501

Kidd, Flora. Meeting at midnight / by Flora Kidd. — London : Mills & Boon, 1981. — 186p ; 20cm
ISBN 0-263-09979-2 : £4.55 B82-09228

Kidd, Flora. Night on the mountain. — Large print ed. — Bath : Chivers, Feb.1983. — [304] p. — (Atlantic large print)
Originally published: London : Mills and Boon, 1973
ISBN 0-85119-522-9 : £5.75 : CIP entry B82-39574

Kidd, Flora. Tangled shadows / Flora Kidd. — Large print ed. — Bath : Chivers, 1982, c1979. — 225p ; 23cm. — (A Seymour book)
Originally published: London : Mills and Boon, 1979
ISBN 0-85119-457-5 : Unpriced : CIP rev. B82-01440

Kidd, Russell. Battle for Bear Head Creek / by Russ Kidd. — London : Hale, 1982. — 159p ; 20cm
ISBN 0-7091-9793-4 (corrected) : £5.50 B82-37239

Kilworth, Garry. Gemini god / Garry Kilworth. — Harmondsworth : Penguin, 1982, c1981. — 240p ; 18cm. — (Penguin science fiction)
Originally published: London : Faber, 1981
ISBN 0-14-005874-5 (pbk) : £1.75 B82-32577

Kincaid, Stephanie. Highland lovesong / Stephanie Kincaid. — London : Hale, 1981, c1978. — 188p ; 20cm
ISBN 0-7091-8735-1 : £6.25 B82-22866

King, Ames. Man-hunter in town / by Ames King. — London : Hale, 1981. — 160p ; 19cm
ISBN 0-7091-9526-5 : £4.95 B82-07207

King, Betty. The French countess / Betty King. — London : Hale, 1982. — 223p ; 20cm
ISBN 0-7091-9677-6 : £7.50 B82-15487

Kingston, Guy. The boys of Coastal / Guy Kingston. — London : Granada, 1982. — 223p ; 18cm. — (A Mayflower book)
ISBN 0-583-13164-6 (pbk) : £1.25 B82-19977

Kingston, Syd. Boot Hill bandit / Syd Kingston. — London : Hale, 1982. — 176p ; 20cm
ISBN 0-7091-9744-6 : £5.50 B82-28920

Kirst, Hans Hellmut. Heroes for sale / Hans Hellmut Kirst ; translated by J. Maxwell Brownjohn. — London : Collins, 1982. — 350p ; 22cm
Translation of: Ausverkauf der Helden
ISBN 0-00-222396-1 : £7.95 : CIP rev. B81-35930

Kirsten, Angela. Sweet sister Ann / Angela Kirsten. — London : Hale, 1982. — 189p ; 20cm
ISBN 0-7091-9818-3 : £7.25 B82-37294

Knight, Alanna. Castle Clodha / by Alanna Knight. — Large print ed. — Long Preston : Magna, 1981, c1972. — 308p : ill ; 23cm
Originally published: London : Hurst and Blackett, 1972. — Published in large print
ISBN 0-86009-336-0 : Unpriced : CIP rev. B81-16908

Knight, Alanna. Castle of foxes / Alanna Knight. — London : Prior, c1981. — 499p ; 25cm
Published in large print
ISBN 0-86043-681-0 : Unpriced B82-28218

Knight, Alanna. Colla's children / Alanna Knight. — London : Macdonald, 1982. — 524p ; 21cm
ISBN 0-356-08533-3 : £8.95 B82-12664

Knowles, Anne. Matthew Ratton / Anne Knowles. — London : Magnum, 1981, c1980. — 158p ; 20cm
Originally published: London : Eyre Methuen, 1980
ISBN 0-417-04960-9 (pbk) : £1.95 B82-15543

Knowles, Anne. Matthew Ratton. — Large print ed. — Long Preston : Magna Print, Nov.1982. — [320]p
Originally published: London : Eyre Methuen, 1980
ISBN 0-86009-438-3 : £5.50 : CIP entry B82-26339

Knox, Bill. Bloodtide / Bill Knox. — London : Hutchinson, 1982. — 232p ; 21cm
ISBN 0-09-147880-4 : £6.95 : CIP rev. B82-14224

Knox, Bill. Bombship / Bill Knox. — Large print ed. — Leicester : Ulverscroft, 1982, c1980. — 329p : 1map ; 23cm. — (Ulverscroft large print)
Originally published: London : Hutchinson, 1980
ISBN 0-7089-0816-0 : Unpriced : CIP rev. B82-15956

Knox, Bill. A killing in antiques. — Large print ed. — Anstey : Ulverscroft, Feb.1983. — 1v.. — (Ulverscroft large print series)
Originally published: London : Long, 1981
ISBN 0-7089-0919-1 : CIP entry B82-38881

Knox-Mawer, June. Marama / June Knox-Mawer. — [London] : Corgi, 1982, c1972. — 267p ; 17cm
Originally published: London : Hamilton, 1972
ISBN 0-552-11889-3 (pbk) : £1.50 B82-12586

Konrad, Klaus. Front swine / Klaus Konrad. — London : Macdonald, 1982. — 208p ; 21cm. — ([Russian series] ; [3])
ISBN 0-354-04827-9 : £4.95 B82-36289

Konrad, Klaus. Front swine / Klaus Konrad. — London : Futura, 1982. — 208p ; 18cm. — (Russian series ; 3)
ISBN 0-7088-2197-9 (pbk) : £1.25 B82-32786

Korda, Michael. Worldly goods. — London : Bodley Head, Aug.1982. — [353]p
ISBN 0-370-30932-4 : £6.95 : CIP entry B82-15778

Kostov, K. N.. Baptism of blood / K.N. Kostov. — London : Severn House, 1981, c1980. — 221p : 1map ; 21cm
Originally published: London : Arrow, 1980
ISBN 0-7278-0739-0 : £5.95 : CIP rev. B81-24637

Kostov, K. N.. Cossack attack / K.N. Kostov. — London : Arrow, 1982. — 216p ; 18cm. — (Punishment battalion 333 ; no.5)
ISBN 0-09-927430-2 (corrected : pbk) : £1.25 B82-13870

Kostov, K. N.. The Gulag rats / K.N. Kostov. — London : Severn House, 1982, c1981. — 206p ; 20cm
Originally published: London : Arrow, 1981
ISBN 0-7278-0786-2 : £6.50 B82-25983

Kostov, K. N.. The steppe wolves / K.N. Kostov. — London : Arrow, 1981. — 194p ; 18cm
ISBN 0-09-926700-4 (pbk) : £1.25 B82-03688

Kraus, Bruno. Shark raid / Bruno Kraus. — London : Sphere, 1982. — 121p ; 18cm. — (Sea wolf)
ISBN 0-7221-5283-3 (pbk) : £1.25 B82-18168

Krauss, Bruno. Shark America / Bruno Krauss. — London : Sphere, 1982, c1981. — 120p ; 18cm. — (Sea wolf ; 7)
ISBN 0-7221-5279-5 (pbk) : £1.25 B82-33913

Kroll, Burt. Ambush Range / by Burt Kroll. — London : Hale, 1981. — 160p ; 19cm
ISBN 0-7091-9339-4 : £4.95 B82-02156

Kroll, Burt. Fight or die / by Burt Kroll. — London : Hale, 1982. — 160p ; 20cm
ISBN 0-7091-9672-5 : £5.25 B82-18317

Kruse, John. Red Omega. — London : Bodley Head, Oct.1981. — [288]p
ISBN 0-370-30336-9 : £6.95 : CIP entry B81-25768

Kyle, Duncan. Black Camelot. — Large print ed. — Long Preston : Magna Print, Nov.1982. — [500]p
Originally published: London : Collins, 1978
ISBN 0-86009-439-1 : £5.50 : CIP entry B82-26340

Kyle, Duncan. Green river high / by Duncan Kyle. — Large print ed. — Long Preston : Magna Print, 1981, c1979. — 489p ; 22cm
Originally published: London : Collins, 1979. — Published in large print
ISBN 0-86009-348-4 : Unpriced : CIP rev. B81-27383

Kyle, Elisabeth. The burning hill / by Elisabeth Kyle. — Long Preston : Magna, 1981, c1977. — 319p ; 23cm
Originally published: London : Davies, 1977. — Published in large print
ISBN 0-86009-343-3 : Unpriced : CIP rev. B81-22460

Lacey, Pat. Austrian inheritance / by Pat Lacey. — London : Hale, 1982. — 190p ; 20cm
ISBN 0-7091-9705-5 : £6.25 B82-18319

Lake, Nara. The traitor heart / by Nara Lake. — London : Hale, 1982. — 208p ; 20cm
ISBN 0-7091-9493-5 : £6.95 B82-11073

Lake, Patricia. Heartless love / by Patricia Lake. — London : Mills & Boon, 1982. — 188p ; 19cm
ISBN 0-263-10079-0 : £5.25 B82-30946

Lake, Patricia. Perfect passion / by Patricia Lake. — London : Mills & Boon, 1981. — 187p ; 19cm
ISBN 0-263-09957-1 : £4.55 B82-04635

Lake, Patricia. Wipe away the tears / by Patricia Lake. — London : Mills & Boon, 1982. — 186p ; 19cm
ISBN 0-263-10030-8 : £5.25 B82-18115

Laker, Rosalind. Banners of silk. — London : Eyre Methuen, Sept.1981. — [480]p
ISBN 0-413-48120-4 : £6.95 : CIP entry B81-23910

Laker, Rosalind. Gilded splendour / Rosalind Laker. — London : Methuen, 1982. — 382p ; 23cm
ISBN 0-413-49730-5 : £7.95 : CIP rev. B82-19231

823'.914[F] — Fiction in English, *1945-* — *Texts continuation*

Laker, Rosalind. Ride the blue riband / by Rosalind Laker. — Large print ed. — Bolton-by-Bowland : Magna, 1980, c1977. — 552p ; 23cm
Originally published: Garden City, N.Y. : Doubleday, 1977 ; London : Hale, 1978. — Published in large print
ISBN 0-86009-219-4 : £5.50 : CIP rev. B79-37482

Laker, Rosalind. The Warwycks of Easthampton / Rosalind Laker. — London : Methuen Paperbacks, 1981, c1980. — 350p ; 18cm. — (Magnum books)
Originally published: London : Eyre Methuen, 1980
ISBN 0-417-05550-1 (pbk) : £1.75 B82-15505

Lamark, Drew. The snake orchards / Drew Lamark. — London : Futura, 1982. — 192p ; 18cm
Originally published: London : Macdonald, 1982
ISBN 0-7088-2182-0 (pbk) : £1.35 B82-30773

Lamb, Charlotte. The girl from nowhere / by Charlotte Lamb. — London : Mills & Boon, 1981. — 187p ; 20cm
ISBN 0-263-09952-0 : £4.55 B82-04655

Lamb, Charlotte. Midnight lover / by Charlotte Lamb. — London : Mills & Boon, 1982. — 187p ; 20cm
ISBN 0-263-10060-x : £5.25 B82-27277

Lamb, Charlotte. Midnight lover / by Charlotte Lamb. — London : Mills & Boon, 1982. — 187p ; 18cm
ISBN 0-263-73858-2 (pbk) : £0.85 B82-36285

Lamb, Charlotte. Storm centre / Charlotte Lamb. — Large print ed. — Bath : Chivers, 1981, c1980. — 211p ; 23cm. — (A Seymour book)
Originally published: London : Mills & Boon, 1980
ISBN 0-85119-445-1 : Unpriced : CIP rev. B81-31727

Lamb, Charlotte. A wild affair / by Charlotte Lamb. — London : Mills & Boon, 1982. — 188p ; 19cm
ISBN 0-263-10107-x : £5.95 B82-37443

Lambert, Derek. The red dove. — London : Hamilton, Sept.1982. — [320]p
ISBN 0-241-10867-5 : £7.95 : CIP entry B82-18840

Lambert, Derek. The Saint Peter's plot / Derek Lambert. — [London] : Corgi, 1981, c1978. — 279p ; 18cm
Originally published: London : Arlington Books, 1978
ISBN 0-552-11853-2 (pbk) : £1.50 B82-09001

Lambert, Lee. The Balinese pearls / by Lee Lambert. — London : Hale, 1982. — 160p ; 20cm
ISBN 0-7091-9565-6 : £6.50 B82-15478

Lampitt, Dinah. Getty's mansion. — London : Muller, Feb.1983. — [320]p
ISBN 0-584-31159-1 : £7.95 : CIP entry B82-37654

Lancaster, Graham. The nuclear letters / by Graham Lancaster. — Long Preston : Magna Print, 1982, c1979. — 422p ; 22cm
Originally published: London : Eyre Methuen, 1979. — Published in large print
ISBN 0-86009-392-1 : Unpriced : CIP rev. B82-04827

Lancaster, Sheila. Mistress of fortune / Sheila Lancaster. — London : Hodder and Stoughton, 1982. — 318p ; 23cm
ISBN 0-340-26333-4 : £7.95 : CIP rev. B82-15720

Lance, Leslie. Cousins by courtesy / Leslie Lance. — Large print ed. — Bath : Chivers, 1982, c1977. — 228p ; 23cm. — (A Lythway book)
Originally published: London : Hale, 1977
ISBN 0-85119-818-x : Unpriced : CIP rev. B82-09862

Lance, Leslie. Hawk's head / by Leslie Lance. — London : Hale, 1981. — 207p ; 20cm
ISBN 0-7091-9422-6 : £6.95 B82-06324

Lance, Leslie. Someone who cares / by Leslie Lance. — London : Hale, 1982. — 176p ; 20cm
ISBN 0-7091-9566-4 : £6.25 B82-17475

Landy, Mary. October gold / by Mary Landy. — London : Hale, 1982. — 157p ; 20cm
ISBN 0-7091-9766-7 : £6.50 B82-30273

Lane, Roumelia. Desert haven / by Roumelia Lane. — London : Mills & Boon, 1981. — 191p ; 20cm
ISBN 0-263-09968-7 : £4.55 B82-09363

Lane, Roumelia. Lupin valley / by Roumelia Lane. — London : Mills & Boon, 1982. — 189p ; 20cm
ISBN 0-263-10098-7 : £5.95 B82-37445

Lang, Frances. To be a fine lady / by Frances Lang. — London : Hale, 1982. — 191p ; 20cm
ISBN 0-7091-9578-8 : £6.95 B82-11069

Langford, David. The space eater / David Langford. — London : Arrow, 1982. — 301p ; 18cm
ISBN 0-09-928820-6 (pbk) : £1.75 B82-31613

Langley, Bob. Traverse of the gods. — Large print ed. — Anstey : Ulverscroft Large Print Books, Nov.1982. — [464]p. — (Ulverscroft large print series)
Originally published: New York : Morrow, 1980 ; London : Joseph, 1980
ISBN 0-7089-0879-9 : £5.00 : CIP entry B82-29098

Langley, Bob. Traverse of the gods / Bob Langley. — London : Sphere, 1982, c1980. — xi,242p ; 18cm
Originally published: London : Joseph, 1980
ISBN 0-7221-5410-0 (pbk) : £1.50 B82-17433

Laurance, Andrew. Ouija / Andrew Laurance. — London : W.H. Allen, 1982. — 154p ; 18cm. — (A Star book)
ISBN 0-352-31048-0 (pbk) : £1.50 B82-34179

Lauren, Linda. Pretties. — London : New English Library, Sept.1982. — [224]p
ISBN 0-450-05199-4 (pbk) : £1.50 : CIP entry B82-19687

Lawrence, John, *1920-*. Love is the victim / John Lawrence. — Bongnor : New Horizon, c1982. — 289p ; 21cm
ISBN 0-86116-826-7 : £6.75 B82-15601

Lawrence, Juliet. Atlantic serenade / by Juliet Lawrence. — London : Hale, 1982. — 190p ; 20cm
ISBN 0-7091-9713-6 : £6.25 B82-22861

Lawrence, Louise. The earth witch / Louise Lawrence. — London : Collins, 1982. — 214p ; 21cm
ISBN 0-00-184205-6 : £5.25 B82-18271

Lawton, Cedric. The Master Theron / Cedric Lawton. — [Bognor Regis] : New Horizon, c1981. — 204p ; 21cm
ISBN 0-86116-752-x : £5.75 B82-05535

Layberry, L. G. J.. To be a farmer's girl / L.G.J. Layberry. — Tunbridge Wells : Midas, 1982. — 148p ; 23cm
ISBN 0-85936-289-2 : £5.95 B82-34959

Le Carré, John. Call for the dead / John le Carré. — Bath : Chivers, 1982, c1961. — 203p ; 23cm. — (A New Portway large print book)
Originally published: London : Gollancz, 1961
ISBN 0-85119-175-4 : Unpriced : CIP rev. B82-13088

Le Carré, John. The little drummer girl. — London : Hodder & Stoughton, Feb.1983. — [512]p
ISBN 0-340-32847-9 : £8.95 : CIP entry B82-38033

Le Carré, John. A murder of quality. — Large print ed. — Bath : Chivers, Nov.1982. — [256] p. — (A New Portway large print book)
Originally published: London : Gollancz, 1962
ISBN 0-85119-190-8 : £5.90 : CIP entry B82-26427

Le Carre, John. The quest for Karla. — London : Hodder and Stoughton, Sept.1982. — [992]p
ISBN 0-340-28376-9 : £8.95 : CIP entry B82-18795

Leach, Christopher, *1925-*. A killing frost : a novel / Christopher Leach. — London : Dent, 1982. — 234p ; 25cm
ISBN 0-460-04537-7 : £7.50 : CIP rev. B82-09710

Lear, Peter. Spider girl / Peter Lear. — London : Granada, 1982, c1980. — 292p ; 18cm. — (A Mayflower book)
Originally published: London : Cassell, 1980
ISBN 0-583-13462-9 (pbk) : £1.50 B82-14110

Leasor, James. Follow the drum / James Leasor. — Leicester : Charnwood, 1982, c1972. — 631p ; 22cm
Originally published: London : Heinemann, 1972. — Published in large print
ISBN 0-7089-8033-3 : Unpriced : CIP rev. B82-08111

Leasor, James. Green Beach / James Leasor. — London : Corgi, 1982, c1975. — 288p ; 18cm
Originally published: London : Heinemann, 1975
ISBN 0-552-11922-9 (pbk) : £1.75 B82-23911

Leasor, James. Open secret. — London : Collins, July 1982. — [320]p
ISBN 0-00-222336-8 : £7.95 : CIP entry B82-12427

Leasor, James. Passport for a pilgrim. — Large print ed. — Anstey : Ulverscroft, Aug.1982. — [400]p. — (Ulverscroft large print series)
Originally published: London : Heinemann, 1968
ISBN 0-7089-0837-3 : £5.00 : CIP entry B82-27000

Leasor, James. The unknown warrior. — Large print ed. — Long Preston : Magna Print, Sept.1982. — [550]p
Originally published: London : Heinemann, 1980
ISBN 0-86009-429-4 : £6.75 : CIP entry B82-20852

Leasor, James. X-Troop / James Leasor. — London : Corgi, 1982, c1980. — 287p ; 18cm
Originally published: London : Heinemann, 1980
ISBN 0-552-11921-0 (pbk) : £1.50 B82-23910

Leather, Edwin. The Duveen letter / Edwin Leather. — Large print ed. — Bath : Chivers, 1982, c1980. — 268p ; 23cm. — (A Lythway book)
Originally published: London : Macmillan, 1980
ISBN 0-85119-795-7 : Unpriced : CIP rev. B82-01431

Lee, Tanith. Death's master / Tanith Lee. — Feltham : Hamlyn Paperbacks, 1982, c1979. — 320p ; 18cm
ISBN 0-600-20191-0 (pbk) : £1.50 B82-37126

823'.914[F] — Fiction in English, *1945-* — *Texts continuation*

Lee, Tanith. Night's master / Tanith Lee. — London : Hamlyn Paperbacks, 1981, c1978. — 188p ; 18cm. — (Hamlyn science fiction)
Originally published: S.l. : s.n., 1978
ISBN 0-600-20130-9 (pbk) : £1.10 B82-03689

Lees, Marguerite. Affair in Provence / Marguerite Lees. — Large print ed. — Bath : Chivers, 1982, c1978. — 237p ; 23cm. — (A Lythway book)
Originally published: London : Mills and Boon, 1978
ISBN 0-85119-837-6 : Unpriced : CIP rev. B82-15869

Legat, Michael. Mario's vineyard / Michael Legat. — London : Corgi, 1981, c1980. — 477p ; 18cm
Originally published: London : Souvenir, 1980
ISBN 0-552-11814-1 (pbk) : £1.75 B82-06417

Legat, Michael. Mario's vineyard. — Large print ed. — Anstey : Ulverscroft, Feb.1983. — 1v.. — (Charnwood library series)
Originally published: London : Souvenir, 1980
ISBN 0-7089-8099-6 : £7.95 : CIP entry B82-38890

Legat, Michael. The Silver Fountain / Michael Legat. — London : Souvenir, 1982. — 345p ; 23cm
ISBN 0-285-62494-6 : £7.95 B82-22111

Leigh, James. The ludi victor / James Leigh. — [St. Albans] : Triad, 1982, c1981. — 287p ; 18cm
Originally published: New York : Coward, McCann & Geoghegan, 1980 ; London : Bodley Head, 1981
ISBN 0-586-05397-2 (pbk) : £1.50 B82-36054

Leigh, Robert. The cheap dream / Robert Leigh. — London : Macmillan, 1982. — 170p ; 23cm
ISBN 0-333-32136-7 : £6.95 B82-13592

Leigh, Roberta. Cupboard love / Roberta Leigh. — London : Mills & Boon, c1976 (1982 [printing]). — 189p ; 18cm
ISBN 0-263-73921-x (pbk) : £0.85 B82-40466

Leitch, Maurice. Silver's city / Maurice Leitch. — London : Secker & Warburg, 1981. — 180p ; 23cm
ISBN 0-436-24413-6 : £6.95 : CIP rev. B81-25319

Lemarchand, Elizabeth. Change for the worse / Elizabeth Lemarchand. — Large print ed. — Leicester : Ulverscroft, 1982, c1980. — 314p : 1ill ; 22cm. — (Ulverscroft Large print series)
Originally published: Loughton : Piatkus, 1980
ISBN 0-7089-0773-3 : £5.00 : CIP rev. B81-36934

Lemarchand, Elizabeth. Nothing to do with the case. — Large print ed. — Anstey : Ulverscroft, Sept.1982. — [336]p. — (Ulverscroft large print series)
Originally published: Loughton : Piatkus, 1981
ISBN 0-7089-0843-8 : £5.00 : CIP entry B82-27174

Lemarchand, Elizabeth. Troubled waters / Elizabeth Lemarchand. — Loughton : Piatkus, 1982. — 214p : 1map ; 21cm
ISBN 0-86188-133-8 : £6.50 : CIP rev. B81-34639

Leopold, Christopher. Looneyhime. — London : Hodder & Stoughton, July 1982. — [256]p. — (Coronet books)
Originally published: London : Hamilton, 1979
ISBN 0-340-25088-7 (pbk) : £1.50 : CIP entry B82-12249

Leslie, Richard. The bloodied hawks / by Richard Leslie. — London : Hale, 1981. — 192p ; 20cm
ISBN 0-7091-9351-3 : £6.95 B82-02811

Leslie, Richard. Dusk patrol / Richard Leslie. — Large print ed. — Bath : Chivers, 1982, c1980. — 230p ; 23cm. — (A Lythway book)
Originally published: London : Hale, 1980
ISBN 0-85119-786-8 : Unpriced : CIP rev. B81-35860

Leslie, Richard. Night raiders / Richard Leslie. — London : Hale, 1982. — 206p ; 20cm
ISBN 0-7091-9431-5 : £7.50 B82-31623

Leslie, Richard. Sunset flight / Richard Leslie. — London : Hale, 1982. — 191p ; 21cm
ISBN 0-7091-9385-8 : £6.95 B82-13850

Lessing, Doris. The golden notebook / Doris Lessing. — Rev. ed. — London : Joseph, 1972 (1982 [printing]). — 638p ; 23cm
ISBN 0-7181-0970-8 : £9.95 B82-36229

Lessing, Doris. The making of the representative for Planet 8 / Doris Lessing. — London : Cape, 1982. — 144p ; 23cm. — (Canopus in Argos)
ISBN 0-224-02008-0 : £6.50 : CIP rev. B82-06493

Lessing, Doris. the marriages between Zones Three, Four, and Five : as narrated by the Chroniclers of Zone Three / Doris Lessing. — London : Granada, 1981, c1980. — 299p ; 18cm. — (Canopus in Argos)
Originally published: London : Cape, 1980
ISBN 0-586-05338-7 (pbk) : £1.95 B82-02996

Leverson, Ada. The little Ottleys. — London : Virago, Nov.1982. — [528]p. — (Virago modern classics)
Originally published: London : MacGibbon & Kee, 1962
ISBN 0-86068-300-1 (pbk) : £3.95 : CIP entry B82-26347

Levey, Michael. Tempting fate : a novel / by Michael Levey. — London : Hamilton, 1982. — 220p ; 23cm
ISBN 0-241-10801-2 : £7.95 : CIP rev. B82-18832

Lewis, Colin. Acid test / Colin Lewis. — Feltham : Hamlyn, 1982. — 221p ; 18cm
ISBN 0-600-20308-5 (pbk) : £1.50 B82-28546

Lewis, J. R. (John Royston). A certain blindness. — Large print ed. — Bath : Chivers Press, Dec.1982. — [256]p. — (A Lythway book)
Originally published: London : Collins, 1980
ISBN 0-85119-872-4 : £6.90 : CIP entry B82-30227

Lewis, J. R. (John Royston). Dwell in danger / Roy Lewis. — London : Collins, 1982. — 186p ; 20cm
ISBN 0-00-231897-0 : £6.50 : CIP rev. B82-07222

Lewis, Maynah. Before the darkness falls / Maynah Lewis. — London : Hamlyn Paperbacks, 1981. — 155p ; 18cm. — (A Sapphire romance)
ISBN 0-600-20413-8 (pbk) : £0.75 B82-00645

Lewis, Maynah. Hour of the siesta / Maynah Lewis. — London : Hale, 1982. — 158p ; 20cm
ISBN 0-7091-9636-9 : £6.25 B82-15479

Lewis, Norman. Cuban passage / Norman Lewis. — London : Collins, 1982. — 250p ; 22cm
ISBN 0-00-222620-0 : £7.50 : CIP rev. B82-03702

Lewis, Richard, *1945-*. Parasite / Richard Lewis. — Feltham : Hamlyn Paperbacks, 1980 (1981 [printing]). — 187p ; 18cm
ISBN 0-600-20066-3 (pbk) : £1.25 B82-38089

Lewis, Richard, *1945-*. The web / Richard Lewis. — London : Hamlyn Paperbacks, 1981. — 204p ; 18cm. — (A Hamlyn original)
ISBN 0-600-20271-2 (pbk) : £1.10 B82-00644

Lewis, Roy. A gathering of ghosts. — London : Collins, Nov.1982. — [224]p. — (The Crime Club)
ISBN 0-00-231412-6 : £6.75 : CIP entry B82-27798

Lewty, Marjorie. A girl bewitched / by Marjorie Lewty. — London : Mills & Boon, 1981. — 186p ; 20cm
ISBN 0-263-09966-0 : £4.55 B82-09227

Lewty, Marjorie. Makeshift marriage / by Marjorie Lewty. — London : Mills & Boon, 1982. — 188p ; 19cm
ISBN 0-263-10110-x : £5.95 B82-37275

Ley, Alice Chetwynd. [Letters for a spy]. The sentimental spy / Alice Chetwynd Ley. — South Yarmouth, Mass. : Curley, 1979, c1970 ; [Long Preston] : Distributed by Magna. — 331p ; 23cm
Originally published: London : Hale, 1970. — Published in large print
ISBN 0-89340-175-7 : £4.75 B82-17032

Ley, Alice Chetwynd. [The tenant of Chesdene Manor]. Beloved Diana / Alice Chetwynd Ley. — South Yarmouth, Mass. : Curley, 1979, c1974 ; [Long Preston] : Distributed by Magna. — 377p ; 23cm
Originally published: London : Hale, 1974. — Published in large print
ISBN 0-89340-176-5 : £4.75 B82-17034

Lilley, Mike. Night gossip. — Telford (84 Wolverley Court, Woodside, Telford, Shropshire) : Woody Books, Mar.1982. — [72]p
ISBN 0-907751-03-2 (pbk) : £1.20 : CIP entry B82-07134

Lillis, Molly. By love bewitched / by Molly Lillis. — London : Hale, 1981. — 160p ; 20cm
ISBN 0-7091-9192-8 : £5.95 B82-11070

Lillis, Molly. That special love / by Molly Lillis. — London : Hale, 1982. — 187p ; 20cm
ISBN 0-7091-9847-7 : £6.50 B82-31624

Linaker, Michael R.. Scorpion: Second generation / Michael R. Linaker. — London : New English Library, 1982. — 158p ; 18cm
ISBN 0-450-05363-6 (pbk) : £1.25 : CIP rev. B81-36203

Lind, Jakov. Travels to the Enu. — London : Eyre Methuen, Mar.1982. — [128]p
ISBN 0-413-46780-5 : £6.50 : CIP entry B82-01993

Lindsay, Kathleen. For ever you'll be mine / Kathleen Lindsay. — Large print ed. — Leicester : Ulverscroft, 1982, c1958. — 392p ; 23cm. — (Ulverscroft large print series)
Originally published: London : Hurst & Blackett, 1958
ISBN 0-7089-0792-x : Unpriced : CIP rev. B82-18554

Lindsay, Paula. The bounds of love. — Large print ed. — Bath : Chivers, Oct.1982. — [288]p. — (A Lythway book)
Originally published: London : Wright and Brown, 1960
ISBN 0-85119-855-4 : £7.20 : CIP entry B82-25761

Lindsay, Rachel. Mask of gold / Rachel Lindsay. — Large print ed. — Leicester : Ulverscroft, 1981, c1969. — 404p ; 23cm. — (Ulverscroft large print series)
Originally published: London : Oliphant, 1953
ISBN 0-7089-0706-7 : £5.00 : CIP rev. B81-30505

Lindsay, Rachel. Second best wife / by Rachel Lindsay. — London : Mills & Boon, 1982. — 186p ; 20cm
ISBN 0-263-10095-2 : £5.95 B82-37438

823'.914[F] — Fiction in English, *1945- — Texts continuation*

Lindsey, Johanna. Paradise wild / Johanna Lindsey. — Feltham : Hamlyn, 1982, c1981. — 288p ; 18cm
ISBN 0-600-20613-0 (pbk) : £1.50 B82-30766

Lindsey, Olive. September spring / by Olive Lindsey. — London : Hale, 1982. — 170p ; 20cm
ISBN 0-7091-9767-5 : £6.50 B82-30398

Linegar, Adrian H. G.. The first chronicle of the Sylm / Adrian H.G. Linegar. — Bognor Regis : New Horizon, c1982. — 291p,[10]leaves of plates : ill,1map ; 22cm
ISBN 0-86116-592-6 : £6.75 B82-10299

Lingard, Joan. The gooseberry / Joan Lingard. — London : Beaver, 1982, c1978. — 159p ; 18cm
Originally published: London : Hamilton, 1978. — For adolescents
ISBN 0-600-20482-0 (pbk) : £0.95 B82-10363

Lingard, Joan. Joan Lingard's Maggie : The clearance, The resettling, The pilgrimage. — London : Hamilton, 1982. — 479p ; 23cm
The clearance originally published: 1974 — The resettling originally published : 1975 — The pilgrimage originally published : 1976
ISBN 0-241-10773-3 : £5.95 : CIP rev.
B82-01826

Little, Patrick. A court for owls / Patrick Little. — London : Macmillan, 1981. — 192p ; 21cm
For adolescents
ISBN 0-333-31076-4 : £5.50 : CIP rev.
B81-25780

Lively, Penelope. Judgement day / Penelope Lively. — Harmondsworth : Penguin, 1982, c1980. — 167p ; 19cm
Originally published: London : Heinemann, 1980
ISBN 0-14-006118-5 (pbk) : £1.75 B82-40374

Lively, Penelope. Next to nature, art / Penelope Lively. — London : Heinemann, 1982. — 185p ; 22cm
ISBN 0-434-42739-x : £6.95 B82-22094

Livette, Jeanne. Sweet Bryony / Jeanne Livette. — London : Macdonald, 1981. — 248p ; 21cm. — (A Minstrel book ; 23)
ISBN 0-354-04741-8 (cased) : £4.95
ISBN 0-7088-2115-4 (pbk) : £0.95 B82-05815

Llewellyn, Sam. Gurney's release / Sam Llewellyn. — Large print ed. — Leicester : Ulverscroft, 1981, c1979. — 554p ; 23cm. — (Ulverscroft large print series)
Originally published: London : Arlington, 1979
ISBN 0-7089-0727-x : £5.00 : CIP rev.
B81-32609

Llewellyn, Sam. Gurney's reward / Sam Llewellyn. — Large print ed. — Leicester : Ulverscroft, 1981, c1978. — 466p ; 23cm. — (Ulverscroft large print series)
Originally published: London : Arlington, 1978
ISBN 0-7089-0699-0 : £5.00 : CIP rev.
B81-28100

Llewellyn, Sam. Hell Bay. — London : Hodder and Stoughton, June 1982. — [496]p. — (Coronet books)
Originally published: London : Arlington Books, 1980
ISBN 0-340-26791-7 (pbk) : £2.50 : CIP entry
B82-10008

Llewellyn, Sam. The last will and testament of Robert Louis Stevenson / Sam Llewellyn. — London : Arlington, c1981. — 284p ; 22cm
ISBN 0-85140-544-4 : £6.95 : CIP rev.
B81-20096

Lloyd, A. R.. Kine / A.R. Lloyd. — [Feltham] : Hamlyn Paperbacks, 1982. — 255p : 1map ; 18cm
ISBN 0-600-20467-7 (pbk) : £1.50 B82-36079

Lloyd, Levanah. Dark surrender / Levanah Lloyd. — London : Macdonald & Co., 1982. — 252p ; 21cm
ISBN 0-356-08503-1 : £4.95 B82-15326

Lodge, David. Changing places : a tale of two campuses / David Lodge. — Harmondsworth : Penguin, 1978, c1975 (1981 [printing]). — 250p ; 18cm
Originally published: London : Secker & Warburg, 1975
ISBN 0-14-004656-9 (pbk) : £1.50 B82-01399

Lodge, David. Ginger, you're barmy. — London : Secker & Warburg, Aug.1982. — [232]p
Originally published: London : Macgibbon and Kee, 1962
ISBN 0-436-25662-2 : £6.95 : CIP entry
B82-15795

Long, Freda M.. The apprentice monarchs / by Freda M. Long. — London : Hale, 1982. — 172p ; 20cm
ISBN 0-7091-9730-6 : £6.95 B82-27319

Long, Freda M.. The boy from Corsica / by Freda M. Long. — London : Hale, 1981. — 192p ; 21cm
Based on the life of Napolean Bonaparte
ISBN 0-7091-9530-3 : £6.95 B82-07193

Long, Jean M.. Passport to happiness / Jean M. Long. — London : Hale, 1982. — 175p ; 19cm
ISBN 0-7091-9669-5 : £6.25 B82-22117

Longrigg, Roger. Bad bet / Roger Longrigg. — London : Hamilton, 1982. — 374p ; 23cm
ISBN 0-241-10760-1 : £7.95 : CIP rev.
B82-04308

Loraine, Philip. Sea-change / Philip Loraine. — London : Collins, 1982. — 190p ; 21cm. — (Collins crime club)
ISBN 0-00-231725-7 : £6.50 : CIP rev.
B82-10569

Lord, Shirley. Golden hill. — London : Muller, Feb.1983. — [544]p
ISBN 0-584-31160-5 (pbk) : £7.95 : CIP entry
B82-38861

Lorrimer, Claire. Chantal / Claire Lorrimer. — London : Corgi, 1981, c1980 (1982 [printing]). — x,429p ; 18cm
Originally published: London : Arlington, 1980
ISBN 0-552-11726-9 (pbk) : £1.95 B82-39336

Lorrimer, Claire. The chatelaine. — London : Arlington Books, May 1981. — [496]p
ISBN 0-85140-531-2 : £6.95 : CIP entry
B81-08806

Lorrimer, Claire. The chatelaine / Claire Lorrimer. — London : Corgi, 1982, c1981. — 523p ; 18cm
Originally published: London : Arlington, 1981
ISBN 0-552-11959-8 (pbk) : £1.95 B82-23908

Lorrimer, Claire. Mavreen : a novel / by Claire Lorrimer. — London : Corgi, 1977, c1976 (1982 [printing]). — 561p ; 18cm
Originally published: London : Arlington Books, 1976
ISBN 0-552-10584-8 (pbk) : £1.95 B82-35480

Lorrimer, Claire. The wilderling. — London : Arlington Books, Apr.1982. — [480]p
ISBN 0-85140-576-2 : £7.50 : CIP entry
B82-04787

Lovell, Marc. The last seance / by Marc Lovell. — London : Hale, 1982. — 190p ; 20cm
ISBN 0-7091-9778-0 : £6.75 B82-31625

Lovesey, Peter. The false Inspector Dew / Peter Lovesey. — London : Macmillan, 1982. — 251p ; 23cm
ISBN 0-333-32748-9 : £6.95 B82-27331

Lowe-Watson, Dawn. The good morrow / by Dawn Lowe-Watson. — Long Preston : Magna, 1982, c1980. — 448p ; 23cm
Originally published: London : Heinemann, 1980. — Published in large print
ISBN 0-86009-370-0 : Unpriced : CIP rev.
B81-33768

Lowe-Watson, Dawn. A sound of water / Dawn Lowe-Watson. — London : Hodder and Stoughton, 1982. — 207p ; 23cm
ISBN 0-340-28166-9 : £7.95 : CIP rev.
B82-12236

Lowing, Anne. The branch and the briar / Anne Lowing. — Large print ed. — Bath : Chivers, 1982, c1976. — 188p ; 23cm. — (A Lythway book)
Originally published: London : Hale, 1976
ISBN 0-85119-787-6 : Unpriced : CIP rev.
B81-35859

Lucas, Jeremy. Whale / Jeremy Lucas. — Bath : Chivers, 1982, c1981. — x,199p ; 23cm. — (A Lythway general novel)
Originally published: London : Cape, 1981
ISBN 0-85119-811-2 : Unpriced : CIP rev.
B82-07015

Luellen, Valentina. Prince of deception / Valentina Luellen. — London : Mills & Boon, 1982. — 191p ; 20cm. — (Masquerade)
ISBN 0-263-10024-3 : £5.25 B82-13882

Luellen, Valentina. The silver salamander / Valentina Luellen. — London : Mills & Boon, 1982. — 190p ; 19cm. — (Masquerade)
ISBN 0-263-10130-4 : £5.95 B82-37267

Lutz, Gunther. Panzer platoon : invade Russia! / Gunther Lutz. — London : Severn House, 1980, c1977. — 174p ; 20cm
Originally published: London : Sphere, 1977
ISBN 0-7278-0630-0 : £4.95 : CIP rev.
B80-10300

Lyall, Gavin. A slightly private war. — London : Hodder and Stoughton, Oct.1982. — [240]p
ISBN 0-340-28587-7 : £7.95 : CIP entry
B82-24834

Lyle, Elizabeth. Cassy. — London : Hodder & Stoughton, Aug.1982. — [304]p
Originally published: London : Joseph, 1981
ISBN 0-340-28108-1 (pbk) : £1.95 : CIP entry
B82-15735

Lyle, Elizabeth. Cassy. — Large print ed. — Anstey : Ulverscroft, Oct.1982. — [512]p. — (Ulverscroft large print series)
Originally published: London : Joseph, 1981
ISBN 0-7089-0862-4 : £5.00 : CIP entry
B82-26683

Lynch, Francis. In the house of dark music. — London : Coronet, Dec.1982. — [320]p
Originally published: London : Hodder and Stoughton, 1979
ISBN 0-340-28652-0 (pbk) : £1.95 : CIP entry
B82-29646

Lynch, Liam. Shell, sea shell. — Dublin : Wolfhound Press, June 1982. — [192]p
ISBN 0-905473-80-9 : £7.50 : CIP entry
B82-12018

Lynn, Vince. The Circle C war / by Vince Lynn. — London : Hale, 1982. — 176p ; 20cm
ISBN 0-7091-9869-8 : £5.50 B82-34191

Lynn, Vince. Debts to repay / by Vince Lynn. — London : Hale, 1982. — 188p ; 21cm
ISBN 0-7091-9525-7 : £4.95 B82-11393

Lynne, James Broom. Rogue diamond / James Broom Lynne. — Leicester : Charnwood, 1982, c1980. — 533p ; 23cm. — (Charnwood library series)
Originally published: London : Joseph, 1980. — Published in large print
ISBN 0-7089-8044-9 : Unpriced : CIP rev.
B82-15944

823'.914[F] — Fiction in English, *1945-* **—** *Texts continuation*

Lyons, Elena. The haunting of Abbotsgarth / Elena Lyons. — Large print ed. — Bath : Chivers, 1981, c1980. — 238p ; 23cm. — (A Lythway book)
Originally published: Loughton : Piatkus, 1980
ISBN 0-85119-758-2 : Unpriced : CIP rev.
B81-31248

MacArthur, Catherine. The flight of the dove / Catherine MacArthur. — Large print ed. — Leicester : Ulverscroft, 1982, c1980. — 340p ; 22cm. — (Ulverscroft Large print series)
Originally published: Feltham : Hamlyn, 1980
ISBN 0-7089-0791-1 : £5.00 : CIP rev.
B81-36933

MacBeth, George. A kind of treason : a novel : based on the war diaries of John Beeby / George MacBeth. — London : Hodder and Stoughton, 1981. — 239p ; 23cm
ISBN 0-340-26490-x (corrected) : £6.95 : CIP rev. B81-38329

McCaffrey, Mary. One way to Rome / Mary McCaffrey. — London : Abelard, 1982. — 125p ; 21cm
ISBN 0-200-72777-x : £5.25 : CIP rev.
B82-07525

McCrum, Robert. A loss of heart : a novel / by Robert McCrum. — London : Hamilton, 1982. — 282p ; 22cm
ISBN 0-241-10705-9 : £7.95 : CIP rev.
B81-35818

McCulloch, Sarah. A lady for Ludovic. — Bath : Firecrest, Jan.1983. — [160]p
Originally published: London : Corgi, 1981
ISBN 0-85997-509-6 : £5.50 : CIP entry
B82-33126

McCulloch, Sarah. Merely a gentleman / Sarah McCulloch. — [London] : Corgi, 1982. — 203p ; 18cm
ISBN 0-552-11908-3 (pbk) : £1.25 B82-19466

McCutchan, Philip. Cameron in the gap / Philip McCutchan. — London : Barker, 1982. — 155p ; 23cm
ISBN 0-213-16837-5 : £6.50 B82-37574

McCutchan, Philip. Cameron's convoy / Philip McCutchan. — London : Barker, c1982. — 156p ; 23cm
ISBN 0-213-16822-7 : £5.95 B82-22048

McCutchan, Philip. Halfhyde on Zanatu / Philip McCutchan. — London : Weidenfeld and Nicolson, c1982. — 165p ; 23cm
ISBN 0-297-78144-8 : £6.50 B82-32967

McCutchan, Philip. Skyprobe. — Large print ed. — Long Preston : Magna, Feb.1983. — [400]p
Originally published: London : Harrap, 1966
ISBN 0-86009-458-8 : £5.75 : CIP entry
B82-39611

McCutchan, Philip. Sunstrike / by Philip McCutchan. — Large print ed. — Long Preston : Magna, 1981, c1979. — 381p ; 23cm
Originally published: London : Hodder & Stoughton, 1979. — Published in large print
ISBN 0-86009-347-6 : Unpriced : CIP rev.
B81-27384

McCutchan, Philip. Werewolf : a 'Commander Shaw' novel / Philip McCutchan. — London : Hodder and Stoughton, c1982. — 187p ; 23cm
ISBN 0-340-25005-4 : £6.95 : CIP rev.
B82-01835

McDermott, Brian. Who killed Robin Cock? / by Brian McDermott. — London : Hale, 1981. — 192p ; 20cm
ISBN 0-7091-9425-0 : £6.25 B82-02140

MacDonald, Malcolm, *1932-*. Abigail. — London : Coronet, Apr.1981. — [448]p
Originally published: 1979
ISBN 0-340-26216-8 (pbk) : £1.95 : CIP entry
B81-01459

Macdonald, Peter, *1928-*. Exit / Peter Macdonald. — London : Hale, 1982. — 176p ; 21cm
ISBN 0-7091-9411-0 : £6.95 B82-16179

MacDougall, Carl. The one legged tap dancer / by Carl MacDougall. — Glasgow : Glasgow Print Studio, 1981. — 13p : ill ; 26cm
ISBN 0-906112-18-4 (pbk) : £0.95
ISBN 0-906112-19-2 (signed copies) : £1.95
B82-24526

McEvoy, Marjorie. The wych stone / by Marjorie McEvoy. — Long Preston : Magna, 1982, c1974. — 290p ; 22cm
Originally published: Great Britain : s.n., 1974. — Published in large print
ISBN 0-86009-396-4 : Unpriced : CIP rev.
B82-07049

McGill, Gordon. See no evil. — Bath : Firecrest, Jan.1983. — [160]p
Originally published: London : Sphere, 1981
ISBN 0-85997-510-x : £5.50 : CIP entry
B82-33127

McGiveny, Maura. Duquesa by default / by Maura McGiveny. — London : Mills & Boon, 1982. — 190p ; 20cm
ISBN 0-263-10052-9 : £5.25 B82-27279

McGrath, Laura. Mayan magic / by Laura McGrath. — London : Mills & Boon, 1982. — 191p ; 20cm
ISBN 0-263-10103-7 : £5.95 B82-37441

McGuire, Sarah. Dance to a different drum / Sarah McGuire. — London : Hale, 1982. — 208p ; 21cm
ISBN 0-7091-9895-7 : £7.50 B82-37250

McInniss, Jean. Ghosts at Rycote Hall / by Jean McInniss. — Birkenhead : Countyrise, [1982?]. — 153p : ill ; 21cm
ISBN 0-907768-05-9 (pbk) : Unpriced
B82-37296

Macintyre, Lorn. Cruel in the shadow. — Large print ed. — Anstey : Ulverscroft, Oct.1982. — [576]p. — (Ulverscroft large print series)
Originally published: London : Collins, 1979
ISBN 0-7089-0867-5 : £5.00 : CIP entry
B82-26688

MacKenzie, Lee. The homecoming / Lee MacKenzie ; based on the successful Yorkshire Television series originated by Kevin Laffan. — [London] : Fontana, 1982. — 156p ; 18cm. — (Emmerdale Farm ; book 16)
ISBN 0-00-616439-0 (pbk) : £1.00 B82-09400

Mackenzie, Lee. Old flames / Lee Mackenzie ; based on the successful Yorkshire Television series originated by Kevin Laffan. — [Glasgow] : Fontana, c1982. — 160p ; 18cm. — (Emmerdale Farm ; bk.17)
ISBN 0-00-616440-4 (pbk) : £1.00 B82-38635

McKew, Robert. Death list / Robert McKew and Reed de Rouen. — London : Futura, 1979. — 251p ; 18cm
ISBN 0-7088-1503-0 (pbk) : £0.90 B82-10548

Mackie, Mary. Nightflower / by Mary Mackie. — London : Hale, 1981. — 159p ; 20cm
ISBN 0-7091-9363-7 : £5.95 B82-12620

MacLachlan, Margie. Redcoat for a Jacobite / by Margie MacLachlan. — London : Hale, 1982. — 159p ; 19cm
ISBN 0-7091-9690-3 : £6.95 B82-22120

McLaren, Colin Andrew. A twister over the Thames / Colin Andrew McLaren. — London : Collings, c1981. — 172p : maps ; 23cm
Maps on lining papers
ISBN 0-86036-160-8 : £5.00 B82-03673

MacLaverty, Bernard. Cal. — London : Cape, Jan.1983. — [170]p
ISBN 0-224-02062-5 : £6.95 : CIP entry
B82-32849

MacLean, Alistair. Four great adventure stories / by Alistair MacLean ; introduction by Carl Foreman. — London : Collins, 1981. — 848p ; 23cm. — (Collins' collectors' choice)
Contents : When eight bells toll — The Golden Gate — Caravan to Vaccarès — Circus
ISBN 0-00-243347-8 : £6.95 : CIP rev.
B81-28765

MacLean, Alistair. Partisans / Alistair MacLean. — London : Collins, 1982. — 224p ; 21cm
ISBN 0-00-222690-1 : £7.50 : CIP rev.
B82-23078

MacLean, Alistair. River of death / Alistair MacLean. — Large print ed. — Leicester : Ulverscroft, 1982, c1981. — 250p ; 23cm. — (Ulverscroft large print series)
Originally published: London : Collins, 1981
ISBN 0-7089-0823-3 : Unpriced : CIP rev.
B82-15962

MacLean, Alistair. Seawitch / Alistair MacLean. — [London] : Fontana, 1979, c1977 (1982 [printing]). — 192p ; 18cm
ISBN 0-00-616474-9 (pbk) : £1.25 B82-09321

MacLean, Alistair. South by Java Head / Alistair MacLean. — [London] : Fontana, 1961, c1958 (1982 [printing]). — 253p ; 18cm
Originally published: London : Collins, 1958
ISBN 0-00-616587-7 (pbk) : £1.50 B82-33551

MacLean, Jan. All our tomorrows / by Jan MacLean. — London : Mills & Boon, 1982. — 188p ; 19cm
ISBN 0-263-10117-7 : £5.95 B82-37272

MacLeod, Jean S.. Meeting in Madrid / Jean S. MacLeod. — Large print ed. — Bath : Chivers, 1981, c1979. — 267p ; 23cm. — (A Lythway book)
Originally published: London : Mills & Boon, 1979
ISBN 0-85119-759-0 : Unpriced : CIP rev.
B81-31247

MacLeod, Jean S.. Moreton's kingdom / by Jean S. MacLeod. — London : Mills & Boon, 1981. — 190p ; 19cm
ISBN 0-263-09938-5 : £4.55 B82-00048

MacLeod, Jean S.. The valley of palms / Jean S. MacLeod. — Large print ed. — Bath : Chivers, 1982, c1977. — 256p ; 23cm. — (Atlantic large print)
Originally published: London : Mills & Boon, 1977
ISBN 0-85119-467-2 : Unpriced : CIP rev.
B82-07620

MacLeod, Robert, *1928-*. A problem in Prague. — London : Hutchinson, Aug.1981. — [184]p
ISBN 0-09-145800-5 : £6.50 : CIP entry
B81-19141

McMaster, Mary. Highland inheritance / Mary McMaster. — London : Hale, 1982. — 159p ; 20cm
ISBN 0-7091-9567-2 : £5.95 B82-12605

McNab, Tom. Flanagan's run : a novel / Tom McNab. — London : Hodder and Stoughton, 1982. — 472p ; 23cm
ISBN 0-340-24393-7 (cased) : £7.95 : CIP rev.
ISBN 0-340-27482-4 (pbk) : £4.95 B82-01169

MacNeil, Duncan. A matter for the regiment : a 'James Ogilvie' novel / Duncan MacNeil. — London : Hodder and Stoughton, 1982. — 191p ; 21cm
ISBN 0-340-28338-6 : £6.95 : CIP rev.
B82-12309

McQueen, Ronald A.. Mardoc / by Ronald A. McQueen. — London : Hale, 1981. — 205p ; 20cm. — (Hale SF)
ISBN 0-7091-9310-6 : £6.25 B82-06329

823'.914[F] — Fiction in English, *1945- — Texts continuation*

McShane, Mark. The halcyon way / Mark McShane. — London : Hale, 1982, c1979. — 219p : ill ; 20cm
Originally published: New York : Manor, 1979
ISBN 0-7091-8672-x : £7.950 B82-27314

Madison, Hank. Bullet justice / by Hank Madison. — London : Hale, 1982. — 160p ; 20cm
ISBN 0-7091-9714-4 : £5.25 B82-17520

Madison, Hank. Hard law / Hank Madison. — London : Hale, 1982. — 160p ; 20cm
ISBN 0-7091-9870-1 : £5.50 B82-34187

Magdalen, I. I.. The search for Anderson : chronicles of the exchange 1963 / I.I. Magdalen. — Tadworth : World's Work, 1982. — 224p ; 23cm
ISBN 0-437-09200-3 : £6.95 B82-30875

Maitland, Derek. Breaking out / Derek Maitland. — Harmondsworth : Penguin, 1982, c1979. — 432p ; 19cm
Originally published: New York : St Martin's Press ; London : Allen Lane, 1979
ISBN 0-14-005339-5 (pbk) : £1.95 B82-39367

Malcolm, Aleen. Ride out the storm / Aleen Malcolm. — [London] : Futura, 1982, c1981. — 554p : 1map ; 18cm. — (A Troubadour book)
ISBN 0-7107-3030-6 (pbk) : £2.25 B82-35717

Malloy, Lester. Beware the yellow Packard / by Lester Malloy. — London : Hale, 1982. — 190p ; 20cm
ISBN 0-7091-9805-1 : £6.75 B82-34192

Malloy, Lester. The happiest ghost in town : a Martin Moon novel / by Lester Malloy. — London : Hale, 1981. — 222p ; 20cm
ISBN 0-7091-9346-7 : £6.25 B82-06330

Malpass, Eric. The long long dances / Eric Malpass. — Large print ed. — Leicester : Ulverscroft, 1982, c1978. — 353p ; 23cm. — (Ulverscroft large print)
Originally published: London : Corgi, 1978
ISBN 0-7089-0825-x : Unpriced : CIP rev. B82-15964

Malpass, Eric. Oh, my darling daughter. — Large print ed. — Anstey : Ulverscroft, Nov.1982. — [384]p. — (Ulverscroft large print series)
Originally published: London : Eyre and Spottiswoode, 1970
ISBN 0-7089-0881-0 : £5.00 : CIP entry B82-29092

Man, John, *1941-*. Gold-dive / John Man and Ann Tweedy. — London : Corgi, 1982. — 189p ; 18cm
ISBN 0-552-12018-9 (pbk) : £1.50 B82-37552

Man, John, *1941-*. The lion's share / John Man. — London : Corgi, 1982. — 317p : 1map,1plan ; 18cm
ISBN 0-552-11886-9 (pbk) : £1.50 B82-16739

Man, Pat. The wall / Pat Man. — Bognor Regis : New Horizon, c1982. — 244p ; 21cm
ISBN 0-86116-691-4 : £5.75 B82-36121

Manley-Tucker, Audrie. The piper in the hills / by Audrie Manley-Tucker. — Long Preston : Magna Print, 1981, c1974. — 341p ; 22cm
Originally published: London : Mills and Boon, 1974. — Published in large print
ISBN 0-86009-346-8 : Unpriced : CIP rev. B81-27385

Manley-Tucker, Audrie. Shadow of yesterday : Audrie Manley-Tucker. — Long Preston : Magna Print, 1982, 1965. — 351p ; 22cm
Originally published: London : Mills & Boon, 1965. — Published in large print
ISBN 0-86009-375-1 : Unpriced : CIP rev. B81-35699

Manley-Tucker, Audrie. Shetland summer / by Audrie Manley-Tucker. — Long Preston : Magna, 1982, c1973. — 361p ; 22cm
Originally published: London : Mills & Boon, 1973. — Published in large print
ISBN 0-86009-395-6 : Unpriced : CIP rev. B82-07048

Mann, James. Endgame. — London : New English Library, Jan.1983. — [256]p
Originally published: 1981
ISBN 0-450-05400-4 (pbk) : £1.50 : CIP entry B82-36138

Mann, Jessica. Funeral sites / Jessica Mann. — London : Macmillan, 1981. — 167p ; 21cm
ISBN 0-333-31812-9 : £5.95 B82-05732

Mann, Phillip. The eye of the queen / by Phillip Mann. — London : Gollancz, 1982. — 264p ; 21cm
ISBN 0-575-03106-9 : £7.95 : CIP rev. B82-07829

Manning, Olivia. The Balkan trilogy / Olivia Manning. — Harmondsworth : Penguin, 1981. — 924p ; 20cm
Contents: The great fortune. Originally published: London : Heinemann, 1960 — The spoilt city. Originally published: London : Heinemann, 1962 — Friends and heroes. Originally published: London : Heinemann, 1965
ISBN 0-14-005936-9 (pbk) : £3.95 B82-06437

Manning, Olivia. School for love / Olivia Manning. — Harmondsworth : Penguin, 1982, c1951. — 191p ; 18cm
Originally published: London : Heinemann, 1951
ISBN 0-14-005932-6 (pbk) : £1.50 B82-29578

Manning, Olivia. The sum of things / Olivia Manning. — Harmondsworth : Penguin, 1982, c1980. — 196p ; 18cm
Originally published: London : Weidenfeld and Nicolson, 1980
ISBN 0-14-005787-0 (pbk) : £1.75 B82-29584

Mansfield, Helene. Contessa. — London : Methuen, Feb.1983. — [494]p
ISBN 0-413-48080-1 : £7.95 : CIP entry B82-38258

Mapleston, Emily. Forget-me-not / Emily Mapleston. — [London] : Fontana, 1982. — 191p ; 18cm. — (Nightshades)
ISBN 0-00-616216-9 (pbk) : £1.00 B82-33836

March, Stella. Barrier to love. — Large print ed. — Bath : Chivers, Sept.1982. — [256]p. — (A Lythway book)
Originally published: London : Wright and Brown, 1965
ISBN 0-85119-847-3 : £6.90 : CIP entry B82-20516

March, Stella. Silk for my lady / by Stella March. — London : Hale, 1982. — 160p ; 20cm
ISBN 0-7091-9549-4 : £6.75 B82-15489

March, Stella. A song in the darkness / by Stella March. — London : Hale, 1982. — 160p ; 20cm
ISBN 0-7091-9886-8 : £7.25 B82-37293

Mark, Jan. Aquarius / Jan Mark. — Harmondsworth : Kestrel, 1982. — 223p ; 23cm
ISBN 0-7226-5793-5 : £5.95 B82-33831

Markstein, George. The ultimate issue. — London : New English Library, Aug.1982. — [384]p
ISBN 0-450-05381-4 (pbk) : £1.75 : CIP entry B82-15804

Marlowe, Derek. Nancy Astor : the lady from Virginia : a novel / by Derek Marlowe. — London : Weidenfeld and Nicolson, 1982. — viii,246p ; 23cm
ISBN 0-297-77866-8 : £6.95 B82-06552

Marsh, Carol. For the love of Lucy / by Carol Marsh. — London : Hale, 1981. — 190p ; 20cm
ISBN 0-7091-9348-3 : £5.75 B82-02158

Marsh, Carol. A primrose for Sarah / by Carol Marsh. — London : Hale, 1982. — 188p ; 20cm
ISBN 0-7091-9733-0 : £6.25 B82-22862

Marshall, Ellis. Return to darkness / Ellis Marshall. — London : Methuen Paperbacks, 1981. — 238p ; 18cm. — (Magnum books)
ISBN 0-417-06860-3 (pbk) : £1.50 B82-15498

Marshall, James Vance. Still waters / James Vance Marshall. — London : Joseph, 1982. — 150p ; 23cm
ISBN 0-7181-2179-1 : £7.95 B82-39209

Martin, Caroline. The chieftain / Caroline Martin. — London : Mills & Boon, 1982. — 191p ; 19cm. — (Masquerade historical romances)
ISBN 0-263-10085-5 : £5.25 B82-30944

Martin, Caroline. The chieftain / Caroline Martin. — London : Mills & Boon, 1982. — 191p ; 18cm. — (Masquerade historical romances)
ISBN 0-263-73906-6 (pbk) : £0.95 B82-36068

Martin, Caroline. The king's favourite / Caroline Martin. — London : Mills & Boon, 1982. — 189p ; 19cm. — (Masquerade)
ISBN 0-263-10039-1 : £5.25 B82-18133

Martin, Netta. Cruise / Netta Martin. — London : Granada, 1981. — 492p ; 18cm. — (A Mayflower book)
ISBN 0-583-13147-6 (pbk) : £1.95 B82-00542

Martin, Rhona. Mango walk / Rhona Martin. — London : Corgi, 1981. — 334p ; 18cm
Originally published: London : Bodley Head, 1981
ISBN 0-552-11872-9 (pbk) : £1.50 B82-16742

Mason, Chuck. Gunman's law / by Chuck Mason. — London : Hale, 1981. — 158p ; 20cm
ISBN 0-7091-9320-3 : £4.95 B82-02155

Massie, Allan. The death of men. — London : Bodley Head, Sept.1981. — [256]p
ISBN 0-370-30339-3 : £6.50 : CIP entry B81-21618

Masters, Anthony. Tenko : a novel / by Anthony Masters ; basd on the BBC-TV series created by Lavinia Warner .... — London : British Broadcasting Corporation, 1981. — 255p ; 22cm
ISBN 0-563-17987-2 : £7.50 B82-04685

Masters, Anthony. Tenko / a novel by Anthony Masters ; based on the BBC-TV series created by Lavinia Warner and scripted by Paul Wheeler, Jill Hyem, Anne Valery. — London : British Broadcasting Corporation, 1981. — 255p ; 18cm
ISBN 0-563-17988-0 (pbk) : £1.50 B82-04214

Masters, John. By the green of the spring : a novel / by John Masters. — London : Joseph, 1981. — 599p : 4geneal.tables ; 23cm
ISBN 0-7181-2057-4 : £8.95 B82-00813

Masters, John. The deceivers / John Masters. — London : Sphere, 1982, c1952. — 285p ; 18cm
Originally published: London : Joseph, 1952
ISBN 0-7221-5873-4 (pbk) : £1.75 B82-34116

Mather, Anne. The autumn of the witch / by Anne Mather. — Long Preston : Magna Print, 1981, c1978. — 363p ; 23cm
Originally published: London : Mills & Boon, 1972. — Published in large print
ISBN 0-86009-341-7 : Unpriced : CIP rev. B81-22463

823'.914[F] — Fiction in English, *1945-* — *Texts continuation*

Mather, Anne. Beware of the beast. — Large print ed. — Long Preston : Magna Print, Sept.1982. — [352]p
Originally published: London : Mills and Boon, 1976
ISBN 0-86009-430-8 : £5.50 : CIP entry
B82-20857

Mather, Anne. Captive destiny / by Anne Mather. — Long Preston : Magna, 1982, c1978. — 312p ; 22cm
Originally published: London : Mills & Boon, 1978. — Published in large print
ISBN 0-86009-388-3 : Unpriced : CIP rev.
B82-04823

Mather, Anne. Charlotte's hurricane / Anne Mather. — Long Preston : Magna Print, 1982, c1970. — 289p ; 22cm
Originally published: London : Mills & Boon, 1970. — Published in large print
ISBN 0-86009-376-x : Unpriced : CIP rev.
B81-35698

Mather, Anne. Duelling fire / by Anne Mather. — London : Mills & Boon, 1981. — 189p ; 20cm
ISBN 0-263-09967-9 : £4.55 B82-09226

Mather, Anne. Edge of temptation / by Anne Mather. — London : Mills & Boon, 1982. — 188p ; 19cm
ISBN 0-263-10046-4 : £5.25 B82-22502

Mather, Anne. For the love of Sara / by Anne Mather. — Long Preston : Magna, 1982, c1975. — 321p ; 23cm
Originally published: London : Mills and Boon, 1976. — Published in large print
ISBN 0-86009-402-2 : Unpriced : CIP rev.
B82-10229

Mather, Anne. Images of love / Anne Mather. — Large print ed. — [Bath] : Chivers, 1982, c1980. — 269p ; 23cm. — (A Seymour large print romance)
Originally published: London : Mills & Boon, 1980
ISBN 0-85119-479-6 : Unpriced : CIP rev.
B82-13091

Mather, Anne. Impetuous masquerade / by Anne Mather. — London : Mills & Boon, 1982. — 188p ; 19cm
ISBN 0-263-10066-9 : £5.25 B82-30934

Mather, Anne. Innocent obsession. — Large print ed. — Bath : Chivers, Nov.1982. — [272]p. — (Atlantic large print)
Originally published: London : Mills & Boon, 1981
ISBN 0-85119-503-2 : £5.25 : CIP entry
B82-26432

Mather, Anne. Lure of eagles / Anne Mather. — Large print ed. — Bath : Chivers, 1981, c1979. — 271p ; 23cm. — (A Lythway book)
Originally published: London : Mills & Boon, 1979
ISBN 0-85119-760-4 : Unpriced : CIP rev.
B81-31273

Mather, Anne. Moon witch / Anne Mather. — Large print ed. — Bath : Chivers, 1982, c1970. — 214p ; 23cm. — (A Lythway romance)
Originally published: London : Mills & Boon, 1970
ISBN 0-85119-803-1 : Unpriced : CIP rev.
B82-05010

Mather, Anne. Season of mists / by Anne Mather. — London : Mills and Boon, 1982. — 188p ; 20cm
ISBN 0-263-10091-x : £5.95 B82-37112

Mather, Anne. Smokescreen / by Anne Mather. — London : Mills & Boon, 1982. — 185p ; 20cm
ISBN 0-263-10012-x : £5.25 B82-13898

Mather, Anne. Stormspell / by Anne Mather. — London : Worldwide Romance, 1982. — 379p ; 19cm
ISBN 0-263-10096-0 : £6.95 B82-24521

Mather, Arthur. The mindbreaker / Arthur Mather. — London : Methuen, 1982, c1980. — 284p ; 18cm
Originally published: Hodder and Stoughton, 1980
ISBN 0-417-06510-8 (pbk) : £1.50 B82-34369

Mather, Berkely. Hour of the dog / Berkely Mather. — London : Collins, 1982. — 346p : 1maps ; 22cm
ISBN 0-00-222670-7 : £7.95 : CIP rev.
B82-15618

Mather, Berkely. The pagoda tree / Berkely Mather. — [London] : Corgi, 1982, c1979. — 287p ; 18cm
Originally published: London : Collins, 1979
ISBN 0-552-11870-2 (pbk) : £1.50 B82-12589

Matthew, Christopher. The Crisp report / Christopher Matthew. — London : Hutchinson, 1981. — 143p ; 23cm
ISBN 0-09-146350-5 : £5.50 : CIP rev.
B81-27373

Matthew, Christopher. Loosely engaged / Christopher Matthew. — London : Arrow, 1981, c1980. — 149p : ill ; 18cm
Originally published: London : Hutchinson, 1980
ISBN 0-09-926520-6 (pbk) : £1.25 B82-03540

Matthews, John, *19---*. Basikasingo / John Matthews. — London : Arrow, 1982. — 485p ; 18cm
ISBN 0-09-927570-8 (pbk) : £1.75 B82-14878

May, Gideon Scott. The croft and ; The Ceilidh / Gideon Scott May ; with sketches by Sandy Cheyne. — Perth : Melven Press, 1981. — 198p : ill ; 23cm
ISBN 0-906664-08-x : £6.50 B82-35469

May, Helen. Sea-Raven's bride / Helen May. — London : Mills & Boon, 1981. — 192p : ill ; 20cm. — (Masquerade)
ISBN 0-263-09988-1 : £4.55 B82-09221

May, Marjorie. The Cockermouth mail / Marjorie May. — London : Mills & Boon, 1982. — 191p ; 20cm. — (Masquerade)
ISBN 0-263-10106-1 : £5.95 B82-37436

May, Marjorie. That sweet enemy / by Marjorie May. — London : Mills & Boon, 1982. — 190p ; 19cm. — (Masquerade)
ISBN 0-263-09998-9 : £5.25 B82-10369

May, Wynne. Peacock in the jungle / by Wynne May. — London : Mills & Boon, 1982. — 189p ; 19cm
ISBN 0-263-10047-2 : £5.25 B82-22504

May, Wynne. Wayside flower / by Wynne May. — London : Mills & Boon, 1982. — 189p ; 19cm
ISBN 0-263-10112-6 : £5.95 B82-37269

Maybury, Anne. Jessamy Court / Anne Maybury. — Large print ed. — Leicester : Ulverscroft, 1982, c1974. — 429p ; 22cm. — (Ulverscroft large print)
Originally published: New York : Random House, 1974 ; London : Collins, 1975
ISBN 0-7089-0737-7 : £5.00 : CIP rev.
B81-33960

Mayhew, Elizabeth. The torn banners / Elizabeth Mayhew. — London : Hale, 1981. — 192p ; 21cm
ISBN 0-7091-9229-0 : £6.75 B82-02812

Mayhew, Margaret. The flame and the furnace. — Large print ed. — Anstey : Ulverscroft Large Print Books, Dec.1982. — 1v.. — (Ulverscroft large print series)
Originally published: London : Hamilton, 1981
ISBN 0-7089-0888-8 : £5.00 : CIP entry
B82-30799

Maynard, Nan. One for the stairs / by Nan Maynard. — London : Hale, 1982. — 175p ; 20cm
ISBN 0-7091-9548-6 : £6.95 B82-18309

Mayne, Cora. Hawkesworth / by Cora Mayne. — London : Hale, 1982. — 176p ; 20cm
ISBN 0-7091-9457-9 : £5.95 B82-13839

Mayo, Margaret. Afraid to love / Margaret Mayo. — Large print ed. — Bath : Chivers, 1981, c1978. — 241p ; 23cm. — (A Seymour book)
Originally published: London : Mills & Boon, 1978
ISBN 0-85119-438-9 : Unpriced : CIP rev.
B81-25804

Mayo, Margaret. Bitter reunion / by Margaret Mayo. — London : Mills & Boon, 1982. — 191p ; 19cm
ISBN 0-263-10072-3 : £5.25 B82-30936

Mayo, Margaret. Diamond stud / by Margaret Mayo. — London : Mills & Boon, 1981. — 198p ; 20cm
ISBN 0-263-09974-1 : £4.55 B82-09362

Mayo, Margaret. Divided loyalties / by Margaret Mayo. — London : Mills & Boon, 1981. — 189p ; 19cm
ISBN 0-263-09936-9 : £4.55 B82-00042

Mayo, Margaret. The emerald coast / by Margaret Mayo. — London : Mills & Boon, 1982. — 191p ; 20cm
ISBN 0-263-10014-6 : £5.25 B82-13890

Mayo, Margaret. Mistaken marriage / Margaret Mayo. — Large print ed. — Bath : Chivers, 1981, c1979. — 226p ; 23cm. — (A Seymour book)
Originally published: London : Mills & Boon, 1979
ISBN 0-85119-446-x : Unpriced : CIP rev.
B81-31728

Mayo, Margaret. Stormy affair / Margaret Mayo. — Large print ed. — Bath : Chivers, 1981, c1979. — 219p ; 23cm. — (A Seymour book)
Originally published: London : Mills & Boon, 1979
ISBN 0-85119-441-9 : Unpriced : CIP rev.
B81-31253

Meadmore, Susan. Mary Mary / by Susan Meadmore. — London : Hale, 1982. — 176p ; 20cm
ISBN 0-7091-9848-5 : £6.50 B82-36781

Meadmore, Susan. [A time for everything]. Thunder in the hills / by Susan Meadmore. — London : Hale, 1981. — 218p ; 20cm
Originally published: New York : Harper & Row, 1979
ISBN 0-7091-9451-x : £7.50 B82-00442

Melville, Anne. Lorimers in love / Anne Melville. — London : Heinemann, 1981. — 253p : 1geneal.table ; 23cm
ISBN 0-434-46274-8 : £7.50 B82-02169

Melville, James, *1931-*. The chrysanthemum chain / James Melville. — Large print ed. — Leicester : Ulverscroft, 1982, c1980. — 369p ; 23cm. — (Ulverscroft large print series)
Originally published: London : Secker and Warburg, 1980
ISBN 0-7089-0758-x : Unpriced : CIP rev.
B82-01748

823'.914[F] — Fiction in English, *1945-* — *Texts continuation*

Melville, James, *1931-*. The ninth netsuke / James Melville. — London : Secker & Warburg, 1982. — 151p ; 23cm
ISBN 0-436-27693-3 : £6.95 : CIP rev.
B82-03576

Melville, James, *1931-*. A sort of samurai / James Melville. — London : Methuen London, 1982, c1981. — 167p ; 18cm
Originally published: London : Secker & Warburg: 1981
ISBN 0-417-07240-6 (pbk) : £1.50 B82-33294

Melville, James, *1931-*. A sort of Samurai. — Large print ed. — Anstey : Ulverscroft, Nov.1982. — [336]p. — (Ulverscroft large print series)
Originally published: London : Secker & Warburg, 1981
ISBN 0-7089-0872-1 : £5.00 : CIP entry
B82-29088

Melville-Ross, Anthony. Tightrope / Anthony Melville-Ross. — London : Fontana, 1982, c1981. — 251p ; 18cm
Originally published: London : Collins, 1981
ISBN 0-00-616507-9 (pbk) : £1.50 B82-25445

Melville-Ross, Anthony. Trigger / Anthony Melville-Ross. — London : Collins, 1982. — 288p ; 22cm
ISBN 0-00-221969-7 : £7.50 : CIP rev.
B81-36980

Melville-Ross, Antony. Blindfold / Antony Melville-Ross. — [London] : Fontana, 1979, c1978. — 224p ; 18cm
Originally published: London : Collins, 1978
ISBN 0-00-616548-6 (pbk) : £1.50 B82-36255

Melvin, Frances. Camberwell beauty / Frances Melvin. — London : Hutchinson, 1982. — 188p ; 23cm
ISBN 0-09-146920-1 : £6.95 : CIP rev.
B82-02655

Melwood, Mary. The watcher bee / Mary Melwood. — London : Deutsch, 1982. — 260p ; 20cm
ISBN 0-233-97432-6 (pbk) : £4.50 : CIP rev.
B81-36389

Merlin, Christina. Sword of Mithras / Christina Merlin. — London : Hale, 1982. — 192p ; 21cm
ISBN 0-7091-9681-4 : £6.95 B82-17526

Mewburn, Robert. Through the fog / Robert Mewburn. — Bognor Regis : New Horizon, c1981. — 99p ; 21cm
ISBN 0-86116-363-x : £3.25 B82-02941

Meyrick, Bette. Cockles is convenient / Bette Meyrick. — [Llandysul] : Gomer, 1981. — 160p ; 23cm
ISBN 0-85088-615-5 : £4.95 B82-09530

Middleton, Stanley. Blind understanding / Stanley Middleton. — London : Hutchinson, 1982. — 159p ; 23cm
ISBN 0-09-146990-2 : £7.50 : CIP rev.
B82-01149

Middleton, Stanley. Entry into Jerusalem. — London : Hutchinson, Jan.1983. — [160]p
ISBN 0-09-150950-5 : £7.50 : CIP entry
B82-33457

Midgley, John, *1931-*. The stone killer / by John Midgley. — London : Hale, 1982. — 192p ; 20cm
ISBN 0-7091-9804-3 : £6.75 B82-30427

Miles, Keith. We'll meet again : a novel / by Keith Miles ; based on the London Weekend Television series created by David Butler. — London : Macdonald, 1982. — 380p ; 21cm
ISBN 0-356-08630-5 : £5.95 B82-14098

Miles, Keith. We'll meet again : a novel / by Keith Miles ; based on the London Weekend Television series created by David Butler. — London : Futura, 1982. — 380p ; 18cm
ISBN 0-7088-2146-4 (pbk) : £1.75 B82-10540

Miller, Hugh. Casualty!. — London : Severn House, Sept.1982. — [192]p
ISBN 0-7278-3002-3 : £7.50 : CIP entry
B82-20400

Miller, Jill. Happy as a dead cat. — London : Women's Press, Jan.1983. — 1v.
ISBN 0-7043-3898-x : £2.75 : CIP entry
B82-32524

Miller, John, *19---*. The Chamdo raid / John Miller. — London : Arrow, 1982. — 269p ; 18cm
ISBN 0-09-927940-1 (corrected : pbk) : £1.50
B82-25356

Milne, John. Tyro. — London : Hamilton, Nov.1982. — [160]p
ISBN 0-241-10860-8 : £7.95 : CIP entry
B82-27373

Milne, Paula. John David / Paula Milne. — London : Virago, 1982. — 195p ; 21cm
ISBN 0-86068-236-6 (cased) : £6.95 : CIP rev.
ISBN 0-86068-237-4 (pbk) : £2.95 B82-10236

Milne, Roseleen. The major's lady. — London : Coronet, July 1981. — [224]p
Originally published: London : Hodder & Stoughton, 1979
ISBN 0-340-26672-4 (pbk) : £1.40 : CIP entry
B81-13818

Minghella, Anthony. On the line / Anthony Minghella. — London : Sphere, 1982. — 184p ; 18cm
ISBN 0-7221-6119-0 (pbk) : £1.25 B82-27892

Minghella, Anthony. On the line / Anthony Minghella. — London : Severn House, 1982. — 184p ; 21cm
ISBN 0-7278-0775-7 : £6.50 B82-35460

Mitchell, Gladys. The mudflats of the dead. — Large print ed. — Long Preston : Magna Print, Oct.1982. — [384]p
Originally published: London : Joseph, 1979
ISBN 0-86009-436-7 : £5.50 : CIP entry
B82-24131

Mitchell, James, *1926-*. The evil ones / by James Mitchell. — London : Hamilton, 1982. — 288p ; 23cm
ISBN 0-241-10837-3 : £7.95 : CIP rev.
B82-12573

Mo, Timothy. Sour sweet / Timothy Mo. — London : Deutsch, 1982. — 251p ; 23cm
ISBN 0-233-97365-6 : £7.95 : CIP rev.
B82-11267

Moffat, Gwen. The buckskin girl : a novel of the California trail in the mid-nineteenth century / by Gwen Moffat. — London : Gollancz, 1982. — 191p : 1map ; 22cm
ISBN 0-575-03049-6 : £6.95 : CIP rev.
B81-37571

Moffat, Gwen. Die like a dog : a novel / by Gwen Moffat. — London : Gollancz, 1982. — 160p ; 21cm
ISBN 0-575-03118-2 : £6.95 : CIP rev.
B82-09439

Moggach, Deborah. Hot water man / Deborah Moggach. — London : Cape, 1982. — 251p ; 21cm
ISBN 0-224-01994-5 : £6.95 : CIP rev.
B82-08427

Montague, Jeanne. Flower of my heart / Jeanne Montague. — London : Macdonald, 1981. — 255p ; 21cm
ISBN 0-354-04816-3 : £4.95 B82-00536

Moorcock, Michael. The brothel in Rosenstrasse : an extravagant tale / Michael Moorcock. — London : New English Library, 1982. — 191p ; 22cm
ISBN 0-450-04877-2 : £6.95 : CIP rev.
B82-01977

Moorcock, Michael. Byzantium endures. — London : Secker & Warburg, May 1981. — [420]p
ISBN 0-436-28459-6 : £6.95 : CIP entry
B81-10507

Moorcock, Michael. The great rock 'n' roll swindle / by Michael Moorcock. — 2nd ed. — London : Virgin, 1981. — 128p ; 20cm
Previous ed.: 1980
ISBN 0-907080-13-8 (pbk) : £1.50 B82-36112

Moorcock, Michael. The steel tsar : third volume in the Oswald Bastable trilogy / Michael Moorcock. — London : Granada, 1981. — 153p ; 18cm. — (A Mayflower book)
ISBN 0-583-13432-7 (pbk) : £1.25 B82-09536

Moorcock, Michael. The sword and the stallion / Michael Moorcock. — London : Granada, 1981, c1974. — 171p ; 18cm. — (The Chronicle of Prince Corum and the silver hand ; vol.3)
Originally published: London : Allison and Busby, 1974
ISBN 0-583-12986-2 (pbk) : £1.25 B82-02997

Moorcock, Michael. The war hound and the world's pain / Michael Moorcock. — Sevenoaks : New English Library, 1982, c1981. — vii,198p ; 23cm
Originally published: New York : Timescape Books, 1981
ISBN 0-450-04912-4 : £6.95 B82-38799

Moore, Mary, *1928-*. Run before the wind / by Mary Moore. — London : Mills & Boon, 1982. — 190p ; 20cm
ISBN 0-263-10056-1 : £5.25 B82-27276

Moore, Melissa. The agency : Susan. — London : Severn House, Sept.1982. — [160]p
ISBN 0-7278-0818-4 : £6.50 : CIP entry
B82-23865

Moore, Melissa. The agency: Susan / Melissa Moore. — London : Sphere, 1982, c1981. — 150p ; 18cm
ISBN 0-7221-5087-3 (pbk) : £1.25 B82-22591

Moray, Helga. Carla / Helga Moray. — London : Methuen, 1982. — 459p ; 18cm
ISBN 0-417-06870-0 (pbk) : £2.50 B82-34183

Morgan, Alun, *1918-*. Elizabeth : fair maid of Sker / by Alun Morgan. — Cowbridge : Brown, 1979. — 152p ; 18cm
ISBN 0-905928-02-4 (pbk) : £1.35 B82-25429

Morgan, Anna. Shine on Harvey Moon. — London : Severn House, Sept.1982. — [192]p
ISBN 0-7278-0826-5 : £6.95 : CIP entry
B82-23868

Morgan, Denise. The house in Knightrider Street / by Denise Morgan. — London : Hale, 1982. — 192p ; 20cm
ISBN 0-7091-9948-1 : £7.25 B82-39180

Morgan, Geoffrey. Summer of the seals. — Large print ed. — Long Preston : Magna Print, Sept.1982. — [380]p
Originally published: London : Collins, 1975
ISBN 0-86009-428-6 : £5.50 : CIP entry
B82-20856

Morgan, Geoffrey. The view from Prospect / by Geoffrey Morgan. — Long Preston : Magna Print, 1982, c1980. — 315p ; 22cm
Originally published: London : Collins, 1980. — Published in large print
ISBN 0-86009-414-6 : Unpriced : CIP rev.
B82-13158

823'.914[F] — Fiction in English, *1945-* — *Texts continuation*

Morgan, Stanley. Too rich to live / Stanley Morgan. — Feltham : Hamlyn Paperbacks, 1981, c1980. — 293p ; 18cm
ISBN 0-600-20138-4 (pbk) : £1.50 B82-03537

Morice, Anne. Death in the round / Anne Morice. — Large print ed. — Bath : Chivers, 1981, c1980. — 235pp ; 23cm. — (A Lythway book)
Originally published: London : Macmillan, 1980
ISBN 0-85119-770-1 : Unpriced : CIP rev. B81-31801

Morice, Anne. Hollow vengeance / Anne Morice. — London : Macmillan, 1982. — 173p ; 21cm
ISBN 0-333-32631-8 : £5.95 B82-13597

Moriconi, Virginia. Black Annis. — London : Duckworth, Sept.1982. — [256]p
ISBN 0-7156-1673-0 : £9.95 : CIP entry B82-20188

Morrison, Humphrey R.. The masque of St. Eadmundsburg. — London : Blond & Briggs, Oct.1982. — [224]p
ISBN 0-85634-127-4 : £7.50 : CIP entry B82-24115

Morrow, John. The Essex factor / John Morrow. — Dundonald : Blackstaff, c1982. — 135p ; 21cm
ISBN 0-85640-262-1 (pbk) : £4.50 : CIP rev. B82-11124

Mortimer, Carole. Burning obsession / by Carole Mortimer. — London : Mills & Boon, 1982. — 188p ; 19cm
ISBN 0-263-10017-0 : £5.25 B82-18127

Mortimer, Carole. Deceit of a pagan / Carole Mortimer. — Large print ed. — Bath : Chivers, 1981, c1980. — 226p ; 23cm. — (A Seymour book)
Originally published: London : Mills & Boon, 1980
ISBN 0-85119-442-7 : Unpriced : CIP rev. B81-31252

Mortimer, Carole. Elusive lover / by Carole Mortimer. — London : Mills & Boon, 1982. — 188p ; 19cm
ISBN 0-263-10078-2 : £5.25 B82-30943

Mortimer, Carole. Forbidden surrender / by Carole Mortimer. — London : Mills & Boon, 1982. — 186p ; 20cm
ISBN 0-263-10100-2 : £5.95 B82-37444

Mortimer, Carole. Forgotten lover / by Carole Mortimer. — London : Mills & Boon, 1982. — 187p ; 20cm
ISBN 0-263-10049-9 : £5.25 B82-27274

Mortimer, Carole. Forgotten lover / by Carole Mortimer. — London : Mills & Boon, 1982. — 187p ; 18cm
ISBN 0-263-73848-5 (pbk) : £0.85 B82-36279

Mortimer, Carole. Golden fever / by Carole Mortimer. — London : Mills & Boon, 1982. — 187p ; 19cm
ISBN 0-263-10116-9 : £5.95 B82-37277

Mortimer, Carole. Love's duel / by Carole Mortimer. — London : Mills & Boon, 1982. — 188p ; 19cm
ISBN 0-263-09990-3 : £5.25 B82-10376

Mortimer, Carole. Red rose for love / by Carole Mortimer. — London : Mills & Boon, 1982. — 187p ; 19cm
ISBN 0-263-10036-7 : £5.25 B82-22643

Mortimer, Carole. Shadowed stranger / by Carole Mortimer. — London : Mills & Boon, 1982. — 188p ; 20cm
ISBN 0-263-10011-1 : £5.25 B82-13896

Mortimer, John, *1923-*. Rumpole's return / John Mortimer. — Large print ed. — Bath : Chivers Press, 1982, c1980. — 227p ; 23cm. — (A New Portway large print book)
Originally published: London : Allen Lane, 1980
ISBN 0-85119-156-8 : Unpriced : CIP rev. B81-36051

Morton, Moira. Blossoming romance / by Moira Morton. — London : Hale, 1981. — 159p ; 20cm
ISBN 0-7091-9388-2 : £5.95 B82-00445

Mosco, Maisie. Children's children / Maisie Mosco. — London : New English Library, 1981 (1982 [printing]). — 382p : 2geneal.tables 18cm
ISBN 0-450-05397-0 (pbk) : £1.95 : CIP rev. B82-12351

Mosley, Nicholas. Serpent : a novel / by Nicholas Mosley. — London : Secker & Warburg, 1981. — 187p ; 23cm
ISBN 0-436-28847-8 : £6.95 : CIP rev. B81-25320

Moss, Robert, *1946-*. Death beam : a novel / by Robert Moss. — London : Weidenfeld and Nicolson, 1981. — 408p ; 22cm
ISBN 0-297-78022-0 : £6.50 B82-02280

Moules, Joan. Richer than diamonds / by Joan Moules. — London : Hale, 1982. — 159p ; 20cm
ISBN 0-7091-9849-3 : £6.50 B82-34167

Moyes, Patricia. Angel death / Patricia Moyes. — Large print ed. — Leicester : Ulverscroft, 1982, c1980. — 456p ; 22cm. — (Ulverscroft large print)
Originally published: London : Collins, 1980
ISBN 0-7089-0746-6 : £5.00 : CIP rev. B81-33954

Moyes, Patricia. Dead men don't ski : a famous first : the Inspector Tibbett novel / Patricia Moyes. — London : Collins, 1959, c1958 (1981 [printing]). — 280p ; 21cm. — (The Crime Club)
ISBN 0-00-231686-2 : £6.50 B82-03080

Mullen, Michael. Kelly. — Dublin : Wolfhound Press, Oct.1981. — [176]p
ISBN 0-905473-69-8 : £6.00 : CIP entry B81-27478

Muller, Robert. Virginities / Robert Muller. — London : Hutchinson, 1982. — 248p ; 23cm
ISBN 0-09-147710-7 : £7.95 : CIP rev. B82-15660

Mullin, Chris. A very British coup / Chris Mullin. — London : Hodder and Stoughton, 1982. — 220p ; 23cm
ISBN 0-340-28586-9 : £6.95 : CIP rev. B82-21088

Murari, Timeri. Field of honour / Timeri Murari. — London : Eyre Methuen, 1982. — 318p ; 23cm
ISBN 0-413-49410-1 : £7.95 : CIP rev. B82-01996

Murdoch, Iris. The bell / Iris Murdoch. — [London] : Triad/Granada, 1981, c1958. — 317p ; 18cm
Originally published: London : Chatto & Windus, 1958
ISBN 0-586-04427-2 (pbk) : £1.95 B82-12519

Murdoch, Iris. A fairly honourable defeat / Iris Murdoch. — Harmondsworth : Penguin in association with Chatto & Windus, 1972, c1970 (1982 [printing]). — 446p ; 18cm
ISBN 0-14-003332-7 (pbk) : £1.95 B82-25118

Murphy, Christopher. The Jericho rumble / Christopher Murphy. — London : Secker & Warburg, 1982. — 222p ; 23cm
ISBN 0-436-29686-1 (corrected) : £6.95 : CIP rev. B82-10756

Murray, Annabel. Master of Camariguo / by Annabel Murray. — London : Mills and Boon, 1982. — 191p ; 20cm
ISBN 0-263-10088-x : £5.95 B82-37107

Murray, Hal. Death deals in diamonds / by Hal Murray. — London : Hale, 1982. — 192p ; 20cm
ISBN 0-7091-9611-3 : £6.50 B82-10752

Murray, Julia. The adventuress / Julia Murray. — London : Hale, 1982. — 207p ; 19cm
ISBN 0-7091-9757-8 : £7.50 B82-27317

Murrey, Jeneth. A time of wanting / by Jeneth Murrey. — London : Mills & Boon, 1982. — 190p ; 20cm
ISBN 0-263-10045-6 : £5.25 B82-22503

Nabb, Magdalen. Death of a Dutchman / Magdalen Nabb. — London : Collins, 1982. — 216p ; 21cm. — (The Crime Club)
ISBN 0-00-231327-8 : £6.75 : CIP rev. B82-12430

Nabb, Magdalen. Death of an Englishman / Magdalen Nabb. — London : Collins, 1981. — 172p ; 21cm. — (The Crime Club)
ISBN 0-00-231298-0 : £6.25 : CIP rev. B81-31525

Nash, Padder. Grass / by Padder Nash. — London : Hale, 1982. — 176p ; 20cm
ISBN 0-7091-9798-5 : £6.75 B82-30407

Nash, Walter, *1926-*. Kettle of roses / Walter Nash. — London : Hutchinson, 1982. — 140p ; 23cm
ISBN 0-09-147130-3 : £5.95 : CIP rev. B82-04121

Neels, Betty. All else confusion / by Betty Neels. — London : Mills and Boon, 1982. — 187p ; 20cm
ISBN 0-263-10094-4 : £5.95 B82-37106

Neels, Betty. A girl to love / by Betty Neels. — London : Mills & Boon, 1982. — 186p ; 19cm
ISBN 0-263-10038-3 : £5.25 B82-22645

Neels, Betty. Judith / by Betty Neels. — London : Mills & Boon, 1982. — 188p ; 20cm
ISBN 0-263-09992-x : £5.25 B82-10381

Neels, Betty. Midnight sun's magic / Betty Neels. — Large print ed. — Bath : Chivers, 1982, c1979. — 209p ; 23cm. — (A Seymour book)
Originally published: London : Mills and Boon, 1979
ISBN 0-85119-458-3 : Unpriced : CIP rev. B82-01439

Neels, Betty. Sister Peters in Amsterdam / Betty Neels. — Large print ed. — Bath : Chivers, 1982, c1969. — 209p ; 23cm. — (A Lythway book)
Originally published: London : Mills & Boon, 1969
ISBN 0-85119-796-5 : Unpriced : CIP rev. B82-01430

Neiderman, Andrew. Pin / Andrew Neiderman. — London : Arrow, 1982, c1981. — 264p ; 18cm
ISBN 0-09-927460-4 (pbk) : £1.50 B82-19017

Neilan, Sarah. An air of glory / Sarah Neilan. — South Yarmouth, Mass. : Curley, 1978, c1977 ; [Long Preston] : Distributed by Magna. — 452p ; 23cm
Originally published: New York : Morrow ; London : Hodder and Stoughton, 1977. — Published in large print
ISBN 0-89340-159-5 : Unpriced B82-17036

Neilson, Marguerite. The dark path. — Large print ed. — Long Preston : Magna Print, Sept.1982. — [480]p
Originally published: London : Wingate, 1976
ISBN 0-86009-426-x : £5.50 : CIP entry B82-20855

823'.914[F] — Fiction in English, ***1945- — Texts continuation***

Nelson, Dorothy. In night's city. — Dublin : Wolfhound Press, Nov.1982. — [122]p
ISBN 0-905473-88-4 (cased) : £7.00 : CIP entry
ISBN 0-905473-89-2 (pbk) : £3.00 B82-31318

Neville, Anne. Lindsay's escape / by Anne Neville. — London : Hale, 1982. — 159p ; 20cm
ISBN 0-7091-9850-7 : £6.50 B82-34174

Neville, Anne. Sandy's father / by Anne Neville. — London : Hale, 1982. — 160p ; 21cm
ISBN 0-7091-9568-0 : £5.95 B82-11387

Newby, P. H.. Feelings have changed / P.H. Newby. — London : Faber, 1981. — 266p ; 21cm
ISBN 0-571-11823-2 : £6.95 : CIP rev. B81-25330

Newman, Andrea. Alexa / Andrea Newman. — Harmondsworth : Penguin, 1976, c1968 (1982 [printing]). — 157p ; 18cm
Originally published: London : Triton Books, 1968
ISBN 0-14-004091-9 (pbk) : £1.25 B82-21065

Newman, G. F.. Charlie and Joanna / G.F. Newman. — London : Granada, 1982, c1981. — 199p ; 18cm
ISBN 0-586-05184-8 (pbk) : £1.50 B82-37215

Newman, G. F.. The men with the guns / G.F. Newman. — London : Secker & Warburg, 1982. — ix,241p ; 23cm
ISBN 0-436-30535-6 : £7.95 : CIP rev. B82-01545

Newton, William. Death is for losers / by William Newton. — London : Hale, 1981. — 160p ; 20cm
ISBN 0-7091-9232-0 : £6.50 B82-06323

Newton, William. The Rio contract / by William Newton. — London : Hale, 1982. — 159p ; 20cm
ISBN 0-7091-9831-0 : £6.75 B82-33199

Newton, William. The way to get dead / by William Newton. — London : Hale, 1982. — 173p ; 20cm
ISBN 0-7091-9544-3 : £6.75 B82-17522

Nichols, Leigh. The eyes of darkness / Leigh Nichols. — [London] : Fontana, c1982, c1981. — 312p ; 18cm
Originally published: New York : Pocket Books, 1981
ISBN 0-00-616508-7 (pbk) : £1.50 B82-38636

Nichols, Leigh. The eyes of darkness. — Loughton : Piatkus, Aug.1982. — [320]p
ISBN 0-86188-201-6 : £6.95 : CIP entry B82-17218

Nichols, Mary. The hand you hold / by Mary Nichols. — London : Hale, 1982. — 160p ; 20cm
ISBN 0-7091-9648-2 : £6.25 B82-18310

Nicole, Christopher. The Friday spy / Christopher Nicole. — London : Severn House, 1981, c1980. — 410p ; 21cm
Originally published: under the name of C.R. Nicholson. London : Corgi, 1980
ISBN 0-7278-0743-9 : £6.95 : CIP rev. B81-30588

Nicole, Christopher. Haggard's inheritance / Christopher Nicole. — [London] : Corgi, 1982, c1981. — 389p ; 18cm
Originally published: London : Joseph, 1981
ISBN 0-552-11923-7 (pbk) : £1.75 B82-28364

Nicole, Christopher. The queen of Paris. — London : Severn House, Sept.1982. — [448]p
Originally published: London : Corgi, 1979
ISBN 0-7278-0825-7 : £7.95 : CIP entry B82-23867

Niven, David. Go slowly, come back quickly. — London : Hodder and Stoughton, Sept.1982. — [384]p. — (Coronet books)
Originally published: London : Hamilton, 1981
ISBN 0-340-28347-5 (pbk) : £1.95 : CIP entry B82-18794

Norman, Barry. Have a nice day / Barry Norman. — London : Quartet, 1981. — 182p ; 23cm
ISBN 0-7043-2292-7 : £6.50 : CIP rev. B81-25764

Norman, Barry. Have a nice day / Barry Norman. — London : Arrow, 1982, c1981. — 219p ; 18cm
Originally published: London : Quartet, 1981
ISBN 0-09-929130-4 (pbk) : £1.50 B82-35590

Norman, Diana. King of the last days / Diana Norman. — London : Hodder and Stoughton, 1981. — 189p : 1map ; 23cm
ISBN 0-340-27039-x : £6.95 : CIP rev. B81-30131

Norman, Frank. The Baskerville caper / Frank Norman. — London : Macdonald, 1981. — 251p ; 21cm
ISBN 0-356-08530-9 : £6.95 B82-10080

North, Elizabeth. Ancient enemies. — London : Cape, Nov.1982. — [236]p
ISBN 0-224-02052-8 : £6.95 : CIP entry B82-26219

Northan, Irene. The incomparable Lydia / by Irene Northan. — London : Hale, 1981. — 176p ; 20cm
ISBN 0-7091-9452-8 : £6.75 B82-07200

Nye, Robert. The voyage of the Destiny. — London : Hamilton, Mar.1982. — [288]p
ISBN 0-241-10742-3 : £7.95 : CIP entry B82-00918

O'Donnell, Michael. The devil's prison : a novel / by Michael O'Donnell. — London : Gollancz, 1982. — 216p ; 21cm
ISBN 0-575-03102-6 : £6.95 : CIP rev. B82-04608

O'Faolain, Julia. The obedient wife / Julia O'Faolain. — [London] : Lane, 1982. — 229p ; 22cm
ISBN 0-7139-1467-x : £7.50 B82-25978

Ogle, Josephine. Call me Sebastian / Josephine Ogle. — Bognor Regis : New Horizon, c1982. — 172p ; 21cm
ISBN 0-86116-534-9 : £5.25 B82-06364

O'Hara, Kenneth. Nightmares' nest. — London, Gollancz, Oct.1982. — [160]p
ISBN 0-575-03191-3 : £6.95 : CIP entry B82-23346

Olbrich, Freny. Sweet and deadly / Freny Olbrich. — Feltham : Hamlyn, 1982, c1979. — 189p ; 18cm. — (A Hamlyn whodunnit)
Originally published: London : Heinemann, 1979
ISBN 0-600-20368-9 (pbk) : £1.25 B82-11329

Oldfield, Elizabeth. Submission / by Elizabeth Oldfield. — London : Mills & Boon, 1982. — 188p ; 19cm
ISBN 0-263-10118-5 : £5.95 B82-37274

Oldfield, Pamela. After the storm / Pamela Oldfield. — London : Futura, 1981, c1982. — 395p ; 18cm. — (The Heron saga ; 3)
ISBN 0-7088-2140-5 (pbk) : £1.95 B82-06610

Oldfield, Pamela. After the storm / Pamela Oldfield. — London : Macdonald, 1982. — 395p ; 21cm. — (The Heron saga ; 3)
Originally published: 1981
ISBN 0-356-08500-7 : £6.95 B82-12667

Oldfield, Pamela. The rich earth / Pamela Oldfield. — London : Macdonald, 1982, c1980. — 461p ; 21cm. — (The Heron saga ; 1)
ISBN 0-356-08514-7 : £6.95 B82-12669

Oldfield, Pamela. This ravished land / Pamela Oldfield. — London : Macdonald, 1982, c1981. — 428p ; 21cm. — (The Heron saga ; 2)
ISBN 0-356-08520-1 : £6.95 B82-12668

Oldfield, Pamela. White water / Pamela Oldfield. — London : Futura, 1982. — 415p ; 18cm. — (The Heron saga ; 4)
ISBN 0-7088-2209-6 (pbk) : £2.25 B82-38606

Oliver, Winifred. Laid her soiled glove by / Winifred Oliver. — Maidstone : Mann, 1981. — 148p ; 21cm
ISBN 0-7041-0201-3 : £6.95 B82-00954

Oram, Neil. The warp / Neil Oram. — London : Sphere
3: The balustrade paradox. — 1982. — 204p ; 18cm
ISBN 0-7221-6554-4 (pbk) : £1.95 B82-09388

Orford, Margaret. The king's daughter / by Margaret Orford. — London : Hale, 1982. — 192p ; 20cm
ISBN 0-7091-9423-4 : £6.95 B82-10753

Ormsby, Patricia. Bridal path / Patricia Ormsby. — London : Mills & Boon, 1982. — 192p ; 20cm
ISBN 0-263-10068-5 : £5.25 B82-27606

Ormsby, Patricia. The elusive marriage / by Patricia Ormsby. — Long Preston : Magna, 1981, c1979. — 389p ; 23cm
Originally published: London : P. Davies, 1979. — Published in large print
ISBN 0-86009-356-5 : Unpriced : CIP rev. B81-31814

Orr, Chris. Arthur : a story / by Chris Orr. — London (Level F3, New Crane Wharf, Garnet St., E.1) : Signford, c1979. — 50p : ill ; 22x24cm
£4.95 (pbk) B82-00608

Osman, George. Une affaire mysterieuse / George Osman. — Bognor Regis : New Horizon, c1981. — 194p ; 21cm
ISBN 0-86116-528-4 : £5.75 B82-04558

Osmond, Andrew. War without frontiers. — London : Hodder and Stoughton, Sept.1982. — [672]p
ISBN 0-340-25140-9 : £8.95 : CIP entry B82-18802

Ouspensky, P. D.. Strange life of Ivan Osokin. — 4th ed. — London : Routledge & Kegan Paul, Jan.1983. — [200]p
Previous ed.: London : Faber, 1971
ISBN 0-7100-9419-1 (pbk) : £3.95 : CIP entry B82-32554

Padfield, Peter. Gold chains of Empire / Peter Padfield. — London : Hutchinson, 1982. — 310p : 1map ; 23cm
ISBN 0-09-148940-7 : £7.95 : CIP rev. B82-07966

Page, Emma. Every second Thursday. — Large print ed. — Anstey : Ulverscroft, Feb.1983. — 1v.. — (Ulverscroft large print series)
Originally published: London : Gollancz, 1981
ISBN 0-7089-0922-1 : CIP entry B82-38884

Page, Emma. Last walk home. — London : Collins, Oct.1982. — [224]p. — (The Crime Club)
ISBN 0-00-231411-8 : £6.75 : CIP entry B82-23082

Page, Nicola. Bride of the sun / Nicola Page. — London : Macdonald, 1982, c1981. — 251p ; 21cm
ISBN 0-356-08502-3 : £4.95 B82-10078

823'.914[F] — Fiction in English, ***1945-*** **— *Texts continuation***

Page, Vicki. Arabian love story / by Vicki Page. — London : Hale, 1981. — 175p ; 20cm
ISBN 0-7091-9107-3 : £5.75 B82-00446

Page, Vicki. Nurse at Tye Towers / by Vicki Page. — London : Hale, 1982. — 154p ; 20cm
ISBN 0-7091-9162-6 : £5.95 B82-11071

Page, Vicki. Shadows on the snow / Vicki Page. — Large print ed. — Bath : Chivers, 1982, c1978. — 182p ; 23cm. — (A Lythway book)
Originally published: London : Hale, 1978
ISBN 0-85119-838-4 : Unpriced : CIP rev. B82-15870

Pargeter, Margaret. Not far enough / by Margaret Pargeter. — London : Mills & Boon, 1982. — 188p ; 19cm
ISBN 0-263-09994-6 : £5.25 B82-10370

Pargeter, Margaret. Prelude to a song / by Margaret Pargeter. — London : Mills and Boon, 1982. — 186p ; 20cm
ISBN 0-263-10087-1 : £5.95 B82-37109

Pargeter, Margaret. Storm cycle / by Margaret Pargeter. — London : Mills & Boon, 1982. — 188p ; 20cm
ISBN 0-263-10065-0 : £5.25 B82-27605

Pargeter, Margaret. Storm cycle / by Margaret Pargeter. — London : Mills & Boon, 1982. — 188p ; 18cm
ISBN 0-263-73872-8 (pbk) : £0.85 B82-36278

Parker, Gordon, *1940-*. The action of the tiger / Gordon Parker. — London : Macdonald, 1981. — 272p ; 21cm
ISBN 0-354-04673-x : £6.95 B82-03073

Parker, Olwen. Wednesday's child / by Olwen Parker. — London : Hale, 1982. — 160p ; 20cm
ISBN 0-7091-9920-1 : £6.50 B82-35898

Parkin, Molly. A bite of the apple / Molly Parkin. — London : Star, 1982, c1981. — 165p ; 18cm
Originally published: London : W.H. Allen, 1981
ISBN 0-352-31035-9 (pbk) : £1.35 B82-16096

Parrish, Frank. Snare in the dark / Frank Parrish. — London : Constable, 1982. — 216p ; 23cm
ISBN 0-09-464380-6 : £6.95 B82-16192

Parv, Valerie. Love's greatest gamble / by Valerie Parv. — London : Mills & Boon, 1982. — 190p ; 19cm
ISBN 0-263-10076-6 : £5.25 B82-30937

Patterson, Harry. Brought in dead / Harry Patterson. — Large print ed. — Bath : Chivers Press, 1981, c1967. — 211p : 23cm. — (A Lythway book)
Originally published: London : John Long, 1967
ISBN 0-85119-761-2 : Unpriced : CIP rev. B81-31272

Patterson, Harry. The graveyard shift. — Large print ed. — Bath : Chivers, Feb.1983. — [264] p. — (A Lythway book)
Originally published: London : Long, 1965
ISBN 0-85119-899-6 : £6.90 : CIP entry B82-39587

Pattinson, James. A fatal errand / by James Pattinson. — London : Hale, 1982. — 192p ; 21cm
ISBN 0-7091-8000-4 : £7.25 B82-37256

Pattinson, James. Lethal orders / James Pattinson. — London : Hale, 1982. — 191p ; 21cm
ISBN 0-7091-7766-6 : £6.95 B82-22909

Pattinson, James. The seven sleepers / James Pattinson. — London : Hale, 1981. — 190p ; 21cm
ISBN 0-7091-7462-4 : £6.95 B82-12624

Paul, Barbara, *1931-*. First gravedigger / Barbara Paul. — London : Collins, c1982, c1980. — 190p ; 20cm. — (The Crime Club)
Originally published: Garden City, N.Y. : Doubleday, 1980
ISBN 0-00-231299-9 : £6.50 : CIP rev. B81-35936

Paul, Barbara, *1931-*. Your eyelids are growing heavy / Barbara Paul. — London : Collins, 1982, c1981. — 211p ; 20cm. — (The Crime club)
Originally published: Garden City, N.Y. : Published for the Crime Club by Doubleday, 1981
ISBN 0-00-231689-7 : £6.75 : CIP rev. B82-15622

Payne, Laurence. Take the money and run. — London : Hodder and Stoughton, Nov.1982. — [256]p
ISBN 0-340-28232-0 : £7.50 : CIP entry B82-27347

Peake, Lilian. Bitter revenge / Lilian Peake. — London : Mills & Boon, 1982. — 188p ; 20cm
ISBN 0-263-10005-7 : £5.25 B82-13895

Peake, Lilian. Capture a stranger / by Lilian Peake. — London : Mills & Boon, 1981. — 188p ; 19cm
ISBN 0-263-09941-5 : £4.55 B82-00046

Peake, Lilian. Stay till morning / by Lilian Peake. — London : Mills & Boon, 1982. — 188p ; 19cm
ISBN 0-263-10082-0 : £5.25 B82-33807

Pearce, Mary E.. Apple tree saga / Mary E. Pearce. — London : Granada, 1982. — 254,224,176p ; 18cm
Contents: Apple tree lean down. Originally published: London : Macdonald & Janes, 1973. — The Sorrowing wind. Originally published: London : Macdonald & Janes, 1974. — Jack Mercybright. Originally published: London : Macdonald & Janes, 1974
ISBN 0-583-13608-7 (pbk) : £1.95 B82-30956

Pearce, Mary E.. The land endures / Mary E. Pearce. — Large print ed. — Leicester : Ulverscroft, 1982, c1978. — 432p ; 23cm. — (Ulverscroft large print)
Originally published: London : Macdonald & Jane's, 1978
ISBN 0-7089-0811-x : Unpriced : CIP rev. B82-18551

Pearsall, Ronald. The iron sleep / by Ronald Pearsall. — Long Preston : Magna, 1982, c1979. — 591p ; 22cm
Originally published: London : Joseph, 1979. — Published in large print
ISBN 0-86009-398-0 : Unpriced : CIP rev. B82-07050

Pearsall, Ronald. Tides of war / by Ronald Pearsall. — Long Preston : Magna, 1982, c1978. — 764p ; 23cm
Originally published: London : Joseph, 1978. — Published in large print
ISBN 0-86009-365-4 : Unpriced : CIP rev. B81-33771

Pearson, John, *1930-*. The kindness of Doctor Avicenna / John Pearson. — London : Macmillan, 1981, c1982. — 243p ; 21cm
ISBN 0-333-33118-4 : £6.50 B82-35912

Pearson, Michael, *1924-*. The store / Michael Person. — [London] : Fontana, 1981, c1980. — 506p ; 18cm
Originally published: London : Macmillan, 1980
ISBN 0-00-616359-9 (pbk) : £1.95 B82-03010

Peel, Colin D.. Snowtrap / Colin D. Peel. — London : Hale, 1981. — 189p ; 21cm
ISBN 0-7091-9323-8 : £6.75 B82-02142

Pemberton, Margaret. The flower garden / Margaret Pemberton. — London : Macdonald, 1982. — 442p ; 23cm
ISBN 0-356-08545-7 : £7.95 B82-22569

Pemberton, Margaret. The guilty secret. — Large print ed. — Bath : Chivers, Sept.1982. — [280] p. — (A Lythway book)
Originally published: London : Hale, 1979
ISBN 0-85119-848-1 : £6.90 : CIP entry B82-20517

Pemberton, Margaret. The mystery of Saligo Bay / Margaret Pemberton. — Large print ed. — Bath : Lythway, 1980, c1976. — 269p ; 23cm
Originally published: London : Macdonald and Jane's, 1976
ISBN 0-85046-915-5 : Unpriced : CIP rev. B80-32452

Pemberton, Margaret. Pioneer girl / Margaret Pemberton. — London : Mills & Boon, 1982. — 192p : 1map ; 19cm. — (Masquerade)
ISBN 0-263-10040-5 : £5.25 B82-18114

Penn, John. Notice of death / John Penn. — London : Collins, 1982. — 191p ; 21cm. — (The Crime club)
ISBN 0-00-231921-7 : £6.50 : CIP rev. B82-00902

Penn, Margaret. The foolish virgin / Margaret Penn. — London : Futura, 1982. — 243p ; 18cm. — (Heritage)
Originally published: London : Cape, 1951
ISBN 0-7088-2138-3 (pbk) : £1.95 B82-12755

Penn, Margaret. Manchester fourteen miles / Margaret Penn. — London : Futura, 1982, c1979. — xx,230p ; 18cm. — (Heritage)
Originally published: Cambridge : Cambridge University Press, 1947
ISBN 0-7088-2136-7 (pbk) : £1.95 B82-12754

Penn, Margaret. Young Mrs Burton / Margaret Penn. — London : Futura, 1982. — 250p : ill ; 18cm. — (Heritage)
Originally published: London : Cape, 1954
ISBN 0-7088-2137-5 (pbk) : £1.95 B82-12756

Perriam, Wendy. After purple / Wendy Perriam. — London : Joseph, 1982. — 382p ; 23cm
ISBN 0-7181-2096-5 : £7.95 B82-15600

Perriam, Wendy. Cuckoo / Wendy Perriam. — London : Futura, 1982, c1981. — 318p ; 18cm
Originally published: London : Joseph, 1981
ISBN 0-7088-2164-2 (pbk) : £1.60 B82-18266

Perry, Anne. Callander Square / Anne Perry. — Large print ed. — Leicester : Ulverscroft, 1981, c1980. — 446p ; 23cm
Originally published: London : Hale, 1980
ISBN 0-7089-0718-0 : £5.00 : CIP rev. B81-32033

Perry, Hilda. Jealous love / Hilda Perry. — London : Hale, 1982. — 160p ; 20cm
ISBN 0-7091-9851-5 : £6.50 B82-33419

Perry, Hilda. A tower of strength / by Hilda Perry. — London : Hale, 1981. — 160p ; 20cm
ISBN 0-7091-9429-3 : £5.95 B82-02162

Perry, Ritchie. Bishop's pawn. — Large print ed. — Bath : Chivers, Nov.1982. — [344]p. — (A Lythway book)
Originally published: London : Collins, 1979
ISBN 0-85119-862-7 : £7.50 : CIP entry B82-26305

Peters, Maureen. The dragon and the rose / Maureen Peters. — London : Hale, 1982. — 187p ; 21cm
ISBN 0-7091-9789-6 : £7.25 B82-33197

Peters, Maureen. Frost on the rose / by Maureen Peters. — London : Hale, 1982. — 208p ; 20cm
ISBN 0-7091-9538-9 : £7.25 B82-18316

823'.914[F] — Fiction in English, *1945- — Texts continuation*

Peters, Natasha. The enticers. — London : New English Library, Jan.1983. — [512]p
ISBN 0-450-05542-6 (pbk) : £1.95 : CIP entry B82-34604

Peters, Sue. Jade / by Sue Peters. — London : Mills & Boon, 1982. — 188p ; 19cm
ISBN 0-263-10080-4 : £5.25 B82-30945

Peters, Sue. Man of teak / by Sue Peters. — London : Mills & Boon, 1982. — 187p ; 19cm
ISBN 0-263-09986-5 : £5.25 B82-10371

Petri, David. Curtain of the night. — Henley on Thames : Aidan Ellis, Oct.1982. — [208]p
ISBN 0-85628-115-8 : £6.95 : CIP entry B82-24113

Petty, Elizabeth. Nurse at Whispering Pines. — London : Severn House, Aug.1982. — [192]p
ISBN 0-7278-0815-x : £5.50 : CIP entry B82-21106

Petty, Elizabeth. Nurse at Whispering Pines. — Large print ed. — Long Preston : Magna, Feb.1983. — [320]p
Originally published: London : Mills and Boon, 1980
ISBN 0-86009-487-1 : £5.75 : CIP entry B82-39614

Peyton, K. M.. Dear Fred / K.M. Peyton. — [London] : Pavanne, 1982, c1981. — 250p ; 18cm
Originally published: London : Bodley Head, 1981
ISBN 0-330-26810-4 (pbk) : £1.50 B82-35743

Phillips, Dee. The coconut kiss / Dee Phillips. — London : Hodder and Stoughton, 1982. — 191p ; 23cm
ISBN 0-340-27468-9 : £6.95 : CIP rev. B81-34138

Phillips, Dee. No, not I. — Large print ed. — Bath : Chivers, Jan.1983. — [336]p. — (A Lythway book)
Originally published: London : Robin Clark, 1980
ISBN 0-85119-886-4 : £7.50 : CIP entry B82-33100

Phillips, Mary, *1915-*. Catchee Chinaman / by Mary Phillips. — Hornchurch : Ian Henry, 1982, c1973. — 188p ; 21cm
Originally published: s.l. : El Greco, 1973
ISBN 0-86025-204-3 : £5.45 B82-18232

Phillips, Patricia. Captive flame / Patricia Phillips. — London : Futura, 1982, c1980. — 384p ; 18cm. — (Troubadour)
ISBN 0-7107-3027-6 (pbk) : £1.75 B82-30777

Phipps, Grace M.. The tenants of Linden Lodge / by Grace M. Phipps. — London : Hale, 1982. — 188p ; 20cm
ISBN 0-7091-9917-1 : £6.50 B82-37255

Pickering, R. E.. The word game / R.E. Pickering. — London : Deutsch, 1982. — 306p ; 22cm
ISBN 0-233-97430-x : £7.95 : CIP rev. B82-10688

Pike, Charles R.. Bloody Christmas / Charles R. Pike. — London : Granada, 1981. — 141p ; 18cm. — (Jubal Cade ; 18) (A Mayflower book)
ISBN 0-583-13261-8 (pbk) : £0.95 B82-09534

Pike, Charles R.. Jubal Cade : the killing trail / Charles R. Pike. — Large print ed. — Bath : Chivers, 1982, c1974. — 175p ; 23cm. — (A Lythway book)
Originally published: St. Albans : Mayflower, 1974
ISBN 0-85119-839-2 : Unpriced : CIP rev. B82-15871

Pike, Charles R.. Time of the damned / Charles R. Pike. — London : Granada, 1982. — 127p ; 18cm. — (Jubal Cade ; 18) (A Mayflower book)
ISBN 0-583-13262-6 (pbk) : £0.95 B82-19980

Pike, Charles R.. The waiting game / Charles R. Pike. — London : Granada, 1982. — 128p ; 18cm. — (Jubal Cade ; 19) (A Mayflower book)
ISBN 0-583-13412-2 (pbk) : £0.95 B82-30955

Pincher, Chapman. The private world of St John Terrapin : a novel of the Café Royal / by Chapman Pincher. — London : Sidgwick & Jackson, 1982. — 332p ; 24cm
ISBN 0-283-98849-5 : £7.95 B82-23525

Pitstow, Margaret. Restored to love / Margaret Pitstow. — London : Hale, 1982. — 192p ; 20cm
ISBN 0-7091-9787-x : £6.25 B82-27427

Pitt, Ingrid. The Perons. — London : Methuen London, Nov.1982. — [400]p
ISBN 0-423-00410-7 : £7.95 : CIP entry B82-27511

Polland, Madeleine. All their kingdom / Madeleine Polland. — [London] : Fontana, 1982, c1981. — 352p ; 18cm
Originally published: London : Collins, 1981
ISBN 0-00-616483-8 (pbk) : £1.65 B82-16822

Polland, Madeleine. The heart speaks many ways : a novel / by Madeleine A. Polland. — London : Collins, 1982. — 375p ; 24cm
ISBN 0-00-222617-0 : £7.50 B82-37123

Pollock, Rosemary. The sun and Catriona / by Rosemary Pollock. — London : Mills & Boon, 1981. — 190p ; 19cm
ISBN 0-263-09963-6 : £4.55 B82-04639

Pope, Dudley. Admiral : a novel / by Dudley Pope. — London : Secker & Warburg, 1982. — 309p : 1map ; 23cm. — (An Alison Press book)
ISBN 0-436-37743-8 : £7.50 : CIP rev. B82-09198

Pope, Dudley. Buccaneer / Dudley Pope. — Feltham : Hamlyn, 1982, c1981. — 277p : 1map ; 18cm
Originally published: London : Secker & Warburg, 1981
ISBN 0-600-20600-9 (pbk) : £1.50 B82-27051

Pope, Dudley. Ramage and the renegades : a novel / by Dudley Pope. — London : Secker & Warburg, 1981. — 290p : 1map ; 23cm
ISBN 0-436-37741-1 : £6.95 : CIP rev. B81-25321

Pope, Dudley. Ramage and the renegades / Dudley Pope. — [London] : Fontana, 1982, c1981. — 304p : 1map ; 18cm
Originally published: London : Secker & Warburg, 1981
ISBN 0-00-616639-3 (pbk) : £1.50 B82-38638

Pope, Dudley. Ramage's devil. — London : Secker & Warburg, Oct.1982. — [288]p. — (An Alison Press book)
ISBN 0-436-37742-x : £7.95 : CIP entry B82-28452

Pope, Dudley. Ramage's prize / Dudley Pope. — [London] : Fontana, 1982, c1974. — 344p : 1map ; 18cm
Originally published: London : Alison Press, 1974
ISBN 0-00-616343-2 (pbk) : £1.75 B82-25443

Pope, Pamela. The magnolia siege / by Pamela Pope. — London : Mills & Boon, 1982. — 190p ; 20cm
ISBN 0-263-10009-x : £5.25 B82-13885

Pope, Pamela. The magnolia siege / by Pamela Pope. — London : Mills & Boon, 1982. — 190p ; 18cm
ISBN 0-263-73966-x (pbk) : £0.85 B82-36271

Porteous, R. S.. Cattleman. — Large print ed. — Anstey : Ulverscroft, Sept.1982. — [368]p. — (Charnwood library series)
Originally published: London : Harrap, 1960
ISBN 0-7089-8070-8 : £4.50 : CIP entry B82-27009

Porter, Alvin. Range justice / by Alvin Porter. — London : Hale, 1982. — 159p ; 20cm
ISBN 0-7091-9572-9 : £4.95 B82-15482

Potter, Dennis. Pennies from heaven / Dennis Potter. — London : Quartet, 1981. — 196p ; 23cm
ISBN 0-7043-2300-1 : £6.50 : CIP rev. B81-30407

Potter, Dennis. Pennies from heaven / Dennis Potter. — London : Quartet Books, 1981. — 196p,[8]p of plates : ports ; 20cm
ISBN 0-7043-3394-5 (pbk) : £2.50 B82-12064

Potter, Jay Hill. Call me Pilgrim / by Jay Hill Potter. — London : Hale, 1981. — 160p ; 19cm
ISBN 0-7091-9394-7 : £4.95 B82-07214

Potter, Jay Hill. Pilgrim's trail / by Jay Hill Potter. — London : Hale, 1982. — 160p ; 20cm
ISBN 0-7091-9716-0 : £5.25 B82-17523

Potter, Jay Hill. Young Joe Pilgrim / by Jay Hill Potter. — London : Hale, 1982. — 156p ; 20cm
ISBN 0-7091-9871-x : £5.50 B82-34188

Potter, Sarah. Brimstone and treacle. — London : Quartet, May 1982. — 1v.
ISBN 0-7043-3414-3 (pbk) : £3.95 : CIP entry B82-13497

Powell, Margaret. The housekeeper / Margaret Powell. — London : Joseph, 1982. — 205p ; 23cm
ISBN 0-7181-2155-4 : £7.95 B82-34221

Powell, Margaret. Maids and mistresses. — Large print ed. — Bath : Chivers, Nov.1982. — [264]p. — (A Lythway book)
Originally published: London : Joseph, 1981
ISBN 0-85119-864-3 : £6.90 : CIP entry B82-26307

Powell, Roberta. The apothecary's child / Roberta Powell. — London : Hale, 1982. — 206p ; 19cm
ISBN 0-7091-9494-3 : £6.95 B82-10754

Pratchett, Terry. Strata / Terry Pratchett. — London : New English Library, 1982, c1981. — 192p ; 19cm
Originally published: Gerrards Cross : Smythe, 1981
ISBN 0-450-04977-9 (pbk) : £1.50 : CIP rev. B82-06821

Pratten, Gordon. The saga of O'Rorke (1) / Gordon Pratten. — Bognor Regis : New Horizon, c1982. — 141p ; 22cm
ISBN 0-86116-817-8 : £5.25 B82-08820

Preston, Faith. Fragrant harbour / by Faith Preston. — London : Hale, 1982. — 159p ; 20cm
ISBN 0-7091-9852-3 : £6.50 B82-33420

Preston, Ivy. Interlude in Greece / by Ivy Preston. — London : Hale, 1982. — 155p ; 20cm
ISBN 0-7091-9806-x : £6.50 B82-34169

823′.914[F] — Fiction in English, *1945- — Texts continuation*

Price, Anthony. The labyrinth makers / Anthony Price. — Large print ed. — Leicester : Ulverscroft, 1981, c1970. — 368p ; 23cm. — (Ulverscroft large print series)
Originally published: London : Gollancz, 1970
ISBN 0-7089-0711-3 : £5.00 : CIP rev.
B81-30498

Price, Anthony. The old Vengeful. — London : Gollancz, Oct.1982. — [256]p
ISBN 0-575-03192-1 : £6.95 : CIP entry
B82-23347

Price, Anthony. Other paths to glory / Anthony Price. — London : Futura, 1982, c1974. — 220p ; 18cm
Originally published: London : Gollancz, 1974
ISBN 0-7088-2187-1 (pbk) : £1.50 B82-27057

Price, Anthony. Our man in Camelot / Anthony Price. — London : Futura, 1982, c1975. — 223p ; 18cm
Originally published: London : Gollancz, 1975
ISBN 0-7088-2189-8 (pbk) : £1.50 B82-27058

Prole, Lozania. The two Queen Annes. — Large print ed. — Bath : Chivers, Feb.1983. — [288] p. — (A Lythway book)
Originally published: London : Hale, 1971
ISBN 0-85119-895-3 : £7.20 : CIP entry
B82-39584

Pullein-Thompson, Christine. Father unknown / Christine Pullein-Thompson. — London : Dobson, 1981. — 120p ; 21cm
ISBN 0-234-72282-7 : Unpriced B82-13595

Pulman, Jack. Fixation / Jack Pulman. — London : Arrow, 1981, c1978. — 281p ; 18cm
Originally published: London : Hamish Hamilton, 1978
ISBN 0-09-921910-7 (pbk) : £1.75 B82-06573

Pyatt, Rosina. To catch an earl / Rosina Pyatt. — London : Mills & Boon, 1982. — 223p ; 19cm. — (Masquerade historical romances)
ISBN 0-263-10086-3 : £5.25 B82-30947

Pyatt, Rosina. To catch an earl / Rosina Pyatt. — London : Mills & Boon, 1982. — 223p ; 18cm. — (Masquerade historical romances)
ISBN 0-263-73907-4 (pbk) : £0.95 B82-36067

Pym, Barbara. A few green leaves / Barbara Pym. — London : Granada, 1981, c1980. — 220p ; 18cm. — (A Panther book)
Originally published: London : Macmillan, 1980
ISBN 0-586-05425-1 (pbk) : £1.50 B82-09545

Pym, Barbara. An unsuitable attachment / Barbara Pym. — London : Macmillan, 1982. — 256p ; 21cm
ISBN 0-333-32654-7 : £6.95 B82-18242

Quinn, Paul. The tormentors / Paul Quinn. — Bognor Regis : New Horizon, c1979. — 109p ; 21cm
ISBN 0-86116-052-5 : £3.95 B82-18343

Quinnell, A. J.. The Mahdi / A.J. Quinnell. — London : Macmillan, 1981. — 252p ; 23cm
ISBN 0-333-32671-7 : £6.95 B82-05736

Quinnell, A. J.. Man on fire / A.J. Quinnell. — London : Futura, 1982, c1980. — 318p ; 18cm
Originally published: New York : Morrow, 1980 ; London : Macmillan, 1981
ISBN 0-7088-2147-2 (pbk) : £1.60 B82-27056

Quinnell, A. J.. Man on fire / A.J. Quinnell. — Leicester : Charnwood, 1982,c1980. — 421p ; 23cm. — (Charnwood library series)
Originally published: New York : Morrow, 1980 ; London : Macmillan, 1981. — Published in large print
ISBN 0-7089-8045-7 : Unpriced : CIP rev.
B82-15943

Radley, Sheila. A talent for destruction / Sheila Radley. — London : Constable, 1982. — 160p ; 23cm
ISBN 0-09-464430-6 : £5.95 B82-22756

Rae, Douglas. The last fisherman / by Douglas Rae. — London : Hale, 1982. — 206p ; 23cm
ISBN 0-7091-9679-2 : £7.25 B82-33904

Rae, Hugh C.. Privileged strangers / Hugh Rae. — London : Hodder and Stoughton, 1982. — 332p ; 23cm
ISBN 0-340-25588-9 : £7.95 : CIP rev.
B82-12251

Rance, Joseph. Bullet train / Joseph Rance and Arei Kato. — Large print ed. — Leicester : Ulverscroft, 1981, c1980. — 409p : 1ill ; 23cm. — (Ulverscroft large print series)
Originally published: London : Souvenir, 1980
ISBN 0-7089-0697-4 : £5.00 : CIP rev.
B81-28092

Randall, Rona. The ladies of Hanover Square / Rona Randall. — London : Hamilton, 1981. — 322p ; 24cm
ISBN 0-241-10661-3 : £7.95 : CIP rev.
B81-20514

Rankin, Robert. The antipope / Robert Rankin. — London : Pan, 1981. — 248p ; 18cm. — (Pan original)
ISBN 0-330-26503-2 (pbk) : £1.50 B82-00779

Raphael, Frederic. Richard′s things / Frederic Raphael. — London : New English Library, 1981, c1973. — 175p ; 19cm
Originally published: London : Cape, 1973
ISBN 0-450-05223-0 (pbk) : £1.25 B82-37211

Raven, James. The Venice ultimatum / by James Raven. — London : Hale, 1982. — 192p ; 20cm
ISBN 0-7091-9694-6 : £6.75 B82-22128

Raven, Simon. An inch of fortune / Simon Raven. — London : Hamlyn, 1981, c1980. — 188p ; 18cm
Originally published: London : Blond and Briggs, 1980
ISBN 0-600-20432-4 (pbk) : £1.25 B82-12057

Raymond, Diana. Emma Pride / by Diana Raymond. — Loughton : Piatkus, c1981. — 345p ; 21cm
ISBN 0-86188-128-1 : £6.95 : CIP rev.
B81-31637

Raymond, Mary. Grandma Tyson′s legacy. — Loughton : Piatkus, Nov.1982. — [192]p
ISBN 0-86188-207-5 : £6.95 : CIP entry
B82-26060

Rayner, Claire. Bedford Row / Claire Rayner. — London : Weidenfeld and Nicolson, 1982, c1977. — 278p ; 23cm. — (The Performers ; bk.5)
Originally published: London : Cassell, 1977
ISBN 0-297-78132-4 : £6.95 B82-27755

Rayner, Claire. Charing Cross / Claire Rayner. — London : Weidenfeld and Nicolson, 1982, c1979. — 306p : 2geneal.tables ; 23cm. — (The Performers ; bk.7)
Originally published: London : Cassell, 1979
ISBN 0-297-78134-0 : £6.95 B82-30289

Rayner, Claire. Gower Street / Claire Rayner. — London : Weidenfeld and Nicolson, 1982, c1973. — 320p ; 23cm. — (The Performers ; bk.1)
Originally published: London : Cassell, 1973
ISBN 0-297-78128-6 : £6.95 B82-22726

Rayner, Claire. The house on the fen / by Claire Rayner. — Loughton : Piatkus, 1982, c1967. — 123p ; 21cm
Originally published: London : Transworld, 1967
ISBN 0-86188-138-9 : £5.50 : CIP rev.
B82-10244

Rayner, Claire. Lady mislaid. — Loughton : Piatkus, Oct.1982. — [128]p
ISBN 0-86188-136-2 : £5.95 : CIP entry
B82-24574

Rayner, Claire. Long Acre / Claire Rayner. — London : Weidenfeld and Nicolson, 1982, c1978. — 276p ; 23cm. — (The Performers ; bk.6)
Originally published: London : Cassell, 1978
ISBN 0-297-78133-2 : £6.95 B82-27756

Rayner, Claire. Paddington Green / Claire Rayner. — London : Weidenfeld and Nicolson, 1982, c1975. — 317p ; 23cm. — (The Performers ; bk.3)
Originally published: London : Cassell, 1975
ISBN 0-297-78130-8 : £6.95 B82-27753

Rayner, Claire. The running years / Claire Rayner. — London : Hutchinson, 1981. — 618p : 1map,geneal.tables ; 23cm
ISBN 0-09-146510-9 : £7.95 : CIP rev.
B81-24618

Rayner, Claire. Soho Square / Claire Rayner. — London : Weidenfeld and Nicolson, 1982, c1976. — 311p ; 23cm. — (The Performers ; bk.4)
Originally published: London : Cassell, 1976
ISBN 0-297-78131-6 : £6.95 B82-27754

Rayner, Claire. The Strand / Claire Rayner. — London : Weidenfeld and Nicolson, 1982, c1980. — 259p : 2geneal.tables ; 23cm. — (The Performers ; bk.8)
Originally published: London : Cassell, 1980
ISBN 0-297-78135-9 : £6.95 B82-30288

Rayner, Claire. A time to heal : a novel / by Claire Rayner. — Loughton : Piatkus, 1982, c1972. — 281p ; 21cm
Originally published: London : Cassell, 1972
ISBN 0-86188-105-2 : £5.95 : CIP rev.
B81-30626

Read, ***Miss***. Gossip from Thrush Green / by Miss Read ; illustrated by J.S. Goodall. — London : Joseph, c1981. — 246p : ill ; 21cm
Ill on lining papers
ISBN 0-7181-2046-9 : £6.95 B82-00812

Read, ***Miss***. The market square / Miss Read ; drawings by Harry Grimley. — Harmondsworth : Penguin, 1969, c1966 (1981 [printing]). — 204p : ill ; 18cm
Originally published: London : Joseph, 1966
ISBN 0-14-003007-7 (pbk) : £1.25 B82-01400

Read, ***Miss***. Miss Clare remembers / by ′Miss Read′ ; illustrated by J.S. Goodall. — Harmondsworth : Penguin, 1981, c1962. — 208p : ill ; 18cm
Originally published: London : Michael Joseph, 1962
£1.25 (pbk) B82-06433

Read, ***Miss***. Over the gate / ′Miss Read′ ; illustrated by J.S. Goodall. — Harmondsworth : Penguin, 1968, c1964 (1981 [printing]). — 202p : ill ; 18cm
Originally published: London : Joseph, 1964
ISBN 0-14-002900-1 (pbk) : £1.25 B82-01398

Read, ***Miss***. Return to Thrush Green / by Miss Read ; illustrations by J.S. Goodall. — Bolton-by-Bowland : Magna, 1980, c1978. — 368p : ill ; 23cm
Originally published: London : Joseph, 1978. — Published in large print
ISBN 0-86009-221-6 : £5.25 : CIP rev.
B79-37487

Read, ***Miss***. Village centenary / ′Miss Read′ ; illustrated by J.S. Goodall. — Harmondsworth : Penguin, 1982, c1980. — 221p : ill ; 18cm
Originally published: London : Joseph, 1980
ISBN 0-14-005788-9 (pbk) : £1.75 B82-29576

823'.914[F] — Fiction in English, *1945-* — *Texts continuation*

Read, *Miss*. Village centenary. — Large print ed. — Long Preston : Magna Print, Aug.1982. — [380]p
Originally published: London : Joseph, 1980
ISBN 0-86009-422-7 : £5.50 : CIP entry B82-16672

Read, *Miss*. The white robin / by Miss Read. — Bolton-by-Bowland : Magna, 1980, c1979. — 192p : ill ; 23cm
Originally published: London : Joseph, 1979. — Published in large print
ISBN 0-86009-284-4 : £5.25 : CIP rev. B80-34124

Read, *Miss*. The white robin / 'Miss Read'. — Harmondsworth : Penguin, 1981, c1979. — 110p : ill ; 18cm
Originally published: London : Michael Joseph, 1979
ISBN 0-14-005470-7 (pbk) : £1.25 B82-06432

Read, *Miss*. Winter in Thrush Green / Miss Read ; illustrated by J.S. Goodall. — Harmondsworth : Penguin, 1975 (1981 [printing]). — 194p : ill ; 19cm
Originally published: London : Michael Joseph, 1961
£1.25 (pbk) B82-08661

Redgrove, Peter. The facilitators, or, Mr Hole-in-the-Day. — London : Routledge & Kegan Paul, Sept.1982. — [128]p
ISBN 0-7100-9214-8 (pbk) : £4.95 : CIP entry B82-20022

Reeman, Douglas. Badge of glory. — London : Hutchinson, Oct.1982. — [304]p
ISBN 0-09-150470-8 : £7.50 : CIP entry B82-24978

Reeman, Douglas. Surface with daring / Douglas Reeman. — Large print ed. — Leicester : Ulverscroft, 1982, c1976. — 504p ; 23cm. — (Ulverscroft large print series)
Originally published: London : Hutchinson, 1976
ISBN 0-7089-0795-4 : Unpriced : CIP rev. B82-18557

Reeman, Douglas. To risks unknown. — Large print ed. — Anstey : Ulverscroft, Dec.1982. — 1v.. — (Ulverscroft large print series)
Originally published: London : Hutchinson, 1969
ISBN 0-7089-0893-4 : £5.00 : CIP entry B82-30787

Reeman, Douglas. Torpedo run / Douglas Reeman. — London : Arrow, 1982, c1981. — 290p ; 18cm
Originally published: London : Hutchinson, 1981
ISBN 0-09-928380-8 (pbk) : £1.50 B82-30457

Rees, David. The milkman's on his way. — London (27 Priory Ave., N8 7RN) : Gay Men's Press, Mar.1982. — [120]p
For adolescents
ISBN 0-907040-12-8 (pbk) : £2.50 : CIP entry B82-01159

Rees, David, *1936-*. The Exeter blitz / David Rees. — London : Heinemann Educational, 1981, c1978. — 116p ; 20cm. — (New windmill series)
Originally published: London : Hamilton, 1978. — For adolescents
ISBN 0-435-12258-4 : £1.50 B82-05288

Rees, Lucy. Take it to the limit : a novel / by Lucy Rees and Alan Harris. — London : Diaden, 1981. — 197p : ill ; 23cm
ISBN 0-906371-80-5 : £5.95 : CIP rev. B81-28173

Reid, Henrietta. New boss at Birchfields / by Henrietta Reid. — London : Mills & Boon, 1982. — 190p ; 20cm
ISBN 0-263-10050-2 : £5.25 B82-27275

Rendell, Ruth. The best man to die / Ruth Rendell. — London : Arrow, 1981, c1969. — 183p ; 18cm
Originally published: London : Long, 1969
ISBN 0-09-925910-9 (pbk) : £1.25 B82-06569

Rendell, Ruth. A dragon in their palaces. — London : Hutchinson, Feb.1983. — [288]p
ISBN 0-09-151060-0 : £6.95 : CIP entry B82-36568

Rendell, Ruth. Master of the moor. — London : Hutchinson, Apr.1982. — [220]p
ISBN 0-09-146930-9 : £6.95 : CIP entry B82-04723

Rendell, Ruth. A new lease of death / Ruth Rendell. — London : Arrow, 1981, c1969. — 183p ; 18cm
Originally published: London : Long, 1967
ISBN 0-09-925920-6 (pbk) : £1.25 B82-03542

Rendell, Ruth. Put on by cunning / Ruth Rendell. — London : Arrow, 1982, c1981. — 207p ; 18cm
Originally published: London : Hutchinson, 1981
ISBN 0-09-927730-1 (pbk) : £1.25 B82-22078

Rendell, Ruth. Put on by cunning. — Large print ed. — Bath : Chivers, Nov.1982. — [320]p. — (A New Portway large print book)
Originally published: London : Hutchinson, 1981
ISBN 0-85119-192-4 : £5.90 : CIP entry B82-26429

Rendell, Ruth. The secret house of death / Ruth Rendell. — London : Arrow, 1982, c1968. — 184p ; 18cm
Originally published: London : Long, 1968
ISBN 0-09-928660-2 (pbk) : £1.25 B82-35565

Rendell, Ruth. Wolf to the slaughter / Ruth Rendell. — London : Arrow, 1982, c1967. — 183p ; 18cm
Originally published: London : Long, 1967
ISBN 0-09-927740-9 (pbk) : £1.25 B82-31606

Renwick, John. The hungry guns / by John Renwick. — London : Hale, 1981. — 158p ; 20cm
ISBN 0-7091-9524-9 : £4.95 B82-00515

Rhea, Nicholas. Constable across the moors / Nicholas Rhea. — London : Hale, 1982. — 172p ; 23cm
ISBN 0-7091-9879-5 : £6.95 B82-34874

Rhea, Nicholas. Constable on the prowl / Nicholas Rhea. — Sevenoaks : New English Library, 1982, c1980. — 192p ; 18cm
Originally published: London : Hale, 1980
ISBN 0-450-05356-3 (pbk) : £1.50 : CIP rev. B82-15803

Rhodes, Leland. The danger trail / by Leland Rhodes. — London : Hale, 1981. — 155p ; 20cm
ISBN 0-7091-9356-4 : £4.95 B82-02818

Rhodes, Leland. Morning gun / by Leland Rhodes. — London : Hale, 1982. — 158p ; 20cm
ISBN 0-7091-9392-0 : £4.95 B82-12611

Richards, Alun. Barque whisper / Alun Richards. — Harmondsworth : Penguin, 1982, c1979. — 221p ; 19cm
Originally published: London : Joseph, 1979
ISBN 0-14-005441-3 (pbk) : £1.50 B82-25422

Richards, Alun. Ennal's point / Alun Richards. — Harmondsworth : Penguin, 1979, c1977 (1981 [printing]). — 255p ; 18cm
Originally published: London : Joseph, 1977
ISBN 0-14-004803-0 (pbk) : £1.50 B82-09164

Richards, Guy. The Canaris papers / Guy Richards. — London : Arrow, 1982. — 295p ; 18cm
ISBN 0-09-929030-8 (pbk) : £1.75 B82-35593

Richards, Vicki. Home is where the heart is / by Vicki Richards ; illustrated by Barbara Gordon ; editors Sheila Clark, Valerie Piacentini. — Strathmartine by Dundee (c/o 6 Craigmill Cottages, Strathmartine by Dundee, Scotland) : Scotpress, 1982. — 53p : ill ; 30cm
Unpriced (unbound) B82-22378

Richardson, Julia. Angel's cove / by Julia Richardson. — London : Hale, 1982. — 155p ; 20cm
ISBN 0-7091-9853-1 : £6.50 B82-32719

Richardson, Julia. Dragonhead / by Julia Richardson. — London : Hale, 1981. — 189p ; 20cm
ISBN 0-7091-9413-7 : £5.95 B82-03158

Richardson, Julia. Under a Dartmoor heaven / by Julia Richardson. — London : Hale, 1982. — 192p ; 20cm
ISBN 0-7091-9540-0 : £6.25 B82-13834

Richmond, Fiona. From here to virginity / Fiona Richmond. — London : W.H. Allen, 1981. — 145p ; 18cm. — (A Star book)
ISBN 0-352-30964-4 (pbk) : £1.25 B82-02674

Riems, David Alexander. Tibetan queen / David Alexander Riems ; illustrated by Jane Drotsky. — St. Ives : United Writers, c1982. — 109p : ill ; 22cm
ISBN 0-901976-75-x : £4.25 B82-17494

Rigby, Ray. Hill of sand / Ray Rigby. — London : W.H. Allen, 1981 (1982 [printing]). — 286p ; 18cm. — (A Star book)
ISBN 0-352-31141-x (pbk) : £1.75 B82-29191

Rimmer, W. S.. Son of a gun / by W.S. Rimmer. — London : Hale, 1982. — 159p ; 20cm
ISBN 0-7091-9546-x : £4.95 B82-13851

Roberts, Irene. Jasmine for a nurse / by Irene Roberts. — London : Hale, 1982. — 174p ; 20cm
ISBN 0-7091-9569-9 : £5.95 B82-15492

Roberts, Irene. Sister on leave / Irene Roberts. — London : Hale, 1982. — 176p ; 20cm
ISBN 0-7091-9581-8 : £6.50 B82-30498

Roberts, Janet Louise. Silver jasmine / Janet Louise Roberts. — London : Sphere, 1982, c1980. — 346p ; 18cm
ISBN 0-7221-7405-5 (pbk) : £1.95 B82-14905

Robins, Denise. Meet me in Monte Carlo. — Large print ed. — Bath : Chivers, Feb.1983. — [184]p. — (A Lythway book)
Originally published: London : Hutchinson, 1953
ISBN 0-85119-901-1 : £6.40 : CIP entry B82-39589

Robinson, Robert. Landscape with dead dons / by Robert Robinson. — London : Gollancz, c1956 (1982 [printing]). — 200p ; 21cm
Originally published: 1956
ISBN 0-575-03137-9 : £6.95 : CIP rev. B82-12985

Roe, Sue. Estella : her expectations : a novel / by Sue Roe. — Brighton : Harvester, 1982. — 154p ; 21cm
ISBN 0-7108-0465-2 : £6.95 : CIP rev. B82-07122

Rogers, Jane. Separate tracks. — London : Faber, Jan.1983. — [208]p
ISBN 0-571-11995-6 : £7.50 : CIP entry B82-32447

Rollo, Bill. Olympus gambit. — London : New English Library, Jan.1983. — [320]p
ISBN 0-450-05538-8 (pbk) : £1.75 : CIP entry B82-34603

823'.914[F] — Fiction in English, *1945- — Texts continuation*

Rome, Margaret. Isle of Calypso / Margaret Rome. — Large print ed. — Bath : Chivers, 1981, c1979. — 199p ; 23cm. — (A Seymour book)
Originally published: London : Mills & Boon, 1979
ISBN 0-85119-447-8 : Unpriced : CIP rev. B81-31794

Rome, Margaret. King Kielder / by Margaret Rome. — London : Mills & Boon, 1981. — 188p ; 19cm
ISBN 0-263-09951-2 : £4.55 B82-04634

Rome, Margaret. Miss High and Mighty / Margaret Rome. — Large print ed. — Bath : Chivers, 1981, c1980. — 236p ; 23cm
Originally published: London : Mills & Boon, 1980
ISBN 0-85119-439-7 : Unpriced : CIP rev. B81-25805

Rome, Margaret. Rapture of the deep / by Margaret Rome. — London : Mills & Boon, 1982. — 188p ; 20cm
ISBN 0-263-10108-8 : £5.95 B82-37439

Rome, Margaret. Son of Adam / Margaret Rome. — Large print ed. — Bath : Chivers Press, 1982, c1978. — 208p ; 23cm. — (A Seymour book)
Originally published: London : Mills & Boon, 1978
ISBN 0-85119-451-6 : Unpriced : CIP rev. B81-33805

Rome, Margaret. Valley of gentians / by Margaret Rome. — London : Mills & Boon, 1982. — 188p ; 19cm
ISBN 0-263-10027-8 : £5.25 B82-18109

Roos, Kelley. Murder on Martha's Vineyard / by Kelley Roos. — London : Hale, 1982, c1981. — 197p ; 20cm
Originally published: New York : Walker, 1981
ISBN 0-7091-9732-2 : £6.75 B82-27425

Roscoe, Charles. Sixgun showdown / by Charles Roscoe. — London : Hale, 1982. — 175p ; 20cm
ISBN 0-7091-9755-1 : £5.50 B82-30274

Ross, Cameron. The scaffold / by Cameron Ross. — London : Hale, 1981. — 155p ; 19cm
ISBN 0-7091-9427-7 : £6.50 B82-07208

Ross, Catherine. The colours of the night / Catherine Ross. — London : Magnum : 1981, c1962. — 215p ; 18cm
Originally published: London : Joseph, 1962
ISBN 0-417-06070-x (pbk) : £1.50 B82-15551

Ross, Edwina. Bequest of love / by Edwina Ross. — London : Hale, 1982. — 189p ; 20cm
ISBN 0-7091-9709-8 : £6.25 B82-30401

Ross, Frank. The shining day / Frank Ross. — London : Macmillan, 1981. — 339p ; 23cm
Originally published: New York : Atheneum, 1981
ISBN 0-333-30109-9 : £6.95 B82-05735

Ross, Frank, *1914-*. Dead runner. — Large print ed. — Long Preston : Magna, Feb.1983. — [440]p
Originally published: London : Macmillan, 1977
ISBN 0-86009-437-5 : £5.75 : CIP entry B82-39610

Ross, Maggie. Milena. — London : Collins, Jan.1983. — [288]p
ISBN 0-00-222602-2 : £8.50 : CIP entry B82-36123

Ross, Malcolm. The dukes. — Loughton : Piatkus, Feb.1983. — [512]p
ISBN 0-86188-241-5 : £8.50 : CIP entry B82-39812

Ross, Norman. Squadron. — London : Coronet, Oct.1982. — [192]p
ISBN 0-340-32050-8 (pbk) : £1.50 : CIP entry B82-28448

Ross, Raymond K.. One hundred miles above earth / by Raymond J. Ross. — London : Hale, 1981. — 192p ; 20cm. — (Hale SF)
ISBN 0-7091-9438-2 : £6.25 B82-12607

Ross, Stella. Sad flowers of winter / by Stella Ross. — London : Hale, 1981. — 160p ; 20cm
ISBN 0-7091-9443-9 : £5.95 B82-03174

Ross, Stella. A sprig of white heather / by Stella Ross. — London : Hale, 1982. — 158p ; 20cm
ISBN 0-7091-9765-9 : £6.50 B82-33901

Ross, Stella. Wildfire summer / by Stella Ross. — London : Hale, 1982. — 160p ; 20cm
ISBN 0-7091-9559-1 : £6.25 B82-15488

Rouch, James. Overkill. — London : New English Library, Mar.1982. — [160]p. — (The Zone ; 5)
ISBN 0-450-05402-0 (pbk) : £1.25 : CIP entry B82-01984

Rowe, Ron. Bye-bye blackbird / Ron Rowe. — Bognor Regis : New Horizon, c1982. — 112p ; 22cm
ISBN 0-86116-610-8 : £4.50 B82-10298

Rowe, Sydney T.. Foxhouse / Sydney T. Rowe. — Irchester : Saunders, 1982, c1981. — 144p ; 22cm
ISBN 0-907877-25-7 : £4.50 B82-35888

Rowland, Iris. Moonlight and roses / by Iris Rowland. — London : Hale, 1982. — 160p ; 20cm
ISBN 0-7091-9855-8 : £6.50 B82-33422

Rowland, Iris. Weave me a moonbeam / by Iris Rowland. — London : Hale, 1982. — 189p ; 20cm
ISBN 0-7091-9638-5 : £6.25 B82-15483

Rowlands, V. M. D.. The convenient wife / by V.M.D. Rowlands. — London : Hale, 1981. — 207p ; 20cm
ISBN 0-7091-9412-9 : £6.95 B82-03172

Royce, Kenneth. 10,000 days / Kenneth Royce. — London : Hodder and Stoughton, 1981. — 282p : 1map ; 22cm
ISBN 0-340-26249-4 (corrected) : £6.95 : CIP rev. B81-10471

Royce, Kenneth. 10,000 days. — London : Coronet, Dec.1982. — [288]p
Originally published: London : Hodder and Stoughton, 1981
ISBN 0-340-28648-2 (pbk) : £1.50 : CIP entry B82-29644

Royce, Kenneth. Channel assault / Kenneth Royce. — London : Hodder and Stoughton, 1982. — 252p ; 23cm
ISBN 0-340-28133-2 : £7.50 : CIP rev. B82-15741

Royce, Kenneth. The third arm. — London : Hodder & Stoughton, Nov.1981. — [208]p
Originally published: 1980
ISBN 0-340-26671-6 (pbk) : £1.50 : CIP entry B81-30542

Rubens, Bernice. Madame Sousatzka / Bernice Rubens. — London : Hamilton, 1982, c1962. — 187p ; 23cm
Originally published: London : Eyre & Spottiswoode, 1962
ISBN 0-241-10844-6 : £7.95 : CIP rev. B82-23452

Rubens, Bernice. Madame Sousatzka / Bernice Rubens. — London : Abacus, 1982. — 187p ; 20cm
Originally published: London : Eyre & Spottiswoode, 1962
ISBN 0-349-13015-9 (pbk) : £2.25 B82-34229

Rubens, Robert. A night at the Odeon / Robert Rubens. — Maidstone : Bachman & Turner, 1981. — 158p ; 23cm
ISBN 0-85974-106-0 : £5.95 B82-03213

Rush, Robert. The birthday treat / Robert Rush. — London : Macdonald Futura, c1981. — 286p ; 18cm. — (A Futura book)
ISBN 0-7088-2104-9 (pbk) : £1.50 B82-00457

Rushforth, P. S.. Kindergarten / P.S. Rushforth. — London : Abacus, 1981, c1979. — 151p ; 20cm
Originally published: London: Hamilton, 1979
ISBN 0-349-13019-1 (pbk) : £1.95 B82-06008

Russell, Martin, *1934-*. All part of the service / Martin Russell. — London : Collins, 1982. — 178p ; 20cm. — (The Crime Club)
ISBN 0-00-231032-5 : £6.50 : CIP rev. B82-19071

Russell, Martin, *1934-*. Death fuse / by Martin Russell. — Long Preston : Magna, 1982, c1980. — 330p ; 23cm
Originally published: London : Collins, 1980. — Published in large print
ISBN 0-86009-373-5 : Unpriced : CIP rev. B81-33765

Russell, Martin, *1934-*. Rainblast / Martin Russell. — London : Collins, 1982. — 191p ; 21cm. — (The Crime Club)
ISBN 0-00-231721-4 : £6.50 : CIP rev. B81-35937

Russell, Martin, *1934-*. Touchdown / by Martin Russell. — Long Preston : Magna, 1982, c1979. — 305p ; 22cm
Originally published: London : Collins, 1979. — Published in large print
ISBN 0-86009-409-x : Unpriced : CIP rev. B82-07838

Rutherford, Douglas. Porcupine basin / Douglas Rutherford. — London : Macmillan, 1981. — 191p ; 21cm
ISBN 0-333-32230-4 : £5.95 B82-05896

Ryan, David Stuart. The affair is all. — London (48A Astonville St., SW18 5AL) : Kozmik Press Centre, Feb.1982. — [256]p
ISBN 0-905116-06-2 : £6.50 : CIP entry B82-04717

Ryan, David Stuart. Looking for Kathmandu. — London (48A Astonville St., SW18 5AL) : Kozmik Press Centre, Feb.1982. — [256]p
ISBN 0-905116-05-4 : £6.50 : CIP entry B82-04716

Sadler, Geoff. Black revenge. — London : New English Library, Oct.1982. — [208]p. — (Justus)
ISBN 0-450-05458-6 (pbk) : £1.25 : CIP entry B82-24721

Sadler, Jeff. Sonora lode / by Jeff Sadler. — London : Hale, 1982. — 176p ; 20cm
ISBN 0-7091-9584-2 : £5.25 B82-17470

Sadler, Jeff. Tamaulipas guns / by Jeff Sadler. — London : Hale, 1982. — 160p ; 20cm
ISBN 0-7091-9873-6 : £5.50 B82-38555

Sager, Esther. Chasing rainbows : a novel / by Esther Sager. — Loughton : Piatkus, 1981. — 346p ; 21cm
ISBN 0-86188-157-5 : £7.50 : CIP rev. B82-00347

823'.914[F] — Fiction in English, *1945-* — *Texts continuation*

Sager, Esther. Chasing rainbows / Esther Sager. — London : Corgi, 1982, c1981. — 335p ; 18cm
Originally published: New York : Jove, 1981
ISBN 0-552-11981-4 (pbk) : £1.50 B82-35477

Salisbury, Carola. Count Vronsky's daughter. — Large print ed. — Anstey : Ulverscroft, Feb.1983. — 1v.. — (Ulverscroft large print series)
Originally published: London : Collins, 1981
ISBN 0-7089-0924-8 : CIP entry B82-38886

Salisbury, Ray. Say goodbye, Simon. — London : Deutsch, Aug.1982. — [260]p
ISBN 0-233-97469-5 : £6.95 : CIP entry B82-15688

Salway, Lance. Second to the right, and straight on till morning / Lance Salway. — Basingstoke : Macmillan 1980, c1979. — 103p ; 18cm. — (Topliners)
For adolescents
ISBN 0-333-26218-2 (pbk) : £0.70 : CIP rev. B80-18013

Sandon, J. D.. Survivors / J.D. Sandon. — London : Granada, 1982. — 123p ; 18cm. — (A Mayflower book)
ISBN 0-583-13415-7 (pbk) : £0.95 B82-36060

Sandon, J. D.. Wheels of thunder / J.D. Sandon. — London : Granada, 1981. — 144p ; 18cm. — (Gringos ; 8) (A Mayflower book)
ISBN 0-583-13263-4 (pbk) : £0.95 B82-09539

Sargent, Ruth. Waterbrook / by Ruth Sargent. — London : Hale, 1981. — 192p ; 20cm
ISBN 0-7091-9430-7 : £5.95 B82-02136

Saunders, Jean. The kissing time. — London : Hodder & Stoughton, Dec.1982. — [192]p. — (Silhouette romance)
ISBN 0-340-32694-8 (pbk) : £0.75 : CIP entry B82-29664

Savarin, Julian J.. Waterhole. — London : Allison & Busby, June 1982. — [256]p
ISBN 0-85031-458-5 : £6.95 : CIP entry B82-14214

Saxton, Judith. The glory / Judith Saxton. — Feltham : Hamlyn Paperbacks, 1982. — 350p ; 18cm
ISBN 0-600-20436-7 (pbk) : £1.50 B82-34031

Scanlan, Nelle M.. Pencarrow / Nelle M. Scanlan. — Large print ed. — Leicester : Ulverscroft, 1982. — 464p ; 23cm. — (Ulverscroft large print)
ISBN 0-7089-0820-9 : Unpriced : CIP rev. B82-15959

Scanlan, Nelle M.. Tides of youth. — Large print ed. — Anstey : Ulverscroft, Sept.1982. — [576] p. — (Ulverscroft large print series)
ISBN 0-7089-0849-7 : £5.00 : CIP entry B82-27179

Scanlan, Nelle M.. Winds of heaven. — Large print ed. — Anstey : Ulverscroft, Oct.1982. — [544]p. — (Ulverscroft large print series)
ISBN 0-7089-0863-2 : £5.00 : CIP entry B82-26684

Scarman, George. The victim / George Scarman. — London : Corgi, 1982. — 234p ; 18cm
ISBN 0-552-11926-1 (pbk) : £1.50 B82-23909

Schlee, Ann. Rhine journey / Ann Schlee. — Harmondsworth : Penguin in association with Macmillan, 1981, c1980. — 165p ; 20cm
Originally published: London : Macmillan, 1980
ISBN 0-14-006215-7 (pbk) : £2.25 B82-03211

Scholefield, Alan. The stone flower / by Alan Scholefield. — London : Hamilton, 1982. — 501p ; 23cm
ISBN 0-241-10739-3 : £7.95 : CIP rev. B81-37588

Scott, Alexandra. Love me again / by Alexandra Scott. — London : Mills & Boon, 1982. — 190p ; 20cm
ISBN 0-263-10008-1 : £5.25 B82-13886

Scott, Alexandra. This side of heaven / by Alexandra Scott. — London : Mills & Boon, 1982. — 189p ; 20cm
ISBN 0-263-10059-6 : £5.25 B82-27603

Scott, Douglas, *1926-*. The burning of the ships / Douglas Scott. — London : Fontana, 1981, c1980. — 319p ; 18
Originally published: London : Secker and Warburg, 1980
ISBN 0-00-616238-x (pbk) : £1.50 B82-03161

Scott, Douglas, *1926-*. In the face of the enemy / Douglas Scott. — London : Secker & Warburg, 1982. — 312p ; 23cm
ISBN 0-436-44427-5 : £6.95 : CIP rev. B81-35725

Scott, Hardiman. Operation 10 / Hardiman Scott. — London : Bodley Head, 1982. — 218p ; 22cm
ISBN 0-370-30462-4 : £6.95 : CIP rev. B82-00904

Scott, Hardiman. Operation 10. — London : Coronet Books, Feb.1983. — [240]p
Originally published: London : Bodley Head, 1982
ISBN 0-340-32114-8 (pbk) : £1.50 : CIP entry B82-38067

Scott, Isobel. Enchanted desert / by Isobel Scott. — London : Hale, 1981. — 159p ; 20cm
ISBN 0-7091-9058-1 : £6.25 B82-15474

Scott, Isobel. The scent of wild thyme / by Isobel Scott. — London : Hale, 1982. — 175p ; 20cm
ISBN 0-7091-9405-6 : £6.50 B82-30400

Scott, Isobel. That halcyon summer / by Isobel Scott. — London : Hale, 1981. — 176p ; 20cm
ISBN 0-7091-8748-3 : £5.95 B82-00449

Scott, Jack. An uprush of mayhem. — London : Collins, Feb.1982. — [204]p. — (The Crime Club)
ISBN 0-00-231894-6 : £6.95 : CIP entry B81-35938

Scott, Jack, *1922-*. A clutch of vipers. — Large print ed. — Bath : Chivers, Jan.1983. — [288] p. — (Atlantic large print)
Originally published: London : Collins, 1979
ISBN 0-85119-520-2 : £5.25 : CIP entry B82-36336

Scott, Jack, *1922-*. A distant view of death / Jack Scott. — Large print ed. — [Bath] : Chivers, 1982, c1981. — 319p ; 23cm. — (A Midnight large print thriller) (Atlantic large print)
Originally published: London : Collins, 1981
ISBN 0-85119-465-6 : Unpriced : CIP rev. B82-05003

Scott, Jack, *1922-*. The local lads. — London : Collins, Dec.1982. — [224]p. — (The Crime Club)
ISBN 0-00-231035-x : £6.75 : CIP entry B82-29858

Scott, Jeremy. The king of money / Jeremy Scott. — London : W.H. Allen, 1982. — 255p ; 23cm
ISBN 0-491-02677-3 : £7.95 B82-34120

Scott, Norford. Gun wranglers / by Norford Scott. — London : Hale, 1982. — 160p ; 19cm
ISBN 0-7091-9929-5 : £5.50 B82-39186

Secombe, Harry. Twice brightly / Harry Secombe. — London : Robson, 1974 (1981 [printing]). — 224p ; 23cm
ISBN 0-903895-23-4 : £6.95 B82-01512

Seeber, Gerd Christian. The abduction. — London : Secker and Warburg, Aug.1982. — [268]p
ISBN 0-436-44460-7 : £6.95 : CIP entry B82-15796

Sela, Owen. Triple factor / Owen Sela. — London : Collins, 1982. — 377p ; 22cm
ISBN 0-00-222372-4 : £7.95 : CIP rev. B82-06019

Selwyn, Francis. Sergeant Verity and the swell mob / Francis Selwym. — London : Deutsch, 1981. — 275p ; 21cm
ISBN 0-233-97217-x : £5.95 B82-03210

Serafin, David. Christmas rising. — London : Collins, Dec.1982. — [224]p
ISBN 0-00-231033-3 : £6.75 : CIP entry B82-29857

Serafin, David. Madrid underground : a superintendent Bernal novel / David Serafin. — London : Collins, 1982. — 211p : 1map ; 21cm. — (The Crime Club)
ISBN 0-00-231664-1 : £6.75 : CIP rev. B82-00899

Seton, Marie. Song of the atom / Marie Seton. — London : Dobson, 1981. — 126p ; 23cm
ISBN 0-234-72243-6 : £4.95 B82-05329

Sewart, Alan. Close your eyes and sleep my baby / by Alan Sewart. — London : Hale, 1981. — 190p ; 20cm
ISBN 0-7091-8784-x : £6.75 B82-30405

Sewart, Alan. The letter-box man / by Alan Sewart. — London : Hale, 1981. — 191p ; 20cm
ISBN 0-7091-8299-6 : £6.25 B82-00517

Sewart, Alan. Smoker's cough / by Alan Sewart. — London : Hale, 1982. — 190p ; 20cm
ISBN 0-7091-8629-0 : £6.75 B82-15480

Seymour, Arabella, *1948-*. The white and scarlet girl / Arabella Seymour. — London : Hale, 1981. — 239p ; 20cm
ISBN 0-7091-9437-4 : £6.95 B82-07203

Seymour, Gerald. Battleground. — London : Collins, May 1982. — [224]p
ISBN 0-00-222621-9 : £7.50 : CIP entry B82-07221

Seymour, Gerald. The contract / Gerald Seymour. — [London] : Fontana, 1981, c1980. — 347p ; 18cm
Originally published: London : Collins, 1980
ISBN 0-00-616253-3 (pbk) : £1.50 B82-03011

Seymour, Gerald. The glory boys / Gerald Seymour. — [London] : Fontana, 1977, c1976 (1982 [printing]). — 286p ; 18cm
ISBN 0-00-616436-6 (pbk) : £1.50 B82-09316

Shakespeare, Brian. Fox / Brian Shakespeare ; based on a series for television written by Trevor Preston. — London : Severn House Pt.1. — 1980. — 189p ; 21cm
ISBN 0-7278-0624-6 : £5.95 : CIP rev. B80-18903

Shaldon, Nina. The Sun God's island / by Nina Shaldon. — London : Hale, 1981. — 188p ; 20cm
ISBN 0-7091-9520-6 : £5.95 B82-07204

Shaldon, Nina. Thunder over Etna / by Nina Shaldon. — London : Hale, 1982. — 173p ; 19cm
ISBN 0-7091-9957-0 : £6.50 B82-39181

823′.914[F] — Fiction in English, *1945-* — *Texts continuation*

Shand, Linda. Sister in opposition / by Linda Shand. — London : Mills & Boon, 1979. — 188p ; 20cm
ISBN 0-263-09993-8 : £4.55 B82-09359

Shannon, Jade. Flowers in the valley / Jade Shannon. — London : Macdonald, 1981. — 251p ; 21cm. — (A Minstrel book ; 22)
ISBN 0-354-04761-2 (cased) : £4.95
ISBN 0-7088-2116-2 (pbk) : £0.95 B82-03144

Sharp, Roger. Quarmby / by Roger Sharp. — London : Hale, 1981. — 189p ; 20cm
ISBN 0-7091-9454-4 : £6.50 B82-06326

Sharpe, Tom. Vintage stuff. — London : Secker & Warburg, Oct.1982. — [224]p
ISBN 0-436-45810-1 : £7.95 : CIP entry B82-25517

Shaul, Frank. Uneasy range / by Frank Shaul. — London : Hale, 1982. — 159p ; 20cm
ISBN 0-7091-9770-5 : £5.50 B82-33198

Shaw, Howard. Death of a don / Howard Shaw. — London : Hodder and Stoughton, 1982, c1981. — 187p ; 23cm
ISBN 0-340-27643-6 : £6.50 : CIP rev. B81-34123

Sheard, John. Ebony, ivory / John Sheard. — Feltham : Hamlyn, 1982. — 220p ; 18cm
ISBN 0-600-20344-1 (pbk) : £1.25 B82-11330

Shears, Sarah. Deborah Hammond / Sarah Shears. — Loughton : Piatkus, 1981. — 215p ; 21cm
ISBN 0-86188-110-9 : £6.50 : CIP rev. B81-21617

Shears, Sarah. The landlady. — Large print ed. — Anstey : Ulverscroft, Sept.1982. — [352]p. — (Ulverscroft large print series)
Originally published: Littlehampton: Piatkus, 1980
ISBN 0-7089-0852-7 : £5.00 : CIP entry B82-27181

Shears, Sarah. Martha Craddock / Sarah Shears. — Loughton : Piatkus, c1982. — 189p ; 21cm
ISBN 0-86188-175-3 : £6.50 : CIP rev. B82-06261

Shears, Sarah. The neighbours. — Loughton : Piatkus, Nov.1982. — [600]p
ISBN 0-86188-214-8 : £8.95 : CIP entry B82-26061

Shears, Sarah. Tapioca for tea. — Loughton (17 Brook Rd, Loughton, Essex) : Piatkus, June 1981. — [256]p
Originally published: London : Elek, 1971
ISBN 0-86188-100-1 : £6.95 : CIP entry B81-09475

Sheffield, Charles. The web between the worlds / Charles Sheffield. — London : Arrow, 1981, c1979. — 274p ; 18cm
Originally published: New York : Ace, 1979 ; London : Sidgwick and Jackson, 1980
ISBN 0-09-926670-9 (pbk) : £1.60 B82-06570

Shelley, Elizabeth. Caravan of desire / Elizabeth Shelley. — London : Futura, 1982, c1980. — 30p ; 18cm. — (A Troubadour book)
ISBN 0-7107-3028-4 (pbk) : £1.75 B82-27078

Sherrell, Ted. The lonely and lost / Ted Sherrell. — St. Ives : United Writers, c1980. — 144p ; 22cm
ISBN 0-901976-57-1 : £4.50 B82-17495

Sherwood, John. A shot in the arm / by John Sherwood. — London : Gollancz, 1982. — 172p ; 21cm
ISBN 0-575-03197-2 : £6.95 : CIP rev. B82-18765

Short, Christopher. Leslie Charteris′ The Saint and the Hapsburg necklace / written by Christopher Short. — Sevenoaks : Hodder and Stoughton, 1976, c1975 (1980 [printing]). — 192p ; 18cm. — (Coronet books)
Originally published: Garden City, N.Y. : Doubleday ; London : Hodder and Stoughton, 1976
ISBN 0-340-23252-8 (pbk) : £0.75 : CIP rev. B78-30075

Sillitoe, Alan. Her victory. — London : Granada, Sept.1982. — [544]p
ISBN 0-246-11872-5 : £8.95 : CIP entry B82-18863

Sillitoe, Alan. The second chance and other stories. — Large print ed. — Bath : Chivers, Oct.1982. — [320]p. — (A Lythway book)
Originally published: London : Cape, 1981
ISBN 0-85119-858-9 : £7.50 : CIP entry B82-20524

Silvester, Frank. Greenhorn Gorge / by Frank Silvester. — London : Hale, 1981. — 160p ; 19cm
ISBN 0-7091-9460-9 : £4.95 B82-07206

Simms, Jacqueline. Unsolicited gift / Jacqueline Simms. — London : Chatto & Windus, 1982. — 151p ; 21cm
ISBN 0-7011-2616-7 : £6.95 B82-16937

Simpson, Dorothy, *1933-*. Six feet under / Dorothy Simpson. — London : Joseph, c1982. — 192p ; 23cm
ISBN 0-7181-2082-5 : £6.95 B82-13686

Simpson, Jane, *1923-*. The soldier from the fire / Jane Simpson. — London : Hale, 1981. — 174p ; 21cm
ISBN 0-7091-9386-6 : £6.50 B82-02139

Simpson, John. A fine and private place. — London : Robson, Sept.1982. — [296]p
ISBN 0-86051-189-8 : £6.95 : CIP entry B82-20867

Sims, George, *1923-*. The keys of death / George Sims. — London : Macmillan, 1982. — 189p ; 21cm
ISBN 0-333-32632-6 : £5.95 B82-18241

Sisson, Rosemary Anne. The Manions of America / by Rosemary Anne Sisson ; based on a story by Agnes Nixon. — Loughton : Piatkus, 1982, c1981. — 395p ; 21cm
ISBN 0-86188-173-7 : £8.50 : CIP rev. B82-10247

Skelton, C. L.. The Maclarens / C.L. Skelton. — Leicester : Charnwood, 1982, c1978. — 464p ; 23cm. — (Charnwood library series)
Originally published: London : Granada, 1978. — Published in large print
ISBN 0-7089-8040-6 : Unpriced : CIP rev. B82-08100

Skelton, C. L.. Sweethearts and wives / C.L. Skelton. — Leicester : Charnwood, 1982, c1979. — 483p ; 23cm. — (Charnwood library series)
Originally published: London : Granada, 1979. — Published in large print
ISBN 0-7089-8052-x : Unpriced : CIP rev. B82-15951

Skidmore, Ian. Island fling / Ian Skidmore. — London : W.H. Allen, 1982, c1981. — 172p ; 19cm
ISBN 0-491-02795-8 : £4.95 B82-11443

Skinner, Michael, *1924-*. Raiders of Spanish Creek / by Mike Skinner. — London : Hale, 1982. — 155p ; 20cm
ISBN 0-7091-9931-7 : £5.50 B82-37253

Skinner, Michael, *1924-*. Ride into hell / Mike Skinner. — London : Hale, 1982. — 174p ; 20cm
ISBN 0-7091-9718-7 : £5.25 B82-22863

Slaughter, Carolyn. Dreams of the Kalahari / Carolyn Slaughter. — London : Granada, 1982, c1981. — 394p ; 18cm. — (A Panther book)
ISBN 0-586-05394-8 (pbk) : £1.95 B82-28373

Slaughter, Carolyn. Heart of the river. — London : Granada, Oct.1982. — [288]p
ISBN 0-246-11902-0 : £7.95 : CIP entry B82-25155

Smethurst, William. Ambridge : an English village through the ages / Jennifer Aldridge & John Tregorran. — London : Borchester in association with Eyre Methuen. By arrangement with the British Broadcasting Corporation, 1981. — 150p : ill,maps,facsims,port ; 26cm
Written by William Smethurst. — Includes index
ISBN 0-413-48350-9 : £6.95 B82-17542

Smethurst, William. Ambridge : an English village through the ages / Jennifer Aldridge & John Tregorran. — London : Borchester Press in association with Methuen by arrangement with the British Broadcasting Corporation, 1982, c1981. — 150p : ill,facsims,maps ; 26cm
Written by William Smethurst. — Originally published: London : Borchester Press in association with Eyre Methuen, 1981. — Includes index
ISBN 0-413-50170-1 (pbk) : £3.50 B82-33928

Smith, Colin, *1944-*. Cut-out / Colin Smith. — London : Deutsch, 1980. — 200p ; 21cm
ISBN 0-233-97279-x : £5.95 B82-16193

Smith, Doris E.. Marmalade witch / by Doris E. Smith. — London : Mills & Boon, 1982. — 189p ; 19cm
ISBN 0-263-10021-9 : £5.25 B82-18112

Smith, Doris E.. Noah′s daughter / by Doris E. Smith. — London : Hale, 1982. — 160p ; 20cm
ISBN 0-7091-9708-x : £6.25 B82-31615

Smith, Frederick E. (Frederick Edward). 633 Squadron — Operation Titan / Frederick E. Smith. — London : Severn House, 1982. — 238p ; 21cm
ISBN 0-7278-0802-8 : £6.95 B82-30469

Smith, Frederick E. (Frederick Escreet). 633 Squadron — Operation Cobra / Frederick E. Smith. — [London] : Corgi, 1981. — 235p ; 18cm
ISBN 0-552-11824-9 (pbk) : £1.35 B82-03228

Smith, Frederick E. (Frederick Escreet). 633 Squadron, Operation Cobra / Frederick E. Smith. — London : Severn House, 1981. — 235p ; 21cm
ISBN 0-7278-0744-7 : £6.95 : CIP rev. B81-30254

Smith, Frederick E. (Frederick Escreet). A killing for the hawks / Frederick E. Smith. — London : Corgi, 1982, c1966. — 253p ; 18cm
Originally published: London : Harrap, 1966
ISBN 0-552-11784-6 (pbk) : £1.50 B82-16746

Smith, Frederick E. (Frederick Escreet). Lydia Trendennis / F.E. Smith. — [Feltham] : Hamlyn Paperbacks, 1982, c1957. — 190p ; 18cm
Originally published: London : Hutchinson, 1957
ISBN 0-600-20558-4 (pbk) : £1.25 B82-35724

Smith, Frederick E. (Frederick Escreet). [The other cousin]. The dark cliffs / F.E. Smith. — Feltham, Hamlyn, 1982, c1962. — 156p ; 18cm
Originally published: Henley-on-Thames : Gresham, 1962
ISBN 0-600-20557-6 (pbk) : £1.25 B82-30763

Smith, Guy N.. Blood circuit. — London : New English Library, Jan.1983. — [176]p. — (Sabat ; 3)
ISBN 0-450-05552-3 (pbk) : £1.25 : CIP entry B82-34605

823'.914[F] — Fiction in English, *1945- — Texts continuation*

Smith, Guy N.. The blood merchants / Guy N. Smith. — London : New English Library, 1982. — 160p ; 18cm. — (Sabat ; 2)
ISBN 0-450-05414-4 (pbk) : £1.25 : CIP rev. B82-06826

Smith, Guy N.. Cannibal cult. — London : New English Library, Nov.1982. — [160]p. — (Sabat ; 3)
ISBN 0-450-05548-5 (pbk) : £1.25 : CIP entry B82-27520

Smith, Guy N.. Entombed / Guy N. Smith. — Feltham : Hamlyn, 1982. — 191p ; 18cm
ISBN 0-600-20353-0 (pbk) : £1.25 B82-13045

Smith, Guy N.. The graveyard vultures / Guy N. Smith. — London : New English Library, 1982. — 160p ; 18cm. — (Sabat ; 1)
ISBN 0-450-05413-6 (pbk) : £1.25 : CIP rev. B82-06825

Smith, Guy N.. The Pluto pact / Guy N. Smith. — Feltham : Hamlyn, 1982. — 187p ; 18cm
ISBN 0-600-20488-x (pbk) : £1.25 B82-30985

Smith, Guy N.. Warhead / Guy N. Smith. — London : New English Library, 1981. — 256p ; 18cm
ISBN 0-450-05279-6 (pbk) : £1.50 B82-08657

Smith, Harriet. First love, last love / by Harriet Smith. — London : Hale, 1982. — 159p ; 19cm
ISBN 0-7091-9977-5 : £6.50 B82-39185

Smith, Henry T.. The necessary peace / Henry T. Smith. — London : Hale, 1982. — 191p ; 20cm
ISBN 0-7091-9905-8 : £7.25 B82-35896

Smith, Iain Crichton. A field full of folk : a novel / by Iain Crichton Smith. — London : Gollancz, 1982. — 144p ; 22cm
ISBN 0-575-03110-7 : £6.95 : CIP rev. B82-06934

Smith, Jasper. Sledgehammer / Jasper Smith. — London : Hamlyn Paperbacks, 1981. — 250p ; 18cm
ISBN 0-600-20359-x (pbk) : £1.25 B82-00649

Smith, Molly. The turning of the tide / Molly Smith. — Bognor Regis : New Horizon, c1982. — 248p ; 21cm
ISBN 0-86116-869-0 : £6.25 B82-13603

Smith, Rukshana. Sumitra's story / Rukshana Smith. — London : Bodley Head, 1982. — 159p ; 20cm. — (A Book for new adults)
ISBN 0-370-30466-7 (pbk) : £3.50 : CIP rev. B82-03842

Smith, Wilbur. The angels weep / Wilbur Smith. — London : Heinemann, 1982. — 506p ; 23cm
ISBN 0-434-71414-3 : £8.50 B82-26002

Smith, Wilbur. Cry wolf / by Wilbur Smith. — Long Preston : Magna, 1982, c1976. — 803p ; 23cm
Originally published: London : Heinemann, 1976. — Published in large print
ISBN 0-86009-407-3 : Unpriced : CIP rev. B82-12171

Smith, Wilbur. Men of men / Wilbur Smith. — London : Pan in association with Heinemann, 1982, c1981. — 524p ; 18cm
Originally published: London : Heinemann, 1981
ISBN 0-330-26711-6 (pbk) : £1.95 B82-34252

Smith, Wilbur. The sound of thunder / Wilbur Smith. — Long Preston : Magna Print, 1982, c1966. — 839p ; 22cm
Originally published: London : Heinemann, 1966. — Published in large print
ISBN 0-86009-367-0 : Unpriced : CIP rev. B81-33995

Sonny, St. Clair. The St. Lucian affair / St. Clair Sonny. — Bognor Regis : New Horizon, c1982. — 195p ; 21cm
ISBN 0-86116-774-0 : £5.75 B82-36118

Spark, Muriel. The comforters / Muriel Spark. — Harmondsworth : Penguin, 1963, c1957 (1982 [printing]). — 203p ; 18cm
Originally published: London : Macmillan, 1957
ISBN 0-14-001911-1 (pbk) : £1.75 B82-29607

Spark, Muriel. The hothouse by the East River / Muriel Spark. — London : Granada, 1982, c1973. — 139p ; 18cm
Originally published: London : Macmillan, 1973
ISBN 0-586-05559-2 (pbk) : £1.25 B82-40248

Spark, Muriel. The public image / Muriel Spark. — Harmondsworth : Penguin, 1970, c1968 (1982 [printing]). — 124p ; 18cm
Originally published: London : Macmillan, 1968
ISBN 0-14-003131-6 (pbk) : £1.50 B82-28632

Spark, Muriel. Robinson / Muriel Spark. — Harmondsworth : Penguin, 1964, c1958 (1982 [printing]). — 174p : 1map ; 19cm
Originally published: London : Macmillan, 1958
ISBN 0-14-002157-4 (pbk) : £1.75 B82-32575

Sparks, Christine. Triangle : question of command : a novel / by Christine Sparks ; from the BBC-TV series created by Ted Rhodes and Bill Sellars ; based on storylines by Ben Steed and scripts by Colin Davis ... [et al.]. — London : British Broadcasting Corporation, 1982. — 255p ; 18cm
ISBN 0-563-20061-8 (pbk) : £1.95 B82-27768

Spendlove, Jean. For freedom to be equal / Jean Spendlove. — Helmdon (54 Wappenham Rd., Helmdon, Brackley, Northants.) : J. Spendlove, c1982. — xi,143p : 2maps ; 23cm
Maps on lining papers
ISBN 0-9507986-0-6 (cased) : Unpriced
ISBN 0-9507986-1-4 (pbk) : Unpriced B82-27991

Spurr, Clinton. Hostile hills / by Clinton Spurr. — London : Hale, 1982. — 159p ; 20cm
ISBN 0-7091-9554-0 : £4.95 B82-11059

Spurr, Clinton. Killer on the range / by Clinton Spurr. — London : Hale, 1982. — 159p ; 20cm
ISBN 0-7091-9742-x : £5.50 B82-31622

Squire, Lilian Stella. Jan / by Lilian Stella Squire. — London : Hale, 1982. — 160p ; 20cm
ISBN 0-7091-9703-9 : £6.25 B82-18306

St Aubin de Terán, Lisa. Keepers of the house / Lisa St Aubin de Terán. — London : Cape, 1982. — 183p ; 23cm
ISBN 0-224-02001-3 : £6.95 : CIP rev. B82-14228

St. George, Edith. West of the moon / Edith St. George. — London : Silhouette, 1981. — 189p ; 18cm. — (Silhouette romance ; 69)
ISBN 0-340-27124-8 (pbk) : £0.65 : CIP rev. B81-26774

St. James, Ian. The Balfour conspiracy / Ian St. James. — [London] : Fontana, 1982, c1981. — 317p ; 18cm
Originally published: London : Heinemann, 1981
ISBN 0-00-616298-3 (pbk) : £1.50 B82-16820

St. James, Ian. The money stones. — Large print ed. — Anstey : Ulverscroft, Feb.1983. — 1v.. — (Ulverscroft large print series)
Originally published: London : Heinemann, 1980
ISBN 0-7089-0923-x : CIP entry B82-38885

St. James, Ian. Winner Harris / Ian St. James. — London : Heinemann, 1982. — 342p ; 22cm
ISBN 0-434-66622-x : £7.95 B82-26005

Stafford, Lee. Royalist enchantress / Lee Stafford. — London : Hale, 1982. — 190p ; 20cm
ISBN 0-7091-9822-1 : £7.25 B82-33194

Stall, Mike. The Bormann judgement / by Mike Stall. — London : Hale, 1981. — 160p ; 20cm
ISBN 0-7091-9311-4 : £6.50 B82-07199

Stall, Mike. The killing mask / by Mike Stall. — London : Hale, 1982. — 186p ; 20cm
ISBN 0-7091-9610-5 : £6.75 B82-22132

Stall, Mike. The wet job / by Mike Stall. — London : Hale, 1982. — 188p ; 20cm
ISBN 0-7091-9796-9 : £6.75 B82-36524

Standish, Caroline. Sweet temptation / Caroline Standish. — London : Macdonald, 1982, c1981. — 253p ; 21cm
Originally published: London : Futura, 1981
ISBN 0-356-08652-6 : £4.95 B82-26007

Stearn, Kelly. Best friends / Kelly Stearn. — London : W.H. Allen, 1982. — 284p ; 18cm. — (Star)
ISBN 0-352-31086-3 (pbk) : £1.75 B82-22064

Steele, Addison E.. Buck Rogers in the 25th century / Addison E. Steele ; based on the story and teleplay by Glen A. Larson and Leslie Stevens. — London : Severn House, 1979, c1978. — 256p ; 21cm
Originally published: London : Sphere, 1979
ISBN 0-7278-0538-x : £4.95 : CIP rev. B79-32061

Steele, Jassica. The other brother / by Jessica Steele. — London : Mills & Boon, 1981. — 191p ; 19cm
ISBN 0-263-09962-8 : £4.55 B82-04633

Steele, Jessica. But know not why / by Jessica Steele. — London : Mills & Boon, 1982. — 189p ; 19cm
ISBN 0-263-10020-0 : £5.25 B82-18113

Steele, Jessica. Dishonest woman / by Jessica Steele. — London : Mills & Boon, 1982. — 188p ; 20cm
ISBN 0-263-09997-0 : £5.25 B82-10385

Steele, Jessica. The other brother / Jessica Steele. — London : Mills & Boon, c1981 (1982 [printing]). — 191p ; 18cm
ISBN 0-263-73967-8 (pbk) : £0.85 B82-36103

Stephens, Kay. Journey no more. — Large print ed. — Anstey : Ulverscroft, Feb.1983. — 1v.. — (Ulverscroft large print series)
Originally published: London : Collins, 1978
ISBN 0-7089-0925-6 : CIP entry B82-38887

Stephenson, Maureen. Autumn of deception / by Maureen Stephenson. — London : Hale, 1982. — 207p ; 20cm
ISBN 0-7091-9500-1 : £6.95 B82-11067

Stern, G. B.. Dolphin Cottage / G.B. Stern. — London : Remploy, 1981, c1962. — 190p ; 22cm
Originally published: London : Collins, 1962
ISBN 0-7066-0910-7 : £4.90 B82-03683

Stevens, Lynsey. Play our song again / by Lynsey Stevens. — London : Mills & Boon, 1981. — 188p ; 20cm
ISBN 0-263-09969-5 : £4.50 B82-09358

Stevens, Lynsey. Race for revenge / by Lynsey Stevens. — London : Mills & Boon, 1981. — 188p ; 19cm
ISBN 0-263-09942-3 : £4.55 B82-00043

Stevens, Lynsey. Starting over / by Lynsey Stevens. — London : Mills & Boon, 1982. — 187p ; 20cm
ISBN 0-263-10053-7 : £5.25 B82-27282

823'.914[F] — Fiction in English, *1945-* **—** *Texts continuation*

Stevens, Lynsey. Starting over / by Lynsey Stevens. — London : Mills & Boon, 1982. — 187p ; 18cm
ISBN 0-263-73854-x (pbk) : £0.85 B82-36284

Stevens, Lynsey. Tropical knight / by Lynsey Stevens. — London : Mills & Boon, 1982. — 188p ; 20cm
ISBN 0-263-10006-5 : £5.25 B82-13892

Stevens, Robert Tyler. The fields of yesterday / Robert Tyler Stevens. — [Feltham] : Hamlyn Paperbacks, 1982. — 239p : 1map ; 18cm
ISBN 0-600-20578-9 (pbk) : £1.50 B82-33682

Stevenson, Anne. Mask of treason. — Large print ed. — Anstey : Ulverscroft Large Print Books, Nov.1982. — [416]p. — (Ulverscroft large print series)
Originally published: New York : Putnam, 1979 ; Loughton : Piatkus, 1981
ISBN 0-7089-0875-6 : £5.50 : CIP entry B82-29095

Stevenson, Anne. Turkish rondo / by Anne Stevenson. — Loughton : Piatkus, 1982, c1981. — 238p ; 21cm
ISBN 0-86188-096-x : £6.95 : CIP rev. B81-21616

Stewart, A. J.. Falcon. — Glasgow : MacLellan, Dec.1981. — [248]p
Originally published: London : P. Davies, 1970
ISBN 0-85335-246-1 : £6.95 : CIP entry B81-33881

Stewart, Bruce. The hot and copper sky / Bruce Stewart. — London : Arrow, 1981. — 398p ; 18cm
ISBN 0-09-926710-1 (pbk) : £1.95 B82-03535

Stewart, Bruce. The hot and copper sky / Bruce Stewart. — London : Severn House, 1982, c1981. — 398p ; 21cm
Originally published: London : Arrow, 1981
ISBN 0-7278-0812-5 : £7.95 B82-35458

Stewart, Isobel. Believe in me / by Isobel Stewart. — London : Hale, 1981. — 160p ; 20cm
ISBN 0-7091-9447-1 : £5.95 B82-07198

Stewart, Isobel. The laird of Glenlochan / by Isobel Stewart. — London : Hale, 1982. — 173p ; 20cm
ISBN 0-7091-9888-4 : £6.50 B82-36522

Stewart, Isobel. Trust in tomorrow / Isobel Stewart. — London : Hale, 1982. — 174p ; 19cm
ISBN 0-7091-9582-6 : £6.25 B82-22131

Stewart, Jean, *19---*. Escape to Hong Kong / Jean Stewart. — London : Hamlyn Paperbacks, 1981. — 139p ; 18cm. — (A Sapphire romance)
ISBN 0-600-20070-1 (pbk) : £0.75 B82-00648

Stewart, Susan. Master of Ashwood / by Susan Stewart. — London : Hale, 1982. — 160p ; 20cm
ISBN 0-7091-9609-1 : £6.75 B82-39080

Stonehouse, John. Ralph / John Stonehouse. — London : Cape, 1982. — 318p ; 23cm
ISBN 0-224-02019-6 : £6.95 : CIP rev. B82-01132

Stoneley, Jack. The Reichling affair / Jack Stoneley. — Feltham : Hamlyn Paperbacks, 1982. — 318p ; 18cm
ISBN 0-600-20430-8 (pbk) : £1.75 B82-22393

Storey, David. Flight into Camden. — London : Cape, Nov.1982. — [224]p
Originally published: London : Longman, 1960
ISBN 0-224-02033-1 : £7.50 : CIP entry B82-26867

Storey, David. Radcliffe. — London : Cape, Nov.1982. — [376]p
Originally published: London : Longman, 1963
ISBN 0-224-02032-3 : £8.50 : CIP entry B82-26866

Storey, David, *1933-*. A prodigal child / David Storey. — London : Cape, 1982. — 319p ; 23cm
ISBN 0-224-02027-7 : £7.50 : CIP rev. B82-14064

Storr, Catherine. The Chinese egg / Catherine Storr. — London : Faber Fanfares, 1982, c1975. — 266p ; 19cm
Originally published: London : Faber, 1975
ISBN 0-571-11871-2 (pbk) : £2.50 : CIP rev. B82-04595

Strachan, Ian, *1938-*. The Soutar retrospective / Ian Strachan. — Oxford : Oxford University Press, 1982. — 176p ; 23cm
ISBN 0-19-271464-3 : £5.95 : CIP rev. B82-04163

Stranger, Joyce. The curse of Seal Valley / Joyce Stranger. — London : Carousel, 1982, c1979. — 127p ; 18cm
Originally published: London : Dent, 1979
ISBN 0-552-52207-4 (pbk) : £0.95 B82-37553

Stranger, Joyce. Double trouble : vet up the wall / Joyce Stranger. — London : Severn House, 1982, c1981. — 116p ; 21cm
Originally published: London : Carousel, 1981
ISBN 0-7278-0759-5 : £4.25 B82-30474

Stranger, Joyce. No more horses : vet in a muddle! / Joyce Stranger. — [London] : Carousel, 1982. — 127p ; 17cm
ISBN 0-552-52168-x (pbk) : £0.95 B82-24176

Stratton, Rebecca. Charade / by Rebecca Stratton. — London : Mills & Boon, 1982. — 188p ; 19cm
ISBN 0-263-10019-7 : £5.25 B82-18128

Stratton, Rebecca. The golden Spaniard / by Rebecca Stratton. — London : Mills & Boon, 1982. — 186p ; 20cm
ISBN 0-263-09984-9 : £5.25 B82-10382

Stratton, Rebecca. The man from nowhere / by Rebecca Stratton. — London : Mills & Boon, 1982. — 184p ; 19cm
ISBN 0-263-10113-4 : £5.95 B82-37270

Street, Pamela. The stepsisters / by Pamela Street. — London : Hale, 1982. — 192p ; 22cm
ISBN 0-7091-9563-x : £6.95 B82-22114

Streib, Dan. The deadly crusader / Dan Streib. — London : Sphere, 1982, c1980. — 183p ; 17cm. — (Hawk ; 1)
ISBN 0-7221-8188-4 (pbk) : £1.25 B82-36542

Streib, Dan. The mind twisters / Dan Streib. — London : Sphere, 1982, c1980. — 184p ; 17cm. — (Hawk ; 2)
ISBN 0-7221-8189-2 (pbk) : £1.25 B82-36541

Streib, Dan. The predators / Dan Streib. — London : Sphere, 1982, c1980. — 187p ; 17cm. — (Hawk ; 4)
ISBN 0-7221-8191-4 (pbk) : £1.25 B82-36543

Strong, Susan, *1927-*. By love cast out / by Susan Strong. — London : Hale, 1982. — 188p ; 20cm
ISBN 0-7091-9923-6 : £6.50 B82-35871

Strong, Susan, *1927-*. Drama of love / by Susan Strong. — London : Hale, 1981. — 176p ; 20cm
ISBN 0-7091-9349-1 : £5.75 B82-02154

Strong, Susan, *1927-*. Will to love / by Susan Strong. — London : Hale, 1982. — 206p ; 20cm
ISBN 0-7091-9639-3 : £6.25 B82-15495

Strong, Terence. The fifth hostage. — London : Coronet Books, Feb.1983. — [352]p
ISBN 0-340-32120-2 (pbk) : £1.75 : CIP entry B82-39275

Strong, Terence. Whisper who dares. — Bath : Chivers, Nov.1982. — [352]p. — (Firecrest books)
ISBN 0-85997-505-3 : £7.50 : CIP entry B82-26337

Strong, Terence. Whisper who dares. — Large print ed. — Bath : Chivers, Feb.1983. — [512] p. — (A Lythway book)
Originally published: London : Hodder and Stoughton, 1982
ISBN 0-85119-902-x : £7.90 : CIP entry B82-39590

Strong, Terry. Whisper who dares. — London : Hodder and Stoughton, Mar.1982. — [336]p. — (Coronet books)
ISBN 0-340-27908-7 (pbk) : £1.75 : CIP entry B82-00254

Strutt, Sheila. Stamp of possession / by Sheila Strutt. — London : Mills & Boon, 1982. — 186p ; 20cm
ISBN 0-263-09948-2 : £5.25 B82-10384

Stuart, Blair. Bloodwealth / Blair Stuart. — Feltham : Hamlyn Paperbacks, 1982, c1980. — 284p ; 18cm
Originally published: London : Macmillan, 1980
ISBN 0-600-20568-1 (pbk) : £1.50 B82-34030

Stuart, Dee. Wings of morning / Dee Stuart. — London : Futura, 1982, c1980. — 391p ; 18cm. — (Troubadour)
ISBN 0-7107-3020-9 (pbk) : £1.95 B82-18264

Stuart, Ian, *1927-*. The garb of truth / by Ian Stuart. — London : Hale, 1982. — 176p ; 20cm
ISBN 0-7091-9833-7 : £6.75 B82-37295

Stuart, Vivian. The exiles. — Large print ed. — Anstey : Ulverscroft, Dec.1982. — 1v.. — (Charnwood library series)
Originally published: New York : Dell ; London : Futura, 1980
ISBN 0-7089-8088-0 : £7.50 : CIP entry B82-30794

Stuart, Vivian. The traitors / Vivian Stuart writing as William Stuart Long. — London : Futura, 1982, c1981. — 621p : 2maps ; 18cm. — (The Australians)
ISBN 0-7088-2186-3 (pbk) : £2.50 B82-27055

Stuart, Vivian. The traitors. — Henley-on-Thames : Ellis, Sept.1982. — [624]p. — (The Australians ; v.3)
ISBN 0-85628-106-9 : £9.50 : CIP entry B82-21766

Stubbington, Ann. The devil's dress. — Loughton : Piatkus, Nov.1982. — [224]p
ISBN 0-86188-203-2 : £6.95 : CIP entry B82-26059

Stubbs, Jean. The ironmaster / Jean Stubbs. — London : Pan Books in association with Macmillan London, 1982, c1981. — 414p ; 18cm. — (Brief chronicles ; v.2)
Originally published: London : Macmillan, 1981
ISBN 0-330-26636-5 (pbk) : £1.75 B82-22150

Stubbs, Jean. The ironmaster. — Large print ed. — Anstey : Ulverscroft, Sept.1982. — [672]p. — (Ulverscroft large print series)
Originally published: London : Macmillan, 1981
ISBN 0-7089-0853-5 : £5.00 : CIP entry B82-27013

823'.914[F] — Fiction in English, *1945-* — *Texts continuation*

Stubbs, Jean. Kit's Hill / Jean Stubbs. — London : Pan Books in association with Macmillan London, 1980, c1978. — 286p ; 18cm. — (Brief chronicles ; v.1)
Originally published: London : Macmillan, 1978
ISBN 0-330-25955-5 (pbk) : £1.50 B82-26913

Sturrock, Jeremy. Captain Bolton's corpse / by Jeremy Sturrock. — London : Hale, 1982. — 175p ; 21cm
ISBN 0-7091-9823-x : £7.25 B82-34193

Styles, Showell. The Baltic convoy / Showell Styles. — Large print ed. — Bath : Chivers, 1981, c1979. — 245p ; 23cm. — (A Lythway book)
Originally published: London : Faber, 1979
ISBN 0-85119-771-x : Unpriced : CIP rev. B81-31802

Styles, Showell. Mr Fitton's commission / Showell Styles. — Large print ed. — Bath : Chivers, 1981, c1977. — 284p : 1map ; 23cm. — (A Lythway book)
Originally published: London : Faber, 1977
ISBN 0-85119-755-8 : Unpriced : CIP rev. B81-25812

Styles, Showell. The quarterdeck ladder / Showell Styles. — London : Kimber, 1982. — 173p ; 23cm
ISBN 0-7183-0029-7 : £5.95 B82-27259

Sullivan, Jo. Suspicion / by Jo Sullivan. — London : Mills & Boon, 1982. — 189p ; 20cm
ISBN 0-263-10099-5 : £5.95 B82-37442

Summerson, Rachel. Hearts are trumps, or, She would be a lady : a novel / by Rachel Summerson. — London : Sidgwick & Jackson, 1981 (1982 [printing]). — 295p ; 18cm
ISBN 0-283-98834-7 (pbk) : £1.75 B82-13046

Suson, Marlene. Desire's command / Marlene Suson. — London : Futura, 1982, c1981. — 392p ; 18cm. — (A Troubador book)
ISBN 0-7107-3029-2 (pbk) : £1.95 B82-33313

Suster, Gerald. The offering / Gerald Suster. — Feltham : Hamlyn, 1982. — 156p ; 18cm
ISBN 0-600-20358-1 (pbk) : £1.25 B82-25316

Swan, Rose. The promise of the daffodils / Rose Swan. — London : Hale, 1982. — 158p ; 20cm
ISBN 0-7091-9641-5 : £6.25 B82-18311

Swan, Rose. The shining thread / by Rose Swan. — London : Hale, 1982. — 159p ; 20cm
ISBN 0-7091-9858-2 : £6.50 B82-34168

Swanne, E. S.. Gemma / by E.S. Swanne. — London : Hale, 1982. — 192p ; 20cm
ISBN 0-7091-9640-7 : £6.25 B82-17472

Swift, Graham. Shuttlecock / Graham Swift. — Harmondsworth : Penguin, 1982, c1981. — 219p ; 20cm
Originally published: London : Allen Lane, 1981
ISBN 0-14-006322-6 (pbk) : £2.25 B82-40673

Swift, Michael. The Bedouin tent. — London : New English Library, Sept.1982. — [224]p
ISBN 0-450-05288-5 (pbk) : £1.50 : CIP entry B82-19688

Tabor, Margaret. [Unity Penfold]. Eclipse / Margaret Tabor. — London : Hamlyn, 1982, c1980. — 192p ; 18cm
Originally published: London : Heinemann, 1980
ISBN 0-600-20445-6 (pbk) : £1.35 B82-22713

Tannahill, Reay. A dark and distant shore. — London : Century Publishing, Oct.1982. — [608]p
ISBN 0-7126-0001-9 : £8.95 : CIP entry B82-23872

Tarrant, John, *1927-*. China gold / John Tarrant. — London : Macdonald & Co., 1982. — 252p ; 23cm
ISBN 0-356-08532-5 : £7.95 B82-15327

Tattersall, Jill. Chanters Chase / Jill Tattersall. — South Yarmouth, Mass. : Curley ; [Skipton] : Magna Print [distributor], 1978. — 429p ; 22cm
Originally published: New York : Morrow ; London : Hodder and Stoughton, 1978. — Published in large print
ISBN 0-89340-158-7 : Unpriced B82-17038

Tattersall, Jill. Damnation reef. — London : Hodder & Stoughton, Mar.1982. — [288]p. — (Coronet books)
Originally published: 1980
ISBN 0-340-27543-x (pbk) : £1.25 : CIP entry B82-01099

Tattersall, Jill. [Lady Ingram's retreat]. Lady Ingram's room / Jill Tattersall. — South Yarmouth, Mass. : Curley ; [Skipton] : Magna Print [distributor], 1979, c1971. — 416p ; 22cm
Originally published: London : Collins, 1970. — Published in large print
ISBN 0-89340-179-x : Unpriced B82-17039

Tattersall, Jill. The shadows of Castle Fosse / Jill Tattersall. — South Yarmouth, Mass. : Curley ; [Skipton] : Magna Print [distributor], 1979, c1976. — 520p ; 22cm
Originally published: New York : Morrow ; London : Hodder and Stoughton, 1976. — Published in large print
ISBN 0-89340-177-3 : Unpriced B82-17040

Tattersall, Jill. The wild hunt / Jill Tattersall. — South Yarmouth, Mass. : Curley ; [Skipton] : Magna Print [distributor], 1979, c1974. — 469p ; 22cm
Originally published: London : Hodder and Stoughton, 1974. — Published in large print
ISBN 0-89340-178-1 : Unpriced B82-17041

Taylor, Andrew, *1951-*. Caroline Minuscule : a novel / by Andrew Taylor. — London : Gollancz, 1982. — 184p ; 21cm
ISBN 0-575-03142-5 : £6.95 : CIP rev. B82-12987

Taylor, Bernard, *1934-*. The Moorstone sickness / Bernard Taylor. — Loughton : Piatkus, 1982. — 161p ; 21cm
ISBN 0-86188-155-9 : £6.50 : CIP rev. B82-07846

Taylor, Elizabeth, *1912-1975*. Mrs Palfrey at the Claremont / Elizabeth Taylor ; with a new introduction by Paul Bailey. — London : Virago, 1982, c1975. — ix,205p ; 20cm. — (Virago modern classics)
Originally published: London : Chatto and Windus, 1971
ISBN 0-86068-263-3 (pbk) : £2.95 : CIP rev. B82-10238

Taylor, Elizabeth, *1912-1975*. The sleeping beauty / Elizabeth Taylor ; with a new introduction by Susannah Clapp. — London : Virago, 1982, c1975. — xiii, 250p ; 20cm. — (Virago modern classics)
Originally published: London : Peter Davies, 1953
ISBN 0-86068-262-5 (pbk) : £2.95 : CIP rev. B82-10237

Taylor, Graham, *19---*. Lifetimes / Graham Taylor. — Braunton : Merlin Books, 1981. — 22p ; 21cm
ISBN 0-86303-006-8 (pbk) : £0.60 B82-19411

Taylor, L. E.. Thyme cottage ; and Bessie in black / by L.E. Taylor. — London : New Horizon, c1981. — 201p ; 21cm
ISBN 0-86116-629-9 : £5.75 B82-00655

Taylor, May. Bird watchers / by May Taylor. — London : Regency, c1982. — 148p ; 21cm
ISBN 0-7212-0607-7 : £6.00 B82-41010

Tennant, Emma. Alice fell / Emma Tennant. — London : Pan, 1982, c1980. — 123p ; 20cm. — (Picador)
Originally published: London : Cape, 1980
ISBN 0-330-26597-0 (pbk) : £1.95 B82-13637

Tennant, Emma. Queen of stones. — London : Cape, Nov.1982. — 1v.
ISBN 0-224-02061-7 : CIP entry B82-29114

Thomas, Alexandra. The weeping desert / Alexandra Thomas. — London : Hamlyn Paperbacks, 1981. — 143p ; 18cm. — (A Sapphire romance)
ISBN 0-600-20173-2 (pbk) : £0.75 B82-00646

Thomas, Craig. Jade tiger / Craig Thomas. — London : Joseph, 1982. — 326p ; 23cm
ISBN 0-7181-2130-9 : £7.95 B82-30911

Thomas, Craig. Sea leopard / Craig Thomas. — London : Sphere, 1981 (1982 [printing]). — 370p ; 18cm
ISBN 0-7221-8453-0 (pbk) : £1.95 B82-18167

Thomas, D. M.. Birthstone / D.M. Thomas. — Rev. ed.. — Harmondsworth : Penguin, 1982, c1980. — 157p ; 20cm
Previous ed.: Gollancz, 1980
ISBN 0-14-006414-1 (pbk) : £1.95 B82-35614

Thomas, D. M.. The white hotel / D.M. Thomas. — Harmondsworth : Penguin, 1981. — 240p ; 20cm. — (King Penguin)
Originally published: London : Gollancz, 1981
ISBN 0-14-006032-4 (pbk) : £2.25 B82-16762

Thomas, Leslie. The magic army / Leslie Thomas. — London : Eyre Methuen, 1981. — 464p ; 23cm
ISBN 0-413-46560-8 : £7.50 : CIP rev. B81-25316

Thomas, Leslie, *1931-*. Ormerod's landing / Leslie Thomas. — Long Preston : Magna Print, 1982, c1978. — 483p ; 22cm
Originally published: London : Eyre Methuen, 1978. — Published in large print
ISBN 0-86009-378-6 : Unpriced : CIP rev. B81-35700

Thomas, Rosie. Celebration / Rosie Thomas. — [London] : Fontana, 1982. — 317p ; 18cm
ISBN 0-00-616524-9 (pbk) : £1.50 B82-25442

Thomas, Rosie. Celebration / Rosie Thomas. — Loughton : Piatkus, 1982. — 317p ; 21cm
ISBN 0-86188-195-8 : £7.50 : CIP rev. B82-13524

Thompson, Anne Armstrong. The Swiss legacy. — London : Hodder and Stoughton, Aug.1981. — [256]p
Originally published: New York : Simon and Schuster, 1974 ; London : Hodder and Stoughton, 1979
ISBN 0-340-26684-8 (pbk) : £1.50 : CIP entry B81-18135

Thompson, E. V.. Ben Retallick / E.V. Thompson. — London : Pan in association with Macmillan, 1982, c1980. — 399p ; 17cm
Originally published: London : Macmillan, 1980
ISBN 0-330-26607-1 (pbk) : £1.75 B82-18098

Thompson, E. V.. Ben Retallick. — Large print ed. — Leicester : Ulverscroft, Dec.1982. — 1v.. — (Charnwood library series)
Originally published: London : Macmillan, 1980
ISBN 0-7089-8087-2 : £6.50 : CIP entry B82-30803

Thompson, E. V.. The dream traders / E.V. Thompson. — London : Macmillan, 1981. — 392p ; 23cm
ISBN 0-333-32409-9 : £6.95 B82-08767

823'.914[F] — Fiction in English, *1945- — Texts continuation*

Thomson, Daisy. The talisman of love / by Daisy Thomson. — London : Hale, 1982. — 192p ; 20cm
ISBN 0-7091-9750-0 : £6.25 B82-30402

Thomson, June. Alibi in time / June Thomson. — Large print ed. — Leicester : Ulverscroft, 1982, c1980. — 434p ; 23cm. — (Ulverscroft large print)
Originally published: London : Constable, 1980
ISBN 0-7089-0800-4 : Unpriced : CIP rev. B82-18454

Thomson, June. Shadow of a doubt / June Thomson. — London : Constable, 1981. — 221p ; 23cm. — (Constable crime)
ISBN 0-09-464350-4 : £6.95 B82-02273

Thorne, Nicola. The daughters of the house / Nicola Thorne. — London : Granada, 1982, c1981. — 684p ; 18cm. — (A Mayflower book)
Bibliography: p682-684
ISBN 0-583-13317-7 (pbk) : £1.95 B82-28370

Thorne, Nicola. The perfect wife and mother / Nicola Thorne. — London : Granada, 1982, c1980. — 248p ; 18cm. — (A Mayflower book)
Originally published: London : Heinemann, 1980
ISBN 0-583-13182-4 (pbk) : £1.50 B82-14111

Thorne, Nicola. Where the rivers meet. — London : Granada, Aug.1982. — [544]p
ISBN 0-246-11409-6 : £7.95 : CIP entry B82-15704

Thorne, Victoria. Longsword / Victoria Thorne. — [London] : Corgi, 1982. — 224p ; 18cm
ISBN 0-552-11906-7 (pbk) : £1.50 B82-28359

Thorne, Victoria. The siege of Salwarpe / by Victoria Thorne. — London : Hale, 1982. — 239p ; 20cm
ISBN 0-7091-9491-9 : £7.25 B82-15485

Thornley, Richard. Zig-zag / Richard Thornley. — London : Picador, 1982, c1981. — 171p ; 20cm
Originally published: London : Cape, 1981
ISBN 0-330-26646-2 (pbk) : £1.95 B82-22145

Thorpe, Kay. The last of the Mallorys / Kay Thorpe. — Bath : Chivers, 1982, c1977. — 222p ; 23cm. — (A Lythway romance)
Originally published: London : Mills and Boon, 1968
ISBN 0-85119-812-0 : Unpriced : CIP rev. B82-07016

Thorpe, Kay. The new owner / by Kay Thorpe. — London : Mills & Boon, 1982. — 188p ; 19cm
ISBN 0-263-10031-6 : £5.25 B82-18111

Thorpe, Kay. Temporary marriage / by Kay Thorpe. — London : Mills & Boon, 1981. — 188p ; 19cm
ISBN 0-263-09940-7 : £4.55 B82-00044

Thorpe, Sylvia. Fair shine the day / Sylvia Thorpe. — South Yarmouth, Mass. : Curley, 1978, c1964 ; [Long Preston] : Distributed by Magna. — 358p ; 23cm
Originally published: London : Hurst & Blackett, 1964. — Published in large print
ISBN 0-89340-148-x : Unpriced B82-17024

Thorpe, Sylvia. A flash of scarlet / Sylvia Thorpe. — Sth. Yarmouth, [Mass.] : Curley ; [Long Preston] : Distributed in the U.K. by Magna Print, c1976. — 352p ; 22cm
Published in large print
ISBN 0-89340-399-7 (corrected) : Unpriced B82-39651

Thorpe, Sylvia. Rogues' covenant / Sylvia Thorpe. — South Yarmouth : Curley ; [Skipton] : Magna Print [distributor], 1978 c1957. — 478p ; 22cm
Originally published: London : Hurst and Blackett, 1957. — Published in large print
ISBN 0-89340-150-1 (corrected) : Unpriced B82-19791

Thorpe, Sylvia. Smugglers' moon / Sylvia Thorpe. — London : Corgi, 1982. — 252p ; 18cm
Originally published: London : Rich & Cowan, 1982
ISBN 0-552-11928-8 (pbk) : £1.50 B82-23905

Thorpe, Sylvia. Spring will come again / Sylvia Thorpe. — South Yarmouth : Curley ; [Skipton] : Magna Print [distributor], 1978, c1965. — 363p ; 22cm
Originally published: London : Hurst and Blackett, 1965. — Published in large print
ISBN 0-89340-149-8 : Unpriced B82-19792

Thorpe, Sylvia. Sword of vengeance / Sylvia Thorpe. — London : Corgi, 1981, c1957. — 287p ; 18cm
Originally published: London : Rich & Cowan, 1957
ISBN 0-552-11837-0 (pbk) : £1.25 B82-06422

Thwaite, Eric. Funny man / Eric Thwaite. — London : Severn House, 1980. — 181p ; 21cm
ISBN 0-7278-0758-7 : £6.95 B82-12077

Thynn, Alexander. Pillars of the establishment / Alexander Thynn. — [Feltham] : Hamlyn Paperbacks, 1982, c1980. — 283p : music,1geneal.table ; 18cm
Originally published: London : Hutchinson, 1980
ISBN 0-600-20483-9 (pbk) : £1.50 B82-17478

Tilbury, Quenna. Island of rapture / by Quenna Tilbury. — London : Hale, 1982. — 160p ; 20cm
ISBN 0-7091-9799-3 : £6.50 B82-31638

Timperley, Rosemary. The face in the leaves / by Rosemary Timperley. — London : Hale, 1982. — 191p ; 20cm
ISBN 0-7091-9687-3 : £6.95 B82-27318

Tinniswood, Peter. Collected tales from a long room. — London : Hutchinson, Oct.1982. — [272]p
ISBN 0-09-150140-7 : £6.95 : CIP entry B82-24971

Tinsley, Nina. The bridge between / by Nina Tinsley. — London : Hale, 1982. — 159p ; 20cm
ISBN 0-7091-9702-0 : £6.25 B82-17524

Tonkin, Peter. The journal of Edwin Underhill / Peter Tonkin. — London : Hodder and Stoughton, 1981. — 192p ; 22cm
ISBN 0-340-26242-7 : £6.95 : CIP rev. B82-07433

Tonkin, Peter. The journal of Edwin Underhill. — London : Coronet Books, Feb.1983. — [192]p
Originally published: London : Hodder & Stoughton, 1981
ISBN 0-340-32045-1 (pbk) : £1.25 : CIP entry B82-38062

Toomey, Colleen. Bird of prey : a novel / by Colleen Toomey ; based on the BBC-TV serial scripts by Ron Hutchinson. — London : British Broadcasting Corporation, 1982. — 205p ; 18cm
ISBN 0-563-20063-4 (pbk) : £1.75 B82-26581

Tovey, Doreen. Life with grandma. — Large print ed. — Bath : Chivers, Jan.1983. — [240]p
Originally published: 1964
ISBN 0-85119-202-5 : £6.30 : CIP entry B82-33086

Townley, Pamela. Foxy lady / Pamela Townley. — London : Futura, 1981. — 417p ; 18cm
ISBN 0-7088-2080-8 (pbk) : £1.75 B82-00454

Townley, Pamela. The image / Pamela Townley. — London : Futura, 1980 (1981 [printing]). — 447p ; 18cm
ISBN 0-7088-1835-8 (pbk) : £1.95 B82-00458

Townsend, John Rowe. Noah's castle / John Rowe Townsend. — Harmondsworth : Puffin in association with Oxford University Press, 1980, c1975 (1981 [printing]). — 184p ; 19cm
Originally published: London : Oxford University Press, 1975
ISBN 0-14-031294-3 (pbk) : £1.00 B82-09142

Trapido, Barbara. Brother of the more famous Jack / by Barbara Trapido. — London : Gollancz, 1982. — 218p ; 23cm
ISBN 0-575-03112-3 : £6.95 : CIP rev. B82-04611

Treacy, Maura. Scenes from a country wedding / Maura Treacy. — Swords : Poolbeg, 1981. — 176p ; 23cm
ISBN 0-905169-49-2 : Unpriced B82-08741

Tremayne, Peter. Destroyers of Lan-Kern. — London : Methuen London, Nov.1982. — [192]p
ISBN 0-413-50730-0 : £6.95 : CIP entry B82-28294

Tremayne, Peter. The Morgow rises! / Peter Tremayne. — London : Sphere, 1982. — 183p ; 18cm
ISBN 0-7221-8615-0 (pbk) : £1.25 B82-14903

Tremayne, Peter. The return of Raffles / Peter Tremayne. — London : Magnum, 1981. — 188p ; 18cm
ISBN 0-417-06620-1 (pbk) : £1.50 B82-15546

Trenhaile, John. Kyril : a novel of espionage / John Trenhaile. — London : Severn House, 1981. — 279p ; 21cm
ISBN 0-7278-0741-2 : £6.95 : CIP rev. B81-24636

Tresillian, Richard. The bondmaster fury. — London : Arlington Books, Apr.1982. — [288]p
ISBN 0-85140-574-6 : £6.95 : CIP entry B82-05013

Trevelyan, Robert. Pendragon — seeds of mutiny. — London : Hodder & Stoughton, Oct.1981. — [192]p. — (Coronet books)
Originally published: 1979
ISBN 0-340-26682-1 (pbk) : £1.10 : CIP entry B81-26728

Treves, Kathleen. Touchstone of love / by Kathleen Treves. — London : Hale, 1981. — 173p ; 20cm
ISBN 0-7091-9390-4 : £5.95 B82-00443

Trevor, Elleston. The Damocles sword / Elleston Trevor. — [London] : Fontana, 1982, c1981. — 314p ; 18cm
Originally published: London : Collins, 1981
ISBN 0-00-616492-7 (pbk) : £1.75 B82-36259

Trevor, Meriol. The wanton fires / Meriol Trevor. — Large print ed. — Leicester : Ulverscroft, 1981, c1979. — 355p : geneal.table ; 23cm
Originally published: New York : Dutton, 1979
ISBN 0-7089-0722-9 : £5.00 : CIP rev. B81-32034

Trevor, William. The children of Dynmouth / William Trevor. — Harmondsworth : Penguin, 1979, c1976 (1982 [printing]). — 188p ; 20cm. — (A King Penguin)
Originally published: London : Dynmouth, 1976
ISBN 0-14-006263-7 (pbk) : £1.95 B82-32235

823'.914[F] — Fiction in English, *1945-* **— Texts** *continuation*

Trevor, William. Mrs Eckdorf in O'Neill's Hotel / William Trevor. — Harmondsworth : Penguin, 1973, c1969 (1982 [printing]). — 264p ; 20cm. — (A King Penguin)
Originally published: London : Bodley Head, 1969
ISBN 0-14-006014-6 (pbk) : £2.25 B82-29821

Trevor, William. A standard of behaviour / William Trevor. — London : Abacus, 1982, c1958. — 122p ; 20cm
Originally published: London : Hutchinson, 1958
ISBN 0-349-13389-1 (pbk) : £1.95 B82-22600

Trew, Antony. The Antonov project / by Antony Trew. — Long Preston : Magna, 1982, c1979. — 412p ; 23cm
Originally published: London : Collins, 1979. — Published in large print
ISBN 0-86009-405-7 : Unpriced : CIP rev. B82-10232

Trew, Antony. Kleber's convoy / by Antony Trew. — Long Preston : Magna, 1981, c1973. — 408p ; 23cm
Originally published: New York : St. Martin's Press, 1973 ; London : Collins, 1974. — Published in large print
ISBN 0-86009-352-2 : Unpriced : CIP rev. B81-30433

Trew, Antony. Sea fever / Antony Trew. — [London] : Fontana, 1982, c1980. — 220p : 1map ; 18cm
Originally published: London : Collins, 1980
ISBN 0-00-616560-5 (pbk) : £1.50 B82-30764

Trollope, Joanna. The city of gems / Joanna Trollope. — London : Hutchinson, 1981. — 300p : 1map ; 23cm
ISBN 0-09-145690-8 : £6.95 : CIP rev. B81-22598

Trollope, Joanna. Eliza Stanhope / Joanna Trollope. — London : Arrow, 1979, c1978 (1981 [printing]). — 223p ; 18cm
Originally published: London : Hutchinson, 1978
ISBN 0-09-919420-1 (pbk) : £1.50 B82-17435

Trollope, Joanna. Eliza Stanhope / by Joanna Trollope. — Long Preston : Magna, 1981, c1978. — 438p ; 23cm
Originally published: London : Hutchinson, 1978. — Published in large print
ISBN 0-86009-342-5 : Unpriced : CIP rev. B81-22462

Trollope, Joanna. Leaves from the valley / Joanna Trollope. — London : Arrow, 1982, c1980. — 253p ; 18cm
Originally published: London : Hutchinson, 1980
ISBN 0-09-927490-6 (pbk) : £1.50 B82-14917

Trollope, Joanna. Parson Harding's daughter / by Joanna Trollope. — Long Preston : Magna, 1982, c1979. — 533p ; 23cm
Originally published: London : Hutchinson, 1979. — Published in large print
ISBN 0-86009-382-4 : Unpriced : CIP rev. B82-00313

Troy, Una. So true a fool / Una Troy. — London : Hale, 1981. — 158p ; 23cm
ISBN 0-7091-9398-x : £6.95 B82-03180

Tubb, E. C.. The Quillian Sector / E.C. Tubb. — London : Arrow, 1982, c1978. — 158p ; 18cm. — (The Dumarest saga ; 19)
ISBN 0-09-929050-2 (pbk) : £1.25 B82-33312

Tucker, James, *1929-*. The king's friends / James Tucker. — London : Arrow, 1982. — 239p ; 18cm
ISBN 0-09-928390-5 (pbk) : £1.75 B82-30452

Turnbull, Peter. Dead knock / Peter Turnbull. — London : Collins, 1982. — 205p ; 21cm. — (The Crime Club)
ISBN 0-00-231688-9 : £6.50 : CIP rev. B82-10568

Turnbull, Peter. Deep and crisp and even. — Large print ed. — Anstey : Ulverscroft, Aug.1982. — [352]p. — (Ulverscroft large print series)
Originally published: London : Collins, 1981
ISBN 0-7089-0830-6 : £5.00 : CIP entry B82-26674

Turner, Janet, *1952-*. The changing wind / by Janet Turner. — London : Hale, 1982. — 175p ; 20cm
ISBN 0-7091-9891-4 : £6.50 B82-37252

Turner, Judy. Triple tangle / Judy Turner. — London : Mills & Boon, 1981. — 190p ; 20cm
ISBN 0-263-09989-x : £4.55 B82-09361

Twemlow, C.. The pike / Cliff Twemlow. — Feltham : Hamlyn, 1982. — 160p ; 18cm
ISBN 0-600-20664-5 (pbk) : £1.25 B82-27050

Underwood, Michael. A clear case of suicide / Michael Underwood. — Large print ed. — Leicester : Ulverscroft, 1982, c1980. — 336p ; 23. — (Ulverscroft large print)
Originally published: London : Macmillan, 1980
ISBN 0-7089-0801-2 : Unpriced : CIP rev. B82-18453

Underwood, Michael. Crime upon crime. — Large print ed. — Bath : Chivers, Jan.1983. — [280]p. — (A Lythway book)
Originally published: London : Macmillan, 1980
ISBN 0-85119-889-9 : £6.90 : CIP entry B82-33102

Underwood, Michael. Double jeopardy. — Large print ed. — Anstey : Ulverscroft, Dec.1982. — 1v.. — (Ulverscroft large print series)
Originally published: London : Macmillan, 1981
ISBN 0-7089-0885-3 : £5.00 : CIP entry B82-30785

Underwood, Michael. Goddess of death / Michael Underwood. — London : Macmillan, 1982. — 187p ; 21cm
ISBN 0-333-33071-4 : £5.95 B82-32558

Underwood, Michael. Hand of fate / Michael Underwood. — London : Macmillan, 1981. — 220p ; 21cm
ISBN 0-333-32233-9 : £5.95 B82-05584

Underwood, Michael. Murder with malice / Michael Underwood. — Large print ed. — Leicester : Ulverscroft, 1981, c1977. — 341p ; 23cm. — (Ulverscroft large print)
Originally published: London : Macmillan, 1977
ISBN 0-7089-0704-0 : £5.00 : CIP rev. B81-30500

Unsworth, Barry. The rage of the vulture. — London : Granada, Aug.1982. — [384]p
ISBN 0-246-11416-9 : £7.95 : CIP entry B82-15705

Ure, Jean. Bid time return / Jean Ure. — London : Severn House, 1981, c1977. — 170p ; 21cm
Originally published: London : Corgi, 1978
ISBN 0-7278-0740-4 : £5.95 B82-03674

Ure, Jean. A girl like that / Jean Ure. — Large print ed. — Leicester : Ulverscroft, 1982, c1979. — 310p ; 23cm. — (Ulverscroft large print series)
Originally published: London : Corgi, 1979
ISBN 0-7089-0763-6 : Unpriced : CIP rev. B82-01738

Ure, Jean. If it weren't for Sebastian — / Jean Ure. — London : Bodley Head, 1982. — 187p ; 20cm
ISBN 0-370-30490-x (pbk) : £3.75 : CIP rev. B82-19205

Ure, Jean. A proper little Nooryeff / Jean Ure. — London : Bodley Head, 1982. — 157p ; 20cm
For adolescents
ISBN 0-370-30470-5 (pbk) : £3.50 : CIP rev. B82-00905

Ure, Jean. See you Thursday / Jean Ure. — Harmondsworth : Puffin, 1982, c1981. — 174p ; 19cm. — (Puffin plus)
Originally published: London : Kestrel, 1981
ISBN 0-14-031335-4 (pbk) : £1.10 B82-33019

Uren, Rhona. The heir of Boskellow Manor / by Rhona Uren. — London : Hale, 1981. — 188p ; 20cm
ISBN 0-7091-9345-9 : £6.95 B82-12603

Uren, Rhona. Love and Nurse Sinclair / Rhona Uren. — London : Hale, 1982. — 190p ; 20cm
ISBN 0-7091-9786-1 : £6.50 B82-27428

Uren, Rhona. Nurse Foster / by Rhona Uren. — London : Mills & Boon, 1982. — 160p ; 18cm. — (Doctor nurse romance)
Originally published: London : Hale, 1980
ISBN 0-263-73924-4 (pbk) : £0.85 B82-36272

Vale, Brenda. Albion / Brenda Vale. — Barnstaple : Spindlewood, 1982. — 181p ; 24cm
ISBN 0-907349-15-3 : £6.95 B82-26020

Valenti, Justine. Love notes / Justine Valenti. — London : Sphere, 1982, c1981. — 311p ; 18cm
ISBN 0-7221-8721-1 (pbk) : £1.75 B82-27894

Valenti, Justine. Twin connections. — Loughton : Piatkus, Feb.1983. — [320]p
ISBN 0-86188-224-5 : £7.95 : CIP entry B82-39807

Van Atta, Winfred. The Adam sleep / Winfred Van Atta. — London : Hale, 1981, c1980. — 180p ; 20cm
Originally published: Garden City : Doubleday, 1980
ISBN 0-7091-9275-4 : £6.25 B82-02141

Van der Zee, Karen. Waiting / by Karen van der Zee. — London : Mills & Boon, 1982. — 188p ; 19cm
ISBN 0-263-10043-x : £5.25 B82-22506

Van Greenaway, Peter. The Lazarus lie : a novel / by Peter Van Greenaway. — London : Gollancz, 1982. — 192p ; 21cm
ISBN 0-575-03048-8 : £6.95 : CIP rev. B82-12980

Van Greenaway, Peter. Manrissa man : by Peter Van Greenaway. — London : Gollancz, 1982. — 208p ; 21cm
ISBN 0-575-03100-x : £6.95 : CIP rev. B81-40244

Van Hassen, Amy. Menace. — London : New English Library, Nov.1982. — [192]p
ISBN 0-450-05238-9 (pbk) : £1.50 : CIP entry B82-27523

Vance, Jack. The face. — Sevenoaks : Coronet Books, June 1981. — [224]p
ISBN 0-340-26666-x (pbk) : £1.10 : CIP entry B81-12348

Vance, Jack. Space opera. — London : Hodder and Stoughton, Mar.1982. — [176]p. — (Coronet books)
Originally published: New York : Daw Books, 1979
ISBN 0-340-26775-5 (pbk) : £1.10 : CIP entry B82-01541

823'.914[F] — Fiction in English, *1945-* — *Texts continuation*

Vanner, Lyn. Guardian of Rannoch / Lyn Vanner. — London : Corgi, 1982. — 223p ; 18cm
ISBN 0-552-11985-7 (pbk) : £1.50 B82-35475

Vaughan, Carol. Flight of fancy / Carol Vaughan. — London : Hale, 1982. — 208p ; 20cm
ISBN 0-7091-9692-x : £7.25 B82-25986

Vern, Sarah. Surrender to the night / by Sarah Vern. — London : Hale, 1982. — 188p ; 20cm
ISBN 0-7091-9758-6 : £6.50 B82-25985

Vernon, Henry. At home to terror / Henry Vernon. — Bognor Regis : New Horizon, c1981. — 238p ; 21cm
ISBN 0-86116-261-7 : £5.75 B82-02944

Vernon, Marjorie. Love, come to my castle / Marjorie Vernon. — London : Hale, 1982. — 190p ; 20cm
ISBN 0-7091-9791-8 : £6.50 B82-31949

Veryan, Patricia. [Love's duet]. A perfect match / Patricia Veryan. — London : Fontana, 1982, c1979. — 317p ; 18cm
Originally published: New York : Walker, 1979
ISBN 0-00-616542-7 (pbk) : £1.75 B82-19739

Veryan, Patricia. Mistress of Willowvale / Patricia Veryan. — London : Souvenir, 1982, c1980. — 274p ; 23cm
Originally published: New York : Walker, 1980
ISBN 0-285-62518-7 : £7.95 B82-22113

Vincent, Peter. Sorry. — London : Severn House, Nov.1982. — [160]p
ISBN 0-7278-0844-3 : £6.95 : CIP entry B82-34068

Wain, John. Lizzie's floating shop / John Wain. — London : Bodley Head, 1981. — 210p ; 20cm
For adolescents
ISBN 0-370-30906-5 (pbk) : £3.50 : CIP rev. B81-27956

Wainwright, John, *1921-*. Anatomy of a riot / John Wainwright. — London : Macmillan, 1982. — 168p ; 21cm
ISBN 0-333-32987-2 : £5.95 B82-32565

Wainwright, John, *1921-*. Blayde R.I.P. / John Wainwright. — London : Macmillan, 1982. — 251p ; 21cm
ISBN 0-333-32826-4 : £5.95 B82-18240

Wainwright, John, *1921-*. Landscape with violence / John Wainwright. — Large print ed. — Leicester : Ulverscroft, 1981, c1975. — 486p ; 23cm. — (Ulverscroft large print)
Originally published: London : Macmillan, 1975
ISBN 0-7089-0690-7 : £5.00 : CIP rev. B81-28101

Wainwright, John, *1921-*. Man of law / John Wainwright. — Large print ed. — Leicester : Ulverscroft, 1982, c1980. — 352p ; 23cm. — (Ulverscroft large print)
Originally published: London : Macmillan, 1980
ISBN 0-7089-0802-0 : Unpriced : CIP rev. B82-18452

Wainwright, John, *1921-*. The reluctant sleeper / John Wainwright. — Large print ed. — Bath : Chivers, 1982, c1979. — 222p ; 23cm. — (A Lythway book) (A Lythway thriller)
Originally published: London : Macmillan, 1979
ISBN 0-85119-779-5 : Unpriced : CIP rev. B81-33794

Wainwright, John, *1921-*. The tainted man. — Large print ed. — Bath : Chivers, Jan.1983. — [320]p. — (A Lythway book)
Originally published: London : Macmillan, 1980
ISBN 0-85119-890-2 : £7.20 : CIP entry B82-33103

Walker, Lucy. Love in a cloud. — Large print ed. — Anstey : Ulverscroft Large Print Books, Nov.1982. — [448]p. — (Ulverscroft large print series)
Originally published: London : Collins, 1960
ISBN 0-7089-0877-2 : £5.00 : CIP entry B82-29097

Walker, Lucy. Sweet and faraway. — Large print ed. — Anstey : Ulverscroft, Jan.1983. — [416] p. — (Ulverscroft large print series)
Originally published: London : Collins, 1955
ISBN 0-7089-0911-6 : £6.25 : CIP entry B82-32539

Walker, Martin. The Eastern question / Martin Walker. — London : Granada, 1982. — 208p ; 18cm. — (A Panther book)
ISBN 0-586-05435-9 (pbk) : £1.25 B82-33679

Walker, Peter N.. Teenage cop / by Peter N. Walker. — London : Hale, 1982. — 190p ; 19cm
ISBN 0-7091-9834-5 : £6.75 B82-34189

Wall, Mervyn. Hermitage. — Dublin : Wolfhound Press, July 1982. — [256]p
ISBN 0-905473-82-5 (cased) : £7.00 : CIP entry
ISBN 0-905473-83-3 (pbk) : £3.00 B82-13170

Wallace, Jane. Fugitive summer. — London : New English Library, Mar.1982. — [256]p
Originally published: 1981
ISBN 0-450-05234-6 (pbk) : £1.50 : CIP entry B82-01980

Wallace, Pamela. Malibu colony / Pamela Wallace. — London : Sphere, 1981. — 311p ; 18cm
ISBN 0-7221-8888-9 (pbk) : £1.50 B82-06009

Wallis, Roy A.. Charlie / Roy A. Wallis. — Bognor Regis : New Horizon, c1982. — 210p ; 21cm
ISBN 0-86116-556-x : £5.75 B82-19997

Walsh, Bill, *1933-*. Cheat / by Bill Walsh. — London : Hale, 1981. — 192p ; 20cm
ISBN 0-7091-9550-8 : £6.50 B82-10745

Walthew, Beryl. A queen betrayed / by Beryl Walthew. — London : Hale, 1981. — 191p ; 20cm
ISBN 0-7091-9421-8 : £6.95 B82-03178

Ward, Edmund. The Baltic emerald / Edmund Ward. — London : Methuen London, 1982, c1981. — 217p ; 18cm. — (A Methuen paperback)
Originally published: London : Eyre Methuen, 1981
ISBN 0-417-06800-x (pbk) : £1.50 B82-34007

Ward, Kate. Heart of danger / Kate Ward. — London : Hale, 1982. — 206p ; 20cm
ISBN 0-7091-9904-x : £7.50 B82-36523

Ward, Kate. To remember forever / Kate Ward. — London : Hale, 1982. — 192p ; 21cm
ISBN 0-7091-9518-4 : £5.95 B82-11388

Wark, Geoffrey. Judgement postponed / Geoffrey Wark. — London : Hale, 1982. — 207p ; 20cm
ISBN 0-7091-9501-x : £6.95 B82-26025

Warmington, Mary Jane. Bride in sables / Mary Jane Warmington. — London : Macdonald, 1981. — 252p ; 21cm
ISBN 0-354-04799-x : £4.95 B82-00537

Warmington, Mary Jane. Midsummer madness / by Mary Jane Warmington. — London : Hale, 1982. — 160p ; 20cm
ISBN 0-7091-9516-8 : £5.95 B82-11058

Warmington, Mary Jane. Silver stardust / Mary Jane Warmington. — London : Macdonald, 1982. — 256p ; 21cm
ISBN 0-356-08516-3 : £4.95 B82-17308

Warner, Marina. The skating party / Marina Warner. — London : Weidenfeld and Nicolson, c1982. — 180p ; 23cm
ISBN 0-297-78113-8 : £6.95 B82-19797

Waterhouse, Keith. The bucket shop / Keith Waterhouse. — London : Sphere, 1982, c1968. — 158p ; 18cm
Originally published: London : Joseph, 1968
ISBN 0-7221-8925-7 (pbk) : £1.25 B82-18177

Waterhouse, Keith. There is a happy land / Keith Waterhouse. — London : Sphere, 1981, c1957. — 153p ; 18cm
Originally published: London : Joseph, 1957
ISBN 0-7221-8924-9 (pbk) : £1.25 B82-02300

Watson, Colin. Whatever's been going on at Mumblesby. — London : Methuen, Oct.1982. — [160]p
ISBN 0-413-48950-7 : £7.50 : CIP entry B82-24477

Watson, Ian. Chekhov's journey. — London : Gollancz, Feb.1983. — [184]p
ISBN 0-575-03213-8 : £7.95 : CIP entry B82-38682

Watson, Ian. The gardens of delight / Ian Watson. — [London] : Corgi, 1982, c1980. — 184p ; 17cm
Originally published: London : Gollancz, 1980
ISBN 0-552-11878-8 (pbk) : £1.50 B82-12587

Watson, Robert. Rumours of fulfilment / Robert Watson. — London : Heinemann, 1982. — 200p ; 23cm
ISBN 0-434-84201-x : £6.95 B82-16687

Watson, William, *1931-*. The knight on the bridge. — London : Chatto & Windus, Sept.1982. — [224]p
ISBN 0-7011-2635-3 : £7.95 : CIP entry B82-20302

Way, Margaret. Blue lotus / Margaret Way. — Large print ed. — Bath : Chivers, 1982, c1979. — 219p ; 23cm. — (A Seymour book)
Originally published: London : Mills & Boon, 1979
ISBN 0-85119-459-1 : Unpriced : CIP rev. B82-01438

Way, Margaret. Broken rhapsody / by Margaret Way. — London : Mills & Boon, 1982. — 188p ; 20cm
ISBN 0-263-10054-5 : £5.25 B82-27281

Way, Margaret. Broken rhapsody / by Margaret Way. — London : Mills & Boon, 1982. — 188p ; 18cm
ISBN 0-263-73855-8 (pbk) : £0.85 B82-36281

Way, Margaret. Home to Morning Star / by Margaret Way. — London : Mills & Boon, 1981. — 188p ; 20cm
ISBN 0-263-09980-6 : £4.55 B82-09225

Way, Margaret. North of Capricorn / by Margaret Way. — London : Mills & Boon, 1981. — 189p ; 19cm
ISBN 0-263-09939-3 : £4.55 B82-00047

Way, Margaret. The silver veil / by Margaret Way. — London : Mills and Boon, 1982. — 189p ; 20cm
ISBN 0-263-10092-8 : £5.95 B82-37110

Way, Peter. Belshazzar's feast / by Peter Way. — London : Gollancz, 1982. — 272p ; 21cm
ISBN 0-575-03032-1 : £6.95 B82-22363

823'.914[F] — Fiction in English, *1945-* **—** *Texts continuation*

Weale, Anne. Antigua kiss / Anne Weale. — London : Worldwide Romance, 1982. — 380p ; 19cm
ISBN 0-263-10097-9 : £6.95 B82-30987

Weale, Anne. Passage to Paxos / by Anne Weale. — London : Mills & Boon, 1981. — 187p ; 20cm
ISBN 0-263-09950-4 : £4.55 B82-04658

Weale, Anne. Portrait of Bethany / by Anne Weale. — London : Mills & Boon, 1982. — 188p ; 19cm
ISBN 0-263-10070-7 : £5.25 B82-30940

Webb, Forrest. Chieftains / Bob Forrest Webb. — London : Futura, 1982. — 256p ; 18cm
ISBN 0-7088-2150-2 (pbk) : £1.60 B82-15310

Webb, Forrest. Circle of Ra / Forrest Webb. — [London] : Corgi, 1982. — 238p ; 18cm
ISBN 0-552-11945-8 (pbk) : £1.50 B82-28362

Webb, Forrest. The sealing / Forrest Webb. — London : Corgi, 1982. — 316p ; 18cm
ISBN 0-552-11718-8 (pbk) : £1.75 B82-35473

Webb, Neil. Gun hatred / by Neil Webb. — London : Hale, 1981. — 174p ; 20cm
ISBN 0-7091-9379-3 : £4.95 B82-00448

Webster, Ernest. Cossack hide-out / by Ernest Webster. — London : Hale, 1981. — 175p ; 20cm
ISBN 0-7091-9360-2 : £6.25 B82-02137

Webster, Jan. Beggarman's country / Jan Webster. — Large print ed. — Leicester : Ulverscroft, 1981, c1979. — 522p ; 23cm. — (Ulverscroft large print series)
Originally published: London : Collins, 1979. — Geneal.tables on lining papers
ISBN 0-7089-0713-x : £5.00 : CIP rev.
B81-30366

Webster, Jan. Due south / Jan Webster. — London : Collins, 1982. — 320p ; 22cm
ISBN 0-00-221435-0 : £7.95 : CIP rev.
B81-33966

Weigh, Iris. Harmony for two / Iris Weigh. — London : Hale, 1982. — 174p ; 20cm
ISBN 0-7091-9614-8 : £6.25 B82-12614

Weldon, Fay. The fat woman's joke. — London : Hodder and Stoughton, May 1982. — [160]p. — (Coronet books)
Originally published: 1967
ISBN 0-340-27914-1 (pbk) : £1.10 : CIP entry
B82-06723

Weldon, Fay. The president's child. — London : Hodder and Stoughton, Sept.1982. — [256]p
ISBN 0-340-24564-6 : £7.95 : CIP entry
B82-18800

Weldon, Fay. Puffball. — London : Hodder and Stoughton, May 1981. — [272]p
Originally published: 1980
ISBN 0-340-26662-7 (pbk) : £1.25 : CIP entry
B81-03819

Weldrick, Jane. Suffer me gladly / by Jane Weldrick. — London : Hale, 1982. — 175p ; 20cm
ISBN 0-7091-9521-4 : £5.95 B82-11068

Wendorf, Patricia. Peacefully : in Berlin. — London : Hamilton, Jan.1983. — [192]p
ISBN 0-241-10885-3 : £7.95 : CIP entry
B82-33501

Wentworth, Sally. The sea master / Sally Wentworth. — London : Mills & Boon, 1982. — 186p ; 20cm
ISBN 0-263-10004-9 : £5.25 B82-13891

Wentworth, Sally. Semi-detached marriage / by Sally Wentworth. — London : Mills & Boon, 1982. — 187p ; 19cm
ISBN 0-263-10074-x : £5.25 B82-30939

West, Hilary. A husband for Susannah / by Hilary West. — London : Hale, 1981. — 205p ; 20cm
ISBN 0-7091-9315-7 : £6.75 B82-02813

West, Hilary. A mission for Charles / by Hilary West. — London : Hale, 1982. — 188p ; 20cm
ISBN 0-7091-9688-1 : £6.95 B82-18318

West, Nicola. Carver's bride / by Nicola West. — London : Mills and Boon, 1982. — 188p ; 20cm
ISBN 0-263-10084-7 : £5.95 B82-37108

West, Nicola. Devil's gold / by Nicola West. — London : Mills & Boon, 1982. — 189p ; 19cm
ISBN 0-263-10071-5 : £5.25 B82-30938

Westall, Robert. Break of dark / Robert Westall. — London : Chatto & Windus, 1982. — 182p ; 21cm
ISBN 0-7011-2614-0 : £5.50 : CIP rev.
B82-01196

Westwood, A. B.. The life & adventures of Charles Shuttleworth / A.B. Westwood. — Bognor Regis : New Horizon, c1981. — 209p ; 21cm
ISBN 0-86116-651-5 : £5.75 B82-02943

Westwood, Gwen. Keeper of the heart / Gwen Westwood. — Large print ed. — Leicester : Ulverscroft, 1981, c1969. — 364p ; 23cm
Originally published: London : Mills & Boon, 1969
ISBN 0-7089-0721-0 : £5.00 : CIP rev.
B81-32036

Whalen, Steve. Deep water. — London : Arlington Books, Sept.1981. — [320]p
ISBN 0-85140-546-0 : £6.95 : CIP entry
B81-20095

Whalen, Steve. POB 2. — London : Arlington Books, Aug.1982. — [208]p
ISBN 0-85140-581-9 : £6.95 : CIP entry
B82-15873

Wheeler, Guy. Cato's war / Guy Wheeler. — London : Pan, 1982, c1980. — 331p ; 18cm
Originally published: London : Chatto and Windus, 1980
ISBN 0-330-26609-8 (pbk) : £1.50 B82-18207

Whitby, Sharon. Nine days a-dying / Sharon Whitby. — London : Hale, 1982. — 172p ; 20cm
ISBN 0-7091-9399-8 : £7.25 B82-26024

Whitby, Sharon. Shiver me a story / by Sharon Whitby. — London : Hale, 1982. — 191p ; 21cm
ISBN 0-7091-9328-9 : £6.95 B82-15476

White, Alan, *1924-*. Cassidy's Yard / Alan White. — Large print ed. — Bath : Chivers Press, 1981, c1980. — 273p ; 23cm. — (A Lythway book)
Originally published: London : Granada, 1980
ISBN 0-85119-763-9 : Unpriced : CIP rev.
B81-31270

White, Alan, *1924-*. The homeward tide / A.L. White. — London : Granada, 1981 (1982 [printing]). — 443p ; 18cm. — (A Mayflower book)
ISBN 0-583-13295-2 (pbk) : £1.95 B82-30951

White, Alan, *1924-*. The vanishing land. — London : Granada, May 1982. — [368]p
ISBN 0-246-11465-7 : £8.95 : CIP entry
B82-07405

Whitehead, Ted. World's End : a novel / by Ted Whitehead ; based on the BBC-TV serial. — London : British Broadcasting Corporation, 1981. — 204p ; 22cm
ISBN 0-563-17963-5 (cased) : £6.75
ISBN 0-563-17964-3 (pbk) : £1.50 B82-04515

Whitnell, Barbara. The ring of bells / Barbara Whitnell. — London : Hodder and Stoughton, c1982. — 479p ; 22cm
ISBN 0-340-26489-6 : £7.95 : CIP rev.
B82-07436

Whittal, Yvonne. Bitter-sweet waters / by Yvonne Whittal. — London : Mills & Boon, 1982. — 188p ; 19cm
ISBN 0-263-10041-3 : £5.25 B82-22499

Whittal, Yvonne. Dance of the snake / by Yvonne Whittal. — London : Mills & Boon, 1981. — 188p ; 20cm
ISBN 0-263-09970-9 : £4.55 B82-09360

Whittal, Yvonne. East to Barryvale / Yvonne Whittal. — Large print ed. — Bath : Chivers, 1982, c1975. — 200p ; 23cm. — (A Lythway book)
Originally published: London : Mills and Boon, 1975
ISBN 0-85119-788-4 : Unpriced : CIP rev.
B81-35858

Whittal, Yvonne. House of mirrors / by Yvonne Whittal. — London : Mills and Boon, 1982. — 187p ; 20cm
ISBN 0-263-10093-6 : £5.95 B82-37111

Whittal, Yvonne. Late harvest / by Yvonne Whittal. — London : Mills & Boon, 1982. — 186p ; 20cm
ISBN 0-263-10051-0 : £5.25 B82-27280

Whittal, Yvonne. Late harvest / by Yvonne Whittal. — London : Mills & Boon, 1982. — 186p ; 17cm
ISBN 0-263-73853-1 (pbk) : £0.85 B82-36282

Whittle, Norah. In search of a name / Norah Whittle. — Large print ed. — Bath : Chivers Press, 1982, c1972. — 200p ; 23cm. — (A Seymour book)
Originally published: London : Arrow, 1972
ISBN 0-85119-455-9 : Unpriced : CIP rev.
B81-36058

Wiat, Philippa. Bride in darkness / Philippa Wiat. — London : Hale, 1982. — 205p ; 20cm
ISBN 0-7091-9316-5 : £7.25 B82-18315

Wiat, Philippa. The King's vengeance. — Large print ed. — Bath : Chivers Press, Dec.1982. — [288]p. — (A Lythway book)
Originally published: London : Hale, 1980
ISBN 0-85119-874-0 : £7.20 : CIP entry
B82-30229

Wiat, Philippa. The mistletoe bough / Philippa Wiat. — London : Hale, 1981. — 245p ; 23cm
ISBN 0-7091-8938-9 : £7.25 B82-02817

Wibberley, Mary. A dangerous man / Mary Wibberley. — Large print ed. — Bath : Chivers, 1981, c1979. — 225p ; 23cm. — (A Seymour book)
Originally published: London : Mills & Boon, 1979
ISBN 0-85119-443-5 : Unpriced : CIP rev.
B81-31251

Wibberley, Mary. Law of the jungle / by Mary Wibberley. — London : Mills & Boon, 1982. — 188p ; 19cm
ISBN 0-263-09982-2 : £5.25 B82-10372

Wibberley, Mary. Master of Saramanca. — Large print ed. — Bath : Chivers, Jan.1983. — [280] p. — (Atlantic large print)
Originally published: London : Mills and Boon, 1973
ISBN 0-85119-516-4 : £5.25 : CIP entry
B82-33088

823'.914[F] — Fiction in English, *1945-* — *Texts continuation*

Wibberley, Mary. The wilderness hut / Mary Wibberley. — London : Mills & Boon, c1975 (1982 [printing]). — 187p ; 18cm
ISBN 0-263-73922-8 (pbk) : £0.85 B82-36105

Wilde, Jennifer. Love me, Marietta / Jennifer Wilde. — London : Futura, 1982, c1981. — 582p ; 18cm. — (A Troubadour book)
ISBN 0-7107-3024-1 (pbk) : £2.50 B82-15316

Wiles, Domini. Pay-off / Domini Wiles. — London : Constable, 1982. — 189p ; 23cm. — (Constable crime)
ISBN 0-09-464410-1 : £5.95 B82-10546

Williams, David, *1926-*. Copper, Gold & Treasure : a Mark Treasure novel / David Williams. — London : Collins, 1982. — 213p ; 20cm. — (The Crime Club)
ISBN 0-00-231297-2 : £6.75 : CIP rev. B82-03703

Williams, David, *1931-*. Atlantic convoy / David Williams. — London : Pan, 1982, c1979. — 236p ; 18cm
Originally published: London : Cassell, 1979
ISBN 0-330-26171-1 (pbk) : £1.50 B82-10022

Williams, David, *1931-*. Bluebirds over / David Williams. — London : Severn House, 1981. — 158p ; 21cm. — (Fighter ; 1)
Originally published: London : New English Library, 1981
ISBN 0-7278-0753-6 : £5.95 : CIP rev. B81-31626

Williams, David, *1931-*. Fighter 2 vendetta / David Williams. — London : Severn House, 1982, c1981. — 135p ; 21cm
Originally published: London : New English Library, 1981
ISBN 0-7278-0800-1 : £6.50 B82-30472

Williams, Eric, *1911 July 13-*. The borders of barbarism / Eric Williams. — London : Remploy, 1979. — viii,230p ; 22cm
Originally published: London : Heinemann, 1961
ISBN 0-7066-0828-3 : £4.50 B82-02261

Williams, Irene M.. Riverlea / by Irene M. Williams. — London : Hale, 1981. — 160p ; 20cm
ISBN 0-7091-9446-3 : £5.95 B82-06318

Williams, Louie. Romance at St. Margaret's / by Louie Williams. — London : Hale, 1982. — 160p ; 20cm
ISBN 0-7091-9571-0 : £5.95 B82-11074

Williams, Malcolm. Another time, another place / by Malcolm Williams. — London : Hale, 1982. — 159p ; 20cm
ISBN 0-7091-9915-5 : £6.50 B82-35895

Williams, Malcolm. Debt of friendship / by Malcolm Williams. — London : Hale, c1981. — 174p ; 20cm
Originally published: 1980
ISBN 0-7091-9305-x : £5.95 B82-00451

Williams, Mary. Louise : a romantic novel of Cornwall / Mary Williams. — London : Kimber, 1981. — 219p ; 23cm
ISBN 0-7183-0228-1 : £6.50 B82-04682

Williams, Mary. The Tregellis inheritance / Mary Williams. — London : Kimber, 1982. — 236p ; 23cm
ISBN 0-7183-0388-1 : £6.50 B82-30508

Williams, Mary. Trenhawk / Mary Williams. — London : Sphere, 1982, c1980. — 317p ; 18cm
Originally published: London : Kimber, 1980
ISBN 0-7221-9123-5 (pbk) : £1.75 B82-34223

Williams, Mary-Beth. Doctor Devine / Mary-Beth Williams. — London : Hale, 1982. — 192p ; 19cm
ISBN 0-7091-9670-9 : £6.25 B82-22118

Williams, Nigel. Jack be nimble. — London : Hodder and Stoughton, Apr.1982. — [256]p. — (Coronet books)
Originally published: London : Secker & Warburg, 1980
ISBN 0-340-26783-6 (pbk) : £1.25 : CIP entry B82-03807

Williams, Roger, *1947-*. Aftermath / Roger Williams. — London : W.H. Allen, 1982. — 185p ; 18cm. — (A Star book)
ISBN 0-352-31041-3 (pbk) : £1.60 B82-22065

Williams, Timothy. Converging parallels : a novel / by Timothy Williams. — London : Gollancz, 1982. — 250p ; 21cm
ISBN 0-575-03125-5 : £6.95 : CIP rev. B82-09442

Williams, Veronica. Merlinston / Veronica Williams. — London : Hale, 1982. — 223p ; 19cm
ISBN 0-7091-9774-8 : £7.95 B82-27316

Williams, Veronica. Wildashe / by Veronica Williams. — London : Hale, 1981. — 206p ; 20cm
ISBN 0-7091-9419-6 : £6.95 B82-02160

Williamson, Leslie. The crowded cemetery / by Leslie Williamson. — London : Hale, 1981. — 158p ; 20cm
ISBN 0-7091-9324-6 : £3.25 B82-03155

Williamson, Leslie. Death of a portrait / by Leslie Williamson. — London : Hale, 1982. — 159p ; 20cm
ISBN 0-7091-9668-7 : £6.75 B82-15496

Williamson, Tony. Doomsday contract / Tony Williamson. — [London] : Fontana, 1978, c1977. — 192p ; 18cm
Originally published: London : Collins, 1977
ISBN 0-00-616378-5 (pbk) : £1.25 B82-06307

Williamson, Tony. Warhead / Tony Williamson. — London : Collins, 1982. — 222p ; 22cm
ISBN 0-00-222626-x : £7.25 : CIP rev. B81-34584

Willock, Colin. In the rut / Colin Willock. — London : Sphere, 1982. — 184p ; 18cm
ISBN 0-7221-9194-4 (pbk) : £1.25 B82-14902

Wilson, A. N.. The healing art / A.N. Wilson. — Harmondsworth : Penguin, 1982, c1980. — 269p ; 19cm
Originally published: London : Secker and Warburg, 1980
ISBN 0-14-006122-3 (pbk) : £1.95 B82-40675

Wilson, A. N.. Who was Oswald Fish? / A.N. Wilson. — London : Secker & Warburg, 1981. — 313p ; 23cm
ISBN 0-436-57606-6 : £6.95 : CIP rev. B81-25324

Wilson, A. N.. Wise virgin. — London : Secker and Warburg, Oct.1982. — [224]p
ISBN 0-436-57608-2 : £7.50 : CIP entry B82-24008

Wilson, Alan, *1932-*. Arthur : the war king / by Alan Wilson and A.T. Blackett. — Cardiff : Byrd
Founder of Britain and his people of the Dark Ages. — 1982, c1981. — 315p : ill,maps,2ports ; 31cm
ISBN 0-86285-004-5 : Unpriced B82-33272

Wilson, Angus, *1913-*. Setting the world on fire / Angus Wilson. — London : Granada, 1981, c1980. — 336p ; 18cm. — (A Granada book)
Originally published: London : Secker & Warburg, 1980. — Port on inside covers
ISBN 0-586-05339-5 (pbk) : £1.95 B82-09548

Wilson, Derek. Bear rampant : the autobiography of Robert Dudley, Duke of Northumberland, Earl of Warwick and Earl of Leicester in the Holy Roman Empire, part two, 1598-1603 / Derek Wilson. — London : Hamilton, 1981. — 236p ; 21cm
ISBN 0-241-10147-6 : £7.95 : CIP rev. B81-20580

Wilson, Jacqueline. Nobody's perfect / Jacqueline Wilson. — Oxford : Oxford University Press, 1982. — 104p ; 23cm
For adolescents
ISBN 0-19-271463-5 : £5.95 : CIP rev. B82-04162

Wilson, Steve. Dealer's move / Steve Wilson. — London : Granada, 1982, c1978. — 224p ; 18cm. — (A Panther book)
Originally published: London : Macmillan, 1978
ISBN 0-586-05420-0 (pbk) : £1.50 B82-14109

Wilson, Steve. Dealer's war / Steve Wilson. — London : Granada, 1982, c1980. — 254p ; 18cm. — (A Panther book)
Originally published: London : Macmillan, 1980
ISBN 0-586-05421-9 (pbk) : £1.50 B82-14108

Wilson, Steve. Dealer's wheels / Steve Wilson. — London : Macmillan, 1982. — 187p ; 21cm
ISBN 0-333-32232-0 : £5.95 B82-18243

Wilson, Steve. Dealer's wheels. — Large print ed. — Bath : Chivers, Feb.1983. — [288]p. — (A Lythway book)
Originally published: London : Macmillan, 1982
ISBN 0-85119-903-8 : £7.20 : CIP entry B82-39591

Wingate, John. Carrier / John Wingate. — London : Sphere Books, 1982, c1981. — 191p : maps ; 18cm
Originally published: London : Weidenfeld & Nicolson, 1981
ISBN 0-7221-9111-1 (pbk) : £1.50 B82-33899

Wingate, John. Frigate / John Wingate. — London : Sphere Books, 1982, c1980. — 215p : ill,maps ; 18cm
Originally published: London : Weidenfeld & Nicolson, 1980
ISBN 0-7221-9110-3 (pbk) : £1.50 B82-33898

Wingate, John. Submarine / John Wingate. — London : Weidenfeld and Nicolson, c1982. — 212p : 2charts ; 23cm
ISBN 0-297-78004-2 : £6.50 B82-14877

Wingate, John. Submarine / John Wingate. — London : Sphere Books, 1982, c1982. — 211p : ill,maps ; 18cm
Originally published: London : Weidenfeld & Nicolson, 1982
ISBN 0-7221-9113-8 (pbk) : £1.50 B82-33900

Winslow, Pauline Glen. Coppergold / Pauline Glen Winslow. — London : Fontana, 1982, c1978. — 253p ; 18cm
Originally published: London : Collins, 1978
ISBN 0-00-616484-6 (pbk) : £1.50 B82-17068

Winslow, Pauline Glen. I, Martha Adam. — London : Arlington, Sept.1982. — [288]p
ISBN 0-85140-585-1 : £7.50 : CIP entry B82-20526

Winslow, Pauline Glen. The Rockefeller gift : a Superintendent Capricorn novel / Pauline Glen Winslow. — London : Collins, 1982. — 272p ; 21cm. — (The Crime Club)
ISBN 0-00-231720-6 : £6.95 : CIP rev. B82-00901

823'.914[F] — Fiction in English, *1945-* — *Texts continuation*

Winspear, Violet. Bride's dilemma / Violet Winspear. — Large print ed. — [Bath] : Chivers, 1982, c1965. — 285p ; 23cm. — (A Seymour large print romance) (Atlantic large print)
Originally published: London : Mills and Boon, 1965
ISBN 0-85119-461-3 : Unpriced : CIP rev. B82-04999

Winspear, Violet. A girl possessed. — Large print ed. — Bath : Chivers, Sept.1982. — [280]p. — (Atlantic large print)
Originally published: London : Mills and Boon, 1980
ISBN 0-85119-491-5 : £5.25 : CIP entry B82-20508

Winspear, Violet. The kisses and the wine / Violet Winspear. — Large print ed. — [Bath] : Chivers, 1982, c1973. — 286p ; 23cm. — (Atlantic large print) (A Seymour large print romance)
Originally published: London : Mills & Boon, 1973
ISBN 0-85119-473-7 : Unpriced : CIP rev. B82-09851

Winspear, Violet. Love is the honey. — Large print ed. — Bath : Chivers, Dec.1982. — [256] p. — (Atlantic large print)
Originally published: London : Mills and Boon, 1980
ISBN 0-85119-509-1 : £5.25 : CIP entry B82-30237

Winspear, Violet. No man of her own / by Violet Winspear. — London : Mills & Boon, 1981. — 188p ; 20cm
ISBN 0-263-09978-4 : £4.55 B82-09224

Winspear, Violet. Satan took a bride / Violet Winspear. — London : Mills & Boon, c1975 (1982 [printing]). — 186p ; 18cm
ISBN 0-263-73923-6 (pbk) : £0.85 B82-36104

Winter, Patrick. The Brack report : a report / by Patrick Winter ; based on the scripts of the Thames Television series The Brack report by Christopher Penfold. — London : Arrow, 1982. — 189p ; 18cm
ISBN 0-09-927160-5 (pbk) : £1.50 B82-19010

Winter, Patrick. The Brack report : a novel / by Patrick Winter ; based on the scripts of the Thames Television series The Brack report by Christopher Penfold. — London : Severn House, 1982. — 189p ; 21cm
Originally published: London : Arrow, 1982
ISBN 0-7278-0781-1 : £6.50 B82-31422

Winter, Sarah. Pamela's passions / Sarah Winter. — London : Macdonald, 1982, c1981. — 251p ; 21cm
Originally published: London : Futura, 1981
ISBN 0-356-08651-8 : £4.95 B82-26006

Winton, John. Aircraft carrier / John Winton. — London : Sphere, 1982, c1980. — 303p ; 18cm
Originally published: London : Joseph, 1980
ISBN 0-7221-9232-0 (pbk) : £1.75 B82-22594

Winward, Walter. The ball bearing run / Walter Winward. — [London] : Corgi, 1982, c1981. — 303p ; 18cm
Originally published: London : Hamilton, 1981
ISBN 0-552-11940-7 (pbk) : £1.50 B82-28365

Winward, Walter. The Canaris fragments / by Walter Winward. — London : Hamilton, 1982. — 264p,[2]leaves of plates : 1map ; 23cm
ISBN 0-241-10795-4 : £7.95 : CIP rev. B82-01827

Wood, Bridget. Mask of the fox / Bridget Wood. — London : Hale, 1982. — 206p ; 20cm
ISBN 0-7091-9994-5 : £7.50 B82-39174

Wood, Christopher, *1935-*. Dead centre / Christopher Wood. — London : Futura, 1982, c1980. — 276p ; 18cm
Originally published: London : Joseph, 1980
ISBN 0-7088-1807-2 (pbk) : £1.75 B82-15317

Wood, Flora Maitland. Philippa of the Vendée / by Flora Maitland Wood. — London : Hale, 1981. — 208p ; 20cm
ISBN 0-7091-9420-x : £6.95 B82-06327

Wood, Kenneth, *1922-*. Shining armour / Kenneth Wood. — London : Julia MacRae, 1982. — 144p ; 23cm
ISBN 0-86203-059-5 : £6.25 : CIP rev. B81-33758

Woodman, Richard. A King's cutter / Richard Woodman. — London : John Murray, 1982. — 169p ; 22cm
ISBN 0-7195-3946-3 : £7.50 : CIP rev. B82-09834

Woods, Fredric. Rundown / Fredric Woods. — London : Hale, 1982. — 208p ; 20cm
ISBN 0-7091-9835-3 : £6.75 B82-33192

Woods, Sara. Enter a gentlewoman / Sara Woods. — London : Macmillan, 1982. — 218p ; 21cm
ISBN 0-333-32393-9 : £5.95 B82-22521

Woods, Sara. Proceed to judgement / Sara Woods. — London : Macmillan, 1979. — 191p ; 21cm
ISBN 0-333-27411-3 : £4.95 B82-05328

Woods, Sara. Villains by necessity / Sara Woods. — London : Macmillan, 1982. — 190p ; 21cm
ISBN 0-333-33072-2 : £6.50 B82-35913

Woods, Sara. Weep for her / Sara Woods. — Large print ed. — Leicester : Ulverscroft, 1982, c1980. — 366p ; 23cm. — (Ulverscroft large print series)
Originally published: London : Macmillan, 1980
ISBN 0-7089-0760-1 : Unpriced : CIP rev. B82-01737

Worboys, Anne. Run, Sara, run / Anne Worboys. — London : Severn House, 1982. — 234p ; 21cm
ISBN 0-7278-0774-9 : £6.50 B82-17492

Wright, Meg. The female of the species is more deadly than the male / by Meg Wright ; cover by Ann Humphrey. — Strathmartine (Sheila Clark, 6 Craigmill Cottages, Strathmartine by Dundee, Scotland) : Scotpress, 1982. — 70p ; 30cm. — (A Star trek fanzine)
Unpriced (pbk) B82-17391

Wright, Melinda. Love at 30,000 feet. — London : Arlington Books, Aug.1982. — [224]p
ISBN 0-85140-557-6 : £6.95 : CIP entry B82-15872

Wright, Wade. Death at nostalgia street / Wade Wright. — London : Hale, 1982. — 189p ; 20cm
ISBN 0-7091-9836-1 : £6.75 B82-33423

Wright, Wade. It leads to murder / Wade Wright. — London : Hale, 1981. — 192p ; 20cm
ISBN 0-7091-9440-4 : £6.50 B82-06328

Yorke, Katherine. The enchantress / Katherine Yorke. — London : Futura, 1979. — 407p ; 18cm. — (A Troubadour spectacular)
ISBN 0-7088-1458-1 (pbk) : £1.25 B82-10549

Yorke, Margaret. Devil's work / Margaret Yorke. — London : Hutchinson, 1982. — 169p ; 23cm
ISBN 0-09-147580-5 : £6.95 : CIP rev. B82-04725

Yorke, Margaret. The hand of death / Margaret Yorke. — London : Arrow, 1982, c1981. — 217p ; 18cm
Originally published: London : Hutchinson, 1981
ISBN 0-09-928490-1 (pbk) : £1.25 B82-33314

Yorke, Margaret. No medals for the major / by Margaret Yorke. — Long Preston : Magna, 1981, c1974. — 345p ; 23cm
Originally published: London : Bles, 1974. — Published in large print
ISBN 0-86009-357-3 : Unpriced : CIP rev. B81-31816

Yorke, Margaret. The scent of fear / Margaret Yorke. — London : Arrow, 1982, c1980. — 220p ; 18cm
Originally published: London : Hutchinson, 1980
ISBN 0-09-927420-5 (pbk) : £1.25 B82-14918

Yorke, Margaret. The small hours of the morning / Margaret Yorke. — Long Preston : Magna Print, 1982, c1975. — 345p ; 22cm
Originally published: London : Bles, 1975. — Published in large print
ISBN 0-86009-384-0 : Unpriced : CIP rev. B82-00358

Young, Arthur, *1925-*. The surgeon's knot / Arthur Young. — London : Collins, 1982. — 280p ; 22cm
ISBN 0-00-222061-x : £7.95 : CIP rev. B82-07655

823'.914[F] — Short stories in English, *1945-* — *Texts*

Adams, Tessa. Kathryn of Oak Hill Farm / Tessa Adams. — [Irchester] : Castle, 1982, c1981. — 89p ; 21cm
ISBN 0-907877-10-9 (pbk) : £1.10 B82-22913

Archer, Jeffrey. A quiver full of arrows. — London : Hodder & Stoughton, Nov.1981. — [192]p. — (Coronet books)
Originally published: 1980
ISBN 0-340-27272-4 (pbk) : £1.25 : CIP entry B81-30136

Ballard, J. G.. Myths of the near future / J.G. Ballard. — London : Cape, 1982. — 205p ; 21cm
ISBN 0-224-02936-3 : £6.95 : CIP rev. B82-25521

Bannon, J. M.. M62 / J.M. Bannon. — Bognor Regis : New Horizon, c1981. — 179p ; 21cm
ISBN 0-86116-604-3 : £5.75 B82-02942

Barrington, Margaret. David's daughter, Tamar. — Dublin : Wolfhound Press, Sept.1982. — [176]p
ISBN 0-905473-74-4 (cased) : £7.50 : CIP entry B82-21568

Behan, Brendan. After the wake : twenty-one prose works including previously unpublished material / Brendan Behan ; edited by Peter Fallon. — Dublin : O'Brien, 1981. — 156p ; 21cm. — (Classic Irish fiction series, ISSN 0332-1347)
ISBN 0-905140-97-4 : Unpriced : CIP rev. B81-20653

Bell, Mal. The black rose : and other stories / Mal Ball ; illustrated by Ossie Murray. — Birmingham : Affor, 1982. — 30p : ill ; 21x30cm
ISBN 0-907127-07-x (pbk) : £1.00 : CIP rev. B82-16209

Boyd, Neil. Bless me again, Father / Neil Boyd. — [London] : Corgi, 1982, c1981. — 255p ; 18cm
Originally published: London : Joseph, 1981
ISBN 0-552-11903-2 (pbk) : £1.50 B82-19372

Boyle, Patrick. The port wine stain. — Dublin : O'Brien Press, June 1982. — [196]p. — (Classic Irish fiction, ISSN 0332-1347 ; 3)
ISBN 0-86278-010-1 : £8.00 : CIP entry B82-14070

823'.914[F] — Short stories in English, *1945-* **—** *Texts* *continuation*

Cavendish, Arabella. The other woman / Arabella Cavendish. — Irchester : Mark Saunders, 1982, c1981. — 68p ; 21cm. — (Castle books)
ISBN 0-907877-05-2 (pbk) : £1.00 B82-13873

Chetwynd-Hayes, R.. Tales of darkness / R. Chetwynd-Hayes. — London : Kimber, 1981. — 188p ; 23cm
ISBN 0-7183-0138-2 : £5.95 B82-02270

Clarke, Arthur C.. Tales from the White Hart / Arthur C. Clarke. — London : Sidgwick & Jackson, 1972 (1980 [printing]). — 156p ; 18cm
ISBN 0-283-98624-7 (pbk) : £0.95 B82-39230

Cooper, Jilly. Love and other heartaches. — London : Arlington, Oct.1981. — [224]p
ISBN 0-85140-558-4 : £6.50 : CIP entry B81-27388

Cornish, Margaret. Still waters : mystery tales of the canals / by Margaret Cornish ; with illustrations by Valerie Croker. — London : Hale, 1982. — 186p : ill ; 22cm
ISBN 0-7091-9625-3 : £7.60 B82-22164

Dearnley, Moira. Icarus : and other stories / Moira Dearnley. — Port Talbot : Alun, c1981. — 23p ; 19cm. — (Alun stories ; no.4)
ISBN 0-907117-04-x (pbk) : £0.75 B82-02952

Ellis, David B.. The deadly hunger and other stories / David B. Ellis. — Bognor Regis : New Horizon, c1982. — 73p ; 21cm
ISBN 0-86116-960-3 : £3.25 B82-36120

Elson, Jenny. Worlds apart : a study of Earth and Vulcan in fiction and article / by Jenny Elson. — Dundee (6 Craigmill Cottages, Strathmartine, Dundee) : Star Trek Action Group, c1979. — 57p ; 30cm. — (A STAG publication)
£0.95 (unbound) B82-40825

Enderby, Mavis. Enderby's anecdotes. — Lincoln (1 Stonefield Ave., Lincoln) : Asgill, 1981. — 31p ; 80x110mm
£0.30 (pbk) B82-09653

Enderby, Mavis. Enderby's book of very short stories. — Lincoln (1 Stonefield Ave., Lincoln) : Asgill, 1981. — 31p ; 80x110mm
£0.30 (pbk) B82-09652

Fleming, Ian, *1908-1964.* For your eyes only : five secret occasions in the life of James Bond / Ian Fleming. — Large print ed. — Bath : Chivers, 1982, c1960. — 252p ; 23cm. — (A New Portway large print book)
Originally published: London : Cape, 1960
ISBN 0-85119-161-4 : Unpriced : CIP rev. B82-04994

Forsyth, Frederick. No comebacks : collected short stories / Frederick Forsyth. — London : Hutchinson, 1982. — 255p ; 23cm
ISBN 0-09-147870-7 : £6.95 : CIP rev. B82-01705

Forsyth, Frederick. No comebacks. — Large print ed. — Bath : Chivers, Jan.1983. — [400] p. — (A Lythway book)
Originally published: London : Hutchinson, 1982
ISBN 0-85119-880-5 : £7.90 : CIP entry B82-33093

Freddi, Chris. Pork / Chris Freddi. — London : Routledge & Kegan Paul, 1982, c1981. — 209p ; 21cm
ISBN 0-7100-9230-x : £6.95 B82-35916

Friel, Brian. The diviner. — Dublin : O'Brien Press, June 1982. — [196]p. — (Classic Irish fiction, ISSN 0332-1347 ; 2)
ISBN 0-86278-021-7 : £8.00 : CIP entry B82-11120

Gardam, Jane. Black faces, white faces / Jane Gardam. — London : Abacus, 1982. — 117p ; 20cm
Originally published: London : Hamish Hamilton, 1975
ISBN 0-349-11407-2 (pbk) : £1.95 B82-32111

Gardam, Jane. The pangs of love and other stories. — London : Hamilton, Feb.1983. — [160]p
ISBN 0-241-10942-6 : £7.95 : CIP entry B82-37854

Geras, Adèle. The green behind the glass. — London : Hamilton, Sept.1982. — [144]p
For adolescents
ISBN 0-241-10808-x : £5.25 : CIP entry B82-21758

Gettings, Fred. The salamander tales / Fred Gettings. — Edinburgh : Floris, c1981. — 94p : ill ; 22cm
ISBN 0-903540-48-7 : £3.95 : CIP rev. B81-25124

Greig, Francis. The bite : and other apocryphal tales / Francis Greig. — London : Cape, 1981. — x,166p ; 23cm
ISBN 0-224-01904-x : £5.95 : CIP rev. B81-20623

Haynes, Dorothy K.. Peacocks and pagodas : and the best of Dorothy K. Haynes / introduction by Trevor Royle. — Edinburgh : Harris, 1981. — 151p ; 23cm. — (The Scottish fiction reprint library)
ISBN 0-86228-020-6 : £6.95 B82-13944

Healy, Dermot. Banished misfortune : and other stories / by Dermot Healy. — London : Allison & Busby, 1982. — 111p ; 23cm
ISBN 0-85031-456-9 : £6.95 : CIP rev.
ISBN 0-86322-003-7 (Brandon) B82-11104

Hill, Susan. The albatross : and other stories / Susan Hill. — Harmondsworth : Penguin, 1974, c1971 (1982 [printing]). — 174p ; 18cm
Originally published: London : Hamilton, 1971
ISBN 0-14-003649-0 (pbk) : £1.25 B82-32492

Hind, Graham. A table for two : and other stories / Graham Hind. — Bognor Regis : New Horizon, c1981. — 160p ; 21cm
ISBN 0-86116-530-6 : £5.25 B82-02948

Hogan, Desmond. Stories : The diamonds at the bottom of the sea, Children of Lir / Desmond Hogan. — London : Pan, 1982, c1981. — 254p ; 20cm. — (Picador)
The diamonds at the bottom of the sea. Orginally published: London : Hamilton, 1979 ; Children of Lir. Originally published: London : Hamilton, 1981
ISBN 0-330-26624-1 (pbk) : £1.95 B82-09945

Holdstock, Robert. In the valley of the statues : a collection of short stories / by Robert Holdstock. — London : Faber, 1982. — 223p ; 21cm
ISBN 0-571-11858-5 : £6.95 : CIP rev. B82-06232

Jones, G. O.. THe lecture / G.O. Jones. — Port Talbot : Alun, c1980. — 24p ; 19cm. — (Alun stories ; no.3)
Partial contents: The committee / G.O. Jones
ISBN 0-907117-00-7 (pbk) : £0.75 B82-02953

Judkins, Rod. City sync. — [24]p : ill ; 30cm. — (A neue, neue, neue publication)
Author: Rod Judkins. — Contents: Laundrette love — Lindastic — Shitopolis
ISBN 0-902490-56-7 (unbound) : £0.60 B82-22627

Lurie, Morris. Dirty friends : stories / by Morris Lurie. — Harmondsworth : Penguin, 1981. — 192p ; 18cm
Originally published: Ringwood, Vic. : Penguin Australia, 1981
ISBN 0-14-005825-7 (pbk) : £1.10 B82-19904

Mac Intyre, Tom. The harper's turn / Tom Mac Intyre ; with an introduction by Seamus Heaney. — Dublin : Gallery, 1982. — 65p : ill ; 22cm
ISBN 0-904011-29-1 (cased) : Unpriced B82-36177

Mac Laverty, Bernard. A time to dance : and other stories / Bernard Mac Laverty. — London : Cape, 1982. — 174p ; 21cm
ISBN 0-224-02018-8 : £6.50 : CIP rev. B82-14051

McAughtry, Sam. Blind spot : and other stories / Sam McAughtry. — Belfast : Blackstaff, c1979. — 116p ; 22cm
ISBN 0-85640-179-x : £5.95 B82-16936

Meakin, Viola. The ghost ring and other tales of telepathy / by Viola Meakin. — Ipswich : East Anglian Magazine, c1981. — 48p ; 21cm
ISBN 0-900227-57-5 (pbk) : £2.50 B82-01014

Miller, Mona. Part of a theme : and other stories / by Mona Miller. — [London] ([The Daisy House, 30, Carmichael Court, Barnes, SW13 OHA]) : Archer, 1981. — 48p ; 21cm
£1.25 (pbk) B82-10344

Milner, Dorothy Levien. When you've time to read / Dorothy Levien Milner. — Bognor Regis : New Horizon, c1982. — 122p ; 21cm
ISBN 0-86116-444-x : £3.50 B82-06365

Morgan, Clare. Hill of stones : and other stories / Clare Morgan. — [Great Britain] : The White Friar Press, 1980. — 31p ; 18cm
Unpriced (pbk) B82-13600

Mortimer, John. Rumpole of the Bailey. — Large print ed. — Bath : Chivers Press, Feb.1982. — [256]p. — (A New Portway large print book)
ISBN 0-85119-154-1 : £5.25 : CIP entry B81-36053

Mortimer, John, *1923-.* Regina v. Rumpole / John Mortimer. — London : Allen Lane, 1981. — 344p ; 23cm
Contents: Rumpole for the defence - Rumpole's return. Originally published: Harmondsworth : Penguin, 1980
ISBN 0-7139-1443-2 : £6.95 B82-05583

Mortimer, John, *1923-.* Rumpole / John Mortimer. — Bath : Chivers Press, 1982, c1979. — 196p ; 23cm. — (A New Portway large print book)
Originally published: as part of Rumpole of the Bailey. Harmondsworth : Penguin, 1978
ISBN 0-85119-153-3 : Unpriced : CIP rev. B81-35836

Mortimer, John, *1923-.* The trials of Rumpole / John Mortimer. — Bath : Chivers Press, 1982, c1979. — 199p ; 23cm. — (A New Portway large print book)
Originally published: as part of The trials of Rumpole. Harmondsworth : Penguin, 1979
ISBN 0-85119-155-x : Unpriced : CIP rev. B81-36052

Needle, Jan. A sense of shame : and other stories / Jan Needle. — London : Fontana, 1982, c1980. — 125p ; 18cm. — (Lions)
Originally published: London : Deutsch, 1980. — For adolescents
ISBN 0-00-671901-5 (pbk) : £1.00 B82-19737

O'Brien, Edna. Returning : tales / Edna O'Brian. — London : Weidenfeld and Nicolson, 1982. — 158p ; 23cm
ISBN 0-297-78052-2 : £6.50 B82-22727

Race, Mary. Convent tales / Mary Race. — Ilfracombe : Stockwell, 1981. — 104p ; 19cm
ISBN 0-7223-1496-5 (pbk) : £2.20 B82-05495

Reeman, Douglas. Against the sea / Douglas Reeman. — London : Sparrow, 1981, c1971. — 173p ; 18cm
Originally published: London : Hutchinson, 1971. — Includes index
ISBN 0-09-927180-x (pbk) : £0.95 B82-03541

823'.914[F] — Short stories in English, *1945-* — *Texts* *continuation*

Rendell, Ruth. The fever tree : and other stories / Ruth Rendell. — London : Hutchinson, 1982. — 191p ; 23cm
ISBN 0-09-149730-2 : £6.95 : CIP rev.
B82-19154

Scott, Andy. Portrait of a smalltime crooner / Andy Scott ; [illustrations by Derek Taylor]. — London : Editions Ecosse, c1981. — 14p : ill ; 21cm
ISBN 0-907720-00-5 (pbk) : £0.35 B82-03977

Scupham, A. G.. Duty to the devil : and other ghost stories / A.G. Scupham. — London : Kimber, 1981. — 207p ; 23cm
ISBN 0-7183-0108-0 : £5.95 B82-05285

Serraillier, Ian. The road to Canterbury : tales from Chaucer / retold by Ian Serraillier ; illustrated with wood engravings by John Lawrence. — London : Heinemann Educational, 1981. — 144p : ill ; 20cm. — (New windmill series)
Originally published: Harmondsworth : Kestrel, 1979
ISBN 0-435-12259-2 : £1.50 B82-05286

Shaw, Bob. A better mantrap : nine science fiction and fantasy stories / by Bob Shaw. — London : Gollancz, 1982. — 192p ; 21cm
ISBN 0-575-03083-6 : £6.95 : CIP rev.
B81-35885

Sillitoe, Alan. The second chance : and other stories / Alan Sillitoe. — [London] : Triad, 1982, c1981. — 203p ; 18cm
Originally published: London : Cape, 1981
ISBN 0-586-05504-5 (pbk) : £1.50 B82-37209

Sinclair, Clive, *1948-*. Bedbugs / by Clive Sinclair. — London : Allison & Busby, 1982. — 109p ; 23cm
ISBN 0-85031-454-2 : £6.95 : CIP rev.
B82-07113

Sinclair, David, *1935-*. Willick o'Pirliebraes : tales of Flotta / by David Sinclair ; illustrated by Jim Baikie. — Stromness : Orkney Press, 1981. — 166p : ill ; 23cm
ISBN 0-907618-00-6 : £4.95 B82-22712

Stewart, Mary, *1916-*. Touch not the cat ; The Gabriel hounds ; Nine coaches waiting ; Madam, will you talk? / Mary Stewart. — London : Heinemann, 1981. — 792p ; 24cm
ISBN 0-905712-65-x : £6.95 B82-03189

Sykala, U.. Mystical encounters / Ursula Sykala. — Irchester : Castle Books, 1982, c1981. — 102p ; 21cm
ISBN 0-907877-20-6 (pbk) : £1.45 B82-33260

Tindall, Gillian. The China egg and other stories. — Large print ed. — Bath : Chivers, Nov.1982. — [366]p. — (A Lythway book)
Originally published: London : Hodder & Stoughton, 1981
ISBN 0-85119-867-8 : £7.20 : CIP entry
B82-26310

Tinniswood, Peter. More tales from a long room / Peter Tinniswood. — London : Arrow, 1982. — 139p : ill ; 20cm
ISBN 0-09-928800-1 (pbk) : £1.50 B82-30451

Toulmin, David. Hard shining corn / David Toulmin. — Edinburgh : Harris, 1982. — 134p ; 22cm. — (The Scottish fiction reprint library)
Originally published: Aberdeen : Impulse Books, 1972
ISBN 0-86228-039-7 (pbk) : £4.95 B82-32974

Trevor, William. Beyond the pale and other stories. — London : Bodley Head, Oct.1981. — [256]p
ISBN 0-370-30442-x : £6.95 : CIP entry
B81-28829

Watson, Ian. Sunstroke : and other stories / by Ian Watson. — London : Gollancz, 1982. — 190p ; 21cm
ISBN 0-575-03138-7 : £7.95 : CIP rev.
B82-12986

Webb, Colin David. Best bitter / by Colin David Webb. — [Millbrook] ([Knill Cross House, Higher Anderton Rd., Millbrook, Cornwall]) : Kawabata, 1981. — 19p ; 21cm
ISBN 0-906110-33-5 (pbk) : £0.60 B82-06446

Weldon, Fay. Watching me, watching you. — London : Hodder and Stoughton, May 1982. — [208]p. — (Coronet books)
Originally published: 1981
ISBN 0-340-27915-x (pbk) : £1.50 : CIP entry
B82-06724

Wilson, Angus, *1913-*. A bit off the map : and other stories / Angus Wilson. — London : Granada, 1982, c1957. — 173p ; 18cm. — (A Panther book)
Originally published: London : Secker & Warburg, 1957
ISBN 0-586-04896-0 (pbk) : £1.50 B82-14107

Wilson, Angus, *1913-*. Such darling dodos : and other stories / Angus Wilson. — London : Panther, 1980, c1950. — 188p : 1port ; 18cm
Originally published: London : Secker & Warburg, 1950. — Port on inside cover
ISBN 0-586-04904-5 (pbk) : £1.50 B82-31784

Wilson, Angus, *1913-*. The wrong set : and other stories / Angus Wilson. — London : Granada, 1982, c1949. — 200p ; 18cm
Originally published: London : Secker & Warburg, 1949
ISBN 0-586-04905-3 (pbk) : £1.95 B82-19979

Wyndham, John. Jizzle. — London : New English Library, Sept.1982. — [192]p
Originally published: London : Dobson, 1954
ISBN 0-450-02250-1 : £1.25 : CIP entry
B82-19685

823'.914[J] — Children's short stories in English, *1945-* — *Texts*

Aiken, Joan. A whisper in the night : stories of horror, suspense and fantasy / Joan Aiken. — London : Gollancz, 1982. — 189p ; 21cm
ISBN 0-575-03105-0 : £5.95 : CIP rev.
B82-06932

Ainsworth, Ruth. The phantom roundabout : and other ghostly tales / Ruth Ainsworth ; illustrated by Shirley Hughes. — [Sevenoaks] : Knight, 1981, c1977. — 127p : ill ; 18cm
Originally published: London : Deutsch, 1977
ISBN 0-340-25505-6 (pbk) : £0.95 : CIP rev.
B80-24882

Ambrus, Victor. Dracula's bedtime storybook. — Oxford : Oxford University Press, Sept.1981. — [32]p
ISBN 0-19-279762-x : £4.50 : CIP entry
B81-22498

Archer, Jeffrey, *1940-*. Willy and the killer kipper / Jeffrey Archer ; art by Derek Matthews. — London : Hodder and Stoughton, 1981. — 42p : col.ill ; 29cm
ISBN 0-340-27057-8 : £3.95 : CIP rev.
B81-25695

Ashley, Bernard. I'm trying to tell you / Bernard Ashley ; illustrated by Lyn Jones. — [Harmondsworth] : Puffin, 1982, c1981. — 78p : ill ; 19cm
Originally published: Harmondsworth : Kestrel, 1981
ISBN 0-14-031337-0 (pbk) : £0.85 B82-40802

Berthoud, Michael. Precisely Pig / Michael Berthoud ; with illustrations by John Lawrence. — London : Collins, 1982. — 95p : ill ; 24cm
ISBN 0-00-183146-1 : £4.95 B82-32270

Bird, Maria. Andy Pandy story book. — Sevenoaks : Hodder and Stoughton Children's Books, Aug.1981. — [64]p
ISBN 0-340-26764-x : £2.50 : CIP entry
B81-18143

Bishop, Joyce. Toby the water baby and his friends of the riverside / Joyce Bishop ; illustrated by Tracy Lavercombe. — Braunton : Merlin Books, 1982. — 28p : ill ; 21cm
ISBN 0-86303-019-x (pbk) : £0.80 B82-38609

Black, Peter, *19---*. Mirabel, once upon a time / by Peter Black. — Cambridge (50 Kingston St., Cambridge CB1 2NU) : Pembgate Christian, 1980. — 35p : ill ; 21cm
£0.95 (pbk) B82-00814

Body, Wendy. A cat called Rover ; A dog called Smith / Wendy Body ; [illustrated by Mairi Hedderwick]. — Harlow : Longman, 1981. — 32p : ill(some col.) ; 21cm. — (Whizz bang)
Cover title
ISBN 0-582-18294-8 (cased) : Unpriced
ISBN 0-582-18293-x (pbk) : £0.80 B82-13599

Bond, Michael. Olga takes charge / Michael Bond ; illustrated by Hans Helweg. — Harmondsworth : Kestrel, 1982. — 127p : ill ; 21cm
ISBN 0-7226-5779-x : £4.95 B82-38154

Bond, Ruskin. Tales and legends from India / Ruskin Bond ; illustrated by Sally Scott. — London : MacRae, 1982. — 153p : ill ; 24cm
ISBN 0-86203-044-7 : £6.50 : CIP rev.
B82-04713

Bowles, Steve. Jamie / by Steve Bowles. — London : Gollancz, 1981. — 118p ; 21cm
ISBN 0-575-03015-1 : £4.95 B82-02262

Brett, Molly. Goodnight time tales / by Molly Brett. — [London] : Medici, c1982. — 24p : col.ill ; 18x21cm
ISBN 0-85503-067-4 (pbk) : £0.75 B82-34694

Broomsticks and beasticles : stories and verse about witches and strange creatures / chosen by Barbara Sleigh ; illustrated by John Patience. — London : Hodder and Stoughton, 1981. — 153p : ill ; 23cm
ISBN 0-340-25948-5 : £5.95 : CIP rev.
B81-28055

Byrne, Anna. The magic tinderbox and other bedtime stories / Anna Byrne. — Bognor Regis : New Horizon, c1981. — 43p : ill ; 21cm
ISBN 0-86116-810-0 : £3.50 B82-00654

Callan, Michael Feeney. Jockey school / Michael Feeney Callan ; based on the television series by Alan Janes. — London : British Broadcasting Corporation, 1982. — 143p ; 22cm
ISBN 0-563-20035-9 : £5.50 B82-22720

Chandler, Robert. The magic ring and other Russian folktales. — London : Faber, Feb.1983. — [90]p
Originally published: 1979
ISBN 0-571-13006-2 (pbk) : CIP entry
B82-38696

Clifford, Martin, *1875-1961*. High jinks at St Jim's / by Martin Clifford. — London : Howard Baker, 1981. — 1v.(various pagings) : ill(some col.),facsims(some col.) ; 28cm. — (Howard Baker Gem ; v.12)
Facsim of: selected weekly issues of the Gem, 1922-1923
ISBN 0-7030-0207-4 : £7.95 B82-37151

Coren, Alan. Arthur and the purple panic. — London : Robson, Sept.1981. — [64]p. — (Arthur books)
ISBN 0-86051-141-3 : £1.95 : CIP entry
B81-22457

823'.914[J] — Children's short stories in English, *1945- — Texts* *continuation*

Cox, Godfrey. Salt of the earth / by Godfrey Cox. — Ilkeston : Moorley's Bible & Bookshop, [1982]. — 38p : ill ; 21cm
Bibliography: p38
ISBN 0-86071-130-7 (pbk) : £0.55 B82-27328

Craig, Wendy. Happy endings : stories old and new / Wendy Craig ; illustrated by Gillian Chapman. — London : Granada, 1982. — 91p : ill ; 18cm. — (A Dragon book)
Originally published: London : Hutchinson, 1972
ISBN 0-246-11786-9 (cased) : Unpriced
ISBN 0-583-30519-9 (pbk) : £0.85 B82-17348

Cresswell, Helen. The secret world of Polly Flint. — London : Faber, Sept.1982. — 1v.
ISBN 0-571-11939-5 : £5.25 : CIP entry B82-28463

Davidson, Allan. Annabel. — London : Granada, Nov.1982. — [128]p. — (The Adventures of Annabel)
ISBN 0-246-11945-4 : £4.95 : CIP entry B82-27363

Dean's enchanting stories from the magic castle / illustrated by Gillian Embleton and Ronald Embleton. — London : Dean, 1981. — [42]p : col.ill ; 27cm
ISBN 0-603-00248-x : Unpriced B82-26111

Dean's enchanting stories from the magic forest / illustrated by Gillian Embleton and Ronald Embleton. — London : Dean, 1981. — [42]p : col.ill ; 27cm
ISBN 0-603-00245-5 : Unpriced B82-26110

Dean's enchanting stories from the magic lake / illustrated by Gillian Embleton and Ronald Embleton. — London : Dean, 1981. — [42]p : col.ill ; 28cm
ISBN 0-603-00246-3 : Unpriced B82-26112

Dean's enchanting stories from the magic mountain / illustrated by Gillian Embleton and Ronald Embleton. — London : Dean, 1981. — [42]p : col.ill ; 28cm
ISBN 0-603-00247-1 : Unpriced B82-26113

Dent, Jenny. The adventures of Hoppy the gnome : a story and colouring book for young children / by Jenny Dent ; drawings by Rosemary Young. — Liss : White Eagle, c1981. — 16p : ill ; 21cm
Cover title. — Text on inside cover
ISBN 0-85487-048-2 (pbk) : Unpriced B82-02255

Dicks, Terrance. Doctor Who and the auton invasion : based on the BBC television serial Doctor Who and the spearhead from space by Robert Holmes ... / Terrance Dicks ; illustrated by Chris Achilleos. — London : W.H. Allen, 1981, c1974. — 156p : ill ; 21cm
Originally published: London : Tandem Books, 1974
ISBN 0-491-02895-4 : £4.95 B82-06562

Doherty, Berlie. How green you are!. — London : Methuen Children's Books, Jan.1982. — [144] p. — (A Pied piper book)
ISBN 0-416-20940-8 : £3.95 : CIP entry B81-33789

Dowling, Patrick. The big match / Patrick Dowling ; illustrated by Peter Lord. — London : Heinemann, 1981. — [52]p : col.ill ; 23cm. — (The Amazing adventures of Morph)
Bound tête-bêche with: Poor old Morph!
ISBN 0-434-98020-x : £3.95 B82-11365

Eadington, Joan. Tales of Appleby fair / Joan Eadington ; illustrated by David Eaton. — London : Hamlyn, 1982. — 188p : ill(some col.) ; 13cm. — (Bumblebee books)
ISBN 0-600-36675-8 : £0.99 B82-36263

Firmin, Peter. Two tales of Basil Brush / Peter Firmin. — London : Fontana, 1982, c1969. — 94p : ill ; 20cm. — (Lions)
Contents: Basil Brush goes boating. Originally published : London : Kaye & Ward, 1969 — Basil Brush goes flying. London : Kaye & Ward, 1969
ISBN 0-00-672016-1 (pbk) : £0.90 B82-18089

Fisk, Nicholas. Sweets from a stranger : and other SF stories / Nicholas Fisk ; illustrated by David Barlow. — Harmondsworth : Kestrel, 1982. — 155p : ill ; 23cm
ISBN 0-7226-5759-5 : £4.95 B82-33830

Foreman, Michael. Winter's tales / written by Michael Foreman ; illustrated by Freire Wright. — London : Benn, 1979. — [32]p : col.ill ; 30cm
Ill on lining papers
ISBN 0-510-00054-1 : £3.75 B82-12522

Gavin, Jamila. Double dare and other stories / Jamila Gavin ; illustrated by Simon Willby. — London : Methuen Children's, 1982. — 143p : ill ; 20cm. — (A Pied Piper book)
ISBN 0-416-21540-8 : £3.95 : CIP rev. B82-04047

Gifford, Griselda. Pete and the doodlebug and other stories. — London : Macmillan Children's, Feb.1983. — [128]p
ISBN 0-333-33636-4 : £5.95 : CIP entry B82-38060

Grender, Iris. Did I ever tell you about my Irish great grandmother? / Iris Grender ; illustrated by Tony Ross. — London : Hutchinson, 1981. — 63p : ill ; 23cm
ISBN 0-09-146570-2 : £3.95 : CIP rev. B81-28170

Jones, Geraldine. One hundred and one Arabian nights. — Oxford : Oxford University Press, Apr.1982. — [192]p
ISBN 0-19-274530-1 : £5.50 : CIP entry B82-04838

Jones, Terry. Fairy tales / Terry jones ; illustrated by Michael Foreman. — London : Pavilion, 1981. — 127p : ill(some col.) ; 29cm
ISBN 0-907516-03-3 : £6.95 : CIP rev. B81-20188

Julie-Dawn. Ramsbottom stories : a collection of children's stories / Julie-Dawn. — Bognor Regis : New Horizon, c1982. — 24p : ill ; 21cm
ISBN 0-86116-537-3 : £3.50 B82-13605

Kenward, Jean. Ragdolly Anna : two stories / by Jean Kenward ; illustrated by Zoë Hall. — London : Warne, 1979. — 32p : ill ; 22cm
Cover title
ISBN 0-7232-2279-7 : £0.75(net)
ISBN 0-7232-2280-0 (non net) : £0.55 B82-20973

Kenward, Jean. Ragdolly Anna and the river picnic : two stories / by Jean Kenward ; illustrated by Zoë Hall. — London : Warne, 1979. — p35-63 : ill ; 20cm
Cover title
ISBN 0-7232-2283-5 : £0.75 (net)
ISBN 0-7232-2284-3 (non net) : £0.55 B82-20972

Kenward, Jean. Ragdolly Anna goes to the fair : two stories / by Jean Kenward ; illustrated by Zoë Hall. — London : Warne, 1979. — p67-95 : ill ; 20cm
Cover title
ISBN 0-7232-2281-9 : £0.75 (net)
ISBN 0-7232-2282-7 (non net) : £0.55 B82-20974

Kohler, Charles. April sunshine : stories / by Charles Kohler ; illustrations by Sabine Price. — Dorking : Kohler & Coombes, 1982. — 71p : ill ; 22cm
ISBN 0-903967-21-9 (pbk) : £1.00 B82-22103

McBratney, Sam. Jimmy Zest / Sam McBratney ; illustrated by Thelma Lambert. — London : Hamish Hamilton, 1982. — 147p : ill ; 23cm
ISBN 0-241-10807-1 : £4.95 : CIP rev. B82-15692

Mahy, Margaret. The chewing-gum rescue and other stories / Margaret Mahy ; illustrated by Jan Ormerod. — London : Dent, 1982. — 141p : ill ; 23cm
ISBN 0-460-06084-8 : £4.95 : CIP rev. B81-38337

Mayne, William. All the king's men / William Mayne. — London : Cape, 1982. — 182p ; 23cm
ISBN 0-224-02026-9 : £5.95 : CIP rev. B82-14063

Morgan, Helen, *1921-*. Mary Kate and the jumble bear : and other stories / Helen Morgan ; illustrated by Shirley Hughes. — Harmondsworth : Puffin, 1982, c1967. — 77p : ill ; 20cm. — (A Young Puffin book)
Originally published: London : Faber, 1967
ISBN 0-14-031271-4 (pbk) : £0.85 B82-29593

Oldfield, Pamela. Melanie Brown climbs a tree / Pamela Oldfield ; illustrated by Carolyn Dinan. — London : Faber Fanfares, 1980, c1972. — 63p : ill ; 19cm
Originally published: London : Faber, 1972
ISBN 0-571-11488-1 (pbk) : £0.95 : CIP rev. B80-18053

Palmer, Geoffrey, *1912 Aug.22-*. Haunting stories of ghosts and ghouls / Geoffrey Palmer and Noel Lloyd ; illustrated by Ivan Lapper. — London : Hamlyn, 1982. — 256p : ill(some col.) ; 22cm. — (Falcon Fiction Club)
ISBN 0-600-36676-6 : £1.75 B82-35383

Prince, Alison. Haunted children / Alison Prince ; illustrated by Michael Bragg. — [London] : Methuen, 1982. — 125p : ill ; 21cm
ISBN 0-416-22230-7 : £4.95 : CIP rev. B82-19234

Rainbow orange storybook. — London : Thames, 1982. — 118p : col.ill ; 25cm
ISBN 0-423-00360-7 : Unpriced B82-38801

Rawson, Christopher. Dragons / Christopher Rawson ; illustrated by Stephen Cartwright. — London : Usborne, 1979. — 32p : col.ill ; 21cm. — (Usborne story books)
ISBN 0-86020-336-0 (pbk) : Unpriced B82-33945

Rawson, Christopher. Dragons, giants and witches / Christopher Rawson ; illustrated by Stephen Cartwright. — London : Usborne, 1979. — 96p : col.ill ; 22cm
ISBN 0-86020-342-5 : £2.95 B82-32476

Rawson, Christopher. Giants / Christopher Rawson ; illustrated by Stephen Cartwright. — London : Usborne Publishing, 1979. — 32p : col.ill ; 21cm. — (Usborne story books)
ISBN 0-86020-339-5 : £1.99 B82-08840

Rawson, Christopher. Witches / Christopher Rawson ; illustrated by Stephen Cartwright. — London : Usborne Publishing, 1979. — 32p : col.ill ; 21cm. — (Usborne story books)
ISBN 0-86020-341-7 : £1.99 B82-08841

Redmond, Phil. Tucker and Co : stories of life in and out of Grange Hill : based on the BBC television series Grange Hill / Phil Redmond. — [London] : Fontana, 1982. — 111p ; 18cm. — (Lions)
ISBN 0-00-672017-x (pbk) : £0.85 B82-13641

Redmond, Phil. Tucker and Co : stories from Grange Hill : based on the BBC television series Grange Hill / Phil Redmond. — London : British Broadcasting Corporation, 1982. — 111p ; 22cm
ISBN 0-563-20053-7 : £4.50 B82-22182

823'.914[J] — Children's short stories in English, *1945- — Texts continuation*

Riordan, James. Tales of King Arthur / James Riordan ; illustrated by Victor Ambrus. — London : Hamlyn, 1982. — 124p : col.ill ; 29cm
ISBN 0-600-35352-4 : £4.95 B82-25993

Schweitzer, Iris. Hilda's restful chair / Iris Schweitzer. — London : Collins, 1981. — [26]p : col.ill ; 21cm
ISBN 0-00-183763-x (corrected) : £3.95 B82-05115

Swindells, Robert. The Wheaton book of science fiction stories / Robert Swindells ; illustrated by Gary Long. — Exeter : Wheaton, 1982. — 67p : col.ill ; 22cm
ISBN 0-08-026425-5 : £3.95 B82-31492

Trueman, Brian. Stories from Cockleshell Bay. — [London] : Thames Methuen, 1982. — [102p] : col.ill ; 23cm
Author: Brian Trueman. — Also available individually. — Contents: Bucket and spade — Dressing up — The pirate seagull — Lost and found
ISBN 0-423-00500-6 : Unpriced B82-33269

Tubby, *Uncle*. Three bedtime stories / by Uncle Tubby. — Crawley : Wren, c1982
Bk.3. — 11p : ill,1map ; 21cm
At head of title: Gatwick Garden Aviaries and Children's Zoo
ISBN 0-907820-05-0 (pbk) : Unpriced B82-36498

White, Brenda Margaret. The adventures of Julie and Bluebell / Brenda Margaret White. — Bognor Regis : New Horizon, c1982. — 39p : ill ; 20cm
ISBN 0-86116-815-1 : £3.50 B82-22161

Wood, Anne, *1937-*. A first fairy story book. — London : Hodder and Stoughton Children's Books, July 1981. — [192]p
ISBN 0-340-25297-9 : £3.95 : CIP entry B81-14939

Woodward, Ken. Telling the time : the king's clocks / written and illustrated by Ken Woodward. — Bristol : Purnell, 1976 (1982 [printing]). — [28]p : col.ill ; 25cm. — (My first colour library)
ISBN 0-361-03490-3 : Unpriced B82-25853

823'.914[J] — Children's stories in English, *1945- — Texts*

Adams, Georgie. Tubby Tin and the footies / written by Georgie Adams ; illustrated by Mike Shepherd. — London : Thurman, 1982. — [32]p : col.ill ; 17cm
ISBN 0-85985-143-5 (pbk) : £0.60 B82-16689

Adams, Georgie. Tubby Tin and the munching moon / written by Georgie Adams ; illustrated by Mike Shepherd. — London : Thurman, 1982. — [32]p : col.ill ; 17cm
ISBN 0-85985-144-3 (pbk) : £0.60 B82-16690

Adams, Georgie. Tubby Tin and the no such things / written by Georgie Adams ; illustrated by Mike Shepherd. — London : Thurman, 1982. — [32]p : col.ill ; 17cm
ISBN 0-85985-145-1 (pbk) : £0.60 B82-16691

Adams, Georgie. Tubby Tin and the runaway rainbow / written by Georgie Adams ; illustrated by Mike Shepherd. — London : Thurman, 1982. — [32]p : col.ill ; 17cm
ISBN 0-85985-147-8 (pbk) : £0.60 B82-16688

Adams, Richard, *1920-*. Watership Down / Richard Adams. — Leicester : Charnwood, 1981, c1972. — 683p : 1maps ; 23cm. — (Charnwood library series) (Charnwood large type)
Originally published: London : Rex Collings, 1972. — Map on lining papers
ISBN 0-7089-8012-0 : £6.50 : CIP rev. B81-22669

Adamson, Jean. Topsy and Tim can garden / Jean and Gareth Adamson. — Glasgow : Blackie, c1980. — [24]p : col.ill ; 25cm. — (Topsy and Tim activity books)
ISBN 0-216-90985-6 (cased) : £2.75 : CIP rev.
ISBN 0-216-90984-8 (pbk) : £0.95 B80-18908

Adamson, Jean. Topsy and Tim can help birds / Jean and Gareth Adamson. — Glasgow : Blackie, c1982. — [24]p : col.ill ; 25cm. — (Topsy and Tim activity books)
ISBN 0-216-91177-x (cased) : £2.75 : CIP rev.
ISBN 0-216-91176-1 (pbk) : £0.95 B82-01078

Adamson, Jean. Topsy and Tim can make music / Jean and Gareth Adamson. — Glasgow : Blackie, c1982. — [24]p : col.ill ; 25cm. — (Topsy and Tim activity books)
ISBN 0-216-91175-3 (cased) : £2.75 : CIP rev.
ISBN 0-216-91174-5 (pbk) : £0.95 B82-01077

Adamson, Jean. Topsy and Tim can print in colour / Jean and Gareth Adamson. — Glasgow : Blackie, c1980. — [24]p : col.ill ; 25cm. — (Topsy and Tim activity books)
ISBN 0-216-90991-0 (cased) : £2.75 : CIP rev.
ISBN 0-216-90990-2 (pbk) : £0.95 B80-18504

Adamson, Jean. Topsy and Tim go fishing. — London : Blackie, Feb.1983. — [24]p. — (Topsy and Tim handy books ; 1)
ISBN 0-216-91397-7 (cased) : £1.95 : CIP entry
ISBN 0-216-91398-5 (pbk) : £0.75 B82-37843

Adamson, Jean. Topsy and Tim go on holiday. — London : Blackie, Feb.1983. — [24]p. — (Topsy and Tim handy books ; 3)
ISBN 0-216-91399-3 (cased) : £1.95 : CIP entry
ISBN 0-216-91400-0 (pbk) : £0.75 B82-37844

Adamson, Jean. Topsy and Tim go riding. — London : Blackie, Feb.1983. — [24]p. — (Topsy and Tim handy books ; 2)
ISBN 0-216-91401-9 (cased) : £1.95 : CIP entry
ISBN 0-216-91402-7 (pbk) : £0.75 B82-37845

Adamson, Jean. Topsy and Tim go safely. — London : Blackie, Sept.1982. — [24]p
ISBN 0-216-91314-4 (cased) : £1.75 : CIP entry
ISBN 0-216-91313-6 (pbk) : £0.75 B82-19000

Adamson, Jean. Topsy and Tim go to hospital / Jean and Gareth Adamson. — Glasgow : Blackie, c1982. — [22]p : col.ill ; 19cm. — (Topsy and Tim handy books)
ISBN 0-216-91137-0 : £1.95 : CIP rev.
ISBN 0-216-91136-2 (pbk) : Unpriced B81-36031

Adamson, Jean. Topsy and Tim go to the dentist / Jean and Gareth Adamson. — Glasgow : Blackie, c1982. — [22]p : col.ill ; 19cm. — (Topsy and Tim handy books)
ISBN 0-216-91135-4 : £1.95 : CIP rev.
ISBN 0-216-91134-6 (pbk) : Unpriced B81-36030

Adamson, Jean. Topsy and Tim go to the doctor / Jean and Gareth Adamson. — Glasgow : Blackie, c1982. — [22]p : col.ill ; 19cm. — (Topsy and Tim handy books)
ISBN 0-216-91133-8 : £1.95 : CIP rev.
ISBN 0-216-91132-x (pbk) : Unpriced B81-36029

Adamson, Jean. Topsy and Tim have their eyes tested / Jean and Gareth Adamson. — Glasgow : Blackie, c1982. — [22]p : col.ill ; 19cm. — (Topsy and Tim handy books)
ISBN 0-216-91154-0 : £1.95 : CIP rev.
ISBN 0-216-91155-9 (pbk) : Unpriced B81-36390

Adamson, Jean. Topsy and Tim help the dustmen. — London : Blackie, July 1982. — [24]p
ISBN 0-216-91261-x (cased) : £1.95 : CIP entry
ISBN 0-216-91260-1 (pbk) : £0.75 B82-12557

Adamson, Jean. Topsy and Tim learn to dance. — London : Blackie, July 1982. — [24]p
ISBN 0-216-91265-2 (cased) : £1.95 : CIP entry
ISBN 0-216-91264-4 (pbk) : £0.75 B82-12559

Adamson, Jean. Topsy and Tim take no risks. — London : Blackie, Feb.1983. — [24]p. — (Topsy and Tim handy books ; 4)
ISBN 0-216-91403-5 (cased) : £1.95 : CIP entry
ISBN 0-216-91404-3 (pbk) : £0.75 B82-37846

Adamson, Jean. Topsy and Tim's new playground. — London : Blackie, July 1982. — [24]p
ISBN 0-216-91259-8 (cased) : £1.95 : CIP entry
ISBN 0-216-91258-x (pbk) : £0.75 B82-12556

Adamson, Jean. Topsy and Tim's school play. — London : Blackie, July 1982. — [24]p
ISBN 0-216-91263-6 (cased) : £1.95 : CIP entry
ISBN 0-216-91262-8 (pbk) : £0.75 B82-12558

Ahlberg, Allan. Ten in a bed. — London : Granada, Oct.1982. — [96]p
ISBN 0-246-11551-3 : £4.95 : CIP entry B82-23467

Ahlberg, Janet. Funnybones / Janet and Allan Ahlberg. — London : Fontana, 1982, c1980. — [28]p : col.ill ; 22cm. — (Picture lions)
Originally published: London : Heinemann, 1980
ISBN 0-00-661953-3 (pbk) : £0.95 B82-28005

Aiken, Joan. Mortimer's portrait on glass / John Aiken ; illustrated by Quentin Blake. — London : BBC, 1982. — 64p : ill ; 20cm
'As told in Jackanory'
ISBN 0-563-17883-3 (pbk) : £0.95 : CIP rev.
ISBN 0-340-27534-0 (Knight) B82-01138

Aiken, Joan. The mystery of Mr Jones's disappearing taxi : as told in Jackanory / Joan Aiken ; illustrated by Quentin Blake. — London : B.B.C., 1982. — 64p : ill ; 20cm
ISBN 0-563-17882-5 (pbk) : £0.95 : CIP rev.
ISBN 0-340-27533-2 (Knight) B82-03810

Aiken, Joan. The shadow guests / Joan Aiken. — Harmondsworth : Puffin, 1982, c1980. — 168p ; 18cm
Originally published: London : Cape, 1980
ISBN 0-14-031388-5 (pbk) : £1.10 B82-34159

Akrill, Caroline. A hoof in the door. — London : Arlington Books, June 1982. — [192]p
ISBN 0-85140-577-0 : £4.95 : CIP entry B82-09867

Alcock, Vivien. The haunting of Cassie Palmer / Vivien Alcock. — London : Fontana, 1982, c1980. — 154p ; 18cm
Originally published: London : Methuen, 1980
ISBN 0-00-671895-7 (pbk) : £0.90 B82-16821

Alcock, Vivien. The Sylvia game / Vivien Alcock. — London : Methuen, 1982. — 157p ; 21cm
ISBN 0-416-21930-6 : £5.50 : CIP rev. B82-10789

Aldridge, James. The broken saddle. — London : MacRae, Oct.1982. — [128]p
ISBN 0-86203-112-5 : £5.95 : CIP entry B82-24590

Allan, Mabel Esther. Alone at Pine Street. — London : Abelard-Schuman, Feb.1983. — [112]p
ISBN 0-200-72802-4 (cased) : £4.95 : CIP entry
ISBN 0-200-72801-6 (pbk) : £1.50 B82-37864

823'.914[J] — Children's stories in English, *1945- — Texts* *continuation*

Allan, Mabel Esther. Goodbye to Pine Street / Mabel Esther Allan ; illustrated by Patricia Drew. — London : Abelard, 1982. — 107p : ill ; 21cm. — (A Grasshopper book)
ISBN 0-200-72770-2 (cased) : £3.95 : CIP rev.
ISBN 0-200-72771-0 (pbk) : Unpriced
B81-36228

Allan, Mabel Esther. Growing up in Wood Street. — London : Methuen Children's Books, Apr.1982. — [128]p. — (A Pied Piper book)
ISBN 0-416-24430-0 : £3.95 : CIP entry
B82-04048

Allan, Mabel Esther. The night wind / Mabel Esther Allan. — London : Severn House, 1982, c1974. — 212p ; 21cm
ISBN 0-7278-0787-0 : £4.95 B82-31427

Allen, Judy. Barriers : based on the Tyne Tees television series by William Corlett from an idea by Margaret Bottomley / Judy Allen. — [London] : Hamilton, 1981. — 212p ; 23cm
ISBN 0-241-10718-0 : £5.25 : CIP rev.
B81-30206

Allen, Judy. Barriers : based on the Tyne Tees Television series by William Corlett, from an idea by Margaret Bottomley / Judy Allen. — London : Sphere, 1981. — 212p ; 18cm
ISBN 0-7221-2558-5 (pbk) : £1.25 B82-02122

Allen, Peter M.. The bag of salt / by Peter M. Allen ; illustrated by Gabrielle Stoddart. — London : Hodder and Stoughton, 1982. — [28]p : col.ill ; 25cm
ISBN 0-340-25293-6 : £3.95 : CIP rev.
B81-01306

Althea. Adventures of Desmond the dinosaur / by Althea and some children. — Cambridge : Dinosaur, c1981. — 62p : col.ill ; 28cm
ISBN 0-85122-318-4 : £5.50 B82-31210

Althea. Desmond at the zoo : by Althea / illustrated by the author. — Cambridge : Dinosaur, c1981. — [24]p : col.ill ; 16x19cm. — (Dinosaur's Althea books)
ISBN 0-85122-301-x (cased) : £2.25
ISBN 0-85122-300-1 (pbk) : £0.70 B82-07171

Althea. Desmond starts school / by Althea ; based on a story by Mark Cooper (7). — Cambridge : Dinosaur, c1982. — [24]p : col.ill ; 16x19cm
ISBN 0-85122-349-4 (cased) : Unpriced
ISBN 0-85122-348-6 (pbk) : Unpriced
B82-31024

Althea. Jeremy Mouse : by Althea / illustrated by the author. — Cambridge : Dinosaur, c1981. — [24]p : ill(some col.) ; 16x19cm. — (Dinosaur's Althea books)
ISBN 0-85122-304-4 : £2.25 B82-07173

Althea. Peter pig / by Althea ; illustrated by the author. — Cambridge : Dinosaur, c1981. — [24]p : col.ill ; 16x19cm
ISBN 0-85122-327-3 (cased) : £1.85
ISBN 0-85122-036-3 (pbk) : Unpriced
B82-31023

Althea. Riding on a roundabout : by Althea / illustrated by Helen Herbert. — Cambridge : Dinosaur, c1981. — [24]p : col.ill ; 16x19cm. — (Dinosaur's Althea books)
ISBN 0-85122-280-3 (cased) : £2.25
ISBN 0-85122-264-1 (pbk) : £0.70 B82-07172

Althea. Smith the lonely hedgehog / by Althea ; illustrated by the author ; based on a story by Helena Moore. — Cambridge : Dinosaur, c1981. — [24]p : col.ill ; 16x19cm. — (Dinosaur's Althea books)
ISBN 0-85122-310-9 (cased) : Unpriced
ISBN 0-85122-137-8 (pbk) : Unpriced
B82-38093

Alverson, Charles. Time bandits / Charles Alverson ; based on a screenplay by Michael Palin and Terry Gilliam. — London : Severn House, 1981. — 123p ; 21cm
ISBN 0-7278-0737-4 : £5.95 : CIP rev.
B81-30177

Ambrus, Victor. Blackbeard the Pirate. — Oxford : Oxford University Press, Sept.1982. — [32]p
ISBN 0-19-279771-9 : £4.50 : CIP entry
B82-19194

Anang, George K.. Moon legend : from Malaysia / retold by George K. Anang ; illustrated by Marjorie Lee Claus. — London : Nile & Mackenzie, c1979. — [16]p : col.ill ; 26cm. — (The Selene collection)
ISBN 0-86031-029-9 : £1.95 B82-30980

Anderson, Verily. Brownies on wheels. — London : Hodder and Stoughton, Apr.1981. — [128]p
ISBN 0-340-26546-9 (pbk) : £0.85 : CIP entry
B81-01307

Antrobus, John. Ronnie and the Great Knitted Robbery. — London : Robson Books, Sept.1982. — [64]p
ISBN 0-86051-180-4 : £3.95 : CIP entry
B82-20866

Antrobus, John. Ronnie and the haunted Rolls Royce. — London : Robson Books, Sept.1982. — [64]p
ISBN 0-86051-179-0 : £3.95 : CIP entry
B82-20865

Appleton, Victor. The Alien probe / by Victor Appleton. — London : Transworld, 1981. — 127p ; 18cm. — (Tom Swift ; 3) (A Carousel book)
ISBN 0-552-52156-6 (pbk) : £0.85 B82-06607

Appleton, Victor. The astral fortress / by Victor Appleton. — [London] : Carousel, 1982, c1981. — 155p ; 18cm. — (Tom Swift ; 5)
Originally published: New York : Wanderer, 1981
ISBN 0-552-52165-5 (pbk) : £0.85 B82-19369

Appleton, Victor. The city in the stars / by Victor Appleton. — London : Transworld, 1981. — 192p ; 18cm. — (Tom Swift ; 1) (A Carousel book)
ISBN 0-552-52154-x (pbk) : £0.85 B82-06605

Appleton, Victor. Terror on the moons of Jupiter / by Victor Appleton. — London : Transworld, 1981. — 157p ; 18cm. — (Tom Swift ; 2) (A Carousel book)
ISBN 0-552-52155-8 (pbk) : £0.85 B82-06606

Appleton, Victor. The war in outer space / Victor Appleton. — London : Transworld, 1981. — 127p ; 18cm. — (Tom Swift ; 4) (A Carousel book)
ISBN 0-552-52157-4 (pbk) : £0.85 B82-06608

Arthur, Ruth M.. Requiem for a princess / Ruth M. Arthur ; illustrated by Margery Gill. — [Sevenoaks] : Knight, 1981, c1967. — 182p : ill ; 18cm
Originally published: London : Gollancz, 1967
ISBN 0-340-26597-3 (pbk) : £0.95 : CIP rev.
B81-31737

Ashley, Bernard. Linda's lie. — London : MacRae, Sept.1982. — [48]p. — (Blackbird books)
ISBN 0-86203-099-4 : £2.95 : CIP entry
B82-22439

Augarde, Steve. January Jo and friends / Steve Augarde. — London : Deutsch, 1981. — [28]p : col.ill ; 26cm
ISBN 0-233-97364-8 : £4.95 : CIP rev.
B81-28839

Baby Tod and baby Copper. — Bristol : Purnell, c1981. — [12]p : chiefly col.ill ; 19cm. — (The Fox and the hound)
ISBN 0-361-05293-6 (unbound) : £0.75
B82-13286

Bain, Janet. Never trust the Tinnyman / Janet Bain. — London : Dobson, 1981. — 191p : 1map ; 23cm
ISBN 0-234-72248-7 : £4.95 B82-05330

Baker, Alan. Benjamin's book. — London : Deutsch, Mar.1982. — [32]p
ISBN 0-233-97464-4 : £1.95 : CIP entry
B82-01860

Baker, Jeannie. One hungry spider / words and pictures by Jeannie Baker. — London : Deutsch, 1982. — [29]p : col.ill ; 25x27cm
ISBN 0-233-97429-6 : £4.95 : CIP rev.
B82-12567

Baker, Margaret J.. Catch as catch can. — London : Hodder & Stoughton Children's Books, Feb.1983. — [96]p
ISBN 0-340-28615-6 : £2.95 : CIP entry
B82-38053

Baker, Nick. The one-eyed lion. — London : Methuen Children's Books, Feb.1983. — [32]p
ISBN 0-416-26730-0 : £3.95 : CIP entry
B82-38261

Bambi's friends. — Bristol : Purnell, 1982. — [8]p : chiefly col.ill ; 11x14cm
ISBN 0-361-05308-8 (unbound) : £0.40
B82-26039

Banks, Lynne Reid. One more river / Lynne Reid Banks. — Harmondsworth : Puffin, 1980, c1973 (1982 [printing]). — 253p : 1map ; 18cm
Originally published: London : Vallentine, Mitchell, 1973
ISBN 0-14-031296-x (pbk) : £1.35 B82-29586

Barrie, J. M.. Peter Pan. — London : Hodder & Stoughton, Sept.1982. — [64]p
ISBN 0-340-28747-0 : £2.95 : CIP entry
B82-25179

Barry, Margaret Stuart. Simon and the witch / Margaret Stuart Barry ; illustrated by Linda Birch. — London : Fontana Lions, [1978], c1976 (1982 [printing]). — 77p : ill ; 20cm
Originally published: London : Collins, 1976
ISBN 0-00-672064-1 (pbk) : £0.95 B82-25435

Baum, Willi. Angelito / Willi Baum. — London : Dent, 1981. — [30]p : ill(some col.) ; 26cm
ISBN 0-460-06083-x : £3.95 : CIP rev.
B81-22606

Bawden, Nina. A handful of thieves / Nina Bawden. — Harmondsworth : Puffin, 1970, c1967 (1982 [printing]). — 139p ; 18cm
Originally published: London : Gollancz, 1967
ISBN 0-14-030472-x (pbk) : £0.95 B82-28629

Bawden, Nina. Kept in the dark / Nina Bawden. — London : Gollancz, 1982. — 141p ; 21cm
ISBN 0-575-03113-1 : £5.50 : CIP rev.
B82-04609

Bawden, Nina. On the run / Nina Bawden. — Harmondsworth : Puffin, 1967, c1964 (1982 [printing]). — 189p ; 19cm
Originally published: London : Gollancz, 1964
ISBN 0-14-030337-5 (pbk) : £1.00 B82-25539

Bawden, Nina. The robbers / Nina Bawden. — Harmondsworth : Puffin, 1981, c1979. — 136p ; 18cm
Originally published: London : Gollancz, 1979
ISBN 0-14-031317-6 (pbk) : £0.95 B82-05950

Bawden, Nina. The robbers / Nina Bawden. — London : Heinemann Educational, 1981, c1979. — 143p : ill ; 20cm. — (The New windmill series ; 257)
Originally published: London : Gollancz, 1979
ISBN 0-435-12257-6 : £1.60 B82-03678

Bawden, Nina. The runaway summer / Nina Bawden. — Harmondsworth : Puffin, 1972, c1969 (1981 printing). — 174p ; 18cm
Originally published: London : Gollancz, 1969
ISBN 0-14-030539-4 (pbk) : £0.95 B82-09163

823'.914[J] — Children's stories in English, ***1945-*** **—** ***Texts*** *continuation*

Bawden, Nina. The runaway summer / Nina Bawden. — Basingstoke : Macmillan Education, 1981, c1969 (1982 [printing]). — 174p ; 21cm. — (M books)
Originally published: London : Gollancz, 1969
ISBN 0-333-29487-4 : Unpriced B82-39210

Bawden, Nina. The secret passage / Nina Bawden. — (Opening chapters shortened). — [Harmondsworth] : Puffin, 1979 (1982 [printing]). — 153p ; 19cm
Previous ed.: London : Gollancz, 1963
ISBN 0-14-031166-1 (pbk) : £0.95 B82-40503

Bawden, Nina. The White Horse Gang / Nina Bawden. — Harmondsworth : Puffin, 1972, c1966 (1981 [printing]). — 154p ; 18cm
Originally published: London : Gollancz, 1966
ISBN 0-14-030508-4 (pbk) : £0.95 B82-09141

Bawden, Nina. The witch's daughter / Nina Bawden ; with drawings by Shirley Hughes. — Harmondsworth : Puffin, 1969, c1966 (1981 [printing]). — 158p : ill ; 18cm
Originally published: London : Gollancz, 1966
ISBN 0-14-030407-x (pbk) : £0.95 B82-09160

Baxter, Gillian. Pantomime ponies / Gillian Baxter ; illustrated by Elisabeth Grant. — London : Magnet, 1982, c1969. — 141p : ill ; 18cm
Originally published: London : Methuen, 1969
ISBN 0-416-57120-4 (pbk) : £0.95 B82-37244

Baxter, Gillian. Ponies in harness / Gillian Baxter ; illustrated by Elisabeth Grant. — London : Magnet, 1982, c1977. — 126p : ill ; 18cm
Originally published: London : Methuen Children's Books, 1977
ISBN 0-416-58210-9 (pbk) : £0.95 B82-37242

'BB'. Bill Badger and the pirates. — London : Methuen Children's Books, Oct.1982. — [144]p
ISBN 0-416-26760-2 : £3.95 : CIP entry
B82-24489

Benabo, Brian. Ace of diamonds. — London : Hodder & Stoughton Children's Books, Nov.1982. — [64]p
ISBN 0-340-28620-2 : £4.25 : CIP entry
B82-27356

Benabo, Brian. Moonlight kingdom. — London : Hodder & Stoughton Children's Books, Nov.1982. — [64]p
ISBN 0-340-28621-0 : £4.25 : CIP entry
B82-27357

Bennett, Thea. A little silver trumpet / Thea Bennett ; illustrated by Priscilla Lamont. — London : BBC/Knight, 1980. — 110p : ill ; 18cm
Originally published: London : BBC, 1980
ISBN 0-563-17886-8 (pbk) : £0.95 : CIP rev.
ISBN 0-340-28041-7 (Knight Books)
B81-33930

Benney, H. P.. Ferryman's folly / by H.P. Benney. — Eastbourne : Kingsway, 1982, c1972. — 119p ; 18cm
Originally published: London : Victory, 1972
ISBN 0-86065-173-8 (pbk) : £1.00 B82-27750

Bentley, Roy, *19---*. Lift off to danger / Roy Bentley. — London : Deutsch, 1982. — [32]p : col.ill ; 27cm. — (Spacers)
ISBN 0-233-97443-1 : £4.50 : CIP rev.
B82-07532

Beowulf. — Oxford : Oxford University Press, Sept.1982. — [481]p
ISBN 0-19-279770-0 : £4.50 : CIP entry
B82-19193

Beresford, Elisabeth. The arrivals nobody wanted. — London : Methuen Children's Books, Mar.1982. — [144]p
ISBN 0-416-21450-9 : £3.95 : CIP entry
B82-01997

Beresford, Elisabeth. Jack and the magic stove. — London : Hutchinson, Oct.1982. — [32]p
ISBN 0-09-150530-5 : £4.50 : CIP entry
B82-24981

Beresford, Elisabeth. The Tovers. — London : Methuen Children's Books, Sept.1982. — [150]p
ISBN 0-416-26660-6 : £4.95 : CIP entry
B82-20182

Beresford, Elisabeth. The treasure hunters / Elisabeth Beresford ; illustrated by Joanna Carey. — London : Magnet, 1982, c1980. — 110p : ill ; 18cm
Originally published: London : Methuen, 1980
ISBN 0-416-24600-1 (pbk) : £0.95 B82-34952

Berrisford, Judith M.. Jackie and the missing showjumper / Judith M. Berrisford ; illustrated by Geoffrey Whittam. — London : Hodder and Stoughton, 1982. — 116p : ill ; 20cm
ISBN 0-340-26193-5 : £3.50 : CIP rev.
B82-01867

Berrisford, Judith M.. Jackie and the moonlight pony / Judith M. Berrisford ; illustrated by Geoffrey Whittam. — London : Armada, 1982, c1980. — 108p : ill ; 18cm
Originally published: Sevenoaks : Hodder & Stoughton, 1977
ISBN 0-00-691958-8 (pbk) : £0.85 B82-19730

Berrisford, Judith M.. Pony-trekkers, go home!. — London : Hodder & Stoughton, July 1981. — [128]p
ISBN 0-340-26599-x (pbk) : £0.85 : CIP entry
B81-14915

Berrisford, Judith M.. Pony-trekkers, go home! / Judith M. Berrisford. — London : Severn House, 1982. — 124p ; 21cm
ISBN 0-7278-0750-1 : £4.25 B82-30462

Berrisford, Judith M.. Sabotage at Stableways / Judith M. Berrisford. — [Sevenoaks] : Knight Books, 1982. — 121p : ill ; 18cm
ISBN 0-340-26812-3 (pbk) : £0.95 : CIP rev.
B82-03808

Berrisford, Judith M.. Sabotage at Stableways. — London : Severn House, Aug.1982. — [128]p
Originally published: London : Hodder & Stoughton, 1982
ISBN 0-7278-0828-1 : £4.95 : CIP entry
B82-21374

Billington, Rachel. Rosanna and the wizard-robot / Rachel Billington ; illustrated by Kate Mellor. — London : Methuen Children's Books, 1981. — 175p : ill ; 21cm
ISBN 0-416-21840-7 : £4.95 : CIP rev.
B81-25838

Biro, Val. Gumdrop and Horace / Val Biro. — London : Hodder and Stoughton, c1982. — [24]p : col.ill ; 14cm
ISBN 0-340-27963-x (pbk) : £0.40 : CIP rev.
B82-03831

Biro, Val. Gumdrop and the steamroller / Val Biro. — London : Hodder and Stoughton, c1982. — [24]p : col.ill ; 14cm
Originally published: Leicester : Hodder and Stoughton, 1976
ISBN 0-340-27964-8 (pbk) : £0.50 : CIP rev.
B82-03832

Biro, Val. Gumdrop makes a start / story and pictures by Val Biro. — London : Hodder and Stoughton Children's Books, 1982. — [28]p : col.ill ; 25cm
Text, ill on lining paper
ISBN 0-340-26275-3 : £3.95 : CIP rev.
B82-10006

Biro, Val. Gumdrop posts a letter / Val Biro. — London : Hodder and Stoughton, c1982. — [24]p : col.ill ; 14cm
Originally published: Leicester : Knight Books, 1976
ISBN 0-340-27962-1 (pbk) : £0.50 : CIP rev.
B82-03830

Biro, Val. Gumdrop races a train / Val Biro. — London : Hodder and Stoughton, c1982. — [24]p : col.ill ; 14cm
ISBN 0-340-27961-3 (pbk) : £0.50 : CIP rev.
B82-03829

Biro, Val. The magic doctor / Val Biro. — Oxford : Oxford University Press, 1982. — [32]p : col.ill ; 29cm
ISBN 0-19-279752-2 : £4.50 : CIP rev.
B81-06050

Bisset, Donald. The joyous adventures of Snakey Boo. — London : Methuen Children's Books, Sept.1982. — [96]p. — (A read aloud book)
ISBN 0-416-22410-5 : £3.95 : CIP entry
B82-19245

Black Beauty's family. — [London] : Beaver 2 / Josephine, Diana and Christine Pullein-Thompson. — 1982. — 159p ; 18cm
ISBN 0-600-20464-2 (pbk) : £0.95 B82-13044

The **black** hole / Walt Disney Productions. — Maidenhead : Purnell, 1980, c1979. — 47p : col.ill,col.ports ; 26cm. — (A Purnell colour book)
ISBN 0-361-04871-8 : £1.95 B82-40574

Blakeley, Peggy. Two little ducks / Peggy Blakeley, Kenzo Kobayashi. — London : Neugebauer Press, c1981. — [26]p : col.ill ; 22x24cm
ISBN 0-907234-07-0 : £3.50 B82-02278

Bloomfield, Emily, *1959-*. The adventures of Moppett / by Emily Bloomfield. — [London] ([6A Sydenham Hill, S.E.26]) : [E. Bloomfield], c1981. — [47]p : ill ; 21cm
ISBN 0-9507863-0-6 (pbk) : Unpriced
B82-08836

Bloomfield, Emily, *1959-*. The further adventures of Moppett / by Emily Bloomfield. — [London] ([6A Sydenham Hill, S.E.26]) : [E. Bloomfield], [1981]. — 42p : ill ; 21cm
ISBN 0-9507863-2-2 (pbk) : Unpriced
B82-08837

Bloomfield, Emily, *1959-*. Moppett's royal assignment / by Emily Bloomfield. — [London] ([6A Sydenham Hill, S.E.26]) : [E. Bloomfield], [1981]. — 19p : ill ; 21cm
ISBN 0-9507863-1-4 (pbk) : Unpriced
B82-08838

Body, Wendy. The globe of Zelkon / Wendy Body & Derek Cheshire. — London : Longman, 1980. — 32p : ill(some col.) ; 21cm. — (Whizz bang books)
ISBN 0-582-18254-9 (cased) : £2.25
ISBN 0-582-18249-2 (pbk) : Unpriced
B82-33450

Bolliger, Max. Three little bears. — London : Hutchinson, Apr.1982. — [32]p
ISBN 0-09-148980-6 : £4.95 : CIP entry
B82-04127

Bond, Michael. Here comes Thursday! / Michael Bond ; illustrated by Daphne Rowles. — Harmondsworth : Puffin, 1968, c1966 (1982 [printing]). — 129p : ill ; 18cm
Originally published: London : Harrap, 1966
ISBN 0-14-030383-9 (pbk) : £0.85 B82-34162

Bond, Michael. J.D. Polson and the great unveiling. — London : Hodder and Stoughton Children's Books, July 1982. — [32]p
ISBN 0-340-27977-x : £3.95 : CIP entry
B82-12268

Bond, Michael. Paddington at the seaside / Michael Bond ; illustrated by Fred Banbery. — London : Piccolo in association with Collins, 1982, c1975. — 32p : col.ill ; 22cm. — (Piccolo picture books)
Originally published: London : Collins, 1975
ISBN 0-330-26727-2 (pbk) : £1.25 B82-35434

823′.914[J] — Children′s stories in English, *1945-* **—** *Texts* *continuation*

Bond, Michael. Paddington at the Tower / Michael Bond ; illustrated by Fred Banbery. — London : Piccolo in association with Collins, 1982, c1975. — 32p : col.ill ; 22cm. — (Piccolo picture books)
Originally published: London : Collins, 1975
ISBN 0-330-26728-0 (pbk) : £1.25 B82-35435

Bond, Michael. Paddington bear / Michael Bond ; illustrated by Fred Banbery. — London : Pan in association with Collins, 1981, c1972. — 32p : col.ill ; 22cm. — (A Paddinton picture book) (Piccolo)
Originally published: London : Collins, 1972
ISBN 0-330-26572-5 (pbk) : £0.95 B82-03193

Bond, Michael. Paddington on screen / Michael Bond ; illustrated by Barry Macey. — London : British Broadcasting Corporation, 1981. — 128p : ill ; 20cm. — (A second Blue Peter storybook)
ISBN 0-563-17967-8 : £3.95
ISBN 0-00-182173-3 (Collins) B82-02789

Bond, Michael. Paddington′s garden / by Michael Bond ; illustrated by Fred Banbery. — London : Pan in association with Collins, 1981, c1972. — 32p : col.ill ; 22cm. — (A Paddington picture book) (Piccolo)
Originally published: London : Collins, 1972
ISBN 0-330-26573-3 (pbk) : £0.95 B82-03194

Bond, Michael. Thursday rides again / Michael Bond ; illustrated by Beryl Sanders. — Harmondsworth : Puffin, 1970, c1968 (1982 [printing]). — 136p : ill ; 18cm. — (A Puffin book)
Originally published: London : Harrap, 1968
ISBN 0-14-030454-1 (pbk) : £0.95 B82-33017

Boreham, Dennis W.. Prisoners of the sea / Dennis W. Boreham. — Eastbourne : Kingsway, 1982, c1968. — 119p ; 18cm
Originally published: London : Victory, 1968
ISBN 0-86065-176-2 (pbk) : £1.00 B82-27748

Bosanquet, Reginald. Filboyd′s frogs. — London : Quartet, Sept.1982. — [32]p
ISBN 0-7043-2340-0 : £4.95 : CIP entry B82-21980

Box, Janette Marie. The rock monster / Janette Marie Box. — Bognor Regis : New Horizon, c1981. — 43p : ill ; 22cm
ISBN 0-86116-577-2 : £3.50 B82-03498

Bradenburg, Franz. Leo and Emily′s big ideas. — London : Bodley Head, Sept.1982. — [64]p
ISBN 0-370-30936-7 : £3.50 : CIP entry B82-19204

Brandreth, Gyles. Frankenstein′s monster fun book. — London : Hodder & Stoughton, July 1981. — [128]p
ISBN 0-340-26532-9 (pbk) : £0.85 : CIP entry B81-13508

Branfield, John. Brown cow. — London : Gollancz, Jan.1983. — [160]p
ISBN 0-575-03223-5 : £5.95 : CIP entry B82-32458

Branfield, John. The fox in winter / by John Branfield. — London : Collins, 1981, c1980. — 158p ; 18cm. — (Fontana lions)
Originally published: London : Gollancz, 1980
ISBN 0-00-671932-5 (pbk) : £1.00 B82-06363

Brassey, Richard. The famous lion / Richard Brassey. — London : Cape, 1980. — [32]p : col.ill ; 27cm
ISBN 0-224-01688-1 : £3.50 : CIP rev. B80-05089

Brett, Molly. The runaway fairy / by Molly Brett. — [London] : [Medici Society], c1982. — 24p : ill(some col.) ; 19x22cm. — (Medici books for children)
ISBN 0-85503-066-6 (pbk) : £0.75 B82-32999

Brierley, Louise. King Lion and his cooks / Louise Brierley. — London : Hutchinson, c1981. — [26]p : col.ill ; 24cm
ISBN 0-86264-008-3 : £3.50 : CIP rev. B81-27416

Briggs, Raymond. Fungus the bogeyman plop-up book. — London : Hamilton, Oct.1982. — [12]p
ISBN 0-241-10811-x : £5.95 : CIP entry B82-23448

Briggs, Raymond. Gentleman Jim / Raymond Briggs. — London : Hamilton, 1981, c1980. — [32p] : col.ill ; 30cm
Originally published: 1980
ISBN 0-241-10698-2 (pbk) : £1.95 B82-00007

Broughton, John. The wild man of the four winds. — London : Hamilton, Sept.1982. — [32]p
ISBN 0-241-10816-0 : £4.75 : CIP entry B82-18838

Brown, Lindsay. The secret of the silver lockets / Lindsay Brown. — London : Piccolo, 1982, c1980. — 159p ; 18cm
Originally published: London : Hale, 1980
ISBN 0-330-26628-4 (pbk) : £1.25 B82-13719

Brown, Roy, *1921-*. Chips and the black moth / Roy Brown ; illustrated by Victoria Cooper. — London : Andersen, 1982. — 94p : ill ; 21cm. — (Andersen young readers′ library)
ISBN 0-86264-012-1 : £3.95 : CIP rev. B82-07690

Brown, Roy, *1921-*. Chips and the river rat / Roy Brown ; illustrated by Victoria Cooper. — London : Andersen Press, 1981. — 94p : ill ; 21cm. — (Andersen young reader′s library)
ISBN 0-86264-007-5 : £3.95 : CIP rev. B81-27415

Brown, Ruth. A dark, dark tale / Ruth Brown. — London : Andersen, 1981. — [26]p : chiefly col.ill ; 27cm
ISBN 0-86264-001-6 : £3.95 : CIP rev. B81-23899

Brown, Ruth. If at first you do not see. — London : Andersen Press, Oct.1982. — [32]p
ISBN 0-86264-021-0 : £4.50 : CIP entry B82-24592

Browne, Anthony. Bear goes to town. — London : Hamilton, Sept.1982. — [34]p
ISBN 0-241-10817-9 : £4.25 : CIP entry B82-18833

Browne, Anthony. Bear hunt / Anthony Browne. — London : Scholastic, 1982, c1979. — [26]p : chiefly col.ill ; 20x23cm. — (A Hippo book)
Originally published: London : H. Hamilton, 1979
ISBN 0-590-70090-1 (pbk) : £0.95 B82-14129

Bruce, Dorita Fairlie. Dimsie goes to school. — Wendover : John Goodchild, Jan.1983. — [176]p
ISBN 0-903445-61-1 : £5.95 : CIP entry B82-37626

Bull, Angela. The accidental twins / Angela Bull ; illustrated by Jill Bennett. — London : Faber, 1982. — 63p : ill ; 21cm
ISBN 0-571-11761-9 : £3.50 : CIP rev. B82-03625

Burch, T. R.. The mercury cup. — London : Granada, Nov.1982. — [160]p
ISBN 0-246-11900-4 : £4.95 : CIP entry B82-27362

Burch, T. R.. Tipper Wood′s revenge. — London : Hodder & Stoughton Children′s Books, Jan.1983. — [64]p
ISBN 0-340-28618-0 : £4.95 : CIP entry B82-33743

Burnett, David, *1946-*. The priestess of Henge : a novel / David Burnett. — London : Hamilton, 1982. — 434p ; 23cm
Map on lining paper
ISBN 0-241-10753-9 : £8.50 : CIP rev. B82-07397

Burnham, Jeremy. Break point. — London : BBC/Knight, Nov.1982. — [192]p
ISBN 0-563-20046-4 (pbk) : £1.25 : CIP entry
ISBN 0-340-28084-0 (Hodder & Stoughton) : Unpriced B82-26575

Burningham, John. Avocado baby / John Burningham. — London : Cape, 1982. — [24]p : chiefly col.ill ; 27cm
ISBN 0-224-02004-8 : £3.95 : CIP rev. B82-14052

Burningham, John. Mr Grumpy′s outing / John Burningham. — Harmondsworth : Puffin, 1978, c1970 (1981 [printing]). — [32]p : ill (some col.) ; 23cm
Originally published: London : Cape, 1970
ISBN 0-14-050254-8 (pbk) : £0.95 B82-01391

Burns, Peggy. Secret of the driftwood elephant / Peggy Burns. — Tring : Lion, 1982. — 119p : ill ; 18cm
ISBN 0-85648-331-1 (pbk) : £1.25 B82-35439

Byron, May. A first Peter Pan / J.M. Barrie ; retold by May Byron ; illustrations by Mabel Lucie Attwell. — London : Hodder and Stoughton, c1962 (1979 [printing]). — 31p : ill (some col.) ; 14cm
ISBN 0-340-03357-6 (pbk) : £0.40 B82-00059

Callan, Michael Fenney. Jockey school. — London : Hodder and Stoughton, Mar.1982. — [144]p. — (Knight books)
ISBN 0-340-28040-9 (pbk) : £0.95 : CIP entry
ISBN 0-563-20036-7 (BBC) B82-01543

Cameron, Joan. King Solomon′s mines / H. Rider Haggard ; retold in simple language by Joan Cameron ; with illustrations by Frank Humphris. — Loughborough : Ladybird, c1982. — 51p : col.ill,1col.map ; 18cm. — (Ladybird children′s classics)
ISBN 0-7214-0720-x : £0.50 B82-32946

Cameron, Joan. The three musketeers / Alexandre Dumas ; retold in simple language by Joan Cameron ; with illustrations by Frank Humphris. — Loughborough : Ladybird, c1981. — 51p : col.ill ; 18cm. — (Ladybird children′s classics)
Col.ill on lining papers
ISBN 0-7214-0633-5 : Unpriced B82-14719

Campbell, Rod. Charlie Clown. — London : Abelard-Schuman, July 1981. — [16]p. — (Little people)
ISBN 0-200-72753-2 (pbk) : £0.50 : CIP entry B81-14802

Campbell, Rod. Eddie Engine-driver. — London : Abelard-Schuman, July 1981. — [16]p. — (Little people)
ISBN 0-200-72755-9 (pbk) : £0.50 : CIP entry B81-14846

Campbell, Rod. Freddie Fireman. — London : Abelard-Schuman, July 1981. — [16]p. — (Little people)
ISBN 0-200-72756-7 (pbk) : £0.50 : CIP entry B81-14847

Campbell, Rod. Gertie Gardener. — London : Abelard-Schuman, July 1981. — [16]p. — (Little people)
ISBN 0-200-72758-3 (pbk) : £0.50 : CIP entry B81-14805

Campbell, Rod. Nancy Nurse. — London : Abelard-Schuman, July 1981. — [16]p. — (Little people)
ISBN 0-200-72754-0 (pbk) : £0.50 : CIP entry B81-14804

823'.914[J] — Children's stories in English, ***1945-*** ***— Texts*** ***continuation***

Campbell, Rod. Nigel Knight. — London : Abelard-Schuman, July 1981. — [16]p. — (Little people)
ISBN 0-200-72757-5 (pbk) : £0.50 : CIP entry
B81-14803

Carpenter, Humphrey. The Captain Hook affair / Humphrey Carpenter ; illustrated by Posy Simmonds. — [Harmondsworth] : Puffin, 1982, c1979. — 196p : ill ; 19cm
Originally published: London : Allen & Unwin, 1979
ISBN 0-14-031330-3 (pbk) : £1.00 B82-35497

Carter, Peter, ***1929-***. The children of the book. — Oxford : Oxford University Press, Oct.1982. — [256]p
ISBN 0-19-271456-2 : £5.95 : CIP entry
B82-23666

Cartlidge, Michelle. A mouse's diary / Michelle Cartlidge. — London : Heinemann, 1981. — [32]p : col.ill ; 21cm
ISBN 0-434-93142-x : £3.95 B82-02167

Carus, Zena. The mysterious schoolmaster. — London : Blackie, Feb.1983. — [105]p
ISBN 0-216-91374-8 : £5.50 : CIP entry
B82-37842

Carus, Zena. Mystery at Foxhill / Zena Carus. — London : Blackie, 1982. — 96p ; 20cm
ISBN 0-216-91171-0 : £4.50 : CIP rev.
B82-04299

Carus, Zena. Smuggler's castle. — Sevenoaks : Hodder & Stoughton, Aug.1981. — [192]p
Originally published: London : Blackie, 1980
ISBN 0-340-26536-1 (pbk) : £0.85 : CIP entry
B81-18132

Caveney, Sylvia. Fred feels fed up / story by Sylvia Caveney ; pictures by Simon Stern. — London : Pelham, 1982. — [16]p : col.ill ; 16cm. — (Fred & Bixby)
Text on inside cover
ISBN 0-7207-1358-7 (pbk) : £0.75 : CIP rev.
B82-14384

Caveney, Sylvia. Little zip's night-time book / by Sylvia Caveney ; pictures by Simon Stern. — London : Pelham, 1980. — [24]p : col.ill ; 24x25cm
ISBN 0-7207-1187-8 : £3.50 B82-02257

Caveney, Sylvia. Speckles. — London : Pelham, July 1982. — [16]p. — (Fred & Bixby)
ISBN 0-7207-1361-7 : £0.75 : CIP entry
B82-14386

Caveney, Sylvia. Spoilsports. — London : Pelham, July 1982. — [16]p. — (Fred & Bixby)
ISBN 0-7207-1360-9 : £0.75 : CIP entry
B82-14385

Caveney, Sylvia. Who do you think you are? / story by Sylvia Caveney ; pictures by Simon Stern. — London : Pelham, 1982. — [16]p : col.ill ; 16cm. — (Fred & Bixby)
Text on inside cover
ISBN 0-7207-1359-5 (pbk) : £0.75 : CIP rev.
B82-14527

Cecil, Mirabel. The bears' Christmas. — London : Methuen/Walker Books, Sept.1982. — [24]p
ISBN 0-416-06440-x : £2.95 : CIP entry
B82-19237

Cecil, Mirabel. Blue Bear's race. — London (17 Hanway House, Hanway Place, W.1) : Methuen/Walker, Aug.1982. — [24]p
ISBN 0-416-06110-9 : £3.50 : CIP entry
B82-16640

Cecil, Mirabel. Speedy bears. — London : Methuen/Walker Books, Sept.1982. — [24]p
ISBN 0-416-06430-2 : £2.95 : CIP entry
B82-19236

Cecil, Mirabel. The surprise bear. — London (17 Hanway House, Hanway Place, W.1.) : Methuen/Walker, Aug.1982. — [24]p
ISBN 0-416-06100-1 : £3.50 : CIP entry
B82-16639

Chant, Joy. Red moon and black mountain. — London : Allen & Unwin, Oct.1982. — [288]p
Originally published: 1970
ISBN 0-04-823220-3 (pbk) : £2.50 : CIP entry
B82-23100

Chapman, Elizabeth. Marmaduke goes to Wales / Elizabeth Chapman ; pictures by Douglas Hall. — London : Hodder and Stoughton, 1982. — 89p : ill ; 20cm
ISBN 0-340-26891-3 : £2.95 : CIP rev.
B82-10010

Chichester, Imogen. Mr Teago and the magic slippers. — London : Kestrel Books, Feb.1983. — 1v.
ISBN 0-7226-5824-9 : CIP entry B82-39423

Childs, Rob. Sandford on the run / Rob Childs. — London : Blackie, 1981. — 123p ; 21cm
ISBN 0-216-91131-1 : £4.95 : CIP rev.
B81-27354

Christopher, John, ***1922-***. New found land. — London : Gollancz, Jan.1983. — [192]p
ISBN 0-575-03222-7 : £5.95 : CIP entry
B82-32457

Clark, Dorothy. Shepherd's pie. — London : MacRae, Sept.1982. — [48]p. — (Blackbird books)
ISBN 0-86203-098-6 : £2.95 : CIP entry
B82-22438

Cleary, Beverly. Ralph S. Mouse. — London : Hamilton, Oct.1982. — [142]p
ISBN 0-241-10883-7 : £4.95 : CIP entry
B82-23112

Cleveland-Peck, Patricia. William the wizard / Patricia Cleveland-Peck ; illustrated by Sophie Kittredge. — London : Hamlyn, 1982, c1980. — 77p : ill ; 18cm. — (Beaver books)
Originally published: London : Hamilton, 1980
ISBN 0-600-20446-4 (pbk) : £0.85 B82-09004

Cockett, Mary. The cat and the castle / Mary Cockett ; illustrated by Doreen Caldwell. — London : Hodder and Stoughton, 1982. — 46p : ill ; 23cm. — (Hopscotch)
ISBN 0-340-26575-2 : £2.50 : CIP rev.
B81-26710

Cockett, Mary. Enough is enough / by Mary Cockett ; illustrated by Nancy Petley-Jones. — London : Hodder and Stoughton, 1980. — [29]p : col.ill ; 25cm
ISBN 0-340-24624-3 : £3.95 : CIP rev.
B80-18511

Cockett, Mary. Hoo-Ming's discovery / Mary Cockett ; illustrated by Valerie Littlewood. — London : H. Hamilton, 1982. — 48p : ill ; 20cm. — (Gazelle books)
ISBN 0-241-10775-x : £1.95 : CIP rev.
B82-07401

Cockett, Mary. The school donkey / Mary Cockett ; illustrated by Valerie Littlewood. — London : Hamish Hamilton Children's Books, 1982. — 46p : ill ; 20cm. — (Gazelle books)
ISBN 0-241-10824-1 : £1.95 : CIP rev.
B82-15695

Cockett, Mary. Shadow at Applegarth / Mary Cockett ; illustrated by Gavin Rowe. — London : Hodder and Stoughton, 1981. — 133p : ill ; 23cm
ISBN 0-340-25708-3 : £4.95 B82-39535

Codd, Carol. Chooki and the ptarmigan / Carol Codd ; illustrated by Michael Codd. — London : Robson, c1976. — [32]p : col.ill ; 24cm
ISBN 0-903895-96-x : £2.95 B82-25839

Cole, Adrian. Moorstones. — Barnstaple (70 Lynhurst Ave., Barnstaple, Devon EX31 2HY) : Spindlewood, May 1982. — [160]p
ISBN 0-907349-30-7 : £5.95 : CIP entry
B82-09219

Cole, Babette. Beware of the vet. — London : Hamilton, Oct.1982. — [40]p
ISBN 0-241-10813-6 : £4.75 : CIP entry
B82-23107

Cole, Babette. Don't go out tonight : a creepy concertina pop up / Babette Cole. — London : Hamilton, 1982. — 1folded sheet(8p) : col.ill ; 31cm
ISBN 0-241-10732-6 : £5.95 B82-29319

Cole, Joanne. Gran gliding. — London : Blackie, July 1982. — [32]p. — (Gran)
ISBN 0-216-91274-1 (cased) : £2.50 : CIP entry
ISBN 0-216-91275-x (pbk) : £0.75 B82-12560

Cole, Joanne. Gran's good news. — London : Blackie, July 1982. — [32]p. — (Gran)
ISBN 0-216-91280-6 (cased) : £2.50 : CIP entry
ISBN 0-216-91281-4 (pbk) : £0.75 B82-12563

Cole, Joanne. Gran's old bones. — London : Blackie, July 1982. — [32]p. — (Gran)
ISBN 0-216-91276-8 (cased) : £2.50 : CIP entry
ISBN 0-216-91277-6 (pbk) : £0.75 B82-12561

Cole, Joanne. Gran's pets. — London : Blackie, July 1982. — [32]p. — (Gran)
ISBN 0-216-91278-4 (cased) : £2.50 : CIP entry
ISBN 0-216-91279-2 (pbk) : £0.75 B82-12562

Cole, Michael, ***1933-***. The flood / [by Michael Cole and Alan Rogers]. — London : Hamilton, 1982. — [26]p : col.ill ; 17cm. — (Pigeon Street)
Ill on lining papers
ISBN 0-241-10727-x : £1.75 : CIP rev.
B82-01828

Cole, Michael, ***1933-***. Gerald kicks off! / [by Michael Cole and Alan Rogers]. — London : Hamilton, 1982. — [26]p : col.ill ; 17cm. — (Pigeon Street)
Ill on lining papers
ISBN 0-241-10728-8 : £1.75 : CIP rev.
B82-01832

Cole, Michael, ***1933-***. A light in the sky / [by Michael Cole and Alan Rogers]. — London : Hamilton, 1982. — [26]p : col.ill ; 17cm. — (Pigeon Street) (A Pigeon Street book)
Ill on lining papers
ISBN 0-241-10729-6 : £1.75 : CIP rev.
B82-01829

Cole, Michael, ***1933-***. Pigeon at sea / [by Michael Cole and Alan Rogers]. — London : Hamilton, 1982. — [26]p : col.ill ; 17cm. — (Pigeon Street) (A Pigeon Street book)
Ill on lining papers
ISBN 0-241-10730-x : £1.75 : CIP rev.
B82-00919

Cooper, Jilly. Little Mabel wins. — London : Granada, July 1982. — [32]p. — (Little Mabel books ; 3)
ISBN 0-246-11159-3 : £3.95 : CIP entry
B82-13232

Copper and Tod make friends. — Bristol : Purnell, c1981. — [12]p : chiefly col.ill ; 19cm. — (The Fox and the hound)
ISBN 0-361-05293-6 (unbound) : £0.75
B82-13287

Corbett, W. J.. The song of Pentecost. — London : Methuen Children's Books, Oct.1982. — [192]p
ISBN 0-416-24730-x : £5.50 : CIP entry
B82-24485

823'.914[J] — Children's stories in English, *1945-* *— Texts* *continuation*

Coren, Alan. Arthur v the rest. — London : Robson, Sept.1981. — [64]p. — (Alan Coren's Arthur books ; 10th)
ISBN 0-86051-142-1 : £1.95 : CIP entry
B81-22467

Crèche, Sylvia. Hooray for Mervyn Mouse!. — London : Methuen, July 1982. — [96]p
ISBN 0-416-24870-5 : £3.50 : CIP entry
B82-12332

Creche, Sylvia. Mervyn mouse at the fair / by Sylvia Creche ; illustrated by Roger Twinn. — [London] : Magnet, 1982. — [24]p : ill(some col.) ; 19cm
ISBN 0-416-24770-9 (pbk) : £0.95 B82-39198

Creche, Sylvia. Mervyn mouse at the zoo / by Sylvia Creche ; illustrated by Roger Twinn. — [London] : Magnet, 1982. — [24]p : col.ill ; 19cm
ISBN 0-416-24860-8 (pbk) : £0.95 B82-39197

Creche, Sylvia. Mervyn mouse goes camping / by Sylvia Creche ; illustrated by Roger Twinn. — [London] : Magnet, 1982. — [24]p : col.ill ; 19cm
ISBN 0-416-24790-3 (pbk) : £0.95 B82-39196

Creche, Sylvia. Mervyn Mouse joins the sports club / by Sylvia Creche ; illustrated by Roger Twinn. — London : Magnet, 1982. — [23]p : col.ill ; 20cm
ISBN 0-416-24780-6 (pbk) : £0.95 B82-38966

Cresswell, Helen. Bagthorpes v. the world : being the fourth part of the Bagthorpe saga / Helen Cresswell ; illustrated by Jill Bennett. — Harmondsworth : Puffin in association with Faber, 1982, c1979. — 191p : ill ; 18cm. — (The Bagthorpe saga ; pt.4)
Originally published: London : Faber, 1979
ISBN 0-14-031324-9 (pbk) : £1.00 B82-35543

Cresswell, Helen. My aunt Polly / Helen Cresswell ; illustrated by Margaret Gordon. — Exeter : Wheaton, 1979. — 24p : col.ill ; 21cm
ISBN 0-08-024998-1 (cased) : Unpriced
ISBN 0-08-024997-3 (pbk) : £0.90 B82-13689

Cross, Gillian. The demon headmaster / Gillian Cross ; illustrated by Gary Rees ; cover illustration by Mark Thomas. — Oxford : Oxford University Press, 1982. — 174p : ill ; 20cm. — (An Eagle book)
ISBN 0-19-271460-0 : £3.50 : CIP rev.
B82-04160

Cross, Gillian. The Mintyglo kid. — London : Methuen Children's, Jan.1983. — [128]p. — (A Pied piper book)
ISBN 0-416-25420-9 : £3.95 : CIP entry
B82-34449

Cross, Peter. Trouble for Trumpets / Peter Cross ; story by Peter Dallas-Smith. — London : Ernest Benn, 1982. — [32]p : col.ill ; 33cm
ISBN 0-510-00122-x : £5.95 B82-36614

Crouch, Marcus. Rainbow warrior's bride / Marcus Crouch ; illustrated by William Stobbs. — London : Pelham Books, 1981. — [24]p : col.ill ; 24x25cm
ISBN 0-7207-1296-3 : £3.95 : CIP rev.
B81-27888

Cunliffe, John. Postman Pat's difficult day. — London : Deutsch, Oct.1982. — [32]p
ISBN 0-233-97507-1 : £1.95 : CIP entry
B82-23487

Cunliffe, John. Postman Pat's foggy day. — London : Deutsch, Oct.1982. — [32]p
ISBN 0-233-97473-3 : £1.95 : CIP entry
B82-23484

Cunliffe, John. Postman Pat's rainy day / story by John Cunliffe ; pictures by Celia Berridge from the original television design by Ivor Wood. — London : Deutsch, 1982. — [36]p : col.ill ; 17x20cm
ISBN 0-233-97438-5 : £1.95 : CIP rev.
B82-03359

Cunliffe, John. Postman Pat's secret / story by John Cunliffe ; pictures by Celia Berridge from the original televison designs by Ivor Wood. — London : Deutsch, 1982. — [36]p : col.ill ; 17x20cm
ISBN 0-233-97437-7 : £1.95 : CIP rev.
B82-02654

Curley, Chris. The wood within the wall. — London : Macmillan Children's Books, Sept.1982. — [160]p
ISBN 0-333-32853-1 : £5.50 : CIP entry
B82-18827

Curtis, Philip. Mr Browser and the comet crisis. — London : Andersen, Aug.1981. — [128]p. — (Andersen young readers' library)
ISBN 0-86264-004-0 : £3.95 : CIP entry
B81-23788

Curtis, Philip. The revenge of the Brain Sharpners. — London : Andersen Press, Apr.1982. — [128]p. — (Andersen young readers' library)
ISBN 0-86264-013-x : £3.95 : CIP entry
B82-04836

Curtis, Richard. The story of Elsie and Jane. — London : Bodley Head, Oct.1982. — [32]p
ISBN 0-370-30505-1 : £3.50 : CIP entry
B82-24451

Dahl, Roald. The BFG. — London : Cape, Oct.1982. — [224]p
ISBN 0-224-02040-4 : £6.50 : CIP entry
B82-25524

Dalton, Pamela. How the world was won for mice : the dramatic story of supermouse Raffles / Pamela Dalton ; drawings by Jean de Lemos. — Kingswood : Kaye & Ward, 1982. — 102p : ill ; 24cm
ISBN 0-7182-2110-9 : £4.95 B82-30436

Daly, Niki. Joseph's other red sock / written and illustrated by Niki Daly. — London : Gollancz, 1982. — [32]p : chiefly col.ill ; 23cm
ISBN 0-575-03008-9 : £3.95 : CIP rev.
B82-00202

Daniels, Meg. Out of doors. — London : Blackie, Feb.1982. — [12]p. — (Blackie concertina books)
ISBN 0-216-91130-3 : £0.95 : CIP entry
B81-36028

Daniels, Ursula. Something from space. — London : Hamilton, Jan.1983. — [48]p. — (Gazelle books)
ISBN 0-241-10918-3 : £1.95 : CIP entry
B82-33505

Dann, Colin. Fox's feud. — London : Hutchinson, Sept.1982. — [172]p
ISBN 0-09-149400-1 : £5.50 : CIP entry
B82-21080

Dann, Colin. In the grip of winter / Colin Dann ; illustrated by Terry Riley. — London : Hutchinson, 1981. — 168p ; 23cm
ISBN 0-09-146340-8 : £5.50 : CIP rev.
B81-26763

Davies, Andrew. [Marmalade and Rufus]. Marmalade Atkin's dreadful deeds / Andrew Davies ; illustrated by John Laing. — [London] : Thames/Magnet, 1982, c1979. — 96p : ill ; 18cm
Originally published: London : Abelard-Schuman, 1979
ISBN 0-423-00560-x (pbk) : £0.95 B82-36171

Davies, Andrew. Marmalade Atkins in space / Andrew Davies ; illustrated by John Laing. — London : Abelard, 1982. — 87p : ill ; 21cm
ISBN 0-200-72773-7 : £4.50 : CIP rev.
B81-30220

Davies, Anita. Green fingers & grit / by Anita Davies. — Winchester : Hambleside, c1981. — 120p ; 18cm. — (A Terrapin book)
ISBN 0-86042-037-x (pbk) : £1.20 B82-06439

Davies, David. Gilbert and the bicycle. — London : Hutchinson Junior Books, Sept.1982. — [32]p
ISBN 0-09-142260-4 : £3.95 : CIP entry
B82-21737

Davies, Hunter. Flossie Teacake's fur coat. — London : Bodley Head, Oct.1982. — [128]p
ISBN 0-370-30933-2 : £3.95 : CIP entry
B82-24454

De Fossard, Esta. Monty : learns to fly / story by Esta de Fossard ; photography by Haworth Bartram. — Leeds : Arnold, 1982. — [30]p : col.ill ; 27cm. — (Scamps)
ISBN 0-560-03478-4 (pbk) : Unpriced
B82-31215

De Morgan, Mary. The necklace of Princess Fiorimonde. — Abridged ed. — London : Evans, Apr.1982. — [32]p
ISBN 0-237-45511-0 : £4.50 : CIP entry
B82-04841

Dehn, Olive. Goodbye day / by Olive Dehn. — London : Fontana, 1981, c1980. — 125p ; 18cm. — (Lions)
Originally published: London : Gollancz, 1980
ISBN 0-00-671810-8 (pbk) : £0.95 B82-03008

Denton, Derek. Don't go near the magic shop!. — Wendover : John Goodchild, Jan.1983. — [176]p
ISBN 0-903445-58-1 : £5.95 : CIP entry
B82-37627

Denton, Michael. The eggbox brontosaurus / Michael Denton ; illustrated by Hilda Offen. — London : Granada, 1981 (1982 [printing]). — 94p : ill ; 18cm. — (A Dragon book)
ISBN 0-583-30476-1 (pbk) : £0.85 B82-17351

Denton, Michael. Glitter city / Michael Denton ; illustrated by Hilda Offen. — London : Granada, 1982. — 91p : ill(some col.) ; 23cm
ISBN 0-246-11738-9 : £4.50 B82-22704

Derwent, Lavinia. Macpherson's Highland fling. — London : Knight, Nov.1982. — [128]p
Originally published: London : Burke, 1963
ISBN 0-340-28043-3 (pbk) : £0.95 : CIP entry
B82-27376

Devlin, Polly. The far side of the lough. — London : Gollancz, Feb.1983. — [128]p
ISBN 0-575-03244-8 : £4.95 : CIP entry
B82-38690

Diack, Anne. Winking witch / Anne Diack. — London : Longman, 1980. — 32p : ill(some col.) ; 21cm. — (Whizz bang books)
ISBN 0-582-18074-0 (cased) : £2.25
ISBN 0-582-18415-0 (pbk) : Unpriced
B82-33449

Dickens, Frank. Teddy pig and Julia's birthday / by Frank Dickens. — London : Quartet, 1981. — [48]p : col.ill ; 29cm
ISBN 0-7043-2307-9 : £4.95 B82-08983

Dickinson, Mary. Alex and the baby / story by Mary Dickinson ; pictures by Charlotte Firmin. — London : Deutsch, 1982. — [30]p : col.ill ; 18x22cm
ISBN 0-233-97465-2 : £3.95 : CIP rev.
B82-12566

823'.914[J] — Children's stories in English, *1945-* *— Texts* *continuation*

Dickinson, Mike. My dad doesn't even notice / words and pictures by Mike Dickinson. — London : Deutsch, 1982. — [32]p : col.ill ; 18x22cm
ISBN 0-233-97385-0 : £3.50 : CIP rev.
B81-37579

Dickinson, Peter, *1927-*. The devil's children / Peter Dickinson ; illustrated by Robert Hales. — Harmondsworth : Puffin, 1972, c1970 (1982 [printing]). — 156p : ill ; 19cm. — (The Changes trilogy)
Originally published: London : Gollancz, 1970
ISBN 0-14-030546-7 (pbk) : £1.10 B82-28630

Dickinson, Peter, *1927-*. Heartsease / Peter Dickinson ; illustrated by Robert Hales. — Harmondsworth : Puffin in association with Gollancz, 1971, c1969 (1982 [printing]). — 187p : ill ; 18cm. — (The Changes trilogy)
Originally published: London : Gollancz, 1969
ISBN 0-14-030498-3 (pbk) : £1.10 B82-25563

Dickinson, Peter, *1927-*. The weathermonger / Peter Dickinson. — Harmondsworth : Puffin, 1970, c1969 (1982 [printing]). — 171p ; 19cm. — (The Changes trilogy)
Originally published: London : Gollancz, 1969
ISBN 0-14-030433-9 (pbk) : £1.10 B82-28628

Dicks, Terrance. The case of the ghost grabbers / Terrance Dicks. — Glasgow : Blackie, 1980. — 127p ; 21cm
ISBN 0-216-90888-4 : £3.95 : CIP rev.
B80-13098

Dicks, Terrance. Cry vampire! / Terrance Dicks. — Glasgow : Blackie, 1981. — 111 ; 21cm
ISBN 0-216-91126-5 : £5.25 : CIP rev.
B81-26760

Dicks, Terrance. Doctor Who and an unearthly child : based on the BBC television serial by Anthony Coburn ... / Terrance Dicks. — London : W.H. Allen, 1981. — 128p ; 18cm. — (A Star book)
ISBN 0-426-20144-2 (pbk) : £1.25 B82-02669

Dicks, Terrance. Doctor Who and an unearthly child : based on the BBC television serial by Anthony Coburn by arrangement with the British Broadcasting Corporation / Terrance Dicks. — London : W.H. Allen, 1981. — 128p ; 21cm
ISBN 0-491-02748-6 : £4.95 B82-03669

Dicks, Terrance. Doctor Who and the destiny of the Daleks : based on the BBC television serial by Terry Nation by arrangement with the British Broadcasting Corporation / Terrance Dicks. — London : W.H. Allen, 1979 ([1981 printing]). — 110p ; 18cm. — (A Target book)
ISBN 0-426-20096-9 (pbk) : £0.90 B82-16092

Dicks, Terrance. Doctor Who and the Keeper of Traken / based on the BBC television serial by Johnny Byrne by arrangement with the British Broadcasting Corporation ; Terrance Dicks. — London : W.H. Allen, 1982. — 124p ; 18cm. — (A Target book)
ISBN 0-426-20148-5 (pbk) : £1.25 B82-29950

Dicks, Terrance. Doctor Who and the monster of Peladon : based on the BBC television serial by arrangement with the British Broadcasting Corporation / Terrance Dicks. — London : W.H. Allen, 1980. — 124p ; 21cm
ISBN 0-491-02823-7 : £3.95 B82-39249

Dicks, Terrance. Doctor Who and the state of decay / based on the BBC television serial by Terrance Dicks by arrangement with the British Broadcasting Corporation ; Terrance Dicks. — London : W.H. Allen, 1981. — 125p ; 21cm
ISBN 0-491-02953-5 : £4.50 B82-00052

Dicks, Terrance. Doctor Who and the terror of the Autons : based on the BBC television serial by Robert Holmes by arrangement with the British Broadcasting Corporation / Terrance Dicks ; illustrated by Alan Willow. — London : W.H. Allen, 1981. — 127p ; 21cm
ISBN 0-491-02864-4 : £4.25

Dicks, Terrance. Marvin's monster / Terrance Dicks. — Glasgow : Blackie, 1982. — 114p ; 21cm
ISBN 0-216-91179-6 : £5.25 : CIP rev.
B82-01079

Dicks, Terrance. The mystery of the missing diamond / by Terrance Dicks ; illustrated by Valerie Littlewood. — [London] : Pepper Press, 1982. — 55p : ill ; 21cm. — (Ask Oliver)
ISBN 0-237-45636-2 : £3.95 B82-35572

Dicks, Terrance. Wereboy. — London : Blackie, Oct.1982. — [128]p
ISBN 0-216-91308-x : £5.95 : CIP entry
B82-23706

Digby, Anne, *1935-*. The quicksilver horse / Anne Digby. — London : Granada, 1979. — 74p ; 23cm
ISBN 0-246-11163-1 : £3.95 B82-22648

Digby, Anne, *1935-*. Summer camp at Trebizon / Anne Digby ; illustrated by Gavin Rowe. — London : Granada, 1982. — 124p : ill ; 19cm
ISBN 0-246-11764-8 (cased) : Unpriced
ISBN 0-583-30515-6 (pbk) : £0.85 B82-33675

Digby, Anne, *1942-*. Into the fourth at Trebizon. — London : Granada, Nov.1982. — [160]p. — (Trebizon school series ; 8)
ISBN 0-246-11866-0 : £4.95 : CIP entry
B82-27361

Dobson, Julia. The animal rescuers : a Crisp twins adventure / Julia Dobson ; illustrated by Gary Rees. — London : Methuen Children's Books, 1982. — 95p : ill ; 19cm. — (A Magnet book)
ISBN 0-416-24610-9 (cased) : £3.95 : CIP rev.
ISBN 0-416-24620-6 (pbk) : £0.95 B82-11524

Dobson, Julia. The wreck finders / Julia Dobson ; illustrated by Gary Rees. — London : Methuen Children's, 1982. — 94p : ill ; 18cm. — (A Crisp twins adventure) (A Magnet book)
ISBN 0-416-24630-3 (cased) : £3.95 : CIP rev.
ISBN 0-416-24640-0 (pbk) : £0.95 B82-11761

Docherty, Hugh. The day Ollie broke down. — Glasgow : MacLellan, Jan.1982. — [20]p. — (Embryo)
ISBN 0-85335-253-4 : £2.50 : CIP entry
B81-38830

Dodd, Lynley. The smallest turtle. — Barnstaple (70 Lynhurst Ave., Barnstaple, Devon EX31 2HY) : Spindlewood, Sept.1982. — [32]p
ISBN 0-907349-35-8 : £3.50 : CIP entry
B82-21574

Dodd, Maurice. Merrymole the magnificent / written and illustrated by Maurice Dodd. — London : Hodder and Stoughton, 1982. — 110p : ill ; 22cm
ISBN 0-340-27972-9 : £3.95 : CIP rev.
B82-15727

Donald's adventure. — Bristol : Purnell, 1982. — [8]p : chiefly col.ill ; 11x14cm
ISBN 0-361-05308-8 (unbound) : £0.40
B82-26037

Douglas-Home, Felicity. Mrs B's farm. — London : Methuen Children's Books, Sept.1982. — [96]p
ISBN 0-416-24740-7 : £3.50 : CIP entry
B82-20180

Drazin, Judith. The midsummer picnic / by Judith Drazin ; illustrated by Gavin Rowe. — London : Hamilton, 1982. — 86p : ill ; 19cm. — (Antelope books)
ISBN 0-241-10716-4 : £2.50 : CIP rev.
B81-34322

Dunlop, Eileen. The maze stone. — Oxford : Oxford University Press, Sept.1982. — [144]p
ISBN 0-19-271458-9 : £5.95 : CIP entry
B82-19183

Dunn, Miriam. Kim and Ting / Miriam Dunn. — Sevenoaks : OMF, 1981. — 104p ; 21cm
ISBN 0-85363-137-9 (pbk) : £0.95 B82-08818

Dyke, John. Pigwig and the crusty diamonds. — London : Methuen Children's Books, Feb.1982. — [32]p
ISBN 0-416-21380-4 : £3.50 : CIP entry
B81-35713

Dyke, John. Pigwig and the pirates / John Dyke. — London : Methuen, 1979. — [30]p : col.ill ; 30cm
ISBN 0-416-88570-5 : £3.50 : CIP rev.
B79-26687

Eadington, Joan. Jonny Briggs and the galloping wedding. — London : BBC/Knight Books, Feb.1983. — [96]p
ISBN 0-340-33022-8 (pbk) : £0.95 : CIP entry
B82-38304

Eadington, Joan. Jonny Briggs and the giant cave / Joan Eadington ; illustrated by William Marshall ; as told in Jackanory by Bernard Holley. — London : British Broadcasting Corporation, c1982. — 95p : ill ; 21cm
ISBN 0-563-20033-2 : £4.75 B82-14099

Eadington, Joan. Jonny Briggs and the giant cave / Joan Eadington ; illustrated by William Marshall ; as told in Jackanory by Bernard Holley. — London : BBC/Knight, 1982. — 95p : ill ; 20cm
ISBN 0-563-20034-0 (pbk) : £0.95 : CIP rev.
ISBN 0-340-28042-5 (Knight Books)
B81-37573

Eadington, Joan. Jonny Briggs and the great razzle dazzle / Joan Eadington ; illustrated by William Marshall ; as told in Jackanory by Bernard Holley. — [Sevenoaks] : Knight Book/B.B.C., 1981. — 95p : ill ; 20cm. — (Jackanory)
ISBN 0-340-27532-4 (pbk) : £0.85
ISBN 0-563-20024-3 (B.B.C.) B82-03027

Eadington, Joan. Jonny Briggs and the great Razzle dazzle / Joan Eadington ; illustrated by William Marshall ; as told in Jackanory by Bernard Holley. — London : British Broadcasting Corporation, 1981. — 95p : ill ; 21cm
ISBN 0-563-17931-7 : £4.75 B82-00607

Edwards, Dorothy. A strong and willing girl / Dorothy Edwards ; illustrated by Robert Micklewright. — [London] : Magnet, 1982, c1980. — 110p : ill ; 18cm
Originally published: London : Methuen, 1980
ISBN 0-416-24590-0 (pbk) : £1.25 B82-36176

Egan, Frank. The fairy Isle of Coosanure. — Dublin : Wolfhound Press, Oct.1981. — [96]p
ISBN 0-905473-70-1 : £3.75 : CIP entry
B81-27479

Elkin, Judith. Nowhere to play. — London : A. & C. Black, Oct.1982. — [48]p
ISBN 0-7136-2236-9 : £3.95 : CIP entry
B82-22991

Elliott, Janice. The incompetent dragon. — London : Blackie, Aug.1982. — [32]p
ISBN 0-216-91252-0 : £4.95 : CIP entry
B82-15685

Elvey, Amy. The day the animals talk : a book / written & illustrated by Amy Elvey. — Telford : Woody, c1981. — 16p : ill ; 30cm
ISBN 0-907751-01-6 (pbk) : £1.50 : CIP rev.
B81-32052

823'.914[J] — Children's stories in English, *1945-* — *Texts* *continuation*

Erickson, Russell E.. Warton and Morton. — London : Hodder and Stoughton, Aug.1981. — [64]p
Originally published: New York : Lothrop, Lee and Shepard, 1976 ; London : Hodder and Stoughton, 1979
ISBN 0-340-26535-3 (pbk) : £0.85 : CIP entry B81-18136

Evans, Betty. The golden goose / retold for easy reading by Betty Evans ; illustrated by Frank Humphris. — Loughborough : Ladybirds, c1981. — 51p : col.ill ; 18cm. — (Well loved tales)
ISBN 0-7214-0626-2 : £0.50 B82-16601

Fair, Sylvia. The bedspread. — London : Macmillan Children's Books, Mar.1982. — [32]p
ISBN 0-333-32655-5 : £3.95 : CIP entry B82-01856

Faraday, Joyce. Around the world in eighty days / by Jules Verne ; retold in simple language by Joyce Faraday ; illustrated by Kathie Layfield. — Loughborough : Ladybird, c1982. — 51p : col.ill,1col.map ; 18cm. — (Ladybird children's classics)
ISBN 0-7214-0721-8 : £0.50 B82-32948

Farmer, Ruth. Angie's fairies / Ruth Farmer. — Bognor Regis : New Horizon, c1982. — 60p : ill ; 21cm
ISBN 0-86116-658-2 : £3.50 B82-14102

Fell, Alison. The grey dancer / Alison Fell. — London : Fontana Lions, 1982, c1981. — 89p ; 18cm
Originally published: London : Collins, 1981
ISBN 0-00-671946-5 (pbk) : £0.95 B82-25433

Fenby, Terry Pitts. The Piper of dreams. — London : Hodder & Stoughton Children's Books, Oct.1982. — [48]p
ISBN 0-340-28606-7 : £4.95 : CIP entry B82-27355

Fine, Anne. Round behind the ice-house / Anne Fine. — London : Methuen, 1981. — 107p ; 21cm
ISBN 0-416-20820-7 : £4.95 B82-15565

Firmin, Peter. The winter diary of a country rat : some pages from the diary of Branwell a rat ... / by Peter Firmin. — Tadworth : Kay & Ward, 1981. — 136p : ill(some col.),2col maps ; 23cm
Maps on lining papers
ISBN 0-7182-2541-4 : £4.95 B82-06163

Fisher, David, *1929 Apr.13-*. Doctor Who and the leisure hive : based on the BBC television serial by David Fisher by arrangement with the British Broadcasting Corporation / David Fisher. — London : W.H. Allen, 1982. — 127p ; 18cm. — (A Star book)
ISBN 0-426-20147-7 (pbk) : £1.25 B82-34118

Fisk, Nicholas. Antigrav / Nicholas Fisk. — Harmondsworth : Puffin, 1982, c1978. — 125p ; 19cm
Originally published: Harmondsworth : Kestrel, 1978
ISBN 0-14-031416-4 (pbk) : £0.95 B82-32648

Fisk, Nicholas. Calfang. — London : Hodder & Stoughton, July 1981. — [112]p
ISBN 0-340-26529-9 (pbk) : £0.85 : CIP entry B81-13820

Fisk, Nicholas. Evil eye. — London : Knight Books, Nov.1982. — [112]p
ISBN 0-340-27076-4 (pbk) : £0.95 : CIP entry B82-28735

Fisk, Nicholas. Leadfoot / Nicholas Fisk. — Sevenoaks : Knight Books, 1982, c1980. — 126p ; 18cm. — (Knight books)
Originally published: London : Pelham, 1980
ISBN 0-340-26809-3 (pbk) : £0.95 : CIP rev. B82-12256

Fisk, Nicholas. On the flipside. — London : Kestrel Books, Feb.1983. — 1v.
ISBN 0-7226-5825-7 : CIP entry B82-39422

Fisk, Nicholas. Trillions / Nicholas Fisk. — London : Macmillan Education, 1982, c1971. — 118p ; 21cm. — (M books)
Originally published: London : Hamilton, 1971
ISBN 0-333-28407-0 : Unpriced : CIP rev. B82-01848

Flynn, Frank. Bernie's bird. — London : Hamilton, Jan.1983. — [96]p. — (Antelope books)
ISBN 0-241-10927-2 : £2.75 : CIP entry B82-33706

Foreman, Michael, *1938-*. Land of dreams. — London : Anderson Press, Sept.1982. — [32]p
ISBN 0-86264-022-9 : £4.95 : CIP entry B82-21558

Forest, Antonia. The attic term / Antonia Forest. — [Harmondsworth] : Puffin in association with Faber, 1982, c1976. — 261p ; 19cm
Originally published: London : Faber, 1976
ISBN 0-14-031309-5 (pbk) : £1.50 B82-35493

Forest, Antonia. Run away home / Antonia Forest. — London : Faber, 1982. — 221p ; 21cm
ISBN 0-571-11837-2 : £5.25 : CIP rev. B82-04594

Forsyth, Anne. Monster Monday. — London : Hamilton, Jan.1983. — [48]p. — (Gazelle books)
ISBN 0-241-10910-8 : £1.95 : CIP entry B82-33504

Forsyth, Anne. Sam's wonderful shell / Anne Forsyth ; illustrated by Linda Birch. — London : Hamilton, 1982. — 48p : ill ; 19cm. — (Gazelle books)
ISBN 0-241-10708-3 : £1.95 : CIP rev. B81-34321

Fox, Margaret. The street of the starving cats / by Margaret Fox. — Winchester : Hambleside, c1981. — 77p ; 18cm. — (A Terrapin book)
ISBN 0-86042-038-8 (pbk) : £1.00 B82-06440

Francis, Frank. Pog / story and pictures by Frank Francis. — London : Hodder & Stoughton, 1982. — [32]p : col.ill ; 30cm
ISBN 0-340-27024-1 : £4.95 : CIP rev. B82-10768

French, Fiona. John Barleycorn. — London : Abelard-Schuman, May 1982. — [32]p
ISBN 0-200-72769-9 : £4.95 : CIP entry B82-10772

Fripp, Arthur. Stories of the fishfolk / Arthur Fripp ; illustrated by L.M. Butler. — St. Ives : United Writers, c1981. — 96p : ill ; 22cm
ISBN 0-901976-73-3 : £3.95 B82-17491

Furminger, Jo. Blackbirds' pony trek. — London : Hodder and Stoughton, July 1981. — [120]p
Originally published: 1977
ISBN 0-340-26528-0 (pbk) : £0.85 : CIP entry B81-13866

Furminger, Jo. Oh no, Aunt Belladonna! / by Jo Furminger ; illustrated by Sally Holmes. — London : Hodder and Stoughton, 1982. — 88p : ill ; 20cm. — (Leapfrog)
ISBN 0-340-27145-0 : £3.95 : CIP rev. B82-12265

Furminger, Justine. Bobbie's sponsored ride. — London : Hodder & Stoughton Children's Books, Oct.1982. — [128]p
ISBN 0-340-28150-2 : £4.95 : CIP entry B82-24360

Galdone, Joanna. The little girl and the big bear / retold by Joanna Galdone ; pictures by Paul Galdone. — Kingswood : World's Work, 1982, c1980. — [40]p : col.ill ; 23cm
Originally published: New York : Houghton Mifflin, 1980
ISBN 0-437-42534-7 : £4.50 B82-32559

Gard, Elizabeth. Billy Boot's brainwave / Elizabeth Gard ; illustrated by David Mostyn. — [London] : Beaver, 1982. — 125p : ill ; 18cm
ISBN 0-600-20490-1 (pbk) : £0.95 B82-36179

Gardam, Jane. Horse / Jane Gardam ; illustrated by Janet Rawlins. — London : Julia MacRae, 1982. — 46p : ill ; 21cm. — (Blackbird books)
ISBN 0-86203-066-8 : £2.75 : CIP rev. B81-36044

Garfield, Leon. John Diamond / Leon Garfield ; illustrated by Anthony Maitland. — Harmondsworth : Puffin, 1981, c1980. — 179p : ill ; 19cm
Originally published: Harmondsworth : Kestrel, 1980
ISBN 0-14-031366-4 (pbk) : £0.95 B82-06426

Garfield, Leon. King Nimrod's tower / Leon Garfield & Michael Bragg. — London : Methuen Children's, c1982. — [30]p : col.ill ; 28cm
ISBN 0-416-24410-6 : £3.95 : CIP rev. B82-10501

Garner, Alan. Elidor / Alan Garner ; illustrated by Charles Keeping. — London : Macmillan Education, 1982, c1965. — 160p : ill ; 21cm. — (M books)
Originally published: London : Collins, 1965
ISBN 0-333-31553-7 : Unpriced : CIP rev. B82-01850

Garner, Alan. The owl service / Alan Garner. — London : Macmillan Education, 1982, c1967. — 172p ; 21cm. — (M books)
Originally published: London : Collins, 1967
ISBN 0-333-31554-5 : Unpriced : CIP rev. B82-01851

Gascoigne, Bamber. Fearless Freddy's magic wish. — London : Methuen/Walker, Sept.1982. — [32]p
ISBN 0-416-06520-1 : £2.95 : CIP entry B82-19243

Gascoigne, Bamber. Fearless Freddy's sunken treasure. — London : Methuen/Walker, Sept.1982. — [32]p
ISBN 0-416-06510-4 : £2.95 : CIP entry B82-19242

Gascoigne, Bamber. Why the rope went tight / words by Bamber Gascoigne ; pictures by Christina Gascoigne. — London : Methuen, 1981. — [28]p : col.ill ; 24cm
Ill on lining papers
ISBN 0-416-05700-4 : £3.95 : CIP rev. B81-14387

Gerlings, Charlotte. The ghosts of Greywethers. — London : Hodder & Stoughton Children's Books, Feb.1983. — [128]p
ISBN 0-340-28607-5 : £4.95 : CIP entry B82-38046

Gervaise, Mary. The distance enchanted. — Wendover : John Goodchild, Feb.1983. — [176]p
ISBN 0-903445-64-6 : £5.95 : CIP entry B82-39291

Gibson, Enid. Night of the lemures / Enid Gibson. — Winchester : Hambleside, 1982. — 154p ; 18cm. — (A Terrapin book)
ISBN 0-86042-041-8 (pbk) : £1.40 B82-35734

Gifford, Griselda. The magic mitre / by Griselda Gifford ; illustrated by Sally Holmes. — London : Hamilton, 1982. — 48p : ill ; 20cm. — (Gazelle books)
ISBN 0-241-10802-0 : £1.95 : CIP rev. B82-10802

823'.914[J] — Children's stories in English, *1945-* **— Texts** *continuation*

Gilham, Bill. A place to hide. — London : Deutsch, Feb.1983. — [32]p
ISBN 0-233-97496-2 : £4.95 : CIP entry
B82-37847

Gillham, Bill. My brother Barry. — London : Deutsch, Sept.1981. — [96]p
ISBN 0-233-97358-3 : £4.50 : CIP entry
B81-22666

Gilmore, Maeve. Captain Eustace and the magic room / Maeve Gilmore/Kenneth Welfare. — London : Metheun Children's, 1981. — [28]p : chiefly col.ill ; 23cm. — (A Methuen picture story book)
ISBN 0-416-89020-2 : £3.50 : CIP rev.
B81-25282

Goffe, Toni. Toby's animal rescue service / Toni Goffe. — London : Hamilton, 1981. — [42p] : col.ill ; 29cm
ISBN 0-241-10580-3 : £3.50 : CIP rev.
B81-02557

Gordon, Margaret. Wilberforce goes on a picnic / Margaret Gordon. — London : Kestrel, 1982. — [32]p : col.ill ; 20x24cm
ISBN 0-7226-5750-1 : £3.95 B82-25317

Grange, R. M. D.. Mauve mountains : an allegorical fairy story / by R.M.D. Grange ; illustrated by Hilary Schofield with vignettes by the author. — [London] : Signet Press, 1982. — 77p : ill ; 18cm
ISBN 0-946167-00-1 (pbk) : Unpriced
B82-35568

Grant, Edwin C.. The dark sun / Edwin C. Grant ; illustrated by Susan Bradley and Philip Pestell. — Ilfracombe : Stockwell, 1981. — 160p : ill ; 19cm
ISBN 0-7223-1498-1 : £5.50 B82-05539

Grant, Gwen. The Lily Pickle band book / Gwen Grant ; illustrated by Margaret Chamberlain. — London : Heinemann, 1982. — 159p : ill ; 23cm
ISBN 0-434-94137-9 : £5.50 B82-33834

Grant, John. Littlenose the marksman. — London : BBC/Knight, Oct.1982. — [96]p
ISBN 0-340-28653-9 (pbk) : £0.95 : CIP entry
ISBN 0-563-20083-9 (BBC) B82-25927

Grant, John, *1930-*. Littlenose's birthday / John Grant. — Sevenoaks : Knight, 1981, c1979. — 93p : ill ; 20cm
Originally published: London : British Broadcasting Corporation, 1979
ISBN 0-340-27531-6 (pbk) : £0.85 : CIP rev.
ISBN 0-563-20023-5 (BBC) B81-30125

Gray, John, *1947-*. There are dragons / by John Gray. — Belfast : Appletree, c1981. — [24]p : col.ill ; 14x16cm
ISBN 0-904651-85-1 (pbk) : £0.95 : CIP rev.
B81-30997

Gray, Nigel. The deserter / Nigel Gray. — London : Fontana, 1982, c1977. — 124p ; 18cm
Originally published: London : Harper and Row, 1977
ISBN 0-00-672029-3 (pbk) : £1.00 B82-38402

Greaves, Jeanne R.. Mr Clutterbuck Jones / Jeanne R. Greaves ; illustrated by Linda Birch. — London : Hodder and Stoughton, 1982. — 90p : ill ; 20cm. — (Brock books)
ISBN 0-340-27214-7 : £3.50 : CIP rev.
B82-03814

Greaves, Margaret. Charlie, Emma and the dragon family. — London : Methuen Children's Books, Feb.1982. — [96]p. — (Read aloud books)
ISBN 0-416-21580-7 : £3.50 : CIP entry
B81-35712

Green, Wendy. The steel band / Wendy Green ; illustrated by Jennifer Northway. — London : Hamilton, 1982. — 80p : ill ; 19cm. — (Antelope books)
ISBN 0-241-10777-6 : £2.50 : CIP rev.
B82-01711

Greenway, Shirley. Hansel and Gretel / the Brothers Grimm ; retold by Shirley Greenway ; pictures by Peter Richardson. — London : Pan, 1981. — [24]p : col.ill ; 21cm. — (Piccolo picture classics) (A Piccolo original)
ISBN 0-330-26548-2 (pbk) : £0.90 B82-03195

Grender, Iris. But that's another story. — London : Hodder & Stoughton, Mar.1982. — [64]p
Originally published: London : Hutchinson, 1978
ISBN 0-340-26814-x (pbk) : £0.85 : CIP entry
B82-01093

Grender, Iris. Did I ever tell you about my birthday party?. — London : Hutchinson, Jan.1983. — [64]p
ISBN 0-09-151230-1 : £3.95 : CIP entry
B82-33458

Grice, Frederick. The courage of Andy Robson / Frederick Grice ; illustrated by Victor G. Ambrus. — Oxford : Oxford University Press, 1969 (1982 [printing]). — 131p : ill ; 21cm
ISBN 0-19-271469-4 : £3.95 B82-36555

Grice, Frederick. The courage of Andy Robson / Frederick Grice. — Harmondsworth : Puffin, in association with Oxford University Press, 1982, c1969. — 127p ; 18cm
Originally published: Oxford : Oxford University Press, 1969
ISBN 0-14-031528-4 (pbk) : £0.85 B82-34166

Griffiths, Helen. Dancing horses. — London : Hutchinson, Sept.1981. — [160]p
ISBN 0-09-146160-x : £5.50 : CIP entry
B81-20184

Griffiths, Helen. Hari's pigeon. — London : Hutchinson, Oct.1982. — [96]p
ISBN 0-09-149410-9 : £4.50 : CIP entry
B82-24964

Griffiths, Helen. The wild horse of Santander / Helen Griffiths ; illustrated by Victor G. Ambrus. — Sevenoaks : Hodder and Stoughton, 1982, c1966. — 157p : ill ; 18cm
Originally published: London : Hutchinson, 1966
ISBN 0-340-25544-7 (pbk) : £1.10 : CIP rev.
B82-12250

Groves, Sheila. [More tortoise tales. Selections]. The greatest / by Sheila Groves ; illustrations by Gordon Stowell. — Eastbourne : Kingsway, c1976 [i.e. 1981, c1976]. — [24]p : col.ill ; 15cm. — (Tortoise tales)
Originally published: Eastbourne: Victory, 1976
ISBN 0-86065-142-8 (pbk) : Unpriced
B82-08832

Groves, Sheila. [More tortoise tales. Selections]. Hedgehog law / by Sheila Groves ; illustrations by Gordon Stowell. — Eastbourne : Kingsway, c1976 [i.e. 1981, c1976]. — [24]p : col.ill ; 15cm. — (Tortoise tales)
Originally published: Eastbourne: Victory, 1976
ISBN 0-86065-143-6 (pbk) : Unpriced
B82-08833

Groves, Sheila. [More tortoise tales. Selections]. Leapalong / by Sheila Groves ; illustrations by Gordon Stowell. — Eastbourne : Kingsway, c1976 [i.e. 1981, c1976]. — [24]p : col.ill ; 15cm. — (Tortoise tales)
Originally published: Eastbourne: Victory, 1976
ISBN 0-86065-144-4 (pbk) : Unpriced
B82-08834

Groves, Sheila. [More tortoise tales. Selections]. All change! / by Sheila Groves ; illustrations by Gordon Stowell. — Eastbourne : Kingsway, c1976 [i.e. 1981, c1976]. — [24]p : col.ill ; 15cm. — (Tortoise tales)
Originally published: Eastbourne: Victory, 1976
ISBN 0-86065-145-2 (pbk) : Unpriced
B82-08831

Groves, Sheila. [More tortoise tales. Selections]. Whisperings / by Sheila Groves ; illustrations by Gordon Stowell. — Eastbourne : Kingsway, c1976 [i.e. 1981, c1976]. — [24]p : col.ill ; 15cm. — (Tortoise tales)
Originally published: Eastbourne: Victory, 1976
ISBN 0-86065-146-0 (pbk) : Unpriced
B82-08829

Groves, Sheila. [More tortoise tales. Selections]. Dolly's revenge / by Sheila Groves ; illustrations by Gordon Stowell. — Eastbourne : Kingsway, c1976 [i.e. 1981, c1976]. — [24]p : col.ill ; 15cm. — (Tortoise tales)
Originally published: Eastbourne: Victory, 1976
ISBN 0-86065-147-9 (pbk) : Unpriced
B82-08830

Haas, Irene. The Little Moon Theatre / by Irene Haas. — London : Collins, 1981. — [32]p : col.ill ; 24x27cm
ISBN 0-00-195539-x : Unpriced B82-04681

Haigh, Sheila. The little gymnast. — London : Blackie, Oct.1982. — [96]p
ISBN 0-216-91284-9 : £4.95 : CIP entry
B82-23705

Haldane, David. The zoo goes to France. — London : Methuen Children's Books, Mar.1982. — [32]p
ISBN 0-416-22100-9 : £3.50 : CIP entry
B82-01999

Hale, Irina. Donkey's dreadful day / written and illustrated by Irina Hale. — London : Macmillan Children's Books, 1982. — [30]p : col.ill ; 22x26cm
ISBN 0-333-33014-5 : £3.95 B82-31420

Hall, Fergus. Groundsel. — London : Cape, Oct.1982. — [32]p
ISBN 0-224-01938-4 : £4.95 : CIP entry
B82-24365

Hall, Willis. The last vampire. — London : Bodley Head, Oct.1982. — [160]p
ISBN 0-370-30503-5 : £4.50 : CIP entry
B82-24447

Hanbury Tenison, Marika. A boy and a dolphin. — St. Albans : Granada, Feb.1983. — [64]p
ISBN 0-246-11930-6 : £4.95 : CIP entry
B82-36339

Hanna, Ron. The quest of the dragonslayer. — London : Methuen Children's Books, Feb.1983. — [32]p. — (Methuen picture-story books)
ISBN 0-416-26690-8 : £3.95 : CIP entry
B82-38260

Hardcastle, Michael. Attack! : a Mark Fox story. — London : Fontana, 1982. — 111p ; 18cm
ISBN 0-00-691758-5 (pbk) : £0.85 B82-19734

Hardcastle, Michael. Away from home / Michael Hardcastle ; illustrated by Trevor Stubley. — London : Methuen Children's, 1974 (1982 [printing]). — 127p : ill ; 18cm. — (A Magnet book)
ISBN 0-416-79860-8 (pbk) : £0.95 B82-34008

Hardcastle, Michael. Fast from the gate. — London : Methuen Children's, Feb.1983. — [128]p
ISBN 0-416-23420-8 : £3.95 : CIP entry
B82-38259

Hardcastle, Michael. Free kick / Michael Hardcastle ; illustrated by Trevor Stubley. — London : Methuen Children's, 1974 (1982 [printing]). — 126p : ill ; 18cm. — (A Magnet book)
ISBN 0-416-79880-2 (pbk) : £0.95 B82-34012

823'.914[J] — Children's stories in English, ***1945-*** **—** ***Texts*** *continuation*

Hardcastle, Michael. The gigantic hit / Michael Hardcastle. — London : Pelham, 1982. — 121p ; 21cm
ISBN 0-7207-1305-6 : £4.95 : CIP rev. B82-01113

Hardcastle, Michael. Half a team / Michael Hardcastle ; illustrated by Trevor Stubley. — London : Methuen Children's, 1980 (1982 [printing]). — 108p : ill ; 18cm. — (A Magnet book)
ISBN 0-416-25210-9 (pbk) : £0.95 B82-38392

Hardcastle, Michael. In the net / Michael Hardcastle ; illustrated by Trevor Stubley. — London : Methuen Children's, 1971, (1982 [printing]). — 123p : ill ; 18cm. — (A Magnet book)
ISBN 0-416-79900-0 (pbk) : £0.95 B82-34009

Hardcastle, Michael. Roar to victory. — London : Methuen Children's Books, Jan.1982. — [128] p. — (A Pied Piper book)
ISBN 0-416-20960-2 : £3.95 : CIP entry B81-34398

Hardcastle, Michael. Shooting star. — London : Severn House, Nov.1982. — [128]p. — (Mark Fox ; v.4)
ISBN 0-7278-0843-5 : £4.95 : CIP entry B82-34067

Hardcastle, Michael. Soccer special / Michael Hardcastle ; illustrated by Paul Wright. — London : Methuen Children's, 1978 (1982 [printing]). — 127p : ill ; 18cm. — (A Magnet book)
ISBN 0-416-58000-9 (pbk) : £0.95 B82-34011

Hardcastle, Michael. United! / Michael Hardcastle ; illustrated by Trevor Stubley. — London : Methuen Children's, 1973 (1982 [printing]). — 127p : ill ; 18cm. — (A Magnet book)
ISBN 0-416-79840-3 (pbk) : £0.95 B82-34010

Hargreaves, Roger. Hippo leaves home. — London : Hodder & Stoughton Children's Books, June 1982. — [24]p
ISBN 0-340-27981-8 : £0.50 : CIP entry B82-10469

Hargreaves, Roger. Hippo Potto & mouse. — London : Hodder & Stoughton Children's Books, June 1982. — [24]p
ISBN 0-340-27978-8 : £0.50 : CIP entry B82-10466

Hargreaves, Roger. Mouse gets caught. — London : Hodder and Stoughton Children's Books, June 1982. — [24]p
ISBN 0-340-27980-x : £0.50 : CIP entry B82-10468

Hargreaves, Roger. Once upon a worm. — London : Hodder and Stoughton Children's Books, Sept.1982. — [32]p
ISBN 0-340-28491-9 : £3.95 : CIP entry B82-18809

Hargreaves, Roger. Potto finds a job. — London : Hodder & Stoughton Children's Books, June 1982. — [24]p
ISBN 0-340-27979-6 : £0.50 : CIP entry B82-10467

Hargreaves, Roger. Things / Roger Hargreaves. — London : Hodder and Stoughton, 1981. — [40]p : col.ill ; 23x30cm
ISBN 0-340-27445-x : £2.50 : CIP rev. B81-20581

Harris, Geraldine. Seven citadels / Geraldine Harris. — London : Macmillan
Pt.1: Prince of the godborn. — 1982. — 186p : ill,maps ; 20cm
Maps on lining papers
ISBN 0-333-32849-3 : £5.50 : CIP rev. B82-18826

Harris, Geraldine. Seven citadels. — London : Macmillan Children's Books
Pt.2: The children of the wind. — Oct.1982. — [192]p
ISBN 0-333-32850-7 : £5.50 : CIP entry B82-24805

Harris, Rosemary. Zed. — London : Faber, Oct.1982. — 1v.
ISBN 0-571-11947-6 : £5.95 : CIP entry B82-28477

Harris, Rosemary, *1923-*. Janni's stork. — London : Blackie, Aug.1982. — [32]p
ISBN 0-216-91253-9 : £3.95 : CIP entry B82-15686

Harvey, Anne. A present for Nellie / Anne Harvey ; illustrated by Victoria Cooper. — London : Julia MacRae, 1982. — 44p : ill ; 21cm. — (Blackbird books)
ISBN 0-86203-067-6 : £2.75 : CIP rev. B81-36043

Harvey, John, *19---*. What about it, Sharon? / John Harvey. — Harmondsworth : Puffin, 1982, c1979. — 124p ; 18cm. — (Puffin plus)
Originally published: Harmondsworth : Penguin, 1979
ISBN 0-14-031375-3 (pbk) : £0.85 B82-16781

Hastings, Selina. Sir Gawain and the Green Knight / words by Selina Hastings ; illustrations by Juan Wijngaard. — London : Methuen/Walker, 1981. — [26]p : col.ill ; 22cm
ISBN 0-416-05860-4 : £3.95 : CIP rev. B81-20642

Hawkins, Colin. Vampires. — London : Granada, Sept.1982. — 1v.
ISBN 0-246-11713-3 : £3.95 : CIP entry B82-18856

Haynard, Julia. Percival's party / by Julia Haynard ; illustrated by Frances Thatcher. — Winchester : Hambleside, c1981. — [32]p : col.ill ; 23x26cm. — (A Terrapin book)
ISBN 0-86042-036-1 : Unpriced B82-08917

Heffron, Dorris. Rain and I / Dorris Heffron. — London : Macmillan Children's Books, 1982. — 157p ; 21cm
ISBN 0-333-32851-5 : £5.50 : CIP rev. B82-11754

Heide, Florence Parry. Treehorn's treasure. — London : Kestrel Books, Feb.1983. — 1v.
ISBN 0-7226-5827-3 : CIP entry B82-39421

Henri, Adrian. Eric the punk cat / Adrian Henri ; illustrated by Roger Wade Walker. — London : Hodder and Stoughton, 1982. — [25]p : col.ill ; 25cm
ISBN 0-340-27969-9 : £4.50 : CIP rev. B82-18808

Hersom, Kathleen. Maybe it's a tiger / Kathleen Hersom ; illustrated by Niki Daly. — London : Macmillan Children's Books, 1981. — [32]p : chiefly col.ill ; 21cm
ISBN 0-333-32382-3 : £3.95 : CIP rev. B81-15815

Hersom, Kathleen. The spitting image. — London : Macmillan Children's Books, Aug.1982. — [160]p
ISBN 0-333-32852-3 : £5.50 : CIP entry B82-15715

Hickson, Joan. The seven sparrows and the motor car picnic / story and pictures by Joan Hickson. — London : Deutsch, 1981. — [32]p : col.ill ; 25cm
ISBN 0-233-97363-x : £4.95 : CIP rev. B81-26716

Higgs, Mike. Moonbird / ; Mike Higgs. — London : Granada, 1981. — [32]p : col.ill ; 19cm. — (A Dragon book)
ISBN 0-583-30487-7 (pbk) : £0.85 B82-03002

Higgs, Mike. Moonbird & the unicorn / Mike Higgs. — London : Granada, 1981. — [32]p : col.ill ; 19cm. — (A Dragon book)
ISBN 0-583-30489-3 (pbk) : £0.85 B82-03004

Higgs, Mike. Moonbird and the space pirates / Mike Higgs. — London : Granada, 1981. — [32]p : col.ill ; 19cm. — (A Dragon book)
ISBN 0-583-30490-7 (pbk) : £0.85 B82-03005

Higgs, Mike. Moonbird to the rescue / Mike Higgs. — London : Granada, 1981. — [32]p : col.ill ; 19cm. — (A Dragon book)
ISBN 0-583-30488-5 (pbk) : £0.85 B82-03003

Higham, David, *1949-*. G was a giant who knocked down a house. — London : Methuen Children's Books, Oct.1981. — [32]p. — (A Methuen picture-story book)
ISBN 0-416-21790-7 : £3.25 : CIP entry B81-25728

Hill, Denise. The golden bicycle. — London : Hamilton, Aug.1982. — [96]p. — (Antelope books)
ISBN 0-241-10846-2 : £2.75 : CIP entry B82-15698

Hill, Douglas. Young legionary. — London : Gollancz, Nov.1982. — [128]p
ISBN 0-575-03201-4 : £4.95 : CIP entry B82-26561

Hill, Eric. Spot's first walk / Eric Hill. — London : Heinemann, 1981. — [20]p : col.ill ; 22cm
Text, ill on lining papers
ISBN 0-434-94289-8 : £3.95 B82-03215

Hinton, Nigel. The witch's revenge / Nigel Hinton ; illustrated by Peter Rush. — London : Abelard, 1981. — 103p : ill,2maps ; 21cm
Maps on lining papers
ISBN 0-200-72765-6 : £4.50 : CIP rev. B81-26758

Holiday, Jane. Victor the vulture / Jane Holiday ; illustrated by Jo Worth. — Harmondsworth : Puffin, 1981, c1978. — 76p : ill ; 18cm. — (A young Puffin)
Originally published: London : Hamilton, 1978
ISBN 0-14-031255-2 (pbk) : £0.80 B82-06465

Hollander, Neil. The chocolate feast / by Neil Hollander ; illustrations by Tim Jaques. — London : Warne, 1982. — [28]p : col.ill ; 20x27cm
ISBN 0-7232-2905-8 : Unpriced B82-30003

Hollander, Neil. The great zoo break. — London : Hodder & Stoughton Children's Books, Nov.1982. — [32]p
ISBN 0-340-28448-x : £4.95 : CIP entry B82-27358

Hooper, J. K.. Kaspar and the iron poodle. — London : Andersen Press, Oct.1982. — [144]p. — (Andersen young readers' library)
ISBN 0-86264-034-2 : £4.95 : CIP entry B82-24595

Hooper, Mary. Love Emma XXX / Mary Hooper ; illustrated by Garry Cobb. — [London] : Piccolo, 1982. — 125p : ill ; 17cm
ISBN 0-330-26587-3 (pbk) : £0.95 B82-18095

Hoover, H. M.. This time of darkness. — London : Methuen, Mar.1982. — [160]p
ISBN 0-416-21770-2 : £4.95 : CIP entry B82-01990

Hoyle, Fred. The energy pirate / by Fred and Geoffrey Hoyle ; illustrated by Martin Aitchison. — Loughborough : Ladybird, c1982. — 51p : col.ill ; 18cm. — (Science fiction)
ISBN 0-7214-0725-0 : £0.60 B82-37116

823'.914[J] — Children's stories in English, *1945-* *— Texts* *continuation*

Hoyle, Fred. The frozen planet of Azuron / by Fred and Geoffrey Hoyle ; illustrated by Martin Aitchison. — Loughborough : Ladybird, c1982. — 51p : col.ill ; 18cm. — (Science fiction)
ISBN 0-7214-0726-9 : £0.60 B82-37119

Hoyle, Fred. The giants of universal park / by Fred and Geoffrey Hoyle ; illustrated by Martin Aitchison. — Loughborough : Ladybird, c1982. — 51p : col.ill ; 18cm. — (Science fiction)
ISBN 0-7214-0727-7 : £0.60 B82-37117

Hoyle, Fred. The planet of death / by Fred and Geoffrey Hoyle ; illustrated by Martin Aitchison. — Loughborough : Ladybird, c1982. — 51p : col.ill ; 18cm
ISBN 0-7214-0728-5 : £0.60 B82-37118

Hughes, Monica. The Isis pedlar. — London : Hamilton, Sept.1982. — [144]p
ISBN 0-241-10834-9 : £5.25 : CIP entry
B82-20163

Hughes, Shirley. Alfie's feet. — London : Bodley Head, July 1982. — [32]p
ISBN 0-370-30416-0 : £3.50 : CIP entry
B82-12316

Hughes, Shirley. Charlie Moon and the big bonanza bust-up / written and illustrated by Shirley Hughes. — London : Bodley Head, 1982. — 123p : ill ; 23cm
ISBN 0-370-30918-9 : £4.25 : CIP rev.
B82-12318

Hughes, Shirley. Here comes Charlie Moon / written and illustrated by Shirley Hughes. — London : Fontana, 1982, c1980. — 142p : ill ; 20cm. — (Lions)
Originally published: London : Bodley Head, 1980
ISBN 0-00-671934-1 (pbk) : £0.95 B82-18090

Hughes, Shirley. Lucy & Tom's Christmas / Shirley Hughes. — London : Gollancz, 1981. — [32]p : col.ill ; 21x23cm
ISBN 0-575-02970-6 : £3.95 B82-01047

Hunt, Helen. A bath for Biscuit / story by Helen Hunt ; photography Haworth. — Leeds : Arnold, 1982. — [30]p : col.ill ; 27cm. — (Scamps)
ISBN 0-560-03468-7 (pbk) : Unpriced
B82-31216

Hunt, Peter. The maps of time. — London : MacRae Books, Jan.1983. — [148]p
ISBN 0-86203-119-2 : £5.95 : CIP entry
B82-33230

Hurford, John. The dormouse. — Barnstaple : Spindlewood, Nov.1981. — [25]p
Originally published: London: Cape, 1974
ISBN 0-907349-20-x (cased) : £3.95 : CIP entry
ISBN 0-907349-25-0 (pbk) : £1.35 B81-35891

Hurford, John. Fredgehog / by John Hurford. — Barnstaple : Spindlewood, 1980. — [27]p : ill (some col.) ; 22x30cm
ISBN 0-907349-00-5 : £4.80 : CIP rev.
B80-35471

Hutchins, Pat. Titch / by Pat Hutchins. — Harmondsworth : Penguin in association with Bodley Head, 1974, c1971 (1981 [printing]). — [30]p : col.ill ; 23cm. — (Picture puffins)
Originally published: New York : Macmillan, 1971 ; London : Bodley Head, 1972. — Text on inside cover
ISBN 0-14-050096-0 (pbk) : £0.95 B82-01402

Hutton, Warwick. The Nose tree / adapted from an old German story and illustrated by Warwick Hutton. — London : MacRae, 1981. — [32]p : col.ill ; 28cm
ISBN 0-86203-040-4 : £4.95 : CIP rev.
B80-12133

Ibbotson, Eva. Which witch? / Eva Ibbotson ; illustrated by Annabel Large. — [London] : Piccolo in association with Macmillan London, 1981, c1979. — 169p : ill ; 18cm
Originally published: London : Macmillan, 1979
ISBN 0-330-26586-5 (pbk) : £1.25 B82-10171

Jackson, Steve. The Warlock of Firetop Mountain / Steve Jackson and Ian Livingtone ; illustrated by Russ Nicholson. — Harmondsworth : Puffin, 1982. — 21,[170]p : ill ; 19cm
ISBN 0-14-031538-1 (pbk) : £1.25 B82-40671

Jaques, Faith. Tilly's house / written and illustrated by Faith Jaques. — London : Fontana, 1981, c1979. — [32]p : col.ill ; 21cm. — (Picture lions)
Originally published: London : Heinemann, 1979
ISBN 0-00-661791-3 (pbk) : £0.90 B82-03191

Jeffries, Roderic. Eighteen desperate hours / Roderic Jeffries. — Harmondsworth : Puffin, 1982, c1979. — 107p ; 19cm
Originally published: London : Hodder & Stoughton, 1979
ISBN 0-14-031299-4 (pbk) : £0.85 B82-25540

Jeffries, Roderic. The missing man / Roderic Jeffries. — London : Beaver Books, 1982, c1980. — 126p ; 18cm
Originally published: London : Hodder and Stoughton, 1980
ISBN 0-600-20475-8 (pbk) : £0.95 B82-25310

Jenkins, Alan C.. The ghost elephant : an African story / Alan C. Jenkins ; illustrated by Nelda Prins. — Harmondsworth : Puffin, 1981. — 60p : ill ; 20cm
ISBN 0-14-031301-x (pbk) : £0.85 B82-06084

Johnston, Derek. Normy Dormy / by Derek Johnston ; illustrated by Harry Johnston. — Bury : D. & H. Johnston, 1982. — [31]p : ill ; 22cm
ISBN 0-9508049-0-8 (pbk) : Unpriced
B82-38617

Jones, Diana Wynne. The time of the ghost / Diana Wynne Jones. — London : Macmillan Children's Books, 1981. — 192p ; 21cm
ISBN 0-333-32012-3 : £4.95 : CIP rev.
B81-26759

Jones, Diana Wynne. Witch week / Diana Wynne Jones. — London : Macmillan, 1982. — 210p ; 21cm
ISBN 0-333-33189-3 : £5.50 : CIP rev.
B82-07427

Jones, Ivan. Zot and Mrs Mouse / written by Ivan Jones ; illustrated by Jenny Holden. — Upton : Gemini Books, 1981. — 30p : col.ill ; 16x18cm
ISBN 0-9507748-0-4 (pbk) : £0.65 B82-09335

Jones, Olive. A little box of fairy tales / told by Olive Jones and illustrated by Francesca Crespi. — [London] : Methuen, [1982]. — 1case : col.ill ; 11cm
Contents: Beauty and the Beast — The elves and the shoemaker — Rumpelstiltskin — Snow White and the seven dwarfs
ISBN 0-416-24690-7 : Unpriced : CIP rev.
B82-12330

Joy, Margaret. Monday magic. — London : Faber, Sept.1982. — [128]p
ISBN 0-571-11924-7 : £3.95 : CIP entry
B82-19548

Kayani, M. S.. The brave boy. — London : Islamic Foundation, Nov.1982. — [36]p. — (Muslim children's library ; 10)
ISBN 0-86037-112-3 (pbk) : £0.95 : CIP entry
B82-36297

Kaye, Geraldine. The plum tree party / Geraldine Kaye ; illustrated by Gabrielle Stoddart. — London : Hodder and Stoughton, 1981. — 47p : ill ; 23cm. — (Hopscotch)
ISBN 0-340-26574-4 : £2.50 : CIP rev.
B81-26711

Kaye, Geraldine. The sky-blue dragon. — London : Hodder and Stoughton Children's Books, Jan.1983. — [64]p. — (Hopscotch series)
ISBN 0-340-28215-0 : £2.75 : CIP entry
B82-33732

Kaye, M. M.. Thistledown / written and illustrated by M.M. Kaye. — London : Quartet, 1981. — [24]p : col.ill ; 20x29cm
ISBN 0-7043-2303-6 : Unpriced B82-08982

Kellogg, Steven. Tallyho, Pinkerton!. — London : Hutchinson Junior, Feb.1983. — [32]p
ISBN 0-09-150580-1 : £4.95 : CIP entry
B82-36569

Kemp, Gene. The clock tower ghost / Gene Kemp ; illustrated by Carolyn Dinan. — London : Faber, 1981. — 89p : ill ; 20cm
ISBN 0-571-11767-8 : £3.95 : CIP rev.
B81-25327

Kemp, Gene. Tamworth Pig saves the trees / Gene Kemp ; illustrated by Carolyn Dinan. — [London] : Faber Fanfares, 1980, c1973. — 103p : ill ; 19cm
Originally published: London : Faber, 1973
ISBN 0-571-11493-8 (pbk) : £1.15 : CIP rev.
B80-18050

Kemp, Jo. Sam's birthday cake : a story about 5 / by Jo Kemp and John Coop ; drawings by Pete Beard. — St Albans : Hart-Davis Educational for Granada Television, c1980. — 15p : col.ill ; 22cm. — (Sam and Squeak stories. Set one)
With: One more makes 6 / by Jo Kemp and John Coop
ISBN 0-247-13194-6 (unbound) : Unpriced
ISBN 0-247-13156-3 (set) : Unpriced
B82-38600

Kemp, Jo. A touch of magic : a story about 7 / by Jo Kemp ; drawings by Pete Beard. — St. Albans : Hart-Davis Educational for Granada Television, c1980. — 15p : col.ill ; 22cm. — (Sam and Squeak stories. Set one)
With: The missing button / by Sybil Marshall and John Coop
ISBN 0-247-13195-4 (unbound) : Unpriced
ISBN 0-247-13156-3 (set) : Unpriced
B82-38596

Kennemore, Tim. Wall of words / Tim Kennemore. — London : Faber, 1982. — 173p ; 20cm
ISBN 0-571-11856-9 : £5.25 : CIP rev.
B82-02645

Kent, Jack. Clotilda's magic / by Jack Kent. — London : Scholastic, 1981, c1978. — [32]p : col.ill ; 20cm. — (A Hippo book)
Originally published: New York : Random House, 1969
ISBN 0-590-72055-4 (pbk) : £0.75 B82-16602

Kerr, Judith. Mog and the baby / Judith Kerr. — London : Fontana Picture Lions, 1982, c1980. — [32]p : col.ill ; 22cm
Originally published: Glasgow : Collins, 1980
ISBN 0-00-661799-9 (pbk) : £0.90 B82-16829

Kerr, Judith. When Willy went to the wedding / written and illustrated by Judith Kerr. — Glasgow : Collins, 1972 (1982 [printing]). — [40]p : chiefly col.ill ; 27cm
ISBN 0-00-195906-9 : Unpriced B82-25233

Kidd, Meg. Dobbin days / by Meg Kidd ; with drawings by Olive Scott. — London : Silver Streak, c1982. — 15p : ill ; 17cm
Cover title
ISBN 0-9508200-0-8 (pbk) : Unpriced
B82-38632

823'.914[J] — Children's stories in English, *1945-* — *Texts* *continuation*

Killingley, Siew-yue. The pottery ring : a fairy tale for the young and old / Siew-yue Killingley. — [Gosforth] ([9 Rectory Drive, Gosforth, Newcastle upon Tyne NE3 1XT]) : S. Killingley, 1981, c1977. — 27p ; 30cm
£0.50 (unbound) B82-02027

Kincaid, Lucy. Jack and the beanstalk / story adapted by Lucy Kincaid ; illustrated by Eric Rowe. — Cambridge : Brimax Books, 1979 (1981 printing). — [20]p : col.ill ; 27cm. — (Now you can read)
ISBN 0-86112-049-3 : Unpriced B82-16295

King, Deborah. Sirius and Saba. — London : Hamilton, Apr.1981. — [32]p
ISBN 0-241-10599-4 : £4.50 : CIP entry B81-01325

King-Smith, Dick. Daggie Dogfoot / Dick King-Smith ; illustrated by Mary Rayner. — Harmondsworth : Puffin, 1982. — 155p : ill ; 18cm
Originally published: London : Gollancz, 1980
ISBN 0-14-031391-5 (pbk) : £0.95 B82-22303

King-Smith, Dick. Magnus Powermouse / by Dick King-Smith ; illustrated by Mary Rayner. — London : Gollancz, 1982. — 125p : ill ; 21cm
ISBN 0-575-03116-6 : £4.95 : CIP rev. B82-12981

King-Smith, Dick. The Queen's nose. — London : Gollancz, Feb.1983. — [128]p
ISBN 0-575-03228-6 : £4.95 : CIP entry B82-38683

Klein, Robin. Thing / Robin Klein ; illustrated by Alison Lester. — Melbourne ; Oxford : Oxford University Press, 1982. — [32]p : ill (some col.) ; 23cm
ISBN 0-19-554330-0 : £3.50 B82-24994

Knights, Roger. The lettermen go on a picnic / by Roger Knights. — [London] : Hathercliff, [1980]. — [32]p : chiefly col.ill ; 14x15cm
ISBN 0-907048-03-x (pbk) : £0.45 B82-39255

Knights, Roger. The lettermen go to the circus / by Roger Knights. — [London] : Hathercliff, [1980]. — [32]p : chiefly col.ill ; 14x15cm
ISBN 0-907048-01-3 (pbk) : £0.45 B82-39254

Knights, Roger. The lettermen go to the seaside / by Roger Knights. — [London] : Hathercliff, [1980]. — [32]p : chiefly col.ill ; 14x15cm ; pbk
ISBN 0-907048-00-5 : £0.45 B82-39253

Knights, Roger. The lettermen go to the shops / by Roger Knights. — [London] : Hathercliff, [1980]. — [32]p : chiefly col.ill ; 14x15cm
ISBN 0-907048-02-1 (pbk) : £0.45 B82-39252

Knowles, Anne. The stirrup and the ground. — London : Granada, Feb.1983. — [160]p
ISBN 0-246-11940-3 : £4.95 : CIP entry B82-37828

Knowles, Tony. The book mice / Tony Knowles ; pictures by Stephen Forster. — London : Evans Brothers, 1980. — 30p : ill ; 16cm
ISBN 0-237-44992-7 : £2.25 : CIP rev. B80-21133

Koralek, Jenny. Toad Tuesday / story by Jenny Koralek ; pictures by Martin Ursell. — Kingswood : Kaye & Ward, 1982. — [32]p : col.ill ; 23cm
ISBN 0-7182-3631-9 : £4.50 B82-34205

Krailing, Tessa. Washington and the marrow raiders / Tessa Krailing ; illustrated by Hilda Offen. — London : Scholastic, 1981. — 120p : ill ; 18cm. — (Hippo books)
ISBN 0-590-70092-8 (pbk) : £0.80 B82-02267

Kraus, Robert. Herman the helper lends a hand / by Robert Kraus ; pictures by Jose Aruego & Ariane Dewey. — London : Methuen's Children, 1982. — [12]p : chiefly col. ; 21cm. — (A Methuen picture puppet book)
Cover title. — Finger puppet attached to lining paper
ISBN 0-416-22120-3 : £1.95 B82-33920

Kraus, Robert. Milton the early riser takes a trip / by Robert Kraus ; pictures by Jose Aruego & Ariane Dewey. — London : Methuen Children's, 1982. — [12]p : chiefly col. ; 21cm. — (A Methuen picture puppet book)
Cover title. — Finger puppet attached to inside cover
ISBN 0-416-22140-8 : £1.95 B82-33921

Kraus, Robert. Owliver the actor takes a bow / by Robert Kraus ; pictures by Jose Aruego & Ariane Dewey. — London : Methuen Children's, 1982. — [12]p : chiefly col. ; 21cm. — (A Methuen picture book)
Finger puppet attached to lining paper
ISBN 0-416-22130-0 : £1.95 B82-33919

Lane, Margaret, *1907-*. Operation hedgehog / by Margaret Lane ; illustrations by Patricia Casey. — London : Methuen, 1981. — [28]p : col.ill ; 22cm
ISBN 0-416-05920-1 : £3.95 : CIP rev. B81-28119

Lang, Andrew. The chronicles of Pantouflia. — London : Methuen Children's Books, Jan.1982. — [196]p
ISBN 0-416-21940-3 : £4.95 : CIP entry B81-34397

Langholm, A. D.. The bewitching of Alison Allbright / A.D. Langholm. — [London] : Carousel, 1982, c1979. — 190p ; 17cm
Originally published: London : W.H. Allen, 1979
ISBN 0-552-52160-4 (pbk) : £0.95 B82-12579

Lavelle, Sheila. The fiend next door / Sheila Lavelle ; illustrated by Linda Birch. — London : Hamilton, 1982. — 108p : ill ; 23cm
ISBN 0-241-10774-1 : £4.95 : CIP rev. B82-07398

Lavelle, Sheila. Mr Ginger's potato / words by Sheila Lavelle ; with pictures by Anni Axworthy. — London : Black, 1981. — [26]p : col.ill ; 20x27cm. — (Fact and fancy books ; 28)
ISBN 0-7136-2092-7 : £2.95 B82-06087

Lavelle, Sheila. Myrtle turtle / words by Sheila Lavelle ; with pictures by Anni Axworthy. — London : Black, 1981. — [24]p : col.ill ; 20x27cm. — (Fact and fancy books ; 27)
ISBN 0-7136-2093-5 : £2.95 B82-06088

Lavelle, Sheila. Ursula flying. — London : H. Hamilton, July 1981. — [48]p. — (Gazelle series)
ISBN 0-241-10651-6 : £1.80 : CIP entry B81-14956

Law, Felicia. Lost baggage / Felicia Law ; art: Lynn Breeze. — London : Hodder and Stoughton Children's Books, 1982. — 44p : col.ill ; 26cm
ISBN 0-340-27973-7 : £4.95 : CIP rev. B82-15728

Leavy, Una. Shoes for Tom / Una Leavy ; pictures by Nita Sowter. — London : Abelard, 1981. — [28]p : col.ill ; 19cm
ISBN 0-200-72767-2 : £3.50 : CIP rev. B81-23870

Leavy, Una. Tom's garden / Una Leavy ; pictures by Nita Sowter. — London : Abelard, 1981. — [28]p : col.ill ; 19cm
ISBN 0-200-72766-4 : £3.50 : CIP rev. B81-23869

Lee, Samantha. The path through the circle of time / Samantha Lee ; with illustrations by Pat Hannah. — London : Arlington, 1980. — 140p : ill ; 25cm. — (The Lightbringer trilogy)
ISBN 0-85140-508-8 : £4.50 : CIP rev. B80-18051

Lee, Tanith. Prince on a white horse / Tanith Lee. — London : Macmillan Children's Books, 1982. — 157p ; 21cm
ISBN 0-333-32929-5 : £5.50 : CIP rev. B82-03802

Leeson, Robert. Grange Hill for sale / Robert Leeson ; based on the BBC television series Grange Hill by Phil Redmond. — London : British Broadcasting Corporation, 1981. — 128p ; 22cm
ISBN 0-563-20025-1 : £4.75 B82-03019

Leeson, Robert. Harold and Bella, Jammy and me / Robert Leeson. — London : Hamilton in association with Fontana, 1982, c1980. — 125p ; 21cm
Originally published: London : Fontana : 1980
ISBN 0-241-10722-9 : £4.95 : CIP rev. B81-36383

Leeson, Robert. 'Maroon boy / Robert Leeson. — London : Fontana, 1982, c1974. — 190p ; 18cm
Originally published: London : Collins, 1974
ISBN 0-00-672097-8 (pbk) : £1.25 B82-36063

Leitch, Patricia. The Magic pony / Patricia Leitch. — London : Fontana, c1982. — 127p ; 18cm. — (An Original Armada)
ISBN 0-00-691929-4 (pbk) : £0.85 B82-19735

Letts, Barry. Doctor Who and the dæmons : based on the BBC television serial by Guy Leopold by arrangement with the British Broadcasting Corporation / Barry Letts ; illustrated by Alan Willow. — London : W.H. Allen, 1982, c1974. — 170p : ill ; 21cm
Originally published: London : Target Books, 1974
ISBN 0-491-02687-0 : £4.95 B82-11369

Levy, Elizabeth. The case of the mile high race. — London : Knight Books Feb.1983. — [112]p
ISBN 0-340-32812-6 (pbk) : £0.95 : CIP entry B82-38072

Lewis, Naomi. Come with us. — London : Andersen Press, Feb.1982. — [32]p
ISBN 0-86264-011-3 : £3.95 : CIP entry B81-36962

Lewis, Naomi. Once upon a rainbow / story by Naomi Lewis ; pictures by Gabriele Eichenauer. — London : Cape, 1981. — [32]p : col.ill ; 28cm
ISBN 0-224-01842-6 : £4.95 : CIP rev. B81-27339

Lillington, Kenneth. What beckoning ghost?. — London : Faber, Jan.1983. — [128]p
ISBN 0-571-11959-x : CIP entry B82-32446

Lindsay, Gillian. Fox Barn / by Gillian Lindsay ; illustrated by Janet Duchesne. — London : Hamilton, 1982. — 88p : ill ; 20cm. — (Antelope books)
ISBN 0-241-10826-8 : £2.75 : CIP rev. B82-10800

Line, David. Under Plum Lake / David Line (Lionel Davidson) ; decorations by Mike Wilks. — London : Heinemann Educational, 1982, c1980. — 144p : ill ; 20cm
Originally published: under the name Lionel Davidson. London : Cape, 1980
ISBN 0-435-12263-0 : Unpriced B82-35733

Lingard, Joan. Strangers in the house / by Joan Lingard. — London : Hamish Hamilton, 1981. — 131p ; 23cm
ISBN 0-241-10671-0 : £4.95 : CIP rev. B81-25701

823'.914[J] — Children's stories in English, *1945-* **—** *Texts* *continuation*

Lingard, Joan. The twelfth day of July / Joan Lingard. — Harmondsworth : Puffin in association with Hamilton, 1973, c1970 (1981 [printing]). — 127p ; 18cm. — (A Kevin and Sadie story) (Puffin plus)
Originally published: London : Hamilton, 1970
ISBN 0-14-030635-8 (pbk) : £0.85 B82-09144

Little, Patrick. Knight of swords / Patrick Little. — London : Macmillan, 1982. — 206p : 1map ; 21cm
ISBN 0-333-32855-8 : £5.50 : CIP rev.
B82-11755

Lively, Penelope. The revenge of Samuel Stokes / by Penelope Lively. — London : Heinemann, 1981. — 122p ; 22cm
ISBN 0-434-94889-6 : £4.95 B82-11364

Lloyd, Errol. Nandy's bedtime. — London : Bodley Head, June 1982. — [32]p
ISBN 0-370-30395-4 : £3.50 : CIP entry
B82-10477

Locke, Angela. Mr. Mullet owns a cloud. — London : Chatto & Windus, Sept.1982. — [128]p
ISBN 0-7011-2639-6 : £5.50 : CIP entry
B82-19812

Lockwood, Jennifer. Friday every day. — London : H. Hamilton, July 1981. — [48]p. — (Gazelle series)
ISBN 0-241-10652-4 : £1.80 : CIP entry
B81-17523

Longden, Peter. The missing ambassador / written and illustrated by Peter Longden. — Loughborough : Ladybird, 1982. — 51p : col.ill ; 18cm. — (Adventures of Major Tom)
ISBN 0-7214-0708-0 : £0.50 B82-16172

Longden, Peter. The planet of the elves / written and illustrated by Peter Longden. — Loughborough : Ladybird, 1982. — 51p : col.ill ; 18cm. — (Adventures of Major Tom)
ISBN 0-7214-0698-x : £0.50 B82-16173

Longden, Peter. The space pirates / written and illustrated by Peter Longden. — Loughborough : Ladybird, 1982. — 51p : col.ill ; 18cm. — (Adventures of Major Tom)
ISBN 0-7214-0709-9 : £0.50 B82-16174

Lucie-Smith, Edward. Bertie and the big red ball. — London : J. Murray, Oct.1982. — [32]p
ISBN 0-7195-3976-5 : £4.95 : CIP entry
B82-23021

Lydecker, John. Doctor Who and warriors' gate / based on the BBC television serial by Steve Gallagher by arrangement with the British Broadcasting Corporation ; John Lydecker. — London : W.H. Allen, 1982. — 124p ; 18cm. — (A Target book)
ISBN 0-426-20146-9 (pbk) : £1.25 B82-29947

MacBeth, George. The rectory mice. — London : Hutchinson, Sept.1982. — [208]p
ISBN 0-09-147940-1 : £5.95 : CIP entry
B82-19107

McCaffrey, Mary. Smoke-drift to heaven / Mary McCaffrey. — London : Abelard, 1981. — 96p ; 21cm
ISBN 0-200-72763-x : £4.25 : CIP rev.
B81-23867

McCann, Sean. Hot shot!. — London : Hodder & Stoughton, Sept.1981. — [96]p
Originally published: 1979
ISBN 0-340-26539-6 (pbk) : £0.85 : CIP entry
B81-23926

McCann, Sean. Shooting stars / Sean McCann ; illustrated by Barry Raynor. — [Sevenoaks] : Knight Books, 1980, c1978. — 92p : ill ; 18cm
Originally published: Sevenoaks : Hodder and Stoughton, 1978
ISBN 0-340-25497-1 (pbk) : £0.75 : CIP rev.
B80-12620

McCann, Sean. The team that nobody wanted / Sean McCann ; illustrated by Barry Raynor. — London : Hodder and Stoughton, 1982. — 94p : ill ; 21cm
ISBN 0-340-27883-8 : £4.25 : CIP rev.
B82-15725

McClure, Gillian. What's the time, Rory Wolf? / story and pictures by Gillian McClure. — London : Deutsch, 1982. — [30]p : col.ill ; 26cm
ISBN 0-233-97439-3 : £4.95 : CIP rev.
B82-08076

McCrum, Robert. The magic mouse and the millionaire / Robert McCrum ; illustrated by Michael Foreman. — London : Hamilton Children's, 1982. — [34]p : col.ill ; 29cm
ISBN 0-241-10720-2 : £4.25 : CIP rev.
B82-01831

McCullagh, Sheila K.. Captain Rasha and the golden dragon / Sheila K. McCullagh ; illustrated by Derek Collard. — Rev. ed. — Leeds : E.J. Arnold, 1981, c1980. — 72p : col.ill ; 20cm. — (Buccaneers ; 7)
Previous ed.: 1980. — Text on front inside cover
ISBN 0-560-04334-1 (pbk) : Unpriced
B82-31165

McCullagh, Sheila K.. The fight for Ramir / Sheila K. McCullagh ; illustrated by Derek Collard. — Rev. ed. — Leeds : E.J. Arnold, 1981, c1980. — 64p : col.ill ; 20cm. — (Buccaneers ; 5)
Previous ed.: 1980. — Text on front inside cover
ISBN 0-560-04332-5 (pbk) : Unpriced
B82-31170

McCullagh, Sheila K.. The island of fire / Sheila K. McCullagh ; illustrated by Derek Collard. — Rev. ed. — Leeds : E.J. Arnold, 1981, c1980. — 72p : col.ill ; 20cm. — (Buccaneers ; 8)
Previous ed.: 1980. — Text on front inside cover
ISBN 0-560-04335-x (pbk) : Unpriced
B82-31166

McCullagh, Sheila K.. The island of Solomon Dee / Sheila K. McCullagh ; illustrated by Derek Collard. — Rev. ed. — Leeds : E.J. Arnold, 1981, c1980. — 63p : col.ill ; 20cm. — (Buccaneers ; 2)
Previous ed.: 1980. — Text on front inside cover
ISBN 0-560-04329-5 (pbk) : Unpriced
B82-31172

McCullagh, Sheila K.. The journey through the strange land / Sheila K. McCullagh ; illustrated by Derek Collard. — Rev. ed. — Leeds : E.J. Arnold, 1981, c1980. — 64p : col.ill ; 20cm. — (Buccaneers ; 4)
Previous ed.: 1980. — Text on front inside cover
ISBN 0-560-04331-7 (pbk) : Unpriced
B82-31169

McCullagh, Sheila K.. The mystery of the blue whale / Sheila K. McCullagh ; illustrated by Derek Collard. — Rev. ed. — Leeds : E.J. Arnold, 1981, c1980. — 63p : col.ill ; 20cm. — (Buccaneers ; 3)
Previous ed.: 1980. — Text on front inside cover
ISBN 0-560-04330-9 (pbk) : Unpriced
B82-31168

McCullagh, Sheila K.. The silver ship / Sheila K. McCullagh ; illustrated by Derek Collard. — Rev. ed. — Leeds : E.J. Arnold, 1981, c1980. — 64p : col.ill ; 20cm. — (Buccaneers ; 1)
Previous ed.: 1980. — Text on front inside cover
ISBN 0-560-04328-7 (pbk) : Unpriced
B82-31171

McCullagh, Sheila K.. The stolen treasure / Sheila K. McCullagh ; illustrated by Derek Collard. — Rev. ed. — Leeds : E.J. Arnold, 1981, c1980. — 64p : col.ill ; 20cm. — (Buccaneers ; 6)
Previous ed.: 1980. — Text on front inside cover
ISBN 0-560-04333-3 (pbk) : Unpriced
B82-31167

Macdonald, Maryann. Peter gets angry : by Maryann Macdonald / illustrated by Ruth Bartlett. — Cambridge : Dinosaur, c1981. — [24]p : col.ill ; 16x19cm. — (Dinosaur's Althea books)
ISBN 0-85122-278-1 (cased) : £2.25
ISBN 0-85122-262-5 (pbk) : £0.70 B82-07175

McKee, David. I hate my teddy bear. — London : Andersen Press, Oct.1982. — [32]p
ISBN 0-86264-016-4 : £3.95 : CIP entry
B82-24591

McKee, David. King Rollo and King Frank / David McKee. — London : Andersen Press, c1981. — [25]p : chiefly col.ill ; 13cm
ISBN 0-905478-97-5 : £0.95 : CIP rev.
B81-27465

McKee, David. King Rollo and the bath / David McKee. — London : Andersen Press, c1981. — [25]p : chiefly col.ill ; 13cm
ISBN 0-905478-96-7 : £0.95 : CIP rev.
B81-27464

McKee, David. King Rollo and the search / David McKee. — London : Andersen Press, c1981. — [25]p : chiefly col.ill ; 13cm
ISBN 0-905478-98-3 : £0.95 : CIP rev.
B81-27420

Maclean, Colin. My word and picture book. — London : Ward Lock, Sept.1982. — [80]p
ISBN 0-7063-6214-4 : £2.95 : CIP entry
B82-20017

McNaughton, Colin. Fat pig / by Colin McNaughton. — London : Ernest Benn, 1981. — [28]p : col.ill ; 18cm. — (The Little library)
ISBN 0-510-00036-3 : £1.50 B82-00055

McNaughton, Colin. Football crazy / Colin McNaughton. — London : Piccolo Picture Book in association with Heinemann, 1982, c1980. — [32]p : col.ill ; 22cm
Originally published: London : Heinemann, 1980
ISBN 0-330-26747-7 (pbk) : £1.25 B82-22154

Maddocks, Peter. Animal antics. — London : Hodder & Stoughton Children's Books, Sept.1982. — [32]p
ISBN 0-340-28329-7 : £2.95 : CIP entry
B82-18813

Mahy, Margaret. The haunting / Margaret Mahy. — London : Dent, 1982. — 135p ; 23cm
ISBN 0-460-06097-x : £4.95 : CIP rev.
B82-13239

Mahy, Margaret. A lion in the meadow / story by Margaret Mahy ; pictures by Jennie Williams. — Harmondsworth : Puffin, 1972, c1969 (1981 [printing]). — 21p : col.ill ; 18x23cm. — (Picture Puffins)
Originally published: London : Dent, 1969. — Text on inside covers
ISBN 0-14-050043-x (pbk) : £0.95 B82-09162

Main, Carol. The white planet / Carol Main. — London : Hodder and Stoughton, 1982. — 125p ; 23cm
ISBN 0-340-27968-0 : £4.95 : CIP rev.
B82-06727

Manning, Rosemary. Dragon in the harbour / Rosemary Manning ; illustrated by Peter Rush. — Harmondsworth : Puffin, 1982, c1980. — 184p : ill,music ; 19cm
Originally published: Harmondsworth : Kestrel, 1980
ISBN 0-14-031423-7 (pbk) : £1.00 B82-29587

823'.914[J] — Children's stories in English, ***1945-*** ***— Texts*** *continuation*

Maris, Ron. Better move on frog. — London : MacRae Books, May 1982. — [32]p
ISBN 0-86203-083-8 : £4.95 : CIP entry
B82-07684

Mark, Jan. The dead letter box / by Jan Mark ; illustrated by Mary Rayner. — London : Hamilton, 1982. — 90p : ill ; 20cm. — (Antelope books)
ISBN 0-241-10804-7 : £2.75 : CIP rev.
B82-10702

Mark, Jan. Under the autumn garden / by Jan Mark ; illustrated by Colin Twinn. — London : Heinemann Educational, 1982, c1977. — 175p : ill ; 19cm. — (The New windmill series ; 264)
Originally published: Harmondsworth : Kestrel, 1977
ISBN 0-435-12264-9 : £1.70 B82-34222

Marks, Graham. The big surprise. — London : Hodder & Stoughton Children's Books, Jan.1983. — [32]p
ISBN 0-340-28777-2 : £4.50 : CIP entry
B82-33747

Marks, Graham. Stoby Binder. — London : Hodder & Stoughton Children's Books, Sept.1982. — [96]p
ISBN 0-340-28153-7 : £4.25 : CIP entry
B82-18812

Marriott, Jack. A friend for Sam : a story about 1 / drawings by Pete Beard. — St Albans : Hart-Davis Educational for Granada Television, c1980. — 15p : col.ill ; 21cm. — (Sam and Squeak stories. Set one)
With: Two for fun / by Jo Kemp
ISBN 0-247-13191-1 (unbound) : Unpriced
ISBN 0-247-12156-3 (set) : Unpriced
B82-38599

Marriott, Jack. Three bad cats : a story about 3 / by Jack Marriott and John Coop ; drawings by Pete Beard. — St Albans : Hart-Davis Educational for Granada Television, c1983. — 15p : col.ill ; 22cm. — (Sam and Squeak stories. Set one)
With: A bed for Squeak / by Jack Marriott
ISBN 0-247-13193-8 (unbound) : Unpriced
ISBN 0-247-13156-3 (set) : Unpriced
B82-38598

Marshall, Frances. Princess Kalina and the hedgehog / original text by Jeannette B. Flat ; adapted by Frances Marshall ; with pictures by Dorothée Duntze. — London : Faber in association with Nord-Süd, 1981. — [16]p : col.ill ; 30cm
ISBN 0-571-11844-5 : £3.50 : CIP rev.
B81-23756

Marshall, Ray, *1957-*. The crocodile and the dumper truck : a reptilian guide to London : a pop-up book / by Ray Marshall and Korky Paul. — London : Deutsch, 1982. — [12]p : chiefly col.ill ; 26cm
ISBN 0-233-97410-5 : £4.95 B82-22709

Marshall, Sybil. Who stopped the clock? : a story about 9 / by Sybil Marshall and John Coop ; drawings by Pete Beard. — St Albans : Hart-Davis Educational for Granada Television, c1980. — 15p : col.ill ; 22cm. — (Sam and Squeak stories. Set one)
With: Bundles of ten / by Sybil Marshall
ISBN 0-247-13196-2 (unbound) : Unpriced
ISBN 0-247-13156-3 (set) : Unpriced
B82-38597

Marshall, Yvonne. The bird. — London : Evans Bros, Apr.1981. — [24]p. — (Hide-and-seek series)
ISBN 0-237-45535-8 : £1.95 : CIP entry
B81-00611

Marshall, Yvonne. The bumble-bee. — London : Evans Bros, Apr.1981. — [24]p. — (Hide-and-seek series)
ISBN 0-237-45537-4 : £1.95 : CIP entry
B81-00612

Marshall, Yvonne. The cat. — London : Evans Bros, Apr.1981. — [24]p. — (Hide-and-seek series)
ISBN 0-237-45536-6 : £1.95 : CIP entry
B81-00613

Marshall, Yvonne. Nasim. — London : Evans Bros, Apr.1981. — [24]p. — (Hide-and-seek series)
ISBN 0-237-45534-x : £1.95 : CIP entry
B81-00614

Martin, Su. The lion that snored. — Telford (84 Wolverley Court, Woodside, Telford) : Woody Books Cooperative, Dec.1982. — [18]p
ISBN 0-907751-12-1 (pbk) : £0.75 : CIP entry
B82-36334

Martyn, Harriet. Jenny and the syndicate / Harriet Martyn. — London : Deutsch, 1982. — 200p ; 20cm. — (A Balcombe Hall story)
ISBN 0-233-97436-9 (pbk) : £3.95 : CIP rev.
B82-06222

Mattingley, Christopher. The jetty. — Sevenoaks : Hodder & Stoughton, June 1981. — [128]p
ISBN 0-340-26530-2 (pbk) : £0.85 : CIP entry
B81-09989

Mayne, William. The mouse and the egg / William Mayne ; with pictures by Krystyna Turska. — London : Fontana Picture Lions, 1982, c1980. — [32]p : col.ill ; 22cm
Originally published: London : MacRae, 1980
ISBN 0-00-661884-7 (pbk) : £0.90 B82-16830

Mayne, William. Salt Rivers times / William Mayne ; illustrations by Elizabeth Honey. — [Ringwood, Vic.] ; [Harmondsworth] : Puffin, 1982, c1980. — 178p : ill ; 20cm
Originally published: London : Hamilton, 1980
ISBN 0-14-031499-7 (pbk) : £1.25 B82-40674

Mayne, William. Skiffy and the twin planets. — London : Hamilton, Oct.1982. — [144]p
ISBN 0-241-10835-7 : £4.95 : CIP entry
B82-23108

Mayne, William. Winter quarters. — London : Cape, Oct.1982. — [144]p
ISBN 0-224-02035-8 : £5.50 : CIP entry
B82-24363

Meredith, Lucy. The paper aeroplane / Fulvio Testa ; retold by Lucy Meredith. — London : Faber in association with Nord-Süd, 1981. — [26]p : col.ill ; 30cm
ISBN 0-571-11845-3 : £3.95 : CIP rev.
B81-20555

Mickey's film show. — Bristol : Purnell, 1982. — [8]p : chiefly col.ill ; 11x14cm
ISBN 0-361-05308-8 (unbound) : £0.40
B82-26040

Miller, Margaret J.. The mad muddle / Margaret J. Miller ; illustrated by Janina Ede. — London : Hodder and Stoughton, 1982. — 96p : ill ; 20cm
ISBN 0-340-27253-8 : £3.50 : CIP rev.
B81-36358

Milne, Paula. S.W.A.L.K.. — London : Methuen Children's, Feb.1983. — [144]p
ISBN 0-423-00820-x : £3.95 : CIP entry
B82-40889

Mitson, Angela. The Munch Bunch have a party / illustrations by Angela Mitson ; written by Giles Reed. — Ipswich : Studio Publications, 1979. — [32]p : chiefly col.ill ; 21cm
ISBN 0-904584-57-7 (cased) : £1.50
ISBN 0-904584-79-8 (pbk) : Unpriced
B82-00602

Moodie, Fiona. Beauty and the beast / Fiona Moodie. — London : Macdonald Futura, 1981. — [26]p : col.ill ; 21x30cm
These illustrations originally published: with German text
ISBN 0-354-08121-7 : £4.25 B82-35442

Moon, Heather. Winklepicker. — Sevenoaks : Hodder & Stoughton, July, 1981. — [160]p
ISBN 0-340-26534-5 (pbk) : £0.85 : CIP entry
B81-13816

Moon, Heather. Winklepicker goes south / Heather Moon ; illustrated by Gavin Rowe. — London : Hodder and Stoughton, c1982. — 158p : ill,2maps ; 23cm
ISBN 0-340-26577-9 : £4.95 : CIP rev.
B82-07437

Moore, Inga. Atkil's rescue. — Oxford : Oxford University Press, Sept.1982. — [32]p
ISBN 0-19-279772-7 : £4.50 : CIP entry
B82-21383

Moore, John, *1951-*. Granny Stickleback / John Moore and Martin Wright. — London : Hamilton, 1981. — [28]p : col.ill ; 27cm
Ill on lining papers
ISBN 0-241-10635-4 : £4.50 : CIP rev.
B81-26781

Moore, Katharine. The little stolen sweep / by Katharine Moore ; illustrated by Pat Marriott. — London : Allison & Busby, 1982. — 121p : ill ; 23cm
ISBN 0-85031-414-3 : £4.95 : CIP rev.
B81-20130

Moore, Katharine. Moog. — London : Allison & Busby, Aug.1982. — [96]p
ISBN 0-85031-478-x : £4.95 : CIP entry
B82-18580

Moore, Susan. Silvery Cove's peculiar people / Susan Moore. — Bognor Regis : New Horizon, c1982. — 57p,[12]leaves of plates : col.ill ; 21cm
ISBN 0-86116-603-5 : £3.50 B82-26013

Morecambe, Eric. The reluctant vampire / Eric Morecambe ; illustrated by Tony Ross. — London : Methuen Children's Books, 1982. — 135p : ill ; 21cm
ISBN 0-416-25860-3 : £4.95 : CIP rev.
B82-20181

Morgan, David R. (David Richard). The strange case of William Whipper-Snapper / David R. Morgan. — Winchester : Hambleside, c1982. — 151p ; 18cm. — (A Terrapin book)
ISBN 0-86042-042-6 (pbk) : £1.40 B82-35736

Morgensen, Jan. Ted and the Chinese princess. — London : Hamilton, Feb.1983. — [40]p
ISBN 0-241-10912-4 : £4.50 : CIP entry
B82-37851

Morris, Neil. Charlie waits for tea. — London : Hodder & Stoughton Children's Books, Jan.1983. — [24]p
ISBN 0-340-28494-3 : £1.75 : CIP entry
B82-33736

Morris, Neil. Diana makes a playhouse. — London : Hodder & Stoughton Children's Books, Jan.1983. — [24]p
ISBN 0-340-28493-5 : £1.75 : CIP entry
B82-33735

Morris, Neil. Eve plays with her toys. — London : Hodder & Stoughton, Jan.1983. — [24]p
ISBN 0-340-28496-x : £1.75 : CIP entry
B82-33738

Morris, Neil. Find the canary. — London : Hodder and Stoughton Children's Books, Feb.1982. — [24]p. — (Mystery pictures)
ISBN 0-340-27463-8 : £1.75 : CIP entry
B81-36360

Morris, Neil. Hide and seek. — London : Hodder and Stoughton Children's Books, Feb.1982. — [24]p. — (Mystery pictures)
ISBN 0-340-27464-6 : £1.75 : CIP entry
B81-36361

823'.914[J] — Children's stories in English, *1945- — Texts continuation*

Morris, Neil. Sam finds his clothes. — London : Hodder & Stoughton Children's Books, Jan.1983. — [24]p
ISBN 0-340-28495-1 : £1.75 : CIP entry
B82-33737

Morris, Neil. Search for Sam. — London : Hodder and Stoughton Children's Books, Feb.1982. — [24]p. — (Mystery pictures)
ISBN 0-340-27461-1 : £1.75 : CIP entry
B81-36357

Morris, Neil. Where's my hat?. — London : Hodder and Stoughton Children's Books, Feb.1982. — [24]p. — (Mystery pictures)
ISBN 0-340-27462-x : £1.75 : CIP entry
B81-36359

Muir, Frank. Prince What-a-mess / Frank Muir ; illustrated by Joseph Wright. — London : Transworld, 1981, c1979. — [32]p : col.ill ; 28cm. — (A Carousel book)
Originally published: London : Benn, 1979
ISBN 0-552-52146-9 (pbk) : £0.95 B82-03295

Mullen, Michael. Magus the lollipop man / MIchael Mullen ; illustrated by Harry Horse. — Edinburgh : Cannongate, 1981. — 97p : ill ; 23cm
ISBN 0-86241-020-7 : £4.95 B82-08826

Mullen, Michael. Sea wolves from the north. — Dublin : Wolfhound, Nov.1982. — [112]p
ISBN 0-905473-94-9 : £4.95 : CIP entry
B82-37667

Munthe, Adam John. I believe in unicorns / Adam John Munthe, Elizabeth Falconer. — London : Chatto & Windus, 1979. — [32]p : col.ill ; 20x25cm
ISBN 0-7011-2437-7 : £3.50 : CIP rev.
B79-10666

Murphy, Jill. A bad spell for the worst witch / written and illustrated by Jill Murphy. — Harmondsworth : Kestrel, 1982. — 127p : ill ; 23cm
ISBN 0-7226-5763-3 : £4.50 B82-36115

Naughton, Bill. My pal Spadger / Bill Naughton ; illustrated by Charles Mozley. — Harmondsworth : Puffin, 1982, c1977. — 127p : ill ; 19cm
Originally published: London : Dent, 1977
ISBN 0-14-031379-6 (pbk) : £0.90 B82-16772

Needle, Jan. Another fine mess / Jan Needle ; illustrated by Roy Bentley. — London : Deutsch, 1981. — 189p : ill ; 21cm
ISBN 0-233-97370-2 : £4.95 : CIP rev.
B81-28827

Needle, Jan. Losers weepers / Jan Needle ; illustrated by Jane Bottomley. — London : Metheun Children's, 1981. — 126p : ill ; 20cm. — (A Pied Piper book)
ISBN 0-416-21510-6 : £3.95 : CIP rev.
B81-30158

Needle, Jan. Piggy in the middle. — London : Deutsch, Sept.1982. — [32]p
ISBN 0-233-97481-4 : £3.95 : CIP entry
B82-20196

Needle, Jan. Wild wood. — London : Deutsch, May 1981. — [192]p
ISBN 0-233-97346-x : £4.95 : CIP entry
B81-04385

Nesbitt, Jo. The great escape of Doreen Potts / written and illustrated by Jo Nesbitt. — London : Sheba Feminist, 1981. — 80p : ill ; 23cm
ISBN 0-907179-07-x (pbk) : £2.50 B82-02121

Newman, Marjorie. The amazing pet / Marjorie Newman ; illustrated by Janet Duchesne. — London : H. Hamilton, 1982. — 48p : ill ; 20cm. — (Gazelle books)
ISBN 0-241-10776-8 : £1.95 : CIP rev.
B82-07399

Newman, Nanette. That dog! / Nanette Newman ; illustrated by Penny Simon. — [London] : Carousel, 1981, c1980. — [50]p ; 18cm
Originally published: London : Heinemann, 1980
ISBN 0-552-52147-7 (pbk) : £0.85 B82-03237

Nichols, Grace. Trust you, Wriggly!. — Sevenoaks : Hodder and Stoughton, Apr.1981. — [128]p
ISBN 0-340-25555-2 : £3.25 : CIP entry
B81-01331

Nicoll, Helen. Meg's veg / Helen Nicoll and Jan Pieńkowski. — Harmondsworth : Puffin, 1982, c1976. — [36]p : col.ill ; 21cm. — (Picture puffin)
Cover title. — Originally published: London : Heinemann, 1976
ISBN 0-14-050356-0 (pbk) : £1.00 B82-16758

Norton, André. Outside. — London : Hodder and Stoughton, Sept.1982. — [128]p. — (Knight books)
Originally published: London : Blackie, 1976
ISBN 0-340-26810-7 (pbk) : £0.95 : CIP entry
B82-18806

Oakley, Graham. Hetty and Harriet / Graham Oakley. — London : Macmillan Children's Books, 1981. — [32]p : col.ill ; 25x27cm
ISBN 0-333-32373-4 : £3.95 : CIP rev.
B81-27357

O'Brien, Edna. The expedition. — London : Hodder and Stoughton Children's Books, Sept.1982. — [32]p
ISBN 0-340-27971-0 : £3.95 : CIP entry
B82-20752

O'Brien, Robert C.. Mrs Frisby and the rats of NIMH / Robert C. O'Brien. — Harmondsworth : Puffin, in association with Victor Gollancz, 1975, c1971 (1982 [printing]). — 197p ; 18cm. — (A Puffin book)
Originally published: New York : Atheneum, 1971 ; London : Gollancz, 1972
ISBN 0-14-030725-7 (pbk) : £1.10 B82-33026

O'Brine, Rory. Mr Pinkerton's hat / Rory O'Brine ; illustrated by Claire Mumford. — London : H. Hamilton, 1982. — [29]p : col.ill ; 24cm
ISBN 0-241-10819-5 : £4.50 : CIP rev.
B82-15693

O'Brine, Rory. Timmy's dog / Rory O'Brine ; illustrated by Thelma Lambert. — London : Hamish Hamilton Children's Books, 1982. — 48p : ill ; 20cm. — (Gazelle books)
ISBN 0-241-10825-x : £1.95 : CIP rev.
B82-15696

Offen, Hilda. Old William and the seventh sheep. — London : Methuen Children's, Jan.1983. — [32]p. — (Methuen picture story book)
ISBN 0-416-23540-9 : £3.50 : CIP entry
B82-34447

Ogilvy, Angus. Lionel and the secret hat / by Angus Ogilvy & Christine McArthur. — Edinburgh : Saint Andrew Press, 1981. — 40p : col.ill ; 29cm
Folded tricorn hat in plastic bag as insert
ISBN 0-7152-0483-1 : £1.95 B82-02277

O'Hare, Colette. Seven years and a day / Colette O'Hare & Beryl Cook. — London : Fontana, 1981, c1980. — [24]p : col.ill ; 25
Originally published: London : Collins, 1980
ISBN 0-00-661899-5 (pbk) : £1.25 B82-03167

Oldfield, Pamela. The Gumby gang on holiday. — London : Hodder and Stoughton, Jan.1983. — [96]p
Originally published: Glasgow : Blackie, 1980
ISBN 0-340-28561-3 (pbk) : £0.85 : CIP entry
B82-33739

Oldfield, Pamela. More about the Gumby Gang / Pamela Oldfield ; illustrated by Lesley Smith. — London : Hodder and Stoughton, 1982, c1979. — 96p : ill ; 18cm
Originally published: Glasgow : Blackie, 1979
ISBN 0-340-27530-8 (pbk) : £0.95 : CIP rev.
B81-34136

Oldfield, Pamela. Parkin's storm / Pamela Oldfield ; illustrated by Peter Westcott. — London : Abelard, 1982. — 63p : ill ; 21cm. — (A Grasshopper book)
ISBN 0-200-72774-5 (cased) : £3.95 : CIP rev.
ISBN 0-200-72775-3 (pbk) : £1.25 B82-07524

Oldfield, Pamela. The Willerbys' and the old castle. — London : Blackie, Oct.1982. — [64]p
ISBN 0-216-91283-0 : £4.95 : CIP entry
B82-23704

Oldfield, Pamela. The Willerbys and the sad clown / Pamela Oldfield ; illustrated by Shirley Bellwood. — London : Blackie, 1982. — 64p : ill ; 21cm
ISBN 0-216-91167-2 : £4.50 : CIP rev.
B82-04298

Oram, Hiawyn. Angry Arthur / text by Hiawyn Oram ; pictures by Satoshi Kitamura. — London : Anderson, 1982. — [29]p : col.ill ; 24cm
ISBN 0-86264-017-2 : £3.95 : CIP rev.
B82-07691

Orgill, Douglas. Brother Esau. — London : Bodley Head, Apr.1982. — [256]p
ISBN 0-370-30433-0 : £6.95 : CIP entry
B82-03840

Ormerod, Jan. Be brave Billy. — London : Dent, Oct.1982. — [32]p
ISBN 0-460-06093-7 : £3.50 : CIP entry
B82-23322

O'Sullivan, Kay J.. The adventures of Bamfrey / Kay J. O'Sullivan ; illustrated by Wendy R. Duffin. — Ilfracombe : Stockwell, 1981. — 32p : ill ; 19cm
ISBN 0-7223-1542-2 (pbk) : £0.85 B82-10404

Oxenbury, Helen. Animals. — London : Methuen/Walker, Apr.1982. — [14]p
ISBN 0-416-06070-6 : £1.25 : CIP entry
B82-06226

Oxenbury, Helen. Bedtime. — London : Methuen/Walker, Apr.1982. — [14]p
ISBN 0-416-06090-0 : £1.25 : CIP entry
B82-06228

Oxenbury, Helen. Bill and Stanley / Helen Oxenbury. — London : Ernest Benn, 1981. — [28]p : col.ill ; 18cm. — (The Little library)
ISBN 0-510-00111-4 : £1.50 B82-00058

Oxenbury, Helen. Helping. — London : Methuen/Walker, Apr.1982. — [14]p
ISBN 0-416-06080-3 : £1.25 : CIP entry
B82-06227

Oxenbury, Helen. Holidays. — London : Methuen/Walker Books, Apr.1982. — [14]p
ISBN 0-416-06050-1 : £1.25 : CIP entry
B82-06224

Oxenbury, Helen. Shopping. — London : Methuen/Walker, Apr.1982. — [14]p
ISBN 0-416-06060-9 : £1.25 : CIP entry
B82-06225

Oxley, Dorothy. Wheelchair summer / Dorothy Oxley. — Tring : Lion, 1982. — 128p : ill,1map ; 18cm
ISBN 0-85648-330-3 (pbk) : £1.25 B82-35438

Page, Ian. Learning Tree and a terrible tummy ache / Ian Page ; [illustrated by Keith Aldred and Bridget Appleby]. — London : Sackett and Marshall, 1979. — 32p : col.ill ; 20cm
ISBN 0-86109-057-8 (pbk) : £0.50 B82-00008

823'.914[J] — Children's stories in English, *1945-* — *Texts* *continuation*

Page, Ian. Learning Tree and Mrs Blackbird's nest / Ian Page ; [illustrated by Keith Aldred and Bridget Appleby]. — London : Sackett and Marshall, 1979. — 32p : col.ill ; 20cm
ISBN 0-86109-053-5 (pbk) : £0.50 B82-00011

Page, Ian. Learning Tree and the lucky escape / Ian Page ; [illustrated by Keith Aldred and Bridget Appleby]. — London : Sackett and Marshall, 1979. — 32p : col.ill ; 20cm
ISBN 0-86109-056-x (pbk) : £0.50 B82-00012

Page, Ian. Learning Tree and the old tin can / Ian Page ; [illustrated by Keith Aldred and Bridget Appleby]. — London : Sackett and Marshall, 1979. — 32p : col.ill ; 20cm
ISBN 0-86109-054-3 (pbk) : £0.50 B82-00009

Page, Ian. Learning Tree and the Otter / Ian Page ; [illustrated by Keith Aldred and Bridget Appleby]. — London : Sackett and Marshall, 1979. — 32p : col.ill ; 20cm
ISBN 0-86109-055-1 (pbk) : £0.50 B82-00010

Palin, Michael. Small Harry and the toothache pills / Michael Palin ; illustrated by Caroline Holden. — London : Methuen, 1982. — [32]p : col.ill ; 28cm
ISBN 0-416-21760-5 (cased) : Unpriced : CIP rev.
ISBN 0-416-23690-1 (pbk) : Unpriced
B82-19233

Parsons, Virginia. To please the king. — London : Hodder & Stoughton Children's Books, Apr.1982. — [32]p
ISBN 0-340-27251-1 : £3.95 : CIP entry
B82-04844

Partridge, Jenny. Dominic Sly / Jenny Partridge. — Kingswood : World's Work Children's, c1981. — [25]p : col.ill ; 17cm. — ([An Oakapple Wood story])
ISBN 0-437-66175-x : £1.95 B82-07162

Partridge, Jenny. Grandma Snuffles / Jenny Partridge. — Kingswood : World's Work Children's, c1981. — [25]p : col.ill ; 17cm. — ([An Oakapple Wood story])
ISBN 0-437-66176-8 : £1.95 B82-07163

Partridge, Jenny. Harriet Plume / Jenny Partridge. — Kingswood : World's Work Children's, c1981. — [25]p : col.ill ; 17cm. — ([An Oakapple Wood story])
ISBN 0-437-66178-4 : £1.95 B82-07164

Partridge, Jenny. Lop-ear / Jenny Partridge. — Kingswood : World's Work Children's, c1981. — [26]p : col.ill ; 17cm. — ([An Oakapple Wood story])
ISBN 0-437-66177-6 : £1.95 B82-07161

Paton Walsh, Jill. Babylon / story by Jill Paton Walsh ; pictures by Jennifer Northway. — London : Deutsch, 1982, c1981. — [32]p : col.ill ; 26cm
ISBN 0-233-97362-1 : £4.95 : CIP rev.
B81-26714

Paton Walsh, Jill. The green book / Jill Paton Walsh ; illustrated by Joanna Stubbs. — London : Macmillan Children's, c1981. — 112p : ill ; 21cm
ISBN 0-333-31910-9 : £4.95 : CIP rev.
B81-27358

Patterson, Geoffrey. A pig's tale. — London : Deutsch, Sept.1982. — [32]p
ISBN 0-233-97477-6 : £4.95 : CIP entry
B82-20195

Peake, E. C.. The secret citadel of the apemen / by E.C. Peake. — London : Regency Press, c1980. — 89p ; 23cm
ISBN 0-7212-0596-8 : £3.00 B82-15105

Peppé, Rodney. Run rabbit, run! / Rodney Peppé. — London : Methuen Children's Books, 1982. — [10]p : col.ill ; 23cm
A pop-up book
ISBN 0-416-22060-6 : Unpriced B82-34957

Perkins, Janet. Haffertee goes exploring / by Janet and John Perkins ; illustrations by Gillian Gaze. — [New] ed. — Tring : Lion Publishing, 1982, c1977. — 61p : ill ; 16cm. — (A Lion paperback)
Previous ed.: 1979
ISBN 0-85648-492-x (pbk) : £0.85 B82-28007

Perkins, Janet. Haffertee Hamster Diamond / by Janet and John Perkins ; illustrations by Gillian Gaze. — [New] ed. — Tring : Lion Publishing, 1982, c1977. — 60p : ill ; 18cm. — (A Lion paperback)
Previous ed.: 1979
ISBN 0-85648-490-3 (pbk) : £0.85 B82-28008

Perkins, Janet. Haffertee Hamster's new house / by Janet and John Perkins ; illustrations by Gillian Gaze. — [New] ed. — Tring : Lion Publishing, 1982, c1977. — 61p : ill ; 18cm. — (A Lion paperback)
Previous ed.: 1979
ISBN 0-85648-491-1 (pbk) : £0.85 B82-28006

Perkins, Janet. Haffertee's first Christmas / by Janet and John Perkins ; illustrations by Gillian Gaze. — [New] ed. — Tring : Lion Publishing, 1982, c1977. — 61p : ill ; 18cm. — (A Lion paperback)
Previous ed.: 1979
ISBN 0-85648-493-8 (pbk) : £0.85 B82-28009

Peyton, K. M.. The Beethoven medal / K.M. Peyton ; illustration by the author. — London : Magnet, 1982, c1971. — 152p : 1ill ; 18cm
Originally published: Oxford : Oxford University Press, 1971
ISBN 0-416-24720-2 (pbk) : £1.25 B82-33298

Peyton, K. M.. Going home / K.M. Peyton ; illustrated by Chris Molan. — Oxford : Oxford University Press, 1982. — 104p : ill ; 20cm. — (An Eagle book)
ISBN 0-19-271459-7 : £3.50 : CIP rev.
B82-04159

Peyton, K. M.. A midsummer night's death / K.M. Peyton. — Harmondsworth : Puffin in asssociation with Oxford University Press, 1981, c1978. — 148p ; 18cm. — (Puffin plus)
Originally published: Oxford : Oxford University Press, 1978
ISBN 0-14-031355-9 (pbk) : £1.00 B82-05951

Peyton, K. M.. Pennington's seventeenth summer / K.M. Peyton. — London : Magnet, 1982, c1970. — 154p : 1ill ; 18cm
Originally published: Oxford : Oxford University Press, 1970
ISBN 0-416-24710-5 (pbk) : £1.25 B82-33297

Peyton, K. M.. Prove yourself a hero / K.M. Peyton. — Harmondsworth : Puffin, 1982, c1977. — 172p ; 18cm. — (Puffin plus)
Originally published: Oxford : Oxford University Press, 1977
ISBN 0-14-031297-8 (pbk) : £1.10 B82-16780

Peyton, K. M.. The team / K.M. Peyton ; illustrated by the author. — London : Sparrow, 1982, c1975. — 204p ; 18cm
Originally published: London : Oxford University Press, 1975
ISBN 0-09-927680-1 (pbk) : £0.95 B82-14912

Pilgrim, Jane. Blackberry Farm story book. — London : Hodder & Stoughton Children's Books, Oct.1982. — [128]p
ISBN 0-340-28492-7 : £2.25 : CIP entry
B82-27351

Postma, Lidia. Tom Thumb. — London : Hutchinson, Oct.1982. — [32]p
ISBN 0-09-150510-0 : £4.50 : CIP entry
B82-24979

Potts, Richard, *1938-*. Tod's owl / Richard Potts ; illustrated by Maureen Bradley. — Sevenoaks : Knight, 1982, c1980. — 127p : ill ; 18cm
Originally published: London : Hodder & Stoughton, 1980
ISBN 0-340-27865-x (pbk) : £0.95 : CIP rev.
B82-03819

Powling, Chris. Daredevils or scaredycats / Chris Powling ; illustrated by Stephen Lavis. — London : Collins, 1981, c1979. — 112p ; 18cm. — (Fontana lions)
Originally published: London : Abelard-Schuman, 1979
ISBN 0-00-671897-3 (pbk) : £0.95 B82-06361

Powling, Chris. Mog and the Rectifier. — London : Knight, Dec.1982. — [144]p
Originally published: London : Abelard-Schuman, 1980
ISBN 0-340-28046-8 (pbk) : £0.95 : CIP entry
B82-29643

Powling, Chris. The Mustang machine / Chris Powling. — London : Arnold, 1981. — 123p ; 21cm
ISBN 0-200-72764-8 : £5.25 : CIP rev.
B81-23868

Powling, Chris. Under Neptune. — London : Abelard-Schuman, Oct.1982. — [96]p
ISBN 0-200-72781-8 : £5.95 : CIP entry
B82-23701

Pownall, David. The bunch from Bananas / David Pownall ; illustrated by Freire Wright. — Harmondsworth : Puffin, 1982, c1980. — 90p : ill ; 19cm. — (A Puffin book)
Originally published: London : Gollancz, 1980
ISBN 0-14-031343-5 (pbk) : £0.90 B82-33025

Prater, John. On Friday something funny happened / John Prater. — London : Bodley Head, 1982. — [25]p : chiefly col.ill ; 26cm
ISBN 0-370-30449-7 : £6.95 : CIP rev.
B82-09289

Price, Merlin. Edge / Merlin Price. — London : Rex Collings, 1981. — 128p : 1map ; 23cm
ISBN 0-86036-145-4 : £5.00 B82-03256

Prince, Alison. Mill Green on fire / Alison Prince. — London : Armada, 1982. — 128p ; 18cm
ISBN 0-00-691972-3 (pbk) : £0.85 B82-34105

Prince, Alison. The sinister airfield. — London : Methuen Children's Books, Feb.1982. — [128] p. — (A Pied Piper book)
ISBN 0-416-21440-1 : £3.95 : CIP entry
B81-35711

Prince, Maggie. Witch hill / Maggie Prince. — London : Abelard, 1982. — 95p ; 21cm
ISBN 0-200-72776-1 : £4.95 : CIP rev.
B82-10460

Pullein-Thompson, Christine. Phantom horse goes to Scotland. — London : Severn House, Dec.1982. — [128]p
ISBN 0-7278-0853-2 : £4.95 : CIP entry
B82-34073

Pullein-Thompson, Christine. Ponies in the park / Christine Pullein-Thompson ; illustrated by Tony Morris. — [London] : Beaver, c1982. — 126p : ill ; 18cm
ISBN 0-600-20457-x (pbk) : £0.95 B82-28793

Pullein-Thompson, Diana. A foal for Candy / Diana Pullein-Thompson. — London : Severn House, 1982, c1981. — 111p ; 21cm
ISBN 0-7278-0773-0 : £4.50 B82-22611

Pullein-Thompson, Diana. Riding with the Lyntons / Diana Pullein-Thompson. — London : Armada, 1982, c1956. — 160p ; 18cm
Originally published: London : Collins, 1956
ISBN 0-00-691986-3 (pbk) : £0.85 B82-19731

823'.914[J] — Children's stories in English, *1945-* *— Texts* *continuation*

Pullein-Thompson, Josephine. [All change]. The hidden horse / Josephine Pullein-Thompson. — London : Armada, 1982, c1961. — 160p : ill ; 19cm
Originally published: London : Benn, 1961
ISBN 0-00-691731-3 (pbk) : £0.85 B82-19732

Pullein-Thompson, Josephine. The no-good pony / Josephine Pullein-Thompson. — London : Severn House, 1982, c1981. — 128p ; 21cm
Originally published: London : Sparrow, 1981
ISBN 0-7278-0751-x : £4.25 : CIP rev. B81-30253

Pullein-Thompson, Josephine. The prize pony / Josephine Pullein-Thompson. — London : Arrow, 1982. — 108p ; 18cm. — (Sparrow books)
ISBN 0-09-928020-5 (pbk) : £0.95 B82-22072

Pullein-Thompson, Josephine. Treasure on the moor / Josephine Pullein-Thompson ; illustrated by Jon Davis. — London : Hodder and Stoughton, 1982. — 111p : ill ; 23cm
ISBN 0-340-26889-1 : £4.95 : CIP rev. B81-36352

Pullman, Philip. Count Karlstein. — London : Chatto & Windus, Oct.1982. — [192]p
ISBN 0-7011-2649-3 : £5.50 : CIP entry B82-23197

Ray, Mary. The windows of Elissa / Mary Ray. — London : Faber, 1982. — 183p ; 21cm
ISBN 0-571-11831-3 : £4.95 : CIP rev. B82-04593

Rees, David. The mysterious rattle. — London : Hamilton, Oct.1982. — [96]p
ISBN 0-241-10878-0 : £1.95 : CIP entry B82-23458

Reith, Angela. The great olympics / written by Angela Reith ; designed and illustrated by Peter Longden. — London : Ark, 1979. — [20]p : col.ill ; 15cm. — (Buddy bear books)
ISBN 0-85421-845-9 (pbk) : £0.40 B82-36780

Reith, Angela. The honey hullabaloo / written by Angela Reith ; designed and illustrated by Peter Longden. — London : Ark, 1979. — [20]p : col.ill ; 15cm. — (Buddy bear books)
ISBN 0-85421-846-7 (pbk) : £0.40 B82-32267

Reith, Angela. The lost bear / written by Angela Reith ; designed and illustrated by Peter Longden. — London : Ark, 1979. — [20]p : col.ill ; 15cm. — (Buddy bear books)
ISBN 0-85421-827-0 (pbk) : £0.40 B82-32268

Reith, Angela. Tiny to the rescue / written by Angela Reith ; designed and illustrated by Peter Longden. — London : Ark, 1979. — [20]p : col.ill ; 15cm. — (Buddy bear books)
ISBN 0-85421-828-9 (pbk) : £0.40 B82-32269

Richardson, Dorothy. Brownie explorers. — London : Hodder & Stoughton Children's Books, Jan.1983. — [96]p
ISBN 0-340-28617-2 : £2.95 : CIP entry B82-33742

Richardson, Dorothy. The Brownie venturers / Dorothy Richardson ; illustrated by Thelma Lambert. — London : Hodder and Stoughton, 1982. — 117p : ill ; 20cm
ISBN 0-340-27215-5 : £2.95 : CIP rev. B82-03813

Richardson, Dorothy. The secret Brownies / Dorothy Richardson ; illustrated by Thelma Lambert. — London : Hodder & Stoughton, 1982, c1979. — 127p : ill ; 18cm. — (Knight books)
Originally published: 1979
ISBN 0-340-27867-6 (pbk) : £0.85 : CIP rev. B82-07442

Richardson, Jean. One foot on the ground. — London : Hodder and Stoughton, Oct.1982. — [160]p
ISBN 0-340-26813-1 (pbk) : £0.95 : CIP entry B82-24815

Rippon, Angela. Victoria Plum and her animal friends / [Angela Rippon]. — Bristol : Purnell, 1982. — [40]p : col.ill ; 15cm. — (A Purnell playmate)
£0.50 (pbk) B82-28924

Rippon, Angela. Victoria Plum goes house hunting / [Angela Rippon]. — Bristol : Purnell, 1982. — [40]p : col.ill ; 15cm. — (A Purnell playmate)
£0.50 (pbk) B82-28925

Rippon, Angela. Victoria Plum has a party / [Angela Rippon]. — Bristol : Purnell, 1982. — [40]p : col.ill ; 15cm. — (A Purnell playmate)
£0.50 (pbk) B82-28926

Rippon, Angela. Victoria Plum plants a garden / [Angela Rippon]. — Bristol : Purnell, 1982. — [40]p : col.ill ; 15cm. — (A Purnell playmate)
£0.50 (pbk) B82-28927

Roberts, Keith H.. Bingo Bones and the boggart. — London : Hodder and Stoughton Children's Books, July 1982. — [64]p
ISBN 0-340-27853-6 : £3.50 : CIP entry B82-12267

Robinson, Martha. The Wheaton book of animal stories / Martha Robinson ; illustrated by Peter Jones. — Exeter : Wheaton, 1981. — 58p : col.ill ; 22cm
ISBN 0-08-026421-2 : £3.95 B82-06006

Robinson, S.. Magpie and the sock / S. Robinson. — Ifracombe : Stockwell, 1982. — 16p : ill ; 18cm
ISBN 0-7223-1577-5 (pbk) : £0.60 B82-36657

Roche, P. K.. Plaid bear : and the rude rabbit gang / by P.K. Roche. — London : Julia MacRae, 1982. — [31]p : col.ill ; 23x28cm
ISBN 0-86203-088-9 : £4.95 : CIP rev. B82-13168

Rogers, Margaret, *1941-*. Cindy and the silver enchantress / Margaret Rogers ; illustrated by Riana Duncan. — [Harmondsworth] : Puffin, 1982, c1978. — 78p : ill ; 19cm
Originally published: London : Andersen, 1978
ISBN 0-14-031283-8 (pbk) : £0.85 B82-35492

Roose-Evans, James. [Elsewhere & the gathering of the clowns]. Elsewhere & the clowns : an Odd & Elsewhere story / James Roose-Evans ; with pictures by Brian Robb. — [London] : Magnet, 1982, c1974. — 101p : ill ; 20cm
Originally published: London : Deutsch, 1974
ISBN 0-416-25260-5 (pbk) : £1.25 B82-39199

Roose-Evans, James. Odd & the Great Bear : an Odd & Elsewhere story / by James Roose-Evans ; with pictures by Brian Robb. — London : Magnet, 1982, c1973. — 111p : ill ; 20cm. — (An Odd and Elsewhere story)
Originally published: London : Deutsch, 1973
ISBN 0-416-25250-8 (pbk) : £1.25 B82-38963

Ropner, Pamela. Helping Mr Paterson / Pamela Ropner. — London : Chatto & Windus, 1982. — 137p ; 21cm
ISBN 0-7011-2605-1 : £4.95 : CIP rev. B81-34297

Rose, Gerald, *1935-*. PB on ice. — London : Bodley Head, Mar.1982. — [32]p
ISBN 0-370-30464-0 : £3.95 : CIP entry B82-00903

Rose, Gerald, *1935-*. PB takes a holiday / Gerald Rose. — London : Bodley Head, c1980. — [32]p : col.ill ; 26cm
ISBN 0-370-30314-8 : £3.95 : CIP rev. B80-20000

Rosen, Michael. A cat and mouse story. — London : Deutsch, Nov.1982. — [32]p
ISBN 0-233-97484-9 : £4.95 : CIP entry B82-27380

Ross, Tony. The enchanted pig : an old Rumanian tale / retold by Tony Ross. — London : Andersen, 1982. — [27]p : col.ill ; 26cm
ISBN 0-86264-002-4 : £3.95 : CIP rev. B81-30616

Ross, Tony. Hugo and Oddsock / Tony Ross. — [London] : Carousel, 1982, c1978. — [28]p : col.ill ; 19cm
Originally published: London : Andersen, 1978
ISBN 0-552-52162-0 (pbk) : £0.95 B82-22571

Ross, Tony. Naughty Nigel. — London : Andersen Press, Oct.1982. — [32]p
ISBN 0-86264-027-x : £3.95 : CIP entry B82-24593

Ross, Tony. Puss in Boots : the story of a sneaky cat / by Tony Ross. — London : Anderson in association with Sparrow, 1981 (1982 [printing]). — [32]p : col.ill ; 24cm
ISBN 0-09-928510-x (pbk) : Unpriced B82-30460

Ruffell, Ann. Dragon earth / Ann Ruffell ; illustrated by Nicole Goodwin. — London : Hamilton, 1981. — 46p : ill ; 19cm. — (Gazelle books)
ISBN 0-241-10532-3 : £1.80 B82-15272

Rush, Alison. The last of Danu's Children / by Alison Rush. — London : Allen & Unwin, 1981. — 238p ; 23cm
ISBN 0-04-823201-7 : Unpriced : CIP rev. B81-25284

Ryan, John, *1921-*. Action stations! / written and illustrated by John Ryan. — London : Hamlyn, 1982. — [32]p : col.ill ; 21cm. — (Beaver books)
ISBN 0-600-20506-1 (pbk) : £0.95 B82-10302

Ryan, John, *1921-*. Captain Pugwash and the mutiny. — London : Bodley Head, May 1982. — [48]p
ISBN 0-370-30453-5 : £3.50 : CIP entry B82-03843

Ryan, John, *1921-*. The frozen ark / written and illustrated by John Ryan. — London : Hamlyn, 1982. — [32]p : col.ill ; 21cm. — (Beaver books)
ISBN 0-600-20505-3 (pbk) : £0.95 B82-10301

Ryan, John, *1921-*. Pugwash and the buried treasure : a pirate story / by John Ryan. — London : Fontana, 1982, c1980. — [30]p : col.ill ; 22cm. — (Picture lions)
Originally published: London : Bodley Head, 1980
ISBN 0-00-661967-3 (pbk) : £0.95 B82-31116

Saddler, Allen. The archery contest / by Allen Saddler ; illustrated by Joe Wright. — Oxford : Oxford University Press, 1982. — [32]p : col.ill ; 16cm. — (King and queen)
ISBN 0-19-279760-3 : £1.95 : CIP rev. B82-00878

Saddler, Allen. The clockwork monster. — Sevenoaks : Hodder and Stoughton Children's Books, Apr.1981
ISBN 0-340-25593-5 : £3.50 : CIP entry B81-01336

Saddler, Allen. The king gets fit / by Allen Saddler ; illustrated by Joe Wright. — Oxford : Oxford University Press, 1982. — [32]p : col.ill ; 16cm. — (King and queen)
ISBN 0-19-279761-1 : £1.95 : CIP rev. B82-00879

823'.914[J] — Children's stories in English, *1945-* — *Texts* *continuation*

Sampson, Derek, *1932-*. Grump and the hairy mammoth / Derek Sampson ; illustrated by Simon Stern. — London : Methuen Children's, 1982, c1971. — 89p : ill ; 20cm. — (A Magnet book)
Originally published: 1971
ISBN 0-416-58020-3 (pbk) : £0.95 B82-38094

Santos, Nina Dolores. Strangers on the mountain / Nina Dolores Santos. — Llandysul : Gwasg Gomer, 1981. — 128p ; 18cm
ISBN 0-85088-665-1 (pbk) : £1.50 B82-27245

Saville, Malcolm. The thin grey man / Malcolm Saville ; illustrated by Desmond Knight. — St. Johns ; London : Breakwater, 1981, c1966. — 127p : ill ; 18cm. — (A Breakwater book)
Originally published: New York : St Martin's, 1966
ISBN 0-919948-17-0 (pbk) : Unpriced B82-35880

Scott, Peter Graham. Return to the labyrinth. — London : Muller, Aug.1982. — [196]p
ISBN 0-584-62065-9 : £5.95 : CIP entry B82-17974

Seabourne, Peter. The little yellow plane adventures / by Peter Seabourne ; [pictures by the writer]. — Alderney : Aurigny Air Services Cover title. — Text and map on inside covers No.1: Thunderstorm!. — c1981. — [28]p : col.ill,1col.map ; 15x21cm
ISBN 0-907825-00-1 (pbk) : Unpriced B82-09943

Seabourne, Peter. The little yellow plane adventures / by Peter Seabourne ; [pictures by the writer]. — Alderney : Aurigny Air Services Cover title. — Text and map on inside covers No.2: 'Test flight!'. — c1981. — [24]p : col.ill,1col.map ; 15x21cm
ISBN 0-907825-01-x (pbk) : Unpriced B82-09942

Sefton, Catherine. The Emma dilemma / Catherine Sefton ; illustrated by Jill Bennett. — London : Faber and Faber, 1982. — 96p : ill ; 20cm
ISBN 0-571-11841-0 : £3.95 B82-13963

Sefton, Catherine. Island of the strangers. — London : Hamilton, Feb.1983. — [160]p
ISBN 0-241-10914-0 : £5.25 : CIP entry B82-36312

Sefton, Catherine. A puff of smoke / Catherine Sefton ; illustrated by Thelma Lambert. — London : Hamilton, 1982. — 48p : ill ; 19cm. — (Gazelle books)
ISBN 0-241-10707-5 : £1.95 : CIP rev. B81-34320

Sharp, Allen. The evil of Mr. Happiness. — Cambridge : Cambridge University Press, Mar.1982. — [93]p. — (Storytrails)
ISBN 0-521-28500-3 (pbk) : £0.95 : CIP entry B82-03370

Sharp, Allen. The haunters of Marsh Hall. — Cambridge : Cambridge University Press, Mar.1982. — [77]p. — (Storytrails)
ISBN 0-521-28499-6 (pbk) : £0.95 : CIP entry B82-03369

Sharp, Allen. Invitation to murder. — Cambridge : Cambridge University Press, Mar.1982. — [77]p. — (Storytrails)
ISBN 0-521-28502-x : £0.95 : CIP entry B82-03372

Sharp, Allen. The king's mission. — Cambridge : Cambridge University Press, Mar.1982. — [93] p. — (Storytrails)
ISBN 0-521-28498-8 (pbk) : £0.95 : CIP entry B82-03368

Sharp, Allen. The stone of Badda. — Cambridge : Cambridge University Press, Mar.1982. — [77]p. — (Storytrails)
ISBN 0-521-28503-8 (pbk) : £0.95 : CIP entry B82-03373

Sharp, Allen. Terror in the fourth dimension. — Cambridge : Cambridge University Press, Mar.1982. — [77]p. — (Storytrails)
ISBN 0-521-28501-1 (pbk) : £0.95 : CIP entry B82-03371

Sheringham, Sally. The adventures of Teddy / Sally Sheringham ; illustrated by Peter Kingston. — London : Hamlyn, 1982. — 187p : ill(some col.) ; 13cm. — (Bumblebee books)
ISBN 0-600-36672-3 : £0.99 B82-36266

Sheringham, Sally. The lonely house / Sally Sheringham ; illustrated by Douglas Hall. — London : Hamlyn, 1982. — 187p : ill(some col.) ; 13cm. — (Bumblebee books)
ISBN 0-600-36674-x : £0.99 B82-36265

Sheringham, Sally. The magic bicycle ride / Sally Sheringham ; illustrated by Robin Lawrie. — London : Hamlyn, 1982. — 189p : ill(some col.) ; 13cm. — (Bumblebee books)
ISBN 0-600-36673-1 : £0.99 B82-36267

Sherry, Sylvia. Street of the Small Night Market / Sylvia Sherry. — London : Cape, 1966 (1982 [printing]). — 159p ; 21cm
ISBN 0-224-01078-6 : £4.95 B82-18407

Sibley, Raymond. The hound of the Baskervilles / by Sir Arthur Conan Doyle ; retold in simple language by Raymond Sibley ; illustrated by Drury Lane Studies. — Loughborough : Ladybird, c1982. — 51p : col.ill ; 18cm. — (Ladybird children's classics)
ISBN 0-7214-0719-6 : £0.50 B82-32947

Siegel, Robert. Alpha Centauri / Robert Siegel. — Tring : Lion, 1981, c1980. — 255p : ill ; 18cm. — (A Lion paperback)
Originally published: Westchester, Ill. : Cornerstone, 1980
ISBN 0-85648-382-6 (pbk) : £1.25 B82-28010

Silcock, Ruth. Posy and Sam / by Ruth Silcock ; illustrated by Lisa Kopper. — Cambridge : Dinosaur, 1982. — [24]p : col ill ; 16x19cm
ISBN 0-85122-315-x (cased) : Unpriced
ISBN 0-85122-314-1 (pbk) : £0.70 B82-31022

Simon, Heather. The fox and the hound / Heather Simon ; based on the Walt Disney Productions film of the same name. — London : New English Library, 1981. — 125p,[8]p of plates : ill(some col.) ; 18cm
ISBN 0-450-05331-8 (pbk) : £1.25 B82-03692

Sinclair, Olga. Gypsy girl / Olga Sinclair ; illustrated by Jane Bottomley. — London : Fontana Lions, 1982, c1981. — 128p : ill ; 20cm
Originally published: London : Collins, 1981
ISBN 0-00-671963-5 (pbk) : £0.95 B82-25434

Sivers, Brenda. The case of the baffling burglary / Brenda Sivers ; illustrated by Frank Rodgers. — London : Beaver, 1982, c1980. — 74p : ill ; 18cm. — (The Adventures of Sherlock Hound)
Originally published: London : Abelard, 1980
ISBN 0-600-20539-8 (pbk) : £0.85 B82-27049

Sivers, Brenda. Count Dobermann of Pinscher / Brenda Sivers ; illustrated by Frank Rodgers. — London : Beaver Books, 1982, c1981. — 91p : ill ; 18cm. — (The Adventures of Sherlock Hound)
Originally published: London : Abelard-Schuman, 1981
ISBN 0-600-20574-6 (pbk) : £0.85 B82-25309

Sivers, Brenda. Hound and the curse of Kali / Brenda Sivers ; illustrations by Frank Rodgers. — London : Abelard, 1982. — 92p : ill ; 21cm. — (The Adventures of Sherlock Hound)
ISBN 0-200-72722-2 : £4.50 : CIP rev. B82-01122

Slater, Jim. Bignose / written by Jim Slater ; illustrated by Christopher Slater. — London : Granada, 1979. — [32]p : col.ill ; 16cm. — (AMazing monsters) (A Dragon original)
ISBN 0-583-30363-3 (corrected : pbk) : £0.40 B82-26176

Slater, Jim. The boy who saved Earth / Jim Slater. — London : Hodder and Stoughton, 1982, c1979. — 94p ; 18cm. — (Knight books)
Originally published: 1979
ISBN 0-340-26541-8 (pbk) : £0.95 : CIP rev. B81-33924

Slater, Jim. Dimmo / written by Jim Slater ; illustrated by Christopher Slater. — London : Granada, 1979. — [32]p : col.ill ; 16cm. — (A.Mazing monsters) (A Dragon original)
ISBN 0-583-30364-1 (pbk) : £0.40 B82-22758

Slater, Jim. Goldenrod and the kidnappers / Jim Slater ; illustrated by Christopher Chamberlain. — Harmondsworth : Puffin, 1980, c1979. — 128p : ill ; 19cm
Originally published: London : Cape, 1979
ISBN 0-14-031229-3 (pbk) : £0.80 B82-13362

Slater, Jim. Grasshopper and the pickle factory / Jim Slater ; illustrated by Babette Cole. — London : Granada, 1980 (1982 [printing]). — 94p : ill ; 18cm. — (A Dragon book)
ISBN 0-583-30369-2 (pbk) : £0.85 B82-17356

Slater, Jim. Grasshopper and the poisoned river / Jim Slater ; illustrated by Babette Cole. — London : Granada, 1982. — 91p : ill ; 23cm
ISBN 0-246-11587-4 : £3.95 B82-22703

Slater, Jim. The great gulper / written by Jim Slater ; illustrated by Christopher Slater. — London : Granada, 1979. — [32]p : ill ; 16cm. — (A. Mazing monsters) (Dragon)
ISBN 0-583-30325-0 (pbk) : £0.40 B82-03556

Slater, Jim. Greeneye / written by Jim Slater ; illustrated by Christopher Slater. — London : Granada, 1979. — [32]p : col.ill ; 16cm. — (AMazing monsters) (A Dragon original)
ISBN 0-583-30366-8 (pbk) : £0.40 B82-22759

Slater, Jim. The tricky troggle / written by Jim Slater ; illustrated by Christopher Slater. — London : Granada, 1979. — [32]p : col.ill ; 16cm. — (A. Mazing monsters) (Dragon)
ISBN 0-583-30324-2 (pbk) : £0.40 B82-03554

Slater, Jim. Webfoot / written by Jim Slater ; illustrated by Christopher Slater. — London : Granada, 1979. — [32]p : ill ; 16cm. — (A. Mazing monsters) (Dragon)
ISBN 0-583-30326-9 (pbk) : £0.40 B82-03555

Slater, Jim. The winkybird / written by Jim Slater ; illustrated by Christopher Slater. — London : Granada, 1979. — [32p : col.ill ; 16cm. — (A.Mazing monsters) (A Dragon original)
ISBN 0-583-30367-6 (corrected : pbk) : £0.40 B82-29902

Slater, Jim. Wormball / written by Jim Slater ; illustrated by Christopher Slater. — London : Granada, 1979. — [32]p : ill ; 16cm. — (A. Mazing monsters) (Dragon)
ISBN 0-583-30327-7 (pbk) : £0.40 B82-03557

Sloan, Carolyn. Shakespeare : theatre cat / Carolyn Sloan ; illustrated by Jill Bennett. — London : Macmillan Children's, 1982. — 127p ; 21cm
ISBN 0-333-32713-6 : £5.50 : CIP rev. B82-11752

Smith, Alexander McCall. The perfect hamburger / by Alexander McCall Smith ; illustrated by Laszlo Acs. — London : Hamilton, 1982. — 86p : ill ; 19cm. — (Antelope books)
ISBN 0-241-10717-2 : £2.50 : CIP rev. B81-34406

Smith, Bryan. The day they stole the FA cup. — London : Blackie, May 1982. — [96]p
ISBN 0-216-91185-0 : £4.95 : CIP entry B82-07528

823'.914[J] — Children's stories in English, ***1945-*** **— *Texts*** *continuation*

Smith, Jim. Nimbus and the crown jewels / Jim Smith. — Tadworth : World's Work, c1981. — [28]p : col.ill ; 20cm. — (A World's Work children's book)
Ill on lining papers
ISBN 0-437-75042-6 : £2.50 B82-09348

Smith, Jim. Nimbus the explorer / Jim Smith. — Tadworth : World's Work, c1981. — [28]p : col.ill ; 20cm. — (A World's Work children's book)
Ill on lining papers
ISBN 0-437-75041-8 : £5.50 B82-09349

Smith, Joan. The gift of Umtal. — London : MacRae, Aug.1982. — [160]p
ISBN 0-86203-101-x : £6.25 : CIP entry B82-17983

Smith, Joan, *19---*. Grandmother's donkey. — London : MacRae Books, Feb.1983. — [48]p. — (Blackbird series)
ISBN 0-86203-116-8 : £2.95 : CIP entry B82-39818

Smith, Joan, *1933-*. The great cube race. — London : Hamilton, Oct.1982. — [96]p
ISBN 0-241-10880-2 : £1.95 : CIP entry B82-23460

Smith, Norman, *1958-*. Bad Friday / by Norman Smith ; (illustrations by the author). — Birmingham (516 Coventry Rd., Small Heath, Birmingham B10 0UN) : Trinity Arts Association, c1982. — 114p : ill ; 21cm
£2.00 (pbk) B82-38630

Smith, Roger. Greta the green cow. — Oxford : Oxford University Press, Sept.1982. — [32]p. — (Umbrella books)
ISBN 0-19-278200-2 : £2.95 : CIP entry B82-19188

Smith, Vian. Come down the mountain / Vian Smith. — [London] : Carousel, 1973, c1967 (1981 [printing]). — 223p ; 18cm
Originally published: London : Constable, 1967
ISBN 0-552-52136-1 (pbk) : £0.95 B82-09114

Smith, Vian. Martin rides the moor : Vian Smith / illustrated by Peter Forster. — [London] : Carousel, 1974, c1964 (1981 [printing]). — 176p : ill ; 18cm
Originally published: London : Constable, 1964
ISBN 0-552-52135-3 (pbk) : £0.95 B82-09115

Snell, Nigel. Clare's new baby brother / Nigel Snell. — London : Hamilton, 1982. — [25]p : col.ill ; 16cm. — (Nigel Snell books)
ISBN 0-241-10790-3 : £2.50 : CIP rev. B82-11751

Snell, Nigel. Danny is afraid of the dark / Nigel Snell. — London : Hamilton, 1982. — [27]p : col.ill ; 16cm. — (Nigel Snell books)
ISBN 0-241-10792-x : £2.50 : CIP rev. B82-09980

Snell, Nigel. Julie stays the night / Nigel Snell. — London : Hamilton, 1982. — [27]p : col.ill ; 16cm. — (Nigel Snell books)
ISBN 0-241-10793-8 : £2.50 : CIP rev. B82-09981

Snell, Nigel. Paul gets lost / Nigel Snell. — London : Hamilton, 1982. — [25]p : col.ill ; 16cm. — (Nigel Snell books)
ISBN 0-241-10791-1 : £2.50 : CIP rev. B82-09979

Softly, Barbara. Place Mill / Barbara Softly ; illustrated by Shirley Hughes. — London : Collins, 1976, c1962 (1981 [printing]). — 158p : ill,1map ; 18cm. — (Fontana lions)
Originally published: London : Macmillan, 1962
ISBN 0-00-671952-x (pbk) : £1.00 B82-06362

Solomon, Helen. Ollie the trolley. — London : Hodder & Stoughton Children's Books, Feb.1983. — [96]p. — (Brock red)
ISBN 0-340-28616-4 : £2.95 : CIP entry B82-38054

Sooty and the flood. — Bristol : Purnell, 1982. — [40]p : col.ill ; 15cm. — (A Purnell playmates)
ISBN 0-361-05462-9 (pbk) : £0.50 B82-36175

Sooty's adventures. — Bristol : Purnell, 1982. — [40]p : col.ill ; 15cm. — (A Purnell playmates)
ISBN 0-361-05469-6 (pbk) : £0.50 B82-36173

Sooty's caravan. — Bristol : Purnell, 1982. — [40]p : col.ill ; 15cm. — (A Purnell playmates)
ISBN 0-361-05460-2 (pbk) : £0.50 B82-36172

Sooty's TV Town train. — Bristol ; London : Purnell, 1982. — [40]p : col.ill ; 15cm. — (Purnell playmates)
ISBN 0-361-05461-0 (pbk) : £0.50 B82-36174

Sooty's world tour. — Bristol : Purnell, 1973 (1982 [printing]). — [20]p : col.ill ; 27cm
Ill on lining papers
ISBN 0-361-02447-9 : £0.99 B82-33536

Southgate, Vera. Cinderella / retold for easy reading by Vera Southgate ; illustrated by Brian Price Thomas. — Loughborough : Ladybird, c1981. — 51p : col.ill ; 18cm. — (Ladybird series ; 606D. Well-loved tales ; grade 3)
ISBN 0-7214-0647-5 : £0.50 B82-15104

Sowter, Nita. Maisie Middleton / Nita Sowter. — London : Fontana, 1982, c1977. — [24]p : col.ill ; 21cm. — (Picture lions)
Originally published: London : Black, 1977
ISBN 0-00-662041-8 (pbk) : £0.95 B82-34133

Speare, Elizabeth George. The bronze bow / Elizabeth George Speare. — Harmondsworth : Puffin, 1970, c1961 (1982 [printing]). — 203p ; 18cm
Originally published: Boston : Houghton Mifflin, 1961 ; London : Gollancz, 1962
ISBN 0-14-030459-2 (pbk) : £1.25 B82-36227

Starbeck, Eleanor. A dragon called Aunt Blanche / Eleanor Starbeck ; illustrated by Maggie Ling. — London : Abelard, 1982. — 96p : ill ; 21cm
ISBN 0-200-72772-9 : £4.95 : CIP rev. B82-07523

Steele, Tommy. Quincy : a story for children / by Tommy Steele ; illustrated by Peter Wingham. — London : Heinemann, c1981. — 74p : ill ; 24cm
ISBN 0-434-96455-7 : £3.95 B82-03216

Stewart, Mary. A walk in Wolf Wood / Mary Stewart ; illustrated by Doreen Caldwell. — [Sevenoaks] : Knight Books, 1981, c1980. — 128p ; 18cm
Originally published: London : Hodder and Stoughton, 1980
ISBN 0-340-26537-x (pbk) : £0.95 : CIP rev. B81-25751

Stinton, Judith. Tom's tale. — London : MacRae, Feb.1983. — [48]p. — (Blackbird series)
ISBN 0-86203-117-6 : £2.95 : CIP entry B82-39819

Stobbs, William. There's a hole in my bucket. — Oxford : Oxford University Press, Sept.1982. — [32]p. — (Umbrella books)
ISBN 0-19-279755-7 : £2.95 : CIP entry B82-19190

Stobbs, William. This little piggy. — London : Bodley Head, Oct.1981. — [32]p
ISBN 0-370-30428-4 : £3.50 : CIP entry B81-27396

Stone, Bernard, *1920-*. Inspector Mouse / by Bernard Stone and Ralph Steadman. — London : Arrow, 1982, c1980. — [28]p : col.ill ; 23cm
Originally published: London : Andersen, 1980
ISBN 0-09-928500-2 (pbk) : £1.35 B82-31951

Stone, Bernard, *1920-*. The tale of Admiral Mouse / story by Bernard Stone ; pictures by Tony Ross. — London : Andersen Press, 1981. — [25]p : col.ill ; 24cm
ISBN 0-86264-009-1 : £3.50 : CIP rev. B81-27463

Storey, Margaret, *1926-*. The dragon's sister ; and Timothy travels / by Margaret Storey ; illustrated by Charles W. Stewart. — [London] : Faber Fanfares, 1980, c1967. — 139p : ill ; 19cm
Originally published: London : Faber, 1967
ISBN 0-571-11490-3 (pbk) : £1.15 : CIP rev. B80-18927

Storr, Catherine. February Yowler / Catherine Storr ; illustrated by Gareth Floyd. — London : Faber, 1982. — 76p : ill ; 21cm
ISBN 0-571-11854-2 : £3.50 : CIP rev. B81-36223

Storr, Catherine. Vicky / Catherine Storr. — London : Faber, 1981. — 152p ; 21cm
ISBN 0-571-11762-7 : £4.90 : CIP rev. B81-24640

Stranger, Joyce. The fox at Drummers' Darkness / Joyce Stranger ; illustrated by William Geldart. — London : Transworld, 1982, c1976. — 95p : ill ; 17cm. — (A Carousel book)
Originally published: London : Dent, 1976
ISBN 0-552-52159-0 (pbk) : £0.85 B82-12584

Stranger, Joyce. Vet on call / Joyce Stranger. — London : Severn House, 1982, c1981. — 123p ; 21cm
Originally published: London : Transworld, 1981
ISBN 0-7278-0738-2 : £4.25 : CIP rev. B81-24635

Stranger, Joyce. Vet riding high / Joyce Stranger. — London : Transworld, 1981. — 124p ; 18cm. — (A Carousel book)
ISBN 0-552-52148-5 (pbk) : £0.85 B82-03238

Strathdee, Jean. The house that grew / Jean Strathdee ; illustrated by Jessica Wallace. — Wellington ; Oxford : Oxford University Press, c1979. — [32]p : col.ill,music ; 24cm
ISBN 0-19-558041-9 : £2.95 B82-22846

Strong, Jeremy. Lightning Lucy / Jeremy Strong ; illustrated by Toni Goffe. — London : Black, 1982. — 80p : ill ; 23cm
ISBN 0-7136-2164-8 : £3.50 : CIP rev. B81-35832

Sussex, Rayner. King Otto's apprentice. — London : Methuen Children's Books, Apr.1982. — [32]p
ISBN 0-416-21410-x : £3.95 : CIP entry B82-04046

Sutcliff, Rosemary. A circlet of oak leaves / Rosemary Sutcliff ; illustrated by Victor Ambrus. — [London] : Beaver, 1982, c1968. — 76p : ill ; 18cm
Originally published: London : Macmillan, 1965
ISBN 0-600-20470-7 (pbk) : £0.80 B82-11326

Sutcliff, Rosemary. Dawn wind / Rosemary Sutcliff. — Harmondsworth : Puffin in association with Oxford University Press, 1982, c1961. — 299p : 2maps ; 18cm
Originally published: Oxford : Oxford University Press, 1961
ISBN 0-14-031223-4 (pbk) : £1.50 B82-35544

823'.914[J] — Children's stories in English, *1945-* — *Texts* *continuation*

Sutcliff, Rosemary. Eagle's egg / Rosemary Sutcliff ; illustrated by Victor Ambrus. — [London] : Beaver, 1982, c1981. — 76p : ill ; 18cm
Originally published: London : Hamilton Children's, 1981
ISBN 0-600-20471-5 (pbk) : £0.80 B82-11327

Sutcliff, Rosemary. Sun horse, moon horse / Rosemary Sutcliff ; decorations by Shirley Felts. — Sevenoaks : Hodder and Stoughton, 1982, c1977. — 111p : ill ; 18cm. — (Knight books)
Originally published: London : Bodley Head, 1977
ISBN 0-340-26815-8 (pbk) : £0.95 : CIP rev. B82-01094

Sutcliffe, Rosemary. The sword and the circle. — London : Knight Books, Jan.1983. — [320]p
Originally published: London : Bodley Head, 1981
ISBN 0-340-28562-1 (pbk) : £1.25 : CIP entry B82-33740

Sutton, Rosalind. Treasure Island / by Robert Louis Stevenson ; abridged by Rosalind Sutton ; illustrated by Eric F. Rowe. — Cambridge : Brimax Books, 1979. — 76p : ill(some col.),1col.map ; 29cm. — (Classics in actions)
Ill on lining papers
ISBN 0-86112-025-6 : Unpriced B82-16296

Swindells, Robert. Norah and the whale / Robert Swindells ; illustrated by Avril Haynes. — Exeter : Wheaton, c1981. — [32]p : col.ill ; 22x27cm
ISBN 0-08-024980-9 : £3.75 B82-10076

Swindells, Robert. Norah to the rescue / Robert Swindells ; illustrated by Avril Haynes. — Exeter : Wheaton, c1981. — [32]p : col.ill ; 22x27cm
ISBN 0-08-024979-5 : £3.75 B82-10077

Swindells, Robert. World-eater / Robert Swindells. — London : Hodder and Stoughton, 1981. — 103p ; 23cm
ISBN 0-340-26576-0 : £4.95 : CIP rev. B81-26709

Taro, Oda. Panda the doctor / Oda Taro. — London : Hamlyn, c1982. — [28]p : col.ill ; 17cm
ISBN 0-600-38841-7 : £0.99 B82-37709

Taro, Oda. Panda the explorer / Oda Taro. — London : Hamlyn, c1982. — [28]p : col.ill ; 17cm
ISBN 0-600-38842-5 : £0.99 B82-37710

Taro, Oda. Panda the racing driver / Oda Taro. — London : Hamlyn, c1982. — [28]p : col.ill ; 17cm
ISBN 0-600-38843-3 : £0.99 B82-37711

Taro, Oda. Panda the soldier / Oda Taro. — London : Hamlyn, c1982. — [28]p : col.ill ; 17cm
ISBN 0-600-38844-1 : £0.99 B82-37712

Taro, Oda. Panda the train driver / Oda Taro. — London : Hamlyn, c1982. — [28]p : col.ill ; 17cm
ISBN 0-600-36700-2 : £0.99 B82-37708

Taro, Oda. Panda the wizard / Oda Taro. — London : Hamlyn, c1982. — [28]p : col.ill ; 17cm
ISBN 0-600-38845-x : £0.99 B82-37707

Tarrant, Audrey. Pip Squeak's trouble / by Audrey Tarrant. — London : Medici Society, c1982. — 24p : ill(some col.) ; 19x22cm. — (Medici books for children)
ISBN 0-85503-068-2 (pbk) : £0.75 B82-33263

Taylor, Jenny. Messy Malcolm's dream / Jenny Taylor and Terry Ingleby ; illustrated by Lynette Hemmant. — Tadworth : World's Work, c1981. — [32]p : col.ill ; 19x26cm. — (A World's Work children's book)
ISBN 0-437-78172-0 (pbk) : £3.95 B82-14097

Taylor, Judy. Sophie and Jack. — London : Bodley Head, Oct.1982. — [32]p
ISBN 0-370-30941-3 : £3.50 : CIP entry B82-24458

Testa, Fulvio. Doory story / Fulvio Testa. — London : Ernest Benn, 1981. — [28]p : col.ill ; 18cm. — (The Little library)
ISBN 0-510-00044-4 : £1.50 B82-00057

Testa, Fulvio. If you take a paint brush. — London : Andersen Press, Feb.1983. — [32]p
ISBN 0-86264-037-7 : £3.95 : CIP entry B82-39825

Testa, Fulvio. Never satisfied. — London : Abelard-Schuman, Sept.1982. — [32]p
Translation of: Ein ganz gewöhnlicher Tag
ISBN 0-200-72789-3 : £4.95 : CIP entry B82-18965

Thomas, Andrew. Baby Baalamb gets into trouble / Andrew Thomas (Bendi) ; illustrated by Michael Huggins ; inked by Elaine Franks. — Ilfracombe : Stockwell, 1981. — 24p : ill ; 19cm
ISBN 0-7223-1544-9 (pbk) : £0.75 B82-05508

Thompson, Brian, *1935-*. Trooper Jackson's story / Brian Thompson. — Harmondsworth : Puffin, 1982, c1979. — 174p ; 19cm. — (Puffin plus)
Originally published: London : Gollancz, 1979
ISBN 0-14-031291-9 (pbk) : £1.10 B82-25541

Thompson, Janice. Marco Polo and Wellington search for Solomon. — London : Cape, Sept.1982. — [32]p
ISBN 0-224-02036-6 : £4.25 : CIP entry B82-19818

Thorne, Jenny. My uncle / by Jenny Thorne. — London : Macmillan Children's, 1981. — [28]p : col.ill ; 18x25cm
ISBN 0-333-32430-7 : £2.95 B82-13596

The **Three** little pigs / with illustrations by Erik Blegvad. — London : Fontana, 1982, c1980. — 31p : col.ill ; 22cm. — (Picture lions)
Originally published: London : MacRae, 1980
ISBN 0-00-661966-5 (pbk) : £0.95 B82-34134

Tinkle, Oliver. The golliwog / Oliver Tinkle. — Ilfracombe : Stockwell, 1982. — 16p : ill ; 19cm
ISBN 0-7223-1578-3 (pbk) : £0.60 B82-30972

Tison, Annette. The Barbapapas' winter / Annette Tison & Talus Taylor. — London : Warne, 1982. — [32]p : col.ill ; 21x27cm
ISBN 0-7232-2902-3 : £2.95 B82-22134

Toby's day. — Woking : Red Balloon, c1979. — [14]p : chiefly col.ill ; 14cm. — (Peek-a-boo series)
Cover title
ISBN 0-906846-00-5 (spiral) : Unpriced B82-06481

Todd, H. E.. Bobby Brewster's lamp post / H.E. Todd ; illustrated by Lilian Buchanan. — London : Hodder and Stoughton, 1982. — 94p : ill ; 20cm
ISBN 0-340-27457-3 : £2.95 : CIP rev. B82-10013

Todd, H. E.. Bobby Brewster's shadow. — London : Knight, Dec.1982. — [96]p
Originally published: Leicester : Brockhampton, 1956
ISBN 0-340-28044-1 (pbk) : £0.85 : CIP entry B82-29642

Todd, H. E.. Changing of the guard ; and Wallpaper holiday / stories by H.E. Todd ; pictures by Val Biro. — Harmondsworth : Puffin, 1982. — 80p : ill ; 20cm. — (A Young Puffin)
Changing of the guard. Originally published: London : Hodder and Stoughton, 1978
ISBN 0-14-031382-6 (pbk) : £0.80 B82-22136

Todd, H. E.. King of beasts / story by H.E. Todd ; pictures by Val Biro. — Harmondsworth : Puffin, 1982, c1979. — [30]p : chiefly col.ill ; 23cm. — (Picture Puffins)
Originally published: London : Hodder & Stoughton Children's Books, 1979
ISBN 0-14-050361-7 (pbk) : £1.10 B82-29591

Todd, Justin. Moonshadow / idea and paintings by Justin Todd ; text by Angela Carter. — London : Gollancz, 1982. — [32]p : col.ill ; 29cm
ISBN 0-575-03026-7 : £4.95 : CIP rev. B82-04602

Townsend, John Rowe. Clever Dick. — Oxford : Oxford University Press, Apr.1982. — [80]p
ISBN 0-19-271462-7 : £4.95 : CIP entry B82-04161

Townson, Hazel. The speckled panic. — London : Andersen Press, Oct.1982. — [80]p. — (Andersen young readers' library)
ISBN 0-86264-031-8 : £3.50 : CIP entry B82-24594

Treece, Henry. The dream time. — London : Hodder and Stoughton, Nov.1981. — [96]p
Originally published: Leicester : Brockhampton Press, 1967
ISBN 0-340-17464-1 (pbk) : £0.95 : CIP entry B81-30249

Tring, A. Stephen. Penny dreadful. — Wendover : John Goodchild, Feb.1983. — [176]p
ISBN 0-903445-65-4 : £5.95 : CIP entry B82-39292

Troop, Kevin. Spike & Co / by Kevin Troop. — [Stamford] : K.T. Publications, [1981?]. — 120p : ill ; 19cm
ISBN 0-907759-00-9 (pbk) : £1.00 B82-02131

Turska, Krystyna. The prince and the firebird / Krystyna Turska ; [text by Linda M. Jennings after an idea by Robert Angles]. — London : Hodder and Stoughton, 1982. — [36]p : col.ill ; 30cm
ISBN 0-340-25557-9 : £4.95 : CIP rev. B81-25779

Ulyatt, Kenneth. Legends of King Arthur. — London : Hodder and Stoughton Children's Books, Oct.1982. — [64]p
ISBN 0-340-27138-8 : £4.95 : CIP entry B82-24817

Uncle Scrooge's magic carpet. — Bristol : Purnell, 1982. — [8]p : chiefly col.ill ; 11x14cm
£0.40 (unbound) B82-26038

Van der Meer, Ron. Who's afraid? / Ron & Atie van der Meer. — London : Hamilton, 1982. — [14]p : chiefly col.ill ; 24cm
ISBN 0-241-10731-8 : £4.95 : CIP rev. B82-09974

Vendrell, Carme Solé. The bandstand / Carme Solé Vendrell-Roc Almirall. — London : Blackie, 1982. — [24]p : col.ill ; 16cm. — (Victor & Maria)
ISBN 0-216-91102-8 (cased) : £2.50 : CIP rev.
ISBN 0-216-91101-x (pbk) : Unpriced B82-04295

Vendrell, Carme Solé. The cherry tree / Carme Solé Vendrell-Roc Almirall. — London : Blackie, 1982. — [24]p : col.ill ; 16cm. — (Victor & Maria)
ISBN 0-216-91098-6 (cased) : £2.50 : CIP rev.
ISBN 0-216-91097-8 (pbk) : Unpriced B82-04296

823'.914[J] — Children's stories in English, *1945-*
— Texts *continuation*

Vendrell, Carme Solé. The climb / Carme Solé Vendrell-Roc Almirall. — London : Blackie, 1982. — [24]p : col.ill ; 16cm. — (Victor & Maria)
ISBN 0-216-91100-1 (cased) : £2.50 : CIP rev.
ISBN 0-216-91099-4 (pbk) : Unpriced
B82-04294

Vendrell, Carme Solé. The coat / Carme Solé Vendrell-Roc Almirall. — London : Blackie, 1982. — [24]p : col.ill ; 16cm. — (Victor & Maria)
ISBN 0-216-91096-x (cased) : £2.50 : CIP rev.
ISBN 0-216-91095-1 (pbk) : Unpriced
B82-20194

Vendrell, Carme Solé. Hide and seek. — London : Blackie, Feb.1983. — [24]p. — (Victor and Maria)
ISBN 0-216-91292-x (cased) : £2.50 : CIP entry
ISBN 0-216-91293-8 (pbk) : £0.95 B82-37840

Vendrell, Carme Solé. Jon's moon. — London : Blackie, Apr.1982. — [32]p
ISBN 0-216-91186-9 : £4.95 : CIP entry
B82-04300

Vendrell, Carme Solé. The moon. — London : Blackie, Feb.1983. — [24]p. — (Victor and Maria)
ISBN 0-216-91288-1 (cased) : £2.50 : CIP entry
ISBN 0-216-91289-x (pbk) : £0.95 B82-37838

Vendrell, Carme Solé. The parcel. — London : Blackie, Feb.1983. — [24]p. — (Victor and Maria)
ISBN 0-216-91290-3 (cased) : £2.50 : CIP entry
ISBN 0-216-91291-1 (pbk) : £0.95 B82-37839

Vendrell, Carme Solé. The sun. — London : Blackie, Feb.1983. — [24]p. — (Victor and Maria)
ISBN 0-216-91286-5 (cased) : £2.50 : CIP entry
ISBN 0-216-91288-1 (pbk) : £0.95 B82-37837

Vonberg, Liz. The quiltmaker's dream / Liz Vonberg. — [London] : Abelard, 1981. — [25]p : col.ill ; 24cm
Col.ill on lining papers
ISBN 0-200-72745-1 : £4.95 B82-06007

Waddell, Martin. Harriet and the crocodiles. — London : Abelard-Schuman, Oct.1982. — [80]p
ISBN 0-200-72780-x : £4.95 : CIP entry
B82-23700

Waddell, Martin. The house under the stairs. — London : Methuen Children's, Jan.1983. — [96]p. — (Read aloud book)
ISBN 0-416-25040-8 : £3.95 : CIP entry
B82-34448

Waddell, Martin. Napper strikes again / Martin Waddell ; illustrated by Barrie Mitchell. — Harmondsworth : Puffin, 1981. — 112p : ill ; 18cm. — (A Puffin original)
ISBN 0-14-031319-2 (pbk) : £0.85 B82-06467

Waller, Jane, *1944-*. Below the green pond / Jane Waller ; illustrated by Frank Rodgers. — London : Abelard, 1982. — 125p : ill ; 23cm
Bibliography: p125
ISBN 0-200-72762-1 : £5.50 : CIP rev.
B81-36246

Walt Disney's Bambi's big day : a mini pop-up book. — Bristol : Purnell, 1977 (1982 [printing]). — [10]p : col.ill ; 16cm
Cover title. — Text and ill on lining papers
ISBN 0-361-03613-2 : £1.25 B82-33538

Walt Disney's Mickey Mouse and the Martian mix up : a mini pop-up book. — Bristol : Purnell, 1979 (1982 [printing]). — [10]p : col.ill ; 16cm
Cover title. — Text and ill on lining papers
ISBN 0-361-04490-9 : £1.25 B82-33537

Walt Disney's Snow White's party : a mini pop-up book. — Bristol : Purnell, 1977 (1982 [printing]). — [10]p : col.ill ; 16cm
Cover title. — Text and ill on lining papers
ISBN 0-361-03614-0 : £1.25 B82-33539

Walt Disney's Winnie the Pooh and the fire alarm : a mini pop-up book. — Bristol : Purnell, 1979 (1982 [printing]). — [10]p : col.ill ; 16cm
Cover title. — Text and ill on lining papers
ISBN 0-361-04489-5 : £1.25 B82-33535

Walters, Hugh. Terror by satellite / Hugh Walters. — [London] : Faber Fanfares, 1980, c1964. — 159p ; 19cm
Originally published: London : Faber, 1974
ISBN 0-571-11492-x (pbk) : £1.25 : CIP rev.
B80-18930

Ward, Nicholas. Giant. — Oxford : Oxford University Press, Sept.1982. — [32]p. — (Umbrella books)
ISBN 0-19-278201-0 : £2.95 : CIP entry
B82-19189

Warner, Marina. The impossible bath / by Marina Warner ; illustrations by Malcolm Livingstone. — London : Methuen, 1982. — [18]p : col.ill ; 22cm
ISBN 0-416-06380-2 : Unpriced : CIP rev.
B82-04044

Warner, Marina. The impossible day / by Marina Warner ; illustrations by Malcolm Livingstone. — London : Methuen, 1981. — [18]p : col.ill ; 22cm
ISBN 0-416-05770-5 : £2.95 : CIP rev.
B81-28081

Warner, Marina. The impossible night / by Marina Warner ; illustrations by Malcolm Livingstone. — London : Methuen, 1981. — [18]p : col.ill ; 22cm
ISBN 0-416-05850-7 : £2.95 : CIP rev.
B81-27931

Warner, Marina. The impossible rocket / by Marina Warner ; illustrations by Malcolm Livingstone. — London : Methuen, 1982. — [20]p : col.ill ; 22cm
ISBN 0-416-06370-5 : Unpriced : CIP rev.
B82-15787

Warner Hooke, Nina. The moon on the water. — London : Methuen Children's Books, Jan.1982. — [144]p. — (A Pied Piper book)
Originally published: London : British Broadcasting Corporation, 1975
ISBN 0-416-88060-6 : £3.50 : CIP entry
B81-34396

Waterhouse, Keith. New television adventures of Worzel Gummidge and Aunt Sally / Keith Waterhouse and Willis Hall. — London : Sparrow, 1981. — 126p ; 18cm
ISBN 0-09-927760-3 (pbk) : £0.90 B82-06567

Waterhouse, Keith. Worzel Gummidge and Aunt Sally. — London : Severn House, Sept.1982. — [128]p
ISBN 0-7278-0827-3 : £4.95 : CIP entry
B82-25916

Waterhouse, Keith. Worzel's birthday / Keith Waterhouse and Willis Hall ; based on the characters created by Barbara Euphan Todd ; illustrated by Andrew Skilleter. — Harmondsworth : Puffin, 1981. — 95p : ill ; 20cm
ISBN 0-14-031487-3 (pbk) : £0.80 B82-05955

Waterman, Jill. Harry's shapes. — London : Burke, Aug.1982. — [32]p
ISBN 0-222-00759-1 : £4.25 : CIP entry
B82-18469

Watkins, E. M.. A friend from the woods / E.M. Watkins. — Eastbourne : Kingsway, 1982, c1972. — 121p ; 18cm
Originally published: London : Victory, 1972
ISBN 0-86065-174-6 (pbk) : £1.00 B82-27752

Watkins, E. M.. Wagon girl / by Eleanor Watkins. — Eastbourne : Kingsway, 1982, c1975. — 122p ; 18cm
Originally published: Eastbourne : Victory, 1975
ISBN 0-86065-178-9 (pbk) : £1.00 B82-27751

Weinberg, Arthur M.. The refuge & the cave / Arthur M. Weinberg ; text illustrations by Mary Jane Rostami. — London : Bahá'í Publishing Trust, c1982. — 111p : ill ; 19cm
ISBN 0-900125-48-9 (pbk) : £4.30 B82-19712

Weller, P. F.. Linda and Lorenzo / by P.F. Weller ; illustrated by Francesca. — Braunton : Merlin Books, 1981. — 54p,[8]p of plates : ill (some col.) ; 21cm
ISBN 0-86303-004-1 (pbk) : £4.00 B82-10085

Westall, Robert. Fathom five / Robert Westall. — Rev. — Harmondsworth : Puffin, 1982, c1979. — 249p ; 19cm
Previous ed.: London : Macmillan, 1979. — Sequel to: The machine gunners
ISBN 0-14-031353-2 (pbk) : £1.25 B82-25536

Westall, Robert. The wind eye / Robert Westall. — Harmondsworth : Puffin, 1982, c1976. — 158p : 1map ; 18cm. — (Puffin plus)
Originally published: London : Macmillan, 1976
ISBN 0-14-031374-5 (pbk) : £1.10 B82-29822

White, Christopher M.. A present from 2B / Christopher M. White ; illustrated by Jane Paton. — London : Hamilton, 1982. — 47p : ill ; 20cm. — (Gazelle books)
ISBN 0-241-10803-9 : £1.95 : CIP rev.
B82-10801

Whitmore, Ken. Jump! / Ken Whitmore ; illustrated by Alan Cracknell. — Oxford : Oxford University Press, 1982. — 144p : ill ; 20cm. — (An Eagle book)
ISBN 0-19-271461-9 : £3.50 : CIP rev.
B82-11749

Wilde, Nicholas. Sir Bertie & the wyvern : a tale of heraldry / by Nicholas Wilde ; preface by the Baroness Trumpington. — London : Debrett's Peerage, c1982. — [56]p : ill ; 24cm
ISBN 0-905649-46-x : £4.95 B82-26119

Wildsmith, Brian. Cat on the mat / Brian Wildsmith. — Oxford : Oxford University Press, 1982. — 16p : chiefly col.ill ; 23cm
ISBN 0-19-272123-2 (pbk) : £0.95 : CIP rev.
B82-04164

Wildsmith, Brian. Pelican. — Oxford : Oxford University Press, Sept.1982. — [32]p
ISBN 0-19-279764-6 : £4.50 : CIP entry
B82-19191

Wildsmith, Brian. The trunk / Brian Wildsmith. — Oxford : Oxford University Press, c1982. — 16p : all col.ill ; 23cm
ISBN 0-19-272124-0 (pbk) : £0.95 : CIP rev.
B82-04165

Willard, Barbara. Spell me a witch. — London : Hodder and Stoughton, Sept.1981. — [144]p
Originally published: 1979
ISBN 0-340-26540-x (pbk) : £0.95 : CIP entry
B81-23927

Williams, Hugh Steadman. Gavin and the monster / by Hugh Steadman Williams ; illustrated by Margaret Gray. — London : Grosvenor, 1981. — 126p : ill ; 20cm
ISBN 0-901269-62-x (cased) : £3.95
ISBN 0-901269-63-8 (pbk) : £1.50 B82-04669

Williams, Jay. The magic grandfather / Jay Williams ; illustrated by Anne Mieke. — Harmondsworth : Puffin, 1982, c1979. — 149p : ill ; 19cm
Originally published: London : Macdonald and Jane's, 1979
ISBN 0-14-031307-9 (pbk) : £1.00 B82-40379

823'.914[J] — Children's stories in English, *1945-* — *Texts* *continuation*

Williams, Kit. Masquerade / Kit Williams. — London : Cape, 1979 (1982 [printing]). — [48]p : ill(some col.) ; 19cm
ISBN 0-224-02937-1 (pbk) : £1.50 : CIP rev. B82-08440

Williams, Susan, *19---*. Lambing at Sheepfold Farm : a story / by Susan Williams. — London : Gollancz, 1982. — 56p : ill ; 21cm
ISBN 0-575-03045-3 : £3.95 : CIP rev. B82-01549

Williams, Ursula Moray. Bellabelinda and the no-good angel. — London : Chatto & Windus, Sept.1982. — [96]p
ISBN 0-7011-2627-2 : £4.95 : CIP entry B82-20299

Willis, Jeanne. Fearsome Fritz. — London : Andersen Press, Nov.1982. — [32]p
ISBN 0-86264-028-8 : £3.95 : CIP entry B82-26077

Willis, Jeanne. The tale of Georgie Grub / words by Jeanne Willis ; pictures by Margaret Chamberlain. — London : Andersen, 1981. — [26]p : chiefly col.ill ; 24cm
ISBN 0-86264-003-2 : £3.95 : CIP rev. B81-30617

Wills, Jean. Stargazers' folly / Jean Wills. — London : Hamilton, 1982. — 134p ; 23cm
ISBN 0-241-10796-2 (corrected) : £4.95 : CIP rev. B82-08137

Willson, Robina Beckles. Secret witch / Robina Beckles Willson ; illustrated by Azalea Sturdy. — London : Hodder and Stoughton, 1982. — 47p : ill ; 22cm. — (Hopskotch)
ISBN 0-340-27813-7 : £2.50 : CIP rev. B82-12264

Willson, Robina Beckles. Square bear. — London : Hamilton, Jan.1983. — [96]p. — (Antelope books)
ISBN 0-241-10928-0 : £2.75 : CIP entry B82-33707

Wilson, Bob, *1942-*. Stanley Bagshaw and the fourteen-foot wheel / by Bob Wilson. — London : Hamilton, 1981. — [28]p : chiefly col.ill ; 22x28cm
ISBN 0-241-10634-6 : £4.50 : CIP rev. B81-26778

Wilson, Forrest. Super Gran / Forrest Wilson ; illustrated by David McKee. — Harmondsworth : Puffin, 1980, c1978 (1981 [printing]). — 152p : ill ; 19cm
Originally published: London : Andersen Press, 1978
ISBN 0-14-031266-8 (pbk) : £0.85 B82-01394

Wilson, Forrest, *1934-*. Super gran / Forrest Wilson ; illustrated by David McKee. — [Harmondsworth] : Puffin, 1980, c1978 (1982 [printing]). — 152p : ill ; 19cm
Originally published: London : Andersen, 1978
ISBN 0-14-031266-8 (pbk) : £0.95 B82-35494

Wilson, Forrest, *1934-*. Super gran rules OK! / Forrest Wilson ; illustrated by David McKee. — [Harmondsworth] : Puffin, 1981 (1982 [printing]). — 142p : ill ; 18cm
ISBN 0-14-031427-x (pbk) : £0.95 B82-35496

Wilson, Forrest, *1934-*. Super gran superstar / Forrest Wilson ; illustrated by David McKee. — [Harmondsworth] : Puffin, 1982. — 153p : ill ; 19cm
ISBN 0-14-031484-9 (pbk) : £0.95 B82-35495

Wilson, Gina. The whisper. — London : Faber, Sept.1982. — [160]p
ISBN 0-571-11930-1 : £5.50 : CIP entry B82-28462

Wilson, Granville, *1912-*. War of the computers / Granville Wilson ; illustrated by Bert Hill. — London : Granada, 1981. — 92p : ill ; 18cm. — (A Dragon book)
ISBN 0-583-30495-8 (pbk) : £0.85 B82-09538

Wilson, May. Smoke away! / May Wilson. — Sevenoaks : Overseas Missionry Fellowship, 1981. — 36p : ill ; 19cm. — (An OMF Oriole book)
ISBN 0-85363-138-7 (pbk) : Unpriced B82-08817

Woolcock, Peter. Busy days. — London : Hodder and Stoughton Children's Books, Aug.1982. — [32]p
ISBN 0-340-27975-3 : £2.95 : CIP entry B82-15730

Woolcock, Peter. Busy people. — London : Hodder & Stoughton Children's Books, Aug.1982. — [32]p
ISBN 0-340-27974-5 : £2.95 : CIP entry B82-15729

Wright, Christopher, *1937-*. The Merlins / by Christopher Wright. — Eastbourne : Kingsway, 1982, c1975. — 121p : 1map ; 18cm
Originally published: Eastbourne : Victory, 1975
ISBN 0-86065-175-4 (pbk) : £1.00 B82-27749

Yates, Paula. A tail of two kitties. — London : Quartet Books, Oct.1982. — [24]p
ISBN 0-7043-2355-9 : £4.95 : CIP entry B82-29009

Yeoman, John. Mouse trouble / story by John Yeoman ; pictures by Quentin Blake. — Harmondsworth : Puffin, 1976, c1972 (1981 [printing]). — [32]p : col.ill ; 23cm. — (Picture Puffins)
Originally published: London : Hamish Hamilton, 1972
ISBN 0-14-050128-2 (pbk) : £0.95 B82-09159

Yeoman, John. Rumbelow's dance. — London : Hamilton, Sept.1982. — [32]p
ISBN 0-241-10815-2 : £4.50 : CIP entry B82-20751

Yeoman, John. The wild washerwomen : a new folk tale / by John Yeoman ; with pictures by Quentin Blake. — Harmondsworth : Puffin, 1982, c1979. — [29]p : col.ill ; 19x23cm. — (Picture Puffins)
Originally published: London : Hamilton, 1979. — Text on inside covers
ISBN 0-14-050367-6 (pbk) : £1.15 B82-22046

Young, Lesley. Camembert and the magic lamp / Lesley Young ; illustrated by José Ramón Sánchez. — London : Octopus, 1979. — 64p : col.ill ; 31cm
ISBN 0-7064-1043-2 : £2.95 B82-05595

Zola, Meguido. Moving. — London : MacRae Books, Feb.1983. — [48]p. — (Blackbird series)
ISBN 0-86203-115-x : £2.95 : CIP entry B82-39817

Zola, Meguido. Only the best / Meguido Zola ; illustrated by Valerie Littlewood. — London : MacRae, c1981. — [32]p : col.ill ; 26cm
ISBN 0-86203-047-1 : £4.95 : CIP rev. B81-28058

823'.914'09 — Fiction in English, *1945-* — *Critical studies*

McEwan, Neil. The survival of the novel : British fiction in the later twentieth century / Neil McEwan. — London : Macmillan, 1981. — ix,188p ; 23cm
Bibliography: p175-183. — Includes index
ISBN 0-333-30092-0 : £15.00 B82-10807

823'.91409 — Fiction in English, *1945-* — *Interviews*

The **Imagination** on trial : British and American writers discuss their working methods / [edited by] Alan Burns and Charles Sugnet. — London : Allison and Busby, 1981. — vi,170p : ports ; 23cm
Includes index
ISBN 0-85031-383-x (cased) : £8.95
ISBN 0-85031-384-8 (pbk) : Unpriced B82-13578

823'.914'099282 — Children's stories in English, *1945-* — *Critical studies*

Children's writers : seven studies of contemporary authors reprinted from the School Librarian with revised bibliographies. — [Oxford] : School Library Association], 1982. — 42p ; 23cm
Includes bibliographies
ISBN 0-900641-41-x (pbk) : £2.25 B82-38346

824 — ENGLISH ESSAYS

824 — Essays in English. South African writers, *1837-1900* — *Texts*

Schreiner, Olive. Dreams. — London : Wildwood House, Jan.1982. — [184]p. — (Rediscovery)
Originally published: 1891
ISBN 0-7045-0454-5 (pbk) : £2.95 : CIP entry B81-37531

824.4 — ENGLISH ESSAYS, 1625-1702

824'.4 — Essays in English, *1625-1702* — *Texts*

Bolingbroke, Henry St. John, *Viscount*. Lord Bolingbroke: contributions to the Craftsman. — Oxford : Clarendon Press, Oct.1982. — [208]p
ISBN 0-19-822386-2 : £17.50 : CIP entry B82-23687

824.7 — ENGLISH ESSAYS, 1800-1837

824'.7 — Essays in English. Lamb, Charles, *1775-1834* — *Biographies*

Courtney, Winifred F.. Young Charles Lamb 1775-1802 / Winifred F. Courtney. — London : Macmillan, 1982. — xviii,411p,[9]p of plates : ill,geneal.tables,ports ; 23cm
Bibliography: p378-386. — Includes index
ISBN 0-333-31534-0 : £25.00 B82-39744

824'.7 — Essays in English. Lamb, Charles, *1775-1834.* **Friends & local associations**

Prance, Claude A.. Companion to Charles Lamb. — London : Mansell, Jan.1983. — [416]p
ISBN 0-7201-1657-0 : £17.50 : CIP entry B82-32624

824'.7 — Essays in English. Smith, Sydney, *1771-1845* — *Biographies*

Bell, Alan, *1942-*. Sydney Smith. — Oxford : Oxford University Press, Oct.1982. — [260]p. — (Oxford paperbacks)
Originally published: 1980
ISBN 0-19-281370-6 (pbk) : £3.95 : CIP entry B82-23671

824.912 — ENGLISH ESSAYS, 1900-1945

824'.912 — Essays in English, *1900-1945* — *Texts*

Lewis, C. S.. Of this and other worlds / C.S. Lewis ; edited by Walter Hooper. — London : Collins, 1982. — 192p ; 22cm
ISBN 0-00-215608-3 : £7.95 : CIP rev. B82-15615

Webb, Mary, *1881-1927*. The spring of joy. — London : Wildwood House, Jan.1982. — [152] p. — (Rediscovery)
Originally published: London : Dent, 1917
ISBN 0-7045-0455-3 (pbk) : £2.95 : CIP entry B81-37545

824.914 — ENGLISH ESSAYS, 1945-

824'.914 — Essays in English, *1945-* — *Texts*

Blythe, Ronald. From the headlands. — London : Chatto & Windus, Oct.1982. — [224]p
ISBN 0-7011-2638-8 : £8.50 : CIP entry B82-23196

824'.914 — Essays in English, *1945- — Texts continuation*

Golding, William. A moving target / William Golding. — London : Faber, 1982. — 202p ; 23cm
ISBN 0-571-11822-4 : £8.95 : CIP rev. B82-09298

Hattersley, Roy. Politics apart : a selection of 'Listener' endpieces / by Roy Hattersley. — London : British Broadcasting Corporation, 1982. — 184p ; 23cm
ISBN 0-563-20058-8 : £7.25 B82-37161

826.912 — ENGLISH LETTERS, 1900-1945

826'.912'08 — Letters in English, *1900- — Anthologies*

The **First** cuckoo : a selection of the most witty, amusing and memorable letters to The Times, 1900-1980 / chosen and introduced by Kenneth Gregory. — 2nd ed. — [London] : Times Books, 1981. — 359p ; 23cm
Previous ed.: 1976. — Includes index
ISBN 0-04-808031-4 : Unpriced : CIP rev. B81-28180

826.914 — ENGLISH LETTERS, 1945-

826'.914'08 — Letters in English, *1945- — Anthologies*

Lyttelton, George. The Lyttelton Hart-Davis letters : correspondence of George Lyttelton and Rupert Hart-Davis / edited and introduced by Rupert Hart-Davis. — London : Murray Vol.4: 1959. — 1982. — vi,186p : 1plan ; 23cm
Includes index
ISBN 0-7195-3941-2 : £12.50 : CIP rev. B82-00356

827 — ENGLISH SATIRE AND HUMOUR

827'.008 — Humour in English, *1641-1979 — Anthologies*

Everyman's book of nonsense / edited by John Davies ; foreword by Spike Milligan. — London : Dent, 1982, c1981. — 253p : ill ; 19cm. — (Everyman's library)
Originally published: 1981
ISBN 0-460-01277-0 (pbk) : £1.95 B82-28917

827'.008'09282 — Children's humour in English — *Anthologies*

Brandreth, Gyles. Gyles Brandreth's big book of jokes / illustrated by David Farris. — London : Macdonald, 1982. — 93p : ill(some col.) ; 27cm
Ill and text on lining papers
ISBN 0-356-07544-3 : £3.50 B82-35467

Rogers, Janet. Even crazier jokes / compiled by Janet Rogers ; illustrated by Robert Nixon. — London : Beaver Books, 1981. — 126p : ill ; 18cm
ISBN 0-600-20384-0 (pbk) : £0.75 B82-00081

Whizz kids book of jokes and riddles / illustrated by Sara Silcock. — London : Macdonald, 1982. — 95p : ill ; 18cm
ISBN 0-356-07836-1 (pbk) : £0.85 B82-35471

827'.008'09282 — Humour in English — *Anthologies — For children*

The **Illustrated** treasury of humour for children / editor Judith Hendra ; with introduction by William Cole. — London : Hodder and Stoughton, 1981, c1980. — 244p : ill(some col.) ; 26cm
Originally published: New York : Grosset and Dunlap, 1980. — Includes index
ISBN 0-340-27456-5 : £4.95 : CIP rev. B81-27362

827'.009 — Humour in English, *to 1979 — Critical studies*

Mikes, George. English humour for beginners / George Mikes ; illustrated by Walter Goetz. — London : Deutsch, 1980. — 149p : ill ; 21cm
ISBN 0-233-97296-x : £5.95 B82-14707

827.912 — ENGLISH SATIRE AND HUMOUR, 1900-1945

827'.912'08 — Humour in English, *1900-1982 — Anthologies*

Frank Muir presents : the book of comedy sketches. — London : Hamilton, Oct.1982. — [192]p
ISBN 0-241-10852-7 (cased) : £9.95 : CIP entry
ISBN 0-241-10870-5 (pbk) : £5.95 B82-25192

827'.912'080355 — Humour in English, *1900-1980.* **Special subjects: Cinema films** — *Anthologies*

Punch at the cinema / presented by Dilys Powell ; [edited by Susan Jeffreys]. — London : Robson, 1981. — 192p : ill ; 29cm
Ill on lining papers. — Includes index
ISBN 0-86051-145-6 : £7.50 : CIP rev. B81-14434

827.914 — ENGLISH SATIRE AND HUMOUR, 1945-

827'.914 — Humour in English. Mikes, George — *Biographies*

Mikes, George. How to be seventy : an autobiography / George Mikes. — London : Deutsch, 1982. — 248p ; 23cm
Includes index
ISBN 0-233-97453-9 : £7.95 B82-16142

827'.914'08 — Humour in English, *1945- — Anthologies*

The **Lowest** form of wit / [compiled by] Leonard Rossiter ; with cartoons by Honeysett. — London : Joseph, 1981. — 154p : ill ; 23cm
ISBN 0-7181-2067-1 : £5.95 B82-03289

'No more curried eggs for me' : a concoction of classic comedy sketches / compiled by Roger Wilmut. — London : Methuen, 1982. — 95p ; 26cm
List of sound discs: p95
ISBN 0-413-49510-8 : £3.95 B82-40710

Present laughter. — London : Robson, Oct.1982. — [352]p
ISBN 0-86051-191-x : £7.95 : CIP entry B82-24141

This England. — London : Allen and Unwin, Jan.1983. — [224]p
ISBN 0-04-827067-9 : £5.95 : CIP entry B82-33595

Trumps. — London : Dent, Sept.1982. — [192]p
ISBN 0-460-04550-4 : £5.95 : CIP entry B82-19699

827'.91408 — Humour in English, *1945- — Anthologies — Serials*

Pick of Punch. — London : Hutchinson, Sept.1981. — [192]p
ISBN 0-09-146580-x : £7.50 : CIP entry B81-25131

827'.914'08 — Humour in English, *1945- — Anthologies — Serials*

Pick of Punch. — 1982. — London : Hutchinson, Oct.1982. — [192]p
ISBN 0-09-150630-1 : £7.95 : CIP entry B82-25920

827'.914'080324278 — Humour in English, *1945-.* **Special subjects: Cumbria. Lake District. Social life** — *Anthologies*

The **Best** of Lakeland humour / compiled by Cumbria magazine. — Clapham, [Lancs.] : Dalesman, c1982. — 64p : ill ; 21cm. — (Dalesman leisure)
ISBN 0-85206-666-x (pbk) : £1.50 B82-23154

827'.914'080352039162 — Humour in English, *1945-.* **Special subjects: Kerry** *(County)* **persons** — *Anthologies*

MacHale, Des. The bumper book of Kerryman jokes / Des MacHale. — Dublin : Mercier, c1981. — 80p : ill ; 24cm
ISBN 0-85342-666-x (pbk) : £2.99 B82-03937

827'.914'080355 — Humour in English, *1945-.* **Special subjects: Education** — *Anthologies*

Up with skool! : children's own choice of the best school jokes / pictures by Quentin Blake. — Harmondsworth : Puffin, 1981. — 160p : ill ; 18cm. — (A Puffin original)
ISBN 0-14-031436-9 (pbk) : £0.80 B82-07391

827'.914'08036 — Humour in English, *1945-.* **Special subjects: Lions** — *Anthologies*

Lions Club of Keynsham. Lion laughs. — London : Muller, Oct.1982. — [80]p
ISBN 0-584-11042-1 : £3.95 : CIP entry B82-25183

827'.914'09353 — Humour in English, *1945-.* **Special themes: Grotesque** — *Critical studies*

Monty Python : complete and utter theory of the grotesque / edited by John O. Thompson. — London : BFI Publishing, 1982. — 58p : ill ; 20x21cm
Bibliography: p58
ISBN 0-85170-119-1 (pbk) : Unpriced : CIP rev. B82-11782

828 — ENGLISH MISCELLANY

828 — English literature. New Zealand writers. Frame, Janet — *Critical studies*

Dalziel, Margaret. Janet Frame / Margaret Dalziel. — Auckland ; Oxford : Oxford University Press, c1980 (1981 [printing]). — 53p ; 22cm. — (New Zealand writers and their work)
Bibliography: p52-53
ISBN 0-19-558068-0 (pbk) : £4.95 B82-41066

828 — Humorous prose in English. Australian writers, *1945- — Texts*

Humphries, Barry. A nice night's entertainment : sketches and monologues 1956-1981 / Barry Humphries ; introduced by R.F. Brissenden. — Illustrated ed. — London : Granada, 1981. — xix, 211p : ill,facsims,ports ; 24cm
Facsims on lining papers. — List of sound discs: p197-200. — Bibliography: p204. — Includes index
ISBN 0-246-11727-3 : £8.95 B82-09825

828 — Humorous prose in English. New Zealand writers, *1907- — Texts*

Brown, Helen. Don't let me put you off : how to survive in New Zealand suburbia / Helen Brown ; illustrated by David Johnstone. — Christchurch [N.Z.] ; London : Whitcoulls, 1981. — 128p : ill ; 22cm
ISBN 0-7233-0660-5 : Unpriced B82-00392

Lowe, Bob. Sin and tonic / Bob Lowe. — Christchurch, [N.Z.] ; London : Whitcoulls, 1981. — 167p ; 22cm
ISBN 0-7233-0662-1 : Unpriced B82-05580

828 — Prose in English. Polish writers, *1945- — Texts*

Podgórecki, Adam. The aphorisms of Si-Tien / Adam Podgórecki. — London : Poet and Painters Press, 1981. — 32p ; 22cm
Unpriced (pbk) B82-26624

Podgórecki, Adam. The enigmas of Si-tien / Adam Podgórecki. — London : Poets and Painters Press, 1982. — 39p ; 22cm
Unpriced (pbk) B82-36554

828'.02 — English literature, *1750-1980.* **Humorous quotations** — *Anthologies*

Bloomers / illustrated by Heath. — London : Unwin Paperbacks, 1982. — 80p : ill ; 17cm
Originally published: / compiled by Edward Gathorne-Hardy. London : Bodley Head, 1966
ISBN 0-04-827058-x (pbk) : £1.50 : CIP rev. B82-07236

828'.02 — Jokes in English. Special subjects: Catholic Church — *Anthologies*

Clerical capers : Catholic fun / edited by John D. Vose. — Wheathampstead : Anthony Clarke Books, c1979. — 59p : ill ; 19cm
Originally published: Blackpool : J.D. Vose, 1979
ISBN 0-85650-063-1 (pbk) : £1.25 B82-26811

828′.02 — Jokes in English. Special subjects: Music — *Anthologies*
The **Musical** joke book : over 300 musical jokes / [compiled by Michael Kilgarriff]. — London (250 Earlham St., WC2H 9LN) : Fentone Music, c1981. — [44]p : ill,music ; 21cm
Unpriced (pbk) B82-12938

828′.02 — Jokes in English, *to 1980.* **Special subjects: Irish persons** — *Anthologies*
The **Official** Irish joke book no.4 / edited by Peter Cagney ; with additional material by Ernest Forbes ; illustrated by Lome Brown. — London : Futura, 1979 (1981 [printing]). — 128p : ill ; 18cm
ISBN 0-7088-1646-0 (pbk) : £0.95 B82-10547

Positively the last Irish joke book / edited by Peter Cagney ; with additional material by Ernest Forbes. — [London] : Futura, 1979 (1981 [printing]). — 128p : ill ; 18cm
ISBN 0-7088-1537-5 (pbk) : £0.95 B82-35865

828′.08 — Prose in English, *1700-1824.* **Special subjects: Ancient Greek culture** — *Anthologies*
Webb, Timothy. English romantic hellenism : 1700-1824 / Timothy Webb. — Manchester : Manchester University Press, 1982. — xxii,253p ; 21cm. — (Literature in context)
Bibliography: p248-253
ISBN 0-7190-0772-0 : £15.75 B82-36426

828′.08 — Prose in English, *1709-1969.* **Criticism** — *Questions & answers — For Irish students*
Deegan, Anne. Prose extracts for learning cert. '83 : with notes, glossary, exam papers, literary terms / Anne Deegan. — Tallaght : Folens, c1981. — vii,117p ; 22cm. — (Succeed in English ; 1)
ISBN 0-86121-160-x : Unpriced B82-01518

828′.08 — Prose in English, *ca 1600-ca 1900.* **Criticism** — *For Irish students*
Murray, Patrick, *1935-*. English prose / Patrick Murray. — Dublin (Ballymount Road, Walkinstown, Dublin 12) : Educational Company, 1982. — 68p ; 21cm. — (Inscapes ; 21)
Text on inside cover
Unpriced (pbk) B82-17160

828′.08 — Prose in English, *to 1980.* **Special subjects: Love** — *Anthologies*
An **Anthology** of erotic prose / edited by Derek Parker. — London : Constable, 1981. — 256p ; 23cm
Includes index
ISBN 0-09-464230-3 : £8.50 B82-00391

828′.08 — Prose in English, *to 1981.* **Special subjects: Alcoholic drinks. Consumption** — *Anthologies*
Drink to me only. — London : Robin Clark, Oct.1982. — [160]p
ISBN 0-86072-058-6 : £6.95 : CIP entry B82-24152

828.2 — ENGLISH MISCELLANY, 1400-1558

828′.2 — Graffiti in English - *Anthologies*
Barker, Mark. The writing on the wall. — Sevenoaks : Hodder & Stoughton, June 1981. — [144]p
ISBN 0-340-26981-2 (pbk) : £0.95 : CIP entry B81-09992

828.3 — ENGLISH MISCELLANY, 1558-1625

828′.308 — Prose in English, *1558-1640.* **Special subjects: England. Social life** — *Critical studies*
Clark, Sandra. The Elizabethan pamphleteers. — London : Athlone Press, Mar.1982. — [320]p
ISBN 0-485-11216-7 : £16.00 : CIP entry B82-01116

828′.308′09 — Prose in English, *1558-1702* — *Critical studies*
Poetry and drama 1570-1700. — London : Methuen, Nov.1981. — [256]p
ISBN 0-416-74470-2 : £13.50 : CIP entry B81-30627

828′.309 — English literature, *1558-1625* — *Texts*
Gascoigne, George. The greenknight. — Manchester : Carcanet Press, Aug.1982. — [160]p. — (Fyfield books)
ISBN 0-85635-279-9 : £5.95 : CIP entry B82-19260

828′.309 — English literature. Hall, Joseph — *Critical studies*
McCabe, Richard A.. Joseph Hall : a study in satire and meditation. — Oxford : Clarendon Press, Nov.1982. — [320]p
ISBN 0-19-812807-x : £20.00 : CIP entry B82-26882

828.4 — ENGLISH MISCELLANY, 1625-1702

828′.408 — England. Physicians. Organisations: Royal College of Physicians of London. Exhibits: Items associated with Browne, ***Sir*** **Thomas,** *1605-1682* — *Catalogues*
Sir Thomas Browne (1605-1682) and the Baroque : with a postscript on his son Edward as Treasurer (1694-1703/4) and President (1704-8) of the College of Physicians : catalogue of an exhibition. — London : Royal College of Physicians of London, 1982. — v,35p ; 30cm
Bibliography: p31-34
Unpriced (pbk) B82-13912

828′.408 — Prose in English. Milton, John, *1608-1674* — *Critical studies*
Corns, Thomas N.. The development of Milton's prose style / Thomas N. Corns. — Oxford : Clarendon, 1982. — xiv,118p ; 23cm. — (Oxford English monographs)
Bibliography: p112-115. — Includes index
ISBN 0-19-811717-5 : £12.50 : CIP rev. B82-10442

828′.409 — English literature. Baxter, Richard, *1615-1691* — *Critical studies*
Keeble, N. H.. Richard Baxter : Puritan man of letters / N.H. Keeble. — Oxford : Clarendon, 1982. — xi,217p ; 22cm. — (Oxford English monographs)
Bibliography: p156-184. — Includes index
ISBN 0-19-811716-7 : £15.00 : CIP rev. B82-07506

828′.409 — Prose in English. Browne, ***Sir*** **Thomas,** *1605-1682* — *Biographies*
Batty Shaw, Anthony. Sir Thomas Browne of Norwich / Anthony Batty Shaw. — Norwich : Browne 300 Committee, 1982. — [29]p : ill (some col.),facsims,maps,ports(some col.) ; 25cm
Bibliography: p[28]
ISBN 0-7117-0031-1 (unbound) : Unpriced B82-35766

828.5 — ENGLISH MISCELLANY, 1702-1745

828′.509 — English literature. Swift, Jonathan — *Critical studies*
Reilly, Patrick. Jonathan Swift : the brave desponder / Patrick Reilly. — Manchester : Manchester University Press, c1982. — viii,287p ; 24cm
Bibliography: p265-277. — Includes index
ISBN 0-7190-0850-6 : £21.00 : CIP rev. B81-23825

828.6 — ENGLISH MISCELLANY, 1745-1800

828′.607 — Satirical prose in English, *1745-1800* — *Texts*
Hume, David, *1711-1776*. Sister Peg : a pamphlet hitherto unknown / by David Hume ; edited with an introduction and notes by David R. Raynor. — Cambridge : Cambridge University Press, 1982. — vii,127p ; 23cm. — (Cambridge studies in the history and theory of politics)
Bibliography: p125-127
ISBN 0-521-24299-1 : £15.50 : CIP rev. B82-11498

828′.608 — Prose in English, *1745-1800* — *Texts*
Cowper, William. The letters and prose writings of William Cowper. — Oxford : Clarendon Press
Vol.3: Letters 1787-1791. — Oct.1982. — [628]p
ISBN 0-19-812608-5 : £35.00 : CIP entry
Also classified at 821′.6 B82-23681

828′.608 — Prose in English. Boswell, James, *1740-1795, 1782-1785* — *Correspondence, diaries, etc.*
Boswell, James, *1740-1795*. Boswell: the applause of the jury 1782-1785 / edited by Irma S. Lustig and Frederick A. Pottle. — London : Heinemann, 1982, c1981. — xxv,419p,[8]p of plates : ill,ports ; 25cm. — (The Yale editions of the private papers of James Boswell)
Originally published: New York : McGraw-Hill, c1980. — Bibliography: p365-372. — Includes index
ISBN 0-434-43945-2 : £15.00 B82-17169

828′.608 — Prose in English. Boswell, James, *1740-1795* — *Critical studies*
Ingram, Allan. Boswell's creative gloom : a study of imagery and melancholy in the writings of James Boswell / Allan Ingram. — London : Macmillan, 1982. — xi,219p ; 23cm
Bibliography: p202-210. — Includes index
ISBN 0-333-29476-9 : £20.00 B82-20913

828′.608 — Prose in English. Boswell, James, *1740-1795.* **Documents associated with Boswell, James,** *1740-1795.* **Discovery,** *1925-1971*
Pottle, Frederick A.. Pride and negligence : the history of the Boswell papers / by Frederick A. Pottle. — New York ; London : McGraw-Hill, c1982. — xiv,290p ; 25cm. — (The Yale editions of the private papers of James Boswell)
Includes index
ISBN 0-07-050564-0 : £15.95 B82-15985

828′.608 — Prose in English. Cobbett, William — *Biographies*
Spater, George. William Cobbett : the poor man's friend / George Spater. — Cambridge : Cambridge University Press, 1982. — 2v.(xv,653p) : ill,facsims,maps,ports ; 24cm
Maps on lining papers. — Bibliography: 17p. — Includes index
ISBN 0-521-22216-8 : Unpriced : CIP rev.
ISBN 0-521-24077-8 (v.2) : £15.00 B81-37552

828′.609 — English literature. Johnson, Samuel, *1709-1784* — *Biographies — Early works*
Boswell, James, *1740-1795*. Life of Johnson / James Boswell ; edited by R.W. Chapman. — Rev. ed. / revised by J.D. Fleeman ; with a new introduction by Pat Rogers. — Oxford : Oxford University Press, 1970 (1980 [printing]). — xxxvi,1492p ; 19cm. — (The World's classics)
Previous ed.: 1953. — Bibliography: pxxxv-xxxvi. — Includes index
ISBN 0-19-281537-7 (pbk) : £4.95 : CIP rev. B80-05111

828′.609 — English literature. Johnson, Samuel, *1709-1784.* **Religious beliefs**
Pierce, Charles E.. The religious life of Samuel Johnson. — London : Athlone Press, Jan.1983. — [190]p
ISBN 0-485-30010-9 : £12.50 : CIP entry B82-32428

828.7 — ENGLISH MISCELLANY, 1800-1837

828′.708 — Prose in English. Coleridge, Samuel Taylor. Style — *Critical studies*
Christensen, Jerome. Coleridge's blessed machine of language. — Ithaca ; London : Cornell University Press, c1981. — 276p ; 23cm
Includes index
ISBN 0-8014-1405-9 : Unpriced B82-16917

828′.709 — English literature, *1800-1837* — *Texts*
Clare, John, *1793-1864*. John Clare's birds / by Eric Robinson & Richard Fitter ; illustrated by Robert Gillmor. — Oxford : Oxford University Press, 1982. — xxii,105p : ill ; 23cm
Includes index
ISBN 0-19-212977-5 : £6.95 : CIP rev. B82-10428

828′.709 — English literature. Wordsworth, Dorothy - *Correspondence, diaries, etc*
Wordsworth, Dorothy. Letters of Dorothy Wordsworth. — Oxford : Oxford University Press, July 1981. — [240]p. — (Oxford paperbacks)
ISBN 0-19-281318-8 (pbk) : £2.50 : CIP entry B81-14867

828′.709 — English literature. Wordsworth, Dorothy — *Correspondence, diaries, etc*

Wordsworth, William, *1770-1850*The letters of William and Dorothy Wordsworth / edited by the late Ernest De Selincourt. — 2nd ed. — Oxford : Clarendon
6: The later years
Previous ed.: 1939
Pt.2: 1835-1839 / revised, arranged and edited by Alan G. Hill. — 1982. — xxv,794p,[3]leaves of plates : 3ports ; 23cm
Bibliography: pvii-ix. — Includes index
ISBN 0-19-812483-x : £35.00 : CIP rev.
Primary classification 821′.7 B82-23680

828.8 — ENGLISH MISCELLANY, 1837-1900

828′.807 — Humorous prose in English, *1837-1900 — Texts*

Thackeray, W. M.. The book of snobs / William Makepeace Thackeray ; edited by John Sutherland. — [St. Lucia, Queensland] : University of Queensland Press ; Hemel Hempstead : Prentice-Hall [distributor], c1978. — 237p : ill ; 22cm. — (Victorian texts ; 5)
Bibliography: p19
ISBN 0-7022-1490-6 (cased) : £9.95
ISBN 0-7022-1484-1 (pbk) : Unpriced
B82-00973

828′.808 — Prose in English. Carlyle, Thomas — *Critical studies*

Le Quesne, A. L.. Carlyle / A.L. Le Quesne. — Oxford : Oxford University Press, 1982. — x,99p ; 19cm. — (Past masters)
Bibliography: p95-96. — Includes index
ISBN 0-19-287563-9 (cased) : £5.50 : CIP rev.
ISBN 0-19-287562-0 (pbk) B82-00884

828.8′08 — Prose in English. Hudson, W. H. — *Critical studies*

Wilson, Jason. W.H. Hudson : the colonial′s revenge / by Jason Wilson. — London : University of London, Institute of Latin American Studies, [1982?]. — 23,iiip ; 25cm. — (Working papers / University of London. Institute of Latin American Studies, ISSN 0142-1875 ; 5)
ISBN 0-901145-37-8 (pbk) : £1.25 B82-23379

828′.808 — Prose in English. Hudson, William Henry — *Biographies*

Tomalin, Ruth. W.H. Hudson. — London : Faber, Sept.1982. — 1v.
ISBN 0-571-10599-8 : £13.95 : CIP entry
B82-28461

828′.808′09 — Prose in English. Carlyle, Jane Welsh & Carlyle, Thomas — *Correspondence, diaries, etc.*

Carlyle, Thomas. Thomas and Jane : selected letters from the Edinburgh University Library collection / edited by Ian Campbell. — Edinburgh : Edinburgh University Library, 1980. — 102p,[8]p of plates : ill,facsims,2ports ; 23cm
Bibliography: p98
ISBN 0-905152-01-8 : Unpriced B82-21527

828′.809 — English literature, *1837-1900 — Texts*

Carroll, Lewis. [Works]. The Penguin complete Lewis Carroll / with an introduction by Alexander Woollcott ; and the illustrations by John Tenniel. — Harmondsworth : Penguin, 1982, c1939. — xiv,1165p : ill ; 21cm
Includes index
ISBN 0-14-009004-5 (pbk) : £3.95 B82-29815

Eliot, George. A George Eliot miscellany : a supplement to her novels / edited with commentary and notes by F.B. Pinion. — London : Macmillan, 1982. — xi,183p ; 23cm
Includes index
ISBN 0-333-29348-7 : £17.50 B82-32383

Wilde, Oscar. [Selections]. The portable Oscar Wilde. — Rev. ed. / edited by Richard Aldington and Stanley Weintraub. — Harmondsworth : Penguin, 1981. — vi,741p ; 18cm. — (The Viking portable library)
Previous ed.: New York : Viking Press, 1946 ; Harmondsworth : Penguin, 1977
ISBN 0-14-015093-5 (pbk) : £2.50 B82-07076

828′.809 — English literature. Carroll, Lewis. Interpersonal relationships with Liddell, Lorina

Shaberman, R. B.. Lewis Carroll and Mrs Liddell : a study of their relationship based on new material together with a review of the unpublished diaries of Lewis Carroll / R.B. Shaberman. — London : [R.B. Shaberman], 1982. — 16p ; 21cm
Limited ed. of 300 copies
Unpriced (pbk)
Also classified at 942.081′092′4 B82-16968

828′.809 — English literature. Ruskin, John — *Biographies*

Hunt, John Dixon. The wider sea. — London : Dent, , Sept.1981. — [320]p
ISBN 0-460-12009-3 : £8.25 : CIP entry
B81-25859

Hunt, John Dixon. The wider sea : a life of John Ruskin / John Dixon Hunt. — London : Dent, 1982. — xv,512p,[32]p of plates : ill,facsims,ports ; 25cm
Includes index
ISBN 0-460-04547-4 : £15.95 B82-14684

828′.809 — English literature. Ruskin, John — *Critical studies*

Fellows, Jay. Ruskin′s maze : mastery and madness in his art / by Jay Fellows. — Princeton ; Guildford : Princeton University Press, c1981. — xxxv,282p ; 25cm
ISBN 0-691-06479-2 : £17.60 B82-11655

New approaches to Ruskin : thirteen essays / edited by Robert Hewison. — London : Routledge & Kegan Paul, 1981. — xiv,229p,[4]p of plates : ill ; 23cm
ISBN 0-7100-0915-1 : £10.95 B82-07917

The **Ruskin** polygon : essays on the imagination of John Ruskin / John Dixon Hunt, Faith M. Holland, editors. — Manchester : Manchester University Press, c1982. — xii,284p : ill,facsims,ports ; 25cm
Facsims on lining papers. — Includes index
ISBN 0-7190-0834-4 : £30.00 : CIP rev.
Also classified at 709′.2′4 B81-19160

828′.809 — English literature. Stevenson, Robert Louis — *Critical studies*

Knight, Alanna. Robert Louis Stevenson treasury. — London : Shepheard-Walwyn, June 1982. — [320]p
ISBN 0-85683-052-6 : £9.95 : CIP entry
B82-10226

828′.809 — English literature. Wilde, Oscar — *Biographies*

Nicholls, Mark. The importance of being Oscar : the wit and wisdom of Oscar Wilde set against his life and times / Mark Nicholls. — London : Robson, 1981, c1980. — xvi,238p ; 23cm
Originally published: New York : St. Martin′s, 1980. — Includes index
ISBN 0-86051-128-6 : £6.50 B82-13945

828.912 — ENGLISH MISCELLANY, 1900-1945

828′.91207 — Humorous prose in English, *1900-1945 — Texts*

Herbert, A. P.. More uncommon law. — London : Methuen, Nov.1982. — [368]p
Contents: Codd′s last case — Bardot MP?
ISBN 0-413-51480-3 (cased) : £9.95 : CIP entry
ISBN 0-413-50880-3 (pbk) : £4.95 B82-28285

Thompson, T.. Lancashire laughter / T. Thompson. — Didsbury : Pride, [c1982?]. — 112p ; 20cm
Originally published: London : Allen & Unwin, 1951
ISBN 0-907592-01-5 : £2.00 B82-18322

828′.91207′08094281 — Humorous prose in English. Yorkshire writers, *1900- — Anthologies*

The **Best** of Yorkshire humour / compiled by The Dalesman. — Clapham, Lancs. : Dalesman Publishing, [1981?]. — 64p : ill ; 21cm
ISBN 0-85206-652-x (pbk) : £1.50 B82-06125

828′.91208 — Prose in English, *1900-1945 — Texts*

Huxley, Aldous. Moksha : writings on psychedelics and the visionary experience 1931-1963 / Aldous Huxley ; edited by Michael Horowitz and Cynthia Palmer ; with introductions by Albert Hofmann and Alexander Shulgin. — London : Chatto & Windus, 1980. — xxii,280p ; 23cm
Includes index
ISBN 0-7011-2319-2 : £12.50 : CIP rev.
B80-14062

Morley, Robert. Morley matters. — London : Hodder & Stoughton, Nov.1981. — [176]p. — (Coronet books)
Originally published: London : Robson, 1980
ISBN 0-340-26774-7 (pbk) : £1.50 : CIP entry
B81-30541

West, Rebecca. The Young Rebecca. — London : Virago, Jan.1983. — [416]p
Originally published: London : Macmillan, 1981
ISBN 0-86068-318-4 (pbk) : £5.50 : CIP entry
B82-33223

828′.91208 — Prose in English. Nicolson, Harold — *Biographies*

Lees-Milne, James. Harold Nicolson : a biography / by James Lees-Milne. — London : Chatto & Windus
Vol.2: 1930-1968. — 1981. — xii,403p,8p of plates : ill,ports ; 23cm
Bibliography: p373-377. — Includes index
ISBN 0-7011-2602-7 : £15.00 : CIP rev.
B81-27927

828′.91208 — Prose in English. Williamson, Henry, *ca 1925-1937 — Biographies*

Farson, Daniel. Henry : an appreciation of Henry Williamson / Daniel Farson. — London : Joseph, c1982. — x,245p,[12]p of plates : ill,ports ; 23cm
Ill on lining papers. — Includes index
ISBN 0-7181-2122-8 : £8.95 B82-29751

828′.91209 — English literature, *1900-1945 — Texts*

Harwood, Cecil. The voice of Cecil Harwood : a miscellany / edited by Owen Barfield. — London : Steiner, 1979. — 320p,[1]leaf of plates : 1port ; 23cm
Includes index
ISBN 0-85440-329-9 : £6.50 B82-03670

Mew, Charlotte. Collected poems & prose / Charlotte Mew ; edited and with an introduction by Val Warner. — London : Virago in association with Carcanet, 1982, c1981. — xxiv,445p ; 20cm
ISBN 0-86068-223-4 (pbk) : £4.95 : CIP rev.
B81-36024

Tolkien, J. R. R.. Poems and stories / J.R.R. Tolkien ; illustrated by Pauline Baynes. — London : Allen & Unwin, 1980. — 342p : ill (some col.) ; 23cm
In slip case
ISBN 0-04-823174-6 : £17.50 : CIP rev.
B80-02230

828′.91209 — English literature. Ackerley, J. R. — *Correspondence, diaries, etc.*

Ackerley, J. R.. My sister and myself : the diaries of J.R. Ackerley / edited and introduced by Francis King. — London : Hutchinson, 1982. — 216p,[8]p of plates : 1facsim,ports ; 24cm
Includes index
ISBN 0-09-147020-x : £8.95 : CIP rev.
B82-03351

828′.91209 — English literature. Baring, Maurice — *Correspondence, diaries, etc.*

Baring, Maurice. Dear animated bust : letter to Lady Juliet Duff, France 1915-1918 / Maurice Baring ; with an introduction by Margaret Fitzherbert. — Salisbury : Michael Russell, 1981. — ix,165p ; 23cm
Includes index
ISBN 0-85955-086-9 : £7.50 B82-11917

828'.91209 — English literature. Beckett, Samuel — *Critical studies*

Baldwin, Hélène L.. Samuel Beckett's real silence / Hélène L. Baldwin. — University Park ; London : Pennsylvania State University Press, c1981. — viii,171p ; 23cm
Bibliography: p161-165. — Includes index
ISBN 0-271-00301-4 : Unpriced
Also classified at 848'.91409 B82-02053

Paine, Sylvia. Beckett, Nabokov, Nin : motives and modernism / Sylvia Paine. — Port Washington ; London : National University Publications : Kennikat, 1981. — x,102p ; 23cm. — (Literary criticism series)
Bibliography: p79-100. — Includes index
ISBN 0-8046-9288-2 : £12.75
Also classified at 813'.54 ; 813'.52 B82-12285

828'.91209 — English literature. Brittain, Vera, *1913-1917 — Biographies*

Brittain, Vera. Chronicle of youth : war diary 1913-1917. — Large print ed. — Anstey : Ulverscroft, Sept.1982. — [656]p. — (Charnwood library series)
Originally published: London : Gollancz, 1981
ISBN 0-7089-8066-x : £6.50 : CIP entry
B82-27006

828'.91209 — English literature. Chesterton, G. K.. Political beliefs

Corrin, Jay P.. G.K. Chesterton & Hilaire Belloc : the battle against modernity / by Jay P. Corrin. — Athens [Ohio] ; London : Ohio University Press, c1981. — xv,262p ; 24cm
Bibliography: p240-250. — Includes index
ISBN 0-8214-0604-3 : £14.70
Also classified at 820.9'00912 B82-19571

828'.91209 — English literature. Evans, Margiad — *Critical studies*

Dearnley, Moira. Margiad Evans. — Cardiff : University of Wales Press, Dec.1982. — [104]p. — (Writers of Wales, ISSN 0141-5050)
ISBN 0-7083-0820-1 (pbk) : £2.50 : CIP entry
B82-30829

828'.91209 — English literature. Harris, Frank, *1855-1931 — Correspondence, diaries, etc.*

Shaw, Bernard. The playwright and the pirate : Bernard Shaw and Frank Harris, a correspondence. — Gerrards Cross : Smythe, Sept.1982. — [276]p
ISBN 0-86140-131-x : £11.00 : CIP entry
Primary classification 822'.912 B82-26058

828'.91209 — English literature. Symons, A. J. A. — *Correspondence, diaries, etc.*

Symons, A. J. A.. A.J.A. Symons to Wyndham Lewis : twenty-four letters / with comments by Julian Symons. — Edinburgh : The Tragara Press, 1982. — 21p[1]leaf of plates : 1facsim,1port ; 24cm
Limited ed. of 120 copies
ISBN 0-902616-76-5 : Unpriced B82-23378

828'.91209 — English literature. Trefusis, Violet — *Biographies*

Sharpe, Henrietta. A solitary woman : a life of Violet Trefusis / Henrietta Sharpe. — London : Constable, 1981. — 205p : ill,ports ; 23cm
Bibliography: p197-198. — Includes index
ISBN 0-09-464140-4 : £7.95 B82-04264

828'.91209 — English literature. Warner, Sylvia Townsend — *Correspondence, diaries, etc.*

Warner, Sylvia Townsend. The letters of Sylvia Townsend Warner. — London : Chatto & Windus, July 1982. — [320]p
ISBN 0-7011-2603-5 : £15.00 : CIP entry
B82-13265

828'.91209 — Humour in English, *1900-1945 — Texts*

Bentley, E. Clerihew. The complete clerihews of E. Clerihew Bentley. — Rev. ed. — Oxford : Oxford University Press, Sept.1982. — [176]p
Previous ed.: 1981
ISBN 0-19-212981-3 : £6.95 : CIP entry
B82-19179

Bentley, E. Clerihew. The first clerihews. — Oxford : Oxford University Press, Sept.1982. — [128]p
ISBN 0-19-212980-5 : £6.95 : CIP entry
B82-19178

828.914 — ENGLISH MISCELLANY, 1945-

828'.91402 — Aphorisms in English, *1945- — Texts*

Ussher, Arland. The juggler : selections from a journal by Arland Ussher : being the second series of From a dark lantern / with a memoir by Mervyn Wall. — Mountrath : Dolmen, 1982. — 110p ; 22cm
ISBN 0-85105-374-2 (pbk) : £5.00 : CIP rev.
B81-20579

828'.91402 — Jokes in English, *1945- — Texts*

Ahlberg, Janet. The ha ha bonk book / Janet and Allan Ahlberg. — Harmondsworth : Puffin, 1982. — 95p : ill ; 20cm. — (A Young Puffin original)
ISBN 0-14-031412-1 (pbk) : £0.85 B82-22972

Kilgarriff, Michael. 1000 more jokes for kids / by Michael Kilgarriff. — London : Ward Lock, 1982. — 112p ; 31x13cm
ISBN 0-7063-6180-6 : £0.99 : CIP rev.
B82-02634

MacHale, Des. The official Kerryman joke book / by Des MacHale. — Dublin : Mercier, 1979 (1982 [printing]). — 48p : ill ; 18cm. — (Mercier mini books)
ISBN 0-85342-609-0 (pbk) : Unpriced
B82-32997

828'.91402'08 — Jokes in English, *1945- — Anthologies*

Sick as a parrot : the world's worst jokes / collected by Nigel Blundell ; pictures by Hillary Hayton. — [London] : Piccolo, 1982. — 89p : ill ; 18cm. — (A Piccolo original)
ISBN 0-330-26588-1 (pbk) : £0.95 B82-10167

The **Small** book of giant jokes. — Mereworth (3 Pleasant Villas, 189 Kent St., Mereworth, Maidstone, Kent ME18 5QN) : The Club, [1982?]. — [18]p : ill ; 11cm
Unpriced (unbound) B82-19427

828'.91402'080355 — Humorous anecdotes in English, *1945-*. **Special subjects: Rugby football** — *Anthologies*

Boots, balls and banter : a collection of rugby stories / edited by David Parry-Jones ; cartoons by Gren. — London : Sphere, 1982, c1980. — vi,88p : ill ; 18cm
Originally published: London : Barker, 1980
ISBN 0-7221-5106-3 (pbk) : £1.00 B82-16572

828'.91402'0809282 — Jokes in English, *1945 — Anthologies — For children*

The **Book** of elephant jokes / [compiled] by Des MacHale. — Dublin : Mercier, c1982. — 48p ; 18cm
ISBN 0-85342-674-0 (pbk) : Unpriced
B82-38627

Markoe, Karen. Nutty knock knocks / Karen Markoe and Louis Phillips ; illustrated by David Gantz. — London : Granada, 1982, c1981. — 63p : ill ; 20cm. — (A Dragon book)
Originally published: New York : Wanderer Books, 1981
ISBN 0-583-30516-4 (pbk) : £0.80 B82-33990

828'.91402'08355 — Jokes in English, *1945-*. **Special subjects: Schools** — *Anthologies*

Skool graffiti / [compiled by] Peter Eldin ; illustrations by John Miller ; design by Shelagh McGee. — London : Sparrow, 1982. — [93]p : ill ; 18cm
ISBN 0-09-928910-5 (pbk) : £0.95 B82-32752

828'.91407 — Experimental writing in English, *1945- — Texts*

Apsley, Jacob. Structural poetic analysis / Jacob Apsley & Denizen Groat. — [Bristol] : Belston Night Works, c1981. — [18]leaves ; 30cm
ISBN 0-907795-03-x (pbk) : Unpriced
B82-36892

Edwards, Ken. Flood / Ken Edwards. — London : Reality Studios, 1981. — [8]p : ill ; 22cm
Cover title. — Limited ed. of 100 copies
ISBN 0-9507018-1-5 (pbk) : Unpriced
B82-05716

Etrog, Sorel. Dream chamber : Joyce and the Dada circus : a collage / Sorel Etrog : an Irish circus on Finnegans Wake / John Cage ; edited by Robert O'Driscoll. — Toronto : Black Brick ; Dublin : Dolmen, 1982. — 91p ; 26cm
Limited ed. of 900 copies of which 150 are numbered and signed by the authors
ISBN 0-85105-397-1 : Unpriced B82-32416

Fisher, Allen. Unpolished mirrors / Allen Fisher. — London (85 Ramilles Close, SW2 5DQ) : Spanner, c1979
Serial A. — 9p ; 30cm
Unpriced (pbk) B82-40827

Fisher, Allen. Unpolished mirrors / Allen Fisher. — London (85 Ramilles Close, SW2 5DQ) : Spanner, c1979
Serial B. — 23p ; 30cm
Unpriced (pbk) B82-40828

Griffiths, Bill. For rediffusion / by Bill Griffiths ; with illustrations by Robert Clark. — London : New London Pride, 1978. — [30]leaves : ill ; 27cm. — (Exclusive mimeograph masterpieces)
Limited ed. of 250 copies
ISBN 0-85652-038-1 (pbk) : Unpriced
ISBN 0-85652-039-x (signed ed.) : Unpriced
B82-34698

828'.91407 — Humorous prose in English, *1945- — Texts*

Bedford, John Russell, *Duke of.* The Duke of Bedford's book of snobs / by John, Duke of Bedford ; illustrated by Nicolas Bentley. — Milton Keynes : Robin Clark, 1979, c1965. — 142p ; 20cm
Originally published: London : Owen, 1965
ISBN 0-86072-019-5 (pbk) : £1.50 B82-24409

Bradbury, Malcolm. All dressed up and nowhere to go. — Revised ed. — London : Pavilion, Oct.1982. — [204]p
Previous ed. separately published as: Phogey, or, How to have class in a classless society. London : Parrish, 1960 ; All dressed up and nowhere to go. London : Parrish, 1962
ISBN 0-907516-16-5 : £7.95 : CIP entry
B82-24369

Buckman, Rob. Jogging from memory : or letters to Sigmund Freud Vol.II / Rob Buckman ; illustrations by Martin Honeysett. — London : Pan in association with Heinemann/Quixote, 1982, c1980. — 158p : ill ; 18cm
Originally published: London : Heinemann/Quixote, 1980
ISBN 0-330-26592-x (pbk) : £1.25 B82-15210

Carrott, Jasper. A little zit on the side / Jasper Carrott ; text illustrations by David English. — London : Arrow, 1979 (1981 [printing]). — 160p : ill ; 18cm
ISBN 0-09-921700-7 (pbk) : £1.00 B82-22770

Cooper, Jilly. Supercooper / Jilly Cooper. — London : Corgi, 1981, c1980. — 167p ; 18cm
Originally published: London : Eyre Methuen, 1980
ISBN 0-552-11832-x (pbk) : £1.25 B82-04178

Cooper, Jilly. Supercooper / Jilly Cooper. — Bath : Chivers, 1981. — 220p ; 23cm. — (A Lythway memoir)
Originally published: London : Eyre Methuen, 1980. — Published in large-print
ISBN 0-85119-767-1 : Unpriced : CIP rev.
B81-31798

Coren, Alan. Tissues for men / Alan Coren. — London : Sphere, 1981, c1980. — 181p : facsims ; 18cm
ISBN 0-7221-2555-0 (pbk) : £1.25 B82-06011

Crampton, Emma Jane. Letters to Emma Jane / Emma Jane Crampton ; with notes by William Donaldson ; and a preface by Kenneth Tynan. — Milton Keynes : Robin Clark, 1979, c1977. — 94p ; 18cm
Originally published: London : Eyre Methuen, 1977
ISBN 0-86072-028-4 (pbk) : £0.95 B82-00087

828'.91407 — Humorous prose in English, *1945-* **—** *Texts* *continuation*

De Courcy, Ken. Ken De Courcy's life lines : a selection of gags specially chosen to get you out of trouble. — Bideford (64 High St., Bideford, Devon) : Supreme Magic, c1982. — 20p : ill ; 25cm
Unpriced (pbk) B82-29322

Foley, Donal. Man bites dog / Donal Foley. — Dublin : Irish Times
No.10. — c1981. — 96p ; 22cm
ISBN 0-907011-07-1 (pbk) : £3.00 B82-29915

Graham, Richard, *1925-*. The good dog's guide to better living / by Richard Graham ; illustrations by Don Grant. — London : Jay Landesman, c1981. — 64p : ill ; 19cm
Bibliography: p63
ISBN 0-905150-37-6 : £3.95 : CIP rev. B81-30198

Green, Michael, *1927-*. Tonight Josephine : and other undiscovered letters / by Michael Green ; drawings by John Jensen. — London : Secker & Warburg, 1981. — 93p : ill ; 21cm
ISBN 0-436-18793-0 : £3.95 B82-08883

Hawkins, Colin. Witches / by Colin Hawkins and an old witch. — St. Albans : Granada, 1981. — [32]p : col.ill ; 25cm
ISBN 0-246-11513-0 : £2.95 B82-09244

Keane, John B.. Unlawful sex and other testy matters / by John B. Keane. — Dublin : Mercier, c1978. — 96p ; 19cm
ISBN 0-85342-527-2 (pbk) : £1.60 B82-20976

Keane, John B.. Unusual Irish careers / John B. Keane. — Dublin : Mercier, c1982. — 100p ; 18cm
ISBN 0-85342-670-8 (pbk) : Unpriced B82-22230

Kington, Miles. Miles and miles. — London : Hamilton, Sept.1982. — [128]p
ISBN 0-241-10901-9 : £4.95 : CIP entry B82-20623

Kington, Miles. Moreover... — London : Robson Books, June 1982. — [160]p
ISBN 0-86051-173-1 : £5.95 : CIP entry B82-10235

Landers, Fred. Short stories of humour / Fred Landers. — Irchester : Mark Saunders, 1981. — 68p ; 21cm. — (A Castle book publication)
ISBN 0-907877-00-1 (pbk) : £0.70 B82-08742

MacNab, Ed. The alien-spotter's handbook / Ed MacNab ; illustrations by Brian Howard-Heaton and John Higgins. — London : Armada, 1982. — 128p : ill ; 19cm
ISBN 0-00-691971-5 (pbk) : £0.90 B82-36111

Marshall, Andrew, *1954-*. Whoops Apocalypse : a state of the world report / Andrew Marshall & David Renwick. — [London] : Unwin, c1982. — 48p : ill,maps(some col.) ; 25cm
ISBN 0-04-827057-1 (pbk) : £1.95 B82-18883

Marshall, Arthur, *1910-*. Smile please : further musings from Myrtlebank / Arthur Marshall ; illustrated by Tim Jaques. — London : Hamilton, 1982. — 197p : ill ; 23cm
ISBN 0-241-10842-x : £6.95 : CIP rev. B82-17195

Mikes, George, *1912-*. Tsi-Tsa : the biography of a cat / George Mikes ; Nicolas Bentley drew the pictures. — Harmondsworth : Penguin, 1981, c1978. — 119p : ill ; 18cm
Originally published: London : Deutsch, 1978
ISBN 0-14-005291-7 (pbk) : £1.25 B82-05941

Milligan, Spike. Indefinite articles : (culled from his newspaper writings) & Scunthorpe / Spike Milligan. — London : M & J Hobbs in association with Michael Joseph, 1981. — 149p : ill,ports ; 22cm
Text and ill on lining papers
ISBN 0-7181-2078-7 : £7.50 B82-03170

Morley, Robert. Robert Morley's second book of bricks. — London : Hodder and Stoughton, Oct.1982. — [144]p
Originally published: London : Weidenfeld & Nicolson, 1981
ISBN 0-340-28443-9 (pbk) : £1.25 : CIP entry B82-24830

Oh, my word! : a fourth collection of stories from My word and panel games devised by Edward J. Mason & Tony Shryane / Frank Muir & Denis Norden. — London : Eyre Methuen, 1980. — 128p ; 23cm
ISBN 0-413-47510-7 : £2.95 : CIP rev. B80-18534

Robinson, Kenneth, *1925-*. Kenneth Robinson at random / with cartoons by Lucy. — London : Barker, c1981. — 138p : ill ; 23cm
ISBN 0-213-16769-7 : £5.50 B82-31835

Sharp, Mary, *1907-*. Seventh book of humour / Mary Sharp. — Ilfracombe : Stockwell, 1982. — 23p ; 19cm
ISBN 0-7223-1573-2 (pbk) : £0.66 B82-19024

Sykes, Eric. Eric Sykes of Sebastopol Terrace / Eric Sykes. — Walton-on-Thames : M & J. Hobbs ; London : Joseph, 1981. — 190p : ports ; 21cm
ISBN 0-7181-2081-7 : £6.95 B82-02298

Ward, Christopher. Our cheque is in the post / Christopher Ward ; illustrated by Frank Dickens. — London : Pan in association with Secker and Warburg, 1982, c1980. — vi,87p : ill ; 20cm
Originally published: London : Secker & Warburg, 1980. — Includes index
ISBN 0-330-26657-8 (pbk) : £1.00 B82-11638

Waterhouse, Keith. Rhubarb, rhubarb and other noises / Keith Waterhouse. — London : Sphere, 1981, c1979. — 215p ; 18cm
Originally published: London : Michael Joseph, 1979
ISBN 0-7221-8923-0 (pbk) : £1.25 B82-02177

Wells, John. The champagne account. — London : Cape, Nov.1982. — 1v.
ISBN 0-224-02005-6 : CIP entry B82-29113

Williams, Kenneth. Back drops. — London : Dent, Feb.1983. — [160]p
ISBN 0-460-04583-0 : £5.95 : CIP entry B82-38299

Williams, Kenneth. Kenneth Williams' acid drops. — London : Hodder & Stoughton, Oct.1981. — [208]p
Originally published: London : Dent, 1980
ISBN 0-340-26782-8 (pbk) : £1.25 : CIP entry B81-26708

Willock, Colin. Town gun / Colin Willock ; illustrated by William Garfit. — London : Deutsch
2. — 1981. — 208p : ill ; 23cm
ISBN 0-233-97399-0 : £7.95 : CIP rev. B81-30217

828'.91407 — Prose in English, *1945-*. **Special subjects: Pets: Cats & donkeys —** *Texts*

Tovey, Doreen. Raining cats and donkeys / Doreen Tovey. — Large print ed. — Bath : Chivers, 1982, c1967. — 172p ; 23cm. — (A New Portway large print book)
Originally published: London : Joseph, 1967
ISBN 0-85119-160-6 : Unpriced : CIP rev. B82-01442

828'.91407'08 — Experimental writing in English, *1945-* **—** *Anthologies*

The **Avant-garde** today : an international anthology / edited by Charles Russell. — Urbana ; London : University of Illinois Press, c1981. — 269p : ill,facsims ; 21cm
ISBN 0-252-00851-0 (cased) : Unpriced
ISBN 0-252-00852-9 (pbk) : £5.30 B82-05712

828'.91407'08 — Humorous prose in English, *1945-* **—** *Anthologies*

High life, low life. — London : Allen & Unwin Paperbacks, Nov.1982. — [224]p
Originally published: London : Jay Landesman, 1981
ISBN 0-04-827068-7 (pbk) : £1.95 : CIP entry B82-27187

828'.91407'08 — Humorous prose in English, *1945-*. **Special subjects: Gaffes —** *Anthologies*

Rees, Nigel. Foot in mouth. — London : Unwin Paperbacks, Oct.1982. — [144]p
ISBN 0-04-827073-3 (pbk) : £1.50 : CIP entry B82-24704

828'.91407'080355 — Humorous prose in English, *1945-*. **Special subjects: Schools. Students: Celebrities. School reports —** *Anthologies*

Could do better / collected by Patrick Dickinson ; illustrated by David English. — London : Arrow, 1982. — 76p : ill ; 18cm
ISBN 0-09-928320-4 (pbk) : £1.00 B82-23161

828'.91408 — Epigrams in English, *1945-* **—** *Texts*

Enderby, Mavis. Enderby's doings. — Lincoln (1 Stonefield Ave., Lincoln) : Asgill, 1979. — [31]p ; 70x120mm
£0.30 (pbk) B82-09656

Enderby, Mavis. Enderby's ifs & buts. — Lincoln (1 Stonefield Ave., Lincoln) : Asgill, 1981. — 31p ; 80x110mm
£0.30 (pbk) B82-09657

Enderby, Mavis. Enderby's stiff sentences. — Lincoln (1 Stonefield Ave., Lincoln) : Asgill, 1981. — [31]p ; 80x110mm
£0.30 (pbk) B82-09655

Foxglove Joe. The sayings of Foxglove Joe. — Lincoln (1 Stonefield Ave., Lincoln) : Asgill, 1980. — [32]p ; 70x110mm
£0.30 (pbk) B82-09651

828'.91408 — Prose in English, *1945-*. **Special subjects: Livestock: Dogs —** *Texts*

Stranger, Joyce. Three's a pack / Joyce Stranger. — London Corgi, 1982, c1980. — 191p ; 18cm
Originally published: London : Joseph, 1980
ISBN 0-552-11951-2 (pbk) : £1.50 B82-29901

828'.91408 — Prose in English, *1945-* **—** *Texts*

Bell-Knight, C. A.. Musings : little stories for lighter reading / C.A. Bell-Knight. — Bath (North Wing, Freshford, Bath BA3 6EF) : British Nostalgia, c1981. — 23p : ill ; 22cm
Cover title
Unpriced (pbk) B82-29529

Enderby, Mavis. Enderby's allsorts. — Lincoln (1 Stonefield Ave., Lincoln) : Asgill, c1979. — [31]p ; 80x110mm
£0.30 (pbk) B82-09654

Podgórecki, Adam. The apophtegms of SI-tien / Adam Podgórecki. — London : Poets' and Painters', 1981. — 30p ; 22cm
Unpriced (pbk) B82-05448

Politics in the Bible / Apostle Paul as troubleshooter. — Penicuik (Jess Cottage, Carlops, Penicuik, Midlothian EH26 9NF) : Scots Secretariat, 1980. — 14p : 1ill ; 21cm. — (Lord for the people, ISSN 0141-4216)
£0.25 (unbound) B82-13225

828'.91408 — Prose in English. Tovey, Doreen — *Biographies*

Tovey, Doreen. Roses round the door / Doreen Tovey ; illustrated by Derek Crowe. — London : Joseph, 1982. — 189p : ill ; 23cm
ISBN 0-7181-2092-2 : £7.95 B82-28541

828'.914'08080353 — Prose in English, *1945-*. **Special subjects: Dislikes —** *Anthologies*

Pieces of hate. — London : Hodder and Stoughton, Oct.1982. — [144]p
ISBN 0-340-28592-3 : £2.50 : CIP entry B82-25076

828′.91409 — English literature, *1945-* — *Texts*

Blagg, Anthony. The apparently magic mind / by Anthony Blagg ; illustrations, Anthony Blagg ; calligraphy, Nicholas Caulkin. — Birmingham : A. Blagg, c1981. — 19p : ill ; 22cm
ISBN 0-907973-00-0 (pbk) : £0.75 B82-17537

Boyce, Max. I was there / Max Boyce ; cartoons by Gren. — London : Arrow, 1980, c1979. — 143p : ill ; 18cm
Originally published: London : Weidenfeld and Nicolson, 1979
ISBN 0-09-924410-1 (pbk) : £1.00 B82-39248

Ground, Hannah. Reflections and new poems / by Hannah Ground. — [Alfreton] ([172 Mansfield Rd., Alfreton, Derbys. DE5 7JQ]) : [H. Ground], [1982]. — 31p : ill,facsims,ports ; 21cm
£2.00 (pbk) B82-40987

Hemmings, Louis. The homecoming : poems & stories / Louis Hemmings. — Blackrock (63 Ardagh Park, Blackrock, Co. Dublin) : Samovar, c1982. — 49p : ill ; 20cm
Limited ed. of 400 copies
£2.50 (pbk) B82-30981

Lyre, Larry. The renascence of being algae : a philosophy of aesthetia / by Larry Lyre. — London : Regency Press, c1982. — 364p ; 23cm
£5.00 B82-22885

Rankin, Andrew, *1942-*. Nothing becomes / Andrew Rankin. — Newcastle upon Tyne (82 Lodore Road, High West Jesmond, Newcastle upon Tyne 2) : Pescador, 1979. — 68p ; 24cm
Unpriced (pbk) B82-19419

Titterington, Oliver. Something different / Oliver Titterington ; illustrated by Andrea Pryor. — Braunton : Merlin Books, 1981. — 23p : ill ; 21cm
ISBN 0-86303-000-9 (pbk) : £0.60 B82-19418

828′.91409 — English literature. Blishen, Edward — *Biographies*

Blishen, Edward. Lizzie Pye / Edward Blishen. — London : Hamish Hamilton, 1982. — 239p ; 23cm
ISBN 0-241-10781-4 : £8.50 : CIP rev. B82-12571

828′.91409 — English literature. Brenan, Gerald, *1894-1920* — *Biographies*

Brenan, Gerald. A life of one′s own : childhood and youth / by Gerald Brenan. — Cambridge : Cambridge University Press, 1979, c1962. — xii,244p,[4]p of plates : ill,ports ; 23cm
Originally published: London : Hamilton, 1962. — Includes index
ISBN 0-521-29734-6 (pbk) : £4.95 B82-08280

828′.91409 — English literature. Brenan, Gerald, *1920-1972* — *Biographies*

Brenan, Gerald. Personal record 1920-1972 / Gerald Brenan. — Cambridge : Cambridge University Press, 1979, c1974. — 381p,[16]p of plates : ports ; 23cm
Originally published: London : Cape, 1974. — Includes index
ISBN 0-521-29735-4 (pbk) : £5.95 B82-08281

828′.91409 — English literature. Mortimer, John, *1923-* — *Biographies*

Mortimer, John, *1923-*. Clinging to the wreckage : a part of life / John Mortimer. — London : Weidenfeld and Nicolson, c1982. — vii,200p,[12]p of plates : ill,ports ; 24cm
ISBN 0-297-78010-7 : £8.50 B82-20426

828′.91409 — English literature. Oakes, Philip — *Biographies*

Oakes, Philip. Dwellers all in time and space : a memory of the 1940s / Philip Oakes. — London : Deutsch, 1982, c1981. — 227p ; 23cm
ISBN 0-233-97434-2 : £8.50 B82-21126

828′.91409 — English literature. Williams, Raymond — *Critical studies*

Ward, J. P.. Raymond Williams / J.P. Ward. — [Cardiff] : University of Wales Press on behalf of the Welsh Arts Council, 1981. — 80p : 1port ; 25cm. — (Writers of Wales, ISSN 0141-5050)
Limited ed. of 1000 copies. — Bibliography: p77-79
ISBN 0-7083-0807-4 (pbk) : £2.50 : CIP rev. B81-32020

828′.91409 — Humour in English, *1945-* — *Texts*

Barker, Ronnie. Sugar and spice / by Ronnie Barker. — London : Hodder & Stoughton, 1981. — 120p : ill(some col.) ; 28cm
ISBN 0-340-27817-x (cased) : Unpriced : CIP rev.
ISBN 0-340-27000-4 (pbk) : £4.50
Primary classification 743′.924′09034 B81-23932

Bostock-Smith, Colin. Metal Mickey′s boogie book / by Metal Mickey and his friends ; with help from Colin Bostock-Smith and Mary Danby ; drawings by Bryan Reading. — [London] : Armada, 1981. — 128p : ill ; 18cm
ISBN 0-00-691955-3 (pbk) : £0.95 B82-03012

The **Complete** works of Shakespeare and Monty Python : volume one — Monty Python. — London : Eyre Methuen, 1981. — [160]p : ill (some col.),maps,music,facsims,ports,1geneal.table ; 29cm
Contents: Monty Python′s big red book. Originally published: 1971. — The brand new Monty Python bok. Originally published: 1973
ISBN 0-413-49450-0 : £9.99 B82-17556

Connolly, Billy. Gullible′s travels. — London (196 Shaftesbury Ave., WC2) : Pavilion Books, Sept.1982. — [192]p
ISBN 0-907516-10-6 : £6.95 : CIP entry B82-21575

Coren, Alan. The Cricklewood diet. — London : Robson Books, Sept.1982. — [164]p
ISBN 0-86051-186-3 : £5.95 : CIP entry B82-20864

Ford, Brian. The cult of the expert. — London : Hamilton, July 1982. — [192]p
ISBN 0-241-10476-9 : £5.95 : CIP entry B82-14087

Green, Michael, *1927-*. The Peterborough book / Michael Green. — London : Sphere, 1982, c1980. — 115p ; 18cm
At head of title: The Daily telegraph. — Originally published: Newton Abbot : David & Charles, 1980
ISBN 0-7221-4083-5 (pbk) : £1.25 B82-37125

Harding, Mike. The 14 1/2lb budgie / by Mike Harding ; illustrated by Chic Jacob. — London : Robson, 1980. — 96p : ill,music ; 22cm
List of sound discs : p95
ISBN 0-86051-118-9 : £3.95 : CIP rev. B80-18067

Harding, Mike. The 14 1/2lb budgie / Mike Harding ; illustrated by Chic Jacob. — London : Arrow Books, 1981, c1980. — 137p : ill,music
Originally published: London : Robson, 1980. — List of sound discs: p136
ISBN 0-09-926540-0 (pbk) : £1.25 B82-04626

Harding, Mike. The armchair anarchist′s almanac. — London : Robson, Oct.1981. — [144]p
ISBN 0-86051-124-3 : £5.95 : CIP entry B81-27451

I′m sorry I haven′t a clue / Tim Brooke-Taylor ... [et al.] ; cartoons by Graeme Garden, William Rushton and Humphrey Lyttelton ; commentary on Mornington Cresent by Graeme Garden. — London : Unwin Paperbacks, 1981. — 122p : ill,music ; 20cm
Originally published: London : Robson, 1980
ISBN 0-04-827047-4 (pbk) : £1.95 : CIP rev. B81-24605

Just joking. — London : Coronet Books, Oct.1982. — [144]p
Originally published: London : Dent, 1981
ISBN 0-340-28444-7 (pbk) : £1.25 : CIP entry B82-24831

Kilroy, Roger. The rules of success : an A to Z of lifelaws / revealed by Roger Kilroy ; illuminated by Ed McLachlan. — London : Futura, c1982. — [128]p : ill ; 20cm
ISBN 0-7088-2199-5 (pbk) : £1.25 B82-37694

Marshall, Andrew, *1954-*. Best seller! : the life & death of Eric Pode of Croydon / by Andrew Marshall & David Renwick. — London : Allen & Unwin, 1981. — 120p : ill ; 26cm
Text, ill on lining papers
ISBN 0-04-827036-9 : Unpriced : CIP rev. B81-20480

Monkhouse, Bob. The book of days / Bob Monkhouse. — London : Arrow Books, 1981. — [375]p ; 18cm
ISBN 0-09-927150-8 (pbk) : £1.75 B82-04628

O′Regan, Peter. The Irish Kama Sutra / by Peter O′Regan & Sean Dunbar ; illustrated by Albert Murfy. — London : Macdonald, c1981. — 112p : ill ; 18cm. — (A Futura book)
ISBN 0-7088-2111-1 (pbk) : £0.90 B82-03136

Over the moon — sick as a parrot : starring Eric Morecambe / photography by David Montgomery ; devised and written by Roddy Bloomfield. — London : Hutchinson, 1982. — [124]p : ill,ports ; 24cm
ISBN 0-09-149511-3 (pbk) : £3.95 : CIP rev. B82-14209

Root, Henry. Henry Root′s world of knowledge. — London : Weidenfeld and Nicolson, c1982. — 192p : ill,maps,ports ; 26cm
ISBN 0-297-78097-2 : £6.50 B82-27465

Salome dear, not with a porcupine. — London : Unwin Paperbacks, Oct.1982. — [144]p
ISBN 0-04-827072-5 (pbk) : £1.95 : CIP entry B82-23101

Smith, Walter Verdun. ′Jest a minute, please′ / Walter Verdun Smith. — Bognor Regis : New Horizon, c1981. — 84p ; 21cm
ISBN 0-86116-265-x : £3.75 B82-04561

Stilgoe, Richard. The Richard Stilgoe letters : a jumble of anagrams / with cartoons by Richard Wilson. — London : Unwin, c1981 (1982 [printing]). — 201p : ill ; 18cm
ISBN 0-04-827053-9 (pbk) : £1.50 : CIP rev. B82-15649

Tarrant, Chris. Beyond the pail / [Chris Tarrant, John Gorman] ; [edited by Nicolas Locke]. — London : Eel Pie, c1982. — [96]p : ill,music ; 30cm
ISBN 0-14-006302-1 (pbk) : £2.50 B82-19930

Time for a few extra items / edited by Ian Davidson ; illustrations by Ian Heath. — London : W.H. Allen, 1981. — 118p : ill ; 18cm. — (A Star book)
Cover title: The two Ronnies
ISBN 0-352-30958-x (pbk) : £1.00 B82-02672

829 — OLD ENGLISH LITERATURE

829′.09 — Old English literature — *Critical studies*

Whitelock, Dorothy. From Bede to Alfred : studies in early Anglo-Saxon literature and history / Dorothy Whitelock. — London : Variorum, 1980. — 368p in various pagings : 1port ; 24cm. — (Collected studies series ; CS 121)
Facsim reprints. — Includes index
ISBN 0-86078-066-x : £22.00 : CIP rev. B80-18073

829'.09 — Old English literature — *Critical studies — Festschriften*
Studies in English language and early literature in honour of Paul Christophersen / edited by P.M. Tilling. — [Coleraine] : New University of Ulster, 1981. — viii,175p ; 21cm. — (Occasional papers in linguistics and language learning, ISSN 0308-2075 ; no.8)
Includes bibliographies
Unpriced (pbk) B82-05639

829'.1 — Poetry in Old English — *Anthologies — English texts*
Anglo-Saxon poetry : an anthology of Old English poems / in prose translation with introduction and headnotes by S.A.J. Bradley. — London : Dent, 1982. — xxvi,559p ; 20cm. — (Everyman's library)
Bibliography: p xxv-xxvi
ISBN 0-460-10794-1 (cased) : £10.95 : CIP rev.
ISBN 0-460-11794-7 (pbk) : £4.95 B82-14079

829'.1 — Poetry in Old English — *English texts*
The **Seafarer** / translated from the Anglo-Saxon by John Wain ; [drawing by Brenda Stones]. — Warwick ([Emscote Lawn] Warwick) : Greville Press, 1980. — [9]p : 1ill ; 23cm
Limited ed. of 275 numbered and signed copies
Unpriced B82-15101

829'.1 — Poetry in Old English. Exodus *(Anglo-Saxon poem) — Critical studies*
Tolkien, J. R. R.. The Old English Exodus : text, translation and commentary / by J.R.R. Tolkien ; edited by Joan Turville-Petre. — Oxford : Clarendon Press, 1981. — x,85p ; 23cm
Bibliography: pix-x. — Includes index
ISBN 0-19-811177-0 : £7.95 : CIP rev. B81-28850

829'.1 — Poetry in Old English. Special themes: Finn & Hengest — *Critical studies*
Tolkien, J. R. R.. Finn and Hengest : the fragment and the episode. — London : Allen & Unwin, Sept.1982. — [76]p
ISBN 0-04-829003-3 : £9.95 : CIP entry B82-19086

829'.1 — Poetry in Old English — *Texts*
The **Battle** of Maldon / edited by D.G. Scragg. — Manchester : Manchester University Press, 1981. — x,110p : 2maps,1facsim ; 19cm. — (Old and Middle English texts)
Anglo-Saxon text, English introduction and commentary. — Bibliography: p85-88
ISBN 0-7190-0843-3 (cased) : Unpriced : CIP rev.
ISBN 0-7190-0838-7 (pbk) : £4.50 B81-25830

Resignation / edited by Lars Malmberg. — Rev. reprint. — Durham : Durham and St. Andrews Medieval Texts, 1982. — 45p ; 21cm. — (Durham and St. Andrews medieval texts, ISSN 0140-4261 ; no.2)
Previous ed.: 1979. — Bibliography: p30-31
ISBN 0-9505989-1-7 (pbk) : Unpriced B82-25836

829'.3 — Poetry in Old English. Beowulf — *Critical studies*
Williams, David, *1939-*. Cain and Beowulf : a study in secular allegory / David Williams. — Toronto ; London : University of Toronto Press, c1982. — 119p : 1facsim ; 24cm
Bibliography: p111-116. — Includes index
ISBN 0-8020-5519-2 : Unpriced B82-39345

829'.3 — Poetry in Old English. Beowulf. Dating
The **Dating** of Beowulf / edited by Colin Chase. — Toronto ; London : Published in association with the Centre for Medieval Studies, University of Toronto by University of Toronto Press, c1981. — ix,220p ; 26cm. — (Toronto Old English series ; 6)
Includes index
ISBN 0-8020-5576-1 : Unpriced B82-16983

829'.3 — Poetry in Old English. Beowulf — *English texts*
Beowulf : the oldest English epic / translated [from the Anglo-Saxon] into alliterative verse with a critical introduction by Charles W. Kennedy. — Oxford : Oxford University Press, 1940 (1978 [printing]). — lxv,121p ; 21cm. — (A Galaxy book)
Bibliography: p105-111
ISBN 0-19-502435-4 (pbk) : £2.50 B82-26798

830 — GERMANIC LITERATURES

830.8 — German literature, *1700-1980 — Anthologies*
Gefunden : an anthology of German literature / compiled by Richard Stokes. — London : Heinemann Educational, 1982. — 186p ; 22cm
German text, English introduction and notes
ISBN 0-435-38860-6 (pbk) : £2.95 : CIP rev. B81-13475

830.8'09436 — German literature. Austrian writers, *1945- — Anthologies — English texts*
Anthology of modern Austrian literature. — London : Oswald Wolff, Oct.1981. — [200]p
ISBN 0-85496-077-5 : £8.00 : CIP entry B81-27462

830.9 — GERMAN LITERATURE. HISTORY AND CRITICAL STUDIES

830.9'142 — German literature, *1740-1815.* **Classicism** — *Critical studies*
Lange, Victor. The classical age of German literature, 1740-1815. — London : Edward Arnold, Sept.1982. — [160]p
ISBN 0-7131-6366-6 (cased) : £9.95 : CIP entry
ISBN 0-7131-6367-4 (pbk) : £4.95 B82-20042

831 — GERMAN POETRY

831'.04'09 — Lyric poetry in German, *1150-1300 — Critical studies*
Sayce, Olive. The medieval German lyric, 1150-1300 : the development of its themes and forms in their European context / Olive Sayce. — Oxford : Clarendon, 1982. — xviii,511p ; 24cm
Bibliography: p483-497. — Includes index
ISBN 0-19-815772-x : £3.50 : CIP rev. B81-16887

831.2 — GERMAN POETRY, 1150-1300

831'.2 — Poetry in German, *1150-1300 — English texts*
Hartmann, *von Aue*. Erec / by Hartmann von Aue ; translated with an introduction by J.W. Thomas. — Lincoln, [Neb.] ; London : University of Nebraska Press, c1982. — 146p ; 23cm
Translation of: Erec
ISBN 0-8032-4408-8 : Unpriced B82-34779

831'.2 — Poetry in German. Wolfram, von Eschenbach. Parzival — *Critical studies*
Green, D. H.. The art of recognition in Wolfram's Parzival. — Cambridge : Cambridge University Press, Sept.1982. — [416]p
ISBN 0-521-24500-1 : £35.00 : CIP entry B82-19832

831.6 — GERMAN POETRY, 1750-1830

831'.6 — Poetry in German, *1750-1830 — German-English parallel texts*
Goethe, Johann Wolfgang von. [Poems. Selections]. Goethe : with plain prose translations of each poem / introduced and edited by David Luke. — Harmondsworth : Penguin, 1964 (1981 [printing]). — xxxix,366p ; 18cm. — (The Penguin poets)
Parallel German text and English translation. — Includes index
ISBN 0-14-042074-6 (pbk) : £2.50 B82-09951

831'.6 — Poetry in German. Goethe, Johann Wolfgang von — *Critical studies*
Goethe revisited : a collection of essays. — London : John Calder, Nov.1982. — [224]p
ISBN 0-7145-3951-1 (pbk) : £4.95 : CIP entry B82-29013

831'.6 — Poetry in German. Goethe, Johann Wolfgang von. Influence of Ancient Greek culture
Trevelyan, Humphry. Goethe & the Greeks / by Humphry Trevelyan ; foreword by Hugh Lloyd-Jones. — Cambridge : Cambridge University Press, 1941 (1981 [printing]). — xlviii,321p ; 23cm
Originally published: 1941. — Bibliography: pxlv-xlvii. — Includes index
ISBN 0-521-24137-5 (cased) : £25.00 : CIP rev.
ISBN 0-521-28471-6 (pbk) : £8.95 B81-31285

831'.6 — Poetry in German. Goethe, Johann Wolfgang von. Items associated with Goethe, Johann Wolfgang von — *Catalogues*
Rowley, Brian A.. Johann Wolfgang von Goethe (1749-1832) : catalogue of an exhibition to mark the 150th anniversary of Goethe's death on 22 March 1832 / by Brian A. Rowley ; organized by the Goethe-Institut, London and designed by Clifford Simmons. — London : Goethe-Institut, London in association with John Calder, 1982. — 71p,[16]p of plates : ill,ports ; 21x23cm
Bibliography: p66-71
ISBN 0-7145-3940-6 (pbk) : £2.95 B82-35352

831.7 — GERMAN POETRY, 1830-1856

831'.7 — Poetry in German, *1830-1856 — English texts*
Heine, Heinrich. [Poems. English]. The complete poems of Heinrich Heine : a modern English version / by Hal Draper. — Boston, [Mass.] : Suhrkamp/Insel ; Oxford : Distributed by Oxford University Press, c1982. — xvi,1032p : 3ports ; 24cm
Translation from the German. — Includes index
ISBN 0-19-815785-1 : £20.00 : CIP rev. B82-02668

831.8 — GERMAN POETRY, 1856-1900

831'.8 — Poetry in German, *1856-1900 — English texts*
Busch, Wilhelm. The genius of Wilhelm Busch : comedy of frustration : an English anthology / edited and translated by Walter Arndt. — Berkeley, [Calif.] ; London : University of California Press, c1982. — 253p : ill,1col.port ; 27cm
Bibliography: p251-252. — Includes index
ISBN 0-520-03897-5 : Unpriced
Also classified at 741.5'943 B82-28299

831.912 — GERMAN POETRY, 1900-1945

831'.912 — Poetry in German, *1900-1945 — German-English parallel texts*
Rilke, Rainer Maria. [Poems]. An unofficial Rilke : poems 1912-1926 / selected, translated and with an introduction by Michael Hamburger. — London : Anvil Press Poetry, 1981. — 117p ; 22cm. — (Poetica ; 12)
Parallel German text and English translation
ISBN 0-85646-077-x (pbk) : £3.95 B82-10293

831'.912 — Poetry in German. Rilke, Rainer Maria — *Biographies*
Hendry, J. F.. The sacred threshold. — Manchester : Carcanet, Sept.1982. — [280]p
ISBN 0-85635-369-8 : £9.95 : CIP entry B82-18483

831.914 — GERMAN POETRY, 1945-

831'.914 — Poetry in German, *1945- — English texts*
Dörflinger, Johannes. Johannes Dörflinger : life cycle, paintings and drawings : 17 October-22 November 1981, Serpentine Gallery London / organised by the Arts Council of Great Britain with the support of the Federal Republic of Germany. — London : Arts Council of Great Britain, c1981. — 36p : ill(some col.) ; 16x21cm
ISBN 0-7287-0305-x (pbk) : Unpriced
Primary classification 760'.092'4 B82-13040

Gernhardt, Almut. A pig that is kind won't be left behind / pictures by Almut Gernhardt ; with verses by Robert Gernhardt ; translated from the German by Kathrine Talbot. — London : Cape, 1981. — [32]p : col.ill ; 22x25cm
Translation of: Ein gutes Schwein bleibt nicht allein
ISBN 0-224-01973-2 : £4.50 : CIP rev. B81-27394

Schondilie / translated from the German by Charles Causley ; illustrated by Robert Tilling. — Leicester : New Broom Private Press, 1982. — [16]p : ill ; 21cm
Translated from the German. — Limited ed. of 120 copies. — Also available in limited ed. of 55 signed copies
ISBN 0-901870-64-1 (pbk) : £5.00 B82-40986

831'.914 — Poetry in German, *1945- — German-English parallel texts*

Celan, Paul. Paul Celan : poems / selected, translated and introduced by Michael Hamburger. — Bilingual ed. — Manchester : Carcanet New Press, 1980. — 307p ; 24cm
Parallel German text and English translation
ISBN 0-85635-313-2 : £7.95 B82-36832

832.6 — GERMAN DRAMA, 1750-1830

832'.6 — Drama in German. Austrian writers, *1750-1830 — Texts*

Grillparzer, Franz. Ein Bruderzwist in Habsburg / Franz Grillparzer ; edited by Bruce Thompson. — Glasgow : Scottish Papers in Germanic Studies, 1982. — xl,111p : 1geneal.table,1map ; 21cm. — (Scottish papers in Germanic studies ; v.2)
Text in German, English introduction and notes. — Bibliography: p xxxix-xl
ISBN 0-907409-01-6 (spiral) : Unpriced
B82-39731

832'.6 — Drama in German. Kleist, Heinrich von, *1803-1804 — Biographies*

Samuel, R. H.. Kleist's lost year and the quest for Robert Guiskard / R.H. Samuel and H.M. Brown. — Leamington Spa : James Hall, 1981. — ix,126p : facsims,ports ; 22cm
Includes index
ISBN 0-907471-02-1 (pbk) : £5.95 : CIP rev.
B81-31238

832'.6 — Drama in German. Schiller, Friedrich. Historical plays. Characters *— Critical studies*

Sharpe, Lesley. Schiller and the historical character : presentation and interpretation in the historiographical works and in the historical dramas / by Lesley Sharpe. — Oxford : Oxford University Press, 1982. — 211p ; 22cm. — (Oxford modern languages and literature monographs)
Bibliography: p201-207. — Includes index
ISBN 0-19-815537-9 : £12.50 : CIP rev.
B82-18984

832.7 — GERMAN DRAMA, 1830-1856

832'.7 — Drama in German, *1830-1856 — English texts*

Büchner, Georg. Danton's death / Georg Büchner ; a new version by Howard Brenton ; from a translation by Jane Fry. — London : Methuen, 1982. — 72p ; 19cm
Translation of : Danton's Tod
ISBN 0-413-51260-6 (pbk) : £2.95 B82-39648

832'.7 — Drama in German. Büchner, Georg *— Critical studies*

Hilton, Julian. George Büchner / Julian Hilton. — London : Macmillan, 1982. — xi,167p,8p of plates : ill,ports ; 20cm. — (Macmillan modern dramatists)
Bibliography: p159-161. — Includes index
ISBN 0-333-29109-3 (cased) : Unpriced
ISBN 0-333-29110-7 (pbk) : Unpriced
B82-24538

832'.7 — Drama in German. Büchner, Georg. Dantons Tod *— Critical studies*

James, Dorothy. Georg Büchner's Dantons Tod : a reappraisal / Dorothy James. — London : Modern Humanities Research Association, 1982. — 138p ; 23cm. — (Texts and dissertations ; v.16)
Bibliography: p127-134. — Includes index
ISBN 0-900547-78-2 (pbk) : Unpriced
B82-36913

832.8 — GERMAN DRAMA, 1856-1900

832'.8 — Drama in German. Austrian writers, *1856-1900 — English texts*

Schnitzler, Arthur. The round dance : and other plays / Arthur Schnitzler ; translated with an introduction by Charles Osborne. — Manchester : Carcanet New Press, 1982. — x,222p ; 23cm
Contents: The round dance. Translation of: Reigen — Anatol — Love games. Translation of: Liebelei
ISBN 0-85635-398-1 : £6.95 : CIP rev.
B81-38832

832.912 — GERMAN DRAMA, 1900-1945

832'.912 — Drama in German, *1900-1945 — English texts*

Brecht, Bertolt. Bertolt Brecht collected plays / edited by John Willett and Ralph Manheim. — London : Eyre Methuen. — (Bertolt Brecht plays, poetry and prose) (A Methuen modern play)
Vol.6
Part 2: The resistible rise of Arturo Ui / translated by Ralph Manheim. — 1981. — xx,123p ; 19cm
ISBN 0-413-47270-1 (cased) : £7.50
ISBN 0-413-47810-6 (pbk) : £2.50 B82-17540

Brecht, Bertolt. Parables for the theatre : two plays / by Bertolt Brecht ; revised English versions by Eric Bentley. — Harmondsworth : Penguin, 1966 (1982 [printing]). — 207p ; 18cm
Translation of: Der gute Mensch von Sezuan, and Der kaukische Kreidekreis, respectively. — Originally published: Minneapolis : University of Minnesota Press, 1948 ; London : Calder, 1958. — Contents: The good woman of Setzuan — The Caucasian chalk circle
ISBN 0-14-048063-3 (pbk) : £1.50 B82-26121

Kaiser, Georg. Plays volume two / Georg Kaiser ; translated from the German by B.J. Kenworthy, H.F. Garten, Elizabeth Sprigg. — London : Calder, 1981. — 205p ; 22cm
Contents: The flight to Venice — One day in October — The raft of the Medusa — David and Goliath — The president
ISBN 0-7145-3763-2 (cased) : Unpriced : CIP rev.
ISBN 0-7145-3899-x (pbk) : Unpriced
B81-18104

832'.912 — Drama in German, *1900-1945 — Texts*

Brecht, Bertolt. Der kaukasische Kreidekreis / Bertold Brecht ; edited by Bruce Thompson. — London : Methuen Educational, 1982, c1955. — xl,152p : ill ; 20cm. — (Methuen's twentieth century texts)
German text, English introduction. — Originally published: Berlin : Edition Suhrkamp, 1955. — Bibliography: p xxxviii-xl
ISBN 0-423-50800-8 (pbk) : Unpriced : CIP rev. B82-23975

832'.912 — Drama in German, *1900-1945 - Texts with commentaries*

Brecht, Bertolt. Der aufhaltsame Aufsteig des Arturo Ui. — London : Methuen, June 1981. — [220]p. — (Methuen's twentieth century texts)
ISBN 0-423-90180-x (pbk) : £2.50 : CIP entry
B81-12868

832'.912 — Drama in German. Austrian writers, *1900-1945 — English texts*

Schnitzler, Arthur. La ronde (Reigen) / Arthur Schnitzler ; adapted by John Barton from a translation by Sue Davies. — Harmondsworth : Penguin, 1982. — vii,67p ; 20cm
Five men, 5 women. — Translation of: Reigen
ISBN 0-14-048171-0 (pbk) : £1.50 B82-13587

832'.912 — Drama in German. Brecht, Bertolt *— Critical studies*

Bentley, Eric. The Brecht commentaries 1943-1980 / Eric Bentley. — New York : Grove ; London : Eyre Methuen, 1981. — 320p : 1port ; 22cm
Includes index
ISBN 0-413-48860-8 (cased) : £9.95
ISBN 0-413-48870-5 (pbk) : Unpriced
B82-17541

Brecht in perspective. — London : Longman, Sept.1982. — [288]p
ISBN 0-582-49205-x (pbk) : £5.95 : CIP entry
B82-20271

McInnes, Edward O'Hara. The morality of doubt : Brecht and the German dramatic tradition / Edward O'Hara McInnes. — [Hull] : University of Hull, 1980. — 16p ; 21cm
An inaugural lecture delivered in the University of Hull on 27th November, 1979
ISBN 0-85958-425-9 (pbk) : £0.75 B82-28382

832'.912 — Drama in German. Swiss writers, *1900-1945 — Texts*

Frisch, Max. Don Juan, oder, Die Liebe zur Geometrie / Max Frisch. — School ed. / edited by D.G. and S.M. Matthews. — London : Methuen Educational, 1979. — xl,117p ; 20cm. — (Methuen's twentieth century texts)
German text, English introduction. — Previous ed.: i.e. Rev. ed. Frankfurt am Main : Suhrkamp Verlag, c1962. — Bibliography: pxxxix-xl
ISBN 0-423-50630-7 (pbk) : £1.95 : CIP rev.
B79-21429

832'.912 — German literature. Austrian writers. Kraus, Karl *— Critical studies*

Grimstad, Kari. Masks of the prophet : the theatrical world of Karl Kraus / Kari Grimstad. — Toronto ; London : University of Toronto Press, c1982. — 296p : ill,ports ; 24cm
Bibliography: p288-289. — Includes index
ISBN 0-8020-5522-2 : Unpriced B82-35660

832.914 — GERMAN DRAMA, 1945-

832'.914 — Drama in German, *1945- — English texts*

König, Karl. An Easter play / Karl König. — Botton Village : Camphill Press, 1981. — 2v. ; 20cm
Translated from the German
ISBN 0-904145-21-2 (pbk) : Unpriced
ISBN 0-904145-22-0 (vol.2) : Unpriced
B82-25577

König, Karl. Plays for Ascensiontide / Karl König. — Botton Village : Camphill Press, 1981. — 62p ; 20cm
Translated from the German. — Contents: Evening in Emmaus — The cup of Zarathustra — Quo vadis, Domine?
ISBN 0-904145-23-9 (pbk) : Unpriced
B82-25576

Lettau, Reinhard. Breakfast in Miami. — London : John Calder, Sept.1982. — [48]p. — (Playscript series)
Translation of: Frühstücks-Gespräche in Miami
ISBN 0-7145-3834-5 (pbk) : £4.95 : CIP entry
B82-25913

Schmidt, Arno. Evening edged in gold / Arno Schmidt ; translated by John E. Woods. — London : Boyars, c1980. — 215p : ill,maps ; 44cm
Translation of Abend mit Goldrand. — In slip case
ISBN 0-7145-2719-x : £60.00 : CIP rev.
B80-22644

Weiss, Peter. The investigation. — London : Boyars, Aug.1982. — [208]p
Translation of: Die Ermittlung. — Originally published: 1966
ISBN 0-7145-0301-0 (pbk) : £4.95 : CIP entry
B82-17211

833 — GERMAN FICTION

833'.009 — Fiction in German, *1700-1980.* **Forms: Novels** *compared with* **English novels,** *1700-1980*

Klieneberger, H. R.. The novel in England and Germany. — London : Wolff, Aug.1981. — [254]p
ISBN 0-85496-079-1 (pbk) : £8.00 : CIP entry
Primary classification 823'.009 B81-18114

833'.009 — Fiction in German, *1750-1945.* **Bildungsromane** *— Critical studies*

Beddow, Michael. The fiction of humanity : studies in the Bildungsroman from Wieland to Thomas Mann / Michael Beddow. — Cambridge : Cambridge University Press, 1982. — x,325p ; 23cm. — (Anglica Germanica. Series 2)
Bibliography: p316-325. — Includes index
ISBN 0-521-24533-8 : £25.00 : CIP rev.
B82-15940

833.6 — GERMAN FICTION, 1750-1830

833′.6 — Fiction in German. Goethe, Johann Wolfgang von — *Critical studies*
Cottrell, Alan P.. Goethe′s view of evil and the search for a new image of man in our time. — Edinburgh : Floris Books, May 1982. — [368]p
ISBN 0-903540-51-7 : £12.95 : CIP entry
B82-11794

833′.6 — Fiction in German. Goethe, Johann Wolfgang von. Leiden des jungen Werthers. Special themes: Philosophy. Idealism
Miller, R. D.. The beautiful soul : a study of eighteeth-century idealism as exemplified by Rousseau′s La Nouvelle Héloïse and Goethe′s Die Leiden des jungen Werthers / by R. D. Miller. — Harrogate (8 Lancaster Rd., Harrogate) : Duchy Press, 1981. — 100p ; 23cm
Includes index
Unpriced
Primary classification 843′.5 B82-06455

833′.6[F] — Fiction in German, *1750-1830 — English texts*
Goethe, Johann Wolfgang von. Wilhelm Meister′s years of travel, or, The renunciants ; Wilhelm Meisters Wanderjahre, oder, Die Entsagenden / by Johann Wolfgang von Goethe. — London : Calder, 1980. — (Wilhelm Meister ; v.4)
Translation of: Wilhelm Meisters Wanderjahre, oder, Die Entsagenden
Bk.1 / translated by H.M. Waidson. — 128p ; 21cm
ISBN 0-7145-3827-2 : £6.95 : CIP rev.
B80-12142

Goethe, Johann Wolfgang von. Wilhelm Meister′s years of travel, or, The renunciants = Wilhelm Meisters Wanderjahre, oder, Die Entsagenden / by Johann Wolfgang von Goethe ; translated by H.M. Waidson. — London : Calder. — (Wilhelm Meister ; v.5)
Bk.2. — 1981. — 140p ; 21cm
Bibliography: p137
ISBN 0-7145-3838-8 (cased) : £6.95 : CIP rev.
ISBN 0-7145-3932-5 (pbk) : £3.95 B81-30597

Goethe, Johann Wolfgang von. Wilhelm Meister′s years of travel, or, The renunciants = Wilhelm Meisters Wanderjahre, oder, Die Entsagenden / by Johann Wolfgang von Goethe ; translated by H.M. Waidson. — London : Calder. — (Wilhelm Meister ; v.6)
Bk.3. — 1982. — 147p ; 21cm
Bibliography: p143
ISBN 0-7145-3840-x (cased) : £6.95 : CIP rev.
ISBN 0-7145-3934-1 (pbk) : £3.95 B82-06045

Wyss, Johann R.. The Swiss family Robinson / by Johann R. Wyss. — Abridged. — London : Dean, [198-?]. — 184p ; 19cm. — (Dean′s classics)
ISBN 0-603-03037-8 (pbk) : Unpriced
B82-27145

833′.6[F] — Short stories in German, *1750-1830 — English texts*
Hoffmann, E. T. A.. Tales of Hoffmann / selected and translated with an introduction by R.J. Hollingdale with the assistance of Stella and Vernon Humphries, and Sally Hayward. — Harmondsworth : Penguin, 1982. — 411p ; 19cm. — (Penguin classics)
Translated from the German
ISBN 0-14-044392-4 (pbk) : £2.25 B82-30531

833.8 — GERMAN FICTION, 1856-1900

833′.8 — Fiction in German. Fontane, Theodor — *Critical studies*
Bance, Alan. Theodor Fontane. — Cambridge : Cambridge University Press, Aug.1982. — [272]p. — (Anglica Germanica. Series 2)
ISBN 0-521-24532-x : £25.00 : CIP entry
B82-19259

833′.8[J] — Children′s short stories in German, *1856-1900 — English texts*
Seidel, Heinrich. The magic inkstand and other stories / by Heinrich Seidel ; translated from the German by Elizabeth Watson Taylor ; illustrated by Wayne Anderson. — London : Cape, 1982. — 160p : ill(some col.) ; 26cm
″The stories first appeared in Wintermärchen ... published in German″
ISBN 0-224-01856-6 : £5.95 B82-39652

833′.8[J] — Children′s stories in German. Swiss writers, *1856-1900 — Texts*
Spyri, Johanna. Heidi / Johanna Spyri. — Abridged. — Bristol : Purnell, 1982. — 150p : ill ; 21cm. — (A Purnell childrens classic)
ISBN 0-361-05334-7 : £0.99 B82-40122

833.912 — GERMAN FICTION, 1900-1945

833′.912 — Fiction in German, *1900-1945 — Polish texts*
Schaper, Edzard. Synowie Hioba / Edzard Schaper ; tlumaczyla z originalu niemieckiego Krystyna Brozozowska. — Londyn : Veritas Foundation Publication Centre, 1982. — 46p ; 19cm. — (Biblioteka ″Gazety niedzielnej″)
Unpriced (pbk) B82-30840

833′.912 — Fiction in German. Czechoslovak writers. Kafka, Franz — *Biographies*
Hayman, Ronald. K : a biography of Kafka / Ronald Hayman. — London : Weidenfeld and Nicolson, c1981. — xviii,349p,349p,[12]p of plates : ill,facsims,ports ; 24cm
Bibliography: p335-339. — Includes index
ISBN 0-297-77996-6 (cased) : £16.50
ISBN 0-297-78031-x (pbk) : £8.50 B82-01628

833′.912 — Fiction in German. Czechoslovak writers. Kafka, Franz *compared with* **Flaubert, Gustave** — *Critical studies*
Bernheimer, Charles. Flaubert and Kafka. — London : Yale University Press, Sept.1982. — [262]p
ISBN 0-300-02633-1 : £17.50 : CIP entry
Primary classification 843′.8 B82-29118

833′.912 — Fiction in German. Czechoslovak writers. Kafka, Franz. Correspondence to Baner, Felice — *Critical studies*
Canetti, Elias. Kafka′s other trial : the letters to Felice / Elias Canetti ; translated by Christopher Middleton. — Harmondsworth : Penguin, 1982, c1974. — 95p ; 20cm
Translation of: Der andere Prozess. — Originally published: London : Calder & Boyars, 1974
ISBN 0-14-006287-4 (pbk) : £1.95
Also classified at 943.08′4′0924 B82-18137

833′.912 — Fiction in German. Czechoslovak writers. Kafka, Franz — *Critical studies*
Robert, Marthe. Franz Kafka′s loneliness. — London : Faber, Sept.1982. — [264]p
Translation of: Seul comme Franz Kafka
ISBN 0-571-11945-x : £9.00 : CIP entry
B82-19551

833′.912 — Fiction in German. Czechoslovak writers. Kafka, Franz. Narrative — *Critical studies*
Pascal, Roy. Kafka′s narrators : a study of his stories and sketches / Roy Pascal. — Cambridge : Cambridge University Press, 1982. — 251p ; 22cm. — (Anglica Germanica. Series 2)
Includes index
ISBN 0-521-24365-3 (cased) : £22.50 : CIP rev.
ISBN 0-521-28965-0 (pbk) : £6.50 B82-09296

833′.912 — Fiction in German. Czechoslovak writers. Kafka, Franz. Prozess, *Der* **. Comedy**
Plaice, Neville. Kafka′s silent comedy / by Neville Plaice. — Portree : Aquila, c1982. — [20]p ; 21cm. — (Aquila essays ; no.15)
ISBN 0-7275-0258-1 (pbk) : £0.60 B82-39868

833′.912 — Fiction in German. Kafka, Franz — *Marxist viewpoints — Collections*
Franz Kafka : an anthology of Marxist criticism / edited and translated by Kenneth Hughes. — Hanover, N.H. ; London : Published for Clark University by University Press of New England, 1981. — xxviii,290p ; 24cm
Translated from several languages including French, German and Russian. — Includes index
ISBN 0-87451-206-9 : Unpriced B82-28091

833′.912 — Fiction in German. Mann, Thomas — *Biographies*
Winston, Richard. Thomas Mann : the making of an artist 1875-1911 / Richard Winston ; with an afterword by Clara Winston. — London : Constable, 1982, c1981. — vi,325p ; 25cm
Includes index
ISBN 0-09-460060-0 : £12.50 B82-21947

833′.912 — Fiction in German. Mann, Thomas. Tonio Kröger — *Study outlines*
Niven, Colin. Tonio Kröger : notes / by Colin Niven. — Harlow : Longman, 1982. — 80p ; 21cm. — (York notes ; 168)
Bibliography: p72-73
ISBN 0-582-78261-9 (pbk) : £0.90 B82-16463

833′.912[F] — Fiction in German, *1900-1945.* **Austrian writers** — *English texts*
Roth, Joseph. Weights and measures / Joseph Roth ; translated by David Le Vay. — London : Peter Owen, 1982. — 150p : 1ill ; 20cm
Translation of: Das falsche Gewicht
ISBN 0-7206-0562-8 : £7.50 B82-10617

833′.912[F] — Fiction in German, *1900-1945 — English texts*
Canetti, Elias. Auto da fé. — London : Cape, Jan.1982. — [464]p
Translation of: Die Blendung. — Originally published: 1946
ISBN 0-224-00568-5 : £7.95 : CIP entry
B82-00158

Mann, Thomas. Joseph and his brothers / Thomas Mann ; translated from the German by H.T. Lowe-Porter ; with an introduction by the author. — London : Secker & Warburg, 1956 (1981 [printing]). — xxi,1207p ; 22cm
Translation of: Joseph und seine Brüder
ISBN 0-436-27234-2 : £12.50 B82-02170

Schmidt, Arno. The egghead republic. — London : Boyars, July 1982. — [174]p
Translation of: Die Gelehrtenrepublik. — Originally published: 1979
ISBN 0-7145-2592-8 (pbk) : £3.95 : CIP entry
B82-13520

Schmidt, Arno. Scenes from the life of a faun. — London : Marion Boyars, Oct.1982. — [160]p
Translation of: Aus dem Leben eines Fauns
ISBN 0-7145-2762-9 : £6.95 : CIP entry
B82-25065

Traven, B.. The carreta / B. Traven. — London : Allison & Busby, 1981, c1970. — 264p ; 23cm
ISBN 0-85031-392-9 (cased) : £6.95 : CIP rev.
ISBN 0-85031-393-1 (pbk) : Unpriced
B80-22645

Traven, B.. Government / B. Traven. — London : Allison & Busby, 1980, c1971. — 231p ; 23cm
Translation of: Regierung. — Originally published: New York : Hill and Wang, c1971
ISBN 0-85031-356-2 (cased) : £6.50 : CIP rev.
ISBN 0-85031-357-0 (pbk) : £2.50 B80-07150

Traven, B.. March to the Montería / B. Traven. — London : Allison & Busby, 1982. — 227p ; 23cm
Translation from the German
ISBN 0-85031-394-5 (cased) : £6.95 : CIP rev.
ISBN 0-85031-395-3 (pbk) : Unpriced
B80-19495

Traven, B.. The treasures of B. Traven. — London : Cape, 1980. — 627p ; 21cm
Contents: The treasures of the Sierra Madre — The death ship — The bridge in the jungle
ISBN 0-224-01830-2 : £7.50 : CIP rev.
B80-05062

Traven, B.. The white rose / B. Traven. — London : Allison & Busby, 1980, c1979. — vii,209p ; 23cm
Translation of Die weisse Rose
ISBN 0-85031-369-4 (cased) : £6.50 : CIP rev.
ISBN 0-85031-370-8 (pbk) : £2.50 B80-07151

Zweig, Stefan. Beware of pity. — London : Cape, Oct.1982. — [368]p
Translation of: Ungeduld des Herzens
ISBN 0-224-02057-9 : £7.95 : CIP entry
B82-25163

833'.912[F] — Fiction in German. Czechoslovak writers, ***1900-1945 — English texts***

Kafka, Franz. The metamorphosis / by Franz Kafka ; translated and edited by Stanley Corngold. — Toronto ; London : Bantam, 1972 (1981 [printing]). — 201p : ill ; 18cm. — (A Bantam classic)
Translation of: Die Verwandlung. — Bibliography: p195-201
ISBN 0-553-21042-4 (pbk) : £0.65 B82-18411

833'.912[F] — Short stories in German, ***1900-1945 — English texts***

Hesse, Hermann. Pictor's metamorphoses : and other fantasies / Hermann Hesse ; edited, and with an introduction, by Theodore Ziolkowski ; translated by Rika Lesser. — London : Cape, 1982. — xxiv,213p ; 23cm
Translations from the German
ISBN 0-224-02025-0 : £7.50 : CIP rev. B82-01130

Marut, Ret. To the Honourable Miss S— : and other stories / by Ret Marut a/k/a B. Traven ; translated from the German by Peter Silcock ; with an introduction by Will Wyatt. — Westport : Hill ; Sanday (Over the Water, Sanday, Orkney) : Cienfuegos Press, 1981. — xvi,151p ; 21cm
ISBN 0-904564-45-2 (pbk) : £5.00 : CIP rev.
ISBN 0-88208-130-6 (U.S.)
ISBN 0-88208-131-4 (U.S.) B81-27423

833'.912[F] — Short stories in German. Austrian writers, ***1900-1945 — English texts***

Zweig, Stefan. The royal game & other stories / Stefan Zweig ; with an introduction by John Fowles ; translated from the German by Jill Sutcliffe. — London : Cape, 1981. — xviii,250p ; 23cm
Translation from the German
ISBN 0-224-01984-8 : £6.95 : CIP rev. B81-30964

833'.912[F] — Short stories in German. Czech writers, ***1900-1945 — English texts***

Kafka, Franz. Stories 1904-1924 / Franz Kafka ; translated from the German by J.A. Underwood ; with a foreword by Jorge Luis Borges. — London : Macdonald, 1981. — 271p ; 23cm
Translations from the German
ISBN 0-354-04639-x : £7.95 B82-03496

Kafka, Franz. Wedding preparations in the country : and other stories / Franz Kafka. — Harmondsworth : Penguin, 1978, c1953 (1982 [printing]). — 190p ; 20cm. — (Penguin modern classics)
Translated from the German
ISBN 0-14-004441-8 (pbk) : £2.25 B82-25121

833'.912[J] — Children's stories in German, ***1900-1945 — English texts***

Salten, Felix. Bambi : a life in the woods / by Felix Salten ; translated from the German by Whittaker Chambers ; with a foreword by John Galsworthy. — London : Cape, 1942 (1982 [printing]). — 223p ; 20cm
Translation of: Bambi
ISBN 0-224-60665-4 : £5.50 B82-40420

833'.912'09 — Fiction in German. Hofmannsthal, Hugo von & Rilke, Rainer Maria ***— Critical studies***

Segal, Naomi. The banal object : theme and thematics in Proust, Rilke, Hofmannsthal, and Sartre / Naomi Segal. — London : Institute of Germanic Studies, University of London, 1981. — ix,147p ; 22cm. — (Bithell series of dissertations ; v.6)
Bibliography: p136-143. — Includes index
ISBN 0-85457-099-3 (pbk) : Unpriced
Also classified at 843'.912'09 B82-20536

833.914 — GERMAN FICTION, 1945-

833'.914 — Children's stories in German, ***1945- — Irish texts***

Scheidl, Gerda Marie. Tibí : agus an fharraige mhór / scéal le Gerda Marie Scheidl ; pictiúir le Bernadette ; Gabriel Rosenstock a rinne an leagan Gaeilge do pháistí 8-10 mbliana. — Baile Átha Cliath [i.e. Dublin] : Oifig an tSoláthair, c1981. — [26]p : col.ill ; 30cm
Translation from the German
Unpriced B82-07763

833'.914 — Fiction in German, ***1945- — Texts***

Schnurre, Wolfdietrich. Man sollte dagegen sein : and other stories / Wolfdietrich Schnurre ; edited with an introduction and notes by Ursula Cairns Smith and Roderick H. Watt. — London : Heinemann, 1982. — 174p ; 19cm. — (Heinemann German texts)
German text, introduction and notes in English. — Bibliography: p160-163
ISBN 0-435-38750-2 (pbk) : Unpriced : CIP rev. B81-38846

833'.914 — Fiction in German. Schmidt, Arno ***— critical studies***

Minden, M. R.. Arno Schmidt : a critical study of his prose. — Cambridge : Cambridge University Press, Sept.1982. — [288]p. — (Anglica Germanica. Series 2)
ISBN 0-521-24515-x : £25.00 : CIP entry B82-21729

833'.914[F] — Fiction in German, ***1945- — English texts***

Abish, Walter. How German is it : Wie Deutsch ist es : a novel / by Walter Abish. — Manchester : Carcanet New Press, 1982. — 252p ; 22cm
Originally published: New York : New Directions, 1980
ISBN 0-85635-396-5 : Unpriced : CIP rev. B82-00310

Berthold, Will. Prinz-Albrecht-Strasse / Will Berthold ; translated by Fred Taylor. — London : Sphere, 1981. — 279p ; 18cm
Translation of: Prinz Albrecht Strasse
ISBN 0-7221-1622-5 (pbk) : £1.50 B82-02123

Betke, Lotte. Lights by the canal / Lotte Betke ; translated by Anthea Bell. — Basingstoke : Macmillan 1980, c1979. — 116p ; 18cm. — (Topliners)
Translation of: Lampen am Kanal. — For adolescents
ISBN 0-333-26430-4 (pbk) : £0.70 : CIP rev. B80-13113

Böll, Heinrich. And never said a word / Heinrich Böll ; translated from the German by Leila Vennewitz. — Harmondsworth : Penguin, 1982, c1978. — 151p ; 20cm
Translation of: Und sagte kein einziges Wort. — Originally published: London : Secker and Warburg, 1978
ISBN 0-14-005208-9 (pbk) : £1.95 B82-40370

Böll, Heinrich. The safety net / Heinrich Böll ; translated from the German by Leila Vennewitz. — London : Secker & Warburg, 1982, c1981. — xi,313p ; 23cm
Translation of: Fürsorgliche Belagerung
ISBN 0-436-05454-x : £7.50 B82-19796

Buchheim, Lothar-Günther. The boat / Lothar-Günther Buchheim ; translated by J. Maxwell Brownjohn. — [London] : Fontana, 1982, c1974. — 480p : ill ; 18cm
Translation of: Das Boot. — Originally published: London : Collins, 1974
ISBN 0-00-616646-6 (pbk) : £1.95 B82-25440

Grass, Günter. Cat and mouse. — London : Secker & Warburg, Aug.1982. — [192]p
ISBN 0-436-18780-9 : £6.95 : CIP entry B82-30566

Grass, Günter. Headbirths, or, The Germans are dying out / Günter Grass ; translated by Ralph Manheim. — London : Secker & Warburg, 1982. — 136p ; 21cm
Translation of: Kopfgeburten
ISBN 0-436-18777-9 : £6.95 B82-22093

Handke, Peter. The left-handed woman / Peter Handke. — London : Abacus, 1982, c1978. — 89p ; 20cm
Translation of: Die linkshändige Frau. — Originally published: New York : Farrar, Straus and Giroux, 1978 ; London : Eyre Methuen, 1980
ISBN 0-349-11631-8 (pbk) : £1.50 B82-37120

Jieschke, Wolfgang. The last day of creation. — London (76 Old Compton St., W.1.) : Century, Nov.1982. — [224]p
Translation of: Der letzte Tag der Schöpfung
ISBN 0-7126-0042-6 (pbk) : £3.95 : CIP entry B82-27971

Kempowski, Walter. Days of greatness / Walter Kempowski ; translated by Leila Vennewitz. — London : Secker & Warburg, 1982, c1981. — 399p ; 22cm
Translation of: Aus grosser Zeit. — Originally published: New York : Knopf, 1981
ISBN 0-436-23290-1 : £7.95 B82-08881

Kirst, Hans Hellmut. Party games / Hans Hellmut Kirst ; translated from the German by J. Maxwell Brownjohn. — [London] : Fontana, 1982, c1980. — 249p ; 18cm
Translation of: 08/15 in der Partei. — Originally published: London : Collins, 1980
ISBN 0-00-616585-0 (pbk) : £1.65 B82-36256

Kirst, Hans Hellmut. Party games. — Large print ed. — Anstey : Ulverscroft, Nov.1982. — [432]p. — (Ulverscroft large print series)
Translation of: 08/15 in der Partei. — Originally published: London : Collins, 1980
ISBN 0-7089-0880-2 : £5.00 : CIP entry B82-29091

Kirst, Hans Hellmut. The return of Gunner Asch / Hans Hellmut Kirst ; translated from the German by Robert Kee. — [London] : Fontana, 1966, c1957 (1982 [printing]). — 286p ; 18cm
Originally published: London : Weidenfeld & Nicolson, 1957
ISBN 0-00-616557-5 (pbk) : £1.50 B82-32103

Kirst, Hans Hellmut. What became of Gunner Asch / Hans Hellmut Kirst ; translated from the German by J. Maxwell Brownjohn. — [London] : Fontana, 1966, c1964 (1982 [printing]). — 285p ; 18cm
Translation of: 08/15 Heute. — Originally published: London : Collins, 1964
ISBN 0-00-616558-3 (pbk) : £1.50 B82-32104

Kirst, Hans Helmut. The night of the generals / Hans Helmut Kirst ; translated from the German by J. Maxwell Brownjohn. — Large print ed. — Leicester : Ulverscroft, 1981, c1963. — 468p ; 23cm. — (Ulverscroft large print series)
Originally published: London : Collins, 1963
ISBN 0-7089-0712-1 : £5.00 : CIP rev. B81-30507

Konsalik, Heinz G.. The damned of the Taiga / Heinz G. Konsalik ; translated by Charles Lewis. — Large print ed. — Leicester : Ulverscroft, 1982. — 420p ; 23cm. — (Ulverscroft large print series)
Translation o: Die Verdammten der Taiga. 4.Aufl. — Originally published: Henley-on-Thames : A. Ellis, 1978
ISBN 0-7089-0797-0 : Unpriced : CIP rev. B82-18559

Konsalik, Heinz G.. Diagnosis. — Henley-on-Thames : A. Ellis, Apr.1981. — [224]p
Translation of: Diagnose
ISBN 0-85628-102-6 : £7.50 : CIP entry B81-04234

Konsalik, Heinz G.. The ravishing doctor / Heinz G. Konsalik ; translated by Anthea Bell. — Large print ed. — Leicester : Ulverscroft, 1981, c1979. — 364p ; 23cm. — (Ulverscroft large print series)
Translation of: Die schoene Aerztin. — Originally published: Henley-on-Thames : Aidan Ellis, 1979
ISBN 0-7089-0691-5 : £5.00 : CIP rev. B81-28099

Konsalik, Heinz G.. The war bride. — Large print ed. — Anstey : Ulverscroft, Jan.1983. — [432]p. — (Ulverscroft large print series)
Translation of: Die Glückliche Ehe. — Originally published: Henley-on-Thames : H. Ellis, 1979
ISBN 0-7089-0906-x : £6.25 : CIP entry B82-32534

833'.914[F] — Fiction in German, *1945- — English texts* *continuation*

Paretti, Sandra. Maria Canossa / by Sandra Paretti ; translated from the German by Ruth Hein. — London : Hodder and Stoughton, 1982, c1981. — 296p ; 23cm
ISBN 0-340-27449-2 : £6.95 : CIP rev.
B81-35684

Simmel. The Sibyl cipher / Simmel ; translated from the German by Catherine Hutter. — London : Hamlym, 1982, c1979. — 220p ; 18cm
Translation of: Gott schuetzt die Liebenden
ISBN 0-600-20498-7 (pbk) : £1.50 B82-12063

Walser, Martin. The swan villa. — London : Secker & Warburg, Feb.1983. — [256]p
Translation of: Das Schwanenhaus
ISBN 0-436-56141-7 : £7.95 : CIP entry
B82-40891

Weitzer, Horst. Genocide at St-Honor / Horst Weitzer ; translated by George Hirst. — London : New English Library, 1981. — 155p ; 18cm. — (Wehrmacht series ; no.2)
Translation from the German
ISBN 0-450-05275-3 (pbk) : £1.25 B82-03694

Weitzer, Horst. Panzergrenadier / Horst Weitzer ; translated by George Hirst. — London : New English Library, 1981. — 157p ; 18cm. — (Wehrmacht series ; no.1)
Translation from the German
ISBN 0-450-05249-4 (pbk) : £1.25 B82-03693

Weitzer, Horst. Sonderkommando. — London : New English Library, Apr.1982. — [160]p. — (Wehrmacht ; no.3)
Translation from the German
ISBN 0-450-05376-8 (pbk) : £1.25 : CIP entry
B82-03595

Wolf, Christa. A model childhood / Christa Wolf ; translated by Ursule Molinaro and Hedwig Rappolt. — London : Virago, 1982, c1980. — 407p ; 22cm
Translation of: Kindheitsmuster. — Originally published: New York : Farrar, Straus and Giroux, c1980
ISBN 0-86068-253-6 : £8.95 : CIP rev.
B81-36021

Wolf, Christa. The quest for Christa T / by Christa Wolf ; translated by Christopher Middleton. — London : Virago, 1982, c1970. — 185p ; 20cm. — (Virago modern classics)
Translation of: Nachdenken über Christa T.. — Originally published: New York : Farrar, Straus and Giroux, 1970 ; London : Hutchinson, 1971
ISBN 0-86068-221-8 (pbk) : £2.95 : CIP rev.
B81-36025

833'.914[F] — Fiction in German. Swiss writers, *1945- — English texts*

Pedretti, Erica. Stones. — London : Calder, Sept.1982. — [224]p. — (The Swiss library)
Translation of: Veränderung
ISBN 0-7145-3929-5 : £7.95 : CIP entry
B82-26048

833'.914[J] — Children's short stories in German, *1945- — English texts*

Ecke, Wolfgang. Be a super sleuth with the case of the invisible witness / Wolfgang Ecke ; illustrated by Rolf Rettich ; by Stella and Vernon Humphries translated from the German. — London : Methuen Children's, 1980. — 141p : ill ; 20cm. — (A Pied piper book)
ISBN 0-416-89330-9 : £3.50 : CIP rev.
B80-10888

Ecke, Wolfgang. The Magnet detective box / [Wolfgang Ecke] ; [translated from the German by Stella and Vernon Humphries]. — [London] : [Methuen Children's Books], [1981]. — 1case : ill ; 19cm
Translation of: Der Schloss der roten Affen, Der Mann in schwarz and Das Gesicht an der Scheibe ; Solo für Melodica, Das Geheimnis der Alten Dschunke and Das Haus der 99 Geister ; Die neuesten und spannendsten Geschichten, Schach bei Vollmund and Der unsichtbare Zeuge. — Title from container. — Contents: Super sleuth 1. Originally published: London : Magnet, 1979 — The Magnet detective book 2. Originally published: London : Methuen, 1979 — The Magnet detective book 3. Originally published: London : Methuen, 1980
ISBN 0-416-86490-2 : £2.40
ISBN 0-416-89540-9 (v.2) : £0.85
ISBN 0-416-21370-7 (v.3) : £0.90 B82-36078

Janosch. Animal antics. — London : Andersen Press, Nov.1982. — [128]p
Translation of: Das Leben der Tiere
ISBN 0-86264-033-4 : £6.95 : CIP entry
B82-26078

833'.914[J] — Children's stories in German, *1945- — English texts*

Ball, Sara. Croguphant. — London : Blackie, Oct.1982. — [24]p
Translation of: Krogufant
ISBN 0-200-72793-1 (spiral) : £2.50 : CIP entry B82-25531

Bartos-Höppner, Barbara. My favourite animals / Barbara Bartos-Höppner ; pictures by Mary Rahn. — Galsgow : Blackie, 1981. — [28]p : col.ill ; 29cm
Translation of: Meine allerliebsten Tiere
ISBN 0-216-91166-4 : £3.95 : CIP rev.
B82-04297

Bauman, Kurt. Puss in Boots. — London : Abelard-Schuman, Sept.1982. — [24]p
Translation of: Der gestiefelte Kater
ISBN 0-200-72790-7 : £4.95 : CIP entry
B82-18966

Beisert, Heide Helene. Poor fish / story and pictures by Heide Helene Beisert ; translated by Marion Koenig. — London : Abelard, 1982. — [24]p : col.ill ; 30cm
Translation of: Der Fisch
ISBN 0-200-72792-3 : £4.95 : CIP rev.
B82-18967

Bohdal, Susi. Selina, the mouse and the giant cat / Susi Bohdal ; translated by Lucy Meredith. — London : Faber, 1982. — [28]p : ill ; 31cm
Translation of: Selina, Pumpernickel und die Katze Flora
ISBN 0-571-11855-0 : £6.95 : CIP rev.
B82-00210

Bolliger, Max. The lonely prince / Max Bolliger ; illustrated by Jürg Obrist. — London : Methuen Children's Books, 1981. — [26]p : col.ill ; 25x27cm
Translation of: Heinrich
ISBN 0-416-21590-4 : £3.95 B82-15608

Böttcher, Cordelia. Felix Finestitch / story told by Cordelia Böttcher ; pictures by Peer Rugland ; [translated by Stanley Drake]. — Edinburgh : Floris, 1982. — [32]p : col.ill ; 25x32cm
Translation of: Felix Nadelfein
ISBN 0-903540-52-5 : £4.95 : CIP rev.
B82-11110

Cantieni, Benita. Little elephant and big mouse / written by Benita Cantieni ; illustrated by Fred Gächten ; and translated by Oliver Gadsby. — London : Neugebauer, c1981. — [30]p : col.ill ; 30cm
Translation of: Der kleine Elefant und die grosse Maus
ISBN 0-907234-09-7 : £3.95 B82-03906

Donnelly, Elfie. Odd stockings / Elfie Donnelly ; translated by Anthea Bell. — London : Anderson, 1982. — 127p ; 21cm
Translation of: Der rote Strumpf
ISBN 0-86264-019-9 : £3.95 : CIP rev.
B82-10255

Ecke, Wolfgang. Be a super sleuth with the case of the bank hold-up. — London : Methuen Children's Books, Mar.1982. — [144]p. — (A Pied piper book)
These stories originally published: in German, in volumes entitled Der Mann in Schwarz, Das Geheimnis der alten Dschunke and Ein Gauner spielte Mundharmonika. Ravensburg : Otto Maier Verlag, 1972, 1973 and 1981
ISBN 0-416-21780-x : £3.95 : CIP entry
B82-01998

Galler, Helga. Little Nerino / Helga Galler. — London : Neugebauer, c1982. — [24]p : col.ill ; 22x24cm
Translation of: Der kleine Nerino
ISBN 0-907234-13-5 : £3.50 B82-19987

Gantschev, Ivan. The moon lake / story and pictures by Ivan Gantschev ; translated by Oliver Gadsby. — London : Neugebauer Press, c1981. — [28]p : col.ill ; 30cm
Translation of: Der Mondsee
ISBN 0-907234-08-9 : £3.95 B82-02275

Heine, Helme. Friends / Helme Heine. — London : Dent, c1982. — [29]p : col.ill ; 28cm
Translation of: Freunde
ISBN 0-460-06100-3 : £4.50 : CIP rev.
B82-13240

Heine, Helme. King Bounce the 1st / Helme Heine. — London : Neugebauer, c1982. — [28]p : col.ill ; 22x24cm
Translation of: König Hupf der 1
ISBN 0-907234-11-9 : £3.95 B82-19992

Kaufmann, Angelika. Pegas the horse / Angelika Kaufmann, Friederike Mayrocker for Philipp. — London : Neugebauer, c1982. — [27]p : col.ill ; 21x29cm
Translation of: Pegas, das Pferd
ISBN 0-907234-14-3 : £3.95 B82-19985

Korschunow, Irina. Johnny's dragon / by Irina Korschunow ; pictures by Mary Rahn ; translated from the German by Anthea Bell. — London : Scholastic, 1982, c1978. — 47p : ill ; 20cm. — (Hippo books)
ISBN 0-590-70088-x (pbk) : £0.70 B82-09334

Laimgruber, Monika. Let's make a play! / Monika Laimgruber. — London : MacRae, 1981. — [28]p : ill(some col.) ; 25x27cm
Translation of: Komm, spiel mit mir Theater. — Ill on lining paper
ISBN 0-86203-082-x : £3.95 B82-13348

Muller, Jorg. The sea people. — London : Gollancz, Aug.1982. — [36]p
Translation of: Die Menschen im Meer
ISBN 0-575-03088-7 : £5.95 : CIP entry
B82-15889

Nickl, Peter. The story of the kind wolf / Peter Nickl wrote it ; Józef Wilkoń painted the pictures ; and Marion Koenig retold the story in English. — London : Faber, 1982. — 28p : col.ill ; 29cm
Translation of: Die Geschichte vom guten Wolf
ISBN 0-571-11897-6 : £4.25 : CIP rev.
B82-03375

Opgenoorth, Winfried. Valerie and the goodnight swing. — Oxford : Oxford University Press, Sept.1982. — [32]p
Translation of: Valerie und die Gute-Nacht Schaukel
ISBN 0-19-279769-7 : £3.95 : CIP entry
B82-19192

Preussler, Otfried. The little water sprite. — London : Knight Books Feb.1983. — [112]p
Translation of: Der kleine Wasserman. — Originally published: London : Abelard-Schuman, 1960
ISBN 0-340-28643-1 (pbk) : £0.95 : CIP entry
B82-38070

Richter, Konrad. Simple Stephen and the magic fish. — London : Abelard-Schuman, Sept.1982. — [32]p
Translation of: Ofkos seltsame Reisen
ISBN 0-200-72787-7 : £4.95 : CIP entry
B82-18963

833'.914[J] — Children's stories in German, *1945- — English texts* *continuation*

Ruck-Pauquet, G.. The singing elephant. — London : Hodder & Stoughton Children's Books, Feb.1983. — [32]p
Translated from the German
ISBN 0-340-28610-5 : £4.95 : CIP entry
B82-38048

Sacré, Marie-José[Konig und Koch. *English*]. King and cook / Marie-José Sacré. — London : Abelard-Schuman, 1980. — [26]p : col.ill ; 30cm
Translation of: Konig und koch
ISBN 0-200-72678-1 : £3.95 : CIP rev.
B80-00448

Sommer-Bodenburg, Angela. The little vampire. — London : Andersen Press, Apr.1982. — [128]p
Translation of: Der kleine Vampir
ISBN 0-86264-018-0 : £3.95 : CIP entry
B82-06262

Sommer-Bodenburg, Angela. The little vampire moves in. — London : Andersen Press, Nov.1982. — [128]p. — (Little vampire series ; 2) (Andersen young readers' library)
Translation of: Der kleine Vampir zieht um
ISBN 0-86264-035-0 : £3.95 : CIP entry
B82-26079

Türk, Hanne. Hieronymus / text and illustrations by Hanne Türk ; translated by Oliver Gadsby. — London : Neugebauer Press, c1981. — [26]p : col.ill ; 30cm
Translation of: Heironymus
ISBN 0-907234-06-2 : £3.95 B82-02276

Ungerer, Tomi. Crictor / Tomi Ungerer. — London : Methuen, 1959, c1958 (1982 [printing]). — 30p : chiefly col.ill ; 28cm
Originally published: New York : Harper, 1958
ISBN 0-416-61700-x (cased) : Unpriced
ISBN 0-416-22440-7 (Unpriced) B82-36117

833'.914[J] — Children's stories in German. Austrian writers, *1945- — English texts*

Nostlinger, Christine. Lollipop. — London : Andersen Press, Feb.1982. — [128]p. — (Andersen young readers' library)
Translation of: Lollipop
ISBN 0-86264-015-6 : £3.95 : CIP entry
B81-36964

833'.914[J] — Children's stories in German. Swiss writers, *1945- — English texts*

Baumann, Kurt. Piro and the fire brigade / by Kurt Baumann ; translated by Marion Koenig ; with pictures by Jiri Bernard. — London : Faber in association with Nord-Süd, 1981. — [25]p : col.ill ; 30cm
Translation of: Piro und die Feuerwehr. — Ill on lining papers
ISBN 0-571-11843-7 : £3.95 : CIP rev.
B81-22623

Nikly, Michelle. The Princess on the nut, or, The curious courtship of the son of the Princess on the Pea / by Michelle Nikly ; translated by Lucy Meredith ; with pictures by Jean Claverie. — London : Faber in association with Nord-Süd, 1981. — [24]p : ill(some col.) ; 30cm
Translation of: Die Prinzessin auf der Nuss
ISBN 0-571-11846-1 : £3.95 : CIP rev.
B81-22624

836.5 — GERMAN LETTERS, 1625-1750

836'.5 — Fiction in Spanish. Pérez Galdós, Benito. La de Bringas — *Critical studies*

Bly, Peter. Péréz Galdós, La de Bringas / Peter Bly. — London : Grant & Cutler in association with Tamesis, 1981. — 100p ; 20cm. — (Critical guides to Spanish texts)
Bibliography: p96-100
ISBN 0-7293-0110-9 (pbk) : £2.00 B82-33976

837.8 — GERMAN SATIRE AND HUMOUR, 1856-1900

837'.8 — Satire in German. Tucholsky, Kurt - *Critical studies*

Grenville, Bryan P.. Kurt Tucholsky. — London : Oswald Wolff, 4une 1981. — [112]p. — (German literature and society ; v.1)
ISBN 0-85496-074-0 (pbk) : £4.00 : CIP entry
B81-10018

838.912 — GERMAN MISCELLANY, 1900-1945

838'.91208 — Prose in German, *1900-1945 — English texts*

Walser, Robert. Selected shorter prose. — Manchester : Carcanet Press, Oct.1981. — [224]p
ISBN 0-85635-370-1 : £6.95 : CIP entry
B81-28848

838.914 — GERMAN MISCELLANY, 1945-

838'.91409 — German literature. Austrian writers. Handke, Peter — *Critical studies*

Schlueter, June. The plays and novels of Peter Handke / June Schlueter. — Pittsburgh : University of Pittsburgh Press ; London : Feffer and Simons, c1981. — xiii,213p ; 24cm. — (Critical essays in modern literature)
Includes appendix in German with English translation. — Bibliography: p195-208. — Includes index
ISBN 0-8229-3443-4 (cased) : Unpriced
B82-23743

839.09 — YIDDISH LITERATURE

839'.0933[F] — Short stories in Yiddish, *1860- — English texts*

Singer, Isaac Bashevis. The collected stories of Isaac Bashevis Singer. — London : Cape, 1982, c1981. — viii,610p ; 23cm
Originally published: New York : Farrar, Strauss, Giroux, 1981
ISBN 0-224-02024-2 : £10.50 : CIP rev.
B82-01129

Singer, Isaac Bashevis. Old love / Isaac Bashevis Singer. — Harmondsworth : Penguin, 1982, c1979. — 253p ; 19cm
Originally published: New York : Farrar, Straus & Giroux, 1979 ; London : Cape, 1980
ISBN 0-14-005768-4 (pbk) : £1.50 B82-16783

839.31 — DUTCH LITERATURE

839.3'1164 — Poetry in Dutch, *1945- — English texts*

Claus, Hugo. Selected poems 1953-1973. — Portree (P.O. Box 1, Portree, Isle of Skye, Scotland IV51 9BT) : Aquila Publishing, Nov.1982. — 1v.
Translation from the Dutch
ISBN 0-7275-0245-x (cased) : £5.95 : CIP entry
ISBN 0-7275-0246-8 (pbk) : £3.50
ISBN 0-7275-0244-1 (signed ed.) : £10.00
B82-29022

839.3'1364[J] — Children's short stories in Dutch, *1945- — English texts*

Biegel, Paul. Crocodile man / Paul Biegel ; translated by Patricia Crampton ; illustrated by Eva Järnerud. — London : Dent, 1982. — ill ; 23cm
Translation of: Jiri
ISBN 0-460-06091-0 : £4.95 : CIP rev.
B82-06848

839.3'1364[J] — Children's stories in Dutch, *1945- — English texts*

Biegel, Paul. Virgil Nosegay and the Hupmobile. — London : Blackie, Feb.1983. — [124]p
Translation of: Virgilius Van Tuil en de oom uit Zweden
ISBN 0-216-91372-1 : £5.95 : CIP entry
B82-37841

Hartman, Evert. War without friends. — London : Chatto & Windus, Oct.1982. — [192]p
Translation of: Oorlog zonder vrienden
ISBN 0-7011-2650-7 : £5.50 : CIP entry
B82-23200

Kooiker, Leonie. The magic stone. — London : Methuen Children's Books, Apr.1982. — [160]p
Translation of: De heksensteen. — Originally published: New York : Morrow, 1978
ISBN 0-416-22170-x : £4.95 : CIP entry
B82-08079

839.36 — AFRIKAANS LITERATURE

839.3'635[F] — Fiction in Afrikaans, *1961- — English texts*

Joubert, Elsa. Poppie. — London : Hodder & Stoughton, Dec.1981. — [368]p
Translation of: Die swerfjare van Poppie Nongena. — Originally published: 1980
ISBN 0-340-27269-4 (pbk) : £1.25 : CIP entry
B81-31365

Joubert, Elsa. To die at sunset / Elsa Joubert ; translated from the Afrikaans by Klaas Steytler. — London : Hodder and Stoughton, 1982. — 141p ; 23cm
Translation of: Ons wag op die kaptein
ISBN 0-340-28129-4 : £5.95 : CIP rev.
B82-10474

839.5 — SCANDINAVIAN LITERATURES

839'.68 — Prose in Old Norse. Kings' sagas. Rhetoric — *Critical studies*

Knirk, James E.. Oratory in the kings' sagas / James E. Knirk. — Oslo : Univesitetsforlaget ; London : Global Book Resources [distributor], 1981. — 247p ; 22cm
Bibliography: p233-242. — Includes index
ISBN 82-00-05685-6 (pbk) : £10.40
B82-05724

839'.68 — Prose in Old Norse — *Texts*

Bandamanna saga / edited by Hallvard Magerøy ; glossary made by Peter Foote ; introduction and notes Englished by Peter Foote and Sue Margeson. — [London] : Viking Society for Northern Research, University College London, c1981. — lx,105p : 3maps ; 21cm
Main text in Icelandic. — Introduction and notes translated from the Norwegian. — Includes index
ISBN 0-903521-15-6 (pbk) : Unpriced
B82-22544

Snorri Sturluson. [Edda. Pt.1]. Edda : prologue and Gylfaginning / Snorri Sturluson ; edited by Anthony Faulkes. — Oxford : Clarendon, c1982. — xxxiv,177p,[1]leaf of plates : 1facsim ; 23cm
Bibliography: pxxxiii-xxxiv. — Includes index
ISBN 0-19-811175-4 : £12.50 B82-31355

839.7 — SWEDISH LITERATURE

839.7'172 — Poetry in Swedish, *1900-1945 — Swedish-English parallel texts*

Ekelöf, Gunnar. Songs of something else : selected poems / of Gunnar Ekelöf ; translated by Leonard Nathan and James Larson. — Princeton ; Guildford : Princeton University Press, c1982. — xiv,168p ; 22cm. — (The Lockert library of poetry in translation)
Parallel English and Swedish texts
ISBN 0-691-06511-x (cased) : £14.10
B82-32985

839.7'1'74 — Poetry in Swedish, *1945- - English texts*

Aspenström, Werner. The blue whale & other pieces. — London (12 Stevenage Rd, SW6 6ES) : Oasis Books, July 1981. — [96]p
ISBN 0-903375-48-6 (pbk) : £1.80 : CIP entry
B81-14401

839.7'174 — Poetry in Swedish, *1945- — English texts*

Edfelt, Johannes. Family tree and other prose poems. — London : Oasis, Sept.1981. — [20]p. — (O books series ; 4)
Translated from the Swedish
ISBN 0-903375-56-7 (pbk) : £0.60 : CIP entry
B81-22604

839.7'26 — Drama in Swedish. Strindberg, August — *Critical studies*

Sprinchorn, Evert. Strindberg as dramatist. — London : Yale University Press, Sept.1982. — [332]p
ISBN 0-300-02731-1 : £20.00 : CIP entry
B82-29120

839.7'374 — Children's stories in Swedish, *1945-* — *Welsh texts*

Bergström, Gunilla. Bydd yn ddewr, Ifan Bifan / Gunilla Bergström ; addasiad Cymraeg gan Juli Phillips ; ymgynghorwr iaith Elen Ogwen. — Caerdydd : Gwasg y Dref Wen, c1982. — [28]p : col.ill ; 24cm
Translation of: Är du feg, Alfons Aberg?. — Text on inside cover
£2.40 B82-33918

Boore, Roger. Dafydd yn fach, Dafydd yn fawr / Gunilla Wolde ; addasiad gan Roger Boore ; ymgynghorwr D. Gwynfor Evans. — Caerdydd : Gwasg y Dref Wen, c1981. — [24]p : col.ill ; 17cm
Adaptation of: Totte är liten. — Text on lining papers
£1.15 B82-10643

Boore, Roger. Dafydd yn gwneud teisen / Gunilla Wolde ; addasiad gan Roger Boore ; ymgynghorwr D. Gwynfor Evans. — Caerdydd : Gwasg y Dref Wen, c1981. — [24]p : col.ill ; 17cm
Adaptation of: Totte bakar. — Text on lining papers
£1.15 B82-10642

839.7'374 — Fiction in Swedish. Delblanc, Sven. Åminne — *Critical studies*

Robinson, Michael. Sven Delblanc: Åminne / by Michael Robinson. — Hull : Department of Scandinavian Studies, University of Hull, 1981. — 79p : 1map ; 21cm. — (Studies in Swedish literature ; no.12)
Bibliography: p77-79
ISBN 0-85958-533-6 (corrected : pbk) : Unpriced B82-08903

839.7'374[F] — Fiction in Swedish, *1945-* — *English texts*

Claesson, Stig, *1928-*. Ancient monuments / Stig Claesson ; translated from the Swedish by Irene Scobbie. — Stornaway : Thule, 1980. — 142p ; 22cm. — (UNESCO collection of representative works. European series)
Translation of: Vem älskar Yngve Frej?
ISBN 0-906191-47-5 (pbk) : £3.50 B82-04239

Rudström, Lennart. Our family / Lennart Rudstrom ; English version by Olive Jones ; pictures by Carl Larsson. — London : Methuen, 1980. — [32]p : ill(some col.),ports (some col.) ; 24x32cm
Translation of: Carl Larsson och bilder av familjen. — Translation and revision of: 'Carl Larsson och hans bilder av familjen'. Stockholm : Bonniers, 1979. — Based on the life of Carl Larsson
ISBN 0-416-88560-8 : £4.50 : CIP rev.
Also classified at 741.64'092'4 B79-37407

839.7'374[F] — Short stories in Swedish, *1945-* — *English texts*

Bergman, Ingmar. Four stories. — London : Boyars, June 1982. — [168]p
Originally published: 1977. — Contents: The touch — Cries and whispers — The hour of the wolf — A passion
ISBN 0-7145-2603-7 (pbk) : £3.95 : CIP entry
B82-14215

839.7'374[J] — Children's stories in Swedish, *1945-* — *English texts*

Beskow, Elsa. Peter in blueberry land / Elsa Beskow. — London : Ernest Benn, 1982. — [17]leaves : col.ill ; 25x32cm
Translation from the Swedish
ISBN 0-510-00129-7 : £3.95 B82-32133

Beskow, Elsa. The sun egg / Elsa Beskow. — London : Ernest Benn, [1980]. — [34]p : ill (some col.) ; 25x32cm
Translated from the Swedish
ISBN 0-510-00078-9 : £3.50 B82-22915

Hansson, Gunilla. Nina. — London : Burke, Aug.1982. — [32]p
Translation of: Nu ska har bli Andra Bular
ISBN 0-222-00837-7 : £4.25 : CIP entry
B82-18470

Löfgren, Ulf. Hans Andersen's The swineherd / [retold and illustrated by] Ulf Löfgren ; English version by Linda M. Jennings. — London : Hodder and Stoughton, c1981. — [26]p : col.ill ; 25x27cm
Translation from the Swedish
ISBN 0-340-27133-7 : £3.50 : CIP rev.
B82-04842

Löfgren, Ulf. Hans Andersen's Tomfool / [retold and illustrated by] Ulf Löfgren ; English version by Linda M. Jennings. — London : Hodder and Stoughton, c1981. — [26]p : col.ill ; 25x27cm
Translation from the Swedish
ISBN 0-340-27134-5 : £3.50 : CIP rev.
B82-04843

Löfgren, Ulf. The thief / Ulf Löfgren ; English text by Linda M. Jennings. — London : Hodder and Stoughton, 1982. — [24]p : col.ill ; 23x27cm
Translated from the Swedish. — Ill on lining papers
ISBN 0-340-27751-3 : £3.50 : CIP rev.
B82-00263

Nilsson, Ulf. Runtle the pig. — London : Methuen Children's Books, Oct.1982. — [32]p
Translation of: Alskade lilla gris
ISBN 0-416-26350-x : £3.95 : CIP entry
B82-24488

Pettersson, Allan Rune. Frankenstein's aunt. — London : Hodder and Stoughton, Sept.1982. — [128]p. — (Knight books)
Translation of: Frakenstein's faster. — Originally published: London : Hodder and Stoughton Children's Books, 1980
ISBN 0-340-28045-x (pbk) : £0.95 : CIP entry
B82-18798

Pettersson, Allan Rune. Frankenstein's aunt / Allan Rune Pettersson ; translated by Joan Tate. — London : Heinemann Educational, 1982, c1980. — 125p ; 20cm. — (The New Windmill series ; 260)
Translation of: Frankensteins faster. — Originally published: London : Hodder & Stoughton, 1980
ISBN 0-435-12260-6 : £1.40 B82-35735

Rydberg, Viktor. The Christmas tomten. — London : Hodder & Stoughton Children's Books, Aug.1981. — [32]p
ISBN 0-340-27065-9 : £3.50 : CIP entry
B81-18031

Stalsjo, Eva. The flyaway bird. — London : Methuen Children's Books, Oct.1982. — [32]p
Translation of: Undulat bortflugen
ISBN 0-416-26240-6 : £3.50 : CIP entry
B82-24487

Swahn, Sven Christer. The twilight visitors / Sven Christer Swahn ; translated from the Swedish by Joan Tate. — London : Methuen, 1980. — 158p ; 21cm
Translation of: Skymningsgästerna
ISBN 0-416-87750-8 : £4.50 B82-22724

839.81 — DANISH LITERATURE

839.8'116 — Poetry in Danish, *1800-1900* — *Danish-English parallel texts*

Andersen, H. C.. The comet / Hans Christian Andersen ; translation & foreword by Anne Born. — Richmond, Surrey : Keepsake in association with Quarto, 1982. — 15p : ill,1port ; 26cm
Parallel Danish text and English translation. — Limited ed. of 200 copies
ISBN 0-901924-56-3 (pbk) : £1.95 B82-29752

839.8'1172 — Poetry in Danish, *1900-1945* — *English texts*

Heinesen, William. Arctis : selected poems, 1921-1972 / William Heinesen ; translated from the Danish by Anne Born. — Findhorn : Thule, 1980. — 56p ; 23cm
ISBN 0-906191-56-4 (cased) : £3.50
ISBN 0-906191-58-0 (pbk) : £1.95 B82-04237

839.8'136[J] — Children's short stories in Danish, *1800-1900* — *English texts*

Andersen, H. C.. Fairy tales of Hans Christian Andersen. — London : Hodder & Stoughton, Oct.1981. — [160]p
Translated from the Danish
ISBN 0-340-27025-x : £6.95 : CIP entry
B81-28164

Andersen, H. C.. Michael Hague's favourite Hans Christian Andersen fairy tales. — London : Methuen Children's, 1981. — 162p : col.ill ; 27cm
Originally published: New York : Holt, Rinehart, and Winston, 1981
ISBN 0-416-22080-0 : £6.95 B82-15611

Andersen, H. C.. The nightingale : and other tales / Hans Christian Andersen ; illustrated by Mary Tozer. — Tadworth : World's Work, c1982. — 106p : ill(some col.) ; 25cm
Translation from the Danish
ISBN 0-437-23062-7 : £5.95 B82-35637

Andersen, H. C.. Three Hans Andersen fairy tales / illustrated by Josef Paleček. — [London] : Dent, [1980]. — 1case : col.ill ; 16cm
Contents: The princess and the pea. Translation of: Die Prinzessin auf der Erbse — Blockhead Hans. Translation of: Der Töpel-Hans — The Swineherd. Translation of: Der Schweine-hirt
ISBN 0-460-06059-7 : £3.95 : CIP rev.
B80-11657

839.8'136[J] — Children's stories in Danish, *1800-1900* — *English texts*

Andersen, H. C.. The little match-girl / Hans Christian Andersen ; translated by L.W. Kingsland ; illustrated by Kaj Beckman. — Kingswood : Kaye & Ward, c1981. — [28]p : col.ill ; 22x27cm
Translation from the Danish. — Originally published: in 'Hans Andersen's Fairy tales'. London : Oxford University Press, 1959
ISBN 0-7182-2930-4 : £3.95 B82-09367

Andersen, H. C.. The little mermaid / Hans Christian Andersen ; illustrated by Joseph Paleček ; translated by M.R. James. — London : Faber in association with Nord-Süd, 1981. — 42p : col.ill ; 33cm
Translation of: Die kleine Seejungfrau
ISBN 0-571-11847-x : £4.95 : CIP rev.
B81-21496

Andersen, H. C.. The swineherd / Hans-Christian Andersen, Lisbeth Zwerger ; translated from the Danish by Anthea Bell. — London : Neugebauer, c1982. — [25]p : col.ill ; 22x24cm
Translation of: Der Schweinehir
ISBN 0-907234-12-7 : £3.95 B82-19986

Andersen, H. C.. The ugly duckling. — London : Hamilton, Sept.1982. — [32]p
Translation of: Den grimme aelling
ISBN 0-241-10836-5 : £4.50 : CIP entry
B82-18835

839.8'1372[F] — Fiction in Danish, *1900-1945* — *English texts*

Heinesen, William. The tower at the edge of the world : a poetic mosaic novel about my earliest youth / William Heinesen ; translated from the Danish by Maja Jackson. — Findhorn : Thule, 1981. — 183p ; 20cm. — (UNESCO collection of representative works. European series)
Translation of: Tårnet ved verdens ende
ISBN 0-906191-64-5 (pbk) : £2.50 B82-04238

839.8'1374[F] — Fiction in Danish, *1945- — English texts*

Stangerup, Henrik. The man who wanted to be guilty / Henrik Stangerup ; translated into English by David Gress-Wright. — London : Boyars, 1982. — 124p ; 23cm
Translation of: Manden der ville vaere skyldig
ISBN 0-7145-2733-5 : £6.95 B82-13683

839.8'1374[J] — Children's stories in Danish, *1945- — English texts*

Haugaard, Erik C.. Chase me, catch nobody!. — London : Granada, Jan.1983. — [200]p
ISBN 0-246-11938-1 : £4.95 : CIP entry B82-33708

Holm, Anne. The hostage / Anne Holm ; translated from the Danish by Patricia Crampton. — London : Magnet, 1982, c1980. — 171p ; 18cm
Originally published: London : Methuen Children's, 1980
ISBN 0-416-24580-3 (pbk) : £1.25 B82-34114

Mogensen, Jan. Just before dawn / Jan Mogensen ; English text by Wendy Wolf. — London : Hamilton, 1982. — [29]p : col.ill ; 26cm
Translation of: Har du sovet godt, Bamse?
ISBN 0-241-10719-9 : £3.95 : CIP rev. B81-35819

Olsen, Mimi Vang. The fur children / Mimi Vang Olsen. — [London] : Collins, 1981, c1979. — [39]p : col.ill ; 23cm
£2.95 B82-17567

Svend, Otto S.. The giant fish / Svend Otto S. ; translated by Joan Tate. — London : Pelham, 1982. — [24]p : col.ill ; 26cm
Translation of: Kaempefisken
ISBN 0-7207-1380-3 : £3.50 B82-11687

839.82 — NORWEGIAN LITERATURE

839.8'226 — Drama in Norwegian, *1800-1900 — English texts*

Ibsen, Henrik. A doll's house / by Henrik Ibsen ; English translation by Michael Meyer. — London : Methuen, 1982, c1965. — 90p ; 21cm. — (A Pit playtext)
Four men, 3 women. — Translation of: Et dukkehjem. — Originally published: London : Hart-Davis, 1965
ISBN 0-413-51230-4 (pbk) : £1.95 B82-33938

839.8'226 — Drama in Norwegian. Ibsen, Henrik *— Critical studies*

Chamberlain, John. Ibsen : the open vision. — London : Athlone Press, May 1982. — [260]p
ISBN 0-485-11227-2 (cased) : £20.00 : CIP entry B82-07667

Durbach, Errol. Ibsen the romantic : analogues of paradise in the later plays / Errol Durbach. — London : Macmillan, 1982. — vii,213p ; 23cm
Bibliography: p206-209. — Includes index
ISBN 0-333-28426-7 : £15.00 B82-28392

839.8'2301'08[FS] — Short stories in Norwegian, *ca 1850-1981 — Anthologies — English texts*

Slaves of love and other Norwegian short stories. — Oxford : Oxford University Press, Oct.1982. — [300]p
ISBN 0-19-212601-6 : £12.50 : CIP entry B82-23658

839.8'2372[F] — Fiction in Norwegian, *1900-1945 — English texts*

Borgen, Johan. Lillelord : a novel / by Johan Borgen ; edited with an introduction by Ronald E. Peterson ; translated by Elizabeth Brown Moen and Ronald E. Peterson. — London : Calder, 1982. — viii,312p ; 21cm
Translation of: Lillelord
ISBN 0-7145-3692-x : £8.95 : CIP rev. B82-04505

Rølvaag, O. E.. Peder victorious : a tale of the pioneers twenty years later / by O.E. Rölvaag ; translated from the Norwegian by Nora O. Solum & the author ; with an introduction by Gudrun Hovde Gvåle ; translated from the Norwegian & adapted by Einer Haugen. — Lincoln, Neb. ; London : University of Nebraska Press, 1982, c1957. — xix,325p ; 21cm. — (A Bison book)
Translation of: Peder Seier
ISBN 0-8032-8906-5 (pbk) : Unpriced B82-36530

839.8'2374[J] — Children's stories in Norwegian, *1945- — English texts*

Lorentzen, Karin. Lanky Longlegs. — London : Dent, Aug.1982. — [96]p
ISBN 0-460-06120-8 : £3.50 : CIP entry B82-16642

Prøysen, Alf. Mrs Pepperpot's Christmas / story by Alf Prøysen ; illustrated by Björn Berg ; translated by Marianne Helweg. — Harmondsworth : Puffin, 1981, c1972. — [32]p : col.ill ; 19x23cm. — (Picture Puffins)
Translation of: Här kommer yag, sa testedsgumman. — Originally published: London : Hutchinson, 1972
ISBN 0-14-050378-1 (pbk) : £0.95 B82-05946

839.83 — NEW NORSE LITERATURE

839.8'3172 — Poetry in New Norse: Poetry in Telemark dialects, *1900-1945 — English texts*

Vesaas, Tarjei. Evening. — London : Oasis, Sept.1981. — [16]p. — (O books series ; 3)
Translation of selections from Dikt i samling
ISBN 0-903375-57-5 : £0.60 : CIP entry B81-23904

840 — ROMANCE LITERATURES

840'.800912 — French literature, *1900- — Anthologies — French texts — For schools*

Variété : passages from modern French literature. — London : Edward Arnold, Feb.1983. — [96]p
ISBN 0-7131-0656-5 (pbk) : £2.25 : CIP entry B82-38903

840.9 — FRENCH LITERATURE. HISTORY AND CRITICAL STUDIES

840'.9 — French literature - *Critical studies*

Barthes, Roland. A Barthes reader. — London : Cape, June 1981. — [450]p
ISBN 0-224-01944-9 : £12.50 : CIP entry B81-11939

840'.9 — French literature. Criticism. Barthes, Roland *— Critical studies*

Lavers, Annette. Roland Barthes : structuralism and after. — London : Methuen, Sept.1982. — [400]p
ISBN 0-416-72380-2 : £15.00 : CIP entry B82-19662

840.9 — French literature. Criticism. Baudelaire, Charles *— Critical studies*

Lloyd, Rosemary. Baudelaire's literary criticism / Rosemary Lloyd. — Cambridge : Cambridge University Press, 1981. — x,338p ; 24cm
Bibliography: p306-330. — Includes index
ISBN 0-521-23552-9 : £29.50 : CIP rev. B81-31830

840'.9 — French literature, *to 1973 — Critical studies*

Genette, Gérard. Figures of literary discourse. — Oxford : Basil Blackwell, Mar.1982. — [320]p
Translation of selections from: Figures. 1966-1972. — Originally published: New York : Columbia University Press, 1981
ISBN 0-631-13089-6 : £15.00 : CIP entry B82-03112

840.9'005 — French literature, *1715-1789 — Critical studies*

Mason, Haydn. French writers and their society 1715-1800 / Haydn Mason. — London : Macmillan, 1982. — vi,261p ; 23cm
Bibliography: p246-248. — Includes index
ISBN 0-333-26465-7 : £20.00 B82-28684

Studies on Voltaire and the eighteenth century, 199. — Oxford : Voltaire Foundation at the Taylor Institution, 1981. — 379p ; 24cm. — (Studies on Voltaire and the eighteenth century, ISSN 0435-2866 ; 199)
Text in English and French
Unpriced B82-19508

840.9'008 — French literature, *1848-1900.* **Decadence** *— Critical studies*

Pierrot, Jean. The decadent imagination : 1880-1900 / Jean Pierrot ; translated by Derek Coltman. — Chicago ; London : University of Chicago Press, 1981. — viii,309p ; 24cm
Translation of: Marveilleux et fantastique. — Includes index
ISBN 0-226-66822-3 : £15.75 B82-17775

840.9'27 — French literature, *1800-1900.* **Characters: Fools. Symbolic aspects**

Fletcher, Dennis. Praise of folly : an inaugural lecture / by Dennis Fletcher. — [Durham] ([Old Shire Hall, Durham DH1 3HP]) : University of Durham, 1981. — 19p ; 22cm
£0.60 (pbk)
Also classified at 704.9'46 B82-07759

840.9'96 — French literature. African writers, *1945- — Critical studies*

Irele, Abiola. The African experience in literature and ideology. — London : Heinemann Educational, Sept.1981. — [224]p. — (Studies in African literature)
ISBN 0-435-91631-9 (pbk) : £5.95 : CIP entry
Primary classification 820.9'96 B81-22601

840.9'96 — French literature. African writers, *1945- — Critical studies — Serials*

African literature today. — London : Heinemann Educational
No.12: New writing, new approaches. — Oct.1981. — [224]p
ISBN 0-435-91648-3 (cased) : £9.95 : CIP entry
ISBN 0-435-91649-1 (pbk) : £4.95
Primary classification 820.9'96 B81-28035

840.9'97294 — French literature. Haitian writers. Cultural aspects, *1915-1961*

Dash, J. Michael. Literature and ideology in Haiti, 1915-1961 / J. Michael Dash. — London : Macmillan, 1981. — xv,213p ; 23cm
Includes index
ISBN 0-333-30013-0 : £15.00 B82-06649

841 — FRENCH POETRY

841 — Poetry in French. Martinique writers. Césaire, Aimé *— Critical studies*

Arnold, A. James. Modernism and negritude : the poetry and poetics of Aimé Césaire / A. James Arnold. — Cambridge, Mass. ; London : Harvard University Press, 1981. — xi,318p ; 24cm
Includes index
ISBN 0-674-58057-5 : £15.00 B82-11874

841'.009 — Poetry in French. Reading. Techniques

Lewis, Roy, *1922-*. On reading French verse. — Oxford : Clarendon, May 1982. — [300]p
ISBN 0-19-815775-4 (cased) : £14.50 : CIP entry
ISBN 0-19-815783-5 (pbk) : £6.95 B82-07510

841.1 — FRENCH POETRY, TO 1400

841'.1 — Poetry in French. Chaucer, Geoffrey. Authorship

Chaucer and the poems of "Ch". — Woodbridge : Brewer, Oct.1982. — [192]p. — (Chaucer studies, ISSN 0261-9822 ; 9)
ISBN 0-85991-130-6 : £19.50 : CIP entry
Primary classification 841'.1 B82-24127

841'.1 — Poetry in French, *to 1400 — French-English parallel texts*

Chaucer and the poems of "Ch". — Woodbridge : Brewer, Oct.1982. — [192]p. — (Chaucer studies, ISSN 0261-9822 ; 9)
ISBN 0-85991-130-6 : £19.50 : CIP entry
Also classified at 841'.1 B82-24127

841'.1 — Poetry in Old French. Aucassin et Nicolete — *Bibliographies*

Sargent-Baur, Barbara Nelson. Aucassin et Nicolette : a critical bibliography / Barbara Nelson Sargent-Baur and Robert Francis Cook. — London : Grant & Cutler, 1981. — 83p ; 23cm. — (Research bibliographies & checklists) Includes index
ISBN 0-7293-0108-7 (pbk) : £4.80 B82-33979

841'.1 — Poetry in Old French. Chrétien, *de Troyes.* **Special themes: Love** — *Critical studies*

Noble, Peter S.. Love and marriage in Chrétien de Troyes. — Cardiff : University of Wales Press, July 1982. — [141]p
ISBN 0-7083-0805-8 : £9.95 : CIP entry
B82-13009

841'.1 — Poetry in Old French — *Old French-English parallel texts*

Chrétien, *de Troyes*. Lancelot, or, The knight of the cart = (Le chevalier de la charrette) / Chrétien de Troyes ; edited and translated by William W. Kibler. — New York ; London : Garland, 1981. — xxxvi,312p : 1ill ; 23cm. — (Garland library of medieval literature. Series A. ; vol.1)
Parallel Old French and English text. — Bibliography: pxxix-xxxvi. — Includes index
ISBN 0-8240-9442-5 : Unpriced B82-27171

Daniel, Arnaut. The poetry of Arnaut Daniel / edited and translated by James J. Wilhelm. — New York ; London : Garland, 1981. — xxxix,131p,4p of plates : ill,facsims,music ; 23cm. — (Garland library of medieval literature. Series A ; vol.3)
Translations from Old French. — Bibliography: pxxxi-xxxix. — Includes index
ISBN 0-8240-9446-8 : Unpriced B82-27170

841'.1'08 — Poetry in English. Chaucer, Geoffrey. Sources: Poetry in Old French — *Anthologies* — *English texts*

Chaucer, Geoffrey. Chaucer's dream poetry : sources and analogues / edited and translated by B.A. Windeatt. — Cambridge : Brewer, 1982. — xviii,168p ; 24cm. — (Chaucer studies ; 7)
Bibliography: p156-163. — Includes index
ISBN 0-85991-072-5 : £19.50 : CIP rev.
B82-07042

841.3 — FRENCH POETRY, 1500-1600

841'.3 — Poetry in French, *1500-1600* — *Texts*

Héroët, Antoine. La parfaicte amye / Antoine Héroët ; édition critique par Christine M. Hill. — [Exeter] : University of Exeter, 1981. — xxxvii,73p : 1facsim ; 21cm. — (Textes littéraires, ISSN 0309-6998 ; 43)
Text in French. — Bibliography: pxxxvi-xxxvii
ISBN 0-85989-177-1 (pbk) : Unpriced
B82-19918

841.4 — FRENCH POETRY, 1600-1715

841'.4 — Poetry in French, *1600-1715* — *French-English parallel texts*

La Fontaine, Jean de. Fables de La Fontaine / peint et écrit [par] Marie Angel. — London : Neugebauer, c1981. — [36]p : col.ill ; 35cm + English translation([16]; 34cm)
Facsim. of ms. held in Harrison collection, San Francisco Public Library. — English translation by Sir Edward March. — In slipcase
ISBN 0-907234-10-0 : £14.95 B82-07468

841.7 — FRENCH POETRY, 1815-1848

841'.7 — Poetry in French, *1815-1848* — *English texts*

Hugo, Victor. The distance, the shadows / Victor Hugo : selected poems / translated by Harry Guest. — London : Anvil Press Poetry in association with Wildwood House, 1981. — 239p ; 22cm. — (Poetica ; 10)
English and French text. — Bibliography: p235-236
ISBN 0-85646-068-0 (pbk) : £6.95 B82-00676

841.8 — FRENCH POETRY, 1848-1900

841'.8 — Poetry in French, *1848-1900* — *French-English parallel texts*

Baudelaire, Charles. Les fleurs du mal. — Brighton : Harvester Press, Oct.1982. — [364]p
Translation of: Les fleurs du mal. — English and French text
ISBN 0-7108-0459-8 : £18.95 : CIP entry
B82-28482

841'.8 — Poetry in French. Baudelaire, Charles — *Biographies*

Hemmings, F. W. J.. Baudelaire the damned. — London : Hamilton, May 1982. — [288]p
ISBN 0-241-10779-2 : £15.00 : CIP entry
B82-07402

841'.8 — Poetry in French. Baudelaire, Charles. Cygne, *Le* — *Critical studies*

Burton, Richard D.. The context of Baudelaire's Le cygne / Richard D. Burton. — [Durham] : University of Durham, 1980. — 101p ; 21cm. — (Durham modern languages series)
ISBN 0-907310-01-x (pbk) : Unpriced
B82-15071

841'.8 — Poetry in French. Mallarmé, Stéphane — *Critical studies*

Bersani, Leo. The death of Stéphane Mallarmé / Leo Bersani. — Cambridge : Cambridge University Press, 1982. — ix,100p ; 23cm. — (Cambridge studies in French)
Includes index
ISBN 0-521-23863-3 : £9.95 : CIP rev.
B81-36240

841'.8'08 — Poetry in French, *1848-1900* — *Anthologies* — *English texts*

Baudelaire, Charles. From the Nineties : some translations of Baudelaire & Verlaine / by Lord Alfred Douglas ... [et al.]. — Edinburgh : Tragara Press, 1982. — 29p ; 23cm
Parallel French and English text. — Limited edition of 95 copies
ISBN 0-902616-78-1 (pbk) : £9.00 B82-35049

841'.8'09 — Poetry in French, *1848-1900.* **Parnassians** — *Critical studies* — *Serials*

Parnasse : a quarterly journal devoted to the study of the French Parnassians and their influence. — Vol.1, no.1 (June 1982)-. — Oxford ([89 Edgeway Rd, Oxford OX3 0HE]) : Parnassian Study Circle, 1982-. — v. ; 21cm
Text in English and French
ISSN 0263-2942 = Parnasse : £5.60 per year
B82-40065

841'.8'09 — Poetry in French, *1848-1945* — *Critical studies* — *Festschriften*

Baudelaire, Mallarmé, Valéry : new essays in honour of Lloyd Austin / edited by Malcolm Bowie, Alison Fairlie and Alison Finch. — Cambridge : Cambridge University Press, 1982. — xxv,456p : ill,1facsim,1port ; 23cm
ISBN 0-521-23443-3 : £30.00 : CIP rev.
B82-29349

841.912 — FRENCH POETRY, 1900-1945

841'.912 — Poetry in French, *1900-1945* — *French-English parallel texts*

Follain, Jean. D'après tout : poems / by Jean Follain ; translated by Heather McHugh. — Princeton ; Guildford : Princeton University Press, c1981. — xiv,184p ; 23cm. — (The Lockert library of poetry in translation)
Parallel French text and English translation
ISBN 0-691-06476-8 : £8.30
ISBN 0-691-01372-1 (pbk) : £4.25 B82-14560

841'.912 — Poetry in French. Jacob, Max. Cornet à dés — *Critical studies*

Lévy, Sydney. The play of the text : Max Jacob's Le Cornet à dés / Sydney Lévy ; with translations of selected poems and prose from Le Cornet à des by Judith Morganroth Schneider. — Madison ; London : University of Wisconsin Press, c1981. — xii,159p ; 22cm
Includes index
ISBN 0-299-08510-4 : £12.60 B82-12771

841'.912 — Poetry in French. Valéry, Paul — *Critical studies*

Crow, Christine M.. Paul Valéry and the poetry of voice / Christine M. Crow. — Cambridge : Cambridge University Press, 1982. — xviii,302p ; 23cm. — (Major European authors)
Bibliography: p292-298. — Includes index
ISBN 0-521-24182-0 : £25.00 : CIP rev.
B82-01719

841'.912'08 — Poetry in French, *1900-1945* — *Anthologies*

Anthology of Second World War French poetry / edited by Ian Higgins. — London : Methuen Educational, 1982. — xviii,236p ; 20cm. — (Methuen's twentieth century texts)
French texts with English introduction and notes
ISBN 0-423-50860-1 (pbk) : Unpriced : CIP rev. B82-10787

841'.912'09 — Poetry in French, *1900-ca 1975* — *Critical studies*

Caws, Mary Ann. A metapoetics of the passage : architectures in surrealism and after / Mary Ann Caws. — Hanover, N.H. ; London : University Press of New England, 1981. — xv,202p : ill ; 23cm
Includes index
ISBN 0-87451-194-1 : Unpriced B82-31118

841.914 — FRENCH POETRY, 1945-

841'.914 — Poetry in French, *1945-* — *English texts*

Bouvard, Hélène. That the gods may remember / Hélène Bouvard ; translated from the French by Jean Overton Fuller. — London : Fuller D'Arch Smith, c1981. — 84p ; 22cm
Translation of: Que les dieux se souviennent
Unpriced (pbk) B82-38755

Lambersy, Werner. Anchors of ink / Werner Lambersy ; translated by Philip Mosley. — London (86 Dresden Rd., N19) : Sceptre, c1982. — [18]p ; 30cm
Translation from the French
Unpriced (pbk) B82-40220

841'.914 — Poetry in French. English writers, *1945-* — *Texts*

Mellanby, John. Un 'crazy' tour de Cambridge / poème par John Mellanby ; dessins par David Urwin. — Cambridge : Cambridge Guide Service, c1981. — [8]p : ill ; 19cm
ISBN 0-907736-03-3 (unbound) : Unpriced
B82-08134

841'.914'09 — Poetry in French, *1945-* — *Critical studies*

French poetry now. — 2nd ed. — Portree : Aquila, Jan.1983. — [144]p. — (Prospice, ISSN 0308-2776 ; v.3)
Previous ed.: 1974
ISBN 0-903226-91-x (pbk) : £3.75 : CIP entry
B82-33247

842 — FRENCH DRAMA

842'.0512'09 — Drama in French. Corneille, Pierre. Tragedies *compared with* **tragedies of Racine, Jean**

Barnwell, H. T.. The tragic drama of Corneille and Racine : an old parallel revisited / by H.T. Barnwell. — Oxford : Clarendon, 1982. — xxi,275p ; 23cm
Bibliography: p261-270. — Includes index
ISBN 0-19-815779-7 : £17.50 : CIP rev.
B82-07511

842.2 — FRENCH DRAMA, 1400-1500

842'.2 — Drama in French, *1400-1500* — *Texts*

The **Passion** de Semur. — Leeds (University of Leeds, Leeds LS2 9JT) : University of Leeds, Centre for Medieval Studies, Jan.1982. — [276] p. — (Leeds medieval studies, ISSN 0140-8089 ; 3)
ISBN 0-906441-02-1 (pbk) : £12.00 : CIP entry
B82-01351

842′.2 — Drama in French, *1400-1600 — Critical studies*

Knight, Alan E.. Aspects of genre in late medieval French drama. — Manchester : Manchester University Press, June 1982. — [224]p
ISBN 0-7190-0862-x : £17.50 : CIP entry
B82-09631

842.4 — FRENCH DRAMA, 1600-1715

842′.4 — Drama in French, *1600-1715 — Critical studies — Festschriften*

Form and meaning : aesthetic coherence in seventeenth-century French drama. — Amersham : Avebury, Sept.1982. — [256]p
ISBN 0-86127-216-1 : £15.95 : CIP entry
B82-28601

842′.4 — Drama in French, *1600-1715 — English texts*

Racine, Jean. Four Greek plays : Andromache — Iphigenia — Phaedra — Athaliah / Jean Racine ; translated, with introduction and notes by R.C. Knight. — Cambridge : Cambridge University Press, 1982. — xvi,223p ; 22cm
Translation from the French. — Bibliography: pxvi
ISBN 0-521-24415-3 (cased) : £18.50 : CIP rev.
ISBN 0-521-28676-x (pbk) : £5.95 B82-12009

842′.4 — Drama in French, *1600-1715 — Texts*

Cyrano de Bergerac, Savinien. La mort D'Agrippine / Savinien Cyrano de Bergerac. — Ed. critique / Par C.J. Gossip. — [Exeter] : University of Exeter, 1982. — xxiv,90p : 1ill ; 22cm. — (Textes litteraires, ISSN 0309-6998 ; 44)
Bibliography: pxxiii-xxiv
ISBN 0-85989-182-8 (pbk) : Unpriced
B82-29566

842′.4 — Drama in French. Molière — *Critical studies*

Howarth, W. D.. Molière, a playwright and his audience / W.D. Howarth. — Cambridge : Cambridge University Press, 1982. — xiii,325p,viiip of plates : ill ; 22cm. — (Major European authors)
Includes passages in French. — Bibliography: p316-319. — Includes index
ISBN 0-521-24425-0 (cased) : £27.50 : CIP rev.
ISBN 0-521-28679-4 (pbk) : £7.95 B82-12721

842′.4 — Drama in French. Molière. Malade imaginaire — *Critical studies*

Barnwell, H. T.. Molière, Le malade imaginaire / H.T. Barnwell. — London : Grant & Cutler, 1982. — 76p ; 20cm. — (Critical guides to French texts)
Bibliography: p74-76
ISBN 0-7293-0122-2 (pbk) : £1.80 B82-33983

842′.4 — Drama in French. Racine, Jean — *Critical studies*

Drown, Norah K.. Jean Racine : meditations on his poetic art / Norah K. Drown. — [Worthing] (26 Robson Rd, Worthing W. Sussex BN12 4EF]) : N.K. Drown, 1982. — x,179p ; 23cm
Unpriced (pbk) B82-38586

Goldmann, Lucien. Racine / Lucien Goldmann ; translated by Alastair Hamilton ; with an introduction by Raymond Williams. — London : Writers and Readers, 1981. — xxii,105p ; 21cm
Translation of: Racine. — Originally published: Cambridge : River Press, 1972. — Includes index
ISBN 0-906495-77-6 (pbk) : £2.50 B82-09472

842.8 — FRENCH DRAMA, 1848-1900

842′.8 — Drama in French, *1848-1900 — English texts*

Feydeau, Georges. Feydeau, first to last : eight one-act comedies / translated and with an introduction by Norman R. Shapiro. — Ithaca ; London : Cornell University Press, 1982. — 316p : ill ; 25cm
Translated from the French
ISBN 0-8014-1295-1 : Unpriced B82-34960

842′.8′09 — Drama in French. Feydeau, Georges & Labiche, Eugène — *Critical studies*

Pronko, Leonard C.. Eugène Labiche and Georges Feydeau / Leonard C. Pronko. — London : Macmillan, 1982. — ix,181p,[8]p of plates : ill ; 20cm. — (Macmillan modern dramatists)
Bibliography: p172-175. — Includes index
ISBN 0-333-28897-1 (cased) : Unpriced
ISBN 0-333-28899-8 (pbk) : Unpriced
B82-23275

842′.8′09353 — Drama in French, *1800-1900.* **Special subjects: Physiognomy** — *Critical studies*

Wechsler, Judith. A human comedy : physiognomy and caricature in 19th century Paris / Judith Wechsler ; foreword by Richard Sennett. — London : Thames and Hudson, c1982. — 208p : ill,facsims,ports ; 27cm
Bibliography: p201-206. — Includes index
ISBN 0-500-01268-7 : £18.50
Primary classification 741.5′944 B82-31749

842.912 — FRENCH DRAMA, 1900-1945

842′.912 — Drama in French, *1900-1945 — English texts*

Sartre, Jean-Paul. Three plays / Jean-Paul Sartre. — Harmondsworth : Penguin in association with Hamilton, 1969 (1982 [printing]). — 347p ; 20cm. — (Penguin plays)
Contents: Kean / translated by Kitty Black. Originally published: London : Hamish Hamilton, 1954 — Nekrassov / translated by Sylvia and George Leeson. Originally published: London : Hamish Hamilton, 1956 — The Trojan women / English version by Ronald Duncan. Originally published: London : Hamish Hamilton, 1967. Translation of: Les Troyennes
ISBN 0-14-048083-8 (pbk) : £2.95 B82-16779

842′.912 — Drama in French, *1900-1945 — Texts*

Genet, Jean. Le balcon. — London : Methuen Educational, Sept.1982. — [180]p. — (Methuen's twentieth century texts)
ISBN 0-423-50980-2 (pbk) : £3.50 : CIP entry
B82-19671

842.914 — FRENCH DRAMA, 1945-

842′.914 — Drama in French, *1945- — English texts*

Obaldia, René de. Obaldia plays. — London : John Calder
Translated from the French
Vol.3. — Jan.1982. — [256]p
ISBN 0-7145-3559-1 (pbk) : £4.95 : CIP entry
B81-33835

842′.914 — Drama in French. Beckett, Samuel. En attendant Godot & Fin de partie — *Critical studies*

Little, J. P.. En attendant Godot and Fin de partie / J.P. Little. — London : Grant & Cutler, 1981. — 83p ; 19cm. — (Critical guides to French texts ; 6)
Bibliography: p81-83
ISBN 0-7293-0104-4 (pbk) : £1.80 B82-17579

843 — FRENCH FICTION

843[F] — Fiction in French. Belgian writers, *1830-1900 — English texts*

Rosny, J. H., *1856-1940.* Quest for fire / J.H. Rosny-Aîné ; translated by Harold Talbott. — Harmondsworth : Penguin, 1982, c1967. — 143p ; 19cm
Originally published: New York : Pantheon, 1967
ISBN 0-14-006434-6 (pbk) : £1.25 B82-26188

843[F] — Fiction in French. Benin *(People's Republic)* **writers,** *1960- — English texts*

Bhêly-Quénum, O.. Snares without end / Olympe Bhêly-Quénum ; translated by Dorothy S. Blair. — Harlow : Longman, 1981. — 206p ; 18cm. — (Drumbeat)
Translation of: Un piège sans fin
ISBN 0-582-64262-0 (pbk) : £1.50 B82-00495

843[F] — Fiction in French. Cameroon writers, *1960- — English texts*

Beti, Mongo. Remember Ruben / Mongo Beti ; translated from the French by Gerald Moore. — London : Heinemann, 1980. — 252p ; 19cm. — (African writers series ; 214)
Translation of: Remember Ruben. — Originally published: Ibadan : New Horn, 1980
ISBN 0-435-90214-8 (pbk) : £3.40 : CIP rev.
B80-26116

843[F] — Fiction in French. Guadeloupean writers, *1945- — English texts*

Schwarz-Bart, Simone. The bridge of beyond / Simone Schwarz-Bart ; translated from the French by Barbara Bray ; introduction by Bridget Jones. — London : Heinemann, 1982, c1974. — xviii,174p ; 19cm
Translation of: Pluie et vent sur Télumée miracle. — Originally published: London : Gollancz, 1975
ISBN 0-435-98770-4 (pbk) : £1.95 : CIP rev.
B81-31163

843[F] — Fiction in French. Senegalese writers, *1960- — English texts*

Bâ, Mariama. So long a letter / Mariama Bâ ; translated from the French by Modupé Bodé-Thomas. — London : Virago, 1982, c1981. — 90p ; 21cm
Translation of: Une si longue lettre. — Originally published: London : Heinemann, 1981
ISBN 0-86068-295-1 (cased) : Unpriced : CIP rev.
ISBN 0-86068-296-x (pbk) : £2.50 B82-16680

Bâ, Mariana. So long a letter / Mariana Bâ ; translated from the French by Modupé Bodé-Thomas. — London : Heinemann, 1981. — 90p ; 19cm. — (African writers series ; 248)
Translated fron the French
ISBN 0-435-90248-2 (pbk) : £1.95 B82-00952

843′.008′03538 — Erotic fiction in French, *1464-1927 — Anthologies — English texts*

The **Body** and the dream. — London : Quartet, Jan.1983. — 1v.
Translation from the French
ISBN 0-7043-2364-8 : CIP entry B82-40308

843′.01′08 — Short stories in French, *1789-1815 — Anthologies*

Contes revolutionnaires / textes établis et présentés par Malcolm Cook. — [Exeter] : University of Exeter, 1982. — xxiii,71p : ill ; 21cm. — (Textes littéraires, ISSN 0309-6998 ; 45)
Bibliography: pxxii-xxiii
ISBN 0-85989-187-9 (pbk) : Unpriced
B82-34632

843′.01′08 — Short stories in French. Anthologies de contes et nouvelles modernes. Vocabulary — *Lists*

Moran, John F.. Vocabulary and comprehension tests on Anthologie de contes et nouvelles modernes / John F. Moran. — Dublin : Helicon, 1981 : Distributed by Educational Company. — 32p ; 21cm. — (Helicon notes)
French and English text. — Cover title
Unpriced (pbk) B82-02555

843.1 — FRENCH FICTION, TO 1400

843′.1 — Fiction in Old French — *English texts*

Troyes, Chrétien. [Perceval le Gallois. English]. Perceval : the story of the Grail. — Woodbridge : Brewer, June 1982. — [288]p. — (Arthurian series, ISSN 0261-9814 ; 5)
Translation of: Perceval le Gallois
ISBN 0-85991-092-x : £15.00 : CIP entry
B82-10227

843′.1 — Fiction in Old French — *Middle French texts — Facsimiles*

Meliadus de Leonnoys, 1532 / introduction by C.E. Pickford. — London : Scolar, 1980. — ca 486p : ill,1facsim ; 29cm
Middle French text. — Facsimile reprint of 1532 ed. Paris : Janot, 1532
ISBN 0-85967-563-7 : Unpriced : CIP rev.
B80-03400

843.5 — FRENCH FICTION, 1715-1789

843′.5 — Fiction in French, *1715-1789 — English texts — Facsimiles*

Marivaux, Pierre Carlet de Chamblain de. The virtuous orphan : or, the life of Marianne, Countess of * * * * * / Pierre Carlet de Chamblain de Marivaux. — New York ; London : Garland, 1979. — 4v. ; 19cm. — (The Novel, 1720-1805)
Translation of: Vie de Marianne. — Facsim. of: edition published : London : Robinson, 1743
ISBN 0-8240-3652-2 : Unpriced B82-09326

843′.5 — Fiction in French. Diderot, Denis. Religieuse, *La — Critical studies*

Mylne, Vivienne. Le Religieuse / Vivienne Mylne. — London : Grant & Cutler, 1981. — 72p ; 19cm. — (Critical guides to French texts ; 10)
Bibliography: p71-72
ISBN 0-7293-0106-0 (pbk) : £1.50 B82-17577

843′.5 — Fiction in French. Rousseau, Jean-Jacques. Nouvelle Héloïse. Special themes: Philosophy. Idealism

Miller, R. D.. The beautiful soul : a study of eighteeth-century idealism as exemplified by Rousseau's La Nouvelle Héloïse and Goethe's Die Leiden des jungen Werthers / by R. D. Miller. — Harrogate (8 Lancaster Rd., Harrogate) : Duchy Press, 1981. — 100p ; 23cm
Includes index
Unpriced
Also classified at 833′.6 B82-06455

843′.5′09 — Fiction in French, *1715-1789 — Critical studies*

Mylne, Vivienne. The eighteenth-century French novel : techniques of illusion / by Vivienne Mylne. — 2nd ed. — Cambridge : Cambridge University Press, 1981. — viii,293p ; 23cm
Previous ed.: Manchester : Manchester University Press, 1965. — Bibliography: p282-288. — Includes index
ISBN 0-521-23864-1 (cased) : £19.50 : CIP rev.
ISBN 0-521-28266-7 (pbk) : £6.95 B81-31261

843.6 — FRENCH FICTION, 1789-1815

843′.6 — Fiction in French. Sade, D. A. F., *marquis de — Critical studies*

Gallop, Jane. Intersections : a reading of Sade with Bataille, Blanchot and Klossowski / Jane Gallop. — Lincoln [Neb.] ; London : University of Nebraska Press, c1981. — vii,135p ; 23cm
Bibliography: p125-127. — Includes index
ISBN 0-8032-2110-x : £9.80 B82-09772

843.7 — FRENCH FICTION, 1815-1848

843′.7 — Fiction in French. Balzac, Honoré de. Illusions perdues *— Critical studies*

Adamson, Doanld, *1939-*. Illusions perdues / Donald Adamson. — London : Grant & Cutler, 1981. — 90p ; 19cm. — (Critical guides to French texts ; 7)
Bibliography: p88-90
ISBN 0-7293-0105-2 (pbk) : £1.80 B82-17582

843′.7[F] — Fiction in French, *1815-1848 — English texts*

Dumas, Alexandre, *1802-1870.* The man in the iron mask / by Alexandre Dumas. — Abridged ed. — London : Dean, [198-?]. — 188p ; 19cm. — (Dean's classics)
ISBN 0-603-03021-1 : Unpriced B82-26098

Dumas, Alexandre, *1802-1870.* The three musketeers / by Alexandre Dumas. — Abridged ed. — London : Dean, [198-?]. — 184p ; 19cm. — (Dean's classics)
ISBN 0-603-03010-6 : Unpriced B82-26097

Hugo, Victor. Les Misérables / Victor Hugo ; translated and with an introduction by Norman Denny. — Harmondsworth : Penguin, 1980,c1976 (1982 [printing]). — 1231p ; 18cm. — (Penguin classics)
Translation of: Les Misérables. — Originally published: in 2 vols. London : Folio Press, 1976
ISBN 0-14-044430-0 (pbk) : £3.95 B82-19908

843.8 — FRENCH FICTION, 1848-1900

843′.8 — Fiction in French. Flaubert, Gustave, *1830-1857 — Correspondence, diaries, etc.*

Flaubert, Gustave. The letters of Gustave Flaubert 1830-1857 / selected, edited and translated by Francis Steegmuller. — London : Faber, 1981, c1980. — xvii,250p,[4]p of plates : ill,ports ; 24cm
Originally published: Cambridge, Mass. : Belknapp Press, 1980. — Bibliography: p246. — Includes index
ISBN 0-571-11814-3 (pbk) : £3.50 : CIP rev. B81-21463

843′.8 — Fiction in French. Flaubert, Gustave *— Biographies*

Sartre, Jean-Paul. The family idiot : Gustave Flaubert, 1821-1857 / Jean-Paul Sartre ; translated by Carol Cosman. — Chicago ; London : University of Chicago Press
Vol.1. — 1981. — x,627p ; 24cm
Translation of: L'idiot de la famille, pt.1
ISBN 0-226-73509-5 : £17.50 B82-13706

843′.8 — Fiction in French. Flaubert, Gustave. Biographies: Sartre, Jean-Paul. Idiot de la famille *— Critical studies*

Barnes, Hazel E.. Sartre & Flaubert / Hazel E. Barnes. — Chicago ; London : University of Chicago Press, 1981. — x,449p ; 24cm
Bibliography: p437-441. — Includes index
ISBN 0-226-03720-7 : £17.50 B82-13705

843′.8 — Fiction in French. Flaubert, Gustave *compared with* **Kafka, Franz** *— Critical studies*

Bernheimer, Charles. Flaubert and Kafka. — London : Yale University Press, Sept.1982. — [262]p
ISBN 0-300-02633-1 : £17.50 : CIP entry
Also classified at 833′.912 B82-29118

843′.8 — Fiction in French. Flaubert, Gustave *— Critical studies — Conference proceedings — French texts*

Flaubert : la dimension du texte : communications du congrès international du centenaire organisé en mai 1980 par la Délégation Culturelle Française et la Section d'études Françaises de l'Université de Manchester / présentées par P.M. Wetherill. — Manchester : Manchester University Press, c1982. — 272p ; 22cm
ISBN 0-7190-0842-5 (pbk) : £8.50 : CIP rev. B81-34553

843′.8 — Fiction in French. Flaubert, Gustave. Madame Bovary *— Critical studies*

LaCapra, Dominick. Madame Bovary on trial / Dominick LaCapra. — Ithaca ; London : Cornell University Press, 1982. — 219p ; 23cm
Includes index
ISBN 0-8014-1477-6 : £14.75 B82-36988

843′.8 — Fiction in French. Flaubert, Gustave. Salammbô *— Concordances*

Carlut, Charles. A concordance to Flaubert's Salammbô / Charles Carlut, Pierre H. Dubé, J. Raymond Dugan. — New York ; London : Garland, 1979. — 2v. ; 24cm. — (Garland reference library of the humanities ; v.148)
ISBN 0-8240-9794-7 : Unpriced B82-31069

843′.8 — Fiction in French. Flaubert, Gustave. Salammbô *— Critical studies*

Green, Anne. Flaubert and the historical novel : Sallammbô reassessed / Anne Green. — Cambridge : Cambridge University Press, 1982. — vi,185p ; 23cm
Appendix in French. — Bibliography: p167-180. — Includes index
ISBN 0-521-23765-3 : £19.50 : CIP rev. B82-04857

843′.8 — Fiction in French. Loti, Pierre *— Biographies*

Blanch, Lesley. Pierre Loti. — London : Collins, Nov.1982. — [368]p
ISBN 0-00-211649-9 : £14.50 : CIP entry B82-27790

843′.8 — Fiction in French. Mallarmé, Stéphane. Igitur *— Critical studies*

Cohn, Robert Greer. Mallarmé Igitur / Robert Greer Cohn. — Berkeley ; London : University of California Press, c1981. — xii,189p ; 21cm
Includes the French text of Igitur. — Bibliography: p187-189
ISBN 0-520-04188-7 : £17.25 B82-13753

843′.8[F] — Fiction in French, *1848-1900 — English texts*

Flaubert, Gustave. Madame Bovary : life in a country town / Gustave Flaubert. — Rev. translation / translated by Gerard Hopkins ; with an introduction by Terence Cave ; and notes by Mark Overstall. — Oxford : Oxford University Press, 1981. — xxvii,362p ; 19cm. — (The World's classics)
Translation of: Madame Bovary. — Previous ed.: London : Hamilton, 1949. — Bibliography: pxxiii-xxiv
ISBN 0-19-281564-4 (pbk) : £1.75 : CIP rev. B81-30514

Verne, Jules. Around the world in eighty days / by Jules Verne. — Abridged ed. — London : Dean, [198-?]. — 183p ; 19cm. — (Dean's classics)
ISBN 0-603-03013-0 : Unpriced B82-26106

Verne, Jules. Twenty thousand leagues under the sea / by Jules Verne. — Abridged. — London : Dean, [198-?]. — 183p ; 19cm. — (Dean's classics)
ISBN 0-603-03019-x : Unpriced B82-26105

843′.8[F] — Short stories in French, *1848-1900 — English texts*

Schwob, Marcel. The King in the golden mask and other stories. — Manchester : Carcanet, Aug.1982. — [192]p
ISBN 0-85635-403-1 : £6.95 : CIP entry B82-23842

843.912 — FRENCH FICTION, 1900-1945

843′.912 — Fiction in French, *1900-1945 — Texts*

Bernanos, Georges. Nouvelle histoire de Mouchette. — London : Methuen, Nov.1982. — [250]p. — (Methuen's twentieth century texts)
ISBN 0-423-90120-6 (pbk) : £2.95 : CIP entry B82-27512

Camus, Albert. L'Exil et le Royaume / Albert Camus ; edited with an introduction and notes by David H. Walker. — London : Harrap, 1981. — lxvii,226p : 1map,1port ; 17cm. — (Modern world literature series)
French text, English introduction and notes. — Bibliography: plxiii-lxvii
ISBN 0-245-53508-x (pbk) : £3.50 B82-00634

843′.912 — Fiction in French, *1900-1945 — Texts with commentaries*

Sartre, Jean-Paul. Les mots. — London : Methuen Educational, Sept.1981. — [200]p. — (Methuen's twentieth century texts)
ISBN 0-423-50560-2 (pbk) : £2.50 : CIP entry B81-22642

843′.912 — Fiction in French. Bataille, Georges *— Critical studies*

Richman, Michèle H.. Reading Georges Bataille : beyond the gift / Michèle H. Richman. — Baltimore ; London : Johns Hopkins University Press, c1982. — xii,177p ; 24cm
Bibliography: p168-173. — Includes index
ISBN 0-8018-2593-8 : £11.25 B82-34984

843′.912 — Fiction in French. Beauvoir, Simone de *— Biographies*

Ascher, Carol. Simone de Beauvoir : a life of freedom / Carol Ascher. — Brighton : Harvester, 1981. — vi,254p ; 24cm
Includes index
ISBN 0-7108-0313-3 : £8.95 B82-08277

843′.912 — Fiction in French. Camus, Albert *— Biographies*

McCarthy, Patrick. Camus : a critical study of his life and work / by Patrick McCarthy. — London : Hamilton, 1982. — 359p ; 22cm
Bibliography: p343-346. — Includes index
ISBN 0-241-10603-6 : £12.50 : CIP rev. B81-35820

843'.912 — Fiction in French. Colette — *Correspondence, diaries, etc.*

Colette. [Correspondence. English. Selections]. Letters from Colette / selected and translated by Robert Phelps. — London : Virago, 1982, c1980. — x,214p ; 22cm
Translation from the French. — Originally published: New York : Farrar, Straus and Giroux, 1980
ISBN 0-86068-252-8 : £6.95 : CIP rev. B82-00389

843'.912 — Fiction in French. Duras, Marguerite. Moderato cantabile — *Critical studies*

Coward, David. Moderato cantabile / David Coward. — London : Grant & Cutler, 1981. — 83p ; 19cm. — (Critical guides to French texts ; 8)
Bibliography: p79-80
ISBN 0-7293-0107-9 (pbk) : £1.80
ISBN 84-499-4882-7 (Spain) B82-17581

843'.912 — Fiction in French. Gide, André. Faux-monnayeurs, *Les — Critical studies*

Tilby, M. J.. Gide, Les faux-monnayeurs / Michael Tilby. — London : Grant & Cutler, 1981. — 105p ; 20cm
Bibliography: p102-105
ISBN 0-7293-0112-5 (pbk) : £1.80 B82-33980

843'.912 — Fiction in French. Malraux, André. Voie royale — *Critical studies*

Fallaize, Elizabeth. Malraux, La voie royale / Elizabeth Fallaize. — London : Grant & Cutler, 1982. — 86p ; 20cm. — (Critical guides to French texts)
Bibliography: p85-86
ISBN 0-7293-0124-9 (pbk) : £1.80 B82-33982

843'.912 — Fiction in French. Proust, Marcel — *Correspondence, diaries, etc.*

Proust, Marcel. Time for Proust : selected correspondence of Marcel Proust, 1880-1903. — London : Collins, June 1982. — [500]p
Translation of: Correspondence générale de Marcel Proust
ISBN 0-00-211872-6 : £10.00 : CIP entry B82-10562

843'.912 — Fiction in French. Proust, Marcel — *Critical studies*

Cocking, J. M.. Proust : collected essays on the writer and his art / J.M. Cocking. — Cambridge : Cambridge University Press, 1982. — xxii,307p,[13]p of plates : ill ; 23cm. — (Cambridge studies in French)
Bibliography: p298-301. — Includes index
ISBN 0-521-23790-4 (cased) : £27.50 : CIP rev.
ISBN 0-521-28799-5 (pbk) : £7.95 B82-12142

843'.912[F] — Fiction in French, *1900-1945 — English texts*

Bataille, Georges. L'abbé C. — London : Marion Boyars, Nov.1982. — [160]p
Translated from the French
ISBN 0-7145-2709-2 : £7.95 : CIP entry B82-28753

Bataille, Georges. Story of the eye / by Lord Auch [i.e.] Georges Bataille ; translated by Joachim Neugroschel ; with essays by Susan Sontag and Roland Barthes. — Harmondsworth : Penguin, 1982, c1977. — 127p ; 20cm. — (Penguin modern classics)
Translation of: Histoire de l'oeil. — Originally published: London : Boyars, 1979
ISBN 0-14-005359-x (pbk) : £1.95 B82-32238

Beauvoir, Simone de. Les belles images / Simone de Beauvoir ; translated by Patrick O'Brian. — [London] : Fontana, 1969, c1968 (1982 [printing]). — 154p ; 18cm
Translation of: Les belles images
ISBN 0-00-616475-7 (pbk) : £1.25 B82-09320

Beauvoir, Simone de. The blood of others / Simone de Beauvoir ; translated by Yvonne Moyse and Roger Senhouse. — Harmondsworth : Penguin in association with Secker & Warburg, 1964 (1981 [printing]). — 239p ; 20cm
Translation of: Le sang des autres. — Originally published: London : Secker & Warburg, 1945
ISBN 0-14-001830-1 (pbk) : £2.75 B82-05963

Beauvoir, Simone de. The mandarins / Simone de Beauvoir ; translated by Leonard M. Friedman. — [London] : Fontana, 1960 (1982 [printing]). — 763p : ill ; 18cm
Originally published: London : Collins, 1957
ISBN 0-00-616550-8 (pbk) : £2.50 B82-25441

Beauvoir, Simone de. The woman destroyed / Simone de Beauvoir ; translated by Patrick O'Brien. — London : Fontana, 1971, c1969 (1981 [printing]). — 220p ; 19cm
Translation of: La femme rompue. — Originally published: London : Collins, 1969
ISBN 0-00-613598-6 (pbk) : £1.50 B82-05695

Camus, Albert. The outsider / Albert Camus ; translated from the French by Joseph Laredo. — London : Hamilton, 1982, c1981. — 96p ; 23cm
Translation of: L'étranger
ISBN 0-241-10778-4 : £5.95 : CIP rev. B81-34567

Cendrars, Blaise. Gold : the marvellous history of General John Augustus Sutter / Blaise Cendrars ; translated from the French by Nina Rootes. — London : Peter Owen, 1982. — 128p ; 20cm
Translation of: L'or, ou, La merveilleuse histoire du General Johann August Sutter
ISBN 0-7206-0597-0 : £7.50 B82-40244

Genêt, Jean. The thief's journal / Jean Genet ; translated by Bernard Frechtman. — Harmondsworth : Penguin, 1967, c1965 (1982 [printing]). — 223p ; 20cm. — (Penguin modern classics)
Translation of: Journal du voleur. — Originally published: London : Blond, 1965
ISBN 0-14-002582-0 (pbk) : £2.75 B82-36231

Gide, André. The counterfeiters / André Gide ; translated from the French by Dorothy Bussy. — Harmondsworth : Penguin, 1966, c1931 (1982 [printing]). — 345p ; 20cm. — (Penguin modern classics)
Translation of: Les Faux-monnayeurs
ISBN 0-14-002415-8 (pbk) : £2.95 B82-22139

Gide, André. Fruits of the earth ; Later fruits of the earth / André Gide. — Harmondsworth : Penguin in association with Secker & Warburg, 1970 (1982 [printing]). — 220p ; 20cm. — (Penguin modern classics)
Fruits of the earth. Translation of: Les nourritures terrestres. — Originally published: London : Secker & Warburg, 1949
ISBN 0-14-003178-2 (pbk) : £2.75 B82-32494

Guillaumin, Emile. The life of a simple man. — London (10 Archway Close, N19 3TD) : Sinclair Browne, June 1982. — [240]p
Translation of: La vie d'un simple
ISBN 0-86300-011-8 (cased) : £9.95 : CIP entry
ISBN 0-86300-012-6 (pbk) : £3.95 B82-10256

Queneau, Raymond. [Zazie dans le métro. English]. Zazie in the metro. — London : Calder, June 1982. — [208]p
Translation of: Zazie dans le métro
ISBN 0-7145-3872-8 : £6.95 : CIP entry B82-10870

Radiguet, Raymond. The devil in the flesh. — London : Boyars, June 1982. — [128]p
Translation of: Le diable au corps
ISBN 0-7145-0192-1 (cased) : CIP entry
ISBN 0-7145-0913-x (pbk) : £3.95 B82-12158

Roché, Henri-Pierre. Jules and Jim / Henri-Pierre Roché ; translated by Patrick Evans. — [London] : Pavanne, 1982, c1963. — 185p ; 18cm
Translation of: Jules et Jim. — Originally published: London : Calder, 1963
ISBN 0-330-26809-0 (pbk) : £1.50 B82-35744

Sartre, Jean-Paul. The age of reason / Jean-Paul Sartre ; translated by Eric Sutton. — Harmondsworth : Penguin in association with H. Hamilton, 1961 (1982 [printing]). — 299p ; 18cm. — (Penguin modern classics)
Translation of: L'âge de raison. — Originally published: London : H. Hamilton, 1947
ISBN 0-14-001521-3 (pbk) : £1.95 B82-35389

Sartre, Jean-Paul. Nausea / Jean-Paul Sartre ; translated from the French by Robert Baldick. — Harmondsworth : Penguin, 1965 (1982 [printing]). — 252p ; 18cm. — (Penguin modern classics)
Translation of: La nausée
ISBN 0-14-002276-7 (pbk) : £1.75 B82-40663

Simenon, Georges. Maigret and the flea / by Georges Simenon. — Long Preston : Magna, 1981, c1971. — 227p ; 23cm
Translation of: Maigret et l'indicateur. — Originally published: London : Hamilton, 1972. — Published in large print
ISBN 0-86009-353-0 : Unpriced : CIP rev. B81-30432

Troyat, Henri. Sylvie / Henri Troyat ; translated by Anthea Bell. — Henley-on-Thames : Ellis, 1982. — 150p ; 23cm
Translation of: Viou
ISBN 0-85628-101-8 : £6.95 B82-22718

Yourcenar, Marguerite. Memoirs of Hadrian / Marguerite Yourcenar ; translated from the French by Grace Frick in collaboration with the author. — Harmondsworth : Penguin in association with Secker and Warburg, 1959 (1982 [printing]). — 252p : 1map ; 20cm. — (A King Penguin)
Translation of: Mémoires d'Hadrien. — Originally published: London : Secker and Warburg, 1955
ISBN 0-14-006171-1 (pbk) : £2.25 B82-29814

843'.912[F] — Fiction in French. Belgian writers, *1900-1945 — English texts*

Simenon, Georges. The long exile. — London : Hamilton, Jan.1983. — [352]p
ISBN 0-241-10762-8 : £8.95 : CIP entry B82-36301

843'.912[F] — Short stories in French, *1900-1945 — English texts*

Duras, Marguerite. Whole days in the trees. — London : Calder, June 1982. — [144]p. — (Riverrun writers)
Translation of: Les journées entières dans les arbres
ISBN 0-7145-3820-5 (cased) : £6.95 : CIP entry
ISBN 0-7145-3854-x (pbk) : £2.95 B82-14503

Simenon, Georges. Maigret's Christmas / George Simenon ; translated from the French by Jean Stewart. — Harmondsworth : Penguin, 1981, c1976. — 435p ; 20cm
Originally published: London : Hamilton, 1976
ISBN 0-14-004931-2 (pbk) : £2.50 B82-08030

Yourcenar, Marguerite. Fires / Marguerite Yourcenar ; translated from the French by Dori Katz in collaboration with the author. — Henley-on-Thames : Aidan Ellis, 1982, c1981. — xxi,129p ; 21cm
Translation of: Feux
ISBN 0-85628-109-3 : £7.50 : CIP rev. B81-31650

843'.912[J] — Children's stories in French, *1900-1945 — English texts*

Blond, Georges. The girl who lost her shadow / Georges and Germaine Blond ; illustrated by Françoise Clabots. — [Exeter] : Wheaton, 1981. — 60p : col.ill ; 24cm
Translation of: La petite fille qui avait perdu son ombre
ISBN 0-08-027865-5 : £4.50 B82-01760

Saint-Exupéry, Antoine de. The little prince / written and drawn by Antoine de Saint-Exupéry ; translated from the French by Katherine Woods. — London : Piccolo in association with Heinemann, 1974, c1945 (1982 printing). — 89p : ill ; 18cm
Translation of: Le Petit prince
ISBN 0-330-26832-5 (pbk) : £0.95 B82-18116

843'.912'09 — Fiction in French. Proust, Marcel & Sartre, Jean-Paul — *Critical studies*

Segal, Naomi. The banal object : theme and thematics in Proust, Rilke, Hofmannsthal, and Sartre / Naomi Segal. — London : Institute of Germanic Studies, University of London, 1981. — ix,147p ; 22cm. — (Bithell series of dissertations ; v.6)
Bibliography: p136-143. — Includes index
ISBN 0-85457-099-3 (pbk) : Unpriced
Primary classification 833'.912'09 B82-20536

843.914 — FRENCH FICTION, 1945-

843'.914 — Children's stories in French, *1945- — Welsh texts*

Delahaye, Gilbert. Siani ar lan y môr / stori gan Gilbert Delahaye ; lluniau gan Marcel Marlier. — Caerdydd : Gwasg y Dref Wen, c1981. — 19p : col.ill ; 26cm. — (Cyfres cadi-mi-dawns)
Translation of: Martine à la mer
£1.60 B82-10644

Delahaye, Gilbert. Siani yn helpu mam / stori gan Gilbert Delahaye ; lluniau gan Marcel Marlier. — Caerdydd : Gwasg y Dref Wen, c1981. — 19p : col.ill ; 26cm. — (Cyfres cadi-mi-dawns)
Translation of: Martine à la maison
£1.60 B82-10645

843'.914 — Fiction in French, *1945- — Texts*

Rochefort, Christiane. Les petits enfants du siècle / Christiane Rochefort ; edited with an introduction and notes by P.M.W. Thody. — London : Harrap, 1982. — xxv,177p : 1port ; 17cm. — (Modern world literature series)
French text, English introduction and notes. — Originally published: Paris : Grasset, 1961
ISBN 0-245-53684-1 (pbk) : £2.35 B82-25286

843'.914 — Fiction in French, *1945- — Texts with commentaries*

Lainé, Pascal. La dentellière. — London : Methuen, Nov.1981. — [250]p. — (Methuen's twentieth century French texts)
ISBN 0-423-50820-2 (pbk) : £2.50 : CIP entry B81-30156

843'.914[F] — Fiction in French, *1945- — English texts*

Benson, Bernard. The peace book / Bernard Benson. — London : Cape, 1981, c1980. — 223p : col.ill ; 27cm
Translation of: Le livre de la paix
ISBN 0-224-01989-9 (pbk) : £4.95 : CIP rev. B81-27363

Benzoni, Juliette. The devil's diamonds / Juliette Benzoni ; translated by Anne Carter. — London : Sphere, 1982, c1980. — 399p ; 18cm
Originally published: London : Heinemann, 1980
ISBN 0-7221-1629-2 (pbk) : £1.95 B82-22589

Bonnecarrère, Paul. The golden triangle / translated by Oliver Coburn. — Large print ed. — Leicester : Ulverscroft, 1982, c1977. — 432p ; 23cm. — (Ulverscroft large print)
Translation of: Le triangle d'or. — Originally published: Henley-on-Thames : Ellis, 1977
ISBN 0-7089-0808-x : Unpriced : CIP rev. B82-18445

Curval, Philippe. Brave old world / Philippe Curval ; translated from French by Steve Cox. — London : Allison & Busby, 1981. — 262p ; 22cm
Translation of: Cette chère humanité
ISBN 0-85031-407-0 : £6.95 : CIP rev. B81-18097

Hemingway, Joan. Roesbud / Joan Hemingway, Paul Bonnecarrère ; translated from the French by Joan Hemingway. — Large print ed. — Leicester : Ulverscroft, 1981, c1974. — 432p ; 23cm
Translation of: Rosebud. — Originally published: New York : Morrow ; Henley-on-Thames : Aidan Ellis, 1974
ISBN 0-7089-0725-3 : £5.00 : CIP rev. B81-32604

Hollander, Xaviera. Madame l'ambassadrice / Xaviera Hollander ; translated by Anthea Bell. — Nuffield : Ellis, c1982. — 175p ; 23cm
Translated from the French
ISBN 0-85628-110-7 : £7.50 : CIP rev. B82-00232

Ionesco, Eugène. The hermit. — London : Calder, Jan.1983. — [176]p
Translation of: Le solitaire
ISBN 0-7145-3894-9 (pbk) : £7.95 : CIP entry B82-37469

Jacquemard, Yves. The body vanishes / Jacquemard-Sénécal ; translated by Gordon Latta. — Large print ed. — Bath : Chivers, 1981, c1980. — 197p ; 23cm. — (A Lythway book)
Translation of: La Crime de la Maison Grün. — Originally published: London : Collins, 1980
ISBN 0-85119-762-0 : Unpriced : CIP rev. B81-31271

Japrisot, Sébastien. One deadly summer / Sébastien Japrisot ; translated by Alan Sheridan. — Harmondsworth : Penguin, 1981, c1980. — 297p ; 18cm. — (Penguin crime fiction)
Translation of: L'Été meurtrier. — Originally published: New York : Harcourt Brace Jovanovich, 1980
ISBN 0-14-005846-x (pbk) : £1.25 B82-19909

Maillet, Antonine. Pélagie-la-charrette / by Antonine Maillet ; translated by Philip Stratford. — London : Calder, 1982. — 251p ; 21cm
ISBN 0-7145-3945-7 : £6.95 : CIP rev. B82-10871

Oh wicked country! / Anonymous ; translated by Celeste Piano. — London : W.H. Allen, 1982. — 138p ; 18cm. — (A Star book)
Translation of: Cruelle Zélande
ISBN 0-352-31135-5 (corrected : pbk) : £1.50 B82-32898

Pinget, Robert. Fable / Robert Pinget ; translated by Barbara Wright. — London : Calder, 1980. — 58p ; 22cm. — (Riverrun writers ; 6)
Translated from the French
ISBN 0-7145-3792-6 (pbk) : £2.95 : CIP rev. B80-23812

Robbe-Grillet, Alain. Djinn. — London : Calder, Jan.1983. — [128]p
Translation of: Djinn
ISBN 0-7145-3978-3 (pbk) : £7.95 : CIP entry B82-37468

Sagan, Françoise. The red setter. — Henley-on-Thames : Aidan Ellis, Apr.1982. — [192]p
Translation of : Le chien couchant
ISBN 0-85628-104-2 : £6.50 : CIP entry B82-04805

Tournier, Michel. The four wise men. — London : Collins, Nov.1982. — [264]p
Translation of: Gaspard, Melchior et Balthazar
ISBN 0-00-221436-9 : £7.95 : CIP entry B82-27795

Volkoff, Vladimir. The turnaround / Vladimir Volkoff ; translated from the French by Alan Sheridan. — London : Corgi, 1982, c1981. — 410p ; 18cm
Translation of: Le retournement. — Originally published: London : Bodley Head, 1981
ISBN 0-552-11941-5 (pbk) : £1.75 B82-23907

Yourcenar, Marguerite. A coin in nine hands. — Henley on Thames : Aidan Ellis, Nov.1982. — [192]p
Translation of: Denier du rêve
ISBN 0-85628-123-9 : £7.50 : CIP entry B82-26325

843'.914[F] — Short stories in French, *1945- — English texts*

Beauvoir, Simone de. When things of the spirit come first : five early tales / Simone de Beauvoir ; translated by Patrick O'Brian. — London : Deutsch, 1982. — 212p ; 23cm
Translation of: Quand prime le spirituel
ISBN 0-233-97462-8 : £6.95 B82-30004

843'.914[J] — Children's short stories in French, *1945- — English texts*

Stories of the Arabian Nights. — London : Hodder and Stoughton Children's Books, Aug.1982. — [128]p
ISBN 0-340-25806-3 : £4.95 : CIP entry B82-15719

843'.914[J] — Children's stories in French, *1945- — English texts*

Brisville, Jean-Claude. King Oleg / story by Jean-Claude Brisville ; illustrations by Daniele Bour. — London : Gollancz, 1982. — [24]p : col.ill ; 29cm
Translation of: Oleg retrouve son royaume
ISBN 0-575-03074-7 : £3.95 B82-12948

Brunhoff, Laurent de. Babar and the Christmas tree / Laurent de Brunhoff. — London : Magnet, 1982, c1972. — [20]p : col.ill ; 19cm
Translation of: Babar et l'arbre de Noël. — Originally published: London : Methuen, 1972
ISBN 0-416-25730-5 (pbk) : £0.95 B82-34956

Brunhoff, Laurent de. Babar and the doctor / Laurent de Brunhoff. — London : Magnet, 1982, c1972. — [20p] : col.ill ; 19cm
Translation of: Babar et le docteur. — Originally published: London : Methuen, 1972
ISBN 0-416-25720-8 (pbk) : £0.95 B82-34953

Brunhoff, Laurent de. Babar and the ghost / Laurent de Brunhoff. — London : Methuen Children's Books, 1981. — [28]p : col.ill ; 27cm
Ill on lining papers
ISBN 0-416-21480-0 : £3.95 : CIP rev. B81-04249

Brunhoff, Laurent de. Babar the cook / Laurent de Brunhoff. — London : Magnet, 1982, c1973. — [20]p : col.ill ; 19cm
Translation of: Babar patissier. — Originally published: London : Methuen, 1973
ISBN 0-416-25740-2 (pbk) : £0.95 B82-34954

Brunhoff, Laurent de. Babar the musician / Laurent de Brunhoff. — London : Magnet, 1982, c1973. — [22]p : col.ill ; 19cm
Translation of: Babar musicien. — Originally published: London : Methuen, 1973
ISBN 0-416-25750-x (pbk) : £0.95 B82-34955

Demez, Colette. Tom and Tina in Topsy-turvy Town / Colette Demez ; illustrated by Marie-José Sacré. — [Exeter] : Wheaton, c1981. — [28]p : col.ill ; 29cm
Translation of: Pirouette et Réséda à Chaos-la-Folie
ISBN 0-08-027866-3 : £3.95 B82-00956

Dumas, Philippe. Laura and the bandits / Philippe Dumas. — London : Fontana, 1982, c1979. — [61]p : ill ; 20cm. — (Lions)
Translation of: Laura et les bandits. — Originally published: London : Gollancz, 1980
ISBN 0-00-672043-9 (pbk) : £0.95 B82-30783

Felix, Monique. The story of a little mouse trapped in a book / story and pictures by Monique Felix. — [London] : Moonlight, c1981. — [28]p : allill ; 15cm
Translation from the French
ISBN 0-907144-28-4 : £1.25 B82-06441

Goscinny. Curing the Daltons. — London : Hodder & Stoughton Children's Books, Jan.1982. — [48]p
Translation of: La guérison des Dalton
ISBN 0-340-27473-5 : £1.50 : CIP entry B81-34125

843'.914[J] — Children's stories in French, *1945- — English texts* *continuation*

Goscinny. The dashing white cowboy. — London : Hodder & Stoughton Children's Books, Jan.1982. — [48]p
Translation of: Le cavalier blanc
ISBN 0-340-27474-3 : £1.50 : CIP entry
B81-34124

Lamorisse, Albert. Trip in a balloon / Albert Lamorisse ; the photographs in this book were taken while making the film trip in a balloon by Claude Lamorisse and Alain Duparc ; translated by Malcolm Barnes. — London : Unwin paperbacks, 1980. — [61]p : ill(some col.) ; 19cm
Translation of: Le Voyage en ballon. — Originally published: 1961
ISBN 0-04-823181-9 (pbk) : £1.50 : CIP rev.
B80-18537

Lebrun, Claude. Little brown bear is cross / Claude Lebrun and Danièle Bour. — London : Methuen, 1982. — [12]p : col.ill ; 16cm. — (Little brown bear books)
Translation from the French. — Cover title
ISBN 0-416-24950-7 : £1.50 B82-33884

Lebrun, Claude. Little brown bear won't eat! / Claude Lebrun and Danièle Bour. — London : Methuen, 1982. — [12]p : col.ill ; 16cm. — (Little brown bear books)
Translation from the French. — Cover title
ISBN 0-416-24940-x : £1.50 B82-33888

Lebrun, Claude. Little brown bear's cold / Claude Lebrun and Danièle Bour. — London : Methuen, 1982. — [12]p : col.ill ; 16cm. — (Little brown bear books)
Translation from the French. — Cover title
ISBN 0-416-24930-2 : £1.50 B82-33886

Lebrun, Claude. Little brown bear's story / Claude Lebrun and Danièle Bour. — London : Methuen, 1982. — [12]p : col.ill ; 16cm. — (Little brown bear books)
Translation from the French. — Cover title
ISBN 0-416-24900-0 : £1.50 B82-33887

Lebrun, Claude. Little brown bear's tricycle / Claude Lebrun and Danièle Bour. — London : Methuen, 1982. — [12]p : col.ill ; 16cm. — (Little brown bear books)
Translation from the French. — Cover title
ISBN 0-416-24920-5 : £1.50 B82-33885

Lebrun, Claude. Little brown bear's walk / Claude Lebrun and Danièle Bour. — London : Methuen, 1982. — [12]p : col.ill ; 16cm. — (Little brown bear books)
Translation from the French. — Cover title
ISBN 0-416-24910-8 : £1.50 B82-33883

Nikly, Michelle. The Emperor's plum tree. — London : J. MacRae, Aug.1982. — [32]p
Translation of: Le prunier
ISBN 0-86203-089-7 : £4.95 : CIP entry
B82-17220

Timmermans, Gommaar. The rabbit who tried / Gommaar Timmermans. — London : Methuen Children's Books, 1981. — [26]p : col.ill ; 22cm
Translation of: Albin le lapin
ISBN 0-416-21750-8 : £3.50 : CIP rev.
B81-23774

Vincent, Gabrielle. Bravo, Ernest and Celestine! / Gabrielle Vincent. — London : MacRae, 1982. — [26]p : col.ill ; 22x25cm
Translation of: Ernest et Célestine, musiciens des rues
ISBN 0-86203-074-9 : £3.50 : CIP rev.
B82-00372

Vincent, Gabrielle. Ernest and Celestine / Gabrielle Vincent. — London : MacRae, 1982. — [26]p : col.ill ; 22x25cm
Translation of: Ernest et Célestine ont perdu Siméon
ISBN 0-86203-072-2 : £3.50 : CIP rev.
B82-00371

Vincent, Gabrielle. A picnic for Ernest and Celestine. — London : MacRae, Sept.1982. — [32]p
Translation of: Ernest et Celestine vont pique-niquer
ISBN 0-86203-094-3 : £3.50 : CIP entry
B82-21553

Vincent, Gabrielle. Smile please, Ernest and Celestine. — London : MacRae, Sept.1982. — [32]p
Translation of: Ernest et Celestine chez le photographe
ISBN 0-86203-093-5 : £3.50 : CIP entry
B82-21552

Voilier, Claude. The Famous Five and the golden galleon : a new adventure of the characters created by Enid Blyton / told by Claude Voilier ; translated by Anthea Bell ; illustrated by John Cooper. — Sevenoaks : Hodder and Stoughton, 1982. — 121p : ill ; 18cm. — (Knight books)
Translation of: Les Cinq et le galion d'or
ISBN 0-340-27866-8 (pbk) : £0.85 : CIP rev.
B82-12243

Voilier, Claude. The Famous Five and the missing cheetah : a new adventure of the characters created by Enid Blyton / told by Claude Voilier ; translated by Anthea Bell ; illustrated by John Cooper. — [Sevenoaks] : Knight, 1981. — 140p : ill ; 18cm
Translation of: Les Cinq au Cap des Tempêtes
ISBN 0-340-27248-1 (pbk) : £0.75 : CIP rev.
B81-30250

Voilier, Claude. The famous five and the mystery of the emeralds. — London : Hodder and Stoughton, Apr.1981. — 1v.
Translation of: Les cinq sont les plus forts
ISBN 0-340-26524-8 : £0.75p : CIP entry
B81-00637

Voilier, Claude. The Famous Five and the stately homes gang. — London : Hodder and Stoughton, Apr.1981. — [128]p
Translation of: Le marquis appelle les cinq
ISBN 0-340-26525-6 (pbk) : £0.85 : CIP entry
B81-02562

Voilier, Claude. The Famous Five go on television : a new adventure of the characters created by Enid Blyton / told by Claude Voilier ; translated by Anthea Bell ; illustrated by John Cooper. — [Sevenoaks] : Knight, 1981. — 142p : ill ; 18cm
Translation of: Les Cinq à la télévision
ISBN 0-340-27247-3 (pbk) : £0.75 : CIP rev.
B81-30251

Voilier, Claude. The Famous Five versus the Black Mask : a new adventure of the characters created by Enid Blyton / told by Claude Voilier ; translated by Anthea Bell ; illustrated by John Cooper. — Sevenoaks : Hodder and Stoughton, 1982. — 138p : ill ; 18cm. — (Knight books)
Translation of: Les Cinq contre le Masque Noir
ISBN 0-340-27864-1 (pbk) : £0.85 : CIP rev.
B82-12242

844.3 — FRENCH ESSAYS, 1500-1600

844'.3 — Essays in French. Montaigne, Michel de *— Critical studies*

O'Neill, John, *1933-*. Essaying Montaigne : a study of the Renaissance institution of writing and reading / John O'Neill. — London : Routledge & Kegan Paul, 1982. — ix,244p : 1facsim ; 23cm. — (The International library of phenomenology and moral sciences)
Bibliography: p229-241. — Includes index
ISBN 0-7100-0937-2 : £12.50 B82-23254

844'.3 — Essays in French. Montaigne, Michel de *— Festschriften*

Montaigne : essays in memory of Richard Sayce. — Oxford : Clarendon Press, Oct.1982. — [250]p
ISBN 0-19-815769-x : £17.50 : CIP entry
B82-23683

844.912 — FRENCH ESSAYS, 1900-1945

844'.912 — Essays in French, *1900-1945 — English texts*

Sarraute, Nathalie. The use of speech. — London : J. Calder, Nov.1982. — [96]p
Translation of: L'usage de la parole
ISBN 0-7145-3904-x : £6.95 : CIP entry
B82-26391

848 — FRENCH MISCELLANY

848'.08 — Prose in French, *ca 1500-ca 1980.* **Rhetoric** *— Critical studies*

Houston, John Porter. The traditions of French prose style : a rhetorical study / John Porter Houston. — Baton Rouge ; London : Louisiana State University Press, 1981. — xii,278p ; 24cm
Includes index
ISBN 0-8071-0858-8 : £21.00 B82-09916

848.4 — FRENCH MISCELLANY, 1600-1715

848'.409 — French literature. Gueudeville, Nicolas *— Biographies*

Rosenberg, Aubrey. Nicholas Gueudeville and his work (1652-172?) / by Aubrey Rosenberg. — The Hague ; London : Nijhoff, 1982. — 285p ; 25cm. — (Archives internationales d'histoire des idées = International archives of the history of ideas ; 99)
Bibliography: p214-220. — Includes index
ISBN 90-247-2533-x : Unpriced
ISBN 90-247-2433-3 B82-30622

848.5 — FRENCH MISCELLANY, 1715-1789

848'.503 — Memoirs in French, *1715-1789 — English texts*

Saint-Simon, Louis de Rouvroy, *duc de*. Saint-Simon at Versailles / edited and translated by Lucy Norton. — London : Hamilton, 1980. — 255p,[8]p of plates : ill (some col.),1facsim,ports(some col.),1geneal.table ; 26cm
Translation of: Mémoires. — Previous ed.: 1978. — Includes index
ISBN 0-241-10284-7 : £9.95 : CIP rev.
B80-09498

848'.5'08 — Prose in French, *1715-1789 — English texts*

Rousseau, Jean-Jacques. Reveries of a solitary walker : and essay on the origin of languages. — London : John Calder, Sept.1982. — [224]p. — (The Swiss library)
Translation of: Les rêveries du promeneur solitaire
ISBN 0-7145-3936-8 : £6.95 : CIP entry
B82-28573

848'.508 — Prose in French. Rousseau, Jean-Jacques. Style. Semiotic aspects

De Man, Paul. Allegories of reading. — London : Yale University Press, Mar.1982. — [320]p
Originally published: 1979
ISBN 0-300-02845-8 (pbk) : £4.95 : CIP entry
Also classified at 808'.009'034 B82-12136

848'.509 — France. Paris. Visits by Voltaire, *1694-1778 — French texts*

Fahmy, Jean Mohsen. Voltaire et Paris / Jean Mohsen Fahmy. — Oxford : Voltaire Foundation, 1981. — 265p ; 25cm. — (Studies on Voltaire and the eighteenth century, ISSN 0435-2866 ; 195)
French text. — Bibliography: p247-249. — Includes index
ISBN 0-7294-0257-6 : Unpriced B82-17346

848'.509 — French literature. Crébillon, Claude Prosper Julyot de *— Critical studies — French texts*

Siemek, Andrzej. La recherche morale et esthétique dans le roman de Crébillon fils / Andrzej Siemek. — Oxford : Voltaire Foundation at the Taylor Institution, 1981. — 266p ; 24cm. — (Studies on Voltaire and the eighteenth century, ISSN 0435-2866 ; 200)
French text. — Bibliography: p253-261. — Includes index
ISBN 0-7294-0265-7 : Unpriced B82-19505

848′.509 — French literature. Loaisel de Tréogate, Joseph Marie — *Critical studies*

Bowling, Townsend Whelen. The life, works, and literary career of Loaisel de Tréogate / Townsend Whelen Bowling. — Oxford : Voltaire Foundation, 1981. — 254p ; 25cm. — (Studies on Voltaire and the eighteenth century, ISSN 0435-2866 ; 196)
Bibliography: p229. — Includes index
ISBN 0-7294-0261-4 : Unpriced B82-17347

848′.509 — French literature. Voltaire. Influence of Ancient Greek culture — *French texts*

Mat-Hasquin, Michèle. Voltaire et l'antiquité grecque / Michèle Mat-Hasquin. — Oxford : Voltaire Foundation at the Taylor Institution, c1981. — 324p ; 24cm. — (Studies on Voltaire and the eighteenth century, ISSN 0435-2866 ; 197)
French text. — Bibliography: p295-306. — Includes index
ISBN 0-7294-0259-2 : Unpriced B82-19507

848.7 — FRENCH MISCELLANY, 1815-1848

848′.709 — French literature. Gautier, Théophile — *Biographies*

Snell, Robert. Théophile Gautier : a romantic critic of the visual arts / Robert Snell. — Oxford : Clarendon, 1982. — xiii,273p,[8]p of plates : ill ; 23cm
Bibliography: p257-263. — Includes index
ISBN 0-19-815768-1 : £15.00 : CIP rev.
B81-28859

848.912 — FRENCH MISCELLANY, 1900-1945

848′.91209 — French literature. Camus, Albert — *Critical studies*

Fitch, Brian T.. The narcissistic text : a reading of Camus' fiction / Brian T. Fitch. — Toronto ; London : University of Toronto Press, c1982. — xvii,128p ; 23cm. — (University of Toronto romance series ; 42)
Bibliography: p121-125. — Includes index
ISBN 0-8020-2426-2 : Unpriced B82-27906

848′.91209 — French literature. Gide, André, *to 1900* — *Biographies*

Gide, André. If it die — / André Gide ; translated by Dorothy Bussy. — Harmondsworth : Penguin in association with Secker & Warburg, 1977, c1950 (1982 [printing]). — 304p ; 20cm. — (Penguin modern classics)
Translation of: Si le grain ne meurt. — Originally published: London : Secker & Warburg, 1950
ISBN 0-14-001234-6 (pbk) : £3.50 B82-33635

848.914 — FRENCH MISCELLANY, 1945-

848′.91407 — Humorous prose in Franglais, *1945-* — *Texts*

Kington, Miles. Let's parler Franglais. — London : Robson Books, Sept.1982. — [96]p
ISBN 0-86051-178-2 : £3.50 : CIP entry
B82-20863

848′.91409 — French literature, *1945-* — *English texts*

Félix, Monique. Stories : with and without words / Monique Félix. — London : Evans, 1982. — [32]p : col.ill ; 22cm. — (Busy books)
ISBN 0-237-45598-6 : £2.25 B82-25019

848′.91409 — French literature. Beckett, Samuel — *Critical studies*

Baldwin, Hélène L.. Samuel Beckett's real silence / Hélène L. Baldwin. — University Park ; London : Pennsylvania State University Press, c1981. — viii,171p ; 23cm
Bibliography: p161-165. — Includes index
ISBN 0-271-00301-4 : Unpriced
Primary classification 828′.91209 B82-02053

849 — PROVENCAL LITERATURE

849′.34 — Fiction in Provençal. Favre, Jean Baptiste Castor. Istória de Joan l'an-pres — *Critical studies*

Le Roy Ladurie, Emmanuel. Love, death and money in the pays d'oc. — London : Scolar, Sept.1982. — [512]p
Translation of: L'argent, l'amour et la mort en pays d'oc
ISBN 0-85967-655-2 : £15.00 : CIP entry
B82-20847

849.9 — CATALAN LITERATURE

849′.933[F] — Fiction in Catalan, *1450-1500* — *English texts*

Curial and Guelfa / translated from Catalan by Pamela Waley. — London : Allen & Unwin, 1982. — xii,287p ; 23cm
ISBN 0-04-823217-3 : Unpriced : CIP rev.
B82-14507

851.1 — ITALIAN POETRY, TO 1375

851′.1 — Poetry in Italian, *1492-1542* — *English texts*

Ariosto, Ludovico. Orlando Furioso. — Oxford : Oxford University Press, Feb.1983. — [647]p. — (The World's classics)
Originally published: 1974
ISBN 0-19-281636-5 (pbk) : £3.95 : CIP entry
B82-36594

851′.1 — Poetry in Italian. Dante Alighieri — *Critical studies*

Boyde, Patrick. Dante, philomythes and philosopher. — Cambridge : Cambridge University Press, June 1981. — [404]p
ISBN 0-521-23598-7 : £30.00 : CIP entry
B81-13795

851′.1 — Poetry in Italian. Dante Alighieri. Divina commedia — *Critical studies*

Cambridge readings in Dante's Comedy / edited by Kenelm Foster and Patrick Boyde. — Cambridge : Cambridge University Press, 1981. — x,213p ; 24cm
ISBN 0-521-24140-5 : £19.50 : CIP rev.
B82-01356

851′.1 — Poetry in Italian. Dante Alighieri. Vita nuova — *Critical studies*

Mazzaro, Jerome. The figure of Dante : an essay on the 'Vita nuova' / by Jerome Mazzaro. — Princeton ; Guildford : Princeton University Press, c1981. — xix,150p ; 23cm
Bibliography: p139-145. — Includes index
ISBN 0-691-06474-1 : £9.00 B82-03283

851′.1 — Poetry in Italian, *to 1375* — *English texts*

Jacopone, *da Todi*. The Lauds / Jacopone da Todi ; translated by Serge and Elizabeth Hughes ; introduction by Serge Hughes ; preface by Elémire Zolla. — London : SPCK, 1982. — xxi,296p ; 23cm. — (The Classics of western spirituality)
Translation of: Laude. — Includes index
ISBN 0-281-03849-x (pbk) : £8.50 B82-34555

Petrarca, Francesco. Sonnets for Laura / Petrarch ; translated by G.R. Nicholson ; introduced by G.S. Fraser. — London (14, Barlby Rd., W10 6AR) : Autolycus, [1981?]. — 31p ; 21cm
Translation from the Italian
Unpriced (pbk) B82-04668

851′.1 — Poetry in Italian, *to 1375* — *Italian-English parallel texts*

Dante Alighieri. The divine comedy of Dante Alighieri : a verse translation / with introductions & commentary by Allen Mandelbaum ; drawings by Barry Moser. — Berkeley ; London : University of California Press, c1982. — xxviii,303p : ill ; 29cm
Spine title: Purgatorio
ISBN 0-520-04516-5 : £17.00 B82-38631

Dante Alighieri. The divine comedy of Dante Alighieri / with translation and comment by John D. Sinclair. — New York ; Oxford : Oxford University Press
Parallel Italian text and English translation of: La divina commedia ; introduction and notes in English
3: Paradiso. — 1961 (1981 [printing]). — 504p ; 21cm
Includes index
ISBN 0-19-500414-0 (pbk) : £3.95 B82-33175

Latini, Brunetto. Il tesoretto : (The little treasure) / Brunetto Latini ; edited and translated by Julia Bolton Holloway. — New York ; London : Garland, 1981. — xliii,164p : facsims,port ; 23cm. — (Garland library of medieval literature. Series A ; vol.2)
Parallel Italian and English texts. — Bibliography: pxxxv-xliii. — Includes index
ISBN 0-8240-9376-3 : Unpriced B82-27169

Petrarca, Francesco. Petrarch's lyric poems : the Rime sparse and other lyrics / translated and edited by Robert M. Durling. — Cambridge, Mass. ; London : Harvard University Press, c1976 (1979 printing). — xii,657p ; 24cm
Parallel Italian text and English translation. — Bibliography: p637—646. - Includes index
ISBN 0-674-66348-9 (pbk) : £6.30 B82-19371

851′.1′08 — Poetry in Italian, *to 1375* — *Anthologies — English texts*

The **Early** Italian poets / [translated by] Dante Gabriel Rossetti ; edited by Sally Purcell. — London : Anvil Press Poetry in association with Wildwood House, 1981. — xxiii,320p ; 19cm. — (Poetica ; 7)
Translation from the Italian. — Bibliography: p305-306. — Includes index
ISBN 0-85646-054-0 (pbk) : £4.95 B82-33185

851.6 — ITALIAN POETRY, 1748-1814

851′.6 — Poetry in Italian. Foscolo, Ugo. Dei sepolcri — *Critical studies*

O'Neill, Tom, *1942-*. Of virgin muses and of love : a study of Foscolo's Dei sepolcri / Tom O'Neill. — Dublin : Published for the Foundation for Italian Studies, University College Dublin [by] Irish Academic Press, c1981. — xviii,219p ; 22cm
Includes index
ISBN 0-7165-0508-8 (corrected : pbk) : Unpriced B82-06414

851.7 — ITALIAN POETRY, 1814-1859

851′.7 — Poetry in Italian, *1814-1859* — *Italian-English parallel texts*

Belli, Giuseppe Gioachino. Sonnets of Giuseppe Belli / translated, with an introduction, by Miller Williams. — Bilingual ed. — Baton Rouge ; London : Louisiana State University Press, c1981. — xxiii,159p : 2ports ; 22cm
Parallel Italian and English text
ISBN 0-8071-0762-x : £12.20 B82-00493

851.912 — ITALIAN POETRY, 1900-1945

851′.912 — Poetry in Italian. Montale, Eugenio — *Critical studies*

West, Rebecca J.. Eugenio Montale : poet on the edge / Rebecca J. West. — Cambridge, Mass. ; London : Harvard University Press, 1981. — x,200p ; 24cm
Bibliography: p191-192. — Includes index
ISBN 0-674-26910-1 : £11.55 B82-11870

851.914 — ITALIAN POETRY, 1945-

851′.914 — Poetry in Italian, *1945-* — *English texts*

Pascoli, Giovanni. Selected poems. — Manchester : Manchester University Press, May 1982. — [240]p. — (Italian texts)
ISBN 0-7190-0870-0 (pbk) : £3.95 : CIP entry
B82-07590

Pasolini, Pier Paolo. Poems. — London : Calder, June 1982. — [256]p
Translated from the Italian
ISBN 0-7145-3889-2 (pbk) : £4.95 : CIP entry
B82-09612

851′.914 — Poetry in Italian, *1945- — English texts* *continuation*

Sanesi, Roberts. In visible ink. — Isle of Skye : Aquila, Dec.1982. — [96]p. — (Prospice, ISSN 0308-2776 ; v.13)
Translation from the Italian
ISBN 0-7275-0255-7 (pbk) : £2.75 : CIP entry B82-30307

852.912 — ITALIAN DRAMA, 1900-1945

852′.912 — Drama in Italian. Pirandello, Luigi — *Critical studies — Serials*

British Pirandello Society. The Yearbook of the British Pirandello Society. — No.2. — Bristol : The Society, May 1982. — [110]p
ISBN 0-907564-01-1 (pbk) : £3.50 : CIP entry
ISSN 0260-9215 B82-12832

852′.9′12 — Drama in Italian. Pirandello, Luigi - *Critical studies - Serials*

The **Yearbook** of the British Pirandello Society. — No.1 (1981)-. — Bristol (c/o Dept. of Italian, University of Bristol, 95 Woodland Rd, Bristol BS8 1US) : British Pirandello Society, Apr.1981. — [110]p
ISBN 0-907564-00-3 (pbk) : £2.95 : CIP entry
ISSN 0260-9215 B81-10503

852′.912 — Drama in Italian. Pirandello, Luigi — *Critical studies — Serials*

The **Yearbook** of the British Pirandello Society. — No.1 (1981)-. — Bristol (c/o Felicity Firth, Department of Italian, University of Bristol, 95 Woodland Rd., Bristol BS8 1US) : The Society, 1981-. — v. : ill,ports ; 21cm
Text in English and Italian. — Spine title: Pirandello yearbook
ISSN 0260-9215 = Yearbook of the British Pirandello Society : Unpriced B82-12477

852.914 — ITALIAN DRAMA, 1945-

852′.914 — Drama in Italian, *1945- — English texts*

Fo, Dario. Female parts : one woman plays / by Dario Fo and Franca Rame ; adapted by Olwen Wymark. — London : Pluto, 1981. — v,40p ; 21cm. — (Pluto plays)
Contents: Waking up — A woman alone — The same old story / translated by Margaret Kunzle — Medea / translated by Stuart Hood
ISBN 0-86104-220-4 (pbk) : £1.95 B82-20715

853.1 — ITALIAN FICTION, TO 1375

853′.1 — Short stories in Italian. Boccaccio, Giovanni. Decamerone — *Critical studies*

Potter, Joy Hambuechen. Five frames for the Decameron : communications and social systems in the cornice / Joy Hambuechen Potter. — Princeton ; Guildford : Princeton University Press, c1982. — ix,230p ; 23cm
Bibliography: p216-224. — Includes index
ISBN 0-691-06503-9 : £14.10 B82-40617

853.8 — ITALIAN FICTION, 1859-1900

853′.8[F] — Fiction in Italian, *1859-1900 — English texts*

Svevo, Italo. Confessions of Zeno / Italo Svevo ; translated from the Italian by Beryl de Zoete ; with a note on Svevo by Édouard Roditi. — Harmondsworth : Penguin in association with Secker & Warburg, 1964, c1930 (1982 [printing]). — 377p ; 20cm. — (Penguin modern classics)
Translation of: La coscienza di Zeno
ISBN 0-14-002171-x (pbk) : £3.50 B82-25226

Svevo, Italo. A life / Italo Svevo ; translated from the Italian by Archibald Colquhoun. — Harmondsworth : Penguin, 1982, c1963. — 297p ; 20cm. — (Penguin modern classics)
Translation of: Una vita. — Originally published: London : Secker & Warburg, 1963
ISBN 0-14-006030-8 (pbk) : £2.95 B82-40666

853′.8[J] — Children's stories in Italian, *1859-1900 — English texts*

Collodi, Carlo. The adventures of Pinocchio / by Carlo Collodi ; retold by Neil Morris ; illustrated by Frank Baber. — [London] : Peter Lowe, c1982. — 83p : ill(some col.) ; 28cm
Translation of: Pinocchio
ISBN 0-85654-042-0 : £3.50 B82-35989

853.912 — ITALIAN FICTION, 1900-1945

853′.912 — Fiction in Italian, *1900-1945 — Texts*

Ginzburg, Natalia. Le voci della sera / Natalia Ginzburg ; edited with introduction, notes and vocabulary by Alan Bullock. — Manchester : Manchester University Press, c1982. — xxxxiii,158p ; 19cm. — (Italian texts)
Text in Italian; introduction and notes in English. — Bibliography: pxxx-xxxiii
ISBN 0-7190-0857-3 (pbk) : £4.95 : CIP rev. B82-00305

Pitigrilli. Cocaine / Pitigrilli ; translated from the Italian by Eric Mosbacher. — [Feltham] : Hamlyn Paperbacks, 1982. — 205p ; 18cm
Translation of: Cocaina
ISBN 0-600-20327-1 (pbk) : £1.50 B82-33684

853′.912[F] — Fiction in Italian, *1900-1945 — English texts*

Moravia, Alberto. Time of desecration / Alberto Moravia ; translated from the Italian by Angus Davidson. — London : Granada, 1982, c1980. — 375p ; 18cm. — (A Panther book)
Translation of: La vita interiore. — Originally published: London : Secker & Warburg, 1980
ISBN 0-586-05364-6 (pbk) : £1.95 B82-14104

Moravia, Alberto. Two women / Alberto Moravia ; translated by Angus Davidson. — Harmondsworth : Penguin in association with Secker & Warburg, 1961, c1958 (1982 [printing]). — 339p ; 18cm
Translation of: La ciociara. — Originally published: London : Secker & Warburg, 1958
ISBN 0-14-001603-1 (pbk) : £2.25 B82-32491

Moravia, Alberto. The woman of Rome : a novel / by Alberto Moravia ; translated by Lydia Holland. — Harmondsworth : Penguin in association with Secker & Warburg, 1952 (1982 [printing]). — 380p ; 18cm
Translation from the Italian
ISBN 0-14-000880-2 (pbk) : £2.25 B82-32490

853.914 — ITALIAN FICTION, 1945-

853′.914[F] — Fiction in Italian, *1945- — English texts*

Sciascia, Leonardo. Candido : or a dream dreamed in Sicily / Leonardo Sciascia. — Manchester : Carcanet New Press, 1982, c1979. — 132p ; 21cm
Translation of the Italian
ISBN 0-85635-404-x : Unpriced : CIP rev. B81-40262

853′.914[F] — Fiction in Italian. Swiss writers, *1945- — English texts*

Martini, Plinio. The bottom of the barrel. — London : Calder, Sept.1982. — [224]p. — (The Swiss library)
Translation of: Il fondo del sacco
ISBN 0-7145-3935-x : £6.95 : CIP entry B82-28572

853′.914[F] — Short stories in Italian, *1945- — English texts*

Calvino, Italo. Adam, one afternoon and other stories. — London : Secker & Warburg, Dec.1982. — [192]p
Translation of: Ultimo viene il corvo
ISBN 0-436-08273-x : £7.50 : CIP entry B82-33336

853′.914[J] — Children's stories in Italian, *1945- — English texts*

The **Falling** star / [illustrations by Carlo A. Michelini]. — London : Methuen, 1982, c1980. — [24]p : chiefly col.ill ; 22x25cm
These illustrations originally published with Italian text, 1980
ISBN 0-416-22760-0 (spiral) : Unpriced B82-40712

858.7 — ITALIAN MISCELLANY, 1814-1859

858′.708 — Prose in Italian, *1814-1859 — Italian-English parallel texts*

Leopardi, Giacomo. Pensieri / Giacomo Leopardi ; translated by W.S. Di Piero. — A bilingual ed. — Baton Rouge ; London : Louisiana State University Press, c1982. — 172p ; 23cm
Text in English and Italian. — Translation of: Pensieri
ISBN 0-8071-0885-5 : Unpriced B82-34769

858′.709 — Italian literature, *1814-1859 — English texts*

Leopardi, Giacomo. A Leopardi reader / editing and translations by Ottavio M. Casale. — Urbana ; London : University of Illinois Press, c1981. — xv,271p ; 24cm
Includes the text of original poems by Leopardi in Italian. — Bibliography: p223-225
ISBN 0-252-00824-3 (cased) : £17.50
ISBN 0-252-00892-8 (pbk) : Unpriced B82-09766

858.912 — ITALIAN MISCELLANY, 1900-1945

858′.91209 — Italian literature. Pavese, Cesare — *Critical studies*

Thompson, Doug. Cesare Pavese : a study of the major novels and poems / Doug Thompson. — Cambridge : Cambridge University Press, 1982. — x,292p : 1port ; 23cm
Includes bibliographies and index
ISBN 0-521-23602-9 : £22.50 : CIP rev. B82-13260

859 — ROMANIAN LITERATURE

859′.134 — Poetry in Romanian, *1945- — Romanian-English parallel texts*

Caraion, Ion. Ion Caraion, poems / English translation by Marguerite Dorian and Elliott B. Urdang. — Athens, Ohio ; London : Ohio University Press, c1981. — 109p : 1port ; 24cm
Parallel Romanian text and English translation
ISBN 0-8214-0608-6 (cased) : Unpriced
ISBN 0-8214-0620-5 (pbk) : Unpriced B82-30839

859′.134 — Poetry in Romanian, *1945- — Texts*

Michael-Titus, C.. Poeme de ieri şi de azi / C. Michael-Titus ; comentate şi editate de George Alexe. — London : Panopticum, 1981. — 95p ; 21cm
ISBN 0-907256-03-1 (pbk) : Unpriced B82-09013

861 — SPANISH POETRY

861 — Ballads in Ladino. Words — *Anthologies*

Judeo-Spanish ballads from New York / collected by Maír José Benardete ; edited with introduction and notes by Samuel G. Armistead and Joseph H. Silverman. — Berkeley ; London : University of California Press, 1981. — viii,149p ; 24cm
English text with ballads in Spanish. — Bibliography: p121-138. — Includes index
ISBN 0-520-04348-0 : £13.50 B82-31093

861 — Poetry in Spanish. Chilean writers, *1900-1945 — English texts*

Neruda, Pablo. Selections : poems from Canto general / Pablo Neruda ; translated by J.C.R. Green. — Isle of Skye : Aquila, c1982. — [24]p ; 21cm
Translations from: Canto general
ISBN 0-7275-0235-2 (pbk) : £0.75
ISBN 0-7275-0236-0 (signed, limited ed.) : £1.50 B82-33766

861 — Poetry in Spanish. Cuban writers. Guillén, Nicholás — *Critical studies*

Williams, Lorna V.. Self and society in the poetry of Nicholás Guillén / Lorna V. Williams. — Baltimore ; London : Johns Hopkins University Press, c1982. — x,177p ; 24cm. — (Johns Hopkins studies in Atlantic history and culture)
Bibliography: p163-174. — Includes index
ISBN 0-8018-2666-7 : Unpriced B82-36869

861 — Poetry in Spanish. Peruvian writers, *1910-* — *Critical studies*

Higgins, James. The poet in Peru : alienation and the quest for a super-reality / James Higgins. — Liverpool : Cairns, 1982. — vii,166p ; 23cm. — (Liverpool monographs in hispanic studies, ISSN 0261-1538 ; 1)
ISBN 0-905205-10-3 : £7.50 B82-22200

861 — Poetry in Spanish. Venezuelan writers. Bello, Andrés — *Biographies*

Andres Bello : the London years / edited by John Lynch. — Richmond : Richmond Publishing, 1982. — 167p ; 22cm
ISBN 0-85546-005-9 (pbk) : Unpriced
B82-38325

861.1 — SPANISH POETRY, TO 1369

861'.1 — Poetry in Spanish, *to 1369* — *Texts*

Berceo, Gonzalo de. El sacrificio de la misa ; La vida de Santa Oria ; El martirio de San Lorenzo / Gonzalo de Berceo ; estudio y edición crítica por Brian Dutton. — London : Tamesis, c1981. — 208p ; 25cm. — (Colección Támesis. Serie A — monografías ; 80) (Obras completas ; 5)
Bibliography: p191-195. — Includes index
ISBN 0-7293-0099-4 (pbk) : Unpriced
B82-35245

861.2 — SPANISH POETRY, 1369-1516

861'.2'09 — Poetry in Spanish, *1369-1516* — *Critical studies* — *Spanish texts*

Whinnom, Keith. La poesía amatoria de la época de los Reyes Católicos / Keith Whinnom. — [Durham] : University of Durham, 1981. — 112p ; 21cm. — (Durham modern languages series ; hm.2)
Spanish text
ISBN 0-907310-02-8 (pbk) : Unpriced
B82-27433

861.3 — SPANISH POETRY, 1516-1700

861'.3 — Poetry in Spanish, *1516-1700* — *Spanish-English parallel texts*

Alcázar, Baltasar del. Three things I love / Baltasar del Alcázar ; English version by Ivor Waters. — Chepstow : Moss Rose, 1982. — 9p : 1ill ; 23cm
Parallel Spanish text and English translation. — Limited ed. of 100 copies
ISBN 0-906134-18-8 (pbk) : £12.00
B82-28792

Quevedo, Francisco de. Lord Cash = Letrilla Satirica / Francisco de Quevedo Villegas ; translation by Ivor Waters. — Chepstow (41 Hardwick Avenue, Chepstow, Gwent, NP6 5DS) : Moss Rose, 1982. — 11p ; 23cm
Parallel English and Spanish text
ISBN 0-906134-16-1 (pbk) : Unpriced
B82-23962

861'.3 — Poetry in Spanish. Garcilaso de la Vega, *1503-1536* — *Critical studies*

Fernandez-Morera, Dario. The lyre and the oaten flute : Garcilaso and the pastoral / Dario Fernandez-Morera. — London : Tamesis, c1982. — 128p ; 25cm. — (Colección Támesis. Serie A — monografías ; 81)
Includes index
ISBN 0-7293-0114-1 : Unpriced B82-35240

861'.3 — Poetry in Spanish. Montemayor, Jorge de — *Critical studies*

Creel, Bryant L.. The religious poetry of Jorge de Montemayor / Bryant L. Creel. — London : Tamesis, c1981. — 270p : 1facsim ; 25cm. — (Colección Támesis. Serie A — monografías ; 78)
Bibliography: p265-270
ISBN 0-7293-0103-6 : Unpriced B82-35243

861'.3 — Poetry in Spanish. Quevedo, Francisco de — *Critical studies* — *Spanish texts*

Snell, Ana Maria. Hacia el verbo : signos y transignificacion en la poesia de Quevedo / Ana Maria Snell. — London : Tamesis, c1981. — 99p ; 25cm. — (Colección Támesis. Serie A — monografías ; 84)
Bibliography: p95-99
ISBN 0-7293-0117-6 (pbk) : Unpriced
B82-35241

861'.3 — Sonnets in Spanish. Gongora, Luis de — *Critical studies*

Calcraft, R. P.. The sonnets of Luis de Góngora / R.P. Calcraft. — [Durham] : University of Durham, 1980. — 127p ; 21cm. — (Durham modern languages series)
Bibliography: p123-127
ISBN 0-907310-00-1 (pbk) : Unpriced
B82-17714

861.5 — SPANISH POETRY, 1800-1900

861'.5 — Poetry in Spanish, *1800-1900* — *Texts*

Mesa, Enrique de. Seven poems / Enrique de Mesa ; English versions by Ivor Waters. — Chepstow : Moss Rose, c1982. — 19p : 1ill ; 23cm
Parallel Spanish text and English translation. — Limited ed. of 100 copies
ISBN 0-906134-17-x (pbk) : £1.00 B82-28802

861.62 — SPANISH POETRY, 1900-1945

861'.62 — Poetry in Spanish, *1900-1945* — *English texts*

Jiménez, Juan Ramon. The flower scenes / Juan Ramon Jimenez ; trans. J.C.R. Green. — Isle of Skye : Aquila, 1982. — 22p ; 21cm
Translations from the Spanish
ISBN 0-7275-0237-9 (pbk) : £0.75
ISBN 0-7275-0238-7 (signed, limited ed)
B82-33759

Machado, Antonio. The Castilian camp / Antonio Machado ; trans. J.C.R. Green. — Isle of Skye : Aquila, 1982. — 22p ; 21cm
Translations from the Spanish
ISBN 0-7275-0239-5 (pbk) : £0.75
ISBN 0-7275-0240-9 (signed limited ed.) : £1.50 B82-32650

861'.62 — Poetry in Spanish. Prados, Emilio — *Critical studies*

Ellis, P. J.. The poetry of Emilio Prados : a progression towards fertility / P.J. Ellis. — Cardiff : University of Wales Press, 1981. — 332p ; 23cm
English text, Spanish verse. — Bibliography: p295-299. — Includes index
ISBN 0-7083-0786-8 : Unpriced B82-00718

862.3 — SPANISH DRAMA, 1516-1700

862'.3 — Drama in Spanish, *1516-1700* — *English texts*

Calderón de la Barca, Pedro. The Mayor of Zalamea, or, The best garrotting ever done / by Calderon de la Barca ; adapted by Adrian Mitchell. — Edinburgh : Salamander Press, 1981. — ix,110p : music ; 21cm
Translation of: El alcalde de Zalamea
ISBN 0-907540-11-2 (cased) : Unpriced
ISBN 0-907540-12-0 (pbk) : £3.75 B82-15436

862.62 — SPANISH DRAMA, 1900-1945

862'.62 — Drama in Spanish, *1900-1945* — *Texts*

García Lorca, Federico. Bodas de sangre / Federico Garcia Lorca ; edited with introduction, notes and vocabulary by H. Ramsden. — [Manchester] : Manchester University Press, [1980]. — li,96p : music ; 20cm. — (Spanish texts)
Spanish text, English introduction. — Bibliography: pl-li
ISBN 0-7190-0764-x (pbk) : £3.50 : CIP rev.
B79-34601

863 — SPANISH FICTION

863 — Fiction in Spanish. Argentinian writers. Arlt, Roberto — *Critical studies* — *Spanish texts*

Hayes, Aden W.. Roberto Arlt : la estrategia de su ficcion / Aden W. Hayes. — London : Tamesis, c1981. — 82p ; 25cm. — (Colección Tamesis. Serie A — monografías ; 83)
Bibliography: p77-82
ISBN 0-7293-0116-8 (pbk) : Unpriced
B82-35242

863 — Fiction in Spanish. Latin American writers, *1826-1888* — *Critical studies*

Brushwood, John S.. Genteel barbarism : experiments in analysis of nineteenth-century Spanish-American novels / John S. Brushwood. — Lincoln, Neb. ; London : University of Nebraska Press, c1981. — xi,241p : ill ; 23cm
Bibliography: p225-232 . — Includes index
ISBN 0-8032-1165-1 : £13.30 B82-22624

863 — Fiction in Spanish. Latin American writers, *1910-1975* — *Critical studies*

Kapschutschenko, Ludmila. El laberinto en la narrativa hispanoamericano contemporanea / Ludmila Kapschutschenko. — London : Tamesis, c1981. — 115p ; 25cm. — (Colección Támesis. Serie A — monografías ; 85)
Bibliography: p111-115
ISBN 0-7293-0118-4 : Unpriced B82-35244

863[F] — Fiction in Spanish. Colombian writers, *1945-* — *English texts*

García Márquez, Gabriel. Chronicle of a death foretold / Gabriel García Márquez ; translated from the Spanish by Gregory Rabassa. — London : Cape, 1982. — 122p ; 21cm
Translation of: Crónica de una muerte anunciada
ISBN 0-224-01990-2 : £5.95 : CIP rev.
B82-25519

863[F] — Fiction in Spanish. Colombian writers, *1945* — *English texts*

García Márquez, Gabriel. In evil hour / Gabriel García Márquez ; translated from the Spanish by Gregory Rabassa. — [London] : Picador, 1982, c1979. — 183p ; 20cm
Translation of: La mala hora. — Originally published: New York : Harper and Row, 1979 ; London : Cape, 1980
ISBN 0-330-26596-2 (pbk) : £2.50 B82-34254

García Márquez, Gabriel. One hundred years of solitude / Gabriel García Márquez ; translated from the Spanish by Gregory Rabassa. — [London] : Picador, 1978, c1970 (1981 [printing]). — 335p : 1geneal.table,1port ; 20cm
Translation of: Cien años de soledad. — Originally published: New York : Harper and Row ; London : Cape, 1970. — Port on inside cover
ISBN 0-330-25559-2 (pbk) : £2.25 B82-06406

863[F] — Fiction in Spanish. Mexican writers, *1945-* — *English texts*

Fuentes, Carlos. Distant relations / Carlos Fuentes ; translated from the Spanish by Margaret Sayers Peden. — London : Secker & Warburg, 1982. — 225p ; 21cm
Translation of: Una familia lejana
ISBN 0-436-16764-6 : £7.95 B82-26004

Ibargüengoitia, Jorge. The dead girls. — London : Chatto & Windus, Feb.1983. — [160]p
Translation from the Spanish
ISBN 0-7011-2656-6 (cased) : £7.95 : CIP entry
ISBN 0-7011-2687-6 (pbk) : £3.50 B82-38867

863[F] — Fiction in Spanish. Peruvian writers, *1945-* — *English texts*

Vargas Llosa, Mario. Aunt Julia and the script writer. — London : Faber, Jan.1983. — [361]
Translation of: La tía Julia y le escribidor
ISBN 0-571-13021-6 : CIP entry B82-32449

863.3 — SPANISH FICTION, 1516-1700

863'.3 — Fiction in Spanish. Cervantes Saavedra, Miguel de. Don Quixote — *Critical studies*

Mancing, Howard. The chivalric world of Don Quijote : style, structure and narrative technique / Howard Mancing. — Columbia ; London : University of Missouri Press, 1982. — xii,240p,[3]leaves of plates : ill ; 22cm
Bibliography: p226-234. — Includes index
ISBN 0-8262-0350-7 : £15.75 B82-40262

863′.3[F] — Fiction in Spanish, *1516-1700 — English texts*

Cervantes Saavedra, Miguel de. The adventures of Don Quixote / Miguel Cervantes De Saavedra ; translated by J.M. Cohen ; abridged by Olive Jones ; drawings by George Him. — London : Methuen Children′s, c1980. — 206p : ill ; 24cm
Translated from the Spanish
ISBN 0-416-87910-1 : £5.95 : CIP rev. B79-37546

863.5 — SPANISH FICTION, 1800-1900

863′.5 — Fiction in Spanish. Pérez Galdós, Benito — *Critical studies*

Bly, Peter A.. Galdós′s novel of the historical imagination. — Liverpool : Francis Cairns, Jan.1983. — [196]p. — (Liverpool monographs in Hispanic studies ; 2)
ISBN 0-905205-14-6 : £12.50 : CIP entry B82-32859

Gilman, Stephen. Galdós and the art of the European novel : 1867-1887 / Stephen Gilman. — Princeton ; Guildford : Princeton University Press, c1981. — x,413p ; 24cm
Includes index
ISBN 0-691-06456-3 : £21.10 B82-06973

Urey, Diane F.. Galdós and the irony of language / Diane F. Urey. — Cambridge : Cambridge University Press, 1982. — vi,138p ; 24cm. — (Cambridge Iberian and Latin American studies)
Bibliography: p134-136. — Includes index
ISBN 0-521-23756-4 : £17.50 : CIP rev. B81-39209

863′.5[F] — Fiction in Spanish, *1800-1900 — English texts*

Alas, Leopoldo. His only son / Leopoldo Alas ; translated from the Spanish, with an introduction, by Julie Jones. — Baton Rouge ; London : Louisiana State University Press, c1981. — x,256p ; 24cm
Translation of: Su único hijo
ISBN 0-8071-0759-x : £15.70 B82-00492

863.62 — SPANISH FICTION, 1900-1945

863′.62 — Fiction in Spanish. Pérez de Ayala, Ramón. Tigre Juan & Curandero de su honra — *Critical studies*

Macklin, J. J.. Tigre Juan and El curandero de su honra / J.J. Macklin. — London : Grant & Cutler in association with Tamesis, 1980. — 100p ; 19cm. — (Critical guides to Spanish texts ; 28)
Bibliography: p98-100
ISBN 0-7293-0100-1 (pbk) : £1.80 B82-17578

863′.62 — Fiction in Spanish. Unamuno, Miguel de. San Manuel Bueno, mártir — *Critical studies*

Butt, John, *1943-*. San Manuel Bueno, mártir / John Butt. — London : Grant & Cutler in association with Tamesis, 1981. — 84p ; 19cm. — (Critical guides to Spanish texts ; 31)
Bibliography: p82-84
ISBN 0-7293-0111-7 (pbk) : £1.80 B82-17576

863.64 — SPANISH FICTION, 1945-

863′.64[J] — Children′s stories in Spanish, *1945- — English texts*

Calders, Pere. Brush. — London : Blackie, Sept.1982. — [32]p
Translation of: Cepillo
ISBN 0-216-91332-2 : £4.95 : CIP entry B82-18999

Pacheco, M. A.. A million stories about a miller and his three sons. — London : Blackie, Oct.1982. — [32]p
Translation of: Un millón de cuentos de un molinero y sus tres hijos
ISBN 0-216-91347-0 : £4.50 : CIP entry B82-23492

Puncel, Maria. I want to be a reporter / [text by Maria Puncel] ; [illustrator Alexandra Hellwagner]. — London : Macdonald Educational, 1981. — 46p : col.ill ; 27cm. — (When I grow up)
Translation from the Spanish
ISBN 0-356-07142-1 : £3.75 B82-00616

Puncel, Maria. I want to be a shopkeeper / [text by Maria Puncel] ; [illustrator Maria Rius]. — London : Macdonald Educational, 1981. — 46p : col.ill ; 27cm. — (When I grow up)
Translation from the Spanish
ISBN 0-356-07143-x : £3.25 B82-00617

868.62 — SPANISH MISCELLANY, 1900-1945

868′.6202 — Aphorisms in Spanish, *1900-1945 — English texts*

Gómez de la Serna, Ramón. Greguerías. — Cambridge : Oleander, Dec.1982. — [224]p. — (Oleander language and literature ; 13)
Translated from the Spanish
ISBN 0-900891-45-9 (cased) : £13.50 : CIP entry
ISBN 0-900891-49-1 (pbk) : £6.95 B82-30739

868′.6209 — Spanish literature. Unamuno, Miguel de — *Critical studies*

Nozick, Martin. Miguel de Unamuno : the agony of belief / Martin Nozick. — Princeton ; Guildford : Princeton University Press, 1982, c1971. — 238p ; 21cm
Originally published: New York : Twayne, 1971. — Bibliography: p222-229. — Includes index
ISBN 0-691-06498-9 (cased) : Unpriced
ISBN 0-691-01366-7 (pbk) : £5.60 B82-27492

869.09 — PORTUGUESE LITERATURE. HISTORY AND CRITICAL STUDIES

869.09 — Portuguese literature, *ca 1550-1940 — Critical studies*

Sousa, Ronald W.. The rediscoverers : major writers in the Portuguese literature of national regeneration / Ronald W. Sousa. — University Park ; London : Pennsylvania State University Press, c1981. — 192p : ports ; 24cm
Bibliography: p183-189. — Includes index
ISBN 0-271-00300-6 : Unpriced B82-02048

869.1 — PORTUGUESE POETRY

869.1 — Poetry in Portuguese. Mozambican writers, *1945- — Anthologies — English texts*

Sunflower of hope : poems from the Mozambican revolution / compiled by Chris Searle. — London : Allison & Busby, 1982. — xii,148p ; 23cm
Translated from the Portugese
ISBN 0-85031-412-7 : £7.95 : CIP rev.
ISBN 0-85031-419-4
ISBN 0-85031-420-8 (pbk) : Unpriced B81-30574

869′.1 — Poetry in Portuguese. Pessoa, Fernando — *Biographies*

Green, J. C. R.. Fernando Pessoa. — Isle of Skye : Aquila, Dec.1982. — [48]p. — (Prospice, ISSN 0308-2776 ; v.12)
ISBN 0-7275-0241-7 (pbk) : £1.50 : CIP entry B82-30308

869.1′044′09 — Ballads in Portuguese. Brazilian writers, *1921- — Critical studies*

Slater, Candace. Stories on a string : the Brazilian literature de cordel / Candace Slater. — Berkeley ; London : University of California Press, 1982. — xvii,313p,[23]p of plates : ill,1map,ports ; 24cm
Bibliography: p275-300. — Includes index
ISBN 0-520-04154-2 : £22.50 B82-31091

869.2 — PORTUGUESE DRAMA

869.2′2 — Drama in Portuguese. Vicente, Gil. Casandra & Don Duardos — *Critical studies*

Hart, Thomas R.. Gil Vicente, Casandra and Don Duardos / Thomas R. Hart. — London : Grant & Cutler in association with Tamesis, 1981. — 88p ; 20cm. — (Critical guides to Spanish texts)
ISBN 0-7293-0109-5 (pbk) : £2.00 B82-33981

869.3 — PORTUGUESE FICTION

869.3 — Fiction in Portuguese. Brazilian writers. Veríssimo, Érico — *Critical studies*

Richards, B. A. (Basil Anthony). The Brazilian novels of Érico Veríssimo : assessed in the context of modernism and Latin American fiction / B.A. Richards. — Pinner (35 St. Lawrence Drive, Pinner, Middx HA5 2RW) : ITP, 1981. — 68p : ill ; 30cm
Bibliography: p66-68
Unpriced (pbk) B82-08000

869.3[F] — Fiction in Portuguese. Brazilian writers, *1921- — English texts*

Olinto, Antonio. The water house / Antonio Olinto ; translated by Dorothy Heapy. — Walton-on-Thames : Nelson, 1982. — 410p ; 19cm. — (Panafrica library)
Translation of: A casa de agua. — Originally published: London : Collings, 1970
ISBN 0-17-511622-9 (pbk) : £2.75 : CIP rev. B81-34391

Souza, Márcio. The Emperor of the Amazon / Márcio Souza ; translated by Thomas Colchie. — London : Abacus, 1982, c1980. — 189p ; 20cm
Translation of: Galvez, imperador do acre. — Originally published: New York : Avon Books, 1980
ISBN 0-349-13332-8 (pbk) : £2.50 B82-18276

869.3[F] — Short stories in Portuguese. Angolan writers, *1945- — Texts*

Vieira, José Luandino. Luuanda / Jose Luandino Vieira ; translated by Tamara L. Bender with Donna S. Hill. — Ibadan ; London : Heinemann, 1980. — x,118p ; 19cm. — (African writers series ; 222)
Translated from the Portuguese
ISBN 0-435-90222-9 (pbk) : £1.50 : CIP rev. B80-01889

869.3[F] — Short stories in Portuguese. Brazalian writers, *1830-1921 — English texts*

Machado de Assis, Joaquim Maria. The Devil′s church and other stories / by Machado de Assis ; translated by Jack Schmitt and Lorie Ishimatsu. — Austin ; London : University of Texas Press, c1977. — xiii,152p : ill ; 23cm. — (The Texas pan American series)
ISBN 0-292-77535-0 : £8.25 B82-34900

871 — LATIN POETRY

871′.01 — Poetry in Latin. Horace — *Critical studies*

Bailey, D. R. Shackleton. Profile of Horace / D.R. Shackleton Bailey. — London : Duckworth, 1982. — x,142p ; 23cm. — ([Classical life and letters])
Includes Latin text and appendix of passages in Latin. — Includes index
ISBN 0-7156-1591-2 : £18.00 : CIP rev. B82-09626

871′.01 — Poetry in Latin. Juvenal — *Critical studies*

Jenkyns, Richard. Three classical poets : Sappho, Catullus and Juvenal / Richard Jenkyns. — London : Duckworth, 1982. — ix,243p ; 24cm
Bibliography: p231-234. — Includes index
ISBN 0-7156-1636-6 : £24.00 : CIP rev.
Also classified at 874′.01 ; 884′.01 B82-07826

871′.01 — Poetry in Latin. Ovid. Texts with French imprints, *to 1600 — Critical studies*

Moss, Ann. Ovid in Renaissance France : a survey of the Latin editions of Ovid and commentaries printed in France before 1600 / by Ann Moss. — London : Warburg Institute, University of London, 1982. — 89p ; 25cm. — (Warburg Institute surveys, ISSN 0083-7202 ; 8)
Includes index
ISBN 0-85481-059-5 (pbk) : Unpriced B82-38931

871′.01 — Poetry in Latin. Statius, Pablius Papinius. Silvae — *Critical studies*

Hardie, Alex. Statius and the Silvae. — Liverpool (The University, P.O. Box 147, Liverpool L69 3BX) : Francis Cairns, Jan.1983. — [250]p. — (ARCA classical and medieval texts. Papers and monographs, ISSN 0309-5541 ; v.9)
ISBN 0-905205-13-8 : £15.00 : CIP entry B82-35235

871′.01 — Poetry in Latin, *to ca 500* **—** *English texts*

Catullus, Gaius Valerius. Gaius Valerius Catullus : an introduction together with a foreword by Robert Philip of Fettes College, Edinburgh and twenty-eight poems in English verse / J.A.B. Harrisson. — [Southwold] ([4 The Rest, Covert Rd., Reydon, Southwold, Suffolk IP18 6RB]) : J.A.B. Harrisson, c1980. — 22p ; 21cm
Translated from the Latin
Unpriced (pbk) B82-20975

Horace. Rhymes after Horace : six verse translations / William Johnson Cory. — Edinburgh : Tragara Press, 1982. — [19]p ; 25cm
Limited ed. of 115 numbered copies
ISBN 0-902616-75-7 (pbk) : £8.00 B82-17405

Juvenal. Sixteen satires upon the ancient harlot. — Manchester : Carcanet Press, June 1982. — [320]p
ISBN 0-85635-324-8 : £5.95 : CIP entry B82-12923

Persius Flaccus, Aulus. [Satires. English]. The satires of Persius / translated by W.S. Merwin ; introduction & notes by William S. Anderson. — London : Anvil Press Poetry in association with Wildwood House, 1981. — 109p ; 22cm. — (Poetica ; 3)
Translated from the Latin
ISBN 0-85646-019-2 (pbk) : £3.95 B82-33186

Virgil. The georgics / Virgil ; translated with an introduction by Robert Wells. — Manchester : Carcanet, 1982. — 95p ; 23cm
Translated from the Latin
ISBN 0-85635-422-8 : Unpriced : CIP rev. B82-13272

871′.01 — Poetry in Latin, *to ca 500* **—** *Latin-English parallel texts*

Catullus, Gaius Valerius. Catullus. — London : Duckworth, Apr.1982. — [272]p
ISBN 0-7156-1435-5 : £18.00 : CIP entry B82-04875

Catullus, Gaius Valerius. The poems of Catullus / translated by James Michie ; introduction by Gavin Ewart. — [London] : Folio Society, c1981. — 224p ; 23cm
Parallel Latin text and English translation, English introduction and notes. — Originally published: London : Hart-Davis, 1969. — In slip case
£8.50 B82-05997

Claudian. Claudian's panegyric on the fourth consulate of Honorius / introduction, text, translation and commentary by William Barr. — Liverpool : Cairns, 1981. — 96p ; 22cm. — (Liverpool Latin texts (classical and medieval) ; 2)
Latin text, English introduction, translation and commentary. — Bibliography: p95-96
ISBN 0-905205-11-1 (pbk) : £4.00 B82-19778

Johnson, Samuel, *1709-1784*. Johnson's Juvenal / edited with introduction, notes, Latin texts and translations by Niall Rudd. — Bristol : Bristol Classical Press, 1981. — xvi,106p ; 21cm
English text with some chapters in Latin with English translations. — Bibliography: pxv-xvi. — Contents: London — The vanity of human wishes
ISBN 0-906515-64-5 (pbk) : Unpriced
Primary classification 821′.6 B82-05338

Tibullus, Albius. [Elegiae. English]. Tibullus : elegies / introduction, text, translation and notes by Guy Lee. — 2nd ed. — Liverpool : Francis Cairns, 1982. — 157p ; 22cm. — (Liverpool Latin texts (classical and medieval) ; 3)
Parallel Latin text and English translation with English introduction, and notes. — Previous ed.: Cambridge : Guy Lee, 1975. — Bibliography: p155-157
ISBN 0-905205-09-x (pbk) : £5.00 B82-19957

871′.01 — Poetry in Latin, *to ca 500* **—** *Texts*

Virgil. The Eclogues ; & Georgics / Virgil ; edited with introduction and notes by R.D. Williams. — New York : St. Martins Press ; London : Macmillan Education, 1979. — xvii,222p ; 22cm. — (Classical series)
Latin text, English introduction and notes. — Bibliography: pxvi-xvii. — Includes index
ISBN 0-333-25881-9 (pbk) : £7.95 : CIP rev. B79-23527

871′.01 — Poetry in Latin, *to ca 500* **—** *Texts with commentaries*

Juvenal. Satires I, III, X / Juvenal ; text, with introduction and notes by Niall Rudd and Edward Courtney. — Bristol : Bristol Classical Press, c1977 ([1980 printing]). — 86p ; 21cm
Latin text, English introduction and notes. — Bibliography: p9
ISBN 0-906515-03-3 (pbk) : Unpriced B82-05090

Ovid. Metamorphoses III / Ovid ; with introduction, notes and vocabulary by A.A.R. Henderson. — Bristol : Bristol Classical Press, 1979 (1981 printing). — 137p : ill ; 21cm
Latin text, English introduction and notes. — Bibliography: p16
ISBN 0-906515-02-5 (pbk) : Unpriced B82-05091

871′.01 — Poetry in Latin. Virgil — *Critical studies*

Pattie, T. S.. Virgil : his poetry through the ages. — London : British Library Reference Division, Sept.1982. — [120]p
ISBN 0-7123-0006-6 (cased) : £7.50 : CIP entry
ISBN 0-7123-0005-8 (pbk) : £4.00 B82-19802

871′.01 — Poetry in Latin. Virgil. Eclogues — *Critical studies*

Segal, Charles. Poetry and myth in ancient pastoral : essays on Theocritus and Virgil / by Charles Segal. — Princeton ; Guildford : Princeton University Press, c1981. — xii,348p ; 25cm. — (Princeton series of collected essays)
Bibliography: pxi-xii. — Includes index
ISBN 0-691-06475-x (cased) : £17.40
ISBN 0-691-01383-7 (pbk) : £6.30
Primary classification 881′.01 B82-06970

871′.01′09 — Poetry in Latin, *to ca 500* **—** *Critical studies*

Putnam, Michael C. J.. Essays on Latin lyric, elegy, and epic / Michael C.J. Putnam. — Princeton ; Guildford : Princeton University Press, c1982. — xiii,354p ; 25cm. — (Princeton series of collected essays)
Includes index
ISBN 0-691-06497-0 (cased) : £21.20
ISBN 0-691-01388-8 (pbk) : £5.60 B82-25334

871′.01′09354 — Poetry in Latin, *to 1200.* **Special themes: Courtly love —** *Critical studies — Latin-English parallel texts*

Andreas, *Capellanus*. [De amore. English & Latin]. Andreas Capellanus on love. — London : Duckworth, July 1982. — [384]p. — (Duckworth classical, medieval and renaissance editions)
ISBN 0-7156-1436-3 : £24.00 : CIP entry B82-13073

871′.01′09354 — Poetry in Latin, *to ca 500.* **Special subjects: Love —** *Critical studies*

Lyne, R. O. A. M.. Latin love poets : from Catullus to Horace / by R.O.A.M. Lyne. — Oxford : Clarendon, 1980. — xiv,316p ; 21cm
Bibliography: pxii-xiv. — Includes index
ISBN 0-19-814453-9 (cased) : £13.50 : CIP rev.
ISBN 0-19-814454-7 (pbk) : Unpriced B80-23820

871′.03 — Poetry in Latin, *ca 750-1350* **—** *English texts*

Alcuin. The bishops, kings and saints of York. — Oxford : Oxford University Press, Jan.1983. — [250]p
Translated from the Latin
ISBN 0-19-822262-9 : £28.00 : CIP entry B82-33475

871′.04 — Poetry in Latin. Scottish writers. Buchanan, George, *1506-1582 — Critical studies*

Ford, Philip J.. George Buchanan. — Aberdeen : Aberdeen University Press, Apr.1982. — [224]p
Includes an edition and translation of the Miscellaneorum liber
ISBN 0-08-028458-2 : £16.00 : CIP entry B82-03738

872 — LATIN DRAMATIC POETRY AND DRAMA

872′.01 — Drama in Latin, *to ca 500* **—** *English texts*

Plautus, Titus Maccius. Rudens ; Curculio ; Casina. — Cambridge : Cambridge University Press, Nov.1981. — [157]p. — (Translations from Greek and Roman authors)
ISBN 0-521-28046-x (pbk) : £2.50 : CIP entry B81-38813

Seneca, Lucius Annaeus, *ca. 4 B.C.-65*. Thyestes : a tragedy / Lucius Annaeus Seneca ; translated by Jane Elder. — Ashington : Mid Northumberland Arts Group, 1982. — 58p ; 21cm
Translation of: Thyestes
ISBN 0-904790-19-3 (pbk) : £2.95
ISBN 0-85635-434-1 (Carcanet New) B82-30009

Seneca, Lucius Annaeus, *ca 4 B.C.-65*. [Thyestes. English]. Thyestes / Lucius Annaeus Seneca ; translated by Jasper Heywood ; edited by Joost Daalder. — London : E. Benn, 1982. — lvi,88p : facsims ; 20cm. — (The New mermaids) (A Benn study drama)
Translation of: Thyestes. — Bibliography: plv
ISBN 0-510-39010-2 (pbk) : £3.50 : CIP rev.
ISBN 0-393-95237-1 (U.S.) B82-11764

872′.04 — Drama in Latin. English writers, *1350-* **—** *Latin-English parallel texts*

Legge, Thomas. Thomas Legge's Richardus Tertius / a critical edition with a translation [by] Robert J. Lordi. — New York ; London : Garland, 1979. — xlvi,539p : ill,music ; 24cm. — (Renaissance drama)
Latin text, English translation and introduction
ISBN 0-8240-9741-6 : Unpriced B82-15186

873 — LATIN EPIC POETRY AND FICTION

873′.01 — Epic poetry in Latin, *to ca 500* **—** *English texts*

Virgil. [Aeneid. English]. The Aeneid of Virgil : a verse translation / by Allen Mandelbaum. — [New ed.] / with thirteen drawings by Barry Moser. — Berkeley ; London : University of California Press, c1981. — xvi,413p : ill ; 26cm
Translation of: Aeneid. — Previous ed.: 1971. — Bibliography: p409-413
ISBN 0-520-04439-8 : £19.25 B82-13761

873′.01 — Epic poetry in Latin, *to ca 500* **—** *Latin-English parallel texts*

Lucan. [Pharsalia. English & Latin]. Civil War VIII / Lucan ; edited with a commentary by R. Mayer. — Warminster : Aris & Phillips, c1981. — x,197p ; 22cm
Parallel Latin text and English translation. — Includes index
ISBN 0-85668-155-5 (cased) : Unpriced
ISBN 0-85668-176-8 (pbk) : Unpriced B82-31268

873′.01 — Epic poetry in Latin, *to ca 500* **—** *Texts*

Virgil. [Aeneid. Book 4]. Aeneidos, liber quartus / P. Vergili Maronis ; edited with a commentary by R.G. Austin. — Oxford : Clarendon Press, 1955 (1982 [printing]). — xix,212p ; 19cm
Latin text, English introduction and commentary. — Includes index
ISBN 0-19-872111-0 (pbk) : £5.25 : CIP rev. B82-02442

Virgil[Aeneid. Book 6. *English & Latin. Selections*]. Virgil : selections from Aeneid VI. — Cambridge : Cambridge University Press, Feb.1983. — [62]p. — (Cambridge Latin texts)
ISBN 0-521-28694-8 (pbk) : £1.50 : CIP entry B82-40902

873′.01 — Epic poetry in Latin. Virgil. Aeneid — *Critical studies*

Pollard, John. Virgil and the Sibyl / by John Pollard. — Exeter : University of Exeter, 1982. — 17p ; 22cm. — (Jackson Knight memorial lecture ; 14th)
ISBN 0-85989-148-8 (pbk) : Unpriced B82-31553

873′.04 — Fiction in Latin, *1350- — English texts — Texts with commentaries*

Hall, Joseph. Another world and yet the same : Bishop Joseph Hall's Mundus alter et idem / translated and edited by John Millar Wands. — New Haven ; London : Yale University Press, c1981. — lviii,230p : ill,maps,facsims ; 24cm
Translation of: Mundus alter et idem. — Bibliography: p201-215. — Includes index
ISBN 0-300-02613-7 : Unpriced B82-09967

874 — LATIN LYRIC POETRY

874′.008 — Lyric poetry in Latin, *B.C.70-A.D.1674 — Anthologies — Latin-English parallel texts*

Songs of the wandering scholars / [compiled and translated by] Helen Waddell ; edited and with a preface by Felicitas Corrigan ; wood-engraving by Joan Freeman. — London : Folio Society, 1982. — 371p : ill,music ; 26cm
Parallel Latin text and English translations. — In slip case. — Includes index
Unpriced B82-25471

874′.008 — Lyric poetry in Latin, *to 1350 — Anthologies — English texts*

The **Dancing** girl : an anthology of late Roman poetry and prose / [compiled by S.D.P. Clough]. — Enl. — [Malvern Wells] ([16 Eaton Rd., Malvern Wells, Worcs.]) : S.D.P. Clough, c1982. — 96p ; 21cm
Previous ed.: 1975
£1.50 (pbk) B82-26814

874′.01 — Lyric poetry in Latin. Catullus, Gaius Valerius — *Critical studies*

Bardon, Henry. L'art de la composition chez Catulle / Henry Bardon. Meter and diction in Catullus' hendecasyllabics / Thomas Cutt. — New York ; London : Garland, 1979. — 76,iii,67p : ill ; 23cm. — (The Garland library of Latin poetry)
Text in English and French. — L'art de la composition chex Catulle originally published: Paris : société D'Édition, 1973. — Bibliography: p75-76
ISBN 0-8240-2961-5 : Unpriced B82-10716

Jenkyns, Richard. Three classical poets : Sappho, Catullus and Juvenal / Richard Jenkyns. — London : Duckworth, 1982. — ix,243p ; 24cm
Bibliography: p231-234. — Includes index
ISBN 0-7156-1636-6 : £24.00 : CIP rev.
Primary classification 871′.01 B82-07826

874′.01 — Lyric poetry in Latin. Propertius, Sextus — *Critical studies — Italian texts*

Alfonsi, Luigi. L'elegia di Properzio / Luigi Alfonsi. — New York ; London : Garland, 1979. — vii,89p ; 23cm. — (The Garland library of Latin poetry)
Facsim of: ed. published Milan : Società editrice 'Vita e pensiero', 1945
ISBN 0-8240-2960-7 : Unpriced B82-08745

874′.01′08 — Elegiac love poetry in Latin, *to ca 500 — Anthologies*

Latin love elegy / selected and edited with introduction and notes by Robert Maltby. — Bristol : Bristol Classical Press, 1980. — v,143p ; 21cm
Latin texts with English introduction and notes. — Bibliography: p17-22
ISBN 0-906515-01-7 (pbk) : Unpriced B82-05334

874′.03′08 — Pastoral poetry in Latin, *ca 750-1350 — Anthologies*

Seven versions of Carolingian pastoral / edited and annotated by R.P.H. Green. — Reading : Department of Classics, University of Reading, c1980. — 149p ; 21cm. — (Medieval and renaissance Latin texts)
Latin text, English introduction, notes and commentary
ISBN 0-7049-0527-2 (pbk) : Unpriced B82-14137

876 — LATIN LETTERS

876′.01 — Letters in Latin. Jerome, *Saint — Critical studies*

A **Leaf** from the letters of St. Jerome : first printed by Sixtus Reissinger, Rome c1466-1467 / with an historical essay by Jeremy Duquesnay Adams and a bibliographical essay by John L. Sharpe III ; edited by Bennett Gilbert. — Los Angeles : Zeitlin & Ver Brugge ; London ([27 Cecil Court, Charing Cross Rd, WC2N 4EZ]) : Fletcher, 1981. — 30p ; 40cm
Limited ed. of 300 numbered copies. — One sheet from Epistolae Hieronymi in pocket
Unpriced B82-21489

876′.01 — Letters in Latin, *to ca 500 — Texts*

Cicero, Marcus Tullius. M. Tulli Ciceronis epistulae. — 2nd ed. — Oxford : Clarendon, July 1982. — (Oxford classical texts)
Previous ed.: 1901
Vol.1: Epistulae ad familiares. — [544]p
ISBN 0-19-814660-4 : £7.95 : CIP entry B82-19247

876′.01 — Letters in Latin, *to ca 500 — Texts — For schools*

Pliny. [Epistolae. Selections]. Pliny on himself. — London : Bell & Hyman, June 1982. — [108]p. — (Alpha classics)
Originally published: 1965
ISBN 0-7135-0046-8 (pbk) : £2.40 : CIP entry B82-22772

877 — LATIN SATIRE AND HUMOUR

877′.01′09 — Satire in Latin, *to ca 500 — Critical studies*

Anderson, William S.. Essays on Roman satire / William S. Anderson. — Princeton ; Guildford : Princeton University Press, c1982. — xviii,494p ; 25cm. — (Princeton series of collected essays)
Includes index
ISBN 0-691-05347-2 (cased) : £19.40
ISBN 0-691-00791-8 (pbk) : £6.30 B82-28350

878 — LATIN MISCELLANY

878′.0108 — Prose in Latin, *to ca 500 — Texts with commentaries*

Seneca, Lucius Annaeus, *ca 4 B.C. - 65*. Selected prose / the younger Seneca ; text, with introduction and notes by H. MacL. Currie. — 2nd ed. — Bristol : Bristol Classical Press, 1980. — vi,120p ; 21cm
Latin text, English introduction and notes. — Bibliography: p11-12
ISBN 0-906515-05-x (pbk) : Unpriced B82-05093

878′.0108′08 — Declamatory prose in Latin, *to ca 500 — Anthologies*

Roman declamation / extracts edited with commentary by Michael Winterbottom. — Bristol : Bristol Classical Press, 1980. — x,110p ; 21cm
Latin text, English introduction and notes. — Bibliography: pviii-x.— Includes index
ISBN 0-906515-10-6 (pbk) : Unpriced B82-05094

880 — CLASSICAL AND MODERN GREEK LITERATURES

880.09 — Classical literatures. Classical criticism

Russell, D. A.. Criticism in antiquity / D.A. Russell. — London : Duckworth, 1981. — 219p : 1ill ; 23cm. — (Classical life and letters)
Bibliography: p209-216. — Includes index
ISBN 0-7156-1516-5 : £18.00 B82-00563

880′.09 — Classical literatures, *to ca 500 — Critical studies*

The **Cambridge** history of classical literature. — Cambridge : Cambridge University Press
2: Latin literature / edited by E.J. Kenney, W.V. Clausen. — 1982. — xviii,973p,[4]p of plates : ill,2facsims ; 24cm
Bibliography: p940-958. — Includes index
ISBN 0-521-21043-7 : £40.00 B82-21450

880.9 — CLASSICAL GREEK LITERATURE. HISTORY AND CRITICAL STUDIES

880.9′001 — Greek literature, *to ca 500 — Critical studies*

Later Greek literature / edited by John J. Winkler and Gordon Williams. — Cambridge : Cambridge University Press, 1982. — ix,344p ; 24cm. — (Yale classical studies ; v.27)
ISBN 0-521-23947-8 : £27.50 : CIP rev. B82-12007

880.9′001 — Greek literature, *to ca 500.* **Origins: Oral traditions**

Havelock, Eric A.. The literate revolution in Greece and its cultural consequences / Eric A. Havelock. — Princeton ; Guildford : Princeton University Press, c1982. — viii,362p ; 23cm. — (Princeton series of collected essays)
Includes index
ISBN 0-691-09396-2 : £17.70
ISBN 0-691-00026-3 (pbk) : Unpriced B82-31196

880.9′352042 — Greek literature, *to ca 500.* **Special subjects: Women —** *Critical studies*

Lefkowitz, Mary R.. Heroines and hysterics / Mary R. Lefkowitz. — London : Duckworth, 1981. — ix,96p ; 23cm
Includes index
ISBN 0-7156-1518-1 : £8.95
Primary classification 305.4′2′0938 B82-08759

881 — CLASSICAL GREEK POETRY

881′.008 — Poetry in classical languages. Translations into English language, *ca 1370-1981 — Anthologies*

Daphne into laurel : translations of classical poetry from Chaucer to the present. — London : Duckworth, June 1982. — [338]p
ISBN 0-7156-1646-3 : £24.00 : CIP entry B82-10874

881′.009 — Poetry in Greek, *to 1600 — Critical studies*

Trypanis, C. A.. Greek poetry : from Homer to Seferis / C.A. Trypanis. — London : Faber and Faber, 1981. — 896p ; 25cm
Bibliography: p789-885. — Includes index
ISBN 0-571-08346-3 : £25.00 : CIP rev.
Also classified at 889′.1′009 B81-12821

881′.01 — Poetry in Greek. Theocritus. Idylls — *Critical studies*

Segal, Charles. Poetry and myth in ancient pastoral : essays on Theocritus and Virgil / by Charles Segal. — Princeton ; Guildford : Princeton University Press, c1981. — xii,348p ; 25cm. — (Princeton series of collected essays)
Bibliography: pxi-xii. — Includes index
ISBN 0-691-06475-x (cased) : £17.40
ISBN 0-691-01383-7 (pbk) : £6.30
Also classified at 871′.01 B82-06970

881′.01 — Poetry in Greek, *to ca 500 — English texts*

Colotes. The fragments of Colotes / versions by Gordon Jackson. — Lincoln (1 Stonefield Ave., Lincoln) : Asgill, 1981. — 31p : 1ill ; 21cm
Translated from the Greek. — Limited ed. of 400 numbered copies
£0.75 (pbk) B82-09650

Meleager. Heliodora and some others : some amatory epigrams / Meleager ; English versions by Frederic Vanson. — Stevenage : Ore, 1979. — 8p ; 21cm. — (The Chariot poets ; no.8)
Translations from the classical Greek
ISBN 0-904838-04-8 (unbound) : £0.25 B82-34964

881′.01′08 — Epigrammatic poetry in Greek, *to ca 500 — Anthologies*

Further Greek epigrams : epigrams before A.D. 50 from the Greek anthology and other sources not included in Hellenistic epigrams or the Garland of Philip / edited by D.L. Page ; revised and prepared for publication by R.D. Dawe and J. Diggle. — Cambridge : Cambridge University Press, 1981. — xiv,598p ; 24cm
Includes index
ISBN 0-521-22903-0 : £82.50 : CIP rev. B81-40269

881′.01′09 — Poetry in Greek, *to ca 700.* **Metre —** *Critical studies*

West, M. L.. Greek metre. — Oxford : Clarendon Press, Jan.1983. — [224]p
ISBN 0-19-814018-5 : £15.00 : CIP entry
B82-33489

882 — CLASSICAL GREEK DRAMATIC POETRY AND DRAMA

882′.01 — Drama in Greek. Aeschylus — *Critical studies*

Rosenmeyer, Thomas G.. The art of Aeschylus / Thomas G. Rosenmeyer. — Berkeley ; London : University of California Press, c1982. — 393p : 1facsim ; 25cm
Bibliography: p377-384. — Includes index
ISBN 0-520-04440-1 : £26.25 B82-40219

882′.01 — Drama in Greek. Sophocles. Stagecraft

Seale, David. Vision and stagecraft in Sophocles. — London : Croom Helm, June 1982. — [320]p
ISBN 0-7099-2328-7 : £15.95 : CIP entry
B82-09593

882′.01 — Drama in Greek, *to ca 500 — English texts*

Aeschylus. The Oresteia / Aeschylus ; translated by Tony Harrison. — London : Collings, 1981. — 120p ; 22cm
Translated from the Greek
ISBN 0-86036-178-0 (pbk) : £3.50 B82-08946

Euripides. The children of Herakles / Euripides ; translated by Henry Taylor and Robert A. Brooks. — New York ; Oxford : Oxford University Press, 1981. — xi,85p ; 24cm. — (The Greek tragedy in new translations)
Translation from the classical Greek
ISBN 0-19-502914-3 : £9.95 B82-08994

Euripides. The Phoenician women / Euripides ; translated by Peter Burian and Brian Swann. — New York ; Oxford : Oxford University Press, 1981. — ix,100p ; 25cm. — (The Greek tragedy in new translations)
Translation from the classical Greek
ISBN 0-19-502923-2 : £9.95 B82-08995

Euripides. The Trojan women ; Helen ; The Bacchae / Euripides ; translated by Neil Curry. — Cambridge : Cambridge University Press, 1981. — 166p : 1plan ; 22cm. — (Translations from Greek and Roman authors)
ISBN 0-521-28047-8 (pbk) : Unpriced : CIP rev. B81-30312

882′.01 — Drama in Greek, *to ca 500 — Esperanto texts*

Aeschylus. [Prometheus vinctus. Esperanto]. Prometeo ligita / Esĥilo (Aeschylus) ; elhelenigis Albert Goodheir. — Glasgow : Eldonejo Kardo, 1982. — 54p ; 22cm
Translation of: Prometheus vinctus
ISBN 0-905149-16-5 (pbk) : £2.60 B82-13584

882′.01 — Drama in Greek, *to ca 500 — Greek-English parallel texts*

Aristophanes. [Clouds. English & Greek (Classical Greek)]. Clouds / [Aristophanes] ; edited with translation and notes by Alan H. Sommerstein. — Warminster : Aris & Phillips, c1982. — x,232p ; 22cm. — (The Comedies of Aristophanes ; v.3)
Parallel Classical Greek text and English translation
ISBN 0-85668-209-8 (cased) : Unpriced: CIP rev.
ISBN 0-85668-210-1 (pbk) : Unpriced
B82-10222

Aristophanes. [Knights. English & Greek (Classical Greek)]. Knights / [Aristophanes] ; edited with translation and notes by Alan H. Sommerstein. — Warminster : Aris & Phillips, c1981. — ix,220p ; 22cm. — (The Comedies of Aristophanes ; v.2)
Parallel Classical Greek text and English translation
ISBN 0-85668-177-6 (cased) : Unpriced : CIP rev.
ISBN 0-85668-178-4 (pbk) : Unpriced
B81-30405

Ezekiel. The Exagoge of Ezekiel. — Cambridge : Cambridge University Press, Jan.1983. — [268]p
ISBN 0-521-24580-x : £25.00 : CIP entry
B82-40894

882′.01 — Drama in Greek, *to ca 500 — Texts*

Euripides. Euripidis fabulae / editit J. Diggle. — Oxonii : E typographeo Clarendoniano, 1981. — (Scriptorum classicorum bibliotheca Oxoniensis)
Tomus II. — xiii,373p ; 19cm
Greek text, Latin preface
ISBN 0-19-814590-x : £6.25 B82-13899

Euripides. Heracles / Euripides ; with introduction and commentary by Godfrey W. Bond. — Oxford : Clarendon Press, 1981. — xxxv,429p ; 20cm
Greek text, English introduction and commentary. — Includes index
ISBN 0-19-814012-6 : £25.00 : CIP rev.
B80-23821

882′.01 — Drama in Greek, *to ca 500 — Texts with commentaries*

Sophocles. Trachiniae. — Cambridge : Cambridge University Press, Nov.1982. — [272]p. — (Cambridge Greek and Latin classics)
ISBN 0-521-20087-3 (cased) : £19.50 : CIP entry
ISBN 0-521-28776-6 (pbk) : £7.50 B82-29396

882′.01′09 — Drama in Greek. Tragedies, *to ca 500 — Critical studies*

Bain, David, *19---*. Masters, servants and orders in Greek tragedy : a study of some aspects of dramatic technique and convention / David Bain. — Manchester : Manchester University Press, c1981. — 72p ; 23cm
Bibliography: p68-70. — Includes index
ISBN 0-7190-1296-1 : £12.50 : CIP rev.
B81-31244

Oxford readings in Greek tragedy. — Oxford : Oxford University Press, Feb.1983. — [528]p
ISBN 0-19-872110-2 (pbk) : £7.50 : CIP entry
B82-39271

883 — CLASSICAL GREEK EPIC POETRY AND FICTION

883′.01 — Epic poetry in Greek. Homer. Hymns. Linguistic aspects

Janko, Richard. Homer, Heriod and the Hymns. — Cambridge : Cambridge University Press, Aug.1982. — [340]p. — (Cambridge classical studies)
ISBN 0-521-23869-2 : £25.00 : CIP entry
B82-29352

883′.01 — Epic poetry in Greek, *to ca 500 — English texts*

Homer. The Odyssey / Homer ; translated by Walter Shewring with an epilogue on translation ; introduced by G.S. Kirk. — Oxford : Oxford University Press, 1980. — xx,349p : 2maps ; 19cm
Translated from the Greek. — Includes index
ISBN 0-19-251019-3 (cased) : Unpriced : CIP rev.
ISBN 0-19-281542-3 (pbk) : £1.50 B80-13620

883′.01 — Epic poetry in Greek, *to ca 500 — Texts*

Hesiod. Essential Hesiod : Theogony 1-232, 453-733 Works and Days 1-307 / with introduction and notes by C.J. Rowe. — [Bristol] : Bristol Classical Press, [c1978]. — 141p ; 21cm
Greek text, English introduction and notes. — Bibliography: p11-14
ISBN 0-906515-15-7 (pbk) : Unpriced
B82-05098

Homer. [Iliad. Bk.24]. Iliad, book XXIV / Homer ; edited by C.W. Macleod. — Cambridge : Cambridge University Press, 1982. — ix,161p ; 20cm. — (Cambridge Greek and Latin classics)
Text in English and Greek. — Bibliography: p58-60. — Includes index
ISBN 0-521-24353-x (cased) : £15.00 : CIP rev.
ISBN 0-521-28620-4 (pbk) : £5.95 B82-03364

Homer. Iliad III / Homer ; with introduction, notes & vocabulary by J.T. Hooker. — Bristol : Bristol Classical Press, [1980?]. — v,89p : ill ; 21cm
Greek text, English introduction and notes. — Bibliography: p4-5
ISBN 0-906515-14-9 (pbk) : Unpriced
B82-05099

Homer. Odyssey IX / Homer ; with introduction and running vocabulary by J.V. Muir. — Bristol : Bristol Classical Press, c1980. — xiv,67p : ill ; 21cm
Greek text, English introduction and notes. — Bibliography: pxiii-xiv
ISBN 0-906515-61-0 (pbk) : Unpriced
B82-05097

884 — CLASSICAL GREEK LYRIC POETRY

884′.01 — Lyric poetry in Greek. Pindar — *Critical studies*

Crotty, Kevin. Song and action : the victory odes of Pindar / Kevin Crotty. — Baltimore ; London : Johns Hopkins University Press, c1982. — xii,173p ; 24cm
Includes short classical Greek passages, with English translations. — Bibliography: p161-167. — Includes index
ISBN 0-8018-2746-9 : £11.25 B82-34986

884′.01 — Lyric poetry in Greek. Pindar. Special subjects: Ancient Greek legends & Ancient Greek myths — *Critical studies*

Huxley, George. Pindar′s vision of the past / George Huxley. — Belfast : [the Queen′s University of Belfast], 1975 (1982 [printing]). — 48p : geneal.tables ; 21cm
Bibliography: p44-48. — Includes index
£1.00 (pbk) B82-30502

884′.01 — Lyric poetry in Greek. Sappho — *Critical studies*

Jenkyns, Richard. Three classical poets : Sappho, Catullus and Juvenal / Richard Jenkyns. — London : Duckworth, 1982. — ix,243p ; 24cm
Bibliography: p231-234. — Includes index
ISBN 0-7156-1636-6 : £24.00 : CIP rev.
Primary classification 871′.01 B82-07826

884′.01′08 — Lyric poetry in Greek, *to ca 500 — Anthologies*

Delectus ex iambis et elegis Graecis / edidit M.L. West. — Oxonii : Typograppeo Clarendoniano, 1980. — ix,295p ; 20cm. — (Scriptorum classicorum bibliotheca Oxoniensis)
Classical Greek text, Latin notes and headings. — Includes index
ISBN 0-19-814589-6 : £7.95 : CIP rev.
B78-13923

884′.01′08 — Lyric poetry in Greek, *to ca 500 — Anthologies — English texts*

Campbell, D. A.. The golden lyre. — London : Duckworth, Sept.1981. — [300]p
ISBN 0-7156-1563-7 : £24.00 : CIP entry
B81-22576

884′.01′08 — Lyric poetry in Greek, *to ca 500 — Anthologies — Greek-English parallel texts*

Greek lyric. — Cambridge, Mass. : Harvard University Press ; London : Heinemann, 1982. — (The Loeb classical library)
1 / Sappho [and] Alcaeus ; with an English translation by David A. Campbell. — xix,492,8p ; 17cm
Classical Greek text, English translation, introduction and notes, short Latin passages. — Bibliography: pxviii-xix. — Includes index
ISBN 0-434-99142-2 : £5.00 B82-24434

888 — CLASSICAL GREEK MISCELLANY

888′.0108 — Prose in Greek, *to ca 500 — English texts*

Aesop. [Fables. English. Selections]. Aesop′s fables / illustrated by Heidi Holder. — London : Macmillan Children′s Books, 1981. — 25p : col.ill ; 28cm
Originally published: New York : Viking, 1981
ISBN 0-333-32202-9 : £4.95 : CIP rev.
B81-23948

888′.0108 — Prose in Greek, *to ca 500* — *English texts* *continuation*

Crampton, Patricia. Aesop's fables / illustrated by Bernadette ; retold by Patricia Crampton. — London : Dent, 1980. — [42]p : ill(some col.) ; 33cm
Translation of: Zwanzig fabeln des Aesop
ISBN 0-460-06058-9 : £4.50 : CIP rev.
B80-10896

Plato. [Parmenides. English]. Plato's Parmenides. — Oxford : Blackwell, Aug.1982. — [384]p
ISBN 0-631-13121-3 : £21.00 : CIP entry
B82-15900

888′.0108 — Prose in Greek, *to ca 500* — *Texts with commentaries*

Plato. The Atlantis story : Timaeus 17-27, Critias / Plato ; with introduction, notes and vocabulary by Christopher Gill. — Bristol : Bristol Classical Press, 1980. — xxvii,95p : maps,1plan ; 21cm
Greek text, English introduction and notes. — Bibliography: pxxv-xxvii
ISBN 0-906515-59-9 (pbk) : Unpriced
B82-05092

888′.0109 — Satire in Greek, *to ca 500* — *Texts*

Lucian. [Works]. Luciani opera / recognovit brevique adnotatione critica instruiut M.D. MacLeod. — Oxonii : E. Typographeo Clarendoniano. — (Scriptorum classicorum bibliotheca Oxoniensis)
Tomus 3: Libelli 44-68. — 1980. — 391p ; 19cm
Greek text, Latin titlepage
ISBN 0-19-814592-6 : £7.95 : CIP rev.
B79-34602

889 — MODERN GREEK LITERATURE

889′.1′009 — Poetry in Modern Greek, *to 1980* — *Critical studies*

Trypanis, C. A.. Greek poetry : from Homer to Seferis / C.A. Trypanis. — London : Faber and Faber, 1981. — 896p ; 25cm
Bibliography: p789-885. — Includes index
ISBN 0-571-08346-3 : £25.00 : CIP rev.
Primary classification 881′.009 B81-12821

889′.132 — Poetry in Modern Greek, *1900-1945* — *English texts*

Elytēs, Odysseas. Odysseus Elytis : selected poems / chosen and introduced by Edmund Keeley and Philip Sherrard ; translated by Edmund Keeley ... [et al.]. — London : Anvil Press Poetry, 1981. — xiv,114p ; 25cm
Translated from the Greek
ISBN 0-85646-076-1 : £6.95 B82-10294

Elytis, Odysseus. Odysseus Elytis : selected poems / chosen and introduced by Edmund Keeley and Philip Sherrard ; translated by Edmund Keeley ... [et al.]. — Harmondsworth : Penguin, 1981. — xiv,114p ; 24cm
ISBN 0-14-042289-7 (pbk) : £2.95 B82-19950

Sikelíanos, Angelos. Selected poems / Angelos Sikelianos ; translated by Edmund Keeley and Philip Sherrard with an introduction and notes. — London : Allen & Unwin, 1980, c1979. — 75p ; 22cm
Translated from the Greek. — Originally published: Princeton : Princeton University Press, c1979
ISBN 0-04-889001-4 (pbk) : £3.95 : CIP rev.
B80-11242

889′.134 — Poetry in Modern Greek, *1945-* — *Texts*

Constantinides, Erricos. Poems and chapter verse / by Erricos Constantinides. — London (24 Conway St. W.1.) : E. Constantinides, 1982. — 101 leaves : ill ; 23cm
Text in English and Greek
Unpriced (unbound)
Primary classification 821 B82-20142

890 — LITERATURES(OTHER THAN GERMANIC, ROMANCE AND GREEK)

890 — Oriental literatures. Criticism & translation. Waley, Arthur — *Biographies*

Waley, Alison. A half of two lives / Alison Waley. — London : Weidenfeld and Nicolson, c1982. — xxviii,326p,[8]p of plates : ill,1facsim,ports ; 23cm
ISBN 0-297-78156-1 : £10.95 B82-39947

891.2/4 — INDIC LITERATURES

891′.42′05 — Punjabi literature — *Serials* — *Punjabi texts*

Racanā : Iṅgalaiṇḍa coṃ nikaladā iko ika sāhitaka manthalī. — Vol.1, no.1 (Jan. 1981)-. — London (367 Katherine Rd, Forestgate, E7 8LT) : Rachna Publishers, 1981. — v. : ill ; 25cm
Monthly. — English title: Rachna (Punjabi monthly). — Description based on: Vol.1, no.7 (July 1981)
ISSN 0262-7132 = Racanā : £0.50 per issue
B82-10117

891′.43915 — Poetry in Urdu, *1895-1920* — *English texts*

Rāma Tīrtha, *Swāmī*. Yoga and the supreme bliss : songs of enlightenment / by Rāma Tīrtha ; translated from the Urdu and Persian by A.J. Alston. — London : A.Z. Alston, 1982. — x,214p ; 25cm
Bibliography: p207-208
ISBN 0-9508019-0-9 (pbk) : £3.90 : CIP rev.
Also classified at 891′.5512 B82-11106

891′.43915 — Poetry in Urdu, *1895-1920* — *Polyglot texts*

Iqbal, Muhammad. Shikwa and Jawab-i-Shikwa = Complaint and answer : Iqbal's dialogue with Allah / Muhammad Iqbal ; translated from the Urdu, with an introduction, by Khushwant Singh and a foreword by Rafiq Zakaria. — Delhi ; Oxford : Oxford University Press, 1981. — 96p ; 22cm
Parallel Urdu text with English and Hindi translations, and introduction in English
ISBN 0-19-561324-4 (pbk) : £2.50 B82-26622

891′.43917 — Poetry in Urdu, *1940-* — *Texts*

Madnī, Jamīl. Fikr-i jamīl / Jamīl Madnī. — Bār avval. — London : 44 Lynton Ave., W13 0EB (Kul Barṭāniyah Anjuman-i Taraqqī-yi Urdū), [1981]. — 40p ; 22cm
Unpriced (pbk) B82-19890

Madnī, Jamīl. Ḳhalish-i ārzū / Jamīl Madanī. — Bār avval. — London (44 Lynton Ave., W13 0EB) : Kul Barṭāniyah Anjuman-i Taraqqī-yi Urdū, [1981]. — 159p ; 22cm
Unpriced B82-19891

891′.44′05 — Bengali literature — *Bengali texts* — *Serials*

Prabāsī samācāra. — 1386 [1979]-. — London (45 Sedgwick Rd, E10 6QP) : Probashi Samachar, [1979]-. — v. : ill ; 25cm
Two issues yearly. — Also entitled: Probashi samachar. — Size varies. — Description based on: Nababarsha saṅkhyā (1387 [1980])
ISSN 0262-8635 = Prabāsī samācāra : £1.50 per year B82-11143

891.5 — IRANIAN LITERATURES

891′.5511 — Poetry in Persian, *1000-1389* — *English texts*

Omar Khayyám. [Rubaiyat. English]. The ruba'iyat of Omar Khayyam / translated by Peter Avery and John Heath-Stubbs. — Harmondsworth : Penguin, 1981, c1979. — 128p : col.ill ; 24cm
Translated from the Persian. — This translation originally published: London : Allen Lane, 1979. — Bibliography: p128
ISBN 0-14-005954-7 (pbk) : £3.95 B82-08132

Omar Khayyám. Rubáiyát of Omar Khayyám. — London : Holsworthy, 1982. — vi,90p : col.ill ; 16cm
Translated from the Persian. — Based upon a translation from the original by Edward Fitzgerald
ISBN 0-907333-04-4 (cased) : Unpriced
ISBN 0-907333-03-6 (leather) : Unpriced
B82-10388

891′.5511 — Poetry in Persian, *1000-1389.* **Omar Khayyám. Rubáiyát. Translations** — *Critical studies* — *Welsh texts*

Williams, John Griffith, *1915-*. Omar / John Griffith Williams. — Dinbych [Denbigh] : Gwasg Gee, c1981. — 237p,[3]leaves of plates : 3ports ; 23cm
Includes the text of Sir John Morris-Jones' translation of the Rubáiyat of Omar Khayyám
£4.50 B82-13769

891′.5512 — Poetry in Persian, *1389-1900* — *English texts*

Rāma Tīrtha, *Swāmī*. Yoga and the supreme bliss : songs of enlightenment / by Rāma Tīrtha ; translated from the Urdu and Persian by A.J. Alston. — London : A.Z. Alston, 1982. — x,214p ; 25cm
Bibliography: p207-208
ISBN 0-9508019-0-9 (pbk) : £3.90 : CIP rev.
Primary classification 891′.43915 B82-11106

891.6 — CELTIC LITERATURES

891.6 — Poetry in Celtic languages, *to 1982* — *Critical studies* — *Festschriften* — *Welsh texts*

Bardos / cyflwynedig i J.E. Caerwyn Williams ; golygwyd gan R. Geraint Gruffydd. — Caerdydd : Gwasg Prifysgol Cymru, 1982. — x,235p,[1]leaf of plates : 1port ; 23cm
Bibliography: p214-226. — Includes index
ISBN 0-7083-0799-x : Unpriced : CIP rev.
B81-12833

891.62 — IRISH LITERATURE

891.6′2′09004 — Irish literature, *1850-* — *Critical studies*

Contemporary Irish studies. — Manchester : Manchester University Press, Nov.1982. — [200]p
ISBN 0-7190-0919-7 : £19.50 : CIP entry
B82-26403

891.6′2′0923 — Orally transmitted Irish narrative literature, *to ca 1171.* **Lists** — *Critical studies*

Mac Cana, Proinsias. The learned tales of medieval Ireland / by Proinsias Mac Cana. — Dublin (10 Burlington Rd., Dublin 4) : Dublin Institute for Advanced Studies, 1980. — ix,159p ; 22cm
English and Irish text. — Includes index
Unpriced B82-18608

891.6′2′099287 — Irish literature, *to 1980.* **Special themes: Women** — *Critical studies* — *Irish texts*

Léachtai cholm cille XII : na mná sa litriocht / in eagar ag Pádraig Ó Fiannachta. — Maigh Muad : An Sagart, 1982. — 198p ; 21cm
Includes bibliographies
£1.00 (pbk) B82-30689

891.6′214 — Poetry in Irish, *1850-* — *Texts*

Ní Dhomhnaill, Nuala. An dealg droighin / Nuala Ní Dhomhnaill. — Baile Átha Cliath [Dublin] : Cló Mercier, c1981. — 96p ; 18cm
ISBN 0-85342-655-4 (pbk) : £2.00 B82-02945

891.6′214′0809282 — Children's poetry in Irish, *1850-* — *Anthologies* — *For schools*

Duanaire nua do pháistí (sinear) / eagarthóir Breandán Ó Conaire. — Tamhlacht : Folens, c1980. — 32p ; 22cm
ISBN 0-86121-139-1 (pbk) : Unpriced
B82-37902

891.6′234 — Children's stories in Irish, *1850-* — *Texts*

Mac Uistín, Liam. Deirdre : Seanscéal Gaelige / arna chur in oiriúint do leanaí 8-11 bliana ag Liam Mac Uistín ; Kathy Moore a mhaisigh. — Baile Átha Cliath : Oifig An tSoláthair, c1982. — [25]p : col.ill ; 26cm
Unpriced B82-37916

891.6′234 — Fiction in Irish, *1850-* — *Texts*

Ó Grianna, Séamus. Saol corrach / Séamus Ó Grianna, 'Máire' ; Niall Ó Dónaill a chuir in eagar. — Baile Átha Cliath [Dublin] : Cló Mercier, c1981. — 260p ; 19cm
ISBN 0-85342-633-3 (pbk) : £2.70 B82-03945

891.6′234 — Fiction in Irish. Ó Grianna, Séamus — *Critcal studies — Irish texts*

Mac Congáil, Nollaig. Léargas ar 'Cith is dealán', Mháire / Nollaig Mac Congáil. — Baile Átha Cliath [Dublin] (29 Sráid Uí Chonaill Íoch, Baile Átha Cliath 1) : Foilseacháin Náisiúnta Teoronta, 1982. — 121p,[4]p of plates : ill,ports ; 19cm
Bibliography: p119-121
£2.50 (pbk) B82-31981

891.6′234 — Short stories in Irish, *1850-*

Ó Conaola, Dara. Mo chathair ghríobháin ; agus scéalta eile / Dara Ó Conaola. — Baile Áthe Cliath [Dublin] : Oifig an tSoláthair, c1981. — 60p ; 19cm
£1.00 (pbk) B82-18689

891.6′234 — Short stories in Irish. Ni Chéileachair, Síle. Bullaí Mhártain — *Study outlines — Irish texts*

Ó Maonaigh, Tomás. Bullaí mhártain : eolas agus léumbeas ar / Tómas Ó Maonaigh. — Baile Átha Cliath : Helicon, c1981. — 62p ; 21cm. — (Nótaí Helicon)
Unpriced (pbk) B82-07371

891.6′234 — Short stories in Irish. Ó Cadhain, Máirtín. Idir shúgradh agus dáiríre — *Concordances — Irish texts*

Ó Murchú, Séamas. Liosta focal : as idir shúgradh agus dáiríre / Séamas Ó Murchú. — Baile Átha Cliath : Acadamh Ríoga na hÉireann, 1982. — ix,25p ; 25cm. — (Deascán foclóireachta ; 2)
Bibliography: pviii
ISBN 0-901714-20-8 (pbk) : Unpriced
B82-29843

891.6′28409 — Irish literature, *1850- — Texts*

Behan, Brendan. Poems and a play in Irish / Brendan Behan. — Dublin : Gallery, 1981. — 75p ; 22cm. — (Gallery books)
ISBN 0-904011-14-3 (cased) : £5.40
ISBN 0-904011-15-1 (pbk) : £3.00 B82-13906

891.63 — GAELIC LITERATURE

891.6′333 — Children's stories in Scottish Gaelic, *1830-*

Cunliffe, John. [Postman Pat's difficult day. Gaelic]. Padraig Post air latha doirbh. — Portree (P.O. Box 1, Portree, Isle of Skye IV51 9BT) : Club Leabhar, Nov.1982. — [32]p
Translation of: Postman Pat's difficult day
ISBN 0-902706-50-0 : £1.95 : CIP entry
B82-30320

Cunliffe, John. [Postman Pat's foggy day. Gaelic]. Padraig Post air latha ceothach. — Portree (P.O. Box 1, Portree, Isle of Skye IV51 9BT) : Club Leabhar, Nov.1982. — [32]p
Translation of: Postman Pat's foggy day
ISBN 0-902706-51-9 : £1.95 : CIP entry
B82-30321

891.6′333 — Children's stories in Scottish Gaelic, *1830- — Texts*

Chaimbeul, Ceana. Leagsaidh Luchag agus am baidhsagal / Ceana Chaimbeul ; dealbhan le Priscilla Chaimbeul. — Steòrnabhagh [Stornoway] : Acair, 1982. — 33p : col.ill ; 21cm
ISBN 0-86152-037-8 (pbk) : Unpriced
B82-38735

891.66 — WELSH LITERATURE

891.6′6′09 — Welsh literature — *Critical studies — Welsh texts*

Ysgrifau beirniadol. — Dinbych [Denbigh] : Gwasg Gee
12 / golygydd J.E. Caerwyn Williams. — 1982. — 336p ; 22cm
£6.00 B82-30849

891.6′6′09001 — Welsh literature, *to 1600 — Critical studies — Welsh texts*

Evans, D. Simon. Llafar a llyfr yn yr hen gyfnod. — Cardiff : University of Wales Press, July 1982. — [24]p. — (Darlith goffa G.J. Williams)
ISBN 0-7083-0817-1 (unbound) : £0.95 : CIP entry B82-19272

891.6′6′0994299 — Welsh literature. Gwent writers, *1600- — Critical studies — Welsh texts*

Thomas, Mair Elvet. Agweddau ar weithgarwch llenyddol Gwent yn y ganrif ddiwethaf : darlith goffa Islwyn a draddodwyd yn Adeilad y Dynoliaethau, Coleg y Brifysgol, Caerdydd, ddydd Sadwrn, 17 Mai 1980. Cadeiriwyd y ddarlith gan yr Athro Ceri W. Lewis, Pennaeth Adran y Gymraeg yn y Coleg / Mair Elvet Thomas. — Caerdydd : Gwasg Prifysgol Cymra, 1981. — 36p ; 22cm. — (Darlith goffa Islwyn ; 1980)
ISBN 0-7083-0800-7 (pbk) : Unpriced : CIP rev. B81-07416

891.6′611 — Poetry in Welsh, *to 1600 — Texts*

Kedymdeithyas Amlyn ac Amic / gyda rhagymadrodd a nodiadau gan Patricia Williams. — Caerdydd : Cyhoeddwyd ar ran Bwrdd Gwybodau Celtaidd Prifysgol Cymru [gan] Wasg Prifysgol Cymru, 1982. — xxxvii,84p : 1map ; 23cm
Bibliography: p81-84. — Includes index
ISBN 0-7083-0751-5 : Unpriced : CIP rev.
B81-30374

Llyfr Du Caerfyrddin. — Cardiff : University of Wales Press, Nov.1982. — [258]p
ISBN 0-7083-0629-2 : £8.00 : CIP entry
B82-27974

891.6′611 — Poetry in Welsh, *to 1600 — Welsh-English parallel texts*

Dafydd, *ap Gwilym*. Dafydd ap Gwilym. — Llandysul : Gower Press, Sept.1982. — [240]p. — (The Welsh classics)
ISBN 0-85088-815-8 : £9.75 : CIP entry
B82-22434

891.6′611′08 — Poetry in Welsh, *to 1600 — Anthologies*

Cywyddau serch y tri bedo. — Cardiff : University of Wales Press, Sept.1981. — [85]p. — (Clasuron yr academi ; 3)
ISBN 0-7083-0795-7 : £4.95 : CIP entry
B81-21495

891.6′611′080355 — Poetry in Welsh, *to 1600.* **Special subjects: Food. Welsh dishes** — *Anthologies — English texts*

Roberts, Enid. Food of the bards 1350-1650 / by Enid Roberts. — Cardiff : Image, c1982. — [24]p : ill ; 20cm
Translation of: Bwyd y beirdd
ISBN 0-9507254-3-9 (pbk) : Unpriced : CIP rev.
Primary classification 641.59429 B82-11969

891.6′611′09 — Poetry in Welsh, *to 1600 — Critical studies*

Jarman, A. O. H.. The Cynfeirdd : early Welsh poets and poetry / A.O.H. Jarman. — [Cardiff] : University of Wales Press on behalf of the Welsh Arts Council, 1981. — 133p : 1facsim ; 25cm. — (Writers of Wales)
Limited ed. of 1000 numbered copies. — Bibliography: p125-132
ISBN 0-7083-0813-9 (pbk) : £2.50 : CIP rev.
B81-35890

891.6′612 — Poetry in Welsh, *1600- — English texts*

Eifion Wyn. [Telynegion y misoedd. English]. The months : a lyric sequence from the Welsh / by Eifion Wyn ; Dewi Hopkins. — Liverpool (80 Lark La., Liverpool L17 8UU) : 'Old Police Station', c1982. — 15p ; 21cm. — (Lark Lane poetry books ; no.1)
£0.20 (pbk) B82-21045

891.6′612 — Poetry in Welsh, *1600- — Texts*

Bowen, Euros. Gwynt yn y canghennau / Euros Bowen. — Dinbych [Denbigh] : Gwasg Gee, c1982. — 104p ; 22cm
£2.50 B82-37868

Bowen, Euros. Masg Minos / Euros Bowen. — Dinbych [Denbigh] : Gwasg Gee, c1981. — 47p,[1]leaf of plates : 1port ; 23cm
£1.75 B82-10390

Englynwyr Glannau Mersi / [golygwyd gan] O. Trevor Roberts (Llanowain). — Dinbych [Denbigh] : Gwasg Gee, c1980. — 52p : ports ; 22cm
£1.75 (pbk) B82-11721

Griffiths, J. Gwyn. Cerddi'r holl eneidiau / J. Gwyn Griffiths. — Dinbych [Denbigh] : Gwasg Gee, c1981. — 63p,[1] leaf of plate : 1port ; 23cm
£1.75 B82-10393

Gruffydd, *o Fôn*. Cerddi Gruffydd o Fôn (R.H. Gruffydd). — [Nant Peris] ([Old School, Nant Peris, Caernarfon, Gwynedd]) : Gwasg Gwynedd, 1981. — 77p ; 19cm
£1.00 (pbk) B82-25981

Healy, Desmond. Geiriau / Desmond Healy. — 2 argraffiad. — [Denbigh] : Gwasg Gee, 1981. — 55p : ill ; 21cm
Previous ed.: 1971
Unpriced (pbk) B82-10392

Jones, Einir. Gwellt medi / Einir Jones. — [Nant Peris] ([Old School, Nant Peris, Caernarfon, Gwynedd]) : Gwasg Gwynedd, 1980. — 45p ; 22cm
Unpriced B82-11432

Jones, Gwilym. Cerddi eisteddfodol y diweddar Gwilym Jones / golygydd D. Ben Rees. — Lerpwl [Liverpool] (32 Garth Drive, Liverpool L18 6HW) : Cyhoeddiadau Modern Cymreig, 1981. — 44p ; 22cm
£1.50 (pbk) B82-27773

Jones, William, *b.1908*. Tannau'r cawn / William Jones ; wedi eu dethol gan D. Tecwyn Lloyd. — 2 argraffiad. — [Denbigh] : Gwasg Gee, 1981. — 101p ; 19cm
Previous ed.: 1965
£1.75 (pbk) B82-10395

Lewis, D. Glyn. Cerddi Glyn o Faldwyn / D. Glyn Lewis. — Dinbych [Denbigh] : Gwasg Gee, c1980. — 54p ; 22cm
£1.50 (pbk) B82-11720

Lewis, Stanley G.. Y chwalfa : a cherddi eraill / Stanley G. Lewis. — Lerpwl [Liverpool] (32 Garth Drive, Liverpool L18 6HW) : Cyhoeddiadau Modern Cymreig, 1981. — 60p ; 19cm
Unpriced (pbk) B82-27772

Lloyd, Iorwerth H.. Cerddi Talfryn / Iorwerth H. Lloyd (Talfryn). — [Nant Peris] ([Old School, Nant Peris, Caernarfon, Gwynedd]) : Gwasg Gwynedd, 1980. — 49p ; 19cm
Unpriced B82-11431

Llwyd, Alan. Cerddi'r cyfannu a cherddi eraill / Alan Llwyd. — Abertawe [Swansea] : C. Davies, c1980. — 64p ; 22cm
ISBN 0-7154-0575-6 (pbk) : £1.95 B82-17455

Morris, William, *1889-1979*. Canu oes / William Morris ; golygwyd gan Glennys Roberts. — [Nant Peris] ([Old School, Nant Peris, Caernarfon, Gwynedd]) : Gwasg Gwynedd, 1981. — 191p : 1port ; 23cm
Unpriced B82-26744

Roberts, O. Trevor. Trydydd cerddi Llanowain / O. Trevor Roberts. — Dinbych [Denbigh] : Gwasg Gee, c1981. — 78p ; 19cm
£1.50 (pbk) B82-21476

Thomas, Gwyn, *1936-*. Symud y lliwiau / Gwyn Thomas. — [Denbigh] : Gwasg Gee, c1981. — 62p ; 21cm
£1.75 (pbk) B82-10391

White, Katie. Rhigwm neu ddau : cyfrol o adroddiadau i blant / Katie White. — Dinbych [Denbigh] : Gwasg Gee, c1981. — 42p ; 19cm
£0.90 (pbk) B82-10394

Williams, Gwyn, *1904-*. Y ddefod goll : cerddi / gan Gwyn Williams. — Port Talbot (3 Crown St., Port Talbot, [W. Glamorgan SA13 1BG]) : Llyfrau Alun, c1980. — [28]p ; 22cm
ISBN 0-907117-03-1 (pbk) : £1.00 B82-02956

891.6′612 — Poetry in Welsh. Jones, T. Gwynn (Thomas Gwynn), *1871-1949 — Critical studies — Welsh texts*

Thomas Gwynn Jones / golygydd Gwynn ap Gwilym. — Llandybïe : C. Davies, c1982. — 525p : 1port ; 21cm. — (Cyfres y meistri ; 3) Includes index. — Includes poems by T. Gwynn Jones
£6.95 (pbk) B82-21154

891.6′612 — Poetry in Welsh. Moelwyn *— Critical studies — Welsh texts*

Evans, Meredydd. Moelwyn, y bardd / Meredydd Evans. — [Caernarfon] : Cyngor Sir Gwynedd Gwasanaeth Llyfrgell, 1982. — 30p : 1port ; 21cm. — (Darlith flynyddol Llyfrgell Blaenau Ffestiniog ; 1982)
ISBN 0-904852-26-1 (pbk) : £0.60 B82-22893

891.6′612 — Poetry in Welsh. Parry, R. Williams *— Personal observations — Welsh texts*

Hughes, Mathonwy. Perlau R. Williams Parry / gan Mathonwy Hughes. — [Denbigh] : Gwasg Gee, c1981. — 48p ; 18cm
£1.50 (pbk) B82-13767

891.6′612′08 — Poetry in Welsh, *1600- — Anthologies — English texts*

Twentieth century Welsh poets. — Llandysul : Gomer Press, Feb.1983. — [253]p
ISBN 0-85088-406-3 : £9.75 : CIP entry B82-40915

891.6′622 — Drama in Welsh, *1600- — Texts*

Evans, John R.. Brawd am byth : buddugol yng nghystadleuaeth y fedal ddrama, Eisteddfod Maldwyn a′i Chyffiniau / J.R. Evans. — Llanrwst ([Old Electricity Works House, Owens Terrace, Llanrwst, Gwynedd]) : Argraffwyd a chyhoeddwyd ar ran Pwyllgor Gwaith Eisteddfod Maldwyn a′i Chyffiniau gan Wasg Carreg Gwalch, 1981. — 62p : ill ; 18cm
£1.00 (pbk) B82-26949

Isaac, Norah. Cwpaned : drama / gan Norah Isaac. — Llandysul : Gwasg Gomer, 1982. — 52p : ill ; 21cm
ISBN 0-85088-716-x (pbk) : £1.00 B82-17385

891.6′6301′08[FS] — Short stories in Welsh, *1600- — Anthologies — English texts*

The **Penguin** book of Welsh short stories / edited by Alun Richards. — Harmondsworth : Penguin, 1976 (1982 [printing]). — 358p ; 20cm
Includes some stories translated from the Welsh
ISBN 0-14-004061-7 (pbk) : £2.50
Primary classification 823′.01′089429[FS]
B82-30530

891.6′6301′08[FS] — Short stories in Welsh, *to 1600 — Anthologies — English texts — Facsimiles*

The **Mabinogion** : from the Welsh of the Llyfr coch o Hergest (The red book of Hergest) in the library of Jesus College, Oxford / translated, with notes, by Lady Charlotte Guest. — Ruthin : Spread Eagle, 1981. — xx,504p : ill ; 22cm
Facsim originally published: Cardiff : John Jones (Cardiff), 1977. — Facsim of: 2nd ed. London : Quaritch, 1877
ISBN 0-907207-04-9 : Unpriced B82-18211

891.6′631 — Fiction in Welsh, *to 1600 — Texts*

Y **Mabinogion** / diweddariad gan Dafydd Ifans a Rhiannon Ifans ; ynghyd â rhagymadrodd gan Brynley F. Roberts. — Llandysul : Gwasg Gomer, 1980 (1981 [printing]). — 237p ; 22cm
Bibliography: pxxx-xxxi
ISBN 0-85088-722-4 : £5.95 B82-37616

891.6′632 — Children′s short stories in Welsh, *1600- — Texts*

Edwards, Eirwen. Y drol : a storïau eraill / Eirwen Edwards ; arluniwyd y gyfrol gan Gaynor Owen. — Llandysul : Gwasg Gomer, 1982. — 55p : col.ill ; 18x24cm
ISBN 0-85088-975-8 (pbk) : £1.60 B82-29297

Storïau awr hamdden i blant / gol. Norah Isaac. — Llandybie : C. Davies
2. — c1982. — 132p ; 19cm
£2.50 (pbk) B82-38802

891.6′632 — Children′s stories in Welsh, *1600- — Texts*

Chilton, Irma. Yr iâr goch : a storïau eraill i′w darllen i blant meithrin / Irma Chilton. — [Nant Peris] ([Old School, Nant Peris, Caernarfon, Gwynedd]) : Gwasg Gwynedd, 1980. — 20p : col.ill ; 21cm
Unpriced (pbk) B82-11428

Davies, Haydn. Breuddwydio / Haydn Davies ; lluniau gan Bernadette Watts. — Caerdydd : Gwasg y Dref Wen, c1981. — 62p : ill ; 19cm. — (Cyfres y wiwer)
£1.70 (pbk) B82-32116

Huws, Emily. Y Tomosiaid a′r cybydd / Emily Huws ; arluniwyd y gyfrol gan Alan Williams. — Llandysul : Gwasg Gomer, 1981. — 57p : ill ; 21cm
ISBN 0-85088-624-4 (pbk) : £1.75 B82-27252

Huws, Emily. Y Tomosiaid a′r trên / Emily Huws ; arluniwyd y gyfrol gan Alan Williams. — Llandysul : Gwasg Gomer, 1981. — 52p : ill ; 21cm
ISBN 0-85088-953-7 (pbk) : £1.75 B82-27251

Huws, Emily. Y Tomosiaid ar yr ynys / Emily Huws ; arluniwyd y gyfrol gan Alan Williams. — Llandysul : Gwasg Gomer, 1981. — 56p : ill ; 21cm
ISBN 0-85088-734-8 (pbk) : £1.75 B82-27250

Huws, Emily. Y Tomosiaid yn yr ysgol / Emily Huws ; arluniwyd y gyfrol gan Alan Williams. — Llandysul : Gwasg Gomer, 1981. — 55p : ill ; 21cm
ISBN 0-85088-714-3 (pbk) : £1.75 B82-27249

Ifans, Alun. Nathaniel / Alun Ifans ; arlunydd Lin Jenkins. — Llandysul : Gwasg Gomer, 1981. — 28p : col.ill ; 20cm. — (Cyfres y môr-ladron ; 4)
ISBN 0-85088-914-6 (pbk) : £0.95 B82-08973

Ifans, Alun. Ralff Greulon / Alun Ifans ; arlunydd Lin Jenkins. — Llandysul : Gwasg Gomer, 1981. — 28p : col.ill ; 20cm. — (Cyfres y môr-ladron ; 5)
ISBN 0-85088-924-3 (pbk) : £0.95 B82-08971

Jones, Dyfed Glyn. Y ddraig werdd / Dyfed Glyn Jones. — Aberystwyth : Urdd Gobaith Cymru, c1982. — 77p ; 21cm
Originally published: in Cymru′r plant, Sept.1975-June 1976
Unpriced (pbk) B82-26948

Jones, Eluned. Y ceffyl cudd / Eluned Jones. — Llandybie : C. Davies, c1982. — 102p ; 19cm
£2.50 (pbk) B82-38803

Jones, Geraint V.. Antur yr Allt / Geraint V. Jones ; arluniwyd y gyfrol gan John Shackell. — [Denbigh] : Gwasg Gee, c1981. — 72p : ill ; 22cm
£1.60 (pbk) B82-18209

Jones, Geraint V.. Antur yr Alpau / Geraint V. Jones ; arluniwyd y gyfrol gan John Shackell. — Dinbych [Denbigh] : Gwasg Gee, c1981. — 66p : ill ; 22cm
£1.60 (pbk) B82-11722

Jones, R. D.. Anturiaethau′r Gwenyn / R.D. Jones ; arluniwyd y gyfrol gan Anne Lloyd Morris. — Llandysul : Gwasg Gomer, 1982. — 97p : ill ; 22cm
ISBN 0-85088-875-1 (pbk) : £1.95 B82-29300

Lewis, Gwenda. Dau a dwy ar daith / Gwenda Lewis ; arluniwyd y gyfrol gan Helen Hywel. — Llandysul : Gwasg Gomer, 1982. — 84p : ill ; 19cm
ISBN 0-85088-616-3 (pbk) : £1.80 B82-29299

Lilly, Gweneth. Y gragen a′r drych / ysgrifennwyd ac arluniwyd gan Gweneth Lilly. — Llandysul : Gwasg Gomer, 1982. — 118p : ill ; 19cm
ISBN 0-85088-825-5 (pbk) : £2.10 B82-29296

Roberts, Iago. Moti a′r frechdan jam hud / Iago Roberts ; arlunydd Lin Jenkins. — Llandysul : Gwasg Gomer, 1982. — 32p : col.ill ; 15x22cm
ISBN 0-85088-606-6 (pbk) : £1.60 B82-29298

Williams, Enid Wynne. Storïau Tomos Dafis / gan Enid Wynne Williams ; arluniwyd gan Jones Graphics. — Y Bontfaen [Cowbridge] : D. Brown a′i Feibion, [1981?]. — 32p : ill ; 23cm
£0.95 (pbk) B82-25428

Williams, Ifor Wyn. Gwesty′r llygaid aflan / Ifor Wyn Williams. — [Aberystwyth] ([Swyddfa′r Urdd, Aberystwyth, Dyfed]) : Urdd Gobaith Cymru, c1981. — 79p ; 21cm
Originally published: in instalments in Cymru′r plant, Sept.1972 to June 1973
Unpriced (pbk) B82-18229

891.6′632 — Fiction in Welsh, *1600- — Irish texts*

Lloyd, J. Selwyn. [Trysor Bryniau Caspar. Irish]. Saibhreas Chnoic Chaspair / J. Selwyn Lloyd ; léaráidí le Catherine Thomas ; Liam Mac Cóil a rinne an leagan Gaeilge. — Baile Átha Cliath [Dublin] : Oifig an tSoláthair, c1981. — 111p : ill ; 21cm
Translation of: Trysor Bryniau Caspar
Unpriced (pbk) B82-19423

891.6′632 — Fiction in Welsh, *1600- — Texts*

Hughes, Beti. Pontio′r pellter : buddugol yng nghystadleuaeth Gwobr Goffa Daniel Owen yn Eisteddfod Genedlaethol Caernarfon 1979 / Beti Hughes. — Abertawe [Swansea] : Tŷ John Penry, 1981. — 115p ; 19cm
ISBN 0-903701-40-5 (pbk) : £2.00 B82-16383

Humphreys, Emyr. [A man′s estate. Welsh]. Etifedd y Glyn / Emyr Humphreys ; trosiad Cymraeg gan W.J. Jones (Gwilym Fychan). — Llandysul : Gwasg Gomer, 1981. — 317p ; 22cm
Translation of: A man′s estate
ISBN 0-85088-935-9 : £5.95 B82-27248

Jones, Gerallt. Torri′r cadwynau / Gerallt Jones ; arluniwyd y gyfrol hon gan Alwyn Dempster Jones. — [Caernarfon] ([St. David′s Rd., Caernarfon, Gwynedd]) : Gwasg Tŷ ar y Graig, 1980. — 88p : ill ; 19cm
For adolescents
Unpriced (pbk) B82-22630

Jones, Hugh D.. Glas y Don / Hugh D. Jones. — Llandysul : Gwasg Gomer, 1981. — 149p ; 18cm
ISBN 0-85088-795-x (pbk) : £1.95 B82-17386

Jones, R. Emyr. Ni allaf ddianc / R. Emyr Jones. — Caernarfon ([Llyfrfa′r Methodistiaid Calfinaidd, Heol Ddewi, Caernarfon, Gwynedd LL55 1ER]) : Gwasg Pantycelyn, c1981. — 101p ; 18cm
£2.00 (pbk) B82-01015

Jones, Rhiannon Davies. Eryr Pengwern / Rhiannon Davies Jones. — Llandysul : Gwasg Gomer, 1981. — 226p : 2maps ; 22cm
ISBN 0-85088-595-7 : £4.95 B82-09778

Jones, Stephen, *1911-*. Dirgelwch Lisa Lân / Stephen Jones. — Dinbych [Denbigh] : Gwasg Gee, c1982. — 80p : 3forms ; 22cm
£1.75 (pbk) B82-18210

Owen, Geraint Dyfnallt. Cwymp y blaid wreiddiol / Geraint Dyfnallt Owen. — [Nant Peris] ([Old School, Nant Peris, Caernarfon, Gwynedd]) : Gwasg Gwynedd, 1981. — 181p ; 19cm
£3.00 B82-25980

Owen, Ivor. Trysor y mynydd / Ivor Owen. — Dinbych [Denbigh] ([Chapel St., Denbigh, Clwyd]) : Gwasg Gee, c1981. — 143p ; 19cm
£1.75 (pbk) B82-12197

Watkin-Jones, Elizabeth. Lois / Elizabeth Watkin Jones ; wedi ei diweddaru gan Hugh D. Jones. — Llandysul : Gwasg Gomer, 1981. — 133p ; 19cm
ISBN 0-85088-506-x (pbk) : £1.50 B82-10613

891.6′632 — Short stories in Welsh, *1600- — Texts*

Chilton, Irma. Y cwlwm gwaed : a storïau eraill / Irma Chilton. — Llandysul : Gwasg Gomer, 1981. — 113p ; 18cm
ISBN 0-85088-855-7 (pbk) : £1.75 B82-17306

Parri, Dafydd. Bwrw hiraeth / Dafydd Parri. — Talybont, Ceredigion : Y Lolfa, 1981. — 80p ; 19cm. — (Pocedlyfrau′r Lolfa)
ISBN 0-86243-006-2 (pbk) : £1.45 B82-26030

Roberts, Kate. Haul a drycin : a storïau eraill / Kate Roberts. — Dinbych [Denbigh] ([Chapel St., Denbigh, Clwyd]) : Gwasg Gee, c1981. — 63p : ill ; 22cm
£1.00 (pbk) B82-12195

891.6′632 — Short stories in Welsh. Owen, Daniel. Straeon y pentan — *Critical studies*

Elis, Islwyn Ffowc. Daniel Owen′s Straeon y pentan / by Islwyn Ffowc Elis. — [Mold] ([Bethesda Chapel, Mold, Clwyd]) : Daniel Owen Memorial Room Committee, 1981. — 24,24p ; 21cm. — (Daniel Owen memorial lecture = Darlith goffa Daniel Owen ; 6)
Includes the text in Welsh, printed tête-bêche under the title ′Straeon y pentan ′Daniel Owen
£0.85 (pbk) B82-06128

891.6′642 — Essays in Welsh, *1600- — Texts*

Hughes, Mathonwy. Gwin y gweunydd / gan Mathonwy Hughes. — [Denbigh] ([Castle St., Denbigh, Clwyd]) : Gwasg Gee, c1981. — 47p ; 19cm
£1.00 (pbk) B82-12193

891.6′68209 — Welsh literature. Davies, Pennar — *Festschriften*

Pennar Davies : cyfrol deyrnged / golygydd Dewi Eirug Davies. — Abertawe [Swansea] : Tŷ John Penry, 1981. — 151p ; 23cm
Bibliography: p151. — Includes a selection of essays and poems by Pennar Davies
ISBN 0-903701-45-6 : £3.20 B82-16385

891.6′68209 — Welsh literature. Williams, Gwyn, *1904- — Biographies*

Williams, Gwyn, *1904-*. ABC of (D.) G.W. : a kind of autobiography / by Gwyn Williams. — Llandysul : Gomer, 1981. — 232p,[8]p of plates : ill ; 23cm
Bibliography: p232
ISBN 0-85088-854-9 : £6.95 B82-10273

891.67 — CORNISH LITERATURE

891.6′73 — Short stories in Cornish — *Texts*

Smith, A. S. D.. Nebes whethlow ber / A.S.D. Smith (Caradar). — Redruth (Trewolsta, Trewirgie Hill, Redruth, Cornwall) : Dyllansow Truran, [1981?]. — 32p ; 19cm
Originally published: Camborne : An Lef Kernewek, 1963
Unpriced (pbk) B82-12790

891.68 — BRETON LITERATURE

891.6′82′3 — Drama in Breton, *1900- — Welsh texts*

Malmanche, Tanguy. Dramâu o′r Llydaweg / Tangi Malmanche ; trosiadau gan Rita Williams a Gwyn Griffiths. — Llandybie : Gwasg Christopher Davies, c1982. — 280p ; 22cm
Translations of: Gurvan ar marc′heg estrañjour, Ar baganiz, An intanvez Arzhur, Gwreg an toer respectively. — Contents: Gurvan y marchog dieithr — Ysbail y môr — Y weddw — Gwraig y töwr
£2.95 (pbk) B82-34901

891.7 — RUSSIAN LITERATURE

891.708′0042 — Russian literature, *1917- — Anthologies — English texts*

Soviet Russian literature : 1917-1977 : poetry and prose : selected reading / [compiled by Yuri Andreyev]. — Moscow : Progress ; [London] : Central [distributor], c1980. — 878p ; 21cm
Translation of: Russkaîa sovetskaîa literatura. — Ill on lining papers
ISBN 0-7147-1728-2 : £7.95 B82-29459

891.709′001 — Russian literature, *1015-1700 — Critical studies*

Kuskov, V.. A history of old Russian literature / Vladimir Kuskov ; [translated from the Russian by Ronald Vroon]. — Moscow : Progress, c1980 ; [London] : Distributed by Central Books. — 354p ; 21cm
Translation of: Istoriîa drevenerusskoĭ literatury
ISBN 0-7147-1749-5 : £4.95 B82-39308

Likhachev, Dmitriĭ. The great heritage : the classical literature of Old Rus / Dmitry Likhachev. — Moscow : Progress ; [London] : distributed by Central, 1981. — 348p ; 21cm
Translation of: Velikoe nasledie. — Includes index
ISBN 0-7147-1734-7 : £4.50 B82-29717

891.709′003 — Russian literature, *1800-1917 — Critical studies*

Nabokov, Vladimir. Lectures on Russian literature / Vladimir Nabokov ; edited, with an introduction, by Fredson Bowers. — London : Weidenfeld and Nicolson, 1982, c1981. — xvii,324p : ill,facsims ; 26cm
ISBN 0-297-77886-2 : £16.50 B82-10973

891.709′003 — Russian literature, *1800-1917.* **Influence of society,** *1840-1890*

Andrew, Joe. Russian writers and society in the second half of the nineteenth century / Joe Andrew. — London : Macmillan, 1982. — xvii,238p ; 23cm
Bibliography: p220-228. — Includes index
ISBN 0-333-25911-4 : £20.00 B82-20914

891.709′003 — Russian literature, *1800-1980 — Questions & answers*

Stableford, Tom. The literary appreciation of Russian writers / Tom Stableford. — Cambridge : Cambridge University Press, 1981. — x,227p ; 23cm
ISBN 0-521-23498-0 (cased) : £14.50 : CIP rev.
ISBN 0-521-28003-6 (pbk) : Unpriced B81-36948

891.7′09′0042 — Russian literature, *1917-1978 — Sociological perspectives*

Hingley, Ronald. Russian writers and Soviet society 1917-1978. — London : Methuen, July 1981. — [320]p
Originally published: London : Weidenfeld and Nicolson, 1979
ISBN 0-416-31390-6 (pbk) : £5.50 : CIP entry B81-13869

891.709′0044 — Russian literature, *1945-1977 — Critical studies*

Brown, Deming. Soviet Russian literature since Stalin / Deming Brown. — Cambridge : Cambridge University Press, 1978 (1979 [printing]). — vi,394p ; 24cm
Bibliography: p.387-390. — Includes index
ISBN 0-521-29649-8 (pbk) : £6.95 B82-07533

891.709′0044 — Russian literature. Influence of political events, *1952-1958 — Sources of data: Novy Mir*

Frankel, Edith Rogovin. Novy mir : a case study in the politics of literature 1952-1958 / Edith Rogovin Frankel. — Cambridge : Cambridge University Press, 1981. — xvii,206p : ill,ports ; 23cm. — (Cambridge studies in Russian literature)
Bibliography: p194-200. — Includes index
ISBN 0-521-23438-7 : £19.50 : CIP rev. B81-34728

891.71′3 — Poetry in Russian. Akhmatova, Anna — *Critical studies*

Rosslyn, Wendy. The prince, the fool and the nunnery : the early poetry of Anna Akhmatova. — Amersham : Avebury Publishing, Sept.1982. — [256]p
ISBN 0-86127-217-x (pbk) : £9.95 : CIP entry B82-21545

891.71′3 — Poetry in Russian. Esenin, Sergeĭ — *Biographies — Russian texts*

Mariengof, Anatoliĭ. Roman bez vran′ya / Anatoly Mariengof ; introduction, annotations, appendices by Gordon McVay. — Oxford : Meeuws, 1979. — 157,lxxxp,20p of plates : ports ; 21cm. — (Esenin reprint series ; v.8)
Russian text, English introduction and notes. — Originally published: Leningrad : ′Priboĭ′, 1928
ISBN 0-902672-33-9 (pbk) : Unpriced B82-24529

891.71′3 — Poetry in Russian. Pushkin, A. S. — *Critical studies*

Briggs, A. D. P.. Alexander Pushkin. — London : Croom Helm, Oct.1982. — [224]p
ISBN 0-7099-0688-9 : £12.95 : CIP entry B82-23189

891.71′3 — Poetry in Russian. Pushkin, A. S. — *Critical studies — Russian texts*

Pokrovskiĭ, V. I.. Aleksandr Sergeevich Pushkin, ego zhizn i sochineniîa. — 3rd ed. — Oxford : Meeuws, July 1982. — [802]p
Reprint of Moscow ed. of 1912
ISBN 0-902672-53-3 : £37.50 : CIP entry B82-19283

891.71′3 — Poetry in Russian. Tîutchev, F. I. — *Critical studies — Russian texts*

Pokrovskiĭ, V.. Fedor Ivanovich Tyutchev : ego zhizn i sochineniya : sbornik istoriko-literaturnykh statei / sostavil V.I. Pokrovskii. — 2-e izdanie, dopolnennoe. — Oxford : Meeuws, 1980. — 86p ; 25cm. — (Mouette reprint series ; v.27)
Facsim of: 3rd ed., supplement. Moscow : V. Spiridonova i A. Mikhailova, 1911
ISBN 0-902672-42-8 (pbk) : Unpriced B82-14764

891.7′1′309 — Poetry in Russian, *1880-1935 — Critical studies*

France, Peter. Poets of modern Russia. — Cambridge : Cambridge University Press, Dec.1982. — [256]p. — (Cambridge studies in Russian literature)
ISBN 0-521-23490-5 (cased) : £20.00 : CIP entry
ISBN 0-521-28000-1 (pbk) : £7.50 B82-30301

891.71′42 — Poetry in Russian, *1917-1945 — English texts*

Tsvetayeva, Marina. Selected poems / Marina Tsvetayeva ; translated by Elaine Feinstein ; with literal versions provided by Angela Livingstone ... [et al.]. — Rev. enl. ed. — Oxford : Oxford University Press, 1981. — xviii,108p ; 22cm
Translated from the Russian. — Previous ed.: 1971
ISBN 0-19-211894-3 (pbk) : £4.95 : CIP rev. B81-14413

Tvardovskiĭ, Aleksandr. Alexander Tvardovsky : selected poetry / [compiled by M. Tvardovskaya]. — Moscow : Progress ; [London] : Central [distributor], c1981. — 478p,[48]p of plates : ill,ports ; 21cm. — (Progress Soviet authors library)
Translation of: Aleksandr Tvardovskiĭ
ISBN 0-7147-1733-9 : £3.95 B82-28204

891′.71′42 — Poetry in Russian. Maîakovskiĭ, V. V. — *Critical studies*

Briggs, A. D. P.. Vladimir Mayakovsky : a tragedy / A.D.P. Briggs. — Oxford : Meeuws, 1979. — 127p : 1port ; 21cm. — (Russian literary profiles ; v.7)
Bibliography: 123-124. — Includes index
ISBN 0-902672-35-5 (pbk) : £2.75 B82-21426

891.71′42 — Poetry in Russian. Pasternak, Boris — *Critical studies*

Gifford, Henry. Pasternak : a critical study / by Henry Gifford. — Cambridge : Cambridge University Press, 1977 (1981 [printing]). — xiii,280p ; 22cm. — (Major European authors)
Bibliography: p271-274. — Includes index
ISBN 0-521-28677-8 (pbk) : £7.95 : CIP rev. B81-28174

891.71′42′080351 — Poetry in Russian, *1917-1970.* **Special subjects: Lenin, V. I.** — *Anthologies — English texts*

Lenin in Soviet poetry : a poetical chronicle / [compiled by B.V. Yakovlev] ; [translated from the Russian]. — Moscow : Progress Publishers ; [London : distributed by Central Books, 1980. — 318p,[15]p of plates : ill,facsims,ports ; 27cm
Translation of: Lenin v sovetskoĭ poèzii
Unpriced B82-37154

891.71′42′09 — Poetry in Russian, *1917-1945 — Critical studies*

Hingley, Ronald. Nightingale fever : Russian poets in Revolution / Ronald Hingley. — London : Weidenfeld and Nicolson, c1982. — xiii,269p ; 24cm
Bibliography: p260-262. — Includes index
ISBN 0-297-77902-8 : £12.95 B82-12044

891.71′44 — Poetry in Russian, *1945- — English texts*

Berestov, Valentin. My basket / Valentin Berestov ; illustrated by S. Pynina ; translated by Fainna Solasko. — Moscow : Malysh ; [London] : distributed by Central, [1981?]. — [16]p : col.ill ; 21cm
Translated from the Russian
ISBN 0-7147-1722-3 (pbk) : £0.60 B82-17383

Brodsky, Joseph. A part of speech / Joseph Brodsky. — Oxford : Oxford University Press, 1980. — 151p ; 23cm
Translated from the Russian. — Originally published: New York : Farrar, Straus and Giroux, 1980
ISBN 0-19-211939-7 (pbk) : £4.95 : CIP rev. B80-20020

Brodsky, Joseph. Verses on the winter campaign 1980 / Joseph Brodsky ; translated by Alan Myers. — London : Anvil Press Poetry, 1981. — [8]p ; 18cm
Translation from the Russian. — Limited ed. of 500 numbered copies, of which nos. 1-250 are signed by the poet and translator
ISBN 0-85646-083-4 (pbk) : Unpriced B82-10290

Evtushenko, Evgeniĭ. A dove in Santiago. — London : Secker & Warburg, May 1982. — [64]p
Translated from the Russian
ISBN 0-436-59221-5 : £4.95 : CIP entry B82-10681

Maiakovskiĭ, Vladimir. What shall I be? / Vladimir Mayakovsky. — Moscow : Progress ; [London] : distributed by Central, c1981. — [32]p : col.ill ; 26cm
Translation of: Kem byt′?. — Ill on inside covers
ISBN 0-7147-1721-5 (pbk) : £0.75 B82-17384

891.71′44′08 — Poetry in Russian, *1945- — Anthologies — English texts*

Soviet Russian poetry of the 1950s-1970s / compiled by Nina Kupriyanova [sic] and Ariadna Ivanovskaya. — Moscow : Progress ; [London] : Central [distributor], c1981. — 253p ; 21cm
Translation of: Iz russkoĭ sovetskoĭ poezii 50-70-kh godov
ISBN 0-7147-1701-0 : £2.95 B82-29837

891.7′1′4408 — Poetry in Russian, *1945-. - Anthologies - Russian-English parallel texts*

The **new** Russian poets 1953-1968. — London : Marian Boyars, Apr.1981. — [320]p
Parallel Russian text and English translation
ISBN 0-7145-2715-7 (pbk) : £3.50 : CIP entry B81-07929

891.72′3 — Drama in Russian, *1800-1917 — English texts*

Chekhov, A. P.. Five plays / Anton Chekhov ; translated and with an introduction by Ronald Hingley. — Oxford : Oxford University Press, 1980. — xxxi,294p ; 19cm. — (The World′s classics)
Translated from the Russian. — Contents: Ivanov — The Seagull — Uncle Vanya — Three sisters — The Cherry orchard
ISBN 0-19-281548-2 (pbk) : £1.50 : CIP rev. B80-13622

Turgenev, I. S.. A month in the country : a comedy in five acts / by Ivan Turgenev ; translated and introduced by Isaiah Berlin. — London : Hogarth, 1981. — 127p ; 23cm
Translation of: Mesiats v derevnie
ISBN 0-7012-0540-7 : £5.50 : CIP rev. B81-25836

891.72′3 — Drama in Russian. Chekhov, A. P. — *Critical studies*

Chekhov′s great plays : a critical anthology / edited and with an introduction by Jean-Pierre Barricelli. — New York ; London : New York University Press, 1981. — xvii,268p : 1ill,port ; 24cm. — (The Gotham library of the New York University Press)
Includes index
ISBN 0-8147-1036-0 : £20.50 B82-35943

891.72′3 — One-act plays in Russian. Chekhov, A. P. — *Critical studies*

Gottlieb, Vera. Chekhov and the vaudeville : a study of Chekhov′s one-act plays / Vera Gottlieb. — Cambridge : Cambridge University Press, 1982. — xii,224p : ill,1port ; 23cm
Bibliography: p217-220. — Includes index
ISBN 0-521-24170-7 : £24.00 : CIP rev. B82-26238

891.72′42 — Drama in Russian, *1917-1945 — English texts*

Arbuzov, Alekseĭ. Selected plays of Aleksei Arbuzov. — Oxford : Pergamon, Sept.1982. — [336]p
Translated from the Russian
ISBN 0-08-024548-x : CIP entry B82-19089

Erdman, Nikolaĭ. The suicide : a play / by Nikolai Erdman ; translation by Peter Tegel. — London : French, c1979. — 90p ; 19cm
Nine men, 5 women, supers. — Translation from the Russian
ISBN 0-573-61628-0 (pbk) : £2.75 B82-36074

891.72′44 — Drama in Russian, *1945- — English texts*

Solzhenitsyn, Aleksandr. Prisoners. — London : Bodley Head, Oct.1982. — [144]p
Translation of: Plenniki
ISBN 0-370-30487-x : £5.95 : CIP entry B82-24449

Solzhenitsyn, Aleksandr. Victory celebrations. — London : Bodley Head, Oct.1982. — [80]p
Translation of: Pir pobeditelej
ISBN 0-370-30486-1 : £4.95 : CIP entry B82-24450

891.73′01′08[FS] — Short stories in Russian, *1917-1970 — Anthologies — English texts*

Vasili and Vasilissa : Siberian stories / [compiled by Nina Kupreyanova]. — Moscow : Progress ; [London] : Central [distributor], c1981. — 388p ; 21cm
Translated from the Russian
ISBN 0-7147-1735-5 : £3.50 B82-29838

891.73′01′088924[FS] — Short stories in Russian. Jewish writers, *1917-1980 — Anthologies — English texts*

Native land : a selection of Soviet Jewish writers / [compiled by Chaim Beider]. — Moscow : Progress ; [London] : distributed by Central Books, c1980. — 304p : ports ; 18cm
Translation of: Rodnaia zemlia
ISBN 0-7147-1689-8 : £2.25 B82-19613

891.73′01′09 — Short stories in Russian, *1800-1917 — Critical studies*

O′Toole, L. M.. Structure, style and interpretation in the Russian short story / L. Michael O′Toole. — New Haven ; London : Yale University Press, 1982. — viii,272p ; 24cm
English and Russian text. — Bibliography: p265-267. — Includes index
ISBN 0-300-02730-3 : Unpriced : CIP rev. B82-13489

891.73′0876′08[FS] — Science fiction stories in Russian, *1945- — Anthologies — English texts*

World′s spring / edited by Vladimir Gakov ; translated from the Russian by Roger DeGaris. — New York : Macmillan ; London : Collier Macmillan, c1981. — xiv,297p ; 22cm. — (Macmillan′s best of Soviet science fiction)
ISBN 0-02-542180-8 : £8.95 B82-25465

891.73′3 — Fiction in Russian, *1800-1917 — Texts*

Gor′kiĭ, Maksim. Dvadtsat′ shest′ i odna / Maksim Gor′kiĭ = Twenty six men and a girl / Maxim Gorky ; edited by B. Faden. — Letchworth : Prideaux, 1982. — 45p ; 21cm. — (Russian texts for students ; no.12)
£0.90 (pbk) B82-21604

Tolstoĭ, L. N.. Childhood / L.N. Tolstoy = Detstvo / L.N. Tolstoĭ ; edited by B. Faden ; resunke K. Klemenmeloĭ. — Letchworth : Bradda, 1975 (1982 [printing]). — 120p : ill ; 21cm. — (Library of Russian classics)
Russian text, English notes
£2.40 (pbk) B82-32747

Tolstoĭ, L. N.. Kavkazskiĭ plennik / L.N. Tolstoĭ = A captive in the Caucasus / L.N. Tolstoy ; edited by B. Faden. — Letchworth : Prideaux, 1982. — 54p ; 20cm. — (Russian texts for students ; 14)
Russian title transliterated
£0.90 (pbk) B82-31684

891.73′3 — Fiction in Russian. Dostoevskiĭ, F. M. — *Critical studies*

F.M. Dostoevsky (1821-1881) : a centenary collection / edited by Leon Burnett. — [Colchester] : [University of Essex], 1981. — vi,134p ; 21cm
ISBN 0-9507939-0-6 (pbk) : £3.00 B82-25459

Jackson, Robert Louis. The art of Dostoevsky / deliriums and nocturnes ; Robert Louis Jackson. — Princeton ; Guildford : Princeton University Press, c1981. — xii,380p ; 23cm
Includes index
ISBN 0-691-06484-9 : £17.60 B82-12508

Jones, John. Dostoevsky. — Oxford : Clarendon Press, Feb.1983. — [256]p
ISBN 0-19-812645-x : £12.50 : CIP entry B82-36326

891.73′3 — Fiction in Russian. Dostoevskiĭ, F. M. — *Critical studies — Russian texts*

F.M. Dostoevskiĭ : 1881-100-1981 / Sergeĭ Askol′dov ... [et al.]. — London (40 Elsham Rd, W14 8HB) : Overseas Publications Interchange, 1981. — 188p : 1port ; 22cm
Russian text. — Added t.p. in English
ISBN 0-903868-36-9 (pbk) : £4.50 B82-08172

891.73′3 — Fiction in Russian. Dostoevskiĭ, Fedor Mikhaĭlovich. Idiot — *Critical studies*

Miller, Robin Feuer. Dostoevsky and The Idiot : author, narrator, and reader / Robin Feuer Miller. — Cambridge, Mass. ; London : Harvard University Press, 1981. — ix,296p ; 24cm
Includes index
ISBN 0-674-21490-0 : £14.00 B82-03873

891.73′3 — Fiction in Russian. Tolstaia, S. A. — *Biographies*

Edwards, Anne, *1927-*. Sonya : the life of Countess Tolstoy. — London : Hodder & Stoughton, Sept.1982. — [528]p. — (Coronet books)
Originally published: 1981
ISBN 0-340-28447-1 (pbk) : £2.95 : CIP entry B82-18789

891.73′3 — Fiction in Russian. Tolstoĭ, L. N. — *Critical studies*

Gifford, Henry. Tolstoy / Henry Gifford. — Oxford : Oxford University Press, 1982. — 88p ; 19cm. — (Past masters)
Bibliography: p84-85. — Includes index
ISBN 0-19-287545-0 (cased) : Unpriced : CIP rev.
ISBN 0-19-287544-2 (pbk) : £1.25 B82-00881

891.73′3 — Fiction in Russian. Turgenev, I. S. — *Correspondence, diaries, etc.*

Turgenev, I. S.. Turgenev′s letters. — London : Athlone Press, July 1982. — [320]p
Translated from the Russian
ISBN 0-485-11210-8 : £16.00 : CIP entry B82-25903

891.73'3 — Fiction in Russian. Turgenev, I. S.. Interpersonal relationships with Gissing, George

Coustillas, Pierre. George Gissing and Ivan Turgenev : including two letters from Turgenev / Pierre Coustillas. — London : Enitharmon, 1981. — 12p ; 22cm. — (Enitharmon Press Gissing series)
Limited ed. of 250 copies
ISBN 0-905289-77-3 (corrected : pbk) : £3.75
Primary classification 823'.8 B82-26095

891.73'3[F] — Fiction in Russian, *1800-1917 — English texts*

Aksakov, Sergeĭ. A Russian gentleman / Sergei Aksakov ; translated by J.D. Duff ; with an introduction by Edward Crankshaw. — Oxford : Oxford University Press, 1982. — xviii,208p ; 19cm. — (The world's classics)
Translation of: Semeinaia khronika
ISBN 0-19-281573-3 (pbk) : £2.50 : CIP rev. B82-10436

Chekhov, A. P.. The kiss : and other stories / Chekhov ; translated with an introduction by Ronald Wilks. — Harmondsworth : Penguin, 1982. — 216p ; 19cm. — (The Penguin classics)
Translation from the Russian
ISBN 0-14-044336-3 (pbk) : £1.95 B82-32581

Chernyshevskiĭ, N. G.. What is to be done?. — London : Virago, Nov.1982. — [320]p. — (Virago Russian classics)
ISBN 0-86068-336-2 (pbk) : £3.95 : CIP entry B82-26350

Dostoevskiĭ, F. M.. The brothers Karamazov / Fyodor Dostoyevsky ; translated and with an introduction by David Magarshack. — Harmondsworth : Penguin, 1958 (1982 [printing]). — xxvi,913p ; 18cm. — (Penguin classics)
Translation of: Brat'ia Karamazovy
ISBN 0-14-044416-5 (pbk) : £2.95 B82-29820

Dostoevskiĭ, F. M.. Crime and punishment / Fedor Dostoevsky ; translated by Jessie Coulson ; with an introduction by John Jones. — Oxford : Oxford University Press, 1953 (1980 [printing]). — xviii,530p : plan ; 19cm
Translation of: Prestuplenie i nakazanie
ISBN 0-19-251028-2 (cased) : £5.00 : CIP rev.
ISBN 0-19-281549-0 (pbk) : £1.75 B80-18937

Dostoevskiĭ, F. M.. The Karamazov brothers : a novel in four parts with an epilogue / Fyodor Dostoyevsky ; translated by Julius Katzer. — Moscow : Progress ; London : distributed by Central, c1980. — 2v.(493,680p) : ill,1port ; 21cm. — (Progress Russian classics series)
Translation of: Brat'ia Karamazovy
ISBN 0-7147-1753-3 : £7.50 B82-36533

Dostoevskiĭ, F. M.. Memoirs from the house of the dead. — Oxford : Oxford University Press, Feb.1983. — [384]p. — (The World's classics)
ISBN 0-19-281613-6 (pbk) : £1.95 : CIP entry B82-36593

Dostoevskiĭ, F. M.. Notes from underground / by Fyodor Dostoevsky ; translated by Mirra Ginsburg ; with an introduction by Donald Fanger. — Toronto ; London : Bantam, 1974 (1981 [printing]). — xxvi,158p ; 17cm. — (A Bantam classic)
ISBN 0-553-21043-2 (pbk) : £0.85 B82-24178

Gor'kiĭ, Maksim. Maxim Gorky : collected works in ten volumes. — Moscow : Progress ; [London] : distributed by Central Books
Vol.7: My apprenticeship / [translated by Margaret Wettlin] ; My universities / [translated by Helen Altschuler]. — c1981. — 548p ; 18cm
Translation from the Russian
ISBN 0-7147-1671-5 : £3.50 B82-06891

Gor'kiĭ, Maksim. Maxim Gorky : collected works in ten volumes / [translated from the Russian by Helen Altschuler]. — Moscow : Progress ; [London] : distributed by Central Books
Vol.8: The Artamonovs. — c1981. — 335p ; 18cm
£3.50 B82-05899

Gor'kiĭ, Maksim. Twenty six men and a girl / Maxim Gorky ; translated by B. Faden. — Letchworth (P.O. Box 1, Letchworth, Herts, SG6 1DN) : Prideaux, 1982. — 32p ; 20cm. — (English translations of Russian classics ; no.1)
Translated from the Russian
£0.90 (pbk) B82-18284

Tolstoĭ, L. N.. Childhood, adolescence, youth / Lev Tolstoy ; translated by Fainna Solasko. — Moscow : Progress ; [London] : distributed by Central, c1981. — 456p : ill,ports ; 21cm
Translation of: Detstvo, otrochestvo, iunost'
ISBN 0-7147-1759-2 : £5.50 B82-36532

Tolstoĭ, L. N.. The death of Ivan Ilyich / by Leo Tolstoy ; translated by Lynn Solotaroff. — Toronto ; London : Bantam, 1981. — 134p ; 18cm. — (A Bantam classic)
Translation from the Russian
ISBN 0-553-21035-1 (pbk) : £0.85 B82-19385

Tolstoĭ, L. N.. War and peace / L.N. Tolstoy ; translated and with an introduction by Rosemary Edmonds. — [1st ed.], reprinted with revisions. — Harmondsworth : Penguin, 1978 (1982 [printing]). — xix,1443p ; 19cm. — (Penguin classics)
Translation of: Voĭna i mir
ISBN 0-14-044417-3 (pbk) : £3.95 B82-29955

Turgenev, I. S.. Fathers and sons / by Ivan Turgenev ; translated by Barbara Makanowitzky ; with an introduction by Alexandra Tolstoy. — Toronto ; London : Bantam, 1959 (1981 [printing]). — x,208p ; 18cm. — (A Bantam classic)
Translation of: Ottsy i deti
ISBN 0-553-21036-x (pbk) : £0.85 B82-12582

Turgenev, I. S.. First love; and, A fire at sea. — London : Hogarth Press, Oct.1982. — [160]p
ISBN 0-7012-0545-8 : £5.95 : CIP entry B82-23207

891.73'3[F] — Short stories in Russian, *1800-1917 — English texts*

Chekhov, A. P.. Chekhov : the early stories 1883-88 / chosen and translated by Patrick Miles & Harvey Pitcher. — London : Murray, 1982. — 203p ; 23cm
Translations from the Russian
ISBN 0-7195-3936-6 : £9.50 : CIP rev. B82-04883

Tolstoĭ, L. N.. [Short stories. English. Selections]. The raid and other stories / Leo Tolstoy ; translated by Louise and Aylmer Maude ; with an introduction by P.N. Furbank. — Oxford : Oxford University Press, 1982. — xiv,286p ; 19cm. — (The World's classics)
Translation from the Russian
ISBN 0-19-281584-9 (pbk) : £2.50 : CIP rev. B81-35766

891.73'3'08 — Fiction in Russian, *1800-1917 — Anthologies — English texts*

Russian authors. — Leicester : Windward, c1981. — 961p ; 22cm
Translated from the Russian
ISBN 0-7112-0215-x : £4.95 B82-06001

891.73'42 — Fiction in Russian. Platonov, Andreĭ. Influence of Fedorov, N. F.

Teskey, Ayleen. Platonov and Fyodorov : the influence of Christian philosophy on a Soviet writer / Ayleen Teskey. — [Amersham] : Avebury, 1982. — 182p ; 22cm. — (Avebury monographs on Russian literature)
Bibliography: p155-182
ISBN 0-86127-214-5 (pbk) : Unpriced : CIP rev. B81-31812

891.73'42 — Fiction in Russian. Sholokhov, Mikhail — *Critical studies*

Ermolaev, Herman. Mikhail Sholokhov and his art / Herman Ermolaev. — Princeton ; Guildford : Princeton University Press, c1982. — xvi,375p,[4]p of plates : ill,2maps,ports ; 24cm
Bibliography: p351-363. — Includes index
ISBN 0-691-07634-0 : £20.10 B82-21004

891.73'42 — Fiction in Russian. Zoschenko, Mikhail — *Critical studies*

Murphy, A. B.. Mikhail Zoshchenko : a literary profile / A.B. Murphy. — Oxford : Meeuws, 1981. — 163p : 1port ; 21cm. — (Russian literary profiles ; 8)
Bibliography: p159-163
ISBN 0-902672-44-4 (pbk) : Unpriced B82-03520

891.73'42 — Short stories in Russian, *1917-1945 — Texts*

Babel', I.. Chetyre rasskaza = Four stories / I. Babel' ; with an introduction, notes and vocabulary by A.B. Murphy. — Letchworth : Prideaux, 1981, c1965. — 116p : ill ; 20cm. — (Russian texts for students ; no.6)
Russian text, introduction and notes in English. — Originally published: Letchworth : Bradda, 1965
£1.50 (pbk) B82-10176

Pasternak, Boris. Zhenia's childhood : and other stories / Boris Pasternak. — London : Allison & Busby, 1982. — 115p ; 23cm
Translated from the Russian
ISBN 0-85031-466-6 (cased) : £6.95 : CIP rev.
ISBN 0-85031-467-4 (pbk) : Unpriced B82-11129

891.73'42[F] — Fiction in Russian, *1917-1945 — English texts*

Bulgakov, Mikhail. The Master and Margarita / Mikhail Bulgakov ; translated from the Russian by Michael Glenny. — London : Fontana, 1969, c1967 (1981 [printing]). — 415p ; 18cm
Translated from the Russian. — Originally published: London : Collins, 1967
ISBN 0-00-616454-4 (pbk) : £1.95 B82-03007

Gladkov, F.. Cement : a novel / Fyodor Gladkov ; [translated from the Russian by Liv Tadge]. — Moscow : Progress Publishers ; [London] : distributed by Central Books, c1981. — 405p ; 17cm. — (The Working class in Soviet literature)
Translation of: TSement
Unpriced (pbk) B82-36805

Nabokov, Vladimir. Laughter in the dark / Vladimir Nabokov. — Harmondsworth : Penguin, 1963, c1961 (1982 [printing]). — 186p ; 20cm
ISBN 0-14-001932-4 (pbk) : £2.25 B82-40508

Pasternak, Boris. The last summer / Boris Pasternak ; translated by George Reavey ; with an introducution by Lydia Slater. — Harmondsworth : Penguin, 1960, c1959 (1982 [printing]). — 92p ; 20cm. — (Penguin modern classics)
Translation of: Povest'. — Originally published: London : Owen, 1959
ISBN 0-14-001547-7 (pbk) : £1.75 B82-32493

891.73'42[J] — Children's short stories in Russian, *1917-1945 — English texts*

Grin, Aleksandr. Crimson sails / Alexander Grin. — Moscow : Progress ; [London] : Central [distributor], c1978. — 106p : ill ; 23cm
Translation of: Adye parusa. — Ill. on lining papers
ISBN 0-7147-1729-0 : £2.50 B82-28210

Nosov, Nikolaĭ. Eleven stories for boys and girls : translated from the Russian / Nikolai Nosov ; drawings by Georgi Yudin. — Moscow : Progress ; [London] : distributed by Central, c1981. — 184p : ill(some col.) ; 26cm
Translation of: Veselye druz'ia. — Ill on lining papers
ISBN 0-7147-1723-1 : £2.95 B82-17399

Perovskaia, O.. Kids and cubs / O. Perovskaya ; [drawings by V. Vatagin and I. Godin] ; [translated from the Russian by Fainna Glagoleva]. — Moscow : Progress ; [London] : Central [distributor], 1966 (1981 printing). — 261p : ill ; 23cm
Translation of: Rebiata i zveriata
ISBN 0-7147-1695-2 : £2.25 B82-28206

891.73'42'09353 — Fiction in Russian, *1917-.* **Special subjects: Man. Irrationality** — *Critical studies*

Edwards, T. R. N.. Three Russian writers and the irrational : Zamyatin, Pil'nyak and Bulgakov / T.R.N. Edwards. — Cambridge : Cambridge University Press, 1982. — xi,220p ; 23cm
Bibliography: p206-212. — Includes index
ISBN 0-521-23670-3 : £22.50 : CIP rev. B82-02449

891.73'44 — Fiction in Russian, *1945-* — *Texts*

Kandel', Feliks. Pervyĭ ėtazh : (roman) / Feliks Kandel' ; posleslovie N. Gorbanevskiĭ. — London : Overseas Publications Interchange, c1982. — 223p ; 19cm
ISBN 0-903868-41-5 (pbk) : Unpriced B82-36353

891.73'44 — Fiction in Russian. Solzhenit͡syn, Aleksandr — *Critical studies*

Marion, Corinne. Who's afraid of Solzhenitsyn?. — London : Wildwood House, June 1982. — [200]p
Translation of: Qui a peur de Soljenitsyne?
ISBN 0-7045-0468-5 (pbk) : £4.95 : CIP entry B82-09584

891.73'44[F] — Fiction in Russian, *1945-* — *English texts*

Erofeev, Venedikt. Moscow circles / Benedict Erofeev ; translated from the Russian by J.R. Dorrell. — London : Writers and Readers Publishing Cooperative, 1981. — 188p ; 22cm
ISBN 0-906495-26-1 (cased) : £6.95
ISBN 0-906495-74-1 (pbk) : Unpriced B82-32968

Kochetov, Vsevolod. The Zhurbins / Vsevolod Kochetov ; [translated from the Russian by Robert Daglish] ; [illustrated by Igor Pehelko]. — Moscow : Progess, 1953 (1980 printing) ; [London] : Distributed by Central Books. — 461p,[11]leaves of plates : ill ; 21cm
Translation of: Zhurbiny
ISBN 0-7147-1643-x : £4.50 B82-02096

Krotkov, I͡Uriĭ. The Nobel prize : a novel / by Yuri Krotkov ; translated from the Russian by Linda Aldwinckle. — London : Hamilton, 1980. — 249p ; 23cm
ISBN 0-241-10240-5 : £5.95 : CIP rev. B80-09502

Krotkov, Yuri. The Nobel Prize / Yuri Krotkov ; translated from the Russian by Linda Aldwinckle. — London : Sphere, 1982, c1980. — 310p ; 18cm
Originally published: London : Hamilton, 1980
ISBN 0-7221-5345-7 (pbk) : £1.95 B82-09397

Rybakov, Anatoliĭ. Heavy sand / Anatoli Rybakov ; translated from the Russian by Harold Shukman. — Harmondsworth : Penguin, 1982, c1981. — 380p ; 20cm
Translation of: T͡i͡azhelyĭ pesok. — Originally published: London : Allen Lane, 1981
ISBN 0-14-005535-5 (pbk) : £2.95 B82-32237

Voronov, Nikolaĭ. The crest of the summer / Nikolai Voronov ; [translated from the Russian by Yuri Nemetsky and Sergei Syrovatkin. — Moscow : Progress, c1976 ; [London] : Distributed by Central Books. — 359p ; 21cm
Translation of: Makushka leta
ISBN 0-7147-1641-3 : Unpriced B82-02095

891.73'44[F] — Short stories in Russian, *1945-* — *English texts*

Mikhanovskiĭ, V.. The doubles / fantastic stories ; Vladimir Mikhanovsky. — Moscow : Progress ; [London] : distributed by Central Books, 1981. — 511p ; 18cm
Translation of the Russian. — Contents: The doubles — The land of Inforia — Ends and means — The violet
£3.50 B82-05892

891.73'44[J] — Children's stories in Russian, *1945-* — *English texts*

Dat͡skevich, V.. The green island / Victor Datskevich ; translated from the Russian by Jan Butler. — Moscow : Progress ; [London] : Central [distributor], 1980. — 56p : col.ill ; 29cm
Translation of: Zelenyĭ ostrov
ISBN 0-7147-1664-2 : £2.25 B82-28207

Dombrovskiĭ, A.. In the white stone's shadow / A. Dombrovsky ; [translated from the Russian by Doris Bradbury]. — Moscow : Progress, c1979 ; [London] : Distributed by Central Books. — 70p : ill ; 23cm
Translation of: Golubai͡a ten' velogo kamni͡a. — Ill on lining papers
ISBN 0-7147-1667-7 : £1.95 B82-02097

Dragunskiĭ, V.. The adventures of Dennis / Victor Dragunsky ; [translated from the Russian by Fainna Glagoleva]. — Moscow : Progress ; [London] : distributed by Central Books, c1981. — 236p : col.ill ; 22cm
Translation of: Deniskiny rasskazy
£2.95 B82-05895

Kuprin, A.. The elephant / A. Kuprin ; drawings by D. Borovsky ; translated from the Russian by Fainna Solasko. — Moscow : Progress ; [London] : Central [distributor], c1975 (1981 printing). — 20p : col.ill ; 28cm
Translation of: Slon. — Ill on inside covers
ISBN 0-7147-1724-x (pbk) : £0.55 B82-28209

Nosov, Nikolaĭ. The adventures of Dunno and his friends / Nikolai Nosov ; illustrated by A. Laptev ; [translated from the Russian by Margaret Wettlin]. — Moscow : Progress, [1980?] ; [London] : Distributed by Central Books. — 186p : ill(some col.) ; 27cm
Translation from the Russian
ISBN 0-7147-1642-1 : £3.50 B82-02098

Sviridov, A.. Champions in the making / Alexander Sviridov ; [translated from the Russian by Jan Butler]. — Moscow : Progress ; [London] : Central [distributor], c1980. — 67p : col.ill ; 29cm
Translation of: Put' v chempiony
ISBN 0-7147-1665-0 (pbk) : £1.00 B82-28208

891.77'4'08 — Humour in Russian, *1917-* — *Anthologies — English texts*

Russia dies laughing : jokes from Soviet Russia / compiled and classified by A.N., R.N., and K.S. ; edited and introduced by Z. Dolgopolova ; illustrated by JAK. — London : Deutsch, 1982. — 125p : ill ; 21cm
ISBN 0-233-97402-4 : £4.95 : CIP rev. B82-00308

891.78'209 — Russian literature. Karamzin, N. M. — *Critical studies — Russian texts*

Pokrovskiĭ, V.. Nikolai Mikhailovich Karamzin : ego zhizn i sochineniia : sbornik istoriko-literaturnykh statei / sostavil V.I. Pokrovskii. — 3-e, izdanie, dopolnennoe. — Oxford : Meeuws, 1981. — 171p ; 24cm
Facsim of: 3rd ed., supplement. Moscow : V. Spiridonova i A. Milhaĭlova, 1912
ISBN 0-902672-47-9 (pbk) : Unpriced B82-14765

891.78'308 — Prose in Russian. Belyĭ, Andreĭ — *Critical studies*

Steinberg, Ada. Word and music in the novels of Andrey Bely. — Cambridge : Cambridge University Press, Oct.1982. — [324]p. — (Cambridge studies in Russian literature)
ISBN 0-521-23731-9 : £29.50 : CIP entry B82-29382

891.78'309 — Russian literature, *1800-1917* — *English texts*

Gogol', N. V.. Nikolai Gogol : a selection / [translated from the Russian by Christopher English] ; [illustrations compiled by Nina Glazunova]. — Moscow : Progress ; [London] : Distributed by Central, c1980
1. — 396p : ill(some col.),facsims,ports(some col.) ; 21cm
£4.50 B82-21635

Shevchenko, Taras. Taras Shevchenko : selected works : poetry and prose. — Moscow : Progress ; [London] : Central [distributor], c1979. — 533p : ill(some col.),facsims,ports (some col.) ; 21cm. — (Classics series)
Translated from the Ukrainian
ISBN 0-7147-1730-4 : £5.50 B82-28205

891.78'309 — Russian literature. Gogol', N. V. — *Critical studies*

Peace, Richard. The enigma of Gogol : an examination of the writings of N.V. Gogol and their place in the Russian literary tradition / Richard Peace. — Cambridge : Cambridge University Press, 1981. — viii,344p : 1port ; 22cm. — (Cambridge studies in Russian literature)
Includes index
ISBN 0-521-23824-2 : £22.50 : CIP rev. B82-00234

891.78'309 — Russian literature. Leont'ev, K. N. — *Correspondence, diaries, etc. — Russian texts*

Leont'ev, K. N.. Pis'ma k Vasilii͡u Rozanovu / vstuplenie, kommentarii i posleslovie V.V. Rozanova ; vstupitel'nai͡a stat'i͡a B.A. Filippova. — London : Nina Karsov, 1981. — 136p : port ; 19cm
Originally published under the title: Iz perepiski K.N. Leont'eva in Russkiĭ Vestnik, 1903, no.4-6
ISBN 0-9502324-9-1 (cased) : £7.50 : CIP rev.
ISBN 0-907652-00-x (pbk) : £5.40 B81-20479

891.78'4209 — Russian literature, *1917-1945* — *English texts*

Mikhalkov, Sergeĭ. A choice for children / Sergei Mikhalkov. — Moscow : Progress ; [London] : distributed by Central, c1980. — 189p : col.ill ; 26cm
Translation of: Izbrannoe. — Ill on lining papers
ISBN 0-7147-1714-2 : £2.95 B82-19475

891.78'4408 — Prose in Russian, *1945-* — *Texts*

Gal'perin, I͡Uriĭ. Most cherez letu : (praktika prozy) / I͡Uriĭ Gal'perin. — London : Overseas Publications Interchange, 1982. — 111p ; 19cm
ISBN 0-903868-40-7 (pbk) : £4.80 B82-29291

891.8 — SLAVIC LITERATURES

891.8'113 — Poetry in Bulgarian, *1900-* — *English texts*

Bozhilov, Bozhidar. American pages / Bozhidar Bozhilov ; translated by Cornelia Bozhilova. — Chicago ; London : Ohio University Press, 1980. — 27p : ill ; 24cm. — (International poetry series ; v.5)
Translation of: Amerikanska tetradka
ISBN 0-8214-0596-9 (cased) : Unpriced
ISBN 0-8214-0597-7 (pbk) : £4.90 B82-13957

Levchev, Li͡ubomir. The mysterious man / Lyubomir Levchev ; translated by Vladimir Phillipov. — Chicago ; London : Ohio University Press, 1980. — 30p ; 24cm. — (International poetry series ; v.4)
Translated from the Bulgarian
ISBN 0-8214-0594-2 (cased) : Unpriced
ISBN 0-8214-0595-0 (pbk) : £4.90 B82-13958

891.82 — SERBO-CROATIAN LITERATURE

891.8'215 — Poetry in Serbo-Croatian, *1900-* — *English texts*

Lalić, Ivan V.. The works of love / selected poems of Ivan V. Lalić ; translated by Francis R. Jones. — London : Anvil, 1981. — 78p ; 22cm
Translated from the Serbo-Croatian
ISBN 0-85646-078-8 (pbk) : £3.50 B82-10168

891.85 — POLISH LITERATURE

891.8'5'09007 — Polish literature, *1919-* — *Critical studies — Polish texts*

Pamiętnik literacki / [komitet redakcyjny Józef Garliński et al.]. — Londyn ([9 Charleville Rd., W14 9JL]) : Związek Pisarzy Polskich na Obczyźnie
Tom 4. — 1981. — 171p : 1port ; 21cm
Bibliography: p122-151. — Includes index
Unpriced (pbk) B82-06371

Pamiętnik literacki / [komitet redakcyjny Józef Garliński ... et al.]. — Londyn [London] (c/o Polish Cultural Foundation, 9, Charleville Rd., W14 9JL) : Zwi azek Pisarzy Polskich na Obczyźnie
Tom 4. — 1981. — 171p : 1port ; 21cm
Includes bibliographies and index
Unpriced (pbk) B82-08211

891.8'517 — Poetry in Polish, *1919- — English texts*

John Paul II, *Pope.* Collected poems / Karol Wojtyla ; translated with an introductory essay and notes by Jerzy Peterkiewicz. — London : Hutchinson, 1982. — 191p ; 22cm
Translation from the Polish
ISBN 0-09-149361-7 (pbk) : £4.95 : CIP rev.
B82-09278

Różewicz, Tadeusz. Conversation with the prince : and other poems / Tadeusz Różewicz ; introduced and translated by Adam Czerniawski. — London : Anvil Press Poetry, 1982. — 206p ; 22cm
Translations from the Polish. — Includes index
ISBN 0-85646-079-6 (pbk) : £4.95 B82-33996

891.8'517 — Poetry in Polish, *1919- — Texts*

Bednarczyk, Czesław. Z religijnych zamyśleń / Czesław Bednarczyk. — Londyn ([146 Bridge Arch, Sutton Walk, SE1]) : Oficyna Poetów i Malarzy, 1982. — 30p ; 23cm
Unpriced (pbk) B82-24301

Bednarczyk, Czesław. Z religijnych zamyśleń / Czesław Bednarczyk. — Londyn : Oficyna Poetów i Malarzy, 1982. — 30p ; 23cm
Unpriced (pbk) B82-36893

Cybulski, Kazimierz. Trzy drogi : wybór wierszy / Kazimierz Cybulski. — Londyn : Oficyna Poetów i Malarzy, 1982. — 60p,[1]leaf of plates : ports ; 22cm
Unpriced (pbk) B82-28358

Hebda, Jerzy Romuald. Temat i wariacje : wiersze wybrane 1978-1981 / Jerzy Romuald Hebda. — Londyn : OPiM, 1982. — 56p ; 22cm
Includes index
Unpriced (pbk) B82-18296

891.8'517 — Poetry in Polish. Janta, Aleksander — *Biographies — Polish texts*

Janta : człowiek i pisarz / praca zbiorowa pod redakcj a Jerzego R. Krzyżanowskiego. — Londyn : Polska Fundacja Kulturalma, 1982. — 363p : facsims,ports ; 22cm
Bibliography: p348-357. — Includes index
Unpriced (pbk) B82-40121

891.8'5'17 — Poetry in Polish. Milosz, Czeslaw - *Biographies*

Milosz, Czesław. Native realm. — Manchester : Carcanet Press, May 1981. — [300]p
Translation of the Polish
ISBN 0-85635-378-7 : £6.95 : CIP entry
B81-07918

891.8'527 — Drama in Polish, *1919- — English texts*

Rozewicz, Tadeusz. Mariage blanc ; and, The hunger artist departs. — London : Boyars, Sept.1982. — [160]p
ISBN 0-7145-2775-0 (cased) : £6.95 : CIP entry
ISBN 0-7145-2776-9 (pbk) : £3.95 B82-19804

891.8'527 — Drama in Polish. Witkiewicz, Stanisław Ignacy — *Biographies*

Gerould, Daniel. Witkacy : Stanisław Ignacy Witkiewicz as an imaginative writer / by Daniel Gerould. — Seattle ; London : University of Washington Press, c1981. — xviii,362p,[22]p of plates : ill,ports ; 25cm
Ill on lining papers. — Bibliography: p343-350. — Includes index
ISBN 0-295-95714-x : £17.50 B82-19488

891.8'537 — Fiction in Polish, *1919- — Russian texts*

Woroszylski, Wiktor. Sny pod snegom : povest'o zhizni Mikhaila Sattykova-Shchedrina / Viktor Voroshil'skiĭ ; anonimnyĭ perevod ... — London : Overseas Publications Exchange, 1980. — 175p ; 19cm
Translation of: Sny pod śniegiem. — Title on added t.p.: Dreams under the snow. — Originally circulated in samizdat, Moscow, 1977
ISBN 0-903868-27-x (pbk) : £5.00 B82-03220

891.8'537 — Fiction in Polish, *1919- — Texts*

Andrzejewski, Jerzy. Miazga / Jerzy Andrzejewski. — Londyn [London] : Polonia Book Fund, c1980. — 407p ; 22cm
Polish text
ISBN 0-902352-18-0 (pbk) : £10.00
B82-09318

Gołuszko, Wiktor. Ulisses / Wiktor Gołuszko. — Londyn : Oficyna Poetów i Malarzy, 1981. — 63p ; 22cm
Unpriced (pbk) B82-02802

Gonczyński, Franciszek. Harsha / Franciszek Gonczyński. — Londyn : OPiM, 1982. — 367p ; 22cm
Unpriced (pbk) B82-14900

Kessler-Pawlak, Ada. Kariera Marianny Lind / Ada Kessler-Pawlak. — Londyn : Poets and Painters Press, 1982. — 182p ; 22cm
Unpriced (pbk) B82-18297

Mackiewicz, Józef. Kontra. — London (28 Lanacre Ave., NW9 5FN) : Kontra, Jan.1983. — [272]p
Translation of: Kontra. — Originally published: Paris : Institute Litteraire, 1957
ISBN 0-907652-04-2 : £7.95 : CIP entry
B82-34097

Mackiewicz, Józef. Lewa wolna / Józef Mackiewicz. — Londyn : Kontra, 1981. — 458p ; 22cm
Originally published: Londyn : Polska Fundacja Kulturalna, 1965
ISBN 0-907652-02-6 (pbk) : £7.95 : CIP rev.
B81-28296

Poray-Biernacki, Janusz. Stan Łaski : kompozycje o zakochaniach i o miłości / Janusz Poray-Biernacki (Janusz Jasienczyk). — Londyn : Oficyna Poetów i Malarzy, 1982. — 208p ; 22cm
Unpriced (pbk) B82-37370

Rodziewiczówna, Maria. Anima vilis / Maria Rodziewiczówna. — Londyn : Veritas Foundation Publication Centre, 1982. — 164p ; 19cm. — (Biblioteka "Gazety niedzielnej")
Unpriced (pbk) B82-29187

Sobotkiewicz, Stanisław. Syn Człowieczy : opowieść biblijna / Stanisław Sobotkiewicz. — Londyn : Veritas Foundation Publication Centre, 1982. — 343p,[2]leaves of plates : 1map,1plan ; 19cm. — (Biblioteka Polska. Seria czerwona ; tom 95)
Unpriced (pbk) B82-29183

Tarnawski, Wit. Ucieczka : mini-powieści i opowiadania / Wit Tarnawski. — Wyd. 2 przejrzane i rozsz. — Londyn : Oficyna Poetów i Malarzy, 1982. — 259p,[2]leaves of plates : 2maps ; 22cm
Unpriced (pbk) B82-35455

891.8'537[F] — Fiction in Polish, *1919- — English texts*

Szechter, Szymon. A stolen biography. — London (28 Lanacre Ave., NW9 5FN) : Nina Karsov, Feb.1983. — [160]p
Translation of: Czas zatrzymany do wyjaśnienia
ISBN 0-907652-05-0 : £6.00 : CIP entry
B82-39293

891.8'537[F] — Short stories in Polish, *1919- — English texts*

Lem, Stanisław. Memoirs of a space traveller : further reminiscences of Ijon Tichy / Stanislaw Lem ; drawings by the author ; translated by Joel Stern and Maria Swiecicka-Ziemianek. — London : Secker & Warburg, 1982. — 152p ; 22cm
Translation of: Dzienniki gwiazdowe
ISBN 0-436-24412-8 : £6.95 : CIP rev.
B82-01974

891.8'547 — Essays in Polish, *1919- — Texts*

Chrzanowski, Feliks. W oczach felietonisty : historia i kultura : wspomnienia, reportaże, szkice / Feliks Chrzanowski. — Londyn : Nakładem Polskiej Funadcji Kulturalnej, [1981?]. — 208p : ill,ports ; 22cm
Unpriced (pbk) B82-03912

891.8'58707 — Satirical prose in Polish, *1919- — Texts*

Paporisz, Romuald. Milion piastrów : humoreski, satyry, parodie, plagiaty, imitacje, kapitalistyczne, groźne dla światowego obozu pokoju, socrealistyczne z prawicowolewicowymi odchyleniami od linii marksizmuleninizmu, niepozytywnie krytyczne oraz takie sobie / Romuald Paporisz. — Londyn (146 Bridge Arch, Sutton Walk, London SE1 8XU) : OPiM, 1982. — 252p ; 21cm
Includes index
Unpriced (pbk) B82-27901

891.86 — CZECH LITERATURE

891.8'635 — Fiction in Czech. Hašek, Jaroslav — *Critical studies*

Parrott, Cecil. Jaroslav Hašek : a study of Švejk and the short stories / Cecil Parrott. — Cambridge : Cambridge University Press, 1982. — xi,219p,[8]p of plates : ill,ports ; 23cm. — (Major European authors)
Bibliography: p214-215. — Includes index
ISBN 0-521-24352-1 : £18.00 : CIP rev.
B82-06864

891.8'635[F] — Fiction in Czech, *1900- — English texts*

Gruša, Jiří. The questionnaire. — London : Blond & Briggs, Aug.1982. — [257]p
Translated from the Czech
ISBN 0-85634-134-7 : £8.95 : CIP entry
B82-25907

891.8'635[F] — Fiction in Czech, *1900- - English texts*

Kohout, Pavel. The hangwoman. — London : Hutchinson, July 1981. — [272]p
Translation of : Die Henkerin
ISBN 0-09-139370-1 : £7.50 : CIP entry
B81-13423

891.8'635[F] — Fiction in Czech, *1900- — English texts*

Kundera, Milan. The book of laughter and forgetting / Milan Kundera ; translated from the Czech by Michael Henry Heim. — London : Faber, 1982, c1980. — 228p ; 23cm
Translation of: Kniha smíchu a zapomnění. — Originally published: New York : Penguin, 1981
ISBN 0-571-11830-5 : £7.95 : CIP rev.
B82-00238

Kundera, Milan. The joke. — London : Faber, Feb.1983. — [288]p
Translation of: Zert. — Originally published: New York : Harper & Row, 1982
ISBN 0-571-13019-4 : £8.95 : CIP entry
B82-38697

891.8'635[F] — Short stories in Czech, *1900- — English texts*

Hašek, Jaroslav. The red commissar : including further adventures of the good soldier Švejk and other stories / Jaroslav Hašek ; translated by Cecil Parrott ; original illustrations by Josef Lada. — London : Heinemann, c1981. — xvi,283p : ill ; 23cm
ISBN 0-434-31376-9 : £8.95 B82-04104

891.8'635[J] — Children's stories in Czech, *1900- — English texts*

Sopko, Eugen. Townsfolk and countryfolk. — London : Abelard-Schuman, Sept.1982. — [32]p
Translation of: Drei Städter auf dem Land
ISBN 0-200-72788-5 : £4.95 : CIP entry
B82-18964

891.9 — BALTIC AND OTHER INDO-EUROPEAN LITERATURES

891'.9 — Short stories in Baltic languages, *1900- — Anthologies — English texts*

The **Glade** with life-giving water : stories from the Soviet Baltic Republics. — [Moscow] : Progress ; [London] : distributed by Central, c1981. — 430p ; 20cm
Translation of: Polîana, gde zhivitel'naîa voda. — Ill on lining papers
ISBN 0-7147-1713-4 : £3.95 B82-19719

891.92 — LITHUANIAN LITERATURE

891′.9213 — Poetry in Lithuanian, *1900- — Texts*

Tenisonaitė, Zenta. Vienišì vėjo vaikai / Zenta Tenisonaitė. — London (2 Ladbroke Gdns. W11 2PT) : [Nida], 1979. — 47p ; 18cm
Unpriced (pbk) B82-19473

Timmermans, Felix. Adagio / Felix Timmermans. — London (2 Ladbroke Gdns. W11 2PT) : [Nida], [1979?]. — 45p ; 18cm
Translated from the Dutch
Unpriced (pbk) B82-19474

891.99 — ALBANIAN, ARMENIAN AND OTHER INDO-EUROPEAN LITERATURES

891′.99235[F] — Fiction in Armenian, *1850- — English texts*

Shahnour, Shahan. Retreat without song / Shahan Shahnour ; translated from the Armenian and edited by Mischa Kudian. — London : Mashpots, 1982. — 155p ; 21cm
ISBN 0-903039-10-9 (pbk) : £4.80 B82-37539

892.4 — HEBREW LITERATURE

892.4′35′09352927 — Fiction in Hebrew, *1885-1947.* **Special subjects: Arabs** *— Critical studies*

Domb, Risa. The Arab in Hebrew prose 1911-1948 / Risa Domb. — London : Vallentine, Mitchell, c1982. — xii,180p ; 23cm
Bibliography: p170-174. — Includes index
ISBN 0-85303-203-3 : £13.50 : CIP rev.
B81-27404

892.4′36[F] — Fiction in Hebrew, *1947- — English texts*

Appelfeld, Aron. The age of wonders. — London (45 Blackfriars Rd., SE1 8NZ) : Kudos & Godine, May 1982. — [224]p
Translated from the Hebrew
ISBN 0-906293-25-1 : £6.50 : CIP entry
B82-09312

892.7 — ARABIC LITERATURE

892′.7′0935203933 — Arabic literature, *to ca 1500.* **Special subjects: Berbers** *— Critical studies*

Norris, H. T.. The Berbers in Arabic literature. — London : Longman, Mar.1982. — [320]p. — (Arab background series)
ISBN 0-582-78303-8 : £14.95 : CIP entry
B82-00216

892′.71509 — Poetry in Arabic, *1800- — Critical studies*

'Abdul-Hai, Muhammad. Tradition and English and American influence in Arabic romantic poetry : a study in comparative literature / by Muhammad 'Abdul-Hai. — London : Published for the Middle East Centre, St Antony's College, Oxford [by] Ithaca, 1982. — 269p : 1facsim ; 23cm. — (St Antony's Middle East monographs ; no.12)
Bibliography: p252-266. — Includes index
ISBN 0-903729-70-9 : £12.50 B82-33286

892′.716′08 — Poetry in Arabic, *1945- — Anthologies — English texts*

The **Diwans** of the Darqawa / Shaykh Ibn al-Habib ... [et al]. — Norwich : Diwan, c1980. — 363p : 3ports ; 18cm
ISBN 0-906512-10-7 (pbk) : Unpriced
B82-28635

892′.72041′08962 — One-act plays in Arabic. Egyptian writers, *1945- — Anthologies — English texts*

Egyptian one-act plays / selected and translated from the Arabic by Denys Johnson-Davies. — London : Heinemann, 1981. — x,118p ; 19cm. — (African writers series ; 232)
Translated from the Arabic
ISBN 0-435-90232-6 (pbk) : £2.25
ISBN 0-435-99418-2 B82-02239

Egyptian one-act plays / selected and translated from the Arabic by Denys Johnson-Davies. — London : Heinemann, 1981. — x,118p ; 19cm. — (Arab authors ; 18)
Translated from the Arabic
ISBN 0-435-99418-2 (pbk) : £2.95
ISBN 0-435-90232-6 B82-02238

892′.726 — Drama in Arabic, *1945- — Texts*

'Abd al-Muṭṭalib, Sāmiyyah. Dīk muḥammar wa-ad'i li-Mu'ammar : masraḥiyyah min al-wāqi' / Sāmuyyah 'Abd al-Muṭṭalib. — London (P.O. Box 80, W4 3HE) : Al-Shark Al-Jadid, 1981. — [72]p : ill ; 21cm
Text in Arabic. — Cover title
Unpriced (pbk) B82-40992

892′.7334[F] — Fiction in Arabic. Spanish writers, *750-1258 — English texts*

Abū Bakr ibn al-Ṭufail, Abū Ja'far, *al-Ishbīlī*. The journey of the soul : the story of Hai bin Yaqzan / as told by Abu Bakr Muhammad bin Tufail ; a new translation by Riad Kocache. — London : Octagon, c1982. — x,62p ; 23cm
Translated from the Arabic
ISBN 0-900860-90-1 : £5.00 B82-29266

892′.736[F] — Fiction in Arabic. Egyptian writers, *1945- — English texts*

Hetata, Sherif. The eye with the iron lid. — London : Onyx Press, Sept.1982. — [409]p
ISBN 0-906383-16-1 : £8.95 : CIP entry
B82-33366

892′.78509 — Arabic literature. Lebanese writers. Gibran, Kahlil, *1883-1931 — Biographies*

Hawi, Khalil S.. Kahlil Gibran : his background, character and works / by Khalil S. Hawi. — [2nd ed.]. — [London] : [Third World Centre for Research & Publishing], [1982]. — 311p,[8] leaves of plates : ill,facsims,1port ; 25cm
Previous ed.: Arab Institute for Research and Publishing, 1972. — Bibliography: p285-297. — Includes index
ISBN 0-86199-011-0 : £8.00 B82-22263

893 — HAMITIC AND CHAD LITERATURES

893′.5 — Orally transmitted poetry in Somali. Political aspects *— Study examples: Hasan, Sayyid Maḥammad 'Abdille*

Samatar, Said S.. Oral poetry and Somali nationalism. — Cambridge : Cambridge University Press, June 1982. — [224]p. — (African studies series ; 32)
ISBN 0-521-23833-1 : £19.50 : CIP entry
B82-12005

893′.5[F] — Fiction in Somali *- English texts*

Cawl, Faarax. Ignorance is the enemy of love. — London : Zed, Sept.1981. — [144]p
Translation of: Aqoondarro waa u nacab jacayr
ISBN 0-905762-86-x : £4.50 : CIP entry
B81-20523

893′.723 — Fiction in Hausa *— Texts*

Fulani, Dan. Duniya budurwa wawa. — London : Hodder & Stoughton, Sept.1982. — [128]p
ISBN 0-340-28384-x (pbk) : £1.50 : CIP entry
B82-18788

894 — URAL-ALTAIC, PALAEOSIBERIAN, DRAVIDIAN LITERATURES

894′.3[FS] — Short stories in Kazakh, *1945- — Anthologies — English texts*

The **Voice** of the steppe : modern Kazakh short stories / [author of biographical notes and compiler I. Kramov]. — Moscow : Progress ; [London] : Central [distributor], c1981. — 478p ; 18cm
Translation of: Ispoved′ stepi
ISBN 0-7147-1704-5 : £3.95 B82-29458

894′.51113 — Poetry in Hungarian, *1900- — Texts*

Siklós, István. Csönd erdeje elött / Siklós István. — London : Szepsi Csombor Kör, 1981. — [28]p ; 21cm
ISBN 0-903565-09-9 (pbk) : £2.00 B82-05441

894′.51133 — Short stories in Hungarian, *1900- — Texts*

Ferdinandy, Georges. A mosoly albuma : elbeszélések / Ferdinandy György. — London : Szepsi Csombor Kör, 1982. — 207p ; 21cm. — (A Szepsi Csombor kör kiadványa)
ISBN 0-903565-08-0 (pbk) : Unpriced
B82-37971

894′.51133[F] — Fiction in Hungarian, *1900- — English texts*

Nyíri, János. Streets / János Nyiri ; translated from the Hungarian by Jim O'Malley and Tom Winnifrith. — London : Wildwood House, 1979. — 290p ; 23cm
ISBN 0-7045-3040-6 : £5.95 B82-04344

894′.51133[J] — Children's stories in Hungarian, *1900- — English texts*

Galdone, Paul. The amazing pig : an old Hungarian tale / retold and illustrated by Paul Galdone. — Tadworth : World's Work, c1981. — [32]p : col.ill ; 23cm. — (A World's Work children's book)
ISBN 0-437-42532-0 : £4.50 B82-32696

894′.54133[F] — Fiction in Finnish, *1900- — English texts*

Kurtén, Björn. Dance of the tiger : a novel of the Ice Age / Björn Kurtén ; introduction by Stephen Jay Gould. — [London] : Abacus, 1982, c1980. — xxv,255p ; 20cm
Translation of: Svarta tigern. — Originally published: New York : Pantheon, 1980
ISBN 0-349-12121-4 (pbk) : £1.95 B82-11206

894′.54133[J] — Children's stories in Finnish, *1900- — English texts*

Kunnas, Mauri. Santa Claus / Mauri Kunnas. — London : Methuen Childrens, 1982. — [48]p : col.ill ; 30cm
Translation of: Joulupukki
ISBN 0-416-25310-5 : Unpriced : CIP rev.
B82-19246

894.8 — DRAVIDIAN LITERATURES

894′.81111 — Poetry in Tamil, *to 1345 — English texts*

Nammāḻvār. [Tiruvāymoḻi. English. Selections]. Hymns for the drowning : poems for Viṣṇu / by Nammāḻvār ; translated from Tamil by A.K. Ramanujan. — Princeton ; Guildford : Princeton University Press, c1981. — xviii,176p ; 23cm. — (Princeton library of Asian translations)
Translation of: selections from Tiruvāymoḻi and Tiruvirattam. — Bibliography: p170-176
ISBN 0-691-06492-x (cased) : £13.10
ISBN 0-691-01385-3 (pbk) : Unpriced
B82-21006

894′.8271 — Orally transmitted epic poetry in Telugu *— English texts*

[Palnāti Vīrula Katha. *English***]**. The epic of Palnāḍu. — Oxford : Clarendon Press, Apr.1982. — [300]p
ISBN 0-19-815456-9 : £17.50 : CIP entry
B82-04285

895 — LITERATURES OF EAST AND SOUTHEAST ASIA

895 — Short stories in South-east Asian languages, *to 1981 — Critical studies*

The **Short** story in South East Asia : aspects of a genre / edited by Jeremy H.C.S. Davidson and Helen Cordell. — London : School of Oriental and African Studies, University of London, 1982. — xi,270p : ill ; 25cm. — (Collected papers in Oriental and African studies)
Bibliography: p229-264. — Includes index
ISBN 0-7286-0095-1 (pbk) : £5.00 : CIP rev.
B82-07609

895.1 — CHINESE LITERATURE

895.1′09′005 — Chinese literature, *1912- — Critical studies*

Zhong guo wen xue yishu gung zuo zhe dai biao da hui *(4th : Beijing)*. Chinese literature for the 1980s : the fourth Congress for Writers & Artists / edited with an introduction by Howard Goldblatt. — New York ; Sharpe ; London : European [[distributor]], c1982. — xviii,175p : ports ; 24cm
ISBN 0-87332-208-8 : £25.95 B82-39664

895.1′1′008 — Poetry in Chinese, *B.C. 900-A.D. 1645 — Anthologies — English texts*

Chinese poems. — London : Unwin Paperbacks, Nov.1982. — [192]p
Translated from the Chinese. — Originally published: 1946
ISBN 0-04-895027-0 (pbk) : £2.95 : CIP entry
B82-27827

895.1′12′08 — Poetry in Chinese, *B.C.200-A.D.700 — Anthologies — English texts*
[**Yu tai xin yong.** *English*]. New songs from a jade terrace : an anthology of early Chinese love poetry / translated with annotations and an introduction by Anne Birrell. — London : Allen & Unwin, 1982. — xxvii,374p : 1map ; 24cm
Translation of: Yu tai xin yong. — Originally compiled by Xu Ling
ISBN 0-04-895026-2 : Unpriced : CIP rev. B81-33898

895.1′1′308 — Poetry in Chinese, *700-1000 — Anthologies — English texts*
Zhao, Chongzuo[**Hua jian ji.** *English*]. Among the flowers / translation by Lois Fusek. — New York ; Guildford : Columbia University Press, 1982. — viii,232p : 1ill ; 24cm. — (Translations from the Oriental classics)
Translation from the Chinese. — Compiler: Chao Ch′ung-tso. — Bibliography: p217-219. — Includes index
ISBN 0-231-04986-2 : £18.10 B82-35078

895.1′35′09 — Popular fiction in Chinese, *1912- — Critical studies*
Link, E. Perry. Mandarin ducks and butterflies : popular fiction in early twentieth-century Chinese cities / E. Perry Link, Jr. — Berkeley ; London : University of California Press, c1981. — x,313p : ports ; 24cm
Bibliography: p290-300. — Includes index
ISBN 0-520-04111-9 : £19.50 B82-06996

895.6 — JAPANESE LITERATURE

895.6′09 — Japanese literature, *to 1902 — Critical studies*
Keene, Donald. Some Japanese portraits / Donald Keene ; illustrations by Motoichi Izawa. — Tokyo : Kodansha International ; Oxford : Phaidon [distributor], 1978. — 228p : ill ; 22cm
Bibliography: p209. — Includes index
ISBN 0-87011-298-8 : £9.00 B82-02058

895.6′11 — Poetry in Japanese. Ōtomo, Yakamochi *— Critical studies*
Doe, Paula. A warbler′s song in the dusk : the life and work of Otomo Yakamochi (718-785) / Paula Doe. — Berkeley ; London : University of California Press, c1982. — ix,260p : ill,maps ; 24cm
Bibliography: p241-246. — Includes index
ISBN 0-520-04346-4 : £21.50 B82-37065

895.6′11′08 — Poetry in Japanese, *to 1185 — Anthologies — Japanese-English parallel texts*
The **Little** treasury of one hundred people, one poem each / compiled by Fujiwara no Sadaie ; translated by Tom Galt. — New Jersey ; Guildford : Princeton University Press, c1982. — xii,106p ; 23cm. — (The Lockert library of poetry in translation)
Translation of: Ogura Hyaku nin isshu. — Includes transliterations. — Includes index
ISBN 0-691-06514-4 (cased) : £9.60
ISBN 0-691-01392-6 (pbk) : £5.60 B82-41001

895.6′13′08 — Haikai in Japanese, *1603-1868 — Anthologies — Romanised Japanese-English parallel texts*
The **Monkey′s** straw raincoat : and other poetry of the Bashō School / introduced and translated by Earl Miner and Hiroko Odagiri. — Princeton ; Guildford : Princeton University Press, c1981. — xviii,394p : maps,facsims,1port ; 22cm. — (Princeton library of Asian translations)
Translations from the Japanese. — Bibliography: p351-355. — Includes index
ISBN 0-691-06460-1 : £20.90 B82-07355

895.6′31 — Fiction in Japanese. Murasaki Shikibu *— Correspondence, diaries, etc.*
Murasaki Shikibu. [Murasaki Shikibu nikki. English]. Murasaki Shikibu : her diary and poetic memoirs : a translation and study / by Richard Bowring. — Princeton ; Guildford : Princeton University Press, c1982. — ix,290p,8p of plates : ill,plans ; 25cm. — (Princeton library of Asian translations)
Translation of: Murasaki Shikibu nikki and Murasaki Shikibu shū. — Bibliography: p275-278. — Includes index
ISBN 0-691-06507-1 : £17.70 B82-39032

895.6′34 — Fiction in Japanese. Higuchi, Ichiyō *— Biographies*
Danly, Robert Lyons. In the shade of spring leaves : the life and writings of Higuchi Ichiyō, a woman of letters in Meiji Japan / Robert Lyons Danly. — New Haven ; London : Yale, c1981. — ix,355p,[16]p of plates : ill,maps,ports ; 24cm
Bibliography: p333-337. — Includes index
ISBN 0-300-02614-5 : Unpriced : CIP rev.
Also classified at 895.6′34[F] B81-30245

895.6′34[F] — Fiction in Japanese, *1868-1945 — English texts*
Tanizaki, Junichirō. The secret history of the lord of Musashi ; and, Arrowroot. — London : Secker & Warburg, Jan.1983. — [212]p
Translated from the Japanese
ISBN 0-436-51602-0 : £7.95 : CIP entry B82-34593

895.6′34[F] — Short stories in Japanese, *1868-1945 — English texts*
Danly, Robert Lyons. In the shade of spring leaves : the life and writings of Higuchi Ichiyō, a woman of letters in Meiji Japan / Robert Lyons Danly. — New Haven ; London : Yale, c1981. — ix,355p,[16]p of plates : ill,maps,ports ; 24cm
Bibliography: p333-337. — Includes index
ISBN 0-300-02614-5 : Unpriced : CIP rev.
Primary classification 895.6′34 B81-30245

895.6′35[F] — Fiction in Japanese, *1945- — English texts*
Endō, Shūsaku. The samurai : a novel / Shusaku Endo ; translated by Van C. Gessel. — London : Peter Owen, 1982. — 272p ; 23cm
Translation of: Samurai
ISBN 0-7206-0559-8 : £8.95 B82-25571

Mishima, Yukio. The sailor who fell from grace with the sea / Yukio Mishima ; translated from the Japanese by John Nathan. — Harmondsworth : Penguin in association with Secker & Warburg, 1970, c1966 (1982 [printing]). — 142p ; 20cm. — (King penguin)
Translation of: Gogo no-eiko. — Originally published: London : Secker & Warburg, 1966
ISBN 0-14-006023-5 (pbk) : £1.95 B82-40662

Yamasaki, Toyoko. Bonchi. — London : Gollancz, Sept.1982. — [416]p
Translation from the Japanese
ISBN 0-575-03179-4 : £8.95 : CIP entry B82-18761

895.6′35[J] — Children′s stories in Japanese, *1945- — English texts*
Akaba, Suekichi. Suho and the white horse. — London : Dent, Sept.1982. — [48]p
Translated from the Japanese
ISBN 0-460-06119-4 : £4.95 : CIP entry B82-19707

Iguchi, Bunshu. An elephant′s tale / Bunshu Iguchi. — London : Dent, 1981. — [28]p : chiefly col.ill ; 25cm
ISBN 0-460-06090-2 : £3.95 : CIP rev. B81-25819

Iwamura, Kazuo. Nat′s braces / Kazuo Iwamura ; English text written by Kaye Webb. — Harmondsworth : Kestrel, 1982. — [40]p : col.ill ; 19cm
Translated from the Japanese
ISBN 0-7226-5769-2 : £3.50 B82-37577

Iwamura, Kazuo. Nat′s hat / Kazuo Iwamura ; English text written by Kaye Webb. — Harmondsworth : Kestrel, 1982. — [40]p : col.ill ; 19cm
Translated from the Japanese
ISBN 0-7226-5765-x : £3.50 B82-37576

Kitada, Taxi. The night express. — London : Dent, Nov.1982. — [28]p
ISBN 0-460-06122-4 : £4.25 : CIP entry B82-27532

Sueyoshi, Akiko. Ladybird on a bicycle / by Akiko Sueyoshi ; illustrated by Viv Allbright. — London : Faber, 1982. — 40p : col.ill ; 26cm
ISBN 0-571-11802-x : £4.95 : CIP rev. B82-04597

Watanabe, Shigeo. I can do it! / Shigeo Watanabe ; illustrated by Yasuo Ohtomo. — London : Bodley Head, 1982, c1981. — 28p : col.ill ; 22cm
Translated from the Japanese
ISBN 0-370-30911-1 : £3.25 B82-15011

Watanabe, Shigeo. I′m the King of the Castle / Shigeo Watanabe ; illustrated by Yasuo Ohtomo. — London : Bodley Head, 1982. — 28p : chiefly col.ill ; 22cm
Translated from the Japanese
ISBN 0-370-30912-x : £3.25 B82-15602

895.6′35′09 — Fiction in Japanese, *1945- — Critical studies*
Miyoshi, Masao. Accomplices of silence : the modern Japanese novel / Masao Miyoshi. — Berkeley ; London : University of California Press, 1974 (1982 [printing]). — xviii,194p ; 25cm
Includes index
ISBN 0-520-04609-9 : £17.00 B82-34358

895.7 — KOREAN LITERATURE

895.7′301′08[FS] — Short stories in Korean, *1945- — Anthologies — English texts*
The **Rainy** spell and other Korean short stories. — London : Onyx Press, Dec.1982. — [252]p
Translation from the Korean
ISBN 0-906383-17-x : £7.95 : CIP entry B82-33367

896 — AFRICAN LITERATURES

896 — African literatures. Orally transmitted literature, *to 1979 — Critical studies*
Genres, forms, meanings : essays in African oral literature : papers in French and English / edited by Veronika Görög-Karady ; with a foreword by Ruth Finnegan. — Oxford (51 Banbury Rd., Oxford OX2 6PF) : JASO, 1982. — vi,122p : ill ; 24cm. — (JASO occasional papers ; no.1)
Conference papers. — Includes bibliographies
Unpriced (pbk) B82-39561

896 — Literature in African languages, *to 1980 — Critical studies*
Gérard, Albert S.. African language literatures : an introduction to the literary history of sub-Saharan Africa / Albert S. Gérard. — Harlow : Longman, 1981. — xv,398p : maps ; 23cm
Includes index
ISBN 0-582-64352-x (pbk) : £7.50 B82-14615

896′.34 — Orally transmitted literature in Mende *— Critical studies*
Cosentino, Donald. Defiant maids and stubborn farmers : tradition and invention in Mende story performance / Donald Cosentino. — Cambridge : Cambridge University Press, 1982. — xii,226p : ill,maps,music,ports ; 24cm. — (Cambridge studies in oral and literate culture ; 4)
Bibliography: p221-222. — Includes index
ISBN 0-521-24197-9 : £19.50 : CIP rev. B82-12694

896′.39 — Drama in Kikuyu, *1960- — English texts*
Ngũgĩ wa Thiong′o. I will marry when I want / Ngũgĩ wa Thiong′o and Ngũgĩ wa Mĩriĩ ; translated from the Gĩkũyũ by the authors. — London : Heinemann, c1982. — 122p ; 19cm
Eight men, 5 women, supers. — Translation of: Ngaahika ndeenda
ISBN 0-435-90246-6 (pbk) : £1.95 B82-33984

896′.39 — Poetry in Zulu *— English texts*
Kunene, Mazisi. The ancestors & the sacred mountain : poems / Mazisi Kunene. — London : Heinemann, 1982. — xix,75p ; 19cm. — (African writers series ; 235)
Translated from the Zulu
ISBN 0-435-90235-0 (pbk) : £1.95 B82-35728

896′.39[F] — Fiction in Kikuyu *— English texts*
Ngũgĩ wa Thiong′o. Devil on the cross / Ngũgĩ wa Thiong′o ; translated from the Gĩkũyũ by the author. — London : Heinemann, 1982. — 254p ; 20cm
ISBN 0-435-90651-8 (cased) : £7.50
ISBN 0-435-90200-8 (pbk) : £2.25 B82-22525

896′.39212 — Poetry in Swahili, *1960-* — *Texts*

Karama, Said. Urembo wa Kiswahili / Said Karama. — Ibadan ; London : Evans, 1981. — viii,96p ; 22cm
ISBN 0-237-50590-8 (pbk) : Unpriced
B82-21636

899 — AUSTRONESIAN AND OTHER LITERATURES

899′.22 — Orally transmitted narrative poetry in Minangkabau — *Critical studies*

Phillips, Nigel. Sijobang : sung narrative poetry of West Sumatra / Nigel Phillips. — Cambridge : Cambridge University Press, 1981. — ix,255p : ill,maps,ports ; 24cm. — (Cambridge studies in oral and literate culture ; 1)
Includes poems in Minangkabau, together with English translations. — Bibliography: p251-253. — Includes index
ISBN 0-521-23737-8 : £22.50 : CIP rev.
B81-21566

900 — GEOGRAPHY, HISTORY, AND THEIR AUXILIARIES

900 — History — *For schools*

Thornton, David, *1935-*. History around you / series editor A. Waplington. — Edinburgh : Oliver & Boyd
[Bk.] 1 / D. Thornton ; [illustrations by Terry Gabbey]. — c1981. — 64p : ill(some col.),facsims,forms,ports(some col.) ; 27cm
Includes index
ISBN 0-05-002426-4 (pbk) : £1.75 B82-11534

Thornton, David, *1935-*. History around you / series editor A. Waplington. — Edinburgh : Oliver & Boyd
[Bk.] 2 / L.E. Snellgrove ; [illustrations by Terry Gabbey and Hamish Gordon]. — c1982. — 64p : ill(some col.),col.coats of arms,facsims,col.maps,2col.plans,ports(some col.) ; 27cm
Text on inside cover. — Includes index
ISBN 0-05-002427-2 (pbk) : Unpriced
B82-36513

901 — HISTORY. PHILOSOPHY AND THEORY

901 — Historical events — *Philosophical perspectives*

Miller, John William. The philosophy of history : with reflections and aphorisms / John William Miller. — New York ; London : Norton, c1981. — 192p ; 22cm
ISBN 0-393-01464-9 : £12.95 B82-35677

901 — Historical events — *Philosophical perspectives* — *Facsimiles*

Volney, C.-F.. A new translation of Volney′s Ruins / Constantin Francois Volney ; introduction by Robert D. Richardson, Jr. — New York ; London : Garland, 1979. — 2v. : 1ill,1chart,1port ; 19cm. — (Myth & romanticism ; 25)
Translation of: Les ruines, ou, Meditation sur les révolutions des Empires. — Facsim of: 1802 ed. Paris : Levrault
ISBN 0-8240-3574-7 : Unpriced B82-15181

901 — Historical events. Philosophical perspectives. Theories of Voegelin, Eric

Sandoz, Ellis. The Vogegelinian revolution : a biographical introduction / Ellis Sandoz. — Baton Rouge ; London : Louisiana State University Press, c1981. — xvi,271p : 1port ; 24cm
Includes index
ISBN 0-8071-0870-7 : Unpriced B82-34774

901 — Historiology. Explanation — *Philosophical perspectives*

Porter, Dale H.. The emergence of the past : a theory of historical explanation / Dale H. Porter. — Chicago ; London : University of Chicago Press, c1981. — x,205p ; 23cm
Includes index
ISBN 0-226-67550-5 (pbk) : £9.95 B82-09582

901 — Historiology — *Philosophical perspectives*

Gorman, J. L.. The expression of historical knowledge / J.L. Gorman. — Edinburgh : Edinburgh University Press, c1982. — viii,123p ; 23cm
Bibliography: p114-118. — Includes index
ISBN 0-85224-427-4 : £12.00 : CIP rev.
B82-06524

Heller, Agnes. A theory of history / Agnes Heller. — London : Routledge & Kegan Paul, 1982. — viii,333p ; 23cm
ISBN 0-7100-9010-2 : £15.00 B82-23258

901 — Historiology — *Philosophical perspectives* — *Festschriften*

Substance and form in history : a collection of essays in philosophy of history / edited by L. Pompa and W.H. Dray for the University of Edinburgh Press. — Edinburgh : Edinburgh University Press, c1981. — xii,198p ; 23cm
′And presented to W.H. Walsh′ — cover. — Includes bibliographies and index
ISBN 0-85224-413-4 : £12.00 B82-12031

901 — Historiology. Philosophical perspectives. Theories of Collingwood, R. G.

Dussen, W. J. van der. History as a science : the philosophy of R.G. Collingwood / by W.J. van der Dussen. — The Hague ; London : Nijhoff, 1981. — xiv,480p ; 25cm. — (Martinus Nijhoff philosophy library ; v.3)
Bibliography: p445-471. — Includes index
ISBN 90-247-2453-8 : Unpriced
ISBN 90-247-2344-2 (set) : Unpriced
B82-05346

901 — Philosophy of history

Graham, Gordon. Historical explanation reconsidered. — Aberdeen : Aberdeen University Press, Jan.1983. — [96]p. — (Scots philosophical monographs, ISSN 0144-3062 ; 4)
ISBN 0-08-028478-7 (pbk) : £6.00 : CIP entry
B82-33629

904 — HISTORY. COLLECTED ACCOUNTS OF SPECIAL KINDS OF EVENTS

904 — Disasters

Perham, Molly. The Pepper Press book of catastrophes / by Molly Perham and Elizabeth Holt ; illustrations by Ian Pollock. — Leeds : Pepper Press, 1981. — 64p : ill ; 19x23cm
Cover title: Catastrophes
ISBN 0-560-74525-7 : £3.75 B82-08698

904 — Disasters — *Forecasts*

Asimov, Isaac. A choice of catastrophes / Isaac Asimov. — London : Arrow, 1981, c1979. — 365p ; 18cm
Originally published: New York : Simon and Schuster, 1979 ; London : Hutchinson, 1980. — Includes index
ISBN 0-09-926570-2 (pbk) : £1.95 B82-04743

907 — HISTORY. STUDY AND TEACHING

907 — Historical sources — *For schools*

Nichol, Jon. What is history? / Jon Nichol. — Oxford : Blackwell, 1981. — 32p : ill,2maps,1facsim,ports ; 30cm. — (Evidence in history)
ISBN 0-631-93320-4 (pbk) : £1.35 B82-08582

907′.1142 — England. Further & higher education institutions. Curriculum subjects: History. Teaching — *Conference proceedings*

Teaching of history in further and higher education : report of a conference held at St. Mary′s College, Strawberry Hill, Twickenham, 11-14 July 1978 / edited by Joan Blyth and Joan Lewin. — [London] : NATFHE History Section, [1979?]. — 54p ; 30cm
Bibliography: p49-53
Unpriced (spiral) B82-08489

907′.2 — Historiography

Making histories. — London : Hutchinson Education, Oct.1982. — [352]p
ISBN 0-09-145210-4 (cased) : £15.00 : CIP entry
ISBN 0-09-145211-2 (pbk) : £6.95 B82-24961

Oakeshott, Michael. On history and other essays. — Oxford : Basil Blackwell, Oct.1982. — [192]p
ISBN 0-631-13114-0 : £9.50 : CIP entry
B82-23174

907′.2 — Historiography, *700-1500*

Medieval historical writing in the Christian and Islamic worlds. — London : University of London, School of Oriental and African Studies, Sept.1982. — [150]p
ISBN 0-7286-0098-6 (pbk) : £5.00 : CIP entry
B82-20483

907′.2 — Historiography. Role of biography

Beales, Derek. History and biography : an inaugural lecture / Derek Beales. — Cambridge : Cambridge University Press, 1981. — 36p ; 19cm
Cover title
ISBN 0-521-28474-0 (pbk) : Unpriced
B82-32123

907′.2 — Historiography. Theories of Marxists

McLennan, Gregor. Marxism and the methodologies of history / Gregor McLennan. — London : NLB, c1981. — xiii,272p ; 23cm
Includes index
ISBN 0-86091-045-8 (cased) : £14.00 : CIP rev.
ISBN 0-86091-743-6 (pbk) : Unpriced
B81-34211

907′.2 — Historiology

Tuchman, Barbara W.. Practicing history : selected essays / by Barbara W. Tuchman. — London : Macmillan, 1982, c1981. — vi,306p ; 25cm
Originally published: New York : Knopf, 1981
ISBN 0-333-32757-8 : £9.95 B82-14868

907′.2 — Historiology *related to* **sociology**

Tilly, Charles. As sociology meets history / Charles Tilly. — New York ; London : Academic Press, c1981. — xiii,237p : ill ; 24cm. — (Studies in social discontinuity)
Bibliography: p217-232. — Includes index
ISBN 0-12-691280-7 : £16.60
Primary classification 301 B82-30132

907.2 — Oral history

Henige, David. Oral historiography. — London : Longman, Oct.1982. — [208]p
ISBN 0-582-64364-3 (cased) : £12.50 : CIP entry
ISBN 0-582-64363-5 (pbk) : £4.95 B82-20266

907′.2 — Oral history. Projects — *Manuals*

Lance, David. An archive approach to oral history / by David Lance. — London ([Lambeth Rd., SE1 6HZ]) : Imperial War Museum in association with International Association of Sound Archives, 1978. — viii,64p : 2facsims ; 21cm
Cover title. — Bibliography: p60-62
Unpriced (pbk) B82-25130

907′.2024 — Arab historiography. Ibn Khaldūn — *Critical studies*

Al-Azmeh, Aziz. Ibn Khaldūn : an essay in reinterpretation / Aziz Al-Azmeh. — London : Cass, 1982. — xv,176p ; 23cm
Bibliography: p166-170. — Includes index
ISBN 0-7146-3130-2 : £15.00 : CIP rev.
B81-08861

907′.2024 — Historiography. Gooch, G. P. — *Biographies*

Eyck, Frank. G.P. Gooch : a study in history and politics / Frank Eyck. — London : Macmillan, 1982. — xv,498p : 1port ; 23cm
Includes index
ISBN 0-333-30849-2 : £8.95 B82-20948

907′.2024 — Historiography. Josephus, Flavius — *Critical studies*

Rajak, Tessa. Josephus. — London : Duckworth, Jan.1983. — [256]p
ISBN 0-7156-1502-5 : £18.00 : CIP entry
B82-32614

907′.2042 — Engligh historiography, *1900-1970*
Tawney, R. H.. The attack. — Nottingham : Spokesman, May 1981. — [200]p
Originally published: London : Allen & Unwin, 1953
ISBN 0-85124-311-8 (cased) : £8.00 : CIP entry
ISBN 0-85124-312-6 (pbk) : £3.00 B81-08838

907′.2042 — English historiography, *1848-1878*
Burrow, J. W.. A liberal descent : Victorian historians and the English past / J.W. Burrow. — Cambridge : Cambridge University Press, 1981. — x,308p ; 24cm
Includes index
ISBN 0-521-24079-4 : £19.50 B82-00977

907′.2′042 — English historiography, *ca 1066-ca 1485*
Galbraith, V. H.. Kings and chroniclers. — London (35 Gloucester Ave., NW1 7AX) : Hambledon Press, Nov.1981. — [320]p. — (History series ; 4)
ISBN 0-9506882-4-x : £20.00 : CIP entry
B81-30622

907′.2042843 — Great Britain. Universities. Curriculum subjects: History. Research. Use of information sources — *Study examples: University of York*
Smith, Carole. Information officer in history at York University 1978-1980 : report to the British Library Research and Development Department on Project S1/G/282 / Information officer Carole Smith ; Project head Norman Hampson. — York : University of York, History Department, 1980. — iv,95leaves ; 30cm
Bibliography: leaves 81-84
Unpriced (pbk) B82-23249

907′.8 — Great Britain. Schools. Curriculum subjects: History. Visual aids
Unwin, Robert. The visual dimension in the study and teaching of history / by Robert Unwin. — London : Historical Association, 1981. — 64p : ill ; 30cm. — (Teaching history series ; 49)
ISBN 0-85278-241-1 (pbk) : Unpriced
B82-03639

909 — WORLD HISTORY, CIVILIZATION

909 — Castles — *For children*
Woodlander, David. Castles. — London : Black, Jan.1983. — [32]p. — (History explorers)
ISBN 0-7136-2271-7 (cased) : £2.95 : CIP entry
ISBN 0-7136-2272-5 (pbk) : £1.45 B82-32596

909 — Civilization — *For children*
Crush, Margaret. What's in our world. — London : Granada, July 1982. — [64]p
ISBN 0-246-11552-1 (pbk) : £2.95 : CIP entry
B82-14086

909 — Civilization — *History*
World civilizations : their history and their culture. — 6th ed. / Edward McNall Burns ... [et al.]. — New York ; London : Norton
Previous ed.: / Edward McNall Burns, Philip Lee Ralph
Vol.2. — c1982. — xvii,p661-1384,xxv,[30]p of plates : ill(some col.),maps(some col.),ports ; 24cm
Includes bibliographies and index
ISBN 0-393-95095-6 (pbk) : £10.25
B82-32728

909 — Civilization — *History* — *For children*
Sandford, Ron. Picture the past / Ron Sandford & L.E. Snellgrove. — Harlow : Longman
5: War, welfare & science. — 1982. — 95p : ill (some col.),facsims,2maps,ports ; 28cm
Includes index
ISBN 0-582-20694-4 (cased) : £5.95
ISBN 0-582-22130-7 B82-24103

909 — Civilization, *to 1976* — *For schools*
Guest, George. The march of civilization. — 3rd ed. — London : Bell & Hyman, Apr.1982. — [230]p
Originally published: 1977
ISBN 0-7135-0039-5 (pbk) : £2.40 : CIP entry
B82-14201

909 — Civilization, *to 1978*
Velikovsky, Immanuel. Mankind in amnesia / Immanuel Velikovsky. — London : Sidgwick & Jackson, 1982. — xiii,225p ; 23cm
Includes index
ISBN 0-283-98844-4 : £7.95 B82-18888

909 — Civilizations
Service, Alastair. Lost worlds / Alastair Service. — London : Collins, 1981. — 201p : ill(some col.),maps,plans ; 30cm
Maps on lining papers. — Includes index
ISBN 0-00-216461-2 : Unpriced : CIP rev.
B81-24621

World civilizations : their history and their culture. — 6th ed. / Edward McNall Burns ... [et al.]. — London : Norton, c1982
Previous ed.: 1974
Vol.1. — xv,660,xxxvp, [28]p of plates : ill (some col.),maps(some col.),ports(some col.) ; 24cm
Includes bibliographies and index
ISBN 0-393-95083-2 (pbk) : £10.25
B82-40781

909 — Historical events. Influence of climatic changes
Climate and history : studies in past climates and their impact on man / edited by T.M.L. Wigley, M.J. Ingram and G. Farmer. — Cambridge : Cambridge University Press, 1981. — xii,530p ; 24cm
Includes bibliographies and index
ISBN 0-521-23902-8 : £30.00 : CIP rev.
B81-32521

International Conference on Climate and History *(1979 : University of East Anglia)*. International Conference on Climate and History, 8-14 July 1979 / [compiled and edited by G. Farmer ... et al.]. — [Norwich] : University of East Anglia, Climatic Research Unit, [1980?]. — 2v. : ill,charts,maps ; 21cm
Cover title. — Includes bibliographies
Unpriced (pbk) B82-38114

909 — Human geography — *For Malaysian students*
Goh, Cheng Leong. Human and economic geography / Goh Cheng Leong, Gillian C. Morgan. — 2nd ed. — Kuala Lumpur ; Oxford : Oxford University Press, 1982. — xxvi,662p : ill,maps ; 25cm. — (Oxford in Asia)
Previous ed.: 1973. — Bibliography: 638. — Includes index
ISBN 0-19-582816-x (pbk) : Unpriced
B82-40498

909 — World events, *to 1980*
Lewis, Brenda Ralph. Purnell's pictorial encyclopedia of world history / Brenda Ralph Lewis. — Maidenhead : Purnell, 1981. — 187p : ill(some col.),maps,facsims,ports(some col.) ; 31cm
Includes index
ISBN 0-361-04826-2 (corrected) : £5.99
B82-02043

909 — World, *to 1980*
Thomas, Hugh. An unfinished history of the world. — Rev. ed. — London : Hamish Hamilton, Jan.1982. — [816]p
Previous ed.: 1979
ISBN 0-241-10696-6 : £17.50 : CIP entry
B81-34405

909 — World, *to 1981* — *For children*
Millard, Anne. Children's atlas of world history. — London : Ward Lock, May 1982. — [96]p
ISBN 0-7063-6191-1 : £5.95 : CIP entry
B82-12147

909 — World, *to 1981* — *For schools*
Hobley, L. F.. Steps in history / L.F. Hobley. — London : Hutchinson
1. — 1982. — 96p : ill,maps ; 30cm
Includes index
ISBN 0-09-146721-7 (pbk) : Unpriced : CIP rev. B82-04118

Hobley, L. F.. Steps in history. — London : Hutchinson Education
2. — Sept.1982. — [96]p
ISBN 0-09-148991-1 (pbk) : £2.50 : CIP entry
B82-20191

909.04924 — Jewish civilization. Origins
Raphael, Chaim. The springs of Jewish life. — London : Chatto & Windus, Nov.1982. — [304]p
ISBN 0-7011-2335-4 : £12.50 : CIP entry
B82-27037

909′.04927 — Arab culture, *ca 900-ca 1600*
Bosworth, Clifford Edmund. Medieval Arabic culture and administration. — London : Variorum, Sept.1982. — [358]p. — (Collected studies series ; CS165)
ISBN 0-86078-113-5 : £26.00 : CIP entry
B82-21407

909′.04927 — Arabs. Attitudes of Britons, *to 1976*
Nasir, Sari J.. The Arabs and the English / Sari J. Nasir. — 2nd ed. — London : Longman, 1979. — xii,186p,[20]p of plates : ill,ports
Previous ed.: 1976. — Includes index
ISBN 0-582-78305-4 (cased) : £8.75 : CIP rev.
ISBN 0-582-78306-2 (pbk) : £3.95 B79-18786

909.07 — Colonisation by European countries, *ca 800-1650*
Scammell, G. V.. The world encompassed : the first European maritime empires c.800-1650 / G.V. Scammell. — London : Methuen, 1981. — xiv,538p : ill,maps ; 24cm
Includes index
ISBN 0-416-76280-8 : £14.95 B82-17559

909.07 — Crusades — *For children* — *Irish texts*
Cyrille, George. Na crosáidí / George Cyrille ; a mhaisigh Ghislaine Joos ; a rinne an leagan Gaeilge Peadar Ó Casaide. — Baile Átha Cliath : Oifig an tSoláthair, c1981. — [26]p : ill (some col.),maps ; 23cm. — (Leabhair staire le léaraidí)
£0.70 B82-19589

909.07 — Crusades — *Serials*
Society for the Study of the Crusades and the Latin East. Bulletin / Society for the Study of the Crusades and the Latin East. — No.1 (1981)-. — [Cambridge] ([c/o Dr. N.J. Housley, Girton College, Cambridge CB3 0JG]) : [The Society], 1981-. — v. ; 21cm
Annual
ISSN 0262-6322 = Bulletin - Society for the Study of the Crusades and the Latin East : Unpriced B82-06796

909.07 — World, *500-1500* — *For children*
Atlas of the world in the Middle Ages / [authors Brian Adams ... et al. ...]. — London : Longman, 1980. — 61p : col.ill,col.maps ; 33cm
Includes index
ISBN 0-582-39074-5 : £3.95 : CIP rev.
B80-10399

909.08 — Land battles, *1066-1944*
Seymour, William, *1914-*. Yours to reason why : decision in battle / William Seymour ; maps and battle-plans by W.F.N. Watson. — London : Sidgwick & Jackson, 1982. — x,338p,[16]p of plates : ill,maps,plans,ports ; 24cm
Bibliography: p321-324. — Includes index
ISBN 0-283-98788-x : £9.95 B82-14016

909.08 — Social conditions, *1400-1800*
Braudel, Fernand. The wheels of commerce. — London : Collins, Oct.1982. — [720]p. — (Civilization and capitalism ; v.2)
Translation of: Les jeux de l'échange
ISBN 0-00-216132-x : CIP entry B82-23066

909.08 — World, *1450-1950*
The **New** Cambridge modern history. — Cambridge : Cambridge University Press, 1979 (1980 [printing])
13: Companion volume / edited by Peter Burke. — Dec. 1980. — vi,378p ; 23cm
Includes index
ISBN 0-521-28017-6 (pbk) : £5.95 : CIP rev.
B80-28844

909.08 — World events, *1440-1750* — *For schools*
Millard, Anne. Exploration & discovery : from AD 1450 to AD 1750 / Anne Millard ; illustrated by Joseph McEwan ; designed by Graham Round ; edited by Robyn Gee. — London : Usborne, 1979. — 32p : col.ill,col.maps,col.ports ; 29cm. — (The Children's picture world history)
Bibliography: p32. — Includes index
ISBN 0-86020-260-7 : £2.50 B82-08955

909'.09182202 — Mediterranean region, *1250-1300*
Runciman, Steven. The Sicilian Vespers : a history of the Mediterranean world in the later thirteenth century / by Stephen Runciman. — Cambridge : Cambridge University Press, 1958 (1982 [printing]). — xiii,355p,[16]p of plates : ill,facsims,ports ; 22cm
Bibliography: p331-338. — Includes index
ISBN 0-521-28652-2 (pbk) : £8.95 : CIP rev. B82-01720

909'.0971241'0072042574 — Commonwealth. Historiography in University of Oxford
Oxford and the idea of Commonwealth : essays presented to Sir Edgar Williams / edited by Frederick Madden and D.K. Fieldhouse. — London : Croom Helm, c1982. — vii,167p : 1port ; 23cm
ISBN 0-7099-1021-5 : £11.95 : CIP rev. B82-09179

909'.0971241081 — Commonwealth, *1837-1973*
Gallagher, John. The decline, revival and fall of the British Empire. — Cambridge : Cambridge University Press, Aug.1982. — [224]p
ISBN 0-521-24642-3 : £16.00 : CIP entry B82-29351

909'.0971241081 — Commonwealth, *1897*
Morris, Jan. The spectacle of Empire. — London : Faber, Sept.1982. — [260]p
ISBN 0-571-11957-3 : £12.50 : CIP entry B82-28466

909'.097170828 — Communist countries. Unity — *Soviet viewpoints*
Consolidation of the socialist countries' unity : problems of theory / [translated from the Russian by Nicholas Bobrov]. — Moscow : Progress Publishers ; [London] : Distributed by Central Books, 1981. — 268p ; 18cm. — (Practical problems and prospects of socialism)
Translation of: Ukreplenie edinstva sot͡sialisticheskikh stran. Rev. ed.. — At head of title: USSR Academy of Sciences Institute of the Economics of the World Socialist System
ISBN 0-7147-1677-4 (pbk) : £1.95 B82-06709

909'.09724'00321 — Developing countries — *Encyclopaedias*
The **Current** history encyclopedia of developing nations / [edited by Carol L. Thompson, Mary M. Anderberg, Joan B. Antell] ; [consulting editors Marvin Alisky ... [et al.]]. — New York ; London : McGraw-Hill, c1982. — viii,395p : ill ; 28cm
Includes index
ISBN 0-07-064387-3 : £29.95 B82-22763

Kurian, George Thomas. Encyclopedia of the Third World / by George Thomas Kurian. — Rev. ed. — London : Mansell, 1982. — 3v.(xxvii,2125p) : ill,maps,coats of arms ; 29cm
Previous ed.: New York : Facts on File, 1978 ; London : Mansell, 1979. — Includes bibliographies and index
ISBN 0-7201-1628-7 : £67.50 : CIP rev. B81-33844

909'.097240828 — Developing countries
Third world lives of struggle. — London : Heinemann Educational, Dec.1982. — [272]p. — (Open University Third World readers ; 1)
ISBN 0-435-96130-6 (pbk) : £5.95 : CIP entry B82-29772

909'.097240828 — Developing countries — *For schools*
Bale, John, *1940-*. Patterns of underdevelopment / John Bale. — Walton-on-Thames : Nelson for the Schools Council, 1982. — 48p : ill(some col.),maps(some col.),2ports ; 28cm. — (Geography and change)
ISBN 0-17-434185-7 (pbk) : Unpriced B82-29551

Life in developing countries. — London : Longman, 1981. — 47p : ill,maps,plans ; 27cm. — (Enquiries)
Bibliography: p47
ISBN 0-582-23031-4 (pbk) : £1.40 B82-34027

909'.097240828 — Developing countries. Social conditions
MacPherson, Stewart. Social policy in the Third World : the social dilemmas of underdevelopment / Stewart MacPherson. — Brighton : Wheatsheaf, 1982. — 220p ; 23cm
Bibliography: p192-211. — Includes index
ISBN 0-7108-0195-5 : £15.95 : CIP rev. B82-06951

909'.0973'2 — Urban regions *History - Serials*
Urban history yearbook. — 1981. — Leicester : Leicester University Press, July 1981. — [248]p
ISBN 0-7185-6081-7 (pbk) : £14.00 : CIP entry
ISSN 0306-0845 B81-16388

909'.0973'2 — Urban regions — *History* — *Serials*
Urban history yearbook. — 1982. — Leicester : Leicester University Press, Sept.1982. — [208]p
ISBN 0-7185-6082-5 (pbk) : £15.00 : CIP entry
ISSN 0306-0845 B82-21395

909'.097320828 — Cities. Social life — *For schools*
Bennett, Olivia. City life / Olivia Bennett. — London : Macmillan Education in association with the Save the Children Fund and the Commonwealth Institute, 1982. — 48p : ill (some col.),2col.plans ; 26cm. — (Patterns of living)
Text on lining papers. — Includes index
ISBN 0-333-31192-2 : Unpriced B82-33385

909'.09734 — Rural regions. Social conditions, *to 1980*
Our forgotten past : seven centuries of life on the land / edited by Jerome Blum ; texts by Jerome Blum ... [et al.]. — London : Thames and Hudson, c1982. — 240p : ill(some col.),maps ; 28cm
Bibliography: p233-234. — Includes index
ISBN 0-500-25080-4 : £12.50 B82-21918

909'.097340828 — Villages. Social life — *For schools*
Bennett, Olivia. Village life / Olivia Bennett. — London : Macmillan Education in association with the Save the Children Fund and the Commonwealth Institute, 1982. — 48p : col.ill,1col.plan ; 26cm. — (Patterns of living)
Text on lining papers. — Includes index
ISBN 0-333-31193-0 : Unpriced B82-33384

909'.0974927 — Arab countries. Social change
Ibrahim, Saad Eddin. The new Arab social order : a study of the social impact of oil wealth / Saad Eddin Ibrahim. — Boulder : Westview ; London : Croom Helm, 1982. — xiv,208p : ill,maps ; 24cm. — (Westview's special studies on the Middle East)
Bibliography: p193-199. — Includes index
ISBN 0-7099-1305-2 : £13.95 B82-31740

909'.09749270828'05 — Arab Islamic countries — *Serials*
[Arabia *(London)*]. Arabia : the Islamic world review. — No.1 (Sept 1981)-. — London (104 Great Russell St., WC1B 3LA) : Islamic Press Agency, 1981-. — v. : ill,ports ; 30cm
Monthly
ISSN 0260-4272 = Arabia (London) : Unpriced B82-03427

909'.09761 — Islamic civilization, *1500-1980*
Robinson, Francis. Atlas of the Islamic world since 1500. — Oxford : Phaidon Press, Oct.1982. — [240]p
ISBN 0-7148-2200-0 : £17.95 : CIP entry B82-20370

909'.097671 — Islamic civilization, *to 1958*
Gibb, *Sir* **Hamilton**. Studies on the civilization of Islam / by Hamilton A.R. Gibb ; edited by Stanford J. Shaw and William R. Polk. — Princeton ; Guildford : Princeton University Press, 1982, c1962. — xiv,369p ; 22cm
Includes two chapters in Arabic. — Originally published: London : Routledge & Kegan Paul, 1962. — Includes index
ISBN 0-691-05354-5 (cased) : Unpriced
ISBN 0-691-00786-1 (pbk) : Unpriced B82-31199

909'.0976710827 — Islamic countries. Revolutions, *1976-1980*
Siddiqui, Kalim. 'Al-Harakah Al-Islamiyah : Qadāya wa Ahdāf'. — London (6 Endsleigh St., WC1H 0DS) : Open Press, Sept.1981. — [96]p
ISBN 0-905081-09-9 (pbk) : £2.50 : CIP entry B81-20470

909'.097'6710828 — Islamic countries. Political events, *1980-1981*
Issues in the Islamic movement 1980-1981. — London : Open Press, Dec.1981. — [200]p
ISBN 0-905081-10-2 (cased) : £10.00 : CIP entry
ISBN 0-905081-11-0 (pbk) B81-31544

909'.0976710828 — Islamic culture
Islam and contemporary society. — London : Longman in association with the Islamic Council of Europe, 1982. — x,279p ; 22cm
Includes index
ISBN 0-582-78323-2 (cased) : Unpriced : CIP rev.
ISBN 0-582-78322-4 (pbk) : £3.50 B82-00217

909'.0976710828'05 — Islamic countries. Political events — *Islamic viewpoints* — *Serials*
The **Monitor** Weekly. — Vol.1, no.1 (Sept. 24 to Oct. 1 1981)-. — London (70 Leathwaite Rd, SW11) : Muslim Monitor Ltd., 1981-. — v. : ill,ports ; 27cm
ISSN 0262-6845 = Monitor weekly : £25.00 per year B82-07650

909'.09812 — Western civilization. Influence of Ancient Egyptian civilization, *to 1981*
Curl, James Stevens. The Egyptian revival : an introductory study of a recurring theme in the history of taste / James Stevens Curl. — London : Allen & Unwin, 1982. — xviii,249p : ill,facsims,plans ; 26cm
Bibliography: p221-239. — Includes index
ISBN 0-04-724001-6 : £30.00 : CIP rev. B82-00896

909'.09812 — Western civilization, *to 1955*
Borkenau, Franz. End and beginning : on the generations of cultures and the origins of the West / Franz Borkenau ; edited with an introduction by Richard Lowenthal. — New York ; Guildford : Columbia University Press, 1981. — ix,493p : 1port ; 24cm. — (European perspectives)
Includes index
ISBN 0-231-05066-6 : £17.50 B82-10649

909'.098120828 — Western world. Society
Changing images of man / by the following staff of and consultants to the Center for the Study of Social Policy — SRI International: Joseph Cambell [i.e. Campbell] ... [et al.] ; edited by O.W. Markley and Willis W. Harman. — Oxford : Pergamon, 1982. — xxiv,255p : ill ; 23cm. — (Systems science and world order library) (Pergamon international library)
Bibliography: p207-218. — Includes index
ISBN 0-08-024314-2 (cased) : Unpriced : CIP rev.
ISBN 0-08-024313-4 (pbk) : £7.95 B81-00653

909'.09821 — Caribbean region, *1450-1960* — *For Caribbean students*
Hall, Douglas, *1920-*. The Caribbean experience : an historical survey, 1450-1960 / Douglas Hall. — Kingston, [Jamaica] ; London : Heinemann Educational, 1982. — xi,146p : ill,3maps,ports ; 25cm. — (Heinemann CXC history)
Bibliography: p138-141. — Includes index
ISBN 0-435-98300-8 (pbk) : £2.75 : CIP rev. B81-30259

909'.09821 — Caribbean region — *Serials*
Latin America & Caribbean. — 1980-. — Saffron Walden : World of Information, 1980-. — v. : ill ; 27cm
Annual. — Continues: Latin America annual review and the Caribbean. — Description based on: 1981-82 issue
ISSN 0262-5415 = Latin America & Caribbean : Unpriced
Primary classification 980'.038'05 B82-24764

909'.09821 — Caribbean region, *to 1980 — For Caribbean students*

Claypole, William. Caribbean story / William Claypole, John Robottom. — Trinidad : Longman Caribbean ; London : Longman
Bk.1: Foundations. — 1980. — 198p : ill,maps,ports ; 25cm
Bibliography: p190-191. — Includes index
ISBN 0-582-76534-x (pbk) : £2.15 : CIP rev.
B79-36614

Honychurch, Lennox. The Caribbean people / Lennox Honychurch. — Walton-on-Thames : Nelson
Includes index
Book 3. — 1981. — 183p : ill(some col.),maps (somecol.),ports(some col.) ; 25cm
ISBN 0-17-566242-8 (pbk) : £2.75 B82-00939

909'.09821 — Western culture, *to 1981*

Cunningham, Lawrence. Culture and values : a survey of the Western humanities / Lawrence Cunningham, John Reich. — New York ; London : Holt, Rinehart and Winston
Includes bibliographies and index
Vol.1. — c1982. — xi,483p : ill(some col.),maps,music,facsims,plans,ports ; 26cm
ISBN 0-03-054001-1 (pbk) : £14.95
B82-19056

Cunningham, Lawrence. Culture and values : a survey of the Western humanities / Lawrence Cunningham, John Reich. — New York ; London : Holt, Rinehart and Winston
Vol.2. — c1982. — ix,486p : ill(some col.),ports ; 26cm
Includes index
ISBN 0-03-054011-9 (pbk) : £14.95
B82-25403

909'.09822'006041 — Mediterranean studies. Organisations: Society for Mediterranean Studies *— Serials*

[Bulletin *(Society for Mediterranean Studies)*]. Bulletin / Society for Mediterranean Studies. — No.1 (Spring 1981)-. — [Aberdeen] ([c/o Ms A. Williams, Department of History, King's College, Aberdeen AB9 2VB]) : The Society, 1981-. — v. ; 30cm
Two issues yearly
ISSN 0262-9062 = Bulletin - Society for Mediterranean Studies : Free to Society members only B82-11152

909'.098220828 — Mediterranean region

Rosenthal, Glenda Goldstone. The Mediterranean Basin : its political economy and changing international relations / Glenda G. Rosenthal. — London : Butterworth Scientific, 1982. — 146p : ill,maps ; 24cm. — (Butterworths European studies)
Includes index
ISBN 0-408-10711-1 : Unpriced : CIP rev.
B82-10495

909'.1 — Civilization, *476-816*

Grant, Michael, *1914-*. Dawn of the Middle Ages / Michael Grant. — London : Weidenfeld and Nicolson, 1981. — 224p : ill(some col.),maps (some col.),facsims(some col.),ports(some col.) ; 31cm
Includes index
ISBN 0-297-78026-3 : £20.00 B82-00660

909'.1 — World, *1100-1300 — For children*

Millard, Anne. The age of the Crusades : c. AD 1100-AD 1300 / Anne Millard. — [London] : Macmillan Children's, c1980. — 46p : ill(some col.),maps,ports(some col.) ; 33cm. — (History in pictures ; bk.8)
Includes index
ISBN 0-333-25545-3 : £3.95 B82-25203

909'.5 — Political events, *1500-1980*

Woodruff, William. The struggle for world power 1500-1980 / William Woodruff. — London : Macmillan, 1981. — xvi,371p : maps ; 23cm
Bibliography: p336-342. — Includes index
ISBN 0-333-29087-9 : £20.00 B82-15251

909.7 — Colonisation by European countries, *1700-1900*

Cairns, Trevor. Europe round the world / Trevor Cairns. — Cambridge : Cambridge University Press, 1981. — 96p : ill(some col.),maps(some col.),ports(some col.) ; 21x22cm. — (Cambridge introduction to the history of mankind ; Book 9)
ISBN 0-521-22710-0 (pbk) : £3.00 : CIP rev.
B81-03150

909.7 — Non-European civilizations. Attitudes of Britons, *1700-1800*

Marshall, P. J.. The great map of mankind : British perceptions of the world in the age of enlightenment / P.J. Marshall & Glyndwr Williams. — London : Dent, 1982. — 314p : maps ; 24cm
Maps on lining papers. — Includes index
ISBN 0-460-04554-7 : £16.50 : CIP rev.
B82-03601

909.7 — Sea battles, *1794-1805 - Readings from contemporary sources*

Jackson, T. Sturges. Logs of the great sea fights 1794-1805. — Havant : K. Mason, Aug.1981
Vol.1. — [346]p
Originally published: London : Navy Records Society, 1899
ISBN 0-85937-266-9 : £15.00 : CIP entry
B81-18054

Jackson, T. Sturges. Logs of the great sea fights 1794-1805. — Havant : K. Mason, Aug.1981
Vol.2. — [348]p
Originally published: London : Navy Records Society, 1900
ISBN 0-85937-267-7 : £15.00 : CIP entry
B81-18055

909.7 — World events, *1700-1914 — For schools*

Millard, Anne. The age of revolution : from AD 1750 to AD 1914 / Anne Millard ; illustrated by Joseph McEwan ; designed by Graham Round ; edited by Robyn Gee. — London : Usborne, 1979. — 32p : col.ill,col.maps,col.ports ; 29cm. — (The Children's picture world history)
Bibliography: p32. — Includes index
ISBN 0-86020-262-3 : £2.50 B82-08956

909.8'076 — World events, *1756-1918 — Questions & answers*

Revise your 'O' history / compiled by C.M. Thomson ... [et al.]. — Glasgow : Robert Gibson, c1981. — 63p : ill,maps ; 21cm
ISBN 0-7169-6951-3 (pbk) : Unpriced
B82-08013

909.82 — Adventures, *1946-1981*

Bonington, Chris. Quest for adventure / Chris Bonington. — London : Hodder and Stoughton, 1981. — 448p : ill(some col.),maps,ports ; 29cm
Bibliography: p442-443. — Includes index
ISBN 0-340-25599-4 : £14.95 : CIP rev.
B81-26753

909.82 — Scandals, *1900-1981*

Street-Porter, Janet. Scandal! / Janet Street-Porter. — London : Allen Lane, 1981. — 240p : ill,facsims ; 25cm
Bibliography: p240
ISBN 0-7139-1432-7 : £6.95 B82-00795

909.82 — World, *1900-1979 — For schools*

Poulton, Richard. A history of the modern world / Richard Poulton. — Oxford : Oxford University Press, 1981 (1982 [printing]). — 360p : ill,maps,ports ; 24cm
Includes index
ISBN 0-19-913265-8 (pbk) : £3.95 B82-34773

909.82 — World, *1900-1980*

Grenville, J. A. S.. A world history of the twentieth century / J.A.S. Grenville. — London : Fontana
Vol.1: Western dominance 1900-45. — 1980. — 605p ; 18cm
Also published: Hassocks : Harvester, 1980. — Bibliography: p572-589. — Includes index
ISBN 0-00-635208-1 (pbk) : £2.95 B82-14131

909.82 — World, *1914-1980 — For schools*

Neville, Peter, *1944-*. World history : 1914-80 / Peter Neville. — London : Heinemann Educational, 1982. — 218p : ill,maps,ports ; 25cm
Bibliography: p212. — Includes index
ISBN 0-435-31670-2 (pbk) : £3.95 : CIP rev.
B82-06772

909.82 — World, *1919-1981 — For schools*

Rayner, E. G.. International affairs. — London : E. Arnold, Nov.1982. — [224]p. — (A History of the 20th century world)
ISBN 0-7131-0678-6 (pbk) : £3.95 : CIP entry
B82-27952

909.82 — World, *1950-1974*

Mid-century world / editor Roger Morgan. — Repr. with amendments. — London : Reader's Digest in association with Newsweek Books, 1980. — 160p : ill(some col.),col.maps,ports (some col.) ; 30cm. — (Milestones of history ; 12)
Originally published: London : Weidenfeld and Nicolson, 1979. — Ill. on lining papers. — Includes index
£7.95 B82-23777

909.82 — World, *1955-1980*

From our own correspondent / edited by Roger Lazar. — Large print ed. — Bath : Chivers, 1982, c1980. — (A Lythway book)
Originally published: London : British Broadcasting Corporation, 1980
Vol.1: 1955-1968. — May 1982. — xiii,175p ; 23cm
ISBN 0-85119-810-4 : Unpriced : CIP rev.
B82-07014

From our own correspondent / edited by Roger Lazar. — Large print ed. — Bath : Chivers. — (A Lythway book)
Vol.2: 1969-1980. — 1982, c1980. — xiii,180p ; 23cm
Originally published: London : British Broadcasting Corporation, 1980
ISBN 0-85119-819-8 : Unpriced : CIP rev.
B82-09863

909.82 — World events, *1900-1980 — For schools*

Heater, Derek. Our world this century / Derek Heater. — Oxford : Oxford University Press, 1982. — 183p : ill,maps,ports ; 28cm
Includes index
ISBN 0-19-913276-3 (pbk) : £3.50 B82-20111

909.82 — World events, *1914-1980*

Lowe, Norman. Mastering modern world history / Norman Lowe. — London : Macmillan, 1982. — xvii,370p : ill,maps ; 23cm. — (Macmillan master series)
Bibliography: p357-362. — Includes index
ISBN 0-333-31295-3 (cased) : Unpriced
ISBN 0-333-30449-7 (pbk) : Unpriced
ISBN 0-333-31069-1 (export ed.) : Unpriced
B82-17299

909.82'022'2 — World events, *1956-1980 — Illustrations*

Eye witness : 25 years through world press photos / [edited by] Harold Evans. — London (11a Albemarle St., W.1) : Quiller Press, 1981. — 192p : chiefly ill,facsims,ports ; 28cm
'Published to celebrate the 25th anniversary of the World Press Photo Holland Foundation. — Includes index
ISBN 0-907621-00-7 : £9.95 B82-02191

909.82'092'2 — Politicians, *1900-1980 — Personal observations*

Berlin, Isaiah. Personal impressions. — Oxford : Oxford University Press, Oct.1982. — [256]p. — (Selected writings / Isaiah Berlin) (Oxford paperbacks)
Originally published: London : Hogarth Press, 1980
ISBN 0-19-283029-5 (pbk) : £2.95 : CIP entry
Primary classification 305.5'52'0924
B82-23673

909.82'1 — Social conditions, *1900*

West, Rebecca. 1900 / Rebecca West. — London : Weidenfeld and Nicolson, c1982. — 190p : ill (1col.),2facsims,ports ; 22x26cm
Includes index
ISBN 0-297-77963-x : £10.00 B82-16432

909.82′2 — Political events, *1920-1921 — Readings from contemporary sources — Facsimiles*

Weekly summaries : November 13, 1920-January 22, 1921 / introduction by Richard D. Challener. — New York ; London : Garland, 1979. — vii,p5736-7117,[1]folded leaf of plates : maps ; 24cm. — (United States military intelligence ; v.16)
Facsim. of: Weekly intelligence summaries. United States War Dept. General Staff, 1920-1921
ISBN 0-8240-3015-x : Unpriced B82-19607

909.82′2 — Political events, *1921 — Readings from contemporary sources — Facsimiles*

Weekly summaries : June 14-August 16, 1921 / introduction by Richard D. Challener. — New York ; London : Garland, 1979. — vip,p8129-8675,[3]folded p of plates : 3maps ; 24cm. — (United States military intelligence ; v.19)
Facsims of: documents issued by the Military Intelligence Branch of the United States Army, which had the title Weekly intelligence summary
ISBN 0-8240-3018-4 : Unpriced B82-14346

909.82′2′0207 — Political events, *1920-1922 — Communist viewpoints — Cartoons*

Communist cartoons. — 2nd rev. ed. — London (10 St. John St., EC1M 4AL) : James Klugmann Pictorials, Oct.1982. — [52]p
Previous ed.: London : Communist Party of Great Britain, 1922
ISBN 0-946114-00-5 (pbk) : £4.95 : CIP entry B82-30327

909.82′7 — Political events, *1977-1979 — Communist viewpoints*

Documents in communist affairs. — London : Butterworth Scientific, 1982
1981 / edited by Bogdan Szajkowski. — vii,347p ; 25cm
Includes index
ISBN 0-408-10821-5 : Unpriced : CIP rev. B82-01971

909.82′7′05 — Political events *— Communist viewpoints — Serials*

Documents in communist affairs. — 1977. — London : Butterworths, Jan.1982. — [364]p
Originally published: Cardiff : University College Cardiff Press, 1978
ISBN 0-408-10818-5 : £15.00 : CIP entry B81-37542

Documents in communist affairs. — 1979. — London : Butterworths, Jan.1982. — [572]p
Originally published: Cardiff : University College Cardiff Press, 1979
ISBN 0-408-10819-3 : £20.00 : CIP entry B81-37543

909.82′8′05 — Political events *— Communist viewpoints — Serials*

[Communist affairs *(Woburn, Mass.)***]**.
Communist affairs : documents and analysis. — Vol.1, no.1 (Jan. 1982)-. — Woburn, Mass. ; Sevenoaks : Butterworths, 1982-. — v. ; 25cm
Quarterly. — Continues: Documents in communist affairs
ISSN 0260-9819 = Communist affairs (Woburn, Mass.) : £30.00 per year to multiple reader institutions (£12.50 to individuals) B82-15163

909.82′8′05 — Political events *— Left-wing political viewpoints — Serials*

Red Action. — No.1 (Feb. 1982)-. — London (136 Kingsland High Rd, E8) : Red Action, 1982-. — v. : ill,ports ; 43cm
Monthly
£3.00 per year B82-38495

909.82′8′05 — Political events *— Marxist viewpoints — Serials*

[October *(London)***]**. October : theoretical journal of the Revolutionary Communist League of Britain (Marxist-Leninist). — Vol.1, no.1-. — [London] ([c/o New Era Books, 203 Seven Sisters Rd, N.4]) : The League, [198-]-. — v. ; 30cm
Continues: Revolution
ISSN 0263-6026 = October (London) : £0.30 B82-28856

909.82′8′05 — World events *— Arabic texts — Serials*

Al-**Muslimūn** : al-mağallah al-usbū'iyyah ad-duwaliyyah : usbū'iyyah, iaqāfiyyah, ğāmi'ah : Islamic international weekly. — Al-'Adad al-awwal (al-Ğum'ah 2 Muḥarram 1403 A.H. al-muwāfiq 30 Tišrīn al-awwal (Oktūbir) 1981 A.D.)-. — London (1 Bolt Court, Fleet St., EC4A 3DJ) : Saudi Research and Marketing (UK) Ltd, 1981-. — v. : ill(some col.),ports ; 29cm
Also entitled: Al-Muslimoon
ISSN 0262-7175 = Al-Muslimūn : £0.60 per issue B82-10126

909.82′8′05 — World events *— Serials*

The **Annual** register. — 1981. — London : Longman, July 1982. — [576]p
ISBN 0-582-50303-5 : £27.00 : CIP entry B82-16471

909.82′8′05 — World *— Serials*

The **Europa** year book. — 1982 (Vol.1, pt.1, International organizations, pt.2, Europe, pt.3, Afghanistan-Burundi). — London : Europa, Feb.1982. — [1800]p
ISBN 0-905118-71-5 : CIP entry
ISSN 0071-2302 B81-38838

The **Europa** year book. — 1982 (Vol.2, Cameroon-Zimbabwe). — London : Europa, Apr.1982. — [1840]p
ISBN 0-905118-72-3 : CIP entry
ISSN 0071-2302 B82-04718

The **Europa** year book 1983. — Vol.1. — London : Europa, Feb.1983. — [1790]p
ISBN 0-905118-84-7 : £44.00 : CIP entry
ISSN 0071-2302 B82-39832

World view. — 1983. — London : Pluto Press, Nov.1982. — [448]p
ISBN 0-86104-150-x (pbk) : £6.95 : CIP entry B82-32872

World view. — 82. — London : Pluto Press, May 1982. — [320]p
ISBN 0-86104-367-7 (pbk) : £5.95 : CIP entry B82-14206

909.82′8′076 — Current affairs *— Humour — Questions & answers*

The **News** quiz book / compiled by John Langdon, Danny Greenstone and Alan Nixon ; illustrated by Mac. — London : Robson, 1981. — 108p : ill ; 24cm
ISBN 0-86051-155-3 : £4.50 : CIP rev. B81-27454

910 — GEOGRAPHY, TRAVEL

910 — Applied geography

Sant, Morgan. Applied geography : practice, problems and prospects / Morgan Sant. — London : Longman, 1982. — x,152p : ill,maps ; 25cm
Bibliography: p138-145. — Includes index
ISBN 0-582-30040-1 (cased) : Unpriced : CIP rev. (pbk) : £5.95 B81-25878

910 — Geographical features

Hartley, G.. Geography 'O' level : a course leading to the University of London GCE O level examination in geography (syllabus B — subject no.210). — Cambridge : National Extension College, 1977. — 3v. : ill,charts,maps ; 30cm. — (National Extension College correspondence texts ; course no.G4)
Volume 2 and 3 joint author R.J. Davies
ISBN 0-902404-96-2 (pbk) : Unpriced
ISBN 0-902404-94-6 (v.2)
ISBN 0-902404-95-7 (v.3) B82-40130

910 — Geographical features *— For children*

Bowler, L.. Exploring geography / L. Bowler and B. Waites ; illustrated by Barry and Tim Davies. — Huddersfield : Schofield & Sims
4. — 1982. — 88p : ill(some col.),col.maps,1plan,port ; 26cm
ISBN 0-7217-1047-6 (pbk) : Unpriced B82-18947

Woodcock, Roy. My favourite picture atlas / Roy Woodcock. — London : Hamlyn, 1982. — 71p : col.ill,col.maps ; 33cm
Includes index
ISBN 0-600-39500-6 : £3.50 B82-37313

910 — Geographical features *— For Irish students*

Mcgillicuddy, T. N.. Primary geography / Tim McGillicuddy. — Dublin : Educational Company of Ireland
4 / [maps and diagrams Bob Rogan]. — 1981. — 128p : ill,col.maps ; 26cm
Cover title
Unpriced (pbk) B82-00420

MacNamara, William. Geography / William MacNamara. — Dublin : Helicon : Distributed by Educational Company
1: Maps and physical geography / [maps and diagrams Ann Murphy, Bob Rogan, Tommy McCann]. — 1980. — 142p : ill(some col.),charts(some col.),maps(some col.) ; 26cm
Six maps on folded sheets in pocket
Unpriced (pbk) B82-02558

910 — Geographical features *— For schools*

Ballance, Denis. Geography now / D. and H. Ballance. — Welwyn : Nisbet
1: The empty lands. — 1982. — 95p : ill(some col.),maps(some col.) ; 22cm
ISBN 0-7202-1350-9 (pbk) : £1.85 B82-34823

Ballance, Denis. Geography now / D. and H. Ballance. — Welwyn : Nesbit
2: The crowded lands. — 1982. — 95p : ill (some col.),maps(some col.) ; 22cm
ISBN 0-7202-1351-7 (pbk) : £1.85 B82-34824

Beddis, R. A.. Places, resources and people / Rex Beddis. — Oxford : Oxford University Press, 1982. — 128p : ill(some col.),1facsim,col.maps,1col.port ; 28cm. — (A Sense of place : bk.2)
ISBN 0-19-833434-6 (pbk) : £2.95 B82-29684

Gadsby, Jean. Looking at the world / Jean and David Gadsby ; general editor R.J. Unstead. — 5th ed. — London : Black, 1980. — 365p in various pagings : ill(some col.),charts(some col.),maps(some col.),col.plans ; 26cm
Previous ed.: 1971. — Includes index
ISBN 0-7136-2099-4 : £7.95 B82-14192

Long, M.. World problems : a topic geography / M. Long, B.S. Roberson. — 3rd ed. — London : Hodder and Stoughton, 1981. — vii,216p : ill,maps,plans ; 17x24cm. — (Secondary school series)
Previous ed.: 1977. — Includes index
ISBN 0-340-26148-x (pbk) : Unpriced B82-05549

Lowry, J. H.. A course in world geography. — London : Edward Arnold, Oct.1982
Book 11: The British Isles : a systematic geography. — [192]p
ISBN 0-7131-0689-1 (pbk) : £4.00 : CIP entry B82-22985

910 — Geography *— For schools*

Bateman, R.. Steps in geography. — London : Hutchinson Education
Bk.3. — Sept.1982. — [96]p
ISBN 0-09-149131-2 (pbk) : £2.65 : CIP entry B82-19152

Clarke, Calvin. Farming, towns, water. — London : Edward Arnold, Aug.1982. — [64]p. — (Geography alive ; 1)
ISBN 0-7131-0661-1 (pbk) : £2.00 : CIP entry B82-15912

Clarke, Calvin. Industry, power and transport. — London : Edward Arnold, Aug.1982. — [64]p. — (Geography alive ; 2)
ISBN 0-7131-0662-x (pbk) : £2.00 : CIP entry B82-15913

Cole, J. P.. New ways in geography / J.P. Cole, N.J. Beynon. — Oxford : Basil Blackwell
Book 1. — 2nd ed. — 1982. — 60p : ill(some col.),maps(some col.),plans(some col.) ; 25cm
Previous ed.: 1968
ISBN 0-631-91820-5 (pbk) : Unpriced B82-36828

910 — Geography — *For schools*
continuation

Cole, J. P.. New ways in geography / J.P. Cole, N.J. Beynon. — Oxford : Basil Blackwell
Books 1 and 2. — 2nd ed
Teachers' notes. — 1982. — 35p ; 21cm
Cover title. — Previous ed.: 1969
ISBN 0-631-91830-2 (pbk) : Unpriced
B82-35297

Cole, J. P.. New ways in geography / J.P. Cole, N.J. Beynon. — Oxford : Basil Blackwell
Book 2. — 2nd ed. — 1982. — 64p : ill(some col.),maps(some col.),plans(some col.) ; 25cm
Previous ed.: 1968
ISBN 0-631-91840-x (pbk) : Unpriced
B82-36829

Cole, J. P.. New ways in geography / J.P. Cole, N.J. Beynon. — Oxford : Basil Blackwell
Book 3. — 2nd ed. — 1982. — 61p : ill(some col.),col.maps,plans(some col.) ; 25cm
Previous ed.: 1972
ISBN 0-631-91870-1 (pbk) : Unpriced
B82-36830

Cole, J. P.. New ways in geography / J.P. Cole, N.J. Beynon. — Oxford : Basil Blackwell
Book 3. — 2nd ed
Teachers' notes. — 1982. — 30p ; 21cm
Cover title. — Previous ed.: 1972
ISBN 0-631-91880-9 (pbk) : Unpriced
B82-35295

Cole, J. P.. New ways in geography / J.P. Cole, N.J. Beynon. — Oxford : Basil Blackwell
Introductory book. — 2nd ed. — 1982. — 46p : ill(some col.),maps(some col.),plans(some col.) ; 25cm
Previous ed.: 1970
ISBN 0-631-91780-2 (pbk) : Unpriced
B82-36831

Cole, J. P.. New ways in geography / J.P. Cole, N.J. Beynon. — Oxford : Basil Blackwell
Introductory book. — 2nd ed
Teachers' notes. — 1982. — 7p ; 21cm
Cover title. — Previous ed.: 1970
ISBN 0-631-91790-x (pbk) : Unpriced
B82-35296

Elliott, Gordon. Oxford new geography : a course for juniors / Gordon Elliott. — Oxford : Oxford University Press
1. — 1980 (1982 [printing]). — 96p : col.ill ; 30cm
ISBN 0-19-917023-1 (pbk) : Unpriced
B82-37530

Geography in a changing world. — London : Hodder and Stoughton
Bk.3: Understanding developed places / David P. Jones. — c1982. — 128p : ill(some col.),maps(some col.) ; 25cm
ISBN 0-340-23446-6 (pbk) : Unpriced
B82-39027

Lines, C. J.. Revise geography : a complete revision course for O level and CSE / Clifford Lines, Laurie Bolwell. — Rev. [ed.]. — London : Letts, 1981, c1979. — 190p,[2]folded p of plates : ill,maps(some col.) ; 30cm. — (Letts study aids)
Previous ed.: 1979. — Includes index
ISBN 0-85097-347-3 (pbk) : £3.65 B82-19114

Martin, F.. Work. — London : Hutchinson Education, Sept.1982. — [128]p. — (Core geography ; 2)
ISBN 0-09-144461-6 (pbk) : £3.25 : CIP entry
B82-19102

Murphey, Rhoads. The scope of geography. — London : Methuen, Nov.1982. — [336]p
ISBN 0-416-33410-5 : £5.00 : CIP entry
B82-28290

Oxford geography project. — 2nd ed. — Oxford : Oxford University Press
Previous ed.: 1974-1977
Teacher's guide / John Rolfe ... [et al.]. — 1980. — 150p : ill,maps ; 22cm
Includes bibliographies
ISBN 0-19-914232-7 (pbk) : £2.95 B82-22199

Pantling, Norman. Understanding geography. — Huddersfield : Schofield & Sims
2: People and environments / by Norman Pantling ; illustrated by Geoff Bucktrout. — 1982. — 120p : ill(some col.),col.maps ; 24cm
Includes index
ISBN 0-7217-1053-0 (pbk) : Unpriced
B82-25558

Punnett, Neil. Man, land and resources / Neil Punnett. — Basingstoke : Macmillan Education, 1982. — 68p : ill,maps ; 25cm. — (Geography in focus)
Includes index
ISBN 0-333-28978-1 (pbk) : Unpriced : CIP rev. B82-03799

Slater, Frances. Skills in geography / Frances Slater & Michael Weller. — London : Cassell
Text on inside back cover. — Includes index
Level 1. — 1982. — 63p : ill(some col.),facsims,1col.map,plan(some col.) ; 28cm
ISBN 0-304-30377-1 (pbk) : £2.25 : CIP rev.
B81-34140

Slater, Frances. Skills in geography. — London : Cassell
Level 2. — Feb.1982. — [64]p
ISBN 0-304-30378-x (pbk) : £2.25 : CIP entry
B81-35786

Slater, Frances. Skills in geography Level 3. — London : Cassell, Sept.1982. — [64]p
ISBN 0-304-30379-8 (pbk) : £2.25 : CIP entry
B82-18824

Slater, Frances. Skills in geography Level 4. — London : Cassell, Jan.1983. — [64]p
ISBN 0-304-30380-1 (pbk) : £2.25 : CIP entry
B82-33724

Thomas, Spencer. The developed world. — London : Bell & Hyman, Sept.1982. — [144]p
Originally published: 1980
ISBN 0-7135-1095-1 (pbk) : £3.95 : CIP entry
B82-22810

910 — Geography — *Marxist viewpoints*

Quaini, Massimo. Geography and Marxism / Massimo Quaini ; translated by Alan Braley ; edited and with an annotated bibliography by Russell King. — Oxford : Basil Blackwell, 1982. — 204p : 1ill ; 23cm
Translation of: Marxismo e geografia. — Bibliography: p172-200. — Includes index
ISBN 0-631-12565-5 (cased) : Unpriced : CIP rev.
ISBN 0-631-12816-6 (pbk) : Unpriced
B81-34289

910 — Industrialised countries. Geographical features — *For schools*

Clare, Roger. The industrial world / Roger Clare. — London : Edward Arnold, 1981. — 32p : ill,maps ; 30cm. — (Meet the world!)
ISBN 0-7131-0611-5 (pbk) : £1.95 B82-08962

910 — Travel by businessmen — *Serials*

Executive travel : incorporating Executive travel & leisure : the magazine for the frequent business traveller. — Vol.4. no.7 (July/Aug. 1982)-. — London (21 Fleet St., EC4Y 1AP) : Business Magazines International, 1982-. — v. : ill(some col.),ports ; 29cm
Monthly. — Continues: Executive travel & leisure
ISSN 0263-7685 = Executive travel : £11.00 per year B82-32361

910 — World. Geographical features

Boyce, Ronald Reed. Geographic perspectives on global problems : an introduction to geography / Ronald Reed Boyce. — New York ; Chichester : Wiley, c1982. — x,362p : ill,maps ; 25cm
Includes bibliographies and index
ISBN 0-471-09336-x : £16.60 B82-24218

Philips' international atlas / [edited by B.M. Willett]. — London : George Philip, 1981. — 1v.(various pagings) : col.ill,col.charts,col.maps,ports ; 36cm
ISBN 0-540-05372-4 : £29.95 B82-11019

910 — World. Geographical features — *For children*

James, Paul. It's a weird world / Paul James ; illustrated by David Mostyn. — [London] : Beaver, 1982. — 127p : ill,maps ; 18cm
ISBN 0-600-20289-5 (pbk) : £0.95 B82-17872

Longman chidren's illustrated world atlas. — London : Longman, Aug.1982. — [128]p
ISBN 0-582-25059-5 : £7.95 : CIP entry
B82-15893

Thornford, Charles. A first atlas : of the world / compiled by Charles Thornford ; designed by T.H.B. Russell ; illustrated by P.S. Walker. — Huddersfield : Schofield & Sims, 1982. — 32p : col.ill,col.maps,col.plans ; 32cm
ISBN 0-7217-1057-3 (pbk) : Unpriced
ISBN 0-7217-1058-1 (net ed.) : Unpriced
B82-26271

Tyler, Jenny. Children's atlas of the world / Jenny Tyler and Lisa Watts ; illustrated by Bob Hersey ; consultant editor Ray Pask. — London : Usborne, 1979. — 64p : col.ill,col.maps ; 28cm
Includes index
ISBN 0-86020-264-x : £2.99 B82-17795

910'.01 — Geography. Theories, *1600-1860*

Bowen, Margarita. Empiricism and geographical thought : from Francis Bacon to Alexander von Humboldt / Margarita Bowen. — Cambridge : Cambridge University Press, 1981. — xv,351p : ill,facsims,1port ; 24cm. — (Cambridge geographical studies ; 15)
Bibliography: p312-336. — Includes index
ISBN 0-521-23653-3 : £25.00 : CIP rev.
B81-32596

910'.01 — Travel. Behavioural aspects — *Conference proceedings*

New approaches to analysing travel behaviour. — Aldershot : Gower, Jan.1983. — [488]p
Conference papers
ISBN 0-566-00601-4 : £25.00 : CIP entry
B82-32440

910'.01'5142 — Geography. Q-analysis

Beaumont, John R.. An introduction to Q-analysis / by John R. Beaumont and Anthony C. Gatrell. — Norwich : Geo Abstracts, c1982. — 55p : ill ; 21cm. — (Concepts and techniques in modern geography, ISSN 0306-6142 ; no.34)
Bibliography: p52-55
ISBN 0-86094-106-x (pbk) : Unpriced
B82-33254

910'.01'8 — Geography. Quantitative methods

Quantitative geography : a British view / edited by N. Wrigley and R.J. Bennett. — London : Routledge & Kegan Paul, 1981. — vi,419p : ill,maps,plans ; 25cm
Includes bibliographies and index
ISBN 0-7100-0731-0 : £30.00 : CIP rev.
B81-25731

910'.01'8 — Geography. Quantitative methods — *Case studies* — *For teaching*

Assignments in geography / Roger Dalton ... [et al.]. — London : George Philip, c1978. — 68p : ill ; 25cm. — (Modern techniques in geography)
ISBN 0-540-01024-3 (pbk) : £1.85 : CIP rev.
B78-25673

910'.01'8 — Geography. Spatial analysis — *Conference proceedings*

European progress in spatial analysis / edited by R.J. Bennett. — London : Pion, c1981. — 305p : ill,maps ; 24cm
Conference papers. — Includes bibliographies
ISBN 0-85086-091-1 : £12.50 B82-17602

910'.01'8 — Geography. Spatial aspects. Systems analysis

Coffey, William J.. Geography : towards a general spatial systems approach / William J. Coffey. — London : Methuen, 1981. — xviii,270p : ill,maps ; 24cm
Bibliography: p242-259. — Includes index
ISBN 0-416-30970-4 (cased) : £12.95 : CIP rev.
ISBN 0-416-30980-1 (pbk) : Unpriced
B81-30552

910'.02 — Physical geographical features

Essentials of physical geography / Robert E. Gabler ... [et al.]. — 2nd ed. — Philadelphia ; London : Saunders College, c1982. — vii,568p,[32]p of plates : ill(some col.),col.maps ; 25cm
Previous ed.: New York : Holt, Rinehart and Winston, 1977. — Maps on lining papers. — Includes index
ISBN 0-03-058551-1 : £21.95 B82-25405

910'.02 — Physical geographical features — *For children*

Lambert, David, *1932-*. The active earth. — London : Methuen/Walker, Aug.1981. — [48] p. — (All about earth)
ISBN 0-416-05650-4 : £3.95 : CIP entry B81-20640

910'.02 — Physical geography

Bryant, Richard H.. Physical geography made simple / Richard H. Bryant. — 2nd ed. — London : Heinemann, 1979, c1976 (1982 [printing]). — xi,320p : ill,maps ; 22cm. — (Made simple books)
Previous ed.: London : W.H. Allen, 1976. — Includes bibliographies and index
ISBN 0-434-98520-1 (pbk) : £2.95 B82-18083

910'.02 — Physical geography — *For schools*

Cattell, Tim. This earth / written and illustrated by Tim Cattell. — London : Edward Arnold, 1982. — 2v. : ill ; 25cm
Previous control numbers ISBN 0-7131-0690-5 ; ISBN 0-7131-0691-3
ISBN 0-7131-0690-5 (pbk) : Unpriced : CIP rev.
ISBN 0-7131-0691-3 (Bk.2) : £1.25 B82-04482

Curtis, John. Weather, rocks and landforms. — London : Hutchinson Education, Nov.1982. — [32]p. — (Down to earth)
ISBN 0-09-149141-x (pbk) : £0.80 : CIP entry B82-28724

Knapp, Brian. Earth and man / B.J. Knapp. — London : Allen & Unwin, 1982. — 241p : ill (some col.),charts,maps(some col.) ; 25cm
Includes index
ISBN 0-04-551055-5 (pbk) : Unpriced : CIP rev. B81-35918

Newson, Malcolm D.. Systematic physical geography / Malcolm Newson, James Hanwell. — Basingstoke : Macmillan Education, 1982. — x,246p : ill,maps ; 26cm
Bibliography: p238-239. — Includes index
ISBN 0-333-27619-1 : £5.95 B82-38474

Webber, Peter. Physical geography and man. — London : Macmillan Education, June 1982. — [88]p. — (Geography in focus ; 4)
ISBN 0-333-32728-4 (pbk) : £1.95 : CIP entry B82-10000

910'.02 — Physical geography — *For West African students*

Waters, Grahame H.C.. First lessons in physical geography / Grahame H.C. Waters. — West African ed. — Harlow : Longman, 1982. — iv,140p : ill(some col.),col.maps ; 22cm
Previous ed.: i.e. metric ed. 1977. — Includes index
ISBN 0-582-60399-4 (pbk) : £1.75 B82-30193

910'.091 — Regional geography

Jackson, Richard H.. World regional geography : issues for today / Richard H. Jackson, Lloyd E. Hudman. — New York ; London : Wiley, c1982. — ix,534p,[8]p of plates : ill(some col.),maps ; 29cm
Includes bibliographies and index
ISBN 0-471-06214-6 : £17.50 B82-30268

910'.0913 — Tropical regions. Travel — *Practical information*

Hatt, John. The tropical traveller : an essential guide to travel in hot climates / by John Hatt ; illustrated by Angela Antrim. — London : Pan, 1982. — 253p : ill ; 20cm
Bibliography: p232-234. — Includes index
ISBN 0-330-26577-6 (pbk) : £2.25 B82-11643

910'.09142 — Islands. Description & travel — *Personal observations*

Wiggins, Norah. A raft of small islands / Norah Wiggins. — Braunton : Merlin Books, 1982. — 77p : ill ; 22cm
ISBN 0-86303-001-7 : £4.00 B82-24038

910'.09163 — Atlantic Ocean. Voyages by Halley, Edmond, *1698-1701* — *Correspondence, diaries, etc.*

Halley, Edmond. The three voyages of Edmond Halley in the Paramore, 1698-1701 / edited by Norman J.W. Thrower. — London : Hakluyt Society, 1981. — 2v.(392p, 15p of plates) : ill,charts,maps,facsims,1port ; 23cm. — (Works issued by the Hakluyt Society. Second series ; no.156-157)
Vol.2 consists of portfolio of maps and charts (3 folded sheets). — Bibliography: p373-378. — Includes index
ISBN 0-904180-02-6 : £20.00 (free to members) B82-21858

910'.091631 — North Atlantic Ocean. Voyages by American merchant ships — *Personal observations*

Buckley, Christopher. Steaming to Bamboola : the world of a tramp freighter / Christopher Buckley. — London : Collins, 1982. — xiv,222p ; 24cm
ISBN 0-00-216665-8 : £7.95 : CIP rev. B82-15617

910'.09'1631 — North Atlantic Ocean. Voyages by replica Viking longships, *1979:* **Odin's Raven** *(Ship)*

Ingram, Michael. The voyage of Odin's Raven. — Surby : Clearwater, Dec.1982. — [192]p
ISBN 0-946363-00-5 : £8.50 : CIP entry B82-36169

910'.091631 — North Atlantic Ocean. Voyages by small sailing boats — *Personal observations*

Spiess, Gerry. Alone against the Atlantic / Gerry Spiess with Marlin Bree. — London : Souvenir, 1982, c1981. — 224p,[33]p of plates : ill(some col.),maps(some col.),ports ; 24cm
Originally published: Minneapolis : Control Data Arts, 1981. — Maps on lining papers
ISBN 0-285-62528-4 : £7.50 B82-25326

910'.091632 — Arctic Ocean. Voyages by Soviet nuclear powered ice-breakers, *1977:* **Arktika** *(Ship)* — *Personal observations*

Zakhar'ko, V.. A special mission / V. Zakharko ; [translated from the Russian by Joseph Shapiro]. — Moscow : Progress ; [London] : distributed by Central Books, c1981. — 164p,[16]p of plates : ill,1map,ports ; 17cm
Translation of: Reĭs osobogo naznacheniia
ISBN 0-7147-1686-3 (pbk) : £1.50 B82-19612

910'.0916324 — Barents Sea. Great Britain. *Royal Navy.* **Warships: Edinburgh** *(Ship).* **Cargoes: Gold. Underwater salvage,** *1981*

Penrose, Barrie. Stalin's gold : the story of HMS Edinburgh and its treasure. — London : Granada, May 1982. — [256]p
ISBN 0-246-11778-8 : £8.95 : CIP entry B82-09286

910'.09164 — Pacific Ocean. Exploration by ships, *1769-1770:* **St Jean-Baptiste** *(Ship)* — *Correspondence, diaries, etc*

The **Expedition** of the St Jean-Baptiste to the Pacific 1769-1770 : from journals of Jean de Surville and Guillaume Labé / translated and edited by John Dunmore. — London : Hakluyt Society, 1981. — x,310p,[9]p of plates : ill,maps,facsims ; 23cm. — (Works issued by the Hakluyt Society. Second series ; no.158)
Translated from the French. — Bibliography: p294-301. — Includes index
ISBN 0-904180-11-5 : £12.00 : CIP rev. B81-28037

910'.09164 — Pacific Ocean. Exploration, *to 1836*

Gilbert, John, *1926-*. Charting the vast Pacific / by John Gilbert. — London : Reader's Digest Association, 1980, c1971. — 191p : ill(some col.),facsims(some col.),col.maps,ports(some col.) ; 27cm. — (Discovery and exploration)
Originally published: London : Aldus, 1971. — Includes index
£6.97 B82-31538

910'.09164 — Pacific Ocean. Exploration. Voyages by Cook, James, *1728-1779, 1772-1775* — *Correspondence, diaries, etc.* — *Facsimiles*

Cook, James, *1728-1779*. The journal of HMS Resolution 1772-1775 / by James Cook. — Guildford : Genesis Publications in association with Hedley Fine Art Books, 1981. — 806p : ill(some col.),maps,facsims,ports ; 36cm
Facsimile of: British Library Add. MSS 27886. — Limited ed. of 500 numbered copies, bound in half leather, in slip case
ISBN 0-904351-06-8 : £230.00 B82-05939

910'.09164 — Pacific Ocean. Voyages by rafts, *1947:* **Kon-Tiki** *(Raft)* — *Personal observations*

Heyerdahl, Thor. The Kon-Tiki Expedition : by raft across the South Seas / Thor Heyerdahl ; translated by F.H. Lyon ; with 16 pages of photographs. — London : Unwin Paperbacks, 1982. — 235p,[16]p of plates : ill,1map,ports ; 20cm
Translation of: Kon-Tiki ekspedisjonen. — Originally published: London : Allen and Unwin, 1950. — Includes index
ISBN 0-04-910073-4 (pbk) : £1.95 : CIP rev. B82-03727

910'.0916451 — Bering Sea. Voyages by Dezhnev, Semen, *1648*

Fisher, Raymond H.. The voyage of Semen Dezhnev in 1648 : Bering's precursor : with selected documents / by Raymond H. Fisher. — London : Hakluyt Society, 1981. — xiii,326p,[1]folded leaf of plates : ill,maps ; 23cm. — (Works issued by the Hakluyt Society. Second series ; no.15)
Bibliography: p290-306. — Includes index
ISBN 0-904180-12-3 : £11.00 B82-02770

910'.091647 — South-West Pacific Ocean. Voyages by Vietnamese refugees

Townsend, Peter, *1914-*. The girl in the white ship : a story of the Vietnamese boat people / Peter Townsend. — London : Collins, 1981. — 175p : ill,maps ; 23cm
Maps on lining papers
ISBN 0-00-216726-3 : £8.95 : CIP rev. B81-28163

910'.091648 — South Pacific Ocean. Exploration. Voyages by sailing ships, *1699-1701:* **Roebuck** *(Ship)* — *Personal observations*

Dampier, William. A voyage to New Holland : the English voyage of discovery to the South Seas in 1699 / William Dampier ; edited with an introduction by James Spencer. — Gloucester : Alan Sutton, 1981. — 256p,[8]p of plates : ill,facsims,maps,1port ; 26cm
Facsim of: ed. in 1 vol. London : Knapton, 1729. — Includes index
ISBN 0-904387-75-5 : Unpriced : CIP rev. B81-31099

910'.09165 — Indian Ocean. Voyages by reed ships, *1978:* **Tigris** *(Ship)* — *Personal observations*

Heyerdahl, Thor. The Tigris expedition : in search of our beginnings / Thor Heyerdahl. — London : Unwin Paperbacks, 1982. — 379p : col.ill,1map,col.ports ; 20cm
Originally published: London : Allen and Unwin, 1980. — Includes index
ISBN 0-04-572024-x (pbk) : £2.95 : CIP rev. B82-03726

910'.09165 — Indian Ocean. Voyages by sailing ships, *1980.* **Sohar** *(Ship)* — *Personal observations*

Severin, Tim. The Sindbad voyage. — London : Hutchinson, Oct.1982. — [256]p
ISBN 0-09-150560-7 : £9.95 : CIP entry B82-24706

910'.091724 — Developing countries. Geographical features — *For schools*

Clare, Roger. The developing world / Roger Clare. — London : Edward Arnold, 1981. — 32p : ill,maps ; 30cm. — (Meet the world!)
ISBN 0-7131-0612-3 (pbk) : £1.95 B82-08961

Kimpton, Lawrence. Geography in a changing world. — London : Hodder & Stoughton
Bk.5: Understanding our decisions. — Feb.1983. — [144]p
ISBN 0-340-23448-2 (pbk) : £3.45 : CIP entry B82-38041

910′.09173 — Human settlements. Geographical aspects — *For schools*

Meyer, Iain R.. Settlements / Iain R. Meyer & Richard J. Huggett. — Repr. with amendments. — London : Harper & Row, 1981, c1979. — 201p : ill,charts,maps ; 25cm. — (Geography ; bk.1)
Includes bibliographies
ISBN 0-06-318096-0 (pbk) : £4.50 B82-27325

910′.091732 — Cities. Description & travel

Cities : from the television series conceived by John McGreevy. — [London] : Angus & Robertson, 1981. — 265p : ill(some col.),ports (some col.) ; 26cm
ISBN 0-207-14175-4 : £9.95 B82-32568

Morris, Jan. Destinations. — Oxford : Oxford University Press, Nov.1982. — [256]p
ISBN 0-19-281367-6 (pbk) : £2.95 : CIP entry B82-28726

910′.091732 — Urban regions. Geographical aspects

Carter, Harold. The study of urban geography / Harold Carter. — 3rd ed. — London : E. Arnold, 1981. — xiv,434p : ill,maps ; 23cm
Previous ed.: 1976. — Includes bibliographies and index
ISBN 0-7131-6235-x (pbk) : £6.95 : CIP rev. B80-23845

Clark, David. Urban geography. — London : Croom Helm, June 1982. — [288]p. — (Croom Helm series in geography and environment)
ISBN 0-7099-0732-x (cased) : £14.95 : CIP entry
ISBN 0-7099-0733-8 (pbk) : £6.95 B82-10864

Geography and the urban environment. — Chichester : Wiley
Vol.4. — Dec.1981. — [336]p
ISBN 0-471-28051-8 : £19.30 : CIP entry B81-34225

Progress in urban geography. — London : Croom Helm, Dec.1982. — [288]p
ISBN 0-7099-2027-x : £15.95 : CIP entry B82-30806

910′.091732 — Urban regions. Geographical aspects — *Serials*

Geography and the urban environment. — Vol.5. — Chichester : Wiley, Jan.1983. — [400]p
ISBN 0-471-10225-3 : £20.50 : CIP entry B82-34615

910′.091732 — Urban regions. Geography

Herbert, David T.. Urban geography : a first approach. — Chichester : Wiley, Sept.1982. — [600]p
ISBN 0-471-10137-0 (cased) : £30.00 : CIP entry
ISBN 0-471-10138-9 (pbk) : £9.00 B82-19520

910′.091734 — Rural regions. Geographical aspects

Progress in rural geography. — London : Croom Helm, Dec.1982. — [256]p
ISBN 0-7099-2021-0 : £15.95 : CIP entry B82-30804

910′.091811 — Eastern hemisphere. Running journeys, *1974-1975* — *Personal observations*

Bowers, Kelvin. Closing the distance / Kelvin Bowers. — Stoke-on-Trent : Andy Ridler, c1980. — 225p : ill,maps,ports ; 18cm
ISBN 0-905074-03-3 (pbk) : £1.50 B82-18612

910′.091821 — Caribbean region. Voyages by sailing boats

Robinson, Bill. South to the Caribbean : how to carry out the dream of sailing your own boat to the Caribbean / Bill Robinson. — New York ; London : Norton, c1982. — 342p : ill,1map,ports ; 24cm
ISBN 0-393-03265-5 : £13.50 B82-35676

910′.091821 — Western world. Geographical features — *For Irish students*

Kennedy, Bernard. Revision atlas : for Intermediate Certificate geography / Bernard Kennedy, William MacNamara. — Dublin : Educational Company of Ireland, c1982. — 72p : maps ; 26cm
Text on inside covers
Unpriced (pbk) B82-25668

910′.2 — Overland travel

Hewat, Theresa. Overland and beyond / Theresa & Jonathan Hewat. — 5th ed. — London : Lascelles, 1981. — 160p : ill,1map,2ports ; 19cm
Previous ed.: 1980?. — Includes index
ISBN 0-903909-13-8 (pbk) : £2.50 B82-40627

910′.2′02 — Northern Ireland. International vacations for young persons. Organisation — *Practical information — For youth work*

Hope, Roger. Getting away : a handbook for organising international holidays and exchanges for young people / prepared by Roger Hope and Arthur Dempster. — Belfast : Standing Conference of Youth Organisations in Northern Ireland, 1980. — 38p : forms ; 30cm
Cover title
ISBN 0-906797-06-3 (spiral) : Unpriced
Also classified at 370.19′62 B82-00098

910′.2′02 — Overseas residence — *Practical information — For expatriate British personnel*

The **expatriate** survival kit / prepared by Resident Abroad. — [London] : Financial Times Business, [1982]. — 1portfolio : ill,forms,ports ; 30cm
ISBN 0-902101-22-6 : Unpriced B82-30021

910′.2′02 — Travel — *Practical information*

The **Traveller′s** handbook : incorporating The independent traveller′s handbook / edited by Ingrid Cranfield in association with Richard Harrington. — London : Heinemann, 1982. — xxiv,695p : maps ; 19cm
Bibliography: p454-495. — Includes index
ISBN 0-434-14827-x (pbk) : £8.50 B82-15432

Wright, Carol. The travel survival guide. — Newton Abbot : David & Charles, Jan.1983. — [192]p
ISBN 0-7153-8310-8 : £6.50 : CIP entry B82-32612

910′.2′02 — Travel — *Practical information — Serials*

Travelnews diary and yearbook. — 1982-. — Sutton : IPC Transport Press, 1981-. — v. ; 22cm
ISSN 0263-0710 = Travelnews diary and yearbook : Unpriced B82-15151

910′.3′21 — Geography — *Encyclopaedias*

Walker, Ann. A basic dictionary of geography. — London : Bell and Hyman, June 1981. — [48]p
ISBN 0-7135-1245-8 (pbk) : £1.60 : CIP entry B81-11919

910′.3′9171 — Geographical features — *Russian & English dictionaries*

Geographical names in Russian / edited by B. Faden. — Letchworth : Prideaux, 1982. — 38p ; 21cm. — (Russian texts for students ; no.13)
£0.90 (pbk) B82-21682

910.4 — Antiquities. Sites. Description & travel, *1955-1968 — Occult viewpoints*

Von Harten, Marjorie. Walking in the world / by Marjorie Von Harten. — Sherborne : Coombe Springs, c1978. — 208p : ill,1plan,1port ; 30cm
ISBN 0-900306-46-7 (pbk) : £2.00 B82-12779

910.4 — England. Emigration to Australia. Voyages by sailing ships, *1874:* **Northumberland** *(Ship)* — *Correspondence, diaries, etc*

Sams, Joseph. The diary of Joseph Sams : an emigrant in the ′Northumberland′ 1874 / edited with additional material by Simon Braydon and Robert Songhurst. — London : H.M.S.O., 1982. — vii,102p,[8]p of plates : ill,1map,facsims ; 23cm. — ([Recollections])
ISBN 0-11-290341-x : £4.25 B82-17766

910.4 — Expeditions by primary school parties — *Renewals*

Evans, John. So you want to go abroad — / by John Evans & Sybil Camsey. — Worthing : Travel plus, c1981. — 137p : ill,2maps ; 30cm
Unpriced (spiral) B82-01269

910.4 — Expeditions: Operation Drake *(1978-1980)*

Chapman, Roger, *1945-*. In the eye of the wind : the story of Operation Drake / Roger Chapman. — London : Hamilton, 1982. — 128p,[8]p of plates : ill(some col.),maps,ports ; 26cm
ISBN 0-241-10764-4 : £5.95 : CIP rev. B82-04310

Operation Drake *(1978-1980)*. Operation Drake : voyage of discovery / written & edited by Andrew W. Mitchell. — London : Severn House, c1981. — 224p : ill(some col.),maps,1coat of arms,ports(some col.) ; 28cm
Ill on lining papers. — Bibliography: p221. — Includes index
ISBN 0-7278-2007-9 : £12.95 : CIP rev. B81-24665

910.4 — Expeditions — *Practical information*

The **Expeditioner′s** handbook. — London : Macmillan, June 1982. — [192]p
ISBN 0-333-29376-2 : £8.95 : CIP entry B82-09998

Planning a small expedition : course notes for seminars to be held at Royal Geographical Society, London, 6th November ... [and elsewhere]. — London (Royal Geographical Society, 1 Kensington Gore [SW7 2AR]) : Expedition Advisory Centre, 1981. — 64,xxp : ill ; 30cm
Cover title. — Includes bibliographies
£3.00 (spiral) B82-11737

910.4 — International travel, *1891-1913 — Personal observations — Correspondence, diaries, etc*

Fountaine, Margaret. Love among the butterflies : the travels and adventures of a Victorian lady / Margaret Fountaine ; edited by W.F. Cater. — Harmondsworth : Penguin, 1982, c1980. — 203p ; 20cm
Originally published: London : Collins, 1980
ISBN 0-14-006066-9 (pbk) : £1.95 B82-33970

910.4 — Travel, *1946-1981 — Personal observations*

Castle, Ronald. Can teach, will travel / Ronald Castle. — Bognor Regis : New Horizon, c1982. — 114p ; 22cm
ISBN 0-86116-478-4 : £4.50 B82-27156

910.4 — Travel, *ca 1200-1450*

Labarge, Margaret Wade. Medieval travellers. — London : Hamilton, Oct.1982. — [224]p
ISBN 0-241-10886-1 : £12.50 : CIP entry B82-23461

910.4 — Travel — *Personal observations*

De Gaury, G.. Traces of travel. — London : Quartet Books, Jan.1983. — 1v.
ISBN 0-7043-2363-x : CIP entry B82-40309

910.4 — Travel — *Personal observations — Welsh texts*

Griffith, John Ffrancon. Crwydro / John Ffrancon Griffith. — [Caernarfon] : Gwasanaeth Llyfrgell Gwynedd, 1982. — 25p : 1port ; 22cm. — (Darlith flynyddol Llyfrgell Bethesda ; 1981)
′Darlith a draddodwyd yn Ysgol Penybryn, Bethesda, Mawrth 18ed, 1981′
ISBN 0-904852-28-8 (pbk) : £0.50 B82-26992

910.4 — World. Description & travel — *Personal observations*

Visions of paradise / Bernhard Grzimek ... [et al.]. — [London] : Hodder & Stoughton, 1981. — 236p : ill(some col.),ports(some col.) ; 30cm
Translation of the German. — Ill on lining papers
ISBN 0-340-27220-1 : £8.50 : CIP rev. B81-27391

910.4′025 — Overseas expeditions. Organisations — *Directories*

Winser, Nigel. Joining an expedition / compiled by Nigel Winser. — London (Royal Geographical Society, 1 Kensington Gore, SW7 2AR) : Expedition Advisory Centre, [1981?]. — 12p : ill ; 21cm
Cover title
Unpriced (pbk) B82-11732

910.4′07 — Expeditions. Information sources — *Directories*

Hemming, John, *1935-*. Reference sources for expeditions / compiled by John Hemming. — London : Expedition Advisory Centre, 1981. — 30p ; 21cm
ISBN 0-907649-02-5 (spiral) : Unpriced
B82-11735

910.4′079 — Expeditions. Grants. Organisations — *Directories*

Hemming, John, *1935-*. Grant-giving organisations for expeditions / [compiled by John Hemming]. — London : Expedition Advisory Centre, [1981]. — 17p ; 21cm
Cover title. — Bibliography: p17
ISBN 0-907649-01-7 (spiral) : Unpriced
B82-11734

910.4′092′4 — Travel. Newby, Eric — *Biographies*

Newby, Eric. A traveller′s life / Eric Newby. — London : Collins, 1982. — 302p,[12]p of plates : ill ; 23cm
ISBN 0-00-211874-2 : £8.95 : CIP rev.
B81-24606

910.4′092′4 — Travel. Price, Willard — *Biographies — For children*

Price, Willard. My own life of adventure. — London : Cape, Oct.1982. — 1v.
ISBN 0-224-02069-2 : CIP entry B82-27196

910.4′092′4 — Travel. Stark, Freya — *Personal observations*

Maitland, Alexander. A tower in a wall : a portrait of Dame Freya Stark. — Edinburgh : Blackwood, Oct.1982. — [140]p
ISBN 0-85158-159-5 : CIP entry B82-28586

910.4′092′4 — Travel. Van der Post, Laurens — *Biographies*

Van der Post, Laurens. Yet being someone other. — London : Hogarth Press, Oct.1982. — [352]p
ISBN 0-7012-1900-9 : £9.50 : CIP entry
B82-23208

910.4′1 — Journeys round the world by bicycles, *1896-1898 — Personal observations*

Fraser, John Foster. Round the world on a wheel : being the narrative of a bicycle ride of nineteen thousand two hundered and thirty-seven miles through seventeen countries and across three continents by John Foster Fraser, S. Edward Lunn and F.H. Lowe / by John Foster Fraser. — Abridged ed. — London : Chatto & Windus, 1982. — 325p : ill,1facsim,ports ; 23cm
Full ed. originally published: London : Methuen, 1899
ISBN 0-7011-2609-4 : £7.95 : CIP rev.
B82-16196

910.4′1 — World. Circumnavigation by sailing catamarans, *1978-1980:* **Ocean Winds II** *(Ship) — Correspondence, diaries, etc.*

Patterson, Pat. In the wake of Drake / Pat Patterson. — St. Ives, Cornwall : United Writers, c1981. — 255p,[40]p of plates : ill,maps,ports ; 22cm
Maps on lining papers
ISBN 0-901976-74-1 : £7.95 B82-20116

910.4′1 — World. Circumnavigation by warships, *1772-1775:* **Resolution** *(Ship) - Personal observations*

Forster, Johann Reinhold. The Resolution Journal of Johann Reinhold Forster, 1772-1775. — London (c/o Map Library, British Library, Great Russell St., WC1B 3DG) : Hakluyt Society, July 1981. — 4v.[(786)]p. — (Hakluyt Society second series ; 152-5)
ISBN 0-904180-10-7 : CIP entry B81-13721

910.4′1′0924 — World. Circumnavigation by Drake, *Sir Francis, 1540?-1596, 1577-1580*

Quinn, David B.. Drake′s circumnavigation of the globe : a review : the fifteenth Harte Lecture, delivered in the University of Exeter on 14 November 1980 / David B. Quinn. — [Exeter] : University of Exeter, 1981. — 21p : 2maps ; 21cm
ISBN 0-85989-197-6 (pbk) : £0.60 B82-06454

910.4′5 — Exploration. Voyages by Cook, James, *1728-1779, 1776-1779*

Gilbert, George. Captain Cook′s final voyage : the journal of Midshipman George Gilbert / introduced and edited by Christine Holmes. — [Horsham] : Caliban, c1982. — 158p,[8]p of plates : ill,1facsim,maps,2col.ports ; 24cm
ISBN 0-904573-33-8 : £10.00 B82-28297

910.4′5 — Seafaring. Nutritional factors, *1700-1945 — Conference proceedings*

Starving sailors : the influence of nutrition upon naval and maritime history / edited by J. Watt, E.J. Freeman, and W.F. Bynum. — [London] : National Maritime Museum, 1981. — 212p,[8]p of plates : ill(some col.),1map,ports ; 21cm
Conference papers. — Includes index
ISBN 0-905555-53-8 (pbk) : Unpriced
B82-10034

910.4′5 — Seafaring — *Questions & answers*

Muncaster, Martin. The yachtsman′s quizbook. — Newton Abbot : David & Charles, Nov.1982. — [128]p
ISBN 0-7153-8291-8 : £4.50 : CIP entry
B82-26397

910.4′5 — Voyages by converted fishing boats, *ca 1960-1980:* **Sanu** *(Boat) — Personal observations*

Baker, Denys Val. A family at sea / Denys Val Baker. — London : Kimber, 1981. — 206p ; 23cm
ISBN 0-7183-0358-x : £5.95 B82-05912

910.4′5 — Voyages by sailing boats, *1972-1977:* **Seraffyn** *(Yacht) — Personal observations*

Pardey, Lin. Seraffyn′s European adventure / by Lin and Larry Pardey. — New York ; London : Norton, c1979. — 311p : ill,1map,ports ; 24cm
ISBN 0-393-03231-0 : £9.95 B82-40954

910.4′5 — Voyages by sailing boats, *1974-1980:* **Sea Dart** *(Ship) — Personal observations*

Jones, Tristan. Adrift. — London : Bodley Head, May 1981. — [284]p
ISBN 0-370-30422-5 : £6.95 : CIP entry
B81-06587

910.4′5 — Voyages by sailing boats: Barbara *(Ship)* **& Sea Dart** *(Ship), 1969-1974 — Personal observations*

Jones, Tristan. The incredible voyage : a personal odyssey / Tristan Jones ; foreword by John Hemming. — Leicester : Charnwood, 1981, c1977. — 557p : maps ; 23cm
Originally published: Mission, Kan. : Sheed Andrews and McMeel, 1977 ; London : Bodley Head, 1978. — Published in large print
ISBN 0-7089-8002-3 : £6.50 : CIP rev.
B81-25665

910.4′5 — Voyages by sailing boats, *ca 1950-1977 — Personal observations*

Tilman, H. W.. Adventures under sail. — London : Gollancz, Oct.1982. — [256]p
ISBN 0-575-03159-x : £9.95 : CIP entry
B82-23344

910.4′5 — Voyages by steamships, *1837-1856 — Correspondence, diaries, etc.*

Cree, Edward H.. The Cree journals : the voyages of Edward H. Cree, Surgeon R.N., as related in his private journals, 1837-1856 / edited with an introduction by Michael Levien. — Exeter : Webb & Bower, 1981. — 276p : ill(some col.),maps(some col.),ports ; 25cm
Maps on lining papers
ISBN 0-906671-36-1 : £12.50 : CIP rev.
B81-25887

910.4′5 — Voyages by yachts, *1968-1971 — Personal observations*

Moitessier, Bernard. The long way. — London : Granada, Sept.1982. — [256]p
Translation of: La longue route. — Originally published: St Albans : Coles, 1974
ISBN 0-246-10987-4 : £6.95 : CIP entry
B82-18845

910.4′5 — Voyages from Great Britain to Australia by British immigrants, *1800-1900 — Readings from comtemporary sources*

The **Long** farewell / [compiled by] Don Charlwood. — Victoria ; [London] : Allen Lane, 1981. — x,338p : ill,2maps,facsims,plans,ports ; 23cm
Bibliography: p320-327. — Includes index
ISBN 0-7139-1428-9 : £10.00 B82-16137

910.4′5 — Voyages from Great Britain to New Zealand by sailing ships, *1850-1851 — Correspondence, diaries, etc.*

Burnett, *Mr*. A passenger′s diary of a voyage from London to New Zealand 1850-1851. — [Workington] ([22, Calva Brow, Workington, Cumbria]) : Workington & District Local History Society, [1981]. — 30p : ill,1map ; 21cm
Cover title. — Author: Mr Burnett
Unpriced (pbk) B82-01900

910.4′5 — Voyages from Greece to China by boats, *1979-1980 — Personal observations*

Young, Gavin. Slow boats to China / Gavin Young ; illustrations by Salim. — London : Hutchinson, 1981. — 488p : ill,maps ; 25cm
Map on lining papers
ISBN 0-09-146050-6 : £8.95 : CIP rev.
B81-20583

910.4′5 — Voyages, *to 1980*

A **Book** of sea journeys / compiled by Ludovic Kennedy. — London : Collins, 1981. — xix,395p : ill,ports ; 24cm
ISBN 0-00-216310-1 : £7.95 : CIP rev.
B81-24587

910.4′5′0924 — American seafaring, *1834-1836 — Personal observations*

Dana, Richard Henry. Two years before the mast : a personal narrative of life at sea / by Richard Henry Dana, Jr ; with an introduction by Sir Wilfred Grenfell ; and illustrations by Charles Pears. — London : Macmillan, 1980. — viii,415p,[11]leaves of plates : col.ill ; 20cm
Facsim of: edition published 1911
ISBN 0-333-30785-2 : £5.95 B82-16024

Dana, Richard Henry. Two years before the mast : a personal narrative of life at sea / by Richard Henry Dana, Jr ; edited with an introduction by Thomas Philbrick. — Harmondsworth : Penguin, 1981. — 572p : 1port ; 19cm. — (The Penguin American library)
Originally published: New York : Harper, 1840 ; London : Moxon, 1841. — Port on inside cover. — Bibliography: p31-32
ISBN 0-14-039008-1 (pbk) : £2.95 B82-22258

910.4′53 — Hidden treasure

Wilson, Derek. The world atlas of treasure / Derek Wilson. — London : Pan, 1982, c1981. — 256p : ill,maps(some col.),facsims,ports ; 30cm
Originally published: London : Collins, 1981. — Bibliography: p250-251. — Includes index
ISBN 0-330-26450-8 (pbk) : £6.50 B82-15120

910′.5 — Travel — *Serials*

Adventure sports & travel. — No.11-. — London (17 South Molton St., W1) : Danpalm, [1981]-. — v. : ill ; 30cm
Six issues yearly. — Continues: Adventure sports
ISSN 0262-5768 = Adventure sports & travel : £6.50 per year
Primary classification 796′.05 B82-07646

910′.68 — Tourism. Management — *Serials*

[Tourism management *(1982)*]. Tourism management : research, policies, planning. — Vol.3, no.1 (Mar. 1982)-. — Guildford (PO Box 63, Westbury House, Bury St., Guildford GU2 5BH) : Butterworth Scientific, 1982-. — v. ; 28cm
Quarterly. — Continues: International journal of tourism management. — Also available on microfiche
ISSN 0261-5177 = Tourism management (1982) : £50.00 per year B82-27644

910′.7′1 — Schools. Curriculum subjects: Geography. Curriculum, *1579-1961*

Historical perspectives on geographical education : research papers prepared for the 24th Congress of the International Geographical Union, Tokyo, 1980 / edited by William E. Marsden. — [London] (N.J. Greaves, International Geographical Union, c/o Institute of Education, University of London, Bedford Way, WC1H 0AL) : University of London Institute of Education, c1980. — iii,86p ; 21cm
At head of title: International Geographical Union Commission on Geographical Education
£2.00 (pbk) B82-09239

910′.7′1 — Schools. Curriculum subjects: Geography — *For teaching*

Slater, Frances. Learning through geography. — London : Heinemann Educational, Sept.1982. — [192]p
ISBN 0-435-35715-8 (pbk) : £4.95 : CIP entry B82-19674

910′.7′1 — Schools. Curriculum subjects: Geography. Teaching. Bias

Bias in geographical education / edited by Ashley Kent. — London : Dept. of Geography, University of London Institute of Education, 1982. — ii,46p : ill ; 30cm
Includes bibliographies
ISBN 0-85473-127-x (unbound) : Unpriced B82-28407

910′.7′1 — Schools. Curriculum subjects: Geography. Use of graphicacy — *For teaching*

Boardman, David. Graphicacy and geography teaching. — London : Croom Helm, Nov.1982. — [208]p
ISBN 0-7099-0644-7 : £12.95 : CIP entry B82-28747

910′.7′1241 — Great Britain. Secondary schools. Curriculum subjects: Geography. Teaching

Our landscapes. — Edinburgh : Oliver & Boyd, 1982. — (Outlook geography)
Teaching guide / Thomas H. Masterton. — 31p : ill,maps ; 30cm
Cover title
ISBN 0-05-003402-2 (pbk) : £1.25 B82-34972

910′.7′1241 — Great Britain. Secondary schools. Curriculum subjects: Geography. Teaching — *Conference proceedings*

Signposts for geopgraphy teaching : papers from the Charney Manor Conference 1980 / edited by Rex Walford. — Harlow : Longman, 1981. — 222p : ill,maps ; 23cm
ISBN 0-582-35334-3 (cased) : Unpriced
ISBN 0-582-35335-1 (pbk) : £4.95 B82-08896

910′.7′1242 — England. Secondary schools. Students, 16-19 years. Curriculum subjects: Geography. Local studies. Teaching methods: Inquiry methods

Rawling, Eleanor. Local issues and enquiry-based learning / by Eleanor Rawling. — London : Schools Council Curriculum Development Project, 1981. — 42p : ill ; 21cm. — (Occasional paper / Schools Council Curriculum Development Geography 16-19 ; no.2)
ISBN 0-85473-120-2 (pbk) : Unpriced B82-11739

910′.76 — Geography - *Questions & answers - For African students - For schools*

Pritchard, J. M.. Africa. — London : Edward Arnold, July 1981. — [80]p
ISBN 0-7131-8071-4 (pbk) : £1.75 : CIP entry B81-14396

910′.76 — Geography — *Questions & answers — For schools*

Catling, Simon. Outset geography / Simon Catling, Tim Firth, David Rowbothom. — London : Oliver & Boyd
Text and ill on inside covers
2 / mapping consultant Jane Thake ; illustrated by Moira Chesmur, Jon Davis and Hamish Gordon. — 1981. — 56p : col.ill,col.maps,facsims(some col.) ; 27cm
ISBN 0-05-003295-x (pbk) : £1.75 B82-02042

Catling, Simon. Outset geography / Simon Catling, Tim Firth, David Rowbotham. — Edinburgh : Oliver & Boyd, 1982
3 / mapping consultant Jane Thake ; illustrated by Moira Chesmur, Jon Davis and Hamish Gordon. — 64p : col.ill,col.map ; 27cm
ISBN 0-05-003296-8 : Unpriced B82-36238

Foster, I. D. L.. Data response exercises. — London : Edward Arnold, Oct.1982. — [64]p
ISBN 0-7131-0676-x (pbk) : £2.50 : CIP entry B82-22984

The **Whole** world : exercises : answers. — Huddersfield : Schofield & Sims, 1982. — [44]p : ill,maps ; 30cm
ISBN 0-7217-1059-x (unbound) : Unpriced B82-31814

910′.88042 — Travel by women, *1700-1900 — Personal observations — Collections*

Ladies on the loose : women travellers of the 18th and 19th centuries / edited, with an introduction by Leo Hamalian. — South Yarmouth, Mass. : Curley ; [Skipton] : distributed by Magna Print, c1981. — xviii,586p ; 22cm
Published in large print
ISBN 0-89340-513-2 : Unpriced B82-39722

910′.880621 — Travel by British royal families, *to 1981*

Garrett, Richard. Royal travel. — Poole : Blandford Press, Sept.1982. — [238]p
ISBN 0-7137-1182-5 : £8.95 : CIP entry B82-23870

910′.9 — Exploration, *to ca 1970 — For schools*

Case, S. L.. Explorers / S.L. Case. — London : Evans, 1982. — 48p : ill,maps,ports ; 25cm. — (Knowing world history)
ISBN 0-237-29263-7 (pbk) : Unpriced B82-16620

910′.902 — Exploration, *1254-1780 — For children*

Grant, Neil, *1938-*. Discovering the world / [author Neil Grant] ; [editors Jo Jones, Trisha Pike]. — London : Marshall Cavendish, 1981. — 29p : col.ill,col.maps,col.ports ; 30cm. — (Enigma) (An All colour fact book)
Text, ill, port on lining papers
ISBN 0-85685-969-9 : Unpriced B82-06078

910′.9′024 — World. Exploration, *1422-1522*

Castlereagh, Duncan. The great age of exploration / by Duncan Castlereagh. — London : Reader's Digest Association, 1979, c1971. — 191p : ill(some col.),col.coat of arms,facsims,maps(some col.),ports(some col.) ; 27cm. — (Discovery and exploration)
Originally published: London : Aldus, 1971. — Includes index
£6.97 B82-31536

910′.92′2 — Eccentric British travellers, *1700-1900 — Biographies*

Keay, John. Eccentric travellers / John Keay. — London : Murray, c1982. — 216p,[16]p of plates : ill,maps,ports ; 23cm
Includes index
ISBN 0-7195-3868-8 : £9.50
ISBN 0-563-17973-2 (BBC) B82-39037

910′.92′2 — Geographers — *Biographies — Serials*

Geographers : biobibliographical studies. — Vol.5. — London : Mansell, Nov.1981. — [150]p
ISBN 0-7201-1635-x : £17.00 : CIP entry B81-30633

910′.92′4 — Exploration. Cook, James, *1728-1779 — Biographies*

Gould, R. T.. Captain Cook / R.T. Gould. — New ed. with introduction. — London : Duckworth, 1978. — 128p,[1]leaf of plates : 3maps,1port ; 22cm
Previous ed.: 1935. — Includes index
ISBN 0-7156-1665-x : £4.95 B82-39804

910′.9469 — Exploration. Attitudes of Portuguese, *1500-1600*

Hooykaas, R.. Humanism and the voyages of discovery in 16th century Portuguese science and letters / R. Hooykaas. — Amsterdam ; Oxford : North-Holland, 1979. — 67p ; 24cm. — (Mededelingen der Koninklijke Nederlandse akademie van Wetenschappen, Afd Letterkunde. Nieuwe reeks ; d.42, no.4)
Pages also numbered 99-159
ISBN 0-7204-8487-1 (pbk) : Unpriced
Primary classification 144′.09469 B82-05450

911 — HISTORICAL GEOGRAPHY

911 — Historical geography

Guelke, Leonard. Historical understanding in geography. — Cambridge : Cambridge University Press, Oct.1982. — [109]p. — (Cambridge studies in historical geography ; 3)
ISBN 0-521-24678-4 : £15.00 : CIP entry B82-29371

911 — World, *to 500 — Atlases*

Muir, Ramsay. Muir's atlas of ancient and classical history. — London : G. Philip, July 1982. — [36]p
ISBN 0-540-05433-x (pbk) : £3.00 : CIP entry B82-13264

911 — World, *to 1980 — Atlases*

Muir, Ramsay. Muir's historical atlas : ancient, medieval and modern. — London : G. Philip, July 1982. — [168]p
ISBN 0-540-05435-6 : £7.50 : CIP entry B82-14234

Muir, Ramsay. Muir's historical atlas : medieval and modern. — London : G. Philip, July 1982. — [136]p
ISBN 0-540-05434-8 : £5.95 : CIP entry B82-14233

The **Times** concise atlas of world history. — London : Times Books, Oct.1982. — [192]p
ISBN 0-7230-0247-9 : £12.50 : CIP entry B82-24263

911′.0722 — Historical geography. Methodology — *Case studies*

Period and place : research methods in historical geography / edited by Alan R.H. Baker and Mark Billinge. — Cambridge : Cambridge University Press, 1982. — x,377p : ill,maps ; 24cm. — (Cambridge studies in historical geography)
Bibliography: p363-372. — Includes index
ISBN 0-521-24272-x : £25.00 : CIP rev. B82-14496

911′.41 — Great Britain. Goegraphical features. Historical sources: Directories

Shaw, Gareth. British directories as sources in historical geography / by Gareth Shaw. — Norwich : Geo Abstracts, c1982. — 60p : ill,maps ; 21cm. — (Historical geography research series, ISSN 0143-683x ; no.8)
Text on inside cover
ISBN 0-86094-109-4 (pbk) : Unpriced B82-32714

911′.411 — Scotland. Historical geography, *to 1981*

An **Historical** geography of Scotland. — London : Academic Press, Feb.1983. — [350]p
ISBN 0-12-747360-2 (cased) : CIP entry
ISBN 0-12-747362-9 (pbk) B82-36578

911′.415 — Ireland, *to 1980 — Atlases*

Edwards, Ruth Dudley. An atlas of Irish history. — 2nd ed. — London : Methuen, July 1981. — [280]p
Previous ed.: 1973
ISBN 0-416-74820-1 (cased) : £11.00 : CIP entry
ISBN 0-416-74050-2 (pbk) : £5.50 B81-13498

911′.42 — England. Geographical features, *1066-1485*

The **English** medieval landscape / edited by Leonard Cantor. — London : Croom Helm, c1982. — 225p : ill,1facsim,maps ; 23cm. — (Croom Helm historical geography series)
Includes index
ISBN 0-7099-0707-9 : £12.95 : CIP rev. B82-04461

911′.4238 — Somerset. Geographical features, *to ca 1980*

Havinden, Michael. The Somerset landscape / by Michael Havinden. — London : Hodder and Stoughton, 1981. — 272p,[28]p of plates : ill,maps ; 22cm. — (The Making of the English landscape)
Includes index
ISBN 0-340-20116-9 (pbk) : £7.95 : CIP rev. B81-35689

911′.42574 — Oxfordshire. Oxford. Green belts. Geographical features, *ca 1600-1974*

The **Landscape** of Oxford′s green belt. — [Oxford] : Oxford University Department for External Studies, c1981. — v,88p : maps ; 30cm
Includes bibliographies
ISBN 0-903736-13-6 (pbk) : Unpriced B82-08214

911′.4271 — Cheshire. Geographical features. Historical sources: Fields. Ridges & furrows

Thompson, Patience. Ploughlands and pastures : the imprint of agrarian history in four Cheshire townships — Peckforton, Haughton, Bunbury, Huxley / Patience Thompson, Laurie McKenna, Jenny Mackillop ; study co-ordinator Oliver Bott ; forestry and landscape advisors Bob Price and Bill Williams. — Chester : [Cheshire] Libraries & Museums in conjunction with the County Planning Dept., 1982. — 112p : ill,maps ; 20x21cm. — (Cheshire monographs ; 4)
Bibliography: p107-112
ISBN 0-906767-05-9 (pbk) : Unpriced B82-36942

911′.6 — Africa, *1000-1980 — Atlases*

African history in maps. — London : Longman, Mar.1982. — [80]p
ISBN 0-582-60331-5 (pbk) : £1.90 : CIP entry B82-00215

911′.73 — United States. Geographical features, *1580-1845*

Stilgoe, John R.. Common landscape of America, 1580 to 1845 / John R. Stilgoe. — New Haven ; London : Yale University Press, c1982. — xi,429p : ill,1plan ; 25cm
Bibliography: p381-424. — Includes index
ISBN 0-300-02699-4 : Unpriced : CIP rev. B82-17896

912 — ATLASES AND MAPS

912 — Maps — *Collectors′ guides*

Gohm, D. C.. Maps and prints : for pleasure and investment / by D.C. Gohm. — 2nd rev. ed. — London : Gifford, 1978. — 196p,[16]p of plates : ill(some col.),maps(some col.),ports ; 24cm
Previous ed.: 1969. — Bibliography: p196. — Includes index
ISBN 0-7071-0567-6 : £7.50
Primary classification 769 B82-23656

912 — Maps — *For schools*

Proctor, Dena. Mapwork. — London : E. Arnold, Nov.1982. — [64]p. — (Foundation geography)
ISBN 0-7131-0667-0 (pbk) : £2.00 : CIP entry B82-26045

912 — World — *Atlases*

The **Atlas** of world geography / consultant editor Emrys Jones ; introduction by Magnus Magnusson. — London : Octopus, 1981, c1977. — 80,64p,112p of plates : col.ill,col.maps ; 29cm
Originally published: London : Sundial, 1977. — Ill on lining papers. — Includes index
ISBN 0-7064-1677-5 : £4.99 B82-03928

Bartholomew, John. The observer′s world atlas / John Bartholomew. — London : Warne, 1981. — 128,32p : col.ill,col.maps ; 15cm. — (The Observer′s series ; 41)
Includes index
ISBN 0-7232-1624-x : £1.95 B82-19401

Basic world atlas. — Edinburgh : Bartholomew, 1981. — 22p : all col.maps ; 29cm
Text on inside cover. — Includes index
ISBN 0-7028-0391-x (pbk) : Unpriced B82-03469

The **Library** atlas. — 16th ed. — London : Philip, Dec.1982. — [376]p
Previous ed.: 1981
ISBN 0-540-05431-3 : £12.50 : CIP entry B82-30072

Modern home atlas. — 5th ed. — London : G. Philip, May 1981. — [56]p
ISBN 0-540-05390-2 : £1.95 : CIP entry B81-06875

Philips′ concise atlas of the world. — 2nd ed. — London : George Philip & Son, Oct.1981. — [232]p
Previous ed.: 1980
ISBN 0-540-05407-0 : £5.95 : CIP entry B81-28811

912 — World - *Atlases*

Philip′s new practical atlas. — 9th ed. — London : G. Philip, Aug.1981. — [152]p
Previous ed.: 1980
ISBN 0-540-05394-5 : £4.95 : CIP entry B81-16366

912 — World — *Atlases*

Philips′ new reference atlas. — 2nd ed. — London : Philip, Apr.1981. — [264]p
Previous ed.: 1980
ISBN 0-540-05386-4 : £7.95 : CIP entry B81-02112

Philips′ new world atlas. — 4th ed. — London : George Philip, Oct.1981. — [280]p
Previous ed.: 1980
ISBN 0-540-05406-2 : £7.95 : CIP entry B81-25734

Philips′ universal atlas. — 4th ed. — London : Philip, Dec.1982. — [400]p
Previous ed.: 1981
ISBN 0-540-05430-5 : £15.00 : CIP entry B82-30071

Philips′ world atlas / [edited by Harold Fullard, B.M. Willett]. — 2nd ed. — London : George Philip, 1981. — 80,64p : maps(some col.) ; 29cm
Previous ed.: 1979. — Includes index
ISBN 0-540-05385-6 : £5.50 : CIP rev. B81-02111

Philips′ world atlas. — 3rd ed. — London : Philip, Jan.1983. — [152]p
Previous ed: 1981
ISBN 0-540-05443-7 : £5.50 : CIP entry B82-32432

Pocket atlas of the world. — New ed. — London : G. Philip, Jan.1982. — [124]p
Previous ed.: Published as Philips′ pocket atlas of the world, 1971
ISBN 0-540-05410-0 (pbk) : £1.50 : CIP entry B81-34278

The **University** atlas. — 22nd ed. — London : Philip, Dec.1982. — [344]p
Previous ed.: 1981
ISBN 0-540-05432-1 : £10.00 : CIP entry B82-30073

912 — World — *Atlases — For Caribbean students*

Philips′ certificate atlas : for the Caribbean / [edited by B.M. Willett ... et al.] ; [maps prepared by George Philip Cartographic Services Ltd. under the direction of A.G. Poynter]. — London : George Philip, 1982. — 137p : ill(some col.),col.maps ; 29cm
Maps on lining papers. — Includes index
ISBN 0-540-05424-0 : Unpriced B82-34735

912 — World — *Atlases — For children*

Tivers, Jacqueline. The Bartholomew children′s world atlas : a book of maps for young children / Jacqueline Tivers and Michael Day. — Edinburgh : Bartholomew, 1980. — 47p : col.ill,col.maps ; 31cm
ISBN 0-7028-8250-x : £3.50 : CIP rev. B80-18093

Townson, W. D.. Illustrated atlas of the modern world. — London : Longman, Sept.1981. — [64]p
ISBN 0-582-39128-8 : £4.95 : CIP entry B81-25876

912 — World — *Atlases — For schools*

First atlas of the environment. — Edinburgh : Bartholomew, 1980. — 41p : col.ill,col.maps ; 30cm
Cover title. — Includes index
ISBN 0-7028-0063-5 (pbk) : Unpriced B82-34140

Philips′ certificate atlas for secondary schools / [prepared under the direction of H. Fullard, B.M. Willett, D. Gaylard]. — London : George Philip, c1979. — 143p : col.ill,col.maps ; 29cm
Text, ill on lining papers. — Includes index
ISBN 0-540-05348-1 : Unpriced B82-04772

Philips′ middle school atlas / edited by Harold Fullard. — 3rd ed. — London : George Philip, c1982. — 32p : col.ill,col.maps ; 28cm
Cover title. — Includes index
ISBN 0-540-05413-5 (pbk) : Unpriced B82-10841

Philips′ modern school atlas. — 78th ed. / edited by Harold Fullard. — London : George Philip, c1981. — xiv,100,32p : col.ill,col.maps ; 29cm
Previous ed.: 1978. — Ill on lining papers. — Includes index
ISBN 0-540-05395-3 : Unpriced
ISBN 0-540-05384-3 (pbk) : Unpriced B82-04774

Philips′ modern school economic atlas : comprising the Modern school atlas and maps of economic resources / edited by Harold Fullard. — London : George Philip, c1981. — xii,100,32p,[32]p of plates : ill,col.maps ; 29cm
Ill on lining papers. — Includes index
ISBN 0-540-05402-x : Unpriced B82-04773

Philips′ new school atlas / edited by Harold Fullard. — 63rd ed. — London : George Philip, c1981. — viii,64,24p : ill,chiefly maps (some col.) ; 28cm
Includes index
ISBN 0-540-05408-9 (pbk) : Unpriced B82-10842

Philips′ secondary school atlas / edited by Harold Fullard. — New impression. — London : George Philip, 1980, c1979. — xvi,55p : col.ill,col.maps ; 28cm
Includes index
ISBN 0-540-05317-1 (pbk) : Unpriced B82-04775

Second atlas of the environment. — Edinburgh : Bartholomew, 1977 (1980 [printing]). — 41p : col.ill,chiefly col.maps ; 30cm
Cover title. — Includes index
ISBN 0-7028-0075-9 (pbk) : Unpriced B82-34141

912′.01′4 — Map reading

Keates, J. S.. Understanding maps / J.S. Keates. — London : Longman, 1982. — xi,139p : ill,maps ; 24cm
Bibliography: p129-133. — Includes index
ISBN 0-582-30039-8 (pbk) : £5.95 : CIP rev. B81-37602

912′.01′4 — Map reading — *For West African students*

Nimako, D. Annor. Map reading for West Africa / D.A. Nimako. — Rev. ed. with metric examples. — Harlow : Longman, 1982. — 76p : ill,maps ; 28cm
Previous ed.: ie New ed. 1977
ISBN 0-582-60391-9 (pbk) : £2.20 B82-35335

912′.01′4 — Map reading — *Manuals*

Matkin, Robert B.. The Dalesman′s guide to map reading / by Robert B. Matkin ; illustrations by R. Martyn Jones. — Clapham (via Lancaster) : Dalesman, 1979. — 32p : ill,maps ; 22cm
Ill, map on lining papers
ISBN 0-85206-519-1 (pbk) : £0.75 B82-23614

912'.01'4 — Western Europe. Maps. Map reading — *For schools*

Knowles, R.. Western Europe in maps : topographical map studies / R. Knowles, P.W.E. Stowe. — Rev. ed. — Harlow : Longman, 1982. — 128p : ill(some col.),maps (some col.),1plan ; 21x33cm
Previous ed.: published as Europe in maps in 2 vols. 1969. — Includes bibliographies
ISBN 0-582-35260-6 (pbk) : £5.95 B82-14435

912'.0148 — Shipping. Navigational aids: British Admiralty charts. Symbols — *Lists*

Symbols and abbreviations used on Admiralty charts. — Taunton (Hydrographic Department, Ministry of Defence, Taunton, Somerset) : Hydrographer of the Navy, c1979. — [38]p : ill (some col.) ; 30cm. — (Chart ; 5011)
Includes index
Unpriced (pbk) B82-40573

912'.01'8 — Maps. Spatial analysis

Unwin, David J.. Introductory spatial analysis / David Unwin. — London : Methuen, 1981. — xii,212p : ill,maps ; 24cm
Includes bibliographies and index
ISBN 0-416-72190-7 (cased) : Unpriced : CIP rev.
ISBN 0-416-72200-8 (pbk) : £5.50 B81-31715

912'.074'02142 — Great Britain. National libraries: British Library. *Map Library.* **Exhibits: Unusual maps**

Hill, Gillian. Cartographical curiosities / Gillian Hill. — London : British Library Reference Division, c1978. — 63p : ill,maps,facsims ; 19x25cm
Originally published: London : British Museum Publications for the British Library, 1978
ISBN 0-904654-42-7 (pbk) : £2.50 B82-12786

912'.13046'0941 — Great Britain. Population. Census data — *Atlases*

People in Britain : a census atlas / prepared by Census Research Unit, Department of Geography, University of Durham in collaboration with Office of Population Censuses and Surveys and General Register Office (Scotland). — [London] : H.M.S.O., 1980. — 132p : col.maps ; 30cm
ISBN 0-11-690618-9 (pbk) : Unpriced
B82-19391

912'.1554 — Europe. Geological features — *Atlases*

Ziegler, Peter Alfred. Geological atlas of western and central Europe. — Oxford : Elsevier Scientific, Apr.1982. — [125]p
ISBN 0-444-42084-3 : CIP entry B82-14369

912'.158194256 — Bedfordshire. Plants. Distribution — *Atlases*

Dony, John G.. Bedfordshire plant atlas / by John G. Dony. — [Luton] ([Wardown Park, Luton LU2 3HA]) : Borough of Luton Museum and Art Gallery, 1976 (chiefly maps), 25cm (two overlays) [pbk]
Includes index
Unpriced B82-08499

912'.158213'094223 — Kent. Flowering plants. Distribution — *Atlases*

Philp, Eric G.. Atlas of the Kent flora / Eric G. Philp. — [Maidstone?] : Kent Field Club, 1982. — xii,211p : ill,maps ; 30cm
Ill on lining papers. — Bibliography: p198. — Includes index
ISBN 0-905155-37-8 (corrected) : £12.00
B82-39334

912'.1592094 — Europe. Invertebrates. Distribution — *Atlases*

Provisional atlas of the invertebrates of Europe : maps 1-27 / edited by John Heath & Jean Leclercq. — Abbots Ripton : Institute of Terrestrial Ecology, Monks Wood Experimental Stn., 1981. — 27leaves : chiefly maps ; 21x30cm
At head of title: European Invertebrate Survey. — Includes index
ISBN 0-904282-58-9 (pbk) : Unpriced
B82-05886

912'.159318 — Great Britain. Coastal waters. Marine Dinoflagellata. Distribution — *Atlases*

Provisional atlas of the marine dinoflagellates of the British Isles / edited by John D. Dodge. — Huntingdon : Biological Records Centre, 1981. — vii,125p : chiefly maps ; 30cm
Includes index
ISBN 0-904282-53-8 (spiral) : £4.00
B82-05887

912'.15954'0941 — Great Britain. Arachnida. Distribution — *Atlases*

Provisional atlas of the Arachnida of the British Isles. — Huntingdon : Biological Records Centre Pt.1: Pseudoscorpiones / edited by Philip E. Jones. — 1980. — [357] : chiefly maps ; 30cm
At head of title: European Invertebrate Survey. — Bibliography: p6-7. — Includes index
ISBN 0-904282-50-3 (spiral) : £2.00
B82-31763

912'.1598294 — Europe. Birds. Distribution — *Atlases*

Harrison, C. J. O.. An atlas of the birds of the Western Palaearctic / Colin Harrison ; design and cartography by Crispin Fisher. — London : Collins, 1982. — 322p : ill(some col.),col.maps ; 25cm
Bibliography: p314. — Includes index
ISBN 0-00-219729-4 : £12.95 B82-20551

912'.1967 — Antarctic Ocean — *Atlases*

Gordon, Arnold L.. Southern ocean atlas. — New York ; [Guildford, Surrey] : Columbia University Press, 1982. — 1v.(various pagings) : chiefly ill(some col.),chiefly maps(some col.) ; 32x46cm + 42 microfiche(11x15cm)
Microfiche in 4 envelopes. — Includes bibliographies. — Contents: Thermohaline and chemical distributions and the atlas data set / by Arnold L. Gordon and Eugene J. Molinelli — Objective contouring and the grid point data set / by Arnold L. Gordon and Ted N. Baker
ISBN 0-231-05214-6 (spiral) : Unpriced
B82-35786

912'.4 — Europe — *Atlases — For motoring*

Road atlas Europe. — Edinburgh : Bartholomew, 1980. — 136p : all col.maps ; 30cm
Text, map on lining papers. — Includes index
ISBN 0-7028-0242-5 : Unpriced B82-03464

912'.4 — North-western Europe. Coastal waters — *Atlases*

Atlas of the seas around the British Isles / compiled in the Directorate of Fisheries Research ; drawn by the Survey Section, Agricultural Development and Advisory Service. — [London] : Ministry of Agriculture, Fisheries and Food, 1981. — [102]p : ill,col.charts,maps(some col.) ; 31x43cm
Ill on inside covers
ISBN 0-907545-00-9 (spiral) : Unpriced
B82-02869

912'.41 — Great Britain — *Atlases*

The **Ordnance** Survey atlas of Great Britain. — Southampton : Ordnance Survey, 1982. — 224p : col.ill,col.maps ; 31cm
Bibliography: p177. — Includes index
ISBN 0-600-35005-3 : £12.95 B82-37804

912'.41 — Great Britain — *Atlases — For motoring*

AA big road atlas of Britain. — Basingstoke : Automobile Association, c1981. — 76,[16]p : col.maps ; 39cm
Includes index
ISBN 0-86145-067-1 (pbk) : £2.95 B82-24869

AA big road atlas of Britain. — 2nd ed. — Basingstoke : Automobile Association, c1982. — 76p : col.ill,chiefly col.maps,plans(chiefly col.) ; 39cm
Previous ed.: 1981. — Map and text on inside covers. — Includes index
ISBN 0-86145-122-8 (pbk) : Unpriced
B82-25017

Atlas Britain. — Edinburgh : Bartholomew, c1979. — 128p,viiip : col.ill,col.maps ; 30cm
Cover title: Road atlas Britain. — Ill and text on lining papers. — Includes index
ISBN 0-7028-0303-0 : Unpriced B82-21848

Bartholomew, John C. (John Christopher). The observer's tourist atlas of Great Britain and Ireland / John Bartholomew. — London : Warne, 1976 (1981 [printing]). — 121p : chiefly col.maps ; 16cm. — (The Observer's series ; 63)
Col.map on lining papers. — Includes index
ISBN 0-7232-1623-1 : £1.95 B82-00865

BP road atlas of Great Britain. — 1982 ed. — London : G. Philip, Apr.1982. — [148]p
ISBN 0-540-05418-6 : £2.95 : CIP entry
B82-03618

Drivers road atlas of Britain. — London : AA, 1981. — xiii,98p : chiefly ill(some col.),col.maps ; 31cm
Maps on lining papers. — Includes index
ISBN 0-7064-1691-0 : £5.95 B82-03924

Great Britain road atlas / general editor Roger Edwards ; editor Pat Sorton. — 2nd ed. — [London] : Map Production, [1982?]. — 96p : chiefly col.maps ; 29cm
English text, English, French, German introduction and key to maps. — At head of title: RAC. — Previous ed.: published as RAC Great Britain road atlas. 1977. — Text on inside cover. — Includes index
ISBN 0-540-03175-5 (corrected : pbk) : £3.25
B82-32902

Haynes road atlas of Great Britain : with special London section. — Yeovil : Haynes, c1982. — 80,61p : chiefly col.maps ; 29cm
Includes index
ISBN 0-85696-819-6 : £5.95 B82-26364

National road atlas of Great Britain : road maps & town plans. — [London] : George Philip, c1981. — 120,[61]p : col.ill,col.maps ; 29cm
Includes index
ISBN 0-540-05391-0 : £4.95 B82-04776

National road atlas of Great Britain. — 1982 ed. — London : G. Philip, Apr.1982. — [184]p
ISBN 0-540-05419-4 : £4.95 : CIP entry
B82-03619

New-fold touring atlas. — Edinburgh : Bartholomew, 1980. — 48p(some folded) : col.ill,col.maps ; 30cm
Text, ill on inside cover
ISBN 0-7028-0356-1 (pbk) : £1.95 B82-03466

Philips' road atlas of Great Britain : with special London section. — [London] : George Philip, c1980. — viii,60p : col.ill,col.maps ; 29cm
Includes index
ISBN 0-540-05364-3 : £4.50 : CIP rev.
B80-04587

Philips' road atlas of Great Britain : with special London section. — [London] : George Philip, c1981. — viii,80,[61]p : col.ill,col.maps ; 29cm
Includes index
ISBN 0-540-05392-9 : £3.95 B82-04777

Reader's digest AA new book of the road / [edited and designed by the Readers Digest Association]. — 4th ed. — London : Readers' Digest Association in collaboration with the Automobile Association, c1982. — 415p : ill (chiefly col.),charts,col.maps,col.plans ; 29cm
Spine title: New book of the road. — Page width varies. — Col. maps on lining papers. — Includes index
£11.95 B82-31737

Road atlas Britain. — New ed. rev. — Edinburgh : Bartholomew, c1981. — 1v.(various pagings) : col.ill,col.charts,col.maps ; 31cm
Previous ed.: 1976. — Includes index
ISBN 0-7028-0419-3 : Unpriced B82-03465

Roadmaster atlas. — Edinburgh : Bartholomew, 1981. — xi,89,[24]p : ill,chiefly col.maps ; 30cm
Maps on inside covers. — Includes index
ISBN 0-7028-0433-9 (pbk) : Unpriced
B82-03467

912′.41 — Great Britain — *Atlases — For motoring* *continuation*

The **Shell** road atlas of Great Britain / [maps and map index edited by R.W. Lidbetter, with research by H. Snape, and prepared by the cartographic staff of Goerge Philip Cartographic Services Ltd. under the direction of Alan Poynter]. — [London] : George Philip, c1982. — 142p : col.maps ; 32cm
Includes index
ISBN 0-540-05420-8 : £6.95 : CIP rev. B82-03620

Shell touring atlas of Great Britain. — London : George Philip, c1981. — 128p : ill(some col.),col.maps ; 29cm
Includes index
ISBN 0-540-05383-x : £9.95 B82-04778

Shell touring atlas of Great Britain. — 2nd ed. — London : George Philip, Sept.1982. — [256]p
Previous ed.: 1981
ISBN 0-540-05440-2 : £9.95 : CIP entry B82-22425

912′.41 — Great Britain. British maps, *ca 1570-ca 1870 — Collectors′ guides*

Booth, John, *1926-*. Looking at old maps / John Booth. — Westbury : Cambridge House, 1979. — xiii,167p : ill(some col.),maps,coats of arms,facsims ; 26cm
Includes index
ISBN 0-906853-00-1 : Unpriced B82-02609

Smith, David, *1943 July 15-*. Antique maps of the British Isles / David Smith. — London : Batsford, 1982. — 243p,[4]p of plates : ill,maps (some col.) ; 26cm
Includes index
ISBN 0-7134-1694-7 : £25.00 B82-33822

912′.41 — Great Britain. Towns — *Atlases*

AA big atlas of town plans. — Basingstoke : Automobile Association, c1982. — 96p : ill,maps,plans ; 39cm
Plans on inside covers. — Includes index
ISBN 0-86145-111-2 (pbk) : £2.95 B82-25016

912′.41 — Maps of counties of Great Britain — *Collectors′ guides*

Beresiner, Yasha. British county maps. — Woodbridge : Antique Collectors′ Club, May 1982. — [300]p
ISBN 0-902028-97-9 : £22.50 : CIP entry B82-07698

912′.42 — England — *Atlases — For motoring*

Navigator / RAC. — London : Map Productions 4: Northern England, Lakes, Borders, Leeds and Manchester / [editors Roger Edwards, Pat Sorton] ; [cartography Map Productions Limited]. — [1980]. — 104p : ill(some col.),col.maps ; 32cm
Cover title. — Includes index
ISBN 0-540-03168-2 (pbk) : £4.50 B82-13318

912′.42 — England. Maps, *to 1860*

Hodgkiss, Alan G.. Discovering antique maps / Alan G. Hodgkiss. — 1981 ed. — Princes Risborough : Shire, 1981. — 72p : ill,facsims,maps ; 18cm
Previous ed.: i.e. [New ed.]. 1977. — Bibliography: p67. — Includes index
ISBN 0-85263-581-8 (pbk) : £1.25 B82-31010

912′.421 — Central London — *Atlases*

Geographia London visitors atlas. — London : Geographia, [1982?]. — 31,[16]p : ill,chiefly maps(some col.),plans ; 29cm
Text on inside covers
ISBN 0-09-202730-x (pbk) : Unpriced B82-37952

912′.421 — London, *1739 — Atlases — Facsimiles*

Rocque, John. [A plan of the cities of London and Westminster, and Borough of Southwark, with the contiguous buildings]. The A to Z of Georgian London / introductory notes by Ralph Hyde. — Lympne Castle : Published for the London Topographical Society by Harry Margary in association with Guildhall Library, London, 1982. — viii,88p : chiefly maps,facsims ; 31cm. — (Publication / London Topographical Society ; no.126)
Facsim. of: John Rocque′s work published: London : John Pine ; John Tinney, 1747. — Bibliography: pviii. — Includes index
ISBN 0-902087-16-9 : Unpriced B82-16725

912′.421 — London, *1747 — Maps — Facsimiles*

Rocque, John. [A plan of the cities of London and Westminster, and Borough of Southwark, with the contiguous buildings]. The A to Z of Georgian London / introductory notes by Ralph Hyde. — Lympne Castle : Harry Margary in association with Guildhall Library, London, 1981. — viii,88p : chiefly maps,facsims ; 31cm
Facsim. of: John Rocque′s work published: London : John Pine ; John Tinney, 1747. — Bibliography: pviii. — Includes index
ISBN 0-903541-34-3 : Unpriced B82-10993

912′.421 — London, *1862 — Maps — Facsimiles*

Stanford′s library map of London and its suburbs : 24 sheets on the scale of six inches to a mile / introductory notes by Ralph Hyde. — Lympne Castle : Margary in association with Guildhall Library London, 1980. — [28]leaves : 1ill,chiefly maps ; 38x45cm
Originally published: London : Stanford, 1862. — Bibliography: leaf 3
ISBN 0-903541-33-5 (pbk) : Unpriced B82-25051

912′.421 — London — *Atlases*

AA Greater London street atlas. — 3rd rev. ed. — Basingstoke : Automobile Association, 1981. — 403p in various pagings : ill,chiefly col.maps ; 31cm
Previous ed.: 1978. — Maps on lining papers. — Includes index
ISBN 0-86145-070-1 : £14.95 B82-24870

Francis Chichester′s map & guide of London. — London : F. Chichester, [1982?]. — 119p : col.maps ; 15cm
Map on lining paper. — Includes index
Unpriced B82-37880

912′.4212 — London *(City), 1553-1667 — Maps — Facsimiles*

A **Collection** of early maps of London 1553-1667 / introduction by John Fisher. — [Hythe] (Lympne Castle [Lympne, Hythe], Kent) : Harry Margary in association with Guildhall Library, London, 1981. — [4],21leaves : ill,maps,coats of arms,facsims,1port ; 45x58cm
Bibliography: 4th prelim. leaf
£30.00 (cased) (pbk) : £15.00 (loose sheets) : £10.00 B82-06188

912′.422′1 — Surrey — *Atlases*

Surrey street atlas : 3 inches to the mile. — 8th ed. — London : George Philip, 1981. — 160,61p : chiefly maps ; 28cm
Previous ed.: published as Round and about Surrey. 1978. — Includes index
ISBN 0-540-05368-6 : £5.95 : CIP rev. B80-02972

912′.422′1 — Surrey. Roads — *Atlases*

Surrey street altas. — 9th ed. — London : G. Philip, Apr.1982. — [218]p
Previous ed.: 1980
ISBN 0-540-05417-8 : £5.95 : CIP entry B82-06231

912′.42296 — Berkshire. Windsor and Maidenhead *(District) — Atlases*

Windsor and Maidenhead official street and area map : containing street plans of Windsor, Maidenhead, Cookham, Ascot, and Sunninghill. — Wallington : Forward Publicity, [1981?]. — 54p : ill,maps ; 21cm
Cover title. — Map on folded sheet attached to inside cover. — Includes index
Unpriced (pbk) B82-09903

912′.4238 — Somerset, *1782-1822 — Maps — Facsimiles — Collections*

Somerset maps : Day & Masters 1782, Greenwood 1822 / introduction by J.B. Harley & R.W. Dunning. — Taunton : Somerset Record Society, 1981. — 1case : maps ; 26cm. — (Somerset Record Society ; v.76)
Facsims of: maps of Somerset by William Day and Charles Harcourt Masters, 1782 and Christopher Greenwood, 1822
ISBN 0-901732-23-0 (unbound) : Unpriced
ISBN 0-901732-24-9 (in plastic envelope) B82-11688

912′.42464 — Staffordshire. Stafford *(District) — Atlases*

Stafford Borough : official guide. — Gloucester : British Publishing, [1981?]. — 20p,[2]folded p of plate : ill,maps,1coat of arms ; 21cm
ISBN 0-7140-1940-2 (pbk) : Unpriced B82-08615

912′.42567 — Bedfordshire. Luton — *Atlases*

Borough of Luton : official street & area map. — Wallington : Forward Publicity, [1981?]. — 16p : ill,maps ; 21cm
Cover title. — Map on folded sheet attached to inside cover. — Includes index
Unpriced (pbk) B82-09901

912′.427645 — Lancashire. Pendle *(District) — Atlases*

Borough of Pendle official map. — Wallington : Forward Publicity, [1981?]. — 55p : ill,maps ; 24cm
Cover title. — Includes index
Unpriced (pbk) B82-09902

912′.42815 — West Yorkshire *(Metropolitan County)*. **Wakefield** *(District) — Atlases*

Wakefield. *Metropolitan District Council.* City of Wakefield Metropolitan District / [official map] ; issued by authority of the Wakefield Metropolitan District Council. — Wallington : Forward Publicity, [1981]. — 92p : chiefly maps ; 24cm
Includes index
Unpriced (pbk) B82-05846

912′.42995 — Gwent. Blaenau Gwent *(District) — Atlases*

The **Borough** of Blaenau Gwent : official street plan. — Gloucester : British Publishing, [1981?]. — 16p,1 folded leaf of plate : 2maps ; 21cm
Cover title
ISBN 0-7140-1852-x (pbk) : Unpriced B82-08616

912′.47 — Soviet Union — *Atlases*

Dewdney, John C.. USSR in maps. — London : Hodder & Stoughton, June 1982. — [128]p
ISBN 0-340-24414-3 : £6.50 : CIP entry B82-11522

912′.669 — Nigeria — *Atlases*

Nigeria in maps. — London : Hodder & Stoughton, Aug.1982. — [144]p
ISBN 0-340-18425-6 (pbk) : £6.95 : CIP entry B82-15717

913 — ANCIENT WORLD

913′.04 — Ancient world. Exploration

Barker, Felix. The first explorers / by Felix Barker in collaboration with Anthea Barker. — London : Reader′s Digest Association, 1980, c1971. — 191p : ill(some col.),facsims(some col.),col. maps,ports(some col.) ; 27cm. — (Discovery and exploration)
Originally published: London : Aldus, 1971. — Includes index
£6.97 B82-31535

913.61′0014 — Great Britain. Place names, *to 410*

Rivet, A. L. F.. The place-names of Roman Britain / by A.L.F. Rivet and Colin Smith. — London : Batsford, 1979. — xviii,526p,2p of plates : maps,facsims ; 26cm
Includes index
ISBN 0-7134-2077-4 B82-09257

914 — EUROPE

914 — Europe. Geographical features — *For schools*
Jackson, Nora. Europe / Nora Jackson, Philip Penn. — Metric ed. — London : George Philip, c1979. — viii,336p : ill,maps ; 22cm. — (Groundwork geographies)
Previous ed. i.e. 5th ed.: 1974
ISBN 0-540-01042-1 (pbk) : Unpriced : CIP rev. B78-34945

914 — European Community countries. Geographical features — *For schools*
Bamford, C. G.. Geography of the EEC. — Plymouth : Macdonald & Evans, Jan.1983. — [288]p. — (Aspect geographies)
ISBN 0-7121-0732-0 : £6.50 : CIP entry B82-32855

914'.042'0922 — Europe. Description & travel, *1458-ca 1910 — Personal observations — Collections*
Hindley, Geoffrey, *1935-*. Tourists, travellers and pilgrims. — London : Hutchinson, Oct.1982. — [192]p
ISBN 0-09-149460-5 : £9.95 : CIP entry B82-24966

914'.0452 — Europe. Description & travel, *1931-1939 — Personal observations*
Fisher, Kathleen. Sun and shadows : holidays in Hitler's Reich / Kathleen Fisher ; edited by Eileen V. Smith. — Ilfracombe : Stockwell, 1982. — 153p,[8]p of plates : ill,ports ; 22cm
ISBN 0-7223-1545-7 : £7.50 B82-22207

914'.04557 — Europe. Description & travel, *1979-1981 — Personal observations*
Hone, Joseph. Gone tomorrow : some more collected travels / Joseph Hone. — London : Secker & Warburg, 1981. — 144p ; 23cm
ISBN 0-436-20084-8 : £6.95 : CIP rev. B81-27375

914'.04558 — Europe. Description & travel, *ca 1980 — Personal observations — Spanish texts*
Farrando, Julio. El valle de la joda / Julio Farrando. — Fareham : J. Farrando, 1982. — 79p ; 22cm
ISBN 0-9506701-2-x (pbk) : £2.90 B82-37978

914'.04558 — Europe. Hitch-hiking — *Practical information*
Calder, Simon. Europe : a manual for hitch-hikers / by Simon Calder, Colin Brown and Roger Brown. — Oxford : Vacation Work, 1980. — 176p : ill,maps ; 22cm
ISBN 0-901205-82-6 (cased) : Unpriced
ISBN 0-901205-83-4 (pbk) : £2.95 B82-12952

914'.04558 — Europe — *Practical information*
Brown, Roger, *19---*. Travellers survival kit Europe / Roger Brown. — Oxford : Vacation-Work, 1976 (1978 [printing]). — 192p : ill ; 23cm
ISBN 0-901205-46-x (cased) : £2.95
ISBN 0-901205-51-6 B82-34548

914'.04558 — Europe. Travel — *Practical information*
Brown, Roger, *1949-*. Travellers survival kit Europe / by Roger Brown. — 3rd ed. / revised by David Woodworth. — Oxford : Vacation Work, c1980. — 208p : ill ; 22cm
Previous ed.: 1978
ISBN 0-901205-80-x (cased) : Unpriced
ISBN 0-901205-72-9 (pbk) : £2.95 B82-12951

Brown, Roger, *1949-*. Travellers survival kit Europe / by Roger Brown. — 4th ed. / revised by Simon Calder. — Oxford : Vacation-Work, c1982. — 215p ; 21cm
Previous ed.: 1980
ISBN 0-907638-08-2 (cased) : Unpriced
ISBN 0-907638-07-4 (pbk) : £3.95 B82-24651

914'.04558 — Europe — *Visitors' guides*
Lo Bello, Nino. European detours : a travel guide to unusual sights / by Nino Lo Bello. — Edinburgh : Bartholomew, 1981. — 163p : ill,maps,ports ; 24cm. — (A Giniger book)
Maps on lining papers
ISBN 0-7028-8081-7 : £5.25 B82-03463

914'.04558 — Europe — *Visitors' guides — For motoring*
RAC continental motoring guide. — Croydon : Royal Automobile Club, 1982. — 207p : ill,maps ; 22cm
ISBN 0-86211-031-9 (pbk) : £3.50 B82-19301

914'.04558 — Western Europe. National parks — *Visitors' guides*
Duffey, Eric. National parks : and reserves of Western Europe / Eric Duffey. — London : Macdonald, 1982. — 288p : ill(some col.),maps (some col.) ; 32cm
Bibliography: p287. — Includes index
ISBN 0-356-08586-4 : £14.95 B82-25693

914'.04558'05 — Western Europe — *Practical information — Serials — For motoring*
Travellers' guide to Europe. — 1982-3-. — Basingstoke : Automobile Association, 1982-. — v. : ill,maps(some col.) ; 23cm
Annual. — Cover title: AA travellers' guide to Europe. — Continues: Motoring in Europe
ISSN 0263-600X = Travellers' guide to Europe : £3.95 B82-28860

914.1 — GREAT BRITAIN

914.1 — Great Britain. Adam country houses — *Visitors' guides*
Beard, Geoffrey. Robert Adam's country houses / Geoffrey Beard ; illustrated by A.F. Kersting. — Edinburgh : Bartholomew, 1981. — 31p : ill (some col.),1col.map,ports ; 26cm
Text, ill on inside covers. — Bibliography: on inside cover
ISBN 0-7028-8061-2 (pbk) : £1.95 : CIP rev. B81-07927

914.1 — Great Britain. Buildings of historical importance & gardens open to the public — *Directories*
Johnstone, Clive. The Which? heritage guide / Clive Johnstone and Winifred Weston. — London : Consumers' Association and Hodder & Stoughton, c1981. — 458p : ill,maps ; 21cm
Includes index
ISBN 0-340-26585-x (pbk) : £4.95
Also classified at 069'.025'41 B82-02587

914.1 — Great Britain. Gardens open to the public — *Directories*
Saville, Diana. The observer's book of gardens of England, Scotland & Wales / Diana Saville. — London : Warne, 1982. — 184p,[8]p of plates : ill(some col.) ; 15cm. — (The Observer's pocket series ; 96)
Includes index
ISBN 0-7232-1629-0 : Unpriced B82-30673

914.1 — Great Britain. Geographical features — *For schools*
Bryant, D. (David), *19---*. Regional geography : British Isles / D. Bryant and R. Knowles. — London : Letts, 1982. — 224p : maps ; 19cm. — (GCE O-level passbooks)
Bibliography: p194. — Includes index
ISBN 0-85097-448-8 (pbk) : £1.75 B82-31587

Hardy, A. V.. The British Isles / A.V. Hardy. — New ed. — Cambridge : Cambridge University Press, 1981. — 163p : ill,charts,maps ; 25cm. — (Geography of the British Isles)
Previous ed.: 1973
ISBN 0-521-22258-3 (pbk) : £3.75 B82-32325

Jackson, Nora. The British Isles / Nora Jackson, Philip Penn. — Metric ed. — London : George Philip, c1981. — vii,296p : ill,maps ; 22cm. — (Groundwork geographies)
Previous ed. i.e. 7th ed.: 1978
ISBN 0-540-01065-0 (pbk) : £2.95 : CIP rev. B81-12309

Our landscapes / authors: Allan C. Ayers ... [et al.] ; general editor: T.H. Masterton ; illustrated by: Tim Smith, Barry Adamson. — Edinburgh : Oliver & Boyd, 1982. — v,121p : ill(some col.),facsims,maps(some col.),col.plans ; 25cm. — (Outlook geography)
ISBN 0-05-003453-7 (pbk) : £3.15 B82-30191

Stephenson, Kenneth B.. Geography of the British Isles in colour / Kenneth B. Stephenson. — 4th rev. ed. — Poole : Blandford, 1982. — 320p : ill(some col.),maps (some col.) ; 21cm
Previous ed.: 1978. — Includes index
ISBN 0-7137-1256-2 (pbk) : Unpriced : CIP rev. B82-07839

914.1 — Great Britain. National Trust properties — *Directories*
The **National** Trust atlas / The National Trust and the National Trust for Scotland ; foreword by Nigel Nicolson. — [London] : The National Trust, c1981. — 224p : ill(some col.),maps (some col.) ; 29cm
Includes index
ISBN 0-540-05398-8 : £9.95 : CIP rev. B81-25837

914.1'0068'8 — Great Britain. Marketing by tourist industries — *Manuals*
Bishop, John, *1944-*. Travel marketing / John Bishop. — Folkestone : Bailey & Swinfen, 1981. — 268p ; 23cm
ISBN 0-561-00313-0 : £17.50 B82-07708

914.1'04857 — Great Britain. Long-distance footpaths. Description & travel, *1970-1979 — Personal observations*
Peel, J. H. B.. Along the green roads of Britain / J.H.B. Peel. — Newton Abbot : David & Charles, 1982. — 214p,[16]p of plates : ill ; 23cm
Includes index
ISBN 0-7153-8327-2 : £8.95 : CIP rev. B82-09625

914.1'04858 — Great Britain. Buildings of historical importance, *1500-1640 — Visitors' guides*
Airs, Malcolm. Tudor and Jacobean : a guide and gazetteer / Malcolm Airs. — London : Barrie & Jenkins, 1982. — 192p : ill,maps,plans ; 22cm. — (The Buildings of Britain)
Bibliography: p190
ISBN 0-09-147830-8 (cased) : £9.50 : CIP rev.
ISBN 0-09-147831-6 (pbk) : £4.95 B82-07257

914.1'04858 — Great Britain. Buildings of historical importance, *1603-1714 — Visitors' guides*
Morrice, Richard. Stuart and Baroque. — London : Barrie and Jenkins, Sept.1982. — [192]p. — (The Buildings of Britain)
ISBN 0-09-150430-9 (cased) : £9.50 : CIP entry
ISBN 0-09-150431-7 (pbk) : £4.95 B82-28440

914.1'04858 — Great Britain. Buildings of historical importance, *ca 400-1100 — Visitors' guides*
Service, Alastair. Anglo-Saxon and Norman. — London : Barrie and Jenkins, Sept.1982. — [192]p. — (The Buildings of Britain)
ISBN 0-09-150130-x (cased) : £9.50 : CIP entry
ISBN 0-09-150131-8 (pbk) : £4.95 B82-28439

914.1'04858 — Great Britain. Buildings of historical importance — *Visitors' guides*
Cole, Roger. Family guide to the stately homes of Britain. — Oxford : Phaidon, Apr.1982. — [288]p
ISBN 0-7148-2238-8 : £12.95 : CIP entry B82-04509

914.1'04858 — Great Britain. Castles — *Visitors' guides*
Mills, John FitzMaurice. The Mitchell Beazley pocket guide to stately homes and castles in Great Britain and Ireland / John FitzMaurice Mills. — London : Mitchell Beazley, c1982. — 192p : ill,1map ; 20cm
Includes index
ISBN 0-85533-269-7 : £3.95
Primary classification 914.1'04858 B82-33580

914.1'04858 — Great Britain. Description & travel
AA illustrated guide to Britain. — 4th ed., repr. with amendments. — London : Drive Publications for the Automobile Association, 1982, c1981. — 543p : col.ill,col.maps,col.ports ; 27cm
Includes index
£10.95 B82-28982

914.1′04858 — Great Britain. Description & travel *continuation*

Burton, Anthony. The Shell book of curious Britain / Anthony Burton. — Newton Abbot : David & Charles, c1982. — 304p,[8]p of plates : ill(some col.) ; 22cm
Bibliography: p300. — Includes index
ISBN 0-7153-8083-4 : £9.95 : CIP rev. B81-27972

Darke, Jo. What you must see in the British Isles / [authors Jo Darke, Tim Finn] ; [editor Elizabeth Longley] ; [designer Annie Tomlin]. — New York : Exeter Books ; London : Enigma, 1981. — 184p : ill(some col.),2col.maps ; 30cm
Maps on lining papers
ISBN 0-85685-939-7 : Unpriced B82-06105

914.1′04858 — Great Britain. Islands. Description & travel — *Personal observations*

Thomas, Leslie, *1931-*. Some lovely islands. — Rev. ed. — London : Arlington, Oct.1982. — [256]p
Previous ed.: 1968
ISBN 0-85140-586-x : £11.95 : CIP entry B82-24261

914.1′04858 — Great Britain. Islands — *Visitors′ guides*

The **Observer** Island Britain / edited by Peter Crookston. — London : Macdonald, 1982, c1981. — 252p : col.ill,col.maps,col.ports ; 27cm
Includes index
ISBN 0-356-08540-6 : £12.95 B82-17874

914.1′04858 — Great Britain. Mountains — *Walkers′ guides*

Wilson, Ken, *1941-*. The big walks : challenging mountain walks and scrambles in the British Isles / compiled by Ken Wilson and Richard Gilbert ; with editorial assistance from Mike Pearson ; maps by Don Sargeant. — London : Diadem, 1980. — 255p : ill(some col.),maps ; 29cm
Includes index
ISBN 0-906371-60-0 : £16.95 : CIP rev. B80-22406

914.1′04858 — Great Britain — *Practical information — For businessmen*

Businessman′s guide to the UK. — London : The Financial Times Business Publishing Ltd, c1981. — 256p : maps ; 24x21cm
ISBN 0-902101-13-7 : £6.95 B82-07060

Businessman′s guide to the UK / [edited by Johanna Darke & Michael Hampshire. — London : New Burlington, c1981. — 256p : maps,plans ; 23cm
Spine title: Financial Times businessman′s guide to the UK
ISBN 0-906286-11-5 (pbk) : £4.25 B82-07061

914.1′04858 — Great Britain — *Practical information — For Commonwealth immigrants*

Introduction to Britain : a guide for Commonwealth immigrants / [prepared for the Home Office by Central Office of Information]. — [London] : [Home Office], [1982?]. — [12]p ; 23cm
Unpriced (unbound) B82-33375

914.1′04858 — Great Britain. Rural regions — *Walkers′ guides*

Butler, Liz, *1948 June 12-*. The seasons : an exploration of twelve country walks / watercolours by Liz Butler ; text by Michael Chinery. — London : Collins, 1982. — 200p : col.ill,col.maps ; 26cm
Includes index
ISBN 0-00-216319-5 : £9.95 : CIP rev. B82-03698

914.1′04858 — Great Britain. Stately homes — *Visitors′ guides*

Mills, John FitzMaurice. The Mitchell Beazley pocket guide to stately homes and castles in Great Britain and Ireland / John FitzMaurice Mills. — London : Mitchell Beazley, c1982. — 192p : ill,1map ; 20cm
Includes index
ISBN 0-85533-269-7 : £3.95
Also classified at 914.1′04858 B82-33580

914.1′04858 — Great Britain. Unnavigable inland waterways — *Visitors′ guides*

Russell, Ronald. Lost canals and waterways of Britain / Ronald Russell. — Expanded and updated version. — Newton Abbot : David & Charles, c1982. — 272p : ill,maps ; 24cm
Previous ed.: published as Lost canals of England and Wales. 1971. — Bibliography: p265-266. — Includes index
ISBN 0-7153-8072-9 : £12.50 : CIP rev. B81-33823

914.1′04858 — Great Britain — *Visitors′ guides*

Darke, Jo. Colourful Britain / Jo Darke. — London : Batsford, 1982. — 79p : col.ill ; 26cm
ISBN 0-7134-3821-5 : £4.95 B82-27494

Discovering Britain : an illustrated guide to more than 500 selected locations in Britain′s unspoiled countryside. — London (Berkeley Square House, W1X 5PD) : Drive Publications for the Automobile Association, c1982. — 415p : col.ill,maps(some col.) ; 22cm
Map on lining papers. — Includes index
£12.95 B82-23785

Jennings, Paul. Paul Jenning′s companion to Britain. — London : Cassell, 1981. — 207p : ill,maps ; 25cm. — (The Schweppes Leisure Library. Travel)
Includes index. — Maps on lining papers
ISBN 0-304-30459-x : £5.95 B82-32783

Nicholson′s historic Britain / [edited by Rosemarie McCabe] ; [drawings by Towler Cox]. — London : Nicholson, 1982. — 288p : ill,maps(some col.) ; 24cm
Includes index
ISBN 0-905522-53-2 (pbk) : Unpriced B82-35418

On route : what to see in Great Britain and how to get there / [maps and map index edited by R.W. Lidbetter, with research by H. Snape, and prepared by the cartographic staff of George Philip Cartographic Services Ltd. under the direction of Alan Poynter]. — [London] : George Philip, c1982. — 216p : ill(some col.),col.maps ; 35cm
Includes index
ISBN 0-540-05414-3 (pbk) : £6.95 : CIP rev. B82-06866

Swengley, Nicole. Britain : welcome to Britain / Nicole Swengley. — Glasgow : Collins, 1982. — 128p : col.ill,col.maps ; 19cm. — (A Collins travel guide)
Includes index
ISBN 0-00-447320-5 (pbk) : £1.95 B82-10522

914.1′04858 — Great Britain — *Visitors′ guides — For motoring*

Alternative routes in Britain / [editor Julia Brittain]. — Basingstoke : Automobile Association, 1981. — 288p : ill(some col.),maps ; 28cm
Includes index
ISBN 0-86145-063-9 : Unpriced B82-24999

Brereton, Peter. Through Britain on country roads / Peter Brereton. — London : Barker, 1982. — 320p : ill(some col.),maps,ports ; 25cm
Includes index
ISBN 0-213-16829-4 : £7.50 B82-26367

Eperon, Arthur. Travellers′ Britain / Arthur Eperon ; introduction by Cliff Michelmore ; maps and drawings by Ken Smith. — London : Pan in association with the British Broadcasting Corporation, 1981. — xiv,241p : ill(some col.),col.maps ; 21cm
Includes index
ISBN 0-563-17993-7 (cased) : £5.95
ISBN 0-330-26559-8 (pbk) : £2.95 B82-12032

914.1′04858 — Great Britain — *Visitors′ guides — For rail travel*

Goldring, Patrick. Britain by train / Patrick Goldring. — Feltham : Hamlyn, 1982. — 202p : 2maps ; 20cm
Maps on inside covers
ISBN 0-600-20502-9 (pbk) : £1.75 B82-30670

914.1′04858 — Great Britain — *Walkers′ guides*

Classic walks : mountain and moorland walks in Britain and Ireland / compiled by Ken Wilson and Richard Gilbert ; with editorial assistance from Jim Perrin ; maps by Don Sargeant. — London : Diadem, 1982. — 272p : ill(some col.),maps ; 29cm
Includes index
ISBN 0-906371-11-2 : £17.95 : CIP rev. B82-11795

Merrill, John N.. John Merrill′s favourite walks / maps by Paul Boyes ; photographs by John N. Merrill. — Clapham : Dalesman, 1982. — 96p : ill,maps ; 21cm
Bibliography: p94-96
ISBN 0-85206-669-4 (pbk) : £2.95 B82-31384

Smith, Roger, *1938-*. Weekend walking / Roger Smith. — Yeovil : Oxford Illustrated, 1982. — 250p : ill,maps ; 21cm
Includes index
ISBN 0-902280-76-7 : Unpriced B82-36379

914.1′04858 — Great Britian. Description & travel — *Personal observations*

Thomas, Leslie. The hidden places of Britain / Leslie Thomas ; photographed by Peter Chèze-Brown ; decorated by Shirley Felts. — London : Arlington, 1981. — 256p : ill(some col.),2maps ; 25cm
Maps on lining papers. — Includes index
ISBN 0-85140-542-8 : £9.95 : CIP rev. B81-20097

914.1′04858′0222 — Great Britain. Description & travel — *Illustrations*

Gentleman, David. David Gentleman′s Britain. — London : Weidenfeld and Nicolson, c1982. — 224p : ill(some col.) ; 30cm
Includes index
ISBN 0-297-78126-x : £12.50 B82-39948

914.1′04858′0247966 — Great Britain. Rural regions — *Visitors′ guides — For cycling*

Gausden, Christa. Weekend cycling / Christa Gausden. — Yeovil : Oxford Illustrated Press, 1981. — 256p : ill,maps ; 21cm
Includes index
ISBN 0-902280-75-9 : £6.95 B82-17591

914.1′04858′0247966 — Great Britain — *Visitors′ guides — For cycling*

Gausden, Christa. Weekend cycling / Christa Gausden. — Feltham : Hamlyn, 1982. — 256p : ill,maps ; 20cm
Includes index
ISBN 0-600-20444-8 (pbk) : £1.95 B82-30671

914.1′04858′05 — Great Britain — *Visitors′ guides — Serials*

The **Which?** guide to holidays in Britain. — 1982-. — London : Consumers′ Association, 1981-. — v. : ill,maps ; 21cm
ISSN 0262-7302 = Which? guide to holidays in Britain : £5.95 B82-11832

914.11 — SCOTLAND

914.11 — Scotland. Geographical features — *For schools*

Gilchrist, Peter. Scottish studies : O-grade geography. — London : Edward Arnold, Jan.1983. — [160]p
ISBN 0-7131-0672-7 (pbk) : £3.00 : CIP entry B82-32590

Macgregor, Alan. Looking at Scotland / Alan Macgregor. — London : A. & C. Black, c1981. — 64p : ill,maps ; 26cm. — (Looking at geography ; 5)
Includes bibliographies and index
ISBN 0-7136-2143-5 (cased) : £3.95 : CIP rev.
ISBN 0-7136-2142-7 (pbk) : £1.95 B81-30465

914.11 — Scotland. Haunted castles — *Visitors′ guides*

Guide to the haunted castles of Scotland. — East Kilbride (62, New Plymouth, East Kilbride G75 8QB) : Leyline, c1981. — 48p : ill,1map,1port ; 21cm
£1.25 (pbk) B82-35640

914.11'0014 — Scotland. Place names

Johnstone, Fiona. Place names / Fiona Johnstone ; drawings by Catriona Millar. — Edinburgh : Spurbooks, c1982. — 64p : ill ; 19cm. — (Introducing Scotland)
Bibliography: p63. — Includes index
ISBN 0-7157-2086-4 (pbk) : £1.25 B82-20593

914.11'0472 — Scotland. Description & travel, *1746-1770 — Personal observations*

Stott, Louis. Smollett's Scotland : an illustrated guide for visitors : by Louis Stott. — [Dumbarton] : Dumbarton District Libraries, 1981. — 32p : ill,1map,1facsim,1port,1geneal.table ; 21cm
Text on inside covers
ISBN 0-906927-08-0 (pbk) : £2.95 B82-01898

914.11'04858 — Scotland. Description & travel — *Personal observations*

Tranter, Nigel. Nigel Tranter's Scotland : a very personal review / by Nigel Tranter. — Glasgow : Drew, 1981. — 190p : ill,ports ; 24cm
ISBN 0-904002-73-x : £8.95 B82-28992

Weir, Tom. Weir's way / Tom Weir. — Edinburgh : Gordon Wright, c1981. — 207,[32]p of plates : ill,ports ; 23cm
ISBN 0-903065-34-7 : £7.50 B82-10204

914.11'04858 — Scotland. Lowlands. Description & travel — *Personal observations*

Fenwick, Hubert. View of the Lowlands / described and photographed by Hubert Fenwick. — London : Hale, [1981]. — 208p : ill,1map ; 23cm
Includes index
ISBN 0-7091-9322-x : £8.95 B82-09124

914.11'04858 — Scotland — *Visitors' guides*

Complete Scotland. — 13th ed. / [edited by] Reginald J.W. Hammond ; edited and revised by Kenneth E. Lowther. — London : Ward Lock, c1980. — 449p,16p of plates : ill(some col.),maps(some col.) ; 20cm. — (Red guide)
Previous ed.: 1978?. — Includes index
ISBN 0-7063-5905-4 : £6.95 : CIP rev.
B80-04588

Scotland. — 8th ed. / [editor] John Tomes ; with 22 maps and plans and atlas. — London : Benn, 1980. — 451p,16p of plates : maps(some col.),plans ; 21cm. — (Blue guide)
Previous ed.: 1977. — Bibliography: p5. — Includes index
ISBN 0-510-01625-1 (cased) : £12.95
ISBN 0-510-01626-x (pbk) : Unpriced
B82-24783

914.11'04858 — Scotland — *Visitors' guides — For motoring*

Scotland : where to go, what to do / [editor, Barry Francis]. — Basingstoke : Automobile Association, c1982. — 240p : ill,col.maps ; 21cm
ISBN 0-86145-104-x (pbk) : £2.95 B82-28824

914.11'04858 — Scotland — *Walkers' guides*

The **Sunday** post walks : twelve Scottish walks for all the family to enjoy. — London : D.C. Thompson, c1981. — [16]p : ill(some col.),facsims,maps ; 27x31cm
Unpriced (unbound) B82-26383

Walking in Scotland / edited by Roger Smith ; with a foreword by W.H. Murray. — Edinburgh : Spurbooks in association with the Ramblers' Association (Scottish Area), c1981. — 216p,[24]p of plates : ill,maps ; 22cm
Includes bibliographies and index
ISBN 0-7157-2094-5 (pbk) : £4.95 B82-20584

914.11'04858 — Western Scotland. Coastal regions — *Practical information — For sailing*

Faux, Ronald. The West. — Edinburgh : Bartholomew, Sept.1982. — [176]p
ISBN 0-7028-8101-5 : £12.95 : CIP entry
B82-22808

914.11'04858'0222 — Scotland. Description & travel — *Illustrations*

Scotland / with an introduction by Lord Home of the Hirsel ; photographs: Douglas Corrance ; editorial consultant: John Hutchinson. — [London] : Fontana, 1982, c1980. — ca.130p : ill(chiefly col.),1map,1port ; 25cm
Originally published: London : Collins, 1980. — Published for the Scottish Tourist Board
ISBN 0-00-636495-0 (pbk) : £4.95 B82-29534

914.11'04858'0222 — Scotland. Mountains. Description & travel — *Illustrations*

Wainright, A.. Scottish mountain drawings / A. Wainwright. — Kendal : Westmorland Gazette
Vol.6: The Islands. — [1981?]. — [173]p : chiefly ill,maps ; 19x24cm
£3.30 B82-10531

914.111 — Scotland. Highlands & Islands. Geographical features — *For schools*

Condie, Ian H.. The Highlands and Islands : by Ian H. Condie. — 4th ed. — London : Heinemann Educational, 1982. — 44p : ill,maps ; 20x22cm. — (Contemporary Scotland ; 5)
Previous ed.: 1976. — Bibliography: p44
ISBN 0-435-34204-5 (pbk) : Unpriced
B82-28412

914.11'4 — Scotland. Western Isles. Barra & Vatersay — *Visitors' guides*

A **Short** guide to — the island of Barra. — Stornoway (4 South Beach St., Stornoway, Isle of Lewis) : Western Isles Tourist Organisation, [1982?]. — 1folded sheet[8]p : ill ; 21cm
Unpriced (unbound) B82-20964

914.11'4 — Scotland. Western Isles. Benbecula & South Uist — *Visitors' guides*

A **Short** guide to — the islands of South Uist and Benbecula. — Stornoway (4 South Beach St., Stornoway, Isle of Lewis) : Western Isles Tourist Organisation, [1982?]. — 1folded sheet [8]p : ill ; 21cm
Unpriced (unbound) B82-20966

914.11'4 — Scotland. Western Isles. Isle of Harris — *Visitors' guides*

A **Short** guide to — the island of Harris. — Stornoway (4 South Beach St., Stornoway, Isle of Lewis) : Western Isles Tourist Organisation, [1982?]. — 1folded sheet[8]p : ill ; 21cm
Unpriced (unbound) B82-20965

914.11'4 — Scotland. Western Isles. Isle of Lewis — *Visitors' guides*

A **Short** guide to — the island of Lewis. — Stornoway (4 South Beach St., Stornoway, Isle of Lewis) : Western Isles Tourist Organisation, [1982?]. — [16]p : ill ; 21cm
Unpriced (unbound) B82-20963

914.11'4 — Scotland. Western Isles. North Uist — *Visitors' guides*

A **Short** guide to — the island of North Uist. — Stornoway (4 South Beach St., Stornoway, Isle of Lewis) : Western Isles Tourist Organisation, [1982?]. — 1folded sheet[8]p : ill ; 21cm
Unpriced (unbound) B82-20967

914.11'4 — Scotland. Western Isles. St Kilda — *Visitors' guides*

Quine, David A.. St. Kilda revisited / by David A. Quine. — Frome : Dowland Press, 1982. — ix,230p : ill(some col.),maps,ports ; 15x22cm
Bibliography: p221-227. — Includes index
ISBN 0-9508135-0-8 (pbk) : Unpriced
B82-37676

914.11'65 — Scotland. Highland Region. Golspie. Country houses: Dunrobin Castle — *Visitors' guides*

Dunrobin Castle : Golspie, Sutherland : seat of the Countess of Sutherland. — [Derby] : Pilgrim, c1982. — 16p : ill(some col.),2coats of arms,1geneal.table,ports(some col.) ; 24cm
Also available in French and German. — Cover title. — Text, ill on inside covers
ISBN 0-900594-69-1 (pbk) : £0.60 B82-37541

914.11'65 — Scotland. Highland Region. Golspie. Country houses: Dunrobin Castle — *Visitors' guides — German texts*

Schloss Dunrobin : Golspie, Sutherland : Wohnsitz der Gräfin von Sutherland. — [Derby] : Pilgrim, c1982. — 16p : ill(some col.),2coats of arms,1geneal.table,ports(some col.) ; 24cm
Also available in English and French. — Cover title. — Text, ill on inside covers
ISBN 0-900594-70-5 (pbk) : £0.60 B82-37543

914.11'72 — Scotland. Highland Region. Cromarty. Parish churches: Cromarty East Church — *Visitors' guides*

Cromarty East Church. — [Cromarty] ([Church St, Cromarty, Ross-shire, Scotland]) : [Cromarty East Church], [1981?]. — 20p : ill ; 21cm
£1.00 (pbk) B82-27710

914.11'804858 — Scotland. Western Highlands. Description & travel — *Personal observations*

Davidson, Andrew. From the sea to the land : a journey in two parts / by Andrew Davidson. — [London] : Lion and Unicorn, c1982. — [62]p : ill ; 20x25cm
Limited ed. of 150 copies. — Text, ill on lining papers
ISBN 0-902490-57-5 : Unpriced B82-35336

914.11'804858 — Scotland. Western Highlands. Long-distance footpaths: West Highland Way — *Walkers' guides*

Aitken, Robert, *1948-*. The West Highland Way : official guide / Robert Aitken. — Edinburgh : Published for the Countryside Commission for Scotland by H.M.S.O., 1980. — 174p : ill,col.maps ; 21cm + 1 map in 4 sections(col. ; 66x85cm folded to 17x13cm)
Bibliography: p169-171
ISBN 0-11-491664-0 (pbk) : £4.75 B82-16406

914.11'82 — Scotland. Highland Region. Skye — *Walkers' guides*

Reid, Donald, *1905-*. Walks from Sligachan / by Donald Reid. — [Skye] ([Sligachan Hotel, Skye]) : [Skye Mountain Rescue Association], [1982?]. — [15]p : ill ; 21cm
Cover title
£0.50 (pbk) B82-38493

914.11'8504858 — Scotland. Highland Region. Lochaber *(District) — Visitors' guides*

MacDonald, Màiri. Historic hill routes of Lorn and Lochaber / compiled and illustrated by Màiri MacDonald. — [Scotland] : [West Highland Publications], c1981. — 24p : ill,maps ; 22cm. — (West Highland series ; no.2)
Ill on inside cover
Unpriced (pbk)
Primary classification 914.14'23 B82-35791

914.12'104858 — Scotland. Grampian Region — *Visitors' guides*

Peck, *Sir* Edward. North-East Scotland / Sir Edward Peck. — Edinburgh : Bartholomew, 1981. — x,181,8p : ill,maps(some col.) ; 26cm
Bibliography: p172-173. — Includes index
ISBN 0-7028-8021-3 : £8.95 : CIP rev.
Also classified at 914.12'504858 B81-04251

914.12'32 — Scotland. Grampian Region. Kemnay. Castles: Castle Fraser — *Visitors' guides*

National Trust for Scotland. Castle Fraser : a masterpiece of native genius / a guidebook with text by Cuthbert Graham. — [Edinburgh] ([Carlton House, 30 Dean St., Edinburgh]) : National Trust for Scotland, c1982. — 35p,[12]p of plates : ill(some col.),1geneal.table,plans,ports ; 21cm
Bibliography: p35
Unpriced (pbk) B82-29704

914.12'3204858 — Scotland. Grampian Region. Aberdeenshire — *Visitors' guides — For motoring*

Car tours : around & about the north east. — Aberdeen : Department of Development & Tourism, [1982?]. — 64p : ill,maps,ports ; 21cm
Ill on inside cover
Unpriced (pbk) B82-27496

914.12′4 — Scotland. Grampian Region. Braemar. Castles: Braemar Castle — *Visitors′ guides*

Braemar Castle. — Derby : Pilgrim, c1981. — 12p : ill(some col.),ports ; 20cm
Cover title. — Ill on inside covers
ISBN 0-900594-60-8 (pbk) : £0.30 B82-19414

914.12′504858 — Scotland. Tayside Region — *Visitors′ guides*

Peck, *Sir* **Edward**. North-East Scotland / Sir Edward Peck. — Edinburgh : Bartholomew, 1981. — x,181,8p : ill,maps(some col.) ; 26cm
Bibliography: p172-173. — Includes index
ISBN 0-7028-8021-3 : £8.95 : CIP rev.
Primary classification 914.12′104858
B81-04251

914.12′95 — Scotland. Fife Region. Kirkcaldy *(District).* **Coastal region. Buildings of historical importance** — *Walkers′ guides* — *For teaching*

Aberdour Castle trail. — [West Wemyss] : West Wemyss Environmental Education Centre, [1982]. — 50p : ill,1map ; 22cm. — (Castle & heritage trail of Fife)
Cover title. — Text on inside cover
Unpriced (pbk) B82-19485

914.12′95 — Scotland. Fife Region. West Wemyss. Buildings of historical importance — *Walkers′ guides*

Conservation of built-up environment of West Wemyss : West Wemyss village. — [West Wemyss] : West Wemyss Environmental Education Centre, [1982]. — 32p,[2]leaves of plates : ill,3maps,2plans ; 21cm
Cover title. — Bibliography: p32. — Text on inside cover
Unpriced (pbk) B82-19634

914.12′95 — Scotland. Fife Region. West Wemyss — *Walkers′ guides*

The **Chapel** Shore trail. — [West Wemyss] : West Wemyss Environmental Education Centre, [1982]. — 28p,[2]leaves of plates : ill,3maps ; 21cm
Cover title. — Text on inside cover
Unpriced (pbk) B82-19479

From Macduff Castle to Wemyss Castle. — [West Wemyss] : West Wemyss Environmental Education Centre, [1982]. — 28p,[2]leaves of plates : ill,1map ; 22cm
Cover title
Unpriced (pbk) B82-19478

West Wemyss village trail : from 14th century to 20th century walkabout. — West Wemyss : West Wemyss Environmental Education Centre, 1980. — 32p,[2]leaves of plates : ill,1map ; 22cm
Cover title. — Text and ill on inside covers
Unpriced (pbk) B82-19632

914.13′104858 — Scotland. Central Region — *Visitors′ guides*

Scotland′s Central Region. — [Gloucester] : [British Publishing], [1981]. — 136p : ill(some col.),maps(some col.),ports ; 30cm
Cover title. — Designed and compiled by the Public Relations Unit, Central Regional Council
ISBN 0-7140-1913-5 (pbk) : Unpriced
B82-03950

914.13′12 — Scotland. Central Region. Doune. Castles: Doune Castle — *Visitors′ guides*

Simpson, W. Douglas. Doune Castle / [text by the late W. Douglas Simpson]. — Derby : Pilgrim, c1982. — 28p : ill,2plans,ports ; 20cm
Cover title. — Ill on inside covers
ISBN 0-900594-68-3 (pbk) : Unpriced
B82-37540

914.13′12 — Scotland. Central Region. Dunblane, *1875-1975* — *Illustrations*

Portrait of Dunblane 1875-1975 / written and compiled by A.C. McKerracher. — Dunblane (Holmcroft, Claredon Place, Dunblane, Perthshire) : A.C. McKerracher, 1980. — 44p : chiefly ill,ports ; 18x23cm
Text on inside cover
Unpriced (pbk) B82-28707

914.13′18 — Scotland. Central Region. Bo′ness — *Visitors′ guides*

Burgh of Borrowstounness : Bo′ness town guide / produced by Bo′ness Community Council. — [Bo′ness] ([26 East Pier St., Bo′ness]) : Bo′ness Town Trust, [1982?]. — [56]p : ill,2maps ; 22cm
Cover title. — Text on inside cover. — Includes index
Unpriced (pbk) B82-37403

914.13′1804858 — Scotland. Central Region. Falkirk *(District)* — *Visitors′ guides*

Falkirk District Council : official guide. — Gloucester : British Publishing, [1981?]. — 64p : ill(some col.),1map ; 21cm
ISBN 0-7140-1995-x (pbk) : Unpriced
B82-08614

914.13′3 — Scotland. Lothian Region. Bathgate Hills — *Visitors′ guides*

The **Bathgate** Hills. — Linlithgow (Old Country Buildings, Linlithgow) : West Lothian District Council, Leisure and Recreation Dept., 1982. — [34]p : ill(some col.),1col.map ; 21cm
Unpriced (pbk) B82-33441

914.13′4 — Edinburgh. Craigmillar. Castles: Craigmillar Castle — *Visitors′ guides*

Simpson, W. Douglas. Craigmillar Castle / W. Douglas Simpson. — 2nd ed. — Edinburgh, H.M.S.O., 1980, c1954. — 28p : ill,plans,2ports ; 21cm
Previous ed.: 1954
ISBN 0-11-491616-0 (pbk) : £0.60 B82-13739

914.13′4 — Edinburgh. Royal Mile — *Visitors′ guides*

Goodchild, Doris Ann. The Royal Mile : souvenir guide / from the original manuscript by Doris Ann Goodchild. — Edinburgh : Harris, c1978. — 20p : ill(some col.),2maps,coats of arms ; 26cm
Ill on inside cover
ISBN 0-904505-51-0 (cased) : Unpriced
ISBN 0-904505-52-9 (pbk) : Unpriced
B82-27071

914.13′40481 — Edinburgh. Description & travel, *1847*

Edinburgh : the grand panorama of Edinburgh : as seen in a walk round the Calton Hill in 1847. — Edinburgh : Harris, 1982. — 7p : ill ; 15x21cm
Cover title. — Facsim of ed. published: London : Ackermann, 1847. — Folded sheet (ill) attached to inside front cover
ISBN 0-86228-048-6 : £2.25 B82-35121

914.13′404858 — Edinburgh — *Visitors′ guides*

Edinburgh. — Huntingdon : Photo Precision, [1982]. — 32p : chiefly col.ill,2col.maps ; 24cm. — (Colourmaster international)
Cover title: Souvenir of England
ISBN 0-85933-207-1 (pbk) : Unpriced
B82-36351

Royle, Trevor. Edinburgh / Trevor Royle ; drawings by Richard Hook. — Edinburgh : Spurbooks, c1982. — 64p : ill,ports ; 19cm. — (Introducing Scotland)
Bibliography: p63. — Includes index
ISBN 0-7157-2087-2 (pbk) : £1.25 B82-20589

914.13′7 — Scotland. Borders Region. Buildings of historical importance & gardens open to the public — *Directories*

Gardens and historic houses. — Newtown St. Boswells (Newtown St. Boswells, Roxburghshire) : Borders Regional Council, 1982. — 1folded sheet([6]p) ; 21cm. — (The Scottish Borders)
Unpriced B82-32910

914.13′704858 — Scotland. Borders Region — *Visitors′ guides* — *German texts*

Britain : the Scottish borders. — London : British Tourist Authority, c1980. — 1folded sheet : col.ill,col.map ; 63x44cm. folded to 21x15cm
German text
ISBN 0-7095-0447-0 : Unpriced B82-32906

914.13′704858 — Scotland. Borders Region — *Walkers′ guides*

About the Scottish Borders. — [St. Boswells] ([Regional Headquarters, Newtown, St. Boswells]) : Borders Regional Council, Tourism Division,, 1982. — 28p : ill(some col.),col.maps ; 21cm
£0.30 (unbound) B82-33667

914.13′85 — Scotland. Borders Region. Melrose — *Visitors′ guides*

The **Little** guide to Melrose. — [Melrose] ([Newtown St., Boswells, Melrose, TD6 0SA]) : Borders Regional Council, Planning & Development Department, c1978. — 40p : ill,maps ; 15cm
Cover title
£0.20 (pbk) B82-17819

914.14′23 — Scotland. Strathclyde Region. Cowal. Description & travel

Stirling, Nancy. Through the glens of Cowal / Nancy Stirling. — Kirn (Rosemount Park Rd., Kirn, Argyll) : Argyll Reproductions, [1982?]. — 47p,[8]p of plates : ill,2maps ; 20cm
Maps on inside covers
Unpriced (pbk) B82-29708

914.14′23 — Scotland. Strathclyde Region. Cowal. Place names. Etymology

McLean, Angus. The place names of Cowal : their meaning and history / by Angus McLean. — Dunoon (84 John St., Dunoon) : Dunoon Observer, [1982]. — 137p,[4]p of plates : ill,maps ; 20cm
Cover title
Unpriced (pbk) B82-29541

914.14′23 — Scotland. Strathclyde Region. Lorn — *Visitors′ guides*

MacDonald, Màiri. Historic hill routes of Lorn and Lochaber / compiled and illustrated by Màiri MacDonald. — [Scotland] : [West Highland Publications], c1981. — 24p : ill,maps ; 22cm. — (West Highland series ; no.2)
Ill on inside cover
Unpriced (pbk)
Also classified at 914.11′8504858 B82-35791

914.14′23 — Scotland. Strathclyde Region. Nether Lorn — *Visitors′ guides*

MacDonald, Màiri. The islands of Nether Lorn / compiled and illustrated by Màiri MacDonald. — [Scotland] : [West Highland Publications], c1982. — 24p : ill,maps ; 22cm. — (West Highland series ; no.3)
Ill and text on inside cover
Unpriced (pbk) B82-35790

914.14′25 — Scotland. Strathclyde Region. Helensburgh. Country houses: Hill House — *Visitors′ guides*

National Trust for Scotland. The Hill House, Helensburgh. — Edinburgh (5 Charlotte Sq, Edinburgh EH2 4DU) : National Trust for Scotland, [1982?]. — 20p : ill(some col.),col.maps,plans,ports(some col.) ; 21cm
Maps and plans on inside covers
Unpriced (pbk) B82-35353

914.14′43 — Scotland. Strathclyde Region. Glasgow. Streets — *Lists*

Alphabetical list of streets, roads, etc. in the City of Glasgow District. — Glasgow ([40 Cochrane St., Glasgow G1 1IJB]) : Strathclyde Regional Council. Department of Assessor and Electoral Registration Officer. Glasgow Sub-Region, 1982. — 384p ; 30cm
Unpriced (pbk) B82-14341

914.14′61 — Scotland. Strathclyde Region. Arran. Antiquities. Sites — *Visitors′ guides*

Fairhurst, Horace. Exploring Arran′s past. — Brodick (Ivy Cottage, Brodick, Isle of Arran KA27 8DD) : Kilbrannan Publishing, Aug.1982. — [144]p
Originally published: Isle of Arran : The author, 1981
ISBN 0-907939-05-8 (pbk) : £3.00 : CIP entry
B82-27022

914.15 — IRELAND

914.15'04 — Ireland. Description & travel, *ca 1600-1981*
Somerville-Large, Peter. The grand Irish tour. — London : Hamilton, Oct.1982. — [288]p
ISBN 0-241-10871-3 : £12.50 : CIP entry B82-23456

914.15'04824 — Ireland — *Visitors' guides*
Harrison, John, *1928-*. Ireland : welcome to Ireland / John and Shirley Harrison. — Glasgow : Collins, 1982. — 128p : col.ill,col.maps ; 19cm. — (A Collins travel guide)
Includes index
ISBN 0-00-447318-3 (pbk) : £1.95 B82-10518

Oram, Hugh. Outings in Ireland. — Belfast : Appletree Press, Mar.1982. — [200]p
ISBN 0-904651-79-7 (pbk) : £3.95 : CIP entry B82-01732

914.16'1804824 — Newtownabbey *(District)* — *Visitors' guides*
Borough of Newtownabbey : official guide / issued with the authority of Newtownabbey Borough Council. — Wallington : Home Publishing, [1981]. — 44p : ill(some col.),1map ; 21cm
Unpriced (pbk) B82-01664

914.16'4504824 — Dungannon *(District)* — *Visitors' guides*
Dungannon district : official guide / issued by authority of the Dungannon District Council. — Wallington : Home Publishing, [1981]. — 64p : ill(some col.),1map ; 21cm
Unpriced (pbk) B82-01660

914.169'304824 — Donegal *(County)* — *Walkers' guides*
Campbell, Patrick. Rambles round Donegal / Patrick Campbell. — Dublin : Mercier, c1981. — 128p : 1map ; 18cm
ISBN 0-85342-642-2 (pbk) : £2.30 B82-05814

914.17 — Ireland *(Republic).* **Midland region. Description & travel**
The **Midlands** / editor Leo Daly ; assisted by Tom Kennedy, Gearoid O'Brien. — Dublin (5 Henrietta St., Dublin) : Albertine Kennedy, 1979. — 71p : ill,1map,ports ; 30cm
Text on inside covers
Unpriced (pbk) B82-37265

914.17'04824 — Ireland *(Republic).* **Buildings of historical importance & gardens open to the public** — *Visitors' guides*
Irish houses castles and gardens : open to the public. — Dublin : Published by Eason for Historic Irish Tourist Houses and Gardens Association (H.I.T.H.A.), c1979. — 32p : ill,1map ; 25cm
Text, ill on inside covers
ISBN 0-900346-34-5 (pbk) : Unpriced B82-00580

914.17'04824 — Ireland *(Republic)* — *Practical information*
Facts about Ireland. — 5th ed. — Dublin : Department of Foreign Affairs, 1981. — 259p : ill(some col.),col.maps,col.facsims,ports(some col.) ; 20cm
Previous ed.: 197-?. — Bibliography: p245-256
ISBN 0-906404-10-x (pbk) : Unpriced
ISBN 0-906404-12-6 (pbk) : Unpriced B82-15253

914.17'04824 — Ireland *(Republic)* — *Practical information — For British businessmen*
The **Republic** of Ireland. — [London] : British Overseas Trade Board, 1981. — 42p : ill ; 21cm. — (Hints to exporters)
Text on inside front cover. — Bibliography: p36-38
Unpriced (pbk) B82-18661

914.17'04824 — Ireland *(Republic).* **Shannon River. Description & travel** — *Personal observations*
Moran, Roger. The wildfowler. — Belfast : Blackstaff Press, Nov.1982. — [132]p
ISBN 0-85640-277-x (cased) : £8.95 : CIP entry
ISBN 0-85640-278-8 (pbk) : £4.95 B82-28758

914.17'04824 — Ireland *(Republic).* **Shannon River** — *Practical information — For boating*
Shell guide to the Shannon. — 2nd ed. — [Dublin] ([Shell House, 20-22 Lower Hatch St., Dublin 2]) : Irish Shell Limited, [1981?]. — [46]p : ill(some col.),col.maps ; 31cm
Parallel English, French and German text
Unpriced (spiral) B82-01817

914.17'04824'0240652 — Ireland *(Republic)* — *Practical information — For single women*
Hogg, Lorna. A handbook for single women in Ireland / Lorna Hogg. — Dublin : Mercier, c1981. — 128p : forms ; 18cm
ISBN 0-85342-662-7 (pbk) : £2.75 B82-03442

914.17'4 — Galway *(County).* **Gort. Country houses: Coole Park** — *Visitors' guides*
Smythe, Colin. A guide to Coole Park, Co. Galway. — 2nd rev. and enl. ed. — Gerrards Cross : Smythe, July 1982. — [64]p
Previous ed.: 1973
ISBN 0-86140-013-5 (cased) : £4.75 : CIP entry
ISBN 0-86140-014-3 (pbk) : £1.50 B82-18468

914.18'35 — Dublin. Embassies: United States. *Embassy (Ireland).* **Official residences** — *Visitors' guides*
Shannon, Elizabeth. The American Ambassador's residence, Dublin / written by Elizabeth Shannon. — [Dublin] : [Eason], c1979. — [24]p : ill(some col.),2plans,ports ; 25cm. — (The Irish heritage series ; 28)
Ill on inside covers
ISBN 0-900346-30-2 (pbk) : Unpriced B82-20673

914.18'6 — Offaly *(County).* **Birr. Castles: Birr Castle. Gardens** — *Visitors' guides*
Girouard, Mark. Birr Castle demesne : the home of the Earl and Countess of Rosse / [Mark Girouard and Lanning Roper]. — [London?] : [National Trust?], [1981?]. — 32p : ill(some col.) ; 25cm
£1.40 (pbk) B82-16382

914.19'2 — Tipperary *(County).* **Nenagh** — *Visitors' guides — For industrial development*
Feehily, Patricia. Why Ireland, why North Tipperary, why Nenagh for your industry? / [text originated by Patricia Feehily] ; [updated by D.A. Murphy]. — [Nenagh] : Nenagh Chamber of Commerce, 1981. — 20p : ill,1map,music,ports ; 30cm
Cover title. — Text, ill, map on covers
Unpriced (pbk) B82-12960

914.19'304824 — Clare *(County).* **Caves** — *Visitors' guides — For exploration*
Caves of County Clare / compiled by C.A. Self. — [Bristol] (University Rd, Bristol BS8 1SP) : University of Bristol Spelaeological Society, [1981]. — 225p,[18]p of plates(some folded) : ill(some col.),maps ; 25cm
Includes index
Unpriced B82-08171

914.2 — ENGLAND

914.2 — England. Gardens open to the public — *Directories — Serials*
Visit an English garden / English Tourist Board. — 1979-. — London : The Board, 1979-. — v. : col.ill,maps ; 30cm
Annual. — Description based on: 1980 issue
ISSN 0262-9550 = Visit an English garden : Unpriced B82-11806

914.2 — Great Britain. Physical geographical features. Information sources
Historical change in the physical environment : a guide to sources and techniques. — London : Butterworths, May 1982. — [256]p. — (Studies in physical growth)
ISBN 0-408-10743-x : £16.00 : CIP entry B82-06742

914.2'0014 — England. Place names
Addison, *Sir* **William.** Understanding English place names / Sir William Addison. — London : Futura, 1979, c1978. — 190p,[8]p of plates : ill ; 18cm
Originally published: London : Batsford, 1978. — Bibliography: p174-175. — Includes index
ISBN 0-7088-1594-4 (pbk) : £1.25 B82-33064

914.2'003'21 — England. Prehistoric antiquities — *Gazetteers*
Dyer, James. The Penguin guide to prehistoric England and Wales / James Dyer. — Harmondsworth : Penguin, 1982, c1981. — 384p,[16]p of plates : ill,maps,plans ; 20cm. — (Penguin handbooks)
Originally published: London : Allen Lane, 1981. — Bibliography: p363-366. — Includes index
ISBN 0-14-046351-8 (pbk) : £3.95 B82-33150

914.2'0455 — England. Description & travel, *1588 — Personal observations — Early works*
Smith, William. The particular description of England in 1588. — Gloucester : Alan Sutton, Nov.1982. — [124]p
ISBN 0-86299-015-7 : £36.00 : CIP entry B82-26083

914.2'0468 — England. Description & travel, *ca 1685-1712 — Personal observations*
Fiennes, Celia. The illustrated journeys of Celia Fiennes 1685-c1712 / edited by Christopher Morris. — London : Macdonald, 1982. — 248p : ill(some col.),coats of arms,1geneal.table,maps ; 26cm
Maps on lining papers. — Includes index
ISBN 0-356-08631-3 : £12.95 B82-40510

914.2'0481 — England. Description & travel, *1852 — Personal observations*
Tuckerman, Henry T.. A month in England / Henry T. Tuckerman. — Gloucester : Sutton, 1982. — 156p : ill ; 19cm
Originally published: Redfield, 1853 ; London, 1854
ISBN 0-86299-020-3 (pbk) : £1.50 : CIP rev. B82-07814

914.2'0481 — England. Inland waterways. Journeys by rowing boats, *1875 — Personal observations — Correspondence, diaries, etc.*
Williams, Howard, *1854-1933.* The diary of a rowing tour : from Oxford to London via Warwick, Gloucester, Hereford & Bristol August 1875 / Howard Williams. — Gloucester : Sutton, 1982. — 166p : ill,maps,1port ; 23cm
ISBN 0-904387-69-0 (cased) : £7.95 : CIP rev.
ISBN 0-904387-69-0 (pbk) : Unpriced B82-07809

914.2'0482 — England. Description & travel, *ca 1905 — Personal observations*
Thomas, Edwards, *1878-1917.* The heart of England / by Edward Thomas ; with wood-engravings by Eric Fitch Daglish. — Oxford : Oxford University Press, 1982. — 227p : ill,music ; 20cm
Originally published: London : Dent, 1906
ISBN 0-19-281353-6 (pbk) : £2.95 : CIP rev. B82-12542

914.2'0482 — England. Description & travel, *ca 1908 — Personal observations*
Hudson, W. H.. Afoot in England. — Oxford : Oxford University Press, Sept.1982. — [316]p. — (Oxford paperbacks)
Originally published: London : Hutchinson, 1909
ISBN 0-19-281356-0 (pbk) : £2.95 : CIP entry B82-19195

914.2'0485 — England. Description & travel
Entwisle, Frank. Abroad in England. — London : Deutsch, Sept.1982. — [350]p
ISBN 0-233-97334-6 : £10.00 : CIP entry B82-20620

914.2'04857 — England. Description & travel, *1975 — Personal observations — Correspondence, diaries, etc*
West, Richard, *1930-*. An English journey / Richard West. — London : Chatto & Windus, 1981. — ix,196p ; 23cm
ISBN 0-7011-2584-5 : £8.50 : CIP rev. B81-23844

914.2'04858 — England. Anglo-Saxon antiquities — *Visitors' guides*
Kerr, Nigel. A guide to Anglo-Saxon sites. — London : Granada, Aug.1982. — [256]p
ISBN 0-246-11775-3 : £9.95 : CIP entry B82-15708

914.2′04858 — England. Buildings of historical importance. Guidebooks — *Critical studies*
Tinniswood, Adrian. Guide books and historic buildings / Adrian Tinniswood. — Nottingham : Department of Adult Education, University of Nottingham, c1981. — xiv,128p : forms ; 29cm
ISBN 0-902031-66-x (spiral) : Unpriced B82-17006

914.2′04858 — England. Castles — *Visitors′ guides*
Forde-Johnston, James. A guide to the castles of England and Wales / James Forde-Johnston. — London : Constable, 1981. — 348p : ill,maps,plans ; 18cm
Bibliography: p348. — Includes index
ISBN 0-09-463730-x : £5.95 B82-01785

914.2′04858 — England. Coastal regions — *Visitors′ guides*
Gundrey, Elizabeth. England by the sea : where to go, what to see and things to do / Elizabeth Gundrey. — London : Severn House, c1982. — 160p,[8]p of plates : ill(some col.),2maps ; 25cm
Includes index
ISBN 0-7278-2016-8 : £8.95 : CIP rev. B82-07608

914.2′04858 — England. Description & travel
Hallman, Robert. The beauty of England / Robert Hallman ; text by Derek Temple. — London : Batsford, 1982. — 64p : col.ill ; 20cm
Includes index
ISBN 0-7134-3828-2 (pbk) : £2.25 B82-38391

914.2′04858 — England. Description & travel — *For children*
Fairclough, Chris. Let′s go to England / text and photographs by Chris Fairclough ; general editor Henry Pluckrose. — London : Watts, c1982. — 32p : col.ill,2col.maps,col.ports ; 22cm
Includes index
ISBN 0-85166-961-1 : £2.99 B82-23303

914.2′04858 — England. National parks — *Walkers′ guides*
Mattingly, Alan. Walking in the national parks / Alan Mattingly. — Newton Abbot : David & Charles in collaboration with the Ramblers′ Association, c1982. — 192p : ill,maps ; 23cm
Bibliography: p170-188. — Includes index
ISBN 0-7153-8144-x : £6.95 : CIP rev. B82-07583

914.2′04858 — England. Parish churches — *Visitors′ guides*
The **Good** church guide : a church-goer′s companion / edited and compiled by C.A. Anthony Kilmister with Audrey Rich. — London : Blond & Briggs in association with Penguin, 1982. — 392p : ill,maps ; 21cm
ISBN 0-85634-120-7 : £10.95 : CIP rev. B82-09310

914.2′04858 — England — *Visitors′ guides*
Leeds, Christopher A.. England : a traveller′s guide to history / Christopher A. Leeds. — 2nd rev. ed. — Ormskirk : Hesketh, 1981. — 212p : ill ; 22cm
Previous ed.: published as Historical guide to England. Swanage : Croxton, 1976. — Includes index
ISBN 0-905777-21-2 (pbk) : £3.90 B82-05260

The **New** Shell guide to England / edited by John Hadfield ; preface by J.B. Priestley. — 2nd ed. / introductory essays by John Arlott ... [et al.], gazetteer entries by Therèse Appleby ... [et al.], revised for this edition by Anthony Brode ... [et al.]. — London : Joseph in association with Rainbird, 1981. — 864p,[44]p of plates : ill (some col.),col.maps ; 25cm
Previous ed.: published as The Shell guide to England, 1970. — Text, map on lining papers. — Bibliography: p852-855. — Includes index
ISBN 0-7181-2027-2 : £12.50 B82-07354

914.21 — London. Celebrities. Residences — *Visitors′ guides*
Carter, Katy. London & the famous : an historical guide to fifty famous people and their London homes / Katy Carter ; photographs by Helen Douglas-Cooper and Sandy Young. — London : Frederick Muller, 1982. — 157p : ill,maps,ports ; 24cm
ISBN 0-584-95005-5 (cased) : £5.95 : CIP rev.
ISBN 0-584-95006-3 (pbk) : £3.95 B81-34288

914.21 — London. Cemeteries — *Visitors′ guides*
Meller, Hugh. London cemeteries : an illustrated guide and gazetteer / Hugh Meller. — Amersham : Avebury, 1981. — xv,318p : ill,map ; 26cm
Bibliography: p295-298. — Includes index
ISBN 0-86127-003-7 (cased) : £14.95 : CIP rev.
ISBN 0-86127-004-5 (pbk) : Unpriced B81-31644

914.21′04858 — London. Catholic Church. Churches — *Visitors′ guides*
Usherwood, Stephen. Visit some London Catholic churches : (in the diocese of Westminster) / Stephen & Elizabeth Usherwood ; illustrations by Ush ; foreword by Cardinal Basil Hume. — Great Wakering : Mayhew McCrimmon, c1982. — 104p : ill,maps ; 21cm
ISBN 0-85597-329-3 (pbk) : £1.95 B82-25389

914.21′04858 — London. Description & travel
Housego, Fred. London : a portrait of Britain′s historic capital / Fred Housego. — London : Hamlyn, c1982. — 125p : col.ill,1col.map ; 33cm
Ill on lining papers. — Includes index
ISBN 0-600-34294-8 : £4.95 B82-32415

914.21′04858 — London — *Visitors′ guides*
Alternative London 6. — London : Wildwood House, Aug.1981. — [256]p
ISBN 0-7045-0427-8 (pbk) : £2.95 : CIP entry B81-20574

Banks, F. R.. The new Penguin guide to London / F.R. Banks. — 8th ed. — Harmondsworth : Penguin, 1982. — 607p : maps,plans ; 18cm
Previous ed.: published ed.: published as The Penguin guide to London, 1977. — Includes index
ISBN 0-14-070419-1 (pbk) : £2.95 B82-30513

Blogg, Keith. Free (or nearly free) London / [Keith Blogg]. — London : London Transport, 1982. — 63p : col.ill,col.maps, 1port ; 21x10cm. — (A Visitor′s London guide)
Text and ill on inside covers
ISBN 0-85329-113-6 (pbk) : £0.99 B82-39547

Blogg, Keith. Royal & historic London / [Keith Blogg]. — London : London Transport, 1982. — 63p : col.ill,col.maps,1port ; 21x10cm. — (A Visitor′s London guide)
Text and ill on inside covers
ISBN 0-85329-114-4 (pbk) : £0.99 B82-39548

Blogg, Keith. Young London / [Keith Blogg]. — London : London Transport, 1982. — 63p : col.ill,col.ill,1port ; 21x10cm. — (A Visitor′s London guide)
Text and ill on inside covers
ISBN 0-85329-111-x (pbk) : £0.99 B82-39546

Francis Chichester′s 5 language guide to London. — London : Chichester, [1981?]. — 80,119p : col.maps ; 14cm
Map on lining papers. — Includes index
Unpriced (pbk) B82-05885

Francis Chichester′s map & guide of London. — London : Francis Chichester, [1981?]. — 119p : chiefly col.maps,1facsim,1col.plan ; 14cm
Plan on inside cover. — Includes index
Unpriced (pbk) B82-00021

Hammond, Reginald. London in your pocket. — London : Ward Lock, Apr.1982. — [256]p
ISBN 0-7063-6146-6 (pbk) : £4.95 : CIP entry B82-04615

Powell, Anton. Discovering London. — London : Ward Lock, Apr.1981. — [96]p
ISBN 0-7063-6099-0 : £2.95 : CIP entry B81-00657

914.21′04858 — London — *Visitors′ guides — For children*
Ivory, Lesley Ann. A day in London. — London : Burke Publishing, July 1982. — [24]p. — (Headstart books)
ISBN 0-222-00785-0 (cased) : £1.60 : CIP entry
ISBN 0-222-00787-7 (pbk) : £0.95 B82-17926

914.21′04858 — London — *Visitors′ guides — For young persons*
Cobban, Alex. Young persons′ handbook to London / Alex Cobban. — Melksham : Venton, c1981. — 184p,33p of plates(some col.) : ill,1map ; 21cm
Includes index
ISBN 0-85993-031-9 : £7.95 B82-08796

914.21′04858 — London — *Visitors′ guides — French texts*
Les **Nombreux** visages de Londres. — Norwich : Jarrold Colour Publications, 1981. — [64]p : ill (some col.),1map,ports ; 29cm
Also available in German and Italian versions. — Ill on inside covers
ISBN 0-85306-982-4 (pbk) : Unpriced B82-01488

914.21′04858 — London — *Visitors′ guides — German texts*
Farbeprächtiges London. — Norwich : Jarrold Colour Publications, 1981. — [64]p : ill(some col.),1map,ports ; 29cm
Also available in French and Italian versions. — Ill on inside covers
ISBN 0-85306-980-8 (pbk) : Unpriced B82-01486

914.21′04858 — London — *Visitors′ guides — Italian texts*
Londra giorno e notte / Giuseppe Scimone, editorial director. — London : Canal, c1980. — 119p : ill(some col.),maps(some col.),col.plans,1col.port ; 22cm
ISBN 0-907237-00-2 (pbk) : £3.50 B82-13745

I **Numerosi** aspetti di Londra. — Norwich : Jarrold Colour Publications, 1981. — [64]p : ill (some col.),1map,ports ; 29cm
Also available in German and French versions. — Ill on inside covers
ISBN 0-85306-981-6 (pbk) : Unpriced B82-01487

914.21′04858′0240313 — London — *Visitors′ guides — For American tourists*
Newson, Gerald. American London : people and places of popular and historic interest / Gerald Newson. — Kingston upon Thames : Q Books, 1982. — 90p : ill,2maps ; 22cm
Ill on lining papers
ISBN 0-907943-00-4 : £4.50 B82-28976

914.21′04858′0240431 — London — *Visitors′ guides — For parents*
Miles, Vanessa. A capital guide for kids : a London guide for parents with small children / by Vanessa Miles. — London : Allison & Busby, 1982. — 120p : 1map ; 23cm
Includes index
ISBN 0-85031-441-0 (cased) : £4.95 : CIP rev.
ISBN 0-85031-438-0 (pbk) : Unpriced B82-11103

914.21′04858′0247 — London — *Practical information — For visual artists*
London art and artists guide / editor Heather Waddell. — 2nd ed. — London (89 Notting Hill Gate, W.11) : Art Guide Publications, 1981. — 120p : ill,maps ; 21cm
Previous ed.: London : ACME Housing Association for International Visual Artists Exchange Programme, 1979. — Maps on inside covers
ISBN 0-9507160-0-6 (pbk) : £1.95 B82-03034

914.21′04858′0247 — London — *Visitors′ guides — For visual arts*
Boyle, Sandy. Checkbook / written by Sandy Boyle and Antonia Williams. — London : Designer Publications, 1981. — [104]p : 2col.maps ; 19cm
Maps on inside cover. — Includes index
ISBN 0-86306-000-5 (pbk) : £3.00 B82-17409

914.21′04858′0247966 — London — *Visitors′ guides — For cycling*
Cycling in and around London / compiled by the North London, South-West London, West Kent and West London District Associations of the Cyclists′ Touring Club ; edited by John Franklin. — Edinburgh : Bartholomew, 1981. — 128p : ill,maps(some col.) ; 21cm
ISBN 0-7028-8051-5 (pbk) : £2.95 : CIP rev. B81-13550

914.21'04858'05 — London — *Visitors' guides — Serials*

I guide : the recommended guide of the hotel hall porters, members of the Society of the Golden Keys of Great Britain and the Commonwealth. — Summer 1981-. — London (48 Rochester Row, SW1P 1JU) : Brombacher Pub. Co., 1981-. — v. : ill,maps,plans,ports ; 30cm
Quarterly. — Continues: Golden Keys magazine
ISSN 0261-4359 = I guide : £3.80 per year (Free to members of the Society) B82-10353

914.21'204858 — London *(City) — Visitors' guides*

Jarvis, S. M.. Around the historic City of London / Stan Jarvis ; illustrated by David Baker. — London : Bell & Hyman, 1981. — 127p : ill,maps ; 19x22cm
ISBN 0-7135-1249-0 : £5.95 B82-18906

Lowe, Jacques. Living city. — London : Quartet, Oct.1982. — [192]p
ISBN 0-7043-2346-x : £18.50 : CIP entry B82-29080

914.21'3204858 — London. Westminster *(London Borough) — Visitors' guides*

City of Westminster. — London : Burrow, [1981]. — 60p : ill(some col.),1coat of arms,1col.port ; 25cm
Unpriced (pbk) B82-14587

914.21'3404858 — London. Kensington and Chelsea *(London Borough) — Visitors' guides*

Kensington and Chelsea. The Royal Borough of Kensington and Chelsea : 1982-1983 official guide / published by authority of the Royal Borough of Kensington and Chelsea. — [London] (Publicity House, Streatham Hill, SW2 4TR) : Burrow, [1982]. — 76p,1folded leaf of plates : ill,1col.coat of arms,1map ; 21cm
Unpriced (pbk) B82-37410

914.21'4204858 — London. Camden *(London Borough) — Visitors' guides*

London Borough of Camden : official guide. — Gloucester : British Publishing, [1981]. — 112p : ill,1map ; 26cm
ISBN 0-7140-1927-5 (pbk) : Unpriced B82-03952

914.21'43 — London. Islington *(London Borough).* **Barnsbury. Buildings of historical importance** — *Walkers' guides*

Cosh, Mary. An historical walk through Barnsbury / by Mary Cosh. — [London] : Islington Archaeology History Society, 1981. — 29p : ill,1map ; 22cm
Map on inside cover. — Bibliography: p29
ISBN 0-9507532-0-3 (pbk) : £0.95 B82-02411

914.21'7304858 — London. Redbridge *(London Borough) — Visitors' guides*

London borough of Redbridge : the official guide and directory. — Gloucester : Published for the Council by British Publishing, [1981]. — 108p : ill(some col.),1coat of arms ; 24cm
ISBN 0-7140-1951-8 (pbk) : Unpriced B82-02917

914.21'7504858 — London. Barking and Dagenham *(London Borough) — Visitors' guides*

Barking and Dagenham. London Borough of Barking and Dagenham : official guide / issued by authority of the London Borough of Barking and Dagenham. — Wallington (Falcon House, 20-22 Belmont Rd., Wallington, Surrey SM6 8TA) : Home Publishing, [1982?]. — 72p : ill ; 24cm
Unpriced (pbk) B82-28542

914.21'8204858 — London. Hounslow *(London Borough) — Visitors' guides*

Hounslow. *Borough Council.* Hounslow : Borough guide / issued by authority of the Hounslow Borough Council. — Wallington : Home Publishing, 1981. — 92p : ill,maps ; 19x24cm
Unpriced (pbk) B82-05844

914.21'8504858 — London. Brent *(London Borough) — Visitors' guides*

Official guide to Brent borough : its industry and commerce. — London : Burrow with the co-operation of Brent London Borough Council, 1981. — 84p : ill(some col.),2coats of arms,1map ; 21cm
Sixth ed. — Previous ed.: i.e. New ed. 1977
Unpriced (pbk) B82-16251

914.21'9304858 — London. Merton *(London Borough) — Visitors' guides*

London Borough of Merton. — Wallington : Home Publishing, [1982?]. — 72p : ill(some col.),1coat of arms,1port ; 24cm
Unpriced (pbk) B82-24049

914.21'9404858 — London. Kingston upon Thames *(London Borough) — Visitors' guides*

Royal Borough of Kingston upon Thames official guide. — Wallington : Home Publishing, [1982?]. — 104p : ill(some col.),1col.coat of arms,maps,ports ; 21cm
£0.50 (pbk) B82-36031

914.21'9504858 — London. Richmond upon Thames *(London Borough) — Visitors' guides*

Dunbar, Janet. Richmond upon Thames : a short guide / Janet Dunbar. — Richmond [Surrey] : J. Dunbar, c1978. — 40p : 2maps ; 21cm
Ill on inside covers
ISBN 0-9506110-0-x (pbk) : £1.75 B82-23384

London Borough of Richmond upon Thames : official guide 1982 / issued by authority of the Council of the London Borough of Richmond upon Thames ; editorial copy produced by the Reference and Information Service of the Libraries Department ; photographs by Michael Murnane. — Wallington (20 Belmont Rd., Wallington, Surrey, SM6 8TA) : Home Publishing, 1982. — 116p : ill(some col.),1col.coat of arms,maps ; 21cm
Unpriced (pbk) B82-37095

914.21'9504858 — London. Richmond upon Thames *(London Borough) — Visitors' guides — For children*

Law, Felicia. Children's Richmond : a children's guide to the London Borough of Richmond upon Thames : for children, for teachers, for parents, for visitors / by Felicia Law ; illustrated by Stephen Cartwright. — Richmond : Ferry Book, 1979. — 95p : ill ; 20cm
Includes index
ISBN 0-9506536-0-8 (pbk) : Unpriced B82-24320

914.21'9504858'0240816 — London. Richmond upon Thames *(London Borough) — Visitors' guides — For physically handicapped persons*

Richmond upon Thames access guide and handbook for the disabled. — Richmond ([Central Library, Little Green, Richmond, Surrey TW9 1QL]) : Richmond upon Thames, Library and Information Services, 1981. — 108p : maps ; 21cm
Cover title
Unpriced (pbk) B82-09043

914.22 — South-east England. Trackways: Pilgrim's Way — *Walkers' guides — Early works*

Cartwright, Julia. The Pilgrim's Way from Winchester to Canterbury. — London : Wildwood House, Feb.1982. — [168]p. — (Rediscovery)
Originally published: London : Virtue, 1893
ISBN 0-7045-0453-7 (pbk) : £3.50 : CIP entry B81-36973

914.22 — Southern England. Trackways: Icknield Way. Description & travel — *Personal observations*

Thomas, Edward, *1878-1917*. The Icknield Way / by Edward Thomas ; with illustrations by A.L. Collins. — London : Wildwood House, 1980. — 320p : ill,1map ; 22cm. — (A Wildwood rediscovery)
Originally published: London : Constable, 1913. — Includes index
ISBN 0-7045-0407-3 (pbk) : £2.95 B82-17154

914.22'0483 — Southern England. Description & travel, *1913 — Personal observations*

Thomas, Edward, *1878-1917*. In pursuit of spring / by Edward Thomas. — London : Wildwood House, 1981. — 301p ; 22cm. — (A Wildwood rediscovery)
Facsim. of ed. published: Walton-on-Thames : Nelson, 1914
ISBN 0-7045-0423-5 (pbk) : £3.95 B82-30033

914.22'04858 — England. Thames River region. Description & travel

Chaplin, Peter. The Thames from source to tideway. — Weybridge : Whittet Books, Oct.1982. — [192]p
ISBN 0-905483-27-8 : £11.95 : CIP entry B82-24601

914.22'04858 — London & Home Counties. Canals: Grand Junction Canal — *Visitors' guides*

Elwin, Geoff. Braunston to Brentford : a guide to the towns and villages to be found near the canal, descibing features of canal and railway engineering, local industries and present, parish churches and country houses / written by Geoff Elwin ; illustrated by Cathleen King. — Northolt : Blackthorn, c1980. — 56p : ill,maps ; 30cm
Text on inside front cover. — Bibliography: p56. — Includes index
ISBN 0-9507303-0-0 (pbk) : £3.90 B82-20137

914.22'04858 — London & Home Countries. Canals: Grand Junction Canal — *Visitors' guides*

Elwin, Geoff. The Grand Union Canal : from the Chilterns / to the Thames / Geoff Elwin & Cathleen King. — Northolt (44 Moat Farm Rd, Northolt, Middx UB5 5DR) : Blackthorn, c1981. — 16p : ill,maps ; 21cm
Cover title. — Text on inside cover
ISBN 0-9507303-2-7 (pbk) : £0.95 B82-00859

914.22'04858 — South-east England — *Visitors' guides*

South East England. — Huntingdon : Photo Precision, [1982]. — 32p : chiefly col.ill ; 24cm. — (Colourmaster international)
ISBN 0-85933-206-3 (pbk) : Unpriced B82-36350

914.22'04858 — Southern England — *Visitors guides*

Hamlyn leisure atlas : southern England / [compiled and edited by Colin Wilson]. — London : Hamlyn, 1982. — 128p : ill(some col.),maps(some col.),plans ; 31cm
Maps on lining papers. — Includes index
ISBN 0-600-34998-5 : £5.95 B82-27142

914.22'04858'0222 — England. Thames River region. Description & travel — *Illustrations*

Winter, Gordon, *1912-*. The Country life picture book of the Thames / Gordon Winter. — London : Country Life, 1982. — 128p : col.ill ; 31cm
ISBN 0-600-36829-7 : £7.95 B82-28782

914.22'1 — Surrey. Navigable rivers: River Wey Navigation & Godalming Navigation — *Visitors' guides*

Elwin, Geoff. The River Wey & Godalming navigations : Weybridge to Godalming / compiled by Geoff Elwin ; illustrated by Cathleen King. — Northolt : Published in conjunction with the Inland Waterways Association by Blackthorn Publications, c1981. — 17p : ill,maps ; 21cm
Cover title
ISBN 0-9507303-3-5 (pbk) : £1.25 B82-16091

914.22'1 — Surrey. North Downs. Long-distance footpaths: North Downs Way — *Walkers' guides*

Wright, Christopher John, *1943-*. A guide to the Pilgrim's Way and North Downs Way / Christopher John Wright. — 3rd ed. — London : Constable, 1981, c1971. — 325p : ill,maps,plans ; 18cm
Previous ed.: 1977. — Bibliography: p317. — Includes index
ISBN 0-09-464180-3 : £5.95
Primary classification 914.22'3 B82-13349

914.22′16 — Surrey. Guildford *(District)*. Country houses: Hatchlands — *Visitors′ guides*
National Trust. Hatchlands : Surrey. — [London] : National Trust, c1978 (1982 [printing]). — 15p,[4]p of plates : ill,1facsim ; 22cm
Originally published: S.l. : s.n., 1947
Unpriced (pbk) B82-25777

914.22′16204858 — Surrey. Guildford *(District)* — *Visitors′ guides*
Guildford Borough official guide. — Wallington : Home Publishing
1982/84. — 1982. — 64p : ill(some col.),1map,1port ; 24cm
Unpriced (pbk) B82-40202

914.22′16504858 — Surrey. Mole Valley *(District)* — *Visitors′ guides*
Mole Valley District guide. — Gloucester : British Publishing, [1981]. — 144p : ill(some col.),maps(some col.),1coat of arms ; 21cm
ISBN 0-7140-1924-0 (pbk) : Unpriced
B82-03949

914.22′3 — Kent. North Downs. Long-distance footpaths: North Downs Way — *Walkers′ guides*
Wright, Christopher John, *1943-*. A guide to the Pilgrim′s Way and North Downs Way / Christopher John Wright. — 3rd ed. — London : Constable, 1981, c1971. — 325p : ill,maps,plans ; 18cm
Previous ed.: 1977. — Bibliography: p317. — Includes index
ISBN 0-09-464180-3 : £5.95
Primary classification 914.22′3 B82-13349

914.22′3 — South-east England. North Downs. Trackways: Pilgrims′ Way — *Walkers′ guides*
Wright, Christopher John, *1943-*. A guide to the Pilgrim′s Way and North Downs Way / Christopher John Wright. — 3rd ed. — London : Constable, 1981, c1971. — 325p : ill,maps,plans ; 18cm
Previous ed.: 1977. — Bibliography: p317. — Includes index
ISBN 0-09-464180-3 : £5.95
Also classified at 914.22′3 ; 914.22′1
B82-13349

914.22′304858 — Kent. Castles — *Visitors′ guides*
Guy, John, *1952-*. Kent castles : a comprehensive guide to sixty castles and castle sites for both the visitor and the historian / John Guy ; plan and line drawings by Colin Guy. — Gillingham : Meresborough, 1980. — 264p : ill,1map,plans ; 22cm
Map on lining papers. — Bibliography: p257. — Includes index
ISBN 0-905270-15-0 : £7.50 B82-36971

914.22′304858′0247966 — Kent — *Visitors′ guides* — *For cycling*
Guy, John, *1952-*. Cycle tours of Kent / John Guy. — Rainham : Meresborough
No.1: Medway-Gravesend-Maidstone-Sittingbourne-Sheppey areas. — c1982. — 48p : ill,maps ; 21cm
Text on inside front cover
ISBN 0-905270-51-7 (pbk) : £1.50 B82-36402

914.22′323 — Kent. Cooling. Redundant churches: St. James *(Church : Cooling)* — *Visitors′ guides*
Guide to St James′, Cooling. — London (St Andrew-by-Wardrobe, Queen Victoria St., EC4V 5DER) : Redundant Churches Fund, 1980. — [4]p : ill ; 22cm. — (RCF guides. Series 2 ; no.10)
Ill on inside covers
£0.25 (pbk) B82-15007

914.22′323 — Kent. Rochester — *Visitors′ guides*
Pilcher, Derek. Rochester′s heritage trail / [by Derek Pilcher] ; [illustrated by Robert Ratcliffe]. — Rainham : Published for the City of Rochester Society by Meresborough Books, c1980. — 32p : ill,maps ; 21cm
Text on inside front cover. — Bibliography: p32
ISBN 0-905270-16-9 (pbk) : £0.95 B82-36408

914.22′323′04858 — Medway River region. Description & travel
Penn, Roger. Portrait of the River Medway / by Roger Penn. — London : Hale, 1981. — 192p,[24]p of plates : ill,1map ; 23cm
Includes index
ISBN 0-7091-9434-x : £7.95 B82-03282

914.22′32504858 — Kent. Gillingham — *Visitors′ guides*
Gillingham. *Borough Council*. Gillingham Borough Council : official guide. — [London] : Published with the authority of the Council [by] Burrow, [1981?]. — 48p,[2]p of plates : ill,1map ; 21cm
Unpriced (pbk) B82-14567

914.22′3404858 — Kent. Canterbury *(District)* — *Visitors′ guides*
Guide to local services and amenities / Canterbury City Council. — [Wallington, Surrey] : Home Publishing, [1981]. — 68p : ill (some col.),maps,1col.coat of arms ; 21cm
Bibliography: p21
Unpriced (pbk) B82-13304

914.22′352 — Kent. Dover. Ancient Roman houses: Painted House — *Visitors′ guides*
Philp, Brian. The Roman painted house at Dover / by Brian Philp. — [Dover] ([C.I.B. Headquarters, Dover Castle, Kent]) : Kent Archaeological Rescue Unit, [1981?]. — 16p : ill(some col.),1plan ; 21cm
Cover title. — Text on inside covers
£0.30 (pbk) B82-09474

914.22′36 — Kent. Edenbridge — *Visitors′ guides*
Edenbridge : official guide / issued by authority of the Edenbridge Parish Council. — Wallington : Forward Publicity, [1982?]. — 32p : ill,1map ; 19cm
Unpriced (pbk) B82-32768

914.22′37204858 — Kent. Tonbridge and Malling *(District)* — *Visitors′ guides*
Official guide / issued by authority of the Tonbridge and Malling District Council. — Wallington : Home Publishing, [1982?]. — 92p : ill(some col.),1col.coat of arms,1col.map ; 21cm
Unpriced (pbk) B82-24080

914.22′38 — Kent. Lamberhurst. Castles: Scotney Castle — *Visitors′ guides*
National Trust. Scotney Castle, Kent. — [London] : The National Trust, 1979 (1982 [printing]). — 26p : ill ; 22cm
Unpriced (pbk) B82-39518

914.22′38 — Kent. Sissinghurst. Country houses: Sissinghurst Castle — *Visitors′ guides*
National Trust. Sissinghurst Castle & garden, Kent. — Rev. — [London] : The National Trust, 1982, c1978. — 28p,[4]p of plates : ill (some col.),1plan,1port ; 22cm
Previous ed.: 1979
Unpriced (pbk) B82-38909

914.22′38 — Kent. Southborough — *Visitors′ guides*
Southborough official guide. — London (Publicity House, Streatham Hill, SW2 4TR) : Burrow, [1982]. — 82p : ill,1map ; 19cm
Unpriced (pbk) B82-37411

914.22′3804858 — Kent. Tunbridge Wells *(District)* — *Visitors′ guides*
Tunbridge Wells official guide. — [Gloucester] : [Published for Tunbridge Wells Borough Council by British Publishing], [1982]. — 76p : ill[some col.),1map ; 20cm
ISBN 0-7140-2045-1 (pbk) : Unpriced
B82-28953

914.22′392 — Kent. Chilham. Castles: Chilham Castle — *Visitors′ guides*
Chilham Castle. — [Derby] : English Life, c1982. — 24p : ill(some col.),1col.coat of arms,1geneal.table,1plan ; 20cm
Ill and plan on inside covers
ISBN 0-85101-192-6 (pbk) : £0.45 B82-28235

914.22′395 — Kent. Romney Marsh — *Visitors′ guides*
Godwin, Fay. Romney Marsh / photographs by Fay Godwin ; written by Richard Ingrams. — London : Wildwood House, 1980 (1981 [printing]). — 192p : ill,maps,ports ; 20cm
Bibliography: p189. — Includes index
ISBN 0-7045-0441-3 : £4.95 B82-38153

914.22′504858 — East Sussex — *Visitors′ guides*
The **1066** country : a guide and pictorial souvenir. — Lewes : Economic Promotion Group East Sussex County Planning Department, c1982. — 40p : col.ill,maps(some col.) ; 21cm
ISBN 0-86147-011-7 (pbk) : Unpriced
B82-40566

914.22′504858 — East Sussex — *Walkers′ guides*
On foot in East Sussex. — 8th ed., fully rev. — Eastbourne (c/o Mr. H. Comber, 28 Kinfauns Ave., Eastbourne, E. Sussex, BN22 8SS) : Eastbourne Rambling Club, 1982. — 67p,[4]p of plates : ill,maps ; 19cm. — (An Eastbourne Rambling Club publication)
Cover title. — Previous ed.: 1979
£1.50 (pbk) B82-24039

914.22′504858 — England. Weald. Long-distance footpaths: Wealdway — *Walkers′ guides*
Wealdway. — [Tonbridge] ([c/o M. Temple, 1 Tudeley La., Tonbridge, Kent]) : Wealdway Steering Group, 1981. — 36p : ill(some col.),maps ; 21cm
Ill on inside covers
Unpriced (pbk) B82-15201

914.22′504858′0222 — East & West Sussex. Description & travel — *Illustrations*
Bloemendal, F. A. H.. Sussex / photographs by F.A.H. Bloemendal ; text by Alan Hollingsworth. — London : Ian Allan, 1981. — 110p : chiefly col.ill,maps ; 30cm. — (England in cameracolour)
Maps on lining papers. — Bibliography: p4
ISBN 0-7110-1167-2 : £8.95 B82-11220

914.22′51 — East Sussex. Fletching. Country houses: Sheffield Park. Gardens — *Visitors′ guides*
Sheffield Park Garden, Sussex. — [London] : National Trust, c1979 (1981 [printing]). — 21p,[8]p of plates : col.ill,1plan ; 21cm
Unpriced (pbk) B82-05647

914.22′52 — East Sussex. Bodiam. Castles: Bodiam Castle — *Visitors′ guides*
Morton, Catherine. Bodiam Castle, Sussex / Catherine Morton. — [London] : National Trust, 1981. — 24p,[4]p of plates : ill,1map,coats of arms,1plan ; 22cm
Ill on inside cover
Unpriced (pbk) B82-05645

914.22′5604858 — East Sussex. Brighton — *Visitors′ guides*
Borough of Brighton : residents′ handbook : 1982 / issued by authority of the Brighton Borough Council. — Wallington : Home Publishing, [1982]. — 85p : ill(some col.),1map,1coat of arms ; 24cm
Unpriced (pbk) B82-24047

914.22′57 — East Sussex. Newhaven — *Visitors′ guides*
Newhaven : official guide / issued by authority of Newhaven Town Council. — Wallington : Forward, [1982?]. — 32p : ill,1map ; 22cm
Map on folded sheet attached to inside cover
Unpriced (pbk) B82-24075

914.22′5804858 — East Sussex. Eastbourne — *Walkers′ guides*
Eight town walks in Eastbourne / Eastbourne Civic Society. — Eastbourne ([c/o M. Barber, The Butts, Butts La., Willingdon, Eastbourne BN20 9EN]) : The society, c1981. — 63p : ill,map ; 23cm
Map on inside cover
£2.00 (pbk) B82-20934

914.22′62 — West Sussex. Midhurst region — *Visitors′ guides*
Midhurst. *Town Council*. Midhurst and District : official guide / issued by authority of the Midhurst Town Council. — Wallington : Forward Publicity, [1981?]. — 44p : ill,maps ; 19cm
Map attached to inside cover
Unpriced (pbk) B82-05849

914.22′62 — West Sussex. Petworth. Country houses: Petworth House — *Visitors′ guides*

National Trust. Petworth House : West Sussex. — Rev [ed.]. — [London] ([42 Queen Anne′s Gate, SW1H 9AS]) : National Trust, 1981, c1978 (1982 [printing]). — 47p,[12]p of plates : ill,1geneal.table,1plan,ports ; 25cm
Bibliography: p47
Unpriced (pbk) B82-39625

914.22′62 — West Sussex. Petworth region — *Visitors′ guides*

Petworth. *Parish Council*. Petworth and surrounding District Essex : official guide / issued by authority of the Petworth Parish Council. — Wallington (Falcon House, 20-22 Belmont Rd., Wallington) : Forward Publicity, [1982?]. — 36p : ill,1map ; 19cm
Unpriced (pbk) B82-33303

914.22′6204858 — West Sussex. Chichester *(District)* — *Visitors′ guides*

Chichester : district guide / issued by authority of the Chichester District Council. — 3rd ed. — Wallington : Home Publishing, [1982?]. — 96p : ill(some col.),1col.map ; 21cm
Previous ed.: 1980. — Map (1 folded sheet) attached to inside cover
Unpriced (pbk) B82-36026

914.22′64 — West Sussex. Pulborough. Country houses: Parham Park — *Visitors′ guides*

Tritton, *Mrs* **P. A.**. Parham : Pulborough, West Sussex / [text by Mrs. P.A. Tritton] ; [photography by D.W. Gardiner]. — Derby : English Life, c1982. — 28p : ill(some col.),1geneal.table,ports(some col.) ; 20cm
Cover title. — Originally published: 1981. — Port, geneal.table on inside covers
ISBN 0-85101-194-2 (pbk) : £0.75 B82-27304

914.22′6504858 — West Sussex. Mid Sussex *(District)* — *Visitors′ guides*

Mid Sussex : official guide. — Gloucester : British Publishing, [1981?]. — 80p : ill(1 col.),maps(1col.),1col.coat of arms ; 21cm
Street maps (3 folded sheets) as inserts
ISBN 0-7140-1975-5 (pbk) : Unpriced B82-08612

914.22′6804858 — West Sussex. Worthing — *Visitors′ guides*

Historical notes on Worthing. — [Worthing] ([Town Hall, Worthing, Sussex BN11 1HQ]) : [Worthing Borough Council] Borough Amenities Department, c1980. — 15p : ill ; 21cm
Cover title. — Bibliography: p15. — Includes index
£0.20 (pbk) B82-16528

914.22′7 — Hampshire. Long-distance footpaths: Inkpen Way — *Walkers′ guides*

Ward, Ian, *1953-*. The Inkpen way / Ian Ward. — Cheltenham : Thornhill, c1979. — 51p : ill,maps ; 21cm
ISBN 0-904110-78-8 (pbk) : £1.10
Also classified at 914.23′1 B82-05556

914.22′71 — Hampshire. Tadley region — *Walkers′ guides*

Searing, Roger. Tadley tracks, Tadley facts : eight country rambles, a little history and somewhat more conjecture, based on Tadley and its surroundings / written and published by Roger Searing, Pat Minter. — Tadley (49 Mount Pleasant, Tadley, Basingstoke, Hants. RG26 6BN) : [R. Searing, P. Minter], [1982]. — 52p : ill,maps ; 21cm
ISBN 0-9508027-0-0 (pbk) : £1.20 B82-30872

914.22′725 — Hampshire. Aldershot — *Visitors′ guides — Facsimiles*

Sheldrake, W.. A guide to Aldershot : and its neighbourhood / by W. Sheldrake. — Farnborough : Saint Michael′s Abbey Press, 1981. — vi,116p : ill ; 17cm
Facsim of: 1st ed. Aldershot : Sheldrake, 1859
ISBN 0-907077-06-4 : Unpriced : CIP rev. B80-20032

914.22′72504858 — Hampshire. Rushmoor *(District)* — *Visitors′ guides*

Rushmoor official guide. — London (Publicity House, Streatham Hill, SW2 4TR) : Burrow, [1982]. — 68p : ill(some col.),maps ; 21cm
Unpriced (pbk) B82-37413

914.22′73204858 — Hampshire. Test River region. Description & travel

O′Dell, Noreen. The River Test : the delightful story of the Test from its beginnings in the beautiful Hampshire countryside to Southampton / by Noreen O′Dell ; photographs Gerd Franklin. — Southampton : Cave, 1979 (1981 [printing]). — 72p : ill ; 22cm
Ill on inside covers
ISBN 0-86146-008-1 (pbk) : £1.00 B82-14340

914.22′735 — Hampshire. Bishop′s Waltham — *Visitors′ guides*

Bishop′s Waltham : official guide / issued by authority of the Bishop′s Waltham Parish Council. — Wallington (20 Belmont Rd., Wallington, Surrey, SM6 8TA) : Forward Publicity, [1982]. — 16p : ill,1map ; 19cm
Map (1 folded sheet) attached to inside back cover
Unpriced (pbk) B82-37096

914.22′75 — Hampshire. Lyndhurst — *Visitors′ guides*

Lyndhurst, Hampshire : official guide / issued by authority of the Lyndhurst Parish Council. — Wallington (20 Belmont Rd., Wallington, Surrey SM6 8TA) : Forward Publicity, [1982]. — 20p : ill,1map ; 19cm
Unpriced (pbk) B82-36619

914.22′7504858 — Hampshire. New Forest — *Walkers′ guides*

Edwards, Anne-Marie. New Forest walks / Anne-Marie Edwards. — New rev. ed. — Southampton : Arcady, 1982. — 64p : maps ; 21cm
Previous ed.: London : British Broadcasting Corporation, 1975. — Bibliography: p6
ISBN 0-907753-03-5 (pbk) : £1.95 B82-17747

914.22′792 — Hampshire. Portsmouth. Buckland. New Road area — *Walkers′ guides*

The **New** Road trail : a town trail from Kingston Road to Kingston Cemetery, Portsmouth / [compiled by the members of the W.E.A. Local History Group]. — Buckland (Adult Education Centre, Balliol Rd., Buckland) : The Group, 1980. — [38]p : ill,1map ; 21cm
Cover title
£0.20 (pbk) B82-19935

914.22′792 — Hampshire. Portsmouth. Coastal waters. Shipwrecks: Mary Rose *(Ship), 1545*

Bradford, Ernle. The story of the Mary Rose / Ernle Bradford. — London : Published in association with the Mary Rose Trust by Hamish Hamilton, 1982. — 207p : ill(some col.),1map,2plans,ports(some col.) ; 26cm
Includes index
ISBN 0-241-10768-7 : £9.95 : CIP rev. B82-15691

914.22′804858 — Isle of Wight — *Visitors′ guides*

McInnes, Robin. A guide to the Isle of Wight / by Robin McInnes. — New and enl. ed. — Havant : Pallant, 1981. — 111p : ill,maps ; 22cm
Previous ed.: London : Collins, 1974. — Includes index
ISBN 0-9507141-2-7 (pbk) : £2.00 B82-07358

Where to go in the Isle of Wight : what to do, what to see. — [London] : [Wessex Publications], [c1981]. — 44p : ill(some col.),maps(some col.) ; 21cm
Includes index
ISBN 0-86207-017-1 (pbk) : £0.65 B82-38992

914.22′8081′0924 — Isle of Wight. Visits by Marx, Karl, *1874-1883*

Laurence, A. E.. Prometheus bound : Karl Marx on the Isle of Wight / by A.E. Laurence with A.N. Insole. — [Newport, I.o.W.] : Cultural Services Department, Isle of Wight County Library HQ.], [1981?]. — 20p : ill,2ports ; 21cm. — (Island biographies ; no.1)
Text on inside covers. — Bibliography: on inside cover
ISBN 0-906328-15-2 (pbk) : Unpriced B82-12087

914.22′904858 — Berkshire — *Visitors guides*

Royal County of Berkshire : official guide / compiled and written by the County Public Relations Unit. — Gloucester : Published with the authority of Berkshire County Council by British Publishing Co., [1981]. — 108p : ill (some col.),maps(some col.), 1col.coat of arms,2ports ; 21x30cm
ISBN 0-7140-1947-x (pbk) : Unpriced B82-04098

914.22′9104858 — Berkshire. Newbury *(District)* — *Visitors′ guides*

Newbury District : official guide / issued by authority of the Newbury District Council. — [Wallington] ([Falcon House, 20-22 Belmont Rd., Wallington, Surrey SM6 8TA]) : Home Publishing, [1982?]. — 120p : ill(some col.),maps ; 21cm
Unpriced (pbk) B82-21040

914.22′96 — Berkshire. Windsor & Eton. Street names

The **Streets** of Windsor and Eton / [Windsor Local History Publications Group]. — [Windsor] : The Group, c1980. — 53p : ill,maps,coats of arms,1port ; 21cm
Cover title. — Text on inside covers
ISBN 0-9505567-1-8 (pbk) : Unpriced B82-15305

914.22′9704858 — Berkshire. Slough — *Visitors′ guides*

Slough. *Borough Council*. The Borough of Slough official guide : published with the approval of Slough Borough Council. — London (Publicity House, Streatham Hill, SW2 4TR) : Burrow, [1982?]. — 88p,1folded leaf of plates : ill,coat of arms,1map ; 21cm
Unpriced (pbk) B82-37414

914.22′9804858 — Berkshire. Bracknell *(District)* — *Visitors′ guides*

Bracknell District : official guide. — Wallington : Home Publishing, [1982]. — 120p : ill(some col.),2maps,2ports ; 21cm
Unpriced (pbk) B82-40205

914.23′04858 — South-west England. Coastal regions — *Visitors′ guides — For motoring*

Titchmarsh, Peter. Exploring England′s south west coast / by Peter and Helen Titchmarsh ; photography by Alan and Peter Titchmarsh. — Norwich : Jarrold Colour, [1982?]. — 128p : ill,maps(some col.) ; 21cm. — (The Jarrold ′White Horse′ series)
Map on inside cover. — Includes index
ISBN 0-7117-0000-1 : Unpriced B82-24891

914.23′04858 — South-west England. Gardens open to the public — *Visitors′ guides*

Sales, John, *1933-*. West Country gardens : the gardens of Gloucestershire, Avon, Somerset and Wiltshire / John Sales. — Gloucester : Sutton, 1980. — 270p,[4]p of plates : ill(some col.) ; 23cm
Includes index
ISBN 0-904387-55-0 : £7.95 B82-25352

Sales, John, *1933-*. West country gardens : the gardens of Gloucestershire, Avon, Somerset and Wiltshire / John Sales. — Gloucester : Sutton, 1980 ([1981 printing]). — 270p,[4]p of plates : ill(some col.),maps,plans ; 22cm
Includes index
ISBN 0-904387-84-4 (pbk) : £3.95 B82-40408

914.23′04858 — South-west England — *Visitors′ guides — For motoring*

Le Messurier, Brian. The West Country / Brian Le Messurier. — London : Ward Lock, 1982. — 160p : ill,col.maps ; 23cm. — (Regional guides to Britain)
Includes index
ISBN 0-7063-5893-7 (cased) : £4.95 : CIP rev.
ISBN 0-7063-5892-9 (pbk) : £2.95 B81-31648

Mason, John, *1914-*. Southwest England : Avon, Dorset, Somerset, Wiltshire / John Mason. — London : Travellers Realm, 1981. — 128p : ill,maps ; 19cm. — (RAC going places ; 4)
Includes index
ISBN 0-86211-005-x (pbk) : £2.95 B82-03957

914.23′1 — Wiltshire. Long-distance footpaths: Inkpen Way — *Walkers′ guides*

Ward, Ian, *1953-*. The Inkpen way / Ian Ward. — Cheltenham : Thornhill, c1979. — 51p : ill,maps ; 21cm
ISBN 0-904110-78-8 (pbk) : £1.10
Primary classification 914.22′7 B82-05556

914.23′104858 — Wiltshire. Villages. Description & travel

Woodruffe, Brian J.. Wiltshire villages / Brian J. Woodruffe ; photographs by the author and Patricia M. Woodruffe. — London : Hale, 1982. — 208p,[32]p of plates : ill,1map ; 23cm. — (The Village series)
Bibliography: p200. — Includes index
ISBN 0-7091-9745-4 : £8.50 B82-32750

914.23′104858 — Wiltshire — *Visitors′ guides*

Leete-Hodge, Lornie. Moonraker county : a Wiltshire guide / Lornie Leete-Hodge. — Gloucester : Alan Sutton, 1982. — 144p : ill ; 22cm
Includes index
ISBN 0-904387-92-5 (pbk) : £3.95 : CIP rev. B82-07810

Where to go in Wiltshire : what to do, what to see. — London : Wessex, c1981. — 44p : ill (some col.),1col.map ; 21cm
Includes index
ISBN 0-86207-016-3 (pbk) : £0.65 B82-30509

Wiltshire county handbook / issued by Wiltshire County Council. — Wallington : Home Publishing, [1982]. — 80p : ill(some col.),1map ; 24cm
Map on folded sheet attached to inside cover. — Bibliography: p73-79
Unpriced (pbk) B82-24046

914.23′1504858 — Wiltshire. West Wiltshire *(District)* — *Visitors′ guides*

The **District** of West Wiltshire official guide. — Wallington : Home Publishing, [1982]. — 92p : ill,1coat of arms,1map ; 22cm
Unpriced (pbk) B82-40206

914.23′17 — Wiltshire. Devizes — *Visitors′ guides*

Devizes : official guide. — Newbury : Kingsclere on behalf of Devizes Town Council, 1981. — 36p : ill,1coat of arms,1map ; 21cm
ISBN 0-86204-013-2 (pbk) : Unpriced B82-38993

914.23′3 — Dorset. Coastal regions. Long-distance footpaths: Dorset Coast Path — *Walkers′ guides*

Gant, Roland. A guide to the south Devon and Dorset coast paths / Roland Gant. — London : Constable, 1982. — 242p : ill,maps ; 18cm. — (A Constable guide)
Bibliography: p230-231. — Includes index
ISBN 0-09-462440-2 : £5.95
Primary classification 914.23′5 B82-34624

914.23′30481 — Dorset. Description and travel, *ca 1900*

Treves, *Sir* **Frederick**. Highways and byways in Dorset / by Sir Frederick Treves, Bart. ; with illustrations by Joseph Pennell. — Re-issued / introduction by Roland Grant. — London : Wildwood House, 1981. — 376p : ill,1map ; 22cm. — (A Wildwood rediscovery)
Facsims of: ed. published London : Macmillan, 1906. — Includes index
ISBN 0-7045-0430-8 (pbk) : £4.50 B82-36251

914.23′3504858 — Dorset. Weymouth and Portland *(District)* — *Visitors′ guides*

Weymouth and Portland. — Weymouth : Leisure and Entertainments Department for the Leisure and Recreation Committee of the Weymouth and Portland Borough Council, [1982]. — 150p : ill(some col.),col.maps ; 23cm
Maps on folded sheet as insert
Unpriced (pbk) B82-11609

914.23′38 — Dorset. Bournemouth region — *Visitors′ guides — For children*

Banks, Rodney. Children′s Bournemouth and Poole : a guide for all the family / Rodney Banks ; illustrations by Alan Hurst. — Bristol : Redcliffe, 1977. — 64p : ill ; 19cm
ISBN 0-905459-03-2 (pbk) : £0.75 B82-21820

914.23′38 — Dorset. North Bournemouth — *Visitorss′ guides*

Parsons, J. F.. A companion guide to north Bournemouth : Redhill to Kinson / by J.F. Parsons. — Bournemouth : The Teacher′s Centre, 1981. — 52p : 1map ; 21cm. — (Bournemouth local studies publications ; no.658)
Bibliography: p52
ISBN 0-906287-35-9 (pbk) : £0.50 B82-06453

914.23′404858 — Channel Islands — *Visitors′ guides*

Fane-Gladwin, Mary. Channel Island hopping : a handbook for the independent traveller / Mary Fane-Gladwin. — London : Sphere, 1982. — 267p : maps ; 24cm. — (Island hopping series)
Bibliography: p267
ISBN 0-7221-3816-4 (pbk) : £5.95 B82-21271

914.23′5 — South Devon. Coastal regions. Long-distance footpaths: South Devon Coast Path — *Walkers′ guides*

Gant, Roland. A guide to the south Devon and Dorset coast paths / Roland Gant. — London : Constable, 1982. — 242p : ill,maps ; 18cm. — (A Constable guide)
Bibliography: p230-231. — Includes index
ISBN 0-09-462440-2 : £5.95
Also classified at 914.23′3 B82-34624

914.23′504858 — Devon — *Visitors′ guides*

Jellicoe, Ann. Devon / by Ann Jellicoe and Roger Mayne. — London : Faber, 1975 (1982 [printing]). — 180p : ill,1col.map ; 23cm. — (A Shell guide)
Includes index
ISBN 0-571-11818-6 (pbk) : £2.95 : CIP rev. B81-22619

914.23′504858 — Devon — *Visitors′ guides — For motoring*

Mead, Robin. West Country : Cornwall, Devon / Robin Mead. — London : Travellers Realm, 1981. — 128p : ill,maps ; 19. — (RAC going places ; 3)
Includes index
ISBN 0-86211-004-1 (pbk) : £2.95
Also classified at 914.23′704858 B82-03956

914.23′5204858 — North Devon — *Visitors′ guides*

Lowther, Kenneth E.. North Devon and Exmoor : Clovelly, Bideford, Barnstaple, Ilfracombe, Combe Martin, Lynton and Lynmouth, Minehead / Kenneth Lowther and Reginald Hammond. — London : Ward Lock, 1982. — 159p : ill,maps ; 18cm. — (A Ward Lock red guide)
Includes index
ISBN 0-7063-6076-1 (pbk) : £2.95
Primary classification 914.23′8504858 B82-25883

914.23′530481 — Devon. Dartmoor. Description & travel, *ca 1900 — Personal observations*

Baring-Gould, S.. A book of Dartmoor. — London : Wildwood House, Feb.1982. — [304] p. — (Rediscovery)
Originally published: London : Methuen, 1900
ISBN 0-7045-0465-0 (pbk) : £3.95 : CIP entry B81-36972

914.23′53′0483 — Devon. Dartmoor - *Visitors′ guides - Early works - Facsimiles*

Crossing, William. Crossing′s guide to Dartmoor. — Newton Abbott : David & Charles, Apr.1981. — [530]p
Originally published: 1965. - Facsim. of: 2nd ed. of Guide to Dartmoor. Plymouth : Western Morning News, 1912
ISBN 0-7153-4034-4 : £4.95 : CIP entry B81-08926

914.23′5304857 — Devon. Dartmoor. Description & travel, *1970-1979 — Personal observations*

Gunnell, Clive. My Dartmoor / Clive Gunnell ; introduced by Jeremy Thorpe. — Enl. ed. — Bodmin : Bossiney, 1980. — 140p : ill,ports ; 21cm
′Based on Westward TV′s Dartmoor series′. — Previous ed.: 1977
ISBN 0-906456-24-x (pbk) : £1.50 B82-18614

914.23′5304858 — Devon. Dartmoor — *Visitors′ guides*

Dartmoor. — Postbridge (Pencroft, Widecombe Rd., Postbridge, Devon) : Dartmoor Tourist Association, c1980. — 64p : ill,1map ; 21x10cm
English text, introduction in several languages
£0.15 (pbk) B82-21928

Dartmoor. — Tavistock (c/o 8, Fitzford Cottage, Tavistock, Devon PL19 8DB) : Dartmoor Tourist Association, c1982. — 64p : ill,2maps ; 22cm
English text, introduction in English, French, German and Dutch
£0.25 (pbk) B82-20094

914.23′5304858 — Devon. Dartmoor — *Walkers′ guides*

Starkey, F. H. (Harry). Exploring Dartmoor / F.H (Harry) Starkey. — [Newton Abbot] : F.H. Starkey, 1980. — 144p : ill,1map ; 21cm
Map attached to inside back cover
ISBN 0-9507240-0-9 (pbk) : £2.45 B82-34473

Starkey, F. H. (Harry). Exploring Dartmoor again / F.H. (Harry) Starkey. — [Newton Abbot] : F.H. Starkey, 1981. — 182p : ill,1map ; 21cm
Map attached to inside back cover
ISBN 0-9507240-1-7 (pbk) : £2.45 B82-34474

914.23′57 — Devon. Axminster region — *Visitors′ guides*

Axminster and district official guide. — 1981-1982 ed. / edited by Ann Waller. — Abergavenny : Published for the Axminster Town Council by Regional Publications (Bristol), c1981. — xvi,88p : ill,1coat of arms,maps ; 19cm
Previous ed.: 19--?. — Includes index
ISBN 0-906570-06-9 (pbk) : £0.45 B82-22327

914.23′57 — Devon. Ottery St Mary — *Visitors′ guides*

Ottery St. Mary official guide. — London : Burrow, [1981]. — 32p : ill,maps ; 19cm
Unpriced (pbk) B82-14590

914.23′595 — Devon. Paignton. Houses: Kirkham House — *Visitors′ guides*

Great Britain. *Department of the Environment*. Kirkham House / Department of the Environment. — 2nd ed. — [London?] : H.M.S.O., 1980. — [4]p : 1ill,2plans ; 21cm
Previous ed.: 1963
ISBN 0-11-671064-0 (unbound) : £0.10 B82-16407

914.23′704858 — Cornwall — *Visitors′ guides — For motoring*

Mead, Robin. West Country : Cornwall, Devon / Robin Mead. — London : Travellers Realm, 1981. — 128p : ill,maps ; 19. — (RAC going places ; 3)
Includes index
ISBN 0-86211-004-1 (pbk) : £2.95
Primary classification 914.23′504858 B82-03956

914.23′72 — Cornwall. Newquay. Country houses: Trerice House — *Visitors′ guides*

National Trust. Trerice, Cornwall / [illustrated by] Rena Gardiner for the National Trust. — New and revised ed. — [London] : [National Trust], 1982. — [35]p : ill(chiefly col.) ; 29cm
Previous ed.: 1974. — Ill on inside covers
Unpriced (pbk) B82-28230

914.23′74 — Cornwall. Cotehele — *Visitors′ guides*

National Trust. Cotehele / [illustrated by] Rena Gardiner [for] the National Trust. — 2nd revised ed. — [London] : [National Trust], 1979. — 57p : ill(chiefly col.),1plan ; 22cm
Previous ed.: 1979. — Ill on inside covers
Unpriced (pbk) B82-28227

914.23'750482 — Cornwall. Penwith *(District)*. **Description & travel,** *1905 — Personal observations*

Hudson, W. H.. The Land's End : a naturalist's impressions in West Cornwall / by W.H. Hudson ; introduction by Ian Niall. — London : Wildwood House, 1981. — 307p ; 22cm. — (A Wildwood rediscovery)
Originally published: London : Hutchinson, 1908. — Includes index
ISBN 0-7045-0420-0 (pbk) : £3.50 B82-39472

914.23'78 — Cornwall. Truro region. Stately homes *— Visitors' guides*

Barratt, Rex. Stately homes in and around Truro / Rex Barratt. — Redruth : Dyllansow Truran, [1980?]. — 48p : ill,1map ; 21cm
Cover title
Unpriced (pbk) B82-17996

914.23'78 — Cornwall. Truro *— Visitors' guides*

Truro. *Council*. City of Truro official guide / issued by authority of City of Truro Council. — Wallington (Falcon House, 20-22 Belmont Rd., Wallington, Surrey SM6 8TA) : Forward Publicity, [1982?]. — 80p : ill(some col.),1col.coat of arms,1map ; 21cm
Unpriced (pbk) B82-33304

914.23'8'00321 — Somerset, *1821 — Gazetteers — Early works*

Greenwood, C.. Somersetshire delineated / C. & J. Greenwood. — Gloucester : Sutton, 1980. — 215p ; 23cm
Facsim of: edition published London : C. & J. Greenwood, 1822
ISBN 0-904387-53-4 : £6.00 : CIP rev.
B80-22685

914.23'83 — Somerset. Mendip region. Ancient Roman antiquities. Sites *— Visitors' guides*

Jones, Barri. Roman sites on Mendip / Barri Jones. — Bristol : Bristol and Avon Archaeological Research Group, c1982. — 1sheet ; 22x30cm folded to 22x8cm : ill,2maps (some col.). — (Folder guide ; no.2)
Includes bibliography
ISBN 0-900198-07-9 (unbound) : £0.20
B82-40786

914.23'83 — Somerset. Mendip region. Prehistoric antiquities. Sites *— Visitors' guides*

Grinsell, L. V.. Prehistoric sites on Mendip / Leslie Grinsell. — Bristol : Bristol and Avon Archaeological Research Group, c1982. — 1sheet ; 22x30cm folded to 22x8cm : ill,2col.maps. — (Folder guide ; no.1)
Includes bibliographies
ISBN 0-900198-06-0 (unbound) : £0.20
B82-40785

914.23'83 — Somerset. Stratton-on-the-Fosse. Abbeys: Downside Abbey *— Visitors' guides*

Fitzgerald-Lombard, Charles. Downside Abbey : a guide to the Church of St. Gregory the Great : Stratton-on-the-Fosse, nr. Bath, Somerset / [text by Charles Fitzgerald-Lombard]. — Bath (Stratton-on-the-Fosse, Bath, Somerset) : Downside Abbey Trustees, c1981. — 24p : ill (some col.),1map,1plan,2ports ; 25cm
Text, map and plan on inside covers
Unpriced (pbk) B82-25960

914.23'8304858 — Somerset. Mendip region *— Walkers' guides*

Elkin, Tom. Mendip walks / Tom Elkin ; drawings by Marigold Elkin. — Wells : Mendip, [1981?]. — 44p : ill,2maps ; 22cm
ISBN 0-905903-11-0 (pbk) : £1.25 B82-00727

914.23'85 — Somerset. Winsford *— Walkers' guides*

A **Quick** guide to Winsford on Exmoor : what to see, where it is, and a map : a walk over Winsford's eight bridges, & notes on Winsford Hill & Tarr Steps. — Minehead : Nether Halse, c1982. — 7p : 1map ; 21cm
ISBN 0-9507469-1-6 (unbound) : £0.25 : CIP rev. B82-09315

914.23'8504858 — England. Exmoor *— Visitors' guides*

Lowther, Kenneth E.. North Devon and Exmoor : Clovelly, Bideford, Barnstaple, Ilfracombe, Combe Martin, Lynton and Lynmouth, Minehead / Kenneth Lowther and Reginald Hammond. — London : Ward Lock, 1982. — 159p : ill,maps ; 18cm. — (A Ward Lock red guide)
Includes index
ISBN 0-7063-6076-1 (pbk) : £2.95
Also classified at 914.23'5204858 B82-25883

914.23'8504858 — Somerset. Quantocks *— Visitors' guides*

Lawrence, Berta. Discovering the Quantocks / Berta Lawrence. — 3rd ed. — Aylesbury : Shire, 1980. — 48p : ill,1map ; 18cm
Previous ed.: 1977. — Bibliography: p47. — Includes index
ISBN 0-85263-526-5 (pbk) : £0.75 B82-15062

914.23'89 — Somerset. Barrington. Country houses: Barrington Court *— Visitors' guides*

National Trust. Barrington Court : Somerset. — [London] : National Trust, c1979 (1982 [printing]). — 19p,[4]p of plates : ill,1plan ; 22cm
Bibliography: p19
Unpriced (pbk) B82-25776

914.23'89 — Somerset. Ilminster *— Visitors' guides*

Ilminster official guide / issued by authority of Ilminster Town Council. — 2nd ed. — Wellington : Forward Publicity, [1981?]. — 32p : ill,1map ; 21cm
Previous ed.: 1979
Unpriced (pbk) B82-09896

914.23'89 — Somerset. South Petherton *— Walkers' guides*

Waldock, M. F.. Explore South Petherton past & present : suggested walks & notes / illustrated & compiled by M.F. Waldock. — [South Petherton] ([M.F. Waldock, Yarn Barton, South Petherton, Som]) : [M.F. Waldock], c1982. — 28p : ill,coats of arms,1map ; 21cm
Unpriced (unbound) B82-31397

914.23'8904858 — Somerset. Yeovil *(District) — Visitors' guides*

Yeovil. *District Council*. Yeovil District : official guide / issued by authority of the Yeovil District Council. — Wallington : Home Publishing, [1981]. — 114p : ill(some col.),maps ; 15x21cm
English text, French and German introductions. — Maps attached to inside cover
Unpriced (pbk) B82-05845

914.23'904858 — Avon *— Visitors' guides*

The **County** of Avon : official handbook. — Wallington : Home Publishing, [1982]. — 160p : ill(some col.),maps(some col.),ports ; 30cm
Unpriced (pbk) B82-40207

914.23'91 — Avon. Snowshill. Country houses: Snowshill Manor *— Visitors' guides*

National Trust. Snowshill Manor : Gloucestershire. — 11th ed. rev. / [Aidan J. de la Mare]. — London ([42 Queen's Gate SW1H 9AS]) : The National Trust, 1982, c1965. — 32p,[8]p of plates : ill,1plan ; 22cm
Previous ed.: 1978
Unpriced (pbk) B82-27998

914.23'93 — Avon. Bristol. Clifton *— Visitors' guides*

Pascoe, Michael. The Clifton guide / Michael Pascoe. — Bristol : Redcliffe, [1982?]. — 55p : ill,1map ; 21cm
ISBN 0-905459-26-1 (pbk) : £0.50 B82-21826

914.23'93 — Avon. Bristol. Town houses: Georgian House *— Visitors' guides*

The **Georgian** house. — [Bristol] ([Queen's Rd, Bristol BS8 1RL]) : City of Bristol Museum and Art Gallery, 1982. — [8]p ; 30cm
Unpriced (unbound) B82-35928

914.23'9304858 — Avon. Bristol. Buildings of historical importance *— Walkers' guides*
Bristol past revisited with Sperry Local History Group : a series of 16 walks and talks. — [Bristol] ([Sperry House, Temple Back, Bristol BS1 6EZ]) : [Sperry Local History Group], [1981]. — 61leaves : ill,maps,2facsims ; 30cm
Cover title
£1.50 (pbk) B82-03885

914.23'9804858 — Avon. Bath *— Visitors' guides — For children*
Children's Bath : a guide for all the family / compiled and written by Judy Boyd ... [et al.] ; illustrated by Alan Hurst. — Bristol : Redcliffe in association with Tridias, 1977. — 80p : ill ; 19cm
Includes index
ISBN 0-905459-01-6 (pbk) : £0.75 B82-21823

914.24'04858 — England. Midlands *— Visitors' guides — For motoring*
Lindley, Kenneth. Central England : Gloucestershire, Hereford & Worcestershire, Warwickshire, West Midlands, Shropshire, Staffordshire / Kenneth Lindley. — London : Travellers Realm, 1982. — 128p : ill,maps ; 19cm. — (RAC going places ; 9)
Includes index
ISBN 0-86211-010-6 (pbk) : £2.95 B82-29517

914.24'04858 — England. West Midlands. Gardens open to the public *— Visitors' guides*
Sidwell, Ron. West Midland gardens : the gardens of Hereford & Worcester, Shropshire, Staffordshire, Warwickshire & West Midlands / Ron Sidwell. — Gloucester : Sutton, 1981. — 252p,[10]p of plates : ill(some col.),maps,plans ; 23cm
Includes index
ISBN 0-904387-71-2 (cased) : £7.95
ISBN 0-86299-001-7 (pbk) B82-25379

914.24'04858 — Welsh Marches. Long-distance footpaths: Offa's Dyke Path *— Walkers' guides*
Noble, Frank. The O.D.A. book of Offa's Dyke Path / Frank Noble. — Repr. with new preface and minor changes. — Knighton : Offa's Dyke Association, 1972 (1981 [printing]). — 81p : ill,maps,3ports ; 22cm
Previous ed.: published as Shell book of Offa's Dyke Path, 1969. — Bibliography: p78-79. — Includes index
ISBN 0-9507227-0-7 (pbk) : Unpriced
B82-08488

914.24'12 — Gloucestershire. Hailes. Parish churches: Hailes Church *— Visitors' guides*
Sudeley, Merlin Charles Sainthill Hanbury-Tracy, *Baron*. A guide to Hailes Church : near Winchombe, Gloucestershire / by Lord Sudely. — Gloucester : British Publishing, [1982?]. — 24p,[2]p of plates : ill,1plan ; 19cm
Cover title. — Text on inside covers
ISBN 0-7140-2058-3 (pbk) : Unpriced
B82-21431

914.24'16 — Gloucestershire. Cheltenham region. Prehistoric antiquities & Ancient Roman antiquities. Sites *— Visitors' guides*
Cox, W. L.. Prehistoric and Roman sites of the Cheltenham area / W.L. Cox ; designed and illustrated by Richard M. Bryant. — 2nd ed. — [Gloucester] : Gloucestershire County Library, 1981. — [48]p : ill,maps ; 22cm
Previous ed.: Cheltenham : Borough of Cheltenham Libraries and Arts Committee, 1972. — Bibliography: p[48]
ISBN 0-904950-42-5 (pbk) : £0.85 B82-11565

914.24'160481 — Gloucestershire. Cheltenham, *1845 — Visitors' guides — Facsimiles*
Rowe, George. George Rowe's Illustrated Cheltenham guide 1845. — Gloucester : Sutton, 1981. — ix,100,xlviii : ill ; 22cm
Facsim of ed. published: 1845. — Includes index
ISBN 0-904387-95-x (pbk) : £3.95 : CIP rev.
B81-33879

914.24'17 — Gloucestershire. Hidcote Bartrim. Country houses: Hidcote Manor. Gardens *— Visitors' guides*
Hidcote Manor garden, Gloucestershire. — Repr. with revisions. — [London] : National Trust, 1981, c1979. — 34p,[8]p of plates : col.ill,1plan ; 22cm
Originally published: 1979
Unpriced (pbk) B82-05646

914.24′1704858 — England. Cotswolds — *Visitors′ guides*

The **Cotswolds**. — Huntington : Photo Precision, [1982]. — 32p : chiefly col.ill,1map ; 24cm. — (Colourmaster international)
Map on inside cover
ISBN 0-85933-208-x (pbk) : Unpriced
B82-36349

Hall, Michael, *1957-*. The Cotswolds / text by Michael Hall ; with photographs by Ernest Frankl. — Cambridge : Pevensey, 1982. — 85p : col.ill,1map,1plan ; 26cm
Map on inside cover
ISBN 0-907115-07-1 (cased) : Unpriced
ISBN 0-907115-08-x (pbk) : £2.25 B82-27704

Hall, Michael, *1957-*. Stratford-upon-Avon and surrounding places of interest, and, The Cotswolds / text by Michael Hall ; with photographs by Ernest Frankl. — Cambridge : Pevensey, c1982. — 113p : col.ill,maps(some col.) ; 26cm
'The Cotswolds' also available separately. — Maps on inside covers
ISBN 0-907115-05-5 (cased) : Unpriced
ISBN 0-907115-06-3 (pbk) : £2.95
Also classified at 914.24′89 B82-27703

Sale, Richard, *1946-*. A visitor's guide to the Cotswolds / Richard Sale. — Ashbourne : Moorland, c1982. — 144p : ill,maps ; 22cm
Includes index
ISBN 0-86190-048-0 (cased) : Unpriced : CIP rev.
ISBN 0-86190-047-2 (pbk) : £3.95 B82-12892

914.24′1704858 — England. Cotswolds — *Visitors′ guides — For motoring*

Bird, Vivian. The Shakespeare country and Cotswolds / Vivian Bird. — London : Ward Lock, 1982. — 160p : ill,col.maps ; 23cm. — (Regional guides to Britain)
Includes index
ISBN 0-7063-6152-0 (cased) : £4.95 : CIP rev.
ISBN 0-7063-6153-9 (pbk) : £2.95 B82-00222

914.24′1704858′0222 — England. Cotswolds. Description & travel — *Illustrations*

Newbury, Hugh. The Country life picture book of the Cotswolds and surrounding country / Hugh Newbury. — [London] : Country Life Books ; London : Hamlyn [distributor], 1982. — 128p : col.ill ; 30cm
ISBN 0-600-36768-1 : £7.95 B82-19313

914.24′4104858 — Hereford and Worcester. Wyre Forest *(District)* — *Visitors′ guides*

Wyre Forest District official guide / issued by authority of the Wyre Forest District Council. — Wallington : Home Publishing, [1981?]. — 80p : ill(some col.),maps(some col.),1port ; 15x21cm
Maps on folded sheet attached to inside cover
Unpriced (pbk) B82-09899

914.24′42 — Hereford and Worcester. Bromsgrove *(District).* **Hagley. Country houses: Hagley Hall** — *Visitors′ guides*

Jackson-Stops, Gervase. Hagley Hall : seat of the Viscount Cobham / [Gervase Jackson-Stops]. — Derby : English Life, c1982. — 16p : ill (some col.),ports ; 20cm
Cover title. — Ill, text on inside covers
ISBN 0-85101-188-8 (pbk) : £0.50 B82-27305

914.24′44 — Hereford and Worcester. Leominster *(District).* **Castles: Croft Castle** — *Visitors′ guides*

National Trust. Croft Castle : Herefordshire. — [London] : National Trust, c1982, c1979. — 34p,[8]p of plates : ill,1map,1plan,ports ; 22cm
Originally published: 1979. — Bibliography: p34
Unpriced (pbk) B82-25779

914.24′4604858 — Hereford and Worcester. Hereford — *Visitors′ guides*

City of Hereford official guide. — 5th ed. — Hereford : Hereford City Council, 1980. — 156p : ill,maps(some col.),facsims,1plan,ports ; 24cm
Previous ed.: 1974
ISBN 0-902350-09-9 (pbk) : Unpriced
B82-00983

914.24′47 — Hereford and Worcester. Great Malvern. Parish churches: Malvern Priory — *Visitors′ guides*

Winsor, John. Malvern Priory guide / written and photographed by John Winsor. — [Malvern] : Malvern Priory Parochial Church Council, c1981. — 15p : ill(some col.),1col.plan ; 22cm
ISBN 0-9507546-1-7 (cased) : Unpriced
ISBN 0-9507546-0-9 (pbk) : Unpriced
B82-09816

914.24′4704858 — Hereford and Worcester. Malvern Hills — *Visitors′ guides*

Winsor, John. What to see in Malvern / by John Winsor. — 5th ed. — [Malvern] : [Winsor Fox Photos], c1981. — [16]p : ill(some col.),1col.map ; 21cm
Previous ed.: 197-?
ISBN 0-9507540-0-5 (unbound) : Unpriced
B82-03269

914.24′49 — Hereford and Worcester. Hanbury. Country houses: Hanbury Hall — *Visitors′ guides*

Hanbury Hall, Worcestershire. — Rev. — [London] : National Trust, 1981. — 42p : ill,1plan,1port,1geneal.table ; 22cm
Previous ed.: 1979. — Bibliography: p40
Unpriced (pbk) B82-05649

914.24′4904858 — Hereford and Worcester. Wychavon *(District).* **Long-distance footpaths: Wychavon Way** — *Walkers′ guides*

The **Wychavon** Way : an illustrated guide / edited by Mark Richards. — London : Social Science Research Council, [1982?]. — 80p : ill (some col.),col.maps ; 24cm
Cover title. — Text on inside cover. — Includes index
ISBN 0-9508099-0-x (pbk) : £1.50 B82-38936

914.24′4904858 — Hereford and Worcester. Wychavon *(District)* — *Visitors′ guides*

Wychavon district : official guide / issued by authority of the Wychavon District Council. — Wallington : Home Publishing, [1981]. — 93p : ill,maps ; 21cm
Unpriced (pbk) B82-01661

914.24′51 — Shropshire. Oswestry — *Visitors′ guides*

Oswestry and district guide / edited by M. Bennett ; photographs by Bernard Mitchell. — Gloucester : British Publishing, [1981?]. — 56p,[1] folded leaf of plate : ill,2maps ; 21cm
ISBN 0-7140-1944-5 (pbk) : Unpriced
B82-08617

914.24′5104858 — Shropshire. Oswestry *(District).* **Canals** — *Walkers′ guides*

Spencer, Alexandra. About the Montgomery Canal — / [prepared by Alexandra Spencer, Phil Horsley and Janet Cooper]. — [Welshpool] ([2 Canal Yard, Welshpool, Powys SY21 7AQ]) : [Prince of Wales′ Committee and Powys County Council], [1981]. — 4v. : ill,col.maps ; 25x12cm
£0.20 per V. (unbound)
Primary classification 914.29′5104858
B82-21664

914.24′54 — Shropshire. Shrewsbury. Country houses: Attingham Park — *Visitors′ guides*

Attingham Park, Shropshire. — Rev. — [London] : National Trust, 1981. — 34p : ill,1plan,ports,1geneal.table ; 25cm
Previous ed.: 1979. — Bibliography: p34
Unpriced (pbk) B82-05648

914.24′56 — Shropshire. Stokesay. Manor houses: Stokesay Castle — *Visitors′ guides*

Magnus-Allcroft, *Sir* **Philip**. Stokesay Castle, Shropshire / Sir Philip and Lady Magnus-Allcroft. — Derby : English Life, 1982. — [16]p,[4]p of plates : ill,1maps ; 14x21cm
ISBN 0-85101-184-5 (pbk) : Unpriced
B82-24377

914.24′5704858 — Shropshire. South Shropshire *(District)* — *Visitors′ guides*

The **Official** guide to South Shropshire / compiled in the Office of the Chief Executive, South Shropshire District Council. — Gloucester : British Publishing Co., [1982?]. — 112p : ill(some col.),1map ; 15x21cm
ISBN 0-7140-1983-6 (pbk) : £0.50 B82-20309

914.24′61 — Staffordshire. Leek — *Visitors′ guides*

Warrender, Keith. Exploring Leek / written and illustrated by Keith Warrender. — Altrincham : Willow, 1982. — 33p : ill,2maps ; 15x21cm
Text on inside cover. — Bibliography: p33
ISBN 0-9506043-6-4 (pbk) : Unpriced
B82-24274

914′.24′66 — Staffordshire. Pattingham — *Visitors′ guides*

Pattingham : a guide and a brief history of the parish. — 2nd ed. — [Pattingham] : Pattingham Parish Council, 1981. — 82p : ill,2maps ; 19cm
Previous ed.: 1970
ISBN 0-9500848-1-6 : £1.00 B82-09888

914.24′6704858 — Staffordshire. Cannock Chase *(District)* — *Visitors guides*

Cannock Chase : official guide / published by the authority of the District Council. — Gloucester : British Publishing, [1982]. — 80p : ill(some col.),2maps ; 20cm
Streetplans and index on folded sheet attached to inside cover
ISBN 0-7140-1982-8 (pbk) : Unpriced
B82-28952

914.24′8104858 — Warwickshire. North Warwickshire *(District)* — *Visitors′ guides*

North Warwickshire : official guide / issued by authority of the North Warwickshire Borough Council. — Wallington : Home Publishing, [1982]. — 56p : ill,maps,1coat of arms ; 21cm
Unpriced (pbk) B82-17153

914.24′87 — Warwickshire. Leamington Spa region — *Walkers′ guides*

Roth, Daniel. A pocket guide to Royal Leamington Spa / by Daniel Roth ; with illustrations by the author. — Warwick : Gould, 1978. — vii,56p,[10]p of plates : ill,maps ; 19cm + 1sheet(2maps ; 45x62cm folded to 8x11cm)
Street map and index (1 folded sheet) in pocket
ISBN 0-9506270-0-3 (pbk) : £1.50 B82-20533

914.24′89 — Warwickshire. Alcester. Country houses: Ragley Hall — *Visitors′ guides*

Hertford, Hugh Edward Conway Seymour, *Marquess of*. Ragley Hall / [text ... written by the Marquess of Hertford]. — Derby : English Life, c1982. — 24p : ill(some col.),1col.map,1col.coat of arms,ports ; 24cm
Cover title. — New ed. — Previous ed.: 1979. — Text, ill, coat of arms, map on inside covers
ISBN 0-85101-190-x (pbk) : £0.60 B82-27667

914.24′89 — Warwickshire. Stratford-on-Avon *(District).* **Country houses: Upton House** — *Visitors′ guides*

National Trust. Upton House : Warwickshire. — [London] : National Trust, c1980 (1982 [printing]). — 27p,[8]p of plates : ill ; 22cm
Unpriced (pbk) B82-25775

914.24′89 — Warwickshire. Stratford-upon-Avon. Buildings associated with Shakespeare, William — *Visitors′ guides*

Fox, Levi. The Shakespearian properties / described by Levi Fox. — Norwich : Jarrold in association with the Shakespeare Birthplace Trust, 1981. — [28]p : ill(some col.),1col.map,1col.port ; 25cm
Ill,port on inside covers
ISBN 0-85306-967-0 (pbk) : Unpriced
B82-01366

914.24′89 — Warwickshire. Stratford-upon-Avon region — *Visitors′ guides*

Coster, E. L.. The Shakespeare country : a guide to Stratford-upon-Avon and surrounding areas / written by E.L. Coster. — London : Geographia, 1981. — 40p : ill(some col.),maps ; 22cm. — (A Geographia guide)
ISBN 0-09-205680-6 (pbk) : £1.50 B82-08316

914.24′89 — Warwickshire. Stratford-upon-Avon region — *Visitors′ guides* *continuation*
Hall, Michael, *1957-*. Stratford-upon-Avon and surrounding places of interest, and, The Cotswolds / text by Michael Hall ; with photographs by Ernest Frankl. — Cambridge : Pevensey, c1982. — 113p : col.ill,maps(some col.) ; 26cm
'The Cotswolds' also available separately. — Maps on inside covers
ISBN 0-907115-05-5 (cased) : Unpriced
ISBN 0-907115-06-3 (pbk) : £2.95
Primary classification 914.24′1704858
B82-27703

914.24′9404858 — West Midlands *(Metropolitan County)*. **Sandwell** *(District)* — *Visitors′ guides*
Sandwell Metropolitan Borough official guide / issued by authority of the Sandwell Metropolitan Borough Council. — Wallington : Home Publishing, [1982?]. — 132p : ill(some col.),1col.coat of arms,maps(some col.) ; 30cm
Unpriced (pbk) B82-36032

914.24′96 — West Midlands *(Metropolitan County)*. **Birmingham. Country houses: Aston Hall** — *Visitors′ guides*
Fairclough, Oliver. Aston Hall : a general guide / [Oliver Fairclough]. — Birmingham : Birmingham Museums and Art Gallery, 1981. — 32p,[4]p of plates : ill(some col.),1map,plans,ports,1geneal.table ; 21cm
Bibliography: p32
Unpriced (pbk) B82-15401

914.24′9604857 — West Midlands *(Metropolitan County)*. **Birmingham**, *1970-1979* — *Visitors′ guides*
Welcome to Birmingham. — 3rd ed. — Birmingham : Information Bureau, National Exhibition Centre Limited, 1979. — 48p : ill,maps ; 15cm
Unpriced (pbk) B82-40684

914.25′04858 — England. Chilterns. Description & travel
Cull, Elizabeth. Portrait of the Chilterns / by Elizabeth Cull. — London : Hale, 1982. — 208p,[24]p of plates : ill,1map ; 23cm
Bibliography: p196-198. — Includes index
ISBN 0-7091-9738-1 : £8.25 B82-28963

914.25′04858 — England. Chilterns — *Visitors′ guides*
Lands, Neil. A visitor's guide to the Chilterns / Neil Lands. — Ashbourne : Moorland, c1982. — 126p : ill,maps ; 22cm
Bibliography: p119. — Includes index
ISBN 0-86190-029-4 (cased) : £3.95 : CIP rev.
ISBN 0-86190-028-6 (pbk) : £3.95 B81-38834

914.25′04858 — England. East Midlands — *Visitors′ guides*
Westacott, H. D.. East Midlands : Derbyshire, Leicestershire, Lincolnshire, Northamptonshire, Nottinghamshire / Hugh Westacott. — London : Travellers Realm, 1982. — 128p : ill,maps ; 19cm. — (RAC going places ; 10)
Includes index
ISBN 0-86211-011-4 (pbk) : £2.95 B82-29516

914.25′104858 — Derbyshire. Churches — *Visitors′ guides*
Innes-Smith, Robert. Notable churches of Derbyshire / by Robert Innes-Smith. — Derby : Derbyshire Countryside, c1981. — 24p : ill,1coat of arms ; 24cm
Cover title. — Text, ill on inside covers
ISBN 0-85100-072-x (pbk) : £0.50 B82-04575

914.25′104858 — Derbyshire — *Visitors′ guides* — *For motoring*
Merrill, John N.. Explore Derbyshire by car / by John N. Merrill. — 3rd ed. — Clapham, North Yorkshire : Dalesman, 1979. — 63p : ill,maps ; 21cm
Previous ed.: 1976
ISBN 0-85206-546-9 (pbk) : £1.25 B82-14852

914.25′1104858 — England. Peak District — *Visitors′ guides*
Porter, Lindsey. A visitor's guide to the Peak District / Lindsey Porter. — Ashbourne : Moorland, c1982. — 129p : ill,maps ; 22cm
Bibliography: p120-121. — Includes index
ISBN 0-86190-038-3 (cased) : £3.95 : CIP rev.
ISBN 0-86190-037-5 (pbk) : £3.95 B81-39242

914.25′1104858 — England. Peak District — *Visitors′ guides* — *For motoring*
Titchmarsh, Peter. The Peak district by car / compiled by Peter, Helen and David Titchmarsh ; photography by Alan and Peter Titchmarsh. — Norwich : Jarrold [Colour], [1982?]. — 32p : ill,maps(some col.) ; 21cm. — (The Jarrold White Horse series)
Map and text on inside covers. — Includes index
ISBN 0-85306-854-2 (pbk) : Unpriced
B82-24623

914.25′13 — Derbyshire. Ashbourne region — *Visitors′ guides*
Ashbourne : Dovedale and the Manifold Valley : official guide to Ashbourne and District. — Derby : Derbyshire Countryside in collaboration with Ashbourne Town Council, [1982?]. — 56p : ill,1map,ports ; 22cm
ISBN 0-85100-077-0 (pbk) : £0.50 B82-34558

914.25′13 — Derbyshire. Edensor. Country houses: Chatsworth House. Gardens — *Visitors′ guides*
The **Garden** at Chatsworth : the Derbyshire home of the Duke and Duchess of Devonshire. — Derby : Derbyshire Countryside, c1982. — 28p : ill(some col.),2maps ; 19x26cm
Ill on inside covers. — Bibliography: p28
ISBN 0-85100-076-2 (pbk) : Unpriced
B82-25545

914.25′1704858 — Derbyshire. Derby — *Visitors′ guides*
City of Derby : official guide. — Gloucester : British Publishing, [1981?]. — 152p : ill(some col.),col.maps,col.coat of arms ; 24cm
ISBN 0-7140-1930-5 (pbk) : Unpriced
B82-08618

914.25′19 — Derbyshire. Repton. Parish churches: St. Wystan's Church — *Visitors′ guides*
Taylor, H. M. (Harold McCarter). St. Wystan's Church, Repton : a guide and history / [H.M. Taylor]. — [Repton] ([c/o St. Wystan's Church, Repton, Derbys.]) : H.M. Taylor. — 29p : ill,plans ; 21cm
Unpriced (pbk) B82-14414

914.25′24 — Nottinghamshire. Newark — *Visitors′ guides*
Newark-on-Trent : official guide / compiled by D.A. Graham. — Wallington : Published for the Newark Town Trustees by Forward Publicity, [1982?]. — 44p : ill,1map ; 22cm
One folded sheet (map) attached to inside back cover
Unpriced (pbk) B82-32771

914.25′2504858 — Nottinghamshire. Ashfield *(District)* — *Visitors′ guides*
Ashfield official guide / issued by authority of Ashfield District Council. — [Wallington] ([Falcon House, 20-22 Belmont Rd., Wallington, Surrey SM6 8TA]) : Home Publishing, [1982?]. — 56p : ill,maps(some col.) ; 21cm
Map attached to inside back cover
Unpriced (pbk) B82-21038

914.25′29 — Nottinghamshire. Ruddington. Parish churches: St. Peter's Church *(Ruddington)* — *Visitors′ guides*
St. Peter's Church *(Ruddington)*. A guide to St. Peter's Church Ruddington / [produced by the Ruddington Local History of Amenity Society Publications Committee on behalf of the Parish Church]. — [Nottingham] : [The Committee], [1981]. — [16]p : 1ill,1plan ; 21cm
Plan (1 folded sheet) as insert
ISBN 0-903929-04-x (unbound) : Unpriced
B82-10274

914.25′304858 — Lincolnshire — *Practical information* — *For businessmen*
The **County** of Lincolnshire : the official industrial and commercial guide to the county issued by the authority of the Lincolnshire County Council. — Gloucester : British Publishing, [1982]. — 80p : ill,1col.coat of arms,2col.maps ; 24cm
ISBN 0-7140-2018-4 (pbk) : Unpriced
B82-28954

914.25′32 — Lincolnshire. Louth — *Walkers′ guides*
Redmore, Ken. Louth town trail / written by Ken Redmore ; based on research by Stuart Sizer and observations by Gill Foot ; illustrated by Anne Keward. — 2nd ed. — Lincoln : Lincolnshire Library Service, 1981. — 24p : ill,1map ; 21cm
Cover title. — Originally published: Louth : Louth Teachers Centre, 1979. — Text and ill on inside covers
ISBN 0-86111-104-4 (pbk) : Unpriced
B82-16594

914.25′32 — Lincolnshire. Spilsby — *Visitors′ guides*
Spilsby, official guide / issued by authority of the Spilsby Town Council. — Wallington : Forward Publicity, [1981?]. — 24p : ill,1map ; 21cm
Unpriced (pbk) B82-09900

914.25′3404858 — Lincolnshire. Lincoln — *Visitors′ guides*
City of Lincoln official guide. — [Wallington] ([Falcon House, 20-22 Belmont Rd., Wallington, Surrey SM6 8TA]) : Home Publishing, [1982?]. — 120p : ill(some col.),maps ; 24cm
English text with summary in Dutch, French German and Swedish
Unpriced (pbk) B82-21036

914.25′44 — Leicestershire. West Langton. Country houses: Langton Hall — *Visitors′ guides*
Langton Hall : near Market Harborough, Leicestershire. — Derby : English Life, c1982. — [12]p : ill,1coat of arms,1geneal.table,1map ; 15x21cm
Ill on inside covers
ISBN 0-85101-187-x (pbk) : £0.40 B82-28234

914.25′4404858 — Leicestershire. Harborough *(District)* — *Visitors′ guides*
Harborough District Council : official guide. — Gloucester : British Publishing, [1981]. — 104p : ill(some col.),maps(some col.) ; 21cm
Plan on folded sheet attached to inside cover
ISBN 0-7140-1884-8 (pbk) : Unpriced
B82-03947

914.25′45 — Leicestershire. Lyddington. Almshouses: Lyddington Bedehouse — *Visitors′ guides*
Great Britain. *Department of the Environment*. Lyddington Bedehouse / Department of the Environment. — [London?] : H.M.S.O., c1979 (1980 printing). — [4]p : 1ill,1plan ; 21cm
ISBN 0-11-671068-3 (unbound) : £0.10
B82-16408

914.25′57 — Northamptonshire. Sulgrave. Country houses: Sulgrave Manor — *Visitors′ guides*
Sulgrave Manor : Northamptonshire : home of George Washington's ancestors. — [Derby] : [English Life], c1982. — 16p : ill(some col.),facsims,1geneal.table,ports(some col.) ; 20cm
Cover title. — Ill on inside covers
ISBN 0-85101-186-1 (pbk) : £0.40 B82-33061

914.25′59 — Northamptonshire. Towcester — *Visitors′ guides*
Towcester. *Parish Council*. Towcester : official guide / issued by authority of the Towcester Parish Council. — Wallington : Forward Publicity, [1981?]. — 24p : ill,maps ; 19cm
Unpriced (pbk) B82-05847

914.25′7′04858 — Oxfordshire. Description & travel
Scargill, D. I.. Oxford and its countryside / Ian Scargill and Alan Crosby ; with original art by Laura Potter. — Oxford : Walter L. Meagher, 1982. — 92p : ill,maps,ports ; 23cm. — (Oxford books)
Ports and text on inside cover
ISBN 0-907933-00-9 (cased) : Unpriced : CIP rev.
ISBN 0-907933-01-7 (pbk) : £3.95 B82-14400

914.25′704858 — Oxfordshire — *Visitors′ guides*
Oxfordshire county handbook. — London : Burrow, [1981?]. — 52p : ill(some col.),1coat of arms,1map ; 25cm
Unpriced (pbk) B82-16252

914.25'7404858'0240816 — Oxfordshire. Oxford — *Visitors' guides — For physically handicapped persons*
Oxford for the disabled / edited by Jane Turner and Neil Hicks on behalf of the Oxfordshire Council for Voluntary Service. — Oxford (Pratten Building, New Rd., Oxford) : The Council, 1981. — 47p : 1map ; 21cm
Map (1 folded leaf) attached to inside cover. — Bibliography: p46-47
£0.50 (pbk) B82-26742

914.25'76 — Oxfordshire. Faringdon. Country houses: Buscot Park — *Visitors' guides*
National Trust. The Faringdon collection : Buscot Park. — [London] ([42 Queen Anne's Gate, SW1H 9AS]) : [National Trust], 1982. — 39p,[12]p of plates : ill(some col.),ports ; 25cm
Includes index
Unpriced (pbk) B82-39779

914.25'7604858 — Oxfordshire. Vale of White Horse *(District) — Visitors' guides*
The **Vale** of White Horse : official guide / issued by authority of the Vale of White Horse District Council. — 3rd ed. — Wallington : Home Publishing, 1982. — 104p : ill(some col.),1col.coat of arms,maps ; 19cm
Previous ed.: 1979. — Map (1 folded sheet) attached to inside cover
Unpriced (pbk) B82-36028

914.25'79 — Oxfordshire. Henley-on-Thames. Country houses: Greys Court — *Visitors' guides*
National Trust. Greys Court : Henley-on-Thames. — [London] : National Trust, c1970 (1982 [printing]). — 14p,[4]p of plates : ill,1map ; 22cm
Unpriced (pbk) B82-25778

914.25'79 — Oxfordshire. Stonor. Country houses: Stonor House — *Visitors' guides*
Stonor. — [Henley-on-Thames] : [Stonor Enterprises], [198-?]. — 20p : ill(some col.) ; 21cm
Cover title
Unpriced (pbk) B82-26187

914.25'804858 — Hertfordshire — *Visitors' guides*
Healey, R. M.. A Shell guide to Hertfordshire. — London : Faber, Sept.1982. — [192]p
ISBN 0-571-11801-1 : £7.95 : CIP entry B82-25168

914.25'81 — Hertfordshire. Oughton Head — *Walkers' guides*
James, Trevor J.. Oughton Head : guided walk. — Baldock (High St., Baldock, Herts.) : North Hertfordshire Museums Service, 1981. — 20p : ill,1map ; 21cm
Cover title. — Written by Trevor J. James. — Ill on inside covers
Unpriced (pbk) B82-18891

914.25'8104858 — Hertfordshire. North Hertfordshire *(District) — Visitors' guides*
North Hertfordshire district : official guide / issued by authority of the North Hertfordshire District Council. — 2nd ed. — Wallington : Home Publishing, [1982?]. — 92p : ill(some col.),1coat of arms,1map ; 21cm
Previous ed.: 1979
Unpriced (pbk) B82-24079

914.25'83 — Hertfordshire. Sawbridgeworth — *Visitors' guides*
Sawbridgeworth : offical guide. — [Sawbridgeworth] : [Sawbridgeworth & District Round Table], [1978]. — 71p : ill,1map ; 21cm
Cover title. — Map, folded, attached to inside back cover
£0.50 (pbk) B82-38494

Sawbridgeworth, town guide / issued by authority of the Sawbridgeworth Town Council. — Wallington : Forward Publicity, [1981?]. — 36p : ill,1map ; 21cm
Unpriced (pbk) B82-09895

914.25'84 — Hertfordshire. Berkhamsted — *Visitors' guides*
Berkhamsted : official guide. — Wallington : Forward Publicity, [1982]. — 32p : ill,1col.map ; 21cm
Col. map on folded sheet tipped in
Unpriced (pbk) B82-40204

914.25'89504858 — Hertfordshire. Hertsmere *(District) — Walkers' guides*
Walks in Hertsmere. — [Borehamwood] ([Civic Offices, Elstree Way, Borehamwood, Herts. WD6 1WA]) : [Hertsmere Borough Council], [1980]. — 4v. : ill,maps ; 29x42cm folded to 21x10cm
Unpriced B82-08885

914.25'904858 — Buckinghamshire — *Visitors' guides*
Watkin, Bruce. Buckinghamshire / by Bruce Watkin. — London : Faber, 1981. — 192p : ill,1col.map ; 24cm. — (A Shell guide)
Ill on lining papers. — Includes index
ISBN 0-571-11784-8 : £5.95 : CIP rev. B81-21532

914.25'91 — Buckinghamshire. Olney — *Visitors' guides*
Olney, Buckinghamshire : official guide / issued by authority of Olney Town Council. — Wallington : Forward Publicity, 1981. — 19p : ill ; 19cm
Unpriced (pbk) B82-01659

914.25'93 — Buckinghamshire. Buckingham — *Visitors' guides*
Buckingham, official guide : with 2 maps / photos by R. & H. Chapman ; issued by authority of the Buckingham Town Council. — Wallington : Forward Publicity, [1981?]. — 24p : ill,2maps ; 19cm
Maps on folded sheet attached to inside cover
Unpriced (pbk) B82-09898

914.25'93 — Buckinghamshire. Middle Claydon. Country houses: Claydon House — *Visitors' guides*
Claydon House, Buckinghamshire. — [London] : National Trust, c1978 (1981 [printing]). — 38p : ill,2plans,ports,1geneal.table ; 22cm
Bibliography: p38
Unpriced (pbk) B82-05650

914.25'98 — Buckinghamshire. Burnham — *Visitors' guides*
Burnham. *Parish Council*. Burnham : official guide / issued by authority of the Burnham Parish Council. — Wallington (Falcon House, 20-22 Belmont Rd., Wallington, Surrey SM6 8TA) : Forward Publicity, [1982?]. — 24p : ill,maps(some col.) ; 19cm
Map (folded sheet) attached to inside back cover
Unpriced (pbk) B82-28545

914.25'98 — Buckinghamshire. Denham — *Visitors' guides*
A **Guide** to Denham, Buckinghamshire : with general information, street map and footpaths map. — [Maidenhead] ([c/o G.A. Perry, 'Augustine', 8A Cresswells Mead, Holyport, Maidenhead, Berks. SL6 2YP]) : Denham Parish Council, [1981]. — 20p : ill,maps ; 21cm
Cover title
Unpriced (pbk) B82-11656

914.26'04858 — East Anglia — *Walkers' guides*
Galloway, Bruce. Walks in East Anglia / Bruce Galloway. — Woodbridge : Boydell Press
2: Cambridgeshire and Essex. — c1982. — 192p : maps ; 25cm
Bibliography: p189. — Includes index
ISBN 0-85115-163-9 : £9.95 : CIP rev. B82-10694

914.26'104858 — Norfolk — *Visitors' guides*
Harrod, Wilhelmine. Norfolk / by Wilhelmine Harrod. — 4th ed. — London : Faber, 1982. — 192p : ill(some col.),1map ; 24cm. — (A Shell guide)
Previous ed.: 1966. — Ill on lining papers. — Includes index
ISBN 0-571-18057-4 : £6.95 : CIP rev. B82-04621

914.26'1404858 — Norfolk. Breckland *(District) — Visitors' guides*
Breckland District Council : official guide. — Gloucester : British Publishing, [1981?]. — 100p : ill(some col.),maps(1col.) ; 21cm
ISBN 0-7140-1988-7 (pbk) : Unpriced B82-08613

914.26'17 — Norfolk. Blickling. Country houses: Blickling Hall — *Visitors' guides*
National Trust. Blickling Hall : Norfolk. — [London] : National Trust, c1980, c1978 (1982 [printing]). — 62p : ill,plans,1port ; 25cm
Originally published: 1978
Unpriced (pbk) B82-25780

914.26'40474 — Suffolk. Description & travel, *1823-1844 — Correspondence, diaries, etc.*
Davey, David English. A journal of excursions through the county of Suffolk 1823-1844. — Woodbridge : Boydell Press for the Suffolk Records Society, Apr.1982. — [208]p. — (Suffolk Records Society ; v.24)
ISBN 0-85115-162-0 : £12.00 : CIP entry B82-04992

914.26'404858 — Suffolk — *Visitors' guides*
Scarfe, Norman. Suffolk / by Norman Scarfe. — 3rd ed. — London : Faber, 1976 (1982 [printing]). — 192p : ill,1col.map ; 23cm. — (A Shell guide)
Previous ed.: 1966. — Includes index
ISBN 0-571-11821-6 (pbk) : £2.95 : CIP rev. B81-22622

914.26'41 — Suffolk. Southwold region — *Walkers' guides*
Alcott, Michael. Walks in & around Southwold / by Michael Alcott. — St. Ives, Cambs. : Cromwell, 1980. — 36p : ill,maps ; 15cm
Maps on inside covers
£0.50 (pbk) B82-26183

914.26'44 — Suffolk. Horringer. Country houses: Ickworth — *Visitors' guides*
Ickworth, Suffolk. — [London] : National Trust, c1979 (1981 [printing]). — 34p,[24]p of plates : ill,1plan,ports,1geneal.table ; 25cm
Bibliography: p34
Unpriced (pbk) B82-05651

914.26'46 — Suffolk. Aldeburgh region — *Walkers' guides*
Alcott, Michael. Walks in and around Aldeburgh / by Michael Alcott. — St. Ives, Cambs. : Cromwell, 1981. — 40p : ill,maps ; 15cm
Maps on inside covers
ISBN 0-907397-04-2 (pbk) : £0.50 B82-26180

914.26'46 — Suffolk. Woodbridge region — *Walkers' guides*
Alcott, Michael. Walks in and around Woodbridge / by Michael Alcott. — St. Ives, Cambs. : Cromwell, c1981. — 40p : ill,maps ; 15cm
Maps on inside covers
ISBN 0-907397-03-4 (pbk) : £0.50 B82-29681

914.26'48 — Suffolk. Sudbury. Museums: Gainsborough's House — *Visitors' guides*
Coke, David. Gainsborough's House : Sudbury, Suffolk : an illustrated history of the house and its contents / [text by David Coke]. — [Sudbury, Suffolk] : [Gainsborough's House], [1982?]. — [23]p : ill(some col.),1facsims,col.ports ; 26cm
Unpriced (pbk) B82-28332

914.26'49 — Suffolk. Ipswich. Buildings of historical importance — *Walkers' guides*
Underwood, Peter, *19---*. Town trail / [written by Peter Underwood and Bob Allen] ; [artwork by Bill Haward]. — Ipswich : Ipswich Society, c1980. — [24]p : ill,col.maps ; 30x11cm
Cover title. — Ill on inside back cover
ISBN 0-9507328-0-x (pbk) : Unpriced B82-23251

914.26'4904858 — Suffolk. Ipswich. Parish churches — *Visitors' guides*
Tricker, Roy. Ipswich churches ancient & modern / by Roy Tricker. — Ipswich : Brechinset, c1982. — 90p : ill,maps ; 21cm
Text on inside covers
ISBN 0-9507064-1-8 (pbk) : £2.25 B82-40164

914.26'5104858 — Cambridgeshire. Peterborough *(District) — Visitors' guides*
Peterborough city guide 1982/83. — London : Burrow, [1981?]. — 96p : ill(some col.),maps (some col.),1coat of arms,1port ; 25cm
Unpriced (pbk) B82-14572

914.26'54 — Cambridgeshire. St. Ives region — *Walkers' guides*

Alcott, Michael. Walks in around near St. Ives / by Michael Alcott. — St. Ives, Cambs. : M. Alcott, 1980. — 44p : ill,maps ; 15cm
Maps on inside covers
£0.50 (pbk) B82-26184

Alcott, Michael. [Walks in around near St. Ives]. Walks in and around St. Ives / by Michael Alcott. — St. Ives, Cambs. : Cromwell, c1980 (1981 [printing]). — 44p : ill,maps ; 15cm
ISBN 0-907397-00-x (pbk) : £0.50 B82-29682

914.26'54 — Cambridgeshire. St. Neots region — *Walkers' guides*

Alcott, Michael. Walks in and around St. Neots / by Michael Alcott. — St. Ives, Cambs. : Cromwell, c1981. — 40p : ill,maps ; 15cm
Maps on inside covers
ISBN 0-907397-05-0 (pbk) : £0.50 B82-29683

914.26'54 — Cambridgeshire. St Neots — *Visitors' guides*

St. Neots : official guide. — Wallington : Forward Publicity, [1982]. — 40p : ill,2maps ; 21cm
Unpriced (pbk) B82-40203

914.26'5404858 — Cambridgeshire. Huntingdon *(District)* **—** *Visitors' guides*

Huntingdon District official guide / issued by authority of the Huntingdon District Council. — 2nd ed. — [Wallington] ([Falcon House, 20-22 Belmont Rd., Wallington, Surrey SM6 8TA]) : Home Publishing, [1982?]. — 67p : ill (some col.) ; 21cm
Previous ed.: 1979. — Map attached to p67
Unpriced (pbk) B82-21041

914.26'57 — Cambridgeshire. Wimpole. Country houses: Wimpole Hall. Visits by Victoria, *Queen of Great Britain, 1843*

Wimpole amuses Victoria : from contemporary sources including Her Majesty's own diary October 1843. — Orwell (41 High St., Orwell, Cambs.) : Ellison's Editions, [1981?]. — 16p,[4]p of plates : ill,facsims,ports ; 21cm
Edited by David Ellison. — Ill on inside covers. — Limited ed. of 500 numbered copies
£1.25 (pbk) B82-08798

914.26'59 — Cambridgeshire. Cambridge. Chesterton. Parish churches: Parish Church of St. Andrews *(Chesterton)* **—** *Visitors' guides*

Parish Church of St. Andrew *(Chesterton)*. A history and guide to the Parish Church of St. Andrew, Chesterton, Cambridge / [text and layout by Barry Eaden]. — [Chesterton] ([64, Green End Rd., Chesterton, Cambridge, CB4 1RY]) : [The Parish Church], c1981. — 16p : ill ; 26cm
Text on inside covers
£0.30 (pbk) B82-14288

914.26'59 — Cambridgeshire. Cambridge region — *Walkers' guides*

Alcott, Michael. Walks in and around Cambridge / by Michael Alcott. — St. Ives, Cambs. : Cromwell, 1980. — 48p : ill,maps ; 15cm
Maps on inside covers
ISBN 0-907397-02-6 (pbk) : £0.50 B82-26181

914.26'59 — Cambridgeshire. Cambridge. Universities: University of Cambridge. Colleges — *Visitors' guides — German texts*

Mellanby, Ruth. Kleiner Führer durch Cambridge / Ruth Mellanby. — Rev. ed. / by John Mellanby and Ingrid Woitschik. — Cambridge : Cambridge Guide Service, 1980. — 32p : 1ill,1map,coats of arms ; 18cm
Translation of : Cambridge in brief. — Also available in French, Spanish and Italian versions. — Previous ed.: Cambridge : Heffer, 1967
ISBN 0-907736-00-9 (unbound) : £0.40 B82-07892

914.26'59 — Cambridgeshire. Cambridge. Universities: University of Cambridge. Colleges — *Visitors' guides — Italian texts*

Mellanby, Ruth. Cambridge in un giorno / Ruth Mellanby. — Cambridge : Cambridge Guide Service, 1980. — 32p : 1ill,1map,coats of arms ; 18cm
Translation of: Cambridge in brief. — Also available in French, Spanish and German versions. — Revised by John Mellanby et al.
ISBN 0-907736-01-7 (unbound) : £0.40 B82-07891

914.26'59 — Cambridgeshire. Cambridge. Universities: University of Cambridge. Colleges — *Visitors' guides — Spanish texts*

Mellanby, Ruth. Cambridge en un día / Ruth Mellanby. — Rev. / John Mellanby, Fioretta Blyde, Helen Grant. — Cambridge : Cambridge Guide Service, c1981. — 32p : 1ill,1map,coats of arms ; 18cm
Translation of: Cambridge in brief. — Also available in French, German and Italian versions. — Previous ed.: Cambridge : Heffer, 1973
ISBN 0-907736-02-5 (unbound) : £0.40 B82-07893

914.26'59 — Cambridgeshire. Cambridge. Universities: University of Cambridge — *Visitors' guides*

Hall, Michael, *1957-*. Cambridge / text by Michael Hall ; with photographs by Ernest Frankl. — 2nd ed. — Cambridge : Pevensey, 1981. — 89p : col.ill,maps ; 26cm
Previous ed.: 1980. — Maps on lining papers
ISBN 0-907115-01-2 (cased) : £4.95
ISBN 0-907115-02-0 (pbk) : Unpriced B82-34991

914.26'704857 — Essex. Description & travel, *1970-1979*

Day, James Wentworth. The James Wentworth Day book of Essex / photographs by Dennis Mansell. — Letchworth : Egon, 1979. — 132p : ill ; 25cm
Includes index
ISBN 0-905858-09-3 : £5.95 B82-06975

914.26'704858 — Essex — *Visitors' guides*

Scarfe, Norman. Essex / by Norman Scarfe. — Repr. with corrections. — London : Faber, 1975 (1982 [printing]). — 211p : ill,1 col.map ; 23cm. — (A Shell guide)
Previous ed.: 1968. — Includes index
ISBN 0-571-11819-4 (pbk) : £2.95 : CIP rev. B81-22620

914.26'704858 — Essex — *Visitors' guides — For business firms*

Enterprise in Essex. — [Chelmsford] : The Planning Department of Essex County Council, [1982]. — [60]p : ill(some col.),3maps(some col.) ; 21x30cm
Cover title
Unpriced (spiral) B82-29513

914.26'723 — Essex. Colchester. Castles: Colchester Castle — *Visitors' guides*

Clarke, David T.-D.. Colchester Castle : a history, description and guide / [written by David T.-D. Clarke] ; [modern photographs by Charles Seely and Dennis Mansell] ; [plans and drawing by D.G. Davies and R.E. Boustred] ; [plan by Tony Young]. — [Colchester] ([Town Hall, Colchester CO1 1PJ]) : Colchester Borough Council, Cultural Activities Committee, 1980. — 32p : ill(some col.),plans ; 21cm
Previous ed.: 1966?. — Ill on inside covers. — Bibliography: p32
Unpriced (pbk) B82-17396

914.26'725 — Essex. Elmstead Market. Gardens: Beth Chatto Gardens — *Visitors' guides*

The **Beth** Chatto gardens. — Derby : English Life Publications, 1982. — 12p : ill(some col.),1plan ; 20cm
Cover title. — Ill and text on inside cover
ISBN 0-85101-193-4 (pbk) : £0.35 B82-31014

914.26'74 — Essex. Epping — *Visitors' guides*

Epping. *Town Council*. Epping Town : official guide / issued by authority of the Epping Town Council. — Wallington (Falcon House, 20-22 Belmont Rd., Wallington, Surrey SM6 8TA) : Forward Publicity, [1982?]. — 42p : ill,1map ; 21cm
Unpriced (pbk) B82-28544

914.26'7404858 — Essex. Epping Forest — *Walkers' guides*

Brimble, James. Brimble's guide to Epping Forest : for ramblers and riders. — [London] ([62, Wilson St., EC2A 2BU]) : Field Studies Council, 1982. — 15p : maps ; 21cm
Cover title. — 'Based on the original work of James Brimble and completely revised by Mandy Johnson for the Field Studies Council'
Unpriced (pbk) B82-28843

914.26'77504858 — Essex. Rochford *(District)* **—** *Visitors' guides*

Rochford : official guide / issued by authority of the Rochford District Council. — Wallington : Home Publishing, [1982]. — 52p : ill(some col.),1map,1col.coat of arms ; 21cm
Unpriced (pbk) B82-17152

914.26'79204858 — Essex. Castle Point *(District)* **—** *Visitors guides*

The **Official** guide to Castle Point : illustrated. — Gloucester : British Publishing, [1982]. — 64p : ill,2maps ; 20cm
Streetplans on folded sheet attached to inside cover. — Includes index
ISBN 0-7140-1880-5 (pbk) : Unpriced B82-28955

914.27'04858 — North-west England — *Visitors' guides — For motoring*

Ward, Ken, *1926-*. Northwest England : Cumbria, Cheshire, Greater Manchester, Lancashire, Merseyside / Ken Ward. — London : Travellers Realm, 1981. — 128p : ill,maps. — (RAC going places ; 5)
Includes index
ISBN 0-86211-006-8 (pbk) : £2.95 B82-03958

914.27'04858 — Northern England. Caves — *Visitors' guides*

Northern caves. — Clapham, North Yorkshire : Dalesman
Vol.2: Penyghent and Malham / by A & D Brook, G.M. Dvies, M.H. Long. — 2nd ed. — 1982. — 128p : maps,plans ; 19cm
Previous ed.: 1976. — Includes index
ISBN 0-85206-659-7 (pbk) : £2.95 B82-14848

Northern caves. — Clapham, North Yorkshire : Dalesman
Vol.3: Ingleborough / by A & D Brook, G.M. Davies, M.H. Long. — 2nd ed. — 1981. — 144p : maps,plans ; 19cm
Previous ed.: 1975. — Includes index
ISBN 0-85206-654-6 (pbk) : £3.25 B82-14849

914.27'04858 — Northern England — *Visitors' guides*

Hamlyn leisure atlas : north country / [compiled and edited by Colin Wilson]. — London : Hamlyn, 1982. — 128p : ill(some col.),maps (some col.),1plan,1col.port ; 31cm
Maps on lining papers. — Includes index
ISBN 0-600-34997-7 : £5.95 B82-27143

914.27'04858 — Northern England — *Walkers' guides*

Emett, Charlie. Walking through northern England / Charlie Emett & Mike Hutton ; illustrations by Jean Marshall. — Newton Abbot : David & Charles, c1982. — 207p : ill,maps ; 23cm
Bibliography: p202. — Includes index
ISBN 0-7153-8285-3 : £6.95 : CIP rev. B82-07584

914.27'1'0014 — Cheshire. Place names

Dodgson, J. McN.. The place-names of Cheshire / by McN. Dodgson. — Nottingham : English Place-Name Society
Pt.5
1. — 1981. — 2v.(li,426p) ; 23cm. — (English Place-Name Society ; v.48, 54)
Includes index
ISBN 0-304-88907-6 : Unpriced
ISBN 0-904889-08-4 (v.2) B82-14685

914.27'1804858 — Cheshire. Halton *(District)* **—** *Visitors' guides*

The **Borough** of Halton official guide / [Halton Borough Council]. — Gloucester : British Publishing Co. by authority of the Council, 1981. — 104p : ill(some col.),maps(some col.) ; 21cm
Bibliography: p73
ISBN 0-7140-1935-6 (pbk) : Unpriced B82-20306

914.27′32 — Greater Manchester *(Metropolitan County).* **Salford** — *Directories — Facsimiles*
Raffald, Elizabeth. Elizabeth Raffald′s directory of Manchester and Salford 1772 : an illustrated reprint of the first Manchester and Salford directory. — Swinton (375 Chorley Rd, Swinton M27 2AY) : Neil Richardson, [1981]. — [20]p : facsims ; 30cm
Facsim of: 1889 ed
£1.00 (pbk)
Primary classification 914.27′33′0025
B82-02871

914.27′33 — Greater Manchester *(Metropolitan County).* **Manchester region** — *Visitors′ guides — For children*
Thomas, Anne, *1930-*. Children′s Manchester : a guide to things to see and do in and around Manchester / Anne Thomas ; with illustrations and special material by Philip Atkins. — Bristol : Redcliffe, 1977. — 96p : ill ; 19cm
Includes index
ISBN 0-905459-04-0 (pbk) : £0.95 B82-21821

914.27′33′0025 — Greater Manchester *(Metropolitan County).* **Manchester** — *Directories — Facsimiles*
Raffald, Elizabeth. Elizabeth Raffald′s directory of Manchester and Salford 1772 : an illustrated reprint of the first Manchester and Salford directory. — Swinton (375 Chorley Rd, Swinton M27 2AY) : Neil Richardson, [1981]. — [20]p : facsims ; 30cm
Facsim of: 1889 ed
£1.00 (pbk)
Also classified at 914.27′32 B82-02871

914.27′3504858 — Greater Manchester *(Metropolitan County).* **Canals: Huddersfield Narrow Canal** — *Walkers′ guides*
The **Huddersfield** canals : towpath guide / [editor Diane Charlesworth] ; [contributors Ivy Lodge ... [et al.]. — Huddersfield (c/o General Secretary, 28 Cinderhills Rd., Holmfirth, Huddersfield HD7 1EH) : Huddersfield Canal Society, c1981. — 80p : ill(some col.),maps ; 21cm
Cover title. — Ill on inside covers
Unpriced (pbk)
Primary classification 914.28′1304858
B82-07570

914.27′36 — Greater Manchester *(Metropolitan County).* **Leigh** — *Walkers′ guides*
Bond, Richard. Walks around Leigh / by Richard Bond. — Leigh : [Leigh Local History Society], 1981. — 24p : 2ill,1map ; 21cm. — (Publication / Leigh Local History Society ; no.9)
£0.75 (pbk) B82-14481

914.27′37 — Greater Manchester *(Metropolitan County).* **Horwich** — *Visitors′ guides*
Horwich : illustrated official guide. — Gloucester : British Publishing, [1981]. — 40p : ill,1map,1coat of arms ; 21cm
Plan on folded sheet attached to inside cover
ISBN 0-7140-1990-9 (pbk) : Unpriced
B82-03948

914.27′37′00142 — Great Manchester *(Metropolitan County).* **Bolton** *(District).* **Place names. Etymology**
Billington, William Derek. From Affetside to Yarrow. — Egerton : Ross Anderson Publications, Dec.1982. — [70]p
ISBN 0-86360-003-4 (pbk) : £2.95 : CIP entry
B82-36331

914.27′3804858 — Greater Manchester *(Metropolitan County).* **Bury** *(District)* — *Practical information*
Information handbook / issued by authority of the Bury Metropolitan Borough Council. — Wallington : Home Publishing, [1982?]. — 72p : ill ; 21cm
Unpriced (pbk) B82-32770

914.27′392 — Greater Manchester *(Metropolitan County).* **Littleborough region** — *Walkers′ guides*
Through the Summit Gap / Littleborough Local Historical Society. — 2nd ed. — Rochdale (Denehurst, Edenfield Rd., Rochdale) : Rochdale Recreation and Amenities Department, c1980. — [15]p,[2]leaves of plates : ill,1facsim ; 21cm. — (History trail ; no.1)
Cover title. — Previous ed.: 197-
£0.20 (pbk) B82-12055

914.27′392 — Greater Manchester *(Metropolitan County).* **Rochdale** — *Walkers′ guides*
Further trails around Rochdale 1982 : parks and conservation areas. — [Rochdale] ([10 Ashley Close, Rochdale OL11 3EP]) : Rochdale Civic Society, [1982]. — [9]p : ill,1map ; 30cm
Unpriced (unbound) B82-41141

914.27′5104858 — Merseyside *(Metropolitan County).* **Wirral** *(District)* — *Visitors′ guides*
Wirral : a great place to live and work. — Wallington : Home Publishing, [1982?]. — 100p : ill(some col.),1col.coat of arms,maps ; 24cm
Unpriced (pbk) B82-36027

914.27′5304858′05 — Merseyside *(Metropolitan County).* **Liverpool** — *Practical information — Serials*
Survive in the city : a guide to alternative Liverpool. — [No.1]-. — Liverpool (Lark Lane Community Centre, 80 Lark La., Liverpool L17) : Creative Mind (Arts Association), [1982]-. — v. ; 21cm
ISSN 0263-5836 = Survive in the city : Unpriced B82-38497

914.27′604858 — Lancashire. Waterside regions — *Walkers′ guides*
Bearshaw, Brian. Waterside walks in Lancashire / by Brian Bearshaw ; illustrations by David Chesworth. — London : Hale, 1982. — 160p : ill,maps ; 21cm
Bibliography: p9. — Includes index
ISBN 0-7091-9449-8 : £6.95 B82-19782

914.27′61504858 — Lancashire. Chorley *(District)* — *Visitors′ guides*
Borough of Chorley : official guide & industrial handbook / [issued by the authority of Chorley Borough Council]. — Wallington : Home Publishing, [1982?]. — 72p : ill,1map ; 21cm
Cover title
Unpriced (pbk) B82-36025

914.27′682 — Lancashire. Wyre River region. Description & travel — *Illustrations*
Wainwright, A.. A Wyre sketchbook : A. Wainwright. — Kendal : Westmorland Gazette, 1982. — xi,[154]p : ill,maps ; 19x24cm
£3.80 B82-33642

914.27′69 — Lancashire. Carnforth. Country houses: Leighton Hall — *Visitors′ guides*
Leighton Hall. — Derby : English Life, c1982. — [18]p : ill(some col.) ; 20cm
Ill on inside covers
ISBN 0-85101-185-3 (pbk) : £0.50 B82-27120

914.27′804858 — Cumbria. Lake District. Description & travel
Presences of nature : words and images of the Lake District. — Carlisle : Carlisle Museum & Art Gallery ; London (62 West Hill, SW18 1RU) : Travelling Light [distributor], July 1982. — [224]p
ISBN 0-907852-00-9 (pbk) : £7.95 : CIP entry
ISBN 0-9502457-9-8 (limited ed.) : Unpriced
B82-13175

914.27′804858 — Cumbria. Lake District. Description & travel — *Personal observations*
Lofthouse, Jessica. The curious traveller : Lancaster to Lakeland, being present-day journeys on ancient and historic routes around Morecambe Bay, through Cartmel and Low and High Furness, to the Lakes / Jessica Lofthouse ; illustrations by the author. — 2nd ed. — London : Hale, 1981. — 224p : ill,1map ; 23cm
Previous ed.: 1956. — Includes index
ISBN 0-7091-9529-x : £7.25 B82-09126

914.27′804858 — Cumbria. Lake District — *Visitors′ guides*
Heart of Lakeland. — Clapham : Dalesman, 1982. — 32p : ill,maps ; 21cm. — (A Dalesman white rose guide)
ISBN 0-85206-671-6 (pbk) : £0.75 B82-31378

Wyatt, John, *1925-*. Discover the Lake District : the tourist and holiday guide to the area / written by John Wyatt. — Barnard Castle (35 Galgate, Barnard Castle, Co. Durham, DL12 8EJ) : Discovery Guides, c1981. — 63p : ill,col.maps ; 29cm. — (The Discovery Guides series)
Cover title. — Maps on inside covers. — Includes index
Unpriced (pbk) B82-00465

Young, Geoffrey. Enjoy a day in the Lake District / [written by Geoffrey Young]. — Norwich : Jarrold, c1981. — 32p : col.ill,1col.map ; 20cm. — (Watch ; bk.10)
Cover title. — Text on inside covers. — Includes index
ISBN 0-85306-976-x (pbk) : Unpriced
B82-01368

914.27′804858′0222 — Cumbria. Lake District. Description & travel — *Illustrations*
Poucher, W. A.. The Lake District / W.A. Poucher. — London : Constable, 1982. — 207p : chiefly col.ill ; 27cm
ISBN 0-09-464480-2 : £10.95 B82-23728

914.27′804858′0222 — Cumbria. Lake District. Mountains. Description & travel — *Illustrations*
Wainwright, A.. Lakeland mountain drawings / A. Wainwright. — Kendal : Westmorland Gazette
Vol.2. — 1981. — [110]p : all ill ; 23x28cm
£6.00 B82-08136

914.27′83 — Cumbria. Grasmere — *Visitors′ guides*
Guide to Grasmere : walks — hotels — shops, places of interest, street plan. — [Grasmere] ([c/o Hon. Sec., Sunny Bank, Grasmere, Ambleside LA22 9QX]) : [Grasmere Publicity Association], [1982?]. — 64p : ill(some col.),1map ; 21cm
Unpriced (unbound) B82-18391

914.27′8304858′0222 — Cumbria. South Lakeland *(District).* **Rivers. Description & travel** — *Illustrations*
Wainright, A.. Three Westmorland rivers : the Kent, the Sprint and the Mint / A. Wainwright. — Kendal : Westmorland Gazette, 1979. — [174]p : chiefly ill,maps ; 20x26cm
£4.00 B82-10532

914.27′8604857 — Cumbria. Eden Valley, *1970-1979* — *Visitors′ guides*
Wood, Gordon. Exploring the Eden Valley / by Gordon Wood. — Clapham, N. Yorkshire : Dalesman, 1979. — 63p : ill,maps ; 19cm. — (A Dalesman mini-book)
ISBN 0-85206-514-0 (pbk) : £1.00 B82-03626

914.27′87 — Cumbria. Derwentwater region. Places associated with Potter, Beatrix — *Walkers′ guides*
Bartlett, Wynne. Lakeland walks from Beatrix Potter / by Wynne Bartlett. — London : Warne, 1982. — 23p : ill ; 19cm
ISBN 0-7232-2899-x (pbk) : £0.75 B82-22955

914.27′89 — Cumbria. Carlisle — *Visitors′ guides*
Lakescene guide to Carlisle : Lakeland′s cathedral city and famous border fortress. — [S.l.] : [s.n.], [1982] (Carlisle : Charles Thuman & Sons). — 48p : ill,maps ; 21cm
Unpriced (pbk) B82-40184

914.28′04857 — England. Pennines. Long-distance footpaths: Pennine Way, *1970-1979* — *Walkers′ guides*
Oldham, Kenneth. The Pennine Way : Britain′s longest continuous footpath / by Kenneth Oldham. — 8th ed. — Clapham, N. Yorkshire : Dalesman, 1979. — 80p : ill,maps ; 21cm
Previous ed.: 1977. — Bibliography: p80
ISBN 0-85206-508-6 (pbk) : £1.75 B82-03631

914.28′04858 — North-east England. Description & travel — *Personal observations*
Wright, Geoffrey N.. View of Northumbria / described and photographed by Geoffrey N. Wright. — London : Hale, 1981. — 224p : ill,1map ; 23cm
Includes index
ISBN 0-7091-9321-1 : £8.95 B82-09125

914.28′1′0014 — Yorkshire. Place names
Morris, R. W.. Yorkshire through place names / R.W. Morris. — Newton Abbot : David & Charles, c1982. — 224p : ill,maps ; 23cm
Bibliography: p217-218. — Includes index
ISBN 0-7153-8230-6 : £10.95 : CIP rev. B81-35824

914.28′104858 — Yorkshire. Buildings of historical importance, *ca 1200-1500* — *Visitors′ guides*
Ryder, Peter F.. Medieval buildings of Yorkshire. — Ashbourne : Moorland, Apr.1982. — [160]p
ISBN 0-86190-035-9 : £8.95 : CIP entry B82-09171

914.28′104858 — Yorkshire — *Visitors′ guides*
Complete Yorkshire / the coast resorts, the dales, main centres and places of interest ; edited by Reginald J.W. Hammond. — London : Ward Lock, 1973 (1982 [printing]). — 356p : ill,maps ; 19cm. — (Red guide)
Includes index
ISBN 0-7063-6147-4 (pbk) : £4.95 B82-25882

914.28′1304858 — West Yorkshire *(Metropolitan County).* **Kirklees** *(District).* **Canals: Huddersfield Broad Canal & Huddersfield Narrow Canal** — *Walkers′ guides*
The **Huddersfield** canals : towpath guide / [editor Diane Charlesworth] ; [contributors Ivy Lodge ... [et al.]. — Huddersfield (c/o General Secretary, 28 Cinderhills Rd., Holmfirth, Huddersfield HD7 1EH) : Huddersfield Canal Society, c1981. — 80p : ill(some col.),maps ; 21cm
Cover title. — Ill on inside covers
Unpriced (pbk)
Also classified at 914.27′3504858 B82-07570

914.28′17 — West Yorkshire *(Metropolitan County).* **Bradford region** — *Walkers′ guides*
Sheldon, Paul. Bradford ringwalks / by Paul Sheldon ; maps by Arthur Gemmell. — Otley : Stile with financial assistance from the Countryside Commission, 1982. — 28p : col.maps ; 20cm. — (Stile maps)
Cover title
ISBN 0-906886-12-0 (pbk) : £1.00 B82-28956

914.28′17 — West Yorkshire *(Metropolitan County).* **Keighley. Houses: East Riddlesden Hall** — *Visitors′ guides*
National Trust. East Riddlesden Hall : Keighley, Yorkshire. — [London] : National Trust, c1979 (1982 [printing]). — 17p,[4]p of plates : ill ; 22cm
Bibliography: p17
Unpriced (pbk) B82-25774

914.28′2304858 — South Yorkshire *(Metropolitan County).* **Rotherham** *(District)* — *Visitors′ guides*
Rotherham : official guide / issued by the authority of Rotherham Borough Council. — Wallington : Home Publishing, [1982]. — 88p : ill(some col.),2maps,1coat of arms ; 24cm
Unpriced (pbk) B82-17151

914.28′3 — North Humberside. Long-distance footpaths: Wolds Way — *Walkers′ guides*
Rubinstein, David. The Wolds Way / by David Rubinstein. — Clapham, N. Yorkshire : Dalesman, 1979. — 79p : ill,maps ; 21cm
Bibliography: p78-79
ISBN 0-85206-504-3 (pbk) : £1.75
Primary classification 914.28′404857 B82-03630

914.28′3204858 — Humberside. Glanford *(District)* — *Visitors′ guides*
Glanford Borough : official guide / issued by authority of the Glanford Borough Council. — 3rd ed. — [Wallington] ([Falcon House, 20-22 Belmont Road, Wallington, Surrey]) : Home Publishing, [1982?]. — 56p : ill(some col.),maps,ports ; 21cm
Previous ed.: 1980. — Map attached to inside back cover
Unpriced (pbk) B82-21039

914.28′3704858 — Humberside. Hull — *Visitors′ guides*
Kingston upon Hull : official guide 1981-82. — Kingston upon Hull : Kingston upon Hull City Council, [1981]. — 92p : ill(some col.),1col.map ; 30cm
Unpriced (pbk) B82-01657

914.28′3904858 — Humberside. East Yorkshire *(District).* **Coastal regions** — *Visitors′ guides*
Yorkshire coast : Straithes to Bridlington. — Clapham (N. Yorks) : Dalesman, 1982. — 32p : ill,1map ; 21cm. — (A Dalesman white rose guide)
ISBN 0-85206-672-4 (pbk) : £0.75
Primary classification 914.28′4704858 B82-31958

914.28′3904858 — Humberside. East Yorkshire *(District)* — *Visitors′ guides*
The **Borough** of East Yorkshire : official handbook. — London : Burrow, [1981?]. — 52p,[2]p of plates : ill(some col.),maps,1coat of arms ; 21cm
Unpriced (pbk) B82-14571

914.28′404857 — North Yorkshire. Long-distance footpaths: Wolds Way, *1970-1979* — *Walkers′ guides*
Rubinstein, David. The Wolds Way / by David Rubinstein. — Clapham, N. Yorkshire : Dalesman, 1979. — 79p : ill,maps ; 21cm
Bibliography: p78-79
ISBN 0-85206-504-3 (pbk) : £1.75
Also classified at 914.28′3 B82-03630

914.28′404858 — North Yorkshire. Dales — *Visitors′ guides*
Parker, Malcolm. Discover the Yorkshire Dales : the tourist and holiday guide to the area / designed and written by Malcolm Parker. — Barnard Castle (35 Galgate, Barnard Castle, Co. Durham, DL12 8EJ) : Discovery Guides, c1980. — 63p : ill,col.maps ; 29cm. — (The Discovery Guides series)
Cover title. — Maps on inside covers. — Includes index
Unpriced (pbk) B82-00467

Spencer, Brian, *1931-*. A visitor′s guide to the Yorkshire Dales : Teesdale & Weardale / Brian Spencer. — Ashbourne : Moorland, [1982?]. — 153p : ill,maps ; 21cm
Bibliography: p146. — Includes index
ISBN 0-86190-040-5 (cased) : £3.95 : CIP rev.
ISBN 0-86190-039-1 (pbk) : £3.95 B82-12925

914.28′404858 — North Yorkshire. Dales. Walkers′ guides
Speakman, Colin. Walking in the Yorkshire Dales / by Colin Speakman. — London : Hale, 1982. — 207p,[16]p of plates : ill,maps ; 23cm
Includes bibliographies and index
ISBN 0-7091-9617-2 : £7.95 B82-31154

914.28′41 — North Yorkshire. Three Peaks region — *Visitors′ guides*
Yorkshire′s Three Peaks. — Clapham : Dalesman, 1982. — 32p : ill,2maps ; 21cm. — (A Dalesman white rose guide)
ISBN 0-85206-673-2 (pbk) : £0.75 B82-31380

914.28′4104858 — North Yorkshire. Craven *(District)* — *Visitors′ guides*
Craven Dales. — Clapham : Dalesman, 1982. — 32p : ill,maps ; 21cm. — (A Dalesman white rose guide)
ISBN 0-85206-674-0 (pbk) : £0.75 B82-31379

Craven district : official guide / issued by authority of the Craven District Council. — Wallington : Home Publishing, [1982?]. — 60p : ill(some col.),1coat of arms,2maps ; 21cm
Unpriced (pbk) B82-24081

914.28′42 — North Yorkshire. Harrogate — *Visitors′ guides*
Kellett, Arnold. Harrogate and district : a guide for visitors and residents / by Arnold Kellett ; illustrated by Peter Kearney. — 2nd ed. — Clapham, [North Yorkshire] : Dalesman, 1982. — 32p : ill,2maps ; 19cm. — (Dalesman leisure)
Previous ed.: 1978. — Maps on inside covers. — Bibliography: p17
ISBN 0-85206-662-7 (pbk) : £0.60 B82-14845

914.28′43 — North Yorkshire. York. Cathedrals: York Minster — *Visitors′ guides*
Beckett, Lucy. York Minster / Lucy Beckett & Angelo Hornak. — Firenze : Scala Istituto Fotografico ; London : Philip Wilson, 1981. — 96p : ill(some col.),1plan ; 28cm
ISBN 0-85667-090-1 (cased) : Unpriced
ISBN 0-85667-089-8 (pbk) : £3.95 B82-08285

914.28′4304858 — North Yorkshire. York — *Visitors′ guides — For children*
Waites, Bryan. Children′s York : a guide for all the family / Bryan Waites. — Bristol : Redcliffe, 1981. — 112p : ill,1map ; 19cm
ISBN 0-905459-35-0 (pbk) : £1.95 B82-21822

914.28′45 — North Yorkshire. Tadcaster — *Walkers′ guides*
Nuttall, Barry. A walk by the Wharfe / Barry Nuttall ; with illustrations by Pauline Hawthorne. — Tadcaster : Tadcaster Civic Society, c1980. — 30p : ill,1map ; 21cm. — (Tadcaster walk ; no.2)
ISBN 0-9507275-0-4 (pbk) : £0.65 B82-16887

914.28′46 — North Yorkshire. Ryedale *(District).* **Landscape gardens: Duncombe Terrace & Rievaulx Terrace** — *Visitors′ guides*
National Trust. The Rievaulx Terrace : North Yorkshire. — [London] ([42 Queen′s Gate SW1H 9AS]) : The National Trust, c1978 (1982 [printing]). — 17p,[8]p of plates : ill ; 22cm
Bibliography: p17
Unpriced (pbk) B82-27997

914.28′4604858 — North Yorkshire. North York Moors — *Visitors′ guides*
The **Dalesman** guide to the North York Moors. — Clapham : Dalesman, 1982. — 96p : ill (some col.),maps ; 21cm
ISBN 0-85206-665-1 (pbk) : £1.25 B82-31385

Staniforth, Pat. Discover the North York Moors : and Yorkshire heritage coast : the tourist and holiday guide to the area / written by Pat and Alan Staniforth. — Barnard Castle (35 Galgate, Barnard Castle, Co. Durham, DL12 8EJ) : Discovery Guides, c1980. — 62p : ill,col.maps ; 29cm. — (The Discovery Guides series)
Cover title. — Maps on inside covers. — Includes index
Unpriced (pbk) B82-00468

914.28′4604858 — North Yorkshire. Ryedale *(District)* — *Visitors′ guides*
The **Ryedale** District of North Yorkshire : official guide book / issued by the Ryedale District Council ; text and illustrations by Norman Appleton. — [4th ed.]. — [Malton] ([Ryedale House, Malton, N. Yorks. YO17 OHH]) : [The Council], c1982. — 48p : ill,2maps ; 24cm
Previous ed.: 1980?. — Map on inside cover
Unpriced (pbk) B82-38937

Top attractions in Ryedale : in the heart of the Yorkshire countryside. — Malton (Ryedale House, Malton, N. Yorks. [YO17 0HH]) : Ryedale District Council, [1982]. — 1folded sheet([12]p) : ill,col.maps ; 21cm
Unpriced (unbound) B82-38938

914.28′4704858 — North Yorkshire. Scarborough *(District).* **Coastal regions** — *Visitors′ guides*
Yorkshire coast : Straithes to Bridlington. — Clapham (N. Yorks) : Dalesman, 1982. — 32p : ill,1map ; 21cm. — (A Dalesman white rose guide)
ISBN 0-85206-672-4 (pbk) : £0.75
Also classified at 914.28′3904858 B82-31958

914.28′604858 — Durham *(County).* **Description & travel**
Parker, Malcolm. Durham / designed and written by Malcolm and Elizabeth Parker ; drawings by Brian Sutherland. — Barnard Castle (35 Galgate, Barnard Castle, Co. Durham, DL12 8EJ) : Discovery Guides, c1980. — 48p : ill ; 30x21cm. — (Stories, sketches and places to visit)
Cover title. — Text on inside covers
Unpriced (pbk) B82-00464

914.28′604858 — Durham *(County)* — *Visitors′ guides*
Parker, Malcolm. Discover Durham : historic city, beautiful county : the tourist and holiday guide to the area / designed and written by Malcolm Parker. — Barnard Castle (35 Galgate, Barnard Castle, Co. Durham, DL12 8EJ) : Discovery Guides, c1980. — 63p : ill,col.maps ; 29cm. — (The Discovery Guides series)
Cover title. — Maps on inside covers. — Includes index
Unpriced (pbk) B82-00469

914.28′6104858 — Durham *(County).* **Teesdale. Description & travel**

Parker, Malcolm. Teesdale / designed and written by Malcolm and Elizabeth Parker ; drawings by Brian Sutherland. — Barnard Castle (35 Galgate, Barnard Castle, Co. Durham, DL12 8EJ) : Discovery Guides, c1980. — 48p : ill ; 30x21cm. — (Stories, sketches and places to visit)
Cover title. — Text on inside covers
Unpriced (pbk) B82-00463

914.28′6104858 — Durham *(County).* **Teesdale** — *Visitors′ guides*

Parker, Malcolm. Discover Teesdale : and its surrounding areas of the beautiful High Penines : the tourist and holiday guide to the area / written by Malcolm Parker. — Barnard Castle (35 Galgate, Barnard Castle, Co. Durham, DL12 8EJ) : Discovery Guides, c1981. — 63p : ill,col.maps ; 29cm. — (The Discovery Guides series)
Cover title. — Maps on inside covers. — Includes index
Unpriced (pbk) B82-00466

914.28′64 — Durham *(County).* **Weardale** — *Visitors′ guides*

Wood, Chris Foote. Discover Weardale, Allendale, S. Tynedale : the tourist and holiday guide to the area / written by Chris Foote Wood. — [Barnard Castle] ([35 Galgate, Barnard Castle, Co. Durham]) : [Discovery Guides], c1981. — 59p : ill,col.maps ; 29cm. — (The Discovery Guides series)
Cover title. — Maps on inside covers. — Includes index
Unpriced (pbk)
Also classified at 914.28′81 B82-00462

914.28′65 — Durham *(County).* **Durham. Buildings of historical importance** — *Visitors′ guides*

Caring for historic buildings : listed buildings in the City of Durham : two architectural trails. — [Durham] ([City Planning Office, Byland Lodge, Hawthorn Terrace, Durham DH1 4TD]) : City of Durham, c1977. — 20p : ill,1map,1plan ; 30cm
Cover title
£0.20 (pbk) B82-35030

914.28′65 — Durham *(County).* **Durham** — *Visitors′ guides*

Durham *(Durham, England). Council.* Historic city of Durham tourist guide & central area street plan / prepared by Anthony R.N. Scott. — [Durham] ([City Planning Office, Byland Lodge, Hawthorn Terrace, Durham DH1 4TD]) : Council of the City of Durham, c1981. — 1sheet : ill,maps(some col.) ; 60x43cm folded to 30x22cm
Includes index
Unpriced (unbound) B82-35029

Johnson, Margot. Durham City : a pictorial history and guide / by Margot Johnson. — 3rd ed. rev. and re-arranged with additions. — Durham : Turnstone Ventures, 1982. — 32p : ill,1map ; 22cm
Previous ed.: Whinway : Northern Notes, 1974. — Text on inside covers
ISBN 0-946105-00-6 (pbk) : £0.95 B82-40456

914.28′6704858 — Durham *(County).* **Easington** *(District)* — *Visitors′ guides*

Easington. *District Council.* Easington District information handbook. — London (Publicity House, Streatham Hill, SW2 4TR) : Burrow in association with Easington District Council, [1982]. — 40p : ill ; 19cm
Unpriced (pbk) B82-37405

914.28′7604858 — Tyne and Wear *(Metropolitan County).* **Newcastle upon Tyne. Parish churches** — *Visitors′ guides*

The **Newcastle** Diocesan gazetteer : a guide to the Anglican church in Newcastle upon Tyne and Northumberland / edited by Stanley Prins, Roger Massingberd-Mundy. — Newcastle upon Tyne : by the Newcastle Diocesan Bishop′s Editorial Committee of the Link, 1982. — 142p : ill ; 21cm
Ill on inside covers. — Includes index
ISBN 0-902080-01-6 (pbk) : £0.90
Also classified at 914.28′804858 B82-28888

914.28′804858 — Northumberland. Parish churches — *Visitors′ guides*

The **Newcastle** Diocesan gazetteer : a guide to the Anglican church in Newcastle upon Tyne and Northumberland / edited by Stanley Prins, Roger Massingberd-Mundy. — Newcastle upon Tyne : by the Newcastle Diocesan Bishop′s Editorial Committee of the Link, 1982. — 142p : ill ; 21cm
Ill on inside covers. — Includes index
ISBN 0-902080-01-6 (pbk) : £0.90
Primary classification 914.28′7604858 B82-28888

914.28′81 — Northumberland. Allendale region — *Visitors′ guides*

Wood, Chris Foote. Discover Weardale, Allendale, S. Tynedale : the tourist and holiday guide to the area / written by Chris Foote Wood. — [Barnard Castle] ([35 Galgate, Barnard Castle, Co. Durham]) : [Discovery Guides], c1981. — 59p : ill,col.maps ; 29cm. — (The Discovery Guides series)
Cover title. — Maps on inside covers. — Includes index
Unpriced (pbk)
Primary classification 914.28′64 B82-00462

914.28′81 — Northumberland. Alnmouth-Hexham road region. Description & travel

Rowland, T. H.. The Alemouth or Corn Road : Alnwick-Alnmouth : Hexham, Wall, Chollerton, Rothbury / T.H. Rowland. — Morpeth (4, De Merley Rd., Morpeth, Northumberland NE61 1HZ) : T.H. Rowland, [1982?]. — 72p : ill,maps ; 22cm
Bibliography: p72
£1.20 (pbk) B82-35579

914.28′81 — Northumberland. Hexham — *Visitors′ guides*

Hexham : Northumberland : official town guide. — Wallington (20, Belmont Rd., Wallington, Surrey SM6 8TA) : Forward Publicity, [1981]. — 36p : ill,1map ; 21cm
Street map (39x39cm folded to 20x13cm) as insert
Unpriced (pbk) B82-01649

914.28′8104858 — Northern England. Ancient Roman fortifications: Hadrian′s Wall — *Visitors′ guides*

Webster, Peter, *1943-*. Hadrian′s Wall / Peter Webster. — Cardiff : University College Cardiff Department of Extra-Mural Studies, 1981. — 72p : ill,maps,plans ; 30cm
Cover title. — Bibliography: p69-70. — Includes index
ISBN 0-946045-16-x (pbk) : Unpriced B82-31776

914.28′89 — Northumberland. Holy Island. Castles: Lindisfarne Castle — *Visitors′ guides*

National Trust. Lindisfarne Castle / by Peter Orde. — [London] : National Trust, c1978 (1982 [printing]). — 15p,[4]p of plates : ill,2plans,ports ; 25cm
Unpriced (pbk) B82-25773

914.29 — WALES

914.29 — Wales. Geographical features — *For schools*

Davies, Margaret, *1914-*. Looking at Wales / Margaret Davies. — London : Black, c1981. — 64p : ill,maps(some col.),2facsims,1port ; 26cm. — (Looking at geography ; 6)
Previous ed.: 1977. — Includes index
ISBN 0-7136-2085-4 (cased) : £2.95 : CIP rev.
ISBN 0-7136-2074-9 (pbk) : £1.75 B80-21200

914.29 — Wales. Geographical features — *Welsh texts*

Daearyddiaeth / paratowyd ... gan Broject Defnyddiau ac Adnoddau Y Swyddfa Gymreig ; cyfarwyddwr Carl Dodson. — [Llandysul] : Gwasg Gomer
Diwydiant 1 / awdur ... Siân Jones. — c1981. — 34p : ill,col.maps,col.plans ; 30cm
ISBN 0-85088-786-0 (pbk) : £1.50 B82-30854

Daearyddiaeth / paratowyd ... gan Broject Defnyddiau ac Adnoddau Y Swyddfa Gymreig ; cyfarwyddwr Carl Dodson. — [Llandysul] : Gwasg Gomer
Ffermio 1 / awdur ... D.J.O. Williams â chymorth M. Eluned Rowlands. — c1981. — 22p : ill,col.maps,1col.plan,ports ; 30cm
ISBN 0-85088-796-8 (pbk) : £1.50 B82-30851

Daearyddiaeth / paratowyd ... gan Broject Defnyddiau ac Adnoddau Y Swyddfa Gymreig ; cyfarwyddwr Carl Dodson. — [Llandysul] : Gwasg Gomer
Hamddena 1 / awdur ... Siân Jones. — c1981. — 28p : ill,facsims,col.maps ; 30cm
ISBN 0-85088-776-3 (pbk) : £1.50 B82-30852

Daearyddiaeth / paratowyd ... gan Broject Defnyddiau ac Adnoddau Y Swyddfa Gymreig ; cyfarwyddwr Carl Dodson. — [Llandysul] : Gwasg Gomer
Poblogaeth 1 / awdur ... Siân Jones. — c1981. — 20p : ill,facsims,1geneal.table,maps(some col.),ports ; 30cm
ISBN 0-85088-806-9 (pbk) : £1.50 B82-30853

Daearyddiaeth / paratowyd ... gan Broject Defnyddiau ac Adnoddau Y Swyddfa Gymreig ; cyfarwyddwr Carl Dodson. — [Llandysul] : Gwasg Gomer
Trafnidiaeth / awdur ... Nia Hall Williams. — c1981. — 28p : ill,facsims,maps(some col.) ; 30cm
ISBN 0-85088-816-6 (pbk) : £1.50 B82-30850

914.29′003′21 — Wales. Place names — *Dictionaries*

Jones, Gwen Pritchard. Welsh place names / by Gwen Pritchard Jones. — Cardiff : J. Jones, 1979. — 40p : ill,1map ; 21cm
ISBN 0-902375-58-x (pbk) : £0.50 B82-21223

914.29′04858 — Wales. Description & travel

Barber, W. T.. Exploring Wales / W.T. Barber. — Newton Abbot : David & Charles, c1982. — 208p : ill,maps ; 22cm
Bibliography: p204-205. — Includes index
ISBN 0-7153-8179-2 : £7.95 : CIP rev. B82-01174

914.29′04858 — Wales. Mountains — *Walkers′ guides*

Mulholland, H.. Guide to Wales′ 3000-foot mountains : the Welsh Munros / H. Mulholland. — Wirral : Mulholland, 1982. — 96p : ill,maps ; 21cm. — (The Furth Munro books)
Bibliography: p94. — Includes index
ISBN 0-9507121-1-6 (pbk) : £1.65 B82-23604

914.29′04858 — Wales — *Visitors′ guides*

Tingey, Frederick. Wales / Frederick Tingey. — London : Travellers Realm, 1982. — 128p : ill,maps ; 19cm. — (RAC going places ; 11)
Includes index
ISBN 0-86211-012-2 (pbk) : £2.95 B82-29518

914.29′104858 — North Wales. Lakes — *Walkers′ guides*

Jones, Jonah. The lakes of North Wales. — London : Wildwood House, June 1982. — [224]p. — (Wildwood walking guides)
ISBN 0-7045-3056-2 : £8.95 : CIP entry B82-12146

914.29′104858 — North Wales — *Visitors′ guides*

Macdonlad, Colin. A visitor′s guide to North Wales & Snowdonia. — Ashbourne : Moorland, May 1982. — [144]p
ISBN 0-86190-050-2 (cased) : £6.50 : CIP entry
ISBN 0-86190-049-9 (pbk) : £3.95 B82-12893

914.29′104858′0222 — North Wales. Description & travel — *Illustrations*

Wainwright, A.. A North Wales sketchbook / A. Wainwright. — Kendal : Engraved, printed and published by Westmorland Gazette, 1982. — [177]p : chiefly ill,1map ; 19x24cm
£3.80 B82-21665

914.29′23 — Gwynedd. Lleyn Peninsula. Description & travel

Bowen, Alwynne. The Llŷn peninsula / by Alwynne Bowen ; illustrated by the author. — Denbigh ([Chapel St., Denbigh, Clwyd]) : Gee and Son, c1980. — [23]p : ill ; 21cm
£0.90 (pbk) B82-12194

914.29′25 — Gwynedd. Bangor. Country houses: Penrhyn Castle — *Visitors′ guides*

National Trust. Penrhyn Castle : Gwynedd. — [London] ([42 Queen′s Gate SW1H 9AS]) : The National Trust, c1979 (1982 [printing]). — 16p,[4]p of plates : ill,1plan ; 25cm
Unpriced (pbk) B82-27999

914.29′2504858 — Gwynedd. National parks: Snowdonia National Park — *Walkers′ guides*

Duerden, Frank. Great walks of North Wales / Frank Duerden. — London : Ward Lock, 1982. — 192p : ill,maps ; 18cm
Includes index
ISBN 0-7063-6156-3 (pbk) : £3.95 : CIP rev.
B82-00221

914.29′5 — Powys. Caerfanell Valley — *For environmental studies*

Caerfanell : study resources. — Brecon (7 Glamorgan St., Brecon, Powys LD3 7DP) : Brecon Beacons National Park Committee with the support of the Welsh Water Authority, [1981]. — 1portfolio : ill,maps ; 23x32cm
Unpriced B82-30920

914.29′51 — Powys. Welshpool. Country houses: Powis Castle — *Visitors′ guides*

Powis Castle, Powys. — [London] : National Trust, c1978 (1981 [printing]). — 17p,[8]p of plates : ill,1geneal.table ; 25cm
Bibliography: p17
Unpriced (pbk) B82-05644

914.29′5104858 — Powys. Montgomery *(District)*. **Canals: Montgomery Canal** — *Walkers′ guides*

Spencer, Alexandra. About the Montgomery Canal — / [prepared by Alexandra Spencer, Phil Horsley and Janet Cooper]. — [Welshpool] ([2 Canal Yard, Welshpool, Powys SY21 7AQ]) : [Prince of Wales′ Committee and Powys County Council], [1981]. — 4v. : ill,col.maps ; 25x12cm
£0.20 per V. (unbound)
Also classified at 914.24′5104858 B82-21664

914.29′6 — Southern Dyfed — *Visitors′ guides*

Rees, Vyvyan. South-west Wales : part of Dyfed. The old counties of Carmarthenshire and Pembrokeshire / by Vyvyan Rees. — 2nd ed. — London : Faber, 1976 (1982 [printing]). — 189p : ill,1 col.map ; 23cm. — (A Shell guide)
Previous ed.: 1963. — Includes index
ISBN 0-571-11820-8 (pbk) : £2.95 : CIP rev.
B81-22621

914.29′62 — Dyfed. Dale Peninsula. Long-distance footpaths: Pembrokeshire Coast Path — *Walkers′ guides*

Barrett, John H.. A plain man′s guide to the path round the Dale Peninsula / by John Barrett. — 2nd ed. — [Haverfordwest] : Pembrokeshire Coast National Park Authority, 1981. — 31p : ill,col.maps ; 21cm. — (Pembrokeshire Coast National Park area guide)
Previous ed.: 1966?
ISBN 0-86075-005-1 (pbk) : Unpriced
B82-14476

914.29′62 — Dyfed. Milford Haven *(Estuary)* **region** — *Visitors′ guides*

John, Brian. Milford Haven waterway / Brian John. — Newport, Dyfed : Published by Greencroft for the Pembrokeshire Coast National Park Authority, 1981. — 32p : ill,maps ; 21cm. — (Pembrokeshire Coast National Park area guide, ISSN 0144-090x)
Text on inside covers. — Bibliography: on inside covers
ISBN 0-905559-07-x (pbk) : Unpriced
B82-02848

914.29′6204858 — Dyfed. Preseli *(District)* **& South Pembrokeshire** *(District)*. **National parks: Pembrokeshire Coast National Park** — *Visitors′ guides*

Official handbook of the Pembrokeshire Coast National Park Authority / prepared by the Pembrokeshire Coast National Park Information Service. — [Newport, Dyfed] : Pembrokeshire Coast National Park Authority, [1981?]. — 52p : ill(some col.),maps(some col.) ; 21cm
Includes index
ISBN 0-86075-002-7 (pbk) : Unpriced
B82-08003

914.29′7204858 — Mid Glamorgan. Rhondda — *Visitors′ guides*

Rhondda. *Borough Council*. The Borough of Rhondda official guide / issued by authority of Rhondda Borough Council. — 11th ed. — London (Publicity House, Streatham Hill, SW2 4TR) : Burrow, 1982. — 80p : ill,1map ; 19cm
Previous ed.: 1978
Unpriced (pbk) B82-37412

914.29′82 — West Glamorgan. Gower. Parish churches — *Visitors′ guides*

Toft, L. A.. Noteworthy Gower Churches / text by L.A. Toft ; photographs by Harold Grenfell. — [Swansea] : [Gower Society], 1981. — 16p : ill,1map ; 21cm. — (A Gower Society publication)
Text on inside cover
Unpriced (pbk) B82-10199

914.29′85 — West Glamorgan. Port Talbot. Country parks: Afan Argoed Country Park — *Visitors′ guides*

Afan Argoed Country Park, Cynonville, Port Talbot, West Glamorgan : an introduction to the history, ecology and forestry of the delightful Afan Valley. — Swansea (12 Orchard St., Swansea) : West Glamorgan County Council, Planning Department in conjunction with the Forestry Commission, 1979. — 30p : ill(some col.),1col.map,1plan ; 15x21cm
Ill on lining papers
Unpriced (pbk) B82-17502

914.29′87 — South Glamorgan. Tongwynlais — *Walkers′ guides*

Brown, Roger Lee. The Tongwynlais walk / text: Roger Lee Brown ; graphics: Kevin Morgan ; map: Jonathan Smith. — Tongwynlais ([The Vicarage, Merthyr Rd, Tongwynlais, Cardiff, CF4 7LF]) : Tair Eglwys, 1982. — 10p : ill,1map ; 21cm
Unpriced (unbound) B82-35597

914.29′904858 — Gwent — *Visitors′ guides*

The **Gwent** County guide. — Gloucester : British Publishing, [1981]. — 144p : ill(some col.),3maps(some col.) ; 19x24cm
Map on folded sheet attached to inside cover
ISBN 0-7140-1987-9 (pbk) : Unpriced
B82-03951

914.29′98 — Gwent. Llangattock Lingoed. Parish churches: St Cadoc *(Church : Llangattock Lingoed)* — *Visitors′ guides*

Williams, David H.. Parish of Llangattock Lingoed alias Llangatwg Celennig / [D. H. W.]. — [Abergavenny] ([The rectory, Llanddewi Ysgyryd, Abergavenny, Gwent NP7 8AG]) : [D.H. Williams], 1982. — [4]p : ill,1port ; 22cm
Unpriced (unbound) B82-35828

914.3 — CENTRAL EUROPE, GERMANY

914.3′0484 — Germany. Description & travel, *1890* — *Personal observations*

Jerome, Jerome K.. Diary of a pilgrimage / Jerome K. Jerome. — Gloucester : Sutton, 1982. — 166p : ill ; 20cm
ISBN 0-86299-010-6 (pbk) : £1.95 : CIP rev.
B82-07812

914.3′04878 — West Germany — *Practical information* — *For British businessmen*

The **Federal** Republic of Germany and West Berlin. — [London] : British Overseas Trade Board, 1981. — 84p : ill,1map ; 21cm. — (Hints to exporters)
Text on inside front cover. — Bibliography: p70-73
Unpriced (pbk) B82-18662

914.31′04877 — East Germany. Description & travel, *1978* — *Personal observations*

Holford, Harry W.. Package pilgrimage / Harry W. Holford. — Bristol (St. Anne′s Drive, Oldland Common, Bristol) : H.W. Holford, 1981. — iv,72p,[8]p of plates : ill,1map ; 21cm
ISBN 0-9507465-0-9 (pbk) : £1.70 B82-09491

914.3′4 — Europe. Rhine River Basin. Geographical features — *For schools*

Waters, Grahame H.C.. Certificate notes : the geography of the Rhine Basin and North America / Grahame Waters. — Nairobi ; Harlow : Longman, 1982. — 92p : ill,maps ; 22cm. — (Study for success)
ISBN 0-582-60387-0 (pbk) : £1.10
Primary classification 917 B82-24404

914.38 — POLAND

914.38′6 — Poland. Tatra Mountains. Mountaineering expeditions, *1980* — *Personal observations*

Northern Ireland Youth Expedition *(1980)*. Polish peaks : an account of the 1980 Northern Ireland Youth Expedition to the Polish Tatra′s. — Belfast : Published for the 1980 Northern Ireland Youth Expedition by the Standing Conference of Youth Organisations in Northern Ireland, 1981. — 43p ; 30cm
ISBN 0-906797-07-1 (spiral) : £0.50
B82-00101

914.4 — FRANCE

914.4 — France. Paris Basin. Geographical features

Thompson, Ian B.. The Paris Basin / Ian B. Thompson. — 2nd ed. — Oxford : Oxford University Press, 1981. — 48p : ill,maps ; 24cm. — (Problem regions of Europe)
Previous ed.: 1973. — Bibliography: p46-47. — Includes index
ISBN 0-19-913278-x (pbk) : £2.50 B82-17584

914.4′0434 — France. Description & travel, *1763-1765* — *Correspondence, diaries, etc.*

Smollett, Tobias. Travels through France and Italy / Tobias Smollett ; edited by Frank Felsenstein. — Oxford : Oxford University Press, 1981, c1979. — xxvi,425p : 1map,1facsim ; 19cm. — (The World′s classics)
Originally published: Oxford : Clarendon, 1979. — Bibliography: pxxii-xxiv. — Includes index
ISBN 0-19-281569-5 (pbk) : £2.95 : CIP rev.
Also classified at 914.5′047 B81-30566

914.4′04837 — France. Battles, *1914-1918*. **Battlefields,** *1970-1979* — *Visitors′ guides*

Coombs, Rose E. B.. Before endeavours fade : a guide to the battlefields of the First World War / by Rose E.B. Coombs ; [edited by Winston G. Ramsey]. — 3rd ed. — London (3 New Plaistow Rd., E15 3JA) : Battle of Britain Prints International, 1979, c1976. — 136p : ill,maps,ports ; 31cm
Previous ed.: 1977. — Maps on lining papers. — Includes index
£5.95
Also classified at 914.93′0443 B82-20803

914.4′04838 — France. Description & travel

Feifer, Maxine. Everyman′s France / Maxine Feifer ; photographs by Harold Chapman. — London : Dent, 1982. — xiv,305p,[32]p of plates : ill(some col.),maps ; 26cm
Includes index
ISBN 0-460-04463-x : £12.50 : CIP rev.
B82-01989

914.4′04838 — France. Journeys by bicycles, *1980* — *Personal observations*

Vernon, Tom. Fat man on a bicycle : a discovery of France / by Tom Vernon who pedalled his nineteen stone from Muswell Hill in London to the Mediterranean the summer of 1979, the journey described in BBC Radio 4′s series of the same name. — London : Joseph, 1981. — 288p : ill,maps ; 23cm
Maps on lining papers. — Includes index
ISBN 0-7181-2072-8 : £7.95 B82-02311

914.4′04838 — France — *Practical information*

Harris, John, *1923-*. Easy living in France : how to cope with the French way of life / John Harris. — London : Arrow, 1982, c1981. — 146p ; 18cm
Includes index
ISBN 0-09-928770-6 (pbk) : £1.50 B82-22771

914.4'04838 — France — *Visitors' guides — For motoring*

Eperon, Arthur. Travellers' France : a guide to six major routes through France / Arthur Eperon ; maps and drawings by Ken Smith ; introduction by John Carter. — London : Pan, 1979 (1981 printing). — 160p : ill(some col.),col.maps ; 20cm
Includes index
ISBN 0-330-25982-2 (pbk) : £2.95 B82-10514

914.4'04838 — France — *Walkers' guides*

Hunter, Rob. Walking in France / Rob Hunter. — [Yeovil] : Oxford Illustrated, 1982. — vi,218p : ill,maps ; 21cm
Includes index
ISBN 0-902280-83-x : £6.95 B82-34868

914.4'04838'05 — France — *Visitors' guides — Serials*

Fodor's budget France. — '79-. — London : Hodder and Stoughton, 1979-. — v. : maps ; 18cm
Annual. — Description based on: '81 issue
ISSN 0194-4150 = Fodor's budget France : £3.50 B82-04929

914.4'104838 — France. Brittany. Description & travel

Deschamps, Marion. Portrait of Brittany / by Marion Deschamps. — London : Hale, 1980. — 176p,[24]p of plates : ill,1map,ports ; 23cm
Includes index
ISBN 0-7091-8118-3 : £8.50 B82-04185

914.4'204838 — Northern France — *Visitors' guides*

Fen, Patricia. French entrée : the Townsend Thoresen guide to Calais, Le Havre, Cherbourg and environs / Patricia Fenn. — London : Quiller, 1982. — 176p : ill,maps ; 20cm
Includes index
ISBN 0-907621-03-1 (pbk) : £2.95 B82-20804

914.4'25 — France. Dieppe. Description & travel

Ardizzone, Edward. Visiting Dieppe / Edward Ardizzone ; with an introduction by Lynton Lamb. — [London] : Warren Editions, [1981]. — [23]p : ill ; 28cm
Limited ed. of 175 copies
ISBN 0-9505969-1-4 : Unpriced B82-32690

914.4'25 — France. Dieppe. Discription & travel — *Personal observations*

Harte, Glynn Boyd. A weekend in Dieppe / by Glynn Boyd Harte. — [London] : Warren, 1981. — [34]p : ill(some col.) ; 28cm
Limited ed. of 150 signed and numbered copies
ISBN 0-9505969-5-7 : Unpriced B82-32689

914.4'3604838 — France. Paris — *Visitors' guides*

Corbierre, Anne-Marie. Paris : welcome to Paris / Anne-Marie Corbierre ; [photographs Van Phillips, J. Allan Cash] ; [illustrations Peter Joyce] ; [maps M. and R. Piggott]. — Glasgow : Collins, 1981. — 128p : ill(some col.),col.maps ; 18cm. — (A Collins travel guide)
Includes index
ISBN 0-00-447312-4 (pbk) : £1.95 B82-15074

De Stroumillo, Elisabeth. The observer's book of Paris / Elisabeth de Stroumillo. — London : Warne, 1982. — 192p,6p of plates : ill(some col.) ; 15cm. — (The Observer's pocket series ; 94)
Map on lining papers. — Bibliography: p182. — Includes index
ISBN 0-7232-1630-4 : £1.95 B82-22821

Turner, Miles. Paupers' Paris / Miles Turner. — London : Pan, 1982. — 249p : 2maps ; 20cm
Includes index
ISBN 0-330-26595-4 (pbk) : £1.95 B82-15207

914.4'3604838'0240664 — France. Paris — *Visitors' guides — For homosexuals*

Gay guide to Paris. — 1982-. — [London] ([c/o A. Weaver, BM Paris Guide, WC1N 3XX]) : [s.n.], 1982-. — v. : maps ; 15cm
Annual
ISSN 0263-2578 = Gay guide to Paris : Unpriced B82-23602

914.4'4804838 — France. Savoy — *Visitors' guides*

Scola, Paul. Savoy / Paul Scola. — London : Harrap, 1981. — 32p : ill,2maps ; 14x22cm. — (The Regions of France)
ISBN 0-245-53504-7 (pbk) : £0.95 B82-32665

914.4'72'0484 — France. Dordogne — *Visitors' guides*

Lands, Neil. A visitors guide to the Dordogne. — Ashbourne : Moorland, Dec.1982. — [144]p
ISBN 0-86190-042-1 (cased) : £6.50 : CIP entry
ISBN 0-86190-041-2 (pbk) : £3.95 B82-37498

914.4'8604838 — France. Midi-Pyrénées — *Visitors' guides*

Barbanneau, Jean-Luc. Midi-Pyrenees : and Languedoc-Roussillon / by Jean-Luc Barbanneau and Gisèle Barbanneau. — London : Harrap, 1982. — 32p : ill,maps,1port ; 14x22cm. — (The Regions of France)
ISBN 0-245-53503-9 (pbk) : £0.95 B82-32664

914.5 — ITALY

914.5'047 — Italy. Description & travel, *1763-1765 — Correspondence, diaries, etc.*

Smollett, Tobias. Travels through France and Italy / Tobias Smollett ; edited by Frank Felsenstein. — Oxford : Oxford University Press, 1981, c1979. — xxvi,425p : 1map,1facsim ; 19cm. — (The World's classics)
Originally published: Oxford : Clarendon, 1979. — Bibliography: pxxii-xxiv. — Includes index
ISBN 0-19-281569-5 (pbk) : £2.95 : CIP rev.
Primary classification 914.4'0434 B81-30566

914.5'04928 — Italy — *Visitors' guides — For youth hostelling*

Youth hosteller's guide to Europe. — 10th ed. — London (14 Southampton St., WC2E 7HY) : YHA Services
Italy / [written by R.M. Stuttard]. — 1980. — 32p : maps ; 19cm
Cover title: Youth hosteller's guide to Italy. — Previous ed.: 1977. — Includes index
£0.40 (pbk) B82-18659

914.5'04928'05 — Italy — *Visitors' guides — Serials*

Fodor's budget Italy. — '80-. — London : Hodder and Stoughton, 1980-. — v. : maps ; 18cm
Annual. — Description based on: '81 issue
ISSN 0270-787x = Fodor's budget Italy : £3.50 B82-04928

914.5'31 — Italy. Venice. Description & travel

McCarthy, Mary, *1912-*. The stones of Florence ; and, Venice observed / Mary McCarthy. — Harmondsworth : Penguin, 1972, c1956 (1982 [printing]). — 280p ; 20cm
The stones of Florence originally published: New York : Harcourt, Brace ; London : Heinemann, 1959
£2.25 (pbk)
Primary classification 914.5'51 B82-33634

Morris, Jan. Venice. — New and rev. ed. — London : Faber, Jan.1983. — 1v.
Previous ed.: 1960
ISBN 0-571-18067-1 (pbk) : CIP entry B82-32451

914.5'385 — Italy. Brenta Dolomites — *Climbers' guides*

Anderson, Michael, *1930-*. Brenta Dolomites : scramblers' guide / Michael Anderson. — Reading : West Col, 1982. — 56p : ill,maps ; 18cm. — (Alpine guides)
Includes index
ISBN 0-906227-21-6 (pbk) : Unpriced B82-31204

914.5'51 — Italy. Florence. Description & travel

McCarthy, Mary, *1912-*. The stones of Florence ; and, Venice observed / Mary McCarthy. — Harmondsworth : Penguin, 1972, c1956 (1982 [printing]). — 280p ; 20cm
The stones of Florence originally published: New York : Harcourt, Brace ; London : Heinemann, 1959
£2.25 (pbk)
Also classified at 914.5'31 B82-33634

914.5'604928 — Central Italy. Description & travel — *Personal observations*

Knox, Oliver. From Rome to San Marino : a walk in the steps of Garibaldi / Oliver Knox. — London : Collins, 1982. — 204p : 1map ; 23cm
Bibliography: p202. — Includes index
ISBN 0-00-216297-0 : £9.95 : CIP rev. B82-12426

914.5'63204928 — Italy. Rome. Description & travel

Hofmann, Paul. Rome. — London : Harvill Press, Feb.1983. — [245]p
ISBN 0-00-262775-2 : £7.95 : CIP entry B82-37664

914.5'63204928 — Italy. Rome — *Visitors' guides*

Masson, Georgina. The companion guide to Rome / Georgina Masson. — 6th ed. — London : Collins, 1980, c1965. — 541p,[12]p of plates : ill,maps ; 21cm. — (The Companion guides)
Previous ed.: 1974. — Bibliography: p513-515. — Includes index
ISBN 0-00-216277-6 (pbk) : £6.50 B82-21237

914.5'63204928'0222 — Italy. Rome. Description & travel — *Illustrations*

Mansione, E.. Rome : and the Vatican / E. Mansione, L. Pazienti. — London : Frederick Muller, 1981. — 127p : chiefly col.ill,1col.map,col.ports ; 28cm
Includes index
ISBN 0-584-95012-8 (cased) : £7.50
ISBN 0-584-95004-7 (pbk) : Unpriced B82-20322

914.5'63204928'05 — Italy. Rome — *Visitors' guides — Serials*

Fodor's Rome. — [1980]-. — London : Hodder and Stoughton, 1980-. — v. : maps ; 18cm
Annual. — Description based on: [1981] issue
ISSN 0276-2560 = Fodor's Rome : £3.95 B82-04923

914.5'73049 — Italy. Naples region. Description & travel, *ca 1910 — Personal observations*

Douglas, Norman. Siren land / by Norman Douglas. — London : Secker & Warburg in association with the Arts Council of Great Britain, 1982. — 198p ; 23cm
Originally published: London : Dent, 1911
ISBN 0-436-13204-4 : £6.50 B82-31050

914.6 — IBERIAN PENINSULA, SPAIN

914.6'0483 — Spain — *Visitors' guides*

Morris, Jan. Spain / Jan Morris. — Rev. ed. — Harmondsworth : Penguin, 1982, c1979. — 155p : ill,1map ; 20cm
Originally published: London : Faber, 1979. — Includes index
ISBN 0-14-005463-4 (pbk) : £1.75 B82-10138

914.6'0483'05 — Spain — *Visitors' guides — Serials*

Fodor's budget Spain. — '80-. — London : Hodder and Stoughton, 1980-. — v. : maps ; 18cm
Annual. — Description based on: '81 issue
ISSN 0270-7888 = Fodor's budget Spain : £3.50 B82-04930

914.69 — PORTUGAL

914.69'80444 — Portugal. Madeira — *Visitors' guides*

Hayter, Judith. Canary Island hopping : the Azores/Madeiira : a handbook for the independent traveller / Judith Hayter. — London : Sphere, 1982. — 319p : maps ; 24cm. — (Island hopping series)
Bibliography: p303-304
ISBN 0-7221-4496-2 (pbk) : £5.95
Primary classification 916.4'90483 B82-21270

914.69'90444 — Portugal. Azores — *Visitors' guides*

Hayter, Judith. Canary Island hopping : the Azores/Madeiira : a handbook for the independent traveller / Judith Hayter. — London : Sphere, 1982. — 319p : maps ; 24cm. — (Island hopping series)
Bibliography: p303-304
ISBN 0-7221-4496-2 (pbk) : £5.95
Primary classification 916.4'90483 B82-21270

914.7 — EASTERN EUROPE, SOVIET UNION

914.7 — Soviet Union. Geographical features
The **Soviet** Union : a systematic geography. — London : Hodder and Stoughton, Sept.1982. — [352]p
ISBN 0-340-26279-6 (cased) : £10.75 : CIP entry
ISBN 0-340-26280-x (pbk) : £6.95 B82-18803

914.7′04 — Eastern Europe. Description & travel, *1844 — Personal observations — Correspondence, diaries, etc.*
Borrow, George. A journey to Eastern Europe in 1844 : (thirteen letters) / by George Borrow ; edited by Angus M. Fraser. — Edinburgh : Tragara, 1981. — 33p ; 24cm
Limited ed. of 140 numbered copies
ISBN 0-902616-74-9 (pbk) : £10.50
B82-13118

914.7′04′05 — Eastern Europe — *Visitors′ guides — Serials*
Fodor′s Eastern Europe. — 1980-. — London : Hodder and Stoughton, 1980-. — v. : ill,maps ; 21cm
Annual. — Description based on: 1981 issue
£7.95 B82-04927

914.7′04853 — Soviet Union. Journeys by railways, *1975 — Personal observations*
Pennington, Michael. Rossya. — Cambridge : Oleander, June 1982. — [96]p. — (Oleander travel books ; v.12)
Originally published: England : Red Man, 1977
ISBN 0-906672-10-4 (pbk) : £4.95 : CIP entry
B82-25752

914.7′31204853 — Russia *(RSFSR).* **Moscow** — *Visitors′ guides*
Dvinskiĭ, Emmanuil. Moscow and its environs : a guide / Emmanuil Dvinsky ; [translated from the Russian by Barry Jones]. — Moscow : Progress ; [London] : distributed by Central, c1981. — 429p,[32]p of plates : col.ill,col.maps,2ports ; 21cm
Translation of: Moskva i ee prigorody. — Ill on lining papers. — Street map and index (1 folded sheet) as insert. — Includes index
ISBN 0-7147-1737-1 : £4.50 B82-29287

Moscow and Leningrad / edited by Evan and Margaret Mawdsley. — London : Benn, 1980. — 389p,16p of plates : maps,plans ; 21cm. — (Blue guides)
Includes index
ISBN 0-510-01627-8 (cased) : £12.95
ISBN 0-510-01628-6 (pbk) : Unpriced
Also classified at 914.7′45304853 B82-20729

914.7′45304853 — Russia *(RSFSR).* **Leningrad** — *Visitors′ guides*
Moscow and Leningrad / edited by Evan and Margaret Mawdsley. — London : Benn, 1980. — 389p,16p of plates : maps,plans ; 21cm. — (Blue guides)
Includes index
ISBN 0-510-01627-8 (cased) : £12.95
ISBN 0-510-01628-6 (pbk) : Unpriced
Primary classification 914.7′31204853
B82-20729

914.7′9 — Soviet Union. Caucasus. Coastal regions — *Visitors′ guides*
Khutsishvili, G.. The Black Sea coast of the Caucasus : a guide / G. Khutsishvili ; [translated from the Russian by Galina Glagoieva] ; [maps by Vladislav Sokolov] ; [editors of the English text Alexandra Bouianovskaya, Galina Ryumshina]. — Moscow : Progress ; [London] : Distributed by Central, c1980. — 207p : ill(some col.) ; 21cm
Translation of: Chernomorskoe poberezh′e Kavkaza
Unpriced B82-21929

914.92 — LOW COUNTRIES, NETHERLANDS

914.92′0473 — Benelux countries — *Visitors′ guides*
Baedeker′s Holland, Belgium and Luxembourg. — [Basingstoke] : Automobile Association, [1982?]. — 328p : col.ill,col.maps ; 27cm + 1map(74x84cm folded to 26x13cm)
Translation of the German. — Includes index
ISBN 0-86145-099-x : Unpriced B82-27466

Chester, Carole. Holland, Belgium & Luxembourg : welcome to Holland, Belgium and Luxembourg / Carole Chester. — Glasgow : Collins, 1982. — 128p : col.ill,col.maps ; 19cm. — (A Collins travel guide)
Includes index
ISBN 0-00-447316-7 (pbk) : £1.95 B82-10525

914.92′0473 — Netherlands. Description & travel — *For children*
Fairclough, Chris. Let′s go to Holland / text and photographs by Chris Fairclough ; general editor Henry Pluckrose. — London : Watts, c1982. — 32p : col.ill,2col.maps ; 22cm
Includes index
ISBN 0-85166-962-x : £2.99 B82-23293

914.93 — BELGIUM

914.93′0443 — Belgium. Battles, *1914-1918.* **Battlefields** — *Visitors′ guides*
Coombs, Rose E. B.. Before endeavours fade : a guide to the battlefields of the First World War / by Rose E.B. Coombs ; [edited by Winston G. Ramsey]. — 3rd ed. — London (3 New Plaistow Rd., E15 3JA) : Battle of Britain Prints International, 1979, c1976. — 136p : ill,maps,ports ; 31cm
Previous ed.: 1977. — Maps on lining papers. — Includes index
£5.95
Primary classification 914.4′04837 B82-20803

914.93′0443 — Belgium. Description & travel
Richmond, Fiona. An inside story / by Fiona Richmond ; illustrated by Liz Reber. — London (2a Chester Close, Chester St., SW1X 7BQ) : Time Off, c1982. — 15p : col.ill ; 22x9cm
Unpriced (unbound) B82-35403

914.95 — GREECE

914.95 — Southern Greece — *Visitors′ guides*
Dicks, Brian. Portrait of Southern Greece / by Brian Dicks. — London : Hale, 1982. — 239p,[24]p of plates : ill,1map ; 23cm
Bibliography: p229. — Includes index
ISBN 0-7091-9623-7 : £8.50 B82-27045

914.95′0476 — Greece. Coastal regions — *Visitors′ guides — For sailing*
Denham, H. M.. The Ionian Islands to the Anatolian coast : a sea-guide. — London : Murray, Sept.1982. — [248]p. — (Denham sea guides)
ISBN 0-7195-3949-8 : £20.00 : CIP entry
Also classified at 915.64 B82-20384

914.95′0476 — Greece — *Visitors′ guides*
Ellingham, Mark. The rough guide to Greece / written and researched by Mark Ellingham, Natania Jansz and John Fisher ; with additional research and accounts by Sarah Peel ... [et al.] ; edited by Mark Ellingham. — London : Routledge & Kegan Paul, 1982. — 224p : maps,plans ; 22cm
Includes index
ISBN 0-7100-9206-7 (pbk) : £3.95 B82-30119

914.95′0476 — Greece — *Visitors′ guides — For youth hostelling*
Youth hosteller′s guide to Europe. — 8th ed. — London (14 Southampton St., WC2E 7HY) : YHA Services
Greece and Yugoslavia / [written by John Parfitt, Richard Quilter and R.M. Stuttard]. — 1980. — 40p : 2maps ; 19cm
Cover title: Youth hosteller′s guide to Greece and Yugoslavia. — Previous ed.: [1974?]. — Includes index
£0.45 (pbk)
Also classified at 914.97′0423 B82-18660

914.95′5 — Greece. Corfu — *Visitors′ guides*
Young, Martin. Corfu and the other Ionian Islands / by Martin Young. — 3rd ed. — London : Cape, 1981. — 327p : maps(some col.) ; 18cm. — (Travellers′ guide)
Previous ed.: 1976. — Maps on inside covers. — Bibliography: p310-313. — Includes index
ISBN 0-224-01952-x (pbk) : £5.95 : CIP rev.
B81-15908

914.95′60476 — Greece. Macedonia — *Visitors′ guides*
Crossland, John. Macedonian Greece / John Crossland and Diana Constance. — London : Batsford, 1982. — 189p,[28]p of plates : ill (some col.),maps,plans ; 24cm
Bibliography: p183-184. — Includes index
ISBN 0-7134-3809-6 : £8.95 B82-17659

914.965 — ALBANIA

914.96′5043 — Albania — *Visitors′ guides*
Bland, William B.. A short guide to the People′s Socialist Republic of Albania / by William B. Bland. — Bristol (13 Small St., Bristol BS1 1DE) : Regent Holidays (UK) in co-operation with the Albanian Society, c1981. — iv,39p : 2maps ; 21cm
Unpriced (pbk) B82-03265

Ward, Philip. Touring Albania. — Cambridge : Oleander, Feb.1983. — [160]p. — (Oleander travel books series ; v.10)
ISBN 0-906672-41-4 (cased) : £12.50 : CIP entry
ISBN 0-906672-42-2 (pbk) : £5.95 B82-39836

914.97 — YUGOSLAVIA

914.97′0421 — Yugoslavia. Description & travel, *1936-1941 — Personal observations*
West, Rebecca. Black lamb and grey falcon : a journey through Yugoslavia / by Rebecca West. — Rev. ed. — London : Papermac, 1982, c1941. — 1181p ; 20cm
Previous ed.: London : Macmillan, 1942. — Bibliography: p1153-1158. — Includes index
ISBN 0-333-33492-2 (pbk) : £6.95 B82-35079

914.97′0423 — Yugoslavia — *Visitors′ guides — For youth hostelling*
Youth hosteller′s guide to Europe. — 8th ed. — London (14 Southampton St., WC2E 7HY) : YHA Services
Greece and Yugoslavia / [written by John Parfitt, Richard Quilter and R.M. Stuttard]. — 1980. — 40p : 2maps ; 19cm
Cover title: Youth hosteller′s guide to Greece and Yugoslavia. — Previous ed.: [1974?]. — Includes index
£0.45 (pbk)
Primary classification 914.95′0476 B82-18660

914.99 — AEGEAN ISLANDS

914.99 — Greece. Skiathos — *Visitors′ guides*
Skiathos : the shaded isle / edited by Jack Causton. — 3rd ed. — Send : Cartbridge, 1979. — 80p : ill,3maps,port ; 22cm
Previous ed.: 1974. — Includes index
ISBN 0-903223-03-1 (pbk) : Unpriced
B82-24860

915 — EURASIA, ASIA

915 — Asia. Geographical features — *For schools*
Jackson, Nora. North America and Asia / Nora Jackson, Philip Penn. — Metric ed. — London : George Philip, c1980. — ix,278p : ill,maps ; 22cm. — (Groundwork geographies)
Previous ed.: i.e. 6th ed. 1976
ISBN 0-540-01047-2 (pbk) : Unpriced : CIP rev.
Primary classification 917 B80-04593

915 — South-west Asia. Travel — *Practical information*
Griffith, Susan. Travellers survival kit to the East. — 2nd ed. / by Susan Griffith. — Oxford : Vacation-Work, 1982. — 176p : ill,maps ; 21cm
Previous ed.: / by Nigel Clarke. 1979. — Includes bibliographies and index
ISBN 0-907638-04-x (cased) : Unpriced
ISBN 0-907638-03-1 (pbk) : £2.95 B82-24873

915.1 — CHINA AND ADJACENT AREAS

915.1′0425′0924 — China. Description & travel, *ca 1270-1295.* **Polo, Marco** — *For schools*
Tulloch, Jill. At the time of Marco Polo / Jill Tulloch. — Harlow : Longman, 1982. — 63p : ill,maps,facsims,1plan,ports ; 24cm. — (Focus on history)
Text on inside cover. — Includes index
ISBN 0-582-18225-5 (pbk) : £1.45 B82-17725

915.1'0458 — China — *Visitors' guides*

Schwartz, Brian. China off the beaten track. — London : Harvill Press, Jan.1983. — [256]p
ISBN 0-00-272114-7 (pbk) : £5.95 : CIP entry B82-33591

Youde, Pamela. China / Pamela Youde. — London : Batsford, 1982. — 176p,[28]p of plates : ill(some col.),maps,plans ; 25cm
Bibliography: p166-167. — Includes index
ISBN 0-7134-3795-2 : £8.95 B82-17661

915.1'0458'05 — China — *Visitors guides — Serials*

Fodor's People's Republic of China. — [1979]-. — London : Hodder and Stoughton, 1979-. — v. : ill,maps ; 21cm
Description based on: 1981 ed.
ISSN 0192-2378 = Fodor's People's Republic of China : £6.95 B82-04926

915.1'504 — Tibet. Description & travel

Allen, Charles. Always a little further. — London : André Deutsch, Sept.1981. — [240]p
ISBN 0-233-97281-1 : £9.95 : CIP entry B81-21627

915.1'504 — Tibet. Description & travel, *ca 1950 — Personal observations*

Harrer, Heinrich. Seven years in Tibet. — Large print ed. — Anstey : Ulverscroft, Sept.1982. — [528]p. — (Ulverscroft large print series)
Originally published: London : Hart-Davis, 1953
ISBN 0-7089-0854-3 : £5.00 : CIP entry B82-27014

915.1'504 — Tibet. Exploration, *1800-1950*

Hopkirk, Peter. Trespassers on the roof of the world : the race for Lhasa / Peter Hopkirk. — London : Murray, 1982. — x,274p,[20]p of plates : ill,maps,ports ; 23cm
Bibliography: p267-269. — Includes index
ISBN 0-7195-3938-2 : £9.75 : CIP rev. B82-07593

915.1'6 — China. Mount Kongur. Mountaineering expeditions, *1981 — Personal observations*

Bonington, Chris. Kongur, China's elusive summit. — London : Hodder & Stoughton, Oct.1982. — [224]p
ISBN 0-340-26514-0 : £9.95 : CIP entry B82-24813

915.19'50443 — South Korea — *Practical information — For British businessmen*

The **Republic** of Korea. — [London] : British Overseas Trade Board, 1981. — 52p : ill,2maps ; 21cm. — (Hints to exporters)
Text on inside front cover. — Bibliography: p45-46
Unpriced (pbk) B82-18664

915.2 — JAPAN

915.2'044 — Japan. Description & travel, *1954-1979 — Personal observations*

Crosthwaite, Helen. Song of Japan / Helen Crosthwaite. — Bognor Regis : New Horizon, c1982. — 76p,[9]p of plates : ill,ports ; 21cm
ISBN 0-86116-728-7 : £3.75 B82-11251

915.2'1350448 — Japan. Tokyo — *Visitors' guides*

Kuroki, Junichirō. Touring Tokyo / Junichirō Kuroki, Shinzō Uchida. — Tokyo : Kodansha ; Oxford : Phaidon [distributor], 1979. — 154p : col.ill,maps ; 19cm. — (This beautiful world ; v.63)
ISBN 0-87011-358-5 (pbk) : £2.95 B82-20101

915.3 — ARABIAN PENINSULA AND ADJACENT AREAS

915.3'04 — Arabia. Exploration, *to ca 1950*

Hamilton, Paul, *19---*. Seas of sand / by Paul Hamilton. — London : Reader's Digest Association, 1980, c1971. — 191p : ill(some col.),col.facsims,col.maps,ports(some col.) ; 27cm. — (Discovery and exploration)
Originally published: London : Aldus, 1971. — Includes index
£6.97 B82-31532

915.3'5 — United Arab Emirates. Description & travel

UAE. — London (21 John St., WC1N 2BP) : Middle East Economic Digest, Nov.1981. — [240]p
ISBN 0-7103-0014-x (pbk) : £12.50 : CIP entry B81-30881

915.3'530453 — Oman. Description & travel

Graz, Liesl. The Omanis. — London : Longman, Sept.1982. — [216]p
ISBN 0-582-78348-8 : £12.00 : CIP entry B82-20276

915.3'530453 — Oman — *Practical information — For British businessmen*

Oman / edited by John Whelan. — London : Middle East Economic Digest, c1981. — viii,198p : ill(some col.),maps,ports(some col.) ; 21cm. — (A MEED practical guide)
Includes index
ISBN 0-7103-0013-1 (pbk) : £10.00 : CIP rev. B81-30882

915.3'60453'05 — Arabia. Gulf States — *Practical information — For British businessmen — Serials*

Gulf guide & diary. — 1977-. — Saffron Walden : Middle East Review Co., 1976-. — v. : ill (some col.),maps,ports ; 22cm
Annual. — Continues: Gulf diary. —
Description based on: 1980 issue
ISSN 0308-8693 = Gulf guide & diary : £3.50 B82-11131

915.3'80453 — Saudi Arabia — *Practical information — For British businessmen*

Living in Saudi Arabia : a brief guide. — [London] : Foreign & Commonwealth Office Consular Department, [1982?]. — 15p ; 21cm
Cover title
Unpriced (pbk) B82-33407

915.4 — SOUTH ASIA, INDIA

915.4'042 — South Asia. Exploration, *ca B.C.340-A.D.1610*

Napier, William, *1914-*. Lands of spice and treasure / by William Napier. — London : Reader's Digest Association, 1980, c1971. — 191p : ill(some col.),maps(some col.),ports(some col.) ; 27cm. — (Discovery and exploration)
Originally published: London : Aldus Books, 1971. — Includes index
Unpriced B82-34304

915.4'0435'0924 — South Asia. Exploration. Morshead, Henry — *Biographies*

Morshead, Ian. The life and murder of Henry Morshead : a true story from the days of the Raj / Ian Morshead ; with an introduction by Mark Tully. — Cambridge : Oleander Press, c1982. — xiv,207p : ill,facsims,1form,1geneal.table,maps,ports ; 22cm
Map on lining paper. — Bibliography: p200-201. — Includes index
ISBN 0-900891-76-9 : £10.50 : CIP rev. B82-10890

915.4'6 — Asia. Karakoram Range. Mountaineering expeditions, *1980 — Personal observations*

Miller, Keith, *19---*. Continents in collision : the International Karakoram Project / Keith Miller ; foreword by Lord Hunt. — London : George Philip, c1982. — xi,212p,[32]p of plates : ill(some col.),maps,col.ports ; 29cm
Bibliography: p205. — Includes index
ISBN 0-540-01066-9 : £12.50 : CIP rev. B82-00228

915.4'6 — Kashmir. K2. Mountaineering expeditions, *1979 — Personal observations — Collections*

Messner, Reinhold. K2 : mountain of mountains / Reinhold Messner, Alessandro Gogna ; translated by Audrey Salkeld. — London : Kaye & Ward, 1981. — 176p : ill(chiefly col.),maps,ports ; 27cm
Translated from the German. — Ill on lining papers. — Bibliography: p176
ISBN 0-7182-3940-7 : £12.50 B82-09241

915.4'799 — India *(Republic)*. **Goa. Description & travel**

Richards, J.M.. Goa / J.M. Richards. — London : Hurst, 1981. — xii,143p,20p of plates : ill,2maps,1plan,1port ; 23cm + 1sheet (22x28cm folded to 17x11cm)
'Plan of the city of Goa' (1 folded sheet) as insert. — Bibliography: p134. — Includes index
ISBN 0-905838-46-7 : £7.50 B82-22278

915.491 — PAKISTAN

915.49'1045 — Pakistan. Description & travel

Amin, Mohamed. Journey through Pakistan / Mohamed Amin, Duncan Willetts, Graham Hancock. — London : Bodley Head, 1982. — 254p : col.ill,1col.map,col.ports ; 33cm
ISBN 0-370-30489-6 : £14.95 B82-37903

915.49'13 — Kashmir. Zaskar. Description & travel

Peissel, Michel. Zanskar : the hidden kingdom / Michel Peissel. — Large print ed. — Leicester : Ulverscroft, 1981, c1979. — 396p : 3maps ; 23cm. — (Ulverscroft large print series)
Originally published: London : Collins, 1979
ISBN 0-7089-0714-8 : £5.00 : CIP rev. B81-30501

915.492 — BANGLADESH

915.49'2 — Bangladesh. Geographical features

Johnson, B. L. C.. Bangladesh / B.L.C. Johnson. — 2nd ed. — London : Heinemann Educational, c1982. — ix,133p : ill,maps ; 26cm
Previous ed.: 1975. — Bibliography: p127. — Includes index
ISBN 0-435-35490-6 : £9.50 : CIP rev. B82-01121

915.496 — NEPAL

915.49'6 — Asia. Everest. Expeditions, *1980-1981 — Personal observations*

Tasker, Joe. Everest the cruel way / Joe Tasker. — London : Eyre Methuen, 1981. — 166p,12p of plates : ill,ports ; 23cm
ISBN 0-413-48750-4 : £6.95 : CIP rev. B81-25312

915.49'6 — Eastern Nepal. Himalayas. Mountaineering expeditions, *1952 — Personal observations*

Weir, Tom. East of Katmandu / by Tom Weir. — Edinburgh : Gordon Wright, c1981. — 138p,[32]p of plates : ill,1map,ports ; 23cm
Originally published: Edinburgh : Oliver & Boyd, 1955
ISBN 0-903065-35-5 : £6.95 B82-10205

915.6 — MIDDLE EAST

915.6'041 — Middle East. Description & travel, *1834 — Personal observations*

Kinglake, Alexander. Eothen, or, Traces of travel brought home from the East. — Oxford : Oxford University Press, Nov.1982. — [304]p. — (Oxford paperbacks)
Originally published: London : s.n., 1844
ISBN 0-19-281361-7 (pbk) : £2.95 : CIP entry B82-26894

915.6'043 — Middle East. Description & travel, *1929-1969 — Illustrations*

Stark, Freya. Rivers of time : the photographs of Dame Freya Stark. — Edinburgh : Blackwood, Oct.1982. — [248]p
ISBN 0-85158-147-1 : £25.00 : CIP entry B82-24266

915.64 — Turkey. Southern coastal regions — *Visitors' guides — For sailing*

Denham, H. M.. The Ionian Islands to the Anatolian coast : a sea-guide. — London : Murray, Sept.1982. — [248]p. — (Denham sea guides)
ISBN 0-7195-3949-8 : £20.00 : CIP entry
Primary classification 914.95'0476 B82-20384

915.64'0437'0924 — Southern Turkey. Visits by Grant, Duncan, *1973 — Personal observations*

Roche, Paul. With Duncan Grant in southern Turkey / Paul Roche. — [London] : Honeyglen, 1982. — ix,134p,[8]p of plates : col.ill ; 26cm
Includes index
ISBN 0-907855-00-8 : £9.95 : CIP rev.
B82-21584

915.66'2 — Turkey. Mount Ararat. Expeditions to discover Noah's Ark, *to ca 1975*

LaHaye, Tim F.. The ark on Ararat / Tim F. LaHaye and John D. Morris. — Abridged ed. — [London] : Lakeland, 1979. — 160p ; 18cm
Previous ed.: Nashville : T. Nelson, c1976
ISBN 0-551-00802-4 (pbk) : £1.50 : CIP rev.
B79-08365

915.694'0453 — Israel. Description & travel — *Personal observations — Ukrainian texts*

Zhyzhka, Mariīā. Svīāta zemlīā : reportazh iz podorozhi / Mariīā Zhyzhka. — Kembridzh : Nakladom avtora, 1977. — 128p : ill,1facsim,ports ; 19cm
Unpriced B82-03941

915.694'0454 — Israel. Description & travel — *Personal observations*

Stewart, Desmond. The Palestinians : victims of expediency. — London : Quartet, Aug.1982. — [160]p
ISBN 0-7043-2294-3 : £7.95 : CIP entry
B82-21960

915.694'0454 — Palestine — *Visitors' guides — For Christians*

Richards, Hubert J.. Pilgrim to the Holy Land : a practical guide / H.J. Richards ; drawings and maps by Clare Richards. — Great Wakering : Mayhew McCrimmon, 1982. — 224p : ill,maps,plans ; 21cm
Map in pocket on inside back cover. — Includes index
ISBN 0-85597-321-8 (pbk) : £3.75 B82-25382

915.694'40454 — Jerusalem. Holy places — *Walkers' guides*

Freeman-Grenville, G. S. P.. The beauty of Jerusalem. — London : East-West Publications, Apr.1982. — [128]p
ISBN 0-85692-079-7 (pbk) : £2.95 : CIP entry
B82-06053

915.8 — CENTRAL ASIA

915.8'04 — Central Asia. Exploration, *to 1915*

Ettinger, Nathalie. The heartland of Asia / by Nathalie Ettinger. — London : Reader's Digest Association, 1981, c1971. — 191p : ill(some col.),facsims(some col.),col.maps,ports(some col.) ; 27cm. — (Discovery and exploration)
Originally published: London : Aldus, 1971. — Includes index
£6.97 B82-31533

915.8'10443 — Afghanistan. Hindu Kush. Description & travel, *1956 — Personal observations*

Newby, Eric. A short walk in the Hindu Kush / Eric Newby ; preface by Evelyn Waugh. — London : Pan, 1974, c1958 (1981 [printing]). — 247p,[8]p of plates : ill,maps,ports ; 20cm. — (Picador)
ISBN 0-330-26623-3 (pbk) : £1.95 B82-08253

915.93 — THAILAND

915.93'0444 — Thailand — *Visitors' guides*

Clarac, Achille. Guide to Thailand / Achille Clarac ; edited and translated by Michael Smithies ; photographs by Achille Clarac and Henri Pagau-Clarac ; maps and plans by Henri Pagau-Clarac. — Kuala Lumpur : Duang Kamol Book House ; Oxford : Oxford University Press, 1981. — 219,35p,32p of plates : ill,maps,plans ; 22cm
Translation from the French. — Maps on inside covers. — Bibliography: p217-219. — Includes index
ISBN 0-19-580417-1 (pbk) : £12.00
B82-05419

915.95 — MALAYSIA, BRUNEI, SINGAPORE

915.95'1043 — Peninsular Malaysia. Description & travel, *1854-1862 — Personal observations*

Wallace, Alfred Russel. The Malay Archipelago. — 5th ed. — London : Wildwood House, June 1982. — [640]p
Facsim. of: 5th ed. London : Macmillan, 1874
ISBN 0-7045-0456-1 (pbk) : £4.95 : CIP entry
B82-09465

915.95'1043 — Peninsular Malaysia. Description & travel, *1879 — Personal observations — Facsimiles*

Bird, Isabella L.. The golden Chersonese and the way thither / Isabella L. Bird ; with an introduction by Wang Gungwa. — Kuala Lumpur ; Oxford : Oxford University Press, 1980. — 384p,[1]folded leaf of plates : ill,facsims,1map ; 20cm
Facsimile reprint of: London : Murray, 1883. — Includes index
ISBN 0-19-580490-2 (pbk) : £5.50 B82-36849

915.97 — VIETNAM

915.97'044 — Indo-China. Description & travel, *1950 — Personal observations*

Lewis, Norman, *1918-*. A dragon apparent : travels in Cambodia, Laos and Vietnam / Norman Lewis. — London : Eland, 1982, c1951. — 317p,[24]p of plates : ill,1map ; 22cm
Originally published: London : Cape, 1951
ISBN 0-907871-00-3 (pbk) : £3.95 B82-26185

915.98 — INDONESIA

915.98'30437 — Borneo. Description & travel, *ca 1972 — Personal observations*

Macdonald, David. Expedition to Borneo / the search for Proboscis monkeys and other creatures ; David Macdonald ; line drawings by Priscilla Barrett. — London : Dent, 1982. — 180p,[8]p of plates : ill(some col.) ; 24cm
ISBN 0-460-04517-2 : £9.95 : CIP rev.
B82-03600

915.98'30438 — Borneo. Description & travel

Barclay, James. A stroll through Borneo / James Barclay. — Large print ed. — Leicester : Ulverscroft, 1982, c1980. — 375p : 2maps ; 23cm. — (Ulverscroft large print series : non-fiction)
Originally published: London : Hodder and Stoughton, 1980
ISBN 0-7089-0742-3 : £5.00 : CIP rev.
B81-33955

915.99 — PHILIPPINES

915.99'0446 — Philippines — *Practical information — For British businessmen*

Philippines. — [London] : British Overseas Trade Board, 1981. — 48p : ill,1map ; 21cm. — (Hints to exporters)
Text on inside front cover. — Bibliography: p40-41
Unpriced (pbk) B82-18665

916 — AFRICA

916 — Africa. Geographical features — *For schools*

Hickman, Gladys. The new Africa. — 3rd ed. / Gladys Hickman assisted by Richard Hickman and Lorna Hickman. — London : Hodder and Stoughton, 1980. — 192p,[4]p of plates : ill,maps(some col.) ; 25cm
Previous ed.: 1976. — Includes index
ISBN 0-340-25343-6 (pbk) : £3.95 : CIP rev.
B80-06223

916'.04 — Africa. Exploration, *to 1877*

Huxley, Elspeth. The challenge of Africa / by Elspeth Huxley. — London : Reader's Digest Association, 1980, c1971. — 191p : ill(some col.),facsims(some col.),col.maps,ports(some col.) ; 27cm. — (Discovery and exploration)
Originally published: London : Aldus, 1971. — Includes index
£6.97 B82-31531

916'.04327 — Africa. Description & travel, *1970-1979 — Personal observations*

Oliver, Dorothy. Four wheels across Africa / Dorothy Oliver. — St. Ives, Cornwall : United Writers, c1980. — 156p,[9]p of plates : ill,ports ; 22cm
ISBN 0-901976-59-8 : £5.20 B82-20114

916.11 — TUNISIA

916.1'1 — Tunisia. Geographical features

Field studies in Tunisia / edited by Ray Harris and Dick Lawless. — Durham (South Rd., Durham DH1 3LE) : Department of Geography, University of Durham, c1981. — 96p : ill,maps ; 30cm
Includes bibliographies
Unpriced (pbk) B82-08209

916.1'1045 — Tunisia — *Visitors' guides*

Tomkinson, Michael. Tunisia : a holiday guide / [Michael Tomkinson]. — 8th ed. — London : M. Tomkinson, 1980. — 144p : ill(some col.) ; 21cm
Previous ed.: 197-. — Includes index
ISBN 0-905500-02-4 (pbk) : Unpriced
B82-14430

916.2 — EGYPT

916.2'0455 — Egypt — *Visitors' guides*

Von Haag, Michael. Guide to Egypt / by Michael von Haag. — London : Travelaid, 1981 (1982 printing). — 347p,[4]p of plates : ill (some col.),maps,plans,1port ; 22cm
Port on inside cover. — Includes index
ISBN 0-902743-14-7 (pbk) : £6.50 B82-29515

916.24 — SUDAN

916.24'044 — Sudan. Description & travel

Hoagland, Edward. African calliope : a journey to the Sudan / Edward Hoagland. — Harmondsworth : Penguin, 1981, c1979. — 272p : ill,maps ; 20cm
Originally published: New York : Random House, 1979
ISBN 0-14-005806-0 (pbk) : £1.95 B82-18143

916.4 — MOROCCO

916.4'6 — Morocco. Marrakesh. Description & travel — *Personal observations*

Canetti, Elias. The voices of Marrakesh. — London : Boyars, July 1982. — [104]p
Translation of: Die Stimmen von Marrakesch. — Originally published: 1978
ISBN 0-7145-2580-4 (pbk) : £3.95 : CIP entry
B82-13519

916.49 — CANARY ISLANDS

916.4'90483 — Canary Islands — *Visitors' guides*

Hayter, Judith. Canary Island hopping : the Azores/Madeiira : a handbook for the independent traveller / Judith Hayter. — London : Sphere, 1982. — 319p : maps ; 24cm. — (Island hopping series)
Bibliography: p303-304
ISBN 0-7221-4496-2 (pbk) : £5.95
Also classified at 914.69'80444 ; 914.69'90444
B82-21270

916.6 — WEST AFRICA

916.6'04 — West Africa. Description & travel, *1893-1900 — Personal observations*

Kingsley, Mary H.. Travels in West Africa : Congo Français, Corisco and Cameroons / Mary H. Kingsley. — 4th ed. / with a new introduction by Elizabeth Claridge. — London : Virago, 1982. — xxiv,741p,[16]p of plates : ill,2maps,ports ; 20cm
Previous ed.: London : Cass, 1965. — Includes index
ISBN 0-86068-266-8 (pbk) : £5.95 : CIP rev.
B82-13162

916.6'04 — West Africa — *Practical information — For British businessmen*

Senegal, Guinea, Mali, Mauritania, Guinea-Bissau and Cape Verde. — [London] : British Overseas Trade Board, 1981. — 115p : ill,1map ; 21cm. — (Hints to exporters)
Text on inside front cover. — Bibliography: p108-111
Unpriced (pbk) B82-18666

916.662 — LIBERIA

916.66′2042 — Liberia. Description & travel, *1935 — Personal observations*
Greene, Graham. Journey without maps / Graham Greene. — Harmondsworth : Penguin, 1971 ([1981 printing]). — 249p : 1map ; 18cm
Originally published: London : Heinemann, 1936
ISBN 0-14-003280-0 (pbk) : £1.75 B82-08150

916.69 — NIGERIA

916.69′043′0924 — Nigeria. Exploration. Slessor, Mary — *Biographies — For children*
Mary Slessor and the 'white man's grave'. — London : Marshall, Morgan & Scott, Feb.1982. — [96]p. — (Heroes of the cross)
ISBN 0-551-00943-8 (pbk) : £0.95 : CIP entry B82-07804

916.69′045′05 — Nigeria — *Practical information — For businessmen — Serials*
The **Guardian** Nigerian handbook. — 1982-3-. — Glasgow : Collins, 1982-. — v. : ill,maps,ports ; 22cm
Annual. — Also entitled: Nigerian handbook
ISSN 0263-4864 = Guardian Nigerian handbook : Unpriced B82-28115

916.69′4 — Nigeria. Niger Delta. Canoeing expeditions: 1st St Austell Boy Scout & Nigerian Boy Scout Canoe Expedition to the Niger Delta 1981 — *Personal observations*
Sheen, Brian. 1st. St. Austell Scout & Nigerian Boy Scout Canoe expedition to the Niger Delta 1981 / by Brian Sheen. — Par (92 Par Green, Cornwall PL24 2AG) : B. Sheen, c1981. — iv,48p : ill,2maps ; 21cm
£1.45 (pbk) B82-24858

916.7 — CENTRAL AFRICA

916.7′04 — Africa south of the Sahara. Exploration. Livingstone, David, *1813-1873 — Biographies — For children*
David Livingstone. — London : Marshall, Morgan & Scott, Feb.1982. — [96]p. — (Heroes of the cross)
ISBN 0-551-00942-x (pbk) : £0.95 : CIP entry B82-07803

916.76 — EAST AFRICA

916.76 — East Africa. Geographical features — *For East African students*
Senior, M. W.. Certificate notes : the geography of East Africa / Mike Senior. — Harlow : Longman, 1982. — 96p : ill,maps ; 22cm. — (Study for success)
ISBN 0-582-60383-8 (pbk) : £1.10 B82-23063

916.76′044 — East Africa — *Visitors' guides*
Travellers' guide to East Africa : a concise guide to the wildlife and tourist facilities of Kenya, Tanzania, Uganda, Zambia and Zanzibar. — 5th ed., fully rev. / contributors to the text include Richard Beeston ... [et al.] ; revised by Richard Cox ; maps by Tom Stalker Miller. — London : Thornton Cox, 1980. — 164p : ill (some col.),maps ; 22cm
Previous ed.: 1972. — Includes index
ISBN 0-902726-33-1 (pbk) : Unpriced B82-04528

916.76′044 — East Africa. Wildlife reserves: National parks — *Visitors' guides*
Williams, John G. (John George). A field guide to the national parks of East Africa. — New ed. / John G. Williams and Norman Arlott ; with 24 colour plates and 5 black and white plates by Norman Arlott and Rena Fennessy. — London : Collins, c1981. — 336p : ill(some col.),maps ; 20cm
Previous ed.: 1967. — Includes index
ISBN 0-00-219215-2 : £7.95 B82-07394

916.762 — KENYA

916.76′2044 — Kenya. Description & travel — *Personal observations*
Tetley, Brian. A journey through Kenya. — London : Bodley Head, Oct.1982. — [192]p
ISBN 0-370-30485-3 : £14.95 : CIP entry B82-24851

916.78 — TANZANIA

916.78′25 — Tanzania. Game reserves: Selous Game Reserve. Travel
Matthiessen, Peter. Sand rivers / Peter Matthiessen ; photographs by Hugo van Lawick. — London : Aurum, c1981. — 213p : ill(some col.),maps,ports ; 26cm
Maps on lining papers
ISBN 0-906053-22-6 : £9.95 B82-17679

916.78′26 — Tanzania. Mount Kilimanjaro. Description & travel
Reader, John. Kilimanjaro : an exploration of Africa's highest mountain. — London : Hamilton, Aug.1982. — [128]p
ISBN 0-241-10683-4 : £12.95 : CIP entry B82-15690

916.8 — SOUTHERN AFRICA

916.8 — South Africa. Geographical features
Christopher, A. J.. South Africa / A.J. Christopher ; with a foreword by J.M. Houston. — London : Longman, 1982. — xvii,237p : ill,maps ; 23cm. — (The World's landscapes)
Bibliography: p221-228. — Includes index
ISBN 0-582-49001-4 (pbk) : £7.95 : CIP rev. B82-09449

916.8′0463 — Southern Africa — *Visitors' guides*
Travellers' guide to Southern Africa : a concise guide to the wildlife and tourist facilities of South Africa, Botswana, Lesotho, Namibia, Swaziland and Zimbabwe / [orginally compiled by Richard Cox]. — 3rd ed. / revisions by Clive Wilson and Mike Nicol ; drawings of animals by David Cook ; line drawings by Philip Bawcombe ; maps by Tom Stalker-Miller ; edited by Richard Cox. — London : Geographia, 1981. — 176p,[12]p of plates : ill(some col.),maps ; 22cm. — (Thornton Cox travellers' guides)
Previous ed.: London : Thornton Cox, 1973. — Includes index
ISBN 0-09-208200-9 (pbk) : £3.50 B82-14163

916.81′1043 — Southern Africa. Kalahari Desert. Description & travel — *Personal observations*
Luard, Nicholas. The last wilderness : a unique journey across the Kalahari Desert / Nicholas Luard. — Feltham : Hamlyn Paperbacks, 1982, c1981. — 222p ; 18cm
Originally published: London : Elm Tree, 1981
ISBN 0-600-20635-1 (pbk) : £1.50 B82-38107

916.891 — ZIMBABWE

916.891′044 — Zimbabwe. Description & travel, *ca 1975 — Personal observations*
Loveday, Thomas T.. Rhodesian ramble / by Thomas T. Loveday. — St. Peter Port : Toucan, 1980. — 40p : ill,2ports ; 22cm
ISBN 0-85694-216-2 (pbk) : Unpriced B82-17503

917 — NORTH AMERICA

917 — North America. Geographical features — *For schools*
Goh, Cheng Leong. North America / Goh Cheng Leong, Soo Fong Beng. — Kuala Lumpur ; Oxford : Oxford University Press, c1977 (1981 [printing]). — v,106p : ill,maps ; 25cm. — (Modern certificate guides) (Oxford in Asia)
ISBN 0-19-581082-1 (pbk) : £1.75 B82-33038

Jackson, Nora. North America and Asia / Nora Jackson, Philip Penn. — Metric ed. — London : George Philip, c1980. — ix,278p : ill,maps ; 22cm. — (Groundwork geographies)
Previous ed.: i.e. 6th ed. 1976
ISBN 0-540-01047-2 (pbk) : Unpriced : CIP rev.
Also classified at 915 B80-04593

Waters, Grahame H.C.. Certificate notes : the geography of the Rhine Basin and North America / Grahame Waters. — Nairobi ; Harlow : Longman, 1982. — 92p : ill,maps ; 22cm. — (Study for success)
ISBN 0-582-60387-0 (pbk) : £1.10
Also classified at 914.3′4 B82-24404

917′.04 — North America. Exploration, *to ca 1860*
Dresner, Simon. Rivers of destiny / by Simon Dresner. — London : Reader's Digest Association, 1981, c1971. — 191p : ill(some col.),coat of arms,col.facsims,col.maps,ports (some col.) ; 27cm. — (Discovery and exploration)
Originally published: London : Aldus, 1971. — Includes index
£6.97 B82-31541

917′.04537 — North America, *1970-1979 — Visitors' guides*
Verstappen's economy USA & Canada. — London : Pitman, 1980. — 1023p : maps ; 20cm
Includes index
ISBN 0-273-01290-8 (pbk) : £4.95 B82-07474

917.2 — MIDDLE AMERICA, MEXICO

917.2′04833′05 — Mexico — *Visitors' guides — Serials*
Fodor's budget Mexico. — '79-. — London : Hodder and Stoughton, 1979-. — v. : maps ; 18cm
Annual. — Description based on: '81 issue
ISSN 0196-1829 = Fodor's budget Mexico : £3.50 B82-04931

917.28 — CENTRAL AMERICA

917.28′04 — Central America. Spanish exploration, *to ca 1540*
Hordern, Nicholas. God, gold and glory / by Nicholas Hordern. — London : Reader's Digest Association, 1980, c1971. — 191p : ill (some col.),maps,ports ; 27cm. — (Discovery and exploration)
Originally published: London : Aldus Books, 1971. — Includes index
Unpriced B82-34303

917.29 — WEST INDIES

917.29′042′0924 — West Indies. Voyages by Drake, *Sir* **Francis,** *1540?-1596, 1585-1586 — Early works*
Sir Francis Drake's West Indian voyage 1585-86 / edited by Mary Frear Keeler. — London : Hakluyt Society, 1981. — xiv,358p,[23]p of plates(some folded) : maps,facsims ; 23cm. — (Hakluyt Society. Second series ; v.148)
Bibliography: p321-327. — Includes index
ISBN 0-904180-01-8 : £12.00 (free to members) B82-03055

917.29′0452 — West Indies — *Visitors' guides*
Bellamy, Frank. Caribbean island hopping : a handbook for the independent traveller / Frank Bellamy. — London : Sphere, 1981, c1979. — 294p : maps ; 24cm. — (Island hopping series)
Originally published: London : Gentry, 1979. — Includes index
ISBN 0-7221-1564-4 (pbk) : £5.95 B82-08163

917.29′0452′05 — West Indies — *Visitors' guides — Serials*
Fodor's Caribbean and the Bahamas. — 1980-. — London : Hodder and Stoughton, 1980-. — v. : some col.ill,maps ; 22cm
Annual. — Cover title: Fodor's ... guide to Caribbean and the Bahamas. — Also entitled: Fodor's Caribbean. — Continues in part: Fodor's Caribbean, Bahamas and Bermuda. — Description based on: 1981 issue
ISSN 0271-4760 = Fodor's Caribbean and the Bahamas : £6.95 B82-18535

917.298′3 — Trinidad and Tobago. Geographical features — *For schools*
Beddoe, I. B.. Trinidad and Tobago : a social and economic geography / I.B. Beddoe. — New ed. — Trinidad ; Harlow : Longman, 1981. — 155p : ill,maps ; 25cm
Previous ed.: 1970
ISBN 0-582-76579-x (pbk) : £3.00 B82-24405

917.298′3044 — Trinidad and Tobago — *Practical information — For British businessmen*
Trinidad and Tobago. — [London] : British Overseas Trade Board, 1981. — 42p : ill ; 21cm. — (Hints to exporters)
Text on inside front cover. — Bibliography: p35-36
Unpriced (pbk) B82-18668

917.3 — UNITED STATES

917.3 — United States. Geographical features

Watson, J. Wreford. The United States. — London : Longman, Feb.1982. — [304]p. — (Geographies for advanced study)
ISBN 0-582-30004-5 (cased) : £18.00 : CIP entry
ISBN 0-582-30005-3 (pbk) : £9.95 B81-35920

917.3′0488 — United States. National parks. Description & travel, *1897-1901*

Muir, John, *1838-1914*. Our national parks / John Muir ; with a foreword by Richard F. Fleck. — Madison ; London : University of Wisconsin Press, 1981. — xvii,370p,[11] leaves of plates : ill,1map ; 22cm
Facsim of: 1st ed. Boston, Mass. : Houghton Mifflin, 1901. — Includes index
ISBN 0-299-08590-2 (cased) : Unpriced
ISBN 0-299-08594-5 (pbk) : £4.55 B82-01303

917.3′04927 — United States — *Practical information*

Trudgill, Peter. Coping with America : a beginner's guide to the USA / Peter Trudgill. — Oxford : Basil Blackwell, 1982. — ix,148p : ill ; 21cm
Includes index
ISBN 0-631-12557-4 (cased) : £9.95 : CIP rev.
ISBN 0-631-12969-3 (pbk) : £2.95 B82-04592

917.4 — UNITED STATES. NORTH-EASTERN STATES

917.4′0443 — Eastern United States — *Visitors' guides*

Facaros, Dana. Around America : New York and the Mid-Atlantic states : a handbook for the independent traveller / Dana Facaros and Michael Pauls. — London : MacDonald, 1982. — 377p : maps ; 24cm
Bibliography: p368-369. — Includes index
ISBN 0-356-07869-8 (cased) : £8.95
ISBN 0-356-07870-1 (pbk) : £4.95 B82-20217

917.4′0443 — New England. Description & travel

Chamberlain, Samuel. New England in colour : a collection of colour photographs / by Samuel Chamberlain ; with an introductory text and notes on the illustrations by Stewart Beach. — London : Thorton Cox, 1979. — 94p : col.ill ; 25cm. — (Profiles of America)
Originally published: New York: Hastings House, 1969
ISBN 0-902726-34-x (pbk) : Unpriced
B82-33653

917.4′0443 — New England — *Visitors' guides*

Facaros, Dana. Around America : New England : a handbook for the independent traveller / by Dana Facaros and Michael Pauls. — London : Macdonald, 1982. — 250p : maps ; 24cm
Bibliography: p244-245. — Includes index
ISBN 0-356-07867-1 (cased) : £8.50
ISBN 0-356-07688-x (pbk) : £4.50 B82-19591

917.4′0443 — United States. Eastern states — *Visitors' guides*

Destination U.S.A. East / AA. — Basingstoke : Automobile Association, c1982. — 96p : col.ill,col.maps
ISBN 0-86145-106-6 (28cmpbk) : £2.95
B82-28484

917.47′10443 — New York *(City)* — *Visitors' guides — For children*

Ivory, Leslie Ann. A day in New York. — London : Burke Publishing, July 1982. — [24] p. — (Headstart books)
ISBN 0-222-00788-5 (cased) : £1.60 : CIP entry
ISBN 0-222-00790-7 (pbk) : £0.95 B82-17925

917.5 — UNITED STATES. SOUTH-EASTERN STATES

917.59′0463 — Florida — *Visitors' guides*

Chester, Carole. Florida / Carole Chester. — London : Batsford, 1982. — 153p : ill,maps ; 25cm
Includes index
ISBN 0-7134-3807-x : £7.95 B82-17662

917.8 — UNITED STATES. WESTERN STATES

917.8′042 — United States. Rocky Mountains. Description & travel, *1873-1880 — Correspondence, diaries, etc.*

Bird, Isabella L.. A lady's life in the Rocky Mountains / Isabella L. Bird. — [3rd ed.] / with a new introduction by Pat Barr. — London : Virago, 1982. — xxii,296p,[8]p of plates : ill ; 20cm
Facsim. of ed. published: London : John Murray, 1880
ISBN 0-86068-267-6 (pbk) : £4.50 : CIP rev.
B82-13163

917.8′0433 — United States. Western states. Overland travel to California — *Personal observations*

Moffat, Gwen. Hard road west. — Large print ed. — Anstey : Ulverscroft, Jan.1983. — [448] p. — (Ulverscroft large print series)
Originally published: London : Gollancz, 1981
ISBN 0-7089-0908-6 : £6.25 : CIP entry
B82-32536

917.8′0433 — United States. Western states — *Visitors' guides*

Destination U.S.A. West / AA. — Basingstoke : Automobile Association, c1982. — 96p : col.ill,col.maps ; 28cm
ISBN 0-86145-107-4 (pbk) : £2.95 B82-28485

917.9 — UNITED STATES. PACIFIC COAST STATES

917.94′04′4 — California. Gold deposits. Prospecting. Expeditions, *1849-1851*

Holliday, J. S.. The world rushed in. — London : Gollancz, Feb.1983. — [560]p
ISBN 0-575-03236-7 : £12.50 : CIP entry
B82-38684

918 — SOUTH AMERICA

918 — South America. Geographical features

Bromley, R. D. F.. South American development. — Cambridge : Cambridge University Press, Oct.1982. — [121]p. — (Cambridge topics in geography. 2nd series)
ISBN 0-521-23496-4 (cased) : £6.95 : CIP entry
ISBN 0-521-28008-7 (pbk) : £3.25 B82-23331

Morris, Arthur S.. South America / Arthur S. Morris. — 2nd ed. — Sevenoaks : Hodder & Stoughton, 1981. — xii,276p : ill,maps ; 25cm
Previous ed.: 1979. — Bibliography: p265-270. — Includes index
ISBN 0-340-27205-8 (pbk) : £6.95 : CIP rev.
B81-22493

918 — South America. Geographical features — *For schools*

Paor, Seán de. South America for intermediate certificate / Seán de Paor. — Dublin : Folens, c1979. — 72p : ill,maps ; 20x30cm
ISBN 0-86121-058-1 (pbk) : Unpriced
B82-01234

918′.04 — South America. Exploration, *to 1925*

Willis, Marcia. Jungles, rivers & mountain peaks / by Marcia Willis. — London : Reader's Digest Association, 1979, c1971. — 191p : ill (some col.),facsims,col.maps,ports(some col.) ; 27cm. — (Discovery and exploration)
Originally published: London : Aldus, 1971. — Includes index
£6.95 B82-31540

918.1 — BRAZIL

918.1′0463 — Brazil — *Practical information — For British businessmen*

Brazil. — 3rd ed. — [London] ([1 Little New St., EC4R 3TR]) : Touche Ross International, 1981. — viii,76p : 1map ; 23cm. — (Business study)
Previous ed.: 1976. — Map on inside cover
Unpriced (pbk) B82-08156

918.1′0463′05 — Brazil — *Visitors' guides — Serials*

Fodor's Brazil. — [No.1]-. — London : Hodder and Stoughton, [197-]-. — v. : ill,maps ; 18cm
Annual. — Description based on: [1981] issue
ISSN 0163-0628 = Fodor's Brazil : £5.50
B82-04925

918.2 — ARGENTINA

918.2′0464 — Argentina — *Practical information — For British businessmen*

Argentina. — [London] : British Overseas Trade Board, 1981. — 55p : ill,1map ; 21cm. — (Hints to exporters)
Text on inside front cover. — Bibliography: p47-50
Unpriced (pbk) B82-18667

918.5 — PERU

918.5′04633 — Peru. Andes. Description & travel — *Personal observations*

Brown, Michael, *1948-*. The weaver and the abbey : the quest for a secret monastery in the Andes / Michael Brown. — London : Barker, c1982. — 223p : 2maps ; 25cm
ISBN 0-213-16831-6 : £7.95 B82-21673

918.6 — NORTH-WESTERN SOUTH AMERICA

918.6′04 — North-western South America. Description & travel — *Personal observations*

Tchira, S. E.. Holiday & travel narratives : Columbia, Venezuela, Barbados, Luxembourg / by S.E. Tchira. — [Cheadle] ([Brook Lodge, Schools Hill, Cheadle, Cheshire]) : [S.E. Tchira], [1981]. — 20p : ill,maps ; 21cm
Unpriced (unbound) B82-12861

919.3 — MELANESIA, NEW ZEALAND

919.31′04 — New Zealand. Exploration, *1606-1875*

Holland, Julian. Lands of the Southern Cross / by Julian Holland. — London : Reader's Digest Association, 1980, c1971. — 191p : ill (some col.),facsims(some col.),col.maps,ports (some col.) ; 27cm. — (Discovery and exploration)
Originally published: London : Aldus, 1971. — Includes index
£6.97
Also classified at 919.4′04 B82-31534

919.31′0437 — New Zealand — *Practical information — For British businessmen*

New Zealand. — [London] : British Overseas Trade Board, 1981. — 52p : ill,1map ; 21cm. — (Hints to exporters)
Text on inside front cover. — Bibliography: p43-45
Unpriced (pbk) B82-18663

919.4 — AUSTRALIA

919.4′04 — Australia. Exploration, *1606-1875*

Holland, Julian. Lands of the Southern Cross / by Julian Holland. — London : Reader's Digest Association, 1980, c1971. — 191p : ill (some col.),facsims(some col.),col.maps,ports (some col.) ; 27cm. — (Discovery and exploration)
Originally published: London : Aldus, 1971. — Includes index
£6.97
Primary classification 919.31′04 B82-31534

919.4′0463 — Australia. Deserts. Description & travel — *Personal observations*

Davidson, Robyn. Tracks / Robyn Davidson. — London : Granada, 1982, c1980. — 247p,[16]p of plates : ill,1map,ports ; 18cm. — (A Paladin book)
Originally published: London : Cape, 1980. — Bibliography: 249-250
ISBN 0-586-08392-8 (pbk) : £1.95 B82-16152

Davidson, Robyn. Tracks / Robyn Davidson. — Large print ed. — Leicester : Ulverscroft, 1982, c1980. — 395p : maps ; 22cm. — (Ulverscroft large print)
Originally published: London : Cape, 1980. — Map on lining papers. — Bibliography: p394-395
ISBN 0-7089-0756-3 : £5.00 : CIP rev.
B81-36944

919.4′0463′0222 — Australia. Description & travel — *Illustrations*

Burt, Jocelyn. Spectacular Australia / Jocelyn Burt. — Adelaide ; London : Rigby, 1981. — 80p : chiefly col.ill ; 31cm
ISBN 0-7270-1479-x : £9.25 B82-27138

919.4′0463′0247 — Australia — *Practical information — For visual artists*

Australian arts guide / editor Roslyn Kean. — London : Art Guide Publications, 1981. — 82p : ill,maps ; 21cm
Maps on inside covers
ISBN 0-9507160-3-0 (pbk) : £2.50 B82-35650

919.7 — ATLANTIC OCEAN ISLANDS

919.7′11 — South Georgia & South Sandwich Islands. Place names. Etymology

Hattersley-Smith, G.. The history of place-names in the Falkland Islands dependencies (South Georgia and the South Sandwich Islands) / by G. Hattersley-Smith. — Cambridge : British Antarctic Survey, 1980. — 112p ; 31cm. — (Scientific reports / British Antarctic Survey ; no.101)
Maps in pocket. — Bibliography: p99-112
ISBN 0-85665-060-9 : Unpriced B82-05876

919.8 — POLAR REGIONS

919.8 — Polar regions. Geographical features — *For schools*

Sugden, David. Arctic and Antarctic : a modern geographical synthesis. — Oxford : Basil Blackwell, Sept.1982. — [256]p
ISBN 0-631-13085-3 : £25.00 : CIP entry B82-20290

919.8′04 — Arctic. Expeditions, *1977 — Personal observations*

Fiennes, Ranulph. Hell on ice / Ranulph Fiennes. — Large print ed. — Leicester : Ulverscroft, 1982, c1979. — 464p ; 23cm. — (Ulverscroft large print)
Originally published: London : Hodder & Stoughton, 1979
ISBN 0-7089-0784-9 : Unpriced : CIP rev. B82-08095

919.8′04 — Polar regions. Exploration, *to 1970*

Scott, J. M.. The private life of polar exploration / J.M. Scott. — Edinburgh : Blackwood, 1982. — xi,177p,[36]p of plates : ill,maps,ports ; 22cm
ISBN 0-85158-153-6 : £7.95 B82-28836

Willis, Thayer. The frozen world / by Thayer Willis. — London : Reader's Digest Association, 1980, c1971. — 191p : ill(some col.),facsims(some col.),col.maps,ports(some col.) ; 27cm. — (Discovery and exploration)
Originally published: London : Aldus, 1971. — Includes index
£6.97 B82-31537

919.8′904 — Antarctic. Exploration by Scott, R. F., *1902-1912 — Correspondence, diaries, etc*

Wilson, Edward, *1872-1912*. South Pole odyssey : selections from the Antarctic diaries of Edward Wilson / edited by Harry King. — Poole : Blandford, c1982. — 176p,[8]p of plates : ill (some col.),maps,2ports(some col.) ; 22cm
Bibliography: p168-169. — Includes index
ISBN 0-7137-1206-6 (pbk) : £3.95 : CIP rev. B82-04502

919.8′904 — Antarctic. Exploration, *to 1980 — For schools*

McCullagh, Sheila K.. Discovery in the Antarctic / Sheila McCullagh and Lois Myers. — Harlow : Longman, 1981. — 33p : ill(some col.),maps ; 21cm
Includes index
ISBN 0-582-18425-8 (cased) : Unpriced
ISBN 0-582-19341-9 (pbk) : £0.80 B82-16549

919.9 — EXTRATERRESTRIAL WORLDS

919.9′04 — Outer space. Exploration

Sevast′īanov, V.. The universe and civilisation / V. Sevastyanov, A. Ursul, Yu. Shkolenko ; [translated from the Russian by Sergei Syrovatkin]. — Moscow : Progress ; London : distributed by Central Books, c1981. — 239p ; 17cm
Translation of: Vselennaīa i TSivilizatsiia
ISBN 0-7147-1688-x (pbk) : £1.95 B82-19975

919.9′04 — Outer space. Exploration & research — *Conference proceedings*

Alternative Space futures and the human condition. — Oxford : Pergamon, Aug.1982. — [150]p
Conference papers
ISBN 0-08-029969-5 : £7.50 : CIP entry B82-25164

919.9′04 — Outer space. Exploration — *For children*

Couper, Heather. All about space / [authors Heather Couper Nigel Henbest] ; [editor Christopher Cooper]. — London : Marshall Cavendish, 1981. — 29p : col.ill ; 30cm. — (An All colour fact book) (Enigma)
Text, ill on lining papers
ISBN 0-85685-968-0 : Unpriced B82-06074

919.9′04 — Solar system. Exploration, *to 1981*

Appel, Fred. The moon and beyond / by Fred Appel and James Wollek. — Repr. with amendments. — London : Reader's Digest Association, 1981, c1971. — 191p : ill(some col.),facsims,ports ; 27cm. — (Discovery and exploration)
Previous ed.: London : Aldus, 1971. — Includes index
£6.97 B82-31539

920 — BIOGRAPHY

920′.009033 — Obituaries, *ca 1700-ca 1900 — Collections*

The **Last** word. — London : Deutsch, Sept.1982. — [140]p
ISBN 0-233-97474-1 : £4.95 : CIP entry B82-18843

920′.009′034 — Western culture. Persons, *1800-1914*

Makers of nineteenth century culture 1800-1914. — London : Routledge and Kegan Paul, Nov.1982. — [736]p
ISBN 0-7100-9295-4 : £15.00 : CIP entry B82-29134

920′.009′045 — Obituaries, *1951-1960 — Collections*

Obituaries from 'The times' 1951-1960 : including an index to all obituaries and tributes appearing in 'The times' during the years 1951-1960 / compiler Frank C. Roberts. — Reading : Newspaper Archive Developments, 1979. — 896p ; 31cm
ISBN 0-903713-96-9 : Unpriced B82-13311

920′.009′047 — Celebrities — *Biographies*

Cartland, Barbara. Barbara Cartland's book of celebrities. — London : Quartet Books, Apr.1982. — [160]p
ISBN 0-7043-3395-3 (pbk) : £4.95 : CIP entry B82-06237

920′.02 — Eponymous persons — *Biographies*

Hellicar, Eileen. The real McCoy / by Eileen Hellicar. — London : Reader's Digest, c1982. — 48p : ports ; 19cm
Unpriced (pbk) B82-38730

920′.02 — Persons, *1660-1978*

Foot, Michael. Debts of honour / Michael Foot. — London : Pan, 1981, c1980. — 222p ; 20cm. — (Picador)
Originally published: London : Poynter, 1980. — Includes index
ISBN 0-330-26551-2 (pbk) : £2.50 B82-01594

920′.02 — Persons, *to 1980 — Biographies*

More of who said that? : quotations and biographies of famous people / selected and compiled by Renie Gee. — Newton Abbot : David & Charles, c1981. — 64p ; 22cm
Bibliography: p61. — Includes index
ISBN 0-7153-8275-6 : £2.95 : CIP rev.
Primary classification 080 B81-28073

920′.02 — Persons, *to 1981 — Biographies*

Jones, Barry, *1932-*. The Macmillan dictionary of biography / Barry Jones and M.V. Dixon. — London : Macmillan, 1981. — 854p ; 24cm
ISBN 0-333-27274-9 : £14.95 B82-06658

920′.02 — Postage stamps. Special subjects: Persons — *Biographies — For children — Welsh texts*

Jones, Robert Emrys. Cymwynaswyr mawr y byd / Robert Emrys Jones. — Llandybie : C. Davies
[Cyfrol 2]. — c1982. — 136p : ill,maps,ports ; 21cm
ISBN 0-7154-0590-x (pbk) : £2.50 B82-16425

920′.02′05 — Persons — *Biographies — Serials*

The **International** who's who. — 45th ed. (1981-82). — London : Europa, June 1981. — [1400]p
ISBN 0-905118-63-4 : £35.00 : CIP entry
ISSN 0074-9613 B81-13807

The **International** who's who. — 45th ed. (1982-83). — London : Europa, June 1982. — [1400]p
ISBN 0-905118-73-1 : CIP entry
ISSN 0074-9613 B82-10891

920′.041 — Britons, *1550-1625 — Biographies*

Barkley, Harold. Likenesses in line : an anthology of Tudor and Stuart engraved portraits / Harold Barkley. — London : H.M.S.O., 1982. — 87p : ill,ports ; 19x25cm
ISBN 0-11-290352-5 (pbk) : £4.95 B82-14992

920′.041 — Britons — *Biographies*

The **Dictionary** of national biography : the concise dictionary. — Oxford : Oxford University Press
Part 2: 1901-1970. — 1982. — 747p ; 25cm
ISBN 0-19-865303-4 : £17.50 : CIP rev. B81-36247

The **Dictionary** of national biography. — Oxford : Oxford University Press, 1981
Includes index
1961-1970 : with an index covering the years 1901-1970 in one alphabetical series / edited by E.T. Williams and C.S. Nicholls. — xviii,1178p ; 25cm
ISBN 0-19-865207-0 : £70.00 : CIP rev. B81-30180

Watkins, Alan. Brief lives. — London : Hamilton, Sept.1982. — [192]p
ISBN 0-241-10890-x : £6.95 : CIP entry B82-18741

920′.041 — Britons, *ca 1530-ca 1695 — Biographies — Early works*

Aubrey, John. Brief lives. — Woodbridge : Boydell, Sept.1982. — [288]p
ISBN 0-85115-206-6 (pbk) : £4.95 : CIP entry B82-19841

920′.0411 — Scots — *Biographies*

Hanley, Clifford. The Scots / Clifford Hanley. — London : Sphere, 1982, c1980. — xi,276p ; 18cm
Originally published: Newton Abbot : David and Charles, 1980. — Bibliography: p266-268. — Includes index
ISBN 0-7221-4223-4 (pbk) : £1.75 B82-16578

920′.0421 — Londoners — *Humour*

Roberts, Glenys. Metropolitan myths. — London : Gollancz, Oct.1982. — [192]p
ISBN 0-575-03232-4 (cased) : £7.95 : CIP entry
ISBN 0-575-03154-9 (pbk) : £4.95 B82-23354

920'.042732 — Greater Manchester persons: Salfordians — *Biographies*

O'Brien, E.. Eminent Salfordians / by E. O'Brien. — [Salford] ([7 St George's Crescent, Pendleton, Salford, M6 8JL]) : Salford Local History Society
Vol.1: Langworthy and Brotherton. — 1982. — 36p : ill,2ports ; 21cm
Cover title
£1.50 (pbk) B82-37955

920'.071 — Canadians — *Biographies*

Dictionary of Canadian biography. — Toronto ; London : University of Toronto Press
Index, volumes I to IV, 1000 to 1800 / [prepared under the direction of Mary McD. Maude and Michel Paquin with the assistance ... of Margaret Filshie ... et al.]. — c1981. — vii,254p : 2maps ; 27cm
Issued also in French
ISBN 0-8020-3326-1 : £18.75 B82-34724

920'.073'088055 — United States. Persons, 15-30 yrs — *Biographies*

International youth in achievement. — Raleigh : American Biographical Institute ; Cambridge : International Biographical Centre, c1981. — xii,946p ; 25cm
ISBN 0-934544-10-7 : Unpriced B82-10311

920.72 — Women — *Biographies*

Plante, David. Difficult women. — London : Gollancz, Jan.1983. — [176]p
ISBN 0-575-03189-1 : £8.95 : CIP entry B82-32454

920.72'0941 — Great Britain. Women — *Biographies*

Putting the pieces together. — London : Women's Lives and Writings, 1981. — 63p : ill ; 21cm
'This book grew out of the Women's Lives and Writings course at Thames Poly' — Preface
ISBN 0-9507767-0-x (pbk) : £0.50 B82-03472

920.72'0942 — England. Women, ***1816-1933*** — *Biographies*

Longford, Elizabeth. Eminent Victorian women / Elizabeth Longford. — London : Papermac, 1982, c1981. — 256p : ill(some col.),facsims,1map,ports(some col.) ; 25cm
Originally published: London : Weidenfeld and Nicolson, 1981. — Bibliography: p249-250. — Includes index
ISBN 0-333-32638-5 (pbk) : £4.95 B82-39988

920.72'0973 — United States. Women, ***1900-1975*** — *Biographies*

Notable American women : the modern period : a biographical dictionary / edited by Barbara Sicherman, Carol Hurd Green with Ilene Kantrov, Harriette Walker. — Cambridge, Mass. ; London : Belknap, c1980. — xxii,773p ; 27cm
ISBN 0-674-62732-6 : £24.50 B82-27552

929 — GENEALOGY AND HERALDRY

929'.06'0424 — England. Midlands. Genealogy & heraldry. Organisations: Birmingham and Midland Society for Genealogy and Heraldry — *Directories*

Midland genealogical directory. — [Solihull] : [Birmingham and Midland Society for Genealogy and Heraldry]
Supplement no.1. — 1981. — 100p ; 30cm
Cover title
ISBN 0-905105-54-0 (pbk) : £2.00 B82-12111

929.1 — GENEALOGY

929'.1 — Genealogy

Beale, G. A.. The uses of genealogy / G.A. Beale. — London : [Cadenza], 1981. — ix,62,55p ; 20cm
Limited ed. of 60 copies. — Includes the Familial historian and the Beales of Blandford
Unpriced
Also classified at 929'.2'0942 B82-02495

929'.1 — Genealogy — *Amateurs' manuals*

Currer-Briggs, Noel. Worldwide family history / Noel Currer-Briggs. — London : Routledge & Kegan Paul, 1982. — ix,230p : maps ; 24cm
Bibliography: p219-223. — Includes index
ISBN 0-7100-0934-8 : £9.95 B82-38375

929'.1'024092 — Genealogy — *For librarianship*

Harvey, Richard. Genealogy for librarians. — London : Bingley, Nov.1982. — [160]p
ISBN 0-85157-335-5 : £11.50 : CIP entry B82-26311

929'.1'072041 — Great Britain. Genealogy. Research — *Amateurs' manuals*

Buckley, Kenneth A.. British ancestry tracing : a D.I.Y. guide for beginners / [Kenneth A. Buckley]. — Sutton Coldfield : K.A. Buckley, c1982. — 32p : facsims ; 21cm
ISBN 0-9506081-2-2 (sprial) : Unpriced B82-31954

Pelling, George. Beginning your family history / George Pelling. — 2nd ed. — Plymouth : Federation of Family History Societies, 1982. — 48p ; 21cm
Previous ed.: 1980. — Text on inside covers. — Bibliography: p47
ISBN 0-907099-17-3 (pbk) : £0.95 B82-40642

929'.1'0941 — Great Britain. Genealogy — *Amateurs' manuals*

Currer-Briggs, Noel. Debrett's family historian : a guide to tracing your ancestry / Noel Currer-Briggs and Royston Gambier ; introduction by Sir Iain Moncreiffe ; foreword by Lord Teviot. — London : Debrett, 1981. — 208p : ill(some col.),maps(some col.),coats of arms(some col.),facsims(some col.),forms,ports (some col.),geneal.tables(some col.) ; 26cm
ISBN 0-905649-51-6 : £9.95 B82-02498

Field, D. M.. Step-by-step guide to tracing your ancestors / D.M. Field. — London : Hamlyn, c1982. — 64p : ill,facsims,forms,1geneal.table,maps ; 26cm
Includes index
ISBN 0-600-34271-9 : £2.99 B82-32759

929.2 — FAMILY HISTORIES

929'.2 — Family trees — *For children*

Totten, Eileen. My family tree book : (for colouring in too) / Eileen Totten ; illustrated by Ann Doolen. — London : Evans, 1980. — 32p : ill,maps ; 25x37cm
Bibliography: p32
ISBN 0-237-45525-0 (spiral) : £2.95 B82-21346

929'.2'0604121 — Scotland. Grampian Region. Families. Genealogical aspects. Organisations: Aberdeen and North East Scotland Family History Society. Members. Interests — *Lists*

Aberdeen and North East Scotland Family History Society. Aberdeen & North East Scotland Family History Society : directory of members interests. — [Aberdeen] : [The Society], 1981. — 33p ; 22cm
ISBN 0-9507828-0-7 (unbound) : £1.25 B82-06886

929'.2'0604227 — Hampshire. Families. Genealogical aspects. Organisations: Hampshire Genealogical Society. Members. Interests — *Lists*

Hampshire Genealogical Society. Addendum no.2 to a catalogue of members' interests / Hampshire Genealogical Society. — [Southampton] ([c/o 12 Woodlands Way, North Baddesley, Southampton S05 9HE]) : [The Society], 1980. — 40p ; 21cm
£1.20 (pbk) B82-22739

929'.2'0604253 — Lincolnshire. Families. Genealogical aspects. Organisations: Society for Lincolnshire History and Archaeology. ***Family History Sub-committee*** — *Serials*

Lincolnshire family historian / Society for Lincolnshire History and Archaeology, Family History Sub-committee. — Vol.1, no.1 (Oct. 1981)-. — Sleaford (c/o Community Council of Lincolnshire, 25 Westgate, Sleaford, Lincs. NG34 7PL) : The Society, 1981-. — v. ; 30cm
Quarterly. — Continues: Family history newsletter (Society for Lincolnshire History and Archaeology). — Description based on: Vol.1, no.2 (Jan. 1982)
ISSN 0261-3565 = Lincolnshire family historian : Unpriced B82-14790

929'.2'0604258 — Hertfordshire. Families. Genealogical aspects. Organisations: Hertfordshire Family and Population History Society — *Directories* — *Serials*

Hertfordshire Family and Population History Society. Directory of members' interests / Hertfordshire Family and Population History Society. — Issue no.1 (1981)-. — Stevenage (c/o Mrs J. Laidlaw, 155 Jessop Rd, Stevenage, Herts.) : The Society, 1981-. — v. ; 21cm
Unpriced B82-15139

929'.2'06042651 — Cambridgeshire. Peterborough. Families. Genealogical aspects. Organisations: Peterborough & District Family History Society — *Serials*

Peterborough & District Family History Society journal. — Vol.1, part 1 (Dec. 1981)-. — Peterborough (c/o J. Gunn, 4 Setchfield Pl., New Rd, Woodston, Peterborough, Cambs.) : The Society, 1981-. — v. ; 30cm
Cover title: Peterborough Family History Society journal
ISSN 0262-4427 : Unpriced B82-17248

929'.2'0604295 — Powys. Families. Genealogical aspects. Organisations: Powys Family History Society — *Serials*

Powys chronicle = Chronicl Powys : cylchgrawn Cymdeithas Hanes Teuluoedd Powys / Powys Family History Society. — Vol.1, no.1 (Spring 1981)-. — [Knutsford] ([c/o Mrs. D.R. Glover, 34 Glebelands Rd., Knutsford, Cheshire WA16 9DZ]) : The Society, 1981-. — v. ; 30cm
ISSN 0261-1104 = Chronicl Powys : Unpriced B82-09685

929'.2'0604299 — Gwent. Families. Genealogical aspects. Organisations: Gwent Family History Society — *Serials*

[Journal *(Gwent Family History Society)*]. Journal / Gwent Family History Society. — No.1 (Aug.1981)-. — [Newport, Gwent] ([c/o Mr. C.J. Pitt-Lewis, 17 Graig Park La., Newport, Gwent]) : The Society, 1981-. — v. ; 30cm
ISSN 0262-4672 = Journal - Gwent Family History Society : Free to Society members B82-04078

929'.2'07204257 — Oxfordshire. Families. Genealogical aspects. Organisations: Oxfordshire Family History Society. Research projects — *Directories* — *Serials*

Oxfordshire Family History Society. Directory of members' research / Oxfordshire Family History Society. — 1976-1980-. — Oxford (c/o Ms K.M. Beck, 90 Hockmore Tower, Cowley Centre, Oxford OX4 3YG) : The Society, 1981-. — v. ; 21cm
Continues: Oxfordshire Family History Society. Research in progress
ISSN 0262-5121 = Directory of members' research - Oxfordshire Family History Society : £1.50 B82-04896

929'.2'0941 — Great Britain. Armstrong ***(Family).*** **Genealogical aspects** — *Serials*

The **Milnholm** Cross newsletter. — Vol.1, no.1 (Autumn 1980)-. — Edinburgh (6 St. Colme St., Edinburgh) : The Armstrong Trust, 1980-. — v. ; 30cm
Two issues yearly. — Description based on: Vol.1, no.3 (Christmas 1981)
ISSN 0261-3158 = Milnholm Cross Newsletter : £2.50 per year B82-31733

929'.2'0941 — Great Britain. Families. Genealogical sources: Methodist Church. Archives

Leary, William. My ancestor was a methodist : how can I find out more about him? / by William Leary ; edited by Michael Gandy. — London : Society of Genealogists, c1982. — 12p ; 22cm
ISBN 0-901878-49-9 (pbk) : £1.00 B82-21840

929'.2'0941 — Great Britain. Guinness ***(Family)*** — *Biographies*

Mullally, Frederic. The silver salver : the story of the Guinness family / Frederic Mullally. — London : Granada, 1981. — xii,255p,[40]p of plates : ill,ports,geneal.tables ; 25cm
Includes index
ISBN 0-246-11271-9 : £9.95 B82-09525

929′.2′0941 — Great Britain. Leithead *(Family).* **Genealogical aspects** — *Serials*

The **Leithead** family newsletter. — Vol.1, no.1 (Mar. 1982)-. — Mansfield (87 Chatsworth Drive, Mansfield, Notts. NG18 4QU) : D. Leithead, 1982-. — v. : maps ; 30cm
Two issues yearly
ISSN 0262-4435 = Leithead family newsletter : Unpriced B82-26145

929′.2′0941 — Great Britain. Pulvertaft *(Family)* **& Pulvertoft** *(Family)* — *History* — *Serials*

Pulvertaft papers : a newsletter on the Pulvertofts & Pulvertafts. — Vol.1 no.1 (Dec. 1981)-. — Newton Abbot (Tucketts, Trusham, Newton Abbot, Devon TQ13 ONR) : Captain D. Pulvertaft, 1981-. — v. : geneal.tables ; ; 21cm
Two issues yearly
ISSN 0261-118X = Pulvertaft papers : Unpriced B82-17246

929′.2′09411 — Scotland. Clans

Moncreiffe, *Sir* **Iain**. The Highland clans : the dynastic origins, chiefs and background of the clans of some other families connected with Highland history / Sir Iain Moncreiffe of that Ilk. — New rev. ed. — London : Barrie & Jenkins, 1982. — 248p,[16]p of plates : ill(some col.),coats of arms,geneal.tables,maps,ports ; 29cm
Previous ed.: 1967. — Geneal.tables on lining papers. — Includes index
ISBN 0-09-144740-2 : £12.95 : CIP rev. B81-12384

929′.2′09411 — Scotland. Clans. Tartans. Authenticity

Stewart, Donald C.. Scotland′s forged tartans : an analytical study of the Vestiarium Scoticum / Donald C. Stewart and J. Charles Thompson ; edited by James Scarlett. — Edinburgh : Harris, 1980. — 157p,12p of plates : 2col.ill,facsims ; 23cm
Includes index
ISBN 0-904505-67-7 : £10.00 B82-17055

929′.2′09411 — Scotland. Clans, *to 1981*

Martine, Roderick. Clans and Tartans / Roderick Martine ; drawings by Richard Hook. — Edinburgh : Spurbooks, c1982. — 64p : ill,ports ; 19cm. — (Introducing Scotland)
Bibliography: p63. — Includes index
ISBN 0-7157-2082-1 (pbk) : £1.25 B82-20586

929.2′09411 — Scotland. Clars. Tartans — *Serials*

Tartans : the journal of the Scottish Tartans Society. — Vol.1, no.1 (Summer 1980)-. — Comrie (Comrie, Perthshire PH6 2DW) : [The Society], 1980-. — v. : ill,ports ; 28cm
Description based on: Vol.2, no.1 (Spring 1981)
ISSN 0263-4791 = Tartans : £1.00 per issue B82-25481

929′.2′09411 — Scotland. Dunbar *(Family), to 1884*

Dunbar of Kilconzie, William. A short record of the ancient family of Dunbar / compiled from his larger Dunbar miscellany by Wiliam Dunbar of Kilconzie. — Herne Bay (Greenways, Oxenden Square, Herne Bay, Kent CT6 8TW) : [W. Dunbar], [1982?]. — 106p ; 21cm
Cover title: Dunbar′s 1000 years
Unpriced B82-28788

929′.2′09411 — Scotland. Macnair *(Family), to 1980*

Macnair, A. A.. Macnair genealogies : McNoyare. 1454 ... / compiled by A.A. Macnair. — [Gloucester] ([8, Healthville Rd., Gloucester GL1 3EW]) : [A.A. Macnair], 1981. — 109p,xiii,30leaves of plates : ill,1map,ports,1geneal.table ; 30cm
Includes index
Unpriced (pbk) B82-10023

929′.2′09411 — Scotland. Strathclyde Region. Glasgow. West End. Paterson *(Family).* **Daughters,** *ca 1870- ca 1960* — *Personal observations*

Dickson, Mora. The aunts / Mora Dickson. — Edinburgh : Saint Andrew Press, 1981. — 123p : ill,1geneal.table ; 22cm
Geneal.table on lining papers
ISBN 0-7152-0491-2 : £3.25
Also classified at 929′.2′09411 B82-02774

929′.2′09411 — Scotland. Strathclyde Region. Glasgow. West End. Sloan *(Family).* **Daughters,** *ca 1870-1960* — *Personal observations*

Dickson, Mora. The aunts / Mora Dickson. — Edinburgh : Saint Andrew Press, 1981. — 123p : ill,1geneal.table ; 22cm
Geneal.table on lining papers
ISBN 0-7152-0491-2 : £3.25
Primary classification 929′.2′09411 B82-02774

929′.2′094115 — Scotland. Highlands. Families. Genealogical aspects — *Serials*

[Journal *(Highland Family History Society)*]. Journal / Highland Family History Society. — Vol.1, no.1 (Dec. 1981)-. — [Inverness] ([c/o D. Evans, 53 Ballifeary Rd, Inverness]) : The Society, 1981-. — v. ; 22cm
Quarterly
ISSN 0262-6659 = Journal - Highland Family History Society : Unpriced B82-20895

929′.2′09415 — Ireland. Families. Genealogical sources

Irish genealogy : a record finder / edited by Donal F. Begley. — Dublin : Heraldic Artists, c1981. — 252p : ill,maps,facsims,ports ; 21cm. — (Heraldry and genealogy series)
Includes index
ISBN 0-9502455-7-7 (pbk) : Unpriced B82-22558

929′.2′09415 — Ireland. Families, *to 1981.* **Genealogical aspects**

MacLysaght, Edward. More Irish families. — Blackrock : Irish Academic Press, Nov.1982. — [256]p
ISBN 0-7165-0126-0 : £20.00 : CIP entry B82-35228

929′.2′09415 — Ireland. O′Neill *(Clan), to 1982*

O′Neill *(Clan).* O′Neill commemorative journal of the first international gathering of the Clan, 20th to 27th June 1982 / compiled by Kathleen Neill. — Belfast : Irish Genealogical Association, c1982. — 55p : ill,facsims,forms,1geneal.table,ports ; 30cm
ISBN 0-9508193-0-1 (pbk) : Unpriced B82-41019

929′.2′0942 — Braund *(Family).* **Genealogical aspects** — *Serials*

The **Braund** Society. — No.1 (Summer 1982)-. — [Bideford] ([c/o Mrs J.H. Braund, Little Stanmore, Lily Close, Northam, Bideford, Devon]) : The Society, 1982-. — v. : geneal.table,port ; 21cm
Quarterly
ISSN 0264-0368 = Braund Society (Newsletter) : Free to Society members only B82-38545

929′.2′0942 — Crimp *(Family).* **Genealogical aspects** — *Serials*

The **Crimp** journal / the Crimp Family History Society. — No.1 (Aug. 1981)-. — [Runcorn] ([c/o Mr. R.A. Crimp, 43 Porthleven Rd., Brookvale, Runcorn, Ches. WA7 6BE]) : The Society, 1981-. — v. ; 30cm
ISSN 0261-1171 = Crimp journal : Unpriced B82-10350

929′.2′0942 — Dorset. Blandford. Beale *(Family, to 1980.* **Genealogical aspects**

Beale, G. A.. The uses of genealogy / G.A. Beale. — London : [Cadenza], 1981. — ix,62,55p ; 20cm
Limited ed. of 60 copies. — Includes the Familial historian and the Beales of Blandford
Unpriced
Primary classification 929′.1 B82-02495

929′.2′0942 — East Sussex. Gladwish *(Family), 1225-1980.* **Genealogical aspects**

Gladwish, Victor E. R.. The rape of Hastings family of de Gladwyshe 1225-1980 / by Victor E.R. Gladwish. — [Somersham, Cambs.] ([1 High St., Somersham, Cambs.]) : [U.P.E.C. Publications], [1981]. — 182p : ill,3maps,coats of arms,facsims,ports,geneal.tables ; 30cm
Cover title. — Includes index
£14.72 B82-05689

929′.2′0942 — England. Denning *(Family)*

Denning, Alfred Denning, *Baron.* The family story / Lord Denning. — Feltham : Hamlyn Paperbacks, 1982, c1981. — 270p,[8]p of plates : ill,ports,1geneal.table ; 18cm
Originally published: London : Butterworths, 1981. — Includes index
ISBN 0-600-20592-4 (pbk) : £1.95 B82-28011

929′.2′0942 — England. Eyre *(Family), 1415-1856*

Hulbert, Martin F. H.. Legends of the Eyres : [fact and fiction] / collected by M.F.H. Hulbert. — Sheffield : Hathersage Parochial Church Council, c1981. — 16p : ill,1map,coats of arms,ports,1geneal.table ; 22cm
Bibliography: p16
ISBN 0-907602-08-8 (pbk) : Unpriced B82-27838

929′.2′0942 — England. Fitzalan-Howard *(Family), to 1981*

Robinson, John Martin. The Dukes of Norfolk. — Oxford : Oxford University Press, Jan.1983. — [288]p
ISBN 0-19-215869-4 : £12.50 : CIP entry B82-33474

929.2′0942 — England. Garland *(Family).* **Genealogical aspects** — *Serials*

Garlandhayes. — Rept. no.1 (Spring 1981)-. — Ilford (53 Spearpoint Gardens, Newbury Pk, Ilford, Essex IG2 7SZ) : Mrs N. Furlong, 1981-. — v. : maps,ports,geneal.tables ; 21cm
ISSN 0263-1458 = Garlandhayes : Unpriced B82-18491

929′.2′0942 — England. Gibbs *(Family), to 1980* — *Genealogies*

Gibbs, Rachel. Pedigree of the family of Gibbs of Pytte in the parish of Clyst St. George. — 4th ed. / by Rachel Gibbs. — [London] ([21 Albion Sq., E8 4ES]) : [Mrs. R.E. Gibbs], 1981. — xxi,170p,[28]folded leaves of plates : ill,ports,geneal.tables ; 35cm
Previous ed.: / by John Arthur Gibbs. London : Mitchell Hughes & Clark, 1932. — Includes index
Unpriced B82-12525

929′.2′0942 — England. Hungerford *(Family), to 1822* — *Early works* — *Facsimiles*

Hoare, *Sir* **Richard Colt**. Hungerfordiana : or memoirs of the family of Hungerford / collected by Sir Richard Colt Hoare. — [Great Britain] : J. & R. Hungerford ; Bristol : R.N. Hungerford [[distributor]], 1981. — 149p,[8]p of plates : ill,1coat of arms,1plan,port ; 23cm
Facsim of: ed. published Shastoniae: typis Rutterianis, 1823. — Limited ed. of 50 numbered copies. — Includes index
ISBN 0-9593944-0-0 : Unpriced B82-21239

929′.2′0942 — England. Koe *(Family), to 1900*

Koe, Wendy Stuart. The jackdaws : a history of the Scandinavian family named Kaae, anglicised to Koe, and its connections / by Wendy Stuart Koe ; illustrated by the author with many photographs by her and her husband Raymond Garrett Taylor. — Buckland : R.G. Taylor, 1981. — xi,144p : ill,coats of arms,facsims,ports,geneal.tables ; 30cm
Limited edition of 100 numbered copies. — Bibliography: p121-133. — Includes index
ISBN 0-9507542-0-x (pbk) : Unpriced B82-01266

929′.2′0942 — England. Mond *(family), 1830-1981*

Goodman, Jean. The Mond legacy : a family saga / Jean Goodman. — London : Weidenfeld and Nicolson, c1982. — xv,272p,[8]p of plates : ill,ports,1geneal.table ; 23cm
Bibliography: p250-256. — Includes index
ISBN 0-297-78055-7 : £11.50 B82-19765

929′.2′0942 — England. Paston *(Family)* — *Correspondence, diaries, etc.*

The **Paston** letters. — Oxford : Oxford University Press, Feb.1983. — [320]p. — (The World′s classics)
Originally published: 1956
ISBN 0-19-281615-2 (pbk) : £1.95 : CIP entry B82-36587

929'.2'0942 — England. Rowntree *(Family), to 1982.* **Genealogical aspects**

Rowntree, C. Brightwen. The Rowntrees of Riseborough / by C. Brightwen Rowntree. — [York] : [Sessions], [1982]. — 84p : ill,ports,1geneal.table ; 21cm
Previous ed.: / with manuscript and typed additions by Margaret E. Sessions. 1979. — Includes index
ISBN 0-900657-67-7 (pbk) : Unpriced
B82-24632

929'.2'0942 — England. Warwick *(Earl of), to ca 1485 — Early works*

Rous, John[Rous roll]. The Rous roll / John Rous ; with an historical introduction on John Rous and the Warwick roll by Charles Ross. — Gloucester : Sutton, 1980. — [150]p : ill,coats of arms,ports ; 26cm
Facsim. reprint of ed. orginally published: S.l. : H.G. Bohn, 1859. — Includes index
ISBN 0-904387-43-7 : £12.00 : CIP rev.
B79-30435

929'.2'0942 — Harwell *(Family).* **Genealogical aspects**

Fletcher, John, *19---*. The Harwell Trail / by John Fletcher and Jan Whittaker. — Abingdon ([20 Tullis Close, Sutton Courtenay, Abingdon OX14 4BD]) : J. Fletcher, c1981. — vi,29p : ill,maps,facsims,geneal.tables ; 21cm
£2.50 (pbk) B82-07742

929'.2'0942 — Leicestershire. Rutland *(District).* **Hardy** *(Family), to 1900*

Hardy, Eric B.. A family out of Rutland : (an account of a family called Hardy who lived in Rutland for 400 years) / [Eric B. Hardy]. — [Burton on Trent] ([c/o 71 Scalpcliffe Rd., Burton on Trent, Staffs. DE15 9AB]) : [Halcyon Private Press], [1981]. — 100leaves : 1ill,1col.map,1geneal.table ; 31cm
Limitied ed. of 55 numbered copies
Unpriced (pbk) B82-01491

929'.2'0942 — South-west England. Lobb *(Family), to 1600.* **Genealogical aspects**

Lobb, Douglas H. V.. 20,000 Lobbs around the world : Lobb genealogical records / Douglas H.V. Lobb. — Truro : D.H.V. Lobb, [1982?]. — 26p : ill,maps,coat of arms,geneal.table ; 30cm
Bibliography: p26
ISBN 0-9508071-0-9 (unbound) : Unpriced
B82-26974

929'.2'0942 — Staffordshire. Beresford *(Family), to ca 1700*

Beresford, William. Beresford of Beresford. — Didsbury : Morten
Part 1: A History of the Manor of Beresford in the County of Stafford / by William Beresford and the late Samuel B. Beresford. — 1981. — vi,106p,[4]p of plates : ill,1facsim ; 27cm
Facsim of ed. published: Leek : Moorlands Press, [1908?]
ISBN 0-85972-049-7 : Unpriced B82-17715

929'.2'0942 — Staffordshire. North Staffordshire. Mason *(Family), ca 1750-1860*

Mason : a family of potters / [edited Deborah S. Skinner]. — Stoke-on-Trent : City Museum & Art Gallery, [1982]. — 36p : ill,coats of arms,facsims,1port ; 20x22cm
Published to accompany an exhibition at the City Museum and Art Gallery, 1982. — Bibliography: p35
ISBN 0-905080-17-3 (pbk) : Unpriced
Also classified at 738.2'3 B82-33686

929'.2'094221 — West Surrey. Families. Genealogical aspects — *Serials*

[Record series *(West Surrey Family History Society)*]. Record series / West Surrey Family History Society. — No. 1-. — Frimley Green (c/o A. Bevins, Wykeham Lodge, St. Catherine's Rd, Frimley Green, Surrey) : The Society, 1981-. — v. ; 21cm
Irregular
ISSN 0261-5681 = Record series - West Surrey Family History Society : £1.80
B82-38522

[Research aids *(West Surrey Family History Society)*]. Research aids / West Surrey Family History Society. — No.3-. — [Farnborough, Hants.] ([109 West Heath Rd, Farnborough, Hants. GU14 8QZ]) : The Society, 1981-. — v. ; 22cm
Irregular. — Numbering irregular
ISSN 0261-5673 = Research aids - West Surrey Family History Society : Unpriced
B82-36710

929'.2'094253 — Lincolnshire. Families. Genealogical aspects

Birth briefs / contributed by members of SLHA. — Sleaford : Society for Lincolnshire History and Archaeology, Family History Sub-committee, 1982. — 100p : geneal.table ; 22x31cm
Cover title. — Includes index
ISBN 0-904680-18-5 (spiral) : Unpriced
B82-40598

929'.2'09429 — South Glamorgan. Llanblethian. Thomas *(Family), to 1981*

Thomas, Robert, *1887-1965*. Llanblethian in 1895 : a boyhood walk / by Robert Thomas. Memories of father. & Family roots / by Derek Thomas. — [Cowbridge] ([5 Westgate St., Cowbridge, Glam. CF7 7YW]) : Robert Thomas (Cowbridge) Ltd, c1982. — 50p : ill,facsims,map,ports ; 16x23cm
Cover title. — Bibliography: p47
Unpriced (pbk) B82-36890

929'.2'09429 — Wales. Trefan *(Family), to 1980.* **Genealogical aspects** — *Welsh texts*

Gresham, Colin A.. Teulu'r Trefan / Colin Gresham ; cyfieithwyd gan Guto Roberts. — [Caernarfon] : Gwasanaeth Llyfrgell Gwynedd, 1982. — 30p : 1port ; 22cm. — (Darlith flynyddol Eifionydd)
'Darlith a draddodwyd yng Ngwesty'r Marine, Criccieth, tachwedd 13ed, 1981'
ISBN 0-904852-27-x (pbk) : £0.60 B82-26986

929'.2'09436 — Austria. Klaar *(Family), 1842-1942 — Biographies*

Clare, George. Last waltz in Vienna : the destruction of a family 1842-1942 / George Clare. — London : Macmillan, 1981. — 274p,[8]p of plates : ill,ports,geneal.tables ; 23cm
Originally published: in German translation as Das waren die Klaars. 1980. — Bibliography: p261-265. — Includes index
ISBN 0-333-32212-6 : £8.95 B82-06639

929'.2'0973 — Texas. Dallas. Hunt *(Family), to 1980*

Hurt, Harry. Texas rich : the story of the Hunt dynasty of Dallas / Harry Hurt III. — London : Orbis, 1982, c1981. — 446p,[10]p of plates : ill,ports ; 24cm
Originally published: New York : W.W. Norton, 1981. — Includes index
ISBN 0-85613-400-7 : Unpriced B82-36653

929'.2'0973 — Texas. Hunt *(Family), to 1980*

Hurt, Harry. Texas rich : the Hunt dynasty from the early oil days through the silver crash / Harry Hurt III. — New York ; London : Norton, c1981. — 446p : ill,geneal.tables,ports ; 24cm
Includes index
ISBN 0-393-01391-x : Unpriced B82-33166

929'.2'0973 — United States. Truman *(Family) — Correspondence, diaries, etc.*

Truman, Harry S.. Letters from father : the Truman family's personal correspondence / edited and annotated by Margaret Truman. — South Yarmouth : John Curley ; [Long Preston] : Magna Print [distributor], c1981. — 428p ; 22cm
Published in large print
ISBN 0-89340-365-2 : Unpriced B82-14673

929.3 — GENEALOGICAL SOURCES

929'.342162 — London. Greenwich *(London Borough).* **Charlton. Parish registers,** *1813-1840 — Texts*

St. Luke's *(Church : Charlton).* Charlton parish register 1813-1840. — [London] ([c/o J.G. Smith, 7, Crown Court, Horn Park Lane, Lee SE12]) : Charlton Society]
Cover title. — Register of St. Lukes, Charlton Baptisms. — [1981?]. — [69]leaves ; 25cm
Unpriced (pbk) B82-03063

929'.342262 — West Sussex. Chichester. Record repositories: West Sussex Record Office. Stock: Genealogical sources

Wilkinson, Peter M.. Genealogists guide to the West Sussex Record Office / by Peter M. Wilkinson. — Chichester : West Sussex County Council, 1979. — 109p : 1map ; 21x30cm
ISBN 0-900801-45-x (spiral) : Unpriced
B82-41157

929'.342447 — Hereford and Worcester. Clifton upon Teme. Parish registers, *1598-1837 — Texts*

Registers of St. Kenelm's, Clifton-Upon-Teme, Worcestershire : 1598-1837. — Sedgley : Birmingham and Midland Society for Genealogy and Heraldry, [1982]. — 149p ; 29cm
Cover title. — Includes index
ISBN 0-905105-56-7 (pbk) : £3.25 B82-24631

929'.342447 — Hereford and Worcester. Little Witley. Parish registers, *1680-1846 — Texts*

Registers of the Chapelry of St. Michael & All Angels, Little Witley, Worcestershire : baptisms 1680-1846, marriages 1680-1836, burials 1680-1744. — [Birmingham] : [Birmingham and Midland Society for Genealogy and Heraldry], [1982?]. — i,47,3p ; 30cm
Cover title. — Includes index
ISBN 0-905105-58-3 (pbk) : Unpriced
B82-37457

929'.342447 — Hereford and Worcester. Woolhope. Parish registers, *1558-1812 — Texts*

Woolhope register. — Trowbridge (47 Victoria Rd, Trowbridge, Wiltshire BA14 7LD) : R.E. Sparry, [1982]
Limited ed. of 100 copies. — Includes index
Vol.2: Marriages 1755 to 1812 / extracted by Stella and Erle Sparry. — [31]p ; 21cm
Unpriced (pbk) B82-29218

929'.342462 — Staffordshire. Newcastle-under-Lyme. Parish registers, *1563-1812 — Texts*

Newcastle under Lyme parish register / Staffordshire Parish Registers Society. — [Birmingham] : Birmingham & Midland Society for Genealogy & Heraldry, 1981
Cover title. — Includes index
Newcastle under Lyme 1771-1812 / hon. editor Norman W. Tildesley. — 354,34p ; 22cm
ISBN 0-905105-55-9 (pbk) : £5.00 B82-31272

929'.342464 — Staffordshire. Adbaston. Parish churches: St. Michael and All Angels *(Church : Adbaston).* **Parish registers** — *Texts*

St. Michael and All Angels *(Church : Adbaston).* Registers of St. Michael & All Angels, Adbaston Staffordshire. — [Sedgley] : [Birmingham and Midland Society for Genealogy and Heraldry], [1980]
Pt.2: Baptisms, marriages and burials 1727-1839. — i,89,9p ; 30cm
Cover title. — Includes index
ISBN 0-905105-43-5 (pbk) : £1.90 B82-23250

929'.342496 — West Midlands *(Metropolitan County).* **Birmingham. Parish churches: St. Philip's** *(Church : Birmingham).* **Marriages. Parish registers** — *Texts*

St. Philip's *(Church : Birmingham).* Registers of St Philip's, the cathedral church of Birmingham : marriages 1715-1800 (inc.) / transcribed by P. Shellis. — [Sedgley] : [Birmingham and Midland Society for Genealogy and Heraldry], [1981?]. — 111,28p ; 30cm
Includes index
ISBN 0-905105-48-6 (pbk) : £2.10 B82-15420

929'.342496 — West Midlands *(Metropolitan County).* **Sheldon. Parish registers** — *Texts*

St Giles *(Church : Sheldon).* Registers of the Church of St Giles, Sheldon. — Sedgley : Birmingham and Midland Society for Genealogy and Heraldry
Pt.2: Baptisms 1683-1839, marriages 1684-1858, burials 1683-1841. — [1980?]. — 124p,12p ; 30cm
Includes index
ISBN 0-905105-42-7 (pbk) : Unpriced
B82-22854

929′.342584 — Hertfordshire persons: Kings Langley persons. Wills, ***1498-1659.*** **Collections**

Life and death in Kings Langley : wills and inventories 1498-1659 / edited by Lionel M. Munby. — Kings Langley : Kings Langley Local History & Museum Society in association with Kings Langley W.E.A., 1981. — xxxiv,166p ; 26cm
Bibliography: p147. — Includes index
ISBN 0-9507647-0-1 : Unpriced
Primary classification 942.5′84 B82-09817

929′.342757 — Merseyside ***(Metropolitan County).*** **Rainford. Marriages. Parish registers,** ***1813-1837 — Texts***

The registers of Rainford Chapel / transcribed, edited and indexed by Douglas J. Browning and Frank R. Pope ; assisted by April D. Turner. — Henham ([5, Vernons Close, Henham, Bishops Stortford, Herts.]) : D.J. Browning, 1981. — iv,54p ; 30cm
ISBN 0-9507753-0-4 (pbk) : Unpriced
B82-32941

929′.3428′15 — West Yorkshire persons: Horbury persons. Wills, ***1404-1800 — Collections***

The Will of Horbury / transcribed and edited by K.S. Bartlett. — Wakefield : City of Wakefield Metropolitan District Council
[Vol.3]: 1757-1800. — 1981. — 117p : geneal.tables ; 26cm
ISBN 0-86169-008-7 (pbk) : £3.00 B82-19117

929′.342821 — South Yorkshire ***(Metropolitan County).*** **Sheffield. Parish registers** ***— Texts***

The Parish register of Sheffield. — [Leeds] ([Claremont, 23 Clarendon Rd., Leeds LS2 9NZ]) : Yorkshire Archaeological Society, Parish Register Section
Vol.6: 1720-1736 / edited by W.S. Owen and Mary Walton. — 1981. — viii,384p ; 21cm. — (The Publications of the Yorkshire Archaeological Society. Parish Register Section ; 143)
Includes index
Private circulation (pbk) B82-22023

929′.342837 — Humberside. Hull. Parish churches: Sculcoates All Saints ***(Church : Hull).*** **Marriages. Parish registers** ***— Texts***

Sculcoates All Saints, index to marriages January 1813-April 1817 / compiled by P.M. Pattinson. — Cottingham (1 Creyke Close, Cottingham, N. Humberside HU16 4DH) : East Yorkshire Family History Society, [1981]. — 26p ; 21cm
Unpriced (unbound) B82-06191

929′.342843 — North Yorkshire. York. Parish registers, ***1813-1837 — Texts***

The Parish registers of St. Mary, Bishophill Junior, York 1813-1837 / transcribed by members of the York Family History Society. — York (c/o 9 The Paddock, Boroughbridge Rd., York YO2 6AW) : York Family History Society, 1981. — iii,123p : ill ; 23cm. — (York Family History Society publications, ISSN 0141-5344 ; 5)
Unpriced (pbk) B82-16558

929.4 — PERSONAL NAMES

929.4 — Pseudonyms, ***to 1980***

Room, Adrian. Naming names : stories of pseudonyms and name changes, with a who's who / by Adrian Room. — London : Routledge & Kegan Paul, 1981. — ix,349p ; 24cm
Bibliography: p346-349
ISBN 0-7100-0920-8 : £9.75 B82-02717

929.4′2′0941 — British surnames. Etymology

Verstappen, Peter. The book of surnames : origins and oddities of popular names / Peter Verstappen. — London : Sphere Books, 1982. — 254p ; 18cm
Originally published: London : Pelham, 1980. — Includes index
ISBN 0-7221-8743-2 (pbk) : £1.75 B82-37362

929.4′2′09415 — Irish surnames. Etymology & distribution ***— Dictionaries***

De Breffny, Brian. Irish family names : arms, origins, and locations / Brian de Breffny ; colour photographs by George Mott. — Dublin : Gill and Macmillan, 1982. — 192p : col.ill,coats of arms(some col.),col.maps,ports (some col.) ; 25cm
Bibliography: p191
ISBN 0-7171-1232-2 (cased) : Unpriced
ISBN 0-7171-1225-x (pbk) : £7.50 B82-34554

929.4′2′094253 — Lincolnshire surnames, ***1851 — Lists***

Ratcliffe, Richard. Alphabetical index of surnames in the 1851 census of Lincolnshire. — Sleaford : Society for Lincolnshire History and Archaeology, Family History Sub-committee
Pt.1: Gainsborough registration district. — 1982. — 78p ; 30cm
Compiled by Richard Ratcliffe
ISBN 0-904680-17-7 (pbk) : Unpriced
B82-40597

929.4′2′094276 — Lancashire surnames. Etymology

McKinley, Richard. The surnames of Lancashire / by Richard McKinley. — London : Leopard's Head, 1981. — xiii,501p : maps ; 23cm. — (English surnames series ; 4)
Includes index
ISBN 0-904920-05-4 : £12.00 B82-28336

929.4′4′094237 — Cornish forenames — ***Dictionaries***

Names for the Cornish. — [Redruth] : [Dyllansow Truran], [1981?]. — 32p : ill,facsims ; 26cm
ISBN 0-907566-03-0 (pbk) : Unpriced
B82-12788

929.5 — EPITAPHS

929.5 — Epitaphs in English ***— Anthologies***

Lamont-Brown, Raymond. A book of epitaphs. — Newton Abbot : David & Charles, Sept.1982. — [64]p
ISBN 0-7153-8311-6 : £3.50 : CIP entry
B82-20373

929.5 — Humorous epitaphs in English — ***Anthologies***

A Small book of grave humour / collected by Fritz Spiegl and recreated by Jane Knights. — London : Pan by arrangement with Scouse Press, 1971 (1981 printing). — [183]p : chiefly ill ; 18cm
Top edge curved
ISBN 0-330-02871-5 (pbk) : £1.25 B82-10516

929.5′09414′23 — Scotland. Strathclyde Region. Islay. Gravestones. Inscriptions, ***to 1855***

Booth, C. G.. Index of pre 1855 gravestone inscriptions in Islay / compiled for the Islay Museum by C.G. Booth. — [Port Charlotte] ([Isle of Islay, Argyll]) : [Islay Museums Trust], 1981. — 32leaves ; 30cm
Unpriced (unbound) B82-25050

929.5′09416′1 — Antrim ***(County).*** **Graveyards. Monumental inscriptions** ***— Collections***

Gravestone inscriptions : County Antrim / general editor: R.S.J. Clarke. — Belfast (66 Balmoral Ave, Belfast BT9 6NY) : Ulster Historical Foundation
Vol.2: Parishes of Glynn, Kilroot, Raloo and Templecorran / compiled by George Rutherford. — 1981. — xv,174p : ill,maps,facsims,2plans,1port ; 25cm
Bibliography: pxiii
ISBN 0-901905-26-7 (pbk) : Unpriced
B82-09121

929.5′09422′145 — Surrey. Weybridge. Parish churches: Saint James ***(Church : Weybridge).*** **Monumental inscriptions** ***— Collections***

Saint James Weybridge : monumental inscriptions. — [Walton-on-Thames] ([65 Welsey Drive, Walton-on-Thames, Surrey] [Walton and Weybridge Local History Society]), 1979. — 75p : 1plan ; 21cm. — (Walton and Weybridge Local History Society paper ; no.19)
Includes index
Unpriced (pbk) B82-24191

929.5′09423′7 — Cornwall. Graveyards. Monumental inscriptions: Epitaphs, ***ca 1100-ca 1900 — Collections***

Cornish epitaphs / edited by John Keast and Renée Keast. — Redruth : Dyllansow Truran
[Vol.1]. — 1981. — 64p : ill ; 22cm
ISBN 0-907566-16-2 (cased) : Unpriced
ISBN 0-907566-15-4 (pbk) : Unpriced
B82-12789

929.5′09425′2 — Nottinghamshire. Churchyards. Monumental inscriptions ***— Collections***

Monumental inscriptions : East Leake, East Leake (Baptist), Rempstone, Sandiacre (Derbyshire), South Muskham, West Leake. — [Nottingham] : [Nottinghamshire Family History Society], c1981 (Nottingham : Technical Print Services). — 63p ; 22cm. — (Records series / Nottinghamshire Family History Society, ISSN 0142-5099 ; v.13)
ISBN 0-906614-14-7 (pbk) : Unpriced
B82-00946

929.5′09425′86 — Hertfordshire. Ayot St. Lawrence. Graveyards. Monumental inscriptions ***— Collections***

Ruston, Alan R.. Ayot St. Lawrence : monumental inscriptions / edited & arranged by Alan Ruston. — [Watford] : Hertfordshire Family and Population History Society, 1982. — 17p : ill ; 21cm
Text on inside cover
ISBN 0-9507043-5-0 (pbk) : Unpriced
B82-21224

929.6 — HERALDRY

929.6 — Heraldry

Summers, Peter G.. How to read a coat of arms / by Peter G. Summers ; illustrated by Anthony Griffiths. — 2nd ed. reset. — London : Published for the Standing Conference for Local History by the Bedford Square Press of the National Council of Social Service, 1979. — 23p : ill,coats of arms ; 22cm
Previous ed.: 1967. — Bibliography: p23
ISBN 0-7199-1025-0 (pbk) : £0.95 B82-34727

929.6′09 — Heraldry, ***to 1982***

Dennys, Rodney. Heraldry and the heralds / Rodney Dennys. — London : Cape, 1982. — xviii,285p,[8]p of plates : ill(some col.),coats of arms(some col.),ports(some col.) ; 24cm
Includes index
ISBN 0-224-01643-1 : £12.95 : CIP rev.
B81-26720

929.6′09426′4 — Suffolk. Churches. Heraldry

The Heraldry of Suffolk churches / [F. Steward, general editor]. — [Ipswich] ([219 Valley Rd, Ipswich, Suffolk IP4 3AH]) : Suffolk Heraldry Society
No.12: Brandeston, Bruisyard, Cransford, Dennington, Earl Soham, Framlingham, Rendham, Saxtead, Sweffling. — [1980]. — [25]p : ill ; 30cm
Cover title. — Includes index
Unpriced (pbk) B82-22855

The Heraldry of Suffolk churches / [F. Steward, general editor]. — [Ipswich] (219 Valley Rd, Ipswich, Suffolk IP4 3AH]) : Suffolk Heraldry Society
No.13: Badley, Buxhall, Combs, Drinkstone, Felsham, Gt Finborough, Lt Finborough, Gedding, Harleston, Hessett, Onehouse, Rattlesden, Shelland, Woolpit. — [1980]. — [28]p : ill ; 30cm
Cover title. — Includes index
Unpriced (pbk) B82-22856

The Heraldry of Suffolk churches / [F. Steward, general editor]. — [Ipswich] (219 Valley Rd, Ipswich, Suffolk IP4 3AH]) : Suffolk Heraldry Society
No.14: Assington, Chilton, Gt Cornard, Lt Cornard, Newton, Sudbury churches, All Saints, St Gregory, St Peter. — [1980]. — [21]p : ill ; 30cm
Cover title. — Includes index
Unpriced (pbk) B82-22857

929.6'09426'4 — Suffolk. Churches. Heraldry
continuation

The **Heraldry** of Suffolk churches / [F. Steward, general editor]. — [Ipswich] : Suffolk Heraldry Society
No.15: Barnby, Carlton, Colville, Corton, Flixton, Gisleham, Gorleston, Gunton, Hopton, Kirkley, Lowestoft, Mutford, Oulton, Pakefield, Rushmere. — [1981]. — 19p : ill ; 30cm
Cover title. — Includes index
ISBN 0-907593-00-3 (pbk) : Unpriced
B82-38551

The **Heraldry** of Suffolk churches / [F. Steward, general editor]. — [Ispwich] : Suffolk Heraldry Society
No.16: Ashby, Belton, Blundeston, Bradwell, Burgh Castle, Fritton, Herringfleet, Lound, Somerleyton. — [1981]. — 18p : ill ; 30cm
Cover title. — Includes index
ISBN 0-907593-01-1 (pbk) : Unpriced
B82-38552

The **Heraldry** of Suffolk churches / [F. Steward general editor]. — [Ispwich] : Suffolk Heraldry Society
No.17: Badingham, Brundish, Heveningham, Huntingfield, Laxfield, Ubberston, Wilby. — [1981]. — 18p : ill ; 30cm
Cover title. — Includes index
ISBN 0-907593-02-x (pbk) : Unpriced
B82-38549

The **Heraldry** of Suffolk churches / [F. Steward, general editor]. — [Ispwich] : Suffolk Heraldry Churches
Cover title
No.18: Alderton, Bawdsey, Boyton, Butley, Capel, St. Andrew, Chillesford, Hollesley, Iken, Orford, Ramsholt, Rendlesham, Shottisham, Sudbourne, Sutton, Tunstall, Wantisden. — [1981]. — 17p : ill ; 30cm
Includes index
ISBN 0-907593-03-8 (pbk) : Unpriced
B82-38550

929.7 — ROYAL HOUSES, PEERAGE, LANDED GENTRY

929.7 — Royal families. Genealogical aspects

Burke's Royal families of the world / [editor Hugh Montgomery-Massingberd]. — London : Burke's Peerage
Vol.2: Africa & the Middle East. — 1980. — xv,320p : maps,coats of arms,ports,geneal.tables ; 26cm
Maps on lining papers. — Bibliography: p297-299. — Includes index
ISBN 0-85011-029-7 : £32.00 B82-15471

929.7'094 — Europe. Royal families. Genealogical aspects

Louda, Jiří. Lines of succession : heraldry of the royal families of Europe / tables by Jiří Louda ; text by Michael Maclagan. — London : Orbis, 1981. — 308p : ill,col.coat of arms,ports,geneal.tables ; 30cm
ISBN 0-85613-276-4 : £12.50 B82-04763

929.7'2 — Great Britain. Bowes-Lyon *(Family)*, *1767-1978*

Day, James Wentworth. The Queen Mother's family story / James Wentworth Day. — 2nd ed., Large print ed. — Bath : Chivers, 1981, c1979. — xxii,367p,[8]p of plates : ill,ports ; 23cm. — (A New Portway large print book)
Originally published: London : Hale, 1979
ISBN 0-85119-165-7 : Unpriced : CIP rev.
B81-28019

929.7'2 — Great Britain. Royal families. Children, *1819-1982 — Biographies*

Courtney, Nicholas. Royal children / Nicholas Courtney. — London : Dent, 1982. — 216p : ill,coat of arms,1facsim,geneal.tables,ports(some col.) ; 27cm
Bibliography: p211-212. — Includes index
ISBN 0-460-04567-9 : £8.95 : CIP rev.
B82-16641

929.7'2 — Great Britain. Royal families, *to 1981 — Genealogies*

Moncreiffe of that Ilk, *Sir* Iain. Royal Highness. — London : Hamilton, July 1982. — [128]p
ISBN 0-241-10840-3 : £6.95 : CIP entry
B82-16238

929.7'2 — Great Britain. Stuart *(Family)*

Morrah, Patrick. A Royal family : Charles I and his family / Patrick Morrah. — London : Constable, 1982. — 292p : ill,ports ; 22cm
Bibliography: p275-277. — Includes index
ISBN 0-09-463560-9 : £9.95 B82-24399

929.7'2'025 — Great Britain. Nobility — *Directories*

G.E.C.. The complete peerage of England, Scotland, Ireland, Great Britain and the United Kingdom, extant, extinct or dormant. — New ed., rev. and much enl. — Gloucester : Alan Sutton, Dec.1981. — 6v.
Facsim. of: New ed., rev. and much enl. London : St Catherine's Press, 1910-1959. — Previous ed.: London : G. Bell & Sons, 1887-1898
ISBN 0-904387-82-8 : £300.00 : CIP entry
B81-31543

929.7'5 — Italy. Borgia *(Family)*

Johnson, Marion, *d.1980*. The Borgias / Marion Johnson. — London : Macdonald Futura, 1981. — 232p : ill(some col.),2maps,ports,2geneal.tables ; 25cm
Ill on lining papers. — Bibliography: p225. — Includes index
ISBN 0-354-04791-4 : £9.95 B82-03961

929.7'999'538 — Saudi Arabia. Al Sa'ud *(Family)* — *Genealogies*

Lees, Brian. A handbook of the Al Sa'ud ruling family of Saudi Arabia / Brian Lees. — London : Royal Genealogies, 1980. — 64p : geneal.tables ; 30cm
ISBN 0-905743-17-2 : £25.00 B82-21152

929.8 — ORDERS AND DECORATIONS, ARMORIAL BEARINGS, AUTOGRAPHS

929.8'2'0941 — British royal coats of arms, *to 1977*

Brooke-Little, J. P.. Royal heraldry : beasts and badges of Britain / by J.P. Brooke-Little. — Derby : Pilgrim, 1977, c1981 ([1981 printing]). — 24p : ill(some col.),coats of arms(some col.),col.ports ; 24cm
ISBN 0-900594-59-4 (pbk) : Unpriced
B82-01819

929.8'2'094237 — Cornwall. Churches. Royal coats of arms

Pardoe, Rosemary A.. Royal Arms in the churches of Cornwall / compiled ... by Rosemary Pardoe. — Runcorn (11B Cote Lea Sq., Southgate, Runcorn, Cheshire WA7 2SA) : R. Pardoe, c1982. — 14p,[1]folded leaf of plates : coat of arms ; 21cm
£1.25 (pbk) B82-38548

929.9 — FLAGS AND OTHER FORMS OF INSIGNIA AND IDENTIFICATION

929.9'7 — Houses. Names

Miles, Joyce. The house names book : Ackybotha to Zeelust / Joyce Miles. — London : Unwin Paperbacks, 1982. — 123p ; 17cm
Includes index
ISBN 0-04-827046-6 (pbk) : £1.50 : CIP rev.
B82-03721

930 — ANCIENT HISTORY, TO CA 500 A. D.

930 — Ancient civilizations

Hollister, C. Warren. Roots of the Western tradition : a short history of the ancient world / C. Warren Hollister. — 4th ed. — New York ; Chichester : Wiley, c1982. — xii,244p : ill,maps ; 21cm
Previous ed.: 1977. — Includes bibliographies and index
ISBN 0-471-08900-1 (pbk) : Unpriced
B82-35992

930 — Ancient civilizations — *For children*

Gibson, Michael, *1936-*. Discovering ancient mysteries / [author Michael Gibson] ; [editors Su Box, Jo Jones]. — London : Marshall Cavendish, 1981. — 29p : col.ill,col.maps ; 30cm. — (Enigma) (An All colour fact book)
Text, ill on lining papers
ISBN 0-85685-970-2 : Unpriced B82-06077

Millard, Anne. Ancient civilizations / by Anne Millard ; editor Anne Priestley. — London : Kingfisher, 1982. — 89p : ill(some col.),maps (some col.) ; 19cm. — (A Kingfisher factbook)
Includes index
ISBN 0-86272-034-6 : £2.50 : CIP rev.
B82-01405

Pullman, Philip. Ancient civilizations / P. Pullman ; illustrated by Gary Long. — Exeter : Wheaton, 1981. — 88p : ill(some col.),maps,ports ; 23cm
Includes index
ISBN 0-08-021920-9 : £4.50 B82-08010

930 — Ancient world

The **Cambridge** ancient history. — Cambridge : Cambridge University Press
Vol.3. — 2nd ed
Previous ed.: 1925
Pt.1: The prehistory of the Balkans : and the Middle East and the Aegean world, tenth to eighth centuries B.C. / edited by John Boardman ... [et al.]. — 1982. — xx,1059p : ill,maps ; 24cm
Bibliography: p906-1007. — Includes index
ISBN 0-521-22496-9 : £40.00 : CIP rev.
B82-12682

The **Cambridge** ancient history. — Cambridge : Cambridge University Press
Previous ed.: chapters published individually as fascicles, 1961-1968
Vol.3. — Apr.1982
The expansion of the Greek world, eighth to sixth centuries B.C.. — [544]p
ISBN 0-521-23447-6 : £25.00 : CIP entry
B82-08425

930'.072024 — Ancient world. Historiography. Hieronymus, *of Cardia — Critical studies*

Hornblower, Jane. Hieronymus of Cardia / Jane Hornblower. — Oxford : Oxford University Press, 1981. — xi,301p ; 23cm. — (Oxford classical & philosophical monographs)
Bibliography: p282-287. — Includes index
ISBN 0-19-814717-1 : £18.50 : CIP rev.
B81-25843

930'.091822 — Eastern Mediterranean region countries. Cultural processes, *B.C.2000-A.D.100*

The **Book** of Bible knowledge. — London : Scripture Union, [c1982]. — 288p : ill(some col.),col.maps,col.facsims,col.plans ; 30cm
Contributors Arnold Anderson et al. ; editors Elrose Hunter, Paul Marsh ; illustrations & maps Fred Apps et al.. — Ill on lining papers. — Includes index
ISBN 0-86201-121-3 : Unpriced B82-13544

930'.09'732 — Ancient civilizations. Cities. Social life — *For children*

Unstead, R. J.. How they lived in cities long ago / R.J. Unstead. — London : Hutchinson, 1980. — 77p : col.ill,col.maps ; 33cm
Includes index
ISBN 0-09-142460-7 : £4.95 : CIP rev.
B80-18542

930.1 — ARCHAEOLOGY

930.1 — Archaeology

Hester, James J.. Introduction to archaeology / James J. Hester, James Grady. — 2nd ed. — New York ; London : Holt, Rinehart and Winston, c1982. — vii,496p : ill,maps,plans ; 25cm
Previous ed.: 1976. — Text on lining papers. — Bibliography: p466-483. — Includes index
ISBN 0-03-046291-6 : Unpriced B82-28666

Sharer, Robert J.. Fundamentals of archaeology / Robert J. Sharer, Wendy Ashmore. — Menlo Park ; London : Benjamin/Cummings, c1979 (1980 printing). — xxii,614p : ill,maps,plans ; 25cm
Bibliography: p577-600. — Includes index
ISBN 0-8053-8760-9 : Unpriced B82-14167

930.1 — Archaeology — *Conference proceedings*

Symbolic and structural archaeology / edited by Ian Hodder for the Cambridge Seminar on Symbolic and Structural Archaeology. — Cambridge : Cambridge University Press, 1982. — viii,188p : ill,maps,plans ; 29cm. — (New directions in archaeology)
Conference papers. — Includes bibliographies and index
ISBN 0-521-24406-4 : £19.50 : CIP rev. B82-19256

930.1 — Archaeology — *For children*

Rollin, Sue. The illustrated atlas of archaeology. — London : Longman, June 1982. — [64]p
ISBN 0-582-39200-4 : £4.95 : CIP entry B82-09448

930.1 — Environmental archaeology

Butzer, Karl W.. Archaeology as human geology : method and theory for a contextual approach / Karl W. Butzer. — Cambridge : Cambridge University Press, 1982. — xiii,364p : ill,maps ; 24cm
Bibliography: p321-357. — Includes index
ISBN 0-521-24652-0 (cased) : £22.50
ISBN 0-521-28877-0 (pbk) : Unpriced B82-38918

Evans, John G.. An introduction to environmental archaeology / John G. Evans. — London : Elek, 1978 (1981 [printing]). — xii,154p : ill,maps ; 23cm
Bibliography: p140-148. — Includes index
ISBN 0-246-11595-5 (cased) : £6.95
ISBN 0-246-11596-3 (pbk) : Unpriced B82-40622

Shackley, Myra. Environmental archaeology / Myra Shackley. — London : Allen & Unwin, 1981. — xv,213p : ill,maps ; 26cm
Includes bibliographies and index
ISBN 0-04-913020-x (cased) : Unpriced : CIP rev.
ISBN 0-04-913021-8 (pbk) : Unpriced B81-24604

930.1 — Ley systems

Fidler, J. Havelock. Ley lines. — Wellingborough : Turnstone, Feb.1983. — [144]p
ISBN 0-85500-173-9 (pbk) : £3.95 : CIP entry B82-39608

930.1 — Prehistoric burial places. Archaeological investigation

The **Archaeology** of death / edited by Robert Chapman, Ian Kinnes, Klaus Randsborg. — Cambridge : Cambridge University Press, 1981. — vii,159p : ill,maps ; 28cm. — (New directions in archaeology)
Bibliography: p145-155. — Includes index
ISBN 0-521-23775-0 : £17.50 : CIP rev. B81-28822

930.1 — Prehistoric man — *For children*

Delluc, Brigitte. Prehistoric hunters. — London : Hart-Davis Educational, May 1982. — [64]p. — (Signposts series)
Translation of: Les chasseurs de la préhistoire
ISBN 0-247-13040-0 : £3.50 : CIP entry B82-07414

930.1'01'51 — Archaeology. Applications of mathematics

Orton, Clive. Mathematics in archaeology / Clive Orton. — Cambridge : Cambridge University Press, 1982, c1980. — 248p : ill,maps ; 23cm
Originally published: London : Collins, 1980. — Bibliography: p225-240. — Includes index
ISBN 0-521-28922-x (pbk) : £5.95 : CIP rev. B82-26255

930.1'01'8 — Archaeology. Spatial analysis

Hodder, Ian. Spatial analysis in archaeology / Ian Hodder and Clive Orton. — Cambridge : Cambridge University Press, 1976 (1979 [printing]). — viii,270p : ill,maps ; 23cm. — (New studies in archaeology)
Bibliography: p249-263. — Includes index
ISBN 0-521-29738-9 (pbk) : £6.50 B82-04529

930.1'028 — Archaeology. Applications of aerial photography

Wilson, D. R.. Air photo interpretation for archaeologists. — London : Batsford, Nov.1982. — [224]p
ISBN 0-7134-1085-x : £14.95 : CIP entry B82-27965

930.1'028 — Environmental archaeological investigation. Techniques

Ganderton, Paul S.. Environmental archaeology : site methods and interpretation / by Paul S. Ganderton. — Highworth : VORDA, c1981. — 42p : ill,maps,forms ; 30cm. — (VORDA research series ; 2) (VORDA archaeological and historical publications)
Bibliography: p42
ISBN 0-907246-01-x (pbk) : Unpriced B82-25047

930.1'028 — Great Britain. Archaeology. Applications of aerial photography

Riley, D. N.. Aerial archaeology in Britain / D.N. Riley. — Princes Risborough : Shire, 1982. — 56p : ill,maps ; 21cm. — (Shire archaeology ; 22)
Bibliography: p54-55. — Includes index
ISBN 0-85263-592-3 (pbk) : £1.95 B82-39397

930.1'028'04 — Shipwrecks. Archaeological investigation — *Personal observations*

Wignall, Sydney. In search of Spanish treasure : a diver's story / Sydney Wignall. — Newton Abbot : David & Charles, c1982. — 252p : ill,maps,ports ; 24cm
Bibliography: p237-240. — Includes index
ISBN 0-7153-8244-6 : £9.50 : CIP rev. B81-33816

930.1'028'3 — Man. Bones. Excavation of remains. Techniques

Brothwell, D. R.. Digging up bones : the excavation, treatment and study of human skeletal remains / D.R. Brothwell. — 3rd ed. — London : British Museum (Natural History) : Oxford University Press, 1981. — 208p : ill ; 26cm
Previous ed.: 1972. — Bibliography: p179-199. — Includes index
ISBN 0-19-858504-7 (cased) : £16.00 : CIP rev.
ISBN 0-19-858510-1 (pbk) : Unpriced B81-30457

930.1'03'21 — Archaeology — *Encyclopaedias*

Bray, Warwick. The Penguin dictionary of archaeology / Warwick Bray, David Trump ; drawings by Judith Newcomer. — Harmondsworth : Penguin, 1982. — 283p : ill,maps ; 20cm. — (Penguin reference books)
Previous ed.: London : Allen Lane, 1970
ISBN 0-14-051116-4 (pbk) : £3.50 B82-22089

930.1'05 — Antiquities. Serials: Reliquary, *The*, *1860-1886* — *Indexes*

Riden, Philip. An index to The Reliquary : first series, volumes 1-26, 1860-86 / compiled by Philip Riden. — Matlock : Derbyshire Record Society, 1979. — 70p ; 21cm. — (Occasional paper / Derbyshire Record Society ; no.2)
Includes index
£1.00 (pbk) B82-25355

930.1'05 — Archaeology — *Serials*

Archaeological reviews from Cambridge. — Vol.1 : 1 (July '81)-. — Cambridge (c/o Dept. of Archaeology, Downing St., Cambridge) : [s.n.], 1981-. — v. : ill,maps ; 30cm
Two issues yearly
ISSN 0261-4332 = Archaeological reviews from Cambridge : £8.00 per year B82-07638

930.1'07'1041 — Great Britain. Schools. Curriculum subjects. Archaeology — *Serials* — *For teaching*

Bulletin of archaeology for schools / Council for British Archaeology. — No.1 (1977)-. — London : CBA, 1977-. — v. ; 30cm
Two issues yearly. — Bulletin of: CBA Schools Committee
ISSN 0263-0079 = Bulletin of archaeology for schools : Unpriced B82-12468

930.1'0724 — Experimental archaeology. Research — *Serials*

Bulletin of experimental archaeology. — No.1 (1980)-. — Southampton ([University Rd, Highfield, Southampton, Hants.]) : Department of Adult Education, University of Southampton, 1980-. — v. ; 30cm
Annual. — Indexes: Nos.1-2 in no.2 (1981)
ISSN 0262-4176 = Bulletin of experimental archaeology : £1.00 B82-15762

930.1'092'2 — Archaeology. Dawkins, W. Boyd & Jackson, J. Wilfrid — *Biographies*

The **Cave** hunters : biographical sketches of the lives of Sir William Boyd Dawkins (1837-1929) and Dr. J. Wilfrid Jackson (1880-1978) / edited by M.J. Bishop. — [Derby] : Derbyshire Museum Service, [1982]. — 48p : ill,ports ; 22cm
Accompanies an exhibition held at Buxton Museum, 1982. — Includes bibliographies. — Contents: Sir William Boyd Dawkins (1837-1929) / by J. Wilfrid Jackson. Originally published: in Cave science. 1966 — Dr. J. Wilfrid Jackson (1880-1978) / by Michael J. Bishop
ISBN 0-906753-02-3 (pbk) : Unpriced B82-35782

930.1'092'4 — Archaeology. Wheeler, *Sir* Mortimer — *Biographies*

Hawkes, Jacquetta. Mortimer Wheeler : adventurer in archaeology / Jacquetta Hawkes. — London : Weidenfeld and Nicolson, c1982. — xii,387p,[16]p of plates : ill,1map,1plan,ports ; 25cm
Bibliography: p378. — Includes index
ISBN 0-297-78056-5 : £10.95 B82-21124

930.1'2 — Palaeolithic civilization

Wymer, John. The palaeolithic age / John Wymer. — London : Croom Helm, c1982. — 310p,[10]p plates : ill ; 24cm. — (Croom Helm studies in archaeology)
Bibliography: p273-293. — Includes index
ISBN 0-7099-2710-x : £16.95 : CIP rev. B81-08830

931 — ANCIENT HISTORY. CHINA

931 — Ancient China — *For children*

Gibson, Michael. Ancient China. — London : Granada, July 1982. — [64]p. — (Granada guide series ; 17)
ISBN 0-246-11799-0 : £1.95 : CIP entry B82-13236

931 — Ancient Chinese antiquities

Rawson, Jessica. Ancient China : art and archaeology / Jessica Rawson. — London : Published for the Trustees of the British Museum by British Museum Publications, c1980. — 240p,[8]p of plates : ill(some col.),maps,plans ; 24cm
Bibliography: p221-228. — Includes index
ISBN 0-7141-1415-4 (cased) : £8.95 : CIP rev.
ISBN 0-7141-1414-6 (pbk) : Unpriced B80-06228

931 — China. Antiquities, *B.C.1300-A.D.900*. Excavation of remains

Qian, Hao. Out of China's earth : archaeological discovereis in the People's Republic of China / Qian Hao, Chen Heyi, and Ru Suichu. — London : Muller, 1981. — 206p : ill(some col.),1map ; 34cm
Includes index
ISBN 0-584-95003-9 : £25.00 B82-08812

931 — China. Shenshi *(Province)*. Ancient Chinese antiquities

Cotterell, Arthur. The first Emperor of China / Arthur Cotterell ; introduction by Yang Chen Ching. — London : Macmillan, 1981. — 208p,[16]p of plates : ill(some col.),maps,plans,ports ; 26cm
Ill on lining papers. — Bibliography: p198-201. — Includes index
ISBN 0-333-32444-7 : £9.95 : CIP rev.
Primary classification 931'.04'0924 B81-26749

931'.02 — Chinese civilization, *B.C. 1776-B.C. 1122*

Chang, Kwang-chih. Shang civilization. — London : Yale University Press, Aug.1982. — [417]p. — (Early Chinese civilization series)
ISBN 0-300-02885-7 (pbk) : £8.50 : CIP entry B82-26699

931'.04 — Ancient Chinese civilization, *B.C.202-A.D.220*
Wang, Zhongshu. Han civilization. — London : Yale University Press, May 1982. — [312]p. — (Chinese civilization series ; 2)
Translated from the Chinese
ISBN 0-300-02723-0 : £24.50 : CIP entry
B82-17893

931'.04 — Chinese civilization, *B.C.202-A.D.220*
Pirazzoli-t'Serstevens, Michèle. The Han civilization of China. — Oxford : Phaidon, Oct.1982. — [224]p
Translation of: La chine des Han
ISBN 0-7148-2213-2 : £40.00 : CIP entry
B82-23002

931'.04'0924 — Ancient China. Qin Shi Huang Di, *Emperor of China — Biographies*
Cotterell, Arthur. The first Emperor of China / Arthur Cotterell ; introduction by Yang Chen Ching. — London : Macmillan, 1981. — 208p,[16]p of plates : ill(some col.),maps,plans,ports ; 26cm
Ill on lining papers. — Bibliography: p198-201. — Includes index
ISBN 0-333-32444-7 : £9.95 : CIP rev.
Also classified at 931 B81-26749

932 — ANCIENT HISTORY. EGYPT

932 — Ancient Egypt. Deir el Medineh. Working classes. Social life, *ca B.C.1570-ca B.C.1075*
Bierbrier, Morris. Tomb-builders of the Pharaohs. — London : British Museum Publications, Sept.1982. — [160]p. — (A Colonnade book)
ISBN 0-7141-8044-0 : £10.95 : CIP entry
B82-22432

932 — Ancient Egypt, *to 640*
Kamil, Jill. Upper Egypt. — London : Longman, Sept.1982. — [224]p
ISBN 0-582-78314-3 (pbk) : £3.95 : CIP entry
B82-20274

932 — Ancient Egyptian civilization — *For children*
Millard, Anne. Ancient Egypt. — London : Granada, July 1982. — [64]p. — (Granada guide series ; 18)
ISBN 0-246-11798-2 : £1.95 : CIP entry
B82-13235

Ruffle, John. The ancient Egyptians / [text by John Ruffle] ; [photographs by Michael Smith]. — [Durham] ([Old Shire Hall, Durham DH1 3HP]) : Gulbenkian Museum of Oriental Art, University of Durham, 1980. — 26p : ill,1map ; 21cm
Unpriced (pbk) B82-17060

932 — Ancient Egyptian civilization — *For schools*
Crystal, David. The ancient Egyptians. — London : Edward Arnold, 1981. — 23p : ill,2maps ; 21cm. — (Databank)
Authors: David Crystal and John L. Foster. — Text on inside covers. — Includes index
ISBN 0-7131-0555-0 (pbk) : £0.90 B82-08965

932 — Egypt. Luxor. Ancient Egyptian antiquities
Kamil, Jill. Luxor : a guide to ancient Thebes. — 3rd ed. — London : Longman, Apr.1982. — [182]p
ISBN 0-582-78339-9 (pbk) : £3.95 : CIP entry
B82-04708

932 — Egypt. Qaṣr Ibrîm. Cemeteries. Ancient Nubian antiquities. Excavation of remains, *1961*
Mills, A. J.. The cemeteries of Qaṣr Ibrîm : a report of the excavations conducted by W.B. Emery in 1961. — London : Egypt Exploration Society, Jan.1982. — [94]p. — (Excavation memoirs, ISSN 0307-5109 ; 51)
ISBN 0-85698-078-1 : £60.00 : CIP entry
B81-38844

932 — Egypt. Saqqara. Ancient Egyptian tombs: Tomb of Rē-wer
el-Fikey, Said. The tomb of the Vizier Rē'-Wer at Saqqara / Said el-Fikey. — Warminster : Aris & Phillips, c1980. — viii,55p : ill,plans ; 30cm. — (Egyptology today ; no.4, 1980)
ISBN 0-85668-158-x (pbk) : £7.50 : CIP rev.
B80-02606

932'.006'041 — Ancient Egypt. Archaeological investigations. British organisations: Egyptian Exploration Society, *1882-1982*
Excavating in Egypt. — London : British Museum Publications, Feb.1982. — [192]p
ISBN 0-7141-0932-0 : £5.95 : CIP entry
B81-35829

932'.0074 — Antiquities *Ancient Egyptian — Catalogues*
British Museum. Catalogue of Egyptian antiquities in the British Museum. — London : Published for the Trustees of the British Museum by British Museum Publications
6: Jewellery I : from the earliest times to the seventeenth dynasty / by Carol A.R. Andrews ; based on material collected by Alex Wilkinson ; drawings by Marion Cox. — c1981. — 102p,48p of plates : ill ; 37cm
Includes index
ISBN 0-7141-0928-2 : £75.00 B82-39872

932'.0074'02134 — London. Camden *(London Borough).* **Museums: British Museum.** *Department of Egyptian Antiquities, to 1980*
James, T. G. H.. The British Museum and Ancient Egypt. — London : British Museum Publications, Aug.1981. — [32]p
ISBN 0-7141-0930-4 (pbk) : £3.95 : CIP entry
B81-18106

932'.0074'02142 — London. Camden *(London Borough).* **Museums: British Museum. Exhibits: Ancient Egyptian antiquities**
British Museum. Egyptian Sculpture Gallery : teachers notes / British Museum Education Service. — [London] : [British Museum Publications], [1982]. — 16,[21]leaves : ill,plans ; 30cm
Unpriced (unbound) B82-39024

932'.0074'02142 — London. Camden *(London Borough).* **Museums: British Museum. Stock: Ancient Egyptian antiquities** — *Catalogues*
British Museum. Catalogue of Egyptian antiquities in the British Museum. — London : British Museum Publications
5: Early dynastic objects. — Sept.1981. — [192]p
ISBN 0-7141-0927-4 : £25.00 : CIP entry
B81-28201

932'.0074'02716 — Cheshire. Macclesfield. Museums: Macclesfield Museum. Stock: Ancient Egyptian antiquities — *Catalogues*
David, Rosalie. The Macclesfield collection of Egyptian antiquities / Rosalie David ; with a foreword by the late C.D.F.P. Brocklehurst. — Warminster : Aris & Phillips, c1980. — vii,77p,[32]p of plates : ill ; 26cm
A collection in the Macclesfield Museum
ISBN 0-85668-129-6 : £15.00 : CIP rev.
B80-02607

932'.01'0924 — Ancient Egypt. Nefertiti, *Queen of Egypt — Biographies*
Vandenberg, Philip. Nefertiti. — London : Hodder & Stoughton, Mar.1982. — [160]p. — (Coronet books)
Originally published: 1978
ISBN 0-340-27544-8 (pbk) : £1.50 : CIP entry
B82-01100

932'.014'0924 — Ancient Egypt. Rameses II, *Pharaoh of Egypt — Biographies*
Kitchen, K. A.. Pharaoh triumphant. — Warminster : Aris and Phillips, Feb.1983. — [220]p
ISBN 0-85668-215-2 (pbk) : £12.00 : CIP entry
B82-39599

932'.022 — Ancient Egyptian civilization, *B.C.30-A.D.324*
Lewis, Naphtali. Life in Egypt under Roman rule. — Oxford : Clarendon, Feb.1983. — [256]p
ISBN 0-19-814848-8 : £12.50 : CIP entry
B82-36600

933 — ANCIENT HISTORY. PALESTINE

933 — Ancient Israel. Society
Robinson, H. Wheeler. Corporate personality in ancient Israel / H. Wheeler Robinson. — Rev. ed. — Edinburgh : T. & T. Clark, 1981. — 64p ; 22cm
Previous ed.: Philadelphia : Fortress, 1964. — Bibliography: p61-64
ISBN 0-567-29109-x (corrected : pbk) : £1.95
B82-17010

933 — Ancient Palestine. Philistine antiquities. Excavation of remains
Dothan, Trude. The Philistines and their material culture. — London : Yale University Press, July 1982. — [352]p
Translated from the Hebrew
ISBN 0-300-02258-1 : £30.00 : CIP entry
B82-22787

933 — England. Hebrew studies, *1485-1603*
Jones, G. Lloyd. The discovery of Hebrew in Tudor England. — Manchester : Manchester University Press, Aug.1982. — [300]p
ISBN 0-7190-0875-1 : £25.00 : CIP entry
B82-17976

933 — Israel *B.C.538-B.C.332*
Stern, Ephraim. The material culture of the land of the Bible in the Persian period 538-332 B.C.. — Warminster : Aris & Phillips, June 1982. — [304]p
Translation from the Hebrew
ISBN 0-85668-137-7 (pbk) : £25.00 : CIP entry
B82-12169

933 — Jordan. Jerash. Antiquities, *B.C. 150-A.D. 300*
Browning, Iain. Jerash and the Decapolis. — London : Chatto and Windus, Oct.1982. — [224]p
ISBN 0-7011-2591-8 : £10.00 : CIP entry
B82-27963

933 — Jordan. Jericho. Cultural processes, *B.C.9200-A.D.100 — Sources of data: Antiquities*
Bartlett, John R.. Jericho / John R. Bartlett. — Guildford : Lutterworth, 1982. — 128p : ill,maps,plans ; 21cm. — (Cities of the Biblical world)
Includes bibliographies and index
ISBN 0-7188-2456-3 (pbk) : £4.95 B82-21131

933 — Jordan. Khirbat Qumran. Antiquities, *B.C.125-A.D.68*
Qumrân grotte 4. — Oxford : Clarendon. — (Discoveries in the Judaean Desert ; 7)
3: (4Q482-4Q520) / par Maurice Baillet. — 1982. — xiv,339p,lxxxp of plates : ill ; 33cm
French text, index in Hebrew
ISBN 0-19-826321-x : £60.00 : CIP rev.
B81-23880

933 — Jordan. Khirbet Qumran. Cultural processes, *B.C.780-A.D.135 — Sources of data: Antiquities*
Davies, Philip R.. Qumran / Philip R. Davies. — Guildford : Lutterworth, 1982. — 128p : ill,maps,plans ; 21cm. — (Cities of the Biblical world)
Includes bibliographies and index
ISBN 0-7188-2458-x (pbk) : £4.95 B82-21129

933 — Jordan. Tell es-Sultan. Antiquities. Excavation of remains, *1952-1958*
Kenyon, Kathleen M.. Excavations at Jericho / Kathleen M. Kenyon. — London : British School of Archaeology in Jerusalem
Vol.3: The architecture and stratigraphy of the Tell / [edited by] Thomas A. Holland with contributions by R. Burleigh ... [et al.]. — 1981. — 2v. : ill,plans ; 29cm
ISBN 0-9500542-3-2 : Unpriced B82-02610

933 — Palestine. Antiquities. Archaeological investigation
Moorey, P. R. S.. Excavation in Palestine / Roger Moorey. — Guildford : Lutterworth, 1981. — 128p : ill,1map,plans ; 21cm. — (Cities of the Biblical world)
Includes bibliographies and index
ISBN 0-7188-2432-6 (pbk) : £4.95 B82-21130

933'.04 — Palestine, *B.C.150-A.D.100 — Readings from contemporary sources*

Kee, Howard Clark. The origins of Christianity : sources and documents / Howard Clark Kee. — London : S.P.C.K., 1980, c1973. — xii,270p : ill ; 24cm
Originally published: Englewood Cliffs : Prentice-Hall, 1973. — Bibliography: p266-267. — Includes index
ISBN 0-281-03791-4 (pbk) : £4.95 B82-16576

934 — ANCIENT HISTORY. INDIA

934 — Indian civilization, *to ca B.C.100*

Allchin, Bridget. The rise of civilization in India and Pakistan / Bridget and Raymond Allchin. — Cambridge : Cambridge University Press, 1982. — xiv,379p : ill,maps,plans ; 26cm. — (Cambridge world archaeology)
Bibliography: p362-371. — Includes index
ISBN 0-521-24244-4 (cased) : £25.00 : CIP rev.
ISBN 0-521-28550-x (pbk) : £8.95 B82-21722

934 — Pakistan. Peshawar Valley. Buddhist antiquities. Excavation of remains

Zwalf, W.. The shrines of Gandhara / W. Zwalf. — London : British Museum Publications, c1979. — 32p : ill,1map,1plan ; 24cm
Cover title. — Bibliography: p32
ISBN 0-7141-1416-2 (pbk) : Unpriced
B82-12226

934'.01 — Harappan civilization

The **Harappan** civilisation. — Warminster : Aris & Phillips, June 1982. — [430]p
ISBN 0-85668-211-x : £16.00 : CIP entry
B82-12170

934'.01 — Lower Palaeolithic & Iron Age Indian civilization. Archaeological sources

Agrawal, D. P.. The archaeology of India / D.P. Agrawal. — London : Curzon, 1982. — 294p : ill,maps,1plan ; 23cm. — (Scandinavian Institute of Asian Studies monograph series, ISSN 0069-1712 ; no.46)
Bibliography: p281-290. — Includes index
ISBN 0-7007-0140-0 (pbk) : Unpriced : CIP rev. B82-08406

935 — ANCIENT HISTORY. NEAR EAST

935 — Ancient Mesopotamian antiquities. Excavation of remains, *1932-1982*

British School of Archaeology in Iraq. Fifty years of Mesopotamian discovery : the work of the British School of Archaeology in Iraq 1932-1982 / with an introduction by Seton Lloyd ; edited by John Curtis. — London : British School of Archaeology in Iraq, c1982. — 123p,[8]p of plates : ill(some col.),maps,plans ; 25cm
ISBN 0-903472-05-8 (pbk) : Unpriced
B82-35577

935 — Iraq. Ur. Antiquities. Excavation of remains, *1922-ca 1935*

Woolley, *Sir* Leonard. Ur 'of the Chaldees'. — Rev. ed. — London (65 Belsize Lane, NW3 5AU) : Herbert Press, Apr.1982. — [256]p
Previous ed.: 1954
ISBN 0-906969-21-2 : £3.95 : CIP entry
B82-04721

935'.05 — Iran, *B.C.560-B.C.330*

Cook, J. M.. The Persian Empire. — London : Dent, Jan.1983. — [320]p
ISBN 0-460-04448-6 : £12.95 : CIP entry
B82-34611

935'.05'0924 — Ancient Iran. Army operations by Ancient Greek mercenaries, *B.C.401-B.C.399 — Personal observations — Greek texts*

Xenophon. [Anabasis. Selections]. The Persian expedition / Xenophon ; text, with introduction and notes by Jeremy Antrich and Stephen Usher. — Bristol : Bristol Classical Press, [1981?]. — 200p : ill,maps,plans ; 21cm
Classical Greek text with English introduction and summaries. — Bibliography: p198-200
ISBN 0-906515-11-4 (pbk) : Unpriced
B82-05337

936 — ANCIENT HISTORY. EUROPE NORTH AND WEST OF ITALIAN PENINSULA

936 — North-western Europe. Megalithic monuments. Scientific aspects

Heggie, Douglas C.. Megalithic science : ancient mathematics and astronomy in North-West Europe / Douglas C. Heggie. — London : Thames and Hudson, c1981. — 256p : ill,maps,plans ; 25cm
Bibliography: p248-251. — Includes index
ISBN 0-500-05036-8 : £12.00 B82-04002

936 — Western Europe. Megalithic monuments. Theories, *to 1981*

Michell, John. Megalithomania : artists, antiquarians and archaeologists at the old stone monuments / John Michell ; with 220 illustrations, 8 in colour. — London : Thames and Hudson, c1982. — 156,[10]p : ill(some col.),1map,ports ; 25cm
Includes index
ISBN 0-500-01261-x : £8.50 B82-19969

936.1 — Great Britain. Antiquities. Excavation of remains & preservation

Our past before us : why do we save it? / edited by David Lowenthal and Marcus Binney. — London : Temple Smith, 1981. — 253p : ill ; 22cm
Includes bibliographies and index
ISBN 0-85117-219-9 (pbk) : £6.00 : CIP rev.
B81-28563

936.1 — Great Britain, *B.C.55-A.D.410 — For schools*

Farnworth, Warren. Roman Britain. — London : Bell & Hyman, Jan.1982. — [80]p. — (History around us)
Originally published: London : Mills & Boon, 1980
ISBN 0-7135-2112-0 (pbk) : £3.95 : CIP entry
B82-01337

936.1 — Great Britain. Celtic antiquities, *ca B.C.700-ca A.D.800*

Laing, Lloyd. Celtic Britain / Lloyd Laing. — London : Granada, 1981, c1979. — 254p : ill,maps ; 20cm. — (Britain before the conquest) (A Paladin book)
Originally published: London : Routledge & Kegan Paul, 1979. — Bibliography: p245-247. — Includes index
ISBN 0-586-08373-1 (pbk) : £2.50 B82-04013

936.1'003'21 — Great Britain. Archaeology — *Encyclopaedias*

Adkins, Lesley. A thesaurus of British archaeology / Lesley Adkins & Roy A. Adkins. — Newton Abbot : David & Charles, c1982. — 319p : ill,maps,plans ; 24cm
Bibliography: p285-296. — Includes index
ISBN 0-7153-7864-3 : £14.95 : CIP rev.
B81-30388

936.1'009'732 — Great Britain. Ancient Roman towns

Wacher, John. The towns of Roman Britain / John Wacher. — London : Batsford, 1975, c1974 (1978 [printing]). — 460p : ill,maps ; 25cm
Includes index
ISBN 0-7134-2790-6 (pbk) : £9.50 B82-07317

936.1'009'732 — Great Britain. Towns. Archaeological investigation — *Conference proceedings*

Environmental archaeology in the urban context. — London : Council for British Archaeology, Apr.1982. — [144]p. — (CBA research report, ISSN 0589-9036 ; 43)
Conference proceedings
ISBN 0-906780-12-8 (pbk) : £12.50 : CIP entry
B82-09195

936.1'01 — Great Britain. Prehistoric antiquities, *to ca B.C.1000*

Laing, Lloyd. The origins of Britain / Lloyd and Jennifer Laing. — London : Granada, 1982, c1980. — 256p : ill,1map ; 20cm. — (Britain before the conquest)
Originally published: London : Routledge and Kegan Paul, 1980. — Bibliography: p251-252. — Includes index
ISBN 0-586-08370-7 (pbk) : £2.50 B82-22253

936.1'01 — Great Britain, *to B.C.700 — For schools*

Herdman, Margaret. Hunters and early farmers in Britain / Margaret Herdman. — London : Harrap, 1982. — 48p : ill,2maps,2plans ; 19x21cm. — (History in evidence)
Cover title. — Text and ill on inside covers
ISBN 0-245-53564-0 (pbk) : £1.65 B82-31016

936.1'04 — Great Britain, *B.C.55-A.D.410*

Wacher, John. The coming of Rome / John Wacher. — London : Granada, 1981, c1979. — 255p : ill,maps ; 20cm. — (Britain before the conquest) (A Paladin book)
Originally published: London : Routledge & Kegan Paul, 1979. — Bibliography: p243-247. — Includes index
ISBN 0-586-08369-3 (pbk) : £2.50 B82-04011

936.1'04 — Great Britain. Social life, *43-410 — For schools*

Bodey, Hugh. Roman people / Hugh Bodey. — London : Batsford Academic and Educational, 1981. — 72p : ill,maps ; 26cm. — (People in period)
Bibliography: p70-71. — Includes index
ISBN 0-7134-3568-2 : £5.95 B82-06274

Roman Britain. — [Stockport] ([c/o Town Hall, Stockport SK1 3XE]) : Stockport Museum Education Service, [1981?]. — 1portfolio : ill,1map ; 30cm
ISBN 0-905164-40-7 : £0.75 B82-05275

936.1'04'0924 — Great Britain. Agricola, Gnaeus Julius. Biographies: Tacitus, Cornelius. Agricola — *Critical studies*

Soulsby, D. E.. Selections from Tacitus, Agricola : handbook / D.E. Soulsby. — Cambridge : Cambridge University Press, 1982. — 50p ; 22cm. — (Cambridge Latin texts)
ISBN 0-521-20488-7 (pbk) : £3.25 B82-23610

936.1'1'006 — Scotland. Archaeology. Organisations: Society of Antiquaries of Scotland, *to 1980 — Festschriften*

The **Scottish** antiquarian tradition : essays to mark the bicentenary of the Society of Antiquaries of Scotland and its museum, 1780-1980 / edited by A.S. Bell. — Edinburgh : Donald, c1981. — x,286p,[9]p of plates : ill,1coat of arms,ports ; 25cm
Includes bibliographies and index
ISBN 0-85976-080-4 : £15.00 B82-24852

936.1'101 — Scotland, *to 500B.C.*

Piggott, Stuart. Scotland before history. — Edinburgh : Edinburgh University Press, Sept.1982. — [208]p
ISBN 0-85224-348-0 (pbk) : £5.75 : CIP entry
B82-25940

936.1'104'0924 — Scotland. Army operations by Ancient Roman armies. Role of Agricola, Gnaeus Julius

Scottish Archaeological Forum *(12th : 1980 : University of Edinburgh)*. Agricola's campaigns in Scotland : Scottish Archaeological Forum 12 / edited by James Kenworthy. — Edinburgh : Edinburgh University Press, c1981. — 114p : ill,maps,plans ; 24cm
Includes bibliographies
ISBN 0-85224-418-5 : £4.00 B82-12030

936.1'11'00723 — Northern Scotland. Antiquities. Sites. Field surveys

Archaeological field survey in Northern Scotland. — [Edinburgh] ([Edinburgh EH8 9YL]) : [University of Edinburgh, Department of Archaeology]
Vol.2: 1980-1981 / by R.J. Mercer. — 1981. — viii leaves, 170p,[1]folded leaf of plates : ill,maps,2plans ; 30cm. — (Occasional paper / University of Edinburgh Department of Archaeology, ISSN 0144-3313 ; no.7)
Bibliography: p168-170
Unpriced (pbk) B82-00681

936.1'132 — Scotland. Orkney. Birsay. Antiquities. Excavation of remains, *1934-1974*

Curle, C. L.. Pictish and Norse finds from the Brough of Birsay 1934-74. — Edinburgh (c/o National Museum of Antiquities of Scotland, Queen St., Edinburgh) : Society of Antiquaries of Scotland, July 1982. — [140]p. — (Society of Antiquaries of Scotland monograph series, ISSN 0263-3191 ; 1)
ISBN 0-903903-01-6 (pbk) : £14.95 : CIP entry
B82-25098

936.1'14 — Scotland. Western Isles. Isle of Lewis. Achmore. Megalithic circles. Excavation of remains

Ponting, Margaret. Achmore stone circle / by Margaret & Gerald Ponting. — Callanish : G. & M. Ponting, 1981. — 57p,[1]folded leaf of plates : ill,maps,plans,ports ; 30cm
Cover title. — Limited ed. of 200 copies. — Text on inside covers. — Bibliography: p57
ISBN 0-9505998-3-2 (pbk) : £2.00 B82-12080

936.1'28 — Scotland. Tayside Region. Kinross region. Archaeology. Organisations: Kinross-shire Antiquarian Society, *to 1981*

Kinross-shire Antiquarian Society. An account of the first twenty-one years of the Kinross-shire Antiquarian Society. — Kinross ([Lynallan, Kinnesswood, KV13 7HN]) : Kinross-shire Antiquarian Society, c1981. — 24p ; 30cm
Unpriced (pbk) B82-26991

936.1'292 — Scotland. Fife Region. Crail. Archaeological investigation — *Proposals*

Simpson, Anne Turner. Historic Crail : the archaeological implications of development / Anne Turner Simpson, Sylvia Stevenson. — [Glasgow] : Department of Archaeology, University of Glasgow, 1981. — 26leaves,[3] leaves of plates(some col.) : maps,1coat of arms ; 30cm. — (Scottish burgh survey)
Bibliography: leaves 24-26
Unpriced (pbk) B82-15259

936.1'33 — Scotland. Lothian Region. Linlithgow. Archaeological investigation — *Proposals*

Simpson, Anne Turner. Historic Linlithgow : the archaeological implications of development / Anne Turner Simpson, Sylvia Stevenson. — [Glasgow] : Department of Archaeology, University of Glasgow, 1981. — 31leaves,[3] leaves of plates(some folded) : maps,1coat of arms ; 30cm. — (Scottish burgh survey)
Bibliography: leaves 29-31
Unpriced (pbk) B82-15256

936.1'36 — Scotland. Lothian Region. Dunbar. Archaeological investigation — *Proposals*

Simpson, Anne Turner. Historic Dunbar : the archaeological implications of development / Anne Turner Simpson, Sylvia Stevenson. — [Glasgow] ([The University, Glasgow, G12 8QG]) : Department of Archaeology, University of Glasgow, 1981. — 27leaves,[3] leaves of plates(some folded) : maps,coat of arms ; 30cm. — (Scottish burgh survey)
Bibliography: p26-27
Unpriced (pbk) B82-00738

936.1'423 — Scotland. Strathclyde Region. Argyll and Bute *(District).* **Antiquities**

Argyll : an inventory of the monuments / the Royal Commission of the Ancient and Historical Monuments of Scotland. — [Edinburgh] : H.M.S.O.
Vol.4: Iona. — 1982. — xvi,296p,[7]folded p of plates : ill,maps(some col.),plans(some col.) ; 29cm
Maps on lining papers. — Bibliography: p259-264. — Includes index
ISBN 0-11-491728-0 : £45.00 B82-34393

Royal Commission on the Ancient and Historical Monuments of Scotland. The ancient and historical monuments of Argyll / The Royal Commission on the Ancient and Historical Monuments of Scotland. — Edinburgh : H.M.S.O.. — (Cmnd. ; 8420) (Report ; 22)
Vol.4: Iona. — [1982]. — 3p ; 25cm
ISBN 0-10-184200-7 (unbound) : £1.25
B82-29622

936.1'423 — Scotland. Strathclyde Region. Mid Argyll. Antiquities

Mackenna, F. S.. Unfamiliar sites in Mid-Argyll / F.S. Mackenna. — [Curran] ([c/o Secretary, Harbain House, Curran, Argyll]) : Natural History & Antiquarian Society of Mid-Argyll, 1982. — [28]p : ill ; 23cm
Cover title. — Text and ill on inside covers
Unpriced (pbk) B82-24437

936.1'461 — Scotland. Strathclyde Region. Irvine. Archaeological investigation — *Proposals*

Simpson, Anne Turner. Historic Irvine : the archaeological implications of development / Anne Turner Simpson, Sylvia Stevenson. — [Glasgow] : Department of Archaeology, University of Glasgow, 1980. — 27leaves,[3] leaves of plates(some col.) : maps,1coat of arms ; 30cm. — (Scottish burgh survey)
Bibliography: leaves 25-26
Unpriced (pbk) B82-15258

936.1'461 — Scotland. Strathclyde Region. Kilwinning. Archaeological investigation — *Proposals*

Simpson, Anne Turner. Historic Kilwinning : the archaeological implications of development / Anne Turner Simpson, Sylvia Stevenson. — [Glasgow] : Department of Archaeology, University of Glasgow, 1981. — 18leaves,[3] leaves of plates (some col.) : maps,1coat of arms ; 30cm. — (Scottish burgh survey)
Bibliography: leaves 17-18
Unpriced (pbk) B82-15257

936.1'483 — Scotland. Dumfries and Galloway Region. Annan. Archaeological investigation — *Proposals*

Simpson, Anne Turner. Historic Annan : the archaeological implications of development / Anne Turner Simpson, Sylvia Stevenson. — [Glasgow] ([The University, Glasgow, G12 8QG]) : Department of Archaeology, University of Glasgow, 1981. — 27leaves,[3] leaves of plates(some folded) : maps,coat of arms ; 30cm. — (Scottish burgh survey)
Bibliography: p25-27
Unpriced (pbk) B82-00739

936.1'483 — Scotland. Dumfries and Galloway Region. Upper Eskdale. Antiquities — *Lists*

The **Archaeological** sites and monuments of Upper Eskdale, Annanda and Eskdale District Dumfries and Galloway Region / [Society of Antiquaries of Scotland, Archaeological Field Survey]. — [Edinburgh] ([54 Melville St., Edinburgh EH3 7HF]) : [Royal Commission on the Ancient and Historical Monuments of Scotland], [1980]. — 28p,[3]leaves of plates (some folded) : maps ; 30cm
Bibliography: p27-28
Unpriced (pbk) B82-23437

936.2'01 — Dorset. Simons Ground. Bronze age burials. Archaeological investigation

White, D. A.. The Bronze Age cremation cemeteries at Simons Ground, Dorset. — Dorchester (Dorset County Museum, High West St., Dorchester, Dorset DT1 1AX) : Dorset Natural History and Archaeological Society, June 1982. — [72]p. — (Dorset Natural History & Archaeological Society monograph ; no.3)
ISBN 0-900341-11-4 (pbk) : £6.50 : CIP entry
B82-10888

936.2'02 — England. Celtic civilization, *ca B.C.55 — For schools*

Reynolds, Peter J.. Cassivellaunus, the Celtic king / by Peter Reynolds ; illustrated by Peter Kesteven. — Cambridge : Cambridge University Press, 1980. — 1case : ill(some col.),1col.map ; 25cm. — (History first)
Contents: Cassivellaunus — Caesar's landing — Danebury — Teacher's notes — 12 work cards
ISBN 0-521-22557-4 : £4.50
ISBN 0-521-22557-4 (work cards)
ISBN 0-521-22554-x (Caesar's landing)
ISBN 0-521-22555-8 (Danebury)
ISBN 0-521-22556-6 (Cassivellaunus)
B82-40287

936.2'04 — England. Military campaigns by Ancient Roman military forces, *48-58*

Webster, Graham. Rome against Caratacus : the Roman campaigns in Britain AD48-58 / [Graham Webster]. — London : Batsford, 1981. — 181p,16p of plates : ill,maps,plans ; 24cm
Includes index
ISBN 0-7134-3627-1 : £9.95 : CIP rev.
B81-30359

936.2'104 — London, *43-592*

Morris, John, *d. 1977.* Londinivm : London in the Roman empire / John Morris ; revised by Sarah Macready. — London : Weidenfeld and Nicolson, c1982. — xvi,384p,[8]p of plates : ill,maps,plans,ports ; 24cm
Bibliography: p363-368. — Includes index
ISBN 0-297-78093-x : £15.00 B82-20425

936.2'192 — London. Sutton *(London Borough).* **Beddington, Carshalton & Wallington. Antiquities. Archaeological investigation**

The **Past**, our future : studies in local archaeology and history presented to Keith Pryer on the occasion of the diamond jubilee of Beddington, Carshalton and Wallington Archaeological Society / edited by Clive Orton. — [Sutton] : [The Society], c1980. — 48p : ill,maps,plans,1port ; 25cm. — (Beddington, Carshalton and Wallington Archaeological Society occasional paper, ISSN 0307-5710 ; no.4)
Bibliography: p47-48
ISBN 0-9501481-3-x (pbk) : Unpriced
B82-20797

936.2'23 — East Kent. Ancient Roman settlements

Scoffham, Stephen. The Romans in East Kent : a brief guide / by Stephen Scoffham. — [Maidstone] : North Kent, [1982?]. — 34p : ill,1facsim,maps ; 21cm
Bibliography: p30-32
ISBN 0-9505733-7-x (pbk) : Unpriced
B82-35628

936.22'3 — Kent. Antiquities. Archaeological investigation — *Festschriften — Conference proceedings*

Archaeology in Kent to AD 1500. — London : Council for British Archaeology, Sept.1982. — [106]p. — (Research report / Council for British Archaeology, ISSN 0589-9036 ; no.48)
Conference papers
ISBN 0-906780-18-7 (pbk) : £14.00 : CIP entry
B82-23854

936.2'259'005 — East Sussex. Hastings. Archaeology — *Serials*

[News letter and journal *(Hastings Area Archaeological Research Group)*]. News letter and journal / Hastings Area Archaeological Research Group. — Vol.1, no.1 [(198-?)]-. — [Hastings] : c/o Priory Road Adult Education Centre, [Hastings, E. Sussex] : The Group, [198-?]-. — v. : ill,maps ; 30cm
Description based on: Vol.2, no.4 (Oct. 1981)-
ISSN 0263-6108 = News letter and journal - Hastings Area Archaeological Research Group : Unpriced B82-23589

936.2'27 — Hampshire. Antiquities — *Lists*

Hampshire treasures survey. — [Winchester] ([County Planning Officer, The Castle, Winchester, Hants.]) : [Hampshire County Council]
Vol.1: Winchester City district. — [1979]. — vi,343p,[10]leaves of plates : ill,1map ; 29cm
Unpriced (pbk) B82-11893

Hampshire treasures survey. — [Winchester] ([County Planning Officer, The Castle, Winchester, Hants.]) : [Hampshire County Council]
Vol.2: Basingstoke and Deane. — [1979]. — vi,359p,[28]leaves of plates : ill,1map ; 29cm
£4.00 (pbk) B82-11892

Hampshire treasures survey. — [Winchester] ([County Planning Officer, The Castle, Winchester, Hants.]) : [Hampshire County Council]
Vol.3: Hart and Rushmoor. — [1980]. — v,225p,[23]leaves of plates : ill,1map ; 29cm
Unpriced (pbk) B82-11894

936.2'27 — Hampshire. Antiquities — *Lists*
continuation

Hampshire treasures survey. — [Winchester] ([County Planning Officer, The Castle, Winchester, Hants.]) : [Hampshire County Council]
Vol.4: Winchester. — [1980]. — v,133p,[56]p of plates : ill,maps(some col.) ; 29cm
£4.95 (pbk) B82-11895

Hampshire treasures survey. — [Winchester] ([County Planning Officer, The Castle, Winchester, Hants.]) : [Hampshire County Council]
Vol.5: New Forest. — [1981]. — vi,324p,[22] leaves of plates : ill,1map ; 29cm
Unpriced (pbk) B82-11896

Hampshire treasures survey. — [Winchester] : Hampshire County Council
Vol.6: East Hampshire. — 1982. — vi,331p : ill,1map ; 29cm
ISBN 0-900908-72-6 (pbk) : Unpriced
B82-32497

936.2'29 — Berkshire. Berkshire Downs. Archaeological investigations — *Proposals*

Richards, Julian C.. The archaeology of the Berkshire downs : an introductory survey / Julian C. Richards. — Reading : [Berkshire Archaeological Unit], 1978. — iv,95p : ill,maps (some col.) ; 30cm. — (Berkshire Archaeological Committee publication ; no.3)
Ill on inside covers. — Bibliography: p85-87
ISBN 0-904989-02-x (pbk) : Unpriced
B82-07275

936.2'312 — Wiltshire. Nettleton. Ancient Roman shrines: Shrine of Apollo. Excavation of remains

Wedlake, W. J.. The excavation of the shrine of Apollo at Nettleton, Wiltshire, 1956-1971 / by W.J. Wedlake with contributions by the late D.F. Allen ... [et al.]. — London : Society of Antiquaries of London, 1982. — xx,267p,47p of plates : ill(some col.),maps,ports ; 28cm. — (Reports of the Research Committee of the Society of Antiquaries of London ; no.40)
ISBN 0-500-99032-8 : £30.00 B82-35977

936.2'319 — Wiltshire. Amesbury. Megalithic henge monuments: Stonehenge

Shaw, Philip. The hidden face of Stonehenge : new avenues upon an old mystery / by Philip Shaw. — Bognor Regis : New Horizon, c1982. — 194p,[6]p of plates : ill,charts,maps,plans ; 21cm
Bibliography: p193-194. — Includes index
ISBN 0-86116-557-8 : £6.25 B82-37770

936.2'33 — Dorset. Rural regions. Antiquities. Archaeological investigation

Groube, Les. The archaeology of rural Dorset. — Dorchester : Dorset Natural History and Archaeological Society, Oct.1982. — [52]p. — (Dorset Natural History and Archaeological Society monograph series ; no.4)
ISBN 0-900341-12-2 (pbk) : £5.50 : CIP entry
B82-24622

936.2'3301 — Dorset. Burial places: Barrows

Grinsell, L. V.. Dorset barrows supplement. — Dorchester (Dorset County Museum, High West St., Dorchester DT1 1XA) : Dorset Natural History and Archaeological Society, Oct.1982. — [48]p
ISBN 0-900341-14-9 (pbk) : £3.00 : CIP entry
B82-24749

936.2'331 — Dorset. Dorchester. Antiquities. Excavations of remains

Dorchester excavations. — Dorchester : Dorset Natural History and Archaeological Society. — (Dorset Natural History and Archaeological Society monograph series ; no.2)
Vol.1: Excavations at Wadham House 1968, Dorchester Prison 1970, 1975 and 1978, and Glyde Path Road 1966 / by Jo Draper and Christopher Chaplin with contributions by Hedley Pengelly and Elizabeth Watkins. — 1982. — vi,112p : ill,1map,plans ; 30cm
Bibliography: p111-112
ISBN 0-900341-10-6 (pbk) : Unpriced : CIP rev. B82-02476

936.2'339 — Dorset. Christchurch. Archaeological investigation, *1969-1980*

Jarvis, K. S.. Excavations in Christchurch 1969-1980. — Dorchester : Dorset Natural History & Archaeological Society, Feb.1983. — [160]p. — (Dorset Natural History and Archaeological Society monographs ; 5)
ISBN 0-900341-18-1 (pbk) : £12.00 : CIP entry
B82-36340

936.2'353 — Devon. Dartmoor. Antiquities. Archaeological investigation

Price, D. G.. Dartmoor's past in the present : some research problems / D.G. Price. — London : Polytechnic of Central London, School of Social Sciences and Business Studies, 1981. — 23p ; 30cm. — (Research working paper / Polytechnic of Central London. School of Social Sciences and Business Studies ; no.14)
Unpriced (spiral) B82-11601

936.2'3701 — Cornwall. Megalithic monuments

Barnatt, John. Prehistoric Cornwall : the ceremonial monuments / by John Barnatt. — Wellingborough : Turnstone, 1982. — 288p : ill,maps,plans ; 22cm
Bibliography: p277-283. — Includes index
ISBN 0-85500-129-1 (pbk) : £4.95 : CIP rev.
B82-07030

936.2'375 — Cornwall. Penwith *(District).* **Megalithic monuments**

Michell, John. The old stones of Land's End : an enquiry into the mysteries of the megalithic science / John Michell. — [New ed.]. — Bristol (6, Perry Rd., Bristol 1) : Pentacle, 1979. — 95p : ill,charts,maps,1plan,ports ; 21cm. — (Ley hunter's library ; 3)
Previous ed.: Port Eliot, Cornwall : Elephant ; London : Garnstone, 1974. — Bibliography: p95
Unpriced (pbk) B82-32040

936.2'379 — Isles of Scilly. Antiquities — *Lists*

Russell, Vivien. Isles of Scilly Survey / Vivien Russell. — St Mary's ([Church St., St Mary's, Isles of Scilly]) : Isles of Scilly Museum and Institute of Cornish Studies, 1980. — 61p ; 16x21cm. — (Parochial checklist survey ; 2)
Bibliography: p8-9
ISBN 0-903686-29-5 (pbk) : Unpriced
B82-18610

936.2'381 — Somerset. Bridgewater region. Archaeology — *Serials*

[Report *(Bridgwater & District Archaeological Society)***]**. Report / Bridgwater & District Archaeological Society. — 1981-. — [Bridgwater] ([6 Greenacre, Wembdon, Bridgwater, Somerset TA6 7RD]) : The Society, 1981-. — v. : ill,maps,plans ; 21cm
ISSN 0263-7014 = Report - Bridgwater & District Archaeological Society : £1.25
B82-31720

936.2'39'005 — Avon. Antiquities. Archaeological investigation — *Serials*

BAARG bulletin. — No.4 (Spring 1981)-. — Bristol (Bristol Museum, Queen's Rd, Bristol BS8 1RL) : Bristol and Avon Archaeological Research Group, 1981-. — v. ; 30cm
Continues: BARG bulletin. — Description based on: No.5 (Autumn 1981)
ISSN 0262-9828 = BAARG bulletin : Free to Group members B82-12472

936.2'391 — Avon. Cattybrook. Romano-British antiquities. Excavation of remains

Bennett, Julian. A Romano-British settlement at Cattybrook, Almondsbury, Avon / Julian Bennett. — Bristol (The Archaeological Centre, Mark La,, Bristol BS1 4XR) : Committee for Rescue Archaeology in Avon, Gloucestershire and Somerset, c1980. — p159-181 : ill,plans ; 30cm. — (Occasional papers ; no.5)
Cover title. — Bibliography: p181
Unpriced (pbk) B82-35985

936.2'396 — Avon. Weston-super-Mare. Iron Age hill forts: Worlebury. Excavation of remains, *1851-1881*

Evans, Jane, *1937-*. Worlebury : the story of the Iron Age hill-fort at Weston-super-Mare / [text compiled by Jane Evans]. — Weston-super-Mare (Town Hall, Weston-super-Mare [Avon BSQ3 1UJ]) : Woodspring District Council, Leisure Services Department, 1980. — 20p : ill ; 15x21cm
Cover title. — Ill on inside cover. — Bibliography: p20
£0.50 (pbk) B82-16525

936.2'4104 — Gloucestershire, *43-410*

McWhirr, Alan. Roman Gloucestershire / Alan McWhirr. — Gloucester : Sutton, 1981. — 183p : ill,maps,plans ; 23cm
Bibliography: p173-175. — Includes index
ISBN 0-904387-63-1 (cased) : £7.95 : CIP rev.
ISBN 0-904387-60-7 (pbk) : unpriced
B81-19123

936.2'417 — Gloucestershire. Guiting Power. Iron Age settlements. Excavation of remains

Saville, Alan. Excavations at Guiting Power Iron Age site, Gloucestershire, 1974 / Alan Saville. — Bristol (The Archaeological Centre, Mark La., Bristol BS1 4XR) : Council for Rescue Archaeology in Avon, Gloucestershire and Somerset, c1979. — p125-153,[3]p of plates : ill,maps,plans ; 30cm. — (Occasional papers ; no.7)
Cover title. — Bibliography: p150-152
Unpriced (pbk) B82-35987

936.2'417 — Gloucestershire. Lower Swell. Burial places: Bronze Age barrows. Excavation of remains

Saville, Alan. Recent work at Cow Common Bronze Age cemetery, Gloucestershire / Alan Saville. — Bristol (The Archaeological Centre, Mark La., Bristol BS1 4XR) : Committee for Rescue Archaeology in Avon, Gloucesershire and Somerset, c1979. — p83-119,[3]p of plates : ill,maps,plans ; 30cm. — (Occasional papers ; no.6)
Cover title. — Bibliography: p117-119
Unpriced (pbk) B82-35986

936.2'446 — Hereford and Worcester. Hereford. Antiquities. Excavation of remains

Shoesmith, R.. Hereford City excavations. — London : Council for British Archaeology
Vol.2: Excavations on and close to the defences. — July 1982. — [120]p. — (CBA research report, ISSN 0589-9036 ; 46)
ISBN 0-906780-16-0 : £14.50 : CIP entry
ISBN 0-900312-95-5 (set) : Unpriced
B82-21740

936.2'513 — Derbyshire. Hathersage, *ca B.C.100-B.C.75*

Tomlinson, Tom D.. Hathersage in prehistoric times / by Tom D. Tomlinson. — [Hathersage] : Hathersage Parochial Church Council, c1981. — 11p : ill ; 21cm
ISBN 0-907602-07-x (pbk) : £0.50 B82-06890

936.2'534 — Lincolnshire. Lincoln. Ancient Roman fortifications. Excavation of remains, *1938-1979*

Jones, M. J. (Michael John), *1938-*. The defences of the upper Roman enclosure / Michael J. Jones with Margaret J. Darling ... [et al.] ; final drawings by Carol Peel. — London : Council for British Archaeology for the Lincoln Archaeological Trust, 1980. — 62p,[1] folded leaf of plates : ill,2maps,plans ; 30cm. — (The Archaeology of Lincoln ; v.VII-1)
English text, English, French and German summaries. — Text on inside front cover. — Bibliography: p62
ISBN 0-906780-00-4 (pbk) : Unpriced
B82-17617

936.2'54 — Leicestershire. Antiquities. Archaeological investigation

Liddle, Peter, *1951-*. Leicestershire archaeology : the present state of knowledge / by Peter Liddle. — Leicester : Leicestershire Museums, Art Galleries and Records Service. — (Leicestershire Museums publication ; no.31) (Archaeological reports series ; no.4)
Vol.1: To the end of the Roman period. — 1982. — 52p : ill,maps ; 30cm
Bibliography: p48-52
ISBN 0-85022-103-x (pbk) : Unpriced
B82-34398

936.2′545 — Leicestershire. Whitwell. Romano-British antiquities. Excavation of remains

Todd, Malcolm, *1939-*. The Iron Age and Roman settlement at Whitnell, Leicestershire / by Malcolm Todd. — [Leicester] : Leicestershire Museums, Art Galleries and Records Service, 1981. — 44p : ill,maps,plans ; 30cm. — (Archaeological reports series / Leicestershire Museums, Art Galleries and Records Service ; no.1)
Ill on inside covers
ISBN 0-85022-088-2 (pbk) : £1.50 B82-14657

936.2′546 — Leicestershire. Eaton & Sproxton. Burial places: Bronze age barrows. Excavation of remains

Clay, Patrick. Two multi-phase barrow sites at Sproxton and Eaton, Leicestershire / by Patrick Clay. — [Leicester] : Leicestershire Museums, Art Galleries and Records Service, [1981]. — 48p : ill,maps,plans ; 30cm. — (Archaeological reports series / Leicestershire Museums, Art Galleries and Records Service ; no.2)
Ill on inside covers. — Bibliography: p45-46
ISBN 0-85022-095-5 (pbk) : £1.50 B82-14658

936.2′55 — Northamptonshire. Antiquities

An **inventory** of the historical monuments in the County of Northampton / Royal Commission on Historical Monuments (England). — London : H.M.S.O.
Vol.4: Archaeological sites in Northamptonshire. — 1982. — xxii,226p,8p of plates : ill,maps(some col.),plans ; 28cm
Map on folded sheet 77x83cm folded to 19x85cm in pocket. — Includes index
ISBN 0-11-700997-0 : £40.00 (red binding) : Unpriced B82-34394

936.2′55 — Northamptonshire. Nene Valley. Iron Age settlements & Ancient Roman settlements

Windell, David. The Upper Nene valley in the Iron Age and Roman periods : Upper Nene 400BC-400AD / compiled by David Windell. — [Northampton] : Northamptonshire County Council, [1981]. — 23p : ill,col.maps,plans ; 22x30cm
Compiled for the County′s Archaeology Unit
ISBN 0-9500633-8-x (unbound) : £1.00 B82-09551

936.2′574 — Oxfordshire. Oxford region. Antiquities. Excavation of remains, *1950-ca 1965*

Settlement patterns in the Oxford region. — London : Council for British Archaeology, Sept.1982. — [160]p. — (CBA research report, ISSN 0589-9036 ; 44)
ISBN 0-906780-14-4 (pbk) : £20.00 : CIP entry B82-20789

936.2′583 — Hertfordshire. Puckeridge. Skeleton Green. Romano-British antiquities. Excavation of remains, *1971-1972*

Partridge, Clive. Skeleton Green a Late Iron Age and Romano-British site / by Clive Partridge with contributions from R. Ashdown ... [et al.]. — London : Society for the Promotion of Roman Studies, 1981. — 359p,[12]p of plates : ill,maps,plans ; 30cm. — (Britannia monograph series ; no.2)
Bibliography: p15-21. — Includes index
ISBN 0-907764-00-2 (pbk) : Unpriced B82-14483

936.2′6 — East Anglia. Antiquities. Archaeological investigation

East Anglian archaeology. — Dereham : Norfolk Archaeological Unit
Report no.11: Norfolk
Spong Hill
Pt.2. — 1981. — viii,287p,[10]p of plates : ill ; 30cm
Bibliography: p26. — Includes index
Unpriced (pbk) B82-12729

East Anglian archaeology. — Dereham (Union House, Gressenhall, Dereham, Norfolk NR20 4DR) : Norfolk Archaeological Unit
Report no.14: Norfolk
Trowse, Horning, deserted medieval villages, Kings Lynn / [editor Peter Wade-Martins]. — 1982. — viii,133p,[30]p of plates (some col.) : ill,maps,plans ; 30cm
Includes bibliographies and index
Unpriced (pbk) B82-34395

936.2′614 — Norfolk. Weeting. Prehistoric flint mines: Grimes Graves. Excavation of remains, *1971-1972*

Grimes Graves, Norfolk : excavations 1971-72. — London : H.M.S.O.. — (Department of the Environment archaeological reports ; no.11)
Vol.2. — 1981. — ix,182p,1folded leaf of plate : ill ; 30cm
Bibliography: p177-178. — Includes index. — Contents: Summary of the excavations / R.J. Mercer — The flint assemblage / A. Saville
ISBN 0-11-671084-5 (pbk) : £19.00 B82-06089

936.2′651 — Cambridgeshire. Fengate. Antiquities. Excavation of remains

Pryor, Francis. Excavation at Fengate, Peterborough, England : the third report / Francis Pryor ; with illustrations by Robert Powell, Maisie Taylor and the author. — [Leicester] : Northamptonshire Archaeological Society, 1980. — xiv,272p : ill ; 25cm. — (Northamptonshire Archaeological Society monograph, ISSN 0144-5391 ; 1) (Royal Ontario Museum Archaeology monograph ; 6)
Bibliography: p249-257
Unpriced (pbk) B82-10916

Pryor, Francis. Fengate / Francis Pryor. — Princes Risborough : Shire, 1982. — 56p : ill,maps,plans ; 21cm. — (Shire archaeology)
Bibliography: p53-54. — Includes index
ISBN 0-85263-577-x (pbk) : £1.95 B82-31006

936.2′653 — Cambridgeshire. Grandford. Romano-British antiquities. Excavation of remains

Potter, T. W.. A Romano-British village at Granford, March, Cambridgeshire / T.W. Potter and C.F. Potter. — London : British Museum, 1982. — viii,133p : ill,maps,plans ; 30cm. — (Occasional paper / British Museum, ISSN 0142-4815 ; no.35)
Bibliography: p128-129
ISBN 0-86159-035-x (pbk) : Unpriced B82-25624

936.2′6712 — Essex. Saffron Walden. Archaeological investigation

Bassett, S. R.. Saffron Walden : excavations and research 1972-80. — London : Council for British Archaeology, Oct.1982. — [140]p. — (Chelmsford Archaeological Trust report ; 2) (CBA research report, ISSN 0589-9036 ; 45)
ISBN 0-906780-15-2 (pbk) : £15.00 : CIP entry B82-28614

936.2′713 — Cheshire. Congleton. Antiquities. Sites

Thompson, Patience. Congleton : the archaeological potential of a town / Patience Thompson. — Chester : Cheshire County Concil in conjunction with Cheshire County Record Office, 1981. — 12p : 5maps ; 30cm. — (Cheshire monographs ; 3)
Bibliography: p10-12
ISBN 0-906767-04-0 (spiral) : Unpriced B82-17858

936.2′789 — Cumbria. Carlisle *(District)*. **Ancient Roman fortifications: Hadrian′s Wall. Forts**

Graham, Frank, *1913-*. Birdoswald, Bewcastle and Castleheads in the days of the Romans / by Frank Graham ; illustrated by Ronald Embleton. — Newcastle upon Tyne : F. Graham, 1982. — 31p : ill(some col.),plans ; 24cm
ISBN 0-85983-137-x (pbk) : £1.20 B82-26910

936.2′843 — North Yorkshire. York. Antiquities. Archaeological investigation

The **Archaeology** of York / [general editor P.V. Addyman]. — London : Published for the York Archaeological Trust by the Council for British Archaeology
Vol.17: [The small finds]. — 1982
English text, English, French and German summary. — Bibliography: p171-174
Fasc.3: Anglo-Scandinavian finds from Lloyds Bank, pavement, and other sites. — p67-174,[4]p of plates : ill,1map,1plan ; 24cm
ISBN 0-906780-02-0 (pbk) : Unpriced : CIP rev. B81-35021

936.2′93′005 — Clwyd. Antiquities. Excavation of remains — *Serials*

Clwyd-Powys Archaeological Trust. Projects in the year to ... / the Clwyd-Powys Archaeological Trust. — Oct. 1978-. — [Welshpool] ([7a Church St., Welshpool, Powys SY21 7DL]) : The Trust, 1978. — 1v. : ill,maps,plans
Annual. — Continued by: Clwyd-Powys Archaeological Trust. Review of projects. — Only one issue published under this title
Unpriced
Also classified at 936.2′95′005 B82-19886

Clwyd-Powys Archaeological Trust. Review of projects / Clwyd-Powys Archaeological Trust. — Oct. 1979-. — Welshpool (7a Church St., Welshpool, Powys SY21 7DL) : The Trust, 1979-. — v. : ill,maps,plans ; 30cm
Annual. — Continues: Clwyd-Powys Archaeological Trust. Projects in the year to ..
ISSN 0263-4074 = Review of projects - Clwyd-Powys Archaeological Trust : Unpriced
Also classified at 936.2′95′005 B82-19887

936.2′95′005 — Powys. Antiquities. Excavation of remains — *Serials*

Clwyd-Powys Archaeological Trust. Projects in the year to ... / the Clwyd-Powys Archaeological Trust. — Oct. 1978-. — [Welshpool] ([7a Church St., Welshpool, Powys SY21 7DL]) : The Trust, 1978. — 1v. : ill,maps,plans
Annual. — Continued by: Clwyd-Powys Archaeological Trust. Review of projects. — Only one issue published under this title
Unpriced
Primary classification 936.2′93′005 B82-19886

Clwyd-Powys Archaeological Trust. Review of projects / Clwyd-Powys Archaeological Trust. — Oct. 1979-. — Welshpool (7a Church St., Welshpool, Powys SY21 7DL) : The Trust, 1979-. — v. : ill,maps,plans ; 30cm
Annual. — Continues: Clwyd-Powys Archaeological Trust. Projects in the year to ..
ISSN 0263-4074 = Review of projects - Clwyd-Powys Archaeological Trust : Unpriced
Primary classification 936.2′93′005 B82-19887

936.2′998 — Gwent. Usk. Ancient Roman forts. Excavation of remains, *1968-1971*

Manning, W. H.. The Fortress excavations 1968-1971 / W.H. Manning. — Cardiff : published on behalf of the Board of Celtic Studies of the University of Wales [by] University of Wales Press, 1981. — xvii,233p,[59]p of plates (some folded) : ill,maps(some col.),plans (some col.) ; 30cm. — (Report on the excavations at 1965-1976)
Bibliography: p217-221. — Includes index
ISBN 0-7083-0774-4 : Unpriced
ISBN 0-7083-0741-8 (set) : Unpriced B82-07999

936.3 — Central Europe. Antiquities. Archaeological investigation, *to 1981*

Sklenar, Karel. Archaeology in Central Europe. — Leicester : Leicester University Press, Jan.1983. — [192]p
Translation from the Czech
ISBN 0-7185-1204-9 : £16.00 : CIP entry B82-32856

936.3 — Denmark, *to B.C.500*

Jensen, Jørgen. The prehistory of Denmark. — London : Methuen, Nov.1982. — [325]p
ISBN 0-416-34190-x (cased) : £18.00 : CIP entry
ISBN 0-416-34200-0 (pbk) : £8.50 B82-28291

936.4′0074′02142 — London. Camden *(London Borough)*. **Museums: British Museum. Exhibits: Celtic antiquities from France** — *Catalogues*

Stead, Ian. The Gauls. — London : British Museum Publications Ltd, May 1981. — [80]p
ISBN 0-7141-2008-1 (pbk) : £3.95 : CIP entry B81-07429

937 — ANCIENT HISTORY. ROME

937 — Ancient Roman civilization — *For schools*

Crystal, David. The Romans. — London : Edward Arnold, 1981. — 23p : ill,2maps,2plans,1port ; 21cm. — (Databank)
Authors: David Crystal and John L. Foster. — Text on inside covers. — Includes index
ISBN 0-7131-0554-2 (pbk) : £0.90 B82-08964

937 — Ancient Roman civilization, *to 330 — For children*
Trump, David. Ancient Rome. — London : Granada, July 1982. — [64]p. — (Granada guide series ; 19)
ISBN 0-246-11797-4 : £1.95 : CIP entry
B82-13234

937 — Ancient Rome. Social life — *Readings from contemporary sources*
Society in Imperial Rome : selections from Juvenal, Petronius, Martial, Tacitus, Seneca and Pliny / translated and edited by Michael Massey. — Cambridge : Cambridge University Press, 1982. — 107p : ill,maps ; 22cm. — (Translations from Greek and Roman authors)
Translations from Roman authors. — Includes index
ISBN 0-521-28036-2 (pbk) : £2.20 : CIP rev.
B82-03366

937 — Italy. Antiquities. Excavation of remains
Lancaster in Italy : archaeological research undertaken in Italy by the Dept. of Classics & Archaeology in 1981. — [Lancaster] : University of Lancaster, 1982. — 34p : ill,1map,plans ; 30cm
Cover title. — Includes bibliographies
ISBN 0-901699-89-6 (pbk) : Unpriced
B82-37951

937'.0072024 — Ancient Rome. Historiography. Gibbon, Edward — *Biographies*
Craddock, Patricia B.. Young Edward Gibbon : gentleman of letters / Patricia B. Craddock. — Baltimore ; London : Johns Hopkins University Press, c1982. — xvi,380p : 1port ; 24cm
Includes index
ISBN 0-8018-2714-0 : £18.75 B82-34344

937'.007'8 — Schools. Curriculum subjects: Ancient Roman civilization. Teaching aids — *Lists*
Roman studies handbook / the Scottish Classics Group. — Edinburgh : Oliver & Boyd, 1982. — 55p ; 22cm
ISBN 0-05-003552-5 (pbk) : £1.25 B82-23056

937'.02 — Italian civilization. Influence of Ancient Roman civilization, *B.C.350-B.C.90*
Salmon, E. T.. The Making of Roman Italy / E.T. Salmon. — London : Thames and Hudson, c1982. — xi,212p : ill,maps ; 23cm. — (Aspects of Greek and Roman life)
Includes index
ISBN 0-500-40042-3 : £12.00 B82-21915

937'.03 — Ancient Rome, *B.C.390-B.C.292 — Early works*
Livy. [Ab urbe condita. Book 6-10. English]. Rome and Italy : book VI-X of The history of Rome from its foundation / Livy ; translated and annotated by Betty Radice ; with an introduction by R.M. Ogilvie. — Harmondsworth : Penguin, 1982. — 376p : maps ; 18cm. — (Penguin classics)
Translation of: Ab urbe condita. — Includes index
ISBN 0-14-044388-6 (pbk) : £2.95 B82-30356

937'.05 — Ancient Rome, *B.C.133-A.D.68*
Scullard, H. H.. From the Gracchi to Nero : a history of Rome from 133 B.C. to A.D. 68 / H.H. Scullard. — 5th ed. — London : Methuen, 1982. — xxii,500p : 1geneal.table,2maps ; 21cm
Previous ed.: 1976. — Bibliography: p485. — Includes index
ISBN 0-416-32890-3 (cased) : Unpriced : CIP rev.
ISBN 0-416-32900-4 (pbk) : Unpriced
B82-12334

937'.05 — Catiline's War — *Latin texts*
Sallust. Bellum Catilinae / Sallust ; text with introduction and notes by Patrick McGushin. — Bristol : Bristol Classical Press, 1980. — 154p ; 21cm
Latin text, English introduction and notes. — Bibliography: p10-11
ISBN 0-906515-19-x (pbk) : Unpriced
B82-05096

937'.05'0924 — Ancient Rome. Sulla, Lucius Cornelius — *Biographies*
Keaveney, Arthur. Sulla. — London : Croom Helm, Aug.1982. — [256]p
ISBN 0-7099-1507-1 : £12.95 : CIP entry
B82-15908

937'.06 — Ancient Rome, *138-476*
Gibbon, Edward. The decline and fall of the Roman Empire / Edward Gibbon. — An abridged version / edited and with an introduction by Dero A. Saunders ; preface by Charles Alexander Robinson, Jr. — Harmondsworth : Penguin, 1981, c1952. — x,691p : ill,1map ; 18cm. — (The Penguin English library)
Originally published: New York : Viking, 1952
ISBN 0-14-043189-6 (pbk) : £2.95 B82-18140

937'.06 — Ancient Rome, *B.C. 60-A.D. 410*
Cornell, Tim. Atlas of the Roman world. — Oxford : Phaidon Press, Mar.1982. — [240]p
ISBN 0-7148-2152-7 : £17.95 : CIP entry
B82-01219

937'.07 — Ancient Roman civilization, *B.C.31-A.D.14*
Rome : the Augustan age. — Milton Keynes : Open University Press. — (Arts : a second level course)
At head of title: The Open University
Unit 5: Roman painting and sculpture / [prepared for the Course Team by Beryl Bowen]. — 1982. — 40p ; 30cm. — (A293 ; block IV, unit 5)
Bibliography: p38-40
ISBN 0-335-11093-2 (pbk) : Unpriced
B82-31989

Rome : the Augustan age. — Milton Keynes : Open University Press. — (Arts : a second level course)
At head of title: The Open University
[Block 6]
Unit 9: Tiberius, Gaius and Claudius. — 1982. — 31p : ill ; 30cm. — (A293 ; Block 6, unit 9)
Bibliography: p30-31
ISBN 0-335-11095-9 (pbk) : Unpriced
B82-39130

Rome : the Augustan age. — Milton Keynes : Open University Press. — (Arts : a second level course)
At head of title: The Open University
Units 6-8: Augustan poetry / [prepared for the Course Team by Chris Emlyn-Jones]. — 1982. — 68p : ill,1facsim ; 30cm. — (A293 ; block V, units 6-8)
Bibliography: p67-68
ISBN 0-335-11094-0 (pbk) : Unpriced
B82-31988

Rome : the Augustan age. — Milton Keynes : Open University Press. — (Arts : a second level course)
At head of title: The Open University
[Block 7]
Units 10-12: Social history, architecture and town planning. — 1982. — 87p : ill ; 30cm. — (A293 ; Block 7, units 10-12)
Bibliography: p85-87
ISBN 0-335-11096-7 (pbk) : Unpriced
B82-39131

Rome : the Augustan age. — Milton Keynes : Open University Press. — (Arts : a second level course)
At head of title: The Open University
[Block 8]
Units 13 and 14: Provincial case studies I : Gaul, Germany and Britain. — 1982. — 93p : ill,maps ; 30cm. — (A293 ; Block 8, units 13 and 14)
Maps on inside cover. — Includes bibliographies
ISBN 0-335-11097-5 (pbk) : Unpriced
B82-40136

Rome : the Augustan age. — Milton Keynes : Open University Press. — (Arts : a second level course)
At head of title: The Open University
Unit 15 & 16: Provincial case studies 2 : Judaea. — 1982. — 58p : ill ; 30cm. — (A293 ; block 9, units 15-16)
Bibliography: p58
ISBN 0-335-11098-3 (pbk) : Unpriced
B82-40658

937'.07 — Ancient Rome, *B.C.44-A.D.14*
Rome, the Augustan age. — Oxford : Oxford University Press, Nov.1981. — [800]p
ISBN 0-19-872108-0 (cased) : £28.00 : CIP entry
ISBN 0-19-872109-9 (pbk) : £13.00
B81-30218

937'.07 — Ancient Rome. Social conditions, *B.C.28-A.D.117*
Garnsey, Peter. The early Principate : Augustus to Trajan / by Peter Garnsey and Richard Saller. — Oxford : Published for the Classical Association at the Clarendon Press, 1982. — 42p ; 24cm. — (New surveys in the classics ; no.15)
Bibliography: p41-42
ISBN 0-903035-12-x (pbk) : £2.50 B82-25359

937'.07 — Ancient Rome. Social life, *ca 50-138*
Carcopino, Jérôme. Daily life in Ancient Rome : the people and the city at the height of the Empire / by Jérôme Carcopino ; edited with bibliography and notes by Henry T. Rowell ; translated from the French by E.O. Lorimer. — Harmondsworth : Penguin, 1962, c1941 (1981 [printing]). — 365p ; 20cm. — (Pelican books)
Translation of: La vie quotidienne à Rome à l'apogee de l'empire. — Originally published: New Haven : Yale University Press, 1940 ; London : Routledge, 1941. — Bibliography: p303-313. — Includes index
ISBN 0-14-055023-2 (pbk) : £3.50 B82-09949

937'.07'0922 — Ancient Rome. Germanicus. Interpersonal relations with Piso, Gnaeus Calpurnius — *Early works*
Tacitus, Cornelius. [Annals. English and Latin]. Selections from Tacitus, Annals II-III : Germanicus and Piso / [edited by] David C. Chandler. — Cambridge : Cambridge University Press, 1980. — 78p : 1geneal.table,maps ; 22cm. — (Cambridge Latin texts)
Text in English and Latin
ISBN 0-521-22650-3 (pbk) : £1.50 B82-38836

937'.07'0924 — Ancient Rome. Nero, *Emperor of Rome — Biographies — Latin texts*
Suetonius. Nero / Suetonius ; text, with introduction and notes by B.H. Warmington. — Bristol : Bristol Classical Press, c1977. — 118p ; 21cm
Latin text, English introduction and notes. — Bibliography: p15-16
Unpriced (pbk) B82-05095

937'.08'072 — Ancient Rome, *270-491.* **Historiography,** *400-500*
Blockley, R. C.. The fragmentary classicising historians of the later Roman Empire : Eunapius, Olympiodorus, Priscus and Malchus / by R.C. Blockley. — Liverpool : Cairns, c1981. — ix,196p ; 23cm. — (Arca ; 6)
Bibliography: p175-182. — Includes index
ISBN 0-905205-07-3 : £12.50 B82-09569

937'.08'0924 — Ancient Rome. Julian, *Emperor of Rome — Biographies*
Athanassiadi-Fowden, Polymnia. Julian and Hellenism : an intellectual biography / Polymnia Athanassiadi-Fowden. — Oxford : Clarendon Press, 1981. — vii,245p ; 23cm
Bibliography: p233-238. — Includes index
ISBN 0-19-814846-1 : £17.50 B82-12957

937'.09 — Ancient Rome. Invasion by Dacian & Germanic tribes, *ca 400-ca 600*
Wilcox, Peter. Rome enemies. — London : Osprey, Nov.1982. — [40]p. — (Men-at-arms series ; 129)
ISBN 0-85045-473-5 (pbk) : £3.50 : CIP entry
B82-26419

937'.8 — Italy. Morgantina. Classical antiquities
Bell, Malcolm. Morgantina studies : results of the Princeton University Archaeological Expedition to Sicily. — New Jersey ; Guildford : Princeton University Press. — (Morgantina studies ; v.1)
Vol.1: The terracottas / by Malcolm Bell, III. — 1981. — xxvii,266p,[150]p of plates : ill,1map,1plan ; 29cm
Includes index
ISBN 0-691-03946-1 : £38.70 B82-20092

938 — ANCIENT HISTORY. GREECE

938 — Ancient Greece, *B.C. 478-B.C. 404*
Quinn, T. J.. Athens and Samos, Lesbos and Chios 478-404 B.C.. — Manchester : Manchester University Press, Nov.1981. — [96] p. — (Publications of the Faculty of Arts of the University of Manchester ; no.27)
ISBN 0-7190-1297-x : £10.00 : CIP entry
B81-40274

938 — Ancient Greece, *B.C.350-B.C.100*
Walbank, F. W.. The Hellenistic world. — Brighton : Harvester Press, June 1981. — [288] p. — (Fontana history of the ancient world)
ISBN 0-7108-0310-9 : £18.95 : CIP entry
B81-12807

938 — Ancient Greece, *to B.C.30*
Burn, A. R.. [A traveller's history of Greece]. The Pelican history of Greece / A.R. Burn. — Repr. with revisions. — Harmondsworth : Penguin, 1982, c1965. — 414p : maps ; 19cm
Originally published: London : Hodder & Stoughton, 1965. — Bibliography: p395-400. — Includes index
ISBN 0-14-020792-9 (pbk) : £2.75 B82-40771

938 — Ancient Greek civilization
Gernet, Louis. The anthropology of ancient Greece / Louis Gernet ; translated by John Hamilton and Blaise Nagy. — Baltimore ; London : Johns Hopkins University Press, c1981. — xiii,378p ; 24cm
Translation of: Anthropologie de la grèce antique. — Includes index
ISBN 0-8018-2112-6 : Unpriced B82-22605

938 — Ancient Greek civilization, ca *B.C.500- ca B.C.300*
Dover, K. J.. The Greeks / Kenneth Dover. — Oxford : Oxford University Press, 1982, c1980. — viii,160p,[24]p of plates : ill,maps ; 20cm
Originally published: London : British Broadcasting Corporation, 1980. — Bibliography: p155-156. — Includes index
ISBN 0-19-285114-4 (pbk) : £3.50 : CIP rev.
B82-04280

938 — Ancient Greek civilization — *For children*
Millard, Anne. Ancient Greece. — London : Granada, July 1982. — [64]p. — (Granada guide series ; 20)
ISBN 0-246-11796-6 : £1.95 : CIP entry
B82-13233

938 — Ancient Greek civilization — *For schools*
Crystal, David. The Greeks. — London : Edward Arnold, 1981. — 23p : ill,3maps,2ports ; 21cm. — (Databank)
Authors: David Crystal and John L. Foster. — Includes index
ISBN 0-7131-0556-9 (pbk) : £0.90 B82-08966

938 — Ancient Greek culture — *Sources of data: English language. Words. Greek elements*
Humez, Alexander. Alpha to omega : the life & times of the Greek alphabet. — London : Kudos & Godine, Apr.1982. — [208]p
ISBN 0-906293-20-0 : £9.95 : CIP entry
B82-09194

938 — Classical antiquity — *For schools*
Cambridge School Classics Project foundation course. — Cambridge : Cambridge University Press for the Schools Council
The Roman world
Unit 1 / compiled by Mike Hughes and Martin Forrest. — 1978. — 73pieces : ill(some col.),1map
Includes material translated from the Latin, Greek and Irish. — One leaflet, 4 books, 12 A4 cards, 56 A5 cards
ISBN 0-521-21313-4 : Unpriced
ISBN 0-521-21601-x (Bk.1) : £0.75
ISBN 0-521-21599-4 (Bk.2) : £0.75
ISBN 0-521-21603-6 (Bk.3) : £0.75
ISBN 0-521-21600-1 (Bk.4) : £0.75
B82-38760

Cambridge School Classics Project foundation course. — Cambridge : Cambridge University Press for the Schools Council
The Roman world
Teacher's handbook 1. — 1978 (1979 [printing]). — iii,24p : 1map ; 25cm
ISBN 0-521-22378-4 (pbk) : Unpriced
B82-40515

938 — Classical civilization
Lloyd-Jones, Hugh. Classical survivals : the classics in the modern world / Hugh Lloyd-Jones. — London : Duckworth, 1982. — 184p ; 24cm
Includes index
ISBN 0-7156-1517-3 : £18.00 : CIP rev.
B81-36224

938 — Classical civilization — *For schools*
Cunningham, J. F. C.. Classical notes / J.F.C. Cunningham. — Braunton : Merlin, 1982. — 94p ; 20cm
ISBN 0-86303-013-0 (pbk) : £2.00 B82-28949

938 — Greece. Ancient Greek antiquities
Burn, A. R.. The living past of Greece : a time-traveller's tour of historic and prehistoric places / A.R. and Mary Burn ; foreword by Lawrence Durrell. — Harmondsworth : Penguin, 1982, c1980. — 288p : ill,maps,plans ; 24cm
Originally published: London : Herbert Press, 1980. — Bibliography: p278-279. — Includes index
ISBN 0-14-006086-3 (pbk) : £4.95 B82-10137

938'.007 — Classical studies, *1800-1980*
Lloyd-Jones, Hugh. Blood for the ghosts : classical influences in the nineteenth and twentieth centuries / Hugh Lloyd-Jones. — London : Duckworth, 1982. — 312p ; 24cm
Includes index
ISBN 0-7156-1500-9 : £24.00 B82-29453

938'.007 — Classical studies, *to ca 1900*
Wilamowitz-Moellendorff, U. von. History of classical scholarship / U. von Wilamowitz-Moellendorff ; translated from the German by Alan Harris ; edited with an introduction and notes by Hugh Lloyd-Jones. — London : Duckworth, 1982. — xxxii,189p ; 23cm
Translation of: Geschichte der Philologie. — Bibliography: p179-181. — Includes index
ISBN 0-7156-0976-9 : £18.00 : CIP rev.
B81-36975

938'.0072024 — Ancient Greece. Historiography. Herodotus, *b.484 B.C.? compared with* **Thucydides**
Hunter, Virginia. Past and process in Herodotus and Thucydides / Virginia Hunter. — Princeton ; Guildford : Princeton University Press, c1982. — xviii,371p ; 23cm
Bibliography: p339-353. — Includes index
ISBN 0-691-03556-3 : £19.40
Also classified at 938'.05'072024 B82-24311

938'.0072024 — Ancient Greece. Historiography. Herodotus, *b.484 B.C.? — Critical studies*
Hart, John, *1936-*. Herodotus and Greek history / John Hart. — London : Croom Helm, c1982. — 227p : ill,geneal.tables,maps ; 23cm
Bibliography: p209-211. — Includes index
ISBN 0-7099-1224-2 : £13.95 : CIP rev.
B81-37558

938'.0074'02142 — London. Camden *(London Borough).* **Museums: British Museum.** *Department of Greek and Roman Antiquities.* **Stock: Acqusitions** — *Catalogues*
British Museum. *Department of Greek and Roman Antiquities.* Department of Greek and Roman Antiquities : new acquisitions no.1 (1976-1979). — London : British Museum, 1981. — iv,51p : ill ; 30cm. — (Occasional paper / British Museum, ISSN 0142-021x ; no.22)
Includes bibliographies
Unpriced (pbk) B82-11551

938'.0092'2 — Ancient Greece — *Biographies*
Bowder, Diana. Who was who in the Greek world. — Oxford : Phaidon, Oct.1982. — [256]p
ISBN 0-7148-2207-8 : £18.00 : CIP entry
B82-23001

938'.03 — Persian Wars — *Early works*
Herodotus, *b.484 B.C.?*. [History. English. Selections]. The Persian War / Herodotus ; translated by William Shepherd. — Cambridge : Cambridge University Press, 1982. — 136p : maps ; 22cm. — (Translations from Greek and Roman authors)
Translation from the Greek. — Includes index
ISBN 0-521-28194-6 (pbk) : £2.25 B82-18055

938'.05 — Peloponnesian War, *B.C.421-B.C.413*
Kagan, Donald. The Peace of Nicias and the Sicilian expedition / Donald Kagan. — Ithaca ; London : Cornell University Press, c1981. — 393p : maps ; 24cm
Bibliography: p373-378. — Includes index
ISBN 0-8014-1367-2 : Unpriced B82-16916

938'.05 — Peloponnesian War. Causes — *Greek texts*
Thucydides. [History of the Peloponnesian War. Book 1, chapters 1-55]. Thucydides, book I, ch.1-55 / edited by E.C. Marchant ; with new introduction and bibliography by Thomas Wiedemann. — Bristol : Bristol Classical Press, 1978. — xxxvii,198p : ill,1map ; 21cm
Greek text with English introduction and notes. — Originally published: London : Macmillan, 1905. — Bibliography: pxxxv-xxxvii
ISBN 0-906515-13-0 (pbk) : Unpriced
B82-05335

938'.05 — Peloponnesian War, *to B.C. 428 — Greek texts*
Thucydides. [History of the Peloponnesian War. Book 2]. Thucydides, book II / edited by E.C. Marchant ; with a new introduction by Thomas Wiedemann. — Bristol : Bristol Classical Press, 1978. — xxxix,239p : ill,maps ; 21cm
Greek text with English introduction and notes. — Originally published: London : Macmillan, 1891. — Bibliography: pxxxvi-xxxix
ISBN 0-906515-20-3 (pbk) : Unpriced
B82-05336

938'.05'072024 — Peloponnesian War. Historiography. Thucydides *compared with* **Herodotus,** *b.484 B.C.?*
Hunter, Virginia. Past and process in Herodotus and Thucydides / Virginia Hunter. — Princeton ; Guildford : Princeton University Press, c1982. — xviii,371p ; 23cm
Bibliography: p339-353. — Includes index
ISBN 0-691-03556-3 : £19.40
Primary classification 938'.0072024
B82-24311

938'.07 — Ancient Greece, *B.C. 362-B.C. 146 — Readings from contemporary sources*
The **Hellenistic** world from Alexander to the Roman conquest : a selection of ancient sources in translation / [edited by] M.M. Austin. — Cambridge : Cambridge University Press, 1981. — xv,488p : ill,maps ; 24cm
Bibliography: p467-470. — Includes index
ISBN 0-521-22829-8 (cased) : £30.00 : CIP rev.
ISBN 0-521-29666-8 (pbk) : £9.95 B81-31262

938'.07'0924 — Ancient Macedonia. Alexander III, *King of Macedonia*
Tarn, W. W.. Alexander the Great / by W.W. Tarn. — Cambridge : Cambridge University Press
1: Narrative. — 1948 (1979 [printing]). — x,160p ; 23cm
Includes index
ISBN 0-521-22584-1 (cased) : Unpriced
ISBN 0-521-29563-7 (pbk) : £2.75 B82-24193

938'.07'0924 — Ancient Macedonia. Alexander III, *King of Macedonia.* **Arrian. Anabasis** — *Commentaries*
Bosworth, A. B.. A historical commentary on Arrian's History of Alexander / by A.B. Bosworth. — Oxford : Clarendon
Vol.1: Commentary on Books 1-3. — 1980. — xv,396p : maps ; 23cm
Bibliography: pxi-xv. — Includes index
ISBN 0-19-814828-3 : £30.00 : CIP rev.
B80-18547

938'.07'0924 — Ancient Macedonia. Alexander III, *King of Macedonia — Biographies*
Lane Fox, Robin. The search for Alexander / Robin Lane Fox. — London : Allen Lane, 1980. — 448p : ill(some col.),maps(some col.),facsims ; 26cm
Map on lining papers. — Bibliography: p443-448. — Includes index
ISBN 0-7139-1395-9 : £12.95 B82-09087

938'.07'0924 — Ancient Macedonia. Alexander III, *King of Macedonia — Biographies — Early works*
Arrian. Alexander the Great : selections from Arrian / [translated by] J.G. Lloyd. — Cambridge : Cambridge University Press, 1981. — 104p : maps,plans ; 22cm. — (Translations from Greek and Roman authors)
Includes index
ISBN 0-521-28195-4 (pbk) : £2.20 : CIP rev.
B81-30524

938'.107 — Ancient Macedonia, *B.C.359-B.C.336.* **Archaeological sources**
Wynne-Thomas, Joan L.. Proud-voiced Macedonia : a background for King Philip II and and the Royal Burial Ground at Vergina / Joan L. Wynne-Thomas. — London : Springwood, 1979. — 96p,1leaf of plates : ill (some col.),1map ; 22cm
Bibliography: p96
ISBN 0-905947-56-8 : £4.95 B82-05654

938'.16 — Greece. Rhodes, *B.C.3000-B.C.2000*
Mee, Christopher. Rhodes in the bronze age. — Warminster : Aris & Phillips, Oct.1982. — [160]p
ISBN 0-85668-143-1 : £25.00 : CIP entry B82-24120

938'.5 — Ancient Greece. Athens. Rich families. Children. Social life, *ca B.C.470-ca B.C.430 — For schools*
Jenkins, Ian. An Athenian childhood / by Ian Jenkins ; with drawings by Sue Bird. — London (31 Gordon) : Joint Association of Classical Teachers, [1982?]. — 21p : ill,1plan ; 30cm
Bibliography: p21
Unpriced (spiral) B82-14334

938'.7 — Ancient Greece. Sicyon, *to B.C.146*
Griffin, Audrey. Sikyon / Audrey Griffin. — Oxford : Clarendon, 1982. — 171p,[8]p of plates : ill,2maps ; 23cm. — (Oxford classical and philosophical monographs)
Bibliography: p165-167. — Includes index
ISBN 0-19-814718-x : £15.00 : CIP rev. B81-33651

939.1 — ANCIENT HISTORY. AEGEAN ISLANDS

939'.15 — Greece. Melos *(Island), ca 400*
An **Island** polity : the archaeology of exploitation in Melos / edited by Colin Renfrew and Malcolm Wagstaff. — Cambridge : Cambridge University Press, 1982. — xiv,361p : ill,maps ; 29cm
Bibliography: p329-347. — Includes index
ISBN 0-521-23785-8 : Unpriced : CIP rev.
Also classified at 949.9 B82-03107

939'.18 — Greece. Crete. Ancient Roman antiquities
Sanders, I. F.. Roman Crete : an archaeological survey and gazetteer of late Hellenistic, Roman and early Byzantine Crete / I.F. Sanders. — Warminster : Aris & Phillips, c1982. — xiii,185p : ill,maps,plans,1port ; 30cm
One map on folded sheet attached to back inside cover. — Bibliography: p183-185
ISBN 0-85668-150-4 (pbk) : Unpriced : CIP rev. B80-34296

939.2 — ANCIENT HISTORY. ASIA MINOR

939'.21 — Turkey. Attalid Kingdom, *ca.B.C.241-B.C.133*
Allen, R. E.. The Attalid Kingdom. — Oxford : Clarendon Press, Sept.1981. — [288]p
ISBN 0-19-814845-3 : £15.00 : CIP entry B81-23750

939'.24 — Turkey. Geyre. Human settlements: Aphrodisias, *B.C.100-A.D.300 — Correspondence, diaries, etc.*
Aphrodisias and Rome : documents from the excavation of the theatre at Aphrodisias conducted by Kenan T. Erim : together with some related texts / [compiled and annotated by] Joyce Reynolds. — London : Society for the Promotion of Roman Studies, 1982. — xviii,214,[35]p of plates : ill,facsims,1map ; 28cm. — (Journal of Roman studies monographs ; no.1)
English and Greek Text. — Bibliography: pviii-x. — Includes index
ISBN 0-907764-01-0 : Unpriced B82-39333

939'.24'00994 — Ancient Karia. Hellenisation. Role of Mausolus, *B.C.377-B.C.352*
Hornblower, Simon. Mausolus / Simon Hornblower. — Oxford : Clarendon, 1982. — xxiv,[18]p of plates : ill,maps ; 23cm
Includes index
ISBN 0-19-814844-5 : £35.00 : CIP rev. B81-35804

939.37 — ANCIENT HISTORY. CYPRUS

939'.37 — Cyprus. Antiquities. Archaeological investigation, *1969-1973*
Paltenburg, E. J.. Vrysi : a subterranean settlement in Cyprus : excavation at Ayios Epiktitos Vrysi 1969-1973. — Warminster : Aris & Phillips, Dec.1982. — [132]p
ISBN 0-85668-217-9 (pbk) : £15.00 : CIP entry B82-37499

939.4 — ANCIENT HISTORY. SYRIA AND ARABIA

939'.4 — Arabia. Conquest by Muslims, *570-632*
Donner, Fred McGraw. The early Islamic conquests / by Fred McGraw Donner. — Princeton ; Guildford : Princeton University Press, c1981. — xviii,489p : maps ; 24cm
Bibliography: p439-457. — Includes index
ISBN 0-691-05327-8 : £24.50 B82-14675

939'.4 — Arabia. Tribes. Cultural processes, *500-700*
Kister, M. J.. Studies in Jāhiliyya and early Islam / M.J. Kister. — London : Variorum, 1980. — 360p in various pagings ; 24cm. — (Collected studies series ; CS 123)
Facsim reprints. — Includes index
ISBN 0-86078-068-6 : £22.00 : CIP rev. B80-18103

939'.4 — Saudi Arabia. Qaryat al-Fau. Antiquities
al-Ansary, A. R.. Qaryat al-Fau : a portrait of Pre-Islamic civilisation in Saudi Arabia / by A.R. al-Ansary. — London : Croom Helm, 1982. — 147,[59]p : col.ill,maps(some col.),plans,ports(some col.) ; 34cm
English & Arabic texts. — Added t.p. in Arabic. — Central pagination sequence p58-147, in both westernised Arabic & Arabic numerals. — Maps on lining papers. — Bibliography: p30
ISBN 0-7099-0517-3 : £14.95 B82-33637

939'.4004924 — Ancient Middle East. Jews, *ca B.C.1500-ca B.C.1400.* **Dating**
Bimson, John J.. Redating the Exodus and Conquest / John J. Bimson. — 2nd ed. — Sheffield : Almond, 1981. — 288p : 2maps ; 22cm. — (Journal for the study of the Old Testament supplement series, ISSN 0309-0787 ; 5)
Previous ed.: Sheffield : Department of Biblical Studies, University of Sheffield, 1978. — Bibliography: p252-275. — Includes index
ISBN 0-907459-04-8 (pbk) : £8.95 B82-35561

939'.48 — Jordan. Petra. Antiquities
Browning, Iain. Petra / by Iain Browning. — New and rev. ed. — London : Chatto & Windus, 1982. — 255p,6leaves of plates : ill (some col.),maps,plans ; 26cm
Previous ed.: 1973. — Bibliography: p247. — Includes index
ISBN 0-7011-2622-1 : £12.50 : CIP rev. B82-06513

939.5 — ANCIENT HISTORY. BLACK SEA AND CAUCASUS REGIONS

939'.55 — Armenia, *451-454 — Early works*
Eliseus, *Saint, Vardapet.* [Vasn Vardanay ew Hayots' Paterazmin. English]. History of Vardan and the Armenian war / Eḷishē ; translation and commentary by Robert W. Thomson. — Cambridge, Mass. ; London : Harvard University Press, 1982. — viii,353p : 1map ; 25cm. — (Harvard Armenian texts and studies ; 5)
Translation of: Vasn Vardanay ew Hayots' Paterazmin. — Bibliography: p329-337. — Includes index
ISBN 0-674-40335-5 : Unpriced B82-35394

939.6 — ANCIENT HISTORY. CENTRAL ASIA

939'.6 — Soviet Central Asia. Bronze Age antiquities
The **Bronze** Age civilization of Central Asia : recent Soviet discoveries / edited with an introduction by Philip L. Kohl ; afterword by C.C. Lamberg-Karlovsky ; [translated by Philip L. Kohl and William Mandel]. — Armonk, N.Y. : Sharpe ; London : distributed by Eurospan, c1981. — xl,399p : ill,maps,plans ; 24cm
Translation from the Russian. — Includes bibliographies
ISBN 0-87332-169-3 : £26.50 B82-17304

939.7 — ANCIENT HISTORY. NORTH AFRICA

939'.73'0924 — Ancient Carthage. Hannibal — *Biographies*
Bradford, Ernle. Hannibal / Ernle Bradford. — London : Macmillan, 1981. — 223p : maps,plans ; 24cm
Bibliography: p215. — Includes index
ISBN 0-333-28191-8 : £7.95 B82-06700

939'.78 — Nubia, *to 640 — Conference proceedings*
Nubian studies. — Warminster : Aris & Phillips, July 1982. — [272]p
Conference papers
ISBN 0-85668-198-9 (pbk) : £20.00 : CIP entry B82-13146

940 — HISTORY. EUROPE

940 — Europe, *to 1914 — Festschriften*
History and imagination : essays in honour of H.R. Trevor-Roper / edited by Hugh Lloyd-Jones, Valerie Pearl & Blair Worden. — London : Duckworth, 1981. — ix,386p,[1]leaf of plates : 1port ; 26cm
Includes index
ISBN 0-7156-1570-x : Unpriced : CIP rev. B81-22675

940 — Europe, *to 1935*
Fisher, H. A. L.. A History of Europe / H.A.L. Fisher. — [Glasgow] : Fontana/Collins, 1960, c1935 (1982 [printing]). — 2v.(ix,1376p) : maps,geneal.tables ; 18cm
Originally published: London : Eyre & Spottiswoode, 1935. — Includes bibliographies and index
ISBN 0-00-636506-x (pbk) : Unpriced
ISBN 0-00-636507-8 (v.2) : £2.95 B82-15245

940 — European civilization. Influence of Ancient Greek civilization, *to 1980*
The **Legacy** of Greece : a new appraisal / edited by M.I. Finley. — Oxford : Clarendon, 1981. — 479p : ill,1map,plans ; 23cm
Includes bibliographies and index
ISBN 0-19-821915-6 : £8.95 : CIP rev. B80-23884

940 — European civilization. Influence of Islamic civilization, *700-1866*
Lewis, Bernard. The Muslim discovery of Europe / by Bernard Lewis. — London : Weidenfeld and Nicolson, c1982. — 350p : ill ; 24cm
Includes index
ISBN 0-297-78140-5 : £12.50 B82-35843

940 — European civilization, *to 1939*
Bowle, John, *1905-*. A history of Europe : a cultural and political survey / John Bowle. — London : Pan in association with Secker and Warburg, 1982, c1979. — xi,626p : maps ; 20cm
Originally published: London : Secker and Warburg ; Heinemann, 1979. — Includes index
ISBN 0-330-26598-9 (pbk) : £3.95 B82-15212

940 — Western Europe. Society. Theories, *800-1980*
Fink, Hans. Social philosophy / Hans Fink. — London : Methuen, 1981. — 122p ; 20cm. — (Ideas)
Includes bibliographies and index
ISBN 0-416-71990-2 (cased) : Unpriced : CIP rev.
ISBN 0-416-71000-5 (pbk) : £2.50 B81-28082

940′.01 — European civilization. Theories of French intellectuals. Influence of World War 1
Cruickshank, John. Variations on catastrophe : some French responses to the Great War / John Cruickshank. — Oxford : Clarendon Press, 1982. — vii,219p ; 23cm
Bibliography: p210-213. — Includes index
ISBN 0-19-212599-0 : £15.00 : CIP rev. B82-10427

940′.04916 — Celtic civilization, *395-1500 — Serials*
Cambridge medieval Celtic studies. — No.1 (Summer 1981)-. — Leamington Spa (2a Upper Grove St., Leamington Spa, Warwickshire CV32 5AN) : James Hall (Publishing) in association with the Department of Anglo-Saxon, Norse, & Celtic, University of Cambridge, 1981-. — v. : maps ; 22cm
Two issues yearly
ISSN 0260-5600 = Cambridge medieval Celtic studies : £14.00 per year B82-05223

940′.04′916 — Celtic civilization, *to 1980*
The **Celtic** consciousness. — Portlaoise : Dolmen Press, Apr.1982. — [672]p
ISBN 0-85105-375-0 : £40.00 : CIP entry B82-04988

940′.07′1041 — Great Britain. Educational institutions. Curriculum subjects: European studies
European studies : a report from the European Association of Teachers, United Kingdom Section. — [London] ([20 c/o Brookfield, Highgate West Hill, N6 6AS]) : European Association of Teachers, [c1981]. — 70,[24]p : ill,2maps ; 30cm
£2.00 (pbk) B82-10325

940′.072073 — Europe, *ca 1300-1660.* **American historiography**
Hexter, J. H.. Reappraisals in history : new views on history and society in early modern Europe / J.H. Hexter. — 2nd ed. — Chicago ; London : University of Chicago Press, c1979. — xix,278p ; 21cm
Previous ed.: Evanston, Ill. : Northwestern University Press ; London : Longmans, 1961
ISBN 0-226-33232-2 (cased) : Unpriced
ISBN 0-226-33233-0 (pbk) : £4.90 B82-22706

940.1 — HISTORY. EUROPE, 476-1453

940.1 — Europe, *476-1492 — German texts*
Elze, Reinhard. Päpste-Kaiser-Könige und die mittelalterliche Herrschaftssymbolik / Reinhard Elze ; ausgewählte Aufsätze herausgegeben von Bernhard Schimmelpfennig und Ludwig Schmugge. — London : Variorum Reprint, 1982. — 302p in various pagings : ill,1port ; 24cm. — (Collected studies series ; CS152)
Includes 2 papers in Italian and 1 text in Latin. — Facsimile reprints. — Includes index
ISBN 0-86078-098-8 : Unpriced : CIP rev. B82-01570

940.1 — Europe, *ca 300-ca 1450*
Claster, Jill N.. The medieval experience : 300-1400 / Jill N. Claster. — New York ; London : New York University Press, 1982. — xvi,398p : ill,4maps,ports ; 24cm
Bibliography: p385-389. — Includes index
ISBN 0-8147-1384-x (cased) : £24.15
ISBN 0-8147-1381-5 (pbk) : £11.15 B82-36363

Medieval Europe : a short sourcebook / edited by C. Warren Hollister ... [et al.]. — New York ; Chichester : Wiley, c1982. — ix,246p ; 23cm
ISBN 0-471-08369-0 (pbk) : £7.00 B82-28076

940.1 — European civilization, *476-1500*
Hollister, C. Warren. Medieval Europe : a short history / C. Warren Hollister. — 5th ed. — New York ; Chichester : Wiley, c1982. — x,348p : ill,maps ; 22cm
Previous ed.: 1978. — Includes bibliographies and index
ISBN 0-471-08447-6 (pbk) : £8.00 B82-21532

940.1 — European civilization, *1000-1800*
Gerhard, Dietrich. Old Europe : a study of continuity, 1000-1800 / Dietrich Gerhard. — New York ; London : Academic Press, 1981. — xii,147p ; 24cm. — (Studies in social discontinuity)
ISBN 0-12-280720-0 : £8.40 B82-30148

940.1 — European civilization, *ca B.C. 50-ca A.D. 1300 — For children*
Caselli, Giovanni. The Roman Empire and the Dark Ages / Giovanni Caselli. — London : Macdonald, 1981. — 48p : col.ill,col.maps ; 29cm. — (History of everyday things)
Bibliography: p48
ISBN 0-356-05975-8 : £3.95 B82-02896

940.1 — Western Europe. Islands. Christian hermitages, *ca 500-1200.* **Archaeological investigation**
Cramp, Rosemary. The hermitage and the offshore island / by Rosemary Cramp. — [London] : Trustees of the National Maritime Museum, [1980?]. — ii,23p : ill,2maps,3plans ; 21cm. — (Second Paul Johnstone memorial lecture) (Occasional lecture / National Maritime Museum, ISSN 0141-1268 ; no.3)
ISBN 0-905555-54-6 (pbk) : Unpriced B82-14179

940.1′4 — European culture. Effects of Vikings, *700-1100*
Sawyer, P. H.. Kings and Vikings : Scandinavia and Europe AD 700-1100. — London : Methuen, Nov.1982. — [190]p
ISBN 0-416-74180-0 (cased) : £11.95 : CIP entry
ISBN 0-416-74190-0 (pbk) : £5.95 B82-29441

940.1′7 — Europe. Courtly life. Cultural aspects, *1350-1525 — Conference proceedings*
English court culture in the later Middle Ages. — London : Duckworth, Aug.1982. — [224]p
Conference papers
ISBN 0-7156-1637-4 : £18.00 : CIP entry B82-15843

940.1′82 — Europe, *1100-1199*
Renaissance and renewal in the twelfth century. — Oxford : Clarendon Press, Oct.1982. — [832]p
ISBN 0-19-821934-2 : £28.00 : CIP entry B82-23686

940.1′92 — Western European civilization. Role of chivalry, *1270-1350*
Vale, Juliet. Edward III and chivalry. — Woodbridge : Boydell Press, Nov.1982. — [256]p
ISBN 0-85115-170-1 : £19.50 : CIP entry B82-26426

940.2 — HISTORY. EUROPE, 1453-

940.2 — Europe, *1770-1870*
Best, Geoffrey. War and society in revolutionary Europe, 1770-1870 / Geoffrey Best. — [London] : Fontana, 1982. — 336p ; 20cm. — (Fontana history of European war and society)
Bibliography: p321-332. — Includes index
ISBN 0-00-634747-9 (pbk) : £2.95 B82-22561

940.2 — Europe. Political events, *1870-1974 — For schools*
Morales, A. C.. Europe : the last hundred years / A.C. Morales. — Basingstoke : Macmillan Education, 1979 (1982 [printing]). — 226p : ill,maps,ports ; 25cm
Bibliography: p221. — Includes index
ISBN 0-333-33114-1 (pbk) : Unpriced B82-28649

940.2′1 — European culture, *1453-1517*
Renaissance. — London : Methuen, Nov.1982. — [400]p
Translation of: Il Rinascimento
ISBN 0-416-31130-x : £12.50 : CIP entry B82-28287

940.2′32 — Europe, *1500-1600 — For schools*
Maland, David. Europe in the sixteenth century. — 2nd ed. — London : Macmillan Education, May 1982. — [460]p
Previous ed.: 1973
ISBN 0-333-32712-8 (pbk) : £2.95 : CIP entry B82-07426

940.2′32 — Europe. Social life, *1500-1600 — For children*
Middleton, Haydn. Everyday life in the sixteenth century / Haydn Middleton. — London : Macdonald, 1982. — 61p : ill(some col.),1geneal.table, col.maps,1plan ; 27cm. — (Peoples of the past)
Includes index
ISBN 0-356-07534-6 (cased) : £3.50
ISBN 0-356-07528-1 (pbk) : Unpriced B82-35128

940.2′4 — Thirty Years′ War
Langer, Herbert. The Thirty Years′ War / Herbert Langer. — Poole : Blandford, 1980. — 278p : ill(some col.),maps,facsims,ports ; 28cm
Translation of: Hortus Bellicus. — Text, ill on lining papers. — Bibliography: p279. — Includes index
ISBN 0-7137-1098-5 : £19.95 : CIP rev. B80-14085

Wedgwood, C. V.. The Thirty Years War / C.V. Wedgwood. — London : Methuen, 1981. — 542p : ill,2maps,2geneal.tables ; 20cm
Originally published: London : Cape, 1938. — Bibliography: p527-528. — Includes index
ISBN 0-416-32020-1 (pbk) : £4.95 : CIP rev. B81-30551

940.2′52 — Europe. Social life, *1600-1700 — For children*
Taylor, Laurence. Everyday life in the seventeenth century / Laurence Taylor. — London : Macdonald, 1982. — 61p : ill(some col.),1facsim,1col.map ; 27cm. — (Peoples of the past)
Includes index
ISBN 0-356-07535-4 (cased) : £3.50
ISBN 0-356-07529-x (pbk) : Unpriced B82-35129

940.2′52′076 — Europe, *1600-1700 — Questions & answers — For schools*
Best, Gary Martin. Seventeenth-century Europe / Gary Martin Best. — Basingstoke : Macmillan Education, 1982. — iv,124p ; 22cm. — (Documents and debates)
ISBN 0-333-31222-8 (pbk) : Unpriced : CIP rev. B82-10769

940.2′53 — Europe. Social conditions, *1715-1789*
Woloch, Isser. Eighteenth-century Europe : tradition and progress 1715-1789 / Isser Woloch. — New York ; London : Norton, c1982. — xvii,364p : ill,maps,ports ; 22cm. — (The Norton history of modern Europe)
Bibliography: p339-354. — Includes index
ISBN 0-393-01506-8 (cased) : Unpriced
ISBN 0-393-95214-2 (pbk) : Unpriced B82-39005

940.2′7 — Europe. Wars, *1770-1870*
Best, Geoffrey. War and society in revolutionary Europe 1770-1870 / Geoffrey Best. — [Leicester] : Leicester University Press in association with Fontana, 1982. — 336p ; 23cm. — (Fontana history of European war and society)
Bibliography: p321-328. — Includes index
ISBN 0-7185-1226-x : £12.00 : CIP rev. B82-04879

940.2′7 — Napoleonic Wars. Army operations by Austria. *Armee, 1792-1814*
Rothenberg, Gunther E.. Napoleon′s great adversaries : the Archduke Charles and the Austrian army, 1792-1814 / Gunther E. Rothenberg. — London : Batsford, 1982. — 219p,[16]p of plates : ill,maps,ports ; 25cm
Bibliography: p202-2106. — Includes index
ISBN 0-7134-3758-8 : £9.95 B82-27497

940.2′7 — Napoleonic Wars. Army operations by German allies of France, *1800-1815*
Pivka, Otto von. Napoleon′s German allies / text by Otto von Pivka. — London : Osprey. — (Men-at-arms series)
3: Saxony 1806-1815 / colour plates by Richard Hook. — 1979. — 40p,A-Hp of plates : ill(some col.),maps ; 25cm
English text, English, French and German captions to plates
ISBN 0-85045-309-7 (pbk) : Unpriced B82-10732

940.2'7 — Napoleonic Wars. Army operations by German allies of France, *1800-1815*
continuation

Pivka, Otto von. Napoleon's German allies / text by Otto von Pivka. — London : Osprey. — (Men-at-arms series ; 122)
5: Hessen-Darmstadt & Hessen-Kassel / colour plates by Bryan Fosten. — 1982. — 40p,A-H p of plates : ill(some col.),coats of arms,1maps,ports ; 25cm
English text, with notes on the plates in French and German. — Bibliography: p39-40
ISBN 0-85045-431-x (pbk) : Unpriced
B82-37338

940.2'7 — Napoleonic Wars. Army operations by Great Britain. *Army. King's German Legion* **& Hanover.** *Harroverschen Armee.* **Decorations: Guelphic Medal**

Vigors, D. D.. The Hanoverian Guelphic Medal of 1815 : a record of Hanoverian bravery during the Napoleonic Wars / by D.D. Vigors. — Salisbury (Apshill House, Lower Chicksgrove, Tisbury, Salisbury, Wilts. SP3 6NB) : D.D. Vigors, c1981. — 14,[664]p : 1ill ; 22cm
Limited ed. of 7 numbered copies
Unpriced B82-01798

940.2'7 — Napoleonic Wars. Battle of Leipzig — *For war games*

Parker, Jeff. The campaign of Leipzig 1813 / text by Jeff Parker ; colour plates arranged by Peter Gilder ; colour map by Christine Howes. — London : Osprey, 1979. — 40p,A-Gp of plates : ill(some col.),maps(some col.),plans ; 25cm. — (Wargames series ; 2)
ISBN 0-85045-338-0 (pbk) : Unpriced
B82-10734

940.2'7 — Napoleonic Wars. Peninsular campaign

Tranie, J.. Napoleon's war in Spain : the French Peninsular Campaigns, 1807-1814 / J. Tranie and J.-C. Carmigniani from the notes and manuscripts of Henry Lachouque ; with original illustrations by Louis de Beaufort ; translated by Janet S. Mallender and John R. Clements ; foreword by David G. Chandler. — London : Arms and Armour, 1982. — 191p : ill(some co.),maps,ports ; 28cm
Translation of: Napoleon et la Campagne d'Espagne. — Bibliography: p185-186. — Includes index
ISBN 0-85368-506-1 : £16.50 : CIP rev.
B81-33778

940.2'7'0924 — Europe. Social life, *1789-1820 — Personal observations — Correspondence, diaries, etc*

Wynne, Elizabeth. The Wynne diaries 1789-1820 / passages selected and edited by Anne Fremantle ; with an introduction by Christopher Hibbett. — Oxford : Oxford University Press, 1982. — xxiv,551p : geneal.tables ; 20cm
ISBN 0-19-281304-8 (pbk) : £3.50 : CIP rev.
B82-00880

940.2'7'0924 — Napoleonic Wars. Army operations by Great Britain. *Army. 95th (Rifle) Regiment — Personal observations*

Kincaid, *Sir* **John**. Adventures in the Rifle Brigade ; and, Random shots from a rifleman. — Glasgow (20 Park Circus, Glasgow G3 6BE) : Richard Drew, Nov.1981. — [304]p
Contents: Adventures in the Rifle Brigade. Originally published: London : s.n., 1830 — Random shots from a rifleman. Originally published: London : s.n., 1835
ISBN 0-904002-83-7 : £9.50 : CIP entry
B81-30892

940.2'7'0924 — Napoleonic wars. Army operations by Great Britain. *Army — Personal observations — Correspondence, diaries, etc. — Facsimiles*

Robertson, D.. The journal of Sergeant D. Robertson, late 92d foot : comprising the different campaigns, between the years 1797 and 1818, in Egypt, Walcheren, Denmark, Sweden, Portugal, Spain, France, and Belgium. — London : Maggs, 1982. — vii,164p ; 19cm
Facsim. of: ed. published Perth: printed by J. Fisher, 1842. — Limited ed. of 100 numbered copies
ISBN 0-901953-03-2 : Unpriced B82-22225

940.2'8 — Europe, *1763-1850 — For Irish students*

Collins, M. E. (Mary Elizabeth). A time of revolution / M.E. Collins, H. Gough, P. Holohan ; [Maps and diagrams Bob Rogan]. — Dublin : Educational Company, 1981. — 291p : ill,maps,music,facsims,1plan,ports ; 22cm
Includes index
Unpriced (pbk) B82-02549

940.2'8 — Europe, *1789-1978 — For schools*

Jennings, A.. Ireland and Europe, 1800-1980 : concise history / A. Jennings. — Dublin (Ballymount Rd., Walkinstown, Dublin 12) : Helicon, 1982. — 182p : ill,facsims,maps,ports ; 26cm
Unpriced (pbk) B82-34490

940.2'8 — Europe, *1789-1980*

Lee, Stephen J.. Aspects of European history 1789-1980. — London : Methuen, Oct.1982. — [340]p
ISBN 0-416-73170-8 (cased) : £10.50 : CIP entry
ISBN 0-416-73180-5 (pbk) : £5.95 B82-23985

940.2'8 — Europe, *1800-1900*

Brooks, Christopher. Nineteenth century Europe. — London : Macmillan Education, May 1982. — [112]p. — (Documents and debates)
ISBN 0-333-28406-2 (pbk) : £2.45 : CIP entry
B82-07423

940.2'8 — Europe, *1815-1945*

History A Level : a course leading to the Associated Examining Board Advanced Level. — Cambridge : National Extension College, c1981-c1982. — 3v. : maps ; 30cm. — (National Extension College correspondence texts ; course no.HS15)
Includes bibliographies
ISBN 0-86082-225-7 (pbk) : Unpriced
ISBN 0-86082-222-2 (v.1)
ISBN 0-86082-223-0 (v.2)
ISBN 0-86082-224-9 (v.3) B82-38350

940.2'8 — Europe, *1848-1950 — For Irish students*

Ó Broin, Art. European history 1848-1950 / Art Ó Broin. — [Dublin] : Folens, [c1979]. — 64p ; 22cm. — (Folen's student aids leaving certificate)
Cover title
ISBN 0-86121-065-4 (pbk) : Unpriced
B82-01232

940.2'8 — Europe, *1871-1979*

Perry, K.. Modern European history made simple 1871-1979. — London : Heinemann, Jan.1983. — [304]p. — (Made simple books)
Originally published: London : W.H. Allen, 1976
ISBN 0-434-98569-4 (pbk) : £2.95 : CIP entry
B82-34583

940.2'8 — Europe. Political events, *1815-1871 — Welsh texts*

Jones, Marian Henry. Hanes Ewrop, 1815-1871 / Marian Henry Jones. — Caerdydd : Gwasg Prifysgol Cymru, 1982. — xvii,355p : col.maps ; 22cm
Includes bibliographies and index
ISBN 0-7083-0801-5 : £9.95 : CIP rev.
B81-12832

940.2'8 — Europe. Political events, *1870-1980 — For schools*

Jamieson, Alan. Europe in conflict : a history of Europe 1870-1980. — 3rd ed. — London : Hutchinson Education, June 1982. — [352]p
Previous ed.: 1972
ISBN 0-09-149301-3 (pbk) : £3.75 : CIP entry
B82-10416

940.2'8 — Europe. Revolutions, *1789-1917*

Taylor, A. J. P.. Revolutions and revolutionaries / A.J.P. Taylor. — Oxford : Oxford University Press, 1981, c1980. — 165p : ill,ports ; 24cm. — (Oxford paperbacks)
Originally published: London : Hamilton, 1980. — Includes index
ISBN 0-19-285102-0 (pbk) : £3.50 : CIP rev.
B81-31068

940.2'84 — Europe. Revolutions, *1848*

Jones, Peter, *19---*. The 1848 revolution / Peter Jones. — Harlow : Longman, 1981. — vi,98p : 1map ; 20cm. — (Seminar studies in history)
Bibliography: p90-95. — Includes index
ISBN 0-582-35312-2 (pbk) : £1.75 : CIP rev.
B81-30291

940.3 — HISTORY. WORLD WAR 1, 1914-1918

940.3 — World War 1

Cruttwell, C. R. M. F.. A history of the Great War : 1914-1918 / C.R.M.F. Cruttwell. — 2nd ed. — London : Granada, 1982, c1934. — xii,655p,[16]p of plates : ill,maps,ports ; 20cm. — (A Paladin book)
Originally published: Oxford : Clarendon, 1936. — Includes index
ISBN 0-586-08398-7 (pbk) : £3.95 B82-41098

Stokesbury, James L.. A short history of World War I / by James L. Stokesbury. — London : Hale, 1982, c1981. — 348p : maps ; 25cm
Originally published: New York : Morrow, 1981. — Bibliography: p325-336. — Includes index
ISBN 0-7091-9735-7 : £11.95 B82-21058

940.3 — World War 1 — *For schools*

Evans, David, *1931-*. The Great War 1914-1918 / David Evans. — London : Edward Arnold, 1981. — 64p : ill,maps,ports ; 25cm. — (Links)
Text on inside cover. — Bibliography: p64. — Includes index
ISBN 0-7131-0539-9 (pbk) : £1.95 : CIP rev.
B81-06594

Mair, Craig. Britain at war 1914-1919 / Craig Mair. — London : Murray, 1982. — 122p : ill,facsims,maps,ports ; 25cm
Includes index
ISBN 0-7195-3877-7 (pbk) : £2.60 : CIP rev.
B82-00352

Simkin, John. Contemporary accounts of the First World War / [written by John Simkin] ; [illustrated by David Simkin]. — Brighton : Tressell, 1981. — 32p : ill,1map,ports ; 24cm. — (Active learning in the humanities)
Cover title. — Text on inside covers
Unpriced (pbk) B82-15386

940.3'092'2 — World War 1 — *Personal observations — Collections*

Voices from the Great War / [selected by] Peter Vansittart. — London : Cape, 1981. — xv,303p : ill ; 23cm
Bibliography: p289-294. — Includes index
ISBN 0-224-01915-5 : £7.95 : CIP rev.
B81-30300

940.3'1 — Europe. Social change. Influence of World War 1

Leed, Eric J.. No man's land : combat & identity in World War I / Eric J. Leed. — Cambridge : Cambridge University Press, 1981, c1979. — xii,257p ; 23cm
Bibliography: p233-245. — Includes index
ISBN 0-521-28573-9 (pbk) : £6.50
Also classified at 970.051 B82-13750

940.3'41 — Great Britain. Resources. Mobilisation, *1914-1918 — Conference proceedings*

Mobilization for total war : the Canadian, American and British experience 1914-1918, 1939-1945 / edited by N.F. Dreisziger. — Ontario : Wilfrid Laurier University Press ; Gerrards Cross : Smythe [distributor], 1981. — xvi,115p ; 24cm
Includes index
ISBN 0-88920-109-9 : Unpriced
Primary classification 940.3'7 B82-08602

940.3'7 — North America. Resources. Mobilisation, *1914-1918 — Conference proceedings*

Mobilization for total war : the Canadian, American and British experience 1914-1918, 1939-1945 / edited by N.F. Dreisziger. — Ontario : Wilfrid Laurier University Press ; Gerrards Cross : Smythe [distributor], 1981. — xvi,115p ; 24cm
Includes index
ISBN 0-88920-109-9 : Unpriced
Also classified at 940.3'41 ; 940.53'7 ; 940.53'41 B82-08602

940.4 — World War 1. Military operations, *1914-1918*

Wigginton, John. The Great War 1914-1918 / John Wigginton. — Bognor Regis : New Horizon, c1982. — 28p,[13]p of plates : ill,maps,ports ; 21cm
ISBN 0-86116-571-3 : £3.25 B82-17486

940.4 — World War 1. Role of technology

Terraine, John. White heat : the new warfare 1914-18 / John Terraine. — London : Sidgwick & Jackson, 1982. — 352p : ill,maps ; 24cm
Ill on lining papers. — Includes index
ISBN 0-283-98828-2 : £9.95 B82-26521

940.4′12′41 — World War 1. Army operations by Great Britain. *Army. Post Office Rifles*

Messenger, Charles. Terriers in the trenches : the Post Office Rifles at war 1914-1918 / Charles Messenger. — [Chippenham] : Picton, 1982. — xii,170p : ill,facsims,maps,ports ; 22cm
ISBN 0-902633-82-1 : £12.95 B82-28657

940.4′144 — World War 1. Western Front. Mining operations by Allied forces

Barrie, Alexander. War underground / Alexander Barrie ; with an introduction by Sir John Hackett. — London : W.H. Allen, 1981. — 272p : ill,1map ; 18cm. — (War in the twentieth century) (A Star book)
Originally published: London : Muller, 1962. — Bibliography: p262-263. — Includes index
ISBN 0-352-30970-9 (pbk) : £1.95 B82-03041

940.4′144′06041 — World War 1. Western Front. Army operations by Great Britain. *Army.* **Organisations: Western Front Association** — *Serials*

[Bulletin *(Western Front Association)***]**. Bulletin / the Western Front Association. — No.1 (1981)-. — [Rainham] ([c/o Mr P. Foster, 224 Lonsdale Drive, Rainham, Gillingham, Kent ME8 9JN]) : The Association, 1981-. — v. ; 30cm
Irregular
ISSN 0263-8479 = Bulletin - Western Front Association : Free to Association members B82-32364

940.4′147 — Soviet Union. Military operations by Great Britain. *Royal Naval Air Service. Russian Armoured Car Division, 1915-1981*

Perrett, Bryan. The Czar′s British squadron / Bryan Perrett and Anthony Lord ; foreword by HRH The Duke of Edinburgh. — London : Kimber, 1981. — 192,[16]p of plates : ill,ports ; 24cm
Includes index
ISBN 0-7183-0268-0 : £8.95 B82-06069

940.4′15′0924 — World War 1. Arabian campaign. Lawrence, T. E. — *Serials*

T.E. Lawrence studies newsletter. — Vol.1 no.1 (1981)-. — Lymington (11 Stanford Rd., Lymington, Hants. S04 9GF) : Helari, 1981-. — v. ; 21cm
Two issues yearly
ISSN 0260-9835 = T.E. Lawrence studies newsletter : Unpriced B82-04889

940.4′15′0924 — World War 1. Mesopotamian campaign. Leachman, Gerard — *Biographies*

Winstone, H. V. F.. Leachman. — London : Quartet, Aug.1982. — [256]p
ISBN 0-7043-2330-3 : £11.95 : CIP entry B82-21965

940.4′16′0924 — World War 1. East African campaign. Army operations by Germany. *Heer.* **Lettow-Vorbeck, Paul von**

Hoyt, Edwin P.. Guerilla : Colonel von Lettow-Vorbeck and Germany′s East African empire / Edwin P. Hoyt. — New York : Macmillan ; London : Collier Macmillan, c1981. — 216p ; 25cm
Bibliography: p204-208. — Includes index
ISBN 0-02-555210-4 : £8.95 B82-26198

940.4′21 — World War 1. Army operations by Great Britain. *Army. British Expeditionary Force, 1914 (August-November)*

Ascoli, David. The Mons Star : the British Expeditionary Force, 5th Aug.-22nd Nov. 1914 / David Ascoli. — London : Harrap, 1981. — xxii,250p : ill,maps,facsims,plans,ports ; 24cm
Includes index
ISBN 0-245-53785-6 : £9.95 B82-07473

Simpson, Keith, *1949-*. The Old Contemptibles : a photographic history of the British Expeditionary Force August to December 1914 / Keith Simpson. — London : Allen & Unwin, 1981. — xvi,143p : ill,maps,ports ; 23cm
Bibliography: p139. — Includes index
ISBN 0-04-940062-2 : Unpriced : CIP rev. B81-15868

940.4′3 — World War 1. Military operations, *1918 (November)*

Brook-Shepherd, Gordon. November 1918 : the last act of the Great War / Gordon Brook-Shepherd. — London : Collins, 1981. — 461p,[12]p of plates : ill,1map,ports ; 24cm
Map on lining papers. — Bibliography: p423-429. — Includes index
ISBN 0-00-216558-9 : £12.50 : CIP rev. B81-30322

940.4′31 — World War 1. Battle of Ypres. Battlefields, *1914-1918 compared with* **battlefields,** *1970-1979*

Giles, John. The Ypres Salient : Flanders then and now / John Giles. — Rev. ed. — London : Picardy, c1979. — 229p : ill,maps,facsims,ports ; 21x27cm
Previous ed.: London : Leo Cooper, 1970
ISBN 0-906725-00-3 (pbk) : £8.50 B82-10920

940.4′31′0924 — World War 1. Army operations by Great Britain. *Army. King′s Shropshire Light Infantry. Battalion, 4th, 1917.* **Role of Morley, G. H.**

Allwood, Arthur. Morley of the Fourth / by Arthur Allwood. — Shrewsbury (4 Cross Hill Court, Shrewsbury SY1 1JH) : A. Allwood, 1966 (1982 [printing]). — 8p ; 21cm
Bibliography: p8
Unpriced (unbound) B82-27909

940.4′31′0924 — World War 1. Western Front. Military operations, *1917 — Personal observations — Correspondence, diaries, etc.*

Vaughan, Edwin Campion. Some desperate glory : the diary of a young officer, 1917 / Edwin Campion Vaughan ; with a foreword by John Terraine. — [London] : Warne, 1981. — xi,232p : 1map ; 22cm
ISBN 0-7232-2773-x : £9.95 B82-05173

940.4′34 — World War 1. Amiens campaign. Army operations by Great Britain. *Army, 1918*

Blaxland, Gregory. Amiens : 1918 / Gregory Blaxland ; with an introduction by Sir John Hackett. — London : W.H. Allen, 1981. — xiv,274p : maps ; 18cm. — (War in the twentieth century) (A Star book)
Originally published: London : Muller, 1968. — Includes index
ISBN 0-352-30833-8 (pbk) : £1.95 B82-03038

940.4′4 — World War 1. Western Front. Air operations

Simkins, Peter. Air fighting 1914-18 : the struggle for air superiority over the Western Front / by Peter Simkins. — [London] ([Lambeth Rd, SE1 6HZ]) : Imperial War Museum, 1978. — 80p : ill,1map,ports ; 20x21cm
Cover title. — Bibliography: p78-79
Unpriced (pbk) B82-03982

940.4′41 — World War 1. Air operations by fighter aeroplanes. Pilots

Winter, Denis. The first of the few : fighter pilots of the First World War / Denis Winter. — London : Allen Lane, 1982. — 223p,[24]p of plates : ill,1map,ports ; 23cm
Includes index
ISBN 0-7139-1278-2 : £8.95 B82-17590

940.4′4941′0222 — Kent. Air operations by Great Britain. *Royal Naval Air Services, 1914-1918 — Illustrations*

Flying : the First World War in Kent / compiled by David Collyer. — Rochester : North Kent, c1982. — [64]p : chiefly ill,1map,2ports ; 16x21cm
ISBN 0-9505733-6-1 (pbk) : £1.80 B82-29846

940.4′4941′0924 — World War 1. Air operations by Great Britain. *Royal Air Force — Personal observations — Correspondence, diaries, etc.*

Wortley, Rothesay Stuart. Letters from a flying officer / Rothesay Stuart Wortley. — Gloucester : Sutton, 1982. — vii,[8]p of plates : ill,1port ; 19cm
Originally published: London : Milford, 1928
ISBN 0-86299-017-3 (pbk) : £3.95 : CIP rev. B82-07813

940.4′5 — British ships. Losses, *1914-1918 — Lists — Early works*

British vessels lost at sea 1914-18. — Cambridge : Stephens, 1977 (1979 [printing]). — vi,184p ; 23cm
Facsim of: Navy losses and Merchant shipping (losses). London : H.M.S.O., 1919. — Includes index
ISBN 0-85059-384-0 (pbk) : £2.25 B82-08778

940.4′514 — Steam liners: Lusitania *(Ship).* **Sinking,** *1915*

Hickey, Des. Seven days to disaster : the sinking of the Lusitania / Des Hickey and Gus Smith. — [London] : Fontana, 1982, c1981. — 336p,[8]p of plates : ill,facsims,1map,ports ; 18cm
Originally published: London : Collins, 1981. — Bibliography: p325-331. — Includes index
ISBN 0-00-636514-0 (pbk) : £2.50 B82-39134

940.4′55′0924 — World War 1. Dardanelles campaign. Naval operations by Great Britain. *Royal Navy, 1915-1916 — Personal observations — Correspondence, diaries, etc.*

Denham, H. M.. Dardanelles : a midshipman′s diary 1915-16 / H.M. Denham. — London : Murray, 1981. — 200p : ill,maps,ports ; 25cm
Includes index
ISBN 0-7195-3858-0 : £11.00 : CIP rev. B81-27350

940.4′5943 — Scotland. Orkney. Scapa Flow. Germany. *Kriegsmarine.* **Warships. Scuttling,** *1919*

Van der Vat, Dan. The grand scuttle : the sinking of the German fleet at Scapa Flow in 1919 / Dan van der Vat. — London : Hodder and Stoughton, 1982. — 240p,[16]p of plates ; 24cm
Maps on lining papers. — Includes index
ISBN 0-340-27580-4 : £9.95 : CIP rev. B82-10014

940.4′65′4426 — France. Colincamps. Commonwealth World War 1 military cemeteries: Euston Road Cemetry. Graves — *Lists*

Great Britain. *Commonwealth War Graves Commission.* War graves of the British Commonwealth : the register of the names of those who fell in the Great War and are buried in Euston Road Cemetery, Colincamps, France / compiled and published by order of the Imperial War Graves Commission, London. — Amended version. — Maidenhead : Commonwealth War Graves Commission, 1981. — 56p : 1map,1plan ; 26cm. — (France ; 156)
Previous ed.: 1924
Unpriced (pbk) B82-03318

940.4′65′4427 — France. Aire. World War 1 military Commonwealth cemeteries: Aire Communal Cemetery. Graves — *Lists*

Great Britain. *Commonwealth War Graves Commission.* War graves of the British Commonwealth : the register of the names of those who fell in the Great War and are buried in Aire Communal Cemetery, Aire, France / compiled and published by order of the Imperial War Graves Commission. — Amended version. — Maidenhead : Commonwealth War Graves Commission, 1981. — 48p : 1map,1plan ; 26cm. — (France ; 31)
Previous ed.: 1922
Unpriced (pbk) B82-14176

940.4'65'5456 — India *(Republic).* **Delhi. Commonwealth World War 1 military cemeteries. Graves** — *Lists*

Great Britain. *Commonwealth War Graves Commission*. War dead of the British Commonwealth : the register of the names of those who fell in the 1914-1918 war and whose graves can no longer be maintained / compiled and published by the Commonwealth War Graves Commission. — Maidenhead : The Commission, 1981. — (Memorial registers ; 67, 68, 69)
The Karachi, Taukkyan and Delhi 1914-1918 war memorials. — x,32p ; 27cm
Unpriced (pbk)
Also classified at 940.4'65'549183 ; 940.4'65'591 B82-02926

940.4'65'549183 — Pakistan. Karachi. Commonwealth World War 1 military cemeteries. Graves — *Lists*

Great Britain. *Commonwealth War Graves Commission*. War dead of the British Commonwealth : the register of the names of those who fell in the 1914-1918 war and whose graves can no longer be maintained / compiled and published by the Commonwealth War Graves Commission. — Maidenhead : The Commission, 1981. — (Memorial registers ; 67, 68, 69)
The Karachi, Taukkyan and Delhi 1914-1918 war memorials. — x,32p ; 27cm
Unpriced (pbk)
Primary classification 940.4'65'5456 B82-02926

940.4'65'563 — Turkey. Hellas. Commonwealth World War 1 military cemeteries: Skew Bridge Cemetery & 'V' Beach Cemetery. Graves — *Lists*

Great Britain. *Commonwealth War Graves Commission*. War graves of the British Commonwealth : the register of the names of those who fell in the Great War and are buried in Skew Bridge Cemetery and "V" Beach Cemetery, Helles, Gallipoli / compiled and published by order of the Imperial War Graves Commission, London. — Amended version. — Maidenhead : Commonwealth War Graves Commission, 1982. — 31p : 1map,2plans ; 26cm
Previous ed.: London : Imperial War Graves Commission, 1925
£2.00 (pbk) B82-35147

940.4'65'591 — Burma. Taukkyan. Commonwealth World War 1 military cemeteries. Graves — *Lists*

Great Britain. *Commonwealth War Graves Commission*. War dead of the British Commonwealth : the register of the names of those who fell in the 1914-1918 war and whose graves can no longer be maintained / compiled and published by the Commonwealth War Graves Commission. — Maidenhead : The Commission, 1981. — (Memorial registers ; 67, 68, 69)
The Karachi, Taukkyan and Delhi 1914-1918 war memorials. — x,32p ; 27cm
Unpriced (pbk)
Primary classification 940.4'65'5456 B82-02926

940.4'81'41 — Army operations by Great Britain. *Army. Shropshire Royal Horse Artillery, 1913-1918 — Personal observations*

Allwood, Arthur. The lighter side of war 1914-18, 1939-45 / by Arthur Allwood. — Shrewsbury (4 Cross Hill, Shrewsbury SY1 1JH) : [A. Allwood], 1981. — 9p ; 21cm
Cover title
Unpriced (pbk) B82-05279

940.4'81'71 — World War 1. Role of Canadians — *Personal observations*

Craig, Grace Morris. But this is our war / Grace Morris Craig. — Toronto ; London : University of Toronto Press, c1981. — xii,148p,[16]p of plates : ill,ports ; 24cm. — (Social history of Canada, ISSN 0085-6207 ; 35)
ISBN 0-8020-2442-4 : £10.50 B82-13937

940.4'86'41 — World War I. Naval intelligence operations by Great Britain. *Admiralty. Room 40*

Beesly, Patrick. Room 40 : British naval intelligence 1914-18. — London : Hamilton, Oct.1982. — [320]p
ISBN 0-241-10864-0 : £12.95 : CIP entry B82-23464

940.4'886'41 — World War 1. British airdropped propaganda, *1916-1918:* **Facsimiles of correspondence from German prisoners of war in Great Britain**

Catalogue of airdropped facsimile postal stationery World War 1 1916-1918 / compiled by R.G. Auckland. — [Sandridge] ([Sandridge, via St. Albans, Herts.]) : Published for the Psywar Society [by R.G. Auckland], 1981. — 32p : ill,facsims,forms,ports ; 21cm. — (Blatter catalogue ; no.14)
Unpriced (pbk) B82-05812

940.5 — HISTORY. EUROPE, 1918-

940.5 — Europe, *1900-1978.* **Historical sources: Oral traditions** — *Conference proceedings*

Our common history : the transformation of Europe. — London : Pluto Press, Aug.1982. — [334]p
ISBN 0-86104-378-2 (cased) : £16.50 : CIP entry
ISBN 0-86104-361-8 (pbk) : £7.50 B82-16682

940.5'092'4 — Europe. Social life, *ca 1870-1956 — Personal observations*

Marie Louise, *Princess.* My memories of six reigns / Princess Marie Louise. — London : Evans, 1956 (1979 [printing]). — 328p,[34]p of plates : ill,1facsim,ports,1geneal.table ; 23cm
Includes index
ISBN 0-237-44948-x : £8.50 B82-24192

940.5'2'0924 — Europe. Political events, *1934-1939 — Personal observations*

Duff, Sheila Grant. The parting of ways : a personal account of the thirties / Sheila Grant Duff. — London : Owen, 1982. — 223p,[8]p of plates : ill,ports ; 23cm
Includes index
ISBN 0-7206-0586-5 : £10.50 B82-15417

940.53 — HISTORY. WORLD WAR 2, 1939-1945

940.53 — World War 2

Arnold-Foster, Mark. The world at war. — 2nd ed. — London : Thames Methuen, Oct.1981. — [340]p
Previous ed.: London : Collins, 1973
ISBN 0-423-00150-7 : £7.50 : CIP entry B81-28038

The **Second** World War : essays in military and political history. — London : Sage, Apr.1982. — [420]p. — (Sage readers in 20th century history ; 4)
ISBN 0-8039-9780-9 (cased) : £17.00 : CIP entry
ISBN 0-8039-9781-7 (pbk) : £7.50 B82-04973

Stokesbury, James L.. A short history of World War II / James L. Stokesbury. — London : Hale, 1982, c1980. — 420p ; 25cm
Originally published: New York : Morrow, 1980. — Bibliography: p390-406. — Includes index
ISBN 0-7091-9736-5 : £11.95 B82-21063

Weinberg, Gerhard L.. World in the balance : behind the scenes of World War II / Gerhard L. Weinberg. — Hanover, N.H. ; London : Published for Brandeis University Press by University Press of New England, 1981. — xvii,165p,[1]folded leaf of plates : 1map ; 23cm. — (Tauber Institute series ; no.1)
Bibliography: p149-157. — Includes index
ISBN 0-87451-216-6 (cased) : Unpriced
ISBN 0-87451-217-4 (pbk) : Unpriced B82-28088

940.53 — World War 2, *1939-1940*

Shachtman, Tom. The phony war : 1939-1940 / Tom Shachtman. — New York ; London : Harper & Row, c1982. — xii,289p ; 24cm
Bibliography: p265-269. — Includes index
ISBN 0-06-038036-5 : Unpriced B82-38724

940.53 — World War 2, *1941*

Collier, Richard. 1941 : Armageddon / Richard Collier. — London : Hamilton, 1981. — 310p,16p of plates : ill,ports ; 25cm
Bibliography: p281-299. — Includes index
ISBN 0-241-10611-7 : £9.95 : CIP rev. B81-08905

940.53 — World War 2. Attitudes of right-wing political movements in Great Britain, *1940-1941 — Socialist viewpoints*

Fingal, Marc. The contradictories / Marc Fingal. — Sunderland : Cairns, [1981?]. — [12]p ; 21cm. — (The Right wing of evil ; 2)
ISBN 0-907066-06-2 (unbound) : Unpriced B82-03222

940.53'022'2 — World War 2 — *Illustrations*

Beaton, Cecil. War photographs 1939-45 / Cecil Beaton ; foreword by Peter Quennell ; introduction by Gail Buckland. — London : Imperial War Museum : Jane's, 1981. — 189p : chiefly ill,ports ; 30cm
ISBN 0-7106-0136-0 : £12.95 B82-00103

940.53'03'21 — World War 2 — *Encyclopaedias*

Marshall Cavendish encyclopedia of World War II. — London : Marshall Cavendish, June 1981. — 11v.
ISBN 0-85685-948-6 : CIP entry B81-11928

940.53'144 — Europe. Reconstruction, *1946*

Rostow, W. W.. The division of Europe after World War II : 1946. — Aldershot : Gower, Apr.1982. — [220]p
ISBN 0-566-00535-2 (cased) : £13.50 : CIP entry
ISBN 0-566-00536-0 (pbk) : £6.00 B82-03623

940.53'15'03924 — Belorussia. Nesvizh. Jews. Persecution, *1939-1945 — Personal observations*

Cholawski, Shalom. Soldiers from the ghetto / Shalom Cholawski. — San Diego : Barnes ; London : Tantivy, c1980. — 182p : ill,facsims,ports ; 24cm
ISBN 0-498-02382-6 : £3.25 B82-36373

940.53'15'03924 — Europe. Jews. Persecution. Attitudes of Pius XII, *Pope, 1939-1945*

Holmes, J. Derek. Pius XII, Hitler and the Jews / J. Derek Holmes. — London : Catholic Truth Society, 1982. — 18p ; 19cm
ISBN 0-85183-458-2 (pbk) : £0.40 B82-19046

940.53'15'03924 — Hungary. Jews. Escapes. Role of Wallenberg, Raoul, *1944*

Bierman, John. Righteous gentile : the story of Raoul Wallenberg, missing hero of the holocaust / John Bierman. — London : Allen Lane, 1981. — xii,218p,[8]p of plates : ill,1facsim ports ; 22cm
Bibliography: p217-218
ISBN 0-7139-1387-8 : £6.95 B82-06206

940.53'15'03924 — Jews. Genocide, *1939-1942.* **Information. Disclosure**

Laqueur, Walter. The terrible secret : suppression of the truth about Hitler's "final solution" / Walter Laqueur. — Harmondsworth : Penguin, 1982, c1980. — 262p ; 20cm
Originally published: London : Weidenfeld and Nicolson, 1980. — Includes index
ISBN 0-14-006136-3 (pbk) : £1.95 B82-40768

940.53'15'03924 — Jews. Genocide, *1939-1945.* **Historiography**

Dawidowicz, Lucy S.. The holocaust and the historians / Lucy S. Dawidowicz. — Cambridge, Mass. ; London : Harvard University Press, 1981. — x,187p ; 24cm
Includes index
ISBN 0-674-40566-8 : £10.50 B82-03869

940.53'15'03924 — Jews. Genocide, *1939-1945 — National Socialist viewpoints*

Degrelle, Léon. Letter of the Pope on his visit to Auschwitz / Léon Degrelle. — Ladbroke : Historical Review Press, 1979. — 12p ; 22cm
ISBN 0-906879-00-0 (pbk) : Unpriced B82-38584

Harwood, Richard. Did six million really die? : the truth at last. — [New ed.]. — Ladbroke (Chapel Ascote, Ladbroke, Southam, Warwickshire) : Historical Review, 1978?. — 28p : ill,1map,3facisms,ports ; 29cm. — (Historical fact ; no.1)
Written by Richard Harwood. — Previous ed.: 1974
£0.40 (unbound) B82-04331

940.53'15'03924 — Jews. Genocide, *1939-1945 — National Socialist viewpoints continuation*
Harwood, Richard. Six million lost and found : the truth at last / [Richard Harwood]. — Ladbroke : Historical Review Press, [1982?]. — 28p : ill,ports ; 28cm. — (Historical fact ; no.1)
£0.40 (unbound) B82-38583

940.53'15'03924 — Jews. Genocide, *1939-1945.* **Theories**
The **Six** million reconsidered : is the Nazi Holocaust story a Zionist propaganda ploy? / by the Committee for Truth in History. — Southam : Historical Review Press
Vol.1: In an examination of the Jewish genocide claim versus the disaster of the twentieth century. — 1979, c1977. — 134p : ill,1map,facsims,ports ; 28cm
Originally published: S.l. : Media Research Associates, 1977
ISBN 0-9505505-7-4 (pbk) : Unpriced B82-04781

940.53'15'03924 — Poland. Jews. Escapes. Role of Schindler, Oskar, *1939-1945*
Keneally, Thomas. Schindler's ark. — London : Hodder & Stoughton, Oct.1982. — [576]p
ISBN 0-340-27838-2 : £7.95 : CIP entry B82-24845

940.53'15'03924 — Poland. Warsaw. Jewish ghettos: Warsaw Ghetto, *1939-1943 — Personal observations*
Eisner, Jack. The survivor / Jack Eisner ; edited by Irving A. Leitner. — London : Sphere, 1982, c1980. — 263p : ill,ports ; 17cm
Originally published: New York : Morrow, 1980
ISBN 0-7221-3267-0 (pbk) : £1.75 B82-33820

940.53'15'039240922 — Eastern Europe. Jews. Genocide, *1939-1945.* **Survivors** *— Biographies*
Wiesenthal, Simon. Max and Helen. — London : Granada, Oct.1982. — [122]p
ISBN 0-246-11922-5 : £5.95 : CIP entry B82-23471

940.53'15'03956085 — Peru. Japanese. Policies of government, *1939-1945*
Gardiner, C. Harvey. Pawns in a triangle of hate : the Peruvian Japanese and the United States / C. Harvey Gardiner. — Seattle ; London : University of Washington Press, c1981. — x,222p : 2maps ; 23cm
Bibliography: p209-213. — Includes index
ISBN 0-295-95855-3 : £17.50
Also classified at 940.53'15'03956085 B82-20410

940.53'15'03956085 — Peru. Japanese. Policies of United States government, *1939-1945*
Gardiner, C. Harvey. Pawns in a triangle of hate : the Peruvian Japanese and the United States / C. Harvey Gardiner. — Seattle ; London : University of Washington Press, c1981. — x,222p : 2maps ; 23cm
Bibliography: p209-213. — Includes index
ISBN 0-295-95855-3 : £17.50
Primary classification 940.53'15'03956085 B82-20410

940.53'159 — United States. Soviet refugees. Repatriation, *1946*
Elliott, Mark R.. Pawns of Yalta : Soviet refugees and America's role in their repatriation / Mark R. Elliott. — Urbana ; London : University of Illinois Press, c1982. — xiii,287p,[10]p of plates : ill,ports ; 24cm
Bibliography: p253-277. — Includes index
ISBN 0-252-00897-9 : Unpriced B82-38423

940.53'162 — Great Britain. World War 2. Conscientious objection
Barker, Rachel. Conscience, government and war : conscientious objection in Great Britain 1939-45 / Rachel Barker. — London : Rougledge & Kegan Paul, 1982. — x,174p ; 24cm. — (Routledge direct editions)
Bibliography: p159-165. — Includes index
ISBN 0-7100-9000-5 (pbk) : £6.95 B82-28427

940.53'163 — World War 2. Collaboration
Rings, Werner. Life with the enemy : collaboration and resistance in Hitler's Europe : 1939-1945 / Werner Rings ; translated by J. Maxwell Brownjohn. — London : Weidenfeld and Nicolson, c1982. — 351p,[46]p of plates : ill,maps,ports ; 24cm
Translation of: Leben mit dem Feind. — Bibliography: p329-342. — Includes index
ISBN 0-297-77970-2 : £9.95
Primary classification 940.53'4 B82-19570

940.53'22 — Allied countries. Foreign relations, *1942-1948*
Douglas, Roy, *1924-*. From war to cold war, 1942-1948 / Roy Douglas. — London : Macmillan, 1981. — 224p,[8]p of plates : ill,1facsim,ports ; 23cm
Bibliography: p196-198. — Includes index
ISBN 0-333-25346-9 : £20.00 B82-06646

940.53'22'41 — Great Britain. Exile of Sozialdemokratische Partei Deutschlands, *1941-1945*
Glees, Anthony. Exile politics during the Second World War : the German Social Democrats in Britain. — Oxford : Clarendon, Sept.1982. — [340]p. — (Oxford historical monographs)
ISBN 0-19-821893-1 : £17.50 : CIP entry B82-18997

940.53'22'41 — Great Britain. Foreign relations with France, *1939-1940*
Gates, Eleanor M.. End of the affair : the collapse of the Anglo-French alliance, 1939-40 / Eleanor M. Gates. — London : Allen & Unwin, 1981. — xviii,630p : plans ; 24cm
Bibliography: p573-602. — Includes index
ISBN 0-04-940063-0 : Unpriced : CIP rev.
Also classified at 940.53'22'44 B81-20116

940.53'22'44 — France. Foreign relations with Great Britain, *1939-1940*
Gates, Eleanor M.. End of the affair : the collapse of the Anglo-French alliance, 1939-40 / Eleanor M. Gates. — London : Allen & Unwin, 1981. — xviii,630p : plans ; 24cm
Bibliography: p573-602. — Includes index
ISBN 0-04-940063-0 : Unpriced : CIP rev.
Primary classification 940.53'22'41 B81-20116

940.53'24'45 — Italy. Foreign relations. Policies of government, *1939-1941*
Knox, MacGregor. Mussolini unleashed, 1939-1941 : politics and strategy in fascist Italy's last war / MacGregor Knox. — Cambridge : Cambridge University Press, 1982. — x,385p : maps ; 24cm
Bibliography: p368-373. — Includes index
ISBN 0-521-23917-6 : £22.50 B82-21448

940.53'4 — Europe. Resistance movements, *1939-1945*
Rings, Werner. Life with the enemy : collaboration and resistance in Hitler's Europe : 1939-1945 / Werner Rings ; translated by J. Maxwell Brownjohn. — London : Weidenfeld and Nicolson, c1982. — 351p,[46]p of plates : ill,maps,ports ; 24cm
Translation of: Leben mit dem Feind. — Bibliography: p329-342. — Includes index
ISBN 0-297-77970-2 : £9.95
Also classified at 940.53'163 B82-19570

940.53'41 — Great Britain. Proposed invasion by Germany, *1940*
Macksey, Kenneth. Invasion : the German invasion of England, July 1940 / Kenneth Macksey. — [London] : Corgi, 1981, c1980. — 287p,[16]p of plates : ill,maps,facsims,ports ; 18cm
Originally published: London : Arms and Armour, 1980. — Bibliography: p279-280. — Includes index
ISBN 0-552-11830-3 (pbk) : £1.50 B82-08041

940.53'41 — Great Britain. Resources. Mobilisation, *1939-1945 — Conference proceedings*
Mobilization for total war : the Canadian, American and British experience 1914-1918, 1939-1945 / edited by N.F. Dreisziger. — Ontario : Wilfrid Laurier University Press ; Gerrards Cross : Smythe [distributor], 1981. — xvi,115p ; 24cm
Includes index
ISBN 0-88920-109-9 : Unpriced
Primary classification 940.3'7 B82-08602

940.53'42341 — Jersey. Occupation by German military forces, *1940-1945*
Lewis, John, *1907-*. A doctor's occupation / John Lewis. — [London] : Corgi, 1982. — 238p ; 18cm
ISBN 0-552-11946-6 (pbk) : £1.50 B82-29572

940.53'4253'0924 — England. Wash region. Military operations, *1939-1945 — Personal observations*
Rhodes, Eric. The Wash in wartime : a personal history / Eric Rhodes. — Newport Pagnell : Enthusiasts Publications, 1981. — 25p : ill,maps ; 21cm
ISBN 0-907700-02-0 (pbk) : Unpriced B82-09050

940.53'438 — Poland. Resistance movements: Szare Szeregi, *to 1945 — Polish texts*
Szare Szeregi : Zwj azek Harcerstwa Polskiego w czasie II wojny Swiatowej : Główna Kwatera Harcerzy "Pasieka" : ocalałe dokumenty / [dokumenty ze zbiorów orchiwalnych w Warszawie i w Londynie Skomentowane przez Jana Rossmana]. — Londyn : Polonia Book Fund, 1982. — 275p ; 22cm
Title translated: Polish Scouts Movement during the Second World War. — Includes index
ISBN 0-902352-19-9 (pbk) : £8.00 B82-25132

940.53'44 — France. Occupation by German military forces, *1940-1944 — Personal observations*
Hunt, Antonia. Little resistance : a teenage English girl's adventures in occupied France / Antonia Hunt ; with a foreword by M.R.D. Foot. — London : Cooper, 1982. — vi,149p,[8]p of plates : ill,facsims,1map,ports ; 23cm
ISBN 0-436-20987-x : £6.50 B82-37288

940.53'44'0924 — France. Resistance movements, *1939-1945.* **Rousseeuw, Charles D. C.** *— Biographies*
Rousseeuw, Charles D. C.. The story of Jean Bart, resistance leader / as told to Geoffrey Moore. — Huntingdon : G. Moore, c1982. — 64p : ill,facsims,1map,ports ; 22cm
Includes index
ISBN 0-9506360-9-6 (pbk) : £2.95 B82-35774

940.53'4585 — World War 2. Siege of Malta, *1940-1943*
Attard, Joseph. The battle of Malta / Joseph Attard. — London : Hamlyn Paperbacks, 1982, c1980. — 252p,[4]p of plates : ill,1map,ports ; 18cm
Originally published: London : Kimber, 1980. — Bibliography: p241. — Includes index
ISBN 0-600-20548-7 (pbk) : £1.50 B82-23273

940.53'47 — Soviet Union. Occupation by German military forces, *1941-1945*
Dallin, Alexander. German rule in Russia, 1941-1945 : a study in occupation politics / by Alexander Dallin. — 2nd ed. — London : Macmillan, 1981. — xx,707p : maps ; 25cm
Previous ed.: 1957. — Includes index
ISBN 0-333-21695-4 : £30.00 : CIP rev. B80-09025

940.53'492'0924 — Netherlands. Resistance movements, *1940-1945 — Personal observations*
Roelfzema, Erik Hazelhoff. Soldier of Orange / Erik Hazelhoff Roelfzema. — London : Sphere, 1982, c1981. — 280p ; 18cm
ISBN 0-7221-4493-8 (pbk) : £1.75 B82-29178

Schaepman, Antoinette. Clouds : an episode of Dutch wartime resistance 1940-1945 / Antoinette Schaepman. — Ilfracombe : Stockwell, 1981. — 36p ; 19cm
ISBN 0-7223-1528-7 (pbk) : £1.98 B82-12277

940.53'5125 — Hong Kong. Resistance movements. Role of Great Britain. *Army. British Army Aid Group, 1942-1945*
Ride, Edwin. BAAG : Hong Kong resistance 1942-1945 / Edwin Ride. — Hong Kong ; Oxford : Oxford University Press, 1981. — xiv,347p,[20]p of plates : ill,facsims,maps,1plan,ports ; 23cm
Maps on lining papers. — Bibliography: p333-334. — Includes index
ISBN 0-19-581325-1 : £14.00 B82-37006

940.53′7 — North America. Resources. Mobilisation, *1939-1945 — Conference proceedings*

Mobilization for total war : the Canadian, American and British experience 1914-1918, 1939-1945 / edited by N.F. Dreisziger. — Ontario : Wilfrid Laurier University Press ; Gerrards Cross : Smythe [distributor], 1981. — xvi,115p ; 24cm
Includes index
ISBN 0-88920-109-9 : Unpriced
Primary classification 940.3′7 B82-08602

940.54′012 — World War 2. Grand strategy of Australia

Horner, D. M.. High Command : Australia and allied strategy 1939-1945. — London : Allen & Unwin, Apr.1982. — [384]p
ISBN 0-86861-076-3 : £20.00 : CIP entry
B82-10855

940.54′05′094384 — Poland. Warsaw. Jewish ghettos: Warsaw Ghetto, *1939-1943*

Gutman, Yisrael. The Jews of Warsaw, 1939-1943. — Brighton : Harvester Press, May 1982. — [512]p
Translated from the Hebrew
ISBN 0-7108-0411-3 : £15.95 : CIP entry
B82-10697

940.54′1 — World War 2. Army operations by Allied forces. Armoured combat vehicles: Sherman tanks

Zaloga, Steven J.. The Sherman tank : in US and Allied service / text and colour plates by Steven J. Zaloga. — London : Osprey, 1982. — 40p,A-H p of plates : ill(some col.),1port ; 25cm. — (Vanguard series ; 26)
English text, with notes on the plates in French and German
ISBN 0-85045-427-1 (pbk) : £3.50 B82-37331

940.54′1 — World War 2. Military operations by suicide squads

O′Neill, Richard. Suicide squads : Axis and Allied special attack weapons of World War II : their development and their missions / Richard O′Neill. — London : Salamander, 1981. — 296p : ill,maps,ports ; 24cm
Maps on lining papers. — Bibliography: p282-283. — Includes index
ISBN 0-86101-098-1 : £7.95 B82-05284

940.54′1′0202 — World War 2. Military operations *— Chronologies*

2194 days of war : an illustrated chronology of the Second World War with 620 illustrations and 84 maps / compiled by Cesare Salmaggi and Alfredo Pallavisini ; [translated from the Italian by Hugh Young]. — New York ; London : Windward, c1979. — 754p : ill,maps,ports ; 29cm
Translation of: 2194 giorni di guerra. — Bibliography: p743. — Includes index
ISBN 0-7112-0005-x : £11.95 B82-05910

940.54′12′41 — World War 2. Army operations by Great Britain. *Army. Royal Artillery. Durham Survey Regiment, 4th*

Whetton, J. T.. Z location, or, Survey in war : the story of the 4th Durham Survey Regiment, R.A., T.A. / by J.T. Whettton and R.H. Ogden ; with a foreword by Sir Brian G. Horrocks. — Bolton ([6, Woods Lea, Heaton, Bolton, Lancs, BL1 5DU]) : R.H. Ogden, [1982]. — [195]p : ill,facsims,maps ; 21cm
Bibliography: p195
Unpriced (pbk) B82-25544

940.54′12′41 — World War 2. Military operations by Great Britain. *Army.* **Airborne forces. Generals**

Dover, Victor, *1919-*. The sky generals / Victor Dover. — London : Cassell, 1981. — xiv,215p : ill,maps,ports ; 23cm
Bibliography: p205. — Includes index
ISBN 0-304-30480-8 : £7.95 B82-23129

940.54′12′41 — World War 2. Military operations by Great Britain. *Royal Marines*

Dear, Ian. Marines at war / Ian Dear. — London : Ian Allan, 1982. — 128p : ill,1map,plans,ports ; 30cm
ISBN 0-7110-1147-8 : £9.95
Also classified at 940.54′26 B82-30636

940.54′12′73 — World War 2. Army operations by United States. *Army. Infantry Division, 27th*

Love, Edmund G.. The 27th Infantry Division in World War II / by Edmund G. Love. — Nashville : Battery ; Walpole, Suffolk : Quorn [distributor], 1982. — viii,677p,[32]p of plates : ill,maps,ports ; 24cm
Originally published: Washington, D.C. : Infantry Journal Press, 1949
ISBN 0-89839-056-7 : £16.50 B82-17749

940.54′12′73 — World War 2. Army operations by United States. *Army. Special Service Force, First, 1942-1944*

Burhans, Robert D.. The First Special Service Force : a war history of the North Americans 1942-1944 / by Robert D. Burhans. — Nashville, Tenn. : Battery Press ; Walpole : Patrick Quorn [distributor], 1981, c1975. — xiii,376p : ill,maps,ports ; 24cm
Originally published: Washington : Infantry Journal Press, 1947. — Maps on lining papers
ISBN 0-89839-050-8 : Unpriced B82-00107

940.54′13′43 — World War 2. Army operations by Germany. *Heer.* **Armoured cars & military half-tracked vehicles**

Perrett, Bryan. German armoured cars : and reconnaissance half-tracks : 1939-45 / text by Bryan Perrett ; colour plates by Bruce Culver. — London : Osprey, 1982. — 40p,A-H p of plates : ill(some col.) ; 25cm. — (Vanguard series ; 25)
English text, with notes on the plates in French and German
ISBN 0-85045-426-3 (pbk) : £3.50 B82-37330

940.54′13′43 — World War 2. Army operations by Germany. *Heer.* **Armoured combat vehicles: PzKpfw V tanks**

Perrett, Bryan. The PzKpfw V Panther / text by Bryan Perrett ; colour plates by David E. Smith. — London : Osprey, 1981. — 40p,A-Hp of plates : ill(some col.),facsims,ports ; 25cm. — (Vanguard series ; 21)
ISBN 0-85045-397-6 (pbk) : £2.95 B82-05032

940.54′13′43 — World War 2. Army operations by Germany. *Heer.* **Generals**

Kemp, Anthony. German commanders of World War II / text by Anthony Kemp ; colour plates by Angus McBride. — London : Osprey, 1982. — 39p,A-H p of plates : ports(some col.) ; 25cm. — (Men-at-arms series ; 124)
English text, with notes on the plates in French and German
ISBN 0-85045-433-6 (pbk) : Unpriced
B82-37335

940.54′13′43 — World War 2. Army operations by Germany. *Heer. Panzerdivision, 6*

Ritgen, Helmut. The 6th Panzer Division 1937-45 / text by Helmut Ritgen ; with colour photographs by the author. — London : Osprey, 1982. — 40p,A-H p of plates : ill(some col.),maps,ports(some col.) ; 25cm. — (Vanguard series ; 28)
ISBN 0-85045-453-0 (pbk) : £3.50 B82-37332

940.54′13′43 — World War 2. Army operations by Germany. *Heer. Panzerjäger* **& Germany.** *Heer. Sturmartillerie*

Perrett, Bryan. Sturmartillerie and panzerjäger / text by Bryan Perrett ; colour plates by Mike Chappell. — London : Osprey, 1979. — 40p,A-Hp of plates : ill(some col.),ports ; 25cm. — (Vanguard series ; 12)
English text, English, French and German captions to plates. — Bibliography: p2
ISBN 0-85045-332-1 (pbk) : Unpriced
B82-10740

940.54′21 — East Germany. Dresden. Air raids by Great Britain. *Royal Air Force. Bomber Command, 1945*

McKee, Alexander. Dresden 1945 : the devil′s tinderbox / by Alexander McKee. — London : Souvenir, 1982. — 334p,[24]p of plates : ill,2maps,1plan,ports ; 23cm
Maps on lining papers. — Bibliography: p327-329. — Includes index
ISBN 0-285-62515-2 : £8.95 B82-29674

940.54′21 — Germany. Air raids by Allied air forces, *1944-1945.* **Strategy**

Rostow, W. W.. Pre-invasion bombing strategy : General Eisenhower′s decision of March 25, 1944 / W.W. Rostow. — Aldershot : Gower, c1981. — xiii,166p ; 22cm
Includes index
ISBN 0-566-00482-8 (cased) : £12.50 : CIP rev.
ISBN 0-566-00483-6 (pbk) : Unpriced
B81-21534

940.54′21 — Hampshire. Southampton. Air raids by Germany. *Luftwaffe, 1940-1944*

Brode, Anthony. The Southampton blitz / Anthony Brode. — Rev. ed. — Newbury (3 Catherine Rd, Newbury, Berks.) : Countryside, 1982. — 96p : ports ; 15x21cm
Previous ed.: Winchester : Shurlock, 1977
ISBN 0-905392-15-9 (pbk) : £2.95 B82-31065

940.54′21 — Steam liners: Wilhelm Gustloff *(Ship).* **Sinking,** *1945 — Survivors′ experiences*

Dobson, Christopher. The cruellest night. — Large print ed. — Long Preston : Magna Print, Aug.1982. — [380]p
Originally published: London : Hodder and Stoughton, 1979
ISBN 0-86009-444-8 : £5.50 : CIP entry
B82-16675

940.54′21 — World War 2: Air operations over Benelux Countries, *1945*

Franks, Norman L. R.. The battle of the airfields : 1st January 1945 / Norman L.R. Franks. — London : Kimber, 1982. — 224p : ill,1map,ports ; 24cm
Bibliography: p216. — Includes index
ISBN 0-7183-0448-9 : £9.50 B82-30647

940.54′21 — World War 2. Atlantic campaign. Naval air operations by escort aircraft carriers

Poolman, Kenneth. The sea hunters. — London : Arms and Armour, Sept.1982. — [208]p
ISBN 0-85368-544-4 : £9.95 : CIP entry
B82-20835

940.54′21 — World War 2. Balkan campaigns & Italian campaigns. Army operations by Germany. *Heer.* **Tank units** *— Illustrations*

Panzers in the Balkans and Italy. — Cambridge : Stephens, May 1981. — [96]p. — (World War 2 photo albums ; no.19)
ISBN 0-85059-456-1 (cased) : £5.50 : CIP entry
ISBN 0-85059-457-x (pbk) : £3.95 B81-12823

940.54′21 — World War 2. Battle of Walcheren

Rawling, Gerald. Cinderella Operation : the Battle for Walcheren 1944 / Gerald Rawling. — London : Cassell, 1980. — xi,164p,[8]p of plates : ill ; 23cm
Bibliography: p155. — Includes index
ISBN 0-304-30641-x : £7.95 B82-19149

940.54′21 — World War 2. Cretan campaign, *1941*

Simpson, Tony, *1945-*. Operation Mercury : the battle for Crete, 1941 / Tony Simpson. — London : Hodder and Stoughton, 1981. — 316p,[8]p of plates : ill,maps,ports ; 24cm
Bibliography: p305-306. — Includes index
ISBN 0-340-23118-1 : £8.50 : CIP rev.
B81-15821

940.54′21 — World War 2. Dunkirk campaign. Evacuation of Great Britain. *Army. British Expeditionary Force, 1940*

Goddard, *Sir* **Victor**. Skies to Dunkirk : a personal memoir / Sir Victor Goddard. — London : Kimber, 1982. — 269p,[12]p of plates : ill,1facsim,ports ; 24cm
Includes index
ISBN 0-7183-0498-5 : £9.95 B82-35855

Harman, Nicholas. Dunkirk. — London : Coronet, May 1981. — [304]p
Originally published: 1980
ISBN 0-340-26660-0 (pbk) : £1.95 : CIP entry
B81-07625

940.54′21 — World War 2. English Channel campaign. Naval operations by warships: Gneisenau *(Ship),* Prinz Eugen *(Ship)* & Scharnhurst *(Ship), 1942*

Cooksley, Peter G.. Operation Thunderbolt : the Nazi warships′ escape 1942 / by Peter G. Cooksley. — London : Hale, 1981. — 190p,[16]p of plates : ill,maps,coats of arms,plans,ports ; 23cm
Includes index
ISBN 0-7091-9435-8 : £8.25 B82-03285

940.54′21 — World War 2. European campaigns. Air operations

Bowyer, Chaz. Air war over Europe : 1939-1945 / Chaz Bowyer. — London : Kimber, 1981. — 235p,[30]p of plates : ill,ports ; 24cm
Bibliography: p223-224. — Includes index
ISBN 0-7183-0238-9 : £11.50 B82-02582

940.54′21 — World War 2. French campaign. Army operations by Germany. *Heer. Panzerdivision, 2, 'Das Reich', 1944- (June)*

Hastings, Max. Das Reich : resistance and the march of the 2nd SS Panzer Division through France, June 1944 / Max Hastings. — London : Joseph, 1981. — vi,264p,[16]p of plates : ill,maps,facsim,ports ; 24cm
Maps on lining papers. — Bibliography: p237-239. — Includes index
ISBN 0-7181-2074-4 : £9.95 B82-03047

940.54′21 — World War 2. German campaign. Military operations, *1944-1945*

Whiting, Charles. Siegfried : the Nazis′ last stand. — London : Secker & Warburg, Nov.1982. — [288]p. — (A Leo Cooper book)
ISBN 0-436-57093-9 : £8.95 : CIP entry B82-28738

940.54′21 — World War 2. Italian campaign. Army operations by Allied forces, *1944*

Trevelyan, Raleigh. Rome ′44 : the battle for the Eternal City / Raleigh Trevelyan. — London : Secker & Warburg, 1981. — xvi,366p,[16]p of plates : ill,maps,ports ; 24cm
Includes index
ISBN 0-436-53400-2 : £8.95 : CIP rev. B81-25323

940.54′21 — World War 2. Italian campaign. Army operations by United States. *Army. Infantry Regiment, 350th, 1944-1945*

Wallace, John E.. The Blue Devil ″Battle Mountain″ Regiment in Italy : a history of the 350th Infantry Regiment 1944-1945 / John E. Wallace. — 2nd ed. — Nashville, Tenn. : Battery Press ; Walpole : Patrick Quorn [distributor], 1981, c1977. — vi,266p : ill,maps,ports ; 24cm
Previous ed.: 1977. — Bibliography: p265-266
ISBN 0-89839-052-4 : Unpriced B82-00106

940.54′21 — World War 2. Metz campaign

Kemp, Anthony. The unknown battle : Metz, 1944 / by Anthony Kemp. — London : Warne, 1981, c1980. — xiv,261p,[28]p of plates : ill,maps,plans ; 24cm. — (A Leo Cooper book)
Originally published: New York : Stein and Day, 1979. — Bibliography: p245-247. — Includes index
ISBN 0-7232-2758-6 : £7.95 B82-02400

940.54′21 — World War 2. Normandy campaign

Keegan, John, *1934-*. Six armies in Normandy : from D-Day to the liberation of Paris, June 6th-August 25th, 1944 / John Keegan. — London : Cape, 1982. — xvii,365p,[24]p of plates : ill,maps,ports ; 22cm
Bibliography: p345-349. — Includes index
ISBN 0-224-01541-9 : £8.95 : CIP rev. B81-40241

940.54′21 — World War 2. Normandy campaign. Army operations by Great Britain. *Army. Parachute Regiment, Battalion, 9th, 1944 (June)*

Golley, John. The big drop : the guns of Merville, June 1944 / John Golley. — London : Jane′s, 1982. — 174p,[32]p of plates : ill,facsims,maps,ports ; 24cm
Bibliography: p170. — Includes index
ISBN 0-7106-0193-x : £8.95 B82-32411

940.54′21 — World War 2. Normandy campaign. D-Day, *1944*

Gilchrist, Donald. Dont cry for me : the Commandos : D-Day and after / by Donald Gilchrist. — London : Hale, 1982. — 192p,[32]p of plates : ill,maps,ports ; 23cm
Includes index
ISBN 0-7091-9148-0 : Unpriced B82-28960

940.54′21 — World War 2. Normandy campaign. D-Day, *1944.* **Army operations by Great Britain.** *Army. Airborne Division, 6th*

Wheldon, Huw. Red Berets into Normandy : 6th Airborne Division′s assault into Normandy, D Day 1944 / Sir Huw Wheldon. — Norwich : Jarrold, c1982. — 27p : ill(some col.),col.maps,1port ; 25cm
ISBN 0-7117-0032-x (unbound) : Unpriced B82-36921

940.54′21 — World War 2. Normandy campaign. D-Day, *1944.* **Combined operations by Allied forces**

Paine, Lauran. D-Day. — Large print ed. — Long Preston : Magna, Jan.1983. — [432]p
Originally published: London : Hale, 1981
ISBN 0-86009-454-5 : £6.95 : CIP entry B82-36158

Ryan, Cornelius. The longest day / Cornelius Ryan. — Sevenoaks : New English Library, 1969, c1959 (1982 [printing]). — 256p : 3maps ; 18cm
Originally published: New York : Simon & Schuster, 1959 ; London : Gollancz, 1960. — Bibliography: p249-253
ISBN 0-450-05453-5 (pbk) : £1.95 : CIP rev. B82-09693

940.54′21 — World War 2. Polish campaign

Nowak, Jan. Courier from Warsaw. — London : Collins, Nov.1982. — [480]p
Translation of: Zuraer z Warszawy
ISBN 0-00-262121-5 : £12.50 : CIP entry B82-27800

940.54′21 — World War 2. Russian campaigns. Army operations by Germany

Abbot, Peter. Germany′s Eastern Front allies, 1941-45. — London : Osprey, Nov.1982. — [40]p. — (Men-at-arms series ; 131)
ISBN 0-85045-475-1 (pbk) : £3.50 : CIP entry B82-26422

940.54′21 — World War 2. Western European campaigns. Air operations by Great Britain. *Royal Air Force. Squadron, No.617, 1943:* **Operation Chastise**

Sweetman, John. Operation chastise : the dams raid: epic or myth / John Sweetman. — London : Jane′s, 1982. — xiv,218p,[32]p of plates : ill,maps,ports ; 24cm
Bibliography: p208-215. — Includes index
ISBN 0-7106-0124-7 : £9.95 B82-25869

940.54′21 — World War 2. Western European campaigns. Combined operations by United States. *Army. Parachute Infantry, 501st, 1944-1945*

Critchell, Laurence. Four stars of hell / by Laurence Critchell ; with a foreword by Lewis Brereton. — Nashville : Battery Press ; Walpole, Suffolk : Quorn [distributor], c1974 (1982 printing). — xii,353p,1leaf of plates : ill,maps,ports ; 22cm
ISBN 0-89839-059-1 : £11.00 B82-29924

940.54′21′0222 — World War 2. Mediterranean campaign. Air operations by Germany. *Luftwaffe.* **Fighter aeroplanes** — *Illustrations*

German fighters over the Med : a selection of German wartime photographs from the Bundesarchiv, Koblenz / [compiled by] Bryan Philpott. — Cambridge : Stephens, 1979. — 95p : chiefly ill,1map,ports ; 24cm. — (World War 2 photo album ; no.6)
ISBN 0-85059-343-3 (cased) : £3.95 : CIP rev.
ISBN 0-85059-323-9 (pbk) : £3.50 B78-40636

940.54′21′0222 — World War 2. Normandy campaign. Army operations by Germany. *Heer, 1944.* **Armoured combat vehicles: Tanks** — *Illustrations*

Panzers in North-West Europe : a selection of German wartime photographs from the Bundesarchiv, Koblenz / [conpiled by] Bruce Quarrie. — Cambridge : Stephens, 1979. — 94p : chiefly ill,1map,ports ; 25cm. — (World War 2 photo album ; no.5)
Includes index
ISBN 0-85059-342-5 (cased) : £3.95 : CIP rev.
ISBN 0-85059-322-0 (pbk) : £3.50 B78-40635

940.54′21′0922 — France. Coastal regions. Army operations by Cuthberton, Leslie & King, Peter, *1942*

Foxall, Raymond. [The amateur commandos]. Against all odds / Raymond Foxall. — London : Sphere, 1982, c1980. — 151p,[8]p of plates : ill,1chart,1facsim,ports ; 18cm
Originally published: London : Hale, 1980
ISBN 0-7221-3633-1 (pbk) : £1.50 B82-11197

940.54′21′0924 — World War 2. Western European campaigns. Air operations by Canada. *Royal Canadian Air Force. Squadron, 418, 1943-1944.* **De Havilland Mosquito aeroplanes** — *Personal observations*

McIntosh, Dave. [Terror in the starboard seat]. Mosquito intruder / Dave McIntosh. — London : John Murray, 1982, c1980. — 184p,[8]p of plates : ill,1map,ports ; 23cm
Originally published: Don Mills, Ont. : General, 1980
ISBN 0-7195-3918-8 : £7.50 B82-19316

940.54′23 — World War 2. Battle of El Alamein

Lucas, James. War in the desert. — London : Arms and Armour, Oct.1982. — [288]p
ISBN 0-85368-549-5 : £9.95 : CIP entry B82-24109

940.54′23 — World War 2. North African campaign

Pitt, Barrie. The crucible of war. — London : Cape, Oct.1982
Year of Alamein 1942. — [528]p
ISBN 0-224-01827-2 : £12.50 : CIP entry B82-25159

Pitt, Barrie. The crucible of war / Barrie Pitt. — London : Futura
Western Desert 1941. — 1981, c1980. — xix,506p,[16]p of plates : ill,maps,ports ; 20cm
Originally published: London : Cape, 1980. — Includes index
ISBN 0-7088-2079-4 (pbk) : £3.95 B82-06374

940.54′23 — World War 2. North African campaign. Army operations by Great Britain. *Army.* **Armoured combat vehicles: Tanks**

Perrett, Bryan. British tanks in N. Africa 1940-42 / text by Bryan Perrett ; colour plates by Peter Sarson and Tony Bryan. — London : Osprey, 1981. — 40p,A-Hp of plates : ill(some col.) ; 25cm. — (Vanguard series ; 23)
English text, English, French and German captions to plates. — Bibliography: p2
ISBN 0-85045-421-2 (pbk) : Unpriced B82-10736

940.54′23 — World War 2. Tunisian campaign

Messenger, Charles. The Tunisian Campaign / Charles Messenger. — London : Ian Allan, 1982. — 128p : ill,maps,ports ; 25cm
Bibliography: p128
ISBN 0-7110-1192-3 : £8.95 B82-38012

940.54′23 — World War 2. Western Desert campaign. Military operations by Great Britain. *Army, 1939-1943*

Barnett, Corelli. The desert generals. — 2nd ed. — London : Allen and Unwin, Dec.1982. — [352]p
Previous ed.: London : Kimber, 1960
ISBN 0-04-355018-5 : £12.50 : CIP entry B82-29863

940.54′23′0924 — World War 2. North African campaign, *1942-1943 — Officers′ personal observations*

Messenger, Charles. The unknown Alamein / Charles Messenger. — London : Ian Allan, 1982. — 64p : ill,maps,ports ; 24cm. — (Crucial battles of World War 2)
Bibliography: p62-64
ISBN 0-7110-1186-9 (pbk) : £3.50 B82-38011

940.54'25 — Japan. Hiroshima & Nagasaki. Nuclear bombing, ***1945.*** **Effects**

Unforgettable fire : pictures drawn by atomic bomb survivors / edited by the Japanese Broadcasting Corporation (NHK). — London : Wildwood House, 1981, c1977. — 109p : ill (some col.),facsims,1map ; 26cm
Originally published: Tokyp : Nippon Hoso Shuppan Kyokai, 1977. — Includes index
ISBN 0-7045-0439-1 (pbk) : £4.95 B82-30032

940.54'25 — Sino-Japanese War, ***1937-1945***

Wilson, Dick. When tigers fight : the story of the Sino-Japanese war 1937-45 / Dick Wilson. — London : Hutchinson, 1982. — 269p,[8]p of plates : ill,maps,ports ; 23cm
Bibliography: p258-260. — Includes index
ISBN 0-09-145710-6 : £10.95 B82-20806

940.54'25 — World War 2. Burma campaign. Army operations by Great Britain. ***Army. South-east Asia Command. Special Force***

Forty, George. XIV Army at war / George Forty. — London : Ian Allan, 1982. — 144p : ill,maps,ports ; 30cm
Bibliography: p144
ISBN 0-7110-1161-3 : £11.95 B82-34788

940.54'25 — World War 2. Burma campaign. Army operations by Great Britain. ***Army. South-east Asia Command. Special Force, 1944***

Bidwell, Shelford. The Chindit war : the campaign in Burma, 1944 / Shelford Bidwell. — Large print ed. — Leicester : Ulverscroft, 1982. — 513p ; 22cm. — (Ulverscroft large print)
Originally published: London : Hodder and Stoughton, 1979. — Bibliography: p496-499
ISBN 0-7089-0770-9 : Unpriced : CIP rev.
B82-01749

940.54'25 — World War 2. Far Eastern campaigns, ***1940-1945***

Reynoldson, Fiona. War in the Far East. — London : Heinemann Educational, Sept.1982. — [80]p
ISBN 0-435-31882-9 (pbk) : £1.75 : CIP entry
B82-19673

940.54'25 — World War 2. Leyte campaigne & Okinawa campaign. Army operations by United States. ***Army. Infantry Division, 96th***

Davidson, Orlando R.. The Deadeyes : the story of the 96th Infantry Division / by Orlando R. Davidson, J. Carl Willems, Joseph A. Kahl. — Nashville, Tenn. : Battery Press ; Walpole (Sunnybank, Halesworth Rd, Walpole Suffolk) : Patrick Quorn, 1981. — xvi,310p : ill,plans,ports ; 29cm
Originally published: Washington : Infantry Journal Press, 1947. — Maps on lining papers
ISBN 0-89839-051-6 : £13.25 B82-02961

940.54'25 — World War 2. Philippines campaign

Morris, Eric. Corregidor : the nightmare in the Philippines / Eric Morris. — London : Hutchinson, 1982. — xvii,528p,[14]p of plates : ill,1facsim,3maps,1plan,ports ; 24cm
Facsim on inside covers. — Bibliography: p511-512. — Includes index
ISBN 0-09-146490-0 : £12.95 : CIP rev.
B82-06491

940.54'25 — World War 2. Singapore campaign

Holmes, Richard, *1946-*. The bitter end / Richard Holmes and Anthony Kemp. — Strettington : Bird, 1982. — 212p,[8]p of plates : ill,maps,ports ; 24cm
Bibliography: p204-205. — Includes index
ISBN 0-907319-03-3 : £9.50 : CIP rev.
B81-36055

940.54'25'0924 — World War 2. Japanese campaign, ***1941-1945 — Personal observations***

Guillain, Robert. I saw Tokyo burning : an eyewitness narrative from Pearl Harbor to Hiroshima / by Robert Guillain ; translated by William Byron. — London : Murray, 1981. — xii,298p : maps ; 23cm
Translation of: La guerre au Japon. — Maps on lining papers. — Includes index
ISBN 0-7195-3862-9 : £9.50 : CIP rev.
B81-21539

940.54'26 — Hawaii. Pearl Harbor. Air raids by Japan. ***Nihon Rikugun Kōkū-butai*** **& Japan.** ***Nihon Kaigun Kōkū-bu, 1941***

Prange, Gordon W.. At dawn we slept : the untold story of Pearl Harbor / Gordon W. Prange in collaboration with Donald M. Goldstein and Katherine V. Dillon. — London : Joseph, 1982, c1981. — xvi,873p,[8]p of plates : ill,ports ; 25cm
Originally published: New York : McGraw-Hill, 1981. — Bibliography: p827-838. — Includes index
ISBN 0-7181-2090-6 : £14.95 B82-16319

Toland, John, *1912-*. Infamy : Pearl Harbor and its aftermath / John Toland. — London : Methuen, 1982. — xvi,366p,[16]p of plates : ill,facsims,col.plans,ports ; 24cm
Includes index
ISBN 0-413-49820-4 : £9.50 B82-34764

940.54'26 — World War 2. Battle of Okinawa. Naval operations by Japan. ***Kaigun, 1945.*** **Battleships: Yamato** ***(Ship)***

Spurr, Russell. A glorious way to die : the kamikaze mission of the battleship Yamato, April 1945 / Russell Spurr. — London : Sidgwick & Jackson, 1982, c1981. — x,341p,[16]p of plates : ill,maps,plans,ports ; 24cm
Originaly published: New York : Newmarket Press, 1981. — Bibliography: p331-336. — Includes index
ISBN 0-283-98850-9 : £8.95 B82-22262

940.54'26 — World War 2. Pacific campaigns, ***1941-1945***

Castello, John, *1943-*. The Pacific war / John Castello. — London : Collins, 1981. — xiv,242p,[40]p of plates : ill,maps,ports ; 24cm
Maps on lining papers. — Bibliography: p709-720. — Includes index
ISBN 0-00-216046-3 : £12.95 : CIP rev.
B81-30214

940.54'26 — World War 2. Pacific campaigns. Air operations by United States. ***Army Air Force. Air Force, Thirteenth***

Rust, Kenn C.. Thirteenth Air Force : story : — in World War II / Kenn C. Rust and Dana Bell. — Temple City : Historical Aviation Album ; London : Hersant [distributor], c1981. — 64p : ill,maps,ports ; 28cm. — (A Historical Aviation Album publication)
ISBN 0-911852-90-5 (pbk) : £5.45 B82-07869

940.54'26 — World War 2. Pacific campaigns. Military cryptology by American military forces

Lewin, Ronald. The other Ultra / Ronald Lewin. — London : Hutchinson, 1982. — xv,332p,[16]p of plates : ill,1facsim,ports ; 24cm
Bibliography: p309-311. — Includes index
ISBN 0-09-147470-1 : £10.95 : CIP rev.
B82-01704

940.54'26 — World War 2. Pacific campaigns. Military operations by United States. ***Marine Corps***

Dear, Ian. Marines at war / Ian Dear. — London : Ian Allan, 1982. — 128p : ill,1map,plans,ports ; 30cm
ISBN 0-7110-1147-8 : £9.95
Primary classification 940.54'12'41 B82-30636

940.54'26 — World War 2. Pacific campaigns. Naval operations by United States. ***Navy, 1941-1945.*** **Submarines**

Blair, Clay. Combat patrol : abridged from Silent victory / by Clay Blair, Jr ; [maps by Alan McKnight] ; [drawings Robert Blanchard]. — Toronto ; London : Bantam, 1978. — xvi,397p,[1]folded leaf of plate : ill(some col.),maps ; 18cm
Includes index
ISBN 0-553-12279-7 (pbk) : £0.95 B82-18599

940.54'26 — World War 2. Pacific campaigns. Naval operations by United States. ***Navy. Fifth Fleet.*** **Flagships: Indianapolis** ***(Ship).*** **Sinking**

Newcomb, Richard F.. Abandon ship! : the death of the U.S.S. Indianapolis / Richard F. Newcomb. — [New ed.]. — South Yarmouth, Mass. : Curley, c1976 ; [Long Preston] : Distributed by Magna Print. — xi,563p ; 23cm
Originally published: Bloomington, London : Indiana University Press, 1976. — Published in large print
ISBN 0-89340-242-7 : £5.50 B82-21465

940.54'26 — World War 2. Pacific campaigns. Naval operations by United States. ***Navy.*** **Submarines: Batfish** ***(Submarine)***

Lowder, Hughston E.. Batfish : the champion 'submarine-killer' submarine of World War II / Hughston E. Lowder with Jack Scott. — London : Sphere, 1982, c1980. — 276p,[8]p of plates : ill,ports ; 18cm
Originally published: Englewood Cliffs : Prentice-Hall, 1980. — Includes index
ISBN 0-7221-5649-9 (pbk) : £1.95 B82-33664

940.54'26 — World War 2. Pacific campaigns. Night air operations by United States. ***Navy.*** **PBY Catalina aeroplanes**

Knott, Richard C.. [Black Cat raiders of World War II]. The Black Cats / Richard C. Knott. — Cambridge : Stephens, 1981. — x,198p : ill,maps,1facsim,ports ; 24cm
Originally published: Annapolis : Nautical & Aviation Pub. Co. of America, c1981. — Includes index
ISBN 0-85059-568-1 : £8.95 B82-18329

940.54'4 — World War 2. Air operations by Allied air forces. Boeing B17 aeroplanes

Willmott, H. P.. B-17 flying fortress / H.P. Willmott. — London : Arms and Armour Press, 1980. — 64p : ill(some col.),ports(some col.) ; 29cm. — ([War planes in colour] ; 4) (A bison book)
ISBN 0-85368-444-8 : £2.95 : CIP rev.
B80-18106

940.54'4 — World War 2. Air operations by Commonwealth air forces

Great Britain. *Commonwealth War Graves Commission*. The Runnymede Memorial to airmen who have no known grave : 1939-1945 / compiled and published by order of the Imperial War Graves Commission. — Amended version. — Maidenhead : Commonwealth War Graves Commission, 1982. — 20p,[14]p of plates : ill,1map,1plan ; 26cm. — (Memorial register ; 7)
Previous ed.: 1953
Unpriced (pbk)
Also classified at 940.54'65'42211 B82-21809

940.54'41 — World War 2. Air photographic operations

Stanley, Roy M.. World War II photo intelligence / Roy M. Stanley. — London : Sidgwick & Jackson, 1982, c1981. — x,374p : ill,maps,plans ; 29cm
Originally published: New York : Scribner, 1981. — Bibliography: p365-367. — Includes index
ISBN 0-283-98824-x : £12.50 B82-12071

940.54'4941 — World War 2. Air operations by Great Britain. ***Royal Air Force. Bomber Command***

Messenger, Charles. Cologne : the first 1000-bomber raid / Charles Messenger. — London : Ian Allan, 1982. — 64p : ill,maps,plans,ports ; 24cm. — (Crucial battles of World War 2)
Bibliography: p62-64
ISBN 0-7110-1199-0 (pbk) : £2.95 B82-30642

940.54'4941 — World War 2. Air operations by Great Britain. ***Royal Air Force. Desert Air Force, 1940-1945***

Bowyer, Chaz. Desert Air Force : at war / Chaz Bowyer & Christopher Shores. — London : Ian Allan, 1981. — 128p : ill,ports ; 30cm
Bibliography: p128
ISBN 0-7110-1154-0 : £9.95 B82-11214

940.54'4941 — World War 2. Air operations by Great Britain. ***Royal Air Force.*** **Hawker Hurricane aeroplanes**

Stewart, Adrian. Hurricane : the war exploits of the fighter aircraft / Adrian Stewart. — London : Kimber, 1982. — 336p,[16]p of plates : ill,maps ; 24cm
Bibliography: p315-320. — Includes index
ISBN 0-7183-0009-2 : £11.50 B82-35351

940.54'4941 — World War 2. Air operations by Great Britain. *Royal Air Force. Squadron, No.76, 1941-1945*

Chorley, W. R.. To see the dawn breaking : 76 Squadron operations / W.R. Chorley. — [Ottery St. Mary] : W.R. Chorley, 1981. — 272p : ill,ports ; 22cm
Bibliography: p188. — Includes index
ISBN 0-9507467-0-3 (pbk) : Unpriced B82-27068

940.54'4941 — World War 2. Air operations by Great Britain. *Royal Air Force. Squadron, No.161, 1942-1945*

McCall, Gibb. Flight most secret : air missions for SOE and SIS / Gibb McCall. — London : Kimber, 1981. — 270p,[12]p of plates : ill,ports ; 25cm
Bibliography: p261-262. — Includes index
ISBN 0-7183-0038-6 : £8.95 B82-14660

940.54'4941 — World War 2. Air operations by Great Britain. *Royal Air Force. Squadron, No.617*

Cooper, Alan W.. The men who breached the dams : 617 squadron 'The dambusters' / Alan W. Cooper. — London : Kimber, 1982. — 223p : ill,1map,ports ; 24cm
Includes index
ISBN 0-7183-0308-3 : £9.50 B82-35854

940.54'4941 — World War 2. Air operations by Great Britain. *Royal Air Force.* **Supermarine Spitfire aeroplanes**

Bowyer, Chaz. Supermarine Spitfire / Chaz Bowyer. — London : Arms and Armour, 1980. — 64p : ill(some col.),ports(some col.) ; 29cm. — (A bison book) ([War planes in colour] ; 1)
Bibliography: p64
ISBN 0-85368-464-2 : £2.95 : CIP rev. B80-18107

940.54'4941 — World War 2. Naval air operations by Great Britain. *Royal Navy. Fleet Air Arm*

Sturtivant, Ray. Fleet air arm at war / Ray Sturtivant. — London : Ian Allan, 1982. — 144p : ill,maps,ports ; 30cm
ISBN 0-7110-1084-6 : £8.95 B82-25645

940.54'4941'0922 — World War 2. Air operations by Royal Air Force Great Britain, *1943-1945.* **Halifax aeroplanes** — *Personal observations — Collections*

Jones, Geoffrey P.. Night flight : Halifax squadrons at war / Geoffrey P. Jones. — London : Kimber, 1981. — 224p : ill,maps,ports ; 25cm
Includes index
ISBN 0-7183-0338-5 : £9.50 B82-06617

940.54'4941'0924 — Great Britain. *Royal Air Force. Ferry Command, to 1942 — Personal observations*

McVicar, Don. Ferry command / Don McVicar ; illustrated by L.R. Williams. — Shrewsbury : Airlife, 1981. — 213p,[8]p of plates : ill,ports ; 23cm
Maps on lining papers
ISBN 0-906393-12-4 : £7.95 B82-03944

940.54'4941'0924 — Malta. Air operations by Great Britain. *Royal Air Force, 1942 — Personal observations*

Douglas-Hamilton, *Lord* **James**. The air battle for Malta : the diaries of a fighter pilot / Lord James Douglas-Hamilton ; introduction by Laddie Lucas. — Edinburgh : Mainstream, 1981. — 208p,[24]p of plates : ill,1facsim,ports ; 23cm
Bibliography: p195-202. — Includes index
ISBN 0-906391-20-2 : £7.95 B82-31398

940.54'4941'0924 — World War 2. Air operations, *1943-1944.* **Great Britain.** *Royal Air Force. Bomber Command.* **Avro Lancaster aeroplanes** — *Personal observations*

Currie, Jack. Lancaster target : the story of a crew who flew from Wickenby / Jack Currie. — London : Goodall, 1981, c1977. — 175p ; 17cm
Originally published: London : New English Library, 1977
ISBN 0-907579-00-0 (pbk) : £1.50 B82-40631

940.54'4941'0924 — World War 2. Air operations by Great Britain. *Royal Air Force. Squadron, No. 217, 1941 — Personal observations*

Nesbit, Roy Conyers. Woe to the unwary : a memoir of low level bombing operations 1941 / Roy Conyers Nesbit. — London : Kimber, 1981. — 192p : ill,maps,facsims,ports ; 25cm
Includes index
ISBN 0-7183-0348-2 : £8.95 B82-06615

940.54'4941'0924 — World War 2. Air operations by Great Britain. *Royal Air Force.* **Supermarine Spitfire aeroplanes** — *Personal observations*

Smith, W. G. G. Duncan. Spitfire into battle / W.G.G. Duncan Smith. — Feltham : Hamlyn, 1982, c1981. — 235p,[8]p of plates : ill,maps,ports ; 18cm
Originally published: London : Murray, 1981. — Includes index
ISBN 0-600-20606-8 (pbk) : £1.75 B82-39073

940.54'4943 — World War 2. Air operations by Germany. *Luftwaffe.* **Junkers Stuka aeroplanes**

Vanags-Baginskis, Alex. Stuka Ju87 / text by Alex Vanags-Baginskis ; illustrations by Rikyu Watanabe. — London : Jane's, 1982. — 55p,8folded : ill(some col.) ; 33cm. — (Jane's aircraft spectaculars)
ISBN 0-7106-0191-3 : £6.95 B82-40634

940.54'4943 — World War 2. Air operations by Germany. *Luftwaffe. Kampfgruppe 100, 1939-1941*

Wakefield, Kenneth. The first pathfinders : the operational history of Kampfgruppe 100, 1939-1941 / Kenneth Wakefield. — London : Kimber, 1981. — 256p : ill,maps,facsims,ports ; 24cm
Includes index
ISBN 0-7183-0318-0 : £9.75 B82-06616

940.54'4943'0222 — World War 2. Air operations by Germany. *Luftwaffe.* **Night fighter forces** — *Illustrations*

The **Defence** of the Reich : Hitler's nightfighter planes and pilots / [compiled by] Werner Held and Holger Nauroth ; translated by David Roberts. — London : Arms and Armour, 1982. — 230p : ill,1map,facsims,ports ; 25cm
Translation of : Die deutsche Nachtjagd
ISBN 0-85368-414-6 : £9.95 : CIP rev. B81-33783

940.54'4973 — World War 2. Air operations by United States. *Army Air Force. Air Force, 8th*

Freeman, Roger A. (Roger Anthony). Mighty Eighth war diary / Roger A. Freeman with Alan Crouchman and Vic Maslen. — London : Jane's, 1981. — 508p : ill,ports ; 29cm
Includes index
ISBN 0-7106-0038-0 : £12.95 B82-00112

940.54'4973 — World War 2. Air operations by United States. *Army Air Force. Bombardment Group, 306th, 1942-1946*

Bove, Arthur P.. First over Germany : a story of the 33th Bombardment Group / by Arthur P. Bove. — [S.l.] : [s.n.] ; Walpole (Sunnybank, Halesworth Road, Walpole, Suffolk) : Patrick Quorn [distributor], [1981?]. — [148]p : chiefly ill,facsim,ports ; 28cm
Originally published: San Angelo, Tex. : News Foto Publishing Co., 1946
Unpriced B82-00102

940.54'4973 — World War 2. Air operations by United States. *Army Air Force. Bomber Command.* **Documents**

A **Guide** to the reports of the United States Strategic Bombing Survey. — Woodbridge : Boydell Press, Sept.1981. — [224]p. — (Royal Historical Society guides and handbooks. Supplementary series ; no.2)
ISBN 0-901050-71-7 : £15.00 : CIP entry B81-20602

940.54'5 — World War 2. Naval operations by destroyers

Haines, Gregory, *d. 1981.* Destroyers at war / Gregory Haines. — London : Ian Allan, 1982. — 128p : ill ; 29cm
ISBN 0-7110-1110-9 : £9.95 B82-17809

940.54'51 — World War 2. Naval operations by submarines

Compton-Hall, Richard. The underwater war 1939-1945 / Richard Compton-Hall ; artwork by John Batchelor. — Poole : Blandford, 1982. — 160p : ill,facsims,1map,ports ; 29cm
Includes index
ISBN 0-7137-1131-0 : £8.95 : CIP rev. B82-04500

940.54'51'0924 — World War 2. Naval operations by Great Britain. *Royal Navy, 1940-1945.* **Submarines** — *Personal observations*

Young, Edward, *1913-*. One of our submarines / Edward Young. — London : Granada, 1982, c1952. — 336p,[16]p of plates : ill,maps,ports ; 18cm. — (A Mayflower book)
Originally published: London : Hart-Davis, 1952
ISBN 0-583-13531-5 (pbk) : £1.95 B82-19603

940.54'5941 — Norway. Coastal waters. Germany. *Kriegsmarine.* **Supply ships: Altmark** *(Ship).* **British prisoners of war. Rescue by Great Britain.** *Royal Navy, 1940.* **Destroyers: Cossack** *(Ship)*

Wiggan, Richard. Hunt the Altmark / by Richard Wiggan. — London : Hale, 1982. — 176p,[16]p of plates : ill,facsims,maps,ports ; 23cm
Bibliography: p165. — Includes index
ISBN 0-7091-9737-3 : Unpriced B82-37021

940.54'5941 — South-east England. Coastal waters. Colliers. Convoys, *1940-1943*

McKee, Alexander. The Coal Scuttle Brigade / Alexander McKee. — Abridged ed. — [London] : Hamlyn Paperbacks, 1981. — 131p ; 18cm
Originally published: London : New English Library, 1973
ISBN 0-600-20275-5 (pbk) : £1.10 B82-05854

940.54'5941 — World War 2. Naval operations by Great Britain. *Royal Navy, 1942.* **Cruisers: Edinburgh** *(Ship)*

Pearce, Frank, *1909-*. Last call for HMS Edinburgh : a story of the Russian convoys / Frank Pearce. — London : Collins, 1982. — 200p,[8]p of plates : ill,maps,1port ; 22cm
Bibliography: p195. — Includes index
ISBN 0-00-216677-1 : £8.95 : CIP rev. B82-00900

940.54'5941 — World War 2. Naval operations by Great Britain. *Royal Navy.* **Cruisers**

Smith, Peter C. (Peter Charles), *1940-*. Cruisers in action 1939-1945 / Peter C. Smith and John R. Dominy. — London : Kimber, 1981. — 320p,[12]p of plates : ill ; 25cm
Includes index
ISBN 0-7183-0218-4 : £11.95 B82-08752

940.54'5941 — World War 2. Naval operations by Great Britain. *Royal Navy. Destroyer Flotilla, 17th*

Connell, G. G.. Arctic destroyers : the 17th flotilla / G.G. Connell. — London : Kimber, 1982. — 237p,[16]p of plates : ill,1facsim,maps,ports ; 25cm
Bibliography: p223-224. — Includes index
ISBN 0-7183-0428-4 : £9.95 B82-37222

940.54'59'410924 — World War 2. Naval operations by Great Britain. *Royal Navy — Officers' personal observations*

Brooke, Geoffrey. Alarm starboard!. — Cambridge : Patrick Stephens, May 1982. — [224]p
ISBN 0-85059-578-9 : £8.95 : CIP entry B82-07612

940.54'5941'0924 — World War 2. Naval operations by Great Britain. *Royal Navy — Personal observations*

Holmes, David, *1923-*. Not beyond recall / David Holmes. — Bognor Regis : New Horizon, c1982. — 81p,[10]p of plates : ill ; 21cm
ISBN 0-86116-838-0 : £4.25 B82-22459

940.54′5943 — World War 2. Naval operations by Germany. ***Kriegsmarine.*** **Destroyers & escort ships**

German destroyers and escorts. — Cambridge : Stephens, May 1981. — [96]p. — (World War 2 photo albums ; no.20)
ISBN 0-85059-458-8 (cased) : £3.95 : CIP entry
ISBN 0-85059-459-6 (pbk) : £3.95 B81-12824

940.54′5943′0924 — World War 2. Naval operations by Germany. ***Kriegsmarine.*** **Battleships: Bismarck** ***(Ship) - Personal observations***

Müllenheim-Rechberg, Burkard, *Freiherr von*. Battleship Bismarck. — London : Bodley Head, May 1981. — [288]p
This translation originally published: Annapolis : Naval Institute Press, 1980
ISBN 0-370-30390-3 : £7.95 : CIP entry
B81-06038

940.54′65′41 — Great Britain. Commonwealth World War 2 naval war memorials

Great Britain. *Commonwealth War Graves Commission*. Naval memorials in the United Kingdom 1939-1945 : introduction to the registers / compiled and published by order of the Imperial War Graves Commission. — Amended version. — Maidenhead (Maidenhead, Berks.) : Commonwealth War Graves Commission, 1982. — 15,vip,[4]p of plates : ill,maps ; 27cm. — (Memorial register ; 4)
Previous ed.: 1952. — Contents refer to Liverpool
Unpriced (pbk) B82-30878

940.54′65′42211 — Surrey. Runnymede. World War 2 Commonwealth air force war memorials: Runnymede Memorial

Great Britain. *Commonwealth War Graves Commission*. The Runnymede Memorial to airmen who have no known grave : 1939-1945 / compiled and published by order of the Imperial War Graves Commission. — Amended version. — Maidenhead : Commonwealth War Graves Commission, 1982. — 20p,[14]p of plates : ill,1map,1plan ; 26cm. — (Memorial register ; 7)
Previous ed.: 1953
Unpriced (pbk)
Primary classification 940.54′4 B82-21809

940.54′65′43515 — West Germany. Hamburg. Ohlsdorf. Commonwealth World War 2 military cemeteries: Hamburg War Cemetery. Graves — ***Lists***

Great Britain. *Commonwealth War Graves Commission*. War graves of the British Commonwealth : the register of the names of those who fell in the 1939-1945 War and are buried in cemeteries in Germany : Hamburg Cemetery, Ohlsdorf : Part II (Lai-You) / compiled and published by order of the Imperial War Graves Commission. — Amended version. — Maidenhead ([2, Marlow Rd] Maidenhead, Berkshire) : Commonwealth War Graves Commission, 1981. — xii,[32]p ; 26cm. — (Germany ; 11)
Previous ed.: 1957. — Pages also numbered 33-63
£2.00 (pbk) B82-15086

940.54′65′4359 — West Germany. Becklingen. Commonwealth World War 2 military cemeteries: Becklingen War Cemetery. Graves — ***Lists***

Great Britain. *Commonwealth War Graves Commission*. War graves of the British Commonwealth : the register of the names of those who fell in the 1939-1945 War and are buried in cemeteries in Germany : Becklingen War Cemetery, Soltau : Part III (Pa-Za), Visselhövede Civil Cemetery / compiled and published by order of the Imperial War Graves Commission. — Amended version. — Maidenhead : Commonwealth War Graves Commission, 1981. — xii,77-110p : 1map,1plan ; 26cm. — (Germany ; 9)
Previous ed.: 1957
Unpriced (pbk) B82-05640

940.54′65′436 — Austria. Ukrainian World War 2 war memorials — ***Ukrainian texts***

Voīaky — voīakam / [zahal′na redaktsiīa Svīatomyr M. Fostun]. — London : Ob′īednannīa buvshykh Voīakiv Ukraïntsiv u Velykiĭ Brytaniï, 1981. — 64p : ill,ports ; 22cm
Added title: Soldiers to soldiers
Unpriced (pbk) B82-08786

940.54′65′4422 — France. Bayeux. Commonwealth World War 2 military cemeteries: Bayeux War Cemetery. Graves — ***Lists***

Great Britain. *Commonwealth War Graves Commission*. War graves of the British Commonwealth : the register of the names of those who fell in the 1939-1945 war and are buried in cemeteries in France : Bayeux War Cemetery, part III (Lai-Roy) / compiled and published by order of the Imperial War Graves Commission. — Maidenhead : Commonwealth War Graves Commission, 1981. — xxiv,99p,[2] leaves of plates : maps,plans ; 26cm. — (France ; 1058)
Previous ed.: 1955
Unpriced (pbk) B82-21810

940.54′65′4422 — France. Calvados. Commonwealth World War 2 military cemeteries: Secqueville-en-Bessin War Cemetery. Graves — ***Lists***

Great Britain. *Commonwealth War Graves Commission*. War graves of the British Commonwealth : the register of the names of those who fell in the 1939-1945 War and are buried in cemeteries in France : Secqueville-en-Bessin War Cemetery, Fontenay-le-Pesnel War Cemetery, Tessel / compiled and published by order of the Imperial War Graves Commission. — Amended version. — Maidenhead : Commonwealth War Graves Commission, 1981. — xxii,29p : 2maps,2plans ; 26cm. — (France ; 1077-1078)
Previous ed.: 1956
Unpriced (pbk)
Also classified at 940.54′65′4422 B82-16788

940.54′65′4422 — France. Ranville. Commonwealth World War 2 military cemeteries: Ranville War Cemetery. Graves — ***Lists***

Great Britain. *Commonwealth War Graves Commission*. War graves of the British Commonwealth : the register of the names of those who fell in the 1939-1945 war and are buried in cemeteries in the [sic] France : Ranville War Cemetery : Part II (Hac-Ped) / compiled and published by order of the Imperial War Graves Commission. — Amended version. — Maidenhead : Commonwealth War Graves Commission, 1981. — xxivp,p37-70 : maps,1plan ; 26cm. — (France ; 1071)
Previous ed.: 1955
Unpriced (pbk) B82-24699

940.54′65′4422 — France. Tessel. Commonwealth World War 2 military cemeteries: Fontenay-le-Pesnel War Cemetery. Graves — ***Lists***

Great Britain. *Commonwealth War Graves Commission*. War graves of the British Commonwealth : the register of the names of those who fell in the 1939-1945 War and are buried in cemeteries in France : Secqueville-en-Bessin War Cemetery, Fontenay-le-Pesnel War Cemetery, Tessel / compiled and published by order of the Imperial War Graves Commission. — Amended version. — Maidenhead : Commonwealth War Graves Commission, 1981. — xxii,29p : 2maps,2plans ; 26cm. — (France ; 1077-1078)
Previous ed.: 1956
Unpriced (pbk)
Primary classification 940.54′65′4422
B82-16788

940.54′65′4427 — France. Pas-de-Calais. Commonwealth World War 2 military cemeteries. Graves — ***Lists***

Great Britain. *Commonwealth War Graves Commission*. War graves of the British Commonwealth : the register of the names of those who fell in the 1939-1945 war and are buried in cemeteries in France : Boulogne Eastern Cemetery and minor cemeteries in Pas-de-Calais 1 / compiled and published by order of the Imperial War Graves Commission. — Amended verision. — Maidenhead : Commmonwealth War Graves Commission, 1982. — xxiii,77p,[3]leaves of plates(1 folded) : 2maps,1plan ; 26cm. — (France ; 184-293)
Previous ed.: 1958
Unpriced (pbk) B82-21811

940.54′65′4428 — France. Nord. Commonwealth World War 2 military cemeteries. Graves — ***Lists***

Great Britain. *Commonwealth War Graves Commission*. War graves of the British Commonwealth : the register of the names of those who fell in the 1939-1945 War and are buried in cemeteries in France : minor cemeteries in Nord-II / compiled and published by order of the Imperial War Graves Commission. — Amended version. — Maidenhead : Commonwealth War Graves Commission, 1981. — xxiv,37p : maps,plans ; 26cm. — (France ; 72-101)
Previous ed.: 1958
Unpriced (pbk) B82-02715

940.54′65′492 — Netherlands. Commonwealth World War 2 military cemeteries. Graves — ***Lists***

Great Britain. *Commonwealth War Graves Commission*. War graves of the British Commonwealth : the register of the names of those who fell in the 1939-1945 War and are buried in cemeteries in the Netherlands : Venray War Cemetery, Sittard War Cemetery, Sittard General Cemetery / compiled and published by order of the Imperial War Graves Commission. — Amended version. — Maidenhead : Commonwealth War Graves Commission, 1981. — xvi,47p : 1map,plans ; 26cm. — (Netherlands ; 161-163)
Previous ed.: 1955
Unpriced (pbk) B82-02716

940.54′65′4924 — Netherlands. North Brabant ***(Province).*** **Commonwealth World War 2 military cemeteries. Graves —** ***Lists***

Great Britain. *Commonwealth War Graves Commission*. War Graves of the British Commonwealth : the register of the names of those who fell in the 1939-1945 war and are buried in cemeteries in The Netherlands : Uden War Cemetery, minor cemeteries in the province of North Brabant / compiled and published by order of the Imperial War Graves Commission. — Amended version. — Berkshire : Commonwealth War Graves Commission, 1981. — xvi,69p : ill,1map ; 26cm. — (Netherlands ; 88-148)
Previous ed.: 1957
Unpriced (pbk) B82-03486

940.54′65′5332 — Yemen ***(People′s Democratic Republic).*** **Commonwealth World War 2 military cemeteries. Graves —** ***Lists***

War dead of the British Commonwealth : the register of the names of those who fell in the 1939-1945 War and are buried in cemeteries in Yemen (including the Maala Memorial) and Saudi Arabia. — [Maidenhead] ([2 Marlow Rd., Maidenhead, SL6 7DX]) : Commonwealth War Graves Commission, 1981. — vii,17p ; 26cm. — (Yemen ; 1, 1a, 1b) (Saudi Arabia ; Arab 1)
Unpriced (pbk)
Also classified at 940.54′65′538 B82-05461

940.54′65′538 — Saudi Arabia. Commonwealth World War 2 military cemeteries. Graves — ***Lists***

War dead of the British Commonwealth : the register of the names of those who fell in the 1939-1945 War and are buried in cemeteries in Yemen (including the Maala Memorial) and Saudi Arabia. — [Maidenhead] ([2 Marlow Rd., Maidenhead, SL6 7DX]) : Commonwealth War Graves Commission, 1981. — vii,17p ; 26cm. — (Yemen ; 1, 1a, 1b) (Saudi Arabia ; Arab 1)
Unpriced (pbk)
Primary classification 940.54′65′5332
B82-05461

940.54′65′611 — Tunisia. Medjez-el-Bab. Commonwealth World War 2 military cemeteries: Medjez-el-Bab War Cemetery. Graves — ***Lists***

Great Britain. *Commonwealth War Graves Commision*. War graves of the British Commonwealth : the register of the names of those who fell in the 1939-1945 War and are buried in cemeteries in Tunisia : Medjez-el-Bab War Cemetery, Part 1 (Abb-Fur) / compiled and published by order of the Imperial War Graves Commission. — Amended version. — Maidenhead : Commonwealth War Graves Commission, 1981. — xiii,40p : 1map,1plan ; 26cm. — (Tunisia ; 6)
Previous ed.: 1957
Unpriced (pbk) B82-17345

940.54'65'6811 — Botswana. Commonwealth World War 2 military cemeteries. Graves — *Lists*
Great Britain. *Commonwealth War Graves Commission*. War dead of the British Commonwealth : the register of the names of those who fell in the 1939-1945 war and have no known grave, or whose graves can no longer be maintained : the Botswana, Lesotho and Swaziland 1939-1945 war memorials / compiled and published by the Commonwealth War Graves Commission. — Maidenhead ([2 Marlow Rd., Maidenhead, Berks. SL6 7DX]) : The Commission, 1981. — viii,45p : ill ; 26cm. — (Memorial registers Bot1, Les1, Swa1)
Unpriced (pbk)
Also classified at 940.54'65'6813 ; 940.54'65'6816 B82-07775

940.54'65'6813 — Swaziland. Commonwealth World War 2 military cemeteries. Graves — *Lists*
Great Britain. *Commonwealth War Graves Commission*. War dead of the British Commonwealth : the register of the names of those who fell in the 1939-1945 war and have no known grave, or whose graves can no longer be maintained : the Botswana, Lesotho and Swaziland 1939-1945 war memorials / compiled and published by the Commonwealth War Graves Commission. — Maidenhead ([2 Marlow Rd., Maidenhead, Berks. SL6 7DX]) : The Commission, 1981. — viii,45p : ill ; 26cm. — (Memorial registers Bot1, Les1, Swa1)
Unpriced (pbk)
Primary classification 940.54'65'6811 B82-07775

940.54'65'6816 — Lesotho. Commonwealth World War 2 military cemeteries. Graves — *Lists*
Great Britain. *Commonwealth War Graves Commission*. War dead of the British Commonwealth : the register of the names of those who fell in the 1939-1945 war and have no known grave, or whose graves can no longer be maintained : the Botswana, Lesotho and Swaziland 1939-1945 war memorials / compiled and published by the Commonwealth War Graves Commission. — Maidenhead ([2 Marlow Rd., Maidenhead, Berks. SL6 7DX]) : The Commission, 1981. — viii,45p : ill ; 26cm. — (Memorial registers Bot1, Les1, Swa1)
Unpriced (pbk)
Primary classification 940.54'65'6811 B82-07775

940.54'65'729 — West Indies. Commonwealth World War 2 military cemeteries. Graves — *Lists*
The **War** dead of the British Commonwealth : the register of the names of those who fell in the 1939-1945 War and are buried in cemeteries in Bermuda, the West Indies, Central and South America and those who have no known grave and are commemorated on the Nassau, Timehri, Kingston (Up Park Camp) and Port of Spain memorials / compiled and published by the Commonwealth War Graves Commission. — Maidenhead ([2 Marlow Rd., Maidenhead SL6 7DX]) : Commonwealth War Graves Commission, 1982. — xi,34p ; 26cm
Unpriced (pbk)
Also classified at 940.54'65'8 B82-23264

940.54'65'8 — Latin America. Commonwealth World War 2 military cemeteries. Graves — *Lists*
The **War** dead of the British Commonwealth : the register of the names of those who fell in the 1939-1945 War and are buried in cemeteries in Bermuda, the West Indies, Central and South America and those who have no known grave and are commemorated on the Nassau, Timehri, Kingston (Up Park Camp) and Port of Spain memorials / compiled and published by the Commonwealth War Graves Commission. — Maidenhead ([2 Marlow Rd., Maidenhead SL6 7DX]) : Commonwealth War Graves Commission, 1982. — xi,34p ; 26cm
Unpriced (pbk)
Primary classification 940.54'65'729 B82-23264

940.54'72'43 — Germany. British prisoners of war. Escapes, *1940-1944*
Castle, John. The password is courage / by John Castle. — Long Preston : Magna, 1982, c1954. — 466p ; 22cm
Originally published: London : Souvenir, 1954. — Published in large print
ISBN 0-86009-400-6 : Unpriced : CIP rev. B82-07047

940.54'72'430924 — Austria. Karawanken Mountains. Road tunnels: Loibl Pass tunnel. Construction by prisoners of war, *1942-1945 — Personal observations*
Lacaze, André. The tunnel / André Lacaze ; translated from the French by Barrett W. Dower, Julian Evans and Anne Gray. — [London] : Corgi, 1982, c1980. — 638p ; 17cm
Translation of: Le tunnel. — Originally published: London : Hamilton, 1980
ISBN 0-552-11867-2 (pbk) : £1.95 B82-14451

940.54'72'430924 — East Germany. Concentration camps: Dora *(Concentration camp), 1943-1945 — Personal observations*
Michel, Jean. Dora / Jean Michel written in association with Louis Nucera ; translated by Jennifer Kidd. — London : Sphere, 1981, c1979. — viii,308p,[8]p of plates : ill,2maps ; 18cm
Translation of: Dora. — Originally published: London : Weidenfeld and Nicolson, 1979
ISBN 0-7221-6067-4 (pbk) : £1.75 B82-08372

940.54'72'430924 — Germany. British prisoners of war, *1939-1945 — Personal observations*
Edgar, Donald. The Stalag men / by Donald Edgar. — London : Clare, c1982. — 192p ; 23cm
ISBN 0-906549-27-2 : £9.95 B82-33781

Kee, Robert. A crowd is not company / Robert Kee. — London : Cape, 1982. — 240p ; 23cm
Originally published: London : Eyre & Spottiswoode, 1947
ISBN 0-224-02003-x : £7.50 : CIP rev. B82-14059

940.54'72'430924 — Germany. Canadian prisoners of war, *1942-1945 — Personal observations*
Prouse, A. Robert. Ticket to hell via Dieppe : from a prisoner's wartime log 1942-1945 / A. Robert Prouse. — Exeter : Webb & Bower, 1982. — 192p,[8]p of plates : ill(some col.),facsims(some col.),maps,ports ; 25cm
Ill on lining papers
ISBN 0-906671-62-0 : £8.95 : CIP rev. B82-17233

940.54'72'430924 — Poland. Oświęcim. Concentration camps: Auschwitz *(Concentration camp), to 1945 — Personal observations*
Kielar, Wieslaw. Anus mundi : five years in Auschwitz / Wieslaw Kielar ; translated from the German by Susanne Flatauer. — Harmondsworth : Penguin, 1982, c1980. — 312p : plans ; 20cm
Translation of: Anus mundi. — Originally published: New York : Times Books, 1980 ; London : Allen Lane, 1981
ISBN 0-14-005385-9 (pbk) : £2.50 B82-30248

940.54'72'430924 — West Germany. Belsen. Concentration camps: Belsen *(Concentration camp), 1944-1945 — Personal observations — Correspondence, diaries, etc.*
Lévy-Hass, Hanna. Inside Belsen / Hanna Lévy-Hass ; translated from the German by Ronald Taylor ; with an introduction by Jane Caplan. — Brighton : Harvester Press, 1982. — xvi,134p : map ; 21cm
Translation of: Vielleicht war das alles erst der Anfang. — Bibliography: pxv-xvi
ISBN 0-7108-0355-9 : £12.95 : CIP rev. B82-04733

940.54'72'43094 — Germany. British prisoners of war, *1941-1945 — Personal observations*
Passmore, Richard. Moving tent / Richard Passmore. — London : Harmsworth, 1982. — vii,240p,[16]p of plates : ill,1map,ports ; 23cm
ISBN 0-9506012-3-3 : £7.95 B82-30120

940.54'72'43094321 — East Germany. Colditz. Prisoners of war. Escapes, *1941-1944*
Baybutt, Ron. Camera in Colditz / Ron Baybutt ; [photographs by Johannes Lange]. — London : Hodder and Stoughton, 1982. — 127p : ill,facsims,1plan,ports ; 26cm
ISBN 0-340-24823-8 : £7.95 : CIP rev. B82-03803

940.54'72'43094426 — France. Amiens. Prisons: Prison d'Amiens. Organised mass escapes, *1944:* **Operation Jericho**
Fishman, Jack. And the walls came tumbling down / Jack Fishman. — London : Souvenir, 1982. — 448p,[16]p of plates : ill,1map,1plan,ports ; 23cm
Maps on lining papers. — Bibliography: p442. — Includes index
ISBN 0-285-62519-5 : £8.95
Also classified at 940.54'86 B82-26980

940.54'72'470924 — Poland. Population. Deportation by Soviet military forces, *1939-1942 — Polish texts*
Tęczarowska, Danuta. Deportacja w nieznane : wspomnienia 1939-1942 / Danuta Tęczarowska. — London : Veritas Foundation Publication Centre, 1981. — 195p ; 22cm
Unpriced (pbk) B82-12181

940.54'72'520924 — Far East. British prisoners of war, *1942-1945 — Personal observations*
MacCarthy, Aidan. A doctor's war / Aidan MacCarthy. — [London] : Magnum, 1980, c1979. — 159p : 1map,facsims ; 18cm
Originally published: London : Robson, 1979
ISBN 0-417-03690-6 (pbk) : £1.25 B82-21031

940.54'72'520924 — Japan. British prisoners of war, *1941-1945 — Personal observations*
Fletcher-Cooke, John. The Emperor's guest / John Fletcher-Cooke. — [London] : Corgi, 1982, c1972. — 380p : 3maps,ports ; 18cm
Originally published: London : Hutchinson, 1971. — Ports on inside cover
ISBN 0-552-11919-9 (pbk) : £1.95 B82-29573

940.54'72'520924 — Malaysia. Kuala Lumpur. Australian prisoners of war, *1941-1945 — Personal observations*
Braddon, Russell. The naked island / Russell Braddon ; with drawings made in Changi Prison Camp by Ronald Searle. — Large print ed. — Leicester : Charnwood, 1982, c1952. — 465p : ill,ports ; 23cm. — (Charnwood library series)
Originally published: London : Laurie, 1952. — Published in large print
ISBN 0-7089-8024-4 : £5.25 : CIP rev. B81-36956

940.54'72'520924 — South-east Asia. Scottish prisoners of war: Gordon, Ernest — *Biographies — For schools*
Owen, R. J.. Death camp on the River Kwai : the story of Ernest Gordon / Roger J. Owen. — Exeter : Religious Education Press, 1981. — 29p : ill,2maps,2ports ; 21cm. — (Faith in action series)
Bibliography: p29
ISBN 0-08-025643-0 (pbk) : £0.65
ISBN 0-08-025642-2 (pbk) : Unpriced (non net) B82-12069

940.54'72'520951156 — China. Peking. Japanese prisons. American prisoners of war. Prison life, *1942-1945*
Glines, Carroll V.. Four came home / Carroll V. Glines. — New York ; London : Van Nostrand Reinhold, 1966, c1981 (1981 [printing]). — xiv,226p : ill,ports ; 23cm
Includes index
ISBN 0-442-21924-5 (pbk) : £5.90 B82-13196

940.54'72'520959 — South-east Asia. Allied prisoners of war. Prison life, *1941-1945*
Lindsay, Oliver. At the going down of the sun : Hong Kong and South-East Asia 1941-45 / Oliver Lindsay. — London : Sphere, 1982, c1981. — 280p,[8]p of plates : ill,1map,ports ; 18cm
Originally published: London : Hamilton, 1981. — Bibliography: p271. — Includes index
ISBN 0-7221-5543-3 (pbk) : £1.95 B82-16575

940.54'72'52095981 — Indonesia. Sumatra. Allied women prisoners of war. Prison life, *1942-1945*
Warner, Lavinia. Women beyond the wire : a story of prisoners of the Japanese 1942-45 / Lavinia Warner and John Sandilands. — London : Joseph, 1982. — xiii,289p,[32]p of plates : ill,1map,facsims,ports ; 25cm
Includes index
ISBN 0-7181-1934-7 : £9.95 B82-21278

940.54'7541'0924 — World War 2. Army operations by Great Britain. *Army. Royal Army Medical Corps — Personal observations*

Petty, Gerald F.. Mad Gerry : Welsh wartime medical officer : a true story by a major in the Royal Army Medical Corps 1939-1945 / Gerald F. Petty. — Newport : Starling, 1982. — 143p,[22]p of plates : ill,ports ; 22cm
ISBN 0-903434-47-4 : £6.50 B82-17286

940.54'81 — World War 2. Military operations by Allied forces — *Personal observations — Collections*

True stories of World War II / [editor Nancy J. Sparks]. — Pleasantville ; London : Reader's Digest Association, c1981. — 447p : ill(some col.),maps(some col.),ports ; 25cm
At head of title: Reader's digest. — Originally published: 1980
ISBN 0-89577-081-4 : £8.95 B82-23781

940.54'81'41 — World War 2. Army operations by Great Britain. *Army. Field Regiment, 92nd — Personal observations*

Willis, Donald. Eggshells and tea-leaves : memories of an ordinary man / Donald Willis. — Oxford : Dugdale, 1981. — xv,220p : ill,maps,ports ; 20cm
ISBN 0-9503880-7-6 (pbk) : £2.95 B82-31191

940.54'81'41 — World War 2. Army operations by Great Britain. *Army. Royal Army Service Corps — Personal observations*

Merritt, Maurice. Eighth Army driver / Maurice Merritt. — Tunbridge Wells : Midas, 1981. — 181p ; 23cm
ISBN 0-85936-282-5 : £6.25 B82-11597

940.54'81'41 — World War 2 — *British personal observations — Correspondence, diaries, etc.*

Eccles, David Eccles, *Viscount*. By safe hand : the wartime letters of David and Sybil Eccles. — London : Bodley Head, Oct.1982. — [384]p
ISBN 0-370-30482-9 : £11.95 : CIP entry B82-24850

940.54'81'41 — World War 2. Military operations by Great Britain. *Army.* **Broad, Richard**

Woods, Rex. A talent to survive : the wartime exploits of Lt.-Col. Richard Lowther Broad, M.C., Légion d'Honneur, Croix de Guerre / Rex Woods. — London : Kimber, 1982. — 205p,[16]p of plates : ill,2facsims,maps,ports ; 24cm
Includes index
ISBN 0-7183-0488-8 : £8.95 B82-26517

940.54'81'41 — World War 2. Military operations by Great Britain. *Army. Royal Tank Regiment, 5th, 1941-1943 — Personal observations*

Wardrop, Jake. Tanks across the desert : the war diary of Jake Wardrop / edited by George Forty ; foreword by W.M. Hutton. — London : Kimber, 1981. — 222p : ill,1map,ports ; 24cm
Bibliography: p213. — Includes index
ISBN 0-7183-0288-5 : £8.95 B82-06613

940.54'81'71 — World War 2. Military operations by Canadian military forces, *1942-1945 — Personal observations*

Mowat, Farley. And no birds sang / Farley Mowat. — London : Cassell, 1980, c1979. — 250p ; 22cm
Originally published: Boston, Mass. : Little, Brown, 1979
ISBN 0-304-30747-5 : £5.95 B82-14089

940.54'82'43 — World War 2, *1939-1940 — German viewpoints — Correspondence, diaries, etc.*

Roubiczek, Paul. Across the abyss. — Cambridge : Cambridge University Press, Aug.1982. — [344]p
Translation of: Über den Abgrund
ISBN 0-521-24288-6 : £15.00 : CIP entry B82-14531

940.54'83 — Allied armies. Generals. Interpersonal relationships, *1943-1945*

Irving, David. The war between the generals / David Irving. — Harmondsworth : Penguin, 1982, c1981. — 446p : ill,1map,ports ; 19cm
Originally published: London : Allen Lane, 1981. — Includes index
ISBN 0-14-005534-7 (pbk) : £2.25 B82-26445

940.54'83 — Allied armies. Soldiers. Army life, *1940-1945*

Ellis, John, *1945-*. The sharp end of war : the fighting man in World War II / John Ellis. — London : Corgi, 1982, c1980. — 410p,[32]p of plates ; 18cm
Originally published: Newton Abbot : David and Charles, 1980. — Bibliography: p386-399. — Includes index
ISBN 0-552-11902-4 (pbk) : £1.95 B82-24559

940.54'86 — France. Amiens. Secret service operations by Allied forces, *1944:* **Operation Jericho**

Fishman, Jack. And the walls came tumbling down / Jack Fishman. — London : Souvenir, 1982. — 448p,[16]p of plates : ill,1map,1plan,ports ; 23cm
Maps on lining papers. — Bibliography: p442. — Includes index
ISBN 0-285-62519-5 : £8.95
Primary classification 940.54'72'43094426 B82-26980

940.54'86 — World War 2. Intelligence operations by Allied forces

Collier, Basil. Hidden weapons : Allied secret or undercover services in World War II / Basil Collier ; with a foreword by R.V. Jones. — London : Hamilton, 1982. — xviii,386p ; 23cm
Bibliography: p335-342. — Includes index
ISBN 0-241-10788-1 : £15.00 : CIP rev. B82-04312

940.54'86 — World War 2. Military operations. Effects of possession by Allied forces of Axis forces' Enigma cipher machines — *Personal observations*

Welchman, Gordon. The hut six story : breaking the enigma codes / Gordon Welchman. — London : Allen Lane, 1982. — ix,326p : ill,maps ; 24cm
Bibliography: p315-317. — Includes index
ISBN 0-7139-1294-4 : £8.95 B82-36415

940.54'86'41 — World War 2. Army operations by Great Britain. *Army. Special Operations Executive*

Beevor, John G.. SOE : recollections and reflections 1940-1945 / J.G. Beevor. — London : Bodley Head, 1981. — 269p : maps ; 23cm
Bibliography: p240-243. — Includes index
ISBN 0-370-30414-4 : £8.95 B82-31350

940.54'86'41 — World War 2. Intelligence operations by British military forces

Hampshire, A. Cecil. Undercover sailors : secret operations of World War II / A. Cecil Hampshire. — London : Kimber, 1981. — 208p : ill,maps,ports ; 24cm
Bibliography: p203. — Includes index
ISBN 0-7183-0368-7 : £9.50 B82-05911

940.54'86'41 — World War 2. Military operations by Great Britain. *Army. Special Operations Executive. Scandinavian Section*

Baden-Powell, Dorothy. Operation Jupiter : SOE's secret war in Norway / by Dorothy Baden-Powell. — London : Hale, 1982. — 208p,[12]p of plates : ill,maps,2facsims,ports ; 23cm
Bibliography: p199-200. — Includes index
ISBN 0-7091-9367-x : Unpriced B82-14628

940.54'86'41 — World War 2. Strategy. Role of British intelligence services

Hinsley, F. H.. British intelligence in the Second World War : its influence on strategy and operations / by F.H. Hinsley with E.E. Thomas, C.F.G. Ransom, R.C. Knight. — London : H.M.S.O.. — (History of the Second World War)
Vol.2. — 1981. — xv,850p,[4]folded leaves of plates : maps(some col.) ; 25cm
Includes index
ISBN 0-11-630934-2 : £15.95 B82-05274

940.54'86'410924 — World War 2. Intelligence operations by British military forces — *Personal observations*

Hyde, H. Montgomery. Secret intelligence agent / H. Montgomery Hyde. — London : Constable, 1982. — xviii,281p : ill,facsims,ports ; 23cm
Includes index
ISBN 0-09-463850-0 : £8.95 B82-31547

940.54'86'410924 — World War 2. Italian campaigns. Military operations by Great Britain. *Army. Special Operations Executive. Special Force, No.1, 1943-1945 — Personal observations*

Macintosh, Charles. From cloak to dagger : an SOE agent in Italy 1943-1945 / Charles Macintosh. — London : Kimber, 1982. — 189p,[12]p of plates : ill,maps,plans,ports ; 24cm
Includes index
ISBN 0-7183-0019-x : £8.95 B82-35853

940.54'86'481 — Norway. Gold reserves. Rescue by resistance movements, *1940*

Baden-Powell, Dorothy. Pimpernel gold : how Norway foiled the Nazis / Dorothy Baden-Powell ; foreword by Sir Laurence Collier. — Large print ed. — Leicester : Ulverscroft, 1981, c1978. — 352p : 2maps ; 23cm. — (Ulverscroft large print series)
Originally published: New York : St. Martin's Press ; London : Hale, 1978
ISBN 0-7089-0700-8 : £5.00 : CIP rev. B81-30365

940.54'87'430924 — World War 2. Anti-British espionage. Druid

Mosley, Leonard. The Druid. — London : Eyre Methuen, Jan.1982. — [256]p
ISBN 0-413-40280-0 : £7.50 : CIP entry B81-34399

940.55 — HISTORY. EUROPE, 1945-

940.55 — Europe, *1945-1981*

The **Successor** generation. — London : Butterworth, Jan.1983. — [224]p
ISBN 0-408-10817-7 : £20.00 : CIP entry B82-34435

940.55 — Western Europe. Political events, *1945-1980*

Urwin, Derek W.. Western Europe since 1945 : a short political history / Derek W. Urwin. — 3rd ed. — London : Longman, 1981. — xiv,376p ; 22cm
Previous ed.: 1972. — Bibliography: p361-367. — Includes index
ISBN 0-582-49071-5 (pbk) : £5.95 : CIP rev. B81-15935

940.55 — Western Europe. Political events. Role of United States. *Central Intelligence Agency, 1950-1980*

Dirty work : the CIA in Western Europe / edited by Philip Agee and Louis Wolf. — London : Zed, 1981, c1978. — 318p ; 22cm
Originally published: Secaucus : L. Stuart, 1978
ISBN 0-86232-045-3 (pbk) : £4.95 B82-01767

940.55'8 — Europe — *For schools*

Darton, Nicholas. Europe in the world / Nicholas Darton. — London : Harrap, 1981. — 48p : ill(some col.),col.maps ; 30cm. — (Harrap's European studies course ; pt.1)
ISBN 0-245-53476-8 (pbk) : £1.95 B82-01815

940.55'8'0922 — Western Europe. Persons — *Biographies — Serials*

Who's who in Western Europe. — 1981 ed.-. — Cambridge (Cambridge CB2 3QP) : International Biographical Centre, 1981-. — v. ; 24cm
Irregular
ISSN 0262-4486 = Who's who in Western Europe : Unpriced B82-04917

941 — HISTORY. GREAT BRITAIN

941 — Great Britain, *60-1970 — For schools*

Page, Philip. Who? what? why? / Philip Page. — London : Edward Arnold, 1981. — 3v.(96p) : ill,maps ; 19x25cm
ISBN 0-7131-0471-6 (pbk) : Unpriced : CIP rev.
ISBN 0-7131-0607-7 (v.2) : £1.25
ISBN 0-7131-0608-5 (v.3) : £1.25 B81-23833

941 — Great Britain, *1450-1980 — For schools*

Johnston, Marjorie. Centuries of change : British history since 1450 / Marjorie Johnston. — South Melbourne ; London : Macmillan, 1981. — 226p : ill,maps,ports ; 24cm
Includes index
ISBN 0-333-33775-1 (pbk) : £3.95 B82-33839

941 — Great Britain, *1600-1980*
Ridley, Nancy. Nancy Ridley's love affair with history / by Nancy Ridley. — Stocksfield : Oriel, 1982. — ix,133p ; 23cm
ISBN 0-85362-191-8 : £6.95 B82-30177

941 — Great Britain. Abbeys & priories — *Encyclopaedias*
Bottomley, Frank, *1920-*. The abbey explorer's guide : a guide to abbeys and other religious houses / Frank Bottomley ; illustrated by Paul Bottomley. — London : Kaye & Ward, c1981. — vii,284p : ill,plans ; 18cm
Bibliography: p194
ISBN 0-7182-1280-0 (pbk) : £4.95 B82-15290

941 — Great Britain. Archives
Harvey, P. D. A.. The historian and the written word : an inaugural lecture by / P.D.A. Harvey. — Durham : University of Durham, [1982?]. — 12p ; 22cm
£0.60 (pbk) B82-31226

941 — Great Britain, *B.C.100-A.D.1977* **—** *For schools*
Moss, Peter, *1921-*. History scene / by Peter Moss. — St. Albans : Hart-Davis Educational 3 / illustrated and designed by Ray Fishwick. — c1981. — 112p : ill,maps,facsims,plans,ports ; 28cm
ISBN 0-247-12765-5 (pbk) : Unpriced B82-24516

941 — Great Britain, *ca 1300-ca 1782*
Sayles, G. O.. Scripta diversa. — London : Hambledon, Sept.1982. — [360]p. — (History series ; 15)
ISBN 0-907628-12-5 : £22.00 : CIP entry B82-21583

941 — Great Britain. Castles — *For children*
Davison, Brian. Explore a castle / Brian Davison. — London : Hamilton, 1982. — 120p : ill,1map ; 24cm
Includes index
ISBN 0-241-10763-6 : £4.95 : CIP rev. B82-07400

941 — Great Britain. Castles, *to ca 1540* **—** *For children*
Sancha, Sheila. The castle story / Sheila Sancha. — Harmondsworth : Penguin, 1981, c1979. — 224p : ill,maps,plans ; 24cm
Originally published: Harmondsworth : Kestrel, 1979. — Includes index
ISBN 0-14-005747-1 (pbk) : £3.95 B82-07303

941 — Great Britain. Country houses. Organisations: Historic Houses Association — *Directories — Serials*
Historic Houses Association. Yearbook & list of members / Historic Houses Association. — 1982-. — Letchworth (PO Box 21, 71 Leys Ave., Letchworth, Herts. SG6 3EY) : M. McCartney for the Association, 1982-. — v. : maps ; 30cm
Continues: Historic Houses Association. List of members
ISSN 0262-7590 = Yearbook & list of members - Historic Houses Association : Unpriced B82-25478

941 — Great Britain — *History — For schools*
Cowie, Evelyn E.. History in close-up. — London : Cassell
Britain and the world 1901-75. — Dec.1981. — [224]p
ISBN 0-304-30645-2 : £3.50 : CIP entry B81-31463

941 — Great Britain. Literary associations
Daiches, David. Literary landscapes of the British Isles. — 2nd ed. — London : Bell & Hyman, Sept.1981. — [287]p
Previous ed.: London : Paddington Press, 1979
ISBN 0-7135-1244-x : £7.95 : CIP entry B81-22522

941 — Great Britain. Local studies — *For schools*
Evans, Frederic. Local studies for schools / Frederic Evans, V.F. Searson, G.H. Williams. — 6th ed. — London : George Philip, c1979. — iv,124p ; 21cm
Previous ed.: 1972
ISBN 0-540-01045-6 (pbk) : £1.50 : CIP rev. B79-07673

941 — Great Britain. Lost country houses, *to 1981*
Sproule, Anna. Lost houses of Britain. — Newton Abbot : David & Charles, Oct.1982. — [256]p
ISBN 0-7153-8104-0 : £10.95 : CIP entry B82-23006

941 — Great Britain. Places associated with music composers
Burke, John. Musical landscape. — Exeter : Webb & Bower, Feb.1983. — [192]p
ISBN 0-906671-60-4 : £10.95 : CIP entry B82-39815

941 — Great Britain. Places associated with musicians — *Encyclopaedias*
Norris, Gerald. A musical gazetteer of Great Britain and Ireland / Gerald Norris. — Newton Abbot : David & Charles, c1981. — 352p : ill,2maps,ports ; 23cm
Includes index
ISBN 0-7153-7845-7 : £10.95 : CIP rev. B81-27947

941 — Great Britain. *Royal Commission on Historical Manuscripts — Proposals*
Caplan, D.. Independent review of the work of the Royal Commission on Historical Manuscripts / report by D. Caplan. — London (Whitehall, SW1 2AZ) : Civil Service Department Library, 1980. — [66]p ; 30cm
With comments of the Commission and extracts from Hansard
Unpriced (sprial) B82-17331

941 — Great Britain. Royal residences
Adair, John, *1934-*. The royal palaces of Britain / John Adair. — London : Thames and Hudson, 1981. — 192p : ill(some col.),ports(some col.) ; 30cm
Bibliography: p188. — Includes index
ISBN 0-500-25077-4 : £8.50 B82-03996

Montague-Smith, Patrick. The Country life book of royal palaces, castles & homes : including vanished palaces and historic houses with royal connections / by Patrick Montague-Smith and Hugh Montgomery-Massingberd. — [London] : Country life, 1981. — 176p : ill(some col.),plans,3ports ; 31cm
Bibliography: p176
ISBN 0-600-36808-4 : £12.50 B82-04460

941 — Great Britain. Social life. Historical sources: Sound tape recordings. Collections — *Directories*
Directory of British oral history collections / compiled by Anne McNulty and Hilary Troop. — Colchester : Oral History Society
Includes index
Vol.1. — c1981. — [60]p ; 30cm
ISBN 0-9507804-0-5 (pbk) : Unpriced B82-01905

941 — Great Britain. Social life, *to 1981* **—** *For schools*
Hodgson, Pat. Home life / Pat Hodgson. — London : Batsford Academic and Educational, 1982. — 71p : ill ; 26cm. — (History in focus)
ISBN 0-7134-4085-6 : £5.95 B82-22245

941 — Great Britain. Stately homes
Flower, Sibylla Jane. The stately homes of Britain. — Exeter : Webb & Bower, Sept.1982. — [240]p
ISBN 0-905649-55-9 : £12.50 : CIP entry B82-21570

941 — Great Britain. Structures of historical importance — *Manuscripts — Facsimiles*
Aubrey, John. Monumenta Britannica, or, A miscellany of British antiquities / by John Aubrey ; illustrated with notes of Thomas Gale and John Evelyn ... ; annotated by Rodney Legg ; archaeological consultant William Hoade ; language adviser Robert J. Briggs ; literary editor John Fowles. — [Sherborne] : [Dorset Publishing]
Part 3 and Index. — 1982. — p605-1143 : ill,maps,facsims,1geneal.table ; 31cm
Limited ed. of 595 copies
ISBN 0-902129-50-3 : £95.00 B82-20989

941 — Great Britain, *to 1980*
Historical atlas of Britain / [general editors] Malcolm Falkus, John Gillingham. — London : Granada, 1981. — 223p : ill(some col.),col.maps,facsims(some col.),plans(some col.),ports,geneal.tables (some col.) ; 30cm
Includes index
ISBN 0-246-11614-5 : £15.00 B82-09236

941 — Great Britain, *to 1981*
Rose, Richard, *1933-*. Understanding the United Kingdom. — London : Longman, Sept.1982. — [256]p
ISBN 0-582-29591-2 (pbk) : £3.95 : CIP entry B82-20259

941'.003'21 — Great Britain. Social life, *to 1980* **—** *Encyclopaedias — For children*
Cowie, Leonard W.. [A dictionary of British social history]. Life in Britain : a junior encyclopaedia of social history / L.W. Cowie. — London : Bell & Hyman, 1980. — vi,326p : ill,1map,plans ; 24cm
Originally published: London : Bell, 1973. — Bibliography: p326
ISBN 0-7135-1212-1 (pbk) : £5.95 B82-38363

941'.00491497 — Great Britain. Gypsies
Okely, Judith. The traveller-gypsies. — Cambridge : Cambridge University Press, Feb.1983. — [272]p
ISBN 0-521-24641-5 (cased) : £19.50 : CIP entry
ISBN 0-521-28870-3 (pbk) : £6.50 B82-40896

941'.00491497 — Great Britain. Gypsy civilization
Borrow, George. Romano Lavo-Lil. — Gloucester : Alan Sutton, Aug.1982. — [192]p
ISBN 0-86299-024-6 (pbk) : £2.95 : CIP entry B82-19267

941'.004951 — Great Britain. Chinese families. Social life — *For children*
Tsow, Ming. A day with Ling. — London : Hamilton, Oct.1982. — [32]p
ISBN 0-241-10828-4 : £3.50 : CIP entry B82-23450

941'.007 — Great Britain. Local history. Information sources: Census data. Use
Boreham, John M.. The census and how to use it / John M. Boreham. — Brentwood : Essex Society for Family History, c1982. — 20p : 2forms ; 21cm
Bibliography: p20
ISBN 0-9504327-1-7 (pbk) : £0.50 : CIP rev. B81-32018

941'.007'1141 — Great Britain. Higher education institutions. Curriculum subjects: Local history. Teaching — *Serials*
[Newsletter *(Conference of Teachers of Regional and Local History in Tertiary Education)***]**. Newsletter / Conference of Teachers of Regional and Local History in Tertiary Education. — Issue no.11 (Spring 1980)-. — Lancaster (Engineering Block, University of Lancaster, Bailrigg, Lancaster) : Centre for N.W. Regional Studies, 1980-. — v. ; 30cm
Two issues yearly. — Continues: Regional history newsletter. — Description based on: Issue no.14
ISSN 0262-7582 = Newsletter - Conference of Teachers of Regional and Local History in Tertiary Education : Free to CORAL members only B82-24771

941'.0072 — Great Britain. Local history. Research — *Manuals*
Ravensdale, J. R.. The local history kit / Jack Ravensdale, Sallie Purkis. — Cambridge : National Extension College, [1982?]. — 120p : ill,facsims,plans ; 21cm. — (National Extension College correspondence texts ; course no.HS31)
Includes bibliographies
ISBN 0-86082-317-2 (pbk) : Unpriced B82-38355

941'.0072 — Great Britain. Rural regions. Settlement. Historiology. Research
Roberts, Brian K.. Rural settlement : an historical perspective / by Brian K. Roberts. — Norwich : Geo Abstracts, c1982. — 46p : ill,maps ; 21cm. — (Historical geography research series, ISSN 0143-683x ; no.9)
Text on inside cover
ISBN 0-86094-110-8 (pbk) : Unpriced B82-32713

941'.007'23 — Great Britain. Local history. Field studies — *Manuals*
Hoskins, W. G.. Fieldwork in local history / W.G. Hoskins. — 2nd ed. — London : Faber, 1982. — 202p,[8]p of plates : ill,maps ; 20cm
Previous ed.: 1967. — Bibliography: p185-192. — Includes index
ISBN 0-571-18050-7 (cased) : £9.50 : CIP rev.
ISBN 0-571-18051-5 (pbk) : Unpriced
B81-38839

941'.0075 — British artefacts. Collecting — *Serials*
The **Bell-Knight** collection of British nostalgia : bulletin of the Bell Knight Trust. — Issue no.1 (1st Jan. 1981)-issue no.3 (Summer 1981). — Bath (c/o C.A. Bell Knight, North Wing, Freshford, Bath BA3 6EP) : The Trust, 1981-1981. — 3v. : ill ; 21cm
Quarterly. — Continued by: British nostalgia
£1.50 per year B82-29051

British nostalgia. — No.4 (Autumn 1981)-. — Bath (c/o C.A. Bell Knight, North Wing, Freshford, Bath BA3 6EP) : Bell Knight Trust, 1981-. — v. : ill ; 21cm
Quarterly. — Issued for: Friends of British Nostalgia. — Continues: The Bell-Knight collection of British nostalgia
ISSN 0263-6859 = British nostalgia : £1.75 per year B82-29052

941'.009'732 — Great Britain. Cities. Inner areas. Social conditions
Battye, Nicholas. Survival programmes. — Milton Keynes : Open University Press, Aug.1982. — [216]p
ISBN 0-335-10111-9 (pbk) : £6.95 : CIP entry
B82-15716

Crowder, Roy B.. Inner city issues / by Roy B. Crowder and John J. Vincent. — Liverpool : Liverpool Institute of Socio-Religious Studies, c1980. — 41p ; 21cm. — (LISS occasional papers ; no.1)
ISBN 0-905052-19-6 (pbk) : £1.00 B82-16526

The **Inner** city in context : the final report of the Social Science Research Council Inner Cities Working Party / edited by Peter Hall. — London : Heinemann, 1981. — viii,175p ; 23cm
Bibliography: p154-163. — Includes index
ISBN 0-435-35717-4 (cased) : £12.50 : CIP rev.
ISBN 0-435-35718-2 (pbk) : Unpriced
B81-30162

941'.009'732 — Great Britain. Deserted villages
Muir, Richard, *1943-*. The lost villages of Britain / Richard Muir. — London : Joseph, 1982. — 285p,[16]p of plates : ill(some col.),maps,1facsim,1plan ; 26cm
Ill on lining papers. — Bibliography: p271-272. — Includes index
ISBN 0-7181-2036-1 : £11.95 B82-25329

941'.009'732 — Great Britain. Towns, *1450-1700*
The **Urban** experience. — Manchester : Manchester University Press, Feb.1983. — [224]p
ISBN 0-7190-0900-6 : £19.50 : CIP entry
B82-39458

941'.009'734 — Great Britain. Countryside
Norton-Taylor, Richard. Whose land is it anyway?. — Wellingborough : Thorsons, Nov.1982. — [224]p
ISBN 0-85500-095-3 (pbk) : £4.95 : CIP entry
B82-26323

Young, Geoffrey. Enjoy a day in the countryside / [written by Geoffrey Young]. — Norwich : Jarrold, c1981. — 32p : col.ill ; 20cm. — (Watch ; bk.9)
Cover title. — Text on inside covers. — Includes index
ISBN 0-85306-975-1 (pbk) : Unpriced
B82-01367

941'.009'734 — Great Britain. Countryside — *Encyclopaedias*
Grigson, Geoffrey. [The Shell country alphabet]. Geoffrey Grigson's countryside : the classic companion to rural Britain. — London : Ebury, 1982. — 263p : ill(some col.) ; 27cm
Text originally published: London : Joseph in association with Rainbird, 1966. — Ill on lining papers. — Includes index
ISBN 0-85223-223-3 : £12.95 B82-24988

941'.009'734 — Great Britain. Rural regions, *1880-1914*
Marsh, Jan. Back to the land. — London : Quartet, June 1982. — 1v.
ISBN 0-7043-2276-5 : £10.95 : CIP entry
B82-13506

941'.009'734 — Great Britain. Rural regions. Social life
Belonging : identity and social organisation in British rural cultures / edited by Anthony P. Cohen. — Manchester : Manchester University Press, c1982. — x,325p : ill,1map ; 24cm
Includes bibliographies and index
ISBN 0-7190-0859-x : £21.00 : CIP rev.
B82-01424

941'.009'92 — Great Britain. Country houses. Social life, *to ca 1939* — *Personal observations — Collections*
The **Country** house. — Oxford : Oxford University Press, Nov.1982. — [120]p. — (Small Oxford books)
ISBN 0-19-214139-2 : £3.95 : CIP entry
B82-26888

941'.009'92 — Great Britain. Kings & queens, *to 1980*
Delderfield, Eric R.. Kings and Queens of England and Great Britain. — 3rd ed. — Newton Abbot : David and Charles, Oct.1981. — [160]p
Previous ed.: 1970
ISBN 0-7153-8299-3 (pbk) : £1.95 : CIP entry
B81-30195

941'.009'92 — Great Britain. Persons, *1650-1977* — *Biographies*
Sewell, Brocard. Like black swans : some people and themes / by Brocard Sewell ; with an introduction by Colin Wilson. — Padstow : Tabb House, 1982. — xviii,232p : ports ; 23cm
Limited ed. of 500 numbered and signed copies
ISBN 0-907018-13-0 : £11.95 B82-35817

941'.009'92 — Great Britain. Royal families, *1301-1981* — *Illustrations*
Leete-Hodge, Lornie. A souvenir of the royal wedding / Lornie Leete-Hodge. — [London] : Optimum, 1981. — 192p : chiefly ill(some col.),coats of arms(some col.),1facsim,ports (some col.),1geneal.table ; 31cm
Ill on lining papers
ISBN 0-600-37811-x : £4.95 B82-11856

941'.009'92 — Great Britain. Royal families, *to 1981* — *For children*
Hichens, Phoebe. All about the Royal Family / Phoebe Hichens ; [illustrated by Leslie Marshall]. — London : Macmillan Children's, 1981. — 128p : ill(some col.),1col.map,coats of arms,ports(some col.) ; 22x28cm
Ill on lining papers. — Includes index
ISBN 0-333-31562-6 : £4.95 : CIP rev.
B81-23945

941'.009'92 — Great Britain. Royal families, *to 1982*
Brown, Craig. The book of royal lists. — London : Routledge & K. Paul, Sept.1982. — [320]p
ISBN 0-7100-9358-6 : £7.95 : CIP entry
B82-20770

941'.009'92 — Great Britain. Rulers, *to 1305*
Kightly, Charles. Folk heroes of Britain / Charles Kightly. — London : Thames and Hudson, c1982. — 208p : ill,maps,ports ; 25cm
Bibliography: p192-199. — Includes index
ISBN 0-500-25082-0 : £8.50 B82-21921

941.01 — Great Britain, *410-1100* — *For schools*
Pluckrose, Henry. Saxon and Norman Britain. — London : Bell & Hyman, Jan.1982. — [80]p. — (History around us)
Originally published: London : Mills & Boon, 1980
ISBN 0-7135-2113-9 (pbk) : £3.95 : CIP entry
B82-02457

941.01 — Great Britain, *to 1086* — *For schools*
Burrell, Roy. The invaders / Roy Burrell. — Oxford : Oxford University Press by arrangement with the British Broadcasting Corporation, 1980. — 128p : ill(some col.),col.maps,facsims,ports ; 28cm. — (Oxford junior history ; 1)
ISBN 0-19-918119-5 (pbk) : £2.25 B82-14139

941.01 — Great Britain, *to ca 1000*
Newbigin, Edith. British roots. — Liverpool (47 Reeds Rd., Huyton, Liverpool L36 7SL) : Edith Newbigin, [1982?]. — 119p ; 21cm
Bibliography: p119
Unpriced (pbk) B82-33688

941.01'092'2 — Great Britain. Monarchs, *to 901*
Ashe, Geoffrey. Kings and queens of early Britain. — London : Eyre Methuen, Apr.1982. — [224]p
ISBN 0-413-47920-x : £8.50 : CIP entry
B82-04043

941.06 — England. Social conditions, *1580-1680*
Wrightson, Keith. English society 1580-1680 / Keith Wrightson. — London : Hutchinson, 1982. — 264p ; 24cm. — (Hutchinson social history of England)
Includes index
ISBN 0-09-145170-1 (cased) : £12.00 : CIP rev.
ISBN 0-09-145171-x (pbk) : Unpriced
B81-28794

941.06 — Great Britain, *1603-1688* — *For schools*
Nichol, Jon. The Stuarts / Jon Nichol. — Oxford : Blackwell, 1982. — 64p : ill,maps,plans,ports ; 30cm. — (Evidence in history)
ISBN 0-631-93360-3 (pbk) : Unpriced
B82-36804

941.06 — Great Britain, *1603-1714*
Farmer, D. L.. Britain and the Stuarts. — London : Bell and Hyman, Oct.1981. — [436]p
Originally published: 1965
ISBN 0-7135-0445-5 (pbk) : £5.50 : CIP entry
B81-32086

941.06'1'0924 — Great Britain. Northampton, Henry Howard, *Earl of* — *Biographies*
Peck, Linda Levy. Northampton : patronage and policy at the court of James I. — London : Allen & Unwin, Nov.1982. — [288]p
ISBN 0-04-942177-8 : £18.50 : CIP entry
B82-28997

941.07 — Great Britain, *1700-1800* — *For schools*
Farnworth, Warren. Eighteenth century Britain. — London : Bell & Hyman, Oct.1981. — [80] p. — (History around us)
ISBN 0-7135-1288-1 (pbk) : £3.95 : CIP entry
B81-25723

941.07 — Great Britain, *1714-1815* — *For schools*
Titley, Paul. The Georgian age. — London : Bell & Hyman, May 1982. — [180]p. — (Look and remember history series)
Originally published: 1971
ISBN 0-7135-2117-1 (pbk) : £1.95 : CIP entry
B82-13499

941.07 — Great Britain, *1714-1980*
Cook, Cris. The Longman handbook of modern British history 1714-1980. — London : Longman, Feb.1983. — [400]p
ISBN 0-582-48581-9 (cased) : £13.95 : CIP entry
ISBN 0-582-48582-7 (pbk) : £7.95 B82-38680

941.07 — Great Britain, *1760-1914* — *For schools*
Tucker, Elizabeth M. M.. British history 1760-1914 / Elizabeth M.M. Tucker. — London : Edward Arnold, 1981, c1982. — ix,308p : ill,maps ; 22cm
Bibliography: p297-298. — Includes index
ISBN 0-7131-0601-8 (pbk) : £4.25 : CIP rev.
B82-04478

941.07 — Great Britain, *1780-1981*
Harrison, Brian. Peaceable kingdom : stability and change in modern Britain. — Oxford : Clarendon Press, Sept.1982. — [400]p
ISBN 0-19-822603-9 : £17.50 : CIP entry
B82-18978

941.07 — Great Britain. Social conditions, *1815-1851* — *For schools*
McNab, Colin. From Waterloo to the Great Exhibition : Britain 1815-1851 / Colin McNab, Robert Mackenzie. — Edinburgh : Oliver & Boyd, 1982. — 186p : ill,1map,facsims ; 21cm
Bibliography: p181-183. — Includes index
ISBN 0-05-003351-4 (pbk) : Unpriced
B82-20125

941.07 — Great Britain. Social conditions, *1815-1851 — For schools* *continuation*

Patrick, John, *1931-*. Waterloo to the Great Exhibition : British society 1815-1851 / John Patrick. — London : Murray, c1981. — 92p : ill,maps,facsims,ports ; 25cm
Includes index
ISBN 0-7195-3880-7 (pbk) : £1.95 : CIP rev.
B81-31534

941.07 — Great Britain. Social life, *1750-1914 — For children*

Pollard, Michael, *1931-*. Empires and ideas 1750-1914 / Michael Pollard ; illustrated by Robert G. Hunter. — Glasgow : Blackie, 1981. — 94p : ill(some col.) ; 21cm. — (The story of life ; 6)
ISBN 0-216-90735-7 (pbk) : £2.95 B82-05311

941.07'092'2 — Great Britain, *1730-1970 — Biographies*

Larkin, P. J. (Patrick John). The history makers 1730-1970 : a biographical history of Britain / P.J. Larkin ; illustrated by Jennifer J. Moore. — Amersham : Hulton Educational, 1982. — 95p : ill,maps,ports ; 25cm
ISBN 0-7175-1004-2 (pbk) : £2.50 B82-21498

941.07'092'4 — Great Britain. Frederick, *Prince of Wales — Biographies*

Frederick, Prince of Wales and his circle. — Sudbury (Sudbury, Suffolk) : Gainsborough's House, [1981]. — 27p : ill,ports ; 30cm
Published to accompany an exhibition
Unpriced (pbk) B82-30879

941.07'092'4 — Great Britain. Granville, Harriet Granville, *Countess — Biographies*

Askwith, Betty. Piety and wit : a biography of Harriet Countess Granville, 1785-1862 / Betty Askwith. — London : Collins, 1982. — 207p : ill,3geneal.tables ; 24cm
Bibliography: p183-184. — Includes index
ISBN 0-00-216258-x : £14.50 : CIP rev.
B81-37581

941.07'1 — Great Britain. Jacobitism, *1689-1759*

Ideology and conspiracy : aspects of Jacobitism, 1689-1759 / edited by Eveline Cruickshanks. — Edinburgh : Donald, c1982. — xi,231p ; 24cm
Includes index
ISBN 0-85976-084-7 : £15.00 B82-37193

941.07'1'0924 — Great Britain. Wharton, Phillip, *Duke of — Biographies*

Blackett-Ord, Mark. Hell-fire Duke. — Windsor (Shooters Lodge, Windsor Forest, Windsor, Berks. SL4 4SY) : Kensal Press, Oct.1982. — [290]p
ISBN 0-946041-02-4 : £12.50 : CIP entry
B82-29042

941.07'2 — Great Britain. Jacobite Rebellion, *1745.* **Suppression by William,** *Duke of Cumberland*

Speck, W. A.. The butcher : the Duke of Cumberland and the suppression of the 45 / W.A. Speck. — Oxford : Blackwell, 1981. — x,230p : ill,maps,facsims,plans,ports,1geneal.table ; 26cm
Includes index
ISBN 0-631-10501-8 : £12.50 : CIP rev.
B81-21461

941.07'3 — Great Britain, *1760-1820*

Christie, Ian R.. Wars and revolutions : Britain 1760-1815 / Ian R. Christie. — London : Edward Arnold, 1982. — 359p : maps ; 24cm. — (The New history of England ; 7)
Bibliography: p327. — Includes index
ISBN 0-7131-6157-4 (cased) : Unpriced : CIP rev.
ISBN 0-7131-6158-2 : £6.95 B82-13515

941.081 — Great Britain, *1815-1914*

Wood, Anthony, *1923-*. Nineteenth century Britain : 1815-1914 / Anthony Wood. — 2nd ed. — Harlow : Longman, 1982. — viii,470p : 1geneal.table,maps ; 23cm
Previous ed: 1960. — Bibliography: p450-456. — Includes index
ISBN 0-582-35311-4 (cased) : Unpriced
ISBN 0-582-35310-6 (pbk) : £5.25 B82-30902

941.081 — Great Britain, *1815-1914 — For schools*

Helm, P. J.. Modern British history. — London : Bell & Hyman
Originally published: 1965
Pt.1: 1815-1914. — Nov.1981. — [269]p
ISBN 0-7135-1803-0 (pbk) : £2.75 : CIP entry
B81-34714

941.081 — Great Britain, *1837-1901 — For schools*

Pluckrose, Henry. Victorian Britain. — London : Bell & Hyman, Apr.1982. — [80]p. — (History around us)
ISBN 0-7135-1290-3 (pbk) : £3.95 : CIP entry
B82-04492

941.081 — Great Britain, *1860-1980 — For schools*

Speed, P. F.. The modern age / Peter & Mary Speed. — Oxford : Oxford University Press by arrangement with the British Broadcasting Corporation, 1980 (1981 [printing]). — 128p : ill(some col.),col.maps,facsims(some col.),ports (some col.) ; 28cm. — (Oxford junior history ; 5)
ISBN 0-19-918122-5 (corrected : pbk) : £2.50
B82-13876

941.081 — Great Britain. Intellectual life, *1860-1900.* **Influence of theories of evolution of Darwin, Charles**

Ebbatson, Roger. The evolutionary self : Hardy, Forster, Lawrence. — Brighton : Harvester Press, Nov.1982. — [192]p
ISBN 0-7108-0491-1 : £18.95 : CIP entry
B82-27932

941.081 — Great Britain. Riots, *1837-1901*

Richter, Donald C.. Riotous Victorians / by Donald C. Richter. — Athens ; London : Ohio University Press, c1981. — xi,185p : ill,1map,ports ; 23cm
Map tipped in. — Bibliography: p171-178. — Includes index
ISBN 0-8214-0571-3 (cased) : Unpriced
ISBN 0-8214-0618-3 (pbk) : £4.50 B82-30757

941.081 — Great Britain. Social conditions, *1800-1900 — For schools*

A **Social** history of Britain. — London (Ealing Abbey, W5 2DY) : A-V for Schools
The nineteenth century / Robin Nonhebel. — 1977. — 68p : ill(some col.),2ports ; 24cm
£0.90 (pbk) B82-13612

941.081 — Great Britain. Social conditions, *1837-1980 — For schools*

Middleton, Geoffrey. Victorian times and the twentieth century / Geoffrey Middleton ; illustrated with contemporary pictures and by Peter Dennis and Kathy Deeks. — Harlow : Longman, 1982. — 78p : ill(some col.),maps (some col.),facsims(some col.),ports(some col.) ; 27cm. — (History in focus ; 5)
Text on inside covers. — Includes index
ISBN 0-582-18317-0 (pbk) : £2.25 B82-17728

941.081 — Great Britain. Social conditions, *ca 1830-1900 — Readings from contemporary sources*

Everitt, Alastair. The papers and transactions of the Manchester Statistical Society. — Brighton : Harvester Press Microform Publications
Pt.1: The papers 1833-1845; and, The transactions for sessions 1853/54 to 1875/76. — May 1982. — [62]p
ISBN 0-86257-012-3 (pbk) : £6.00 : CIP entry
B82-16505

941.081 — Great Britain. Social conditions, *ca 1870-1918*

Adams, Carol. Ordinary lives : a hundred years ago / Carol Adams. — London : Virago, 1982. — 228p : ill,facsims,ports ; 21cm
Bibliography: p223-228
ISBN 0-86068-239-0 (pbk) : £4.50 : CIP rev.
B82-00382

941.081 — Great Britain. Social life, *1837-1901*

Bloom, Ursula. Victorian vinaigrette / Ursula Bloom. — Large print ed. — Bath : Chivers, 1982. — ix,327p ; 23cm. — (A Lythway chronicle)
Originally published: London : Hutchinson, 1956
ISBN 0-85119-833-3 : Unpriced : CIP rev.
B82-15865

941.081 — Great Britain. Social life, *1898-1899 — Correspondence, diaries, etc.*

Dearest Beatie — my darling Jack. — London : Collins, Feb.1983. — [192]p
ISBN 0-00-218015-4 : £7.95 : CIP entry
B82-36459

941.081 — Great Britain. Social life, *ca 1825-ca 1940*

Body, Geoffrey. The railway era. — Ashbourne : Moorland, Nov.1982. — [160]p
ISBN 0-86190-072-3 : £7.95 : CIP entry
B82-30600

941.081 — Great Britain. Society. Role of chivalry, *1790-1914*

Girouard, Mark. The return to Camelot : chivalry and the English gentleman / Mark Girouard. — New Haven ; London : Yale, 1981. — 312p : ill(some col.),coats of arms,facsims,ports(some col.) ; 27cm
Includes index
ISBN 0-300-02739-7 : £12.50 : CIP rev.
B81-28808

941.081'05 — Great Britain. Social conditions, *1881 — Serials — Facsimiles*

The **Englishwoman's** review of social and industrial questions, 1881. — New York ; London : Garland, 1979. — iv,576p ; 23cm
Facsim. of: Vol.12, January to December, 1881. London : Engwoman's Review, 1891
ISBN 0-8240-3738-3 : Unpriced B82-14153

941.081'05 — Great Britain. Social conditions, *1891 — Serials — Facsimiles*

The **Englishwoman's** review of social and industrial questions, 1891. — New York ; London : Garland, 1979. — v,292p : facsims ; 23cm
Facsim. of: Vol.22, January to October, 1891 London : Englishwoman's Review, 1891
ISBN 0-8240-3748-0 : Unpriced B82-05862

941.08'1092'4 — Great Britain. Churchill, Randolph S. *— Biographies*

Foster, R. F.. Lord Randolph Churchill. — Oxford : Clarendon Press, Nov.1981. — [440]p
ISBN 0-19-822679-9 : £15.00 : CIP entry
B81-28852

941.081'092'4 — Great Britain. Churchill, Randolph S. *— Biographies*

Foster, R. F.. Lord Randolph Churchill. — Oxford : Clarendon Press, Nov.1982. — [431]p
Originally published: 1981
ISBN 0-19-822756-6 (pbk) : £9.95 : CIP entry
B82-29001

941.081'092'4 — Great Britain. Disraeli, Benjamin *— Correspondence, diaries, etc*

Disraeli, Benjamin. Benjamin Disraeli letters / edited by J.A.W. Gunn [... et al.]. — Toronto ; London : University of Toronto Press
1815-1834. — c1982. — lxviii,482p : maps ; 26cm
Includes index
ISBN 0-8020-5523-0 : £40.20 B82-35658

Disraeli, Benjamin. Benjamin Disraeli letters / edited by J.A.W. Gunn [... et al.]. — Toronto ; London : University of Toronto Press
1815-1837. — c1982. — xliii,458p ; 26cm
Includes index
ISBN 0-8020-5587-7 : £40.20 B82-35659

941.081'092'4 — Great Britain. Gladstone, W. E. (William Ewart) *— Biographies*

Gladstone, W. E. (William Ewart). W.E. Gladstone : [papers] / edited by John Brooke and Mary Sorensen. — London : H.M.S.O.. — (The Prime Ministers' papers series)
Includes index
4: Autobiographical memoranda 1868-1894. — 1981. — viii,165p ; 25cm
ISBN 0-11-440113-6 : £15.00 B82-31153

Shannon, Richard. Gladstone. — London : Hamilton, Sept.1982
Vol.1: 1809-1865. — [480]p
ISBN 0-241-10780-6 : £15.00 : CIP entry
B82-18738

941.081′092′4 — Great Britain. Gladstone, W. E. (William Ewart) — *Correspondence, diaries, etc*

Gladstone, W. E.. The Gladstone diaries with cabinet minutes and Prime-Ministerial correspondence. — Oxford : Clarendon Press
Vol.7: 1869-June 1871. — Sept.1982. — [700]p
ISBN 0-19-822638-1 : £40.00 : CIP entry
B82-18977

Gladstone, W. E.. The Gladstone diaries with cabinet minutes and Prime-Ministerial correspondence. — Oxford : Clarendon Press
Vol.8: July 1871-December 1874. — Sept.1982. — [750]p
ISBN 0-19-822639-x : £40.00 : CIP entry
B82-18976

941.081′092′4 — Great Britain. Gladstone, W. E. (William Ewart). Local associations: Clwyd. Hawarden

Veysey, A. G.. Mr Gladstone and Hawarden / [compiled by A. Geoffrey Veysey]. — Hawarden : Clwyd Record Office, 1982. — [20] : ill,ports ; 21cm
Cover title. — Text, ill on covers. — Bibliography: p20
ISBN 0-904444-63-5 (pbk) : Unpriced
B82-38243

941.081′092′4 — Great Britain. Gladstone, W. E. (William Ewart). Religious beliefs, *1809-1859*

Butler, Perry. Gladstone : church, state, and Tractarianism : a study of his religious ideas and attitudes, 1809-1859 / by Perry Butler. — Oxford : Clarendon, 1982. — 246p ; 23cm. — (Oxford historical monographs)
Bibliography: p236-241. — Includes index
ISBN 0-19-821890-7 : £17.50 : CIP rev.
B81-35762

941.081′092′4 — Great Britain. Heckford, Sarah — *Biographies*

Allen, Vivien. Lady trader : a biography of Mrs. Sarah Heckford / Vivien Allen. — Large print ed. — Leicester : Ulverscroft, 1981, c1979. — 475p ; 22cm
Originally published: London : Collins, 1979
ISBN 0-7089-0728-8 : £5.00 : CIP rev.
B81-32037

941.081′092′4 — Great Britain. Palmerston, Henry John Temple, *Viscount* — *Biographies*

Bourne, Kenneth. Palmerston : the early years 1784-1841 / by Kenneth Bourne. — London : Allen Lane, 1982. — xiv,749p,[16]p of plates : ill,facsims,ports ; 25cm
Bibliography: p698-708. — Includes index
ISBN 0-7139-1083-6 : £25.00 B82-38334

941.081′092′4 — Great Britain. Politics. Chamberlain, Joseph

Jay, Richard. Joseph Chamberlain : a political study / Richard Jay. — Oxford : Clarendon, 1981. — lx,383p : 1port ; 23cm
Bibliography: p369-371. — Includes index
ISBN 0-19-822623-3 : £16.95 B82-15094

941.081′092′4 — Great Britain. Politics. Ripon, George Frederick Samuel Robinson, *Marquis of* — *Biographies*

Denholm, Anthony. Lord Ripon 1827-1909 : a political biography / Anthony Denholm. — London : Croom Helm, c1982. — 287p ; 23cm
Bibliography: p263-280. — Includes index
ISBN 0-7099-0805-9 : £12.95 : CIP rev.
B82-11307

941.081′092′4 — Great Britain. Politics. Spencer, John Poyntz Spencer, *Earl* — *Correspondence, diaries, etc*

Spencer, John Poyntz Spencer, *Earl*. The red Earl : the papers of the fifth Earl Spencer 1835-1910 / edited by Peter Gordon. — Northampton : Northamptonshire Record Society
Vol.1: 1835-1885. — 1981. — x,328p,8p of plates : ill,1facsim, ports ; 26cm. — (The Publications of the Northamptonshire Record Society ; v.31)
Includes index
ISBN 0-901275-45-x : Unpriced B82-14423

941.081′092′4 — Great Britain. Victoria, *Queen of Great Britain, 1878-1885* — *Correspondence, diaries, etc.*

Victoria, *Queen of Great Britain*. Beloved mama : private correspondence of Queen Victoria and the German Crown Princess, 1878-1885 / edited by Roger Fulford. — London : Evans, 1981. — xiii,209p,[16]p of plates : ports,2geneal.tables ; 23cm
Includes index
ISBN 0-237-44997-8 : £10.95 : CIP rev.
Also classified at 943.08′3′0924 B81-25777

941.081′092′4 — Middle East. Visits by Disraeli, Benjamin, *1830-1831*

Blake, Robert Blake, *Baron*. Disraeli′s grand tour : Benjamin Disraeli and the Holy Land, 1830-31 / Robert Blake. — London : Weidenfeld and Nicolson, c1982. — xvi,141p,[13]p of plates : ill,1map,ports ; 25cm
Includes index
ISBN 0-297-77910-9 : £8.95 B82-12380

941.081′092′4 — West Glamorgan. Swansea. Visits by Gladstone, W. E. (William Ewart), *1887*

Shannon, Richard. Mr Gladstone and Swansea 1887 : inaugural lecture delivered at the College on 18 November 1980 / by Richard T. Shannon. — Swansea : University College of Swansea, 1982. — 15p ; 21cm
ISBN 0-86076-029-4 (pbk) : Unpriced
B82-25038

941.082 — Great Britain, *1870-1975*

Robbins, Keith. The eclipse of a great power 1870-1975. — London : Longman, Oct.1982. — [416]p. — (Foundations of modern Britain)
ISBN 0-582-48971-7 (cased) : £14.95 : CIP entry
ISBN 0-582-48972-5 (pbk) : £7.50 B82-23356

941.082 — Great Britain, *1900-1965* — *For schools*

Brown, Richard, *1948-*. Twentieth-century Britain / Richard Brown, Christopher Daniels. — Basingstoke : Macmillan Education, 1982. — v,137p ; 21cm. — (Documents and debates)
ISBN 0-333-31285-6 (pbk) : Unpriced
B82-37933

941.082 — Great Britain, *1900-1982* — *For schools*

Pluckrose, Henry. Twentieth century Britain. — London : Bell & Hyman, Sept.1982. — [80]p. — (History around us series ; 9)
ISBN 0-7135-1291-1 (pbk) : £3.95 : CIP entry
B82-20773

941.082 — Great Britain, *1901-1910*

Edwardian realities. — London : Croom Helm, Aug.1982. — [192]p
ISBN 0-7099-1223-4 (cased) : £12.95 : CIP entry
ISBN 0-7099-1237-4 (pbk) : £6.95 B82-15906

941.082 — Great Britain. Political events, *1896-1955* — *Correspondence, diaries, etc.*

Amery, Leo. The Leo Amery diaries / edited by John Barnes and David Nicholson ; introduced by Julian Amery. — London : Hutchinson
Vol.1: 1869-1929. — 1980. — 652p ; 25cm
Includes index
ISBN 0-09-131910-2 : £27.50 : CIP rev.
B79-24814

941.082 — Great Britain. Social change, *1900-1980*

Halsey, A. H.. Change in British society : based on the Reith Lectures / A.H. Halsey. — 2nd ed. — Oxford : Oxford University Press, 1981. — vii,198p : ill ; 20cm. — (OPUS) (Open University set book)
Previous ed.: 1978. — Bibliography: p189-193.— Includes index
ISBN 0-19-289156-1 (pbk) : £2.95 : CIP rev.
B81-22563

941.082′0880623 — Great Britain. Working class young persons. Social life, *1889-1939*

Humphries, Stephen. Hooligans or rebels? : an oral history of working-class childhood and youth 1889-1939 / Stephen Humphries. — Oxford : Blackwell, 1981. — viii,279p : ill,maps,facsims ; 24cm
Facsim on lining papers. — Includes index
ISBN 0-631-12982-0 : £12.50 : CIP rev.
B81-30170

941.082′092′2 — Great Britain. Monarchs. Boradcast Christmas speeches, *to 1981* — *Collections*

George V, *King of Great Britain*. Voices out of the air : the royal Christmas broadcasts 1932-1981 / introduced by Tom Fleming. — London : Heinemann, 1981. — 157p : ill,facsims,ports ; 26cm
Texts of speeches written and delivered by King George V, King George VI and Queen Elizabeth II
ISBN 0-434-26680-9 : £7.95 B82-08699

941.082′092′4 — Great Britain. Alexandra, *Queen, consort of Edward VII, King of Great Britain* — *Biographies*

Duff, David. Alexandra : princess and queen / David Duff. — London : Sphere, 1981, c1980. — 327p,[8]p of plates : ill,ports,geneal,tables ; 20cm
Originally published: London : Collins, 1980. — Bibliography: p305-310. — Includes index
ISBN 0-7221-3080-5 (pbk) : £2.50 B82-08374

941.082′092′4 — Great Britain. Alice, *Princess, Duchess of Gloucester* — *Biographies*

Alice, *Princess, Duchess of Gloucester*. The memoirs of Princess Alice, Duchess of Gloucester. — London : Collins, Nov.1982. — [256]p
ISBN 0-00-216646-1 : £9.95 : CIP entry
B82-27793

941.082′092′4 — Great Britain. Churchill, Winston S. (Winston Spencer), *1874-1965* — *Biographies*

Morgan, Ted. Churchill : 1874-1915. — London : Cape, Oct.1982. — [576]p
ISBN 0-224-02044-7 : £12.50 : CIP entry
B82-25162

941.082′092′4 — Great Britain. Churchill, Winston S. (Winston Spencer), *1874-1965* **World crisis 1911-1918** — *Critical studies*

Prior, Robin. Churchill′s World crisis as history. — London : Croom Helm, Jan.1983. — [352]p
ISBN 0-7099-2011-3 : £15.95 : CIP entry
B82-33350

941.082′092′4 — Great Britain. Cooper, Diana, *1892-* — *Biographies*

Ziegler, Philip. Diana Cooper / Philip Ziegler. — Leicester : Charnwood, 1982, c1981. — 597p ; 22cm. — (Charnwood library series)
Originally published: London : Hamilton, 1981. — Published in large print
ISBN 0-7089-8059-7 : Unpriced : CIP rev.
B82-15966

941.082′092′4 — Great Britain. Hill, Archie — *Biographies*

Hill, Archie. The second meadow. — London : Hutchinson, Apr.1982. — [118]p
ISBN 0-09-147570-8 : £4.95 : CIP entry
B82-04724

941.082′092′4 — Great Britain. Leslie, Anita — *Biographies*

Leslie, Anita. A story half told. — London : Hutchinson, Feb.1983. — [224]p
ISBN 0-09-151210-7 : £9.95 : CIP entry
B82-36562

941.082′092′4 — Great Britain. Margerison, H. — *Biographies*

Margerison, H.. Memoirs of a dilittante [i.e. dilettante] / H. Margerison. — Bognor Regis : New Horizon, c1982. — 134p,[7]p of plates : ill,ports ; 21cm
ISBN 0-86116-129-7 : £5.25 B82-06384

941.082′092′4 — Great Britain. Mosley, *Lady Cynthia* — *Biographies*

Mosley, Nicholas. Rules of the game. — London : Secker & Warburg, Sept.1982. — [266]p
ISBN 0-436-28849-4 : £8.95 : CIP entry
Also classified at 941.082′092′4 B82-19821

941.082′092′4 — Great Britain. Mountbatten, Louis Mountbatten, *Earl* — *Biographies*

Hough, Richard. Mountbatten, hero of our time / by Richard Hough. — Long Preston : Magna, 1981, c1980. — 723p ; 23cm
Originally published: London : Weidenfeld and Nicholson, 1980. — Published in large print
ISBN 0-86009-362-x : Unpriced : CIP rev.
B81-27440

941.082′092′4 — Great Britain. Mountbatten, Louis Mountbatten, *Earl — Biographies — For children*

Dobson, Julia. Mountbatten, sailor hero / Julia Dobson ; illustrated by Michael Ogden. — London : MacRae, 1982. — 42p : ill,ports ; 21cm. — (Blackbird books)
ISBN 0-86203-062-5 : £2.75 : CIP rev.
B81-36046

941.082′092′4 — Great Britain. Paul, G. C. P. — *Biographies*

Paul, G. C. P.. Never say die / by G.C.P. Paul. — Ilfracombe : Stockwell, 1978. — 92p : ill,ports ; 22cm
ISBN 0-7223-1588-0 (pbk) : £2.50 B82-21773

941.082′092′4 — Great Britain. Politicians, *1929-1960 — Personal observations*

Butler, Richard Austen Butler, *Baron*. The art of memory : friends in perspective / Lord Butler. — London : Hodder and Stoughton, c1982. — 175p ; 24cm
Bibliography: p164-165. — Includes index
ISBN 0-340-26497-7 : £7.95 : CIP rev.
B82-03806

941.082′092′4 — Great Britain. Politics. Astor, Nancy — *Biographies*

Collis, Maurice. Nancy Astor / Maurice Collis. — London : Futura, 1982, c1960. — 254p : 1geneal.table ; 18cm
Originally published: London : Faber, 1960. — Includes index
ISBN 0-7088-2166-9 (pbk) : £1.75 B82-12752

Grigg, John. Nancy Astor / John Grigg. — Feltham : Hamlyn, 1982, c1980. — 192p : ill,ports ; 25cm
Includes index
ISBN 0-600-20594-0 (pbk) : £2.95 B82-14469

941.082′092′4 — Great Britain. Politics. Longford, Frank Pakenham, *Earl of — Correspondence, diaries, etc.*

Longford, Frank Pakenham, *Earl of*. Diary of a year / Lord Longford. — London : Weidenfeld and Nicolson, c1982. — v,234p ; 23cm
Includes index
ISBN 0-297-78049-2 : £10.00 B82-37195

941.082′092′4 — Great Britain. Politics. Mosley, *Sir* **Oswald** — *Biographies*

Mosley, Nicholas. Rules of the game. — London : Secker & Warburg, Sept.1982. — [266]p
ISBN 0-436-28849-4 : £8.95 : CIP entry
Primary classification 941.082′092′4
B82-19821

941.082′092′4 — Great Britain. Politics. Swinton, Philip Cunliffe-Lister, *Earl of — Biographies*

Cross, J. A.. Lord Swinton. — Oxford : Clarendon, Feb.1983. — [350]p
ISBN 0-19-822602-0 : £19.50 : CIP entry
B82-36604

941.082′092′4 — Great Britain. Politics. Wilkinson, Ellen — *Biographies*

Vernon, Betty D.. Ellen Wilkinson 1891-1947 / Betty D. Vernon. — London : Croom Helm, c1982. — 254p ; 23cm
Bibliography: p243-247. — Includes index
ISBN 0-85664-984-8 : £14.95 : CIP rev.
B81-33773

941.082′092′4 — Great Britain. Woodhouse, C. M. — *Biographies*

Woodhouse, C. M.. Something ventured. — London : Granada, June 1982. — [304]p
ISBN 0-246-11061-9 : £12.00 : CIP entry
B82-09983

941.082′092′4 — Political events, *1894-1948*. **Attitudes of Churchill, Winston S. (Winston Spencer),** *1874-1965*

Gilbert, Martin. Churchill's political philosophy : thank-offering to Britain Fund Lectures 24, 25 and 27 November 1980 / by Martin Gilbert. — Oxford : Published for the British Academy by Oxford University Press, 1981. — 119p ; 22cm
Includes index
ISBN 0-19-726005-5 : £8.00 B82-05661

941.082′3 — Great Britain. Children. Social life, *1901-1914*

Smith, Joanna. Edwardian children. — London : Hutchinson, Sept.1982. — [192]p
ISBN 0-09-147910-x : £8.95 : CIP entry
B82-19106

941.083 — Great Britain. Society, *1914*

McLeod, Kirsty. The last summer. — London : Collins, May 1982. — [206]p
ISBN 0-00-216456-6 : £10.95 : CIP entry
B82-12709

941.083′092′4 — Great Britain. Asquith, Henry Herbert, *Earl of Oxford & Asquith*. **Correspondence with Stanley, Venetia,** *1912-1917*

Asquith, Herbert Henry, *Earl of Oxford & Asquith*. H.H. Asquith : letters to Venetia Stanley. — Oxford : Oxford University Press, Oct.1982. — [672]p
ISBN 0-19-212200-2 : £17.50 : CIP entry
B82-23657

941.083′092′4 — Great Britain. Dalton, Hugh — *Correspondence, diaries, etc.*

Dalton, Hugh. The political diaries of Hugh Dalton. — London : Cape, Feb.1983. — [940]p
ISBN 0-224-01912-0 : £20.00 : CIP entry
B82-37831

941.083′092′4 — Great Britain. Moore, Aubrey — *Biographies*

Moore, Aubrey. A son of the rectory. — Gloucester : Alan Sutton, Dec.1982. — [144]p
ISBN 0-86299-035-1 (cased) : £7.95 : CIP entry
ISBN 0-86299-036-x (pbk) : £3.95 B82-35231

941.083′092′4 — Great Britain. Politics. Isaacs, Rufus, *Marquess of Reading — Biographies*

Judd, Denis. Lord Reading : Rufus Isaacs, first Marquess of Reading, Lord Chief Justice and Viceroy of India, 1860-1935 / Denis Judd. — London : Weidenfeld and Nicolson, 1982. — x,316p,[8]p of plates : 1facsim,ports ; 25cm
Bibliography: p303-307. — Includes index
ISBN 0-297-78014-x : £15.00 B82-26817

941.083′092′4 — Great Britain. Social life, *1930-1939 — Personal observations*

Blake, Beryl. Ankle-strap shoes on Sundays / Beryl Blake. — Bognor Regis : New Horizon, c1982. — 68p : ill ; 21cm
ISBN 0-86116-551-9 : £3.25 B82-13974

941.084 — Great Britain. Social life, *1936-1953*

Kelsall, Freda. How we used to live : 1936-1953 / Freda Kelsall. — London : Macdonald by arrangement with Yorkshire Television, 1981. — 48p : ill(some col.),facsims,ports(some col.) ; 29cm
Bibliography: p46. — Includes index
ISBN 0-356-06298-8 (cased) : £3.50
ISBN 0-356-06299-6 (pbk) : Unpriced
B82-00104

941.084′092′2 — Great Britain. Social life, *1938-1945 — Personal observations — Collections*

The **Home** front : an anthology of personal experience 1938-1945 / selected and edited by Norman Longmate. — London : Chatto & Windus, 1981. — xiii,242p,[8]p of plates : ill ; 23cm
Includes index
ISBN 0-7011-2553-5 : £9.95 : CIP rev.
B81-12386

941.084′092′2 — Great Britain. Social life, *1940-1945 — Personal observations — Collections*

You, you & you : the people out of step with World War II / [compiled by] Pete Grafton. — London : Pluto, 1981. — 169p ; 19cm
ISBN 0-86104-360-x (pbk) : £2.95 B82-20687

941.084′092′2 — Great Britain. Windsor, Edward, *Duke of* **& Windsor, Wallis Windsor,** *Duchess of — Biographies*

Bryan, Joe. The Windsor story / J. Bryan III and Charles J.V. Murphy. — London : Granada, 1979 (1981 [printing]). — 751p : ill,ports ; 18cm
Bibliography: p719-725. — Includes index
ISBN 0-586-05181-3 (pbk) : £2.95 B82-04014

941.084′092′4 — Great Britain. Elizabeth, *Queen, consort of George VI, King of Great Britain — Biographies*

Cathcart, Helen. The Queen Mother herself / by Helen Cathcart. — Large print ed. — Long Preston : Magna Print, 1982, c1979. — 572p,[16]p of plates : ports ; 22cm
Originally published: London : W.H. Allen, 1979. — Published in large print. — Bibliography: p565-572
ISBN 0-86009-366-2 : Unpriced : CIP rev.
B81-33770

941.084′092′4 — Great Britain. Elizabeth, *Queen, consort of George VI, King of Great Britain — Biographies — For children*

Morrison, Ian A.. H.M. Queen Elizabeth the Queen Mother / by Ian A. Morrison. — Loughborough : Ladybird, c1982. — 51p : ill (some col.),1col.coat of arms,1facsim,1col.geneal.table,ports(some col.) ; 18cm
ISBN 0-7214-0713-7 : £0.60 B82-37070

941.084′092′4 — Great Britain. Social life, *1939-1953 — Personal observations*

Harvie, Alida. The rationed years : sequel to Those glittering years / by Alida Harvie. — London : Regency, c1982. — 151p : ill,ports ; 21cm
ISBN 0-7212-0602-6 : £5.50 B82-35516

941.085 — Great Britain, *1945-1980 — For schools*

Madgwick, P. J.. Britain since 1945 / P.J. Madgwick, D. Steeds, L.J. Williams. — London : Hutchinson, 1982. — 382p : 2ill ; 24cm
Bibliography: p365-369. — Includes index
ISBN 0-09-147371-3 (pbk) : Unpriced : CIP rev. B82-04123

941.085 — Great Britain. Social change, *ca 1930-ca 1980*

The **Changing** geography of the United Kingdom. — London : Methuen, Jan.1983. — [350]p
ISBN 0-416-74800-7 (cased) : £15.00 : CIP entry
ISBN 0-416-74810-4 (pbk) : £7.50 B82-34573

941.085 — Great Britain. Social conditions, *1945-1980*

Custom and conflict in British society / edited by Ronald Frankenberg. — Manchester : Manchester University Press, c1982. — 361p ; 25cm
Includes bibliographies and index
ISBN 0-7190-0855-7 : £25.00 : CIP rev.
B82-01425

Marwick, Arthur. British society since 1945 / Arthur Marwick. — Harmondsworth : Penguin, 1982. — 303p ; 19cm. — (The Pelican social history of Britain)
Bibliography: p278-286. — Includes index
ISBN 0-14-021906-4 (pbk) : £2.95 B82-23931

Marwick, Arthur. British society since 1945 / Arthur Marwick. — London : Allen Lane, 1982. — 303p ; 23cm. — (The Pelican social history of Britain)
Bibliography: p278-286. — Includes index
ISBN 0-7139-1075-5 : £12.50 B82-23930

941.085′022′2 — Great Britain. Social life, *1953-1970 — Illustrations*

Yesterday : a photographic album of daily life in Britain 1953-1970 / introduced by Benny Green. — London : Dent, 1982. — [288]p : chiefly ill,ports ; 26cm
ISBN 0-460-04549-0 : £10.50 : CIP rev.
B82-19698

941.085′092′2 — Great Britain. Charles, *Prince of Wales;* **Anne,** *Princess, daughter of Elizabeth II* **; Andrew,** *Prince, son of Elizabeth II* **& Edward,** *Prince, son of Elizabeth II — Biographies*

Metcalfe, James. All the Queen's children / James Metcalfe. — London : W.H. Allen, 1982, c1981. — 184p : ill,ports ; 18cm. — (A Star book)
Originally published: 1981
ISBN 0-352-31143-6 (pbk) : £1.75 B82-35258

941.085'092'2 — Great Britain. Charles, *Prince of Wales*. Interpersonal relationships with Diana, *Princess of Wales*

Craven, John. Charles and Diana. — London : Severn House, Oct.1982. — [128]p
ISBN 0-7278-0854-0 : £4.95 : CIP entry
B82-28582

Craven, John, *1940-*. Charles & Diana : their story / told by John Craven ; including children's memories of the Royal wedding ; research by Katie Griffiths. — London : Sparrow Books, 1982. — 127p,[16]p of plates : ill,coat of arms,ports ; 18cm
ISBN 0-09-928790-0 (pbk) : £0.95 B82-31348

941.085'092'2 — Great Britain. Politics. Bevan, Aneurin & Lee, Jennie — *Biographies*

Lee, Jennie. My life with Nye / Jennie Lee. — Harmondsworth : Penguin, 1981, c1980. — 326p,[8]p of plates : ill,ports ; 18cm
Originally published: London : Cape, 1980. — Includes index
ISBN 0-14-005933-4 (pbk) : £1.75 B82-07289

941.085'092'4 — Great Britain. Alexandra, *Princess* — *Biographies*

Elborn, Geoffrey. Princess Alexandra. — London : Sheldon Press, Oct.1982. — [280]p
ISBN 0-85969-376-7 : £7.95 : CIP entry
B82-24125

941.085'092'4 — Great Britain. Bingham, Charlotte — *Biographies*

Bingham, Charlotte. Coronet among the weeds. — Bath : Chivers, Sept.1982. — [60]p. — (A New Portway book)
Originally published: London : Heinemann, 1963
ISBN 0-86220-506-9 : £4.95 : CIP entry
B82-21993

941.085'092'4 — Great Britain. Brindley, Louise — *Biographies*

Brindley, Louise. There's one born every minute. — London : Muller, Nov.1982. — [256]p
ISBN 0-584-31154-0 : £7.50 : CIP entry
B82-26568

941.085'092'4 — Great Britain. Diana, *Princess of Wales* — *Biographies*

Courtney, Nicholas. Diana, Princess of Wales / Nicholas Courtney. — London (40 Park St., W1Y 4DE) : Park Lane Press, 1982. — 79p : ill(some col.),ports(some col.) ; 30cm
£1.50 (pbk) B82-36023

Junor, Penny. Diana : Princess of Wales : a biography / by Penny Junor. — London : Sidgwick and Jackson, 1982. — 224p,[16]p of plates : ill(some col.),1coat of arms,ports ; 24cm
Includes index
ISBN 0-283-98843-6 : £5.95 B82-33033

Junor, Penny. Diana, Princess of Wales. — Large print ed. — Bath : Chivers, Sept.1982. — [336] p. — (A Lythway book)
Originally published: London : Sidgwick and Jackson, 1982
ISBN 0-85119-878-3 : £7.90 : CIP entry
B82-23861

Lacey, Robert. Princess. — London : Hutchinson, May 1982. — [128]p
ISBN 0-09-149170-3 : £6.95 : CIP entry
B82-09277

Leete-Hodge, Lornie. The Country Life book of Diana, Princess of Wales / Lornie Leete-Hodge. — [London] : Country Life, c1982. — 192p : ill(some col.),ports(some col.) ; 31cm
ISBN 0-600-37853-5 : £8.95 B82-24436

Maxwell, Susan. The Princess of Wales : an illustrated biography / by Susan Maxwell. — London : Queen Anne Press, 1982. — 128p : ill(some col.),1coat of arms,plan ; 26cm
ISBN 0-356-07871-x : £6.95 B82-27993

Montgomery-Massingberd, Hugh. Diana : the Princess of Wales / Hugh Montgomery-Massingberd. — [London] : Fontana Paperbacks, 1982. — 95p : ill(some col.),1col.coat of arms ; 27cm
ISBN 0-00-636538-8 (pbk) : £1.95 B82-27992

941.085'092'4 — Great Britain. Diana, *Princess of Wales* — *Biographies* — *For children*

Lewis, Brenda Ralph. HRH the Princess of Wales / by Brenda Ralph Lewis. — Loughborough : Ladybird, c1982. — 50p : col.ill,ports,1geneal.table ; 18cm
ISBN 0-7214-0740-4 : £0.50 B82-21263

941.085'092'4 — Great Britain. Diana, *Princess of Wales* — *Illustrations*

God bless the Princess of Wales / text by Christopher Bentham-Smith. — [London] : Corgi, 1982. — 126p : col.ill,chiefly col.ports ; 29cm
Port on folded sheet as insert
ISBN 0-552-99008-6 (pbk) : Unpriced
B82-29540

Lewis, Brenda Ralph. Diana : Princess of Wales : our future Queen / Brenda Ralph Lewis. — Bristol : Purnell, 1982. — [46]p : col.ill,geneal.table,ports ; 27cm
Text, ill on lining papers. — Includes index
ISBN 0-361-05433-5 : £2.95 B82-36215

941.085'092'4 — Great Britain. Elizabeth II, *Queen of Great Britain* — *Biographies*

Cathcart, Helen. The Queen herself / Helen Cathcart. — Large print ed. — Bath : Chivers, 1982. — ix,382p ; 23cm. — (A New Portway large print book)
Originally published: London : W.H. Allen, 1982
ISBN 0-85119-194-0 : Unpriced : CIP rev.
B82-13271

Hamilton, Alan. Queen Elizabeth II. — London : Hamilton, Oct.1982. — [64]p. — (Profiles)
ISBN 0-241-10850-0 : £3.25 : CIP entry
B82-25921

941.085'092'4 — Great Britain. Foley, Winifred, *1945-1980* — *Biographies*

Foley, Winifred. Back to the Forest / Winifred Foley. — London : Futura, 1982, c1981. — 206p ; 18cm
Originally published: London : Macdonald, 1981
ISBN 0-7088-2183-9 (pbk) : £1.25 B82-31496

Foley, Winifred. Back to the forest. — Large print ed. — Bath : Chivers, Sept.1982. — [320] p. — (A New Portway large print book)
Originally published: London : Macdonald, 1981
ISBN 0-85119-182-7 : £5.95 : CIP entry
B82-20501

941.085'092'4 — Great Britain. Macmillan, Harold — *Biographies*

Fisher, Nigel. Harold Macmillan : a biography / by Nigel Fisher. — London : Weidenfeld and Nicolson, 1982. — xi,404p,[8]p of plates : ports ; 24cm
Bibliography: p371-373. — Includes index
ISBN 0-297-77914-1 : £12.95 B82-20422

941.085'092'4 — Great Britain. Margaret, *Princess, Countess of Snowdon* — *Biographies*

Dempster, Nigel. H.R.H. The Princess Margaret : a life unfulfilled / Nigel Dempster. — London : Quartet, 1981. — xi,192p,[12]p of plates : ports ; 24cm
ISBN 0-7043-2314-1 : £7.95 : CIP rev.
B81-31091

Dempster, Nigel. H.R.H. the Princess Margaret. — London : Quartet, July 1982. — 1v.
Originally published: 1981
ISBN 0-7043-3413-5 (pbk) : CIP entry
B82-14075

Dempster, Nigel. H.R.H. the Princess Margaret : a life unfulfilled / Nigel Dempster. — Large print ed. — Bath : Chivers, 1982, c1981. — x,322p,[8]p of plates : ports ; 22cm. — (A Lythway book)
Originally published: London : Quartet, 1981
ISBN 0-85119-840-6 : Unpriced : CIP rev.
B82-07676

941.085'092'4 — Great Britain. Philip, *Prince, consort of Elizabeth II, Queen of Great Britain* — *Biographies*

Fisher, Graham. Consort : the life and times of Prince Philip / Graham and Heather Fisher. — Large print ed. — Bath : Chivers, 1982, c1980. — xi,244p ; 23cm. — (A Lythway book)
Originally published: London : W.H. Allen, 1980
ISBN 0-85119-830-9 : Unpriced : CIP rev.
B82-13102

941.085'092'4 — Great Britain. Phillips, Mark, *1948-* — *Biographies*

Rippon, Angela. Mark Phillips : the man and his horses / Angela Rippon. — Newton Abbot : David & Charles, 1982. — 320p : ill(some col.),2maps,ports ; 24cm
Includes index
ISBN 0-7153-8224-1 : £8.95 : CIP rev.
B82-04870

941.085'092'4 — Great Britain. Politics. Benn, Tony — *Biographies*

Benn, Tony. Parliament and power. — London : Verso/NLB, Oct.1982. — [176]p
ISBN 0-86091-057-1 (cased) : £15.00 : CIP entry
ISBN 0-86091-758-4 (pbk) : £3.50 B82-28597

941.085'092'4 — Great Britain. Politics. Bevan, Aneurin — *Biographies*

Foot, Michael. Aneurin Bevan. — London : Granada
Originally published: London : MacGibbon and Kee, 1962
Vol.1: 1897-1945. — Feb.1982. — [536]p
ISBN 0-246-11847-4 : £10.00 : CIP entry
B82-03099

941.085'092'4 — Great Britain. Politics. Crosland, Anthony — *Biographies*

Crosland, Susan. Tony Crosland / Susan Crosland. — London : Cape, 1982. — xvii,422p,[24]p of plates : ill,ports ; 23cm
Includes index
ISBN 0-224-01787-x : £10.95 : CIP rev.
B82-14062

941.085'092'4 — Great Britain. Politics. Foot, Michael — *Biographies*

Hoggart, Simon. Michael Foot : a portrait / Simon Hoggart and David Leigh. — London : Hodder and Stoughton, 1981. — 216p : ill,ports,1geneal.table ; 22cm
Bibliography: p202-204. — Includes index
ISBN 0-340-27040-3 (cased) : Unpriced : CIP rev.
ISBN 0-340-27600-2 (pbk) : £4.95 B81-21581

941.085'092'4 — Great Britain. Politics. Grimond, Jo — *Biographies*

Grimond, Jo. Memoirs / Jo Grimond. — London : Heinemann, 1979. — 315p,[16]p of plates : ill,ports ; 24cm
Includes index
ISBN 0-434-30600-2 : £7.95 B82-27099

941.085'092'4 — Great Britain. Politics. Parker, John, *1906-* — *Biographies*

Parker, John, *1906-*. Father of the House : fifty years in politics / John Parker. — London : Routledge & Kegan Paul, 1982. — xii,203p,[4]p of plates : ports ; 24cm
Includes index
ISBN 0-7100-9220-2 : £10.50 B82-35775

941.085'092'4 — Great Britain. Politics. Redcliffe-Maud, *Lord* — *Biographies*

Redcliffe-Maud, *Lord*. Experience of an optimist. — London : Hamilton, July 1981. — [256]p
ISBN 0-241-10569-2 : £12.50 : CIP entry
B81-19187

941.085'092'4 — Great Britain. Politics. Steel, David, *1938 Mar.31- — Biographies*
Bartram, Peter. David Steel : his life and politics / Peter Bartram ; with a foreword by Ludovic Kennedy. — London : W.H. Allen, 1981. — 200p,[8]p of plates : ports ; 23cm
Includes index
ISBN 0-491-02736-2 : £7.95 B82-00111

941.085'092'4 — Great Britain. Politics. Thomas, George *- Biographies*
Hunston, Ramon. "Order, order". — London : Lakeland, Apr.1981. — [160]p
ISBN 0-551-00882-2 (pbk) : £1.60 : CIP entry B81-08938

941.085'5'0922 — Great Britain. Royal families, *ca 1950-1981 — Illustrations*
Lichfield, Patrick. A royal album. — London : Hamilton, Oct.1982. — [160]p
ISBN 0-241-10856-x : £12.50 : CIP entry B82-23109

941.085'5'0924 — Great Britain. Politics. Gaitskell, Hugh *— Biographies*
Williams, Philip. Hugh Gaitskell. — Oxford : Oxford University Press, Oct.1982. — [500]p
Originally published: London : Cape, 1979
ISBN 0-19-285115-2 (pbk) : £5.95 : CIP entry B82-23674

941.085'6 — British culture, *1960-1980*
Hoggart, Richard. An English temper : essays on education, culture and communications / Richard Hoggart. — London : Chatto & Windus, 1982. — 207p ; 23cm
Includes index
ISBN 0-7011-2581-0 : £9.50 : CIP rev.
Primary classification 370'.941 B82-01194

941.085'6 — Great Britain. Social life, *1960-1970*
Wheen, Francis. The sixties. — London : Century Publishing, Oct.1982. — [176]p
ISBN 0-7126-0018-3 (cased) : £8.95 : CIP entry
ISBN 0-7126-0014-0 (pbk) : £6.95 B82-23883

941.085'7 — Great Britain, *ca 1976-1981 — Readings from contemporary sources*
Peterborough, *Newspaper columnist*. The 'Peterborough' book II. — Newton Abbot : David & Charles, Sept.1982. — [64]p
ISBN 0-7153-8338-8 : £2.95 : CIP entry B82-20374

941.085'7 — Great Britain. Social life, *1977-1981*
Toynbee, Polly. The way we live now / Polly Toynbee. — London : Eyre Methuen, 1981. — xvi,157p ; 23cm
Collection of articles originally published in The Guardian
ISBN 0-413-49090-4 : £6.95 : CIP rev. B81-25308

941.085'7'0880623 — Great Britain. Urban regions. Working class adolescent boys. Social life, *1973-1978 — Case studies*
Williamson, Howard. Five years / by Howard and Pip Williamson. — Leicester : National Youth Bureau, 1981. — 115p : ill ; 21cm
ISBN 0-86155-046-3 (pbk) : £2.25 B82-10923

941.085'8 — British civilization *— For foreign students*
Musman, Richard. Britain today / Richard Musman. — 3rd ed. — Harlow : Longman, 1982. — xi,179p : ill,2maps,ports ; 24cm. — (Longman background books)
Previous ed.: 1977
ISBN 0-582-74912-3 (pbk) : Unpriced B82-36000

941.085'8 — Great Britain
Davies, Hunter. Great Britain. — London : Hamilton, June 1982. — [288]p
ISBN 0-241-10755-5 : £12.50 : CIP entry B82-09977

941.085'8 — Great Britain *— For children*
Penny, Malcolm. Great Britain / Malcolm Penny. — London : Macdonald Educational, 1981. — 46p : ill(some col.),col.maps ; 29cm. — (Looking at lands)
Includes index
ISBN 0-356-07101-4 : £3.50 B82-02898

941.085'8 — Great Britain *— For schools*
Thompson, Kenneth, *1920-*. About Great Britain / by Kenneth Thompson. — London : Cassell, 1982. — 64p : ill(some col.),maps(some col.),ports(some col.) ; 28cm. — (Skills in research)
Maps on inside cover. — Bibliography: p62. — Includes index
ISBN 0-304-30646-0 (pbk) : Unpriced : CIP rev. B81-34141

941.085'8 — Great Britain. Social change *— Proposals*
Saunders, James H.. Laying the foundations for change / James H. Saunders. — Hythe (21 Fisher Close, Hythe, Kent, CT21 6AB) : New Creation Enterprises, [1982]. — 16p ; 21cm. — (The Orpington initiative ; pamphlet no.9)
£1.00 (pbk) B82-30662

941.085'8 — Great Britain. Social conditions
Dahrendorf, Ralf. On Britain / Ralf Dahrendorf. — London : University of Chicago Press, 1982. — 200p ; 21cm
ISBN 0-226-13410-5 (pbk) : Unpriced B82-40082

Dahrendorf, Ralf. On Britain / Ralf Dahrendorf. — London : B.B.C., 1982. — 200p ; 22cm
ISBN 0-563-20037-5 (cased) : £6.95
ISBN 0-563-20072-3 (pbk) : Unpriced B82-40081

Sampson, Anthony. The changing anatomy of Great Britain. — London : Hodder and Stoughton, Sept.1982. — [576]p
ISBN 0-340-20964-x : £8.95 : CIP entry B82-18743

Saunders, James H.. New perspectives on pressing problems / James H. Saunders. — Hythe (21 Fisher Close, Hythe, Kent CT21 6AB) : New Creation Enterprises, [1982?]. — 17p ; 17cm. — (The Orpington initiative ; pamphlet no.8)
£1.00 (pbk) B82-35606

941.085'8 — Great Britain. Social conditions *— For schools*
Sanday, A. P.. Understanding industrial society. — London : Hodder and Stoughton
[Pupil's book]. — Jan.1983. — [176]p
ISBN 0-340-28735-7 (pbk) : £4.95 : CIP entry B82-33745

Sanday, A. P.. Understanding industrial society. — London : Hodder and Stoughton
Teacher's guide. — 3rd ed. — Jan.1983. — [160]p
Previous ed.: 1979
ISBN 0-340-28736-5 (pbk) : £6.95 : CIP entry B82-33746

941.085'8 — Great Britain. Society *— For school leavers*
Jamieson, Wilson. The individual in society / Wilson Jamieson. — Glasgow : Blackie, 1981. — 23p : ill ; 22cm. — (Insight)
Cover title. — Bibliography on inside cover
ISBN 0-216-90794-2 (pbk) : Unpriced B82-05679

941.085'8 — Great Britain. Society *— Liberal Party viewpoints*
Saunders, James H.. Towards a substantial society / James H. Saunders. — Hythe (21 Fisher Close, Hythe, Kent, CT21 6AB) : New Creation Enterprises, [1982]. — 13p ; 21cm. — (The Orpington initiative ; pamphlet no.6)
£1.00 (pbk) B82-30660

Saunders, James H.. Translating radicalism into realistic policies / James H. Saunders. — Hythe (21 Fisher Close, Hythe, Kent, CT21 6AB) : New Creation Enterprises, [1982]. — 17p ; 21cm. — (The Orpington initiative ; pamphlet no.7)
£1.00 (pbk) B82-30661

941.085'8 — Great Britain. Society. Role of television drama in English *— Conference proceedings*
Television Play and Contemporary Society *(Conference : 1980 : Goldsmith's College)*. Report of the seminar The Television Play and Contemporary Society / [held in The George Wood Theatre, Drama Department, University of London Goldsmith's College on 20th November 1980] ; [report by Janet Morgan]. — [London] ([New Cross, SE14 6NW]) : [University of London Goldsmith's College], [1981?]. — 40p ; 21cm
Cover title
£1.00 (pbk) B82-18387

941.085'8'0222 — Great Britain *— Aerial photographs*
Stonehouse, Bernard. The Aerofilms book of Britain from the air / Bernard Stonehouse ; foreword by Sir Huw Wheldon. — London : Weidenfeld and Nicolson, c1982. — 160p : chiefly ill(some col.),1col.map ; 27x37cm
Includes index
ISBN 0-297-78121-9 : £14.95 B82-39693

941.085'8'0222 — Great Britain *— Illustrations — For children*
Anno, Mitsumasa. [Anno's journey III]. Anno's Britain / Mitsumasa Anno. — London : Bodley Head, 1982, c1981. — [48]p : chiefly col.ill ; 26cm
Originally published: Tokyo : Fukuinkan Shoten, 1981
ISBN 0-370-30916-2 : Unpriced : CIP rev. B82-00907

941.085'8'024055 — Great Britain. Social conditions *— For adolescents*
May, John, *1931-*. Living in Britain / John May. — Birmingham : Clearway, c1979. — 128p : ill,2maps ; 21cm. — (Britain today series)
ISBN 0-902336-64-9 (pbk) : Unpriced B82-11640

941.085'8'076 — Great Britain. Society *— Questions & answers*
Fitzgerald, Mike. Know your own society / Mike Fitzgerald, Karen Margolis, Jock Young. — London : Pan, 1981. — 95p : ill ; 18cm. — (Pan information) (A Pan original)
Bibliography: p95
ISBN 0-330-26448-6 (pbk) : £1.25 B82-01593

941.085'8'0924 — Great Britain. Countryside *— Personal observations*
Page, Robin. Journeys into Britain / Robin Page ; illustrations : Fiona Silver. — London : Hodder and Stoughton, 1982. — 272p : ill,1map ; 23cm
Includes index
ISBN 0-340-26327-x : £8.50 : CIP rev. B82-12253

941.085'8'0924 — Great Britain. McLeod, Enid *— Biographies*
McLeod, Enid. Living twice. — London : Hutchinson, June 1982. — [244]p
ISBN 0-09-149600-4 : £8.50 : CIP entry B82-18457

941.1 — HISTORY. SCOTLAND

941.1 — Scotland. Castles
Ainslie, Alan D.. Historic Castles of Scotland / by Alan D. Ainslie. — Friockheim ([The Manse, Friockheim, Arbroath]) : A.D. Ainslie, c1982. — 30p ; 22cm
£1.00 (pbk) B82-24438

Ward, Desmond. Castles / Desmond Ward ; drawings by John Marshall. — Edinburgh : Spurbooks, c1982. — 64p : ill ; 19cm. — (Introducing Scotland)
Bibliography: p63. — Includes index
ISBN 0-7157-2081-3 (pbk) : £1.25 B82-20590

941.1 — Scotland. Coal mining communities. Working life, *ca 1830 — For schools*
Scottish Central Committee on Social Subjects. *History Working Party S1 and S2*. Life and work in a mining community about 150 years ago / Scottish Central Committee on Social Subjects, History Working Party SI and SII. — [Glasgow] : [The Party]
Set C. — [1980?]. — 37p : ill ; 30cm
Cover title. — Bibliography: p5
Unpriced (spiral) B82-22853

941.1 — Scotland. Coal mining communities. Working life, *ca 1830* **—** *For schools*

continuation

Scottish Central Committee on Social Subjects. *History Working Party S1 and S2.* Life and work in a mining community about 150 years ago / Scottish Central Committee on Social Subjects, History Working Party SI and SII. — [Glasgow] : [The Party]
Set D. — [1980?]. — 51p : ill,2maps ; 30cm
Cover title. — Bibliography: p9
Unpriced (pbk) B82-22852

941.1 — Scotland, *to 1979*

Mitchison, Rosalind. A history of Scotland / Rosalind Mitchison ; illustrated by George Mackie. — 2nd ed. — London : Methuen, 1982. — x,472p : ill,2geneal.tables,3maps ; 22cm
Previous ed.: 1970. — Bibliography: p431-445. — Includes index
ISBN 0-416-33220-x (cased) : Unpriced : CIP rev.
ISBN 0-416-33080-0 (pbk) : Unpriced B82-04050

941.1 — Scottish culture, *to 1979*

The **Scottish** world : history and culture of Scotland / edited by Harold Orel, Henry L. Snyder, Marilyn Stokstad ; texts by the editors ... [et al.]. — London : Thames and Hudson, 1981. — 328p : ill(some col.),maps,facsims,ports(some col.) ; 31cm
Ill on lining papers. — Bibliography: p321-324. — Includes index
ISBN 0-500-25079-0 : £16.00 B82-04662

941.1 — Scottish culture, *to 1980*

A **Companion** to Scottish culture / edited by David Daiches. — London : Edward Arnold, 1981. — 441p : ill,maps ; 26cm
Bibliography: p408-418. — Includes index
ISBN 0-7131-6344-5 : £14.95 : CIP rev. B81-22520

941.1'009'734 — Scotland. Rural regions. Social conditions, *1458-1603*

Sanderson, Margaret H. B.. Scottish rural society in the sixteenth century / Margaret H.B. Sanderson. — Edinburgh : Donald, c1982. — ix,286p : ill,maps ; 24cm
Bibliography: p257-260. — Includes index
ISBN 0-85976-027-8 : £15.00 B82-14578

941.1'009'734 — Scotland. Rural regions. Social conditions, *to 1780*

Dodgshon, Robert A.. Land and society in early Scotland / by Robert A. Dodgshon. — Oxford : Clarendon Press, 1981. — xii,345p,6p of plates : ill,maps,plans ; 23cm
Bibliography: p321-330. — Includes index
ISBN 0-19-822660-8 : £22.50 : CIP rev. B81-35761

941.102'092'4 — Scotland. Robert I, *King of Scots — Biographies*

Scott, Ronald McNair. Robert the Bruce : King of Scots / Ronald McNair Scott. — London : Hutchinson, 1982. — xviii,253p : geneal.tables,maps ; 24cm
Includes index
ISBN 0-09-149630-6 : £9.95 : CIP rev. B82-17192

941.102'092'4 — Scotland. Wallace, *Sir* **William,** *1272?-1305 — Biographies*

Scott, Tom, *1918-*. Tales of Sir William Wallace : guardian of Scotland / freely adapted from The Wallas of Blin Hary by Tom Scott. — Edinburgh : Gordon Wright, c1981. — 118p : ill ; 23cm
ISBN 0-903065-32-0 : £4.95 B82-03778

941.104'092'4 — Scotland. James III, *King of Scotland — Biographies*

Macdougall, Norman. James III : a political study / Norman Macdougall. — Edinburgh : Donald, c1982. — 338p ; 24cm
Bibliography: p316-323. — Includes index
ISBN 0-85976-078-2 : £18.00 B82-35822

941.105 — Scotland, *1572-1580*

Hewitt, George R.. Scotland under Morton 1572-80 / George R. Hewitt. — Edinburgh : Donald, c1982. — vii,232p : 2maps ; 24cm
Bibliography: p212-219. — Includes index
ISBN 0-85976-077-4 : £14.00 B82-27705

941.105'092'4 — Scotland. James I, *King of England, to 1603 — Biographies*

Bingham, Caroline. Relations between Mary Queen of Scots and her son King James VI of Scotland / by Caroline Bingham. — London (10, Uphill Grove, London NW7 4NJ) : Royal Stuart Society, 1982. — 14p ; 21cm. — (Royal Stuart papers, ISSN 0307-997x ; 19)
Text on inside cover
Unpriced (pbk) B82-27231

941.105'092'4 — Scotland. Mary, *Queen of Scots — Biographies*

Cheetham, J. Keith. Mary Queen of Scots "the captive years" : the story of Mary Queen of Scots with particular reference to the buildings and monuments connected with her captivity in England / J. Keith Cheetham. — Sheffield : J.W. Northend Ltd., 1982. — ix,66p : ill,1geneal.table,1map,ports ; 21cm
Bibliography: p62. — Includes index
£2.75 (pbk) B82-28242

Lamont-Brown, Raymond. Mary Queen of Scots / Raymond Lamont-Brown ; drawings by Richard Hook. — Edinburgh : Spurbooks, c1982. — 64p : ill,ports ; 19cm. — (Introducing Scotland)
Bibliography: p63. — Includes index
ISBN 0-7157-2084-8 (pbk) : £1.25 B82-20585

941.106'8 — Glencoe Massacre

Linklater, Magnus. Massacre : the story of Glencoe / Magnus Linklater ; photographs by Anthony Gascoigne. — London : Collins, 1982. — 159p : ill(some col.),maps(some col.),facsim,col.ports,geneal.tables(some col.) ; 26cm
Bibliography: p152-153. — Includes index
ISBN 0-00-435669-1 : £7.95 B82-14690

941.107 — Scotland, *1746-1832*

Lenman, Bruce. Integration, enlightenment and industrialization : Scotland 1746-1832 / Bruce Lenman. — London : Edward Arnold, 1981. — vi,182p ; 21cm. — (The New history of Scotland ; 6)
Bibliography: p168-179. — Includes index
ISBN 0-7131-6314-3 (cased) : Unpriced : CIP rev.
ISBN 0-7131-6315-1 (pbk) : £4.95 B81-30596

941.107 — Scottish civilization, *1680-1800*

The **Origins** and nature of the Scottish Enlightenment / essays edited by R.H. Campbell and Andrew S. Skinner. — Edinburgh : Donald, c1982. — vii,231p ; 25cm
Includes index
ISBN 0-85976-076-6 : £15.00 B82-31551

941.107'2'0924 — Scotland. Charles Edward Stuart, *Prince — Biographies*

Bailey, Kenneth. Bonnie Prince Charlie / Kenneth Bailey ; drawings by Richard Hook. — Edinburgh : Spurbooks, c1982. — 64p : ill,ports ; 19cm. — (Introducing Scotland)
Bibliography: p63. — Includes index
ISBN 0-7157-2079-1 (pbk) : £1.25 B82-20587

941.107'2'0924 — Scotland. MacEachen, Neil — *Biographies*

Maclean, Alasdair, *1918-*. A Macdonald for the prince : the story of Neil MacEachen / Alasdair Maclean. — Stornoway : Acair, 1982. — 104p : ill,1map,facsims,1port,1geneal.table ; 22cm
Bibliography: p97-99. — Includes index
ISBN 0-86152-002-5 (pbk) : Unpriced B82-27775

941.107'3 — Scotland. Rural regions. Working life, *ca 1780 — For schools*

Scottish Central Committee on Social Subjects. *History Working Party S1 and S2.* Life in the countryside in Scotland about 200 years ago / Scottish Central Committee on Social Subjects, History Working Party SI and SII. — [Glasgow] : [The Party]
Set A. — [1980?]. — 43p : ill ; 30cm
Cover title. — Bibliography: p10
Unpriced (spiral) B82-22848

941.1082 — Scotland, *1914-1980*

Harvie, Christopher. No gods and precious few heroes : Scotland 1914-1980 / Christopher Harvie. — London : Edward Arnold, 1981. — ix,182p ; 21cm. — (The New history of Scotland ; 8)
Bibliography: p166-170. — Includes index
ISBN 0-7131-6318-6 (cased) : Unpriced : CIP rev.
ISBN 0-7131-6319-4 (pbk) : £4.95 B81-23834

941.1082'092'4 — Scotland. Fforde, *Lady* **Jean —** *Biographies*

Fforde, *Lady* **Jean.** Castles in the air : the memories of a childhood in two castles / by the Lady Jean Fforde. — Brodick : Kilbrannan, 1982. — 202p : ill,1geneal.table,ports ; 22cm
ISBN 0-907939-01-5 : £8.50 B82-32975

941.1082'092'4 — Scotland. MacVicar, Angus — *Biographies*

MacVicar, Angus. Bees in my bonnet / Angus MacVicar. — London : Hutchinson, 1982. — 182p,[8]p of plates : ill,ports ; 23cm
Includes index
ISBN 0-09-147070-6 : £6.95 : CIP rev. B82-00273

MacVicar, Angus. Bees in my bonnet. — Large print ed. — Bath : Chivers, Feb.1983. — [272] p. — (A Lythway book)
Originally published: London : Hutchinson, 1982
ISBN 0-85119-898-8 : £7.20 : CIP entry B82-39586

MacVicar, Angus. Rocks in my scotch / Angus MacVicar. — London : Arrow, 1982, c1977. — 182p ; 18cm
Originally published: London : Hutchinson, 1977. — Includes index
ISBN 0-09-928010-8 (corrected : pbk) : £1.25 B82-24898

941.1082'092'4 — Scotland. Sutherland, Millicent Fanny Sutherland-Leveson-Gower, *Duchess of — Biographies*

Stuart, Denis. Dear Duchess : Millicent Duchess of Sutherland 1867-1955 / Denis Stuart. — London : Gollancz, 1982. — 215p,[15]p of plates : ill,ports,2geneal.tables ; 23cm
Bibliography: p197-203. — Includes index
ISBN 0-575-03020-8 : £10.95 : CIP rev. B81-35883

941.1085'8 — Scotland. Local communities. Social conditions. Influence of dominant ideologies — *Conference proceedings*

Way of life : dominant ideologies and local communities / edited by Anthony Jackson. — London : Social Science Research Council, [1982?]. — 77p ; 21cm. — (North Sea Oil Panel occasional paper ; no.11)
Conference papers. — Includes bibliographies
ISBN 0-86226-081-7 (pbk) : £1.80 B82-38928

941.1085'8'05 — Scotland — *Serials*

Radical Scotland : a socialist quarterly. — Issue no.1 (Summer '82)-. — Edinburgh (52 Broughton St., Edinburgh) : Radical Scotland Publications, 1982-. — v. : ill,facsims,maps,ports ; 30cm
Continues: Crann-Tàra (Aberdeen)
ISSN 0262-6993 = Radical Scotland : £0.60 B82-31722

941.1'10858'05 — Scotland. Highlands & Islands — *Serials*

The **Highlands** and Islands today = Leasachadh an diugh. — Issue no.1 (Jan./Feb. 1982)-. — Inverness (Bridge House, Bank St., Inverness IV1 1QR) : Highlands and Islands Development Board, 1982-. — v. : ill(some col.),ports ; 42cm
Six issues yearly. — Text in English and Gaelic. — Continues: North 7. — Description based on: Issue no.2 (Mar./Apr. 1982)
ISSN 0263-5771 = Highlands and Islands today : Unpriced B82-28131

941.1′305′0924 — Scotland. Orkney & Shetland. Orkney, Robert Stewart, *Earl of — Biographies*

Anderson, Peter D.. Robert Stewart : Earl of Orkney, Lord of Shetland 1533-1593 / Peter D. Anderson. — Edinburgh : Donald, c1982. — viii,245p : ill,3geneal.tables,maps,1plan ; 24cm
Bibliography: p218-222. — Includes index
ISBN 0-85976-082-0 : £15.00 B82-37196

941.1′32 — Scotland. Orkney. North Isles. Social conditions — *For environment planning*

North Isles local plan. — Kirkwall (Orkney Islands Council, Council Offices, Kirkwall) : [Dept.] of Physical Planning & Development
Consultative document no.1: Shapinsay. — 1981. — 13leaves : 3ill,2maps ; 30cm
Unpriced (unbound) B82-34124

North Isles local plan. — Kirkwall (Orkney Islands Council, Council Offices, Kirkwall) : [Dept.] of Physical Planning & Development
Consultative document no.2: Rousay, Egilsay and Wyre. — 1981. — 28leaves : ill,2maps ; 30cm
Unpriced (unbound) B82-34125

North Isles local plan. — Kirkwall (Orkney Islands Council, Council Offices, Kirkwall) : [Dept.] of Physical Planning & Development
Consultative document no.4: Westray & Papa Westray. — 1982. — 27p : ill,3maps ; 30cm
Unpriced (unbound) B82-34126

941.1′32′005 — Scotland. Orkney — *History — Serials*

Orkney heritage. — Vol.1 (1981)-. — Kirkwall ([c/o W.P.L. Thomson, Papdale House, Kirkwall, Orkney]) : Orkney Heritage Society, 1981-. — v. : ill,maps,ports ; 22cm
Annual
ISSN 0263-7049 = Orkney heritage : £2.90 B82-31727

941.1′320858 — Scotland. Orkney. Social conditions — *For structure planning*

Orkney Islands Council structure plan monitoring. — Kirkwall (Council Offices, Kirkwall) : Department of Physical Planning and Development, Orkney Islands Council
Study no.1: Industry and employment. — 1981. — 31p : ill,2maps ; 30cm
Unpriced (unbound) B82-40981

941.1′35 — Scotland. Shetland, *1469-1969 — Conference proceedings*

Shetland and the outside world 1469-1969. — Oxford : Oxford University Press, Sept.1982. — [248]p
Conference papers
ISBN 0-19-714107-2 : £15.00 : CIP entry B82-18994

941.1′4 — Scotland. Western Isles. Isle of Harris. Social life, *1914-1925 — Childhood reminiscences*

Macdonald, Finlay J.. Crowdie and cream / Finlay J. Macdonald. — London : Macdonald, 1982. — 176p ; 23cm
ISBN 0-356-08587-2 : £6.95 B82-26723

941.1′4 — Scotland. Western Isles. South Uist, *to 1980 — Gaelic texts*

MacDhòmhnaill, Dòmhnall Iain. Uibhist & Deas : beagan mu eachdraidh is mu bheul-aithris an eilein / Dòmhnall Iain MacDhòmhnaill ; na dealbhan le Anndra MacMhorein. — Steòrnabhagh [Stornoway] : Acair, 1981. — 64p : ill ; 21cm
ISBN 0-86152-021-1 (pbk) : Unpriced B82-17841

941.1′4 — Scotland. Western Isles. St Kilda, *to 1981 — Illustrations*

A **St Kilda** album. — Edinburgh : Blackwood, Oct.1982. — [120]p
ISBN 0-85158-151-x : £6.95 : CIP entry B82-28585

941.1′5081′0924 — Scotland. Highlands. Social life, *1842-1882 — Personal observations*

Victoria, *Queen of Great Britain* **[Leaves from the journal of our life in the Highlands of Scotland. Selections]**. Queen Victoria's Highland journal. — New and rev. ed. — Exeter : Webb & Bower, Feb.1983. — [240]p
Originally published: 1980
ISBN 0-906671-74-4 (pbk) : £4.95 : CIP entry B82-37485

941.1′50857 — Scotland. Highland Region. Social conditions. Effects of large-scale industrial development, *ca 1970-1980*

Scott, Angus. The social impact of large-scale industrial developments / by Angus Scott. — London : Social Science Research Council, [1982?]. — 53p ; 21cm. — (North Sea Oil Panel occasional paper ; no.10)
ISBN 0-86226-071-x (pbk) : £1.80 B82-38929

941.1′50858 — Scotland. Highland Region — *For industrial development*

The **Highland** connection. — Inverness, Highland Regional Council [in association with] Bank of Scotland, [1981?]. — [13]p : col.ill,maps ; 30cm
Unpriced (pbk) B82-07344

941.1′50858 — Scotland. Highland Region — *For petroleum industries*

The **North** Sea connection. — Inverness : Highland Regional Council, [1981?]. — 1folded sheet([6]p) : col.ill,4maps ; 30cm
Unpriced B82-07342

941.1′50858 — Scotland. Highland Region — *For tourist industries*

Development opportunities in tourism, the Highland Region of Scotland. — [Inverness] : [Highland Regional Council], [1981?]. — [92],[18]p : 3maps ; 30cm
Unpriced (spiral) B82-07343

941.1′50858 — Scotland. Highland Region. Social conditions — *For investors*

[Highland connection]. Profile of the Highland Region. — [Edinburgh] : Bank of Scotland ; [Inverness] ([Regional Buildings, Glenurquhart Rd., Inverness IV3 5NX]) : Highland Regional Council, Development Department, [1982]. — [12]p : col.ill,col.maps ; 30cm
Cover title. — Originally published: 1979. — Text, ill on inside covers
Unpriced (pbk) B82-30865

941.1′65 — Scotland. Highland Region. Dornoch, *to 1900*

Dornoch / illustrations by Graeme Nairn. — 2nd ed. — Dornoch (Town Jail, Cathedral Sq., Dornoch, Sutherland) : Dornoch Craft Centre, [1982?]. — [31]p : ill,2maps ; 21cm
£0.35 (pbk) B82-26740

941.1′75 — Scotland. Highland Region. Glen Urquhart. Social life, *to 1961*

Mackell, Alastair. The Glen Urquhart story : a brief survey of the history of Urquhart. — Inverness : Inverness Field Club, 1982. — 58p,[8]p of plates : ill ; 21cm
Written by Alastair Mackell
ISBN 0-9502612-2-x (pbk) : Unpriced B82-24313

941.1′75 — Scotland. Highland Region. Inverness *(District), to ca 1970 — Stories, anecdotes*

MacDonald, Mairi A.. By the banks of the Ness : tales of Inverness and district / Mairi A. MacDonald. — Edinburgh : Paul Harris, 1982. — 159p,[8]p of plates : ill,geneal.tables,maps,ports ; 23cm
ISBN 0-86228-043-5 : £4.95 B82-34364

941.1′75 — Scotland. Highland Region. Loch Ness region. Social life, *to ca 1880*

MacDonald, Alexander, *1860-1928*. Story and song from Loch Ness-side / by Alexander MacDonald ; a reprint with an English translation of the stories and songs and also the tunes of a number of the songs. — [New ed.]. — Inverness (c/o [Inverness County Council, Department of Education, Inverness]) : Gaelic Society of Inverness, 1982. — xi,445p,[3]leaves of plate : ill,ports ; 20cm
English and Gaelic text. — Previous ed.: Inverness : Northern Counties Newspaper and Printing and Publishing, 1914
Unpriced B82-35356

941.1′92 — Scotland. Highland Region. Badenoch. Agricultural industries. Farms. Social life, *1769-1782*

Grant, I. F.. Every-day life on an old Highland farm 1769-1782 / I.F. Grant. — London : Shepheard-Walwyn, c1981. — ix,292p,[16]p of plates : ill,facsims,plans,ports ; 25cm
Originally published: London : Longmans & Co., 1924. — Includes index
ISBN 0-85683-058-5 : £8.95 B82-12882

941.2′23 — Scotland. Grampian Region. Dyke. Parish churches: Dyke Parish Church, *to 1981*

Dyke Parish Church. Dyke Parish Church : bicentenary book : 1781-1981 / editor, T. Williamson ; contributors, Margaret McKay ... [et al.] ; cover & illustrations Flora MacLeod. — [Dyke] ([Dyke Parish Church, Dyke, Scotland]) : [T. Williamson], [1981]. — 28p : ill ; 26cm
Text on inside cover
Unpriced (pbk) B82-28839

941.2′23 — Scotland. Grampian Region. Moray *(District)*. **Churches,** *to 1980*

Howat, Angus J.. Churches of Moray / Angus J. Howat, Mike Seton. — [Elgin] ([c/o Department of Libraries, 21 Tyock, Elgin, IV30 1XY]) : Moray District Publications, 1981. — 50[i.e.107]p : ill ; 20x22cm
Bibliography: p106-107
Unpriced (pbk) B82-10201

941.2′23 — Scotland. Grampian Region. Moray *(District)*. **Religious buildings,** *to 1980*

Keillar, Ian. Cathedrals, abbeys and priories in Moray / text Ian Keillar ; illustrations Crispin Worthington. — [Elgin] ([c/o Moravian Press Ltd, 31 South St, Elgin]) : Moray Field Club, [1982?]. — [24]p : ill ; 15x21cm
Bibliography: p[24]
£0.70 (pbk) B82-31895

941.2′25 — Scotland. Grampian Region. Peterhead. Social conditions. Effects of exploitation of North Sea natural gas deposits & petroleum deposits

Moore, Robert, *1936-*. The social impact of oil : the case of Peterhead / Robert Moore. — London : Routledge & Kegan Paul, 1982. — 189p : ill ; 23cm
Includes index
ISBN 0-7100-0903-8 : £12.50 B82-27047

941.2′35 — Scotland. Grampian Region. Aberdeen. Antiquities, *ca 1100-1400*. **Archaeological investigations,** *1973-1982*

Excavations in the medieval Burgh of Aberdeen 1973-82. — Edinburgh : Society of Antiquaries of Scotland, Nov.1982. — 1v.. — (Society of Antiquaries of Scotland monograph series, ISSN 0263-3191 ; 2)
ISBN 0-903903-02-4 (pbk) : CIP entry B82-32318

941.2′350858′05 — Scotland. Grampian Region. Aberdeen — *Serials*

[Scene *(Aberdeen)***]**. Scene. — Issue no.1-. — Aberdeen ([P.O. Box 43] Lang Stracht, Mastrict, Aberdeen AB9 8AF) : Aberdeen Journals, [1981]-. — v. : ill,ports ; 42cm
Description based on: Issue no.4
Unpriced B82-36727

941.2′4 — Scotland. Grampian Region. Birse. Social conditions, *1500-1981*

Callander, Robin. History in Birse / compiled and published by Robin Callander. — Finzean (Haughend, Finzean, Aberdeenshire) : R. Callander, [1981]. — 49p : ill,1map,ports ; 25cm
Text on inside cover. — Bibliography: p48-49
£1.00 (pbk) B82-08600

941.2′6 — Scotland. Tayside Region. Arbroath. Social conditions — *For environment planning*

Arbroath local plan : report of survey and issues / Angus District Planning Department. — [Forfar] ([County Buildings, Market St., Forfar DD8 3LG]) : [The Department], 1979. — 63p : 1map ; 30cm
Map (1 folded sheet) as insert
Unpriced (spiral) B82-12641

941.2′6 — Scotland. Tayside Region. Brechin. Social conditions — *For environment planning*

Brechin local plan : summary of survey findings and issues / Angus District Council. — [Forfar] ([County Buildings, Market St., Forfar DD8 3LG]) : [The Council], 1981. — 25p : 2maps ; 30cm
Unpriced (spiral) B82-12646

941.2′6 — Scotland. Tayside Region. Forfar. Social conditions — *For environment planning*

Forfar local plan : summary of survey findings and potential issues / Angus District Council. — [Forfar] ([County Buildings, Market St., Forfar DD8 3LG]) : [The Council], 1980. — 27p,[1]folded leaf of plates : 1map ; 30cm
Unpriced (sprial) B82-12648

941.2′6 — Scotland. Tayside Region. Kirriemuir. Social conditions — *For environment planning*

Kirriemuir local plan : summary of survey findings and issues / Angus District Council. — [Forfar] ([County Buildings, Market St., Forfar DD8 3LG]) : [The Council], 1981. — 22p : 1map ; 30cm
Unpriced (spiral) B82-12647

941.2′6 — Scotland. Tayside Region. Monikie. Social life, *to 1981*

Chisholm, W. Douglas. The Monikie story / W. Douglas Chisholm. — [Monikie] : W.D. Chisholm, c1982. — 153p : ill,maps,1plan ; 21cm
Bibliograph: p151-153
ISBN 0-9508163-0-2 (pbk) : Unpriced
B82-38960

941.2′7 — Scotland. Tayside Region. Broughty Ferry. Castles: Broughty Castle, *to 1981*

Broughty Castle and its history. — [Dundee] : Dundee Museums and Art Galleries, c1981. — [4]p : ill ; 30cm
Bibliography: p[4]
Unpriced (unbound) B82-34498

941.2′7 — Scotland. Tayside Region. Dundee. Broughty Ferry & Monifieth, *1900-1940 — Illustrations*

Old Broughty Ferry and Monifieth / [compiled by] A.W. Brotchie and J.J. Herd. — Dundee : N.B. Traction Group, 1980. — 48p : chiefly ill,3ports ; 22cm
ISBN 0-905069-15-3 (pbk) : £0.95 B82-35558

941.2′7 — Scotland. Tayside Region. Lochee, *1900-1940 — Illustrations*

Old Lochee and round about / [compiled by] A.W. Brotchie and J.J. Herd. — Dundee : N.B. Traction Group, 1981. — 48p : chiefly ill,2ports ; 22cm
ISBN 0-905069-17-x (pbk) : £0.95 B82-35557

941.2′7081′0222 — Scotland. Tayside Region. Dundee. Social life, *1837-1910 — Illustrations*

Victorian and Edwardian Dundee and Broughty Ferry from rare photographs / [compiled by] Raymond Lamont-Brown and Peter Adamson ; foreword by Ron Thompson. — St. Andrews : Published on behalf of the Dundee Museums and Art Galleries by Alvie, 1981. — 106,[14]p : chiefly ill,ports ; 26cm
ISBN 0-9506200-2-5 : £6.90 B82-20820

941.2′8 — Scotland. Tayside Region. Atholl region & Breadalbane region — *Serials*

Atholl & Breadalbane community comment. — Vol.1, no.1-. — [Aberfeldy] ([Dunkeld St., Aberfeldy, Tayside]) : [s.n.], [1981]-. — v. : ill ; 30cm
Six issues yearly
ISSN 0262-5113 = Atholl & Breadalbane community comment : £0.15 per issue
B82-04897

941.2′8 — Scotland. Tayside Region. Comrie. Parish churches: Comrie Church, *1881-1981*

One hundred years : in the life of our church building : 1881-1981. — [Comrie] ([The Church, Burrell Street, Comrie, Perthshire]) : [Comrie Church Centenary Committee], [1982]. — 20p : ill ; 20cm
Cover title
Unpriced (pbk) B82-29700

941.2′8 — Scotland. Tayside Region. Perth, *ca 1850-1925 — Illustrations*

Reflections of old Perth. — [Perth] : Perth Museum & Art Gallery, 1979. — 43p : chiefly ill,1facsim,1map ; 21cm
ISBN 0-9505884-4-x (pbk) : £0.95 B82-31667

941.2′9′00946 — Scotland. Fife Region. Coastal regions. Buildings of historical importance — *For teaching*

Ravenscraig Castle trail. — [West Wemyss] : West Wemyss Environmental Education Centre, [1982]. — 49p,[2]leaves of plates : ill,1map,2coats of arms ; 21cm. — (Castles & heritage trail of Fife)
Cover title. — Text on inside covers
Unpriced (pbk) B82-19637

941.2′92 — Scotland. Fife Region. Isle of May

The **Isle** of May. — [West Wemyss] : West Wemyss Environmental Education Centre, [1982]. — 32p,[2]leaves of plates : ill,2maps ; 21cm
Text and map on inside cover
Unpriced (pbk) B82-19633

941.2′92 — Scotland. Fife Region. Lower Largo. Social life, *1850-1980 — Illustrations*

Jardine, Ivy. Seatoun of Largo : (a collection of Victorian photographs and Largo today) / Ivy Jardine. — St. Andrews : W.C. Henderson, [1982?]. — 135p : chiefly ill,1map,facsims,ports,1geneal.table ; 25cm
Limited ed. of 1000 copies. — Bibliography: p134
ISBN 0-9507803-0-8 : £6.95 B82-21896

941.2′92 — Scotland. Fife Region. Newport-on-Tay. Social life, *1900-1966 — Personal observations*

Scrymgeour, James T.. Tales of Newport / told by James T. Scrymgeour. — East Newport-on-Tay (Rosedene [11A Kilnburn] East Newport-on-Tay) : J.T. Scrymgeour, 1981. — 55p : ill ; 19cm
Unpriced (pbk) B82-11006

941.2′92 — Scotland. Fife Region. North East Fife *(District).* **Buildings of historical importance** — *For teaching*

St. Andrews Castle trail. — [West Wemyss] : West Wemyss Environmental Education Centre, [1982]. — 56p : ill,1map,1coat of arms ; 21cm. — (Castles & heritage trail of Fife)
Cover title
Unpriced (pbk) B82-19635

941.2′95 — Scotland. Fife Region. Kirkcaldy. Social conditions — *For environment planning*

Kirkcaldy local plan : report of survey / [Kirkcaldy District Council]. — Kirkcaldy (Town House, Kirkcaldy) : [The Council], 1980. — 175p,31folded leaves of plates : ill,maps ; 30cm
Unpriced (spiral) B82-21647

Kirkcaldy local plan : planning issues / [Kirkcaldy District Council]. — Kirkcaldy (Town House, Kirkcaldy) : [The Council], 1980. — 36p,5folded leaves of plates : ill,maps ; 30cm
Unpriced (spiral) B82-21648

941.2′95 — Scotland. Fife Region. Levenmouth. Social conditions — *For environment planning*

Levenmouth local plan : report of survey / Kirkcaldy District Council. — Kirkcaldy (Town House, Kirkcaldy) : [The Council], 1980. — iv,124p,27leaves of plates(some col.) : maps ; 30cm
Unpriced (spiral) B82-21649

Levenmouth local plan : planning issues / Kirkcaldy District Council. — Kirkcaldy (Town House, Kirkcaldy) : [The Council], 1980. — 41p,1leaf of plates : 1ill,1map ; 30cm
Unpriced (spiral) B82-21650

941.2′95 — Scotland. Fife Region. Markinch region. Buildings of historical importance — *For teaching*

Dunn, Garry. Wemyss to Markinch Walk. — [West Wemyss] : West Wemyss Environmental Education Centre, [1982]. — 28p : ill,maps ; 22cm
Cover title. — Author: Garry Dunn. — Ill and text on inside cover
Unpriced (pbk) B82-19636

941.2′95 — Scotland. Fife Region. Methil. Social life, *1981 — Personal observations — Collections*

1981 on reflection / [edited by Henry G. McGuire and Alastair H. Gray]. — [Methil] ([The Manse, 14 Methilbrae, Methil, Fife]) : [A.H. Gray], [1982?]. — 44p ; 20cm
Unpriced (unbound) B82-29207

941.2′98 — Scotland. Fife Region. Dalgety, *to 1979*

Simpson, Eric. Dalgety : the story of a parish / by Eric Simpson. — Dalgety Bay : Dalgety Bay Community Council, c1980. — 66p,[12] folded leaf of plates : ill,maps,1facsim ; 24cm
Maps on inside covers
Unpriced (pbk) B82-08530

941.2′98 — Scotland. Fife Region. Dunfermline. Social conditions, *1750-1800*

Everyday life in Dunfermline in the late 18th century. — [Dunfermline] ([Central Library, Abbot St., Dunfermline]) : Dunfermline District Libraries, 1978. — 11p ; 30cm
Cover title. — Bibliography: p11
Unpriced (pbk) B82-08886

941.2′98 — Scotland. Fife Region. North Queensferry, *to 1980*

Dean, Peter, *1939-*. Passage of time / text Peter Dean ; design and illustration Carol Dean. — North Queensferry : P. & C. Dean, c1981. — 79p : ill,maps ; 30cm
Bibliography: p78-79
ISBN 0-9507858-0-6 (pbk) : Unpriced
B82-28807

941.2′98 — Scotland. Fife Region. Rosyth, *to 1981*

The **Story** of Rosyth / Inverkeithing High School. — [Rev. ed.]. — [Inverkeithing] ([Hillend Rd, Inverkeithing, Fife]) : [Inverkeithing High School], [1982]. — 240p : ill,facsims,maps ; 31cm
Previous ed.: 1979
£2.50 (pbk) B82-40636

941.2′98081′0222 — Scotland. Fife Region. Dunfermline *(District), ca 1870-1940 — Illustrations*

Dunfermline Central Library. *Local History Department*. Old Dunfermline : photographs of Dunfermline and West Fife from the Local History Department of the Central Library. — Dunfermline : Dunfermline District Library and Museum, 1982. — 48p : col.ill,ports ; 25cm
ISBN 0-946082-00-6 (pbk) : £2.25 B82-31151

941.3′10857 — Scotland. Central Region. Households. Social conditions, *1976 — Statistics*

Central Region. *Department of Planning*. Household survey 1976, summary report / Central Regional Council, Department of Planning. — [Stirling] ([Viewforth, Stirling FK8 2ET]) : [Central Regional Council], 1978. — 39leaves : ill,maps ; 30cm
Unpriced (unbound) B82-15456

941.3′15 — Scotland. Central Region. Clackmannan *(District).* **Buildings of historical importance**

Stewart, Alan George. Buildings of architectural and historic interest in Clackmannan District : a selection of listed buildings in the District / [text and photographs by Alan George Stewart]. — Alloa (The Whins, Alloa) : Planning Department, Clackmannan District Council, 1981. — 48p : ill ; 21cm
£1.00 (pbk) B82-10323

941.3′18 — Scotland. Central Region. Vale of Bonny, *to 1980*

Waugh, James. The Vale of Bonny in history and legend / by J. Waugh. — Falkirk : Falkirk District Council Department of Libraries and Museums, 1981. — 211p,xip of plates : ill ; 30cm
Bibliography: p208-209. — Includes index
ISBN 0-906586-18-6 (pbk) : £1.75 B82-39052

941.3′3 — Scotland. Lothian Region. Linlithgow, *to 1878 — Early works*

Waldie, George. A history of the town and palace of Linlithgow : with notices, historical and antiquarian of places of interest in the neighbourhood / by George Waldie. — Bathgate : West Lothian District Council, Department of Libraries, 1982. — 116p : ill,1map,music,2plans ; 18cm
Facsim of: 3rd ed. Linlithgow : G. Waldie, 1879. — Includes index
ISBN 0-907952-00-3 (pbk) : Unpriced B82-33174

941.3′4 — Edinburgh. Buildings of historical importance *— Illustrations*

Kersting, Anthony F.. The buildings of Edinburgh / Anthony F. Kersting and Maurice Lindsay. — London : Batsford, 1981. — 184p : chiefly ill,2plans ; 26cm
Ill. on lining papers
ISBN 0-7134-0874-x : £12.50 B82-06211

941.3′4 — Edinburgh. Coltbridge, Murrayfield & Roseburn, *to 1982*

Picturesque notes of an Edinburgh suburb : Coltbridge, Murrayfield, Roseburn. — [Edinburgh] ([c/o N. Macleod Nicol, 'Muiravonside', 25 Coltbridge Ave., Edinburgh EH12 6AF]) : [Murrayfield Residents' Association], [1982?]. — 20p : ill,maps ; 21cm
Unpriced (pbk) B82-40641

941.3′4 — Edinburgh. Duddingston, *to 1981*

Cruickshank, W. G.. Duddingston Kirk and village : a short history of the parish / W.G. Cruickshank. — [Edinburgh] ([37, The Causeway, Duddingston Village, Edinburgh EH15 3QA]) : [W.G. Cruickshank], [1980?]. — 32p,[4]p of plates : ill,ports ; 22cm
Unpriced (pbk) B82-26585

941.3′4 — Edinburgh. Houses: Kirkbrae House, *to 1982*

Skinner, Basil C.. The house on the bridge / Basil Skinner. — [Great Britain] : Pavilion Press, 1982. — 12p : ill,1map ; 22cm
Unpriced (pbk) B82-37402

941.3′4 — South Edinburgh, *to 1980*

Smith, Charles J.. Historic south Edinburgh / by Charles J. Smith. — Edinburgh : Charles Skilton
Vol.2. — 1979. — x,548p : ill,maps,facsims,ports ; 22cm
Maps on lining papers. — Bibliography: p515-523. — Includes index
£7.50 B82-01880

941.3′4073 — Edinburgh. Social life, *1763-1793 — Early works*

Creech, William. [Letters addressed to Sir John Sinclair, Bart, respecting the mode of living, arts, commerce, literature, manners &c. of Edinburgh in 1763]. Letters respecting the trade, manners, &c. of Edinburgh / [William Creech]. — Edinburgh : Harris, 1982. — 52p ; 23cm
Facsim of ed. published: Edinburgh : [s.n.], 1793
ISBN 0-86228-002-8 : £12.50 B82-39928

941.3′40858′0222 — Edinburgh *— Illustrations*

Bell, Frank, *1939-*. Edinburgh : sketches to colour & mount, hints on techniques, notes on the city / by Frank Bell. — [Edinburgh] ([41 Willowbrae Avenue, Edinburgh EH8 7HF]) : [F. Bell], [1982]. — [14]p : ill,maps ; 21x30cm
Maps on inside covers
£1.20 (pbk) B82-40497

941.3′5 — Scotland. Lothian Region. Midlothian *(District).* **Lasswade,** *1650-1750*

Houston, Rab. Records of a Scottish village, Lasswade 1650-1750. — Cambridge : Chadwyck-Healey, Nov.1982. — [30]p
ISBN 0-85964-118-x : CIP entry B82-31313

941.3′6 — Scotland. Lothian Region. Haddington. Abbeys: Nunraw Abbey, *to 1981*

Nunraw, past and present. — [Haddington] ([Haddington, East Lothian]) : [Nunraw Abbey], [1982]. — [8]p : ill ; 18cm
Unpriced (unbound) B82-26636

941.3′60858 — Scotland. Lothian Region. East Lothian *(District).* **Social conditions** *— For environment planning*

West Sector local plan : survey & possible policies consultations report. — [Haddington] : East Lothian District Council, Department of Physical Planning, 1979. — 36p : 1map ; 30cm
Cover title
£1.00 (pbk) B82-27266

941.3′85 — Scotland. Borders Region. St. Mary's Loch region. Social conditions *— For environment planning*

Borders Region. *Department of Physical Planning and Development.* St. Mary's Loch-Tweedsmuir Hills management plan / Borders Regional Council, Department of Physical Planning and Development. — [St. Boswells] ([Regional Hq., Newtown, St. Boswells TD6 0SA]) : [The Department], 1980. — 18p : ill,maps(some col.) ; 30cm
Unpriced (pbk) B82-23440

941.3′92 — Scotland. Cheviot Hills. Social life, *ca 1915-1930 — Childhood reminiscences*

Derwent, Lavinia. God bless the borders! / Lavinia Derwent ; illustrated by Elizabeth Haines. — London : Arrow, 1982, c1981. — 143p : ill ; 18cm
Originally published: London : Hutchinson, 1981
ISBN 0-09-928030-2 (pbk) : £1.25 B82-21351

941.3′95 — Scotland. Borders Region. Cockburnspath. Social conditions, *1600-1800*

Rankin, Eric. Cockburnspath : a documentary social history of a Border parish / by Eric Rankin ; edited by James Bulloch. — Edinburgh : T. & T. Clark, 1981. — xv,149p,[12]p of plates : ill,maps ; 23cm
Includes index
ISBN 0-567-09316-6 : £6.95 B82-00425

941.4′10858 — Scotland. Strathclyde Region *— For industrial development*

Strathclyde industrial guide. — 2nd ed. — London : Burrow, [1981]. — 184p : ill ; 25cm
Unpriced (pbk) B82-14593

941.4′23 — Scotland. Strathclyde Region. Islay, *to 1980*

Storrie, Margaret C.. Islay : biography of an island / Margaret C. Storrie. — Port Ellen : Oa, 1981. — 260p : ill,maps,plans,ports ; 21cm
Bibliography: p239-245. — Includes index
ISBN 0-907651-01-1 (pbk) : £5.45 B82-13350

941.4′23 — Scotland. Strathclyde Region. Lorn, *to 1981*

A **Lorn** miscellany of history and tradition / compiled by the Lorn Archaeological and Historical Society ; with a foreword by his Grace the Duke of Argyll and Madam MacDougal of MacDougal ; edited and illustrated by Mairi MacDonald. — [Oban] : Lorn Archaeological and Historical Society, [1982?]. — 76p : ill,1map ; 21cm
£1.50 (pbk) B82-36394

941.4′23 — Scotland. Strathclyde Region. Mull. Social life, *1895-1918 — Childhood reminiscences*

Fairfax-Lucy, Norah, *Lady.* Hebridean childhood : an autobiography / by Norah, Lady Fairfax-Lucy ; illustrated by Mary Clare Foa. — Glasgow : Molendinar, 1981. — 125p : col.ill,1col.port ; 24cm
ISBN 0-904002-56-x : £8.50 B82-39929

941.4′25 — Scotland. Strathclyde Region. Dumbarton. Social life, *ca 1940 — Personal observations*

Gallacher, Tom. Hunting shadows / by Tom Gallacher. — Helensburgh ([East King St., Helensburgh, Strathclyde]) : Craig M. Jeffrey, c1981. — 42p : ill,1port ; 21cm
Unpriced (pbk) B82-31107

941.4′25 — Scotland. Strathclyde Region. Vale of Leven, *ca 1900-ca 1980 — Illustrations*

Jones, Arthur F.. The old Vale and the new / by Arthur F. Jones and Graham N. Hopner. — Dumbarton : Dumbarton District Libraries, 1981. — 48p : ill,facsims ; 15x22cm
Facsims on inside cover
ISBN 0-906927-09-9 (pbk) : £1.50 B82-06401

941.4′25′005 — Scotland. Strathclyde Region. Dumbarton *(District) — History — Serials*

The **Lennox** guardian. — Issue no.1 (Spring 1982)-. — Dumbarton (c/o David Harvie, 82 Bonhill Rd, Dumbarton) : Lennox Heritage Society, 1982-. — v. : ill ; 22cm
Irregular
ISSN 0263-5461 = Lennox guardian : £0.40 B82-27650

941.4′28 — Scotland. Strathclyde Region. Kilmacolm & Port Glasgow, *1860-1970*

Port Glasgow and Kilmacolm / [compiled by] Joy Monteith, Robert McPherson. — Greenock : Inverclyde District Libraries, c1981. — 59p : chiefly ill,1map ; 20x21cm
Map on inside cover. — Bibliography: p59
ISBN 0-9500687-3-x (pbk) : £2.00 B82-09956

941.4′28′00992 — Scotland. Strathclyde Region. Inverclyde *(District), 1645-1961 — Biographies*

Macdougall, Sandra. Profiles from the past / Sandra Macdougall. — Greenock : Inverclyde District Libraries, c1982. — 60p : ill,facsims,music,ports ; 20x21cm
Bibliography: p58
ISBN 0-9500687-4-8 (pbk) : £2.00 B82-35990

941.4′34 — Scotland. Strathclyde Region. Bearsden. Social conditions *— For environment planning*

Bearsden and Milngavie. *District Council.* Bearsden urban area comprehensive local plan : report of survey June 1980. — Milngavie (2 Grange Ave., Milngavie) : Department of Technical Services Planning Group, [1980]. — 63p,[7]leaves of plates : maps ; 30cm
Unpriced (spiral) B82-34755

941.4′43 — Scotland. Strathclyde Region. Glasgow. Baillieston, *to 1981*

Jackson, Stewart. My ain folk : history of Baillieston and district with illustrations / by Stewart Jackson. — [Baillieston] : Baillieston Community Council, [c1981]. — 148p : ill,ports ; 21cm
Cover title. — Bibliography: p148
£1.25 (pbk) B82-13799

941.4′43 — Scotland. Strathclyde Region. Glasgow. Carmyle. Social conditions *— For environment planning*

Carmyle local plan : report of survey / City of Glasgow District Council. — Glasgow (84 Queen St., Glasgow G1 3DP) : [The Council] : 1980. — 41p,[12]leaves of plates(some col.) : ill,maps ; 30cm
Cover title
£1.50 (pbk) B82-21637

Carmyle local plan : issues document / the City of Glasgow District Council. — Glasgow (84 Queen St., Glasgow G1 3DP) : The Council, 1980. — 9p,[2]folded leaves of plates : ill,2maps ; 30cm
Unpriced (unbound) B82-23428

941.4′43 — Scotland. Strathclyde Region. Glasgow. Castlemilk. Social conditions *— For environment planning*

Castlemilk local plan : issues document / City of Glasgow District Council. — Glasgow (84 Queen St., Glasgow G1 3DP) : The Council, 1980. — 14p : ill,maps ; 30cm
Cover title. — Maps on inside covers
Unpriced (pbk) B82-21644

Castlemilk local plan : survey report / City of Clasgow District Council. — [Glasgow] ([84 Queen St., Glasgow G1 3DP]) : [The Council], [1980]. — 89p,[20]leaves of plates(some folded) : maps ; 30cm
Cover title
£1.50 (pbk) B82-21645

941.4′43 — Scotland. Strathclyde Region. Glasgow. Farme Cross. Social conditions *— For environment planning*

Farme Cross local plan : survey report / City of Glasgow District Council. — [Glasgow] ([84 Queen St., Glasgow G1 3DP]) : [The Council], [1980]. — i,58p,[12]leaves of plates : ill,maps ; 30cm
Cover title
Unpriced (spiral) B82-21638

941.4′43 — Scotland. Strathclyde Region. Glasgow. Farme Cross. Social conditions — *For environment planning* *continuation*

Farme Cross local plan : issues document / City of Glasgow District Council. — Glasgow (84 Queen St., Glasgow G1 3DP) : [The Council], [1980]. — 7p : 2maps ; 30cm
Cover title
Unpriced (pbk) B82-21639

941.4′43 — Scotland. Strathclyde Region. Glasgow. Social life, *to 1976*

Daiches, David. Glasgow / David Daiches. — London : Granada, 1982, c1977. — xiv,272p,[16]p of plates : ill,maps,facsims,ports ; 20cm
Originally published: London : Deutsch, 1977. — Bibliography: p256-258. — Includes index
ISBN 0-586-05357-3 (pbk) : £2.50 B82-29734

941.4′43 — Scotland. Strathclyde Region. Glasgow, *to 1979* — *For children*

Scott, Ann. Sam sees old Glasgow / [words and pictures by Ann Scott]. — Glasgow : Morland Print, c1980. — [32]p : ill ; 21cm
Cover title. — Ill on inside cover
£0.45 (pbk) B82-12737

941.4′43 — Scotland. Strathclyde Region. Glasgow, *to 1982*

Gibb, A.. Glasgow. — London : Croom Helm, Jan.1983. — [224]p
ISBN 0-7099-0161-5 : £12.95 : CIP entry B82-33346

941.4′43 — Scotland. Strathclyde Region. Glasgow. Whiteinch. Social conditions — *For environment planning*

Whiteinch local plan : survey report / the City of Glasgow District Council. — Glasgow (84 Queen St., Glasgow G1 3DP) : [The Council], 1979. — 58p,12leaves of plates(some col.) : maps ; 30cm
£1.50 (spiral) B82-21640

941.4′43 — Scotland. Strathclyde Region. Glasgow. Woodlands. Social conditions — *For environment planning*

Woodlands local plan : survey report / the City of Glasgow District Council. — Glasgow (84 Queen St., Glasgow G1 3DP) : The Council, 1979. — 53p,[15]leaves of plates(some col.) : maps ; 30cm
£1.50 (pbk) B82-21646

941.4′43 — Scotland. Strathclyde Region. Rutherglen — *Serials*

[Rutherglen reformer *(1981)***]**. Rutherglen reformer. — Friday 16th Oct. 1981-. — [Glasgow] (Press Buildings, Hamilton, [Glasgow]) : Scottish & Universal Newspapers, 1981-. — v. : ill,ports ; 44cm
Weekly. — Continues: South Glasgow and Rutherglen reformer
£0.15 per issue B82-40042

941.4′43082 — Scotland. Strathclyde Region. Glasgow. Social conditions, *1875-1981*

Checkland, S. G.. The upas tree Glasgow 1875-1975 : — and after 1975-1980 / S.G. Checkland ; with eight illustrations by Muirhead Bone. — 2nd enl. ed. — [Glasgow] : University of Glasgow Press, 1981. — 160p,[8]p of plates : ill,2maps ; 21cm
Previous ed.: 1976. — Bibliography: p134-143. — Includes index
ISBN 0-85261-168-4 (pbk) : Unpriced B82-08283

941.4′430858′0222 — Scotland. Strathclyde Region. Glasgow — *Illustrations*

Corrance, Douglas. Glasgow / photographed by Douglas Corrance ; with commentary by Edward Boyd. — Glasgow : Collins, 1981. — 128p : chiefly col.ill,col.ports ; 26cm
ISBN 0-00-435667-5 : £7.95 B82-31982

941.4′46 — Scotland. Strathclyde Region. Coatbridge, *to 1982*

Drummond, Peter. Coatbridge : three centuries of change / by Peter Drummond and James Smith ; pen and ink drawings by Ian Allan. — [Glasgow] : Monklands Library Services Department, [1982]. — 64p : ill,facsims,maps,plans ; 30cm
Bibliography: p59
ISBN 0-946120-00-5 (pbk) : Unpriced B82-33176

941.4′49 — Scotland. Strathclyde Region. Motherwell *(District)*. **Buildings of historical importance**

Historic buildings in Motherwell district : a descriptive record / Motherwell District Council, Department of Planning. — [Motherwell] (c/o Motherwell District Libraries, 35 Hamilton Rd, Motherwell ML1 3BZ) : [The Council], c1981. — 47p : ill(some col.),maps,1coat of arms,plans,1port ; 21x30cm
ISBN 0-903207-13-3 (pbk) : Unpriced B82-12293

941.4′49 — Scotland. Strathclyde Region. Motherwell. Social life, *1920-1930* — *Childhood reminiscences*

Moir, Norman. A Motherwell childhood : a personal memory / by Norman Moir. — Motherwell : Motherwell District Libraries, 1981. — 14p,[7]leaves of plates : ill ; 21cm
ISBN 0-903207-09-5 (pbk) : Unpriced B82-11882

941.4′57 — Scotland. Strathclyde Region. Bothwell. Social conditions — *For environment planning*

Bothwell Local Plan : report of survey : the summary. — Hamilton (123 Cadzow St., Hamilton) : Director of Planning & Development, [1981]. — [4]p : ill,1map ; 30cm
Unpriced (unbound) B82-25716

941.4′57 — Scotland. Strathclyde Region. Hamilton. Social conditions — *For environment planning*

Hamilton Local Plan : report of survey : the summary. — Hamilton (123 Cadzow St., Hamilton) : Director of Planning and Development, Hamilton District Council, 1980. — [8]p : ill,1col.map ; 30cm
Unpriced (pbk) B82-25718

Hamilton Local Plan : report of survey. — Hamilton (123 Cadzow St., Hamilton) : Director of Planning and Development, Hamilton District Council, 1980. — 81p,4leaves of plates(1 folded) : maps ; 30cm
Two folded sheets (maps) in pocket
Unpriced (pbk) B82-25719

941.4′57 — Scotland. Strathclyde Region. Stonehouse. Social conditions — *For environment planning*

Stonehouse Local Plan : report of survey : the summary. — Hamilton ([123 Cadzow St.], Hamilton) : Hamilton District Council, [1979]. — [8]p : ill,1map ; 21cm
Response card (1 sheet) as insert
Unpriced (pbk) B82-25717

Stonehouse Local Plan : report of survey. — Hamilton (123 Cadzow St., Hamilton) : Director of Planning and Development, Hamilton District Council, 1979. — 41p,5leaves of plates (4 folded) : maps ; 30cm
Unpriced (pbk) B82-25721

941.4′57 — Scotland. Strathclyde Region. Uddingston. Social conditions — *For environment planning*

Uddingston Local Plan : report of survey. — Hamilton (123 Cadzow St., Hamilton) : Director of Planning and Development, Hamilton District Council, 1979. — 54p,4leaves of plates(3 folded) : maps ; 22x30cm
Unpriced (pbk) B82-25720

941.4′61 — Scotland. Strathclyde Region. Ardrossan, Saltcoats & Stevenston. Social conditions — *For environment planning*

Survey report : Ardrossan, Saltcoats, Stevenston local plan. — Irvine (Cunninghame House, Irvine) : Cunninghame District Council, [1978]. — [29]p ; 30cm + technical appendices (121leaves ; 30cm)
Cover title
Unpriced (spiral) B82-11349

Survey report : technical appendices : Ardrossan, Saltcoats, Stevenston local plan. — [Irvine] ([Cunninghame House, Irvine]) : Cunninghame District Council, [1981?]. — 121leaves ; 30cm
Cover title. — Originally published: as a part of Survey report. 1978
Unpriced (spiral) B82-20903

941.4′61 — Scotland. Strathclyde Region. Arran, *to 1981*

The **Book** of Arran. — Brodick (Ivy Cottage, Brodick, Isle of Arran KA27 8DD) : Kilbrannan Publishing, Aug.1982. — 2v. ([683] p)
Originally published: Glasgow : Arran Society of Glasgow, 1910-14
ISBN 0-907939-04-x : £40.00 : CIP entry B82-27021

941.4′63 — Scotland. Strathclyde Region. Kilmarnock, *to 1800*. **Archaeological investigation** — *Proposals*

Simpson, Anne Turner. Historic Kilmarnock : the archaeological implications of development / Anne Turner Simpson, Sylvia Stevenson. — [Glasgow] ([The University, Glasgow G12 8QG]) : Department of Archaeology, University of Glasgow, 1981. — [24]leaves (some folded) : maps ; 30cm. — (Scottish burgh survey)
Bibliography: leaves 20-21
Unpriced (pbk) B82-22837

941.4′64 — Scotland. Strathclyde Region. Ayr region. Social conditions — *For environment planning*

Kyle and Carrick. *Planning Department*. Ayr and Prestwick local plan : report of survey and draft plan : summary / Kyle and Carrick District Council. — [Ayr] ([Burns House, Burns Statue Sq., Ayr]) : [Kyle and Carrick District Council, Planning Department], 1982. — 50p ; 30cm
Cover title
Unpriced (spiral) B82-29922

Kyle and Carrick. *Planning Department*. Ayr and Prestwick local plan : report of survey and draft plan / Kyle and Carrick District Council. — [Ayr] ([Burns House, Burns Statue Sq., Ayr]) : [Kyle and Carrick District Council, Planning Department], 1982. — iii,234p + 3 maps : ill,maps ; 30cm
Unpriced (spiral) B82-29923

941.4′64 — Scotland. Strathclyde Region. Troon region. Social conditions — *For environment planning*

North Kyle local plan : survey draft plan. — Ayr (Burns House, Burns Statue Sq., Ayr) : Kyle and Carrick District Council, [1982?]. — 163p : ill ; 30cm + 2folded sheets(147x120cm folded to 26x21cm)
Cover title
Unpriced (spiral) B82-25615

941.4′640858′05 — Scotland. Strathclyde Region. Kyle and Carrick *(District)* — *Serials*

Troon times : Ayr advertiser & Prestwick times. — No.4168 (Friday Mar. 5 1982)-. — Ayr (3 Arthur St, Ayr) : Arthur Guthrie & Sons, 1982-. — v. : ill,ports ; 43cm
Weekly. — Continues: Troon & Prestwick times
£0.12 per issue B82-40040

941.4′67 — Scotland. Strathclyde Region. Doon Valley region. Social conditions, *1963-1972*

Moore, John, *1937-*. Doon Valley diary : the critical decade 1963-72 / John Moore. — Alloway : J. Moore, c1980. — 111p,viiip of plates : ill,1map,ports ; 21cm
ISBN 0-9507273-0-x (pbk) : £4.95 B82-16021

941.4′69 — Scotland. Strathclyde Region. Crossford. Social life, *1910-1920* — *Correspondence, diaries, etc.*

Scott, Gavin, *1841-1917*. Your loving father, Gavin Scott : letters from a Lanarkshire farmer / edited by Ruth Richens. — Cambridge (11 Barton Close, Cambridge CB3 9LQ) : R. Richens
1912. — c1982. — ix,p78-140 : ill,geneal.tables,maps,ports ; 22cm
Cover title
£1.20 (pbk) B82-32663

941.4'69 — Scotland. Strathclyde Region. Crossford. Social life, *1911 — Personal observations — Correspondence, diaries, etc.*

Scott, Gavin, *1841-1917*. Your loving father, Gavin Scott : letters from a Lanarkshire farmer / edited by Ruth Richens. — Cambridge (11 Barton Close, Cambridge CB3 9LQ) : R. Richens
1911. — 1981. — 77p : ill,maps,ports,geneal.table ; 21cm
£1.20 (pbk) B82-00582

941.4'69 — Scotland. Strathclyde Region. Lanark, *to ca 1800*. **Archaeological investigation** — *Proposals*

Simpson, Anne Turner. Historic Lanark : the archaeological implications of development / Anne Turner Simpson, Sylvia Stevenson. — [Glasgow] ([The University, Glasgow G12 8QG]) : Department of Archaeology, University of Glasgow, 1981. — [37]leaves (some folded) : maps ; 30cm. — (Scottish burgh survey)
Bibliography: leaves 31-33
Unpriced (pbk) B82-22838

941.4'7 — Great Britain. Solway Firth region, *to 1981*

Blake, Brian. The Solway Firth / Brian Blake. — 3rd ed. — London : Hale, 1982. — x,232p,[16]p : ill,1map ; 23cm
Previous ed.: 1974. — Bibliography: p220-221. — Includes index
ISBN 0-7091-9747-0 : £7.95 B82-24784

941.4'7081'0924 — Scotland. Dumfries and Galloway Region. Social life, *ca 1900 — Personal observations*

Niall, Ian. A Galloway childhood / Ian Niall ; with illustrations by C.F. Tunnicliffe. — London : Wildwood, 1981, c1967. — 182p : ill ; 20cm
Originally published: London : Heinemann, 1967
ISBN 0-7045-0440-5 (pbk) : £3.95 B82-02845

941.4'86 — Scotland. Dumfries and Galloway Region. Dumfries. Grierson, William — *Correspondence, diaries, etc*

Grierson, William. Apostle to Burns : the diaries of William Grierson / edited by John Davies. — Edinburgh : Blackwood, 1981. — xxi,327p,[16]p of plates : ill(some col.),ports ; 23cm
Ill on lining papers. — Bibliography: p323-324. — Includes index
ISBN 0-85158-152-8 : £8.95 B82-19592

941.4'86 — Scotland. Dumfries and Galloway Region. Dumfries, *to 1981*

Urquhart, James. Dumfries : the remarkable story of its common seal and coat of arms with a wealth of local history / by James Urquhart ; illustrated by John Williamson and David Ferguson. — Dumfries : J. Urquhart, 1981. — xiii,168p : ill,maps,coats of arms,music,facsims,2plans,1port ; 30cm
Maps on folded sheet attached to inside cover. — Includes index
ISBN 0-9507033-2-x (pbk) : £15.00
B82-00947

941.4'95 — Scotland. Dumfries and Galloway Region. Wigtown, *to ca 1850*. **Archaeological investigation** — *Proposals*

Simpson, Anne Turner. Historic Wigtown : the archaeological implications of development / Anne Turner Simpson, Sylvia Stevenson. — [Glasgow] ([The University, Glasgow, G12 8QG]) : Department of Archaeology, University of Glasgow, 1981. — 25p,[3]leaves of plates(some folded) : 3maps,1coat of arms ; 31cm. — (Scottish burgh survey)
Bibliography: p23-25
Unpriced (pbk) B82-09264

941.5 — HISTORY. IRELAND

941.5 — Ireland — *History*

Plunkett, Horace. Ireland in the new century. — Blackrock : Irish Academic Press, Nov.1982. — 1v.
ISBN 0-7165-0294-1 : £3.50 : CIP entry
B82-37666

941.5 — Ireland. Political events, *1318-1541*

Cosgrove, Art. Late medieval Ireland 1370-1541 / Art Cosgrove. — Dublin (Ballymount Rd., Walkinstown, Dublin 12) : Helicon, 1981. — vii,134p : 4maps,1geneal.table ; 21cm. — (Helicon history of Ireland)
Includes index
Unpriced (pbk) B82-08207

941.5 — Ireland. Social conditions, *1600-1922 — Festschriften*

Irish population, economy, and society : essays in honour of the late K.H. Connell / edited by J.M. Goldstrom and L.A. Clarkson. — Oxford : Clarendon, 1981. — x,322p : 1port ; 23cm
Bibliography: p308. — Includes index
ISBN 0-19-822499-0 : £17.50 : CIP rev.
B81-34379

941.5 — Ireland. Social conditions — *History — For children — Irish texts*

Coolahan, John. [Discover the past. Irish]. Ar lorg na staire / Seán Ó Cúlacháin. — Baile Átha Cliath : Oifig an tSoláthair
3: Ionradh agus plandáil 1169-1691. — c1981. — 95p : ill,maps,1facsims,plans,ports ; 22x24cm
Translation of: Discover the past, 3. — Originally published: Dublin : Gill and Macmillan, 1973. — Bibliography: 2p
Unpriced (pbk) B82-19587

941.5 — Ireland, *to 1969*

O'Brien, Máire. A concise history of Ireland / Máire and Conor Cruise O'Brien. — 2nd ed. rev. — [London] : Thames and Hudson, 1973 (1980 [printing]). — 192p : ill,facsims,maps,music,ports ; 23cm
Previous ed.: 1972. — Bibliography: p175-177. — Includes index
ISBN 0-500-27199-2 (pbk) : £2.95 B82-25105

941.5 — Ireland, *to 1975*

MacCall, Seamus. A little history of Ireland / Seamus MacCall. — New ed. / with a final chapter by Catherine MacCall and Börje Thilman. — Portlaoise : Dolmen Press, 1982. — 63p ; 22cm
Previous ed.: 1973. — Includes index
ISBN 0-85105-400-5 (pbk) : £2.50 B82-41022

941.5 — Ireland, *to 1978*

Johnson, Paul. Ireland : a history from the twelfth century to the present day / Paul Johnson. — London : Granada, 1981. — 272p,[16]p of plates : ill,maps,ports ; 18cm. — (A Panther book)
Originally published: London : Eyre Methuen, 1980. — Includes index
ISBN 0-586-05453-7 (pbk) : £1.50 B82-00794

941.5 — Irish civilization, *to 1980 — Irish texts*

Breathnach, Diarmuid. Almanag Éireannach / Diarmuid Breathnach. — Baile Átha Cliath : Oifig an tSoláthair, c1981. — vii,135p : ill ; 24cm
Includes index
Unpriced B82-27469

941.5 — Irish culture — *History*

Irish studies. — 1. — Cambridge : Cambridge University Press, Apr.1981. — [176]p
ISBN 0-521-23336-4 : £16.50 : CIP entry
B81-03358

941.5

Wallace, Martin. A short history of Ireland. — Newton Abbot : David & Charles, Apr.1981. — [166]p
Originally published: 1973
ISBN 0-7153-6974-1 (pbk) : £2.95 : CIP entry
B81-07444

941.5'0072024 — Ireland. Political events, *to 1882*. **Historiography. Marx, Karl** — *Critical studies*

Cronin, Sean. Marx and the Irish question / Sean Cronin. — Dublin : Repsol, c1977. — 48p ; 18cm
ISBN 0-86064-012-4 (pbk) : £0.55 B82-16999

941.503 — Ireland. Political events, *1318-1361*

Frame, Robin. English lordship in Ireland 1318-1361 / Robin Frame. — Oxford : Clarendon Press, 1982. — xiv,381p : maps,geneal.tables ; 23cm
Bibliography: p347-359. — Includes index
ISBN 0-19-822673-x : £19.50 : CIP rev.
B81-35760

941.503 — Ireland. Settlement by Anglo-Normans, *1169-1369*

Frame, Robin. Colonial Ireland, 1169-1369 / Robin Frame. — Dublin (Ballymount Rd., Walkinstown, Dublin 12) : Helicon, 1981. — x,149p : maps ; 21cm. — (Helicon history of Ireland)
Includes index
Unpriced (pbk) B82-08206

941.507 — Ireland. Invasion by French, *1798 — Personal observations*

Stock, Joseph. Bishop Stock's 'narrative' from the year of the French. — Ballina (Terrybaun, Bofeenaun, Ballina, County Mayo) : Irish Humanities Centre, May 1982. — [126]p
Originally published: Dublin : Printed by and for R.E. Mercier & Co. & John Jones, 1800
ISBN 0-906462-08-8 : £8.00 : CIP entry
B82-14399

941.507 — Ireland. United Irishmen Rebellion

Elliott, Marianne. Partners in revolution. — London : Yale University Press, Nov.1982. — [430]p
ISBN 0-300-02770-2 : £15.00 : CIP entry
B82-40334

941.508 — Ireland, *1790-1970 — For schools — Irish texts*

Cullen, L. M.. Sé ghlúin Éireannacha : cúrsaí an tSaoil in Éirinn 1790-1970 : bunaithe ar an sraithchlár, Six Generations, de chuid RTÉ / le L.M. Ó Cuileáin (L.M. Cullen) ; Livín Ó Murchú a d'aistrigh. — [Baile Átha Cliath] : Oifig an tSoláthair, 1981, c1970. — 137p : ill,1facsim,maps,ports ; 23cm
Unpriced (pbk) B82-30873

941.5081 — Ireland, *1848-1950 — For Irish students*

Ó Broin, Art. Irish history 1848-1950 / Art Ó Broin. — Dublin : Folens, c1979. — 45p ; 22cm. — (Folen's student aids leaving certificate)
ISBN 0-86121-060-3 (pbk) : Unpriced
B82-01230

941.5081 — Ireland, *1850-1950 — For Irish students*

Gray, E. C.. History, Ireland 1850-1950 / E.C. Gray. — Dublin : Helicon, 1981 : Distributed by Educational Company. — 32p ; 21cm. — (Notes on Leaving Certificate)
Unpriced (pbk) B82-02557

941.5081 — Ireland. Political events, *1813-1835 — Correspondence, diaries, etc.*

Gregory, William. Mr. Gregory's letter-box 1813-1835 / edited by Lady Gregory. — 2nd ed. / with a foreword by Jon Stallworthy. — Gerrards Cross : Smythe, 1981. — 242p : 1port ; 23cm. — (The Coole edition ; v.20)
Previous ed.: 1898. — Includes index
ISBN 0-900675-41-1 : £15.00 : CIP rev.
B80-22741

941.5081 — Ireland. Political events. Role of Catholic Church, *1841-1846*

Kerr, Donal A.. Peel, priests and politics. — Oxford : Clarendon Press, Oct.1982. — [450]p. — (Oxford historical monographs)
ISBN 0-19-821891-5 : £19.50 : CIP entry
B82-23685

941.5081'092'4 — Ireland. Politics. O'Connell, Daniel — *Biographies*

The World of Daniel O'Connell / edited by Donal McCartney. — Dublin : Published for the Cultural Relations Committee of Ireland by Mercier, c1980. — viii,185p : ill,1port ; 20cm
Includes bibliographies
ISBN 0-85342-589-2 (pbk) : £3.95 B82-03648

941.5081'0924 — Ireland. Taaffe, Julia. Interpersonal relationships with Gagarin, Grégoire

Brophy, Brigid. The prince and the wild geese. — London : Hamilton, Feb.1983. — [64]p
ISBN 0-241-10894-2 : £5.95 : CIP entry
Primary classification 947'.07'0924 B82-37849

941.5082 — Ireland. Political events, *1897-1923 — Interviews*

Griffith, Kenneth. Curious journey : an oral history of Ireland's unfinished revolution / Kenneth Griffith and Timothy E. O'Grady. — London : Hutchinson, 1982. — xxxvii,376p ; 20cm
Bibliography: p362-366. — Includes index
ISBN 0-09-145301-1 (pbk) : £3.95 : CIP rev.
B82-10413

941.5082 — Ireland. Political events. Attitudes of Labour Party *(Great Britain), ca 1880-1981*

Bell, Geoffrey. Troublesome business : the Labour Party and the Irish question. — London : Pluto, Aug.1982. — [176]p
ISBN 0-86104-373-1 : £4.50 : CIP entry
B82-22407

941.5082'092'4 — Ireland. Political events, *1916-1981 — Personal observations*

O'Brien, Nora Connolly. We shall rise again / Nora Connolly O'Brien. — London : Mosquito, 1981. — 121p,viiip of plates : ill,facsims,ports ; 18cm
£1.95 (pbk) B82-05905

941.5082'1 — Ireland. Political events, *1890-1939.* Cultural factors

Lyons, F. S. L.. Culture and anarchy in Ireland 1890-1939. — Oxford : Oxford University Press, Sept.1982. — [160]p
Originally published: 1979
ISBN 0-19-285121-7 (pbk) : £2.95 : CIP entry
B82-18991

941.5082'1 — Ireland. Social conditions, *ca 1911*

A. E.. Cooperation and nationality : a guide for rural reformers from this to the next generation / by George W. Russell (AE). — Blackrock : Irish Academic Press, c1982. — 103p ; 22cm. — (Cooperative studies ; 1)
Originally published: Dublin : Maunsel, 1912
ISBN 0-7165-0335-2 (pbk) : £3.00 B82-29758

941.5082'2 — Ireland. Political events, *1922-1923*

Morrison, George, *1922-*. The Irish Civil War / George Morrison. — Dublin : Gill and Macmillan, 1981. — 142p : ill,ports ; 31cm
ISBN 0-7171-1045-1 : £17.25 B82-08551

941.5082'2'0924 — Ireland. Political events, *1922-1923 — Personal observations*

Deasy, Liam. Brother against brother / Liam Deasy. — Dublin : Mercier, c1982. — 126p ; 18cm
ISBN 0-85342-668-6 (pbk) : Unpriced
B82-22231

941.5082'2'0924 — Ireland. Social life, *1920-1950 — Personal observations*

Gogarty, Oliver St. John. Rolling down the lea / Oliver St. John Gogarty. — London : Sphere, 1982, c1950. — 182p ; 18cm
Originally published: London : Constable, 1950
ISBN 0-7221-3916-0 (pbk) : £1.75 B82-29174

941.5082'4 — Ireland. Social development. Political aspects

Power conflict and inequality : studies in Irish society. — Dublin : Turoe Press, May 1982. — [200]p
ISBN 0-905223-34-9 (pbk) : £10.00 : CIP entry
B82-17890

941.50824 — Ireland. Society

Peillon, Michel. Contemporary Irish society : an introduction / Michel Peillon. — Dublin : Gill and Macmillan, 1982. — 231p : 1ill ; 22cm
Bibliography: p212-224. — Includes index
ISBN 0-7171-1141-5 (pbk) : £5.95 B82-36378

941.50824'05 — Ireland. Social conditions — *Socialist viewpoints — Serials*

Gralton. — No.1 (Apr./May 1982)-. — Dublin (25 Mountainview Court, Harold's Cross, Dublin 6) : Gralton Co-operative Society, 1982-. — v. : ill,ports ; 29cm
Six issues yearly
Unpriced B82-27640

941.6 — Northern Ireland, *1000-1550*

Sheane, Michael. Ulster and the Middle Ages / Michael Sheane. — Stockport : Highfield, c1982. — 195p ; 20cm
Bibliography: p193-195
ISBN 0-906221-04-8 (pbk) : £5.50 B82-39082

941.6 — Northern Ireland. Social conditions, *to 1981.* Geographical aspects

Integration and division : geographical perspectives on the Northern Ireland problem / edited by Frederick W. Boal and J. Neville H. Douglas, with the assistance of Jenitha A. E. Orr. — London : Academic Press, 1982. — xii,368p : ill,maps ; 24cm
Includes bibliographies and index
ISBN 0-12-108080-3 : £19.80 : CIP rev.
B82-04133

941.6 — Northern Ireland, *to ca 1945*

O'Byrne, Cathal. As I roved out. — Belfast : Blackstaff, Oct.1982. — [464]p
Facsim. of: ed. published Belfast : Irish News, 1946
ISBN 0-85640-204-4 : £7.95 : CIP entry
B82-31309

941.608 — Northern Ireland, *1800-1980*

Longford, Frank Pakenham, *Earl of.* Ulster / Lord Longford and Anne McHardy. — London : Weidenfeld and Nicolson, c1981. — viii,260p : maps ; 23cm
Bibliography: p251-252. — Includes index
ISBN 0-297-77971-0 : £10.95 B82-01627

941.6081 — Northern Ireland. Political events, *1800-1920*

Sheane, Michael. Ulster & the British connection / Michael Sheane. — Stockport : Highfield, c1979. — 185p ; 20cm
Bibliography: p181-185
ISBN 0-906221-02-1 (pbk) : £4.25 B82-39083

941.60824 — Northern Ireland. Army operations by Great Britain. *Army, 1969-1975*

Barzilay, David. The British army in Ulster / David Barzilay. — Belfast : Century
Vol.1. — 1973 (1978 [printing]). — 254p : ill,maps,2ports ; 25cm
£8.00 B82-23528

Barzilay, David. The British army in Ulster / David Barzilay. — Belfast : Century
Vol.2. — 1975 (1978 [printing]). — 256p : ill,1port ; 25cm
ISBN 0-903152-12-6 : £8.00 B82-23529

941.60824 — Northern Ireland. Army operations by Great Britain. *Army, 1969-1980*

Barzilay, David. The British army in Ulster / David Barzilay. — Belfast (51-59 Donegall St., Belfast BT1 2GB) : Century
Vol.3. — 1978. — 240p : ill,3maps,facsims ; 25cm
£8.00 B82-27716

Barzilay, David. The British army in Ulster / David Barzilay. — Belfast (51-59 Donegall St., Belfast BT1 2GB) : Century
Vol.4. — 1981. — 256p : ill,1map,ports ; 25cm
£8.95 B82-27717

941.60824 — Northern Ireland. Army operations by Great Britain. *Army, 1969-1982 — Committee for Withdrawal from Ireland viewpoints*

Ireland : voices for withdrawal / [edited and produced by the Committee for Withdrawal from Ireland]. — London (1 North End Road, London W14) : Information on Ireland, [1980]. — 64p : ill ; 30cm
Cover title. — Bibliography: p64
£0.75 (pbk) B82-13459

941.60824 — Northern Ireland. Army operations by Great Britain. *Army, 1969-1982 — Information on Ireland viewpoints*

British soldiers speak out on Ireland / [edited by Alistair Renwick]. — [London] ([1 North End Road, London W.14]) : [Information on Ireland], [1978]. — 31p : ill ; 30cm. — (Information on Ireland ; no.1)
£0.40 (unbound) B82-13460

941.60824 — Northern Ireland. Army operations by Great Britain. *Army, 1973-1976*

Clarke, A. F. N.. Contact. — London : Secker and Warburg, Sept.1982. — [208]p
ISBN 0-436-09998-5 : £7.50 : CIP entry
B82-32292

941.6082'4 — Northern Ireland. Army operations by Great Britain. *Army, 1978-1980.* Mascots: Dogs: Rats

Halstock, Max. Rats : the story of a dog soldier / by Max Halstock. — London : Gollancz, 1981. — 119p,[8]p of plates : ill,ports ; 21cm
ISBN 0-575-03018-6 : £4.95 B82-04937

941.6082'4 — Northern Ireland. Policies of British government, *1969-1979*

Faligot, Roger. Britain's military strategy in Ireland. — London : Zed Press, Sept.1982. — [256]p
Translation of: Guerre speciale en Europe
ISBN 0-86232-047-x (cased) : £14.95 : CIP entry
ISBN 0-86232-049-6 (pbk) : £6.50 B82-21409

941.60824 — Northern Ireland. Political events, *1969-1980 — Ulster Special Constabulary Association viewpoints*

Ulster Special Constabulary Association. Why? : 6,700 explosions, 2,000 murdered, 21,000 injured, 12,000 shootings / Ulster Special Constabulary Association. — [Northern Ireland] : U.S.C.A., 1980. — 71p : ill,ports ; 21cm
Cover title
£1.00 (pbk) B82-14427

941.6082'4 — Northern Ireland. Political events, *1969-1981 — Labour Party (Great Britain). Young Socialists viewpoints*

Northern Ireland : the way forward. — [London] ([144 Walworth Rd, SE17]) : [Labour Party Young Socialists National Committee], [1982]. — 19p ; 30cm. — (LPYS conference document ; 1982)
£0.25 (unbound) B82-25254

941.60824 — Northern Ireland. Political events. Role of Christian church, *1968-1980*

Gallagher, Eric. Christians in Ulster, 1968-1980 / Eric Gallagher and Stanley Worrall. — Oxford : Oxford University Press, 1982. — 241p ; 22cm
Bibliography: p225-231. — Includes index
ISBN 0-19-213237-7 : £10.00 : CIP rev.
B82-04149

941.60824 — Northern Ireland. Political events. Role of Irish Republican Army, *1969-1981*

Kelley, Kevin. Britain's longest war : Northern Ireland and the IRA. — London : Zed Press, Oct.1982. — [336]p
ISBN 0-86232-023-2 (cased) : £16.95 : CIP entry
ISBN 0-86232-024-0 (pbk) : £6.95 B82-24583

941.60824 — Northern Ireland. Social conditions

McCreary, Alf. Profiles of hope / by Alf McCreary. — Belfast : Christian Journals, 1981. — 96p ; 22cm
ISBN 0-904302-73-3 (pbk) : Unpriced
B82-31783

Northern Ireland observed / photographs Anderson McMeekin ... [et al.]. — [Belfast] (Stormont Castle, Belfast BT4 3ST]) : Northern Ireland Information Service, [1982?]. — 24p : ill(some col.),1col.map,col.ports ; 30cm
Unpriced (unbound) B82-37972

941.60824'092'4 — Northern Ireland. Politics. Paisley, Ian — *'Workers Weekly' viewpoints*

Paisley on the Lundy Trail. — Belfast (10 Athol St., Belfast, 12) : Workers' Weekly, 1981. — 20p ; 26cm
Cover title
Unpriced (pbk) B82-04226

941.6′12081 — Antrim *(District)*. Antrim. Social life, *ca 1865-ca 1880 — Childhood reminiscences*

Irvine, Alexander. The souls of poor folk. — Belfast : Appletree Press, Oct.1981. — [160]p
ISBN 0-904651-86-x : £4.50 : CIP entry
B81-30189

941.6′18 — Newtownabbey *(District)*. Carnmoney region. Agricultural industries. Farms: Sentry Hill. Social life, *to 1981*

Walker, Brian Mercer. Sentry Hill : an Ulster farm and family / Brian M. Walker. — Dundonald : Blackstaff, c1981. — xii,167p : ill,1map,facsims,forms,ports ; 24cm
ISBN 0-85640-254-0 (pbk) : £5.95 : CIP rev.
B81-34962

941.6′19 — Lisburn *(District)*. Drumbo, *to 1980*

Rankin, J. Fred. The heritage of Drumbo / J. Fred Rankin. — [Drumbo] : [Parish of Drumbo in the Diocese of Down], [1982?]. — iv,125p : ill,1map,facsims,plans,ports,1geneal.table ; 21cm
Unpriced (pbk) B82-20218

941.6′7 — Belfast, *to 1982*

Bardon, Jonathan. Belfast. — Belfast : Blackstaff, Oct.1982. — [304]p
ISBN 0-85640-272-9 (cased) : £12.95 : CIP entry
ISBN 0-85640-271-0 (pbk) : £7.50 B82-28590

941.6′7081 — Belfast, *1800-1914*

Beckett, J. C.. Belfast : the making of the city 1800-1914. — Belfast : Appletree Press, Oct.1982. — [200]p
ISBN 0-86281-100-7 : £10.00 : CIP entry
B82-29411

941.6′70821 — Belfast. Social life, *1901-1910*

Gribbon, Sybil. Edwardian Belfast. — Belfast : Appletree Press, June 1982. — [64]p. — (Explorations in Irish history)
ISBN 0-86281-104-x (pbk) : £2.95 : CIP entry
B82-17222

941.69′3081′0924 — Donegal *(County)*. Social life, *1850-1900 — Personal observations*

McCarron, Edward. Life in Donegal 1850-1900 / Edward McCarron. — Dublin : Mercier, c1981. — 140p ; 18cm
ISBN 0-85342-654-6 (pbk) : £2.50 B82-03441

941.69′8′005 — Cavan *(County)*. Social life — *History — Serials*

The **Heart** of Breifne : traditions, ballads, legends and folklore from mid-Cavan = I gceartlár Breifne. — Vol.1, no.1-. — [Bailieboro, Co. Cavan] : Cumann Staire Leathrátha, 1978-. — v. : ill,maps,music,ports ; 22cm
Annual. — Description based on: Vol.1, no.4
£2.25 B82-22655

941.708 — Ireland *(Republic)*. Social life, *1800-1981*

Dillon, Eilís. Inside Ireland / Eilís Dillon ; photographs by Tom Kennedy. — London : Hodder and Stoughton, 1982. — 207p : ill,1map ; 26cm
Ill on lining papers
ISBN 0-340-26342-3 : Unpriced : CIP rev.
B82-18804

941.7082′092′4 — Ireland *(Republic)*. Politics. Andrews, C. S. — *Biographies*

Andrews, C. S.. Dublin made me : an autobiography / C.S. Andrews. — Dublin : Mercier, c1979. — 312p ; 23cm
Includes index
ISBN 0-85342-606-6 : £9.00 B82-22924

941.7082′1′0924 — Ireland *(Republic)*. Mac Eoin, Seán — *Biographies*

O'Farrell, Padraic. The Seán Mac Eoin story / Padraic O'Farrell. — Dublin : Mercier, 1981. — 129p ; 18cm
Includes index
ISBN 0-85342-664-3 (pbk) : £2.60 B82-05685

941.7082′1′0924 — Ireland *(Republic)*. Political events. Role of Collins, Michael, *1890-1922, 1917-1922*

Dwyer, T. Ryle. Michael Collins and the Treaty : his differences with de Valera / T. Ryle Dwyer. — Dublin : Mercier, c1981. — 172p ; 18cm
Bibliography: p169-170. — Includes index
ISBN 0-85342-667-8 (pbk) : Unpriced
B82-09818

941.7082′2′0924 — Ireland *(Republic)*. Breen, Dan — *Biographies*

Ambrose, Joseph G.. The Dan Breen story / Joseph G. Ambrose. — Dublin : Mercier, 1981. — 119p ; 18cm
Bibliography: p117. — Includes index
ISBN 0-85342-663-5 (pbk) : £2.60 B82-14534

941.7082′3′0924 — Ireland *(Republic)*. Political events, *1960-1975 — Personal observations*

Boland, Kevin. Up Dev! / by Kevin Boland. — Rathcoole (Red Gap, Rathcoole, Co. Dublin) : K. Boland, [1981?]. — 147p : ill,ports ; 22cm
£1.75 (pbk) B82-14409

941.70824 — Ireland *(Republic)*. Social conditions

The **Economic** and social state of the nation : a series of public lectures / given by James F. Meenan ... [et al.]. — Dublin : The Economic and Social Research Institute, c1982. — 110p ; 21cm
Bibliography: p102
ISBN 0-7070-0048-3 (pbk) : £4.00(Irish)
B82-37802

941.70824′072 — Ireland *(Republic)*. Social conditions. Research organisations: Economic and Social Research Institute. Research, *1981-1985 — Proposals*

Kennedy, Kieran A.. The ESRI research plan 1981-85 and background analysis / compiled by Kieran A. Kennedy. — Dublin : Economic and Social Research Institute, 1981. — viii,100p ; 21cm
Bibliography: p51-59
ISBN 0-7070-0043-2 (pbk) : £3.00 B82-01907

941.7′101′0924 — Ireland *(Republic)*. Connacht. Guaire, *King of Connaught — Biographies*

Hynes, James Patrick. White sheeted fort : a history of Guaire, the Hospitable, King of Connaught, and his descendants / James Patrick Hynes. — [Mold] : [J.P. Hynes], [c1980]. — 92p : ill,coats of arms,maps ; 22cm
Cover title. — Bibliography: 92
ISBN 0-9508227-0-1 (pbk) : Unpriced
B82-36035

941.7′2 — Sligo *(County)*. Inishmurray, *to 1948*

Heraughty, Patrick. Inishmurray. — Dublin : O'Brien Press, July 1982. — [128]p. — (Island series, ISSN 0332-1932 ; 5)
ISBN 0-905140-98-2 : £8.00 : CIP entry
B82-19284

941.7′3 — Mayo *(County)*. Killala. Political events, *1798 — Personal observations*

Stock, Joseph. [A narrative of what passed at Killalla in the county of Mayo and the parts adjacent during the French invasion in the summer of 1798]. Bishop Stock's 'Narrative' of the Year of the French: 1798 / edited by Grattan Freyer ; foreword by Michael Garvey. — Terrybaun : Irish Humanities Centre, 1982. — xxiv,118p,[4p] of plates : ill,2maps ; 19cm
Originally published: Dublin : Mercier, 1800
ISBN 0-906462-07-x : £5.85(Irish) B82-39765

941.7′3 — Mayo *(County)*. Killasser, *to 1980*

O'Hara, Bernard. Killasser : a history / edited by Bernard O'Hara. — Galway (2, Seaman Drive, Riverside, Galway) : B. O'Hara, c1981. — 104p : ill,maps,ports ; 24cm
£3.00 (pbk) B82-00961

941.7′3 — Mayo *(County)*, *to 1981*

County Mayo. — Galway (c/o 2 Seaman Drive, Riverside, Galway, Ireland) : Regional Technical College, Archaeological, Historical and Folklore Society, Aug.1982. — [250]p
ISBN 0-9508233-0-9 (cased) : CIP entry
ISBN 0-9508233-1-7 (pbk) : Unpriced
B82-25748

941.7′3 — Mayo *(County)*. Westport. Country houses: Westport House, *to 1981*

Sligo, Denis Browne, *Marquess of*. Westport House and the Brownes. — Ashbourne : Moorland Publishing, Jan.1982. — [112]p
ISBN 0-86190-045-6 : £5.95 : CIP entry
B81-38833

941.7′3 — Mayo *(County)*. Westport — *History — Serials*

Cathair na Mart : journal of Westport Historical Society. — Vol.1, no.1-. — [Westport] ([c/o Carrowholly Lodge, Westport, Co. Mayo]) : [The Society], 1981-. — v. : ill,facsims,maps ; 21cm
Unpriced B82-22671

941.7′4 — Galway *(County)*. Lough Corrib region, *1800-1980*

Semple, Maurice. By the Corribside / by Maurice Semple. — [Galway] ([Rock Lown, St. Mary's Park, Galway, Ireland]) : M. Semple, 1981. — 181p,7folded leaves of plates : ill,maps(some col.),facsims,plans,ports ; 25cm
Unpriced (pbk) B82-12943

941.8 — Church of Ireland. *United Dioceses of Meath and Kildare*. Parish churches, *to 1980*

Meath and Kildare : an historical guide / edited by John Paterson ; drawings by John Flinn. — Kingscourt : G. Corrigan, 1981. — 46p,[19]p of plates : ill ; 22cm
Bibliography: p44
ISBN 0-900346-46-9 (pbk) : £2.00 B82-14289

941.8′3 — Dublin *(County)*. Blackrock, *to ca 1900*

Mac Cóil, Liam. The book of Blackrock / by Liam Mac Cóil. — 2nd ed. — Blackrock : Carraig, 1981. — 155p : ill,2maps ; 21cm
Previous ed.: 1977. — Map (1 folded sheet) attached to inside cover. — Bibliography: p142-145. — Includes index
£4.00 (pbk) B82-10971

941.8′350821 — Dublin, *1913 — For schools*

[Divided city]. Dublin 1913 : a divided city / Curriculum Development Unit ; [researched and edited by Gary Granville]. — Dublin : O'Brien, 1978 (1982 [printing]). — 112p : ill,facsims,ports ; 22cm
Includes index
ISBN 0-86278-023-3 (pbk) : £3.25 B82-32397

941.8′350821 — Dublin. Social conditions, *1899-1916*

O'Brien, Joseph V.. "Dear dirty Dublin" : a city in distress, 1899-1916 / Joseph V. O'Brien. — Berkeley ; London : University of California Press, c1982. — xiv,338p : ill,1map ; 27cm
Map on lining paper. — Bibliography: p325-332. — Includes index
ISBN 0-520-03965-3 : £24.50 B82-40217

941.8′350821′0222 — Dublin, *1904 — Illustrations*

Faithful departed : the Dublin of James Joyce's Ulysses / recaptured from classic photographs and assembled by Kieran Hickey ; with an introductory essay by Des Hickey. — Swords : Ward River Press, 1982. — xxxi,73p : chiefly ill ; 27cm
Includes index
ISBN 0-907085-26-1 (pbk) : Unpriced
B82-40454

941.8′350821′0924 — Dublin. Social life, *1915-1930 — Childhood reminiscences*

Crosbie, Paddy. 'Your dinner's poured out!' boyhood in the twenties in a Dublin that has disappeared / Paddy Crosbie ; introduction by James Plunkett. — Dublin : O'Brien, 1981. — 224p : ill,2facsims,ports ; 23cm
Bibliography: p221. — Includes index
ISBN 0-905140-92-3 : Unpriced B82-10197

941.8′350822′0924 — Dublin. Social life, *1924-1939 — Personal observations*

O'Beirne, Michael. And the moon at night : a Dubliner's story / Michael O'Beirne. — Belfast : Blackstaff, c1981. — 200p ; 22cm
ISBN 0-85640-242-7 (pbk) : £3.95 B82-08128

941.8′38 — Dublin *(County).* **Dún Laoghaire,** *to 1980*

Pearson, Peter, *1955-.* Dun Laoghaire : Kingstown / Peter Pearson assisted by Anne Brady and Daniel Gillman. — Dublin : O'Brien, 1981. — 176p : ill,maps,facsims ; 26cm. — (Urban heritage series, ISSN 0332-1886 ; 2)
Bibliography: p172-173. — Includes index
ISBN 0-905140-83-4 : £12.00 : CIP rev. B81-12887

941.8′6 — Southern *Offaly (County), to 1915*

Gleeson, John. History of the Ely O'Carroll. — Kilkenny (St. Kieran St., Kilkenny, Ireland) : Roberts Books, Mar.1982. — 2v. [644]p
Originally published: Dublin : Gill, 1915
ISBN 0-907561-06-3 : CIP entry
Primary classification 941.9′2 B82-05792

941.8′85 — Wexford *(County).* **Courtown Harbour,** *to 1981*

Kinsella, Anna. The windswept shore : a history of the Courtown district / Anna Kinsella. — [Dublin] ([133, Silchester Park, Glenageary, Dublin]) : [A. Kinsella], c1982. — 163p : ill,1facsim,geneal.tables,2maps,1plan,2ports ; 21cm
Map attached inside back cover. — Includes index
Unpriced (pbk) B82-35537

941.8′9 — Kilkenny *(County).* **Callan. Social life,** *1827-1835 — Correspondence, diaries, etc.*

O'Sullivan, Humphrey, *1780-1838.* The diary of Humphrey O'Sullivan : 1827-1835 : a translation of Cín lae Amhlaoibh / by Tomás de Bhaldraithe. — Dublin : Mercier, c1979. — 139p : ill ; 19cm
Originally published: Dublin : An Clóchomhar Teoranta, 1970
ISBN 0-85342-588-4 (pbk) : £2.30 B82-22925

941.9′1 — Waterford *(County), to 1814 — Early works — Facsimiles*

Ryland, R. H.. The history, topography and antiquities of the county and city of Waterford. — Kilkenny (Freshwood, Kilkenny, Ireland) : Wellbrook Press, Sept.1982. — [420]p
Facsim of ed. published: London : Murray, 1814
ISBN 0-946198-00-4 : CIP entry
ISBN 0-946198-01-2 (limited ed.) : Unpriced B82-24352

941.9′2 — Tipperary *(County), to 1915*

Gleeson, John. History of the Ely O'Carroll. — Kilkenny (St. Kieran St., Kilkenny, Ireland) : Roberts Books, Mar.1982. — 2v. [644]p
Originally published: Dublin : Gill, 1915
ISBN 0-907561-06-3 : CIP entry
Also classified at 941.8′6 B82-05792

941.9′2081 — Ireland, *1800-1900 — Study regions: Tipperary (County)*

O'Shea, James. The priest, society and politics in nineteenth century Ireland. — Dublin : Wolfhound Press, Oct.1981. — [300]p
ISBN 0-905473-71-x : £12.00 : CIP entry B81-27477

941.9′3 — Clare *(County).* **Inishkillane. Social change**

Brody, Hugh. Inishkillane. — London : Norman & Hobhouse, Sept.1982. — [224]p
Originally published: London : Allen Lane, 1973
ISBN 0-906908-79-5 (pbk) : £3.95 : CIP entry B82-22000

941.9′3082 — Clare *(County).* **Social life,** *1930-1981 — Stories, anecdotes*

Armstrong, Jimmy. Long ago by Shannon side / [Jimmy Armstrong] ; [as told to] Edmund Lenihan. — Dublin : Mercier, c1982. — 127p ; 19cm
Includes index
ISBN 0-85342-671-6 (pbk) : £2.70 B82-29531

941.9′40824′05 — Limerick *(County) — Serials*

Limerick echo and Shannon news. — Vol.86, no.15 (Saturday Apr. 11 1981)-. — [Limerick] ([51 O'Connell St., Limerick]) : [Limerick Weekly Echo], 1981-. — v. : ill,ports ; 44cm
Weekly. — Continues: Limerick weekly echo and Shannon news
Unpriced B82-38517

941.9′6 — Kerry *(County).* **Blasket Islands. Social life,** *1904- ca 1930 — Personal observations*

O'Guiheen, Micheál. A pity youth does not last : reminiscences of the last of the Great Blasket Island's poets and storytellers / Micheál O'Guiheen ; translated from the Irish by Tim Enright. — Oxford : Oxford University Press, 1982. — 137p : ill,1map,3ports ; 20cm
Includes selections from Coinnle corra
ISBN 0-19-281320-x (pbk) : £2.50 : CIP rev. B82-03094

941.9′6 — Kerry *(County).* **Castleisland,** *to 1980*

O'Shea, Kieran. Castleisland : church and people / Kieran O'Shea. — Repr. with additions. — [Castleisland] ([College Rd, Castleisland, Co. Kerry]) : [K. O'Shea], 1982, c1981. — 88p : ill,coats of arms,facsims,2maps,ports ; 22cm
Previous ed.: 1981. — Map attached to inside cover
Unpriced (pbk) B82-36419

941.9′6 — Kerry *(County).* **Great Blasket Island. Social life,** *ca 1904-ca 1924 — Personal observations*

O'Sullivan, Maurice. Twenty years a-growing. — Oxford : Oxford University Press, Feb.1983. — [320]p
Translation of: Fiche blian ag fás
ISBN 0-19-281325-0 (pbk) : £2.95 : CIP entry B82-36590

942 — HISTORY. ENGLAND

942 — England, *1066-1485*

Saul, Nigel. The Batsford companion to medieval England. — London : Batsford, Nov.1982. — [272]p
ISBN 0-7134-1345-x : £14.95 : CIP entry B82-27966

942 — England, *1066-1977 — For schools*

Smith, Barry A.. History by questions / by Barry A. Smith ; cartoons from originals by Alexander Drew. — Thirsk : Crake Hill
Originally published: Helperby : Cundall Manor Publications, 1978
Normans and Plantagenets. — c1981. — 48p : ill ; 21cm
ISBN 0-907105-11-4 (pbk) : Unpriced B82-33566

942 — England. Churches. Archaeological investigation, *to 1980*

Rodwell, Warwick. The archaeology of the English church : the study of historic churches and churchyards / Warwick Rodwell. — London : Batsford, 1981. — 192p : ill,maps,plans,forms ; 26cm
Bibliography: p183-187. — Includes index
ISBN 0-7134-2590-3 : £14.95 B82-14090

942 — England. Hill figures

Marples, Morris. White horses and other hill figures / Morris Marples. — Gloucester : Alan Sutton, 1981. — 223p : ill,1map ; 22cm
Originally published: London : Country Life, 1949. — Includes bibliographies and index
ISBN 0-904387-59-3 (pbk) : £3.95 B82-25400

942 — England *— History — For schools*

Pictorial history. — Huddersfield : Schofield & Sims
Bk.4. — Rev. ed. / by J.E. Allen ; drawings by W.M. Ireland and Neville Swaine. — 1982. — 95p : ill(some col.),col.maps,ports(some col.),1geneal.table ; 25cm
Previous ed.: / by H.E. Hounsell and D.W. Airne, 1961
ISBN 0-7217-1602-4 (pbk) : £2.05 B82-24037

942 — England. Local history

Ravensdale, J. R.. History on your doorstep / by J.R. Ravensdale ; edited by Bryn Brooks. — London : British Broadcasting Corporation, 1982. — 152p : ill,maps,facsims,plans ; 23cm
Published in conjunction with the BBC Television series History on your doorstep, produced by Bryn Brooks and first transmitted on 2 January 1982. — Bibliography: p147-150. — Includes index
ISBN 0-563-16495-6 (cased) : Unpriced
ISBN 0-563-16464-6 (pbk) : £4.50 B82-08872

942 — England. Seaside resorts. Social life, *1750-1914*

Walton, John K.. The English seaside resort. — Leicester : Leicester University Press, Jan.1983. — [263]p
ISBN 0-7185-1217-0 : £25.00 : CIP entry B82-36338

942 — England. Seaside resorts. Social life, *to 1981 — For children*

Hudson, Kenneth. Waterside furniture / Kenneth Hudson. — London : Bodley Head, 1982. — 48p : ill ; 25cm
Includes index
ISBN 0-370-30393-8 : £3.95 : CIP rev.
Also classified at 620 B82-03837

942 — England, *to 1981*

Bryant, Arthur. Spirit of England. — London : Collins, Dec.1982. — [1v.]
ISBN 0-00-217084-1 : £6.95 : CIP entry B82-30342

942 — English civilization, *1066-1500*

Partridge, A. C.. A companion to Old and Middle English studies / A.C. Partridge. — London : Deutsch, 1982. — x,462p ; 22cm. — (The language library)
Bibliography: p439-452. — Includes index
ISBN 0-233-97411-3 (pbk) : £12.95 B82-37264

942 — English culture. Patronage by middle classes, *1300-1500 — Festschriften*

Profession, vocation, and culture in later medieval England : essays dedicated to the memory of A.R. Myers / edited by Cecil H. Clough. — Liverpool : Liverpool University Press, 1982. — xi,262p(2 folded),[1]leaf of plates : ill,1geneal.table,1port ; 24cm
Bibliography: p245-248. — Includes index
ISBN 0-85323-324-1 : £18.50 : CIP rev. B81-31512

942′.004395′074 — England. Viking antiquities, *793-1035 — Catalogues*

The Vikings in England : and in their Danish homeland. — London : Anglo-Danish Viking Project, c1981. — 192p : ill(some col.),maps (some col.) ; 25cm
Published to accompany an exhibition held at the Danish National Museum, Brede-Copenhagen, April 11-August 16 1981 ; The Prehistoric Museum, Moesgård, Arhus, September 5-December 31 1981 ; The Yorkshire Museum, York, April 3-September 30 1982. — Bibliography: p187-188. — Includes index
ISBN 0-9507432-0-8 (pbk) : Unpriced B82-27674

942′.0072024 — England. Historiography. Paris, Matthew *— Critical studies*

Vaughan, Richard, *1927-.* Matthew Paris / Richard Vaughan. — Reissued with supplementary bibliography. — Cambridge : Cambridge University Press, 1958 (1979 [printing]). — xii,287p,[22]p of plates : ill,facsims ; 23cm. — (Cambridge studies in medieval life and thought. 2nd series ; v.6)
Bibliography: p267-276. — Includes index
ISBN 0-521-22612-0 (cased) : £17.50
ISBN 0-521-29575-0 (pbk) : Unpriced B82-04527

942′.009′732 — England. Towns, *1485-1714 — For children*

Jones, Madeline. Tudor and Stuart towns / Madeline Jones. — London : Batsford, 1982. — 48p : ill,2maps,1facsim ; 26cm. — (Finding out about)
Bibliography: p46. — Includes index
ISBN 0-7134-4293-x : £4.50 B82-41038

942′.009′732 — England. Towns, *1500-1800*

Country towns in pre-industrial England / edited by Peter Clark. — [Leicester] : Leicester University Press, 1981. — xiii,258p : ill,maps,plans ; 24cm. — (Themes in urban history)
Includes bibliographies and index
ISBN 0-7185-1175-1 : £14.00 : CIP rev. B81-23850

942'.009'732 — England. Towns, *1700-1800*
Corfield, P. J.. The impact of English towns 1700-1800 / P.J. Corfield. — Oxford : Oxford University Press, 1982. — vi,206p : ill,maps ; 21cm. — (OPUS)
Bibliography: p193-198. — Includes index
ISBN 0-19-215830-9 (cased) : Unpriced : CIP rev.
ISBN 0-19-289093-x (pbk) : £3.95 B82-04156

942'.009'732 — England. Towns, *1837-1901 — For children*
Rawcliffe, Michael. Victorian towns / Michael Rawcliffe. — London : Batsford, 1982. — 48p : ill,facsims,maps ; 26cm. — (Finding out about)
Bibliography: p47. — Includes index
ISBN 0-7134-4289-1 : £4.50 B82-41039

942'.009'732 — England. Towns. Social life, *400-1500*
Reynolds, Susan. An introduction to the history of English medieval towns / Susan Reynolds. — Oxford : Clarendon Press, 1977 (1982 [printing]). — xiii,234p : maps ; 22cm
Includes index
ISBN 0-19-822697-7 (pbk) : £5.95 : CIP rev. B82-12686

942'.009'734 — England. Countryside — *Illustrations*
Mannes-Abbott, Sheila. Four seasons : the life of the English countryside / the pictures of Sheila Mannes-Abbott ; with text by Phil Drabble. — London : Eyre Methuen, 1981. — [28]p : col.ill ; 32cm
Ill on lining papers
ISBN 0-413-39920-6 : £4.95 : CIP rev. B81-27933

942'.009'734 — England. Deserted villages
Rowley, Trevor. Deserted villages / Trevor Rowley and John Wood. — Princes Risborough : Shire, 1982. — 72p : ill,facsims,maps,plans ; 21cm. — (Shire archaeology)
Bibliography: p64-65. — Includes index
ISBN 0-85263-593-1 (pbk) : £1.95 B82-31002

942'.009'734 — England. Rural regions. Social change, *1735-1910*
Sturgess, R. W.. The rural revolution in an English village / Roy Sturgess. — Cambridge : Cambridge University Press, 1981. — 48p : ill,facsims,maps,plans,ports ; 21x22cm. — (Cambridge introduction to the history of mankind. Topic book)
ISBN 0-521-22800-x (pbk) : £1.95 : CIP rev. B81-33617

942'.009'734 — England. Rural regions. Social life, *1850-1914 — Readings from contemporary sources*
Seasons of change. — London : Allen & Unwin, Nov.1982. — [192]p
ISBN 0-04-630009-0 : £10.95 : CIP entry B82-27822

942'.009'734 — England. Rural regions. Social life, *1900-1980*
Cullingford, Ada. Happenings and poems in country life / Ada Cullingford. — Ilfracombe : Stockwell, 1982. — 116p ; 19cm
ISBN 0-7223-1552-x : £4.35 B82-31758

Watkins, Michael. The English : the countryside and its people / Michael Watkins ; photographs by Peter Pugh-Cook. — London : Elm Tree, 1981. — 254p : ill(some col.),ports (some col.) ; 25cm
ISBN 0-241-10547-1 : £9.95 B82-17636

942.01 — Anglo-Saxon culture, *to 1066*
The **Anglo-Saxons**. — Oxford : Phaidon, Oct.1981. — [272]p
ISBN 0-7148-2149-7 : £19.50 : CIP entry B81-30468

942.01'05 — England, *450-1066 — Serials*
Anglo-Saxon England. — 10. — Cambridge : Cambridge University Press, Feb.1982. — [324]p
ISBN 0-521-24177-4 : £25.00 : CIP entry B81-40272

942.02 — England, *1066-1154*
Chambers, James. The Norman kings / James Chambers ; introduction by Antonia Fraser. — London : Weidenfeld and Nicolson, c1981. — 224p : ill,2maps,facsims,ports(some col.),1geneal.table ; 26cm. — ([Kings and queens of England])
Bibliography: p218-220. — Includes index
ISBN 0-297-77964-8 : £7.50 B82-02289

942.02 — England, *1066-ca 1200 — Conference proceedings*
Battle Conference on Anglo-Norman Studies *(4th : 1981)*. Proceedings of the Battle Conference on Anglo Norman Studies IV 1981 / edited by R. Allen Brown. — Woodbridge : Boydell, 1982. — 237p : ill,facsims,plans ; 25cm
Includes index
ISBN 0-85115-161-2 : £25.00 : CIP rev. B82-07614

942.02'1 — England. Norman Conquest
Loyn, H. R.. The Norman Conquest. — 3rd ed. — London : Hutchinson Education, Oct.1982. — [224]p
Previous ed.: 1967
ISBN 0-09-149530-x (cased) : £10.00 : CIP entry
ISBN 0-09-149531-8 (pbk) : £4.95 B82-24967

942.02'1'0924 — England. Norman Conquest. Resistance by Saxons. Role of Hereward, *the Wake*
Bevis, Trevor A.. Hereward the siege of the Isle of Ely and involvement of Peterborough and Ely monasteries ; together with De gestis Herewardi Saxonis (The exploits of Hereward the Saxon) / researched and compiled in the 12th century by monastery historians ; revised and rewritten in modern English by Trevor A. Bevis. — March : Westrydale Press, c1982. — 38p : ill ; 21cm
Hereward originally published: 1979
ISBN 0-901680-16-8 (pbk) : £1.75 B82-28951

942.03 — England. Political events, *1272-1377*
Prestwich, Michael. The three Edwards : war and state in England 1272-1377 / Michael Prestwich. — London : Methuen, 1981, c1980. — 336p,[16]p of plates : ill,maps,facsims,ports,geneal.tables ; 22cm
Originally published: London : Weidenfeld and Nicolson, 1980. — Includes bibliographies and index
ISBN 0-416-30450-8 (pbk) : £5.95 : CIP rev. B81-31713

942.03 — England. Relations with Papacy, *1100-1300*
Cheney, C. R.. The papacy and England 12th-14th centuries : historical and legal studies / C.R. Cheney. — London : Variorum Reprints, 1982. — 346p in various pagings : ill,1facsim ; 24cm. — (Collected studies series ; CS154)
Includes Latin texts. — Facsimile reprints. — Includes index
ISBN 0-86078-099-6 : Unpriced : CIP rev.
Also classified at 262'.13 B82-01571

942.03'1'0924 — England. Becket, Thomas, *Saint — Biographies*
Harvey, Margaret, *1941-*. St. Thomas of Canterbury / Margaret Harvey. — London : Catholic Truth Society, 1981. — 13p ; 19cm. — (B537)
ISBN 0-85183-441-8 (pbk) : £0.30 B82-06354

942.03'3 — England. Magna Carta, *1215*
British Library. Magna Carta. — London : British Library Reference Division Publications, Sept.1982. — [40]p
Originally published: London : British Museum, 1963
ISBN 0-7123-0014-7 (pbk) : £1.95 : CIP entry B82-20026

942.03'8 — England, *1377-1399*
Senior, Michael. The life and times of Richard II / Michael Senior ; introduction by Antonia Fraser. — London : Weidenfeld and Nicolson, 1981. — 223p : ill,facsims,geneal.tables,maps,ports(some col.) ; 26cm
Ill on lining papers. — Bibliography: p219. — Includes index
ISBN 0-297-77975-3 : £7.50 B82-36492

942.03'8 — England. Peasants' Revolt
Jones, Leslie S. A.. The Peoples Uprising 1381 / Leslie S.A. Jones. — London (Limehouse Town Hall, E14) : Museum of Labour History, 1981. — 20p ; 21cm
Cover title. — Bibliography: p20
Unpriced (pbk) B82-12747

942.03'8'0202 — England, *1381-1394 — Chronologies — Early works*
[The Westminster chronicle. *English & Latin*]. The Westminster chronicle : 1381-1394 / edited and translated by the late L.C. Hector and Barbara F. Harvey. — Oxford : Clarendon, 1982. — lxxvii,563p,[1]leaf of plates : 1facsim ; 22cm. — (Oxford medieval texts)
Parallel Latin text and English translation. — Includes index
ISBN 0-19-822255-6 : £48.00 : CIP rev. B81-30324

942.04 — England, *1399-1485*
Patronage, the Crown and the provinces : in later medieval England / edited by Ralph A. Griffiths. — Gloucester : Sutton, 1981. — 190p : 1map ; 23cm
Includes index
ISBN 0-904387-45-3 : £7.95 : CIP rev. B80-32692

942.04 — England, *1400-1500*
Armstrong, C. A. J.. England, France and Burgundy in the fifteenth century. — London : Hambledon, Oct.1982. — [450]p. — (History series ; 16)
ISBN 0-907628-13-3 : £24.00 : CIP entry
Primary classification 944'.4026 B82-25743

McFarlane, K. B.. England in the fifteenth century. — London (35 Gloucester Ave., NW1 7AX) : Hambledon Press, Oct.1981. — [320]p. — (History series ; 5)
ISBN 0-9506882-5-8 : £15.00 : CIP entry B81-27367

942.04 — England, *1450-1509*
Lander, J. R.. Government and community : England 1450-1509 / J.R. Lander. — London : Edward Arnold, 1980. — vii,406p : 1geneal.table ; 24cm. — (The New history of England ; 1)
Bibliography: p370-386. — Includes index
ISBN 0-7131-6151-5 (cased) : £12.95 : CIP rev.
ISBN 0-7131-6152-3 (pbk) : £5.95 B79-30447

942.04 — Wars of the Roses
Gillingham, John. The Wars of the Roses : peace and conflict in fifteenth-century England / John Gillingham. — London : Weidenfeld and Nicolson, c1981. — xv,274p,[16]p of plates : ill,1facsim,plans,ports,1geneal.table ; 24cm
Bibliography: p258-265. — Includes index
ISBN 0-297-77630-4 : £12.50 B82-25819

942.04'092'4 — England. Lovel, Francis Lovel, *Viscount — Biographies*
Robottam, J.. The life and times of Francis Lovel / [J. Robottam, P. Workman, R. Carty]. — Warley (124, Lewisham Rd., Smethwick, Warley, West Midlands) : Richard III Society West Midlands Branch, 1982. — 24p : ill,1map,1coat of arms ; 21cm
Unpriced (pbk) B82-28988

942.04'4'0924 — England. Edward IV, *King of England — Biographies*
Falkus, Gila. The life and times of Edward IV / Gila Falkus ; introduction by Antonia Fraser. — London : Weidenfeld and Nicolson, 1981. — 224p : ill(some col.),facsims,ports(some col.),3geneal.tables ; 26cm
Ill on lining papers. — Bibliography: p217. — Includes index
ISBN 0-297-78009-3 : £7.50 B82-04230

942.04'6'0924 — England. Richard III, *King of England*
Ross, Charles, *1924-*. Richard III / Charles Ross. — London : Eyre Methuen, 1981. — liii,265p,[16]p of plates : ill,maps,facsims,ports,geneal.table ; 25cm
Bibliography: p243-252. — Includes index
ISBN 0-413-29530-3 : £9.95 : CIP rev. B81-28833

942.04'6'0924 — England. Richard III, *King of England — Biographies — Early works*

Buck, *Sir* **George**. The history of King Richard. — Gloucester : Alan Sutton, July 1982. — [512]p
Text reconstructed from the original MS. of 1619
ISBN 0-86299-008-4 (pbk) : £16.00 : CIP entry
B82-19266

942.05 — England, *1485-1603*

The **Tudor** constitution. — 2nd ed. — Cambridge : Cambridge University Press, Aug.1982. — [514]p
Previous ed.: 1960
ISBN 0-521-24506-0 (cased) : £30.00 : CIP entry
ISBN 0-521-28757-x (pbk) : £9.95 B82-19258

Williams, Penry. The Tudor regime / by Penry Williams. — Oxford : Clarendon, 1979 (1981 [printing]). — xii,486p ; 22cm
Includes index
ISBN 0-19-822678-0 (pbk) : £6.95 B82-38766

942.05 — England. Buildings of historical importance, *1485-1603*

Helm, P. J.. Exploring Tudor England / P.J. Helm. — London : Hale, 1981. — 192p,[16]p of plates : ill,ports ; 23cm
Bibliography: p179-180. — Includes index
ISBN 0-7091-9461-7 : £8.95 B82-09127

942.05'2'0924 — England. More, *Sir* **Thomas,** *Saint — Biographies*

Chambers, R. W.. Thomas More / by R.W. Chambers. — Brighton : Harvester, 1982, c1981. — 416p ; 21cm
Originally published: London : Cape, 1935. — Bibliography: p403-404. — Includes index
ISBN 0-7108-0337-0 (pbk) : £6.95 B82-35562

942.05'2'0924 — England. More, *Sir* **Thomas,** *Saint — Marxist viewpoints*

Fox, Alistair. Thomas More : history and providence. — Oxford : Blackwell, Sept.1982. — [320]p
ISBN 0-631-13094-2 : £17.50 : CIP entry
B82-20284

942.05'3'0924 — England. Edward VI, *King of England — Biographies*

Chapman, Hester W.. The last Tudor King. — Bath : Chivers, Sept.1982. — [312]p. — (A New Portway book)
Originally published: London : Cape, 1958
ISBN 0-86220-507-7 : £5.95 : CIP entry
B82-21994

942.05'5 — England. Political events. Attitudes of Catholics, *1558-1603*

Holmes, P. J. (Peter John), *1949-*. Resistance and compromise : the political thought of the Elizabethan Catholics / Peter Holmes. — Cambridge : Cambridge University Press, 1982. — viii,279p ; 23cm. — (Cambridge studies in the history and theory of politics)
Bibliography: p262-270. — Includes index
ISBN 0-521-24343-2 : £22.50 : CIP rev.
B82-12008

942.05'5 — England. Social life, *1558-1603*

Plowden, Alison. Elizabethan England : life in an age of adventure / Alison Plowden. — London : Reader's Digest, c1982. — 320p : ill(some col.),facsims,col.maps,ports(some col.) ; 26cm. — (Life in Britain)
Map on lining paper. — Includes index
ISBN 0-340-23464-4 : £7.95 B82-39006

942.05'5 — England. War with Spain, *1588.* **Spanish Armada**

The **Great** enterprise. — London : Bell & Hyman, Mar.1982. — [192]p
Originally published: London : Folio Society, 1978
ISBN 0-7135-1309-8 : £8.00 : CIP entry
B82-01215

942.05'5 — England. War with Spain, *1588.* **Spanish Armada** — *Correspondence, diaries, etc.*

State papers relating to the defeat of the Spanish Armada, anno 1588 / edited by John Knox Laughton. — 2nd ed. — Havant : Mason for the Navy Records Society
Vol.1. — 1981. — lxxxiv,365p : 1map ; 25cm. — (Publications of the Navy Records Society ; v.1)
Facsim. of: 1st ed. 1895
ISBN 0-85937-264-2 : Unpriced : CIP rev.
B81-26685

State papers relating to the defeat of the Spanish Armada, anno 1588 / edited by John Knox Laughton. — 2nd ed. — Havant : Mason for the Navy Records Society
Vol.2. — 1981. — 418p ; 25cm. — (Publications of the Navy Records Society ; v.2)
Facsim of: 1st ed. 1900. — Includes index
ISBN 0-85937-265-0 : Unpriced : CIP rev.
B81-26696

942.05'5'0922 — England. Dane, Margaret & Dane William — *Biographies*

Ormerod, S. C. L.. In search of Margaret and William Dane / by S.C.L. Ormerod. — [Enfield] ([Parsonage La., Enfield, Middx]) : [Margaret Dane School], [1981?]. — 34p : ill,1port,1geneal.table
£0.35 (pbk) B82-10986

942.05'5'0924 — England. Cork, Richard Boyle, *Earl of — Biographies*

Canny, Nicholas P.. The upstart Earl : a study of the social and mental world of Richard Boyle first Earl of Cork 1566-1643 / Nicholas Canny. — Cambridge : Cambridge University Press, 1982. — xii,211p ; 23cm
Includes index
ISBN 0-521-24416-1 : £18.50 : CIP rev.
B82-25491

942.05'5'0924 — England. Unton, *Sir* **Henry** — *Biographies*

Cox, Angela, *1945-*. Sir Henry Unton : Elizabethan gentleman / Angela Cox. — Cambridge : Cambridge University Press, 1982. — 32p : ill,ports,2geneal.tables ; 20x21cm. — (Cambridge introduction to the history of mankind. Topic book)
ISBN 0-521-22549-3 (pbk) : £1.95 : CIP rev.
B81-33883

942.05'5'0924 — England. Willoughby de Eresby, Peregrine Bertie, *Baron — Biographies*

Lupton, Lewis. Courage / Lewis Lupton. — London (2 Milnthorpe Rd., W4 3DX) : Olive Tree, 1978. — 192p : ill,maps ; 23cm. — (A History of the Geneva Bible ; v.10)
Ill on lining papers
£9.24 (£6.77 to subscribers) B82-11645

942.06 — England, *1600-1700 — Festschriften*

Puritans and revolutionaries : essays in seventeenth-century history presented to Christopher Hill / edited by Donald Pennington and Keith Thomas. — Oxford : Clarendon Press, 1978 (1982 [printing]). — xii,419p,[1]leaf of plates : 1 port ; 20cm
Bibliography: p382-402. — Includes index
ISBN 0-19-822686-1 (pbk) : £9.95 : CIP rev.
B82-06024

942.06 — England, *1618-1689*

Seventeenth-century England : a changing culture, 1618-1689. — Milton Keynes : Open University Press. — (Arts : a second level course)
At head of title: The Open University
[Block 5]: Political ideas / prepared for the course team by Dianė Collinson ... [et al.]. — 1981. — 68p : ports ; 30cm. — (A203 ; block 5)
Includes bibliographies
ISBN 0-335-11039-8 (pbk) : Unpriced
B82-04962

Seventeenth-century England : changing culture, 1618-1689. — Milton Keynes : Open University Press. — (Arts : a second level course)
At head of title: The Open University
[Block 7] : Milton and Marvell / prepared for the course team by Joan Bellamy ... [et al.]. — 1981. — 82p : ill,2facsims ; 30cm. — (A203 ; block 9)
Bibliography: p73
ISBN 0-335-11041-x (pbk) : Unpriced
B82-04964

Seventeenth-century England : a changing culture, 1618-1689. — Milton Keynes : Open University Press. — (Arts : a second level course)
At head of title: The Open University
[Block 9]: Restoration culture / prepared for the course team by Tim Benton ... [et al.]. — 1981. — 72p : ill,ports ; 30cm. — (A203 ; block 9)
Includes bibliographies
ISBN 0-335-11043-6 (pbk) : Unpriced
B82-04963

942.06 — English civilization, *1600-1700*

Seventeenth-century England : a changing culture. — London : Ward Lock Educational in association with the Open University Press
Vol.1: Primary sources / edited by Ann Hughes at the Open University. — 1980. — xiv,401p ; 25cm
Includes index
ISBN 0-7062-4090-1 (cased) : £10.00
ISBN 0-7062-4088-x (pbk) : £4.95 B82-41042

Seventeenth-century England : a changing culture. — London : Ward Lock Educational in association with the Open University Press
Vol.2: Modern studies / edited by W.R. Owens at the Open University. — 1980. — iv,337p ; 25cm
Includes index
ISBN 0-7062-4091-x (cased) : £8.50
ISBN 0-7062-4089-8 (pbk) : £4.50 B82-41043

942.06'092'4 — England. Evelyn, John, *1620-1706 — Correspondence, diaries, etc.*

Evelyn, John, *1620-1706*. [The diary of John Evelyn. Selections]. The diary of John Evelyn. — Oxford : Oxford University Press, Feb.1983. — [360]p
ISBN 0-19-251011-8 : £12.50 : CIP entry
B82-36589

942.06'2 — English Civil War

Roots, Ivan. The Great Rebellion 1642-1660 / Ivan Roots. — London : Batsford, 1966 (1979 [printing]). — x,326p ; 23cm
Bibliography: p304-314. — Includes index
ISBN 0-7134-1353-0 (cased) : Unpriced
ISBN 0-7134-1399-9 (pbk) : £6.50 B82-07318

942.06'2 — English Civil War. Army operations by England and Wales. *Army, 1642-1646*

Hutton, Ronald. The Royalist war effort 1642-1646 / Ronald Hutton. — London : Longman, 1981. — xvi,271p ; 23cm
Bibliography: p241-264. — Includes index
ISBN 0-582-50301-9 : £12.00 : CIP rev.
B81-27978

942.06'3 — England, *1649-1660*

Barnard, T. C.. The English Republic 1649-1660 / Toby Barnard. — Harlow : Longman, 1982. — vii,111p ; 20cm. — (Seminar studies in history)
Bibliography: p99-107. — Includes index
ISBN 0-582-35231-2 (pbk) : £1.80 B82-34752

Woolrych, Austin. Commonwealth to Protectorate / by Austin Woolrych. — Oxford : Clarendon, 1982. — xii,446p : 1map ; 23cm
Bibliography: pxi-xii. — Includes index
ISBN 0-19-822659-4 : £22.50 : CIP rev.
B82-01083

942.06′4′0924 — Cambridgeshire. Huntingdon. Museums: Cromwell Museum. Exhibits — *Catalogues*
Cromwell Museum. Guide to the Cromwell Museum, Huntingdon / [edited by : Mac Dowdy] ; [artwork by : Mac Dowdy]. — 2nd ed. — Ely : EARO, for the Cromwell Museum Management Committee, 1981. — 40p : ill,2plans,1ports ; 21cm
Previous ed.: 1975
ISBN 0-904463-80-x (pbk) : Unpriced B82-38940

942.06′6′0922 — England. Charles II, *King of England.* **Mistresses**
Masters, Brian. The mistresses of Charles II / Brian Masters. — London : Blond & Briggs, 1979. — 192p,[16]p of plates : ill,ports
Includes index
ISBN 0-85634-099-5 : £6.95 B82-14416

942.06′6′0924 — England. Chandos, Cassandra Brydges, *Duchess of — Biographies*
Johnson, Joan, *1915-*. Excellent Cassandra : the life and times of the Duchess of Chandos / Joan Johnson. — Gloucester : Alan Sutton, 1981. — 160p : ill,maps,facsims,ports,1geneal.table ; 23cm
Bibliography: p155-156. — Includes index
ISBN 0-904387-76-3 : £7.95 : CIP rev. B81-20571

942.06′6′0924 — England. Charles II, *King of England — Biographies*
Fraser, Antonia. King Charles II / Antonia Fraser. — London : Macdonald Futura, 1980, c1979. — xi,524p,[16]p of plates : ill,ports ; 20cm. — (A Contract book)
Originally published: London : Weidenfeld & Nicolson, 1979. — Bibliography: p486-499. — Includes index
ISBN 0-7088-1933-8 (pbk) : £3.50 B82-04255

942.06′6′0924 — England. Henrietta, *duchesse d'Orléans — Biographies*
Bevan, Bryan. Charles II's Minette : Princess Henriette-Anne, Duchess of Orleans / Bryan Bevan. — London : Ascent, 1979. — ix,206p,[12]p of plates : ports ; 23cm
Bibliography: p197-200. — Includes index
ISBN 0-906407-03-6 : £6.95 B82-19468

942.06′6′0924 — England. Pepys, Samuel — *Correspondence, diaries, etc.*
Pepys, Samuel. [Diary. Selections]. The illustrated Pepys. — London : Bell & Hyman, Mar.1982. — [338]p
Originally published: 1978
ISBN 0-7135-1328-4 (pbk) : £5.95 : CIP entry B82-03117

Pepys, Samuel. The diary of Samuel Pepys. — London : Bell and Hyman
Vol.10: Companion. — Feb.1983. — [576]p
ISBN 0-7135-1993-2 : £18.50 : CIP entry B82-39427

Pepys, Samuel. The diary of Samuel Pepys. — London : Bell and Hyman
Vol.11: Index. — Feb.1983. — [384]p
ISBN 0-7135-1994-0 : £19.50 : CIP entry B82-39428

942.06′7′0924 — England. Stuart, Louise Marie — *Biographies*
Cole, Susan. Princess over the water : a memoir of Louise Marie Stuart (1692-1712) / by Susan Cole. — London (10, Uphill Grove, Mill Hill, NW7 4NJ) : Royal Stuart Society, 1981. — 20p ; 21cm. — (Royal Stuart papers, ISSN 0307-997x ; 18)
Bibliography: p21
Unpriced (pbk) B82-09811

942.07 — England, *1680-1730*
Holmes, Geoffrey. Augustan England. — London : Allen and Unwin, Oct.1982. — [352]p
ISBN 0-04-942178-6 : £18.50 : CIP entry B82-23102

942.07 — England. Social conditions, *1700-1800*
Porter, Roy, *1946-*. English society in the eighteenth century / Roy Porter. — Harmondsworth : Penguin, 1982. — 424p ; 19cm. — (The Pelican social history of Britain)
Bibliography: p393-403. — Includes index
ISBN 0-14-022099-2 (pbk) : £2.95 B82-23932

Porter, Roy, *1946-*. English society in the eighteenth century / Roy Porter. — London : Allen Lane, 1982. — 424p ; 23cm. — (The Pelican social history of Britain)
Bibliography: p393-403. — Includes index
ISBN 0-7139-1417-3 : £12.50 B82-23929

942.07′07′8 — Secondary schools. Curriculum subjects: England, *1700-1900.* **Teaching aids: Role-playing exercises —** *Collections*
Wood, Tim. Playback : history roleplays / Tim Wood. — London : Edward Arnold, 1982. — 96p : ill,plans ; 22cm
ISBN 0-7131-0592-5 (pbk) : £1.75 : CIP rev. B82-04477

942.07′3′0924 — England. Pentrich Rising. Role of Brandreth, Jeremiah
Young, John, *19---*. Jeremiah Brandreth : the Nottingham captain and the Derbyshire rising / [text and photography John Young] ; [concept and songs Keith Jones and John Young]. — [Belper] ([23 Mill Lane, Belper, Derbyshire, DE5 1LG]) : [Liberty Tree Projects], c1981. — 37p : ill,music ; 26cm
Cover title
£1.00 (pbk) B82-10904

942.081 — England. Intellectual life, *1830-1900*
Heyck, Thomas William. The transformation of intellectual life in Victorian England / T.W. Heyck. — London : Croom Helm, c1982. — 262p ; 23cm. — (Croom Helm studies in society and history)
Bibliography: p240-254. — Includes index
ISBN 0-7099-1206-4 : £14.50 : CIP rev. B81-30536

942.081 — England. Intellectual life. Influence of Hulme, T. E., *1883-1917*
Roberts, Michael. T.E. Hulme. — Manchester : Carcanet Press, June 1982. — [320]p
Originally published: London : Faber, 1938
ISBN 0-85635-411-2 : £6.95 : CIP entry B82-10220

942.081′0924 — England. Countryside, *ca 1860-ca 1880 — Personal observations*
Jefferies, Richard. The open air. — London : Wildwood House, Aug.1981. — [288]p
ISBN 0-7045-0422-7 (pbk) : £2.95 : CIP entry B81-25125

942.081′092′4 — England. Countryside, *ca 1880 — Personal observations*
Jefferies, Richard. The life of the fields. — Oxford : Oxford University Press, Feb.1983. — [228]p. — (Oxford paperbacks)
Originally published: London : Chatto & Windus, 1884
ISBN 0-19-281358-7 (pbk) : £2.95 : CIP entry B82-36586

942.081′092′4 — England. Grove, Agnes Geraldine, *Lady — Biographies*
Hawkins, Desmond. Concerning Agnes : Thomas Hardy's 'Good little pupil' / Desmond Hawkins. — Gloucester : A. Sutton, 1982. — xi,148p,[8]p of plates : ill,1facsim,1map,ports ; 23cm
Includes index
ISBN 0-904387-97-6 : £7.95 : CIP rev. B82-11507

942.081′092′4 — England. Liddell, Alice — *Biographies*
Gordon, Colin, *1944-*. Beyond the looking glass. — London : Hodder and Stoughton, Sept.1982. — [256]p
ISBN 0-340-26378-4 : £12.50 : CIP entry B82-18805

942.081′092′4 — England. Liddell, Lorina. Interpersonal relationships with Carroll, Lewis
Shaberman, R. B.. Lewis Carroll and Mrs Liddell : a study of their relationship based on new material together with a review of the unpublished diaries of Lewis Carroll / R.B. Shaberman. — London : [R.B. Shaberman], 1982. — 16p ; 21cm
Limited ed. of 300 copies
Unpriced (pbk)
Primary classification 828′.809 B82-16968

942.081′092′4 — England. Morris, Jane, *b.1840.* **Interpersonal relationships with Blunt, Wilfrid Scawen**
Faulkner, Peter. Wilfrid Scawen Blunt and the Morrises : the first annual Kelmscott Lecture of the William Morris Society given at the Society of Antiquaries on Tuesday 30th September 1980 / by Peter Faulkner. — London : William Morris Society, 1981. — 45p ; 22cm
ISBN 0-903283-01-8 (pbk) : £2.50
Primary classification 821′.8 B82-06596

942.081′092′4 — England. Oliphant, Laurence — *Biographies*
Taylor, Anne. Laurence Oliphant : 1829-1888 / Anne Taylor. — Oxford : Oxford University Press, 1982. — vii,306p,[8]p of plates : ill,ports ; 23cm
Bibliography: p287-291. — Includes index
ISBN 0-19-812676-x : £12.50 : CIP rev. B82-10443

942.081′092′4 — England. Ridley, John — *Biographies*
Sergeant, Xher John. To whom in part we owe our daily bread : the life of John Ridley / by Xher John Sergeant. — [Easington] ([Homelea, Durham Rd., Easington, Peterlee, Durham]) : C.J. Sergeant, c1981. — 20p : ill ; 21cm
£1.14 (pbk) B82-06889

942.081′092′4 — England. Riley, Athelstan — *Correspondence, diaries, etc.*
Park, Jo. Athelstan Riley : patron of St. Petroc Minor, Little Petherick. — Truro : [Jo Park], c1982. — v,59p,[1]p leaf of plates : 2ill,1facsims,2ports ; 21cm
Compiled and written by Jo Park
ISBN 0-9508074-0-0 (pbk) : £1.65 B82-35082

942.082 — England. Social conditions, *1880-1980*
Perkin, Harold. Professionalism, property and English society since 1880 / by Harold Perkin. — [Reading] : University of Reading, 1981. — 24p ; 23cm. — (The Stenton lecture)
ISBN 0-7049-0211-7 (pbk) : £1.00 B82-17799

942.082′092′2 — England. Butler, Daisy. Family & friends — *Personal observations*
Bulter, Daisy. Relatively speaking / by Daisy Butler. — [Cambridge] ([3, Long Road, Cambridge CB2 2PP]) : [D. Butler], c1981. — [48]p : ill,facsims,ports,1geneal.table ; 22cm
Unpriced (pbk) B82-01936

942.082′092′2 — England. Social life, *1901-1910 — Childhood reminiscences — Collections*
Edwardian childhoods / [compiled by] Thea Thompson. — London : Routledge & Kegan Paul, 1981 (1982 [printing]). — xiii,232p,[32]p of plates : ill,ports ; 24cm
ISBN 0-7100-9335-7 (pbk) : £4.95 B82-39668

942.082′092′4 — England. Best, Ann — *Biographies*
Best, Ann. No limit to my sight / Ann Best. — Bognor Regis : New Horizon, c1982. — 327p ; 19cm
ISBN 0-86116-641-8 : £6.75 B82-22234

942.082′092′4 — England. Bratley, Bertha Harlington — *Biographies*
Bratley, Bertha Harlington. Arthritic, scholastic and exotic / Bertha Harlington Bratley. — Ilfracombe : Stockwell, 1982. — 125p ; 19cm
ISBN 0-7223-1576-7 : £4.35 B82-31757

942.082′092′4 — England. Bruce, Nina — *Biographies*
Bruce, Nina. Live a little, die a little / Nina Bruce. — Bognor Regis : New Horizon, c1982. — 95p ; 21cm
ISBN 0-86116-553-5 : £3.75 B82-17485

942.082′092′4 — England. Malcolm, Gwen — *Biographies*
Malcolm, Gwen. Gwen Malcolm's memories : 80 years in Somerset, Wiltshire and Wimbledon. — [London] ([30A Parkside, SW19 5NB]) : [G. Malcolm], [1982?]. — 48p : ill,ports ; 21cm
Unpriced (pbk) B82-25794

942.082′092′4 — England. Morris, Mary F. — *Biographies*

Morris, Mary F. "Round and roundabout" / by Mary F. Morris (Mary Bune). — [Llandysul] ([Gomer Press, Llandysul, Dyfed SA44 4BQ]) : [J.D. Lewis & Sons], 1982. — 188p : 1ill ; 22cm
Unpriced B82-19621

942.082′092′4 — England. Morton, John C. — *Biographies*

Morton, John C. With the tide, or, The tale of a lifetime / John C. Morton. — Bognor Regis : New Horizon, c1982. — 257p : ill ; 22cm
ISBN 0-86116-385-0 : £5.75 B82-14753

942.082′092′4 — England. Moss, Les — *Biographies*

Moss, Les. Live and learn : a life and struggle for progress / by Les Moss. — Brighton (71 Richmond St., Brighton) : QueenSpark, 1979. — 137p : ill,facsims,ports ; 21cm. — (QueenSpark book ; 7)
£0.60 (pbk) B82-36038

942.082′092′4 — England. Nickols, Nick — *Biographies*

Nickols, Nick. Fifty years on the road / Nick Nickols. — Bognor Regis : New Horizon, c1982. — 277p ; 21cm
ISBN 0-86116-550-0 : £5.75 B82-10142

942.082′092′4 — England. Westwater, T. A. — *Biographies*

Westwater, T. A. The early life of T.A. Westwater : railway signalman, trade unionist and town councillor in County Durham / T.A. Westwater. — Oxford (Ruskin College, Oxford OX1 2HE) : Ruskin College Library, 1979. — 64p ; 26cm. — (Ruskin College Library occasional publication ; no.1)
£1.50 (pbk) B82-07350

942.082′092′4 — England. Zscherpel, Marion — *Biographies*

Zscherpel, Marion. True life story / Marion Zscherpel. — Bognor Regis : New Horizon, c1982. — 76p ; 21cm
ISBN 0-86116-197-1 : £3.50 B82-11257

942.083′092′4 — England. Smiley, Lavinia, *1919-1931 — Biographies*

Smiley, Lavinia. A nice clean plate : recollections 1919-1931 / Lavinia Smiley. — Salisbury : Michael Russell, 1981. — 96p : ill,ports ; 25cm
Geneal. tables on lining papers. — Includes index
ISBN 0-85955-082-6 : £6.50 B82-03955

942.083′092′4 — England. Social life, *1910-1920 — Childhood reminiscences*

Maddocks, Margaret. An unlessoned girl / Margaret Maddocks ; illustrations by Margaret Wetherbee. — Large print ed. — Bath : Chivers, 1982, c1977. — 188p : ill ; 23cm. — (A Lythway autobiography)
Originally published: London : Hutchinson, 1977
ISBN 0-85119-827-9 : Unpriced : CIP rev. B82-13100

942.083′092′4 — England. Thomas, Myfanwy — *Biographies*

Thomas, Myfanwy. One of these fine days : memoirs / Myfanwy Thomas ; drawings by Henry Croly. — Manchester : Carcanet New Press with Mid Northumberland Arts Group, 1982. — 164p : ill,ports ; 23cm
ISBN 0-85635-387-6 : Unpriced : CIP rev.
ISBN 0-904790-23-1 (MidNAG) B82-04807

942.084 — England. Demonstrations against unemployment in Great Britain. Protest marches: Jarrow Crusade *(1936) — Personal observations*

Pickard, Tom. Jarrow march / Tom Pickard ; design by Joanna Voit. — London : Allison & Busby, 1982. — 120p : ill,facsims,ports ; 21cm
Ill on lining papers. — Bibliography: p6-7
ISBN 0-85031-397-x (cased) : £6.50 (pbk) : Unpriced B82-38020

942.084′092′4 — England. Social life, *1939-1941 — Personal observations*

Brittain, Vera. England's hour / Vera Brittain. — London : Futura, 1981. — xi,226p ; 18cm
Originally published: London : Macmillan, 1941
ISBN 0-7088-2127-8 (pbk) : £1.50 B82-06375

942.0854′092′4 — England. Buildings of historical importance. Organisations: National Trust. Lees-Milne, James, *1946-1947 — Correspondence, diaries, etc.*

Lees-Milne, James. Caves of ice. — London : Chatto & Windus, Feb.1983. — [304]p
ISBN 0-7011-2657-4 : £12.50 : CIP entry B82-38866

942.085′6′0222 — England. Social life, *1965-1981 — Illustrations*

Kasterine, Dmitri. England and the English / Dmitri Kasterine. — Tadworth : World's Work, c1981. — 128p : chiefly ill(some col.),ports(some col.) ; 31cm
ISBN 0-437-08050-1 : £9.95 B82-05267

942.085′7′0924 — England. Leonard, Tim — *Biographies*

Leonard, Tim. Braces and boots / [Tim Leonard]. — Cambridge : Basic Skills Unit, c1980. — 25p : ill,ports ; 21cm
ISBN 0-86082-196-x (pbk) : Unpriced B82-18597

942.085′7′0924 — England. Rural regions. Social life, *1970-1979 — Personal observations*

Peel, J. H. B. Latest country talk / J.H.B. Peel ; illustrated by B.S. Biro. — London : Hale, 1981. — 204p : ill ; 23cm
ISBN 0-7091-9418-8 : £7.95 B82-04181

942.085′8′0924 — England. Rural regions — *Personal observations*

Whitlock, Ralph. The countryside : random gleanings / by the Countryman, Ralph Whitlock. — Dorchester, Dorset : Gavin Press, 1982. — xiii,178p : ill ; 23cm
ISBN 0-905868-07-2 (cased) : £6.50
ISBN 0-905868-08-0 (pbk) : £2.75 B82-37024

942.1/8 — HISTORY. ENGLAND. SPECIAL LOCALITIES

942.1 — London. Mews, — *to 1980*

Rosen, Barbara. The mews of London. — Exeter : Webb & Bower, May 1982. — [160]p
ISBN 0-906671-50-7 : £8.95 : CIP entry B82-07700

942.1′007′10421 — London. Schools. Curriculum subjects: London, *to 1980.* **Teaching**

Veale, Elspeth M. Teaching the history of London / by Elspeth Veale. — London : Historical Association, 1981. — 40p : 1map ; 21cm. — (Teaching of history series ; no.50)
ISBN 0-85278-245-4 (pbk) : Unpriced B82-12054

942.1′009′92 — Persons commemorated by blue plaques in London. Local associations: London. Residences

Dakers, Caroline. The blue plaque guide to London / Caroline Dakers. — London : Macmillan, 1981. — 318p : ill ; 23cm
Includes indexes
ISBN 0-333-28462-3 : £7.95 B82-09122

942.107′3′0924 — London. Social life, *1762-1763 — Personal observations — Correspondence, diaries, etc.*

Boswell, James, *1740-1795.* Boswell's London journal 1762-1763 / edited by Frederick A. Pottle. — London : Futura, 1982, c1950. — xi,404p ; 18cm. — (Heritage)
Originally published: London : Heinemann, 1950. — Includes index
ISBN 0-7088-2180-4 (pbk) : £2.50 B82-24318

942.1′074′0924 — London. Social life, *1826-1839 — Personal observations — Early works*

Tristan, Flora. The London journal of Flora Tristan, 1842. — London : Virago, Jan.1982. — [320]p
Translation of: Promenades dans Londres
ISBN 0-86068-214-5 (pbk) : £3.95 : CIP entry B81-33764

942.1′081 — London. Social conditions, *1869 — Early works*

Greenwood, James, *1832-1929.* The seven curses of London / James Greenwood ; introduction by Jeffrey Richards. — Oxford : Blackwell, 1981. — xxvi,293p ; 24cm
Originally published: London : Stanley Rivers, 1869
ISBN 0-631-12778-x : Unpriced : CIP rev. B81-34292

942.1081′092′4 — London. Social life, *1840 — Correspondence, diaries, etc. — Facsimiles*

Doyle, Richard, *1824-1883.* Richard Doyle's journal, 1840 / introduction and notes by Christopher Wheeler. — Edinburgh : Bartholomew in association with British Museum Publications, 1980. — xvii,156p : ill ; 27cm
Facsim reprint
ISBN 0-7028-8280-1 : £6.95 : CIP rev. B80-18946

942.1083′092′4 — London, *1930-1935 — Personal observations*

Woolf, Virginia. The London scene : five essays / by Virginia Woolf. — London : Hogarth, 1982, c1975. — 44p ; 23cm
Originally published: New York : Hallman, 1975
ISBN 0-7012-0542-3 : £4.95 : CIP rev. B82-00225

942.1′083′0924 — London. Henrey, Madeleine, *ca 1930-ca 1945 — Biographies*

Henrey, Madeleine. Green leaves ; London under fire. — London : Dent, Aug.1982. — [432]p
Green leaves originally published: 1976. — London under fire originally published: 1969
ISBN 0-460-04563-6 : £7.95 : CIP entry B82-15810

942.1′083′0924 — London. Social life, *1903-ca 1920 — Childhood reminiscences*

Rolph, C. H. London particulars / C.H. Rolph. — Oxford : Oxford University Press, 1980 (1982 [printing]). — 202p ; 20cm
ISBN 0-19-281351-x (pbk) : £2.98 : CIP rev. B82-12540

942.1′083′0924 — London. Social life, *1914-ca 1940 — Personal observations*

Youens, Irene. Sis's tribe / Irene Youens. — Bognor Regis : New Horizon, c1981. — 65p ; 21cm
ISBN 0-86116-587-x : £3.75 B82-00929

942.1085′092′4 — London. Woodward, Kathleen — *Biographies*

Woodward, Kathleen. Jipping Street. — London : Virago, Jan.1983. — [168]p
Originally published: London : Longmans, 1928
ISBN 0-86068-390-7 (pbk) : £2.95 : CIP entry B82-33224

942.1085′7 — London. Celebrities. Social life, *1977-1981*

Young, Richard, *1947-.* By invitation only / Richard Young and Christopher Wilson. — London : Quartet, 1981. — 123p : ports ; 28cm
ISBN 0-7043-3387-2 (pbk) : £4.95 B82-10187

942.1085′8′0222 — London — *Illustrations*

Hidalgo, Francisco. London / Francisco Hidalgo. — New York ; London : Proteus, 1981. — [184]p : chiefly ill(some col.) ; 32cm
ISBN 0-906071-45-3 : £18.00 B82-02212

942.1085′8′0924 — London. Social life — *Personal observations*

Romano, Nicola Maria. The Dippy D.P.'s deep diary / Nicola Maria Romano. — Ilfracombe : Stockwell
Pt.1. — 1980. — 119p ; 19cm
ISBN 0-7223-1399-3 (pbk) : £1.50 B82-17621

942.1′32 — London. Westminster *(London Borough).* **Royal parks: Hyde Park. Demonstrations,** *1855-1867*

Jones, Leslie S. A. Hyde Park and free speech / by Leslie Jones. — [London] (Limehouse Town Hall, E14) : Museum of Labour History, [1981?]. — [10]p ; 21cm. — (Hyde Park pamphlet ; no.2)
Originally published: in the 'Hyde Park socialist', Winter 1976-77. No.34
Unpriced (unbound) B82-15122

942.1'33 — London. Hammersmith and Fulham *(London Borough).* **Fulham,** *to 1939*
Hasker, Leslie. The place which is called Fulanham : an outline history of Fulham from Roman times until the start of the Second World War / by Leslie Hasker. — [London] (c/o Fulham Library, 598 Fulham Rd., SW6 5NX) : Fulham and Hammersmith Historical Society, 1981. — ii,220p,[6]p of plates : ill ; 21cm
Includes index
£4.50 (pbk) B82-16145

942.1'34083'0924 — London. Kensington and Chelsea *(London Borough).* **Social life,** *1910-1920 — Childhood reminiscences*
Morrell, Josef. Tell me grandpa / Josef Morrell. — Easthill : Merlin, c1981. — 149p ; 22cm
ISBN 0-86303-005-x : £5.00 B82-10840

942.1'42 — London. Camden *(London Borough).* **Fitzrovia,** *to 1981*
Bailey, Nick. Fitzrovia / by Nick Bailey. — New Barnet : Historical Publications in association with Camden History Society, 1981. — 72p : ill,maps,ports ; 24cm
Bibliography: p70. — Includes index
ISBN 0-9503656-2-9 (pbk) : £2.90 B82-13624

942.1'42 — London. Camden *(London Borough).* **Hampstead. Places of historical importance** — *Lists*
Wade, Ralph. The plaques of Hampstead / by Ralph Wade ; drawings by Eric Wade. — London (6a Hampstead High St., NW3) : High Hill Press, 1980. — 20p : ports ; 22cm
£1.00 (pbk) B82-09053

942.1'42 — London. Camden *(London Borough).* **Hampstead,** *to 1980*
Norrie, Ian. Hampstead. — London : Wildwood House, July 1981. — [208]p
ISBN 0-7045-3060-0 : £7.95 : CIP entry B81-15903

942.1'42 — London. Camden *(London Borough).* **Local history. Historical sources**
Guide to London local history resources : London Borough of Camden / Local History Library. — [London] : London Borough of Camden Libraries and Arts Department, 1982. — 34p ; 30cm. — (Camden libraries and arts information)
Unpriced (pbk) B82-31221

942.1'42 — London. Camden *(London Borough).* **West Hampstead. Social life,** *ca 1900-1981 — Childhood reminiscenses — Collections*
A Child's eye view of West Hampstead / edited by Caroline Woollett ; illustrations by Susie Joyce ... [et al.]. — [London] : West Hampstead Community Centre, [1981?]. — 73p,[4]p of plates : ill,1map,1facsim,ports ; 21cm
£1.75 (pbk) B82-11728

942.1'430858'0222 — London. Islington *(London Borough) — Illustrations*
Usborne, Ann. A portrait of Islington. — London (4 Canonbury Mansions, N.1.) : Damien Tunnacliffe, Oct.1981. — [64]p
ISBN 0-9506284-1-7 : £3.95 : CIP entry B81-30513

942.1'44 — London. Hackney *(London Borough).* **Hoxton. Social life,** *1910-1926 — Childhood reminiscences*
Jasper, A. S.. A Hoxton childhood / A.S. Jasper ; line drawings by James Boswell. — Large print ed. — Bath : Chivers, 1982, c1969. — 139p : ill ; 23cm. — (A New Portway large print book)
Originally published: London : Barrie & Rockliff, 1969
ISBN 0-85119-169-x : Unpriced : CIP rev. B82-07615

942.1'440858 — London. Hackney *(London Borough).* **Social conditions**
Hackney. The London Borough of Hackney 1978-'82. — [London] ([Hackney Central Library, Mare St., E8 1HG]) : London Borough of Hackney, [1982]. — [40]p : ill ; 15x21cm
Cover title
Unpriced (pbk) B82-27481

942.1'5 — London. Tower Hamlets *(London Borough).* **Bethnal Green. Social life,** *1922-1937 — Childhood reminiscences*
Bailey, Doris M.. Children of the Green : a true story of childhood in Bethnal Green 1922-1937 / by Doris M. Bailey ; illustrated by Jonathan Bailey. — London : Stepney Books, 1981. — 128p : ill ; 21cm
ISBN 0-9505241-4-x (pbk) : £2.40 B82-17629

942.1'5 — London. Tower Hamlets *(London Borough).* **Poplar. Social life,** *ca 1914- ca 1935 — Childhood reminiscences*
Scannell, Dorothy. Mother knew best : an East End childhood / Dorothy Scannell. — Large print ed. — Bath : Chivers, 1981, c1974. — 305p ; 23cm. — (A New Portway large print book)
Originally published: London : Macmillan, 1974
ISBN 0-85119-139-8 : Unpriced : CIP rev. B81-25799

942.1'5 — London. Tower Hamlets *(London Borough), to 1980*
Kerrigan, Colm. A history of Tower Hamlets / Colm Kerrigan. — London : London Borough of Tower Hamlets Coummunity Services, Libraries Department, 1982. — viii,95p : ill,maps,ports ; 25cm
Includes bibliographies and index
ISBN 0-902385-06-2 (pbk) : Unpriced B82-35274

942.1'5'007 — London. Tower Hamlets *(London Borough).* **Information sources** — *Directories*
Marcan, Peter. Tower Hamlets 1979-1982 : a supplement to an East End directory : amending information and describing new publications (articles, reports, pamphlets, books) initiatives and significant events / Peter Marcan. — High Wycombe (31 Rowliff Rd, High Wycombe, Bucks) : P. Marcan, c1982. — 13p ; 30cm
Unpriced (unbound) B82-40257

942.1'5082'0924 — London. East End. Working classes. Social life, *1902 — Personal observations*
Southgate, Walter. That's the way it was : a working class autobiography 1890-1950 / Walter Southgate ; edited with an afterword 1950-1981 by Terry Philpot. — Oxted : New Clarion in association with History Workshop, Centre for London History, 1982. — 148p : 1port ; 22cm
ISBN 0-9507961-0-7 (pbk) : £2.95 B82-32923

942.1'50858'0924 — London. East End. Social life *— Personal observations*
Bickerstaff, Dennis. How much did you take yesterday? / Dennis Bickerstaff. — Bognor Regis : New Horizon, c1982. — 212p ; 21cm
ISBN 0-86116-201-3 : £5.75 B82-23609

942.1'63 — London. Lewisham *(London Borough).* **Grove Park,** *to 1982*
King, John, *1945-.* Grove Park : a history of a community / John King. — London : Grove Park Community Group, c1982. — i,25p,[4]p of plates : ill,port ; 21cm
Cover title
ISBN 0-9508216-0-8 (pbk) : Unpriced B82-38169

942.1'63 — London. Lewisham *(London Borough).* **Lee,** *ca 1600-1981*
Birchenough, Josephine. Some farms and fields in Lee / Josephine Birchenough with John King. — Rev. ed. — Lee : J. Birchenough, 1981. — vi,42p : ill,2maps,ports ; 21cm
Cover title. — Previous ed.: 1981. — Text on inside cover. — Bibliography: pvi. — Includes index
ISBN 0-9507525-1-7 (pbk) : Unpriced B82-31561

942.1'63 — London. Lewisham *(London Borough).* **Lee. Country houses: Manor House,** *to 1980*
A Brief history of the manor house, Lee. — [London] : [Josephine Birchenough], c1982. — [4]p ; 21cm
ISBN 0-9507525-2-5 (unbound) : Unpriced B82-34894

942.1'63'005 — London. Lewisham *(London Borough) — History — Serials*
Facts about Lewisham. — No.1-. — [London] ([c/o Ms. J. Birchenough, 116 Manor La., Lee SE12 8LR]) : Lewisham Local History Society, 1981-. — v. ; 21x30cm folded to 21x10cm
Irregular
ISSN 0261-9911 = Facts about Lewisham : Unpriced B82-12459

942.1'64 — London. Southwark *(London Borough).* **Peckham. Social life** — *Personal observations*
Roberts, Florrie. The ups and downs of Florrie Roberts. — London : Peckham Publishing Project, c1980. — 20p ; 20cm
ISBN 0-906464-65-x (pbk) : £0.30 B82-36007

942.1'640855'0924 — London. Southwark *(London Borough).* **Social life,** *1955-1959 — Personal observations*
Avery, Valerie. London shadows / by Valerie Avery. — London : Kimber, 1981. — 190p ; 22cm
ISBN 0-7183-0328-8 : £5.95 B82-04007

942.1'640855'0924 — London. Southwark *(London Borough).* **Social life,** *ca 1955 — Personal observations*
Avery, Valerie. London spring / Valerie Avery. — London : Kimber, 1982. — 208p ; 23cm
ISBN 0-7183-0398-9 : £5.95 B82-27221

942.1'65 — London. Lambeth *(London Borough).* **Brixton. Riots,** *1981 (April) — Inquiry reports*
Scarman, Leslie George, *Baron.* The Brixton disorders 10-12 April 1981 : report of an enquiry / by Lord Scarman. — London : H.M.S.O., 1981. — viii,168p : 1map ; 25cm. — (Cmnd. ; 8427)
Map on folded sheet attached to inside cover. — Bibliography: p164-168
ISBN 0-10-184270-8 (pbk) : £8.00 B82-10317

Scarman, Leslie George, *Baron.* [The Brixton disorders 10-12 April 1981]. The Scarman report : the Brixton disorders 10-12 April 1981 : report of an inquiry / by Lord Scarman. — Harmondsworth : Penguin, 1982. — 255p : 1map ; 18cm. — (Pelican books)
Originally published: London : HMSO, 1981. — Bibliography: p249-253
ISBN 0-14-022455-6 (pbk) : £1.95 B82-30512

942.1'65073'0924 — London. Lambeth *(London Borough).* **Social life,** *1808-1815 — Personal observations — Correspondence, diaries, etc.*
Reynolds *(Family).* Letters from Lambeth : the correspondence of the Reynolds family with John Freeman Milward Dovaston 1808-1815 / introduced and edited by Joanna Richardson. — Woodbridge : Published for the Royal Society of Literature by the Boydell Press, 1981. — 212p : ill,ports ; 22cm
Bibliography: p205-206. — Includes index
ISBN 0-85115-150-7 : £12.00 : CIP rev. B81-18091

942.1'66 — London. Wandsworth *(London Borough).* **Social conditions,** *1600-1950*
A Prospect of Wandsworth : an exhibition presented by the Wandsworth Society to mark the 10th anniversary of its foundation. — [Wandsworth] ([2 Melody Rd, SW18]) : [Wandsworth Society], [1981?]. — 20p : ill ; 21x30cm
Published to accompany an exhibition at Book House, Wandsworth, 1981. — Ill on inside covers
Unpriced (pbk) B82-08598

942.1'66081 — London. Wandsworth *(London Borough).* **Battersea. Social conditions,** *1866-1982*
Living in South London. — Aldershot : Gower, Dec.1982. — [240]p
ISBN 0-566-00600-6 : £12.50 : CIP entry B82-30055

942.1'72 — London. Waltham Forest *(London Borough).* **Walthamstow,** *1800-1850*
Smith, Richard S.. Walthamstow in the early nineteenth century / by Richard S. Smith. — London : Walthamstow Antiquarian Society, 1938 (1981 [printing]). — 36p,8p of plates : ill ; 21cm. — (Monograph. (New series) ; no.24)
ISBN 0-85480-040-9 (pbk) : £1.20 B82-06304

942.1′73 — London. Redbridge *(London Borough).* **Ilford,** *to 1965*
Caunt, George. Ilford′s yesterdays : the village that became a town / [by George Caunt]. — Enl. ed. — [Ilford] : Caunt, 1980. — 120p : ill,1map,ports ; 22cm
Previous ed.: 1964. — Ill on lining papers
ISBN 0-907128-00-9 : Unpriced B82-35807

942.1′73 — London. Redbridge *(London Borough).* **Woodford,** *to 1981 — Illustrations*
Fowkes, Reginald L.. Woodford : then and now : a photographic commentary / compiled by Reginald L. Fowkes. — London : Battle of Britain Prints International, c1981. — 192p : chiefly ill,maps,1coat of arms,facsims ; 31cm
′Text based on the Victoria History of Essex′, 1973. — Ill on lining papers
ISBN 0-900913-23-1 : Unpriced B82-04222

942.1′74 — London. Havering *(London Borough).* **Havering-atte-Bower. Social life,** *ca 1910-ca 1920 — Childhood reminiscences*
Brazier, Winifred. A childhood in Haverin-atte-Bower / Winifred Brazier. — Hornchurch : Ian Henry, c1981. — 52p : ill,ports ; 15x21cm
ISBN 0-86025-810-6 (pbk) : £2.55 B82-14011

942.1′740858′05 — London. Havering *(London Borough) — Serials*
The **Advertiser**. Romford and Havering. — [Ed. no.1 (197-)?]-. — Ilford (98 Goodmayes Rd, Goodmayes, Ilford, Essex) : Adnews Publications, [197-]-. — v. : ill ; 42cm
Weekly. — Description based on: Ed. no.130 (9th-15th Sept. 1981)
ISSN 0262-4664 = Advertiser. Romford and Havering : Unpriced B82-03407

942.1′750858′05 — London. Barking and Dagenham *(London Borough) — Serials*
The **Advertiser** weekly news. — Ed. no.85 (24th-30th June 1981)-. — Goodmayes (98 Goodmayes Rd, Goodmayes, Ilford, Essex IG3 8BR) : Adnews Publications, 1981-. — v. : ill,facsims,ports ; 42cm
Weekly. — Continues: The Advertiser. [Barking and Dagenham]. — Description based on: Ed. no.95 (2nd-8th Sept. 1981)
ISSN 0262-3390 = Advertiser weekly news : Unpriced B82-03415

Dagenham & Barking advertiser & Barking recorder. — No.4296 (Friday Aug. 21 1981)-. — Romford (3 River Chambers, High St., Romford, Essex) : South Essex Recorders Ltd., 1981-. — v. : ill,ports ; 44cm
Weekly. — Continues: Barking & Dagenham advertiser & Barking recorder
ISSN 0262-3382 = Dagenham & Barking advertiser & Barking recorder : £0.10 per issue B82-03414

942.1′78 — London. Bromley *(London Borough).* **Hayes,** *to 1981*
Harrold, Elinor. Hayes remembered / Elinor Harrold. — [Bromley] ([58 West Common Rd, Hayes, Bromley, Kent BR2 7BX]) : [E. Harrold], [1982]. — 56p : ill,ports ; 21cm
Cover title
Unpriced (pbk) B82-31255

942.1′8 — London. Middlesex *— History*
A **History** of the county of Middlesex. — Oxford : Published for the Institute of Historical Research by Oxford University Press
Vol.7: Acton, Chiswick, Ealing and Willesden parishes / edited by T.F.T. Baker. — 1982. — xx,280p,[16]p of plates : ill,maps,coats of arms ; 32cm. — (The Victoria history of the counties of England)
Title of part: A history of Middlesex. — Includes index
ISBN 0-19-722756-2 : £60.00 B82-21344

942.1′830858′05 — London. Hillingdon *(London Borough) — Serials*
[Middlesex weekly post *(Harrow edition)*]. Middlesex weekly post. — [Harrow ed.]. — No.1873 (Thursday Sept. 10, 1981)-. — Ruislip Manor (Newspaper House, P.O. Box 17, Shenley Ave., Ruislip Manor, Middx HA4 6DQ) : Weekly Post Newspapers, 1981-. — v. : ill,ports ; 42cm
Continues: Harrow - Southall - Ealing weekly post
£0.05 per issue B82-38516

[Middlesex weekly post *(Ruislip, Eastcote, Ickenham, Northwood edition)*]. Middlesex weekly post. — [Ruislip, Eastcote, Ickenham, Northwood ed.]. — No.1873 (Thursday Sept. 10 1981)-. — Ruislip Manor (Newspaper House, P.O.Box 17, Shenley Ave., Ruislip Manor, Middx. HA4 6DQ) : Weekly Post Newspapers, 1981-. — v. : ill,ports ; 42cm
Continues: Ruislip - Uxbridge - Hayes weekly post
Unpriced B82-40041

942.1′84 — London. Ealing *(London Borough).* **Acton,** *1872-1928 — Illustrations*
Acton as it was : a selection of photographs / compiled and annotated by London Borough of Ealing Library Service and R.N.G. Rowland. — Nelson : Hendon Publishing, c1981. — [44]p : chiefly ill,ports ; 21x29cm
ISBN 0-86067-067-8 (pbk) : £2.60 B82-08509

942.1′84 — London. Ealing *(London Borough).* **Farmers. Social life,** *1897-1919 — Personal observations*
Crees, F. W.. The life story of F.W. Crees / edited by C.H. Keene. — London : London Borough of Ealing Library Service, 1979. — xi,34p : ill,maps ; 30cm
Includes index
ISBN 0-86192-002-3 (pbk) : £0.50 B82-40583

942.1′840858′05 — London. Ealing *(London Borough) — Serials*
[The Leader *(Greenford & Northolt edition)*]. The Leader. — Greenford & Northolt ed. — No.1 (Friday Sept. 11 1981)-. — Uxbridge (Cricketfield Rd., Uxbridge [Middx UB8 1TB]) : King and Hutchings (Westminster Press) Ltd, 1981-. — v. : ill,ports ; 42cm
Weekly
ISSN 0262-9186 = Leader. Greenford & Northolt edition : Unpriced B82-14775

942.1′85 — London. Brent *(London Borough).* **Wembley Stadium,** *to 1980*
Bass, Howard. Glorious Wembley : the official history of Britain′s foremost entertainment centre. — Enfield : Guinness Superlatives, Feb.1982. — [176]p
ISBN 0-85112-237-x (pbk) : £5.95 : CIP entry B81-38829

942.1′86 — London. Harrow *(London Borough).* **Scandals,** *to 1981*
Brown, R. S.. Harrow′s historical scandals / by R.S. Brown. — Harrow : B.K.R.A., c1982. — 65p : ill,ports,1geneal.table ; 25cm
Bibliography: p4
ISBN 0-907925-00-6 (pbk) : £2.00 B82-27110

942.1′86 — London. Harrow *(London Borough), to 1981*
Brown, R. S.. Histories of Harrow Weald highways / R.S. Brown. — [London] : [Bishop Ken Residents Association], [1974-1981]. — 12v. : ill,maps,ports ; 21cm
Cover title. — Vols. 3-12 have title: Histories of Harrow highways. — Includes index
Unpriced (pbk) B82-14614

942.1′86′00222 — London. Harrow *(London Borough), 1685-1950 — Illustrations*
Ball, Alan W.. The countryside lies sleeping 1685-1950 : paintings, prints and drawings of Pinner, Stanmore and other former villages now in the London Borough of Harrow / Alan W. Ball. — [Orpington] : Riverhill, 1981. — 352p : chiefly ill,facsims,plans,ports ; 30cm
Bibliography: p349-350. — Includes index
ISBN 0-902119-27-3 (cased) : £9.00
ISBN 0-902119-28-1 (pbk) : £6.00 B82-13277

942.1′860858′05 — London. Harrow *(London Borough) — Serials*
Harrow view. — [19—]-. — Harrow (18a Hamilton Rd., Harrow) : Hindes Road Neighbours, [19—]-. — v. : ill,maps,ports rc 30cm
Description based on: June ′81
Unpriced B82-32149

942.1′87 — London. Barnet *(London Borough).* **Manor houses: Finchley Manor. Occupiers,** *to 1981*
Davis, Fred, *1929-*. Finchley Manor : influential families / by Fred Davis. — London : Barnet Libraries Local History, c1982. — [16]p : ill,1coat of arms,1plan,2ports ; 20x21cm
Cover title. — Text, plan on inside covers
ISBN 0-903431-08-4 (pbk) : £0.50 B82-20610

942.1′880858′05 — London. Haringey *(London Borough) — Serials*
The **Haringey** independent. — Issue no. 1 (27th May 1982)-. — London (65 North Sq., Edmonton, N.9) : Billington & Wright, 1982-. — v. : ill,ports ; 43cm
Weekly
ISSN 0263-8983 = Haringey independent : Unpriced B82-38533

942.1′89 — London. Enfield *(London Borough).* **Southgate & Palmers Green** *— Serials*
Southgate and Palmers Green gazette. — [No.4435 (Friday 2 Apr. 1982)?]-. — Enfield (45 Silver St, Enfield, Middx.) : Enfield Newspapers, 1982-. — v. : ill,ports ; 44cm
Weekly. — Continues: Palmers Green and Southgate gazette
£0.15 B82-40050

942.1′9 — London. Wandle River *— Serials*
Bulletin of the Wandle Group. — No.1 [197-?]-. — Wallington (c/o Janet Monk, 11 Lakeside, Wallington, Surrey) : The Group, [197-?]-. — v. ; 30cm
Description based on: No.8 (June 1980)
ISSN 0262-7248 = Bulletin of the Wandle Group : Unpriced B82-11134

942.1′93 — London. Merton *(London Borough).* **Manor houses: Ravensbury Manor House,** *to 1960*
Ravensbury manor house and park. — [London] : Merton Historical Society, 1981. — 12p : ill,1map ; 22cm
Cover title. — Text on inside covers
Unpriced (pbk) B82-23382

942.1′94 — London. Kingston-upon-Thames *(London Borough).* **Kingston. Political events,** *1653-1661 — Sources of data: Kingston-upon-Thames. Archives*
Scandal on the Corporation : Royalist and Puritans in mid-17th century Kingston, from the Kingston Borough Archives. — Kingston-upon-Thames ([c/o Honorary Borough Archivist, Surrey Record Office, County Hall, Kingston-upon-Thames, Surrey KT1 2DN]) : Heritage Unit Recreation Department, Royal Borough of Kingston upon Thames, 1982. — xviii,51p,[2]leaves of plates : facsims ; 30cm
Bibliography: pxviii
ISBN 0-903183-10-2 (pbk) : Unpriced B82-31067

942.1′95 — London. Richmond upon Thames *(London Borough).* **Twickenham,** *704-948 — Sources of data: Charters*
Urwin, A. C. B.. Saxon Twickenham : the evidence of the Charters 704-948 AD / by A.C.B. Urwin. — [Twickenham] : Twickenham Local History Society, 1981. — 17p ; 20cm. — (Paper / Borough of Twickenham Local History Society ; no.48)
Bibliography: p17
ISBN 0-903341-33-6 : £0.75 B82-07267

942.1′95′005 — London. Richmond upon Thames *(London Borough) — History — Serials*
Richmond history : journal of the Richmond Society History Section. — No.1 (May 1981)-. — Twickenham (c/o Mrs E. Barrett, 6 Amyand Cottages, Amyand Park Rd, Twickenham, Middx) : The Section, 1981-. — v. : ill,maps,plans ; 26cm
ISSN 0263-0958 = Richmond history : Unpriced B82-17247

942.1′950858′05 — London. Richmond upon Thames *(London Borough) — Serials*
Fly on the wall : Richmond′s other scurrilous rag. — [No.1]-. — Richmond [Surrey] (P.O. Box 41, Richmond, [Surrey]) : Fly on the Wall Collective, [1981]-. — v. ; 30cm
Irregular
ISSN 0262-3307 = Fly on the wall : Unpriced B82-02384

942.2 — South-east England. Battles, *to 1980*
Blaxland, Gregory. South-East Britain eternal battleground / by Gregory Blaxland ; with sketches by the author. — Rainham : Meresborough, 1981. — 160p : ill,maps ; 22cm
Bibliography: p151-152. — Includes index
ISBN 0-905270-44-4 : £5.95 B82-36403

942.2′005 — Southern England - *History. Periodicals*
Southern history. — Vol.3. — Gloucester (17a Brunswick Rd, Gloucester GL1 1HG) : Alan Sutton, May 1981. — [272]p
ISBN 0-904387-65-8 (cased) : £12.50 : CIP entry
ISBN 0-904387-66-6 (pbk) : £7.50
ISSN 0142-4688 B81-12370

942.2′084′0924 — South-east England. Social life, *ca 1935-ca 1950 — Personal observations*
Scannell, Dorothy. Dolly′s war. — Large print ed. — Bath : Chivers, Jan.1983. — [336]p. — (A New Portway large print book)
Originally published: London : Macmillan, 1975
ISBN 0-85119-201-7 : £6.90 : CIP entry B82-33092

942.2′10858′05 — Surrey — *Serials*
[Mid Surrey news *(Mole Valley & Epsom edition)*]. Mid Surrey news. — Mole Valley & Epsom ed. — No.93 (Jan. 5th 1982)-. — [Redhill] ([19 Ladbroke Rd, Redhill, Surrey]) : [Argus Newspapers], 1982-. — v. : ill,ports ; 44cm
Weekly. — Continues: Mid Surrey mirror (Mole Valley edition)
Unpriced B82-38519

[Mid Surrey news *(Redhill, Reigate, Horley & Caterham edition)*]. Mid Surrey news. — Redhill, Reigate, Horley & Caterham ed. — No.125 (Jan 5th 1982)-. — [Redhill] ([19 Ladbroke Rd, Redhill, Surrey]) : [Argus Newspapers], 1982-. — v. : ill,ports ; 43cm
Weekly. — Continues: Mid Surrey mirror (1979)
Unpriced B82-38520

Surrey style magazine. — No.1 (Nov. 1981)-. — Weybridge (Haland House, York Rd, Weybridge, Surrey) : Polewick, 1981-. — v. : ill,ports ; 30cm
Monthly
ISSN 0263-2616 = Surrey style magazine : Unpriced B82-22675

942.2′12 — Surrey. Staines, *to 1981*
Smithers, M. M.. Staines : an illustrated record / M.M. Smithers. — Shepperton : Ian Allan, 1982. — 63p : ill,coats of arms,facsims,maps,port ; 24cm. — (Town & country books)
Bibliography: p63
ISBN 0-7110-1125-7 (pbk) : £1.95 B82-40521

942.2′13 — Surrey. Camberley — *Serials*
The **Camberley** shopper. — Apr. ′82-. — Aldershot (2 The Grove, Aldershot, Hants.) : Aldershot News Ltd., 1982-. — v. : ill,maps (some col.),ports
Monthly
ISSN 0263-8967 = Camberley shopper : Unpriced B82-38530

942.2′145 — Surrey. Esher — *Serials*
[Courier *(Esher edition)*]. Courier. — Esher ed. — No.188 (Mar. 1981)-no.194(Sept. 1981). — Esher (79A High St., Esher, Surrey KT10 9QA) : Esher & Leatherhead Courier Ltd., 1981-1981. — 7v. : ill,ports ; 45cm
Monthly. — Continues: Esher courier & Molesey review. — Continued by: Courier (Elmbridge edition)
Unpriced B82-03419

942.2′145 — Surrey. Walton-on-Thames & Weybridge. Thames River, *to 1980*
Stonebanks, John Archer. The Thames at Walton and Weybridge / John Archer Stonebanks. — [Weybridge] ([c/o Hon. Sec., Lobswood, Cedar Grove, Weybridge, Surrey]) : [Walton and Weybridge Local History Society], 1980. — 27p,xiip of plates : ill,maps ; 21cm. — (Paper / Walton and Weybridge Local History Society ; no.18)
Unpriced (pbk) B82-13783

942.2′1450858′05 — Surrey. Elmbridge *(District) — Serials*
[Courier *(Elmbridge edition)*]. Courier. — Elmbridge ed. — No.195 (Oct. 1981)-. — Esher (79A High St., Esher, Surrey KT10 9QA) : Esher & Leatherhead Courier Ltd., 1981-. — v. : ill,ports ; 44cm
Monthly. — Continues: Courier (Esher edition)
ISSN 0262-3404 = Courier. Elmbridge edition : Unpriced B82-03420

942.2′165 — Surrey. Holmbury St Mary, *to 1978*
Mackinder, Margaret. Holmbury St Mary : one hundred years / by Margaret Bird. — Dorking (The Glade, Holmbury St. Mary, Dorking, Surrey) : M. Bird, c1979. — 47p : ill ; 21cm
Bibliography: p47
£1.25 (pbk) B82-18908

942.2′165 — Surrey. Leatherhead — *Serials*
[Courier *(Leatherhead edition)*]. Courier. — Leatherhead ed. — No.188(Mar. 1981)-no.194 (Sept. 1981). — Esher (79A High St., Esher, Surrey KT10 9QA) : Esher & Leatherhead Courier Ltd., 1981-. — 7v. : ill,ports ; 45cm
Monthly. — Continues: Leatherhead & Cobham Courier. — Continued by: Courier (Mole Valley edition)
Unpriced B82-03421

942.2′1650858′05 — Surrey. Mole Valley *(District) — Serials*
[Courier *(Mole Valley edition)*]. Courier. — Mole Valley ed. — No.195 (Oct. 1981)-. — Esher (79A High St., Esher, Surrey KT10 9QA) : Esher & Leatherhead Courier Ltd., 1981-. — v. : ill,ports ; 44cm
Monthly. — Continues: Courier (Leatherhead edition)
ISSN 0262-3412 = Courier. Mole Valley edition : Unpriced B82-03418

942.2′19 — Surrey. Cranleigh — *Serials*
Cranleigh times. — [1979?]-. — Guildford (Martyr Rd, Guildford, Surrey GU1 4LQ) : Surrey Advertiser, [1979?]-. — v. : ill,ports ; 45cm
Weekly. — Description based on: No.8799 (Apr. 17, 1982)
Unpriced B82-36731

942.2′19 — Surrey. Farnham — *Serials*
[Surrey & Hants news *(1980)*]. Surrey & Hants news. — [1980?]-. — Farnham (104a West St., Farnham, Surrey) : Surrey and Hants News Ltd., [1980?]-. — v. : ill,ports ; 44cm
Weekly. — Continues: Surrey and Hants news and mail. — Description based on: No.6446 (Tuesday May 18th, 1982)
Unpriced B82-36728

942.2′19 — Surrey. Farnham. Social life, *1200-1560*
Robo, Etienne. Medieval Farnham : everyday life in an episcopal manor / by Etienne Robo. — Farnborough, Hants. : St Michael′s Abbey Press, 1980. — xiii,326p,[24]leaves of plates : ill,2facsims ; 22cm
Originally published: Farnham : E. W. Langham, 1935. — Includes index
ISBN 0-907077-04-8 : Unpriced : CIP rev. B80-09044

942.2′19 — Surrey. Godalming — *Serials*
Godalming times. — [1979?]-. — Guildford (Martyr Rd, Guildford, Surrey GU1 4LQ) : Surrey Advertiser, [1979?]-. — v. : ill,ports ; 45cm
Weekly. — Description based on: No.8799 (Apr. 17, 1982)
Unpriced B82-36730

942.2′19 — Surrey. Haslemere region — *Serials*
County border times. — No.1 (Dec. 1981)-. — Haslemere (70c High St., Haslemere, Surrey) : County Border Times, 1981-. — v. : ill,ports ; 44cm
Weekly
ISSN 0263-015x = County border times : Unpriced B82-14259

942.2′3 — Kent, *to 1800 — Early works — Facsimiles*
Hasted, Edward. [The history and topographical survey of the County of Kent. Selections]. The history and topography of Kent : reprinted from the second edition of 1797 / Edward Hasted. — Sidcup : P.M.E. Erwood
Part 1: Hayes, West Wickham, Keston, Farnborough. — 1981. — viii,32p,[4]p of plates : 2maps ; 21cm
Facsim of: 2nd ed., (p22-53), Canterbury : Simmons & Kirkby, 1797-1801. — Bibliography: pviii
ISBN 0-907322-08-5 (pbk) : £1.50 B82-08586

942.2′3′005 — Kent. Local history — *Serials*
Bygone Kent : a monthly journal on all aspects of local history. — [Introductory issue] (Oct. 1979) ; Vol.1, no.1 (Jan. 1980)-. — Rainham : Meresborough Books, 1979-. — v. : ill,geneal.tables,ports ; 21cm
Introductory issue published Oct. 1979. — Description based on: Vol.2, no.12 (Dec. 1981)
ISSN 0262-5342 = Bygone Kent : £10.50 per year B82-15764

942.2′30858 — Kent. Social conditions — *For structure planning*
Kent structure plan 1980 review : report of survey / Kent County Council. — Maidstone (Springfield, Maidstone, Kent ME14 2LX) : The Council, 1980. — 394p in various pagings : maps ; 30cm
£8.00 (pbk) B82-21652

Kent structure plan 1980 review : summary report of survey / Kent County Council. — Maidstone (Springfield, Maidstone, Kent ME14 2LX) : The Council, 1980. — [65]p : ill,maps ; 30cm
£1.50 (pbk) B82-21653

942.2′30858′05 — Kent. North Downs — *Serials*
The **North** Downs news. — No.1 (Thursday 27 May 1982)-. — Longfield (6A Station Rd, Longfield, Kent) : Toltingtrow Ltd., 1982-. — v. : ill,forms,ports ; 42cm
Weekly
ISSN 0263-8959 = North Downs news : £0.10 B82-38532

942.2′310858′05 — Kent. Dartford *(District) & Gravesham (District) — Serials*
Dartford reporter. — Friday Feb. 26 1982-. — Gravesend (44 Harmer St, Gravesend, Kent DA12 2AY) : Reporter Newspapers, 1982-. — v. : ill,ports ; 45cm
Weekly. — Continues in part: Gravesend & Dartford reporter
£0.15 per issue B82-40046

Gravesend reporter. — Friday Feb. 26 1982-. — Gravesend (44 Harmer St, Gravesend, Kent DA12 2AY) : Reporter Newspapers, 1982-. — v. : ill,ports ; 45cm
Weekly. — Continues in part: Gravesend & Dartford reporter
£0.15 per issue B82-40047

942.2′312 — Kent. Dartford, *1800-1945 — Illustrations*
Porteus, Geoff. Dartford : from country town to industrial borough / by Geoff Porteus. — Buckingham : Barracuda, 1981. — 140p : ill,maps,facsims,ports ; 27cm. — (Yesterday′s town)
Ill on lining papers. — Includes index
ISBN 0-86023-135-6 : £11.50 B82-07911

942.2′323 — Kent. Medway River region, *to ca 1980*
Biggs, Howard. The River Medway / by Howard Biggs. — Lavenham : Dalton, 1982. — ix,150p : ill,1form,maps,ports ; 23cm
Text on inside front cover. — Bibliography: p147. — Includes index
ISBN 0-86138-005-3 (pbk) : £5.95 B82-31485

942.2′323 — Kent. Rochester upon Medway *(District), to 1979*
Clout, Norman. Medway memories / Norman Clout. — Rainham : Meresborough, c1980. — 40p : ill,ports ; 21cm
Text on inside front cover
ISBN 0-905270-14-2 (pbk) : £1.50 B82-36407

942.2'3230858'05 — Kent. Medway River — *Serials*

River news : [Tonbridge to the Medway Buoy]. — Vol.1, no.1 (Nov./Dec. 1981)-. — Rochester (316 City Way, Rochester-upon-Medway, Kent) : J. Lacey, 1981-. — v. : ill ; 21cm
Quarterly
ISSN 0261-0000 = River news : £0.50 per issue B82-18516

942.2'33 — Kent. Murston, *to 1971*

Twist, Sydney James. Murston village & parish : a history / by Sydney James Twist. — [Sittingbourne] ([4 Stanhope Ave., Sittingbourne, Kent]) : [The Sittingbourne Society], [1981]. — 25p : 1map ; 30cm
Cover title. — Map on inside cover
Unpriced (pbk) B82-11729

942.2'34 — Kent. Herne Bay region — *Serials*

Kentish gazette. Herne Bay. — Friday Oct. 9 1981-. — Canterbury (9 St George's Place, Canterbury CT1 1UU) : Kent County Newspapers, 1981-. — v. : ill,ports ; 44cm
Weekly. — Continues: Herne Bay press
£0.20 per issue B82-40045

942.2'34 — Kent. Kingston & Bishopsbourne. Social life, *1700-1981 — Readings from contemporary sources*

An **Anthology** of Kingston and Bishopsbourne. — [Canterbury] ([3 Whitelocks Close, Kingston, Canterbury, Kent CT4 6JG]) : [Kingston Village Society]. — (A Kingston Village Society publication)
Book 1. — 1982. — 50p,[13]p of plates : ill,1map,ports ; 21cm
Cover title. — Compiler and editor Ian Taylor
Unpriced (pbk) B82-11883

942.2'357 — Kent. Birchington, *to 1980*

Walker, Alfred T.. The ville of Birchington : its history and bygones / by Alfred T. Walker. — Margate : Birchington Secretarial Service, 1981. — 202p : ill,1map,facisms ; 21cm
Bibliography: p202
ISBN 0-9507605-0-1 (pbk) : Unpriced B82-11313

942.2'36 — Kent. Sevenoaks region, *ca 1850-1950 — Illustrations*

A **Sevenoaks** camera : Sevenoaks, Westerham and surrounding villages in old photographs / [compiled by] Gordon Anckorn. — Sevenoaks : Ashgrove, 1979. — [127]p : chiefly ill,ports ; 25cm
ISBN 0-906798-00-0 : £6.95 B82-36511

942.2'372 — Kent. Snodland. Parish churches: Parish Church of All Saints *(Snodland), to 1982*

Ashbee, Andrew. A history of the Parish Church of All Saints Snodland / by Andrew Ashbee ; incorporating material by Charles de Rocfort Wall. — Snodland : A. Ashbee, 1980. — 55p : ill,1map,1plan ; 30cm
Limited ed. of 500 numbered copies
ISBN 0-9507207-0-4 (pbk) : £1.65 B82-25125

942.2'3750858'05 — Kent. Maidstone *(District) — Serials*

Adscene. Maidstone, Ashford, Tenterden. — No.1 (1976)-. — Canterbury (Newspaper House, Wincheap, Canterbury, Kent) : Kent Free Press, 1976-. — v. : ill,ports ; 45cm
Weekly. — Description based on: No.284 (Wednesday Sept. 2nd 1981)
ISSN 0262-3420 = Adscene. Maidstone, Ashford, Tenterden : Unpriced
Also classified at 942.2'3920858'05 B82-03413

942.2'392 — Kent. High Halden, *to 1980*

Mitchell, Marcia. High Halden, the parish and the people / by Marcia Mitchell and Ian Murdoch. — Ashford ('Napchester', High Halden, Ashford, Kent TN26 3TY) : M. Mitchell & I. Murdoch, c1981. — 108p,[1] folded leaf of plates : ill,1map,ports ; 30cm
ISBN 0-9507690-0-2 (pbk) : £3.50 B82-03770

942.2'392 — Kent. Woodchurch. Parish churches: Parish Church of All Saints *(Woodchurch), to 1982*

Mansell, M. H.. The Parish Church of All Saints, Woodchurch, Kent / M.H. Mansell. — 2nd ed. — [Ashford] ([24 Kirkwood Ave., Woodchurch, Ashford, Kent]) : [M.H. Mansell], 1982. — 32p : ill,2coats of arms,1plan ; 22cm
Previous ed.: 1972. — Bibliography: p32
Unpriced (pbk) B82-40606

942.2'3920858'05 — Kent. Ashford *(District) — Serials*

Adscene. Maidstone, Ashford, Tenterden. — No.1 (1976)-. — Canterbury (Newspaper House, Wincheap, Canterbury, Kent) : Kent Free Press, 1976-. — v. : ill,ports ; 45cm
Weekly. — Description based on: No.284 (Wednesday Sept. 2nd 1981)
ISSN 0262-3420 = Adscene. Maidstone, Ashford, Tenterden : Unpriced
Primary classification 942.2'3750858'05 B82-03413

942.2'5'005 — East Sussex & West Sussex — *History — Serials*

Sussex vanguard. — No.1 (Summer 1981)-. — Bexhill-on-Sea (23 London Rd, Town Hall Sq., Bexhill-on-Sea, Sussex) : Sussex vanguard, 1981-. — v. : ill ; 29cm
Quarterly
ISSN 0262-513x = Sussex vanguard : £0.20 per issue B82-04894

942.2'5081 — East and West Sussex. Social life, *1830-1930*

Wales, Tony. A day out in old Sussex / by Tony Wales. — [Horsham] : [A. Wales], c1982. — 28p : ill ; 22cm. — (Field and furrow book ; no.1)
Cover title
ISBN 0-9508166-0-4 (pbk) : Unpriced B82-35515

942.2'5083'0924 — East & West Sussex. Social life, *1906-ca 1920 — Childhood reminiscences*

Gaster, Harold. A morning without clouds. — Large print ed. — Bath : Chivers, Oct.1982. — [240]p. — (A Lythway book)
Originally published: London : Cape, 1981
ISBN 0-85119-853-8 : £6.90 : CIP entry B82-20504

942.2'51 — East Sussex. Hailsham, *1870-1914*

The **String** Town : Hailsham 1870-1914 / edited by Brian Short. — Brighton (Education Development Building, University of Sussex, Falmer, Brighton BN1 9RG) : University of Sussex, Centre for Continuing Education, [1980]. — 86p : ill,maps ; 30cm. — (Occasional paper / University of Sussex. Centre for Continuing Education ; no.11)
Cover title
ISBN 0-904242-13-7 (pbk) : £1.50 B82-17507

942.2'51 — East Sussex. Wealden *(District).* **Abbeys: Bayham Abbey. Turnham, Robert de. Biographies**

Elvins, Mark Turnham. Bayham Abbey 1182-1982 : its founder and his family / by Mark Turnham Elvins. — Hove (9 Brunswick Sq., Hove, E. Sussex BN3 1EN) : Chichester Diocesan Fund and Board of Finance, [1981]. — 5p : 1coat of arms ; 21cm
Unpriced (unbound) B82-05934

942.25'11081 — England. South Pennines. Social conditions, *ca 1800-1980*

Breakell, Bill. People who made the Pennines / [written and designed by Bill Breakell]. — Hebden Bridge : Pennine Heritage Network, c1982. — 1folded sheet : ill(some col.) ; 59x21cm folded to 21x15cm
ISBN 0-907613-05-5 : Unpriced B82-37741

942.2'54 — East Sussex. Portslade, *to 1980*

Portslade. — Lewes : East Sussex County Library, [1982?]. — 11p : ill ; 22cm. — (An East Sussex County Library brief history)
ISBN 0-900348-83-6 (pbk) : £0.50 B82-40229

942.2'56083'0924 — East Sussex. Brighton. Social life, *1915-1939 — Personal observations*

Healey, Bert. Hard times and easy terms : and other tales by a Queens Park Cockney / by Bert Healey. — Brighton (13 West Drive, Brighton) : QueenSpark, 1980. — 164p : ill,ports ; 21cm. — (QueenSpark book ; 9)
£0.90 (pbk) B82-05688

942.2'57 — East Sussex. Lewes. Social life, *1906-1934 — Personal observations*

Noakes, George. To be a farmer's boy / by George Noakes. — Brighton (13 West Drive, Brighton) : QueenSpark, 1977. — 46p : ill,ports ; 21cm. — (QueenSpark books ; 5)
£0.30 (pbk) B82-05687

942.2'62 — West Sussex. Kingsley Green. Social life, *ca 1905-1914 — Childhood reminiscences*

Hutchinson, Margaret M.. A childhood in Edwardian Sussex : the making of a naturalist / by Margaret Hutchinson. — Hindhead : Saiga, c1981. — vii,150p : ill,1facsim,ports ; 23cm
ISBN 0-86230-040-1 : £6.00 B82-08708

942.2'67 — West Sussex. Rustington — *History*

Taylor, Mary, *1930-*. This was Rustington / Mary Taylor. — Rustington (The Squirrels, 25 North La., Rustington, West Sussex, BN16 3PL) : M. Taylor
No.3: In times of war. — 1981. — 60p : ill,2maps,facsims,ports ; 21cm
Cover title. — Map on folded sheet attached to inside cover
Unpriced (pbk) B82-14541

942.2'67 — West Sussex. Southwick, *to 1982*

Elliot, A. G.. A portrait of Southwich / by A.G. Elliot. — Portslade ([22 Hurst Cresc., Portslade, East Sussex, BN4 1SG]) : A.G. Elliot, 1982. — 32p : ill ; 21cm
ISBN 0-9506387-5-7 (pbk) : £1.25 B82-29243

942.2'68081 — West Sussex. Worthing. Salvation Army. Processions. Opponents. Riots, *1884*

Homan, Roger. Skeletons and salvationists : the riots in Worthing / by Roger Homan. — Hove (Diocesan Church House, 9 Brunswick Sq., Hove, E. Sussex BN3 1EN) : [Diocese of Chichester], [1981]. — 8p : 1ill ; 21cm
Bibliography: p8
Unpriced (unbound) B82-04376

942.2'69 — West Sussex. Henfield, *1939-1946 — Readings from contemporary sources*

Bishop, Lucie. Henfield in battledress. — Henfield (Highfield, Henfield, West Sussex) : L. Bishop, Dec.1981. — [120]p
ISBN 0-9507841-0-9 (pbk) : £2.95 : CIP entry B81-34967

942.2'69 — West Sussex. Lancing. Social life, *ca 1935-ca 1945 — Childhood reminiscences*

Walker, Ted. The high path. — London : Routledge, Oct.1982. — [180]p
ISBN 0-7100-9302-0 : £6.95 : CIP entry B82-23203

942.2'7 — Hampshire, *to 1918 — Festschriften*

Hampshire studies : presented to Dorothy Dymond on the occasion of her ninetieth birthday / edited by John Webb, Nigel Yates and Sarah Peacock. — Portsmouth : Portsmouth City Records Office, 1981. — xxv,333p : ill,maps,ports(some col.) ; 23cm
Map on lining papers. — Bibliography: p309. — Includes index
ISBN 0-901559-44-x : £12.00 B82-37165

942.2'70858'05 — Hampshire — *Serials*

Style magazine. Hampshire & Dorset. — No.1 (1982)-Oct.1982. — Weybridge (66 York Rd, Weybridge, Surrey) : Polewick Ltd, 1982-. — v. : ill(some col.),ports ; 30cm
Monthly. — Continued by: County style magazine. Hampshire & Dorset
ISSN 0263-9130 = Style magazine. Hampshire & Dorset : £0.60 per issue
Also classified at 942.3'30858'05 B82-32371

942.2′70858′05 — Hampshire. Social conditions — *For structure planning — Serials*

Hampshire strategic monitoring report. — 1978-. — Winchester (The Castle, Winchester, Hants.) : Hampshire County Council, County Planning Department, 1978-. — v. : maps ; 30cm. — (Strategic planning paper / Hampshire County Council)
Annual
ISSN 0263-9068 = Hampshire strategic monitoring report : £0.50 B82-38539

942.2′725 — Hampshire. Farnborough, *1890-1930 — Illustrations*

Farnborough and Cove in camera. — Farnborough : Saint Michael's Abbey Press, Dec.1982. — [40]p
ISBN 0-907077-20-x (cased) : £6.95 : CIP entry
ISBN 0-907077-21-8 (pbk) : £2.25 B82-40340

942.2′732 — Hampshire. Andover. Town houses: Savoy Chambers, *to 1982*

Emery, V.. The story of Savoy Chambers 1770-1982 / written by V. Emery. — [Weybridge] : Crest Estates, [1982?]. — 2p : ill (some col.),plans ; 21x30cm
Back cover title. — Text and ill on inside covers
Unpriced (pbk) B82-40196

942.2′732 — Hampshire. East Wellow & West Wellow, *1870-1980*

'Wellow that were' / by the Wellow History Society. — [Romsey] : Lower Test Valley Archaeological Study Group, 1981. — 52p : ill,1map,ports ; 21cm
Map attached to inside cover
ISBN 0-906921-02-3 (pbk) : £1.90 B82-37159

942.2′732 — Hampshire. Romsey, *1800-1900*

Berrow, Phoebe. A tour of old Romsey / by Phoebe Berrow. — [Romsey] : Lower Test Valley Archaeological Study Group, c1980. — 48p,[1]folded leaf of plates : ill,2maps ; 21cm
ISBN 0-906921-01-5 (pbk) : £1.80 B82-15061

942.2′735 — Hampshire. Winchester, *ca 1845-1900*

Carpenter Turner, Barbara. Winchester : 100 years ago / by Barbara Carpenter Turner. — Southampton : Cave, [1981]. — 48p : ill,ports ; 21cm
Text, ill on inside covers
ISBN 0-86146-007-3 (pbk) : £0.60 B82-04001

942.2′75 — Hampshire. Beaulieu, *1939-1945*

Elsworth, Walter. Beaulieu in World War II. — Christchurch (6 Drake Cl., Christchurch, Dorset BH23 3ET) : Linda Philpott, Jan.1983. — [48]p
ISBN 0-946396-00-0 (pbk) : £2.00 : CIP entry B82-39305

942.2′75 — Hampshire. New Forest *(District)*. **Milton,** *1888-1977*

Handscomb, E. C. G.. Focus on Milton : a lifetime of development. — [New Milton] ([c/o 44, Barton Court Ave, Barton-on-Sea, New Milton, Hants. BH25 7HG]) : [New Milton, Barton and District Ratepayers' and Residents' Association], [1978]. — [28]p : ill ; 21cm
Cover title. — Compiled by E.C.G. Handscomb for the Association
£0.50 (pbk) B82-11333

942.2′76 — Hampshire. Southampton. Melbourne Street. Anglo-Saxon antiquities. Excavation of remains, *1971-1976*

Holdsworth, Philip. Excavations at Melbourne Street Southampton, 1971-1976 : by Philip Holdsworth with contributions on the Hamwih brickearths by Myra L. Shackley and on Hamtvn alias Hamwic (Saxon Southampton) : the place-name traditions and their significance by Alexander R. Rumble / edited for SARC by David A. Hinton. — London : Published for the Southampton Archaeological Research Committee by the Council for British Archaeology, 1980. — viii,140p : ill,maps,plans ; 30cm. — (Southampton Archaeological Research Committee report ; 1) (CBA research report, ISSN 0589-9036 ; 33)
Bibliography: p135-137. — Includes index
ISBN 0-900312-82-3 (pbk) : £15.00 : CIP rev.
ISSN 0589-9036 B79-37099

942.2′760858′05 — Hampshire. Southampton — *Serials*

[The Advertiser *(Southampton)***]**. The Advertiser. — No.1 (1979)-. — Southampton (47 Millbrook Rd, Southampton, Hants.) : [Southern Newspapers], 1979-. — v. : ill ; 42cm
Weekly. — Description based on: No.132 (26th Nov. 1981)
ISSN 0263-0443 = Advertiser (Southampton) : Unpriced B82-14249

942.2′775 — Hampshire. Titchfield, *to 1981*

Titchfield : a history / contributors Christine Bartlett ... [et al.] ; maps and drawings Vernon Belding ; edited by George Watts for the Titchfield History Society. — [Titchfield] : Titchfield History Society, c1982. — 143p : ill,coats of arms,facsims,maps,plans ; 21cm
Bibliography: p141
ISBN 0-9508131-1-7 (pbk) : Unpriced B82-37527

942.2′792 — Hampshire. Portsmouth. Lake Road. Social life, *1900-1960 — Childhood reminiscences — Collections*

Memories of Lake Road / [compiled by John Barker ... et al. with contributions from Mrs. Adams ... et al.]. — Buckland (New Road Centre, Balliol Rd., Buckland) : W.E.A. Local History Group, 1980. — [48]p : ill ; 21cm
£0.20 (pbk) B82-18605

942.2′792 — Hampshire. Southsea. Riots, *1874*

Field, J. L.. The battle of Southsea / [J.L. Field]. — Portsmouth : Portsmouth City Council, 1981. — 3-18p : ill,facsims,1map ; 25cm. — (The Portsmouth papers ; 34)
Cover title
ISBN 0-901559-42-3 (pbk) : £0.75 B82-40518

942.2′792083′0924 — Hampshire. Portsmouth. Social life, *1933 — Childhood reminiscences*

Ford, Frank, *1923-*. Saturday and Sunday : a childhood memory / by Frank Ford. — Buckland (New Road Centre, Balliol Rd., Buckland) : W.E.A. Local History Group, 1980. — [8]p ; 21cm
£0.10 (pbk) B82-18604

942.2′795 — Hampshire. Havant *(District)*. **Country houses: Stakes Hill Lodge,** *to 1973*

Newton, Marion. The rise and fall of Stakes Hill Lodge, 1800-1973 / by Marion Newton and G.H.M. Jackson. — 2nd ed. — [Cirencester] ([Poulton Priory Estate Office, Cirencester, Glos.]) : [G.H.M. Jackson], c1981. — 65p,[26]p of plates : ill(some col.),facsims,3plans,ports (some col.),2geneal.tables ; 24cm
Previous ed.: 1977. — Geneal. tables on lining papers
Unpriced B82-23162

942.2′8 — Isle of Wight. Anglo-Saxon cemeteries. Excavation of remains, *1815-1855*

Arnold, C. J.. The Anglo-Saxon cemeteries of the Isle of Wight. — London : British Museum Publications, July 1982. — [208]p
ISBN 0-7141-1359-x : £25.00 : CIP entry B82-14072

942.2′85 — Isle of Wight. Yarmouth, *to 1981*

Winter, C. W. R.. The ancient town of Yarmouth / by C.W.R. Winter. — Newport : Isle of Wight County Press, c1981. — 208p,[28]p of plates : ill,ports ; 22cm
ISBN 0-9501779-7-0 : Unpriced B82-04203

942.2′9′009732 — Berkshire. Towns. Archaeological investigation — *Proposals*

Astill, Grenville G.. Historic towns in Berkshire : an archaeological appraisal / Grenville G. Astill. — Reading : [Berkshire Archaeological Unit], 1978. — iii,113p(4fold.) : maps,plans (some col.) ; 30cm. — (Berkshire Archaeological Committee publication ; no.2)
Maps on inside covers. — Bibliography: p109-113
ISBN 0-904989-01-1 (pbk) : £2.50 B82-07274

942.2′9081′0222 — Berkshire, *1845-1920 — Illustrations*

Read, Susan. Berkshire in camera : Berkshire and the Vale of the White Horse, 1845-1920 / Susan Read. — Newbury : Countryside Books, 1981. — 95p : ill,ports ; 21x30cm
Includes index
ISBN 0-905392-10-8 (pbk) : £4.95 B82-06580

942.2′93 — Berkshire. Reading. Ort Farm, *to 1981*

Padley, F. C.. A village in the town / by F.C. Padley. — Rev. ed. / with additional photographs. — Reading : Reading Branch Workers' Educational Association, 1981. — 26p : ill,1map,ports ; 21cm
Cover title. — Previous ed.: 1973
ISBN 0-903810-03-4 (pbk) : Unpriced B82-16146

942.2′94 — Berkshire. Three Mile Cross. Social life, *1820-1830 — Personal observations*

Mitford, Mary Russell. Our village / Mary Russell Mitford ; with an introduction by Margaret Lane ; and wood engravings by Joan Hassall. — Oxford : Oxford University Press, 1982. — xi,208p : ill,1port ; 20cm. — (Oxford paperbacks)
Originally published: London : Harrap, 1947
ISBN 0-19-281334-x (pbk) : £2.95 : CIP rev. B82-10433

942.2′97081 — Berkshire. Slough, *1851*

A Town in the making : Slough 1851 / by the WEA (Slough & Eton Branch) Local History Class. — Reading : Berkshire County Council, [1981?]. — 156p : ill,maps,facsims,1form ; 24cm
Bibliography: p146-153. — Includes index
ISBN 0-905538-38-2 (pbk) : Unpriced B82-03446

942.2′98 — Berkshire. Bracknell, *1949-1981*

Parris, Henry. Bracknell : the making of our new town / Henry and Judith Parris. — [Bracknell] : Bracknell Development Corporation, c1981. — 80p : ill(some col.),col.maps ; 20cm
Includes index
ISBN 0-9507672-0-4 (pbk) : £1.50 B82-05706

942.3′1 — Wiltshire, *to 1800 — Stories, anecdotes*

Millson, Cecilia. Tales of old Wiltshire / Cecilia Millson ; with illustrations by Don Osmond. — Newbury : Countryside Books, 1982. — 96p : ill,1map ; 22cm
ISBN 0-905392-12-4 (pbk) : £2.95 B82-24560

942.3′1082′0922 — Wiltshire. Social life, *ca 1900-1930 — Personal observations — Collections*

Wiltshire lives / collected and edited by Jennifer Curry ... [et al.]. — Salisbury : St Edmunds Arts Centre, 1981. — [48]p : ill,ports ; 21cm
ISBN 0-906984-01-7 (pbk) : Unpriced B82-01520

942.3′13 — Wiltshire. South Marston. Social life, *ca 1885-1912 — Personal observations*

Williams, Alfred. In a Wiltshire village : scenes from rural Victorian life / selected from the writings of Alfred Williams by Michael Justin Davis. — Gloucester : Sutton, 1981. — 192p : ill,1map,ports ; 23cm
Includes index
ISBN 0-904387-62-3 (pbk) : Unpriced : CIP rev. B81-20570

942.3′13 — Wiltshire. Swindon, *1840-1901*

Silto, J.. A Swindon history 1840-1901 / by J. Silto. — Swindon : J. Silto, c1981. — 109p,[9] leaves of plates : ill,maps,1coat of arms,facsims,1port ; 30cm
Bibliography: p103-106. — Includes index
ISBN 0-9507186-1-0 (pbk) : £2.50 B82-01297

942.3′17 — Wiltshire. Marlborough, *ca 1850-ca 1910 — Illustrations*

Gray, Michael. Marlborough in old photographs. — Gloucester : Sutton, Nov.1982. — [96]p
ISBN 0-86299-018-1 (pbk) : £3.95 : CIP entry B82-26084

942.3′17 — Wiltshire. Seend, *to 1980*

Bradby, Edward. Seend : a Wiltshire village past and present / Edward Bradby ; commissioned by the Seend Trust with the support of the Carnegie U.K. Trust. — Gloucester : Sutton, 1981. — xii,243p : ill,maps,facsims,plans,ports ; 23cm
Bibliography: p233. — Includes index
ISBN 0-904387-74-7 (cased) : Unpriced : CIP rev.
ISBN 0-904387-81-x (pbk) : £3.95 B81-32590

942.3'19 — Wiltshire. Salisbury. Buildings of historical importance

Royal Commission on Historical Monuments (England). Ancient and historical monuments in the city of Salisbury / Royal Commission on Historical monuments (England). — London : H.M.S.O.
Vol.1. — 1980. — lxiv,199p,104p,[4]p of plates : ill,maps,plans ; 29cm
Three maps on 3 folded leaves in pocket. — Includes index
ISBN 0-11-700849-4 : £33.00
ISBN 0-11-700850-8 (grey binding) : Unpriced B82-19395

942.3'3 — Dorset, *to 1624 — Early works — Facsimiles*

Coker, John. Coker's survey of Dorsetshire. — Sherborne : Dorset Publishing, 1980. — 175p,[7]leaves of plates : ill,coats of arms ; 23cm
Facsim of: A Survey of Dorsetshire containing the antiquities and natural history of that county. London : J. Wilcox, 1732. — Includes index
ISBN 0-902129-20-1 : Unpriced B82-24930

942.3'3'00222 — Dorset, *1539-1855 — Illustrations*

Burnett, David, *1946-*. Dorset before the camera : 1539-1855 / David Burnett. — Wimborne : Dovecote, 1982. — [96]p : chiefly ill ; 27cm
ISBN 0-9503518-7-3 : £5.95 B82-25350

942.3'3'009734 — Dorset. Deserted villages, *to ca 1920*

Good, Ronald. The lost villages of Dorset / Ronald Good. — Wimborne : Dovecote, 1979. — 85p,[4]p of plates : ill,maps ; 26cm
Includes index
ISBN 0-9503518-5-7 : £6.95 B82-25349

942.3'30858'05 — Dorset — *Serials*

Style magazine. Hampshire & Dorset. — No.1 (1982)-Oct.1982. — Weybridge (66 York Rd, Weybridge, Surrey) : Polewick Ltd, 1982-. — v. : ill(some col.),ports ; 30cm
Monthly. — Continued by: County style magazine. Hampshire & Dorset
ISSN 0263-9130 = Style magazine. Hampshire & Dorset : £0.60 per issue
Primary classification 942.2'70858'05
B82-32371

942.3'31 — Dorset. Dorchester, *to 1980*

Adlam, Brian. The book of Dorchester : County town of Dorset / by Brian Adlam. — Buckingham : Barracuda, 1981. — 136p : ill,maps,facsims,ports ; 27cm
Facsim. maps on lining papers. — Bibliography: p130. — Includes index
ISBN 0-86023-128-3 : £12.50 B82-04221

942.3'31 — Dorset. Sherborne, *to 1733*

Barker, Katherine. Sherborne : St Aldhelm and before : an illustrated guide to the early growth of a Dorset country town / Katherine Barker. — [Sherborne] ([Wallace House, South St., Sherborne, Dorset DT9 3NE]) : [K. Barker], c1982. — 1folded sheet([6]p) : ill,plans ; 28cm
Unpriced B82-38245

942.3'31 — Dorset. West Dorset *(District)*. **Bride Valley,** *ca 1765-1982*

Bailey, C. J.. The Bride Valley. — Dorchester (Dorset County Museum, High West St., Dorchester, Dorset DT1 1XA) : Dorset Natural History & Archaeological Society, Oct.1982. — [112]p
ISBN 0-900341-16-5 (cased) : £7.50 : CIP entry
ISBN 0-900341-15-7 (pbk) : £4.70 B82-25757

942.3'31 — Dorset. Winterbourn St Martins. Social life, *1872 — Correspondence, diaries, etc. — Facsimiles*

Dallas, Berry. Our journal at Winterbourn St Martins. — Dorchester : Dorset Natural History & Archaeological Society, Nov.1982. — [60]p
Facsim. of manuscript diary
ISBN 0-900341-17-3 (pbk) : £3.25 : CIP entry
B82-28761

942.3'32 — Dorset. Springhead, *to 1982*

Brocklebank, Joan. Springhead, Fontmell Magna : some historical notes / Joan Brocklebank. — [Dorchester] : Published for the Springhead Trust by J. Brocklebank, c1982. — 13p : 1ill,1map ; 21cm
Unpriced (unbound) B82-21286

942.3'34 — Kent. Canterbury. Castles: Canterbury Castle. Excavation of remains

Bennett, P. (Paul). Excavations at Canterbury Castle / by P. Bennett, S.S. Frere and S. Stow with contributions by J. Anstee ... [et al.]. — Maidstone : Published for the Canterbury Archaeological Trust by the Kent Archaeological Society, 1982. — 236p,[3]folded leaves of plates : ill,1map,plans ; 28cm. — (The Archaeology of Canterbury ; v.1)
Bibliography: p13-16. — Includes index
ISBN 0-906746-01-9 : £9.50 (£7.50 to members of the Kent Archaeological Society)
B82-23570

942.3'35 — Dorset. Weymouth, *1842 — Illustrations*

Weld, Charles. Weymouth sketches, 1842 : from a sketch book by Weld found by the editor in a second-hand bookshop in New York in 1960 / by Charles Weld ; edited by J. Stevens Cox. — [St. Peter's Port] : Toucan, c1982. — [8]p : chiefly ill ; 22cm
Limited ed. of 10 copies
ISBN 0-85694-254-5 (pbk) : Unpriced
B82-10031

942.3'36 — Dorset. Swanage — *Serials*

Swanage & Dorset times. — [No.8708 (Friday 16 Oct. 1981)?]-. — Poole (71 High St, Poole) : W.H. Hallett Ltd., 1981-. — v. : ill,ports ; 45cm. — (Times-Herald series)
Weekly. — Continues: Swanage times
£0.12 B82-40051

942.3'37 — Dorset. Poole. Branksome Park & Canford Cliffs, *1882-1932 — Illustrations*

Hawkes, Andrew. Memories of old Poole / compiled from postcards of Poole by Andrew Hawkes. — Poole : A. Hawkes, 1981. — p237-264 : ill ; 21cm
Includes index
ISBN 0-9506404-7-6 (pbk) : £1.45 B82-08688

942.3'38 — Dorset. Bournemouth. West Howe. Social life, *1900-1945 — Personal observations — Collections*

'West Howe proper' : a part of Dorset remembered by local people / Charlie Bowles ... [et al.]. — Wimborne : Word and Action (Dorset) 1982. — 120p : ill,facsims,2maps,ports ; 21cm
ISBN 0-904939-28-6 (pbk) : £1.70 (£1.50 in Dorset) : CIP rev. B82-17947

942.3'38 — Dorset. Bournemouth. Winton. Social life, *1900-1978 — Personal observations*

Hoare, Nellie. A Winton story / by Nellie Hoare. — Bournemouth (The Teachers' Centre, 40 Lowther Rd., Bournemouth) : Bournemouth Local Studies Publications, 1982. — 46p : ill,1map,ports ; 22cm
ISBN 0-906287-44-8 (pbk) : £0.60 B82-29248

942.3'38082'0924 — Dorset. Bournemouth region, *ca 1890-1958 — Personal observations*

Marshall, Pascoe. My story : memories of Bournemouth and district in the late 19th and early 20th centuries / by Pascoe Marshall. — Bournemouth : Bournemouth Local Studies, 1981. — 59p : ill,ports ; 21cm
ISBN 0-906287-42-1 (pbk) : £0.65 B82-15193

942.3'39 — Dorset. Christchurch — *Serials*

[The Advertiser *(Christchurch)*]. The Advertiser. — No.1 (1979)-. — Christchurch (1 High St., Christchurch, Dorset) : [Southern Newspapers], 1979-. — v. : ill,ports ; 42cm
Weekly. — Description based on: No.141 (26th Nov. 1981)
ISSN 0263-0435 = Advertiser (Christchurch) : Unpriced B82-14248

942.3'45 — Sark, *to 1981*

Coysh, Victor. Sark : the last stronghold of feudalism / by Victor Coysh. — Mount Durand : Toucan, 1982. — 46p : ill,facsims,ports ; 22cm
ISBN 0-85694-252-9 (pbk) : Unpriced
B82-10096

942.3'5 — Devon, *to 1981*

Clements, Pauline. The Devon book : capturing the flavour of Devon in a nutshell / design, drawings and concept by Pauline Clements ; written and researched by James Robertson. — Brompton Regis : Clover, 1981. — 64p : ill,1map ; 25cm. — (Nutshell series)
ISBN 0-907682-00-6 : £2.95 B82-06885

942.3'5'009734 — Devon. Countryside, *1914-1918 — Stories, anecdotes*

Williamson, Henry. Tales of moorland and estuary / Henry Williamson. — London : Macdonald Futura, 1981. — viii,210p ; 18cm. — (Heritage) (A Futura book)
Originally published: London : Macdonald, 1953
ISBN 0-7088-2107-3 (pbk) : £1.75 B82-00839

942.3'5082'0924 — Devon. Carter, Brian — *Biographies*

Carter, Brian. Yesterday's harvest. — London : Dent, Sept.1982. — [192]p
ISBN 0-460-04562-8 : £6.95 : CIP entry
B82-20640

942.3'5082'0924 — Devon. Social life, *ca 1908-1914 — Childhood reminiscences*

Garnett, Eve. First affections. — London : Muller, Oct.1982. — [176]p
ISBN 0-584-11003-0 : £6.95 : CIP entry
Also classified at 942.4'4082'0924 B82-23362

942.3'50858'0222 — Devon — *Illustrations*

Bloemendal, F. A. H.. Devon & Cornwall / photographs by F.A.H. Bloemendal ; text by Alan Hollingsworth. — London : Ian Allan, 1982. — 110p : chiefly col.ill,2maps ; 30cm. — (England in cameracolour)
Maps on lining papers
ISBN 0-7110-1223-7 : £8.95
Also classified at 942.3'70858'0222 B82-38008

Pettit, Paul. The Country life picture book of Devon and Cornwall / Paul Pettit. — London : Country Life, 1982. — 128p : chiefly col.ill ; 31cm
ISBN 0-600-36822-x : £7.95
Also classified at 942.3'70858'0222 B82-27040

942.3'50858'05 — Devon. Social conditions — *For structure planning — Serials*

Devon. *Planning Department*. Settlement : topic report / County Planning Department. — 1981-. — Exeter (County Hall, Topsham Rd, Exeter EX2 4QH) : Devon County Council Planning Department, 1981-. — v. : ill ; 30cm
Annual
ISSN 0261-247x = Settlement topic report : £0.40 B82-09687

942.3'53 — Devon. Buckland Monachorum. Social life, *ca 1910-ca 1930*

Lakeman, Joy. Them days, : from the memories of Joan Bellan / by Joy Lakeman. — Padstow : Tabb House, 1982. — x,118p : ill,ports ; 21cm
ISBN 0-907018-15-7 (pbk) : £2.95 B82-35818

942.3'54 — Devon. Bridwell. Social life, *1844 — Correspondence, diaries, etc.*

Clarke, John Were. Diary of a Devonshire squire—1844 : the journal of John Were Clarke, Esquire, of Bridwell, Uffculme / [edited and annotated by W. P. Authers]. — Tiverton : W.P. Authers, c1982. — 48p : ill,1geneal.table,ports ; 21cm
Bibliography: p48
ISBN 0-9506087-5-0 (pbk) : £1.20 B82-36856

942.3'55 — Devon. Moretonhampstead, *to 1900*

Heath, R. O.. Sparrowhawk : the story of Moretonhampstead : one thousand years from 700AD to 1700AD or thereabouts with a few further episodes of interest / collected and explained by R.O. Heath. — [Newton Abbot] ([Greenhill House, Moretonhamptead, Newton Abbot, Devon TQ13 8LL]) : R.O. Heath, 1977. — 95p : ill,1plan ; 22cm
Unpriced (pbk) B82-26605

942.3'56 — Devon. Exeter. Buildings of historical importance

Hardy, Paul, *1924-*. Exeter : profile of a city / Paul Hardy. — Bristol : Redcliffe, 1982. — 64p : ill ; 22cm
ISBN 0-905459-47-4 (pbk) : £1.75 B82-33784

942.3'56081'0222 — Devon. Exeter, *ca 1880-ca 1935 — Illustrations*

Isca Collection. Old Exeter : a portfolio of photographs from the Isca Collection / [compiled by] Peter D. Thomas. — Exeter : Webb & Bower, 1981, c1977. — 173p : chiefly ill,coats of arms,facsims,1plan,ports ; 31cm
Originally published: Plymouth : Baron Jay, 1977. — Ill on lining papers
ISBN 0-906671-66-3 : £7.95 : CIP rev.
B81-34209

942.3'57 — Devon. Sidmouth. Fishing communities. Social life, *1900-1905 — Personal observations*

Reynolds, Stephen. A poor man's house / Stephen Reynolds ; with an introduction by Roy Hattersley. — Oxford : Oxford University Press, 1982. — xviii,205p ; 20cm
Originally published: London : J. Lane, 1908
ISBN 0-19-281326-9 (pbk) : £2.95 : CIP rev.
B82-07502

942.3'58 — Devon. Tamerton Foliot. Parish churches: Saint Mary's Church *(Tamerton Foliot), to 1981*

Bebbington, P. S.. Saint Mary's Church, Tamerton Foliot : a history guide / by P.S. Bebbington. — [Tamerton Foliot] : Published by the Vicar and Churchwardens of Tamerton Foliot Parish Church, [1981?]. — 32p : ill,1map,1facsim ; 30cm
Cover title. — Text and map on inside covers
ISBN 0-9507852-0-2 (pbk) : Unpriced
B82-24678

942.3'592 — Devon. Dart River region, *to 1981*

Hemery, Eric. Historic Dart / Eric Hemery. — Newton Abbot : David & Charles, c1982. — 268p : ill,facsims,maps,ports ; 23cm
Bibliography: p256-257. — Includes index
ISBN 0-7153-8142-3 : £12.95 : CIP rev.
B82-07580

942.3'592082'0924 — Devon. South Hams *(District).* **Social life,** *1916-1960 — Personal observations*

Burner, Bill. Blue skies / [Bill Burner]. — [Salcombe] ([The Victoria Inn, Salcombe, Devon]) : [Bill Burner], 1979. — 31p : ill ; 20x21cm
Unpriced (unbound) B82-14417

942.3'7 — Cornwall. Churches, *to 1981*

Rendell, Joan. Cornish churches / Joan Rendell. — Bodmin : Bossiney, 1982. — 104p : ill,ports ; 21cm
ISBN 0-906456-60-6 (pbk) : £1.75 B82-28712

942.3'7 — Cornwall. Coastal waters *— Stories, anecdotes*

Tangye, Nigel. Cornwall and the tumbling sea / Nigel Tangye. — London : Kimber, 1981. — 192p : 2maps ; 23cm
Bibliography: p184-186. — Includes index
ISBN 0-7183-0258-3 : £5.95 B82-04265

942.3'7'005 — Cornwall *— History — Serials*

Cornish bedside book. — No.1-. — Redruth (Trewolsta, Trewirgie, Redruth [Cornwall TR15 2TB]) : Dyllansow Truran-Cornish Publications, 1980-. — v. : ill,facsims,ports ; 21cm
Irregular
ISSN 0263-3124 = Cornish bedside book : £1.65 B82-19881

942.3'7082 — Cornwall. Social conditions, *1901-1910*

Mudd, David. The Cornish Edwardians / David Mudd. — Bodmin : Bossiney, 1982. — 120p : ill,ports ; 21cm
ISBN 0-906456-59-2 (pbk) : £1.95 B82-20336

942.3'7085'0222 — Cornwall. Social life, *1939-1981 — Illustrations*

Ellis, George, *1900-*. A Cornish camera : photographs / George Ellis ; text Sarah Foot. — Bodmin : Bossiney Books, 1982. — 119p : of ill,ports ; 30cm
ISBN 0-906456-63-0 (pbk) : £3.90 B82-41120

942.3'7085'0924 — Cornwall. Prynn, Edward *— Biographies*

Prynn, Edward. No problem : the story of a Cornishman, part 2 / Edward Prynn ; edited by Jo Park. — Padstow : Tabb House, 1982. — 92p,[8]p of plates : ill,ports ; 21cm
ISBN 0-907018-16-5 (pbk) : £2.95 B82-41076

942.3'70857'0924 — Cornwall. Rural regions. Social life, *1970-1979 — Personal observations*

Tangye, Derek. Sun on the lintel / Derek Tangye. — Large print ed. — Bath : Chivers Press, 1982, c1976. — 248p ; 23cm. — (A New Portway large print book)
Originally published: London : Joseph, 1976
ISBN 0-85119-152-5 : Unpriced : CIP rev.
B81-33814

Tangye, Derek. When the winds blow / Derek Tangye ; illustrated by Jean Tangye. — London : Sphere, 1982, c1980. — 172p : ill ; 18cm
Originally published: London : Joseph, 1980
ISBN 0-7221-8385-2 : £1.50 B82-26942

942.3'70858'0222 — Cornwall *— Illustrations*

Bloemendal, F. A. H.. Devon & Cornwall / photographs by F.A.H. Bloemendal ; text by Alan Hollingsworth. — London : Ian Allan, 1982. — 110p : chiefly col.ill,2maps ; 30cm. — (England in cameracolour)
Maps on lining papers
ISBN 0-7110-1223-7 : £8.95
Primary classification 942.3'50858'0222
B82-38008

Pettit, Paul. The Country life picture book of Devon and Cornwall / Paul Pettit. — London : Country Life, 1982. — 128p : chiefly col.ill ; 31cm
ISBN 0-600-36822-x : £7.95
Primary classification 942.3'50858'0222
B82-27040

942.3'71'01 — Cornwall. Bodmin Moor. Megalithic circles

O'Brien, C. A. E.. The megalithic odyssey. — Wellingborough : Aquarian Press, Feb.1983. — [192]p
ISBN 0-85030-309-5 (pbk) : £4.95 : CIP entry
B82-39465

942.3'72 — Cornwall. Newquay region *— Serials*

Newquay courier. — 1980-. — Bodmin (The Friaries, Mount Folly, Bodmin, [Cornwall]) : Cornwall Courier, 1980-. — v. : ill,ports ; 45cm
Weekly. — Numbering and chronological designation follow that of Cornwall courier. — Description based on: No.255 (Thursday Jan. 15, 1981)
ISSN 0262-3749 = Newquay courier : £0.12 per issue B82-03409

942.3'74 — Cornwall. Caradon *(District).* **Country parks: Mount Edgcumbe Country Park. Countryside interpretation**

The **Interpretation** of a country park : final report of the Mount Edgcumbe project, 1980-81 / edited by Bryan J.H. Brown. — [Plymouth] : [College of St. Mark & St. John Foundation], c1981. — 88p : ill,1coat of arms,facsims,forms,1map,1port ; 30cm
Bibliography: p77-80
£2.00 (pbk) B82-26458

942.3'75 — Cornwall. St Ives. Knill, John *— Biographies*

James, Beryl. John Knill : his life and times / by Beryl James ; with illustrations by Laura Rowe. — [Redruth] ([Trewolsta, Trewirgie, Redruth]) : [Dyllansow Truran-Cornish Publications], [1981?]. — 68p : ill,1map,facsims,ports,1geneal.table ; 21cm
Unpriced (pbk) B82-03773

942.3'75 — Cornwall. St Ives region. Social life, *to 1945*

Bray, Lena. St. Ives heritage : recollections and records of St. Ives, Carbis Bay and Lelant / by Lena and Donald Bray. — Redruth : Dyllansow Truran, [1981?]. — 108p : ill,1map,1facsim,1plan,ports ; 21cm
Bibliography: p108
ISBN 0-907566-07-3 (cased) : Unpriced
ISBN 0-907566-08-1 (pbk) : Unpriced
B82-12792

942.3'76 — Cornwall. Carn Brea, *to 1951*

Tangye, Michael. Carn Brea : brief history and guide / by Michael Tangye. — [Redruth] : [Dyllansow Truran], [1981?]. — 69p : ill,1map,ports ; 23cm
Cover title
ISBN 0-907566-12-x (cased) : Unpriced
ISBN 0-907566-11-1 (pbk) : Unpriced
B82-12791

942.3'78 — Cornwall. Falmouth & Penryn, *1870-1980 — Illustrations*

Yesterday and today around Falmouth and Penryn / [compiled by] Fisher Barham. — Falmouth : Glasney Press, 1981. — 96p : chiefly ill,ports ; 28cm
ISBN 0-906354-05-6 (cased) : £5.50
ISBN 0-906354-04-8 (pbk) : £4.25 B82-10530

942.3'78 — Cornwall. Falmouth, *to 1961*

Whetter, James. The history of Falmouth / by James Whetter. — Redruth : Dyllansow Truran, c1981. — 190p : ill,maps,1facsim,plans ; 21cm
Bibliography: p101-102. — Includes index
ISBN 0-907566-01-4 (cased) : Unpriced
ISBN 0-907566-02-2 (pbk) : Unpriced
B82-03759

942.3'78 — Cornwall. Truro, *1914-1980 — Personal observations*

Barratt, Rex. Memories of Truronian in war and peace / by Rex Barratt. — [Redruth] : [Dyllansow Truran], [198-?]. — 60p : ill,ports ; 22cm
ISBN 0-907566-00-6 (pbk) : Unpriced
B82-03758

942.3'8 — Somerset. Human settlements, *to 1500. Archaeological investigation*

The **Archaeology** of Somerset. — Taunton (County Hall, Taunton TA1 4DY, Somerset) : Somerset County Council, Nov.1982. — [160]p
ISBN 0-86183-028-8 (pbk) : £7.50 : CIP entry
B82-30318

942.3'8 — Somerset, *to 1981*

Hawkins, Desmond. Avalon and Sedgemoor. — New ed. — Gloucester : A. Sutton, Apr.1982. — [192]p
Previous ed.: 1967
ISBN 0-86299-016-5 (pbk) : £4.50 : CIP entry
B82-11978

942.3'83 — Somerset. Glastonbury. Abbeys: Glastonbury Abbey, *to ca 1350 — Early works*

William, *of Malmesbury*. [De antiquitate Glastonie Ecclesie. English]. The early history of Glastonbury : an edition, translation and study of, William of Malmesbury's De antiquitate Glastonie Ecclesie / John Scott. — Woodbridge : Boydell, c1981. — viii,224p ; 25cm
Parallel Latin text and English translation, notes. — Bibliography: p211-215. — Includes index
ISBN 0-85115-154-x : £25.00 : CIP rev.
B81-25748

942.3'83 — Somerset. Wells. Cathedrals: Wells Cathedral. Closes, *to 1981*

Bailey, Sherwin. Canonical houses of Wells. — Gloucester : Alan Sutton, July 1982. — [192]p
ISBN 0-904387-91-7 : £8.95 : CIP entry
B82-17908

942.3'85 — Somerset. Williton. Parish churches: St. Peter *(Church : Williton), to 1980*

Armstrong, Harry, *1920-*. The parish of St. Peter, Williton / by Harry Armstrong. — [Watchet] ([Outmoor, Five Bells, Watchet, Somerset TA23 0HZ]) : [H. Armstrong], 1982. — 33p : ill,1facsim,1geneal.table,3maps ; 22cm
Unpriced (pbk) B82-36637

942.3'87 — Somerset. Wellington, *to 1981*

Bush, Robin. The book of Wellington : the story of a market town / by Robin Bush & Gillian Allen. — Buckingham : Barracuda, 1981. — 140p : ill,maps,facsims,ports ; 27cm
Maps on lining papers. — Bibliography: p133. — Includes index
ISBN 0-86023-099-6 : £12.50 B82-00932

942.3'89 — Somerset. Castle Cary, *to 1980*
McGarvie, Michael. Castle Cary : a sketch of its industrial and social history with special reference to Boyd's Hair Factory / by Michael McGarvie. — [Castle Cary] : Avalon Industries, 1980. — 48p,[8]p of plates : ill(some col.),1map,ports ; 24cm
Unpriced (pbk) B82-36342

942.3'89 — Somerset. Yeovil, *ca 1965 — Illustrations*
Yeovil : the changing scene. — Yeovil (c/o L.E.J. Brooke, 18, Stilby Rd., Yeovil BA21 3EF) : Yeovil Archaeological and Local History Society, 1981. — 42p : chiefly ill ; 20x26cm
£2.00 (pbk) B82-01908

942.3'89 — Somerset. Yeovil *(District).* **Country houses: Brympton d'Evercy,** *1974-1979*
Clive-Ponsonby-Fane, Charles. We started a stately home / Charles Clive-Ponsonby-Fane. — Yeovil (Brympton d'Evercy, Yeovil, Somerset) : C. Clive-Ponsonby-Fane, 1980. — viii,142p,[10]p of plates : ill,1facsim,1geneal.table,ports ; 23cm
Unpriced B82-36006

942.3'9'009734 — Avon. Villages, *to 1981*
Mason, Edmund J.. Avon villages / Edmund J. Mason and Dorrien Mason ; photographs by John H. Barrett. — London : Hale, 1982. — 192p,[32]p of plates : ill,maps ; 23cm
Bibliography: p179-181. — Includes index
ISBN 0-7091-9585-0 : £8.50 B82-31158

942.3'90858 — Avon. Social conditions *— For structure planning*
County of Avon structure plan : supplement report of survey / [County of Avon, Planning Department]. — [Bristol] : [The Department], 1980. — 7p ; 30cm
Cover title
ISBN 0-86063-108-7 (pbk) : Unpriced B82-26943

Report of survey supplement November 1981 : Avon county structure plan. — Bristol : Avon County Planning Department, [1981]. — 15p ; 30cm
ISBN 0-86063-131-1 (pbk) : Unpriced B82-12219

942.3'93 — Avon. Bristol. Bedminster. Social life, *1918-1939 — Childhood reminiscences*
Vear, Leonard G. W.. Bedminster between the wars : profile of a local community 1918-1939 / Leonard Vear. — Bristol : Published for Bristol & West Building Society by Redcliffe Press, 1981. — 47p : ill,ports ; 21cm
ISBN 0-905459-38-5 (pbk) : £1.50 B82-13608

942.3'93 — Avon. Bristol. Buildings of historical importance, *to 1976*
Shipsides, Frank. Bristol impressions / by Frank Shipsides ; with text compiled by John Sansom. — Bristol : Redcliffe, 1977 (1979 [printing]). — viii,83p : ill ; 25cm
Bibliography: p83
ISBN 0-905459-19-9 (pbk) : £3.50 B82-21829

942.3'93 — Avon. Bristol. Buildings of historical importance, *to 1978*
Shipsides, Frank. Bristol : profile of a city / Shipsides and Eason. — Bristol : Redcliffe, 1979 (1980 [printing]). — 87p : ill(some col.) ; 26cm
ISBN 0-905459-21-0 : £5.95 B82-21830

942.3'93 — Avon. Bristol. Totterdown. Social life, *1922-1936 — Childhood reminiscences*
Lawrance, Elsie. Growing up in Totterdown 1922-1936 / by Elsie Lawrance. — Bristol : Redcliffe Press, 1979. — 30p ; 21cm
ISBN 0-905459-18-0 (pbk) : £0.75 B82-13609

942.3'93 — Avon. Clifton & Westbury. Personal property. Probate inventories, *1609-1761 — Collections*
Clifton and Westbury probate inventories 1609-1761 / edited by John S. Moore. — [Bristol] : Avon Local History Association, c1981. — xlix,247p ; 30cm
Cover title. — At head of title: University of Bristol, Department of Extra-Mural Studies. — Includes index
£6.50 (pbk) B82-01904

942.3'93'00992 — Avon. Bristol. Celebrities, *to 1970*
Foot, David, *1929-*. Famous Bristolians : and others having strong associations with the city / by David Foot. — Bristol : Redcliffe, 1979. — [32]p : ports ; 22cm. — (The Bristol series)
ISBN 0-905459-13-x (pbk) : £0.75 B82-21832

942.3'93062 — Avon. Bristol, *1642-1646*
McGrath, Patrick, *1914-*. Bristol and the Civil War / Patrick McGrath. — [Bristol] ([74 Bell Barn Rd., Stoke Bishop, Bristol BS9 2DG]) : Bristol Branch of the Historical Association, 1981. — 50p,[4]p of plates : ill,maps,ports ; 22cm. — (Local history pamphlets / Bristol Branch of the Historical Association ; 50)
£1.00 (pbk) B82-07477

942.3'93081'0222 — Avon. Bristol, *1880-1890 — Illustrations*
Bristol in the 1880's / the photographs collected by and the book written, designed and published by Reece Winstone. — 2nd ed. — Bristol : R. Winstone, 1978. — 64p : chiefly ill,1map,ports ; 26cm
Previous ed.: 1962. — Includes index
ISBN 0-900814-55-1 : Unpriced B82-12376

942.3'93083'0222 — Avon. Bristol, *1914-1942 — Illustrations*
Bristol as it was 1939-1914 / the photographs taken or collected by and the book written, designed and published by Reece Winstone. — 5th ed. — Bristol : R. Winstone, 1978. — 56p : all ill,1map,ports ; 26cm
Previous ed.: 1969. — Includes index
ISBN 0-900814-54-3 : Unpriced B82-12377

942.3'96 — Avon. Clevedon. Piers: Clevedon Pier, *to 1980*
Mallory, Keith. Clevedon Pier / by Keith Mallory. — Bristol : Redcliffe, 1981. — 77p : ill ; 21cm
Maps on lining papers
ISBN 0-905459-24-5 : £6.50 B82-21828

942.3'96 — Avon. Western-super-Mare. Parish churches: Parish Church of Emmanuel *(Western-super-Mare), to 1982*
Bizley, Joyce. Looking backward — looking forward : the parish church of Emmanuel, Weston-super-Mare, 1847-1982 / Joyce Bizley. — [Weston-super-Mare] ([Emmanuel Vicarage, Walliscote Road, Weston-super-Mare, Avon BS23 1XE]) : [J.L. Ruffle], c1982. — 24p : ill,1map,2plans ; 21cm
£0.35 (pbk) B82-29509

942.3'98 — Avon. Bath. Buildings of historical importance: Royal Crescent, *to 1980*
Lowndes, William. The Royal Crescent in Bath : a fragment of English life / William Lowndes. — Bristol : Redcliffe, 1981. — 96p,[12]p of plates : ill(some col.),ports ; 22cm
Bibliography: p92. — Includes index
ISBN 0-905459-34-2 : £5.95 B82-21825

942.3'980858'05 — Avon. Bath *— Serials*
Bath and district advertiser. — No.76 (5th Nov. 1981)-. — Bath (Beau Nash House, Union Passage, Bath, [Avon]) : [Clownfield Ltd], 1981-. — v. : ill,ports ; 39cm
Continues: Bath weekly advertiser
ISSN 0263-0184 = Bath and district weekly advertiser : Unpriced B82-14245

Bath spark. — No.1 (Mar. '78)-. — [Bath] ([2 Longacre, London Rd, Bath, Avon]) : [Bath Spark], 1978-. — v. : ill,ports ; 30cm
Irregular. — Description based on: No.19 (Nov./Dec. '80)
£0.15 per issue B82-22684

942.4 — England. Severn River region, *to ca 1980*
Kissack, Keith. The River Severn / by Keith Kissack. — Lavenham : Dalton, 1982. — x,150p : ill,1map ; 23cm
Text, map on inside covers. — Bibliography: p144-145. — Includes index
ISBN 0-86138-004-5 (pbk) : £5.95 B82-31484

942.4083'092'4 — England. Midlands. Rural regions. Social life, *1918-1924 — Childhood reminiscences*
England, Daisy. Daisy Daisy / Daisy England ; illustrations by William Andrew Low and Stephen James England. — London : Regency Press, c1981. — 102p : ill ; 21cm
ISBN 0-7212-0666-2 : £3.00 B82-13310

942.4'0858'05 — England. Midlands *— Serials — Punjabi texts*
Dī Aishiana posaṭa pandaravārā = The Asian post fortnightly : a Punjabi fortnightly magazine from the Midlands for your social, political, literary, religious needs and interests. — Issue no.1 (29th Jan.-12th Feb. 1982)-. — [Birmingham] ([183 Rookery Rd, Handsworth, Birmingham B21 9QZ]) : [Design & Print Services], 1982-. — v. : ill,ports ; 30cm
Numerous editions
ISSN 0263-4473 = Asian post fortnightly (Punjabi edition) : £0.15 per issue B82-24755

942.4'10858'0222 — Gloucestershire. Winter, *1981-1982 — Illustrations*
A Winter to remember : December 1981-January 1982. — [Dursley] ([Reliance Works, Dursley, Glos.]) : F. Bailey and Son/Derek Archer], [1982]. — 24p : chiefly ill,ports ; 21x30cm
Cover title
£1.00 (pbk) B82-20734

942.4'13 — Gloucestershire. Forest of Dean, *to 1981*
Phelps, Humphrey. The Forest of Dean. — Gloucester : Alan Sutton, Nov.1982. — [192]p
ISBN 0-904387-86-0 (pbk) : £3.95 : CIP entry B82-26720

942.4'140858'05 — Gloucestershire. Gloucester *— Serials*
Gloucester news shopper. — No.1 (1980)-. — Gloucester (8 Southgate St., Gloucester) : Gloucestershire Newspapers Ltd, 1980-. — v. : ill,ports ; 42cm
Weekly. — Description based on: Friday Sept. 4th 1981
ISSN 0262-9178 = Gloucester news shopper : Unpriced B82-14772

Gloucester weekly news : incorporating the Brockworth and Churchdown news. — No.1055 (Thursday 22 Apr. 1982)-. — Gloucester (Addison House, Greyfriars, Gloucester, GL1 1TS) : [Stroud News & Journal Ltd.], 1982-. — v. : ill,ports ; 60cm
Weekly. — Continues: Brockworth and Churchdown news
£0.10 B82-40056

942.4'16 — Gloucestershire. Cheltenham, *to 1965*
Hart, Gwen. A history of Cheltenham / Gwen Hart. — 2nd ed. — Gloucester : Sutton, 1981. — 349p : ill(some col.),1map,ports ; 23cm
Previous ed.: Leicester ; Leicester University Press, 1965
ISBN 0-904387-87-9 (corrected) : £12.50 : CIP rev. B81-32589

942.4'160858'05 — Gloucestershire. Cheltenham *— Serials*
[The Town crier *(Cheltenham)***]**. The Town crier : the mid-week free newspaper for Cheltenham and district. — No.1 (27th May 1981)-. — Cheltenham (3 Crescent Place, Cheltenham, Glos.) : J & M Publications, 1981-. — v. : ill,ports ; 42cm
Weekly
ISSN 0262-6810 = Town crier (Cheltenham) : Unpriced B82-07652

942.4'17 — Gloucestershire. Cotswold *(District).* **Country houses: Highgrove & Gatcombe Park,** *to 1980*
Sanders, Geoffrey. Royal homes in Gloucestershire / Geoffrey Sanders and David Verey. — Gloucester : Sutton, 1981. — [36]p : ill(some col.),1col.map,ports(some col) ; 21x23cm
ISBN 0-904387-89-5 (pbk) : £1.95 : CIP rev.
Also classified at 942.4'19 B81-19122

942.4'17 — Gloucestershire. Fairford, *to 1980*
Lewis, June R.. A history of Fairford / by June R. Lewis. — Nelson : Hendon Publishing, c1982. — 32p : ill,maps,ports ; 19cm
Maps on inside covers
ISBN 0-86067-071-6 (pbk) : £0.95 B82-06448

942.4′19 — Gloucestershire. Bisley-with-Lypiatt. Country houses: Nether Lypiatt Manor, *to 1980*

Sanders, Geoffrey. Royal homes in Gloucestershire / Geoffrey Sanders and David Verey. — Gloucester : Sutton, 1981. — [36]p : ill(some col.),1col.map,ports(some col) ; 21x23cm
ISBN 0-904387-89-5 (pbk) : £1.95 : CIP rev.
Primary classification 942.4′17 B81-19122

942.4′19 — Gloucestershire. Cam & Dursley, *1860-1973 — Illustrations*

Evans, David E.. Dursley & Cam / David E. Evans. — Gloucester : Sutton, 1981. — 125p : chiefly ill,facsims,ports ; 23cm
ISBN 0-904387-88-7 (pbk) : £3.95 : CIP rev. B81-32591

942.4′19 — Gloucestershire. Painswick, *to 1928*

St. Clair Baddeley, Welbore. A Cotteswold manor being the history of Painswick / by Welbore St. Clair Baddeley ; with a new introduction by Geoffrey Sanders. — [2nd ed.]. — Gloucester : Sutton, 1980. — xiv,261p,[40]p of plates : ill,maps,facsims,geneal.tables ; 23cm
Originally published: London : Longmans & Co., 1929. — Includes index
ISBN 0-904387-54-2 : Unpriced B82-25381

942.4′19 — Gloucestershire. Wotton-under-Edge. Social life, *1800-1970*

Wotton-under-Edge : a century of change / edited for the Wotton-under-Edge Historical Society by G.B. Masefield. — Gloucester : Alan Sutton, 1980. — 112p : ill,ports ; 22cm
ISBN 0-904387-51-8 (pbk) : £3.95 : CIP rev. B80-18125

942.4′4082′0924 — Hereford and Worcester. Worcestershire. Social life, *ca 1908-1914 — Childhood reminiscences*

Garnett, Eve. First affections. — London : Muller, Oct.1982. — [176]p
ISBN 0-584-11003-0 : £6.95 : CIP entry
Primary classification 942.3′5082′0924 B82-23362

942.4′41 — Hereford and Worcester. Rock. Parish churches: Church of SS. Peter and Paul *(Rock), to ca 1970*

Thompson, Robert D.. Rock : together with references to Abberley, Alveley, Astley, Bewdley, Bliss Gate, Bredwardine, Buckeridge, Callow Hill, Chaddesley Corbett, Cleobury Mortimer, Clows Top, Droitwich, Finstall, Furnace Mill, Gorst Hill, Mitre Oak, Neen Sollars, Pensax, Ribbesford, Rock, Rock Moor, Shelf Head, The Shelslies, Thumpers Hole, Worcester, Wrekin, Wyre Forest / by Robert D. Thompson. — Kidderminster : Kenneth Tomkinson, c1981. — xviii,159p,[79]leaves of plates : ill,maps,facsims,ports,geneal.tables ; 21cm
Bibliography: p152. — Includes index
ISBN 0-907083-05-6 (pbk) : Unpriced B82-13951

942.4′45 — Hereford and Worcester. Ross-on-Wye region. Agricultural industries. Farms. Social life, *1796-1797 — Correspondence, diaries, etc.*

Hughes, Anne. The diary of a farmer′s wife 1796-1797 / illustrations by Brian Walker. — Harmondsworth : Penguin, 1981, c1980. — 162p : ill ; 22cm
Author: Ann Hughes. — Originally published: London : Countrywise, 1964
ISBN 0-14-005457-x (pbk) : £2.75 B82-07276

942.4′47 — Hereford and Worcester. Malvern. Social life, *1918-1939*

Malvern between the wars : a reminiscence / compiled by Frederick Covins. — Malvern (Como Road, Malvern WR14 2TJ) : Book Production Services, 1981. — 89p : 1map,music,facsims,ports ; 16x22cm
Map on lining papers
ISBN 0-9507839-0-0 : £4.95 B82-07899

942.4′49 — Hereford and Worcester. Ashton-under-Hill. Social life, *1911*

Archer, Fred, *1915-*. When Adam was a boy. — London : Hodder & Stoughton, Sept.1981. — [224]p. — (Coronet books)
Originally published: London : Hodder & Stoughton, 1979
ISBN 0-340-27104-3 (pbk) : £1.50 : CIP entry B81-22537

942.4′51 — Shropshire. Oswestry, *1850-1950 — Illustrations*

Oswestry : a pictorial history 1850-1950. — Oswestry (Trinity House, 6 Roft St., Oswestry, Shropshire) : Bernard Mitchell, Nov.1982. — [80]p
ISBN 0-9508275-0-9 (pbk) : £4.75 : CIP entry B82-27031

942.4′51 — Shropshire. Oswestry, *to 1981*

Pryce-Jones, John. Historic Oswestry. — Shrewsbury (7 London Rd, Shrewsbury, Shropshire) : Shropshire Libraries, Aug.1982. — [50]p
ISBN 0-903802-21-x (pbk) : £1.30 : CIP entry B82-17224

942.4′53 — Shropshire. Market Drayton — *Serials*

Market Drayton advertiser. — Friday Jan. 16 1981-. — Market Drayton (Chronicle House, Shrewsbury, Shropshire) : Shropshire Weekly Newspapers, 1981-. — v. : ill,ports ; 44cm
Weekly. — Continues in part: Newport & Market Drayton advertiser. — Description based on: Friday July 24, 1981
£0.15 per issue B82-36734

942.4′53 — Shropshire. Market Drayton, *to 1909*

Rowley, N.. Market Drayton : a new history / N. Rowley. — Expanded [version]. — [Weston Lullingfields] ([Blue Gates, Weston Lullingfields, Shrewsbury SY4 2AA]) : [N. Rowley], [1982, c1980]. — 28,9p : ill,2maps,facsims,plans ; 30cm
Cover title. — Previous ed.: 1980
£1.20 (pbk) B82-17634

Rowley, N.. Market Drayton : a new history / N. Rowley. — 3rd ed. — [Weston Lullingfields] ([Blue Gates, Weston Lullingfields, Shrewsbury, SY4 2AA]) : [N. Rowley], [1982]. — 36leaves : ill,facsims,1map,plans ; 30cm
Previous ed.: 1980
£1.35 (unbound) B82-31900

942.4′53 — Shropshire. Market Drayton, *to 1910*

Rowley, N.. Market Drayton : a new history / [N. Rowley]. — Shrewsbury (Blue Gates, Weston Lullingields, Shrewsbury SY4 2AA) : N. Rowley, [c1980]. — 28p : ill,1map,2facsims,1plan ; 30cm
Bibliography: p27. — Includes index
£0.90 (pbk) B82-20132

942.4′54 — Shropshire. Pontesbury, *to 1967*

Gaydon, A. T.. A history of Pontesbury. — Shrewsbury (Column House, 7 London Rd., Shrewsbury, Shropshire) : Shropshire Libraries, Nov.1982. — [56]p
Extracted from: A history of Shropshire, vol.8. Oxford : Oxford University Press for the Institute of Historical Research, 1968
ISBN 0-903802-23-6 (pbk) : £1.50 : CIP entry B82-29154

942.4′54 — Shropshire. Shrewsbury, *to 1979*

Priestley, E. J.. An illustrated history of Shrewsbury / E.J. Priestley. — [Shrewsbury] : Shrewsbury and Atcham Borough Council, 1982. — 48p : ill,2maps,facsims,ports ; 21cm
Maps on inside covers. — Bibliography: p48
ISBN 0-9500122-4-6 (pbk) : £1.00 B82-24305

942.4′56 — Shropshire. Hadley. Social life, *ca 1900-1980 — Personal observations — Collections*

The **Hadley** book : a view of the Hadley district based on the memories and photographs of Hadley people / [edited and compiled by] Telford Community Arts Hadley Book Group. — Telford : Telford Community Arts, 1982. — 162p : ill,facsims,maps,ports ; 26cm
Edited by Martin Humphrey et al.. — Includes index
ISBN 0-946076-00-6 (pbk) : £2.50 B82-36900

942.4′56 — Shropshire. Ironbridge. Social life, *ca 1895-1940 — Stories, anecdotes*

Jones, Billy. Ironbridge tales / by Billy Jones ; illustrations by Lionel Marrion. — Telford : Woody, 1981. — 24p : ill,1map,ports ; 29cm
ISBN 0-907751-00-8 (pbk) : £1.75 B82-06601

942.4′56 — Shropshire. Newport — *Serials*

Newport advertiser. — Friday 16 Jan. 1981-. — Shrewsbury (Chronicle House, Shrewsbury) : Shropshire Weekly Newspapers, 1981-. — v. : ill,ports ; 67cm
Weekly. — Continues in part: Newport & Market Drayton advertiser
£0.15 B82-40053

942.4′56 — Shropshire. Oakengates region, *to 1935*

Cartlidge, J. E. Gordon. ″The vale and gates of Usc-con", or, A history of Oakengates and surrounding district / [by J.E. Gordon Cartlidge]. — Rev. and enl. / [by Jean Beard]. — Telford : J. Beard, 1980, c1982. — xxxix,121p : ill,plans,1port ; 24cm
Previous ed.: S.l : s.n., 1935. — Includes index
ISBN 0-9508085-0-4 : Unpriced B82-37977

942.4′59 — Shropshire. Bridgnorth, *to 1700*

Pee, Ernest H.. Bridgnorth dates and places. — Shrewsbury (7 London Rd., Shrewsbury) : Shropshire Libraries, Dec.1982. — [33]p
ISBN 0-903802-22-8 (pbk) : £0.75 : CIP entry B82-40342

942.4′6 — North Staffordshire — *Stories, anecdotes*

Byrne, Tom. Tales from the past : anecdotes and incidents of North Staffordshire history / by Tom Byrne ; foreword by Robert Copeland. — London : Remploy, 1981, c1977. — 241p : ill,1map,ports,2geneal.tables ; 22cm
Originally published: Newcastle, Staffs. : Ironmarket Press, 1977
ISBN 0-7066-0907-7 : £6.00 B82-05908

942.4′63 — Staffordshire. Stoke-on-Trent. Abbeys: Hulton Abbey, *to 1980*

Lancaster, Thelma W.. Hulton Abbey : Stoke-on-Trent′s cistercian Abbey / Thelma W. Lancaster ; with drawings by Jane Fern. — Stoke-on-Trent ([Hanley, Stoke-on-Trent, ST1 4HS]) : City Museum and Art Gallery, 1981. — iv,25p : ill,2maps,1plan ; 22cm
Bibliography: p25
Unpriced (pbk) B82-11576

942.4′63 — Staffordshire. Stoke-on-Trent. Social conditions, *to 1961*

Warrillow, Ernest J. D.. A sociological history of the city of Stoke-on-Trent / by Ernest J.D. Warrillow ; with 380 illustrations by and from the author′s collection of photographs and engravings. — [Silver Jubilee ed.]. — Newcastle : Ironmarket, 1977. — 727p,[1]leaf of plates : ill,1map,facsims,ports(some col.) ; 32cm
Previous ed.: Stoke-on-Trent : Etruscan, 1960. — Limited ed. of 1000 numbered and signed copies. — Bibliography: p727. — Includes index
ISBN 0-905680-08-1 : Unpriced B82-21529

942.4′640858′05 — Staffordshire. Stafford *(District) — Serials*

Staffordshire market. — No.1 (Tuesday, Apr.14, 1981)-. — Stafford (22 Mill St., Stafford ST16 2AL) : Hourds Publications, 1981-. — v. : ill,ports ; 42cm
Weekly. — Continues: Staffordshire mid-week
ISSN 0263-0400 = Staffordshire market : Unpriced B82-14253

Staffordshire mid-week. — 1980-Apr.7, 1981. — Stafford (22 Mill St., Stafford ST16 2AL) : Hourds Publications, 1980-1981. — ?v. : ill,ports ; 41cm
Weekly. — Continued by: Staffordshire market. — Description based on: Tuesday, July 1, 1980 issue
Unpriced B82-14252

942.4′66 — Staffordshire. Lapley & Wheaton Aston, *to 1981*

Weate, Mary. The parish of Lapley-with-Wheaton Aston / Mary Weate. — [Wheaton Aston] : Lapley Parish Council, c1982. — iii,59p,[18]p of plates : ill,1facsim,1map,ports ; 25cm
Limited ed. of 500 copies. — Bibliography: p57
ISBN 0-9507997-0-x (pbk) : Unpriced
ISBN 0-9507997-1-8 B82-39050

942.4′69 — Staffordshire. Tamworth, *to 1700*

Smith, Christine, *1941-*. The early families of Tamworth : capital of Mercia / by Christine Smith. — [Tamworth] ([10 Drayton Lane, Drayton Bassett, Tamworth]) : [C. Smith], [1982]. — 45p : ill,coats of arms,3geneal.tables,2maps ; 22cm
Cover title. — Preface on 1 leaf as insert. — Bibliography: p45
Unpriced (pbk) B82-38573

942.4′81 — Warwickshire. Coleshill. Castles: Maxstoke Castle, *to 1981*

Fetherston-Dilke, C. B.. A short history of Maxstoke Castle and its owners. — [Coleshill] ([Maxstoke Castle, Coleshill, Warwickshire]) : [C.B. Fetherston-Dilke], 1982. — 19p : 1col.ill ; 22cm
Compiled by C.B. Fetherston-Dilke. — Photgraph attached to inside cover
Unpriced (pbk) B82-17638

942.4′89 — Warwickshire. Bishop′s Itchington, *to 1981*

James, Peter, *1932-*. Icetone : the story of a Warwickshire village / by Peter James. — [Kenilworth] ([6 Borrowell Terrace, Kenilworth]) : [P. James], [1982?]. — 108p : ill,maps,ports ; 21x30cm
Cover title
£5.50 (spiral) B82-28791

942.4′89 — Warwickshire. Stratford-upon-Avon. Social life, *1878-1920 — Personal observations*

Hewins, George. The Dillen : memories of a man of Stratford-upon-Avon / [George Hewins] ; edited by Angela Hewins ; with a foreword by Ronald Blythe. — Oxford : Oxford University Press, 1982. — ix,180p : ill,1geneal.table,1map,ports ; 20cm. — (Oxford paperbacks)
Originally published: London : Elm Tree, 1981
ISBN 0-19-281345-5 (pbk) : £2.95 : CIP rev.
B82-15673

942.4′90857′0880623 — England. West Midlands. Working classes. Social life, *ca 1970-1980*

Hedges, Nick. Born to work. — London : Pluto Press, Oct.1982. — [96]p
ISBN 0-86104-382-0 (pbk) : £3.95 : CIP entry
B82-26704

942.4′93 — West Midlands *(Metropolitan County)*. **Harts Hill, Holly Hall & Woodside,** *to 1980*

Lavender, A. T. C.. The villages of Holly Hall, Woodside and Harts Hill in the Parish of Dudley County of Worcester / A.T.C. and E.M. Lavender. — Wolverhampton (91 Brenton Rd, Wolverhampton) : A.T.C. and E.M. Lavender, 1979. — 31p,[3]leaves of plates : ill,1map ; 30cm
Unpriced (pbk) B82-40962

942.4′96081′0222 — West Midlands *(Metropolitan County)*. **Birmingham,** *1837-1910 — Illustrations*

Victorian and Edwardian Birmingham from old photographs / introduction and commentaries by Dorothy McCulla. — London : Batsford, 1973 (1978 [printing]). — [118]p : chiefly ill,ports ; 25cm
ISBN 0-7134-0150-8 (pbk) : £3.95 B82-06210

942.4′96082′0924 — West Midlands *(Metropolitan County)*. **Birmingham. Working classes. Social life,** *1903-1914 — Personal observations*

Dayus, Kathleen. Her people / Kathleen Dayus ; with an introduction by John Rudd. — London : Virago, 1982. — xxx,194p,[8]p of plates : ill,ports ; 20cm
ISBN 0-86068-275-7 (pbk) : £4.50 : CIP rev.
B82-21540

942.4′96083′0924 — West Midlands *(Metropolitan County)*. **Birmingham** *(District)*. **Social life,** *1920-1939 — Personal observations*

Jones, Douglas V.. Memories of a ′twenties child / Douglas V. Jones. — Sutton Coldfield (Print Shop, 44 Boldmere Rd., Sutton Coldfield, W. Midlands) : Westwood Press, 1981. — 112p : ill,1facsim,ports ; 21cm
£2.95 (pbk) B82-04428

942.4′960858′05 — West Midlands *(Metropolitan County)*. **Birmingham** *— Serials*

ABC adviser. Birmingham East & Chelmsley Wood. — Sept. 1978-issue 763(B) (Sept. 25 1981). — Birmingham (24 Priory Queensway, Birmingham B4 6BS) : ABC Advertiser Ltd, 1978-1981. — ?v. : ill,ports ; 45cm
Weekly. — Continued by: Chelmsley Wood and Castle Bromwich ABC shopper. — Description based on: Issue 753(B) (July 17 1981)
Unpriced B82-03408

942.4′98 — International reconciliation. Role of Coventry

Hodgkinson, George. Coventry and the movement for world peace : writings and speeches, 1971-1975 / George Hodgkinson. — Coventry : The Chapelfield Press, 1981. — 28p ; 21cm
ISBN 0-86279-014-x (pbk) : £1.50 B82-03509

942.4′98 — West Midlands *(Metropolitan County)*. **Coventry,** *to 1981*

Newbold, E. B.. Portrait of Coventry / E.B. Newbold. — 2nd ed. — London : Hale, 1982. — 208p,[24]p of plates : ill,1map ; 23cm
Previous ed.: 1972. — Includes index
ISBN 0-7091-9751-9 : £7.95 B82-31163

942.4′9803 — West Midlands *(Metropolitan County)*. **Coventry,** *1140-1355 — Conference proceedings*

Medieval Coventry- a city divided?. — [Coventry] : University of Warwick, Open Studies & Coventry Branch of the Historical Association, 1981. — iii,58p,[1]leaf of plates : 1map ; 20cm. — (Coventry and Warwickshire pamphlet ; no.11)
Unpriced (pbk) B82-06133

942.4′980855′0924 — West Midlands *(Metropolitan County)*. **Coventry. Social life,** *1953-1962 — Personal observations*

Steane, Leonard. Coventry cameos : a collection of reminiscences / Leonard Steane. — New ed. — Coventry : L. Steane, 1981. — 24p : ill,ports ; 21cm
Previous ed.: 1972
ISBN 0-9502238-2-4 (pbk) : £0.60 B82-12748

942.5′1 — Derbyshire. Derwent Valley, *to 1952*

Byford, James S.. Moorland heritage : the story of Derwent, Ladybower and the Woodlands Valley / by James S. Byford. — [Bamford] ([Wood Cottage, Snake Pass Rd., Bamford]) : J.S. Byford, 1981. — 52p : ill,1map ; 21cm
Unpriced (pbk) B82-17846

942.5′1 — Derbyshire, *to ca 1700 — Early works*

Woolley, William. William Woolley′s History of Derbyshire / edited by Catherine Glover and Philip Riden. — Chesterfield : Derbyshire Record Society, 1981. — lviii,276p,4p of plates : ill,1geneal.table ; 22cm. — (Derbyshire Record Society ; v.6)
Microfiche supplement in pocket. — Includes index
ISBN 0-9505940-7-5 : Unpriced B82-14896

942.5′1 — Northern Derbyshire. Antiquities, *to 1500*. **Archaeological investigation,** *to 1980*

Hart, C. R. (Clive R.). The North Derbyshire archaeological survey : to a.d. 1500 / by C.R. Hart ; illustrated by S. Connock ... [et al.]. — Chesterfield : North Derbyshire Archaeological Trust, 1981. — xiv,179p : ill,maps,plans,1form ; 30cm
Bibliography: p170-174. — Includes index
ISBN 0-9507707-0-1 (pbk) : Unpriced
B82-12070

942.5′11 — Derbyshire. Chapel-en-le-Frith region. Social life, *1708-1755 — Correspondence, diaries, etc.*

Clegg, James. The diary of James Clegg of Chapel en le Frith 1708-1755 / edited by Vanessa S. Doe. — Chesterfield : Derbyshire Record Society. — (Derbyshire Record Society ; v.5)
Pt.3: [1748-1755]. — 1981. — p672-1026 ; 22cm
Includes index
ISBN 0-9505940-8-3 : £8.00 B82-14895

942.5′12 — Derbyshire. Newbold. Parish churches: St. John the Evangelist *(Church : Newbold), to 1982*

Riden, Philip. Building a parish : a history of St John the Evangelist, Newbold 1857-1982 / by Philip Riden. — Newbold (c/o G. Lee, 16 Craven Road, Newbold, Chesterfield) : The Rector, Churchwardens and Parochial Church Council of St John the Evangelist, c1982. — 120p : ill,ports ; 22cm
£2.00 (pbk) B82-29841

942.5′13 — Derbyshire. Darley Dale. Country houses: Sydnope Hall, *to 1982*

Abrahams, Simon. Sydnope Hall and Darley Dale / [Simon Abrahams]. — [Sheffield] : Sheffield City Council, Family and Community Services Committee, 1980, c1978. — 21p : 2ill,geneal.tables ; 21cm
Cover title: A short account to the history of Sydnope Hall and Darley Dale
ISBN 0-900660-56-2 (pbk) : Unpriced
B82-21703

942.5′13 — Derbyshire. Hathersage. Parish churches: St. Michael and All Angels *(Church : Hathersage), to 1980*

Hulbert, Martin F. H.. Let these stones live : Little John and St. Michaels and All Angels, Hathersage / by Martin F.H. Hulbert. — [Sheffield] : [M.F.H. Hulbert], [1982?]. — 20p : ill ; 21cm
ISBN 0-907602-05-3 (pbk) : Unpriced
Primary classification 398′.352 B82-35762

942.5′14 — Derbyshire. Wingerworth. Country houses: Wingerworth Hall, *to 1921*

Eisenberg, Elizabeth. Wingerworth manor & estate / Elizabeth Heathcote Eisenberg. — [Derby] ([20, Evans Ave, Allestree Park, Derby, DE3 2EJ]) : [E. Eisenberg], [1981]. — 20p : ill,1facsim ; 21cm
£0.85 (pbk) B82-15194

942.5′16 — Derbyshire. Shottle, *1086-1981*

Fletcher, Mary. Shottle : a short account of its history 1086-1981 / by Mary Fletcher. — [Belper] ([Ash Farm, Shottle, Belper, Derbyshire DE5 2DR]) : [M. Fletcher?], [1981]. — 16p[i.e.27]p : ill,1map,1port ; 21cm
Cover title
Unpriced (pbk) B82-13327

942.5′17081′0222 — Derbyshire. Derby, *1874-1914 — Illustrations*

Yesterday′s Derby : 1874-1914 through the camera. — Derby : Breedon Books, c1982. — 48p : of ill,ports ; 15x21cm
ISBN 0-907969-01-1 (pbk) : Unpriced
B82-35534

942.5′19 — Derbyshire. Repton. Parish churches: St. Wystan′s Church *(Repton)*. **Anglo-Saxon antiquities. Excavation of remains,** *1974-1976*

Taylor, H. M. (Harold McCarter). The Anglo-Saxon crypt and church / H.M. Taylor. — Cambridge : [H.M. Taylor], 1979. — 21p : ill ; 21cm. — (Repton studies ; 2)
Unpriced (pbk) B82-17343

942.5′19 — Derbyshire. Repton. Parish churches: St. Wystan′s Church *(Repton)*. **Crypts. Anglo-Saxon antiquities. Excavation of remains,** *1974-1976*

Taylor, H. M. (Harold McCarter). The Anglo-Saxon crypt 1974-76 / H.M. Taylor. — [Cambridge] : [H.M. Taylor], 1977. — 12p : ill ; 21cm. — (Repton studies ; 1)
Text on inside cover. — Bibliography: p12
Unpriced (pbk) B82-17342

942.5′1907 — Derbyshire. South Derbyshire *(District)*. **Social conditions,** *1800-1850*

Pits, pots & people : South Derbyshire in 1851 / edited by Janet Spavold. — [Woodville] : [South Derbyshire Local History Research Group], c1981. — 108p : ill,facsims,maps ; 30cm
Cover title
ISBN 0-9507633-0-6 (spiral) : £1.50
B82-35332

942.5′24 — Nottinghamshire. Bulcote, *to 1977*

Burton Joyce & Bulcote remembered : the two villages recorded in photographs and reminiscences. — Burton Joyce (12, Lambley La., Burton Joyce, NG14 5BG) : Burton Joyce Local History Group, c1981. — 56p : ill,facsims,ports ; 30cm
Facsims on inside covers
Unpriced (pbk)
Primary classification 942.5′28 B82-09028

942.5′28 — Nottinghamshire. Burton Joyce, *to 1977*

Burton Joyce & Bulcote remembered : the two villages recorded in photographs and reminiscences. — Burton Joyce (12, Lambley La., Burton Joyce, NG14 5BG) : Burton Joyce Local History Group, c1981. — 56p : ill,facsims,ports ; 30cm
Facsims on inside covers
Unpriced (pbk)
Also classified at 942.5′24 B82-09028

942.5′29 — Nottinghamshire. Hickling, *to 1979*

The **Scrapbook** of Hickling : a collection of notes and photographs of Hickling′s past / compiled by Hazel M. Wadkin. — Hickling (Hickling, Melton Mowbray) : H.M. Wadkin, c1982. — [104]p : ill,ports ; 30cm
£3.00 (unbound) B82-22041

942.5′3′009734 — Lincolnshire. Rural regions. Services, *1980*

Lincolnshire rural facilities survey 1980 : analysis by district. — [Lincoln] ([Planning Dept., County Offices, Lincoln]) : Lincolnshire County Council, 1982. — [16]p ; 30cm
Cover title
Unpriced (pbk) B82-30035

942.5′31 — Lincolnshire. Fonaby. Anglo-Saxon cemeteries. Antiquities

Cook, Alison M.. The Anglo-Saxon cemetery at Fonaby, Lincolnshire / Alison M. Cook ; based on a catalogue of the material by Sonia C. Hawkes. — Sleaford : Society for Lincolnshire History and Archaeology, 1981. — 108p : ill,maps,1plan ; 30cm. — (Occasional papers in Lincolnshire history and archaeology ; 6)
ISBN 0-904680-13-4 (pbk) : £4.50 (£3.20 to Society members) B82-02426

942.5′32 — Lincolnshire. Binbrook. Agricultural industries. Farms. Social life, *1871-1875 — Correspondence, diaries, etc.*

Stovin, Cornelius. Journals of a Methodist farmer 1871-1875 / [Cornelius Stovin] ; edited by Jean Stovin. — London : Croom Helm, c1982. — 251p : maps,2facsims,1geneal.table ; 23cm
Bibliography: p243-244. — Includes index
ISBN 0-7099-2324-4 : £12.95 : CIP rev.
B81-31431

942.5′34 — Lincolnshire. Lincoln. Antiquities, *ca 800-1300.* **Excavations of remains**

Early medieval finds from Flaxengate. — London : Council for British Archaeology. — (The archaeology of Lincoln ; v.14 ; 1)
1: Objects of antler, bone, stone, horn, ivory, amber and jet. — Dec.1982. — [68]p
ISBN 0-906878-20-9 (pbk) : £7.95 : CIP entry
B82-40923

942.5′34 — Lincolnshire. Lincoln. Flaxengate. Antiquities, *800-1100.* **Archaeological investigation,** *1972-1976*

Perring, Dom. Early medieval occupation at Flaxengate, Lincoln / Dom Perring. — London : [Council for British Archaelogy for the Lincoln Archaeological Trust], c1981. — 46p,[3]folded leaves of plates : ill,maps ; 30cm. — (The Archaeology of Lincoln ; v.IX-1)
Bibliography: p87
ISBN 0-906780-10-1 (pbk) : Unpriced : CIP rev. B81-23794

942.5′34 — Lincolnshire. Lincoln. Flaxengate. Houses, *ca 1100-1400.* **Archaeological investigation**

Jones, R. H. (Robert Hugh). Medieval houses at Flaxengate, Lincoln / R.H. Jones ; [photos by H.N. Hawley and Christina Colyer] ; [drawings by Jayne Peacock, Claire Thorne and Helen Gandy]. — London : Council for British Archaeology for the Lincoln Archaeological Trust, 1980. — 56p : ill(some col.),plans ; 30cm. — (The Archaeology of Lincoln ; v.XI-1)
English text, English, French and German summaries. — Text on inside front cover. — Bibliography: p56
ISBN 0-906780-01-2 (pbk) : Unpriced
B82-17616

942.5′34081′0222 — Lincolnshire. Lincoln, *1850-1960 — Illustrations*

Lincoln as it was / compiled on behalf of Lincolnshire Library Service by Laurence Elvin. — Nelson : Hendon Publishing
Vol.4. — c1981. — [44]p : chiefly ill,facsims,ports ; 21x29cm
Ill on inside cover
ISBN 0-86067-069-4 (pbk) : £2.60 B82-03273

942.5′35 — Lincolnshire. Sleaford, *1851-1871*

Mid-Victorian Sleaford 1851-1871 / compiled by members of a W.E.A. class in Sleaford ; edited by Charles Ellis. — Lincoln : Lincolnshire Library Service, 1981. — 196p : ill,maps,facsims ; 21cm. — (Lincolnshire history series ; 4)
Includes index
ISBN 0-86111-102-8 (pbk) : £2.75 B82-11459

942.5′38 — Lincolnshire. Boothby Graffoe, *to 1979*

Ruddock, J. G.. Boothby Graffoe and Somerton Castle / by J.G. Ruddock. — Lincoln : J. Ruddock, c1980. — 96p : ill,3maps,1plan ; 24cm
Maps on folded sheet attached to inside cover. — Includes index
ISBN 0-904327-03-5 (pbk) : £5.75 B82-26485

942.5′38 — Lincolnshire. Irnham. Social life, *1328*

Sancha, Sheila. The Luttrell village : country life in the early fourteenth century. — London : Collins, 1982. — 64p : ill ; 29cm
ISBN 0-00-195838-0 : £5.95 B82-34848

942.5′39 — Lincolnshire. Long Sutton region, *to 1980*

Robinson, F. W. (Frank William). A history of Long Sutton and district (South Lincolnshire) / compiled, edited and written by F.W. & B.A. Robinson. — [Long Sutton, Lincs.] : [Long Sutton and District Civic Trust], c1981. — xvii,303p : ill,3maps,2facsims ; 22cm
Bibliography: piv-vii
ISBN 0-9507703-0-2 (pbk) : Unpriced
B82-08296

942.5′41 — Leicestershire. Littlethorpe & Narborough, *to 1980*

Jarrett, V. N.. The history of Narborough and Littlethorpe / by V.N. & R.P. Jarrett. — Narborough : Narborough Parish Council, 1981. — 64p : ill,2maps,1facsim,ports ; 21cm
Bibliography: p63
ISBN 0-9507776-0-9 (pbk) : Unpriced
B82-08242

942.5′41 — Leicestershire. Sapcote. Parish churches: Parish Church of All Saints *(Sapcote), to 1980*

Tyldesley, Douglas W.. A history of the parish church of All Saints, Sapcote, Leicestershire / written and illustrated by Douglas W. Tyldesley. — Sapcote, Leics. : D.W. Tyldesley, 1981. — 49p : ill,1map ; 21cm
Bibliography: p48. — Includes index
ISBN 0-9507831-0-2 (pbk) : Unpriced
B82-08298

942.5′42 — Leicestershire. Leicester. Friaries: Austin Friary *(Leicester).* **Archaeological investigation,** *1973-1978*

The **Austin** Friars, Leicester / [edited] by Jean E. Mellor and T. Pearce. — [Leicester] : Leicestershire County Council, 1981. — viii,175p,[10]p of plates : ill,maps,plans ; 30cm. — (CBA research report, ISSN 0589-9036 ; 35) (Leicestershire Archaeological Field Unit report)
One folded sheet (1plan) and 2 microfiche in pocket attached to inside cover. — Includes bibliographies
ISBN 0-900312-94-7 (pbk) : Unpriced
B82-06347

942.5′49 — Leicestershire. Desford, *to 1973*

Dickson, Elisabeth M.. History in Desford / Elisabeth M. Dickson. — Desford (26 High St., Desford, Leicester LE9 9JF) : [E.M. Dickson?], 1974. — 69p : ill ; 21cm : maps
Unpriced (pbk) B82-12375

942.5′52 — Northamptonshire. Kettering region. Social life, *1910-1939 — Personal observations*

Sturgess, Arthur, *1905-1979.* A Northamptonshire lad / Arthur Sturgess. — Northampton : Northamptonshire Libraries, 1982. — 84p : ill,ports ; 22cm
ISBN 0-905391-09-8 : £1.75 B82-26730

942.5′54 — Northamptonshire. Raunds. Antiquities, *600-1400.* **Excavation of remains**

Raunds / [Northamptonshire County Council Archaeology Unit] ; [design and illustration by Paul Goff]. — [Northampton] ([Guildhall, Northampton, NN1 1DE]) : Northamptonshire County Council Archaeology Unit, 1979. — 12p : ill,maps,plans ; 29cm. — (Northamptonshire County Council archaeological occasional papers)
Text and maps on inside covers
£0.40 (pbk) B82-25557

942.5′57 — Northamptonshire. Northampton, *to 1540.* **Archaeological sources**

Williams, John H.. Saxon and medieval Northampton / by John H. Williams. — Northampton : Publicity and Information Section of Northampton Development Corporation, c1982. — 52p : ill,maps,plans ; 26cm
Bibliography: p51
ISBN 0-902711-11-3 (pbk) : Unpriced
B82-33783

942.5′57081 — Northamptonshire. Northampton. Social conditions, *1869 — Early works*

"Shobopolis" : Northampton in 1869. — 3rd ed. enl. — [Northampton] ([Central Museum, Guildhall Rd., Northampton, NN1 1DP]) : Museums & Art Gallery of the Northampton Borough Council′s Leisure Activities Department, 1976. — 10p : ill ; 23cm
Previous ed.: Northampton : Northampton Historical Series, 1968
Unpriced (unbound) B82-09746

942.5′61 — Bedfordshire. Bedford. Parish churches: All Saints *(Church : Bedford), to 1980*

All Saints′ *(Church : Bedford).* All Saints′, Bedford : a brief history 1895-1980 / by J.H. Bass. — [Bedford] ([c/o J.H. Bass, 38 Lansdowne Rd., Bedford MK40 2BU]) : All Saints′ Entertainments Committee, c1980. — [20]p,[4]p of plates : ill ; 21cm
Bibliography: p20
Unpriced (pbk) B82-01494

942.5′61 — Bedfordshire. Kempston. Social conditions *— For environment planning*

Kempston district plan : report of survey / North Bedfordshire Borough Council. — [Bedford] ([37-45 Goldington Rd, Bedford MK40 3LQ]) : [The Council], 1978. — 52,xiip,13folded leaves of plate : maps ; 30cm
Unpriced (pbk) B82-41052

942.5'65 — Bedfordshire. Dunstable & Houghton Regis — *Serials*
Dunstable & Houghton Regis plus : distributed free to homes in Dunstable, Houghton Regis, Leighton Linslade. — Issue no.1 (1981)-. — Hemel Hempstead (Mark Rd, Hemel Hempstead, Herts. HP2 7BU) : Evening Post-Echo Ltd., 1981-. — v. : ill,ports ; 41cm
Weekly. — Description based on: Issue no.29 (Oct.29 1981)
ISSN 0263-0427 = Dunstable & Houghton Regis plus : Unpriced B82-14250

942.5'65 — Bedfordshire. Leighton Buzzard & Linslade — *Serials*
Leighton Linslade plus : distributed free to homes in Dunstable, Houghton Regis, Leighton Linslade. — Issue no.1 (1981)-. — Hemel Hempstead (Mark Rd, Hemel Hempstead, Herts. HP2 7BU) : Evening Post-Echo Ltd., 1981-. — v. : ill,ports ; 41cm
Weekly. — Description based on: Issue no.29 (Oct.29, 1981)
ISSN 0263-0419 = Leighton Linslade plus : Unpriced B82-14251

942.5'7 — Oxfordshire, *to 1981*
Bloxham, Christine G.. Portrait of Oxfordshire / by Christine G. Bloxham. — London : Hale, 1982. — 224p,[24]p of plates : ill,1map ; 23cm
Bibliography: p211-213. — Includes index
ISBN 0-7091-9448-x : £8.25 B82-31157

942.5'7'005 — Oxfordshire — *History — Serials*
The **Blowing** stone. — Vol.1, no.1 (Spring 1982)-. — Wantage (c/o F. and S. McDonald, 12 Portway, Wantage, OX12 9BU) : Vale & Downland Museum Trust, 1982-. — v. : ill ; 22cm
Quarterly
ISSN 0263-5631 = Blowing stone : Unpriced B82-33853

942.5'7081'0924 — England. Middle Thames Valley. Villages. Social life, *ca 1885 — Personal observations*
Williams, Alfred. Round about middle Thames. — Gloucester : Alan Sutton, Nov.1982. — [192]p
ISBN 0-86299-032-7 (pbk) : £3.95 : CIP entry B82-26085

942.5'70858'0924 — Oxfordshire. Villages. Social life, *1980-1981 — Personal observations*
Hill, Susan. The magic apple tree : a country year / Susan Hill ; with engraving by John Lawrence. — London : Hamilton, 1982. — 198p : ill ; 24cm
Ill on lining papers
ISBN 0-241-10784-9 : £7.50 : CIP rev. B82-07403

942.5'71 — Oxfordshire. Eynsham. Social life, *1900-1925 — Personal observations — Collections*
Harris, Mollie. From Acre End : portrait of a village / Mollie Harris. — London : Chatto & Windus, 1982. — 153p : ill,3maps,ports ; 25cm
Maps on lining papers
ISBN 0-7011-2630-2 : £7.50 : CIP rev. B82-16222

942.5'73 — Oxfordshire. Charlton-on-Otmoor. Social life, *1918-1959 — Personal observations*
Coulthard, L. B.. This side of the bridge / L.B. Coulthard. — Bognor Regis : New Horizon, c1982. — 247p,[12]leaves of plates : ill ; 21cm
ISBN 0-86116-713-9 : £6.25 B82-15273

942.5'74 — Oxfordshire. Oxford, *to ca 1980*
Town and gown : eight hundred years of Oxford life : an exhibition at the Bodleian Library, Oxford 1982. — Oxford : Bodleian Library, c1982. — 65p : ill,facsims,maps,1plan,1port ; 25cm
ISBN 0-900177-85-3 (pbk) : Unpriced B82-31273

942.5'79 — Oxfordshire. Wallingford. Parish churches: Church of St. Peter *(Wallingford), to 1979*
Taggart, Imelda. History of the Church of St Peter, Wallingford / [Imelda Taggart]. — London (St Andrew-by-the-Wardrobe, Queen Victoria St., EC4V 5DE) : Redundant Churches Fund, [1980?]. — [4]p : 2ill ; 22cm
Cover title. — Ill on inside covers
£0.30 (pbk) B82-18607

942.5'79 — Oxfordshire. Whitchurch region, *to 1979*
Burmah-Castrol Company. Whitchurch & Bozedown House : a short history / John A. Goodall. — Swindon : Burmah-Castrol, 1980. — [16]p : ill,maps(some col.),2col.plans ; 21x30cm
Unpriced (pbk) B82-24386

942.5'8061 — Hertfordshire. Personal property. Probate inventories, *1610-1650 — Collections*
Lock, stock and barrel : some Hertfordshire inventories 1610-1650. — Hertford : [Hertfordshire County Council], 1978. — 69p : ill,facsims ; 30cm. — (Hertfordshire sources ; no.12)
Cover title
£1.50 (pbk) B82-12877

942.5'81 — Hertfordshire. Ashwell. Social life, *1920-1940 — Personal observations — Collections*
I was born in the High Street wasn't I? : Ashwell remembered fifty years ago : a recorded evening of reminiscence / edited by David Short and Peter Greener. — Ashwell : Friends of Ashwell Village Museum, 1981. — 32p : ill,1map,ports ; 25cm
ISBN 0-9507664-0-2 (pbk) : £1.95 B82-12040

942.5'81 — Hertfordshire. Hitchin, *1840-1977 — Illustrations*
Hitchin past and present / [compiled] by Pat Gadd. — Hitchin : Howells, 1978. — 71p : ill,facsims,1port ; 22cm
ISBN 0-9506427-0-3 (pbk) : £1.95 B82-00764

942.5'81 — Hertfordshire. Hitchin region, *1737-1951*
Pigram, Ron. Strange happenings : in Hitchin and North Hertfordshire being an account of local UFO's, ghosts, arson, railway accidents, crime & punishment, Victorian electioneering and carnivals / Ron Pigram. — Hitchin : R. Pigram (1978). — 27p,[8]p of plates : ill,2facsims ; 21cm
Facsims on inside covers
ISBN 0-9506356-0-x (pbk) : Unpriced B82-24647

942.5'83 — Hertfordshire. Bishop's Stortford, *to 1980*
Sparrow, Violet. Yesterday's Stortford : an album of memories and curiosities / by Violet Sparrow. — Buckingham : Barracuda, 1981. — 144p : ill,maps,facsims, ports ; 24cm
Map on lining papers. — Bibliography: p137. — Includes index
ISBN 0-86023-155-0 : £9.50 B82-08605

942.5'83 — Hertfordshire. Little Berkhamsted, *to 1957*
Millington, Gerald. Little Berkhamsted : (a history of a Hertfordshire village) / by Gerald Millington. — [Welwyn Garden City] ([c/o Mrs. O. South, 7 Swanhill, Haldens, Welwyn Garden City, Herts.]) : Little Berkhamsted Local History Group, 1981. — 59p : ill,maps ; 21cm
Unpriced (pbk) B82-22042

942.5'84 — Hertfordshire. Kings Langley. Personal property. Probate inventories, *1498-1659 — Collections*
Life and death in Kings Langley : wills and inventories 1498-1659 / edited by Lionel M. Munby. — Kings Langley : Kings Langley Local History & Museum Society in association with Kings Langley W.E.A., 1981. — xxxiv,166p ; 26cm
Bibliography: p147. — Includes index
ISBN 0-9507647-0-1 : Unpriced
Also classified at 929'.342584 B82-09817

942.5'85 — Hertfordshire. Bricket Wood, *to 1981*
A **Souvenir** of Bricket Wood. — St. Albans ([c/o J.J. Cheal, 30 West Riding,] Bricket Wood, St. Albans [AL2 3QW]) : The Bricket Wood Society, c1982. — 32p : ill,facsims,map ; 21cm
Text on inside covers. — Bibliography: p32
£1.00 (pbk) B82-35321

942.5'85 — Hertfordshire. Harpenden. Social life, *1890-1930 — Illustrations*
Harpenden & District Local History Society. Bygone Harpenden : a pictorial record. — [Harpenden] : Harpenden & District Local History Society, c1980. — [48]p : chiefly ill,1map,2ports ; 21cm
ISBN 0-9505941-2-1 (pbk) : £1.50 B82-16886

942.5'85 — Hertfordshire. Harpenden. Social life, *ca 1900-1914 — Childhood reminiscences*
Gregory, Ronald. The Harpenden I remember : — before 1914 : a prizewinning essay / by Ronald Gregory. — Harpenden : Harpenden & District Local History Society, c1981. — 12p : ill,ports ; 251cm. — (Harpenden and district local history series ; no.3)
Cover title. — Text on inside cover
ISBN 0-9505941-4-8 (corrected : pbk) : Unpriced B82-22191

942.5'85 — Hertfordshire. Park Street & Frogmore, *to 1980*
Martin, Cyril H.. The book of Park Street & Frogmore / by Cyril H. Martin. — Buckingham : Barracuda, 1981. — 104p : ill,2maps,facsims,ports ; 24cm
Map on lining papers. — Bibliography: p99. — Includes index
ISBN 0-86023-139-9 : Unpriced B82-05133

942.5'87 — Hertfordshire. Cheshunt, *1890-1960 — Illustrations*
Cheshunt past : north and west : a selection of old photographs with notes / by Jack Edwards. — London (69, Millcrest Rd., Goff's Oak, Waltham Cross, EN7 5NU) : J. Edwards, [1981]. — [58]p : chiefly ill 30cm
£2.50 (pbk) B82-11192

942.5'87 — Hertfordshire. Cheshunt, *to 1960*
Goff's Oak and Theobalds past : a selection of photographs and engravings / with notes by Jack Edwards. — Waltham Cross (69 Millcrest Rd., Goff's Oak, Waltham Cross EN7 5NU) : J. Edwards, [1982]. — [60]p : chiefly ill,ports ; 30cm
£2.50 (pbk) B82-30867

942.5'8920858'05 — Hertfordshire. Watford — *Serials*
Watford plus : distributed free to homes in Watford, Garston, South Oxhey, Croxley, part of Rickmansworth. — Issue no.1 (1980)-. — Hemel Hempstead (Mark Rd, Hemel Hempstead, Herts. HP2 7BU) : Evening Post-Echo, 1980-. — v. : ill,ports ; 41cm
Weekly. — Supplement to: Evening post-echo. Watford. — Description based on: Issue no.65 (Nov.27, 1981)
ISSN 0263-0192 = Watford plus : Unpriced B82-14258

942.5'9 — Buckinghamshire, *to 1970*
Camp, John. Portrait of Buckinghamshire / John Camp ; photographs by Ronald Goodearl. — London : Hale, 1972 (1982 [printing]). — 240p,[24]p of plates : ill,1map ; 23cm
Includes index
ISBN 0-7091-3232-8 : £8.50 B82-23053

942.5'91 — Buckinghamshire. Milton Keynes region — *Serials*
[Weekender *(Bedford)*]. Weekender : a new face focusing on life in and around Milton Keynes. — No.1 (16 Oct. 1981)- 1982. — Bedford (Caxton House, Caxton Rd, Bedford MK41 0EL) : Bedford County Press, 1981-1982. — v. : ill,ports ; 43cm
Weekly. — Description based on: No.13 (15 Jan. 1982)
Unpriced B82-38531

942.5'91 — Buckinghamshire. Olney. Social life, *1885-1948 — Personal observations — Collections*
Olney album / [compiled by Elizabeth Knight ... [et al.]. — Milton Keynes : People's Press, c1978. — [60]p : ill,facsims,ports ; 15x22cm
ISBN 0-904847-06-3 (pbk) : £0.90 B82-12797

942.5'93 — Buckinghamshire. Aylesbury Vale *(District), to 1981*
Parrott, Hayward. Aylesbury Vale yesterdays / Hayward Parrott. — Waddesdon : Kylin, 1981. — 128p : ill ; 24cm
ISBN 0-907128-01-7 : Unpriced B82-09810

942.5'95 — Buckinghamshire. Frieth. Social conditions, *1860-1930*

Barksfield, Joan. Frieth : a Chiltern village. — Frieth (Frieth, Henley-on-Thames, Oxon) : Frieth Village Society, 1981. — [36]p : ill,1map,facsims,ports ; 30cm
Text by: Joan Barksfield
Unpriced (pbk) B82-21778

942.5'95 — Buckinghamshire. High Wycombe — *Serials*

Wycombe star. — No.1 (Sept. 25 1981)-. — High Wycombe (Gomm Rd, High Wycombe [Bucks.]) : Bucks Free Press, 1981-. — v. : ill,ports ; 42cm
Weekly
ISSN 0262-6829 = Wycombe star : Unpriced B82-07653

942.6082 — East Anglia. Coastal regions. Fishing communities. Social life, *1900-1981 — Interviews*

Butcher, David. Living from the sea. — Sulhamstead (13 Wise's Firs, Sulhamstead, Berkshire RG7 4EH) : Tops'l Books, Oct.1982. — 1v.
ISBN 0-906397-09-x : CIP entry
ISBN 0-906397-10-3 (pbk) B82-28612

942.6'084 — East Anglia. Social conditions, *1940*

Brown, R. Douglas. East Anglia 1940 / by R. Douglas Brown. — Lavenham : Dalton, 1981. — x,166p : ill ; 24cm
Bibliography: p160. — Includes index
ISBN 0-86138-008-8 : £8.95 B82-10207

942.6'085'5 — Eastern England. Coastal regions. Floods, *1953*

Pollard, Michael. North Sea surge : the story of the East Coast floods of 1953 / by Michael Pollard. — Lavenham : Terence Dalton, 1978 (1982 [printing]). — 136p : ill,maps,ports ; 23cm
Map on inside cover. — Includes index
ISBN 0-86138-021-5 (pbk) : £4.95 B82-38821

942.6'1'009734 — Norfolk. Rural regions. Services, *1950-1980*

Packman, John. Services in rural Norfolk : 1950-1980 : a survey of the changing pattern of services in rural Norfolk over the last thirty years / [report ... prepared by J. Packman and M.H.C. Terry] ; [illustrations ... by J. Skinner] ; [maps by S.R. Coe]. — Norwich : Norfolk County Council, 1981. — vi,34p : ill,maps ; 20x21cm
£0.75 (pbk) B82-13953

942.6'1'009734 — Norfolk. Rural regions. Social life — *Stories, anecdotes*

Douglas, Peter, *1932-*. Village life / Peter Douglas ; illustrated by Martin Honeysett. — Woodbridge : Boydell, c1981. — 178p : ill ; 21cm
ISBN 0-85115-155-8 : £5.50 : CIP rev. B81-30483

942.6'12 — Norfolk. Blakeney, *to 1981*

Brooks, Peter, *1927-*. Have you heard about Blakeney? / Peter Brooks. — Norfolk : Poppyland Publishing, 1981. — 24p : ill,1facsim ; 21cm
Cover title. — Text on inside covers
£0.90 (pbk) B82-01524

942.6'12 — Norfolk. Cromer. Country houses: Felbrigg Hall, *to 1969*

Ketton-Cremer, R. W.. Felbrigg : the story of a house / R.W. Ketton-Cremer. — London : Futura, 1982, c1962. — 365p : 1geneal.table,1map ; 18cm. — (Heritage)
Originally published: London : Hart Davis, 1962. — Bibliography: p350-356. — Includes index
ISBN 0-7088-2195-2 (pbk) : £2.25 B82-35419

942.6'13 — Norfolk. Castle Acre. Social life, *ca 1920 — Illustrations*

Farley, Viola. Pictures from a village / Viola Farley. — Woodbridge : Boydell, c1981. — [95]p : chiefly ill,ports ; 19cm. — (Bygones books ; 2)
ISBN 0-85115-157-4 (pbk) : £3.95 B82-02922

942.6'14 — Norfolk. Gressenhall. Social life — *Serials*

Gressenhall news & views. — 1977-. — Gressenhall (c/o A. & B. Carrington, 10 Halls Drive, Gressenhall [Norfolk]) : [S.n.], 1977-. — v. : ill ; 21cm
Monthly. — Description based on: Royal Wedding issue (July 1981)
ISSN 0261-4308 = Gressenhall news & views : £2.00 per year B82-10357

942.6'4 — Suffolk. Social life, *to 1978*

Roberts, Bob. A slice of Suffolk / by Bob Roberts ; foreword by John Seymour. — Lavenham : Terence Dalton, 1978 (1982 [printing]). — x,102p : ill,1port ; 23cm
Includes index
ISBN 0-86138-020-7 (pbk) : £4.95 B82-38813

942.6'4083'0924 — Suffolk. Rural regions. Social life, *ca 1920 — Personal observations*

Bell, Adrian. Corduroy / Adrian Bell ; with an introduction by Susan Hill. — Oxford : Oxford University Press, 1982. — xii,265p ; 20cm. — (Oxford paperbacks)
ISBN 0-19-281343-9 (pbk) : £2.50 : CIP rev. B82-07504

942.6'41 — Suffolk. Lowestoft, *to 1981*

Jack Rose's Lowestoft / [compiled by Jack Rose]. — Lowestoft : Panda Books, c1981. — 118p : chiefly ill,1map,ports ; 26cm
ISBN 0-9507775-1-x (pbk) : £3.95 B82-06184

Malster, Robert. Lowestoft : East Coast port / by Robert Malster. — Lavenham : Terence Dalton, 1982. — 125p : ill,facsims,ports ; 23cm
Includes index
ISBN 0-86138-013-4 (pbk) : £4.95 B82-38814

942.6'43 — Suffolk. Newmarket, *to 1600*

May, Peter, *1913-*. Newmarket : medieval and Tudor / by Peter May with an appendix on the archaeology of Newmarket by Ivan E. Moore ; foreword by David Dymond. — Newmarket : P. May, 1982. — x,74p : ill,facsims,maps,plans ; 21cm
Text, ill on inside covers. — Includes index
ISBN 0-9503024-5-7 (pbk) : £3.50 B82-35518

942.6'46 — Suffolk. Framlingham, *to 1981*

Sitwell, O. R.. Framlingham : a short history and guide / by O.R. Sitwell. — Further rev. and enl. — [Framlingham] ([The Ancient House, Framlingham, Woodbridge, Suffolk]) : O.R. Sitwell, 1982. — 39p : ill,1map ; 24cm
Previous ed. i.e. Rev. and enl. ed.: 1974. — Map on inside cover. — Includes index
Unpriced (pbk) B82-41133

942.6'46 — Suffolk. Sutton Hoo. Anglo-Saxon antiquities — *For children*

East, Katherine. A king's treasure : the Sutton Hoo ship burial / Katherine East ; illustrated by Dinah Cohen. — Harmondsworth : Kestrel in association with British Museum Publications, 1982. — [32]p : ill(some col.),1map ; 25cm
ISBN 0-7226-5738-2 : £4.50 B82-25239

942.6'48 — Suffolk. Sudbury region — *Serials*

[Suffolk and Essex free press *(1981)*]. Suffolk and Essex free press. — No.5951 (Thursday, Dec.3, 1981)-. — Sudbury ('Free Press' Office, Borehamgate Precinct, Sudbury, Suffolk CO10 6EE) : EMAP Provincial Newspapers Ltd, 1981-. — v. : ill,ports ; 41cm
Weekly. — Continues: Suffolk free press
ISSN 0263-0168 = Suffolk and Essex free press (1981) : £0.14 per issue B82-14260

942.6'49055 — Suffolk. Ipswich. Personal property. Probate inventories, *1583-1631 — Texts*

The Ipswich probate inventories 1583-1631 / edited by Michael Reed. — Woodbridge, Suffolk : Published by the Boydell Press for the Suffolk Records Society, 1981. — 122p ; 25cm. — (Vol.22)
ISBN 0-85115-148-5 : £12.00 : CIP rev. B81-14907

942.6'5 — Eastern Cambridgeshire — *History*

A History of the County of Cambridge : and the Isle of Ely. — Oxford : Published for the Institute of Historical Research by Oxford University Press. — (The Victoria history of the counties of England)
Vol.8: Armingford and Thriplow Hundreds / edited by A.P.M. Wright. — 1982. — xvi,301p,[17]p of plates : ill,maps,plans ; 31cm
Bibliography: pxv-xvi. — Includes index
ISBN 0-19-722757-0 : £60.00 B82-22238

942.6'54 — Cambridgeshire. Buckden, *to ca 1980*

Edgington, S. B.. Buckden : a short history and plan / by S.B. Edgington. — Huntingdon (40 Manor Gdns, Buckden, Huntingdon, Cambs.) : S.B. Edgington, c1980. — 24p : 1ill,1map ; 21cm
£0.85 (pbk) B82-17185

942.6'54 — Cambridgeshire. Huntingdon. Places associated with Cromwell, Oliver

Dickinson, Philip G. M.. Oliver Cromwell and Huntingdon / by Philip G.M. Dickinson. — 2nd ed. rev. — Huntingdon : Cambridgeshire County Council, 1981. — vi,23p : ill,1map,1facsim,1plan,1port,1geneal.table ; 22cm
Previous ed.: published as Oliver Cromwell and the town of Huntingdon. Peterborough : Printed by Peterborough Central, 1973
ISBN 0-902436-21-x (pbk) : Unpriced B82-20725

942.6'54081'0922 — Cambridgeshire. Huntingdon *(District)*. **Fens. Social life,** *1800-1900 — Personal observations — Collections*

Edwards, William Henry, *19---*. Fenland chronicle : recollections of William Henry and Kate Mary Edwards / collected and edited by their daughter Sybil Marshall ; with drawings by Ewart Oakeshott. — Cambridge : Cambridge University Press, 1967 (1980 [printing]). — vii,280p : ill ; 23cm
ISBN 0-521-28043-5 (pbk) : £5.95 B82-38833

942.6'56 — Cambridgeshire. Littleport, *1770-1899 — Chronologies*

Littleport chronicle 1770-1899 : some extracts from The Cambridge chronicle / compiled by Roger I. Ruderham ; introduction by Mike Petty. — Wisbech : Standard Project, 1981. — [87]p : ill,maps,ports ; 30cm
Maps on inside covers
ISBN 0-902436-20-1 (pbk) : Unpriced B82-02026

942.6'56 — Cambridgeshire. Stretham, *1770-1899*

Petty, Mike, *1946-*. Stretham chronicle : a record of life in a Cambridgeshire village between 1770 & 1899 with a check-list of national & international happenings / compiled from the files of the Cambridge chronicle & University Journal by Mike & Pat Petty. — Stretham (The Rectory, Stretham [Cambs.]) : St. James' Church, 1980. — ii,55p ; 21cm
£1.00 (pbk) B82-13905

942.6'56 — England. Villages. Social conditions, *1525-1700 — Study regions: Cambridgeshire. Chippenham*

Spufford, Margaret. Contrasting communities : English villagers in the sixteenth and seventeenth centuries / Margaret Spufford. — Cambridge : Cambridge University Press, 1974 (1979 [Printing]). — xxiii,374p : ill,maps,1facsim,1geneal.table ; 23cm
Includes index
ISBN 0-521-29748-6 (pbk) : Unpriced
Also classified at 942.6'57 B82-17643

942.6'57 — England. Villages. Social conditions, *1525-1700 — Study regions: Cambridgeshire. Orwell & Willingham*

Spufford, Margaret. Contrasting communities : English villagers in the sixteenth and seventeenth centuries / Margaret Spufford. — Cambridge : Cambridge University Press, 1974 (1979 [Printing]). — xxiii,374p : ill,maps,1facsim,1geneal.table ; 23cm
Includes index
ISBN 0-521-29748-6 (pbk) : Unpriced
Primary classification 942.6'56 B82-17643

942.6'59 — Cambridgeshire. Cherry Hinton. Parish churches: Cherry Hinton Church, *to 1982*
Cherry Hinton Church. The story of Cherry Hinton Church / by Alice Eleanor Parsons. — 3rd ed. — [Cherry Hinton) ([4 Chelwood Rd., Cherry Hinton, Cambridge, CB1 4LX]) : [St Andrew's Cherry Hinton], 1982. — 26p : ill ; 20cm
Previous ed.: 1961
Unpriced (pbk) B82-31698

942.6'7 — Essex. Parish churches
Clarke, Vernon. The churches dedicated to St Andrew : in the Chelmsford diocese / Vernon Clarke. — Colchester (V. Clarke, The Lodge, Mill Lane, Colne Engaine, Colchester, Essex) : V. Clarke, c1982. — 16p : ill,1map ; 21cm
£0.40 (unbound) B82-31894

942.6'7'007 — Essex, *to 1981.* **Historical sources**
History on your Essex doorstep. — [Chelmsford] : [Essex County Library], 1982. — 12p ; 30cm. — (Essex libraries local studies)
Cover title. — Text on inside cover
ISBN 0-903630-15-x (pbk) : £0.10 B82-14608

942.6'7081'0222 — Essex, *1890-1920 — Illustrations*
Frith, Francis. Grandpa's Essex : as seen by Victorian photographer Francis Frith / compiled by Philip Gifford and Jane Dansie. — [Chelmsford] : [Essex County Library], c1981. — 42p : ill ; 21x30cm
ISBN 0-903630-11-7 (pbk) : £2.00 B82-01026

942.6'7085 — Essex. Social life, *1945-1980 — Stories, anecdotes*
Lynn, B. S.. Short true stories / B.S. Lynn. — Ilfracombe : Stockwell, 1981. — 86p ; 19cm
ISBN 0-7223-1504-x : £4.00 B82-12279

942.6'712 — Essex. Ashdon. Social life, *1910-1920 — Childhood reminiscences*
Mays, Spike. Reuben's Corner : an English country boyhood / Spike Mays ; foreword by Richard Church. — London : Robin Clark, 1981, c1980. — xiii,223p : 1map ; 20cm
Originally published: Andover : Eyre and Spottiswoode, 1969
ISBN 0-86072-055-1 (pbk) : £3.50 B82-10160

942.6'715 — Essex. Bocking. Parish churches: St. Peter's in the Fields *(Church : Bocking), to 1980*
Long, Robert. St. Peter's in the Fields, Bocking : a history and description / Robert Long. — [Braintree] ([46 Rosemary Ave., Bocking, Braintree, Essex CM7 7SZ]) : [R. Long], c1981. — 24p,[12]p of plates : ill,1map,1plan,ports ; 22cm
Cover title: The history of St. Peter's Bocking
£1.00 (pbk) B82-35018

942.6'715 — Essex. Little Yeldham, *to 1980*
Birch, Adrian Corder. A history of Little Yeldham / by Adrian Corder Birch. — Little Yeldham (c/o A.C. Birch, 77 Hyde Wood Rd., Little Yeldham, Halstead, Essex CO9 4QX) : Little Yeldham Parochial Church Council, 1981. — 47p : ill,maps,ports ; 21cm
Bibliography: p46
£1.50 (pbk) B82-03571

942.6'723 — Essex. Colchester. Dutch Quarter, *to 1979*
Bird, Brian, *1902-*. Guide to Colchester's Dutch Quarter / by Brian Bird. — Chelmsford : Essex Libraries, 1981. — 12p : ill ; 21cm. — (Essex Libraries local studies)
ISBN 0-903630-13-3 (pbk) : £0.20 B82-12482

942.6'725 — Essex. Kirby le Soken. Parish churches: Parish Church of Kirby le Soken, *to 1981*
Johnson, Irene. Turning point : the story of Kirby le Soken, Essex, 1823 to 1862 / by Irene Johnson. — London : Regency Press, c1982. — 115p : ill,1coat of arms,1geneal.table,maps,2plans,ports ; 21cm
Map on lining paper. — Includes index
ISBN 0-7212-0651-4 : £5.00 B82-25691

942.6'74 — Essex. Epping Forest, *to 1980*
Green, Georgina. Epping Forest through the ages / by Georgina Green. — Woodford Bridge : G. Green, 1982. — 56p : ill,maps ; 21cm
ISBN 0-9507915-0-4 (pbk) : £1.75 B82-26923

942.6'76 — Essex. Brentwood. Country houses: Pilgrim's Hall. Social life, *1912-1939 — Personal observations*
Lewis, Lesley. The private life of a country house, 1912-1939 / Lesley Lewis. — London : Futura, 1982, c1980. — 189p,[8]p of plates : ill,ports ; 18cm
Originally published: Newton Abbot : David and Charles, 1980. — Includes index
ISBN 0-7088-2184-7 (pbk) : £1.60 B82-28224

942.6'78 — Essex. Coryton, *to 1970*
Scott, Winifred N.. Coryton : the history of a village / Winifred N. Scott. — London : Mobil, 1981. — 47p : ill,col.maps,facsims,ports ; 25cm
Includes index
ISBN 0-9507934-1-8 (pbk) : Unpriced B82-13625

942.6'795 — Essex. Southend-on-Sea. Piers: Southend Pier, *to 1976*
Shepherd, E. W.. The story of Southend Pier — and its associations / E.W. Shepherd. — Letchworth : Egon, 1979. — 120p : ill,coats of arms,facsims,ports ; 25cm
Bibliography: p118. — Includes index
ISBN 0-905858-11-5 : £5.50 B82-06619

942.7 — Northern England. Buildings — *Illustrations*
Thursby, Alan. Northumbria & the Lake District : an architect's sketchbook. — Chester-le-Street : Castle View Fine Arts, c1981. — [32]p : chiefly ill ; 22x30cm
Cover title. — Author: Alan Thursby
ISBN 0-9507743-0-8 (pbk) : £1.80 B82-02197

942.7'038 — North-west England. Social life, *1377-1400*
Bennett, Michael J.. Community, class and careerism : Cheshire and Lancashire society in the Age of Sir Gawain and the Green Knight. — Cambridge : Cambridge University Press, Jan.1983. — [286]p. — (Cambridge studies in medieval life and thought. 3rd series ; v.18)
ISBN 0-521-24744-6 : £28.50 : CIP entry B82-40899

942.7'13 — Cheshire. Sandbach — *Serials*
[The Chronicle *(Sandbach edition)***]**. The Chronicle. — Sandbach ed. — No.5582 (Thursday Sept. 10 1981)-. — Crewe (2 High St., Crewe CW3 7BY) : Chester Chronicle and Associated Newspapers Ltd., 1981-. — v. : ill,ports ; 59cm
Weekly. — Continues: Crewe chronicle (Sandbach edition)
ISSN 0262-3374 = Chronicle. Sandbach edition : £0.18 per issue B82-03416

942.7'14 — Cheshire. Farndon, *to 1980*
Farndon : the history of a Cheshire village / [research organiser and editor Frank A. Latham]. — [Farndon] ([Mrs. H. Morgan, 16 Dee Crescent, Farndon, Nr. Chester]) : [Farndon Local History Society], 1981. — 126p,[8]p of plates : ill,maps,ports,1geneal.table ; 22cm
Maps on inside covers. — Also available in a cased limited ed. (£6.95) and in a limited ed. of 20 copies bound in full leather (£19.50). — Includes index
£5.95 (pbk) B82-16147

942.7'16 — Cheshire. Wilmslow. Social conditions, *1851-1871*
Three Sundays in Wilmslow : 1851-1871 / [editors J.H. Hodson, J.H. Smith]. — Cheadle : Wilmslow Historical Society, c1981. — viii,66p : 1map ; 21cm
ISBN 0-9501384-4-4 (pbk) : £2.95 B82-09904

942.7'17 — Cheshire. Ellesmere Port — *Serials*
Ellesmere port mail. — No.1 (1980)-. — Chester (27 Bridge St., Chester) : Chester Chronicle and Associated Newspapers, 1980-. — v. : ill,ports ; 41cm
Weekly. — Description based on: No.66 (W/E Nov.27, 1981)
ISSN 0262-7469 = Ellesmere port mail : £0.01 1/2 per issue B82-14246

942.7'17 — Cheshire. Ellesmere Port, *to 1971*
Aspinall, Peter J.. Ellesmere Port : the making of an industrial borough / by Peter J. Aspinall and Daphne M. Hudson ; (edited and with contributions by Richard Lawton). — Neston : Borough Council of Ellesmere Port, 1982. — 328p,[16]p of plates : ill,1col.coat of arms,maps ; 25cm
Includes index
ISBN 0-9507666-0-7 : Unpriced B82-29546

942.7'19 — Cheshire. Warrington, *1855-1957 — Illustrations*
Warrington Museum and Art Gallery. Warrington in camera : 1850's-1950's : a photographic portrait / selected from the collections of Warrington Museum and Art Gallery by Janice Hayes and Peter Williams. — [Warrington] : Museum and Art Gallery, Warrington Borough Council, 1981. — 79p : chiefly ill,1map,ports ; 21cm
ISBN 0-907531-01-6 (pbk) : Unpriced B82-08330

942.7'19 — Cheshire. Warrington, *to 1891 — Early works — Facsimiles*
[Warrington as it was, as it is, and as it might be]. Chronicles of Warrington. — Warrington (67 Sankey St., Warrington, Cheshire) : Aquarius, 1981. — 68p : ill,2maps ; 30cm
Facsim of: ed. published Warrington : Sunrise Publishing, 1892
£2.95 (pbk) B82-23654

942.7'19 — Cheshire. Warrington, *to 1980*
Hayes, Janice. Warrington the gateway town : an introduction to Warrington's history / by Janice Hayes. — [Warrington] : Museum and Art Gallery, 1981. — 39p : ill,maps ; 22cm
ISBN 0-907531-00-8 (pbk) : Unpriced B82-08329

942.7'3 — Greater Manchester *(Metropolitan County).* **Tame Valley —** *For environment planning*
Tame Valley : report of survey and issues / prepared by Greater Manchester Council ... [et al.]. — [Manchester] ([County Hall, Piccadilly Gardens, Manchester M60 3HS]) : The Council, 1981. — 56p,[12]folded leaves of plates : ill,col.maps ; 30cm
Unpriced (spiral) B82-11017

942.7'32 — Greater Manchester *(Metropolitan County).* **Eccles,** *to 1981*
Carroll, Brian, *1951-*. Eccles in times past / Brian Carroll. — Chorley : Countryside, [1982?]. — 48p : ill,1coat of arms,1map ; 20x22cm
ISBN 0-86157-066-9 (pbk) : £2.00 (£2.40 including postage) B82-40449

942.7'32 — Greater Manchester *(Metropolitan County).* **Worsley,** *to 1981*
Culpin, Robin. Worsley and the Bridgewater Canal : an introduction / by Robin Culpin. — [Salford] : City of Salford Cultural Services, c1982. — [8]p : ill,maps ; 30cm
Cover title. — Text, ill on inside covers
ISBN 0-901952-09-5 (pbk) : Unpriced B82-25397

942.7'33 — Greater Manchester *(Metropolitan County).* **Wythenshawe,** *to 1980*
Riley, Peter, *1946-*. The story of Wythenshawe / by Peter Riley and Susan Hall. — Warrington (67 Sankey St., Warrington, Cheshire) : Aquarius Publications, c1981. — 34p : ill,ports ; 21cm
£0.60 (pbk) B82-01929

942.7'34 — Greater Manchester *(Metropolitan County).* **Stockport —** *History — Questions & answers*
Hughes, Margaret, *1923-*. A Stockport quiz book / compiled by Margaret Hughes. — Stockport : Stockport Historical Society in association with Stockport Metropolitan Borough, Recreation and Culture Division, 1982. — [31]p : ill ; 21cm
'21st anniversary publication'
ISBN 0-905164-55-5 (pbk) : Unpriced B82-12223

942.7'35 — Greater Manchester *(Metropolitan County).* **Ashton-under-Lyne,** *1890-1940 — Illustrations*

Tameside Local Studies Library. Ashton in old photographs / [compiled] by Alice Lock. — [Ashton-under-Lyne] : Libraries and Arts Committee, Tameside Metropolitan Borough, 1981. — [48]p : all ill,facsims,ports ; 21x29cm
All the photographs are taken from the collection at Tameside's Local Studies Library, Stalybridge
ISBN 0-904506-07-x (pbk) : £1.95 B82-06122

942.7'37 — Greater Manchester *(Metropolitan County).* **Bolton,** *1900-1982*

Readyhough, Gordon. Bolton town centre : a modern history : Deansgate, Victoria Square, Churchgate & adjoining areas from 1900 to 1982 / by Gordon Readyhough. — Manchester : Neil Richardson, [1982]. — 44p : ill,maps ; 30cm
Cover title. — Text, map on inside cover
ISBN 0-9506257-5-2 (pbk) : £2.00 B82-27669

942.7'37 — Greater Manchester *(Metropolitan County).* **Bolton** *(District).* **Churchgate. Social life,** *1930-1940*

Hill, Fred. Churchgate : a biography of life in the early 1930s / by Fred Hill. — [Bolton] : [Bolton Museum and Art Gallery], c1982. — 64p : ill,1map,3ports ; 20x21cm
ISBN 0-906585-04-x (pbk) : £3.00 B82-32921

942.7'37 — Greater Manchester *(Metropolitan County).* **Halliwell region. Social life,** *1783-1786 — Correspondence, diaries, etc.*

Dewhurst, *Captain*. [Local fragments from the diary of Roger, otherwise Captain Dewhurst]. Captain Dewhurst & his diary / edited by W.D. Billington. — [Bolton] ([80 Crosby Rd., Bolton BL1 4EJ]) : [W.D. Billington], [1981]. — [179]p,[2]folded leaves of plates : 2maps,1facsim,1geneal.table ; 20cm
Cover title. — Originally published: in 2v. Bolton : Chronicle, 1880 and 1881. — Includes index
£2.50 (pbk) B82-14997

942.7'38 — Greater Manchester *(Metropolitan County).* **Radcliffe,** *1830-1880 — Personal observations — Early works*

Owd Linthrin Bant. Bits of local history / by 'Owd Linthrin Bant' (Mrs Leah Smith). — [2nd ed.]. — [Radcliffe] ([Radcliffe Library, Radcliffe, Lancs.]) : Radcliffe Local History Society, 1981. — 40p : ill ; 21cm
Cover title. — Previous ed.: 1971
Unpriced (pbk) B82-17263

942.7'392 — Greater Manchester *(Metropolitan County).* **Rochdale. Social life,** *ca 1920-1939 — Childhood reminiscences*

Wilde, Fred. The clatter of clogs in the early morning / Fred Wilde ; foreword by Edward Woodward. — London : Collins, 1982. — 62p : col.ill ; 22x27cm
ISBN 0-00-216527-9 : £4.95 : CIP rev.
B82-19066

942.7'393 — Greater Manchester *(Metropolitan County).* **Oldham,** *1760-1832*

McPhillips, K.. Oldham : the formative years / by K. McPhillips. — Swinton (375 Chorley Rd., Swinton M27 2AY) : Neil Richardson, [1981?]. — 32p : ill,maps,facsims,ports ; 30cm
Cover title
£1.50 (pbk) B82-10322

942.7'393 — Greater Manchester *(Metropolitan County).* **Oldham,** *to 1855 — Early works*

Butterworth, Edwin. Historical sketches of Oldham / by the late Edwin Butterworth ; with an appendix containing the history of the town to the present time. — Didsbury : Morten, 1981. — iv,255p : ill ; 18cm
Facsim of: new ed., Oldham : John Hirst, 1856
ISBN 0-85972-048-9 : Unpriced B82-17266

942.7'5 — Merseyside *(Metropolitan County).* **Social conditions,** *to 1982*

The **Resources** of Merseyside / edited by William T.S. Gould and Alan G. Hodgkiss. — Liverpool : Liverpool University Press, 1982. — xiii,198p : ill,maps ; 25cm
Bibliography: p191-195. — Includes index
ISBN 0-85323-384-5 (pbk) : £6.00 : CIP rev.
B82-20827

942.7'5004924'05 — Merseyside *(Metropolitan County).* **Jews** *— Serials*

[Jewish telegraph *(Liverpool and Merseyside edition)*]. Jewish telegraph : the Jewish weekly for Liverpool and Merseyside. — [Liverpool and Merseyside ed.]. — [Vol.31, no.24 (Friday May 15 1981)?]-. — Manchester (11 Park Hill, Bury Old Rd, Prestwich, Manchester M25 8HH) : Jewish Telegraph, [1981?]-. — v. : ill,ports ; 45cm
Absorbed: Liverpool Jewish gazette, 1981. — Description based on: Vol.31, no.28 (Friday June 12 1981
ISSN 0262-4222 = Jewish telegraph (Liverpool and Merseyside edition) : £0.12 per issue
B82-03412

942.7'51 — Merseyside *(Metropolitan County).* **Bebington,** *ca 1870-ca 1930*

Bidston, Carol E.. Bebington : of yesteryear / Carol E. Bidston. — Birkenhead : Metropolitan Borough of Wirral, Central Library, [1981]. — [32]p : ill ; 21x30cm
Ill and bibliography on inside covers. — Bibliography on inside back cover
ISBN 0-904582-03-5 (pbk) : Unpriced
B82-16960

942.7'51081'0222 — Merseyside *(Metropolitan County).* **Wirral** *(District), ca 1840-1950 — Illustrations*

Boumphrey, Ian. Yesterday's Wirral, Birkenhead, Prenton & Oxton / [compiled] by Ian & Marilyn Boumphrey. — [Great Britain] : I. & M. Boumphrey, c1981. — 63p : chiefly ill
Cover title
ISBN 0-9507255-1-x (pbk) : £2.50 B82-19308

942.7'53 — Merseyside *(Metropolitan County).* **Liverpool. Buildings,** *1207-1727*

The **Changing** face of Liverpool 1207-1727 : archaeological survey of Merseyside / [editor Susan Nicholson]. — Liverpool : Merseyside Archaeological Society, [1982]. — 48p : ill,maps,3facsims,1plan ; 19x25cm
Bibliography: p45-46. — Includes index
ISBN 0-906479-04-5 (pbk) : Unpriced
B82-20345

942.7'53 — Merseyside *(Metropolitan County).* **Liverpool. Toxteth. Riots,** *1981.* **Causes**

Bedford, Colin. Weep for the city / Colin Bedford. — Tring : Lion, 1982. — 127p ; 18cm
ISBN 0-85648-396-6 (pbk) : £1.50 B82-24168

942.7'53083'0924 — Merseyside *(Metropolitan County).* **Liverpool. Working class communities. Social life,** *1933-1937 — Childhood reminiscences*

Forrester, Helen. [Minerva's stepchild]. Liverpool miss / Helen Forrester. — [London] : Fontana, 1982, c1974. — 289p ; 18cm
Originally published: London : Bodley Head, 1979
ISBN 0-00-636494-2 (pbk) : £1.75 B82-15171

942.7'530858'0924 — Merseyside *(Metropolitan County).* **Liverpool. Social life** *— Personal observations*

Cornelius, John. Liverpool 8. — London : J. Murray, Sept.1982. — [224]p
ISBN 0-7195-3975-7 (pbk) : £4.50 : CIP entry
B82-20387

942.7'54 — Merseyside *(Metropolitan County).* **Knowsley. Parish churches: Knowsley Church,** *to 1980*

Carr, Mark. A short history of Knowsley Church and the Derby family / by Mark Carr. — [Knowsley] ([c/o Rev. S.M. Munns, The Vicarage, Tithebarn Rd., Knowsley, Merseyside L34 0JA]) : [M. Carr], [1982?]. — xiv,101p : ill,coats of arms,facsims,2geneal.tables,maps,plans,ports ; 29cm
Unpriced (pbk) B82-32839

942.7'54 — Merseyside *(Metropolitan County).* **Whiston** *— History*

Knowles, Jack. A history of Whiston. — Huyton (Central Library, Derby Rd., Huyton, Liverpool L36 9UJ) : Knowsley Libraries, 1982
Part 1 1100-1900 / by Jack Knowles with a section on craft and industry by Wm.K. Blinkhorn. — vii,137p : ill,facsims,geneal.tables,maps,ports ; 30cm
Includes index
Unpriced (pbk) B82-28672

942.7'570858 — Merseyside *(Metropolitan County).* **St. Helens** *(District).* **Social conditions** *— For industrial development*

St. Helens industrial handbook. — London : Burrow, [1980]. — 80p : ill,maps ; 25cm
Unpriced (pbk) B82-14589

942.7'6 — Lancashire. Fylde, *to 1980*

Davies, R. K.. Companion to the Fylde / by R.K. Davies. — Birkenhead : Countyvise, c1982. — 68p : ill(some col.),maps ; 21cm
Bibliography: p68
ISBN 0-907768-25-3 (pbk) : £1.75 B82-39487

942.7'6081 — Lancashire. Cotton manufacturing industries. Personnel. Social life, *1862 — Correspondence, diaries, etc.*

Ryley, Richard. My days are swifter than a weaver's shuttle. — Orpington (6 Stanbrook House, Orchard Grove, Orpington, Kent BR6 0SR) : Clement, Oct.1982. — [100]p
ISBN 0-907027-09-1 (cased) : £8.50 : CIP entry
ISBN 0-907027-07-5 (pbk) : £4.95 B82-29157

942.7'623 — Lancashire. Hawkshaw. Social life, *ca 1885-1900 — Childhood reminiscences*

Shearer, Ellen. Victorian children at Turton Tower / by Ellen Shearer. — [Blackburn] ([Town Hall, Blackburn, Lancs. BB1 7DY]) : Borough of Blackburn, Recreation Department, 1982. — 32p : ill(some col.),1map,1col.facsim,ports ; 21cm
Cover title. — Text, map on inside covers
Unpriced (pbk) B82-22274

942.7'6230858'05 — Lancashire. Blackburn *(District) — Serials*

Blackburn & Darwen mail. — Issue no.1 (Thursday 10 June 1982)-. — Blackburn (High St, Blackburn BB1 1HT) : North Western Newspaper Co., 1982-. — v. : ill,forms,ports ; 39cm
Weekly
ISSN 0263-8975 = Blackburn & Darwen mail : Unpriced B82-38529

942.7'63 — Lancashire. Higher Cloughfold. Social life, *1921-1939 — Childhood reminiscences*

Gillett, John W.. Once upon hard times : life in the village of Higher Cloughfold / John W. Gillett. — Rawtenstall : Rawtenstall Civic Society, [1981]. — 44p : ill,1map ; 26cm
Cover title
ISBN 0-9507925-0-0 (pbk) : Unpriced
B82-14662

942.7'69 — Lancashire. Bolton-le-Sands, *to 1981*

Entwistle, Kenneth. From Bodeltone to Bolton-le-Sands : the story of a village / by Kenneth Entwistle. — London : Euromonitor, c1982. — xi,241p,[1]folded leaf of plates : ill,facsims,maps,plans ; 23cm
Includes index
ISBN 0-903706-76-8 : £4.95 B82-29179

942.7'8 — Cumbria, *to 1982*

Bragg, Melvyn. Land of the lakes. — London : Secker & Warburg, Feb.1983. — [224]p
ISBN 0-436-06715-3 : £10.95 : CIP entry
B82-38294

942.7'801 — Cumbria, *to 945*

Carruthers, F. J.. People called Cumbri : the heroic age of the Cumbrian Celts / F.J. Carruthers. — London : Hale, 1979. — 208p,[16]p of plates : ill ; 23cm
Bibliography: p199-200. — Includes index
ISBN 0-7091-7245-1 : £6.50 B82-26770

942.7'8052 — Cumbria. Pilgrimage of Grace

Harrison, Scott Michael. The Pilgrimage of Grace in the Lake Counties, 1536-7 / Scott Michael Harrison. — London : Royal Historical Society, 1981. — viii,158p : 3maps ; 23cm. — (Royal Historical Society studies in history series ; no.27)
Bibliography: p141-144. — Includes index
ISBN 0-901050-81-4 : Unpriced B82-15995

942.7′80858′05 — Cumbria. Lake District — *Serials*
Lakeland echo. — No.1 (1979)-. — Bowness-on-Windermere (2 Westmorland House, Lake Rd, Bowness-on-Windermere, [Cumbria] LA23 3BJ) : Windermere Pub., 1979-. — v. : ill,ports ; 43cm
Weekly. — Description based on: No.136 (Apr. 8, 1982)
Unpriced B82-36732

942.7′84 — Cumbria. Arlecdon. Farmhouses: Bigcroft, *to 1975*
Phillipson, David, *1916-*. History of Bigcroft / David Phillipson. — 2nd ed. — Frizington (Bigcroft, Arlecdon, Frizington, Cumbria) : D. Phillipson, 1982. — 6leaves,[5]leaves of plates : ill,ports ; 30cm
Previous ed.: 1976
£1.00 (pbk) B82-28689

942.7′84 — Cumbria. Whitehaven, *1642-1980 — Illustrations*
Moon, Michael. Bygone Whitehaven / by Michael and Sylvia Moon. — Beckermet : M. Moon
Vol.1. — c1980. — 64p : ill,2facsims,port ; 23cm
Bibliography: p64
ISBN 0-904131-23-8 (pbk) : £2.80 B82-18647

Moon, Michael. Bygone Whitehaven / by Michael and Sylvia Moon. — Beckermet : M. Moon
Vol.3. — c1980. — 64p : ill,ports ; 23cm
Bibliography: p64.
ISBN 0-904131-24-6 (pbk) : £2.80 B82-18648

942.8′1 — Yorkshire. Manor houses, *to 1700*
Ambler, Louis. The old halls & manor houses of Yorkshire. — Ashbourne : Moorland Publishing, Nov.1981. — [256]p
Facsim. of 1st ed. London : Batsford, 1913
ISBN 0-86190-025-1 : £13.95 : CIP entry B81-30383

942.8′1081 — Yorkshire, *1830-1900*
Thackrah, J. R.. Victorian Yorkshire / by J.R. Thackrah. — Clapham, N. Yorkshire : Dalesman, 1979. — 70p : ill,1map,1facsim,3ports ; 21cm
Bibliography: p69-70
ISBN 0-85206-506-x (pbk) : £1.00 B82-03632

942.8′1082′0924 — Yorkshire. Bond, Alice — *Biographies*
Bond, Alice. Life of a Yorkshire girl / by Alice Bond. — Hull (39 High St., Hull [N. Humberside]) : Bradley, 1981. — v,120p,[26]p of plates : ill,1map,ports ; 23cm
Limited ed. of 500 copies
£3.60 B82-09379

942.8′1083′0924 — Yorkshire. West Riding. Agricultural industries. Farms. Social life, *ca 1905-1933 — Personal observations*
Kitchen, Fred. Brother to the ox : the autobiograhy of a farm labourer / by Fred Kitchen ; with a prefatory letter by the Duke of Portland and eight photographs. — Horsham : Caliban Books, 1981. — viii,243p,[8]leaves of plates : ill,1port ; 21cm
Originally published: London : Dent, 1940
ISBN 0-904573-54-0 : £9.00 B82-12037

942.8′12 — West Yorkshire *(Metropolitan County)*. **Halifax. Social life,** *1881-1882 — Correspondence, diaries, etc*
Turner, James, *1857-1909*. Hard up husband : James Turner's diary Halifax 1881/2. — Orwell (41, High St., Orwell, Cambs. SG8 5QN) : Ellison's Editions, c1981. — 72p : ill,1map,2facsims,ports ; 22cm
Includes index
Unpriced (spiral) B82-21133

942.8′120858′05 — West Yorkshire *(Metropolitan County)*. **Calderdale** *(District) — For executives — Serials*
Executive living : Brading & Calderdale. — Vol.1, no.1 (June-July 1981)-. — Stockport (Chapel St., Hazel Grove, Stockport SK7 4HW) : G.W. Foster Associates, 1981-. — v. : ill,ports ; 30cm
Six issues yearly
ISSN 0262-7876 = Executive living : £4.50 per year
Primary classification 942.8′170858′05
B82-08460

942.8′13 — West Yorkshire *(Metropolitan County)*. **Colne Valley** — *Serials*
Colne Valley chronicle. — No.1 (Friday Sept. 25th 1981)-. — Holmfirth (54 Huddersfield Rd., Holmfirth, [Huddersfield] HD7 1BA) : Huddersfield District Newspapers (1975) Ltd., 1981-. — v. : ill,ports ; 43cm
Weekly. — Continues: Colne Valley news
ISSN 0262-6802 = Colne Valley chronicle : £0.10 per issue B82-07649

942.8′15 — West Yorkshire *(Metropolitan County)*. **Ryhill,** *to 1982*
Ryhill in history. — [Wakefield] : Ryhill Parish Council
Vol.1. — 1981. — 104p : ill,2maps,ports ; 22cm
ISBN 0-86169-007-9 (pbk) : Unpriced B82-19120

942.8′15 — West Yorkshire *(Metropolitan County)*. **Wakefield,** *ca 1680-1926 — Illustrations*
The **Development** of Wakefield in maps, plans and views c.1680-1926 : selection / made and described by John Goodchild. — [Wakefield] : [Wakefield Historical Publications], [1981]. — 1portfolio : ill,maps,plans ; 32x46cm. — (Wakefield historical publications ; 7)
ISBN 0-901869-09-0 : £3.50 B82-13791

942.8′15 — West Yorkshire *(Metropolitan County)*. **Wakefield. Places associated with wool industries & trades,** *to 1980*
Goodchild, John. Wakefield and wool : a wool trail illustrating some aspects of the textile industries in Wakefield / by John Goodchild. — [Wakefield] : Wakefield Historical Publications, c1981. — 48p : ill,maps,facsims,plans,1port ; 21cm. — (Wakefield historical publications ; 8)
Maps on inside covers. — Includes index
ISBN 0-901869-10-4 (pbk) : £2.00 B82-13792

942.8′17 — West Yorkshire *(Metropolitan County)*. **Bradford,** *ca 1800-ca 1900 — Festschriften*
Victorian Bradford. — Bradford (Bradford Central Library, Princess Way, Bradford, West Yorkshire BD1 1NN) : City of Bradford Metropolitan Council, Libraries Division, Apr.1982. — [250]p
ISBN 0-907734-01-4 (pbk) : £8.00 : CIP entry B82-05793

942.8′170858′05 — West Yorkshire *(Metropolitan County)*. **Bradford** *(District) — For executives — Serials*
Executive living : Brading & Calderdale. — Vol.1, no.1 (June-July 1981)-. — Stockport (Chapel St., Hazel Grove, Stockport SK7 4HW) : G.W. Foster Associates, 1981-. — v. : ill,ports ; 30cm
Six issues yearly
ISSN 0262-7876 = Executive living : £4.50 per year
Also classified at 942.8′120858′05 B82-08460

942.8′19 — West Yorkshire *(Metropolitan County)*. **Harewood. Country houses: Harewood House,** *to 1980*
Kennedy, Carol. Harewood House : the life and times of an English country house. — London : Hutchinson, Mar.1982. — [192]p
ISBN 0-09-146870-1 : £9.95 : CIP entry B82-06219

942.8′19 — West Yorkshire (Metropolitan County). Leeds. Parish churches: St. John's Church *(Leeds), to 1980*
Douglas, Janet, *1943-*. St John's Church Leeds : a history / by Janet Douglas and Ken Powell. — London (St. Andrew by the Wardrobe, Queen Victoria St., E.C.4) : Redundant Churches Fund, [1982?]. — 24p : ill ; 21cm
Cover title. — Text on inside cover. — Bibliography: p24
Unpriced (pbk) B82-22211

942.8′19 — West Yorkshire *(Metropolitan County)*. **Leeds** — *Serials*
Leeds Skyrack express. — Friday May 7 1982-. — Wakefield (Express House, Southgate, Wakefield, W. Yorkshire WF1 1TE) : Yorkshire Weekly Newspaper Group, 1982-. — v. : ill,ports ; 59cm
Weekly. — Continues: Skyrack & East Leeds express
£0.13 per issue B82-36736

942.8′19 — West Yorkshire *(Metropolitan County)*. **Pudsey** — *Serials*
The **Pudsey** news. — Friday 12 June 1981-Mar. 1982. — Harrogate (101 Montpellier St, Harrogate, N. Yorkshire) : R. Ackrill Ltd., 1981-1982. — ?v. : ill,ports ; 45cm
Weekly. — Continues: The News (Pudsey). — Continued by: The Pudsey times
Unpriced B82-40052

942.8′19 — West Yorkshire *(Metropolitan)*. **Harewood. Country houses: Harewood House,** *to 1981 — Illustrations*
Thornton, David, *1935-*. The picture story of Harewood House / by David Thornton. — Leeds (101 Blue Hill La., Leeds LS12 4NX) : D.J. Thornton, [1982]. — 16p : chiefly ill ; 22cm
£0.50 (pbk) B82-25949

942.8′19004924 — West Yorkshire *(Metropolitan County)*. **Leeds. Jewish tailors. Social conditions,** *1880-1914*
Buckman, Joseph. Immigrants and the class struggle. — Manchester : Manchester University Press, Jan.1983. — [224]p
ISBN 0-7190-0908-1 : £19.50 : CIP entry B82-30219

942.8′21 — South Yorkshire *(Metropolitan County)*. **Sheffield. Crookes,** *to 1981*
Crookes : the history of a Sheffield village / [compiled and written by the Crookes Local History Group] ; [joint editors Judy Hague and Margaret Robinson]. — Sheffield : Crookes Residents' Association, 1982. — 77p : ill,maps ; 24cm
Maps on inside covers. — Bibliography: p75. — Includes index
ISBN 0-9508064-0-4 (pbk) : £2.00 B82-39674

942.8′21 — South Yorkshire *(Metropolitan County)*. **Sheffield. Social conditions** — *Serials*
[City trends *(Sheffield. Corporate Management Unit)*]. City trends-. — 1980-. — Sheffield (Town Hall, Sheffield S1 2HH) : Corporate Management Unit, Chief Executive's Dept., Sheffield City Council, 1980-. — v. ; 30cm
Annual. — Description based on: 1981 issue
ISSN 0263-1415 = City trends - Corporate Management Unit, Chief Executive's Department, Sheffield City Council : Unpriced B82-18524

942.8′23 — South Yorkshire *(Metropolitan County)*. **Wentworth. County houses: Wentworth Castle,** *to 1981*
Humphrey, Jean. Wentworth Castle : a short history / by Jean Humphrey. — Derby : English Life, c1982. — 16p : ill(some col.),col.coats of arms,1geneal.table,ports ; 24cm
Ill on inside covers
ISBN 0-85101-189-6 (pbk) : £0.50 B82-25688

942.8′3 — North Humberside. Coastal regions. Social life
Mitchell, W. R. (William Reginald). Life on the Yorkshire coast / compiled by W.R. Mitchell. — Clapham (via Lancaster) : Dalesman, 1982. — 70p : ill,ports ; 18x22cm. — (Dalesman heritage)
ISBN 0-85206-664-3 (pbk) : £2.95
Primary classification 942.8′4′00946
B82-23615

942.8′30858′05 — Humberside — *Serials*
Humberside life. — July 1981-. — Grimsby (384 Cleethorpe Rd, Grimsby, South Humberside DN31 3DE) : T. Aspinall (Holdings) Ltd., 1981-. — v. : ports ; 30cm
Monthly
ISSN 0263-3051 = Humberside life : £9.00 per year B82-22700

942.8′31 — Humberside. Scunthorpe, *to 1974*
An **Industrial** island : a history of Scunthorpe / edited by M. Elizabeth Armstrong. — [Scunthorpe] : Scunthorpe Borough Museum and Art Gallery, 1981. — xiv,218p,[2]leaves of plates : ill,maps,1coat of arms,facsims,ports ; 31cm
Bibliography: p196-202. — Includes index
ISBN 0-9501569-3-0 (cased) : Unpriced
ISBN 0-9501569-4-9 (pbk) : Unpriced
B82-04448

.8′32 — Humberside. Barton-upon-Humber, *to 1086*

Bryant, Geoffrey F.. The early history of Barton upon Humber : prehistory to the Norman Conquest / Geoffrey F. Bryant. — [Barton-Upon-Humber] ([c/o Workers' Educational Association, 8 Queen St., Barton-Upon-Humber, S. Humberside DN18 5QP]) : Barton Civic Society, 1981. — 73p : ill,maps,plans ; 30cm. — (A History of Barton upon Humber ; pt.1)
Ill on inside covers. — Bibliography: p.72-73
£2.10 (pbk) B82-05656

942.8′37082′0924 — Humberside. Hull. Pearson, Kay — *Biographies*

Pearson, Kay. Life in Hull from then till now / by Kay Pearson. — Hull (39 High St., Hull [N. Humberside]) : Bradley, 1979. — 192p : ill,facsims,ports ; 22cm
£2.40 B82-09375

942.8′4 — North Yorkshire. Dales, *to ca 1980*

Barringer, J. C.. The Yorkshire Dales / by J.C. Barringer. — Clapham : Dalesman, 1982. — 175p : ill,maps ; 21cm
Includes index
ISBN 0-85206-668-6 (pbk) : £4.75 B82-31383

942.8′4 — North Yorkshire. Derwent Valley, *1740-1980*

Cooper, Brian. Transformation of a valley. — London : Heinemann Educational, Sept.1981. — [272]p
ISBN 0-435-32973-1 : £13.50 : CIP entry
B81-22637

942.8′4 — North Yorkshire. Ouse River region, *to 1981*

Broadhead, Ivan E.. Portrait of the Yorkshire Ouse / by Ivan E. Broadhead ; illustrated by the author. — London : Hale, 1982. — 188p,[24]p : ill,1map ; 23cm
Includes index
ISBN 0-7091-9605-9 : £8.50 B82-24787

942.8′4′00946 — North Yorkshire. Coastal regions. Social life

Mitchell, W. R. (William Reginald). Life on the Yorkshire coast / compiled by W.R. Mitchell. — Clapham (via Lancaster) : Dalesman, 1982. — 70p : ill,ports ; 18x22cm. — (Dalesman heritage)
ISBN 0-85206-664-3 (pbk) : £2.95
Also classified at 942.8′3 B82-23615

942.8′407 — Yorkshire. North Riding. Social conditions, *1780-1850*

Hastings, R. P.. Essays in North Riding history 1780-1850 / by R.P. Hastings. — [Northallerton] : North Yorkshire County Council, 1981. — 214p : maps ; 30cm. — (North Yorkshire County Record Office publications ; no.28)
Includes index
ISBN 0-906035-17-1 (pbk) : Unpriced
B82-27447

942.8′4082 — North Yorkshire. Dales. Social life, *1900-1935*

Mitchell, W. R. (William Reginald). Yorkshire dalesfolk / by W.R. Mitchell. — Clapham, Lancs. : Dalesman, 1981. — 80p : ill ; 21cm
ISBN 0-85206-653-8 (pbk) : £1.75 B82-06127

942.8′43 — North Yorkshire. York, *1066-1560*

Butler, R. M.. Medieval York / by R.M. Butler ; with illustrations by Stewart Lack and by Ken and Rita Booth. — York : Yorkshire Architectural and York Archaeological Society in association with the Sessions Book Trust, 1982. — 24p : ill ; 22x20cm
ISBN 0-900657-69-3 (pbk) : Unpriced
B82-40460

942.8′43 — North Yorkshire. York, *to 1980*

Willis, Ronald. Portrait of York / Ronald Willis ; photography by Thelma Willis. — 3rd ed. — London : Hale, 1982. — 208p,[24]p of plates : ill,1map ; 23cm
Previous ed.: 1977. — Includes index
ISBN 0-7091-9746-2 : £7.95 B82-24788

942.8′46082 — North Yorkshire. North York Moors. Social life, *1900-1980*

Life on the North York moors : a pictorial review / compiled by W.R. Mitchell. — Clapham, N. Yorkshire : Dalesman, 1981. — 72p : ill,ports ; 18cm
ISBN 0-85206-645-7 (pbk) : £2.95 B82-03635

942.8′460858 — North Yorkshire. North York Moors. Agricultural industries. Farms. Social life, *ca 1980 — Personal observations*

Drysdale, Ann. Faint heart never kissed a pig / Ann Drysdale. — London : Routledge & Kegan Paul, 1982. — 170p ; 23cm
ISBN 0-7100-0972-0 : £6.95 : CIP rev.
B81-37577

942.8′48 — North Yorkshire. Wensleydale. Calvert, Kit — *Biographies*

Calvert, Kit. Kit Calvert of Wensleydale : the complete Dalesman. — Clapham, [North Yorkshire] : Dalesman, 1981. — 80p : ill,ports ; 20cm. — (Dalesman heritage)
ISBN 0-85206-655-4 (pbk) : £1.85 B82-14847

942.8′49 — North Yorkshire. Great Ayton. Buildings of historical importance, *to 1981*

Gaudie, Ruth. A visual history of Great Ayton / by Ruth Gaudie ; drawings by Ruth Gaudie. — Whitby (c/o Bleach Mill Farm, Kildale, Whitby, North Yorks, YO21 2EL) : R. Gaudie in association with Stokesley & District Local History Study Group, 1982. — 32p : ill,maps ; 21x30cm
Unpriced B82-40008

942.8′49 — North Yorkshire. Stokesley region, *to 1900*

Stokesley selection / collected and edited by Alec Wright and John Mawer. — Great Ayton : Studio Print, c1982. — 429p : ill(some col.),facsims,maps,ports ; 28cm
ISBN 0-907922-00-7 : Unpriced B82-35809

942.8′54 — Cleveland. Guisborough, *to 1900*

Guisborough before 1900 / editors B.J.D. Harrison, G. Dixon. — Guisborough (13 Farndale Drive, Guisborough, Cleveland) : G. Dixon, 1981. — xvi,270p,[24]p of plates : ill,maps,facsims,1port ; 21cm
Includes index
ISBN 0-9507827-0-x (pbk) : £5.85 B82-10517

942.8′570855′0924 — Cleveland. Hartlepool. Social life, *ca 1950 — Personal observations*

Caldecourt, Barbara. Home to Hartlepool / Barbara Caldecourt. — Pontefract (17, Linden Terrace, Pontefract) : Brian Lewis, c1981. — 47p : ill,1port ; 21cm. — (Peoples history of the North ; 1)
£1.50 (pbk) B82-17832

942.8′62 — Durham *(County)*. **Spennymoor. Beavis, Dick** — *Biographies*

Beavis, Dick. What price happiness? : my life from coal hewer to shop steward / Dick Beavis. — Whitley Bay : Strong Words, c1980. — 88p : ill,ports ; 21cm
ISBN 0-905274-12-1 (pbk) : £0.75 B82-31636

942.8′64 — Durham *(County)*. **Bishop Auckland,** *1730-1830*

Hebden, Derek J.. When Bishop Auckland was a village / by Derek J. Hebden. — Bishop Auckland (30 Cockton Hill Rd., Bishop Auckland) : D.J. Hebden, 1974. — 44p : ill,maps,2facsims,ports ; 21cm
£0.80 (pbk) B82-21700

942.8′64 — Durham *(County)*. **Bishop Auckland** — *Serials*

[Auckland chronicle *(Wear Valley edition)*]. Auckland chronicle. — Wear Valley ed. — Jan. 1981-. — Durham (Saddler St., Durham) : North of England Newspapers, 1981-. — v. : ill,ports ; 60cm
Weekly. — Continues in part: Auckland chronicle (1935). — Description based on: Thursday, Oct.15, 1981
ISSN 0263-0176 = Auckland chronicle. Wear Valley edition : £0.12 per issue B82-14244

942.8′64 — Durham *(County)*. **Bishop Auckland. Social conditions,** *ca 1800-1960*

Hebden, Derek J.. Bishop Auckland remembered / by Derek J. Hebden. — Bishop Auckland (30 Cockton Hill Rd., Bishop Auckland) : D.J. Hebden, 1979. — 40p : ill,facsims,ports ; 22cm
£1.00 (pbk) B82-17499

942.8′65 — Durham *(County)*. **Durham** — *Serials*

[Durham chronicle *(Chester-le-Street, Birtley edition)*]. Durham chronicle. — Chester-le-Street, Birtley ed.. — 6553 (Friday Sept. 25 1981)-. — Durham (Saddler St., Durham) : North of England Newspapers, 1981-. — v. : ill,ports ; 60cm
Weekly. — Continues in part: Durham chronicle. — Description based on: 6554 (Friday Oct. 2 1981)
ISSN 0262-6837 = Durham chronicle. Chester-le-Street, Birtley edition : £0.12 per issue B82-07651

942.8′65 — Durham *(County)*. **Durham. Social conditions** — *For environment planning*

City of Durham district plan : report of survey. — Durham ([City Planning Officer, Byland Lodge, Hawthorn Terrace, Durham DH1 4TD]) : [City of Durham Council], [1982?]. — 311p,[16]p of plates(some folded) : ill(some col.),maps(some col.),plans ; 30cm
Unpriced (spiral) B82-35033

942.8′75 — Tyne and Wear *(Metropolitan County)*. **Boldon. Social life,** *1900-1945 — Illustrations*

Picture of Boldon. — [South Shields] : South Tyneside Borough Council Library Service, 1979. — 24p : all ill ; 21cm
Also available in limited presentation edition
ISBN 0-906617-00-6 (pbk) : £0.50 B82-40434

942.8′75 — Tyne and Wear *(Metropolitan County)*. **South Shields. Social life,** *1860-1900 — Illustrations*

Picture of South Shields. — [South Shields] : South Tyneside Borough Council Library Service, 1979. — 48p : all ill,facsims ; 21cm
Also available in limited presentation edition
ISBN 0-906617-01-4 (pbk) : £0.75 B82-40435

942.8′76 — Tyne and Wear *(Metropolitan County)*. **Newcastle upon Tyne. Jesmond. Parish churches: Jesmond Parish Church,** *to ca 1960*

Munden, A. F.. Jesmond parish church Newcastle upon Tyne / Alan Munden. — Newcastle upon Tyne : Clayton, 1981. — 30p : ill,1facsim,1port ; 21cm
Text on inside cover
ISBN 0-9507592-0-1 (pbk) : £1.50 B82-04201

942.8′76 — Tyne and Wear *(Metropolitan County)*. **Throckley. Coal industries. Miners. Social life,** *1890-1940*

Williamson, Bill, *1944-*. Class, culture and community : a biographical study of social change in mining / Bill Williamson. — London : Routledge & Kegan Paul, 1982. — xiv,245p,[8]p of plates : ill,1map,ports ; 22cm
Bibliography: p233-239. — Includes index
ISBN 0-7100-0991-7 (pbk) : £6.95 B82-27706

942.8′79082′0222 — Tyne and Wear *(Metropolitan County)*. **North Tyneside** *(District)*, *1900-1960 — Illustrations*

As they were : from old photographs / compiled and published by R. Thompson Dix. — Tynemouth : R.T. Dix, 1981. — [116]p : chiefly ill,1facsim,ports ; 25cm
ISBN 0-9507789-0-7 (cased) : Unpriced
ISBN 0-9507789-1-5 (pbk) : Unpriced
B82-11474

942.8′8 — Northumberland, *to 1975*

Ridley, Nancy. Northumbrian heritage / Nancy Ridley ; foreword by Viscount Ridley. — 2nd ed. — London : Hale, 1982. — 192p,[18]p of plates : ill,1map,1facsim ; 23cm
Previous ed: 1968. — Includes index
ISBN 0-7091-9627-x : £7.95 B82-28962

942.8′84 — Northumberland. Cramlington. Coal miners. Social life, *1913-1965 — Personal observations*

Muckle, William. No regrets / William Muckle. — Newcastle upon Tyne : People's Publications, 1981. — 78p : ill,facsims,ports ; 19cm
ISBN 0-906917-06-9 (cased) : Unpriced
ISBN 0-906917-07-7 (pbk) : £1.50 B82-21843

942.8′84 — Northumberland. Plessey region, ***to 1980***

Bleay, Janet. Plessey : the story of a Northumbrian woodland / text by Janet Bleay ; designed and illustrated by Noel McCready ; maps compiled by Peter Howe. — Hexham : Northumberland County Council. National Park and Countryside Department, c1981. — 38p : ill,maps,facsims ; 20cm
ISBN 0-907632-03-3 (pbk) : £0.75 B82-17316

942.9 — HISTORY. WALES

942.9 — Wales, ***400-1200***

Davies, Wendy. Wales in the early Middle Ages. — Leicester : Leicester University Press, Sept.1982. — [280]p. — (Studies in the early history of Britain)
ISBN 0-7185-1163-8 (cased) : £22.00 : CIP entry
ISBN 0-7185-1235-9 (pbk) : £9.75 B82-19844

942.9 — Wales, ***1200-1928 — Sources of data: Seals***

Williams, David H.. Welsh history through seals / this book was written by David H. Williams. — Cardiff : Amgueddfa Genedlaethol Cymru, 1982. — 48p : ill(some col.) ; 16x24cm
Bibliography: p46-47
ISBN 0-7200-0242-7 (pbk) : £2.25 B82-30549

942.9 — Wales, ***1530-1760 — Welsh texts***

Jenkins, Geraint H.. Hanes Cymru yn y cyfnod modern cynnar 1530-1760. — Cardiff : University of Wales Press, Nov.1982. — [360]p
ISBN 0-7083-0823-6 : £12.95 : CIP entry B82-28743

942.9 — Wales. Castles, ***to 1981 — For children — Welsh texts***

Jones, Gwen Redvers. Herio′r cestyll. — Cardiff : University of Wales Press, Sept.1982. — [80]p
ISBN 0-7083-0826-0 (pbk) : £2.95 : CIP entry B82-20019

942.9 — Wales. Chapels. Names ***— Welsh texts***

Rees, J. Derfel. Ar eu talcennau : enwau capeli yng Nghymru / J. Derfel Rees. — Abertawe [Swansea] : Tŷ John Penry, 1981. — 112p ; 21cm
ISBN 0-903701-50-2 (pbk) : £2.00 B82-16384

942.9 — Wales, ***to 1976***

Williams, Gwyn A.. The Welsh in their history / Gwyn A. Williams. — London : Croom Helm, c1982. — 206p : ill,1map ; 23cm
Includes index
ISBN 0-7099-2711-8 : £11.95 : CIP rev. B82-14944

942.9′0072024 — Wales. Historiography. Giraldus, ***Cambrensis — Critical studies***

Bartlett, Robert. Gerald of Wales : 1145-1223 / Robert Bartlett. — Oxford : Clarendon, 1982. — 246p : 1geneal.table ; 23cm. — (Oxford historical monographs)
Bibliography: p226-236. — Includes index
ISBN 0-19-821892-3 : £19.50 : CIP rev. B82-10447

Roberts, Brynley F.. Gerald of Wales / Brynley F. Roberts. — [Cardiff] : University of Wales Press on behalf of the Welsh Arts Council, 1982. — 107p,[1]leaf of plates : 1map ; 25cm. — (Writers of Wales)
Limited ed. of 1000 numbered copies. — Bibliography: p97-105
ISBN 0-7083-0816-3 (pbk) : £2.50 : CIP rev. B82-11769

942.9′009′52 — Wales. Woodlands, ***to 1981***

Linnard, William. Welsh woods and forests : history and utilization / by William Linnard ; foreword by Douglas A. Bassett. — Cardiff : National Museum of Wales, 1982. — xxi,203p : ill,maps ; 23cm
Bibliography: p167-171. — Includes index
ISBN 0-7200-0245-1 : £7.00 B82-30871

942.9′034′0924 — Wales. Llywelyn ap Gruffydd — ***Biographies — For schools — Welsh texts***

Carr, A. D.. Llywelyn ap Gruffydd : ?-1282 / A.D. Carr. — Caerdydd : Gwasg Prifysgol Cymru, 1982. — 84p,[5]p of plates : ill,maps ; 22cm
Parallel Welsh and English text. — Bibliography: p84
ISBN 0-7083-0815-5 (pbk) : Unpriced : CIP rev. B82-05401

942.9′034′0924 — Wales. Llywelyn ap Gruffydd — ***Biographies — Welsh texts***

Jones, Tecwyn. Llywelyn ein Llyw Olaf : ei gyfnod a′i fywyd / Tecwyn Jones. — Caerdydd : Gwasg Prifysgol Cymru, 1982. — 71p : ill,maps,1coat of arms,1geneal.table ; 20cm
Bibliography: p70
ISBN 0-7083-0818-x (pbk) : Unpriced : CIP rev. B82-05402

942.907 — Wales. Social change, ***1700-1800***

Morgan, Prys. The eighteenth century renaissance / Prys Morgan. — Llandybïe : Christopher Davies, 1981. — 174p,15p of plates : ill,facsims,ports ; 21cm. — (A New history of Wales)
Bibliography: p162-165. — Includes index
£3.95 (pbk) B82-17102

942.9082 — Wales, ***1880-1980***

Morgan, Kenneth O.. Wales 1880-1980 : rebirth of a nation / Kenneth O. Morgan. — Oxford : Oxford University Press, 1982, c1981. — xiii,463p ; 20cm
Originally published: Oxford : Clarendon, 1981. — Bibliography: p422-445. — Includes index
ISBN 0-19-821760-9 (pbk) : £4.95 : CIP rev. B82-07514

942.9′082′0924 — Wales. Morgan, Stella — ***Biographies***

Morgan, Stella. Chase the clouds away / by Stella Morgan. — Oulton : Teecoll, c1981. — 167p ; 22cm
ISBN 0-7109-0004-x : Unpriced B82-34700

942.9′082′092′4 — Wales. Parry, Ann — ***Biographies — Welsh texts***

Parry, Ann. [Thirty thousand yesterdays. Welsh]. Lle henc eira llynedd? / gan Ann Parry ; trosiad gan R. Wallis Evans ... — Llandysul : Gwasg Gomer, 1979. — 158p,[9]p of plates : ports ; 22cm
Translation of: Thirty thousand yesterdays
ISBN 0-85088-811-5 (pbk) : £1.75 B82-25964

942.9′10856′0924 — North Wales. Rural regions. Social life, ***1965-1974 — Personal observations***

West, Elizabeth. Garden in the hills. — Large print ed. — Anstey : Ulverscroft, Nov.1982. — [352]p. — (Ulverscroft large print series)
Originally published: London : Faber, 1980
ISBN 0-7089-0882-9 : £5.00 : CIP entry B82-29093

West, Elizabeth. Hovel in the hills : an account of ″the simple life″ / Elizabeth West. — Large print ed. — Leicester : Ulverscroft, 1982, c1977. — 327p ; 23cm. — (Ulverscroft large print)
Originally published: London : Faber, 1977
ISBN 0-7089-0798-9 : Unpriced : CIP rev. B82-18560

942.9′23 — Gwynedd. Rhoshirwaun. Social life, ***1909-ca 1920 — Childhood reminiscences — Welsh texts***

Roberts, Meurig. Mi Glywais a gwelais : darlith flynyddol Llŷn 1981 / gan Meurig Roberts. — [Caernarfon] : Cyngor Sir Gwynedd, Gwasanaeth Llyfrgell, c1982. — 23p ; 21cm. — (Darlith flynyddol Llŷn ; 1981)
ISBN 0-904852-25-3 (pbk) : £0.40 B82-21304

942.9′25 — Gwynedd. Bethesda. Social life, ***ca 1850-1955 — Personal observations — Welsh texts***

Roberts, John Alun. Cofio′r gorffennol / gan John Alun Roberts. — [Caernarfon] : Gwasanaeth Llyfrgell Gwynedd, Rhanbarth Arfon/Dwyfor, 1980. — 41p : 1port ; 21cm. — (Darlith flynyddol Llyfrgell Bethesda ; 1980)
'Darlith a draddodwyd yn Ysgol Penybryn, Bethesda, Mawrth 19eg, 1980'
ISBN 0-904852-18-0 (pbk) : £0.25 B82-26507

942.9′25 — Gwynedd. Nantlle Valley. Social life, ***ca 1920-1975 — Personal observations — Welsh texts***

Hughes, Mathonwy. Atgofion mab y mynydd / gan Mathonwy Hughes. — [Denbigh] : Gwasg Gee, c1982. — 69p ; 18cm
£1.50 (pbk) B82-39557

942.9′25 — Gwynedd. Snowdonia, ***to 1981***

Hall, Vernon, ***1904-***. A scrapbook of Snowdonia / Vernon Hall. — Ilfracombe : Stockwell, 1982. — 312p,[24]p of plates : ill,ports ; 22cm
ISBN 0-7223-1622-4 (pbk) : £2.95 B82-40752

942.9′39 — Clwyd. Rhosllanerchrugog. Social life, ***ca 1950-1970 — Personal observations***

Portmadoc-Jones, Bill. Through these windows — : a place and its people / by Bill Portmadoc-Jones. — [Denbigh] ([Chapel St., Denbigh, Clwyd]) : [Gwasg Gee], [1981]. — 89p,[13]p of plates : ill,ports ; 19cm
£1.50 (pbk) B82-12202

942.9′4 — South Wales. Coal mining communities. Working life, ***1900-1930***

Keen, Richard. Coalface / ... written by Richard Keen. — [Cardiff] : [National Museum of Wales], c1982. — 51p : ill,ports ; 16x23cm
At head of title: Amgueddfa Genedlaethol Cymru, National Museum of Wales
ISBN 0-7200-0243-5 (pbk) : £1.50 B82-32644

942.9′4′00944 — South Wales. Valleys, ***1840-1870 — Conference proceedings***

Jones, Ieuan Gwynedd. The valleys in the mid-nineteenth century : a lecture / given by Ieuan Gwynedd Jones. — [Gwent] ([Park Buildings, Pontypool, Gwent NP4 6JH]) : Standing Conference on the History of the South Wales Valleys in association with the Torfaen Museum Trust, 1981. — 30p : ill ; 21cm
ISBN 0-85088-525-6 (pbk) : £1.25 B82-00858

942.9′61 — Dyfed. Llangrannog. Cranogwen — ***Biographies — Welsh texts***

Jones, Gerallt. Cranogwen : portread newydd / Gerallt Jones. — Llandysul : Gwasg Gomer, 1981. — 97p : ili,ports ; 19cm
ISBN 0-85088-664-3 (pbk) : £1.50 B82-28309

942.9′61081 — Dyfed. Ceredigion ***(District).*** **Social life,** ***1800-1900 — Welsh texts***

Jones, Mary, ***19---***. Ddoe / Mary Jones. — Llandysul : Gwasg Gomer, 1981. — 115p ; 19cm
ISBN 0-85088-874-3 (pbk) : £1.95 B82-02427

942.9′62 — Dyfed. Preseli ***(District), to 1980***

John, Brian. Presely Hills / Brian John. — Newport, Dyfed : Published by Greencroft for the Pembrokeshire Coast National Park Authority, 1981. — 32p : ill,maps ; 21cm. — (Pembrokeshire Coast National Park area guide, ISSN 0144-090x)
Text on inside covers. — Bibliography: on inside cover
ISBN 0-905559-45-2 (pbk) : Unpriced B82-02849

942.9′63 — Dyfed. Llanreath. Petroleum storage containers. Fires, ***1940***

Scott, Vernon. Inferno 1940 / Vernon Scott. — [Haverfordwest] : [Western Telegraph], [1980]. — iv,76p : ill,ports ; 15x21cm
ISBN 0-9507372-0-8 (pbk) : £2.00 B82-39562

942.9′63 — Dyfed. Tenby, ***ca 1850-1980 — Illustrations***

Tenby : old & new / [compiled by] Roscoe Howells. — Llandysul : Gomer, 1981. — 91p : ill,ports ; 22cm
ISBN 0-85088-835-2 : £3.95 B82-12798

942.9′65 — Dyfed. Carmarthen. Social conditions, ***1800-1900***

Molloy, Pat. Four cheers for Carmarthen : the other side of the coin / Pat Molloy. — Llandysul : Gomer Press, 1981. — 218p : ill,maps,facsims,ports ; 22cm
Maps on lining papers. — Includes index
ISBN 0-85088-925-1 : £5.95 B82-28307

942.9′7 — Glamorgan. Antiquities, *to 1750*
Royal Commission on Ancient and Historical Monuments in Wales. An inventory of the ancient monuments in Glamorgan / The Royal Commission on Ancient and Historical Monuments in Wales. — Cardiff : H.M.S.O.
Vol.4: Domestic architecture from the Reformation to the Industrial Revolution
Part 1: The greater houses. — 1981. — xl,379p,[12]leaves of plates(some folded), 71p of plates : ill(some col.),maps,plans ; 29cm
Maps on lining papers. — Includes index
ISBN 0-11-700754-4 : £45.00 B82-05643

942.9′71 — Mid Glamoran. Gilfach Goch, *to 1980*
Davies, Meirion. Glynogwr and Gilfach Goch : a history / by Meirion Davies. — Cowbridge : D. Brown, 1981. — 229p : ill,geneal.tables,maps,ports ; 26cm
Bibliography: p222-226. — Includes index
ISBN 0-905928-14-8 : £7.95 B82-26299

942.9′71 — Mid Glamorgan. Llynfi Valley, *to 1980*
Richards, Brinley, *1904-1981.* History of the Llynfi Valley / Brinley Richards. — Cambridge : D. Brown, 1982. — 366p : ill,facsims,maps,ports ; 25cm
Includes index
ISBN 0-905928-16-4 : £7.95 B82-35852

942.9′71082′0222 — Mid Glamorgan. Ogwr *(District), 1900-1960 — Illustrations*
Llynfi, Garw & Ogmore valleys : in old photographs / [compiled] by Richard G. Keen ; foreword by H. Vernon Chilcott. — Barry : Stewart Williams, 1981. — [120]p : chiefly ill,ports ; 25cm
ISBN 0-900807-49-0 : £6.50 B82-08068

942.9′75 — Mid Glamorgan. Merthyr Tydfil, *to 1980*
Merthyr Tydfil : drawn from life / edited with an introduction by Huw Williams. — [Dowlais] ([17, Morlais St., Dowlais, Merthyr Tydfil, Mid. Glam. CF48 3AY]) : [H. Williams], [1981]. — 120p : ill,facsims, ports ; 22cm
£1.00 (pbk) B82-06372

Merthyr Tydfil : a valley community / Merthyr Teachers Centre Group. — Merthyr Tydfil : Merthyr Teachers Centre Group, c1981. — viii,496p : ill,maps,plans ; 25cm
Ill on lining papers. — Includes bibliographies and index
ISBN 0-905928-15-6 : £10.95 B82-26304

942.9′76 — Mid Glamorgan. Caerphilly *— History*
Jones, Glyndwr G.. Cronicl Caerffili : a collection of notes relating to Caerphilly′s past / Glyndwr G. Jones. — Bromley (197, Mead Way, Haynes, Bromley, Kent BR2 9ES) : G.G. Jones
No.8. — [1981]. — 2v.(94 leaves) : ill,maps ; 30cm
Includes index
£3.00 (pbk) B82-11886

942.9′78 — Mid Glamorgan. Llantrisant, *to 1981*
Lewis, Dillwyn. The history of Llantrisant / Dillwyn Lewis. — 2nd ed. — Pontypridd : D. Lewis, 1982. — 144p,[84]p of plates : ill,3coats of arms,facsims,1map,ports ; 22cm
Previous ed.: Risca : Starling Press, 1975
ISBN 0-9500567-3-1 : Unpriced B82-34033

942.9′78 — Mid Glamorgan. Pontypridd. Social conditions, *1794-1938*
Pontypridd : essays on the history of an industrial community / edited by Huw Williams. — [Cardiff] : Department of Extra-Mural Studies, University College, Cardiff, 1981. — 63p,[8]p of plates : ill,1map ; 21cm. — (Park Place papers ; no.11)
Includes bibliographies
£1.00 (pbk) B82-05479

942.9′82 — West Glamorgan. Bishopston, *to ca 1980*
Orrin, Geoffrey R.. A history of Bishopston / by Geoffrey R. Orrin. — Llandysul : Gomer, 1982. — 138p : ill,facsims,maps ; 22cm
Bibliography: p135-138
ISBN 0-85088-507-8 (pbk) : £2.95 B82-35517

942.9′82 — West Glamorgan. Gower. Social life, *1950-1980 — Stories, anecdotes*
Thomas, J. Mansel. The sea beneath my feet / by J. Mansel Thomas. — [Swansea] : Gower Society, 1981. — 70 : ill,1port ; 20cm. — (A Gower Society publication)
Text, port on inside cover
Unpriced (pbk) B82-10198

942.9′82 — West Glamorgan. Lower Swansea Valley, *1742-1982*
Lower Swansea valley : legacy and future. — [Swansea] : Swansea City Council, c1982. — 84p : ill(some col.),maps(some col.),facsims,plans(some col.),ports(some col.) ; 20x22cm
Cover title
ISBN 0-946001-00-6 (pbk) : £3.95 B82-21139

942.9′82 — West Glamorgan. Lower Swansea Valley, *1742-1982 — French texts*
La **Vallée** Inférieure de Swansea : l′heritage et l′avenir. — [Swansea] : Swansea City Council, c1982. — 84p : ill(some col.),maps(some col.),facsims,plans(some col.),ports(some col.) ; 20x22cm
Cover title
ISBN 0-946001-02-2 (pbk) : £3.95 B82-21140

942.9′82 — West Glamorgan. Lower Swansea Valley, *1742-1982 — German texts*
Niederes Tal von Swansea : Geschichte und Zukunft. — [Swansea] : Swansea City Council, c1982. — 84p : ill(some col.),maps(some col.),facsims,plans(some col.),ports(some col.) ; 20x22cm
Cover title
ISBN 0-946001-01-4 (pbk) : £3.95 B82-21141

942.9′82 — West Glamorgan. Swansea. Official residences: Mansion House, *to 1978*
Alban, J. R.. The Mansion House, Swansea. — Swansea (Chief Executive and Town Clerk′s Department, Guildhall, Swansea SA1 4PE) : Swansea City Council, 1979. — [12]p : ill(some col.),1facsim,plans(some col.),ports ; 15x21cm. — (City archives publication ; B.7)
Cover title. — Author: J.R. Alban. — Text on inside cover
Unpriced (pbk) B82-18075

942.9′82 — West Glamorgan. Swansea region, *to 1980 — Welsh texts*
Abertawe a′r cylch / golygwyd gan Ieuan M. Williams. — Llandybie : C. Davies, c1982. — 206p : ill,maps,ports(some col.) ; 22cm. — (Bro′r Eisteddfod ; 2)
£5.95 B82-40015

942.9′85 — West Glamorgan. Margam. Country houses: Margam Castle, *to 1980*
Hughes, John Vivian. Margam Castle / John Vivian Hughes. — [Port Talbot] ([29 Arthur St., Port Talbot, W. Glamorgan, SA12 6EH]) : [J.V. Hughes], [1981?]. — [64]p : ill,1plan,ports ; 23cm
Bibliography: p64
£1.75 (pbk) B82-12123

942.9′85 — West Glamorgan. Margam. Country parks: Margam Park, *to 1977*
Margam Park. — Swansea (The Guildhall, Swansea) : West Glamorgan County Council, [1980?]. — 31p : ill(some col.),ports ; 15x21cm
Unpriced (pbk) B82-22744

942.9′85′005 — West Glamorgan. Afan *(District) — History — Serials*
Afan uchaf : the journal of the Cymer Afan and District Historical Society. — Vol.1 (1978)-. — Port Talbot (c/o The Revd. R.L. Brown, The Rectory, Cymer Afan, Port Talbot) : The Society, 1978-. — v. : ill,maps,plans ; 21cm
Annual
ISSN 0263-5607 = Afan uchaf : Unpriced B82-33858

942.9′87 — South Glamorgan. Tongwynlais, *to ca 1930*
Turn of the century Ton : something about the history of Tongwynlais. — Tongwynlais (The Vicarage, 1, Merthyr Rd, Tongwynlais, Cardiff) : R.L. Brown, 1982. — 40p,[4]p of plates : ill,1facsim,1geneal.table ; 21cm
Cover title. — Editor: Roger Brown
Unpriced (pbk) B82-35598

942.9′87081′0222 — Cardiff, *1880-1980 — Illustrations*
Stewart Williams′ Cardiff yesterday. — Barry : Stewart Williams
foreword by Geoff Rich. — 1982. — [120]p : all ill,ports ; 24cm
Ill on lining papers
ISBN 0-900807-50-4 : £6.50 B82-25628

942.9′93 — Gwent. Blackwood region. Social life, *1900-1950 — Illustrations*
Old Blackwood & lower Sirhowy valley : in photographs / [compiled] by Brian Collins and Terry Powell ; foreword by G.A. Davies. — Barry : Williams, 1982. — [118]p : chiefly ill,ports ; 26cm
ISBN 0-900807-51-2 : £6.50 B82-27387

942.9′93 — Gwent. Western Valley, *ca 1900-1979*
Collins, Brian. Old Crumlin to Pontymister in photographs / by Brian Collins and Terry Powell ; foreword by G.A. Davies. — Barry : Stewart Williams, 1981. — [120]p : chiefly ill,ports ; 25cm
ISBN 0-900807-47-4 : £6.50 B82-05056

942.9′95 — Gwent. Blaina, Brynmawr & Nantyglo. Social life, *1794-1981 — Illustrations*
Old Brynmawr, Nantyglo & Blaina in photographs / [compiled] by Edwin Jones and Trevor Rowson ; foreword by Peter J. Law. — Barry : Stewart Williams
Vol.2. — 1981. — [116]p : chiefly ill,ports ; 26cm
ISBN 0-900807-48-2 : £6.50 B82-04426

942.9′98 — Gwent. Llantilio Crossenny. Parish churches: Llanfair Cilgoed Church, *to 1982*
Williams, David H.. Llanfair Cilgoed church / [D.H.W.]. — [Abergavenny] ([The Rectory, Llanddewi Ysgyryd (Skirrid), Abergavenny, Gwent NP7 8AG]) : [D.H. Williams], 1982. — [4]p : ill,1map ; 22cm
Unpriced (unbound) B82-38242

943 — HISTORY. CENTRAL EUROPE, GERMANY

943 — German civilization, *to 1981*
Germany : a companion to German studies. — 2nd ed. — London : Methuen, Sept.1982. — [700]p. — (Methuen′s companions to modern studies)
Previous ed.: 1975
ISBN 0-416-33650-7 (cased) : £15.00 : CIP entry
ISBN 0-416-33660-4 (pbk) : £9.50 B82-20176

943′.004924 — Germany. Jews: Senger, Valentin, *to 1945 — Biographies*
Senger, Valentin. The invisible Jew / Valentin Senger. — [London] : Magnum, 1981, c1980. — vii,238p,[8]p of plates : ill,ports ; 17cm
Translation of: Kaiserhofstrasse zwolfe. — Originally published: New York : Dutton ; London : Eyre Methuen, 1980
ISBN 0-417-06890-5 (pbk) : £1.50 B82-17573

943′.005 — German culture *— History — Serials*
London German studies. — 1-. — London : Institute of Germanic Studies, University of London, 1980-. — v. ; 22cm. — (Publications of the Institute of Germanic Studies, ISSN 0076-0811)
Irregular. — Text in English and German
ISSN 0263-3140 = London German studies : Unpriced B82-19880

943′.02 — Germany, *900-1250*
Leyser, Karl J.. Medieval Germany and its neighbours, 900-1250. — London : Hambledon, Oct.1982. — [300]p. — (History series ; 12)
ISBN 0-907628-08-7 : £18.00 : CIP entry B82-24580

943′.02 — Germany, *1200-1500*
Leuschner, Joachim. Germany in the late Middle Ages / by Joachim Leuschner ; translated by Sabine MacCormack. — Amsterdam ; Oxford : North-Holland, 1980. — xxxii,226p ; 23cm. — (Europe in the Middle Ages ; v.17)
Translation of: Deutschland im Späten Mittelalter. — Bibliography: p205-216. — Includes index
ISBN 0-444-85135-6 : Unpriced B82-01038

943'.031 — Germany. Peasants' War, *1525*

Blickle, Peter. The revolution of 1525 : the German Peasants' War from a new perspective / Peter Blickle ; translated by Thomas A. Brady, Jr. and H.C. Erik Midelford. — Baltimore, Md. ; London : Johns Hopkins University Press, c1981. — xxvi,246p : ill,maps ; 24cm
Translation of: Die Revolution von 1525. — Bibliography: p227-233. — Includes index
ISBN 0-8018-2472-9 : Unpriced B82-28089

943'.07 — Germany, *1800-1914*

Ramm, Agatha. Germany 1789-1919 : a political history / Agatha Ramm. — London : Methuen, 1967 (1981 [printing]). — 517p : maps ; 24cm
Bibliography: p473-486. — Includes index
ISBN 0-416-33990-5 : Unpriced : CIP rev. B82-07969

943.08 — Germany, *1890-1981*

Berghahn, Volker R.. Modern Germany. — Cambridge : Cambridge University Press, Sept.1982. — [314]p
ISBN 0-521-23185-x (cased) : £20.00 : CIP entry
ISBN 0-521-29859-8 (pbk) : £6.95 B82-29365

943.08'092'4 — Germany. Bismarck, Otto, *Fürst von — Biographies*

Crankshaw, Edward. Bismarck / Edward Crankshaw. — London : Macmillan, 1981. — x,451p,[16]p of plates : ill,2maps,ports ; 24cm
Bibliography: p433-438. — Includes index
ISBN 0-333-18364-9 : £9.95 B82-06894

943.08'3'0924 — Germany. Victoria, *Empress, consort of Friedrich III, Emperor of Germany, 1878-1885 — Correspondence, diaries, etc.*

Victoria, *Queen of Great Britain*. Beloved mama : private correspondence of Queen Victoria and the German Crown Princess, 1878-1885 / edited by Roger Fulford. — London : Evans, 1981. — xiii,209p,[16]p of plates : ports,2geneal.tables ; 23cm
Includes index
ISBN 0-237-44997-8 : £10.95 : CIP rev.
Primary classification 941.081'092'4 B81-25777

943.08'4'0922 — Germany. Wilhelm II, *Emperor of Germany.* **Personal advisers**

Hull, Isabel V.. The entourage of Kaiser Wilhelm II : 1888-1918 / Isabel V. Hull. — Cambridge : Cambridge University Press, 1982. — xii,413p : ports ; 24cm
Bibliography: p387-402. — Includes index
ISBN 0-521-23665-7 : £27.50 : CIP rev. B82-13129

943.08'4'0924 — Germany. Bauer, Felice. Correspondence from Kafka, Franz *— Critical studies*

Canetti, Elias. Kafka's other trial : the letters to Felice / Elias Canetti ; translated by Christopher Middleton. — Harmondsworth : Penguin, 1982, c1974. — 95p ; 20cm
Translation of: Der andere Prozess. — Originally published: London : Calder & Boyars, 1974
ISBN 0-14-006287-4 (pbk) : £1.95
Primary classification 833'.912 B82-18137

943.08'4'0924 — Germany. Frederick III, *Emperor of Germany — Biographies*

Van der Kiste, John. Frederick III : German Emperor 1888 / John Van der Kiste. — Gloucester : Alan Sutton, 1981. — 242p : ill,2geneal.tables,ports ; 23cm
Bibliography: p231-233. — Includes index
ISBN 0-904387-77-1 : £8.95 : CIP rev. B81-08933

943.08'4'0924 — Germany. Wilhelm II, *Emperor of Germany — Biographies — Conference proceedings*

Kaiser Wilhelm II : new interpretations : the Corfu papers / edited by John C.G. Röhl and Nicolaus Sombart. — Cambridge : Cambridge University Press, 1982. — xiii,319p : ill,ports ; 24cm
Conference papers. — Includes index
ISBN 0-521-23898-6 : £19.50 : CIP rev. B81-36950

943.085 — Germany. Nationalsozialistische Deutsche Arbeiter-Partei. *Schutzstaffel, to 1945*

Reider, Frederic. The order of the S.S. / by Frederic Reider. — London : Foulsham, c1981. — 256p,[8]p of plates : ill(some col.),maps,facsims,ports ; 24cm
Translation of: L'ordre S.S.. — Includes index
ISBN 0-572-01063-x : £9.50 B82-11860

943.085 — Germany. Political events, *1918-1924.* **Hitler, Adolf. Mein Kampf** *— Critical studies*

Staudinger, Hans. The inner Nazi : a critical analysis of Mein Kampf / Hans Staudinger ; edited, with an introduction and a biographical afterword, by Peter M. Rutkoff and William B. Scott. — Baton Rouge ; London : Louisiana State University Press, c1981. — 153p : 1port ; 23cm
ISBN 0-8071-0882-0 : Unpriced B82-34770

943.085 — Germany. Political events, *1918-1933*

Taylor, Simon. Germany 1918-1933. — London : Duckworth, Jan.1983. — [128]p
ISBN 0-7156-1689-7 (pbk) : £6.95 : CIP entry B82-36299

943.085 — Germany. Political events, *1919-1945 — For schools*

Corkery, J. F.. Weimar Germany and the Third Reich / J.F. Corkery, R.C.J. Stone. — Auckland ; London : Heinemann, 1981, c1980. — 68p : ill,maps ; 24cm
Maps on inside covers
ISBN 0-435-31161-1 (pbk) : £1.95 B82-15274

Gray, Ronald. Hitler and the Germans. — Cambridge : Cambridge University Press, Nov.1981. — [45]p. — (Cambridge introduction to the history of mankind)
ISBN 0-521-22702-x (pbk) : £1.95 : CIP entry B81-32525

943.085'092'4 — Germany. Politics. Role of Stresemann, Gustav, *1919-1929*

Erdmann, Karl Dietrich. Gustav Stresemann : the revision of Versailles and the Weimar parliamentary system / by Karl Dietrich Erdmann. — London ([42, Russell Sq. WC1]) : German Historical Institute, [1981?]. — 24p ; 22cm. — (The 1980 Annual lecture)
Bibliography: p23-24
Unpriced (pbk) B82-12768

943.086 — Germany, *1933-1945*

Williamson, D. G.. The Third Reich / D.G. Williamson. — Harlow : Longman, 1982. — iv,108p ; 20cm. — (Seminar studies in history)
Bibliography: p98-105. — Includes index
ISBN 0-582-35306-8 (pbk) : £1.80 B82-33652

943.086 — Germany, *1939-1945 — National Socialist viewpoints*

McLaughlin, Michael, *1942-*. For those who cannot speak / by Michael McLaughlin. — Ladbroke : Historical Review, c1979. — 35p : ill,facsims,ports ; 29cm. — (Historical fact ; no.3)
ISBN 0-906879-05-1 (unbound) : £1.00 B82-04330

943.086 — Germany. Political events. Influence of occultism, *1933-1945*

Pennick, Nigel. Hitler's secret sciences : his quest for the hidden knowledge of the ancients / Nigel Pennick. — Suffolk, Spearman, 1981. — 182p,[16]p of plates : ill,maps,ports ; 23cm
Bibliography: p178-182
ISBN 0-85435-464-6 : £6.50 B82-25134

943.086'092'4 — Germany. Goebbels, Joseph, *1939-1941 — Correspondence, diaries, etc.*

Goebbels, Joseph. The Goebbels diaries 1939-41. — London : Hamilton, Oct.1982. — [576]p
Translated from the German
ISBN 0-241-10893-4 : £9.95 : CIP entry B82-24713

943.086'0924 — Germany. Hitler, Adolf *— Biographies*

Stone, Norman. Hitler. — London : Hodder and Stoughton, Jan.1982. — [240]p
Originally published: 1980
ISBN 0-340-27538-3 (pbk) : £1.25 : CIP entry B81-34137

943.087 — West Germany, *1945-1980*

Balfour, Michael, *1908-*. West Germany : a contemporary history / Michael Balfour. — London : Croom Helm, c1982. — 307p : 1map ; 23cm
Bibliography: p293-300. — Includes index
ISBN 0-7099-0664-1 : £14.95 : CIP rev. B82-04462

943.087'7 — West Germany. Escapes from East Germany, *1979*

Petschull, Jürgen. Night crossing. — London : Hodder and Stoughton, Mar.1982. — [160]p. — (Coronet books)
Translation of: Mit dem Wind nach Westen
ISBN 0-340-27907-9 (pbk) : £1.50 : CIP entry B82-00253

943.087'7 — West Germany. Escapes in balloons from East Germany, *1979*

Petschull, Jürgen. With the wind to the West : the great balloon escape / Jürgen Petschull ; translated by Courtney Searls. — London : Hodder and Stoughton, 1981. — 180p : ill,1map,ports ; 22cm
Translation of: Mit dem wind nach Westen
ISBN 0-340-25895-0 : £6.95 B82-00524

943.087'8 — West Germany. Social life *— For schools*

Hawkins, Terry. Look at West Germany / Terry Hawkin. — Harlow : Longman, 1981. — 32p : ill,maps ; 16x22cm. — (Longman German workbooks)
Cover title. — Ill and text on inside covers
ISBN 0-582-20070-9 (pbk) : Unpriced
Primary classification 438 B82-05153

943.1087'7 — East Germany. Social conditions, *1971-1981 — Conference proceedings*

The **GDR** under Honecker 1971-1981 / [edited by Ian Wallace]. — Dundee (1 Richmond Terrace, Dundee DD2 1BQ) : GDR monitor, 1981. — iii,115p ; 21cm. — (GDR monitor special series, ISSN 0262-1789 ; no.1)
Conference proceedings
Unpriced (pbk) B82-19347

943.1087'8 — East Germany

Childs, David. The GDR : Moscow's German ally. — London : Allen & Unwin, Nov.1982. — [352]p
ISBN 0-04-354029-5 (cased) : £18.00 : CIP entry
ISBN 0-04-354030-9 (pbk) : £7.95 B82-26209

943'.21 — Germany. Leipzig. Social life, *1914-1918 — Correspondence, diaries, etc.*

Cooper, Ethel. Behind the lines : one woman's war 1914-1918. — London : Jill Norman & Hobhouse, June 1982. — [320]p
ISBN 0-906908-82-5 : £9.95 : CIP entry B82-10899

943.6 — HISTORY. AUSTRIA

943.6'03 — Austria. Habsburg *(House of), 1658-1918 — For schools*

Ambrus, Victor. Under the double eagle : three centuries of history in Austria and Hungary / [illustrations by] Victor G. Ambrus ; text by Victor G. Ambrus and Donald Lindsay. — Oxford : Oxford University Press, 1980, c1979. — 47p : ill(some col.),ports(some col.) ; 29cm
Includes index
ISBN 0-19-279722-0 : £4.95 : CIP rev. B79-09913

943.6'04 — Austria. Habsburg *(House of), 1848-1918*

Crankshaw, Edward. The fall of the House of Hapsburg / by Edward Crankshaw. — [London] : Papermac, 1981, c1963. — ix,459p : 1map ; 20cm
Originally published: London : Longman, 1963. — Includes index
ISBN 0-333-31926-5 (pbk) : £3.95 B82-32652

943.6′04′0924 — Austria. Franz Joseph, *Emperor of Austria.* **Interpersonal relationships with Schratt, Katharina**

Haslip, Joan. The Emperor & the actress : the love story of Emperor Franz Josef & Katharina Schratt / Joan Haslip. — London : Weidenfeld and Nicolson, 1982. — x,284p,[8]p of plates : ill,1geneal.table,ports ; 23cm
Bibliography: p273-274. — Includes index
ISBN 0-297-78102-2 : £9.95
Also classified at 792′.028′0924 B82-38941

943.6′04′0924 — Austria. Rudolf, *Crown Prince of Austria.* **Suicide**

Morton, Frederic. A nervous splendour : Vienna 1888-1889 / by Frederic Morton. — Harmondsworth : Penguin, 1980, c1979 (1981 [printing]). — x,340p : ill,1facsim,ports ; 20cm
Originally published: Boston, Mass. : Little, Brown, 1979 ; London : Weidenfeld and Nicolson, 1980. — Bibliography: p320-329. — Includes index
ISBN 0-14-005667-x (pbk) : £2.50
Primary classification 943.6′1304 B82-01802

943.6′13 — Austrian culture: Viennese culture, *to 1980*

Grunfeld, Frederic V.. Vienna / by Frederic V. Grunfeld and the editors of the Newsweek Book Division. — London : Reader's Digest Association in association with Newsweek Books, 1981. — 172p : ill(some col.),1map,ports ; 30cm. — (Wonders of man)
Bibliography: p168. — Includes index
£7.95 B82-31556

943.6′1304 — Austria. Vienna. Intellectual life, *1888-1889*

Morton, Frederic. A nervous splendour : Vienna 1888-1889 / by Frederic Morton. — Harmondsworth : Penguin, 1980, c1979 (1981 [printing]). — x,340p : ill,1facsim,ports ; 20cm
Originally published: Boston, Mass. : Little, Brown, 1979 ; London : Weidenfeld and Nicolson, 1980. — Bibliography: p320-329. — Includes index
ISBN 0-14-005667-x (pbk) : £2.50
Also classified at 943.6′04′0924 B82-01802

943.7 — HISTORY. CZECHOSLOVAKIA

943.7′021 — London. Camden *(London Borough).* **Museums: British Museum. Exhibits: Moravian antiquities,** *800-900 — Catalogues*

Beeby, Susan. Great Moravia : the archaeology of ninth-century Czechoslovakia. — London : British Museum Publications, Sept.1982. — [48]p
ISBN 0-7141-0520-1 (pbk) : £3.75 : CIP entry
B82-21096

943.7′042′0924 — Czechoslovakia. Hirschmann, Maria Anne *— Biographies*

Hirschmann, Maria Anne. Hansi : captive of the swastika / by Maria Anne Hirschmann. — Eastbourne : Kingsway, 1981, c1973. — 224p ; 18cm
Originally published: Wheaton : Tyndale House, 1973 ; London : Coverdale House, 1974
ISBN 0-902088-60-2 (pbk) : £1.40 B82-32396

943.7′1200431 — Czechoslovakia. Prague. German immigrants. Social life, *1861-1914*

Cohen, Gary B.. The politics of ethnic survival : Germans in Prague, 1861-1914 / Gary B. Cohen. — Princeton ; Guildford : Princeton University Press, c1981. — xvii,344p : ill,2maps ; 24cm
Bibliography: p307-335. — Includes index
ISBN 0-691-05332-4 : £19.30 B82-13391

943.8 — HISTORY. POLAND

943.8 — Poland, *to 1864*

A **Republic** of nobles : studies in Polish history to 1864 / edited and translated by J. K. Fedorowicz ; co-editors Maria Bogucka, Henryk Samsonowicz. — Cambridge : Cambridge University Press, 1982. — xvi,293p : ill,maps,1plan,ports ; 24cm
Includes bibliographies and index
ISBN 0-521-24093-x : £22.00 : CIP rev.
B82-14516

943.8 — Poland, *to 1980*

Davies, Norman. God's playground : a history of Poland in two volumes / by Norman Davies. — Oxford : Clarendon, 1981. — 2v. : ill,maps,music,ports ; 23cm
Includes index
ISBN 0-19-822555-5 : Unpriced : CIP rev.
ISBN 0-19-822592-x (v.2) : £27.50 B81-01397

943.8′004924 — Poland. Jews. Social life, *1939-1946 — Childhood reminiscences*

David, Janina. A square of sky ; and A touch of earth : a wartime childhood in Poland / Janina David. — Harmondsworth : Penguin, 1981. — 349p ; 20cm
Originally published: London : New Authors, 1964
ISBN 0-14-004810-3 (pbk) : £2.25 B82-07286

Rubinowicz, Dawid. The diary of Dawid Rubinowicz / translated by Derek Bowman. — Edinburgh : Blackwood, 1981. — xiv,87p,[4] leaves of plates : facsims ; 20cm
Translation of: Pamíetnik Dawida Rubinowicza
ISBN 0-85158-157-9 : £3.95 B82-28838

943.8′03′0924 — Poland. Piłsudski, Józef *— Biographies — Polish texts*

Jędrzejewicz, Wacław. Józef Piłsudski : 1867-1935 : życiorys / Wacław Jędrzejewicz. — Londyn : Polska Fundacja Kulturalna, 1982. — 303p,[14]p of plates : ill,ports ; 18cm
Includes index
Unpriced (pbk) B82-40458

943.8′04 — Poland. Political events, *1918-1944 — Polish texts*

Ciechanowski, Jan. O genezie i upadku II Rzeczypospolitej / Jan Ciechanowski. — Londyn : Odnowa, 1981. — 44p ; 21cm
ISBN 0-903705-41-9 (pbk) : £2.40 B82-23547

943.8′04′0924 — Poland, *1914-1945 — Personal observations — Polish texts*

Kozarynowa, Zofia. Sto lat : gawęda o kulturze środowiska / Zofia Kozarynowa. — Londyn : Polska Fundacja Kulturalna, 1982. — 310p,[14]p of plates : ports ; 22cm
Unpriced (pbk) B82-38445

943.8′04′0924 — Poland. Piłsudski, Józef *— Biographies — Polish texts*

Droga życia Józefa Piłsudskiego / [redakcja i układ albumu Jan Z.E. Berek i Mieczysław Paszkiewicz]. — Londyn (163 Wargrave Ave. N15) : Wydawnictwo Funduszu im. Aleksandry Piłsudskiej, 1977. — 272p : ill,map,facsims,ports ; 30cm
Unpriced (pbk) B82-24155

943.8′04′0924 — Poland. Rural regions. Social life, *ca 1939 — Personal observations — Correspondence, diaries, etc. — Polish texts*

Sendor, Leokadia. Pamiętnik wiejskiej dziewczyny / Leokadia Sendor. — Londyn : Polska Fundacja Kulturalna, 1982. — 197p ; 22cm
Unpriced (pbk) B82-38447

943.8′05 — Poland, *1920-1981*

Szczypiorski, Andrzej. The Polish ordeal / the view from within ; Andrzej Szczypiorski ; translated by Celina Wieniewska. — London : Croom Helm, c1982. — 154p ; 22cm
Translated from the Polish
ISBN 0-7099-2323-6 : £7.95 : CIP rev.
B82-06517

943.8′05′0924 — Poland. Lubomirski, Eugeniusz *— Biographies*

Lubomirski, Eugeniusz. Kartki z mego życia / Eugeniusz Lubomirski. — Londyn : Polska Fundacja Kulturalna, 1982. — 159p : 1ill,1facsim,ports ; 22cm
Unpriced (pbk) B82-38446

943.8′05′0924 — Poland. Politics. Hoppe, Jan *— Biographies — Polish texts*

Braun, Jerzy. Człowiek ze spiżu / Jerzy Braun, Karol Popiel, Konrad Sieniewicz. — Londyn : Odnowa, 1981. — 223p ; 21cm
Droga ideowego piłsudczyka / Karol Popiel — Jan — pragmatyk / Konrad Sieniewicz — Jan Hoppe — Polityk w służbie idei / Jerzy Braun
ISBN 0-903705-42-7 (pbk) : Unpriced
B82-23546

943.8′053′0924 — Poland. Social life, *1939-1940 — Personal observations — Correspondence, diaries, etc.*

Phillips, Janine. My secret diary / Janine Phillips. — London : Shepheard Walwyn, 1982. — 152p ; 23cm
ISBN 0-85683-062-3 : £4.95 B82-28932

943.8′054 — Poland. Social conditions, *1950-1965 — Dissident viewpoints*

Kuron, J.. Solidarnosc : the missing link? : a new edition of Poland's classic revolutionary socialist manifesto : Kuron & Modzelewski's Open letter to the party / [by Jacek Kuron and Karol Modzelewski]. — New ed. / introduction by Colin Barker. — London : Bookmarks, 1982. — 88p : ill ; 21cm
Translation of: List otwarty do Partii. — Previous ed.: published as Revolutionary socialist manifesto. London : International Socialist, 1967
ISBN 0-906224-07-1 (pbk) : £2.50 B82-26800

943.8′055 — Poland. Political events, *1945-1982 — Communist viewpoints*

Mackiewicz, Józef. Zwycięstwo prowokaczi. — London (28 Lanacre Ave., NW9 5FN) : Kontra, Jan.1983. — [240]p
Translation of: Zwycięstwo prowokaczi. — Originally published: Munich : J. Mackiewicz, 1962
ISBN 0-907652-03-4 (pbk) : £6.90 : CIP entry
Also classified at 947.084 B82-34096

943.8′055 — Poland. Political events, *1970-1981*

Policy and politics in contemporary Poland : reform, failure, crisis, 1970-1981. — London : Frances Pinter, Apr.1982. — [256]p
ISBN 0-86187-221-5 : £15.95 : CIP entry
B82-04834

943.8′055 — Poland. Political events, *1980-1981*

Ruane, Kevin. The Polish challenge / Kevin Ruane. — London : British Broadcasting Corporation, 1982. — xvi,328p,[16]p of plates : ill,ports ; 23cm
Includes index
ISBN 0-563-20054-5 (cased) : £9.95
ISBN 0-563-20041-3 (pbk) : £5.95 B82-31200

943.8′055 — Poland. Political events, *1980-1981 — Partito comunista italiano viewpoints*

Berlinguer, Enrico. After Poland : towards a new internationalism / Enrico Berlinguer with the decisions and resolutions of the Communist Party of Italy ; edited and translated by Antonio Bronda and Stephen Bodington. — Nottingham : Spokesman, 1982. — 114p ; 19cm
ISBN 0-85124-344-4 (cased) : Unpriced : CIP rev.
ISBN 0-8412-4342-8 (pbk) : £2.25 B82-12907

943.8′055 — Poland. Political events *— Revolutionary Communist Party viewpoints*

Poland's black December / [Revolutionary Communist Party]. — London (BCM, JPLTD, WC1N 3XX) : Junius, c1982. — 27p : ill ; 22cm. — (Revolutionary Communist pamphlets, ISSN 0141-8874 ; no.12)
£0.35 (pbk) B82-21807

943.8′055 — Poland. Social conditions *— Dissident viewpoints*

Poland : the state of the republic / reports by the Experience and Future Discussion Group. (DiP) Warsaw ; edited by Michael [i.e. Michel] Vale. — London : Pluto, 1981. — xiii,231p ; 20cm
Translation from the Polish
ISBN 0-86104-343-x (pbk) : £4.95 B82-20691

943.8′055 — Poland. Social conditions *— Trotskyist viewpoints*

Posadas, J.. Poland : the advance of socialist democracy and of socialist influence in the world / J. Posadas. — London : Scientific, Cultural and Political Editions [Vol.1]. — 1982. — 162p ; 21cm
ISBN 0-907694-01-2 (pbk) : £1.35 B82-39898

943.8′055′0924 — Poland. Political events, *1980-1981 — Personal observations*

Yardley, Michael. Poland : a tragedy / Michael Yardley. — Sherborne : Dorset Publishing, 1982. — 98p : ill,facsims,1map,ports ; 26cm
ISBN 0-902129-38-4 (pbk) : £3.50 B82-24871

943.8′055′0924 — Poland. Social life, ***1968-1979*** **—** *Personal observations — Polish texts*

Świderski, Jan. Autobiografie / Jan i Bronisław Świderski. — Londyn : Poets and Painters Press, 1981. — 62p ; 22cm
(pbk) B82-05882

943.8′2 — Poland. Gdańsk. Political events, *1980-1981 — Personal observations*

Potel, Jean-Yves. The summer before the frost : Solidarity in Poland / Jean-Yves Potel ; translated by Phil Markham. — London : Pluto, 1982. — xxviii,229p : 1map ; 19cm
Translation of: Scènes de Grèves en Pologne
ISBN 0-86104-366-9 (pbk) : £3.95 B82-20688

943.9 — HISTORY. HUNGARY

943.9′05 — Hungary. Political events, ***1919-1957***

Trory, Ernie. Hungary 1919 and 1956 : the anatomy of counter-revolution / by Ernie Trory. — Hove : Crabtree Press, 1981. — 88p ; 21cm
Bibliography: p88
£1.40 (pbk) B82-03512

943.9′052′0922 — Hungarian Revolution, ***1956*** **—** *Personal observations — Collections*

. Eye-witness in Hungary : the Soviet invasion of 1956 / edited by Bill Lomax. — Nottingham : Spokesman, 1980 (1981 [printing]). — 183p ; 22cm. — (Spokesman University paperback ; no.34)
Bibliography: p182-183
ISBN 0-85124-327-4 (pbk) : £2.95 B82-10162

943.9′053′0924 — Hungary, ***1981*** **—** *Personal observations*

Porter, Monica. The paper bridge : a return to Budapest / Monica Porter. — London : Quartet, 1981. — xiii,232p : maps ; 25cm
Maps on lining papers
ISBN 0-7043-2296-x : £8.95 : CIP rev.
B81-25708

944 — HISTORY. FRANCE

944 — France, ***1800-1970***

Wright, Gordon, *1912-*. Insiders and outliers : the individual in history / Gordon Wright. — Oxford : Freeman, c1981. — 147p : ill,facsims,ports ; 24cm
Originally published: Stanford : Stanford Alumni Association, 1980. — Bibliography: p136-139. — Includes index
ISBN 0-7167-1339-x (cased) : £11.00
ISBN 0-7167-1340-3 (pbk) : £5.50 B82-23935

944 — France. Cathedrals, ***to 1981***

Dunlop, Ian, *1925 Aug.19---*. The cathedrals′ crusade : the rise of the Gothic style in France / by Ian Dunlop. — London : Hamilton, 1982. — xvi,235p,16p of plates : ill,1map,plans ; 24cm
Bibliography: p223-229. — Includes index
ISBN 0-241-10689-3 : £12.50 : CIP rev.
B81-35792

944 — France. Social conditions, ***1789-1870.*** **Influence of theories of French philosophers,** ***ca 1750-1789***

Lough, John. The Philosophes and post-revolutionary France / by John Lough. — Oxford : Clarendon Press, 1982. — 284p ; 23cm
Bibliography: p271-273. — Includes index
ISBN 0-19-821921-0 : £19.50 : CIP rev.
B82-03356

944 — French civilization, ***ca 1500-1978***

France : a companion guide to French studies. — 2nd ed. — London : Methuen, Feb.1983. — [704]p. — (University paperbacks ; 604)
Originally published: 1979
ISBN 0-416-72310-1 (pbk) : £8.95 : CIP entry
B82-38257

944′.004924 — France. Jews. Goldberg, Michel — *Biographies*

Goldberg, Michel. Namesake. — London : Yale University Press, Sept.1982. — [192]p
Translation of: Ecorché juif
ISBN 0-300-02790-7 : £7.95 : CIP entry
B82-29402

944′.007 — French studies — *Serials*

French studies bulletin : a quarterly supplement. — Autumn 1981 ; No.1 (Winter 1981/82)-. — [Hull] ([c/o G. Chesters, Dept. of French, University of Hull, Hull HU6 7RX]) : Society for French Studies, 1981-. — v. ; 23cm
Supplement to: French studies. — Introductory no., called Special members′ issue, published Autumn 1981
ISSN 0262-2750 = French studies bulletin : Unpriced B82-18487

944′.01 — France, ***ca 486-591*** **—** *Early works*

Gregory, *Saint, Bishop of Tours*. [Historiae Francorum. English]. The history of the Franks / Gregory of Tours ; translated with an introduction by Lewis Thorpe. — Harmondsworth : Penguin, 1974 (1982 [printing]). — 709p : 1map ; 20cm. — (Penguin classics)
Translation of: Historiae Francorum. — Bibliography: p56-58. — Includes index
ISBN 0-14-044295-2 (pbk) : £3.95 B82-33633

944′.021′0922 — France. Royal families. Succession, ***987-1328***

Lewis, Andrew W.. Royal succession in Capetian France : studies on familial order and the state / Andrew W. Lewis. — Cambridge, Mass. ; London : Harvard University Press, 1981. — 356p : 1geneal.table ; 24cm. — (Harvard historical studies ; v.100)
Bibliography: p311-336. — Includes index
ISBN 0-674-77985-1 : £25.90 B82-27092

944′.025 — Hundred Years′ War. Battle of Agincourt

Rothero, Christopher. The armies of Agincourt / text and colour plates by Christopher Rothero. — London : Osprey, 1981. — 40p,A-Hp of plates : ill(some col.),1map ; 25cm. — (Men-at-arms series ; 113)
Notes in French and German
ISBN 0-85045-394-1 (pbk) : £2.95 B82-05041

944′.026′0924 — France. Joan, ***of Arc, Saint*** **—** *Biographies*

Gies, Frances. Joan of Arc : the legend and the reality / Frances Gies. — New York ; London : Harper & Row, c1981. — 306p : ill,maps,facsims,ports ; 22cm
Bibliography: p292-294. — Includes index
ISBN 0-690-01942-4 : Unpriced B82-02193

944′.026′0924 — France. Joan, ***of Arc, Saint*** **-** *Biographies*

Scott, Leonard E.. Joan of Arc. — Oxford (107 Marlborough Rd., Oxford, OX1 4LX) : Alder, Aug.1981. — [128]p
ISBN 0-907162-01-0 (cased) : £8.95 : CIP entry
ISBN 0-907162-02-9 (pbk) : £4.95 B81-17518

944′.026′0924 — France. Joan, ***of Arc, Saint*** **—** *Biographies — For children*

Boutet de Monvel, Maurice. Joan of Arc / Maurice Boutet De Monvel ; introduction by Gerald Gottlieb. — London : Hodder and Stoughton, 1981, c1980. — 55p : col.ill ; 23x28cm
Translation of: Jeanne d′Arc. — Originally published: New York : Viking, 1980
ISBN 0-340-25734-2 : £6.95 : CIP rev.
B80-25009

944′.028 — France, ***1500-1600***

Lloyd, Howell A.. The state, France and the sixteenth century. — London : Allen and Unwin, Feb.1983. — [255]p. — (Early modern Europe today)
ISBN 0-04-940066-5 : £12.50 : CIP entry
B82-36439

944′.028′0924 — France. Political events. Role of François, ***King of France, 1515-1547***

Knecht, R. J.. Francis I / R.J. Knecht. — Cambridge : Cambridge University Press, 1982. — xv,480p,[16]p of plates : ill,maps,1plan,ports ; 24cm
Bibliography: p425-448. — Includes index
ISBN 0-521-24344-0 : £25.00 : CIP rev.
B81-36952

944′.03 — France. Courtly life, ***1589-1789*** **—** *Sociological perspectives*

Elias, Norbert. The court society. — Oxford : Blackwell, Feb.1983. — [320]p
Translation of: Die höfische Gesellschaft
ISBN 0-631-19670-6 : £15.00 : CIP entry
B82-38862

944′.03 — French civilization, ***1700-1799***

Hobson, Marian. The object of art. — Cambridge : Cambridge University Press, Aug.1982. — [400]p. — (Cambridge studies in French)
ISBN 0-521-24350-5 : £25.00 : CIP entry
B82-15825

944′.033′0924 — France. Visits by Bernini, Gian Lorenzo, ***1665***

Gould, Cecil. Bernini in France : an episode in seventeenth-century history / Cecil Gould. — London : Weidenfeld and Nicolson, c1981. — xvi,158p,[16]p of plates : ill,plans,ports ; 24cm
Bibliography: p149-151. — Includes index
ISBN 0-297-77944-3 : £12.95 B82-14634

944.04′072 — France. Political events, ***1789-1799.*** **Historiography**

Furet, François. Interpreting the French Revolution / François Furet ; translated by Elborg Forster. — Cambridge : Cambridge University Press, 1981. — x,204p ; 24cm
Translation of: Penser la révolution française
ISBN 0-521-23574-x (cased) : £15.00 : CIP rev.
ISBN 0-521-28049-4 (pbk) : £4.95 B81-25816

944.04′088042 — France. Political events. Role of women, ***1789-1795*** **—** *Readings from contemporary sources*

Women in revolutionary Paris 1789-1795 / selected documents translated with notes and commentary by Darline Gay Lavy, Harriet Branson Applewhite, Mary Durham Johnson. — Urbana ; London : University of Illinois Press, c1979. — xi,325p ; 23cm
Bibliography: p313-315. — Includes index
ISBN 0-252-00855-3 (pbk) : £7.00 B82-05711

944.04′4 — France. Political events, ***1792-1794***

Hampson, Norman. The terror in the French Revolution / Norman Hampson. — London : Historical Association, c1981. — 32p ; 22cm. — (General series ; 103)
Bibliography: p32
Unpriced (pbk) B82-03505

944.05 — France. Social conditions, ***1799-1815***

Bergeron, Louis. France under Napoleon / by Louis Bergeron ; translated by R.R. Palmer. — Princeton ; Guildford : Princeton University Press, c1981. — xiv,230p : maps ; 23cm
Translation of: L′Episode napoléonien. — Includes index
ISBN 0-691-05333-2 (cased) : £13.40
ISBN 0-691-00789-6 (pbk) : £5.30 B82-05298

944.05′092′4 — France. Napoléon I, ***Emperor of the French, 1814-1815*** **—** *Biographies*

MacKenzie, Norman, *1921-*. The escape from Elba : the fall and flight of Napoleon 1814-1815 / Norman MacKenzie. — Oxford : Oxford University Press, 1982. — xv,299p,[8]p of plates : ill,maps,ports ; 24cm
Includes index
ISBN 0-19-215863-5 : £12.50 : CIP rev.
B82-10429

944.05′092′4 — France. Napoléon I, ***Emperor of the French.*** **Death**

Weider, Ben. The murder of Napoleon / Ben Weider and David Hapgood. — London : Robson, 1982. — viii,266p,[18]p of plates : ill,ports ; 22cm
Includes index
ISBN 0-86051-172-3 : £7.50 : CIP rev.
B82-01731

944.07 — French civilization, ***1848-1945***

Zeldin, Theodore. France 1848-1945. — Oxford : Oxford University Press, May 1981. — (Oxford paperbacks)
Originally published: as the Third section of ′France 1848-1945. Vol.2 : Intellect, taste and anxiety : Oxford : Clarendon Press, 1977
Anxiety & hypocrisy. — [448]p
ISBN 0-19-285106-3 (pbk) : £4.50 : CIP entry
B81-06609

944.07 — French civilization, ***1848-1945***
continuation

Zeldin, Theodore. Intellect & pride / by Theodore Zeldin. — Oxford : Oxford University Press, 1980. — 356p ; 20cm. — (France 1848-1945)
Originally published: as the 1st section of Intellect, taste and anxiety. Oxford : Clarendon Press, 1977. — Bibliography: p347-348. — Includes index
ISBN 0-19-285096-2 (pbk) : £3.50 : CIP rev. B80-00984

944.081'2 — France. Political events. Role of Blanquists, ***1864-1893***

Hutton, Patrick H.. The cult of the revolutionary tradition : the Blanquists in French politics, 1864-1893 / Patrick H. Hutton. — Berkeley ; London : University of California Press, c1981. — xv,218p : ill,1facsim,ports ; 23cm
Bibliography: p201-210. — Includes index
ISBN 0-520-04114-3 : £17.25 B82-22621

944.081'2 — France. Political events. Role of France. ***Armée, 1870-1914***

Porch, Douglas. The march to the Marne : the French army 1871-1914 / Douglas Porch. — Cambridge : Cambridge University Press, 1981. — viii,294p ; 24cm
Bibliography: p281-290. — Includes index
ISBN 0-521-23883-8 : £22.50 B82-08358

944.081'2'0924 — France. Politics. Gambetta, Léon, ***1877-1882***

Bury, J. P. T.. Gambetta's final years : the era of difficulties 1877-1882 / J.P.T. Bury. — London : Longman, 1982. — xi,393p ; 22cm
Bibliography: p366-378. — Includes index
ISBN 0-582-50302-7 : £18.50 : CIP rev. B82-01155

944.081'5'0924 — France. Political events, ***1934-1939 — Personal observations***

Trotskiĭ, L.. Leon Trotsky on France / [edited by David Salner]. — New York : Monad Press, 1979 ; New York ; London : Distributed by Pathfinder Press. — 271p ; 22cm
Includes index
ISBN 0-913460-65-6 (cased) : Unpriced
ISBN 0-913460-66-4 (pbk) : £2.95 B82-14635

944.082 — France. Society, ***1945-1978***

Ardagh, John. France in the 1980s / John Ardagh. — London : Secker & Warburg, 1982. — 672p : 1map ; 25cm
Bibliography: p659-661. — Includes index
ISBN 0-436-01747-4 : £15.00 : CIP rev. B82-11296

944.083 — France. Social conditions, ***1968-1980***

Social movement and protest in France. — London : Frances Pinter, Jan.1982. — [270]p
ISBN 0-86187-213-4 : £14.75 : CIP entry B81-40255

944.083'092'4 — France. Social life, ***1945-1980 — Personal observations***

Ardagh, John. France in the 1980s / John Ardagh. — Harmondsworth : Penguin in association with Secker & Warburg, 1982. — 672p ; 20cm. — (Pelican books)
Bibliography: p659-661. — Includes index
ISBN 0-14-022409-2 (pbk) : £4.95 B82-37614

944.083'6 — France. Political events, ***1968-1980***

Pickles, Dorothy. Problems of contemporary French politics. — London : Methuen, Apr.1982. — [190]p
ISBN 0-416-73230-5 (cased) : £9.00 : CIP entry
ISBN 0-416-73240-2 (pbk) : £4.50 B82-04053

944.083'8 — France — ***For schools***

Houldsworth, P. B.. All about France / Peter Houldsworth. — London : Hodder and Stoughton, c1982. — iv,124p : ill,1coat of arms,maps,ports ; 25cm
ISBN 0-340-25595-1 (pbk) : Unpriced : CIP rev. B81-37589

944.083'8 — France. Social life

Zeldin, Theodore. The French. — London : Collins, Oct.1982. — [572]p
ISBN 0-00-216806-5 : £10.95 : CIP entry B82-23072

944.083'8 — France. Social life — ***For schools***

Hawkin, Terry. Look at France / Terry Hawkin. — Harlow : Longman, 1981. — 32p : ill,maps ; 16x22cm. — (Longman French workbooks. Level 1)
English and French text. — Cover title. — Text and ill on inside covers
ISBN 0-582-20069-5 (pbk) : £0.60 B82-11535

944.083'8 — France. Society

Crozier, Michel. Strategies for change : the future of French society / Michel Crozier ; translated by William R. Beer. — Cambridge, Mass. ; London : MIT, c1982. — xii,230p ; 22cm
Translation of: On ne change pas la société par décret
ISBN 0-262-03082-9 : £12.25 B82-37516

944.083'8'0922 — France. Social life — ***Personal observations — Collections***

Tomlins, James. We live in France / James Tomlins. — Hove : Wayland, 1981. — 64p : col.ill,1col.map,col.ports ; 26cm. — (Living here)
Includes index
ISBN 0-85340-861-0 : £4.50 B82-03879

944.083'8'0924 — France. Mitterand, François — ***Biographies***

MacShane, Denis. François Mitterand : the political odyssey. — London : Quartet, May 1982. — 1v.
ISBN 0-7043-2344-3 (cased) : £9.95 : CIP entry
ISBN 0-7043-3417-8 (pbk) : Unpriced B82-11989

944'.201 — France. Normandy, ***to 1066***

Bates, David. Normandy before 1066. — London : Longman, Oct.1982. — [304]p
ISBN 0-582-48492-8 (pbk) : £6.95 : CIP entry B82-25181

944'.360812 — France. Paris. Political events, ***1870-1871 — Readings from contemporary sources***

Paris under siege : a journal of the events of 1870-1871 kept by contemporaries and translated and presented by Joanna Richardson. — London : Folio Society, 1982. — 221p,[12]leaves of plates : ill ; 23cm
Includes translations from French and German. — In slip case. — Bibliography: p211-218. — Includes index
£9.95 B82-20344

944'.360812 — Paris ***(Commune, 1871)***

Images of the Commune = Images de la Commune / edited by James A. Leith. — Montreal ; London : McGill-Queen's University Press, 1978. — xxviii,349p : ill ; 25cm
English and French text. — Includes index
ISBN 0-7735-0297-1 : Unpriced B82-22456

Tombs, Robert. The war against Paris 1871 / Robert Tombs. — Cambridge : Cambridge University Press, 1981. — xii,256p : ill,maps,ports ; 24cm
Ill on lining papers. — Bibliography: p246-252. — Includes index
ISBN 0-521-23551-0 (cased) : £22.50 : CIP rev.
ISBN 0-521-28784-7 (pbk) : £8.50 B81-32598

944'.36'0816 — France. Paris. Social life, ***1940-1944***

Pryce-Jones, David. Paris in the Third Reich. — London : Collins, Aug.1981. — [320]p
ISBN 0-00-216645-3 : £12.50 : CIP entry B81-15896

944'.361 — France. Paris. Abbeys: St. Germain des Prés ***(Abbey), 1600-1700***

Ultee, Maarten. The Abbey of St. Germain des Prés in the seventeenth century / Maarten Ultee. — New Haven ; London : Yale University Press, c1981. — ix,210p,[7]p of plates : ill,1plan,ports ; 25cm
Bibliography: p193-204. — Includes index
ISBN 0-300-02562-9 : Unpriced : CIP rev. B81-32085

944'.3610815 — France. Paris. Intellectual life, ***1930-1950***

Lottman, Herbert R.. The Left Bank : writers, artists, and politics from the Popular Front to the Cold War / Herbert R. Lottman. — London : Heinemann, 1982. — xiv,319p ; 24cm
Bibliography: p291-307. — Includes index
ISBN 0-434-42943-0 : £12.50 B82-26789

944'.3835 — France. Saverne. Civilians. Abuse by Germany. ***Heer, 1913.*** **Officers**

Schoenbaum, David. Zabern 1913 : consensus politics in imperial Germany / David Schoenbaum. — London : Allen & Unwin, 1982. — 197p ; 23cm
Bibliography: p187-192. — Includes index
ISBN 0-04-943025-4 : Unpriced : CIP rev. B82-03723

944'.3835 — France. Strasbourg. Intellectual life, ***1480-1599***

Chrisman, Miriam Usher. Lay culture, learned culture. — London : Yale University Press, Nov.1982. — [464]p
ISBN 0-300-02530-0 : £25.00 : CIP entry B82-40338

944'.4026 — France. Burgundy, ***ca 1400-ca 1500***

Armstrong, C. A. J.. England, France and Burgundy in the fifteenth century. — London : Hambledon, Oct.1982. — [450]p. — (History series ; 16)
ISBN 0-907628-13-3 : £24.00 : CIP entry
Also classified at 942.04 B82-25743

944'.93 — France. Var. Social conditions, ***1815-1851***

Agulhon, Maurice. The republic in the village. — Cambridge : Cambridge University Press, Sept.1982. — [412]p
Translation of: La République au village
ISBN 0-521-23693-2 : £27.50 : CIP entry B82-19833

944'.945 — Corsica, ***to 1981***

Ramsay, Robert. The Corsican time-bomb. — Manchester : Manchester University Press, Sept.1982. — [192]p
ISBN 0-7190-0893-x : £16.50 : CIP entry B82-20383

944'.949 — Monaco. Grace, ***Princess, consort of Rainier, Prince of Monaco — Biographies***

Hart-Davis, Phyllida. Grace. — London : Collins, Nov.1982. — [144]p
ISBN 0-00-218089-8 (pbk) : £4.95 : CIP entry B82-32274

944'.98 — France. Romans. Rebellions, ***1579-1580***

Le Roy Ladurie, Emmanuel. Carnival : a people's uprising at Romans 1579-1580 / Emmanuel le Roy Ladurie ; translated by Mary Feeney. — London : Scolar, 1980, c1979. — xx,.426p : maps,facsims ; 24cm
Translation of: Le carnaval de Romans. — Originally published: New York : Braziller, 1979. — Bibliography: p413-426
ISBN 0-85967-591-2 : £12.50 : CIP rev. B80-05159

945 — HISTORY. ITALY

945'.006'042134 — Italian civilization. British organisations: British-Italian Society, ***to 1981***

British-Italian Society. 40 Years : the British-Italian Society 1941-1981. — London (c/o J.W. Anson, Kensington Palace Barracks, Kensington Church St., W.8 4EP) : The Society, [1981]. — 18p ; 21cm
£1.00 (pbk) B82-17262

945'.04 — Italy, ***1216-1380***

Larner, John. Italy in the age of Dante and Petrarch, 1216-1380 / John Larner. — London : Longman, 1980. — 278p,[16]p of plates : ill,maps,ports ; 24cm. — (A Longman history of Italy ; v.2)
Includes index
ISBN 0-582-48366-2 : £17.50 : CIP rev. B80-10416

945′.04 — Italy. Christians. Crusades by papacy, *1254-1343*

Housley, Norman. The Italian crusades : the Papal-Angevin alliance and the crusades against Christian lay powers, 1254-1343 / Norman Housley. — Oxford : Clarendon, 1982. — 293p : 2maps ; 22cm
Bibliography: p260-279. — Includes index
ISBN 0-19-821925-3 : £293p : CIP rev. B82-04286

945′.05 — Italian civilization, *ca 1300-ca 1600*

Burckhardt, Jacob. The civilization of the Renaissance in Italy : an essay / Jacob Burckhardt. — 2nd ed. (photographically reprinted). — Oxford : Phaidon, 1981. — xxiii,462p : ill,music,ports ; 21cm. — (Landmarks in art history)
Translation of: Die Cultur der Renaissance in Italien. — Previous ed.: 1944. — Includes index
ISBN 0-7148-2140-3 (pbk) : £7.50 : CIP rev. B81-18115

Chamberlin, E. R.. The world of the Italian Renaissance. — London : Allen & Unwin, June 1982. — [320]p
ISBN 0-04-900035-7 : £8.95 : CIP entry B82-09733

Plumb, J. H.. [The Penguin book of the Renaissance]. The Pelican book of the Renaissance / by J.H. Plumb with essays by Garrett Mattingly ... [et al.]. — [New ed.]. — Harmondsworth : Penguin, 1964 (1982 [printing]). — 333p : ill,ports ; 20cm
Previous ed.: published as The 'Horizon' book of the Renaissance. London : Collins, 1961. — Includes index
ISBN 0-14-022405-x (pbk) : £3.95 B82-40950

945′.06′0924 — Italy. Borgia, Cesare, *duca di Valentino — Biographies*

Bradford, Sarah. Cesare Borgia : his life and times / Sarah Bradford. — London : Futura, 1981, c1976. — viii,327p,[4]p of plates : ill,maps,ports ; 20cm
Originally published: London : Weidenfeld & Nicolson, 1976. — Bibliography: p301-311. — Includes index
ISBN 0-7088-2008-5 (pbk) : £2.95 B82-04258

945′.08 — Italy. Risorgimento, *1830-1876*

Lovett, Clara M.. The democratic movement in Italy 1830-1876 / Clara M. Lovett. — Cambridge, Mass. ; London : Harvard University Press, 1982. — x,285p ; 24cm
Bibliography: p270-274. — Includes index
ISBN 0-674-19645-7 : £19.25 B82-27093

945′.08 — Italy. Risorgimento, *to 1870*

Beales, Derek. The Risorgimento and the unification of Italy / Derek Beales. — London : Longman, 1981. — 176p : maps ; 22cm
Originally published: London : Allen and Unwin, 1971. — Includes index
ISBN 0-582-49217-3 (pbk) : £3.95 : CIP rev. B81-31825

945.091′092′4 — Italy. Mussolini, Benito — *Biographies*

Mack Smith, Denis. Mussolini / Denis Mack Smith. — London : Weidenfeld and Nicolson, c1981. — xiv,429p,[16]p of plates : ports ; 24cm
Bibliography: p389-416. — Includes index
ISBN 0-297-78005-0 : £12.95 B82-16433

945.092′8 — Italy — *For children*

Baker, Susan. Italy / Susan Baker. — London : Macdonald Educational, 1981. — 46p : ill (some col.),col.maps ; 29cm. — (Looking at lands)
Includes index
ISBN 0-356-07102-2 : £3.50 B82-02897

945.092′8 — Italy — *For schools*

Bethemont, Jacques. Italy : a geographical introduction. — London : Longman, Sept.1982. — [224]p
Translation of: L'Italie
ISBN 0-582-30073-8 (cased) : £13.50 : CIP entry
ISBN 0-582-30072-x (pbk) : £6.50 B82-20261

945.092′8 — Italy. Social life — *For schools*

De Zulueta, Tana. We live in Italy / Tana de Zulueta. — Hove : Wayland, 1982. — 64p : col.ill,1col.map,col.ports ; 26cm. — (Living here)
Includes index
ISBN 0-85340-862-9 : £4.95 B82-34828

945′.31 — Italy. Venice, *to 1980*

Bull, George, *1929-*. Venice : the most triumphant city / by George Bull. — London : Joseph, 1982, c1981. — 192p : ill(some col.),facsims(some col.) ; 24cm
Originally published: London : Folio Society, 1981. — Ill on lining papers
ISBN 0-7181-2099-x : £7.95 B82-17551

945′.39 — Italy. Friuli. Earthquakes, *1976 — Sociological perspectives*

Geipel, Robert. Disaster and reconstruction. — Chichester : Wiley, Oct.1982. — [224]p
Translated from the German
ISBN 0-04-904006-5 (cased) : £25.00 : CIP entry (pbk) : £9.95 B82-25095

945′.500421 — Italy. Tuscany. Britons, *1372-1980*

Hamilton, Olive. The divine country : the British in Tuscany 1372-1980 / Olive Hamilton. — London : Deutsch, 1982. — xiv,190p,[16]p of plates : ill,ports ; 24cm
Bibliography: p181-182. — Includes index
ISBN 0-233-97425-3 : £9.95 B82-21844

945′.51 — Italy. Florence. Medici *(Family), ca 1400-1743*

Hibbert, Christopher. The rise and fall of the house of Medici / Christopher Hibbert. — Harmondsworth : Penguin, 1979, c1974 (1981 [printing]). — 368p,[24]p of plates : ill,ports,geneal.tables ; 20cm
Originally published: London : Allen Lane, 1974. — Bibliography: p338-345. — Includes index
ISBN 0-14-005090-6 (pbk) : £2.95 B82-09950

945′.51 — Italy. Florence. Palaces: Palazzo Rucellai, *to 1980*

Giovanni Rucellai ed il suo Zibaldone. — London : Warburg Institute, University of London. — (Studies of the Warburg Institute ; v.24, II)
2: A Florentine patrician and his palace / studies by F.W. Kent ... [et al.] ; with an introduction by Nicolai Rubinstein. — 1981. — xiv,258p,[66]p of plates : ill,plans,2geneal.tables ; 30cm
Includes three chapters and documentary material in Italian. — Includes index
ISBN 0-85481-057-9 : £35.00
Primary classification 338.7′617′00924 B82-09051

945′.58 — Italy. Siena, *1287-1355*

Bowsky, William M.. A medieval Italian commune : Siena under the Nine, 1287-1355 / William M. Bowsky. — Berkeley ; London : University of California Press, c1981. — xxii,327p,16p of plates : ill(some col.),maps,facsims ; 25cm
Map on folded leaf attached to inside cover. — Includes index
ISBN 0-520-04256-5 : £18.00 B82-12188

945′.634 — Vatican, *to 1981*

Bull, George, *1929-*. Inside the Vatican / George Bull. — London : Hutchinson, 1982. — 293p,[8]p of plates : ill,2maps,ports ; 23cm
Bibliography: p271-273. — Includes index
ISBN 0-09-140070-8 : £8.95 : CIP rev. B81-17515

Lo Bello, Nino. The Vatican papers / by Nino Lo Bello. — Sevenoaks : New English Library, 1982. — ix,246p ; 23cm
Bibliography: p237-242. — Includes index
ISBN 0-450-04882-9 : £7.95 B82-30190

945′.700441 — Southern Italy. Normans, *1016-1130*

Norwich, John Julius. The Normans in the south : 1016-1130 / John Julius Norwich. — London : Solitaire, 1981, c1967. — xvi,355p : 3maps ; 20cm
Originally published: London : Longmans, 1967. — Bibliography: p339-345. — Includes index
ISBN 0-907387-00-4 (pbk) : £4.50 : CIP rev. B81-14410

945′.772 — Italy. Gagliano. Peasants. Social life, *1935-1936 — Personal observations*

Levi, Carlo. Christ stopped at Eboli / Carlo Levi ; translated by Frances Frenaye. — Harmondsworth : Penguin, 1982, c1963. — 254p : 1map ; 20cm. — (A King penguin)
Translation of: Cristo sè fermento a Ebali. — Originally published: New York : Farrar, Strauss, 1947
ISBN 0-14-005555-x (pbk) : £2.50 B82-22489

946 — HISTORY. IBERIAN PENINSULA, SPAIN

946 — Spain, *1000-1600*

Bishko, Charles Julian. Studies in medieval Spanish frontier history / Charles Julian Bishko. — London : Variorum, 1980. — 336p : 2maps ; 24cm. — (Collected studies series ; CS 124)
Facsim reprints. — Includes index
ISBN 0-86078-069-4 : £22.00 : CIP rev. B80-18132

946′.004924 — Marranism. Cardoso, Isaac

Yerushalmi, Yosef Hayim. From Spanish court to Italian ghetto : Isaac Cardoso : a study in seventeenth-century Marranism and Jewish apologetics / Yosef Hayim Yerushalmi. — Seattle ; London : University of Washington Press, 1981, c1971. — xxii,524p : facsims ; 22cm
Originally published: New York : Columbia University Press, 1971. — Bibliography: p481-584. — Includes index
ISBN 0-295-95824-3 (pbk) : Unpriced B82-19574

946′.02′0924 — Spain. John II, *King of Castile and Leon — Biographies — Spanish texts — Early works*

Cosas sacadas de la historia del rey Don Juan el Segundo : (BL MS Egerton 1875) / edited by Angus Mackay and Dorothy Sherman Severin. — [Exeter] : University of Exeter, 1981. — xxix,69p ; 21cm. — (Exeter Hispanic texts, ISSN 0305-8700 ; xxix)
Spanish text, English introduction and notes. — Cover title: Historia de Juan II. — Bibliography: p61-65
ISBN 0-85989-127-5 (pbk) : Unpriced B82-32206

946′.08 — Spain, *1808-1975*

Carr, Raymond. Spain 1808-1975. — 2nd ed. — Oxford : Clarendon Press, June 1982. — [800] p. — (Oxford history of modern Europe)
Previous ed.: 1966
ISBN 0-19-822127-4 (cased) : £19.50 : CIP entry
ISBN 0-19-822128-2 (pbk) : £8.95 B82-10448

946.081 — Spanish Civil War

Mitchell, David. The Spanish Civil War. — London : Granada, Dec.1982. — [224]p
ISBN 0-246-11916-0 : £9.95 : CIP entry B82-29634

946.083 — Spain. Social conditions — *For schools*

Jump, J. R.. How Spain is run / J.R. Jump. — London : Harrap, 1981. — 32p : ill,1map,ports ; 14x22cm. — (Discovering Spain)
ISBN 0-245-53417-2 (pbk) : £1.10 B82-08390

946′.202 — Spain. Castile *(Kingdom), 1109-1126*

Reilly, Bernard F.. The kingdom of León-Castilla under Queen Urraca, 1109-1126 / Bernard F. Reilly. — Princeton ; Guildford : Princeton University Press, c1982. — xx,401p,[7]p of plates : ill,1facsim,maps ; 23cm
Bibliography: p371-388. — Includes index
ISBN 0-691-05344-8 : £23.00
Primary classification 946′.302 B82-38418

946′.302 — Spain. Castile. Social conditions, *900-1400 — French texts*

Gautier Dalché, Jean. Economie et société dans les pays de la Couronne de Castille / Jean Gautier Dalché. — London : Variorum Reprints, 1982. — 352p in various pagings : geneal.tables,maps,1port ; 24cm. — (Collected studies series ; CS149)
Facsimile reprints. — Includes index
ISBN 0-86078-096-1 : Unpriced : CIP rev. B82-01568

946′.302 — Spain. León *(Kingdom), 1109-1126*

Reilly, Bernard F.. The kingdom of León-Castilla under Queen Urraca, 1109-1126 / Bernard F. Reilly. — Princeton ; Guildford : Princeton University Press, c1982. — xx,401p,[7]p of plates : ill,1facsim,maps ; 23cm
Bibliography: p371-388. — Includes index
ISBN 0-691-05344-8 : £23.00
Also classified at 946′.202 B82-38418

946′.35 — Spain. Castile, *1400-1521*

Haliczer, Stephen. The Comuneros of Castile : the forging of a revolution, 1475-1521 / Stephen Haliczer. — Madison ; London : University of Wisconsin Press, c1981. — ix,305p : 1map ; 24cm
Bibliography: p273-281. — Includes index
ISBN 0-299-08500-7 : £15.00 B82-12773

946′.82 — Spain. Granada region. Civil wars, *1568-1570*

Hurtado de Mendoza, Diego. The war in Granada / Diego Hurtado de Mendoza ; translated and with an introduction by Martin Shuttleworth. — London : The Folio Society, 1982. — 272p,[12]leaves of plates : ill,maps,ports ; 23cm
Translation of: Guerra de Granada. — Map on lining papers. — In slip case. — Includes index
Unpriced B82-39685

946′.8403 — Spain. Córdoba region, *1479-1516*

Edwards, John. Christian Córdoba : the city and its region in the late Middle Ages. — Cambridge : Cambridge University Press, Nov.1982. — [235]p. — (Cambridge Iberian and Latin American studies)
ISBN 0-521-24320-3 : £24.00 : CIP entry
B82-27535

946.9 — HISTORY. PORTUGAL

946.9′042 — Portugal, *1900-1980*

Gallagher, Tom. Portugal. — Manchester : Manchester University Press, Dec.1982. — [240]p
ISBN 0-7190-0876-x : £16.50 : CIP entry
B82-30216

947 — HISTORY. EASTERN EUROPE, SOVIET UNION

947 — Eastern Europe

Summerscale, Peter. The East European predicament. — Aldershot : Gower, Aug.1982. — [156]p
ISBN 0-566-00518-2 : £11.50 : CIP entry
B82-15880

947 — Eastern Europe, *1740-1980*

Okey, Robin. Eastern Europe 1740-1980 : feudalism to communism / Robin Okey. — London : Hutchinson, 1982. — 264p : maps ; 23cm
Bibliography: p241-253. — Includes index
ISBN 0-09-145000-4 (cased) : £12.00 : CIP rev.
ISBN 0-09-145001-2 (pbk) : £4.95 B81-22667

947 — Russia, *1300-1900*

Baron, Samuel H.. Muscovite Russia : collected essays / Samuel H. Baron. — London : Variorum, 1980. — 362p in various pagings : 1port ; 24cm. — (Collected studies series ; CS 118)
Facsim reprints. — Includes index
ISBN 0-86078-063-5 : £22.00 : CIP rev.
B80-17577

947 — Soviet Union. Influence of Islam, *to 1982*

Bennigsen, Alexandre. The Islamic threat to the Soviet state. — London : Croom Helm, Oct.1982. — [192]p. — (Croom Helm series on the Arab world)
ISBN 0-7099-0619-6 : £14.95 : CIP entry
B82-23188

947 — Soviet Union. Republics, *1917-1978 — Russian texts*

Carrère d'Encausse, Hélène. Raskolotaīā imperiīā : natsīonal'nyĭ bunt v SSSR / Elen Karrer d'Ankoss ; perevela s frantsuzskogo Nina Staviskaīā. — London : Overseas Publications Interchange, 1982. — 381p : maps ; 19cm
Translation of: L'Empire éclaté. — Title page transliterated. — Title on added t.p.: Decline of an empire. — Bibliography: p375-376
ISBN 0-903868-37-7 (pbk) : £9.00 B82-35584

947 — Soviet Union, *to 1981*

The **Cambridge** Encyclopedia of Russia and the Soviet Union / general editors Archie Brown ... [et al.]. — Cambridge : Cambridge University Press, 1982. — 492p : ill(some col.),maps(some col.),ports(some col.) ; 27cm
Bibliography: p485-491. — Includes index
ISBN 0-521-23169-8 : £18.50 B82-15244

947′.0005 — Eastern Europe *— Serials*

Oxford Slavonic papers. New series. — Vol.14. — Oxford : Clarendon Press, Dec.1981. — [144]p
ISBN 0-19-815657-x : £15.00 : CIP entry
B81-31449

Oxford Slavonic papers. New series. — Vol.15. — Oxford : Clarendon Press, Dec.1982. — [144]p
ISBN 0-19-815658-8 : £17.50 : CIP entry
B82-29897

947′.043′0924 — Russia. Ivan IV, *Tsar of Russia*

Yanov, Alexander. The origins of autocracy : Ivan the Terrible in Russian history / Alexander Yanov ; translated by Stephen Dunn. — Berkeley ; London : University of California Press, c1981. — xvi,339p ; 24cm
Bibliography: p325-334. — Includes index
ISBN 0-520-04282-4 : Unpriced B82-16925

947′.046 — Russia. Romanov *(House of), to 1918*

Lincoln, W. Bruce. The Romanovs : autocrats of all the Russias / W. Bruce Lincoln. — London : Weidenfeld and Nicolson, c1981. — xii,852p,[16]p of plates : ill,maps,ports ; 25cm
Bibliography: p815-840. — Includes index
ISBN 0-297-77917-6 : £10.95 B82-08633

947′.048 — Russia, *1645-1676 — Russian texts — Early works*

Kotoshikhin, Grigoriĭ. O Rossii v carstvovanie Alekseja Mixajloviča / Grigorij Kotošixin ; text and commentary A.E. Pennington. — Oxford : Clarendon, 1980. — xvi,775p,[2]leaves of plates : 2facsims ; 24cm
Russian text, English commentary. — Bibliography: p763-775. — Includes index
ISBN 0-19-815639-1 : £60.00 : CIP rev.
B79-06946

947′.07 — Crimean War

. Crimea, 1854-56. — Thame (103, High St., Thame, Oxfordshire OX9 3D2) : Hayes Kennedy, June 1981. — [200]p
ISBN 0-86269-001-3 : £15.00 : CIP entry
B81-14469

947′.07′0924 — Russia. Gagarin, Grégoire. Interpersonal relationships with Taaffe, Julia

Brophy, Brigid. The prince and the wild geese. — London : Hamilton, Feb.1983. — [64]p
ISBN 0-241-10894-2 : £5.95 : CIP entry
Also classified at 941.5081′0924 B82-37849

947′.07′0924 — Russia. Lieven, Dorothea, *Princess — Biographies*

Bingham, Madeleine. Princess Lieven : Russian intriguer / by Madeleine Bingham. — London : Hamish Hamilton, 1982. — x,261p : ill,ports ; 24cm
Bibliography: p249-251. — Includes index
ISBN 0-241-10269-3 : £15.00 : CIP rev.
B82-19003

947′.073 — Crimean War. Peace. Treaties: Treaty of Paris *(1856)*

Baumgart, Winfried. The Peace of Paris 1856 : studies in war, diplomacy, and peacemaking / Winfried Baumgart ; translated by Ann Pottinger Saab. — Santa Barbara ; Oxford : ABC-Clio, c1981. — xx,230p : maps,plans ; 24cm
Bibliography: p213-224. — Includes index
ISBN 0-87436-309-8 : £19.85 B82-27402

947′.073′0924 — Russian civilization. Slavophilism. Theories of Aksakov, K. S.

Christoff, Peter K.. K.S. Aksakov : a study in ideas / by Peter K. Christoff. — Princeton ; Guildford : Princeton University Press, c1982. — ix,475p : ill,ports ; 24cm. — (An introduction to nineteenth-century Russian Slavophilism ; v.3)
Bibliography: p447-465. — Includes index
ISBN 0-691-05334-0 : £26.50 B82-24312

947.08 — Russia, *1900-1953*

Fitzpatrick, Sheila. The Russian Revolution. — Oxford : Oxford University Press, Nov.1982. — [250]p. — (Opus)
ISBN 0-19-219162-4 : £9.95 : CIP entry
B82-26890

947.08 — Soviet Union, *1812-1980*

Westwood, J. N.. Endurance and endeavour : Russian history 1812-1980 / J.N. Westwood. — 2nd ed. — Oxford : Oxford University Press, 1981. — xiv,514p : maps ; 25cm. — (The Short Oxford history of the modern world)
Previous ed.: 1973. — Includes index
ISBN 0-19-822855-4 (cased) : Unpriced : CIP rev.
ISBN 0-19-822856-2 (pbk) : £7.95 B81-18065

947.083′088042 — Soviet Union. Political events. Role of women, *1905-1922 — Stories, anecdotes*

Morozova, Vera. The red carnation : stories / Vera Morozova. — Moscow : Progress ; [London] : distributed by Central, [1981?]. — 231p ; 21cm
Translation of: Zhenshchiny revolīūtsii
ISBN 0-7147-1698-7 : £2.95 B82-29720

947.08′3′088054 — Russia. Political events. Role of young persons, *ca 1900 — Russian texts*

Izgoev, A. S.. Ob intelligentnoĭ molodezhi = On intelligent youth / A.S. Isgoev. — Letchworth : Prideaux, 1981. — 30p ; 27cm. — (Russian titles for the specialist, ISSN 0305-3741 ; no.226)
Originally published: S.l. : S.n., 1909
£0.90 (pbk) B82-00702

947.08′3′0924 — Russia. Political events, *1905 — Personal observations*

Lenin, V. I.. The revolutionary army and the revolutionary government / Lenin. — Moscow : Progress, c1980 ; [London] : Distributed by Central Books. — 15p ; 21cm
Translation of: Revolīūtsionnaīā armiīā i revolīūtsionnoe pravitelstvo
£0.20 (pbk) B82-34677

947.08′3′0924 — Russia. Rasputin, Grigoriĭ — *Biographies*

De Jonge, Alex. The life and times of Grigorii Rasputin / by Alex de Jonge. — London : Collins, 1982. — 368p,[16]p of plates : ill,1facsim,ports ; 24cm
Bibliography: p357-361. — Includes index
ISBN 0-00-216723-9 : £9.95 : CIP rev.
B82-12708

947.084 — Soviet culture, *1917-1980 — Soviet viewpoints*

Gurevich, P.. Culture for the millions / Pavel Gurevich ; [translated from the Russian by Lenina Ilitskaya]. — Moscow : Progress Publishers ; [London] : distributed by Central Books, c1981. — 152p : ill ; 20cm
Translation of: Kul'tura dlīā millionov
ISBN 0-7147-1768-1 (pbk) : £1.95 B82-38234

947.084 — Soviet Union, *1917-1980*

McCauley, Martin. The Soviet Union since 1917 / Martin McCauley. — London : Longman, 1981. — xiv,290p : maps ; 24cm. — (Longman history of Russia)
Bibliography: p265-275. — Includes index
ISBN 0-582-48979-2 (cased) : Unpriced : CIP rev.
ISBN 0-582-48980-6 (pbk) : £6.95 B81-31083

947.084 — Soviet Union, *1917-1982 compared with* **China,** *1949-1982*

Short, Philip. The dragon and the bear : inside China and Russia today / Philip Short. — London : Hodder and Stoughton, c1982. — xi,519p,[8]p of plates : ill,maps,ports ; 24cm
Includes index
ISBN 0-340-25458-0 : £10.95 : CIP rev.
Primary classification 951.05 B82-07431

947.084 — Soviet Union. Political events, *1917-1980 — Dissident viewpoints*

An **End** to silence : uncensored opinion in the Soviet Union : from Roy Medvedev's underground magazine Political diary / edited and with introductions by Stephen F. Cohen ; translated by George Saunders. — New York ; London : Norton, c1982. — 375p ; 24cm
Translated from the Russian. — Includes index
ISBN 0-393-01491-6 : £14.25 B82-33700

947.084 — Soviet Union. Political events, *1917-1982 — Communist viewpoints*

Mackiewicz, Józef. Zwycięstwo prowokaczi. — London (28 Lanacre Ave., NW9 5FN) : Kontra, Jan.1983. — [240]p
Translation of: Zwycięstwo prowokaczi. — Originally published: Munich : J. Mackiewicz, 1962
ISBN 0-907652-03-4 (pbk) : £6.90 : CIP entry
Primary classification 943.8′055 B82-34096

947.084 — Soviet Union. Society, *1918-1980 — Dissident viewpoints*

The **Samizdat** register / edited by Roy Medvedev. — London : Merlin
2. — c1981. — xi,323p ; 23cm
Translation from the Russian
ISBN 0-85036-245-8 (cased) : Unpriced
ISBN 0-85036-246-6 (pbk) : Unpriced
B82-04454

947.084 — Soviet Union. Society. Political aspects

Zaslavsky, Victor. The neo-Stalinist state : class, ethnicity and consensus in Soviet society. — London : Harvester Press, Dec.1982. — [200]p
ISBN 0-7108-0419-9 : £16.95 : CIP entry
B82-30081

947.084′092′4 — Soviet Union, *1917-1939 — Personal observations*

Kopelev, Lev. The education of a true believer / Lev Kopelev ; translated from the Russian by Gay Kern. — London : Wildwood House, 1981, c1980. — 328p ; 24cm
Translation of: I sotvoril sebe kumira. — Originally published: New York : Harper & Row, 1980. — Includes index
ISBN 0-7045-3050-3 : £9.95 B82-17147

947.084′092′4 — Soviet Union. Tolstoy, Alexandra *— Biographies*

Tolstoy, Alexandra. Out of the past / Alexandra Tolstoy ; translated by various hands ; edited by Katharine Strelsky and Catherine Wolkonsky. — New York ; Guildford : Columbia University Press, 1981. — xl,430p : ill,2maps,1facsim,ports ; 24cm
Includes index
ISBN 0-231-05100-x : £14.00 B82-10650

947.084′1 — Russia. Political events, *1917 — Early works*

Lenin, V. I.. Marxism and insurrection / Lenin. — Moscow : Progress, 1980 ; [London] : Distributed by Central Books. — 48p ; 21cm
Translation of: Marksizm i vosstanie. — Includes index
£0.40 (pbk) B82-34678

947.084′1 — Soviet Union. Political events, *1917-1929*

Carrère d'Encausse, Hélène. Lenin : revolution and power / Hélène Carrère d'Encausse ; translated by Valence Ionescu. — London : Longman, 1981. — 279p ; 20cm. — (A History of the Soviet Union 1917-1753 ; v.1)
Translation of: Lénine, révolution et le pouvoir. — Bibliography: p241-268. — Includes index
ISBN 0-582-29559-9 (pbk) : £4.95 : CIP rev.
B81-31821

947.084′1 — Soviet Union. Political events. Role of American international banks, *1917-1920*

Sutton, Antony C.. Wall Street and the Bolshevik Revolution / Antony C. Sutton. — Morley : Veritas ; Sudbury : Bloomfield, c1981. — 228p : 1ill,1facsim,2maps ; 22cm
Originally published: Sandton : Valiant, 1975. — Bibliography: p213-217. — Includes index
£3.50 (pbk) B82-37691

947.084′1′0924 — Russia *(RSFSR).* **Moscow. Museums: T͡Sentral'nyĭ muzeĭ V.I. Lenina** *— Visitors' guides*

Central V.I. Lenin Museum : a guide. — Moscow : Progress, c1979 ; [London] : Distributed by Central Books. — 108p : ill(some col.),maps (some col.),facsims,plans ; 17cm
Translated from the Russian. — Ill on lining papers
£0.95 B82-24527

947.084′1′0924 — Soviet Union. Lenin, V. I., *1917-1924 — Personal observations — Collections*

About Lenin. — Moscow : Progress Publishers, 1980 ; [London] : Distributed by Central Books. — 275p,[15]p of plates : ill,1facsim,ports ; 27cm. — (Lenin in Soviet literature)
Translation of: Rasskazy o Lenine
ISBN 0-7147-1650-2 : £4.25 B82-02533

947.084′1′0924 — Soviet Union. Lenin, V. I. *— Biographies — Welsh texts*

Rees, W. J.. Lenin / W.J. Rees. — [Denbigh] ([Chapel St., Denbigh, Clwyd]) : Gwasg Gee, 1981. — 88p ; 19cm. — (Y Meddwl modern)
Bibliography: p87-88
£1.50 (pbk) B82-12201

947.084′1′0924 — Soviet Union. Lenin, V. I. *— Stories, anecdotes*

Prilezhayeva, M.. A remarkable year / M. Prilezhayeva. The blue notebook / E. Kazakevich. Retracing Lenin's steps / M. Shaginyan. — Moscow : Progress Publishers ; [London] : Distributed by Central Books, c1980. — 265p,[16]p of plates : ill,ports ; 27cm
Translation from the Russian
ISBN 0-7147-1649-9 : £4.25 B82-02700

947.084′1′0924 — Soviet Union. Makhno, Nestor *— Biographies*

Malet, Michael. Nestor Makhno in the Russian civil war / Michael Malet. — London : Macmillan, 1982. — xxvii,232p : 1map ; 23cm
Bibliography: p198-211. — Includes index
ISBN 0-333-25969-6 : Unpriced B82-32410

947.084′1′0924 — Soviet Union. Political events, *1917 — Personal observations*

Raskolnikov, F. F.. Kronshtadt and Petrograd in 1917 / by F.F. Raskolnikov ; translated and annotated by Brian Pearce. — London : New Park, 1982. — xiv,367p,[l]folded leaf of plate : ill,maps,ports ; 21cm
Translation of: Kronshtadt i Piter v 1917 godu. — Map attached to inside back cover. — Includes index
ISBN 0-86151-023-2 (pbk) : £5.00 B82-31004

947.084′1′0924 — Soviet Union. Political events. Role of Kornilov, Lavr Georgievich, *1917*

Katkov, George. The Kornilov Affair : Kerensky and the break-up of the Russian army / George Katkov. — London : Longman, 1980. — xiv,210p : 1map ; 22cm. — (Russia 1917)
Includes index
ISBN 0-582-49101-0 (cased) : £9.95 : CIP rev.
ISBN 0-582-49102-9 (pbk) : £4.95 B80-13657

947.084′2 — Soviet Union. Political events, *1929-1953*

Carrère d'Encausse, Hélène. Stalin : order through terror / Hélène Carrère d'Encausse ; translated by Valence Ionescu. — London : Longman, 1981. — ix,269p ; 20cm. — (A History of the Soviet Union 1917-1953 ; v.2)
Translation of: Staline, l'ordre par la terreur. — Bibliography: p232-260. — Includes index
ISBN 0-582-29560-2 (pbk) : £4.95 : CIP rev.
B81-37601

947.084′2′0924 — Soviet Union. Stalin, I. *— Biographies*

Grey, Ian. Stalin : man of history / Ian Grey. — [London] : Abacus, 1982, c1979. — xxii,547p ; 20cm
Originally published: London : Weidenfeld and Nicolson, 1979. — Bibliography: p511-516. — Includes index
ISBN 0-349-11548-6 (pbk) : £3.95 B82-28846

947.085 — Soviet Union, *1945-1980*

Mooney, Peter J.. The Soviet superpower : the Soviet Union 1945-80 / Peter J. Mooney. — London : Heinemann Educational, 1982. — 210p : maps ; 23cm. — (Studies in modern history)
Includes index
ISBN 0-435-31600-1 (cased) : £10.50 : CIP rev.
ISBN 0-435-31601-x (pbk) : Unpriced
B81-28078

947.085′0924 — Soviet Union. Patolichev, N. S. *— Biographies*

Patolichev, N. S.. Measures of maturity : my early life. — Oxford : Pergamon Press, Dec.1982. — [320]p
ISBN 0-08-024545-5 : £35.00 : CIP entry
B82-40883

947.085′3 — Soviet Union

Chernenko, K. U.. Selected speeches and writings / Konstantin Chernenko ; translated by Y.S. Shirkov. — Oxford : Pergamon, 1982. — x,296p ; 22cm
Translation from the Russian. — Includes index
ISBN 0-08-025848-4 : £15.00 : CIP rev.
B82-11272

Tikhonov, N. A.. Selected speeches and writings / by N.A. Tikhonov. — Oxford : Pergamon, 1982. — xxii,421p ; 22cm
Translation from the Russian. — Includes index
ISBN 0-08-023613-8 : £25.00 : CIP rev.
B82-09184

947.085′3 — Soviet Union. Political events, *1970-1981 — Conference proceedings*

Russia at the crossroads : the 26th Congress of CPSU / edited by Seweryn Bialer and Thane Gustafson. — London : Published under the auspices of the Rand Corporation and the Russian Institute, Columbia University by Allen & Unwin, 1982. — 223p ; 24cm
Includes index
ISBN 0-04-329039-6 : £17.50 : CIP rev.
B82-03716

947.085′3 — Soviet Union. Social conditions *— Soviet viewpoints*

The **Fundamental** law of the USSR / [General editor P.N. Fedoseeva] ; [translated from the Russian by Lenina Ilitskaya]. — Moscow : Progress ; [London] : Distributed by Central, c1980. — 372p ; 21cm
Translation of: Osnovnoĭ zakon SSSR
£2.95 B82-21718

Zolotarevskiĭ, L.. Invitation to a dialogue / L. Zolotarevsky ; [translated from the Russian by Lyudmila Lezhneva]. — Moscow : Progress ; [London] : distributed by Central Books, c1981. — 144p ; 20cm. — (Progress books about the USSR)
Translation of: Priglashenie k dialogu
ISBN 0-7147-1712-6 (pbk) : £0.95 B82-19615

947.085′3 — Soviet Union. Social life *— For children*

Barlow, Pamela. Through the year in the USSR / Pamela Barlow. — London : Batsford Academic and Educational, 1981. — 72p : ill ; 26cm
Includes index
ISBN 0-7134-3555-0 : £5.50 B82-01809

947.085'3'0922 — Soviet Union. Adolescents. Social life — *Personal observations — Collections*

Out into the big wide world / [compiled by Tatyana Yakovleva and Alexei Ivkin] ; [translated from the Russian by Inna Medova]. — Moscow : Progress Publishers, c1980 ; [London] : Distributed by Central Books. — 155p ; 23cm
Translation of: Shagi v bol'shoĭ mir
ISBN 0-7147-1668-5 : £2.25 B82-02695

947.085'3'0924 — Soviet Union. Andropov, Y. Y.. Essays & speeches, *1964-1982 — Collections*

Andropov, Y. Y.. Selected speeches and writings. — Oxford : Pergamon, Dec.1982. — [192]p
ISBN 0-08-028177-x : £25.00 : CIP entry
B82-37507

947.085'3'0924 — Soviet Union. Brezhnev, L. I. — *Biographies*

Brezhnev, L. I.. Memoirs / Leonid Ilyich Brezhnev ; translated by Penny Dole. — Oxford : Pergamon, 1982. — v,41p ; 21cm
Translation of: Vospominaniīa
ISBN 0-08-028164-8 (pbk) : £4.95 : CIP rev.
B82-12898

Leonid I. Brezhnev : pages from his life / written under the auspices of the Academy of Sciences of the USSR ; with a foreword by Leonid I. Brezhnev. — Oxford : Pergamon, 1982. — xi,239,[32]p of plates : ill,ports ; 24cm
Includes index
ISBN 0-08-028150-8 (cased) : Unpriced
ISBN 0-08-028151-6 (pbk) : £5.00 B82-14692

947.085'3'0924 — Soviet Union. Social life, *1978 — Personal observations*

Lee, Andrea. Russian journal / Andrea Lee. — London : Faber, 1982, c1981. — viii,238p ; 23cm
ISBN 0-571-11904-2 : £8.95 : CIP rev.
B82-09299

947.085'3'0924 — Soviet Union. Social life — *Personal observations*

Vaneck, Ludo. The USSR, a dictatorship or a democracy? / Ludo van Eck. — Moscow : Progress Publishers ; [London] : Distributed by Central Books, 1981. — 213p,[64]p of plates : ill,ports ; 21cm. — (Impressions of the USSR series)
Translation of: SSSR, diktatura ili demokratiīa
ISBN 0-7147-1679-0 : £2.50 B82-06712

947'.3120841'0880623 — Soviet Union. Political events. Role of working classes, *1917 — Study regions: Russia (RSFSR). Moscow*

Koenker, Diane. Moscow workers and the 1917 revolution / by Diane Koenker. — Princeton ; Guildford : Princeton University Press, c1981. — xiv,420p : ill ; 25cm. — (Studies of the Russian Institute, Columbia University)
Bibliography: p388-409. — Includes index
ISBN 0-691-05323-5 : £21.30 B82-01023

947'.3120853 — Russia *(RSFSR).* **Moscow. Social life,** *1969-1974 — Correspondence, diaries, etc.*

Davidow, Mike. Moscow diary / Mike Davidow. — Moscow : Progress Publishers, 1980 ; [London] : Distributed by Central Books. — 198p,[80]p of plates : ill(some col.) ; 21cm. — (Impressions of the USSR series)
ISBN 0-7147-1637-5 : £1.95 B82-02536

947'.4084 — Baltic States, *1917-1945*

The **Baltic** States in peace and war 1917-1945 / edited by V. Stanley Vardys, Romuald J. Misiunas. — University Park ; London : Pennsylvania State University Press, c1978. — viii,240p : 1map ; 24cm
Includes index
ISBN 0-271-00534-3 : £11.50 B82-27385

947'.4084 — Baltic States, *1940-1980*

Misiunas, Romuald J.. The Baltic states : years of dependence 1940-1980. — London : Hurst, Jan.1983. — [316]p
ISBN 0-905838-75-0 : £12.50 : CIP entry
B82-33243

947'.453 — Russia *(RSFSR).* **Leningrad. Political events,** *1703-1917 — Readings from contemporary sources*

St Petersburg : a travellers' companion / selected and introduced by Laurence Kelly. — London : Constable, 1981. — 303p : ill,1map,ports ; 23cm
Bibliography: p295-297. — Includes index
ISBN 0-09-463530-7 (cased) : £8.95
ISBN 0-09-463980-9 (pbk) : £5.95 B82-04186

947'.4530841'0924 — Russia *(RSFSR).* **Leningrad. Political events,** *1917 (November) — Personal observations*

Reed, John, *1887-1920.* Ten days that shook the world / John Reed. — Harmondsworth : Penguin, 1966 (1982 [printing]). — xix,351p ; 18cm
Originally published: New York : Boni & Liveright, 1919 ; London : Modern Books, 1928
ISBN 0-14-002433-6 (pbk) : £1.95 B82-25849

947'.5084'0924 — Lithuania. Politics. Škirpa, Kazys — *Biographies — Lithuanian texts*

Gerutis, A.. Pulk. Kazys Škirpa : sukilmo inspiratorius / A. Gerutis. — Londonas : [Nida], 1981. — 32p ; 19cm
Unpriced B82-18708

947'.718 — Ukraine. Beregovo. Jews. Social life, *1939-1944 — Childhood reminiscences*

Siegal, Aranka. Upon the head of the goat. — London : Dent, Sept.1982. — [208]p
ISBN 0-460-04574-1 : £5.50 : CIP entry
B82-19702

948 — HISTORY. SCANDINAVIA

948'.02 — Viking artefacts — *Catalogues*

Graham-Campbell, James. Viking artefacts : a select catalogue / James Graham-Campbell. — London : Published for the Trustees of the British Museum by British Museum Publications, c1980. — 312p : ill ; 29cm
Published in connection with an exhibition at the British Museum. 1980. — Bibliography: p163-171. — Includes index
ISBN 0-7141-1354-9 : £45.00 : CIP rev.
B80-02323

948'.02 — Vikings — *Questions & answers — For schools*

Jordan, Chris. The Vikings / Chris Jordan and Tim Wood. — London : Edward Arnold, 1982. — 15p : ill,2maps ; 30cm. — (History action pack)
Role playing exercise instructions (7 sheets) as inserts
ISBN 0-7131-0702-2 (unbound) : Unpriced : CIP rev. B82-06241

948.1 — HISTORY. NORWAY

948.1'03'0924 — Norway. Haakon VII, *King of Norway — Biographies*

Greve, Tim. Haakon VII of Norway. — London : Hurst, June 1982. — 1v.
Translated from the Norwegian
ISBN 0-905838-66-1 : £12.50 : CIP entry
B82-11119

948.4'5 — Norway. Karasjok. Lapps. Social life — *For children*

Benson, Barbara. Following the reindeer / [by Barbara Benson] ; [adapted from the Dutch of Francis Brewer] ; [illustrated by The Tjong Khing]. — Cambridge : Cambridge University Press, 1980. — 16p : ill(some col.),2maps(some col.) ; 22cm. — (Pole star series. People)
Cover title
ISBN 0-521-23003-9 (pbk) : Unpriced
ISBN 0-521-23220-1 (set) : Unpriced
B82-39477

948.9 — HISTORY. DENMARK AND FINLAND

948.9'01 — Denmark, *909-1134 — Early works*

Saxo Grammaticus. [Gesta Danorum. English. Book 1-9]. The history of the Danes : books 1-9 / Saxo Grammaticus. — Cambridge : Brewer
Vol.2: Commentary / Hilda Ellis Davidson & Peter Fisher. — 1980. — 209p : 1ill,maps,2geneal.tables ; 24cm
Bibliography: p167-178. — Includes index
ISBN 0-85991-062-8 : £15.00 : CIP rev.
B80-24967

948.9'01 — Denmark. Vikings. Social life

Roesdahl, Else. Viking age Denmark. — London : British Museum Publications, Apr.1982. — [272]p. — (A Colonnade book)
Translation of: Danmark Vikingetid
ISBN 0-7141-8027-0 : £16.95 : CIP entry
B82-07111

949.2 — HISTORY. LOW COUNTRIES, NETHERLANDS

949.2'03 — Netherlands. War with Spain, *1559-1659*

Israel, Jonathan I.. The Dutch Republic and the Hispanic world 1606-1661 / Jonathan I. Israel. — Oxford : Clarendon, 1982. — xvi,478p,4p of plates : ill,4maps ; 22cm
Bibliography: p442-463. — Includes index
ISBN 0-19-826534-4 : £22.50 : CIP rev.
B82-12551

949.3 — HISTORY. BELGIUM

949.3'041'0924 — Belgium. Elisabeth, *Queen, consort of Albert, King of the Belgians — Biographies*

Nicholas, Alison. Elisabeth, Queen of the Belgians : her life and times / Alison Nicholas. — Bognor Regis : New Horizon, c1982. — 274p ; 21cm
ISBN 0-86116-233-1 : £6.75 B82-10133

949.3'3 — Belgium. Brussels — *Practical information — For British European Community personnel*

Brussels briefing / [prepared by the] Civil Service Department, Personnel Management Division. — 1981 ed. — [London] : Civil Service Department, 1981. — v,56p : 2maps ; 21cm
ISBN 0-7115-0039-8 (pbk) : Unpriced
B82-17330

949.4 — HISTORY. SWITZERLAND

949.4'5 — Switzerland. Zurich. Intellectual life, *1500-1550*

Lupton, Lewis. Paint & print : a story of reformers, artists, and printers during the life and times of Christopher Froschover of Zurich / Lewis Lupton. — London : Olive Tree, 1982. — 176p : ill,ports ; 23cm. — (The History of the Geneva Bible ; v.14)
Ill. on lining papers. — Limited ed. of autographed copies. — Includes index
ISBN 0-902093-19-3 : £13.77 (£10.00 to subscribers) B82-36223

949.4'7 — Switzerland. Törbel. Cultural processes

Netting, Robert McC.. Balancing on an Alp : ecological change and continuity in a Swiss mountain community / Robert McC. Netting. — Cambridge : Cambridge University Press, 1981. — xxiii,278p : ill,maps ; 24cm
Bibliography: p258-272. — Includes index
ISBN 0-521-23743-2 (cased) : £22.00
ISBN 0-521-28197-0 (pbk) : £7.95 B82-07392

949.5 — HISTORY. GREECE

949.5 — Byzantine civilization, *to 1453*

Ševčenko, Ihor. Ideology, letters and culture in the Byzantine world / Ihor Ševčenko. — London : Variorum Reprints, 1982. — 368p in various pagings : ill,facsims,maps,1port ; 24cm. — (Collected studies series ; CS155)
Includes 1 paper in French. — Facsimile reprints. — Includes index
ISBN 0-86078-101-1 : Unpriced : CIP rev.
B82-01573

949.5 — Greek civilization, *to 1980*

Toynbee, Arnold, *1889-1975.* The Greeks : and their heritages / Arnold Toynbee. — Oxford : Oxford University Press, 1981. — x,334p ; 25cm
Bibliography: p315-320. — Includes index
ISBN 0-19-215256-4 : £12.50 B82-00997

949.5′04 — Byzantine Empire, *1204-1453*

Dennis, George T.. Byzantium and the Franks 1350-1420 / George T. Dennis. — London : Variorum Reprints, 1982. — 320p in various pagings : ill,facsims,1port ; 24cm. — (Collected studies series ; CS150)
Includes 2 papers in Italian and texts in Latin and Greek. — Facsimile reprints
ISBN 0-86078-097-x : Unpriced : CIP rev. B82-01569

949.5′074 — Greece. Political events, *1940-1952 — Conference proceedings*

Greece in the 1940s : a nation in crisis / edited by John O. Iatrides ; editorial committee Peter Bien, Julia W. Loomis, A. Lily Macrakis. — Hanover, N.H. : University Press of New England, 1981. — xvi,444p : maps(some col.) ; 23cm. — (Modern Greek Studies Association series ; 4)
Conference papers. — Maps on lining papers. — Includes index
ISBN 0-87451-198-4 : £24.50 B82-13930

949.5′074′0924 — Greece. Karamanlēs, Kōnstantinos

Woodhouse, C. M.. Karamanlis : the restorer of Greek democracy. — Oxford : Clarendon Press, Oct.1982. — [330]p
ISBN 0-19-822584-9 : £17.50 : CIP entry B82-23688

949.5′075 — Greece. Civil war, *1944-1947.* **Policies of British government. International political aspects**

Alexander, G. M.. The prelude to the Truman Doctrine : British policy in Greece 1944-1947. — Oxford : Clarendon Press, Oct.1982. — [380]p
ISBN 0-19-822653-5 : £19.50 : CIP entry B82-23689

949.5′076′05 — Greece *— Serials — For expatriate Greeks*

[The Greek review *(London : 1982)*]. The Greek review. — Vol.1, no.1 (27 Feb. 1982)-. — London (21 Earl St., EC2A 2HY) : Linnerlake, 1982-. — v. : ill,ports ; 30cm
Weekly
ISSN 0262-8864 = Greek review (London. 1982) : £25.00 per year
Also classified at 956.45′04′05 B82-20887

949.6 — HISTORY. BALKAN PENINSULA

949.6 — Ottoman Empire, *1281-1918 — French texts*

Wittek, Paul. La formation de l'Empire Ottoman / Paul Wittek ; edited by V.L. Ménage. — London : Variorum Reprints, 1982. — 360p in various pagings : ill,facsims,1port ; 24cm. — (Collected studies series ; CS153)
Includes 2 papers in German. — Facsimile reprints. — Includes index
ISBN 0-86078-100-3 : Unpriced : CIP rev. B82-01572

949.7 — HISTORY. YUGOSLAVIA

949.7′023′0924 — Yugoslavia. Political events, *1944-1957 — Personal observations*

Kardelj, Edvard. Reminiscences : the struggle for recognition and independence : the new Yugoslavia 1944-1957 / Edvard Kardelj. — London : Blond & Briggs in association with Summerfield Press, 1982. — 279p,8p of plates : ports ; 22cm
Translation of: Borba za priznanje i nezavisnost nove Jugoslavije 1944-1957. — Includes index
ISBN 0-85634-135-5 : £11.95 B82-35687

949.77 — HISTORY. BULGARIA

949.7′703′0924 — Bulgaria. Zhivkov, Todor *— Biographies*

Zhivkov, Todor. [Selections]. Statesman and builder of new Bulgaria / Todor Zhivkov. — Oxford : Pergamon, 1982. — xxxiii,414p,[33]p of plates : ill,ports(some col.) ; 26cm. — (Leaders of the world)
Translations from the Bulgarian. — Includes index
ISBN 0-08-028205-9 : £10.00 : CIP rev. B81-35889

949.7′703′0924 — Bulgaria. Zhivkova, Ludmila. Essays & speeches, *1972-1982 — Collections*

Zhivkova, Ludmila. Ludmila Zhivkova. — Oxford : Pergamon Press, Dec.1982. — [400]p
ISBN 0-08-028171-0 : £10.00 : CIP entry B82-37508

949.8 — HISTORY. ROMANIA

949.8′02 — Romania, *1859-1918 — Romanian texts*

Alecse, Constantin. Din istoria pămîntului străbun / Constantin Alecse. — [London] ([St Dunstan's-in-the-West, Fleet St., E.C.4.]) : [Publicatie culturală a Parohiei Ortodore Române din Londra], [1979]. — 56p : ill,1map,1port ; 21cm. — (Orizonturi româneşti. Colecţia literară ; nr.2)
Unpriced (pbk) B82-25391

949.9 — HISTORY. AEGEAN ISLANDS

949.9 — Greece. Melos, *B.C. 1000-A.D. 1977.* **Socioeconomic aspects**

An **Island** polity : the archaeology of exploitation in Melos / edited by Colin Renfrew and Malcolm Wagstaff. — Cambridge : Cambridge University Press, 1982. — xiv,361p : ill,maps ; 29cm
Bibliography: p329-347. — Includes index
ISBN 0-521-23785-8 : Unpriced : CIP rev.
Primary classification 939′.15 B82-03107

950 — HISTORY. EURASIA, ASIA

950′.07 — Asian studies *— Serials*

Asian and African studies. — Vol.18. — London : Curzon Press, Aug.1982. — [324]p
ISBN 0-7007-0156-7 : £6.50 : CIP entry
ISSN 0571-2742
Also classified at 960′.07 B82-23845

950′.4 — Asia, *1919-1981 — For schools*

Taylor, J. K. G.. Asia and Australasia. — London : E. Arnold, Nov.1982. — [128]p. — (A History of the 20th century world)
ISBN 0-7131-0679-4 (pbk) : £2.95 : CIP entry
Also classified at 990 B82-27951

950′.428′05 — Asia *— Serials*

Asian and African studies. — 17 (1981). — London : Curzon Press, Nov.1981. — [360]p
ISBN 0-7007-0145-1 : £6.00 : CIP entry
ISSN 0571-2742
Also classified at 960′.328′05 B81-39229

The **Far** East and Australasia. — 13th ed. (1981-82). — London : Europa, Oct.1981. — [1385]p
ISBN 0-905118-66-9 : CIP entry
ISSN 0071-3791 B81-27349

The **Far** East and Australasia. — 14th ed. (1982-83). — London : Europa, Oct.1982. — [1420]p
ISBN 0-905118-76-6 : CIP entry
ISSN 0071-3791 B82-24612

951 — HISTORY. CHINA AND ADJACENT AREAS

951 — China. Modernisation, *ca 1750-1980*

The **Modernization** of China / edited by Gilbert Rozman ; [contributing authors Thomas P. Bernstein ... et al.]. — New York : Free Press ; London : Collier Macmillan, c1981. — xv,551p : maps ; 24cm
Bibliography: p517-529. — Includes index
ISBN 0-02-927480-x : £15.95 B82-18012

951 — China. Modernisation, *to 1982*

Pannell, Clifton W.. China : the geography of development and modernization. — London : Edward Arnold, Nov.1982. — [352]p. — (Scripta series in geography)
ISBN 0-7131-6302-x : £14.95 : CIP entry B82-28752

951 — China, *to 1949*

Rodzinski, Witold. A history of China. — Oxford : Pergamon
Vol.2. — Oct.1982. — [288]p
ISBN 0-08-026060-8 : £25.00 : CIP entry B82-24950

951 — China, *to 1976*

Gernet, Jacques. A history of Chinese civilization / Jacques Gernet ; translated by J.R. Foster. — Cambridge : Cambridge University Press, 1982. — xxiii,772p : ill,maps,ports ; 24cm
Translation of: Le monde chinois. —
Bibliography: p736-757. — Includes index
ISBN 0-521-24130-8 : £25.00 : CIP rev. B82-25933

951 — Chinese civilization, *to 1980*

Bodde, Derk. Essays on Chinese civilization / Derk Bodde ; edited and introduced by Charles Le Blanc and Dorothy Borei. — Princeton, N.J. ; Guildford : Princeton University Press, c1981. — xvii,454p : ill ; 25cm
Bibliography: p427-438. — Includes index
ISBN 0-691-03129-0 (cased) : £17.70
ISBN 0-691-00024-7 (pbk) : £7.00 B82-20219

951′.002′02 — China, *1842-1981 — Chronologies*

Mackerras, Colin. Modern China : a chronology : from 1842 to the present = Zhong guo nian biao / Colin Mackerras with the assistance of Robert Chan. — London : Thames and Hudson, c1982. — 703p : 3maps ; 23cm
Includes index
ISBN 0-500-25084-7 : £20.00 B82-34912

951′.026 — China, *1587*

Huang, Ray. 1587 : a year of no significance : the Ming dynasty in decline. — London : Yale University Press, July 1982. — [293]p
ISBN 0-300-02884-9 (pbk) : £6.95 : CIP entry B82-22778

951′.03 — China. Boxer rebellion. Military operations

Bodin, Lynn E.. The Boxer rebellion / text by Lynn E. Bodin ; colour plates by Chris Warner. — London : Osprey, 1979. — 40p,A-Hp of plates : ill(some col.),maps,2ports ; 25cm. — (Men-at-arms series)
English text, English, French and German captions to plates
ISBN 0-85045-335-6 (pbk) : Unpriced B82-10731

951′.03 — China. Nien Rebellion

Chinese perspectives on the Nien Rebellion / edited with an introduction by Elizabeth J. Perry. — New York : M.E. Sharpe ; London : Eurospan [distributor], c1981. — viii,139p ; 24cm
Translated from the Chinese
ISBN 0-87332-191-x : £13.50 B82-14630

951′.03 — China. Political events, *1895-1980*

Spence, Jonathan D.. The Gate of Heavenly Peace : the Chinese and their revolution, 1895-1980 / Jonathan D. Spence. — London : Faber, 1982, c1981. — xxii,465p : ill,map,ports ; 24cm
Originally published: New York : Viking, 1981. — Map on lining papers. — Bibliography: p423-444. — Includes index
ISBN 0-571-11868-2 : £11.50 : CIP rev. B82-00206

951′.03′0924 — China. Huang, Zunxian *— Biographies*

Kamachi, Noriko. Reform in China : Huang Tsun-hsien and the Japanese model / Noriko Kamachi. — [Cambridge, Mass.] : Council on East Asian Studies, Harvard University ; Cambridge, Mass. ; London : distributed by Harvard University Press, 1981. — xvi,384p : 1facsim,1geneal.table ; 24cm. — (Harvard East Asian monographs ; 95)
Facsim on lining papers. — Bibliography: p323-356. — Includes index
ISBN 0-674-75278-3 : £10.50 B82-04576

951.04 — China, *1911-1975*
Herdan, Innes. Introduction to China / Innes Herdan. — 2nd ed. — London : Anglo-Chinese Educational Institute, c1979. — 83p : ill,1map ; 21cm. — (Modern China series ; no.7)
Previous ed.: 1976. — Bibliography: p81-82
ISBN 0-903193-15-9 (pbk) : £1.00 B82-39373

951.04 — China. Political events, *1900-1979 — For schools*
Dunster, Jack. Mao Zedong and China. — Cambridge : Cambridge University Press, Sept.1982. — [30]p. — (Cambridge introduction to the history of mankind)
ISBN 0-521-23148-5 (pbk) : £1.95 : CIP entry B82-19537

951.04 — China. Political events, *1926-1949*
Zhou, Enlai. Selected works. — Oxford : Pergamon, May 1981. — [430]p. — (Leaders of the world)
ISBN 0-08-024550-1 (cased) : £12.00 : CIP entry
ISBN 0-08-024551-x (pbk) : £5.95 B81-04290

951.04'2 — China. Long March
Wilson, Dick. The Long March, 1935 : the epic of Chinese communism's survival / by Dick Wilson. — Harmondsworth : Penguin, 1977, c1971. — xx,331p : maps ; 20cm
Originally published: London : Hamilton, 1971. — Bibliography: p307-310. — Includes index
ISBN 0-14-006113-4 (pbk) : £2.95 B82-40769

951.04'2 — Sino-Japanese War, *1937-1945*
Wilson, Dick. When tigers fight. — London : Hutchinson, Oct.1981. — 1v.
ISBN 0-09-146571-0 : £9.95 : CIP entry B81-26767

951.04'2'0922 — China. Political events, *1925-1945 — Personal observations — Collections*
Soviet volunteers in China, 1925-1945 : articles and reminiscences / [translated from the Russian by David Fidlon]. — Moscow : Progress Publishers ; [London] : Distributed by Central Books, 1980. — 319p ; 21cm
Translation of: Sovetskie dobrovol'ts͡y v Kitae 1925-1945. — Includes index
ISBN 0-7147-1683-9 : £2.95 B82-06710

951.04'2'0924 — China. Political events, *1932-1939 — Personal observations*
Braun, Otto. A Comintern agent in China 1932-1939. — London : Hurst, Aug.1982. — [299]p
Translation of: Chinesische Aufzeichnungen (1932-1939)
ISBN 0-905838-32-7 : £12.50 : CIP entry B82-17227

951.05 — China, *1949-1981 — For schools*
Pask, Raymond. China / Raymond Pask and Gina Corrigan. — London : Heinemann Educational, 1982. — 58p : ill(some col.),maps (some col.) ; 25cm
Bibliography: p57-58
ISBN 0-435-34689-x (pbk) : £2.50 : CIP rev. B81-34497

951.05 — China, *1949-1982 compared with* **Soviet Union,** *1917-1982*
Short, Philip. The dragon and the bear : inside China and Russia today / Philip Short. — London : Hodder and Stoughton, c1982. — xi,519p,[8]p of plates : ill,maps,ports ; 24cm
Includes index
ISBN 0-340-25458-0 : £10.95 : CIP rev.
Also classified at 947.084 B82-07431

951.05 — China. Political events, *1949-1980*
Shaozhi, Su. Socialist democracy and development in China. — Nottingham : Spokesman, Apr.1982. — [60]p
ISBN 0-85124-343-6 (pbk) : £1.50 : CIP entry B82-12160

951.05 — China. Political events. Role of intellectuals, *1950-1980*
Goldman, Merle. China's intellectuals : advise and dissent / Merle Goldman. — Cambridge, Mass. ; London : Harvard University Press, 1981. — 276p ; 24cm
Includes index
ISBN 0-674-11970-3 : £14.00 B82-03874

951.05 — China. Social conditions, *1949-1981 — For schools*
Long, Gillian. China : portrait of a superpower / Gillian Long, Vincent Oates. — London : Blackie, 1981. — 87p : ill,2maps,ports ; 21cm. — (Crossroads) (Approaches in modern studies)
Bibliography: p87
ISBN 0-216-91065-x (pbk) : Unpriced B82-04360

951.05'092'4 — China, *1932-1981 — Personal observations*
Fairbank, John King. Chinabound : a fifty-year memoir / John King Fairbank. — New York ; London : Harper & Row, c1982. — xiv,480p,[16]p of plates : ill,maps,ports ; 25cm
Maps on inside covers. — Includes index
ISBN 0-06-039005-0 : £12.50 B82-27697

951.05'092'4 — China, *1949-1979 — Personal observations*
Han Suyin. The crippled tree / Han Suyin. — [London] : Triad, 1982, c1965. — 447p : 1map ; 18cm. — (China: autobiography, history ; bk.1)
Originally published: London : Cape, 1965
ISBN 0-586-03836-1 (pbk) : £2.50 B82-39078

Han Suyin. My house has two doors / Han Suyin. — [London] : Triad, 1982, c1980. — 524p ; 18cm. — (China: autobiography, history ; bk.4)
ISBN 0-586-05413-8 (pbk) : £2.50 B82-33993

951.05'092'4 — China. Alley, Rewi *— Biographies*
Chapple, Geoff. Rewi Alley of China. — London : Hodder & Stoughton, July 1981. — [230]p
ISBN 0-340-25687-7 : £8.95 : CIP entry B81-21649

951.05'092'4 — China. Hua, Guofeng *— Biographies*
Wang, Ting. Chairman Hua : leader of the Chinese Communists / by Ting Wang. — London : Hurst, 1980. — xiv,181p,[8]p of plates : ill,1map,ports ; 23cm
Bibliography: p172-177. — Includes index
ISBN 0-905838-22-x : £7.00 : CIP rev. B80-10915

951.05'6 — China. Political events, *1956-1966*
MacFarquhar, Roderick. The origins of the Cultural Revolution. — Oxford : Oxford University Press
2: The great leap forward, 1958-1960. — Feb.1983. — [420]p
ISBN 0-19-214996-2 : £19.50 : CIP entry B82-36584

951.05'7 — China. Social conditions, *1970-1980*
Bonavia, David. The Chinese / David Bonavia. — Rev. ed. — Harmondsworth : Penguin, 1982. — 317p : 1map ; 19cm. — (Pelican books)
Previous ed.: New York : Lippincott & Crowell, 1980 ; London : Allen Lane, 1981. — Includes index
ISBN 0-14-022394-0 (pbk) : £1.95 B82-33153

951.05'7'0924 — China, *1966-1979 — Personal observations*
Han, Suyin. [My house has two doors (v.2)]. Phoenix harvest : volume 2 of My house has two doors / Han Suyin. — [St. Albans] : Triad, 1982, c1980. — 318p ; 18cm. — (China : autobiography, history ; bk.5)
Originally published: London : Cape, 1980
ISBN 0-586-05414-6 (pbk) : £1.95 B82-38353

951.05'7'0924 — China. Social life, *1977-1979 — Personal observations*
Fraser, John, *1944-*. The Chinese : portrait of a people / John Fraser. — [London] : Fontana, 1982, c1980. — 474p,[8]p of plates : ill,1map,3ports ; 18cm
Originally published: Toronto ; London : Collins, 1980. — Includes index
ISBN 0-00-636428-4 (pbk) : £2.50 B82-12085

951.05'8 — China
The **Cambridge** encyclopedia of China / general editor Brian Hook. — Cambridge : Cambridge University Press, 1982. — 492p : ill(some col.),maps(some col.),ports ; 27cm
Bibliography: p488-491. — Includes index
ISBN 0-521-23099-3 : £18.80 : CIP rev. B82-13128

This is China. — Auckland ; London : Hamlyn, 1982. — 382p : ill(some col.) ; 32cm
Editor: Derek Maitland. — Originally published: Sydney : Lansdowne, 1981. — Includes index
ISBN 0-600-38460-8 : £15.00 B82-02611

951.05'8 — China *— For children*
Hickman, Gladys. Introducing the new China. — London : Hodder and Stoughton, Jan.1983. — [48]p
ISBN 0-340-25715-6 (pbk) : £1.75 : CIP entry B82-33727

951.05'8 — China. Social life
China : all provinces and autonomous regions / authors: Zheng Shifeng ... [et al.] ; [translations by Lo Chaotien ... et al.]. — London : Frederick Muller in association with Summerfield Press, 1980. — 285p : chiefly ill (some col.),col.maps ; 31cm
Translated from the Chinese. — Ill on lining papers
ISBN 0-584-97069-2 : £19.50 B82-20323

951.05'8 — China. Social life *— For children*
Fyson, Nance Lui. Chun Ling in China / Nance Lui Fyson and Richard Greenhill. — London : Black, c1982. — 25p : col.ill,1facsim,1col.map ; 22cm. — (Beans)
ISBN 0-7136-2215-6 : £2.95 : CIP rev. B82-13517

Wood, Frances. Through the year in China / Frances Wood. — London : Batsford Academic and Educational, 1981. — 72p : ill,3maps ; 26cm
Bibliography: p70. — Includes index
ISBN 0-7134-3968-8 : £5.50 B82-01810

951.05'8'0922 — China. Social life *— Personal observations — Collections*
We live in China / China Features. — Hove : Wayland, 1981. — 64p : col.ill,1col.map,1facsim,ports ; 25cm. — (Living here)
Includes index
ISBN 0-85340-864-5 : £4.50 B82-16418

951.05'8'0924 — China *— Personal observations*
Butterfield, Fox. China : alive in a bitter sea. — London : Hodder and Stoughton, Oct.1982. — [480]p
ISBN 0-340-26239-7 : £9.95 : CIP entry B82-25075

951.05'8'0924 — China. Social life *— Personal observations*
Kahn-Ackermann, Michael. China : within the outer gate / Michael Kahn Ackermann ; translated by David Fernbach. — London : Marco Polo, 1982. — 158p ; 20cm
Translation of: China. — Bibliography: p158
ISBN 0-907856-00-4 (pbk) : £2.75 B82-31373

951'.1 — Northern China. Ancient Chinese fortifications: Great Wall of China, *to 1981*
The **Great** Wall / foreword by Jacques Gernet ; texts by Luo Zewen ... [et al.]. — London : Joseph, 1982, c1981. — 191p : ill(some col.),maps(some col.) ; 29cm
Originally published: New York : McGraw-Hill, 1981. — Bibliography: p188. — Includes index
ISBN 0-7181-2086-8 : £14.95 B82-17549

951'.156 — China. Ming Valley. Royal tombs: Shih-san-ling
Paludan, Ann. The Imperial Ming tombs / text and photographs by Ann Paludan ; foreword by L. Carrington Goodrich. — New Haven ; London : Yale University Press, c1981. — xvi,251p,[16]p of plates : ill(some col.),1map,plans ; 29cm
Bibliography: p239-243. — Includes index
ISBN 0-300-02511-4 : Unpriced : CIP rev. B81-35024

951′.5 — Tibetan civilization, *to 1967*

Snellgrove, David L.. A cultural history of Tibet / David Snellgrove, Hugh Richardson. — [Rev. ed.]. — London : Routledge & Kegan Paul, 1980, c1968. — 307p : ill,2maps ; 24cm
Originally published: Boulder : Prajñā, 1980. — Bibliography: p293-297. — Includes index
ISBN 0-87773-740-1 (pbk) : £8.75 B82-10263

951′.5 — Tibetan civilization, *to 1980*

Zwalf, W.. Heritage of Tibet. — London : British Museum Publications, Oct.1981. — [144]p
ISBN 0-7141-1420-0 : £5.95 : CIP entry B81-28001

951′.5058 — Tibet. Cultural processes

Paul, Robert A.. The Tibetan symbolic world : psychoanalytic explorations / Robert A. Paul. — Chicago ; London : University of Chicago Press, 1982. — x,347p : ill,geneal.tables ; 23cm. — (Chicago originals)
Bibliography: p321-330. — Includes index
ISBN 0-226-64987-3 (pbk) : Unpriced B82-35313

Tibet / authors Ngapo Ngawang Jigmei ... [et al.] ; [photographs by Yang Kelin ... et al.]. — London : Muller in association with Summerfield Press, 1981. — 296p : ill(some col.),col.maps,col.ports ; 30cm
Ill on lining papers. — Bibliography: p294-296
ISBN 0-584-97077-3 : £19.50 B82-02211

951′.5058′0222 — Tibet. Social life — *Illustrations*

Bonavia, David. Tibet / David Bonavia and Magnus Bartlett. — London : Thames and Hudson, 1981. — 127p : chiefly ill (some col.),1col.map ; 27x35cm
Bibliography: p126-127
ISBN 0-500-54076-4 : £16.00 B82-04663

951.9′042 — Korean War. Air operations by United Nations

Scutts, Jerry. Air war over Korea. — London : Arms and Armour Press, Oct.1982. — [68]p. — (Warbirds illustrated ; 11)
ISBN 0-85368-562-2 (pbk) : £3.95 : CIP entry B82-24748

951.9′042 — Korean War. Army operations by Great Britain. *Army. Agryll and Sutherland Highlanders. Battalion, 1st, 1951*

Mc.Leod, Alistair Sinclair. Banzai attack Korea 1951 / Alistair Sinclair Mc.Leod. — Bognor Regis : New Horizon, c1981. — 283p ; 21cm
ISBN 0-86116-470-9 : £5.75 B82-05351

951.9′042 — Korean War. Army operations by United States. *Army* **& United Nations.** *Emergency Force.* **Armoured combat vehicles: Tanks**

Dunstan, Simon. Armour of the Korean War 1950-53 / text by Simon Dunstan ; colour plates by Terry Hadler. — London : Osprey, 1982. — 40p,A-H p of plates : ill(some col.) ; 25cm. — (Vanguard series ; 27)
English text, with notes on the plates in French and German
ISBN 0-85045-428-x (pbk) : £3.50 B82-37333

951.9′042 — Korean War. Causes

Cumings, Bruce. The origins of the Korean War : liberation and the emergence of separate regimes 1945-1947 / Bruce Cumings. — Princeton ; Guildford : Princeton University Press, c1981. — xxxi,606p : ill,maps,ports ; 25cm
Bibliography: p565-591. — Includes index
ISBN 0-691-09383-0 (cased) : £28.10
ISBN 0-691-10113-2 (pbk) : £10.30 B82-05297

951.9′042′0924 — Korea. British prisoners of War, *1951-1953 — Personal observations*

Farrar-Hockley, *Sir* **Anthony.** The edge of the sword / Sir Anthony Farrar-Hockley ; with an introduction by Sir John Hackett. — London : W.H. Allen, 1981, c1954. — 286p ; 18cm. — (War in the twentieth century) (A star book)
Originally published: London : Muller, 1954
ISBN 0-352-30977-6 (pbk) : £1.95 B82-07894

951.9′042′0924 — Korean War — *Personal observations*

Forty, George. At war in Korea / George Forty. — London : Ian Allan, 1982. — 160p : ill,maps,ports ; 30cm
Bibliography: p160
ISBN 0-7110-1116-8 : £11.95 B82-40538

952 — HISTORY. JAPAN

952 — Japan, *1800-1980*

Storry, Richard. A history of modern Japan / Richard Storry. — Harmondsworth : Penguin, 1960, c1968 (1982 [printing]). — 304p : 1map ; 18cm. — (Pelican books)
Bibliography: p288-297. — Includes index
ISBN 0-14-020475-x (pbk) : £1.95 B82-30522

952 — Japan. Modernisation, *1600-1981*

Lehmann, Jean-Pierre. The roots of modern Japan / Jean-Pierre Lehmann. — London : Macmillan, 1982. — xviii,352p ; 25cm. — (Macmillan Asian histories series)
Bibliography: p332-342. — Includes index
ISBN 0-333-26604-8 (cased) : £16.00
ISBN 0-333-26605-6 (pbk) : Unpriced B82-32377

952′.01 — Japan. Social conditions, *to 700.* **Archaeological sources**

Aikens, C. Melvin. Prehistory of Japan / C. Melvin Aikens, Takayasu Higuchi. — New York ; London : Academic Press, c1982. — xv,354p : ill,maps,plans ; 24cm. — (Studies in archaeology)
Map on lining paper. — Bibliography: p339-347. — Includes index
ISBN 0-12-045280-4 : £24.80 B82-29977

952′.02′088054 — Japan. Children. Social life, *ca 1270-1870 — For schools*

Lewis, Brenda Ralph. Growing up in samurai Japan / Brenda Ralph Lewis. — London : Batsford Academic and Educational, 1981. — 72p : ill,maps,ports ; 26cm
Bibliography: p70. — Includes index
ISBN 0-7134-3572-0 : £5.95 B82-06276

952′.021 — Japan, *1185-1344*

Court and Bakufu in Japan : essays in Kamakura history / edited, with an introduction, by Jeffrey P. Mass. — New Haven ; London : Yale University Press, c1982. — xviii,322p : 1map ; 25cm
Includes Japanese-English glossary. — Bibliography: p299-309. — Includes index
ISBN 0-300-02653-6 : Unpriced : CIP rev. B82-17898

952′.025′0924 — Japan. Tokugawa, Ieyasu — *Biographies*

Sadler, A. L.. The maker of modern Japan : the life of Tokugawa Ieyasu / A.L. Sadler. — Rutland, Vt. : Tuttle ; London : Prentice-Hall [distributor], 1978, c1937 (1981 printing). — 429p,[1]folded leaf of plates : 1geneal.table ; 19cm
Cover title: The maker of modern Japan, the life of Shogun Tokugawa Ieyasu. — Originally published: London : Allen & Unwin, 1937. — Bibliography: p411-412. — Includes index
ISBN 0-8048-1297-7 (pbk) : £5.10 B82-07058

952.03 — Japan. Social conditions, *1868-1941*

Hane, Mikiso. Peasants, rebels and outcastes. — London : Scolar, Sept.1982. — [336]p
ISBN 0-85967-670-6 : £12.50 : CIP entry B82-26057

952.03 — Japan. Social conditions, *ca 1900-1980 — For schools*

Tames, Richard. Japan : in the twentieth century / Richard Tames. — London : Batsford Academic and Educational, 1981. — 96p : ill,maps,ports ; 26cm. — (Twentieth century world history)
Bibliography: p94. — Includes index
ISBN 0-7134-3966-1 : £5.95 B82-06273

953 — HISTORY. ARABIAN PENINSULA AND ADJACENT AREAS

953 — South Arabia. Antiquities

Doe, D. Brian. Monuments of South Arabia. — Cambridge : Oleander Press, Dec.1982. — [288]p. — (Arabia past and present series ; v.12)
ISBN 0-900891-17-3 : £29.95 : CIP entry B82-30738

953′.02′0922 — Arabia. Khalifs, *ca 600-813 — For children*

Murad, Khurram. Stories of the caliphs. — Leicester : Islamic Foundation, Oct.1982. — [48]p. — (Muslim children's library ; 8)
ISBN 0-86037-116-6 (pbk) : £1.00 : CIP entry B82-28593

953′.32 — Yemen *(Arab Republic), to 1981*

Bidwell, Robin L.. The two Yemens. — Harlow : Longman, Sept.1982. — [320]p
ISBN 0-582-78321-6 : £13.95 : CIP entry B82-20277

953′.32052 — Yemen *(Arab Republic), 1930-1981*

Peterson, J. E.. Yemen : the search for a modern state / J.E. Peterson. — London : Croom Helm, c1982. — 221p : 1map ; 23cm
Bibliography: p197-210. — Includes index
ISBN 0-7099-2003-2 : £11.95 : CIP rev. B81-33892

953′.53 — Oman, *to 1979*

Oman and the Sinbad Project : the record of an exhibition at the Gulbenkian Museum, Durham from Nov. 1980 to Feb. 1981 / [edited by John Ruffle]. — Durham : The Gulbenkian Museum of Oriental Art, University of Durham, c1980. — 24p : ill,2maps ; 31cm
Unpriced (pbk) B82-19338

953′.53′009734 — Oman. Rural regions. Social life *— For children — Welsh texts*

Dutton, Roderic. [Arab village. Welsh]. Mohammed yr Arab / Roderic Dutton ; lluniau gan John B. Free ; paratowyd yr addasiad Cymraeg gan Islwyn Griffiths. — Truro : Ivan Corbett, c1982. — [28]p : col.ill,col.maps,1col.port ; 22cm. — (Pobl y byd)
Translation of: Arab village. — Ill on lining papers
ISBN 0-904836-14-2 : Unpriced B82-33251

953′.57 — United Arab Emirates. Social conditions, *to 1980*

Heard-Bey, Franke. From Trucial States to United Arab Emirates. — London : Longman, Jan.1982. — [320]p
ISBN 0-582-78032-2 : £12.75 : CIP entry B81-34287

953′.6053 — Persian Gulf countries. Policies of United States government, *1968-1980*

Conflict in the Persian Gulf / edited by Murray Gordon. — London : Macmillan, 1981. — 173p : maps ; 24cm
Includes index
ISBN 0-333-28592-1 : £15.00 : CIP rev. B79-37106

953′.8 — Saudi Arabia. Hā'il, *to 1980*

Ward, Philip. Hail : oasis city of Saudi Arabia. — Cambridge : Oleander Press, Dec.1981. — [350]p. — (Arabia past & present ; v.11)
ISBN 0-900891-75-0 : £24.75 : CIP entry B81-31541

953′.8 — Saudi Arabia. Mecca

Stewart, Desmond. Mecca / by Desmond Stewart ; photographs by Mohamed Amin. — London : Reader's Digest in association with Newsweek Books, [1980?]. — 172p : ill(some col.) ; 30cm. — (Wonders of man)
Ill on lining papers. — Bibliography: p169. — Includes index
£7.95 B82-27085

953′.8 — Saudi Arabia, *to 1981*
The **Kingdom** of Saudi Arabia / [principal contributors Sir Norman Anderson ... et al.]. — 6th ed. (rev.). — London : Stacey International, c1982. — 256p : ill(some col.),1geneal.table,maps(some col.),ports(some col.) ; 32cm
Previous ed.: 1980. — Bibliography: p248. — Includes index
ISBN 0-905743-28-8 : £25.00 B82-23520

953′.8 — Saudi Arabia, *to 1982*
Al-Farsy, Fouad. Saudi Arabia : a case study in development / Fouad Al-Farsy. — London : Kegan Paul, 1982. — 224p,[8]p of plates : ill,maps,ports ; 23cm
Bibliography: p205-217. — Includes index
ISBN 0-7103-0005-0 (pbk) : £7.95 B82-19121

953′.805 — Saudi Arabia, *1900-1980*
Lacey, Robert. The Kingdom / Robert Lacey. — London : Hutchinson, c 1981. — xv,630p,[48]p of plates : ill,maps,ports ; 24cm
Maps on lining papers. — Bibliography: p539-558. — Includes index
ISBN 0-09-145790-4 : £9.95 : CIP rev. B81-26796

953′.805 — Saudi Arabia, *1902-1980*
Holden, David. The House of Saud / David Holden, Richard Johns. — London : Pan, 1982, c1981. — xiv,582p,[16]p of plates : ill,maps ports ; 18
Originally published: London : Sidgwick and Jackson, 1981. — Bibliography: p539-541. — Includes index
ISBN 0-330-26834-1 (pbk) : £2.95 B82-23287

953′.805′0922 — Saudi Arabia. Royal families, *1902-1981*
Holden, David. The House of Saud / David Holden, Richard Johns. — London : Sidgwick & Jackson, 1981. — xiv,569p,[20]p of plates : ill,3maps,ports ; 25cm
Bibliography: p539-541. — Includes index
ISBN 0-283-98436-8 : £12.50 B82-02499

953′.8′050924 — Saudi Arabia. Ibn Sa'ūd, Abd al-'Azīz ibn 'Abd ar-Rahmān, *King of Saudi Arabia — Biographies*
Almana, Mohammed. Arabia unified : a portrait of Ibn Saud / Mohammed Almana. — Rev. ed. — London : Hutchinson Benham, 1982. — 321p,[16]p of plates : ill,maps,ports ; 22cm
Previous ed.: 1980. — Maps on lining papers. — Includes index
ISBN 0-09-147290-3 : Unpriced
ISBN 0-09-147291-1 (pbk) : £3.95 B82-36241

953′.8053 — Saudi Arabia. Social conditions — *Conference proceedings*
State, society and economy in Saudi Arabia / edited by Tim Niblock. — London : Croom Helm ; Exeter : Centre for Arab Gulf Studies, c1982. — 314p : ill,maps ; 23cm
Includes index
ISBN 0-7099-1806-2 : £13.95 : CIP rev. B81-31170

954 — HISTORY. SOUTH ASIA, INDIA

954 — India. Portuguese colonies, *1550-1800 — Conference proceedings*
Indo-Portuguese history : sources and problems / edited by John Correia-Afonso. — Bombay ; Oxford : Oxford University Press, 1981. — xii,201p : 1map,1plan ; 23cm
Conference papers. — Ill on lining papers. — Includes index
ISBN 0-19-561261-2 : £7.75 B82-21589

954 — India *(Republic), to 1975*
Smith, Vincent A.. The Oxford history of India / by the late Vincent A. Smith. — 4th ed. / edited by Percival Spear. — Delhi ; London : Oxford University Press, 1981. — xv,945p,41p of plates : ill,maps,ports ; 19cm
Previous ed.: 1958. — Includes index
ISBN 0-19-561297-3 (pbk) : Unpriced B82-35002

954 — India *(Republic), to 1980*
Durrans, Brian. India : past into present. — London : British Museum Publications, Apr.1982. — [96]p
ISBN 0-7141-1422-7 (pbk) : £6.95 : CIP entry B82-36251

Wolpert, Stanley. A new history of India / Stanley Wolpert. — 2nd ed. — New York ; Oxford : Oxford University Press, 1982. — 472p : maps ; 24cm
Previous ed.: 1977. — Bibliography: p417-442. — Includes index
ISBN 0-19-502949-6 (cased) : £16.50
ISBN 0-19-502950-x (pbk) : Unpriced B82-31500

954 — India, *to 1935*
Subaltern studies : writings on south Asian history and society / edited by Ranajit Guha. — Delhi ; Oxford : Oxford University Press 1. — 1982. — viii,241p : ill,maps ; 23cm
Includes index
ISBN 0-19-561355-4 : Unpriced B82-40543

954 — India, *to 1973*
Watson, Francis. A concise history of India / Francis Watson. — London : Thames and Hudson, 1974 (1979 [printing]). — 192p : ill,4maps,1facsim,ports ; 24cm
Bibliography: p178-182. — Includes index
ISBN 0-500-27164-x (pbk) : £2.95 B82-08157

954 — South & South-east Asia. Independence, *to 1963*
Asia - the winning of independence / edited by Robin Jeffrey. — London : Macmillan, 1981. — xv,337p : ill,maps ; 23cm
Bibliography: p301-320. — Includes index
ISBN 0-333-27856-9 (cased) : Unpriced
ISBN 0-333-27857-7 (pbk) : Unpriced B82-06652

954 — South Asia. Political events. Foreign relations between Soviet Union & United States
Wolpert, Stanley. Roots of confrontation in South Asia : Afghanistan, Pakistan, India and the superpowers / Stanley Wolpert. — New York ; Oxford : Oxford University Press, 1982. — viii,222p : 2maps ; 22cm
Bibliography: p209-213. — Includes index
ISBN 0-19-502994-1 : £10.50 B82-31504

954′.0072 — South Asia. Research — *Serials*
South Asia research. — No.1 (May 1981)-. — London (c/o South Asia Centre, Room 253, School of Oriental and African Studies, Malet St., WC1E 7HP) : [s.n.], 1981-. — v. ; 25cm
Two issues yearly
ISSN 0262-7280 = South Asia research : £3.00 per year B82-11834

954′.0074′02134 — London. Kensington and Chelsea *(London Borough.* **Museums: India Museum,** *to 1879*
Desmond, Ray. The India Museum 1801-1879 / Ray Desmond. — London : H.M.S.O., 1982. — xv,215p : ill(some col.),1facsim,ports ; 26cm
At head of title: India Office Library and Records. — Includes index
ISBN 0-11-580088-3 : £25.00 B82-26732

954′.024372 — India, *to 1980 — For teaching*
Bahree, Particia. India, Pakistan and Bangladesh : a handbook for teachers / by Patricia Bahree. — London : Extramural Division, School of Oriental and African Studies, University of London, c1982. — v,297p : ill,1map ; 30cm
Includes bibliographies
ISBN 0-7286-0096-x (pbk) : Unpriced B82-35511

954.03′5′0222 — India, *1860-1900 — Illustrations*
Desmond, Ray. Victorian India in focus : a selection of early photographs from the collection in the India Office Library and Records / Ray Desmond. — London : H.M.S.O., 1982. — 100p : ill,ports ; 23x29cm
ISBN 0-11-580227-4 (cased) : £9.95
ISBN 0-11-580228-2 (pbk) : £5.95 B82-28410

954.03′5′0924 — India. Gandhi, M. K. — *Biographies*
Nanda, B. R.. Mahatma Gandhi : a biography / B.R. Nanda. — Delhi ; Oxford : Oxford University Press, 1981, c1958. — 542p ; 23cm
Originally published: London : Allen and Unwin, 1958. — Bibliography: p524-529. — Includes index
ISBN 0-19-561357-0 : £9.95 B82-26512

Shirer, William L.. Gandhi : a memoir / William L. Shirer. — [London] : Abacus, 1981, c1979. — 255p,[8]p of plates : ill,ports ; 20cm
Originally published: New York : Simon and Schuster, 1979. — Includes index
ISBN 0-349-13162-7 (pbk) : £1.75 B82-11194

954.03′5′0924 — India. Gandhi, M. K. — *Biographies — For children*
Gibson, Michael, *1936-*. Gandhi and Nehru / Michael Gibson. — Hove : Wayland, 1981. — 71p : ill,2maps,ports ; 22cm. — (Wayland history makers)
Bibliography: p70. — Includes index
ISBN 0-85340-827-0 : £3.95
Also classified at 954.04′2′0924 B82-06546

954.03′5′0924 — India. Gandhi, M. K. — *Biographies — For schools*
Rawding, F. W.. Gandhi / F.W. Rawding. — Cambridge : Cambridge University Press, 1980. — 48p : ill,1facsim,maps,ports ; 21x22cm. — (Cambridge introduction to the history of mankind. Topic book)
ISBN 0-521-20715-0 (pbk) : £1.95 B82-38834

954.03′5′0924 — India. Politics. Bose, Subhas Chandra — *Biographies*
Bose, Mihir. The lost hero. — London : Quartet Books, May 1982. — [320]p
ISBN 0-7043-2301-x : £15.00 : CIP entry B82-13493

954.03′57 — Amritsar Massacre
Draper, Alfred. Amritsar : the massacre that ended the Raj / Alfred Draper. — London : Cassell, 1981. — 301p,[16]p of plates : ill,ports ; 22cm
Bibliography: p289-293. — Includes index
ISBN 0-304-30481-6 : £8.95 B82-23128

954.03′57′0924 — India. Social life, *ca 1920-ca 1930 — Personal observations*
Battye, Evelyn. Costumes and characters of the British Raj / Evelyn Battye ; illustrated by Cecil Elgee ; introduction by M.M. Kaye. — Exeter : Webb & Bower, 1982. — 79p : ill (some col.) ; 24cm
ISBN 0-906671-42-6 : Unpriced : CIP rev. B81-30475

954.03′59 — India. Policies of British government, *1945-1947*
Moore, R. J.. Escape from empire. — Oxford : Clarendon, Feb.1983. — [340]p
ISBN 0-19-822688-8 : £17.50 : CIP entry B82-36599

954.04′2 — India. Political events, *1947-1948*
Collins, Larry. Freedom at midnight / Larry Collins and Dominique Lapierre. — London : Granada, 1982, c1975. — 595p,[8]p of plates : ill ; 18cm
Originally published: London : Collins, 1975. — Bibliography: p565-576. — Includes index
ISBN 0-586-05451-0 (pbk) : £2.50 B82-22057

954.04′2′0924 — India. Nehru, Jawaharlal — *Biographies — For children*
Gibson, Michael, *1936-*. Gandhi and Nehru / Michael Gibson. — Hove : Wayland, 1981. — 71p : ill,2maps,ports ; 22cm. — (Wayland history makers)
Bibliography: p70. — Includes index
ISBN 0-85340-827-0 : £3.95
Primary classification 954.03′5′0924 B82-06546

954.05′2 — India *(Republic)*
Dolder, Ursula. India / photographs by Ursula and Willi Dolder ; text by Dietmar Rothermund ; translation by Arnold J. Pomerans. — London : Muller, 1982. — 216p : ill(some col.),2maps,ports ; 31cm
Translation from the German. — Ill on lining papers. — Bibliography: p212. — Includes index
ISBN 0-584-11021-9 : £25.00 : CIP rev. B82-08445

954.05′2 — India *(Republic).* **Political events,** *1976-1980*
Selbourne, David. Through the Indian looking glass : selected articles on India 1976-1980 / David Selbourne. — London : Zed, c1982. — xv,239p ; 21cm
ISBN 0-86232-091-7 (pbk) : £5.50 B82-32093

954.05′2′0222 — India — *Illustrations*
MacQuitty, William. The glory of India / photographs by William MacQuitty ; introduction by John Masters ; commentary by Chandra Kumar. — London : Collins, 1982. — 64p : chiefly ill(some col.) ; 30cm
ISBN 0-00-216635-6 (pbk) : £4.95 : CIP rev. B81-37591

954.05′2′0922 — India *(Republic).* **Social life** — *Personal observations — Collections*
Dev, Brahm. We live in India / Brahm Dev. — Hove : Wayland, 1981. — 64p : col.ill,1col.map ; 25cm. — (Living here)
Includes index
ISBN 0-85340-858-0 : £4.50 B82-16419

954′.14035′0882971 — India. Bengal. Muslims, *1871-1906*
Ahmed, Rafiuddin. The Bengal Muslims 1871-1906 : a quest for identity / Rafiuddin Ahmed. — Delhi ; Oxford : Oxford University Press, 1981. — xvi,271p : 2maps ; 23cm
Bibliography: p251-263. — Includes index
ISBN 0-19-561260-4 : £12.00 B82-20553

954′.2 — India *(Republic).* **Garhwal. Britons. Social life,** *ca 1905-1920*
Baylis, Audrey. And then Garhwal / by Audrey Baylis. — London : BACSA, 1981. — vii,216p : ill,1map,facsims,ports ; 23cm
ISBN 0-907799-00-0 (corrected : pbk) : Unpriced B82-13814

954′.2 — India *(Republic).* **Uttar Pradesh. Takukibowli. Social life** — *For children*
Tigwell, Tony. Sakina in India. — London : A. & C. Black, Sept.1982. — [32]p. — (Beans)
ISBN 0-7136-2243-1 : £2.95 : CIP entry B82-20362

954′.52 — India *(Republic).* **Simla,** *1820-1910*
Barr, Pat. Simla : a hill station in British India / Pat Barr & Ray Desmond. — London : Scolar Press, 1978 (1982 [printing]). — 108p : ill(some col.),1map,ports ; 25x28cm
Bibliography: p46
ISBN 0-85967-659-5 (pbk) : £7.50 : CIP rev. B81-39231

954′.5603 — India *(Republic).* **Delhi,** *1803-1931*
Gupta, Narayani. Delhi between two empires 1803-1931 : society, government and urban growth / Narayani Gupta. — Delhi ; Oxford : Oxford University Press, 1981. — xiv,260p,[16]p of plates : ill,maps,facsims,ports ; 23cm
Facsims. on lining papers. — Bibliography: p243-252. — Includes index
ISBN 0-19-561259-0 : £9.50 B82-00508

954′.6 — Kashmir culture: Ladakh region culture, *to 1977*
Snellgrove, David L.. The cultural heritage of Ladakh / David L. Snellgrove and Tadeusz Skorupski. — Warminster : Aris & Phillips
2: Zangskar and the cave temples of Ladakh / with part 4 on the inscriptions at Alchi by Philip Denwood. — c1980. — x,166p,[5]p of plates : ill(some col.),1map,2plans ; 31cm
Text in English and Tibetan. — Map on lining papers. — Bibliography: p164. — Includes index
ISBN 0-85668-148-2 : Unpriced : CIP rev. B80-22776

954′.6052′088054 — Kashmir. Children. Social life — *For children*
Hawker, Frances. Search for a magic carpet in Kashmir / Frances Hawker, Bruce Campbell. — London : Evans, 1982, c1981. — 28p : col.ill,1map ; 20x26cm. — (Kids in other countries)
Originally published: Milton, Qld. : Jacaranda Wiley, 1981
ISBN 0-237-45686-9 (cased) : £2.95
ISBN 0-237-29320-x (pbk) : Unpriced B82-36850

954′.792 — India *(Republic).* **Bombay,** *ca 1665-ca 1900*
Tindall, Gillian. City of gold : the biography of Bombay / by Gillian Tindall. — London : Temple Smith, 1982. — 265p,[4]p of plates : ill,maps,ports ; 25cm
Bibliography: p255-258. — Includes index
ISBN 0-85117-215-6 (corrected) : £11.50 B82-26170

954.91 — HISTORY. PAKISTAN

954.9′1′009734 — Pakistan. Rural regions. Social life — *For children — Welsh texts*
Scarsbrook, Ailsa. [Pakistani village. Welsh]. Assim o Pacistan / Ailsa ac Alan Scarsbrook ; paratowyd yr addasiad Cymraeg gan Islwyn Griffiths. — Truro : Ivan Corbett, c1982. — [28]p : col.ill,1map,col.ports ; 22cm. — (Pobl y byd)
Translation of: Pakistani village. — Map on lining papers
ISBN 0-904836-13-4 : Unpriced B82-33252

954.9′105′05 — Pakistan — *Serials*
Pakistan studies : a quarterly journal. — Vol.1, no.1 (Winter 1981)-. — London (5A Bathurst St., W2) : Centre for Pakistan Studies, 1981-. — v. : ill ; 25cm
ISSN 0262-3277 = Pakistan studies : £12.00 per year B82-18515

954.9′105′0924 — Pakistan. Bhutto, Zulfikar Ali — *Biographies*
Taseer, Salmaan. Bhutto : a political biography / by Salmaan Taseer. — London : Ithaca Press, 1979. — 208p,[4]p of plates : ill,ports,1geneal.table ; 23cm
Bibliography: p205-208. — Includes index
ISBN 0-903729-48-2 (cased) : £9.50
ISBN 0-903729-49-0 (pbk) : £3.50 B82-03086

954.9′12035 — Pakistan. North-West Frontier. Army operations by Great Britain. *Army, 1839-1947*
Barthorp, Michael. The North-West frontiers : a pictorial history 1839-1947. — Poole : Blandford Press, Sept.1982. — [192]p
ISBN 0-7137-1133-7 : £8.95 : CIP entry B82-20365

954.9′1505′05 — Pakistan. Baluchistan. Political events, *1973- — Serials*
Nidā-yi Balocistān. — Jild 1, shumārah 1 (Jūn 1980). — London : [s.n.], 1980-. — v. : ill ; 32cm
Text in Urdu and English. — Continues: People′s front
ISSN 0260-2466 = Nidā-yi Balocistān (corrected) : Unpriced B82-07641

954.93 — HISTORY. SRI LANKA

954.9′3 — Sri Lanka, *to 1980*
De Silva, K. M.. A history of Sri Lanka / by K.M. de Silva. — London : Hurst, c1981. — xx,603p,[12]p of plates : ill,7maps,1plan,ports ; 23cm
Bibliography: p577-580. — Includes index
ISBN 0-905838-50-5 : £18.50 : CIP rev. B81-14407

954.9′3′009734 — Sri Lanka. Rural regions. Social life — *For children — Welsh texts*
Bennett, Gay. [Sri Lanka. Welsh]. Nimal o Sri lanka / Gay Bennett ; lluniau gan Christopher Cormack ; paratowyd yr addasiad Cymraeg gan Islwyn Griffiths. — Truro : Ivan Corbett, c1982. — [26]p : col.ill,col.maps,col.ports ; 22cm. — (Pobl y byd)
Translation of: Sri Lanka
ISBN 0-904836-15-0 : Unpriced B82-33253

954.96 — HISTORY. NEPAL

954.9′6′0088054 — Nepal. Children. Social life — *For children*
Hawker, Frances. My home is a monastery in Nepal / Frances Hawker, Bruce Campbell. — London : Evans, 1982, c1981. — 28p : col.ill,1map ; 20x26cm. — (Kids in other countries)
Originally published: Milton, Qld. : Jacaranda Wiley, 1981
ISBN 0-237-45685-0 (cased) : £2.95
ISBN 0-237-29319-6 (pbk) : Unpriced B82-36851

954.98 — HISTORY. BHUTAN

954.9′8′00994 — Bhutan, *1783 — Personal observations — Correspondence, diaries, etc.*
Davis, Samuel, *1760-1819.* Views of medieval Bhutan : the diary and drawings of Samuel Davis 1783 / [selected and edited by] Michael Aris. — London : Serindia, 1982. — 124p : ill (some col.),maps,1facsim,1plan,ports(some col.) ; 20x29cm
Bibliography: p122. — Includes index
ISBN 0-906026-10-5 : £18.00 : CIP rev.
Also classified at 760′.044995498 B81-34642

955 — HISTORY. IRAN

955 — Iran — *History*
Wilber, Donald N.. Iran : past and present : from monarchy to Islamic republic by Donald N. Wilber. — 9th ed. — Princeton, N.J. ; Guildford : Princeton University Press, 1981. — ix,375p,[12]p plates : ill,1map,ports ; 23cm
Previous ed.: 1976. — Bibliography: p353-358. — Includes index
ISBN 0-691-03130-4 (cased) : Unpriced
ISBN 0-691-00025-5 (pbk) : £4.90 B82-32926

955′.003′21 — Iran — *Encyclopaedias*
Encyclopaedia Iranica / edited by Ehsan Yarshater. — London : Routledge & Kegan Paul
Vol.1
Fasc.1: Āb-′Abd-al-Hamīd. — 1982. — 112p : ill,maps ; 28cm
Cover title. — Text on inside covers. — Bibliography: p8-19
ISBN 0-7100-9090-0 (pbk) : £18.00 B82-27287

955′.04 — Iran. Political events, *1796-1981*
Abrahamian, Ervand. Iran between two revolutions / Ervand Abrahamian. — Princeton, N.J. ; Guildford : Princeton University Press, c1982. — xiii,561p : 1map ; 25cm. — (Princeton studies on the Near East)
Bibliography: p541-550. — Includes index
ISBN 0-691-05342-1 (cased) : £31.80
ISBN 0-691-00790-x (pbk) : £10.30 B82-37588

Keddie, Nikki R.. Roots of revolution : an interpretive history of modern Iran / Nikki R. Keddie ; with a section by Yann Richard. — New Haven ; London : Yale University Press, c1981. — xii,321p,[8]p of plates : ill,1map,ports ; 22cm
Bibliography: p299-307. — Includes index
ISBN 0-300-02606-4 (cased) : Unpriced : CIP rev.
ISBN 0-300-02611-0 (pbk) : Unpriced B81-35023

955′.05′0924 — Iran. Pahlavi, Ashraf — *Biographies*
Pahlavi, Ashraf. Faces in a mirror : memoirs from exile / Ashraf Pahlavi. — Englewood Cliffs ; London : Prentice-Hall, c1980. — xv,238p,[32]p of plates : ill,ports ; 24cm
Includes index
ISBN 0-13-299131-4 : £9.70 B82-07155

955′.053 — Iran, *1940-1980*
Heikal, Mohamed. The return of the Ayatollah : the Iranian revolution from Mossadeq to Khomeini / Mohamed Heikal. — London : Deutsch, 1981. — 217p ; 24cm
Includes index
ISBN 0-233-97404-0 : £9.95 : CIP rev. B81-20607

955′.053 — Iran. Political events, *1978-1981*
Zabih, Sepehr. Iran since the revolution. — London : Croom Helm, June 1982. — [240]p
ISBN 0-7099-3000-3 : £11.95 : CIP entry B82-09596

955′.053′0924 — Iran. Political events, *1978-1979 — Personal observations*
Sullivan, William H.. Mission to Iran / William H. Sullivan. — New York ; London : Norton, c1981. — 296p,[8]p of plates : ill,1map,ports ; 22cm
Includes index
ISBN 0-393-01516-5 : £10.50 B82-33702

955′.054 — Iran. American hostages. Release, *1981*

Assersohn, Roy. The biggest deal. — London : Methuen, Nov.1982. — [320]p
ISBN 0-413-50640-1 : £9.50 : CIP entry
B82-28449

955′.054 — Iran. American hostages. Release. Negotiations between United States and Iran, *1979-1981*

Salinger, Pierre. America held hostage : the secret negotiations / Pierre Salinger. — London : Deutsch, 1982, c1981. — x,349p,[16]p of plates : ill,ports ; 24cm
Includes index
ISBN 0-233-97456-3 : £10.95 B82-28013

955′.054 — Iran. Wars with Iraq, *1980-.* **Causes**

Aziz, Tariq. The Iraq-Iran conflict : questions and discussions / Tareq Aziz ; translated by Naji Al-Hadithi. — London : Published by Third World Center for Research and Publishing in cooperation with Translation and Foreign Languages Publishing House, Baghdad, 1981. — 89p ; 22cm
ISBN 0-86199-010-2 : £3.50 B82-06003

956 — HISTORY. MIDDLE EAST

956 — Arab countries. Conflict with Israel, *1913-1981*

Caplan, Neil. Futile diplomacy. — London : Cass
Vol.1: Early Arab-Zionist negotiation attempts 1913-1931. — Oct.1982. — [296]p
ISBN 0-7146-3214-7 : £15.00 : CIP entry
B82-29015

956 — Middle East. Policies of Soviet Union

The **Soviet** Union and the Middle East : perspectives and policies. — London : Heinemann Educational, Mar.1982. — [192]p
ISBN 0-435-83222-0 (cased) : £13.50 : CIP entry
ISBN 0-435-83223-9 (pbk) : £5.50 B82-06032

956 — Middle East. Political events, *to 1981*

Hiro, Dilip. Inside the Middle East / Dilip Hiro. — London : Routledge & Kegan Paul, 1982. — xix,471p ; 25cm
Maps on lining papers. — Bibliography: p445-449. — Includes index
ISBN 0-7100-9039-0 : £12.50 : CIP rev.
B82-04475

956 — Middle East. Social conditions, *1500-1960*

Bear, Gabriel. Fellah and townsman in the Middle East : studies in social history / Gabriel Bear. — London : Cass, 1982. — ix,338p ; 23cm
Includes index
ISBN 0-7146-3126-4 : £22.50 : CIP rev.
B81-24671

956 — Middle East, *to 1979*

Keddie, Nikki R.. The Middle East and beyond. — London : Cass, May 1981. — [248]p
ISBN 0-7146-3151-5 : £12.50 : CIP entry
B81-08856

956′.004927 — Bedouin — *For children*

Peters, Stella. Bedouin / Stella Peters. — London : Macdonald Educational, 1980. — 48p : ill(some col.),2col.maps,1port ; 29cm. — (Surviving peoples)
Bibliography: p47. — Includes index
ISBN 0-356-05955-3 : £3.95 B82-24545

956′.01 — Battle of Lepanto

Beeching, Jack. The galleys at Lepanto / Jack Beeching. — London : Hutchinson, 1982. — 267p,[8]p of plates : ill,1map,1plan,ports ; 25cm
Bibliography: p.253-254. — Includes index
ISBN 0-09-147920-7 : £10.95 : CIP rev.
B82-03740

956′.01 — Middle East, *ca 600-ca 1500*

Minorsky, Vladimir. Medieval Iran and its neighbours. — London : Variorum, Sept.1982. — [336]p. — (Collected studies series ; CS166)
ISBN 0-86078-114-3 : £26.00 : CIP entry
B82-21408

956′.01′0924 — Middle East. Saladin, *Sultan of Egypt and Syria* — *Biographies*

Lyons, Malcolm Cameron. Saladin : the politics of the holy war / Malcolm Cameron Lyons and D.E.P. Jackson. — Cambridge : Cambridge University Press, 1982. — viii,456p : maps ; 23cm. — (University of Cambridge oriental publications ; no.30)
Bibliography: p435-443. — Includes index
ISBN 0-521-22358-x : £25.00 B82-36391

956′.03′0924 — Middle East. Glubb, John Bagot — *Biographies*

Glubb, John Bagot. The changing scenes of life. — London : Quartet, June 1982. — 1v.
ISBN 0-7043-2329-x : CIP entry B82-13504

956′.04 — Arab countries. Conflict with Israel, *1948-1978.* **Attitudes of Arabs & Israelis**

The **Arab-Israeli** conflict : psychological obstacles to peace / by Daniel Heradstveit. — 2. ed. — Oslo : Universitetsforlaget ; London : Global Book Resources [distributor], c1981. — 231p : ill ; 22cm. — (Norwegian foreign policy studies ; no.28)
Previous ed.: 1979. — Bibliography: p220-227. — Includes index
ISBN 82-00-05746-1 (pbk) : £12.00
B82-11844

956′.04 — Arab-Israeli War, *to 1976*

Herzog, Chaim. The Arab-Israeli wars : war and peace in the Middle East / Chaim Herzog. — London : Arms and Armour, 1982. — 368p,[64]p of plates : ill,maps,ports ; 24cm
Bibliography: p347-351. — Includes index
ISBN 0-85368-367-0 : £11.95 : CIP rev.
B82-07029

956′.04 — Middle East. Policies of governments

For the record : selected information relevant to foreign policy. — London (P.O. Box 455, NW5 1DF) : Egyptian runner, 1982. — 17p ; 21cm
Facsim reprints
Unpriced (unbound) B82-41144

956′.04′05 — Middle East — *Serials*

The **Middle** East and North Africa. — 28th ed. (1981-82). — London : Europa, Sept.1981. — [1005]p
ISBN 0-905118-65-0 : CIP entry
ISSN 0076-8205
Also classified at 961′.048′05 B81-20494

The **Middle** East and North Africa. — 29th ed. (1982-83). — London : Europa, Sept.1982. — [1016]p
ISBN 0-905118-75-8 : CIP entry
ISSN 0076-8502
Also classified at 961′.048′05 B82-21567

956.1 — Turkey, *to 1967*

Davison, Roderic H.. Turkey. — Beverley (42 Northgate, Walkington, Beverley, North Humber, HU17 8ST) : Eothen Press, Dec.1981. — [181]p
Originally published: Englewood Cliffs : Prentice-Hall, 1968
ISBN 0-906719-02-x (cased) : £9.95 : CIP entry
ISBN 0-906719-03-8 (pbk) : £5.50 B81-35896

956.1′024′0924 — Turkey. Political events. Role of Atatürk, Kamâl, *1908-1938*

Atatürk : founder of a modern state / Ali Kazancigil and Ergun Özbudun, editors. — London : C. Hurst, 1981. — vi,243p : 1ill ; 23cm
Bibliography: p141-142. — Includes index
ISBN 0-905838-67-x : £8.50 : CIP rev.
B81-33630

956.3 — Turkey. Straits questions. Foreign relations between Europe & Turkey, *1908-1936*

Macfie, Alexander. A struggle for the Turkish straits : a study in international relations 1908-1936. — London : Prior, Oct.1982. — [240]p
ISBN 0-86043-401-x : £8.95 : CIP entry
B82-24134

956.45 — Cyprus. Political events, *to 1981*

Denktash, R. R.. The Cyprus triangle / R.R. Denktash. — Nicosia : Rustem ; London : Allen & Unwin, 1982. — 222p ; 23cm
Includes index
ISBN 0-04-327066-2 : £15.00 : CIP rev.
B82-19078

956.45 — Cyprus, *to 1981*

Footprints in Cyprus. — London (21 Earl St., EC2A 2HY) : Trigraph, May 1982. — [304]p
ISBN 0-9508026-0-3 : £16.50 : CIP entry
B82-14922

956.45′03′0924 — Cyprus. Antoniadou, Sophia — *Biographies*

Antoniadou, Sophia. Seen Jesus Christ my faith within / Sophia Antoniadou. — Bognor Regis : New Horizon, c1982. — 63p,[8]p of plates : ports ; 21cm
ISBN 0-86116-568-3 : £3.25 B82-10141

956.45′04 — Cyprus. Political events, *1974-1976*

Cyprus. — New ed. — London : Minority Rights Group, 1978. — 28p : maps ; 30cm. — (Report / Minority Rights Group, ISSN 0305-6252 ; no.30)
Previous ed.: 1976. — Bibliography: p26
£1.20 (pbk) B82-05429

956.45′04′05 — Cyprus — *Serials* — *For expatriate Greek Cypriots*

[The Greek review *(London : 1982)*]. The Greek review. — Vol.1, no.1 (27 Feb. 1982)-. — London (21 Earl St., EC2A 2HY) : Linnerlake, 1982-. — v. : ill,ports ; 30cm
Weekly
ISSN 0262-8864 = Greek review (London. 1982) : £25.00 per year
Primary classification 949.5′076′05 B82-20887

956.6′2 — Armenia. Political events, *to 1975*

Lang, David Marshall. The Armenians / by David Marshall Lang and Christopher J. Walker. — New. rev. ed. — London : Minority Rights Group, 1978 ([1981 printing]). — 24p : 1ill,2maps ; 30cm. — (Report / Minority Rights Group, ISSN 0305-6252 ; no.32)
Bibliography: p23-24
£1.20 (pbk) B82-05433

956.7′03 — Iraq. Social conditions, *1802-1831*

Nieuwenhuis, Tom. Politics and society in early modern Iraq : Mamlūk pashas, tribal shayks and local rule between 1802 and 1831 / by Tom Nieuwenhuis. — The Hague ; London : Nijhoff, c1982. — xiii,227p : ill,maps ; 25cm. — (Studies in social history ; 6)
Bibliography: p216-223. — Includes index
ISBN 90-247-2576-3 : Unpriced B82-17291

956.7′043 — Iraq, *1958-1981* — *Conference proceedings*

Iraq. — London : Croom Helm, July 1982. — [288]p
Conference papers
ISBN 0-7099-1810-0 : £14.95 : CIP entry
B82-16227

956.7′043′05 — Iraq — *Serials*

Iraq monthly. — Vol.1, no.1 (July 1981)-. — London (177 Tottenham Court Rd, W1P 9LF) : Iraqi Press Office, 1981-. — v. : ill,ports ; 28cm
Description based on: Vol.1, no.4 (Dec. 1981)
ISSN 0262-7485 = Iraq monthly : £0.50 per issue B82-14257

956.7′4 — Iraq. Osirak. Nuclear reactors. Air raids by Israel. *Ḥēl ăvīr, 1981*

Perlmutter, Amos. Two minutes over Baghdad / Amos Perlmutter, Michael Handel and Uri Bar-Joseph. — [London] : Corgi, 1982. — 192p : maps ; 20cm
Originally published: London : Vallentine, Mitchell, 1982
ISBN 0-552-11939-3 (pbk) : £1.75 B82-30646

956.7′4 — Iraq. Tuwaitha. Nuclear reactors. Bombing by Israel. *Ḥēl ăvīr, 1981*

Perlmutter, Amos. Two minutes over Baghdad / Amos Perlmutter, Michael Handel and Uri Bar-Joseph. — London : Vallentine, Mitchell, 1982. — 191p : maps ; 23cm
ISBN 0-85303-208-4 : £7.50 : CIP rev.
B82-11116

956.91′042′05 — Syria. Political events — *Islamic Revolution of Syria viewpoints — Serials*

Abstracts from al-Nazeer. — No.1 (197?)-. — Claawson, Mich. ; London (BM Box 4141, WC1N 3XX) : Islamic Revolution of Syria, [197-]-. — v. : ill,ports ; 22cm
Monthly
Unpriced B82-12452

956.92′044 — Lebanon. Invasion by Israel, *1982*

Background briefing : Israel′s invasion of Lebanon June 1982. — London ([52 Green St., W.1]) : London Office of the Palestine Liberation Organisation, [1982]. — 31p : ill,2ports ; 21cm
Cover title
Unpriced (pbk) B82-40394

Jansen, Godfrey. The battle of Beirut. — London : Zed Press, Dec.1982. — [160]p
ISBN 0-86232-142-5 (cased) : £11.95 : CIP entry
ISBN 0-86232-143-2 (pbk) : £3.95 B82-35215

956.92′044′0924 — Lebanon. Political events, *1975-1977 — Personal observations*

Joumblatt, Kamal. I speak for Lebanon. — London : Zed Press, June 1982. — [128]p
Translation of: Pour le Liban
ISBN 0-86232-097-6 (cased) : £10.95 : CIP entry
ISBN 0-86232-048-8 (pbk) : £3.95 B82-16215

956.94 — Israel, *ca 1880-1980*

Cragg, Kenneth. This year in Jerusalem : Israel in experience / Kenneth Cragg. — London : Darton, Longman and Todd, 1982. — 178p ; 22cm
Includes index
ISBN 0-232-51534-4 (pbk) : £5.95 : CIP rev. B81-20476

956.94′001 — Zionism, *1897-ca 1910*

Vital, David. Zionism : the formative years / David Vital. — Oxford : Clarendon Press, 1982. — xviii,514p : 2maps ; 23cm
Bibliography: p495-506. — Includes index
ISBN 0-19-827443-2 : £22.50 : CIP rev. B81-31455

956.94′001 — Zionism. Attitudes of British labour movements, *1917-1948*

Gorny, Joseph. The British Labour movement and Zionism 1917-1948. — London : Cass, Oct.1982. — [264]p
ISBN 0-7146-3162-0 : £15.00 : CIP entry B82-23879

956.94′001 — Zionism, *ca 1918-1950*

Brenner, Lenni. Zionism in the age of the dictators. — London : Croom Helm, Feb.1983. — [288]p
ISBN 0-7099-0628-5 : £14.95 : CIP entry B82-38894

956.94′001′01 — Zionism. Theories

Avineri, Shlomo. The making of modern Zionism : the intellectual origins of the Jewish state / Shlomo Avineri. — London : Weidenfeld and Nicolson, c1981. — x,244p ; 24cm
Includes index
ISBN 0-297-78015-8 : £9.95 B82-01456

956.94′001′06041 — Great Britain. Zionist movements: British Aliya Movement — *Serials*

BILU : journal of the British Aliya Movement. — [No.1 (1981)?]-. — London (741 High Rd., N12 0BQ) : The Movement, 1981-. — v. : ill,facsims,ports ; 44cm
Ten issues yearly. — Description based on: No.2 (Dec. 1981)
ISSN 0263-7626 = BILU : £3.00 per year B82-32172

956.94′001′0924 — Zionism. Magnes, Judah L. — *Biographies*

Magnes, Judah L.. Dissenter in Zion / from the writings of Judah L. Magnes ; edited by Arthur A. Goren. — Cambridge, Mass. ; London : Harvard University Press, 1982. — xv,554p,[5]p of plates : ports ; 25cm
List of works: p544-545. — Includes index
ISBN 0-674-21283-5 : £21.00 B82-33396

956.94′001′09438 — Poland. Zionism, *1915-1926*

Mendelsohn, Ezra. Zionism in Poland : the formative years, 1915-1926 / Ezra Mendelsohn. — New Haven ; London : Yale University Press, c1981. — xi,373p : 1map ; 25cm
Bibliography: p359-364. — Includes index
ISBN 0-300-02448-7 : Unpriced : CIP rev. B82-14204

956.94′004927 — Israel. Palestinian Arabs. Social life, *1980 — Personal observations*

Shehadeh, Raja. The third way. — London : Quartet, May 1982. — 1v.
ISBN 0-7043-2354-0 : CIP entry B82-14494

956.94′004927 — Israel. Settlement by Palestinian Arabs — *Arabic texts*

Crawford, Willy. Hiğrat al-ʻawdah al-filastīniyyah / Wilī Krūfūrd = Palestinian exodus / Willy Crawford. — [Staines] ([5, Beehive Rd., Staines, Middx]) : W. Crawford, [1981?]. — 60p ; 21cm
Cover title
£1.75 (pbk) B82-14188

956.94′03 — Palestine. Policies of British government, *1100-1917*

Tuchman, Barbara W.. Bible and sword : how the British came to Palestine / Barbara W. Tuchman. — London : Papermac, 1982, c1956. — xiii,412p,[3]leaves of plates : ports ; 20cm
Originally published: New York : New York University Press, 1956 ; London : Redman, 1957. — Bibliography: p351-390. — Includes index
ISBN 0-333-33414-0 (pbk) : £3.95 B82-32327

956.94′03 — Palestine. Political events. Attitudes of Palestinian Arabs, *1881-1939*

Kayyali, A. W.. Palestine : a modern history / A.W. Kayyali. — London : Third World Centre for Research and Publishing, [1981?]. — 243p : 1map ; 23cm
Translation from the Arabic. — Originally published: London : Croom Helm, 1978. — Bibliography: p232-238. — Includes index
ISBN 0-86199-007-2 : £9.95 B82-01385

956.94′04 — Palestine. Political events, *1917-1973*

Palestine and Israel in the 19th and 20th centuries / edited by Elie Kedourie and Sylvia G. Haim. — London : Cass, 1982. — viii,278p : maps ; 24cm
Bibliography: p275-276
ISBN 0-7146-3121-3 : £22.00 B82-32501

956.94′04 — Palestine. Political events, *1921-1967*

Zionism and Arabism in Palestine and Israel / edited by Elie Kedourie and Sylvia G. Haim. — London : Cass, 1982. — x,255p : 1map ; 24cm
ISBN 0-7146-3169-8 : £22.00 : CIP rev. B80-22777

956.94′04′0222 — Palestine. Social life, *1925-1931 — Illustrations*

Granqvist, Hilma. Portrait of a Palestinian village : the photographs of Hilma Granqvist / editor Karen Seger ; with a foreword by Shelagh Weir. — London : Third World Centre, 1981. — 176p : chiefly ill,1map,ports ; 29cm
Bibliography: p176
ISBN 0-86199-006-4 : £11.00 B82-02831

956.94′05′0924 — Israel. Politics. Eban, Abba — *Biographies*

Eban, Abba. Abba Eban : an autobiography. — London : Futura published in association with Stiematsky′s Agency, 1979, c1977. — 636p,[8]p of plates : ports ; 18cm
Originally published: London : Weidenfeld & Nicolson, 1978. — Includes index
ISBN 0-7088-1467-0 (pbk) : £1.95 B82-32815

956.94′05′0924 — Palestine. Shak'a, Bassam — *Biographies*

Woolfson, Marion. Bassam Shak′a : portrait of a Palestinian / Marion Woolfson. — London : Third World Centre, 1981. — 142p ; 23cm
ISBN 0-86199-009-9 : £5.00 B82-17568

956.94′052′0924 — Israel. Politics. Peres, Shimon — *Biographies*

Golan, Matti. Shimon Peres : a biography / Matti Golan ; translated from the Hebrew by Ina Friedman. — London : Weidenfeld and Nicolson, 1982. — ix,275p,[8]p of plates : ports ; 24cm
Includes index
ISBN 0-297-78019-0 : £12.50 B82-37194

956.94′053 — Israel. Attitudes of Unesco — *Jewish viewpoints*

Brasslof, F. L.. Recent developments in Unesco : the World Heritage List, the Jerusalem excavations and the Islamic States Broadcasting Services Organization / [F.L. Brasslof]. — London (11 Herford St., W1Y 7DX) : IJA, 1981. — 8p ; 24cm. — (Research report / Institute of Jewish Affairs ; no.17)
Unpriced (unbound) B82-27691

956.94′054 — Israel

Frankel, William. Israel observed : an anatomy of the state / William Frankel. — [London] : Thames and Hudson, c1980 (1981 [printing]). — 288p ; 24cm
Bibliography: p280-283. — Includes index
ISBN 0-500-27258-1 (pbk) : £4.50 B82-24931

956.94′054 — Israel, *1976 — Correspondence, diaries, etc — Welsh texts*

Jones, Nesta Wyn. Dyddiadur Israel / Nesta Wyn Jones. — Llandysul : Gwasg Gomer, 1981. — 135p,[4]p of plates : ill(some col.),1map ; 21cm
ISBN 0-85088-565-5 (pbk) : £2.95 B82-19146

956.94′054 — Palestine. Arabs. Conflict with Jews. Role of Jordan

Klieman, Aaron S.. Israel, Jordan, Palestine : the search for a durable peace / Aaron S. Klieman ; foreword by Robert G. Neumann. — Beverly Hills ; London : Sage, c1981. — 96p ; 22cm. — (The Washington papers ; vol.IX,83)
'The Center for Strategic and International Studies'. — Bibliography: p95-96
ISBN 0-8039-1684-1 (pbk) : Unpriced B82-08571

956.94′054′0922 — Israel. Social life — *Paersonal observations — Collections*

Levine, Gemma. We live in Israel / Gemma Levine. — Hove : Wayland, 1981. — 64p : col.ill,1col.map,1facsim,col.ports ; 26cm. — (Living here)
Includes index
ISBN 0-85340-865-3 : £4.50 B82-03876

956.94′4 — Jerusalem, *to 1980*

Uris, Leon. Jerusalem : song of songs / Jill and Leon Uris. — London : Deutsch, 1981. — 318p : ill(some col.),maps,ports ; 30cm
Ill on lining papers
ISBN 0-233-97389-3 : £14.95 B82-05320

956.94′4052 — Jerusalem. Political events, *1948*

Collins, Larry. O Jerusalem! / Larry Collins and Dominique Lapierre. — London : Granada, 1982, c1972. — xx,648p,[32]p of plates : ill,3maps,ports ; 18cm. — (A Panther book)
Originally published: London : Weidenfeld and Nicolson, 1972. — Bibliography: p607-617. — Includes index
ISBN 0-586-05452-9 (pbk) : £2.50 B82-31774

956.95 — Jordan. West Bank. Occupation by Israel, *1967-1980*

Metzger, J.. This land is our land. — London : Zed Press, Sept.1982. — [272]p
Translation of: Das ist unser Land
ISBN 0-86232-086-0 (cased) : £15.95 : CIP entry
ISBN 0-86232-073-9 (pbk) : £6.50 B82-21410

956.95044′092′4 — Jordan. Sharaf, Abdul Hamid — *Biographies*

The **Shaping** of an Arab statesman. — London : Quartet, Aug.1982. — 1v.
ISBN 0-7043-2341-9 : CIP entry B82-17975

957 — HISTORY. ASIATIC SOVIET UNION, SIBERIA

957.7 — South Vietnam. Montagnards, *to 1954*

Hickey, Gerald Cannon. Sons of the mountains : ethnohistory of the Vietnamese Central Highlands to 1954 / Gerald Cannon Hickey. — New Haven ; London : Yale University Press, c1982. — xxi,488p : ill,maps,plans,ports,geneal.tables ; 24cm
Includes index
ISBN 0-300-02453-3 : £31.50 : CIP rev.
B82-01316

958 — HISTORY. CENTRAL ASIA

958 — Central Asia. Political events. Foreign relations between Great Britain & Russia, *1810-1895*

Morgan, Gerald, *1902-*. Anglo-Russian rivalry in Central Asia : 1810-1895 / Gerald Morgan ; with an epilogue by Geoffrey Wheeler. — London : Cass, 1981. — xix,264p : maps ; 23cm
Bibliography: p241-246. — Includes index
ISBN 0-7146-3179-5 : Unpriced : CIP rev.
B81-21487

958'.005 — Central Asia — *Serials*

Central Asian survey. — Vol.1, no.1 (July 1982)-. — Oxford : Oxford Microform Publications, 1982-. — v. ; 23cm
Journal of: Society for Central Asian Studies
ISSN 0263-4937 = Central Asian survey : £12.5 per year (£15.00 to institutions)
B82-38498

958'.1 — Afghanistan, *to 1980*

Afghanistan : past and present. — Moscow : Social Sciences Today Editorial Board USSR Academy of Sciences ; [London] : Distributed by Central Books, 1981. — 270p ; 22cm. — (Oriental studies in the USSR ; no.3)
Translation of: Afganistan. — Translated into English by Evgeni Khazanov. — Bibliography: p254-261
ISBN 0-7147-1682-0 (pbk) : £1.95 B82-06704

Shah, *Sirdar* **Ikbal Ali**. Afghanistan of the Afghans / by Sirdar Ikbal Ali Shah. — London : Octagon, c1982. — 272p ; 23cm
£7.50 B82-32899

958'.103'0924 — Afghanistan. 'Abd al-Raḥmān Khān — *Biographies*

'Abd al-Raḥmān Khān. The life of Abdur Rahman : Amir of Afganistan : G.C.B., G.C.S.I. / edited by Sultan Mahomed Khan ; with a new introduction by M.E. Yapp. — Karachi ; Oxford : Oxford University Press, 1980. — 2v. : ill,2maps,1port,1geneal.table ; 23cm. — (Oxford in Asia historical reprints)
Translation from the Persian. — Originally published: London : Murray, 1900. — Includes index
ISBN 0-19-577258-x : £20.00 B82-00407

958'.1044 — Afghanistan. Political events, *1978-1980 — Soviet viewpoints*

The **Undeclared** war : imperialism vs Afghanistan / [compiled by A.S. Grachev] ; [translated from the Russian by Dmitry Belyavsky]. — Moscow : Progress ; [London] : distributed by Central Books, c1980. — 156p,[16]p of plates : ill,1port ; 20cm
Translation of: Neob"i͡avlennai͡a voĭna. — Includes index
ISBN 0-7147-1708-8 (pbk) : £1.50 B82-19614

958'.408 — Soviet Central Asia, *ca 1855-1981*

Rywkin, Michael. Moscow's Muslim challenge. — London : Hurst, Dec.1982. — [184]p
ISBN 0-905838-80-7 : £10.50 : CIP entry
B82-30744

959 — HISTORY. SOUTH-EAST ASIA

959 — South-east Asia, *to 1978*

Hall, D. G. E.. A history of South-east Asia. — 4th ed. — Basingstoke : Macmillan, Apr.1981. — [1072]p
Previous ed.: 1968
ISBN 0-333-24163-0 : £12.95 : CIP entry
ISBN 0-333-24164-9 (pbk) : £5.95 B81-02094

959'.004951 — South-east Asia. Chinese, *to ca 1970*

Purcell, Victor. The Chinese in Southeast Asia / by Victor Purcell. — 2nd ed. — Kuala Lumpur ; Oxford : Issued under the auspices of the Royal Institute of International Affairs [by] Oxford University Press, 1965 (1980 [printing]). — xvi,623p : maps ; 24cm. — (Oxford in Asia paperbacks)
Previous ed.: 1951. — Maps on inside covers. — Bibliography: p574-610. — Includes index
ISBN 0-19-580463-5 (pbk) : £11.95
B82-28623

959.1 — HISTORY. BURMA

959.1'02 — Burma, *to 1044*

Luce, G. H.. Phases of pre-Pagán Burma. — Oxford : Oxford University Press, July 1982. — 2v.
ISBN 0-19-713595-1 : £80.00 : CIP entry
B82-12543

959.1'04'0924 — Burma. Social life, *ca 1935-1955 — Personal observations*

Tales of Burma / compiled and introduced and with biographies by Alistair McCrae ; [contributors] Harold Braund ... [et al.]. — Paisley : Paton, 1981. — 168p : ill,maps,ports ; 22cm
ISBN 0-9506061-3-8 (pbk) : £2.95 B82-31134

959.3 — HISTORY. THAILAND

959.3 — South-east Asia. Kammu. Social life

The **Kammu** year. — London : Curzon Press, Aug.1982. — [220]p. — (Studies in Asian topics, ISSN 0142-6028 ; v.4)
ISBN 0-7007-0151-6 : £4.50 : CIP entry
B82-24342

959.3 — Thailand. Meo Hill region. Children. Social life — *For children*

Hawker, Frances. Children of the Meo hill tribes / Frances Hawker, Bruce Campbell. — London : Evans, 1982, c1981. — 28p : col.ill,1map ; 20x26cm. — (Kids in other countries)
Originally published: Milton, Qld. : Jacaranda Wiley, 1981
ISBN 0-237-45683-4 (cased) : £2.95
ISBN 0-237-29317-x (pbk) : Unpriced
B82-36853

959.5 — HISTORY. MALAYSIA, BRUNEI, SINGAPORE

959.5'1'04 — Malayan Emergency, *1948-1960*

Scurr, John. The Malayan Campaign 1948-60. — London : Osprey, Nov.1982. — [40]p
ISBN 0-85045-476-x (pbk) : £3.50 : CIP entry
B82-26423

959.5'7 — Singapore, *1819-1975*

Turnbull, C. M.. A history of Singapore : 1819-1975 / C.M. Turnbull. — Kuala Lumpur ; Oxford : Oxford University Press, c1977 (1980 [printing]). — xvi,392p,11p of plates : 2maps,music,1plan,ports ; 25cm
Bibliography: p335-371. — Includes index
ISBN 0-19-580376-0 (pbk) : £8.50 B82-00408

959.6 — HISTORY. CAMBODIA

959.6'04 — Cambodia, *1942-1981*

Peasants and politics in Kampuchea 1942-1981. — London : Zed Press, June 1982. — [360]p
ISBN 0-905762-60-6 (cased) : £18.95 : CIP entry
ISBN 0-905762-80-0 (pbk) : £5.95 B82-14924

959.6'04 — Cambodia. Political events, *ca 1930-1980*

Burchett, Wilfred. The China Cambodia Vietnam triangle / Wilfred Burchett. — Chicago : Vanguard ; London : Zed, c1981. — 235p ; 21cm
ISBN 0-86232-085-2 (pbk) : £4.95 : CIP rev.
B81-37549

959.7 — HISTORY. VIETNAM

959.7 — Vietnam, *1925-1975*

Harrison, James Pinckney. The endless war : fifty years of struggle in Vietnam / James Pinckney Harrison. — New York : Free Press ; London : Collier Macmillan, c1982. — xii,372p : ill,maps ; 25cm
Bibliography: p345-361. — Includes index
ISBN 0-02-914040-4 : £13.95 B82-30024

959.7'03 — Vietnam. Tonkin. Description & travel, *1876 — Personal observations*

Truong-Vinh-Ky, P. J. B.. Voyage to Tonking in the year At-hoi (1876). — London (Malet St., WC1E 7HP) : School of Oriental & African Studies, Aug.1982. — [144]p
Translated from the Vietnamese
ISBN 0-7286-0099-4 : £7.00 : CIP entry
B82-20776

959.704'3 — Vietnamese wars, *1954-1973*

Welsh, Douglas. The history of the Vietnam War / Douglas Welsh. — London : Hamlyn, 1981. — 192p : ill(some col.),col.maps ; 31cm. — (A Bison book)
Includes index
ISBN 0-600-34220-4 : £6.95 B82-00934

959.704'32 — Vietnamese wars. Policies of Australian government, *1962-1975*

Australia's Vietnam. — London : Allen & Unwin, Nov.1982. — [288]p
ISBN 0-86861-037-2 : £15.00 : CIP entry
B82-26086

959.704'342 — Vietnamese wars. Army operations by United States. *Army, 1961-1973*

Stanton, Shelby L.. Vietnam order of battle / by Shelby L. Stanton. — Washington, D.C. : U.S. News Books ; Walpole, Suffolk : Quorn [distributor], c1981. — xvii,396p : ill(some col.),maps ; 32cm
Bibliography: p387-390. — Includes index
ISBN 0-89193-700-5 : £30.00 B82-17756

959.704'348 — Vietnamese wars. Air operations by United States. *Air Force, 1964-1975*

Bell, Dana. Air war over Vietnam. — London : Arms and Armour Press
Vol.1. — Oct.1982. — [68]p. — (Warbirds illustrated ; 10)
ISBN 0-85368-548-7 (pbk) : £3.95 : CIP entry
B82-24747

959.704'4 — South Vietnam. Political events, *1975-1981 — Sinn Féin The Workers' Party viewpoints*

Those who leave : the truth about socialist Viet Nam and the "boat people". — Dublin (30 Gardiner Place, Dublin 1) : Sinn Féin The Workers' Party, [1982?]. — 30p ; 21cm
£0.25 (pbk) B82-35958

959.8 — HISTORY. INDONESIA

959.8 — Indonesia, *ca 1300-1980*

Ricklefs, M. C.. A history of modern Indonesia : c.1300 to the present / M.C. Ricklefs. — London : Macmillan, 1981. — xii,335p : maps ; 24cm. — (Macmillan Asian histories series)
Bibliography: p292-307. — Includes index
ISBN 0-333-24378-1 (cased) : Unpriced
ISBN 0-333-24380-3 (pbk) : Unpriced
B82-12098

959.8'03 — Indonesia, *1945-1979*

Wilhelm, Donald. Emerging Indonesia / Donald Wilhelm. — London : Cassell, 1980. — 192p : ill(some col.),maps,ports ; 25cm
Map on lining papers. — Includes index
ISBN 0-304-30501-4 : £9.95 B82-19050

959.8'03 — Indonesia. Political events. Role of military leaders, *1945-1967*

Sundhaussen, Ulf. The road to power : Indonesian military politics 1945-1967 / Ulf Sundhaussen. — Kuala Lumpur ; Oxford : Oxford University Press, 1982. — xii,304p ; 26cm
Bibliography: p275-287. — Includes index
ISBN 0-19-580467-8 (cased) : £28.00
ISBN 0-19-582521-7 (pbk) : Unpriced
B82-41059

959.8′035 — Indonesia. Policies of government of United States, *1945-1949*

McMahon, Robert J.. Colonialism and cold war : the United States and the struggle for Indonesian independence, 1945-49 / Robert J. McMahon. — Ithaca ; London : Cornell University Press, 1981. — 338p : 1map ; 23cm
Includes index
ISBN 0-8014-1388-5 : £15.75 B82-22617

959.8′2 — Indonesia. Java. Buddhist temples: Borobudur

Forman, B.. Borobudur : the Buddhist legend in stone / Bedřich Forman. — London : Octopus, 1980. — 134p : chiefly ill(some col.),maps ; 32cm
Translation from the Czech. — Bibliography: p134
ISBN 0-7064-1444-6 : £9.95 B82-05594

959.8′201 — Indonesia. Java, *ca 1400-1800*

Raffles, SirStamford. The history of Java / Thomas Stamford Raffles ; with an introduction by John Bastin. — Kuala Lumpur ; Oxford : Oxford University Press, 1965 (1978 [printing]). — 2v.(xlviiii,479p,[31]leaves of plates; viii,288,cclxp,[35]leaves of plates) : ill (some col.),maps(some col.),music ; 29cm
Facsim of: London : Black, Parbury and Allen : London : J. Murray, 1817. — Map (106x45cm folded to 26x19cm) attached to lining papers of volume one
ISBN 0-19-580347-7 : Unpriced
ISBN 0-19-580345-0 (v.1)
ISBN 0-19-580346-9 (v.2) B82-01915

959.8′6 — Indonesia. Bali. Children. Social life — *For children*

Hawker, Frances. Festival of the full moon in Bali / Frances Hawker, Bruce Campbell. — London : Evans, 1982, c1981. — 27p : col.ill,1map ; 20x26cm. — (Kids in other countries)
Originally published: Milton, Qld. : Jacaranda Wiley, 1981
ISBN 0-237-45684-2 (cased) : £2.95
ISBN 0-237-29318-8 (pbk) : Unpriced
B82-36852

959.8′6 — Indonesia. East Timor. Political events. Role of Western bloc countries, *1975-1979*

Chomsky, Noam. East Timor and the Western democracies / Noam Chomsky. — Nottingham (Bertrand Russell House, Gamble Street, Nottingham, NG7 4ET) : Bertrand Russell Peace Foundation, [1979]. — 8p ; 21cm. — (Spokesman pamphlet ; no.67)
£0.30 (unbound) B82-17670

Kohen, Arnold. An act of genocide : Indonesia′s invasion of East Timor / by Arnold Kohen and John Taylor ; foreword by Noam Chomsky. — London : Tapol, c1979. — 133p : ill,maps,facsims,ports ; 21cm
ISBN 0-9506751-0-5 (pbk) : £1.75 B82-17678

959.9 — HISTORY. PHILIPPINES

959.9 — Philippines. Social conditions, *ca 1800-1982*

Philippine social history. — London : Allen & Unwin, Jan.1983. — 1v.
ISBN 0-86861-108-5 : £9.95 : CIP entry
B82-33232

959.9′01 — Philippines. Conquest by Spain, *1521-1581*

Noone, Martin J.. The islands saw it : the discovery and conquest of the Philippines 1521-1581 / Martin J. Noone. — Navan (St. Colombans, Navan, Co. Meath) : M. J. Noone. — xii,476p,[22]p of plates : ill,maps,facsims,ports ; 24cm
Bibliography: p453-462. — Includes index
£10.00 (pbk) B82-27065

960 — HISTORY. AFRICA

960 — Africa. Colonisation

Fanon, Frantz. Toward the African revolution / by Frantz Fanon ; translated from the French by Haakon Chevalier. — London : Writers and Readers, 1980, c1967. — x,197p ; 20cm
Translation of: Pour la révolution africaine. — Originally published: London : Monthly Review Press, 1967
ISBN 0-904613-97-6 (pbk) : £2.95 B82-01377

960 — Africa — *History*

The **Cambridge** history of Africa. — Cambridge : Cambridge University Press
Vol.1: From the earliest times to c.500 BC / edited by J. Desmond Clark. — 1982. — xxiii,1157p,[20]p of plates : ill,maps,plans ; 24cm
Includes bibliographies and index
ISBN 0-521-22215-x : £48.00 : CIP rev.
B81-04307

960 — Africa, *to 1980*

African history and culture / edited by Richard Olaniyan. — Lagos : Longman Nigeria ; Harlow : Longman, 1982. — ix,259p : ill,maps,ports ; 23cm
Includes bibliographies and index
ISBN 0-582-64369-4 (pbk) : £3.95 B82-30192

The **Cambridge** encyclopedia of Africa / general editors Roland Oliver, Michael Crowder. — Cambridge : Cambridge University Press, 1981. — 492p : ill(some col.),maps(some col.)ports (some col.) ; 27cm
Bibliography: p485-491. — Includes index
ISBN 0-521-23096-9 : £18.50 B82-07159

Cultural atlas of Africa / edited by Jocelyn Murray. — Oxford : Phaidon, c1981. — 240p : ill(some col.),col.maps,ports ; 31cm
Maps and ill on lining papers. — Bibliography: p227-229. — Includes index
ISBN 0-7148-2045-8 : £17.95 B82-23626

960′.07 — African studies — *Serials*

Asian and African studies. — Vol.18. — London : Curzon Press, Aug.1982. — [324]p
ISBN 0-7007-0156-7 : £6.50 : CIP entry
ISSN 0571-2742
Primary classification 950′.07 B82-23845

960′.07206 — Africa. African historiography

Temu, A. J.. Historians and Africanist history : a critique : post-colonial historiography examined / Arnold Temu and Bonaventure Swai. — London : Zed, c1981. — xiv,187p ; 23cm. — (Africa series)
Bibliography: p177-183. — Includes index
ISBN 0-905762-78-9 (cased) : £16.95 : CIP rev.
ISBN 0-905762-79-7 (pbk) : Unpriced
B81-33627

960′.09′734 — Africa. Villages. Children. Social life — *For children*

Lewin, Hugh. Jafta / by Hugh Lewin ; illustrated by Lisa Kopper. — Cambridge : Dinosaur, c1982. — [24]p : ill ; 15x18cm. — (Dinosaur′s Althea books)
Originally published: London : Evans, 1981
ISBN 0-85122-267-6 (pbk) : £0.70 B82-31056

960′.09′734 — Africa. Villages. Mothers. Social life — *For children*

Lewin, Hugh. Jafta — my mother / by Hugh Lewin ; illustrated by Lisa Kopper. — Cambridge : Dinosaur, c1982. — [24]p : ill ; 15x19cm. — (Dinosaur′s Althea books)
Originally published: London : Evans, 1981
ISBN 0-85122-268-4 (pbk) : £0.70 B82-31057

960′.22 — Africa. Social conditions. Effects of slave trade, *1400-1900*

Forced migration : the impact of the export slave trade on African societies / edited by J.E. Inikori. — London : Hutchinson University Library, 1982. — 349p : 2maps ; 23cm. — (Hutchinson university library for Africa)
Bibliography: p341-343. — Includes index
ISBN 0-09-145900-1 (cased) : Unpriced : CIP rev.
ISBN 0-09-145901-x (pbk) B81-34588

960′.23 — Africa, *1840-1914 — For East African students*

Tidy, Michael. A history of Africa 1840-1914 / Michael Tidy with Donald Leeming. — London : Hodder and Stoughton
Vol.1: 1840-1880. — 1980. — 188p : maps ; 22cm
Bibliography: p178-180. — Includes index
ISBN 0-340-24419-4 (pbk) : £3.25 : CIP rev.
B80-07185

Tidy, Michael. A history of Africa 1840-1914 / Michael Tidy with Donald Leeming. — London : Hodder and Stoughton
Vol.2: 1880-1914. — 1981. — 220p : maps ; 22cm
Bibliography: p211. — Includes index
ISBN 0-340-24411-9 (pbk) : Unpriced : CIP rev. B81-18066

960′.23 — Africa. Colonisation by European countries, *1880-1920 — American negro viewpoints*

Jacobs, Sylvia M.. The African nexus : black American perspectives on the European partitioning of Africa, 1880-1920 / Sylvia M. Jacobs. — Westport, Conn. ; London : Greenwood Press, 1981. — xiv,311p : ill ; 22cm. — (Contributions in Afro-American and African studies, ISSN 0069-9624 ; no.55)
Bibliography: p275-299. — Includes index
ISBN 0-313-22312-2 : Unpriced B82-01946

960′.3 — Africa, *1914-1981*

Davidson, Basil. Modern Africa. — London : Longman, Jan.1983. — [224]p
ISBN 0-582-65525-0 (pbk) : £3.50 : CIP entry
B82-33344

960′.32 — Africa. Decolonisation, *1940-1960 — Conference proceedings*

The **Transfer** of power in Africa. — London : Yale University Press, Nov.1982. — [704]p
Conference papers
ISBN 0-300-02568-8 : £25.00 : CIP entry
B82-40337

960′.32 — Africa. Decolonisation, *1945-1979*

Decolonization and dependency : problems of development of African societies / edited by Aguibou Y. Yansané. — Westport ; London : Greenwood Press, 1980. — xix,321p ; 25cm. — (Contributions in Afro-American and African studies ; no.48)
Bibliography: p291-304. — Includes index
ISBN 0-313-20873-5 : Unpriced B82-14985

960′.32 — Africa. Political events. Role of communist countries & Western bloc countries, *1945-1980*

Gavshon, Arthur. Crisis in Africa : battleground of East and West / Arthur Gavshon. — Harmondsworth : Penguin, 1981. — 320p : ill,maps ; 20cm. — (Pelican books. African affairs)
Includes index
ISBN 0-14-022239-1 (pbk) : £3.95 B82-07296

960′.32′0924 — Africa, *1950-1981 — Personal observations*

Kaplan, Marion. Focus Africa. — London : Hamilton, Oct.1982. — [480]p
ISBN 0-241-10602-8 : £20.00 : CIP entry
B82-23446

960′.328′05 — Africa — *Serials*

Asian and African studies. — 17 (1981). — London : Curzon Press, Nov.1981. — [360]p
ISBN 0-7007-0145-1 : £6.00 : CIP entry
ISSN 0571-2742
Primary classification 950′.428′05 B81-39229

961 — HISTORY. NORTH AFRICA

961 — North-east Africa, *1860-1863 — Illustrations*

Grant, James Augustus. James Augustus Grant in Africa, 1860-63. — [Edinburgh] : National Library of Scotland, 1982. — 1portfolio([3] p,[28]leaves of plates) : col.ill,1col.map,col.facsims ; 38cm
Cover title
ISBN 0-902220-51-9 : Unpriced B82-25844

961 — North-east Africa — *Serials*

N.E.A. : journal of research on north east Africa. — Vol.1, no.1 (Summer ′81)-. — Oxford (P.O. Box 20, Oxford) : N.E.A., 1981-. — v. ; 21cm
Three issues yearly
ISSN 0261-4243 = N.E.A. : £4.00 per year to individuals (£6.00 to institutions) B82-12464

961′.048′05 — North Africa — *Serials*

Fodor′s North Africa : Algeria, Morocco, Tunisia. — 1980-. — London : Hodder and Stoughton, 1980-. — v. : ill,maps ; 21cm
Annual. — Description based on: 1981 issue
ISSN 0197-1271 = Fodor′s North Africa : £7.95 B82-04924

961′.048′05 — North Africa — *Serials*
continuation

The **Middle** East and North Africa. — 28th ed. (1981-82). — London : Europa, Sept.1981. — [1005]p
ISBN 0-905118-65-0 : CIP entry
ISSN 0076-8205
Primary classification 956′.04′05 B81-20494

The **Middle** East and North Africa. — 29th ed. (1982-83). — London : Europa, Sept.1982. — [1016]p
ISBN 0-905118-75-8 : CIP entry
ISSN 0076-8502
Primary classification 956′.04′05 B82-21567

961.1 — HISTORY. TUNISIA

961′.1 — Tunisia. Sidi Ameur. Cultural processes

Abu Zahra, Nadia. Sidi Ameur : a Tunisian village / Nadia Abu Zahra. — London : Published for the Middle East Centre, St Antony′s College, Oxford [by] Ithaca, 1982. — xvii,237p,[14]p of plates : ill,2geneal.tables,1map ; 24cm. — (St Antony′s Middle East monographs ; no.15)
Bibliography: p230-232. — Includes index
ISBN 0-903729-83-0 : £11.50 B82-33280

961.2 — HISTORY. LIBYA

961′.2 — Libya, *1900-1980*

Wright, John, *1937-*. Libya : a modern history / John Wright. — London : Croom Helm, [1982?]. — 306p : 1map ; 23cm
Bibliography: p282-295. — Includes index
ISBN 0-7099-2733-9 : £13.95 : CIP rev.
B81-30539

961′.2′00321 — Libya, *to 1980* — *Encyclopaedias*

Hahn, Lorna. Historical dictionary of Libya / Lorna Hahn with the assistance of Maureen Muirragui. — Metuchen, N.J. ; London : Scarecrow, 1981. — xiii,116p : 1map ; 23cm. — (African historical dictionaries ; no.33)
Bibliography: p85-108
ISBN 0-8108-1442-0 : £8.00 B82-05354

962 — HISTORY. EGYPT

962′.03 — Egypt. Political events, *1878-1882*

Schölch, Alexander. Egypt for the Egyptians! : the socio-political crisis in Egypt 1878-1882 / Alexander Schölch. — London : Published for the Middle East Centre, St Antony′s College, Oxford [by] Ithaca, 1981. — xiv,386p : 2maps ; 24cm. — (St Antony′s Middle East monographs ; no.14)
Translation of: Ägypten den Ägyptern. — Bibliography: p360-374. — Includes index
ISBN 0-903729-82-2 : £14.50 B82-33283

962′.053 — Egypt, *1945-1981*

Hopwood, Derek. Egypt : politics and society 1945-1981. — London : Allen and Unwin, Aug.1982. — [224]p
ISBN 0-04-956011-5 : £12.50 : CIP entry
B82-15651

962′.053 — Egypt, *1967-1977*

Cooper, Mark N.. The transformation of Egypt / Mark N. Cooper. — London : Croom Helm, c1982. — 278p : ill ; 23cm
Includes index
ISBN 0-7099-0721-4 : £13.95 : CIP rev.
B82-04463

962′.053′0924 — Egypt. Nasser, Gamal Abdul, *1952-1970*

Abu Izzeddin, Nejla M.. Nasser of the Arabs : an Arab assessment / by Nejla M. Abu Izzeddin. — London : Third World Centre for Research and Publishing, 1981. — viii,467p : 1port ; 25cm
Bibliography: p445-458. — Includes index
ISBN 0-86199-012-9 : Unpriced B82-22265

962′.054 — Egypt. Political events

Meiring, Desmond. Since Sadat. — London : Wildwood House, June 1982. — [196]p. — (Wildwood specials)
ISBN 0-7045-0474-x (pbk) : £2.95 : CIP entry
B82-09371

962′.054′0924 — Egypt. Political events. Role of Sadat, Anwar el-, *1970-1981*

Shoukri, Ghali. Egypt : portrait of a president, 1971-1981 : the counter-revolution in Egypt, Sadat′s road to Jerusalem / Ghali Shoukri. — London : Zed, 1981. — v,465p ; 23cm. — (Middle East series)
Translation of the Arabic
ISBN 0-86232-062-3 (cased) : Unpriced : CIP rev.
ISBN 0-86232-072-0 (pbk) : £7.95 B81-35867

962′.054′0924 — Egypt. Sadat, Anwar el-, *1981* — *Biographies*

Müller, Konrad. Anwar Sadat : the last hundred days / photographs by Konrad Müller ; text by Mark Blaisse. — London : Thames and Hudson, 1981. — 75p : ill,ports ; 25cm
ISBN 0-500-01277-6 : £6.95 B82-09468

962′.054′0924 — Egypt. Sadat, Anwar el- — *Biographies*

Fernández-Armesto, Felipe. Sadat and his statecraft / Felipe Fernández-Armesto. — London : Kensal, 1982. — 196p ; 24cm
Bibliography: p191-192. — Includes index
ISBN 0-946041-00-8 : £10.50 : CIP rev.
B82-11488

Hirst, David. Sadat / David Hirst and Irene Beeson. — London : Faber, 1981. — 384p ; 23cm
Bibliography: p371-373. — Includes index
ISBN 0-571-11690-6 : Unpriced : CIP rev.
B81-35866

962′.055′05 — Egypt — *Serials*

The **Egyptian** bulletin. — No.1 (June 1982)-. — London (4 Chesterfield Gardens, W1Y 8BR) : Egyptian Education Bureau, 1982-. — v. : ill ; 27cm
ISSN 0264-0252 = Egyptian bulletin : Unpriced B82-40061

962′.16055 — Egypt. Cairo. Social life — *For children*

Munir, Mustafa. Living in Cairo / Mustafa Munir. — Hove : Wayland, 1981. — 52p : ill,1col.map ; 21cm. — (Living in famous cities)
Bibliography: p51. — Includes index
ISBN 0-85340-842-4 : £3.75 B82-16420

962.4 — HISTORY. SUDAN

962.4′03′0924 — Sudan. Political events, *1940-1953* — *Personal observations*

Zulfakar Sabry, Hussein. Sovereignty for Sudan / Hussein Zulfakar Sabry. — London : Ithaca, 1982. — 136p ; 23cm
ISBN 0-903729-80-6 : £9.50 B82-33284

962.7′02 — Sudan. Darfur & Kordofan, *1750-1916*

O′Fahey, R. S.. State and society in Där Für / by R.S. O′Fahey. — London : Hurst, 1980. — xii,210p : maps ; 23cm
Bibliography: p185-197. — Includes index
ISBN 0-905838-04-1 : £12.00 : CIP rev.
B79-35187

963 — HISTORY. ETHIOPIA

963′.003′21 — Ethiopia, *to 1980* — *Encyclopaedias*

Rosenfeld, Chris Prouty. Historical dictionary of Ethiopia / by Chris Prouty and Eugene Rosenfeld. — Metuchen ; London : Scarecrow, 1981. — xv,436p : 1map ; 23cm. — (African historical dictionaries ; no.32)
Bibliography: p192-407. — Includes index
ISBN 0-8108-1448-x : £20.00
Also classified at 016.963 B82-17418

963′.004924 — Ethiopia. Falashas, *to 1981*

Kessler, David. The Falashas : the forgotten Jews of Ethiopia. — London : Allen & Unwin, Apr.1982. — [192]p
ISBN 0-04-963001-6 : £8.95 : CIP entry
B82-03722

963′.06 — Ethiopia. Political events, *1974-1981*

Halliday, Fred. The Ethiopian revolution / Fred Halliday, Maxine Molyneux. — London : NLB, 1981. — 304p : maps ; 23cm
Bibliography: p286-290. — Includes index
ISBN 0-86091-043-1 (cased) : £15.00 : CIP rev.
ISBN 0-86091-741-x (pbk) : Unpriced
B81-30146

963.1′36 — Scotland. Lothian Region. North Berwick. Archaeological investigation — *Proposals*

Simpson, Anne Turner. Historic North Berwick : the archaeological implications of development / Anne Turner Simpson, Sylvia Stevenson. — [Glasgow] ([The University, Glasgow, G12 8QG]) : University of Glasgow, 1981. — 21leaves,[3]leaves of plates(some folded) : maps,coat of arms ; 30cm. — (Scottish burgh survey)
Bibliography: p20-21
Unpriced (pbk) B82-00740

964 — HISTORY. MOROCCO

964′.02 — Morocco, *1576-1774* — *Readings from contemporary sources* — *Arabic-English parallel texts*

Letters from Barbary 1576-1774. — Oxford : Oxford University Press, Mar.1982. — [176]p. — (Oriental documents ; 6)
ISBN 0-19-726010-1 : £14.95 : CIP entry
Also classified at 965′.02 B82-06022

964′.04 — Morocco, *1900-1913*

Porch, Douglas. The conquest of Morocco. — London : Norman & Hobhouse, Feb.1983. — 1v.
ISBN 0-906908-70-1 : £9.95 : CIP entry
B82-39821

964.8 — HISTORY. WESTERN SAHARA

964′.8′00321 — Western Sahara, *to 1981* — *Encyclopaedias*

Hodges, Tony. Historical dictionary of Western Sahara / by Tony Hodges. — Metuchen ; London : Scarecrow Press, 1982. — xxxix, 431p : 1map ; 23cm. — (African historical dictionaries ; no.35)
Bibliography: p378-431
ISBN 0-8108-1497-8 : Unpriced B82-29214

964.9 — HISTORY. CANARY ISLANDS

964′.907 — Canary Islands, *ca 1480-1530*

Fernández-Armesto, Felipe. The Canary Islands after the conquest : the making of a colonial society in the early sixteenth century / Felipe Fernández-Armesto. — Oxford : Clarendon, 1982. — ix,244p : maps ; 23cm. — (Oxford historical monographs)
Bibliography: p225-232. — Includes index
ISBN 0-19-821888-5 : £19.50 : CIP rev.
B82-01081

965 — HISTORY. ALGERIA

965′.02 — Algeria, *1576-1774* — *Readings from contemporary sources* — *Arabic-English parallel texts*

Letters from Barbary 1576-1774. — Oxford : Oxford University Press, Mar.1982. — [176]p. — (Oriental documents ; 6)
ISBN 0-19-726010-1 : £14.95 : CIP entry
Primary classification 964′.02 B82-06022

965′.04 — Algeria. Social conditions, *1954-1959* — *Revolutionary viewpoints*

Fanon, Frantz. A dying colonialism / by Frantz Fanon ; translated from the French by Haakon Chevalier. — London : Writers and Readers, 1980, c1965. — 159p : 1port ; 20cm
Translation of: L′an cinq de la révolution Algérienne. — Originally published: New York : Monthly Review Press, 1965
ISBN 0-904613-98-4 (pbk) : £2.50 B82-06380

965′.3 — Algeria. Algiers. Bombardment by Great Britain. *Royal Navy* **&** *Netherlands. Marine, 1816*

Perkins, Roger. Gunfire in Barbary : Admiral Lord Exmouth's battle with the Corsairs of Algiers in 1816 — the story of the suppression of white Christian slavery / by Roger Perkins and K.J. Douglas-Morris. — Havant : Mason, c1982. — 200p : ill,facsims,maps,ports ; 23cm
Includes index
ISBN 0-85937-271-5 : £12.95 : CIP rev.
B82-10223

966 — HISTORY. WEST AFRICA

966 — West Africa. Social conditions — *For schools*

Green, Malcolm. Through the year in West Africa / Malcolm Green. — London : Batsford Academic and Educational, 1982. — 72p : ill,3maps,ports ; 26cm
Bibliography: p70. — Includes index
ISBN 0-7134-3964-5 : £5.95 B82-33309

966 — West Africa, *to 1980* — *For West African students*

Lucan, Talabi A.. A visual history of West Africa / Talabi A. Lucan. — London : Evans, 1981. — 76p : ill,maps,ports ; 25cm
ISBN 0-237-50145-7 (pbk) : Unpriced
B82-03573

966.3 — HISTORY. SENEGAL

966′.305 — Senegal

Gellar, Sheldon. Senegal. — Aldershot : Gower, Jan.1983. — [160]p. — (Profiles, nations of contemporary Africa)
ISBN 0-566-00551-4 : £10.50 : CIP entry
B82-32436

966.4 — HISTORY. SIERRA LEONE

966′.402 — Battle of Waima

Freestone, Basil. The horsemen from beyond / by Basil Freestone. — London : Dobson, 1981. — 264p,[16]p of plates : ill,maps,facsims,ports ; 24cm
Map on lining papers. — Bibliography: p249-250. — Includes index
ISBN 0-234-77211-5 : £8.95 B82-14709

966.52 — HISTORY. GUINEA REPUBLIC

966′.5205 — Guinea. Political events, *1958-1977*

Sékou Touré. — London : Panaf, c1978. — 208p,[4]p of plates : ill,1port ; 18cm. — (Panaf great lives)
ISBN 0-901787-43-4 (pbk) : £2.25 B82-31049

966.57 — HISTORY. GUINEA-BISSAU

966′.5702 — Guinea-Bissau. Political events, *1963-1980*

Davidson, Basil. No fist is big enough to hide the sky : the liberation of Guinea Bissau and Cape Verde. — London : Zed, July 1981. — [225]p
ISBN 0-905762-93-2 : £12.95 : CIP entry
Also classified at 966′.5802 B81-18047

966.58 — HISTORY. CAPE VERDE ISLANDS

966′.58 — Cape Verde Islands. Social conditions, *to 1976*

Carreira, Antonio. The people of the Cape Verde Islands. — London : Hurst, Sept.1982. — [226]p
Translation of: Migracoes nas Ilhas de Cabo Verde
ISBN 0-905838-68-8 : £11.00 : CIP entry
B82-22441

966′.5802 — Cape Verde Islands. Political events, *1963-1980*

Davidson, Basil. No fist is big enough to hide the sky : the liberation of Guinea Bissau and Cape Verde. — London : Zed, July 1981. — [225]p
ISBN 0-905762-93-2 : £12.95 : CIP entry
Primary classification 966′.5702 B81-18047

966.7 — HISTORY. GHANA

966.7 — Ghana. Ashanti. Cultural processes

McLeod, M. D. (Malcolm D.). The Asante / M.D. McLeod. — London : Published for the Trustees of the British Museum by British Museum Publications, c1981. — 192p,[8]p of plates : ill(some col.),1map,ports(some col.) ; 26cm
Accompanies the exhibition, Asante, Kingdom of gold, held at the Museum of Mankind in 1981. — Bibliography: p187-189. — Includes index
ISBN 0-7141-1564-9 (cased) : £12.95
ISBN 0-7141-1563-0 (pbk) : Unpriced
B82-14585

966.7′01 — Ghana, *to ca 1870.* **Archaeological sources**

Anquandah, James. Rediscovering Ghana's past / James Anquandah. — Harlow : Longman, 1982. — xii,161p : ill,maps,2ports ; 23cm
Bibliography: p145-149. — Includes index
ISBN 0-582-64309-0 (pbk) : £4.40 : CIP rev.
B82-01553

966.7′05 — Ghana. Political events, *1979*

Okeke, Barbara E.. 4 June : a revolution betrayed / Barbara E. Okeke. — Enugu ; Oxford (P.O. Box 83, Oxford OX2 6XD) : Ikenga, c1982. — 185p,[8]p of plates : ill,facsims,ports ; 20cm
£11.50 B82-22326

966.7′05′0924 — Ghana. Nkrumah, Kwame — *Biographies*

Timothy, Bankolé. Kwame Nkrumah from cradle to grave / by Bankole Timothy. — Dorchester, Dorset : Gavin Press, 1981. — viii,258p,[8]p of plates : ill,2maps,ports ; 23cm
Includes index
ISBN 0-905868-06-4 : £8.95 B82-18286

966.9 — HISTORY. NIGERIA

966.9 — Nigeria, *to 1971*

Studies in Southern Nigerian history / edited by Boniface I. Obichere. — London : Cass, 1982. — 265p : 1map ; 23cm
Bibliography: p245-260. — Includes index
ISBN 0-7146-3106-x : £17.50 : CIP rev.
B78-39399

966.9 — Nigeria, *to 1980*

Isichei, Elizabeth. A history of Nigeria. — London : Longman, Sept.1982. — [512]p
ISBN 0-582-64331-7 (cased) : £12.50 : CIP entry
ISBN 0-582-64330-9 (pbk) : £5.95 B82-22428

966.9 — Nigeria, *to 1981*

Morgan, W. T. W.. Nigeria. — London : Longman, Feb.1983. — [176]p. — (The World's landscapes)
ISBN 0-582-30003-7 (pbk) : £5.75 : CIP entry
B82-38675

966.9′004963 — Nigeria. Yoruba. Social life — *Case studies — For children*

Barker, Carol, *19---*. Kayodé and his village in Nigeria / written and illustrated by Carol Barker. — Oxford : Oxford University Press, c1982. — [40]p : col.ill ; 31cm
ISBN 0-19-279737-9 : £5.25 : CIP rev.
B81-12338

966.9′03′0924 — Nigeria. Niven, *Sir* **Rex** — *Biographies*

Niven, *Sir* **Rex**. Nigerian kaleidoscope. — London : Hurst, Sept.1982. — [350]p
ISBN 0-905838-59-9 : £12.50 : CIP entry
B82-22440

966.9′05 — Nigeria

Usman, Yusufu Bala. For the liberation of Nigeria : essays and lectures 1963-1978 / by Yusufu Bala Usman. — London : New Beacon, 1979. — 292p ; 18cm. — (A New Beacon book)
ISBN 0-901241-35-0 (pbk) : £3.45 B82-34722

966.9′05 — Nigeria. Society — *For Nigerian students*

Ogunniyi, 'Dayo. The Nigerian nation / 'Dayo Ogunniyi. — Rev. ed. — London : Evans, 1982. — iv,92p : ill,maps,1coat of arms,ports ; 25cm. — (Social studies for schools and colleges ; bk.2)
Previous ed.: 1979. — Includes bibliographies
ISBN 0-237-50658-0 (pbk) : Unpriced
B82-13397

Ogunniyi, 'Dayo. The Nigerian nation / 'Dayo Ogunniyi. — Ibadan ; London : Evans. — (Social studies for schools and colleges ; 2)
Previous ed.: 1979
Teacher's book. — Rev. ed. — 1982. — 92p ; 22cm
ISBN 0-237-50659-9 (pbk) : Unpriced
B82-06666

966.9′05 — Nigerian civilization. Ethical aspects

Amadi, Elechi. Ethics in Nigerian culture / Elechi Amadi. — Ibadan ; London : Heinemann Educational, 1982. — viii,120p : 1map ; 22cm
Bibliography: p117. — Includes index
ISBN 0-435-89030-1 (pbk) : Unpriced : CIP rev.
ISBN 978-12-9596-1 (Nigeria) B82-04070

966.9′05′0924 — Nigeria. Shagari, Shehu — *Biographies*

Williams, David, *1913-*. The life of Shehu Shagari : President and power in Nigeria / David Williams ; with a foreword by Kurt Waldheim. — London : Cass, 1982. — xxvi,276p,[18]p of plates : ill,ports ; 23cm
Bibliography: p270. — Includes index
ISBN 0-7146-3182-5 (cased) : £12.50 : CIP rev.
ISBN 0-7146-4036-0 (pbk) : £6.00 B82-09305

966.9′2′004963 — Nigeria. Western states. Egba, *to ca 1920*

Gailey, Harry A.. Lugard and the Abẹokuta uprising : the demise of Ẹgba independence / Harry A. Gailey. — London : Cass, 1982. — x,138p : 1map ; 23cm
Bibliography: p129-132. — Includes index
ISBN 0-7146-3114-0 : £15.00 : CIP rev.
B79-04016

966.9′5 — Nigeria. Plateau *(State), to 1949*

Studies in the history of Plateau State, Nigeria / edited by Elizabeth Isichei. — London : Macmillan, 1982. — xvi,288p,[12]p of plates : ill,maps ; 23cm
Includes index
ISBN 0-333-26931-4 : £25.00 : CIP rev.
B80-04032

966.9′5 — Nigeria. Zaria region. Muslim Hausa women. Social life, *1900-1950* — *Personal observations*

Baba, *of Karo*. Baba of Karo : a woman of the Muslim Hausa / [written down by] Mary F. Smith ; introduction and notes by M.G. Smith ; foreword by Hilda Kuper. — New Haven ; London : Yale University Press, c1981. — 299p,[4]p of plates : ill,ports ; 22cm
Originally published: London : Faber, 1954. — Includes index
ISBN 0-300-02734-6 (cased) : £17.50 : CIP rev.
ISBN 0-300-02741-9 (pbk) : Unpriced
B81-32084

966.9′500421 — Nigeria. Northern states. Britons. Social life, *1951-1960* — *Personal observations*

Hollis, Rosemary. A scorpion for tea or to attempt the impossible / Rosemary Hollis. — Ilfracombe : Stockwell, 1981. — 183p : ill ; 22cm
Ill on lining papers
ISBN 0-7223-1538-4 : £7.15 B82-12281

966.9′5004963 — Edinburgh. Museums: Royal Scottish Museum. Exhibits: Northern Nigerian Hausa artefacts. Collections: Miller collection — *Catalogues*

Royal Scottish Museum. The Hausa of northern Nigeria : a catalogue of the R.E. Miller collection and others in the Royal Scottish Museum / by Dale Idiens. — Edinburgh (Chambers St., Edinburgh EH1 1JF) : Royal Scottish Museum, 1981. — 71p,[8]p of plates : ill(some col.),2maps ; 25cm. — (Royal Scottish Museum studies)
ISBN 0-900733-21-7 (pbk) : Unpriced
B82-23971

967 — HISTORY. CENTRAL AFRICA

967 — Africa. Portuguese speaking countries. Political events — *History — Serials*
People's power in Mozambique, Angola and Guinea-Bissau. — No.5 (1976)-. — London (34 Percy St., WIP 9FG) : Mozambique, Angola and Guine Information Centre, 1976-. — v. : ill,ports ; 22cm
Quarterly. — Continues: People's power in Mozambique and Guinea Bissau. — Description based on: No.14 (Summer 1979)
ISSN 0260-6704 = People's power in Mozambique, Angola and Guinea-Bissau : £2.50 per year B82-17260

967 — Africa south of the Sahara. Role of Scottish persons: Grampian Region persons, *ca 1780-ca 1980*
Hargreaves, John D.. Aberdeenshire to Africa. — Aberdeen : Aberdeen University Press, Dec.1981. — [150]p
ISBN 0-08-025764-x : £9.00 : CIP entry B81-31358

967 — Africa south of the Sahara. Social change. Political aspects
Smith, Anthony D.. State and nation in the Third World. — Brighton : Harvester, Dec.1982. — [192]p
ISBN 0-7108-0199-8 (cased) : £15.95 : CIP entry
ISBN 0-7108-0189-0 (pbk) : £4.95 B82-30084

967 — Central & East Africa. Prehistoric settlements. Archaeological investigation
Hodder, Ian. Symbols in action : ethnoarchaeological studies of material culture / Ian Hodder. — Cambridge : Cambridge University Press, 1982. — x,244p : ill,maps ; 24cm. — (New studies in archaeology)
Bibliography: p230-238. — Includes index
ISBN 0-521-24176-6 : £19.50 : CIP rev. B81-36953

967 — Central Africa, *to 1870*
Birmingham, David. Central Africa to 1870 : Zambezia, Zaïre and the South Atlantic : chapters from the Cambridge History of Africa / David Birmingham. — Cambridge : Cambridge University Press, 1981. — vii,177p : maps ; 24cm
Chapters 1-3 originally published in the Cambridge history of Africa vols 3-5 respectively. — Bibliography: p159-164. — Includes index
ISBN 0-521-24116-2 (cased) : £15.00
ISBN 0-521-28444-9 (pbk) : £4.95 B82-15281

967'.005 — Africa south of the Sahara — *Serials*
Africa south of the Sahara. — 11th ed. (1981-82). — London : Europe, Aug.1981. — [1412]p
ISBN 0-905118-64-2 : CIP entry
ISSN 0065-3896 B81-16915

Africa south of the Sahara. — 12th ed. (1982-83). — London : Europa, Aug.1982. — [1407]p
ISBN 0-905118-74-x : CIP entry
ISSN 0065-3896 B82-17225

967.3 — HISTORY. ANGOLA

967'.304 — Angola. Political events. Policies of government of United States, *1975-1981*
Holness, Marga. Memorandum on The Clark Amendment : the U.S. threat to destabilise Angola / by Marga Holness. — London (34 Percy St., W2P 9FG) : Mozambique, Angola & Guiné Information Centre, 1981. — 5p ; 30cm
£0.40 (unbound) B82-01462

967.51 — HISTORY. ZAIRE

967.5'103 — Zaire. Pygmies. Social life — *For children*
Andrews, Ian. Pygmies move camp / [by Ian Andrews] ; [adapted from the Dutch of Francis Brewer] ; [illustrated by The Tjong Khing]. — Cambridge : Cambridge University Press, 1980. — 16p : ill(some col.),2maps(some col.) ; 22cm. — (Pole star series. People)
Cover title
ISBN 0-521-23006-3 (pbk) : Unpriced
ISBN 0-521-23220-1 (set) : Unpriced B82-39479

967.5'103'0924 — Zaire. Political events. Role of Mobutu, Sese Seko, *1965-1981 — Personal observations — French texts*
Nguza, Karl i Bond. Mobutu, ou, L'Incarnation du mal Zaïrois / Nguza Karl i Bond. — London : Collings, 1982. — 201p,[8]p of plates : ill,facsims,ports ; 23cm
ISBN 0-86036-197-7 : £11.00 B82-35956

967.6 — HISTORY. EAST AFRICA

967.6 — East Africa, *1900-1980*
Nabudere, D. Wadada. Imperialism in East Africa / D. Wadada Nabudere. — London : Zed. — (Africa series)
Vol.1: Imperialism and exploitation. — 1981. — 132p ; 23cm
ISBN 0-905762-99-1 : £16.95 : CIP rev. B81-20522

967.6 — East Africa, *ca 1900-1980*
Nabudere, D. Wadada. Imperialism in East Africa. — London : Zed Press
Vol.2: Imperialism and integration. — July 1982. — [192]p
ISBN 0-905762-05-3 : £16.95 : CIP entry B82-19290

967.61 — HISTORY. UGANDA

967.6'1 — Uganda. Teso. Social conditions, *1894-1927*
Vincent, Joan. Teso in transformation : the political economy of peasant and class in Eastern Africa / Joan Vincent. — Berkeley ; London : University of California Press, 1982. — viii,307p ; 23cm
Bibliography: p265-295. — Includes index
ISBN 0-520-04163-1 : £21.50 B82-31099

967.6'104 — Uganda, *1967-1971*
Uganda's first republic. — Cambridge (Cambridge University, Free School La., Cambridge CB2 3RQ) : African Studies Centre, Oct.1982. — [189]p
ISBN 0-902993-08-9 (pbk) : £5.00 : CIP entry B82-36161

967.62 — HISTORY. KENYA

967.6'2 — Kenya, *to 1979*
Tichy, Herbert. The magical world of Kenya / Herbert Tichy. — Innsbruck : Pinguin ; London : distributed by Kaye & Ward, c1980. — 175p : ill(some col.),3maps ; 28cm
Translation from the German. — Maps on lining papers. — Includes index
ISBN 0-7182-5370-1 : £9.95 B82-36668

967.6'2004963 — Kenya. Akamba — *For primary school teaching*
Nzioki, Sammy. Akamba / Sammy Nzioki. — London : Evans Brothers, 1982. — v,42p : ill,2maps,2plans,1port ; 22cm. — (Kenya's people)
ISBN 0-237-50491-x (pbk) : Unpriced B82-39937

967.6'201 — Kenya, *to 1895 — For schools*
Spear, Thomas. Kenya's past : an introduction to historical method in Africa / Thomas Spear. — Harlow : Longman, 1981. — xxiv,155p : ill,maps,1facsim ; 24cm. — (Longman studies in African history)
Bibliography: p145-146. — Includes index
ISBN 0-582-64696-0 (cased) : Unpriced : CIP rev.
ISBN 0-582-64695-2 (pbk) : £4.95 B81-34556

967.6'203 — Kenya. Colonisation by Great Britain. Resistance by Giriama, *1800-1920*
Brantley, Cynthia. The Giriama and colonial resistance in Kenya 1800-1920 / Cynthia Brantley. — Berkeley ; London : University of California Press, c1981. — xvi,196p : maps ; 25cm
Bibliography: p173-189. — Includes index
ISBN 0-520-04216-6 : £22.50 B82-31176

967.6'203 — Kenya. Social change, *1905-1970 — Marxist viewpoints*
Kitching, G. N.. Class and economic change in Kenya. — London : Yale University Press, July 1982. — [448]p
ISBN 0-300-02929-2 (pbk) : £8.95 : CIP entry B82-22776

967.6'203'0924 — Kenya. Ricciardi, Mirella — *Biographies*
Ricciardi, Mirella. African saga / Mirella Ricciardi. — London : Collins, 1981. — 300p : ill,ports,1geneal.table ; 25cm
Ill on lining papers
ISBN 0-00-216191-5 : £9.95 : CIP rev. B81-30261

967.6'204 — Kenya, *1963-1981*
Independent Kenya. — London : Zed Press, Oct.1982. — [160]p
ISBN 0-86232-078-x (cased) : £11.95 : CIP entry
ISBN 0-86232-079-8 (pbk) : £5.95 B82-32876

967.6'204 — Kenya. Cultural processes
Fedders, Andrew. Peoples and cultures of Kenya / text and colour photographs by Andrew Fedders ; black and white photographs by Cynthia Salvadori. — Nairobi : Transafrica ; London : Rex Collins in association with KTDC, [1981]. — 167p : ill,maps ; 30cm
Bibliography: p164. — Includes index
£12.95 B82-01633

967.6'204 — Kenya. Social conditions
Arnold, Guy. Modern Kenya / Guy Arnold. — London : Longman, 1981. — 156p : ill,maps,ports ; 24cm
Includes index
ISBN 0-582-64286-8 (cased) : Unpriced
ISBN 0-582-64287-6 (pbk) : £3.95 B82-07569

967.6'204'0924 — Kenya. Politics. Mboya, Tom — *Biographies*
Goldsworthy, David. Tom Mboya : the man Kenya wanted to forget / David Goldsworthy. — Nairobi ; London : Heinemann, 1982. — xii,308p : 1port ; 24cm
List of Mboya's writings: p295-299. — Includes index
ISBN 0-435-96275-2 : £13.00 : CIP rev. B81-34569

967.6'2504 — Kenya. Nairobi. Aircraft. Accidents, *1974.* **Survivors' experiences**
Moorhouse, Earl. Wake Up, it's a crash! : the story of the first 747-jet disaster — a survivor's account / Earl Moorhouse. — London : Corgi, 1982, c1980. — 172p,[16]p of plates : ill,1plan,ports ; 18cm
Originally published: Newton Abbot : David & Charles, 1980. — Includes index
ISBN 0-552-11932-6 (pbk) : £1.50 B82-24933

967.62'7 — Kenya. Koobi Fora region. Prehistoric antiquities. Archaeological investigation
Koobi Fora Research Project. — Oxford : Clarendon Press. — (Koobi Fora researches into geology, palaeontology, and human origins)
Vol.2: The fossil ungulates: proboscidea, perissodactyla, and suidae. — Nov.1982. — [400]p
ISBN 0-19-857398-7 : £40.00 : CIP entry B82-26875

967.6'27 — Kenya. Lake Turkana region. Tribal societies. Cultural processes
Amin, Mohamed. Cradle of mankind / Mohamed Amin ; with a foreword by Richard Leakey. — London : Chatto & Windus, 1981. — 191p : chiefly col.ill,col.maps,col.ports ; 31cm
Ill on lining papers. — Bibliography: p191
ISBN 0-7011-2587-x : £14.95 : CIP rev. B81-23746

967.8 — HISTORY. TANZANIA

967'.8 — Tanzania, *to 1981*
Yeager, Rodger. Tanzania. — Aldershot : Gower, July 1982. — [152]p. — (Profiles, nations of contemporary Africa)
ISBN 0-566-00554-9 : £10.50 : CIP entry B82-10804

967.8'04 — Tanzania. Social conditions
Knights, Ian E.. Tanzania : an outline guide for expatriate contract employees / [Ian E. Knights]. — [16th ed.]. — London : Royal Commonwealth Society, 1981. — 16p : 2maps ; 30cm. — (Notes on conditions)
Previous ed.: 1979. — Bibliography: p15-16
ISBN 0-905067-93-2 (unbound) : Unpriced B82-05458

967.8′1 — Tanzania. Zanzibar. Political events, *to 1972*

Clayton, Anthony. The Zanzibar revolution and its aftermath. — London : Hurst, May 1981. — [170]p
ISBN 0-905838-58-0 : £10.50 : CIP entry
B81-07465

967.9 — HISTORY. MOZAMBIQUE

967′.903 — Mozambique. Political events *ca 1945-1969*

Mondlane, Eduardo. The struggle for Mozambique. — London : Zed Press, Oct.1982. — [256]p
Originally published: Harmondsworth : Penguin, 1969
ISBN 0-86232-016-x (pbk) : £5.95 : CIP entry
B82-33359

968 — HISTORY. SOUTHERN AFRICA

968 — South Africa, *to 1977*

Were, Gideon S.. A history of South Africa / Gideon S. Were. — 2nd ed. — London : Evans Brothers, c1982. — x,230p : ill,maps,facsims,ports ; 21cm
Previous ed.: 1974. — Bibliography: p226. — Includes index
ISBN 0-237-50563-0 (pbk) : Unpriced
B82-10717

968 — Southern Africa, *ca 1800- ca 1970*

The **Societies** of Southern Africa in the 17th and 20th centuries. — London : University of London, Institute of Commonwealth Studies. — (Collected seminar papers / University of London. Institute of Commonwealth Studies ; no.28)
Vol.12. — 1981. — 116p ; 30cm
ISBN 0-902499-29-7 (pbk) : Unpriced
B82-21042

968 — Southern Africa. Frontier life, *to 1900 compared with* **frontier life in North America,** *to 1900*

The **Frontier** in history : North America and Southern Africa compared / edited by Howard Lamar and Leonard Thompson. — New Haven ; London : Yale University Press, c1981. — xii,360p : 8maps ; 25cm
Bibliography: p317-333. — Includes index
ISBN 0-300-02624-2 : Unpriced
Primary classification 970
B82-08941

968 — Southern Africa, *to 1980*

Hull, Richard W.. Southern Africa : civilizations in turmoil / Richard W. Hull. — New York ; London : New York University Press, c1981. — vii,168p : ill,2maps ; 24cm
Includes bibliographies and index
ISBN 0-8147-3410-3 (cased) : £13.00
ISBN 0-8147-3411-1 (pbk) : £6.70 B82-38254

968 — Southern Africa, *to 1980 — For schools*

Leeming, Donald. 'O' level Southern African history / Donald Leeming. — Harlow : Longman, 1981. — 92p : maps ; 22cm. — (Study for success) (Certificate notes)
ISBN 0-582-60392-7 (pbk) : Unpriced
B82-30546

968 — Southern Africa, *to 1980 — For Southern African students*

Junior Certificate history of Southern Africa. — London : Heinemann
Bk.1: Southern African societies before the Scramble / Boleswa History Project ; editor Ngwabi Bhebe ; writing team N. Bhebe ... [et al.]. — 1979. — 144p : ill,maps,ports ; 22cm
Bibliography: p141. — Includes index
ISBN 0-435-94160-7 (pbk) : £2.10 : CIP rev.
B79-34642

Junior Certificate history of Southern Africa. — London : Heinemann Educational
Bk.3: The modern world / Boleswa History Project ; editor P.M. Pule ; writing team N. Bhebe ... [et al.]. — 1982. — xiv,130p : ill,maps,ports ; 22cm
Bibliography: p127. — Includes index
ISBN 0-435-94760-5 (pbk) : £2.40 : CIP rev.
B82-11274

Parsons, Neil, *19---*. A new history of southern Africa / by Neil Parsons. — London : Macmillan Education, 1982. — vi,330p : ill,maps,ports ; 25cm
Bibliography: p321-325. — Includes index
ISBN 0-333-26220-4 (pbk) : £3.95 B82-37762

968 — Southern Africa, *to 1981 — For East African students — For schools*

Parker, Graham. History of Southern Africa. — 2nd ed. — London : Bell & Hyman, Jan.1982. — [308]p
Previous ed.: 1975
ISBN 0-7135-1215-6 (pbk) : £5.95 : CIP entry
B81-33836

968′.0043936 — South Africa. Afrikaners, *1838-1980*

Harrison, David, *19---*. The white tribe of Africa : South Africa in perspective / David Harrison. — London : British Broadcasting Corporation, 1981. — vii,307p : ill,1map,ports ; 24cm
Map on lining papers. — Bibliography: p286-290. — Includes index
ISBN 0-563-17838-8 : £8.95 B82-02598

968.04′092′4 — South Africa. Politics. Merriman, John X. *— Biographies*

Lewsen, Phyllis. John X. Merriman : paradoxical South African statesman. — London : Yale University Press, Apr.1982. — [448]p
ISBN 0-300-02521-1 : £28.00 : CIP entry
B82-14203

968.04′8 — Boer War

Pakenham, Thomas. The Boer War / Thomas Pakenham. — London : Macdonald, 1982, c1979. — xxii,659p,[16]p of plates : ill,1map,plans,ports ; 20cm
Originally published: London : Weidenfeld and Nicolson, 1979. — Bibliography: p587-594. — Includes index
ISBN 0-7088-1892-7 (pbk) : £5.95 B82-20999

968.04′8′0924 — Boer War. Army operations by Boer Army *— Personal observations*

Reitz, Deneys. Commando : a Boer journal of the Boer war / Deneys Reitz ; introduction by Leo Cooper ; preface by J.C. Smuts. — London : Folio Society, 1982. — xv,276p,12leaves of plates : ill,1map,ports ; 23cm
'The text of this edition is taken from the revised edition of 1932'—t.p. verso. — Map on inside covers. — In slip case. — Includes index
Unpriced B82-31271

968.06′2 — South Africa. Political events, *1974-1976*

Nolutshungu, Sam C.. Changing South Africa : political considerations / Sam C. Nolutshungu. — Manchester : Manchester University Press, c1982. — xvii,219p ; 23cm
Bibliography: p208-212. — Includes index
ISBN 0-7190-0860-3 : £19.50 : CIP rev.
B82-00385

968.06′2 — Southern Africa. Political events. Role of Tanzania & United States, *1976*

Nyerere, Julius K.. Crusade for liberation / Julius K. Nyerere ; introductory material by the Press Office, State House, Dar es Salaam. — Dar es Salaam ; Oxford : Oxford University Press, 1978. — 94p,[8]p of plates : ill,ports ; 21cm
ISBN 0-19-572462-3 (pbk) : £1.95 B82-14604

968.06′3 — South Africa. Policies of British government *— Fabian viewpoints*

Against all reason : Britain and South Africa in the eighties / a Fabian group [i.e.] Margaret Legum ... [et al.]. — London : Fabian Society, 1981. — 38p ; 21cm. — (Fabian tract, ISSN 0307-7535 ; 478)
Cover title. — Text on inside cover
£0.90 (pbk) B82-06346

968.06′3 — South Africa. Social conditions

Study Commission on U.S. Policy Toward Southern Africa. South Africa : time running out / the report of the Study Commission on U.S. Policy Toward Southern Africa. — Berkeley ; London : University of California Press, c1981. — xxvii,517p,[24]p of plates : ill,col.maps,ports ; 24cm
Bibliography: p479-490. — Includes index
ISBN 0-520-04594-7 (corrected : cased) : Unpriced
ISBN 0-520-04547-5 (pbk) : Unpriced
Also classified at 327.73068 ; 327.68073
B82-17876

968.06′3′05 — Southern Africa. Political events *— Readings from contemporary sources — Serials*

ANC weekly news briefing. — [Vol.1, issue no.1?]-. — London (PO Box 38, 28 Penton St., N1) : African National Congress, [197-]-. — v. ; 21cm
Description based on: Vol.6, issue no.3 (Jan. 14th 1982)
ISSN 0263-1989 = ANC weekly news briefing : £52.00 per year B82-25486

968.1′103′0924 — Botswana. Kalahari Desert. ! Kung women. Social life *— Personal observations*

Nisa. Nisa : the life and words of a !Kung woman / Marjorie Shostak. — London : Allen Lane, 1982, c1981. — 402p : ill,ports ; 25cm
Originally published: Cambridge, Mass. : Harvard University Press, 1981. — Includes index
ISBN 0-7139-1486-6 : £12.95 B82-38761

968.1′601′0924 — Lesotho. Sotho. Moshoeshoe, *Chief of the Basotho — Biographies*

Becker, Peter. Hill of destiny : the life and times of Moshesh, founder of the Basotho / Peter Becker. — Harmondsworth : Penguin, 1982, c1969. — 304p,[8]p of plates : ill,1map,ports ; 19cm
Originally published: London : Longman, 1969. — Bibliography: p289-292. — Includes index
ISBN 0-14-005978-4 (pbk) : £1.95 B82-26441

968.1′602 — Lesotho, *1871-1884*

Burman, Sandra. Chiefdom politics and alien laws : Basutoland under Cape rule 1871-1884 / Sandra Burman. — London : Macmillan in association with St Antony′s College, Oxford, 1981. — xii,250p,[17]p of plates : ill,maps,ports ; 23cm. — (St Antony′s/Macmillan series)
Bibliography: p229-244. — Includes index
ISBN 0-333-26442-8 : £20.00 : CIP rev.
B80-20289

968.2 — South Africa. North-West Transvaal. Boshier, Adrian *— Biographies*

Watson, Lyall. Lightning bird : the story of one man′s journey into Africa′s past / Lyall Watson. — London : Hodder and Stoughton, c1982. — xiv,241p : ill ; 23cm
Bibliography: p234-235. — Includes index
ISBN 0-340-27999-0 : £7.95 : CIP rev.
B82-12000

968.2′0475 — South Africa. Transvaal. Jameson Raid

Longford, Elizabeth. Jameson′s Raid : the prelude to the Boer War / Elizabeth Longford. — New ed. — London : Weidenfeld and Nicolson, 1982. — xvii,314p,[8]p of plates : ill,facsims,1map,ports ; 24cm
Previous ed.: 1960. — Bibliography: p299-302. — Includes index
ISBN 0-297-78136-7 : £12.50 B82-35673

968.2′2 — South Africa. Randfontein. Gold mining industries. Miners. Social life, *1900-1904 — Personal observations — Correspondence, diaries, etc.*

Tucker, Joseph. Letters of a South African miner, 1898-1904 / written by Joseph Tucker to his son, Joseph Wherry Tucker ; edited by his grandson, Norman E. Hannan. — Romford : N.E. Hannan, c1981. — 37p : 3ports ; 21cm
Limited ed. of 119 numbered copies. — Text on inside cover
ISBN 0-9507912-0-2 (pbk) : Unpriced
B82-22476

968.4'04 — South Africa. Natal. Zulu, *1816-1884*
Morris, Donald R.. The washing of the spears / Donald R. Morris. — London : Sphere, 1968, c1965 (1981 [printing]). — 670p : maps ; 18cm
Originally published: London : Cape, 1966. — Bibliography: p622-630. — Includes index
ISBN 0-7221-6178-6 (pbk) : £2.95 B82-00079

968.4'045 — Zulu War. Army operations by Great Britain. *Army. Regiment of Foot, 24th*
Holme, Norman. The Silver Wreath : being the 24th regiment at Isandhlwana and Rorke's Drift, 1879 / Norman Holme. — London : Samson, c1979. — 95p,[8]p of plates : ill,facsims,plans,ports ; 30cm
Bibliography: p8
ISBN 0-906304-04-0 : £9.50 B82-10998

968.7'00421 — South Africa. Cape Province. British settlers, *1795-1819 — Biographies*
Philip, Peter. British residents at the Cape 1795-1819 : biographical records of 4800 pioneers / Peter Philip. — Cape Town : David Philip ; London : Global [distributor], c1981. — xxiii,484p ; 22cm
Bibliography: p481-484
ISBN 0-908396-46-5 : £14.80 B82-15528

968.8'03 — Namibia. Political events, *ca 1970-1982 — Christian viewpoints*
Namibia in the 1980's. — London : Catholic Institute for International Relations, Oct.1981. — [64]p
ISBN 0-904393-58-5 (pbk) : CIP entry B81-31179

968.8'03 — Namibia. Political events — *SWAPO viewpoints*
To be born a nation : the liberation struggle for Namibia. — London : Zed Press, Dec.1981. — [360]p
ISBN 0-905762-34-7 : £18.95 : CIP entry B82-01350

To be born a nation : the liberation struggle for Namibia / Department of Information and Publicity, SWAPO of Namibia. — London : Zed, 1981. — v,357p : ill,maps,ports ; 22cm
Bibliography: p349-355
ISBN 0-905762-73-8 (pbk) : £4.95 B82-01763

968.8'03 — Namibia. Social conditions
Namibia : the last colony / edited by Reginald H. Green, Kimmo Kiljunen, Marja-Liisa Kiljunen. — Harlow : Longman, 1981. — ix,310p : maps,1plan ; 24cm
Bibliography: p293-303. — Includes index
ISBN 0-582-59734-x (cased) : Unpriced : CIP rev.
ISBN 0-582-59735-8 (pbk) : £5.95 B81-02113

968.91 — HISTORY. ZIMBABWE

968.91 — Zimbabwe. Political events, *1890-1980*
Ndlovu, Kimpton. Zimbabwe is free : a short history of the struggle for national liberation in Southern Rhodesia / by Kimpton Ndlovu ; illustrations by Jan Flavell. — 2nd ed. — London : Liberation, 1980. — 19p : ill,1map,1port ; 21x30cm
Previous ed.: 1979
ISBN 0-905405-02-1 (pbk) : £0.75 B82-19438

968.91 — Zimbabwe, *to 1980*
Past and present in Zimbabwe. — Manchester : Manchester University Press, Nov.1982. — [128]p
ISBN 0-7190-0896-4 (pbk) : £8.50 : CIP entry B82-39260

968.91'04 — Zimbabwe. Political events, *1820-1980*
Martin, David, *1936-*. The struggle for Zimbabwe : the Chimurenga War / David Martin and Phyllis Johnson. — London : Faber, 1981 (1982 [printing]). — xvii,378p,[16]p of plates : ill,2maps,ports ; 20cm
Includes index
ISBN 0-571-11887-9 (pbk) : Unpriced : CIP rev. B82-07848

968.91'04 — Zimbabwe. Political events, *1976-1980*
Caute, David. Under the skin : the death of white Rhodesia. — London : Allen Lane, Feb.1983. — 1v.
ISBN 0-7139-1357-6 : CIP entry B82-39439

968.91'04 — Zimbabwe. Social conditions
Zimbabwe's inheritance / edited by Colin Stoneman. — London : Macmillan, 1981. — xiii,234p : ill,maps ; 23cm. — (Contemporary African issues series)
Bibliography: p220-227. — Includes index
ISBN 0-333-31021-7 (cased) : Unpriced
ISBN 0-333-31022-5 (pbk) : Unpriced B82-21414

968.91'04'0924 — Zimbabwe. Mugabe, Robert — *Biographies*
Smith, David, *19---*. Mugabe / David Smith and Colin Simpson with Ian Davies. — London : Sphere, 1981. — 217p,[16]p of plates : 1ill,ports ; 18cm
ISBN 0-7221-7868-9 (pbk) : £1.50 B82-36381

968.94 — HISTORY. ZAMBIA

968.94'02 — Zambia. Occupation by Great Britain, *1884-1924*
Macpherson, Fergus. Anatomy of a conquest : the British occupation of Zambia, 1884-1924 / Fergus Macpherson. — Harlow : Longman, 1981. — 266p : 2maps ; 22cm
Bibliography: p243-253. — Includes index
ISBN 0-582-64679-0 : £18.75 B82-07458

969 — HISTORY. INDIAN OCEAN ISLANDS

969'.101 — Madagascar. Pirates. Social life, *ca 1690*
Law, Larry. Misson and Libertatia / retold by Larry Law. — London (Box 99, 84b Whitechapel High St., E1 7QX) : Spectacular Times, 1980. — 25p : 1facsim ; 21cm
Unpriced (pbk) B82-25393

969'.6 — Seychelles Islands, *1971-1980*
Franda, Marcus. The Seychelles. — Aldershot : Gower, Dec.1982. — [140]p. — (Nations of contemporary Africa)
ISBN 0-566-00552-2 : £10.50 : CIP entry B82-30053

969'.82'00321 — Mauritius, *to 1980 — Encyclopaedias*
Riviere, Lindsay. Historical dictionary of Mauritius / by Lindsay Riviere. — Metuchen ; London : Scarecrow, 1982. — xxxiv,172p : 1map ; 23cm. — (African historical dictionaries ; no.34)
Bibliography: p141-172
ISBN 0-8108-1479-x : £10.80 B82-29250

970 — HISTORY. NORTH AMERICA

970 — North America. Frontier life, *to 1900 compared with* **frontier life in Southern Africa,** *to 1900*
The Frontier in history : North America and Southern Africa compared / edited by Howard Lamar and Leonard Thompson. — New Haven ; London : Yale University Press, c1981. — xii,360p : 8maps ; 25cm
Bibliography: p317-333. — Includes index
ISBN 0-300-02624-2 : Unpriced
Also classified at 968 B82-08941

970.004'31 — North America. German immigrants. Social life, *1683-1979.* **Historical sources. Collections** — *Directories*
Hobbie, Margaret. Museums, sites and collections of Germanic culture in North America : an annotated directory of German immigrant culture in the United States and Canada / compiled by Margaret Hobbie. — Westport ; London : Greenwood Press, 1980. — xix,155p ; 25cm
Bibliography: p123-127. — Includes index
ISBN 0-313-22060-3 : Unpriced B82-14979

970.004'931 — America. Ancient Egyptian civilization — *Sources of data: Antiquities*
Jairazbhoy, R. A.. Ancient Egyptians in Middle and South America / R.A. Jairazbhoy. — London : Ra, c1981. — vi,101p : ill,1map ; 22cm. — (Old World origins of American civilisation ; v.3)
ISBN 0-9505006-1-5 (pbk) : Unpriced B82-28389

970.004'97 — American Indian artefacts
The **Other** America. — Colchester (Wivenhoe Park, Colchester, Essex) : University of Essex, Aug.1982. — [95]p
ISBN 0-901726-20-6 (pbk) : £0.60 : CIP entry B82-28608

970.004'97 — Arizona. Hopi. Social life — *For children*
Peck, Mary C. E.. Hopi rain dance / [by Mary C.E. Peck] ; [adapted from the Dutch of Francis Brewer] ; [illustrated by Bert Zeijlstra]. — Cambridge : Cambridge University Press, 1980. — 16p : ill(some col.),2maps(some col.) ; 22cm. — (Pole star series. People)
Cover title
ISBN 0-521-23005-5 (pbk) : Unpriced
ISBN 0-521-23220-1 (set) : Unpriced B82-39478

970.004'97 — California. Yahi. Ishi — *Biographies*
Kroeber, Theodora. Ishi in two worlds : a biography of the last wild Indian in North America / Theodora Kroeber. — [Deluxe, illustrated ed.]. — Berkeley ; London : University of California Press, c1976. — 262p,[24]p of plates : ill(some col.),maps,2facsims,ports ; 26cm
Bibliography: p253-259. — Includes index
ISBN 0-520-03153-9 (pbk) : £6.25 B82-06974

970'.004'97 — Eastern North America. Indians of North America. Social life, *1600-1900*
King, J. C. H.. Thunderbird and Lightning : Indian life in northeastern North America 1600-1900. — London : British Museum Publications, June 1982. — [96]p
ISBN 0-7141-1567-3 (pbk) : £5.95 : CIP entry B82-14382

970.004'97 — Eskimo civilization — *For children*
Siska, Heather Smith. People of the ice : how the Inuit lived / Heather Smith Siska ; illustrations by Ian Bateson. — Vancouver ; Edinburgh : Douglas & McIntyre, c1980. — 47p : ill,2maps ; 29cm. — (How they lived in Canada)
ISBN 0-88894-287-7 : £3.95 B82-09054

970.004'97 — Greenland. Eskimos. Social life — *For children*
Benson, Barbara. Hunter in Greenland / [by Barbara Benson] ; [adapted from the Dutch of Francis Brewer] ; [illustrated by Kees de Kiefte]. — Cambridge : Cambridge University Press, 1980. — 16p : ill(some col.),2maps(some col.) ; 22cm. — (Pole star series. People)
Cover title
ISBN 0-521-23004-7 (pbk) : Unpriced
ISBN 0-521-23220-1 (set) : Unpriced B82-39476

970.004'97 — North America. Shawnee. Social life
Howard, James H. (James Henri). Shawnee! : the ceremonialism of a native Indian tribe and its cultural background / James H. Howard. — Athens [Ohio] ; London : Ohio University Press, c1981. — xvi,454p : ill,maps,music,ports ; 24cm
Bibliography: p425-436. — Includes index
ISBN 0-8214-0417-2 (cased) : Unpriced
ISBN 0-8214-0614-0 (pbk) : £11.25 B82-30094

970.004'97 — North American Indian antiquities. Archaeological investigation
Foundations of northeast archaeology / edited by Dean R. Snow. — New York ; London : Academic Press, 1981. — xiv,266p : ill,maps ; 24cm. — (Studies in archaeology)
Includes bibliographies and index
ISBN 0-12-653960-x : £13.00 B82-29600

970.004'97 — North American Indians. Attitudes of Europeans, *1590-1634 — Sources of data: Flemish copperplate engravings. Bry, Theodore de*
Bucher, Bernadette. Icon and conquest : a structural analysis of the illustrations of de Bry's Great voyages / Bernadette Bucher ; translated by Basia Miller Gulati. — Chicago ; London : University of Chicago Press, 1981. — xvii,220p,[20]p of plates : ill,maps,facsims ; 22cm. — (Chicago originals)
Translation of: La Sauvage aux seins pendants. — Bibliography: p203-214. — Includes index
ISBN 0-226-07832-9 (pbk) : £9.95 B82-17776

970.004′97 — North American Indians. Cultural processes. Influence of Christian missions, *1492-1980*

Bowden, Henry Warner. American Indians and Christian missions : studies in cultural conflict / Henry Warner Bowden. — Chicago ; London : University of Chicago Press, 1981. — xix,255p ; 22cm. — (Chicago history of American religion)
Includes index
ISBN 0-226-06811-0 : £10.50 B82-13670

970.004′97 — Pacific Northwest. Nez Percé. Social life, *1889-1892 — Correspondence, diaries, etc.*

Gay, E. Jane. With the Nez Perces : Alice Fletcher in the field, 1889-92 / by E. Jane Gay ; edited, with an introduction, by Frederick E. Hoxie and Joan T. Mark. — Lincoln [Neb.] ; London : University of Nebraska Press, c1981. — xxxvii,188p,[40]p of plates : ill,1map,ports ; 23cm
Includes index
ISBN 0-8032-3062-1 : £13.30 B82-09768

970.004′97 — South-western United States. Navaho, *ca 1500-1980*

Iverson, Peter. The Navajo Nation / Peter Iverson. — Westport, Conn. ; London : Greenwood Press, 1981. — xxxii,273p ; 22cm. — (Contributions in ethnic studies, ISSN 0196-7088 ; no.3)
Bibliography: p245-261. — Includes index
ISBN 0-313-22309-2 : Unpriced B82-01945

970.004′97 — South-western United States. Navaho. Social life, *ca 1885-1890 — Personal observations*

Left Handed. Left Handed : a Navajo autobiography / [edited by] Walter and Ruth Dyk. — New York ; Guildford : Columbia University Press, 1980. — xxv,578p ; 24cm
Translated from the Navaho. — Sequel to: Son of Old Man Hat. — Includes index
ISBN 0-231-04946-3 : £13.80 B82-40808

970.004′97 — United States. North American Indians. Perception by children

Hirschfelder, Arlene B.. American Indian stereotypes in the world of children : a reader and bibliography / by Arlene B. Hirschfelder. — Metuchen ; London : Scarecrow, 1982. — xv,296p : ill ; 22cm
Bibliography: p223-276. — Includes index
ISBN 0-8108-1494-3 : £14.00 B82-31803

970.01 — North America, *to 1612 — Readings from contemporary sources*

New American world : a documentary history of North America to 1612 / edited, with a commentary by David B. Quinn with the assistance of Alison M. Quinn and Susan Hillier. — London : Macmillan, 1979. — 5v. : ill,maps ; 29cm
Originally published: New York : Arno Press ; Hector Bye, 1978. — In slip case. — Bibliography: p513-528(Vol.5). — Includes index
ISBN 0-333-26383-9 : £250.00 : CIP rev.
ISBN 0-333-26384-7 (v.1) : Unpriced
ISBN 0-333-26385-5 (v.2) : Unpriced
ISBN 0-333-26386-3 (v.3) : Unpriced
ISBN 0-333-26387-1 (v.4) : Unpriced
ISBN 0-333-26389-8 (v.5) : Unpriced
B79-09946

970.051 — North America. Social change. Influence of World War 1

Leed, Eric J.. No man's land : combat & identity in World War I / Eric J. Leed. — Cambridge : Cambridge University Press, 1981, c1979. — xii,257p ; 23cm
Bibliography: p233-245. — Includes index
ISBN 0-521-28573-9 (pbk) : £6.50
Primary classification 940.3′1 B82-13750

971 — HISTORY. CANADA

971 — Canada, *to 1979*

Understanding Canada : a multidisciplinary introduction to Canadian studies / edited by William Metcalfe ; introduction by Roger Frank Swanson ; editorial assistance James M. Colthart ; cartographic editor Edward J. Miles. — New York ; London : New York University Press, 1982. — xx,621p : ill,maps ; 24cm
Bibliography: p577-612. — Includes index
ISBN 0-8147-5382-5 (cased) : £26.00
ISBN 0-8147-5383-3 (pbk) : £13.00
B82-36364

971.064′3 — Canada. Social conditions *compared with* **social conditions in United States,** *1964-1974*

Michalos, Alex C.. North American social report : a comparative study of the quality of life in Canada and the USA from 1964 to 1974 / by Alex C. Michalos. — Dordrecht ; London : Reidel
Vol.4: Environment, transportation, and housing. — c1981. — xv,293p : ill,1map ; 23cm
Includes index
ISBN 90-277-1288-3 (pbk) : Unpriced
Also classified at 973.923 B82-01753

Michalos, Alex C.. North American social report : a comparative study of the quality of life in Canada and the USA from 1964 to 1974 / by Alex C. Michalos. — Dordrecht ; London : Reidel
V.5: Economics, religion and morality. — c1982. — xv,215p ; 23cm
Includes index
ISBN 90-277-1358-8 (pbk) : Unpriced
Also classified at 973.923 B82-23504

971.064′4′0924 — Canada. Trudeau, Margaret — *Biographies*

Trudeau, Margaret. Consequences / Margaret Trudeau. — Toronto ; London : Bantam, 1982. — 192p : ports ; 18cm
ISBN 0-553-17053-8 (pbk) : £1.50 B82-36738

971.8′01 — Newfoundland. Colonisation by England, *1610-1630*

Newfoundland discovered : English attempts at colonisation, 1610-1630 / edited by Gillian T. Cell. — London : Hakluyt Society, 1982. — xviii,310p : maps,ports ; 23cm. — (Hakluyt Society. Second series ; no.160)
Bibliography: pxii-xviii. — Includes index
ISBN 0-904180-13-1 : £12.50 B82-34989

972 — HISTORY. MIDDLE AMERICA, MEXICO

972 — Maya civilization

Gallenkamp, Charles. Maya : the riddle and rediscovery of a lost civilization / Charles Gallenkamp. — 2nd rev. ed. — Harmondsworth : Penguin, 1981. — 235p,[48]p of plates : ill,1map,ports
Previous ed.: i.e. Rev. and expanded ed. New York : D. McKay, 1976. — Bibliography: p215-222. — Includes index
ISBN 0-14-005367-0 (pbk) : £2.50 B82-18149

Hammond, Norman. Ancient Maya civilization / Norman Hammond. — Cambridge : Cambridge University Press, 1982. — xii,337p : ill,maps,plans ; 26cm
Bibliography: p305-322. — Includes index
ISBN 0-521-24017-4 (cased) : £22.50 : CIP rev.
ISBN 0-521-28399-x (pbk) : £7.95 B82-12680

Henderson, John S.. The world of the ancient Maya / by John S. Henderson. — London : Orbis, 1981. — 271p : ill,maps ; 25cm
Bibliography: p249-267. — Includes index
ISBN 0-85613-402-3 : £15.00 B82-20155

972′.01 — Central America & Mexico. Social change, *to 1520 — Comparative studies*

Ancient Mesoamerica : a comparison of change in three regions / Richard E. Blanton ... [et al.]. — Cambridge : Cambridge University Press, 1981. — x,300p : ill,maps,plans ; 24cm. — (New studies in archaeology)
Bibliography: p267-291. — Includes index
ISBN 0-521-22858-1 (cased) : £17.50
ISBN 0-521-29682-x (pbk) : £5.95 B82-24223

972′.01 — Pre-Columbian Mexican & Central American civilization

Weaver, Muriel Porter. The Aztecs, Maya, and their predecessors : archaeology of Mesoamerica / Muriel Porter Weaver. — 2nd ed. — New York ; London : Academic Press, c1981. — xxiii,597p : ill,maps,plans,1geneal.table ; 25cm. — (Studies in archaeology)
Previous ed.: New York : London : Seminar Press, 1972. — Bibliography: p537-572. — Includes index
ISBN 0-12-785936-5 : Unpriced B82-10524

972.08′1 — Mexican Revolution, *1910-1920*

Gilly, Adolfo. The Mexican Revolution. — London : Verso/NLB, Nov.1982. — [336]p
Translation: La revolución interrumpida
ISBN 0-86091-756-8 (cased) : £16.50 : CIP entry
ISBN 0-86091-056-3 (pbk) : £5.95 B82-28760

Katz, Friedrich. The secret war in Mexico : Europe, the United States and the Mexican Revolution / Friedrich Katz ; with portions translated by Loren Goldner. — Chicago ; London : University of Chicago Press, 1981. — xii,659p ; 24cm
Includes index
ISBN 0-226-42588-6 : £21.00 B82-13704

972.08′1′0924 — Mexican Revolution, *1910-1925 — Personal observations*

O'Hea, Patrick. Reminiscences of the Mexican revolution / Patrick O'Hea. — London : Sphere, 1981, c1966. — 212p ; 18cm
Originally published: Mexico : Editorial Fournier, 1966
ISBN 0-7221-6515-3 (pbk) : £1.50 B82-02172

972′.65081 — Mexican Revolution — *Study regions: Yucatan region*

Joseph, G. M.. Revolution from without : Yucatán, Mexico and the United States, 1880-1924 / G.M. Joseph. — Cambridge : Cambridge University Press, 1982. — xviii,405p : ill,maps,ports ; 22cm. — (Cambridge Latin American studies)
Bibliography: p373. — Includes index
ISBN 0-521-23516-2 : £29.50 B82-26774

972.8 — HISTORY. CENTRAL AMERICA

972.8′03 — Central America, *1680-1840*

Wortman, Miles L.. Government and society in Central America, 1680-1840 / Miles L. Wortman. — New York ; Guildford, Surrey : Columbia University Press, 1982. — xvii,374p : 1map ; 24cm
Bibliography: p341-358. — Includes index
ISBN 0-231-05212-x : £20.45 B82-36482

972.81 — HISTORY. GUATEMALA

972.81′052 — Guatemala. Political events. Role of United States. *Central Intelligence Agency &* **United Fruit Company,** *1954*

Schlesinger, Stephen. Bitter fruit. — London : Sinclair Browne, Sept.1982. — [352]p
ISBN 0-86300-022-3 (cased) : £7.95 : CIP entry
ISBN 0-86300-023-1 (pbk) : £3.95 B82-18778

972.82 — HISTORY. BELIZE

972.82 — Belize, *to 1980*

Setzekorn, William David. Formerly British Honduras : a profile of the new nation of Belize / William David Setzekorn. — Rev. ed. — Chicago ; London : Ohio University Press, 1981. — ix,299p : 2maps,1port ; 22cm
Previous ed.: Newark, Cal. : Dumbarton Press, 1975. — Bibliography: p289-295. — Includes index
ISBN 0-8214-0568-3 (pbk) : £6.75 B82-30097

972.84 — HISTORY. EL SALVADOR

972.84′052 — El Salvador. Political events. Role of Catholic Church

Catholic Church. *Diocese of San Salvador. Archbishop ((1977-1980 : Romero))*. The church, political organisation and violence : third pastoral letter of Oscar Arnulfo Romero, Archbishop of San Salvador and the first of Arturo Rivera Damos, Bishop of Santiago de Maria. — London : CIIR, [1982?]. — 23p : ill,1map,ports ; 30cm. — (Church in the world ; 5)
Translated from Spanish
ISBN 0-904393-46-1 (unbound) : £0.25
B82-30628

972.85 — HISTORY. NICARAGUA

972.85'05 — Nicaragua. Political events, *1920-1980*

Weber, Henri. Nicaragua : the Sandinist revolution / Henri Weber ; translated by Patrick Camiller. — London : NLB, 1981. — 154p ; 23cm
Translation of: Nicaragua. — Bibliography: p147-148. — Includes index
ISBN 0-86091-044-x (cased) : £10.00 : CIP rev.
ISBN 0-86091-742-8 (pbk) : Unpriced
B81-30147

972.85'051'0924 — Nicaragua. Sandino, Augusto César — *Biographies*

Selser, Gregorio. Sandino / by Gregorio Selser ; translated by Cedric Belfrage. — New York ; London : Monthly Review, c1981. — 250p ; 21cm
Translation of: Sandino, general de hombres libre. — Includes index
ISBN 0-85345-558-9 : £8.70
ISBN 0-85345-559-7 (pbk) : Unpriced
B82-01820

972.85'052 — Nicaragua. Political events, *ca 1930-1980*

Black, George, *1949-*. Triumph of the people : the Sandinistra revolution in Nicaragua / George Black. — London : Zed, 1981. — xv,368p : maps ; 23cm. — (Latin America series)
Bibliography: p363-364. — Includes index
ISBN 0-86232-092-5 (cased) : £18.95 : CIP rev.
ISBN 0-86232-036-4 (pbk) : Unpriced
B81-30342

972.85'052'0222 — Nicaragua. Political events, *1978-1979 — Illustrations*

Meiselas, Susan. Nicaragua : June 1978-July 1979 / Susan Meiselas ; edited with Claire Rosenberg. — London : Writers and Readers Publishing Co-operative, 1981. — 71,[28]p : chiefly ill(some col.) ; 22x29cm
ISBN 0-906495-66-0 (cased) : £12.00
ISBN 0-906495-67-9 (pbk) : Unpriced
B82-28539

972.86 — HISTORY. COSTA RICA

972.86'052 — Costa Rica. Social conditions

Biesanz, Richard. The Costa Ricans / Richard Biesanz, Karen Zubris Biesanz, Mavis Hiltunen Biesanz. — Englewood Cliffs ; London : Prentice-Hall, c1982. — x,246p : ill,maps ; 23cm
Includes index
ISBN 0-13-179606-2 (pbk) : £11.20
B82-16696

972.9 — HISTORY. WEST INDIES

972.9 — West Indies, *1492-1978*

Watson, Jack B.. The West Indian heritage : a history of the West Indies / Jack B. Watson. — 2nd ed. — London : Murray, 1982. — 212p : ill ; 25cm
Previous ed.: 1979. — Bibliography: p203-205. — Includes index
ISBN 0-7195-3960-9 (pbk) : £3.25 : CIP rev.
B82-06049

972.91'064'0924 — Cuba. Policies. Role of Castro, Fidel, *1945-1981 — For schools*

Griffiths, John, *1937-*. Castro / John Griffiths. — London : Batsford Academic and Educational, 1981. — 90p : ill,maps,ports ; 26cm. — (World leaders in context)
Bibliography: p85. — Includes index
ISBN 0-7134-1924-5 : £5.95 B82-06277

972.91'2303 — Cuba. Havana. Capture by British military forces, *1762*

Keppel, Sonia. Three brothers at Havana, 1762 / Sonia Keppel. — Salisbury : Michael Russell, 1981. — 120p,[8]p of plates : ill,2maps,ports ; 23cm
Map on lining papers. — Bibliography: p101-102. — Includes index
ISBN 0-85955-083-4 : £6.50 B82-11919

972.92 — Jamaica. Social conditions, *ca 1500-1981*

Beckford, George. Small garden — bitter weed : the political economy of struggle and change in Jamaica / George Beckford, Michael Witter. — 2nd (exp.) ed. — Jamaica : Maroon Publishing ; London : Zed, 1982. — xxi,167p : ill ; 23cm
Previous ed.: ie.: i.e. limited student & electoral ed. 1980. — Bibliography: p163-167
ISBN 0-86232-003-8 (cased) : £16.95
B82-22705

972.92'06 — Jamaica. Social life — *For children*

Hubley, John, *1948-*. Jamaican village / John and Penny Hubley. — London : Black, c1982. — 25p : col.ill,2col.maps ; 22cm. — (Beans)
ISBN 0-7136-2214-8 : £2.95 : CIP rev.
B82-07576

Saunders, Dave. Through the year in the Caribbean / Dave Saunders. — London : Batsford Academic and Educational, 1981. — 72p : ill,maps,ports ; 26cm
Bibliography: p70. — Includes index
ISBN 0-7134-3974-2 : £5.50 B82-02073

972.93'04 — Dominican Republic. Social conditions, *1850-1900*

Hoetink, H.. The Dominican people, 1850-1900 : notes for a historical sociology / H. Hoetink ; translated by Stephen K. Ault. — Baltimore ; London : Johns Hopkins University Press, c1982. — xi,243p ; 24cm. — (Johns Hopkins studies in Atlantic history and culture)
Translation of: El pueblo dominicano ; includes passages in Spanish. — Bibliography: p239-243
ISBN 0-8018-2223-8 : Unpriced B82-36044

972.94'03 — Haiti. Slaves. Rebellion, *1791-1798*

Geggus, David Patrick. Slavery, war and revolution : the British occupation of Saint Domingue 1793-1798 / by David Patrick Geggus. — Oxford : Clarendon, 1982. — ix,492p : maps ; 23cm
Bibliography: p467-480. — Includes index
ISBN 0-19-822634-9 : £28.00 : CIP rev.
B81-31741

972.96 — Bahamas. Windsor, Edward, *Duke of* **& Windsor, Wallis Windsor,** *Duchess of, 1940-1944 — Biographies*

Pye, Michael, *1946-*. [King over the water]. The Windsors in exile / Michael Pye. — Feltham : Hamlyn, 1982, c1981. — 271p : ill,ports ; 18cm
Originally published: London : Hutchinson, 1981. — Bibliography: p270-272
ISBN 0-600-20593-2 (pbk) : £1.50 B82-17871

972.98'1 — Barbados, *to ca 1980*

Tree, Ronald. A history of Barbados / Ronald Tree. — 2nd ed. / rev. and updated by E.L. Cozier. — London : Granada, 1977 (1981 [printing]). — ix,116p,[16]p of plates : ill,1map,1port ; 23cm
Previous ed.: London : Hart-Davis, 1972. — Map on lining papers. — Includes index
ISBN 0-246-11036-8 : £6.95 B82-40628

972.98'3 — Trinidad and Tobago. Trinidad, *1783-1962*

Brereton, Bridget. A history of modern Trinidad, 1783-1962 / Bridget Brereton. — Kingston, Jamaica ; London : Heinemann, 1981. — x,262p : ill,2maps,ports ; 22cm
Bibliography: p254-258. — Includes index
ISBN 0-435-98116-1 (pbk) : £4.95 B82-06197

973 — HISTORY. UNITED STATES

973 — United States, *ca 1600-1971*

Pole, J. R.. Paths to the American past / J.R. Pole. — New York ; Oxford : Oxford University Press, 1979. — xxiii,348p ; 22cm
Bibliography: p334. — Includes index
ISBN 0-19-502579-2 : £11.25 B82-15227

973 — United States. Intellectual life, *1750-1800*

Fliegelman, Jay. Prodigals and pilgrims : the American revolution against patriarchal authority, 1750-1800 / Jay Fliegelman. — Cambridge : Cambridge University Press, 1982. — vii,328p : ill ; 24cm
Includes index
ISBN 0-521-23719-x : £20.00 B82-34352

973 — United States. Society. Cultural factors, *to ca 1790*

Nash, Gary B.. Red, white, and black : the peoples of early America / Gary B. Nash. — 2nd ed. — Englewood Cliffs ; London : Prentice-Hall, c1982. — xvi,330p : ill,maps,ports ; 24cm
Previous ed.: 1974. — Bibliography: p299-322. — Includes index
ISBN 0-13-769794-5 (cased) : Unpriced
ISBN 0-13-769786-4 (pbk) : £8.20 B82-21018

973 — United States, *to 1976 — For schools*

Beacroft, B. W.. The making of America : from wilderness to world power / B.W. Beacroft and M.A. Smale. — 2nd ed. — Harlow : Longman, 1982. — v,218p : ill,maps,ports ; 24cm
Previous ed.: 1972. — Includes bibliographies and index
ISBN 0-582-33146-3 (cased) : Unpriced
ISBN 0-582-33080-7 (pbk) : £3.50 B82-29315

973 — United States, *to 1981*

America : changing times / Charles M. Dollar, general editor ; Joan Rezner Gundersen ... [et al.], contributors ; Reid A. Holland, assistant editor ; John Hammond Moore, writer. — 2nd ed. — New York ; Chichester : Wiley, c1982. — xiv,1003,[64]p,[16]p of plates : ill(some col.),facsims,maps(some col.),ports ; 26cm
Paperback ed. is in 2v. ; v.1, to 1877 ; v.2, since 1865. — Previous ed.: 1979. — Includes bibliographies and index
ISBN 0-471-09421-8 (cased) : £17.95
ISBN 0-471-09418-8 (v.1 : pbk) : £11.00
ISBN 0-471-09417-x : £11.00 B82-26449

973 — United States, *to 1981 — Quotations*

Quotations in American history. — Brighton : Harvester Press, Dec.1982. — [256]p
ISBN 0-7108-0420-2 : £18.95 : CIP entry
B82-30080

973'.004924 — United States. Jewish families. Social life

The **Jewish** family book / [edited by] Sharon Strassfeld & Kathy Green ; photography by Bill Aron. — Toronto ; London : Bantam, 1981. — 453p : ill,ports ; 23cm
Includes index
ISBN 0-553-01339-4 (pbk) : £3.95 B82-21602

973'.03'21 — United States, *to 1981 — Encyclopaedias*

Encyclopedia of American history / edited by Richard B. Morris ; associate editor Jeffrey B. Morris. — 6th ed. — New York ; London : Harper & Row, c1982. — xiv,1285p : maps ; 24cm
Previous ed.: 1976. — Includes index
ISBN 0-06-181605-1 : Unpriced B82-33816

973'.049163 — United States. Scotsmen, *to 1850*

Rodgers, John, *d. 1977*. The common bond / by John Rodgers ; with a foreword by Mary A. Rodgers. — Paisley : Wilfion, 1980. — 107p ; 21cm. — (The Scotland alive series ; v.1)
ISBN 0-905075-11-0 (pbk) : £2.00 B82-21710

973'.0496073 — American negro culture, *to 1976*

Ostendorf, Berndt. Black literature in white America / Berndt Ostendorf. — Brighton : Harvester, 1982. — ix,171p ; 23cm. — ([Studies in contemporary literature & culture ; no.9])
Includes index
ISBN 0-7108-0041-x : £15.95 : CIP rev.
B82-10700

973'.0496073 — United States. Negroes, *to 1980*

Berry, Mary Frances. Long memory : the black experience in America / Mary Frances Berry, John W. Blassingame. — New York ; Oxford : Oxford University Press, 1982. — xxi,486p : ill,facsims,2ports,1geneal.table ; 24cm
Bibliography: p424-456. — Includes index
ISBN 0-19-502909-7 (cased) : £14.00
ISBN 0-19-502910-0 (pbk) : Unpriced
B82-26514

973.9 — American culture. Role of chivalry, *1880-1981*

Fraser, John, *1928-*. America and the patterns of chivalry / John Fraser. — Cambridge : Cambridge University Press, 1982. — x,301p ; 24cm
Includes index
ISBN 0-521-24183-9 : £15.00 B82-24198

973.9 — United States, *1900-1976 — For schools*

Lane, Peter. The USA in the twentieth century / Peter Lane. — London : Batsford, 1978. — 94p : ill,maps,facsims,ports ; 26cm. — (Twentieth century world history)
Includes index
ISBN 0-7134-0975-4 : £5.95 B82-07316

973.9′092′2 — United States. Rural regions. Women. Social life, *1900-1980 — Personal observations — Collections*

Thomas, Sherry. We didn't have much but we sure had plenty / Sherry Thomas ; illustrations by Judith A. Brown. — South Yarmouth, Mass. : Curley ; [Long Preston] : Distributed by Magna, 1981. — 325p ; 23cm
Originally published: Garden City, N.Y. : Anchor, 1981. — Published in large print
ISBN 0-89340-390-3 : Unpriced B82-21836

973.9′092′2 — United States. Social life, *ca 1900-1979 — Personal observations — Collections*

Terkel, Studs. American dreams : lost and found / Studs Terkel. — London : Granada, 1982, c1980. — 541p ; 20cm. — (A Paladin book)
Originally published: New York : Pantheon, 1980 ; London : Hutchinson, 1981
ISBN 0-586-08408-8 (pbk) : £2.95 B82-40718

973.9′092′4 — United States. Jones, Candy — *Biographies*

Bain, Donald, *1935-*. The control of Candy Jones / Donald Bain. — London : Futura, 1979, c1976. — 267p ; 18cm. — (A Circus book)
Originally published: Chicago : Playboy, 1976
ISBN 0-7088-1539-1 (pbk) : £0.95 B82-36779

973.9′092′4 — United States. Politics. Hays, Brooks, *1898-1980 — Biographies*

Hays, Brooks1898-. Politics is my parish : an autobiography / Brooks Hays ; foreword by Arthur Schlesinger, Jr. — Baton Rouge ; London : Louisiana State University Press, c1981. — viii,291p : ill,ports ; 24cm
Includes index
ISBN 0-8071-0798-0 : £14.00 B82-09914

973.91 — United States. Social life, *1910-1940*

Morris, Wright. God's country and my people / by Wright Morris. — Lincoln [Neb.] ; London : University of Nebraska Press, 1981, c1968. — [175]p : ill ; 30cm
Originally published: New York : Harper & Row, 1968
ISBN 0-8032-3067-2 (pbk) : Unpriced B82-02045

973.91′092′2 — United States. Politics. Role of Brandeis, Louis D. & Frankfurter, Felix, *1916-1962*

Murphy, Bruce Allen. The Brandeis-Frankfurter connection : the secret political activities of two Supreme Court justices / Bruce Allen Murphy. — New York ; Oxford : Oxford University Press, 1982. — x,473p ; 24cm
Bibliography: p453-466. — Includes index
ISBN 0-19-503122-9 : £13.50 B82-37011

973.91′092′4 — United States. Longworth, Alice Roosevelt — *Interviews*

Longworth, Alice Roosevelt. Mrs. L : conversations with Alice Roosevelt Longworth / [interviewed by] Michael Teague. — London : Duckworth, 1981. — xviii,203p : ill,ports ; 27cm
Ill on lining papers
ISBN 0-7156-1602-1 : Unpriced : CIP rev. B81-24633

973.91′092′4 — United States. Luce, Clare Boothe *— Biographies*

Sheed, Wilfrid. Clare Boothe Luce / Wilfrid Sheed. — London : Weidenfeld and Nicolson, 1982. — vii,183p,[32]p of plates : ill,ports ; 24cm
Originally published: New York : Dutton, 1982. — Includes index
ISBN 0-297-78146-4 : £12.95 B82-34723

973.91′3′0924 — United States. Wilson, Woodrow. Health

Weinstein, Edwin A.. Woodrow Wilson : a medical and psychological biography / Edwin A. Weinstein. — Princeton ; Guildford : Princeton University Press, c1981. — xi,399p,[16]p of plates : ill,facsims,ports ; 24cm. — (Supplementary volumes to the papers of Woodrow Wilson)
Bibliography: p379-386. — Includes index
ISBN 0-691-04683-2 : £13.00 B82-04337

973.917 — United States. Social conditions, *1933-1935 — Correspondence, diaries, etc.*

Hickok, Lorena. One third of a nation : Lorena Hickok reports on the Great Depression / edited by Richard Lowitt and Maurine Beasley. — Urbana ; London : University of Illinois Press, c1981. — xxxv,378p,[24]p of plates : ill,ports ; 24cm
Includes index
ISBN 0-252-00849-9 : £13.30 B82-05714

973.917′092′4 — United States. Roosevelt, Franklin D. *— Biographies*

Alsop, Joseph. FDR : 1882-1945 : the life and times of Franklin D. Roosevelt / Joseph Alsop ; picture sections compiled and written by Roland Gelatt ; photo research by Laurie Platt Winfrey. — London : Thames and Hudson, c1982. — 255p : ill,facsims,ports ; 29cm
Includes index
ISBN 0-500-01267-9 : £10.50 B82-10526

Butler, William Vivian. Franklin D. Roosevelt : nothing to fear but fear / by William Vivian Butler. — London : Hodder and Stoughton, 1982. — 128p : ill,1facsim,ports ; 25cm. — (Twentieth century people)
Bibliography: p125-126. — Includes index
ISBN 0-340-27097-7 : £5.95 : CIP rev. B81-34160

973.918′092′4 — United States. McCarthy, Joseph. Relations with press, *1950-1955*

Bayley, Edwin R.. Joe McCarthy and the press / Edwin R. Bayley. — Madison ; London : University of Wisconsin Press, c1981. — x,270p ; 24cm
Bibliography: p245-254. — Includes index
ISBN 0-299-08620-8 (pbk) : £11.55 B82-12772

973.918′092′4 — United States. Politics. Barkley, Alben W. *— Biographies*

Davis, Polly Ann. Alben W. Barkley : Senate majority leader and Vice president / Polly Ann Davis. — New York (London) : Garland, 1979. — xviii,343p : 3ports ; 22cm. — (Modern American history)
Bibliography: p320-335. — Includes index
ISBN 0-8240-3630-1 : Unpriced B82-01268

973.918′092′4 — United States. Politics. McCarthy, Joseph *— Biographies*

Reeves, Thomas C.. The life and times of Joe McCarthy : a biography / Thomas C. Reeves. — London : Blond & Briggs, 1982. — xv,819p : ill,ports ; 24cm
Bibliography: p783-799. — Includes index
ISBN 0-85634-131-2 : £11.95 B82-30978

973.918′092′4 — United States. Truman, Harry S. *— Biographies*

Gosnell, Harold F.. Truman's crises : a political biography of Harry S. Truman / Harold F. Gosnell. — Westport ; London : Greenwood Press, 1980. — xv,656p : ill,maps ; 25cm. — (Contributions in political science, ISSN 0147-1066 ; no.33)
Bibliography: p619-633. — Includes index
ISBN 0-313-21273-2 : Unpriced B82-14980

973.92′092′2 — United States. Presidents. Families, *1961-1981 — Biographies*

Kellerman, Barbara. All the president's kin / Barbara Kellerman. — London : Robson, 1982, c1981. — xiv,288p,[8]p of plates : ill,ports ; 24cm
Originally published: New York : Fress Press ; London : Collier Macmillan, 1981. — Bibliography: p269-277. — Includes index
ISBN 0-86051-167-7 : £7.95 : CIP rev. B82-00346

973.921′092′4 — United States. Eisenhower, Dwight D. *— Biographies*

Wykes, Alan. The biography of General Dwight D. Eisenhower / Alan Wykes. — London : Hamlyn, 1982. — 159p : ill,maps(some col.),ports ; 30cm. — (A Bison book)
Includes index
ISBN 0-86124-073-1 : £6.95 B82-40750

973.921′092′4 — United States. Eisenhower, Dwight D. *— Correspondence, diaries, etc.*

Eisenhower, Dwight D.. The Eisenhower diaries / edited by Robert H. Ferrell. — New York ; London : Norton, c1981. — xvii,445p : ill,facsims,maps,ports ; 25cm
Includes index
ISBN 0-393-01432-0 : £14.25 B82-32726

973.922′092′4 — United States. Kennedy, John F. *— Biographies — Welsh texts*

Morris, Robert M.. John F. Kennedy. — Cardiff : University of Wales Press, Nov.1982. — [28] p. — (Project Defnyddian ac Adnoddau y Swyddfa Gymreig. Hanes ; 3)
ISBN 0-7083-0836-8 (pbk) : £1.50 : CIP entry B82-26722

973.923 — United States. Social conditions *compared with* **social conditions in Canada,** *1964-1974*

Michalos, Alex C.. North American social report : a comparative study of the quality of life in Canada and the USA from 1964 to 1974 / by Alex C. Michalos. — Dordrecht ; London : Reidel
Vol.4: Environment, transportation, and housing. — c1981. — xv,293p : ill,1map ; 23cm
Includes index
ISBN 90-277-1288-3 (pbk) : Unpriced
Primary classification 971.064′3 B82-01753

Michalos, Alex C.. North American social report : a comparative study of the quality of life in Canada and the USA from 1964 to 1974 / by Alex C. Michalos. — Dordrecht ; London : Reidel
V.5: Economics, religion and morality. — c1982. — xv,215p ; 23cm
Includes index
ISBN 90-277-1358-8 (pbk) : Unpriced
Primary classification 971.064′3 B82-23504

973.923′092′4 — United States. Johnson, Lyndon Baines *— Biographies*

Caro, Robert A.. The years of Lyndon Johnson. — London : Collins
Vol.1. — Feb.1983. — [790]p
ISBN 0-00-217062-0 : £12.95 : CIP entry B82-40882

973.926′092′4 — United States. Carter, Jimmy, *1977-1981 — Biographies*

Carter, Jimmy. Keeping faith. — London : Collins, Dec.1982. — [640]p
ISBN 0-00-216648-8 : £12.95 : CIP entry B82-39257

973.927 — United States *— For schools*

Krueger, B.. Life in the USA. — London : Hart-Davis Educational, Sept.1982. — [64]p. — (Signposts series)
Translation of: Vivre aux États-Unis
ISBN 0-247-13041-9 : £3.95 : CIP entry B82-18866

973.927 — United States. Social conditions

Fawcett, Edmund. America, Americans. — London : Collins, Jan.1983. — [448]p
ISBN 0-00-216519-8 : £12.50 : CIP entry B82-33201

973.927 — United States. Social life *— For schools*

Fyson, Nance Lui. Through the year in the USA / Nance Lui Fyson. — London : Batsford Academic and Educational, 1982. — 72p : ill,1map,ports ; 26cm
Bibliography: p70. — Includes index
ISBN 0-7134-4069-4 : £5.95 B82-33308

973.927'0880621 — United States. Upper classes. Social life — *Humour*

The **Official** preppy handbook / edited by Lisa Birnbach ; writers Lisa Birnbach ... [et al.] ; photography Robin Holland ; illustration Oliver Williams ; with a preface by Jilly Cooper. — London : Eyre Methuen, 1981, c1980. — 224p : ill ; 21cm
ISBN 0-413-49200-1 (pbk) : £3.95 B82-17589

973.927'092'2 — United States. Social life — *Personal observations — Collections*

Henderson, Bruce. We live in the U.S.A. / Bruce Henderson. — Hove : Wayland, 1981. — 64p : col.ill,1col.map,col.ports ; 26cm. — (Living here)
Includes index
ISBN 0-85340-863-7 : £4.50 B82-03877

973.927'092'4 — United States. Mayo, Gael Elton — *Biographies*

Mayo, Gael Elton. Mad mosaic. — London : Quartet, Nov.1982. — [2-4v.]
ISBN 0-7043-2360-5 : £7.95 : CIP entry
B82-31297

973.927'092'4 — United States. Politics. Haig, Alexander — *Biographies*

Morris, Roger, *1938-*. Haig : the general's progress / Roger Morris. — London : Robson, 1982. — xxv,454p ; 23cm
Includes index
ISBN 0-86051-188-x : £8.95 : CIP rev.
B82-20872

973.927'092'4 — United States. Reagan, Nancy — *Biographies*

Reagan, Nancy. Nancy / by Nancy Reagan with Bill Libby. — London : Robson, 1981. — 240p : ill,ports ; 24cm
ISBN 0-86051-143-x : £7.95 : CIP rev.
B81-12907

973.927'092'4 — United States. Social life — *Personal observations*

Williams, Hugo. No particular place to go / Hugo Williams. — London : Cape, 1981. — vi,200p : maps ; 23cm
Maps on lining papers
ISBN 0-224-01810-8 : £6.50 : CIP rev.
B81-13858

Williams, Hugo. No particular place to go / Hugo Williams. — London : Picador, 1982, c1981. — 189p ; 20cm
Originally published: London : Cape, 1981
ISBN 0-330-26744-2 (pbk) : £1.95 B82-37350

974 — HISTORY. UNITED STATES. NORTH-EASTERN STATES

974'.041'0924 — New England. Robinson, Harriet Hanson — *Biographies*

Bushman, Claudia L.. 'A good poor man's wife' : being a chronicle of Harriet Hanson Robinson and her family in nineteenth-century New England / Claudia L. Bushman. — Hanover, [N.H.] ; London : University Press of New England, 1981. — xvi,276p : 1port,geneal.tables ; 23cm
Bibliography: p253-265. — Includes index
ISBN 0-87451-193-3 : Unpriced B82-15268

974.7'1 — New York *(City)*. **Harlem,** *1900-1950*

Anderson, Jervis. [This was Harlem]. Harlem : the great black way 1900-1950 / Jervis Anderson. — London : Orbis, 1982. — x,389p : ill,facsims,ports ; 25cm
Originally published: New York : Farrar, Straus & Giroux, 1982. — Includes index
ISBN 0-85613-445-7 : £8.95 B82-39029

974.7'103 — New York *(City), 1840-1857*

Spann, Edward K.. The new metropolis : New York City, 1840-1857 / Edward K. Spann. — New York ; Guildford : Columbia University Press, 1981. — xiii,546p : ill,maps ; 24cm
Maps on lining papers. — Bibliography: p511-533. — Includes index
ISBN 0-231-05084-4 : £14.30 B82-05626

974.7'1041 — New York *(City)*. **Night life,** *1890-1930*. **Social aspects**

Erenberg, Lewis A.. Steppin' out : New York nightlife and the transformation of American culture, 1890-1930 / Lewis A. Erenberg. — Westport, Conn. ; London : Greenwood, 1981. — xix,291p : ill,1facsim,ports ; 22cm. — (Contributions in American studies ; no.50)
Bibliography: p265-273. — Includes index
ISBN 0-313-21342-9 : Unpriced B82-02613

974.7'1041'0222 — New York *(City), 1860-1900 — Illustrations*

Nineteenth-century New York in rare photographic views / edited by Frederick S. Lightfoot. — New York : Dover ; London : Constable, 1981. — vi,151p : ill,1port ; 29cm
ISBN 0-486-24137-8 (pbk) : £5.25 B82-18048

974.7'1043'0922 — New York *(City)*. **Manhattan** — *Personal observations — Interviews — Collections*

Mestdagh, Roberte. Manhattan : people and their space / Roberte Mestdagh. — London : Thames and Hudson, 1981. — 143p : ill,1map ; 28cm
ISBN 0-500-27247-6 (pbk) : £7.95 B82-04661

974.7'1043'0924 — New York *(City)*. **Social life,** *1977-1980 — Personal observations*

Leapman, Michael. Yankee doodles / by Michael Leapman in America. — London : Allen Lane, 1982. — 250p ; 23cm
ISBN 0-7139-1453-x : £7.95 B82-23567

974.7'245041'0222 — New York (State). Long Island. Nassau County, *1869-1940 — Illustrations*

Weidman, Bette S.. Nassau County, Long Island : in early photographs 1869-1940 / Bette S. Weidman & Linda B. Martin. — New York : Dover ; London : Constable, 1981. — xii,131p : ill,1map,ports ; 30cm
Includes index
ISBN 0-486-24136-x (pbk) : £6.00 B82-18049

974.7'8900451 — New York *(State)*. **Rochester. Italian immigrants: Sicilian immigrants. Social life,** *ca 1920-1936 — Personal observations*

Mangione, Jerre. Mount Allegro : a memoir of Italian American life / Jerre Mangione ; introduction by Herbert J. Gans. — New York ; Guildford : Columbia University Press, 1981. — xiii,309p ; 22cm
Originally published: Boston, Mass. : Houghton Mifflin, 1943
ISBN 0-231-05330-4 (cased) : £16.60
ISBN 0-231-05331-2 (pbk) : £6.40 B82-05624

975 — HISTORY. UNITED STATES. SOUTH-EASTERN STATES

975'.04 — United States. Southern states, *1850-1979*

From the Old South to the new : essays on the transitional South / edited by Walter J. Fraser and Winifred B. Moore. — Westport ; London : Greenwood Press, 1981. — xiii,286p ; 25cm. — (Contributions in American history ; no.93)
Bibliography: p265-279. — Includes index
ISBN 0-313-22534-6 : Unpriced B82-18020

975'.042 — United States. Southern states. Social conditions, *1930*. **'I'll take my stand'** — *Critical studies — Conference proceedings*

A **Band** of prophets : the Vanderbilt agrarians after fifty years / edited, with an introduction, by William C. Havard and Walter Sullivan. — Baton Rouge ; London : Louisiana State University Press, c1982. — x,190p : ports ; 23cm. — (Southern literary studies)
ISBN 0-8071-1001-9 : £9.75 B82-40263

975'.043'05 — United States. Southern states. Social conditions — *Serials*

Perspectives on the American South : an annual review of society, politics and culture. — Vol.1-. — New York ; London : Gordon and Breach, c1981-. — v. : ill,maps ; 24cm
ISSN 0275-584x = Perspectives on the American South : Unpriced B82-10125

975.2'6 — Maryland. East Baltimore. Social life — *Illustrations*

Rich, Linda G.. Neighborhood : a state of mind : photographs and interviews from the East Baltimore Documentary Photography Project / Linda G. Rich, Joan Clark Netherwood and Elinor B. Cahn ; foreword by Wright Morris ; introduction by David T. Lewis and David J. Boehlke. — Baltimore ; London : Johns Hopkins University Press, c1981. — 147p : chiefly ill,ports ; 28cm
ISBN 0-8018-2558-x (cased) : Unpriced
ISBN 0-8018-2559-8 (pbk) : Unpriced
B82-16920

975.5'4251 — Virginia. Martin's Hundred. Antiquities. Excavation of remains, *1970-1981*

Noël Hume, Ivor. Martin's Hundred. — London : Gollancz, Aug.1982. — [384]p
ISBN 0-575-03178-6 : £12.50 : CIP entry
B82-15892

975.5'44 — Virginia. Berkeley Plantation. Settlement by English immigrants, *1619-1622*

Gethyn-Jones, Eric. George Thorpe and the Berkeley Company : a Gloucestershire enterprise in Virginia / Eric Gethyn-Jones. — Gloucester : Sutton, 1982. — 296p : ill,1map,1plan,ports,geneal.tables ; 23cm
Bibliography: p287-290. — Includes index
ISBN 0-904387-83-6 : £7.95 B82-25378

975.9'01 — Florida. Antiquities, *to 1700*. **Archaeological investigation**

Milanich, Jerald T.. Florida archaeology / Jerald T. Milanich, Charles H. Fairbanks. — New York ; London : Academic Press, 1980. — xvi,290p : ill,maps ; 25cm. — (New world archaeological record)
Includes index
ISBN 0-12-495960-1 : £13.00 B82-10060

976 — HISTORY. UNITED STATES. SOUTH CENTRAL STATES

976.1'061 — Alabama. Social conditions, *1860-1885*

Wiener, Jonathan M.. Social origins of the new South : Alabama, 1860-1885 / Jonathan M. Wiener. — Baton Rouge ; London : Louisiana State University Press, c1978 (1981 [printing]). — xiii,247p : 1map ; 23cm
Includes index
ISBN 0-8071-0888-x (pbk) : £4.90 B82-09769

976.3'061 — Louisiana. Political events. Role of United States. *Army, 1862-1877*

Dawson, Joseph G.. Army generals and Reconstruction : Louisiana, 1862-1877 / Joseph G. Dawson III. — Baton Rouge ; London : Louisiana State University Press, c1982. — 294p : ports ; 24cm
Bibliography: p267-285. — Includes index
ISBN 0-8071-0896-0 : £18.75 B82-40264

976.4'00496073 — Texas. Negroes, *1865-1875*

Smallwood, James M.. Time of hope, time of despair : black Texans durings reconstruction / James M. Smallwood. — Port Washington ; London : National University Publications, 1981. — x,202p ; 23cm. — (Series in ethnic studies)
Includes index
ISBN 0-8046-9273-4 : £14.85 B82-29217

976.4'96 — Texas. El Paso. Mexicans, *1880-1920*

García, Mario T.. Desert immigrants : the Mexicans of El Paso, 1880-1920. — London : Yale University Press, July 1982. — [316]p. — (Yale Western Americana series ; 32)
ISBN 0-300-02883-0 (pbk) : £7.50 : CIP entry
B82-22779

976.6'14053'0924 — Oklahama. Beaver County. Cowboys. Social life — *Personal observations*

Erickson, John R.. Panhandle cowboy / John R. Erickson ; foreword by Larry McMurtry ; photographs by Bill Ellzey. — Lincoln ; London : University of Nebraska Press, c1980 (1981 printing). — xiii,213p : ill,ports ; 21cm. — (A Bison book)
ISBN 0-8032-1803-6 (cased) : Unpriced
ISBN 0-8032-6702-9 (pbk) : Unpriced
B82-02186

976.6′86 — Oklahoma. Tulsa. Riots, *1921*

Ellsworth, Scott. Death in a promised land : the Tulsa race riot of 1921 / Scott Ellsworth ; foreword by John Hope Franklin. — Baton Rouge ; London : Louisiana State University Press, c1982. — xvii,159p : ill,ports ; 24cm
Includes index
ISBN 0-8071-0878-2 : £15.00 B82-40267

976.8′19 — Tennessee. Memphis. Beale Street. Social life, *1900-1980*

McKee, Margaret. Beale black & blue : life and music on black America′s main street / Margaret McKee, Fred Chisenhall. — Baton Rouge ; London : Louisiana State Uiversity Press, c1981. — xii,265p : ill,1map,ports ; 24cm
Bibliography: p257-258. — Includes index
ISBN 0-8071-0863-4 : £12.50
Primary classification 784.5′3′00922
B82-15449

978 — HISTORY. UNITED STATES. WESTERN STATES

978′.01 — United States. Great Plains, *to ca 1900*

Webb, Walter Prescott. The Great Plains / Walter Prescott Webb. — Lincoln [Neb.] ; London : University of Nebraska Press, c1959 (1981 printing). — 525p : ill,maps ; 21cm. — (A Bison book)
Originally published: Boston, Mass. : Ginn, 1931. — Includes bibliographies and index
ISBN 0-8032-9702-5 (pbk) : £7.00 B82-09662

978′.01 — United States. Western states. Frontier life — *Perception by Europeans, 1700-1900*

Billington, Ray Allen. Land of savagery, land of promise : the European image of the American frontier in the nineteenth century / by Ray Allen Billington. — New York ; London : Norton, c1981. — xv,364p : ill,1map ; 25cm
Bibliography: p333-352. — Includes index
ISBN 0-393-01376-6 : £13.50 B82-35679

978′.02 — United States. Rocky Mountains, *1800-1965*

Lavender, David. The Rockies / by David Lavender. — Lincoln [Neb.] ; London : University of Nebraska Press, 1981. — 404p : maps ; 24cm. — (A Bison book)
Originally published: New York : Harper & Row, 1968. — Bibliography: p371-388. — Includes index
ISBN 0-8032-2857-0 (cased) : Unpriced
ISBN 0-8032-7906-x (pbk) : £7.00 B82-09663

978′.02 — United States. Western states. Gold mining communities. Social life, *1848-1898* — *For schools*

Currie, Barbara. Gold miners in the American West 1848-1898 / Barbara Currie ; illustrated from contemporary sources. — London : Longman, 1980. — 96p : ill,maps ; 20cm. — (Then and there series)
Includes index
ISBN 0-582-20545-x (pbk) : Unpriced
B82-15079

978′.02 — United States. Western states. Reconstruction, *1865-1870*

Berwanger, Eugene H.. The West and reconstruction / Eugene H. Berwanger. — Urbana ; London : University of Illinois Press, c1981. — xiv,294p ; 24cm
Bibliography: p263-284. — Includes index
ISBN 0-252-00868-5 : £13.30 B82-12776

978′.02′088042 — United States. Western states. Women. Frontier life, *1850-1880*

Brown, Dee. The gentle tamers : women of the old Wild West / Dee Brown. — Lincoln, [Neb.] ; London : University of Nebraska Press, 1968, c1958 (1981 [printing]). — 317p,[16]p of plates : ill,ports ; 21cm. — (A Bison book)
Originally published: New York : Putnam, 1958. — Includes index
ISBN 0-8032-5025-8 (pbk) : £4.55 B82-19767

978′.02′0924 — United States. Western states. Frontier life, *1871-1888 — Personal observations — Correspondence, diaries, etc.*

Roe, Frances M. A.. Army letters from an officer′s wife : 1871-1888 / by Frances M.A. Roe ; introduction by Sandra L. Myres ; illustrated by I.W. Talier from contemporary photographs. — Lincoln, [Neb.] ; London : University of Nebraska Press, 1981. — xvii,387p : ill,1port ; 21cm
Facsim. of: ed. published: New York : Appleton, 1909
ISBN 0-8032-3859-2 (cased) : Unpriced
ISBN 0-8032-8905-7 (pbk) : £4.90 B82-19490

978′.02′0924 — United States. Western states. Frontier life, *ca 1800-1864 — Personal observations*

Beckwourth, James P.. The life and adventures of James P. Beckwourth / as told to Thomas D. Bonner ; introduced and with notes and an epilogue by Delmont R. Oswald. — Lincoln [Neb.] ; London : University of Nebraska Press, c1972 (1981 printing). — xiii,649p : ill,1port ; 21cm. — (A Bison book)
Includes index
ISBN 0-8032-6061-x (pbk) : £7.70 B82-09770

978′.032′0222 — United States. Western states, *1935-1940 — Illustrations*

Rothstein, Arthur. The American West in the thirties : 122 photographs / by Arthur Rothstein. — New York : Dover ; London : Constable, 1981. — 121p,[1]p of plates : chiefly ill,3ports ; 28cm. — (Dover pictorial archive series)
ISBN 0-486-24106-8 (pbk) : £4.50 B82-18043

978′.033 — United States. Great Plains — *Conference proceedings*

The **Great** Plains : perspectives and prospects / [a symposium sponsored by the Center for Great Plains Studies and the Old West Regional Commission in Lincoln, Nebraska, on 2 and 3 March 1979] ; edited by Merlin P. Lawson and Maurice E. Baker. — Lincoln : Center for Great Plains Studies, University of Nebraska-Lincoln ; Lincoln ; London : Distributed by University of Nebraska Press, 1981. — ix,284p : ill,maps ; 23cm
Includes bibliographies and index
ISBN 0-938932-00-4 (pbk) : Unpriced
B82-02184

978.1′9 — Kansas. Flint Hills. Social life, *1890-1918 — Personal observations*

Carlson, Avis D.. Small world — long gone / Avis Carlson. — South Yarmouth : Curley ; [Skipton] : Magna Print [distributor], 1979, c1975. — xi,334p ; 23cm
Originally published: Evanston, Ill. : Schori Press, 1975. — Published in large print
ISBN 0-89340-188-9 : £4.75 B82-14862

978.3′91 — South Dakota. Deadwood. Social life, *ca 1875-1925*

Bennett, Estelline. Old Deadwood days / by Estelline Bennett. — Lincoln [Neb.] ; London : University of Nebraska Press, 1982. — 300p,[7] leaves of plates : ill,ports ; 22cm
Originally published: New York : Sears, 1928
ISBN 0-8032-1173-2 (cased) : Unpriced
ISBN 0-8032-6065-2 (pbk) : Unpriced
B82-40115

Parker, Watson. Deadwood : the golden years / Watson Parker. — Lincoln [Neb.] ; London : University of Nebraska Press, c1981. — xiv,302p,[32]p of plates : ill,maps,ports ; 23cm
Bibliography: p265-281. — Includes index
ISBN 0-8032-0973-8 (cased) : Unpriced
ISBN 0-8032-8702-x (pbk) : Unpriced
B82-02052

978.9′55 — New Mexico. Pecos. Pueblo Indian artefacts — *Early works — Facsimiles*

Kidder, Alfred V.. The artifacts of Pecos / Alfred V. Kidder. — New York ; London : Garland, 1979. — xvi,314p : ill ; 29cm. — (Classics of anthropology)
Facsim. of: ed. published New Haven : Yale University Press for Phillips Academy ; London : Humphrey Milford, 1932. — Bibliography: p310-314
ISBN 0-8240-9630-4 : Unpriced B82-14681

979 — HISTORY. UNITED STATES. PACIFIC COAST STATES

979′.00497 — South-western United States. Pueblo Indians, *to 1981*

Upham, Steadman. Polities and power : an economic and political history of the Western Pueblo / Steadman Upham. — New York ; London : Academic, 1982. — xvi,225p : ill ; 24cm. — (Studies in archaeology)
Bibliography: p203-221. — Includes index
ISBN 0-12-709180-7 : £18.20 B82-38075

979.2′02 — Utah, *1861-1865*

Long, E. B.. The saints and the Union : Utah Territory during the Civil War / E.B. Long. — Urbana ; London : University of Illinois Press, c1981. — xiii,310p,[10]p of plates : ill,maps,ports ; 24cm
Map on lining papers. — Bibliography: p279-289. — Includes index
ISBN 0-252-00821-9 : £12.60 B82-09665

979.3′54 — Nevada. Paradise Valley. Livestock: Cattle. Production. Ranches. Social life, *to 1980*

Marshall, Howard W.. Buckaroos in Paradise : cowboy life in Northern Navada / Howard W. Marshall, Richard E. Ahlborn. — Lincoln [Neb.] ; London : University of Nebraska Press, 1981. — xvi,95p : ill,1map,plans,ports ; 26cm. — (A Bison book)
Published to accompany an exhibition at the National Museum of History and Technology, Smithsonian Institute, 1980-1981. — Originally published: Washington : Library of Congress, 1980. — Bibliography: 93-94
ISBN 0-8032-8114-5 (pbk) : £11.20
B82-13111

979.4′053′0924 — California. Chinese immigrants. Social life, *ca 1940-ca 1955 — Childhood reminiscences*

Kingston, Maxine Hong. The woman warrior / Maxine Hong Kingston. — South Yarmouth, Ma[ss]. : Curley, 1978, c1976 ; [Long Preston] : Distributed by Magna Print. — 403p ; 23cm
Originally published: New York : Knopf, 1976 ; London : Allen Lane, 1977. — Published in large print
ISBN 0-89340-130-7 : Unpriced B82-16454

979.5′00497 — London. Westminster *(London Borough).* **Museums: British Museum.** *Department of Ethnography.* **Stock: Pacific Northwest Coast Indian artefacts** — *Catalogues*

King, J. C. H.. Artificial curiosities from the northwest coast of America. — London : British Museum Publications, July 1981. — [216]p
ISBN 0-7141-1562-2 : £30.00 : CIP entry
B81-22574

979.7′77 — Washington *(State).* **Seattle. Social conditions,** *1852-1960*

Morgan, Murray. Skid road : an informal portrait of Seattle / by Murray Morgan. — 1st ill ed. / with a new preface and concluding chapter by the author. — Seattle ; London : University of Washington Press, 1982. — 288p,[24]p of plates : ill,facsims,1map,ports ; 22cm
Previous ed.: 1978. — Includes index
ISBN 0-295-95846-4 (pbk) : £6.00 B82-38138

979.8′2 — Alaska. Long Island. Coastal waters. Shipwrecks: Home *(Ship).* **Survivors′ experiences** — *Personal observations*

Wortman, Elmo. Almost too late / Elmo Wortman. — London : Allen & Unwin, 1982, c1981. — 211p : maps ; 23cm
Originally published: New York : Random House, c1981
ISBN 0-04-910074-2 : Unpriced : CIP rev.
B82-06488

979.8′6 — Bering Strait region. Prehistoric antiquities. Archaeological investigation

West, Frederick Hadleigh. The archaeology of Beringia / Frederick Hadleigh West. — New York ; Guildford : Columbia University Press, 1981. — xviii,268p : ill,maps ; 24cm
Maps on lining papers. — Bibliography: p234-253. — Includes index
ISBN 0-231-05172-7 : £21.00 B82-17720

980 — HISTORY. SOUTH AMERICA

980 — Latin America, *ca 1300-1980*
Burns, E. Bradford. Latin America : a concise interpretive history / E. Bradford Burns. — 3rd ed. — Englewood Cliffs ; London : Prentice-Hall, c1982. — x,310p : ill,maps,ports ; 23cm
Previous ed.: 1977. — Bibliography: p300-303. — Includes index
ISBN 0-13-524322-x (pbk) : £9.70 B82-16841

980 — Latin America, *to 1980*
Latin America : an introductory survey / edited by Brian W. Blouet, Olwyn M. Blouet. — New York ; Chichester : Wiley, c1982. — xii,300p : ill,maps ; 23cm
Includes bibliographies and index
ISBN 0-471-08385-2 (pbk) : £12.15 B82-16015

980'.004'98 — Brazil. Amazon River Basin. Panare
Henley, Paul. The Panare. — London : Yale University Press, June 1982. — [320]p
ISBN 0-300-02504-1 : £15.00 : CIP entry B82-21368

980'.004'98 — Latin America. American Indians. Attitudes of Spain, *1500-1800*
Pagden, A. R.. The fall of natural man : the American Indian and the origins of comparative ethnology / Anthony Pagden. — Cambridge : Cambridge University Press, 1982. — xii,256p ; 24cm. — (Cambridge Iberian and Latin American studies)
Bibliography: p237-252. — Includes index
ISBN 0-521-22202-8 : Unpriced : CIP rev. B82-26224

980'.004'98 — Venezuela. Pemon. Cultural processes
Thomas, David John. Order without government : the society of the Pemon Indians of Venezuela / David John Thomas. — Urbana ; London : University of Illinois Press, c1982. — 265p : ill,maps ; 23cm. — (Illinois studies in anthropology ; no.13)
Bibliography: p250-256. — Includes index
ISBN 0-252-00888-x (pbk) : £11.25 B82-35664

980'.01 — Pre-Columbian Latin American civilization
Milton, Joyce. The feathered serpent and the Cross : the pre-Columbian god-kings : the Papal States / Joyce Milton, Robert A. Orsi, Norman Harrison ; preface by Jeffrey R. Parsons. — London : Cassell, 1980. — 168p : col.ill,col.maps,col.ports ; 31cm. — (The Rise and fall of empires)
Includes index
ISBN 0-304-30724-6 : £7.95
Primary classification 262'.13'09 B82-24800

980'.01 — Pre-Columbian Latin American civilization. Effects of conquest by Western European countries — *For Caribbean students*
Menezes, Mary Noel. The Amerindians and the Europeans / M. Noel Menezes. — London : Collins, c1982. — 80p : ill,maps ; 23cm. — (History topics for the Caribbean Examinations Council syllabus)
Bibliography: p74-76. — Includes index
ISBN 0-00-329540-0 (pbk) : £1.25 B82-21777

980'.033 — Latin America, *1939-1942*
Humphreys, R. A. (Robert Arthur). Latin America and the Second World War / by R.A. Humphreys. — London : Athlone, published for the Institute of Latin American Studies, University of London. — (University of London, Institute of Latin American Studies monographs ; 10)
Includes index
Vol.1: 1939-1942. — 1981. — 232p ; 23cm
ISBN 0-485-17710-2 : £16.00 : CIP rev. B81-19174

980'.033 — Latin America, *1939-1945*
Humphreys, R. A.. Latin America and the Second World War. — London : Athlone Press, Nov.1982
Vol.2: 1942-1945. — [240]p. — (University of London Institute of Latin American Studies monographs, ISSN 0776-0846 ; 11)
ISBN 0-485-17711-0 : £18.00 : CIP entry B82-27501

980'.036 — Latin America. Political events. Role of United States, *1960-1981*
Pearce, Jenny. Under the eagle : U.S. intervention in Central America and the Caribbean / Jenny Pearce ; foreword by Richard Gott. — London : Latin America Bureau, 1981. — xi,273p : ill,2maps,1facsim ; 22cm
Bibliography: p257-262. — Includes index
ISBN 0-906156-12-2 (pbk) : £2.50 B82-12780

980'.038'05 — Latin America. Political events — *Spanish texts — Serials*
América Latina. Informe político. — IP-81-01 (7 de agosto de 1981)-. — Londres [London] (90 Cowcross St., EC1M 6BL) : Latin American Newsletters Ltd, 1981-. — v. ; 30cm
Fortnightly. — Continues in part: América Latina informe semanal
ISSN 0261-3743 = América Latina. Informe político : Unpriced B82-14784

980'.038'05 — Latin America — *Serials*
Bulletin of Latin American research. — Vol.1, no.1 (Oct. 1981)-. — Oxford (19a Paradise St., Oxford OX1 1LD) : Oxford Microform Publications, 1981-. — v. ; 23cm
Two issues yearly. — Journal of: Society for Latin American Studies. — Continues: Bulletin of the Society for Latin American Studies
ISSN 0261-3050 = Bulletin of Latin American research : £15.00 per year B82-10108

Latin America & Caribbean. — 1980-. — Saffron Walden : World of Information, 1980-. — v. : ill ; 27cm
Annual. — Continues: Latin America annual review and the Caribbean. — Description based on: 1981-82 issue
ISSN 0262-5415 = Latin America & Caribbean : Unpriced
Also classified at 909'.09821 B82-24764

981 — HISTORY. BRAZIL

981 — Brazil. Social conditions, *to 1974 — Marxist viewpoints*
Fernandes, Florestan. Reflections on the Brazilian counter-revolution : essays / by Florestan Fernandes ; edited with an introduction by Warren Dean ; [translated from the Portuguese by Michel Vale and Patrick M. Hughes]. — New York : M.E. Sharpe ; London : Eurospan [distributor], c1981. — xii,187p ; 24cm
ISBN 0-87332-177-4 : £16.95 B82-14632

981 — Brazil, *to 1980*
Dickenson, John. Brazil. — London : Longman, Nov.1982. — [240]p. — (The World's landscapes)
ISBN 0-582-30016-9 (cased) : £13.00 : CIP entry
ISBN 0-582-30017-7 (pbk) : £6.95 B82-26529

981'.063 — Brazil. Social life
Perry, Ritchie. Brazil : the land and its people / Ritchie Perry. — London : Macdonald Educational, 1977 (1982 [printing]). — 64p : ill (chiefly col.),col.maps,ports ; 29cm. — (Macdonald countries)
Includes index
ISBN 0-356-05456-x (cased) : Unpriced
ISBN 0-356-06531-6 (pbk) : Unpriced B82-32818

981'.53 — Brazil. Rio de Janeiro. Social life — *For children*
Sedor, Mary. Living in Rio de Janeiro / Mary Sedor. — Hove : Wayland, 1981. — 52p : ill,1col.map ; 21cm. — (Living in famous cities)
Bibliography: p51. — Includes index
ISBN 0-85340-840-8 : £3.75 B82-16423

983 — HISTORY. CHILE

983'.0072083 — Chile. Chilean historiography, *to 1900*
Woll, Allen L.. A functional past : the uses of history in nineteenth-century Chile / Allen Woll. — Baton Rouge ; London : Louisiana State University Press, c1982. — 211p ; 24cm
Bibliography: p193-203. — Includes index
ISBN 0-8071-0977-0 : £18.75 B82-40265

983'.064 — Chile. Political events. Role of United States. *Central Intelligence Agency, ca 1960-ca 1975 — Soviet viewpoints*
Sergeev, F.. Chile : CIA big business / F. Sergeyev ; [translated from the Russian by Lev Bobrov]. — Moscow : Progress Publishers ; [London] : distributed by Central Books, c1981. — 247p ; 21cm
Translation of: Chili, TSRU, bol'shoĭ biznes
ISBN 0-7147-1755-x : £4.50 B82-38231

984 — HISTORY. BOLIVIA

984 — Bolivia, *to 1980*
Klein, Herbert S.. Bolivia : the evolution of a multi-ethnic society / Herbert S. Klein. — New York ; Oxford : Oxford University Press, 1982. — xi,318p : ill,maps ; 21cm. — (Latin American histories)
Bibliography: p275-293. — Includes index
ISBN 0-19-503011-7 (cased) : Unpriced
ISBN 0-19-503012-5 (pbk) : £5.95 B82-37366

984'.052 — Revolutions. Effects — *Study regions: Bolivia*
Kelley, Jonathan. Revolution and the rebirth of inequality : a theory applied to the national revolution in Bolivia / Jonathan Kelley, Herbert S. Klein. — Berkeley ; London : University of California Press, c1981. — xvi,279p : ill ; 25cm
Bibliography: p265-273. — Includes index
ISBN 0-520-04072-4 : £18.50 B82-28105

985 — HISTORY. PERU

985'.02 — Peru. Conquest by Spain, *1530-1550 — Early works*
Zárate, Agustín de. The discovery and conquest of Peru : a translation of books I to IV of Agustín de Zárate's History of these events, supplemented by eye-witness accounts of certain incidents ... / translated with an introduction by J.M. Cohen ; illustrated by Edward Bawden. — London : Folio Society, 1981, c1968. — 271p,[10]leaves of plates : col.ill,maps ; 23cm
Translation of: Historia del descubrimiento y conquista del Peru. — Originally published: Harmondsworth : Penguin, 1968. — In slip-case. — Maps on lining papers. — Includes index
£10.50 B82-08351

985'.02 — Peru. Incas. Conquest by Spain — *For schools*
Tate, Nicholas. Pizarro and the Incas / Nicholas Tate ; illustrated from contemporary sources. — Harlow : Longman, 1982. — 80p : ill,maps,plans,1port ; 20cm. — (Then and there series)
Bibliography: p74-75. — Includes index
ISBN 0-582-20547-6 (pbk) : £0.80 B82-17732

985'.0633 — Peru. Political events, *1950-1980*
Caballero, José-María. From Belaunde to Belaunde : Peru's military experiment in third-roadism / by José-María Caballero. — Cambridge (History Faculty Building, West Rd., Cambridge CB3 9EF) : Centre of Latin American Studies, 1981. — 49p ; 30cm. — (Working papers, ISSN 0306-6290 ; no.36)
Bibliography: p47-49
Unpriced (pbk) B82-21173

985'.37 — Peru. Machu Picchu, *to 1980*
Hemming, John, *1935-*. Machu Picchu / by John Hemming. — London : Reader's Digest in association with Newsweek Books, c1981. — 172p : ill(some col.),maps,ports ; 30cm. — (Wonders of man)
Ill on lining papers. — Bibliography: p169. — Includes index
£7.95 B82-27084

987 — HISTORY. VENEZUELA

987 — Venezuela, *1500-1980*
Lombardi, John V.. Venezuela : the search for order, the dream of progress / John V. Lombardi. — New York ; Oxford : Oxford University Press, 1982. — xv,348p : ill,maps ; 21cm. — (Latin American histories)
Bibliography: p288-314. — Includes index
ISBN 0-19-503013-3 (cased) : Unpriced
ISBN 0-19-503014-1 (pbk) : £5.95 B82-37365

987′.6 — Venezuela. Yanomamö. Social life — *Personal observations*
Donner, Florinda. Shabono. — London : Bodley Head, Oct.1982. — [294]p
ISBN 0-370-30494-2 : £7.95 : CIP entry B82-24445

988.1 — HISTORY. GUYANA

988′.100498 — Guyana. South American Indians, *1803-1870*
The **Amerindians** in Guyana 1803-73 : a documentary history / edited by Mary Noel Menezes ; with a foreword by Donald Wood. — London : Cass, 1979. — xxxi,314p : 1map ; 23cm
Bibliography: p303-306. — Includes index
ISBN 0-7146-3054-3 : £15.00 : CIP rev. B79-06175

988.3 — HISTORY. SURINAM

988′.300496 — Surinam. Negroes. Cultural processes — *Personal observations*
Counter, S. Allen. I sought my brother : an Afro-American reunion / S. Allen Counter and David L. Evans. — Cambridge, Mass. ; London : MIT Press, c1981. — xix,276p : ill (some col.),maps,ports(some col.) ; 27cm
Maps on lining papers
ISBN 0-262-03079-9 : £14.00 B82-09788

990 — HISTORY. OCEANIA, ATLANTIC OCEAN ISLANDS, POLAR REGIONS, ETC

990 — Australasia, *1919-1981 — For schools*
Taylor, J. K. G.. Asia and Australasia. — London : E. Arnold, Nov.1982. — [128]p. — (A History of the 20th century world)
ISBN 0-7131-0679-4 (pbk) : £2.95 : CIP entry
Primary classification 950′.4 B82-27951

990′.07209 — Australasia. Austalasian historiography
Historical disciplines & culture in Australasia : an assessment / edited by John A. Moses. — St. Lucia : University of Queensland Press ; Hemel Hempstead : Prentice-Hall [distributor], 1979. — xiii,291p ; 23cm
Includes bibliographies and index
ISBN 0-7022-1295-4 : £19.50 B82-20071

993 — HISTORY. MELANESIA, NEW ZEALAND

993 — Melanesian artefacts — *Catalogues*
Royal Albert Memorial Museum. Melanesia : a catalogue of the ethnographical collection in Exeter City Museum / compiled by Carolyn A. Straw. — [Exeter] : The City Museum, 1982. — 87p : 2maps ; 30cm
ISBN 0-86114-359-0 (spiral) : Unpriced B82-35341

993.1 — New Zealand, *to 1978*
Sinclair, Keith. A history of New Zealand / Keith Sinclair. — Rev. and enl. ed. — London : Allen Lane, 1980. — 351p ; 23cm
Previous ed.: Harmondsworth : Penguin, 1959. — Bibliography: p335-339. — Includes index
ISBN 0-7139-1251-0 : £7.95 B82-22254

993.1′004994 — New Zealand. Maoris, *to 1980*
Higham, Charles, *1939-*. The Maoris / Charles Higham. — Cambridge : Cambridge University Press, 1981. — 48p : ill,1facsim,maps,ports ; 21x22cm. — (Cambridge introduction to the history of mankind. Topic book)
ISBN 0-521-21931-0 (pbk) : £1.95 B82-36491

Houghton, Philip. The first New Zealanders. — London : Hodder and Stoughton, May 1981. — [156]p
ISBN 0-340-25241-3 : £6.95 : CIP entry B81-04238

Lewis, David, *1919-*. The Maori : heirs of Tane / text by David Lewis ; photographs by Werner Forman ; foreword by D.R. Simmons. — London : Orbis, 1982. — 128p : col.ill ; 31cm
Bibliography: p126. — Includes index
ISBN 0-85613-343-4 : £10.00 B82-39028

993.102′092′2 — New Zealand. Social life, *1839-1900 — Personal observations — Collections*
Life in a young colony : selections from early New Zealand writing / edited by Cherry A. Hankin. — Christchurch ; London : Whitcoulls, 1981. — 287p : ill,ports ; 25cm
Bibliography: p285-287
ISBN 0-7233-0657-5 : Unpriced B82-19299

993.102′3′0222 — New Zealand. Social life, *1885-1916 — Illustrations*
Hammond, Charlie. Charlie Hammond′s sketch-book / introduced by Christopher Fry. — Oxford : Oxford University Press, 1980. — [80]p : chiefly ill(some col.),ports(some col.) ; 19x25cm
ISBN 0-19-212974-0 : £5.95 : CIP rev.
Primary classification 994.03′022′2 B80-18559

993.103′7′0924 — New Zealand. Social life — *Personal observations*
Kennedy, John, *1926-*. Straight from the shoulder / John Kennedy. — Christchurch, [N.Z.] ; London : Whitcoulls, 1981. — 224p ; 22cm
ISBN 0-7233-0664-8 : Unpriced B82-05579

993.15′5′0924 — New Zealand. Canterbury. Bennett, Francis — *Biographies*
Bennett, Francis. A Canterbury tale : the autobiography of Francis Bennett. — Wellington ; Oxford : Oxford University Press, c1980. — 249p : ill,ports ; 25cm
ISBN 0-19-558065-6 : £14.50 B82-00410

994 — HISTORY. AUSTRALIA

994 — Australia, *to 1900*
Blainey, Geoffrey. A land half won / Geoffrey Blainey. — South Melbourne ; London : Macmillan, 1980. — v,388p,[10]p of plates : ill,1map,1port ; 23cm
Bibliography: p364-375. — Includes index
ISBN 0-333-29949-3 : £12.95 B82-28682

994 — Australia, *to 1980*
Clark, Manning. A short history of Australia / Manning Clark. — Illustrated 2nd ed. — South Melbourne ; London : Macmillan, 1981. — 256p : ill,facsims,ports ; 27cm
Previous ed.: i.e. 2nd ed. 1980. — Ill on lining papers. — Bibliography: p248-249. — Includes index
ISBN 0-333-33735-2 : Unpriced B82-31688

994 — Australia, *to 1981*
New history : studying Australia today. — London : Allen & Unwin, Apr.1982. — [184]p
ISBN 0-86861-379-7 : £15.00 : CIP entry B82-05770

994′.004991 — Australian aboriginal artefacts — *Catalogues*
Royal Albert Memorial Museum. Australia : a catalogue of the ethnographical collection in Exeter City Museum / [compiled by] Carolyn A. Straw. — [Exeter] : The City Museum, 1982. — 41p : 1map ; 30cm
ISBN 0-86114-353-1 (pbk) : Unpriced B82-35342

994′.0049915 — Australia. Colonisation by European countries. Attitudes of aborigines, *1788-1980*
Broome, Richard. Aboriginal Australians. — London : Allen & Unwin, Jan.1982. — [224]p. — (The Australian experience)
ISBN 0-86861-043-7 : £10.00 : CIP entry B81-33931

994′.0072024 — Australia. Historiography. Hasluck, Alexandra — *Biographies*
Hasluck, Alexandra. Portrait in a mirror : an autobiography / Alexandra Hasluck. — Melbourne ; Oxford : Oxford University Press, [1982?]. — 329p : ill,1facsim,ports ; 23cm
Bibliography: p323. — Includes index
ISBN 0-19-554298-3 : £18.00 B82-41060

994.02 — Australia, *1788-1800*
Taylor, Peter. Australia : the first twelve years. — London : Allen and Unwin, Sept.1982. — [220]p
ISBN 0-86861-268-5 : £15.00 : CIP entry B82-18779

994.03 — Australia. Settlement, *1844-1926*
Wright, Judith. The cry for the dead / Judith Wright. — Melbourne ; Oxford : Oxford University Press, 1981. — 303p : maps ; 23cm
Bibliography: p281-284. — Includes index
ISBN 0-19-554296-7 : Unpriced B82-37003

994.03 — Australia. Social life, *1850-1980*
Chapple, S. G.. The ramblings of an Australian / S.G. Chapple. — Ilfracombe : Stockwell, 1981. — 58p ; 19cm
ISBN 0-7223-1487-6 : £3.75 B82-12278

994.03′022′2 — Australia. Social life, *1885-1916 — Illustrations*
Hammond, Charlie. Charlie Hammond′s sketch-book / introduced by Christopher Fry. — Oxford : Oxford University Press, 1980. — [80]p : chiefly ill(some col.),ports(some col.) ; 19x25cm
ISBN 0-19-212974-0 : £5.95 : CIP rev.
Also classified at 993.102′3′0222 B80-18559

994.05′092′4 — Australia. Politics. Santamaria, B.A. — *Biographies*
Santamaria, B. A.. Santamaria : against the tide. — Melbourne ; Oxford : Oxford University Press, 1981. — xii,382p : ports ; 23cm
Includes index
ISBN 0-19-550593-x : £18.50 B82-08291

994.06′3 — Australia. Social life — *For schools*
Ellis, Rennie. We live in Australia / Rennie Ellis. — Hove : Wayland, 1982. — 64p : col.ill,1col.map,col.ports ; 26cm
Includes index
ISBN 0-85340-857-2 : £4.95 B82-34829

995 — HISTORY. NEW GUINEA

995′.3 — Papua New Guinea. Karkar Island. Social conditions, *to 1968*
McSwain, Romola. The past and future people : tradition and change on a New Guinea island / McSwain Romola. — Melbourne ; Oxford : Oxford University Press, 1977 (1979 [printing]). — xx,213p,[8]p of plates : ill,maps,ports ; 22cm
Bibliography: p198-207. — Includes index
ISBN 0-19-550563-8 (pbk) : £6.95 B82-14606

996 — HISTORY. POLYNESIA

996′.1100491411 — Fiji. Indians — *Personal observations — Collections*
The **Indo-Fijian** experience / edited and introduced by Subramani. — St. Lucia : University of Queensland Press ; Hemel Hempstead : Distributed by Prentice-Hall, 1979. — xii,207p ; 23cm. — (Asian and Pacific writing ; 12)
ISBN 0-7022-1386-1 (cased) : £7.10
ISBN 0-7022-1387-x (pbk) : Unpriced B82-20105

996′.81′00994 — Kiribati & Tuvalu. Social life, *1914-1933 — Personal observations*
Grimble, Arthur. A pattern of islands / Arthur Grimble. — Harmondsworth : Penguin, 1981, c1952. — 264p : 1map ; 18cm
Originally published : London : Murray, 1952
ISBN 0-14-004950-9 (pbk) : £1.75 B82-08028

996.9′02 — Hawaiian Islands. Prehistoric societies. Social development. Archaeological investigation
Cordy, Ross H.. A study of prehistoric social change : the development of complex societies in the Hawaiian Islands / Ross H. Cordy. — New York ; London : Academic Press, 1981. — xii,274p : ill,maps ; 24cm. — (Studies in archaeology)
Bibliography: p253-267. — Includes index
ISBN 0-12-188450-3 : £19.20 B82-18355

997 — HISTORY. ATLANTIC OCEAN ISLANDS

997.11 — Falkland Islands. Conflict, *1982*
Battle for the Falklands. — London : Osprey, Nov.1982
1: Land forces. — [40]p. — (Men-at-arms series ; 133)
ISBN 0-85045-482-4 (pbk) : £3.50 : CIP entry B82-29427

997.11 — Falkland Islands. Conflict, *1982 continuation*

Battle for the Falklands. — London : Osprey, Nov.1982
2: Naval forces. — [40]p. — (Men-at-arms series ; 134)
ISBN 0-85045-492-1 (pbk) : £3.50 : CIP entry
B82-29426

Battle for the Falklands. — London : Osprey, Nov.1982
3: Air forces. — [40]p. — (Men-at-arms series ; 135)
ISBN 0-85045-493-x (pbk) : £3.50 : CIP entry
B82-29425

997′.11 — Falkland Islands. Conflict, *1982*

Dobson, Christopher. The Falklands conflict. — London : Hodder and Stoughton, June 1982. — [192]p
ISBN 0-340-32408-2 (pbk) : £1.50 : CIP entry
B82-18570

Laffin, John. Fight for the Falklands!. — Large print ed. — Bath : Chivers, Oct.1982. — [320] p. — (A Lythway book)
Originally published: London : Sphere, 1982
ISBN 0-85119-879-1 : £7.50 : CIP entry
B82-25762

997.11 — Falkland Islands. Conflict, *1982*

Perrett, Bryan. Weapons of the Falklands conflict. — Poole : Blandford Press, Nov.1982. — [192]p
ISBN 0-7137-1315-1 : £5.95 : CIP entry
Primary classification 623′.0941 B82-32861

997′.11 — Falkland Islands. Conflict, *1982 — Personal observations*

Bishop, Patrick. The winter war : the Falklands conflict. — London : Quartet, Sept.1982. — [192]p
ISBN 0-7043-3424-0 (pbk) : £2.50 : CIP entry
B82-26701

997′.11 — Falkland Islands. Conflict, *1982 — Personal observations — Collections*

Hanrahan, Brian. 'I counted them all out and I counted them all back'. — Large print ed. — Bath : Chivers, Dec.1982. — [192]p
Originally published: London : BBC, 1982
ISBN 0-85119-203-3 : £6.00 : CIP entry
B82-31304

997′.11 — Falkland Islands. Conflict, *1982. Political aspects*

Barnett, Anthony. Iron Britannia. — London : Allison & Busby, Oct.1982. — [128]p
ISBN 0-85031-494-1 (cased) : £5.95 : CIP entry
ISBN 0-85031-493-3 (pbk) : £2.95 B82-29405

997.11 — Falkland Islands. Conflict, *1982.* **Reporting by mass media**

Harris, Robert, *19---*. Gotcha! : the media, the government and the Falklands crisis. — London : Faber, Jan.1983. — [210]p
ISBN 0-571-13052-6 (pbk) : £5.00 : CIP entry
B82-36146

997′.11 — Falkland Islands. Naval operations, *1982*

Preston, Antony. Sea combat off the Falklands. — London : Collins, Nov.1982. — [160]p
ISBN 0-00-218046-4 : £8.95 : CIP entry
B82-27794

997′.11 — Falkland Islands, *to 1982*

The **Disputed** islands : the Falkland crisis : a history & background. — London : H.M.S.O., 1982. — 36p : maps ; 22cm
Bibliography: p36
ISBN 0-11-580241-x (pbk) : £1.95 B82-34300

997′.11 — Falkland Islands, *to ca 1900*

Goebel, Julius. The struggle for the Falkland Islands. — London : Yale University Press, June 1982. — [300]p
Originally published: 1927
ISBN 0-300-02943-8 (cased) : £10.00 : CIP entry
ISBN 0-300-02944-6 (pbk) : £5.95 B82-21085

997′.11 — Falkland Islands War

Beattie, John, *1941-*. The Falklands story : dramatic account of how a task force of 101 ships sailed into action 8,000 miles from home / by John Beattie of the Daily Star. — London (121 Fleet St, EC4P 4JT) : Express Newspapers, c1982. — 66p : ill(some col.),2col.maps,ports(some col.) ; 30cm
Cover title. — Ill on inside covers
£1.00 (pbk) B82-39787

997′.11 — Falkland Islands War, *1982.* **British decorations: South Atlantic Medal** — *Proposals*

Great Britain. The South Atlantic Medal 1982 : service in the South Atlantic from 2 April 1982. — London : H.M.S.O., 1982. — 3p ; 25cm. — (Cmnd. ; 8601)
ISBN 0-10-186010-2 (unbound) : £0.75
B82-39513

997′.11 — Falkland Islands War — *Trotskyist viewpoints*

Posadist IV International. Resolution of the Posadist IV International : the military aggression of Anglo-Yankee imperialism against Argentina and the rout of the world capitalist system. — London (24 Cranbourn St, WC2) : IV International Publications, [1982]. — 10p ; 21cm
£0.10 (unbound) B82-39897

997′.11′005 — Falkland Islands — *Serials*

Falkland Islands newsletter. — No.1 (1977)-. — London (2 Greycoat Place, S.W.1) : Falkland Islands Office, 1977-. — v. : ill,ports ; 30cm
Quarterly. — Description based on: No.11 (Dec. 1981)
ISSN 0262-9399 = Falkland Islands newsletter : Unpriced B82-15170

997′.3 — Tristan da Cunha, *to 1979*

Crabb, George. The history and postal history of Tristan da Cunha / by George Crabb. — Epsom (Charlwood, Howard Ave., Ewell, Epsom, Surrey) : G. Crabb, 1980. — 347p : ill,maps,facsims,ports ; 31cm
Bibliography: p340-342
Unpriced (spiral)
Primary classification 383′.49973 B82-08863

998 — HISTORY. POLAR REGIONS

998′.2 — Greenland. Eskimo children. Social life — *For children — Welsh texts*

Alexander, Bryan. [Eskimo boy. Welsh]. Otto yr Esgimo / Bryan a Cherry Alexander ; paratowyd yr addasiad Cymraeg gan Islwyn Griffiths. — Truro : Ivan Corbett, c1982. — [28]p : col.ill,1map,col.ports ; 22cm. — (Pobl y byd)
Translation of: Eskimo boy. — Map on lining papers
ISBN 0-904836-16-9 : Unpriced B82-33250

998′.200497 — Greenland. Thule. Eskimos. Social life, *1950-1971 — Personal observations*

Malaurie, Jean. The last kings of Thule. — London : Cape, Nov.1982. — 1v.
Translation and revision of: Les derniers rois de Thule
ISBN 0-224-02028-5 : £15.00 : CIP entry
B82-27208

973'.0496073022 — United States. Negroes — *Personal observations — Collections — For schools*

Being black / [compiled and edited] by Roxy Harris. — London : New Beacon Books, 1981. — 52p : ill,ports ; 21cm
Selections from Soledad brother / George Jackson and Soul on ice / Eldridge Cleaver, with questions and notes
ISBN 0-901241-39-3 (pbk) : Unpriced
B82-00731

973'.0497 — United States. North American Indians, *to 1978*

Hagan, William T.. American Indians / William T. Hagan. — Rev. ed. — Chicago ; London : University of Chicago Press, 1979. — xiii,193p,[10]p of plates : ill,ports ; 21cm. — (The Chicago history of American civilization)
Previous ed.: 1961. — Bibliography: p179-185. — Includes index
ISBN 0-226-31234-8 (cased) : £9.75
ISBN 0-226-31235-6 (pbk) : Unpriced
B82-22634

973'.09'732 — United States. Cities. Social life, *to 1950*

Keller, Morton. Historical sources of urban personality : Boston, New York, Philadelphia : an inaugural lecture delivered before the University of Oxford on 3 March 1981 / by Morton Keller. — Oxford : Clarendon, 1982. — 24p ; 22cm
ISBN 0-19-951534-4 (pbk) : Unpriced : CIP rev.
B82-06026

973'.09'92 — United States, *1800-1945.* **Biographies. Kennedy, John F.. Profiles in courage** — *Critical studies*

Ward, John William. John F. Kennedy : profiles in courage / by John William Ward. — Portree : Aquila, 1982. — [14]p ; 21cm. — (Aquila essays ; no.6)
ISBN 0-7275-0220-4 (pbk) : Unpriced
B82-27843

973'.09'92 — United States. Presidents. Families, *to 1981 — Biographies*

Burke's Presidential families of the United States of America / [edited by Hugh Montgomery-Massingberd]. — 2nd ed. — London : Burke's Peerage, 1981. — xiv,597,A74p : 1ill,ports,geneal.tables ; 26cm
Previous ed.: 1975. — Includes index
ISBN 0-85011-033-5 : £28.00 B82-15470

973'.09'92 — United States. Presidents, *to 1981 — Stories, anecdotes*

Boller, Paul F.. Presidential anecdotes / Paul F. Boller, Jr. — New York ; Oxford : Oxford University Press, 1981. — xvi,410p ; 23cm
Includes index
ISBN 0-19-502915-1 : Unpriced B82-02148

973.2'092'4 — United States. Politics. Franklin, Benjamin — *Correspondence, diaries, etc.*

Franklin, Benjamin. The papers of Benjamin Franklin / William B. Willcox editor ; Douglas M. Arnold ... [et al.] assistant editors. — New Haven ; London : Yale University Press
Vol.22: March 23, 1775, through October 27, 1776. — c1982. — 726p : ill,facsims,1map,1port ; 23cm
Includes index
ISBN 0-300-02618-8 : Unpriced : CIP rev.
B82-12135

973.2'2 — Pilgrim Fathers

Heaton, Vernon. The Mayflower / Vernon Heaton. — Exeter : Webb & Bower, 1980. — 200p : ill(some col.),maps,facsims,ports(some col.) ; 26cm
Bibliography: p194. — Includes index
ISBN 0-906671-14-0 : £7.95 : CIP rev.
B80-12190

973.3 — War of American Independence

Middlekauff, Robert. The glorious cause : the American Revolution, 1763-1789 / Robert Middlekauff. — New York ; Oxford : Oxford University Press, 1982. — xvi,696p,[16]p of plates : 1ill,maps,ports ; 25cm. — (The Oxford history of the United States ; v.2)
Bibliography: p666-674. — Includes index
ISBN 0-19-502921-6 : £15.00 B82-37764

973.3'092'4 — United States. Politics. Lee, Arthur, *1740-1792 — Biographies*

Potts, Louis W.. Arthur Lee : a virtuous revolutionary / Louis W. Potts. — Baton Rouge ; London : Louisiana State University Press, c1981. — xiv,315p,[8]p of plates : ill,1facsim,ports ; 24cm. — (Southern biography series)
Bibliography: p285-306. — Includes index
ISBN 0-8071-0785-9 : £17.50 B82-09915

973.3'092'4 — United States. Social life, *ca 1760-1800 — Personal observations*

Crèvecoeur, J. Hector St. John de. Letters from an American farmer ; and, Sketches of eighteenth-century America / by J. Hector St. John de Crèvecoeur ; edited with an introduction by Albert E. Stone. — Harmondsworth : Penguin, 1981. — 491p : 1map,1port ; 18cm. — (The Penguin American library)
Letters from an American farmer originally published: London : Printed for T. Davies, 1782. — Sketches of eighteenth-century America originally published: New Haven : Yale University Press, 1925. — Port on inside cover. — Bibliography: p27-28. — Includes index
ISBN 0-14-039006-5 (pbk) : £2.50 B82-22086

973.4'092'4 — United States. Hamilton, Alexander, *1757-1804 — Biographies*

Hendrickson, Robert A.. The rise and fall of Alexander Hamilton / Robert A. Hendrickson. — New York ; London : Van Nostrand Reinhold, c1981. — xii,658p ; 26cm
Includes index
ISBN 0-442-26113-6 : £21.20 B82-07877

973.4'1'0924 — United States. Washington, George — *Biographies*

Bourne, Miriam Anne. First family : George Washington and his intimate relations / Miriam Anne Bourne. — New York ; London : Norton, c1982. — 212p,[10]p of plates : 2facsims,ports ; 21cm
Bibliography: p211-212. — Includes index
ISBN 0-393-01531-9 : £10.50 B82-34640

973.4'4'0924 — United States. Adams, Abigail — *Biographies*

Withey, Lynne. Dearest friend : a life of Abigail Adams / Lynne Withey. — New York : Free Press ; London : Collier Macmillan, c1981. — xiv,369p,[8]p of plates : ill,ports ; 25cm
Bibliography: p347-356. — Includes index
ISBN 0-02-934760-2 : £12.75 B82-18901

973.5'5'0924 — United States. Adams, John Quincy — *Correspondence, diaries, etc*

Adams, John Quincy. Diary of John Quincy Adams. — Cambridge, Mass. ; London : Belknap Press of Harvard University Press. — (The Adams papers. Series 1, diaries)
Vol.1: November 1779-March 1786 / David Grayson Allen, associate editor ... [et al.]. — 1981. — lxii,415p : ill,2coats of arms,facsims,ports ; 26cm
ISBN 0-674-20420-4 : Unpriced B82-35395

Adams, John Quincy. Diary of John Quincy Adams. — Cambridge, Mass. ; London : Belknap Press of Harvard University Press. — (The Adams papers. Series 1, diaries)
Vol.2: March 1786-December 1788, index / David Grayson Allen, associate editor ... [et al.]. — 1981. — xiv,521p : ill,facsims,music,ports ; 26cm
Includes index
ISBN 0-674-20420-4 : Unpriced B82-35396

973.7'092'4 — United States. Lincoln, Abraham — *Biographies — For children*

Clark, Philip, *1944-*. Abraham Lincoln / Philip Clark. — Hove : Wayland, 1981. — 71p : ill,1map,ports ; 22cm. — (Wayland history makers)
Bibliography: p70. — Includes index
ISBN 0-85340-814-9 : £3.95 B82-06547

973.7'092'4 — United States. Lincoln, Abraham — *Encyclopedias*

Neely, Mark E.. The Abraham Lincoln encyclopedia / Mark E. Neely, Jr. — New York ; London : McGraw-Hill, c1982. — xii,356p : ill,facsims,ports ; 29cm
Includes index
ISBN 0-07-046145-7 : £29.95 B82-07088

973.7'3 — American Civil War. Army operations

Welsh, Douglas. American Civil War : a complete military history / Douglas Welsh. — London : Hamlyn, 1981. — 192p : ill(some col.),maps(some col.),ports(some col.) ; 32cm. — (A Bison book)
Includes index
ISBN 0-600-34174-7 : £7.95 B82-04332

973.7'3 — American Civil War. Army operations by United States. *Army.* **Cavalry**

Starr, Stephen Z.. The Union cavalry in the Civil War / Stephen Z. Starr. — Baton Rouge ; London : Louisiana State University Press. — xv,526p : ill,maps,2plans,ports ; 24cm
Bibliography: p509-510. — Includes index
ISBN 0-8071-0859-6 : £21.00 B82-22553

973.7'336 — American Civil War. Battle of Antietam

Murfin, James V.. The gleam of bayonets : the Battle of Antietam and the Maryland Campaign of 1862 / by James V. Murfin ; maps by James D. Bowlby ; introduction by James I. Robertson Jr. — Baton Rouge ; London : Louisiana State University Press, 1982, c1965. — 451p,[16]p of plates : ill,facsims,maps,ports ; 23cm
Originally published: New York : Yoseloff, 1965. — Bibliography: p429-436. — Includes index
ISBN 0-8071-0989-4 (cased) : Unpriced
ISBN 0-8071-0990-8 (pbk) : £6.75 B82-40269

973.7'4 — American Civil War. Soldiers. Attitudes

Barton, Michael. Goodmen : the character of Civil War soldiers / Michael Barton. — University Park [Pa.] ; London : Pennsylvania State University Press, c1981. — 135p : ill,1form ; 24cm
Bibliography: p111-131. — Includes index
ISBN 0-271-00284-0 : £4.10 B82-22545

973.7'52 — American Civil War. Naval operations by battleships: Monitor *(Ship)* **& Virginia** *(Ship)*

Davis, William C. (William Charles). Duel between the first ironclads / William C. Davis. — Baton Rouge ; London : Louisiana State University Press, 1981, c1975. — x,201p,[16]p of plates : ill,1map,ports ; 22cm
Originally published: Garden City, N.Y. : Doubleday, 1975. — Bibliography: p187-194. — Includes index
ISBN 0-8071-0868-5 (pbk) : £5.55 B82-01302

973.7'81 — American Civil War. Army operation by United States. *Army, 1863-1865 — Personal observations — Correspondence, diaries, etc.*

Horrocks, James. My dear parents. — London : Gollancz, Sept.1982. — [192]p
ISBN 0-575-03152-2 : £7.95 : CIP entry
B82-19808

973.7'82 — American Civil War - *Confederate viewpoints - Correspondence, diaries, etc*

Chesnut, Mary Boykin. Mary Chesnut's civil war. — London : Yale University Press, Apr.1981. — [960]p
ISBN 0-300-02459-2 : £18.85 : CIP entry
B81-09984

973.8'092'2 — United States. Working life, *ca 1880-1910 — Personal observations — Collections*

Plain folk : the life stories of undistinguished Americans / edited and with an introduciton by David M. Katzman and William M. Tuttle, Jr. — Urbana ; London : University of Illinois Press, c1982. — xx,198p,[7]p of plates : ill,2ports ; 21cm
ISBN 0-252-00884-7 (cased) : Unpriced
ISBN 0-252-00906-1 (pbk) : £5.25 B82-39340

973.8'092'4 — United States. Politics. Foster, John W. — *Biographies*

Devine, Michael J.. John W. Foster : politics and diplomacy in the imperial era, 1837-1917 / by Michael J. Devine. — Athens, Ohio ; London : Ohio University Press, c1981. — x,187p : ports ; 24cm
Bibliography: p162-176. — Includes index
ISBN 0-8214-0437-7 : £10.85 B82-15269